W9-BKU-960

I BUY & SELL the World's Rarest Records!

Blues 78's Our Specialty!

My name is John Tefteller.

I have been buying and selling rare records for the past 30 years.

I have the world's largest inventory of Blues, Rhythm & Blues and Rock & Roll 78's with over 100,000 in stock. I also have over 100,000 45's from the 1950's and early 1960's.

I have a worldwide reputation for my knowledge of rare records and I am always interested in buying more rare records!

Before you sell your records to ANYONE, you should at least talk to me. I consistently pay **the highest prices** for records for my collection and am more than fair when buying for resale.

To contact me: Cell: **(541) 659-7175**
Phone: **(800) 955-1326** (U.S. Only)
Phone: **(541) 476-1326**
Fax: **(541) 476-3523**
P.O. Box 1727
Grants Pass, OR 97528-0200
John@tefteller.com

www.**tefteller**.com

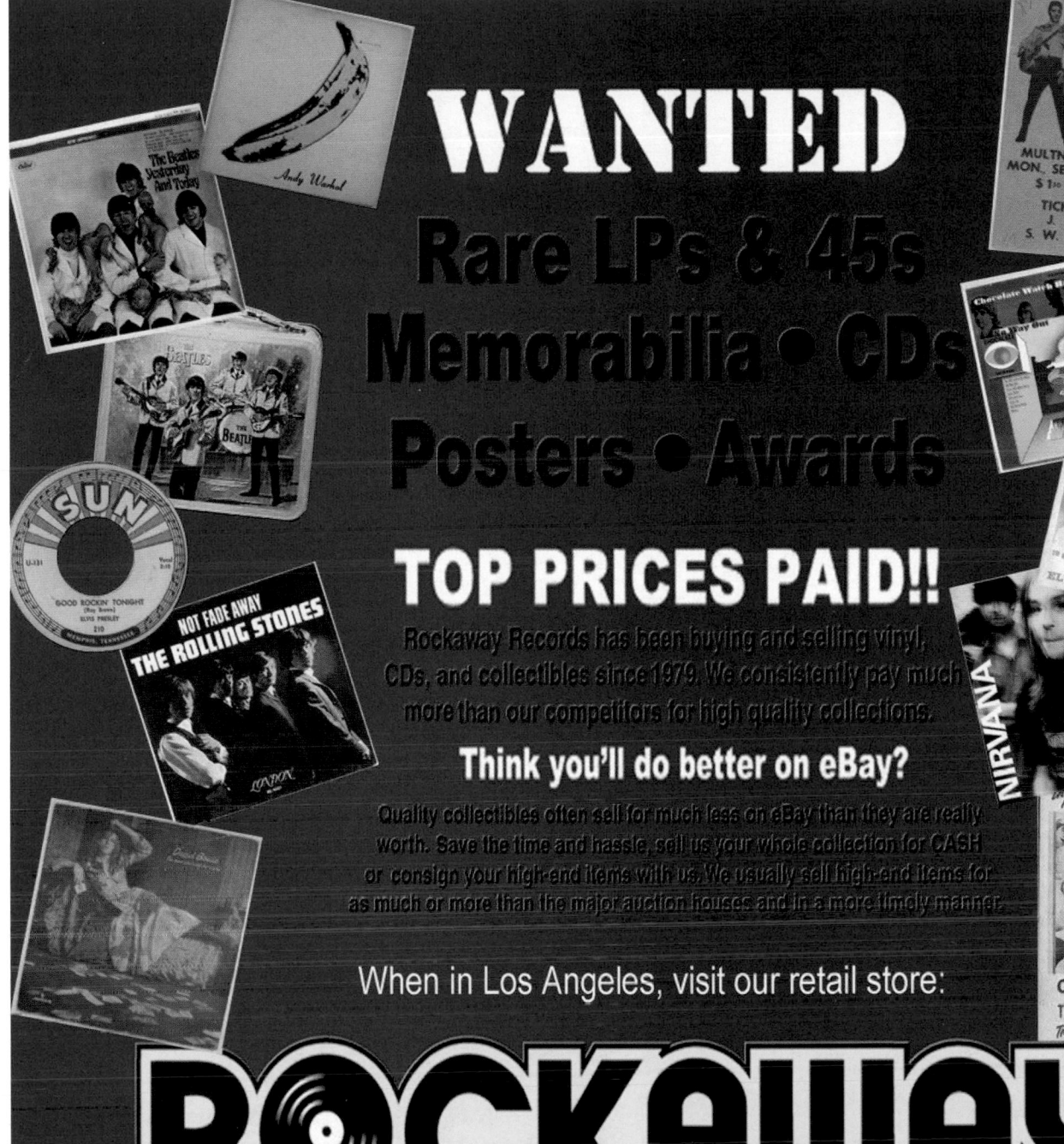

Goldmine® Record Album

PRICE GUIDE
8th Edition

Dave Thompson

Published by

Krause Publications, a division of F+W, A Content + eCommerce Company
700 East State Street • Iola, WI 54990-0001
715-445-2214 • 888-457-2873
www.krausebooks.com

To order books or other products call toll-free 1-800-258-0929
or visit us online at www.krausebooks.com

ISBN-13: 978-1-4402-4372-1
ISBN-10: 1-4402-4372-7

Cover Design by Dane Royer
Book Design by Sandi Carpenter
Edited by Paul Kennedy

Printed in the United States of America

10 9 8 7 6 5 4 3 2 1

Special Acknowledgments to:
- Those who worked on this book, including Database Developer Steve Duberstein; Scanning Supervisor Duayne Kett; Editorial Director Tom Bartsch; Design Manager Sharon Bartsch and Designers Sandi Carpenter and Dane Royer.
- Popsike.com, Heritage Auctions, eBay, Etsy.com, Record Collector magazine, VJM, the Recording Industry Association of America, Shutterstock.com, The Audio Preservation Fund and The Library of Congress.
- The fine advertisers who support this book, as well its sister publication, Goldmine magazine. Please support them with your business. Several are highlighted in a special insert at the back of this book.
- You, the dealers, collectors and readers, for your continued interest in records and your input into this edition.

Connect With Us!

www.goldminemag.com   www.facebook.com/goldminemag   http://twitter.com/Goldmine_mag   http://pinterest.com/goldminemag/

CONTENTS

LISTINGS

INTRODUCTION

Back in Black Collectors welcome vinyl resurgence

If anything has changed since the last edition of this price guide, it is the way the rest of the world now looks at vinyl.

For a long time, some might say too long, LP records were regarded as a dying art, if not a dead issue. The major labels had abandoned them long before, and the handful of independent labels that still kept the faith was shrinking every year. A few established indie labels continued to pump out twelve inches of black (or otherwise) wax, licensing tapes from the majors for the delectation of what seemed an eccentric minority of surviving collectors. But nobody could have foreseen a time when, not only had that minority expanded across the entire spectrum of music fans, but the major labels too had hopped back on the bus.

Record Store Day, the now twice-annual celebration of vinyl that highlights every spring and fall, has played a large part in this renaissance, unleashing a treasure trove of often limited, often fabulous, and always collectible new editions of LPs past and present. Some of the most exquisite modern collectibles now wear the RSD sticker on their jacket, and the lines that form outside participating record stores on the days in question bring a tear of nostalgia to the eye of any fan old enough to remember when so many new releases brought madness to main street.

A new Beatles record, a new Stones release... we used to start blocking the sidewalk at dawn for those, and now we're doing it again.

But if Record Store Day is the biggest, and most visible, symptom of vinyl's resurgence, it is by no means the only one. Every week, it seems, now brings the announcement of a must-have new vinyl release, be it a crop of mainstream catalog reissues from the likes of Rhino, Sony or Universal; a painstakingly curated remaster from Drastic Plastic, Light in the Attic, Sundazed and so on; or a hitherto undreamed of collection of music that was ancient when rock and pop were still infants, exhumed by Tompkins Square, Third Man and so many more.

It's not only on the new release racks that we are seeing such a phenomenal turn around. Record fairs are booming again, vinyl sales are soaring, and Internet dealers are seeing more business than ever. The middle of the second decade of the 21st century might not be the **greatest** time ever to have been a record collector. But in terms of what's available, what's becoming available and what we can dream might one day be reissued, it's close.

What effect has all this activity had on the **Goldmine Album Price Guide**?

A lot.

The great complaint that traditionalists often offer up whenever a new reissue comes around is that it will somehow chip away at the value of an original pressing. And sometimes this is true. Fans who seek a particular rarity because they want to hear the music, and either cannot afford or can't even find a copy of the original, will gratefully snatch up the reissue. But collectors who care for the artifact as well aren't fooled, or deterred

in their quest to pick up a pristine first pressing, or whatever.

A little of the edge might be smoothed off the demand, and maybe a copy listed on an Internet auction will attract a handful less bids than it might have in the past. But they were rarely ever winning bids. Your valuable record remains a valuable record, no matter how often it is reissued, and when you check the prices of rock's most storied investment items, your portfolio continues to perform, as you'd hope.

Even more impressively, the new interest that has been aroused in old vinyl has seen many prices increase. Not for the flotsam and jetsam that have always lived in the dustiest recesses of the dollar box bargain bin - it will take more than a 180-gram reissue of the Idle Race's first album to clear all the scratchy used copies of the Electric Light Orchestra catalog from the basement. But a new audience is discovering the joys of old bands not encountered before, and doing so in a way that compact discs and mp3s never could.

The broader palette that vinyl represents, both in aural and visual terms, has reminded (or maybe even taught) an entire generation that music is something more than merely a noise to be listened to through the speakers on the laptop. It is something to be enjoyed on every level you want it to work at, with packaging and presentation as much a part of the purchase as the songs themselves. The vinyl itself possesses an aesthetic beauty that a coaster-sized silver disc never managed to acquire, and that discovery too has hastened the medium's modern-day rebirth.

Prices are not, however, the only area in which this latest edition for the price guide shows change. The sheer number of new releases (or re-releases) that it contains, too, has seen entire discographies refurbished, and with more reissues arriving, as we said before, every week, accounting for these ensures that this edition can be celebrated as the most up-to-date we have ever published - even as the historic divide between publishing and new release schedules ensures this will forever be a work in progress.

We have not attempted to include **every** reissue. Not every one falls within the pricing parameters set forth in this book; and not every one, sadly, has been traced, falling through the cracks that inevitably dog even the most determined discographer. Others, though widely available in the US, are nevertheless officially regarded as imports - a field that the price guide has never embraced. And, of course, stylistic and chronological concerns also play a role in shaping this edition. Fabulous as it would be to compile **every** long playing record released in the United States since the birth of the medium over 70 years ago, even an e-book style electronic publication would baulk at the sheer behemothic size of it.

So this is it, the new **Goldmine Album Price Guide** and, we believe, the most complete and current edition yet.

Happy browsing, happy collecting, and as always, long live vinyl.

– Dave Thompson

....

TELL US WHAT YOU THINK

We're always working on the "next" edition of Goldmine's price guides and magazines, which means we're always open for business. What would you like to see in the next book or issue? Do you have proof of a heretofore

unknown record? We'd love to hear from you!
- **Via e-mail:** goldminemag@fwmedia.com.
- **Via mail:** Goldmine, Attention: Record Price Guides, 700 E. State St., Iola, WI 54990.
- **Via fax:** 715-445-4087, Attention: Gold-

mine Record Price Guides.

We look forward to reading your suggestions and incorporating as many as possible. Thank you for the time and thought you put in to sharing your viewpoints!

HOW TO USE THIS BOOK

	Number	**Title**	**Yr**	**NM**
artist name —	**QUEEN**			
record label —	ELEKTRA			
catalog number —	❑ 5E-513	The Game	1980	10.00
title —	*With dull gray cover; all copies have custom white labels*			
	❑ 5E-513	The Game	1980	15.00
release year —	*– With shiny, mirrorlike cover; all copies have custom white labels*			
format details —	❑ BB-702 [(2)]	Live Killers	1979	12.00
	❑ EQ-5064 [Q]	Queen	1973	40.00
	❑ EKS-75082	Queen II	1974	10.00
value —	*– Butterfly, red or red/black labels*			
	❑ EKS-75082 [DJ]	Queen II	1974	50.00
recording notes —	*– White label promo*			

To the uninitiated, the Goldmine price guide can seem overwhelming. Here are tips to navigate the listings.

The **artist name** (last name first for solo acts) is the first way we break down the listing information. We strive to provide a cross section of artists, genres and formats within our listings. So while you personally may not care about the 1989 album "You Can't Hold Me Back" by Awesome Dre and The Hardcore Committee, or the 1959 album "Torch Time" by Gogi Grant, there are collectors who do – and who may not be as excited about the Lynyrd Skynyrd, Led Zeppelin or Def Leppard listings as you are.

Each artist's listings are subdivided by the **record label** on which the recording was issued. Records sometimes were issued on more than one label; differ-

ent labels can mean different values.

Individual listings are preceded by a box (which you can use as a handy check-off for what's in your collection), followed by a **catalog number**. The numerical catalog order is what determines the order of the listings – not titles or release dates.

The second column lists the **title** of the album. Few, if any, records in the import, children's, classical, spoken word or various artist genres appear.

If additional **format details** are available (such as whether a recording was pressed in mono, stereo or quadraphonic sound; if it's a deejay or promo copy; if it includes more than one album, etc.), that information appears in brackets and/or parentheses immediately following the catalog number.

The third column lists the **release year**, which is based on record label information or chart date; this may differ from the date noted on the record itself. Release dates of the albums detailed in this book range from the 1940s to the present, but the majority of our listings are for albums released between 1950 and 1989.

The last column lists the Near Mint **value** for the record. In order for an album to be included in this edition of Goldmine's "Record Album Price Guide," its Near Mint value must be at least $10. This means many common records you own may be excluded from our listings.

Some records have an additional line of italic type under the listing. These **recording notes** offer additional details, such as other featured artists, label variations or the color of the vinyl.

COMMON ABBREVIATIONS AND TERMS

Both (B): An album that is listed in stereo, but has some tracks in monaural sound, too.

Cover or Outer Sleeve: A cardboard cover that protects an LP. Double albums may feature gatefold covers, which fold open, like a book.

Dead Wax: The black, grooveless area surrounding the label. It may contain engraved mastering numbers and the mastering agent's initials or company name, or even cryptic messages from the band.

Extended Play (EP): A record with four to six tracks; usually less than half the length of a regular album. Rarely used to describe 12-inch records before the 1980s; before that, it refers to 7-inch records.

Inner Sleeve: A paper, plastic or other lightweight sleeve that protects an album inside the cover. May contain liner notes, lyrics or photos.

Monaural or Mono Sound (M): A single-

channel audio recording. Virtually all records made before the 1950s were in mono; many records were produced in mono until the late 1960s.

Partial Stereo (P): A record listed as stereo, but only part is "true" two-channel stereo.

Picture Disc (PD): A record featuring graphics as part of the record, not merely on the label area

Promo copy (DJ): A promotional pressing not intended for public sale. Often for radio stations, hence DJ for disc jockey. Not meant for public sale.

Quadraphonic (Q): Records – mostly issued from 1972 to 1976 – that were remixed to play on quadraphonic systems, which feature four speakers.

Rechanneled (RE): A recording listed as stereo, but is all or almost all rechanneled, or "fake," stereo. These recordings were marked as "Duophonic" by Capitol and "Enhanced For Stereo" or "Simulated Stereo" by Decca, or may be referred

to as electronically channeled stereo." Typically, these pressings are less in demand than true mono recordings.

Runout Groove: A loop bordering the label where the needle rides after the last song is played.

Stereophonic Sound (S): A two-channel audio recording. Widespread use of stereo record production began in the mid 1960s. Not all monaural phonographs could play stereo records. If we know an album is all or almost all true stereo, we note it as such. This also appears with certain 45s and EPs from the late 1950s and early 1960s, usually when there is also a mono counterpart.

10-Inch Record (10): A 10-inch record, most of which were from the early years of LPs from 1948 to 1954. These records are difficult to find in top condition.

(2), (3), etc.: The number of records in a set.

MASTER GOLDMINE'S GRADING GUIDELINES

BEFORE YOU CAN FIGURE OUT what a record is worth, you need to grade its vinyl, sleeves and labels. Play grading can be a definite advantage for a record that looks much worse than it sounds. When you're visually grading records, use a direct light, such as a 100-watt desk lamp, as less direct lighting can hide defects.

Think like the buyer as you set your grades. If you're on the fence, go with the lower conservative grade under consideration. Records and covers always seem to look better when you're grading them to sell to someone else than when you're on the other side of the table, inspecting a record for purchase. And, if you have a Still Sealed record, subject it to these same grading standards, short of breaking the seal.

MINT (M): Absolutely perfect in every way. Often rumored but rarely seen, Mint should never be used as a grade unless more than one person agrees the item truly is in this condition. There is no hard-and-fast percentage of the Near Mint value these can bring; it is best negotiated between buyer and seller.

- **Overall Appearance:** Looks as if it just came off the manufacturing line.
- **Record:** No scuffs or scratches.
- **Labels:** No writing, stickers or spindle marks. Labels are perfectly placed.
- **Cover/Sleeve:** No blotches, stains, discoloration, stickers, ring wear, dinged corners, sleeve splits or writing.

NEAR MINT (NM) OR MINT MINUS (M-): It's estimated that no more than 2 to 4 percent of all records remaining from the 1950s and 1960s are truly Near Mint. Many dealers won't use a grade higher than this, implying that no record or sleeve is ever truly perfect.

- **Overall Appearance:** Looks as if it were opened for the first time. Includes all original pieces (inner sleeve, lyric sheets, inserts, cover, record, etc.).
- **Record:** Shiny surface, free of visible defects. No surface noise at playback. Records can retain NM condition after many plays provided the record has been played on a properly equipped turntable and has been cared for properly.
- **Labels:** Properly pressed and centered on the record. Free of writing, stickers, spindle marks, blemishes or other markings.
- **Cover/Sleeve:** Free of creases, ring wear and seam splits. Cut-out markings are unacceptable. Picture sleeves look as if no record was ever housed inside. Hint: If you remove a 45 from its picture sleeve and store it separately, you will reduce the potential for damage to the sleeve.

VERY GOOD PLUS (VG+) OR EXCELLENT (E): Except for a few minor condition issues, these records would be Near Mint. Most collectors who want to play their records will be happy with a VG+ record, especially if it is toward the high end of the grade, sometimes called VG++ or E+.

- **Overall Appearance:** Shows slight signs of wear.
- **Record:** May have light scuffs or very light scratches that don't affect the listening experience, or slight warps that don't affect the sound. Expect minor signs of handling, such as telltale marks around the center hole (but the hole is not misshapen). Light ring wear or discoloration may be present, but barely noticeable.
- **Labels:** Free of writing, stickers or major blemishes.
- **Cover/Sleeve:** Outer cover may show some minor seam wear or a split less than one inch long along the bottom, which is the most vulnerable location. A cut-out marking may be present. Picture sleeves may show some slight creasing where it is obvious the record once resided (or still does reside). May show minor seam wear or a split less than 1 inch long along the bottom.

VERY GOOD (VG): VG records have more obvious flaws than records in better condition. That said, VG records – which usually sell for no more than 25 percent of their NM counterparts – are among the biggest bargains in record collecting, because most of the "big money" goes for more perfect copies. For many listeners, a VG record or sleeve will be worth the money. Many collectors who have jukeboxes will use VG records in them and not think twice. They remain a fine listening experience, just not the same as if it were in better shape.

- **Overall Appearance:** Shows signs of wear and handling, including visible groove wear, audible scratches and surface noise, ring wear and seam splits.
- **Record:** Lacks the original glossy finish. Groove wear is evident on sight, and light scratches are deep enough to feel with a fingernail. When played, a VG record has surface noise, and some scratches may be audible, especially during a song's intro and ending, but the noise won't overpower the music otherwise.
- **Labels:** May have minor writing, tape or a sticker.
- **Cover/Sleeve:** Expect obvious signs of human handling and normal wear. Ring wear is expected in the middle or along the edges of the cover where the labels or edges of a record would rest. Seam splits may appear on all three sides, but they won't be obvious. Writing or a price tag may be present. The cover may be dull or discolored, have bent corners, stains or other problems. If the record has more than two of these problems, reduce its grade.

VERY GOOD MINUS (VG–), GOOD PLUS (G+) OR GOOD (G): Good does not necessarily mean bad! A true G to VG- record still plays through without skipping, so it can serve as filler until something better comes along. If the record is common, you may want to pass it up in this condition. If you've sought for a long time, get it cheap and upgrade later. And sellers? Don't expect big profits for records in these grades: They bring 10 to 15 percent of the Near Mint value at most.

- **Overall Appearance:** Shows considerable signs of handling, including groove wear, ring wear, seam splits and damaged labels or covers.
- **Record:** The surface sheen is almost gone, but the record plays through without skipping. Significant surface noise and groove wear..
- **Labels:** Worn, possible stains, heavy writing, or obvious damage caused by someone trying to remove tape or stickers and failing miserably.
- **Cover/Sleeve:** Shows ring wear to the point of distraction, has obvious seam splits and may have even heavier writing, such as huge radio station letters (or the former owner's name) written across the front to deter theft. Expect dinged and dog-eared edges.

FAIR (F) OR POOR (P): These records go for 0 to 5 percent of the Near Mint value – if they go at all. More likely, these records will end up going in the trash, or having their covers, labels or discs turned into kitschy craft items like clocks, journals, purses, jewelry, bowls or coasters.

- **Overall Appearance:** Beat, trashed and dull. Records may lack sleeves or covers (or vice versa). You may want to call a CSI unit to identify "the victim."
- **Record:** Expect the vinyl to be cracked, horrifically scratched and/or impossibly warped. The record will skip and repeat when you attempt to play it.
- **Labels:** Stains, tears, stickers and damage are the least of your problems; the label may be missing some sections altogether.
- **Cover/Sleeve:** So heavily damaged that you almost want to cry. Only the most outrageously rare items ever sell for more than a few cents in this condition– again, if they sell at all.

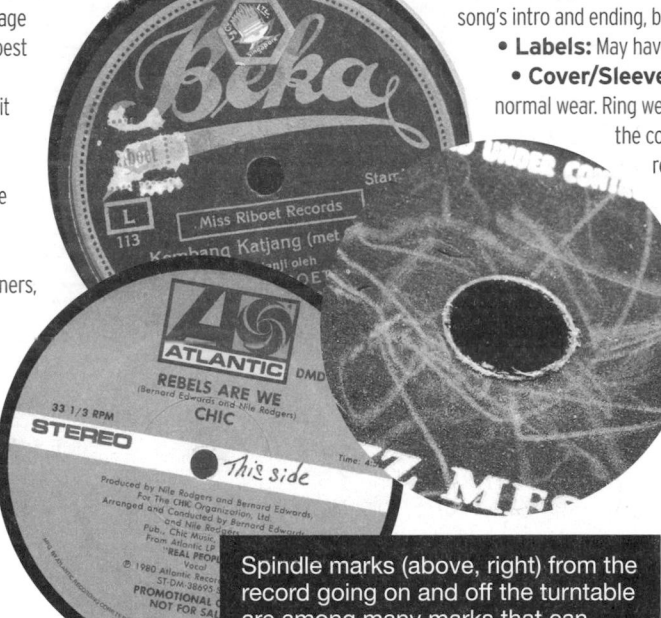

Spindle marks (above, right) from the record going on and off the turntable are among many marks that can help determine a record's grade. The labels also tell a story, and writing (above), stickers and damage (top) all factor into grades.

Number	Title	Yr	NM

A

A.F.O. EXECUTIVES WITH TAMI LYNN

A.F.O.
❏ 5002 [M]	A Compendium	1962	150.00

A-HA

WARNER BROS.
❏ R114779	Hunting High and Low	1985	12.00
—RCA Music Service edition			
❏ 25300	Hunting High and Low	1985	10.00
❏ R163775	Scoundrel Days	1986	12.00
—RCA Music Service edition			
❏ 25501	Scoundrel Days	1986	10.00
❏ R184019	Stay On These Roads	1988	15.00
—BMG Direct Marketing edition			
❏ 25733	Stay On These Roads	1988	12.00

ABBA

ATLANTIC
❏ SD18146	Abba	1975	15.00
❏ PR300 [DJ]	Abba	1978	30.00
❏ 81675	Abba Live	1986	15.00
❏ PR432 [DJ]	A Collection of Hits	1982	30.00
❏ SD19115	Arrival	1977	12.00
❏ SD18207	Arrival	1977	15.00
❏ SD18189	Greatest Hits	1976	15.00
❏ SD19114	Greatest Hits	1977	12.00
❏ SD16009	Greatest Hits, Vol. 2	1979	15.00
❏ 80142	I Love Abba	1984	12.00
❏ SD16023	Super Trouper	1980	12.00
❏ PR436 [DJ]	The Abba Special	1983	50.00
❏ SD19164	The Album	1978	12.00
❏ 80036	The Singles -- The First Ten Years	1982	18.00
❏ SD19332	The Visitors	1981	12.00
❏ SD16000	Voulez-Vous	1979	12.00
❏ SD18101 [B]	Waterloo	1974	18.00

CBS INTERNATIONAL

❏ DAL40301 [B]	Gracias Por La Musica	1980	50.00
—Spanish-language versions of some of their hits, this LP was pressed in the U.S.			

K-TEL
❏ NU9510	The Magic of Abba	1978	18.00

NAUTILUS
❏ NR-20	Arrival	1981	30.00
—Audiophile vinyl			

POLYDOR
❏ 5499701	The Album	2008	25.00

ABC

MERCURY
❏ R143756	Alphabet City	1987	15.00
—BMG Direct Marketing edition			
❏ 832391-1	Alphabet City	1987	12.00
❏ 814661-1	Beauty Stab	1984	12.00
❏ 824904-1	How to Be a Zillionaire	1985	12.00
❏ SRM-1-4059	The Lexicon of Love	1982	12.00
❏ 822890-1	The Lexicon of Love	1984	10.00
—Reissue			
❏ 838646-1	Up	1989	12.00

ABDUL, PAULA

VIRGIN
❏ 90943	Forever Your Girl	1988	12.00
❏ 91362	Shut Up and Dance	1990	15.00
—Red print on cover			
❏ 91362	Shut Up and Dance	1990	15.00
—Yellow print on cover			
❏ 91362	Shut Up and Dance	1990	15.00
—Purple print on cover			
❏ 91362	Shut Up and Dance	1990	15.00

Number	Title	Yr	NM
—Blue print on cover			
❏ IP-8128 [B]	Spellbound	1991	30.00
—Columbia House edition; the only U.S. vinyl of this LP			

ABDUL-MALIK, AHMED

NEW JAZZ
❏ NJLP-8282 [M]	Sounds of Africa	1962	40.00
—Purple label			
❏ NJLP-8282 [M]	Sounds of Africa	1965	30.00
—Blue label, trident logo at right			
❏ NJLP-8266 [M]	The Music of Ahmed Abdul-Malik	1961	40.00
—Purple label			
❏ NJLP-8266 [M]	The Music of Ahmed Abdul-Malik	1965	30.00
—Blue label, trident logo at right			

PRESTIGE
❏ PRLP-16003 [M]	Eastern Moods	1963	30.00

RCA VICTOR
❏ LPM-2015 [M]	East Meets West	1959	30.00
❏ LSP-2015 [S]	East Meets West	1959	40.00

RIVERSIDE
❏ RLP 12-287 [M]	Jazz Sahara	1958	50.00
❏ RLP-1121 [S]	Jazz Sahara	1959	40.00

STATUS
❏ ST-8303 [M]	Spellbound	1965	30.00

ABRAMS, MUHAL RICHARD

ARISTA/NOVUS
❏ 3000	Lifea Blinec	1978	12.00
❏ 3007	Spiral/Live	1979	12.00

BLACK SAINT
❏ BSR 0017	1-OQA + 19	1978	15.00
❏ BSR 0061	Blues Forever	1981	12.00
❏ BSR 0091	Colors in Thirty-Third	1987	12.00
❏ BSR 0051	Duet	1981	12.00
—With Amina Claudine Myers			
❏ BSR 0033	Lifelong Ambitions	1980	12.00
—With Leroy Jenkins			
❏ BSR 0041	Mama and Daddy	1981	12.00
❏ BSR 0071	Rejoicing with the Light	1983	12.00
❏ BSR 0003	Sightsong	1975	15.00
—Featuring Malachi Favors			
❏ BSR 0032	Spihumonesty	1980	12.00
❏ 120103	The Hearinga Suite	1989	15.00
❏ BSR 0081	View From Within	1984	12.00

DELMARK
❏ DS-413	Levels and Degrees of Light	1968	25.00
❏ DS-430	Things to Come From Those Now Gone	1972	18.00
❏ DS-423	Young at Heart, Wise in Time	1970	25.00

INDIA NAVIGATION
❏ IN-1058	Afrisong	1975	18.00

ABSTRACTS, THE

POMPEII
❏ 6002 [M]	The Abstracts	1968	80.00
—Stereo cover with "DJ Copy Monaural" sticker; white label promo record			
❏ 3D6002 [S]	The Abstracts	1968	40.00

ACCEPT

EPIC
❏ FE44368	Eat the Heat	1989	12.00

PASSPORT
❏ 9849	Accept	1982	15.00
❏ PB6010	Breaker	198?	15.00

POLYDOR
❏ 815770-1	Accept	1986	10.00
❏ 815771-1	I'm a Rebel	1986	10.00

PORTRAIT
❏ BFR39241	Balls to the Wall	1984	12.00
❏ PR39241	Balls to the Wall	1986	10.00
❏ BFR39974	Metal Heart	1985	12.00
❏ PR39974	Metal Heart	1986	10.00
❏ BFR39215	Restless and Wild	1983	15.00
❏ PR39215	Restless and Wild	1986	10.00
❏ BFR40354	Russian Roulette	1986	12.00

PVC
❏ 8915	Midnight Highway	198?	15.00

AC/DC

ATCO
❏ SD 36-142	High Voltage	1976	15.00
❏ SD 36-151	Let There Be Rock	1977	15.00
❏ 91413	The Razors Edge	1990	18.00

ATLANTIC
❏ 80178 [EP]	74 Jailbreak	1984	12.00
❏ SD16018	Back in Black	1980	12.00
❏ 81828	Blow Up Your Video	1988	12.00
❏ SD16033	Dirty Deeds Done Dirt Cheap	1981	12.00
❏ 80100	Flick of the Switch	1983	12.00
❏ PR562 [DJ]	Flick of the Switch Interview Album	1983	60.00
❏ 81263	Fly on the Wall	1985	12.00

Number	Title	Yr	NM
❏ SD11111	For Those About to Rock We Salute You	1981	12.00
❏ SD19244	Highway to Hell	1979	12.00
❏ SD19212	If You Want Blood You've Got It	1978	12.00
❏ LAAS-001 [DJ]	Live at the Atlantic Studios	1977	100.00
—This album has been counterfeited			
❏ SD19180	Powerage	1978	12.00
❏ 81650	Who Made Who	1986	12.00

EASTWEST
❏ 61780 [B]	Ballbreaker	1995	25.00

EPIC
❏ E80200 [EP]	74 Jailbreak	2003	12.00
❏ 90643 [B]	AC/DC	2003	200.00
—Box set with 15 albums on 16 LPs in black slipcase			
❏ E290553 [B]	AC/DC	2003	18.00
❏ E80207	Back in Black	2003	15.00
❏ E80212	Blow Up Your Video	2003	15.00
❏ E80202	Dirty Deeds Done Dirt Cheap	2003	15.00
❏ E80209	Flick of the Switch	2003	15.00
❏ E80210	Fly on the Wall	2003	15.00
❏ E80208	For Those About to Rock We Salute You	2003	15.00
❏ E80201	High Voltage	2003	15.00
❏ E80206	Highway to Hell	2003	15.00
❏ E80205	If You Want Blood You've Got It	2003	15.00
❏ E80203	Let There Be Rock	2003	15.00
❏ E80204	Powerage	2003	15.00
❏ E80213	The Razors Edge	2003	30.00
❏ E80211	Who Made Who	2003	15.00

ACE, JOHNNY

ABC DUKE
❏ DLPX-71	Memorial Album	1974	25.00

DUKE
❏ DLP-70 [10]	Memorial Album for Johnny Ace	1955	1200.00
—VG value 400; VG+ value 800			
❏ DLP-71 [M]	Memorial Album for Johnny Ace	1956	500.00
—With no playing card on front cover			
❏ DLP-71 [M]	Memorial Album for Johnny Ace	1961	200.00
—With playing card on front cover			
❏ DLP-71 [M]	Memorial Album for Johnny Ace	1961	4000.00
—Playing card cover; red vinyl; VG value 2000; VG+ value 3000			
❏ LP-71 [R]	Memorial Album for Johnny Ace	196?	50.00
—Orange label; trail-off number is "LRS-71"			

MCA
❏ 27014	Memorial Album	1983	10.00

ACE

ANCHOR
❏ ANCL-2001 [B]	Five-a-Side (An Ace Album)	1975	25.00
❏ ANCL-2020 [B]	No Strings	1977	25.00
❏ ANCL-2013 [B]	Time for Another	1975	30.00

ACE SPECTRUM

ATLANTIC
❏ SD7299	Inner Spectrum	1974	25.00
❏ SD18185	Just Like in the Movies	1976	25.00
❏ SD18143	Low Rent Rendezvous	1975	25.00

ACKLES, DAVID

COLUMBIA
❏ KC32466 [B]	Five & Dime	1973	25.00

ELEKTRA
❏ EKS-75032	American Gothic	1972	15.00
❏ EKS-74022	David Ackles	1968	18.00
❏ EKS-74060	Subway to the Country	1970	15.00

ACKLIN, BARBARA

BRUNSWICK
❏ BL754129	Great Soul Hits	1967	30.00
❏ BL754187	I Call It Trouble	1972	25.00
❏ BL754166	I Did It	1971	25.00
❏ BL754137 [B]	Love Makes a Woman	1968	25.00
❏ BL754148	Seven Days of Night	1969	25.00
❏ BL754156	Someone Else's Arms	1970	25.00

CAPITOL
❏ ST-11377	A Place in the Sun	1975	15.00

ACOUSTIC ALCHEMY

MCA
❏ 6291	Blue Chip	1989	12.00
❏ 42125	Natural Elements	1988	12.00
❏ 5816	Red Dust and Spanish Lace	1987	12.00

ACUFF, ROY

CAPITOL
❏ T617 [M]	Songs of the Smoky Mountains	1955	60.00
❏ T1870 [M]	The Best of Roy Acuff	1963	30.00
❏ DT1870 [R]	The Best of Roy Acuff	1963	25.00

Number	Title	Yr	NM
☐ T2103 [M]	The Great Roy Acuff	1964	30.00
☐ DT2103 [R]	The Great Roy Acuff	1964	18.00
☐ T2276 [M]	The Voice of Country Music	1965	30.00
☐ ST2276 [S]	The Voice of Country Music	1965	40.00
COLUMBIA			
☐ FC39998	Columbia Historic Edition	1985	12.00
☐ CL9010 [10]	Old Time Barn Dance	1949	150.00
☐ CL9013 [10]	Songs of the Saddle	1950	150.00
☐ CL9004 [10]	Songs of the Smoky Mountains	1949	200.00
ELEKTRA			
☐ E-C010-1-78 [DJ]	An Interview with Roy Acuff	1978	30.00
HARMONY			
☐ HL7082 [M]	Great Speckled Bird	1958	30.00
☐ HL7294 [M]	That Glory Bound Train	1961	25.00
☐ HL7342 [M]	The Great Roy Acuff	196?	18.00
☐ HL7376 [M]	Waiting for My Call to Glory	196?	18.00
HICKORY			
☐ LPM-119 [M]	Country Music Hall of Fame	1964	25.00
☐ LPS-139	Famous Opry Favorites	1967	25.00
☐ ST-91297	Famous Opry Favorites	1967	30.00
— Capitol Record Club edition			
☐ LPM-125 [M]	Great Train Songs	1965	25.00
☐ DT-90698 [R]	Great Train Songs	1965	30.00
— Capitol Record Club edition			
☐ LPM-117 [M]	Hand-Clapping Gospel Songs	1963	30.00
☐ LPM-109 [M]	King of Country Music -- All-Time Greatest Hits	1962	30.00
☐ T-90704 [M]	King of Country Music -- All-Time Greatest Hits	1966	30.00
— Capitol Record Club edition			
☐ LPS-145	Living Legend	1968	25.00
☐ LPM-H-101 [M]	Once More It's Roy Acuff	1961	30.00
☐ LPM-115 [M]	Roy Acuff Sings American Folk Songs	1963	30.00
☐ LPM-134 [M]	Roy Acuff Sings Hank Williams	1966	40.00
☐ LPS-134 [S]	Roy Acuff Sings Hank Williams	1966	40.00
☐ LPM-113 [M]	Roy Acuff -- Star of the Grand Ole Opry	1963	30.00
☐ LPS-156	Roy Acuff Time	1970	25.00
☐ LPM-114 [M]	The World Is His Stage	1963	30.00
☐ LPS-147	Treasury of Country Hits	1969	25.00
METRO			
☐ M508 [M]	Roy Acuff	1965	18.00
☐ MS508 [R]	Roy Acuff	1965	12.00
MGM			
☐ E-3707 [M]	Favorite Hymns	1958	50.00
☐ E-4044 [M]	Hymn Time	1962	30.00
☐ SE-4044 [R]	Hymn Time	196?	25.00
ROUNDER			
☐ SS-23	1936-1939: Steamboat Whistle Blues	1985	12.00
☐ SS-24	1939-1941: Fly Birdie Fly	1985	12.00

ADAM AND THE ANTS

Number	Title	Yr	NM
EPIC			
☐ AE1331 [DJ]	Adam and the Ants	1981	12.00
— Five-song promo-only sampler			
☐ FE38698	Dirk Wears White Sox	1983	12.00
— First U.S. issue of U.K. debut			
☐ PE38698	Dirk Wears White Sox	1984	10.00
— Budget-line reissue			
☐ NJE37033	Kings of the Wild Frontier	1981	15.00
☐ PE37033	Kings of the Wild Frontier	1985	10.00
— Budget-line reissue			
☐ ARE37615	Prince Charming	1981	12.00
☐ PE37615	Prince Charming	1984	10.00
— Budget-line reissue			

ADAMS, BRYAN

Number	Title	Yr	NM
A&M			
☐ SP-4800	Bryan Adams	1980	15.00
☐ SP-3100	Bryan Adams	198?	10.00
— Budget-line reissue of 4800			
☐ SP-17231 [EP]	Cuts	1983	30.00
— Promo-only four-song sampler from "Cuts Like a Knife" LP			
☐ SP-6-4919	Cuts Like a Knife	1983	12.00
— Original with "6" as part of the catalog number			
☐ SP-4919	Cuts Like a Knife	1984	10.00
— Reissue withouth the "6" in the catalog number			
☐ SP-3288	Cuts Like a Knife	198?	10.00
— Budget-line reissue of 4919			
☐ SP-3907	Into the Fire	1987	10.00
☐ R153919	Into the Fire	1987	12.00
— BMG Direct Marketing edition			
☐ SP-5013	Reckless	1984	10.00
☐ R151540	Reckless	1984	12.00
— RCA Music Service edition			
☐ SP-17321 [DJ]	Retail Sampler	1985	30.00
— 10-song collection, a sort of "greatest hits" compilation to that time; promo only			
☐ SP-5327	Waking Up the Neighbours	1991	25.00
— Columbia House edition; the only U.S. vinyl of this LP			
☐ SP-4864	You Want It, You Got It	1981	15.00
☐ SP-3154	You Want It, You Got It	198?	10.00
— Budget-line reissue of 4864			

ADAMS, EDIE

Number	Title	Yr	NM
DECCA			
☐ DL4488 [M]	Behind Those Swingin' Doors	1964	30.00
☐ DL74488 [S]	Behind Those Swingin' Doors	1964	30.00
MGM			
☐ E-3751 [M]	Music to Listen to Records To	1959	50.00
☐ SE-3751 [S]	Music to Listen to Records To	1959	60.00

ADAMS, FAYE

Number	Title	Yr	NM
COLLECTABLES			
☐ COL-5122	Golden Classics	1988	12.00
WARWICK			
☐ W2031 [M]	Shake a Hand	1961	600.00

ADAMS, GEORGE-DANNIE RICHMOND QUARTET

Number	Title	Yr	NM
SOUL NOTE			
☐ SN-1057	Gentleman's Agreement	1983	15.00
☐ SN-1007	Hand to Hand	1980	15.00

ADAMS, GEORGE-DON PULLEN QUARTET

Number	Title	Yr	NM
BLUE NOTE			
☐ BLJ-46907	A Song Everlasting	1987	12.00
☐ BT-85122	Breakthrough	1986	12.00
SOUL NOTE			
☐ SN-1004	Don't Lose Control	198?	15.00
☐ SN-1094	Live at the Village Vanguard	1985	15.00
☐ 121144-1	Live at the Village Vanguard 2	199?	12.00
TIMELESS			
☐ LPSJP-147	Earth Beams	1990	15.00

ADAMS, GEORGE

Number	Title	Yr	NM
BLUE NOTE			
☐ B1-91984	Nightingale	1989	12.00
— Tenor sax			
ECM			
☐ 1141	Sound Suggestions	1979	15.00
TIMELESS			
☐ 322	Paradise Space Shuttle	1981	15.00

ADAMS, JERRI

Number	Title	Yr	NM
COLUMBIA			
☐ CL916 [M]	It's Cool Inside	1956	40.00
☐ CL1258 [M]	Play for Keeps	1958	40.00

ADAMS, JOHNNY

Number	Title	Yr	NM
ANALOGUE PRODUCTIONS			
☐ APP 028	Johnny Adams Sings Doc Pomus -- The Real Me	199?	25.00
ARIOLA AMERICA			
☐ SW50038	After All the Good Is Gone	1978	18.00
CHELSEA			
☐ CHL525	Stand By Me	1977	30.00
HEP ME			
☐ 159	Christmas in New Orleans	197?	18.00
ROUNDER			
☐ 2049	After Dark	1986	15.00
☐ 2044	From the Heart	1984	15.00
☐ 2059	Room with a View of the Blues	1988	15.00
☐ 2095	Walking on a Tightrope	1989	15.00
SSS INTERNATIONAL			
☐ 5	Heart and Soul	1969	25.00

ADAMS, KAY

Number	Title	Yr	NM
TOWER			
☐ ST5087	Alcohol & Tears	1968	25.00
☐ T5069 [M]	Make Mine Country	1967	30.00
☐ ST5069	Make Mine Country	1967	25.00
☐ T5033 [M]	Wheels & Tears	1966	30.00
☐ ST5033 [S]	Wheels & Tears	1966	30.00

ADAMS, MIKE, AND THE RED JACKETS

Number	Title	Yr	NM
CROWN			
☐ CLP-5312 [M]	Surfer's Beat	1963	30.00
☐ CST-312 [S]	Surfer's Beat	1963	30.00
— Black vinyl			
☐ CST-312 [S]	Surfer's Beat	1963	120.00
— Red vinyl			
☐ CLP-5255 [M]	Twist Contest	1962	30.00
☐ CST-255 [S]	Twist Contest	1962	30.00

ADAMS, NANCY

Number	Title	Yr	NM
MEGA			
☐ M31-1018	Nancy Adams and the Deer Creek Fundamentalists	1972	25.00

ADAMS, PEPPER, AND FRANK FOSTER

Number	Title	Yr	NM
MUSE			
☐ MR-5313	Generations	1986	18.00

ADAMS, PEPPER, AND JIMMY KNEPPER

Number	Title	Yr	NM
METROJAZZ			
☐ E-1004 [M]	The Pepper-Knepper Quintet	1958	200.00
☐ SE-1004 [S]	The Pepper-Knepper Quintet	1959	150.00

ADAMS, PEPPER

Number	Title	Yr	NM
BETHLEHEM			
☐ BCP-6056 [M]	Motor City Scene	1961	200.00
ENJA			
☐ 2060	Julian	1976	18.00
☐ 2074	Twelfth and Pingree	1976	25.00
FANTASY			
☐ OJC-031	10 to 4 at the 5 Spot	198?	15.00
— Reissue of Riverside 12-265			
INNER CITY			
☐ IC-3014	Julian	1976	15.00
INTERLUDE			
☐ MO-502 [M]	Pepper Adams 5	1959	80.00
— Reissue of Mode 112			
☐ ST-1002 [S]	Pepper Adams 5	1959	60.00
— Reissue of Mode 112; remixed into stereo; black vinyl			
☐ ST-1002 [S]	Pepper Adams 5	1959	100.00
— Orange vinyl			
MODE			
☐ LP-112 [M]	Pepper Adams 5	1957	150.00
— With Mel Lewis			
☐ 112 [S]	Quintet		100.00
MUSE			
☐ MR-5182	Reflectory	1979	25.00
☐ MR-5213	The Master	1980	18.00
PALO ALTO			
☐ PA-8009	Urban Dreams	1981	18.00
PRESTIGE			
☐ PRST-7677	Encounter	1969	25.00
— With Zoot Sims			
REGENT			
☐ MG-6066 [M]	The Cool Sound of Pepper Adams	1958	180.00
RIVERSIDE			
☐ RLP 12-265 [M]	10 to 4 at the 5 Spot	1958	200.00
☐ RLP-1104 [S]	10 to 4 at the 5 Spot	1959	100.00
— black label			
SAVOY			
☐ MG-12211 [M]	The Cool Sound of Pepper Adams	196?	40.00
— Reissue of Regent 6066			
SAVOY JAZZ			
☐ SJL-1142	Pure Pepper	198?	15.00
— Reissue of Savoy 12211			
WARWICK			
☐ W-2041 [M]	Out of This World	1961	100.00
— With Donald Byrd			
WORKSHOP JAZZ			
☐ WSJ-219 [M]	Pepper Adams Plays the Compositions of Charles Mingus	1964	150.00
☐ WSJS-219 [S]	Pepper Adams Plays the Compositions of Charles Mingus	1964	140.00
☐ 219 [S]	Plays Mingus		100.00
WORLD PACIFIC			
☐ PJM-407 [M]	Critic's Choice	1957	200.00
— With Mel Lewis			
☐ WPM-407 [M]	Critic's Choice	1958	100.00
— With Mel Lewis; reissue with new prefix			
ZIM			
☐ ZLS2000	Ephemera	197?	50.00

ADAMS, RYAN

Number	Title	Yr	NM
LOST HIGHWAY			
☐ B0005872-01	29	2005	25.00
☐ B0004343-01	Cold Roses	2005	30.00
— As "Ryan Adams and the Cardinals"			
☐ 088170333-1	Demolition	2002	30.00
☐ 088170235-1	Gold	2002	150.00
☐ B0004707-01	Jacksonville City Nights	2005	30.00
— As "Ryan Adams and the Cardinals"			
☐ B0001702-01 [10]	Love Is Hell Pts. 1 & 2	2003	80.00
— Combination of two EPs on two 10-inch records in gatefold sleeve			
☐ B0001376-01	Rock N Roll	2003	30.00

ADDEO, LEO

Number	Title	Yr	NM
RCA CAMDEN			
☐ CAL-807 [M]	Calypso and Other Island Favorites	1963	15.00
☐ CAS-807 [S]	Calypso and Other Island Favorites	1963	18.00
☐ CAL-901 [M]	Far Away Places	1965	15.00
☐ CAS-901 [S]	Far Away Places	1965	18.00

Number	Title	Yr	NM
❏ CAL-672 [M]	Great Standards with a Hawaiian Touch	1962	15.00
❏ CAS-672 [S]	Great Standards with a Hawaiian Touch	1962	18.00
❏ CAL-853 [M]	Hawaiian Paradise	1964	15.00
❏ CAS-853 [S]	Hawaiian Paradise	1964	18.00
❏ CAL-510 [M]	Hawaii in Hi-Fi	1960	18.00
❏ CAS-510 [S]	Hawaii in Stereo	1960	25.00
❏ CAL-828 [M]	Hello Dolly" and Other Favorites	1964	15.00
❏ CAS-828 [S]	Hello Dolly" and Other Favorites	1964	18.00
❏ CAL-2134 [M]	Love Is a Hurtin' Thing" and Other Favorites	1966	15.00
❏ CAS-2134 [S]	Love Is a Hurtin' Thing" and Other Favorites	1966	18.00
❏ CAL-594 [M]	More Hawaii in Hi-Fi	1961	18.00
❏ CAS-594 [S]	More Hawaii in Hi-Fi	1961	25.00
❏ CAL-977 [M]	Musical Orchids from Hawaii	1966	15.00
❏ CAS-977 [S]	Musical Orchids from Hawaii	1966	18.00
❏ CAL-726 [M]	Organ and Chimes Play Christmas Carols	1962	15.00
❏ CAS-726 [S]	Organ and Chimes Play Christmas Carols	1962	18.00
❏ CAL-759 [M]	Songs of Hawaii	1963	15.00
❏ CAS-759 [S]	Songs of Hawaii	1963	18.00
❏ CAL-2211 [M]	The Magic of Hawaii	1967	15.00
❏ CAS-2211 [S]	The Magic of Hawaii	1967	18.00

RCA VICTOR

Number	Title	Yr	NM
❏ LPM-2414 [M]	Paradise Regained	1961	18.00
❏ LSA-2414 [S]	Paradise Regained	1961	30.00

ADDERLEY, CANNONBALL

AMBASSADOR

Number	Title	Yr	NM
❏ S-98053	The Love Album	197?	18.00

BLUE NOTE

Number	Title	Yr	NM
❏ BLP-1595 [M]	Somethin' Else	1958	600.00
—Deep groove" version; W. 63rd St. address on label			
❏ BLP-1595 [M]	Somethin' Else	1958	120.00
—Regular version; W. 63rd St. address on label			
❏ BLP-1595 [M]	Somethin' Else	1963	50.00
—New York, USA" address on label			
❏ BST-1595 [S]	Somethin' Else	1959	150.00
—Deep groove" version; W. 63rd St. address on label			
❏ BST-1595 [S]	Somethin' Else	1959	100.00
—Regular version; W. 63rd St. address on label			
❏ BST-81595 [S]	Somethin' Else	1963	30.00
—New York, USA" address on label			
❏ BST-81595 [S]	Somethin' Else	1966	25.00
—With "A Division of Liberty Records" on label			
❏ BN-LA169-F	Somethin' Else	1973	15.00
—Reissue			
❏ LT-169	Somethin' Else	1981	12.00
—Another reissue			
❏ BST-81595	Somethin' Else	1984	12.00
—The Finest in Jazz Since 1939" label			
❏ ST-46338	Somethin' Else	1997	25.00
—Audiophile reissue			
❏ BST-81595	Somethin' Else	199?	30.00
—Classic Records reissue on 180-gram vinyl			
❏ BST-1595 [S]	Somethin' Else	2002	30.00
—Classic Records reissue on 200-gram vinyl			
❏ BLP-1595 [M]	Somethin' Else	2002	30.00
—Classic Records reissue on 200-gram vinyl			
❏ BLP-1595C	Somethin' Else	2002	50.00
—Comparison Pack"; contains both the mono and stereo versions of the LP; Classic Records issue on 200-gram vinyl			

CAPITOL

Number	Title	Yr	NM
❏ T2822 [M]	74 Miles Away -- Walk Tall	1967	40.00
❏ ST2822 [S]	74 Miles Away -- Walk Tall	1967	25.00
❏ ST2987	Accent on Africa	1968	25.00
❏ SWBO-812	Cannonball Adderley and Friends	1971	25.00
❏ SVBB-11233	Cannonball Adderley and Friends	1974	18.00
—Reissue of 812			
❏ SM-11817	Cannonball Adderley and Friends, Vol. 1	1978	12.00
❏ SM-11838	Cannonball Adderley and Friends, Vol. 2	1978	12.00
❏ ST-2877	Cannonball Adderley and the Bossa Rio Sextet with Sergio Mendes	1968	30.00
—Reissue of 8 of the 10 tracks from Riverside 9455			
❏ T2399 [M]	Cannonball Adderley -- Live!	1965	25.00
❏ ST2399 [S]	Cannonball Adderley -- Live!	1965	30.00
❏ SM-2399	Cannonball Adderley -- Live!	1976	12.00
❏ ST-162	Cannonball in Person	1968	25.00
❏ SKAO-404	Country Preacher	1970	30.00
❏ SKAO-80404	Country Preacher	1970	30.00
—Capitol Record Club edition			
❏ T2203 [M]	Domination	1964	25.00
❏ ST2203 [S]	Domination	1964	30.00
❏ ST-484	Experience in E, Tensity, Dialogues	1970	40.00
❏ T2216 [M]	Fiddler on the Roof	1965	25.00
❏ ST2216 [S]	Fiddler on the Roof	1965	30.00
❏ ST-11008	Fiddler on the Roof	1972	18.00
—Reissue of 2216			
❏ T2531 [M]	Great Love Themes	1966	25.00
❏ ST2531 [S]	Great Love Themes	1966	30.00
❏ ST-11121	Happy People	1973	40.00
❏ T2284 [M]	Live Session	1965	25.00
❏ ST2284 [S]	Live Session	1965	30.00

Number	Title	Yr	NM
❏ T2663 [M]	Mercy, Mercy, Mercy!	1967	25.00
❏ ST2663 [S]	Mercy, Mercy, Mercy!	1967	18.00
❏ SM-2663	Mercy, Mercy, Mercy!	1976	12.00
❏ SN-16153	Mercy, Mercy, Mercy!	1981	10.00
—Budget-line reissue			
❏ ST-8-2663 [S]	Mercy, Mercy, Mercy!	1969	25.00
—Capitol Record Club edition			
❏ ST-11484	Music, You All	1975	18.00
❏ SN-16002	The Best of Cannonball Adderley	1979	10.00
❏ SKAO2939	The Best of Cannonball Adderley	1968	18.00
—Black label with colorband			
❏ SKAO-502939	The Best of Cannonball Adderley	1976	18.00
—Columbia House edition; orange labels			
❏ SWBO-846	The Black Messiah	1972	100.00
❏ SWBB-636	The Price You Got to Pay to Be Free	1971	100.00
❏ SABB-11120	The Soul of the Bible	1973	120.00
—Reproductions exist			
❏ STBB-697	Walk Tall/Quiet Nights	1971	25.00
❏ T2617 [M]	Why Am I Treated So Bad?	1966	18.00
❏ ST2617 [S]	Why Am I Treated So Bad?	1966	25.00

DOBRE

Number	Title	Yr	NM
❏ 1008	Cannonball, Volume 1	1977	15.00

EMARCY

Number	Title	Yr	NM
❏ EMS-2-404	Beginnings	1976	25.00
❏ 36043 [B]	Cannonball		200.00
—drummer logo			
❏ MG-36135 [M]	Cannonball's Sharpshooters	1958	60.00
❏ MG-36077 [M]	In the Land of Hi-Fi	1956	100.00
❏ MG-36043 [M]	Julian "Cannonball" Adderley	1955	80.00
❏ MG-36063 [M]	Julian "Cannonball" Adderley and Strings	1956	80.00
❏ MG-36146 [M]	Jump for Joy	1958	80.00
❏ SR-80017 [S]	Jump for Joy	1958	60.00
❏ MG-36110 [M]	Sophisticated Swing	1957	70.00

EVEREST ARCHIVE OF FOLK & JAZZ

Number	Title	Yr	NM
❏ FS-261	Cannonball Adderley and John Coltrane	1973	15.00
—Abridged reissue of Limelight 86009			
❏ FS-291 [B]	Cannonball Adderley with Sergio Mendes	197?	15.00

FANTASY

Number	Title	Yr	NM
❏ OJC-258	African Waltz	1987	12.00
❏ F-79006	Big Man	1976	25.00
❏ OJC-035	Cannonball Adderley Quintet in San Francisco	1982	12.00
❏ OJC-142	Cannonball Adderley Sextet In New York	1985	12.00
❏ F-9435	Inside Straight	1973	25.00
❏ OJC-105	Know What I Mean?	1984	12.00
❏ F-9445	Love, Sex and the Zodiac	1974	100.00
❏ F-9505	Lovers	1975	40.00
❏ FSP2 [DJ]	Musical Highlights from Big Man	1975	30.00
❏ OJC-435	Nippon Soul	1990	18.00
❏ F-79004	Phenix	1975	30.00
❏ OJC-361	Portrait of Cannonball	1989	12.00
❏ F 9455	Pyramid	1974	40.00
❏ OJC-306	The Cannonball Adderley Quintet Plus	1988	12.00
❏ OJC-032	Things Are Getting Better	1982	12.00

LANDMARK

Number	Title	Yr	NM
❏ LLP-1301 [B]	The Cannonball Adderley Collection Vol. 1: Them Dirty Blues	1985	15.00
❏ LLP-1302 [B]	The Cannonball Adderley Collection Vol. 2: Cannonball's Bossa Nova	1985	15.00
❏ LLP-1303 [B]	The Cannonball Adderley Collection Vol. 3: Jazz Workshop Revisited	1985	15.00
❏ LLP-1304 [B]	The Cannonball Adderley Collection Vol. 4: Cannonball and the Poll-Winners	1985	15.00
❏ LLP-1305 [B]	The Cannonball Adderley Collection Vol. 5: At the Lighthouse	1985	15.00
❏ LLP-1306 [B]	The Cannonball Adderley Collection Vol. 6: Cannonball Takes Charge	1985	15.00
❏ LLP-1307 [B]	The Cannonball Adderley Collection Vol. 7: Cannonball in Europe	1985	15.00

LIMELIGHT

Number	Title	Yr	NM
❏ LM82009 [M]	Cannonball and Coltrane	1964	30.00
—Reissue of Mercury 20449			
❏ LS86009 [S]	Cannonball and Coltrane	1964	25.00
—Reissue of Mercury 60134			

MERCURY

Number	Title	Yr	NM
❏ MG-20449 [M]	Cannonball Adderley Quintet in Chicago	1959	100.00
❏ SR-60134 [S]	Cannonball Adderley Quintet in Chicago	1960	40.00
❏ MG-20616 [M]	Cannonball En Route	1961	50.00
❏ SR-60616 [S]	Cannonball En Route	1961	40.00
❏ MG-20531 [M]	Cannonball's Sharpshooters	1960	40.00
—Reissue of EmArcy 36135			
❏ SR-60531 [S]	Cannonball's Sharpshooters	1960	30.00
❏ SR-60530 [S]	Jump for Joy	1960	30.00
❏ MG-20530 [M]	Jump for Joy	1960	40.00
—Reissue of EmArcy 36146			
❏ MG-20652 [M]	The Lush Side of Cannonball Adderley	1961	40.00

Number	Title	Yr	NM
—Reissue of EmArcy 36063			
❏ SR-60652 [R]	The Lush Side of Cannonball Adderley	1961	30.00

MILESTONE

Number	Title	Yr	NM
❏ M-47059	Alabama/Africa	1982	18.00
❏ M-9030	Cannonball Adderley in New Orleans	197?	25.00
❏ M-47039	Coast to Coast	1976	30.00
❏ M-47001	Eight Giants	1973	18.00
❏ M-47029	The Japanese Concerts	1975	30.00
❏ M-9106	The Sextet	198?	18.00
❏ M-47053	What I Mean	1979	18.00

PABLO LIVE

Number	Title	Yr	NM
❏ 2308238	What Is This Thing Called Soul	1984	15.00

PICKWICK

Number	Title	Yr	NM
❏ SPC-3128	I Got It Bad and That Ain't Good	196?	12.00
❏ SPC-3255	Quiet Nights of Quiet Stars	196?	12.00
—Reissue of eight of the 10 tracks on Riverside 9455; co-credited to Sergio Mendes			

RIVERSIDE

Number	Title	Yr	NM
❏ RLP377 [M]	African Waltz	1961	50.00
❏ RS9377 [S]	African Waltz	1961	40.00
❏ RLP355 [M]	Cannonball Adderley and the Poll-Winners	1960	50.00
❏ RS9355 [S]	Cannonball Adderley and the Poll-Winners	1960	40.00
❏ RLP344 [M]	Cannonball Adderley Quintet at the Lighthouse	1960	50.00
❏ RS9344 [S]	Cannonball Adderley Quintet at the Lighthouse	1960	40.00
❏ RLP 12-311 [M]	Cannonball Adderley Quintet in San Francisco	1959	80.00
❏ RLP1157 [S]	Cannonball Adderley Quintet in San Francisco	1959	60.00
❏ 6062	Cannonball Adderley Quintet in San Francisco	197?	18.00
—Reissue of 1157			
❏ RLP388 [M]	Cannonball Adderley Quintet Plus	1961	50.00
❏ RS9388 [S]	Cannonball Adderley Quintet Plus	1961	40.00
❏ RLP404 [M]	Cannonball Adderley Sextet In New York	1962	100.00
—blue label			
❏ RS9404 [S]	Cannonball Adderley Sextet In New York	1962	40.00
❏ 6108	Cannonball Adderley Sextet In New York	197?	18.00
—Reissue of 9404			
❏ RM499 [M]	Cannonball in Europe	1964	40.00
❏ RS9499 [S]	Cannonball in Europe	1964	30.00
❏ RLP455 [M]	Cannonball's Bossa Nova	1963	40.00
❏ RS9455 [S]	Cannonball's Bossa Nova	1963	40.00
❏ RS9416 [S]	Cannonball's Greatest Hits	1962	40.00
❏ RLP416 [M]	Cannonball's Greatest Hits	1962	50.00
❏ RLP 12-303 [M]	Cannonball Takes Charge	1959	100.00
❏ RLP1148 [S]	Cannonball Takes Charge	1959	80.00
❏ RLP444 [M]	Jazz Workshop Revisited	1963	40.00
❏ RS9444 [S]	Jazz Workshop Revisited	1963	40.00
❏ RLP433 [M]	Know What I Mean?	1962	80.00
—blue label			
❏ RS9433 [S]	Know What I Mean?	1962	120.00
—black label			
❏ 6051	Know What I Mean?	197?	18.00
—Reissue of 9433			
❏ RLP477 [M]	Nippon Soul -- Recorded in Concert in Tokyo	1964	40.00
❏ RS9477 [S]	Nippon Soul -- Recorded in Concert in Tokyo	1964	40.00
❏ RS3041	Planet Earth	1969	40.00
❏ RLP 12-269 [M]	Portrait of Cannonball	1958	100.00
❏ RS3038	The Best of Cannonball Adderley	1968	30.00
❏ RLP 12-322 [M]	Them Dirty Blues	1960	80.00
❏ RLP1170 [S]	Them Dirty Blues	1960	60.00
❏ RLP 12-286 [M]	Things Are Getting Better	1959	150.00
—blue label			
❏ RLP1128 [S]	Things Are Getting Better	1959	80.00
❏ 6122	Things Are Getting Better	197?	18.00
—Reissue of 1128			

SAVOY

Number	Title	Yr	NM
❏ MG-12018 [M]	Presenting Cannonball	1955	150.00
—Band pictured on cover, red label			
❏ MG-12018 [M]	Presenting Cannonball	196?	80.00
—Cannonballs pictured on cover with band members merely listed			

SAVOY JAZZ

Number	Title	Yr	NM
❏ SJL-1195	Discoveries	1987	18.00
❏ SJC-401	Presenting Cannonball	1985	15.00
—Reissue of Savoy 12018			
❏ SJL-2206	Spontaneous Combustion	1976	18.00

SEARS

Number	Title	Yr	NM
❏ SPS-460	Jump for Joy	196?	18.00

TRIP

Number	Title	Yr	NM
❏ TLP-5573 [M]	In the Land of Hi-Fi	197?	18.00

WING

Number	Title	Yr	NM
❏ SRW-16362 [S]	Cannonball Adderley Quintet	196?	25.00

WONDERLAND/RIVERSIDE

Number	Title	Yr	NM
❏ RLP1435 [M]	A Child's Introduction to Jazz	196?	50.00
—Adderley narrates an album introducing the works of such artists as Armstrong, Monk, Waller, etc.			

Number	Title	Yr	NM

ADDERLEY, CANNONBALL AND NAT

LIMELIGHT
☐ LM82032 [M]	Them Adderleys	1966	50.00
☐ LS86032 [S]	Them Adderleys	1966	50.00

ADDERLEY, NAT

A&M
☐ SP-3017	Calling Out Loud	1969	18.00
☐ LP-2005 [M]	You, Baby	1968	30.00
—Mono is promo only			
☐ SP-3005	You, Baby	1968	18.00
☐ SP9-3005	You, Baby	1983	18.00
—Audio Master Plus" reissue			

ATLANTIC
☐ 1439 [M]	Autobiography	1965	18.00
☐ SD1439 [S]	Autobiography	1965	25.00
☐ 1475 [M]	Live at Memory Lane	1967	25.00
☐ SD1475 [S]	Live at Memory Lane	1967	18.00
☐ 1460 [M]	Sayin' Something	1966	18.00
☐ SD1460 [S]	Sayin' Something	1966	25.00

CAPITOL
☐ SVBB-11025	Cannonball Adderley Presents Soul Zodiac	1972	100.00

EMARCY
☐ MG-36091 [M]	Introducing Nat Adderley	1955	80.00
☐ MG-36100 [M]	To the Ivy League from Nat	1956	80.00

FANTASY
☐ OJC-255	Branching Out	1987	12.00
—Reissue of Riverside 12-285			
☐ OJC-648	In the Bag	1991	15.00
—Reissue of Jazzland 975			
☐ OJC-363	The Work Song	198?	12.00
—Reissue of Riverside 1167			

GALAXY
☐ 5120	Little New York Midtown Music	197?	12.00

JAZZLAND
☐ JLP-75 [M]	In the Bag	1962	30.00
☐ JLP-975 [S]	In the Bag	1962	40.00
☐ JLP-47 [M]	Naturally!	1961	30.00
☐ JLP-947 [S]	Naturally!	1961	40.00

LITTLE DAVID
☐ LD1012	Hummin'	1975	15.00

MILESTONE
☐ MSP-9009	Natural Soul	1968	18.00
☐ MSP-9016	The Scavenger	1968	18.00
☐ 47047	Work Songs	197?	15.00

PRESTIGE
☐ 10090	Double Exposure	1974	15.00

RIVERSIDE
☐ RLP 12-285 [M]	Branching Out	1958	50.00
☐ RM-474 [M]	Little Big Horn!	1964	30.00
☐ RS-9474 [S]	Little Big Horn!	1964	40.00
☐ RLP 12-301 [M]	Much Brass	1959	50.00
☐ RLP-1143 [S]	Much Brass	1959	50.00
☐ RLP-330 [M]	That's Right!	1960	30.00
☐ RS-9330 [S]	That's Right!	1960	40.00
☐ RLP 12-318 [M]	The Work Song	1960	40.00
☐ RLP-1167 [S]	The Work Song	1960	50.00
☐ 6041	The Work Song	197?	15.00
—Reissue			

SAVOY
☐ MG-12021 [M]	That's Nat	1955	80.00

SAVOY JAZZ
☐ SJL-1128	That's Nat	198?	12.00
—Reissue of Savoy 12021			

STEEPLECHASE
☐ SCS-1059	Don't Look Back	198?	12.00

THERESA
☐ TR-122	Blue Autumn	1987	12.00
☐ TR-117	On the Move	198?	12.00

WING
☐ MGW-60000 [M]	Introducing Nat Adderley	1956	50.00

ADRIAN AND THE SUNSETS

SUNSET
☐ 63-601 [M]	Breakthrough	1963	80.00
—Black vinyl			
☐ 63-601 [M]	Breakthrough	1963	150.00
—Multi-color vinyl			
☐ SD 63-601 [S]	Breakthrough	1963	150.00
—Black vinyl			
☐ SD 63-601 [S]	Breakthrough	1963	300.00
—Multi-color vinyl			

ADVANCEMENT, THE

PHILIPS
☐ PHS600328 [B]	The Advancement	1969	100.00

ADVENTURERS, THE (1)

COLUMBIA
☐ CL1747 [M]	Can't Stop Twistin'	1961	60.00
☐ CS8547 [S]	Can't Stop Twistin'	1961	80.00

ADVENTURES, THE

CHRYSALIS
☐ BFV41488	The Adventures	1985	12.00

ELEKTRA
☐ 60772	Sea of Love	1988	10.00
☐ 60772 [DJ]	Sea of Love	1988	15.00
—Ptomo-only audiophile pressing with sticker on cover			

AEROSMITH

COLUMBIA
☐ PC32005	Aerosmith	1976	12.00
—Without bar code			
☐ KC32005	Aerosmith	1973	25.00
—Orange cover with back cover typo "Walking The Dig			
☐ KC32005	Aerosmith	1973	18.00
—Orange cover with correct title "Walking The Dog			
☐ KC32005 [B]	Aerosmith	1973	15.00
—Light blue cover, most (if not all) of which say "Featuring 'Dream On'" on front			
☐ JC32005	Aerosmith	1977	10.00
☐ PC32005	Aerosmith	1984	10.00
—With bar code			
☐ 88765486131 [B]	Aerosmith	2013	25.00
☐ FC36865	Aerosmith's Greatest Hits	1980	12.00
☐ PC36865	Aerosmith's Greatest Hits	1984	10.00
☐ FC40329	Classics Live	1986	12.00
☐ FC40855	Classics Live, Vol. 2	1987	12.00
☐	Draw The Line	2014	25.00
88883760951 [B]			
☐ JC34856	Draw the Line	1977	15.00
☐ PC34856	Draw the Line	198?	10.00
☐ FC44487	Gems (1973-1982)	1989	12.00
☐ KC32847	Get Your Wings	1974	15.00
☐ PC32847	Get Your Wings	1976	12.00
—Without bar code			
☐ KCQ32847 [Q]	Get Your Wings	1974	30.00
☐ JC32847	Get Your Wings	1977	10.00
☐ PC32847	Get Your Wings	1984	10.00
—With bar code			
☐	Get Your Wings	2013	25.00
88765486151 [B]			
☐ C87025	Honkin' on Bobo	2004	18.00
☐ C62088	Just Push Play	2001	18.00
☐ PC235564	Live! Bootleg	1978	18.00
☐ FC36050	Night in the Ruts	1979	12.00
☐ PC36050	Night in the Ruts	1984	10.00
☐ A3S187 [DJ]	Pure Gold from Rock 'n' Roll's Golden Boys	1976	60.00
—Promo-only compilation of the first three albums			
☐	Rock In A Hard Place	2014	25.00
88883761441 [B]			
☐ FC38061	Rock in a Hard Place	1982	12.00
☐ PC38061	Rock in a Hard Place	1984	10.00
☐ PC34165	Rocks	1976	15.00
—Without bar code. Some copies have "Rocks" in quotes on the cover, others don't; no difference in value			
☐ JC34165	Rocks	1976	12.00
—Some copies have "Rocks" in quotes on the cover, others don't; no difference in value			
☐ PC34165	Rocks	1984	10.00
—With bar code			
☐ PCQ34165 [Q]	Rocks	1976	30.00
☐	Rocks	2014	25.00
88883760941 [B]			
☐	Toys In The Attic	2013	25.00
887654861917 [B]			
☐ PC33479	Toys in the Attic	1975	15.00
—Without bar code			
☐ JC33479	Toys in the Attic	1977	12.00
☐ PC33479	Toys in the Attic	1984	10.00
—With bar code			
☐ PCQ33479 [Q]	Toys in the Attic	1975	30.00

GEFFEN
☐ GHS24091	Done with Mirrors	1985	10.00
☐ GHS24162	Permanent Vacation	1987	12.00
☐ GHS24254	Pump	1989	12.00
☐ GHS24254	Pump	2008	25.00

AESOP'S FABLES

CADET CONCEPT
☐ LPS-323	In Due Time	1969	50.00

AFDEM, JEFF, AND THE SPRINGFIELD FLUTE

BURDETTE
☐ 5162	Something	1969	40.00

AFFECTION COLLECTION, THE

EVOLUTION
☐ 2007	The Affection Collection	1969	25.00

AFFINITY

PARAMOUNT
☐ PAS-5027	Affinity	1970	30.00

AFGHAN WHIGS

COLUMBIA
☐ C69450 [B]	1969	1998	30.00

SUB POP
☐ 353 [B]	Black Love	1996	30.00

☐ 130 [B]	Congregation	1992	30.00
—Import only; made in Germany (no U.S. vinyl)			
☐ 238 [B]	Gentlemen	1993	30.00
☐ 60 [B]	Up In It	1990	35.00
—First pressings have orange vinyl and a different sleeve than the black vinyl version			
☐ 60 [B]	Up In It	1990	18.00

ULTRASUEDE
☐ 001 [B]	Big Top Halloween	1988	80.00
—Approximately 2,000 copies were made			

AFI

ADELINE
☐ ADN30035-1 [B]	Decemberunderground	2006	18.00
☐ 026	Sing the Sorrow	2003	25.00
—All copies on red vinyl			

NITRO
☐ 15811	Answer That and Stay Fashionable	1997	15.00
—Reissue; available on black, white, red, tan or gray vinyl			
☐ 15824	Black Sails in the Sunset	1999	15.00
—Available on black, lilac or gray vinyl			
☐ 15815	Shut Your Mouth and Open Your Eyes	1997	15.00
—Available on black, green, yellow, tan, white or gray vinyl			
☐ 15835	The Art of Drowning	2000	15.00
—Available on black, gray, green and purplish vinyl			
☐ 15805	Very Proud of Ya	1996	15.00
—Black or blue vinyl			
☐ 15805	Very Proud of Ya	1996	12.00
—Any other color vinyl ("Special Colored Vinyl" sticker on cover or shinkwrap)			

WINGNUT
☐ WLRP-1370	Answer That and Stay Fashionable	1995	30.00
—First edition: Black vinyl; title on two lines on front cover; no address next to Wingnut logo on back			
☐ WLRP-1370	Answer That and Stay Fashionable	1995	30.00
—Second edition: Black vinyl; title on one line on front cover; address next to Wingnut logo on back			
☐ WLRP-1370	Answer That and Stay Fashionable	1995	50.00
—Third edition: Same as second edition, except on red vinyl			

AFRIKA CORPS

IRON CROSS/DACOIT
☐ (# unknown)0	Music to Kill By	1977	60.00

KLEEN KUT/LIMP
☐ (# unknown)0	Hello World!	1978	25.00
—As "The Korps"; blue vinyl			

AFTER THE FIRE

EPIC
☐ FE38282	ATF	1983	15.00

AGAPE

MARK
☐ MRS-2170 [B]	Gospel Hard Rock	1971	150.00

RENRUT
☐ 101 [B]	Victims of Tradition	1972	150.00

AGE OF REASON, THE

GEORGETOWNE
☐ (no #)	The Age of Reason	1969	150.00

AGENT ORANGE

CLEOPATRA
☐ 5543 [B]	Surf Punks		25.00

AGGREGATION, THE

LHI
☐ 12008	Mind Odyssey	1967	400.00

AGNOSTIC FRONT

COMBAT
☐ 8204	Liberty and Justice for...	1987	15.00
☐ 3022	One Voice	1992	18.00

COMBAT CORE
☐ CC8049	Cause for Alarm	1986	18.00
☐ CC8046	Victim in Pain	1986	18.00

EPITAPH
☐ 86567	Riot Riot Upstart	1999	15.00
☐ 86536	Something's Gotta Give	1998	15.00

IN EFFECT
☐ 3001	Live at CBGB's	1989	15.00

AGUILERA, CHRISTINA

RCA
☐ 82876-82639-1	Back to Basics	2006	50.00
—In oversize "album-style" packaging with fold-open cover			
☐ 07863-68037-1	Stripped	2002	18.00

AHBEZ, EDEN

DEL-FI
☐ DFLP-1211 [M]	Eden's Island	1960	150.00

Number	Title	Yr	NM
❑ DFST-1211 [S]	Eden's Island	1960	200.00

AIR SUPPLY

ARISTA
Number	Title	Yr	NM
❑ AL-8283	Air Supply	1985	10.00
❑ AL-8024	Greatest Hits	1983	10.00
❑ AL-8426	Hearts in Motion	1986	10.00
❑ AL-4268	Lost in Love	1980	10.00
❑ AL-9587	Now and Forever	1982	10.00
❑ AL-8528	The Christmas Album	1987	12.00
❑ AL-9551	The One That You Love	1981	10.00

COLUMBIA
❑ JC35047	Love and Other Bruises	1977	18.00
❑ PC35047	Love and Other Bruises	1981	10.00

—Budget-line reissue; much more common than the original "JC" version

MOBILE FIDELITY
❑ 1-113	The One That You Love	1983	25.00

—Audiophile vinyl

NAUTILUS
❑ NR-31	Lost in Love	1982	25.00

—Audiophile vinyl

AIRTO

ACCORD
❑ SN-7184	Brazilian Heatwave	1982	12.00

ARISTA
❑ AL4068	Identity	1975	12.00
❑ AL4116	Promises of the Sun	1976	12.00

BUDDAH
❑ BDS-21-SK	Natural Feelings	1970	18.00
❑ BDS-5085	Seeds on the Ground	1971	18.00
❑ BDA-5668	The Essential ... Airto	197?	18.00

CTI
❑ 6028	Fingers	1973	15.00
❑ CTSQ-6028 [Q]	Fingers	1974	25.00
❑ 6020	Free	1972	15.00
❑ 8000	Free	197?	12.00

—Reissue of 6020

SALVATION
❑ 701	Virgin Land	1974	15.00

WARNER BROS.
❑ BS3084	I'm Fine, How Are You?	1977	12.00
❑ BSK3279	Touching You, Touching Me	1979	12.00

AKENS, JEWEL

ERA
❑ EL-110 [M]	The Birds and the Bees	1965	30.00
❑ ES-110 [S]	The Birds and the Bees	1965	100.00

AKIYOSHI, TOSHIKO, AND LEON SASH

VERVE
❑ MGV-8236 [M]	Toshiko and Leon Sash at Newport	1958	60.00
❑ V-8236 [M]	Toshiko and Leon Sash at Newport	1961	30.00

AKIYOSHI, TOSHIKO-LEW TABACKIN BIG BAND

JAM
❑ 003	Farewell to Mingus	1981	12.00
❑ 006	Tanuki's Night Out	1982	12.00

RCA VICTOR
❑ AFL1-2678	Insights	1978	15.00
❑ AFL1-3019	Kogun	1979	15.00

—Recorded in 1974

❑ JPL1-1350	Long Yellow Road	1976	18.00
❑ AFL1-1350	Long Yellow Road	1978	12.00

—Reissue with new prefix

❑ CPL2-2242	Road Time	1977	25.00
❑ JPL1-0723	Tales of a Courtesan	1976	18.00
❑ AFL1-0723	Tales of a Courtesan	1978	12.00

—Reissue with new prefix

AKIYOSHI, TOSHIKO

CANDID
❑ CD-8015 [M]	Toshiko Mariano	1960	40.00
❑ CS-9015 [S]	Toshiko Mariano	1960	50.00
❑ CD-8012 [M]	Toshiko Mariano Quartet	1960	40.00
❑ CS-9012 [S]	Toshiko Mariano Quartet	1960	50.00

CONCORD JAZZ
❑ CJ-69	Finesse	1978	12.00
❑ CJ-324	Interlude	1987	12.00

DAUNTLESS
❑ DM-4308 [M]	The Country and Western Sounds of Jazz	1963	40.00
❑ DS-6308 [S]	The Country and Western Sounds of Jazz	1963	50.00

INNER CITY
❑ 6046	Dedications	1977	15.00
❑ 6066	Notorious Tourist from the East	1978	15.00

METROJAZZ
❑ E-1001 [M]	United Notions	1958	50.00
❑ SE-1001 [S]	United Notions	1959	40.00

NORGRAN
❑ MGN-22 [10]	Toshiko's Piano	1954	150.00

STORYVILLE
Number	Title	Yr	NM
❑ STLP-912 [M]	The Toshiko Trio	1956	200.00
❑ STLP-918 [M]	Toshiko Akiyoshi, Her Trio, Her Quartet	1957	60.00

VEE JAY
❑ LP-2505 [M]	Jazz in Japan	1964	30.00

—As "Toshiko Mariano and Her Big Band"

VERVE
❑ MGV-8273 [M]	The Many Sides of Toshiko	1958	60.00
❑ V-8273 [M]	The Many Sides of Toshiko	1961	30.00

AKKERMAN, JAN

ATCO
❑ SD7032	Tabernakel	1974	15.00

ATLANTIC
❑ SD18210	Eli	1977	12.00
❑ SD19159	Jan Akkerman	1978	12.00

SIRE
❑ SAS7407	Profile	1973	18.00

ALABAMA

ACCORD
❑ SN-7132	Pride of Dixie	1981	12.00

ALABAMA
❑ ALA-78-9-01	The Alabama Band	1978	400.00

HEARTLAND
❑ HL1186/7	The Very Best of Alabama	1992	18.00

LSI
❑ 0177	Deuces Wild	1977	1200.00

—As "Wild Country"

❑ 0275	Wild Country	1975	1500.00

—As "Wild Country"; VG value 750; VG+ value 1125

PLANTATION
❑ 44	Wild Country	1981	60.00

RCA
❑ 6825-1-R	Alabama Live	1988	10.00
❑ 6495-1-R	Just Us	1987	10.00
❑ 9574-1-RDJ [DJ]	Open-Ended Interview	1988	30.00
❑ 8587-1-R	Southern Star	1989	10.00
❑ 5649-1-R	The Touch	1986	10.00

RCA VICTOR
❑ AHL1-5339	40 Hour Week	1985	10.00
❑ ASL1-7014	Christmas	1985	15.00

—Original copies have gold embossed letters on cover

❑ ASL1-7014	Christmas	1986	12.00

—Later copies have white non-embossed letters on cover

❑ AHL1-3930	Feels So Right	1981	10.00
❑ AHL1-7170	Greatest Hits	1986	10.00
❑ AHL1-4229	Mountain Music	1982	10.00
❑ AHL1-3644	My Home's in Alabama	1980	18.00
❑ AYL1-3644	My Home's in Alabama	1986	10.00

—Best Buy Series" reissue

❑ AHL1-4939	Roll On	1984	10.00
❑ AHL1-4663	The Closer You Get	1983	10.00

SOUTHWAYS
❑ 101	Pride of Dixie	1981	12.00

—Same album as on Accord

ALAIMO, STEVE

ABC-PARAMOUNT
❑ 501 [M]	Starring Steve Alaimo	1965	40.00
❑ S-501 [S]	Starring Steve Alaimo	1965	50.00
❑ 551 [M]	Steve Alaimo Sings and Swings	1966	40.00
❑ S-551 [S]	Steve Alaimo Sings and Swings	1966	50.00
❑ 531 [M]	Where the Action Is	1965	40.00
❑ S-531 [S]	Where the Action Is	1965	50.00

CHECKER
❑ LP-2986 [M]	Every Day I Have to Cry	1963	150.00
❑ LP-2983 [M]	Mashed Potatoes	1962	150.00
❑ LP-2981 [M]	Twist with Steve Alaimo	1962	150.00

CROWN
❑ CLP-5382 [M]	Steve Alaimo	1963	30.00
❑ CST-382 [R]	Steve Alaimo	1963	18.00

ALAN, BUDDY, AND DON RICH

CAPITOL
❑ ST-769	We're Real Good Friends	1971	25.00

ALAN, BUDDY

CAPITOL
❑ ST-592	Whole Lot of Somethin'	1970	25.00

ALARM, THE

I.R.S.
❑ 82018	Change	1989	12.00
❑ SP70608	Declaration	1984	12.00
❑ 39108	Electric Folklore Live	1988	12.00
❑ 42001	Eye of the Hurricane	1987	12.00
❑ 5666	Strength	1985	12.00
❑ SP70504 [EP]	The Alarm	1984	14.00

ALBAM, MANNY

ABC IMPULSE!
❑ AS-19 [S]	Jazz Goes to the Movies	196?	15.00

—Reissue of Impulse! AS-19

CORAL
Number	Title	Yr	NM
❑ CRL59102 [M]	A Gallery of Gershwin	1958	40.00
❑ CRL57231 [M]	Sophisticated Lady -- The Songs of Duke Ellington	1958	40.00
❑ CRL59101 [M]	The Blues Is Everybody's Business	195?	40.00
❑ CRL57142 [M]	The Jazz Greats of Our Time	1957	40.00
❑ CRL57173 [M]	The Jazz Greats of Our Time, Volume 2	1957	40.00
❑ CRL57207 [M]	West Side Story	1958	40.00

DECCA
❑ DL4517 [M]	Music from West Side Story	1964	18.00
❑ DL74517 [S]	Music from West Side Story	1964	25.00

DOT
❑ DLP-9004 [M]	Jazz New York	1958	40.00
❑ DLP-9008 [M]	Steve's Song	1958	40.00

IMPULSE!
❑ A-19 [M]	Jazz Goes to the Movies	1962	30.00
❑ AS-19 [S]	Jazz Goes to the Movies	1962	30.00

MCA
❑ 1376	The Jazz Greats of Our Time	198?	15.00

MERCURY
❑ MG-20325 [M]	With All My Love	1958	40.00

RCA VICTOR
❑ LPM-2508 [M]	I Had the Craziest Dream	1962	25.00
❑ LSA-2508 [S]	I Had the Craziest Dream	1962	30.00
❑ LPM-2432 [M]	More Double Exposure	1961	25.00
❑ LSA-2432 [S]	More Double Exposure	1961	30.00
❑ LPM-1279 [M]	The Drum Suite	1956	50.00
❑ LPM-1211 [M]	The RCA Victor Jazz Workshop	1956	50.00

SOLID STATE
❑ SM-17000 [M]	Brass on Fire	1966	18.00
❑ SS-18000 [S]	Brass on Fire	1966	25.00
❑ SM-17009 [M]	The Soul of the City	1966	25.00
❑ SS-18009 [S]	The Soul of the City	1966	18.00

TOP RANK
❑ RM-313 [M]	Double Exposure	1960	40.00

UNITED ARTISTS
❑ UAL-3079 [M]	Drum Feast	1959	30.00
❑ UAS-6079 [S]	Drum Feast	1959	40.00

VOCALION
❑ VL3678 [M]	West Side Story	196?	18.00

ALBANY, JOE, AND NIELS-HENNING ORSTED PEDERSEN

INNER CITY
❑ IC-2019	Two's Company	1976	18.00

STEEPLECHASE
❑ SCS-1019	Two's Company	198?	18.00

—Reissue of Inner City 2019

ALBANY, JOE, AND WARNE MARSH

FANTASY
❑ OJC-1749 [M]	The Right Combination	1990	18.00

—Reissue of Riverside 12-270

RIVERSIDE
❑ RLP 12-270 [M]	The Right Combination	1958	120.00

ALBANY, JOE

ELEKTRA/MUSICIAN
❑ 60161	Portrait of an Artist	1983	15.00

INNER CITY
❑ IC-2003	Birdtown Birds	1976	30.00

INTERPLAY
❑ IP-7723	Bird Lives!	1979	25.00

REVELATION
❑ 25	At Home Alone	197?	30.00
❑ 16	Proto-Bopper	197?	30.00

RIVERSIDE
❑ RS-3023	The Legendary Jazz Pianist	1968	25.00

SEABREEZE
❑ SB-1004	The Albany Touch	1977	30.00

STEEPLECHASE
❑ SCS-1003	Birdtown Birds	198?	18.00

—Reissue of Inner City 2003

ALBERT, EDDIE

COLUMBIA
❑ CL2599 [M]	The Eddie Albert Album	1967	25.00
❑ CS9399 [S]	The Eddie Albert Album	1967	25.00

DOT
❑ DLP-3109 [M]	High Upon a Mountain	1958	25.00
❑ DLP-25109 [S]	High Upon a Mountain	1958	30.00

HAMILTON
❑ HLP-103 [DJ]	Oh, What a Beautiful Mornin'	1959	15.00
❑ HLP-12103 [S]	Oh, What a Beautiful Mornin'	1959	18.00

KAPP
❑ KL-1017 [M]	Eddie Albert and Margo	1956	30.00
❑ KL-1000 [M]	One God	1954	30.00
❑ KL-1083 [M]	September Song	1958	30.00

ALBERT, EDDIE

PICCADILLY

Number	Title	Yr	NM
PIC-3374	Take Me Home	1980	18.00

WONDERLAND

Number	Title	Yr	NM
WLP-5000	Eddie Albert Sings and Narrates Americana	1975	18.00

ALBERT, MORRIS

RCA VICTOR

Number	Title	Yr	NM
APL1-1018	Feelings	1975	10.00
APL1-1496	Morris Albert	1976	10.00

ALBERT, THE

PERCEPTION

Number	Title	Yr	NM
9 [B]	The Albert	1971	30.00

ALBERTS, AL

CORAL

Number	Title	Yr	NM
CRL57259 [M]	A Man Has Got to Sing	1959	30.00
CRL757259 [S]	A Man Has Got to Sing	1959	30.00

ALBRIGHT, LOLA

COLUMBIA

Number	Title	Yr	NM
CL1327 [M]	Dreamsville	1959	40.00
CS8133 [S]	Dreamsville	1959	50.00

ALBRIGHT, MAX

MOTIF

Number	Title	Yr	NM
502 [M]	Mood for Max	1956	60.00

ALCATRAZZ

CAPITOL

Number	Title	Yr	NM
ST-12477	Dangerous Games	1986	25.00
ST-12385	Disturbing the Peace	1985	25.00

CLEOPATRA

Number	Title	Yr	NM
8745 [B]	Live '83		25.00

ROCSHIRE

Number	Title	Yr	NM
22020	Live Sentence	1984	25.00
22016	No Parole from Rock 'n' Roll	1983	30.00

ALCOA SINGERS, THE

ALCOA

Number	Title	Yr	NM
44-4184--J	Old-Fashioned Christmas, An	1979	15.00

ALDA, ROBERT

ROULETTE

Number	Title	Yr	NM
R-25006 [M]	Robert Alda	1959	30.00
SR-25006 [S]	Robert Alda	1959	30.00

LDEN, HOWARD-DAN BARRETT QUINTET

CONCORD JAZZ

Number	Title	Yr	NM
CJ-349	Swing Street	1988	12.00

ALDEN, HOWARD

CONCORD JAZZ

Number	Title	Yr	NM
CJ-378	The Howard Alden Trio	1988	12.00

FAMOUS DOOR

Number	Title	Yr	NM
HL-154	Swinging Into Prominence	1988	12.00

STOMP OFF

Number	Title	Yr	NM
SOS-1200	Howard Alden Plays the Music of Harry Reser	1991	15.00

ALEEM FEATURING LEROY BURGESS

ATLANTIC

Number	Title	Yr	NM
81622	Casually Formal	1986	10.00
81784	Shock!	1987	10.00

ALEONG, ALI, AND THE NOBLES

REPRISE

Number	Title	Yr	NM
R-6020 [M]	C'mon Baby, Let's Dance	1962	30.00
R9-6020 [S]	C'mon Baby, Let's Dance	1962	30.00
R-6011 [M]	Twistin' the Hits	1962	30.00
R9-6011 [S]	Twistin' the Hits	1962	30.00

VEE JAY

Number	Title	Yr	NM
LP-1060 [M]	Come Surf with Me	1963	30.00
SR-1060 [S]	Come Surf with Me	1963	50.00

ALESS, TONY

ROOST

Number	Title	Yr	NM
RST-2202 [M]	Tony Aless and His Long Island Suite	1955	80.00

ALESSI

A&M

Number	Title	Yr	NM
SP-4608	Alessi	1976	12.00
SP-4657	All for a Reason	1977	12.00
SP-4713	Driftin'	1978	12.00
SP-4776	Words and Music	1979	12.00

QWEST

Number	Title	Yr	NM
BSK3670	Long Time Friends	1982	12.00

ALEXANDER, ARTHUR

DOT

Number	Title	Yr	NM
DLP3434 [M]	You Better Move On	1962	100.00
DLP25434 [S]	You Better Move On	1962	160.00

WARNER BROS.

Number	Title	Yr	NM
BS2592	Arthur Alexander	1972	30.00

ALEXANDER, DANIELE

MERCURY

Number	Title	Yr	NM
838352-1	First Move	1989	15.00

ALEXANDER, JOE, AND TIMMONS, BOBBY

JAZZLAND

Number	Title	Yr	NM
JLP-23 [M]	Blue Jubilee	1960	200.00
—orange label			
JLP-923 [S]	Blue Jubilee	1960	40.00

ALEXANDER, MONTY, AND ERNEST RANGLIN

PAUSA

Number	Title	Yr	NM
7110	Just Friends	198?	12.00

ALEXANDER, MONTY

BASF

Number	Title	Yr	NM
20913	Here Comes the Sun	197?	15.00
25352	Rass!	197?	15.00
25103	We've Only Just Begun	1972	15.00

CONCORD JAZZ

Number	Title	Yr	NM
CJ-108	Facets	1980	12.00
CJ-287	Full Steam Ahead	1985	12.00
CJ-231	Reunion in Europe	1984	12.00
— With John Clayton and Jeff Hamilton			

CONCORD PICANTE

Number	Title	Yr	NM
CJP-124	Ivory and Steel	1981	12.00
CJP-359	Jamboree	1988	12.00

MGM

Number	Title	Yr	NM
SE-4736	Taste of Freedom	1971	18.00

PABLO

Number	Title	Yr	NM
2310826	Jamento	1978	15.00
2310836	Monty Alexander in Tokyo	1979	15.00

PACIFIC JAZZ

Number	Title	Yr	NM
PJ-86 [M]	Alexander the Great	1966	25.00
ST-86 [S]	Alexander the Great	1966	30.00
PJ-10094 [M]	Spooky	1966	25.00
ST-20094 [S]	Spooky	1966	30.00

PAUSA

Number	Title	Yr	NM
7083	Montreux Alexander Live	197?	15.00
7032	Now Is the Time	197?	15.00
7129	With Love	198?	12.00

RCA VICTOR

Number	Title	Yr	NM
LPM-3930 [M]	Zing	1968	30.00
LSP-3930 [S]	Zing	1968	18.00

VERVE

Number	Title	Yr	NM
V6-8790	This Is Monty Alexander	1970	18.00

VERVE/MPS

Number	Title	Yr	NM
821151-1	The Duke Ellington Songbook	1984	12.00

ALEXANDER, MONTY / NIELS-HENNING ORSTED PEDERSEN / GRADY TATE

SOUL NOTE

Number	Title	Yr	NM
121152-1	Threesome	198?	15.00

ALEXANDER, MONTY / RAY BROWN / HERB ELLIS

CONCORD JAZZ

Number	Title	Yr	NM
CJ-253	Overseas Special	1983	12.00
CJ-136	Trio	1981	12.00
CJ-193	Triple Treat	1982	12.00
CJ-338	Triple Treat II	1988	12.00
CJ-394	Triple Treat III	1989	12.00

ALEXANDER, ROLAND

NEW JAZZ

Number	Title	Yr	NM
NJLP-8267 [M]	Pleasure Bent	1962	50.00
—Purple label			
NJLP-8267 [M]	Pleasure Bent	1965	30.00
—Blue label, trident at right			

ALEXANDER'S TIMELESS BLOOZBAND

SMASK

Number	Title	Yr	NM
1001 [M]	Alexander's Timeless Bloozband	1967	200.00

UNI

Number	Title	Yr	NM
73021	For Sale	1968	30.00

ALEXANDRIA, LOREZ

ABC IMPULSE!

Number	Title	Yr	NM
AS-62	Alexandria the Great	1968	25.00
—Reissue of Impulse! AS-62			
AS-76 [B]	More of the Great Lorez Alexandria	1968	25.00
—Reissue of Impulse! AS-76			

ARGO

Number	Title	Yr	NM
LP-694 [M]	Deep Roots	1962	70.00
LPS-694 [S]	Deep Roots	1962	100.00
LP-663 [M]	Early in the Morning	1960	70.00
LPS-663 [S]	Early in the Morning	1960	100.00
—With the Ramsey Lewis Trio			

Number	Title	Yr	NM
LP-720 [M]	For Swingers Only	1963	70.00
LPS-720 [S]	For Swingers Only	1963	100.00
LP-682 [M]	Sing No Sad Songs for Me	1961	70.00
LPS-682 [S]	Sing No Sad Songs for Me	1961	100.00

CADET

Number	Title	Yr	NM
LPS-682	Sing No Sad Songs for Me	1966	30.00
—Reissue of Argo 682			

DISCOVERY

Number	Title	Yr	NM
DS-800	A Woman Knows	1979	50.00
DS-905	Harlem Butterfly (Sings the Songs of Johnny Mercer Vol. 2)	1984	25.00
DS-782	How Will I Remember You?	1978	60.00
DS-826	Lorez Alexandria Sings Johnny Mercer	1981	30.00

IMPULSE!

Number	Title	Yr	NM
A-62 [M]	Alexandria the Great	1964	40.00
AS-62 [S]	Alexandria the Great	1964	50.00
A-76 [M]	More of the Great Lorez Alexandria	1965	40.00
AS-76 [S]	More of the Great Lorez Alexandria	1965	50.00

KING

Number	Title	Yr	NM
565 [M]	Lorez Sings Prez	1956	200.00
—Black label, crownless "King			
676 [M]	Singing Songs Everyone Knows	1959	200.00
—Black label, crownless "King			
657 [M]	The Band Swings, Lorez Sings	1959	200.00
—Black label, crownless "King			
S-657 [S]	The Band Swings, Lorez Sings	1959	300.00
—Dark blue label, crownless "King			
542 [M]	This Is Lorez	1956	200.00
—Black label, crownless "King			

MCA

Number	Title	Yr	NM
29000	Alexandria the Great	198?	12.00
—Reissue of ABC Impulse! AS-62			

PZAZZ

Number	Title	Yr	NM
LP-320	Didn't We	1968	50.00
LP-324	In a Different Bag	1969	30.00

TREND

Number	Title	Yr	NM
TR-547	Dear to My Heart	1988	18.00
TR-538	Tangerine (Sings the Songs of Johnny Mercer Vol. 3)	1986	18.00

ALFRED, CHUZ

SAVOY

Number	Title	Yr	NM
MG-12030 [M]	Jazz Young Blood	1955	60.00
—With Ola Hanson and Chuck Lee			

ALIAS

MERCURY

Number	Title	Yr	NM
SRM-1-3800	Contraband	1979	12.00

ALICE IN CHAINS

COLUMBIA

Number	Title	Yr	NM
C267248	Alice in Chains	1995	30.00
C257804 [B]	Jar of Flies/Sap	1994	35.00
—Two cassette/CD EP releases in one vinyl package			
CAS2192 [EP]	We Die Young	1990	60.00
—Five-song promo-only issue predating their first LP			

ALIEN SEX FIEND

CAROLINE

Number	Title	Yr	NM
CAROL1370 [B]	Another Planet	1988	30.00

CLEOPATRA

Number	Title	Yr	NM
CLP2221 [B]	Bat Cave Anthems	2008	30.00

EPITAPH

Number	Title	Yr	NM
ASFLP2 [B]	Acid Bath	1985	30.00

PVC

Number	Title	Yr	NM
PVC8960 [B]	Here Cum Germs	1987	40.00
PVC6917 [B]	The Impossible Mission	1987	25.00

RELATIVITY

Number	Title	Yr	NM
EMC8002 [B]	Who's Been Sleeping In My Brain?	1984	40.00

ALIOTTA-HAYNES-JEREMIAH

AMPEX

Number	Title	Yr	NM
A-10119	Aliotta-Haynes-Jeremiah	1970	25.00
A-10108	Aliotta-Haynes Music	1970	25.00
—As "Aliota-Haynes			

BIG FOOT

Number	Title	Yr	NM
714	Lake Shore Drive	1978	30.00

LITTLE FOOT

Number	Title	Yr	NM
711	Slippin' Away	1977	25.00

ALISHA

MCA

Number	Title	Yr	NM
6378	Bounce Back	1990	12.00

RCA

Number	Title	Yr	NM
6248-1-R	Nightwalkin'	1987	12.00

Number	Title	Yr	NM

VANGUARD
| ❑ VSD-79456 | Alisha | 1985 | 15.00 |

ALIVE AND KICKING

ROULETTE
| ❑ SR42052 | Alive and Kicking | 1970 | 25.00 |

ALL AMERICAN RUMBLERS, THE

GONE
| ❑ LP-5006 [M] | Destination Dixie | 1959 | 50.00 |

ALL STARS, THE

GRAMOPHONE
| ❑ 20192 | Boogie Woogie | 196? | 50.00 |

ALLAN, DAVIE, AND THE ARROWS

TOWER
❑ T5002 [M]	Apache '65	1965	40.00
❑ DT5002 [R]	Apache '65	1965	30.00
❑ T5078 [M]	Blues Theme	1967	50.00
❑ DT5078 [R]	Blues Theme	1967	40.00
❑ DT5094 [R]	Cycle-Delic Sounds	1968	80.00
❑ T5094 [M]	Cycle-Delic Sounds	1968	100.00
❑ T5074 [M]	Devil's Angel	1967	60.00
❑ DT5074 [R]	Devil's Angel	1967	25.00
❑ T5083 [M]	Mondo Hollywood	1968	80.00
❑ DT5083 [R]	Mondo Hollywood	1968	25.00
❑ T5043 [M]	The Wild Angels	1966	30.00
❑ DT5043 [R]	The Wild Angels	1966	25.00
❑ T5056 [M]	The Wild Angels, Vol. II	1967	60.00
❑ DT5056 [R]	The Wild Angels, Vol. II	1967	25.00

ALLEN, BYRON, TRIO

ESP-DISK'
| ❑ 1005 [M] | The Byron Allen Trio | 1965 | 25.00 |
| ❑ S-1005 [S] | The Byron Allen Trio | 1965 | 30.00 |

ALLEN, DAVE

INTERNATIONAL ARTISTS
| ❑ 11 | Color Blind | 1969 | 60.00 |
—Original pressing
| ❑ 11 | Color Blind | 1979 | 25.00 |
—Repressing with "RE2" and "Masterfonics" in dead wax

ALLEN, DAVID

EVEREST
| ❑ LP-5224 [M] | David Allen | 1964 | 18.00 |
| ❑ SD-1224 [S] | David Allen | 1964 | 25.00 |

PACIFIC JAZZ
| ❑ PJM-408 [M] | A Sure Thing | 1957 | 60.00 |
| ❑ ST-1006 [S] | A Sure Thing | 1959 | 60.00 |

WORLD PACIFIC
❑ WP-1295 [M]	David Allen Sings the Jerome Kern Songbook	1960	30.00
❑ ST-1295 [S]	David Allen Sings the Jerome Kern Songbook	1960	30.00
❑ WP-1250 [M]	Let's Face the Music and Dance	1958	40.00

ALLEN, DAYTON

GRAND AWARD
| ❑ GA-33-424 [M] | Why Not? | 1960 | 30.00 |

ALLEN, DEBBIE

MCA
| ❑ 6317 | Special Look | 1989 | 12.00 |

ALLEN, HENRY "RED", AND KID ORY

VERVE
❑ MGV-1018 [M]	Henry "Red" Allen Meets Kid Ory	1957	50.00
❑ V-1018 [M]	Henry "Red" Allen Meets Kid Ory	1961	25.00
❑ MGVS-6076 [S]	Henry "Red" Allen Meets Kid Ory	1959	40.00
❑ V6-1018 [S]	Henry "Red" Allen Meets Kid Ory	1961	25.00
❑ MGV-1020 [M]	We've Got Rhythm	1958	50.00
❑ V-1020 [M]	We've Got Rhythm	1961	25.00
❑ MGVS-6121 [S]	We've Got Rhythm	1959	40.00
❑ V6-1020 [S]	We've Got Rhythm	1961	25.00

ALLEN, HENRY "RED", AND RED NORVO

BRUNSWICK
| ❑ BL58044 [10] | Battle of Jazz, Vol. 6 | 1953 | 60.00 |

ALLEN, HENRY "RED"; JACK TEAGARDEN; KID ORY

VERVE
❑ MGV-8233 [M]	Red Allen, Jack Teagarden & Kid Ory at Newport	1958	50.00
❑ V-8233 [M]	Red Allen, Jack Teagarden & Kid Ory at Newport	1961	25.00
❑ UMV-2624	Verve at Newport	198?	12.00

ALLEN, HENRY "RED

AMERICAN RECORDING SOCIETY
| ❑ G-436 [M] | Traditional Jazz | 195? | 40.00 |

COLUMBIA
| ❑ CL2447 [M] | Feelin' Good | 1966 | 18.00 |
| ❑ CS9247 [S] | Feelin' Good | 1966 | 25.00 |

PRESTIGE
| ❑ PRST-7755 | Memorial Album | 1968 | 18.00 |

RCA VICTOR
| ❑ LPV-556 [M] | Henry "Red" Allen | 1965 | 25.00 |
| ❑ LPM-1509 [M] | Ride, Red, Ride in Hi-Fi | 1957 | 50.00 |

SWINGVILLE
| ❑ SWLP-2034 [M] | Mr. Allen | 1962 | 40.00 |
—Purple label
| ❑ SWLP-2034 [M] | Mr. Allen | 1965 | 25.00 |
—Blue label, trident logo at right
| ❑ SWST-2034 [S] | Mr. Allen | 1962 | 50.00 |
—Red label
| ❑ SWST-2034 [S] | Mr. Allen | 1965 | 30.00 |
—Blue label, trident logo at right

TIME-LIFE
| ❑ STL-J-16 | Giants of Jazz | 1981 | 25.00 |

VERVE
❑ MGV-1025 [M]	Red Allen Plays King Oliver	1959	50.00
❑ V-1025 [M]	Red Allen Plays King Oliver	1961	25.00
❑ V6-1025 [S]	Red Allen Plays King Oliver	1961	30.00

X
| ❑ LVA-3033 [M] | Ridin' with Red | 1955 | 50.00 |

ALLEN, LEE

EMBER
| ❑ ELP-200 [M] | Walkin' with Mr. Lee | 1958 | 200.00 |
—Red label
| ❑ ELP-200 [M] | Walkin' with Mr. Lee | 1959 | 50.00 |
—White "logs" label
| ❑ ELP-200 [M] | Walkin' with Mr. Lee | 1961 | 50.00 |
—Red and black label
—udget-line reissue of 9613

ALLEN, PHYLICIA

CASABLANCA
| ❑ NBLP-7108 [B] | Josephine Superstar | 1978 | 30.00 |

ALLEN, RAY, AND THE UPBEATS

BLAST
| ❑ BLP-6804 [M] | A Tribute to Six | 1962 | 120.00 |

ALLEN, RAY

PARAMOUNT
| ❑ PAS-6060 | Ray Allen and the Yonkers Children's Chorus | 1973 | 18.00 |

ALLEN, REX, JR.

WARNER BROS.
❑ BS2821	Another Goodbye Song	1974	12.00
❑ BSK3190	Brand New	1978	12.00
❑ BSK3300	Me and My Broken Heart	1979	12.00
❑ BSK3403	Oklahoma Rose	1980	12.00
❑ BS3054	Rex	1977	12.00
❑ BS2958	Ridin' High	1976	12.00
❑ BSK3122	The Best of Rex	1977	12.00

ALLEN, REX

BUENA VISTA
| ❑ BV-3307 [M] | Rex Allen Sings 16 Golden Hits | 1961 | 40.00 |

DECCA
❑ DL8776 [M]	Mister Cowboy	1959	40.00
❑ DL78776 [S]	Mister Cowboy	1959	60.00
❑ DL75011	The Smooth Country Sound of Rex Allen	1968	25.00
❑ DL75205	The Touch of God's Hand	1970	25.00
❑ DL8402 [M]	Under Western Skies	1956	50.00

HACIENDA
| ❑ WWLP-101 [M] | Rex Allen Sings | 1960 | 200.00 |

MERCURY
❑ MG-20719 [M]	Faith of a Man	1962	30.00
❑ SR-60719 [S]	Faith of a Man	1962	30.00
❑ MG-20752 [M]	Rex Allen Sings and Tells Tales	1963	30.00
❑ SR-60752 [S]	Rex Allen Sings and Tells Tales	1963	30.00

ALLEN, RICHIE

IMPERIAL
❑ LP-9212 [M]	Stranger from Durango	1962	50.00
❑ LP-12212 [S]	Stranger from Durango	1962	60.00
❑ LP-9243 [M]	Surfer's Slide	1963	100.00
❑ LP-12243 [S]	Surfer's Slide	1963	150.00
❑ LP-9229 [M]	The Rising Surf	1963	100.00
❑ LP-12229 [S]	The Rising Surf	1963	150.00

ALLEN, ROSALIE

GRAND AWARD
| ❑ GA-33-330 [M] | Songs of the Golden West | 1957 | 40.00 |

RCA VICTOR
| ❑ LPM-2313 [M] | Rosalie Allen | 1961 | 25.00 |
| ❑ LSP-2313 [S] | Rosalie Allen | 1961 | 30.00 |

WALDORF
| ❑ 150 [10] | Rosalie Allen Sings Country and Western | 1955 | 80.00 |

ALLEN, STEVE, AND MANNY ALBAM

DOT
| ❑ DLP3194 [M] | ...And All That Jazz | 1959 | 30.00 |
| ❑ DLP25194 [S] | ...And All That Jazz | 1959 | 25.00 |

ALLEN, STEVE

CASABLANCA
| ❑ 811366-1 | Funny Fone Calls | 1983 | 10.00 |
—Reissue of Dot 3472
| ❑ 811367-1 | More Funny Fone Calls | 1983 | 10.00 |
—Reissue of Dot 3517

CORAL
❑ CRL57048 [M]	Allen Plays Allen	1956	30.00
❑ CRL57018 [M]	Jazz for Tonight	1956	30.00
❑ CRL57028 [M]	Let's Dance	1956	30.00
❑ CRL57004 [M]	Music for Tonight	1955	30.00
❑ CRL57138 [M]	Romantic Rendezvous	1957	25.00
❑ CRL57442 [M]	Songs Everybody Knows	1964	18.00
❑ CRL757442 [R]	Songs Everybody Knows	1964	15.00
❑ CRL57019 [M]	Steve Sings	1956	30.00
❑ CRL57070 [M]	The Steve Allen Show	1957	30.00
❑ CRL57015 [M]	Tonight at Midnight	1956	30.00

DECCA
| ❑ DL8151 [M] | Steve Allen's All Star Jazz Concert, Vol. 1 | 1955 | 30.00 |
| ❑ DL8152 [M] | Steve Allen's All Star Jazz Concert, Vol. 2 | 1955 | 30.00 |

DOT
❑ DLP3473 [M]	12 Greatest Hits	1963	25.00
❑ DLP3480 [M]	Bossa Nova Jazz	1963	18.00
❑ DLP25380 [S]	Bossa Nova Jazz	1963	25.00
❑ DLP3538 [M]	Cuano Caliente El Sol and More	1963	18.00
❑ DLP25538 [S]	Cuano Caliente El Sol and More	1963	25.00
❑ DLP3472 [M]	Funny Fone Calls	1963	25.00
❑ DLP3515 [M]	Gravy Waltz and 11 Current Hits!	1963	18.00
❑ DLP25515 [S]	Gravy Waltz and 11 Current Hits!	1963	25.00
❑ DLP3560 [M]	Great Ragtime Hits	1963	18.00
❑ DLP25560 [S]	Great Ragtime Hits	1963	25.00
❑ DLP3624 [M]	I Play for You	1965	15.00
❑ DLP25624 [S]	I Play for You	1965	18.00
❑ DLP3517 [M]	More Funny Fone Calls	1963	25.00
❑ DLP3683 [M]	Rhythm and Blues	1966	15.00
❑ DLP25683 [S]	Rhythm and Blues	1966	10.00
❑ DLP3587 [M]	Songs from the Steve Allen TV Show	1964	15.00
❑ DLP25587 [S]	Songs from the Steve Allen TV Show	1964	18.00
❑ DLP3597 [M]	Steve Allen, His Piano and Orchestra	1964	15.00
❑ DLP25597 [S]	Steve Allen, His Piano and Orchestra	1964	18.00
❑ DLP3519 [M]	Steve Allen Plays the Piano Greats	1963	18.00
❑ DLP25519 [S]	Steve Allen Plays the Piano Greats	1963	25.00
❑ DLP3530 [M]	Steve Allen Sings	1963	18.00
❑ DLP25530 [S]	Steve Allen Sings	1963	25.00

FORUM
| ❑ F-9014 [M] | Steve Allen at the Round Table | 196? | 25.00 |
| ❑ FS-9014 [S] | Steve Allen at the Round Table | 196? | 18.00 |

HAMILTON
| ❑ HLP132 [M] | Some of My Favorites | 196? | 15.00 |
| ❑ HLP12132 [S] | Some of My Favorites | 196? | 18.00 |

ROULETTE
| ❑ R-25053 [M] | Steve Allen at the Round Table | 1959 | 30.00 |
| ❑ SR-25053 [S] | Steve Allen at the Round Table | 1959 | 25.00 |

SIGNATURE
| ❑ SM1004 [M] | Man in the Street | 1959 | 30.00 |
| ❑ SM1021 [M] | Monday Nights | 1960 | 30.00 |

ALLEN, TONY

CROWN
| ❑ CLP-5231 [M] | Rock and Roll with Tony Allen | 1960 | 100.00 |
—Black label
| ❑ CLP-5231 [M] | Rock and Roll with Tony Allen | 1961 | 60.00 |
—Gray label
| ❑ CST-240 [S] | Rock and Roll with Tony Allen | 1961 | 150.00 |

ALLEN, WOODY

BELL
| ❑ 6008 | The Wonderful Wacky World of Woody Allen | 1967 | 25.00 |

CAPITOL
| ❑ ST2986 | The Third Woody Allen Album | 1968 | 30.00 |

CASABLANCA
| ❑ NBLP2-7145 | Woody Allen: Stand-Up Comic 1964-1968 | 1979 | 18.00 |

—Compilation of material from Colpix and Capitol LPs (different from either UA collection)

COLPIX

Number	Title	Yr	NM
❑ CP518 [M]	Woody Allen	1964	30.00
❑ CP488 [M]	Woody Allen 2	1965	30.00
❑ SCP488 [R]	Woody Allen 2	1965	30.00

UNITED ARTISTS

Number	Title	Yr	NM
❑ UA-LA849-J2	Woody Allen: Stand-Up Comic 1964-1968	1977	25.00

—Compilation of material from Colpix and Capitol LPs (different from UA 9968)

Number	Title	Yr	NM
❑ UAS9968	Woody Allen: The Nightclub Years	1972	25.00

—Compilation of material from Colpix and Capitol LPs

ALLEN AND ROSSI

ABC-PARAMOUNT

Number	Title	Yr	NM
❑ ABC-270 [M]	Hello Dere	1962	25.00
❑ ABC-445 [M]	One More Time Hello Dere	1963	25.00

MERCURY

Number	Title	Yr	NM
❑ MG-21077 [M]	The Adventures of Batman and Rubin	1966	40.00
❑ SR-61077 [S]	The Adventures of Batman and Rubin	1966	50.00

—The above LP was written by "Batman" creator Bob Kane as a parody of his own comic book

REPRISE

Number	Title	Yr	NM
❑ R-6104 [M]	Too Funny for Words	1964	25.00

ROULETTE

Number	Title	Yr	NM
❑ R-508 [M]	Dedicated to Our Armed Forces	1967	25.00
❑ R-507 [M]	The Truth About the Green Hornet	1966	25.00

ALLIN, GG

ALIVE

Number	Title	Yr	NM
❑ 0001 [B]	Brutality and Bloodshed for All	199?	30.00
❑ 0012 [B]	Terror in America	199?	40.00

BLACK & BLUE

Number	Title	Yr	NM
❑ 006053-X	Always Was, Is and Always Shall Be	1985	50.00

—Reissue of Orange original

Number	Title	Yr	NM
❑ (# unknown)0 [B]	Banned in Boston	1989	30.00
❑ (# unknown)0 [B]	Eat My Fuc	1988	25.00

—Reissue of Blood LP of the same name

BLOOD

Number	Title	Yr	NM
❑ (# unknown)0 [B]	Eat My Fuc	198?	70.00

—Hand-decorated plain cover

HOMESTEAD

Number	Title	Yr	NM
❑ HMS-069 [B]	You Give Love a Bad Name	1987	50.00

ORANGE

Number	Title	Yr	NM
❑ (# unknown)0	Always Was, Is and Always Shall Be	1980	100.00

ALLISON, GENE

VEE JAY

Number	Title	Yr	NM
❑ LP-1009 [M]	Gene Allison	1959	300.00

—Maroon label

Number	Title	Yr	NM
❑ LP-1009 [M]	Gene Allison	196?	100.00

—Black label, oval or brackets logo

ALLISON, KEITH

COLUMBIA

Number	Title	Yr	NM
❑ CL2641 [M]	Keith Allison In Action	1967	30.00
❑ CS9441 [S]	Keith Allison In Action	1967	30.00

ALLISON, LUTHER

DELMARK

Number	Title	Yr	NM
❑ DS-625	Love Me, Mama	1969	30.00

GORDY

Number	Title	Yr	NM
❑ G-964	Bad News Is Coming	1973	12.00
❑ G-967	Luther's Blues	1974	12.00
❑ G-974	Night Life	1976	12.00

ALLISON, MOSE

ATLANTIC

Number	Title	Yr	NM
❑ SD1550	Hello There, Universe	1971	25.00
❑ 1389 [M]	I Don't Worry About a Thing	1962	25.00
❑ SD1389 [S]	I Don't Worry About a Thing	1962	30.00
❑ SD1511	I've Been Doin' Some Thinkin'	1969	30.00

—1841 Broadway" address on label

Number	Title	Yr	NM
❑ SD1511	I've Been Doin' Some Thinkin'	1976	15.00

—75 Rockefeller Plaza" address on label

Number	Title	Yr	NM
❑ 1450 [M]	Mose Alive!	1966	30.00
❑ SD1450 [S]	Mose Alive!	1966	40.00

—Blue and green label

Number	Title	Yr	NM
❑ SD1450 [S]	Mose Alive!	1969	25.00

—Red and green label with "1841 Broadway" address

Number	Title	Yr	NM
❑ SD1627	Mose in Your Ear	1973	25.00

—1841 Broadway" address on label

Number	Title	Yr	NM
❑ SD1627	Mose in Your Ear	1976	15.00

—75 Rockefeller Plaza" address on label

Number	Title	Yr	NM
❑ 1398 [M]	Swingin' Machine	1963	25.00
❑ SD1398 [S]	Swingin' Machine	1963	30.00
❑ SD1542	The Best of Mose Allison	1970	18.00
❑ 1424 [M]	The Word from Mose	1964	25.00
❑ SD1424 [S]	The Word from Mose	1964	30.00
❑ SD1584	Western Man	1972	18.00
❑ 1456 [M]	Wild Man on the Loose	1966	30.00
❑ SD1456 [S]	Wild Man on the Loose	1966	40.00
❑ SD1691	Your Mind Is on Vacation	1976	18.00

BLUE NOTE

Number	Title	Yr	NM
❑ BLJ-48015	Ever Since the World Ended	1988	18.00
❑ B1-93840	My Backyard	1990	25.00

COLUMBIA

Number	Title	Yr	NM
❑ CL1565 [M]	I Love the Life I Live	1960	30.00

—Red and black label with six "eye" logos

Number	Title	Yr	NM
❑ CS8365 [S]	I Love the Life I Live	1960	30.00

—Red and black label with six "eye" logos

Number	Title	Yr	NM
❑ C30564	Retrospective	1971	18.00
❑ CL1444 [M]	The Transfiguration of Hiram Brown	1960	30.00
❑ CS8240 [S]	The Transfiguration of Hiram Brown	1960	30.00

COLUMBIA SPECIAL PRODUCTS

Number	Title	Yr	NM
❑ P13518	V-8 Ford Blues	197?	18.00

ELEKTRA/MUSICIAN

Number	Title	Yr	NM
❑ 60237	Lessons in Living	1984	15.00
❑ E1-60125	Middle Class White Boy	1983	15.00

EPIC

Number	Title	Yr	NM
❑ LA16031 [M]	Take to the Hills	1962	30.00
❑ BA17031 [S]	Take to the Hills	1962	40.00
❑ LN24183 [M]	V-8 Ford Blues	1966	25.00
❑ BN26183 [S]	V-8 Ford Blues	1966	30.00

FANTASY

Number	Title	Yr	NM
❑ OJC-075	Back Country Suite	198?	15.00

—Reissue of Prestige 7091

Number	Title	Yr	NM
❑ OJC-6004	Greatest Hits	1988	15.00
❑ OJC-457	Local Color	1990	15.00

—Reissue of Prestige 7121

ODYSSEY

Number	Title	Yr	NM
❑ 32160294	Mose Goes	1968	18.00

PRESTIGE

Number	Title	Yr	NM
❑ PRLP-7189 [M]	Autumn Song	1960	50.00

—Yellow label with Bergenfield, NJ address on label

Number	Title	Yr	NM
❑ PRLP-7189 [M]	Autumn Song	196?	25.00

—Blue label, trident logo

Number	Title	Yr	NM
❑ PRLP-7091 [M]	Back Country Suite	1957	100.00

—With "W. 50th St., NYC" address on label

Number	Title	Yr	NM
❑ PRLP-7152 [M]	Creek Bank	1959	80.00

—Yellow label with Bergenfield, NJ address on label

Number	Title	Yr	NM
❑ P-24055	Creek Bank	1975	30.00
❑ PRLP-7152 [M]	Creek Bank	196?	30.00

—Blue label, trident logo

Number	Title	Yr	NM
❑ PRLP-7423 [M]	Down Home Piano	1966	25.00

—Blue label, trident logo at right

Number	Title	Yr	NM
❑ PRST-7423 [S]	Down Home Piano	1966	30.00

—Blue label, trident logo at right

Number	Title	Yr	NM
❑ PRLP-7121 [M]	Local Color	1958	100.00

—With "W. 50th St., NYC" address on label

Number	Title	Yr	NM
❑ PR-24002	Mose Allison	1972	30.00
❑ PRLP-7446 [M]	Mose Allison Plays for Lovers	1967	30.00
❑ PRST-7446 [S]	Mose Allison Plays for Lovers	1967	25.00
❑ PRLP-7279 [M]	Mose Allison Sings (The Seventh Son)	1963	40.00

—Yellow label with Bergenfield, NJ address on label

Number	Title	Yr	NM
❑ PRST-7279 [S]	Mose Allison Sings (The Seventh Son)	1963	50.00

—Silver label

Number	Title	Yr	NM
❑ P-10052	Mose Allison Sings (The Seventh Son)	1973	18.00

—Reissue of PRST-7279

Number	Title	Yr	NM
❑ PRST-7279 [S]	Mose Allison Sings (The Seventh Son)	196?	30.00

—Blue label, trident logo at right

Number	Title	Yr	NM
❑ P-24089	Ol' Devil Mose	1980	30.00
❑ PRLP-7215 [M]	Ramblin' with Mose	1961	60.00

—Yellow label with Bergenfield, NJ address on label

Number	Title	Yr	NM
❑ PRLP-7215 [M]	Ramblin' with Mose	196?	30.00

—Blue label, trident logo

Number	Title	Yr	NM
❑ PRLP-7137 [M]	Young Man Blues	1958	100.00

—With "W. 50th St., NYC" address on label

ALLMAN, DUANE

CAPRICORN

Number	Title	Yr	NM
❑ 2CP 0108	An Anthology	1972	25.00
❑ 2CP 0139	An Anthology, Vol. II	1974	25.00

POLYDOR

Number	Title	Yr	NM
❑ 827563-1	The Best of Duane Allman	1984	10.00
❑ PD-1-6338	The Best of Duane Allman	1981	15.00

ALLMAN, DUANE AND GREGG

BOLD

Number	Title	Yr	NM
❑ 33-301 [B]	Duane and Gregg Allman	1972	30.00

—Gatefold cover

Number	Title	Yr	NM
❑ 33-301	Duane and Gregg Allman	197?	25.00

—Non-gatefold cover

ALLMAN, GREGG

CAPRICORN

Number	Title	Yr	NM
❑ CP 0116	Laid Back	1973	15.00
❑ CP 0181	Playin' Up a Storm	1977	15.00
❑ 2CP 0141	The Gregg Allman Tour	1974	18.00

EPIC

Number	Title	Yr	NM
❑ FE40531	I'm No Angel	1987	12.00
❑ OE44033	Just Before the Bullets Fly	1988	12.00

ALLMAN, SHELDON

DEL-FI

Number	Title	Yr	NM
❑ DFLP-1213 [M]	Sing Along with Drac	1961	40.00

HIFI

Number	Title	Yr	NM
❑ R-415 [M]	Folk Songs for the 21st Century	1960	40.00

ALLMAN AND WOMAN

WARNER BROS.

Number	Title	Yr	NM
❑ BSK3120	Two the Hard Way	1977	12.00

ALLMAN BROTHERS BAND, THE

ARISTA

Number	Title	Yr	NM
❑ AL9564	Brothers of the Road	1981	12.00
❑ AL9535	Reach for the Sky	1980	12.00

ATCO

Number	Title	Yr	NM
❑ SD 2-805 [B]	Beginnings	1973	30.00
❑ SD 33-342 [B]	Idlewild South	1970	25.00
❑ SD 33-308 [B]	The Allman Brothers Band	1969	25.00

CAPRICORN

Number	Title	Yr	NM
❑ 2CX 0132	Beginnings	1974	18.00
❑ CPN2 0132	Beginnings	198?	15.00
❑ CP 0111 [B]	Brothers and Sisters	1973	18.00
❑ CPN 0111	Brothers and Sisters	198?	10.00
❑ 2CP 0102 [B]	Eat a Peach	1972	25.00
❑ CX4 0102 [Q]	Eat a Peach	1974	40.00
❑ CPN2 0102 [B]	Eat a Peach	198?	18.00
❑ CPN 0218	Enlightened Rogues	1979	12.00
❑ CPN 0197	Idlewild South	1978	12.00
❑ CPN 0196	The Allman Brothers Band	1978	12.00
❑ SD 2-802 [S]	The Allman Brothers Band at Fillmore East	1971	25.00
❑ 2CP 0131 [B]	The Allman Brothers Band at Fillmore East	1974	30.00
❑ CX4 0131 [Q]	The Allman Brothers Band at Fillmore East	1974	50.00
❑ CPN2 0131 [B]	The Allman Brothers Band at Fillmore East	198?	25.00
❑ 2-802 [M]	The Allman Brothers Band at Fillmore East	1971	80.00

—Promo only; sticker on front cover says "Promotional DJ Copy Monaural Not for Sale

Number	Title	Yr	NM
❑ 2CX 0164	The Road Goes On Forever	1975	15.00
❑ CP 0156	Win, Lose or Draw	1975	12.00
❑ CPN 0156	Win, Lose or Draw	198?	10.00
❑ 2CX 0177	Wipe the Windows, Check the Oil, Dollar Gas	1976	15.00

EPIC

Number	Title	Yr	NM
❑ E46144	Seven Turns	1990	18.00

EPIC LEGACY

Number	Title	Yr	NM
❑ 88843043521 [B]	Selections From: Play All Night: Live At The Beacon Theatre 1992	2014	30.00

MOBILE FIDELITY

Number	Title	Yr	NM
❑ 1-213	Brothers and Sisters	1994	30.00

—Audiophile vinyl

Number	Title	Yr	NM
❑ MFSL2-398 [B]	Eat A Peach	2013	50.00
❑ 1-157	Eat a Peach	1984	200.00

—Audiophile vinyl

NAUTILUS

Number	Title	Yr	NM
❑ NR-30	The Allman Brothers Band at Fillmore East	1982	100.00

—Audiophile vinyl

POLYDOR

Number	Title	Yr	NM
❑ 825092-1	Brothers and Sisters	1985	10.00
❑ 839417-1	Dreams	1989	40.00
❑ 823654-1	Eat a Peach	1984	12.00
❑ 823653-1	The Allman Brothers Band	1984	10.00
❑ 823273-1	The Allman Brothers Band at Fillmore East	1984	12.00
❑ PD-1-6339	The Best of the Allman Brothers Band	1981	12.00
❑ 823708-1	The Best of the Allman Brothers Band	1984	10.00

—Reissue of PD-1-6339

ALLMAN JOYS, THE

DIAL

Number	Title	Yr	NM
❑ DL6005	Early Allman	1973	18.00

ALLSUP, TOMMY

GRT

Number	Title	Yr	NM
❑ 20004	Tommy Allsup and the Tennessee Saxes Play the Hits of Tammy Wynette	1970	25.00

METROMEDIA

Number	Title	Yr	NM
❑ MM1004	Tommy Allsup and the Nashville Survey Play the Hits of Charley Pride	1969	30.00

REPRISE

Number	Title	Yr	NM
❑ R6182 [M]	Tommy Allsup Plays the Buddy Holly Songbook	1965	40.00
❑ RS6182 [S]	Tommy Allsup Plays the Buddy Holly Songbook	1965	50.00

ALMEIDA, LAURINDO, AND CHARLIE BYRD

CONCORD PICANTE

Number	Title	Yr	NM
❑ CJP-150	Brazilian Soul	1981	12.00
❑ CJP-211	Latin Odyssey	1983	18.00
❑ CP-290	Tango	1985	12.00

ALMEIDA, LAURINDO

ANGEL

Number	Title	Yr	NM
❑ S-36064	Clair de Lune	197?	15.00
❑ S-36050	Duets with the Spanish Guitar	197?	15.00
❑ S-36051	Duets with the Spanish Guitar, Vol. 2	197?	15.00
❑ S-36076	Duets with the Spanish Guitar, Vol. 3	197?	15.00
❑ S-37322	Prelude	197?	18.00

CAPITOL

Number	Title	Yr	NM
❑ T2701 [M]	A Man and a Woman	1967	18.00
❑ ST2701 [S]	A Man and a Woman	1967	18.00
❑ SM-2701	A Man and a Woman	1976	12.00
—Reissue			
❑ T2063 [M]	Broadway Solo Guitar	1964	15.00
❑ ST2063 [S]	Broadway Solo Guitar	1964	18.00
❑ H-193 [10]	Concert Creations for Guitar	1950	80.00
❑ P8625 [M]	Concerto de Copacabana	196?	15.00
❑ SP8625 [S]	Concerto de Copacabana	196?	18.00
❑ SP8636	Concerto for Guitar and Small Orchestra	196?	18.00
❑ P8447 [M]	Contemporary Creations for Spanish Guitar	195?	30.00
❑ P8532 [M]	Conversations with the Guitar	196?	25.00
❑ SP8532 [S]	Conversations with the Guitar	196?	30.00
❑ P8467 [M]	Danzas!	196?	25.00
❑ PAO8406 [M]	Duets with the Spanish Guitar	1958	30.00
—Gatefold cover			
❑ P8406 [M]	Duets with the Spanish Guitar	196?	25.00
—Regular cover			
❑ DP8406 [R]	Duets with the Spanish Guitar	196?	15.00
❑ P8461 [M]	For My True Love	1959	25.00
❑ SP8461 [S]	For My True Love	1959	30.00
❑ T2197 [M]	Guitar from Ipanema	1964	18.00
❑ ST2197 [S]	Guitar from Ipanema	1964	25.00
❑ P8341 [M]	Guitar Music from the Romantic Era	195?	30.00
❑ DP8601 [R]	Guitar Music from the Romantic Era	196?	15.00
❑ P8601 [M]	Guitar Music from the Romantic Era	196?	18.00
—Reissue of 8341			
❑ P8321 [M]	Guitar Music of Latin America	196?	30.00
❑ P8295 [M]	Guitar Music of Spain	195?	30.00
❑ T1263 [M]	Happy Cha Cha Cha	1959	25.00
❑ P8381 [M]	Impressaoes do Brasil	195?	40.00
❑ T1946 [M]	It's a Bossa Nova World	1963	18.00
❑ ST1946 [S]	It's a Bossa Nova World	1963	25.00
❑ SP8497 [S]	Music of the Spanish Guitar	196?	25.00
❑ T2419 [M]	New Broadway-Hollywood Hits	1965	15.00
❑ ST2419 [S]	New Broadway-Hollywood Hits	1965	18.00
❑ T1872 [M]	Ole! Bossa Nova	1963	18.00
❑ ST1872 [S]	Ole! Bossa Nova	1963	25.00
❑ P8571 [M]	Reverie for Spanish Guitars	196?	25.00
❑ SP8571 [S]	Reverie for Spanish Guitars	196?	30.00
❑ P8482 [M]	Songs of Enchantment	196?	18.00
❑ SP8482 [S]	Songs of Enchantment	196?	25.00
❑ T2345 [M]	Suenos (Dreams)	1965	18.00
❑ DP8686 [R]	The Best of Laurindo Almeida	1969	15.00
❑ STER-291	The Guitar of Laurindo Almeida	1969	40.00
❑ P8546 [M]	The Guitar Worlds of Laurindo Almeida	196?	18.00
❑ SP8546 [S]	The Guitar Worlds of Laurindo Almeida	196?	25.00
❑ P8582 [M]	The Intimate Bach: Duets with the Spanish Guitar Vol. 2	196?	18.00
❑ SP8582 [S]	The Intimate Bach: Duets with the Spanish Guitar Vol. 2	196?	25.00
❑ ST2866	The Look of Love	1968	25.00
❑ P8392 [M]	The New World of the Guitar	195?	30.00
❑ P8521 [M]	The Spanish Guitars of Laurindo Almeida	196?	18.00
❑ SP8521 [S]	The Spanish Guitars of Laurindo Almeida	196?	25.00
❑ P8497 [M]	Villa-Lobos: Music for the Spanish Guitar	196?	18.00
❑ P8367 [M]	Vistas d'Espana	195?	30.00
❑ T1759 [M]	Viva Bossa Nova!	1962	18.00
❑ ST1759 [S]	Viva Bossa Nova!	1962	25.00
❑ SM-1759	Viva Bossa Nova!	197?	12.00

CONCORD CONCERTO

Number	Title	Yr	NM
❑ CC-2001	First Concerto for Guitar and Orchestra	1980	12.00
❑ CC-2003	Laurindo Almeida with Bud Shank	198?	12.00

CONCORD JAZZ

Number	Title	Yr	NM
❑ CJ-238	Artistry in Rhythm	1984	12.00
❑ CJ-84	Chamber Jazz	1979	18.00

CORAL

Number	Title	Yr	NM
❑ CRL56049 [10]	A Guitar Recital of Famous Serenades	1952	80.00
❑ CRL57056 [M]	A Guitar Recital of Famous Serenades	1956	50.00
—Maroon label original			
❑ CRL57056 [M]	A Guitar Recital of Famous Serenades	196?	30.00
—Black label with color bars			
❑ CRL56086 [10]	Latin Melodies	1952	80.00

CRYSTAL CLEAR

Number	Title	Yr	NM
❑ CCS-8007	New Directions	1979	40.00
—Direct-to-disc recording			
❑ CCS-8001	Virtuoso Guitar	1978	40.00
—Direct-to-disc recording; plays at 45 rpm; white vinyl			
❑ CCS-8001	Virtuoso Guitar	1978	30.00
—Direct-to-disc recording; plays at 45 rpm; black vinyl			

DAYBREAK

Number	Title	Yr	NM
❑ DR-2013	The Best of Everything	1972	18.00

DOBRE

Number	Title	Yr	NM
❑ DR1000	Latin Guitar	1977	25.00
❑ 1024	Trio	197?	12.00

EVEREST

Number	Title	Yr	NM
❑ SDBR-3287 [R]	Spanish Guitar Recital	196?	12.00

INNER CITY

Number	Title	Yr	NM
❑ IC6031	Concierto de Aranjuez	1979	18.00

ORION

Number	Title	Yr	NM
❑ ORS7259	The Art of Laurindo Almeida	197?	18.00

PACIFIC JAZZ

Number	Title	Yr	NM
❑ PJLP-7 [10]	Laurindo Almeida Quartet	1953	200.00
❑ PJLP-13 [10]	Laurindo Almeida Quartet, Vol. 2	1954	200.00
❑ PJ-1204 [M]	Laurindo Almeida Quartet Featuring Bud Shank	1955	120.00
—Reissue of 10-inch Pacific Jazz LPs; red vinyl			
❑ PJ-1204 [M]	Laurindo Almeida Quartet Featuring Bud Shank	1955	80.00
—Reissue of 10-inch Pacific Jazz LPs; black vinyl			

PAUSA

Number	Title	Yr	NM
❑ PR9009	Brazilliance	1983	12.00
—Reissue			

PICKWICK

Number	Title	Yr	NM
❑ SPC-3172	I Left My Heart in San Francisco	197?	10.00

PRO ARTE

Number	Title	Yr	NM
❑ PAD-235	3 Guitars 3	1985	12.00
—With Sharon Isbin and Larry Coryell			

SUTTON

Number	Title	Yr	NM
❑ SU247 [M]	Flamenco	196?	12.00

TOWER

Number	Title	Yr	NM
❑ T5060 [M]	Acapulco '22	1967	30.00
❑ DT5060 [R]	Acapulco '22	1967	25.00

WARNER BROS.

Number	Title	Yr	NM
❑ WS1803	Classical Current: Electronic Excursions	1969	30.00
—Original U.S. edition is on a green "W7" label			
❑ ST-92083	Classical Current: Electronic Excursions	1969	30.00
—Capitol Record Club edition			

WORLD PACIFIC

Number	Title	Yr	NM
❑ WP-1412 [M]	Brazilliance, Vol. 1	1962	30.00
—Reissue of World Pacific 1204			
❑ WPS-21412 [S]	Brazilliance, Vol. 1	196?	30.00
❑ T90078 [M]	Brazilliance, Vol. 1	196?	30.00
—Capitol Record Club edition			
❑ WP-1419 [M]	Brazilliance, Vol. 2	1962	30.00
❑ ST-1419 [S]	Brazilliance, Vol. 2	1962	30.00
❑ WP-1425 [M]	Brazilliance, Vol. 3	1962	30.00
❑ ST-1425 [S]	Brazilliance, Vol. 3	1962	30.00
❑ PJ-1204 [M]	Laurindo Almeida Quartet Featuring Bud Shank	1958	50.00
—Reissue of Pacific Jazz 1204			

ALMERICO, TONY

IMPERIAL

Number	Title	Yr	NM
❑ LP-9151 [M]	French Quarter Jazz	1961	25.00
❑ LP-12072 [S]	French Quarter Jazz	1961	30.00

ALMOND, MARC

CAPITOL

Number	Title	Yr	NM
❑ C1-94404 [B]	Enchanted	1990	25.00
❑ C1-91042 [B]	The Stars We Are	1988	18.00

ALPERT, HERB, AND THE TIJUANA BRASS

A&M

Number	Title	Yr	NM
❑ SP-5022	Bullish	1984	10.00
❑ SP-4166 [S]	Christmas Album	1968	15.00
❑ SP-3113	Christmas Album	198?	10.00
—Reissue of SP-4166			
❑ LP166 [M]	Christmas Album	1968	30.00
—Mono is white label promo only			
❑ SP-4521	Coney Island	1975	12.00
❑ SP-3521	Foursider	1973	15.00
❑ SP-6011	Foursider	197?	12.00
—Reissue			
❑ LP-112 [M]	Going Places	1965	12.00
❑ SP-4112 [S]	Going Places	1965	15.00
❑ SP-3264	Going Places	1984	10.00
—Reissue			
❑ T-90507 [M]	Going Places	1965	18.00
—Capitol Record Club edition			
❑ ST-90507 [S]	Going Places	1965	25.00
—Capitol Record Club edition			
❑ SP-4245	Greatest Hits	1970	12.00
❑ SP-3267	Greatest Hits	1984	10.00
—Reissue			
❑ SP-4627	Greatest Hits, Vol. 2	1976	12.00
❑ SP-3269	Greatest Hits, Vol. 2	1984	10.00
❑ SP-4134	Herb Alpert's Ninth	1967	12.00
❑ LP-103 [M]	Herb Alpert's Tijuana Brass, Volume 2	1963	18.00
—Brown label with A&M logo at top			
❑ SP-4103 [S]	Herb Alpert's Tijuana Brass, Volume 2	1963	18.00
❑ SP-103 [S]	Herb Alpert's Tijuana Brass, Volume 2	1963	25.00
—Original issues had this number			
❑ LP-103 [M]	Herb Alpert's Tijuana Brass, Volume 2	1964	15.00
—Brown label with A&M logo at left			
❑ T-90074 [M]	Herb Alpert's Tijuana Brass, Volume 2	1964	25.00
—Capitol Record Club edition			
❑ SP-4341	Solid Brass	1972	12.00
❑ SP-3268	Solid Brass	1984	10.00
❑ LP-124 [M]	Sounds Like	1967	12.00
❑ SP-4124 [S]	Sounds Like	1967	15.00
❑ LP-108 [M]	South of the Border	1964	15.00
❑ SP-4108 [S]	South of the Border	1964	18.00
❑ SP-3263	South of the Border	1984	10.00
❑ SP-108 [S]	South of the Border	1964	25.00
—Original issues had this number			
❑ ST-90073 [S]	South of the Border	1964	25.00
—Capitol Record Club edition			
❑ LP-119 [M]	S.R.O.	1966	12.00
❑ SP-4119 [S]	S.R.O.	1966	15.00
❑ SP-4314	Summertime	1971	12.00
❑ SW-93870	Summertime	197?	15.00
—Capitol Record Club edition			
❑ SP-4146	The Beat of the Brass	1968	12.00
❑ SP-3266 [B]	The Beat of the Brass	1984	10.00
—Reissue			
❑ LP-9004 [DJ]	The Best from Herb Alpert & The Tijuana Brass	196?	18.00
—Promo-only compilation			
❑ SP-4228	The Brass Are Comin'	1969	12.00
❑ SP-4101 [S]	The Lonely Bull	1962	18.00
❑ LP-101 [M]	The Lonely Bull	1962	30.00
—Originals on yellowish label with brown print			
❑ SP-3101	The Lonely Bull	198?	10.00
—Reissue			
❑ SP-101 [S]	The Lonely Bull	1962	30.00
—Original editions had this number			
❑ LP-101 [M]	The Lonely Bull	1963	18.00
—Second pressings with brown label and A&M logo at top			
❑ LP-101 [M]	The Lonely Bull	1964	15.00
—Third pressing with brown label and A&M logo at left			
❑ SP-4190	Warm	1969	12.00
❑ LP-114 [M]	What Now My Love	1966	12.00
❑ SP-4114 [S]	What Now My Love	1966	15.00
❑ SP-3265	What Now My Love	1984	10.00
❑ T-90655 [M]	What Now My Love	1966	15.00
—Capitol Record Club edition			
❑ LP-110 [M]	Whipped Cream & Other Delights	1965	12.00
❑ SP-4110 [S]	Whipped Cream & Other Delights	1965	15.00
❑ SP-3157	Whipped Cream & Other Delights	198?	10.00
—Reissue			
❑ ST-90387 [S]	Whipped Cream & Other Delights	1965	18.00
—Capitol Record Club edition			
❑ SP-3620	You Smile -- The Song Begins	1974	12.00

LONGINES SYMPHONETTE

Number	Title	Yr	NM
❑ LWS-500	Treasury of Herb Alpert and the Tijuana Brass	196?	30.00
—Also contains music by the Baja Marimba Band; records are individually numbered from 500 through 504			

ALPERT, HERB

A&M

Number	Title	Yr	NM
❑ SP-3717	Beyond	1980	10.00
❑ SP-4949	Blow Your Own Horn	1983	10.00
❑ SP-3731	Fandango	1982	10.00
❑ SP-4591	Just You and Me	1976	12.00
❑ SP-5125	Keep Your Eye on Me	1987	10.00
❑ SP-3728	Magic Man	1981	10.00
❑ SP-5273	My Abstract Heart	1989	10.00
❑ 7502153451	North on South Street	1991	15.00
❑ SP-4790	Rise	1979	12.00
❑ SP-3714	Rise	1980	10.00
—Reissue of 4790			
❑ SP-5209	Under a Spanish Moon	1988	10.00
❑ SP-5082	Wild Romance	1985	10.00

Number	Title	Yr	NM

MOBILE FIDELITY
- ❑ 1-053 — Rise — 1981 — 30.00
— *Audiophile vinyl*

ALPERT, TRIGGER

RIVERSIDE
- ❑ RLP 12-225 [M] — Trigger Happy! — 1956 — 80.00
— *White label, blue print*
- ❑ RLP 12-225 [M] — Trigger Happy! — 195? — 40.00
— *Blue label with microphone logo*

ALVIN, DANNY

JAZZOLOGY
- ❑ 8 [M] — Danny Alvin and the Kings of Dixieland — 1964 — 25.00
- ❑ S-8 [S] — Danny Alvin and the Kings of Dixieland — 1964 — 25.00

STEPHENY
- ❑ MF-4002 [M] — Club Basin Street — 1957 — 50.00

ALVIN, DAVE

EPIC
- ❑ FE40921 — Romeo's Escape — 1987 — 12.00

AMAZING RHYTHM ACES

ABC
- ❑ AA-1063 — Burning the Ballroom Down — 1978 — 18.00
- ❑ D-913 [B] — Stacked Deck — 1975 — 25.00
- ❑ AA-1123 — The Amazing Rhythm Aces — 1979 — 25.00
- ❑ D-940 — Too Stuffed to Jump — 1976 — 18.00
- ❑ AB-1005 — Toucan Do It Too — 1977 — 18.00

COLUMBIA
- ❑ JC36083 — The Amazing Rhythm Aces — 1979 — 15.00
— *Reissue of ABC 1123*

WARNER BROS.
- ❑ BSK3476 — How the Hell Do You Spell Rythum? — 1980 — 15.00

AMBASSADORS, THE (1)

ARCTIC
- ❑ ALPS-1005 [B] — Soul Summit — 1969 — 30.00

AMBOY DUKES, THE

DISCREET
- ❑ DS2181 — Call of the Wild — 1974 — 18.00
— *As "Ted Nugent and the Amboy Dukes"*
- ❑ DS2203 — Tooth, Fang and Claw — 1974 — 18.00
— *As "Ted Nugent and the Amboy Dukes"*

MAINSTREAM
- ❑ S-414 — Dr. Slingshot — 1975 — 18.00
- ❑ S-2-801 — Journeys and Migrations — 1974 — 30.00
— *Reissue of 6112 and 6118*
- ❑ S-6112 [B] — Journey to the Center of the Mind — 1968 — 50.00
- ❑ S-6118 [B] — Migration — 1968 — 50.00
- ❑ S-421 — Ted Nugent and the Amboy Dukes — 1976 — 30.00
— *Reissue of early material*
- ❑ 56104 [M] — The Amboy Dukes — 1967 — 100.00
- ❑ S-6104 [S] — The Amboy Dukes — 1967 — 50.00
- ❑ S-6125 — The Best of the Original Amboy Dukes — 1969 — 30.00

POLYDOR
- ❑ 24-4012 — Marriage on the Rocks/Rock Bottom — 1970 — 30.00
- ❑ 24-4035 — Survival of the Fittest/Live — 1971 — 30.00
— *As "Ted Nugent and the Amboy Dukes"*

AMBROSE, AMANDA

DUNWICH
- ❑ 668 [M] — Amanda — 1966 — 18.00
- ❑ S-668 [S] — Amanda — 1966 — 25.00

AMBROSIA

20TH CENTURY
- ❑ T-434 — Ambrosia — 1975 — 15.00
— *Original cover with black border*
- ❑ T-434 — Ambrosia — 1975 — 12.00
— *New cover without black border*
- ❑ T-510 — Somewhere I've Never Traveled — 1976 — 15.00
— *Fold-open cover in the shape of a pyramid*
- ❑ T-510 — Somewhere I've Never Traveled — 1976 — 12.00
— *Standard cover*

NAUTILUS
- ❑ NR-23 — Life Beyond L.A. — 1981 — 30.00
— *Audiophile vinyl*

WARNER BROS.
- ❑ BSK3181 — Ambrosia — 1978 — 10.00
— *Reissue of 20th Century 434*
- ❑ BSK3135 — Life Beyond L.A. — 1978 — 12.00
- ❑ BSK3368 — One Eighty — 1980 — 12.00
- ❑ BSK3638 — Road Island — 1982 — 12.00

AMECHE, DON, AND FRANCES LANGFORD

COLUMBIA
- ❑ CL1692 — The Bickersons — 1962 — 25.00
— *Live-in-the-studio recordings from 1961*
- ❑ CL1883 — The Bickersons Fight Back — 1962 — 25.00
— *More live-in-the-studio recordings from 1961*
- ❑ G30523 [B] — The Bickersons Rematch — 1970 — 18.00
— *Compilation of the earlier Columbia LPs*

RADIOLA
- ❑ MR1115 — The Bickersons — 198? — 15.00
— *Compilation of radio shows*

RADIOLA/MURRAY HILL
- ❑ 3MH36721 — Return of the Bickersons — 1987 — 25.00
— *Compilation of radio shows*

AMERICA

CAPITOL
- ❑ SOO-12098 — Alibi — 1980 — 12.00
- ❑ SN-16275 — Alibi — 1982 — 10.00
- ❑ ST-12422 — In Concert — 1985 — 12.00
- ❑ ST-12370 — Perspective — 1984 — 12.00
- ❑ SO-11950 — Silent Letter — 1979 — 12.00
- ❑ ST-12209 — View from the Ground — 1982 — 12.00
- ❑ SN-16350 — View from the Ground — 1985 — 10.00
- ❑ ST-12277 — Your Move — 1983 — 12.00
- ❑ SN-16361 — Your Move — 1985 — 10.00

WARNER BROS.
- ❑ BS2576 — America — 1971 — 30.00
— *First pressings omit "A Horse with No Name"*
- ❑ BS2576 — America — 1972 — 15.00
— *With "A Horse with No Name" mentioned on front cover; green label*
- ❑ BS2576 — America — 1972 — 18.00
— *Transitional edition includes "A Horse with No Name" but doesn't mention it on the front cover*
- ❑ BSK3136 — America/Live — 1977 — 15.00
- ❑ BSK3017 — Harbor — 1977 — 15.00
- ❑ BS2728 — Hat Trick — 1973 — 15.00
- ❑ BS2852 — Hearts — 1975 — 15.00
- ❑ BS42852 [Q] — Hearts — 1975 — 30.00
- ❑ BS2932 — Hideaway — 1976 — 15.00
- ❑ BS2894 — History/America's Greatest Hits — 1975 — 15.00
- ❑ BSK3110 — History/America's Greatest Hits — 1977 — 12.00
— *Reissue of BS 2894 with "Burbank" palm trees label (later white labels are $8 NM)*
- ❑ BS2808 — Holiday — 1974 — 15.00
- ❑ BS42808 [Q] — Holiday — 1974 — 30.00
- ❑ BS2655 — Homecoming — 1972 — 15.00

AMERICAN BLUES, THE

KARMA
- ❑ 1001 [B] — The American Blues Is Here — 1967 — 500.00

UNI
- ❑ 73044 [B] — The American Blues Do Their Thing — 1968 — 100.00

AMERICAN BLUES EXCHANGE, THE

TAYL
- ❑ TLS-1 — Blueprints — 1969 — 400.00

AMERICAN BREED, THE

ACTA
- ❑ 8003 [M] — Bend Me, Shape Me — 1968 — 25.00
- ❑ 38003 [S] — Bend Me, Shape Me — 1968 — 30.00
- ❑ 8008 [M] — Lonely Side of the City — 1969 — 50.00
— *In stereo cover with "Monaural" sticker; record is regular yellow label*
- ❑ 38008 [S] — Lonely Side of the City — 1969 — 25.00
- ❑ 38006 [S] — Pumpkin, Powder, Scarlet & Green — 1968 — 25.00
- ❑ 8006 [M] — Pumpkin, Powder, Scarlet & Green — 1968 — 50.00
— *Stock label; the cover is the same as stereo but with a "Monaural" sticker attached*
- ❑ 8002 [M] — The American Breed — 1967 — 25.00
- ❑ 38002 [S] — The American Breed — 1967 — 30.00

AMERICAN DREAM, THE

AMPEX
- ❑ A-10101 [B] — The American Dream — 1970 — 30.00
— *Produced by Todd Rundgren*

AMERICAN EAGLE

DECCA
- ❑ DL75258 — American Eagle — 1971 — 25.00

AMERICAN JAZZ ENSEMBLE, THE

EPIC
- ❑ LA16040 [M] — New Dimensions — 1962 — 25.00
- ❑ BA17040 [S] — New Dimensions — 1962 — 30.00

RCA VICTOR
- ❑ LPM-2557 [M] — The American Jazz Ensemble in Rome — 1962 — 25.00
- ❑ LSP-2557 [S] — The American Jazz Ensemble in Rome — 1962 — 30.00

AMERICAN MUSIC CLUB

ALIAS
- ❑ A015 [B] — Everclear — 1991 — 18.00

FRONTIER
- ❑ 4619-1-L — California — 1988 — 15.00
- ❑ 4612-1-L — Engine — 1987 — 15.00

REPRISE
- ❑ 45721 — San Francisco — 1994 — 15.00

AMERICAN REVOLUTION, THE

FLICK DISC
- ❑ FL-45,002 [M] — The American Revolution — 1968 — 50.00
— *White label promo in stereo cover with "Not for Sale DJ Monaural" sticker on front*
- ❑ FLS-45,002 [S] — The American Revolution — 1968 — 30.00

AMES, ED

RCA CAMDEN
- ❑ ACL1-0244 — Do You Hear What I Hear? — 1973 — 15.00
- ❑ CAS-2536 — Ed Ames — 1972 — 15.00
- ❑ CAS-2598 — Somewhere, My Love — 1972 — 15.00

RCA VICTOR
- ❑ LPM-4028 [M] — Apologize — 1968 — 25.00
- ❑ LSP-4028 [S] — Apologize — 1968 — 12.00
- ❑ LSP-4128 — A Time for Living, A Time for Hope — 1969 — 12.00
- ❑ LSP-4385 — Christmas Is the Warmest Time of the Year — 1970 — 25.00
- ❑ LPM-3838 [M] — Christmas with Ed Ames — 1967 — 18.00
- ❑ LSP-3838 [S] — Christmas with Ed Ames — 1967 — 15.00
- ❑ LSP-4634 — Ed Ames — 1972 — 18.00
- ❑ LSP-4683 — Ed Ames Remembers Jim Reeves — 1972 — 18.00
- ❑ LPM-3460 [M] — It's a Man's World — 1965 — 15.00
- ❑ LSP-3460 [S] — It's a Man's World — 1965 — 15.00
- ❑ LSP-4249 — Love of the Common People — 1969 — 12.00
- ❑ LPM-3636 [M] — More I Cannot Wish You — 1966 — 12.00
- ❑ LSP-3636 [S] — More I Cannot Wish You — 1966 — 15.00
- ❑ LPM-3774 [M] — My Cup Runneth Over — 1967 — 12.00
- ❑ LSP-3774 [S] — My Cup Runneth Over — 1967 — 15.00
- ❑ LPM-3390 [M] — My Kind of Songs — 1965 — 15.00
- ❑ LSP-3390 [S] — My Kind of Songs — 1965 — 18.00
- ❑ LPM-2781 [M] — Opening Night — 1963 — 15.00
- ❑ LSP-2781 [S] — Opening Night — 1963 — 18.00
- ❑ ANL1-1780 — Pure Gold — 1976 — 12.00
- ❑ LSP-4381 — Sing Away the World — 1970 — 12.00
- ❑ LSP-4808 — Songs from "Lost Horizon" — 1973 — 18.00
- ❑ LSP-4184 — The Best of Ed Ames — 1969 — 12.00
- ❑ LPM-2944 [M] — The Ed Ames Album — 1964 — 15.00
- ❑ LSP-2944 [S] — The Ed Ames Album — 1964 — 18.00
- ❑ LSP-4079 — The Hits of Broadway and Hollywood — 1968 — 12.00
- ❑ ANL1-2891 — The Impossible Dream — 1978 — 12.00
- ❑ LSP-4453 — The Songs of Bacharach and David — 1971 — 12.00
- ❑ LSP-4172 — The Windmills of Your Mind — 1969 — 12.00
- ❑ VPS-6023 — This Is Ed Ames — 1970 — 25.00
- ❑ LPM-3834 [M] — Time, Time — 1967 — 15.00
- ❑ LSP-3834 [S] — Time, Time — 1967 — 12.00
- ❑ LPM-3913 [M] — When the Snow Is On the Roses — 1967 — 15.00
- ❑ LSP-3913 [S] — When the Snow Is On the Roses — 1967 — 12.00
- ❑ LPM-3961 [M] — Who Will Answer? And Other Songs of Our Time — 1968 — 18.00
- ❑ LSP-3961 [S] — Who Will Answer? And Other Songs of Our Time — 1968 — 12.00

AMES, NANCY

EPIC
- ❑ LN24197 [M] — As Time Goes By — 1967 — 15.00
- ❑ BN26197 [S] — As Time Goes By — 1967 — 18.00
- ❑ LN24189 [M] — Latin Pulse — 1966 — 15.00
- ❑ BN26189 [S] — Latin Pulse — 1966 — 18.00
- ❑ BN26378 — Nancy Ames at the Americana — 1968 — 15.00
- ❑ LN24238 [M] — Spiced with Brazil — 1967 — 15.00
- ❑ BN26238 [S] — Spiced with Brazil — 1967 — 18.00

LIBERTY
- ❑ LRP-3329 [M] — I Never Will Marry — 1964 — 18.00
- ❑ LST-7329 [S] — I Never Will Marry — 1964 — 25.00
- ❑ LRP-3400 [M] — Let It Be Me — 1965 — 18.00
- ❑ LST-7400 [S] — Let It Be Me — 1965 — 25.00
- ❑ LRP-3299 [M] — Portrait of Nancy — 1963 — 18.00
- ❑ LST-7299 [S] — Portrait of Nancy — 1963 — 25.00
- ❑ LRP-3276 [M] — The Incredible Nancy Ames — 1963 — 18.00
- ❑ LST-7276 [S] — The Incredible Nancy Ames — 1963 — 25.00
- ❑ LRP-3369 [M] — This Is the Girl That Is — 1964 — 18.00
- ❑ LST-7369 [S] — This Is the Girl That Is — 1964 — 25.00

SUNSET
- ❑ SUM-1109 [M] — The Versatile Nancy Ames — 196? — 15.00
- ❑ SUS-5109 [S] — The Versatile Nancy Ames — 196? — 18.00

AMES BROTHERS, THE

CORAL
- ❑ CRL57031 [M] — Ames Brothers Concert — 1956 — 30.00
- ❑ CRL56097 [10] — Favorite Songs — 1954 — 50.00
- ❑ CRL56050 [10] — Favorite Spirituals — 1952 — 50.00
- ❑ CRL56079 [10] — Home on the Range — 1952 — 50.00
- ❑ CRL56025 [10] — Hoop-De-Hoo — 1951 — 50.00
- ❑ CRL56017 [10] — In the Evening by the Moonlight — 1951 — 50.00
- ❑ CRL57176 [M] — Love Serenade — 1958 — 30.00
- ❑ CRL57054 [M] — Love's Old Sweet Song — 1956 — 30.00

Number	Title	Yr	NM
❑ CRL56080 [10]	Merry Christmas	1952	50.00
❑ CRL57338 [M]	Our Golden Favorites	1960	30.00
❑ CRL56024 [10]	Sentimental Me	1951	50.00
❑ CRL56014 [10]	Sing a Song of Christmas	1950	50.00
❑ CRL57166	Sounds of Christmas Harmony	1957	30.00
❑ CRL56042 [10]	Sweet Leilani	1951	50.00

EPIC

Number	Title	Yr	NM
❑ LN24036 [M]	Hello Italy	1962	18.00
❑ BN26036 [S]	Hello Italy	1962	25.00
❑ LN24069 [M]	Knees Up Mother Brown	1963	18.00
❑ BN26069 [S]	Knees Up Mother Brown	1963	25.00

MCA

Number	Title	Yr	NM
❑ 1510 [R]	The Ames Brothers	197?	12.00

RCA CAMDEN

Number	Title	Yr	NM
❑ CAL-571 [M]	The Ames Brothers -- Sweet and Swing	1958	18.00

RCA SPECIAL PRODUCTS

Number	Title	Yr	NM
❑ DVL2-0207	All Their Greatest Hits	1976	18.00

RCA VICTOR

Number	Title	Yr	NM
❑ LPM-1680 [M]	Destination Moon	1958	30.00
❑ LSP-1680 [S]	Destination Moon	1958	30.00
❑ LPM-2981 [M]	Down Memory Lane with the Ames Brothers	1964	15.00
❑ LSP-2981 [S]	Down Memory Lane with the Ames Brothers	1964	18.00
❑ LPM-1142 [M]	Exactly Like You	1955	30.00
❑ LPM-1954 [M]	Famous Hits of Famous Quartets	1959	25.00
❑ LSP-1954 [S]	Famous Hits of Famous Quartets	1959	30.00
❑ LPM-2876 [M]	For Sentimental Reasons	1964	15.00
❑ LSP-2876 [S]	For Sentimental Reasons	1964	18.00
❑ LPM-1157 [M]	Four Brothers	1955	30.00
❑ LPM-2100 [M]	Hello, Amigos	1960	25.00
❑ LSP-2100 [S]	Hello, Amigos	1960	30.00
❑ LPM-3186 [10]	It Must Be True	1954	50.00
❑ LPM-1855 [M]	Smoochin' Time	1958	30.00
❑ LSP-1855 [S]	Smoochin' Time	1958	30.00
❑ LPM-1487 [M]	Sweet Seventeen	1957	30.00
❑ LPM-1998 [M]	The Ames Brothers Sing the Best in the Country	1959	25.00
❑ LSP-1998 [S]	The Ames Brothers Sing the Best in the Country	1959	30.00
❑ LPM-1228 [M]	The Ames Brothers with Hugo Winterhalter	1956	30.00
❑ LPM-1859 [M]	The Best of the Ames Brothers	1958	30.00
❑ LSP-1859(e) [R]	The Best of the Ames Brothers	196?	25.00
❑ ANL1-1095e	The Best of the Ames Brothers	1975	12.00
❑ LPM-2273 [M]	The Best of the Bands	1960	25.00
❑ LSP-2273 [S]	The Best of the Bands	1960	30.00
❑ LPM-2182 [M]	The Blend and the Beat	1960	25.00
❑ LSP-2182 [S]	The Blend and the Beat	1960	30.00
❑ LPM-1541 [M]	There'll Always Be a Christmas	1957	30.00
❑ VPS-6068	This Is the Ames Brothers	1972	18.00
❑ LPM-2009 [M]	Words and Music	1959	25.00
❑ LSP-2009 [S]	Words and Music	1959	30.00

READER'S DIGEST

Number	Title	Yr	NM
❑ RDA-160	Sentimentally Yours	1981	30.00

VOCALION

Number	Title	Yr	NM
❑ VL73788 [R]	Christmas Harmony	196?	15.00
— Reissue of some Coral tracks			
❑ VL3617 [M]	The Ames Brothers	196?	18.00
❑ VL73818	The Ames Brothers Featuring Ed Ames	196?	12.00

AMISH, THE

SUSSEX

Number	Title	Yr	NM
❑ SUX-7016 [B]	The Amish	1972	30.00

AMMONS, ALBERT, AND PETE JOHNSON

RCA VICTOR

Number	Title	Yr	NM
❑ LPT-9 [10]	8 to the Bar	1952	100.00

AMMONS, ALBERT

BLUE NOTE

Number	Title	Yr	NM
❑ BLP-7017 [10]	Boogie Woogie Classics	1951	300.00

COMMODORE

Number	Title	Yr	NM
❑ XFL-15357 [M]	The Boogie Woogie and the Blues	198?	15.00

MERCURY

Number	Title	Yr	NM
❑ MG-25012 [10]	Boogie Woogie Piano	1950	150.00

AMMONS, ALBERT / MEADE LUX LEWIS

MOSAIC

Number	Title	Yr	NM
❑ MR3-103	The Complete Blue Note Recordings of Albert Ammons and Meade Lux Lewis	198?	50.00
— Limited edition of 5,000			

AMMONS, GENE, AND JAMES MOODY

PRESTIGE

Number	Title	Yr	NM
❑ P-10065	Chicago Concert	1973	30.00

AMMONS, GENE, AND RICHARD "GROOVE" HOLMES

PACIFIC JAZZ

Number	Title	Yr	NM
❑ PJ-32 [M]	Groovin' with Jug	1961	80.00
❑ ST-32 [S]	Groovin' with Jug	1961	60.00

AMMONS, GENE, AND SONNY STITT

CADET

Number	Title	Yr	NM
❑ LP-785 [M]	Jug and Sonny	1967	40.00
❑ LPS-785 [S]	Jug and Sonny	1967	30.00
— Fading blue label			
❑ LPS-785 [S]	Jug and Sonny	197?	18.00
— Yellow and pink label (reissue)			

CHESS

Number	Title	Yr	NM
❑ LP1445 [M]	Jug and Sonny	1960	80.00
❑ CH-91549	Jug and Sonny	198?	12.00

PRESTIGE

Number	Title	Yr	NM
❑ PRST-7823	Blues Up and Down Vol. 1	1969	25.00
❑ PRLP-107 [10]	Gene Ammons vs. Sonny Stitt: Battle of the Saxes	1951	250.00
❑ PRLP-7234 [M]	Soul Summit	1962	50.00
❑ PRST-7234 [S]	Soul Summit	1962	40.00
❑ PRLP-7454 [M]	Soul Summit	1967	25.00
❑ PRST-7454 [S]	Soul Summit	1967	18.00
❑ P-10100	Together Again for the Last Time	197?	25.00
❑ PRST-7606	We'll Be Together Again	1969	40.00
❑ PRST-10019	You Talk That Talk!	1970	40.00

VERVE

Number	Title	Yr	NM
❑ V-8426 [M]	Boss Tenors	1962	30.00
❑ V6-8426 [S]	Boss Tenors	1962	30.00
❑ V-8468 [M]	Boss Tenors in Orbit	1962	30.00
❑ V6-8468 [S]	Boss Tenors in Orbit	1962	30.00
❑ 2V6S-8812 [S]	Prime Cuts	1972	25.00

AMMONS, GENE

ANALOGUE PRODUCTIONS

Number	Title	Yr	NM
❑ AP 038 [M]	The Soulful Moods of Gene Ammons	199?	30.00
— 180-gram reissue of Moodsville 28			

ARGO

Number	Title	Yr	NM
❑ 697 [M]	Dig Him	1962	60.00
❑ S-697 [S]	Dig Him	1962	50.00
❑ 698 [M]	Just Jug	1962	80.00
❑ S-698 [S]	Just Jug	1962	40.00

CADET

Number	Title	Yr	NM
❑ 2CA-60038	Early Visions	1975	18.00
❑ LP-783 [M]	Makes It Happen	1967	40.00
❑ LPS-783 [S]	Makes It Happen	1967	25.00
— Fading blue label (original)			
❑ CA-783 [S]	Makes It Happen	197?	18.00
— Yellow and pink label (reissue)			

CHESS

Number	Title	Yr	NM
❑ CH2-92514	Early Visions	198?	15.00
— Reissue of Cadet 60038			
❑ LP1442 [M]	Soulful Saxophone	1959	70.00
Black vinyl			
❑ LP1442 [DJ]	Soulful Saxophone	1959	150.00
— White label promo; multicolor swirl vinyl			

EMARCY

Number	Title	Yr	NM
❑ EMS-2-400	The "Jug" Sessions	1976	25.00
❑ MG-26031 [10]	With or Without	1954	150.00

ENJA

Number	Title	Yr	NM
❑ 3093	Gene Ammons in Sweden	1981	18.00

FANTASY

Number	Title	Yr	NM
❑ OJC-014	All-Star Sessions	1982	12.00
❑ OJC-351	Bad! Bossa Nova	198?	12.00
❑ OJC-192	Blue Gene	1985	12.00
❑ OJC-297	Boss Tenor	1988	12.00
❑ OJC-244	Funky	1987	12.00
❑ OJC-6005	Gene Ammons' Greatest Hits, Vol. 1: The Sixties	1988	15.00
❑ OJC-129	Jammin' in Hi-Fi	198?	12.00
❑ OJC-211	Jammin' with Gene	1986	12.00
❑ OJC-395	Live in Chicago	198?	12.00
❑ OJC-651	The Big Sound	1991	15.00
❑ OJC-013	The Happy Blues	198?	12.00

MOODSVILLE

Number	Title	Yr	NM
❑ MVLP-18 [M]	Nice and Cool	1961	80.00
— Originals have green label			
❑ MVLP-18 [M]	Nice and Cool	1965	40.00
— Second editions have blue label with trident at right			
❑ MVLP-28 [M]	The Soulful Moods of Gene Ammons	1963	80.00
— Originals have green label			
❑ MVLP-28 [M]	The Soulful Moods of Gene Ammons	1965	40.00
— Second editions have blue label with trident at right			
❑ MVST-28 [S]	The Soulful Moods of Gene Ammons	1963	80.00

PRESTIGE

Number	Title	Yr	NM
❑ PRLP-7369 [M]	Angel Eyes	1965	50.00
— Originals have blue label with trident at right			
❑ PRST-7369 [S]	Angel Eyes	1965	60.00
— Originals have blue label with trident at right			
❑ PRLP-7257 [M]	Bad! Bossa Nova	1962	60.00
— Originals have yellow label, Bergenfield, N.J. address; some copies have a cover calling this "Jungle Soul! (ca' purange)			
❑ PRST-7257 [S]	Bad! Bossa Nova	1962	50.00
— Originals have silver label			
❑ P-10070	Big Bad Jug	1973	40.00
❑ PRST-10006	Black Cat	1970	30.00
— Original on purple label			
❑ PRST-10006	Black Cat	1973	30.00
— Second edition on green label			
❑ PRLP-7146 [M]	Blue Gene	1958	350.00
— Originals have yellow label, Bergenfield, N.J. address			
❑ MPP-2514	Blue Groove	1982	15.00
❑ PRLP-7445 [M]	Boss Soul!	1967	50.00
— Originals have blue label with trident at right			
❑ PRST-7445 [S]	Boss Soul!	1967	50.00
— Originals have blue label with trident at right			
❑ PRLP-7180 [M]	Boss Tenor	1960	80.00
— Originals have yellow label, Bergenfield, N.J. address			
❑ PRST-7180 [S]	Boss Tenor	1960	60.00
— Originals have silver label			
❑ PRLP-7534 [M]	Boss Tenor	1967	50.00
— Reissue of 7180; originals have blue label with trident at right			
❑ PRST-7534 [S]	Boss Tenor	1967	30.00
— Reissue of 7180; originals have blue label with trident at right			
❑ P-10080	Brasswind	1974	30.00
❑ P-10021	Brother Jug	1970	40.00
❑ PRST-10010	Chase!	1970	30.00
❑ P-10040	Free Again	1972	30.00
❑ PRLP-7083 [M]	Funky	1957	250.00
— Originals have yellow label, "W. 50th St., NYC" address			
❑ PRLP-107 [10]	Gene Ammons	1951	300.00
❑ PRLP-7050 [M]	Gene Ammons All Star Session	1956	300.00
— Compilation of Prestige 107 and 127, yellow label			
❑ P-10078	Gene Ammons and Friends at Montreux	1973	18.00
❑ PRLP-127 [10]	Gene Ammons Favorites, Volume 2	1952	300.00
❑ PRLP-149 [10]	Gene Ammons Favorites, Volume 3	1953	300.00
❑ PRLP-211 [10]	Gene Ammons Jazz Session	1955	300.00
❑ PRLP-7495 [M]	Gene Ammons Live in Chicago	1967	50.00
— Originals have blue label with trident at right			
❑ PRST-7495 [S]	Gene Ammons Live in Chicago	1967	40.00
— Originals have blue label with trident at right			
❑ P-10093	Goodbye	1975	25.00
❑ PRST-10058	Got My Own	1973	30.00
❑ P-10084	Greatest Hits	1974	30.00
❑ PRLP-7201 [M]	Groove Blues	1961	100.00
— Originals have yellow label, Bergenfield, N.J. address			
❑ PRLP-7039 [M]	Hi Fidelity Jam Session	1956	150.00
❑ PRLP-7110 [M]	Jammin' in Hi-Fi with Gene Ammons	1957	300.00
— Originals have yellow label, "W. 50th St., NYC" address			
❑ PRLP-7060 [M]	Jammin' with Gene	1956	650.00
❑ PRST-7192 [S]	Jug	1960	80.00
— Originals have silver label			
❑ PRLP-7192 [M]	Jug	1960	100.00
— Originals have yellow label, Bergenfield, N.J. address			
❑ PRST-7192 [S]	Jug	1972	30.00
— Reissue; trident logo at top			
❑ P-24021	Jug and Dodo	1972	25.00
❑ P-24036	Juganthology	197?	25.00
❑ PRST-7552	Jungle Soul	1968	40.00
— Reissue of 7257			
❑ PRLP-7287 [M]	Late Hour Special	1964	40.00
— Originals have yellow label, Bergenfield, N.J. address			
❑ PRST-7287 [S]	Late Hour Special	1964	50.00
— Originals have silver label			
❑ P-10022	My Way	197?	25.00
❑ P-7862	Night Lights	1985	15.00
❑ PRLP-7060 [M]	Not Really the Blues	1960	80.00
— Retitled version of "Jammin' with Gene			
❑ PRLP-7270 [M]	Preachin'	1963	60.00
— Originals have yellow label, Bergenfield, N.J. address			
❑ PRST-7270 [S]	Preachin'	1963	70.00
— Originals have silver label			
❑ PRLP-7400 [M]	Sock!	1966	50.00
— Originals have blue label with trident at right			
❑ PRST-7400 [S]	Sock!	1966	60.00
— Originals have blue label with trident at right			
❑ PRLP-7275 [M]	Soul Summit, Volume 2	1963	60.00
— Originals have yellow label, Bergenfield, N.J. address			
❑ PRST-7275 [S]	Soul Summit, Volume 2	1963	70.00
— Originals have silver label			
❑ PRLP-112 [10]	Tenor Sax Favorites, Volume 1	1951	300.00
❑ PRST-7774	The Best of Gene Ammons	1970	25.00
❑ PRST-7708	The Best of Gene Ammons for Beautiful People	1969	25.00
❑ PRLP-7132 [M]	The Big Sound	1958	250.00
— Originals have yellow label, "W. 50th St., NYC" address			
❑ P-24098	The Big Sound of Gene Ammons	1981	25.00
❑ P-10023	The Boss Is Back	197?	25.00
— Reissue of 7739			
❑ PRST-7739	The Boss Is Back!	1970	30.00
❑ P-24079	The Gene Ammons Story: Gentle Jug	197?	25.00

Number	Title	Yr	NM
❑ P-24071	The Gene Ammons Story: Organ Combos	197?	30.00
❑ P-24058	The Gene Ammons Story: The 78 Era	197?	25.00
❑ PRLP-7039 [M]	The Happy Blues	1960	80.00
—Retitled version of "Hi Fidelity Jam Session			
❑ PRST-7654	The Happy Blues -- Jam Session, Vol. 1	1969	30.00
—Second reissue of 7039			
❑ PRLP-7176 [M]	The Twister	1960	100.00
—Originals have yellow label, Bergenfield, N.J. address; reissue of 7110			
❑ PRLP-7238 [M]	Twistin' the Jug	1962	80.00
—Originals have yellow label, Bergenfield, N.J. address			
❑ PRST-7238 [S]	Twistin' the Jug	1962	60.00
—Originals have silver label			
❑ PRLP-7208 [M]	Up Tight!	1961	80.00
—Originals have yellow label, Bergenfield, N.J. address			
❑ PRST-7208 [S]	Up Tight!	1961	60.00
—Originals have silver label			
❑ PRLP-7320 [M]	Velvet Soul	1964	60.00
—Originals have yellow label, Bergenfield, N.J. address			
❑ PRST-7320 [S]	Velvet Soul	1964	80.00
—Originals have silver label			
❑ PRLP-7320 [M]	Velvet Soul	1965	40.00
—Blue label with tridenr at right			
❑ PRST-7320 [S]	Velvet Soul	1965	50.00
—Blue label with tridenr at right			
❑ PRLP-7050 [M]	Woofin' and Tweetin'	1960	80.00
—Retitled version of "Gene Ammons All Star Session			
ROOTS			
❑ 1002	Swinging the Jugg	1976	25.00
SAVOY			
❑ MG-14033 [M]	Golden Saxophone	1961	50.00
❑ SJL-1103	Red Top	1976	15.00
STATUS			
❑ 18	Nice & Cool	197?	18.00
TRIP			
❑ TLP-5578 [M]	Light, Bluesy and Moody	197?	15.00
UPFRONT			
❑ UPF-116	Nothing But Soul	1968	18.00
—Reissue of Vee-Jay material			
VEE JAY			
❑ LP-3024 [M]	Juggin' Around	1961	80.00
❑ LPS-3024 [S]	Juggin' Around	1961	80.00
WING			
❑ MGW-12156 [M]	Light, Bluesy and Moody	1963	25.00
—Reissue of EmArcy 10-inch LP			
❑ SRW-16156 [R]	Light, Bluesy and Moody	1963	18.00

AMON DUUL

Number	Title	Yr	NM
PROPHESY			
❑ PHS-1003 [B]	Amon Duul	1969	100.00

AMON DUUL II

Number	Title	Yr	NM
ATCO			
❑ SD 36-108	Hijack	1975	18.00
❑ SD 36-119	Made in Germany	1976	18.00
CLEOPATRA			
❑ CLP1712 [B]	Dance of the Lemmings	2014	40.00
❑ CLP1804 [B]	Duulirium	2014	30.00
❑ CLP1715 [B]	Phallus Dei	2014	40.00
❑ CLP1720 [B]	Viva La Trance	2014	40.00
❑ CLP1587LP [B]	Wolf City	2014	40.00
UNITED ARTISTS			
❑ UAS-5586 [B]	Carnival in Babylon	1972	35.00
❑ UAS-9954 [B]	Dance of the Lemmings	1971	40.00
❑ UA-LA198-F [B]	Viva La Trance	1974	35.00
❑ UA-LA017-F [B]	Wolf City	1973	35.00

AMOS, TORI

Number	Title	Yr	NM
ATLANTIC			
❑ 82862	Boys for Pele	1996	25.00
—Clear vinyl			
❑ 83095	From the Choirgirl Hotel	1998	30.00
❑ 82567	Under the Pink	1995	30.00
—Limited edition on pink vinyl			
UNIVERSAL REPUBLIC			
❑ 1290601	Abnormally Attracted to Sin	2009	30.00

AMRAM-BARROW QUARTET, THE

Number	Title	Yr	NM
DECCA			
❑ DL8558 [M]	Jazz Studio No. 6	1957	50.00

AMY, CURTIS, AND DUPREE BOLTON

Number	Title	Yr	NM
PACIFIC JAZZ			
❑ PJ-70 [M]	Katanga!	1963	30.00
❑ ST-70 [S]	Katanga!	1963	60.00
—Red vinyl			
❑ ST-70 [S]	Katanga!	1963	30.00
—Black vinyl			

AMY, CURTIS, AND FRANK BUTLER

Number	Title	Yr	NM
PACIFIC JAZZ			
❑ PJ-19 [M]	Groovin' Blue	1961	30.00
❑ ST-19 [S]	Groovin' Blue	1961	40.00

AMY, CURTIS, AND PAUL BRYANT

Number	Title	Yr	NM
KIMBERLY			
❑ 2020 [M]	This Is the Blues	1963	25.00
❑ 11020 [S]	This Is the Blues	1963	30.00
PACIFIC JAZZ			
❑ PJ-26 [M]	Meetin' Here	1961	30.00
❑ ST-26 [S]	Meetin' Here	1961	40.00
❑ PJ-9 [M]	The Blues Message	1960	30.00
❑ ST-9 [S]	The Blues Message	1960	40.00

AMY, CURTIS, AND VICTOR FELDMAN

Number	Title	Yr	NM
PACIFIC JAZZ			
❑ PJ-46 [M]	Way Down	1962	30.00
❑ ST-46 [S]	Way Down	1962	30.00

AMY, CURTIS

Number	Title	Yr	NM
PACIFIC JAZZ			
❑ PJ-62 [M]	Tippin' On Through -- Recorded "Live" at the Lighthouse	1962	30.00
❑ ST-62 [S]	Tippin' On Through -- Recorded "Live" at the Lighthouse	1962	30.00
PALOMAR			
❑ G-24003 [M]	Sounds of Hollywood and Broadway	1965	18.00
❑ GS-34003 [S]	Sounds of Hollywood and Broadway	1965	25.00
VERVE			
❑ V-8684 [M]	Mustang	1966	18.00
❑ V6-8684 [S]	Mustang	1966	25.00

ANCIENT GREASE

Number	Title	Yr	NM
MERCURY			
❑ SR-61305	Women and Children First	1970	30.00

ANDERS & PONCIA

Number	Title	Yr	NM
WARNER BROS.			
❑ WS1778	The Anders & Poncia Album	1969	30.00

ANDERSON, AL

Number	Title	Yr	NM
TWIN/TONE			
❑ TTR88110	Party Favors	1989	15.00
VANGUARD			
❑ VSD-79324	Al Anderson	1973	25.00

ANDERSON, BILL, AND JAN HOWARD

Number	Title	Yr	NM
DECCA			
❑ DL75293	Bill & Jan (Or Jan & Bill)	1972	25.00
❑ DL4959 [M]	For Loving You	1967	30.00
❑ DL74959 [S]	For Loving You	1967	25.00
❑ DL75184	If It's All the Same to You	1970	25.00

ANDERSON, BILL, AND MARY LOU TURNER

Number	Title	Yr	NM
MCA			
❑ 2298	Billy Boy & Mary Lou	1977	15.00
❑ 2182	Sometimes	1976	15.00

ANDERSON, BILL

Number	Title	Yr	NM
DECCA			
❑ DL75275	Always Remember	1971	15.00
❑ DL75161	Bill Anderson's Christmas	1969	18.00
❑ DL4859 [M]	Bill Anderson's Greatest Hits	1967	25.00
❑ DL74859 [S]	Bill Anderson's Greatest Hits	1967	25.00
❑ DL75315	Bill Anderson's Greatest Hits, Vol. 2	1971	15.00
❑ DL4600 [M]	Bill Anderson Showcase	1964	18.00
❑ DL74600 [S]	Bill Anderson Showcase	1964	25.00
❑ DL4499 [M]	Bill Anderson Sings	1964	18.00
❑ DL74499 [S]	Bill Anderson Sings	1964	25.00
❑ DL4192 [M]	Bill Anderson Sings Country Songs	1962	25.00
❑ DL74192 [S]	Bill Anderson Sings Country Songs	1962	30.00
❑ DL75344	Bill Anderson Sings For "All the Lonely Women in the World	1972	15.00
❑ DL4686 [M]	Bright Lights and Country Music	1965	18.00
❑ DL74686 [S]	Bright Lights and Country Music	1965	25.00
❑ DL75383	Don't She Look Good	1972	15.00
❑ DL4646 [M]	From This Pen	1965	18.00
❑ DL74646 [S]	From This Pen	1965	25.00
❑ DL4855 [M]	Get While the Gettin's Good	1967	18.00
❑ DL74855 [S]	Get While the Gettin's Good	1967	25.00
❑ DL75056	Happy State of Mind	1968	18.00
❑ DL4886 [M]	I Can Do Nothing Alone	1967	30.00
❑ DL74886 [S]	I Can Do Nothing Alone	1967	25.00
❑ DL4771 [M]	I Love You Drops	1966	18.00
❑ DL74771 [S]	I Love You Drops	1966	25.00
❑ DL75206	Love Is a Sometimes Thing	1970	15.00
❑ DL75142	My Life/But You Know I Love You	1969	18.00
❑ DL75339	Singing His Praise	1972	15.00
❑ DL4427 [M]	Still	1963	25.00
❑ DL74427 [S]	Still	1963	30.00
❑ DXSA7198	The Bill Anderson Story	1969	18.00
❑ DL75254	Where Have All Our Heroes Gone?	1971	15.00
❑ DL74998	Wild Weekend	1968	18.00
MCA			
❑ 320	Bill	1973	15.00
❑ 13	Bill Anderson's Greatest Hits	1973	12.00
—Reissue of Decca 74859			
❑ 454	Every Time I Turn the Radio On/Talk to Me Ohio	1974	12.00
❑ 3075	Ladies' Choice	1979	12.00
❑ 694	Ladies' Choice	198?	10.00
—Reissue			
❑ 2371	Love and Other Sad Stories	1977	12.00
❑ 693	Love and Other Sad Stories	198?	10.00
—Reissue			
❑ 3214	Nashville Mirrors	1980	12.00
❑ 766	Nashville Mirrors	198?	10.00
—Reissue			
❑ 2222	Peanuts & Diamonds & Other Jewels	1975	12.00
❑ 2264	Scorpio	1976	12.00
❑ 4001	The Bill Anderson Story	1973	15.00
—Reissue of Decca 7198			
❑ 416	Whispering" Bill Anderson	1974	15.00
❑ 35032	Whispering	197?	12.00
MCA CORAL			
❑ 20002	I Can Do Nothing	1973	12.00
VOCALION			
❑ VL3835 [M]	Bill Anderson's Country Style	196?	15.00
❑ VL73835 [S]	Bill Anderson's Country Style	196?	18.00
❑ VL73927	Just Plain Bill	197?	12.00

ANDERSON, CASEY

Number	Title	Yr	NM
ATCO			
❑ 33-176 [M]	Blues Is a Woman Gone	1965	25.00
❑ SD 33-176 [S]	Blues Is a Woman Gone	1965	30.00
❑ 33-172 [M]	Live at the Ice House	1965	25.00
❑ SD 33-172 [S]	Live at the Ice House	1965	30.00
❑ 33-166 [M]	More Pretty Girls Than One	1964	25.00
❑ SD 33-166 [S]	More Pretty Girls Than One	1964	30.00
❑ 33-149 [M]	The Bag I'm In	1962	25.00
❑ SD 33-149 [S]	The Bag I'm In	1962	30.00
CHELSEA			
❑ CHL551	Passing Time	1976	25.00
EDGE			
❑ ER-742	Good Old Boys	1974	25.00
ELEKTRA			
❑ EKL-192 [M]	Goin' Places	1960	25.00
❑ EKS-7192 [S]	Goin' Places	1960	30.00
FORUM CIRCLE			
❑ FCS-9108 [S]	Casey Anderson Sings Folk Songs	196?	15.00
❑ FC-9108 [M]	Casey Anderson Sings Folk Songs	196?	18.00
—Reissue of Urania album with one track deleted			
SUPERSTAR			
❑ SSR-73-1	The Kind of Man I Am	196?	30.00
URANIA			
❑ UR9024 [M]	Casey Sings Out	196?	40.00

ANDERSON, CAT

Number	Title	Yr	NM
CLASSIC JAZZ			
❑ CJ-142	Cat Speaks	1979	15.00
EMARCY			
❑ MG-36142 [M]	Cat on a Hot Tin Roof	1958	50.00
INNER CITY			
❑ 1143	Cat Anderson	198?	12.00
MERCURY			
❑ MG-20522 [M]	Cat on a Hot Tin Roof	1959	40.00
❑ SR-60199 [S]	Cat on a Hot Tin Roof	1959	40.00

ANDERSON, CHRIS

Number	Title	Yr	NM
JAZZLAND			
❑ JLP-57 [M]	Inverted Images	1961	30.00
❑ JLP-957 [S]	Inverted Images	1961	40.00

ANDERSON, ERNESTINE

Number	Title	Yr	NM
CONCORD JAZZ			
❑ CJ-319	Be Mine Tonight	1987	25.00
❑ CJ-214	Big City	1983	25.00
❑ CJ-31	Hello Like Before	1977	25.00
❑ CJ-54	Live from Concord to London	1978	30.00
❑ CJ-147	Never Make Your Move Too Soon	1982	25.00
❑ CJ-109	Sunshine	1980	25.00
❑ CJ-263	When the Sun Goes Down	1985	25.00
MERCURY			
❑ MG-20400 [M]	Ernestine Anderson	1959	40.00
❑ SR-60074 [S]	Ernestine Anderson	1959	100.00
❑ MG-20492 [M]	Fascinating Ernestine	1959	50.00
❑ SR-60171 [S]	Fascinating Ernestine	1959	80.00
❑ MG-20354 [M]	Hot Cargo	1958	60.00
❑ MG-20582 [M]	Moanin'	1960	40.00
❑ SR-60242 [S]	Moanin'	1960	50.00
❑ MG-20496 [M]	My Kinda Swing	1959	60.00
❑ SR-60175 [S]	My Kinda Swing	1959	80.00
SUE			
❑ LP1015 [M]	The New Sound of Ernestine Anderson	1963	25.00

Number	Title	Yr	NM
WING			
❑ MGW-12281 [M]	My Kinda Swing	1964	18.00
❑ SRW-16281 [S]	My Kinda Swing	1964	25.00

ANDERSON, JOHN

Number	Title	Yr	NM
MCA			
❑ 42218	10	1988	10.00
❑ 42037	Blue Skies Again	1988	10.00
WARNER BROS.			
❑ 23912	All the People Are Talkin'	1983	10.00
❑ 25373	Countrified	1986	10.00
❑ 25099	Eye of a Hurricane	1984	10.00
❑ 25169	Greatest Hits	1984	10.00
❑ BSK3599	I Just Came Home to Count the Memories	1981	12.00
❑ BSK3459	John Anderson	1980	15.00
❑ BSK3547	John Anderson 2	1981	12.00
❑ 25211	Tokyo, Oklahoma	1985	10.00
❑ 23721	Wild & Blue	1982	10.00

ANDERSON, JON

Number	Title	Yr	NM
ATLANTIC			
❑ SD19355	Animation	1982	12.00
❑ SD18180 [B]	Olias of Sunhillow	1976	18.00
❑ SD16021 [B]	Song of Seven	1980	15.00
COLUMBIA			
❑ BFC40910	In the City of Angels	1988	12.00
ELEKTRA			
❑ 60469	3 Ships	1985	15.00

ANDERSON, LAURIE

Number	Title	Yr	NM
WARNER BROS.			
❑ BSK3674	Big Science	1982	12.00
❑ WBMS-134-2 [DJ]	Home of the Brave Interview	1986	30.00
—Part of the Warner Bros. Music Show series			
❑ 25400	Home of the Brave (Soundtrack)	1986	12.00
❑ 25077 [DJ]	Mister Heartbreak	1984	18.00
—Quiex II" audiophile pressing			
❑ 25077	Mister Heartbreak	1984	12.00
❑ PRO-A-2123 [EP]	Selections from Mister Heartbreak	1984	10.00
—Promo-only sampler with three songs (Excellent Birds/Sharkey's Day/Sharkey's Night)			
❑ PRO A 2229 [DJ]	Selections from United States Live	1984	15.00
—Promo-only sampler with eight tracks			
❑ 25900	Strange Angels	1989	15.00
❑ 25192	United States Live	1984	40.00
—Boxed set			

ANDERSON, LEROY

Number	Title	Yr	NM
DECCA			
❑ DL8121 [M]	Blue Tango and Other Favorites	1955	25.00
❑ DL8193 [M]	Christmas Carols	1955	25.00
❑ DL8925 [M]	Christmas Festival	1959	15.00
❑ DL78925 [S]	Christmas Festival	1959	18.00
❑ DL9749 [M]	Leroy Anderson "Pops" Concert	195?	25.00
❑ DL8954 [M]	Leroy Anderson Conducts His Music	1959	25.00
❑ DL78954 [S]	Leroy Anderson Conducts His Music	1959	30.00
❑ DL7509 [10]	Leroy Anderson Conducts His Own Compositions, Volume 1	195?	30.00
❑ DL7519 [10]	Leroy Anderson Conducts His Own Compositions, Volume 2	195?	30.00
❑ DL8865 [M]	Leroy Anderson Conducts Leroy Anderson	1958	18.00
❑ DL78865 [S]	Leroy Anderson Conducts Leroy Anderson	1958	25.00
❑ DL4335 [M]	New Music of Leroy Anderson	1962	18.00
❑ DL74335 [S]	New Music of Leroy Anderson	1962	25.00
MCA			
❑ 531	Leroy Anderson Conducts His Music	197?	15.00
—Reissue of Decca 78954; black label with rainbow			
❑ 555	Leroy Anderson Conducts Leroy Anderson	197?	15.00
—Reissue of Decca 78665; black label with rainbow			
PICKWICK			
❑ SPC-1036	Christmas Festival	197?	18.00

ANDERSON, LIZ

Number	Title	Yr	NM
RCA VICTOR			
❑ LPM-3852 [M]	Cookin' Up Hits	1967	30.00
❑ LSP-3852 [S]	Cookin' Up Hits	1967	25.00
❑ LSP-4346	Husband Hunting	1970	25.00
❑ LSP 4222	If the Creek Don't Rise	1969	25.00
❑ LSP-4014	Like a Merry-Go-Round	1968	25.00
❑ LPM-3769 [M]	Liz Anderson Sings	1967	30.00
❑ LSP-3769 [S]	Liz Anderson Sings	1967	25.00
❑ LPM-3908 [M]	Liz Anderson Sings Her Favorites	1968	40.00
❑ LSP-3908 [S]	Liz Anderson Sings Her Favorites	1968	25.00

ANDERSON, LYNN

Number	Title	Yr	NM
CHART			
❑ CHS-1017	At Home with Lynn	1969	18.00
❑ CHS-1008	Big Girls Don't Cry	1969	18.00
❑ CHS-1037	I'm Alright	1970	15.00
❑ CHS-1050	Lynn Anderson	1972	18.00
❑ CHS-1040	Lynn Anderson's Greatest Hits	1971	15.00
❑ CHS-1043	Lynn Anderson with Strings	1971	15.00
❑ CHM-1004 [M]	Promises, Promises	1968	25.00
❑ CHS-1004 [S]	Promises, Promises	1968	18.00
❑ CHM-1001 [M]	Ride, Ride, Ride	1967	25.00
❑ CHS-1001 [S]	Ride, Ride, Ride	1967	18.00
❑ CHS-1032	Songs My Mother Wrote	1970	15.00
❑ CHS-1022	Songs That Made Country Girls Famous	1970	15.00
❑ CHS-1009	The Best of Lynn Anderson	1969	18.00
❑ CHS-1028	Uptown Country Girl	1970	15.00
❑ CHS-1013	With Love, From Lynn	1969	18.00
COLUMBIA			
❑ PC34089	All the King's Horses	1976	12.00
❑ KC30957	Christmas Album	1971	15.00
❑ 3C30957	Christmas Album	198?	10.00
—Reissue of KC 30957			
❑ KC31316	Cry	1972	12.00
❑ FC37354	Encore	1981	12.00
❑ PC37354	Encore	1983	10.00
—Budget-line reissue			
❑ JC36568	Even Cowgirls Get the Blues	1980	12.00
❑ KC35445	From the Inside	1978	12.00
❑ C30925	How Can I Unlove You	1971	12.00
❑ JC34871	I Love What Love Is Doing to Me/He Ain't You	1977	12.00
❑ KC33691	I've Never Loved Anyone More	1975	12.00
❑ KC32078	Keep Me in Mind	1973	12.00
❑ KC31647	Listen to a Country Song	1972	12.00
❑ KC31641	Lynn Anderson's Greatest Hits	1972	12.00
❑ PC31641	Lynn Anderson's Greatest Hits	197?	10.00
—Reissue			
❑ PC34308	Lynn Anderson's Greatest Hits Volume II	1976	12.00
❑ C30099	No Love at All	1970	15.00
❑ JC35776	Outlaw Is Just a State of Mind	1979	12.00
❑ KC32719	Queens of Country	1974	12.00
❑ C30411	Rose Garden	1970	12.00
❑ PC30411	Rose Garden	197?	10.00
—Reissue			
❑ KC32941	Smile for Me	1974	12.00
❑ CS1025	Stay There 'Til I Get There	1970	15.00
❑ CG30902	The World of Lynn Anderson	1971	15.00
❑ KC32429	Top of the World	1973	12.00
❑ KC33293	What a Man, My Man Is	1974	12.00
❑ PC34439	Wrap Your Love All Around Your Man	1977	12.00
❑ C30793	You're My Man	1971	12.00
COLUMBIA LIMITED EDITION			
❑ LE10053	Stay Here 'Til I Get There	197?	12.00
HARMONY			
❑ KH32433	Singing My Song	1973	10.00
MERCURY			
❑ 834625-1	What She Does Best	1988	10.00
MOUNTAIN DEW			
❑ 7047	Lynn Anderson	197?	12.00
PERMIAN			
❑ 8205	Back	1983	12.00
PICKWICK			
❑ SPC-3267	Flower of Love	197?	10.00
❑ SPC-3296	It Makes You Happy	197?	10.00
❑ PTP-2049	Lynn Anderson	1973	15.00
TIME-LIFE			
❑ STW-112	Country Music	1981	12.00

ANDERSON, MARIAN

Number	Title	Yr	NM
RCA VICTOR RED SEAL			
❑ LRM-7006 [10]	Eleven Great Spirituals	1951	50.00
❑ LSC-2592 [S]	He's Got the Whole World in His Hands	1962	25.00
—Originals with "shaded dog" label			
❑ LM7008 [10]	Marian Anderson Sings Christmas Carols	1954	50.00
❑ LSC-2613 [S]	Marian Anderson Sings Christmas Carols	1961	25.00
—Originals with "shaded dog" label			
❑ LSC-2613 [S]	Marian Anderson Sings Christmas Carols	1965	30.00
—Second pressings with "white dog" label			
❑ LM-110 [10]	Spirituals	1956	50.00
❑ LM-2032 [M]	Spirituals	1956	40.00

ANDERSON, MILDRED

Number	Title	Yr	NM
BLUESVILLE			
❑ BVLP-1017 [M]	No More in Life	1961	50.00
—Blue and silver label			
❑ BVLP-1017 [M]	No More in Life	1964	30.00
—Blue label with trident logo			
❑ BVLP-1004 [M]	Person to Person	1960	50.00
—Blue and silver label			
❑ BVLP-1004 [M]	Person to Person	1964	30.00
—Blue label with trident logo			

ANDERSON, PINK, AND REV. GARY DAVIS

Number	Title	Yr	NM
RIVERSIDE			
❑ RLP 12-611 [M]	Carolina Street Ballads/Harlem Street Spirituals	196?	60.00

ANDERSON, PINK

Number	Title	Yr	NM
BLUESVILLE			
❑ BVLP-1071 [M]	Ballad and Folk Singer	1963	100.00
—Blue label, silver print			
❑ BVLP-1071 [M]	Ballad and Folk Singer	1964	30.00
—Blue label with trident logo			
❑ BVLP-1038 [M]	Carolina Blues Man	1961	120.00
—Blue label, silver print			
❑ BVLP-1038 [M]	Carolina Blues Man	1964	30.00
—Blue label with trident logo			
❑ BVLP-1051 [M]	Medicine Show Man	1962	100.00
—Blue label, silver print			
❑ BVLP-1051 [M]	Medicine Show Man	1964	30.00
—Blue label with trident logo			

ANDERSON BRUFORD WAKEMAN HOWE

Number	Title	Yr	NM
ARISTA			
❑ 90126	Anderson Bruford Wakeman Howe	1989	10.00

ANDERZA, EARL

Number	Title	Yr	NM
PACIFIC JAZZ			
❑ PJ-65 [M]	Outa Sight	1963	30.00
❑ ST-65 [S]	Outa Sight	1963	30.00

ANDRE'S CUBAN ALL-STARS

Number	Title	Yr	NM
CLEF			
❑ MGC-515 [10]	Cubano	1954	100.00
—This was reissued on 12-inch as part of a JACK COSTANZO album.			

ANDREWS, ERNIE

Number	Title	Yr	NM
DISCOVERY			
❑ 825	From the Heart	198?	15.00
GENE NORMAN PRESENTS			
❑ GNP-42 [M]	Ernie Andrews	1959	40.00
❑ GNP-28 [M]	In the Dark	1957	40.00
❑ GNP-43 [M]	Travelin' Light	1959	40.00
❑ GNPS-10008 [S]	Travelin' Light	1959	40.00
GNP CRESCENDO			
❑ GNPS-10008 [S]	Travelin' Light	196?	18.00

ANDREWS, GAYLE

Number	Title	Yr	NM
HI-LIFE			
❑ HL-54 [M]	Love's a Snap	195?	30.00

ANDREWS, JULIE

Number	Title	Yr	NM
COLUMBIA			
❑ CL1712 [M]	Broadway's Fair Julie	1962	25.00
—Red and black label with six "eye" logos			
❑ CS8512 [S]	Broadway's Fair Julie	1962	30.00
—Red and black label with six "eye" logos			
❑ CL1886 [M]	Don't Go In the Lion's Cage Tonight	1963	25.00
❑ CS8686 [S]	Don't Go In the Lion's Cage Tonight	1963	30.00
RCA VICTOR			
❑ LPM-3829 [M]	A Christmas Treasure	1967	18.00
❑ LSP-3829 [S]	A Christmas Treasure	1967	18.00
❑ LPM-1681 [M]	Julie Andrews Sings	1958	30.00
❑ LSP-1681 [S]	Julie Andrews Sings	1958	50.00
❑ LPM-1403 [M]	The Lass with the Delicate Air	1957	40.00
—With pale blue jacket and the words "Julie Andrews" in a picture frame			
❑ LPM-1403 [M]	The Lass with the Delicate Air	1958	30.00
—With altered cover; "RE" on jacket			
❑ LSP-1403 [S]	The Lass with the Delicate Air	1958	60.00

ANDREWS, LEE, AND THE HEARTS

Number	Title	Yr	NM
COLLECTABLES			
❑ COL-5028	Biggest Hits	198?	15.00
❑ COL-5003	Gotham Recording Sessions	1982	15.00
LOST-NITE			
❑ LP-101 [M]	Biggest Hits	1964	100.00
—Yellow vinyl			
❑ LP-101 [M]	Biggest Hits	1964	50.00
—Black vinyl			
❑ LP-113 [M]	Lee Andrews and the Hearts Live	1965	50.00
❑ LLP-1 [10]	The Best of Lee Andrews and the Hearts, Volume 1	1981	15.00
—Red vinyl; in die-cut cover with sticker			
❑ LLP-2 [10]	The Best of Lee Andrews and the Hearts, Volume 2	1981	15.00
—Red vinyl; in die-cut cover with sticker			

Number	Title	Yr	NM

ANDREWS, RUBY

ABC
| ❏ AB-1002 | Genuine Ruby | 1977 | 18.00 |

ICHIBAN
| ❏ 1104 | Kiss This | 1991 | 18.00 |

ZODIAC
| ❏ ZS1001 | Everybody Saw You | 1970 | 80.00 |

ANDREWS SISTERS, THE

ABC
| ❏ 4003 | Sixteen Great Performances | 1975 | 15.00 |

CAPITOL
❏ T860 [M]	Fresh and Fancy Free	1957	30.00
❏ T790 [M]	The Andrews Sisters in Hi-Fi	1957	30.00
❏ T973 [M]	The Dancing Twenties	1957	30.00
❏ T1924 [M]	The Hits of the Andrews Sisters	1963	25.00
❏ DT1924 [R]	The Hits of the Andrews Sisters	1963	15.00

DECCA
❏ DL5264 [10]	Berlin Songs	1951	40.00
❏ DL5282 [10]	Christmas Cheer	1950	40.00
— Also see "Crosby, Bing."			
❏ DL5155 [10]	Club 15	1951	40.00
❏ DL4019 [M]	Curtain Call	1956	30.00
❏ DL5306 [10]	I Love to Tell the Story	1952	40.00
❏ DL8354 [M]	Jingle Bells	1956	30.00
❏ DL5423 [10]	My Isle of Golden Dreams	1953	40.00
❏ DL5438 [10]	Sing, Sing, Sing	1953	40.00
❏ DL5120 [10]	The Andrews Sisters	1951	40.00
❏ DL8360 [M]	The Andrews Sisters -- By Popular Demand	1957	30.00
❏ DL5065 [10]	Tropical Songs	1950	40.00

DOT
❏ DLP3567 [M]	Great Country Hits	1963	15.00
❏ DLP25567 [S]	Great Country Hits	1963	18.00
❏ DLP3452 [M]	Great Golden Hits	1962	18.00
❏ DLP25452 [S]	Great Golden Hits	1962	25.00
❏ DLP3529 [M]	Present	1963	15.00
❏ DLP26620 [S]	Present	1963	18.00
❏ DLP3632 [M]	The Andrews Sisters Go Hawaiian	1964	15.00
❏ DLP25632 [S]	The Andrews Sisters Go Hawaiian	1964	18.00
❏ DLP3406 [M]	The Andrews Sisters' Greatest Hits	1962	18.00
❏ DLP25406 [S]	The Andrews Sisters' Greatest Hits	1962	25.00

HAMILTON
| ❏ HLP124 [M] | Pennsylvania Polka | 196? | 15.00 |
| ❏ HLP12124 [S] | Pennsylvania Polka | 196? | 18.00 |

MCA
❏ 27082	Boogie Woogie Bugle Girls	1980	10.00
— Reissue of Paramount 6075			
❏ 24015	Christmas	1987	10.00
— Reissue			
❏ 739	Near You	198?	10.00
— Reissue of Vocalion album			
❏ 908	Rarities	198?	10.00
❏ 27081	Sixteen Great Performances	1980	10.00
— Reissue of ABC 4003			
❏ 2-4024	The Best of the Andrews Sisters	1973	18.00
❏ 2-4093	The Best of the Andrews Sisters, Vol. 2	197?	18.00

PARAMOUNT
| ❏ PAS-6075 | Boogie Woogie Bugle Girls | 1973 | 15.00 |
| ❏ PAS-1023 | In the Mood | 1974 | 18.00 |

PICKWICK
❏ PC-3094 [M]	Don't Sit Under the Apple Tree	196?	18.00
❏ SPC-3094 [S]	Don't Sit Under the Apple Tree	196?	15.00
❏ SPC-3382	Sing! Sing! Sing!	197?	12.00

VOCALION
| ❏ VL3611 [M] | Near You | 196? | 15.00 |

ANDY AND THE BEY SISTERS

PRESTIGE
❏ PRLP-7346 [M]	Now! Hear!	1964	40.00
❏ PRST-7346 [S]	Now! Hear!	1964	50.00
❏ PRLP-7411 [M]	'Round About Midnight	1965	40.00
❏ PRST-7411 [S]	'Round About Midnight	1965	50.00

ANGEL

CASABLANCA
❏ NBLP7021 [B]	Angel	1975	18.00
❏ NBLP7028 [B]	Helluva Band	1976	18.00
❏ NBLP7203	Live Without a Net	1980	18.00
❏ NBLP7043	On Earth As It Is in Heaven	1977	15.00
❏ NBLP7127	Sinful	1979	15.00
❏ NBLP7085	White Hot	1977	15.00

ANGELI, PIER

ROULETTE
| ❏ R-25051 [M] | Italia Con Pier Angeli | 1959 | 30.00 |
| ❏ SR-25051 [S] | Italia Con Pier Angeli | 1959 | 30.00 |

ANGELOU, MAYA

LIBERTY
| ❏ LRP-3028 [M] | Miss Calypso | 1958 | 100.00 |

ANGELS, THE (1)

ASCOT
| ❏ AM13009 [M] | The Angels Sing -- Twelve of Their Greatest Hits | 1964 | 35.00 |
| ❏ ALS16009 [S] | The Angels Sing -- Twelve of Their Greatest Hits | 1964 | 50.00 |

CAPRICE
| ❏ LP1001 [M] | ...And the Angels Sing | 1962 | 120.00 |
| ❏ SLP1001 [S] | ...And the Angels Sing | 1962 | 200.00 |

COLLECTABLES
| ❏ COL-5085 | My Boyfriend's Back: Golden Classics | 198? | 12.00 |

SMASH
❏ MGS-27048 [M]	A Halo to You	1964	40.00
❏ SRS-67048 [S]	A Halo to You	1964	60.00
— Some copies distributed with Netherlands Philips 842 948 edition vinyl instead of US.			
❏ MGS-27039 [M]	My Boyfriend's Back	1963	40.00
❏ SRS-67039 [S]	My Boyfriend's Back	1963	60.00

ANGRY SAMOANS

BAD TRIP
❏ (# unknown) [B]	Back from Samoa	1982	50.00
❏ 001 [EP]	Different World/Unhinged + 4	1986	60.00
❏ 201 [EP]	Inside My Brain	1981	30.00
❏ 201 [EP]	Inside My Brain	1981	60.00
— Original with heavy gray cardboard cover			
❏ 002 [B]	The Mistaken	1987	60.00
— As "The Mistaken"; 1,000 copies made			

PVC
❏ 8955 [B]	Inside My Brain	1987	30.00
— Reissue			
❏ 8965 [B]	STP Not LSD	1988	25.00
❏ 6915 [B]	Yesterday Started Tomorrow	1987	30.00

ANIMALS, THE

ABKCO
❏ AB-4226	The Best of the Animals	1973	15.00
❏ AB-4324 [M]	The Best of the Animals	1987	12.00
— With alternate version of "We Gotta Get Out of This Place"			

ACCORD
| ❏ SN-7193 | Looking Back | 1981 | 10.00 |
| ❏ SN-7235 | The Animals with Eric Burdon | 1982 | 10.00 |

I.R.S.
| ❏ SP70043 | Rip It to Shreds: Their Greatest Hits Live | 1984 | 12.00 |
| ❏ SP70037 | The Ark | 1983 | 12.00 |

JET/UA
❏ JT-LA790-H	Before We Were So Rudely Interrupted	1977	12.00
— As "The Original Animals"			
❏ JT-LA790-H	Before We Were So Rudely Interrupted	1977	100.00
— White label test pressing with promo letter signed by Danny Goldberg			

MGM
❏ E-4414 [M]	Animalism	1966	100.00
— Yellow label promo			
❏ E-4414 [M]	Animalism	1966	30.00
❏ SE-4414 [S]	Animalism	1966	30.00
❏ E-4384 [M]	Animalization	1966	30.00
❏ E-4384 [M]	Animalization	1966	100.00
— Yellow label promo			
❏ SE-4384 [P]	Animalization	1966	30.00
— All stereo except "Inside Looking Out," which is rechanneled.			
❏ T90923 [M]	Animalization	1966	50.00
— Capitol Record Club edition			
❏ ST90923 [M]	Animalization	1966	50.00
— Capitol Record Club edition			
❏ E-4305 [M]	Animal Tracks	1965	150.00
— Yellow label promo			
❏ E-4305 [M]	Animal Tracks	1965	40.00
❏ SE-4305 [R]	Animal Tracks	1965	30.00
❏ T90571 [M]	Animal Tracks	1965	50.00
— Capitol Record Club edition			
❏ E-4433 [M]	Eric Is Here	1967	18.00
❏ SE-4433 [S]	Eric Is Here	1967	25.00
❏ E-4553 [M]	Every One of Us	1968	50.00
— Mono is promo only (yellow label)			
❏ SE-4553 [S]	Every One of Us	1968	30.00
❏ ST-91550 [S]	Every One of Us	1968	40.00
— Capitol Record Club edition; black label			
❏ SE-4602	Greatest Hits of Eric Burdon and the Animals	1969	18.00
❏ SE-4591 [B]	Love Is	1968	60.00
❏ E-4264 [M]	The Animals	1964	200.00
— Yellow label promo			
❏ E-4264 [M]	The Animals	1964	30.00
— The House of the Rising Sun" is the edited 45 version			
❏ SE-4264 [R]	The Animals	1964	30.00
— The House of the Rising Sun" is the edited 45 version (rechanneled, like the rest of the LP)			
❏ T90687 [M]	The Animals	1966	50.00
— Capitol Record Club edition			
❏ E-4281 [M]	The Animals On Tour	1965	100.00
— Yellow label promo			

❏ E-4281 [M]	The Animals On Tour	1965	30.00
❏ SE-4281 [R]	The Animals On Tour	1965	30.00
❏ T90414 [M]	The Animals On Tour	1965	50.00
— Capitol Record Club edition			
❏ ST90414 [R]	The Animals On Tour	1965	40.00
— Capitol Record Club edition			
❏ E-4454 [M]	The Best of Eric Burdon and the Animals, Vol. 2	1967	25.00
❏ SE-4454 [P]	The Best of Eric Burdon and the Animals, Vol. 2	1967	25.00
❏ T-91156 [M]	The Best of Eric Burdon and the Animals, Vol. 2	1967	30.00
— Capitol Record Club edition			
❏ E-4324 [M]	The Best of the Animals	1966	80.00
— Yellow label promo			
❏ SE-4324 [R]	The Best of the Animals	1966	30.00
❏ E-4324 [M]	The Best of the Animals	1966	25.00
— This album was the first to contain the full-length version of "House of the Rising Sun.			
❏ KAO90622 [M]	The Best of the Animals	1966	40.00
— Capitol Record Club edition			
❏ SKAO90622 [R]	The Best of the Animals	1966	40.00
— Capitol Record Club edition; black label			
❏ SKAO90622 [R]	The Best of the Animals	1969	30.00
— Capitol Record Club edition; blue and gold label			
❏ SE-4537 [S]	The Twain Shall Meet	1968	30.00
❏ E-4537 [M]	The Twain Shall Meet	1968	30.00
❏ E-4484 [M]	Winds of Change	1967	30.00
❏ SE-4484 [S]	Winds of Change	1967	30.00

PICKWICK
| ❏ SPC-3330 | The Early Animals with Eric Burdon | 1971 | 10.00 |

POLYDOR
| ❏ 829091-1 [M] | Animalization | 1986 | 10.00 |

SCEPTER CITATION
| ❏ CTN-18026 | The Best of the Animals | 1972 | 10.00 |

SPRINGBOARD
| ❏ SPB-4025 | The Best of the Animals | 1972 | 10.00 |
| ❏ SPB-4065 | The Night Time Is the Right Time | 1973 | 10.00 |

WAND
| ❏ WDS-690 [B] | In the Beginning | 1970 | 12.00 |

ANIMATED EGG, THE

ALSHIRE
| ❏ SF-32700 [B] | The Animated Egg | 1967 | 150.00 |

ANKA, PAUL

ABC-PARAMOUNT
❏ 353 [M]	Anka at the Copa	1960	30.00
❏ S-353 [S]	Anka at the Copa	1960	40.00
❏ 420 [M]	Diana	1962	30.00
❏ S-420 [S]	Diana	1962	40.00
❏ ABC360 [M]	It's Christmas Everywhere	1960	30.00
❏ ABCS360 [S]	It's Christmas Everywhere	1960	40.00
❏ 296 [M]	My Heart Sings	1959	30.00
❏ S-296 [S]	My Heart Sings	1959	50.00
❏ 240 [M]	Paul Anka	1958	50.00
❏ 409 [M]	Paul Anka Sings His Big, Big 15, Volume III	1962	30.00
❏ S-409 [S]	Paul Anka Sings His Big, Big 15, Volume III	1962	30.00
❏ 323 [M]	Paul Anka Sings His Big 15	1960	50.00
❏ S-323 [R]	Paul Anka Sings His Big 15	196?	30.00
❏ S-390 [S]	Paul Anka Sings His Big 15, Vol. 2	1961	40.00
❏ 390 [M]	Paul Anka Sings His Big 15, Vol. 2	1961	30.00
❏ 347 [M]	Paul Anka Swings for Young Lovers	1960	30.00
❏ S-347 [S]	Paul Anka Swings for Young Lovers	1960	40.00
❏ 371 [M]	Strictly Instrumental	1961	30.00
❏ S-371 [S]	Strictly Instrumental	1961	40.00

ACCORD
| ❏ SN-7117 | She's a Lady | 1981 | 10.00 |

BUDDAH
❏ BDS5114	Jubilation	1972	15.00
❏ BDS5093	Paul Anka	1971	15.00
❏ BDS5667	The Essential Paul Anka	1974	18.00
❏ BDS5622	This Is Anka	1974	18.00

COLUMBIA
| ❏ FC39323 | Paul Anka Live | 1984 | 10.00 |
| ❏ FC38442 | Walk a Fine Line | 1983 | 10.00 |

LIBERTY
❏ LN-10149	Feelings	1982	10.00
— Budget-line reissue			
❏ LN-10000	Paul Anka: His Best	1980	10.00
— Budget-line reissue			
❏ LN-10220	The Painter	1983	10.00
— Budget-line reissue			
❏ LN-10001	The Times of Your Life	1980	10.00
— Budget-line reissue			

PAIR
| ❏ PDL2-1129 | Songs I Write and Sing | 1986 | 15.00 |

PICKWICK
❏ PTP-2087	Paul Anka Way	197?	12.00
❏ SPC-3508	Puppy Love	1975	10.00
❏ SPC-3523	She's a Lady	1975	10.00

Number	Title	Yr	NM
RANWOOD			
❏ 8203	The Very Best of Paul Anka	1981	10.00
RCA CAMDEN			
❏ ACL1-0616	My Way	1974	10.00
RCA VICTOR			
❏ AFL1-3926	Both Sides of Love	1981	12.00
❏ LPM-2996 [M]	Excitement on Park Avenue	1964	18.00
❏ LSP-2996 [S]	Excitement on Park Avenue	1964	25.00
❏ LSP-4142	Goodnight My Love	1969	18.00
❏ AFL1-3382	Headlines	1979	12.00
❏ LPM-2575 [M]	Let's Sit This One Out	1962	25.00
❏ LSP-2575 [S]	Let's Sit This One Out	1962	30.00
❏ LSP-4250	Life Goes On	1969	18.00
❏ AFL1-2892	Listen to Your Heart	1978	12.00
❏ LPM-2614 [M]	Our Man Around the World	1963	25.00
❏ LSP-2614 [S]	Our Man Around the World	1963	30.00
❏ LSP-4300	Paul Anka 70s	1970	18.00
❏ LPM-3875 [M]	Paul Anka Live	1967	18.00
❏ LSP-3875 [S]	Paul Anka Live	1967	25.00
❏ LPM-2691 [M]	Paul Anka's 21 Golden Hits	1963	25.00
❏ LSP-2691 [S]	Paul Anka's 21 Golden Hits	1963	30.00
—LPM/LSP-2691 has re-recorded versions of ABC-Paramount hits			
❏ AYL1-3808	Paul Anka's 21 Golden Hits	1980	10.00
—Best Buy Series" reissue			
❏ ANL1-1584	Paul Anka Sings His Favorites	1976	12.00
❏ ANL1-0896	Remember Diana	1975	12.00
❏ ANL1-1054	She's a Lady	1975	12.00
❏ LSP-4203	Sincerely	1969	18.00
❏ LPM-2744 [M]	Songs I Wish I'd Written	1963	18.00
❏ LSP-2744 [S]	Songs I Wish I'd Written	1963	25.00
❏ ANL1-2482	Songs I Wish I'd Written	1977	12.00
❏ LPM-3580 [M]	Strictly Nashville	1966	18.00
❏ LSP-3580 [S]	Strictly Nashville	1966	25.00
❏ LPM-2502 [M]	Young, Alive and In Love!	1962	30.00
—With portrait of Paul Anka on front cover			
❏ LPM-2502 [M]	Young, Alive and In Love!	1962	18.00
—With portrait of Paul Anka on back cover			
❏ LSP-2502 [S]	Young, Alive and In Love!	1962	30.00
—With portrait of Paul Anka on front cover			
❏ LSP-2502 [S]	Young, Alive and In Love!	1962	25.00
—With portrait of Paul Anka on back cover			
RHINO			
❏ RNLP-70220	The Best of Paul Anka (14 Original Hits, 1957-1961)	1986	12.00
RIVIERA			
❏ 0047 [M]	Paul Anka and Others	1959	150.00
—With Paul Anka's RPM recordings plus tracks by other artists			
SIRE			
❏ SASH-3704	Paul Anka Gold	1974	18.00
❏ SBK6043	The Vintage Years 1957-1961	1978	15.00
UNITED ARTISTS			
❏ UA-LA314-G	Anka	1974	12.00
❏ UA-LA367-G	Feelings	1975	12.00
❏ UA-LA922-H	Paul Anka: His Best	1978	12.00
❏ UA-LA746-H	The Music Man	1977	12.00
❏ UA-LA653-G [Q]	The Painter	1976	15.00
—All copies are quadraphonic			
❏ UA-LA569-G	Times of Your Life	1975	12.00

ANN-MARGRET

Number	Title	Yr	NM
LHI			
❏ S-12007	The Cowboy and the Lady	1969	40.00
—With Lee Hazlewood			
MCA			
❏ 3226	Ann-Margret	1980	15.00

LSP-2659 LIVING STEREO — Bachelors' Paradise — Ann-Margret

Number	Title	Yr	NM
RCA VICTOR			
❏ LPM-2399 [M]	And Here She Is…	1961	30.00
❏ LSP-2399 [S]	And Here She Is…	1961	40.00
❏ LPM-2659 [M]	Bachelor's Paradise	1963	30.00

Number	Title	Yr	NM
❏ LSP-2659 [S]	Bachelor's Paradise	1963	40.00
❏ LPM-2453 [M]	On the Way Up	1961	30.00
❏ LSP-2453 [S]	On the Way Up	1961	40.00
❏ LPM-3710 [M]	Songs from The Swinger and Others	1966	60.00
❏ LSP-3710 [S]	Songs from The Swinger and Others	1966	80.00
❏ LPM-2551 [M]	The Vivacious One	1962	30.00
❏ LSP-2551 [S]	The Vivacious One	1962	40.00

ANNA MARIE

Number	Title	Yr	NM
VESTA			
❏ LP-101 [10]	Anna Marie	1955	80.00

ANNETTE

Number	Title	Yr	NM
BUENA VISTA			
❏ BV-3301 [M]	Annette	1959	120.00
❏ BV-3324 [M]	Annette at Bikini Beach	1964	50.00
❏ STER-3324 [S]	Annette at Bikini Beach	1964	100.00
❏ BV-4037	Annette Funicello	1972	50.00
❏ BV-3320 [M]	Annette on Campus	1964	50.00
❏ STER-3320 [S]	Annette on Campus	1964	100.00
❏ BV-3302 [M]	Annette Sings Anka	1960	100.00
❏ BV-3327 [M]	Annette Sings Golden Surfin' Hits	1964	100.00
❏ STER-3327 [S]	Annette Sings Golden Surfin' Hits	1964	150.00
❏ BV-3325 [M]	Annette's Pajama Party	1964	40.00
❏ STER-3325 [S]	Annette's Pajama Party	1964	100.00
❏ BV-3316 [M]	Beach Party	1963	60.00
❏ STER-3316 [S]	Beach Party	1963	100.00
❏ BV-3305 [M]	Dance Annette	1961	75.00
❏ BV-3303 [M]	Hawaiiannette	1960	75.00
❏ BV-3304 [M]	Italiannette	1960	75.00
❏ BV-3314 [M]	Muscle Beach Party	1963	75.00
❏ STER-3314 [S]	Muscle Beach Party	1963	150.00
❏ BV-3328 [M]	Something Borrowed, Something Blue	1964	60.00
❏ STER-3328 [P]	Something Borrowed, Something Blue	1964	100.00
❏ BV-3313 [M]	Teen Street	1962	75.00
❏ BV-3312 [M]	The Story of My Teens	1962	75.00
RHINO			
❏ RNDF-206	The Best of Annette	1984	15.00
❏ RNLP-702 [PD]	The Best of Annette	1984	30.00

ANNETTE / HAYLEY MILLS

Number	Title	Yr	NM
DISNEYLAND			
❏ DL-3508 [M]	Annette and Hayley Mills (Singing 10 of Their Greatest All-Time Hits)	1964	1000.00
—TV offer; issued with paper jacket. Though the cover says "Buena Vista Records Presents," the label is the yellow Disneyland label			

ANONYMOUS

Number	Title	Yr	NM
A-MAJOR			
❏ AMLS-1002	Inside the Shadow	1976	250.00

ANT, ADAM

Number	Title	Yr	NM
EPIC			
❏ ARE38370	Friend or Foe	1982	12.00
❏ FE39108 [B]	Strip	1984	12.00
❏ BFE40159	Vive Le Rock	1985	10.00
MCA			
❏ 6315	Manners & Physique	1989	12.00

ANT TRIP CEREMONY

Number	Title	Yr	NM
C.R.C.			
❏ 2129	24 Hours	1970	750.00
—Originals have thick cover and black vinyl			

ANTHEM

Number	Title	Yr	NM
BUDDAH			
❏ BDS-5071	Anthem	1971	25.00

ANTHONY, MARC

Number	Title	Yr	NM
COLUMBIA			
❏ C69726	Marc Anthony	1999	15.00

ANTHONY, RAY

Number	Title	Yr	NM
AERO SPACE			
❏ RA1007	Around the World	197?	12.00
❏ RA1028	Let's Go Dancing	197?	15.00
—Green vinyl; Arthur Murray promotional item; add 25 percent if certificate for a free dance lesson is included			
CAPITOL			
❏ T1371 [M]	Arthur Murray Favorites – Fox Trots	1960	15.00
❏ H362 [10]	Campus Rumpus	195?	50.00
❏ T2043 [M]	Charade and Other Top Themes	1964	15.00
❏ ST2043 [S]	Charade and Other Top Themes	1964	18.00
❏ T1420 [M]	Dancing Alone Together	1960	15.00
—Black colorband label, Capitol logo at left			
❏ ST1420 [S]	Dancing Alone Together	1960	18.00
—Black colorband label, Capitol logo at left			
❏ T1420 [M]	Dancing Alone Together	1962	12.00
—Black colorband label, Capitol logo at top			

Number	Title	Yr	NM
❏ ST1420 [S]	Dancing Alone Together	1962	15.00
—Black colorband label, Capitol logo at top			
❏ T1028 [M]	Dancing Over the Waves	1958	18.00
❏ T723 [M]	Dream Dancing	1956	18.00
❏ T1608 [M]	Dream Dancing Medley	1961	15.00
❏ ST1608 [S]	Dream Dancing Medley	1961	18.00
❏ T2457 [M]	Dream Dancing Today	1966	15.00
❏ ST2457 [S]	Dream Dancing Today	1966	18.00
❏ M-11978	Fox Trots	1979	12.00
❏ H258 [10]	Fox Trots	195?	40.00
❏ T563 [M]	Golden Horn	1955	18.00
❏ T2530 [M]	Hit Songs to Remember	1966	15.00
❏ ST2530 [S]	Hit Songs to Remember	1966	18.00
❏ H292 [10]	Houseparty Hop	195?	40.00
—Reissue of L 292; purple label; "This Album Contains 8 Selections" on upper right back cover			
❏ L292 [10]	Houseparty Hop	195?	50.00
—Original issue; maroon label; "In addition to the selections listed, this long playing record contains: PERDIDO - WAGON WHEELS" under the title on back cover			
❏ T1783 [M]	I Almost Lost My Mind	1962	15.00
❏ ST1783 [S]	I Almost Lost My Mind	1962	18.00
❏ H476 [10]	I Remember Glenn Miller	1954	40.00
❏ T749 [M]	Jam Session at the Tower	1956	40.00
❏ T1304 [M]	Like Wild!	1959	15.00
❏ ST1304 [S]	Like Wild!	1959	18.00
❏ T917 [M]	Moments Together	1958	18.00
❏ T1252 [M]	More Dream Dancing	1959	15.00
❏ ST1252 [S]	More Dream Dancing	1959	18.00
❏ T2150 [M]	My Love, Forgive Me	1964	15.00
❏ ST2150 [S]	My Love, Forgive Me	1964	18.00
❏ T1066 [M]	Ray Anthony Plays Steve Allen	1958	18.00
❏ T1917 [M]	Smash Hits of '63	1963	15.00
❏ ST1917 [S]	Smash Hits of '63	1963	18.00
❏ T1200 [M]	Sound Spectacular	1959	18.00
❏ T831 [M]	Star Dancing	1957	18.00
❏ T2188 [M]	Swim, Swim, C'mon, Let's Swim	1964	15.00
❏ ST2188 [S]	Swim, Swim, C'mon, Let's Swim	1964	18.00
❏ T969 [M]	The Dream Girl	1958	18.00
❏ T1477 [M]	The Hits of Ray Anthony	1960	15.00
❏ T1421 [M]	The Now Ray Anthony Show	1960	15.00
❏ ST1421 [S]	The New Ray Anthony Show	1960	18.00
❏ T1668 [M]	Twist with Ray Anthony	1961	15.00
❏ ST1668 [S]	Twist with Ray Anthony	1961	18.00
❏ T1752 [M]	Worried Mind	1962	15.00
❏ ST1752 [S]	Worried Mind	1962	18.00
❏ T866 [M]	Young Ideas	1957	18.00
CIRCLE			
❏ CLP-96	Sweet and Swingin' 1949-1963	1987	12.00
HINDSIGHT			
❏ HSR-240	Young Man with a Horn	1988	12.00
RANWOOD			
❏ 8153	Golden Hits	197?	12.00
❏ 8083	I Get the Blues When It Rains	197?	12.00
❏ 8059	Love Is for the Two of Us	197?	12.00
❏ R.8033	Now	197?	12.00
—Cover uses "R." prefix, label uses "RLP" prefix			

ANTHRAX

Number	Title	Yr	NM
ISLAND			
❏ 90584	Among the Living	1987	10.00
❏ 848804-1 [D]	Attack of the Killer B's	1991	25.00
❏ 90685 [EP]	I'm the Man	1987	10.00
❏ 846480-1 [B]	Persistence of Time	1990	18.00
❏ 90480	Spreading the Disease	1985	10.00
❏ PR2563 [DJ]	Statements of Euphoria	1988	18.00
—Promo-only interview album			
❏ 91004 [B]	State of Euphoria	1988	10.00
MEGAFORCE			
❏ MRS-05 [EP]	Armed & Dangerous	1985	25.00
❏ MRI-469 [B]	Fistful of Metal	1983	25.00
❏ CAROL-1383	Fistful of Metal	198?	10.00
—Reissue of 469			

ANTI NOWHERE LEAGUE

Number	Title	Yr	NM
GWR			
❏ 1238	The Perfect Crime	1987	18.00
WXYZ			
❏ FEP1301 [EP]	I Hate…People	1982	14.00
❏ COPE4	We Are … The League	1982	18.00

ANTISEEN

Number	Title	Yr	NM
BONA FIDE/CHOPPER			
❏ (# unknown)	Honor Among Thieves	1987	15.00
REPO			
❏ (# unknown)	The Raw Shit	1986	15.00
—Pink vinyl			

ANVIL

Number	Title	Yr	NM
ENIGMA/METAL BLADE			
❏ 7-73336 [B]	Pound for Pound	1988	25.00
❏ ST-73267 [B]	Strength of Steel	1987	25.00

AORTA

Number	Title	Yr	NM
COLUMBIA			
❏ CS9785	Aorta	1969	30.00

Number	Title	Yr	NM
HAPPY TIGER			
❑ HT-1010	Aorta 2	1970	40.00
APHRODITE'S CHILD			
VERTIGO			
❑ VEL-2-500	666 (The Apocalypse of John)	1972	25.00
APPLE PIE MOTHERHOOD BAND, THE			
ATLANTIC			
❑ SD8233	Apple Pie	1969	30.00
❑ SD8189	The Apple Pie Motherhood Band	1968	30.00
APPLEJACKS, THE (1)			
CAMEO			
❑ C-1004 [M]	Alone Together	1958	50.00
—As "Dave Appell			
APPLETREE THEATRE CO.			
VERVE FORECAST			
❑ FTS-3042	Playback	1968	50.00
—RICK NELSON appears on this album			
APPLEYARD, PETER			
AUDIO FIDELITY			
❑ AFLP-1901 [M]	The Vibe Sound of Peter Appleyard	1958	40.00
❑ AFSD-5901 [S]	The Vibe Sound of Peter Appleyard	1958	40.00
APRIL WINE			
AQUARIUS			
❑ AQR504	Electric Jewels	1973	18.00
❑ AQR505	Live	1974	18.00
ATLANTIC			
❑ SD19303	Stand Back	1981	12.00
—Reissue of Big Tree 89506			
BIG TREE			
❑ BTS2012	April Wine	1972	25.00
❑ 89506	Stand Back	1975	18.00
CAPITOL			
❑ ST-12311	Animal Grace	1984	12.00
❑ ST-11852	First Glance	1979	15.00
❑ SN-16245	First Glance	1982	10.00
—Budget-line reissue			
❑ ST-12013	Harder...Faster	1979	12.00
❑ SN-16322	Harder...Faster	1984	10.00
—Budget-line reissue			
❑ ST-12218	Power Play	1982	12.00
❑ SN-16344	Power Play	1984	10.00
—Budget-line reissue			
❑ SPRO-9632/3 [DJ]	Summer Tour 1981	1981	25.00
—Promo-only sampler			
❑ SOO-12125	The Nature of the Beast	1981	12.00
❑ SN-16379	The Nature of the Beast	1986	10.00
—Budget-line reissue			
❑ C1-48418	Walking Through Fire	1988	15.00
LONDON			
❑ PS699	Live at the El Mocambo	1977	18.00
❑ PS675	The Whole World's Goin' Crazy	1976	18.00
ELEKTRA			
❑ 6E-205	Chance to Dance	1979	12.00
❑ 6E-152	Fantasy	1978	12.00
AQUATONES, THE			
FARGO			
❑ 3001 [M]	The Aquatones Sing	1964	500.00
RELIC/FARGO			
❑ 5033 [M]	The Aquatones Sing	198?	10.00
ARABIAN PRINCE			
ORPHEUS			
❑ D1-75614	Brother Arab	1989	12.00
ARBORS, THE			
DATE			
❑ TEM3003 [M]	A Symphony for Susan	1967	25.00
❑ TES4003 [S]	A Symphony for Susan	1967	25.00
❑ TES4017 [B]	The Arbors Featuring I Can't Quit Her and The Letter	1969	25.00
❑ TEM3011 [M]	Valley of the Dolls	1967	30.00
❑ TES4011 [S]	Valley of the Dolls	1967	30.00
ARCADIA			
CAPITOL			
❑ R134433	So Red the Rose	1985	15.00
—RCA Music Service edition			
❑ SV-12428	So Red the Rose	1985	12.00
ARCHER, FRANCES, AND BEVERLY GILE			
DISNEYLAND			
❑ EB-1347/8 [10]	A Child's Garden of Verses	1955	150.00

Number	Title	Yr	NM
—The very first LP released on Disneyland Records			
❑ WDL-3004 [M]	A Child's Garden of Verses	1956	30.00
—Reissue of 1347/8			
❑ WDL-1008 [M]	A Child's Garden of Verses	1959	25.00
—Reissue of 3004			
❑ DQ-1241 [M]	A Child's Garden of Verses	1964	25.00
—Reissue of 1008			
❑ ST-3802 [M]	A Child's Garden of Verses	1971	30.00
—Reissue of 1241			
❑ WDL-3023 [M]	Community Concert	1958	30.00
❑ WDL-3006 [M]	Folk Songs from the Far Corners	1957	30.00
❑ DQ-1226 [M]	Songs from All Around the World	1962	25.00
—Black and white back cover (original)			
ARCHIES, THE			
51 WEST			
❑ 16002	The Archies	1979	12.00
ACCORD			
❑ SN-7149	Straight A's	1981	12.00
CALENDAR			
❑ KES-103 [B]	Everything's Archie	1969	30.00
❑ KES-101 [B]	The Archies	1968	30.00
KIRSHNER			
❑ KES-103 [DJ]	Everything's Archie Box	1969	100.00
—Box with LP, photos, press kit and buttons			
❑ KES-105 [B]	Jingle Jangle	1969	30.00
❑ KES-107 [B]	Sunshine	1970	30.00
❑ KES-109 [B]	The Archies Greatest Hits	1970	30.00
❑ KES-110	This Is Love	1971	30.00
ARDEN, TONI			
DECCA			
❑ DL8875 [M]	Besame	1959	25.00
—Black label, silver print			
❑ DL78875 [S]	Besame	1959	30.00
—Maroon label, silver print			
❑ DL4375 [M]	Italian Gold	196?	15.00
❑ DL74375 [S]	Italian Gold	196?	18.00
❑ DL8651 [M]	Miss Toni Arden	1957	30.00
—Black label, silver print			
❑ DL8765 [M]	Sing a Song of Italy	1958	30.00
—Black label, silver print			
❑ DL78765 [S]	Sing a Song of Italy	1959	30.00
—Maroon label, silver print			
HARMONY			
❑ HL7212 [M]	Exciting Toni Arden	196?	25.00
AREA CODE 615			
POLYDOR			
❑ 24-4002 [B]	Area Code 615	1969	30.00
❑ 24-4025 [B]	A Trip in the Country	1970	30.00
ARGENT			
EPIC			
❑ KE31556	All Together Now	1972	25.00
—Yellow label			
❑ KE31556	All Together Now	1973	15.00
—Orange label			
❑ PE33955	Anthology	1976	18.00
—Orange label			
❑ PE33955	Anthology	1979	12.00
—Dark blue label			
❑ BN26525	Argent	1970	25.00
—Yellow label			
❑ BN26525	Argent	1973	15.00
—Orange label			
❑ E30128 [B]	A Ring of Hands	1971	25.00
—Yellow label			
❑ KE30128	A Ring of Hands	1973	15.00
—Orange label			
❑ PE33422	Circus	1975	25.00
—Orange label			
❑ PEG33079 [B]	Encore -- Live in Concert	1975	30.00
—Orange labels			
❑ KE32195	In Deep	1973	25.00
—Orange label			
❑ PEQ32195 [Q]	In Deep	1974	50.00
❑ KE32195	In Deep	1973	30.00
—Yellow label			
❑ PE32573	Nexus	1974	25.00
—Orange label			
UNITED ARTISTS			
❑ UA-LA560-G	Counterpoint	1975	15.00
ARGO, TONY			
SAVOY			
❑ MG-12157 [M]	Jazz Argosy	1960	40.00
ARISTOCATS, THE			
HIFI			
❑ J-610 [M]	Boogie and Blues	1959	30.00
❑ JS-610 [S]	Boogie and Blues	1959	40.00

Number	Title	Yr	NM
ARISTOCRATS OF DIXIELAND, THE			
AUDIOPHILE			
❑ AP-129	Florida Blues	1979	12.00
ARLEN, HAROLD, AND "FRIEND			
COLUMBIA MASTERWORKS			
❑ OL6520 [M]	Harold Sings Arlen	1966	30.00
❑ OS2920 [S]	Harold Sings Arlen	1966	40.00
—Gray label with "360 Sound" in white			
ARMAGEDDON (1)			
AMOS			
❑ 73075	Armageddon	1970	30.00
ARMAGEDDON (2)			
A&M			
❑ SP-4513 [B]	Armageddon	1975	35.00
ARMATRADING, JOAN			
A&M			
❑ SP-4525	Back to the Night	1975	15.00
❑ SP-3141	Back to the Night	1980	10.00
—Reissue			
❑ 7502152981	Hearts and Flowers	1990	18.00
❑ SP-3302 [EP]	How Cruel	1979	10.00
❑ SP-4588	Joan Armatrading	1976	12.00
❑ SP-3228	Joan Armatrading	1984	10.00
—Reissue			
❑ SP-8414 [DJ]	Joan Armatrading Live at the Bijou Café	1977	25.00
—Promo-only "Superstars Radio Network" issue			
❑ SP-4809	Me Myself I	1980	12.00
❑ SP-5040	Secret Secrets	1985	12.00
❑ SP-4663	Show Some Emotion	1977	12.00
❑ SP-3273	Show Some Emotion	1984	10.00
—Reissue			
❑ SP-5130	Sleight of Hand	1986	12.00
❑ SP-4912	The Key	1983	12.00
❑ SP-5211	The Shouting Stage	1988	12.00
❑ 3P-4702	To the Limit	1978	12.00
❑ SP-4987	Track Record	1984	12.00
❑ SP-4876	Walk Under Ladders	1981	12.00
❑ SP-4382	Whatever's For Us	1974	15.00
❑ SP-3227	Whatever's For Us	1984	10.00
—Reissue			
ARMEN, KAY			
DECCA			
❑ DL8835 [M]	Golden Songs of Tin Pan Alley	1959	25.00
❑ DL78835 [S]	Golden Songs of Tin Pan Alley	1959	30.00
MGM			
❑ E-3276 [M]	If You Believe	1955	30.00
❑ E-277 [10]	Kay Armen Sings "For No One But You	1955	40.00
ARMORED SAINT			
CHRYSALIS			
❑ BFV41516	Delirious Nomad	1985	12.00
❑ FV41476	March of the Saint	1984	12.00
❑ BFV41601	Raising Fear	1987	12.00
ENIGMA/METAL BLADE			
❑ 72301 [EP]	Live: Saints Will Conquer	1988	12.00
METAL BLADE			
❑ MBR1009 [EP]	Armored Saint	1983	50.00
ARMS, RUSSELL			
ERA			
❑ EL-20013 [M]	Where Can a Wanderer Go	1957	30.00
ARMSTRONG, LIL HARDIN			
RIVERSIDE			
❑ RLP-401 [M]	Lil Armstrong and Her Orchestra	1962	30.00
❑ RLP-9401 [R]	Lil Armstrong and Her Orchestra	1962	18.00
❑ RLP 12-120 [M]	Satchmo and Me	1956	60.00
—White label, blue print			
❑ RLP 12-120 [M]	Satchmo and Me	195?	40.00
—Blue label with microphone logo at top			
ARMSTRONG, LOUIS, AND DUKE ELLINGTON			
MOBILE FIDELITY			
❑ 2-155	The Great Reunion	1984	80.00
—Audiophile vinyl			
PICKWICK			
❑ PC-3033	Louis Armstrong and Duke Ellington	196?	12.00
ROULETTE			
❑ RE-108	The Duke Ellington-Louis Armstrong Era	1973	18.00
❑ R52103 [M]	The Great Reunion	1963	25.00
❑ SR52103 [S]	The Great Reunion	1963	30.00
❑ R52074 [M]	Together for the First Time	1961	30.00
❑ SR52074 [S]	Together for the First Time	1961	25.00

Number	Title	Yr	NM

ARMSTRONG, LOUIS, AND OSCAR PETERSON

VERVE

Number	Title	Yr	NM
❏ MGV-8322 [M]	Louis Armstrong Meets Oscar Peterson	1959	50.00
❏ MGVS-6062 [S]	Louis Armstrong Meets Oscar Peterson	1960	40.00
❏ V-8322 [M]	Louis Armstrong Meets Oscar Peterson	1961	25.00
❏ V6-8322 [S]	Louis Armstrong Meets Oscar Peterson	1961	18.00

ARMSTRONG, LOUIS, AND SIDNEY BECHET

JOLLY ROGER

Number	Title	Yr	NM
❏ 5029 [M]	Louis Armstrong and Sidney Bechet	195?	40.00

ARMSTRONG, LOUIS, AND THE MILLS BROTHERS

DECCA

Number	Title	Yr	NM
❏ DL5509 [10]	Louis Armstrong and the Mills Brothers	1954	60.00

ARMSTRONG, LOUIS

ABC

Number	Title	Yr	NM
❏ S-650	What a Wonderful World	1968	30.00

ACCORD

| ❏ SN-7161 | Mr. Music | 1982 | 12.00 |

AMSTERDAM

| ❏ AMS12009 | Louis Armstrong and His Friends | 1970 | 18.00 |

AUDIO FIDELITY

❏ AFLP-2128 [M]	Ain't Gonna Give Nobody None of My Jelly Roll	1964	18.00
❏ AFSD-6128 [S]	Ain't Gonna Give Nobody None of My Jelly Roll	1964	25.00
❏ AFLP-1924 [M]	Louie and the Dukes of Dixieland	1960	30.00
❏ AFSD-5924 [S]	Louie and the Dukes of Dixieland	1960	40.00
❏ AFSD-6241	Louis Armstrong	196?	18.00
❏ AFLP-1930 [M]	Louis Armstrong Plays King Oliver	1960	30.00
❏ AFSD-5930 [S]	Louis Armstrong Plays King Oliver	1960	40.00
❏ AFLP-2132 [M]	The Best of Louis Armstrong	1964	18.00
❏ AFSD-6132 [S]	The Best of Louis Armstrong	1964	25.00

BIOGRAPH

| ❏ C-5 | Great Soloists | 1973 | 15.00 |
| ❏ C-6 | Louis Armstrong Plays the Blues | 1973 | 15.00 |

BLUEBIRD

❏ 9759-1-RB	Louis Armstrong & His Orchestra 1932-33: Laughin' Louie	1989	15.00
❏ 5920-1-RB	Pops: The 1940s Small Band Sides	1987	18.00
❏ 8310-1-RB	What a Wonderful World	1988	12.00
❏ AXM2-5519	Young Louis (1932-1933)	1984	15.00

BRUNSWICK

| ❏ BL58004 [10] | Armstrong Classics | 1950 | 100.00 |
| ❏ DL754130 | I Will Wait for You | 1968 | 18.00 |

BUENA VISTA

| ❏ BV-4044 | Disney Swings the Satchmo Way | 1968 | 40.00 |

CHIAROSCURO

❏ 2003	Great Alternatives	1977	15.00
❏ 2002	Snake Rag	1977	15.00
❏ 2006	Sweetheart	1977	15.00

CLEOPATRA

| ❏ 4806 [B] | Live In Paris '65 | | 25.00 |

COLUMBIA

| ❏ CL840 [M] | Ambassador Satch | 1956 | 40.00 |
| ❏ CL591 [M] | Louis Armstrong Plays W.C. Handy | 1954 | 60.00 |

— Maroon label, gold print (original)

| ❏ CL591 [M] | Louis Armstrong Plays W.C. Handy | 1955 | 40.00 |

— Red and black label with six "eye" logos

❏ CL6335 [10]	Louis Armstrong Plays W.C. Handy, Volume 2	1955	40.00
❏ CL2638 [M]	Louis Armstrong's Greatest Hits	1967	25.00
❏ CS9438 [R]	Louis Armstrong's Greatest Hits	1967	15.00
❏ PC9438 [R]	Louis Armstrong's Greatest Hits	198?	10.00

— Budget-line reissue

| ❏ CL1077 [M] | Satchmo the Great | 1957 | 30.00 |
| ❏ CL708 [M] | Satch Plays Fats | 1955 | 40.00 |

— Red and black label with six "eye" logos

| ❏ G30416 | The Genius of Louis Armstrong, Vol. 1 | 1971 | 18.00 |
| ❏ ML4383 [M] | The Louis Armstrong Story, Volume 1: Louis Armstrong and His Hot Five | 1951 | 50.00 |

— Green label, gold or silver print

| ❏ CL851 [M] | The Louis Armstrong Story, Volume 1: Louis Armstrong and His Hot Five | 1956 | 30.00 |

— Red and black label with six "eye" logos; reissue of 4383

| ❏ CL851 [M] | The Louis Armstrong Story, Volume 1: Louis Armstrong and His Hot Five | 197? | 15.00 |

— Orange label

Number	Title	Yr	NM
❏ ML4384 [M]	The Louis Armstrong Story, Volume 2: Louis Armstrong and His Hot Seven	1951	50.00

— Green label, gold or silver print

| ❏ CL852 [M] | The Louis Armstrong Story, Volume 2: Louis Armstrong and His Hot Seven | 1956 | 30.00 |

— Red and black label with six "eye" logos; reissue of 5484

| ❏ ML4385 [M] | The Louis Armstrong Story, Volume 3: Louis Armstrong and Earl Hines | 1951 | 50.00 |

— Green label, gold or silver print

| ❏ CL853 [M] | The Louis Armstrong Story, Volume 3: Louis Armstrong and Earl Hines | 1956 | 30.00 |

— Red and black label with six "eye" logos; reissue of 4385

| ❏ CL853 [M] | The Louis Armstrong Story, Volume 3: Louis Armstrong and Earl Hines | 197? | 15.00 |

— Orange label reissue

| ❏ ML4386 [M] | The Louis Armstrong Story, Volume 4: Louis Armstrong Favorites | 1951 | 50.00 |

— Green label, gold or silver print

| ❏ CL854 [M] | The Louis Armstrong Story, Volume 4: Louis Armstrong Favorites | 1956 | 30.00 |

— Red and black label with six "eye" logos; reissue of 4386

COLUMBIA JAZZ MASTERPIECES

| ❏ CJ40242 | Louis Armstrong Plays W.C. Handy | 1986 | 12.00 |
| ❏ CJ40378 | Satch Plays Fats | 1986 | 12.00 |

COLUMBIA MUSICAL TREASURIES

| ❏ P4M5676 | 40 Greatest Hits | 197? | 25.00 |

COLUMBIA SPECIAL PRODUCTS

| ❏ JCL708 [M] | Satch Plays Fats | 196? | 15.00 |

— Special Collector's Series" reissue

DECCA

❏ DL74330 [R]	A Musical Autobiography, 1928-1930	1962	15.00
❏ DL4227 [M]	I Love Jazz	1962	25.00
❏ DL74227 [R]	I Love Jazz	1962	15.00
❏ DL8284 [M]	Jazz Classics	1956	40.00

— Black label, silver print

| ❏ DL8284 [M] | Jazz Classics | 1960 | 18.00 |

— Black label with color bars

❏ DL5280 [10]	Jazz Concert	1950	75.00
❏ DL4245 [M]	King Louis	1962	25.00
❏ DL74245 [R]	King Louis	1962	15.00
❏ DL5532 [10]	Latter-Day Louis	1954	75.00
❏ DL8488 [M]	Louis and the Angels	1957	40.00

— Black label, silver print

| ❏ DL8488 [M] | Louis and the Angels | 1960 | 18.00 |

— Black label with color bars

| ❏ DL8781 [M] | Louis and the Good Book | 1958 | 40.00 |

— Black label, silver print

| ❏ DL8741 [M] | Louis and the Good Book | 1960 | 18.00 |

— Black label with color bars

| ❏ DL8168 [M] | Louis Armstrong at the Crescendo, Volume 1 | 1955 | 40.00 |

— Black label, silver print

| ❏ DL8169 [M] | Louis Armstrong at the Crescendo, Volume 2 | 1955 | 100.00 |

— Black label, silver print

❏ DL5536 [10]	Louis Armstrong-Gordon Jenkins	1954	75.00
❏ DL5279 [10]	New Orleans Days	1950	75.00
❏ DL8283 [M]	New Orleans Jazz	1956	40.00

— Black label, silver print

| ❏ DL8283 [M] | New Orleans Jazz | 1960 | 18.00 |

— Black label with color bars

| ❏ DL8329 [M] | New Orleans Nights | 1957 | 40.00 |

— Black label, silver print

| ❏ DL8329 [M] | New Orleans Nights | 1960 | 18.00 |

— Black label with color bars

| ❏ DL8329 [M] | New Orleans Nights | 1960 | 18.00 |

— Black label with color bars

❏ DL5225 [10]	New Orleans to New York	1950	75.00
❏ DL9225 [M]	Rare Items (1935-1944)	196?	25.00
❏ DL79225 [R]	Rare Items (1935-1944)	196?	15.00
❏ DX155 [M]	Satchmo, A Musical Autobiography	1956	100.00

— Black labels, silver print

| ❏ DXM155 [M] | Satchmo, A Musical Autobiography | 1960 | 40.00 |

— Black labels with color bars

❏ DL8963 [M]	Satchmo, A Musical Autobiography, 1923-1925	1960	30.00
❏ DL78963 [R]	Satchmo, A Musical Autobiography, 1923-1925	196?	15.00
❏ DL4230 [M]	Satchmo, A Musical Autobiography, 1926-1927	1962	30.00
❏ DL4330 [M]	Satchmo, A Musical Autobiography, 1928-1930	1962	30.00
❏ DL4331 [M]	Satchmo, A Musical Autobiography, 1930-1934	1962	30.00
❏ DL8041 [M]	Satchmo at Pasadena	1954	40.00

— Black label, silver print

| ❏ DL8041 [M] | Satchmo at Pasadena | 1960 | 18.00 |

— Black label with color bars

| ❏ DX108 [M] | Satchmo at Symphony Hall | 1954 | 75.00 |

— Black labels, silver print

| ❏ DL8037 [M] | Satchmo at Symphony Hall, Volume 1 | 1954 | 40.00 |

Number	Title	Yr	NM

— Black label, silver print

| ❏ DL8037 [M] | Satchmo at Symphony Hall, Volume 1 | 1960 | 18.00 |

— Black label with color bars

| ❏ DL8038 [M] | Satchmo at Symphony Hall, Volume 2 | 1954 | 40.00 |

— Black label, silver print

| ❏ DL8038 [M] | Satchmo at Symphony Hall, Volume 2 | 1960 | 18.00 |

— Black label with color bars

| ❏ DL8840 [M] | Satchmo in Style | 1958 | 40.00 |

— Black label, silver print

| ❏ DL8840 [M] | Satchmo in Style | 1960 | 18.00 |

— Black label with color bars

| ❏ DL8330 [M] | Satchmo on Stage | 1957 | 40.00 |

— Black label, silver print

| ❏ DL8330 [M] | Satchmo on Stage | 1960 | 18.00 |

— Black label with color bars

| ❏ DL8327 [M] | Satchmo's Collector's Items | 1957 | 40.00 |

— Black label, silver print

| ❏ DL8327 [M] | Satchmo's Collector's Items | 1960 | 18.00 |

— Black label with color bars

| ❏ DL5401 [10] | Satchmo Serenades | 1952 | 75.00 |
| ❏ DL8211 [M] | Satchmo Serenades | 1956 | 40.00 |

— Black label, silver print

| ❏ DL8211 [M] | Satchmo Serenades | 1960 | 18.00 |

— Black label with color bars

❏ DL4137 [M]	Satchmo's Golden Favorites	1961	25.00
❏ DL74137 [R]	Satchmo's Golden Favorites	1961	15.00
❏ DL8126 [M]	Satchmo Sings	1955	40.00

— Black label, silver print

| ❏ DL8126 [M] | Satchmo Sings | 1960 | 18.00 |

— Black label with color bars

❏ DXB183 [M]	The Best of Louis Armstrong	196?	30.00
❏ DXSB7183 [R]	The Best of Louis Armstrong	196?	18.00
❏ DL9233 [M]	Young Louis the Sideman (1924-1927)	196?	25.00
❏ DL79233 [R]	Young Louis the Sideman (1924-1927)	196?	15.00

DISNEYLAND

| ❏ STER-1341 | The Wonderful World of Walt Disney | 1971 | 25.00 |

— Reissue of Buena Vista 4044

EVEREST

| ❏ 3312 [R] | In Memoriam | 1971 | 12.00 |

EVEREST ARCHIVE OF FOLK & JAZZ

| ❏ 258 | Louis "Satchmo" Armstrong | 197? | 15.00 |
| ❏ 312 | Louis Armstrong, Vol. 2 | 197? | 12.00 |

GNP CRESCENDO

| ❏ 11001 | An Evening with Louis Armstrong | 1977 | 18.00 |
| ❏ 9050 | Pasadena Concert, Vol. II | 1967 | 12.00 |

HARMONY

| ❏ HS11316 | Louis Armstrong | 197? | 15.00 |
| ❏ KH31236 | The Louis Armstrong Saga | 1971 | 15.00 |

IAJRC

| ❏ LP-29 | Oregon State Fair, 1960 | 198? | 12.00 |

JOLLY ROGER

| ❏ 5009 [10] | Louis Armstrong | 1954 | 50.00 |

KAPP

| ❏ KL-1364 [M] | Hello, Dolly! | 1964 | 15.00 |

| ❏ KS-3364 [S] | Hello, Dolly! | 1964 | 18.00 |

MCA

| ❏ 1304 | Back in New York | 197? | 12.00 |
| ❏ 538 | Hello, Dolly! | 197? | 12.00 |

— Reissue of Kapp LP

| ❏ 1300 | Louis and the Good Book | 197? | 12.00 |

— Reissue of Decca 8741

| ❏ 2-4013 | Louis Armstrong at the Crescendo | 197? | 15.00 |

— Reissue of Decca 8168/8169 in one sleeve

| ❏ 42328 | Louis Armstrong of New Orleans | 1990 | 15.00 |
| ❏ 1306 | Louis with Guest Stars | 197? | 12.00 |

Number	Title	Yr	NM
❑ 1335	Old Favorites	197?	12.00
❑ 10006	Satchmo, A Musical Autobiography	197?	30.00
—Reissue of Decca 155			
❑ 2-4057	Satchmo at Symphony Hall	197?	15.00
—Reissue of Decca 108			
❑ 1334	Satchmo For Ever!	197?	12.00
❑ 1322	Satchmo's Collector's Items	197?	12.00
—Reissue of Decca 8327			
❑ 1316	Satchmo Serenades	197?	12.00
—Reissue of Decca 8211			
❑ 1312	Swing That Music!	197?	12.00
❑ 2-4035	The Best of Louis Armstrong	197?	15.00
—Reissue of Decca 7183			
❑ 25204	What a Wonderful World	1988	12.00
—Reissue of ABC 650			
❑ 1301	Young Louis the Sideman	197?	12.00
—Reissue of Decca 9233			

MERCURY

Number	Title	Yr	NM
❑ MG-21081 [M]	Louis Armstrong Sings Louis Armstrong	1965	15.00
❑ SR-61081 [S]	Louis Armstrong Sings Louis Armstrong	1965	18.00

METRO

Number	Title	Yr	NM
❑ M-510 [M]	Hello, Louis	1965	15.00
❑ MS-510 [S]	Hello, Louis	1965	18.00

MILESTONE

Number	Title	Yr	NM
❑ 2010	Early Portrait	1969	12.00
❑ 47017	Louis Armstrong and King Oliver	197?	15.00

MOSAIC

Number	Title	Yr	NM
❑ MQ8-146	The Complete Decca Studio Recordings of Louis Armstrong and the All-Stars	199?	150.00

PABLO

Number	Title	Yr	NM
❑ 2310941	Mack the Knife	1990	15.00

PAIR

Number	Title	Yr	NM
❑ PDL2-1042	The Jazz Legend	1986	15.00

PAUSA

Number	Title	Yr	NM
❑ 9018	The Greatest of Louis Armstrong	1983	12.00

RCA VICTOR

Number	Title	Yr	NM
❑ LPM-2322 [M]	A Rare Batch of Satch	1961	30.00
❑ VPM-6044	July 4, 1900/July 6, 1971	1971	25.00
❑ LPM-2971 [M]	Louis Armstrong in the '30s/in the '40s	1964	25.00
❑ LSP-2971(e) [R]	Louis Armstrong in the '30s/in the '40s	1964	15.00
❑ LJM-1005 [M]	Louis Armstrong Sings the Blues	1954	50.00
❑ LPT7 [10]	Louis Armstrong Town Hall Concert	1951	80.00
❑ LPM-1443 [M]	Town Hall Concert Plus	1957	50.00

RIVERSIDE

Number	Title	Yr	NM
❑ RLP 12-122 [M]	Louis Armstrong 1923	1956	80.00
—White label, blue print			
❑ RLP 12-122 [M]	Louis Armstrong 1923	195?	40.00
—Blue label			
❑ RLP-1001 [10]	Louis Armstrong Plays the Blues	1953	100.00
❑ RLP-1029 [10]	Louis Armstrong with King Oliver's Creole Jazz Band 1923	1953	100.00
❑ RLP 12-101 [M]	The Young Louis Armstrong	1956	80.00
—White label, blue print			
❑ RLP 12-101 [M]	The Young Louis Armstrong	195?	40.00
—Blue label			

SEAGULL

Number	Title	Yr	NM
❑ LG-8206	Greatest Hits: Live in Concert	198?	15.00

STORYVILLE

Number	Title	Yr	NM
❑ 4012	Louis Armstrong and His All-Stars	1980	12.00

SWING

Number	Title	Yr	NM
❑ SW-8450	Louis and the Big Bands	1984	12.00

TIME-LIFE

Number	Title	Yr	NM
❑ STBB-22	Big Bands: Louis Armstrong	1985	18.00
❑ STL-J-01	Giants of Jazz	1978	25.00

VANGUARD

Number	Title	Yr	NM
❑ VSD91/92	Essential Louis Armstrong	1977	18.00
❑ VMS73129	Essential Louis Armstrong, Vol. 1	1986	10.00

VERVE

Number	Title	Yr	NM
❑ MGV-4035 [M]	I've Got the World on a String	1959	50.00
❑ MGVS-6101 [S]	I've Got the World on a String	1960	40.00
❑ V-4035 [M]	I've Got the World on a String	1961	25.00
❑ V6-4035 [S]	I've Got the World on a String	1961	18.00
❑ MGVS-4035	I've Got the World on a String	199?	30.00
—Classic Records reissue			
❑ MGV-4012 [M]	Louis Under the Stars	1957	50.00
❑ MGVS-6044 [S]	Louis Under the Stars	1960	40.00
❑ V-4012 [M]	Louis Under the Stars	1961	25.00
❑ V6-4012 [S]	Louis Under the Stars	1961	18.00
❑ MGV-4012 [S]	Louis Under the Stars	199?	30.00
—180-gram reissue; distributed by Classic Records			
❑ V-8595 [M]	The Best of Louis Armstrong	1964	18.00
❑ V6-8595 [S]	The Best of Louis Armstrong	1964	18.00
❑ SW-90658 [S]	The Best of Louis Armstrong	1964	25.00
—Capitol Record Club edition			
❑ V-8569 [M]	The Essential Louis A.	1963	15.00
❑ V6-8569 [S]	The Essential Louis A.	1963	18.00

VOCALION

Number	Title	Yr	NM
❑ VL73851 [R]	Here's Louis Armstrong	196?	12.00
❑ VL3851 [M]	Here's Louis Armstrong	196?	18.00
❑ VL73871 [R]	The One and Only Louis Armstrong	1968	12.00

WING

Number	Title	Yr	NM
❑ SR-16381	Great Louis	196?	12.00

ARMSTRONG, LOUIS/AL HIRT

MURRAY HILL

Number	Title	Yr	NM
❑ 930633	Louis Armstrong and Al Hirt Play Dixieland Trumpet	197?	25.00

ARMSTRONG, VANESSA BELL

JIVE

Number	Title	Yr	NM
❑ 1251-1-J [EP]	Gospel Sampler	1989	15.00
—Promo-only four-song sampler			
❑ 1074-1-J	Vanessa Bell Armstrong	1987	12.00

ARNAZ, DESI

RCA VICTOR

Number	Title	Yr	NM
❑ LPM-3096 [10]	Babalu!	1954	120.00

ARNELL, GINNY

MGM

Number	Title	Yr	NM
❑ E-4228 [M]	Meet Ginny Arnell	1964	30.00
❑ SE-4228 [S]	Meet Ginny Arnell	1964	40.00

ARNOLD, BUDDY

ABC-PARAMOUNT

Number	Title	Yr	NM
❑ ABC-114 [M]	Wailing	1956	60.00

ARNOLD, EDDY

K-TEL

Number	Title	Yr	NM
❑ WC307	The Living Legend of Eddy Arnold	1974	12.00

MGM

Number	Title	Yr	NM
❑ SE-4916	I Wish I Had Loved You Better	1974	15.00
❑ SE-4912	She's Got Everything I Need	1974	15.00
❑ SE-4878	So Many Ways/If the Whole World Stopped Lovin'	1973	15.00
❑ MG-1-4992	The Wonderful World of Eddy Arnold	1975	15.00
❑ MJB-5107	World of Hits	1976	15.00

PAIR

Number	Title	Yr	NM
❑ PDL2-1000	The Mellow Side of Eddy Arnold	1986	15.00

RCA

Number	Title	Yr	NM
❑ 9963-1-R	Hand-Holdin' Songs	1990	18.00

RCA CAMDEN

Number	Title	Yr	NM
❑ CAL-741 [M]	Country Songs I Love to Sing	1963	18.00
❑ CAS-741(e) [R]	Country Songs I Love to Sing	1966	12.00
❑ CAL-471 [M]	Eddy Arnold (That's How Much I Love You)	1959	25.00
❑ CAS-471(e) [R]	Eddy Arnold (That's How Much I Love You)	1966	12.00
❑ CAL-799 [M]	Eddy's Songs	1964	18.00
❑ CAS-799(e) [R]	Eddy's Songs	1966	12.00
❑ CAL-897 [M]	I'm Throwing Rice (At the Girl That I Love) And Other Favorites	1966	18.00
❑ CAS-897(e) [R]	I'm Throwing Rice (At the Girl That I Love) And Other Favorites	1966	12.00
❑ CAL-563 [M]	More Eddy Arnold	1960	25.00
❑ CAS-563(e) [R]	More Eddy Arnold	1966	12.00
❑ CAS-2501	Then You Can Tell Me Goodbye	197?	12.00

RCA VICTOR

Number	Title	Yr	NM
❑ LPM-1293 [M]	A Dozen Hits	1956	50.00
❑ AHL1-3606	A Legend and His Lady	1980	12.00
❑ LPM-1377 [M]	A Little on the Lonely Side	1956	50.00
❑ LPM-3117 [10]	All-Time Favorites	1953	100.00
❑ LPM-1223 [M]	All-Time Favorites	1955	50.00
—New version of LPM 3117			
❑ LSP-1223(e) [R]	All-Time Favorites	1975	12.00
—Tan label; thin vinyl			
❑ LSP-1223(e) [R]	All-Time Favorites	1967	15.00
—Black label, dog on top			
❑ LPM-3031 [10]	All-Time Hits from the Hills	1952	100.00
❑ AHL1-3914	A Man for All Seasons	1980	12.00
❑ LPM-3230 [10]	An American Institution	1954	100.00
❑ LPM-3230	An American Institution Booklet	1954	50.00
❑ LPM-3027 [10]	Anytime	1952	120.00
—Label calls this "Country Classics			
❑ LPM-1224 [M]	Anytime	1955	50.00
—New version of LPM 3027			
❑ LPM-2578 [M]	Cattle Call	1962	30.00
❑ LSP-2578 [S]	Cattle Call	1962	30.00
❑ LSP-2578 [S]	Cattle Call	1967	18.00
—Reissue with "Country Music Hall of Fame" on front cover and "RE" on back cover; black label			
❑ LSP-2578 [S]	Cattle Call	1969	15.00
—Reissue with "Country Music Hall of Fame" on front cover and "RE" on back cover; orange label			
❑ LPM-2554 [M]	Christmas with Eddy Arnold	1962	25.00
❑ LSP-2554 [S]	Christmas with Eddy Arnold	1962	30.00
—Original cover; "Living Stereo" on label			
❑ PRS-346	Christmas with Eddy Arnold	1971	18.00
—Special-products issue			
❑ LSP-2554 [S]	Christmas with Eddy Arnold	1967	18.00
—Second cover with Eddy standing in front of a Christmas tree; "Country Music Hall of Fame" on front cover and "RE" on back cover			
❑ ANL1-1926	Christmas with Eddy Arnold	1976	12.00
—Reissue of LSP-2554 with similar cover to the second edition			
❑ AHL1-4661	Close Enough to Love	1983	12.00
❑ AHL1-5467	Collector's Series	1985	12.00
❑ AHL1-4263	Don't Give Up on Me	1981	12.00
❑ APL1-1817	Eddy	1976	15.00
❑ LSP-4738	Eddy Arnold Sings for Housewives and Other Ladies	1972	15.00
❑ LPM-2185 [M]	Eddy Arnold Sings Them Again	1960	30.00
❑ LSP-2185 [S]	Eddy Arnold Sings Them Again	1960	30.00
❑ LPM-2629 [M]	Faithfully Yours	1963	30.00
❑ LSP-2629 [S]	Faithfully Yours	1963	30.00
❑ LPM-2811 [M]	Folk Song Book	1964	25.00
❑ LSP-2811 [S]	Folk Song Book	1964	30.00
—Black label, dog on top			
❑ LSP-2811 [S]	Folk Song Book	1971	12.00
—Orange label, thin vinyl			
❑ LPM-1928 [M]	Have Guitar, Will Travel	1959	30.00
❑ LSP-1928 [S]	Have Guitar, Will Travel	1959	30.00
❑ APL1-2277	I Need You All the Time	1977	15.00
❑ LPM-3507 [M]	I Want to Go with You	1966	15.00
❑ LSP-3507 [S]	I Want to Go with You	1966	18.00
—Black label, dog on top			
❑ LSP-3507 [S]	I Want to Go with You	1971	12.00
—Orange label, thin vinyl			
❑ LPM-2337 [M]	Let's Make Memories Tonight	1961	25.00
❑ LSP-2337 [S]	Let's Make Memories Tonight	1961	30.00
❑ LPM-3753 [M]	Lonely Again	1967	25.00
❑ LSP-3753 [S]	Lonely Again	1967	18.00
—Black label, dog on top			
❑ LSP-3753 [S]	Lonely Again	1971	12.00
—Orange label, thin vinyl			
❑ LSP-4304	Love & Guitars	1970	15.00
—Orange label, rigid vinyl			
❑ LSP-4304	Love & Guitars	1971	12.00
—Orange label, thin vinyl			
❑ LSP-4625	Loving Her Was Easier	1971	15.00
❑ LPM-1575 [M]	My Darling, My Darling	1957	40.00
❑ LPM-3466 [M]	My World	1965	15.00
❑ LSP-3466 [S]	My World	1965	18.00
❑ LPM-2471 [M]	One More Time	1961	25.00
❑ LSP-2471 [S]	One More Time	1961	30.00
❑ LSP-2471 [S]	One More Time	1967	18.00
—Reissue with "Country Music Hall of Fame" on front cover and "RE" on back cover			
❑ LPM-2596 [M]	Our Man Down South	1962	30.00
❑ LSP-2596 [S]	Our Man Down South	1962	30.00
❑ LPM-2951 [M]	Pop Hits from the Country Side	1964	25.00
❑ LSP-2951 [S]	Pop Hits from the Country Side	1964	30.00
❑ LSP-2951 [S]	Pop Hits from the Country Side	1967	18.00
—Reissue with "Country Music Hall of Fame" on front cover and "RE" on back cover			
❑ LSP-4471	Portrait of My Woman	1971	15.00
❑ LPM-1733 [M]	Praise Him, Praise Him	1958	40.00
❑ ANL1-1078	Pure Gold	1975	12.00
❑ AHL1-3358	Somebody	1979	12.00
❑ LPM-3715 [M]	Somebody Like Me	1966	15.00
❑ LSP-3715 [S]	Somebody Like Me	1966	18.00
❑ LSP-3715 [S]	Somebody Like Me	1967	15.00
—Reissue with "Country Music Hall of Fame" on front cover and "RE" on back cover			
❑ LPM-2909 [M]	Sometimes I'm Happy, Sometimes I'm Blue	1964	25.00
❑ LSP-2909 [S]	Sometimes I'm Happy, Sometimes I'm Blue	1964	30.00
❑ LSP-4110	Songs of the Young World	1969	18.00
❑ LSP-4390	Standing Alone	1970	15.00
❑ LPM-3565 [M]	The Best of Eddy Arnold	1967	25.00
❑ LSP-3565 [S]	The Best of Eddy Arnold	1967	18.00
❑ AYL1-3675	The Best of Eddy Arnold	1980	10.00
—Best Buy Series" reissue			
❑ LSP-4320	The Best of Eddy Arnold, Volume II	1970	15.00
❑ AYL1-3937	The Best of Eddy Arnold, Volume II	1981	10.00
—Best Buy Series" reissue			
❑ LPM-1225 [M]	The Chapel on the Hill	1955	50.00
—New version of LPM 3031			
❑ LPM-3361 [M]	The Easy Way	1965	18.00
❑ LSP-3361 [S]	The Easy Way	1965	25.00
❑ LPM-3931 [M]	The Everlovin' World of Eddy Arnold	1968	40.00
❑ LSP-3931 [S]	The Everlovin' World of Eddy Arnold	1968	18.00
❑ LSP-4179	The Glory of Love	1969	18.00

Number	Title	Yr	NM
❑ DPL2-0051	The Greatest of Eddy Arnold	1973	18.00
— Special products issue; "Tele House Inc. Presents" on labels			
❑ LPM-3622 [M]	The Last Word in Lonesome	1966	15.00
❑ LSP-3622 [S]	The Last Word in Lonesome	1966	18.00
❑ CPL2-4885	The Legendary Performances (1945-1971)	1983	15.00
❑ LSP-4009 [S]	The Romantic World of Eddy Arnold	1968	18.00
❑ LPM-4009 [M]	The Romantic World of Eddy Arnold	1968	150.00
❑ LSP-4231	The Warmth of Eddy	1969	18.00
❑ APL1-0239	The World of Eddy Arnold	1973	15.00
❑ VPS-6032	This Is Eddy Arnold	1972	18.00
❑ LPM-2036 [M]	Thereby Hangs a Tale	1959	30.00
❑ LSP-2036 [S]	Thereby Hangs a Tale	1959	30.00
❑ LPM-3869 [M]	Turn the World Around	1967	25.00
❑ LSP-3869 [S]	Turn the World Around	1967	18.00
❑ LSP-4089	Walkin' in Love Land	1968	18.00
❑ LPM-1111 [M]	Wanderin' with Eddy Arnold	1955	50.00
❑ LPM-3219 [10]	When It's Roundup Time in Heaven	1954	100.00
❑ LPM-1484 [M]	When They Were Young	1956	50.00
❑ LPM-2268 [M]	You Gotta Have Love	1960	30.00
❑ LSP-2268 [S]	You Gotta Have Love	1960	30.00

READER'S DIGEST

❑ RDA168-A	Welcome to My World	1975	50.00
— Box set with booklet; prefix on labels is "RD 4			

TIME-LIFE

❑ STW-120	Country Music	1981	12.00

ARNOLD, HARRY

ATCO

❑ 33-120 [M]	I Love Harry Arnold (And All That Jazz)	1960	40.00

EMARCY

❑ MG-36139 [M]	Harry Arnold and His Orchestra	1958	50.00
❑ SR-80006 [S]	Harry Arnold and His Orchestra	1958	40.00

JAZZLAND

❑ JLP-65 [M]	Harry Arnold's Great Big Band and Friends	1962	30.00
❑ JLP-965 [S]	Harry Arnold's Great Big Band and Friends	1962	30.00

JAZZTONE

❑ J-1270 [M]	The Jazztone Mystery Band	1957	40.00

RIVERSIDE

❑ RM-7536 [M]	Dancing on Broadway to the Music of Cole Porter	196?	25.00
❑ RS-97536 [S]	Dancing on Broadway to the Music of Cole Porter	196?	30.00
❑ RM-7526 [M]	Let's Dance on Broadway	196?	25.00
❑ RS-97526 [S]	Let's Dance on Broadway	196?	30.00

ARNOLD, P.P.

IMMEDIATE

❑ Z1252016 [B]	Kafunta	1968	30.00

ARRESTED DEVELOPMENT

CHRYSALIS

❑ F1-21929	3 Years, 5 Months, & 2 Days in the Life of...	1992	30.00
❑ F1-29274	Zingalamaduni	1994	25.00

ARS NOVA

ATLANTIC

❑ SD8221	Sunshine and Shadows	1969	25.00

ELEKTRA

❑ EKS-74020	Ars Nova	1968	25.00

ART BEARS

RALPH

❑ RR7905 [B]	Winter Songs	1979	30.00

ART ENSEMBLE OF CHICAGO

AECO

❑ 004	Kabalaba	1978	18.00

ARISTA/FREEDOM

❑ AL1903	The Paris Session	197?	18.00

ATLANTIC

❑ SD1639	Bap-Tizum	1973	18.00
❑ SD1651	Fanfare for the Warriors	1974	18.00
❑ 90046	Fanfare for the Warriors	1983	12.00
— Reissue of 1651			

DELMARK

❑ DS-432/433	Live at Mandel Hall	1974	18.00

DIW

❑ 8014	Ancient to the Future	1987	12.00
❑ 8038	Art Ensemble of Soweto	1990	15.00
❑ 8005	Live in Japan	1986	12.00
❑ 8011	Naked	1987	12.00
❑ 8033	The Alternate Express	1989	15.00
❑ 8021/22	The Complete Live in Japan	198?	18.00

ECM

❑ 1167	Full Force	1980	15.00
❑ 1126	Nice Guys	1979	15.00
❑ 25014	The Third Decade	1985	12.00
❑ 1211	Urban Bushmen	1982	18.00

Number	Title	Yr	NM
INNER CITY			
❑ 1004	Certain Blacks	197?	15.00
NESSA			
❑ N-4	Les Stances a Sophie	1970	30.00
— With Fontella Bass			
❑ N-5	Old/Quartet	1975	25.00
❑ N-3	People in Sorrow	1969	30.00
PAULA			
❑ LPS-4001	Chi-Congo	197?	18.00
PRESTIGE			
❑ 10049	Art Ensemble of Chicago with Fontella Bass	1972	18.00
❑ 10064	Phase One	197?	18.00

ART OF LOVIN'

MAINSTREAM

❑ S-6113	Art of Lovin'	1968	300.00

ART OF NOISE

CHINA

❑ 839404-1	Below the Waste	1989	18.00
❑ R143956	In No Sense? Nonsense!	1987	15.00
— BMG Direct Marketing edition			
❑ OV41570	In No Sense? Nonsense!	1987	12.00
❑ BFV41528	In Visible Silence	1986	12.00
❑ FV41567	Re-Works of The Art of Noise	1986	15.00
❑ R100848	The Best of The Art of Noise	1988	15.00
— BMG Direct Marketing edition			
❑ 837367-1	The Best of The Art of Noise	1988	12.00

ISLAND

❑ 90137	Art of Noise	1984	15.00
❑ 90179	(Who's Afraid of?) The Art of Noise!	1984	12.00
❑ 842473-1	(Who's Afraid of?) The Art of Noise!	1990	12.00
— Reissue of Island 90179			

ARTER, CARL

EARWIG

❑ LPS-4905	Song from Far Away	1986	12.00

ARTHUR, BROOKS

VERVE

❑ V-8650 [M]	Sole Forms	1966	18.00
❑ V6-8650 [S]	Sole Forms	1966	18.00
❑ V6-8779	Traces	1969	18.00

ARTHUR

LHI

❑ 12000	Dreams and Images	1968	75.00

ARTISTICS, THE

BRUNSWICK

❑ BL54123 [M]	I'm Gonna Miss You	1967	30.00
❑ BL754123 [S]	I'm Gonna Miss You	1967	30.00
❑ BL754168	I Want You to Make My Life Over	1970	30.00
❑ BL754195 [B]	Look Out	1973	25.00
❑ BL754139	The Articulate Artistics	1968	30.00
❑ BL754153	What Happened	1969	30.00

OKEH

❑ OKM-12119 [M]	Get My Hands on Some Lovin'	1967	80.00
❑ OKS-14119 [S]	Get My Hands on Some Lovin'	1967	80.00

ARTISTS UNITED AGAINST APARTHEID

MANHATTAN

❑ ST-53019	Sun City	1985	15.00
❑ SPRO-9538 [DJ]	Voices of Sun City	1985	30.00
— Promo album of interviews with participants in the benefit LP			

ARVON, BOBBY

FIRST ARTISTS

❑ 4001	Until Now	1978	15.00

ARZACHEL

ROULETTE

❑ SR42036 [B]	Arzachel	1969	200.00

A'S, THE

ARISTA

❑ AL9554	A Woman's Got the Power	1981	12.00
❑ AB4238	The A's	1979	12.00
❑ CP705 [10]	The A's E.P.	1979	15.00
— Red vinyl with three songs from their first album			

ASGAERD

THRESHOLD

❑ THS6 [B]	In the Realm of Asgaerd	1972	30.00

Number	Title	Yr	NM
ASH, DANIEL			
BEGGARS BANQUET			
❑ 3014-1-R [B]	Coming Home	1991	25.00
ASH, MARVIN			
CAPITOL			
❑ H188 [10]	Honky Tonk Piano	1950	60.00
DECCA			
❑ DL8346 [M]	New Orleans at Midnight	1957	40.00
JAZZ MAN			
❑ LPJM-335 [10]	Marvin Ash	1954	50.00
JUMP			
❑ JL-4 [10]	Marvin Ash	1954	50.00

ASHANTI

MURDER, INC.

❑ 314586830-1	Ashanti	2002	25.00
❑ B0000143-01 [B]	Chapter II	2003	18.00
❑ B0003409-01	Concrete Rose	2004	18.00

ASHBY, DOROTHY

ARGO

❑ LP-690 [M]	Dorothy Ashby	1962	30.00
❑ LPS-690 [S]	Dorothy Ashby	1962	30.00

ATLANTIC

❑ 1447 [M]	The Fantastic Jazz Harp of Dorothy Ashby	1966	18.00
❑ SD1447 [S]	The Fantastic Jazz Harp of Dorothy Ashby	1966	25.00

CADET

❑ LPS-809	Afro-Harping	1968	18.00
❑ LP-690 [M]	Dorothy Ashby	1966	15.00
— Reissue of Argo LP-690			
❑ LPS-690 [S]	Dorothy Ashby	1966	18.00
— Reissue of Argo LPS-690			
❑ LPS-825	Dorothy's Harp	1969	18.00
❑ LPS-841	Rubaiyat	1970	18.00

CHESS

❑ CH-91555	Afro-Harping	198?	12.00
— Reissue of Cadet 809			

JAZZLAND

❑ JLP-61 [M]	Soft Winds	1961	30.00
❑ JLP-961 [S]	Soft Winds	1961	30.00

NEW JAZZ

❑ NJLP-8209 [M]	In a Minor Groove	1958	150.00
— Purple label			
❑ NJLP-8209 [M]	In a Minor Groove	1965	30.00
— Blue label, trident logo at right			

PRESTIGE

❑ PRLP-7639	Dorothy Plays for Beautiful People	1969	18.00
— Reissue of New Jazz 8209			
❑ PRLP-7140 [M]	Hip Harp	1958	200.00
❑ PRLP-7638	The Best of Dorothy Ashby	1969	18.00
— Reissue of 7140			

REGENT

❑ MG-6039 [M]	Dorothy Ashby -- Jazz Harpist	1957	60.00

SAVOY

❑ MG-12212 [M]	Dorothy Ashby -- Jazz Harpist	196?	18.00
— Reissue of Regent 6039			

ASHBY, HAROLD

GEMINI

❑ GMLP-60-1	The Viking	1988	12.00

PROGRESSIVE

❑ PRO-7040	Presenting Harold Ashby	1979	12.00

ASHBY, IRVING

AUDIOPHILE

❑ AP-133	Memoirs	1980	12.00

ASHES

VAULT

❑ 125	Ashes	1971	100.00
— Recorded in 1968 but released in 1971			

ASHFORD AND SIMPSON

CAPITOL

❑ ST-12282	High Rise	1983	10.00
❑ C1-46946	Love Or Physical	1989	12.00
❑ ST-12469	Real Love	1986	10.00
❑ ST-12366	Solid	1984	10.00
❑ ST-12207	Street Opera	1982	10.00

WARNER BROS.

❑ HS3458	A Musical Affair	1980	12.00
❑ BS2858	Come As You Are	1976	12.00
❑ BS2739	Gimme Something Real	1973	12.00
❑ BSK3219	Is It Still Good to Ya	1978	12.00
❑ BS2789	I Wanna Be Selfish	1974	12.00
❑ 2BS3524	Performance	1981	15.00

Number	Title	Yr	NM
❏ BS3088	Send It	1977	12.00
❏ BS2992	So So Satisfied	1977	12.00
❏ BSK3357	Stay Free	1979	12.00

ASHKAN

SIRE
❏ SES-97107	In from the Cold	1970	40.00

ASHLEY, LEON, AND MARGIE SINGLETON

ASHLEY
❏ A-3695	New Brand of Country	197?	18.00

ASHLEY, LEON

ASHLEY
❏ 54001	The Best of Leon Ashley	197?	18.00

HILLTOP
❏ JS-6069	Flower of Love	1968	18.00

RCA VICTOR
❏ LPM-3900 [M]	Laura (What's He Got That I Ain't Got)	1967	30.00
❏ LSP-3900 [S]	Laura (What's He Got That I Ain't Got)	1967	25.00

ASHLEY, STEVE

GULL
❏ GU6406S1 [B]	Speedy Return	1976	35.00
❏ GU401V1 [B]	Stroll On	1975	40.00

ASHTON, GARDNER AND DYKE

CAPITOL
❏ ST-563	Resurrection Shuffle	1971	15.00
❏ SW-827	The Last Rebel	1971	15.00
❏ SMAS-862 [B]	What a Bloody Long Day It's Been	1972	18.00

ASHWORTH, ERNEST

HICKORY
❏ LPM-118 [M]	Hits of Today and Tomorrow	1964	30.00

ASIA

GEFFEN
❏ GHS4008	Alpha	1983	10.00
— White label with pinstripes			
❏ GHS4008 [DJ]	Alpha	1983	30.00
— Promo on "Quiex II" vinyl			
❏ GHS2008 [B]	Asia	1982	10.00
— White label with pinstripes			
❏ GHS2008 [DJ]	Asia	1982	30.00
— Promo on "Quiex II" vinyl			
❏ GHS24072	Astra	1985	10.00
❏ GHS24298	Then and Now	1990	15.00

ASLEEP AT THE WHEEL

ARISTA
❏ AL-8550	Keepin' Me Up Nights	1990	15.00

CAPITOL
❏ SW-11726 [B]	Collision Course	1978	15.00
❏ ST-11945	Served Live	1979	15.00
❏ SN-16306	Served Live	1984	10.00
— Budget-line reissue			
❏ ST-11441	Texas Gold	1975	15.00
❏ ST-11620	The Wheel	1977	15.00
❏ ST-11548	Wheelin' and Dealin'	1976	15.00

CAPITOL SPECIAL MARKETS
❏ SL-8138	Drivin'	1980	15.00

DOT/MCA
❏ 39036	Asleep at the Wheel	1985	12.00

EPIC
❏ BFE40681	10	1987	10.00
❏ KE33097	Asleep at the Wheel	1974	18.00
❏ PE33097	Asleep at the Wheel	197?	10.00
— Reissue			
❏ BG33782	Fathers and Sons	1974	30.00
— With Bob Wills			
❏ EG33782	Fathers and Sons	197?	15.00
— Reissue			
❏ FE44213	Western Standard Time	1988	10.00

LIBERTY
❏ LN-10296	Comin' Right At Ya!	1986	10.00
— Budget-line reissue			

MCA
❏ 5131	Framed	1980	12.00
❏ 742	Framed	1982	10.00
— Reissue of 5131			

UNITED ARTISTS
❏ UA-LA038-F	Comin' Right At Ya!	1973	25.00

ASMUSSEN, SVEND

ANGEL
❏ ANG.60010 [10]	Rhythm Is Our Business	1955	60.00
❏ ANG.60000 [10]	Svend Asmussen and His Unmelancholy Danes	1955	60.00

BRUNSWICK
❏ BL58051 [10]	Hot Fiddle	1953	80.00

Number	Title	Yr	NM

DOCTOR JAZZ
❏ FW39150	June Night	1983	15.00

EPIC
❏ LN3210 [M]	Skol!	1955	50.00

ASMUSSEN, SVEND / STEPHANE GRAPPELLI

STORYVILLE
❏ SLP-4088	Two of a Kind	198?	15.00

ASSAULT AND BATTERY

ATTITUDE
❏ 14001	Assault and Battery	1992	18.00

ASSEMBLED MULTITUDE, THE

ATLANTIC
❏ SD8262 [B]	The Assembled Multitude	1970	18.00

ASSOCIATION, THE

COLUMBIA
❏ KC31348 [B]	Waterbeds in Trinidad	1972	12.00

HITBOUND/REALISTIC
❏ 51-3022	New Memories	1983	15.00

PAIR
❏ PDL2-1061	Songs That Made Them Famous	1986	15.00

VALIANT
❏ VLM-5002 [M]	And Then…Along Comes The Association	1966	25.00
❏ VLS-25002 [S]	And Then…Along Comes The Association	1966	30.00
❏ VLM-5004 [M]	Renaissance	1966	25.00
— With no blurb for "No Fair at All" on cover			
❏ VLM-5004 [M]	Renaissance	1967	18.00
— With blurb for "No Fair at All" on cover			
❏ VLS-25004 [S]	Renaissance	1966	30.00
— With no blurb for "No Fair at All" on cover			
❏ VLS-25004 [S]	Renaissance	1967	25.00
— With blurb for "No Fair at All" on cover			

WARNER BROS.
❏ WS1702 [S]	And Then…Along Comes The Association	1967	15.00
— With "W7" logo on green label			
❏ WS1702 [S]	And Then…Along Comes The Association	1967	25.00
— Gold label			
❏ W1702 [M]	And Then…Along Comes The Association	1967	25.00
❏ WS1733	Birthday	1968	15.00
— With "W7" logo on green label			
❏ WS1786	Goodbye Columbus	1969	15.00
— With "W7" logo on green label			
❏ WS1767	Greatest Hits	1968	15.00
— With "W7" logo on green label			
❏ WS1767 [B]	Greatest Hits	197?	10.00
— Any later pressing (LP in print until the late 1980s)			
❏ ST-91586	Greatest Hits	1968	25.00
— Capitol Record Club edition			
❏ W1696 [M]	Insight Out	1967	18.00
❏ WS1696 [S]	Insight Out	1967	25.00
— Gold label			
❏ WS1696 [S]	Insight Out	1968	15.00
— With "W7" logo on green label			
❏ ST-91317 [S]	Insight Out	1967	30.00
— Capitol Record Club edition			
❏ WS1704	Renaissance	1967	15.00
❏ WS1927	Stop Your Motor	1971	15.00
❏ 2WS1868	The Association "Live	1970	18.00
❏ STBO-93249	The Association "Live	1970	25.00
— Capitol Record Club edition			
❏ WS1800	The Association	1969	15.00
— With "W7" logo on green label			

ASTAIRE, FRED

CHOREO
❏ A-1 [M]	Three Evenings with Fred Astaire	1961	40.00

CLEF
❏ MGC-662 [M]	The Fred Astaire Story, Volume 1	1955	50.00
— Reissue of Mercury 1001			
❏ MGC-663 [M]	The Fred Astaire Story, Volume 2	1955	50.00
— Reissue of Mercury 1002			
❏ MGC-664 [M]	The Fred Astaire Story, Volume 3	1955	50.00
— Reissue of Mercury 1003			
❏ MGC-665 [M]	The Fred Astaire Story, Volume 4	1955	50.00
— Reissue of Mercury 1004			

DRG
❏ DARC-3-1102	The Astaire Story	197?	30.00

EPIC
❏ LN3103 [M]	Nothing Thrilled Us Half As Much	1955	50.00
❏ FLM13103 [M]	Nothing Thrilled Us Half As Much	196?	25.00
— Reissue of 3103			
❏ FLS15103 [R]	Nothing Thrilled Us Half As Much	196?	18.00

Number	Title	Yr	NM
❏ LN3137 [M]	The Best of Fred Astaire	1955	50.00

KAPP
❏ KL-1165 [M]	Fred Astaire Now	1959	30.00
❏ KS-3165 [S]	Fred Astaire Now	1959	30.00

MCA
❏ 1552	Fred Astaire Sings	198?	15.00

MERCURY
❏ MGC-1001/4 [M]	The Fred Astaire Story	1953	1000.00
— Spiral-bound four-record set, pressed on blue vinyl, autographed by Fred Astaire			
❏ MGC-1001 [M]	The Fred Astaire Story, Volume 1	1954	100.00
❏ MGC-1002 [M]	The Fred Astaire Story, Volume 2	1954	100.00
❏ MGC-1003 [M]	The Fred Astaire Story, Volume 3	1954	100.00
❏ MGC-1004 [M]	The Fred Astaire Story, Volume 4	1954	100.00

VERVE
❏ MGV-2114 [M]	Easy to Dance With	1958	50.00
❏ MGV-2010 [M]	Mr. Top Hat	1956	50.00

VOCALION
❏ VL3716 [M]	Fred Astaire	1964	18.00

ASTLEY, JON

ATLANTIC
❏ 81740	Everyone Loves the Pilot (Except the Crew)	1987	10.00
❏ 81882	The Compleat Angler	1988	10.00

ASTLEY, RICK

RCA
❏ 8589-1-R	Hold Me in Your Arms	1989	10.00
❏ 6822-1-R	Whenever You Need Somebody	1988	10.00

ASTRONAUTS, THE (1)

RCA VICTOR
❏ LPM-2858 [M]	Competition Coupe	1964	60.00
❏ LSP-2858 [S]	Competition Coupe	1964	80.00
❏ LPM-3454 [M]	Down the Line	1966	30.00
❏ LSP-3454 [S]	Down the Line	1966	40.00
❏ LPM-2782 [M]	Everything Is A-OK!	1964	50.00
❏ LSP-2782 [S]	Everything Is A-OK!	1964	60.00
❏ LPM-3359 [M]	Favorites for You from Us	1965	30.00
❏ LSP-3359 [S]	Favorites for You from Us	1965	40.00
❏ PRM-183 [M]	Rockin' with the Astronauts	1965	30.00
— Promo only			
❏ LPM-2760 [M]	Surfin' with the Astronauts	1963	60.00
❏ LSP-2760 [S]	Surfin' with the Astronauts	1963	80.00
❏ LPM-3307 [M]	The Astronauts Go, Go, Go	1965	30.00
❏ LSP-3307 [S]	The Astronauts Go, Go, Go	1965	40.00
❏ LPM-2903 [M]	The Astronauts Orbit Kampus	1964	40.00
❏ LSP-2903 [S]	The Astronauts Orbit Kampus	1964	50.00
❏ LPM-3733 [M]	Travelin' Men	1967	50.00
❏ LSP-3733 [S]	Travelin' Men	1967	30.00

ASTRONAUTS, THE (1) / THE LIVERPOOL FIVE

RCA VICTOR
❏ PRS-251 [S]	Stereo Festival	1967	150.00
— Special-prodcuts edition			

ASYLUM CHOIR

MCA
❏ 684	Asylum Choir II	1979	10.00
— Reissue of Shelter 52010			

SHELTER
❏ SW-8910	Asylum Choir II	1971	18.00
❏ 52010	Asylum Choir II	1977	12.00
— Reissue of 2120			
❏ SR2120	Asylum Choir II	1974	15.00
— Reissue of 8910			

SMASH
❏ SRS-67107 [B]	Look Inside the Asylum Choir	1968	50.00
— Front cover has a roll of toilet paper			
❏ SRS-67107	Look Inside the Asylum Choir	197?	18.00
— Front cover has a photo of Leon and Marc			

ATCHER, BOB

COLUMBIA
❏ HL9006 [10]	Early American Folk Songs	1949	80.00
❏ HL9013 [10]	Songs of the Saddle	1949	80.00
❏ CL2232 [M]	The Dean of Cowboy Singers	1964	30.00
❏ CS9032 [R]	The Dean of Cowboy Singers	1964	18.00

HARMONY
❏ HL7313 [M]	Bob Atcher's Best	1964	25.00

ATKINS, CHET, AND DOC WATSON

RCA VICTOR
❏ AHL1-3701	Reflections	1980	12.00

ATKINS, CHET, AND LES PAUL

RCA VICTOR

Number	Title	Yr	NM
❑ APL1-1167	Chester and Lester	1976	15.00
❑ AYL1-3682	Chester and Lester	1980	10.00
— Best Buy Series" reissue			
❑ APL1-2786	Guitar Monsters	1978	15.00

ATKINS, CHET

COLUMBIA

Number	Title	Yr	NM
❑ FC44323	Chet Atkins, C.G.P.	1989	10.00
❑ PC39003	East Tennessee Christmas	1983	12.00
❑ FC40593	Sails	1987	10.00
❑ FC39591	Stay Tuned	1985	12.00
❑ FC40256	Street Dreams	1986	10.00
❑ FC38536	Work It Out with Chet Atkins C.G.P.	1983	12.00
❑ PC38536	Work It Out with Chet Atkins C.G.P.	1985	10.00
— Budget-line reissue			

DOLTON

Number	Title	Yr	NM
❑ BLP-16506 [M]	Play Guitar with Chet Atkins	1967	30.00
❑ BST-17506 [S]	Play Guitar with Chet Atkins	1967	30.00

PAIR

Number	Title	Yr	NM
❑ PDL2-1115	Guitar for All Seasons	1986	15.00
❑ PDL2-1047	Tennessee Guitar Man	1985	15.00

RCA CAMDEN

Number	Title	Yr	NM
❑ CAL-2182 [M]	Chet	1967	15.00
❑ CAS-2182 [S]	Chet	1967	18.00
❑ CAL-659 [M]	Chet Atkins and His Guitar	196?	18.00
❑ CAS-659(e) [R]	Chet Atkins and His Guitar	1964	15.00
❑ CAS-2523	Chet 'n Boots	1972	15.00
❑ CAS-2600	Finger Pickin' Good	1973	12.00
❑ CAL-753 [M]	Guitar Genius	196?	18.00
❑ CAS-753(e) [R]	Guitar Genius	196?	15.00
❑ ACL1-7042	Love Letters	197?	12.00
❑ CAL-981 [M]	Music from Nashville, My Home Town	1966	15.00
❑ CAS-981 [S]	Music from Nashville, My Home Town	1966	18.00
❑ CAS-2555	Nashville Gold	1972	15.00
❑ CAS-2296	Relaxin' with Chet	1969	15.00

RCA RED SEAL

Number	Title	Yr	NM
❑ LSC-3104	Chet Picks On the Pops	1969	18.00
— With the Boston Pops Orchestra, Arthur Fiedler, conductor			
❑ LM-2870 [M]	The "Pops" Goes Country	1966	18.00
❑ LSC-2870 [S]	The "Pops" Goes Country	1966	25.00
— Above two with the Boston Pops Orchestra, Arthur Fiedler, conductor			

RCA VICTOR

Number	Title	Yr	NM
❑ CPL1-2503	A Legendary Performer	1977	15.00
❑ APL1-0159	Alone	1973	15.00
❑ LPM-1090 [M]	A Session with Chet Atkins	1954	60.00
— Red cover			
❑ LPM-1090 [M]	A Session with Chet Atkins	1961	25.00
— Woman and guitars cover			
❑ LSP-1090(e) [R]	A Session with Chet Atkins	1967	12.00
❑ LPM-2601 [M]	Back Home Hymns	1962	25.00
❑ LSP-2601 [S]	Back Home Hymns	1962	30.00
❑ LPM-2549 [M]	Caribbean Guitar	1962	25.00
❑ LSP-2549 [S]	Caribbean Guitar	1962	30.00
❑ APL1-0645	Chat Atkins Goes to the Movies	1973	15.00
❑ LPM-1544 [M]	Chet Atkins at Home	1957	50.00
— Title in block letters on cover			
❑ LPM-1544 [M]	Chet Atkins at Home	1961	25.00
— Title in script on cover			
❑ LSP-1544(e) [R]	Chet Atkins at Home	1967	12.00
❑ LPM-3079 [10]	Chet Atkins' Gallopin' Guitar	1952	150.00
❑ LPM-1993 [M]	Chet Atkins in Hollywood	1959	30.00
— Night-time cover			
❑ LPM-1993 [M]	Chet Atkins in Hollywood	1961	25.00
— Daylight "blonde" cover			
❑ LSP-1993 [S]	Chet Atkins in Hollywood	1959	50.00
— Night-time cover			
❑ LSP-1993 [S]	Chet Atkins in Hollywood	1961	30.00
— Daylight "blonde" cover			
❑ LPM-1197 [M]	Chet Atkins in Three Dimensions	1956	50.00
— Black-and-white guitar cover			
❑ LPM-1197 [M]	Chet Atkins in Three Dimensions	1961	25.00
— Red guitar cover			
❑ LSP-1197(e) [R]	Chet Atkins in Three Dimensions	1967	12.00
❑ APL1-0545	Chet Atkins Picks On Jerry Reed	1974	15.00
❑ LPM-3531 [M]	Chet Atkins Picks On the Beatles	1966	30.00
❑ LSP-3531 [S]	Chet Atkins Picks On the Beatles	1966	30.00
❑ LPM-3818 [M]	Chet Atkins Picks the Best	1967	30.00
❑ LSP-3818 [S]	Chet Atkins Picks the Best	1967	15.00
❑ ANL1-0981	Chet Atkins Picks the Best	1975	12.00
❑ LSP-4754	Chet Atkins Picks the Hits	1973	18.00
❑ LPM-2232 [M]	Chet Atkins' Workshop	1961	25.00
❑ LSP-2232 [S]	Chet Atkins' Workshop	1961	30.00
❑ LPM-2423 [M]	Christmas with Chet Atkins	1961	25.00
❑ LSP-2423 [S]	Christmas with Chet Atkins	1961	30.00
❑ ANL1-1935	Christmas with Chet Atkins	1976	10.00
— Reissue of LSP-2423			
❑ LPM-3885 [M]	Class Guitar	1967	30.00
❑ LSP-3885 [S]	Class Guitar	1967	15.00
❑ AHL1-5495	Collector's Series	1985	12.00
❑ LPM-2450 [M]	Down Home	1962	25.00
❑ LSP-2450 [S]	Down Home	1962	30.00
❑ LPM-1383 [M]	Finger Style Guitar	1956	50.00
— Chet's face not visible on cover			
❑ LPM-1383 [M]	Finger Style Guitar	1961	25.00
— Chet's face visible on cover			
❑ LSP-1383(e) [R]	Finger Style Guitar	1962	15.00
❑ LSP-4464	For the Good Times	1971	18.00
❑ LPM-3647 [M]	From Nashville with Love	1966	15.00
❑ LSP-3647 [S]	From Nashville with Love	1966	18.00
❑ AHL1-4724	Great Hits of the Past	1983	12.00
❑ LPM-2783 [M]	Guitar Country	1964	18.00
❑ LSP-2783 [S]	Guitar Country	1964	25.00
❑ LPM-1577 [M]	Hi-Fi in Focus	1957	50.00
— No guitars on cover			
❑ LPM-1577 [M]	Hi-Fi in Focus	1957	25.00
— Guitar on cover			
❑ LSP-1577(e) [R]	Hi-Fi in Focus	196?	12.00
❑ LPM-4017 [M]	Hometown Guitar	1968	80.00
❑ LSP-4017 [S]	Hometown Guitar	1968	18.00
❑ LPM-2025 [M]	Hum & Strum Along	1959	30.00
— Add $10 NM if instruction book is included			
❑ LSP-2025 [S]	Hum & Strum Along	1959	40.00
— Add $10 NM if instruction book is included			
❑ LPM-3728 [M]	It's a Guitar World	1967	30.00
❑ LSP-3728 [S]	It's a Guitar World	1967	15.00
❑ LSP-4135	Lover's Guitar	1968	18.00
❑ LSP-4396	Me & Jerry	1971	18.00
— With Jerry Reed			
❑ LPM-2103 [M]	Mister Guitar	1959	30.00
— Lone guitar on cover			
❑ LPM-2103 [M]	Mister Guitar	1961	25.00
— Guitar and woman on cover			
❑ LSP-2103 [S]	Mister Guitar	1959	50.00
— Lone guitar on cover			
❑ LSP-2103 [S]	Mister Guitar	1961	30.00
— Guitar and woman on cover			
❑ LPM-3429 [M]	More of That "Guitar Country	1965	18.00
❑ LSP-3429 [S]	More of That "Guitar Country	1965	25.00
❑ LPM-3316 [M]	My Favorite Guitars	1965	18.00
❑ LSP-3316 [S]	My Favorite Guitars	1965	25.00
❑ AHL1-2405	My Guitar	1977	15.00
❑ VPXS-6079	Now & Then	1972	18.00
❑ LPM-2616 [M]	Our Man in Nashville	1963	25.00
❑ LSP-2616 [S]	Our Man in Nashville	1963	30.00
❑ LPM-2908 [M]	Progressive Pickin'	1964	18.00
❑ LSP-2908 [S]	Progressive Pickin'	1964	25.00
❑ LSP-4061	Solid Gold '68	1968	18.00
❑ LSP-4244	Solid Gold '69	1969	15.00
❑ LPM-3992 [M]	Solo Flights	1968	50.00
❑ LSP-3992 [S]	Solo Flights	1968	15.00
❑ AHL1-4044	Still Country -- After All These Years	1981	12.00
❑ LPM-3169 [10]	Stringin' Along with Chet Atkins	1953	100.00
❑ LPM-1236 [M]	Stringin' Along with Chet Atkins	1956	50.00
— Orange cover			
❑ LPM-1236 [M]	Stringin' Along with Chet Atkins	1961	25.00
— Full-color cover			
❑ LSP-1236(e) [R]	Stringin' Along with Chet Atkins	1967	12.00
❑ APL1-0329	Superpickers	1974	15.00
❑ APD1-0329 [Q]	Superpickers	1974	25.00
❑ LPM-2719 [M]	Teen Scene	1963	25.00
❑ LSP-2719 [S]	Teen Scene	1963	30.00
❑ LPM-2161 [M]	Teensville	1960	30.00
— Title overlaps cover photo			
❑ LPM-2161 [M]	Teensville	1961	25.00
— Title in black strip at top of cover photo			
❑ LSP-2161 [S]	Teensville	1960	50.00
— Title overlaps cover photo			
❑ LSP-2161 [S]	Teensville	1961	30.00
— Title in black strip at top of cover photo			
❑ LPM-2887 [M]	The Best of Chet Atkins	1964	18.00
❑ LSP-2887 [S]	The Best of Chet Atkins	1964	25.00
❑ APL1-1985	The Best of Chet Atkins	1975	15.00
❑ LPM-3558 [M]	The Best of Chet Atkins, Volume 2	1966	15.00
❑ LSP-3558 [S]	The Best of Chet Atkins, Volume 2	1966	18.00
❑ AHL1-3505	The Best of Chet On The Road…Live	1980	15.00
❑ AHL1-3302	The First Nashville Guitar Quartet	1979	15.00
❑ AYL1-3741	The First Nashville Guitar Quartet	1981	10.00
— Best Buy Series" reissue			
❑ LPM-2346 [M]	The Most Popular Guitar	1961	25.00
❑ LSP-2346 [S]	The Most Popular Guitar	1961	30.00
❑ APL1-1233	The Night Atlanta Burned	1975	15.00
❑ LPM-2175 [M]	The Other Chet Atkins	1960	25.00
❑ LSP-2175 [S]	The Other Chet Atkins	1960	30.00
❑ VPS-6030	This Is Chet Atkins	1972	18.00
❑ LPM-2678 [M]	Travelin'	1963	25.00
❑ LSP-2678 [S]	Travelin'	1963	30.00
❑ LSP-4331	Yestergroovin'	1970	15.00

TIME-LIFE

Number	Title	Yr	NM
❑ STW-117	Country Music	1981	15.00

ATKINS

WARNER BROS.

Number	Title	Yr	NM
❑ BSK3659	Atkins	1982	12.00

ATLANTA

MCA

Number	Title	Yr	NM
❑ 5576	Atlanta	1985	10.00
❑ 5463	Pictures	1984	10.00

ATLANTA DISCO BAND, THE

ARIOLA AMERICA

Number	Title	Yr	NM
❑ SW-50004	Bad Luck	1975	12.00

ATLANTA RHYTHM SECTION

COLUMBIA

Number	Title	Yr	NM
❑ FC37550 [B]	Quinella	1981	12.00
❑ PC37550	Quinella	1982	10.00
— Budget-line reissue			

DECCA

Number	Title	Yr	NM
❑ DL75265	Atlanta Rhythm Section	1972	30.00
❑ DL75390	Back Up Against the Wall	1973	30.00

MCA

Number	Title	Yr	NM
❑ 2-4114	Atlanta Rhythm Section	1977	15.00
— Combines the two Decca LPs into one package			

MOBILE FIDELITY

Number	Title	Yr	NM
❑ 1-038	Champagne Jam	1981	40.00
— Audiophile vinyl			

POLYDOR

Number	Title	Yr	NM
❑ PD-2-6236	Are You Ready!	1979	15.00
❑ PD-1-6080	A Rock and Roll Alternative	1977	12.00
❑ PD-1-6134 [B]	Champagne Jam	1978	12.00
❑ PD6041	Dog Days	1975	12.00
❑ PD-1-6060	Red Tape	1976	12.00
❑ PD-1-6285	The Boys from Doraville	1980	12.00
❑ PD6027	Third Annual Pipe Dream	1974	12.00
❑ PD-1-6200	Underdog	1979	12.00

ATOMIC ROOSTER

CLEOPATRA

Number	Title	Yr	NM
❑ CLP1772 [B]	Death Walks Behind You	2014	30.00

ELEKTRA

Number	Title	Yr	NM
❑ EKS-75074	Atomic Rooster IV	1973	18.00
❑ EKS-74094	Death Walks Behind You	1971	25.00
❑ EKS-74109	In Hearing Of Atomic Rooster	1971	25.00
❑ EKS-75039 [B]	Made in England	1972	25.00

AU GO-GO SINGERS, THE

ROULETTE

Number	Title	Yr	NM
❑ R25280 [M]	They Call Us the Au Go-Go Singers	1964	50.00
❑ SR25280 [S]	They Call Us the Au Go-Go Singers	1964	70.00

AUDIENCE

ELEKTRA

Number	Title	Yr	NM
❑ EKS-74100 [B]	House on the Hill	1971	35.00
❑ EKS-75026 [B]	Lunch	1972	35.00

AUDIO TWO

FIRST PRIORITY

Number	Title	Yr	NM
❑ 91358	I Don't Care -- The Album	1990	80.00
❑ 90907	What More Can I Say?	1988	80.00

AUGUST SONS

EYES IN THE WOODS

Number	Title	Yr	NM
❑ (# unknown) [EP]	I Am Not a Vampire	1989	40.00

AULD, GEORGIE

ABC-PARAMOUNT

Number	Title	Yr	NM
❑ ABC-287 [M]	Georgie Auld Plays for Melancholy Babies	1958	40.00
❑ ABCS-287 [S]	Georgie Auld Plays for Melancholy Babies	1959	30.00

ALLEGRO

Number	Title	Yr	NM
❑ 3102 [M]	Jazz Concert	1953	40.00

APOLLO

Number	Title	Yr	NM
❑ LAP-102 [10]	Concert in Jazz	1951	80.00

CORAL

Number	Title	Yr	NM
❑ CRL57029 [M]	Lullaby of Broadway	1956	40.00
❑ CRL56085 [10]	Manhattan	1953	80.00
❑ CRL57032 [M]	Misty	1956	40.00
❑ CRL56060 [10]	Tenderly	1952	80.00

DISCOVERY

Number	Title	Yr	NM
❑ DL3007 [10]	That's Auld	1950	80.00

EMARCY

Number	Title	Yr	NM
❑ MG-36090 [M]	Dancing in the Land of Hi-Fi	1956	40.00
❑ MG-36060 [M]	In the Land of Hi-Fi	1955	40.00

JARO

Number	Title	Yr	NM
❑ JAM-5003 [M]	Hawaii on the Rocks	1959	30.00

MUSICRAFT

Number	Title	Yr	NM
❑ 501	Georgie Auld and His Orchestra, Vol. 1	197?	12.00
❑ 509	Georgie Auld and His Orchestra, Vol. 2	197?	12.00

Number	Title	Yr	NM
PHILIPS			
❏ PHM200096 [M]	Georgie Auld Plays to the Winners	1963	18.00
❏ PHS600096 [S]	Georgie Auld Plays to the Winners	1963	25.00
❏ PHM200116 [M]	Here's to the Losers	1963	18.00
❏ PHS600116 [S]	Here's to the Losers	1963	25.00
ROOST			
❏ RST-403 [10]	Georgie Auld Quintet	1951	80.00
TOP RANK			
❏ RM-333 [M]	Good Enough to Keep	1960	40.00
❏ RM-306 [M]	The Melody Lingers On	1959	40.00
UNITED ARTISTS			
❏ UAL-3068 [M]	Manhattan with Strings	1959	40.00
❏ UAS-6068 [S]	Manhattan with Strings	1959	30.00
XANADU			
❏ 190	Homage	197?	12.00

AUM

Number	Title	Yr	NM
FILLMORE			
❏ Z30002 [B]	Resurrection	1970	40.00
SIRE			
❏ SES-97007 [B]	Bluesvibes	1969	50.00

AURRA

Number	Title	Yr	NM
DREAM			
❏ DA-3503	Aurra	1980	18.00
SALSOUL			
❏ SA-8551	A Little Love	1982	15.00
❏ SA-8559	Live and Let Live	1983	15.00
❏ SA-8538	Send Your Love	1981	15.00

AUSTIN, BOBBY

Number	Title	Yr	NM
CAPITOL			
❏ T2773 [M]	Apartment No. 9	1967	30.00
❏ ST2773 [S]	Apartment No. 9	1967	25.00
❏ ST2915	Old Love Never Dies	1968	25.00

AUSTIN, CLAIRE

Number	Title	Yr	NM
CONTEMPORARY			
❏ C-5002 [M]	When Your Lover Has Gone	1956	50.00
FANTASY			
❏ OJC-1711	When Your Lover Has Gone	198?	15.00
—Reissue of Contemporary 5002			
GHB			
❏ S-22	Claire Austin and the Great Excelsior Band	197?	18.00
GOOD TIME JAZZ			
❏ L-24 [10]	Claire Austin Sings the Blues	1954	120.00
JAZZOLOGY			
❏ 52	Goin' Crazy	197?	18.00

AUSTIN, DONALD

Number	Title	Yr	NM
EASTBOUND			
❏ EB-9005	Crazy Legs	1973	30.00

AUSTIN, GENE

Number	Title	Yr	NM
DECCA			
❏ DL8433 [M]	My Blue Heaven	1957	40.00
DOT			
❏ DLP3300 [M]	Great Hits	1960	25.00
❏ DLP25300 [S]	Great Hits	1960	30.00
FRATERNITY			
❏ F-1006 [M]	Gene Austin and His Lonesome Road	1957	25.00
RCA VICTOR			
❏ LPM-3200 [10]	My Blue Heaven	1953	60.00
❏ LPM-2490 [M]	My Blue Heaven	1961	30.00
❏ LPM-1549 [M]	Restless Heart	1957	40.00
❏ VPM-6065	This Is Gene Austin	1972	25.00
X			
❏ LVA-1007 [M]	Gene Austin Sings All-Time Favorites	1954	40.00

AUSTIN, SIL

Number	Title	Yr	NM
MERCURY			
❏ MG-20320 [M]	Everything's Shakin'	1958	70.00
❏ SR-60755 [S]	Folk Songs	1963	25.00
❏ MG-20755 [M]	Folk Songs	1963	18.00
❏ MG-20663 [M]	Golden Saxophone Hits	1961	30.00
❏ SR-60663 [S]	Golden Saxophone Hits	1961	30.00
❏ MG-20424 [M]	Sil Austin Plays Pretty for the People	1959	40.00
❏ SR-60096 [S]	Sil Austin Plays Pretty for the People	1959	60.00
—Black label			
❏ SR-60096 [S]	Sil Austin Plays Pretty for the People	1965	30.00
—Red label, white "MERCURY" at top			
❏ SR-60096 [S]	Sil Austin Plays Pretty for the People	1974	12.00
—Chicago styline" label			
❏ MG-21126 [M]	Sil Austin Plays Pretty for the People Again	1967	25.00
❏ SR-61126 [S]	Sil Austin Plays Pretty for the People Again	1967	30.00

Number	Title	Yr	NM
❏ MG-20925 [M]	Sil Austin Plays Pretty Melodies of the World	1964	25.00
❏ SR-60925 [S]	Sil Austin Plays Pretty Melodies of the World	1964	30.00
❏ MG-20237 [M]	Slow Walk Rock	1957	70.00
❏ MG-20576 [M]	Soft, Plaintive and Moody	1960	40.00
❏ SR-60236 [S]	Soft, Plaintive and Moody	1960	60.00
SSS INTERNATIONAL			
❏ 4 [B]	Honey Sax	1969	25.00
❏ 14	Sil and Silver Screen	1971	18.00
❏ 8	Soft Soul with Strings	1970	18.00
❏ 23	Songs of Gold	1971	18.00
WING			
❏ SRW-16227 [S]	Everything's Shakin'	196?	18.00
❏ SRW-16369 [S]	Sil Austin Again Plays Pretty for the People	196?	18.00

AUSTRALIAN ALL STARS, THE

Number	Title	Yr	NM
BETHLEHEM			
❏ BCP-6070 [M]	Jazz for Beach-Niks	1963	40.00
❏ BCP-6073 [M]	Jazz for Surf-Niks	1963	40.00

AUSTRALIAN JAZZ QUARTET, THE

Number	Title	Yr	NM
BETHLEHEM			
❏ BCP-1031 [10]	The Australian Jazz Quartet	195?	60.00
❏ BCP-6003 [M]	The Australian Jazz Quartet	1955	40.00
❏ BCP-6002	The Australian Jazz Quartet	197?	18.00
—Reissue distributed by RCA Victor			
❏ BCP-6012 [M]	The Australian Jazz Quartet at the Varsity Drag	1956	40.00
❏ BCP-6029 [M]	The Australian Jazz Quartet In Free Style	1959	40.00
❏ BCP-6022 [M]	The Australian Jazz Quartet Plays the Best of Broadway Musical Hits	1957	40.00
❏ BCP-6015 [M]	The Australian Jazz Quartet Plus One	1957	40.00
❏ BCP-6002 [M]	The Australian Jazz Quartet/ Quintet	1955	40.00
❏ BCP-6030 [M]	Three Penny Opera	1959	40.00

AUTOSALVAGE

Number	Title	Yr	NM
RCA VICTOR			
❏ LPM-3940 [M]	Autosalvage	1968	150.00
❏ LSP-3940 [S]	Autosalvage	1968	100.00

AUTRY, GENE

Number	Title	Yr	NM
CHALLENGE			
❏ CHL-600 [M]	Christmas with Gene Autry	1958	50.00
COLUMBIA			
❏ JL8012 [10]	Champion	1950	150.00
❏ CL(# unk) [10]	Easter Favorites	1949	150.00
❏ CL2568 [10]	Easter Favorites	1955	120.00
—House Party Series" issue			
❏ CL677 [M]	Gene Autry and Champion — Western Adventures	1955	120.00
❏ JL8001 [10]	Gene Autry at the Rodeo	1949	150.00
❏ CL1575 [M]	Gene Autry's Greatest Hits	1961	30.00
—Red and black label with six "eye" logos			
❏ CL6020 [10]	Gene Autry's Western Classics	1949	150.00
❏ HL9001 [10]	Gene Autry's Western Classics, Volume 1	1949	150.00
❏ HL9002 [10]	Gene Autry's Western Classics, Volume 2	1949	150.00
❏ CL6137 [10]	Merry Christmas	1950	150.00
❏ CL2547 [10]	Merry Christmas with Gene Autry	1954	120.00
—House Party Series" release			
❏ JL8009 [10]	Stampede	1949	150.00
COLUMBIA SPECIAL PRODUCTS			
❏ P15766	Christmas Favorites	1981	15.00
GRAND PRIX			
❏ KX-11 [M]	The Original Gene Autry Sings Rudolph the Red-Nosed Reindeer and Other Christmas Favorites	1961	18.00
❏ KS-X11 [S]	The Original Gene Autry Sings Rudolph the Red-Nosed Reindeer and Other Christmas Favorites	1961	25.00
GUSTO			
❏ 1038	Christmas Classics	1978	12.00
HARMONY			
❏ HL7376 [M]	Back in the Saddle Again	1966	25.00
❏ HL9505 [M]	Gene Autry and Champion – Western Adventures	1959	30.00
❏ HL7332 [M]	Gene Autry's Great Western Hits	1965	30.00
❏ HL7399 [M]	Gene Autry Sings	1966	25.00
❏ HL9550 [M]	The Original Rudolph the Red-Nosed Reindeer and Other Children's Christmas Favorites	1964	30.00
❏ HS14450 [R]	The Original Rudolph the Red-Nosed Reindeer and Other Children's Christmas Favorites	1964	15.00
MELODY RANCH			
❏ 101 [M]	Melody Ranch	1965	40.00
MURRAY HILL			
❏ 897296	Melody Ranch Radio Show	197?	60.00
—Compilation of some of Gene's radio shows in a box set			

Number	Title	Yr	NM
RCA VICTOR			
❏ LPM-2623 [M]	Gene Autry's Golden Hits	1962	30.00
❏ LSP-2623 [S]	Gene Autry's Golden Hits	1962	40.00
REPUBLIC			
❏ RLP6018 [M]	Christmas with Gene Autry	1976	15.00
❏ 6012	Cowboy Hall of Fame	1976	25.00
❏ 6011	South of the Border, All American Cowboy	1976	25.00

AVALANCHES, THE

Number	Title	Yr	NM
WARNER BROS.			
❏ W1525 [M]	Ski Surfin'	1963	40.00
❏ WS1525 [S]	Ski Surfin'	1963	60.00

AVALON, FRANKIE

Number	Title	Yr	NM
ABC			
❏ ABCX-805 [R]	16 Greatest Hits	1974	15.00
CHANCELLOR			
❏ CHL5022 [M]	And Now About Mr. Avalon	1961	30.00
❏ CHLS5022 [S]	And Now About Mr. Avalon	1961	40.00
❏ CHL5018 [M]	A Whole Lotta Frankie	1961	30.00
❏ CHL5032 [M]	Cleopatra Plus 13 Other Great Hits	1963	30.00
❏ CHLS5032 [S]	Cleopatra Plus 13 Other Great Hits	1963	40.00
❏ CHL5001 [M]	Frankie Avalon	1958	50.00
—Pink label			
❏ CHL5001 [M]	Frankie Avalon	1959	40.00
—Black label			
❏ CHL5031 [M]	Frankie Avalon's Christmas Album	1962	30.00
❏ CHLS5031 [S]	Frankie Avalon's Christmas Album	1962	40.00
❏ CHL5025 [M]	Italiano	1962	30.00
❏ CHLS5025 [S]	Italiano	1962	40.00
❏ CHL5011 [M]	Summer Scene	1960	30.00
❏ CHLS5011 [S]	Summer Scene	1960	40.00
❏ CHLX5004 [M]	Swingin' on a Rainbow	1959	40.00
❏ CHLXS5004 [S]	Swingin' on a Rainbow	1959	50.00
❏ CHL5002 [M]	The Young Frankie Avalon	1959	50.00
—Pink label			
❏ CHL5002 [M]	The Young Frankie Avalon	1959	40.00
—Black label			
❏ CHLS5002 [S]	The Young Frankie Avalon	1959	60.00
—Pink label			
❏ CHLS5002 [S]	The Young Frankie Avalon	1959	50.00
—Black label			
❏ 69801 [M]	Young and In Love	1960	80.00
—LP in felt cover and 3-D portrait, all in box			
❏ 69801 [M]	Young and In Love	1960	40.00
—LP without the box			
❏ CHL5027 [M]	You're Mine	1962	30.00
❏ CHLS5027 [S]	You're Mine	1962	40.00
DE-LITE			
❏ 2020	Venus	1976	18.00
❏ 9504	You're My Life	1977	18.00
EVEREST			
❏ 4187	Greatest Hits	1982	12.00
LIBERTY			
❏ LN-10193	Songs from Muscle Beach Party	1981	10.00
—Budget-line reissue			
MCA			
❏ 27096	The Best of Frankie Avalon	1985	10.00
METROMEDIA			
❏ MD-1034	I Want You Near Me	1970	18.00
SUNSET			
❏ SUS-5244	Frankie Avalon	1969	18.00
TRIP			
❏ 1621	16 Greatest Hits of Frankie Avalon	1977	12.00
UNITED ARTISTS			
❏ UAL-3382 [M]	Frankie Avalon's 15 Greatest Hits	1964	25.00
❏ UAS-6382 [S]	Frankie Avalon's 15 Greatest Hits	1964	30.00
❏ UAL-3371 [M]	Songs from Muscle Beach Party	1964	30.00
❏ UAS-6371 [S]	Songs from Muscle Beach Party	1964	30.00
❏ UA-LA450-F	The Very Best of Frankie Avalon	1975	15.00

AVALON, FRANKIE AND FABIAN

Number	Title	Yr	NM
MCA			
❏ 27097	The Greatest of Frankie Avalon and Fabian	1985	12.00

AVENGERS

Number	Title	Yr	NM
4 MEN WITH BEARDS			
❏ 4M519LP [B]	The Avengers		25.00
CD PRESENTS			
❏ 007	Avengers	1983	30.00
—Red vinyl			
❏ 007	Avengers	1983	25.00
—Black vinyl			
GO			
❏ 005	Avengers	1983	120.00

Number	Title	Yr	NM

LOOKOUT!

| ❏ 217 [B] | The Avengers Died for Your Sins | 1999 | 12.00 |

WHITE NOISE

| ❏ 002 [EP] | Avengers | 1978 | 100.00 |

AVENGERS VI, THE

MARK 56

| ❏ 536 | Good Humor Presents Real Cool Hits | 1966 | 250.00 |

— *Custom pressing for the Good Humor ice cream company*

AVERAGE WHITE BAND

ARISTA

| ❏ AB9594 | Cupid's in Fashion | 1981 | 12.00 |
| ❏ AB9523 | Shine | 1980 | 12.00 |

ATLANTIC

❏ SD7308	Average White Band	1974	12.00
❏ QD7308 [Q]	Average White Band	1975	30.00
❏ SD19116	Average White Band	1977	10.00
— *Reissue*			
❏ SD19105	Benny and Us	1977	12.00
— *With Ben E. King*			
❏ SD18140 [B]	Cut the Cake	1975	12.00
❏ SD19207	Feel No Fret	1979	12.00
❏ SD 2-1002	Person to Person	1977	15.00
❏ SD18179	Soul Searching	1976	12.00
❏ SD19266	Volume VIII	1980	12.00
❏ SD19162	Warmer Communications	1978	12.00

MCA

❏ 475	Put It Where You Want It	1975	12.00
— *Reissue of MCA 345*			
❏ 345	Show Your Hands	1973	30.00

MOBILE FIDELITY

| ❏ 1-245 | Average White Band | 1996 | 25.00 |
| — *Audiophile vinyl* | | | |

TRACK

| ❏ 58830 | Aftershock | 1988 | 12.00 |

AVONS, THE (1)

HULL

| ❏ HLP-1000 [M] | The Avons | 1960 | 700.00 |

AWESOME DRE AND THE HARDCORE COMMITTEE

BENTLEY

| ❏ 12001 | You Can't Hold Me Back | 1989 | 25.00 |

AXTON, HOYT

A&M

❏ SP-4571	Fearless	1976	12.00
❏ SP-4376	Less Than a Song	1973	12.00
❏ SP-4402	Life Machine	1974	12.00
❏ SP-3155	Life Machine	198?	10.00
— *Budget-line reissue*			
❏ SP-4009	Road Songs	1977	12.00
❏ SP-3182	Road Songs	198?	10.00
— *Budget-line reissue*			
❏ SP-4510	Southbound	1975	12.00

ACCORD

| ❏ SN-7197 | Heartbreak Hotel | 1982 | 12.00 |

ALLEGIANCE

| ❏ AV-5023 | Down and Out | 1984 | 12.00 |

BRYLEN

| ❏ BN4400 | Double Dare | 1982 | 15.00 |

CAPITOL

| ❏ SMAS-850 | Country Anthem | 1971 | 15.00 |
| ❏ ST-788 | Joy to the World | 1971 | 15.00 |

COLUMBIA

❏ CS9766	My Griffin Is Gone	1969	18.00
❏ KC33103	My Griffin Is Gone	1975	12.00
❏ PC33103	My Griffin Is Gone	1979	10.00
— *Budget-line reissue*			

EXODUS

❏ EX-301 [M]	Hoyt Axton Sings Bessie Smith	1966	25.00
❏ EXS-321 [M]	Saturday's Child	1966	25.00
— *Cover says stereo, record plays mono*			

HORIZON

❏ WP-1601 [M]	Greenback Dollar	1963	25.00
— *Black label; two fewer songs than "The Balladeer*			
❏ WP-1601 [S]	Greenback Dollar	1963	30.00
— *Blue label; two fewer songs than "The Balladeer*			
❏ WP-1621 [M]	Saturday's Child	1963	30.00
❏ SWP-1621 [S]	Saturday's Child	1963	30.00
❏ WP-1601 [M]	The Balladeer	1962	30.00
— *Black label*			
❏ WP-1601 [S]	The Balladeer	1962	30.00
— *Same number as mono, but with blue label*			
❏ WP-1613 [M]	Thunder 'N Lightnin'	1963	30.00
❏ SWP-1613 [S]	Thunder 'N Lightnin'	1963	30.00

JEREMIAH

| ❏ JH-5000 | A Rusty Old Halo | 1979 | 15.00 |
| ❏ JH-5001 | Where Did the Money Go? | 1980 | 15.00 |

Number	Title	Yr	NM

MCA

❏ 2319	Free Sailin'	1978	12.00
❏ 648	Free Sailin'	198?	10.00
— *Budget-line reissue*			
❏ 2263	Snow Blind Friend	1977	12.00
❏ 647	Snow Blind Friend	198?	10.00
— *Budget-line reissue*			

SURREY

| ❏ S-1005 [M] | Mr. Greenback Dollar Man | 1965 | 25.00 |
| ❏ SS-1005 [S] | Mr. Greenback Dollar Man | 1965 | 30.00 |

VEE JAY

❏ LP-1126 [M]	Greenback Dollar	1965	25.00
❏ LPS-1126 [S]	Greenback Dollar	1965	30.00
❏ LP-1098 [M]	Hoyt Axton Explodes!	1964	30.00
❏ LPS-1098 [R]	Hoyt Axton Explodes!	1964	25.00
❏ LP-1127 [M]	Saturday's Child	1965	25.00
❏ LPS-1127 [S]	Saturday's Child	1965	30.00
— *Reissue of Horizon 1621*			
❏ LP-1118 [M]	The Best of Hoyt Axton	1965	25.00
❏ LPS-1118 [S]	The Best of Hoyt Axton	1965	30.00
❏ LP-1128 [M]	Thunder 'N Lightnin'	1965	25.00
❏ LPS-1128 [S]	Thunder 'N Lightnin'	1965	30.00
— *Reissue of Horizon 1613*			

VEE JAY/DYNASTY

| ❏ VJS-7306 | Bessie Smith... My Way | 1974 | 18.00 |

VEE JAY INTERNATIONAL

❏ VJS-2-1005	Gold	1974	25.00
— *Compilation of older Vee Jay material*			
❏ LP-6001	Long Old Road	1977	18.00

AYCOCK, EARL

MERCURY

| ❏ MG-20282 [M] | Earl Aycock | 1958 | 30.00 |

AYERS, ROY, AND WAYNE HENDERSON

POLYDOR

| ❏ PD-1-6276 | Prime Time | 1980 | 12.00 |
| ❏ PD-1-6179 | Step Into Our Life | 1978 | 12.00 |

AYERS, ROY

ATLANTIC

❏ SD1692	Daddy Bug & Friends	1976	15.00
❏ SD1538	Daddy Bug	1969	25.00
❏ SD1514	Stoned Soul Picnic	1968	25.00
❏ 1488 [M]	Virgo Vibes	1967	25.00
❏ SD1488 [S]	Virgo Vibes	1967	18.00

COLUMBIA

| ❏ FC39422 | In the Dark | 1984 | 12.00 |

ICHIBAN

| ❏ ICH-1028 | Drive | 198? | 12.00 |
| ❏ ICH-1040 | Wake Up | 198? | 12.00 |

POLYDOR

❏ PD-1-6327	Africa, Center of the World	1981	12.00
❏ PD6046	A Tear to a Smile	1975	12.00
❏ PD6032	Change Up the Groove	1974	12.00
❏ PD-1-6070	Everybody Loves the Sunshine	1976	12.00
❏ PD-1-6348	Feeling Good	1982	12.00
❏ PD-1-6204	Fever	1979	12.00
❏ PD5022	He's Coming	1972	16.00
❏ PD-1-6126	Let's Do It	1978	12.00
❏ PD-1-6108	Lifeline	1977	12.00
❏ PD-1-6301	Love Fantasy	1980	12.00
❏ PD6057	Mystic Voyage	1976	12.00
❏ PD-1-6246	No Stranger to Love	1979	12.00
❏ PD5045	Red, Black and Green	1973	15.00
❏ PD-1-6078	Red, Black and Green	1976	12.00
— *Reissue of 5045*			
❏ PD-1-6091	Vibrations	1977	12.00
❏ PD6016	Virgo Red	1973	15.00
❏ PD-1-6159	You Send Me	1978	12.00

UNITED ARTISTS

| ❏ UAL-3325 [M] | West Coast Vibes | 1964 | 25.00 |
| ❏ UAS-6325 [S] | West Coast Vibes | 1964 | 30.00 |

AYLER, ALBERT

ABC IMPULSE!

❏ AS-9155 [S]	Live at the Village Vanguard	1968	15.00
❏ IA-9336	Live at the Village Vanguard	1978	18.00
❏ AS-9165	Love Cry	1968	25.00
❏ AS-9191	Music Is the Healing Force of the Universe	1969	25.00
❏ AS-9175 [B]	New Grass	1969	25.00
❏ AS-9257	Re-evaluations: The Impulse Years	1974	18.00
❏ AS-9208	The Last Album	1971	25.00

ARISTA/FREEDOM

| ❏ AL1000 | Vibrations | 1976 | 18.00 |
| ❏ AL1018 | Witches and Devils | 1977 | 18.00 |

ESP-DISK'

❏ 1010 [M]	Bells	1965	30.00
— *Black vinyl*			
❏ 1010 [M]	Bells	1965	50.00
— *Yellow vinyl*			
❏ S-1010 [M]	Bells	1965	25.00
❏ 1016 [M]	New York Eye and Ear Control	1966	60.00

Number	Title	Yr	NM

❏ S-1016 [S]	New York Eye and Ear Control	1966	100.00
❏ ESP-3030	Prophecy	1975	18.00
❏ 1020 [M]	Spirits Rejoice	1966	30.00
❏ S-1020 [S]	Spirits Rejoice	1966	25.00
❏ 1002 [M]	Spiritual Unity	1965	30.00

FANTASY

| ❏ 6016 [M] | My Name Is Albert Ayler | 196? | 25.00 |
| ❏ 86016 [S] | My Name Is Albert Ayler | 196? | 30.00 |

GNP CRESCENDO

| ❏ GNPS-9022 | The First Recordings | 1973 | 15.00 |

IMPULSE!

| ❏ A-9155 [M] | Live at the Village Vanguard | 1967 | 30.00 |
| ❏ AS-9155 [S] | Live at the Village Vanguard | 1967 | 30.00 |

MCA

| ❏ 4129 | Live at the Village Vanguard | 198? | 15.00 |
| — *Reissue of ABC Impulse 9336* | | | |

AZAMA, ETHEL

LIBERTY

❏ LRP-3142 [M]	Cool Heat	1960	40.00
❏ LST-7142 [S]	Cool Heat	1960	50.00
❏ LRP-3104 [M]	Exotic Dreams	1959	25.00
❏ LST-7104 [S]	Exotic Dreams	1959	30.00

AZITIS

ELCO

| ❏ SC-EC-5555 | Help! | 197? | 500.00 |

AZTEC TWO-STEP

ELEKTRA

| ❏ EKS-75031 [B] | Aztec Two-Step | 1972 | 18.00 |

FLYING FISH

| ❏ 505 | See It Was Like This... An Acoustic Retrospective | 1991 | 12.00 |

RCA VICTOR

❏ AFL1-2453	Adjoining Suites	1978	15.00
❏ APL1-1161	Second Step	1975	15.00
❏ APL1-1497	Two's Company	1976	15.00

REFLEX

| ❏ 8601 | Living in America | 1986 | 12.00 |

WATERHOUSE

| ❏ 9 | The Times of Our Lives | 1980 | 18.00 |

AZTECA

COLUMBIA

❏ KC31776	Azteca	1972	15.00
❏ CQ31776 [Q]	Azteca	1974	30.00
❏ KC32451	Pyramid of the Sun	1973	15.00

AZTECS, THE

WORLD ARTISTS

| ❏ WAM-2001 [M] | Live at the Ad Lib Club of London | 1964 | 60.00 |
| — *Features Beatles on the cover endorsing the band* | | | |

B

B-52'S, THE

REPRISE

❏ 25854 [B]	Cosmic Thing	1989	15.00
❏ 44519	Time Capsule -- The Mixes	1998	18.00
— *Numbered as if it were a 12-inch single, this contains remixes of seven songs from the "best of" CD compilation, so we've listed it under LPs; issued in orange vinyl cover*			

WARNER BROS.

❏ 25504	Bouncing Off the Satellites	1986	12.00
❏ R154582	Bouncing Off the Satellites	1986	15.00
— *RCA Music Service edition*			

Number	Title	Yr	NM
❏ MINI3641 [EP]	Mesopotamia	1982	10.00
❏ MINI3596 [EP]	Party Mix	1981	15.00
❏ BSK3355	The B-52's	1979	12.00
❏ 23819	Whammy!	1983	12.00
❏ BSK3471	Wild Planet	1980	15.00

— Originals have red custom labels (deduct 33% for later pressings)

BABASIN, HARRY

MODE
Number	Title	Yr	NM
❏ LP-119 [M]	Jazz Pickers	1957	100.00

NOCTURNE
Number	Title	Yr	NM
❏ NLP-3 [10]	Harry Babasin Quartet	1954	150.00

BABE RUTH

CAPITOL
Number	Title	Yr	NM
❏ ST-11515	Kids Stuff	1976	25.00

HARVEST
Number	Title	Yr	NM
❏ ST-11515	Amar Caballero	1974	30.00
❏ ST-11367	Babe Ruth	1975	18.00
❏ SW-11151	First Base	1973	40.00
❏ ST-11451	Stealin' Home	1975	18.00

BABES IN TOYLAND

REPRISE
Number	Title	Yr	NM
❏ 45868 [B]	Nemesisters	1995	25.00

TWIN/TONE
Number	Title	Yr	NM
❏ TTR89183 [B]	Spanking Machine	1990	35.00

BABY

CHELSEA
Number	Title	Yr	NM
❏ CHL-517	Where Did All the Money Go	1976	16.00

LONE STARR
Number	Title	Yr	NM
❏ 9782	Baby	1974	30.00

BABY GRAND

ARISTA
Number	Title	Yr	NM
❏ AL4140	Baby Grand	1977	25.00

BABY HUEY

CURTOM
Number	Title	Yr	NM
❏ CRS-8007	The Living Legend	1970	40.00

BABY RAY

IMPERIAL
Number	Title	Yr	NM
❏ LP-9335 [M]	Where Soul Lives	1967	30.00
❏ LP-12335 [S]	Where Soul Lives	1967	30.00

BABYFACE

ARISTA
Number	Title	Yr	NM
❏ 12667	Face2Face	2001	18.00

EPIC
Number	Title	Yr	NM
❏ E53558	For the Cool in You	1993	15.00
❏ E67293	The Day	1996	12.00

SOLAR
Number	Title	Yr	NM
❏ ST-72552	Lovers by Babyface	1987	15.00
❏ FZ45288	Tender Lover	1989	12.00

BABYS, THE

CHRYSALIS
Number	Title	Yr	NM
❏ CHR1351	Anthology	1981	12.00
❏ PV41351	Anthology	198?	10.00

— Reissue of 1351
| ❏ CHR1150 | Broken Heart | 1977 | 12.00 |
| ❏ PV41150 [B] | Broken Heart | 1983 | 10.00 |

— Reissue of 1150
| ❏ CHR1195 | Head First | 1979 | 12.00 |
| ❏ FV41195 | Head First | 1983 | 10.00 |

— Reissue of 1195
| ❏ CHR1305 | On the Edge | 1980 | 12.00 |
| ❏ PV41305 | On the Edge | 1983 | 10.00 |

— Reissue of 1305
| ❏ CHR1129 | The Babys | 1976 | 15.00 |
| ❏ PV41129 | The Babys | 1983 | 10.00 |

— Reissue of 1129
| ❏ CHR1267 | Union Jacks | 1980 | 12.00 |
| ❏ PV41267 | Union Jacks | 1983 | 10.00 |

— Reissue of 1267

BACHARACH, BURT

A&M
Number	Title	Yr	NM
❏ SP-3501	Burt Bacharach	1971	12.00
❏ SP-3661	Burt Bacharach's Greatest Hits	1973	12.00
❏ SP-4622	Futures	1977	12.00
❏ SP-3527	Living Together	1973	12.00
❏ SP-4188	Make It Easy on Yourself	1969	12.00
❏ SP-131 [M]	Reach Out	1967	15.00
❏ SP-4131 [S]	Reach Out	1967	15.00
❏ SP-3709	Woman	1979	12.00

COLUMBIA
Number	Title	Yr	NM
❏ C97734	At This Time	2005	12.00

KAPP
Number	Title	Yr	NM
❏ KS-3577	Burt Bacharach Plays His Hits	1969	15.00

MCA
Number	Title	Yr	NM
❏ 65	Burt Bacharach Plays His Hits	1973	10.00

— Reissue of Kapp LP

BACHELORS, THE (1)

LONDON
Number	Title	Yr	NM
❏ PS528 [S]	Bachelors '68	1968	15.00
❏ LL3528 [M]	Bachelors '68	1968	25.00
❏ LL3393 [M]	Back Again	1964	18.00
❏ PS393 [P]	Back Again	1964	25.00

— I Wouldn't Trade You for the World" is rechanneled.
❏ LL3518 [M]	Golden All Time Hits	1967	18.00
❏ PS518 [P]	Golden All Time Hits	1967	18.00
❏ LL3460 [M]	Hits of the 60's	1966	18.00
❏ PS460 [P]	Hits of the 60's	1966	25.00
❏ LL3435 [M]	Marie	1965	18.00
❏ PS435 [P]	Marie	1965	25.00

— Marie" is rechanneled
❏ LL3418 [M]	No Arms Can Ever Hold You	1965	18.00
❏ PS418 [S]	No Arms Can Ever Hold You	1965	25.00
❏ LL3353 [M]	Presenting the Bachelors	1964	18.00
❏ PS353 [S]	Presenting the Bachelors	1964	30.00
❏ LL3491 [M]	The Bachelors' Girls	1966	15.00
❏ PS491 [P]	The Bachelors' Girls	1966	25.00

— Marie" is rechanneled
| ❏ PS611 | Under and Over | 1972 | 12.00 |

BACHMAN, RANDY

POLYDOR
Number	Title	Yr	NM
❏ PD-1-6141	Survivor	1978	15.00

BACHMAN-TURNER OVERDRIVE

COMPLEAT
Number	Title	Yr	NM
❏ CPL1-1010	Bachman-Turner Overdrive	1984	10.00

MCA/CURB
Number	Title	Yr	NM
❏ 5760	Live! Live! Live!	1986	10.00

MERCURY
Number	Title	Yr	NM
❏ SRM-1-673	Bachman-Turner Overdrive	1973	15.00

— Red label
| ❏ SRM-1-673 | Bachman-Turner Overdrive | 1974 | 12.00 |

— Chicago skyline label
| ❏ SRM-1-696 | Bachman-Turner Overdrive II | 1973 | 15.00 |

— Red label
| ❏ SRM-1-696 | Bachman-Turner Overdrive II | 1974 | 12.00 |

— Chicago skyline label
| ❏ SRM-1-1101 | Best of B.T.O. (So Far) | 1976 | 12.00 |
| ❏ 822786-1 | Best of B.T.O. (So Far) | 1984 | 10.00 |

— Reissue of 1101
❏ SRM-1-1027	Four Wheel Drive	1975	12.00
❏ SRM-1-3700	Freeways	1977	12.00
❏ SRM-1-1067	Head On	1975	12.00
❏ SRM-1-1004 [B]	Not Fragile	1974	15.00
❏ SRM-1-3748	Rock N' Roll Nights	1979	12.00
❏ SRM-1-3713	Street Action	1978	12.00

BACHS, THE

ROTO
Number	Title	Yr	NM
❏ PR-1044	Out of the Bachs	1968	4000.00

— VG value 2000, VG+ value 3000

BACK PORCH MAJORITY, THE

EPIC
Number	Title	Yr	NM
❏ LN24134 [M]	Live from Ledbetter's	1965	18.00
❏ BN26134 [S]	Live from Ledbetter's	1965	25.00
❏ LN24149 [M]	Riverboat Days	1965	18.00
❏ BN26149 [S]	Riverboat Days	1965	25.00
❏ LN24184 [M]	That's the Way It's Gonna Be	1966	18.00
❏ BN26184 [S]	That's the Way It's Gonna Be	1966	25.00
❏ LN24319 [M]	Willy Nilly Wonder of Illusion	1967	25.00
❏ BN26319 [S]	Willy Nilly Wonder of Illusion	1967	18.00

— nyl in plastic sleeve

BACKUS, JIM

RCA VICTOR
Number	Title	Yr	NM
❏ LPM-1362 [M]	Mr. Magoo in Hi-Fi	1957	50.00

BACON FAT

BLUE HORIZON
Number	Title	Yr	NM
❏ BH-4807	Grease One for Me	1970	30.00

BAD AZZ

PRIORITY
Number	Title	Yr	NM
❏ 50741	Word on Tha Streets	1998	15.00

BAD BRAINS

BAD BRAINS
Number	Title	Yr	NM
❏ 003 [EP]	I and I Survive/Destroy Babylon	1983	40.00

CAROLINE
Number	Title	Yr	NM
❏ CAROL-1375 [B]	Quickness	1989	30.00
❏ CAROL-1613	Rock for Light	1990	16.00

— Reissue of PVC 8917 with three bonus tracks
| ❏ CAROL-1617 [B] | The Youth Are Getting Restless | 1990 | 25.00 |

IMPORTANT
Number	Title	Yr	NM
❏ 003 [EP]	I and I Survive/Destroy Babylon	1983	30.00

MAVERICK
Number	Title	Yr	NM
❏ 45882	God of Love	1995	25.00

PVC
Number	Title	Yr	NM
❏ 8917 [B]	Rock for Light	1983	50.00

ROIR
Number	Title	Yr	NM
❏ 8223 [B]	Bad Brains	1997	18.00

— First issued in the early 1980s on cassette only, this is a limited vinyl reissue

SST
Number	Title	Yr	NM
❏ 065	I Against I	199?	12.00

— With back cover bar code
| ❏ 065 [B] | I Against I | 1986 | 40.00 |

— No back cover bar code
| ❏ 160 [B] | Live | 1988 | 30.00 |
| ❏ 228 [10] | Spirit Electricity | 1991 | 12.00 |

VICTORY
Number	Title	Yr	NM
❏ VR64 [10]	The Omega Sessions	1997	18.00

BAD COMPANY

ATCO
Number	Title	Yr	NM
❏ 91371	Holy Water	1990	18.00

ATLANTIC
Number	Title	Yr	NM
❏ 81625	10 from 6 (The Best of Bad Company)	1986	12.00
❏ 81884	Dangerous Age	1988	12.00
❏ 81684	Fame and Fortune	1987	12.00

RHINO
Number	Title	Yr	NM
❏ R18413 [B]	Straight Shooter	2014	25.00

SWAN SONG
Number	Title	Yr	NM
❏ SS8410	Bad Company	1974	12.00
❏ SS8501	Bad Company	1977	10.00
❏ SS8500	Burnin' Sky	1977	12.00
❏ SS8506	Desolation Angels	1979	12.00
❏ 90001	Rough Diamonds	1982	12.00
❏ SS8415	Run with the Pack	1976	12.00
❏ SS8503	Run with the Pack	1977	10.00
❏ SS8413 [B]	Straight Shooter	1975	12.00
❏ SS8502	Straight Shooter	1977	10.00

BAD ENGLISH

EPIC
Number	Title	Yr	NM
❏ OE45083 [B]	Bad English	1989	15.00

BAD MANNERS

MCA
Number	Title	Yr	NM
❏ 5218	Bad Manners	1981	18.00
❏ 5415	Klass	1983	18.00

PORTRAIT
Number	Title	Yr	NM
❏ BFR39413	Forging Ahead	1984	15.00
❏ BFR40070	Mental Notes	1985	15.00

BAD RELIGION

ATLANTIC
Number	Title	Yr	NM
❏ 83094	No Substance	1998	25.00
❏ 82658 [B]	Stranger Than Fiction	1994	30.00

— Issued on red vinyl
| ❏ 82870 | The Gray Race | 1996 | 25.00 |

— Issued on gray vinyl
| ❏ 83303 | The New America | 2000 | 18.00 |

EPITAPH
Number	Title	Yr	NM
❏ 86409 [B]	Against the Grain	1990	30.00
❏ 86443	All Ages	1995	15.00
❏ 86416 [B]	Generator	1992	25.00
❏ E-86416-1 [B]	Generator	2014	30.00
❏ EPI-BRLP-1	How Could Hell Be Any Worse?	1982	100.00

— Original edition with lyric sheet. Some copies have personal notes or autographs scribbled on the inner sleeves by the band members; these can bring significantly more than this.
| ❏ 86407 | How Could Hell Be Any Worse? | 1989 | 30.00 |

— Reissue of Epitaph BRLP-1
❏ EPI-BRLP-2	Into the Unknown	1983	200.00
❏ 86406	No Control	1989	18.00
❏ 86420 [B]	Recipe for Hate	1993	25.00
❏ 86404	Suffer	1988	18.00
❏ 86694	The Empire Strikes First	2004	15.00
❏ 86635	The Process of Belief	2002	18.00

BADFINGER

APPLE
Number	Title	Yr	NM
❏ SW3411	Ass	1973	25.00
❏ ST3364	Magic Christian Music	1970	30.00

— With Capitol logo on Side 2 bottom
| ❏ ST3364 | Magic Christian Music | 1970 | 25.00 |
| ❏ ST-3355 | Maybe Tomorrow | 1969 | 2000.00 |

— As "The Iveys"; album not released in US; price is for an LP slick, which does exist
| ❏ SKAO3367 [B] | No Dice | 1970 | 30.00 |
| ❏ SW3387 | Straight Up | 1971 | 60.00 |

ELEKTRA
Number	Title	Yr	NM
❏ 6E-175	Airwaves	1979	15.00

Number	Title	Yr	NM
RADIO			
❏ RR16030	Say No More	1981	12.00
RYKO ANALOGUE			
❏ RALP10189 [B]	Day After Day	1990	40.00
—Limited edition on clear vinyl with obi			
WARNER BROS.			
❏ BS2762	Badfinger	1974	18.00
❏ BS2827	Wish You Were Here	1974	18.00
BADLANDS			
ATLANTIC			
❏ 81966	Badlands	1989	12.00
CMH			
❏ 6254	Badlands	198?	12.00
BADU, ERYKAH			
MOTOWN			
❏ 012-153287-1	Mama's Gun	2000	18.00
—Comes in generic sleeve with large center hole; red vinyl			
UNIVERSAL/KEDAR			
❏ 53027	Baduizm	1997	12.00
—Comes in generic sleeve with large center hole			
❏ 53109	Live	1997	18.00
—Comes in generic sleeve with large center hole			
BAEZ, JOAN			
A&M			
❏ SP-4339	Come From the Shadows	1972	12.00
❏ QU-54339 [Q]	Come From the Shadows	1974	30.00
❏ SP-3103	Come From the Shadows	198?	10.00
—Budget-line reissue			
❏ SP-4527	Diamonds and Rust	1975	12.00
❏ QU-54527 [Q]	Diamonds and Rust	1975	30.00
❏ SP-3233	Diamonds and Rust	198?	10.00
—Budget-line reissue			
❏ SP-3704	From Every Stage	1976	15.00
❏ SP-6506	From Every Stage	198?	12.00
—Reissue			
❏ SP-3614	Gracias A La Vida	1974	15.00
❏ SP-4603	Gulf Winds	1976	12.00
❏ SP-4068	The Best of Joan C. Baez	1977	12.00
❏ SP-3234	The Best of Joan C. Baez	198?	10.00
—Budget-line reissue			
❏ SP-4390	Where Are You Now, My Son?	1973	12.00
BOOK-OF-THE-MONTH			
❏ 40-5711	Satisfied Mind	1979	30.00
—With booklet			
GOLD CASTLE			
❏ D1-71321	Diamonds and Rust in the Bullring	1989	15.00
❏ D1-71309	Recently	1989	15.00
—Reissue of 171 009			
❏ 171009	Recently	1988	12.00
❏ D1-71324	Speaking of Dreams	1989	15.00
MOBILE FIDELITY			
❏ 1-238	Diamonds and Rust	1996	60.00
—Audiophile vinyl			
NAUTILUS			
❏ NR-12	Diamonds and Rust	1980	40.00
—Audiophile vinyl			
PORTRAIT			
❏ PR34697	Blowin' Away	1977	12.00
❏ JR35766	Honest Lullaby	1979	12.00
SQUIRE			
❏ SQ-33001 [M]	The Best of Joan Baez	1963	25.00
VANGUARD			
❏ VSD-79306/7	Any Day Now	1969	30.00
❏ VSD-79275 [B]	Baptism	1968	25.00
❏ VSD-6570/1	Blessed Are...	1971	18.00
—Add 50 percent if bonus 7-inch single, "Maria Dolores"/"Plane Wreck at Los Gatos (Deportee)," and its special sleeve are still in the package			
❏ VSD6570/1 [B]	Blessed Are...	2014	40.00
❏ VSQ-40001/2 [Q]	Blessed Are	1973	30.00
❏ VSD-79313	Carry It On	1971	30.00
—Soundtrack album			
❏ VSD-79308	David's Album	1969	15.00
❏ VRS-9200 [M]	Farewell, Angelina	1965	18.00
❏ VSD-79200 [S]	Farewell, Angelina	1965	25.00
❏ VSD-79332	Hits/Greatest & Others	1973	12.00
❏ VSQ-40032 [Q]	Hits/Greatest & Others	1973	30.00
❏ VRS-9240 [M]	Joan	1967	18.00
❏ VSD-79240 [S]	Joan	1967	25.00
❏ VRS-9078 [M]	Joan Baez	1960	25.00
❏ VSD-2077 [S]	Joan Baez	1960	30.00
❏ VRS-0004 [M]	Joan Baez, Vol. 2	1961	25.00
❏ VSD-2097 [S]	Joan Baez, Vol. 2	1961	30.00
❏ VRS-9160 [M]	Joan Baez/5	1964	18.00
❏ VSD-79160 [S]	Joan Baez/5	1964	25.00
❏ VRS-9112 [M]	Joan Baez In Concert	1962	25.00
❏ VSD-2122 [S]	Joan Baez In Concert	1962	30.00
❏ VRS-9113 [M]	Joan Baez In Concert, Part 2	1963	25.00

Number	Title	Yr	NM
❏ VSD-2123 [S]	Joan Baez In Concert, Part 2	1963	30.00
❏ VRS-9230 [M]	Noel	1966	18.00
❏ VSD-79230 [S]	Noel	1966	25.00
❏ VSD-79310	One Day at a Time	1970	15.00
❏ VSD-49/50	The Contemporary Ballad Book	1974	15.00
❏ VSD-105/6	The Country Music Album	1979	15.00
❏ VSD-6560/1	The First 10 Years	1970	18.00
❏ VSD-41/42	The Joan Baez Ballad Book	1972	15.00
❏ VMS-73107	The Joan Baez Ballad Book, Vol. 1	1985	12.00
❏ VMS-73115	The Joan Baez Ballad Book, Vol. 2	1985	12.00
❏ VSD-79/80	The Love Song Album	197?	15.00
❏ VMS-73119	The Night They Drove Old Dixie Down	198?	12.00
❏ VSD-79446/7	Very Early Joan	1981	15.00
BAGDASARIAN, ROSS			
LIBERTY			
❏ LRP-3451 [M]	The Crazy, Mixed-Up World of Ross Bagdasarian	1966	40.00
❏ LST-7451 [S]	The Crazy, Mixed-Up World of Ross Bagdasarian	1966	50.00
BAGLEY, DON			
DOT			
❏ DLP-3070 [M]	Basically Bagley	1957	50.00
❏ DLP-25070 [S]	Basically Bagley	1959	40.00
❏ DLP-9007 [M]	The Soft Sell	1959	50.00
❏ DLP-29007 [S]	The Soft Sell	1959	40.00
REGENT			
❏ MG-6061 [M]	Jazz on the Rocks	1957	60.00
SAVOY			
❏ MG-12210 [M]	Jazz on the Rocks	196?	25.00
BAHAMADIA			
CHRYSALIS			
❏ SPRO-10478	Kollage	1996	25.00
—Promo-only full-length vinyl issue			
GOOD VIBE			
❏ 2021	B.B. Queen	2000	18.00
BAILES BROTHERS, THE			
AUDIO LAB			
❏ AL-1511 [M]	Avenues of Prayer	1959	200.00
BAILEY, BENNY			
ARGO			
❏ LP-668 [M]	The Music of Quincy Jones	1961	30.00
❏ LPS-668 [S]	The Music of Quincy Jones	1961	30.00
CANDID			
❏ CD-8011 [M]	Big Brass	1960	30.00
❏ CS-9011 [S]	Big Brass	1960	40.00
GEMINI			
❏ GMLP-69-1	While My Lady Sleeps	1990	15.00
SABA			
❏ 15158 [S]	Soul Eyes	1968	300.00
BAILEY, BUSTER			
FELSTED			
❏ FAJ-7003 [M]	All About Memphis	1959	40.00
❏ SJA-2003 [S]	All About Memphis	1959	40.00
BAILEY, DAVE			
EPIC			
❏ LA16011 [M]	Gettin' Into Something	1960	150.00
❏ BA17011 [S]	Gettin' Into Something	1960	200.00
—yellow label			
❏ LA16008 [M]	One Foot in the Gutter	1960	150.00
❏ BA17008 [S]	One Foot in the Gutter	1960	200.00
❏ BA17008 [S]	One Foot in the Gutter	199?	30.00
—Classic Records reissue			
❏ LA16021 [M]	Two Feet in the Gutter	1961	150.00
❏ BA17021 [S]	Two Feet in the Gutter	1961	40.00
JAZZ LINE			
❏ 33-01 [M]	Bash!	1961	350.00
JAZZTIME			
❏ JT-003 [M]	Reaching Out	1961	350.00
❏ JS-003 [S]	Reaching Out	1961	150.00
—Reissued under GRANT GREEN's name			
BAILEY, MILDRED			
ALLEGRO			
❏ 3119 [M]	Mildred Bailey Sings	1955	60.00
❏ 4009 [10]	Mildred Bailey Songs	1952	80.00
❏ 4040 [10]	Mildred Bailey Songs	1954	80.00
COLUMBIA			
❏ C3L22	Her Greatest Performances	1962	50.00
—With booklet; originals have red labels with "Guaranteed High Fidelity" at bottom			
❏ CL6094 [10]	Serenade	1950	60.00
DECCA			
❏ DL5133 [10]	Mildred Bailey Memorial Album	1950	60.00
❏ DL5387 [10]	The Rockin' Chair Lady	195?	60.00

Number	Title	Yr	NM
EVEREST ARCHIVE OF FOLK & JAZZ			
❏ 269	Mildred Bailey	197?	15.00
HINDSIGHT			
❏ HSR-133	Mildred Bailey 1944	198?	12.00
MONMOUTH-EVERGREEN			
❏ 6814	All of Me	196?	18.00
REGENT			
❏ MG-6032 [M]	Me and the Blues	1957	50.00
ROYALE			
❏ VLP6078 [10]	Mildred Bailey Sings	195?	80.00
SAVOY			
❏ MG-12219 [M]	Me and the Blues	196?	25.00
SAVOY JAZZ			
❏ SJL-1151	The Majestic Mildred Bailey	198?	15.00
SUNBEAM			
❏ 209	Radio Show 1944-45	197?	15.00
BAILEY, PEARL, AND LOUIS BELLSON			
EVEREST ARCHIVE OF FOLK & JAZZ			
❏ FS284 [R]	Pearl Bailey and Louis Bellson	197?	12.00
BAILEY, PEARL			
COLUMBIA			
❏ CL6099 [10]	Pearl Bailey Entertains	1950	50.00
❏ CL985 [M]	The Definitive Pearl Bailey	1957	30.00
CORAL			
❏ CRL57162 [M]	Cultured Pearl	1958	40.00
❏ CRL56078 [10]	I'm with You	1954	50.00
❏ CRL57037 [M]	Pearl Bailey	1957	40.00
❏ CRL56068 [10]	Say Si Si	1953	50.00
MERCURY			
❏ MG-20277 [M]	The Intoxicating Pearl Bailey	1957	40.00
❏ MG-20187 [M]	The One and Only Pearl Bailey Sings	1956	40.00
PROJECT 3			
❏ PR5022SD	The Real Pearl	1968	18.00
RCA VICTOR			
❏ LSP-4529	Pearl's Pearls	1971	18.00
ROULETTE			
❏ R-25195 [M]	All About Good Little Girls and Bad Little Boys	1963	25.00
—Originals have a pink and orange label			
❏ SR-25195 [S]	All About Good Little Girls and Bad Little Boys	1963	30.00
—Originals have a pink and orange label			
❏ R-25222 [M]	C'est La Vie	1963	25.00
—Originals have a pink and orange label			
❏ SR-25222 [S]	C'est La Vie	1963	30.00
—Originals have a pink and orange label			
❏ R-25181 [M]	Come On, Let's Play with Pearlie Mae	1962	25.00
—Originals have a white label with colored spokes			
❏ SR-25181 [S]	Come On, Let's Play with Pearlie Mae	1962	30.00
—Originals have a white label with colored spokes			
❏ R-25300 [M]	For Women Only	1965	18.00
❏ SR-25300 [S]	For Women Only	1965	25.00
❏ R-25167 [M]	Happy Sounds	1962	25.00
—Originals have a white label with colored spokes			
❏ SR-25167 [S]	Happy Sounds	1962	30.00
—Originals have a white label with colored spokes			
❏ R-25101 [M]	More Songs for Adults Only	1960	25.00
—Originals have a white label with colored spokes			
❏ SR-25101 [S]	More Songs for Adults Only	1960	30.00
—Originals have a white label with colored spokes			
❏ R-25125 [M]	Naughty But Nice	1960	25.00
—Originals have a white label with colored spokes			
❏ SR-25125 [S]	Naughty But Nice	1960	30.00
—Originals have a white label with colored spokes			
❏ R-25012 [M]	Pearl Bailey A Broad	1957	30.00
—Black label original			
❏ SR-25012 [R]	Pearl Bailey A Broad	196?	15.00
❏ R-25016 [M]	Pearl Bailey Sings for Adults Only	1959	25.00
—Originals have a white label with colored spokes			
❏ SR-25016 [S]	Pearl Bailey Sings for Adults Only	1959	30.00
—Originals have a white label with colored spokes			
❏ R-25063 [M]	Pearl Bailey Sings Porgy and Bess and Other Gershwin Melodies	1959	25.00
—Originals have a white label with colored spokes			
❏ SR-25063 [S]	Pearl Bailey Sings Porgy and Bess and Other Gershwin Melodies	1959	30.00
—Originals have a white label with colored spokes			
❏ R-25155 [M]	Pearl Bailey Sings Songs of Harold Arlen	1961	25.00
—Originals have a white label with colored spokes			
❏ SR-25155 [S]	Pearl Bailey Sings Songs of Harold Arlen	1961	30.00
—Originals have a white label with colored spokes			
❏ R-25271 [M]	Songs by James Van Heusen	1964	18.00
❏ SR-25271 [S]	Songs by James Van Heusen	1964	25.00
❏ R-25116 [M]	Songs of the Bad Old Days	1960	25.00
—Originals have a white label with colored spokes			

Number	Title	Yr	NM
❑ SR-25116 [S]	Songs of the Bad Old Days	1960	30.00
—Originals have a white label with colored spokes			
❑ SR5004	Songs of the Bad Old Days	1976	15.00
❑ R-25037 [M]	St. Louis Blues	1958	30.00
—Black label original			
❑ SR-25037 [S]	St. Louis Blues	1959	30.00
—Originals have a white label with colored spokes			
❑ R-25144 [M]	The Best of Pearl Bailey	1961	25.00
—Originals have a white label with colored spokes			
❑ SR-25144 [S]	The Best of Pearl Bailey	1961	30.00
—Originals have a white label with colored spokes			
❑ SR-25144 [S]	The Best of Pearl Bailey	1964	18.00
—Orange and yellow "roulette wheel" label			
❑ R-25259 [M]	The Risque World of Pearl Bailey	1964	18.00
❑ SR-25259 [S]	The Risque World of Pearl Bailey	1964	25.00

VOCALION
| ❑ VL3621 [M] | Gems by Pearl Bailey | 1958 | 30.00 |

BAILLARGEON, HELENE

FOLKWAYS
| ❑ FW829 [10] | Christmas Songs of French Canada | 195? | 50.00 |
| ❑ FC7229 | Christmas Songs of French Canada | 195? | 50.00 |

BAIN, BOB

CAPITOL
❑ T1500 [M]	Guitar De Amor	1961	30.00
❑ ST1500 [S]	Guitar De Amor	1961	40.00
❑ T1201 [M]	Latin Love	1959	30.00
❑ ST1201 [S]	Latin Love	1959	40.00
❑ T965 [M]	Rockin', Rollin' and Strollin'	1958	80.00

BAIO, SCOTT

RCA VICTOR
❑ NFL1-8025	Scott Baio	1982	15.00
❑ AYL1-4763	Scott Baio	1983	10.00
—Reissue of 8025			
❑ AFL1-4696	The Boys Are Out Tonight	1983	15.00
❑ AYL1-5111	The Boys Are Out Tonight	1985	10.00
—Reissue of 4696			

BAKER, ANITA

BEVERLY GLEN
| ❑ 10002 | The Songstress | 1983 | 15.00 |

ELEKTRA
❑ 60922	Compositions	1990	12.00
❑ 60827	Giving You the Best That I Got	1988	10.00
❑ 60444	Rapture	1986	10.00

BAKER, BUDDY

VERVE
| ❑ MGV-2006 [M] | Two in Love | 1956 | 50.00 |
| ❑ V-2006 [M] | Two in Love | 1961 | 25.00 |

BAKER, CHET, AND ART PEPPER

PACIFIC JAZZ
❑ PJ-18 [M]	Picture of Health	1961	50.00
❑ PJ-1234 [M]	Playboys	1957	350.00
—Pacific Jazz records come in World Pacific covers			

WORLD PACIFIC
| ❑ WP-1234 [M] | Playboys | 1958 | 80.00 |
| ❑ PJ-1234 [M] | Playboys | 1958 | 120.00 |

BAKER, CHET, AND LEE KONITZ

INDIA NAVIGATION
| ❑ IN-1052 | In Concert | 198? | 15.00 |

BAKER, CHET, AND PAUL BLEY

STEEPLECHASE
| ❑ SCS-1207 | Diane | 198? | 12.00 |

BAKER, CHET, JIM HALL; HUBERT LAWS

CTI
| ❑ 9007 | Studio Trieste | 1983 | 12.00 |

BAKER, CHET

ANALOGUE PRODUCTIONS
| ❑ AAPJ-016 | Chet | 199? | 30.00 |
| —Audiophile reissue | | | |

ARTISTS HOUSE
| ❑ 9411 | Once Upon a Summertime | 1978 | 15.00 |

BAINBRIDGE
| ❑ 1040 | Albert's House | 198? | 12.00 |

BLUEBIRD
| ❑ 2001-1-RB | The Italian Sessions | 1990 | 15.00 |

BLUE NOTE
| ❑ B1-92932 | Let's Get Lost/The Best of Chet Baker | 1989 | 15.00 |

BOPLICITY
| ❑ BOP-13 | Cool Out | 198? | 12.00 |

CADENCE JAZZ
| ❑ CJ-1019 | Improviser | 198? | 12.00 |

COLPIX
| ❑ CP-476 [M] | Chet Baker Sings and Plays | 1964 | 40.00 |
| ❑ SCP-476 [S] | Chet Baker Sings and Plays | 1964 | 50.00 |

COLUMBIA
❑ CL549 [M]	Chet Baker and Strings	1954	80.00
—Maroon label, gold print			
❑ CL549 [M]	Chet Baker and Strings	1955	50.00
—Red and black label with six "eye" logos			

CROWN
| ❑ CLP-5317 [M] | Chet Baker Quintette | 196? | 25.00 |
| ❑ CST-317 [R] | Chet Baker Quintette | 196? | 18.00 |

CTI
| ❑ 6050 | She Was Too Good to Me | 1974 | 15.00 |

ENJA
❑ 4016	Peace	1982	12.00
❑ R1-79600	The Last Great Concert: My Favorite Songs Vol. 1	1989	15.00
❑ R1-79624	The Last Great Concert: My Favorite Songs Vol. 2	1989	15.00

FANTASY
❑ OJC-087	Chet	198?	15.00
—Reissue of Riverside 1135			
❑ OJC-370	Chet Baker in Milan	198?	15.00
—Reissue of Jazzland 18			
❑ OJC-207	Chet Baker in New York	1985	15.00
—Reissue of Riverside 1119			
❑ OJC-137	Chet Baker Plays the Best of Lerner and Loewe	198?	15.00
—Reissue of Riverside 1152			
❑ OJC-492	Chet Baker with Fifty Italian Strings	1991	15.00
—Reissue of Jazzland 921			
❑ OJC-303	It Could Happen to You — Chet Baker Sings	1988	12.00
—Reissue of Riverside 1120			
❑ OJC-405	Once Upon a Summertime	1989	12.00
—Reissue of Galaxy 5150			

GALAXY
| ❑ 5150 | Once Upon a Summertime | 1977 | 18.00 |

HARMONY
| ❑ HL7320 [M] | Love Walked In | 1962 | 25.00 |

HORIZON
| ❑ 726 | You Can't Go Home Again | 1977 | 15.00 |

INNER CITY
| ❑ 1120 | Broken Wing | 198? | 12.00 |

JAZZLAND
❑ JLP-11 [M]	Chet Baker and Orchestra	1960	40.00
❑ JLP-911 [S]	Chet Baker and Orchestra	1960	40.00
❑ JLP-18 [M]	Chet Baker in Milan	1960	40.00
❑ JLP-918 [S]	Chet Baker in Milan	1960	40.00
❑ JLP-21 [M]	Chet Baker with Fifty Italian Strings	1960	40.00
❑ JLP-921 [S]	Chet Baker with Fifty Italian Strings	1960	40.00

LIMELIGHT
❑ LM-82003 [M]	Baby Breeze	1964	30.00
❑ LS-86003 [S]	Baby Breeze	1964	30.00
❑ LM-82019 [M]	Baker's Holiday	1965	30.00
❑ LS-86019 [S]	Baker's Holiday	1965	30.00

MOSAIC
| ❑ MR4-113 | The Complete Pacific Jazz Live Recordings of the Chet Baker Quartet with Russ Freeman | 199? | 80.00 |
| ❑ MR4-122 | The Complete Pacific Jazz Studio Recordings of the Chet Baker Quartet with Russ Freeman | 199? | 120.00 |

PACIFIC JAZZ
❑ PJ-1224 [M]	Chet Baker and Crew	1956	120.00
❑ PJ-1229 [M]	Chet Baker Big Band	1957	120.00
❑ PJLP-9 [10]	Chet Baker Ensemble	1954	200.00
❑ PJ-1218 [M]	Chet Baker in Europe	1956	150.00
❑ PJLP-3 [10]	Chet Baker Quartet	1953	200.00
❑ PJLP-6 [10]	Chet Baker Quartet Featuring Russ Freeman	1953	200.00
❑ PJLP-15 [10]	Chet Baker Sextet	1954	200.00
❑ PJLP-11 [10]	Chet Baker Sings	1954	200.00
❑ PJ-1222 [M]	Chet Baker Sings	1954	400.00
❑ PJ-1202 [M]	Chet Baker Sings and Plays with Bud Shank, Russ Freeman and Strings	1955	120.00
❑ PJ-1203 [M]	Jazz at Ann Arbor	1955	120.00
❑ PJ-1206 [M]	The Trumpet Artistry of Chet Baker	1955	120.00

PAUSA
| ❑ 9011 | The Trumpet Artistry of Chet Baker | 198? | 12.00 |

PRESTIGE
❑ PRLP-7512 [M]	Boppin' with the Chet Baker Quintet	1967	30.00
❑ PRST-7512 [S]	Boppin' with the Chet Baker Quintet	1967	25.00
❑ PRLP-7478 [M]	Comin' On with the Chet Baker Quintet	1967	30.00
❑ PRST-7478 [S]	Comin' On with the Chet Baker Quintet	1967	25.00
❑ PRLP-7496 [M]	Cool Burnin' with the Chet Baker Quintet	1967	30.00
❑ PRST-7496 [S]	Cool Burnin' with the Chet Baker Quintet	1967	25.00
❑ PRLP-7460 [M]	Groovin' with the Chet Baker Quintet	1966	25.00
❑ PRST-7460 [S]	Groovin' with the Chet Baker Quintet	1966	30.00
❑ PRLP-7449 [M]	Smokin' with the Chet Baker Quintet	1966	25.00
❑ PRST-7449 [S]	Smokin' with the Chet Baker Quintet	1966	30.00

RIVERSIDE
❑ RLP 12-299 [M]	Chet	1959	200.00
—blue label			
❑ RLP-1135 [S]	Chet	1959	40.00
❑ RLP 12-281 [M]	Chet Baker in New York	1958	250.00
—blue label			
❑ RLP-1119 [S]	Chet Baker in New York	1959	40.00
❑ 6095	Chet Baker in New York	197?	15.00
—Reissue			
❑ RLP 12-307 [M]	Chet Baker Plays Lerner and Loewe	1959	200.00
—blue label			
❑ RLP-1152 [S]	Chet Baker Plays Lerner and Loewe	1959	40.00
❑ RLP 12-278 [M]	It Could Happen to You — Chet Baker Sings	1958	200.00
❑ RLP-1120 [S]	It Could Happen to You — Chet Baker Sings	1959	40.00

SCEPTER
| ❑ 540 [M] | Angel Eyes | 1966 | 25.00 |
| ❑ S-540 [S] | Angel Eyes | 1966 | 30.00 |

STEEPLECHASE
❑ SCS-1142	Daybreak	1981	15.00
❑ SCS-1131	No Problem	198?	15.00
❑ SCS-1180	Someday My Prince Will Come	198?	12.00
❑ SCS-1122	The Touch of Your Lips	1980	15.00
❑ SCS-1168	This Is Always	198?	12.00

TIMELESS
❑ LPSJP-251	As Time Goes By	1990	15.00
❑ LPSJP-252	Cool Cat: Chet Baker Plays, Chet Baker Sings	1990	15.00
❑ LPSJP-192	Mr. B.	1990	15.00

TRIP
| ❑ 5569 | Chet Baker Sings and Plays Billie Holiday | 197? | 12.00 |

VERVE
| ❑ V6-8798 | Blood, Chet and Tears | 1969 | 18.00 |

WORLD PACIFIC
❑ WP-1224 [M]	Chet Baker and Crew	1958	80.00
—Reissue of Pacific Jazz 1224			
❑ ST-1004 [S]	Chet Baker and Crew	1959	60.00
❑ WP-1229 [M]	Chet Baker Big Band	1958	80.00
—Reissue of Pacific Jazz 1229			
❑ WP-1218 [M]	Chet Baker in Europe	1958	80.00
—Reissue of Pacific Jazz 1218			
❑ WP-1222 [M]	Chet Baker Sings	1958	120.00
—Reissue of Pacific Jazz 1222			
❑ WP-1826 [M]	Chet Baker Sings	1964	30.00
—Reissue of World Pacific 1222			
❑ ST-1826 [R]	Chet Baker Sings	1964	25.00
❑ WP-1202 [M]	Chet Baker Sings and Plays with Bud Shank, Russ Freeman and Strings	1958	80.00
—Reissue of Pacific Jazz 1202			
❑ WP-1852 [M]	Double Shot	1967	25.00
❑ WPS-21852 [S]	Double Shot	1967	30.00
❑ WP-1842 [M]	Hat's Off	1966	25.00
❑ WPS-21842 [S]	Hat's Off	1966	30.00
❑ WP-1859 [M]	In the Mood	1968	25.00
❑ WP-1858 [M]	Into My Life	1967	30.00
❑ WPS-21858 [S]	Into My Life	1967	25.00
❑ WP-1203 [M]	Jazz at Ann Arbor	1958	80.00
—Reissue of Pacific Jazz 1203			
❑ WP-1249 [M]	Pretty/Groovy	1958	100.00
❑ WP-1847 [M]	Quietly, There	1966	25.00
❑ WPS-21847 [S]	Quietly, There	1966	30.00
❑ WP-1206 [M]	The Trumpet Artistry of Chet Baker	1958	80.00
—Reissue of Pacific Jazz 1206			

WORLD PACIFIC JAZZ
| ❑ ST-20138 [R] | Chet Baker Plays and Sings | 1968 | 15.00 |
| —Compilation of 1950s Pacific Jazz material | | | |

BAKER, DAVID, AND HIS 21ST CENTURY BEBOP BAND

LAUREL
❑ LR-503	David Baker and His 21st Century Bebop Band	1984	15.00
❑ LR-504	RSVP	1985	15.00
❑ LR-505	Struttin'	1986	15.00

BAKER, GEORGE, SELECTION

COLOSSUS
| ❑ CS-1002 | Little Green Bag | 1970 | 25.00 |

WARNER BROS.
| ❑ BS2905 | Paloma Blanca | 1975 | 18.00 |

BAKER, GINGER, 'S AIR FORCE

ATCO
| ❑ SD 2-703 | Ginger Baker's Air Force | 1970 | 25.00 |

Number	Title	Yr	NM
❏ SD 33-343	Ginger Baker's Air Force 2	1971	15.00
❏ SD7012	Stratavarious	1972	15.00
AXIOM			
❏ 539864-1	Middle Passage	1990	18.00
CELLULOID			
❏ CEL-6126	Horses and Trees	1986	12.00
POLYDOR			
❏ 3504	Ginger Baker At His Best	1973	18.00
SIRE			
❏ SASD-7532	Eleven Sides of Baker	1977	12.00

BAKER, JOSEPHINE

Number	Title	Yr	NM
COLUMBIA			
❏ FL9533 [10]	Chansons Americaines	1951	100.00
❏ FL9532 [10]	Josephine Baker	1951	100.00
COLUMBIA MASTERWORKS			
❏ ML2609 [10]	Chansons Americaines	1952	80.00
❏ ML2613 [10]	Encores Americaines	1952	80.00
❏ ML2608 [10]	Josephine Baker Sings	1952	80.00
JOLLY ROGER			
❏ 5015 [10]	Josephine Baker	1951	50.00
MERCURY			
❏ MG-25151 [10]	Avec Josephine Baker	1952	80.00
❏ MG-25105 [10]	The Inimitable Josephine Baker	1952	80.00
RCA VICTOR RED SEAL			
❏ LSC-2427 [S]	The Fabulous Josephine Baker	1960	50.00
— Original with "shaded dog" label			
❏ LM-2427 [M]	The Fabulous Josephine Baker	1960	18.00
— Original with "shaded dog" label			

BAKER, LAVERN

Number	Title	Yr	NM
ATCO			
❏ SD 33-372	Her Greatest Recordings	1971	15.00
ATLANTIC			
❏ 8030 [M]	Blues Ballads	1959	200.00
— Black label			
❏ 8030 [M]	Blues Ballads	1960	150.00
— White "bullseye" label			
❏ 8030 [M]	Blues Ballads	1960	30.00
— Red and purple label, "fan" logo in white			
❏ 8030 [M]	Blues Ballads	1963	25.00
— Red and purple label, "fan" logo in black			
❏ 8002 [M]	LaVern	1956	250.00
— Black label			
❏ 8002 [M]	LaVern	1960	30.00
— Red and purple label, "fan" logo in white			
❏ 8002 [M]	LaVern	1963	25.00
— Red and purple label, "fan" logo in black			
❏ 8007 [M]	LaVern Baker	1957	250.00
— Black label			
❏ 8007 [M]	LaVern Baker	1960	30.00
— Red and purple label, "fan" logo in white			
❏ 8007 [M]	LaVern Baker	1963	25.00
— Red and purple label, "fan" logo in black			
❏ 1281 [M]	LaVern Baker Sings Bessie Smith	1958	120.00
— Black label			
❏ 1281 [M]	LaVern Baker Sings Bessie Smith	1960	30.00
— Red and purple label, "fan" logo in white			
❏ 1281 [M]	LaVern Baker Sings Bessie Smith	1963	25.00
— Red and purple label, "fan" logo in black			
❏ SD1281 [S]	LaVern Baker Sings Bessie Smith	1959	150.00
— Green label			
❏ SD1281 [S]	LaVern Baker Sings Bessie Smith	1960	40.00
— Green and blue label, "fan" logo in white			
❏ SD1281 [S]	LaVern Baker Sings Bessie Smith	1963	30.00
— Green and blue label, "fan" logo in black			
❏ 90980	LaVern Baker Sings Bessie Smith	1989	15.00
— Reissue of SD 1281			
❏ 8036 [M]	Precious Memories	1959	200.00
— Black label			
❏ 8036 [M]	Precious Memories	1960	150.00
— White "bullseye" label			
❏ 8036 [M]	Precious Memories	1960	30.00
— Red and purple label, "fan" logo in white			
❏ 8036 [M]	Precious Memories	1963	25.00
— Red and purple label, "fan" logo in black			
❏ SD8036 [S]	Precious Memories	1959	300.00
— Green label			
❏ SD8036 [S]	Precious Memories	1960	200.00
— White "bullseye" label			
❏ SD8036 [S]	Precious Memories	1960	40.00
— Green and blue label, "fan" logo in white			
❏ SD8036 [S]	Precious Memories	1963	30.00
— Green and blue label, "fan" logo in black			
❏ 8050 [M]	Saved	1961	100.00
— Red and purple label, "fan" logo in white			
❏ 8050 [M]	Saved	1963	25.00
— Red and purple label, "fan" logo in black			

Number	Title	Yr	NM
❏ SD8050 [S]	Saved	1961	150.00
— Green and blue label, "fan" logo in white			
❏ SD8050 [S]	Saved	1963	30.00
— Green and blue label, "fan" logo in black			
❏ 8071 [M]	See See Rider	1962	100.00
— Red and purple label, "fan" logo in white			
❏ 8071 [M]	See See Rider	1963	25.00
— Red and purple label, "fan" logo in black			
❏ SD8071 [S]	See See Rider	1962	150.00
— Green and blue label, "fan" logo in white			
❏ SD8071 [S]	See See Rider	1963	30.00
— Green and blue label, "fan" logo in black			
❏ 8078 [M]	The Best of LaVern Baker	1963	150.00
— Red and purple label, "fan" logo in black			
BRUNSWICK			
❏ BL754160	Let Me Belong to You	1970	25.00

BAKER, MICKEY "GUITAR

Number	Title	Yr	NM
ATLANTIC			
❏ 8035 [M]	The Wildest Guitar	1959	150.00
— Black label			
❏ 8035 [M]	The Wildest Guitar	1960	50.00
— Red and purple label, "fan" logo in white			
❏ SD8035 [S]	The Wildest Guitar	1959	250.00
— Green label			
❏ SD8035 [S]	The Wildest Guitar	1960	80.00
— Green and blue label, "fan" logo in white			
KICKING MULE			
❏ 142	The Blues and Jazz Guitar of Mickey Baker	1978	15.00
❏ 140	The Jazz Rock Guitar of Mickey Baker	1978	15.00
KING			
❏ 839 [M]	But Wild	1963	400.00
— Black label, no crown			
❏ 839 [M]	But Wild	196?	80.00
— Blue label with crown			
❏ S-839 [R]	But Wild	196?	40.00

BAKER, RONNIE

Number	Title	Yr	NM
WARNER BROS.			
❏ W1212 [M]	Oh, Johnny!	1958	30.00
❏ WS1212 [S]	Oh, Johnny!	1959	50.00

BAKER, SHORTY, AND DOC CHEATHAM

Number	Title	Yr	NM
SWINGVILLE			
❏ SVLP-2021 [M]	Shorty & Doc	1961	50.00
— Purple label			
❏ SVLP-2021 [M]	Shorty & Doc	1965	30.00
— Blue label with trident logo at right			

BAKER, SHORTY

Number	Title	Yr	NM
KING			
❏ 608 [M]	Broadway Beat	1958	80.00

BAKER GURVITZ ARMY, THE

Number	Title	Yr	NM
ATCO			
❏ SD 36-123	Elysian Encounters	1975	12.00
❏ SD 36-137 [B]	Hearts On Fire	1976	12.00
JANUS			
❏ JXS-7015	The Baker Gurvitz Army	1975	15.00

BALAAM AND THE ANGEL

Number	Title	Yr	NM
VIRGIN			
❏ 90869	Live Free or Die	1988	12.00
❏ 90574	The Greatest Story Ever Told	1986	12.00

BALANCE

Number	Title	Yr	NM
PORTRAIT			
❏ NFR37357	Balance	1981	10.00
❏ ARR38019	In for the Count	1982	10.00

BALDRY, LONG JOHN

Number	Title	Yr	NM
ASCOT			
❏ AM-13022 [M]	Long John's Blues	1965	50.00
❏ AS-16022 [R]	Long John's Blues	1965	40.00
CASABLANCA			
❏ NBLP7012	Good to Be Alive	1975	15.00
❏ NBLP7035	Welcome to the Club	1976	15.00
EMI AMERICA			
❏ SW-17015	Baldry's Out	1979	12.00
❏ SW-17038	Long John Baldry	1980	12.00
UNITED ARTISTS			
❏ UAS-5543 [M]	Long John's Blues	1971	15.00
— Reissue of Ascot 13022			
WARNER BROS.			
❏ BS2614 [B]	Everything Stops for Tea	1973	18.00
❏ WS1921 [B]	It Ain't Easy	1971	18.00

BALDWIN, BOB

Number	Title	Yr	NM
ATLANTIC			
❏ 82098	Rejoice	1990	15.00

Number	Title	Yr	NM
MALACO			
❏ MJ-1501	I've Got a Long Way to Go	1988	12.00

BALES, BURT

Number	Title	Yr	NM
ABC-PARAMOUNT			
❏ ABC-181 [M]	Jazz from the San Francisco Waterfront	1957	40.00
CAVALIER			
❏ 5007 [10]	On the Waterfront	195?	60.00
EUPHONIC			
❏ ESR-1210 [M]	New Orleans Ragtime	196?	30.00
GOOD TIME JAZZ			
❏ L-19 [10]	New Orleans Joys	1954	50.00

BALES & LINGLE

Number	Title	Yr	NM
GOOD TIME JAZZ			
❏ L-12025 [M]	They Tore My Playhouse Down	1955	40.00

BALIN, MARTY

Number	Title	Yr	NM
EMI AMERICA			
❏ SPRO-9673 [DJ]	Balin	1981	25.00
— Red vinyl			
❏ ST-17054	Balin	1981	12.00
❏ ST-17088 [B]	Lucky	1983	12.00

BALL, KENNY

Number	Title	Yr	NM
JAZZOLOGY			
❏ 65	In Concert in the USA, Volume 1	1979	12.00
❏ 66	In Concert in the USA, Volume 2	1979	12.00
KAPP			
❏ KL-1340 [M]	Big Ones	1963	18.00
❏ KS-3340 [S]	Big Ones	1963	25.00
❏ KL-1392 [M]	For the Jet Set	1964	18.00
❏ KS-3392 [S]	For the Jet Set	1964	25.00
❏ KL-1285 [M]	It's Trad	1962	25.00
❏ KS-3285 [S]	It's Trad	1962	25.00
❏ KL-1276 [M]	Midnight in Moscow	1962	25.00
❏ KS-3276 [S]	Midnight in Moscow	1962	25.00
❏ KL-1314 [M]	More	1963	18.00
❏ KS-3314 [S]	More	1963	25.00
❏ KL-1204 [M]	Recorded Live	1962	25.00
❏ KS-3294 [S]	Recorded Live	1962	25.00
❏ KL-1348 [M]	Washington Square and the Best of Kenny Ball	1964	18.00
❏ KS-3348 [S]	Washington Square and the Best of Kenny Ball	1964	25.00

BALL, MARCIA

Number	Title	Yr	NM
CAPITOL			
❏ ST-11752	Circuit Queen	1978	15.00

BALL, ROCKY, AND THE RAZ'MATAZ JAZZ BAND

Number	Title	Yr	NM
BONFIRE			
❏ 502	For Your Listening Pleasure	198?	12.00
❏ 501	Hot Dixieland Jazz	198?	12.00
❏ 503	Salute to Li'l Wally	198?	12.00

BALL, RONNIE

Number	Title	Yr	NM
SAVOY			
❏ MG-12075 [M]	All About Ronnie	1956	40.00

BALLADEERS, THE

Number	Title	Yr	NM
DEL-FI			
❏ DFLP-1204 [M]	Alive-O!	1959	40.00
❏ DFST-1204 [S]	Alive-O!	1959	60.00

BALLARD, FRANK

Number	Title	Yr	NM
PHILLIPS INTERNATIONAL			
❏ 1985 [M]	Rhythm-Blues Party	1962	5000.00
— VG value 2500; VG+ value 3750			

BALLARD, HANK, AND THE MIDNIGHTERS

Number	Title	Yr	NM
KING			
❏ 981 [M]	24 Great Songs	1968	40.00
❏ 950 [M]	24 Hit Tunes	1966	60.00
❏ 896 [M]	A Star in Your Eyes	1964	100.00
❏ 867 [M]	Biggest Hits	1963	100.00
❏ 759 [M]	Dance Along	1961	120.00
❏ 927 [M]	Glad Songs, Sad Songs	1965	70.00
❏ 793 [M]	Jumpin' Hank Ballard	1962	100.00
❏ 748 [M]	Let's Go Again	1961	120.00
❏ 700 [M]	Mr. Rhythm and Blues	1960	150.00
❏ 618 [M]	Singin' and Swingin'	1959	250.00
❏ 740 [M]	Spotlight on Hank Ballard	1961	150.00
❏ KS-740 [S]	Spotlight on Hank Ballard	1961	300.00
❏ 815 [M]	The 1963 Sound of Hank Ballard	1963	100.00
❏ 674 [M]	The One and Only Hank Ballard	1959	250.00
— Brown cover			
❏ 674 [M]	The One and Only Hank Ballard	1960	150.00
— Green cover			
❏ 781 [M]	The Twistin' Fools	1962	100.00

Number	Title	Yr	NM
❏ 913 [M]	Those Lazy, Lazy Days	1965	70.00
❏ KSD-1052	You Can't Keep a Good Man Down	1969	50.00

BALLARD, KAYE

UNITED ARTISTS

Number	Title	Yr	NM
❏ UAL-3165 [M]	Ha-Ha Boo-Hoo	1960	25.00
❏ UAS-6165 [S]	Ha-Ha Boo-Hoo	1960	30.00
❏ UAL-3155 [M]	Kaye Ballard Live?	1960	25.00
❏ UAS-6155 [S]	Kaye Ballard Live?	1960	30.00
❏ UAL-3043 [M]	Kaye Ballard Swings	1959	25.00
❏ UAS-6043 [S]	Kaye Ballard Swings	1959	30.00

BALLARD, RUSS

EMI AMERICA

Number	Title	Yr	NM
❏ ST-17108	Russ Ballard	1984	10.00
❏ ST-17162	The Fire Still Burns	1985	10.00

EPIC

Number	Title	Yr	NM
❏ JE35035	At the Third Stroke	1978	12.00
❏ JE36993	Into the Fire	1981	12.00
❏ JE36186	Russ Ballard & the Barnet Dogs	1980	12.00
❏ KE33252 [B]	Russ Ballard	1974	15.00
❏ PE34093	Winning	1976	12.00

BALLIN' JACK

COLUMBIA

Number	Title	Yr	NM
❏ C30344	Ballin' Jack	1971	12.00
❏ KC31468	Buzzard Luck	1972	12.00

MERCURY

Number	Title	Yr	NM
❏ SRM-1-672	Special Pride	1973	12.00

BALLOU, MONTE, AND HIS NEW CASTLE JAZZ BAND

GHB

Number	Title	Yr	NM
❏ GHB-155	They're Moving Willie's Grave to Dig a Sewer	1986	12.00

BALMER, DAN

CMG

Number	Title	Yr	NM
❏ CML-8013	Becoming Became	1989	15.00

BALTIMORA

MANHATTAN

Number	Title	Yr	NM
❏ ST-53026	Living in the Background	1986	12.00

BALTIMORE AND OHIO MARCHING BAND, THE

JUBILEE

Number	Title	Yr	NM
❏ JGS-8008	Lapland	1968	18.00

BAMA

FREE FLIGHT

Number	Title	Yr	NM
❏ AHL1-3440	Touch Me When We're Dancing	1979	12.00

BAMA BAND

COMPLEAT

Number	Title	Yr	NM
❏ 671013	The Bama Band	1985	10.00

MERCURY

Number	Title	Yr	NM
❏ 834627-1	Solid Ground	1988	10.00

BAMBAATAA, AFRIKA, AND THE SOUL SONIC FORCE

CAPITOL

Number	Title	Yr	NM
❏ C1-90157	The Light	1988	15.00

TOMMY BOY

Number	Title	Yr	NM
❏ TBLP-1008	Beware (The Funk Is Everywhere)	1986	18.00
❏ TBEP-1052 [EP]	Don't Stop...Planet Rock (The Remix EP)	1992	12.00
❏ TBLP-1457	Looking for the Perfect Beat 1980-1985	2001	18.00
❏ TBLP-1007	Planet Rock -- The Album	1986	18.00

BANANA AND THE BUNCH

WARNER BROS.

Number	Title	Yr	NM
❏ BS2626	Mid Mountain Ranch	1972	15.00

BANANA SPLITS, THE

DECCA

Number	Title	Yr	NM
❏ DL75075 [B]	We're the Banana Splits	1969	200.00

BANANARAMA

LONDON

Number	Title	Yr	NM
❏ 820036-1	Bananarama	1984	15.00
— Original edition without "The Wild Life"			
❏ 820165-1	Bananarama	1984	12.00
— Revised edition with "The Wild Life" added			
❏ 810102-1	Deep Sea Skiving	1983	15.00
❏ R100616	The Greatest Hits Collection	1988	15.00
— BMG Direct Marketing edition			
❏ 828158-1	The Greatest Hits Collection	1988	12.00
❏ 828013-1	True Confessions	1986	12.00
❏ R150257	Wow!	1987	15.00
— BMG Direct Marketing edition			
❏ 828061-1	Wow!	1987	12.00

BANCHEE

ATLANTIC

Number	Title	Yr	NM
❏ SD8240	Banchee	1969	50.00
— With insert			

POLYDOR

Number	Title	Yr	NM
❏ 24-4066	Thinkin'	1971	50.00

BAND, THE

CAPITOL

Number	Title	Yr	NM
❏ SKBO-11856	Anthology	1978	18.00
❏ SN-16010	Anthology, Volume 1	1980	10.00
— Budget-line reissue			
❏ SN-16011	Anthology, Volume 2	1980	10.00
— Budget-line reissue			
❏ SMAS-651	Cahoots	1971	18.00
❏ SN-16003 [B]	Cahoots	1980	10.00
— Budget-line reissue			
❏ SO-11602	Islands	1977	15.00
❏ SN-16007	Islands	1980	10.00
— Budget-line reissue			
❏ SW-11214	Moondog Matinee	1973	18.00
— Includes tear-off wraparound cover			
❏ SW-11214	Moondog Matinee	1973	12.00
— Without tear-off wraparound cover			
❏ SN-16004	Moondog Matinee	1980	10.00
— Budget-line reissue			
❏ SKAO2955	Music from Big Pink	1968	30.00
— Black label with colorband			
❏ SKAO2955	Music from Big Pink	1969	18.00
— Lime green label			
❏ SKAO2955	Music from Big Pink	1971	18.00
— Red label, purple "C" logo at top			
❏ ST-11440	Northern Lights-Southern Cross	1975	15.00
❏ SN-16005	Northern Lights-Southern Cross	1980	10.00
— Budget-line reissue			
❏ SABB-11045	Rock of Ages	1972	25.00
❏ SN-16008	Rock of Ages, Volume 1	1980	10.00
— Budget-line reissue			
❏ SN-16009	Rock of Ages, Volume 2	1980	10.00
— Budget-line reissue			
❏ SW-425	Stage Fright	1970	18.00
— Includes tear-off wraparound cover			
❏ SW-425	Stage Fright	1970	12.00
— Without tear-off wraparound cover			
❏ SN-16006	Stage Fright	1980	10.00
— Budget-line reissue			
❏ STAO-132	The Band	1969	18.00
— Lime green label			
❏ SN-16296	The Band	198?	10.00
— Budget-line reissue			
❏ STAO-8-0132	The Band	1969	100.00
— Capitol Record Club edition with black rainbow label; we don't know if any standard versions of this album exist with this label			
❏ ST-11553	The Best of the Band	1976	15.00
❏ SN-16331	The Best of the Band	198?	10.00
— Budget-line reissue			

MOBILE FIDELITY

Number	Title	Yr	NM
❏ 1-039	Music from Big Pink	1981	50.00
— Audiophile vinyl			
❏ MFSL1-346 [B]	Music from Big Pink	2012	40.00
❏ MFSL2-348 [B]	Rock Of Ages: The Band In Concert	2012	60.00
❏ MFSL1-419 [B]	The Band	2013	40.00

RHINO

Number	Title	Yr	NM
❏ R13146 [B]	The Last Waltz	2013	40.00

RHINO HANDMADE

Number	Title	Yr	NM
❏ RHM1-7801	The Last Waltz	2003	60.00
— Box set with remixed version of the album, booklet, facsimiles of tickets, posters and other ephemera, many bonus photos, and a reproduction of the cover signed by Robbie Robertson			

WARNER BROS.

Number	Title	Yr	NM
❏ 3WS3146	The Last Waltz	1978	25.00
❏ PRO-A-737 [DJ]	The Last Waltz Sampler	1978	25.00

BAND OF GOLD

RCA VICTOR

Number	Title	Yr	NM
❏ AFL1-5360	Love Songs Are Back Again	1984	12.00

BANDANA

WARNER BROS.

Number	Title	Yr	NM
❏ 25115	Bandana	1985	10.00

BANDIT

ABC

Number	Title	Yr	NM
❏ ABCD-918	Bandit	1975	15.00

ARIOLA AMERICA

Number	Title	Yr	NM
❏ SW-50042	Partners in Crime	1978	12.00

ARISTA

Number	Title	Yr	NM
❏ AL4113	Bandit	1976	12.00

BANDITS, THE

WORLD PACIFIC

Number	Title	Yr	NM
❏ T-1833 [M]	The Electric 12 String	1964	25.00
❏ ST-1833 [S]	The Electric 12 String	1964	30.00

BANDWAGON, THE

EPIC

Number	Title	Yr	NM
❏ BN26426	Johnny Johnson and the Bandwagon	1969	25.00

BANDY, MOE, AND JOE STAMPLEY

COLUMBIA

Number	Title	Yr	NM
❏ FC38316	Greatest Hits	1983	10.00
❏ FC37003	Hey Joe!/Hey Moe!	1981	10.00
❏ JC36202	Just Good Ol' Boys	1979	12.00
❏ PC36202	Just Good Ol' Boys	198?	10.00
— Budget-line reissue			
❏ FC39955	Live from Bad Bob's, Memphis	1985	10.00
❏ FC39426	The Good Ol' Boys -- Alive and Well	1984	10.00

BANDY, MOE

COLUMBIA

Number	Title	Yr	NM
❏ FC39906	Barroom Roses	1985	10.00
❏ PC34874	Cowboys Ain't Supposed to Cry	1977	15.00
— No bar code on back cover			
❏ FC38726	Devoted to Your Memory	1983	10.00
❏ PC37350	Encore	1981	10.00
❏ JC36789	Following the Feeling	1980	12.00
❏ FC38315	Greatest Hits	1983	10.00
❏ KC34091	Hank Williams, You Wrote My Life	1976	15.00
— No bar code on back cover			
❏ PC34091	Hank Williams, You Wrote My Life	198?	10.00
— With bar code on back cover			
❏ KC34285	Here I Am Drunk Again	1976	15.00
— No bar code on back cover			
❏ PC34443	I'm Sorry for You, My Friend	1977	15.00
— No bar code on back cover			
❏ FC38199	I Still Love You in the Same Ol' Way	1982	10.00
❏ KC35779	It's a Cheating Situation	1979	12.00
❏ PC35779	It's a Cheating Situation	198?	10.00
— Budget-line reissue			
❏ FC40140	Keepin' It Country	1986	10.00
❏ KC35534	Love Is What Life's All About	1978	15.00
❏ PC38652	Moe Bandy Sings the Songs of Hank Williams	1983	10.00
❏ FC39275	Motel Matches	1984	10.00
❏ JC36228	One of a Kind	1980	12.00
❏ FC37568	Rodeo Romeo	1981	10.00
❏ FC38009	She's Not Really Cheatin' (She's Just Gettin' Even)	1982	10.00
❏ KC35288	Soft Lights and Hard Country Music	1978	15.00
❏ PC34715	The Best of Moe Bandy Volume One	1977	15.00
— No bar code on back cover			
❏ PC34715	The Best of Moe Bandy Volume One	198?	10.00
— With bar code on back cover			
❏ JC36487	The Champ	1980	12.00

CURB

Number	Title	Yr	NM
❏ 10609	Many Mansions	1989	12.00
❏ 10600	No Regrets	1988	12.00

GRC

Number	Title	Yr	NM
❏ 10016	Bandy the Rodeo Clown	1975	18.00
❏ 10005	I Just Started Hatin' Cheatin' Songs Today	1974	18.00
❏ 10007	It Was Always So Easy (To Find an Unhappy Woman)	1975	18.00

MCA

Number	Title	Yr	NM
❏ 5914	You Haven't Heard the Last of Me	1987	10.00

BANG, BILLY

CELLULOID

Number	Title	Yr	NM
❏ CELL-5004	Outline #12	198?	15.00

SOUL NOTE

Number	Title	Yr	NM
❏ SN-1036	Invitation	1982	15.00
❏ 121316	Live at Carlos 1	1987	15.00
❏ SN-1016	Rainbow Gladiator	1981	15.00
❏ SN-1086	The Fire from Within	1985	15.00

BANG

CAPITOL

Number	Title	Yr	NM
❏ ST-11015	Bang	1972	30.00
❏ SMAS-11110	Mother/Bow to the Music	1972	30.00
❏ ST-11190	Music	1973	30.00

BANG TANGO

MCA

Number	Title	Yr	NM
❏ 6300 [B]	Psycho Cafe	1989	12.00

WORLD OF HURT

Number	Title	Yr	NM
❏ WEP1000 [EP]	Live Injection	1989	18.00

Number	Title	Yr	NM

BANGLES

COLUMBIA
❑ BFC39220	All Over the Place	1984	15.00
❑ PC39220	All Over the Place	1986	10.00

— *Reissue with new prefix and longer bar code*
❑ BFC40039	Different Light	1986	15.00
❑ FC40039	Different Light	1986	10.00

— *Reissue with new prefix; "02" added to bar code on back cover*
❑ OC44056 [B]	Everything	1988	12.00
❑ CAS2270 [DJ]	Interchords	1986	30.00

— *Promo-only interview album*

FAULTY PRODUCTS
❑ FEP1302 [EP]	Bangles	1982	25.00

I.R.S.
❑ SP-70506 [EP]	Bangles	1983	15.00

— *Reissue of Faulty Products EP*

BANGOR FLYING CIRCUS

ABC DUNHILL
❑ DS-50069	Bangor Flying Circus	1969	18.00

BANJO KINGS, THE

GOOD TIME JAZZ
❑ L-12029 [M]	Nostalgia Revisited	1956	40.00
❑ L-15 [10]	The Banjo Kings	1953	50.00
❑ L-12015 [M]	The Banjo Kings	1955	40.00
❑ L-12015 [M]	The Banjo Kings, Vol. 1	198?	12.00

— *Reissue with revised title and thinner vinyl*
❑ L-25 [10]	The Banjo Kings, Vol. 2	1954	50.00
❑ L-12047 [M]	The Banjo Kings Enjoy the Good Old Days	1958	40.00
❑ S-12047 [S]	The Banjo Kings Enjoy the Good Old Days	1959	30.00
❑ L-12036 [M]	The Banjo Kings Go West	1957	40.00

BANKS, ANT

JIVE
❑ 41496	Sittin' on Something Phat	1993	18.00

— *Vinyl may be promo only*
❑ 41534	The Big Badass	1994	18.00

— *Vinyl may be promo only*

PRIORITY
❑ 50698	Big Thangs	1997	18.00

BANKS, DARRELL

ATCO
❑ 33-216 [M]	Darrell Banks Is Here	1967	30.00
❑ SD 33-216 [S]	Darrell Banks Is Here	1967	30.00

VOLT
❑ VOS-6002	Here to Stay	1969	30.00

BANKS, PATRYCE "CHOC'LET"

T-ELECTRIC
❑ 3243	She's Back and Ready...	1900	10.00

BANKS, PETER

CAPITOL/SOVEREIGN
❑ SMAS-11217	Two Sides of Peter Banks	1973	18.00

BANKS, RON

CBS ASSOCIATED
❑ FZ39148	Truly Bad	1983	12.00

BANKS, ROSE

MOTOWN
❑ M6-845S1	Rose	1976	15.00

BANKS, TONY

ATLANTIC
❑ 82007	Bankstatement	1989	12.00

— *As "Bankstatement*
❑ 81680	Soundtracks	1986	10.00
❑ 80071	The Fugitive	1983	10.00

CHARISMA
❑ CA-1-2207 [B]	A Curious Feeling	1979	15.00

BANKS AND HAMPTON

WARNER BROS.
❑ BS2993	Passport to Ecstasy	1977	12.00

BANNON, R.C.

COLUMBIA
❑ KC35346	R.C. Bannon Arrives	1978	15.00

BANTAMS, THE

WARNER BROS.
❑ W1625 [M]	Beware the Bantams	1966	25.00
❑ WS1625 [S]	Beware the Bantams	1966	30.00

BAR-KAYS, THE

ATCO
❑ SD 33-289	Soul Finger	1968	30.00

MERCURY
❑ 836774-1	Animal	1989	12.00
❑ SRM-1-3844	As One	1980	12.00
❑ 824727-1	Banging the Wall	1985	12.00
❑ 830305-1	Contagious	1987	12.00
❑ 818478-1	Dangerous	1984	12.00
❑ SRM-1-1181	Flying High on Your Love	1977	12.00
❑ SRM-1-3781	Injoy	1979	12.00
❑ SRM-1-3732	Light of Life	1978	12.00
❑ SRM-1-4028	Nightcruising	1981	12.00
❑ SRM-1-4065	Propositions	1982	12.00
❑ SRM-1-1099	Too Hot to Stop	1976	12.00

STAX
❑ MPS-8510	Cold Blooded	1981	12.00
❑ 4130	Gotta Groove	1979	12.00
❑ 4106	Money Talks	1978	12.00
❑ MPS-8542	The Best of the Bar-Kays	1988	12.00

VOLT
❑ 6011	Black Rock	1971	30.00
❑ 9504	Cold Blooded	1974	30.00
❑ VOS-8001	Do You See What I See	1972	30.00
❑ 6004	Gotta Groove	1969	30.00
❑ 417 [M]	Soul Finger	1967	40.00
❑ S-417 [S]	Soul Finger	1967	40.00

BARBARIANS, THE

LAURIE
❑ LLP-2033 [M]	Are You a Boy or Are You a Girl?	1966	100.00
❑ SLP-2033 [S]	Are You a Boy or Are You a Girl?	1966	120.00

RHINO
❑ RNLP 008	The Barbarians	1979	15.00

BARBARIN, PAUL, AND PUNCH MILLER

ATLANTIC
❑ 1410 [M]	Paul Barbarin and Punch Miller	1963	25.00
❑ SD1410 [S]	Paul Barbarin and Punch Miller	1963	30.00

BARBARIN, PAUL

ATLANTIC
❑ 1215 [M]	New Orleans Jazz	1955	50.00

— *Black label*
❑ 1215 [M]	New Orleans Jazz	1961	25.00

— *Multi-color label, white "fan" logo at right*
❑ 1215 [M]	New Orleans Jazz	1963	18.00

— *Multi-color label, black "fan" logo at right*
❑ SD1215 [S]	New Orleans Jazz	1959	50.00

— *Green label*
❑ SD1215 [S]	New Orleans Jazz	1961	25.00

— *Multi-color label, white "fan" logo at right*
❑ SD1215 [S]	New Orleans Jazz	1963	18.00

— *Multi-color label, black "fan" logo at right*

CIRCLE
❑ 408 [10]	Paul Barbarin's New Orleans Band	1951	80.00

CONCERT HALL JAZZ
❑ 1006 [10]	New Orleans Jamboree	1954	50.00

GHB
❑ GHB-140 [M]	Bourbon St. Beat	197?	15.00

— *Reissue of Southland LP*
❑ GHB-2 [M]	Paul Barbarin and His New Orleans Jazz Band	1962	25.00

JAZZTONE
❑ J-1205 [M]	New Orleans Jamboree	1955	40.00

NOBILITY
❑ 708	Last Journey of a Jazzman	196?	25.00

SOUTHLAND
❑ SLP-237 [M]	Bourbon St. Beat	195?	40.00

STORYVILLE
❑ 4049 [M]	Jazz from New Orleans	198?	12.00

BARBARIN, PAUL / JOHNNY ST. CYR

SOUTHLAND
❑ SLP-212 [M]	Paul Barbarin and His Jazz Band/Johnny St. Cyr and His Hot Five	1955	40.00

BARBARIN, PAUL / SHARKEY BONANO

RIVERSIDE
❑ RLP 12-217 [M]	New Orleans Contrasts	1955	60.00

— *White label, blue print*
❑ RLP 12-217 [M]	New Orleans Contrasts	195?	40.00

— *Blue label with microphone logo*

BARBARY, RICHARD

A&M
❑ SP-3010	Soul Machine	1969	25.00

BARBER, AVA

RANWOOD
❑ 8170	Grits	1977	15.00
❑ 8180	You're Gonna Love Love	1978	15.00

BARBER, CHRIS

ATLANTIC
❑ 1292 [M]	Here Is Chris Barber	1959	40.00

COLPIX
❑ CP-404 [M]	Chris Barber Plays "Trad	1959	30.00

GHB
❑ GHB-40 [M]	Collaboration	1967	18.00

LAURIE
❑ LLP-1009 [M]	Chris Barber's "American" Jazz Band	1962	30.00
❑ 1001 [M]	Petite Fleur	1959	40.00
❑ LLP-1003 [M]	Trad Jazz Volume 1	1960	30.00

BARBER, FRANK

VICTORY
❑ 702	Hooked on Big Bands	1982	10.00

BARBER, GLENN

HICKORY
❑ LPS-152	New Star	1970	18.00
❑ LPS-167	The Best of Glenn Barber	1973	18.00

HICKORY/MGM
❑ H3F-4510	Glenn Barber	1974	18.00

BARBER, PATRICIA

PREMONITION
❑ PREM737-1	Café Blue	199?	30.00

— *Audiophile vinyl*
❑ 90747	Companion	1999	30.00

— *Audiophile vinyl*
❑ PREM747-1	Modern Cool	1998	30.00

— *Audiophile vinyl*
❑ 27290	Nightclub	2000	30.00

— *Audiophile vinyl*

BARBIERI, GATO & DOLLAR BRAND

ARISTA FREEDOM
❑ AL1003	Confluence	1975	18.00

BARBIERI, GATO

A&M
❑ SP-4597	Caliente!	1976	12.00
❑ SP-3247	Caliente!	198?	10.00

— *Reissue of 4597*
❑ SP-4774	Euphoria	1979	12.00
❑ SP-3188	Euphoria	198?	10.00

— *Reissue of 4774*
❑ SP-3029	Fire and Passion	1970	30.00
❑ SP-9-3029	Fire and Passion	1984	18.00

— *Audio Master Plus" reissue*
❑ SP-4655	Ruby, Ruby	1977	12.00
❑ SP-4710	Tropico	1978	12.00

ABC IMPULSE!
❑ ASD-9303	Chapter Four -- Alive in New York	1975	25.00
❑ AS-9248	Chapter One -- Latin America	1973	25.00
❑ ASD-9279	Chapter Three -- Viva Emiliano Zapata	1974	25.00
❑ AS-9263	Chapter Two -- Hasta Siempre	1974	25.00

BLUEBIRD
❑ 6995-1-RB	Third World Revisited	1988	15.00

DOCTOR JAZZ
❑ FW40183	Apasionado	1986	12.00
❑ W2X39204	Gato...Para Los Amigos	1985	15.00

ESP-DISK'
❑ 1049	In Search of the Mystery	1968	40.00

FANIA
❑ JM608	Gato = Bahia	1982	15.00

FLYING DUTCHMAN
❑ FD10117	3rd World	1970	25.00
❑ BXL1-2826	3rd World	1978	12.00

— *Reissue of 10117*
❑ AYL1-3815	3rd World	1980	10.00

— *Budget-line reissue*
❑ FD10158	Bolivia	1973	30.00
❑ BXL1-2830	Bolivia	1978	12.00

— *Reissue of 10158*
❑ BDL1-1147	El Gato	1976	15.00
❑ AYL1-3817	El Gato	1980	10.00

— *Budget-line reissue*
❑ FD10151	El Pampero	1973	25.00
❑ BXL1-2828	El Pampero	1978	12.00

— *Reissue of 10151*
❑ FD10144	Fenix	1972	25.00
❑ BXL1-2827	Fenix	1978	12.00

— *Reissue of 10144*
❑ FD10165	The Legend of Gato Barbieri	1974	25.00
❑ FD10156	Under Fire	1973	25.00
❑ BXL1-2829	Under Fire	1978	12.00

— *Reissue of 10156*
❑ BDL1-0550	Yesterdays	1974	15.00
❑ AYL1-3816	Yesterdays	1980	10.00

— *Budget-line reissue*

Number	Title	Yr	NM
MCA			
❑ 29003	Chapter Four -- Alive in New York	1981	12.00
—*Reissue of Impulse 9303*			
❑ 29002	Chapter Two -- Hasta Siempre	1981	10.00
—*Reissue of Impulse 9263*			
QUINTESSENCE			
❑ QJ-25281	Gato Barbieri	1979	12.00
—*Reissue of 1974 recordings*			
UNITED ARTISTS			
❑ UA-LA045-F	Last Tango in Paris	1973	18.00

BARBOSA-LIMA, CARLOS, AND SHARON ISBIN

Number	Title	Yr	NM
CONCORD CONCERTO			
❑ CC-2012	Rhapsody in Blue/West Side Story	1988	12.00
CONCORD PICANTE			
❑ CJP-320	Brazil, With Love	1987	12.00

BARBOSA-LIMA, CARLOS

Number	Title	Yr	NM
CONCORD CONCERTO			
❑ CC-2008	Carlos Barbosa-Lima Plays The Entertainer and Other Works by Scott Joplin	1985	12.00
❑ CC-2005	Carlos Barbosa-Lima Plays the Music of Jobim and Gershwin	1983	12.00
❑ CC-2006	Carlos Barbosa-Lima Plays the Music of Luiz Bonfa and Cole Porter	1984	12.00
❑ CC-2009	Impressions	1991	15.00

BARBOUR, KEITH

Number	Title	Yr	NM
EPIC			
❑ BN26485	Echo Park	1969	25.00

BARCLAY JAMES HARVEST

Number	Title	Yr	NM
HARVEST			
❑ SW-11145 [B]	Baby James Harvest	1973	25.00
MCA			
❑ 2302	Gone to Earth	1977	12.00
❑ 2234 [B]	Octoberon	1976	12.00
POLYDOR			
❑ PD-6508	Everyone Is Everybody Else	1974	15.00
❑ PD-1-6267	Eyes of the Universe	1980	12.00
❑ PD-6517	Time Honoured Ghosts	1975	15.00
❑ PD-1-6173	XII	1978	12.00
SIRE			
❑ SI-4904	Back Again	1971	18.00
❑ SES-97026	Barclay James Harvest	1970	25.00
❑ SI-5904	Other Short Stories	1972	18.00

BARDENS, PETE

Number	Title	Yr	NM
CAPITOL			
❑ ST-12555	Seen One Earth	1987	12.00
❑ C1-48967	Speed of Light	1988	12.00

BARDEUX

Number	Title	Yr	NM
ENIGMA			
❑ D1-73312	Bold As Love	1988	12.00
❑ 7735221	Shangri-La	1989	12.00

BARDOT, BRIGITTE & GAINSBOURG SERGE

Number	Title	Yr	NM
4 MEN WITH BEARDS			
❑ 4M178LP [B]	Bonnie and Clyde		25.00

BARDOT, BRIGITTE

Number	Title	Yr	NM
DOT			
❑ DLP-3120 [M]	La Belle Bardot	1958	100.00
PHILIPS			
❑ PCC204 [M]	Brigitte Bardot Sings	1963	30.00
❑ PCC604 [S]	Brigitte Bardot Sings	1963	40.00

BARE, BOBBY, AND SKEETER DAVIS

Number	Title	Yr	NM
RCA VICTOR			
❑ LPM-3336 [M]	Tunes for Two	1965	25.00
❑ LSP-3336 [S]	Tunes for Two	1965	30.00
❑ LSP-4335	Your Husband, My Wife	1970	18.00

BARE, BOBBY, NORMA JEAN, & LIZ ANDERSON

Number	Title	Yr	NM
RCA VICTOR			
❑ LPM-3764 [M]	The Game of Triangles	1967	30.00
❑ LSP-3764 [S]	The Game of Triangles	1967	25.00

BARE, BOBBY

Number	Title	Yr	NM
COLUMBIA			
❑ FC37719	Ain't Got Nothin' to Lose	1982	12.00
❑ FC37157	As Is	1981	12.00
❑ KC35314	Bare	1977	12.00
❑ FC38311	Biggest Hits	1982	12.00
❑ JC36323	Down & Dirty	1978	12.00
❑ PC36323	Down & Dirty	198?	10.00
—*Budget-line reissue*			
❑ FC38670	Drinkin' from the Bottle, Singin' from the Heart	1983	12.00
❑ JC36785	Drunk & Crazy	1980	12.00
❑ FC37351	Encore	1981	12.00
❑ PC37351	Encore	198?	10.00
—*Budget-line reissue*			
HILLTOP			
❑ 6026	Tender Years	196?	15.00
MERCURY			
❑ SR-61290	This Is Bare Country	1970	25.00
❑ SR-61363	What Am I Gonna Do?	1972	25.00
❑ SR-61316	Where Have All the Seasons Gone	1971	25.00
PICKWICK			
❑ ACL-7003	500 Miles Away from Home	1975	12.00
RCA CAMDEN			
❑ CAS-2290	Folsom Prison Blues	1969	15.00
❑ CAS-2465	I'm a Long Way from Home	1971	15.00
❑ ACL1-0150	Memphis, Tennessee	1973	15.00
RCA VICTOR			
❑ LPM-2835 [M]	500 Miles Away from Home	1964	25.00
❑ LSP-2835 [S]	500 Miles Away from Home	1964	30.00
❑ LPM-3831 [M]	A Bird Named Yesterday	1967	30.00
❑ LSP-3831 [S]	A Bird Named Yesterday	1967	25.00
❑ CPL2-0290	Bobby Bare Sings Lullabys, Legends and Lies	1973	25.00
❑ AHL1-5469	Collector's Series	1985	12.00
❑ LPM-3395 [M]	Constant Sorrow	1965	25.00
❑ LSP-3395 [S]	Constant Sorrow	1965	30.00
❑ APL1-1222	Cowboys and Daddys	1975	15.00
❑ LPM-2776 [M]	Detroit City" and Other Hits	1963	25.00
❑ LSP-2776 [S]	Detroit City" and Other Hits	1963	30.00
❑ AYL1-4118	Greatest Hits	1982	10.00
❑ APL1-0906 [B]	Hard Time Hungrys	1975	15.00
❑ APL1-0040	I Hate Goodbyes/Ride Me Down Easy	1973	18.00
❑ LSP-4177	(Margie's At) The Lincoln Park Inn (And Other Controversial Country Songs)	1969	25.00
❑ APL1-2179	Me and McDill	1977	15.00
❑ LSP-4422	Real Thing	1970	18.00
❑ APL1-0700	Singin' in the Kitchen	1974	18.00
❑ ANL1-0560	Sunday Morning	1974	12.00
❑ LPM-3515 [M]	Talk Me Some Sense	1966	25.00
❑ LSP-3515 [S]	Talk Me Some Sense	1966	30.00
❑ LPM-3479 [M]	The Best of Bobby Bare	1965	25.00
❑ LSP-3479 [S]	The Best of Bobby Bare	1965	30.00
❑ LPM-3994 [M]	The Best of Bobby Bare – Volume 2	1968	40.00
❑ LSP-3994 [S]	The Best of Bobby Bare – Volume 2	1968	25.00
❑ LPM-3896 [M]	The English Country Side	1967	40.00
❑ LSP-3896 [S]	The English Country Side	1967	25.00
❑ LPM-3618 [M]	The Streets of Baltimore	1966	25.00
❑ LSP-3618 [S]	The Streets of Baltimore	1966	30.00
❑ LPM-2955 [M]	The Travelin' Bare	1964	25.00
❑ LSP-2955 [S]	The Travelin' Bare	1964	30.00
❑ APL1-1786	The Winner and Other Losers	1976	15.00
❑ LPM-3688 [M]	This I Believe	1966	25.00
❑ LSP-3688 [S]	This I Believe	1966	30.00
❑ VPS-6090	This Is Bobby Bare	1972	25.00
UNITED ARTISTS			
❑ UA-LA621-G	Bare Country	1977	15.00

BARGE, GENE

Number	Title	Yr	NM
CHECKER			
❑ LP-2994 [M]	Dance with Daddy G	1965	50.00

BARKER, WARREN

Number	Title	Yr	NM
WARNER BROS.			
❑ W1205 [M]	The King and I" for Orchestra	1958	25.00
❑ WS1205 [S]	The King and I" for Orchestra	1958	30.00
❑ W1290 [M]	TV Guide -- Top TV Themes	1959	30.00
❑ WS1290 [S]	TV Guide -- Top TV Themes	1959	40.00
❑ B1308 [M]	William Holden Presents a Musical Touch of Far Away Places	1959	30.00
❑ BS1308 [S]	William Holden Presents a Musical Touch of Far Away Places	1959	40.00

BARLOW, RANDY

Number	Title	Yr	NM
GAZELLE			
❑ 6021	Arrival	1976	18.00
PAID			
❑ 2002	Dimensions	1981	15.00
REPUBLIC			
❑ RLP6023	Fall in Love with Me	1978	15.00
❑ RLP6024	Randy Barlow Featuring Sweet Melinda	1979	15.00

BARNABY BYE

Number	Title	Yr	NM
ATLANTIC			
❑ SD7273	Room to Grow	1973	15.00
❑ SD18104	Touch	1974	15.00

BARNES, CHERYL

Number	Title	Yr	NM
OPTIMISM			
❑ OP-3105	Cheryl	198?	15.00

BARNES, EMIL

Number	Title	Yr	NM
AMERICAN MUSIC			
❑ LP-641 [10]	New Orleans Trad Jazz	1952	50.00
JAZZOLOGY			
❑ JCE-34 [M]	Emil Barnes and His New Orleans Music	197?	15.00
❑ JCE-23 [M]	Too Well Thou Lov'st	1967	15.00

BARNES, GEORGE, AND KARL KRESS

Number	Title	Yr	NM
STASH			
❑ ST-222	Two Guitars	198?	12.00
❑ ST-228	Two Guitars and a Horn	198?	12.00
UNITED ARTISTS			
❑ UAL3335 [M]	Town Hall Concert	1963	30.00
❑ UAS6335 [S]	Town Hall Concert	1963	30.00

BARNES, GEORGE

Number	Title	Yr	NM
DECCA			
❑ DL8658 [M]	Guitars -- By George	1957	40.00
—*Black label, silver print*			
GRAND AWARD			
❑ GA 33-358 [M]	Guitar in Velvet	195?	30.00
MERCURY			
❑ MG-20956 [M]	Guitar Galaxies	1962	30.00
❑ SR-60956 [S]	Guitar Galaxies	1962	30.00
❑ PPS-2011 [M]	Guitar Galaxies	196?	30.00
❑ PPS-6011 [S]	Guitar Galaxies	196?	40.00

BARNES, J.J.

Number	Title	Yr	NM
VOLT			
❑ VOS-6001	Rare Stamps	1969	30.00
—*With Steve Mancha*			

BARNES, JIMMY

Number	Title	Yr	NM
GEFFEN			
❑ GHS24146	Freight Train Heart	1988	10.00
❑ GHS24089	Jimmy Barnes	1986	10.00

BARNES, MAE

Number	Title	Yr	NM
ATLANTIC			
❑ ALS-404 [10]	Fun with Mae Barnes	1953	400.00
VANGUARD			
❑ VRS-9036 [M]	Meet Mae Barnes	1958	50.00

BARNES, SIDNEY

Number	Title	Yr	NM
PARACHUTE			
❑ 9009	Footstomp'n Music	1978	15.00

BARNET, CHARLIE

Number	Title	Yr	NM
AIRCHECK			
❑ 5	Charlie Barnet and His Orchestra 1945	197?	12.00
❑ 30	Charlie Barnet On the Air Vol. 2	198?	12.00
ALAMAC			
❑ QSR2446	Charlie Barnet & His Orchestra 1949	198?	12.00
AVA			
❑ A-10 [M]	Charlie Barnet !?!?!?!?!?!?!	1962	30.00
❑ AS-10 [S]	Charlie Barnet !?!?!?!?!?!?!	1962	30.00
BLUEBIRD			
❑ AXM2-5526	The Complete Charlie Barnet Vol. 1, 1935-37	197?	18.00
❑ AXM2-5577	The Complete Charlie Barnet Vol. 2, 1939	197?	18.00
❑ AXM2-5581	The Complete Charlie Barnet Vol. 3, 1939-40	197?	18.00
❑ AXM2-5585	The Complete Charlie Barnet Vol. 4, 1940	197?	18.00
❑ AXM2-5587	The Complete Charlie Barnet Vol. 5, 1940-41	197?	18.00
❑ AXM2-5590	The Complete Charlie Barnet Vol. 6, 1940-41	197?	18.00
BRIGHT ORANGE			
❑ XBO-706 [S]	The Stereophonic Sound of the Charlie Barnet Orchestra	196?	18.00
CAPITOL			
❑ H235 [10]	Big Bands	195?	60.00
❑ T624 [M]	Classics in Jazz	1955	50.00
❑ T1403 [M]	Jazz Oasis	1960	25.00
❑ ST1403 [S]	Jazz Oasis	1960	30.00
❑ H325 [10]	The Modern Idiom	1952	60.00
CHOREO			
❑ A-10 [M]	Charlie Barnet !?!?!?!?!?!?!	196?	25.00
❑ AS-10 [S]	Charlie Barnet !?!?!?!?!?!?!	196?	25.00
—*Some copies have Choreo logo on front cover, but Ava labels and back cover*			
CIRCLE			
❑ CLP-65	Charlie Barnet and His Orchestra 1941	198?	12.00
CLEF			
❑ MGC-164 [10]	Charlie Barnet Dance Session, Vol. 1	1954	100.00
❑ MGC-165 [10]	Charlie Barnet Dance Session, Vol. 2	1954	100.00

Number	Title	Yr	NM
❏ MGC-114 [10]	Charlie Barnet Plays Charlie Barnet	1953	100.00
❏ MGC-139 [10]	Dance with Charlie Barnet	1953	100.00
❏ MGC-638 [M]	One Night Stand	1955	80.00

COLUMBIA

❏ CL639 [M]	Town Hall Jazz Concert	1955	50.00
—Maroon label, gold print			
❏ CL639 [M]	Town Hall Jazz Concert	195?	40.00
—Black and red label with six "eye" logos			

CREATIVE WORLD

❏ ST1056	Charlie Barnet Big Band 1967	197?	15.00
—Reissue of Vault LPS-9004			

CROWN

❏ CLP-5114 [M]	A Tribute to Harry James	195?	25.00
❏ CLP-5127 [M]	Charlie Barnet Presents a Salute to Harry James	195?	25.00
❏ CLP-5134 [M]	On Stage with Charlie Barnet	1959	25.00

DECCA

❏ DL8098 [M]	Hop on the Skyliner	195?	50.00

EVEREST

❏ LPBR-5008 [M]	Cherokee	1958	30.00
❏ SDBR-1008 [S]	Cherokee	1959	25.00
❏ LPBR-5059 [M]	More Charlie Barnet	196?	25.00
❏ SDBR-5059 [S]	More Charlie Barnet	196?	30.00

HEP

❏ 2005	Live at Basin Street East	198?	12.00

MCA

❏ 2-4069	The Best of Charlie Barnet	1975	15.00
—Black rainbow labels			
❏ 2-4069	The Best of Charlie Barnet	1980	12.00
—Blue rainbow labels			

MERCURY

❏ MGC-114 [10]	Charlie Barnet Plays Charlie Barnet	1952	150.00

RCA VICTOR

❏ LPV-551 [M]	Charlie Barnet (Volume 1)	1968	25.00
❏ LPV-567 [M]	Charlie Barnet (Volume 2)	1969	25.00
❏ LPM-1091 [M]	Redskin Romp	1955	50.00
❏ LPT-3062 [10]	Rockin' in Rhythm	195?	80.00
❏ LPM-2081 [M]	The Great Dance Bands	1960	25.00

SUNSET

❏ SUS-5150	Cherokee	1967	15.00

SWING

❏ 103 [M]	Charlie Barnet and His Orchestra	195?	40.00

TIME-LIFE

❏ STBB 07	Big Bands: Charlie Barnet	1983	18.00

VAULT

❏ LP-9004 [M]	Charlie Barnet Big Band 1967	1967	25.00
❏ LPS-9004 [S]	Charlie Barnet Big Band 1967	1967	18.00

VERVE

❏ MGV-2007 [M]	Dance Bash	1956	50.00
❏ V-2007 [M]	Dance Bash	1961	25.00
❏ MGV-2027 [M]	Dancing Party	1956	50.00
❏ V-2027 [M]	Dancing Party	1961	25.00
❏ MGV-2031 [M]	For Dancing Lovers	1956	50.00
❏ V-2031 [M]	For Dancing Lovers	1961	25.00
❏ MGV-2040 [M]	Lonely Street	1957	50.00
❏ V-2040 [M]	Lonely Street	1961	25.00

BARNETT, BOBBY

SIMS

❏ LP-198 [M]	Bobby Barnett at the World Famous Crystal Palace, Tombstone, Arizona	1964	30.00

BARNUM, H.B.

CAPITOL

❏ T2289 [M]	Big Hits of Detroit	1965	18.00
❏ ST2289 [S]	Big Hits of Detroit	1965	25.00
❏ T2278 [M]	Golden Boy	1965	18.00
❏ ST2278 [S]	Golden Boy	1965	25.00
❏ T2583 [M]	Pop and Ice Cream Sodas	1966	18.00
❏ ST2583 [S]	Pop and Ice Cream Sodas	1966	25.00

BAROQUE ENSEMBLE OF THE MERSEYSIDE KAMMERMUSIKGESELLSCHAFT, THE

ELEKTRA

❏ EKL-306 [M]	The Baroque Beatles Book	1966	30.00
❏ EKS-7306 [S]	The Baroque Beatles Book	1966	30.00

BAROQUES, THE

CHESS

❏ LP-1516 [M]	The Baroques	1967	80.00
❏ LPS-1516 [S]	The Baroques	1967	100.00

BARR, WALT

MUSE

❏ 5238	Artful Dancer	1980	18.00
❏ 5210	East Winds	1979	18.00
❏ 5172	First Visit	1978	18.00

BARRABAS

ATCO

Number	Title	Yr	NM
❏ SD 36-110	Barrabas	1974	12.00
❏ SD 36-118	Heart of the City	1975	12.00
❏ SD 36-136	Watch Out	1976	12.00

RCA VICTOR

❏ LSP-4861	Wild Safari	1973	15.00

BARRACUDAS, THE

JUSTICE

❏ JLP-143	A Plane View	1968	250.00

BARRETT, DAN

CONCORD JAZZ

❏ CJ-331	Strictly Instrumental	1988	12.00

BARRETT, EMMA

GHB

❏ 142 [M]	Emma Barrett at Disneyland	1969	15.00
—Reissue of Southland 242			
❏ 141 [M]	Sweet Emma Barrett and Her New Orleans Music	1969	15.00
—Reissue of Southland 241			

NOBILITY

❏ 711 [M]	The Bell Gal and Her New Orleans Jazz	196?	25.00

RIVERSIDE

❏ RLP-364 [M]	Sweet Emma	1960	40.00
❏ RS-9364 [R]	Sweet Emma	196?	25.00

SOUTHLAND

❏ 242 [M]	Emma Barrett at Disneyland	1967	25.00
❏ 241 [M]	Sweet Emma Barrett and Her New Orleans Music	1964	25.00

BARRETT, RONA

MISS RONA

❏ MRR1001	Miss Rona Sings Hollywood's Greatest Hits	1974	40.00

BARRETT, SUSAN

CAPITOL

❏ T1266 [M]	Mixed Emotions	1959	50.00

RCA VICTOR

❏ LPM-3738 [M]	Susan Barrett	1967	40.00
❏ LSP-3738 [S]	Susan Barrett	1967	30.00

BARRETT, SYD

CAPITOL

❏ C1-91206 [B]	Opel	1989	25.00

HARVEST

❏ RP1543314 [B]	Barrett	2014	30.00
❏ RP1543315 [B]	The Madcap Laughs	2014	30.00
❏ SABB-11314	The Madcap Laughs/Barrett	1974	30.00

BARRETTO, RAY

ATLANTIC

❏ SD19198	Can You	1978	15.00
❏ SD19140	Eye of the Beholder	1977	15.00
❏ SD 2-509	Tomorrow: Ray Barretto Live	197?	18.00

CTI

❏ 9002	La Cuna	198?	12.00

FANIA

❏ SLP-346 [B]	Acid	196?	25.00
❏ SLP-388	Barretto Head Sounds	197?	25.00
❏ SLP-410	From the Beginning	197?	25.00
❏ SLP-362	Hard Hands	1970	25.00
❏ SLP-391	Power	197?	25.00
❏ SLP-403	The Message	197?	25.00
❏ SLP-378	Together	197?	25.00

FANTASY

❏ 24713	Carnaval	197?	18.00

TICO

❏ LP-1087 [M]	Charanga Moderna	1962	25.00
❏ SLP-1087 [S]	Charanga Moderna	1962	30.00
❏ LP-1114 [M]	Guajira y Guaguanco	1964	25.00
❏ SLP-1114 [S]	Guajira y Guaguanco	1964	30.00
❏ LP-1102 [M]	La Moderna De Siempre	1963	25.00
❏ SLP-1102 [S]	La Moderna De Siempre	1963	30.00
❏ CLP-1314	Lo Mejor De Ray Barretto	1973	18.00
❏ SLP-1205	Something to Remember	1969	18.00
❏ LP-1099 [M]	The Hit Latin Style of Ray Barretto	1963	25.00
❏ SLP-1099 [S]	The Hit Latin Style of Ray Barretto	1963	30.00

BARRON, BILL

AUDIO FIDELITY

❏ AFLP-2123 [M]	Now Hear This!	1964	25.00
❏ AFSD-6123 [S]	Now Hear This!	1964	30.00

DAUNTLESS

❏ DM-4312 [M]	West Side Story Bossa Nova	1963	30.00
❏ DS-6312 [S]	West Side Story Bossa Nova	1963	30.00

MUSE

❏ 5235	Jazz Caper	1978	15.00
❏ 5306	Variations in Blue	1983	15.00

SAVOY

Number	Title	Yr	NM
❏ MG-12183 [M]	Hot Line	1965	30.00
❏ MG-12163 [M]	Modern Windows	1962	40.00
❏ MG-12303	Motivation	197?	18.00
❏ MG-12160 [M]	The Tenor Stylings of Bill Barron	1961	40.00

SAVOY JAZZ

❏ SJL-1184	Nebulae	1987	12.00
❏ SJL-1160	The Hot Line	1986	12.00

BARRON, KENNY, AND TED DUNBAR

MUSE

❏ MR-5140	In Tandem	1975	15.00

BARRON, KENNY

BLACK HAWK

❏ 50601	1 + 1 + 1	1986	15.00

CRISS CROSS

❏ 3008	Green Chimneys	1984	15.00

EASTWIND

❏ 709	Spiral	1982	15.00

LIMETREE

❏ 20	Landscape	1984	15.00

MUSE

❏ MR-5220	Golden Lotus	1980	15.00
❏ MR-5080	Lucifer	1975	15.00
❏ MR-5044	Peruvian Blue	1974	15.00
❏ MR-5014	Sunset to Dawn	1973	15.00

WHY NOT

❏ 25032	Imo Live	1982	15.00

WOLF

❏ 1203	Innocence	1978	18.00

XANADU

❏ 188	Kenny Barron at the Piano	1981	15.00

BARROW, KEITH

CAPITOL

❏ ST-12112	Just As I Am	1980	15.00

COLUMBIA

❏ PC34585	Keith Barrow	1976	15.00
❏ JC35597	Physical Attraction	1978	15.00

BARRY, CLAUDJA

CHRYSALIS

❏ CHR1232	Boogie Woogie Dancin' Shoes	1979	15.00
❏ CHR1251	Feel the Fire	1980	15.00

EPIC

❏ FE40622	I, Claudja	1987	12.00

PERSONAL

❏ 59801 [EP]	No La De Da Part 2	1983	15.00

SALSOUL

❏ SA5525	Claudja	1977	15.00
❏ SA5512	Sweet Dynamite	1977	15.00

BARRY, GENE

RCA VICTOR

❏ LPM-2975 [M]	The Star of "Burke's Law" Sings of Love and Things	1964	30.00
❏ LSP-2975 [S]	The Star of "Burke's Law" Sings of Love and Things	1964	30.00

BARRY, JEFF

A&M

❏ SP-4393 [B]	Walkin' in the Sun	1973	30.00

BARRY, JOHN

BULLDOG

❏ BDL-1036 [B]	Bond by Barry	198?	12.00

COLUMBIA

❏ CL2493 [M]	Great Movie Sounds of John Barry	1966	18.00
❏ CS9293 [S]	Great Movie Sounds of John Barry	1966	25.00
❏ C1003	Ready When You Are, Mr. J.B.	1970	12.00
❏ CL2708 [M]	You Only Live Twice	1967	18.00
❏ CS9508 [S]	You Only Live Twice	1967	25.00

UNITED ARTISTS

❏ UAL3424 [M]	Goldfinger and Other Favorites	1965	15.00
❏ UAS6424 [S]	Goldfinger and Other Favorites	1965	18.00

BARRY, LEN

BUDDAH

❏ BDS-5105	Ups & Downs	1972	18.00

DECCA

❏ DL4720 [M]	1-2-3	1965	30.00
❏ DL74720 [P]	1-2-3	1965	40.00
—"Lip Sync" is rechanneled			

RCA VICTOR

❏ LPM-3823 [M]	My Kind of Soul	1967	30.00
❏ LSP-3823 [S]	My Kind of Soul	1967	25.00

Number	Title	Yr	NM

BARRY AND THE TAMERLANES

VALIANT

| ❏ LP-406 [M] | I Wonder What She's Doing Tonight | 1963 | 150.00 |
| ❏ LPS-406 [S] | I Wonder What She's Doing Tonight | 1963 | 300.00 |

BARRY SISTERS, THE

ABC

❏ ABCS-597 [S]	A Time to Remember	1967	15.00
❏ ABC-597 [M]	A Time to Remember	1967	18.00
❏ ABCS-578 [S]	Something Spanish	1966	18.00
❏ ABC-578 [M]	Something Spanish	1966	15.00

ABC-PARAMOUNT

| ❏ ABCS-516 [S] | The Barry Sisters Sing Fiddler on the Roof | 1965 | 18.00 |
| ❏ ABC-516 [M] | The Barry Sisters Sing Fiddler on the Roof | 1965 | 15.00 |

CADENCE

❏ CLP-4001 [M]	The Barry Sisters Sing All Time Yiddish Favorites	1958	18.00
— Reissue of 1017			
❏ CLP-1017 [M]	The Barry Sisters Sing All Time Yiddish Favorites	1957	25.00

ROULETTE

❏ SR-25060 [S]	At Home with the Barry Sisters	1959	25.00
❏ R-25060 [M]	At Home with the Barry Sisters	1959	18.00
❏ R-25157 [M]	Shalom	1962	18.00
❏ SR-25157 [S]	Shalom	1962	25.00
❏ SR-25136 [S]	Side by Side	1960	25.00
❏ R-25136 [M]	Side by Side	1960	18.00
❏ SR-25198 [S]	The Barry Sisters in Israel	1963	25.00
❏ R-25198 [M]	The Barry Sisters in Israel	1963	18.00
❏ R-25258 [M]	The World of the Barry Sisters	1964	15.00
❏ SR-25258 [S]	The World of the Barry Sisters	1964	18.00
❏ SR-25156 [S]	We Belong Together	1961	25.00
❏ R-25156 [M]	We Belong Together	1961	18.00

BARRYMORE, LIONEL, AS EBENEZER SCROOGE

MGM

| ❏ CH112 [10] | A Christmas Carol | 1952 | 40.00 |

BARTEL, JON, THING

CAPITOL

| ❏ ST-274 | The Jon Bartel Thing | 1969 | 30.00 |

BARTHOLOMEW, DAVE

BROADMOOR

| ❏ BR-1201 | Dave Bartholomew's New Orleans Jazz Band | 1981 | 18.00 |

IMPERIAL

❏ LP-9162 [M]	Fats Domino Presents Dave Bartholomew	1961	150.00
❏ LP-12076 [S]	Fats Domino Presents Dave Bartholomew	1961	200.00
❏ LP-9217 [M]	New Orleans House Party	1963	150.00
❏ LP-12217 [S]	New Orleans House Party	1963	200.00

BARTLEY, CHARLENE

RCA VICTOR

| ❏ LPM-1478 [M] | Weekend of a Private Secretary | 1957 | 50.00 |

BARTLEY, CHRIS

VANDO

| ❏ VAS-60000 [S] | The Sweetest Thing This Side of Heaven | 1967 | 40.00 |
| ❏ VA-60000 [M] | The Sweetest Thing This Side of Heaven | 1967 | 50.00 |

BARTON, LOU ANN

ANTONE'S

| ❏ ANT 0009 | Read My Lips | 1989 | 12.00 |

ASYLUM

| ❏ 60032 | Old Enough | 1982 | 18.00 |

SPINDLETOP

| ❏ 107 | Forbidden Tones | 1986 | 15.00 |

BARTZ, GARY

ARISTA

| ❏ AL4263 | Bartz | 1979 | 15.00 |

CAPITOL

| ❏ SW-11789 | Love Affair | 1978 | 15.00 |
| ❏ ST-11647 | My Sanctuary | 1977 | 15.00 |

CATALYST

| ❏ 7610 | Ju Ju Man | 1976 | 15.00 |

MILESTONE

❏ 9018	Another Earth	1969	25.00
❏ 9031	Harlem Bush Music -- Taifa	1971	25.00
❏ 9032	Harlem Bush Music -- Uhuru	1972	25.00
❏ 9027	Home!	1970	25.00
❏ 9006	Libra	1968	25.00

PRESTIGE

| ❏ 10068 | Follow the Medicine Man | 197? | 18.00 |
| ❏ 66001 | I've Known Rivers | 197? | 25.00 |

❏ 10057	Juju St. Songs	197?	18.00
❏ 10083	Singerella -- A Ghetto Fairy Tale	197?	18.00
❏ 10092	The Shadow 'Do	1975	18.00

VEE JAY

| ❏ VJS-3068 | Love Song | 1977 | 15.00 |

BAS NOIR

ATLANTIC

| ❏ 4503 [DJ] | Bas Noir | 1992 | 18.00 |
| *— Vinyl is promo only* | | | |

BASE, ROB, AND D.J. E-Z ROCK

PROFILE

| ❏ PRO-1267 | It Takes Two | 1988 | 15.00 |
| ❏ PRO-1285 | The Incredible Base | 1989 | 15.00 |

BASEMENT JAXX

ASTRALWERKS

| ❏ 6270 | Remedy | 1999 | 18.00 |

BASIA

EPIC

❏ EAS2821 [EP]	Basia	1988	18.00
— Promo-only four-song sampler			
❏ E45472	London Warsaw New York	1990	12.00
❏ FE40767	Time and Tide	1988	10.00

BASIE, COUNT, AND BILLY ECKSTINE

ROULETTE

❏ R52029 [M]	Basie/Eckstine, Incorporated	1959	30.00
❏ SR52029 [S]	Basie/Eckstine, Incorporated	1959	40.00
❏ SR42017	Count Basie and Billy Eckstine	1968	18.00
— Reissue			

BASIE, COUNT, AND DIZZY GILLESPIE

PABLO

| ❏ 2310833 | The Gifted Ones | 1979 | 12.00 |

VERVE

| ❏ V-8560 [M] | The Count Basie Band and the Dizzy Gillespie Band at Newport | 1963 | 25.00 |
| ❏ V6-8560 [S] | The Count Basie Band and the Dizzy Gillespie Band at Newport | 1963 | 30.00 |

BASIE, COUNT, AND DUKE ELLINGTON

ACCORD

| ❏ SN-7200 | Heads of State | 1982 | 12.00 |

BASIE, COUNT, AND JOE WILLIAMS

CLEF

| ❏ MGC-678 [M] | Count Basie Swings/Joe Williams Sings | 1955 | 50.00 |

ROULETTE

❏ R52093 [M]	Back to Basie and Blues	1963	30.00
❏ SR52093 [S]	Back to Basie and Blues	1963	30.00
❏ R52033 [M]	Everyday I Have the Blues	1959	30.00
❏ SR52033 [S]	Everyday I Have the Blues	1959	40.00
❏ R52054 [M]	Just the Blues	1960	30.00
❏ SR52054 [S]	Just the Blues	1960	40.00
❏ R52021 [M]	Memories Ad Lib	1959	30.00
❏ SR52021 [S]	Memories Ad Lib	1959	40.00

VANGUARD

| ❏ VRS-8508 [M] | A Night at Count Basie's | 1955 | 50.00 |

VERVE

❏ MGV-8063 [M]	Count Basie Swings/Joe Williams Sings	1957	40.00
— Reissue of Clef 678			
❏ V-8488 [M]	Count Basie Swings/Joe Williams Sings	1962	30.00
— Reissue of 8063			
❏ V6-8488 [R]	Count Basie Swings/Joe Williams Sings	1962	15.00
❏ UMV-2650	The Greatest	1981	12.00
❏ MGV-2016 [M]	The Greatest! Count Basie Swings/Joe Williams Sings Standards	1956	50.00
❏ MGVS-6006 [S]	The Greatest! Count Basie Swings/Joe Williams Sings Standards	1960	40.00

BASIE, COUNT, AND MAYNARD FERGUSON

ROULETTE

| ❏ R52117 [M] | Big Band Scene '65 | 1965 | 25.00 |
| ❏ SR52117 [S] | Big Band Scene '65 | 1965 | 30.00 |

BASIE, COUNT, AND OSCAR PETERSON

PABLO

❏ 2310843	Night Rider	1979	12.00
❏ 2310722	Satch" and "Josh	1975	15.00
❏ 2310802	Satch and Josh Again	1978	12.00
❏ 2310896	The Timekeepers	198?	15.00
❏ 2310923	Yessir, That's My Baby	1987	12.00

BASIE, COUNT, AND SAMMY DAVIS, JR.

VERVE

| ❏ V-8605 [M] | Our Shining Hour | 1965 | 18.00 |

| ❏ V6-8605 [S] | Our Shining Hour | 1965 | 25.00 |

BASIE, COUNT, AND THE MILLS BROTHERS

DOT

| ❏ DLP-25838 | The Board of Directors | 1968 | 18.00 |

BASIE, COUNT; JOE WILLIAMS; LAMBERT, HENDRICKS AND ROSS

ROULETTE

| ❏ R52018 [M] | Sing Along with Basie | 1959 | 25.00 |
| ❏ SR52018 [S] | Sing Along with Basie | 1959 | 30.00 |

BASIE, COUNT

ABC

| ❏ 4001 | 16 Great Performances | 1974 | 15.00 |
| ❏ AC-30004 | The ABC Collection | 1976 | 15.00 |

ABC IMPULSE!

| ❏ AS-15 [S] | Count Basie and the Kansas City Seven | 1968 | 15.00 |
| ❏ IA-9351 | Retrospective Sessions | 1978 | 15.00 |

ABC-PARAMOUNT

| ❏ ABC-570 [M] | Basie's Swingin' -- Voices Singin' | 1966 | 25.00 |
| ❏ ABCS-570 [S] | Basie's Swingin' -- Voices Singin' | 1966 | 30.00 |

ACCORD

| ❏ SN-7183 | Command Performance | 1981 | 12.00 |

ALAMAC

| ❏ QSR-2412 | Count Basie and His Orchestra 1937 | 198? | 12.00 |

AMERICAN RECORDING SOCIETY

❏ G-422 [M]	Basie's Best	1957	40.00
❏ G-401 [M]	Count Basie	1956	40.00
❏ G-435 [M]	Mainstream Jazz Swing	1957	40.00
❏ G-402 [M]	The Band That Swings the Blues	1956	40.00

BASF

| ❏ 25111 | Basic Basie | 1973 | 18.00 |

BOOK-OF-THE-MONTH CLUB

| ❏ 91-6545 | The Early Years | 1982 | 30.00 |
| *— Alternate number: P3-16389* | | | |

BRIGHT ORANGE

| ❏ XBO-702 | Count Basie Featuring B.B. King | 196? | 25.00 |

BRUNSWICK

❏ BL58019 [10]	Basie's Best	195?	100.00
❏ BL754127	Basie's in the Bag	196?	18.00
❏ BL54012 [M]	Count Basie	1957	40.00

BULLDOG

| ❏ BDL-2020 | 20 Golden Pieces of Count Basie | 1980 | 15.00 |

CLEF

❏ MGC-666 [M]	Basie	1955	100.00
❏ MGC-633 [M]	Basie Jazz	1954	100.00
❏ MGC-729 [M]	Basie Rides Again!	1956	60.00
❏ MGC-723 [M]	Basie Roars Again	1956	60.00
❏ MCG-120 [10]	Count Basie and His Orchestra Collates	1953	250.00
❏ MGC-148 [10]	Count Basie Big Band	1954	250.00
❏ MGC-626 [M]	Count Basie Dance Session #1	1954	100.00
❏ MGC-647 [M]	Count Basie Jazz Session #2	1955	100.00
❏ MCG-146 [10]	Count Basie Sextet	1954	250.00
❏ MGC-722 [M]	The Band of Distinction	1956	60.00
❏ MGC-685 [M]	The Count	1956	80.00
❏ MGC-724 [M]	The King of Swing	1956	60.00
❏ MGC-706 [M]	The Swinging Count	1956	60.00

COLISEUM

| ❏ 51003 [S] | The Happiest Millionaire | 1968 | 18.00 |
| ❏ 41003 [M] | The Happiest Millionaire | 1968 | 40.00 |

COLUMBIA

❏ CL2560 [10]	Basie Bash	1956	80.00
❏ CL901 [M]	Blues By Basie	1956	40.00
❏ CL 754 [M]	Classics	1955	60.00
❏ CL6079 [10]	Dance Parade	1949	100.00
❏ CL997 [M]	One O'Clock Jump	1956	40.00
❏ G31224	Super Chief	1972	18.00

COLUMBIA JAZZ MASTERPIECES

❏ CJ40608	The Essential Count Basie, Volume 1	1987	12.00
❏ CJ40835	The Essential Count Basie, Volume 2	1987	12.00
❏ CJ44150	The Essential Count Basie, Volume 3	1988	12.00

COLUMBIA JAZZ ODYSSEY

| ❏ PC36824 | Blues By Basie | 1981 | 10.00 |

COLUMBIA SPECIAL PRODUCTS

| ❏ P14355 | The Count | 198? | 10.00 |

COMMAND

❏ 33-905 [M]	Broadway Basie's...Way	1966	15.00
❏ RS905SD [S]	Broadway Basie's...Way	1966	18.00
❏ CQ-40004 [Q]	Broadway Basie's...Way	1972	25.00
❏ 33-912 [M]	Hollywood... Basie's Way	1967	18.00
❏ RS912SD [S]	Hollywood... Basie's Way	1967	15.00

DAYBREAK

| ❏ 2005 | Have a Nice Day | 1971 | 15.00 |

Number	Title	Yr	NM
DECCA			
☐ DL8049 [M]	Count Basie and His Orchestra	1954	50.00
☐ DL78049 [R]	Count Basie and His Orchestra	196?	15.00
☐ DL5111 [10]	Count Basie at the Piano	1950	120.00
☐ DXB170 [M]	The Best of Count Basie	196?	30.00
☐ DXSB7170 [R]	The Best of Count Basie	196?	18.00
DOCTOR JAZZ			
☐ FW39520	Afrique	1985	12.00
— Reissue of Flying Dutchman 10138			
DOT			
☐ DLP-25938	Standing Ovation	1969	18.00
☐ DLP-25902	Straight Ahead	1969	18.00
EMARCY			
☐ MG-26023 [10]	Jazz Royalty	1954	70.00
EMUS			
☐ ES12011	Basie at Birdland	197?	12.00
EPIC			
☐ LN3169 [M]	Basie's Back in Town	1955	50.00
☐ LN3107 [M]	Lester Leaps In	1955	50.00
— With Lester Young			
☐ LN3168 [M]	Let's Go to Prez	1955	50.00
— With Lester Young			
☐ LN1117 [10]	Rock the Blues	1955	70.00
☐ LG1021 [10]	The Old Count and the New Count – Basie	1954	70.00
EVEREST ARCHIVE OF FOLK & JAZZ			
☐ FS-318	Savoy Ballroom 1937	197?	12.00
FANTASY			
☐ OJC-416	88 Basie Street	198?	15.00
☐ OJC-379	Basie Big Band Montreux '77	1989	12.00
— Reissue of Pablo Live 2308 209			
☐ OJC-600	Kansas City 3/For the Second Time	1991	15.00
— Reissue of Pablo 2310 878			
☐ OJC-449	Kansas City 6	1990	15.00
— Reissue of Pablo 2310 871			
FLYING DUTCHMAN			
☐ FD10138	Afrique	1972	30.00
FORUM			
☐ F-9032 [M]	Kansas City Suite	196?	15.00
☐ SF-9032 [S]	Kansas City Suite	196?	18.00
— Reissue of Roulette 52056			
☐ F-9063 [M]	Not Now -- I'll Tell You When	196?	15.00
☐ SF-9063 [S]	Not Now -- I'll Tell You When	196?	18.00
— Reissue of Roulette 52044			
☐ F-9060 [M]	One More Time	196?	15.00
☐ SF-9060 [S]	One More Time	196?	18.00
— Reissue of Roulette 52024			
GROOVE MERCHANT			
☐ 2001	Evergreens	1972	15.00
HAPPY TIGER			
☐ 1007	Basie on the Beatles	196?	30.00
HARMONY			
☐ HL7229 [M]	Basie's Best	1960	18.00
☐ HS11371	Just in Time	1970	15.00
IMPULSE!			
☐ A-15 [M]	Count Basie and the Kansas City Seven	1962	30.00
☐ AS-15 [S]	Count Basie and the Kansas City Seven	1962	40.00
INTERMEDIA			
☐ QS-5039	The Classic Count	198?	12.00
☐ QS-5028	The Deacon	198?	12.00
JAZZ ARCHIVES			
☐ JA-41	At the Famous Door, 1938-1939	198?	12.00
☐ JA-16	The Count at the Chatterbox, 1937	198?	12.00
JAZZ MAN			
☐ 5006	Ain't It the Truth	198?	12.00
JAZZ PANORAMA			
☐ 1803 [10]	Count Basie and Lester Young	1951	100.00
MCA			
☐ 718	16 Greatest Performances	198?	10.00
☐ 29003	Count Basie and the Kansas City Seven	198?	10.00
☐ 4108	Good Morning Blues	197?	15.00
☐ 42324	One O'Clock Jump	1990	15.00
☐ 4130	Retrospective Sessions	198?	12.00
☐ 4163	Showtime	198?	12.00
☐ 29005	Standing Ovation	198?	10.00
☐ 29004	Straight Ahead	198?	10.00
☐ 4050	The Best of Count Basie	197?	15.00
MCA/IMPULSE!			
☐ 5656	Count Basie and the Kansas City Seven	1986	10.00
MERCURY			
☐ MG-25105 [10]	Count Basie and His Kansas City Seven	1952	100.00
☐ MGC-120 [10]	Count Basie and His Orchestra Collates	1952	220.00
METRO			
☐ M-516 [M]	Count Basie	1965	18.00

Number	Title	Yr	NM
☐ MS-516 [S]	Count Basie	1965	15.00
MGM			
☐ GAS-126	Count Basie (Golden Archive Series)	1970	18.00
MOBILE FIDELITY			
☐ 1-237	April in Paris	1995	40.00
— Audiophile vinyl			
☐ 1-129	Basie Plays Hefti	1985	80.00
— Audiophile vinyl			
MOSAIC			
☐ MR12-135	The Complete Roulette Live Recordings of Count Basie and His Orchestra	199?	200.00
☐ MQ15-149	The Complete Roulette Studio Recordings of Count Basie and His Orchestra	199?	250.00
PABLO			
☐ 2310901	88 Basie Street	1984	25.00
☐ 2310925	Basie and His Friends	1988	15.00
☐ 2310745	Basie and Zoot	1976	25.00
☐ 2310756	Basie Big Band	1975	25.00
☐ 2310786	Basie Jam #2	1977	18.00
☐ 2310840	Basie Jam #3	1979	15.00
☐ 2310718	Basie Jam	1975	18.00
☐ 2310750	Basie Jam/Montreux '75	1976	15.00
☐ 2310924	Count Basie Get Together	1987	12.00
☐ 2310920	Fancy Pants	1987	12.00
☐ 2310874	Farmers Market Barbecue	1982	12.00
☐ 2310712	For the First Time	1974	15.00
☐ 2310767	I Told You So	1976	15.00
☐ 2310871	Kansas City 6	198?	15.00
☐ 2310859	Kansas City Shout	1980	15.00
— With Joe Turner and Eddie "Cleanhead" Vinson			
☐ 2310891	Me & You	1983	12.00
☐ 2310919	Mostly Blues...And Some Others	1987	12.00
☐ 2310797	Prime Time	1977	15.00
☐ 2310852	The Best of Basie	1980	12.00
☐ 2405408	The Best of the Count Basie Band	198?	12.00
☐ 2310709	The Bosses	1974	15.00
PABLO LIVE			
☐ 2308207	Basie Big Band Montreux '77	1977	15.00
☐ 2308209	Basie Jam/Montreux '77	1977	15.00
☐ 2308246	Live in Japan, 1978	198?	12.00
PABLO TODAY			
☐ 2312126	Kansas City 5	198?	12.00
☐ 2312112	On the Road	1980	12.00
☐ 2312131	Warm Breeze	198?	12.00
PAIR			
☐ PDL2-1045	Basic Basie	1986	15.00
PAUSA			
☐ 7105	High Voltage	198?	12.00
PICKWICK			
☐ SPC-3500	Everything's Coming Up Roses	197?	12.00
☐ SPC-3028 [S]	His Hits of the 60's	196?	15.00
☐ PC 3028 [M]	His Hits of the 60's	196?	10.00
PRESTIGE			
☐ 24109	Reunions	197?	15.00
QUINTESSENCE			
☐ 25151	Everything's Coming Up Roses	197?	12.00
RCA CAMDEN			
☐ CAL-497 [M]	Basie's Basement	1959	30.00
☐ CAL-514 [M]	Count Basie in Kansas City	1959	30.00
☐ CAL-395 [M]	The Count	1958	30.00
RCA VICTOR			
☐ LPM-1112 [M]	Count Basie	1955	600.00
— Andy Warhol cover			
☐ LPV-514 [M]	Count Basie in Kansas City	1965	30.00
☐ AFM1-5180	Kansas City Style	1985	12.00
REPRISE			
☐ R-6153 [M]	Pop Goes the Basie	1965	18.00
☐ RS-6153 [S]	Pop Goes the Basie	1965	25.00
☐ R-6070 [M]	This Time by Basie! Hits of the 50's and 60's	1963	25.00
☐ R9-6070 [S]	This Time by Basie! Hits of the 50's and 60's	1963	30.00
ROULETTE			
☐ R52113 [M]	Back with Basie	1964	25.00
☐ SR52113 [S]	Back with Basie	1964	30.00
☐ R52003 [M]	Basie	1958	50.00
— White label with colored "spokes"			
☐ SR52003 [S]	Basie	1958	60.00
— Black vinyl; white label with colored "spokes"			
☐ SR52003 [S]	Basie	1958	150.00
— Red vinyl; white label with colored "spokes"			
☐ R52003 [M]	Basie	1964	30.00
— Orange and yellow "roulette wheel" label			
☐ R52003 [M]	Basie	2003	30.00
— 200-gram vinyl reissue; distributed by Classic Records			
☐ SR52003 [S]	Basie	1964	40.00
— Orange and yellow "roulette wheel" label			
☐ R52065 [M]	Basie at Birdland	1961	30.00
☐ SR52065 [S]	Basie at Birdland	1961	30.00
☐ R52011 [M]	Basie Plays Hefti	1958	30.00
☐ SR52011 [S]	Basie Plays Hefti	1958	30.00

Number	Title	Yr	NM
☐ R52056 [M]	Benny Carter's Kansas City Suite	1960	30.00
☐ SR52056 [S]	Benny Carter's Kansas City Suite	1960	30.00
☐ R52028 [M]	Breakfast, Dance & Barbeque	1959	30.00
☐ SR52028 [S]	Breakfast, Dance & Barbeque	1959	30.00
☐ R52032 [M]	Chairman of the Board	1959	30.00
☐ SR52032 [S]	Chairman of the Board	1959	30.00
☐ R52099 [M]	Count Basie in Sweden	1963	25.00
☐ SR52099 [S]	Count Basie in Sweden	1963	30.00
☐ R52036 [M]	Dance Along with Basie	1959	30.00
☐ SR52036 [S]	Dance Along with Basie	1959	30.00
☐ R52106 [M]	Easin' It	1963	25.00
☐ SR52106 [S]	Easin' It	1963	30.00
☐ RE-102	Echoes of an Era (The Count Basie Years)	1971	18.00
☐ RE-107	Echoes of an Era (The Vocal Years)	1971	18.00
☐ SR42009	Fantail	1968	18.00
☐ RE-124	Kansas City Suite/Easin' It	1973	18.00
☐ R52044 [M]	Not Now -- I'll Tell You When	1960	30.00
☐ SR52044 [S]	Not Now -- I'll Tell You When	1960	30.00
☐ R52024 [M]	One More Time	1959	30.00
☐ SR52024 [S]	One More Time	1959	30.00
☐ R52051 [M]	String Along with Basie	1960	30.00
☐ SR52051 [S]	String Along with Basie	1960	30.00
☐ R52081 [M]	The Best of Basie	1962	18.00
☐ SR52081 [S]	The Best of Basie	1962	25.00
☐ R52089 [M]	The Best of Basie, Volume 2	1962	18.00
☐ SR52089 [S]	The Best of Basie, Volume 2	1962	25.00
☐ RE-118	The Best of Count Basie	1971	18.00
☐ RB-1 [M]	The Count Basie Story	1960	40.00
☐ SRB-1 [S]	The Count Basie Story	1960	50.00
☐ SR42015	The Kid from Red Bank	1968	18.00
☐ R52086 [M]	The Legend	1962	25.00
☐ SR52086 [S]	The Legend	1962	30.00
☐ R52111/3 [M]	The World of Count Basie	1964	40.00
☐ SR52111/3 [S]	The World of Count Basie	1964	50.00
SOLID STATE			
☐ SS-18032	Basie Meets Bond	1968	18.00
— Reissue of United Artists LP			
TIME-LIFE			
☐ STBB-08	Big Bands: Count Basie	1983	18.00
☐ STL-J-22	Giants of Jazz	1982	25.00
UNITED ARTISTS			
☐ UAL-3480 [M]	Basie Meets Bond	1966	30.00
☐ UAS 6480 [S]	Basie Meets Bond	1966	30.00
UPFRONT			
☐ UPF-142	Count Basie and His Orchestra	1969	15.00
VEE JAY			
☐ VJS-3054	I Got Rhythm	198?	15.00
VERVE			
☐ VE-2-2517	16 Men Swinging	197?	15.00
☐ MGV8012 [M]	April in Paris	1957	50.00
☐ V-8012 [M]	April in Paris	1961	25.00
☐ UMV-1-2641	April in Paris	198?	12.00
☐ 821291-1	Basic Basie	198?	15.00
☐ V6-8783	Basie	1969	18.00
☐ MGV8199 [M]	Basie in London	1957	50.00
☐ V-8199 [M]	Basie in London	1961	25.00
☐ V-8597 [M]	Basie Land	1964	18.00
☐ V6-8597 [S]	Basie Land	1964	25.00
☐ V-8616 [M]	Basie Picks the Winners	1965	18.00
☐ V6-8616 [S]	Basie Picks the Winners	1965	25.00
☐ MGV-8108 [M]	Basie Rides Again!	1957	50.00
— Reissue of Clef 729			
☐ V-8108 [M]	Basie Rides Again!	1961	25.00
☐ MGV-8018 [M]	Basie Roars Again	1957	50.00
— Reissue of Clef 723			
☐ V-8018 [M]	Basie Roars Again	1961	25.00
☐ V-8687 [M]	Basie's Beat	1967	25.00
☐ V6-8687 [S]	Basie's Beat	1967	18.00
☐ V-8659 [M]	Basie's Beatle Bag	1966	30.00
☐ V6-8659 [S]	Basie's Beatle Bag	1966	40.00
☐ MGV-8243 [M]	Count Basie at Newport	1958	50.00
☐ MGVS-6024 [S]	Count Basie at Newport	1960	50.00
☐ V-8243 [M]	Count Basie at Newport	1961	25.00
☐ V6-8243 [S]	Count Basie at Newport	1961	25.00
☐ UMV-1-2619	Count Basie at Newport	198?	12.00
☐ MGV-8291 [M]	Hall of Fame	1958	50.00
☐ V-8291 [M]	Hall of Fame	1961	25.00
☐ 825194-1	High Voltage (Basic Basie Vol. 2)	198?	12.00
☐ VSP-12 [M]	Inside Basie, Outside	1966	18.00
☐ VSPS-12 [S]	Inside Basie, Outside	1966	25.00
☐ V-8549 [M]	Li'l Ol' Groovemaker...Basie!	1963	25.00
☐ V6-8549 [S]	Li'l Ol' Groovemaker...Basie!	1963	30.00
☐ V-8563 [M]	More Hits of the 50's and 60's	1963	25.00
☐ V6-8563 [S]	More Hits of the 50's and 60's	1963	30.00
☐ V-8511 [M]	On My Way and Shoutin' Again!	1963	18.00
☐ V6-8511 [S]	On My Way and Shoutin' Again!	1963	25.00
☐ VE-2-2542	Paradise Squat	197?	15.00
☐ MGV-8103 [M]	The Band of Distinction	1957	50.00
— Reissue of Clef 722			
☐ V-8103 [M]	The Band of Distinction	1961	25.00
☐ MGV-8070 [M]	The Count	1957	50.00
— Reissue of Clef 120			
☐ V-8070 [M]	The Count	1961	25.00
☐ V-8407 [M]	The Essential Count Basie	1961	18.00

Number	Title	Yr	NM
❑ V6-8407 [S]	The Essential Count Basie	1961	25.00
❑ MGV-8104 [M]	The King of Swing	1957	50.00
— Reissue of Clef 724			
❑ V-8104 [M]	The King of Swing	1961	25.00
❑ V6-8831	The Newport Years	1973	15.00
❑ MGV-8090 [M]	The Swinging Count!	1957	50.00
— Reissue of Clef 706			
❑ V-8090 [M]	The Swinging Count!	1961	25.00
❑ V-8596 [M]	Verve's Choice -- Best of Count Basie	1964	18.00
❑ V6-8596 [S]	Verve's Choice -- Best of Count Basie	1964	25.00

BASIL, TONI

CHRYSALIS
❑ FV41449	Toni Basil	1983	12.00
❑ PV41449	Toni Basil	1986	10.00
— Reissue with new prefix			
❑ CHR1410	Word of Mouth	1982	15.00
❑ FV41410	Word of Mouth	1983	12.00
— Reissue of 1410			
❑ PV41410	Word of Mouth	1986	10.00
— Reissue with new prefix			

BASIN STREET SIX, THE

CIRCLE
❑ L-403 [10]	Dixieland from New Orleans	1951	50.00

EMARCY
❑ MG-26012 [10]	The Basin Street Six	1954	50.00

MERCURY
❑ MG-20151 [M]	Strictly Dixie	195?	40.00
❑ MG-25111 [10]	The Basin Street Six	1951	50.00

BASKERVILLE HOUNDS, THE

DOT
❑ DLP-3823 [M]	The Baskerville Hounds (Featuring Space Rock, Part 2)	1967	120.00
❑ DLP-25823 [S]	The Baskerville Hounds (Featuring Space Rock, Part 2)	1967	100.00

BASS, FONTELLA

CHECKER
❑ LP-2997 [M]	The "New" Look	1966	100.00
— Blue label with red and black checkers			
❑ LPS-2997 [S]	The "New" Look	1966	80.00
— Blue label with red and black checkers			
❑ LP-2997 [M]	The "New" Look	1967	40.00
— Blue and white label			
❑ LPS-2997 [S]	The "New" Look	1967	40.00
— Blue and white label			

PAULA
❑ LPS-2203	Free	1971	15.00

BASS, MARTHA AND FONTELLA

SOUL NOTE
❑ SN-1006	From the Root to the Source	197?	15.00

BASSEY, SHIRLEY

APPLAUSE
❑ APLP1005	Shirley Bassey	1982	12.00

EPIC
❑ LN3834 [M]	The Bewitching Shirley Bassey	1962	25.00

LIBERTY
❑ LWB-715	Greatest Hits	198?	12.00
❑ LN-10252	Greatest Hits	198?	10.00
❑ LN-10180	I, Capricorn	198?	10.00
❑ LWB-111	Live at Carnegie Hall	198?	12.00
❑ LN-10262	Shirley Means Bassey	198?	10.00
❑ LM-1013	Something Else	198?	10.00
❑ LN-10104	The Best of Shirley Bassey	1980	10.00
❑ LN-10012	The Magic Is You	1980	10.00
❑ LW-847	Yesterdays	198?	10.00

MERCURY
❑ 838033-1	La Mujer	1989	15.00

MGM
❑ E-4301 [M]	Golden Sound	1965	15.00
❑ SE-4301 [S]	Golden Sound	1965	18.00
❑ E-3862 [M]	The Fabulous Shirley Bassey	1960	25.00
❑ SE-3862 [S]	The Fabulous Shirley Bassey	1960	30.00

PAIR
❑ PDL2-1057	Sassy Bassey	1986	15.00

PHILIPS
❑ PHM200168 [M]	Spectacular Shirley Bassey	1965	15.00
❑ PHS600168 [S]	Spectacular Shirley Bassey	1965	18.00

PICKWICK
❑ SPC-3303	How About You	197?	12.00

SPRINGBOARD
❑ SPB-4045	This Is My Life	197?	10.00

UNITED ARTISTS
❑ UAS5643	And I Love You So	1972	12.00
❑ UAL3565 [M]	And We Were Lovers	1967	15.00
❑ UAS6565 [S]	And We Were Lovers	1967	18.00
❑ UAS6713	Does Anybody Miss Me?	1969	15.00
❑ UA-LA542-G	Good, Bad But Beautiful	1975	12.00
❑ UA-LA715-H2	Greatest Hits	1976	18.00
❑ UAS5565	I, Capricorn	1971	12.00
❑ UAL3463 [M]	In Person	1965	15.00
❑ UAS6463 [S]	In Person	1965	18.00
❑ UA-LA111-H	Live at Carnegie Hall	1973	18.00
❑ UA-LA605-G	Love, Life and Feelings	1976	12.00
❑ UAS6765	Never, Never, Never	1973	12.00
❑ UA-LA214-G	Nobody Does It Like Me	1974	12.00
❑ UAL3169 [M]	Shirley Bassey	1962	18.00
❑ UAS6169 [S]	Shirley Bassey	1962	25.00
❑ UAL3419 [M]	Shirley Bassey Belts the Best	1965	15.00
❑ UAS6419 [S]	Shirley Bassey Belts the Best	1965	18.00
❑ UAS6765	Shirley Bassey Is Really "Something"	1970	12.00
❑ UAL3237 [M]	Shirley Bassey Sings the Hits from "Oliver"	1962	18.00
❑ UAS6237 [S]	Shirley Bassey Sings the Hits from "Oliver"	1962	25.00
❑ UAL3545 [M]	Shirley Means Bassey	1966	15.00
❑ UAS6545 [S]	Shirley Means Bassey	1966	18.00
❑ LM-1013	Something Else	1979	12.00
❑ UAS6797	Something Else *	1971	12.00
❑ UA-LA926-H	The Magic Is You	1978	12.00
❑ UAS6675	This Is My Life	1969	15.00
❑ UA-LA847-H	Yesterdays	1977	12.00
❑ UA-LA751-H	You Take My Heart Away	1977	12.00

BASSO-VALDAMBRINI OCTET, THE

VERVE
❑ MGV-20009 [M]	Jazz Festival, Milan	1960	40.00
❑ V-20009 [M]	Jazz Festival, Milan	1961	25.00
❑ MGV-20011 [M]	The New Sound from Italy	1960	40.00
❑ MGVS-6152 [S]	The New Sound from Italy	1960	40.00
❑ V-20011 [M]	The New Sound from Italy	1961	25.00
❑ V6-20011 [S]	The New Sound from Italy	1961	25.00

BASTARDS, THE

TREEHOUSE
❑ 016	Monticallo	1989	15.00

BAT BOYS, THE

DESIGN
❑ DLP249 [B]	Batman - Batman Theme: as on the ABC T.V. television series Batman!		30.00

BATDORF & RODNEY

ARISTA
❑ AL4041	Life Is You	1975	12.00

ASYLUM
❑ SD5056	Batdorf & Rodney	1972	12.00

ATLANTIC
❑ SD8298	Off the Shelf	1971	15.00

BATORS, STIV

BOMP!
❑ 4015 [B]	Disconnected	1980	30.00
❑ 4043 [10]	Disconnected	1993	18.00
— Reissue of 4015 on 10-inch vinyl			
❑ 4046 [10]	L.A. L.A.	1993	18.00

BATTERED ORNAMENTS

HARVEST
❑ SKAO-422 [B]	Mantle-Piece	1970	150.00

BATTIN, SKIP

SIGNPOST
❑ SP8408	Skip Battin	1972	15.00

BATTLE, KATHLEEN

ANGEL
❑ DS-37363	A Christmas Celebration	1986	12.00

BAUDUC, RAY, AND NAPPY LAMARE

CAPITOL
❑ T877 [M]	Riverboat Dandies	1957	40.00

MERCURY
❑ SR-60186 [S]	On a Swinging Date	1960	30.00
❑ MG-0(# unknown) [M]	On a Swinging Date	1960	30.00

BAUER, BILLY

AD LIB
❑ AAL-5501 [10]	Let's Have a Session	1955	200.00

INTERPLAY
❑ IP-8603	Anthology	198?	15.00

NORGRAN
❑ MGN-1082 [M]	Billy Bauer Plectrist	1956	80.00

VERVE
❑ MGV-8172 [M]	Billy Bauer Plectrist	1957	80.00
— yellow label			
❑ V-8172 [M]	Billy Bauer Plectrist	1961	25.00

BAUGH, PHIL

ERA
❑ ES-801	California Guitar	1969	30.00

LONGHORN
❑ LP-02 [M]	Country Guitar	1965	50.00

TORO
❑ T-502 [M]	Country Guitar II	1965	40.00

BAUHAUS

❑ 4M511LP [B]	The Sky's Gone Out		25.00

A&M
❑ SP-4953	Burning from the Inside	1983	25.00
❑ SP4918 [B]	The Sky's Gone Out	1982	25.00

BEGGARS BANQUET
❑ 9804-1-H	Swing the Heartache/The BBC Sessions	1989	25.00

BAXTER, DUKE

VMC
❑ VS-138	Everybody Knows Matilda	1969	25.00

BAXTER, LES

CAPITOL
❑ T1117 [M]	African Jazz	1958	40.00
❑ T1388 [M]	Baxter's Best	1960	30.00
❑ DT1388 [R]	Baxter's Best	1960	18.00
❑ SM-1388	Baxter's Best	197?	10.00
❑ T733 [M]	Caribbean Moonlight	1956	40.00
❑ T1537 [M]	Jewels of the Sea	1961	30.00
❑ ST1537 [S]	Jewels of the Sea	1961	40.00
❑ T594 [M]	Kaleidoscope	1955	40.00
❑ T10015 [M]	La Femme	1956	40.00
❑ H288 [10]	Le Sacre Du Sauvage	1952	80.00
❑ T288 [M]	Le Sacre Du Sauvage	1954	40.00
❑ T1088 [M]	Love Is a Fabulous Thing	1958	40.00
❑ T843 [M]	Midnight on the Cliffs	1957	40.00
❑ H0(# unknown) [10]	Music for Peace of Mind	1953	80.00
❑ H2000 [10]	Music Out of the Moon	1953	80.00
❑ T390 [M]	Music Out of the Moon/ Music for Peace of Mind	1954	40.00
❑ T868 [M]	Ports of Pleasure	1957	40.00
❑ M-11702	Ritual of the Savage	1977	12.00
❑ DT288 [R]	Ritual of the Savage (Le Sacre Du Sauvage)	196?	15.00
❑ T780 [M]	'Round the World	1957	40.00
❑ T1012 [M]	Selections from "South Pacific	1958	40.00
❑ T774 [M]	Skins!	1957	40.00
❑ T968 [M]	Space Escapade	1958	40.00
❑ T655 [M]	Tamboo!	1955	40.00
❑ T1846 [M]	The Original Quiet Village	1963	25.00
❑ ST1846 [S]	The Original Quiet Village	1963	30.00
❑ LAL486 [M]	The Passions	1954	40.00
❑ T1661 [M]	The Sensational Les Baxter	1962	30.00
❑ ST1661 [S]	The Sensational Les Baxter	1962	30.00
❑ SQBO-90984	The Sounds of Adventure	1967	30.00
— Capitol Record Club exclusive			
❑ T474 [M]	Thinking of You	1954	40.00
❑ H474 [M]	Thinking of You	1954	50.00

GNP CRESCENDO
❑ GNPS-2047	African Blue	1969	15.00
❑ GNP-2036 [M]	Brazil Now	1967	18.00
❑ GNPS-2036 [S]	Brazil Now	1967	15.00
❑ GNPS-2042	Love Is Blue	1968	15.00
❑ GNPS-2053	Moon Rock	1969	15.00

PICKWICK
❑ PC-3048 [M]	I Could Have Danced All Night	196?	18.00
❑ SPC-3048 [S]	I Could Have Danced All Night	196?	15.00
❑ PC-3011 [M]	The Fabulous Sounds of Les Baxter	196?	18.00
❑ SPC-3011 [S]	The Fabulous Sounds of Les Baxter	196?	18.00

REPRISE
❑ R-6079 [M]	Academy Award Winners '63	1963	18.00
❑ R9-6079 [S]	Academy Award Winners '63	1963	25.00
❑ R-6048 [M]	The Primitive and the Passionate	1962	18.00
❑ R9-6049 [S]	The Primitive and the Passionate	1962	25.00
❑ R-6100 [M]	The Soul of the Drums	1963	18.00
❑ R9-6100 [S]	The Soul of the Drums	1963	25.00
❑ R-6036 [M]	Voices in Rhythm	1961	18.00
❑ R9-6036 [S]	Voices in Rhythm	1961	25.00

BAXTER

PARAMOUNT
❑ PAS-6050	Baxter	1973	25.00

BAY CITY JAZZ BAND, THE

GOOD TIME JAZZ
❑ S-10053 [S]	Golden Days	1969	18.00
❑ L-12017 [M]	The Bay City Jazz Band	1955	30.00

BAY CITY ROLLERS

ARISTA
❑ AL4049 [B]	Bay City Rollers	1975	15.00
❑ AL4093 [B]	Dedication	1976	15.00

Number	Title	Yr	NM
❑ AB4241 [B]	Elevator	1979	15.00
—As "The Rollers"			
❑ AB4158	Greatest Hits	1977	12.00
❑ AB7004 [B]	It's a Game	1977	15.00
❑ AL4071 [B]	Rock N' Roll Love Letter	1976	15.00
❑ AB4194 [B]	Strangers in the Wind	1978	15.00

BAYARD, EDDIE, AND THE NEW ORLEANS CLASSIC JAZZ ORCHESTRA

STOMP OFF

Number	Title	Yr	NM
❑ SOS-1145	The Owls' Hoot	1987	15.00

BAYETE

PRESTIGE

Number	Title	Yr	NM
❑ 10062	Seeking Other Beauty	1973	30.00
❑ 10045	Worlds Around the Sun	1972	30.00

BAYSIDERS, THE

EVEREST

Number	Title	Yr	NM
❑ LPBR-5124 [M]	Over the Rainbow	1961	200.00
❑ BRST-1124 [S]	Over the Rainbow	1961	300.00

BAZUKA, TONY CAMILLO'S

A&M

Number	Title	Yr	NM
❑ SP-3406	Tomy Camillo's Bazuka	1975	12.00

BBC SYMPHONY ORCHESTRA (ANTAL DORATI, CONDUCTOR)

MERCURY LIVING PRESENCE

Number	Title	Yr	NM
❑ SR90416 [S]	Bartok: The Miraculous Mandarin	196?	50.00
—Maroon label, no "Vendor: Mercury Record Corporation			
❑ SR90416 [S]	Bartok: The Miraculous Mandarin	196?	30.00
—Maroon label, with "Vendor: Mercury Record Corporation			
❑ SR90416 [S]	Bartok: The Miraculous Mandarin	196?	18.00
—Third edition: Dark red (not maroon) label			

BE-BOP DELUXE

CAPITOL

Number	Title	Yr	NM
❑ SN-16025	Axe Victim	1980	10.00
—Reissue of Harvest 11689			
❑ SN-16023	Drastic Plastic	1980	10.00
—Reissue of Harvest 11750			
❑ SN-16024	Futurama	1980	10.00
—Reissue of Harvest 11432			
❑ SN-16026	Modern Music	1980	10.00
—Reissue of Harvest 11575			
❑ SN-16022 [B]	Sunburst Finish	1980	10.00
—Reissue of Harvest 11478			
❑ SPRO-8486 [DJ]	Sunburst Finish	1975	30.00
—Specially banded version for radio			

HARVEST

Number	Title	Yr	NM
❑ SM-11689	Axe Victim	1977	12.00
—Their first UK album; first US issue has "SM" prefix			
❑ SPRO-8531 [DJ]	Be-Bop's Biggest	1978	30.00
—Promo-only compilation			
❑ SW-11750	Drastic Plastic	1978	12.00
❑ ST-11432	Futurama	1975	12.00
❑ SKBB-11666	Live! In the Air Age	1977	15.00
❑ ST-11575	Modern Music	1976	12.00
❑ ST-11478	Sunburst Finish	1975	12.00
❑ SKBO-11870	The Best Of & The Rest Of Be-Bop Deluxe	1979	15.00

BEACH BOYS, THE

ASYLUM

Number	Title	Yr	NM
❑ R113793	Surf's Up	1972	150.00
—RCA Record Club edition, pressed with wrong labels			

BROTHER

Number	Title	Yr	NM
❑ T9001 [M]	Smiley Smile	1967	40.00
—No mention of Barry Turnbull on cover			
❑ T9001 [M]	Smiley Smile	1967	30.00
—Title for this album by Barry Turnbull" on back cover			
❑ ST9001 [R]	Smiley Smile	1967	25.00
—No mention of Barry Turnbull on cover			
❑ ST9001 [R]	Smiley Smile	1967	18.00
—Title for this album by Barry Turnbull" on back cover			

BROTHER/REPRISE

Number	Title	Yr	NM
❑ MS2251	15 Big Ones	1976	15.00
❑ R130223	15 Big Ones	1976	18.00
—RCA Record Club edition			
❑ 2MS2083	Carl and the Passions "So Tough"/Pet Sounds	1972	30.00
❑ 2MS2083 [DJ]	Carl and the Passions "So Tough"/Pet Sounds	1972	50.00
—White label promo			
❑ 2MS2167	Friends & Smiley Smile	1974	18.00
❑ MS2223	Good Vibrations -- Best of the Beach Boys	1975	15.00
❑ MSK2280	Good Vibrations -- Best of the Beach Boys	1978	12.00
❑ MS2118 [DJ]	Holland	1973	40.00
—White label promo; includes bonus white-label promo EP, "Mount Vernon and Fairway," in picture sleeve, taped to back cover			
❑ MS2118	Holland	1973	18.00
—Includes bonus stock-copy EP, "Mount Vernon and Fairway," in picture sleeve, taped to back cover			
❑ MS2118 [DJ]	Holland	1973	500.00
—Test pressing with "We Got Love," deleted from promos and stock copies			
❑ MSK2258	Love You	1977	15.00
❑ MSK2268	M.I.U. Album	1978	15.00
❑ MS2197 [M]	Pet Sounds	1974	25.00
❑ RS-6382 [DJ]	Sunflower	1970	50.00
—White label promo			
❑ RS-6382 [B]	Sunflower	1970	30.00
❑ SKAO-93352	Sunflower	1970	200.00
—Capitol Record Club edition			
❑ RS6453 [DJ]	Surf's Up	1971	40.00
—White label promo			
❑ RS6453	Surf's Up	1971	25.00
❑ R113793	Surf's Up	1972	30.00
—RCA Record Club edition			
❑ 2RS6484 [DJ]	The Beach Boys In Concert	1973	40.00
—White label promo			
❑ 2RS6484	The Beach Boys In Concert	1973	25.00
❑ R223569	The Beach Boys In Concert	1973	30.00
—RCA Record Club edition			
❑ 2MS2166	Wild Honey & 20/20	1974	18.00

CAPITOL

Number	Title	Yr	NM
❑ SKAO-133	20/20	1969	25.00
—Black label with colorband			
❑ SKAO-133	20/20	1969	18.00
—"Starline" label			
❑ SKAO-8-0133	20/20	1969	30.00
—Capitol Record Club edition; black label			
❑ SKAO-8-0133	20/20	1970	40.00
—Capitol Record Club edition; lime label			
❑ C1-29638	20/20	1994	18.00
❑ T2110 [M]	All Summer Long	1964	50.00
—With "Don't Break Down" erroneously listed on front cover			
❑ T2110 [M]	All Summer Long	1964	30.00
—With "Don't Back Down" correctly listed on front cover			
❑ ST2110 [S]	All Summer Long	1964	50.00
—With "Don't Break Down" erroneously listed on front cover			
❑ ST2110 [S]	All Summer Long	1964	30.00
—With "Don't Back Down" correctly listed on front cover			
❑ SN-16010 [S]	All Summer Long	1980	10.00
❑ C1-29631 [S]	All Summer Long	1994	18.00
❑ SF-501	All Summer Long	1970	12.00
—Individual record from above set			
❑ SF-8-0501	All Summer Long	1971	12.00
—Capitol Record Club edition			
❑ SF-500501	All Summer Long	1971	12.00
—Columbia Record Club edition			
❑ STBB-500	All Summer Long/California Girls	1970	25.00
—Lime labels; "Special Double Play" pack; two separate LPs (abridged versions of "All Summer Long" and "Summer Days [And Summer Nights!!]") bound together			
❑ STBB-500	All Summer Long/California Girls	1971	30.00
—Red labels; "Special Double Play" pack; two separate LPs (abridged versions of "All Summer Long" and "Summer Days [And Summer Nights!!]") bound together			
❑ R233593	American Summer	1975	30.00
—RCA Music Service exclusive			
❑ ST-11584	Beach Boys '69 (The Beach Boys Live in London)	1976	15.00
❑ SN-12011	Beach Boys '69 (The Beach Boys Live in London)	1979	12.00
❑ SN-16134	Beach Boys '69 (The Beach Boys Live in London)	1981	10.00
❑ C1-29634	Beach Boys '69 (The Beach Boys Live in London)	1994	18.00
❑ TAO2198 [M]	Beach Boys Concert	1964	30.00
—With bound-in booklet			
❑ STAO2198 [S]	Beach Boys Concert	1964	30.00
—With bound-in booklet			
❑ STAO-8-2198 [S]	Beach Boys Concert	196?	80.00
—Capitol Record Club edition			
❑ SM-2198	Beach Boys Concert	197?	12.00
❑ C1-90427	Beach Boys Concert	1994	18.00
❑ MAS2398 [M]	Beach Boys Party!	1965	40.00
—With sheet of photos			
❑ MAS2398 [M]	Beach Boys Party!	1965	30.00
—Without sheet of photos			
❑ DMAS2398 [R]	Beach Boys Party!	1965	30.00
—With sheet of photos			
❑ DMAS2398 [R]	Beach Boys Party!	1965	30.00
—Without sheet of photos			
❑ DN-16272 [R]	Beach Boys Party!	1982	10.00
❑ C1-29640 [M]	Beach Boys Party!	1994	18.00
❑ T2545 [M]	Best of the Beach Boys	1966	25.00
—Black label with colorband			
❑ T2545 [M]	Best of the Beach Boys	1966	18.00
—Black "The Star Line" label			
❑ T2545 [M]	Best of the Beach Boys	1967	30.00
—Red and white "Starline" label			
❑ DT2545 [P]	Best of the Beach Boys	1966	18.00
—Black label with colorband			
❑ DT2545 [P]	Best of the Beach Boys	1966	15.00
—Black "The Star Line" label			
❑ DT2545 [P]	Best of the Beach Boys	1967	18.00
—Red and white "Starline" label			
❑ DT2545 [P]	Best of the Beach Boys	1970	15.00
—Green "Starline" label			
❑ DT2545 [P]	Best of the Beach Boys	1973	12.00
—Orange label, "Capitol" on bottom			
❑ DT2545 [P]	Best of the Beach Boys	1978	12.00
—Purple label, large Capitol logo			
❑ DT2545 [P]	Best of the Beach Boys	1983	12.00
—Black label, print in colorband			
❑ C1-91318 [R]	Best of the Beach Boys	1988	15.00
—Purple label, small Capitol logo			
❑ R123946	Best of the Beach Boys	197?	18.00
—RCA Music Service edition			
❑ DT-502545 [P]	Best of the Beach Boys	197?	18.00
—Columbia Record Club edition			
❑ DT2706 [P]	Best of the Beach Boys, Vol. 2	1973	12.00
—Orange label, "Capitol" on bottom			
❑ T2706 [M]	Best of the Beach Boys, Vol. 2	1967	30.00
❑ DT2706 [P]	Best of the Beach Boys, Vol. 2	1967	18.00
—Red and while "Starline" label			
❑ DT2706 [P]	Best of the Beach Boys, Vol. 2	1970	15.00
—Green "Starline" label			
❑ DT2706 [P]	Best of the Beach Boys, Vol. 2	1978	12.00
—Purple label, large Capitol logo			
❑ DN-16318 [R]	Best of the Beach Boys, Vol. 2	1984	10.00
❑ DT-502706 [P]	Best of the Beach Boys, Vol. 2	197?	18.00
—Columbia Record Club edition			
❑ N-16273	Be True to Your School	1983	10.00
❑ DN-16017 [R]	California Girls	1980	10.00
❑ SF-502	California Girls	1970	12.00
—Individual record from above set			
❑ SF-8-0502	California Girls	1971	12.00
—Capitol Record Club edition			
❑ SF-500502	California Girls	1971	12.00
—Columbia Record Club edition			
❑ SWBB 253	Close-Up	1969	30.00
—Reissue of "Surfin' U.S.A." and "All Summer Long" in one package; black labels with colorband			
❑ SWBB-253	Close-Up	1970	40.00
—Lime labels			
❑ DN-16019 [R]	Dance, Dance, Dance	1981	10.00
❑ SF-703	Dance, Dance, Dance	1971	12.00
—Individual record from above set			
❑ SF-8-0703	Dance, Dance, Dance	1971	12.00
—Capitol Record Club edition			
❑ SVBB-11307	Endless Summer	1974	25.00
—Orange labels, "Capitol" on bottom; with poster			
❑ SVBB-511307	Endless Summer	197?	30.00
—Columbia Record Club edition			
❑ R223559	Endless Summer	197?	30.00
—RCA Music Service edition			
❑ SVBB-11307	Endless Summer	1978	18.00
—Purple labels, large Capitol logo			
❑ SVBB-11307	Endless Summer	1983	15.00
—Black labels, print in colorband			
❑ SVBB-11307	Endless Summer	1988	15.00
—Purple labels, small Capitol logo			
❑ ST2895	Friends	1968	30.00
❑ SN-16157	Friends	1981	10.00
❑ C1-29637	Friends	1994	18.00
❑ SN-16018 [P]	Fun, Fun, Fun	1980	10.00
—Reissue of "Shut Down, Vol. 2			
❑ SF-702	Fun, Fun, Fun	1971	12.00
—Individual record from above set			
❑ SF-8-0702	Fun, Fun, Fun	1971	12.00
—Capitol Record Club edition			
❑ STBB-701	Fun, Fun, Fun/Dance, Dance, Dance	1970	25.00
—Lime labels; "Special Double Play" pack; two separate LPs (abridged versions of "Shut Down, Volume 2" and "The Beach Boys Today!") bound together			
❑ STBB-701	Fun, Fun, Fun/Dance, Dance, Dance	1971	30.00
—Red labels; "Special Double Play" pack; two separate LPs (abridged versions of "Shut Down, Volume 2" and "The Beach Boys Today!") bound together			
❑ ST-442	Good Vibrations	1970	25.00
—Lime label (original)			
❑ ST-8-0442	Good Vibrations	1970	30.00
—Capitol Record Club edition			
❑ ST-442	Good Vibrations	1972	30.00
—Red or orange label			
❑ T1998 [M]	Little Deuce Coupe	1963	40.00
❑ ST1998 [S]	Little Deuce Coupe	1963	40.00
❑ SM-1998 [S]	Little Deuce Coupe	197?	12.00
❑ SN-16013 [S]	Little Deuce Coupe	1980	10.00
❑ C1-29630 [S]	Little Deuce Coupe	1994	18.00
❑ STBK-12396	Made in U.S.A.	1986	15.00
❑ T2458 [M]	Pet Sounds	1966	40.00
❑ DT2458 [R]	Pet Sounds	1966	30.00
❑ SN-16156 [M]	Pet Sounds	1981	10.00
❑ C1-48421 [M]	Pet Sounds	1994	18.00
❑ C1-21241 [S]	Pet Sounds	1999	18.00
—True stereo version on heavyweight vinyl			
❑ 09463-51370-1-9	Pet Sounds	2006	30.00
—Limited two-record edition; one record is on yellow vinyl and			

Number	Title	Yr	NM

contains the original mono mix; the other is on green vinyl and contains the 2003 stereo mix

❑ ST-12293	Rarities	1983	18.00
❑ T2027 [M]	Shut Down, Volume 2	1964	40.00
❑ ST2027 [P]	Shut Down, Volume 2	1964	40.00
❑ C1-29629 [M]	Shut Down, Volume 2	1994	18.00
❑ PRO3133 [DJ]	Silver Platter Service from Hollywood: The Beach Boys Christmas Special	1964	200.00
❑ T/DT2580	Smile	1966	1000.00

—Unreleased; price is for cover slick, which has been counterfeited

| ❑ T/DT2580 [B] | Smile Booklet | 1966 | 400.00 |

—Printed for insertion into unreleased "Smile" LP; counterfeits exist

❑ SN-16158 [M]	Smiley Smile	1981	10.00
❑ C1-29635 [M]	Smiley Smile	1994	18.00
❑ ST-8-2891 [R]	Smiley Smile	1968	300.00

—Capitol Record Club edition

| ❑ SVBB-11384 | Spirit of America | 1975 | 18.00 |

—Orange labels, "Capitol" on bottom

| ❑ SVBB-511384 | Spirit of America | 1975 | 25.00 |

—Columbia Record Club edition

| ❑ SVBB-11384 | Spirit of America | 1978 | 15.00 |

—Purple labels, large Capitol logo

| ❑ SVBB-11384 | Spirit of America | 1983 | 12.00 |

—Black labels, print in colorband

| ❑ SVBB-11384 | Spirit of America | 1988 | 12.00 |

—Purple labels, small Capitol logo

| ❑ DKAO2893 [B] | Stack-o-Tracks | 1968 | 125.00 |

—With sheet music booklet

| ❑ DKAO2893 | Stack-o-Tracks | 1968 | 50.00 |

—Without sheet music booklet

| ❑ DKAO-8-2893 | Stack-o-Tracks | 1968 | 200.00 |

—Capitol Record Club edition

❑ C1-29641	Stack-o-Tracks	1994	18.00
❑ C1-92639	Still Cruisin'	1989	15.00
❑ T2354 [M]	Summer Days (And Summer Nights!!)	1965	30.00
❑ DT2354 [R]	Summer Days (And Summer Nights!!)	1965	50.00

—With "New Improved Full Dimensional Stereo" banner

| ❑ DT2354 [R] | Summer Days (And Summer Nights!!) | 1965 | 30.00 |

—With "Duophonic" banner

❑ C1-29633 [M]	Summer Days (And Summer Nights!!)	1994	18.00
❑ SVBB-12220	Sunshine Dream	1982	15.00
❑ T1981 [M]	Surfer Girl	1963	40.00

—With reference to The Four Freshmen in liner notes

| ❑ T1981 [M] | Surfer Girl | 1963 | 40.00 |

—With reference to "their other new single record, 'Little Deuce Coupe'" in liner notes

| ❑ ST1981 [S] | Surfer Girl | 1963 | 50.00 |

—With reference to The Four Freshmen in liner notes

| ❑ ST1981 [S] | Surfer Girl | 1963 | 50.00 |

—With reference to "their other new single record, 'Little Deuce Coupe'" in liner notes

❑ SM-1981 [S]	Surfer Girl	197?	12.00
❑ SN-16014 [S]	Surfer Girl	1980	10.00
❑ C1-29628 [S]	Surfer Girl	1994	18.00
❑ T1808 [M]	Surfin' Safari	1962	40.00
❑ DT1808 [R]	Surfin' Safari	1962	80.00

—With "Capitol Full Dimensional Stereo" banner under the "Duophonic" banner

| ❑ DT1808 [R] | Surfin' Safari | 1962 | 30.00 |

—With only the "Duophonic" banner at top

❑ SM-1808 [R]	Surfin' Safari	197?	12.00
❑ N-16012 [M]	Surfin' Safari	1980	10.00
❑ C1-29661 [M]	Surfin' Safari	1994	18.00
❑ SY-4572 [R]	Surfin' Safari	197?	15.00

—Orange label, Capitol logo at bottom; reissue of DT-1808 with completely different back cover and the words "... A Collector's Item ... Special Collections of Classic Hit Recordings by the Brightest Stars ..."

❑ T1890 [M]	Surfin' U.S.A.	1963	40.00
❑ ST1890 [S]	Surfin' U.S.A.	1963	50.00
❑ SM-1890 [M]	Surfin' U.S.A.	197?	12.00
❑ SN-16015 [S]	Surfin' U.S.A.	1980	10.00
❑ C1-48422 [S]	Surfin' U.S.A.	1994	18.00
❑ 509994 63199 13 [B]	That's Why God Made The Radio	2012	35.00
❑ T2164 [M]	The Beach Boys' Christmas Album	1964	50.00
❑ ST2164 [S]	The Beach Boys' Christmas Album	1964	50.00
❑ SM-2164	The Beach Boys' Christmas Album	197?	12.00
❑ R133854	The Beach Boys' Christmas Album	197?	18.00

—RCA Music Service edition

| ❑ TCL2813 [M] | The Beach Boys Deluxe Set | 1967 | 250.00 |

—Black border on box; albums have "T" prefixes

| ❑ DTCL2813 [R] | The Beach Boys Deluxe Set | 1967 | 50.00 |

—Maroon border on box; custom pressings of LPs with "DTCL" prefixes

| ❑ DTCL-8-2813 [R] | The Beach Boys Deluxe Set | 1967 | 150.00 |

—Capitol Record Club edition; blue border on box; custom pressings of LPs with "DTCL" prefixes

❑ T2269 [M]	The Beach Boys Today!	1965	30.00
❑ DT2269 [R]	The Beach Boys Today!	1965	30.00
❑ DT-8-2269 [R]	The Beach Boys Today!	1965	80.00

—Capitol Record Club edition

| ❑ C1-29632 [M] | The Beach Boys Today! | 1994 | 18.00 |

Number	Title	Yr	NM
❑ DKAO2945 [P]	The Best of the Beach Boys, Vol. 3	1968	18.00

—Black label with colorband

| ❑ DKAO2945 [P] | The Best of the Beach Boys, Vol. 3 | 1969 | 25.00 |

—Starline" label

❑ T2859 [M]	Wild Honey	1967	40.00
❑ ST2859 [S]	Wild Honey	1967	25.00
❑ SN-16159 [S]	Wild Honey	1981	10.00
❑ C1-29636 [S]	Wild Honey	1994	18.00

CAPITOL SPECIAL MARKETS

❑ SL-8114	Beach Boys Super Hits	1978	12.00
❑ SLB-6994	Golden Years of the Beach Boys	1975	25.00
❑ SL-9431	Good Vibrations from the Beach Boys	1986	18.00

—Special issue for Sunkist

| ❑ SLB-8134 | The Beach Boys | 1980 | 25.00 |

CARIBOU

| ❑ FZ36283 [DJ] | Keepin' the Summer Alive | 1980 | 18.00 |

—White label promo

❑ FZ36283	Keepin' the Summer Alive	1980	12.00
❑ JZ35752	L.A. (Light Album)	1979	12.00
❑ JZ35752 [DJ]	L.A. (Light Album)	1979	18.00

—White label promo

| ❑ PZ35752 | L.A. (Light Album) | 1980 | 10.00 |

—Budget-line reissue

❑ Z2X37445	Ten Years of Harmony (1970-1980)	1981	15.00
❑ BFZ39946	The Beach Boys	1985	12.00
❑ PZ39946	The Beach Boys	1988	10.00

—Budget-line reissue

DCC COMPACT CLASSICS

| ❑ LPZ-2006 [M] | Pet Sounds | 1995 | 120.00 |

—Audiophile vinyl

ERA

| ❑ HTE-805 [M] | The Beach Boys' Biggest Beach Hits | 1969 | 18.00 |

—Also contains non-Beach Boys filler

EVEREST

| ❑ 4108 [M] | Rare Early Recordings | 1981 | 10.00 |

GATEWAY

| ❑ GSLP-10104 [M] | Surfing with the Beach Boys, the Marketts and the Frogmen | 1979 | 10.00 |

MOBILE FIDELITY

| ❑ 1-116 | Surfer Girl | 1984 | 30.00 |

—Audiophile vinyl

ORBIT

| ❑ OR688 [M] | The Beach Boys' Greatest Hits 1961-1963 | 1972 | 15.00 |

—Also contains non-Beach Boys filler

PAIR

| ❑ PDL2-1068 | For All Seasons | 1986 | 18.00 |
| ❑ PDL2-1084 | Golden Harmonies | 1986 | 18.00 |

PICKWICK

❑ SPC-3269	Good Vibrations	1971	12.00
❑ PTP-2059 [B]	High Water	1973	15.00
❑ SPC-3562	Little Deuce Coupe	1975	12.00
❑ SPC-3221	Summertime Blues	1970	12.00
❑ SPC-3351	Surfer Girl	1973	12.00
❑ SPC-3309	Wow! Great Concert!	1972	12.00

READER'S DIGEST

| ❑ RBA-178 | Their Greatest Hits and Finest Performances | 1989 | 50.00 |

—Box set

SCEPTER CITATION

| ❑ CTN-18004 [M] | The Best of the Beach Boys (1961-1963) | 1972 | 15.00 |

—Also contains non-Beach Boys filler

SEARS

| ❑ SPS-609 | Summertime Blues | 1970 | 50.00 |

SPRINGBOARD

| ❑ SPB-4021 [M] | The Beach Boys 1961 | 1977 | 10.00 |

—Also contains non-Beach Boys filler

SUNDAZED

| ❑ LP5005 [B] | Lost & Found! | 1991 | 15.00 |

—Colored vinyl (red, yellow and light blue are known); first LP issue of the 1961 sessions from the master tapes; three tracks are stereo

TIME-LIFE

| ❑ SRNR-03 | The Beach Boys: 1963-1967 | 1986 | 18.00 |

—2 LPs in box with fold-open liner notes; second cover has a portrait of the Beach Boys

| ❑ SRNR-03 | The Beach Boys: 1963-1967 | 1986 | 30.00 |

—2 LPs in box with fold-open liner notes; original cover portrays the Beach Boys surfing

WAND

| ❑ WDS-688 [M] | The Beach Boys' Greatest Hits 1961-1963 | 1972 | 15.00 |

—Also contains non-Beach Boys filler

BEACHWOOD SPARKS

SUB POP

| ❑ SP503 [B] | Beachwood Sparks | 2000 | 18.00 |

BEACON STREET UNION, THE

MGM

| ❑ SE-4568 [S] | The Clown Died in Marvin Gardens | 1968 | 30.00 |
| ❑ E-4568 [M] | The Clown Died in Marvin Gardens | 1968 | 50.00 |

—May be promo only (yellow label)

| ❑ E-4517 [M] | The Eyes of the Beacon Street Union | 1967 | 30.00 |
| ❑ SE-4517 [S] | The Eyes of the Beacon Street Union | 1967 | 30.00 |

BEAL, JEFF

ANTILLES

| ❑ 90625 | Liberation | 1987 | 12.00 |
| ❑ 91237 | Perpetual Motion | 1989 | 12.00 |

BEAN, BILLY

RIVERSIDE

| ❑ RLP-380 [M] | The Trio | 1961 | 40.00 |
| ❑ RS-9380 [S] | The Trio | 1961 | 50.00 |

BEANS

AVALANCHE

| ❑ 9200 | Beans | 1971 | 25.00 |

BEARFOOT

EPIC

| ❑ KE32146 | Bearfoot | 1973 | 15.00 |

BEARS, THE

I.R.S.

| ❑ 42139 | Rise and Shine | 1988 | 12.00 |
| ❑ 42011 | The Bears | 1987 | 15.00 |

BEASLEY, JIMMY

CROWN

| ❑ CLP-5014 [M] | The Fabulous Jimmy Beasley | 1957 | 150.00 |

—Black label

| ❑ CLP-5247 [M] | Twist with Jimmy Beasley | 1962 | 40.00 |

—Gray label

MODERN

| ❑ MLP-1214 [M] | The Fabulous Jimmy Beasley | 1956 | 400.00 |

BEASLEY, WALTER

MERCURY

| ❑ 838912-1 | Just Kickin' It | 1989 | 15.00 |

POLYDOR

| ❑ 833866-1 | Walter Beasley | 1987 | 10.00 |

BEASLEY, WATSON

WARNER BROS.

| ❑ BSK3445 | Watson Beasley | 1980 | 12.00 |

BEAST

COTILLION

| ❑ SD9012 | Beast | 1969 | 18.00 |

EVOLUTION

| ❑ 2017 | Beast | 1970 | 18.00 |

BEASTIE BOYS

CAPITOL

❑ C1-98938 [B]	Check Your Head	1992	60.00
❑ C137716 [B]	Hello Nasty	1998	30.00
❑ SPRO79461 [DJ]	Hip Hop Sampler	1994	80.00

—Promo-only compilation of remixes and rarities; 1,250 copies were pressed; only the Side 1 number is listed above (the other three sides are numbered SPRO-79463, SPRO-79472 and SPRO-79473); this album has been counterfeited; there are several differences; most notably that authentic copies have gatefold sleeves, and the counterfeits have single-pocket sleeves

| ❑ SPRO79461 [DJ] | Hip Hop Sampler | 1994 | 80.00 |

—This album has been counterfeited; there are several differences, most notably that authentic copies have gatefold sleeves, and the counterfeits have single-pocket sleeves

| ❑ C1-28599 | III Communications | 1994 | 25.00 |
| ❑ C1-92844 | Paul's Boutique | 1989 | 30.00 |

—Multi-gatefold edition (number on record is 91743, the same as single gatefold edition)

| ❑ C1-91743 [B] | Paul's Boutique | 1989 | 18.00 |

—Single gatefold edition

| ❑ C1-22940 | The Sounds of Science | 2000 | 150.00 |

—Boxed set with hardbound booklet; released a year after a similar CD compilation

| ❑ C1-84571 | To the 5 Boroughs | 2004 | 30.00 |

DEF JAM

| ❑ BFC40238 | Licensed to III | 1986 | 25.00 |
| ❑ FC40238 | Licensed to III | 1986 | 18.00 |

Number	Title	Yr	NM

—Second pressing, with "02" added to bar code on back cover

GRAND ROYAL

| ☐ GR 026 [EP] | Aglio E Olio | 1995 | 18.00 |
| ☐ GR 066 | Check Your Head | 1998 | 30.00 |

—Vinyl reissue of Capitol 98938

| ☐ GR 061 [B] | Hello Nasty | 1998 | 45.00 |

—Limited edition on yellow vinyl

| ☐ GR 006 | III Communication | 1994 | 30.00 |
| ☐ GR 065 | Paul's Boutique | 1999 | 25.00 |

—Reissue of original multi-gatefold edition

| ☐ GR 018 [EP] | Root Down | 1995 | 18.00 |

—Black vinyl

| ☐ GR 018 [EP] | Root Down | 1995 | 30.00 |

—Blue vinyl

| ☐ GR 071 [EP] | Scientists of Sound | 2000 | 15.00 |

—Remix album

| ☐ GR 003 [B] | Some Old Bullshit | 1994 | 30.00 |
| ☐ GR 013 | The In Sound from Way Out! | 1996 | 80.00 |

—Original editions were limited to 5,000 and have a sticker indicating this on the back cover

| ☐ GR 013 | The In Sound from Way Out! | 1999 | 30.00 |

—Second editions were not limited and have no sticker on the back cover

RAT CAGE

| ☐ 026 [EP] | Cookypuss | 1983 | 40.00 |

BEAT, THE

COLUMBIA

| ☐ JC36195 | The Beat | 1979 | 15.00 |
| ☐ ARC36794 | The Kids Are the Same | 1982 | 12.00 |

PASSPORT

| ☐ 5002 [EP] | To Beat or Not to Beat | 1983 | 10.00 |

BEAT FARMERS

MCA CURB

| ☐ L33-17381 [EP] | Home of Country Dick | 1987 | 30.00 |

—Promo-only compilation with four non-LP songs

☐ 6296	Poor and Famous	1989	15.00
☐ 5993 [B]	The Pursuit of Happiness	1987	15.00
☐ 5759 [R]	Van Go	1986	15.00

RHINO

| ☐ RNOR-021 [EP] | Bigger Stones | 1985 | 18.00 |

—Promo-only four-song sampler from RNLP-853

| ☐ RNLP-853 | Tales of the New West | 1985 | 15.00 |

BEAT HAPPENING

K

☐ 1 [B]	Beat Happening		30.00
☐ KLP-06	Black Candy	1989	15.00
☐ KLP-03	Dreamy	199?	12.00

—Reissue

| ☐ KLP-02 | Jamboree | 199? | 12.00 |

—Reissue

| ☐ KLP-07 | You Turn Me On | 199? | 12.00 |

—Reissue

K/ROUGH TRADE

| ☐ ROUGH US30 | Jamboree | 198? | 18.00 |

SUB POP

| ☐ SP98 [B] | Dreamy | 1991 | 30.00 |
| ☐ SP167 [B] | You Turn Me On | 1992 | 30.00 |

—Most copies are on red vinyl

BEAT OF THE EARTH, THE

ARDISH

| ☐ AS-001 | The Beat of the Earth | 1968 | 300.00 |
| ☐ AS-0001 | The Beat of the Earth | 1968 | 400.00 |

BEAT RODEO

COYOTE

| ☐ 002 [EP] | Steve Almaas/Beat Rodeo | 1982 | 15.00 |

I.R.S.

| ☐ 5774 | Home in the Heart of the Beat | 1986 | 12.00 |
| ☐ 39020 | Staying Out Late with Beat Rodeo | 1989 | 15.00 |

BEATLE BUDDIES, THE

DIPLOMAT

| ☐ D-2313 [M] | The Beatle Buddies | 1964 | 18.00 |
| ☐ DS-2313 [S] | The Beatle Buddies | 1964 | 25.00 |

BEATLES, THE

APPLE

| ☐ SO-383 | Abbey Road | 1969 | 75.00 |

—With Capitol logo on Side 2 bottom; "Her Majesty" is NOT listed on either the jacket or the label

| ☐ SO-383 | Abbey Road | 1969 | 40.00 |

—With Capitol logo on Side 2 bottom; "Her Majesty" IS listed on both the jacket and the label

| ☐ SO-383 | Abbey Road | 1969 | 25.00 |

—With "Mfd. by Apple" on label; "Her Majesty" is NOT listed on the label

| ☐ SO-383 [B] | Abbey Road | 1969 | 30.00 |

—With "Mfd. by Apple" on label; "Her Majesty" IS listed on the label

| ☐ SO-383 | Abbey Road | 1975 | 30.00 |

—With "All Rights Reserved" on label, either in black print or in light print along label edge (both versions exist)

| ☐ C1-8-34445 [B] | Anthology 1 | 1995 | 60.00 |

—All copies distributed in the U.S. were manufactured in the U.K. with no distinguishing marks (some LPs imported directly from the U.K. have "Made in England" stickers, which can be removed easily)

| ☐ C1-8-34448 | Anthology 2 | 1996 | 40.00 |
| ☐ SPRO11206/7 [EP] | Anthology 2 Sampler | 1996 | 150.00 |

—Promo-only collection sent to college radio stations

| ☐ C1-8-34451 | Anthology 3 | 1996 | 30.00 |
| ☐ SW-385 [B] | Hey Jude | 1970 | 60.00 |

—Label calls the LP "The Beatles Again"; record is "SO-385" (this could be found in retail stores as late as 1973)

| ☐ SW-385 | Hey Jude | 1970 | 30.00 |

—Label calls the LP "The Beatles Again"; record is "SW-385

| ☐ SW-385 | Hey Jude | 1970 | 75.00 |

—With Capitol logo on Side 2 bottom; label calls the LP "Hey Jude

| ☐ SW-385 | Hey Jude | 1970 | 25.00 |

—With "Mfd. by Apple" on label; label calls the LP "Hey Jude

| ☐ SW-385 | Hey Jude | 1975 | 30.00 |

—With "All Rights Reserved" on label; label calls the LP "Hey Jude

| ☐ AR-34001 | Let It Be | 1970 | 30.00 |

—Red Apple label; originals have "Bell Sound" stamped in trail-off area, counterfeits do not

| ☐ C1-8-31796 [B] | Live at the BBC | 1994 | 80.00 |
| ☐ SWBO-101 [B] | The Beatles | 1968 | 1000.00 |

—Numbered copy; includes four individual photos and large poster (included in value); because the white cover shows ring wear so readily, this is an EXTREMELY difficult album to find in near-mint condition; second pressing labels have Side 1, Song 5 correctly listed as "The Continuing Story of Bungalow Bill"; VG value 37.50; VG+ value 75

| ☐ SWBO-101 | The Beatles | 197? | 60.00 |

—Un-numbered copy; includes four individual photos and large poster (included in value)

| ☐ SWBO-101 | The Beatles | 1975 | 70.00 |

—With "All Rights Reserved" on labels; title in black on cover; photos and poster of thinner stock than originals

| ☐ SKBO-3403 [P] | The Beatles 1962-1966 | 1975 | 50.00 |

—Custom red Apple labels with "All Rights Reserved" on labels

| ☐ SKBO-3403 [P] | The Beatles 1962-1966 | 1973 | 30.00 |

—Custom red Apple labels; "Love Me Do" and "I Want to Hold Your Hand" are rechanneled; "She Loves You," "A Hard Day's Night," "I Feel Fine" and "Ticket to Ride" are mono; "From Me to You," "Can't Buy Me Love" and everything else is stereo.

| ☐ C1-97036 [B] | The Beatles 1962-1966 | 1993 | 30.00 |

—Custom red Apple labels; red vinyl; all copies pressed in U.K.; U.S. versions have a bar-code sticker over the international bar code on back cover; "Love Me Do," "Please Please Me," "From Me to You" and "She Loves You" are mono; all others are stereo.

| ☐ SKBO-3404 [B] | The Beatles 1967-1970 | 1973 | 30.00 |

—Custom blue Apple labels. "Hello Goodbye" and "Penny Lane" are mono, all others stereo.

| ☐ SKBO-3404 [B] | The Beatles 1967-1970 | 1975 | 50.00 |

—Custom blue Apple labels with "All Rights Reserved" on labels

| ☐ C1-97039 | The Beatles 1967-1970 | 1993 | 30.00 |

—Custom blue Apple labels; blue vinyl; all copies pressed in U.K.; U.S. versions have a bar-code sticker over the international bar code on back cover

| ☐ -0 [DJ] | The Beatles Again | 1970 | 8000.00 |

—Prototypes with "The Beatles Again" on cover; not released to the general public

| ☐ SO-385 [DJ] | The Beatles Again | 1970 | 10000.00 |

—Prototype covers with "The Beatles Again" on cover; not released to the general public. This is NOT a standard issue! VG value 4000; VG+ value 6000

| ☐ SBC-100 [M] | The Beatles' Christmas Album | 1970 | 600.00 |

—Fan club issue of the seven Christmas messages; very good counterfeits exist

| ☐ SW-153 [P] | Yellow Submarine | 1969 | 50.00 |

—With Capitol logo on Side 2 bottom. "Only a Northern Song" is rechanneled

| ☐ SW-153 [P] | Yellow Submarine | 1971 | 25.00 |

—With "Mfd. by Apple" on label

| ☐ SW-153 [P] | Yellow Submarine | 1975 | 30.00 |

—With "All Rights Reserved" on label

APPLE/CAPITOL

| ☐ ST2228 [P] | Beatles '65 | 1968 | 40.00 |

—With Capitol logo on Side 2 bottom

| ☐ ST2228 [P] | Beatles '65 | 1971 | 25.00 |

—With "Mfd. by Apple" on label

| ☐ ST2228 [P] | Beatles '65 | 1975 | 30.00 |

—With "All Rights Reserved" on label

| ☐ ST2358 [P] | Beatles VI | 1969 | 40.00 |

—With Capitol logo on Side 2 bottom

| ☐ ST2358 [P] | Beatles VI | 1971 | 25.00 |

—With "Mfd. by Apple" on label

| ☐ ST2358 [P] | Beatles VI | 1975 | 30.00 |

—With "All Rights Reserved" on label

| ☐ SMAS2386 [P] | Help! | 1969 | 40.00 |

—With Capitol logo on Side 2 bottom

| ☐ SMAS2386 [P] | Help! | 1971 | 25.00 |

—With "Mfd. by Apple" on label

| ☐ SMAS2386 [P] | Help! | 1975 | 30.00 |

—With "All Rights Reserved" on label

| ☐ SMAL2835 [P] | Magical Mystery Tour | 1969 | 50.00 |

—With Capitol logo on Side 2 bottom; with 24-page booklet

| ☐ SMAL2835 [P] | Magical Mystery Tour | 1971 | 25.00 |

—With "Mfd. by Apple" on label; with 24-page booklet

| ☐ SMAL2835 [P] | Magical Mystery Tour | 1975 | 30.00 |

—With "All Rights Reserved" on label; with 24-page booklet

| ☐ ST2047 [P] | Meet the Beatles! | 1968 | 40.00 |

—With Capitol logo on Side 2 bottom

| ☐ ST2047 [P] | Meet the Beatles! | 1971 | 25.00 |

—With "Mfd. by Apple" on label

| ☐ ST2047 [P] | Meet the Beatles! | 1975 | 30.00 |

—With "All Rights Reserved" on label

| ☐ ST2576 [S] | Revolver | 1971 | 25.00 |

—With "Mfd. by Apple" on label

| ☐ ST2576 [S] | Revolver | 1969 | 40.00 |

—With Capitol logo on Side 2 bottom

| ☐ ST2576 [S] | Revolver | 1975 | 30.00 |

—With "All Rights Reserved" on label

| ☐ ST2442 [S] | Rubber Soul | 1969 | 40.00 |

—With Capitol logo on Side 2 bottom

| ☐ ST2442 [S] | Rubber Soul | 1971 | 25.00 |

—With "Mfd. by Apple" on label

| ☐ ST2442 [S] | Rubber Soul | 1975 | 30.00 |

—With "All Rights Reserved" on label

| ☐ SMAS2653 [S] | Sgt. Pepper's Lonely Hearts Club Band | 1969 | 40.00 |

—With Capitol logo on Side 2 bottom

| ☐ SMAS2653 [S] | Sgt. Pepper's Lonely Hearts Club Band | 1971 | 30.00 |

—With "Mfd. by Apple" on label

| ☐ SMAS2653 [S] | Sgt. Pepper's Lonely Hearts Club Band | 1975 | 30.00 |

—With "All Rights Reserved" on label

| ☐ ST2108 [S] | Something New | 1968 | 40.00 |

—With Capitol logo on Side 2 bottom

| ☐ ST2108 [S] | Something New | 1971 | 25.00 |

—With "Mfd. by Apple" on label

| ☐ ST2108 [S] | Something New | 1975 | 30.00 |

—With "All Rights Reserved" on label

| ☐ (no #)0 | The Beatles 10th Anniversary Box Set | 1974 | 2000.00 |

—VG value 1000; VG+ value 1500

| ☐ ST2080 [P] | The Beatles' Second Album | 1968 | 40.00 |

—With Capitol logo on Side 2 bottom

| ☐ ST2080 [P] | The Beatles' Second Album | 1971 | 25.00 |

—With "Mfd. by Apple" on label

| ☐ ST2080 [P] | The Beatles' Second Album | 1975 | 30.00 |

—With "All Rights Reserved" on label

| ☐ (no #)0 | The Beatles Special Limited Edition | 1974 | 1200.00 |
| ☐ STBO2222 [P] | The Beatles' Story | 1968 | 60.00 |

—With Capitol logo on bottom of B-side of both records

| ☐ STBO2222 [P] | The Beatles' Story | 1971 | 30.00 |

—With "Mfd. by Apple" on labels

| ☐ STBO2222 [P] | The Beatles' Story | 1975 | 40.00 |

—With "All Rights Reserved" on labels

| ☐ ST2309 [P] | The Early Beatles | 1969 | 40.00 |

—With Capitol logo on Side 2 bottom

| ☐ ST2309 [P] | The Early Beatles | 1971 | 25.00 |

—With "Mfd. by Apple" on label

| ☐ ST2309 [P] | The Early Beatles | 1975 | 30.00 |

—With "All Rights Reserved" on label

| ☐ ST2553 [P] | Yesterday and Today | 1969 | 40.00 |

—With Capitol logo on Side 2 bottom

| ☐ ST2553 [P] | Yesterday and Today | 1971 | 25.00 |

—With "Mfd. by Apple" on label

| ☐ ST2553 [P] | Yesterday and Today | 1971 | 30.00 |

—With "Mfd. by Apple" on label; all 11 tracks are in true stereo. Check for a triangle in the record's trail-off area.

| ☐ ST2553 [P] | Yesterday and Today | 1975 | 30.00 |

—With "All Rights Reserved" on label

APPLE FILMS

| ☐ KAL4 [DJ] | The Yellow Submarine (A United Artists Release) | 1969 | 2000.00 |

Number	Title	Yr	NM
—One-sided LP with radio spots for movie			
❑ KAL 004 [DJ]	The Yellow Submarine (A United Artists Release)	1969	3000.00
—One-sided LP with radio spots for movie; VG value 1000; VG+ value 1500			
ATCO			
❑ -0 [M-DJ]	Ain't She Sweet	1964	1000.00
—White label promo			
❑ 33-169 [M]	Ain't She Sweet	1964	300.00
❑ 33-169 [M]	Ain't She Sweet	1964	1500.00
—White label promo			
❑ SD 33-169 [P]	Ain't She Sweet	1964	500.00
—Tan and purple label; all four Beatles tracks are rechanneled			
❑ SD 33-169 [P]	Ain't She Sweet	1969	500.00
—Yellow label			
AUDIOFIDELITY			
❑ PHX-339 [M]	First Movement	1982	15.00
—Contains eight Decca audition tracks			
❑ PD-339 [M]	First Movement	1982	40.00
—Contains eight Decca audition tracks; picture disc			
AUDIO RARITIES			
❑ AR-2452 [M]	The Complete Silver Beatles	1982	18.00
—Contains 12 Decca audition tracks			
BACKSTAGE			
❑ -0 [DJ]	Like Dreamers Do	1982	50.00
—White vinyl promo in white sleeve			
❑ -0 [DJ]	Like Dreamers Do	1982	50.00
—Gray vinyl promo in white sleeve			
❑ BSR-1111 [M]	Like Dreamers Do	1982	60.00
—Two picture discs (10 of 15 Decca audition tracks on one, interviews on the other) and one white-vinyl record (same contests as musical picture disc)			
❑ BSR-1111 [M]	Like Dreamers Do	1982	100.00
—Same as above, except colored-vinyl LP is gray			
❑ BSR-1111 [DJ]	Like Dreamers Do	1982	50.00
—White vinyl promo in white sleeve			
❑ BSR-1111 [DJ]	Like Dreamers Do	1982	50.00
—Gray vinyl promo in white sleeve			
❑ 2-201 [M]	Like Dreamers Do	1982	60.00
—Non-gatefold package			
❑ 2-201 [M]	Like Dreamers Do	1982	40.00
—Gatefold package, individually numbered (numbers under 100 increase value significantly)			
❑ BSR-1165 [PD]	The Beatles Talk with Jerry G.	1982	30.00
—Picture disc			
❑ BSR-1175 [PD]	The Beatles Talk with Jerry G., Vol. 2	1983	30.00
—Picture disc			
CAPITOL			
❑ SV-12245 [P]	20 Greatest Hits	1982	25.00
—Purple label, large Capitol logo. "Love Me Do" and "She Loves You" are rechanneled, the other 18 tracks are stereo			
❑ SV-12245 [P]	20 Greatest Hits	1983	25.00
—Black label, print in colorband			
❑ SV-12245 [P]	20 Greatest Hits	1988	30.00
—Purple label, small Capitol logo			
❑ SO-383	Abbey Road	1976	15.00
—Orange label			
❑ SO-383 [B]	Abbey Road	1978	12.00
—Purple label, large Capitol logo			
❑ SO-383	Abbey Road	1983	18.00
—Black label, print in colorband			
❑ C1-46446	Abbey Road	1988	30.00
—New number; purple label, small Capitol logo			
❑ C1-46446	Abbey Road	1995	15.00
—Apple logo restored to back cover on reissue			
❑ SEAX-11900 [PD]	Abbey Road	1978	40.00
—Picture disc; deduct 25% for cut-outs			
❑ SJ-383	Abbey Road	1984	30.00
—New prefix; black label, print in colorband			
❑ SW-11921 [P]	A Hard Day's Night	1979	15.00
—Purple label, large Capitol logo			
❑ SW-11921 [P]	A Hard Day's Night	1983	18.00
—Black label, print in colorband			
❑ SW-11921 [P]	A Hard Day's Night	1988	30.00
—Purple label, small Capitol logo			
❑ CLJ-46437 [M]	A Hard Day's Night	1987	25.00
—Black label, print in colorband; first Capitol version of original British LP			
❑ CLJ-46437 [M]	A Hard Day's Night	1988	30.00
—Purple label, small Capitol logo			
❑ C1-46437 [M]	A Hard Day's Night	1995	15.00
—New prefix; Apple logo on back cover			
❑ T2228 [M]	Beatles '65	1964	150.00
❑ ST2228 [P]	Beatles '65	1964	100.00
—Black label with colorband. "She's a Woman" and "I Feel Fine" are rechanneled.			
❑ ST2228 [P]	Beatles '65	1969	40.00
—Lime green label			
❑ ST2228 [P]	Beatles '65	1976	15.00
—Orange label			
❑ ST2228 [P]	Beatles '65	1978	12.00
—Purple label, large Capitol logo			
❑ ST2228 [P]	Beatles '65	1983	18.00
—Black label, print in colorband			

Number	Title	Yr	NM
❑ C1-90446 [P]	Beatles '65	1988	30.00
—New number; purple label, small Capitol logo			
❑ CLJ-46438 [M]	Beatles for Sale	1987	25.00
—Black label, print in colorband; first Capitol version of original British LP			
❑ CLJ-46438 [M]	Beatles for Sale	1988	30.00
—Purple label, small Capitol logo			
❑ C1-46438 [M]	Beatles for Sale	1995	15.00
—New prefix; Apple logo on back cover			
❑ T2358 [M]	Beatles VI	1965	150.00
—With "See label for correct playing order" on back cover			
❑ T2358 [M]	Beatles VI	1965	120.00
—With song titles listed in correct order on back cover			
❑ ST2358 [P]	Beatles VI	1965	80.00
—Black label with colorband; with "See label for correct playing order" on back cover			
❑ ST2358 [P]	Beatles VI	1965	100.00
—Black label with colorband; with song titles listed in correct order on back cover. "Yes It Is" is rechanneled.			
❑ ST-8-2358 [P]	Beatles VI	1965	600.00
—Capitol Record Club edition; black label with colorband			
❑ ST-8-2358 [P]	Beatles VI	1969	500.00
—Capitol Record Club edition; lime green label			
❑ ST2358 [P]	Beatles VI	1969	40.00
—Lime green label			
❑ ST2358 [P]	Beatles VI	1976	15.00
—Orange label			
❑ ST2358 [P]	Beatles VI	1978	12.00
—Purple label, large Capitol logo			
❑ ST2358 [M]	Beatles VI	1983	18.00
—Black label, print in colorband; plays in mono despite label designation			
❑ ST2358 [M]	Beatles VI	1988	80.00
—Purple label, small Capitol logo; plays in mono despite label designation			
❑ C1-90445 [M]	Beatles VI	1988	30.00
—New number; purple label, small Capitol logo; plays in mono despite label designation			
❑ MAS2386 [M]	Help!	1965	200.00
❑ SMAS2386 [P]	Help!	1965	100.00
—Black label with colorband. Has incidental music by George Martin. "Ticket to Ride" is rechanneled.			
❑ SMAS-8-2386 [P]	Help!	1965	500.00
—Capitol Record Club edition; black label with colorband; no "8" on cover			
❑ SMAS-8-2386 [P]	Help!	1965	800.00
—Capitol Record Club edition; black label with colorband; with "8" on cover			
❑ SMAS-8-2386 [P]	Help!	197?	700.00
—Longines Symphonette edition; with "Mfd. by Longines" and "8" on cover			
❑ SMAS-8-2386 [P]	Help!	1969	300.00
—Capitol Record Club edition; lime green label; no "8" on cover			
❑ SMAS-8-2386 [P]	Help!	1969	500.00
—Capitol Record Club edition; lime green label; with "8" on cover			
❑ SMAS2386 [P]	Help!	1969	40.00
—Lime green label			
❑ SMAS2386 [P]	Help!	1976	15.00
—Orange label			
❑ SMAS2386 [P]	Help!	1978	12.00
—Purple label, large Capitol logo			
❑ SMAS2386 [P]	Help!	1983	18.00
—Black label, print in colorband			
❑ C1-90454 [P]	Help!	1988	30.00
—New number; purple label, small Capitol logo			
❑ CLJ-46439 [S]	Help!	1987	25.00
—Black label, print in colorband; first Capitol version of original British LP			
❑ CLJ-46439 [S]	Help!	1988	30.00
—Purple label, small Capitol logo			
❑ C1-46439 [S]	Help!	1995	15.00
—New prefix; Apple logo on back cover			
❑ SW-385	Hey Jude	1976	15.00
—Orange label (all Capitol label versions call the LP "Hey Jude")			
❑ SW-385	Hey Jude	1978	12.00
—Purple label, large Capitol logo			
❑ SW-385	Hey Jude	1983	50.00
—Black label, print in colorband			
❑ SJ-385	Hey Jude	1984	30.00
—New prefix; black label, print in colorband			
❑ C1-90442	Hey Jude	1988	30.00
—New number; purple label, small Capitol logo			
❑ SW-11922	Let It Be	1979	18.00
—Purple label, large Capitol logo; with poster and custom innersleeve			
❑ SW-11922	Let It Be	1983	18.00
—Black label, print in colorband; add 33% if poster is included			
❑ SW-11922	Let It Be	1988	30.00
—Purple label, small Capitol logo; add 20% if poster and custom innersleeve are included			
❑ C1-46447	Let It Be	1995	15.00
—New number (the only 1995 reissue with a completely new number)			

Number	Title	Yr	NM
❑ SKBL-11711 [P]	Love Songs	1977	35.00
—With booklet and embossed, leather-like cover. "P.S. I Love You" and "Yes It Is" are rechanneled.			
❑ SKBL-11711 [P]	Love Songs	1988	30.00
—With booklet, but without embossed cover			
❑ MAL2835 [M]	Magical Mystery Tour	1967	500.00
—With 24-page book bound into center of gatefold			
❑ SMAL2835 [P]	Magical Mystery Tour	1967	200.00
—Black label with colorband; with 24-page booklet. "Penny Lane," "Baby You're a Rich Man" and "All You Need Is Love" is rechanneled, as is the second half of "I Am the Walrus" (every "stereo" version of "Walrus" is this way)			
❑ SMAL2835 [P]	Magical Mystery Tour	1969	60.00
—Lime green label; with 24-page booklet			
❑ SMAL2835 [P]	Magical Mystery Tour	1976	15.00
—Orange label; with 24-page booklet			
❑ SMAL2835 [P]	Magical Mystery Tour	1978	12.00
—Purple label, large Capitol logo; this edition did not come with booklet			
❑ SMAL2835 [P]	Magical Mystery Tour	1983	18.00
—Black label, print in colorband; no booklet			
❑ C1-48062 [P]	Magical Mystery Tour	1988	30.00
—New number; purple label, small Capitol logo; no booklet			
❑ C1-48062 [P]	Magical Mystery Tour	1992	15.00
—With Apple logo on back cover; reissue restores booklet to package			
❑ T2047 [M]	Meet the Beatles!	1964	250.00
—Black label with colorband; "Beatles!" on cover in tan to brown print; label has "ASCAP" after every title except "I Want to Hold Your Hand" (BMI); no producer credit on back cover (this is the second edition of this LP)			
❑ T2047 [M]	Meet the Beatles!	1965	150.00
—Black label with colorband; "Beatles!" on cover in green print; most of these have "Produced by George Martin" on lower left of back cover; many of these have a label giving "BMI" credit to every song except "Don't Bother Me" and "Till There Was You			
❑ ST2047 [P]	Meet the Beatles!	1964	200.00
—Black label with colorband; "Beatles!" on cover in tan to brown print; label has "ASCAP" after every title except "I Want to Hold Your Hand" (BMI); no producer credit on back cover (this is the second edition of this LP)			
❑ ST2047 [P]	Meet the Beatles!	1965	100.00
—Black label with colorband; "Beatles!" on cover in green print; most of these have "Produced by George Martin" on lower left of back cover; many of these have a label giving "BMI" credit to every song except "Don't Bother Me" and "Till There Was You			
❑ ST-8-2047 [P]	Meet the Beatles!	1969	500.00
—Capitol Record Club edition; black label with colorband			
❑ ST-8-2047 [P]	Meet the Beatles!	1969	200.00
—Capitol Record Club edition; lime green label			
❑ ST2047 [P]	Meet the Beatles!	1969	40.00
—Lime green label			
❑ ST2047 [P]	Meet the Beatles!	1976	15.00
—Orange label			
❑ ST2047 [P]	Meet the Beatles!	1978	12.00
—Purple label, large Capitol logo			
❑ ST2047 [P]	Meet the Beatles!	1983	18.00
—Black label, print in colorband			
❑ C1-90441 [P]	Meet the Beatles!	1988	30.00
—New number; purple label, small Capitol logo			
❑ C1-91135 [B]	Past Masters Volume 1 and 2	1988	30.00
—Some early tracks are in mono, but "This Boy," "She's a Woman," "Yes It Is," and "The Inner Light" are in stereo.			
❑ CLJ-46435 [M]	Please Please Me	1987	25.00
—Black label, print in colorband; first Capitol version of original British LP			
❑ CLJ-46435 [M]	Please Please Me	1988	30.00
—Purple label, small Capitol logo			
❑ C1-46435 [M]	Please Please Me	1995	15.00
—New prefix; Apple logo on back cover			
❑ -0 [DJ]	Rarities	1979	300.00
—Green label; withdrawn before official release; all known copies have a plain white sleeve			
❑ SPRO-8969	Rarities	1978	50.00
—Purple label, large Capitol logo; part of the U.S. box set The Beatles Collection (BC-13)			
❑ SN-12009 [DJ]	Rarities	1979	500.00
—Green label; withdrawn before official release; all known copies have a plain white sleeve			
❑ SHAL-12060 [B]	Rarities	1980	25.00
—Black label with colorband. First pressing says that "There's a Place" debuts in stereo (false) and that the screaming at the end of "Helter Skelter" was a "classic Lennon statement" (it's actually Ringo).			
❑ SHAL-12060 [B]	Rarities	1980	18.00
—Same as above, with errors deleted and "Produced by George Martin" added to back cover			
❑ -0 [DJ]	Reel Music	1982	40.00
—Yellow vinyl promo; numbered back cover with 12-page booklet			
❑ -0 [DJ]	Reel Music	1982	25.00
—Yellow vinyl promo; plain white cover with 12-page booklet			
❑ SV-12199 [DJ]	Reel Music	1982	40.00
—Yellow vinyl promo; numbered back cover with 12-page booklet			
❑ SV-12199 [DJ]	Reel Music	1982	25.00
—Yellow vinyl promo; plain white cover with 12-page booklet			
❑ SV-12199	Reel Music	1982	12.00
—Standard issue with 12-page booklet			
❑ T2576 [M]	Revolver	1966	250.00

Number	Title	Yr	NM
❑ ST2576 [S]	Revolver	1966	100.00
—Black label with colorband			
❑ ST-8-2576 [S]	Revolver	1966	400.00
—Capitol Record Club edition; black label with colorband			
❑ ST-8-2576 [S]	Revolver	1969	120.00
—Capitol Record Club edition; lime green label			
❑ ST-8-2576 [S]	Revolver	1973?	200.00
—Longines Symphonette edition; orange label (a very late issue, as the club closed in 1974)			
❑ ST2576 [S]	Revolver	1969	40.00
—Lime green label			
❑ ST2576 [S]	Revolver	1970	300.00
—Red label with "target" Capitol at top (same design as lime green label)			
❑ ST2576 [S]	Revolver	1976	15.00
—Orange label			
❑ SW2576 [S]	Revolver	1978	12.00
—Purple label, large Capitol logo			
❑ SW2576 [S]	Revolver	1983	18.00
—Black label, print in colorband			
❑ C1-90452 [S]	Revolver	1988	30.00
—New number; purple label, small Capitol logo			
❑ CLJ-46441 [S]	Revolver	1987	25.00
—Black label, print in colorband; first Capitol version of original British LP			
❑ CLJ-46441 [S]	Revolver	1988	30.00
—Purple label, small Capitol logo			
❑ C1-46441 [S]	Revolver	1995	15.00
—New prefix; Apple logo on back cover			
❑ SKBO-11537	Rock 'n' Roll Music	1976	30.00
❑ SN-16020 [B]	Rock 'n' Roll Music, Volume 1	1980	15.00
❑ SN-16021 [B]	Rock 'n' Roll Music, Volume 2	1980	15.00
❑ T2442 [M]	Rubber Soul	1965	150.00
❑ ST2442 [S]	Rubber Soul	1965	60.00
—Black label with colorband			
❑ ST-8-2442 [S]	Rubber Soul	1965	400.00
—Capitol Record Club edition; black label with colorband			
❑ ST-8-2442 [S]	Rubber Soul	1969	250.00
—Capitol Record Club edition; lime green label			
❑ ST-8-2442 [S]	Rubber Soul	1969	250.00
—Longines Symphonette edition (will be stated on label); lime green label			
❑ ST2442 [S]	Rubber Soul	1969	40.00
—Lime green label			
❑ ST2442 [S]	Rubber Soul	1976	15.00
—Orange label			
❑ SW2442 [S]	Rubber Soul	1978	12.00
—Purple label, large Capitol logo			
❑ SW2442 [S]	Rubber Soul	1983	18.00
—Black label, print in colorband			
❑ C1-90453 [S]	Rubber Soul	1988	30.00
—New number; purple label, small Capitol logo			
❑ CLJ-46440 [S]	Rubber Soul	1987	25.00
—Black label, print in colorband; first Capitol version of original British LP			
❑ CLJ-46440 [S]	Rubber Soul	1988	30.00
—Purple label, small Capitol logo			
❑ C1-46440 [S]	Rubber Soul	1995	15.00
—New prefix; Apple logo on back cover			
❑ MAS2653 [M]	Sgt. Pepper's Lonely Hearts Club Band	1967	500.00
❑ SMAS2653 [S]	Sgt. Pepper's Lonely Hearts Club Band	1967	200.00
—Black label with colorband			
❑ SMAS2653 [S]	Sgt. Pepper's Lonely Hearts Club Band	1969	60.00
—Lime green label			
❑ SMAS2653 [S]	Sgt. Pepper's Lonely Hearts Club Band	1976	15.00
—Orange label			
❑ SMAS2653 [S]	Sgt. Pepper's Lonely Hearts Club Band	1978	12.00
—Purple label, large Capitol logo. Many copies from 1978 had a "The Original Classic" sticker on shrink wrap; it was added at the time of the release of the bomb movie version of Sgt. Pepper. Double the value if the sticker is still there.			
❑ SMAS2653 [S]	Sgt. Pepper's Lonely Hearts Club Band	1983	18.00
—Black label, print in colorband; some of these had "The Original Classic" stickers, too. Add $10 to value if it is there.			
❑ C1-46442 [S]	Sgt. Pepper's Lonely Hearts Club Band	1988	30.00
—New number; purple label, small Capitol logo			
❑ C1-46442 [S]	Sgt. Pepper's Lonely Hearts Club Band	1995	15.00
—With Apple logo on back cover			
❑ SEAX-11840 [PD]	Sgt. Pepper's Lonely Hearts Club Band	1978	25.00
—Picture disc; deduct 25% for cut-outs			
❑ 2653	Sgt. Pepper's Lonely Hearts Club Band Special Inner Sleeve	1967	18.00
—Red-pink psychedelic sleeve only issued with 1967 (mono and stereo) editions			
❑ T2108 [M]	Something New	1964	200.00
❑ ST2108 [S]	Something New	1964	100.00
—Black label with colorband			
❑ ST-8-2108 [S]	Something New	1964	300.00
—Capitol Record Club edition; black label with colorband			
❑ ST-8-2108 [S]	Something New	1969	150.00
—Capitol Record Club edition; lime green label			

Number	Title	Yr	NM
❑ ST-8-2108 [S]	Something New	1969	300.00
—Longines Symphonette edition (will be stated on label); lime green label			
❑ ST2108 [S]	Something New	1969	40.00
—Lime green label			
❑ ST2108 [S]	Something New	1976	15.00
—Orange label			
❑ ST2108 [S]	Something New	1978	12.00
—Purple label, large Capitol logo			
❑ ST2108 [S]	Something New	1983	18.00
—Black label, print in colorband			
❑ C1-90443 [S]	Something New	1988	30.00
—New number; purple label, small Capitol logo			
❑ SWBO-101	The Beatles	1976	30.00
—Orange label; with photos and poster			
❑ C1-46443	The Beatles	1995	25.00
—With Apple logo on back cover			
❑ SWBO-101	The Beatles	1978	30.00
—Purple label, large Capitol logo; with photos and poster (some copies have four photos as one perforated sheet)			
❑ SWBO-101	The Beatles	1983	40.00
—Black label, print in colorband; with photos and poster (some copies have four photos as one perforated sheet)			
❑ C1-46443	The Beatles	1988	50.00
—New number; purple label, small Capitol logo; with photos and poster (some copies have four photos as one perforated sheet)			
❑ SEBX-11841	The Beatles	1978	50.00
—White vinyl; with photos and poster (with number "SEBX-11841" on each)			
❑ SKBO-3403 [P]	The Beatles 1962-1966	1976	25.00
—Red labels			
❑ SKBO-3403 [P]	The Beatles 1962-1966	1976	30.00
—Blue labels (error pressing)			
❑ SEBX-11842 [P]	The Beatles 1962-1966	1978	40.00
—Red vinyl			
❑ C1-90435 [P]	The Beatles 1962-1966	1988	30.00
—New number; purple labels, small Capitol logo			
❑ SKBO-3404 [B]	The Beatles 1967-1970	1976	25.00
—Blue labels			
❑ SEBX-11843 [B]	The Beatles 1967-1970	1978	40.00
—Blue vinyl			
❑ C1-90438 [B]	The Beatles 1967-1970	1988	30.00
—New number; purple labels, small Capitol logo			
❑ -0 [DJ]	The Beatles at the Hollywood Bowl	1977	500.00
—Advance tan label promo in plain white jacket			
❑ SMAS-11638 [B]	The Beatles at the Hollywood Bowl	1977	30.00
—Originals with embossed title and ticket on front cover			
❑ SMAS-11638 [DJ]	The Beatles at the Hollywood Bowl	1977	500.00
—Advance tan label promo in plain white jacket			
❑ SMAS-11638	The Beatles at the Hollywood Bowl	1980	18.00
—Second pressing without embossed title and ticket			
❑ SMAS-11638	The Beatles at the Hollywood Bowl	1989	40.00
—With UPC code on back cover			
❑ BC-13 [B]	The Beatles Collection	1978	300.00
—American versions have "EMI" and "BC-13" on box spine; imports go for less			
❑ (no #)0	The Beatles Collection Platinum Series	1984	800.00
❑ BBX1 91302	The Beatles Deluxe Box Set	1988	300.00
❑ T2080 [M]	The Beatles' Second Album	1964	250.00
❑ ST2080 [P]	The Beatles' Second Album	1964	100.00
—Black label with colorband. "She Loves You," "I'll Get You" and "You Can't Do That" are rechanneled			
❑ ST-8-2080 [P]	The Beatles' Second Album	1964	600.00
—Capitol Record Club edition; black label with colorband			
❑ ST-8-2080 [P]	The Beatles' Second Album	1969	400.00
—Capitol Record Club edition; lime green label			
❑ ST2080 [P]	The Beatles' Second Album	1969	40.00
—Lime green label			
❑ ST2080 [P]	The Beatles' Second Album	1976	15.00
—Orange label			
❑ ST2080 [P]	The Beatles' Second Album	1978	12.00
—Purple label, large Capitol logo			
❑ ST2080 [P]	The Beatles' Second Album	1983	18.00
—Black label, print in colorband			
❑ C1-90444 [P]	The Beatles' Second Album	1988	30.00
—New number; purple label, small Capitol logo			
❑ TBO2222 [M]	The Beatles' Story	1964	250.00
❑ STBO2222 [P]	The Beatles' Story	1964	250.00
—Black label with colorband. Some of the musical snippets are rechanneled.			
❑ STBO2222 [P]	The Beatles' Story	1969	50.00
—Lime green label			
❑ STBO2222 [P]	The Beatles' Story	1976	25.00
—Orange label			
❑ STBO2222 [P]	The Beatles' Story	1978	25.00
—Purple label, large Capitol logo			
❑ STBO2222 [P]	The Beatles' Story	1983	40.00
—Black label, print in colorband			
❑ T2309 [M]	The Early Beatles	1965	250.00
❑ ST2309 [P]	The Early Beatles	1965	100.00
—Black label with colorband. "Love Me Do" and "P.S. I Love You" are rechanneled.			
❑ ST2309 [P]	The Early Beatles	1969	40.00
—Lime green label			

Number	Title	Yr	NM
❑ ST2309 [P]	The Early Beatles	1976	15.00
—Orange label			
❑ ST2309 [P]	The Early Beatles	1978	12.00
—Purple label, large Capitol logo			
❑ ST2309 [P]	The Early Beatles	1983	30.00
—Black label, print in colorband			
❑ CLJ-46436 [M]	With the Beatles	1987	25.00
—Black label, print in colorband; first Capitol version of original British LP			
❑ CLJ-46436 [M]	With the Beatles	1988	30.00
—Purple label, small Capitol logo			
❑ C1-46436 [M]	With the Beatles	1995	15.00
—New prefix; Apple logo on back cover			
❑ SW-153 [P]	Yellow Submarine	1976	15.00
—Orange label			
❑ SW-153 [P]	Yellow Submarine	1978	12.00
—Purple label, large Capitol logo			
❑ SW-153 [P]	Yellow Submarine	1983	18.00
—Black label, print in colorband			
❑ C1-46445 [P]	Yellow Submarine	1988	30.00
—New number; purple label, small Capitol logo			
❑ C1-46445 [P]	Yellow Submarine	1995	15.00
—Reissue has the British liner notes, which include a review of the White Album.			
❑ T2553 [M]	Yesterday and Today	1966	4000.00
—First state" butcher cover (never had other cover on top); cover will be the same size as other Capitol Beatles LPs; VG value 2000; VG+ value 3000			
❑ T2553 [M]	Yesterday and Today	1966	1500.00
—Second state" butcher cover (trunk cover pasted over original cover)			
❑ T2553 [M]	Yesterday and Today	1966	1200.00
—Third state" butcher cover (trunk cover removed, leaving butcher cover intact); cover will be about 3/16-inch narrower than other Capitol Beatles LPs; value is highly negotiable depending upon the success of removing the paste-over; VG value 400; VG+ value 800			
❑ T2553 [M]	Yesterday and Today	1966	200.00
—Trunk cover			
❑ ST2553 [P]	Yesterday and Today	1966	8000.00
—First state" butcher cover (never had other cover on top); cover will be the same size as other Capitol Beatles LPs; VG value 4000; VG+ value 6000			
❑ ST2553 [P]	Yesterday and Today	1966	1000.00
—Second state" butcher cover (trunk cover pasted over original cover)			
❑ ST-8-2553 [P]	Yesterday and Today	1966	350.00
—Capitol Record Club edition; black label with colorband			
❑ ST2553 [P]	Yesterday and Today	1966	1500.00
—Third state" butcher cover (trunk cover removed, leaving butcher cover intact); cover will be about 3/16-inch narrower than other Capitol Beatles LPs; value is highly negotiable depending upon the success of removing the paste-over			
❑ ST2553 [P]	Yesterday and Today	1966	80.00
—Trunk cover; black label with colorband (all later variations have the trunk cover). "I'm Only Sleeping," "Dr. Robert" and "And Your Bird Can Sing" are rechanneled.			
❑ ST-8-2553 [S]	Yesterday and Today	1969	150.00
—Capitol Record Club edition; lime green label; all 11 tracks are in true stereo! (We don't know if the same is true of the black label version.)			
❑ ST2553 [P]	Yesterday and Today	1969	40.00
—Lime green label			
❑ ST2553 [P]	Yesterday and Today	1976	15.00
—Orange label; it's possible that this and all future pressings have all 11 tracks in true stereo, but we don't know.			
❑ ST2553 [P]	Yesterday and Today	1978	12.00
—Purple label, large Capitol logo			
❑ ST2553 [P]	Yesterday and Today	1983	18.00
—Black label, print in colorband			
❑ C1-90447 [P]	Yesterday and Today	1988	30.00
—New number; purple label, small Capitol logo; stereo content uncertain			

CICADELIC

Number	Title	Yr	NM
❑ 1963	All Our Loving	1986	15.00
❑ 1964	East Coast Invasion	1985	15.00
❑ 1967	From Britain with Beat!	1987	15.00
❑ 1968	Here, There and Everywhere	1988	15.00
❑ 1960	Moviemania	1987	15.00
❑ 1961	Not a Second Time	1987	15.00
❑ 1965	Round the World	1986	15.00
❑ 1962	Things We Said Today	1986	15.00
❑ 1966	West Coast Invasion	1985	15.00

CLARION

Number	Title	Yr	NM
❑ 601 [M]	The Amazing Beatles and Other Great English Group Sounds	1966	100.00
❑ SD601 [P]	The Amazing Beatles and Other Great English Group Sounds	1966	200.00
—All four Beatles tracks are rechanneled			

GREAT NORTHWEST

Number	Title	Yr	NM
❑ GNW4007	Beatle Talk	1978	12.00
❑ GNW4007	Beatle Talk	1978	50.00
—Columbia Record Club edition; "CRC" on spine			

HALL OF MUSIC

Number	Title	Yr	NM
❑ HM-1-2200 [M]	Live 1962, Hamburg, Germany	1981	50.00
—Only American LP with the original Eurpoean contents -- "I Saw Her Standing There," "Twist and Shout," "Ask Me Why" and "Reminiscing" replace the four songs listed with the Lingasong issue			

Number	Title	Yr	NM

I-N-S RADIO NEWS

❑ -0 [DJ] — Beatlemania Tour Coverage — 1964 — 1500.00
—Promo-only open-end interview with script in plain white jacket

❑ DOC-1 [DJ] — Beatlemania Tour Coverage — 1964 — 1500.00
—Promo-only open-end interview with script in plain white jacket; VG value 750; VG+ value 1125

LINGASONG

❑ -07001 [DJ] — Live at the Star Club in Hamburg, Germany, 1962 — 1977 — 300.00
—Promo only on blue vinyl

❑ -07001 [DJ] — Live at the Star Club in Hamburg, Germany, 1962 — 1977 — 200.00
—Promo only on red vinyl

❑ -07001 [DJ] — Live at the Star Club in Hamburg, Germany, 1962 — 1977 — 40.00
—Promo on black vinyl; "D.J. Copy Not for Sale" on labels

❑ LS-2-7001 [R] — Live at the Star Club in Hamburg, Germany, 1962 — 1977 — 25.00
—American version contains "I'm Gonna Sit Right Down and Cry," "Where Have You Been All My Life," "Till There Was You," and "Sheila," not on imports

❑ LS-2-7001 [DJ] — Live at the Star Club in Hamburg, Germany, 1962 — 1977 — 300.00
—Promo only on blue vinyl

❑ LS-2-7001 [DJ] — Live at the Star Club in Hamburg, Germany, 1962 — 1977 — 200.00
—Promo only on red vinyl

❑ LS-2-7001 [DJ] — Live at the Star Club in Hamburg, Germany, 1962 — 1977 — 40.00
—Promo on black vinyl; "D.J. Copy Not for Sale" on labels

LLOYDS

❑ ER-MC-LTD — The Great American Tour -- 1965 Live Beatlemania Concert — 1965 — 600.00
—Another interview album from the Ed Rudy people, with a live Beatles show in the background and the songs poorly overdubbed by the Liverpool Lads

METRO

❑ M-563 [M] — This Is Where It Started — 1966 — 100.00
—Reissue of MGM album with two of the "others" tracks deleted

❑ MS-563 [R] — This Is Where It Started — 1966 — 150.00
—In stereo cover

❑ MS-563 [R] — This Is Where It Started — 1966 — 200.00
—In mono cover with "Stereo" sticker

MGM

❑ E-4215 [M] — The Beatles with Tony Sheridan and Their Guests — 1964 — 200.00
—Without "And Guests" on cover

❑ E-4215 [M] — The Beatles with Tony Sheridan and Their Guests — 1964 — 250.00
—With "And Guests" on cover

❑ SE-4215 [R] — The Beatles with Tony Sheridan and Their Guests — 1964 — 600.00
—With "And Guests" on cover

❑ SE-4215 [R] — The Beatles with Tony Sheridan and Their Guests — 1964 — 800.00
—Without "And Guests" on cover

MOBILE FIDELITY

❑ 1-023 — Abbey Road — 1979 — 50.00
—Audiophile vinyl

❑ 1-103 [S] — A Hard Day's Night — 1987 — 40.00
—Audiophile vinyl; British version of album

❑ 1-104 [S] — Beatles for Sale — 1986 — 40.00
—Audiophile vinyl; British version of album

❑ 1-105 [S] — Help! — 1985 — 40.00
—Audiophile vinyl; British version of album

❑ 1-109 — Let It Be — 1987 — 40.00
—Audiophile vinyl; gatefold cover

❑ 1-109 — Let It Be — 1987 — 200.00
—Audiophile vinyl; regular cover

❑ 1-047 [P] — Magical Mystery Tour — 1980 — 60.00
—Audiophile vinyl; yes, this contains the rechanneled stereo versions of "Penny Lane," "Baby You're a Rich Man" and "All You Need Is Love

❑ 1-101 [P] — Please Please Me — 1986 — 40.00
—Audiophile vinyl; British version of album. "Love Me Do" and "P.S. I Love You" are rechanneled.

❑ 1-107 [S] — Revolver — 1986 — 40.00
—Audiophile vinyl; British version of album

❑ 1-106 [S] — Rubber Soul — 1985 — 40.00
—Audiophile vinyl; British version of album

❑ 1-100 [S] — Sgt. Pepper's Lonely Hearts Club Band — 1985 — 40.00
—Audiophile vinyl

❑ UHQR 1-100 [S] — Sgt. Pepper's Lonely Hearts Club Band — 1982 — 300.00
—Ultra High Quality release with special cover; numbered edition of 5,000; numbers under 100 fetch even more

❑ 2-072 — The Beatles — 1982 — 50.00
—Audiophile vinyl; not issued with photos or poster

❑ BC-1 — The Beatles Collection — 1982 — 500.00

❑ 1-102 [S] — With the Beatles — 1986 — 150.00
—Audiophile vinyl; British version of album. Limited run because of a damaged stamper that was not replaced.

❑ 1-108 [P] — Yellow Submarine — 1987 — 60.00
—Audiophile vinyl

ORANGE

❑ -0 [DJ] — The Silver Beatles — 1985 — 300.00
—Test pressing; white cover with title sticker

❑ -0 [DJ] — The Silver Beatles — 1985 — 400.00
—Test pressing; full cover cover slick folded around a white cover. Both contain all 15 Decca audition tracks

❑ ORC-12880 [DJ] — The Silver Beatles — 1985 — 300.00
—Test pressing; white cover with title sticker

❑ ORC-12880 [DJ] — The Silver Beatles — 1985 — 400.00
—Test pressing; full cover cover slick folded around a white cover. Both contain all 15 Decca audition tracks

PBR INTERNATIONAL

❑ 7005/6 — The David Wigg Interviews (The Beatles Tapes) — 1978 — 80.00
—Blue vinyl

❑ 7005/6 — The David Wigg Interviews (The Beatles Tapes) — 1980 — 60.00
—Black vinyl

PHOENIX

❑ P20-623 — 20 Hits, Beatles — 1983 — 25.00
—With 12 Decca audition tracks, four Beatles/Tony Sheridan tracks, and four Tony Sheridan solo tracks

❑ P20-629 — 20 Hits, Beatles — 1983 — 25.00
—With 20 live Hamburg tracks

❑ PHX-352 [M] — Silver Beatles, Volume 1 — 1982 — 15.00
—Contains seven Decca audition tracks

❑ PHX-353 [M] — Silver Beatles, Volume 2 — 1982 — 15.00
—Contains seven Decca audition tracks (different seven than Phoenix 352)

PICKWICK

❑ BAN-90051 [M] — Recorded Live in Hamburg, Vol. 1 — 1978 — 30.00

❑ BAN-90061 [M] — Recorded Live in Hamburg, Vol. 2 — 1978 — 30.00

❑ BAN-90071 [M] — Recorded Live in Hamburg, Vol. 3 — 1978 — 40.00

❑ SPC-3661 [M] — The Beatles' First Live Recordings, Volume 1 — 1979 — 15.00

❑ SPC-3662 [M] — The Beatles' First Live Recordings, Volume 2 — 1979 — 15.00

❑ PTP-2098 [M] — The Historic First Live Recordings — 1980 — 25.00
—Same contents as Lingasong LP, plus "Hully Gully

POLYDOR

❑ 24-4504 [P] — The Beatles -- Circa 1960 -- In the Beginning Featuring Tony Sheridan — 1970 — 30.00
—Originals have gatefold cover

❑ SKAO-93199 [P] — The Beatles -- Circa 1960 -- In the Beginning Featuring Tony Sheridan — 1970 — 40.00
—Capitol Record Club edition

❑ 24-4504 [P] — The Beatles -- Circa 1960 -- In the Beginning Featuring Tony Sheridan — 197? — 40.00
—Some copies of the record contain only the title "The Beatles -- In the Beginning

❑ PD-4504 [P] — The Beatles -- Circa 1960 -- In the Beginning Featuring Tony Sheridan — 1981 — 15.00
—Reissue without gatefold cover

❑ 825073-1 [P] — The Beatles -- Circa 1960 -- In the Beginning Featuring Tony Sheridan — 1988 — 25.00
—Reissue with new number

RADIO PULSEBEAT NEWS

❑ 3 — 1965 Talk Album -- Ed Rudy with New U.S. Tour — 1965 — 150.00
—The Beatles" in black print under front cover photo (other versions appear to be bootlegs)

❑ 2 — The American Tour with Ed Rudy — 1964 — 100.00
—Yellow label; some copies came with a special edition of Teen Talk magazine (add 50%)

❑ 2 — The American Tour with Ed Rudy — 1980 — 30.00
—Blue label; authorized reissue with Beatles' photo on cover

RAVEN/PVC

❑ 8911 [DJ] — Talk Downunder — 1981 — 80.00
—Promo only in white cover with title sticker. Label reads "For Radio Play Only

❑ 8911 — Talk Downunder — 1981 — 12.00

❑ 8911 [DJ] — Talk Downunder — 1981 — 80.00
—Promo only in white cover with title sticker. Label reads "For Radio Play Only

SAVAGE

❑ BM-69 [M] — The Savage Young Beatles — 1964 — 150.00
—Orange label; no legitimate copy says "Stereo" on cover

❑ BM-69 [M] — The Savage Young Beatles — 1964 — 1500.00
—Yellow label, glossy orange cover

SILHOUETTE

❑ SM-10015 — Golden Beatles — 1985 — 18.00

❑ SM-10015 — Golden Beatles — 1985 — 80.00
—Gold vinyl

❑ -0 [DJ] — The British Are Coming — 1984 — 40.00
—White label promo; no numbered sticker

❑ SM-10013 — The British Are Coming — 1984 — 18.00
—Interview album with numbered sticker (very low numbers increase the value)

❑ SM-10013 — The British Are Coming — 1984 — 80.00
—Same as above, but on red vinyl

❑ SM-10013 [DJ] — The British Are Coming — 1984 — 40.00
—White label promo; no numbered sticker

❑ PD-83010 [PD] — The British Are Coming — 1985 — 30.00
—Picture disc

❑ SM-10004 [PD] — Timeless — 1981 — 25.00
—Picture disc with all interviews

❑ SM-10004 [PD] — Timeless — 1981 — 30.00
—Picture disc with interviews plus remakes of "Imagine" and "Let It Be" (by non-Beatles)

❑ SM-10010 [PD] — Timeless II — 1982 — 25.00
—Picture disc with mostly interviews

STERLING

❑ 8895-6481 — I Apologize — 1966 — 300.00
—Same as above, but without photo

❑ 8895-6481 — I Apologize — 1966 — 400.00
—One-sided LP with John Lennon's "apology" for supposed anti-Christian remarks; includes photo

UNITED ARTISTS

❑ UAL3366 [M-DJ] — A Hard Day's Night — 1964 — 3500.00
—White label promo

❑ UAL3366 [M] — A Hard Day's Night — 1964 — 3000.00
—White label promo

❑ UAL3366 [M] — A Hard Day's Night — 1964 — 300.00
—With "I Cry Instead" listing

❑ UAL3366 [M] — A Hard Day's Night — 1964 — 300.00
—With "I'll Cry Instead" listing

❑ UAS6366 [P] — A Hard Day's Night — 1964 — 250.00
—With "I Cry Instead" listing

❑ UAS6366 [P] — A Hard Day's Night — 1964 — 250.00
—With "I'll Cry Instead" listing. Has incidental music by George Martin. All eight Beatles tracks are rechanneled; Martin's are in true stereo.

❑ UAS6366 [P] — A Hard Day's Night — 1964 — 15000.00
—Pink vinyl; only one copy known, probably privately (and secretly) done by a pressing-plant employee; VG value 6000; VG+ value 9000

❑ UAS6366 [P] — A Hard Day's Night — 1968 — 50.00
—Pink and orange label

❑ UAS6366 [P] — A Hard Day's Night — 1970 — 50.00
—Black and orange label

❑ UAS6366 [P] — A Hard Day's Night — 1971 — 25.00
—Tan label

❑ UAS6366 [P] — A Hard Day's Night — 1975 — 25.00
—Tan label with "All Rights Reserved" in perimeter print

❑ UAS6366 [P] — A Hard Day's Night — 1977 — 25.00
—Sunrise label. Note: Any of the variations from 1968 on can have titles of songs incorrectly listed as "I Cry Instead" and "Tell Me Who," or only one can be wrong, or neither can be wrong. No difference in value at this time.

❑ T-90828 [M] — A Hard Day's Night — 1964 — 1500.00
—Capitol Record Club edition; VG value 750; VG+ value 1125

❑ ST-90828 [P] — A Hard Day's Night — 1964 — 750.00
—Capitol Record Club edition

❑ -0 [DJ] — United Artists Presents A Hard Day's Night — 1964 — 1500.00
—Radio spots for movie

❑ -0 [DJ] — United Artists Presents A Hard Day's Night — 1964 — 2500.00
—Open-end interview with script

❑ SP-2362/3 [DJ] — United Artists Presents A Hard Day's Night — 1964 — 2000.00
—Radio spots for movie

❑ SP-2359/60 [DJ] — United Artists Presents A Hard Day's Night — 1964 — 2000.00
—Open-end interview with script; VG value 1000; VG+ value 1500

❑ -0A/B [DJ] — United Artists Presents Help! — 1965 — 2000.00
—Radio spots for movie

❑ -0INT [DJ] — United Artists Presents Help! — 1965 — 2500.00
—Open-end interview with script (red label)

❑ -0Show [DJ] — United Artists Presents Help! — 1965 — 3500.00
—One-sided interview with script (blue label)

❑ UA-Help-0A/B [DJ] — United Artists Presents Help! — 1965 — 2000.00
—Radio spots for movie; VG value 500; VG+ value 1000

❑ UA-Help-0INT [DJ] — United Artists Presents Help! — 1965 — 2000.00
—Open-end interview with script (red label); VG value 1000; VG+ value 1500

❑ UA-Help-0Show [DJ] — United Artists Presents Help! — 1965 — 3000.00
—One-sided interview with script (blue label); VG value 1500; VG+ value 2250

UNITED DISTRIBUTORS

❑ UDL-2333 [M] — Dawn of the Silver Beatles — 1981 — 50.00
—With numbered registration card (deduct 20% if missing)

❑ UDL-2333 [M] — Dawn of the Silver Beatles — 1981 — 60.00
—Hand-stamped numbers on back cover and label; contains 10 Decca audition tracks

❑ UDL-2382 [M] — Lightning Strikes Twice — 1981 — 60.00
—Side 1 has five Beatles' Decca audition tracks; Side 2 has live Elvis Presley performances from 1955

VEE JAY

❑ PRO202 [DJ] — Hear the Beatles Tell All — 1964 — 10000.00
—White label promo with blue print

❑ PRO202 [M] — Hear the Beatles Tell All — 1964 — 200.00
—With "PRO" prefix on label

❑ 202 [M] — Hear the Beatles Tell All — 1964 — 350.00
—Without "PRO" prefix on label

❑ PRO202 [DJ] — Hear the Beatles Tell All — 1964 — 18000.00
—White label promo with blue print; VG value 6000; VG+ value 12000

Number	Title	Yr	NM
❑ PRO202 [M]	Hear the Beatles Tell All	1979	12.00
—Authorized reissue; every copy with the word "Stereo" on the front cover is this edition, though the record still plays in mono (no 1964 copies have "Stereo" on the cover)			
❑ PRO202 [PD]	Hear the Beatles Tell All	1987	25.00
—Shaped picture disc with same recordings as the black vinyl versions			
❑ LP1062 [M]	Introducing the Beatles	1964	5000.00
—Ad back" cover; with "Love Me Do" and "P.S. I Love You"; oval Vee Jay logo with colorband only!; VG value 1500; VG+ value 2750			
❑ SR1062 [B]	Introducing the Beatles	1964	12000.00
—Ad back" cover; with "Love Me Do" and "P.S. I Love You" (both mono); oval Vee Jay logo with colorband only!; VG value 4000; VG+ value 8000			
❑ LP1062 [M]	Introducing the Beatles	1964	1500.00
—Blank back cover; with "Love Me Do" and "P.S. I Love You"; oval Vee Jay logo with colorband only!; VG value 400; VG+ value 800			
❑ SR1062 [B]	Introducing the Beatles	1964	2500.00
—Blank back cover; with "Love Me Do" and "P.S. I Love You"; oval Vee Jay logo with colorband only!			
❑ LP1062 [M]	Introducing the Beatles	1964	1000.00
—Blank back cover; with "Please Please Me" and "Ask Me Why"; oval Vee Jay logo with colorband only!			
❑ LP1062 [M]	Introducing the Beatles	1964	1000.00
—Song titles cover; with "Love Me Do" and "P.S. I Love You"; oval Vee Jay logo with colorband only!			
❑ SR1062 [B]	Introducing the Beatles	1964	10000.00
—Song titles cover; with "Love Me Do" and "P.S. I Love You"; oval Vee Jay logo with colorband only!; VG value 3000; VG+ value 5500; This album has been heavily counterfeited; please check the label of your copy before contacting the author. If the words "Introducing the Beatles" are above the center hole of the record, and the words "The Beatles" are below, it is automatically a counterfeit and almost worthless.			
❑ LP1062 [M]	Introducing the Beatles	1964	400.00
—Song titles cover; with "Please Please Me" and "Ask Me Why"; oval Vee Jay logo with colorband			
❑ LP1062 [M]	Introducing the Beatles	1964	300.00
—Song titles cover; with "Please Please Me" and "Ask Me Why"; brackets Vee Jay logo with colorband (most common authentic version)			
❑ LP1062 [M]	Introducing the Beatles	1964	250.00
—Song titles cover; with "Please Please Me" and "Ask Me Why"; plain Vee Jay logo on solid black label			
❑ LP1062 [M]	Introducing the Beatles	1964	300.00
—Song titles cover; with "Please Please Me" and "Ask Me Why"; oval Vee Jay logo on solid black label			
❑ LP1062 [M]	Introducing the Beatles	1964	1000.00
—Song titles cover; with "Please Please Me" and "Ask Me Why"; brackets Vee Jay logo on solid black label			
❑ SR1062 [S]	Introducing the Beatles	1964	1600.00
—Song titles cover; with "Please Please Me" and "Ask Me Why"; oval Vee Jay logo with colorband			
❑ SR1062 [S]	Introducing the Beatles	1964	1500.00
—Song titles cover; with "Please Please Me" and "Ask Me Why"; brackets Vee Jay logo with colorband			
❑ SR1062 [S]	Introducing the Beatles	1964	1600.00
—Song titles cover; with "Please Please Me" and "Ask Me Why"; plain Vee Jay logo on solid black label			
❑ LP1085 [M]	Jolly What! The Beatles and Frank Ifield on Stage	1964	350.00
—Man in Beatle wig cover; originals have printing on spine and a dark blue/purple background (counterfeits have a black background and no spine print)			
❑ SR1085 [B]	Jolly What! The Beatles and Frank Ifield on Stage	1964	600.00
—Man in Beatle wig cover; "Stereo" on both cover and label. "From Me to You" is mono.			
❑ LP1092 [M]	Songs, Pictures and Stories of the Fabulous Beatles	1964	500.00
—See above; brackets Vee Jay logo with colorband			
❑ LP1092 [M]	Songs, Pictures and Stories of the Fabulous Beatles	1964	500.00
—See above; plain Vee Jay logo on solid black label			
❑ LP1092 [M]	Songs, Pictures and Stories of the Fabulous Beatles	1964	500.00
—See above; oval Vee Jay logo on solid black label			
❑ VJS1092 [S]	Songs, Pictures and Stories of the Fabulous Beatles	1964	2500.00
—See above; brackets Vee Jay logo with colorband; VG value 800; VG+ value 1600			
❑ LP1092 [M]	Songs, Pictures and Stories of the Fabulous Beatles	1964	500.00
—All copies have gatefold cover with 2/3 width on front; also, all copies have "Introducing the Beatles" records. Oval Vee Jay logo with colorband.			
❑ VJS1092 [S]	Songs, Pictures and Stories of the Fabulous Beatles	1964	2500.00
—All copies have gatefold cover with 2/3 width on front; also, all copies have "Introducing the Beatles" records. Oval Vee Jay logo with colorband; VG value 800; VG+ value 1600			
❑ VJS1092 [S]	Songs, Pictures and Stories of the Fabulous Beatles	1964	2500.00
—See above; plain Vee Jay logo on solid black label. NOTE: Any non gatefold copy or any copy called "Songs and Pictures of the Fabulous Beatles" is a counterfeit; VG value 800; VG+ value 1600			
❑ LP1085 [M]	The Beatles and Frank Ifield on Stage	1964	6000.00
—Portrait of Beatles cover; counterfeits are poorly reproduced and have no spine print; VG value 2000; VG+ value 3500			
❑ SR1085 [B]	The Beatles and Frank Ifield on Stage	1964	12000.00
—Portrait of Beatles cover; "Stereo" on both cover and label; VG value 4000; VG+ value 8000			

Number	Title	Yr	NM
❑ DX-30 [M]	The Beatles vs. The Four Seasons	1964	1000.00
—Combines "Introducing the Beatles" with "Golden Hits of the Four Seasons" (Vee Jay 1065)			
❑ DXS-30 [S]	The Beatles vs. The Four Seasons	1964	5000.00
—Combines "Introducing the Beatles" with "Golden Hits of the Four Seasons" (Vee Jay 1065); VG value 1500; VG+ value 2250			
❑ DX(S)-30 [B]	The Beatles vs. The Four Seasons Poster	1964	350.00

BEATNUTS, THE

LOUD/RELATIVITY

❑ 1722	A Musical Massacre	1999	15.00
❑ 1906	Take It or Squeeze It	2001	15.00

RELATIVITY

❑ 1114 [EP]	Intoxicated Demons	1994	12.00
❑ 1508	Stone Crazy	1997	15.00
❑ 1621 [EP]	The Beatnuts Remix EP: The Spot	1998	12.00
❑ 1179	The Beatnuts (Street Level)	1994	15.00

BEATS INTERNATIONAL

ELEKTRA

❑ 60921	Let Them Eat Bingo	1990	18.00

BEAU BRUMMELS, THE

ACCORD

❑ SN-7175	Just a Little	1982	12.00

AUTUMN

❑ LP103 [M]	Introducing the Beau Brummels	1965	60.00
❑ SLP103 [S]	Introducing the Beau Brummels	1965	80.00
❑ LP104 [M]	The Beau Brummels, Volume 2	1965	60.00
❑ SLP104 [S]	The Beau Brummels, Volume 2	1965	80.00

JAS

❑ 5000	Original Hits of the Beau Brummels	1976	18.00

POST

❑ 6000 [B]	The Beau Brummels Sing	196?	25.00

RHINO

❑ RNLP-104	From the Vaults	1981	15.00
❑ RNLP-102	Introducing the Beau Brummels	1981	12.00
❑ RNLP-101	The Best of the Beau Brummels	1981	12.00
❑ RNLP-70171	The Best of the Beau Brummels (Golden Archive Series)	1980	12.00

SUNDAZED

❑ LP5089	Gentle Wanderin' Ways	2001	15.00
❑ LP5000	North Beach Legends	2001	15.00

VAULT

❑ SLP-121	Beau Brummels, Vol. 44	1968	30.00
❑ LP-114 [M]	Best of the Beau Brummels	1967	30.00
❑ SLP-114 [S]	Best of the Beau Brummels	1967	30.00

WARNER BROS.

❑ W1644 [M]	Beau Brummels '66	1966	25.00
❑ WS1644 [S]	Beau Brummels '66	1966	30.00
❑ WS1760	Bradley's Barn	1968	30.00
❑ BS2842	The Beau Brummels	1975	25.00
❑ W1692 [M]	Triangle	1967	25.00
❑ WS1692 [S]	Triangle	1967	30.00

BEAU COUP

AMHERST

❑ AMH3316	Born and Raised on Rock-n-Roll	1987	18.00

BEAUREGARDE

EMPIRE

❑ (no #)0	Beauregarde	1969	100.00

SOUND

❑ 7104 [B]	Beauregarde	1969	100.00

BEAUTIFUL SOUTH, THE

ELEKTRA

❑ 60917	Welcome to the Beautiful South	1989	18.00

BEAUVOIR, JEAN

COLUMBIA

❑ BFC40403	Drums Along the Mohawk	1986	10.00
❑ BFC40621	Jacknifed	1988	10.00

BEAVER, PAUL

RAPTURE

❑ 11111	Perchance to Dream	196?	50.00

BEAVER AND KRAUSE

LIMELIGHT

❑ 86069	Ragnarok -- Electronic Funk	1969	30.00

WARNER BROS.

❑ BS2624	All Good Men	1972	18.00

Number	Title	Yr	NM
❑ WS1909 [B]	Gandharva	1970	18.00
❑ WS1850	In a Wild Sanctuary	1969	18.00

BEBOP AND BEYOND

CONCORD JAZZ

❑ CJ-244	Bebop and Beyond	1984	18.00

BECHET, SIDNEY, AND BOB WILBER

COMMODORE

❑ 15774	New Orleans Style Old and New	198?	12.00

BECHET, SIDNEY, AND BUNK JOHNSON

JAZZ ARCHIVES

❑ JA-48	Bechet, Bunk and Boston 1945	198?	12.00

BECHET, SIDNEY, AND EDDIE CONDON

SAVOY

❑ MG-12208 [M]	We Dig Dixieland	196?	25.00

BECHET, SIDNEY, AND MARTIAL SOLAL

WORLD PACIFIC

❑ PJ-1236 [M]	Young Ideas	1957	80.00
❑ WP-1236 [M]	Young Ideas	1957	60.00
—Reissue with new prefix			

BECHET, SIDNEY, AND MARTY MARSALA

JAZZ ARCHIVES

❑ JA-44	Jazz from California	198?	12.00

BECHET, SIDNEY, AND MEZZ MEZZROW

CLASSIC JAZZ

❑ 28	Sidney Bechet and Mezz Mezzrow	198?	15.00

JAZZ ARCHIVES

❑ JA-39	Really the Blues Concert	198?	12.00

BECHET, SIDNEY, AND MUGGSY SPANIER

ALLEGRO ELITE

❑ 4123 [10]	Bechet-Spanier Quartet	1956	40.00

BECHET, SIDNEY, AND WINGY MANONE

JAZZ ARCHIVES

❑ JA-29	Together at Town Hall, 1947	198?	12.00

BECHET, SIDNEY

ATLANTIC

❑ 1206 [M]	Sidney Bechet Duets	1956	150.00
—With Muggsy Spanier			
❑ ALS-118 [10]	Sidney Bechet Solos	1952	250.00

BLUEBIRD

❑ AXM2-5516	Master Musician	1976	25.00
❑ 6590-1-RB	The Legendary Sidney Bechet	198?	12.00

BLUE NOTE

❑ BLP-7008 [10]	Days Beyond Recall	1951	500.00
❑ BLP-7026 [10]	Dixie by the Fabulous Sidney Bechet	1953	500.00
❑ BLP-1203 [M]	Giant of Jazz, Volume 1	1955	300.00
—Deep groove" version; Lexington Ave. address on label			
❑ BLP-1203 [M]	Giant of Jazz, Volume 1	1955	200.00
—Deep groove" edition, W. 63rd St. address on label			
❑ BST-81203 [R]	Giant of Jazz, Volume 1	1968	25.00
—With "A Division of Liberty Records" on label			
❑ BLP-1203 [M]	Giant of Jazz, Volume 1	1963	60.00
—New York, USA" on label			
❑ BLP-1204 [M]	Giant of Jazz, Volume 2	1955	150.00
—Deep groove" version (deep indentation under label on both sides)			
❑ BLP-1204 [M]	Giant of Jazz, Volume 2	1955	100.00
—Regular edition, Lexington Ave. address on label			
❑ BST-81204 [R]	Giant of Jazz, Volume 2	1968	25.00
—With "A Division of Liberty Records" on label			
❑ BST-81204 [R]	Giant of Jazz, Volume 2	1971	18.00
—With "A Division of United Artists Records" on label			
❑ BLP-7002 [10]	Jazz Classics, Volume 1	1950	500.00
❑ BLP-1201 [M]	Jazz Classics, Volume 1	1955	300.00
—Deep groove" version; Lexington Ave. address on label			
❑ BLP-1201 [M]	Jazz Classics, Volume 1	1958	200.00
—Deep groove" edition, W. 63rd St. address on label			
❑ BST-81201 [R]	Jazz Classics, Volume 1	1968	25.00
—With "A Division of Liberty Records" on label			
❑ BLP-1201 [M]	Jazz Classics, Volume 1	1963	80.00
—New York, USA" on label			
❑ BLP-7003 [10]	Jazz Classics, Volume 2	1950	500.00
❑ BLP-1202 [M]	Jazz Classics, Volume 2	1955	300.00
—Deep groove" version; Lexington Ave. address on label			
❑ BLP-1202 [M]	Jazz Classics, Volume 2	1958	200.00
—Deep groove" edition, W. 63rd St. address on label			
❑ BST-81202 [R]	Jazz Classics, Volume 2	1968	25.00
—With "A Division of Liberty Records" on label			
❑ BLP-1202 [M]	Jazz Classics, Volume 2	1963	80.00
—New York, USA" on label			
❑ BLP-7024 [10]	Jazz Festival Concert, Paris 1952 -- Volume 1	1953	500.00

Number	Title	Yr	NM
❏ BLP-7025 [10]	Jazz Festival Concert, Paris 1952 -- Volume 2	1953	500.00
❏ BLP-7029 [10]	Olympia Concert, Paris 1954 – Volume 1	1954	500.00
❏ BLP-7030 [10]	Olympia Concert, Paris 1954 – Volume 2	1954	500.00
❏ BLP-7001 [10]	Sidney Bechet's Blue Note Jazz Men	1950	1000.00
❏ BLP-7014 [10]	Sidney Bechet's Blue Note Jazz Men, Volume 2	1951	500.00
❏ BLP-7009 [10]	Sidney Bechet with the Blue Note Jazz Men	1951	500.00
❏ BLP-1207 [M]	The Fabulous Sidney Bechet	1956	250.00
— Deep groove" version; Lexington Ave. address on label			
❏ BLP-1207 [M]	The Fabulous Sidney Bechet	1956	200.00
— Deep groove" edition, W. 63rd St. address on label			
❏ BST-81207 [R]	The Fabulous Sidney Bechet	1968	15.00
— With "A Division of Liberty Records" on label			
❏ BLP-7020 [10]	The Fabulous Sidney Bechet and His Hot Six	1952	500.00
❏ BLP-7022 [10]	The Port of Harlem Six	1952	500.00
BRUNSWICK			
❏ BL54037 [M]	Sidney Bechet in Paris	1958	80.00
❏ BL54048 [M]	The Sidney Bechet Story	1959	60.00
COLUMBIA			
❏ CL836 [M]	Grand Master of the Soprano Sax and Clarinet	1956	60.00
— Red and black label with six "eye" logos			
❏ CL1410 [M]	Sidney Bechet In Concert at the Brussels Fair	1960	40.00
— Red and black label with six "eye" logos			
COMMODORE			
❏ FL-20020 [10]	New Orleans Style, Old and New	1952	250.00
DIAL			
❏ LP-301 [10]	Black Stick	195?	600.00
❏ LP-302 [10]	Sidney Bechet with Wally Bishop's Orchestra	195?	600.00
EVEREST ARCHIVE OF FOLK & JAZZ			
❏ FS-323	Sidney Bechet Volume 2	197?	15.00
❏ FS-228	Sidney Bechet with Guest Artist Lionel Hampton	1969	15.00
GNP CRESCENDO			
❏ GNP-9012	Sidney Bechet	197?	15.00
❏ GNP-9037	The Legendary Sidney Bechet	1976	15.00
GOOD TIME JAZZ			
❏ L-12013 [M]	King of the Soprano Saxophone	1955	50.00
JAZZOLOGY			
❏ J-35	The Genius of Sidney Bechet	197?	15.00
JAZZ PANORAMA			
❏ 1801 [10]	Sidney Bechet, Vol. 1	1951	200.00
❏ 1809 [10]	Sidney Bechet, Vol. 2	1951	200.00
JOLLY ROGER			
❏ 5028 [10]	Sidney Bechet	1954	80.00
LONDON			
❏ WV91050 [10]	La Nuit Est Une Sorciere	1955	80.00
MCA			
❏ 1330	Blackstick	198?	12.00
MOSAIC			
❏ MR6-110	The Complete Blue Note Recordings of Sidney Bechet	198?	250.00
— Limited edition of 7,500			
RCA VICTOR			
❏ LPV-510 [M]	Bechet of New Orleans	1965	30.00
— Purple label original			
❏ LPV-510 [M]	Bechet of New Orleans	1969	25.00
— Orange label reissue			
❏ LPV-535 [M]	Blue Bechet	1966	30.00
❏ LPT-22 [10]	Sidney Bechet	1951	300.00
❏ LPT-31 [10]	Treasury of Immortal Performances	1951	300.00
REPRISE			
❏ R-6076 [M]	The Immortal Sidney Bechet	1963	30.00
❏ R9-6076 [R]	The Immortal Sidney Bechet	1963	25.00
RIVERSIDE			
❏ RLP-2516 [10]	Sidney Bechet and His Soprano Sax	1955	250.00
RONDO-LETTE			
❏ A24 [M]	Jam Session Vintage 1946	1953	30.00
SAVOY			
❏ MG-15013 [10]	Sidney Bechet	1952	250.00
STINSON			
❏ 46 [R]	Haitian Moods	196?	15.00
STORYVILLE			
❏ 4028	Sessions	198?	12.00
❏ STLP-902 [M]	Sidney Bechet at Storyville	1955	50.00
❏ STLP-301 [10]	Sidney Bechet at Storyville, Vol. 1	1954	200.00
❏ STLP-306 [10]	Sidney Bechet at Storyville, Vol. 2	1954	200.00
TIME-LIFE			
❏ STL-J-09	Giants of Jazz	1980	25.00

Number	Title	Yr	NM
X			
❏ LVA-3024 [10]	Sidney Bechet and His New Orleans Feetwarmers	1954	120.00

BECHET, SIDNEY / OMER SIMEON

JAZZTONE

❏ J-1213 [M]	Jazz A La Creole	1955	40.00

BECK, BOGERT & APPICE

EPIC

❏ KE32140	Beck, Bogert & Appice	1973	18.00
— Yellow label			
❏ KE32140	Beck, Bogert & Appice	1973	12.00
— Orange label			
❏ CQ32140 [Q]	Beck, Bogert & Appice	1973	30.00
❏ PE32140	Beck, Bogert & Appice	198?	10.00
— Budget-line reissue			

BECK, JEFF

ACCORD

❏ SN-7141	Early Anthology	1981	12.00

EPIC

❏ BN26478	Beck-Ola	1969	18.00
— Yellow label			
❏ BN26478	Beck-Ola	1973	12.00
— Orange label			
❏ PE26478	Beck-Ola	197?	10.00
— Reissue with new prefix			
❏ PE33409	Blow by Blow	1975	12.00
— Orange label, no bar code on cover			
❏ PEQ33409 [Q]	Blow by Blow	1975	30.00
❏ HE43409	Blow by Blow	1980	30.00
— Half-speed mastered edition			
❏ PE33409	Blow by Blow	198?	10.00
— Reissue with dark blue label and bar code on cover			
❏ AS151 [DJ]	Everything You Always Wanted to Hear by Jeff Beck But Were Afraid to Ask For	1977	25.00
— Promo-only sampler			
❏ AS151 [DJ]	Everything You Always Wanted to Hear by Jeff Beck But Were Afraid to Ask For	1977	25.00
— Promo-only sampler			
❏ FE39483	Flash	1985	12.00
❏ KE31331	Jeff Beck Group	1972	18.00
— Yellow label			
❏ KE31331	Jeff Beck Group	1973	12.00
— Orange label			
❏ EQ31331 [Q]	Jeff Beck Group	1972	30.00
❏ PE31331	Jeff Beck Group	198?	10.00
— Budget-line reissue			
❏ FE44313	Jeff Beck's Guitar Shop	1989	18.00
❏ PE34433	Jeff Beck with the Jan Hammer Group Live	1977	12.00
— Orange label, no bar code on cover			
❏ PE34433	Jeff Beck with the Jan Hammer Group Live	198?	10.00
— Reissue with dark blue label and bar code on cover			
❏ KE30993	Rough and Ready	1971	18.00
— Yellow label			
❏ KE30993	Rough and Ready	1973	12.00
— Orange label			
❏ EQ30993 [Q]	Rough and Ready	1972	30.00
❏ PE30973	Rough and Ready	198?	10.00
— Budget-line reissue			
❏ A2S850 [DJ]	Then and Now	1981	30.00
— Promo-only sampler			
❏ A2S850 [DJ]	Then and Now	1981	30.00
— Promo-only sampler			
❏ FE35684	There and Back	1980	12.00
❏ PE35684	There and Back	1985	10.00
— Budget-line reissue			
❏ BN26413 [S]	Truth	1968	25.00
— Yellow label			
❏ BN26413 [B]	Truth	1973	12.00
— Orange label			
❏ PE26413	Truth	198?	10.00
— Reissue with new prefix			
❏ BN26413 [M]	Truth	1968	80.00
— Mono is promo only with stereo number; cover has "Mono" sticker covering the word "Stereo			
❏ BG33779 [B]	Truth/Beck-Ola	1975	18.00
❏ PE33849	Wired	1976	12.00
— Orange label, no bar code on cover			
❏ PEQ33849 [Q]	Wired	1976	30.00
❏ PE33849	Wired	1979	10.00
— Reissue with dark blue label; with or without bar code on cover			
❏ HE43849	Wired	198?	30.00
— Half-speed mastered edition			

BECK, JOE

CTI

❏ 8002	Beck & Sanborn	1979	12.00
— Reissue of Kudu 21 with new title			

CTI/CBS ASSOCIATED

❏ FZ40805	Beck & Sanborn	1987	12.00

Number	Title	Yr	NM
KUDU			
❏ 21	Beck	1975	15.00
POLYDOR			
❏ PD-1-6092	Watch the Time	1976	12.00

BECK, PIA

EPIC

❏ LN3269 [M]	Dutch Treat	1956	40.00

BECK

BONG LOAD

❏ BL12 [B]	Mellow Gold	1993	60.00
❏ BL46 [B]	Midnite Vultures	2000	80.00
❏ BL39	Mutations	1999	50.00
— Includes bonus 7-inch single with sleeve			
❏ BL30 [B]	Odelay	1996	50.00
DGC			
❏ B0004372-01	Sea Change	2006	18.00
— CD version issued in 2002			
FINGERPAINT			
❏ 02 [10]	A Western Harvest Field by Moonlight	1992	75.00
— First 3,000 contain a unique insert fingerpainted by Beck and friends at the record release party			
❏ 02 [10]	A Western Harvest Field by Moonlight	1995	50.00
— Later pressings do not contain a fingerpainted insert			
FLIPSIDE			
❏ 660 [B]	Stereopathetic Soulmanure	2000	30.00
— Vinyl issue of 1994 CD compilation			
ILIAD/K			
❏ 1282901	One Foot in the Grave	2009	30.00
— Expanded two LP edition			
INTERSCOPE			
❏ B0003546-1	Guero	2005	30.00
❏ B0005650-01	Guerolito	2006	18.00
❏ 1163001 [B]	Modern Guilt	2008	25.00
K			
❏ KLP28	One Foot in the Grave	1994	50.00

BECK FAMILY, THE

LEJOINT

❏ LEJ-17001	Dancin' on the Ceiling	1979	12.00

BECKMEIER BROTHERS

CASABLANCA

❏ NBLP-7147	Beckmeier Brothers	1979	15.00

BEDIENT, JACK

EXECUTIVE PRODUCTIONS

❏ (no #)0 [M]	Jack Bedient	196?	80.00
FANTASY			
❏ 3365 [M]	Live at Harvey's	1965	60.00
SATORI			
❏ LP1001 [M]	Where Did She Go?	1967	200.00
TROPHY			
❏ 101 [M]	Two Sides of Jack Bedient	1964	60.00

BEDLAM

CHRYSALIS

❏ CHR-1048	Bedlam	1973	30.00

BEE, CELI

APA

❏ 77002	Alternating Currents	1978	18.00
❏ 77005	Blow My Mind	1979	18.00
❏ 77001	Celi Bee and the Buzzy Bunch	1977	18.00
❏ 77003	Fly Me on the Wings of Love	1979	18.00

BEE, DAVID

BALLY

❏ BAL-12005 [M]	Belgian Jazz	1956	30.00
JUBILEE			
❏ JLP-1076 [M]	Dixieland at the World's Fair	1958	30.00

BEE, MOLLY

ACCORD

❏ 7901	Sounds Fine to Me	1982	12.00
CAPITOL			
❏ T1097 [M]	Young Romance	1958	40.00
GRANITE			
❏ 1002	Good Golly Ms. Molly	1974	15.00
MGM			
❏ E-4303 [M]	It's Great, It's Molly Bee	1965	25.00
❏ SE-4303 [S]	It's Great, It's Molly Bee	1965	30.00
❏ E-4423 [M]	Swingin' Country	1967	25.00
❏ SE-4423 [S]	Swingin' Country	1967	30.00

Number	Title	Yr	NM

BEE GEES

ATCO
❑ 33-353 [M]	2 Years On	1971	40.00
—White label promo only; "DJ Copy Monaural" sticker on cover
❑ SD 33-353 [S]	2 Years On	1971	15.00
❑ 33-223 [M]	Bee Gees' 1st	1967	40.00
❑ SD 33-223 [S]	Bee Gees' 1st	1967	25.00
—Brown and purple label original
❑ SD 33-223	Bee Gees' 1st	1969	12.00
—Yellow label reissue
❑ 33-292 [M]	Best of Bee Gees	1969	30.00
—White label promo only
❑ SD 33-292	Best of Bee Gees	1969	15.00
❑ SD 33-327	Cucumber Castle	1970	15.00
❑ 33-233 [M]	Horizontal	1968	40.00
❑ SD 33-233 [S]	Horizontal	1968	25.00
—Brown and purple label original
❑ SD 33-233	Horizontal	1969	12.00
—Yellow label reissue
❑ 33-253 [M]	Idea	1968	50.00
—White label promo only
❑ SD 33-253 [S]	Idea	1968	25.00
—Brown and purple label original
❑ SD 33-253	Idea	1969	12.00
—Yellow label reissue
❑ SD 2-702 [B]	Odessa	1969	80.00
—Red felt cover
❑ SD 2-702	Odessa	1969	80.00
—Record club editions with plain red cover
❑ 33-264 [M]	Rare, Precious & Beautiful	1968	30.00
—White label promo only
❑ SD 33-264 [R]	Rare, Precious & Beautiful	1968	18.00
—Brown and purple label original
❑ SD 33-264	Rare, Precious & Beautiful	1969	12.00
—Yellow label reissue
❑ 33-321 [M]	Rare, Precious & Beautiful, Volume 2	1970	30.00
—White label promo only
❑ SD 33-321 [R]	Rare, Precious & Beautiful, Volume 2	1970	15.00
❑ SD7012	To Whom It May Concern	1972	15.00
❑ SD7003	Trafalgar	1971	15.00

MOBILE FIDELITY
❑ 1-263 [B]	Trafalgar	1996	60.00
—Audiophile vinyl

NAUTILUS
❑ NR-42 [B]	Living Eyes	1982	200.00
—Record was never released; value is for test pressings
❑ NR-17	Spirits Having Flown	1981	30.00

PICKWICK
❑ BAN-90021 [R]	Monday's Rain	1978	10.00
—Reissue of Australian recordings
❑ BAN-90041 [R]	Peace of Mind	1978	10.00
—Reissue of Australian recordings; tracks on this LP were making their first appearance in the U.S.
❑ BAN-90031 [R]	Take Hold of That Star	1978	10.00
—Reissue of Australian recordings
❑ BAN-90011 [R]	Turn Around, Look at Me	1978	10.00
—Reissue of Australian recordings

RSO
❑ RS-1-3006	Bee Gees Gold, Volume One	1976	12.00
❑ 823659-1	Bee Gees Gold, Volume One	1984	10.00
❑ RS-2-4200	Bee Gees' Greatest	1979	15.00
❑ 825390-1	Bee Gees' Greatest	1984	12.00
—Gatefold replaced by single-pocket cover
❑ SO874	Best of Bee Gees	1973	12.00
—Reissue of Atco SD 33-292
❑ SO875	Best of Bee Gees, Vol. 2	1973	12.00
❑ RS-1-3003	Children of the World	1976	12.00
❑ 823658-1	Children of the World	1984	10.00
❑ RS-2-3901	Here At Last...Bee Gees... Live	1977	15.00
❑ 823274-1	Here At Last...Bee Gees... Live	1984	12.00
❑ SO870 [S]	Life in a Tin Can	1973	12.00
—Side 1 master number is "ST-SO-722677"; Side 2 master number is "ST-SO-722678"
❑ SO870 [M]	Life in a Tin Can	1973	60.00
—Mono is white label promo only; cover has red "d/j copy monaural" sticker on front; Side 1 master number is "SO-14153"; Side 2 master number is "SO-14154"
❑ RS-1-3098	Living Eyes	1981	12.00
❑ SO4807 [B]	Main Course	1975	12.00
❑ RS-1-3024	Main Course	1977	10.00
❑ SO4800	Mr. Natural	1974	12.00
❑ RS-1-3007	Odessa	1976	12.00
—Condensed version of Atco original
❑ PRO33 [DJ]	Saturday Night Fever Special Disco Versions	1978	50.00
—Promo-only sampler; contains an otherwise unavailable extended version of "Stayin' Alive"
❑ PRO 033 [DJ]	Saturday Night Fever Special Disco Versions	1978	50.00
—Promo-only sampler; contains an otherwise unavailable extended version of "Stayin' Alive"
❑ PRO0 [DJ]	Select Disco Cuts from "Spirits Having Flown"	1979	30.00
❑ RPO1008 [DJ]	Select Disco Cuts from "Spirits Having Flown"	1979	30.00
❑ RS-1-3041	Spirits Having Flown	1979	12.00
—Some pressings have a cardboard innersleeve, others a paper innersleeve. No difference in value.
❑ RS-1-3042 [PD]	Spirits Having Flown	1979	18.00
❑ -0 [DJ]	The Words and Music of Maurice, Barry and Robin Gibb	1979	50.00
—Promo-only publisher's sampler
❑ SMP-1 [DJ]	The Words and Music of Maurice, Barry and Robin Gibb	1979	50.00
—Promo-only publisher's sampler
❑ -0 [DJ]	Unichappell Publisher's Sampler	1980	50.00
❑ PUB-1000 [DJ]	Unichappell Publisher's Sampler	1980	50.00

WARNER BROS.
❑ 25541	E.S.P.	1987	12.00
❑ 25887	One	1989	15.00

BEEBE, JIM, 'S CHICAGO JAZZ

DELMARK
❑ DS-219	Cornet Chop Suey	1980	12.00
—With Tommy Bridges
❑ DS-218	Saturday Night Function	1979	12.00

BEENIE MAN

ARTISTS ONLY
❑ 31	Y2K	1999	15.00

VIRGIN
❑ 49093	Art & Life	2000	18.00

VP
❑ 1413	Beenie Man Meets Mad Cobra	1995	15.00
❑ 1605	Best of Beenie Man	2000	18.00
❑ 1547	Doctor	1999	15.00
❑ 1486	Maestro	199?	15.00
❑ 1513	Many Moods of Moses	1998	15.00

BEERS FAMILY, THE

BIOGRAPH
❑ BLP-12033	The Seasons of Peace -- A Great Family Sings	1971	15.00
—Evelyne and Bob Beers; Martha and Eric Nagler; Bill, Janet, Susan, Joe, Becky and John Boyer (all related). In all, 15 songs are on this LP, the following of which are Christmas-related:

COLUMBIA MASTERWORKS
❑ ML6335 [M]	Christmas with the Beers Family	1966	15.00
—Evelyne, Bob and Martha Beers
❑ MS6935 [S]	Christmas with the Beers Family	1966	18.00
—Same as above, but in stereo

BEETHOVEN SOUL

DOT
❑ DLP-3821 [M]	Beethoven Soul	1967	30.00
❑ DLP-25821 [S]	Beethoven Soul	1967	30.00

BEGINNING OF THE END, THE

ALSTON
❑ SD 33-379 [B]	Funky Nassau	1971	25.00

BEIDERBECKE, BIX

BLUEBIRD
❑ 6845-1-R	Bix Lives!	1989	15.00

COLUMBIA
❑ GL507 [M]	The Bix Beiderbecke Story, Volume 1: Bix and His Gang	1952	50.00
—Black label, silver print
❑ CL507 [M]	The Bix Beiderbecke Story, Volume 1: Bix and His Gang	1953	40.00
—Maroon label, gold print
❑ CL844 [M]	The Bix Beiderbecke Story, Volume 1: Bix and His Gang	1956	30.00
—Red and black label with six "eye" logos
❑ CL844 [M]	The Bix Beiderbecke Story, Volume 1: Bix and His Gang	1963	25.00
—Guaranteed High Fidelity" label
❑ CL844 [M]	The Bix Beiderbecke Story, Volume 1: Bix and His Gang	1966	18.00
—360 Sound" label
❑ CL844 [M]	The Bix Beiderbecke Story, Volume 1: Bix and His Gang	1970	15.00
—Orange label
❑ GL508 [M]	The Bix Beiderbecke Story, Volume 2: Bix and Tram	1952	50.00
—Black label, silver print
❑ CL508 [M]	The Bix Beiderbecke Story, Volume 2: Bix and Tram	1953	40.00
—Maroon label, gold print
❑ CL845 [M]	The Bix Beiderbecke Story, Volume 2: Bix and Tram	1956	30.00
—Red and black label with six "eye" logos
❑ CL845 [M]	The Bix Beiderbecke Story, Volume 2: Bix and Tram	1963	25.00
—Guaranteed High Fidelity" label
❑ CL845 [M]	The Bix Beiderbecke Story, Volume 2: Bix and Tram	1966	18.00
—360 Sound" label
❑ CL845 [M]	The Bix Beiderbecke Story, Volume 2: Bix and Tram	1970	15.00
—Orange label
❑ GL509 [M]	The Bix Beiderbecke Story, Volume 3: The Whiteman Years	1952	50.00
—Black label, silver print
❑ CL509 [M]	The Bix Beiderbecke Story, Volume 3: The Whiteman Years	1953	40.00
—Maroon label, gold print
❑ CL846 [M]	The Bix Beiderbecke Story, Volume 3: The Whiteman Years	1956	30.00
—Red and black label with six "eye" logos
❑ CL846 [M]	The Bix Beiderbecke Story, Volume 3: The Whiteman Years	1963	25.00
—Guaranteed High Fidelity" label
❑ CL846 [M]	The Bix Beiderbecke Story, Volume 3: The Whiteman Years	1966	18.00
—360 Sound" label
❑ CL846 [M]	The Bix Beiderbecke Story, Volume 3: The Whiteman Years	1970	15.00
—Orange label

COLUMBIA MASTERWORKS
❑ ML4811 [M]	The Bix Beiderbecke Story, Volume 1	1950	70.00
❑ ML4812 [M]	The Bix Beiderbecke Story, Volume 2	1950	70.00
❑ ML4813 [M]	The Bix Beiderbecke Story, Volume 3	1950	70.00

EVEREST ARCHIVE OF FOLK & JAZZ
❑ 317	Bix Beiderbecke	197?	12.00

JAZZ TREASURY
❑ S-1003	Bix Beiderbecke with the Wolverines	197?	15.00

JOLLY ROGER
❑ 5010 [10]	Bix Beiderbecke	1954	50.00

MILESTONE
❑ 47019	Bix Beiderbecke and the Chicago Cornets	197?	18.00

OLYMPIC
❑ 7130	Bix Beiderbecke and the Wolverines 1924	198?	12.00

RCA VICTOR
❑ LPM-2323 [M]	The Bix Beiderbecke Legend	1961	30.00
—Long Play" on label
❑ LPM-2323 [M]	The Bix Beiderbecke Legend	1963	18.00
—Mono" or "Monaural" on label

RIVERSIDE
❑ RLP-1050 [10]	Bix Beiderbecke and the Wolverines	1954	80.00
❑ RLP 12-123 [M]	Bix Beiderbecke and the Wolverines	1956	50.00
—White label, blue print
❑ RLP 12-123 [M]	Bix Beiderbecke and the Wolverines	195?	30.00
—Blue label with microphone logo
❑ RLP-1023 [10]	Early Bix	1954	80.00

TIME-LIFE
❑ STL-J-04	Giants of Jazz	1979	25.00

BEIRACH, RICHIE, AND JOHN ABERCROMBIE

PATHFINDER
❑ PTF-8701	Emerald City	1988	12.00

BEIRACH, RICHIE

ECM
❑ 1142	Elm	1979	15.00
❑ 1054	Eon	197?	18.00
❑ 1104	Hubris	1977	15.00

MAGENTA
❑ MA-0202	Breathing of Statues	1985	12.00

PATHFINDER
❑ PTF-8617	Antarctica	1987	12.00

BEL-AIRE GIRLS, THE

EVEREST
❑ LPBR-5081 [M]	The Bel-Aire Girls Sing Along with the Teen-Agers	1960	60.00
❑ STBR-1081 [S]	The Bel-Aire Girls Sing Along with the Teen-Agers	1960	80.00

BEL-AIRE POPS ORCHESTRA, THE

LIBERTY
❑ LRP-3414 [M]	Jan and Dean's Pop Symphony No. 1	1965	120.00
❑ LST-7414 [S]	Jan and Dean's Pop Symphony No. 1	1965	200.00

Number	Title	Yr	NM

BELAFONTE, HARRY

COLUMBIA

❏ FC37489	Loving You Is Where I Belong	1981	12.00

DCC COMPACT CLASSICS

❏ LPZ-2039	Jump Up Calypso	1997	60.00

— Audiophile vinyl

EMI

❏ E1-92247	Belafonte '89	1989	15.00

EMI MANHATAN

❏ E1-46971	Paradise in Gazankulu	1988	15.00

PAIR

❏ PDL2-1060	The Belafonte Song Book	1986	15.00

RCA CAMDEN

❏ ACL1-0502	Abraham, Martin and John	1974	12.00
❏ CAS-2599	Harry	1972	12.00

RCA CUSTOM EDITION

❏ DRL1-0068	I Wish You a Merry Christmas	1973	18.00

— Reissue of LSP-2424 with two tracks deleted

RCA VICTOR

❏ CPL1-2469	A Legendary Performer	1977	12.00
❏ LPM-1402 [M]	An Evening with Belafonte	1957	30.00
❏ LSP-1402(e) [R]	An Evening with Belafonte	1960	15.00
— Dog on top			
❏ LSP-1402(e) [R]	An Evening with Belafonte	1969	12.00
— Orange label			
❏ ANL1-1434	An Evening with Belafonte	1976	12.00
— Reissue of LSP-1402			
❏ LPM-3420 [M]	An Evening with Belafonte/ Makeba	1965	18.00
❏ LSP-3420 [S]	An Evening with Belafonte/ Makeba	1965	25.00
— With Miriam Makeba			
❏ LPM-3415 [M]	An Evening with Belafonte/ Mouskouri	1966	18.00
❏ LSP-3415 [S]	An Evening with Belafonte/ Mouskouri	1966	25.00
— With Nana Mouskouri			
❏ LPM-2309 [M]	At Home and Abroad	1961	25.00
❏ LSP-2309 [S]	At Home and Abroad	1961	30.00
❏ LPM-2953 [M]	Ballads, Blues and Boasters	1964	18.00
❏ LSP-2953 [S]	Ballads, Blues and Boasters	1964	25.00
❏ LPM-1150 [M]	Belafonte	1955	50.00
❏ LSP-1150(e) [R]	Belafonte	196?	15.00
❏ LOC-6006 [M]	Belafonte at Carnegie Hall	1959	30.00
❏ LSO-6006 [S]	Belafonte at Carnegie Hall	1959	100.00
❏ LSO-6006 [S]	Belafonte at Carnegie Hall	1996	40.00
— Classic Records reissue on audiophile vinyl			
❏ LOC-6009 [M]	Belafonte at the Greek Theatre	1964	25.00
❏ LSO-6009 [S]	Belafonte at the Greek Theatre	1964	50.00
❏ VPSX-6077	Belafonte Live	1972	18.00
❏ LPM-3779 [M]	Belafonte on Campus	1967	15.00
❏ LSP-3779 [S]	Belafonte on Campus	1967	18.00
❏ LOC-6007 [M]	Belafonte Returns to Carnegie Hall	1960	25.00
❏ LSO-6007 [S]	Belafonte Returns to Carnegie Hall	1960	50.00
— The above LP also has tracks by Odetta, Miriam Makeba and The Chad Mitchell Trio (the latter for the first time on record)			
❏ LSO-6007	Belafonte Returns to Carnegie Hall	1996	40.00
— Classic Records reissue on audiophile vinyl			
❏ LPM-3938 [M]	Belafonte Sings of Love	1968	18.00
❏ LSP-3938 [S]	Belafonte Sings of Love	1968	18.00
❏ LPM-1505 [M]	Belafonte Sings of the Caribbean	1957	30.00
❏ LSP-1505(e) [R]	Belafonte Sings of the Caribbean	196?	15.00
❏ LOP-1006 [M]	Belafonte Sings the Blues	1958	30.00
— Original issue			
❏ LPM-1972 [M]	Belafonte Sings the Blues	1959	25.00
— Reissue of LOP-1006			

❏ LSP-1972 [S]	Belafonte Sings the Blues	1959	30.00
❏ LSP-1972	Belafonte Sings the Blues	199?	30.00
— Classic Records reissue on audiophile vinyl			
❏ LSP-4301	By Request	1970	15.00
❏ LPM-1248 [M]	Calypso	1956	30.00
❏ LSP-1248(e) [R]	Calypso	196?	15.00
❏ AYL1-3801(e) [R]	Calypso	1980	10.00
❏ AFL1-1248	Calypso	1977	12.00
— Reissue with new prefix			
❏ LSP-4521	Calypso Carnival	1971	15.00
❏ LPM-3658 [M]	Calypso in Brass	1967	15.00
❏ LSP-3658 [S]	Calypso in Brass	1967	18.00
❏ LSP-4255	Homeward Bound	1969	18.00
❏ LPM-3571 [M]	In My Quiet Room	1966	15.00
❏ LSP-3571 [S]	In My Quiet Room	1966	18.00
❏ LPM-2388 [M]	Jump Up Calypso	1961	25.00
❏ LSP-2388 [S]	Jump Up Calypso	1961	30.00
❏ LPM-1927 [M]	Love Is a Gentle Thing	1959	25.00
❏ LSP-1927 [S]	Love Is a Gentle Thing	1959	30.00
❏ LPM-1022 [M]	Mark Twain" and Other Folk Favorites	1954	50.00
❏ LSP-1022(e) [R]	Mark Twain" and Other Folk Favorites	196?	15.00
❏ LPM-2022 [M]	My Lord What a Mornin'	1960	25.00
❏ LSP-2022 [S]	My Lord What a Mornin'	1960	30.00
❏ APL1-0094	Play Me	1973	15.00
❏ LOC-1507 [M]	Porgy and Bess	1959	25.00
❏ LSO-1507 [S]	Porgy and Bess	1959	30.00
— With Lena Horne			
❏ AYL1-3860(e) [R]	Pure Gold	1980	10.00
❏ ANL1-0979	Pure Gold	1975	12.00
❏ LPM-2695 [M]	Streets I Have Walked	1963	25.00
❏ LSP-2695 [S]	Streets I Have Walked	1963	30.00
❏ LPM-2194 [M]	Swing Dat Hammer	1961	25.00
❏ LSP-2194 [S]	Swing Dat Hammer	1961	30.00
❏ LPM-2574 [M]	The Many Moods of Belafonte	1962	25.00
❏ LSP-2574 [S]	The Many Moods of Belafonte	1962	30.00
— Living Stereo" on label, "RCA Victor" in silver			
❏ LSP-2574 [S]	The Many Moods of Belafonte	196?	25.00
— Stereo" on black label, "RCA Victor" in white			
❏ LSP-2574 [S]	The Many Moods of Belafonte	1969	15.00
— Orange label			
❏ LPM-2449 [M]	The Midnight Special	1962	30.00
❏ LSP-2449 [S]	The Midnight Special	1962	40.00
— The above LP features Bob Dylan on harmonica on the title track, his first appearance on record			
❏ ANL2-2324	The Midnight Special	1976	12.00
— Reissue of LSP-2449			
❏ VPS-6024	This Is Harry Belafonte	1970	18.00
❏ LPM-2626 [M]	To Wish You a Merry Christmas	1962	25.00
— Reissue of LPM-1887 with new cover and one additional track			
❏ LSP-2626 [S]	To Wish You a Merry Christmas	1962	30.00
❏ LPM-1887 [M]	To Wish You a Merry Christmas	1958	30.00
❏ LSP-1887 [S]	To Wish You a Merry Christmas	1958	40.00
❏ LSP-4481	Warm Touch	1971	15.00

TIME-LIFE

❏ SLGD-17	Legendary Singers: Harry Belafonte	1986	18.00

BELEW, ADRIAN

ATLANTIC

❏ 81959	Mr. Music Head	1989	12.00
❏ 82099	Young Lions	1990	15.00

ISLAND

❏ 90551	Desire Caught by the Tail	1986	12.00
❏ IL9751	Lone Rhino	1982	15.00
❏ 90108 [B]	Twang Bar King	1983	12.00

BELEW, CARL, AND BETTY JEAN ROBINSON

DECCA

❏ DL75337	When My Baby Sings His Song	1972	18.00

BELEW, CARL

BUCKBOARD

❏ BBS1014	Singing My Song	197?	12.00

DECCA

❏ DL4074 [M]	Carl Belew	1960	30.00
❏ DL74074 [S]	Carl Belew	1960	30.00

HILLTOP

❏ JM-6013 [M]	Another Lonely Night	1965	25.00
❏ JS-6013 [S]	Another Lonely Night	1965	25.00

PICCADILLY

❏ 3356	Big Time Gambling Man	198?	12.00

RCA VICTOR

❏ LPM-3381 [M]	Am I That Easy to Forget?	1965	25.00
❏ LSP-3381 [S]	Am I That Easy to Forget?	1965	30.00
❏ LPM-2848 [M]	Hello Out There	1964	25.00
❏ LSP-2848 [S]	Hello Out There	1964	30.00
❏ LPM-3919 [M]	Twelve Shades of Belew	1968	50.00
❏ LSP-3919 [S]	Twelve Shades of Belew	1968	25.00

VOCALION

❏ VL73774 [S]	Country Songs	196?	15.00
❏ VL3774 [M]	Country Songs	196?	15.00
❏ VL3791 [M]	Lonely Street	1967	18.00
❏ VL73791 [S]	Lonely Street	1967	15.00

WRANGLER

❏ WR1007 [M]	Carl Belew	1962	30.00
❏ WRS31007 [S]	Carl Belew	1962	40.00

BELGRAVE, MARCUS

TRIBE

❏ 2228	Gemini II	1975	18.00

BELL, AARON

HERALD

❏ HLP-0100 [M]	Three Swinging Bells	1955	60.00

LION

❏ L-70111 [M]	Music from "77 Sunset Strip	1959	30.00
❏ L-70112 [M]	Music from "Peter Gunn	1959	30.00
❏ L-70113 [M]	Music from "Victory at Sea	1959	30.00

RCA VICTOR

❏ LPM-1876 [M]	After the Party's Over	1958	50.00

BELL, ARCHIE, AND THE DRELLS

ATLANTIC

❏ SD8204	I Can't Stop Dancing	1968	30.00
❏ SD8226	There's Gonna Be a Showdown	1969	30.00
❏ 8181 [M]	Tighten Up	1968	50.00
❏ SD8181 [S]	Tighten Up	1968	30.00

PHILADELPHIA INT'L.

❏ PZ34855	Hard Not to Like It	1977	12.00
❏ JZ36096 [B]	Strategy	1979	12.00
❏ PZ34323	Where Will You Go When the Party's Over	1976	12.00

TSOP

❏ PZ33844	Dance Your Troubles Away	1975	12.00

BELL, CHARLES

ATLANTIC

❏ 1400 [M]	Another Dimension	1963	18.00
❏ SD1400 [S]	Another Dimension	1963	25.00

COLUMBIA

❏ CL1582 [M]	The Charles Bell Contemporary Jazz Quartet	1961	25.00
❏ CS8382 [S]	The Charles Bell Contemporary Jazz Quartet	1961	30.00

GATEWAY

❏ 7012 [M]	Charles Bell in Concert	1964	18.00
❏ S-7012 [S]	Charles Bell in Concert	1964	25.00

BELL, DEE

CONCORD JAZZ

❏ CJ-206	Let There Be Love	1982	12.00

BELL, DELIA

WARNER BROS.

❏ 23838	Delia Bell	1983	12.00

BELL, FREDDIE, AND THE BELL BOYS

20TH FOX

❏ TF-4146 [M]	Bells Are Swinging	1964	30.00
❏ TFS-4146 [S]	Bells Are Swinging	1964	30.00

MERCURY

❏ MG-20289 [M]	Rock and Roll… All Flavors	1957	200.00

BELL, GRAEME

ANGEL

❏ ANG.60002 [10]	Inside Jazz Down Under	1954	60.00

JAZZOLOGY

❏ J-75	Graeme Bell Jazz	197?	15.00

BELL, JERRY

MCA

❏ 5180	Winter Love Affair	1981	18.00

BELL, MADELINE

PHILIPS

❏ PHS600271	I'm Gonna Make You Love Me	1968	15.00

BELL, MAGGIE

ATLANTIC

❏ SD7293	Queen of the Night	1974	15.00

SWAN SONG

❏ SS8412 [B]	Suicide Sal	1975	18.00

BELL, MARTY

RIVERSIDE

❏ RLP 12-206 [M]	The Voice of Marty Bell	1956	60.00
— White label, blue print			
❏ RLP 12-206 [M]	The Voice of Marty Bell	1957	40.00
— Blue label, microphone logo			

Number	Title	Yr	NM

BELL, VINCENT

DECCA
☐ DL75212	Airport Love Theme	1970	18.00
☐ DL4938 [M]	Pop Goes the Electric Sitar	1967	25.00
☐ DL74938 [S]	Pop Goes the Electric Sitar	1967	18.00

MUSICOR
☐ MM-3009 [M]	51 Motion Picture Favorites	1963	18.00
☐ MS-3009 [S]	51 Motion Picture Favorites	1963	25.00
☐ MM-3047 [M]	Big 16 Guitar Favorites	1965	18.00
☐ MS-3047 [S]	Big 16 Guitar Favorites	1965	25.00

VERVE
☐ V-8574 [M]	Whistle Stop	1964	18.00
☐ V6-8574 [S]	Whistle Stop	1964	25.00

BELL, WILLIAM

KAT FAMILY
☐ FZ38643	Survivor	1983	12.00

MERCURY
☐ SRM-1-1146 [B]	Coming Back for More	1977	12.00
☐ SRM-1-1193	It's Time You Took Another Listen	1978	12.00

STAX
☐ ST-2014 [M]	Bound to Happen	1969	50.00
— Mono is promo only			
☐ STS-2014 [S]	Bound to Happen	1969	30.00
☐ STS-3005	Phases of Reality	1973	25.00
☐ STS-5502	Relating	1974	25.00
☐ 719 [M]	Soul of a Bell	1967	40.00
☐ S-719 [S]	Soul of a Bell	1967	50.00
☐ MPS-8541	The Best of William Bell	1988	12.00
☐ STS-2037	Wow…	1971	30.00

WRC
☐ WL-3007	On a Roll	1986	15.00

BELL & JAMES

A&M
☐ SP-4728	Bell & James	1978	12.00
☐ SP-4834	In Black & White	1981	12.00
☐ SP-4784	Only Make Believe	1979	12.00

BELL BIV DEVOE

MCA
☐ 10682	Hootie Mack	1993	15.00
☐ 6387	Poison	1990	15.00
☐ 10345	WBBD -- Bootcity! The Remix Album	1991	15.00

BELLAMY BROTHERS, THE

ELEKTRA
☐ 60210	Strong Weakness	1982	12.00
☐ E1-60099	When We Were Boys	1982	12.00

MCA CURB
☐ 5721	Country Rap	1987	12.00
☐ 42039	Crazy from the Heart	1987	12.00
☐ 1462	Greatest Hits	1985	10.00
— Reissue of Warner Bros. 23697			
☐ 42298	Greatest Hits Volume III	1989	12.00
☐ 5812	Greatest Hits Volume Two	1986	12.00
☐ 5586	Howard & David	1985	12.00
☐ 42224	Rebels Without a Clue	1988	12.00
☐ 5489	Restless	1984	12.00
☐ 1441	Restless	1985	10.00
— Reissue of MCA 5489			

WARNER BROS.
☐ BSK3176	Friends	1978	12.00
☐ 23697	Greatest Hits	1982	12.00
☐ BS2941	Let Your Love Flow	1976	12.00
☐ BS3034	Plain & Fancy	1977	12.00
☐ BSK3491	Sons of the Sun	1980	12.00
☐ 60210	Strong Weakness	1983	10.00
— Reissue of Elektra 60210			
☐ BSK3347	The Two and Only	1979	12.00
☐ BSK3408	You Can Get Crazy	1980	12.00

BELLE, REGINA

COLUMBIA
☐ BFC40537	All By Myself	1987	10.00
☐ FC44367	Stay with Me	1989	12.00

BELLE AND SEBASTIAN

MATADOR
☐ OLE429 [B]	Fold Your Hands Child, You Walk Like a Peasant	2000	25.00
☐ OLE296 [B]	If You're Feeling Sinister	1996	40.00
☐ OLE311 [B]	The Boy with the Arab Strap	1998	30.00
☐ OLE361 [B]	Tigermilk	1999	40.00
— First U.S. release of their rare U.K. debut; issued in loose bag			

BELLE EPOQUE

BIG TREE
☐ BT76008	Miss Broadway	1978	12.00

SHADY BROOK
☐ SB 33-009	Miss Broadway	1977	15.00

BELLE STARS, THE

WARNER BROS.
☐ 23866	The Belle Stars	1983	12.00

BELLETTO, AL

CAPITOL
☐ T751 [M]	Half and Half	1956	50.00
☐ T6514 [M]	Sounds and Songs	1955	60.00
☐ T6506 [M]	The Al Belletto Sextette	1955	60.00
☐ T901 [M]	Whisper Not	1957	50.00

KING
☐ 716 [M]	The Big Sound	1961	50.00

BELLS, THE (1)

POLYDOR
☐ 24-4510	Fly, Little White Dove, Fly	1971	18.00
☐ 24-5503	Love, Luck & Lollypops	1972	18.00

BELLSON, LOUIS, AND GENE KRUPA

ROULETTE
☐ R-52098 [M]	The Mighty Two	1962	25.00
☐ SR-52098 [S]	The Mighty Two	1962	30.00

BELLSON, LOUIS, AND LALO SCHIFRIN

ROULETTE
☐ R-52120 [M]	Explorations	1964	18.00
☐ SR-52120 [S]	Explorations	1964	25.00

BELLSON, LOUIS, AND WALFREDO DE LOS REYES

FANTASY
☐ OJC-632	Edue Ritmos Cubanos	1991	15.00
— Reissue of Pablo 2310 807			

PABLO
☐ 2310807	Edue Ritmos Cubanos	1978	15.00

BELLSON, LOUIS

ABC IMPULSE!
☐ AS-9107 [S]	Thunderbird	1968	15.00
— Reissue of Impulse AS-9107			

CAPITOL
☐ H348 [10]	Just Jazz All-Stars	1952	200.00

CONCORD JAZZ
☐ CJ-36	150 M P H	1977	15.00
☐ CJ-105	Dynamite!	1979	15.00
☐ CJ-350	Live at the Jazz Showcase	1988	15.00
☐ CJ-157	London Scene	198?	15.00
☐ CJ-64	Primo Time	1978	15.00
☐ CJ-73	Raincheck	1978	15.00
☐ CJ-141	Side Track	198?	15.00
☐ CJ-20	The Louis Bellson 7 Live at the Concord Festival	1977	15.00

DISCWASHER
☐ 002	Note Smoking	1979	30.00
— Direct-to-disc recording			

IMPULSE!
☐ A-9107 [M]	Thunderbird	1966	30.00
☐ AS-9107 [S]	Thunderbird	1966	30.00
☐ MGN-1007 [M]	Journey Into Love	1954	150.00
☐ MGN-1011 [M]	Louis Bellson and His Drums	1954	150.00
☐ MGN-1046 [M]	Skin Deep	1955	100.00
☐ MGN-7 [10]	The Amazing Artistry of Louis Bellson	1954	200.00
☐ MGN-1020 [M]	The Driving Louis Bellson	1955	100.00
☐ MGN-14 [10]	The Exciting Mr. Bellson (And His Big Band)	1954	200.00
☐ MGN-1099 [M]	The Hawk Talks	1956	80.00
— Reissue of 1020			

PABLO
☐ 2310899	Cool, Cool Blue	198?	15.00
☐ 2310755	Explosion	1975	18.00
☐ 2310838	Jam	1979	15.00
☐ 2310880	London Gig	198?	15.00
☐ 2310834	Matterhorn	1979	15.00
☐ 2310813	Sunshine Rock	1978	15.00
☐ 2405407	The Best of Louis Bellson	198?	15.00

PROJECT 3
☐ PR5029SD	Breakthrough!	1968	18.00

ROULETTE
☐ R-65002 [M]	Around the World in Percussion	1962	25.00
☐ SR-65002 [S]	Around the World in Percussion	1962	30.00
☐ R-52087 [M]	Big Band Jazz from the Summit	1962	25.00
☐ SR-52087 [S]	Big Band Jazz from the Summit	1962	30.00

SEAGULL
☐ LG-8208	Louis Bellson and Orchestra	198?	12.00

VERVE
☐ MGV-8016 [M]	Concerto for Drums	1957	50.00
— Reissue of Norgran 1011			
☐ V-8016 [M]	Concerto for Drums	1961	25.00
☐ MGV-8354 [M]	Drummer's Holiday	1959	50.00
☐ V-8354 [M]	Drummer's Holiday	1959	25.00
☐ MGV-8193 [M]	Drumorama!	1957	50.00
☐ V-8193 [M]	Drumorama!	1957	25.00
☐ MGV-8258 [M]	Let's Call It Swing	1958	50.00
☐ V-8258 [M]	Let's Call It Swing	1958	25.00
☐ MGV-8256 [M]	Louis Bellson at the Flamingo	1958	50.00
☐ V-8256 [M]	Louis Bellson at the Flamingo	1958	25.00
☐ MGV-2131 [M]	Louis Bellson Swings Jules Styne	1960	50.00
☐ MGVS-6138 [S]	Louis Bellson Swings Jules Styne	1960	40.00
☐ V-2131 [M]	Louis Bellson Swings Jules Styne	1960	25.00
☐ V6-2131 [S]	Louis Bellson Swings Jules Styne	1960	25.00
☐ MGV-8280 [M]	Music, Romance and Especially Love	1958	50.00
☐ V-8280 [M]	Music, Romance and Especially Love	1958	25.00
☐ MGV-8137 [M]	Skin Deep	1957	50.00
— Reissue of Norgran 1046			
☐ V-8137 [M]	Skin Deep	1957	25.00
☐ MGV-2123 [M]	The Brilliant Bellson Sound	1960	50.00
☐ MGVS-6093 [S]	The Brilliant Bellson Sound	1960	40.00
☐ V-2123 [M]	The Brilliant Bellson Sound	1960	25.00
☐ V6-2123 [S]	The Brilliant Bellson Sound	1960	25.00
☐ MGV-8186 [M]	The Hawk Talks	1957	50.00
— Reissue of Norgran 1099			
☐ V-8186 [M]	The Hawk Talks	1957	25.00

VOSS
☐ VLP1-42936	Note Smoking	1988	12.00
— Reissue of Discwasher 002			

BELLSON, LOUIS/ RAY BROWN/PAUL SMITH

PAUSA
☐ 7167	Intensive Care	1978	15.00

VOSS
☐ VLP1-42933	Intensive Care	1988	12.00
— Reissue			

BELLUS, TONY

NRC
☐ LPA-8 [M]	Robbin' the Cradle	1960	200.00
— Blue label			
☐ LPA-8 [M]	Robbin' the Cradle	1960	100.00
— Black label			

SHI-FI
☐ LP-11 [M]	Gems of Tony Bellus	196?	60.00

BELLY

SIRE
☐ 45833	King	1995	15.00

BELMONTS, THE

BUDDAH

☐ BDS-5123 [B]	Cigars, Acapella, Candy	1972	50.00

DOT
☐ DLP-25949 [B]	Summer Love	1969	30.00

SABINA
☐ SALP-5001 [M]	The Belmonts' Carnival of Hits	1962	150.00

STRAWBERRY
☐ 6001	Cheek to Cheek	1978	18.00

BELOVED, THE

ATLANTIC
☐ 82047	Happiness	1990	15.00

BELVIN, JESSE

CROWN
☐ CLP-5145 [M]	The Casual Jesse Belvin	1959	70.00
— Black label			

Number	Title	Yr	NM
❑ CLP-5145 [M]	The Casual Jesse Belvin	196?	18.00

— Gray label

Number	Title	Yr	NM
❑ CLP-5187 [M]	The Unforgettable Jesse Belvin	1959	70.00

— Black label

Number	Title	Yr	NM
❑ CLP-5187 [M]	The Unforgettable Jesse Belvin	196?	18.00

— Gray label

RCA CAMDEN

Number	Title	Yr	NM
❑ CAL-960 [M]	Jesse Belvin's Best	1966	15.00
❑ CAS-960 [S]	Jesse Belvin's Best	1966	18.00

RCA VICTOR

Number	Title	Yr	NM
❑ LPM-2089 [M]	Just Jesse Belvin	1959	40.00
❑ LSP-2089 [S]	Just Jesse Belvin	1959	60.00
❑ LPM-2105 [M]	Mr. Easy	1960	30.00
❑ LSP-2105 [S]	Mr. Easy	1960	40.00

SPECIALTY

Number	Title	Yr	NM
❑ SP-7003	The Blues Balladeer	1990	18.00

BENATAR, PAT

CHRYSALIS

Number	Title	Yr	NM
❑ F1-21715	Best Shots	1989	15.00
❑ CHE1275	Crimes of Passion	1980	10.00
❑ CHE1275	Crimes of Passion	1980	30.00

— Error pressing: White label (not a promo) with photo of Pat leaning on a barre, as on regular copies, but with no blue at all, and with no butterfly or "Chrysalis" on label

Number	Title	Yr	NM
❑ CHR1396	Get Nervous	1982	10.00
❑ CHR1236 [B]	In the Heat of the Night	1979	10.00
❑ FV41444	Live from Earth	1983	10.00
❑ CHR1346	Precious Time	1981	10.00
❑ FV41507	Seven the Hard Way	1985	10.00
❑ FV41471	Tropico	1984	10.00
❑ FV41628	Wide Awake in Dreamland	1988	10.00

MOBILE FIDELITY

Number	Title	Yr	NM
❑ 1-057	In the Heat of the Night	1981	30.00

— Audiophile vinyl

BENAY, BEN

CAPITOL

Number	Title	Yr	NM
❑ T2484 [M]	The Big Blues Harmonica of Ben Benay	1966	25.00
❑ ST2484 [S]	The Big Blues Harmonica of Ben Benay	1966	30.00

BENDIX, WILLIAM

CRICKET

Number	Title	Yr	NM
❑ CR-30 [M]	William Bendix Sings and Tells Famous Pirate Stories	1959	40.00

BENEDICTINE MONKS OF SANTO DOMINGO DE SILOS, THE

MUSICAL HERITAGE SOCIETY

Number	Title	Yr	NM
❑ 923698X	Chant	1994	18.00

— This is the only U.S. vinyl version of this most surprising hit compilation album

BENEDICTINE MONKS OF ST. PROCOPIUS ABBEY

(NO LABEL)

Number	Title	Yr	NM
❑ U-51773/4	Christmas at St. Procopius Abbey	197?	15.00

BENEKE, TEX/RAY EBERLE/THE MODERNAIRES

COLUMBIA

Number	Title	Yr	NM
❑ CL2392 [M]	Christmas Serenade in the Glenn Miller Style	1965	15.00
❑ CS9192 [S]	Christmas Serenade in the Glenn Miller Style	1965	18.00

BENET, VICKI

DECCA

Number	Title	Yr	NM
❑ DL8381 [M]	The French Touch	1957	40.00
❑ DL8987 [M]	Vicki Benet a Paris	1959	30.00
❑ DL78987 [S]	Vicki Benet a Paris	1959	40.00
❑ DL8233 [M]	Woman of Paris	1956	40.00

LIBERTY

Number	Title	Yr	NM
❑ LRP-3103 [M]	Sing to Me of Love	1960	30.00
❑ LST-7103 [S]	Sing to Me of Love	1960	30.00

BENNETT, BETTY

ATLANTIC

Number	Title	Yr	NM
❑ 1226 [M]	Nobody Else But Me	1956	100.00

— Black label

Number	Title	Yr	NM
❑ 1226 [M]	Nobody Else But Me	1961	40.00

— Multicolor label, white "fan" logo

KAPP

Number	Title	Yr	NM
❑ KL-1052 [M]	Blue Sunday	1957	40.00

TREND

Number	Title	Yr	NM
❑ TL-1006 [10]	Betty Bennett Sings Previn Arrangements	1954	120.00

UNITED ARTISTS

Number	Title	Yr	NM
❑ UAL-3070 [M]	I Love to Sing	1959	40.00
❑ UAS-6070 [S]	I Love to Sing	1959	50.00

BENNETT, BOYD

KING

Number	Title	Yr	NM
❑ 395-594 [M]	Boyd Bennett	1955	4000.00

— VG value 1500; VG+ value 2750

BENNETT, CONNIE, WITH BILL SMITH AND THE HARLEM-AIRES

HOLLYWOOD

Number	Title	Yr	NM
❑ LPH-30 [M]	Rhythm 'N Blues in the Night	1957	500.00

— Photo of Julie "Catwoman" Newmar on front cover

BENNETT, JOE, AND THE SPARKLETONES

MCA

Number	Title	Yr	NM
❑ 1553	Black Slacks	1983	18.00

BENNETT, MAX

BETHLEHEM

Number	Title	Yr	NM
❑ BCP-48 [M]	Johnny Jaguar	1957	70.00
❑ BCP-50 [M]	Max Bennett Plays	1957	120.00
❑ BCP-1028 [10]	Max Bennett Quintet	1955	120.00

PALO ALTO

Number	Title	Yr	NM
❑ TBA-216	The Drifter	1986	12.00

BENNETT, RICHARD RODNEY

AUDIOPHILE

Number	Title	Yr	NM
❑ AP-168	Harold Arlen's Songs	1982	12.00
❑ AP-206	Take Love Easy	1985	12.00

DRG

Number	Title	Yr	NM
❑ SL-5182	A Different Side of Sondheim	1978	12.00
❑ DRG-6102	Special Occasions	1979	12.00

BENNETT, TONY, AND BILL EVANS

DRG

Number	Title	Yr	NM
❑ MRS-901	Together Again	1985	10.00

FANTASY

Number	Title	Yr	NM
❑ F-9489	The Tony Bennett/Bill Evans Album	1975	15.00

IMPROV

Number	Title	Yr	NM
❑ 7117	Together Again	1978	15.00

MOBILE FIDELITY

Number	Title	Yr	NM
❑ 1-117	The Tony Bennett/Bill Evans Album	1981	40.00

— Audiophile vinyl

BENNETT, TONY, AND COUNT BASIE

COLUMBIA

Number	Title	Yr	NM
❑ CL1294 [M]	Tony Bennett In Person	1959	30.00
❑ CS8104 [S]	Tony Bennett In Person	1959	40.00

COLUMBIA LIMITED EDITION

Number	Title	Yr	NM
❑ LE10125	Tony Bennett In Person	197?	15.00

ROULETTE

Number	Title	Yr	NM
❑ R25231 [M]	Bennett and Basie Strike Up the Band	1963	25.00
❑ SR25231 [S]	Bennett and Basie Strike Up the Band	1963	30.00
❑ R25072 [M]	Count Basie Swings/Tony Bennett Sings	1961	30.00
❑ SR25072 [S]	Count Basie Swings/Tony Bennett Sings	1961	30.00

BENNETT, TONY

COLUMBIA

Number	Title	Yr	NM
❑ C30240	All Time Hall of Fame Hits	1971	15.00
❑ PC30240	All Time Hall of Fame Hits	197?	12.00

— Reissue with new prefix

Number	Title	Yr	NM
❑ CL2507 [10]	Alone at Last with Tony Bennett	1955	60.00
❑ CL1471 [M]	Alone Together	1960	30.00
❑ CS8262 [S]	Alone Together	1960	40.00
❑ CL1559 [M]	A String of Harold Arlen	1961	25.00
❑ CS8359 [S]	A String of Harold Arlen	1961	30.00
❑ CL2560 [M]	A Time for Love	1966	15.00
❑ CS9360 [S]	A Time for Love	1966	18.00
❑ CL6221 [10]	Because of You	1952	80.00
❑ CL2550 [10]	Because of You	1956	60.00
❑ FC44029	Bennett/Berlin	1987	12.00
❑ C63668	Bennett Sings Ellington -- Hot and Cool	1999	15.00
❑ CL1292 [M]	Blue Velvet	1958	30.00
❑ CL621 [M]	Cloud Seven	1955	40.00
❑ CL2773 [M]	For Once in My Life	1967	30.00
❑ CS9573 [S]	For Once in My Life	1967	18.00
❑ CL1301 [M]	Hometown, My Hometown	1959	30.00
❑ CS8107 [S]	Hometown, My Hometown	1959	40.00
❑ CL2343 [M]	If I Ruled the World -- Songs for the Jet Set	1965	15.00
❑ CS9143 [S]	If I Ruled the World -- Songs for the Jet Set	1965	18.00
❑ CL1869 [M]	I Left My Heart in San Francisco	1962	18.00
❑ CS8669 [S]	I Left My Heart in San Francisco	1962	25.00
❑ PC8669	I Left My Heart in San Francisco	198?	10.00

— Reissue with new prefix

Number	Title	Yr	NM
❑ CG33612	I Left My Heart in San Francisco/Tony Sings the Great Hits of Today!	1975	18.00
❑ CS9882	I've Gotta Be Me	1969	18.00
❑ CL2000 [M]	I Wanna Be Around	1963	18.00
❑ CS8800 [S]	I Wanna Be Around	1963	30.00
❑ CL1186 [M]	Long Ago and Far Away	1958	30.00
❑ GP14	Love Songs	1969	18.00
❑ C30558	Love Story	1971	15.00
❑ CL1535 [M]	More Tony's Greatest Hits	1961	25.00
❑ CS8335 [S]	More Tony's Greatest Hits	1961	30.00
❑ CL1763 [M]	Mr. Broadway	1962	18.00
❑ CS8563 [S]	Mr. Broadway	1962	25.00
❑ CL1658 [M]	My Heart Sings	1961	25.00
❑ CS8458 [S]	My Heart Sings	1961	30.00
❑ CS9739	Snowfall: The Tony Bennett Christmas Album	1968	15.00
❑ C31219	Summer of '42	1972	15.00
❑ FC40344	The Art of Excellence	1986	12.00
❑ CL1079 [M]	The Beat of My Heart	1957	30.00
❑ CL2141 [M]	The Many Moods of Tony	1964	18.00
❑ CS8941 [S]	The Many Moods of Tony	1964	25.00
❑ CL2472 [M]	The Movie Song Album	1966	15.00
❑ CS9272 [S]	The Movie Song Album	1966	18.00
❑ CL2056 [M]	This Is All I Ask	1963	18.00
❑ CS8856 [S]	This Is All I Ask	1963	25.00
❑ CL1429 [M]	To My Wonderful One	1960	30.00
❑ CS8226 [S]	To My Wonderful One	1960	40.00
❑ CL938 [M]	Tony	1956	30.00
❑ C2L23 [M]	Tony Bennett at Carnegie Hall	1962	25.00
❑ C2S823 [S]	Tony Bennett at Carnegie Hall	1962	30.00
❑ CL1905 [M]	Tony Bennett at Carnegie Hall Vol. 1	1963	18.00
❑ CS8705 [S]	Tony Bennett at Carnegie Hall Vol. 1	1963	25.00
❑ CG40424	Tony Bennett Jazz	1987	15.00
❑ C30280	Tony Bennett's "Something	1971	15.00
❑ KG31494	Tony Bennett's All-Time Greatest Hits	1972	18.00
❑ CS9814	Tony Bennett's Greatest Hits, Volume IV	1969	18.00
❑ CL2653 [M]	Tony Makes It Happen!	1967	18.00
❑ CS9453 [S]	Tony Makes It Happen!	1967	18.00
❑ CL1229 [M]	Tony's Greatest Hits	1958	30.00
❑ CS8652 [R]	Tony's Greatest Hits	1962	18.00
❑ CL2373 [M]	Tony's Greatest Hits, Volume III	1965	15.00
❑ CS9173 [S]	Tony's Greatest Hits, Volume III	1965	18.00
❑ CL1446 [M]	Tony Sings for Two	1960	30.00
❑ CS8242 [S]	Tony Sings for Two	1960	40.00
❑ CS9980	Tony Sings the Great Hits of Today!	1970	15.00
❑ CL2175 [M]	When Lights Are Low	1964	18.00
❑ CS8975 [S]	When Lights Are Low	1964	25.00
❑ CL2285 [M]	Who Can I Turn To	1964	18.00
❑ CS9085 [S]	Who Can I Turn To	1964	25.00
❑ KC31460	With Love	1972	15.00
❑ CS9678	Yesterday I Heard the Rain	1968	18.00

COLUMBIA LIMITED EDITION

Number	Title	Yr	NM
❑ LE10057	For Once in My Life	197?	12.00

COLUMBIA SPECIAL PRODUCTS

Number	Title	Yr	NM
❑ CSR8107 [S]	Hometown, My Town	196?	15.00
❑ CSM552 [M]	Singer Presents Tony Bennett	1966	18.00
❑ CSS552 [S]	Singer Presents Tony Bennett	1966	25.00
❑ C11264	This Is All I Ask	1972	15.00

— Distributed by Arc-Jay-Kay Distributing Co." on upper back cover

DRG

Number	Title	Yr	NM
❑ MRS-910	Make Magnificent Music	1985	12.00
❑ DARC-2-2102	The Rodgers and Hart Songbook	1986	18.00

HARMONY

Number	Title	Yr	NM
❑ HS11340	Just One of Those Things	1969	12.00
❑ KH30758	The Very Thought of You	1971	12.00
❑ KH32171	Tony	1973	12.00

IMPROV

Number	Title	Yr	NM
❑ 7123	Beautiful Music	1979	15.00
❑ 7112	Life Is Beautiful	1975	15.00
❑ 7120	Tony Bennett Sings More Rodgers and Hart	1978	15.00
❑ 7113	Tony Bennett Sings Rodgers and Hart	197?	15.00

MGM

Number	Title	Yr	NM
❑ SE-4929	Greatest Hits, Vol. 7	1973	15.00

PAIR

Number	Title	Yr	NM
❑ PDL2-1102	All-Time Favorites	1986	15.00

TIME-LIFE

Number	Title	Yr	NM
❑ SLGD-10	Legendary Singers: Tony Bennett	1986	18.00

VERVE

Number	Title	Yr	NM
❑ MV-5094	Listen Easy	1973	15.00
❑ MV-5088	The Good Things in Life	1972	15.00

BENNO, MARC

A&M

Number	Title	Yr	NM
❑ SP-4364	Ambush	1972	15.00
❑ SP-4767	Lost in Austin	1979	12.00
❑ SP-4273	Marc Benno	1970	15.00
❑ SP-4303	Minnows	1971	15.00

BENOIT, DAVID

AVI

Number	Title	Yr	NM
❑ AV-6074	Can You Imagine	1980	15.00

Number	Title	Yr	NM
❑ AV-8620	Christmastime	1985	15.00
❑ AV-6138	Digits	1984	15.00
❑ AV-6025	Heavier Than Yesterday	1977	18.00
❑ AV-6214	Stages	1983	15.00
❑ AV-8712	Waves of Raves	1986	15.00
GRP			
❑ 1047	Every Step of the Way	1987	15.00
❑ 1035	Freedom at Midnight	1986	15.00
❑ 9621	Inner Motion	1990	15.00
❑ 9587	Urban Daydreams	1989	15.00
❑ 9595	Waiting for Spring	1989	15.00
SPINDLETOP			
❑ STP-104	This Side Up	1986	15.00

BENSON, GEORGE, AND EARL KLUGH

Number	Title	Yr	NM
WARNER BROS.			
❑ 25580 [B]	Collaboration	1987	12.00

BENSON, GEORGE

Number	Title	Yr	NM
A&M			
❑ SP-3014	Shape of Things to Come	1969	25.00
—Brown label			
❑ SP-3014	Shape of Things to Come	1976	15.00
—Silvery label with fading "A&M" logo			
❑ SP9-3014	Shape of Things to Come	1983	18.00
—Audio Master Plus" reissue			
❑ SP-3020	Tell It Like It Is	1969	25.00
—Brown label			
❑ SP-3020	Tell It Like It Is	1976	15.00
—Silvery label with fading "A&M" logo			
❑ SP9-3020	Tell It Like It Is	1984	18.00
—Audio Master Plus" reissue			
❑ SP-3203	The Best of George Benson	1983	12.00
❑ SP-3028	The Other Side of Abbey Road	1970	30.00
—Brown label			
❑ SP-3028	The Other Side of Abbey Road	1976	15.00
—Silvery label with fading "A&M" logo			
❑ SP9-3028	The Other Side of Abbey Road	1984	18.00
—Audio Master Plus" reissue			
COLUMBIA			
❑ CG33569	Benson Burner	1976	15.00
❑ CL2613 [M]	The George Benson Cook Book	1967	25.00
❑ CS9413 [S]	The George Benson Cook Book	1967	25.00
—Red "360 Sound" label			
❑ CS9413	The George Benson Cook Book	1976	12.00
—Orange label			
❑ PC9413	The George Benson Cook Book	198?	10.00
—Reissue with new prefix			
❑ CL2525 [M]	The Most Exciting New Guitarist on the Jazz Scene Today -- It's Uptown	1966	25.00
❑ CS9325 [S]	The Most Exciting New Guitarist on the Jazz Scene Today -- It's Uptown	1966	25.00
—Red "360 Sound" label			
❑ CS9325	The Most Exciting New Guitarist on the Jazz Scene Today -- It's Uptown	1976	12.00
—Orange label			
❑ PC9325	The Most Exciting New Guitarist on the Jazz Scene Today -- It's Uptown	198?	10.00
—Reissue with new prefix			
CTI			
❑ 6045	Bad Benson	1974	15.00
❑ 6069	Benson & Farrell	1976	15.00
❑ 6009	Beyond the Blue Horizon	1971	15.00
❑ 6033	Body Talk	1973	15.00
❑ CTSQ-6033 [Q]	Body Talk	1973	25.00
❑ 8030	Cast Your Fate to the Wind	1982	12.00
❑ 6072	George Benson In Concert -- Carnegie Hall	1976	15.00
❑ 6062	Good King Bad	1976	15.00
❑ 8031	Summertime: In Concert	198?	12.00
❑ 8014	Take Five	198?	12.00
❑ 6015	White Rabbit	1972	15.00
❑ 8009	White Rabbit	198?	12.00
FANTASY			
❑ OJC-461	The New Boss Guitar of George Benson	1990	15.00
—Reissue of Prestige 7310			
MOBILE FIDELITY			
❑ 1-011	Breezin'	1979	60.00
—Audiophile vinyl			
POLYDOR			
❑ PD-1-6084	Blue Benson	1976	12.00
PRESTIGE			
❑ 24072	George Benson & Jack McDuff	1976	18.00
❑ PRLP-7310 [M]	The New Boss Guitar of George Benson	1964	30.00
❑ PRST-7310 [S]	The New Boss Guitar of George Benson	1964	40.00
VERVE			
❑ V6-8749 [B]	Giblet Gravy	1968	25.00
❑ V6-8771	Goodies	1969	25.00
WARNER BROS.			
❑ 25178	20/20	1985	12.00
❑ 26295	Big Boss Band	1990	18.00
❑ BS2919	Breezin'	1976	18.00
—With no mention of "This Masquerade" on front cover			
❑ BS2919	Breezin'	1976	12.00
—With "Contains This Masquerade" on front cover			
❑ BSK3111	Breezin'	1977	10.00
—Reissue of 2919			
❑ HS3453	Give Me the Night	1980	12.00
❑ BSK2983	In Flight	1977	12.00
❑ 23744	In Your Eyes	1983	12.00
❑ 2BSK3277	Livin' Inside Your Love	1979	15.00
❑ 25907	Tenderly	1989	15.00
❑ 2HS3577	The George Benson Collection	1981	15.00
❑ 25705	Twice the Love	1988	12.00
❑ 2WS3139	Weekend in L.A.	1978	15.00
❑ 25475	While the City Sleeps…	1986	12.00

BENTON, BARBI

Number	Title	Yr	NM
PLAYBOY			
❑ PB406	Barbi Benton	1975	18.00
❑ PB404	Barbi Doll	1974	18.00
❑ PB411	Something New	1976	18.00

BENTON, BROOK

Number	Title	Yr	NM
ALLEGIANCE			
❑ AV-5033	Memories Are Made of This	1986	12.00
ALL PLATINUM			
❑ 3015	This Is Brook Benton	1976	15.00
COTILLION			
❑ SD9018	Brook Benton Today	1970	15.00
❑ SD9002	Do Your Own Thing	1969	15.00
❑ SD9028	Home Style	1970	15.00
❑ SD9050	Story Teller	1971	15.00
❑ SD9058	The Gospel Truth	1972	15.00
EPIC			
❑ LN3573 [M]	Brook Benton At His Best	1959	50.00
HARMONY			
❑ HL7346 [M]	The Soul of Brook Benton	196?	15.00
❑ HS11146 [R]	The Soul of Brook Benton	196?	15.00
HMC			
❑ 830724	Beautiful Memories of Christmas	1983	15.00
MERCURY			
❑ MG-20830 [M]	Best Ballads of Broadway	1963	25.00
❑ SR-60830 [S]	Best Ballads of Broadway	1963	30.00
❑ MG-20886 [M]	Born to Sing the Blues	1964	25.00
❑ SR-60880 [S]	Born to Sing the Blues	1964	30.00
❑ MG-20464 [M]	Endlessly	1959	30.00
❑ SR-60146 [S]	Endlessly	1959	40.00
❑ MG-20607 [M]	Golden Hits	1961	25.00
❑ SR-60607 [S]	Golden Hits	1961	30.00
❑ MG-20774 [M]	Golden Hits, Volume 2	1963	25.00
❑ SR-60774 [S]	Golden Hits, Volume 2	1963	30.00
❑ MG-20619 [M]	If You Believe	1961	25.00
❑ SR-60619 [S]	If You Believe	1961	30.00
❑ MG-20421 [M]	It's Just a Matter of Time	1959	40.00
❑ SR-60077 [S]	It's Just a Matter of Time	1959	50.00
❑ 822321-1	It's Just a Matter of Time: His Greatest Hits	1984	12.00
❑ MG-20918 [M]	On the Country Side	1964	18.00
❑ SR-60918 [S]	On the Country Side	1964	25.00
❑ MG-20740 [M]	Singing the Blues -- Lie to Me	1962	25.00
❑ SR-60740 [S]	Singing the Blues -- Lie to Me	1962	30.00
❑ MG-20565 [M]	So Many Ways I Love You	1960	30.00
❑ SR-60225 [S]	So Many Ways I Love You	1960	40.00
❑ MG-20602 [M]	Songs I Love to Sing	1960	30.00
❑ SR-60602 [S]	Songs I Love to Sing	1960	40.00
❑ MG-20641 [M]	The Boll Weevil Song and 11 Other Great Hits	1961	25.00
❑ SR-60641 [S]	The Boll Weevil Song and 11 Other Great Hits	1961	30.00
❑ MG-20673 [M]	There Goes That Song Again	1962	25.00
❑ SR-60673 [S]	There Goes That Song Again	1962	30.00
❑ MG-20934 [M]	This Bitter Earth	1964	18.00
❑ SR-60934 [S]	This Bitter Earth	1964	25.00
MGM			
❑ SE-4874	Something for Everyone	1973	15.00
MUSICOR			
❑ 4603	The Best of Brook Benton	1977	15.00
PAIR			
❑ PDL2-1100	Brook Benton's Best	1986	15.00
RCA CAMDEN			
❑ CAL-564 [M]	Brook Benton	1960	18.00
❑ CAS-2431	I Wanna Be with You	1970	15.00
RCA VICTOR			
❑ APL1-1044	Book Benton Sings a Love Story	1975	12.00
❑ LPM-3526 [M]	Mother Nature, Father Time	1965	18.00
❑ LSP-3526 [S]	Mother Nature, Father Time	1965	25.00
❑ LPM-3590 [M]	My Country	1966	18.00
❑ LSP-3590 [S]	My Country	1966	25.00
❑ LPM-3514 [M]	That Old Feeling	1966	18.00
❑ LSP-3514 [S]	That Old Feeling	1966	25.00
REPRISE			
❑ R-6268 [M]	Laura (What's He Got That I Ain't Got)	1967	25.00
❑ RS-6268 [S]	Laura (What's He Got That I Ain't Got)	1967	18.00
RHINO			
❑ RNFP71497	The Brook Benton Anthology (1959-1970)	1986	15.00
WING			
❑ MGW-12314 [M]	Brook Benton	1966	15.00
❑ SRW-16314 [S]	Brook Benton	1966	15.00

BENTON, WALTER

Number	Title	Yr	NM
JAZZLAND			
❑ JLP-28 [M]	Out of This World	1960	500.00
—orange label			
❑ JLP-928 [S]	Out of This World	1960	100.00
—black label			

BERBERIAN, JOHN, WITH THE ROCK EAST ENSEMBLE

Number	Title	Yr	NM
MAINSTREAM			
❑ S-6123	Impressions East	1969	120.00
VERVE FORECAST			
❑ FTS-3073 [B]	Middle Eastern Rock	1969	60.00

BERG, BOB

Number	Title	Yr	NM
RED			
❑ VPA-178	Steppin' -- Live in Europe	1985	15.00
XANADU			
❑ 159	New Birth	1978	18.00

BERG, GERTRUDE

Number	Title	Yr	NM
AMY			
❑ 8007 [M]	How to Be a Jewish Mother	1965	30.00

BERGAMO, JOHN

Number	Title	Yr	NM
CMP			
❑ CMP 27-ST	On the Edge	1987	12.00

BERGEN, FRANCES

Number	Title	Yr	NM
COLUMBIA			
❑ CL873 [M]	The Beguiling Miss Bergen	1956	30.00

BERGEN, POLLY

Number	Title	Yr	NM
COLUMBIA			
❑ CL1300 [M]	All Alone by the Telephone	1959	25.00
❑ CS8100 [S]	All Alone by the Telephone	1959	30.00
❑ CL994 [M]	Bergen Sings Morgan	1957	30.00
❑ CL1032 [M]	Do Re Mi" and "Annie Get Your Gun	1961	25.00
❑ CS8432 [S]	Do Re Mi" and "Annie Get Your Gun	1961	30.00
❑ CL1451 [M]	Four Seasons of Love	1960	25.00
❑ CS8246 [S]	Four Seasons of Love	1960	30.00
❑ CL1218 [M]	My Heart Sings	1959	25.00
❑ CS8018 [S]	My Heart Sings	1959	30.00
❑ CL1138 [M]	Polly and Her Pop	1958	30.00
❑ CL1031 [M]	The Party's Over	1957	30.00
JUBILEE			
❑ JGL-14 [10]	Polly Bergen	1955	50.00
PHILIPS			
❑ PHM200084 [M]	Act One -- Sing, Too	1963	18.00
❑ PHS600084 [S]	Act One -- Sing, Too	1963	25.00

BERGER, BENGT

Number	Title	Yr	NM
ECM			
❑ 1179	Bitter Funeral Beer	1981	15.00

BERGER, KARL

Number	Title	Yr	NM
CMC			
❑ 00101	Peace Church	197?	25.00
ENJA			
❑ 2022	With Silence	1974	18.00
ESP-DISK'			
❑ 1041 [M]	Karl Berger	1967	30.00
❑ S-1041 [S]	Karl Berger	1967	25.00
MILESTONE			
❑ MSP-9026	Tune In	1969	18.00

BERGMAN, BORAH

Number	Title	Yr	NM
CHIAROSCURO			
❑ 158	Bursts of Joy	1979	15.00
❑ 125	Discovery	1973	18.00
❑ 118	Solo	1972	18.00
SOUL NOTE			
❑ SN-1030	New Frontier	1984	15.00
❑ SN-1080	Upside Down Visions	1985	15.00

BERIGAN, BUNNY, AND WINGY MANONE

Number	Title	Yr	NM
X			
❑ LVA-3034 [10]	Swing Session 1934	1954	80.00

Number	Title	Yr	NM

BERIGAN, BUNNY

BIOGRAPH
❑ C-10	Bunny Berigan 1932-37	197?	15.00

BLUEBIRD
❑ AXM2-5584	The Complete Bunny Berigan, Volume 1	197?	18.00
❑ 5657-1-RB	The Complete Bunny Berigan, Volume 2	1987	18.00
❑ 9953-1-RB	The Complete Bunny Berigan, Volume 3	1990	18.00

EPIC
| ❑ LA16004 [M] | Bunny Berigan and His Boys | 196? | 25.00 |
| ❑ LN3109 [M] | Take It, Bunny! | 1955 | 50.00 |

HINDSIGHT
| ❑ HSR-239 | Bunny Berigan 1937-38 | 1988 | 12.00 |

JAZZ ARCHIVES
| ❑ JA-11 | Down by the Old Mill Stream | 198? | 12.00 |

MCA
| ❑ 1362 | Decca/Champion Sessions | 198? | 15.00 |

RCA CAMDEN
| ❑ CAL-550 [M] | Bunny | 195? | 25.00 |

RCA VICTOR
❑ LPV-550 [M]	Bunny	1966	25.00
❑ LPT-10 [10]	Bunny Berigan 1937-38	1951	80.00
❑ LPT-1003 [M]	Bunny Berigan Plays Again	1952	50.00
❑ LPM-2078 [M]	Great Dance Bands of the 30s and 40s	1959	40.00

TIME-LIFE
| ❑ STL-J-25 | Giants of Jazz | 1982 | 25.00 |

BERIGAN, BUNNY/JACK TEAGARDEN

FOLKWAYS
| ❑ FJ-2819 | The Big Band Sound of Bunny Berigan and Jack Teagarden | 1982 | 15.00 |

BERK, DICK, AND THE JAZZ ADOPTION AGENCY

DISCOVERY
❑ DS-890	Big Jake	1986	12.00
❑ DS-922	More Birds Less Feathers	1987	12.00
❑ DS-877	The Rare One	1985	12.00

TREND
| ❑ 550 | Lover | 198? | 12.00 |

BERLE, MILTON

FORUM
| ❑ F-9005 [M] | Songs My Mother Loved | 1963 | 25.00 |

ROULETTE
| ❑ R-25018 [M] | Songs My Mother Loved | 1957 | 40.00 |

BERLIN

CLEOPATRA
| ❑ 3741 [B] | Greatest Hits | | 25.00 |

ENIGMA
| ❑ 3 [EP] | Pleasure Victim | 1982 | 30.00 |
—Original issue

GEFFEN
| ❑ R100731 | Best of Berlin 1979-1988 | 1988 | 25.00 |
—BMG Direct Marketing edition
| ❑ GHS24187 | Best of Berlin 1979-1988 | 1988 | 18.00 |
| ❑ R153624 | Count Three and Pray | 1986 | 12.00 |
—RCA Music Service edition
❑ GHS24121	Count Three and Pray	1986	10.00
❑ GHS4025	Love Life	1984	12.00
❑ GHS2036 [EP]	Pleasure Victim	1982	10.00
❑	Selections from Love Life	1984	15.00
❑ PRO-A-2121 [EP]			
—Four-song promo sampler (Touch/Now It's My Turn/In My Dreams/No More Words)

BERLINER, JAY

MAINSTREAM
| ❑ 384 | Bananas Not Equal | 1973 | 18.00 |

BERLINER, PAUL, AND KUDU

FLYING FISH
| ❑ FF-092 | The Sun Rises Later Here | 1979 | 18.00 |

BERMAN, SHELLEY

METRO
| ❑ M-546 [M] | Let Me Tell You a Funny Story | 1965 | 18.00 |
| ❑ MS-546 [R] | Let Me Tell You a Funny Story | 1965 | 15.00 |

VERVE
❑ MGV-15027 [M]	A Personal Appearance	1961	25.00
❑ V-15027 [M]	A Personal Appearance	1962	18.00
❑ V6-15027 [R]	A Personal Appearance	196?	15.00
❑ V-15048 [M]	Great Moments in Comedy	1965	25.00
❑ V6-15048 [R]	Great Moments in Comedy	1965	18.00
❑ MGV-15008-2 [M]	Inside and Outside Shelley Berman	1959	30.00
❑ V-15008-2 [M]	Inside and Outside Shelley Berman	1962	25.00
❑ MGV-15003 [M]	Inside Shelley Berman	1959	30.00

❑ V-15003 [M]	Inside Shelley Berman	1962	18.00
❑ V6-15003 [R]	Inside Shelley Berman	196?	15.00
❑ V-15036 [M]	New Sides	1962	18.00
❑ V6-15036 [R]	New Sides	196?	15.00
❑ MGV-15007 [M]	Outside Shelley Berman	1959	30.00
❑ V-15007 [M]	Outside Shelley Berman	1962	18.00
❑ V6-15007 [R]	Outside Shelley Berman	196?	15.00
❑ MGV-15013 [M]	The Edge of Shelley Berman	1960	30.00
❑ V-15013 [M]	The Edge of Shelley Berman	1962	18.00
❑ V6-15013 [R]	The Edge of Shelley Berman	196?	15.00
❑ V-15043 [M]	The Sex Life of the Primate (And Other Bits of Gossip)	1964	25.00
❑ V6-15043 [R]	The Sex Life of the Primate (And Other Bits of Gossip)	1964	18.00

BERMAN, SONNY

ESOTERIC
| ❑ ES-532 [M] | Sonny Berman 1946 | 1954 | 120.00 |

BERNARD, ROD

JIN
| ❑ LP-4007 [M] | Rod Bernard | 196? | 60.00 |

BERNARDI, HERSCHEL

COLUMBIA
| ❑ C30004 | Show Stopper | 1970 | 25.00 |

COLUMBIA MASTERWORKS
| ❑ OL6610 [M] | Fiddler on the Roof | 1966 | 25.00 |
| ❑ OS3010 [S] | Fiddler on the Roof | 1966 | 30.00 |

BERNE, TIM, AND BILL FRISELL

EMPIRE
| ❑ EPC72K | ...Theoretically | 1984 | 25.00 |

MINOR MUSIC
| ❑ 008 | ...Theoretically | 1986 | 18.00 |

BERNE, TIM

COLUMBIA
| ❑ FC40530 | Fulton Street Maul | 1987 | 15.00 |
| ❑ FC44U/3 | Sanctified Dreams | 1987 | 15.00 |

EMPIRE
❑ EPC36K	7X	1980	25.00
❑ EPC60K-2	Songs and Rituals in Real Time	1982	30.00
❑ EPC48K	Spectres	1981	25.00
❑ EPC24K	The Five Year Plan	1979	25.00

JMT
| ❑ 834431-1 | Fractured Fairy Tales | 1989 | 18.00 |

SOUL NOTE
| ❑ SN-1091 | Mutant Variations | 1984 | 15.00 |
| ❑ SN-1061 | The Ancestors | 1983 | 15.00 |

BERNHARDT, WARREN

ARISTA/NOVUS
❑ AN3011	Floating	1979	15.00
❑ AN3020	Manhattan Update	1980	15.00
❑ AN3001	Solo Piano	1978	15.00

BERNHART, MILT

DECCA
| ❑ DL9214 [M] | The Sounds of Bernhart | 1959 | 30.00 |
| ❑ DL79214 [S] | The Sounds of Bernhart | 1959 | 40.00 |

RCA VICTOR
| ❑ LPM-1123 [M] | Modern Brass | 1955 | 50.00 |

BERNSTEIN, LEONARD

COLUMBIA
| ❑ CL919 [M] | What Is Jazz? | 1956 | 50.00 |
—Red and black label with six "eye" logos

BERRY, BILL

CONCORD JAZZ
| ❑ CJ-27 | Hello Rev | 1977 | 15.00 |
| ❑ CJ-75 | Shortcake | 1978 | 15.00 |

DIRECTIONAL SOUND
| ❑ 5002 [M] | Jazz and Swinging Percussion | 1963 | 25.00 |
| ❑ S-5002 [S] | Jazz and Swinging Percussion | 1963 | 30.00 |

PARADE
| ❑ SP-353 [M] | Broadway Escapades | 196? | 25.00 |

REAL TIME
| ❑ 101 [B] | For Duke | 1980 | 175.00 |
—Direct-to-disc recording

BERRY, BROOKS, AND SCRAPPER BLACKWELL

BLUESVILLE
| ❑ BVLP-1074 [M] | My Heart Struck Sorrow | 1963 | 80.00 |
—Blue label, silver print
| ❑ BVLP-1074 [M] | My Heart Struck Sorrow | 1964 | 30.00 |
—Blue label with trident logo

BERRY, CHU

COMMODORE
| ❑ XFL15353 | A Giant of the Tenor Sax | 198? | 12.00 |

| ❑ DL-30017 [M] | Chu Berry | 1959 | 80.00 |
| ❑ FL-20024 [10] | Chu Berry Memorial | 1952 | 250.00 |

ENCORE
| ❑ EE22007 | Chu (1936-1940) | 1968 | 18.00 |

EPIC
| ❑ LG3124 [M] | Chu | 1955 | 80.00 |

MAINSTREAM
| ❑ 56038 [M] | Sittin' In | 1965 | 30.00 |
| ❑ S-6038 [R] | Sittin' In | 1965 | 18.00 |

BERRY, CHUCK

ACCORD
| ❑ SN-7171 | Toronto Rock 'N' Roll Revival, Vol. 2 | 1982 | 12.00 |
| ❑ SN-7172 | Toronto Rock 'N' Roll Revival, Vol. 3 | 1982 | 12.00 |

ATCO
| ❑ SD 38-118 | Rockit | 1979 | 15.00 |

CHESS
❑ LP-1426 [M]	After School Session	1958	200.00
❑ LPS-1426 [R]	After School Session	196?	15.00
❑ CH-9284	After School Session	1989	12.00
—Reissue of 1426
❑ LPS-1550	Back Home	1970	25.00
❑ CH-50043	Chuck Berry/Bio	1973	25.00
❑ LP-1495 [M]	Chuck Berry in London	1965	30.00
❑ LPS-1495 [S]	Chuck Berry in London	1965	40.00
❑ LP-1435 [M]	Chuck Berry Is On Top	1959	180.00
❑ LPS-1435 [R]	Chuck Berry Is On Top	196?	15.00
❑ CH-9256	Chuck Berry Is On Top	1987	12.00
—Reissue of 1435
❑ LP-1480 [M]	Chuck Berry On Stage	1963	120.00
❑ LPS-1480 [R]	Chuck Berry On Stage	196?	15.00
❑ LP-1514 [M]	Chuck Berry's Golden Decade	1967	40.00
❑ LPS-1514 [R]	Chuck Berry's Golden Decade	1967	25.00
—Old cover does not have a pink radio
| ❑ 2CH-1514 [R] | Chuck Berry's Golden Decade | 1972 | 18.00 |
—New cover has a pink radio
❑ 2CH-60023	Chuck Berry's Golden Decade, Vol. 2	1973	30.00
❑ 2CH-60028	Chuck Berry's Golden Decade, Vol. 3	1974	30.00
❑ LP-1485 [M]	Chuck Berry's Greatest Hits	1964	120.00
❑ LPS-1485 [R]	Chuck Berry's Greatest Hits	196?	15.00
❑ LP-1465 [M]	Chuck Berry Twist	1962	100.00
❑ LP-1498 [M]	Fresh Berry's	1965	30.00
❑ LPS-1498 [S]	Fresh Berry's	1965	40.00
❑ CH-9318	Missing Berries: Rarities, Volume 3	1990	12.00
❑ LP-1465 [M]	More Chuck Berry	1963	120.00
—Retitled version of above
❑ LPS-1465 [R]	More Chuck Berry	196?	15.00
❑ CH-9190	More Rock 'n' Roll Rarities	1986	12.00
❑ LP-1456 [M]	New Juke Box Hits	1961	180.00
❑ CH-9171	New Juke Box Hits	1986	12.00
—Reissue of 1456
❑ LP-1432 [M]	One Dozen Berrys	1958	200.00
❑ LPS-1432 [R]	One Dozen Berrys	196?	15.00
❑ CH-9259	Rockin' at the Hop	1987	12.00
—Reissue of 1448

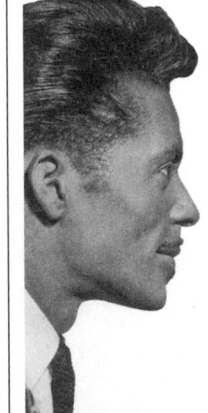

CHESS LP 1448
high-fidelity

CHUCK BERRY

rockin' at the hops

❑ LP-1448 [M]	Rockin' at the Hops	1960	180.00
❑ CH2-92521	Rock 'n' Roll Rarities	1986	18.00
❑ CH-50008	San Fransisco Dues	1971	25.00
❑ LP-1488 [M]	St. Louis to Liverpool	1964	60.00
❑ LPS-1488 [S]	St. Louis to Liverpool	1964	80.00
❑ CH-9186	St. Louis to Liverpool	1988	12.00
—Reissue of 1488
❑ CH6-80001	The Chess Box	1989	50.00
❑ CH2-92500	The Great Twenty-Eight	1983	15.00
❑ CH-60020	The London Chuck Berry Sessions	1972	25.00
❑ CH-9295	The London Chuck Berry Sessions	1989	12.00
—Reissue of 60020

Number	Title	Yr	NM

EVEREST ARCHIVE OF FOLK & JAZZ
| ❏ FS-321 | Chuck Berry's Greatest Hits | 1976 | 12.00 |

GUSTO
| ❏ 0004 | The Best of the Best of Chuck Berry | 198? | 12.00 |

MERCURY
❏ MG-21123 [M]	Chuck Berry in Memphis	1967	18.00
❏ SR-61123 [S]	Chuck Berry in Memphis	1967	18.00
❏ MG-21103 [M]	Chuck Berry's Golden Hits	1967	18.00
❏ SR-61103 [S]	Chuck Berry's Golden Hits	1967	18.00
❏ 826256-1	Chuck Berry's Golden Hits	1985	10.00
—Reissue			
❏ SR-61223	Concerto in B Goode	1969	25.00
❏ SR-61176	From St. Louie to Frisco	1968	25.00
❏ MG-21138 [M]	Love at the Fillmore Auditorium	1967	25.00
❏ SR-61138 [S]	Love at the Fillmore Auditorium	1967	25.00
❏ SRM-2-6501	St. Louis to Frisco to Memphis	1972	25.00

PICKWICK
❏ PTP-2061	Flashback	1975	15.00
❏ SPC-3327	Johnny B. Goode	1973	12.00
❏ SPC-3345	Sweet Little Rock and Roller	1974	12.00
❏ SPC-3392	Wild Berrys	1974	12.00

QUICKSILVER
| ❏ QS-1017 | Live Hits | 198? | 12.00 |

SSS INTERNATIONAL
| ❏ 36 | Chuck Berry Live | 1981 | 12.00 |

BERRY, KEN

BARNABY
| ❏ Z30094 | Ken Berry, R.F.D. | 1970 | 30.00 |
| ❏ Z30014 | R.F.D. | 1970 | 30.00 |

BERRY, RICHARD

CROWN
| ❏ CLP-5371 [M] | Richard Berry and the Dreamers | 1963 | 60.00 |
| ❏ CST-371 [R] | Richard Berry and the Dreamers | 1963 | 40.00 |

PAM
| ❏ 1001 | Live at the Century Restaurant | 1968 | 40.00 |
| ❏ 1002 | Wild Berry | 196? | 40.00 |

BERT, EDDIE

DISCOVERY
| ❏ DL-3020 [M] | Eddie Bert Quintet | 1953 | 100.00 |

JAZZTONE
| ❏ J-1223 [M] | Modern Moods | 1956 | 40.00 |

SAVOY
| ❏ MG-12019 [M] | Encore | 1955 | 120.00 |
| ❏ MG-12015 [M] | Musician of the Year | 1955 | 60.00 |

SAVOY JAZZ
| ❏ SJL-1186 | Kaleidoscope | 198? | 12.00 |

SOMERSET
| ❏ SF-5200 [M] | Like Cool | 1958 | 40.00 |
| —Reissue of Trans World LP | | | |

TRANS WORLD
| ❏ TWLP-208 [M] | Let's Dig Bert | 1955 | 100.00 |

BERTONCINI, GENE, AND MICHAEL MOORE

OMNISOUND
| ❏ GJB-3333 | Bridges | 198? | 15.00 |
| ❏ GJB-3334 | Close Ties | 198? | 15.00 |

STASH
| ❏ ST-258 | O Grande Amor: A Bossa Nova Collection | 1986 | 12.00 |
| ❏ ST-272 | Strollin' | 1987 | 12.00 |

BERTONCINI, GENE

EVOLUTION
| ❏ 3001 | Evolution | 1969 | 18.00 |

BEST, JOHNNY/DICK CATHCART

MERCURY
❏ PPM-2009 [M]	Dixieland	1961	18.00
❏ PPS-6009 [S]	Dixieland (Left and Right)	1961	25.00
—Odd record with Best's band in the left channel and Cathcart's in the right!			

BEST, PETER (1)

PHOENIX
| ❏ PHX-340 | The Beatle That Time Forgot | 1982 | 15.00 |

SAVAGE
| ❏ BM-71 | Best of the Beatles | 1966 | 200.00 |
| —Authentic copies have white circle around the word "Savage" and white circle around Pete Best's head on the album cover. | | | |

BETTER THAN EZRA

ELEKTRA
| ❏ 61944 | Friction, Baby | 1996 | 15.00 |

BETTERS, HAROLD

GATEWAY
❏ GLP-7014 [M]	Do Anything You Wanna	1966	25.00
❏ GS-7014 [S]	Do Anything You Wanna	1966	18.00
❏ GLP-7008 [M]	Even Better	1966	25.00
❏ GS-7008 [S]	Even Better	1966	18.00
❏ GLP-7001 [M]	Harold Betters at the Encore	1964	25.00
❏ GS-7001 [S]	Harold Betters at the Encore	1964	18.00
❏ GLP-7009 [M]	Harold Betters Meets Slide Hampton	1966	25.00
❏ GS-7009 [S]	Harold Betters Meets Slide Hampton	1966	18.00
❏ 7021	Jazz Showcase	197?	15.00
❏ GLP-7015 [M]	Swingin' on the Railroad	1966	25.00
❏ GS-7015 [S]	Swingin' on the Railroad	1966	18.00
❏ GLP-7004 [M]	Take Off	1964	25.00
❏ GS-7004 [S]	Take Off	1964	18.00
❏ 7017	The Best of Betters	197?	15.00

REPRISE
❏ R-6241 [M]	Funk City Express	1966	18.00
❏ RS-6241 [S]	Funk City Express	1966	25.00
❏ R-6208 [M]	Out of Sight and Sound	1966	18.00
❏ RS-6208 [S]	Out of Sight and Sound	1966	25.00
❏ R-6195 [M]	Ram-Bunk-Shush	1965	18.00
❏ RS-6195 [S]	Ram-Bunk-Shush	1965	25.00

BETTS, DICKEY

ARISTA
| ❏ AL4168 | Atlanta's Burning Down | 1978 | 12.00 |
| ❏ AL4123 | Dickey Betts & Great Southern | 1977 | 12.00 |

CAPRICORN
| ❏ CP 0123 | Highway Call | 1974 | 15.00 |
| —As "Richard Betts" | | | |

EPIC
| ❏ FE44289 | Pattern Disruptive | 1988 | 12.00 |

BETTY BOO

SIRE
| ❏ 26360 | Boomania | 1990 | 15.00 |

BEVEL, CHARLES

A&M
| ❏ SP-4412 | Meet "Mississippi Charles | 1973 | 15.00 |

BEVERLY HILL BILLIES, THE

RAR-ARTS
| ❏ 1000 [M] | Those Fabulous Beverly Hill Billies | 1961 | 100.00 |
| —Gold vinyl | | | |

BIANCO

RCA/READER'S DIGEST
| ❏ CPM-104 [M] | Joy to the World | 1962 | 18.00 |
| ❏ CSP-104 [S] | Joy to the World | 1962 | 25.00 |

BICKERT, ED, AND DON THOMPSON

SACKVILLE
| ❏ 4010 | Dance to the Lady | 198? | 12.00 |
| ❏ 4005 | Ed Bickert & Don Thompson | 198? | 12.00 |

BICKERT, ED

CONCORD JAZZ
❏ CJ-232	Bye Bye Baby	1983	12.00
❏ CJ-216	Ed Bickert at Toronto's Bourbon Street	1982	12.00
❏ CJ-284	I Wished on the Moon	1985	12.00
❏ CJ-380	Third Floor Richard	1989	12.00

PM
| ❏ PMR-010 | Ed Bickert | 1976 | 15.00 |

BIDDU ORCHESTRA

EPIC
❏ PE33903	Biddu Orchestra	1975	12.00
❏ PE34723	Eastern Man	1977	12.00
❏ PE34230	Rain Forest	1976	12.00

BIELEFELDER KINDERCHOR, THE

CAPITOL
| ❏ T10308 [M] | A German Christmas | 196? | 18.00 |

BIG AUDIO DYNAMITE

COLUMBIA
❏ FC45212	Megatop Phoenix	1989	12.00
❏ BFC40445	No. 10 Upping Street	1986	15.00
❏ BFC40705	No. 10 Upping Street	1986	12.00
—Reissue with extra track, "Badrock City"			
❏ C46147 [B]	The Globe	1991	25.00
❏ BFC40220	This Is Big Audio Dynamite	1985	12.00
❏ FC44074	Tighten Up Vol. 88	1988	12.00

RADIOACTIVE
| ❏ 11280 | F-Punk | 1995 | 18.00 |

BIG BEATS, THE

LIBERTY
| ❏ LRP-3407 [M] | The Big Beats Live | 1965 | 30.00 |
| ❏ LST-7407 [S] | The Big Beats Live | 1965 | 40.00 |

BIG BLACK

HOMESTEAD
❏ HMS 043 [B]	Atomizer	1986	50.00
❏ HMS 007 [EP]	Racer X	1983	100.00
❏ HMS 044 [B]	The Hammer Party	1986	60.00

RUTHLESS
| ❏ 0(# unknown) [EP] | Bulldozer | 1983 | 80.00 |
| ❏ 0(# unknown) [EP] | Lungs | 1982 | 150.00 |

TOUCH & GO
❏ TG93 [B]	Atomizer	1992	30.00
—Reissue of Homestead 043			
❏ TG111	Boxes	1992	100.00
—Box set containing the Pigpile LP, video, T-shirt and poster			
❏ TG90 [EP]	Bulldozer	1992	30.00
—Reissue			
❏ TG20 [EP]	Headache	1987	30.00
❏ TG20 [EP]	Headache	1987	100.00
—With "gross" cover (different from regular issue), red vinyl record, bonus 7-inch single, book and poster			
❏ TG89 [EP]	Lungs	1992	30.00
—Reissue			
❏ TG81 [B]	Pigpile	1992	30.00
❏ TG91 [EP]	Racer X	1992	30.00
—Reissue of Homestead 007			
❏ TG24 [B]	Songs About Fucking	1987	60.00
❏ 0(no #)? [DJ]	The Incredibly Corporate Whorish Big Black Interview Album	1987	75.00

UNI
❏ 73134	Big Black and the Blues	1972	18.00
❏ 73018	Elements of Now	1968	18.00
❏ 73033	Lion Walk	1969	18.00

BIG BOPPER

MERCURY
❏ MG-20402 [M]	Chantilly Lace	1959	500.00
—Black label			
❏ MG-20402 [M]	Chantilly Lace	1964	200.00
—Red label with black or black & white Mercury logo at top			
❏ MG-20402 [M]	Chantilly Lace	196?	30.00
—Red label with twelve Mercury logos on label edge			
❏ MG-20402 [M]	Chantilly Lace	1975	10.00
—Chicago skyline label			
❏ 832902-1 [M]	Chantilly Lace	1988	18.00
—New number, black label			

PICKWICK
| ❏ SPC-3365 | Chantilly Lace | 1973 | 18.00 |

RHINO
| ❏ R1-70164 | Helloooo Baby! The Best of the Big Bopper 1954-1959 | 1989 | 15.00 |

BIG BOYS

ENIGMA
❏ E-1128	Lullabies Help the Brain Grow	1984	18.00
—Reissue of Moment 002			
❏ 72028	No Matter How Long the Line Is at the Cafeteria, There's Always a Seat	1984	30.00

MOMENT
| ❏ 001 | Fun, Fun, Fun | 1982 | 80.00 |
| ❏ 002 | Lullabies Help the Brain Grow | 1983 | 50.00 |

RAT RACE
| ❏ RRR80351 | Recorded Live at Raul's | 1980 | 80.00 |
| —One side features the Big Boys; the other side, the Dicks | | | |

UNSEEN HAND
| ❏ UHT727-3 | Wreck Collection | 1988 | 18.00 |

WASTED TALENT
| ❏ JWP3405 | Where's My Towel/Industry Standard | 1981 | 60.00 |

BIG BROTHER

ALL-AMERICAN
| ❏ 5770 | Big Brother | 1970 | 250.00 |

BIG BROTHER AND THE HOLDING COMPANY

COLUMBIA
❏ C30222	Be a Brother	1970	25.00
❏ C30631	Big Brother and the Holding Company	1971	25.00
—Reissue of Mainstream LP with two extra tracks			
❏ KCS9700 [M]	Cheap Thrills	1968	100.00
—White label "Special Mono Radio Station Copy" with stereo number			
❏ KCS9700 [S]	Cheap Thrills	1968	30.00
—Red "360 Sound" label			
❏ KCS9700	Cheap Thrills	1970	15.00
—Orange label			
❏ PC9700	Cheap Thrills	198?	10.00
—Reissue with new prefix			
❏ KCL2900 [M]	Cheap Thrills	1968	300.00
—Red label stock copy has been confirmed			
❏ C30738	How Hard It Is	1971	25.00

Number	Title	Yr	NM

COLUMBIA SPECIAL PRODUCTS
| ❏ P13313 | Big Brother and the Holding Company | 197? | 18.00 |

LEGACY
| ❏ KC2900 [B] | Cheap Thrills | 2012 | 30.00 |

MAINSTREAM
| ❏ 56099 [M] | Big Brother and the Holding Company | 1967 | 100.00 |
| ❏ S-6099 [S] | Big Brother and the Holding Company | 1967 | 50.00 |

RHINO
| ❏ RNLP121 | Live | 1984 | 25.00 |
—Recorded 1966

BIG BUB

KEDAR/UNIVERSAL
| ❏ 53074 | Timeless | 1997 | 12.00 |

BIG CHIEF

GET HIP
| ❏ GH-1004 [B] | Drive It Off | 1991 | 18.00 |

SUB POP
| ❏ SP147 [B] | Face | 1992 | 25.00 |

BIG COUNTRY

MERCURY
| ❏ 822831-1 | Steeltown | 1984 | 12.00 |
| ❏ 812870-1 | The Crossing | 1983 | 12.00 |
—Embossed print on front cover
| ❏ 812870-1 | The Crossing | 198? | 10.00 |
—No embossed print on front cover
| ❏ 826844-1 | The Seer | 1986 | 12.00 |
| ❏ 818835-1 [EP] | Wonderland | 1984 | 10.00 |

REPRISE
| ❏ 25787 | Peace in Our Time | 1988 | 12.00 |

BIG DADDY

REGENT
| ❏ MG-6106 [M] | Twist Party | 1962 | 70.00 |

RHINO
| ❏ RNLP-852 | Big Daddy | 198? | 12.00 |
| ❏ RNLP-854 | Meanwhile... Back in the States | 1985 | 12.00 |

BIG ED

NO LIMIT/PRIORITY
| ❏ P1-50729 | The Assassin | 1998 | 15.00 |

BIG FOOT

WINRO
| ❏ 1004 | Big Foot | 1969 | 30.00 |

BIG HEAD TODD AND THE MONSTERS

BIG
| ❏ BR-0001 | Another Mayberry | 1989 | 18.00 |

GIANT
| ❏ 24580 | Strategem | 1994 | 18.00 |

BIG L

COLUMBIA
| ❏ C53795 | Lifestylez Ov Da Poor and Dangerous | 1995 | 18.00 |

RAWKUS
| ❏ RWK1178 | The Big Picture 1974-1999 | 2000 | 18.00 |

BIG MAYBELLE

BRUNSWICK
❏ BL754142	The Gospel Soul of Big Maybelle	1968	40.00
❏ BL54107 [M]	What More Can a Woman Do	1962	50.00
❏ BL754107 [S]	What More Can a Woman Do	1962	70.00

EPIC
| ❏ EE22011 [M] | Gabbin' Blues | 196? | 30.00 |
—Reissue of Okeh recordings

PARAMOUNT
| ❏ PAS-1011 | The Last of Big Maybelle | 1973 | 30.00 |

ROJAC
❏ R522 [M]	Got a Brand New Bag	1967	40.00
❏ RS522 [S]	Got a Brand New Bag	1967	40.00
❏ RS123	Saga of the Good Life and Hard Times	196?	40.00

SAVOY
| ❏ MG-14005 [M] | Big Maybelle Sings | 195? | 300.00 |
| ❏ MG-14011 [M] | Blues, Candy and Big Maybelle | 1958 | 300.00 |

SAVOY JAZZ
| ❏ SJL-1168 | Blues, Candy and Big Maybelle | 1986 | 12.00 |
—Reissue of 14011
| ❏ SJL-1143 | Roots of Rock 'n' Roll Vol. 13: Blues & Early Soul | 1985 | 12.00 |

SCEPTER
| ❏ S-522 [M] | The Soul of Big Maybelle | 1964 | 40.00 |
| ❏ SS-522 [S] | The Soul of Big Maybelle | 1964 | 50.00 |

BIG NOISE

ATCO
| ❏ 91296 | Bang! | 1989 | 12.00 |

BIG NOYD

TOMMY BOY
| ❏ 1156 | Episodes of a Hustla | 1996 | 15.00 |

BIG PIG

A&M
| ❏ SP-6-5185 | Bonk | 1988 | 12.00 |

BIG PUNISHER

LOUD
❏ 67512	Capital Punishment	1998	18.00
❏ 1963	Endangered Species	2001	15.00
❏ C263843	Yeeeah Baby	2000	18.00

BIG RIC

SCOTTI BROTHERS
| ❏ BFZ38864 | Big Ric | 1983 | 12.00 |

BIG STAR

4 MEN WITH BEARDS
| ❏ 4M240 [B] | #1 Record | 2014 | 25.00 |
| ❏ 4M-142 | 3rd | 2006 | 18.00 |
—Reissue on 180-gram vinyl
| ❏ 4M241 [B] | Radio City | 2014 | 25.00 |

ARDENT
| ❏ ADS-2803 [B] | #1 Record | 1972 | 75.00 |
| ❏ ADS-1501 | Radio City | 1974 | 50.00 |

DBK WORKS
| ❏ DBK115 | In Space | 2005 | 18.00 |

PVC
| ❏ 7903 | Big Star's Third | 1978 | 40.00 |
| ❏ 8933 | Sister Lovers | 1985 | 18.00 |
—Reissue of PVC 7903 with new title

BIG THREE, THE

FM
❏ 311 [M]	Live at the Recording Studio	1964	30.00
❏ S-311 [S]	Live at the Recording Studio	1964	40.00
❏ 307 [M]	The Big Three	1963	30.00
❏ S-307 [S]	The Big Three	1963	40.00

ROULETTE
| ❏ R-42000 [M] | The Big Three Featuring Cass Elliot | 1967 | 25.00 |
| ❏ SR-42000 [S] | The Big Three Featuring Cass Elliot | 1967 | 30.00 |

BIG TROUBLE

EPIC
| ❏ BFC40850 | Big Trouble | 1987 | 10.00 |

BIGGS, E. POWER

COLUMBIA MASTERWORKS
| ❏ ML5567 [M] | Joyeaux Noel: Twelve Noels by Louis Clark Daquin | 1960 | 18.00 |
| ❏ MS6167 [S] | Joyeaux Noel: Twelve Noels by Louis Clark Daquin | 1960 | 25.00 |

COLUMBIA SPECIAL PRODUCTS
| ❏ P14076 | Music for a Merry Christmas | 1977 | 12.00 |

BIGGS, RICHARD KEYS

CAPITOL
| ❏ T9013 [M] | Christmas Bells | 1954 | 25.00 |

COLUMBIA
| ❏ CL6076 [10] | An Organ Concert of Carols | 1950 | 40.00 |

BIKINI KILL

KILL ROCK STARS
❏ 204 [EP]	Bikini Kill	1991	18.00
❏ 218 [B]	Pussy Whipped	1993	30.00
❏ 260	Reject All-American	1996	12.00

BILK, ACKER, AND BENT FABRIC

ATCO
| ❏ 33-175 [M] | Together | 1965 | 15.00 |
| ❏ SD 33-175 [S] | Together | 1965 | 18.00 |

BILK, ACKER, AND KEN COLYER

STOMP OFF
| ❏ SOS-1119 | It Looks Like a Big Time Tonight | 198? | 12.00 |

BILK, ACKER

ATCO
❏ 33-144 [M]	Above the Stars	1962	18.00
❏ SD 33-144 [S]	Above the Stars	1962	25.00
❏ 33-181 [M]	Acker Bilk in Paris	1966	15.00
❏ SD 33-181 [S]	Acker Bilk in Paris	1966	18.00
❏ 33-168 [M]	A Touch of Latin	1964	15.00
❏ SD 33-168 [S]	A Touch of Latin	1964	18.00
❏ 33-158 [M]	Call Me Mister	1963	18.00
❏ SD 33-158 [S]	Call Me Mister	1963	25.00
❏ 33-170 [M]	Great Themes from Great Foreign Films	1965	15.00
❏ SD 33-170 [S]	Great Themes from Great Foreign Films	1965	18.00
❏ 33-197 [M]	Mood for Love	1966	15.00
❏ SD 33-197 [S]	Mood for Love	1966	18.00
❏ 33-150 [M]	Only You	1963	18.00
❏ SD 33-150 [S]	Only You	1963	25.00
❏ 33-129 [M]	Stranger on the Shore	1961	18.00
❏ SD 33-129 [S]	Stranger on the Shore	1961	25.00

GNP CRESCENDO
❏ GNPS-2191	Acker Bilk Plays Lennon and McCartney	1988	15.00
❏ GNPS-2116	The Best of Acker Bilk: His Clarinet and Strings	198?	12.00
❏ GNPS-2171	The Best of Acker Bilk: His Clarinet and Strings, Volume 2	198?	12.00

REPRISE
| ❏ R-6031 [M] | A Stranger No More | 1962 | 25.00 |
| ❏ RS-6031 [R] | A Stranger No More | 1962 | 18.00 |

BILLION DOLLAR BABIES

POLYDOR
| ❏ PRO 022 [DJ] | Battle Axe | 1977 | 30.00 |
—Promo-only sampler
| ❏ PD-1-6100 [B] | Battle Axe | 1977 | 30.00 |

BILLY BOY

PRESTIGE
| ❏ PRLP-7389 [M] | Blues on the South Side | 1965 | 40.00 |
—As "Billy Boy Arnold"
| ❏ PRST-7389 [S] | Blues on the South Side | 1965 | 50.00 |
—As "Billy Boy Arnold"

BIRDSONG, EDWIN

ABC DUNHILL
| ❏ DSX-51036 | Can't Stop the Madness | 1974 | 18.00 |

PHILADELPHIA INT'L.
| ❏ JZ35758 [B] | Edwin Birdsong | 1978 | 15.00 |

POLYDOR
| ❏ PD-5057 | Super Natural | 1973 | 15.00 |
| ❏ 24-4071 | What It Is | 1971 | 15.00 |

SALSOUL
| ❏ SA-8550 [B] | Funktaztic | 1981 | 15.00 |

BIRKIN, JANE, AND SERGE GAINSBOURG

FONTANA
| ❏ SRF-67610 | Je T'aime | 1970 | 25.00 |

LIGHT IN THE ATTIC
| ❏ LITA048 [B] | Jane Birkin - Serge Gainsbourg | 2010 | 30.00 |
—includes 7" single

BIRTH CONTROL

PROPHESY
| ❏ PRS-1002 | Birth Control: A New German Rock Group | 1970 | 40.00 |

BIS

CAPITOL
| ❏ 96439 | Social Dancing | 1999 | 12.00 |

GRAND ROYAL
❏ GR 060	Intendo	1998	12.00
❏ GR 045	The New Transistor Heroes	1997	12.00
❏ GR 040 [10]	This Is Teen-C Power	1997	10.00

BISHOP, BOB

ABC
| ❏ ABCS-667 | Somewhere in the Country | 1969 | 18.00 |

BISHOP, ELVIN

ALLIGATOR
| ❏ AL-4767 | Big Fun | 1987 | 12.00 |

CAPRICORN
❏ CPN-0215	Hog Heaven	1978	15.00
❏ CP 0176	Hometown Boy Makes Good!	1976	15.00
❏ CP 0151	Juke Joint Jump	1975	15.00
❏ CP 0134 [B]	Let It Flow	1974	15.00
❏ 2CP 0185	Live! Raisin' Hell	1977	18.00
❏ CP 0165	Struttin' My Stuff	1975	15.00
❏ CPN-0165	Struttin' My Stuff	1980	12.00
—Reissue with revised prefix and Polygram distribution

EPIC
| ❏ KE31563 | Rock My Soul | 1972 | 18.00 |
| ❏ PE33693 | The Best of Elvin Bishop | 1975 | 15.00 |

FILLMORE
| ❏ F30001 | Elvin Bishop Group | 1969 | 25.00 |
| ❏ Z30239 | Feel It | 1970 | 25.00 |

Number	Title	Yr	NM
BISHOP, JOEY			
ABC			
❑ ABCS-656	Joey Bishop Sings Country and Western	1968	30.00
BISHOP, JOHN			
TANGERINE			
❑ TRCS-1508	Bishop's Whirl	1969	18.00
❑ TRCS-1513	John Bishop Plays His Guitar	1970	18.00
BISHOP, STEPHEN			
ABC			
❑ AA-1082	Bish	1977	10.00
❑ ABCD-954	Careless	1976	10.00
ATLANTIC			
❑ PRO(# unk) [DJ]	Bish Is Back!	1989	25.00
—Promo-only interview and music album			
❑ 81970	Bowling in Paris	1989	12.00
RHINO			
❑ R1-70833	The Best of Bish	1988	12.00
WARNER BROS.			
❑ BSK3473	Red Cab to Manhattan	1980	10.00
❑ PRO-A-907 [EP]	Red Cab to Manhattan Sampler	1980	15.00
—Promo-only sampler (Big House; Let Her Go; The Story of a Boy in Love; Sex Kittens Go to College)			
BISHOP, WALTER, JR.			
BLACK JAZZ			
❑ 2	Coral Keys	1972	18.00
❑ QD-14 [Q]	Keeper of My Soul	1974	18.00
COTILLION			
❑ SD236 [B]	Walter Bishop [aka Summertime]	1969	300.00
INTERPLAY			
❑ IP-8605	Just in Time	1988	12.00
JAZZTIME			
❑ JT-002 [M]	Speak Low	1961	700.00
❑ JS-002 [S]	Speak Low	1961	30.00
MUSE			
❑ 5151	Cubicle	1978	15.00
❑ 5183	Hot House	1979	15.00
❑ 5142	Soul Village	1977	15.00
❑ 5066	Speak Low	1976	15.00
—Reissue of Jazztime JS-002			
❑ 5060	Valley Land	1976	15.00
PRESTIGE			
❑ PRST-7730	The Walter Bishop Trio 1965	1969	25.00
SEABREEZE			
❑ 1002	Soliloquy	1975	15.00
XANADU			
❑ 114	Bish Bash	1977	15.00
BIT 'A SWEET			
ABC			
❑ S-640	Hypnotic 1	1968	40.00
BIVONA, GUS			
MERCURY			
❑ MG-20157 [M]	Hey, Dig That Crazy Band	195?	30.00
BIZARROS, THE			
MERCURY			
❑ SRM-1-3776	The Bizarros	1979	18.00
BJOERLING, JUSSI			
RCA VICTOR RED SEAL			
❑ LSC-2570 [S]	The Incomparable Jussi Bjoerling	1962	25.00
—Original with "shaded dog" label			
BJORK			
ELEKTRA			
❑ ED6059 [DJ]	Homogenic	1997	30.00
—WEA Manufacturing test pressing; regular promos are not known to exist; the LP was not issued in the U.S. on vinyl			
❑ 61897	Telegram	1997	15.00
BLAC MONKS			
RAP-A-LOT			
❑ 13153 [EP]	Hot Club Wax	1998	18.00
—Promo-only sampler			
❑ 7082	Secrets of the Hidden Temple	1994	18.00
BLACK, BILL, 'S COMBO			
COLUMBIA			
❑ CS1055	Basic Black	1970	15.00
❑ CS9848	Black with Sugar	1969	15.00
❑ CS9957	Raindrops Keep Fallin' on My Head	1970	15.00
HI			
❑ HL-12032 [M]	All Timers	1966	15.00

Number	Title	Yr	NM
❑ SHL-32032 [S]	All Timers	1966	18.00
❑ 6005	Award Winners	1978	12.00
❑ HL-12015 [M]	Bill Black Plays the Blues	1964	18.00
❑ SHL-32015 [S]	Bill Black Plays the Blues	1964	25.00
❑ HL-12017 [M]	Bill Black Plays Tunes by Chuck Berry	1964	18.00
❑ SHL-32017 [S]	Bill Black Plays Tunes by Chuck Berry	1964	25.00
❑ HL-12020 [M]	Bill Black's Combo Goes Big Band	1964	18.00
❑ SHL-32020 [S]	Bill Black's Combo Goes Big Band	1964	25.00
❑ HL-12013 [M]	Bill Black's Combo Goes West	1963	18.00
❑ SHL-32013 [S]	Bill Black's Combo Goes West	1963	25.00
❑ HL-12012 [M]	Bill Black's Greatest Hits	1963	18.00
❑ SHL-32012 [S]	Bill Black's Greatest Hits	1963	25.00
❑ XSHL-32078	Bill Black's Greatest Hits, Vol. 2	1973	15.00
❑ HL-12006 [M]	Bill Black's Record Hop	1961	30.00
❑ SHL-32006 [S]	Bill Black's Record Hop	1961	30.00
❑ HL-12033 [M]	Black Lace	1966	15.00
❑ SHL-32033 [S]	Black Lace	1966	18.00
❑ SHL-32104	It's Honky Tonk Time	1976	15.00
❑ HL-12036 [M]	King of the Road	1966	15.00
❑ SHL-32036 [S]	King of the Road	1966	18.00
❑ HL-12006 [M]	Let's Twist Her	1961	18.00
—Retitled version of above			
❑ SHL-32006 [S]	Let's Twist Her	1961	25.00
—Retitled version of above			
❑ 8004	Memphis Tennessee	1977	12.00
❑ SHL-32061	More Magic	1971	15.00
❑ HL-12023 [M]	More Solid and Raunchy	1965	18.00
❑ SHL-32023 [S]	More Solid and Raunchy	1965	25.00
❑ HL-12005 [M]	Movin'	1961	25.00
❑ SHL-32005 [S]	Movin'	1961	30.00
❑ HL-12027 [M]	Mr. Beat	1965	18.00
❑ SHL-32027 [S]	Mr. Beat	1965	25.00
❑ HL-12002 [M]	Saxy Jazz	1960	40.00
❑ SHL-32002 [R]	Saxy Jazz	1964	25.00
❑ HL-12001 [M]	Smokie	1960	60.00
—Black label with red and silver logo			
❑ HL-12001 [M]	Smokie	1960	40.00
—Orange and white label			
❑ SHL-32001 [R]	Smokie	1964	25.00
❑ XSHL-32088	Solid and Country	1974	15.00
❑ HL-12003 [M]	Solid and Raunchy	1960	40.00
❑ SHL-32003 [R]	Solid and Raunchy	1964	25.00
❑ SHL-32052	Solid and Raunchy The 3rd	1969	18.00
❑ HL-12047 [M]	Soulin' the Blues	1968	18.00
❑ SHL-32047 [S]	Soulin' the Blues	1968	18.00
❑ HL-12004 [M]	That Wonderful Feeling	1961	25.00
❑ SHL-32004 [S]	That Wonderful Feeling	1961	30.00
❑ HL-12041 [M]	The Beat Goes On	1967	18.00
❑ SHL-32041 [S]	The Beat Goes On	1967	18.00
❑ HL-12009 [M]	The Untouchable Sound of Bill Black	1962	18.00
❑ SHL-32009 [S]	The Untouchable Sound of Bill Black	1962	25.00
❑ SHL-32093	The World's Greatest Honky Tonk Band	1975	15.00
❑ HL-12044 [M]	Turn Your Lovelight On	1967	18.00
❑ SHL-32044 [S]	Turn Your Lovelight On	1967	18.00
MEGA			
❑ MLPS-600	Bill Black Is Back	1973	15.00
❑ 31-1014	Juke Box Favorites	1972	15.00
❑ 51-5008	Rock 'n' Roll Forever	1973	15.00
❑ 31-1008	The Memphis Scene	1971	15.00
BLACK, CILLA			
CAPITOL			
❑ T2308 [M]	Is It Love?	1965	30.00
❑ ST2308 [S]	Is It Love?	1965	40.00
BLACK, CLINT			
RCA			
❑ 9668-1-R	Killin' Time	1989	18.00
❑ R124690	Put Yourself in My Shoes	1990	50.00
—Released on vinyl only through BMG Direct Marketing			
BLACK, FRANK			
SPINART			
❑ spart67	Frank Black and the Catholics	1998	15.00
❑ spart70	Pistolero	1999	15.00
BLACK, JEANNE			
CAPITOL			
❑ T1513 [M]	A Little Bit Lonely	1961	25.00
❑ ST1513 [S]	A Little Bit Lonely	1961	30.00
BLACK BOTTOM STOMPERS (ENGLAND)			
STOMP OFF			
❑ SOS-1045	Stomp Off, Let's Go	1982	12.00
BLACK BOTTOM STOMPERS (SWITZERLAND)			
STOMP OFF			
❑ SOS-1130	Four O'Clock Blues	1987	12.00
BLACK BOX			
RCA			
❑ 2221-1-R	Dreamland	1990	15.00

Number	Title	Yr	NM
BLACK CROWES, THE			
AMERICAN			
❑ 43000 [B]	Amorica	1994	30.00
—All copies of the vinyl LP retained the cover that was censored on most cassette and CD copies			
DEF AMERICAN			
❑ 24278	Shake Your Money Maker	1990	15.00
BLACK EYED PEAS			
INTERSCOPE			
❑ 90152	Behind the Front	1998	15.00
❑ 490661	Bridging the Gap	2000	15.00
BLACK FLAG			
SST			
❑ 081 [EP]	Annihilate This Week	1986	30.00
❑ 007	Damaged	198?	12.00
—Reissue of Unicorn 9502			
❑ 015 [B]	Everything Went Black	1982	40.00
❑ 026 [B]	Family Man	1984	40.00
❑ 226 [EP]	I Can See You	1989	30.00
❑ 045 [B]	In My Head	1985	30.00
❑ 003 [EP]	Jealous Again	1980	40.00
❑ 035 [B]	Loose Nut	1985	35.00
❑ 023 [B]	My War	1984	35.00
❑ 029 [B]	Slip It In	1984	35.00
❑ 021 [B]	The First Four Years	1983	30.00
❑ 037 [EP]	The Process of Weeding Out	1985	30.00
❑ 166 [B]	Wasted Again	1987	30.00
❑ 060	Who's Got the 10 1/2?	1986	15.00
UNICORN/SST			
❑ 9502	Damaged	1981	30.00
—First pressings had stickers on the front and back covers -- the one on the back begins "As a parent...			
❑ 9502 [B]	Damaged	198?	18.00
—With no stickers on cover			
BLACK HEAT			
ATLANTIC			
❑ SD7237	Black Heat	1972	15.00
❑ SD18128	Keep On Burnin'	1975	15.00
❑ SD7294	No Time to Burn	1974	15.00
BLACK ICE			
HDM			
❑ 2001	Black Ice	1977	18.00
❑ 2003	I Judge the Funk	1978	18.00
MONTAGE			
❑ ST-72003	Black Ice	1981	18.00
BLACK IVORY			
BUDDAH			
❑ BDS-5658	Black Ivory	1976	12.00
❑ BDS-5644	Feel It	1975	12.00
❑ BDS-5722	Hangin' Heavy	1979	12.00
TODAY			
❑ 1008	Baby, Won't You Change Your Mind	1972	15.00
❑ 1005	Don't Turn Around	1972	15.00
BLACK KEYS, THE			
FAT POSSUM			
❑ 0371-1 [B]	Thickfreakness	2003	18.00
BLACK LIGHTNING			
TOWER			
❑ ST5129	Shades of Black Lightning	1968	25.00
BLACK MERDA			
CHESS			
❑ LP-1551	Black Merda	1970	50.00
BLACK MOON			
PRIORITY			
❑ 50039	War Zone	1999	15.00
WRECK			
❑ 02002	Enta Da Stage	1993	18.00
BLACK 'N BLUE			
GEFFEN			
❑ GHS24041	Black 'N Blue	1984	10.00
❑ GHS24180	In Heat	1988	10.00
❑ GHS24111	Nasty Nasty	1986	10.00
❑ GHS24075	Without You	1985	10.00
BLACK OAK ARKANSAS			
ATCO			
❑ SD 36-111	Ain't Life Grand	1975	15.00
❑ SD 33-354	Black Oak Arkansas	1971	18.00
❑ SD7035	High on the Hog	1973	18.00
❑ SD7008	If An Angel Came to See You, Would You Make Her Feel at Home?	1972	18.00
❑ SD 33-381 [S]	Keep the Faith	1972	18.00
❑ 33-381 [M]	Keep the Faith	1972	30.00

Number	Title	Yr	NM

— White label promo, "DJ Copy Monaural" sticker on cover; no stock copies were issued in mono

Number	Title	Yr	NM
❑ SD 36-128	Live! Mutha	1976	15.00
❑ SD7019	Raunch 'n' Roll/Live	1973	18.00
❑ QD7019 [Q]	Raunch 'n' Roll/Live	1974	30.00
❑ SD 36-101	Street Party	1974	15.00
❑ SD 36-150	The Best of Black Oak Arkansas	1976	15.00

CAPRICORN

❑ CP 0207	I'd Rather Be Sailing	1978	15.00
❑ CP 0191	Race with the Devil	1977	15.00

MCA

❑ 2224	10 Year Overnight Success	1977	15.00
❑ 2199	Balls of Fire	1976	15.00
❑ 2155	X-Rated	1975	15.00
❑ 704	X-Rated	198?	10.00

— Budget-line reissue

STAX

❑ STS-5504	Early Times	1974	18.00

BLACK PEARL

ATLANTIC

❑ SD8220	Black Pearl	1969	30.00

PROPHESY

❑ PRS-1001	Black Pearl -- Live!	1970	30.00

BLACK RANDY AND THE METROSQUAD

DANGERHOUSE

❑ PCP725	Pass the Dust, I Think I'm Bowie	1980	50.00

BLACK ROB

BAD BOY

❑ 73026	Life Story	2000	18.00

BLACK ROSE

CASABLANCA

❑ NBLP7234	Black Rose	1980	30.00

— Promo copies, with "DJ" and "Promotional Copy Not for Sale" on label, go for less

BLACK SABBATH

I.R.S.

❑ 82002	Headless Cross	1989	12.00

NEMS

❑ NEL6003 [B]	Paranoid	2011	25.00

RHINO

❑ R13186 [B]	Never Say Die!	2013	30.00
❑ R12969 [B]	Technical Ecstasy	2013	30.00
❑ R12923 [B]	We Sold Our Souls for Rock'n'Roll	2013	40.00

WARNER BROS.

❑ WS1871 [B]	Black Sabbath	1970	30.00
— Green label			
❑ WS1871	Black Sabbath	1973	12.00
— Burbank" palm trees label			
❑ WS1871	Black Sabbath	1979	10.00
— White or tan label			
❑ BS2602 [B]	Black Sabbath, Vol. 4	1972	30.00
— Green label			
❑ BS2602	Black Sabbath, Vol. 4	1973	12.00
— Burbank" palm trees label			
❑ BS2602	Black Sabbath, Vol. 4	1979	10.00
— White or tan label			
❑ 23978	Born Again	1983	12.00
❑ BSK3372	Heaven and Hell	1980	15.00
❑ 23742	Live Evil	1983	18.00
❑ BS2562 [B]	Master of Reality	1971	30.00
— Green label			
❑ BS2562	Master of Reality	1973	12.00
— Burbank" palm trees label			
❑ BS2562	Master of Reality	1979	10.00
— White or tan label			
❑ BS2562	Master of Reality Poster	1971	30.00
❑ BSK3605	Mob Rules	1981	15.00
❑ BSK3186	Never Say Die!	1978	15.00
❑ WS1887	Paranoid	1971	18.00
— Green label			
❑ WS1887	Paranoid	1973	12.00
— Burbank" palm trees label			
❑ WS41887 [Q]	Paranoid	1974	50.00
— All quad copies have "Burbank" palm trees label			
❑ BSK3104	Paranoid	1978	12.00
— Reissue; "Burbank" palm trees label			
❑ BSK3104	Paranoid	1979	10.00
— Reissue; white or tan label			
❑ BS2695	Sabbath Bloody Sabbath	1974	18.00
— Burbank" palm trees label			
❑ BS2695	Sabbath Bloody Sabbath	1979	10.00
— White or tan label			
❑ BS2822	Sabotage	1975	18.00
— Burbank" palm trees label			
❑ BS2822	Sabotage	1979	10.00
— White or tan label			
❑ 25337	Seventh Star	1986	12.00
❑ BS2969	Technical Ecstasy	1976	18.00
— Burbank" palm trees label			

Number	Title	Yr	NM
❑ BS2969	Technical Ecstasy	1979	10.00
— White or tan label			
❑ 25548	The Eternal Idol	1987	12.00
❑ 2BS2923	We Sold Our Souls for Rock 'N' Roll	1975	25.00
— Burbank" palm trees label			
❑ 2BS2923	We Sold Our Souls for Rock 'N' Roll	1979	12.00
— White or tan label			

BLACK SHEEP

CAPITOL

❑ ST-11369	Black Sheep	1974	25.00
❑ ST-11447	Encouraging Words	1975	25.00

BLACK SHEEP (1)

MERCURY

❑ 848368-1	A Wolf in Sheep's Clothing	1991	18.00
❑ 522685-1	Non-Fiction	1994	18.00
— May be promo only			

BLACK SHEEP (2)

ENIGMA

❑ 72071	Trouble in the Streets	1985	10.00

BLACK UHURU

HEARTBEAT

❑ HB-18	Guess Who's Coming to Dinner	198?	18.00

ISLAND

❑ 90180	Anthem	1983	12.00
❑ IL-9752	Chill Out	1982	12.00

MANGO

❑ MLPS-9823	Anthem	198?	10.00
— Reissue of Island 90180			
❑ MLPS-9625	Red	1980	12.00
— Black vinyl			
❑ MLPS-9625	Red	1980	18.00
— Red vinyl			
❑ MLPS-9791	Reggae Greats	1984	15.00
❑ MLPS-9593	Sinsimella	1980	12.00
❑ MLPS-9696	Tear It Up	1982	12.00
❑ MLPS-9756	The Dub Factor	1982	15.00

MESA

❑ R1-79021	Now	1990	18.00
❑ R1-79022	Now Dub	1990	18.00

RAS

❑ 3015	Brutal	1986	12.00
❑ 3020	Brutal Dub	1986	15.00
❑ 3025	Positive	1987	15.00

BLACK VELVET

OKEH

❑ OKS14130	Love City	1969	30.00

BLACKBYRDS, THE

FANTASY

❑ F-9535	Action	1977	15.00
❑ F-9602	Better Days	1980	15.00
❑ F-9490	City Life	1975	18.00
❑ F-9472	Flying Start	1974	18.00
❑ FPM-4004 [Q]	Flying Start	1975	30.00
❑ F-9570	Night Grooves	1978	15.00
❑ F-9444	The Blackbyrds	1974	18.00
❑ F-9518	Unfinished Business	1976	18.00

BLACKFOOT, J.

EDGE

❑ 001	U-Turn	1987	15.00

SOUND TOWN

❑ ST8002	City Slicker	1983	15.00
❑ ST8013	Physical Attraction	1984	15.00

BLACKFOOT, J.D.

FANTASY

❑ F-9468	Song of Crazy Horse	1974	25.00
❑ F-9487	Southbound and Gone	1975	25.00

MERCURY

❑ SR-61288	The Ultimate Prophecy	1970	150.00

BLACKFOOT

ANTILLES

❑ AN7076	No Reservations	1975	18.00

ATCO

❑ SD 32-107	Marauder	1981	12.00
❑ 90080	Siogo	1983	12.00
❑ SD 38-112	Strikes	1979	12.00
❑ SD 32-101	Tomcattin'	1980	12.00
❑ 90218	Vertical Smiles	1984	12.00

ATLANTIC

❑ 81743	Rick Medlocke and Blackfoot	1987	15.00

EPIC

❑ PE34378	Flyin' High	1976	18.00
— Orange label			

BLACKHORSE

DSDA

❑ 001	Blackhorse	1979	75.00
— With insert			

BLACKJACK

POLYDOR

❑ PD-1-6215	Blackjack	1979	15.00
❑ PD-1-6279	Worlds Apart	1980	18.00

BLACKMAN, CINDY

MUSE

❑ MR-5341	Arcane	1988	15.00

BLACKMAN, HONOR

LONDON

❑ LL3408 [M]	Everything I've Got	1964	40.00
❑ PS408 [S]	Everything I've Got	1964	60.00

BLACKSMOKE

CHOCOLATE CITY

❑ 2001	Blacksmoke	1976	25.00

BLACKSTREET

INTERSCOPE

❑ INT-90071	Another Level	1996	25.00
❑ INT2-90274	Finally	1999	18.00

BLACKWELL, OTIS

DAVIS

❑ 109 [M]	Singin' the Blues	1956	500.00

INNER CITY

❑ 1032	These Are My Songs	1977	25.00

BLACKWELL, SCRAPPER

BLUESVILLE

❑ BVLP-1047	Mr. Scrapper's Blues	1962	180.00
— Blue label, silver print			
❑ BVLP-1047	Mr. Scrapper's Blues	1964	40.00
— Blue label with trident logo			

BLACKWOOD, R.W.

CAPITOL

❑ ST-11563	We Can Feel Love	1976	12.00

BLACKWOOD BROTHERS, THE

VOICE BOX

❑ VB 0779	Merry Christmas from the Blackwood Brothers	1979	15.00

BLADES, JIMMY, AND CHARLES SMART

LONDON

❑ LB82 [10]	Christmas Chimes	195?	40.00
— Back cover with liner notes and no reference to other LPs			
❑ LB82 [10]	Christmas Chimes	195?	30.00
— Back cover with liner notes and other Christmas LPs mentioned			

RICHMOND

❑ B20063 [M]	Christmas Chimes	196?	15.00
— Reissue of London 82; artist credited only as "Organ and Chimes			

BLADES, RUBEN

ELEKTRA

❑ ED5299 [DJ]	A Conversation with Ruben Blades/Songs and Interview	1988	18.00
❑ 60721	Agua de Luna	1987	12.00
❑ 60795	Antecedente	1988	12.00
❑ 60352	Buscando America	1984	12.00
❑ 60432	Escenas	1985	12.00
❑ 60754	Nothing But the Truth	1988	12.00
❑ 60754 [DJ]	Nothing But the Truth	1988	18.00
— Promo-only white label audiophile edition			

FANIA

❑ JM-576	Maestra Vida	1980	18.00
❑ JM-577	Maestra Vida, Second Part	1980	18.00

BLADES OF GRASS, THE

JUBILEE

❑ JGS-8007	The Blades of Grass Are Not for Smoking	1968	18.00

BLAINE, HAL

ABC DUNHILL

❑ DS-50035	Have Fun!!! Play Drums!!!	1968	50.00
— With instruction booklet			
❑ DS-50035	Have Fun!!! Play Drums!!!	1968	40.00
— Without instruction booklet			

DUNHILL

❑ D-50002 [M]	Drums! Drums! A-Go-Go	1966	30.00
❑ DS-50002 [S]	Drums! Drums! A-Go-Go	1966	40.00
❑ D-50019 [M]	Psychedelic Percussion	1967	40.00
❑ DS-50019 [S]	Psychedelic Percussion	1967	60.00

Number	Title	Yr	NM

RCA VICTOR
| ❑ LPM-2834 [M] | Deuces, "T's," Roadsters & Drums | 1963 | 100.00 |
| ❑ LSP-2834 [S] | Deuces, "T's," Roadsters & Drums | 1963 | 150.00 |

BLAIR, SALLIE

BETHLEHEM
| ❑ BCP-6009 [M] | Squeeze Me | 1957 | 80.00 |

MGM
| ❑ E-3723 [M] | Hello, Tiger! | 1959 | 40.00 |
| ❑ SE-3723 [S] | Hello, Tiger! | 1959 | 50.00 |

BLAKE, BETTY

BETHLEHEM
| ❑ BCP-6058 [M] | Betty Blake Sings in a Tender Mood | 1962 | 400.00 |
—red label
| ❑ BCPS-6058 [S] | Betty Blake Sings in a Tender Mood | 1962 | 250.00 |

BLAKE, EUBIE

BIOGRAPH
| ❑ 1011 | Blues & Ragtime | 1972 | 15.00 |
| ❑ 1012 | Blues & Spirituals | 1972 | 15.00 |

COLUMBIA
| ❑ C2S847 | The Eighty-Six Years of Eubie Blake | 1969 | 25.00 |
—Red "360 Sound" labels
| ❑ C2S847 | The Eighty-Six Years of Eubie Blake | 1970 | 18.00 |
—Orange labels

EUBIE BLAKE MUSIC
❑ EBM-4	Early Rare Recordings	197?	15.00
❑ EBM-7	Early Rare Recordings, Vol. 2	197?	15.00
❑ EBM-8	Eubie Blake and His Proteges	197?	15.00
❑ EBM-1	Eubie Blake Featuring Ivan Harold Browning	197?	15.00
❑ EBM-3	Eubie Blake with Edith Wilson and Ivan Harold Browning	197?	15.00
❑ EBM-6	Introducing Jim Hession	197?	15.00
❑ EBM-5	Live Concert	197?	15.00
❑ EBM-2	Rags to Classics: Charlestown Rag	197?	15.00
❑ EBM-9	Song Hits	197?	15.00

QUICKSILVER
| ❑ QS-9003 | Tricky Fingers | 198? | 12.00 |

BLAKE, HARRIETTE

HARRIETTE BLAKE
| ❑ HBLP-002 | My Way | 1978 | 18.00 |
| ❑ HBLP-001 | This Is My Life | 1976 | 18.00 |

BLAKE, RAN

ARISTA/NOVUS
| ❑ AN3019 | Film Noir | 1980 | 15.00 |
| ❑ AN3006 | Rapport | 1978 | 15.00 |

ESP-DISK'
| ❑ 1011 [M] | Ran Blake Plays Solo Piano | 1965 | 25.00 |
| ❑ S-1011 [S] | Ran Blake Plays Solo Piano | 1965 | 25.00 |

GC
| ❑ 4176 | Take One | 197? | 15.00 |
| ❑ 4177 | Take Two | 197? | 15.00 |

GM RECORDINGS
| ❑ GM-3007 | Painted Rhythms: The Compleat Ran Blake, Vol. 1 | 1987 | 15.00 |
| ❑ GM-3008 | Painted Rhythms: The Compleat Ran Blake, Vol. 2 | 1989 | 15.00 |

IAI
| ❑ 373842 | Breakthru | 1976 | 15.00 |

MILESTONE
| ❑ MSP-9021 | The Blue Potato | 1969 | 18.00 |

OWL
❑ 029	Portrait of Doktor Mabuse	1978	18.00
❑ 012	The Realization of a Dream	1978	18.00
❑ 017	Third Stream Recompositions	1977	18.00
❑ 041	Vertigo	1986	18.00

SOUL NOTE
| ❑ SN-1027 | Duke Dreams | 198? | 15.00 |
| ❑ SN-1077 | Suffield Gothic | 1983 | 15.00 |

BLAKE AND HINES

MOTOWN
| ❑ 6224ML | Blake and Hines | 1987 | 12.00 |

BLAKE BABIES

CHEWBUD
| ❑ CBTW-001 [EP] | Nicely, Nicely | 1987 | 40.00 |
—1,000 copies pressed

MAMMOTH
| ❑ MR0016 [B] | Earwig | 1989 | 18.00 |
| ❑ MR0025 [EP] | Rosy Jack World | 1991 | 18.00 |
—Red vinyl
| ❑ MR0022 [B] | Sunburn | 1990 | 18.00 |

Number	Title	Yr	NM

BLAKEY, ART, AND THE JAZZ MESSENGERS

ABC IMPULSE!
| ❑ AS-45 [S] | A Jazz Message | 1968 | 15.00 |
—Reissue of Impulse AS-45
| ❑ AS-7 [S] | Art Blakey!!!! Jazz Messengers!!!! | 1968 | 15.00 |
—Reissue of Impulse AS-7

BETHLEHEM
❑ BCP-6027 [M]	Art Blakey's Big Band	1958	80.00
❑ BCPS-6027 [S]	Art Blakey's Big Band	1959	50.00
❑ BCP-6023 [M]	Hard Drive	1957	80.00
❑ BCP-6037	Hard Drive	197?	15.00
—Reissue of 6023, distributed by RCA Victor
| ❑ BCP-6015 | The Finest of Art Blakey | 197? | 15.00 |
—Reissue of 6027, distributed by RCA Victor

BLUEBIRD
| ❑ 6286-1-RB | Theory of Art | 1987 | 12.00 |

BLUE NOTE
| ❑ BLP-5037 [10] | A Night at Birdland, Volume 1 | 1954 | 400.00 |
—original cover. Deduct 50% for W 63rd address
| ❑ BLP-1521 [M] | A Night at Birdland, Volume 1 | 1956 | 300.00 |
—Deep groove" version (deep indentation under label on both sides)
| ❑ BLP-1521 [M] | A Night at Birdland, Volume 1 | 1956 | 100.00 |
—Regular version, Lexington Ave. address on label
| ❑ BLP-1521 [M] | A Night at Birdland, Volume 1 | 1957 | 50.00 |
—With W. 63rd St. address on label
| ❑ BLP-1521 [M] | A Night at Birdland, Volume 1 | 1963 | 30.00 |
—With "New York, USA" address on label
| ❑ BST-81521 [R] | A Night at Birdland, Volume 1 | 1968 | 12.00 |
—With "A Division of Liberty Records" on label
| ❑ RLP-1521 [M] | A Night at Birdland, Volume 1 | 1967 | 25.00 |
—A Division of Liberty Records" on label
| ❑ BLP-5038 [10] | A Night at Birdland, Volume 2 | 1954 | 300.00 |
| ❑ BLP-1522 [M] | A Night at Birdland, Volume 2 | 1956 | 300.00 |
—Deep groove" version (deep indentation under label on both sides)
| ❑ BLP-1522 [M] | A Night at Birdland, Volume 2 | 1956 | 100.00 |
—Regular version, Lexington Ave. address on label
| ❑ BLP-1522 [M] | A Night at Birdland, Volume 2 | 1957 | 50.00 |
—With W. 63rd St. address on label
| ❑ BLP-1522 [M] | A Night at Birdland, Volume 2 | 1963 | 30.00 |
—With "New York, USA" address on label
| ❑ BST-81522 [R] | A Night at Birdland, Volume 2 | 1968 | 12.00 |
—With "A Division of Liberty Records" on label
| ❑ BLP-5039 [10] | A Night at Birdland, Volume 3 | 1954 | 300.00 |
| ❑ BLP-4049 [M] | A Night in Tunisia | 1960 | 300.00 |
—Deep groove" version (deep indentation under label on both sides)
| ❑ BLP-4049 [M] | A Night in Tunisia | 1960 | 80.00 |
—Regular version, with W. 63rd St. address on label
| ❑ BLP-4049 [M] | A Night in Tunisia | 1963 | 30.00 |
—With "New York, USA" address on label
| ❑ BST-84049 [S] | A Night in Tunisia | 1960 | 60.00 |
—With W. 63rd St. address on label
| ❑ BST-84049 [S] | A Night in Tunisia | 1963 | 25.00 |
—With "New York, USA" address on label
| ❑ BST-84049 [S] | A Night in Tunisia | 196? | 15.00 |
—With "A Division of Liberty Records" on label
| ❑ B1-84049 | A Night in Tunisia | 1989 | 12.00 |
—The Finest in Jazz Since 1939" reissue
| ❑ BLP-4003 [M] | Art Blakey and the Jazz Messengers | 1958 | 250.00 |
—Deep groove" version (deep indentation under label on both sides)
| ❑ BLP-4003 [M] | Art Blakey and the Jazz Messengers | 1958 | 100.00 |
—Regular version, with W. 63rd St. address on label
| ❑ BLP-4003 [M] | Art Blakey and the Jazz Messengers | 1963 | 30.00 |
—With "New York, USA" address on label
| ❑ BST-4003 [S] | Art Blakey and the Jazz Messengers | 1959 | 200.00 |
—Deep groove" version (deep indentation under label on both sides)
| ❑ BST-4003 [S] | Art Blakey and the Jazz Messengers | 1959 | 80.00 |
—Regular version, with W. 63rd St. address on label
| ❑ BST-4003 [S] | Art Blakey and the Jazz Messengers | 1963 | 25.00 |
—With "New York, USA" address on label
| ❑ BST-84003 [S] | Art Blakey and the Jazz Messengers | 196? | 15.00 |
—With "A Division of Liberty Records" on label
| ❑ BLP-1507 [M] | At the Café Bohemia, Volume 1 | 1956 | 300.00 |
—Deep groove" version (deep indentation under label on both sides)

Number	Title	Yr	NM

| ❑ BLP-1507 [M] | At the Café Bohemia, Volume 1 | 1956 | 100.00 |
—Regular version, Lexington Ave. address on label
| ❑ BLP-1507 [M] | At the Café Bohemia, Volume 1 | 1957 | 50.00 |
—With W. 63rd St. address on label
| ❑ BLP-1507 [M] | At the Café Bohemia, Volume 1 | 1963 | 30.00 |
—With "New York, USA" address on label
| ❑ BST-81507 [R] | At the Café Bohemia, Volume 1 | 1968 | 12.00 |
—With "A Division of Liberty Records" on label
| ❑ BST-81507 [M] | At the Café Bohemia, Volume 1 | 1985 | 12.00 |
—The Finest in Jazz Since 1939" reissue
| ❑ BLP-1508 [M] | At the Café Bohemia, Volume 2 | 1956 | 100.00 |
—Regular version, Lexington Ave. address on label
| ❑ BLP-1508 [M] | At the Café Bohemia, Volume 2 | 1956 | 350.00 |
—Deep groove" version (deep indentation under label on both sides)
| ❑ BLP-1508 [M] | At the Café Bohemia, Volume 2 | 1957 | 50.00 |
—With W. 63rd St. address on label
| ❑ BLP-1508 [M] | At the Café Bohemia, Volume 2 | 1963 | 30.00 |
—With "New York, USA" address on label
| ❑ BST-81508 [R] | At the Café Bohemia, Volume 2 | 1968 | 12.00 |
—With "A Division of Liberty Records" on label
| ❑ B1-81508 | At the Café Bohemia, Volume 2 | 1987 | 12.00 |
—The Finest in Jazz Since 1939" reissue
| ❑ BLP-4015 [M] | At the Jazz Corner of the World, Volume 1 | 1958 | 200.00 |
—Deep groove" version (deep indentation under label on both sides)
| ❑ BLP-4015 [M] | At the Jazz Corner of the World, Volume 1 | 1958 | 80.00 |
—Regular version, with W. 63rd St. address on label
| ❑ BLP-4015 [M] | At the Jazz Corner of the World, Volume 1 | 1963 | 30.00 |
—With "New York, USA" address on label
| ❑ BST-84015 [S] | At the Jazz Corner of the World, Volume 1 | 1959 | 350.00 |
—Deep groove" version (deep indentation under label on both sides)
| ❑ BST-84016 [S] | At the Jazz Corner of the World, Volume 1 | 1959 | 60.00 |
—Regular version, with W. 63rd St. address on label
| ❑ BST-84015 [S] | At the Jazz Corner of the World, Volume 1 | 1963 | 25.00 |
—With "New York, USA" address on label
| ❑ BST-84015 [S] | At the Jazz Corner of the World, Volume 1 | 196? | 15.00 |
—With "A Division of Liberty Records" on label
| ❑ BLP-4016 [M] | At the Jazz Corner of the World, Volume 2 | 1958 | 200.00 |
—Deep groove" version (deep indentation under label on both sides)
| ❑ BLP-4016 [M] | At the Jazz Corner of the World, Volume 2 | 1958 | 80.00 |
—Regular version, with W. 63rd St. address on label
| ❑ BLP-4016 [M] | At the Jazz Corner of the World, Volume 2 | 1963 | 30.00 |
—With "New York, USA" address on label
| ❑ BST-84016 [S] | At the Jazz Corner of the World, Volume 2 | 1959 | 350.00 |
—Deep groove" version (deep indentation under label on both sides)
| ❑ BST-84016 [S] | At the Jazz Corner of the World, Volume 2 | 1959 | 60.00 |
—Regular version, with W. 63rd St. address on label
| ❑ BST-84016 [S] | At the Jazz Corner of the World, Volume 2 | 1963 | 25.00 |
—With "New York, USA" address on label
| ❑ BST-84016 [S] | At the Jazz Corner of the World, Volume 2 | 196? | 15.00 |
—With "A Division of Liberty Records" on label
| ❑ BST-84016 [S] | At the Jazz Corner of the World, Volume 2 | 197? | 12.00 |
—New darker label; with "United Artists Music and Records Group" on label
| ❑ BLP-4104 [M] | Buhaina's Delight | 1962 | 30.00 |
—With "New York, USA" address on label
| ❑ BST-84104 [S] | Buhaina's Delight | 1962 | 40.00 |
—With "New York, USA" address on label
| ❑ BST-84104 [S] | Buhaina's Delight | 196? | 15.00 |
—With "A Division of Liberty Records" on label
| ❑ BLP-4170 [M] | Free for All | 1965 | 30.00 |
| ❑ BST-84170 [S] | Free for All | 1965 | 40.00 |
—With "New York, USA" address on label
| ❑ BST-84170 [S] | Free for All | 196? | 15.00 |
—With "A Division of Liberty Records" on label
| ❑ BLP-4004 [M] | Holiday for Skins, Volume 1 | 1958 | 200.00 |
—Deep groove" version (deep indentation under label on both sides)
| ❑ BLP-4004 [M] | Holiday for Skins, Volume 1 | 1958 | 150.00 |
—Regular version, with W. 63rd St. address on label
| ❑ BLP-4004 [M] | Holiday for Skins, Volume 1 | 1963 | 30.00 |
—With "New York, USA" address on label
| ❑ BST-4004 [S] | Holiday for Skins, Volume 1 | 1959 | 150.00 |
—Deep groove" version (deep indentation under label on both sides)

Number	Title	Yr	NM
❑ BST-4004 [S]	Holiday for Skins, Volume 1	1959	120.00
— Regular version, with W. 63rd St. address on label			
❑ BST-4004 [S]	Holiday for Skins, Volume 1	1963	25.00
— With "New York, USA" address on label			
❑ BST-84004 [S]	Holiday for Skins, Volume 1	196?	15.00
— With "A Division of Liberty Records" on label			
❑ BLP-4005 [M]	Holiday for Skins, Volume 2	1958	200.00
— Deep groove" version (deep indentation under label on both sides)			
❑ BLP-4005 [M]	Holiday for Skins, Volume 2	1958	150.00
— Regular version, with W. 63rd St. address on label			
❑ BLP-4005 [M]	Holiday for Skins, Volume 2	1963	30.00
— With "New York, USA" address on label			
❑ BST-4005 [S]	Holiday for Skins, Volume 2	1959	150.00
— Deep groove" version (deep indentation under label on both sides)			
❑ BST-4005 [S]	Holiday for Skins, Volume 2	1959	120.00
— Regular version, with W. 63rd St. address on label			
❑ BST-4005 [S]	Holiday for Skins, Volume 2	1963	25.00
— With "New York, USA" address on label			
❑ BST-84005 [S]	Holiday for Skins, Volume 2	196?	15.00
— With "A Division of Liberty Records" on label			
❑ BLP-4193 [M]	Indestructible	1966	30.00
❑ BST-84193 [S]	Indestructible	1966	40.00
— With "New York, USA" address on label			
❑ BST-84193 [S]	Indestructible	196?	15.00
— With "A Division of Liberty Records" on label			
❑ BST-84193 [S]	Indestructible	1986	12.00
— The Finest in Jazz Since 1939" reissue			
❑ BLP-4245 [M]	Like Someone in Love	1967	40.00
❑ BST-84245 [S]	Like Someone in Love	1967	40.00
— With "New York, USA" address on label			
❑ BST-84245 [S]	Like Someone in Love	196?	15.00
— With "A Division of Liberty Records" on label			
❑ B1-84245	Like Someone in Love	1989	12.00
— The Finest in Jazz Since 1939" reissue			
❑ BN-LA473-J2	Live Messengers	1975	18.00
❑ BLP-4054 [M]	Meet You at the Jazz Corner of the World, Volume 1	1960	70.00
— With W. 63rd St. address on label			
❑ BLP-4054 [M]	Meet You at the Jazz Corner of the World, Volume 1	1963	30.00
— With "New York, USA" address on label			
❑ BST-84054 [S]	Meet You at the Jazz Corner of the World, Volume 1	1960	60.00
— With W. 63rd St. address on label			
❑ BST-84054 [S]	Meet You at the Jazz Corner of the World, Volume 1	1963	25.00
— With "New York, USA" address on label			
❑ BST-84054 [S]	Meet You at the Jazz Corner of the World, Volume 1	196?	15.00
— With "A Division of Liberty Records" on label			
❑ BLP-4055 [M]	Meet You at the Jazz Corner of the World, Volume 2	1960	70.00
— With W. 63rd St. address on label			
❑ BLP-4055 [M]	Meet You at the Jazz Corner of the World, Volume 2	1963	30.00
— With "New York, USA" address on label			
❑ BST-84055 [S]	Meet You at the Jazz Corner of the World, Volume 2	1960	60.00
— With W. 63rd St. address on label			
❑ BST-84055 [S]	Meet You at the Jazz Corner of the World, Volume 2	1963	25.00
— With "New York, USA" address on label			
❑ BST-84055 [S]	Meet You at the Jazz Corner of the World, Volume 2	196?	15.00
— With "A Division of Liberty Records" on label			
❑ B1-46516	Moanin'	199?	18.00
— Audiophile reissue of 84003			
❑ BLP-4090 [M]	Mosaic	1961	80.00
— With 61st St. address on label			
❑ BLP-4090 [M]	Mosaic	1963	30.00
— With "New York, USA" address on label			
❑ BST-84090 [S]	Mosaic	1961	60.00
— With 61st St. address on label			
❑ BST-84090 [S]	Mosaic	1963	25.00
— With "New York, USA" address on label			
❑ BST-84090 [S]	Mosaic	196?	15.00
— With "A Division of Liberty Records" on label			
❑ B1-46523	Mosaic	199?	18.00
— Audiophile reissue			
❑ LT-1065	Once Upon a Groove	1980	12.00
❑ BLP-1554 [M]	Orgy in Rhythm, Volume 1	1957	150.00
— Deep groove" version (deep indentation under label on both sides)			
❑ BLP-1554 [M]	Orgy in Rhythm, Volume 1	1957	100.00
— Regular version, with W. 63rd St. address on label			
❑ BLP-1554 [M]	Orgy in Rhythm, Volume 1	1963	30.00
— With "New York, USA" address on label			
❑ BST-81554 [R]	Orgy in Rhythm, Volume 1	1968	12.00
— With "A Division of Liberty Records" on label			
❑ BLP-1555 [M]	Orgy in Rhythm, Volume 2	1957	100.00
— Regular version, with W. 63rd St. address on label			
❑ BLP-1555 [M]	Orgy in Rhythm, Volume 2	1957	150.00
— Deep groove" version (deep indentation under label on both sides)			
❑ BLP-1555 [M]	Orgy in Rhythm, Volume 2	1963	30.00
— With "New York, USA" address on label			
❑ BST-81555 [R]	Orgy in Rhythm, Volume 2	1968	12.00
— With "A Division of Liberty Records" on label			
❑ BST-84347	Roots and Herbs	1970	15.00

Number	Title	Yr	NM
— With "Liberty/UA" on label			
❑ BLP-4097 [M]	The African Beat	1961	80.00
— With 61st St. address on label			
❑ BLP-4097 [M]	The African Beat	1963	30.00
— With "New York, USA" address on label			
❑ BST-84097 [S]	The African Beat	1961	60.00
— With 61st St. address on label			
❑ BST-84097 [S]	The African Beat	1963	30.00
— With "New York, USA" address on label			
❑ BST-84097 [S]	The African Beat	196?	15.00
— With "A Division of Liberty Records" on label			
❑ B1-93205	The Best of Art Blakey and the Jazz Messengers	1989	15.00
❑ BLP-4029 [M]	The Big Beat	1960	100.00
— Deep groove" version (deep indentation under label on both sides)			
❑ BLP-4029 [M]	The Big Beat	1960	80.00
— Regular version, with W. 63rd St. address on label			
❑ BLP-4029 [M]	The Big Beat	1963	30.00
— With "New York, USA" address on label			
❑ BST-84029 [S]	The Big Beat	1960	60.00
— With W. 63rd St. address on label			
❑ BST-84029 [S]	The Big Beat	1963	25.00
— With "New York, USA" address on label			
❑ BST-84029 [S]	The Big Beat	196?	15.00
— With "A Division of Liberty Records" on label			
❑ BST-84029 [S]	The Big Beat	1985	12.00
— The Finest in Jazz Since 1939" reissue			
❑ BLP-4156 [M]	The Freedom Rider	1964	30.00
❑ BST-84156 [S]	The Freedom Rider	1964	40.00
— With "New York, USA" address on label			
❑ BST-84156 [S]	The Freedom Rider	196?	15.00
— With "A Division of Liberty Records" on label			
❑ BST-84258 [S]	The Witch Doctor	1969	25.00
— With "A Division of Liberty Records" on label			
CADET			
❑ LP-4049 [M]	Tough!	1966	30.00
❑ LPS-4049 [S]	Tough!	1966	30.00
CATALYST			
❑ 7902	Jazz Messengers '70	197?	15.00
COLUMBIA			
❑ CL1002 [M]	Drum Suite	1957	60.00
— Red and black label with six "eye" logos			
❑ CL1002 [M]	Drum Suite	200?	15.00
— 180-gram reissue			
❑ CL1040 [M]	Hard Bop	1957	60.00
— Red and black label with six "eye" logos			
❑ CL897 [M]	The Jazz Messengers	1956	80.00
— Red and black label with six "eye" logos			
❑ FC38036	The Original Jazz Messengers – A Quarter Century Ago	1982	12.00
CONCORD JAZZ			
❑ CJ-68	In This Korner	1978	18.00
❑ CJ-196	Keystone 3	1982	12.00
❑ CJ-307	Live at Kimball's	1986	12.00
❑ CJ-256	New York Scene	1984	12.00
❑ CJ-168	Straight Ahead	1981	12.00
ELEKTRA			
❑ EKL-120 [M]	A Midnight Session with the Jazz Messengers	1957	80.00
EMARCY			
❑ MG-26030 [10]	Blakey	1954	500.00
EPIC			
❑ LA16017 [M]	Art Blakey in Paris	1961	30.00
❑ BA17017 [S]	Art Blakey in Paris	1961	40.00
❑ LA16009 [M]	Paris Concert	1960	30.00
❑ BA17009 [S]	Paris Concert	1960	40.00
EVEREST ARCHIVE OF FOLK & JAZZ			
❑ 332	Jazz Messengers	197?	12.00
FANTASY			
❑ OJC-038	Caravan	198?	12.00
❑ OJC-145	Kyoto	198?	12.00
❑ OJC-090	Ugetsu	198?	12.00
GNP CRESCENDO			
❑ GNPS-2182	Live at Sweet Basil	1986	12.00
IMPULSE!			
❑ A-45 [M]	A Jazz Message	1963	30.00
❑ AS-45 [S]	A Jazz Message	1963	40.00
❑ A-7 [M]	Art Blakey!!!! Jazz Messengers!!!!	1961	30.00
❑ AS-7 [S]	Art Blakey!!!! Jazz Messengers!!!!	1961	40.00
JOSIE			
❑ JOZ-3501 [M]	Cu-Bop	1962	40.00
— Reissue of Jubilee LP			
❑ JS-3501 [S]	Cu-Bop	1962	30.00
JUBILEE			
❑ JLP-1049 [M]	Cu-Bop	1958	80.00
LIMELIGHT			
❑ LM-82034 [M]	Buttercorn Lady	1966	25.00
❑ LS-86034 [S]	Buttercorn Lady	1966	30.00
❑ LM-82038 [M]	Hold On, I'm Coming	1966	25.00
❑ LS-86038 [S]	Hold On, I'm Coming	1966	30.00
❑ LM-82001 [M]	'S Make It	1965	25.00
❑ LS-86001 [S]	'S Make It	1965	30.00
❑ LM-82019 [M]	Soul Finger	1965	25.00
❑ LS-86019 [S]	Soul Finger	1965	30.00

Number	Title	Yr	NM
MCA IMPULSE!			
❑ MCA-5648	A Jazz Message	1986	10.00
— Reissue			
MILESTONE			
❑ 47008	Thermo	197?	18.00
MOSAIC			
❑ MR10-141	The Complete Blue Note Recordings of Art Blakey's 1960 Jazz Messengers	199?	150.00
ODYSSEY			
❑ PC36809	Hard Bop	1981	12.00
❑ PC37021	The Jazz Messengers	1981	12.00
PACIFIC JAZZ			
❑ PJM-402 [M]	Ritual	1957	80.00
❑ PJ-15 [M]	Ritual	1961	40.00
— Reissue of 402			
PRESTIGE			
❑ 10076	Anthenagin	197?	15.00
❑ 10067	Buhaina	197?	15.00
❑ 10047	Child's Dance	197?	15.00
RCA VICTOR			
❑ LPM-2654 [M]	A Night in Tunisia	1963	40.00
— Reissue of Vik 1115			
❑ LSP-2654 [R]	A Night in Tunisia	1963	25.00
RIVERSIDE			
❑ RS-438 [M]	Caravan	1962	30.00
❑ RS-9438 [S]	Caravan	1962	30.00
❑ 6074	Caravan	197?	15.00
❑ RS-493 [M]	Kyoto	1966	25.00
❑ RS-9493 [S]	Kyoto	1966	30.00
❑ RS-464 [M]	Ugetsu	1963	30.00
❑ RS-9464 [S]	Ugetsu	1963	30.00
❑ RS-3022	Ugetsu	1968	15.00
ROULETTE			
❑ SR-5003	Backgammon	1976	15.00
❑ SR-5008	Gypsy Folk Tales	1977	15.00
SAVOY			
❑ MG-12171 [M]	Art Blakey and the Jazz Messengers	1960	30.00
SAVOY JAZZ			
❑ SJL-1112	Mirage	1977	18.00
SOLID STATE			
❑ SS-18033	Three Blind Mice	1969	15.00
SOUL NOTE			
❑ 121155-1	I Get a Kick Out of You	1990	15.00
❑ 121105-1	Not Yet	1989	15.00
TIMELESS			
❑ SJP-307	Feel the Wind	1990	15.00
❑ 301	In My Prime, Vol. 1	1979	15.00
❑ 317	Reflections in Blue	1980	15.00
TRIP			
❑ 5019	Art Blakey and the Jazz Messengers	197?	12.00
❑ 5034	Art Blakey and the Jazz Messengers Live	197?	12.00
❑ 5505	Buttercorn Lady	197?	12.00
UNITED ARTISTS			
❑ UAJ-14002 [M]	Three Blind Mice	1962	40.00
❑ UAJS-15002 [S]	Three Blind Mice	1962	50.00
❑ UAS-5633	Three Blind Mice	197?	12.00
VEE JAY			
❑ VJS-3066	Bag of Blues Featuring Buddy DeFranco	1977	15.00
VIK			
❑ LX-1115 [M]	A Night in Tunisia	1958	100.00
❑ LX-1103 [M]	Art Blakey and the Jazz Messengers Play Selections from Lerner and Loewe	1957	100.00

BLAKEY, ART, AND THE JAZZ MESSENGERS/ ELMO HOPE

Number	Title	Yr	NM
PACIFIC JAZZ			
❑ PJ-33 [M]	The Jazz Messengers and Elmo Hope	1962	40.00

BLAKEY, ART, AND THE JAZZ MESSENGERS/ MAX ROACH

Number	Title	Yr	NM
CHESS			
❑ CH2-92511	Percussion Discussion	198?	18.00

BLAKEY, ART, AND THE JAZZ MESSENGERS WITH THELONIOUS MONK

Number	Title	Yr	NM
ATLANTIC			
❑ 1278 [M]	Art Blakey's Jazz Messengers with Thelonious Monk	1958	50.00
— Black label			
❑ 1278 [M]	Art Blakey's Jazz Messengers with Thelonious Monk	1960	25.00
— Multicolor label, white "fan" logo			
❑ 1278 [M]	Art Blakey's Jazz Messengers with Thelonious Monk	1963	18.00
— Multicolor label, black "fan" logo			

Number	Title	Yr	NM
❑ SD1278 [S]	Art Blakey's Jazz Messengers with Thelonious Monk	1959	40.00
— Green label			
❑ SD1278 [S]	Art Blakey's Jazz Messengers with Thelonious Monk	1960	18.00
— Multicolor label, white "fan" logo			
❑ SD1278 [S]	Art Blakey's Jazz Messengers with Thelonious Monk	1963	15.00
— Multicolor label, black "fan" logo			

ODYSSEY

Number	Title	Yr	NM
❑ 32160246	Art Blakey with the Original Jazz Messengers	1968	18.00

BLANC, MEL

CAPITOL

Number	Title	Yr	NM
❑ H-436 [10]	Party Panic	1953	100.00

BLANCHARD, JACK, AND MISTY MORGAN

MEGA

Number	Title	Yr	NM
❑ 31-1009	Two Sides	1972	15.00

WAYSIDE

Number	Title	Yr	NM
❑ WWS 33-001	Birds of a Feather	1970	18.00

BLANCHARD, PIERRE

SUNNYSIDE

Number	Title	Yr	NM
❑ SSC-1023	Music for String Quartet, Jazz Trio, Violin and Lee Konitz	1988	12.00

BLANCHARD, TERENCE, AND DONALD HARRISON

COLUMBIA

Number	Title	Yr	NM
❑ FC44216	Black Pearl	1988	12.00
❑ FC40830	Crystal Star	1987	12.00
❑ BFC40335	Nascence	1986	12.00

GEORGE WEIN COLLECTION

Number	Title	Yr	NM
❑ GW-3008	Discernment	1986	15.00
❑ GW-3002	New York Second Line	1984	15.00

BLANCMANGE

ISLAND

Number	Title	Yr	NM
❑ 90053	Happy Families	1983	12.00

SIRE

Number	Title	Yr	NM
❑ 25345	Believe You Me	1985	12.00
❑ 25172	Mange Tout	1984	12.00

BLAND, BOBBY, AND B.B. KING

ABC DUNHILL

Number	Title	Yr	NM
❑ DSY-50190	Together for the First Time... Live	1974	18.00

ABC IMPULSE!

Number	Title	Yr	NM
❑ 9317	Together Again...Live	1976	15.00

COMMAND

Number	Title	Yr	NM
❑ CQDY-40012 [Q]	Together for the First Time... Live	1974	30.00

MCA

Number	Title	Yr	NM
❑ 27012	Together Again...Live	198?	10.00
— Reissue of ABC Impulse! 9317			
❑ 4160	Together for the First Time... Live	198?	12.00
— Reissue of ABC Dunhill 50190			

BLAND, BOBBY

ABC

Number	Title	Yr	NM
❑ AA-1075	Come Fly with Me	1978	12.00
❑ D-895	Get On Down with Bobby Bland	1975	15.00
❑ AB-1018	Reflections in Blue	1977	12.00

ABC DUKE

Number	Title	Yr	NM
❑ DLP-78	Ain't Nothing You Can Do	1974	15.00
❑ DLP-88	A Touch of the Blues	1974	15.00
❑ DLP-77	Call On Me/That's the Way Love Is	1974	15.00
❑ DLP-75	Here's the Man!!!	1974	15.00
❑ DLP92-2	Introspective of the Early Years	1974	25.00
❑ DLP-89	Spotlighting the Man	1974	15.00
❑ DLP-84	The Best of Bobby Bland	1974	15.00
❑ DLP-86	The Best of Bobby Bland, Volume 2	1974	15.00
❑ DLP-79	The Soul of the Man	1974	15.00
❑ DLPS-74	Two Steps from the Blues	197?	15.00

ABC DUNHILL

Number	Title	Yr	NM
❑ DSX-50169	Dreamer	1974	18.00
❑ DSX-50163	His California Album	1973	18.00

BLUESWAY

Number	Title	Yr	NM
❑ BLS-6065	Call On Me	197?	18.00

DUKE

Number	Title	Yr	NM
❑ DLP-78 [M]	Ain't Nothing You Can Do	1964	80.00
❑ DLPS-78 [S]	Ain't Nothing You Can Do	1964	120.00
❑ DLP-88 [M]	A Touch of the Blues	1968	30.00
❑ DLPS-88 [S]	A Touch of the Blues	1968	25.00
❑ DLP-77 [M]	Call On Me/That's the Way Love Is	1963	100.00
❑ DLPS-77 [S]	Call On Me/That's the Way Love Is	1963	150.00
❑ DLP-75 [M]	Here's the Man!!!	1962	200.00
— Purple and yellow label			
❑ DLP-75 [M]	Here's the Man!!!	1962	100.00
— Orange label			
❑ DLPS-75 [S]	Here's the Man!!!	1962	200.00
— With spoken intro to "36-22-36			
❑ DLPS-75 [S]	Here's the Man!!!	196?	100.00
— Without spoken intro to "36-22-36			
❑ DLPS-90	If Loving You Is Wrong	1970	25.00
❑ DLPS-89	Spotlighting the Man	1969	25.00
❑ DLP-84 [M]	The Best of Bobby Bland	1967	25.00
❑ DLPS-84 [P]	The Best of Bobby Bland	1967	30.00
❑ DLP-86 [M]	The Best of Bobby Bland, Volume 2	1968	30.00
❑ DLPS-86 [P]	The Best of Bobby Bland, Volume 2	1968	25.00
❑ DLP-79 [M]	The Soul of the Man	1966	80.00
❑ DLPS-79 [S]	The Soul of the Man	1966	120.00
❑ DLP-74 [M]	Two Steps from the Blues	1961	250.00
— Purple and yellow label			
❑ DLP-74 [M]	Two Steps from the Blues	1962	250.00
— Orange label, red vinyl			
❑ DLP-74 [M]	Two Steps from the Blues	1962	100.00
— Orange label, black vinyl			
❑ DLPS-74 [R]	Two Steps from the Blues	196?	60.00

MCA

Number	Title	Yr	NM
❑ 27040	Ain't Nothing You Can Do	198?	10.00
— Reissue of Duke 78			
❑ 27047	A Touch of the Blues	1984	10.00
— Reissue of Duke 88			
❑ 27042	Call On Me/That's the Way Love Is	1984	10.00
— Reissue of Duke 77			
❑ 27044	Come Fly with Me	1984	10.00
— Reissue of ABC 1075			
❑ 27038	Here's the Man!!!	198?	10.00
— Reissue of Duke 75			
❑ 5297	Here We Go Again	1982	12.00
❑ 3157	I Feel Good, I Feel Fine	1979	12.00
❑ 27073	I Feel Good, I Feel Fine	1985	10.00
— Reissue of MCA 3157			
❑ 4172	Introspective of the Early Years	198?	12.00
— Reissue of Duke 92			
❑ 27043	Reflections in Blue	1984	10.00
— Reissue of ABC 1018			
❑ 27048	Spotlighting the Man	1984	10.00
— Reissue of Duke 89			
❑ 5145	Sweet Vibrations	1980	12.00
❑ 27076	Sweet Vibrations	198?	10.00
— Reissue of 5145			
❑ 5425	Tell Mr. Bland	1983	12.00
❑ 27013	The Best of Bobby Bland	198?	10.00
— Reissue of Duke 84			
❑ 27046	The Best of Bobby Bland, Volume 2	1984	10.00
— Reissue of Duke 86			
❑ 27041	The Soul of the Man	1984	10.00
— Reissue of Duke 79			
❑ 5233	Try Me, I'm Real	1981	12.00
❑ 27036	Two Steps from the Blues	198?	10.00
— Reissue of Duke 74			
❑ 5503	You've Got Me Loving You	1984	12.00

BLASSIE, FRED

RHINO

Number	Title	Yr	NM
❑ RNLP-813 [PD]	I Bite the Songs	1985	25.00

BLAST, C.L.

COTILLION

Number	Title	Yr	NM
❑ SD5222	I Wanna Get Down	1980	15.00

BLASTERS, THE

CROWN

Number	Title	Yr	NM
❑ CLP-5392 [M]	Sounds of the Drags	1963	25.00
❑ CST-392 [S]	Sounds of the Drags	1963	30.00

ROLLIN' ROCK

Number	Title	Yr	NM
❑ 021	American Music	1980	75.00

SLASH

Number	Title	Yr	NM
❑ 25093	Hard Line	1985	12.00
❑ 23818	Non Fiction	1983	12.00
❑ 23735 [EP]	Over There: Live at the Venue, London	1982	12.00
❑ BKS3680	The Blasters	1982	12.00
— With blue labels; reissue of 109			
❑ SR109	The Blasters	1981	18.00

WARNER BROS.

Number	Title	Yr	NM
❑ WBMS-130 [DJ]	Music and Interviews	1985	40.00
— Part of "The Warner Bros. Music Show" series; one side is The Blasters; the other side is The Smiths, which accounts for this piece's value			

BLAZING REDHEADS

REFERENCE RECORDINGS

Number	Title	Yr	NM
❑ RR-26	Blazing Redheads	1988	25.00
❑ RR-41	Crazed Women	1991	25.00

BLESSED END

TNS

Number	Title	Yr	NM
❑ 248	Movin' On	1971	250.00

BLEY, PAUL, AND GARY PEACOCK

ECM

Number	Title	Yr	NM
❑ 1003ST	Paul Bley with Gary Peacock	1973	18.00
— Original issue, made in Germany?			

BLEY, PAUL, AND NIELS-HENNING ORSTED PEDERSEN

INNER CITY

Number	Title	Yr	NM
❑ IC-2005	Paul Bley and Niels-Henning Orsted Pedersen	1973	18.00

STEEPLECHASE

Number	Title	Yr	NM
❑ SCS-1005	Paul Bley and Niels-Henning Orsted Pedersen	198?	15.00

BLEY, PAUL; GARY PEACOCK; BARRY ALTSCHUL

IAI

Number	Title	Yr	NM
❑ 373849	Japan Suite	1977	18.00
❑ 373844	Virtuosi	1976	18.00

BLEY, PAUL

ARISTA/FREEDOM

Number	Title	Yr	NM
❑ AL1901	Copenhagen and Haarlem	197?	25.00

DEBUT

Number	Title	Yr	NM
❑ DLP-7 [10]	Introducing Paul Bley	1954	600.00

ECM

Number	Title	Yr	NM
❑ 1010ST	Ballads	1973	25.00
— Original issue, made in Germany?			
❑ 1320	Fragments	198?	18.00
— Made in Germany			
❑ 1023ST	Open to Love	1974	18.00
— Original issue, made in Germany?			
❑ ECM-1-1023	Open to Love	197?	15.00
— Distributed by Polydor			

EMARCY

Number	Title	Yr	NM
❑ MG-36092 [M]	Paul Bley	1955	200.00

ESP-DISK'

Number	Title	Yr	NM
❑ 1008 [M]	Barrage	1965	30.00
❑ S-1008 [S]	Barrage	1965	40.00
❑ 1021 [M]	Closer	1966	40.00
❑ S-1021 [S]	Closer	1966	50.00

FANTASY

Number	Title	Yr	NM
❑ OJC-201	Introducing Paul Bley	198?	15.00
— Reissue of Debut 7			

GENE NORMAN

Number	Title	Yr	NM
❑ GNP-31 [M]	Solemn Meditation	1957	80.00

GNP CRESCENDO

Number	Title	Yr	NM
❑ GNPS-31 [R]	Solemn Meditation	197?	18.00
❑ GT-3002	Solemn Meditation	198?	18.00

IAI

Number	Title	Yr	NM
❑ 373840	Alone Again	1975	18.00
❑ 373853	Axis	1978	25.00
❑ 373839	Quiet Song	1975	18.00
— With Jimmy Giuffre and Bill Connors			
❑ 373841	Turning Point	1975	15.00
— With John Gilmore			

INNER CITY

Number	Title	Yr	NM
❑ IC-1007	Live at the Hillcrest 1958	197?	18.00

LIMELIGHT

Number	Title	Yr	NM
❑ LS-86060	Mr. Joy	1968	100.00

MILESTONE

Number	Title	Yr	NM
❑ MSP-9046	Paul Bley and Scorpio	1973	60.00
— Reproductions exist			
❑ MSP-9033	Synthesizer Show	1970	150.00

OWL

Number	Title	Yr	NM
❑ 034	Tears	1984	40.00

SAVOY

Number	Title	Yr	NM
❑ MG-12182 [M]	Footloose!	1964	80.00

SAVOY JAZZ

Number	Title	Yr	NM
❑ SJL-1148	Floater	1984	18.00
❑ SJL-1175	Syndrome	1987	18.00
❑ SJL-1192	Turns	1988	18.00

SOUL NOTE

Number	Title	Yr	NM
❑ SN-1140	Paul Bley Group	1986	18.00
❑ SN-1085	Sonor	1984	18.00
❑ SN-1090	Tango Palace	1985	18.00

STEEPLECHASE

Number	Title	Yr	NM
❑ SCS-1214	My Standard	198?	18.00
❑ SCS-1205	Questions	198?	25.00
❑ SCS-1236	Solo Piano	198?	25.00
❑ SCS-1246	The Nearness of You	198?	18.00

TRIP

Number	Title	Yr	NM
❑ TLP-5587	Mr. Joy	197?	18.00

WING

Number	Title	Yr	NM
❑ MGW-60001 [M]	Paul Bley	1956	120.00

Number	Title	Yr	NM

BLEYER, ARCHIE

CADENCE
❏ CLP-3044 [M]	Moonlight Serenade	1962	25.00
❏ CLP-25044 [S]	Moonlight Serenade	1962	30.00

BLIGE, MARY J.

GEFFEN
❏ 1033301	Growing Pains	2008	25.00

MCA
❏ 111929	Mary	1999	18.00
❏ 112616	No More Drama	2001	18.00
— Original edition			
❏ 112808	No More Drama (2002)	2002	15.00
— Revised edition			
❏ 11606	Share My World	1997	18.00

UPTOWN
❏ 11156	My Life	1994	18.00
❏ 10681	What's the 411?	1992	18.00

BLIND FAITH

ATCO
❏ 33-304A [M]	Blind Faith	1969	200.00
— White label promo only			
❏ SD 33-304A [S]	Blind Faith	1969	30.00
— Cover with naked girl on Side 1 and same scene without girl on Side 2			
❏ SD 33-304B [S]	Blind Faith	1969	18.00
— Cover with band photo on Side 1 and song lyrics on Side 2			

MOBILE FIDELITY
❏ 1-186	Blind Faith	1985	40.00
— Audiophile vinyl			

RSO
❏ RS-1-3016	Blind Faith	1977	12.00
— Reissue with naked girl on one side and band photo on the other			
❏ 825094-1	Blind Faith	1986	10.00

BLIND MELON

CAPITOL
❏ 28732	Soup	1995	18.00

BLINK 182

KUNG FU
❏ 78765 [B]	Buddha	1998	18.00
— Reissue of 1995 album			

BLITZ

CLEOPATRA
❏ 8096 [B]	Warriors		25.00

BLOCKER, DAN, AND JOHN MITCHUM

RCA VICTOR
❏ LPM-2896 [M]	Our Land -- Our Heritage	1964	30.00
❏ LSP-2896 [S]	Our Land -- Our Heritage	1964	40.00

BLOCKER, DAN

TREY
❏ TLP-903 [M]	Tales for Young 'Uns	1961	50.00

BLOND

FONTANA
❏ SRF-67067	Blond	1969	25.00

BLONDE ON BLONDE

JANUS
❏ JLP-3003	Contrasts	1969	30.00

BLONDIE

CHRYSALIS
❏ CHS24PDJ [DJ]	At Home with Debbie Harry and Chris Stein	1981	60.00
— Open-end interview with script			
❏ CHE1290	Autoamerican	1980	12.00
❏ PV41290	Autoamerican	1983	10.00
— Reissue			
❏ CHR1165	Blondie	1977	15.00
— Reissue of Private Stock album			
❏ PV41165	Blondie	1983	10.00
— Reissue			
❏ CHE1225	Eat to the Beat	1979	12.00
❏ PV41225	Eat to the Beat	1983	10.00
— Reissue			
❏ R200816	Once More into the Bleach	1988	25.00
— BMG Music Service edition			
❏ V2X41658	Once More into the Bleach	1988	18.00
— Remixes of Blondie and Debbie Harry tracks			
❏ CHR1192	Parallel Lines	1978	18.00
— First pressing, with 3:54 version of "Heart of Glass"			
❏ CHR1192	Parallel Lines	1979	12.00
— Second pressing, with 5:50 version of "Heart of Glass" (Disco Version)			
❏ CHP5001 [PD]	Parallel Lines	1979	30.00
— Picture disc			
❏ FV41192	Parallel Lines	1983	10.00

Number	Title	Yr	NM
— Reissue			
❏ PV41192	Parallel Lines	1986	10.00
— Reissue			
❏ CHR1166	Plastic Letters	1977	25.00
— Green label			
❏ PV41166 [B]	Plastic Letters	1983	10.00
— Reissue			
❏ CHR1166	Plastic Letters	1977	15.00
— Blue and white label			
❏ CHS1337	The Best of Blondie	1981	12.00
❏ FV41337	The Best of Blondie	1983	10.00
— Reissue			
❏ PV41337	The Best of Blondie	1986	10.00
— Reissue			
❏ CHR1384	The Hunter	1982	10.00
❏ PV41384	The Hunter	1983	10.00
— Reissue			
❏ F132748	The Remix Project: Remixed, Remade, Remodeled	1995	18.00

MOBILE FIDELITY
❏ 1-050 [B]	Parallel Lines	1980	40.00
— Audiophile vinyl			

PRIVATE STOCK
❏ PS-2023 [B]	Blondie	1976	35.00

BLOOD, SWEAT AND TEARS

ABC
❏ 1015	Brand New Day	1977	12.00

CBS SPECIAL PRODUCTS
❏ P16660	Musically Speaking	1982	12.00

COLUMBIA
❏ CS9720	Blood, Sweat and Tears	1969	18.00
— Red "360 Sound" label			
❏ CS9720	Blood, Sweat and Tears	1970	12.00
— Orange label			
❏ PC9720	Blood, Sweat and Tears	1980	10.00
❏ CQ30994 [Q]	Blood, Sweat and Tears	1972	30.00
❏ KC30090	Blood, Sweat and Tears 3	1970	12.00
❏ PC30090	Blood, Sweat and Tears 3	1986	10.00
❏ KC31170	Blood, Sweat and Tears' Greatest Hits	1972	12.00
— With the single versions of "You've Made Me So Very Happy," "Spinning Wheel," and "And When I Die" (all in mono)			
❏ CQ31170 [Q]	Blood, Sweat and Tears' Greatest Hits	1972	30.00
❏ PC31170	Blood, Sweat and Tears' Greatest Hits	1980	10.00
❏ PCQ31170 [Q]	Blood, Sweat and Tears' Greatest Hits	1976	25.00
— Reissue with new prefix			
❏ KC30590	BS&T: 4	1971	12.00
❏ CS9616 [S]	Child Is Father to the Man	1968	18.00
— Red "360 Sound" label			
❏ CS9616	Child Is Father to the Man	1970	12.00
— Orange label			
❏ PC9619	Child Is Father to the Man	1980	10.00
❏ HC49619	Child Is Father to the Man	1981	50.00
— Half-speed mastered edition			
❏ CS9616 [M]	Child Is Father to the Man	1968	30.00
— White label promo only, "Special Mono Radio Station Copy" sticker on cover, with same number as stereo edition			
❏ PC32929	Mirror Image	1974	12.00
❏ CQ32929 [Q]	Mirror Image	1974	30.00
❏ PC34233	More Than Ever	1976	12.00
❏ KC31780	New Blood	1972	12.00
❏ PC33484	New City	1975	12.00
❏ PCQ33484 [Q]	New City	1975	30.00
❏ KC32180	No Sweat	1973	12.00

DIRECT DISK
❏ SD-16605	Blood, Sweat and Tears	1981	60.00
❏ L33-1865 [DJ]	Nuclear Blues	1980	18.00
— Promo only on gold vinyl			
❏ 3061	Nuclear Blues	1980	12.00

MOBILE FIDELITY
❏ 1-251	Blood, Sweat and Tears	1996	120.00
— Audiophile vinyl; fewer than 2,000 pressed			

BLOOMFIELD, MIKE, AND AL KOOPER

COLUMBIA
❏ KGP6	The Live Adventures of Mike Bloomfield & Al Kooper	1969	30.00
— Red "360 Sound" labels			
❏ PG6	The Live Adventures of Mike Bloomfield & Al Kooper	197?	15.00
— Reissue with new prefix			

BLOOMFIELD, MIKE, AND NICK GRAVENITES

COLUMBIA
❏ CS9899 [B]	My Labors	1969	18.00
— Red "360 Sound" label			
❏ CS9899 [B]	My Labors	1970	15.00
— Orange label			

BLOOMFIELD, MIKE

COLUMBIA
❏ C237578	Bloomfield	1982	15.00
❏ CS9883	It's Not Killing Me	1969	18.00
— Red "360 Sound" label			

Number	Title	Yr	NM

HARMONY
❏ KH30395	It's Not Killing Me	1971	12.00

SUNDAZED
❏ LP5105	I'm Cutting Out	2001	15.00

TAKOMA
❏ C-1059	Analine	1977	12.00
❏ TAK-7059	Analine	198?	10.00
❏ C-1070	Between a Hard Place and the Ground	1979	12.00
❏ TAK-7070	Between a Hard Place and the Ground	198?	10.00
❏ TAK-7091	Cruisin' for a Bruisin'	198?	10.00
❏ C-1063	Michael Bloomfield	1978	12.00
❏ TAK-7063	Michael Bloomfield	198?	10.00

WATERHOUSE
❏ 11	Living in the Fast Lane	1981	12.00

BLOOMFIELD, MIKE/AL KOOPER/STEVE STILLS

COLUMBIA
❏ CS9701	Super Session	1968	25.00
— Red "360 Sound" label			
❏ CS9701	Super Session	1970	12.00
— Orange label			
❏ CQ30991 [Q]	Super Session	1971	30.00
❏ PC9701	Super Session	198?	10.00
— Reissue with new prefix			

MOBILE FIDELITY
❏ 1-178 [B]	Super Session	198?	60.00
— Audiophile vinyl			

BLOOMFIELD, MIKE/JOHN PAUL HAMMOND/DR. JOHN

COLUMBIA
❏ KC32172	Triumvirate	1973	15.00

BLOSSOMS, THE

LION
❏ 1007	Shockwave	1972	18.00

BLOW, KURTIS

MERCURY
❏ 826141-1	America	1985	12.00
❏ 834692-1	Back by Popular Demand	1988	12.00
❏ SRM-1-4020	Deuce	1981	12.00
❏ 822420-1	Ego Trip	1984	12.00
❏ 830215-1	Kingdom Blow	1986	12.00
❏ SRM-1-3854	Kurtis Blow	1980	15.00
❏ 812757-1	Party Time?	1983	12.00
❏ MX-1-505 [EP]	Tough	1982	12.00

BLOW MONKEYS

RCA
❏ NFL1-8065	Animal Magic	1986	12.00
❏ MFL1-8527 [EP]	Forbidden Fruit	1985	12.00
❏ 6246-1-R	She Was Only a Grocer's Daughter	1987	12.00

BLU, PEGGI

CAPITOL
❏ ST-12550	Blu Blowin'	1987	12.00

BLUE, DAVID

ASYLUM
❏ 7E-1043	Com'n Back for More	1975	12.00
❏ 7E-1077	Cupid's Arrow	1976	12.00
❏ SD5052	Stories	1972	15.00
❏ SD5066	The Nice Baby and the Angel	1973	15.00

ELEKTRA
❏ EKM-4003 [M]	David Blue	1966	30.00
❏ EKS-74003 [S]	David Blue	1966	30.00

REPRISE
❏ RS6296	These 23 Days in September	1968	18.00

BLUE

ROCKET
❏ PIG-2290	Another Night Time Flight	1977	18.00

RSO
❏ SO873	Blue	1973	15.00

BLUE ANGEL

POLYDOR
❏ PD-1-6300	Blue Angel	1980	25.00

BLUE BARONS, THE

PHILIPS
❏ PHM200017 [M]	Twist to the Great Blues Hits	1962	25.00
❏ PHS600017 [S]	Twist to the Great Blues Hits	1962	30.00

BLUE BEATS, THE

A.A.
❏ 133 [M]	The Beatle Beat	1964	40.00

Number	Title	Yr	NM

BLUE BIRD SOCIETY ORCHESTRA, THE

STASH

| ❑ ST-268 | The Blue Bird Society Orchestra | 1987 | 12.00 |

BLUE BOYS, THE

RCA VICTOR

❑ LPM-3794 [M]	Hit After Hit	1967	30.00
❑ LSP-3794 [S]	Hit After Hit	1967	25.00
❑ LPM-3529 [M]	Sounds of Jim Reeves	1966	25.00
❑ LSP-3529 [S]	Sounds of Jim Reeves	1966	30.00
❑ LPM-3696 [M]	The Blue Boys in Person	1967	25.00
❑ LSP-3696 [S]	The Blue Boys in Person	1967	30.00
❑ LPM-3331 [M]	We Remember Jim	1965	30.00
❑ LSP-3331 [S]	We Remember Jim	1965	30.00

BLUE CHEER

CAROLINE

| ❑ CAROL1395 | The Beast Is Back | 1989 | 15.00 |
| — Reissue | | | |

MEGAFORCE

| ❑ MRI1069 | The Beast Is Back | 1984 | 18.00 |

PHILIPS

❑ PHS600333	Blue Cheer	1970	40.00
❑ PHS600305	New! Improved! Blue Cheer	1969	40.00
❑ PHS600350	Oh! Pleasant Hope	1971	40.00
❑ PHS600278	Outsideinside	1968	40.00
❑ PHS600347	The Original Human Being	1970	40.00
❑ PHM200264 [M]	Vincebus Eruptum	1968	80.00
❑ PHS600264 [S]	Vincebus Eruptum	1968	40.00

RHINO

| ❑ RNLP70130 | Louder Than God (The Best of Blue Cheer, 1968-1969) | 1986 | 15.00 |

BLUE DIAMONDS, THE

LONDON

| ❑ LL3235 [M] | Ramona1 | 1963 | 30.00 |

BLUE JAYS, THE (1)

MILESTONE

| ❑ 1001 [M] | The Blue Jays Meet Little Caesar and the Romans | 1962 | 100.00 |

BLUE MAGIC

ATCO

❑ SD7038	Blue Magic	1974	15.00
❑ SD 36-140	Mystic Dragons	1976	15.00
❑ SD 36-103	The Magic of the Blue	1974	15.00
❑ SD 38-104	The Message	1977	15.00
❑ SD 36-120	Thirteen Blue Magic Lane	1975	15.00

CAPITOL

| ❑ ST-12143 | Welcome Back | 1981 | 12.00 |

COLLECTABLES

| ❑ COL-5031 | The Magic of the Blue: Greatest Hits | 198? | 12.00 |

COLUMBIA

| ❑ C45092 | From Out of the Blue | 1989 | 15.00 |

MIRAGE

| ❑ 90074 | Magic # | 1983 | 12.00 |

OMNI

| ❑ 90527 | Greatest Hits | 1986 | 12.00 |

BLUE OYSTER CULT

COLUMBIA

❑ PC34164	Agents of Fortune	1976	12.00
— Original gatefold with no bar code on cover			
❑ PC34164 [B]	Agents of Fortune	198?	10.00
— Budget-line reissue with bar code			
❑ KC31063	Blue Oyster Cult	1972	15.00
❑ PC31063	Blue Oyster Cult	197?	10.00
— Reissue with new prefix			
❑ FC39979	Club Ninja	1986	12.00
❑ JC36550	Cultosaurus Erectus	1980	12.00
❑ PC36550	Cultosaurus Erectus	198?	10.00
— Budget-line reissue			
❑ KG37946	Extraterrestrial Live	1982	15.00
❑ FC37389	Fire of Unknown Origin	1981	12.00
❑ PC37389	Fire of Unknown Origin	1984	10.00
— Budget-line reissue			
❑ FC40618	Imaginos	1988	12.00
❑ JC36009	Mirrors	1979	12.00
❑ PC36009	Mirrors	198?	10.00
— Budget-line reissue			
❑ KG33371	On Your Feet or On Your Knees	1975	18.00
❑ KC32858	Secret Treaties	1974	15.00
❑ CQ32858 [Q]	Secret Treaties	1974	40.00
❑ PC32858	Secret Treaties	197?	10.00
— Reissue with new prefix			
❑ JC35563	Some Enchanted Evening	1978	12.00
❑ PC35563	Some Enchanted Evening	198?	10.00
— Budget-line reissue			
❑ JC35019	Spectres	1977	12.00
❑ PC35019	Spectres	198?	10.00
— Budget-line reissue			
❑ FC38947	The Revolution by Night	1983	12.00
❑ PC38947	The Revolution by Night	1985	10.00

Number	Title	Yr	NM

— Budget-line reissue			
❑ KC32017	Tyranny and Mutation	1973	15.00
❑ CQ32017 [Q]	Tyranny and Mutation	1973	40.00
❑ PC32017	Tyranny and Mutation	197?	10.00
— Reissue with new prefix			

BLUE RIDGE MOUNTAIN BOYS, THE

TIME

❑ T-2103 [M]	Bluegrass Down Home	1963	18.00
❑ ST-2103 [S]	Bluegrass Down Home	1963	25.00
❑ T-2083 [M]	Hootenanny and Bluegrass	1963	18.00
❑ ST-2083 [S]	Hootenanny and Bluegrass	1963	25.00

BLUE RIDGE QUARTET, THE

MARK IV

| ❑ 1118 | Another Christmas with the Blue Ridge Quartet | 197? | 12.00 |
| ❑ 21027 | Christmas with the Blue Ridge Quartet | 197? | 12.00 |

BLUE SKY BOYS, THE

CAPITOL

| ❑ T2483 [M] | Presenting the Blue Sky Boys | 1966 | 25.00 |
| ❑ ST2483 [S] | Presenting the Blue Sky Boys | 1966 | 30.00 |

PINE MOUNTAIN

| ❑ PMR257 | Together Again | 198? | 15.00 |

RCA CAMDEN

| ❑ CAL-797 [M] | The Blue Sky Boys | 1963 | 25.00 |
| ❑ CAS-797(e) [R] | The Blue Sky Boys | 1963 | 18.00 |

ROUNDER

| ❑ 0236 | 1964 | 198? | 18.00 |

STARDAY

❑ SLP-205 [M]	Rare Treasury of Old Song Gems	1962	40.00
❑ SLP-269 [M]	The Blue Sky Boys	1964	40.00
❑ SLP-257 [M]	Together Again	1963	40.00

BLUE STARS

EMARCY

| ❑ MG-36067 [M] | Lullaby of Birdland | 1956 | 40.00 |

BLUE SWEDE

EMI

| ❑ ST-11286 | I looked on a Feeling | 1974 | 12.00 |
| ❑ ST-11346 | Out of the Blue | 1975 | 12.00 |

BLUE THINGS, THE

RCA VICTOR

| ❑ LPM-3603 [M] | The Blue Things | 1966 | 250.00 |
| ❑ LSP-3603 [S] | The Blue Things | 1966 | 300.00 |

BLUE VELVET BAND, THE

WARNER BROS.

| ❑ WS1802 | Sweet Moments | 1969 | 30.00 |

BLUEGRASS HOPPERS, THE

CUCA

| ❑ 1160 | The Country's Come to Town | 196? | 30.00 |

BLUES BROTHERS

ATLANTIC

❑ SD19331	Best of the Blues Brothers	1981	12.00
❑ SD19217	Briefcase Full of Blues	1978	12.00
❑ SD16025	Made in America	1980	12.00
❑ SD16017	The Blues Brothers	1980	12.00
— Movie soundtrack; also includes tracks by Aretha Franklin, Ray Charles and James Brown			

BLUES CLIMAX

HORNE

| ❑ JC-333 | Blues Climax | 1969 | 60.00 |

BLUES IMAGE

ATCO

❑ SD 33-300	Blues Image	1969	30.00
❑ SD 33-317	Open	1970	25.00
❑ SD 33-346	Red, White and Blues Image	1971	25.00

BLUES MAGOOS

ABC

| ❑ S-710 | Gulf Coast Bound | 1970 | 25.00 |
| ❑ S-697 | Never Goin' Back to Georgia | 1969 | 25.00 |

MERCURY

❑ SR-61167	Basic Blues Magoos	1968	30.00
❑ MG-21104 [M]	Electric Comic Book	1967	30.00
❑ SR-61104 [S]	Electric Comic Book	1967	40.00
❑ 21104/61104	Electric Comic Book Comic Book	1967	18.00
❑ MG-21096 [M]	Psychedelic Lollipop	1966	40.00
— With "21096" in trail-off; this record is mono			
❑ SR-61096 [S]	Psychedelic Lollipop	1966	50.00
❑ SR-61096	Psychedelic Lollipop	197?	15.00
— Reissue on Chicago skyline label			
❑ MG-21096 [S]	Psychedelic Lollipop	1966	40.00

Number	Title	Yr	NM

| — With "2/61096" in trail-off; this record plays stereo, though labeled mono | | | |

BLUES PROJECT, THE

CAPITOL

| ❑ ST-782 | Lazarus | 1971 | 15.00 |
| ❑ SMAS-11017 | The Blues Project | 1972 | 15.00 |

MCA

❑ 8003	Reunion in Central Park	1975	18.00
— Reissue of Sounds of the South LP; black rainbow labels			
❑ 25984	Reunion in Central Park	1987	15.00
— Reissue of MCA 8003; blue rainbow labels			

MGM

| ❑ M3G-4953 | Archetypes | 1974 | 15.00 |
| ❑ GAS-118 | The Blues Project | 1970 | 15.00 |

RHINO

| ❑ R1-70165 | No Time Like the Right Time: The Best of the Blues Project | 1989 | 15.00 |

SOUNDS OF THE SOUTH

| ❑ MCA2-8003 | Reunion in Central Park | 1973 | 25.00 |
| — Yellow labels | | | |

VERVE

| ❑ 827918-1 | Projections | 1986 | 10.00 |
| — Reissue | | | |

VERVE FOLKWAYS

❑ FT-3000 [M]	Live at the Café a Go Go	1966	25.00
❑ FTS-3000 [S]	Live at the Café a Go Go	1966	30.00
❑ FT-3008 [M]	Projections	1966	25.00
❑ FTS-3008 [S]	Projections	1966	30.00

VERVE FORECAST

❑ FTS-3077	Best of the Blues Project	1969	18.00
❑ FTS-3069	Flanders/Kalb/Katz, Etc.	1969	18.00
❑ FT-3000 [M]	Live at the Café a Go Go	1967	18.00
— Reissue of Verve Folkways 3000			
❑ FTS-3000 [S]	Live at the Café a Go Go	1967	25.00
— Reissue of Verve Folkways 3000			
❑ FTS-3046	Planned Obsolescence	1968	18.00
❑ FT-3008 [M]	Projections	1967	18.00
— Reissue of Verve Folkways 3008			
❑ FTS-3008 [S]	Projections	1967	25.00
— Reissue of Verve Folkways 3008			
❑ FT-3025 [M]	The Blues Project Live at Town Hall	1967	25.00
❑ FTS-3025 [S]	The Blues Project Live at Town Hall	1967	18.00

BLUES TRAVELER

A&M

| ❑ 7502153081 | Blues Traveler | 1990 | 18.00 |

BLUIETT, HAMIET

BLACK SAINT

| ❑ BSR-0014 | Resolution | 198? | 15.00 |

CHIAROSCURO

| ❑ CH-182 | Orchestra, Duo and Sextet | 1978 | 15.00 |

INDIA NAVIGATION

❑ IN-1030	Birthright	1977	15.00
❑ IN-1025	Endangered Species	1976	15.00
❑ IN-1039	S.O.S.	1979	15.00

SOUL NOTE

| ❑ SN-1018 | Dangerously Suite | 198? | 15.00 |
| ❑ SN-1088 | Ebu | 1985 | 15.00 |

BLUNSTONE, COLIN

4 MEN WITH BEARDS

| ❑ 4M237 [B] | One Year | 2013 | 30.00 |

EPIC

❑ KE31994 [B]	Ennismore	1972	18.00
❑ KE32962 [B]	Journey	1974	18.00
❑ E30974 [B]	One Year	1972	18.00

ROCKET

| ❑ BXL1-2093 | Never Even Thought | 1978 | 12.00 |

BLUNT, JAMES

CUSTARD/ATLANTIC

| ❑ R1-73396 | Back to Bedlam | 2006 | 25.00 |

BLYTH, ANN

EVEREST

| ❑ LPBR-5113 [M] | Hail Mary | 1960 | 30.00 |
| ❑ SDBR-1113 [S] | Hail Mary | 1960 | 40.00 |

BLYTHE, ARTHUR

ADELPHI

| ❑ 5008 | Bush Baby | 1978 | 15.00 |

COLUMBIA

❑ FC37427	Blythe Spirit	1981	12.00
❑ FC40237	Da-Da	1986	12.00
❑ FC38163	Elaborations	1982	12.00
❑ JC36583	Illusions	1980	12.00
❑ PC36583	Illusions	198?	10.00
— Budget-line reissue			
❑ JC36300	In the Tradition	1979	12.00

Number	Title	Yr	NM
❏ JC35638	Lenox Avenue Breakdown	1979	12.00
❏ FC38661	Light Blue	1983	12.00
❏ FC39411	Put Sunshine In It	1984	12.00
INDIA NAVIGATION			
❏ IN-1038	Metamorphosis	1979	15.00
❏ IN-1029	The Grip	1977	15.00

BLYTHE, JIMMY

EUPHORIA
Number	Title	Yr	NM
❏ EES-101	Messin' Around	198?	15.00
❏ EES-102	Messin' Around, Vol. 2	198?	15.00
RIVERSIDE			
❏ RLP-1031 [10]	Chicago Stomps and the Dixie Four	1954	80.00
❏ RLP-1036 [10]	Jimmy Blythe's State Street Ramblers	1954	80.00

BLYTHE, STERLING

CROWN
Number	Title	Yr	NM
❏ CLP-5179 [M]	Sterling Blythe Sings	1963	25.00
SAGE & SAND			
❏ C-14 [M]	A Night at the Showboat	1962	40.00
— Red vinyl; label print is red and black			
❏ C-14 [M]	A Night at the Showboat	196?	30.00
— Red vinyl; label print is multi-colored			

BO GRUMPUS

ATCO
Number	Title	Yr	NM
❏ 33-246 [M]	Bo Grumpus	1968	30.00
❏ SD 33-246 [S]	Bo Grumpus	1968	25.00

BOA

SNAKEFIELD
Number	Title	Yr	NM
❏ SN-001	Wrong Road	1971	500.00

BOB AND EARL

CRESTVIEW
Number	Title	Yr	NM
❏ CRS-3055	Bob & Earl	1969	30.00
TIP			
❏ TLP-1011 [M]	Harlem Shuffle	1964	30.00
❏ TLS-9011 [S]	Harlem Shuffle	1964	50.00

BOB AND RAY

RCA VICTOR
Number	Title	Yr	NM
❏ LPM-2131 [M]	Bob and Ray on a Platter	1960	30.00
❏ LSP-2131 [S]	Bob and Ray on a Platter	1960	50.00
❏ LPM-1773 [M]	Bob and Ray Throw a Stereo Spectacular	1958	30.00
❏ LSP-1773 [S]	Bob and Ray Throw a Stereo Spectacular	1958	80.00
❏ LSP-1773 [S]	Bob and Ray Throw a Stereo Spectacular	199?	30.00
— Classic Records reissue			
UNICORN			
❏ UN1001 [10]	Write If You Get Work	1954	60.00

BOB B. SOXX AND THE BLUE JEANS

PHILLIES
Number	Title	Yr	NM
❏ PHLP-4002 [M]	Zip-a-Dee Doo-Dah	1963	500.00

BOBBY AND THE MIDNITES

ARISTA
Number	Title	Yr	NM
❏ AL9568	Bobby and the Midnites	1981	12.00
COLUMBIA			
❏ BFC39276	Where the Beat Meets the Street	1984	12.00

BOBBY JIMMY AND THE CRITTERS

MACOLA
Number	Title	Yr	NM
❏ MRC 0989	Back and Proud	1987	12.00
❏ MRC 0933	Roaches: The Beginning	1986	12.00
RAPSUR			
❏ RP10009	Ugly Knuckle Butt	1985	30.00

BOBO, WILLIE

BLUE NOTE
Number	Title	Yr	NM
❏ BN-LA711-G	Tomorrow Is Here	1977	40.00
COLUMBIA			
❏ JC36108	Bobo	1979	30.00
— Reproductions exist			
❏ JC35734	Hell of an Act to Follow	1978	40.00
— Reproductions exist			
MGM			
❏ LAT-10012	Spanish Blues Band	197?	40.00
❏ LAT-10007	Spanish Grease	197?	40.00
❏ LAT-10011	Uno, Dos, Tres	197?	40.00
ROULETTE			
❏ R-52097 [M]	Bobo's Beat	1962	60.00
❏ SR-52097 [S]	Bobo's Beat	1962	80.00
SUSSEX			
❏ SXBS-7003	Do What You Want to Do	1971	40.00
— Reproductions exist			
TICO			
❏ T-1108 [M]	Do That Thing	1963	60.00

Number	Title	Yr	NM
❏ ST-1108 [S]	Do That Thing	1963	80.00
— Reproductions exist			
TRIP			
❏ 5013	Latin Beat	1974	12.00
VERVE			
❏ V6-8772	A New Dimension	1969	50.00
❏ V-8699 [M]	Bobo Motion	1967	40.00
❏ V6-8699 [S]	Bobo Motion	1967	40.00
❏ V6-8781	Evil Ways	1969	40.00
❏ V-8669 [M]	Feelin' So Good	1966	40.00
❏ V6-8669 [S]	Feelin' So Good	1966	50.00
❏ V-8685 [M]	Juicy	1967	40.00
❏ V6-8685 [S]	Juicy	1967	40.00
❏ V6-8736 [S]	Spanish Blues Band	1968	40.00
❏ V-8736 [M]	Spanish Blues Band	1968	60.00
— May be promo only			
❏ V-8631 [M]	Spanish Grease	1965	30.00
❏ V6-8631 [S]	Spanish Grease	1965	40.00
❏ V-8648 [M]	Uno, Dos, Tres	1966	30.00
❏ V6-8648 [S]	Uno, Dos, Tres	1966	40.00

BOCAGE, PETER

JAZZOLOGY
Number	Title	Yr	NM
❏ JCE-32	Peter Bocage with His Creole Serenaders	1979	12.00
❏ JCE-29	San Jacinto Hall	1978	12.00
RIVERSIDE			
❏ RLP-379 [M]	Peter Bocage with His Creole Serenaders	1961	30.00
❏ RLP-9379 [S]	Peter Bocage with His Creole Serenaders	1961	30.00

BOCIAN, MICHAEL

GM RECORDINGS
Number	Title	Yr	NM
❏ GM-3002	For This Gift	1982	12.00

BOCK, FRED

IMPACT
Number	Title	Yr	NM
❏ R3479	Upon a Midnight Clear	1977	15.00

BODACIOUS D.F.

RCA VICTOR
Number	Title	Yr	NM
❏ APL1-0206	Bodacious D.F.	1973	18.00
❏ AFL1-0206	Bodacious D.F.	1977	12.00
❏ AYL1-4243	Bodacious D.F.	1982	10.00
— Best Buy Series" reissue			

BODEANS

SLASH
Number	Title	Yr	NM
❏ 25876	Home	1989	15.00
❏ 25403	Love & Hope & Sex & Dreams	1986	12.00
❏ R153192	Outside Looking In	1987	15.00
— BMG Direct Marketing edition			
❏ 25629	Outside Looking In	1987	12.00

BOETCHER, CURT

ELEKTRA
Number	Title	Yr	NM
❏ EKS-75037	There's an Innocent Face	1972	25.00

BOFFALONGO

UNITED ARTISTS
Number	Title	Yr	NM
❏ UAS-6770	Beyond Your Head	1970	25.00
❏ UAS-6726	Boffalongo	1969	25.00

BOFILL, ANGELA

ARISTA
Number	Title	Yr	NM
❏ AL8-8258	Let Me Be the One	1984	12.00
❏ AL9576	Something About You	1981	12.00
❏ AL8-8125	Something About You	198?	10.00
— Reissue of 9576			
❏ AL8-8198	Teaser	1983	12.00
❏ AL8-8396	Tell Me Tomorrow	1985	12.00
❏ AL8-8425	The Best of Angela Bofill	1986	12.00
❏ AL9616	Too Tough	1983	12.00
❏ AL8-8000	Too Tough	198?	10.00
— Reissue of 9616			
ARISTA/GRP			
❏ GL5501	Angel of the Night	1979	15.00
❏ GL8-8060	Angel of the Night	198?	10.00
— Reissue of 5501			
❏ GL5000	Angie	1978	15.00
❏ GLB-8302	Angie	198?	10.00
— Reissue of 5000			
CAPITOL			
❏ C1-48335	Intuition	1988	12.00

BOGARDE, DIRK

LONDON
Number	Title	Yr	NM
❏ LL3187 [M]	Lyrics for Lovers	1960	30.00
❏ PS210 [S]	Lyrics for Lovers	1960	30.00

BOGGUSS, SUZY

CAPITOL
Number	Title	Yr	NM
❏ C1-90237	Somewhere Between	1989	18.00
❏ C1-590237	Somewhere Between	1989	18.00
— Columbia House edition			

BOHANNON, GEORGE
Number	Title	Yr	NM
❏ WSJ-207 [M]	Boss Bossa Nova	1963	80.00

BOHANNON

COMPLEAT
Number	Title	Yr	NM
❏ CPL-1-1003	Make Your Body Move	1983	12.00
❏ CPL-1-1005	The Bohannon Drive	1984	15.00
DAKAR			
❏ DK76917	Bohannon	1975	18.00
❏ DK76919	Dance Your Ass Off	1976	18.00
❏ DK76921	Gittin' Off	1976	25.00
❏ 76916	Insides Out	1974	15.00
❏ 6910	Keep On Dancing	1973	15.00
MCA			
❏ 42310	Here Comes Bohannon	1989	15.00
MERCURY			
❏ SRM-1-3762	Cut Loose	1979	12.00
❏ SRM-1-3813	Music in the Air	1980	12.00
❏ SRM-1-3710	On My Way	1978	12.00
❏ SRM-1-1159	Phase II	1977	12.00
❏ SRM-1-3728	Summertime Groove	1978	12.00
❏ SRM-1-3778	Too Hot to Hold	1979	12.00
PHASE II			
❏ FZ37695	Alive	1981	12.00
❏ FZ38113	Bohannon Fever	1982	12.00
❏ JW36867	One Step Ahead	1980	12.00

BOHEMIAN VENDETTA

MAINSTREAM
Number	Title	Yr	NM
❏ 56106 [M]	Bohemian Vendetta	1968	500.00
❏ S-6106 [S]	Bohemian Vendetta	1968	500.00

BOLCOM, WILLIAM

JAZZOLOGY
Number	Title	Yr	NM
❏ JCE-72	William Bolcom Plays His Own Rags	198?	12.00
NONESUCH			
❏ N-71257	Heliotrope Bouquet (Piano Rags, 1900-70)	1971	15.00
❏ N-71299	Pastimes and Piano Rags	1972	15.00

BOLD

ABC
Number	Title	Yr	NM
❏ ABCS-705	Bold	1969	75.00

BOLDER DAMN

HIT
Number	Title	Yr	NM
❏ HRI-5061	Mourning	1971	1000.00

BOLGER, RAY

DISNEYLAND
Number	Title	Yr	NM
❏ ST-3930 [M]	The Story of the Scarecrow of Oz	1965	30.00

BOLIN, TOMMY

CLEOPATRA
Number	Title	Yr	NM
❏ 2076 [B]	Savannah Woman - Demos And Jam Sessions		25.00
COLUMBIA			
❏ PC34329	Private Eyes	1976	15.00
— Original with no bar code on cover			
❏ PC34329	Private Eyes	198?	10.00
— With bar code on cover			
GEFFEN			
❏ 3GHS24248	The Ultimate Tommy Bolin	1989	30.00
NEMPEROR			
❏ NE436 [B]	Teaser	1975	18.00
❏ PZ37534	Teaser	1982	10.00

BOLL WEEVIL JAZZ BAND

GHB
Number	Title	Yr	NM
❏ 89	Red Hot in Memphis	197?	12.00
❏ 31 [M]	Volume 1	1966	15.00
❏ 32 [M]	Volume 2: Just a Little While	1966	15.00
❏ 33 [M]	Volume 3: One More Time	1966	15.00
❏ 34 [M]	Volume 4: One More Time Again	1966	15.00
❏ 48	Volume 5: A Hot Band Is Hard to Find	1968	12.00

BOLLING, CLAUDE

BALLY
Number	Title	Yr	NM
❏ BAL-12003 [M]	French Jazz	1956	40.00
CBS			
❏ FM42474	Bolling Plays Ellington, Vol. 1	1988	12.00
❏ FM42476	Bolling Plays Ellington, Vol. 2	1988	12.00
❏ FM42318	Suite No. 2 for Flute and Jazz Piano Trio	1987	12.00
CBS MASTERWORKS			
❏ FM39245	Big Band	1985	12.00
❏ M336811	Bolling	1981	30.00
— Combines 33233, 35128, and 35864 in one box			
❏ FM36691	California Suite	1980	12.00
— With Hubert Laws and Shelly Manne; not the same as the original soundtrack recording			

Number	Title	Yr	NM
❑ FM37264	Concerto for Classic Guitar and Jazz Piano	1981	12.00
— With Alexandre Lagoya; reissue of RCA Red Seal 0149			
❑ FM39244	Jazz A La Francaise	1985	12.00
❑ FM39059	Suite for Cello and Jazz Piano Trio	1984	12.00
— With Yo-Yo Ma, others			
❑ FM37798	Suite for Chamber Orchestra and Jazz Piano Trio	1982	12.00
❑ FM36731	Toot Suite for Trumpet and Jazz Piano	1980	12.00
— With Maurice Andre			
COLUMBIA			
❑ PC33277	Original Ragtime	1975	12.00
❑ FM39009	Original Ragtime	1984	10.00
— Reissue of 33277			
COLUMBIA MASTERWORKS			
❑ M35864	Picnic Suite for Flute, Guitar and Jazz Piano	1979	12.00
— With Jean-Pierre Rampal and Alexandre Lagoya			
❑ M33233	Suite for Flute and Jazz Piano	1975	12.00
— With Jean-Pierre Rampal			
❑ M35128	Suite for Violin and Jazz Piano	1978	12.00
— With Pinchas Zuckerman			
DRG			
❑ SL-5201	Nuances	1986	12.00
JAZZ MAN			
❑ 5018	Rolling with Bolling	198?	12.00
— Reissue of Omega OSL-6			
MERCURY			
❑ 812569-1	Bolling Blues	1983	12.00
OMEGA			
❑ OKL-6 [M]	Rolling with Bolling	1960	30.00
❑ OSL-6 [S]	Rolling with Bolling	1960	30.00
PHILIPS			
❑ PHM200204 [M]	Two-Beat Mozart	1966	18.00
❑ PHS600204 [S]	Two-Beat Mozart	1966	25.00
RCA RED SEAL			
❑ FRL1-0149	Concerto for Classic Guitar and Jazz Piano	1973	15.00
— With Alexandre Lagoya			

BOLTON, MICHAEL

Number	Title	Yr	NM
COLUMBIA			
❑ BFC39328	Everybody's Crazy	1985	12.00
❑ BFC38357	Michael Bolton	1983	12.00
❑ OC45012	Soul Provider	1989	12.00
❑ FC40473	The Hunger	1987	10.00
❑ C46771	Time, Love and Tenderness	1991	18.00
RCA VICTOR			
❑ APL1-1551 [B]	Every Day of My Life	1970	30.00
— As "Michael Bolotin			
❑ APL1-0992 [B]	Michael Bolotin	1975	30.00
— As "Michael Bolotin			

BOMBERS

Number	Title	Yr	NM
WEST END			
❑ WE-104	Bombers	1978	18.00
❑ WE-106	Bombers 2	1979	18.00

BON JOVI, JON

Number	Title	Yr	NM
MERCURY			
❑ 846473-1	Blaze of Glory (Young Guns II)	1990	18.00

BON JOVI

Number	Title	Yr	NM
MERCURY			
❑ 824509-1	7800 Fahrenheit	1985	10.00
❑ 814982-1	Bon Jovi	1984	10.00
❑ 836345-1	New Jersey	1988	10.00
❑ 836499-1 [B]	New Jersey	1988	30.00
— Picture disc in plastic sleeve			
❑ 830264-1	Slippery When Wet	1986	10.00
❑ 830822-1 [B]	Slippery When Wet	1986	30.00
— Picture disc in plastic cover			

BONADUCE, DANNY

Number	Title	Yr	NM
LION			
❑ LN-1015	Danny Bonaduce	1973	60.00

BONANO, SHARKEY, AND LIZZIE MILES

Number	Title	Yr	NM
CAPITOL			
❑ T792 [M]	A Night in Old New Orleans	1956	40.00
❑ H367 [10]	Midnight on Bourbon Street	1952	50.00
❑ T367 [M]	Midnight on Bourbon Street	1954	40.00

BONANO, SHARKEY

Number	Title	Yr	NM
CAPITOL			
❑ T266 [M]	Kings of Dixieland	1954	40.00
❑ H266 [10]	Sharkey's Southern Comfort	1951	50.00
CIRCLE			
❑ LP-422 [10]	Sharkey Bonano	1951	50.00
GMB			
❑ 122	Sharkey Bonano and His Kings of Dixieland	198?	12.00
ROULETTE			
❑ R-25112 [M]	Dixieland at the Roundtable	1960	30.00
SOUTHLAND			
❑ 222 [M]	Kings of Dixieland	1959	30.00
❑ SLP-205 [10]	New Orleans Dixieland Session	1954	50.00
❑ 205 [M]	New Orleans Jam Session	1961	30.00

BOND, ANGELO

Number	Title	Yr	NM
ABC			
❑ D-889	Bondage	1975	12.00

BOND, BOBBY

Number	Title	Yr	NM
SOMERSET			
❑ SF24400 [S]	Bobby Bond Sings the Roger Miller Songbook	1966	18.00
❑ P24400 [M]	Bobby Bond Sings the Roger Miller Songbook	1966	15.00
TIME			
❑ 52122 [M]	On the Country Side	1964	15.00
❑ S-2122 [S]	On the Country Side	1964	18.00

BOND, EDDIE

Number	Title	Yr	NM
PHILLIPS INT'L.			
❑ PLP-1980 [M]	The Greatest Country Gospel Hits	1961	400.00

BOND, GRAHAM

Number	Title	Yr	NM
MERCURY			
❑ SR-61327 [B]	Holy Magick	1970	50.00
❑ SRM-1-612 [B]	We Put Our Magick on You	1971	40.00
PULSAR			
❑ 10604 [B]	Love Is the Law	1969	60.00
❑ 10606 [B]	Mighty Graham Bond	1969	50.00
WARNER BROS.			
❑ 2LS2555 [B]	Solid Bond	1971	30.00

BOND, JAMES, SEXTETTE

Number	Title	Yr	NM
MIRWOOD			
❑ M-7001 [M]	The James Bond Songbook	1966	30.00
❑ S-7001 [S]	The James Bond Songbook	1966	30.00

BOND, JOHNNY

Number	Title	Yr	NM
CMH			
❑ 6213	The Return of the Singing Cowboy	1981	12.00
❑ 6212	The Singing Cowboy Again	1981	12.00
HARMONY			
❑ HL7353 [M]	Bottled in Bond	1965	25.00
❑ HL7308 [M]	Johnny Bond's Best	1964	25.00
NASHVILLE			
❑ 2054	Three Sheets to the Wind	196?	18.00
SHASTA			
❑ LP-516	Johnny Bond Rides Again	197?	18.00
STARDAY			
❑ SLP-378 [M]	Bottles Up	1966	30.00
❑ SLP-416	Drink Up and Go Home	1968	18.00
❑ SLP-354 [M]	Famous Hot Rodders I Have Known	1965	40.00
❑ SLP-472	Here Come the Elephants	1971	18.00
❑ SLP-298 [M]	Hot Rod Lincoln	1964	50.00
❑ SLP-456	Old, New, Patriotic and Blue	1970	18.00
❑ SLP-227 [M]	Songs That Made Him Famous	1963	40.00
❑ SLP-333 [M]	Ten Little Bottles	1965	30.00
❑ SLP-402 [M]	Ten Nights in a Barroom	1967	25.00
❑ SLP-147 [M]	That Wild, Wicked But Wonderful Wesy	1961	50.00
❑ SLP-444	The Best of Johnny Bond	1969	18.00
❑ 954	The Best of Johnny Bond	1976	12.00
❑ SLP-388 [M]	The Branded Stock of Johnny Bond	1966	25.00
❑ SLP-368 [M]	The Man Who Comes Around	1966	30.00

BONDS, GARY U.S.

Number	Title	Yr	NM
EMI AMERICA			
❑ SO-17051	Dedication	1981	12.00
❑ SPRO-9666 [EP]	Dedication Sampler	1981	18.00
— Promo-only sampler with limited-edition number on pink sticker			
❑ SO-17068	On the Line	1982	12.00
LEGRAND			
❑ LLP-3001 [M]	Dance 'Til Quarter to Three	1961	100.00
❑ LLP-3003 [M]	Greatest Hits of Gary U.S. Bonds	1962	70.00
❑ LLP-3002 [M]	Twist Up Calypso	1962	70.00
MCA			
❑ 905	The Best of Gary U.S. Bonds	1984	12.00
PHOENIX			
❑ PRT 0072	Standing in the Line of Fire	1984	12.00
RHINO			
❑ RNLP-805	Certified Soul	1981	12.00

BONE THUGS-N-HARMONY

Number	Title	Yr	NM
RUTHLESS			
❑ C263581	BTNH Resurrection	2000	18.00
❑ 5539	E. 1999 Eternal	1995	18.00
❑ 6340	The Art of War	1997	18.00
❑ C69715	The Collection: Volume One	1998	15.00
❑ C285172	The Collection: Volume Two	2000	18.00

BONEY M

Number	Title	Yr	NM
ATCO			
❑ SD 36-143	Take the Heat Off Me	1976	18.00
ATLANTIC			
❑ SD19145	Love for Sale	1977	18.00
SIRE			
❑ SRK6062	Nightflight to Venus	1978	12.00

BONFA, LUIZ

Number	Title	Yr	NM
ATLANTIC			
❑ 8028 [M]	The Fabulous Guitar of Luiz Bonfa/Amor!	1959	40.00
— Black label			
❑ 8028 [M]	The Fabulous Guitar of Luiz Bonfa/Amor!	1960	30.00
— White "bullseye" label			
❑ 8028 [M]	The Fabulous Guitar of Luiz Bonfa/Amor!	1961	25.00
— Multicolor label, white "fan" logo at right			
❑ 8028 [M]	The Fabulous Guitar of Luiz Bonfa/Amor!	1963	18.00
— Multicolor label, black "fan" logo at right			
❑ SD8028 [S]	The Fabulous Guitar of Luiz Bonfa/Amor!	1959	50.00
— Green label			
❑ SD8028 [S]	The Fabulous Guitar of Luiz Bonfa/Amor!	1960	40.00
— White "bullseye" label			
❑ SD8028 [S]	The Fabulous Guitar of Luiz Bonfa/Amor!	1961	30.00
— Multicolor label, white "fan" logo at right			
❑ SD8028 [S]	The Fabulous Guitar of Luiz Bonfa/Amor!	1963	25.00
— Multicolor label, black "fan" logo at right			
CAPITOL			
❑ T10134 [M]	Brazilian Guitar	1958	40.00
— Turquoise label			
DOT			
❑ DLP-25848	Black Orpheus Impressions	1969	18.00
❑ DLP-25881	Bonfa	1969	18.00
❑ DLP-3804 [M]	Luiz Bonfa	1967	25.00
❑ DLP-25804 [S]	Luiz Bonfa	1967	18.00
❑ DLP-25825	Luiz Bonfa Plays Great Songs	1968	18.00
EPIC			
❑ LN24124 [M]	Softly	1964	18.00
❑ BN26124 [S]	Softly	1964	25.00
PHILIPS			
❑ PHM200199 [M]	Braziliana	1965	15.00
❑ PHS600199 [S]	Braziliana	1965	18.00
❑ PHM200087 [M]	Brazil's King of the Bossa Nova and Guitar	1963	18.00
❑ PHS600087 [S]	Brazil's King of the Bossa Nova and Guitar	1963	25.00
❑ PHM200208 [M]	The Brazilian Scene	1966	15.00
❑ PHS600208 [S]	The Brazilian Scene	1966	18.00
RCA VICTOR			
❑ LSP-4376	The New Face of Bonfa	1970	18.00
VERVE			
❑ V-8522 [M]	Luiz Bonfa Plays and Sings Bossa Nova	1963	18.00
❑ V6-8522 [S]	Luiz Bonfa Plays and Sings Bossa Nova	1963	25.00

BONFIRE, MARS

Number	Title	Yr	NM
COLUMBIA			
❑ CS9834	Faster Than the Speed of Life	1969	30.00
— Reissue of Uni 73027 with slight alterations			
UNI			
❑ 73027	Mars Bonfire	1968	40.00

BONHAM, TRACY

Number	Title	Yr	NM
ISLAND			
❑ 524187-1	The Burdens of Being Upright	1996	18.00
— With Jason Bonham, son of John Bonham (Led Zeppelin) on drums.			

BONHAM

Number	Title	Yr	NM
WTG			
❑ P45009	The Disregard of Timekeeping	1989	18.00

BONNEMERE, EDDIE

Number	Title	Yr	NM
PRESTIGE			
❑ PRLP-7354 [M]	Jazz Oriented	1965	25.00
❑ PRST-7354 [S]	Jazz Oriented	1965	30.00

Number	Title	Yr	NM

ROOST
RST-2236 [M]	Piano Bon Bons	1959	30.00
SLP-2236 [S]	Piano Bon Bons	1959	40.00
RST-419 [10]	Piano Mambo with Bonnemere	1954	50.00
RST-2241 [M]	The Sound of Memory	1960	30.00
SLP-2241 [S]	The Sound of Memory	1960	40.00

BONNEVILLES, THE

DRUM BOY
| DLM-1001 [M] | Meet the Bonnevilles | 1963 | 100.00 |
| DLS-1001 [S] | Meet the Bonnevilles | 1963 | 150.00 |
JUSTICE
| JLP-146 | Bringing It Home | 196? | 500.00 |

BONNIE LOU

KING
| 595 [M] | Bonnie Lou Sings | 1958 | 150.00 |

BONNIWELL, T.S.

CAPITOL
| ST-377 | Close | 1969 | 75.00 |

BONOFF, KARLA

COLUMBIA
JC34672	Karla Bonoff	1977	12.00
PC34672	Karla Bonoff	198?	10.00
—Budget-line reissue			
JC35799	Restless Nights	1979	12.00
PC35799	Restless Nights	198?	10.00
—Budget-line reissue			
FC37444	Wild Heart of the Young	1982	10.00
GOLD CASTLE
| 171014-1 | New World | 1987 | 15.00 |

BONZO DOG BAND, THE

IMPERIAL
LP12370 [S]	Gorilla	1968	30.00
—With booklet			
LP12370 [S]	Gorilla	1968	25.00
—Without booklet			
LP9370 [M]	Gorilla	1968	30.00
—With booklet			
LP9370 [M]	Gorilla	1968	25.00
—Without booklet			
LP12457	Keynsham	1969	25.00
LP12445	Tadpoles	1969	25.00
LP12432	Urban Spaceman	1968	30.00
—With booklet			
LP12432	Urban Spaceman	1968	25.00
—Without booklet			
LIBERTY
| LN-10206 | Some of the Best of the Bonzo Dog Band | 1983 | 10.00 |
UNITED ARTISTS
UAS5584	Let's Make Up and Be Friendly	1972	18.00
UAS5517	The Beast of the Bonzos	1971	18.00
UA-LA321-H2	The History of the Bonzos	1974	18.00

BOO-YAA T.R.I.B.E.

4TH & B'WAY
| 4017 | New Funky Nation | 1990 | 18.00 |

BOOGIE BOYS, THE

CAPITOL
ST-12409	City Life	1985	15.00
C1-46917	Romeo Knight	1988	12.00
ST-12488	Survival of the Freshest	1986	15.00

BOOGIE DOWN PRODUCTIONS

B BOY
BB2000	A Man and His Music	1997	18.00
BB4787	Criminal Minded	1987	15.00
—Reissued in 1997 with the same number			
BB5787	Criminal Minded Instrumental	1987	15.00
—Reissued in 1997 with the same number			
JIVE
1097-1-J	By All Means Necessary	1988	12.00
1358-1-J	Edutainment	1990	18.00
1187-1-J	Ghetto Music: The Blueprint of Hip-Hop	1989	12.00
LANDSPEED
| LSR8806 | Best of B-Boy Records | 2000 | 25.00 |

BOOGIE KINGS, THE

MONTEL
| LP-109 [M] | Blue Eyed Soul | 1967 | 30.00 |
| LP-104 [M] | The Boogie Kings | 1966 | 40.00 |

BOOGIEMONSTERS

PENDULUM
| 56045 | God Sound | 1997 | 15.00 |
| E1-29607 | Riders of the Storm: The Underwater Album | 1994 | 18.00 |

Number	Title	Yr	NM

BOOK OF LOVE

SIRE
| 25355 | Book of Love | 1986 | 12.00 |
| 25700 | Lullaby | 1988 | 12.00 |

BOOKER, CHUCKII

ATLANTIC
| 81947 | Chuckii | 1989 | 12.00 |

BOOKER T. AND PRISCILLA

A&M
SP-3504	Booker T. and Priscilla	1971	18.00
SP-4413	Chronicles	1973	12.00
SP-4351	Home Grown	1972	12.00

BOOKER T. AND THE MG'S

A&M
SP-4874	I Want You	1981	12.00
—As "Booker T. Jones			
SP-4798	The Best of You	1979	12.00
—As "Booker T. Jones			
SP-4720	Try and Love Again	1978	12.00
—As "Booker T. Jones			
ASYLUM
| 7E-1093 | Universal Language | 1977 | 12.00 |
ATLANTIC
8202 [M]	The Best of Booker T. and the MG's	1968	50.00
—Mono is white label promo only			
81285	The Best of Booker T. and the MG's	1985	10.00
SD8202 [S]	The Best of Booker T. and the MG's	1968	25.00
EPIC
| KE33143 | Evergreen | 1974 | 15.00 |
MCA
| 6282 | The Runaway | 1989 | 15.00 |
| —As "Booker T. Jones | | | |
STAX
ST-711 [M]	And Now…Booker T. and the MG's	1966	50.00
STS-711 [S]	And Now…Booker T. and the MG's	1966	80.00
STS-2033	Booker T. and the MG's Greatest Hits	1970	18.00
MPS-8505	Booker T. and the MG's Greatest Hits	1981	12.00
STS-724 [S]	Doin' Our Thing	1968	50.00
ST-724 [M]	Doin' Our Thing	1968	80.00
STX-4104	Free Ride	1978	12.00
ST-701 [M]	Green Onions	1962	70.00
STS-701 [R]	Green Onions	1966	50.00

ST-717 [M]	Hip Hug-Her	1967	40.00
STS-717 [S]	Hip Hug-Her	1967	50.00
ST-713 [M]	In the Christmas Spirit	1966	400.00
—Fingers and piano keys cover			
ST-713 [M]	In the Christmas Spirit	1967	200.00
—Same as above; Santa Claus cover			
STS-713 [S]	In the Christmas Spirit	1966	400.00
—Fingers and piano keys cover			
STS-713 [S]	In the Christmas Spirit	1967	200.00
—Santa Claus cover			
STS-2027 [B]	McLemore Avenue	1970	35.00
MPS-8552	McLemore Avenue	1990	15.00
—Reissue of 2027			
STS-2035 [S]	Melting Pot	1971	18.00
MPS-8521 [B]	Melting Pot	198?	12.00
—Reissue of 2035			
STM-2035 [M]	Melting Pot	1971	40.00
—Mono is white label promo only			
ST-705 [M]	Soul Dressing	1965	70.00
STS-705 [R]	Soul Dressing	1966	50.00
STS-2001	Soul Limbo	1968	30.00

Number	Title	Yr	NM

STX-4113	Soul Limbo	198?	12.00
—Reissue of 2001			
STS-2009	The Booker T. Set	1969	30.00
MPS-8531	The Booker T. Set	1987	12.00
—Reissue of 2009			
STS-2006	Uptight	1969	30.00
SUNDAZED
LP5043	And Now! Booker T. and the MG's	2000	18.00
—Reissue on 180-gram vinyl			
LP5079	Green Onions	2002	15.00
—Reissue on 180-gram vinyl			
LP5080	Hip Hug-Her	2002	15.00
—Reissue on 180-gram vinyl			
LP5053	In the Christmas Spirit	2000	18.00
—Reissue on 180-gram vinyl			
LP5042	Soul Dressing	2000	18.00
—Reissue on 180-gram vinyl			

BOOM, TAKA

ARIOLA AMERICA
| SW-50041 | Taka Boom | 1979 | 12.00 |
MIRAGE
| 90290 | Middle of the Night | 1985 | 10.00 |

BOOMERANG

RCA VICTOR
| LSP-4577 | Boomerang | 1971 | 25.00 |

BOOMTOWN RATS, THE

COLUMBIA
JC35750	A Tonic for the Troops	1979	12.00
PC35750	A Tonic for the Troops	198?	10.00
—Budget-line reissue			
FC39335	In the Long Grass	1985	12.00
PC39335	In the Long Grass	198?	10.00
—Budget-line reissue			
JC37062	Mondo Bongo	1981	15.00
—With poster			
PC37062	Mondo Bongo	198?	10.00
—Budget-line reissue			
5C38591 [EP]	Ratrospective	1983	12.00
5C38097 [EP]	The Boomtown Rats	1982	10.00
JC36248	The Fine Art of Surfacing	1979	12.00
PC36248	The Fine Art of Surfacing	198?	10.00
—Budget-line reissue			
FC38195	V Deep	1982	12.00
PC38195	V Deep	198?	10.00
—Budget-line reissue			
MERCURY
| SRM-1-1188 | The Boomtown Rats | 1977 | 18.00 |

BOONE, DANIEL

MERCURY
| SRM-1-649 | Beautiful Sunday | 1972 | 12.00 |

BOONE, DEBBY

CAPITOL
| ST-41005 | Choose Life | 198? | 12.00 |
| ST-41029 | Surrender | 198? | 12.00 |
LAMB & LION
LLR3008	Choose Life	1985	15.00
83011	Friends for Life	198?	15.00
1046	With My Song	1980	15.00
MCA
1457	Best of Debby Boone	198?	10.00
962	You Light Up My Life	198?	10.00
—Reissue of Warner Bros. 3118			
WARNER BROS.
BSK3301	Debby Boone	1979	12.00
BSK3419	Love Has No Reason	1980	12.00
BSK3130	Midstream	1978	12.00
BSK3501	Savin' It Up	1981	12.00
BS3118	You Light Up My Life	1977	12.00

BOONE, LARRY

MERCURY
| 834377-1 | Larry Boone | 1988 | 10.00 |
| 836710-1 | Swingin' Doors, Sawdust Floors | 1989 | 12.00 |

BOONE, PAT, FAMILY

THISTLE
| TR-1001 | The Boone Family Christmas | 1975 | 15.00 |

BOONE, PAT

ABC
| 4006 | 16 Great Performances | 1975 | 10.00 |
BIBLE VOICE
| 7076 | The Solution to Crisis-America | 1970 | 12.00 |
DOT
| DLP-3814 [M] | 15 Hits of Pat Boone | 1967 | 15.00 |
| DLP-25814 [S] | 15 Hits of Pat Boone | 1967 | 12.00 |

Number	Title	Yr	NM
❑ DLP-3601 [M]	Blest Be the Tie That Binds	1965	12.00
❑ DLP-25601 [S]	Blest Be the Tie That Binds	1965	15.00
❑ DLP-3594 [M]	Boss Beat	1964	12.00
❑ DLP-25594 [S]	Boss Beat	1964	15.00
❑ DLP-3770 [M]	Christmas Is a-Comin'	1966	12.00
❑ DLP-25770 [S]	Christmas Is a-Comin'	1966	15.00
❑ DLP-3346 [M]	Great! Great! Great!	1961	15.00
❑ DLP-25346 [S]	Great! Great! Great!	1961	20.00
❑ DLP-3685 [M]	Great Hits of 1965	1965	12.00
❑ DLP-25685 [S]	Great Hits of 1965	1965	15.00
❑ DLP-3234 [M]	He Leadeth Me	1960	15.00
❑ DLP-25234 [S]	He Leadeth Me	1960	20.00
❑ DLP-3030 [M]	Howdy!	1956	50.00
—Maroon label			
❑ DLP-3030 [M]	Howdy!	1957	30.00
—Black label			
❑ DLP-3798 [M]	How Great Thou Art	1967	15.00
❑ DLP-25798 [S]	How Great Thou Art	1967	12.00
❑ DLP-3068 [M]	Hymns We Love	1957	25.00
❑ DLP-25068 [S]	Hymns We Love	1959	30.00
❑ DLP-3399 [M]	I'll See You in My Dreams	1961	12.00
❑ DLP-25399 [S]	I'll See You in My Dreams	1961	15.00
❑ DLP-3475 [M]	I Love You Truly	1962	12.00
❑ DLP-25475 [S]	I Love You Truly	1962	15.00
❑ DLP-3805 [M]	I Was Kaiser Bill's Batman	1967	15.00
❑ DLP-25805 [S]	I Was Kaiser Bill's Batman	1967	12.00
❑ DLP-3876 [M]	Look Ahead	1968	15.00
❑ DLP-25876 [S]	Look Ahead	1968	12.00
❑ DLP-3748 [M]	Memories	1966	12.00
❑ DLP-25748 [S]	Memories	1966	15.00
❑ DLP-3384 [M]	Moody River	1961	12.00
❑ DLP-25384 [S]	Moody River	1961	15.00
❑ DLP-3270 [M]	Moonglow	1960	15.00
❑ DLP-25270 [S]	Moonglow	1960	20.00
—Black vinyl			
❑ DLP-25270 [S]	Moonglow	1960	50.00
—Blue vinyl			
❑ DLP-3650 [M]	My 10th Anniversary with Dot Records	1965	12.00
❑ DLP-25650 [S]	My 10th Anniversary with Dot Records	1965	15.00
❑ DLP-3386 [M]	My God and I	1961	12.00
❑ DLP-25386 [S]	My God and I	1961	15.00
❑ DLP-3606 [M]	Near You	1965	12.00
❑ DLP-25606 [S]	Near You	1965	15.00
❑ DLP-3050 [M]	Pat	1957	25.00
❑ DLP-3012 [M]	Pat Boone	1956	50.00
—Maroon label			
❑ DLP-3012 [M]	Pat Boone	1957	30.00
—Black label			
❑ DLP-25573 [R]	Pat Boone	1964	12.00
❑ DLP-3402 [M]	Pat Boone Reads from the Holy Bible	1962	15.00
❑ DLP-3455 [M]	Pat Boone's Golden Hits	1962	12.00
❑ DLP-25455 [S]	Pat Boone's Golden Hits	1962	15.00
❑ DLP-3504 [M]	Pat Boone Sings "Days of Wine and Roses" and Other Great Movie Themes	1963	12.00
❑ DLP-25504 [S]	Pat Boone Sings "Days of Wine and Roses" and Other Great Movie Themes	1963	15.00
❑ DLP-3158 [M]	Pat Boone Sings	1959	20.00
❑ DLP-25158 [S]	Pat Boone Sings	1959	25.00
❑ DLP-3501 [M]	Pat Boone Sings Guess Who?	1963	50.00
❑ DLP-25501 [S]	Pat Boone Sings Guess Who?	1963	80.00
❑ DLP-3077 [M]	Pat Boone Sings Irving Berlin	1958	20.00
❑ DLP-25077 [S]	Pat Boone Sings Irving Berlin	1959	25.00
❑ DLP-3071 [M]	Pat's Great Hits	1957	25.00
❑ DLP-25071 [P]	Pat's Great Hits	1959	30.00
❑ DLP-3261 [M]	Pat's Great Hits Volume 2	1960	15.00
❑ DLP-25261 [S]	Pat's Great Hits Volume 2	1960	20.00
❑ DLP-3199 [M]	Side by Side	1959	20.00
❑ DLP-25199 [S]	Side by Side	1959	25.00
❑ DLP-3513 [M]	Sing Along Without Pat Boone	1963	12.00
❑ DLP-25513 [S]	Sing Along Without Pat Boone	1963	15.00
❑ DLP-3118 [M]	Star Dust	1958	20.00
❑ DLP-25118 [S]	Star Dust	1959	25.00
❑ DLP-3180 [M]	Tenderly	1959	20.00
❑ DLP-25180 [S]	Tenderly	1959	25.00
❑ DLP-3626 [M]	The Golden Era of Country Hits	1965	12.00
❑ DLP-25626 [S]	The Golden Era of Country Hits	1965	15.00
❑ DLP-3582 [M]	The Lord's Prayer And Other Great Hymns	1964	12.00
❑ DLP-25582 [S]	The Lord's Prayer And Other Great Hymns	1964	15.00
❑ DLP-3520 [M]	The Star Spangled Banner	1963	12.00
❑ DLP-25520 [S]	The Star Spangled Banner	1963	15.00
❑ DLP-3546 [M]	The Touch of Your Lips	1963	12.00
❑ DLP-25546 [S]	The Touch of Your Lips	1963	15.00
❑ DLP-3285 [M]	This and That	1960	15.00
❑ DLP-25285 [S]	This and That	1960	20.00
❑ DLP-3534 [M]	Tie Me Kangaroo Down, Sport	1963	12.00
❑ DLP-25534 [S]	Tie Me Kangaroo Down, Sport	1963	15.00
❑ DLP-3222 [M]	White Christmas	1959	25.00
❑ DLP-25222 [S]	White Christmas	1959	30.00
❑ DLP-3667 [M]	Winner of the Reader's Digest Poll	1965	12.00
❑ DLP-25667 [S]	Winner of the Reader's Digest Poll	1965	15.00
❑ DLP-3764 [M]	Wish You Were Here, Buddy	1966	12.00

Number	Title	Yr	NM
❑ DLP-25764 [S]	Wish You Were Here, Buddy	1966	15.00
❑ DLP-3121 [M]	Yes Indeed!	1958	20.00
❑ DLP-25121 [S]	Yes Indeed!	1959	25.00

HAMILTON

| ❑ HLP-118 [M] | 12 Great Hits | 196? | 12.00 |
| ❑ HLP-12118 [S] | 12 Great Hits | 196? | 12.00 |

HITSVILLE

| ❑ H6-405 | Texas Woman | 1976 | 15.00 |

LAMB & LION

❑ 1008	All in the Boone Family	1972	10.00
❑ 1007	Born Again	197?	10.00
❑ 1005	Christian People, Vol. 1	197?	10.00
❑ 1002	New Songs of the Jesus People	197?	12.00
❑ 1004	Pat Boone and the First Nashville Jesus Band	197?	12.00
❑ 1013	S-A-V-E-D	197?	10.00
❑ 1016	Songs from the Inner Court	197?	10.00
❑ 1006	The Family Who Prays	197?	10.00
❑ 5000	The Pat Boone Family in the Holy Land	197?	10.00

MCA

❑ 658	16 Great Performances	1980	10.00
❑ 6020	The Best of Pat Boone	1980	15.00
❑ 15028 [S]	White Christmas	198?	10.00
—Reissue of Dot LP			

MELODYLAND

| ❑ 6-501 | The Country Side of Pat Boone | 1975 | 15.00 |

MGM

| ❑ SE-4899 | I Love You More and More Every Day | 1973 | 10.00 |

PARAMOUNT

| ❑ 1043 | Pat Boone's Greatest Hits | 1974 | 15.00 |
| ❑ 1024 | Pat Boone's Greatest Hymns | 1974 | 15.00 |

PICKWICK

❑ SPC-3123	Canadian Sunset	196?	10.00
❑ SPC-3145	Favorite Hymns	197?	10.00
❑ SPC-3597	Great Hits	1978	10.00
❑ SPC-3107	Love Me Tender	196?	10.00
❑ SPC-3568	The Old Rugged Cross	1978	10.00
❑ SPC-3079	True Love	196?	10.00
❑ SPC-1024	White Christmas	1979	10.00
❑ SPC-3219	You've Lost That Lovin' Feeling	197?	10.00

SUPREME

| ❑ SS-2060 | Rapture | 1970 | 12.00 |

TETRAGRAMMATON

| ❑ T-110 | Departure | 1969 | 12.00 |

WORD

❑ WST-8711	He Leadeth Me	197?	12.00
❑ WST-8664	Hymns We Love	197?	12.00
❑ WST-8738	I Believe	198?	10.00
❑ WST-8536	The Pat Boone Family	1970	10.00
❑ WST-8725	The Star-Spangled Banner	197?	12.00

BOONE, RANDY

DECCA

❑ DL4663 [M]	Ramblin' Randy	1965	25.00
❑ DL74663 [S]	Ramblin' Randy	1965	30.00
❑ DL4619 [M]	Singing Star of The Virginian	1965	30.00
❑ DL74619 [S]	Singing Star of The Virginian	1965	35.00

BOOT

AGAPE

| ❑ 2601 | Boot | 1972 | 30.00 |

BOOT CAMP CLIK

PRIORITY

| ❑ 50646 | For the People | 1997 | 15.00 |
| ❑ 23052 | Greatest Hits: Basic Training | 2000 | 15.00 |

BOOTEE, DUKE

MERCURY

| ❑ 816667-1 | Bust Me Out | 1984 | 12.00 |

BOOTH, TONY

CAPITOL

❑ ST-11270	Happy Hour	1974	18.00
❑ ST-11126	Lonesone 7-7203	1972	18.00
❑ ST-11076	The Key's in the Mailbox	1972	18.00
❑ ST-11210	This Is Tony Booth	1973	18.00
❑ ST-11160	When a Man Loves a Woman (The Way That I Love You)	1973	18.00
❑ ST-11352	Workin' at the Car Wash Blues	1974	18.00

MGM

| ❑ SE-4704 | On the Right Track | 1970 | 25.00 |

BOOTSY'S RUBBER BAND

WARNER BROS.

❑ BS2972	Ahh... The Name Is Bootsy, Baby!	1977	18.00
❑ BSK3093	Bootsy? Player of the Year	1978	18.00
—With perforated punch-out glasses intact			
❑ BSK3093	Bootsy? Player of the Year	1978	12.00
—Without punch-out glasses			

Number	Title	Yr	NM
❑ BS2920	Stretchin' Out in Bootsy's Rubber Band	1976	18.00
❑ BSK3295	This Boot Is Make for Fonk-n	1979	18.00
—With 8-page coloring book			
❑ BSK3295	This Boot Is Make for Fonk-n	1979	12.00
—Without coloring book			
❑ BSK3433	Ultra Wave	1980	18.00
—As "Bootsy"			

BOOTY PEOPLE

ABC

| ❑ AB-998 | Booty People | 1977 | 18.00 |

BORCHERS, BOBBY

PLAYBOY

| ❑ KZ34829 | Bobby Borchers | 1977 | 15.00 |
| ❑ KZ35027 | Denim and Rhinestones | 1977 | 15.00 |

BORDERSONG

REAL GOOD

| ❑ 1001 | Morning | 1975 | 70.00 |

BORESON, STAN, AND DOUG SETTERBERG

GOLDEN CREST

| ❑ CR31021 | Stan and Doug Yust Go Nuts at Christmas | 1970 | 15.00 |

BORNAND COLLECTION, THE

BORNAND MUSIC BOX

| ❑ AB-3/90-5611 | The Original Music Box Medley of Christmas Songs | 1977 | 15.00 |
| —Book-of-the-Month Club pressing | | | |

BORODIN STRING QUARTET

MERCURY LIVING PRESENCE

| ❑ SR90309 [S] | Shostakovich: String Quartets No. 4 and 8 | 196? | 70.00 |
| —Maroon label, no "Vendor; Mercury Record Corporation | | | |

BOSTIC, EARL

GRAND PRIX

❑ K-404 [M]	The Earl of Bostic	196?	18.00
❑ KS-404 [R]	The Earl of Bostic	196?	15.00
❑ K-416 [M]	Wild Man	196?	18.00
❑ KS-416 [R]	Wild Man	196?	15.00

KING

❑ K-5010X	14 Original Greatest Hits	1977	15.00
❑ 947 [M]	24 Songs That Earl Loved the Most	1966	40.00
❑ 597 [M]	Alto Magic in Hi-Fi	1958	80.00
❑ KS 597 [S]	Alto Magic in Hi-Fi	1959	150.00
❑ 395-515 [M]	Alto-Tude	1956	100.00
❑ 395-503 [M]	Bostic for You	1956	100.00
❑ 613 [M]	Bostic Workshop	1959	50.00
❑ KS 613 [S]	Bostic Workshop	1959	100.00
❑ 786 [M]	By Popular Demand	1961	50.00
❑ 558 [M]	C'mon and Dance with Earl Bostic	1958	80.00
❑ KS-558 [S]	C'mon and Dance with Earl Bostic	1959	150.00
❑ 395-525 [M]	Dance Time	1956	80.00
❑ 395-500 [M]	Dance to the Best of Bostic	195?	80.00
—Second cover with girl in a swimsuit pictured			
❑ 395-500 [M]	Dance to the Best of Bostic	1956	100.00
—Original cover with Earl Bostic pictured			
❑ 295-64 [10]	Earl Bostic and His Alto Sax	1951	200.00
—Black vinyl			
❑ 295-64 [10]	Earl Bostic and His Alto Sax	1951	400.00
—Red vinyl			
❑ 295-65 [10]	Earl Bostic and His Alto Sax	1951	200.00
—Black vinyl			
❑ 295-65 [10]	Earl Bostic and His Alto Sax	1951	400.00
—Red vinyl			
❑ 295-66 [10]	Earl Bostic and His Alto Sax	1951	200.00
—Black vinyl			
❑ 295-66 [10]	Earl Bostic and His Alto Sax	1951	400.00
—Red vinyl			
❑ 295-72 [10]	Earl Bostic and His Alto Sax	1952	200.00
❑ 295-76 [10]	Earl Bostic and His Alto Sax	1952	200.00
❑ 295-77 [10]	Earl Bostic and His Alto Sax	1952	200.00
❑ 295-78 [10]	Earl Bostic and His Alto Sax	1952	200.00
❑ 295-79 [10]	Earl Bostic and His Alto Sax	1952	200.00
❑ 295-103 [10]	Earl Bostic and His Alto Sax	1954	200.00
❑ 827 [M]	Earl Bostic Plays Bossa Nova	1963	50.00
❑ 295-95 [10]	Earl Bostic Plays the Old Standards	1954	200.00
❑ KS-1048 [S]	Harlem Nocturne	1969	30.00
❑ 571 [M]	Hits of the Swing Age	1957	80.00
❑ 705 [M]	Hit Tunes of Big Broadway Shows	1960	50.00
❑ KS-705 [S]	Hit Tunes of Big Broadway Shows	1960	80.00
❑ 395-547 [M]	Invitation to Dance	1956	80.00
❑ 846 [M]	Jazz As I Feel It	1963	50.00
❑ 395-529 [M]	Let's Dance with Earl Bostic	1956	80.00
❑ 662 [M]	Musical Pearls	1960	50.00
❑ KS-662 [S]	Musical Pearls	1960	80.00

Number	Title	Yr	NM
❑ 583 [M]	Showcase of Swinging Dance Hits	1958	80.00
❑ 838 [M]	Songs of the Fantastic Fifties, Volume 2	1963	50.00
❑ 620 [M]	Sweet Tunes from the Roaring Twenties	1959	50.00
❑ KS-620 [S]	Sweet Tunes from the Roaring Twenties	1959	100.00
❑ 602 [M]	Sweet Tunes of the Fantastic Fifties	1959	50.00
❑ KSD-602 [S]	Sweet Tunes of the Fantastic Fifties	1959	100.00
❑ 640 [M]	Sweet Tunes of the Sentimental Forties	1960	50.00
❑ KS-640 [S]	Sweet Tunes of the Sentimental Forties	1960	80.00
❑ 632 [M]	Sweet Tunes of the Swinging Thirties	1959	50.00
❑ KS-632 [S]	Sweet Tunes of the Swinging Thirties	1959	100.00
❑ 881 [M]	The Best of Earl Bostic, Volume 2	1964	50.00
❑ 921 [M]	The Great Hits of 1964	1964	50.00
❑ 900 [M]	The New Sound	1964	50.00

PHILIPS

Number	Title	Yr	NM
❑ PHM200262 [M]	The Song Is Not Ended	1967	30.00
❑ PHS600262 [S]	The Song Is Not Ended	1967	30.00

BOSTIC, EARL/JIMMY LUNCEFORD

ALLEGRO ELITE

Number	Title	Yr	NM
❑ 4053 [10]	Earl Bostic/Jimmy Lunceford Orchestras	195?	40.00

BOSTIC, SAM

ATLANTIC

Number	Title	Yr	NM
❑ 81232	Circuitry Starring Sam Bostic	1985	10.00

BOSTON

EPIC

Number	Title	Yr	NM
❑ HE34188	Boston	1981	50.00
—First edition of the half-speed mastered edition			
❑ HE44188	Boston	1982	40.00
—Second edition of the half-speed mastered edition			
❑ PE34188	Boston	1976	12.00
—Original edition; orange label			
❑ JE34188	Boston	1977	10.00
—Second edition; orange label, different prefix			
❑ E9934188	Boston	1978	25.00
—Picture disc			
❑ HE45050	Don't Look Back	1982	50.00
—Half-speed mastered edition			
❑ FE35050	Don't Look Back	1978	12.00
—Original edition; orange label			
❑ FE35050	Don't Look Back	1979	10.00
—Second edition; dark blue label			

MCA

Number	Title	Yr	NM
❑ 6188	Third Stage	1986	10.00
❑ 10973	Walk On	1994	30.00

MOBILE FIDELITY

Number	Title	Yr	NM
❑ 1-249 [B]	Boston	1996	80.00
—Audiophile vinyl			

BOSTON CAMERATA, THE

NONESUCH

Number	Title	Yr	NM
❑ H-71315	A Medieval Christmas	1975	15.00
❑ H-71354	Sing We Noel: Christmas Music from England and Early America	1978	15.00

BOSTON POPS ORCHESTRA (ARTHUR FIEDLER, CONDUCTOR)

DEUTCHE GRAMMOPHON

Number	Title	Yr	NM
❑ 2584024	White Christmas	198?	12.00
—Reissue of Polydor LP			

FLEETWOOD

Number	Title	Yr	NM
❑ FMS1016	An Evening with Arthur Fiedler and the Boston Pops	1976	15.00
—Side 1: Great Songs for All Seasons; Side 2: Great Songs of Christmas (reissue of Polydor recordings)			

POLYDOR

Number	Title	Yr	NM
❑ 24-5004	A Christmas Festival	1970	12.00

RCA GOLD SEAL

Number	Title	Yr	NM
❑ AGL1-3436	Pops Christmas Party	1979	12.00
—Reissue of LSC-2329			

RCA VICTOR RED SEAL

Number	Title	Yr	NM
❑ LSC-2439 [S]	All-Time Favorites	1960	25.00
—Original with "shaded dog" label			
❑ LSC-2213 [S]	Boston Tea Party	1959	25.00
—Original with "shaded dog" label			
❑ LSC-2621 [S]	Chopin: Les Sylphides; Prokofiev: Love for Three Oranges	1962	30.00
—Original with "shaded dog" label			
❑ LSC-6082 [S]	Everything But the Beer	1959	100.00
—Original with "shaded dog" label			
❑ LSC-2549 [S]	Family Fun	1961	40.00
—Original with "shaded dog" label			
❑ LSC-2586 [S]	Gershwin: Piano Concerto	1962	25.00
—Earl Wild, piano; originals with "shaded dog" label			
❑ LSC-2586 [S]	Gershwin: Piano Concerto	199?	30.00
—Earl Wild, piano; Classic Records reissue			
❑ LSC-2367 [S]	Gershwin: Rhapsody in Blue; An American in Paris	1960	25.00
—Earl Wild, piano; originals with "shaded dog" label			
❑ LSC-2235 [S]	Good Music to Have Fun With	1959	30.00
—Original with "shaded dog" label			
❑ LSC-2125 [S]	Grieg: Music from Peer Gynt	1958	25.00
—Original with "shaded dog" label			
❑ LSC-2100 [S]	Hi-Fi Fiedler	1958	30.00
—Original with "shaded dog" label			
❑ LSC-2240 [S]	Kay, Hershey: Stars and Stripes	1959	40.00
—Original with "shaded dog" label			
❑ LSC-2229 [S]	Marches in Hi-Fi	1959	25.00
—Original with "shaded dog" label			
❑ LSC-2702 [S]	Milhaud: A Frenchman in New York; Gershwin: An American in Paris	1963	30.00
—Original with "shaded dog" label			
❑ LSC-2470 [S]	More Classical Music for People Who Hate Classical Music	1961	40.00
—Original with "shaded dog" label			
❑ LSC-2380 [S]	Music from Million Dollar Movies	1960	25.00
—Original with "shaded dog" label			
❑ LSC-2486 [S]	Music of Frank Loesser	1961	40.00
—Original with "shaded dog" label			
❑ LSC-1817 [S]	Offenbach: Gaite Parisienne	1958	400.00
—Original with "shaded dog" label			
❑ LSC-1817 [S]	Offenbach: Gaite Parisienne	199?	30.00
—Classic Records reissue			
❑ LSC-2267 [S]	Offenbach: Gaite Parisienne; Khachatourian: Gayne Suite	1959	25.00
—Original with "shaded dog" label			
❑ LSC-1990 [S]	Offenbach: In America	1958	40.00
—Original with "shaded dog" label			
❑ LSC-1990 [S]	Offenbach: In America	1964	50.00
—Second pressing with "white dog" label; a rare case where the second edition is more desirable than the first			
❑ LSC-2202 [S]	Pops Caviar	1959	25.00
—Original with "shaded dog" label			
❑ LSC-2329 [S]	Pops Christmas Party	1959	40.00
—Original copies have "shaded dog" with small "RCA Victor" logo; large "Living Stereo" on front cover			
❑ LSC-2329 [S]	Pops Christmas Party	1964	25.00
—Second editions have "white dog" with large "RCA Victor" logo; small "Living Stereo" on front cover			
❑ LSC-3324	Pops Goes Christmas	1972	12.00
—Compilation of older Christmas recordings			
❑ LSC-2270 [S]	Pops Stoppers	1959	25.00
—Original with "shaded dog" label			
❑ LSC-2637 [S]	Rodgers: No Strings; State Fair	1962	25.00
—Original with "shaded dog" label			
❑ LSC-2294 [S]	Rodgers: Slaughter on Tenth Avenue	1959	25.00
—Original with "shaded dog" label			
❑ LSC-2084 [S]	Rossini-Respighi: La Boutique Fantasque	1958	120.00
—Original with "shaded dog" label			
❑ LSC-2596 [S]	Saint-Saens: Carnival of the Animals; Britten: Young Person's Guide to the Orchestra	1962	60.00
—Original with "shaded dog" label			
❑ LSC-2320 [S]	Song of India	1959	25.00
—Original with "shaded dog" label			
❑ LSC-2130 [S]	Strauss, Johann: Orchestral Music from Gypsy Baron and Die Fledermaus	1958	25.00
—Original with "shaded dog" label			
❑ LSC-2052 [S]	Tchaikovsky: The Nutcracker (selections)	1958	25.00
—Original with "shaded dog" label			
❑ LSC-2442 [S]	The Music of Franz Liszt	1960	25.00
—Original with "shaded dog" label			
❑ LSC-2028 [S]	Waltzes by the Strauss Family	1958	25.00
—Original with "shaded dog" label			

READER'S DIGEST

Number	Title	Yr	NM
❑ RBA-060-D	A Christmas Festival	1988	12.00

BOSTON POPS ORCHESTRA (JOHN WILLIAMS, CONDUCTOR)

PHILIPS

Number	Title	Yr	NM
❑ 6302125	We Wish You a Merry Christmas	1981	12.00

BOSTON SYMPHONY ORCHESTRA (AARON COPLAND, CONDUCTOR)

RCA VICTOR RED SEAL

Number	Title	Yr	NM
❑ LSC-2401 [S]	Copland: Appalachian Spring; The Tender Land Suite	1960	25.00
—Original with "shaded dog" label			

BOSTON SYMPHONY ORCHESTRA (CHARLES MUNCH, CONDUCTOR)

RCA VICTOR RED SEAL

Number	Title	Yr	NM
❑ LSC-6140 [S]	Bach: Brandenburg Concertos No. 1-6	196?	150.00
—Original with "shaded dog" label			
❑ LSC-2233 [S]	Beethoven: Symphony No. 3	1959	50.00
—Original with "shaded dog" label			
❑ LSC-2228 [S]	Berlioz: Harold in Italy	1959	25.00
—Original with "shaded dog" label			
❑ LSC-2438 [S]	Berlioz: Overtures	1960	70.00
—Original with "shaded dog" label			
❑ LSC-1900 [S]	Berlioz: Symphonie Fantastique	199?	30.00
—Classic Records issue. This album is not known to have been issued in stereo before this.			
❑ LSC-2608 [S]	Berlioz: Symphonie Fantastique	1962	30.00
—Original with "shaded dog" label			
❑ LSC-2352 [S]	Blackwood: Symphony No. 1; Haieff: Symphony No. 2	1960	60.00
—Original with "shaded dog" label			
❑ LM-2352 [M]	Blackwood: Symphony No. 1; Haieff: Symphony No. 2	1960	25.00
❑ LSC-2097 [S]	Brahms: Symphony No. 1	1958	150.00
—Original with "shaded dog" label			
❑ LSC-2297 [S]	Brahms: Symphony No. 4	1959	30.00
—Original with "shaded dog" label			
❑ LSC-2647 [S]	Chausson: Symphony in B-flat; Franck: Le Chasseur Maudit	1962	40.00
—Original with "shaded dog" label			
❑ LSC-2282 [S]	Debussy: Images	1959	80.00
—Original with "shaded dog" label			
❑ LM-2282 [M]	Debussy: Images	1959	25.00
❑ LSC-2111 [S]	Debussy: La Mer	1958	50.00
—Original with "shaded dog" label			
❑ LSC-2629 [S]	Dvorak: Symphony No. 4 (8) in G	1962	50.00
—Original with "shaded dog" label			
❑ LSC-2131 [S]	Franck: Symphony in D	1958	25.00
—Original with "shaded dog" label			
❑ LSC-2371 [S]	Mahler: Songs of a Wayfarer	1960	30.00
—Original with "shaded dog" label			
❑ LSC-2520 [S]	Mendelssohn: Symphony No. 3 "Scotch"; Scherzo from Octet in E-flat	1961	25.00
—Original with "shaded dog" label			
❑ LSC-2221 [S]	Mendelssohn: Symphony No. 4 and No. 5	1959	25.00
—Original with "shaded dog" label			
❑ LDS-2625 [S]	Milhaud: La Creation du Monde; Suite Provencale	1962	200.00
—Original with "shaded dog" label			
❑ LSC-2625 [S]	Milhaude: La Creation Du Monde	1962	200.00
—With "shaded dog" or "white dog" label			
❑ LSC-2625 [S]	Milhaude: La Creation Du Monde	199?	30.00
—Classic Records reissue			
❑ LSC-2567 [S]	Poulenc: Organ Concerto; Stravinsky: Jeu de Cartes	1961	40.00
—Original with "shaded dog" label			
❑ LSC-1984 [S]	Ravel: Bolero; La Valse; Rapsodie Espagnole; Debussy: Prelude	1958	80.00
—Original with "shaded dog" label			
❑ LSC-2271 [S]	Ravel: Concerto in G; d'Indy: Symphony on a French Mountain Air	1959	100.00
—Original with "shaded dog" label			
❑ LSC-2271 [S]	Ravel: Concerto in G; d'Indy: Symphony on a French Mountain Air	199?	30.00
—Classic Records reissue			
❑ LSC-1893 [S]	Ravel: Daphnis and Chloe	1958	400.00
—Original with "shaded dog" label			
❑ LSC-1893 [S]	Ravel: Daphnis and Chloe	199?	30.00
—Classic Records reissue			
❑ LSC-2568 [S]	Ravel: Daphnis et Chloe	1961	25.00
—Original with "shaded dog" label			
❑ LSC-2341 [S]	Saint-Saens: Symphony No. 3	1960	25.00
—Original with "shaded dog" label			
❑ LSC-2522 [S]	Schubert: Symphony No. 2; Beethoven: Prometheus Ballet Excerpts	1961	25.00
—Original with "shaded dog" label			
❑ LSC-2344 [S]	Schubert: Symphony No. 9	1960	40.00
—Original with "shaded dog" label			
❑ LSC-2344 [S]	Schubert: Symphony No. 9	1964	30.00
—Second edition with "white dog" label			
❑ LSC-2474 [S]	Schumann: Symphony No. 1	1961	25.00
—Original with "shaded dog" label			
❑ LSC-2565 [S]	Tchaikovsky: Romeo and Juliet; Strauss, Richard: Till Eulenspiegel	1961	40.00
—Original with "shaded dog" label			
❑ LSC-2105 [S]	Tchaikovsky: Serenade for Strings	1958	40.00
—Original with "shaded dog" label			
❑ LSC-2683 [S]	Tchaikovsky: Symphony No. 6	1962	25.00
—Original with "shaded dog" label			

Number	Title	Yr	NM
❏ LSC-2292 [S]	The French Touch	1959	200.00
—Original with "shaded dog" label			

BOSTON SYMPHONY ORCHESTRA (ERICH LEINSDORF, CONDUCTOR)

RCA VICTOR RED SEAL

❏ LSC-2707 [S]	Prokofiev: Symphony No. 5	1963	25.00
—Original with "shaded dog" label			

BOSTON SYMPHONY ORCHESTRA (PIERRE MONTEUX, CONDUCTOR)

RCA VICTOR RED SEAL

❏ LSC-2376 [S]	Stravinsky: Petrouchka	1960	100.00
—Original with "shaded dog" label			
❏ LSC-2376 [S]	Stravinsky: Petrouchka	1964	50.00
—Second edition with "white dog" label			
❏ LSC-2369 [S]	Tchaikovsky: Symphony No. 4	1959	50.00
—Original with "shaded dog" label			
❏ LSC-2369 [S]	Tchaikovsky: Symphony No. 4	199?	30.00
—Classic Records reissue			
❏ LSC-2239 [S]	Tchaikovsky: Symphony No. 5	1959	30.00
—Original with "shaded dog" label			
❏ LSC-2239 [S]	Tchaikovsky: Symphony No. 5	1964	25.00
—Second edition with "white dog" label			
❏ LSC-1901 [S]	Tchaikovsky: Symphony No. 6 "Pathetique"	1958	50.00
—Original with "shaded dog" label			
❏ LSC-1901 [S]	Tchaikovsky: Symphony No. 6 "Pathetique"	199?	30.00
—Classic Records reissue			

BOSTON TEA PARTY, THE

FLICK DISC

❏ 45000	The Boston Tea Party	1968	60.00

BOSWELL, CONNEE

DECCA

❏ DL8356 [M]	Connee	1956	50.00
❏ DL5390 [10]	Connee Boswell	1951	80.00
❏ DL5445 [10]	Singing the Blues	1952	80.00

DESIGN

❏ DLP-60 [M]	Connee Boswell Sings Irving Berlin	196?	15.00
❏ DLP3-60 [R]	Connee Boswell Sings Irving Berlin	196?	10.00
❏ DLP-101 [M]	The New Sound of Connee Boswell	196?	15.00
❏ DLPS-101 [R]	The New Sound of Connee Boswell	196?	10.00

RCA VICTOR

❏ LPM-1426 [M]	Connee Boswell and the Original Memphis Five	1957	40.00

BOTHWELL, JOHNNY

BRUNSWICK

❏ BL58033 [10]	Presenting Johnny Bothwell	1953	100.00

BOTICELLI, ANTHONY

CAROLEER

❏ X1702 [M]	Christmas Favorites	196?	15.00
❏ SX1702 [S]	Christmas Favorites	196?	18.00
—Same as above, but in stereo			

BOUNTY KILLER

TVT

❏ 6420	5th Element	1999	15.00
❏ 6370	Next Millennium	1998	15.00

BOURBON STREET STOMPERS, THE

TIME

❏ 52118 [M]	We Like Dixieland	196?	18.00
❏ S-2118 [S]	We Like Dixieland	196?	25.00

BOURGEOIS TAGG

ISLAND

❏ 90496	Bourgeois Tagg	1986	10.00
❏ 90638	YoYo	1987	10.00

BOW STREET RUNNERS, THE

B.T. PUPPY

❏ BTPS-1026	The Bow Street Runners	1969	1000.00

SUNDAZED

❏ LP5029	The Bow Street Runners	199?	12.00
—Reissue of B.T. Puppy LP			

BOW WOW WOW

HARVEST

❏ SK-12234	12 Original Recordings	1982	18.00

RCA VICTOR

❏ AFL1-4375	I Want Candy	1982	15.00
❏ DJL1-4193 [DJ]	RCA Special Radio Series	1981	30.00

Number	Title	Yr	NM
❏ AFL1-4147	See Jungle, See Jungle! Go Join Your Gang, Yeah! City All Over, Go Ape Crazy	1981	15.00
❏ CPL1-4314 [EP]	The Last of the Mohicans	1982	12.00
❏ AFL1-4570	When the Going Gets Tough, the Tough Get Going	1983	12.00

BOWEN, JIMMY

DECCA

❏ DL4816 [M]	Margie Bowes Sings	1967	25.00

REPRISE

❏ R-6210 [M]	Sunday Morning with the Comics	1966	30.00
❏ RS-6210 [S]	Sunday Morning with the Comics	1966	40.00

ROULETTE

❏ R25004 [M]	Jimmy Bowen	1957	300.00
—Black and silver label			
❏ R25004 [M]	Jimmy Bowen	1958	150.00
—Red label			
❏ R25004 [M]	Jimmy Bowen	198?	15.00
—Reissue for Publishers Central Bureau (it says so on the jacket)			

BOWES, MARGIE

DECCA

❏ DL4816 [M]	Margie Bowes Sings	1967	25.00
❏ DL74816 [S]	Margie Bowes Sings	1967	18.00
❏ DL75023	Today's Country Sound	1968	18.00

BOWIE, DAVID

COLUMBIA

❏ C86630	Heathen	2002	15.00
❏ 88765 461861 [B]	The Next Day	2013	50.00

DERAM

❏ DE16003 [M]	David Bowie	1967	200.00
❏ DES18003 [S]	David Bowie	1967	150.00

EMI

❏ DBZSX40 [B]	The Rise And Fall Of Ziggy Stardust And The Spiders From Mars	2012	40.00

EMI AMERICA

❏ R153730	Let's Dance	1983	15.00
—RCA Music Service edition			
❏ SO-17093 [B]	Let's Dance	1983	12.00
❏ SPRO0 [DJ]	Let's Talk	1983	30.00
—Promo-only interview album			
❏ SPRO9960/1 [DJ]	Let's Talk	1983	30.00
—Promo-only interview album			
❏ R174212	Never Let Me Down	1987	15.00
—BMG Direct Marketing edition			
❏ PJ-17267	Never Let Me Down	1987	12.00
❏ -0 [DJ]	Never Let Me Down: The Interview	1987	30.00
❏ SPRO 79112/3 [DJ]	Never Let Me Down: The Interview	1987	30.00
❏ SJ-17138	Tonight	1984	12.00

LONDON

❏ PS628/9	Images 1966-1967	1973	50.00
—Original pressings have dark blue and silver labels. Later pressings, if any, are worth at least 50% less.			
❏ LC50007	Starting Point	1977	15.00

MERCURY

❏ SR61246 [B]	Man of Words, Man of Music	1969	300.00
❏ SR61325	The Man Who Sold the World	1970	40.00
—An often-counterfeited album; originals have matrix numbers stamped in the trail-off area			

MOBILE FIDELITY

❏ 1-083	Let's Dance	1984	30.00
—Audiophile vinyl			
❏ 1-064	The Rise and Fall of Ziggy Stardust and the Spiders from Mars	1983	50.00
—Audiophile vinyl			

RCA RED SEAL

❏ ARL1-2743	Peter and the Wolf	1978	25.00
—With the Philadelphia Orchestra conducted by Eugene Ormandy; green vinyl			
❏ ARL1-2743	Peter and the Wolf	1978	25.00
—With the Philadelphia Orchestra conducted by Eugene Ormandy; black vinyl			

RCA VICTOR

❏ -0 [DJ]	1980 All Clear	1980	30.00
❏ DJL1-3545 [DJ]	1980 All Clear	1980	30.00
—Promo-only compilation			
❏ LSP-4852	Aladdin Sane	1973	25.00
—Orange label is original (deduct 50% for tan labels)			
❏ AFL1-4852	Aladdin Sane	1977	12.00
—Reissue			
❏ AYL1-3890	Aladdin Sane	1980	10.00
—Reissue			
❏ -0 [DJ]	An Evening with David Bowie	1978	50.00
—Live concert for "Superstars Radio Network"			

Number	Title	Yr	NM
❏ DJL1-3016 [DJ]	An Evening with David Bowie	1978	50.00
—Music and interview for "Superstars Radio Network"			
❏ -0 [DJ]	Bowie Now	1978	75.00
❏ DJL1-2697 [DJ]	Bowie Now	1978	60.00
❏ APL1-1732 [B]	Changesonebowie	1976	12.00
❏ AFL1-1732	Changesonebowie	1978	12.00
—Reissue			
❏ AQL1-1732	Changesonebowie	1984	12.00
—Reissue			
❏ AFL1-4202	Changestwobowie	1981	12.00
❏ DJL1-3829 [DJ]	College Radio Series	1980	30.00
❏ CPL1-4346 [EP]	David Bowie in Berthold Brecht's Baal	1982	12.00
❏ CPL2-0771	David Live	1974	25.00
—At time of release, available with either orange or tan labels			
❏ CPL2-0771	David Live	1976	15.00
—Reissue with black label, dog near top			
❏ CPL1-0576	Diamond Dogs	1974	4000.00
—Original copies have cover with dog's genitals clearly visible. Almost all were destroyed prior to release.			
❏ CPL1-0576	Diamond Dogs	1974	25.00
—Standard issue, with dog's genitals airbrushed			
❏ AYL1-3889	Diamond Dogs	1980	10.00
—Reissue			
❏ AFL1-4919	Fame and Fashion	1984	12.00
❏ AFL1-4792	Golden Years	1983	12.00
❏ AFL1-2522	Heroes	1977	12.00
❏ AYL1-3857	Heroes	1980	10.00
—Reissue			
❏ LSP-4623	Hunky Dory	1972	25.00
❏ AYL1-3844	Hunky Dory	1980	10.00
—Reissue			
❏ AQL1-3254	Lodger	1979	12.00
❏ AYL1-4234	Lodger	1981	10.00
—Reissue			
❏ APL1-2030	Low	1977	12.00
❏ AYL1-3856	Low	1980	10.00
—Reissue			
❏ APL1-0291 [B]	Pin Ups	1973	25.00
❏ AFL1-0291	Pin Ups	1978	12.00
—Reissue			
❏ AYL1-4653	Pin Ups	1982	10.00
—Reissue			
❏ AQL1-3647	Scary Monsters	1980	12.00
❏ -0 [DJ]	Scary Monsters Interview	1980	25.00
❏ DJL1-3840 [DJ]	Scary Monsters Interview	1980	25.00
❏ LSP-4813	Space Oddity	1973	25.00
—Reissue of Mercury SR-61246; add 1/3 if bonus poster is enclosed			
❏ DJL1-3829-A [DJ]	Special Radio Series	1980	30.00
—Same material as DJL1-3829			
❏ -0 [DJ]	Special Radio Series, Volume 1	1980	30.00
❏ CPL2-2913	Stage	1978	25.00
❏ APL1-1327	Station to Station	1976	15.00
—Originals have a brown label			
❏ APL1-1327	Station to Station	1976	12.00
—Black label			
❏ AQK1-1327	Station to Station	1984	12.00
—Reissue			
❏ LSP-4816	The Man Who Sold the World	1973	25.00
—Reissue of Mercury SR-61325; add 1/3 if bonus poster is enclosed			
❏ LSP-4702	The Rise and Fall of Ziggy Stardust and the Spiders from Mars	1972	25.00
—Orange label			
❏ AFL1-4702	The Rise and Fall of Ziggy Stardust and the Spiders from Mars	1977	12.00
—Reissue			
❏ AYL1-3843	The Rise and Fall of Ziggy Stardust and the Spiders from Mars	1980	10.00
—Reissue			
❏ LSP-4702	The Rise and Fall of Ziggy Stardust and the Spiders from Mars	1975	15.00
—Tan label			
❏ APL1-0998	Young Americans	1975	15.00
—At time of release, available with either orange or tan label			
❏ APL1-0998	Young Americans	1976	12.00
—Black label			
❏ AQK1-0998	Young Americans	1984	12.00
—Reissue			
❏ -0 [DJ]	Ziggy Stardust, The Motion Picture	1983	50.00
—Promo version on clear vinyl			
❏ CPL2-4862 [DJ]	Ziggy Stardust, The Motion Picture	1983	50.00
—Promo version on clear vinyl			
❏ CPL2-4862	Ziggy Stardust, The Motion Picture	1983	25.00

RYKO ANALOGUE

❏ RALP 0135 [B]	Aladdin Sane	1990	50.00
—Clear vinyl with "Limited Edition" obi			
❏ RALP 0171 [B]	Changesbowie	1990	50.00
—Clear vinyl with "Limited Edition" obi			
❏ RALP 0138/9 [B]	David Live	1990	60.00
—Clear vinyl with "Limited Edition" obi			

Number	Title	Yr	NM

❏ RALP 0137 [B] — Diamond Dogs — 1990 — 50.00
— Clear vinyl with "Limited Edition" obi; genitals on dog are restored

❏ RALP 0133 [B] — Hunky Dory — 1990 — 50.00
— Clear vinyl with "Limited Edition" obi

❏ RALP 0136 [B] — Pin Ups — 1990 — 50.00
— Clear vinyl with "Limited Edition" obi

❏ RALP 0120/1/2 [B] — Sound + Vision — 1989 — 200.00
— Six-LP box set on clear vinyl with three gatefold cardboard inner sleeves

❏ RALP 0131 — Space Oddity — 1990 — 25.00
— Clear vinyl with "Limited Edition" obi

❏ RALP 0132 [B] — The Man Who Sold the World — 1990 — 50.00
— Clear vinyl with "Limited Edition" obi

❏ -0 [DJ] — The Rise and Fall of Ziggy Stardust and the Spiders from Mars — 1990 — 100.00
— Special promo-only package with both the LP and CD versions

❏ RALP 0134 [B] — The Rise and Fall of Ziggy Stardust and the Spiders from Mars — 1990 — 60.00
— Clear vinyl with "Limited Edition" obi

❏ LSD-4702 [DJ] — The Rise and Fall of Ziggy Stardust and the Spiders from Mars — 1990 — 100.00
— Special promo-only package with both the LP and CD versions

BOWIE, LESTER, AND PHILIP WILSON

IAI
❏ 373854 — Duet — 1978 — 15.00

BOWIE, LESTER

BLACK SAINT
❏ BSR-0020 — Fifth Power — 197? — 15.00

ECM
❏ 23789 — All the Magic — 1984 — 12.00
❏ 25034 — I Only Have Eyes for You — 1985 — 12.00
❏ 1209 — The Great Pretender — 1081 — 15.00

MUSE
❏ MR-5055 — Fast Last! — 1975 — 15.00
❏ MR-5337 — Hello Dolly — 1987 — 12.00
❏ MR-5081 — Rope-a-Dope — 1975 — 15.00

NESSA
❏ N-1 — Numbers 1 and 2 — 1968 — 30.00

VENTURE
❏ 90650 — Twilight Dreams — 1988 — 12.00

BOWIE, PAT

PRESTIGE
❏ PRLP-7437 [M] — Feelin' Good — 1967 — 30.00
❏ PRST-7437 [S] — Feelin' Good — 1967 — 30.00
❏ PRLP-7385 [M] — Out of Sight — 1965 — 30.00
❏ PRST-7385 [S] — Out of Sight — 1965 — 30.00

BOWLES, RICK

POLYDOR
❏ PD-1-6352 — Free for the Evening — 1982 — 12.00

BOWMAN, DON

LONE STAR
❏ 4605 — Still Fighting Mental Health — 1979 — 18.00

RCA VICTOR
❏ LPM-3646 [M] — Don Bowman Recorded Almost Live — 1966 — 25.00
❏ LSP-3646 [S] — Don Bowman Recorded Almost Live — 1966 — 30.00
❏ LPM-3345 [M] — Fresh from the Funny Farm — 1965 — 25.00
❏ LSP-3345 [S] — Fresh from the Funny Farm — 1965 — 30.00
❏ LPM-3795 [M] — From Mexico with Laughs Featuring the Tijuana Drum and Bugle Corps — 1967 — 30.00
❏ LSP-3795 [S] — From Mexico with Laughs Featuring the Tijuana Drum and Bugle Corps — 1967 — 25.00
❏ LPM-3920 [M] — Funny Folk Flops — 1968 — 50.00
❏ LSP-3920 [S] — Funny Folk Flops — 1968 — 25.00
❏ LPM-3495 [M] — Funny Way to Make an Album — 1966 — 25.00
❏ LSP-3495 [S] — Funny Way to Make an Album — 1966 — 30.00
❏ LPM-2831 [M] — Our Man in Trouble — 1964 — 25.00
❏ LSP-2831 [S] — Our Man in Trouble — 1964 — 30.00

BOWN, PATTI

COLUMBIA
❏ CL1379 [M] — Patti Bown Plays Big Piano — 1959 — 30.00

BOX OF FROGS

EPIC
❏ BFE39327 [B] — Box of Frogs — 1984 — 15.00
❏ EAS1904 [DJ] — Interchords — 1984 — 25.00
— Promo-only interview album
❏ BFE39923 [B] — Strange Land — 1986 — 15.00

BOX TOPS, THE

BELL
❏ 6017 — Cry Like a Baby — 1968 — 25.00
❏ 6032 — Dimensions — 1969 — 25.00
❏ 6023 — Non-Stop — 1968 — 25.00
❏ 6025 — The Box Tops Super Hits — 1968 — 25.00
❏ 6011 [M] — The Letter/Neon Rainbow — 1967 — 30.00
❏ S-6011 [S] — The Letter/Neon Rainbow — 1967 — 25.00

RHINO
❏ RNLP-161 — The Greatest Hits — 1982 — 15.00

BOXCAR WILLIE

AHMC
❏ AA118 — Marty Martin Sings Country Music — 1976 — 50.00
— As "Marty Martin"; he changed his name to "Boxcar Willie" after one of his early songs

MAIN STREET
❏ 73002 — Best of Boxcar, Vol. 1 — 1982 — 15.00
❏ 73000 — King of the Road — 1981 — 15.00
❏ 73001 — Last Train to Heaven — 1982 — 15.00
❏ 9309 — ... Not the Man I Used to Be — 1984 — 12.00

BOY GEORGE

VIRGIN
❏ R100843 — High Hat — 1989 — 15.00
—BMG Direct Marketing edition
❏ 91022 — High Hat — 1989 — 12.00
❏ R153255 — Sold — 1987 — 15.00
—BMG Direct Marketing edition
❏ 90617 — Sold — 1987 — 12.00

BOY MEETS GIRL

A&M
❏ SP-6-5046 — Boy Meets Girl — 1985 — 12.00
RCA
❏ 8414-1-R — Reel Life — 1988 — 10.00

BOYCE, TOMMY, AND BOBBY HART

A&M
❏ SP-4162 — It's All Happening on the Inside — 1968 — 25.00
❏ LP-143 [M] — I Wonder What She's Doing Tonite? — 1968 — 35.00
❏ SP-4143 [S] — I Wonder What She's Doing Tonite? — 1968 — 25.00
❏ LP-126 [M] — Test Patterns — 1967 — 30.00
❏ SP-4126 [S] — Test Patterns — 1967 — 25.00

BOYCE, TOMMY

RCA CAMDEN
❏ CAL-2202 [M] — Tommy Boyce — 1967 — 25.00
❏ CAS-2202 [S] — Tommy Boyce — 1967 — 30.00

BOYD, BILL, AND HIS COWBOY RAMBLERS

BLUEBIRD
❏ AXM2-5503 — Bill Boyd and His Cowboy Ramblers — 197? — 25.00

BOYD, BILLY

CROWN
❏ CLP-5170 [M] — Twangy Guitars — 1960 — 60.00
— Black label, silver print
❏ CLP-5170 [M] — Twangy Guitars — 1961 — 25.00
— Gray label
❏ CST-196 [R] — Twangy Guitars — 196? — 50.00
— Red vinyl
❏ CST-196 [R] — Twangy Guitars — 196? — 15.00
— Black vinyl

BOYD, EDDIE

EPIC
❏ BN26409 — 7936 South Rhodes — 1968 — 30.00
LONDON
❏ PS554 — I'll Dust My Broom — 1969 — 30.00

BOYD, JIMMY

COLUMBIA
❏ CL6270 [10] — Christmas with Jimmy Boyd — 1953 — 100.00
❏ CL2543 [10] — I Saw Mommy Kissing Santa Claus — 1955 — 40.00
—House Party Series" reissue

BOYD, LIONA

CBS
❏ FM37248 — A Guitar for Christmas — 1981 — 15.00

BOYD, ROCKY

JAZZTIME
❏ JT-001 [M] — Ease It — 1961 — 500.00
— "deep groove"
❏ JS-001 [S] — Ease It — 1961 — 30.00

BOYER, CHARLES

VALIANT
❏ VLM-5001 [M] — Where Does Love Go? — 1966 — 30.00
❏ VLS-25001 [S] — Where Does Love Go? — 1966 — 30.00

BOYER, DAVE

WORD
❏ 8612 — Christmas with Dave Boyer — 198? — 12.00

BOYLAN, TERENCE

ASYLUM
❏ 6E-201 — Suzy — 1980 — 12.00
❏ 7E-1091 — Terence Boylan — 1977 — 12.00

BOYS, THE

MOTOWN
❏ 6260 — Messages from the Boys — 1988 — 12.00
❏ 6302 — The Boys — 1990 — 18.00

BOYS BAND, THE

ELEKTRA
❏ E1-60047 — The Boys Band — 1982 — 15.00

BOYS CLUB

MCA
❏ 42242 — Boys Club — 1988 — 10.00

BOYS DON'T CRY

ATLANTIC
❏ 81795 — Boys Don't Cry — 1987 — 10.00
PROFILE
❏ PRO1219 — Boys Don't Cry — 1986 — 12.00

BOYS ON THE BLOCK

FANTASY
❏ F-9656 — Blockbuster — 1987 — 12.00

BOYS TOWN CHOIR, THE

MASTERTONE
❏ MS-102 — Christmas at Boys Town — 1964 — 25.00
— Some copies contain a concert program

BOYZ II MEN

MOTOWN
❏ 31453 0819-1 — Evolution — 1997 — 15.00
❏ -0 [DJ] — II — 1994 — 30.00
— Vinyl is promo only; in Motown company cover
❏ 31453 0323-1 [DJ] — II — 1994 — 30.00
— Vinyl is promo only; in Motown company cover

BR5-49

ARISTA NASHVILLE
❏ 18862 — Big Backyard Beat Show — 1999 — 15.00
— Originally issued on CD and cassette in 1998
❏ 18818 — BR5-49 — 1999 — 15.00
— Originally issued on CD and cassette in 1996
❏ 10800 [EP] — Live from Robert's — 1999 — 12.00
— Originally issued on CD and cassette in 1996

BRACE, JANET

ABC-PARAMOUNT
❏ ABC-116 [M] — Special Delivery — 1956 — 50.00

BRACKEEN, CHARLES

SILKHEART
❏ SH-110 — Attainment — 198? — 15.00
❏ SH-105 — Bannar — 198? — 15.00
❏ SH-111 — Worshippers Come Nigh — 198? — 15.00
STRATA-EAST
❏ 19736 — Rhythm X — 1974 — 15.00

BRACKEEN, JOANNE

ANTILLES
❏ 1001 — Special Identity — 198? — 12.00
CHOICE
❏ CRS1024 — Prism — 1978 — 15.00
❏ CRS1009 — Snooze — 1976 — 15.00
❏ CRS1016 — Tring-a-Ling — 1977 — 15.00
COLUMBIA
❏ JC36593 — Ancient Dynasty — 1980 — 12.00
❏ JC36075 — Keyed In — 1979 — 12.00
CONCORD JAZZ
❏ CJ-316 — Fi-Fi Goes to Heaven — 1987 — 12.00
❏ CJ-280 — Havin' Fun — 1985 — 12.00
PAUSA
❏ 7045 — Mythical Magic — 1979 — 15.00
TIMELESS
❏ TI-302 — Aft — 1980 — 15.00

BRADDOCK, BOBBY

ELEKTRA
❏ 6E-187 — Between the Lines — 1979 — 15.00
❏ 6E-224 — Love Bomb — 1980 — 15.00
RCA VICTOR
❏ MHL1-8524 [EP] — Hardpore Cornography — 1984 — 10.00

Number	Title	Yr	NM
BRADEN, JOHN			
A&M			
❏ SP-4172	John Braden	1969	18.00
BRADFORD, ALEX			
CHECKER			
❏ LP-10041 [M]	Alex Bradford	196?	30.00
SPECIALTY			
❏ SP-2108 [M]	Too Close to Heaven	1959	100.00
VEE JAY			
❏ LP-5023 [M]	One Step	1962	40.00
❏ LP-5056 [M]	The Soul of Alex Bradford	1964	40.00
BRADFORD, BOBBY			
EMANEM			
❏ 3302	Love's Dream	1976	25.00
NESSA			
❏ N-17	Bobby Bradford with John Stevens and the Spontaneous Music Ensemble, Vol. 1	198?	12.00
❏ N-18	Bobby Bradford with John Stevens and the Spontaneous Music Ensemble, Vol. 2	198?	12.00
SOUL NOTE			
❏ 121168-1	One Night Stand	1990	15.00
BRADFORD, CLEA			
CADET			
❏ LPS-810	Her Point of View	1969	18.00
MAINSTREAM			
❏ 56042 [M]	Clea Bradford Now	1965	30.00
❏ S-6042 [S]	Clea Bradford Now	1965	30.00
STATUS			
❏ ST-8320 [M]	Clea Bradford with Clark Terry	1965	40.00
TRU-SOUND			
❏ TRU-15005 [M]	These Dues	1962	50.00
BRADFORD, PERRY			
CRISPUS ATTUCKS			
❏ 101 [M]	The Perry Bradford Story	1957	60.00
BRADFORD, SCOTT			
PROBE			
❏ 4509	Rock Slides	1969	25.00
BRADLEY, HAROLD			
COLUMBIA			
❏ CS8814 [S]	Bossa Nova Goes to Nashville	1963	18.00
❏ CL2014 [M]	Bossa Nova Goes to Nashville	1963	15.00
❏ CL2456 [M]	Guitar for Lovers Only	1966	15.00
❏ CS9256 [S]	Guitar for Lovers Only	1966	18.00
❏ CL2073 [M]	Misty Guitar	1963	15.00
❏ CS8873 [S]	Misty Guitar	1963	18.00
HARMONY			
❏ H31324	Guitar for Sentimental Lovers	1971	15.00
BRADLEY, JAMES			
MALACO			
❏ 6358	James Bradley	1979	18.00
BRADLEY, OWEN			
CORAL			
❏ CRL56065 [10]	Cherished Hymns	195?	60.00
❏ CRL56012 [10]	Christmas Time	1950	80.00
❏ CRL56035 [10]	Lazy River	195?	60.00
❏ CRL57071 [M]	Organ and Chimes Played by Owen Bradley	1956	30.00
❏ CRL56047 [10]	Singin' in the Rain	195?	60.00
❏ CRL56022 [10]	Strauss Waltzes	195?	60.00
DECCA			
❏ DL8724 [M]	Bandstand Hop	1958	30.00
❏ DL8868 [M]	Big Guitar	1958	30.00
❏ DL78868 [S]	Big Guitar	1958	40.00
❏ DL8652 [M]	Joyous Bells of Christmas	1957	30.00
❏ DL4078 [M]	Paradise Island	1960	25.00
❏ DL74078 [S]	Paradise Island	1960	30.00
BRADLEY, WILL			
EPIC			
❏ LG1005 [10]	Boogie Woogie	1954	120.00
❏ LN3115 [M]	Boogie Woogie	1955	50.00
❏ LN3199 [M]	The House of Bradley	1955	50.00
❏ LN1127 [10]	The House of Bradley	1954	120.00
RCA VICTOR			
❏ LPM-2098 [M]	Big Band Boogie	1960	40.00
❏ LSP-2098 [S]	Big Band Boogie	1960	50.00
WALDORF MUSIC HALL			
❏ MH 33-132 [10]	Jazz – Dixieland and Chicago Style	195?	40.00
❏ MH 33-122 [10]	Jazz Encounter	195?	40.00

Number	Title	Yr	NM
BRADSHAW, EVANS			
RIVERSIDE			
❏ RLP 12-263 [M]	Look Out for Evans Bradshaw	1958	60.00
❏ RLP 12-296 [M]	Pieces of Eighty-Eight	1959	40.00
❏ RLP-1136 [S]	Pieces of Eighty-Eight	1959	30.00
BRADSHAW, TERRY			
BENSON			
❏ R-3702	Until You	1980	18.00
HEART WARMING			
❏ 3735	Here in My Heart	1983	18.00
MERCURY			
❏ SRM-1-1073	I'm So Lonesome I Could Cry	1976	25.00
BRADSHAW, TINY			
KING			
❏ 953 [M]	24 Great Songs	1966	40.00
❏ 653 [M]	Great Composer	1960	300.00
❏ 295-74 [10]	Off and On	1955	1000.00
❏ 395-501 [M]	Selections	1956	700.00
BRADY BUNCH, THE			
PARAMOUNT			
❏ PAS-6032	Meet the Brady Bunch	1972	50.00
❏ PAS-5026	Merry Christmas from the Brady Bunch	1971	80.00
❏ PAS-6058	The Brady Bunch Phonograph Record	1973	80.00
❏ PAS-6037	The Kids from the Brady Bunch	1972	40.00
BRAFF, RUBY, AND DICK HYMAN			
CONCORD JAZZ			
❏ CJ-393	Music from My Fair Lady	1989	15.00
GEORGE WEIN COLLECTION			
❏ GW-3003	America the Beautiful	198?	12.00
BRAFF, RUBY, AND ELLIS LARKINS			
CHIAROSCURO			
❏ 117	The Grand Reunion	1972	18.00
VANGUARD			
❏ VRS-8019 [10]	Inventions in Jazz – Volume 1	1955	80.00
❏ VRS-8020 [10]	Inventions in Jazz – Volume 2	1955	80.00
❏ VRS-8516 [M]	Pocketful of Dreams	1957	40.00
❏ VRS-8507 [M]	Two By Two	1956	40.00
BRAFF, RUBY, AND GEORGE BARNES			
CHIAROSCURO			
❏ 126	Live at the New School	1975	18.00
❏ 121	The Ruby Braff-George Barnes Quartet	1973	18.00
CONCORD JAZZ			
❏ CJ-5	The Ruby Braff-George Barnes Quartet Plays Gershwin	1975	15.00
❏ CJ-7	The Ruby Braff-George Barnes Quartet Salutes Rodgers and Hart	1976	15.00
BRAFF, RUBY, AND SCOTT HAMILTON			
CONCORD JAZZ			
❏ CJ-274	A First	1985	12.00
❏ CJ-296	A Sailboat in the Moonlight	1986	12.00
BRAFF, RUBY; PEE WEE RUSSELL; BOBBY HENDERSON			
VERVE			
❏ MGV-8241 [M]	The Ruby Braff Octet with Pee Wee Russell and Bobby Henderson at Newport	1958	50.00
❏ V-8241 [M]	The Ruby Braff Octet with Pee Wee Russell and Bobby Henderson at Newport	1961	30.00
BRAFF, RUBY			
ABC-PARAMOUNT			
❏ ABC-141 [M]	Ruby Braff Featuring Dave McKenna	1956	40.00
AMERICAN RECORDING SOCIETY			
❏ G-445 [M]	Hey, Ruby	1957	40.00
BETHLEHEM			
❏ BCP-6043	Adoration of the Melody	197?	18.00
— Reissue material, distributed by RCA Victor			
❏ BCP-1034 [10]	Ball at Bethlehem	1955	100.00
❏ BCP-82 [M]	Handful of Cool Jazz	1958	40.00
❏ BCP-1032 [10]	Holiday in Braff	1955	100.00
❏ BCP-5 [M]	Omnibus	1955	50.00
❏ BCP-1005 [10]	Ruby Braff Quartet	1954	120.00
❏ BCP-6043 [M]	The Best of Braff	1960	30.00
BLACK LION			
❏ 127	Hear Me Talkin'	197?	15.00
CHIAROSCURO			
❏ 115	International Quartet Plus Three	1972	18.00

Number	Title	Yr	NM
CONCERT HALL JAZZ			
❏ 1210 [M]	Little Big Horn	1955	50.00
CONCORD JAZZ			
❏ CJ-381	Me, Myself and I	1989	15.00
EPIC			
❏ LN3377 [M]	Braff!	1957	50.00
FINESSE			
❏ FW37988	Very Sinatra	1983	15.00
JAZZTONE			
❏ J-1210 [M]	Little Big Horn	1955	40.00
RCA VICTOR			
❏ LPM-1966 [M]	Easy Now	1959	30.00
❏ LSP-1966 [S]	Easy Now	1959	40.00
❏ LPM-1510 [M]	Hi-Fi Salute to Bunny	1957	40.00
❏ LPM-1332 [M]	The Magic Horn of Ruby Braff	1956	40.00
❏ LPM-1008 [M]	To Fred Astaire with Love	1955	50.00
SACKVILLE			
❏ 3022	Ruby Braff with the Ed Bickert Trio	198?	12.00
STEREO-CRAFT			
❏ RTN-507 [M]	You're Getting to Be a Habit with Me	1959	30.00
❏ RTS-507 [S]	You're Getting to Be a Habit with Me	1959	40.00
STORYVILLE			
❏ STLP-320 [10]	Hustlin' and Bustlin'	1955	80.00
❏ STLP-908 [M]	Hustlin' and Bustlin'	1956	50.00
UNITED ARTISTS			
❏ UAL-3045 [M]	Blowing Around the Around	1959	30.00
❏ UAS-6045 [S]	Blowing Around the Around	1959	40.00
❏ UAL-4093 [M]	Ruby Braff-Marshall Brown Sextet	1960	30.00
❏ UAS-5093 [S]	Ruby Braff-Marshall Brown Sextet	1960	40.00
VANGUARD			
❏ VRS-8504 [M]	The Ruby Braff Special	1955	40.00
WARNER BROS.			
❏ W1273 [M]	Ruby Braff Goes Girl Crazy	1959	30.00
❏ WS1273 [S]	Ruby Braff Goes Girl Crazy	1959	40.00
BRAGG, BILLY, AND WILCO			
ELEKTRA			
❏ 62204 [B]	Mermaid Avenue	1998	18.00
BRAGG, BILLY			
CD PRESENTS			
❏ CD 027	Brewing Up with Billy Bragg	1984	18.00
❏ CD 035 [B]	Life's a Riot Etc. (With the Between the Wars EP)	1985	25.00
ELEKTRA			
❏ 60726	Back to Basics	1987	15.00
❏ 60787 [EP]	Help Save the Youth of America	1988	10.00
❏ 60502	Talking to the Taxman About Poetry	1986	15.00
❏ 61035 [B]	William Bloke	1996	25.00
❏ 60824	Workers Playtime	1988	12.00
BRAINBOX			
CAPITOL			
❏ ST-596	Brainbox	1970	18.00
BRAINS, THE			
LANDSLIDE			
❏ LM1201 [EP]	Dancing Under Streetlights	1982	18.00
MERCURY			
❏ SRM-1-4012	Electronic Eden	1981	12.00
❏ SRM-1-3835	The Brains	1980	15.00
BRAINSTORM			
TABU			
❏ JZ35749	Funky Entertainment	1979	18.00
❏ JZ35327	Journey to the Night	1978	18.00
❏ BQL1-2048	Stormin'	1977	25.00
BRAINTICKET			
CLEOPATRA			
❏ 7058 [B]	Cottonwoodhill		25.00
❏ 6611 [B]	Live in Rome 1973		25.00
❏ 9024 [B]	Psychonaut		25.00
BRAITH, GEORGE			
BLUE NOTE			
❏ BLP-4171 [M]	Extension	1964	60.00
—With "New York, USA" on label			
❏ BST-84171 [S]	Extension	1964	80.00
—With "New York, USA" on label			
❏ BST-84171 [S]	Extension	1966	25.00
—With "A Division of Liberty Records" on label			
❏ BLP-4161 [M]	Soul Stream	1964	70.00
—With "New York, USA" on label			
❏ BST-84161 [S]	Soul Stream	1964	100.00
—With "New York, USA" on label			
❏ BST-84161 [S]	Soul Stream	1966	40.00
—With "A Division of Liberty Records" on label			
❏ BLP-4148 [M]	Two Souls in One	1963	40.00

Number	Title	Yr	NM
— With "New York, USA" on label			
❏ BST-84148 [S]	Two Souls in One	1963	50.00
— With "New York, USA" on label			
❏ BST-84148 [S]	Two Souls in One	1966	25.00
— With "A Division of Liberty Records" on label			

PRESTIGE
❏ PRLP-7474 [M]	Laughing Soul	1967	30.00
❏ PRST-7474 [S]	Laughing Soul	1967	25.00
❏ PRLP-7515 [M]	Musart	1967	30.00
❏ PRST-7515 [S]	Musart	1967	25.00

BRAITHWAITE, DARYL

CBS ASSOCIATED
| ❏ FZ45206 | Edge | 1989 | 12.00 |

BRAM TCHAIKOVSKY

ARISTA
| ❏ AB4292 | Funland | 1981 | 12.00 |

POLYDOR
| ❏ PD-1-6273 | Pressure | 1980 | 12.00 |
| ❏ PD-1-6211 | Strange Man, Changed Man | 1979 | 15.00 |

BRAMLETT, BONNIE

CAPRICORN
❏ CP 0148	It's Time	1975	15.00
❏ CP 0169	Lady's Choice	1976	15.00
❏ CP 0190	Memories	1978	15.00

COLUMBIA
| ❏ KC31786 | Sweet Bonnie Bramlett | 1973 | 18.00 |

BRAMLETT, DELANEY

COLUMBIA
| ❏ KC32420 | Moblus Strip | 1973 | 15.00 |
| ❏ KC31631 | Some Things Coming | 1972 | 15.00 |

MGM
| ❏ M3G-5011 | Giving Birth to a Song | 1975 | 12.00 |

PRODIGAL
| ❏ P6-10017S1 | Class Reunion | 1977 | 12.00 |

BRANCH, CLIFF

SUTRA
| ❏ SUT1020 | All About Love | 1988 | 15.00 |

BRAND, OSCAR

ABC-PARAMOUNT
| ❏ ABC-388 [M] | Oscar Brand Sings for Adults | 1961 | 30.00 |
| ❏ ABCS-388 [S] | Oscar Brand Sings for Adults | 1961 | 30.00 |

AUDIO FIDELITY
❏ AFLP-2121 [M]	Bawdy Hootenanny	1964	25.00
❏ AFSD-6121 [S]	Bawdy Hootenanny	1964	30.00
❏ AFLP-1884 [M]	Bawdy Sea Shanties (Vol. 5)	1959	30.00
❏ AFSD-5884 [S]	Bawdy Sea Shanties (Vol. 5)	1959	30.00
❏ AFLP-1906 [M]	Bawdy Songs and Backroom Ballads, Vol. I	195?	30.00
❏ AFLP-1806 [M]	Bawdy Songs and Backroom Ballads, Vol. II	195?	30.00
❏ AFLP-1824 [M]	Bawdy Songs and Backroom Ballads, Vol. III	195?	30.00
❏ AFSD-5824 [S]	Bawdy Songs and Backroom Ballads, Vol. III	196?	30.00
❏ AFLP-1847 [M]	Bawdy Songs and Backroom Ballads, Vol. IV	195?	30.00
❏ AFSD-5847 [S]	Bawdy Songs and Backroom Ballads, Vol. IV	195?	30.00
❏ AFLP-1952 [M]	Bawdy Songs Goes to College	1961	30.00
❏ AFSD-5952 [S]	Bawdy Songs Goes to College	1961	30.00
❏ AFLP-1920 [M]	Bawdy Western Songs (Vol. VI)	1960	30.00
❏ AFSD-5920 [S]	Bawdy Western Songs (Vol. VI)	1960	30.00
❏ AFLP-1966 [M]	Rollicking Sea Shanties	1962	30.00
❏ AFSD-5966 [S]	Rollicking Sea Shanties	1962	30.00
❏ AFLP-1971 [M]	Sing Along Bawdy Songs and Backroom Ballads	1962	30.00
❏ AFSD-5971 [S]	Sing Along Bawdy Songs and Backroom Ballads	1962	30.00

CAEDMON
| ❏ TC1658 | Singing Is Believing: Songs of the Advent Season | 1980 | 15.00 |

CHESTERFIELD
| ❏ CMS-101 [10] | Backroom Ballads | 195? | 50.00 |

DECCA
| ❏ DL4275 [M] | Folk Songs for Fun | 1962 | 25.00 |
| ❏ DL74275 [S] | Folk Songs for Fun | 1962 | 30.00 |

ELEKTRA
❏ EKL-228 [M]	A Snow Job for Skiers	1963	25.00
❏ EKS-7228 [S]	A Snow Job for Skiers	1963	30.00
❏ EKL-183 [M]	Boating Songs and All That Bilge	1960	25.00
❏ EKS-7183 [S]	Boating Songs and All That Bilge	1960	30.00
❏ EKL-242 [M]	Cough: Army Songs Out of the Barracks Bag	1963	25.00
❏ EKS-7242 [S]	Cough: Army Songs Out of the Barracks Bag	1963	30.00
❏ EKL-169 [M]	Every Inch a Sailor	1960	25.00
❏ EKS-7169 [S]	Every Inch a Sailor	1960	30.00

Number	Title	Yr	NM
❏ EKL-204 [M]	For Doctors Only	1961	25.00
❏ EKS-7204 [S]	For Doctors Only	1961	30.00
❏ EKL-178 [M]	Out of the Blue: Songs of a Fighting Airforce	1960	25.00
❏ EKS-7178 [S]	Out of the Blue: Songs of a Fighting Airforce	1960	30.00
❏ EKL-237 [M]	Songs Fore Golfers	1963	25.00
❏ EKS-7237 [S]	Songs Fore Golfers	1963	30.00
❏ EKL-188 [M]	Sports Car Songs for Big Wheels	1960	25.00
❏ EKS-7188 [S]	Sports Car Songs for Big Wheels	1960	30.00
❏ EKL-174 [M]	Tell It to the Marines	1960	25.00
❏ EKS-7174 [S]	Tell It to the Marines	1960	30.00
❏ EKL-168 [M]	The Wild Blue Yonder	1959	25.00
❏ EKS-7168 [S]	The Wild Blue Yonder	1959	30.00
❏ EKL-198 [M]	Up in the Air: Songs for the Madcap Airman	1961	25.00
❏ EKS-7198 [S]	Up in the Air: Songs for the Madcap Airman	1961	30.00

FOLKWAYS
| ❏ FA5280 [M] | Election Songs of the United States | 1960 | 30.00 |

KAPP
| ❏ KS-3629 | Oscar Brand "Live" On Campus | 1970 | 18.00 |

RIVERSIDE
❏ RLP 12-825 [M]	Absolute Nonsense	195?	30.00
❏ RLP 12-630 [M]	American Drinking Songs	1956	30.00
❏ RLP1419	Everybody Sing, Vol. 2	196?	18.00
❏ RLP 12-639 [M]	G.I. — American Army Songs	195?	30.00
❏ RLP1438	Oscar Brand's Children's Concert	196?	18.00
❏ RLP 12-835 [M]	Songs Inane Only	1959	30.00
❏ RLP 12-844 [M]	Songs of the U.S. Army	1960	30.00

ROULETTE
| ❏ SR-42060 | Brand X | 1971 | 18.00 |

TRADITION
❏ RLP1014 [M]	Laughing America	195?	30.00
❏ TLP1022 [M]	Pie in the Sky	195?	30.00
❏ TLP2053	The Best of Oscar Brand	1967	25.00

BRAND NEW HEAVIES, THE

DELICIOUS VINYL
❏ 14243	Brother Sister	1994	18.00
❏ 71807 [B]	Heavy Rhyme Experience -- Vol. 1	1998	25.00
— Originally issued in 1992			
❏ 71806 [B]	The Brand New Heavies	1998	18.00
— Originally issued in 1991			
❏ 846874-1	The Brand New Heavies	1991	18.00

BRAND NUBIAN

ARISTA
| ❏ 19024 | Foundation | 1998 | 18.00 |

ELEKTRA
❏ 61682	Everything Is Everything	1994	18.00
❏ 61381	In God We Trust	1993	18.00
❏ 60946	One for All	1990	18.00

BRAND X

PASSPORT
❏ PB9845	Do They Hurt?	1980	12.00
❏ PB6016	Is There Anything About?	1982	12.00
❏ PB9824	Livestock	1977	12.00
❏ PB9829	Masques	1978	12.00
❏ PB9822	Moroccan Roll	1977	12.00
— Reissue of 98022			
❏ PP-98022	Moroccan Roll	1977	15.00
❏ PB9840	Product	1979	12.00
❏ PB9819	Unorthodox Behaviour	1977	12.00
— Reissue of 98019			
❏ PPSD-98019 [B]	Unorthodox Behaviour	1976	18.00

BRANDMEIER, JONATHON

BRANDMEIER
| ❏ BPI2004 | Almost Live | 1984 | 25.00 |

BRANDOS, THE

RELATIVITY
| ❏ 88561-8192-1 | Honor Among Thieves | 1987 | 10.00 |

BRANDY

ATLANTIC
❏ PR5970 [DJ]	Brandy	1994	18.00
— Vinyl is promo only			
❏ 83493	Full Moon	2002	18.00
❏ 83039	Never S-a-y Never	1998	18.00

BRANIGAN, LAURA

ATLANTIC
❏ SD19289	Branigan	1982	10.00
❏ 80052	Branigan 2	1983	10.00
❏ 81265	Hold Me	1985	10.00
❏ 82086	Laura Branigan	1990	15.00
❏ 80147	Self Control	1984	10.00
❏ 81747	Touch	1987	10.00

BRANNEN, JOHN

APACHE
| ❏ D1-71650 | Mystery Street | 1988 | 12.00 |

Number	Title	Yr	NM

BRASS COMPANY, THE

SACKVILLE
| ❏ 3006 | Sangoma | 198? | 12.00 |

STRATA-EAST
| ❏ 19752 | Colors | 1974 | 12.00 |

BRASS CONSTRUCTION

CAPITOL
❏ ST-12423	Conquest	1985	10.00
❏ ST-12268	Conversations	1983	10.00
❏ ST-12324	Renegades	1984	10.00

LIBERTY
❏ LT-51121	Attitudes	1982	12.00
❏ LT-1060	Brass Construction 6	1981	10.00
— Reissue of United Artists 1060			

UNITED ARTISTS
❏ UA-LA545-G	Brass Construction	1976	12.00
❏ LT-977	Brass Construction 5	1979	12.00
❏ LT-1060	Brass Construction 6	1980	15.00
❏ UA-LA677-G	Brass Construction II	1976	12.00
❏ UA-LA775-H	Brass Construction III	1977	12.00
❏ UA-LA916-H	Brass Construction IV	1978	12.00

BRASS ENSEMBLE OF THE JAZZ AND CLASSICAL MUSIC SOCIETY, THE

COLUMBIA
| ❏ CL941 [M] | Music for Brass | 1956 | 60.00 |

BRASS FEVER

ABC IMPULSE!
| ❏ ASD-9308 | Brass Fever | 1975 | 18.00 |
| ❏ ASD-9319 | Time Is Running Out | 1976 | 18.00 |

BRASS RING, THE

ABC DUNHILL
❏ DS-50034	Gazpacho	1968	15.00
❏ DS-50044	Only Love	1969	15.00
❏ DS-50051	The Best of the Brass Ring	1970	12.00

DUNHILL
❏ D50012 [M]	Lara's Theme	1966	15.00
❏ DS50012 [S]	Lara's Theme	1966	18.00
❏ ST-91039 [S]	Lara's Theme	1966	25.00
— Capitol Record Club edition			
❏ D50008 [M]	Love Theme from The Flight of the Phoenix	1966	15.00
❏ DS50008 [S]	Love Theme from The Flight of the Phoenix	1966	18.00
❏ D50015 [M]	Sunday Night at the Movies	1967	15.00
❏ DS50015 [S]	Sunday Night at the Movies	1967	18.00
❏ D50017 [M]	The Dis-Advantages of You	1967	15.00
❏ DS50017 [S]	The Dis-Advantages of You	1967	18.00
❏ D50023 [M]	The Now Sound	1967	15.00
❏ DS50023 [S]	The Now Sound	1967	18.00

PROJECT 3
| ❏ 5067 | The Brass Ring | 1972 | 12.00 |

BRASSELLE, KEEFE

CORAL
| ❏ CRL57295 [M] | Minstrel Man | 1959 | 25.00 |
| ❏ CRL757295 [S] | Minstrel Man | 1959 | 30.00 |

BRAUFMAN, ALAN

INDIA NAVIGATION
| ❏ IN-1024 | Valley of Search | 197? | 15.00 |

BRAUN, BOB

DECCA
| ❏ DL4339 [M] | Till Death Do Us Part | 1962 | 25.00 |
| ❏ DL74339 [S] | Till Death Do Us Part | 1962 | 30.00 |

UNITED ARTISTS
| ❏ UAS6664 | Christmas in Your Heart | 1968 | 15.00 |

BRAUTIGAN, RICHARD

HARVEST
| ❏ ST-424 | Listening to Richard Brautigan | 1970 | 30.00 |

BRAVE BELT

REPRISE
❏ MS2210	Bachman-Turner-Bachman As Brave Belt	1974	12.00
❏ RS6447	Brave Belt	1971	15.00
❏ MS2057	Brave Belt II	1972	15.00

BRAXTON, ANTHONY, AND DEREK BAILEY

EMANEM
| ❏ 3313 | Duo 1 | 197? | 18.00 |
| ❏ 3314 | Duo 2 | 197? | 18.00 |

INNER CITY
| ❏ 1041 | Live at Wigmor | 198? | 15.00 |

BRAXTON, ANTHONY, AND MUHAL RICHARD ABRAMS

ARISTA
| ❏ AL4101 | Duets | 1976 | 18.00 |

Number	Title	Yr	NM

BRAXTON, ANTHONY

ANTILLES
| ❏ 1005 | Six Compositions: Quartet | 1981 | 15.00 |

ARISTA
❏ AL4064	5 Pieces 1975	1975	18.00
❏ A2L8602	Alto Sax Improvisations '79	1979	18.00
❏ AL4080	Creative Orchestra Music 1976	1976	18.00
❏ AL4181	For Trio	1978	18.00
❏ AL4032	New York, Fall 1974	1975	18.00
❏ AL5002	The Montreux/Berlin Concerts	1977	25.00

ARISTA FREEDOM
| ❏ AL1902 | The Complete Braxton 1971 | 1978 | 25.00 |

BLACK SAINT
❏ BSR-0066	Four Compositions: Quartet 1983	1983	15.00
❏ BSR-0086	Four Compositions: Quartet 1984	1985	15.00
❏ 120116-1	Six Monk Compositions	1987	15.00

BLUEBIRD
| ❏ 6626-1-RB | Anthony Braxton Live | 1988 | 12.00 |

CONCORD JAZZ
| ❏ CJ-213 | A Ray Brown 3 | 1982 | 15.00 |

DELMARK
❏ DS-420/1	For Alto	1971	30.00
❏ DS-415	Three Compositions of New Jazz	1969	25.00
❏ DS-428	Together Alone	1973	25.00
— With Joseph Jarman			

HAT HUT
❏ 1984	Composition 98	1981	18.00
❏ 1995/96	Open Aspects '82	1982	18.00
❏ 2019	Performance	1983	18.00

INNER CITY
❏ 2015	In the Tradition	197?	18.00
❏ IC2045	In the Tradition, Vol. 2	1976	18.00
❏ 1008	Saxophone Improvisations – Series F	197?	18.00

MAGENTA
| ❏ MA-0203 | Seven Standards 1985 | 1986 | 15.00 |
| ❏ MA-0205 | Seven Standards 1985, Volume 2 | 1986 | 15.00 |

SACKVILLE
| ❏ 3007 | Trio and Duet | 198? | 12.00 |

SOUND ASPECTS
| ❏ SAS-009 | Anthony Braxton with the Robert Schumann Quartet | 1986 | 15.00 |

STEEPLECHASE
| ❏ SCS-1015 | In the Tradition | 198? | 12.00 |
| ❏ SCS-1045 | In the Tradition, Volume 2 | 198? | 12.00 |

BRAXTON, TONI

LAFACE
| ❏ 26069 | The Heat | 2000 | 25.00 |

BRAZOS VALLEY BOYS, THE

WARNER BROS.
❏ W1679 [M]	The Countrypolitan Sound	1967	25.00
❏ WS1679 [S]	The Countrypolitan Sound	1967	30.00
❏ W1686 [M]	The Gold Standard Collection	1967	25.00
❏ WS1686 [S]	The Gold Standard Collection	1967	30.00
❏ W1664 [M]	Where Is the Circus	1966	25.00
❏ WS1664 [S]	Where Is the Circus	1966	30.00

BREAD, LOVE AND DREAMS

LONDON
| ❏ PS566 | Bread, Love and Dreams | 1969 | 30.00 |

BREAD

ELEKTRA
❏ 60414	Anthology of Bread	1985	12.00
❏ EKS-75015	Baby I'm-a Want You	1971	18.00
— Gatefold with raised photo on front			
❏ EKS-75015	Baby I'm-a Want You	197?	12.00
— Front photo is not raised			
❏ EQ-5015 [Q]	Baby I'm-a Want You	1974	30.00
❏ EKS-74044	Bread	1969	18.00
— Red label with large stylized "E			
❏ EKS-74044	Bread	1971	12.00
— Butterfly label			
❏ BRD-1 [DJ]	Bread	1971	25.00
— In-store sampler; very similar to the future LP "The Best of Bread			
❏ EKS-75047	Guitar Man	1972	15.00
❏ 7E-1094	Lost Without Your Love	1976	12.00
❏ EKS-74086	Manna	1971	15.00
❏ EKS-74076	On the Waters	1970	18.00
— Red label with large stylized "E			
❏ EKS-74076	On the Waters	1971	12.00
— Butterfly label			
❏ EKS-75056	The Best of Bread	1973	15.00
❏ 6E-108 [B]	The Best of Bread	1977	10.00
— Reissue of 75056			
❏ EQ-5056 [Q]	The Best of Bread	1973	30.00

❏ 7E-1005	The Best of Bread, Volume 2	1974	15.00
❏ 6E-110	The Best of Bread, Volume 2	1977	10.00
— Reissue of 7E-1005			

BREAKWATER

ARISTA
❏ AB4208	Breakwater	1978	40.00
— Value is for originals; this album has been reissued to look like the original, but has a reissue sticker on the back of sealed copies			
❏ AB4264	Splashdown	1980	40.00

BREAM, JULIAN

RCA VICTOR RED SEAL
❏ LDS-2656 [S]	An Evening of Elizabethan Music	1962	40.00
— Original with "shaded dog" label			
❏ LSC-2487 [S]	Giuliani: Guitar Concerto; Arnold: Guitar Concerto	1961	30.00
— Original with "shaded dog" label			
❏ LSC-2606 [S]	Popular Classics for Spanish Guitar	1962	30.00
— Original with "shaded dog" label			
❏ LSC-2448 [S]	The Art of Julian Bream	1960	30.00
— Original with "shaded dog" label			
❏ LDS-2560 [S]	The Golden Age of English Lute Music	1961	30.00
— Original with "shaded dog" label			

BREATHE

A&M
| ❏ SP-5163 | All That Jazz | 1988 | 10.00 |
| ❏ 7502153201 | Peace of Mind | 1990 | 15.00 |

BREATHLESS

EMI AMERICA
| ❏ SW-17013 | Breathless | 1979 | 18.00 |
| ❏ SW-17041 | Nobody Leaves This Song Alive | 1980 | 18.00 |

BRECKER, MICHAEL

GRP
| ❏ GR-9622 | Now You See It (Now You Don't) | 1990 | 18.00 |

MCA IMPULSE!
| ❏ 42229 | Don't Try This at Home | 1989 | 18.00 |
| ❏ 5980 | Michael Brecker | 1987 | 15.00 |

BRECKER, RANDY, AND ELIANE ELIAS

PASSPORT
| ❏ PJ-88013 | Amanda | 1987 | 12.00 |

BRECKER, RANDY

MCA
| ❏ 6334 | Toe to Toe | 1990 | 18.00 |

PASSPORT
| ❏ PJ-88039 | In the Idiom | 1988 | 18.00 |

SOLID STATE
| ❏ SS-18051 | Score | 1969 | 30.00 |

BRECKER BROTHERS, THE

ARISTA
❏ AL4061	Back to Back	1976	12.00
❏ AQ4061 [Q]	Back to Back	1976	25.00
❏ AB4272	Détente	1979	12.00
❏ AL4122	Don't Stop the Music	1977	12.00
❏ AB4185	Heavy Metal Be-Bop	1978	12.00
❏ AL9550	Straphangin'	1981	15.00
❏ AL4037	The Brecker Brothers	1975	15.00

BREEDLOVE, JIMMY

RCA CAMDEN
| ❏ CAL-430 [M] | Rock 'N' Roll Hits | 1958 | 40.00 |

BREEN, BOBBY

LONDON
| ❏ LB270 [10] | Songs at Yuletide | 1953 | 50.00 |

BREGMAN, BUDDY

VERVE
❏ MGV-2094 [M]	Dig Buddy Bregman in Hi-Fi	1959	50.00
❏ V-2094 [M]	Dig Buddy Bregman in Hi-Fi	1961	25.00
❏ MGV-2064 [M]	Funny Face	1958	50.00
❏ V-2064 [M]	Funny Face	1961	25.00
❏ MGV-2042 [M]	Swingin' Kicks	1957	50.00
❏ MGVS-6013 [S]	Swingin' Kicks	1960	40.00
❏ V-2042 [M]	Swingin' Kicks	1961	25.00
❏ V6-2042 [S]	Swingin' Kicks	1961	18.00
❏ MGV-2093 [M]	The Gershwin Anniversary Album	1959	50.00
❏ V-2093 [M]	The Gershwin Anniversary Album	1961	25.00

WORLD PACIFIC
| ❏ WP-1263 [M] | Swingin' Standards | 1959 | 30.00 |
| ❏ ST-1024 [S] | Swingin' Standards | 1959 | 30.00 |

BREL, JACQUES

COLUMBIA
| ❏ AWS324 [B] | American Debut | 1960 | 25.00 |
| — original release; deduct 25% for 1973 reissue | | | |

PHILIPS
❏ PCC634 [B]	If You Go Away: Jacques Brel Is Alive And Singing In Paris	1967	30.00
— original release; deduct 25% for 1975 reissue			
❏ PCC620 [B]	The Poetic World of Jacques Brel		30.00

REPRISE
| ❏ RS6246 [B] | Encore! | 1967 | 15.00 |
| ❏ RS6187 [B] | Jacques Brel | 1966 | 15.00 |

VANGUARD
| ❏ VSD79265 [B] | Le Formidable | 1967 | 25.00 |

BRENDA AND THE TABULATIONS

CHOCOLATE CITY
| ❏ 2002 | I Keep Coming Back for More | 1977 | 12.00 |

DIONN
| ❏ LPM-2000 [M] | Dry Your Eyes | 1967 | 40.00 |
| ❏ LPS-2000 [S] | Dry Your Eyes | 1967 | 50.00 |

TOP & BOTTOM
| ❏ 100 | Brenda and the Tabulations | 1970 | 25.00 |

BRENNAN, WALTER

DOT
| ❏ DLP-3309 [M] | Dutchman's Gold | 1960 | 30.00 |
| ❏ DLP-25309 [S] | Dutchman's Gold | 1960 | 30.00 |

EVEREST
❏ LPBR-5123 [M]	The President: A Musical Biography of Our Chief Executive	1960	30.00
❏ SDBR-1123 [S]	The President: A Musical Biography of Our Chief Executive	1960	30.00
❏ LPBR-5103 [M]	World of Miracles	1960	30.00
❏ SDBR-1103 [S]	World of Miracles	1960	30.00

HAMILTON
| ❏ HLP-159 [M] | Dutchman's Gold | 1965 | 15.00 |
| ❏ HLP-12159 [S] | Dutchman's Gold | 1965 | 15.00 |

LIBERTY
❏ LRP-3372 [M]	Gunfight at the O.K. Corral	1964	25.00
❏ LST-7372 [S]	Gunfight at the O.K. Corral	1964	30.00
❏ LRP-3266 [M]	Mama Sang a Song	1963	25.00
❏ LST-7266 [S]	Mama Sang a Song	1963	30.00
❏ LRP-3233 [M]	Old Rivers	1962	25.00
❏ LST-7233 [S]	Old Rivers	1962	30.00
❏ LRP-3317 [M]	Talkin' from the Heart	1964	25.00
❏ LST-7317 [S]	Talkin' from the Heart	1964	30.00
❏ LRP-3241 [M]	The President: A Musical Biography of Our Chief Executive	1962	18.00
— Reissue of Everest 5123			
❏ LST-7241 [S]	The President: A Musical Biography of Our Chief Executive	1962	25.00
— Reissue of Everest 1123			
❏ LRP-3257 [M]	'Twas the Night Before Christmas Back Home	1962	25.00
❏ LST-7257 [S]	'Twas the Night Before Christmas Back Home	1962	30.00
❏ LRP-3244 [M]	World of Miracles	1962	18.00
— Reissue of Everest 5103			
❏ LST-7244 [S]	World of Miracles	1962	25.00
— Reissue of Everest 1103			

LONDON
| ❏ PS577 | Yesterday, When I Was Young | 1970 | 18.00 |

R.P.C.
| ❏ 108 [M] | By the Fireside | 1961 | 30.00 |
| ❏ 108S [S] | By the Fireside | 1961 | 40.00 |

SUNSET
❏ SUM-1100 [M]	Country Heart	1966	15.00
❏ SUS-5100 [S]	Country Heart	1966	15.00
❏ SUS-5269	God and Country	1970	12.00

UNITED ARTISTS
| ❏ UA-LA438-E | The Very Best of Walter Brennan | 1975 | 15.00 |

BRESH, TOM

ABC
| ❏ AB-1055 | Portrait | 1978 | 15.00 |

ABC DOT
| ❏ DO-2084 | Kicked Back | 1977 | 15.00 |

FARR
| ❏ FL1000 | Homemade Love | 1976 | 18.00 |

BREWER, TERESA, AND COUNT BASIE

DOCTOR JAZZ
| ❏ FW38836 | Songs of Bessie Smith | 1984 | 10.00 |

FLYING DUTCHMAN
| ❏ FD10161 | Songs of Bessie Smith | 1973 | 15.00 |

Number	Title	Yr	NM

BREWER, TERESA, AND MERCER ELLINGTON

DOCTOR JAZZ
❏ FW40031	The Cotton Connection	1985	12.00

BREWER, TERESA, AND STEPHANE GRAPPELLI

DOCTOR JAZZ
❏ FW38448	On the Road Again	198?	12.00

BREWER, TERESA, AND SVEND ASMUSSEN

DOCTOR JAZZ
❏ FW40233	On the Good Ship Lollipop	1987	12.00

BREWER, TERESA

AMSTERDAM
❏ 12013	Music, Music, Music	1973	12.00
❏ 12015	Teresa Brewer In London	1974	12.00
❏ 12012	The Doo Dah Song	1973	12.00

COLUMBIA
❏ PC37363	A Sophisticated Lady	198?	10.00
—Budget-line reissue			
❏ FC37363	A Sophisticated Lady	1981	12.00

CORAL
❏ CRL56072 [10]	A Bouquet of Hits	1952	40.00
❏ CRL57374 [M]	Aloha from Teresa	1961	25.00
❏ CRL757374 [S]	Aloha from Teresa	1961	30.00
❏ CRL57414 [M]	Don't Mess with Tess	1962	25.00
❏ CRL757414 [S]	Don't Mess with Tess	1962	30.00
❏ CRL57135 [M]	For Teenagers in Love	1957	30.00
❏ 57297 [M]	Heavenly Lover	1959	25.00
❏ CRL57179 [M]	Miss Music	1958	30.00
❏ CRL57027 [M]	Music, Music, Music	1955	30.00
❏ CRL57351 [M]	My Golden Favorites	1960	25.00
❏ CRL757351 [S]	My Golden Favorites	1960	25.00
❏ CRL57329 [M]	Naughty, Naughty, Naughty	1960	25.00
❏ CRL757329 [S]	Naughty, Naughty, Naughty	1960	30.00
❏ CRL57315 [M]	Ridin' High	1960	25.00
❏ CRL757315 [S]	Ridin' High	1960	30.00
❏ CRL57361 [M]	Songs Everybody Knows	1961	25.00
❏ CRL757361 [S]	Songs Everybody Knows	1961	30.00
❏ CRL57053 [M]	Teresa	1956	30.00
❏ CRL57245 [M]	Teresa Brewer and the Dixieland Band	1958	25.00
❏ CRL757245 [S]	Teresa Brewer and the Dixieland Band	1958	30.00
❏ CRL57144 [M]	Teresa Brewer At Christmas Time	1957	30.00
❏ CXB7 [M]	The Best of Teresa Brewer	1965	25.00
❏ CXSB7 [P]	The Best of Teresa Brewer	1965	25.00
❏ CRL56093 [10]	Till I Waltz Again with You	1953	40.00
❏ CRL57232 [M]	Time for Teresa	1958	30.00
❏ CRL57297 [M]	When Your Lover Has Gone	1958	25.00
❏ CRL757297 [S]	When Your Lover Has Gone	1959	30.00

DOCTOR JAZZ
❏ ASLP804	Good News	198?	12.00
❏ FW40951	Good News	198?	10.00
❏ FW38534	I Dig Big Band Singers	1983	12.00
❏ W2X39521	Live at Carnegie Hall and Montreux, Switzerland	1984	15.00
❏ FW40232	Midnight Café	1986	12.00

FLYING DUTCHMAN
❏ BSL1-0577	Good News	1974	15.00

LONDON
❏ APB-1006 [10]	Teresa Brewer	1951	50.00

PHILIPS
❏ PHM200163 [M]	Dear Heart/Goldfinger	1965	15.00
❏ PHS600163 [S]	Dear Heart/Goldfinger	1965	18.00
❏ PHM200216 [M]	Gold Country	1966	15.00
❏ PHS600216 [S]	Gold Country	1966	18.00
❏ PHM200147 [M]	Golden Hits of 1964	1964	15.00
❏ PHS600147 [S]	Golden Hits of 1964	1964	18.00
❏ PHM200119 [M]	Moments to Remember	1964	15.00
❏ PHS600119 [S]	Moments to Remember	1964	18.00
❏ PHM200200 [M]	Songs for Our Fighting Men	1966	15.00
❏ PHS600200 [S]	Songs for Our Fighting Men	1966	18.00
❏ PHM200062 [M]	Teresa Brewer's Greatest Hits	1962	18.00
❏ PHS600062 [S]	Teresa Brewer's Greatest Hits	1962	25.00
❏ PHM200099 [M]	Terrific Teresa	1963	18.00
❏ PHS600099 [S]	Terrific Teresa	1963	25.00
❏ PHM200230 [M]	Texas Leather and Mexican Lace	1967	18.00
❏ PHS600230 [S]	Texas Leather and Mexican Lace	1967	15.00

PROJECT 3
❏ 5108	Come Follow the Band	1982	12.00

RCA VICTOR
❏ ANL1-1131	The Best of Teresa Brewer	1975	12.00

SIGNATURE
❏ PW40113	Teresa Brewer At Christmas Time	1985	12.00
—Reissue of Coral 57144			
❏ FW39421	Teresa Brewer In London	1984	10.00
—Reissue of Amsterdam 12015			

VOCALION
❏ VL73847 [R]	Here's Teresa Brewer	1969	12.00
❏ VL3693 [M]	Teresa Brewer	1966	15.00

BREWER AND SHIPLEY

A&M
❏ SP-4154	Down in L.A.	1968	18.00

CAPITOL
❏ ST-11261	ST-11261	1974	12.00
❏ ST-11402	Welcome to Riddle Bridge	1975	12.00

KAMA SUTRA
❏ KSBS-2058	Rural Space	1972	15.00
❏ KSBS-2039	Shake Off the Demon	1971	15.00
❏ KSBS-2024	Tarkio	1970	15.00
—LP label calls this "Tarkio Road"			
❏ KSBS2613-2	The Best... Brewer & Shipley	1976	18.00
❏ KSBS-2016	Weeds	1969	15.00

BRIAN AND BRENDA

ROCKET
❏ PIG-2291	Supersonic Lover	1977	18.00

BRIARWOOD SINGERS, THE

UNITED ARTISTS
❏ UAL3318 [M]	Well, Well, Well!	1963	15.00
❏ UAS6318 [S]	Well, Well, Well!	1963	18.00

BRICK

BANG
❏ FZ38170	After 5	1982	12.00
❏ BLP-409	Brick	1977	15.00
❏ BLP-408	Good High	1976	15.00
—Beware of sealed copies -- this album has been "reissued" to look exactly like the original			
❏ JZ35969	Stoneheart	1979	12.00
❏ FZ37471	Summer Heat	1981	12.00
❏ JZ36262	Waiting on You	1980	12.00

MAGIC CITY
❏ MCR1001	Too Tuff	1988	12.00

BRICKELL, EDIE, & NEW BOHEMIANS

GEFFEN
❏ GHS24304	Ghost of a Dog	1990	18.00
❏ R100789	Shooting Rubberbands at the Stars	1988	15.00
—BMG Direct Marketing edition			
❏ GHS24192	Shooting Rubberbands at the Stars	1988	12.00

BRICKLIN

A&M
❏ SP-5124	Bricklin	1986	10.00

BRIDES OF FUNKENSTEIN, THE

ATLANTIC
❏ SD19201 [B]	Funk or Walk	1978	25.00
❏ SD19261 [B]	Never Buy Texas from a Cowboy	1980	25.00

BRIDGES, ALICIA

POLYDOR
❏ PD-1-6158	Alicia Bridges	1978	12.00
❏ PD-1-6219	Play It As It Lays	1979	12.00

SECOND WAVE
❏ 22007	Hocus Pocus	1984	15.00

BRIDGEWATER, DEE DEE

ATLANTIC
❏ SD18188	Dee Dee Bridgewater	1976	15.00

ELEKTRA
❏ 6E-188	Bad for Me	1979	12.00
❏ 6E-306	Dee Dee Bridgewater	1980	12.00
❏ 6E-119	Just Family	1978	12.00

MCA/IMPULSE
❏ MCA-6331	Live in Paris	1989	15.00

BRIGADE, THE

BAND'N VOCAL
❏ 1066	Last Laugh	1970	2000.00
— VG value 1000; VG+ value 1500			

BRIGATI

ASYLUM
❏ 7E-1074	Lost in the Wilderness	1976	18.00

BRIGG

SUSQUEHANNA
❏ LP-301	Brigg	1973	200.00

BRIGGS, ANNE

4 MEN WITH BEARDS
❏ 4M164LP [B]	Anne Briggs		25.00
❏ 4M165LP [B]	The Time Has Come		25.00

BRIGGS, KAREN

VITAL
❏ VTL-009	Karen	1996	25.00

BRIGHT, RONNELL

REGENT
❏ MG-6041 [M]	Bright's Spot	1957	100.00

SAVOY
❏ MG-12206 [M]	Bright's Spot	196?	60.00
—Reissue of Regent LP			

VANGUARD
❏ VRS-8512 [M]	Bright's Flight	1957	100.00

BRIGHTER SIDE OF DARKNESS

20TH CENTURY
❏ T-405	Love Jones	1973	30.00

BRIGMAN, GEORGE

SOLID
❏ SR-001	Jungle Rot	1975	120.00

BRIGNOLA, NICK

BEE HIVE
❏ BH-7000	Baritone Madness	1977	15.00
❏ BH-7010	Burn Brigade	1979	15.00

DISCOVERY
❏ DS-917	Northern Lights	1986	12.00

INTERPLAY
❏ IP-7719	New York Bound	198?	15.00

SEA BREEZE
❏ SB-2003	L.A. Bound	198?	15.00

BRILEY, MARTIN

MERCURY
❏ 822423-1	Dangerous Moments	1984	12.00
❏ SRM-1-4026	Fear of the Unknown	1981	15.00
❏ 810332-1	One Night with a Stranger	1983	12.00

BRILL, MARTY

MERCURY
❏ MG-20178 [M]	The Roving Balladeer	1957	30.00

BRIMSTONE

PEPPERMINT
❏ 1022	Paper Winged Dreams	1973	500.00

BRINSLEY SCHWARZ

CAPITOL
❏ ST-589 [B]	Brinsley Schwarz	1970	30.00
❏ SWBC-11869 [B]	Brinsley Schwarz	1978	25.00
❏ ST-744 [B]	Despite It All	1971	30.00

LIBERTY
❏ LN10146	Nervous on the Road	1981	12.00
—10-track reissue			
❏ LN10145	Silver Pistol	1980	12.00
—10-track reissue			

UNITED ARTISTS
❏ UAS-5647 [B]	Nervous on the Road	1972	30.00
❏ UAS-5566 [B]	Silver Pistol	1972	30.00

BRISTOL, JOHNNY

ATLANTIC
❏ SD18197	Bristol's Creme	1976	12.00
❏ SD19184	Strangers	1978	12.00

HANDSHAKE
❏ FW37666	Free to Be Me	1981	12.00

MGM
❏ M3G-4983	Feeling the Magic	1975	15.00
❏ M3G-4959	Hang On In There Baby	1974	15.00

BRITISH LIONS

RSO
❏ RS-1-3032 [B]	British Lions	1978	15.00

BRITNY FOX

COLUMBIA
❏ FC45300	Boys in Heat	1989	15.00
❏ BFC44140	Britny Fox	1988	12.00

BRITT, ELTON

ABC-PARAMOUNT
❏ ABC-322 [M]	Beyond the Sunset	1960	30.00
❏ ABCS-322 [S]	Beyond the Sunset	1960	40.00
❏ ABC-331 [M]	I Heard a Forest Praying	1960	30.00
❏ ABCS-331 [S]	I Heard a Forest Praying	1960	40.00
❏ ABC-566 [M]	Somethin' for Everybody	1966	30.00
❏ ABCS-566 [S]	Somethin' for Everybody	1966	40.00
❏ ABC-521 [M]	The Singing Hills	1965	30.00
❏ ABCS-521 [S]	The Singing Hills	1965	40.00
❏ ABC-293 [M]	The Wandering Cowboy	1959	30.00
❏ ABCS-293 [S]	The Wandering Cowboy	1959	40.00

RCA VICTOR
❏ LPM-2669 [M]	The Best of Elton Britt	1963	30.00
❏ LPM-3222 [10]	Yodel Songs	1954	120.00
❏ LPM-1288 [M]	Yodel Songs	1956	60.00

BROCAS HELM

GARGOYLE
❏ 138801	Black Death	1988	50.00

Number	Title	Yr	NM

BROCK, B., AND THE SULTANS

CROWN
| CLP-5399 [M] | Do the Beetle | 1964 | 40.00 |
| CST-399 [S] | Do the Beetle | 1964 | 50.00 |

BROCK, HERBIE

SAVOY
| MG-12069 [M] | Brock's Tops | 1956 | 40.00 |
| MG-12066 [M] | Herbie Brock Solo | 1956 | 40.00 |

BROKENSHA, JACK

SAVOY
| MG-12180 | And Then I Said | 1962 | 30.00 |

BROLIN, JAMES

ARTCO
| LPC-1099 | James Brolin Sings | 1974 | 30.00 |

BROMBERG, DAVID

COLUMBIA
| C31104 | David Bromberg | 1972 | 15.00 |
| PC31104 | David Bromberg | 198? | 10.00 |
— Budget-line reissue
| KC31753 | Demon in Disguise | 1973 | 15.00 |
| PC31753 | Demon in Disguise | 198? | 10.00 |
— Budget-line reissue
| PC33397 | Midnight on the Water | 1975 | 15.00 |
— Original with no bar code
| PC33397 | Midnight on the Water | 198? | 10.00 |
— Budget-line reissue with bar code
| PC34467 | The Best of David Bromberg: Out of the Blues | 1976 | 15.00 |
— Original with no bar code
| PC34467 | The Best of David Bromberg: Out of the Blues | 198? | 10.00 |
— Budget-line reissue with bar code
| KC32717 | Wanted Dead or Alive | 1974 | 15.00 |

FANTASY
9555	Bandit in a Bathing Suit	1978	12.00
79007	How Late'l Ya Play 'Til?	1976	18.00
9572	My Own House	1979	12.00
9540	Reckless Abandon	1977	15.00
9590	You Should See the Rest of the Band	1980	12.00

ROUNDER
| 3110 | Sideman Serenade | 1989 | 15.00 |

BRONSKI BEAT

MCA
39038 [EP]	Hundreds & Thousands	1985	12.00
5538	The Age of Consent	1984	10.00
5751	Truthdare Doubledare	1986	10.00

BROOKMEYER, BOB, AND BILL EVANS

UNITED ARTISTS
| UAL-3044 [M] | The Ivory Hunters -- Double Barreled Piano | 1959 | 50.00 |
| UAS-6044 [S] | The Ivory Hunters -- Double Barreled Piano | 1959 | 40.00 |

BROOKMEYER, BOB, AND MEL LEWIS

GRYPHON
| 912 | Live at the Village Vanguard | 1980 | 15.00 |

BROOKMEYER, BOB, AND ZOOT SIMS

JAZZTONE
| J-1239 [M] | Bob Brookmeyer and Zoot Sims | 1956 | 40.00 |

STORYVILLE
| STLP-907 [M] | Tonight's Jazz Today | 1956 | 80.00 |
| STLP-914 [M] | Whoo-eeee! | 1956 | 80.00 |

BROOKMEYER, BOB; JIM HALL; JIMMY RANEY

KIMBERLY
| 2021 [M] | Brookmeyer and Guitars | 1963 | 30.00 |
| 11021 [S] | Brookmeyer and Guitars | 1963 | 25.00 |

WORLD PACIFIC
| PJ-1239 [M] | The Street Swingers | 1957 | 200.00 |
| WP-1239 [M] | The Street Swingers | 1958 | 120.00 |
— Reissue with new prefix

BROOKMEYER, BOB

ATLANTIC
| 1320 [M] | Portrait of the Artist | 1960 | 50.00 |
— Black label
| 1320 [M] | Portrait of the Artist | 1961 | 30.00 |
— Multicolor label, white "fan" logo at right
| SD1320 [S] | Portrait of the Artist | 1960 | 50.00 |
— Green label
| SD1320 [S] | Portrait of the Artist | 1961 | 25.00 |
— Multicolor label, white "fan" logo at right

CLEF
| MGC-644 [M] | Bob Brookmeyer Plays Bob Brookmeyer and Some Others | 1955 | 100.00 |

| MGC-732 [M] | The Modernity of Bob Brookmeyer | 1956 | 70.00 |

COLUMBIA
| CL2237 [M] | Bob Brookmeyer and Friends | 1965 | 18.00 |
| CS9037 [S] | Bob Brookmeyer and Friends | 1965 | 25.00 |

CROWN
| CLP-5318 [M] | Bob Brookmeyer | 196? | 18.00 |

FANTASY
| OJC-1729 | The Dual Role of Bob Brookmeyer | 1990 | 15.00 |
— Reissue of Prestige 7066

FINESSE
| FW37488 | Through a Looking Glass | 198? | 12.00 |

GRYPHON
| 785 | Bob Brookmeyer's Small Band | 1978 | 18.00 |

MERCURY
| MG-20600 [M] | Jazz Is a Kick | 1960 | 30.00 |
| SR-60600 [S] | Jazz Is a Kick | 1960 | 30.00 |

NEW JAZZ
| NJLP-8294 [M] | Revelation | 1963 | 50.00 |
— Purple label
| NJLP-8294 [M] | Revelation | 1965 | 30.00 |
— Blue label, trident logo at right

ODYSSEY
| PC36804 | Bob Brookmeyer and Friends | 1980 | 12.00 |
— Reissue of Columbia 9037

PACIFIC JAZZ
| PJLP-16 [10] | Bob Brookmeyer Quartet | 1954 | 150.00 |

PRESTIGE
| PRLP-214 [10] | Bob Brookmeyer with Jimmy Raney | 1955 | 150.00 |
| PRLP-7066 [M] | The Dual Role of Bob Brookmeyer | 1956 | 80.00 |

SONET
| 770 | Back Again | 1979 | 15.00 |

STORYVILLE
| STLP-305 [10] | Bob Brookmeyer Featuring Al Cohn | 1954 | 300.00 |

TODAY'S JAZZ
| J-1239 [M] | Bob Brookmeyer and Zoot Sims | 196? | 30.00 |

TRIP
| 5568 | Jazz Is a Kick | 197? | 12.00 |

UNITED ARTISTS
| UAL-4008 [M] | Kansas City Revisited | 1959 | 50.00 |
| UAS-5008 [S] | Kansas City Revisited | 1959 | 40.00 |

VERVE
V-8413 [M]	7 X Wilder	1961	50.00
V6-8413 [S]	7 X Wilder	1961	50.00
V-8455 [M]	Gloomy Sunday and Other Bright Moments	1962	30.00
V6-8455 [S]	Gloomy Sunday and Other Bright Moments	1962	30.00
MGV-8385 [M]	The Blues, Hot and Cold	1960	80.00
V-8385 [M]	The Blues, Hot and Cold	1961	30.00
V6-8385 [S]	The Blues, Hot and Cold	1961	30.00
MGV-8111 [M]	The Modernity of Bob Brookmeyer	1957	50.00
V-8111 [M]	The Modernity of Bob Brookmeyer	1961	30.00
V-8498 [M]	Trombone Jazz Samba	1962	30.00
V6-8498 [S]	Trombone Jazz Samba	1962	30.00

VIK
| LX-1071 [M] | Brookmeyer | 1957 | 50.00 |

WORLD PACIFIC
| PJ-1233 [M] | Traditionalism Revisited | 1958 | 80.00 |

BROOKS, CECIL, III

MUSE
| MR-5377 | The Collective | 1989 | 15.00 |

BROOKS, DONNA

DAWN
| DLP-1105 [M] | I'll Take Romance | 1956 | 120.00 |

BROOKS, DONNIE

ERA
| EL-105 [M] | The Happiest | 1961 | 150.00 |

BROOKS, GARTH

CAPITOL
| C1-90897 | Garth Brooks | 1989 | 30.00 |
— Non-record club edition
| C1-590897 | Garth Brooks | 1989 | 25.00 |
— Columbia House edition
| 1P-8042 | No Fences | 1990 | 40.00 |
— Columbia House version; cover photo is the size of CD cover

CAPITOL NASHVILLE
| R173266 | No Fences | 1990 | 60.00 |
— BMG Direct Marketing version has a large cover photo

| C1-596330 | Ropin' the Wind | 1991 | 50.00 |
— Only released on U.S. vinyl by Columbia House

BROOKS, HADDA

CROWN
| CLP-5010 [M] | Femme Fatale | 1957 | 60.00 |
— Black label; reissue of Modern LP
| CLP-5374 [M] | Hadda Brooks Sings and Swings | 1963 | 30.00 |
— Gray label

MODERN
| MLP-1210 [M] | Femme Fatale | 1956 | 200.00 |

BROOKS, HADDA / PETE JOHNSON

CROWN
| CLP-5058 [M] | Boogie | 1958 | 50.00 |

BROOKS, JOHN BENSON

DECCA
| DL5018 [M] | Avant Slant | 1968 | 40.00 |
— White label promo only; in stereo cover with "Monaural" sticker on front
| DL75018 [S] | Avant Slant | 1968 | 25.00 |

RIVERSIDE
| RLP 12-276 [M] | The Alabama Concerto | 1958 | 50.00 |
| RLP-1123 [S] | The Alabama Concerto | 1959 | 40.00 |

VIK
| LX-1083 [M] | Folk Jazz U.S.A. | 1957 | 40.00 |

BROOKS, ROY

IM-HOTEP
| CS-030 | Ethnic Expressions | 197? | 18.00 |

MUSE
| MR-5003 | Free Slave | 197? | 18.00 |

WORKSHOP JAZZ
| WSJ-220 [M] | Roy Brooks Beat | 1964 | 50.00 |
| WSJS-220 [S] | Roy Brooks Beat | 1964 | 60.00 |

BROOKS, TINA

BLUE NOTE
| BST-84052 [S] | Back to the Tracks | 199? | 40.00 |
— Classic Records reissue; first U.S. vinyl issue
| BLP-4041 [M] | True Blue | 1960 | 1000.00 |
— Deep Groove, W 63rd address
| B1-28975 | True Blue | 1994 | 25.00 |

MOSAIC
| MR4-106 | The Complete Blue Note Recordings of the Tina Brooks Quintets | 1984 | 150.00 |

BROONZY, BIG BILL

BIOGRAPH
| C-15 | Big Bill Broonzy 1932-1942 | 197? | 12.00 |

CHESS
| LP 1468 [M] | Big Bill Broonzy and Washboard Sam | 1962 | 160.00 |

COLUMBIA
| WL111 [M] | Big Bill's Blues | 1958 | 100.00 |

DIAL
| LP-306 [10] | Blues Concert | 1952 | 150.00 |

EMARCY
| MG-36137 [M] | Blues by Broonzy | 1958 | 100.00 |
| MG-26034 [10] | Folk Blues | 1954 | 120.00 |

EPIC
| EE22017 [M] | Big Bill's Blues | 196? | 25.00 |

EVEREST ARCHIVE OF FOLK & JAZZ
| 213 | Big Bill Broonzy | 1967 | 15.00 |

FOLKWAYS
FA-2315 [M]	Big Bill Broonzy	1957	50.00
31005 [R]	Big Bill Sings Country Blues	196?	18.00
FA-2326 [M]	Country Blues	1957	50.00
FG-3586 [M]	His Songs and Story	195?	50.00

GNP CRESCENDO
| 10004 | Feeling Low Down | 1974 | 12.00 |
| 10009 | Lonesome Road Blues | 1975 | 12.00 |

MERCURY
MG-20822 [M]	Big Bill Broonzy -- Memorial	1963	30.00
SR-60822 [R]	Big Bill Broonzy -- Memorial	1963	25.00
MG-20905 [M]	Remembering Big Bill Broonzy	1964	30.00
SR-60905 [R]	Remembering Big Bill Broonzy	1964	25.00

PERIOD
| SLP-1209 [M] | Big Bill Broonzy Sings and Josh White Comes a-Visiting | 1958 | 70.00 |
| SLP-1114 [M] | Big Bill Broonzy Sings (Blues) | 1956 | 150.00 |

PORTRAIT MASTERS
| RJ44089 | Big Bill's Blues | 1988 | 18.00 |
— Reissue of Columbia 111

SMITHSONIAN FOLKWAYS
| SF-40023 | Big Bill Broonzy Sings Folk Songs | 1989 | 15.00 |

VERVE
| MGV-3001 [M] | Last Session, Vol. 1 | 1959 | 50.00 |

Number	Title	Yr	NM
❑ MGV-3002 [M]	Last Session, Vol. 2	1959	50.00
❑ MGV-3003 [M]	Last Session, Vol. 3	1959	50.00
❑ MGV-3000-5 [M]	The Big Bill Broonzy Story	1959	200.00
YAZOO			
❑ L-1035	Do That Guitar Rag	197?	18.00
❑ L-1011 [B]	The Young Big Bill Broonzy	1969	18.00

BROTHER BONES

Number	Title	Yr	NM
TEMPO			
❑ 7004 [M]	Bones on the Beat	1958	150.00

BROTHER FOX AND TAR BABY

Number	Title	Yr	NM
CAPITOL			
❑ ST-544	Brother Fox and Tar Baby	1970	30.00
ORACLE			
❑ 1001	Brother Fox and Tar Baby	1969	30.00

BROTHER MATTHEW

Number	Title	Yr	NM
ABC-PARAMOUNT			
❑ ABC-121	Brother Matthew	1956	50.00

BROTHERHOOD OF MAN, THE

Number	Title	Yr	NM
DERAM			
❑ DES18046	United We Stand	1970	18.00
PYE			
❑ 12134	Save Your Kisses for Me	1976	15.00

BROTHERS FOUR, THE

Number	Title	Yr	NM
COLUMBIA			
❑ CL2502 [M]	A Beatles' Songbook (The Brothers Four Sing Lennon/ McCartney)	1966	18.00
❑ CS9302 [S]	A Beatles' Songbook (The Brothers Four Sing Lennon/ McCartney)	1966	25.00
❑ CL2702 [M]	A New World's Record	1967	30.00
—Original cover has a flopped image on the front cover, which makes it appear as if the guitarist is left-handed			
❑ CS9502 [S]	A New World's Record	1967	25.00
—Original cover has a flopped image on the front cover, which makes it appear as if the guitarist is left-handed			
❑ CS9502 [S]	A New World's Record	1967	15.00
—Corrected cover, with the guitarist using his right hand, as he does in real life			
❑ CL2702 [M]	A New World's Record	1967	18.00
—Corrected cover, with the guitarist using his right hand, as he does in real life			
❑ CL1578 [M]	B.M.O.C. (Best Music On/ Off Campus)	1961	15.00
❑ CS8378 [S]	B.M.O.C. (Best Music On/ Off Campus)	1961	18.00
❑ CL1946 [M]	Cross Country Concert	1963	15.00
❑ CS8746 [S]	Cross Country Concert	1963	18.00
❑ CS9818	Let's Get Together	1969	15.00
❑ CL2213 [M]	More Big Folk Hits	1964	15.00
❑ CS9013 [S]	More Big Folk Hits	1964	18.00
❑ CL1479 [M]	Rally 'Round the Brothers Four	1960	15.00
❑ CS8270 [S]	Rally 'Round the Brothers Four	1960	18.00
❑ CL1625 [M]	Roamin'	1961	15.00
❑ CS8425 [S]	Roamin'	1961	18.00
❑ CL2033 [M]	The Big Folk Hits	1963	15.00
❑ CS8833 [S]	The Big Folk Hits	1963	18.00
❑ CL1402 [M]	The Brothers Four	1960	15.00
❑ CS8197 [S]	The Brothers Four	1960	18.00
❑ CL1828 [M]	The Brothers Four: In Person	1962	15.00
❑ CS8628 [S]	The Brothers Four: In Person	1962	18.00
❑ CL1803 [M]	The Brothers Four's Greatest Hits	1962	15.00
❑ CS8603 [S]	The Brothers Four's Greatest Hits	1962	18.00
—Red "360 Sound" label			
❑ CS8603	The Brothers Four's Greatest Hits	1970	12.00
—Orange label			
❑ PC8603	The Brothers Four's Greatest Hits	198?	10.00
—Reissue with new prefix			
❑ CL2128 [M]	The Brothers Four Sing of Our Times	1964	15.00
❑ CS8928 [S]	The Brothers Four Sing of Our Times	1964	18.00
❑ CL1697 [M]	The Brothers Four Song Book	1961	15.00
❑ CS8497 [S]	The Brothers Four Song Book	1961	18.00
❑ CL2305 [M]	The Honey Wind Blows	1965	15.00
❑ CS9105 [S]	The Honey Wind Blows	1965	18.00
❑ CL2379 [M]	Try to Remember	1965	15.00
❑ CS9179 [S]	Try to Remember	1965	18.00
FANTASY			
❑ 8400	The Brothers Four 1970	1970	12.00
FIRST AMERICAN			
❑ 7722	Greenfields and Other Gold	1980	15.00
❑ 7728	New Gold	1981	12.00
❑ 7705	The Brothers Four Now	1978	12.00
HARMONY			
❑ HS11341	Four Strong Winds	1969	12.00
❑ H31505	Great Songs of Our Times	1972	12.00

BROTHERS JOHNSON, THE

Number	Title	Yr	NM
A&M			
❑ PR-4714 [DJ]	Blam!!	1978	25.00
—Promo-only picture disc			
❑ SP-4714	Blam!!	1978	12.00
❑ SP-17049 [DJ]	Blam!! Radio Special	1978	25.00
—Promo-only music and interview record			
❑ SP-4927	Blast! (The Latest and the Greatest)	1982	12.00
❑ SP-5162	Kickin'	1988	12.00
❑ SP-3716	Light Up the Night	1980	12.00
❑ SP-4567	Look Out for #1	1976	12.00
❑ SP-4965	Out of Control	1984	12.00
❑ SP-4644	Right on Time	1977	12.00
❑ SP-3724	Winners	1981	12.00

BROWN, AL

Number	Title	Yr	NM
AMY			
❑ A-1 [M]	Madison Dance Party	1960	40.00
❑ AS-1 [S]	Madison Dance Party	1960	60.00

BROWN, ARTHUR, THE CRAZY WORLD OF

Number	Title	Yr	NM
GULL			
❑ GU6-405	Dance	1975	15.00
PASSPORT			
❑ 98003	Journey	1974	15.00
—As Arthur Brown's Kingdom Come			
TRACK			
❑ SD8198	The Crazy World of Arthur Brown	1968	30.00

BROWN, BOBBY

Number	Title	Yr	NM
DESTINY			
❑ 4001	Bobby Brown Live	1972	100.00
❑ 4002	The Enlightening Beam of Axonda	1972	120.00
MCA			
❑ 10417	Bobby	1992	18.00
❑ 6342	Dance! ... Ya Know It!	1989	15.00
❑ 42185	Don't Be Cruel	1988	10.00
❑ 11691	Forever	1997	18.00
❑ 5827	King of Stage	1986	10.00
❑ 10974	Remixes N the Key of B	1993	18.00
—Issued in generic black cardboard sleeve			

BROWN, BOOTS / DAN DREW

Number	Title	Yr	NM
GROOVE			
❑ LG-1000 [M]	Rock That Boat	1955	300.00

BROWN, BUSTER

Number	Title	Yr	NM
COLLECTABLES			
❑ COL-5110	Golden Classics: The New King of the Blues	198?	12.00
FIRE			
❑ FLP-102 [M]	The New King of the Blues	1961	700.00
—White and red label			
❑ FLP-102 [M]	The New King of the Blues	1961	400.00
—Red and black label, purple cover			
❑ FLP-102 [M]	The New King of the Blues	1961	300.00
—Red and black label, white cover			
SOUFFLE			
❑ 2014	Get Down	1973	15.00

BROWN, CHARLES

Number	Title	Yr	NM
ALADDIN			
❑ LP-702 [10]	Mood Music	1952	7500.00
—Red vinyl; VG value 3000; VG+ value 5250			
❑ LP-702 [10]	Mood Music	1952	4000.00
—Black vinyl; VG value 1500; VG+ value 2750			
ALLIGATOR			
❑ AL-4771	One More for the Road	1989	15.00
BIG TOWN			
❑ 1003	Merry Christmas Baby	1977	15.00
❑ 1005	Music Maestro Please	1978	12.00
BLUESWAY			
❑ BLS-6039	Charles Brown -- Legend	1970	30.00
BULLSEYE BLUES			
❑ BB-9501	All My Life	1990	25.00
IMPERIAL			
❑ LP-9178 [M]	Charles Brown Sings Million Sellers	1961	400.00
JEWEL			
❑ 5006	Blues 'N' Brown	1972	15.00
KING			
❑ 775 [M]	Charles Brown Sings Christmas Songs	1961	150.00
❑ KS-775 [S]	Charles Brown Sings Christmas Songs	1963	300.00
—Stereo copies (whether true stereo or rechanneled, we don't know) exist on blue labels with "King" in block letters (no crown)			
❑ 878 [M]	The Great Charles Brown	1963	200.00
MAINSTREAM			
❑ 56035 [M]	Ballads My Way	1965	25.00
❑ S-6035 [S]	Ballads My Way	1965	30.00
❑ 56007 [M]	Boss of the Blues	1965	25.00
❑ S-6007 [S]	Boss of the Blues	1965	30.00
MOSAIC			
❑ MQ7-153	The Complete Aladdin Recordings of Charles Brown	1994	150.00
SCORE			
❑ SLP-4011 [M]	Driftin' Blues	1958	400.00

BROWN, CHUCK AND THE SOUL SEARCHERS

Number	Title	Yr	NM
SOURCE			
❑ SOR-3076	Bustin' Loose	1979	15.00
❑ SOR-3234	Funk Express	1980	18.00
SUSSEX			
❑ SRA-8030 [B]	Salt of the Earth	1974	120.00
—Reproductions exist			
❑ SXBS-7020 [B]	We the People	1972	120.00
—Reproductions exist			

BROWN, CLIFFORD, AND ART FARMER

Number	Title	Yr	NM
PRESTIGE			
❑ PRLP-167 [10]	Clifford Brown and Art Farmer with the Swedish All Stars	1953	300.00

BROWN, CLIFFORD, AND MAX ROACH

Number	Title	Yr	NM
ELEKTRA/MUSICIAN			
❑ 60026	Pure Genius	1982	15.00
EMARCY			
❑ MG-36037 [M]	A Study in Brown	1955	700.00
❑ MG-36008 [M]	Brown and Roach Incorporated	1955	200.00
❑ MG-26043 [10]	Clifford Brown and Max Roach	1954	600.00
❑ MG-36036 [M]	Clifford Brown and Max Roach	1955	200.00
❑ MG-36070 [M]	Clifford Brown and Max Roach at Basin Street	1956	200.00
GENE NORMAN			
❑ GNP-5 [10]	Clifford Brown and Max Roach, Vol. 1	1954	300.00
❑ GNP-7 [10]	Clifford Brown and Max Roach, Vol. 2	1954	300.00
❑ GNP-125 [10]	Gene Norman Presents Max Roach and Clifford Brown	1954	400.00
❑ GNP-18 [M]	The Best of Max Roach and Clifford Brown In Concert	1955	250.00
MAINSTREAM			
❑ MRL-386 [M]	Daahoud	197?	15.00
TRIP			
❑ 5550	All Stars	197?	12.00
❑ 5530	A Study in Brown	197?	12.00
❑ 5537	Best Coast Jazz	197?	12.00
❑ 5520	Brown and Roach Incorporated	197?	12.00
❑ 5511 [B]	Clifford Brown and Max Roach at Basin Street	197?	12.00
❑ 5540	Jordu	197?	12.00

BROWN, CLIFFORD

Number	Title	Yr	NM
BLUE NOTE			
❑ BST-84428	Alternate Takes	198?	15.00
❑ BN-LA267-G	Brownie Eyes	1974	15.00
❑ BLP-1526 [M]	Clifford Brown Memorial Album	1956	800.00
—Deep groove" version (deep indentation under label on both sides)			
❑ BLP-1526 [M]	Clifford Brown Memorial Album	1956	150.00
—Regular edition, Lexington Ave. address on label			
❑ BLP-1526 [M]	Clifford Brown Memorial Album	196?	50.00
—With W. 63rd St. address on label			
❑ BLP-1526 [M]	Clifford Brown Memorial Album	196?	30.00
—With "New York, USA" address on label			
❑ BST-81526 [R]	Clifford Brown Memorial Album	1967	15.00
—With "A Division of Liberty Records" on label			
❑ BST-81526	Clifford Brown Memorial Album	1985	12.00
—The Finest in Jazz Since 1939" reissue			
❑ BLP-5047 [10]	Clifford Brown Quartet	1954	500.00
❑ BLP-5032 [10]	New Star on the Horizon	1953	500.00
COLUMBIA			
❑ KC32284	The Beginning and the End	1973	18.00
❑ C32284	The Beginning and the End	197?	15.00
—Reissue with new prefix			
EMARCY			
❑ 36039 [M]	Best Coast Jazz		120.00
—Blue label, Silver lettering, Deep Groove, small drummer logo.			
❑ MG-36102 [M]	Clifford Brown All Stars	1956	120.00
❑ MG-36005 [M]	Clifford Brown with Strings	1955	200.00
—drummer logo			
FANTASY			
❑ OJC-359	Clifford Brown Big Band in Paris	198?	12.00
❑ OJC-017	Clifford Brown Memorial	198?	12.00

Number	Title	Yr	NM
❑ OJC-357	Clifford Brown Quartet in Paris	198?	12.00
❑ OJC-358	Clifford Brown Sextet in Paris	198?	12.00

JAZZTONE

Number	Title	Yr	NM
❑ J-1281 [M]	Jazz Messages	195?	40.00

LIMELIGHT

Number	Title	Yr	NM
❑ 2-8201 [M]	The Immortal Clifford Brown	1965	40.00
❑ 2-8601 [R]	The Immortal Clifford Brown	1965	30.00

MERCURY

Number	Title	Yr	NM
❑ MG-20827 [M]	Remember Clifford	1963	40.00
❑ SR-60827 [R]	Remember Clifford	1963	30.00

MOSAIC

Number	Title	Yr	NM
❑ MR5-104	The Complete Blue Note and Pacific Jazz Recordings of Clifford Brown	198?	80.00

PACIFIC JAZZ

Number	Title	Yr	NM
❑ PJ-3 [M]	Jazz Immortal	1956	150.00
❑ LN-10126	Jazz Immortal	198?	12.00
❑ PJLP-19 [10]	The Clifford Brown Ensemble	1955	300.00

PRESTIGE

Number	Title	Yr	NM
❑ PRLP-16008 [M]	Clifford Brown	1964	40.00
❑ PRST-7840	Clifford Brown Big Band in Paris	1970	15.00
❑ 24020	Clifford Brown in Paris	1971	18.00
❑ PRLP-7055 [M]	Clifford Brown Memorial	1956	80.00
❑ PRST-7662 [R]	Clifford Brown Memorial Album	1969	15.00
❑ PRST-7761	Clifford Brown Quartet in Paris	1969	15.00
❑ PRST-7794	Clifford Brown Sextet in Paris	1970	15.00

TRIP

Number	Title	Yr	NM
❑ 5502	Clifford Brown with Strings	197?	12.00

BROWN, DENNIS

A&M

Number	Title	Yr	NM
❑ SP-4850	Foul Play	1981	15.00
❑ SP-4886	Love Has Found Its Way	1982	15.00
❑ SP-4964	The Prophet Rides Again	1983	15.00

RAS

Number	Title	Yr	NM
❑ 3207	Brown Sugar	1986	18.00

VP

Number	Title	Yr	NM
❑ 1478	Could It Be	1996	12.00

BROWN, DON

1ST AMERICAN

Number	Title	Yr	NM
❑ 7711	Come On	1978	12.00
❑ 7701	I Can't Say No	1977	12.00

BROWN, HYLO

CAPITOL

Number	Title	Yr	NM
❑ T1168 [M]	Hylo Brown	1959	80.00

STARDAY

Number	Title	Yr	NM
❑ SLP-185 [M]	Bluegrass Balladeer	1962	40.00
❑ SLP-204 [M]	Bluegrass Goes to College	1962	40.00
❑ SLP-220 [M]	Hylo Brown Meets the Lonesome Pine Fiddlers	1963	40.00
❑ SLP-249 [M]	Sing Me a Bluegrass Song	1963	40.00

BROWN, JAMES

CLEOPATRA

Number	Title	Yr	NM
❑ 2061 [B]	Cold Sweat Live		25.00
❑ 3038 [B]	Live In New York 1980		25.00
❑ 7500 [B]	New York City Soul Break Out!		25.00

HRB

Number	Title	Yr	NM
❑ 1004	The Fabulous James Brown	1974	30.00

KING

Number	Title	Yr	NM
❑ KSD-1092	Ain't It Funky	1970	40.00
❑ KS-1040	A Soulful Christmas	1968	80.00
❑ 1010 [M]	Christmas Songs	1966	100.00
— Wreath on gray wall, no song titles on back			
❑ 1010 [M]	Christmas Songs	1967	80.00
— Wreath on white wall, song titles are on back			
❑ KS-1010 [S]	Christmas Songs	1966	150.00
— Wreath on gray wall, no song titles on back			
❑ KS-1010 [S]	Christmas Songs	1967	100.00
— Wreath on white wall, song titles are on back			
❑ 1020 [M]	Cold Sweat	1967	50.00
❑ KS-1020 [S]	Cold Sweat	1967	70.00
❑ 780 [M]	Excitement	1963	150.00
— Third title; "crownless" King label			
❑ 780 [M]	Excitement	1966	50.00
— Third title; "crown" King label			
❑ KS-1051	Gettin' Down To It	1969	50.00
❑ 780 [M]	Good Good Twistin'	1962	200.00
— Good Good Twistin' " on either label or cover, or both			
❑ KSD-1124	Hey America!	1970	40.00
❑ LPS-1030	I Can't Stand Myself (When You Touch Me)	1968	50.00
❑ LPS-1031	I Got the Feelin'	1968	50.00
❑ 946 [M]	I Got You (I Feel Good)	1966	100.00
— Crownless" King label			
❑ 946 [M]	I Got You (I Feel Good)	1966	40.00
— Crown" King label			
❑ LPS-946 [S]	I Got You (I Feel Good)	1966	150.00
— Crownless" King label			
❑ LPS-946 [S]	I Got You (I Feel Good)	1966	50.00
— Crown" King label			
❑ 985 [M]	It's a Man's Man's Man's World	1966	50.00
❑ KS-985 [S]	It's a Man's Man's Man's World	1966	70.00
❑ KSD-1063	It's a Mother	1969	40.00
❑ KSD-1095	It's a New Day So Let a Man Come In	1970	40.00
❑ 804 [M]	James Brown & His Famous Flames Tour the U.S.A.	1962	250.00
— Crownless" King label			
❑ 804 [M]	James Brown & His Famous Flames Tour the U.S.A.	1966	50.00
— Crown" King label			
❑ KSD-1055	James Brown Plays & Directs The Popcorn	1969	40.00
❑ LPS-1034	James Brown Plays Nothing But Soul	1968	50.00
❑ LPS-1024	James Brown Presents His Show of Tomorrow	1968	50.00
— Various-artists album			
❑ 771 [M]	Jump Around	1963	200.00
— Third title			
❑ KS-771 [S]	Jump Around	1963	300.00
— Stereo copies of King 771 only exist with this title			
❑ 826 [M]	Live at the Apollo	1963	200.00
— Custom back cover; "crownless" King label			
❑ 826 [M]	Live at the Apollo	1963	150.00
— Other King albums on back cover; "crownless" King label			
❑ 826 [M]	Live at the Apollo	1966	50.00
— Crown" King label			
❑ KS-826 [S]	Live at the Apollo	1963	300.00
— Custom back cover; "crownless" King label			
❑ KS-826 [S]	Live at the Apollo	1963	200.00
— Other King albums on back cover; "crownless" King label			
❑ KS-826 [S]	Live at the Apollo	1966	70.00
— Crown" King label			
❑ 826 [M]	Live at the Apollo	1963	800.00
— White label promo, banded for airplay			
❑ LPS-1022	Live at the Apollo, Volume II	1968	70.00
❑ 1018 [M]	Live at the Garden	1967	400.00
— Black label promo; banded for airplay			
❑ 1018 [M]	Live at the Garden	1967	80.00
❑ KS-1018 [S]	Live at the Garden	1967	100.00
❑ 961 [M]	Mighty Instrumentals	1966	100.00
❑ LPS-961 [S]	Mighty Instrumentals	1966	150.00
❑ 771 [M]	Night Train	1961	300.00
— Original title			
❑ 938 [M]	Papa's Got a Brand New Bag	1965	80.00
— Red cover; "crownless" King label			
❑ 938 [M]	Papa's Got a Brand New Bag	1966	50.00
— Green cover; "crownless" King label			
❑ 938 [M]	Papa's Got a Brand New Bag	1966	40.00
— Crown" King label			
❑ LPS-938 [P]	Papa's Got a Brand New Bag	1965	100.00
— Red cover; "crownless" King label			
❑ LPS-938 [P]	Papa's Got a Brand New Bag	1966	60.00
— Green cover; "crownless" King label			
❑ LPS-938 [P]	Papa's Got a Brand New Bag	1966	50.00
— Crown" King label			
❑ 610 [M]	Please Please Please	1958	1200.00
— Woman's and man's legs" cover; "King" on label is two inches wide			
❑ 610 [M]	Please Please Please	1961	1000.00
— Woman's and man's legs" cover; "King" on label is three inches wide			
❑ 909 [M]	Please Please Please	1964	100.00
— Reissue of 610; "crownless" King label			
❑ 909 [M]	Please Please Please	1966	50.00
— Crown" King label			
❑ 851 [M]	Prisoner of Love	1963	200.00
— Custom back cover; "crownless" King label			
❑ 851 [M]	Prisoner of Love	1963	100.00
— Other King albums on back cover; "crownless" King label			
❑ 851 [M]	Prisoner of Love	1966	50.00
— Crown" King label			
❑ 883 [M]	Pure Dynamite! Live at the Royal	1964	800.00
— White label promo; banded for airplay			
❑ 883 [M]	Pure Dynamite! Live at the Royal	1964	200.00
— Crownless" King label			
❑ 883 [M]	Pure Dynamite! Live at the Royal	1966	50.00
— Crown" King label			
❑ 1016 [M]	Raw Soul	1967	50.00
❑ KS-1016 [P]	Raw Soul	1967	70.00
❑ KS-1047	Say It Loud -- I'm Black and I'm Proud	1969	50.00
❑ KSD-1115	Sex Machine	1970	50.00
❑ KSD-1110	Sho Is Funky Down Here	1971	40.00
❑ 780 [M]	Shout and Shimmy	1962	250.00
— Shout and Shimmy" on both cover and label			
❑ KSD-1100	Soul on Top	1970	40.00
❑ KSD-1127	Super Bad	1971	40.00
❑ 743 [M]	The Amazing James Brown	1961	500.00
— James Brown in suit" cover			
❑ 743 [M]	The Amazing James Brown	1963	150.00
— White title cover; "crownless" King label			
❑ 743 [M]	The Amazing James Brown	1966	500.00
— White title cover with "James Brown" in huge letters; "crown" King label			
❑ 919 [M]	The Unbeatable James Brown -- 16 Hits	1964	100.00
— Reissue of 635; "crownless" King label			
❑ 919 [M]	The Unbeatable James Brown -- 16 Hits	1966	50.00
— Crown" King label			
❑ 683 [M]	Think!	1960	900.00
— Baby" cover; "King" on label is two inches wide			
❑ 683 [M]	Think!	1961	600.00
— Baby" cover; "King" on label is three inches wide			
❑ 683 [M]	Think!	1963	100.00
— James Brown photo cover; "crownless" King label			
❑ 683 [M]	Think!	1966	50.00
— James Brown photo cover; "crown" King label			
❑ LPS-1038 [B]	Thinking About Little Willie John and a Few Nice Things	1968	50.00
❑ 635 [M]	Try Me!	1959	900.00
— Woman with cigarette and gun" cover; "King" on label is two inches wide			
❑ 635 [M]	Try Me!	1961	600.00
— Woman with cigarette and gun" cover; "King" on label is three inches wide			
❑ 771 [M]	Twist Around	1962	250.00
— Second title			

POLYDOR

Number	Title	Yr	NM
❑ 821231-1	Ain't That a Groove: The James Brown Story 1966-1969	1984	18.00
❑ PD-6014	Black Caesar	1973	50.00
❑ PD-1-6093	Bodyheat	1976	40.00
❑ 827439-1	Dead on the Heavy Funk: The James Brown Story 1974-1978	1985	18.00
❑ 821232-1	Doing It to Death: The James Brown Story 1970-1973	1984	18.00
❑ PD-1-6054	Everybody's Doin' the Hustle & Dead On the Double Bump	1975	40.00
❑ PD2-3004	Get On the Good Foot	1972	60.00
❑ PD 1-6071	Get Up Offa That Thing	1976	40.00
❑ PD-2-9001	Hell	1974	80.00
❑ PD-1-6059	Hot	1976	40.00
❑ 24-4054	Hot Pants	1971	40.00
❑ 829624-1	In the Jungle Groove	1986	18.00
❑ PD-1-6140	Jam/1980s	1978	40.00
❑ PD-2-6290	James Brown…Live/Hot on the One	1980	50.00
❑ 829417-1	James Brown's Funky People	1986	18.00
— Various-artists LP			
❑ 835857-1	James Brown's Funky People 2	1988	18.00
— Various-artists compilation			
❑ SC-5401	James Brown Soul Classics	1972	30.00
❑ 8434791 [S]	Live at the Apollo	2008	25.00
❑ 837126-1	Motherlode	1988	18.00
❑ PD-1-6111	Mutha's Nature	1977	40.00
❑ PD-1-6318	Nonstop!	1981	30.00
❑ PD-1-6258	People	1980	30.00
❑ PD-1-6039	Reality	1975	40.00
❑ 25-3003	Revolution of the Mind -- Live at the Apollo, Volume III	1971	60.00
❑ PD-2-9004	Sex Machine Live	1976	50.00
❑ PD-1-6042 [B]	Sex Machine Today	1975	40.00
❑ PD 6015	Slaughter's Big Rip-Off	1973	50.00
❑ 829254-1	Solid Gold: 30 Golden Hits	1985	25.00
❑ SC-5402	Soul Classics, Volume 2	1973	30.00
❑ PD-1-6181	Take a Look at Those Cakes	1978	30.00
❑ PD-1-6340	The Best of James Brown	1981	25.00
❑ 823275-1	The Best of James Brown	1984	15.00
— Reissue of 6340			
❑ PD-1-6212	The Original Disco Man	1979	30.00
❑ PD2-3007	The Payback	1973	50.00
❑ PD-5028	There It Is	1972	40.00

RHINO

Number	Title	Yr	NM
❑ RNLP-219	Greatest Hits (1964-1968)	1986	18.00
❑ R1-70219	Greatest Hits (1964-1968)	1988	15.00
— Reissue of 219			
❑ RNLP-217	Live at the Apollo, Volume 2, Part 1	1985	18.00
❑ R1-70217	Live at the Apollo, Volume 2, Part 1	1988	15.00
— Reissue of 217			
❑ RNLP-218	Live at the Apollo, Volume 2, Part 2	1985	18.00
❑ R1-70218	Live at the Apollo, Volume 2, Part 2	1988	15.00
— Reissue of 218			
❑ R170194	Santa's Got a Brand New Bag	1986	12.00
— Reissue of King material			

SCOTTI BROTHERS

Number	Title	Yr	NM
❑ FZ40380	Gravity	1986	15.00
❑ FZ44241	I'm Real	1988	15.00
❑ 75225-1	Love Overdue	1991	25.00
❑ FZ45164	Soul Session Live	1989	18.00

SMASH

Number	Title	Yr	NM
❑ MGS-27057 [M]	Grits & Soul	1965	30.00

Number	Title	Yr	NM
❑ SRS-67057 [S]	Grits & Soul	1965	40.00
❑ MGS-27084 [M]	Handful of Soul	1966	30.00
❑ SRS-67084 [S]	Handful of Soul	1966	40.00
❑ MGS-27072 [M]	James Brown Plays James Brown -- Today & Yesterday	1965	30.00
❑ SRS-67072 [S]	James Brown Plays James Brown -- Today & Yesterday	1965	40.00
❑ MGS-27080 [M]	James Brown Plays New Breed	1966	30.00
❑ SRS-67080 [S]	James Brown Plays New Breed	1966	40.00
❑ MGS-27093 [M]	James Brown Plays the Real Thing	1967	30.00
❑ SRS-67093 [S]	James Brown Plays the Real Thing	1967	40.00
❑ SRS-67109	James Brown Sings Out of Sight	1968	30.00
— Abridged reissue of 67058			
❑ MGS-27058 [M]	Out of Sight	1965	100.00
❑ SRS-67058 [S]	Out of Sight	1965	150.00
❑ MGS-27054 [M]	Showtime	1964	30.00
❑ SRS-67054 [S]	Showtime	1964	40.00
❑ MGS-27087 [M]	The James Brown Show	1967	30.00
— Various-artists LP			
❑ SRS-67087 [S]	The James Brown Show	1967	40.00
— Various-artists LP			

SOLID SMOKE

Number	Title	Yr	NM
❑ SS-8013	Can Your Heart Stand It	1981	15.00
❑ SS-8006	Live and Lowdown at the Apollo, Vol. 1	1980	15.00
❑ SS-8023	The Federal Years, Part 1	198?	15.00
❑ SS-8024	The Federal Years, Part 2	198?	15.00

SUNDAZED

Number	Title	Yr	NM
❑ LP5470 [B]	Love Power Peace	2014	60.00

T.K.

Number	Title	Yr	NM
❑ 615	Soul Syndrome	1980	30.00

BROWN, JIM ED

RCA CAMDEN

Number	Title	Yr	NM
❑ CAS-2549	Country Cream	1972	12.00
❑ CAS-2496	Gentle on My Mind	1971	12.00
❑ ACL1-0197	Hey Good Lookin'	1973	12.00
❑ ACL1-0618	The Three Bells	1974	12.00

RCA VICTOR

Number	Title	Yr	NM
❑ LPM-3569 [M]	Alone with You	1966	25.00
❑ LSP-3569 [S]	Alone with You	1966	30.00
❑ LSP-4525	Angel's Sunday	1971	18.00
❑ APL1-0172	Bar-Rooms & Pop-A-Tops	1973	18.00
❑ APL1-0324	Best of Jim Ed Brown	1973	18.00
❑ LPM-3942 [M]	Bottle, Bottle	1968	40.00
❑ LSP-3942 [S]	Bottle, Bottle	1968	25.00
❑ LSP-4755	Brown Is Blue	1972	18.00
❑ LSP-4011	Country's Best on Record	1968	25.00
❑ LSP-4713	Evening	1972	18.00
❑ LPM-3853 [M]	Gems by Jim	1967	30.00
❑ LSP-3853 [S]	Gems by Jim	1967	25.00
❑ LSP-4262	Going Up the Country	1970	18.00
❑ APL1-0572	It's That Time of Night	1974	18.00
❑ ANL1-1215	It's That Time of Night	1975	12.00
— Reissue of 0572			
❑ LSP-4175	Jim Ed Sings the Browns	1969	25.00
❑ LSP-4366	Just for You	1970	18.00
❑ LPM-3744 [M]	Just Jim	1967	30.00
❑ LSP-3744 [S]	Just Jim	1967	25.00
❑ LSP-4461	Morning	1971	18.00
❑ LSP-4614	She's Leavin'	1971	18.00
❑ LSP-4130	This Is My Best!	1968	25.00

BROWN, LAWRENCE

ABC IMPULSE!

Number	Title	Yr	NM
❑ AS-89	Inspired Abandon	1968	15.00

CLEF

Number	Title	Yr	NM
❑ MGC-682 [M]	Slide Trombone	1955	120.00

IMPULSE!

Number	Title	Yr	NM
❑ A-89 [M]	Inspired Abandon	1965	30.00
❑ AS-89 [S]	Inspired Abandon	1965	30.00

VERVE

Number	Title	Yr	NM
❑ MGV-8067 [M]	Slide Trombone	1957	50.00
❑ V-8067 [M]	Slide Trombone	1961	25.00

BROWN, LES, AND VIC SCHOEN

KAPP

Number	Title	Yr	NM
❑ KRL-4504 [M]	Impact! Band Meets Band	196?	25.00
— Reissue of KDL-7003			
❑ KRS-4504 [S]	Impact! Band Meets Band	196?	30.00
— Reissue of KDS-7003			
❑ KDL-7003 [M]	Stereophonic Suite for Two Bands	195?	30.00
❑ KDS-7003 [S]	Stereophonic Suite for Two Bands	195?	40.00

MCA

Number	Title	Yr	NM
❑ 1548	Stereophonic Suite for Two Bands	198?	15.00

BROWN, LES

CAPITOL

Number	Title	Yr	NM
❑ T657 [M]	College Classics	1955	30.00
— Turquoise or gray label			
❑ T886 [M]	Composer's Holiday	1957	30.00
— Turquoise or gray label			
❑ T959 [M]	Concert Modern	1958	30.00
— Turquoise or gray label			
❑ T746 [M]	Les Brown's in Town	1956	30.00
— Turquoise or gray label			
❑ T659 [M]	The Les Brown All Stars	1955	30.00
— Turquoise or gray label			
❑ T1174 [M]	The Les Brown Story	1959	30.00
— Black colorband label, logo at left			
❑ ST1174 [S]	The Les Brown Story	1959	30.00
— Black colorband label, logo at left			
❑ SM-1174	The Les Brown Story	1976	10.00
— Reissue with new prefix			

CIRCLE

Number	Title	Yr	NM
❑ CLP-90	Les Brown and His Orchestra 1946	1986	12.00

COLUMBIA

Number	Title	Yr	NM
❑ CL1497 [M]	Bandland	1960	18.00
— Red and black label with six "eye" logos			
❑ CS8288 [S]	Bandland	1960	25.00
— Red and black label with six "eye" logos			
❑ CL6159 [10]	Classics in Rhythm	195?	40.00
❑ CL6060 [10]	Dance Parade	1949	40.00
❑ CL539 [M]	Dance with Les Brown	1954	30.00
— Maroon label, gold print			
❑ CL2030 [M]	Explosive Sound	1964	18.00
— Guaranteed High Fidelity" on label			
❑ CS8830 [S]	Explosive Sound	1964	25.00
— 360 Sound Stereo" in black on label			
❑ CL2512 [10]	I've Got My Love to Keep Me Warm	1955	40.00
❑ CL1818 [M]	Revolution in Sound	1962	18.00
— Red and black label with six "eye" logos			
❑ CS8618 [S]	Revolution in Sound	1962	25.00
— Red and black label with six "eye" logos			
❑ CL649 [M]	Sentimental Journey	1955	30.00
— Maroon label, gold print			
❑ CL649 [M]	Sentimental Journey	1955	30.00
— Red and black label with six "eye" logos			
❑ CL2561 [10]	The Cool Classics	1955	40.00
❑ CS8394 [S]	The Lerner and Loewe Bandbook	1960	25.00
— Red and black label with six "eye" logos			
❑ CL(# unk) [M]	The Lerner and Loewe Bandbook	1960	18.00
— Red and black label with six "eye" logos			
❑ CL2119 [M]	The Young Beat	1964	18.00
— Guaranteed High Fidelity" on label			
❑ CS8919 [S]	The Young Beat	1964	25.00
— 360 Sound Stereo" in black on label			
❑ CL6123 [10]	Your Dance Date with Les Brown	1950	40.00

COLUMBIA SPECIAL PRODUCTS

Number	Title	Yr	NM
❑ P14361	Sentimental Journey	198?	12.00

CORAL

Number	Title	Yr	NM
❑ CRL56108 [10]	Invitation	1954	50.00
❑ CRL57311 [M]	Jazz Song Book	1959	30.00
❑ CRL757311 [S]	Jazz Song Book	1959	30.00
❑ CX-1 [M]	Les Brown Concert at the Palladium	1953	60.00
❑ CRL57000 [M]	Les Brown Concert at the Palladium, Part 1	1954	30.00
❑ CRL57001 [M]	Les Brown Concert at the Palladium, Part 1	1954	30.00
❑ CRL56094 [10]	Les Dance	1953	50.00
❑ CRL56116 [10]	Les Dream	1954	50.00
❑ CRL57165 [M]	Love Letters in the Sand	1957	30.00
❑ CRL57058 [M]	More from Les	1956	30.00
❑ CRL56077 [10]	Musical Weather Vane	1953	50.00
❑ CRL57051 [M]	Open House	1956	30.00
❑ CRL56026 [10]	Over the Rainbow	1951	50.00
❑ CRL57300 [M]	Swing Song Book	1959	30.00
❑ CRL757300 [S]	Swing Song Book	1959	30.00
❑ CRL56030 [10]	The Sound of Renown	1951	50.00
❑ CRL57030 [M]	The Sound of Renown	1955	30.00
❑ CRL56109 [10]	Time to Dance	1954	50.00
❑ CRL56046 [10]	You're My Everything	1952	50.00

DAYBREAK

Number	Title	Yr	NM
❑ 2007	New Horizons	1972	15.00

DECCA

Number	Title	Yr	NM
❑ DL4768 [M]	A Sign of the Times	1966	15.00
❑ DL74768 [S]	A Sign of the Times	1966	18.00
❑ DL4607 [M]	In Town	1965	15.00
❑ DL74607 [S]	In Town	1965	18.00
❑ DL4965 [M]	The World of the Young	1968	25.00
❑ DL74965 [S]	The World of the Young	1968	15.00

FANTASY

Number	Title	Yr	NM
❑ F-9650	Digital Swing	1987	15.00

GREAT AMERICAN

Number	Title	Yr	NM
❑ 1010	Les Brown Goes Direct to Disc	1981	25.00

HARMONY

Number	Title	Yr	NM
❑ HL7335 [M]	Hits from The Sound of Music, My Fair Lady, Camelot and Others	1965	15.00
❑ HS11135 [S]	Hits from The Sound of Music, My Fair Lady, Camelot and Others	1965	15.00
❑ HL7100 [M]	Les Brown's Greatest	196?	15.00
❑ HL7211 [M]	Sentimental Journey	196?	15.00
❑ KH32015	The Beat of the Bands	1972	12.00

HINDSIGHT

Number	Title	Yr	NM
❑ HSR-103	Les Brown and His Orchestra 1944-45	198?	12.00
❑ HSR-131	Les Brown and His Orchestra 1949	198?	12.00
❑ HSR-199	Les Brown and His Orchestra 1956-57	198?	12.00
❑ HSR-132	Les Brown and His Orchestra Vol. 3	198?	12.00

INSIGHT

Number	Title	Yr	NM
❑ 213	Les Brown and His Orchestra, 1949	198?	12.00

MCA

Number	Title	Yr	NM
❑ 4070	The Best of Les Brown	1974	15.00

TIME-LIFE

Number	Title	Yr	NM
❑ STBB-11	Big Bands: Les Brown	1984	18.00

VOCALION

Number	Title	Yr	NM
❑ VL3618 [M]	Les Dance	196?	15.00

BROWN, MARION, AND ELLIOTT SCHWARTZ

CENTURY

Number	Title	Yr	NM
❑ 41746	Soundways	1973	18.00

BROWN, MARION, AND GUNTER HAMPEL

IAI

Number	Title	Yr	NM
❑ 373855	Reeds 'n Vibes	1978	15.00

BROWN, MARION

ABC IMPULSE!

Number	Title	Yr	NM
❑ AS-9252	Geechee Recollections	1973	15.00
❑ AS-9275	Sweet Earth Flying	1974	15.00
❑ AS-9139	Three for Shepp	1968	15.00
❑ ASD-9304	Vista	1975	15.00

ARISTA FREEDOM

Number	Title	Yr	NM
❑ AL1904	Duets	1975	18.00
❑ AL1001	Porto Novo	1975	15.00

ECM

Number	Title	Yr	NM
❑ 1004	Afternoon of a Georgia Faun	197?	18.00

ESP-DISK'

Number	Title	Yr	NM
❑ 1022 [M]	Marion Brown Quartet	1966	25.00
❑ S-1022 [S]	Marion Brown Quartet	1966	18.00
❑ 1040 [M]	Why Not?	1967	25.00
❑ S-1040 [S]	Why Not?	1967	18.00

IMPULSE!

Number	Title	Yr	NM
❑ A-9139 [M]	Three for Shepp	1967	30.00
❑ AS-9139 [S]	Three for Shepp	1967	25.00

SWEET EARTH

Number	Title	Yr	NM
❑ SER-1001	Solo Saxophone	1978	15.00

TIMELESS

Number	Title	Yr	NM
❑ TI-314	La Placita -- Live in Willisau	197?	15.00

BROWN, MAXINE (1)

COLLECTABLES

Number	Title	Yr	NM
❑ COL-5116	Golden Classics	198?	15.00

COMMONWEALTH UNITED

Number	Title	Yr	NM
❑ CU-6001	We'll Cry Together	1969	25.00

GUEST STAR

Number	Title	Yr	NM
❑ GS-1911 [M]	Maxine Brown	1964	15.00

WAND

Number	Title	Yr	NM
❑ WD-684 [M]	Maxine Brown's Greatest Hits	1967	25.00
❑ WDS-684 [S]	Maxine Brown's Greatest Hits	1967	30.00
❑ WD-663 [M]	Spotlight on Maxine Brown	1965	30.00
❑ WDS-663 [S]	Spotlight on Maxine Brown	1965	40.00
❑ LP-656 [M]	The Fabulous Sound of Maxine Brown	1963	50.00
❑ WDS-656 [S]	The Fabulous Sound of Maxine Brown	1963	60.00
❑ DT-91012 [R]	The Fabulous Sound of Maxine Brown	196?	50.00
— Capitol Record Club edition			

BROWN, MAXINE (2)

CHART

Number	Title	Yr	NM
❑ 1012	Sugar Cane Country	1969	25.00

BROWN, MEL

ABC

Number	Title	Yr	NM
❑ AA-1103	Actor of Music	1978	15.00

ABC IMPULSE!

Number	Title	Yr	NM
❑ AS-9249 [Q]	Big Foot Country Girl	1974	18.00
❑ A-9180 [M]	Blues for We	1969	50.00
❑ AS-9180 [S]	Blues for We	1969	25.00
❑ A-9152 [M]	Chicken Fat	1967	30.00
❑ AS-9152 [S]	Chicken Fat	1967	25.00
❑ AS-9209	Fifth	1971	25.00
❑ AS-9186	I'd Rather Suck My Thumb	1970	25.00
❑ A-9169 [M]	The Wizard	1968	40.00
❑ AS-9169 [S]	The Wizard	1968	25.00

BLUESWAY

Number	Title	Yr	NM
❑ 6064	18 Pounds of Uncleaned Chittlins	1973	18.00

BROWN, NAPPY

BLACK TOP

Number	Title	Yr	NM
❑ BT-1039	Something Gonna Jump Out the Bushes	1987	18.00

ICHIBAN

Number	Title	Yr	NM
❑ ICH-1056	Apples and Lemons	1990	15.00

Number	Title	Yr	NM
KING SNAKE/ICHIBAN			
❑ ICH-9006	Aw! Shucks	1991	18.00
LANDSLIDE			
❑ LD1008	Tore Up	1984	18.00
MELTONE			
❑ 1502	Deep Sea Diver	1989	18.00
SAVOY			
❑ 14427	Nappy Brown	1977	15.00
❑ MG-14002 [M]	Nappy Brown Sings	1958	400.00
❑ MG-14025 [M]	The Right Time	1960	250.00
SAVOY JAZZ			
❑ SJL-1149	Don't Be Angry	1984	12.00

BROWN, OSCAR, JR.

Number	Title	Yr	NM
ATLANTIC			
❑ SD1649	Brother Where Are You	1973	18.00
❑ SD18106	Fresh	1974	15.00
❑ SD1629	Movin' On	1972	18.00
COLUMBIA			
❑ CL1774 [M]	Between Heaven and Hell	1962	30.00
—Red and black label with six "eye" logos			
❑ CS8574 [S]	Between Heaven and Hell	1962	30.00
—Red and black label with six "eye" logos			
❑ CL1873 [M]	In a New Mood	1963	25.00
—Red label, "Guaranteed High Fidelity" in black			
❑ CS8673 [S]	In a New Mood	1963	30.00
—Red label, "360 Sound Stereo" in black			
❑ CL2025 [M]	Oscar Brown Jr. Tells It Like It Is	1964	25.00
—Red label, "Guaranteed High Fidelity" in black			
❑ CS8825 [S]	Oscar Brown Jr. Tells It Like It Is	1964	30.00
—Red label, "360 Sound Stereo" in black			
❑ CL1577 [M]	Sin and Soul	1960	30.00
—Red and black label with six "eye" logos			
❑ CS8377 [S]	Sin and Soul	1960	30.00
—Red and black label with six "eye" logos			
FONTANA			
❑ MGF-27549 [M]	Finding a New Friend	1966	18.00
❑ SRF-67549 [S]	Finding a New Friend	1966	25.00
❑ MGF-27540 [M]	Mr. Oscar Brown Goes to Washington	1965	18.00
❑ SRF-67540 [S]	Mr. Oscar Brown Goes to Washington	1965	25.00

BROWN, PETE

Number	Title	Yr	NM
BETHLEHEM			
❑ BCP-1011 [10]	Peter the Great	1954	120.00
VERVE			
❑ MGV-8365 [M]	From the Heart	1958	50.00
❑ MGVS-6133 [S]	From the Heart	1960	40.00
❑ V-8365 [M]	From the Heart	1962	25.00
❑ V6 8365 [S]	From the Heart	1962	18.00

BROWN, PETE/JONAH JONES

Number	Title	Yr	NM
BETHLEHEM			
❑ BCP-4 [M]	Jazz Kaleidoscope	1957	80.00

BROWN, RAY

Number	Title	Yr	NM
BLUESWAY			
❑ BLS-6056	Hard Times	1971	18.00
CONCORD JAZZ			
❑ CJ-375	Bam Bam Bam	1989	15.00
❑ CJ-19	Brown's Bag	1976	15.00
❑ CJ-293	Don't Forget the Blues	1986	12.00
❑ CJ-213	Ray Brown 3	1982	12.00
❑ CJ-268	Soular Energy	1985	12.00
❑ CJ-102	The Ray Brown Trio Live at the Concord Jazz Festival	1979	15.00
❑ CJ-315	The Red Hot Ray Brown Trio	1987	12.00
CONTEMPORARY			
❑ C-7641	Something for Lester	1978	12.00
FANTASY			
❑ OJC-412	Something for Lester	1990	15.00
VERVE			
❑ MGV-8022 [M]	Bass Hit!	1957	120.00
—yellow label			
❑ V-8022 [M]	Bass Hit!	1961	25.00
❑ MGV-8390 [M]	Jazz Cello	1960	50.00
❑ V-8390 [M]	Jazz Cello	1961	25.00
❑ V-8580 [M]	Much in Common	1964	30.00
❑ V6-8580 [S]	Much in Common	1964	30.00
—With Milt Jackson			
❑ V-8615 [M]	Ray Brown/Milt Jackson	1965	30.00
❑ V6-8615 [S]	Ray Brown/Milt Jackson	1965	30.00
❑ V-8444 [M]	Ray Brown with the All Star Big Band Featuring Cannonball Adderley	1962	30.00
❑ V6-8444 [S]	Ray Brown with the All Star Big Band Featuring Cannonball Adderley	1962	30.00
❑ MGV-8290 [M]	This Is Ray Brown	1958	200.00
❑ V-8290 [M]	This Is Ray Brown	1961	100.00
❑ UMV-2117	This Is Ray Brown	198?	12.00
❑ VSP-10 [M]	Two for the Blues	1966	15.00
❑ VSPS-10 [S]	Two for the Blues	1966	18.00

BROWN, ROY

Number	Title	Yr	NM
BLUESWAY			
❑ BLS-6056	Hard Times	1973	30.00
❑ BLS-6019	The Blues Are Brown	1968	30.00
EPIC			
❑ E30473	Live at Monterey	1971	30.00
INTERMEDIA			
❑ QS-5027	Good Rockin' Tonight	198?	12.00
KING			
❑ KS-1130	Hard Luck Blues	1971	30.00
❑ 956 [M]	Roy Brown Sings 24 Hits	1966	50.00
❑ KS-956 [R]	Roy Brown Sings 24 Hits	1966	50.00

BROWN, ROY / WYNONIE HARRIS

Number	Title	Yr	NM
KING			
❑ 607 [M]	Battle of the Blues	1958	600.00
❑ 627 [M]	Battle of the Blues, Volume 2	1959	800.00

BROWN, ROY / WYNONIE HARRIS / EDDIE VINSON

Number	Title	Yr	NM
KING			
❑ 668 [M]	Battle of the Blues, Volume 4	1960	2500.00

BROWN, RUTH

Number	Title	Yr	NM
ATLANTIC			
❑ 1308 [M]	Last Date with Ruth Brown	1959	200.00
—Black label			
❑ 1308 [M]	Last Date with Ruth Brown	1961	50.00
—Red and purple label, "fan" logo in white			
❑ SD1308 [S]	Last Date with Ruth Brown	1959	300.00
—Green label			
❑ SD1308 [S]	Last Date with Ruth Brown	1961	60.00
—Blue and green label, "fan" logo in white			
❑ 8026 [M]	Miss Rhythm	1959	200.00
—Black label			
❑ 8026 [M]	Miss Rhythm	1960	150.00
—White "bullseye" label			
❑ 8026 [M]	Miss Rhythm	1961	50.00
—Red and purple label, "fan" logo in white			
❑ 8004 [M]	Ruth Brown	1957	200.00
—Black label			
❑ 8004 [M]	Ruth Brown	1960	150.00
—White "bullseye" label			
❑ 8004 [M]	Ruth Brown	1961	50.00
—Red and purple label, "fan" logo in white			
❑ 8080 [M]	The Best of Ruth Brown	1963	40.00
DOBRE			
❑ 1041	You Don't Know Me	1978	15.00
FANTASY			
❑ F-9662	Blues on Broadway	1989	15.00
❑ F-9661	Have a Good Time	1988	15.00
ICHIBAN			
❑ SPEG-4023	Brown, Black and Beautiful	198?	15.00
MAINSTREAM			
❑ 56034 [M]	Ruth Brown '65	1965	30.00
❑ S-6034 [S]	Ruth Brown '65	1965	30.00
❑ 369	Softly	1972	15.00
PHILIPS			
❑ PHM200028 [M]	Along Comes Ruth	1962	40.00
❑ PHS600028 [S]	Along Comes Ruth	1962	50.00
❑ PHM200055 [M]	Gospel Time	1962	30.00
❑ PHS600055 [S]	Gospel Time	1962	40.00
SKYE			
❑ SK-13	Black Is Brown and Brown Is Beautiful	1970	18.00

BROWN, TED

Number	Title	Yr	NM
CRISS CROSS			
❑ 1031	Free Spirit	1988	15.00
VANGUARD			
❑ VRS-8515 [M]	Free Wheeling	1956	500.00

BROWNE, JACKSON

Number	Title	Yr	NM
ASYLUM			
❑ SD5067	For Everyman	1973	15.00
❑ 5E-511	Hold Out	1979	12.00
❑ SD5051	Jackson Browne (Saturate Before Using)	1972	25.00
—Burlap cover, opens at top; white label with "Asylum Records" logo in a circle at top			
❑ SD5051	Jackson Browne (Saturate Before Using)	1972	15.00
—Burlap cover; "clouds" label			
❑ SD5051	Jackson Browne (Saturate Before Using)	1972	16.00
—Burlap cover, opens at right side; white label with "Asylum Records" logo in a circle at top			
❑ SD5051	Jackson Browne (Saturate Before Using)	1972	10.00
—Standard cover			
❑ 7E-1017	Late for the Sky	1974	15.00
❑ EQ-1017 [Q]	Late for the Sky	1974	50.00
❑ 60268	Lawyers in Love	1983	12.00
❑ 60457	Lives in the Balance	1986	12.00
❑ 6E-113	Running on Empty	1977	12.00
❑ 7E-1079	The Pretender	1976	15.00
❑ 6E-107	The Pretender	1977	12.00
—Reissue of 7E-1079			
ELEKTRA			
❑ 60830	World in Motion	1989	12.00
MOBILE FIDELITY			
❑ 1-055	The Pretender	1981	30.00
—Audiophile vinyl			
NINA MUSIC PUBLISHING			
❑ (no #)0 [B]	Songs by Jackson Browne	1967	2500.00
—Publisher's demo in plain cardboard jacket; three sides performed by Jackson Browne, one side by Steve Noonan; VG value 1000; VG+ value 1500			

BROWNS, THE

Number	Title	Yr	NM
RCA CAMDEN			
❑ CAL-2142 [M]	Big Ones from the Country	1967	15.00
❑ CAS-2142 [S]	Big Ones from the Country	1967	12.00
❑ CAL-885 [M]	I Heard the Bluebirds Sing	1965	15.00
❑ CAS-885 [S]	I Heard the Bluebirds Sing	1965	15.00
❑ CAS-2262	The Browns Sing a Harvest of Country Songs	1968	12.00
RCA VICTOR			
❑ LPM-2784 [M]	Grand Ole Opry Favorites	1963	18.00
❑ LSP-2784 [S]	Grand Ole Opry Favorites	1963	25.00
❑ LPM-1438 [M]	Jim Edward, Maxine and Bonnie Brown	1957	50.00
❑ LPM-2333 [M]	Our Favorite Folk Songs	1961	25.00
❑ LSP-2333 [S]	Our Favorite Folk Songs	1961	30.00
❑ LPM-3668 [M]	Our Kind of Country	1966	18.00
❑ LSP-3668 [S]	Our Kind of Country	1966	25.00
❑ LPM-2144 [M]	Sweet Sounds by the Browns	1959	30.00
❑ LSP-2144 [S]	Sweet Sounds by the Browns	1959	40.00
❑ LPM-3561 [M]	The Best of the Browns	1966	18.00
❑ LSP-3561 [S]	The Best of the Browns	1966	25.00
❑ ANL1-1083	The Best of the Browns	1975	12.00
❑ LPM-2260 [M]	The Browns Sing Their Hits	1960	25.00
❑ LSP-2260 [S]	The Browns Sing Their Hits	1960	30.00
❑ LPM-2345 [M]	The Little Brown Church Hymnal	1961	25.00
❑ LSP-2345 [S]	The Little Brown Church Hymnal	1961	30.00
❑ LPM-3798 [M]	The Old Country Church	1967	25.00
❑ LSP-3798 [S]	The Old Country Church	1967	18.00
❑ LPM-2860 [M]	This Young Land	1964	18.00
❑ LSP-2860 [S]	This Young Land	1964	25.00
❑ LPM-2987 [M]	Three Shades of Brown	1964	18.00
❑ LSP-2987 [S]	Three Shades of Brown	1964	25.00
❑ LPM-2174 [M]	Town and Country	1960	25.00
❑ LSP-2174 [S]	Town and Country	1960	30.00
❑ LPM-3423 [M]	When Love Is Gone	1965	18.00
❑ LSP-3423 [S]	When Love Is Gone	1965	25.00

BROWN'S FERRY FOUR, THE

Number	Title	Yr	NM
KING			
❑ 551 [M]	Sacred Songs	1957	80.00
❑ 590 [M]	Sacred Songs	1958	80.00
❑ 943	Wonderful Sacred Songs	1964	30.00

BROWNSVILLE STATION

Number	Title	Yr	NM
BIG TREE			
❑ BTS-2010	A Night on the Town	1972	15.00
❑ BT89510	Motor City Connection	1975	15.00
❑ BT89500	School Punks	1974	15.00
❑ BTS-2102	Yeah!	1973	15.00
EPIC			
❑ JE35606	Air Special	1978	16.00
❑ JE35606 [DJ]	Air Special	1978	25.00
—Orange vinyl promo			
PALLADIUM			
❑ P-1004	Brownsville Station	1970	30.00
PRIVATE STOCK			
❑ PS-2026	Brownsville Station	1977	12.00
WARNER BROS.			
❑ WS1888	No B.S.	1970	18.00

BRUBECK, DAVE

Number	Title	Yr	NM
ATLANTIC			
❑ SD1684	All the Things We Are	1976	15.00
❑ SD1660	Brother, The Great Spirit Made Us All	1974	15.00
❑ SD 2-317	The Art of Dave Brubeck: The Fantasy Years	1975	18.00
❑ SD1607	The Last Set at Newport	1972	15.00
❑ SD1606	Truth Is Fallen	1972	15.00
❑ SD1645	Two Generations of Brubeck	1974	15.00
❑ SD1641	We're All Together Again for the First Time	1973	15.00
BOOK-OF-THE-MONTH			
❑ 80-5547	Early Fantasies	1980	25.00
COLUMBIA			
❑ G30625	Adventures in Time	1971	18.00
❑ KG32761	All-Time Greatest Hits	1974	18.00
❑ CL932 [M]	American Jazz Festival at Newport '56	1956	50.00
—Red/black label with six "eye" logos			
❑ CL932 [M]	American Jazz Festival at Newport '56	1962	25.00
—Red "Guaranteed High Fidelity" label			

Number	Title	Yr	NM
❑ CL2348 [M]	Angel Eyes	1965	25.00
—Red “Guaranteed High Fidelity” label			
❑ CL2348 [M]	Angel Eyes	1966	15.00
—Red “360 Sound” label			
❑ CS9148 [S]	Angel Eyes	1965	30.00
—Red label, “360 Sound” in black			
❑ CS9148 [S]	Angel Eyes	1966	18.00
—Red label, “360 Sound” in white			
❑ CL2602 [M]	Anything Goes! Dave Brubeck Quartet Plays Cole Porter	1966	18.00
❑ CS9402 [S]	Anything Goes! Dave Brubeck Quartet Plays Cole Porter	1966	25.00
—Red “360 Sound” label			
❑ CS9402	Anything Goes! Dave Brubeck Quartet Plays Cole Porter	1971	15.00
—Orange label			
❑ PC9402	Anything Goes! Dave Brubeck Quartet Plays Cole Porter	1981	10.00
—Reissue with new prefix			
❑ PC37022	A Place in Time	1981	12.00
—Reissue of Odyssey LP			
❑ CL1466 [M]	Bernstein Plays Brubeck Plays Bernstein	1960	30.00
—Red/black label with six “eye” logos			
❑ CL1466 [M]	Bernstein Plays Brubeck Plays Bernstein	1962	18.00
—Red “Guaranteed High Fidelity” label			
❑ CL1466 [M]	Bernstein Plays Brubeck Plays Bernstein	1966	15.00
—Red “360 Sound” label			
❑ CS9749	Blues Roots	1969	18.00
—Red “360 Sound” label			
❑ CS9749	Blues Roots	1971	15.00
—Orange label			
❑ CL1998 [M]	Bossa Nova U.S.A.	1963	25.00
—Red “Guaranteed High Fidelity” label			
❑ CL1998 [M]	Bossa Nova U.S.A.	1966	15.00
—Red “360 Sound” label			
❑ CS8798 [S]	Bossa Nova U.S.A.	1963	30.00
—Red label, “360 Sound” in black			
❑ CS8798 [S]	Bossa Nova U.S.A.	1966	18.00
—Red label, “360 Sound” in white			
❑ CL1963 [M]	Brandenburg Gate Revisited	1963	25.00
—Red “Guaranteed High Fidelity” label			
❑ CL1963 [M]	Brandenburg Gate Revisited	1966	15.00
—Red “360 Sound” label			
❑ CS8763 [S]	Brandenburg Gate Revisited	1963	30.00
—Red label, “360 Sound” in black			
❑ CS8763 [S]	Brandenburg Gate Revisited	1966	18.00
—Red label, “360 Sound” in white			
❑ CL2695 [M]	Bravo Brubeck!	1967	25.00
❑ CS9495 [S]	Bravo Brubeck!	1967	18.00
—Red “360 Sound” label			
❑ CS9495	Bravo Brubeck!	1971	15.00
—Orange label			
❑ CL1553 [M]	Brubeck and Rushing	1961	30.00
—Red/black label with six “eye” logos			
❑ CL1553 [M]	Brubeck and Rushing	1962	18.00
—Red “Guaranteed High Fidelity” label			
❑ CL1553 [M]	Brubeck and Rushing	1966	15.00
—Red “360 Sound” label			
❑ CS8353 [S]	Brubeck and Rushing	1961	30.00
—Red/black label with six “eye” logos			
❑ CS8353 [S]	Brubeck and Rushing	1962	25.00
—Red label, “360 Sound” in black			
❑ CS8353 [S]	Brubeck and Rushing	1966	18.00
—Red label, “360 Sound” in white			
❑ KC32143	Brubeck at the Berlin Philharmonic	1973	15.00
❑ CS9897	Brubeck in Amsterdam	1969	18.00
—Red “360 Sound” label			
❑ CS9897	Brubeck in Amsterdam	1971	15.00
—Orange label			
❑ KG31298	Brubeck On Campus	1972	18.00
❑ CS8257 [S]	Brubeck Plays Bernstein Plays Brubeck	1960	30.00
—Red/black label with six “eye” logos			
❑ CS8257 [S]	Brubeck Plays Bernstein Plays Brubeck	1962	25.00
—Red label, “360 Sound” in black			
❑ CS8257 [S]	Brubeck Plays Bernstein Plays Brubeck	1966	18.00
—Red label, “360 Sound” in white			
❑ CS8257	Brubeck Plays Bernstein Plays Brubeck	1971	15.00
—Orange label			
❑ CL878 [M]	Brubeck Plays Brubeck	1956	60.00
—Red/black label with six “eye” logos			
❑ CL878 [M]	Brubeck Plays Brubeck	1962	25.00
—Red “Guaranteed High Fidelity” label			
❑ CL878 [M]	Brubeck Plays Brubeck	1966	15.00
—Red “360 Sound” label			
❑ CL622 [M]	Brubeck Time	1955	60.00
—Red/black label with six “eye” logos			
❑ CL622 [M]	Brubeck Time	1962	25.00
—Red “Guaranteed High Fidelity” label			
❑ CL622 [M]	Brubeck Time	1966	15.00
—Red “360 Sound” label			
❑ CS9704	Compadres	1968	18.00
—Red “360 Sound” label			
❑ CS9704	Compadres	1971	15.00
—Orange label			
❑ CL1775 [M]	Countdown -- Time in Outer Space	1962	30.00
—Red/black label with six “eye” logos			
❑ CL1775 [M]	Countdown -- Time in Outer Space	1962	18.00
—Red “Guaranteed High Fidelity” label			
❑ CL1775 [M]	Countdown -- Time in Outer Space	1966	15.00
—Red “360 Sound” label			
❑ CS8575 [S]	Countdown -- Time in Outer Space	1962	40.00
—Red/black label with six “eye” logos			
❑ CS8575 [S]	Countdown -- Time in Outer Space	1962	25.00
—Red label, “360 Sound” in black			
❑ CS8575 [S]	Countdown -- Time in Outer Space	1966	18.00
—Red label, “360 Sound” in white			
❑ CL590 [M]	Dave Brubeck at Storyville: 1954	1954	80.00
—Dark red label, gold print; released at the same time as 6330 and 6331			
❑ CL590 [M]	Dave Brubeck at Storyville: 1954	1955	50.00
—Red/black label with six “eye” logos			
❑ CL590 [M]	Dave Brubeck at Storyville: 1954	1962	25.00
—Red “Guaranteed High Fidelity” label			
❑ CL590 [M]	Dave Brubeck at Storyville: 1954	1966	15.00
—Red “360 Sound” label			
❑ CL6330 [10]	Dave Brubeck at Storyville: 1954, Volume 1	1954	80.00
❑ CL6331 [10]	Dave Brubeck at Storyville: 1954, Volume 2	1954	80.00
❑ CL2484 [M]	Dave Brubeck's Greatest Hits	1966	18.00
❑ CS9284 [S]	Dave Brubeck's Greatest Hits	1966	25.00
—Red “360 Sound” label			
❑ CS9284	Dave Brubeck's Greatest Hits	1971	15.00
—Orange label			
❑ PC9284	Dave Brubeck's Greatest Hits	1981	10.00
—Reissue with new prefix			
❑ CL1059 [M]	Dave Digs Disney	1957	40.00
—Red/black label with six “eye” logos			
❑ CL1059 [M]	Dave Digs Disney	1962	25.00
—Red “Guaranteed High Fidelity” label			
❑ CL1059 [M]	Dave Digs Disney	1966	15.00
—Red “360 Sound” label			
❑ CS8090 [S]	Dave Digs Disney	1959	50.00
—Red/black label with six “eye” logos			
❑ CS8090 [S]	Dave Digs Disney	1962	30.00
—Red label, “360 Sound” in black			
❑ CS8090 [S]	Dave Digs Disney	1966	18.00
—Red label, “360 Sound” in white			
❑ CL1347 [M]	Gone with the Wind	1959	40.00
—Red/black label with six “eye” logos			
❑ CL1347 [M]	Gone with the Wind	1962	25.00
—Red “Guaranteed High Fidelity” label			
❑ CL1347 [M]	Gone with the Wind	1966	15.00
—Red “360 Sound” label			
❑ CS8156 [S]	Gone with the Wind	1959	50.00
—Red/black label with six “eye” logos			
❑ CS8156 [S]	Gone with the Wind	1962	30.00
—Red label, “360 Sound” in black			
❑ CS8156 [S]	Gone with the Wind	1966	18.00
—Red label, “360 Sound” in white			
❑ CS8156	Gone with the Wind	1971	15.00
—Orange label			
❑ CG33666	Gone with the Wind/Time Out	1975	18.00
❑ CL2712 [M]	Jackpot	1967	25.00
❑ CS9512 [S]	Jackpot	1967	18.00
—Red “360 Sound” label			
❑ CL699 [M]	Jazz: Red Hot and Cool	1955	60.00
—Red/black label with six “eye” logos			
❑ CL699 [M]	Jazz: Red Hot and Cool	1962	25.00
—Red “Guaranteed High Fidelity” label			
❑ CL699 [M]	Jazz: Red Hot and Cool	1966	15.00
—Red “360 Sound” label			
❑ CS8645 [R]	Jazz: Red Hot and Cool	1963	18.00
—Red label, “360 Sound” in black			
❑ CS8645 [R]	Jazz: Red Hot and Cool	1966	15.00
—Red label, “360 Sound” in white			
❑ CL566 [M]	Jazz Goes to College	1954	80.00
—Dark red label, gold print; released at the same time as 6321 and 6322			
❑ CL566 [M]	Jazz Goes to College	1955	50.00
—Red/black label with six “eye” logos			
❑ CL566 [M]	Jazz Goes to College	1962	25.00
—Red “Guaranteed High Fidelity” label			
❑ CL566 [M]	Jazz Goes to College	1966	15.00
—Red “360 Sound” label			
❑ CL6321 [10]	Jazz Goes to College, Volume 1	1954	100.00
❑ CL6322 [10]	Jazz Goes to College, Volume 2	1954	100.00
❑ CL1034 [M]	Jazz Goes to Junior College	1957	40.00
—Red/black label with six “eye” logos			
❑ CL1034 [M]	Jazz Goes to Junior College	1962	25.00
—Red “Guaranteed High Fidelity” label			
❑ CL1034 [M]	Jazz Goes to Junior College	1966	15.00
—Red “360 Sound” label			
❑ CL1251 [M]	Jazz Impressions of Eurasia	1958	40.00
—Red/black label with six “eye” logos			
❑ CL1251 [M]	Jazz Impressions of Eurasia	1962	25.00
—Red “Guaranteed High Fidelity” label			
❑ CL1251 [M]	Jazz Impressions of Eurasia	1966	15.00
—Red “360 Sound” label			
❑ CS8058 [S]	Jazz Impressions of Eurasia	1959	50.00
—Red/black label with six “eye” logos			
❑ CS8058 [S]	Jazz Impressions of Eurasia	1962	30.00
—Red label, “360 Sound” in black			
❑ CS8058 [S]	Jazz Impressions of Eurasia	1966	18.00
—Red label, “360 Sound” in white			
❑ CL2212 [M]	Jazz Impressions of Japan	1964	25.00
—Red “Guaranteed High Fidelity” label			
❑ CL2212 [M]	Jazz Impressions of Japan	1966	15.00
—Red “360 Sound” label			
❑ CS9012 [S]	Jazz Impressions of Japan	1964	30.00
—Red label, “360 Sound” in black			
❑ CS9012 [S]	Jazz Impressions of Japan	1966	18.00
—Red label, “360 Sound” in white			
❑ CS9012	Jazz Impressions of Japan	1971	15.00
—Orange label			
❑ PC9012	Jazz Impressions of Japan	1981	10.00
—Reissue with new prefix			
❑ CL2275 [M]	Jazz Impressions of New York	1965	25.00
—Red “Guaranteed High Fidelity” label			
❑ CL2275 [M]	Jazz Impressions of New York	1966	15.00
—Red “360 Sound” label			
❑ CS9075 [S]	Jazz Impressions of New York	1965	30.00
—Red label, “360 Sound” in black			
❑ CS9075 [S]	Jazz Impressions of New York	1966	18.00
—Red label, “360 Sound” in white			
❑ CS9075	Jazz Impressions of New York	1971	15.00
—Orange label			
❑ PC9075	Jazz Impressions of New York	1981	10.00
—Reissue with new prefix			
❑ CL984 [M]	Jazz Impressions of the U.S.A.	1957	50.00
—Red/black label with six “eye” logos			
❑ CL984 [M]	Jazz Impressions of the U.S.A.	1962	25.00
—Red “Guaranteed High Fidelity” label			
❑ CL984 [M]	Jazz Impressions of the U.S.A.	1966	15.00
—Red “360 Sound” label			
❑ CL2437 [M]	My Favorite Things	1966	18.00
❑ CS9237 [S]	My Favorite Things	1966	25.00
—Red “360 Sound” label			
❑ CL1249 [M]	Newport 1958	1958	40.00
—Red/black label with six “eye” logos			
❑ CL1249 [M]	Newport 1958	1962	25.00
—Red “Guaranteed High Fidelity” label			
❑ CL1249 [M]	Newport 1958	1966	15.00
—Red “360 Sound” label			
❑ CS8082 [S]	Newport 1958	1959	50.00
—Red/black label with six “eye” logos			
❑ CS8082 [S]	Newport 1958	1962	30.00
—Red label, “360 Sound” in black			
❑ CS8082 [S]	Newport 1958	1966	18.00
—Red label, “360 Sound” in white			
❑ CL1439 [M]	Southern Scene	1960	30.00
—Red/black label with six “eye” logos			
❑ CL1439 [M]	Southern Scene	1962	18.00
—Red “Guaranteed High Fidelity” label			
❑ CL1439 [M]	Southern Scene	1966	15.00
—Red “360 Sound” label			
❑ CS8235 [S]	Southern Scene	1960	30.00
—Red/black label with six “eye” logos			
❑ CS8235 [S]	Southern Scene	1962	25.00
—Red label, “360 Sound” in black			
❑ CS8235 [S]	Southern Scene	1966	18.00
—Red label, “360 Sound” in white			
❑ CL2316 [M]	Take Five	1965	25.00
—Red “Guaranteed High Fidelity” label			
❑ CL2316 [M]	Take Five	1966	15.00
—Red “360 Sound” label			
❑ CS9116 [S]	Take Five	1965	30.00
—Red label, “360 Sound” in black			
❑ CS9116 [S]	Take Five	1966	18.00
—Red label, “360 Sound” in white			
❑ C2L26 [M]	The Dave Brubeck Quartet at Carnegie Hall	1963	30.00
—Red “Guaranteed High Fidelity” label			
❑ C2L26 [M]	The Dave Brubeck Quartet at Carnegie Hall	1966	18.00
—Red “360 Sound” label			

Number	Title	Yr	NM
❑ C2S826 [S]	The Dave Brubeck Quartet at Carnegie Hall	1963	30.00
—*Red label, "360 Sound" in black*			
❑ C2S826 [S]	The Dave Brubeck Quartet at Carnegie Hall	1966	25.00
—*Red label, "360 Sound" in white*			
❑ C2S826	The Dave Brubeck Quartet at Carnegie Hall	1971	18.00
—*Orange label*			
❑ CL1168 [M]	The Dave Brubeck Quartet in Europe	1958	40.00
—*Red/black label with six "eye" logos*			
❑ CL1168 [M]	The Dave Brubeck Quartet in Europe	1962	25.00
—*Red "Guaranteed High Fidelity" label*			
❑ CL1168 [M]	The Dave Brubeck Quartet in Europe	1966	15.00
—*Red "360 Sound" label*			
❑ CS9672	The Last Time We Saw Paris	1968	18.00
—*Red "360 Sound" label*			
❑ CS9572	The Last Time We Saw Paris	1971	15.00
—*Orange label*			
❑ CL1454 [M]	The Riddle	1960	30.00
—*Red/black label with six "eye" logos*			
❑ CL1454 [M]	The Riddle	1962	18.00
—*Red "Guaranteed High Fidelity" label*			
❑ CL1454 [M]	The Riddle	1966	15.00
—*Red "360 Sound" label*			
❑ CS8248 [S]	The Riddle	1960	30.00
—*Red/black label with six "eye" logos*			
❑ CS8248 [S]	The Riddle	1962	25.00
—*Red label, "360 Sound" in black*			
❑ CS8248 [S]	The Riddle	1966	18.00
—*Red label, "360 Sound" in white*			
❑ C30522	The Summit Sessions	1971	15.00
❑ CL2127 [M]	Time Changes	1964	25.00
—*Red "Guaranteed High Fidelity" label*			
❑ CL2127 [M]	Time Changes	1966	15.00
—*Red "360 Sound" label*			
❑ CS8927 [S]	Time Changes	1964	30.00
—*Red label, "360 Sound" in black*			
❑ CS8927 [S]	Time Changes	1966	18.00
—*Red label, "360 Sound" in white*			
❑ CL1690 [M]	Time Further Out	1961	30.00
—*Red/black label with six "eye" logos*			
❑ CL1690 [M]	Time Further Out	1962	18.00
—*Red "Guaranteed High Fidelity" label*			
❑ CL1690 [M]	Time Further Out	1966	15.00
—*Red "360 Sound" label*			
❑ CS8490 [S]	Time Further Out	1961	30.00
—*Red/black label with six "eye" logos*			
❑ CS8490 [S]	Time Further Out	1962	25.00
—*Red label, "360 Sound" in black*			
❑ CS8490 [S]	Time Further Out	1966	18.00
—*Red label, "360 Sound" in white*			
❑ CS8490	Time Further Out	1971	15.00
—*Orange label*			
❑ PC8490	Time Further Out	1981	10.00
—*Reissue with new prefix*			
❑ CL2512 [M]	Time In	1966	18.00
❑ CS9312 [S]	Time In	1966	25.00
—*Red "360 Sound" label*			
❑ CS9312	Time In	1971	15.00
—*Orange label*			
❑ PC9312	Time In	1981	10.00
—*Reissue with new prefix*			
❑ CL1397 [M]	Time Out	1960	30.00
—*Red/black label with six "eye" logos*			

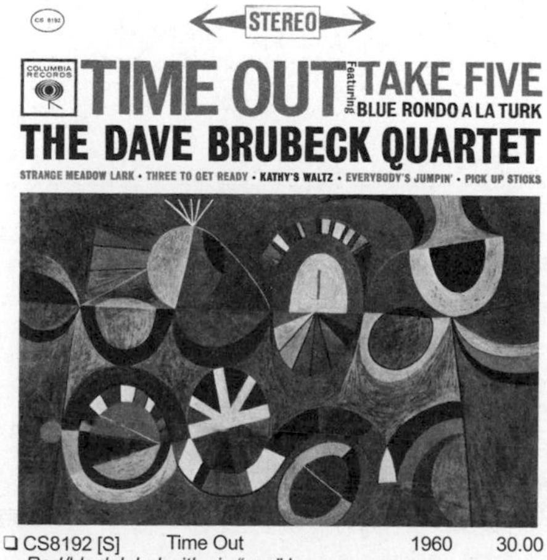

Number	Title	Yr	NM
❑ CS8192 [S]	Time Out	1960	30.00
—*Red/black label with six "eye" logos*			
❑ PC8192	Time Out	1981	10.00
—*Reissue with new prefix*			
❑ CS8192	Time Out	1995	30.00
—*Audiophile vinyl, distributed by Classic Records*			
❑ CL1397 [M]	Time Out Featuring "Take Five"	1962	18.00
—*Red "Guaranteed High Fidelity" label; beginning with this issue, the cover was altered to emphasize the hit*			
❑ CL1397 [M]	Time Out Featuring "Take Five"	1966	15.00
—*Red "360 Sound" label*			
❑ CS8192 [S]	Time Out Featuring "Take Five"	1962	25.00
—*Red label, "360 Sound" in black; beginning with this issue, the cover was altered to emphasize the hit*			
❑ CS8192 [S]	Time Out Featuring "Take Five"	1966	18.00
—*Red label, "360 Sound" in white*			
❑ CS8192	Time Out Featuring "Take Five"	1971	15.00
—*Orange label*			
❑ CL1609 [M]	Tonight Only!	1961	30.00
—*Red/black label with six "eye" logos*			
❑ CL1609 [M]	Tonight Only!	1962	18.00
—*Red "Guaranteed High Fidelity" label*			
❑ CL1609 [M]	Tonight Only!	1966	15.00
—*Red "360 Sound" label*			
❑ CS8409 [S]	Tonight Only!	1961	30.00
—*Red/black label with six "eye" logos*			
❑ CS8409 [S]	Tonight Only!	1962	25.00
—*Red label, "360 Sound" in black*			
❑ CS8409 [S]	Tonight Only!	1966	18.00
—*Red label, "360 Sound" in white*			

COLUMBIA JAZZ MASTERPIECES

Number	Title	Yr	NM
❑ CJ40627	Gone with the Wind	1987	12.00
❑ CJ45149	Jazz Goes to College	1989	12.00
❑ CJ40455	The Dave Brubeck Quartet Plays Music from West Side Story and Other Shows and Films	1987	12.00
❑ CJ40585	Time Out	1987	12.00

COLUMBIA LIMITED EDITION

Number	Title	Yr	NM
❑ LE10013	Gone with the Wind	197?	12.00

CONCORD JAZZ

Number	Title	Yr	NM
❑ CJ-103	Back Home	1979	12.00
❑ CJ-317	Blue Rondo	1987	12.00
❑ CJ-198	Concord on a Summer Night	1982	12.00
❑ CJ-259	For Iola	1985	12.00
❑ CJ-353	Moscow Night	1988	12.00
❑ CJ-178	Paper Moon	1982	12.00
❑ CJ-299	Reflections	1986	12.00
❑ CJ-129	Tritonis	1980	12.00

CROWN

Number	Title	Yr	NM
❑ CLP5470 [M]	Dave Brubeck and the George Nielson Quartet	196?	18.00
❑ CLP-5406 [M]	The Greats	196?	18.00

DECCA

Number	Title	Yr	NM
❑ DL710181	Brubeck/Mulligan/Cincinnati	1971	15.00
❑ DL710175	The Gates of Justice	1969	15.00
❑ DXSA7202	The Light in the Wilderness	1968	18.00
—*Records are individually numbered "DL 710,155" and "DL 710,156"*			

DIRECT DISK

Number	Title	Yr	NM
❑ 106	A Cut Above	1979	30.00

FANTASY

Number	Title	Yr	NM
❑ 3249 [M]	Brubeck & Desmond at Wilshire-Ebell	1957	100.00
—*Dark red vinyl*			
❑ 3249 [M]	Brubeck & Desmond at Wilshire-Ebell	195?	60.00
—*Black vinyl, red label, non-flexible vinyl*			
❑ 3249 [M]	Brubeck & Desmond at Wilshire-Ebell	196?	40.00
—*Black vinyl, red label, flexible vinyl*			
❑ 3301 [M]	Brubeck A La Mode	1960	60.00
—*Red vinyl*			
❑ 3301 [M]	Brubeck A La Mode	1960	40.00
—*Black vinyl, red label, non-flexible vinyl*			
❑ 3301 [M]	Brubeck A La Mode	196?	30.00
—*Black vinyl, red label, flexible vinyl*			
❑ 8047 [S]	Brubeck A La Mode	1962	50.00
—*Blue vinyl*			
❑ 8047 [S]	Brubeck A La Mode	196?	30.00
—*Black vinyl, blue label, non-flexible vinyl*			
❑ 8047 [S]	Brubeck A La Mode	196?	25.00
—*Black vinyl, blue label, flexible vinyl*			
❑ OJC-200	Brubeck A La Mode	1985	12.00
❑ 8095 [S]	Brubeck and Desmond at Wilshire-Ebell	1962	50.00
—*Blue vinyl*			
❑ 8095 [S]	Brubeck and Desmond at Wilshire-Ebell	1962	30.00
—*Black vinyl, blue label, non-flexible vinyl*			
❑ 8095 [S]	Brubeck and Desmond at Wilshire-Ebell	196?	25.00
—*Black vinyl, blue label, flexible vinyl*			
❑ 3229 [M]	Brubeck-Desmond	1956	100.00
—*Dark red vinyl; reissue of 3-5*			
❑ 3229 [M]	Brubeck-Desmond	195?	60.00
—*Black vinyl, red label, non-flexible vinyl*			
❑ 3229 [M]	Brubeck-Desmond	196?	40.00
—*Black vinyl, red label, flexible vinyl*			
❑ 8092 [R]	Brubeck-Desmond	1962	40.00
—*Blue vinyl*			
❑ 8092 [R]	Brubeck-Desmond	1962	25.00
—*Black vinyl, blue label, non-flexible vinyl*			
❑ 8092 [R]	Brubeck-Desmond	196?	18.00
—*Black vinyl, blue label, flexible vinyl*			
❑ 24727	Brubeck-Desmond	1982	18.00
❑ 3240 [M]	Brubeck Desmond: Jazz at Storyville	1957	100.00
—*Dark red vinyl; reissue of 3-8*			
❑ 3240 [M]	Brubeck Desmond: Jazz at Storyville	195?	60.00
—*Black vinyl, red label, non-flexible vinyl*			
❑ 3240 [M]	Brubeck Desmond: Jazz at Storyville	196?	40.00
—*Black vinyl, red label, flexible vinyl*			
❑ 3332 [M]	Brubeck Tjader	1962	60.00
—*Red vinyl*			
❑ 3332 [M]	Brubeck Tjader	1962	40.00
—*Black vinyl, red label, non-flexible vinyl*			
❑ 3332 [M]	Brubeck Tjader	196?	30.00
—*Black vinyl, red label, flexible vinyl*			
❑ 8074 [R]	Brubeck Tjader	1962	40.00
—*Blue vinyl*			
❑ 8074 [R]	Brubeck Tjader	1962	25.00
—*Black vinyl, blue label, non-flexible vinyl*			
❑ 8074 [R]	Brubeck Tjader	196?	18.00
—*Black vinyl, blue label, flexible vinyl*			
❑ 3-3 [10]	Dave Brubeck Octet	1951	150.00
❑ 3239 [M]	Dave Brubeck Octet	1956	100.00
—*Dark red vinyl; reissue of 3-3*			
❑ 3239 [M]	Dave Brubeck Octet	195?	60.00
—*Black vinyl, red label, non-flexible vinyl*			
❑ 3239 [M]	Dave Brubeck Octet	196?	40.00
—*Black vinyl, red label, flexible vinyl*			
❑ 8094 [R]	Dave Brubeck Octet	1962	40.00
—*Blue vinyl*			
❑ 8094 [R]	Dave Brubeck Octet	1962	25.00
—*Black vinyl, blue label, non-flexible vinyl*			
❑ 8094 [R]	Dave Brubeck Octet	196?	18.00
—*Black vinyl, blue label, flexible vinyl*			
❑ 3259 [M]	Dave Brubeck Plays and Plays and Plays and Plays and…	1958	60.00
—*Red vinyl*			
❑ 3259 [M]	Dave Brubeck Plays and Plays and Plays and Plays and…	195?	40.00
—*Black vinyl, red label, non-flexible vinyl*			
❑ 3259 [M]	Dave Brubeck Plays and Plays and Plays and Plays and…	196?	30.00
—*Black vinyl, red label, flexible vinyl*			
❑ 3230 [M]	Dave Brubeck Quartet	1956	100.00
—*Dark red vinyl; reissue of 3-7*			
❑ 3230 [M]	Dave Brubeck Quartet	195?	60.00
—*Black vinyl, red label, non-flexible vinyl*			
❑ 3230 [M]	Dave Brubeck Quartet	196?	40.00
—*Black vinyl, red label, flexible vinyl*			
❑ 8093 [R]	Dave Brubeck Quartet	1962	40.00
—*Blue vinyl*			
❑ 8093 [R]	Dave Brubeck Quartet	196?	25.00
—*Black vinyl, blue label, non-flexible vinyl*			
❑ 8093 [R]	Dave Brubeck Quartet	196?	18.00
—*Black vinyl, blue label, flexible vinyl*			
❑ 3-5 [10]	Dave Brubeck Quartet with Paul Desmond	1952	150.00
❑ 3-7 [10]	Dave Brubeck Quartet with Paul Desmond	1952	150.00
❑ 3-1 [10]	Dave Brubeck Trio	1951	150.00
❑ 3-2 [10]	Dave Brubeck Trio	1951	150.00
❑ 3-4 [10]	Dave Brubeck Trio	1952	150.00
❑ 3204 [M]	Dave Brubeck Trio	1956	100.00
—*Dark red vinyl; reissue of 3-1*			
❑ 3204 [M]	Dave Brubeck Trio	195?	60.00
—*Black vinyl, red label, non-flexible vinyl*			
❑ 3204 [M]	Dave Brubeck Trio	196?	40.00
—*Black vinyl, red label, flexible vinyl*			
❑ 3205 [M]	Dave Brubeck Trio: Distinctive Rhythm Instrumentals	1956	100.00
—*Dark red vinyl; reissue of 3-2*			
❑ 3205 [M]	Dave Brubeck Trio: Distinctive Rhythm Instrumentals	195?	60.00
—*Black vinyl, red label, non-flexible vinyl*			
❑ 3205 [M]	Dave Brubeck Trio: Distinctive Rhythm Instrumentals	196?	40.00
—*Black vinyl, red label, flexible vinyl*			
❑ 3331 [M]	Dave Brubeck Trio Featuring Cal Tjader	1962	60.00
—*Red vinyl*			
❑ 3331 [M]	Dave Brubeck Trio Featuring Cal Tjader	1962	40.00
—*Black vinyl, red label, non-flexible vinyl*			
❑ 3331 [M]	Dave Brubeck Trio Featuring Cal Tjader	196?	30.00
—*Black vinyl, red label, flexible vinyl*			
❑ 8073 [R]	Dave Brubeck Trio Featuring Cal Tjader	1962	40.00
—*Blue vinyl*			
❑ 8073 [R]	Dave Brubeck Trio Featuring Cal Tjader	1962	25.00
—*Black vinyl, blue label, non-flexible vinyl*			

Number	Title	Yr	NM
❏ 8073 [R]	Dave Brubeck Trio Featuring Cal Tjader	196?	18.00
—Black vinyl, blue label, flexible vinyl			
❏ MPF-4528	Greatest Hits from the Fantasy Years	1987	12.00
❏ 3-11 [10]	Jazz at Oberlin	1953	200.00
—Red vinyl			
❏ 3245 [M]	Jazz at Oberlin	1957	100.00
—Dark red vinyl; reissue of 3-11			
❏ 3245 [M]	Jazz at Oberlin	195?	60.00
—Black vinyl, red label, non-flexible vinyl			
❏ 3245 [M]	Jazz at Oberlin	196?	40.00
—Black vinyl, red label, flexible vinyl			
❏ 8069 [R]	Jazz at Oberlin	1962	40.00
—Blue vinyl			
❏ 8069 [R]	Jazz at Oberlin	196?	25.00
—Black vinyl, blue label, non-flexible vinyl			
❏ 8069 [R]	Jazz at Oberlin	196?	18.00
—Black vinyl, blue label, flexible vinyl			
❏ OJC-046	Jazz at Oberlin	198?	12.00
—Reissue of 3245			
❏ 3-11 [10]	Jazz at Oberlin	1953	100.00
—Black vinyl			
❏ 3-8 [10]	Jazz at Storyville	1953	150.00
❏ 8080 [R]	Jazz at Storyville	1962	40.00
—Blue vinyl			
❏ 8080 [R]	Jazz at Storyville	1962	25.00
—Black vinyl, blue label, non-flexible vinyl			
❏ 8080 [R]	Jazz at Storyville	196?	18.00
—Black vinyl, blue label, flexible vinyl			
❏ 3-10 [10]	Jazz at the Blackhawk	1953	150.00
❏ 3210 [M]	Jazz at the Blackhawk	1956	100.00
—Dark red vinyl; reissue of 3-10			
❏ 3210 [M]	Jazz at the Blackhawk	195?	60.00
—Black vinyl, red label, non-flexible vinyl			
❏ 3210 [M]	Jazz at the Blackhawk	196?	40.00
—Black vinyl, red label, flexible vinyl			
❏ 3-13 [10]	Jazz at the College of the Pacific	1954	150.00
❏ 3223 [M]	Jazz at the College of the Pacific	1956	100.00
—Dark red vinyl; reissue of 3 13			
❏ 3223 [M]	Jazz at the College of the Pacific	195?	60.00
—Black vinyl, red label, non-flexible vinyl			
❏ 3223 [M]	Jazz at the College of the Pacific	196?	40.00
—Black vinyl, red label, flexible vinyl			
❏ 8078 [R]	Jazz at the College of the Pacific	1962	40.00
—Blue vinyl			
❏ 8078 [R]	Jazz at the College of the Pacific	196?	25.00
—Black vinyl, blue label, non-flexible vinyl			
❏ 8078 [R]	Jazz at the College of the Pacific	196?	18.00
—Black vinyl, blue label, flexible vinyl			
❏ OJC-047	Jazz at the College of the Pacific	198?	12.00
—Reissue of 3223			
❏ OJC-236	Near Myth	1986	12.00
—Reissue of Fantasy 3319			
❏ 3319 [M]	Near-Myth	1961	60.00
—Red vinyl			
❏ 3319 [M]	Near-Myth	1961	40.00
—Black vinyl, red label, non-flexible vinyl			
❏ 3319 [M]	Near-Myth	196?	30.00
—Black vinyl, red label, flexible vinyl			
❏ 8063 [S]	Near-Myth	1962	50.00
—Blue vinyl			
❏ 8063 [S]	Near-Myth	196?	30.00
—Black vinyl, blue label, non-flexible vinyl			
❏ 8063 [S]	Near-Myth	196?	25.00
—Black vinyl, blue label, flexible vinyl			
❏ 3-16 [10]	Old Sounds from San Francisco	1954	250.00
—Red or purple vinyl			
❏ 3-20 [10]	Paul and Dave's Jazz Interwoven	1955	150.00
❏ 3268 [M]	Re-Union	1958	60.00
—Red vinyl			
❏ 3268 [M]	Re-Union	195?	40.00
—Black vinyl, red label, non-flexible vinyl			
❏ 3268 [M]	Re-Union	196?	30.00
—Black vinyl, red label, flexible vinyl			
❏ 8007 [S]	Re-Union	1962	50.00
—Blue vinyl			
❏ 8007 [S]	Re-Union	196?	30.00
—Black vinyl, blue label, non-flexible vinyl			
❏ 8007 [S]	Re-Union	196?	25.00
—Black vinyl, blue label, flexible vinyl			
❏ OJC-150	Re-Union	198?	12.00
❏ 24728	Stardust	198?	18.00
❏ OJC-101	The Dave Brubeck Octet	198?	12.00
—Reissue of Fantasy 3239			
❏ 24726	The Dave Brubeck Trio	198?	18.00
❏ 3298 [M]	Two Knights at the Black Hawk	1959	60.00
—Red vinyl			
❏ 3298 [M]	Two Knights at the Black Hawk	1959	40.00
—Black vinyl, red label, non-flexible vinyl			

Number	Title	Yr	NM
❏ 3298 [M]	Two Knights at the Black Hawk	196?	30.00
—Black vinyl, red label, flexible vinyl			
❏ 8081 [R]	Two Knights at the Blackhawk	1962	40.00
—Blue vinyl			
❏ 8081 [R]	Two Knights at the Blackhawk	1962	25.00
—Black vinyl, blue label, non-flexible vinyl			
❏ 8081 [R]	Two Knights at the Blackhawk	196?	18.00
—Black vinyl, blue label, flexible vinyl			

HARMONY

❏ HS11336	Gone with the Wind	1969	15.00
❏ HS11253	Instant Brubeck	1968	15.00

HORIZON

❏ SP-703	1975: The Duets	1975	15.00
❏ SP-714	The Dave Brubeck Quartet 25th Anniversary	1976	15.00

JAZZTONE

❏ J-1272 [M]	Best of Brubeck	195?	40.00

MOBILE FIDELITY

❏ 1-216	We're All Together Again for the First Time	1994	60.00
—Audiophile vinyl			

MOON

❏ 028	St. Louis Blues	1992	25.00

ODYSSEY

❏ 32160248	A Place in Time	1968	15.00

TOMATO

❏ 7018	The New Brubeck Quartet at Montreux	1978	15.00

BRUCE, LENNY

BIZARRE

❏ 2XS6329	The Berkeley Concert	1969	30.00

DOUGLAS

❏ 788 [B]	The Essential Lenny Bruce Politics	1968	30.00
❏ 2 [B]	To Is a Preposition, Come Is a Verb	196?	30.00
❏ Z30872	What I Was Arrested For	1971	18.00
—Reissue of 2			

FANTASY

❏ 7007 [M]	I Am Not a Nut, Elect Me	1960	100.00
—Opaque, non-flexible red vinyl			
❏ 7007 [M]	I Am Not a Nut, Elect Me	1960	40.00
—Non-flexible black vinyl			
❏ 7007 [M]	I Am Not a Nut, Elect Me	1962	40.00
—Translucent, flexible red vinyl			
❏ 7007 [M]	I Am Not a Nut, Elect Me	1962	25.00
—Flexible black vinyl			
❏ 7001 [M]	Interviews of Our Times	1959	100.00
—Opaque, non-flexible red vinyl; tan cover with Lenny Bruce's name blacked out throughout the back			
❏ 7001 [M]	Interviews of Our Times	1959	40.00
—Non-flexible black vinyl; cover changed to blue tint			
❏ 7001 [M]	Interviews of Our Times	1962	40.00
—Translucent, flexible red vinyl			
❏ 7001 [M]	Interviews of Our Times	1962	25.00
—Flexible black vinyl			
❏ 7011 [M]	Lenny Bruce, American	1961	100.00
—Opaque, non-flexible red vinyl			
❏ 7011 [M]	Lenny Bruce, American	1961	40.00
—Non-flexible black vinyl			
❏ 7011 [M]	Lenny Bruce, American	1962	40.00
—Translucent, flexible red vinyl			
❏ 7011 [M]	Lenny Bruce, American	1962	25.00
—Flexible black vinyl			
❏ 34201	Lenny Bruce at the Curran Theater	1971	40.00
❏ 7017	Thank You Masked Man	1971	18.00
❏ 7012 [M]	The Best of Lenny Bruce	1962	50.00
—Red vinyl			
❏ 7012 [M]	The Best of Lenny Bruce	1962	25.00
—Black vinyl			
❏ FP-1 [DJ]	The Promo Album	196?	200.00
—Promo-only compilation of material from albums 7001, 7003, 7007 and 7011			
❏ 79003	The Real Lenny Bruce	1975	25.00
❏ 7003 [M]	The Sick Humor of Lenny Bruce	1959	100.00
—Opaque, non-flexible red vinyl			
❏ 7003 [M]	The Sick Humor of Lenny Bruce	1959	40.00
—Non-flexible black vinyl			
❏ 7003 [M]	The Sick Humor of Lenny Bruce	1962	40.00
—Translucent, flexible red vinyl			
❏ 7003 [M]	The Sick Humor of Lenny Bruce	1962	25.00
—Flexible black vinyl			

LENNY BRUCE

❏ LB-3001/2 [M]	Lenny Bruce Is Out Again	196?	300.00
—Privately pressed version with white labels and Lenny's address on cover			
❏ LB-9001/2 [10]	Warning: Sale of This Album...	1962	500.00

Number	Title	Yr	NM
—Privately pressed LP with routines used as evidence in Lenny's obscenity trial			

PHILLIES

❏ PHLP-4010 [M]	Lenny Bruce Is Out Again	1966	100.00
—Reissue of Lenny Bruce 3001/2			

UNITED ARTISTS

❏ UAS9800	Lenny Bruce/Carnegie Hall	1972	30.00
❏ UAL3580 [M]	The Midnight Concert	1967	30.00
❏ UAS6794	The Midnight Concert	1972	18.00
—Reissue of 6580			
❏ UAS6580	The Midnight Concert	1967	25.00

WARNER/SPECTOR

❏ SP9101	The Law, the Language and Lenny Bruce	1975	18.00

BRUEL, MAX

EMARCY

❏ MG-36062 [M]	Cool Bruel	1955	60.00

BRUNIS, GEORG

COMMODORE

❏ FL-20008 [10]	King of the Tailgate Trombone	1950	80.00
❏ DL30015 [M]	King of the Tailgate Trombone	1959	40.00

JAZZOLOGY

❏ J-012	Georg Brunis and His Rhythm Kings	1965	18.00

JOLLY ROGER

❏ 5024 [10]	Georg Brunis and the New Orleans Rhythm Kings	1954	50.00

RIVERSIDE

❏ RLP-1024 [10]	Georg Brunis and the Original New Orleans Rhythm Kings	1954	80.00

BRUNSON, FRANKIE

GEE

❏ GLP-704 [M]	Big Daddy's Blues	1959	80.00
❏ SGLP-704 [S]	Big Daddy's Blues	1959	120.00

BRUNSON, TYRONE

BELIEVE IN A DREAM

❏ FZ39197	Fresh	1984	12.00

MCA

❏ 5968	Love Triangle	1987	12.00
❏ 5810	The Method	1986	12.00

BRUSH ARBOR

CAPITOL

❏ ST-11158	Brush Arbor	1973	18.00
❏ ST-11209	Brush Arbor 2	1973	18.00

LIGHT

❏ LS-5873	Live	1985	15.00

MONUMENT

❏ KZ34251	Page One	1977	18.00
❏ 6637	Page One	1977	15.00
—Reissue of 34251			
❏ 7613	Straight	1978	15.00

MYRRH

❏ MSB-6664	Hero	198?	15.00
❏ MSB-6624	Hide Away	1979	15.00

BRUTE FORCE

B.T. PUPPY

❏ BTPS-1015	Extemporaneous	1971	300.00

COLUMBIA

❏ CL2615 [M]	I, Brute Force -- Confections of Love	1967	30.00
❏ CS9415 [S]	I, Brute Force -- Confections of Love	1967	25.00

EMBRYO

❏ 522	Brute Force	1970	25.00
—Different band			

BRYAN, JOY

CONTEMPORARY

❏ M-3604 [M]	Make the Man Love Me	1961	40.00
❏ S-7604 [S]	Make the Man Love Me	1961	50.00

MODE

❏ LP-108 [M]	Joy Bryan Sings	1957	80.00

BRYANT, BOBBY

CADET

❏ LP-795 [M]	Ain't Doing Too B-A-D, Bad	1967	25.00
❏ LPS-795 [S]	Ain't Doing Too B-A-D, Bad	1967	18.00
❏ CA-50011	Swahili Strut	1972	15.00

VEE JAY

❏ VJS-3059	Big Band Blues	1974	25.00

WORLD PACIFIC

❏ ST-20159	The Jazz Excursion Into "Hair	1969	18.00

Number	Title	Yr	NM

BRYANT, BOUDLEAUX

MONUMENT
❏ MLP-8007 [M]	Boudleaux Bryant's Best Sellers	1963	25.00
❏ SLP-18007 [S]	Boudleaux Bryant's Best Sellers	1963	30.00

BRYANT, CLORA

MODE
❏ LP-106 [M]	Gal with a Horn	1957	150.00

BRYANT, JIMMY

CAPITOL
❏ T1314 [M]	Country Cabin Jazz	1960	80.00
❏ ST1314 [S]	Country Cabin Jazz	1960	100.00

DOLTON
❏ BLP-16505 [M]	Play Country Guitar with Jimmy Bryant	196?	30.00
❏ BST-17505 [S]	Play Country Guitar with Jimmy Bryant	196?	30.00

IMPERIAL
❏ LP-9310 [M]	Bryant's Back in Town	1966	25.00
❏ LP-12310 [S]	Bryant's Back in Town	1966	30.00
❏ LP-9315 [M]	Laughing Guitar, Crying Guitar	1966	25.00
❏ LP-12315 [S]	Laughing Guitar, Crying Guitar	1966	30.00
❏ LP-9360 [M]	That Fastest Guitar in the Country	1967	30.00
❏ LP-12360 [S]	That Fastest Guitar in the Country	1967	25.00
❏ LP-9338 [M]	We Are Young	1967	25.00
❏ LP-12338 [S]	We Are Young	1967	30.00

BRYANT, PAUL

FANTASY
❏ 3363 [M]	Groove Time	1964	25.00
❏ 8363 [S]	Groove Time	1964	30.00
❏ 3357 [M]	Something's Happening	1963	25.00
❏ 8357 [S]	Something's Happening	1963	30.00

PACIFIC JAZZ
❏ PJ-12 [M]	Burnin'	1961	40.00

BRYANT, RAY

ATLANTIC
❏ SD1626	Alone at Montreux	1972	15.00
❏ SD1564	MCMLXX	1970	18.00

CADET
❏ LP-767 [M]	Gotta Travel On	1966	18.00
❏ LPS-767 [S]	Gotta Travel On	1966	25.00
❏ 50052	In the Cut	1974	15.00
❏ 50038	It Was a Very Good Year	1973	18.00
❏ LP-778 [M]	Lonesome Traveler	1966	18.00
❏ LPS-778 [S]	Lonesome Traveler	1966	25.00
❏ LP-781 [M]	Slow Freight	1967	18.00
❏ LPS-781 [S]	Slow Freight	1967	25.00
❏ LPS-830	Sound Ray	1969	18.00
❏ LP-801 [M]	Take a Bryant Step	1967	25.00
❏ LPS-801 [S]	Take a Bryant Step	1967	18.00
❏ LP-793 [M]	The Ray Bryant Touch	1967	25.00
❏ LPS-793 [S]	The Ray Bryant Touch	1967	18.00
❏ LPS-818	Up Above the Rock	1968	18.00

CLASSIC JAZZ
❏ 130	Hot Turkey	198?	12.00

COLUMBIA
❏ CL1633 [M]	Con Alma	1961	25.00
❏ CS8433 [S]	Con Alma	1961	30.00
❏ CL1746 [M]	Dancing the Big Twist	1962	25.00
❏ CS8546 [S]	Dancing the Big Twist	1962	30.00
❏ CL1867 [M]	Hollywood Jazz Beat	1962	25.00
❏ CS8667 [S]	Hollywood Jazz Beat	1962	30.00
❏ CL1449 [M]	Little Susie	1960	25.00
❏ CS8244 [S]	Little Susie	1960	30.00
❏ CL1476 [M]	The Madison Time	1960	30.00
❏ CS8276 [S]	The Madison Time	1960	30.00

COLUMBIA JAZZ MASTERPIECES
❏ CJ44058	Con Alma	1988	12.00

EMARCY
❏ 836368-1	Golden Earrings	1989	15.00
❏ 832235-1	Ray Bryant Plays Basie and Ellington	1987	15.00
❏ 832589-1	The Ray Bryant Trio Today	1988	15.00

EPIC
❏ LN3279 [M]	Ray Bryant Trio	1956	70.00

FANTASY
❏ OJC-213	Alone with the Blues	1987	12.00
—Reissue			
❏ OJC-371	Montreux '77	1989	12.00
—Reissue of Pablo Live 2308 201			

NEW JAZZ
❏ NJLP-8213 [M]	Alone with the Blues	1959	50.00
—Purple label			
❏ NJLP-8213 [M]	Alone with the Blues	1965	30.00
—Blue label with trident logo			
❏ NJLP-8227 [M]	Ray Bryant Trio	1959	150.00
—Purple label; reissue of Prestige 7098			
❏ NJLP-8227 [M]	Ray Bryant Trio	1965	30.00
—Blue label with trident logo			

PABLO
❏ 2310820	All Blues	1978	12.00
❏ 2310764	Here's Ray Bryant	1976	12.00
❏ 2310860	Potpourri	1981	12.00
❏ 2310798	Solo Flight	1977	12.00
❏ 2405402	The Best of Ray Bryant	198?	12.00

PABLO LIVE
❏ 2308201	Montreux '77	1977	12.00

PRESTIGE
❏ PRLP-7837	Alone with the Blues	1971	18.00
—Reissue of New Jazz 8213			
❏ PRT-7837	Alone with the Blues	1973	15.00
—Reissue; "Distributed by Fantasy Records, Berkeley, California" on label			
❏ 24038	Me and the Blues	1973	18.00
❏ PRLP-7098 [M]	Ray Bryant Trio	1957	500.00

SIGNATURE
❏ SM-6008 [M]	Ray Bryant Plays	1960	500.00
❏ SS-6008 [S]	Ray Bryant Plays	1960	250.00

SUE
❏ LP-1032 [M]	Cold Turkey	1964	40.00
❏ LPS-1032 [S]	Cold Turkey	1964	50.00
❏ LP-1016 [M]	Groove House	1963	40.00
❏ LPS-1016 [S]	Groove House	1963	50.00
❏ LP-1019 [M]	Live at Basin Street	1964	40.00
❏ LPS-1019 [S]	Live at Basin Street	1964	50.00
❏ STLP-1036 [M]	Ray Bryant Soul	1965	40.00
❏ STLPS-1036 [S]	Ray Bryant Soul	1965	50.00

BRYANT, RUSTY

DOT
❏ DLP-3006 [M]	All Night Long	1956	40.00
—Maroon label			
❏ DLP-3353 [M]	America's Greatest Jazz	1961	18.00
❏ DLP-25353 [S]	America's Greatest Jazz	1961	25.00
❏ DLP-3079 [M]	Rusty Bryant Plays Jazz	1957	40.00

FANTASY
❏ OJC-331	Rusty Bryant Returns	1988	12.00
—Reissue of Prestige 7626			

PRESTIGE
❏ 10013	Fire Eater	1972	15.00
❏ 10073	For the Good Times	1974	15.00
❏ 10053	Friday Night Funk	1973	15.00
❏ PRST-7735	Night Train Now!	1970	15.00
❏ PRST-7626	Rusty Bryant Returns	1969	15.00
❏ PRST-7798	Soul Liberation	1971	15.00
❏ 10085	Until It's Time for You to Go	1974	15.00
❏ 10037	Wild Fire	1972	15.00

BRYNNER, YUL

VANGUARD
❏ VRS-9256 [M]	The Gypsy and I	1967	30.00
❏ VSD-79256 [S]	The Gypsy and I	1967	40.00

BRYSON, PEABO, AND ROBERTA FLACK

ATLANTIC
❏ SD7000	Live and More	1980	15.00
—As "Roberta Flack and Peabo Bryson"			

CAPITOL
❏ ST-12284	Born to Love	1983	10.00

BRYSON, PEABO

BULLET
❏ 7000	Peabo	1976	25.00

CAPITOL
❏ C1-90461	All My Love	1989	12.00
❏ ST-11875	Crosswinds	1978	12.00
❏ ST-12241	Don't Play with Fire	1982	10.00
❏ ST-12179	I Am Love	1981	12.00
❏ SOO-12063	Paradise	1980	12.00
❏ ST-11729	Reaching for the Sky	1978	12.00
❏ SJ-12348	The Peabo Bryson Collection	1984	12.00
❏ ST-12138	Turn the Hands of Time	1981	12.00

COLUMBIA
❏ C46823	Can You Stop the Rain	1991	18.00

ELEKTRA
❏ 60753	Positive	1988	10.00
❏ 60484	Quiet Storm	1986	10.00
❏ 60362	Straight from the Heart	1983	10.00
❏ 60427	Take No Prisoners	1985	10.00

BUA, GENE

HERITAGE
❏ 35004	Love of Life	1973	25.00

BUBBLE GUM MACHINE, THE

SENATE
❏ 21002 [M]	The Bubble Gum Machine	1968	30.00
❏ S-21002 [S]	The Bubble Gum Machine	1968	30.00

BUBBLE PUPPY, THE

INTERNATIONAL ARTISTS
❏ 10	A Gathering of Promises	1969	100.00
—Original does not have "Masterfonics" in the dead wax			
❏ 10	A Gathering of Promises	1979	30.00
—Reissue has "Masterfonics" in the dead wax			

BUCHANAN, ROY

ALLIGATOR
❏ AL-4747	Dancing on the Edge	1986	12.00
❏ AL-4756	Hot Wires	1988	12.00
❏ AL-4741	When a Guitar Plays the Blues	1985	12.00

ATLANTIC
❏ SD18170	A Street Called Straight	1976	15.00
❏ SD18219	Loading Zone	1977	15.00
❏ SD19138	Loading Zone	1978	10.00
—Reissue of 18219			
❏ SD19170	You're Not Alone	1978	15.00

BIOYA
❏ MM-519	Buch and the Snake Stretchers	1971	300.00

POLYDOR
❏ PD-6035	In the Beginning	1974	18.00
❏ PD-6048	Live Stock	1975	18.00
❏ PD-5033	Roy Buchanan	1972	18.00
❏ PD-5046	Second Album	1973	18.00
❏ PD-6020	That's What I Am Here For	1974	18.00

WATERHOUSE
❏ 12	My Babe	1981	12.00

BUCKAROOS, THE

CAPITOL
❏ T2722 [M]	America's Most Wanted Band	1967	25.00
❏ ST2722 [S]	America's Most Wanted Band	1967	30.00
❏ ST2902	A Night on the Town with Buck Owens' Buckaroos	1968	30.00
❏ ST-194	Anywhere U.S.A.	1969	30.00
❏ ST2973	Meanwhile Back at the Ranch	1968	30.00
❏ ST-322	Roll Your Own with Buck Owens' Buckaroos	1969	30.00
❏ ST-440	Rompin' and Stompin'	1970	25.00
❏ ST-767	The Buckaroos Play the Hits	1971	25.00
❏ ST-860	The Buckaroos Play the Songs of Merle Haggard	1971	30.00
❏ T2828 [M]	The Buck Owens' Buckaroos Strike Again!	1968	40.00
❏ ST2828 [S]	The Buck Owens' Buckaroos Strike Again!	1968	30.00
❏ T2436 [M]	The Buck Owens Song Book	1966	25.00
❏ ST2436 [S]	The Buck Owens Song Book	1966	30.00

BUCKINGHAM, LINDSEY

ASYLUM
❏ 512970	Gift of Screws	2008	25.00
❏ 5E-561	Law and Order	1981	12.00

ELEKTRA
❏ 60363	Go Insane	1984	12.00

BUCKINGHAM NICKS

POLYDOR
❏ PD-5058 [B]	Buckingham Nicks	1973	60.00
—Gatefold cover			
❏ PD-5058	Buckingham Nicks	1975	15.00
Regular cover			

BUCKINGHAMS, THE (1)

COLUMBIA
❏ CS39703	In One Ear and Gone Tomorrow	1968	25.00
❏ KG33333	Made in Chicago	1975	25.00
❏ CS9598 [S]	Portraits	1968	25.00
❏ CL2798 [M]	Portraits	1968	30.00
❏ CS9812	The Buckinghams Greatest Hits	1969	25.00
—Red "360 Sound" label			
❏ CS9812	The Buckinghams Greatest Hits	1970	15.00
—Orange label			
❏ PC9812	The Buckinghams Greatest Hits	198?	10.00
—Reissue with new prefix			
❏ CL2669 [M]	Time & Charges	1967	30.00
❏ CS9469 [S]	Time & Charges	1967	25.00

U.S.A.
❏ 107 [M]	Kind of a Drag	1967	600.00
—With "I'm a Man"			
❏ 107 [M]	Kind of a Drag	1967	30.00
—Without "I'm a Man"			
❏ 107 [S]	Kind of a Drag	1967	40.00
—No known stereo copy has "I'm a Man"			

BUCKLEY, LORD

CRESTVIEW
❏ CRV-801 [M]	The Best of Lord Buckley	1963	50.00
❏ CRV7-801 [S]	The Best of Lord Buckley	1963	60.00

ELEKTRA
❏ EKS-74047	The Best of Lord Buckley	1969	30.00
—Reissue of Crestview 7-801			

Number	Title	Yr	NM

RCA VICTOR
| ❏ LPM-3246 [10] | Hipsters, Flipsters and Finger Poppin' Daddies, Knock Me Your Lobes | 1955 | 600.00 |

REPRISE
| ❏ RS6389 | A Most Immaculately Hip Aristocrat | 1970 | 50.00 |

— Reissue of Straight 1054

STRAIGHT
| ❏ STS-1054 | A Most Immaculately Hip Aristocrat | 1970 | 80.00 |

VAYA
| ❏ 1715 [10] | Euphoria | 195? | 600.00 |

— Red vinyl

| ❏ 101/2 [M] | Euphoria, Volume 1 | 1955 | 300.00 |
| ❏ 107/8 [M] | Euphoria, Volume 2 | 1955 | 400.00 |

WORLD PACIFIC
❏ WPS-21889	Bad Rapping of the Marquis de Sade	1969	80.00
❏ WP-1849 [M]	Blowing His Mind (and Yours, Too)	1966	80.00
❏ WPS-21879	Buckley's Best	1968	40.00
❏ WP-1815 [M]	Lord Buckley in Concert	1964	50.00

— Reissue of 1279

| ❏ WP-1279 [M] | The Way Out Humor of Lord Buckley | 1959 | 250.00 |

— With "Far Out Humor" on the back cover

| ❏ WP-1279 [M] | The Way Out Humor of Lord Buckley | 1959 | 200.00 |

— With correct "Way Out Humor" on the back cover

BUCKNER, MILT

ARGO
❏ LP-702 [M]	Midnight Mood	1962	18.00
❏ LPS-702 [S]	Midnight Mood	1962	25.00
❏ LP-660 [M]	Mighty High	1960	18.00
❏ LPS-660 [S]	Mighty High	1960	25.00
❏ LP-670 [M]	Please Mr. Organ Player	1960	18.00
❏ LPS-670 [S]	Please Mr. Organ Player	1960	25.00

BASF
| ❏ 20631 | Chords | 1972 | 18.00 |

BETHLEHEM
| ❏ BCP-6072 [M] | The New World of Milt Buckner | 1963 | 30.00 |

CAPITOL
| ❏ T722 [M] | Rockin' Hammond | 1956 | 50.00 |

— Turquoise or gray label

| ❏ T642 [M] | Rockin' with Milt | 1955 | 50.00 |

— Turquoise or gray label

| ❏ T938 [M] | Send Me Softly | 1958 | 50.00 |

— Turquoise or gray label

CLASSIC JAZZ
| ❏ 141 | Green Onions | 198? | 12.00 |

JAZZ MAN
| ❏ 5012 | Rockin' Again | 198? | 15.00 |

PRESTIGE
| ❏ PRST-7668 | Milt Buckner in Europe '66 | 1969 | 18.00 |

REGENT
| ❏ MG-6004 [M] | Organ -- Sweet 'n' Swing | 195? | 30.00 |

SAVOY
| ❏ MG-15023 [10] | Milt Buckner Piano | 1953 | 120.00 |

BUCKWHEAT

LONDON
❏ PS595	Buckwheat	1971	18.00
❏ XPS621	Charade	1972	15.00
❏ XPS635	Hot Tracks	1973	15.00
❏ PS609	Movin' On	1972	15.00

BUCKWHEAT ZYDECO

BLACK TOP
| ❏ 1024 [B] | 100% Fortified Zydeco | 1983 | 18.00 |

BLUES UNLIMITED
| ❏ 5006 | Ils Sont Partis | 1981 | 25.00 |
| ❏ 5017 | People's Choice | 1982 | 25.00 |

ISLAND
| ❏ 90622 | On a Night Like This | 1987 | 12.00 |
| ❏ 90968 [B] | Taking It Home | 1988 | 12.00 |

ROUNDER
| ❏ 2045 | Turning Point | 1984 | 18.00 |
| ❏ 2051 | Waitin' for My Ya Ya | 1985 | 18.00 |

BUD AND TRAVIS

LIBERTY
❏ LRP-3125 [M]	Bud and Travis	1959	30.00
❏ LST-7125 [S]	Bud and Travis	1959	40.00
❏ LDM-11001 [M]	Bud and Travis...In Concert	1960	30.00
❏ LDS-12001 [S]	Bud and Travis...In Concert	1960	30.00
❏ LRP-3222 [M]	Bud and Travis In Concert at the Santa Monica Civic Auditorium, Vol. 2	1961	25.00
❏ LST-7222 [S]	Bud and Travis In Concert at the Santa Monica Civic Auditorium, Vol. 2	1961	30.00
❏ LRP-3386 [M]	Bud and Travis In Person (At the Cellar Door)	1964	25.00

Number	Title	Yr	NM
❏ LST-7386 [S]	Bud and Travis In Person (At the Cellar Door)	1964	30.00
❏ LRP-3295 [M]	Naturally	1963	25.00
❏ LST-7295 [S]	Naturally	1963	30.00
❏ LRP-3341 [M]	Perspective on Bud and Travis	1964	25.00
❏ LST-7341 [S]	Perspective on Bud and Travis	1964	30.00
❏ LRP-3138 [M]	Spotlight On Bud and Travis	1960	25.00
❏ LST-7138 [S]	Spotlight On Bud and Travis	1960	30.00
❏ LRP-3398 [M]	The Latin Album	1965	25.00
❏ LST-7398 [S]	The Latin Album	1965	30.00

SUNSET
| ❏ SUM-1154 [M] | Bud and Travis | 1967 | 15.00 |
| ❏ SUS-5154 [S] | Bud and Travis | 1967 | 15.00 |

BUDD, HAROLD

ADVANCE RECORDINGS
| ❏ FGR16 [B] | The Oak Of The Golden Dreams | 1971 | 500.00 |

CANTIL
| ❏ 384 [B] | Abandoned Cities | 1984 | 25.00 |
| ❏ 181 [B] | The Serpent (In Quicksilver) | 1981 | 25.00 |

EDITIONS EG
| ❏ EGED46 [B] | Lovely Thunder | 1986 | 30.00 |
| ❏ EGS301 [B] | The Pavilion of Dreams | 1981 | 30.00 |

— US release for 1978 LP on the UK Obscure label

OPAL
| ❏ 9 25766-1 [B] | The White Arcades | 1988 | 15.00 |

BUDDIES, THE

WING
❏ MGW-12306 [M]	Go Go with the Buddies	1965	50.00
❏ SRW-16306 [S]	Go Go with the Buddies	1965	80.00
❏ MGW-12293 [M]	The Buddies and the Compacts	1965	50.00
❏ SRW-16293 [S]	The Buddies and the Compacts	1965	80.00

BUDGIE

A&M
❏ SP-4618 [B]	Bandolier	1975	25.00
❏ SP-4593 [B]	If I Were Brittania I'd Waive the Rules	1976	18.00
❏ SP-4675 [B]	Impeckable	1978	18.00

KAPP
| ❏ KS-3656 [B] | Budgie | 1971 | 80.00 |
| ❏ KS-3669 [B] | Squawk | 1972 | 40.00 |

MCA
| ❏ 429 [B] | In for the Kill | 1973 | 40.00 |

BUFFALO SPRINGFIELD

ATCO
| ❏ 33-200 [M] | Buffalo Springfield | 1967 | 200.00 |

— With "Baby Don't Scold Me"

| ❏ SD 33-200 [S] | Buffalo Springfield | 1967 | 200.00 |

— With "Baby Don't Scold Me"

| ❏ 33-200A [M] | Buffalo Springfield | 1967 | 30.00 |

— With "For What It's Worth" replacing "Baby Don't Scold Me"

| ❏ SD 33-200A [S] | Buffalo Springfield | 1967 | 30.00 |

— With "For What It's Worth" replacing "Baby Don't Scold Me"; purple and brown label

| ❏ SD 33-200A [S] | Buffalo Springfield | 1969 | 18.00 |

— Reissue on yellow label

| ❏ SD 2-806 | Buffalo Springfield | 1973 | 25.00 |

— Yellow label

| ❏ SD 33-200A [S] | Buffalo Springfield | 197? | 10.00 |

— Later white or gray label

| ❏ SD 2-806 | Buffalo Springfield | 197? | 15.00 |

— Later white or gray label

| ❏ 33-226 [M] | Buffalo Springfield Again | 1967 | 120.00 |
| ❏ SD 33-226 [S] | Buffalo Springfield Again | 1967 | 30.00 |

— Purple and brown label

| ❏ SD 33-226 [S] | Buffalo Springfield Again | 1969 | 18.00 |

— Reissue on yellow label

| ❏ SD 33-226 [S] | Buffalo Springfield Again | 197? | 10.00 |

— Later white or gray label

| ❏ SD 33-256 [S] | Last Time Around | 1968 | 30.00 |

— Purple and brown label

| ❏ 33-256 [M] | Last Time Around | 1968 | 120.00 |

— White label promo only

| ❏ SD 33-256 [S] | Last Time Around | 1969 | 18.00 |

— Reissue on yellow label

| ❏ SD 33-256 [S] | Last Time Around | 197? | 10.00 |

— Later white or gray label

| ❏ 33-283 [M] | Retrospective/The Best of Buffalo Springfield | 1969 | 100.00 |

— White label promo only

| ❏ SD 33-283 [S] | Retrospective/The Best of Buffalo Springfield | 1969 | 25.00 |

— Yellow label

| ❏ SD 38-105 [S] | Retrospective/The Best of Buffalo Springfield | 197? | 10.00 |

— Reissue of 33-283

BUFFALO TOM

SST
| ❏ 250 | Buffalo Tom | 1989 | 18.00 |

Number	Title	Yr	NM

BUFFETT, JIMMY

ABC
❏ AB-990	Changes in Latitudes, Changes in Attitudes	1977	15.00
❏ D-914	Havana Daydreamin'	1976	15.00
❏ AA-1046	Son of a Son of a Sailor	1978	15.00
❏ -0 [DJ]	Special Jimmy Buffett Sampler	1978	25.00
❏ SPDJ-43 [DJ]	Special Jimmy Buffett Sampler	1978	25.00
❏ AK-1008	You Had to Be There	1978	18.00

ABC DUNHILL
❏ DSD-50183	A1A	1975	18.00
❏ DSX-50150	A White Sport Coat and a Pink Crustacean	1974	18.00
❏ DSD-50132	Living and Dying in 3/4 Time	1973	18.00

BARNABY
| ❏ Z30093 | Down to Earth | 1970 | 100.00 |
| ❏ BR-6014 | High Cumberland Jubilee | 1975 | 40.00 |

MCA
❏ 37027	A1A	1981	10.00
❏ 37026	A White Sport Coat and a Pink Crustacean	1981	10.00
❏ 37150	Changes in Latitudes, Changes in Attitudes	1982	10.00
❏ 5169	Coconut Telegraph	1981	12.00
❏ 5730	Floridays	1986	12.00
❏ 37023	Havana Daydreamin'	1981	10.00
❏ 42093	Hot Water	1988	12.00
❏ 5600	Last Mango in Paris	1985	12.00
❏ 37025	Living and Dying in 3/4 Time	1981	10.00
❏ 6314	Off to See the Lizard	1989	12.00
❏ 5447	One Particular Harbour	1983	12.00
❏ 5512	Riddles in the Sand	1984	12.00
❏ 5285	Somewhere Over China	1982	12.00
❏ 37246	Somewhere Over China	1984	10.00
❏ 5633	Songs You Know By Heart -- Jimmy Buffett's Greatest Hit(s)	1985	12.00
❏ 37024	Son of a Son of a Sailor	1981	10.00
❏ 5102	Volcano	1979	12.00
❏ 37156	Volcano	1982	12.00
❏ 2-6005	You Had to Be There	1981	12.00

BUGALOOS, THE

CAPITOL
| ❏ SW-621 | The Bugaloos | 1970 | 30.00 |

BURDON, ERIC, AND WAR

ABC
| ❏ D-988 | Love Is All Around | 1976 | 15.00 |

— As "War Featuring Eric Burdon"

LAX
| ❏ PW37109 | Spill the Wine | 1981 | 12.00 |

— Reissue of MGM 4663 with new title

MGM
| ❏ SE-4663 | Eric Burdon Declares "War" | 1970 | 18.00 |
| ❏ SE-4710-2 | The Black Man's Burdon | 1970 | 25.00 |

— Add 50% if the package includes an "Official War Bond," entitling the bearer to $1 off any Eric Burdon and War concert before December 31, 1973

BURDON, ERIC

CAPITOL
| ❏ S?A?11426 | Stop | 1975 | 25.00 |

— Cover shaped like a hexagon

| ❏ ST-11426 | Stop | 1975 | 15.00 |

— Regular square cover

| ❏ ST-11359 | Sun Secrets | 1974 | 15.00 |

GNP CRESCENDO
| ❏ GNPS-2194 | Wicked Man | 1988 | 12.00 |

LAX
| ❏ PW37110 | Sun Secrets | 1981 | 12.00 |

— Reissue of Capitol 11359

STRIPED HORSE
| ❏ SHL2006 | I Used to Be an Animal | 1988 | 12.00 |

BURGESS, WILMA

DECCA
❏ DL4788 [M]	Don't Touch Me	1966	18.00
❏ DL74788 [S]	Don't Touch Me	1966	25.00
❏ DL75090	Parting Is Such Sweet Sorrow	1968	25.00
❏ DL4935 [M]	Tear Time	1967	30.00
❏ DL74935 [S]	Tear Time	1967	25.00
❏ DL75024	The Tender Lovin' Country Sound	1968	25.00
❏ DL4852 [M]	Wilma Burgess Sings Misty Blue	1967	18.00
❏ DL74852 [S]	Wilma Burgess Sings Misty Blue	1967	25.00

BURKE, SOLOMON

ABC DUNHILL
| ❏ DSX-50161 | I Have a Dream | 1974 | 15.00 |

AMHERST
| ❏ AMH-1018 | Please Don't You Say Goodbye to Me | 1978 | 15.00 |

Number	Title	Yr	NM
APOLLO			
❏ ALP-498 [M]	Solomon Burke	1962	500.00
ATLANTIC			
❏ 8085 [M]	If You Need Me	1963	50.00
❏ SD8085 [S]	If You Need Me	1963	80.00
❏ SD8185	I Wish I Knew	1968	30.00
❏ SD8158	King Solomon	1968	30.00
❏ 8096 [M]	Rock N' Soul	1964	50.00
❏ SD8096 [S]	Rock N' Soul	1964	80.00
❏ 8067 [M]	Solomon Burke's Greatest Hits	1962	50.00
❏ SD8067 [S]	Solomon Burke's Greatest Hits	1962	80.00
❏ 8109 [M]	The Best of Solomon Burke	1965	30.00
❏ SD8109 [S]	The Best of Solomon Burke	1965	40.00
BELL			
❏ 6033	Proud Mary	1969	25.00
CHESS			
❏ CH-19002	Back to My Roots	1976	15.00
❏ CH-60042	Music to Make Love By	1975	15.00
CLARION			
❏ 607 [M]	I Almost Lost My Mind	1966	25.00
❏ SD607 [S]	I Almost Lost My Mind	1966	30.00
DBK WORKS			
❏ 104	Don't Give Up on Me	2003	25.00
INFINITY			
❏ INF-9024	Sidewalks, Fences and Walls	1979	15.00
KENWOOD			
❏ LP-498 [M]	Solomon Burke	1964	200.00
—Reissue of Apollo 498			
MGM			
❏ SE-4767	Electronic Magnetism	1971	18.00
❏ SE-4830	King Heavy	1972	18.00
PRIDE			
❏ 0011	The History of Solomon Burke	1972	18.00
ROUNDER			
❏ 2053	A Change Is Gonna Come	1986	12.00
❏ 2042/3	Soul Alive!	1984	15.00
SAVOY			
❏ 14679	Into My Life	1982	12.00
❏ 14660	Solomon Burke	1981	12.00
❏ 14717	Take Me, Shake Me	1983	12.00
BURKE, VINNIE			
ABC-PARAMOUNT			
❏ ABC-139 [M]	The Vinnie Durke All Stars	1956	50.00
❏ ABC-170 [M]	The Vinnie Burke String Jazz Quartet	1957	50.00
BETHLEHEM			
❏ BCP-1010 [10]	East Coast Jazz 2	1954	120.00
BURNETT, CAROL			
DECCA			
❏ DL4049 [M]	Carol Burnett Remembers How They Stopped the Show	1960	30.00
❏ DL74049 [S]	Carol Burnett Remembers How They Stopped the Show	1960	40.00
❏ DL4437 [M]	Let Me Entertain You	1964	25.00
❏ DL74437 [S]	Let Me Entertain You	1964	30.00
RCA VICTOR			
❏ LPM-3839 [M]	Carol Burnett Sings	1967	25.00
❏ LSP-3839 [S]	Carol Burnett Sings	1967	25.00
BURNETT, T-BONE			
COLUMBIA			
❏ BFC40792	Talking Animals	1988	12.00
MCA			
❏ 5809	T-Bone Burnett	1986	10.00
TAKOMA			
❏ 7080	Truth Decay	1980	12.00
UNI			
❏ 73125	The B-52 Band and the Fabulous Skyhawks	1972	30.00
—As "J. Henry Burnett"			
WARNER BROS.			
❏ 23921 [B]	Proof Through the Night	1983	18.00
—Quiex II vinyl promo			
❏ 23691	Trap Door	1982	12.00
BURNETTE, DORSEY			
CALLIOPE			
❏ CAL7006	Things I Treasure	1977	15.00
CAPITOL			
❏ ST-11219	Dorsey Burnette	1973	18.00
❏ ST-11094	Here and Now	1972	18.00
DOT			
❏ DLP-3456 [M]	Dorsey Burnette Sings	1963	40.00
❏ DLP-25456 [S]	Dorsey Burnette Sings	1963	50.00
ERA			
❏ ES-800 [M]	Dorsey Burnette's Greatest Hits	1969	30.00

Number	Title	Yr	NM
❏ EL-102 [M]	Tall Oak Tree	1960	150.00
❏ ES-102 [S]	Tall Oak Tree	1960	300.00
GUSTO			
❏ 0050	The Golden Hits of Dorsey Burnette	197?	15.00
BURNETTE, DORSEY AND JOHNNY			
SOLID SMOKE			
❏ SS-8005	Together Again	1978	18.00
BURNETTE, JOHNNY			
CORAL			
❏ CRL57080 [M]	Johnny Burnette & the Rock 'N' Roll Trio	1956	6000.00
—Originals have maroon labels, machine-stamped (not engraved) numbers in the dead wax, printing on jacket's spine and "Printed in U.S.A." in lower right of back cover; VG value 2000; VG+ value 4000			
LIBERTY			
❏ LRP-3179 [M]	Dreamin'	1960	40.00
❏ LST-7179 [S]	Dreamin'	1960	60.00
❏ LRP-3183 [M]	Johnny Burnette	1961	40.00
❏ LST-7183 [S]	Johnny Burnette	1961	60.00
❏ LRP-3206 [M]	Johnny Burnette's Hits and Other Favorites	1962	40.00
❏ LST-7206 [S]	Johnny Burnette's Hits and Other Favorites	1962	50.00
❏ LRP-3190 [M]	Johnny Burnette Sings	1961	40.00
❏ LST-7190 [S]	Johnny Burnette Sings	1961	60.00
❏ LRP-3255 [M]	Roses Are Red	1962	40.00
❏ LST-7255 [S]	Roses Are Red	1962	50.00
❏ LRP-3389 [M]	The Johnny Burnette Story	1964	40.00
❏ LST-7389 [S]	The Johnny Burnette Story	1964	50.00
MCA			
❏ 1513	Listen to Johnny Burnette and the Rock 'N' Roll Trio	1982	12.00
SOLID SMOKE			
❏ SS-8001	Tear It Up	1978	30.00
—Blue vinyl			
❏ SS-8001	Tear It Up	1978	18.00
—Black viinyl			
SUNSET			
❏ SUM-1179 [M]	Dreamin'	1967	18.00
❏ SUS-5179 [S]	Dreamin'	1967	25.00
UNITED ARTISTS			
❏ UA-LA432-G	The Very Best of Johnny Burnette	1975	12.00
BURNETTE, SMILEY			
CRICKET			
❏ CR-11 [M]	Rodeo Songaree	1959	30.00
STARDAY			
❏ SLP-191 [M]	Ole Frog	1962	40.00
BURNS, DAVE			
VANGUARD			
❏ 9111 [B]	Dave Burns	1962	200.00
❏ VR9143 [M]	Warming Up	1964	200.00
BURNS, GEORGE			
BUDDAH			
❏ BDS-5127	A Musical Trip with George Burns	1972	15.00
—Reissue of 5027			
❏ BDS-5025	George Burns Sings	1969	18.00
MERCURY			
❏ SRM-1-6001	George Burns in Nashville	1981	12.00
❏ SRM-1-5025	I Wish I Was Eighteen Again	1980	12.00
❏ SRM-1-4061	Young at Heart	1982	12.00
PRIDE			
❏ PRD-0011	An Evening with George Burns	1974	25.00
BURNS, RALPH			
BETHLEHEM			
❏ BCP-68 [M]	Bijou	1957	80.00
CLEF			
❏ MGC-115 [10]	Free Forms	1953	150.00
DECCA			
❏ DL8235 [M]	Jazz Studio 5	1956	80.00
❏ DL9068 [M]	New York's a Song	1959	40.00
❏ DL79068 [S]	New York's a Song	1959	50.00
❏ DL9215 [M]	Porgy and Bess	1959	40.00
❏ DL79215 [S]	Porgy and Bess	1959	50.00
❏ DL8555 [M]	The Masters Revisited	1957	60.00
❏ DL9207 [M]	Very Warm for Jazz	1959	60.00
❏ DL79207 [S]	Very Warm for Jazz	1959	70.00
EPIC			
❏ LN24015 [M]	Swingin' Down the Lane	1962	30.00
❏ BN26015 [S]	Swingin' Down the Lane	1962	40.00
JAZZTONE			
❏ J-1228 [M]	Spring Sequence	1956	50.00
MERCURY			
❏ MGC-115 [10]	Free Forms	1952	200.00
MGM			
❏ E-3616 [M]	The Swinging Seasons	1958	50.00
❏ SE-3616 [S]	The Swinging Seasons	1959	40.00

Number	Title	Yr	NM
NORGRAN			
❏ MGN-1028 [M]	Ralph Burns Among the JATP's	1955	120.00
PERIOD			
❏ SPL-1109 [10]	Bijou	1955	120.00
❏ SPL-1105 [10]	Spring Sequence	1955	120.00
VERVE			
❏ MGV-8121 [M]	Ralph Burns Among the JATP's	1957	50.00
❏ V-8121 [M]	Ralph Burns Among the JATP's	1961	25.00
WARWICK			
❏ W-5001 [M]	Where There's Burns There's Fire	1961	50.00
❏ W-5001ST [S]	Where There's Burns There's Fire	1961	70.00
BURNS, RALPH/BILLIE HOLIDAY			
CLEF			
❏ MGC-718 [M]	The Free Forms of Ralph Burns/The Songs of Billie Holiday	1956	120.00
VERVE			
❏ MGV-8098 [M]	Jazz Recital	1957	50.00
❏ V-8098 [M]	Jazz Recital	1961	25.00
BURNS, RANDY			
ESP-DISK'			
❏ 1089	Evening of the Magician	1968	75.00
❏ 2007	Song for an Uncertain Lady	1971	50.00
❏ 1039	Songs of Love and War	1966	100.00
MERCURY			
❏ SR-61329	Randy Burns and the Skydog Band	1971	30.00
POLYDOR			
❏ PD-5030	I'm a Lover, Not a Fool	1972	15.00
❏ PD-5049	Still On Our Feet	1973	15.00
BURNSIDE, R.L.			
FAT POSSUM			
❏ 80301-1 [B]	Mr Wizard	1997	18.00
❏ 80307-1 [B]	Too Bad Jim	1994	18.00
BURNT SUITE			
B.J.W.			
❏ 9	Burnt Suite	1972	200.00
BURRELL, DAVE			
ARISTA FREEDOM			
❏ AL1906	High Won/High Two	1975	18.00
DOUGLAS			
❏ SD798	High	1969	25.00
HAT ART			
❏ 2025	Windward Passages	1987	18.00
— Reissue of Hat Hut 05			
HAT HUT			
❏ 05	Windward Passages	1979	25.00
BURRELL, KENNY, AND JIMMY RANEY			
PRESTIGE			
❏ PRLP-7119 [M]	Two Guitars	1957	80.00
BURRELL, KENNY, AND JOHN COLTRANE			
FANTASY			
❏ OJC-300	Kenny Burrell and John Coltrane	1987	12.00
❏ OJC-079	The Cats	198?	12.00
— Reissue of New Jazz 8217			
NEW JAZZ			
❏ NJLP-8276 [M]	Kenny Burrell with John Coltrane	1962	60.00
—Purple label			
❏ NJLP-8276 [M]	Kenny Burrell with John Coltrane	1965	30.00
— Blue label with trident logo			
❏ NJLP-8217 [M]	The Cats	1959	80.00
—Purple label			
❏ NJLP-8217 [M]	The Cats	1965	30.00
— Blue label with trident logo			
PRESTIGE			
❏ 24059	Kenny Burrell & John Coltrane	197?	18.00
— Reissue of New Jazz and Prestige LPs in one package			
❏ PRLP-7532 [M]	Kenny Burrell Quintet with John Coltrane	1967	30.00
❏ PRST-7532 [S]	Kenny Burrell Quintet with John Coltrane	1967	25.00
BURRELL, KENNY; TINY GRIMES; BILL JENNINGS			
STATUS			
❏ ST-8318 [M]	Guitar Soul	1965	40.00
BURRELL, KENNY			
ARGO			
❏ LP-655 [M]	A Night at the Vanguard	1959	30.00

Number	Title	Yr	NM
❑ LPS-655 [S]	A Night at the Vanguard	1959	40.00
BLUE NOTE			
❑ BLP-1596 [M]	Blue Lights, Volume 1	1958	800.00
—Deep groove" version (deep indentation under label on both sides). Andy Warhol cover.			
❑ BST-1596 [S]	Blue Lights, Volume 1	1959	400.00
—Deep groove" version (deep indentation under label on both sides)			
❑ BLP-1596 [M]	Blue Lights, Volume 1	1958	300.00
—Regular version, W. 63rd St., NYC address on label			
❑ BST-1596 [S]	Blue Lights, Volume 1	1959	70.00
—Regular version, W. 63rd St., NYC address on label			
❑ BLP-1596 [M]	Blue Lights, Volume 1	1963	30.00
—New York, USA address on label			
❑ BST-1596 [S]	Blue Lights, Volume 1	1963	30.00
—New York, USA address on label			
❑ BST-81596 [S]	Blue Lights, Volume 1	1967	18.00
—A Division of Liberty Records" on label			
❑ BLP-1597 [M]	Blue Lights, Volume 2	1958	750.00
—Deep groove" version (deep indentation under label on both sides). Andy Warhol cover.			
❑ BST-1597 [S]	Blue Lights, Volume 2	1959	400.00
—Deep groove" version (deep indentation under label on both sides)			
❑ BLP-1597 [M]	Blue Lights, Volume 2	1958	70.00
—Regular version, W. 63rd St., NYC address on label			
❑ BST-1597 [S]	Blue Lights, Volume 2	1959	70.00
—Regular version, W. 63rd St., NYC address on label			
❑ BLP-1597 [M]	Blue Lights, Volume 2	1963	30.00
—New York, USA address on label			
❑ BST-1597 [S]	Blue Lights, Volume 2	1963	30.00
—New York, USA address on label			
❑ BST-81597 [S]	Blue Lights, Volume 2	1967	18.00
—A Division of Liberty Records" on label			
❑ B1-85137	Generation	1987	12.00
❑ BLP-1523 [M]	Introducing Kenny Burrell	1956	500.00
—Deep groove" version (deep indentation under label on both sides)			
❑ BLP-1523 [M]	Introducing Kenny Burrell	1956	250.00
—Regular version, Lexington Ave. address on label			
❑ BLP-1523 [M]	Introducing Kenny Burrell	1957	80.00
—W. 63rd St., NYC address on label			
❑ BLP-1523 [M]	Introducing Kenny Burrell	1963	30.00
—New York, USA address on label			
❑ BST-81523 [R]	Introducing Kenny Burrell	1967	15.00
—A Division of Liberty Records" on label			
❑ BLP-1543 [M]	Kenny Burrell, Volume 2	1957	1500.00
—Deep groove" version (deep indentation under label on both sides). Andy Warhol cover.			
❑ BLP-1543 [M]	Kenny Burrell, Volume 2	1957	1000.00
—Regular version, Lexington Ave. address on label. Andy Warhol cover.			
❑ BLP-1543 [M]	Kenny Burrell, Volume 2	1957	800.00
—W. 63rd St., NYC address on label. Andy Warhol cover.			
❑ BLP-1543 [M]	Kenny Burrell, Volume 2	1963	400.00
—New York, USA address on label. Andy Warhol cover.			
❑ BST-81543 [R]	Kenny Burrell, Volume 2	1967	15.00
—A Division of Liberty Records" on label			
❑ BLP-4123 [M]	Midnight Blue	1963	30.00
—New York, USA address on label			
❑ BST-84123 [S]	Midnight Blue	1963	40.00
—New York, USA address on label			
❑ BST-84123 [S]	Midnight Blue	1967	18.00
—A Division of Liberty Records" on label			
❑ BST-84123	Midnight Blue	1985	12.00
—The Finest in Jazz Since 1939" reissue			
❑ BLP-4021 [M]	On View at the Five Spot Café	1960	200.00
—Deep groove" version (deep indentation under label on both sides)			
❑ BLP-4021 [M]	On View at the Five Spot Café	1960	70.00
—Regular version, W. 63rd St., NYC address on label			
❑ BST-84021 [S]	On View at the Five Spot Café	1960	60.00
—W. 63rd St., NYC address on label			
❑ BLP-4021 [M]	On View at the Five Spot Café	1963	30.00
—New York, USA address on label			
❑ BST-84021 [S]	On View at the Five Spot Café	1963	30.00
—New York, USA address on label			
❑ BST-84021 [S]	On View at the Five Spot Café	1967	18.00
—A Division of Liberty Records" on label			
❑ B1-90260	Pieces of Blue and the Blues	1988	12.00
CADET			
❑ LP-779 [M]	Have Yourself a Soulful Little Christmas	1966	18.00
❑ LPS-779 [S]	Have Yourself a Soulful Little Christmas	1966	25.00
❑ LP-769 [M]	Men at Work	1965	18.00
—Reissue of Argo 655			
❑ LPS-769 [S]	Men at Work	1965	25.00
—Reissue of Argo 655			
❑ LP-798 [M]	Ode to 52nd Street	1967	25.00
❑ LPS-798 [S]	Ode to 52nd Street	1967	18.00
❑ LP-772 [M]	The Tender Gender	1966	18.00
❑ LPS-772 [S]	The Tender Gender	1966	25.00
CHESS			
❑ CH-9316	A Night at the Vanguard	1990	15.00

Number	Title	Yr	NM
—Reissue of Argo 655			
❑ CH-60019	Cool Cookin'	1973	18.00
❑ CH2-92509	Recapitulation	198?	15.00
COLUMBIA			
❑ CL1703 [M]	Weaver of Dreams	1961	25.00
❑ CS8503 [S]	Weaver of Dreams	1961	30.00
CONCORD JAZZ			
❑ CJ-121	Moon and Sand	1980	12.00
❑ CJ-45	Tin Tin Deo	1978	12.00
❑ CJ-83	When Lights Are Low	1978	12.00
CONTEMPORARY			
❑ C-14058	Guiding Spirit	1990	15.00
CTI			
❑ 6011	God Bless the Child	1970	15.00
DENON			
❑ 7533	Lush Life	1979	18.00
❑ 7541	'Round Midnight	1979	18.00
FANTASY			
❑ OJC-456	All Day Long	1990	15.00
❑ OJC-427	All Night Long	1990	15.00
❑ F-9427	Both Feet on the Ground	1973	15.00
❑ 79005	Ellington Is Forever	1975	18.00
❑ 79008	Ellington Is Forever, Vol. 2	197?	18.00
❑ MPF-4506	For Duke	1981	12.00
❑ OJC-019	Kenny Burrell	198?	12.00
—Reissue of Prestige 7088			
❑ F-9417	'Round Midnight	1972	15.00
❑ F-9514	Sky Street	1975	15.00
❑ F-9558	Stormy Monday	1978	15.00
❑ OJC-216	Two Guitars	198?	12.00
❑ F-9458	Up the Street	1974	15.00
KAPP			
❑ KL-1326 [M]	Lotta Bossa Nova	1962	25.00
❑ KS-3326 [S]	Lotta Bossa Nova	1962	30.00
MOODSVILLE			
❑ MVLP-29 [M]	Bluesy Burrell	1963	40.00
—Green label			
❑ MVST-29 [S]	Bluesy Burrell	1963	40.00
—Green label			
❑ MVLP-29 [M]	Bluesy Burrell	1965	25.00
—Blue label with trident logo			
❑ MVST-29 [S]	Bluesy Burrell	1965	30.00
—Blue label with trident logo			
MUSE			
❑ 5317	A La Carte	1984	12.00
❑ 5281	Groovin' High	1983	12.00
❑ 5144	Handcrafted	1979	12.00
❑ 5241	Kenny Burrell in New York	1982	12.00
❑ 5264	Listen to the Dawn	1982	12.00
❑ 5216	Live at the Village Vanguard	1979	12.00
PAUSA			
❑ 9000	Midnight	198?	12.00
PRESTIGE			
❑ 24025	All Day Long & All Night Long	197?	18.00
—Reissue of both albums in one package			
❑ PRLP-7081 [M]	All Day Long	1957	400.00
—Actually an all-star session; reissued as a Kenny Burrell album, thus it is listed here			
❑ PRLP-7277 [M]	All Day Long	1963	50.00
—Reissue of 7081			
❑ PRST-7277 [R]	All Day Long	1963	25.00
❑ PRLP-7073 [M]	All Night Long	1957	100.00
—Actually an all-star session; reissued as a Kenny Burrell album, thus it is listed here			
❑ PRLP-7289 [M]	All Night Long	1964	50.00
—Reissue of 7073			
❑ PRST-7289 [R]	All Night Long	1964	25.00
❑ PRLP-7308 [M]	Blue Moods	1964	30.00
—Reissue of 7088			
❑ PRST-7308 [R]	Blue Moods	1964	25.00
❑ PRLP-7347 [M]	Crash	1964	30.00
❑ PRST-7347 [S]	Crash	1964	30.00
❑ PRLP-7088 [M]	Kenny Burrell	1957	80.00
❑ PRST 7578	Out of This World	1968	18.00
—Reissue of Moodsville 29			
❑ PRLP-7315 [M]	Soul Call	1964	30.00
❑ PRST-7315 [S]	Soul Call	1964	30.00
❑ PRLP-7448 [M]	The Best of Kenny Burrell	1967	30.00
❑ PRST-7448 [S]	The Best of Kenny Burrell	1967	25.00
SAVOY JAZZ			
❑ SJL-1120	Monday Stroll	1978	12.00
—Reissue			
VERVE			
❑ V-8656 [M]	A Generation Ago Today	1966	18.00
❑ V6-8656 [S]	A Generation Ago Today	1966	25.00
❑ V6-8773	Asphalt Canyon Suite	1969	18.00
❑ V-8553 [M]	Blue Bash!	1963	25.00
❑ V6-8553 [S]	Blue Bash!	1963	30.00
❑ V-8746 [M]	Blues-- The Common Ground	1968	25.00
❑ V6-8746 [S]	Blues-- The Common Ground	1968	18.00
❑ V-8612 [M]	Guitar Forms	1965	18.00
❑ V6-8612 [S]	Guitar Forms	1965	25.00
❑ UMV-2070	Guitar Forms	198?	12.00
—Reissue of 8612			
❑ V6-8751	Night Song	1968	18.00

Number	Title	Yr	NM
VOSS			
❑ VLP1-42930	Heritage	1988	12.00

BURROUGHS, WILLIAM

Number	Title	Yr	NM
ESP-DISK'			
❑ 1050 [M]	Call Me Burroughs	1967	100.00

BURROWS, ABE

Number	Title	Yr	NM
COLUMBIA			
❑ CL6128 [10]	Abe Burrows Sings?	1950	40.00
DECCA			
❑ DL5288 [10]	The Girl with the 3 Blue Eyes	1951	40.00

BURTON, GARY, AND CHICK COREA

Number	Title	Yr	NM
ECM			
❑ 1024ST	Crystal Silence	1973	15.00
—Original edition; made in Germany?			
❑ 1140	Duet	1978	15.00
❑ ECM2-1182	Gary Burton and Chick Corea In Concert	1979	18.00
—Distributed by Warner Bros.			
❑ 23797	Lyric Suite for Sextet	1983	12.00
—Distributed by Warner Bros.			
❑ 1260	Lyric Suite for Sextet	1983	15.00
—Made in Germany			

BURTON, GARY; SONNY ROLLINS; CLARK TERRY

Number	Title	Yr	NM
RCA VICTOR			
❑ LPM-2725 [M]	Three in Jazz	1963	18.00
❑ LSP-2725 [S]	Three in Jazz	1963	25.00

BURTON, GARY

Number	Title	Yr	NM
ATLANTIC			
❑ SD1598	Alone at Last	1971	15.00
❑ SD1577	Gary Burton with Keith Jarrott	1971	15.00
❑ SD1560	Good Vibes	1970	15.00
❑ SD1597	Paris Encounter	1972	15.00
❑ SD1531	Throb	1969	15.00
❑ SD 2-321	Turn of the Century	1976	18.00
BLUEBIRD			
❑ 6280-1-RB	Artist's Choice	1987	12.00
ECM			
❑ 1072	Dreams So Real	1976	15.00
❑ 1184	Easy As Pie	1979	15.00
❑ 1055	Hotel Hello	1974	15.00
❑ 1092	Passengers	1977	15.00
❑ 1226	Picture This	1980	15.00
❑ 25024	Real Life Hits	1985	12.00
❑ 1051	Ring	1975	15.00
❑ 1040	Seven Songs for Quartet and Chamber Orchestra	1974	15.00
❑ 1030	The New Quartet	1973	15.00
❑ 1111	Times Square	1978	15.00
GRP			
❑ GR-9598	Reunion	1990	15.00
❑ GR-9569	Times Like These	1988	12.00
RCA CAMDEN			
❑ ACL1-0200	Norwegian Wood	1973	12.00
RCA VICTOR			
❑ LSP-3988	A Genuine Tong Funeral	1968	18.00
❑ LSP-4098	Country Roads and Other Places	1969	18.00
❑ LPM-3835 [M]	Duster	1967	25.00
❑ LSP-3835 [S]	Duster	1967	18.00
❑ LPM-3985 [M]	Gary Burton Quartet In Concert	1968	30.00
❑ LSP-3985 [S]	Gary Burton Quartet In Concert	1968	18.00
❑ LPM-3901 [M]	Lofty Fake Anagram	1967	25.00
❑ LSP-3901 [S]	Lofty Fake Anagram	1967	18.00
❑ LPM-2420 [M]	New Vibe Man in Town	1961	25.00
❑ LSP-2420 [S]	New Vibe Man in Town	1961	30.00
❑ LPM-2880 [M]	Something's Coming	1964	25.00
❑ LSP-2880 [S]	Something's Coming	1964	30.00
❑ LPM-3719 [M]	Tennessee Firebird	1966	18.00
❑ LSP-3719 [S]	Tennessee Firebird	1966	25.00
❑ LPM-3360 [M]	The Groovy Sound of Music	1965	18.00
❑ LSP-3360 [S]	The Groovy Sound of Music	1965	25.00
❑ LPM-3642 [M]	The Time Machine	1966	18.00
❑ LSP-3642 [S]	The Time Machine	1966	25.00
❑ LPM-2665 [M]	Who Is Gary Burton?	1963	25.00
❑ LSP-2665 [S]	Who Is Gary Burton?	1963	30.00

BURTON, JAMES

Number	Title	Yr	NM
A&M			
❑ SP-4293	James Burton	1971	30.00

BURTON, JOE

Number	Title	Yr	NM
CORAL			
❑ CRL57175 [M]	Here I Am in Love Again	1958	40.00
❑ CRL757175 [S]	Here I Am in Love Again	1959	30.00
❑ CRL57098 [M]	Joe Burton Session	1957	40.00
JODAY			
❑ J-1000 [M]	The Subtle Sound of Joe Burton	1963	18.00
❑ JS-1000 [S]	The Subtle Sound of Joe Burton	1963	25.00

Number	Title	Yr	NM
REGENT			
❏ MG-6036 [M]	Jazz Pretty	1957	50.00
BUS BOYS			
ARISTA			
❏ AL9569	American Worker	1982	15.00
❏ AL8-8030	American Worker	198?	10.00
—Reissue			
❏ AB4280	Minimum Wage Rock 'n' Roll	1980	15.00
❏ AL5-8324	Minimum Wage Rock 'n' Roll	198?	10.00
—Second reissue of 4280			
❏ AL8-8054	Minimum Wage Rock 'n' Roll	198?	10.00
—First reissue of 4280			
VOSS/CHRYSALIS			
❏ 72915	Money Don't Make No Man	1988	15.00
BUSH, JOHNNY			
HILLTOP			
❏ JS-6081	You Ought to Hear Me Cry	197?	18.00
MILLION			
❏ 1001	The Best of Johnny Bush	1972	30.00
POWER PAK			
❏ PO-217	Bush Country	197?	15.00
RCA VICTOR			
❏ APL1-0216	Here Comes the World Again	1973	18.00
❏ APL1-0369	Texas Dance Hall Girl	1974	18.00
❏ LSP-10002	Whiskey River/There Stands the Glass	1973	18.00
STOP			
❏ 10014	Johnny Bush	1970	25.00
❏ 10002	Sound of a Heartache	1968	30.00
❏ 1028	The Greatest Hits of Johnny Bush	1972	25.00
❏ 10005	Undo the Right	1968	25.00
❏ 10008	You Gave Me a Mountain	1969	25.00
WHISKEY RIVER			
❏ 8024	Live at Dance Town USA	1979	18.00
BUSH, KATE			
COLUMBIA			
❏ OC44164	The Sensual World	1989	15.00
EMI AMERICA			
❏ ST-17171 [B]	Hounds of Love	1985	40.00
—Marbled vinyl			
❏ ST-17171	Hounds of Love	1985	12.00
—Black vinyl			
❏ MLP-19004 [LP]	Kate Bush	1983	18.00
❏ OMAS 17008	Lionheart	1978	18.00
❏ ST-17115	Never for Ever	1983	12.00
❏ ST-17084	The Dreaming	1982	12.00
❏ SW-17003	The Kick Inside	1978	12.00
—Reissue of Harvest release			
❏ PWAS-17242	The Whole Story	1986	18.00
HARVEST			
❏ SW-11761	The Kick Inside	1978	30.00
STEVE STROUT & ASSOC.			
❏ SSA3021	Kate Bush Radio Special: Self-Portrait	1978	450.00
—Uses The Kick Inside cover with special wrapper band			
BUSH			
TRAUMA			
❏ INT2-90161	Deconstructed	1997	18.00
❏ INT-90091	Razorblade Suitcase	1996	18.00
❏ IS-92531	Sixteen Stone	1996	18.00
—Distributed by Revelation			
BUSHKIN, JOE			
ATLANTIC			
❏ ALR-108 [10]	I Love a Piano	1950	50.00
❏ 81621	Play It Again, Joe	1985	12.00
CAPITOL			
❏ T832 [M]	A Fellow Needs a Girl	1957	30.00
—Turquoise or gray label			
❏ T1094 [M]	Blue Angels	1959	25.00
—Black colorband label, logo at left			
❏ ST1094 [S]	Blue Angels	1959	30.00
—Black colorband label, logo at left			
❏ T911 [M]	Bushkin Spotlights Berlin	1958	30.00
—Turquoise or gray label			
❏ T711 [M]	Midnight Rhapsody	1956	30.00
—Turquoise or gray label			
❏ T759 [M]	Skylight Rhapsody	1956	30.00
—Turquoise or gray label			
COLUMBIA			
❏ CL6201 [10]	After Hours	195?	50.00
❏ CS9615	Doctor Dolittle	1968	15.00
❏ CL6152 [10]	Piano Moods	195?	50.00
DECCA			
❏ DL4731 [M]	Night Sounds of San Francisco	1965	15.00
❏ DL74731 [S]	Night Sounds of San Francisco	1965	18.00

Number	Title	Yr	NM
EPIC			
❏ LN3345 [M]	Piano After Midnight	1956	30.00
REPRISE			
❏ R-6119 [M]	In Concert, Town Hall	1964	18.00
❏ RS-6119 [S]	In Concert, Town Hall	1964	25.00
ROYALE			
❏ 18118 [10]	Joe Bushkin	195?	50.00
BUSTA RHYMES			
ELEKTRA			
❏ 62517 [B]	Anarchy	2000	18.00
❏ 62211	E.L.E. (Extinction Level Event)	1998	18.00
❏ 61742	The Coming	1996	18.00
❏ ED6052 [DJ]	When Disaster Strikes	1997	25.00
—Promo-only version			
❏ 62064	When Disaster Strikes	1997	18.00
J			
❏ 20009 [B]	Genesis	2001	25.00
BUTCHER, JON, AXIS			
CAPITOL			
❏ ST-12425	Along the Axis	1985	10.00
❏ C1-90238	Pictures from the Front	1989	15.00
❏ ST-12542	Wishes	1987	10.00
POLYDOR			
❏ 810059-1	Jon Butcher Axis	1983	12.00
❏ 817493-1	Stare at the Sun	1984	12.00
BUTERA, SAM, AND THE WITNESSES			
CAPITOL			
❏ T1098 [M]	The Big Horn	1958	30.00
❏ ST1098 [S]	The Big Horn	1959	40.00
❏ T1521 [M]	The Big Sax and the Big Voice	1960	30.00
❏ ST1521 [S]	The Big Sax and the Big Voice	1960	30.00
DOT			
❏ DLP-3381 [M]	Apache	1961	25.00
❏ DLP-25381 [S]	Apache	1961	30.00
❏ DLP-3272 [M]	The Wildest Clan	1960	25.00
❏ DLP-25272 [S]	The Wildest Clan	1960	30.00
BUTLER, ARTIE			
A&M			
❏ SP-2007 [M]	Have You Met Miss Jones?	1968	50.00
—Mono appears to be promo only, in stereo cover with "Monaural" sticker			
❏ SP-3007 [S]	Have You Met Miss Jones?	1968	30.00
BUTLER, BILLY			
FANTASY			
❏ OJC-334	Guitar Soul	1988	15.00
—Reissue of Prestige 7734			
OKEH			
❏ OKM12115 [M]	Right Track	1966	25.00
❏ OKS14115 [S]	Right Track	1966	30.00
PRESTIGE			
❏ PRST-7734	Guitar Soul	1969	30.00
❏ PRST-7854	Night Life	1971	30.00
❏ PRST-7622	This Is Billy Butler	1968	30.00
❏ PRST-7797	Yesterday, Today and Tomorrow	1970	30.00
BUTLER, CARL, AND PEARL			
CHART			
❏ 1051	Temptation Keeps Twistin' Her Arm	1972	18.00
COLUMBIA			
❏ CL2640 [M]	Avenue of Prayer	1967	25.00
❏ CS9440 [S]	Avenue of Prayer	1967	18.00
❏ CS1039	Carl and Pearl Butler's Greatest Hits	1970	18.00
❏ CS9769	Honky Tonkin'	1969	18.00
❏ CL2125 [M]	Loving Arms	1964	25.00
❏ CS8925 [S]	Loving Arms	1964	30.00
❏ CS9651	Our Country World	1968	18.00
❏ CL2308 [M]	The Old and the New	1965	18.00
❏ CS9108 [S]	The Old and the New	1965	25.00
HARMONY			
❏ H31182	Watch and Pray	1972	15.00
BUTLER, CARL			
COLUMBIA			
❏ CL2002 [M]	Don't Let Me Cross Over	1963	25.00
❏ CS8802 [S]	Don't Let Me Cross Over	1963	30.00
HARMONY			
❏ H30674	For the First Time	1971	15.00
❏ HL7385 [M]	The Great Carl Butler Sings	1966	15.00
❏ HS11185 [S]	The Great Carl Butler Sings	1966	18.00
BUTLER, JERRY, AND BRENDA LEE EAGER			
MERCURY			
❏ SRM-1-660	The Love We Have	1973	18.00
BUTLER, JERRY			
ABNER			
❏ R-2001 [M]	Jerry Butler, Esq.	1959	400.00

Number	Title	Yr	NM
BUDDAH			
❏ BDS-4001	The Very Best of Jerry Butler	1969	18.00
FOUNTAIN			
❏ FR 2-82-1	Ice 'n Hot	1982	12.00
MERCURY			
❏ SR-61234	Ice On Ice	1969	18.00
❏ SR-61151	Jerry Butler's Golden Hits Live	1968	18.00
❏ SR-61320	Jerry Butler Sings Assorted Sounds	1971	18.00
❏ MG-21146 [M]	Mr. Dream Merchant	1967	25.00
❏ SR-61146 [S]	Mr. Dream Merchant	1967	18.00
❏ 822212-1	Only the Strong Survive: The Great Philadelphia Hits	1984	12.00
❏ SRM-1-1006	Sweet Sixteen	1974	18.00
❏ SR-61281	The Best of Jerry Butler	1970	18.00
❏ 810369-1	The Best of Jerry Butler	1983	12.00
❏ SR-61198	The Ice Man Cometh	1968	18.00
❏ SRM-1-689	The Power of Love	1973	18.00
❏ SR-61347	The Sagittarius Movement	1971	18.00
❏ MG-21005 [M]	The Soul Artistry of Jerry Butler	1967	25.00
❏ SR-61005 [S]	The Soul Artistry of Jerry Butler	1967	18.00
❏ SR-61171 [B]	The Soul Goes On	1968	18.00
❏ SRM-2-7502	The Spice of Life	1972	25.00
❏ SR-61269	You & Me	1970	18.00
MOTOWN			
❏ M6-892	It All Comes Out in My Songs	1977	12.00
❏ M6-850	Love's on the Menu	1976	15.00
❏ M6-878	Suite for the Single Girl	1977	12.00
PHILADELPHIA INT'L.			
❏ JZ35510	Nothing Says I Love You Like I Love You	1978	12.00
❏ JZ36413	The Best Love I Ever Had	1979	12.00
RHINO			
❏ RNLP-216	The Best of Jerry Butler (1958-1969)	1984	12.00
TRADITION			
❏ TLP-2068	Starring Jerry Butler	1969	18.00
TRIP			
❏ 8011	All Time Hits	1972	18.00
UNITED ARTISTS			
❏ UA-LA498-E	The Very Best of Jerry Butler	1975	12.00
VEE JAY			
❏ LP-1038 [M]	Aware of Love	1961	40.00
❏ SR-1038 [S]	Aware of Love	1961	50.00
❏ LP-1057 [M]	Folk Songs	1963	30.00
❏ SR-1057 [S]	Folk Songs	1963	30.00
❏ LP-1075 [M]	For Your Precious Love	1963	30.00
❏ SR-1075 [S]	For Your Precious Love	1963	30.00
❏ LP-1076 [M]	Giving Up On Love/Need to Belong	1963	30.00
❏ VJS-1076 [S]	Giving Up On Love/Need to Belong	1963	30.00
❏ LP-1029 [M]	He Will Break Your Heart	1960	80.00
❏ D1-74807	He Will Break Your Heart	1989	15.00
❏ LP-1027 [M]	Jerry Butler, Esquire	1960	150.00
—Reissue of Abner 2001			
❏ VJLP2-1003	Jerry Butler Gold	198?	18.00
❏ LP-1034 [M]	Love Me	1961	50.00
—Reissue of 1027			
❏ LP-1046 [M]	Moon River	1962	40.00
❏ SR-1046 [S]	Moon River	1962	50.00
❏ VJLP-1046	Moon River	1985	12.00
—Reissue of original 1046; has softer vinyl			
❏ LP-1119 [M]	More of the Best of Jerry Butler	1965	30.00
❏ VJS-1119 [S]	More of the Best of Jerry Butler	1965	30.00
❏ LP-1048 [M]	The Best of Jerry Butler	1962	30.00
❏ SR-1048 [P]	The Best of Jerry Butler	1962	30.00
❏ VJLP-1048	The Best of Jerry Butler	1985	12.00
—Reissue of original 1048; has softer vinyl			
BUTTERFIELD, BILLY			
CAPITOL			
❏ H424 [10]	Classics in Jazz	195?	50.00
❏ H201 [10]	Stardusting	1950	50.00
CIRCLE			
❏ CLP-037	Billy Butterfield with Ted Easton's Jazz Band	1977	18.00
COLUMBIA			
❏ CL1514 [M]	Billy Blows His Horn	1960	25.00
❏ CS8314 [S]	Billy Blows His Horn	1960	30.00
❏ CL1673 [M]	The Golden Horn	1961	25.00
—Red and black label with six "eye" logos			
❏ CS8473 [S]	The Golden Horn	1961	30.00
—Red and black label with six "eye" logos			
❏ CS8473 [S]	The Golden Horn	196?	25.00
—"360 Sound Stereo" on label			
EPIC			
❏ LA16026 [M]	Billy Plays Bix	1962	30.00
❏ BA17026 [S]	Billy Plays Bix	1962	40.00
ESSEX			
❏ 403 [M]	Billy Butterfield at Amherst	1955	40.00
❏ 401 [M]	Billy Butterfield at Princeton	1955	40.00
❏ 404 [M]	Billy Butterfield at Rutgers	1955	40.00
❏ 402 [M]	Billy Butterfield Goes to NYU	1955	40.00

Number	Title	Yr	NM
❑ ESLP-111 [10]	Far Away Places	195?	50.00
HINDSIGHT			
❑ HSR-173	Billy Butterfield 1946	198?	12.00
JAZZOLOGY			
❑ J-117	Just Friends	1984	15.00
❑ J-93	Watch What Happens	198?	12.00
JOY			
❑ JL-1003 [M]	The New Dance Sound of Billy Butterfield	196?	40.00
RCA VICTOR			
❑ LPM-1699 [M]	A Lovely Way to Spend an Evening	1958	30.00
❑ LSP-1699 [S]	A Lovely Way to Spend an Evening	1958	40.00
❑ LPM-1566 [M]	A Touch of the Blues	1958	40.00
❑ LPM-1212 [M]	New York Land Dixie	1956	40.00
❑ LPM-1590 [M]	Thank You for a Lovely Evening	1958	30.00
❑ LPM-1441 [M]	They're Playing Our Song	1957	40.00
SOMERSET			
❑ P-2200 [M]	I'm In the Mood for the Magic Trumpet of Billy Butterfield and His Orchestra	196?	18.00
WESTMINSTER			
❑ WL-3020 [10]	Billy Butterfield	1954	50.00
❑ WL-6006 [M]	Dancing for Two in Love	1955	40.00

BUTTERFIELD, PAUL

Number	Title	Yr	NM
AMHERST			
❑ AMH-3305	The Legendary Paul Butterfield Rides Again	1986	15.00
BEARSVILLE			
❑ BR2170	It All Comes Back	1973	15.00
❑ BRK6995	North-South	1978	15.00
❑ BR2119	Paul Butterfield's Better Days	1973	15.00
❑ BR6960	Put It In Your Ear	1976	15.00
ELEKTRA			
❑ EKL-315 [M]	East-West	1966	25.00
— Gold label with guitar player			
❑ EKL-315 [M]	East-West	1967	18.00
— Brown label			
❑ EKS-7315 [S]	East-West	1966	30.00
— Gold label with guitar player			
❑ EKS-7315 [S]	East-West	1967	25.00
— Brown label			
❑ EKS-7315 [S]	East-West	1969	18.00
— Red label with large stylized "E"			
❑ EKS-7315 [S]	East-West	1971	15.00
— Butterfly label			
❑ 7E-2005	Golden Butter/The Best of the Paul Butterfield Blues Band	1972	30.00
❑ EKS-74025	In My Own Dream	1968	25.00
— Brown label			
❑ EKS-74025	In My Own Dream	1969	18.00
— Red label with large stylized "E"			
❑ EKS-74025	In My Own Dream	1971	15.00
— Butterfly label			
❑ EKS-74053	Keep On Moving	1969	25.00
— Red label with large stylized "E"			
❑ EKS-74053	Keep On Moving	1971	15.00
— Butterfly label			
❑ EKS-75013	Sometimes I Just Feel Like Smilin'	1971	25.00
❑ 7E-2001	The Butterfield Blues Band/Live	1970	30.00
❑ EKL-294 [M]	The Paul Butterfield Blues Band	1965	25.00
— Gold label with guitar player			
❑ EKS-7294 [S]	The Paul Butterfield Blues Band	1965	30.00
— Gold label with guitar player			
❑ EKL-294 [M]	The Paul Butterfield Blues Band	1966	18.00
— Brown label			
❑ EKS-7294 [S]	The Paul Butterfield Blues Band	1966	25.00
— Brown label			
❑ EKS-7294 [S]	The Paul Butterfield Blues Band	1969	18.00
— Red label with large stylized "E"			
❑ EKS-7294 [S]	The Paul Butterfield Blues Band	1971	15.00
— Butterfly label			
❑ EKL-4015 [M]	The Resurrection of Pigboy Crabshaw	1967	30.00
❑ EKS-74015 [S]	The Resurrection of Pigboy Crabshaw	1967	25.00
— Brown label			
❑ EKS-74015 [S]	The Resurrection of Pigboy Crabshaw	1969	18.00
— Red label with large stylized "E"			
❑ EKS-74015 [S]	The Resurrection of Pigboy Crabshaw	1971	15.00
— Butterfly label			
RHINO			
❑ RNLP-70878	It All Comes Back	1987	10.00
— Reissue of Bearsville 2170			
❑ RNLP-70880	North-South	1987	10.00
— Reissue of Bearsville 6995			

Number	Title	Yr	NM
❑ RNLP-70877	Paul Butterfield's Better Days	1987	10.00
— Reissue of Bearsville 2119			
❑ RNLP-70879	Put It In Your Ear	1987	10.00
— Reissue of Bearsville 6960			
SUNDAZED			
❑ LP5096	East-West	2001	15.00
— Reissue on 180-gram vinyl			
❑ LP5095 [S]	The Paul Butterfield Blues Band	2001	15.00
— Reissue on 180-gram vinyl			

BUTTHOLE SURFERS

Number	Title	Yr	NM
ALTERNATIVE TENTACLES			
❑ VIRUS32 [EP]	Brown Reason to Live	198?	10.00
— Black vinyl			
❑ VIRUS32 [EP]	Brown Reason to Live	1983	25.00
— Retitled version of debut EP with brown swirl vinyl			
❑ VIRUS32 [EP]	Butthole Surfers	1983	30.00
— Original pressing of debut EP with no title			
❑ VIRUS39 [EP]	Live PCPPEP	1984	10.00
CAPITOL			
❑ C1-29842 [B]	Electriclarryland	1996	30.00
❑ C1-98798	Independent Worm Saloon	1993	18.00
HOLLYWOOD			
❑ 41447-1	Weird Revolution	2001	18.00
— Pressed in Germany for U.S. release			
LATINO BUGGERVEIL			
❑ LBV 07	Humpty Dumpty LSD	2002	25.00
ROUGH TRADE			
❑ R260	Pioughd	1990	25.00
TOUCH & GO			
❑ 14 [EP]	Cream Corn from the Socket of Davis	1985	30.00
— Yellow vinyl in green generic sleeve with sticker			
❑ 14 [EP]	Cream Corn from the Socket of Davis	1985	25.00
— Red vinyl			
❑ 14 [EP]	Cream Corn from the Socket of Davis	1985	12.00
— Black vinyl			
❑ 29	Hairway to Steven	1988	12.00
❑ 19	Locust Abortion Technician	1987	12.00
❑ 5	Psychic...Powerless... Another Man's Sac	1985	12.00
— Reissue on black vinyl			
❑ 5	Psychic...Powerless... Another Man's Sac	1985	25.00
— Original on clear vinyl			
❑ 8	Rembrandt Pussyhorse	1986	12.00
— Black vinyl			
❑ 8	Rembrandt Pussyhorse	1986	40.00
— Red vinyl; supposedly only 100 were pressed			
❑ 50	Widowermaker!	1989	12.00

BUZZCOCKS, THE

Number	Title	Yr	NM
4 MEN WITH BEARDS			
❑ 4M505LP [B]	Singles Going Steady		25.00
GO-KART			
❑ GK 058	Modern	1999	12.00
I.R.S.			
❑ SP-009	A Different Kind of Tension	1980	18.00
— Original issue			
❑ SP-75009	A Different Kind of Tension	1981	12.00
— Reissue of SP-009			
❑ -0 [DJ]	Are Everything/Strange Thing + 4	1980	18.00
— Red vinyl; no cover; some come with numbered sticker			
❑ SP-70507 [EP]	Parts 1-3	1984	12.00
❑ SP-70955 [DJ]	Parts 1-3	1981	30.00
— Original issue; six-song promo on red vinyl in plastic cover with numbered sticker			
❑ SP-001	Singles Going Steady	1979	18.00
— Original issue			
❑ SP-75001	Singles Going Steady	1981	12.00
— Reissue of SP-001			

BYARD, JAKI

Number	Title	Yr	NM
MUSE			
❑ 5173	Family Man	1978	18.00
❑ 5007	There'll Be Some Changes Made	1974	25.00
NEW JAZZ			
❑ NJLP-8256 [M]	Here's Jaki	1961	100.00
— Purple label			
❑ NJLP-8256 [M]	Here's Jaki	1965	30.00
— Blue label with trident logo at right			
❑ NJLP-8273 [M]	Hi-Fly	1962	60.00
— Purple label			
❑ NJLP-8273 [M]	Hi-Fly	1965	30.00
— Blue label with trident logo at right			
PRESTIGE			
❑ PRLP-7463 [M]	Freedom Together	1967	40.00
— Blue label with trident logo at right			
❑ PRST-7463 [S]	Freedom Together	1967	40.00
— Blue label with trident logo at right			

Number	Title	Yr	NM
❑ PRST-7463 [S]	Freedom Together	1968	30.00
— Blue label with trident logo in circle at top			
❑ 24086	Giant Steps	197?	25.00
❑ PRST-7573	Jaki Byard with Strings!	1968	30.00
❑ PRLP-7419 [M]	Live!	1966	30.00
— Blue label with trident logo at right			
❑ PRST-7419 [S]	Live!	1966	40.00
— Blue label with trident logo at right			
❑ PRST-7419 [S]	Live!	1968	30.00
— Blue label with trident logo in circle at top			
❑ PRLP-7477 [M]	Live! Volume 2	1967	40.00
— Blue label with trident logo at right			
❑ PRST-7477 [S]	Live! Volume 2	1967	40.00
— Blue label with trident logo at right			
❑ PRST-7477 [S]	Live! Volume 2	1968	30.00
— Blue label with trident logo in circle at top			
❑ PRLP-7524 [M]	On the Spot	1967	50.00
— Blue label with trident logo at right			
❑ PRST-7524 [S]	On the Spot	1967	40.00
— Blue label with trident logo at right			
❑ PRST-7524 [S]	On the Spot	1968	30.00
— Blue label with trident logo in circle at top			
❑ PRLP-7397 [M]	Out Front	1965	30.00
— Blue label with trident logo at right			
❑ PRST-7397 [S]	Out Front	1965	40.00
— Blue label with trident logo at right			
❑ PRST-7397 [S]	Out Front	1968	30.00
— Blue label with trident logo in circle at top			
❑ PRST-7686	Solo Piano	1969	30.00
❑ PRST-7615	The Jaki Byard Experience	1969	30.00
❑ PRST-7550	The Sunshine of My Soul	1968	30.00
SOUL NOTE			
❑ 121125	Foolin' Myself	199?	15.00
❑ SN-1075	Phantasies	1985	15.00
❑ 121175	Phantasies II	199?	15.00
❑ SN-1031	To Them -- To Us	198?	15.00

BYAS, DON

Number	Title	Yr	NM
ATLANTIC			
❑ ALR-117 [10]	Don Byas Solos	1952	250.00
BATTLE			
❑ B-6121 [M]	April in Paris	1963	30.00
❑ BS-6121 [S]	April in Paris	1963	40.00
BLACK LION			
❑ 160	Anthropology	1973	18.00
DIAL			
❑ LP-216 [10]	Tenor Saxophone Concerto	1951	300.00
DISCOVERY			
❑ 3022 [10]	Don Byas with Beryl Booker	1954	150.00
EMARCY			
❑ MG-26026 [10]	Don Byas Sax	1954	120.00
GNP CRESCENDO			
❑ GNP-9027	Don Byas	197?	15.00
NORGRAN			
❑ MGN-12 [10]	In France "Don Byas Et Ses Rhythmes	1954	150.00
ONYX			
❑ 208	Midnight at Minton's	197?	18.00
PRESTIGE			
❑ PRST-7598	Don Byas In Paris	1969	25.00
❑ PRST-7692	Don Byas Meets Ben Webster	1969	25.00
REGENT			
❑ MG-6044 [M]	Jazz Free and Easy	1957	80.00
SAVOY			
❑ MG-9007 [10]	Don Byas Sax	1952	150.00
❑ MG-12203	Jazz Free and Easy	196?	25.00
❑ SJL-2213	Savoy Jam Party	197?	18.00
❑ MG-15043 [10]	Tenor Sax Solos	1955	120.00
SEECO			
❑ SLP-35 [10]	Don Byas Favorites	1955	120.00

BYAS, DON/ BERNARD PEIFFER

Number	Title	Yr	NM
VERVE			
❑ MGV-8119 [M]	Jazz from Saint-Germain Des Pres	1957	50.00
❑ V-8119 [M]	Jazz from Saint-Germain Des Pres	1961	25.00

BYAS, DON/BUDDY TATE

Number	Title	Yr	NM
ALLEGRO			
❑ 1741 [M]	All Star Jazz	1956	40.00

BYERS, BILLY; JOE NEWMAN; EDDIE BERT

Number	Title	Yr	NM
JAZZTONE			
❑ J-1276 [M]	East Coast Sounds	1959	60.00

BYERS, BILLY

Number	Title	Yr	NM
CONCERT HALL JAZZ			
❑ 1217 [M]	Byers' Guide	1955	80.00
MERCURY			
❑ PPM-2028 [M]	Impressions of Duke Ellington	196?	25.00
❑ PPS-6028 [S]	Impressions of Duke Ellington	196?	30.00

RCA VICTOR

Number	Title	Yr	NM
❑ LPM-1269 [M]	The Jazz Workshop	1956	80.00

WING

Number	Title	Yr	NM
❑ SRW-16398 [S]	Impressions of Duke Ellington	196?	18.00

BYRD, BILLY

REPRISE

Number	Title	Yr	NM
❑ R-6040 [M]	Lonesome Country Songs	1962	25.00
❑ R9-6040 [S]	Lonesome Country Songs	1962	30.00

WARNER BROS.

Number	Title	Yr	NM
❑ W1327 [M]	I Love a Guitar	1960	25.00
❑ WS1327 [S]	I Love a Guitar	1960	30.00
❑ W1576 [M]	The Golden Guitar of Billy Byrd	1964	25.00
❑ WS1576 [S]	The Golden Guitar of Billy Byrd	1964	30.00

BYRD, CHARLIE, AND FATHER MALCOLM BOYD

COLUMBIA

Number	Title	Yr	NM
❑ CL2548 [M]	Are You Running With Me, Jesus?	1966	18.00
❑ CS9348 [S]	Are You Running With Me, Jesus?	1966	25.00
❑ CL2657 [M]	Happening Prayers for Now	1967	18.00
❑ CS9457 [S]	Happening Prayers for Now	1967	18.00

BYRD, CHARLIE, HERB ELLIS & BARNEY KESSEL

CONCORD JAZZ

Number	Title	Yr	NM
❑ CJD-1002	Straight Tracks	1986	25.00
—Direct-to-disc recording			
❑ C-4	The Great Guitars	197?	15.00
❑ C-23	The Great Guitars	197?	15.00
❑ CJ-209	The Great Guitars at Charlie's Georgetown	1982	12.00
❑ CJ-131	The Great Guitars at the Winery	1981	12.00

BYRD, CHARLIE

COLUMBIA

Number	Title	Yr	NM
❑ CS9841	Aquarius	1969	18.00
❑ C30380	A Stroke of Genius	1971	15.00
❑ CL2504 [M]	A Touch of Gold	1966	15.00
❑ CS9304 [S]	A Touch of Gold	1966	18.00
❑ CL2337 [M]	Brazilian Byrd	1965	18.00
—Guaranteed High Fidelity" on label			
❑ CL2337 [M]	Brazilian Byrd	1965	15.00
—360 Sound Mono" on label			
❑ CS9137 [S]	Brazilian Byrd	1965	25.00
—Red label, "360 Sound" in black			
❑ CS9137 [S]	Brazilian Byrd	1965	18.00
—Red label, "360 Sound" in white			
❑ PC9137	Brazilian Byrd	198?	10.00
—Reissue with new prefix			
❑ CS9137	Brazilian Byrd	1971	12.00
—Orange label			
❑ CL2592 [M]	Byrdland	1967	25.00
❑ CS9392 [S]	Byrdland	1967	18.00
❑ CL2555 [M]	Christmas Carols for Solo Guitar	1966	18.00
❑ CS9355 [S]	Christmas Carols for Solo Guitar	1966	25.00
❑ CS9667	Delicately	1968	18.00
❑ G30622	For All We Know	1971	18.00
❑ CS9627 [M]	Hit Trip	1968	30.00
—Special Mono Radio Station Copy" with white label			
❑ CS9627 [S]	Hit Trip	1968	18.00
❑ CL2652 [M]	Hollywood Byrd	1967	25.00
❑ CS9452 [S]	Hollywood Byrd	1967	18.00
❑ CS9869	Let Go	1969	18.00
❑ CS1053	Let It Be	1970	15.00
❑ CL2692 [M]	More Brazilian Byrd	1967	25.00
❑ CS9492 [S]	More Brazilian Byrd	1967	18.00
❑ C31025	Onda Nuevo	1972	15.00
❑ CS9582	Sketches of Brazil (Music of Villa Lobos)	1968	18.00
❑ CS9747	The Great Byrd	1968	18.00
❑ CS9970	The Greatest Hits of the 60's	1970	15.00
❑ CG31967	The World of Charlie Byrd	1972	18.00
❑ CL2435 [M]	Travellin' Man Recorded Live	1966	15.00
❑ CS9235 [S]	Travellin' Man Recorded Live	1966	18.00

CONCORD JAZZ

Number	Title	Yr	NM
❑ CJ-82	Blue Byrd	1979	12.00
❑ CJ-304	Byrd & Brass	1986	12.00
❑ CJ-252	Isn't It Romantic	1984	12.00
❑ CJ-374	It's a Wonderful World	1989	15.00

CONCORD PICANTE

Number	Title	Yr	NM
❑ P-173	Brazilville	1981	12.00
❑ P-114	Sugarloaf Suite	1980	12.00

CRYSTAL CLEAR

Number	Title	Yr	NM
❑ 8002	Charlie Byrd	1979	30.00
—Direct-to-disc recording; plays at 45 rpm			

FANTASY

Number	Title	Yr	NM
❑ OJC-107	Bossa Nova Pelos Passaros	198?	12.00
—Reissue of Riverside 436			
❑ OJC-262	Byrd at the Gate	1987	12.00
—Reissue of Riverside 9467			
❑ F-9466	Byrd by the Sea	1974	15.00
❑ F-9429	Crystal Silence	1973	15.00
❑ F-9496	Top Hat	1975	15.00

IMPROV

Number	Title	Yr	NM
❑ 7116	Charlie Byrd Swings Downtown	1977	15.00

MILESTONE

Number	Title	Yr	NM
❑ 47049	Charlie Byrd in Greenwich Village	1978	18.00
❑ 47005	Latin Byrd	1973	18.00

MOBILE FIDELITY

Number	Title	Yr	NM
❑ 1-515	Byrd at the Gate	1982	40.00
—Audiophile vinyl			

OFFBEAT

Number	Title	Yr	NM
❑ OLP-3009 [M]	Blues Sonata	1960	30.00
❑ OS-93009 [S]	Blues Sonata	1960	30.00
❑ OJ-3007 [M]	Charlie's Choice	1960	30.00
❑ OS-93007 [S]	Charlie's Choice	1960	30.00
❑ OJ-3001 [M]	Jazz at the Show Boat, Volume 1	1959	30.00
❑ OS-93001 [S]	Jazz at the Show Boat, Volume 1	1959	30.00
❑ OJ-3005 [M]	Jazz at the Show Boat, Volume 2	1959	30.00
❑ OS-93005 [S]	Jazz at the Show Boat, Volume 2	1959	30.00
❑ OJ-3006 [M]	Jazz at the Show Boat, Volume 3	1959	30.00
❑ OS-93006 [S]	Jazz at the Show Boat, Volume 3	1959	30.00

PICKWICK

Number	Title	Yr	NM
❑ SPC-3042	Byrd and the Herd	196?	15.00

RIVERSIDE

Number	Title	Yr	NM
❑ RM-453 [M]	Blues Sonata	1963	25.00
❑ RS-9453 [S]	Blues Sonata	1963	30.00
❑ 6054	Blues Sonata	197?	12.00
❑ RM-436 [M]	Bossa Nova Pelos Passaros	1962	25.00
❑ RS-9436 [S]	Bossa Nova Pelos Passaros	1962	30.00
❑ RM-467 [M]	Byrd at the Gate	1964	25.00
❑ RS-9467 [S]	Byrd at the Gate	1964	30.00
❑ RM-449 [M]	Byrd in the Wind	1963	25.00
❑ RS-9449 [S]	Byrd in the Wind	1963	30.00
❑ RS-3044	Byrd Man with Strings	1969	18.00
❑ RM-481 [M]	Byrd Song	1966	18.00
❑ RS-9481 [S]	Byrd Song	1966	25.00
❑ RM-448 [M]	Byrd's Word	1963	25.00
❑ RS-9448 [S]	Byrd's Word	1963	30.00
❑ RM-452 [M]	Charlie Byrd at the Village Vanguard	1963	25.00
❑ RS-9452 [S]	Charlie Byrd at the Village Vanguard	1963	30.00
❑ RM-427 [M]	Latin Impressions	1962	25.00
❑ RS-9427 [S]	Latin Impressions	1962	30.00
❑ RM-450 [M]	Mr. Guitar	1963	25.00
❑ RS-9450 [S]	Mr. Guitar	1963	30.00
❑ RM-454 [M]	Once More! Bossa Nova	1963	25.00
❑ RS-9454 [S]	Once More! Bossa Nova	1963	30.00
❑ RM-498 [M]	Solo Flight	1967	25.00
❑ RS-9498 [S]	Solo Flight	1967	18.00
❑ RM-451 [M]	The Guitar Artistry of Charlie Byrd	1963	25.00
❑ RS-9451 [S]	The Guitar Artistry of Charlie Byrd	1963	30.00
❑ RS-3005	The Guitar Artistry of Charlie Byrd	1968	18.00

SAVOY

Number	Title	Yr	NM
❑ MG-12116 [M]	Blues for Night People	1957	40.00
❑ MG-12099 [M]	Jazz Recital	1957	40.00

SAVOY JAZZ

Number	Title	Yr	NM
❑ SJL-1131	First Flight	1980	12.00
❑ SJL-1121	Midnight Guitar	1980	12.00

BYRD, DONALD; HANY MOBLEY; KENNY BURRELL

STATUS

Number	Title	Yr	NM
❑ ST-8317 [M]	Donald Byrd, Hank Mobley & Kenny Burrell	1965	40.00

BYRD, DONALD

AMERICAN RECORDING SOCIETY

Number	Title	Yr	NM
❑ G-437 [M]	Modern Jazz	1957	40.00

BLUE NOTE

Number	Title	Yr	NM
❑ BLP-4124 [M]	A New Perspective	1964	25.00
❑ BST-84124 [S]	A New Perspective	1964	30.00
—New York, USA" address on label			
❑ BST-84124 [S]	A New Perspective	1967	15.00
—A Division of Liberty Records" on label			
❑ BST-84124	A New Perspective	198?	12.00
—The Finest in Jazz Since 1939" reissue			
❑ BST-84124 [S]	A New Perspective	1973	12.00
—A Division of United Artists Records Inc." on label			
❑ BN-LA047-F	Black Byrd	1973	18.00
❑ LO-047	Black Byrd	1981	10.00
—Reissue of LA047			
❑ BLP-4259 [M]	Blackjack	1967	30.00
❑ BST-84259 [S]	Blackjack	1967	25.00
❑ BLP-4048 [M]	Byrd in Flight	1960	350.00
—Deep groove" version (deep indentation under label on both sides)			
❑ BLP-4048 [M]	Byrd in Flight	1960	80.00
—W. 63rd St., NYC address on label			
❑ BLP-4048 [M]	Byrd in Flight	1963	30.00
—New York, USA" address on label			
❑ BST-84048 [S]	Byrd in Flight	1960	60.00
—W. 63rd St., NYC address on label			
❑ BST-84048 [S]	Byrd in Flight	1963	30.00
—New York, USA" address on label			
❑ BST-84048 [S]	Byrd in Flight	1967	15.00
—A Division of Liberty Records" on label			
❑ BLP-4019 [M]	Byrd in Hand	1959	350.00
—Deep groove" version (deep indentation under label on both sides)			
❑ BLP-4019 [M]	Byrd in Hand	1959	80.00
—W. 63rd St., NYC address on label			
❑ BLP-4019 [M]	Byrd in Hand	1963	30.00
—New York, USA" address on label			
❑ BST-84019 [S]	Byrd in Hand	1959	60.00
—W. 63rd St., NYC address on label			
❑ BST-84019 [S]	Byrd in Hand	1963	30.00
—New York, USA" address on label			
❑ BST-84019 [S]	Byrd in Hand	1967	15.00
—A Division of Liberty Records" on label			
❑ BST-84007 [S]	Byrd in Hand	1967	15.00
—A Division of Liberty Records" on label			
❑ BST-84019	Byrd in Hand	198?	12.00
—The Finest in Jazz Since 1939" reissue			
❑ BN-LA633-G	Caricatures	1976	18.00
❑ LT-991	Chant	1980	15.00
❑ LT-1096	Creeper	1981	15.00
❑ BLP-4060 [M]	Donald Byrd at the Half Note Café, Volume 1	1961	80.00
—W. 63rd St., NYC address on label			
❑ BLP-4060 [M]	Donald Byrd at the Half Note Café, Volume 1	1963	30.00
—New York, USA" address on label			
❑ BST-84060 [S]	Donald Byrd at the Half Note Café, Volume 1	1961	60.00
—W. 63rd St., NYC address on label			
❑ BST-84060 [S]	Donald Byrd at the Half Note Café, Volume 1	1963	30.00
—New York, USA" address on label			
❑ BST-84060 [S]	Donald Byrd at the Half Note Café, Volume 1	1967	15.00
—A Division of Liberty Records" on label			
❑ BLP-4061 [M]	Donald Byrd at the Half Note Café, Volume 2	1961	80.00
—W. 63rd St., NYC address on label			
❑ BLP-4061 [M]	Donald Byrd at the Half Note Café, Volume 2	1963	30.00
—New York, USA" address on label			
❑ BST-84061 [S]	Donald Byrd at the Half Note Café, Volume 2	1961	60.00
—W. 63rd St., NYC address on label			
❑ BST-84061 [S]	Donald Byrd at the Half Note Café, Volume 2	1963	30.00
—New York, USA" address on label			
❑ BST-84061 [S]	Donald Byrd at the Half Note Café, Volume 2	1967	15.00
—A Division of Liberty Records" on label			
❑ BN-LA700-G	Donald Byrd's Best	1976	18.00
❑ BST-84349	Electric	1970	25.00
❑ B1-36195	Electric Byrd	1996	18.00
❑ BST-84380	Ethiopian Nights	1972	25.00
❑ BST-84319	Fancy Free	1969	25.00
❑ B1-89796	Fancy Free	1993	18.00
❑ BLP-4118 [M]	Free Form	1963	25.00
❑ BST-84118 [S]	Free Form	1963	30.00
—New York, USA" address on label			
❑ BST-84118 [S]	Free Form	1967	15.00
—A Division of Liberty Records" on label			
❑ BST-84118	Free Form	1986	12.00
—The Finest in Jazz Since 1939" reissue			
❑ BLP-4026 [M]	Fuego	1960	250.00
—Deep groove" version (deep indentation under label on both sides)			
❑ BLP-4026 [M]	Fuego	1960	80.00
—W. 63rd St., NYC address on label			
❑ BLP-4026 [M]	Fuego	1963	30.00
—New York, USA" address on label			
❑ BST-84026 [S]	Fuego	1959	60.00
—W. 63rd St., NYC address on label			
❑ BST-84026 [S]	Fuego	1963	30.00
—New York, USA" address on label			
❑ BST-84026 [S]	Fuego	1967	15.00
—A Division of Liberty Records" on label			
❑ BLP-4188 [M]	I'm Tryin' to Get Home	1965	25.00
❑ BST-84188 [S]	I'm Tryin' to Get Home	1965	30.00
—New York, USA" address on label			
❑ BST-84188 [S]	I'm Tryin' to Get Home	1967	15.00
—A Division of Liberty Records" on label			
❑ BST-84188	I'm Tryin' to Get Home	1986	12.00
—The Finest in Jazz Since 1939" reissue			
❑ B1-31875	Kofi	1995	18.00
❑ BLP-4238 [M]	Mustang!	1966	25.00
❑ BST-84238 [S]	Mustang!	1966	30.00
—New York, USA" address on label			
❑ BST-84238 [S]	Mustang!	1967	15.00
—A Division of Liberty Records" on label			
❑ BLP-4007 [M]	Off to the Races	1959	120.00
—Deep groove" version (deep indentation under label on both sides)			
❑ BLP-4007 [M]	Off to the Races	1959	80.00
—W. 63rd St., NYC address on label			
❑ BLP-4007 [M]	Off to the Races	1963	30.00
—New York, USA" address on label			

Number	Title	Yr	NM
❑ BST-4007 [S]	Off to the Races	1959	80.00
—Deep groove" version (deep indentation under label on both sides)			
❑ BST-4007 [S]	Off to the Races	1959	60.00
—W. 63rd St., NYC address on label			
❑ BST-4007 [S]	Off to the Races	1963	30.00
—New York, USA" address on label			
❑ BN-LA549-G	Places and Spaces	1975	18.00
❑ LW-549	Places and Spaces	1981	10.00
—Reissue of LA549			
❑ BLP-4101 [M]	Royal Flush	1962	25.00
❑ BST-84101 [S]	Royal Flush	1962	30.00
—New York, USA" address on label			
❑ BST-84101 [S]	Royal Flush	1967	15.00
—A Division of Liberty Records" on label			
❑ BN-LA368-G	Sleeping Into Tomorrow	1975	18.00
❑ BST-84292 [B]	Slow Drag	1968	25.00
❑ BN-LA140-G	Street Lady	1974	18.00
❑ LN-10054	Street Lady	1981	10.00
—Budget-line reissue			
❑ BLP-4075 [M]	The Cat Walk	1961	80.00
—61st St, New York address on label			
❑ BLP-4075 [M]	The Cat Walk	1963	30.00
—New York, USA" address on label			
❑ BST-84075 [S]	The Cat Walk	1961	60.00
—61st St, New York address on label			
❑ BST-84075 [S]	The Cat Walk	1963	30.00
—New York, USA" address on label			
❑ BST-84075 [S]	The Cat Walk	1967	15.00
—A Division of Liberty Records" on label			

DELMARK

Number	Title	Yr	NM
❑ DS-407	First Flight	1990	15.00

DISCOVERY

Number	Title	Yr	NM
❑ 869	September Afternoon	198?	12.00

ELEKTRA

Number	Title	Yr	NM
❑ 6E-247	Donald Byrd and 125th St., N.Y.C.	1980	12.00
❑ 5E-531	Love Byrd	1981	12.00
❑ 6E-144	Thank You for F.U.M.L. (Funking Up My Life)	1978	12.00
❑ 60188	Words, Sounds, Colors and Shapes	1982	12.00

LANDMARK

Number	Title	Yr	NM
❑ LLP-1523	Getting Down to Business	1990	15.00
❑ LLP-1516	Harlem Blues	1988	12.00

SAVOY

Number	Title	Yr	NM
❑ MG-12032 [M]	Byrd's Word	1956	100.00
❑ MG-12064 [M]	The Jazz Message of Donald Byrd	1956	120.00

SAVOY JAZZ

Number	Title	Yr	NM
❑ SJL-1101	Long Green	198?	12.00
❑ SJL-1114	Star Eyes	198?	12.00

TRANSITION

Number	Title	Yr	NM
❑ TRLP-17 [M]	Byrd Blows on Beacon Hill	1956	600.00
❑ TRLP-5 [M]	Byrd Jazz	1956	600.00
❑ TRLP-4 [M]	Byrd's Eye View	1956	600.00

TRIP

Number	Title	Yr	NM
❑ 5000	Two Sides of Donald Byrd	1974	18.00

VERVE

Number	Title	Yr	NM
❑ V-8609 [M]	Up with Donald Byrd	1965	25.00
❑ V6-8609 [S]	Up with Donald Byrd	1965	30.00

BYRD, JERRY

DECCA

Number	Title	Yr	NM
❑ DL8643 [M]	Hi-Fi Guitar	1958	40.00
❑ DL4078 [M]	Paradise Island	1961	25.00
❑ DL74078 [S]	Paradise Island	1961	30.00

MERCURY

Number	Title	Yr	NM
❑ MG-20856 [M]	Blue Hawaiian Steel Guitar	1963	30.00
❑ SR-60856 [S]	Blue Hawaiian Steel Guitar	1963	40.00
❑ MG-25169 [10]	Byrd's Expedition	1954	80.00
❑ MG-25134 [10]	Guitar Magic	1954	80.00
❑ MG-20693 [M]	Hawaiian Golden Hits	1962	30.00
❑ SR-60693 [S]	Hawaiian Golden Hits	1962	40.00
❑ MG-25077 [10]	Nani Hawaii	1953	80.00
❑ MG-20230 [M]	On the Shores of Waikiki	1960	30.00
❑ SR-60230 [S]	On the Shores of Waikiki	1960	40.00
❑ MG-20345 [M]	Steel Guitar Favorites	1961	30.00
❑ SR-60345 [S]	Steel Guitar Favorites	1961	40.00
❑ MG-20932 [M]	The Man of Steel	1964	25.00
❑ SR-60932 [S]	The Man of Steel	1964	30.00

MONUMENT

Number	Title	Yr	NM
❑ MLP-8014 [M]	Admirable Byrd	1963	25.00
❑ SLP-18014 [S]	Admirable Byrd	1963	30.00
❑ MLP-8009 [M]	Byrd of Paradise	1962	25.00
❑ SLP-18009 [S]	Byrd of Paradise	1962	30.00
❑ MLP-4008 [M]	Memories of Maria	1962	25.00
❑ SLP-14008 [S]	Memories of Maria	1962	30.00

BYRD, JOE, AND THE FIELD HIPPIES

COLUMBIA MASTERWORKS

Number	Title	Yr	NM
❑ MS7317	The American Metaphysical Circus	1969	40.00

BYRDS, THE

ASYLUM

Number	Title	Yr	NM
❑ 5058 [M]	Byrds	1973	40.00
—Mono is white label promo only; "dj copy monaural" sticker on stereo cover			
❑ SD5058 [S]	Byrds	1973	15.00

COLUMBIA

Number	Title	Yr	NM
❑ CS9942 [S]	Ballad of Easy Rider	1969	25.00
—Red "360 Sound" label			
❑ CS9942 [S]	Ballad of Easy Rider	1971	12.00
—Orange label			
❑ PC9942	Ballad of Easy Rider	1984	10.00
—Reissue with new prefix			
❑ KC30640	Byrdmaniax	1971	15.00
❑ CS9755 [S]	Dr. Byrds and Mr. Hyde	1969	25.00
—Red "360 Sound" label			
❑ CS9755 [S]	Dr. Byrds and Mr. Hyde	1971	12.00
—Orange label			
❑ PC9755 [S]	Dr. Byrds and Mr. Hyde	198?	10.00
—Reissue with new prefix			
❑ C31050	Farther Along	1971	15.00
❑ CL2549 [M]	Fifth Dimension (5D)	1966	30.00
❑ CS9349 [S]	Fifth Dimension (5D)	1966	30.00
—Red "360 Sound" label			
❑ CS9349 [S]	Fifth Dimension (5D)	1971	12.00
—Orange label			
❑ PC9349 [S]	Fifth Dimension (5D)	198?	10.00
—Reissue with new prefix			
❑ CL2372 [M]	Mr. Tambourine Man	1965	40.00
—Guaranteed High Fidelity" on label			
❑ CL2372 [M]	Mr. Tambourine Man	1966	30.00
—360 Sound Mono" on label			
❑ CS9172 [S]	Mr. Tambourine Man	1965	40.00
—Red label, "360 Sound" in black			
❑ CS9172 [S]	Mr. Tambourine Man	1966	30.00
—Red label, "360 Sound" in white			
❑ CS9172 [S]	Mr. Tambourine Man	1971	12.00
—Orange label			
❑ PC9172 [S]	Mr. Tambourine Man	198?	10.00
—Reissue with new prefix			
❑ CG33645	Mr. Tambourine Man/Turn! Turn! Turn!	1976	18.00
❑ KC32183	Preflyte	1973	15.00
—Reissue of Together LP			
❑ C32183	Preflyte	197?	12.00
—Reissue with new prefix			
❑ CS9670 [M]	Sweetheart of the Rodeo	1968	100.00
—Special Mono Radio Station Copy" with white label			
❑ CS9670 [S]	Sweetheart of the Rodeo	1968	25.00
—Red "360 Sound" label			
❑ CS9670 [S]	Sweetheart of the Rodeo	1971	12.00
—Orange label			
❑ PC9670 [S]	Sweetheart of the Rodeo	198?	10.00
—Reissue with new prefix			
❑ KC31795	The Best of the Byrds (Greatest Hits, Volume II)	1972	15.00
❑ C31795	The Best of the Byrds (Greatest Hits, Volume II)	197?	12.00
—Reissue with new prefix			
❑ PC31795	The Best of the Byrds (Greatest Hits, Volume II)	198?	10.00
—Reissue with another new prefix			
❑ CL2716 [M]	The Byrds' Greatest Hits	1967	30.00
❑ CS9516 [S]	The Byrds' Greatest Hits	1967	25.00
—Red "360 Sound" label			
❑ KCS9516 [S]	The Byrds' Greatest Hits	1971	12.00
—Orange label			
❑ PC9516 [S]	The Byrds' Greatest Hits	197?	10.00
—Reissue with another new prefix			
❑ PC36293	The Byrds Play Dylan	1980	12.00
❑ G30127	The Byrds (Untitled)	1970	25.00
—With "Kathleen" listed on back cover (it is not on the set)			
❑ G30127	The Byrds (Untitled)	1970	18.00
—Without "Kathleen" listed on back cover			
❑ CL2775 [M]	The Notorious Byrd Brothers	1968	50.00
❑ CS9575 [S]	The Notorious Byrd Brothers	1968	25.00
—Red "360 Sound" label			
❑ CS9575 [S]	The Notorious Byrd Brothers	1971	12.00
—Orange label			
❑ PC9575 [S]	The Notorious Byrd Brothers	198?	10.00
—Reissue with new prefix			
❑ FC37335	The Original Singles Volume 1 (1965-1967)	1981	12.00
❑ PC37335	The Original Singles Volume 1 (1965-1967)	1985	10.00
—Budget-line reissue			
❑ CL2454 [M]	Turn! Turn! Turn!	1965	30.00
❑ CS9254 [S]	Turn! Turn! Turn!	1965	30.00
—Red "360 Sound" label			
❑ CS9254 [S]	Turn! Turn! Turn!	1971	12.00
—Orange label			
❑ PC9254 [S]	Turn! Turn! Turn!	198?	10.00
—Reissue with new prefix			
❑ CL2642 [M]	Younger Than Yesterday	1967	30.00
❑ CS9442 [S]	Younger Than Yesterday	1967	30.00
—Red "360 Sound" label			
❑ CS9442 [S]	Younger Than Yesterday	1971	12.00
—Orange label			
❑ PC9442 [S]	Younger Than Yesterday	198?	10.00
—Reissue with new prefix			

COLUMBIA LIMITED EDITION

Number	Title	Yr	NM
❑ LE10215	Farther Along	197?	18.00
—Reissue of 31050			

PAIR

Number	Title	Yr	NM
❑ PDL2-1040	The Very Best of the Byrds	1986	15.00

RE-FLYTE

Number	Title	Yr	NM
❑ MH-70318	Never Before	1987	15.00
—Released by Muuray Hill Records via mail order			

RHINO

Number	Title	Yr	NM
❑ R1-70244	In the Beginning	1988	12.00

SUNDAZED

Number	Title	Yr	NM
❑ LP5059	Fifth Dimension	1999	18.00
—Reissue on 180-gram vinyl			
❑ LP5199 [M]	Fifth Dimension	2006	18.00
—Reissue on 180-gram vinyl			
❑ LP5057	Mr. Tambourine Man	1999	18.00
—Reissue on 180-gram vinyl			
❑ LP5197 [M]	Mr. Tambourine Man	2006	18.00
—Reissue on 180-gram vinyl			
❑ LP5061	Sanctuary	2000	15.00
❑ LP5065	Sanctuary II	2000	15.00
❑ LP5066	Sanctuary III	2001	15.00
❑ LP5090	Sanctuary IV	2002	15.00
❑ LP5130	The Columbia Singles '65-'67	2001	18.00
❑ LP5201 [M]	The Notorious Byrd Brothers	2006	18.00
—Reissue on 180-gram vinyl			
❑ LP5114	The Preflyte Sessions	2001	18.00
❑ LP5058	Turn! Turn! Turn!	1999	18.00
—Reissue on 180-gram vinyl			
❑ LP5198 [M]	Turn! Turn! Turn!	2006	18.00
—Reissue on 180-gram vinyl			
❑ LP5060	Younger Than Yesterday	1999	18.00
—Reissue on 180-gram vinyl			
❑ LP5200 [M]	Younger Than Yesterday	2006	18.00
—Reissue on 180-gram vinyl			

TOGETHER

Number	Title	Yr	NM
❑ ST-T-1001	Preflyte	1969	30.00

BYRNE, BOBBY

COMMAND

Number	Title	Yr	NM
❑ RS 33-894 [M]	1966 -- Magnificent Movie Themes	1966	15.00
❑ RS894SD [S]	1966 -- Magnificent Movie Themes	1966	18.00
❑ RS928SD	Sound in the 8th Dimension	1968	80.00

GRAND AWARD

Number	Title	Yr	NM
❑ GA 33-381 [M]	Great Song Hits of the Glenn Miller Orchestra	1958	30.00
❑ GA207SD [S]	Great Song Hits of the Glenn Miller Orchestra	1958	40.00
❑ GA 33-382 [M]	Great Song Hits of the Tommy and Jimmy Dorsey Orchestras	1958	30.00
❑ GA206SD [S]	Great Song Hits of the Tommy and Jimmy Dorsey Orchestras	1958	40.00
❑ GA 33-392 [M]	Great Themes of America's Greatest Bands	1958	30.00
❑ GA225SD [S]	Great Themes of America's Greatest Bands	1959	40.00
❑ GA 33-416 [M]	The Jazzbone's Connected to the Trombone	1959	40.00
❑ GA248SD [S]	The Jazzbone's Connected to the Trombone	1959	50.00

WALDORF MUSIC HALL

Number	Title	Yr	NM
❑ MH 33-121 [10]	Dixieland Jazz	195?	50.00

BYRNE, DAVID, AND RYUICHI SAKAMOTO

VIRGIN

Number	Title	Yr	NM
❑ 2204 [DJ]	The Making of The Last Emperor: An Interview with...	1988	30.00

BYRNE, DAVID

ECM

Number	Title	Yr	NM
❑ 25022	Music for The Knee Plays	1985	18.00

LUAKA BOP

Number	Title	Yr	NM
❑ 25990	Rei Momo	1989	15.00
❑ 26799	Uh-Oh	1992	15.00

SIRE

Number	Title	Yr	NM
❑ SRK6093	My Life in the Bush of Ghosts	1981	15.00
—With Brian Eno			
❑ SRK3645	The Catherine Wheel	1981	12.00
—Songs and music from the Broadway play of the same name			

VIRGIN

Number	Title	Yr	NM
❑ PR2204 [DJ]	The Making of The Last Emperor: An Interview with David Byrne and Ryuichi Sakamoto	1988	30.00

BYRNES, EDD

WARNER BROS.

Number	Title	Yr	NM
❑ W1309 [M]	Kookie	1959	100.00
❑ WS1309 [S]	Kookie	1959	120.00
❑ W/WS1309	Kookie Bonus Photo	1959	50.00

BYRON, GEORGE

ATLANTIC

Number	Title	Yr	NM
❑ 1293 [M]	Premiere Performance	1958	40.00
—Black label			
❑ SD1293 [S]	Premiere Performance	1958	50.00
—Green label			

Number	Title	Yr	NM

C

C.A. QUINTET, THE

CANDY FLOSS
Number	Title	Yr	NM
❏ 7764	A Trip Through Hell	1969	1500.00

— *VG value 500; VG+ value 1000*

SUNDAZED
| ❏ LP-5037 [B] | Trip Thru Hell | 1997 | 18.00 |

C.C.S.

RAK
| ❏ KZ31569 | C.C.S. | 1972 | 25.00 |
| ❏ Z30559 | Whole Lotta Love | 1971 | 25.00 |

C.K. STRONG

EPIC
| ❏ BN26473 | C.K. Strong | 1969 | 25.00 |

CABLES, GEORGE

CONTEMPORARY
| ❏ C-14030 | By George: The Music of George Gershwin | 1987 | 12.00 |
| ❏ C-14001 | Cables' Vision | 1979 | 18.00 |

— *Pianist.*

| ❏ C-14015 | Circle | 198? | 15.00 |
| ❏ C-14014 | Phantom of the City | 198? | 15.00 |

CABO FRIO

ZEBRA
❏ ZEB-5990	Cabo Frio	198?	12.00
❏ ZR-5002	Just Having Fun	198?	15.00
❏ ZEB-5685	Right On the Money	1986	12.00

CABOT, SEBASTIAN

MGM
| ❏ E-4431 [M] | Sebastian Cabot, Actor; Bob Dylan, Poet: A Dramatic Reading with Music | 1967 | 30.00 |
| ❏ SE-4431 [S] | Sebastian Cabot, Actor; Bob Dylan, Poet: A Dramatic Reading with Music | 1967 | 40.00 |

CACIA, PAUL

HAPPY HOUR
| ❏ HH6001 | Paul Cacia Presents The Alumni Tribute to Stan Kenton | 198? | 12.00 |
| ❏ HH5004 | Quantum Leap | 198? | 12.00 |

— *Trumpeter and bandleader.*

OUTSTANDING
| ❏ OUTS-056 | Quantum Leap | 1986 | 15.00 |

CACTUS

ATCO
❏ SD 33-340	Cactus	1970	25.00
❏ SD 33-356	One Way...Or Another	1971	25.00
❏ SD7011 [B]	'Ot 'N' Sweaty	1972	25.00
❏ SD 33-377	Restrictions	1971	25.00

CLEOPATRA
| ❏ 6804 [B] | Ultra Sonic Boogie | 1971 | 40.00 |

CADETS, THE

CROWN
| ❏ CLP-5015 [M] | Rockin' 'n' Reelin' | 1957 | 250.00 |

— *Black label*

| ❏ CLP-5370 [M] | The Cadets | 1963 | 150.00 |
| ❏ CST-370 [R] | The Cadets | 1963 | 100.00 |

RELIC
| ❏ 5025 | The Cadets' Greatest Hits | 197? | 15.00 |

CADILLACS, THE

HARLEM HIT PARADE
| ❏ 5009 | Cruisin' with the Cadillacs | 197? | 12.00 |

JUBILEE
| ❏ JGM-1089 [M] | The Crazy Cadillacs | 1959 | 300.00 |

— *Flat black label*

| ❏ JGM-1089 [M] | The Crazy Cadillacs | 1960 | 100.00 |

— *Glossy black label*

| ❏ JGM-1045 [M] | The Fabulous Cadillacs | 1957 | 400.00 |

— *Blue label*

| ❏ JGM-1045 [M] | The Fabulous Cadillacs | 1959 | 250.00 |

— *Flat black label*

Number	Title	Yr	NM
❏ JGM-1045 [M]	The Fabulous Cadillacs	1960	100.00

— *Glossy black label*

| ❏ JGM-5009 [S] | Twisting with the Cadillacs | 1962 | 200.00 |

MURRAY HILL
| ❏ 1285 | The Cadillacs | 198? | 40.00 |

— *Box set*

| ❏ 1195 | The Very Best of the Cadillacs | 198? | 18.00 |

CADILLACS, THE/ THE ORIOLES

JUBILEE
| ❏ JGM-1117 [M] | The Cadillacs Meet the Orioles | 1961 | 200.00 |

CAFFERTY, JOHN, AND THE BEAVER BROWN BAND

SCOTTI BROTHERS
| ❏ BFZ38929 | Eddie and the Cruisers (Soundtrack) | 1983 | 15.00 |

— *With original prefix*

| ❏ FZ38929 | Eddie and the Cruisers (Soundtrack) | 1984 | 10.00 |

— *With altered prefix*

| ❏ F740980 | Roadhouse | 1988 | 12.00 |
| ❏ FZ39405 | Tough All Over | 1985 | 10.00 |

CAGLE, BUDDY

IMPERIAL
❏ LP-9361 [M]	Longtime Traveling	1967	30.00
❏ LP-12361 [S]	Longtime Traveling	1967	30.00
❏ LP-9348 [M]	Mi Casa, Tu Casa	1967	25.00
❏ LP-12348 [S]	Mi Casa, Tu Casa	1967	30.00
❏ LP-9318 [M]	The Way You Like It	1966	25.00
❏ LP-12318 [S]	The Way You Like It	1966	30.00
❏ LP-12374	Through a Crack in a Boxcar Door	1968	30.00

CAIN, JACKIE, AND ROY KRAL

ABC-PARAMOUNT
❏ ABC-163 [M]	Bits and Pieces	1957	50.00
❏ ABC-207 [M]	Free and Easy	1958	50.00
❏ ABC-267 [M]	In the Spotlight	1959	40.00
❏ ABCS-267 [S]	In the Spotlight	1959	50.00
❏ ABC-120 [M]	The Glory of Love	1956	50.00

AUDIOPHILE
| ❏ AP-230 | One More Rose (A Tribute to the Lyrics of Alan Jay Lerner) | 1988 | 12.00 |

BRUNSWICK
| ❏ BL54026 [M] | Jackie Cain and Roy Kral | 1957 | 50.00 |

CAPITOL
| ❏ ST2936 | Grass | 1968 | 18.00 |

COLUMBIA
❏ CL1704 [M]	Double Take	1961	30.00
❏ CS8504 [S]	Double Take	1961	30.00
❏ CL1934 [S]	Jackie and Roy Kral Like And Sing Songs by Dory And André Previn	1963	25.00
❏ CS8734 [S]	Like Sing	1963	30.00
❏ CL1469 [M]	Sweet and Low Down	1960	30.00
❏ CS8260 [S]	Sweet and Low Down	1960	30.00

CONCORD JAZZ
❏ CJ-149	East of Suez	1981	15.00
❏ CJ-186	High Standards	198?	15.00
❏ CJ-115	Star Sounds	1979	15.00

CONTEMPORARY
| ❏ C-14046 | Full Circle | 1989 | 15.00 |

CTI
| ❏ 6040 | A Wilder Alias | 1974 | 18.00 |
| ❏ 6019 | Time and Love | 1972 | 18.00 |

DISCOVERY
| ❏ 907 | We've Got It: The Music of Cy Coleman | 1986 | 12.00 |

FANTASY
Number	Title	Yr	NM
❏ F-9643	Bogie	1986	12.00

FINESSE
| ❏ FW38324 | A Stephen Sondheim Collection | 1983 | 12.00 |

MCA
| ❏ 4169 | Jackie & Roy | 198? | 15.00 |

REGENT
| ❏ MG-6057 [M] | Jackie & Roy | 1957 | 50.00 |

ROULETTE
| ❏ R-25278 [M] | By Jupiter & Girl Crazy | 1964 | 25.00 |
| ❏ SR-25278 [S] | By Jupiter & Girl Crazy | 1964 | 30.00 |

SAVOY
| ❏ MG-12198 [M] | Jackie and Roy | 196? | 25.00 |

STORYVILLE
❏ STLP-322 [10]	Jackie & Roy	1955	120.00
❏ STLP-915 [M]	Sing Baby, Sing!	1956	60.00
❏ STLP-904 [M]	Storyville Presents Jackie & Roy	1955	60.00

STUDIO 7
| ❏ 402 | By the Sea | 1978 | 15.00 |

VERVE
❏ V-8668 [M]	Changes	1966	25.00
❏ V6-8668 [S]	Changes	1966	30.00
❏ V-8688 [M]	Lovesick	1967	30.00
❏ V6-8688 [S]	Lovesick	1967	25.00

CAIN

A.S.I.
| ❏ 204 | A Pound of Flesh | 1974 | 75.00 |
| ❏ 214 [B] | Stinger | 1975 | 40.00 |

CAIOLA, AL

ATCO
| ❏ 33-117 [M] | Music for Space Squirrels | 1960 | 30.00 |
| ❏ SD 33-117 [S] | Music for Space Squirrels | 1960 | 30.00 |

AVALANCHE
| ❏ 9201 | The Magnificent Seven | 1972 | 15.00 |
| ❏ AV-LA058-F | The Magnificent Seven Ride '73 | 1973 | 12.00 |

AVCO EMBASSY
| ❏ 33019 | Bonanza Guitars/50 Years of the Greatest Country Music | 1971 | 12.00 |

BAINBRIDGE
❏ 1030	Guitar of Plenty	1980	10.00
❏ 1023	Italian Guitars	198?	10.00
❏ 1010	Soft Guitars	198?	10.00

CHANCELLOR
| ❏ CHL-5008 [M] | Great Pickin' | 1960 | 30.00 |
| ❏ CHS-5008 [S] | Great Pickin' | 1960 | 30.00 |

PICKWICK
| ❏ SPC-3034 | Italian Style | 196? | 15.00 |

RCA CAMDEN
❏ CAS-2569	Music from "The Godfather"	1972	12.00
❏ CAL-710 [M]	The Guitar Style of Al Caiola	1962	15.00
❏ CAS-710 [S]	The Guitar Style of Al Caiola	1962	18.00

RCA VICTOR
| ❏ LPM-2031 [M] | High Strung | 1959 | 30.00 |
| ❏ LSP-2031 [S] | High Strung | 1959 | 30.00 |

ROULETTE
❏ SR-42008	Roman Guitar	1968	12.00
❏ R25108 [M]	Salute Italia	1960	25.00
❏ SR25108 [S]	Salute Italia	1960	30.00

SAVOY
| ❏ MG-12033 [M] | Deep in a Dream | 1955 | 40.00 |
| ❏ MG-12057 [M] | Serenade in Blue | 1956 | 40.00 |

SUNSET
| ❏ SUS-5292 | Guitar in Love | 1970 | 12.00 |

TIME
❏ 52101 [M]	Gershwin and Guitars	1961	25.00
❏ S-2101 [S]	Gershwin and Guitars	1961	30.00
❏ 52000 [M]	Percussion and Guitars	1960	25.00
❏ S-2000 [S]	Percussion and Guitars	1960	30.00
❏ 52006 [M]	Percussion Espanol	1960	25.00
❏ S-2006 [S]	Percussion Espanol	1960	30.00
❏ 52026 [M]	Percussion Espanol, Vol. 2	1960	25.00
❏ S-2026 [S]	Percussion Espanol, Vol. 2	1960	30.00
❏ 52039 [M]	Spanish Guitars	1960	25.00
❏ S-2039 [S]	Spanish Guitars	1960	30.00

UNITED ARTISTS
❏ UAL-3330 [M]	50 Fabulous Guitar Favorites	1964	15.00
❏ UAS-6330 [S]	50 Fabulous Guitar Favorites	1964	18.00
❏ UAL-3354 [M]	50 Fabulous Italian Favorites	1964	15.00
❏ UAS-6354 [S]	50 Fabulous Italian Favorites	1964	18.00
❏ UAL-3256 [M]	Acapulco 1922 and The Lonely Bull	1963	15.00
❏ UAS-6256 [S]	Acapulco 1922 and The Lonely Bull	1963	18.00
❏ UAL-3276 [M]	Ciao	1963	15.00
❏ UAS-6276 [S]	Ciao	1963	18.00
❏ UAL-3255 [M]	City Guy Goes Country	1963	15.00
❏ UAS-6255 [S]	City Guy Goes Country	1963	18.00
❏ UAL-3299 [M]	Cleopatra and All That Jazz	1963	15.00
❏ UAS-6299 [S]	Cleopatra and All That Jazz	1963	30.00
❏ UAL-3280 [M]	Give Me the Simple Life	1963	15.00
❏ UAS-6280 [S]	Give Me the Simple Life	1963	18.00

Number	Title	Yr	NM
❏ UAL-3240 [M]	Golden Guitar	1962	15.00
❏ UAS-6240 [S]	Golden Guitar	1962	18.00
❏ UAL-3142 [M]	Golden Instrumental Hits	1961	15.00
❏ UAS-6142 [S]	Golden Instrumental Hits	1961	18.00
❏ UAL-3403 [M]	Guitar for Lovers	1965	15.00
❏ UAS-6403 [S]	Guitar for Lovers	1965	18.00
❏ UAL-3405 [M]	Have Guitar Will Travel	1965	15.00
❏ UAS-6405 [S]	Have Guitar Will Travel	1965	18.00
❏ UAL-3161 [M]	Hit Instrumentals from TV Westerns	1961	18.00
❏ UAS-6161 [S]	Hit Instrumentals from TV Westerns	1961	25.00
❏ UAS-6712	Let the Sunshine In	1969	12.00
❏ UAL-3228 [M]	Midnight Dance Party	1962	15.00
❏ UAS-6228 [S]	Midnight Dance Party	1962	18.00
❏ UAL-3362 [M]	On the Trail	1964	15.00
❏ UAS-6362 [S]	On the Trail	1964	18.00
❏ UAL-3263 [M]	Paradise Village	1963	15.00
❏ UAS-6263 [S]	Paradise Village	1963	18.00
❏ UAL-3180 [M]	Solid Gold Guitar	1962	15.00
❏ UAS-6180 [S]	Solid Gold Guitar	1962	18.00
❏ UAL-3418 [M]	Solid Gold Guitar Goes Hawaiian	1965	15.00
❏ UAS-6418 [S]	Solid Gold Guitar Goes Hawaiian	1965	18.00
❏ UAL-3435 [M]	Sounds for Spies and Private Eyes	1965	18.00
❏ UAS-6435 [S]	Sounds for Spies and Private Eyes	1965	25.00
❏ UAL-3310 [M]	The Best of Al Caiola	1964	15.00
❏ UAS-6310 [S]	The Best of Al Caiola	1964	18.00
❏ UAL-3133 [M]	The Magnificent Seven	1960	25.00
❏ UAS-6133 [S]	The Magnificent Seven	1960	30.00
❏ UAL-3389 [M]	Tuff Guitar	1965	15.00
❏ UAS-6389 [S]	Tuff Guitar	1965	18.00
❏ UAL-3454 [M]	Tuff Guitar English Style	1966	15.00
❏ UAS-6454 [S]	Tuff Guitar English Style	1966	18.00

CAJUN PETE

MERCURY

Number	Title	Yr	NM
❏ MG-20633 [M]	Tales of the Bayou	1961	25.00
❏ SR-60633 [S]	Tales of the Bayou	1961	30.00

CAKE, THE

DECCA

Number	Title	Yr	NM
❏ DL75039 [S]	A Slice of the Cake	1968	30.00
❏ DL5039 [M]	A Slice of the Cake	1968	50.00
— Mono is white label promo only			
❏ DL4927 [M]	The Cake	1967	25.00
❏ DL74927 [S]	The Cake	1967	30.00

CALDWELL, LOUISE HARRISON

RECAR

Number	Title	Yr	NM
❏ 2012 [M]	All About the Beatles	1965	200.00
— With insert			
❏ 2012 [M]	All About the Beatles	1965	150.00
— Without insert			

CALE, J.J.

MCA

Number	Title	Yr	NM
❏ 37102	5	1981	10.00
— Reissue of Shelter 3163			
❏ 37104	Naturally	1981	10.00
— Reissue of Shelter 52009			
❏ 37106	Okie	1981	10.00
— Reissue of Shelter 52019			
❏ 37105	Really	1981	10.00
— Reissue of Shelter 52012			
❏ 5158	Shades	1981	12.00
❏ 37103	Troubadour	1981	10.00
— Reissue of Shelter 52002			

MERCURY

Number	Title	Yr	NM
❏ 811152-1	#8	1983	12.00
❏ SRM-1-4038	Grasshopper	1982	12.00
❏ 818633-1	Special Edition	1984	12.00

SHELTER

Number	Title	Yr	NM
❏ 3163 [B]	5	1979	15.00
❏ 2122	Naturally	1974	15.00
— Reissue of SW-8908			
❏ SW-8908	Naturally	1971	18.00
❏ 52009	Naturally	1977	12.00
— Reissue of 2122			
❏ 2107	Okie	1974	18.00
❏ 52015	Okie	1977	12.00
— Reissue of 2107			
❏ SW-8912	Really	1972	18.00
❏ 2123	Really	1974	15.00
— Reissue of 8912			
❏ 52012	Really	1977	12.00
— Reissue of 2123			
❏ 52002	Troubadour	1976	18.00

SILVERTONE

Number	Title	Yr	NM
❏ 1306-1-J	Travel-Log	1990	15.00

CALE, JOHN

4 MEN WITH BEARDS

Number	Title	Yr	NM
❏ 4M125LP [B]	Paris 1919		25.00

A&M

Number	Title	Yr	NM
❏ SP-4849 [B]	Honi Soit	1981	18.00

ANTILLES

Number	Title	Yr	NM
❏ AN-7063 [B]	Guts	198?	18.00
— Reissue of Island 9459			

COLUMBIA

Number	Title	Yr	NM
❏ C30131	Church of Anthrax	1971	18.00
❏ CS1037	Vintage Violence	1970	30.00
— Red "360 Sound" label			
❏ CS1037	Vintage Violence	1971	18.00
— Orange label			

ISLAND

Number	Title	Yr	NM
❏ IT-8401 [B]	Caribbean Sunset	1984	18.00
❏ ILPS9301	Fear	1975	25.00
❏ ILPS9459	Guts	1977	25.00
❏ IXP-2 [DJ]	Hear Fear	1975	60.00
— Promo-only interview album			
❏ ILPS9350 [B]	Helen of Troy	1975	30.00
❏ IT-8402 [B]	John Cale Comes Alive	1984	15.00
❏ ILPS9317 [B]	Slow Dazzle	1975	30.00

OPAL/WARNER BROS.

Number	Title	Yr	NM
❏ 26024 [B]	Words for the Dying	1989	18.00

PASSPORT

Number	Title	Yr	NM
❏ PB6019 [B]	Music for a New Society	1982	18.00

PVC

Number	Title	Yr	NM
❏ 8947	Artificial Intelligence	1985	18.00

REPRISE

Number	Title	Yr	NM
❏ MS2131	Paris, 1919	1973	35.00
❏ MS2079	The Academy in Peril	1972	75.00

SPY/I.R.S.

Number	Title	Yr	NM
❏ SP-004 [B]	Sabotage/Live	1980	25.00

CALIFORNIA POPPY PICKERS, THE

ALSHIRE

Number	Title	Yr	NM
❏ S-5153	Blue-Eyed Soul	1969	30.00
❏ S-5167	Honky Tonk Women	1970	40.00
❏ S-5163	Today's Chart Busters	1969	25.00

CALIFORNIA RAMBLERS, THE

BIOGRAPH

Number	Title	Yr	NM
❏ 12021	Hallelujah, Vol. 2 1925-29	197?	12.00
❏ 12020	Miss Annabelle Lee 1925-27	197?	12.00

CALIMAN, HADLEY

CATALYST

Number	Title	Yr	NM
❏ 0(# unknown)	Celebration	1977	15.00
❏ 7604	Projecting	1976	15.00

MAINSTREAM

Number	Title	Yr	NM
❏ MRL-318	Hadley Caliman	1971	25.00
❏ MRL-342	Iapetus	1972	25.00

CALL, THE

ELEKTRA

Number	Title	Yr	NM
❏ 60739	Into the Woods	1987	12.00
❏ R141152	Reconciled	1986	15.00
— RCA Music Service edition			
❏ 60440	Reconciled	1986	12.00

MCA

Number	Title	Yr	NM
❏ 6303	Let the Day Begin	1989	12.00
❏ 10033	Red Moon	1990	15.00

MERCURY

Number	Title	Yr	NM
❏ 810307-1	Modern Romans	1983	12.00
❏ SRM-1-4037	The Call	1982	15.00
❏ 822868-1	The Call	1984	10.00
— Reissue of 4037			
❏ 818793-1	The Scene Beyond Dreams	1984	15.00

CALLENDER, BOBBY

MGM

Number	Title	Yr	NM
❏ SE-4557	Rainbow	1968	150.00

CALLENDER, RED

CROWN

Number	Title	Yr	NM
❏ CLP-5012 [M]	Callender Speaks Low	1957	40.00
❏ CLP-5025 [M]	Swingin' Suite	1957	40.00

LEGEND

Number	Title	Yr	NM
❏ 1005	Basin Street Bass	197?	15.00

METROJAZZ

Number	Title	Yr	NM
❏ E-1007 [M]	The Lowest	1958	50.00
❏ SE-1007 [S]	The Lowest	1959	40.00

MODERN

Number	Title	Yr	NM
❏ MLP-1201 [M]	Swingin' Suite	1956	80.00

RED

Number	Title	Yr	NM
❏ KM2248	Red Callender Speaks Low	1978	18.00

CALLOWAY, CAB

BRUNSWICK

Number	Title	Yr	NM
❏ BL58101 [10]	Cab Calloway	1954	100.00

COLUMBIA

Number	Title	Yr	NM
❏ CG32593	The Hi De Ho Man	1973	25.00

CORAL

Number	Title	Yr	NM
❏ CRL57408 [M]	Blues Make Me Happy	1962	30.00
❏ CRL757408 [S]	Blues Make Me Happy	1962	30.00

EPIC

Number	Title	Yr	NM
❏ LN3265 [M]	Swing Showman	1957	50.00

GLENDALE

Number	Title	Yr	NM
❏ GLS9007	Cab Calloway	1984	12.00

GONE

Number	Title	Yr	NM
❏ LP-101 [M]	Cotton Club Revue '58	1958	80.00

MCA

Number	Title	Yr	NM
❏ 1344	Mr. Hi-De-Ho	198?	12.00

P.I.P.

Number	Title	Yr	NM
❏ 6801	Cab Calloway '68	1968	25.00

RCA VICTOR

Number	Title	Yr	NM
❏ LPM-2021 [M]	Hi De Hi De Ho	1958	30.00
❏ LSP-2021 [S]	Hi De Hi De Ho	1958	40.00

VOCALION

Number	Title	Yr	NM
❏ VL73820	The Blues	196?	15.00

CAMARATA

BUENA VISTA

Number	Title	Yr	NM
❏ BV-3319 [M]	33 Great Walt Disney Motion Picture Melodies	1963	30.00
❏ STER-3319 [S]	33 Great Walt Disney Motion Picture Melodies	1963	30.00
❏ BV-4023 [M]	Camarata Conducts a Modern Interpretation of Snow White and the Seven Dwarfs	1963	30.00
— Gatefold cover			
❏ BV-4023 [M]	Camarata Conducts a Modern Interpretation of Snow White and the Seven Dwarfs	1967	25.00
— Regular cover			
❏ STER-4023 [S]	Camarata Conducts a Modern Interpretation of Snow White and the Seven Dwarfs	1963	40.00
— Gatefold cover			
❏ STER-4023 [S]	Camarata Conducts a Modern Interpretation of Snow White and the Seven Dwarfs	1967	30.00
— Regular cover			
❏ BV-4048	Camarata Featuring Tutti's Trombones	1970	25.00
❏ BV-4047	Camarata Featuring Tutti's Trumpets	1970	25.00
— Reissue of 3011			
❏ BV-3322 [M]	In the Still of the Night	1959	25.00
❏ STER-3322 [S]	In the Still of the Night	1960	30.00
❏ BV-3321 [M]	The Changing Seasons	1964	25.00
❏ STER-3321 [S]	The Changing Seasons	1964	30.00
❏ BV-3330 [M]	Tinpanorama	1965	25.00

DISNEYLAND

Number	Title	Yr	NM
❏ DQ-1232 [M]	A Child's Introduction to Melody and Instruments of the Orchestra	1963	25.00
❏ WDL-3021 [M]	Autumn	1958	25.00
❏ STER-3021 [S]	Autumn	1959	30.00
❏ WDL-4009 [M]	Camarata Interprets Music from Cinderella and Bambi	1957	60.00
❏ (# unknown)0 [M]	Music of the Seasons	1959	40.00
— Box set with mono versions of 3021, 3026, 3027 and 3032			
❏ (# unknown)0 [S]	Music of the Seasons	1959	80.00
— Box set with stereo versions of 3021, 3026, 3027 and 3032			
❏ WDL-3032 [M]	Spring	1958	25.00
❏ STER-3032 [S]	Spring	1959	30.00
❏ WDL-3027 [M]	Summer	1958	25.00
❏ STER-3027 [S]	Summer	1959	30.00
❏ WDL-3011 [M]	Tutti's Trumpets	1957	25.00
❏ STER-3011 [S]	Tutti's Trumpets	1959	30.00
❏ WDL-3026 [M]	Winter	1958	25.00
❏ STER-3026 [S]	Winter	1959	30.00

CAMBRIDGE, GODFREY

EPIC

Number	Title	Yr	NM
❏ FLM13108 [M]	Godfrey Cambridge Toys with the World	1966	25.00
❏ FLS15108 [S]	Godfrey Cambridge Toys with the World	1966	25.00
❏ FLM13101 [M]	Ready or Not…Here's Godfrey Cambridge	1964	25.00
❏ FLS15101 [S]	Ready or Not…Here's Godfrey Cambridge	1964	25.00
❏ FLM13115 [M]	The Godfrey Cambridge Show Live at the Aladdin	1968	25.00
❏ FLS15115 [S]	The Godfrey Cambridge Show Live at the Aladdin	1968	25.00
❏ FLM13102 [M]	Them Cotton Pickin' Days Is Over	1965	25.00
❏ FLS15102 [S]	Them Cotton Pickin' Days Is Over	1965	25.00

CAMP, HAMILTON

ELEKTRA

Number	Title	Yr	NM
❏ EKL-278 [M]	Paths of Victory	1965	40.00
❏ EKS-7278 [S]	Paths of Victory	1965	50.00

WARNER BROS.

Number	Title	Yr	NM
❏ WS1737	Here's to You	1967	30.00
❏ WS1753	Welcome to Hamilton Camp	1969	25.00

CAMP, RED

COOK

Number	Title	Yr	NM
❏ LP-5005 [M]	Camp Has a Ball	1957	40.00

Number	Title	Yr	NM
❏ LP-1087 [10]	Camp Inventions: Bold New Design for Jazz Piano	1955	50.00
❏ LP-1089 [10]	Red Camp	1955	50.00

CAMPBELL, ALEX

STARDAY
❏ SLP-214 [M]	16 Radio Favorites	1963	30.00
❏ SLP-342 [M]	Travel On	1965	30.00

CAMPBELL, ARCHIE, AND LORENE MANN

RCA VICTOR
❏ LSP-4086	Archie and Lorene Tell It Like It Is	1968	25.00

CAMPBELL, ARCHIE

RCA VICTOR
❏ LPM-3504 [M]	Have a Laugh on Me	1966	25.00
❏ LSP-3504 [S]	Have a Laugh on Me	1966	30.00
❏ LPM-3780 [M]	Kids I Love 'Em	1967	30.00
❏ LSP-3780 [S]	Kids I Love 'Em	1967	25.00
❏ LPM-3699 [M]	The Cockfight and Other Tall Tales	1967	25.00
❏ LSP-3699 [S]	The Cockfight and Other Tall Tales	1967	30.00
❏ LPM-3892 [M]	The Golden Years	1967	30.00
❏ LSP-3892 [S]	The Golden Years	1967	25.00

STARDAY
❏ SLP-167 [M]	Bedtime Stories for Adults	1962	30.00
❏ SLP-162 [M]	Make Friends with Archie Campbell	1962	30.00
❏ SLP-377 [M]	The Grand Ole Opry's Good Humor Man	1966	30.00
❏ SLP-223 [M]	The Joker Is Wild	1963	30.00

CAMPBELL, CECIL

STARDAY
❏ SLP-254 [M]	Steel Guitar Jamboree	1963	40.00

CAMPBELL, CHOKER

MOTOWN
❏ M-620 [M]	Hits of the Sixties	1964	100.00
❏ MS-620 [S]	Hits of the Sixties	1964	150.00

CAMPBELL, GLEN, AND BOBBIE GENTRY

CAPITOL
❏ ST2928	Bobbie Gentry & Glen Campbell	1968	18.00
❏ ST 8-2928	Bobbie Gentry & Glen Campbell	1968	25.00
— Capitol Record Club edition			

CAMPBELL, GLEN

ATLANTIC AMERICA
❏ 90483	It's Just a Matter of Time	1985	10.00
❏ 90164	Letter to Home	1984	10.00
❏ 90016	Old Home Town	1983	10.00

CAPITOL
❏ ST2907	A New Place in the Sun	1968	18.00
❏ SW-11407	Arkansas	1975	12.00
❏ SM-11407	Arkansas	1977	10.00
— Reissue with new prefix			
❏ SW-11722	Basic	1978	12.00
❏ T1810 [M]	Big Bluegrass Special	1962	80.00
— As "The Green River Boys Featuring Glen Campbell			
❏ ST1810 [S]	Big Bluegrass Special	1962	100.00
— As "The Green River Boys Featuring Glen Campbell			
❏ SW-11516	Bloodline	1976	12.00
❏ T2679 [M]	Burning Bridges	1967	18.00
❏ ST2679 [S]	Burning Bridges	1967	18.00
❏ T2851 [M]	By the Time I Get to Phoenix	1967	18.00
❏ ST2851 [S]	By the Time I Get to Phoenix	1967	18.00
❏ SM-12040	By the Time I Get to Phoenix	1979	10.00
— Reissue of 2851			
❏ ST-210	Galveston	1969	18.00
❏ T2809 [M]	Gentle on My Mind	1967	18.00
❏ ST2809 [S]	Gentle on My Mind	1967	18.00
❏ SM-11960	Gentle on My Mind	1979	10.00
— Reissue of 2809			
❏ STBO-268	Glen Campbell -- "Live	1969	25.00
❏ SW-752	Glen Campbell's Greatest Hits	1971	15.00
❏ SW-11117	Glen Travis Campbell	1972	12.00
❏ ST2878 [S]	Hey, Little One	1968	18.00
❏ T2878 [M]	Hey, Little One	1968	30.00
❏ SOO-12008	Highwayman	1979	12.00
❏ SW-11293	Houston (I'm Comin' to See You)	1974	12.00
❏ SW-11185	I Knew Jesus (Before He Was a Star)	1973	12.00
❏ SW-11253	I Remember Hank Williams	1973	12.00
❏ SOO-12124	It's the World Gone Crazy	1981	12.00
❏ SWAK-93157	Limited Collector's Edition	1970	25.00
— Capitol Record Club exclusive; includes tour program			
❏ SWBC-11707	Live at the Royal Festival Hall	1977	15.00
❏ SW-443	Oh Happy Day	1970	15.00
❏ SW-11336	Reunion (The Songs of Jimmy Webb)	1974	12.00
❏ SW-11430	Rhinestone Cowboy	1975	12.00
❏ SOO-12075	Somethin' 'Bout You Baby I Like	1980	12.00
❏ SO-11601	Southern Nights	1977	12.00
❏ ST2978	That Christmas Feeling	1968	18.00

Number	Title	Yr	NM
❏ T2023 [M]	The Astounding 12-String Guitar of Glen Campbell	1964	18.00
❏ ST2023 [S]	The Astounding 12-String Guitar of Glen Campbell	1964	25.00
❏ ST-11577	The Best of Glen Campbell	1976	12.00
❏ T2392 [M]	The Big Bad Rock Guitar of Glen Campbell	1965	18.00
❏ ST2392 [S]	The Big Bad Rock Guitar of Glen Campbell	1965	25.00
❏ SW-493	The Glen Campbell Goodtime Album	1970	15.00
❏ SW-733	The Last Time I Saw Her	1971	15.00
❏ SM-733	The Last Time I Saw Her	1977	10.00
— Reissue with new prefix			
❏ T1881 [M]	Too Late to Worry, Too Blue to Cry	1963	25.00
❏ ST1881 [S]	Too Late to Worry, Too Blue to Cry	1963	30.00
❏ SW-389	Try a Little Kindness	1970	15.00
❏ SM-389	Try a Little Kindness	1977	10.00
— Reissue with new prefix			

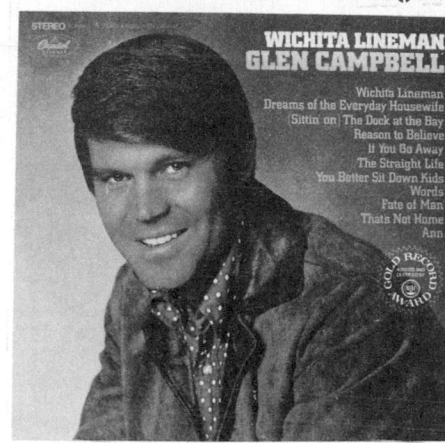

❏ ST-103 [R]	Wichita Lineman	1968	18.00
❏ SM-103	Wichita Lineman	1977	10.00
— Reissue with new prefix			
❏ ST-8-0103	Wichita Lineman	1968	25.00
— Capitol Record Club edition			

LONGINES SYMPHONETTE
❏ LS-218	Glen Campbell's Golden Favorites	1972	30.00

MCA
❏ 42210	Light Years	1988	10.00
❏ 42009	Still Within the Sound of My Voice	1987	10.00

PAIR
❏ PDL2-1089	All-Time Favorites	1980	16.00

PICKWICK
❏ SPC-3134	A Satisfied Mind	197?	10.00
❏ SPC-3346	I'll Paint You a Song	197?	10.00
❏ PTP-2048	Only the Lonely	197?	12.00
❏ PC-3052	The 12 String Guitar of Glen Campbell	196?	15.00
❏ SPC-3052 [S]	The 12 String Guitar of Glen Campbell	196?	12.00
❏ SPC-3274	The Glen Campbell Album	197?	10.00

STARDAY
❏ SLP-437	Country Music Star #1	1969	18.00
❏ SLP-424	Country Soul	1968	18.00

SURREY
❏ S1007 [M]	Country Shindig	196?	15.00

CAMPBELL, JO ANN

ABC-PARAMOUNT
❏ 393 [M]	Twistin' and Listenin'	1962	80.00
❏ S-393 [S]	Twistin' and Listenin'	1962	100.00

CAMEO
❏ C-1026 [M]	All the Hits of Jo Ann Campbell	1962	50.00
❏ SC-1026 [S]	All the Hits of Jo Ann Campbell	1962	100.00

CORONET
❏ CX-199 [M]	Starring Jo Ann Campbell	196?	25.00
❏ CXS-199 [R]	Starring Jo Ann Campbell	196?	15.00

END
❏ LP-306 [M]	I'm Nobody's Baby	1959	150.00

CAMPBELL, JOHN

CONTEMPORARY
❏ C-14053	After Hours	1989	15.00
❏ C-14061	Turning Point	1991	18.00

CAMPER VAN BEETHOVEN

INDEPENDENT PROJECT
❏ 016	Telephone Free Landslide Victory	1985	80.00
— Letterpress cover, "First Edition: June 1985" on back (numbered edition from 1-1,250); the basic color scheme is			

Number	Title	Yr	NM
white, black and flourescent orange on brown chipboard			
❏ 016	Telephone Free Landslide Victory	1985	60.00
— Letterpress cover, "Second Edition: 1175 cp./September 1985" on back (numbered edition from 1251-2425)			
❏ 016	Telephone Free Landslide Victory	1985	70.00
— Letterpress cover, "First Edition: June 1985" on back (un-numbered promo); the basic color scheme is red, black and flourescent orange on brown chipboard			
❏ 016	Telephone Free Landslide Victory	1985	50.00
— Letterpress cover, "Second Edition: 1175 cp./September 1985" on back (un-numbered promo)			
❏ 016	Telephone Free Landslide Victory	1985	30.00
— Manufactured and Distributed within the United States of America by Rough Trade" on back cover; non-letterpress edition; several color schemes exist, all of equal value			

PITCH A TENT
❏ 02	Camper Van Beethoven	1986	18.00
❏ 01	II & III	1985	18.00
❏ 05 [EP]	Vampire Can Mating Oven	1987	18.00

VIRGIN
❏ 91289	Key Lime Pie	1989	12.00
❏ 90918	Our Beloved Revolutionary Sweetheart	1988	12.00

CAMPI, RAY

ROLLIN' ROCK
❏ 023	Rockabilly Music	1979	15.00

ROUNDER
❏ 3047	Gone, Gone, Gone	198?	12.00
❏ 3046	Rockin' at the Ritz	198?	12.00

CAMPUS SINGERS, THE

ARGO
❏ LP-4033 [M]	Road of Blue	1964	25.00
❏ LPS-4033 [S]	Road of Blue	1964	30.00
❏ LP-4023 [M]	The Campus Singers at the Fickle Pickle	1963	25.00
❏ LPS-4023 [S]	The Campus Singers at the Fickle Pickle	1963	30.00

CAN

CLEOPATRA
❏ 3016 [B]	Inner Space		25.00
❏ 3043 [B]	Out Of Reach		25.00

MUTE
❏ 9033-1	Sacrilege	1997	30.00
— Album of remixes			

CANADIAN ALL STARS, THE

DISCOVERY
❏ DL-3025 [10]	The Canadian All Stars	1954	80.00

CANADIAN BEADLES, THE

TIDE
❏ 2005 [M]	Three Faces North	1964	50.00

CANADIAN SWEETHEARTS, THE

A&M
❏ LP-106 [M]	Introducing the Canadian Sweethearts	1964	40.00
❏ SP-4106 [S]	Introducing the Canadian Sweethearts	1964	50.00

CANARIES, THE

B.T. PUPPY
❏ BTS-1007	Flying High with the Canaries	1970	100.00

CANDIDO

ABC-PARAMOUNT
❏ ABC-125 [M]	Candido Featuring Al Cohn	1956	50.00
❏ ABC-453 [M]	Candido's Comparsa	1963	25.00
❏ ABCS-453 [S]	Candido's Comparsa	1963	30.00
❏ ABC-236 [M]	In Indigo	1958	50.00
❏ ABCS-236 [S]	In Indigo	1959	40.00
❏ ABC-286 [M]	Latin Fire	1959	50.00
❏ ABCS-286 [S]	Latin Fire	1959	50.00
❏ ABC-180 [M]	The Volcanic Candido	1957	50.00

BLUE NOTE
❏ BST-84357	Beautiful	1970	18.00

POLYDOR
❏ PD-5063	Drum Fever	1973	15.00

RCA VICTOR
❏ LPM-2027 [M]	Beautiful	1959	30.00
❏ LSP-2027 [S]	Beautiful	1959	40.00

ROULETTE
❏ R-52078 [M]	Conga Soul	1962	25.00
❏ SR-52078 [S]	Conga Soul	1962	30.00

SOLID STATE
❏ SS-18066	The Thousand Finger Man	1969	18.00

CANDLEBOX

MAVERICK
❏ 46076	Lucy/Candlebox	1995	30.00

Number	Title	Yr	NM

—First two albums packaged together in gatefold sleeve (neither available separately in U.S.)

CANDOLI, CONTE, AND STAN LEVEY

BETHLEHEM

Number	Title	Yr	NM
❏ BCP-9 [M]	West Coasting	1956	80.00

CANDOLI, CONTE

ANDEX

❏ A-3002 [M]	Mucho Calor	1958	50.00
❏ AS-3002 [S]	Mucho Calor	1959	40.00

BETHLEHEM

❏ BCP-1016 [10]	Sincerely, Conte Candoli	1954	150.00
❏ BCP-30 [M]	Toots Sweet	1956	80.00

CROWN

❏ CLP-5162 [M]	Little Band, Big Jazz	1960	25.00
❏ CST-190 [R]	Little Band, Big Jazz	196?	15.00
—Black vinyl			
❏ CST-190 [R]	Little Band, Big Jazz	196?	30.00
—Red vinyl			

GROOVE

❏ 1003 [M]	Cool Gabriels	1956	500.00
—Warhol cover			

CANDOLI, PETE

DECCA

❏ DL4761 [M]	Moscow Mule (And Many More Kicks)	1966	18.00
❏ DL74761 [S]	Moscow Mule (And Many More Kicks)	1966	25.00

KAPP

❏ KL-1230 [M]	For Pete's Sake	1960	25.00
❏ KS-3230 [S]	For Pete's Sake	1960	30.00

SOMERSET

❏ SF-17200 [M]	Blues, When Your Lover Has Gone	1963	25.00
❏ SFS-17200 [S]	Blues, When Your Lover Has Gone	1963	30.00

CANDOLI BROTHERS, THE

DOT

❏ DLP-3168 [M]	Bell, Book and Candoli	1959	30.00
❏ DLP-25168 [S]	Bell, Book and Candoli	1959	30.00
❏ DLP-3062 [M]	The Brothers Candoli	1957	50.00

IMPULSE!

❏ 29064	The Brothers Candoli	198?	12.00

MERCURY

❏ MG-20515 [M]	Two for the Money	1959	30.00
❏ SR-60191 [S]	Two for the Money	1959	30.00

WARNER BROS.

❏ W1462 [M]	The Brothers Candoli	1962	25.00
❏ WS1462 [S]	The Brothers Candoli	1962	30.00

CANDY STORE, THE

DECCA

❏ DL75147	Turned-On Christmas	1969	30.00

CANDYMEN, THE

ABC

❏ 616 [M]	The Candymen	1967	30.00
❏ S-616 [S]	The Candymen	1967	25.00
❏ S-633	The Candymen Bring You Candypower	1968	25.00

DIPLOMAT

❏ FM100	The Twist	196?	25.00

CANNED HEAT

ACCORD

❏ SN-7144	Captured Live	1981	12.00

ATLANTIC

❏ SD7289	One More River to Cross	1973	18.00

CLEOPATRA

❏ CLP1790 [B]	Live at Topanga Corral	2014	25.00

DALI

❏ DCLP-89022	Reheated	1990	18.00

JANUS

❏ JLS-3009	Vintage -- Canned Heat	1969	18.00

LIBERTY

❏ LST-7541 [S]	Boogie with Canned Heat	1968	25.00
❏ LN-10105	Boogie with Canned Heat	1981	10.00
—Budget-line reissue			
❏ LRP-3541 [M]	Boogie with Canned Heat	1968	40.00
—Stock copy in stereo cover with "Audition Mono LP Not for Sale" sticker			
❏ LRP-3526 [M]	Canned Heat	1967	30.00
❏ LST-7526 [S]	Canned Heat	1967	25.00
❏ LST-11000	Canned Heat Cook Book (The Best of Canned Heat)	1969	25.00
❏ LN-10106	Canned Heat Cook Book (The Best of Canned Heat)	1981	10.00
—Budget-line reissue			
❏ LST-11002	Future Blues	1970	18.00
❏ LST-7618	Hallelujah	1969	25.00
❏ LST-27200	Living the Blues	1968	30.00

PICKWICK

❏ SPC-3614	Boogie	1978	12.00
❏ SPC-3364	Live at Topanga Canyon	197?	12.00

SCEPTER CITATION

❏ CTN-18017	The Best of Canned Heat	1972	12.00

SUNSET

❏ SUS-5298	Collage	1971	12.00

TAKOMA

❏ 7066	The Human Condition	1980	15.00

UNITED ARTISTS

❏ LM-1015	Boogie with Canned Heat	1980	15.00
—Reissue of Liberty 7541			
❏ UAS-5509	Canned Heat Concert (Recorded Live in Europe)	1971	18.00
❏ UAS-5557	Historical Figures and Ancient Heads	1972	18.00
❏ UAS-9955	Living the Blues	1971	25.00
—Reissue of Liberty 27200			
❏ UA-LA049-F	The New Age	1973	18.00

WAND

❏ WDS-693	Live at Topanga Canyon	1970	30.00

CANNIBAL AND THE HEADHUNTERS

DATE

❏ TEM3001 [M]	Land of 1000 Dances	1966	30.00
❏ TES4001 [S]	Land of 1000 Dances	1966	40.00

RAMPART

❏ RM-3302 [M]	Land of 1000 Dances	1965	50.00
❏ RS-3302 [S]	Land of 1000 Dances	1965	70.00

CANNON, ACE

ALLEGIANCE

❏ AV-5024	Ace in the Whole	1986	10.00

HI

❏ HL-12025 [M]	Ace Cannon Live	1965	18.00
❏ SHL-32025 [S]	Ace Cannon Live	1965	25.00
❏ SHL-32072/3	Aces Back to Back	1972	18.00
❏ HL-12016 [M]	Aces Hi	1964	25.00
❏ SHL-32016 [S]	Aces Hi	1964	30.00
❏ 6006	After Hours	1978	12.00
❏ SHL-32076	Baby Don't Get Hooked on Me	1973	12.00
❏ SHL-32067	Blowing Wild	1971	15.00
❏ SHL-32071	Cannon Country	1972	15.00
❏ 8008	Cannon Country	1979	12.00
❏ HL-12022 [M]	Christmas Cheer	1964	25.00
❏ SHL-32022 [S]	Christmas Cheer	1964	30.00
❏ SHL-32060	Cool 'n Saxy	1971	15.00
❏ SHL-32080	Country Comfort	1974	12.00
❏ SHL-32046	In the Spotlight	1968	18.00
❏ HL-12008 [M]	Looking Back	1962	30.00
❏ SHL-32008 [S]	Looking Back	1962	30.00
❏ HL-12040 [M]	Memphis Golden Hits	1967	25.00
❏ SHL-32040 [S]	Memphis Golden Hits	1967	18.00
❏ HL-12028 [M]	Nashville Hits	1965	18.00
❏ SHL-32028 [S]	Nashville Hits	1965	25.00
❏ SHL-32101	Peace in the Valley	1976	12.00
❏ 8003	Sax Man	1977	12.00
❏ SHL-32090	Super Sax Country Style	1975	12.00
❏ HL-12030 [M]	Sweet and Tuff	1966	18.00
❏ SHL-32030 [S]	Sweet and Tuff	1966	25.00
❏ SHL-32086	That Music City Feeling	1974	12.00
❏ SHL-32051	The Ace of Sax	1969	18.00
❏ HL-12019 [M]	The Great Show Tunes	1964	25.00
❏ SHL-32019 [S]	The Great Show Tunes	1964	30.00
❏ SHL-32057	The Happy and Mellow Sax of Ace Cannon	1970	15.00
❏ SHL-32043	The Incomparable Sax of Ace Cannon	1968	18.00
❏ HL-12035 [M]	The Misty Sax of Ace Cannon	1967	25.00
❏ SHL-32035 [S]	The Misty Sax of Ace Cannon	1967	18.00
❏ HL-12014 [M]	The Moanin' Sax of Ace Cannon	1963	30.00
❏ SHL-32014 [S]	The Moanin' Sax of Ace Cannon	1963	30.00
❏ HL-12007 [M]	Tuff Sax	1962	30.00
❏ SHL-32007 [S]	Tuff Sax	1962	30.00

CANNON, FREDDY

RHINO

❏ RNLP-210	14 Booming Hits	1982	12.00

SWAN

❏ LP-507 [M]	Freddy Cannon at Palisades Park	1962	150.00
❏ LP-511 [M]	Freddy Cannon Steps Out	1963	150.00
❏ LP-504 [M]	Happy Shades of Blue	1960	150.00
❏ LP-505 [M]	Solid Gold Hits	1961	150.00
❏ LP-502 [M]	The Explosive! Freddy Cannon	1960	120.00
❏ LPS-502 [S]	The Explosive! Freddy Cannon	1960	300.00

WARNER BROS.

❏ W1612 [M]	Action!	1965	30.00
❏ WS1612 [S]	Action!	1965	40.00
❏ W1544 [M]	Freddie Cannon	1964	30.00
❏ WS1544 [S]	Freddie Cannon	1964	40.00
❏ W1628 [M]	Freddy Cannon's Greatest Hits	1966	30.00
❏ WS1628 [S]	Freddy Cannon's Greatest Hits	1966	40.00

CANNON, GUS

STAX

❏ ST-702 [M]	Walk Right In	1962	600.00

CANO, EDDIE

ATCO

❏ 33-184 [M]	On Broadway	1966	12.00
❏ SD 33-184 [S]	On Broadway	1966	15.00

DUNHILL

❏ D-50018 [M]	Brought Back Live from P.J.'s	1967	15.00
❏ DS-50018 [S]	Brought Back Live from P.J.'s	1967	12.00

GNP CRESCENDO

❏ GNP-77 [M]	A Taste of Cano	1963	15.00
❏ GNPS-77 [S]	A Taste of Cano	1963	18.00

PICKWICK

❏ SPC-3017	25 Latin Dance Favorites	196?	12.00

RCA VICTOR

❏ LPM-1672 [M]	Time for Cha Cha Cha	1958	18.00

REPRISE

❏ R-6124 [M]	Broadway -- Right Now!	1964	15.00
❏ R9-6124 [S]	Broadway -- Right Now!	1964	18.00
❏ R-6068 [M]	Cano Plays Mancini	1963	15.00
❏ R9-6068 [S]	Cano Plays Mancini	1963	18.00
❏ R-6105 [M]	Danke Schoen	1963	15.00
❏ R9-6105 [S]	Danke Schoen	1963	18.00
❏ R-6030 [M]	Eddie Cano at P.J.'s	1962	15.00
❏ R9-6030 [S]	Eddie Cano at P.J.'s	1962	18.00
❏ R-6055 [M]	Here Is the Fabulous Eddie Cano	1963	15.00
❏ R9-6055 [S]	Here Is the Fabulous Eddie Cano	1963	18.00
❏ R-6145 [M]	The Sound of Music	1965	15.00
❏ RS-6145 [S]	The Sound of Music	1965	18.00

CANTELON, WILLARD

SUPREME

❏ M-113 [M]	L.S.D. Battle for the Mind	1966	30.00
❏ S-113 [S]	L.S.D. Battle for the Mind	1966	40.00

CANTOR, EDDIE

VIK

❏ LXA-1119 [M]	The Best of Eddie Cantor	1957	50.00

CAPITAL CITY ROCKETS

ELEKTRA

❏ EKS-75079	Capital City Rockets	1973	25.00

CAPITOLS, THE (1)

ATCO

❏ 33-190 [M]	Dance the Cool Jerk	1966	40.00
❏ SD 33-190 [S]	Dance the Cool Jerk	1966	50.00
❏ 33-201 [M]	We Got a Thing That's In the Groove	1966	40.00
❏ SD 33-201 [S]	We Got a Thing That's In the Groove	1966	50.00

COLLECTABLES

❏ COL-5105	Golden Classics	1988	12.00

SOLID SMOKE

❏ 8019	The Capitols: Their Greatest Hits	1983	15.00

CAPP-PIERCE JUGGERNAUT, THE

CONCORD JAZZ

❏ CJ-40	Juggernaut	1979	15.00
—Frank Capp and Nat Pierce, leaders			
❏ CJ-336	Live at the Alley Cat	1988	12.00
❏ CJ-72	Live at the Century Plaza	1980	15.00
❏ CJ-183	The Juggernaut Orchestra Strikes Again	1981	15.00

CAPRARO, JOE

SOUTHLAND

❏ 220 [M]	Dixieland	1959	25.00

CAPRIS, THE (1)

AMBIENT SOUND

❏ FW37714	There's a Moon Out Again	1982	18.00

COLLECTABLES

❏ COL-5016	There's a Moon Out Tonight	198?	15.00

CAPRIS, THE (2)

COLLECTABLES

❏ COL-5000	Gotham Recording Stars	198?	15.00

CAPTAIN AND TENNILLE

A&M

❏ SP-4667	Captain & Tennille's Greatest Hits	1977	12.00
❏ SP-3105	Captain & Tennille's Greatest Hits	198?	10.00
—Reissue of 4667			
❏ SP-4700	Come In From the Rain	1977	12.00
❏ SP-4707	Dream	1978	12.00
❏ SP-3405	Love Will Keep Us Together	1975	15.00
❏ SP-4552	Love Will Keep Us Together	1975	12.00

Number	Title	Yr	NM
—Reissue of 3405			
QU-54552 [Q]	Love Will Keep Us Together	1975	18.00
SP-4561	Por Amor Vivremos	1975	15.00
SP-4570	Song of Joy	1976	12.00

CASABLANCA

NBLP7250	Keeping Our Love Warm	1980	12.00
NBLP7188	Make Your Move	1979	12.00

CAPTAIN BEEFHEART

4 MEN WITH BEARDS

4M211LP [B]	Doc At The Radar Station		25.00
4M212LP [B]	Ice Cream For Crow		25.00

A&M

SP-12510 [EP]	The Legendary A&M Sessions	1984	18.00

BLUE THUMB

BTS-1	Strictly Personal	1968	50.00
—Black label, unbanded sides			
BTS-1	Strictly Personal	1969	30.00
—White label, unbanded sides			
BTS-1	Strictly Personal	197?	25.00
—White label, banded sides			

BUDDAH

BDS-5077	Mirror Man	1971	50.00
—Die-cut gatefold cover			
BDS-5077 [B]	Mirror Man	197?	30.00
—Regular cover			
1001/5001 [B]	Safe As Milk "Baby Jesus" Bumper Sticker	1967	30.00
BDM-1001 [M]	Safe As Milk	1967	100.00
BDS-5001 [S]	Safe As Milk	1967	60.00
BDS-5063 [B]	Safe As Milk	1969	30.00

MERCURY

SRM-1-1018	Bluejeans and Moonbeams	1975	25.00
SRM-1-709	Unconditionally Guaranteed	1974	25.00

REPRISE

MS2115	Clear Spot	1972	30.00
RS6420	Lick My Decals Off, Baby	1970	30.00
MS2050	The Spotlight Kid	1971	30.00
2MS2027 [B]	Trout Mask Replica	1970	40.00
—Stock copy with 2027 labels and 2027 jacket			

STRAIGHT

RS6420	Lick My Decals Off, Baby	1970	50.00
2 STS-1053	Trout Mask Replica	1969	250.00
—Stock copy with 1053 labels (this has been confirmed to exist)			
2MS2027 [DJ]	Trout Mask Replica	1969	150.00
—White label promo with 2027 labels inside 1053 jacket			
2MS2027	Trout Mask Replica	1969	60.00
—Stock copy with 2027 labels inside 1053 jacket			
2 STS-1053 [DJ]	Trout Mask Replica	1969	200.00
—White label promo with 1053 labels			

SUNDAZED

LP5460 [B]	Safe As Milk	2013	30.00

VIRGIN

VA13148	Doc at the Radar Station	1980	15.00

VIRGIN/EPIC

ARE38274	Ice Cream for Crow	1982	15.00

WARNER BROS.

(no #)0	Bat Chain Puller	1978	400.00
—Test pressing with different selections than stock version			
BSK3256	Shiny Beast (Bat Chain Puller)	1978	18.00

CAPTAIN BEYOND

CAPRICORN

CP 0105	Captain Beyond	1972	30.00
—Original covers are 3-D			
CP 0105	Captain Beyond	1972	18.00
—Later covers are normal			
CP 0115	Sufficiently Breathless	1973	18.00

CLEOPATRA

CLP1716 [B]	Captain Beyond	2014	25.00
CLP0150 [B]	Captain Beyond	2013	30.00
CLP0296 [B]	Live In Texas October 6, 1973	2013	30.00
CLP0149 [B]	Sufficiently Breathless	2013	30.00

WARNER BROS.

BS3047	Dawn Explosion	1977	15.00

CAPTAIN SKY

AVI

6077	Pop Goes the Captain	1979	18.00
6042	The Adventures of Captain Sky	1978	40.00
6100	The Return of Captain Sky	1981	30.00

TEC

1202	Concerned Party No. 1	1980	25.00

CARAM, ANA

CHESKY

JR-28	Rio After Dark	199?	30.00
—Audiophile vinyl			

CARAMIA, TONY

STOMP OFF

SOS-1209	Hot Ivories	1991	18.00

CARAVAN, JIMMY

TOWER

T5103 [M]	Look Into the Flower	1968	50.00
ST5103 [S]	Look Into the Flower	1968	25.00

VAULT

9007	Hey Jude	1969	25.00

CARAVAN

4 MEN WITH BEARDS

4M237 [B]	If I Could Do It All Over Again, I'd Do It All Over You	2013	25.00

ARISTA

AL4088	Blind Dog at St. Dunstans	1976	12.00

BTM

5000	Cunning Stunts	1975	12.00

LONDON

XPS650	Caravan and the New Symphonia	1974	18.00
XPS637	For Girls Who Grow Plump in the Night	1973	18.00
PS582	If I Could Do It All Over Again…	1971	18.00
PS593	In the Land of the Grey & Pink	1971	18.00
LC50011 [B]	The Best of Caravan	1978	25.00
XPS615	Waterloo Lily	1972	18.00

VERVE FORECAST

FTS-3066 [B]	Caravan	1969	60.00

CARAVELLES, THE (1)

SMASH

MGS-27044 [M]	You Don't Have to Be a Baby to Cry	1963	60.00
SRS-67044 [R]	You Don't Have to Be a Baby to Cry	1963	60.00

CARE PACKAGE

LIBERTY

LST 7647	Keep On Keepin' On	1970	30.00

CAREFREES, THE

LONDON

LL3379 [M]	From England! The Carefrees	1964	80.00
PS379 [S]	From England! The Carefrees	1964	100.00

CAREY, DAVE

LAURIE

LLP-1004 [M]	Bandwagon Plus 2	1959	30.00

CAREY, MARIAH

COLUMBIA

C269670	#1's	1998	25.00
C47980	Emotions	1991	18.00
C45202	Mariah Carey	1990	25.00
C53205	Music Box	1993	18.00
C263800	Rainbow	1999	18.00

ISLAND

440 063467-1	Charmbracelet	2002	18.00
B0003943-01	The Emancipation of Mimi	2005	18.00
B0003943-01	The Emancipation of Mimi	2005	18.00

VIRGIN

SPRO-16452 [DJ]	Glitter	2001	25.00
—Promo-only version			
10797	Glitter	2001	18.00

CAREY, MUTT, AND PUNCH MILLER

SAVOY

MG-12038 [M]	Jazz – New Orleans	1955	50.00
MG-12050 [M]	Jazz – New Orleans, Vol. 2	1955	50.00

SAVOY JAZZ

SJC-415	New Orleans Jazz	1985	12.00

CAREY, MUTT

RIVERSIDE

RLP-1042 [10]	Mutt Carey Plays the Blues	1954	100.00
—on jacket; title on label is "Bring In Christmas			

CARGILL, HENSON

ATLANTIC

SD7279	This Is Henson Cargill Country	1973	15.00

HARMONY

KH31397	Welcome to My World	1972	12.00

MEGA

31-1016	On the Road	1972	18.00

MONUMENT

SLP-18103	Coming On Strong	1968	25.00
SLP-18117	None of My Business	1969	25.00
SLP-18094	Skip a Rope	1968	25.00
SLP-18137	Uncomplicated	1970	25.00

CARISI, JOHN

COLUMBIA

CL1419 [M]	The New Jazz Sound of "Show Boat"	1960	30.00
CS(# unk) [S]	The New Jazz Sound of "Show Boat"	1960	30.00

CARLIN, GEORGE

ATLANTIC

SD19326	A Place for My Stuff	1981	12.00

EARDRUM

1001	Carlin On Campus	1984	12.00
90523	Playin' with Your Head	1986	12.00
90972	What Am I Doing in New Jersey?	1988	12.00

ERA

EL103 [M]	George Carlin and Jack Burns At the Playboy Club Tonight	1960	30.00
E600	The Original George Carlin	1972	15.00

LAFF

A219	Killer Carlin	1981	12.00
—Reissue of Era material			

LITTLE DAVID

LD1008	An Evening with Wally Londo	1975	12.00
LD1004	Class Clown	1972	12.00
LD7214 [B]	FM & AM	1972	12.00
LD1076	Indecent Exposure (Some of the Best of George Carlin)	1978	12.00
LD1005	Occupation: Foole	1973	12.00
LD1075	On the Road	1977	12.00
90241	The George Carlin Collection	1984	10.00
LD3003	Toledo Window Box	1974	12.00
90129	Toledo Window Box	1983	10.00
—Reissue of 3003			

RCA CAMDEN

CAS-2566	Take-Offs and Put-Ons	1972	12.00

RCA VICTOR

LPM-3772 [M]	Take-Offs and Put-Ons	1967	25.00
LSP-3772 [S]	Take-Offs and Put-Ons	1967	18.00

CARLISLE, BELINDA

I.R.S.

R114824	Belinda	1986	15.00
—RCA Music Service edition			
5741	Belinda	1986	12.00

MCA

R143541	Heaven on Earth	1987	15.00
—BMG Direct Marketing edition			
42080	Heaven on Earth	1987	12.00
R173667	Runaway Horses	1989	15.00
—BMG Direct Marketing edition			
6339	Runaway Horses	1989	12.00

CARLISLE, BILL

HICKORY

LPS-129 [S]	The Best of Bill Carlisle	1967	30.00
LPM-129 [M]	The Best of Bill Carlisle	1967	30.00

CARLISLE, CLIFF

OLD TIMEY

103	Cliff Carlisle, Volume 1	198?	15.00
104	Cliff Carlisle, Volume 2	198?	15.00

CARLISLE BROTHERS, THE

KING

643 [M]	Fresh from the Country	1959	50.00

MERCURY

MG-20359 [M]	On Stage with the Carlisles	1958	50.00

CARLOS, WALTER

CBS MASTERWORKS

M39340	Digital Moonscapes	1984	12.00
—As "Wendy Carlos"			

COLUMBIA

KG31236	Sonic Seasonings	1972	18.00
KC31480	Walter Carlos' Clockwork Orange	1972	15.00

COLUMBIA MASTERWORKS

KM32659	More Switched-On Bach	1974	15.00
MS7194	Switched-On Bach	1968	15.00
—Standing Bach" cover; gray label with "360 Sound Stereo			
MS7194	Switched-On Bach	1970	15.00
—Gray label with orange Columbia logos and no "360 Sound Stereo			
HM47194	Switched-On Bach	198?	30.00
—Half-speed mastered edition			
MS7194	Switched-On Bach	1968	50.00
—Sitting Bach" (sometimes called "Constipated Bach") cover that was quickly replaced; gray label with "360 Sound Stereo			
MS7194	Switched-On Bach	198?	18.00

Number	Title	Yr	NM

—Later reissue under the name "Wendy Carlos"; bar code on back cover

Number	Title	Yr	NM
❑ M2X35895	Switched-On Brandenburgs	1979	18.00
❑ HM45950	Switched-On Brandenburgs Vol. 1	1980	100.00

—Half-speed mastered edition

| ❑ MS7286 | The Well-Tempered Synthesizer | 1969 | 18.00 |

—Gray label with "360 Sound Stereo

| ❑ MS7286 | The Well-Tempered Synthesizer | 1970 | 15.00 |

—Gray label with orange Columbia logos and no "360 Sound Stereo

| ❑ M32088 | Walter Carlos By Request | 1973 | 15.00 |

CARLTON, CARL

20TH CENTURY
| ❑ T-628 | Carl Carlton | 1981 | 12.00 |

ABC
| ❑ D-857 | Everlasting Love | 1974 | 15.00 |
| ❑ D-910 | I Wanna Be with You | 1975 | 15.00 |

BACK BEAT
| ❑ BBLX-71 | Can't Stop a Man in Love | 1973 | 18.00 |

CASABLANCA
| ❑ 822705-1 | Private Property | 1985 | 12.00 |

RCA VICTOR
| ❑ AFL1-4425 | The Bad C.C. | 1982 | 12.00 |

CARMEN, ERIC

ARISTA
❑ AB4124	Boats Against the Current	1977	10.00
❑ AB4184	Change of Heart	1978	10.00
❑ AL4057	Eric Carmen	1975	15.00

—Shiny, simulated gold foil cover

| ❑ AL4057 | Eric Carmen | 1975 | 10.00 |

—Regular non-shiny gold cover

| ❑ AQ4057 [Q] | Eric Carmen | 1975 | 25.00 |
| ❑ AL8547 | The Best of Eric Carmen | 1988 | 18.00 |

—Original copies do not contain "Make Me Lose Control

| ❑ AL8547 | The Best of Eric Carmen | 1988 | 10.00 |

—Reissues add "Make Me Lose Control

| ❑ AL9513 | Tonight You're Mine | 1980 | 10.00 |

GEFFEN
| ❑ GHS24042 | Eric Carmen | 1985 | 10.00 |

CARMEN

EPIC
| ❑ BN26479 | Carmen | 1969 | 25.00 |

CARMICHAEL, HOAGY

BIOGRAPH
| ❑ 37 | Stardust (1927-30) | 198? | 12.00 |

BLUEBIRD
| ❑ 8333-1-RB | Stardust, And Much More | 1989 | 15.00 |

BOOK-OF-THE-MONTH
| ❑ 61-5450 | Hoagy Carmichael | 1984 | 30.00 |

DECCA
| ❑ DL5068 [10] | Stardust Road | 1950 | 80.00 |
| ❑ DL8588 [M] | Stardust Road | 1958 | 30.00 |

GOLDEN
| ❑ LP-198-18 [M] | Havin' a Party | 1958 | 30.00 |

JAZZTONE
| ❑ J-1266 [M] | Hoagy Sings Carmichael | 1957 | 30.00 |

KIMBERLY
| ❑ 2023 [M] | The Legend of Hoagy Carmichael | 1962 | 30.00 |
| ❑ 11023 [R] | The Legend of Hoagy Carmichael | 196? | 25.00 |

MCA
| ❑ 20196 | Hong Kong Blues | 198? | 12.00 |
| ❑ 1507 | Stardust Road | 198? | 12.00 |

PACIFIC JAZZ
| ❑ PJ-1223 [M] | Hoagy Sings Carmichael | 1956 | 60.00 |

PAUSA
| ❑ 9006 | Hoagy Sings Carmichael | 1982 | 12.00 |

RCA VICTOR
| ❑ CPL1-3370(e) | A Legendary Performer and Composer | 1979 | 18.00 |
| ❑ LPT-3072 [10] | Old Rockin' Chair | 1953 | 80.00 |

TOTEM
| ❑ 1039 | The 1944-45 V-Disc Sessions | 198? | 12.00 |

CARNES, KIM

A&M
❑ SP-4548	Kim Carnes	1975	15.00
❑ SP-4606	Sailin'	1976	15.00
❑ SP-3114	Sailin'	198?	10.00

—Budget-line reissue

| ❑ SP-3204 | The Best of Kim Carnes | 1982 | 12.00 |

AMOS
| ❑ AAS7016 [B] | Rest on Me | 1971 | 30.00 |

EMI AMERICA
❑ SO-17159	Barking at Airplanes	1985	12.00
❑ SO-17107	Café Racers	1983	12.00
❑ ST-17198	Light House	1986	10.00
❑ SO-17052	Mistaken Identity	1981	12.00
❑ SW-17030	Romance Dance	1980	12.00
❑ SW-17004	St. Vincent's Court	1978	12.00
❑ SO-17078	Voyeur	1982	12.00

MCA
| ❑ 914 | The Early Years | 1984 | 10.00 |
| ❑ 42200 | View from the House | 1988 | 10.00 |

MOBILE FIDELITY
| ❑ 1-073 | Mistaken Identity | 1982 | 30.00 |

—Audiophile vinyl

CARNEY, ART

COLUMBIA
| ❑ CL2595 [10] | Doodle-Li-Boops and Rhinocelopes | 1955 | 80.00 |

CARNEY, HARRY

CLEF
| ❑ MGC-640 [M] | Harry Carney with Strings | 1955 | 150.00 |

VERVE
| ❑ MGV-2028 [M] | Moods for Girl and Boy | 1957 | 50.00 |

—Reissue of Clef 640

| ❑ V-2028 [M] | Moods for Girl and Boy | 1957 | 25.00 |

CAROLINA SLIM

SHARP
| ❑ 2002 [M] | Blues from the Cotton Fields | 195? | 250.00 |

CARP

EPIC
| ❑ E30212 | Carp | 1970 | 30.00 |

CARPENTER, IKE

DISCOVERY
| ❑ DL3003 [10] | Dancers in Love | 1949 | 300.00 |

INTRO
| ❑ 950 [10] | Lights Out | 1952 | 300.00 |

SCORE
| ❑ SLP-4010 [M] | Lights Out | 1957 | 150.00 |

CARPENTER, MARY CHAPIN

COLUMBIA
| ❑ FC40758 | Hometown Girl | 1987 | 12.00 |
| ❑ FC44228 | State of the Heart | 1989 | 12.00 |

CARPENTERS

A&M
| ❑ SP-4581 | A Kind of Hush | 1976 | 15.00 |
| ❑ SP-3197 | A Kind of Hush | 1982 | 10.00 |

—Reissue of 4581

| ❑ SP-5172 | An Old Fashioned Christmas | 1987 | 10.00 |

—Reissue of 3270 (record still says 3270 but cover is 5172)

❑ SP-3270	An Old-Fashioned Christmas	1984	10.00
❑ SP-3511	A Song for You	1972	15.00
❑ SMAS-94398	A Song for You	1972	25.00

—Capitol Record Club edition; unlike the standard edition, the cover is smooth and not textured

❑ SP-3502 [B]	Carpenters	1971	15.00
❑ SP-4726	Christmas Portrait	1978	18.00
❑ SP-3210	Christmas Portrait	198?	10.00

—Reissue of SP-4726

| ❑ SP-4271 | Close to You | 1970 | 15.00 |
| ❑ SP-3184 | Close to You | 1982 | 10.00 |

—Reissue of 4271

❑ SP-4530	Horizon	1975	15.00
❑ QU-54530 [Q]	Horizon	1975	30.00
❑ SP-3723	Made in America	1981	15.00
❑ SP-3519	Now & Then	1973	15.00
❑ QU-53519 [Q]	Now & Then	1974	30.00
❑ SP-4205	Offering	1969	80.00
❑ SP-4703	Passage	1977	15.00
❑ SP-3199	Passage	1982	10.00

—Reissue of 4703

❑ SP-3601	The Singles 1969-1973	1973	15.00
❑ QU-53601 [Q]	The Singles 1969-1973	1974	30.00
❑ SP-4205	Ticket to Ride	1970	15.00

—Reissue of "Offering" with new title and cover

| ❑ SP-4954 | Voice of the Heart | 1983 | 15.00 |
| ❑ SP-6601 | Yesterday Once More | 1985 | 18.00 |

CARR, CATHY

DOT
| ❑ DLP-3674 [M] | Ivory Tower | 1966 | 30.00 |
| ❑ DLP-25674 [S] | Ivory Tower | 1966 | 30.00 |

FRATERNITY
| ❑ 1005 [M] | Ivory Tower | 1957 | 120.00 |

ROULETTE
| ❑ R25077 [M] | Shy | 1959 | 40.00 |
| ❑ SR25077 [S] | Shy | 1959 | 50.00 |

CARR, GEORGIA

TOPS
| ❑ L-1617 [M] | Songs by a Moody Miss | 195? | 30.00 |

VEE JAY
| ❑ LP-1105 [M] | Rocks in My Bed | 1964 | 25.00 |
| ❑ VJS-1105 [S] | Rocks in My Bed | 1964 | 30.00 |

CARR, HELEN

BETHLEHEM
| ❑ BCP-1027 [10] | Down in the Depths on the 90th Floor | 1955 | 120.00 |
| ❑ BCP-45 [M] | Why Do I Love You | 1956 | 100.00 |

CARR, JAMES

GOLDWAX
| ❑ 3002S | A Man Needs a Woman | 1968 | 150.00 |
| ❑ 3001S | You Got My Mind Messed Up | 1968 | 150.00 |

CARR, JOE "FINGERS

CAPITOL
❑ T280 [M]	Bar Room Piano	1952	30.00
❑ T1151 [M]	Fingers" and the Flapper	1959	25.00
❑ ST1151 [S]	Fingers" and the Flapper	1959	30.00
❑ T527 [M]	Fireman's Ball	1954	30.00
❑ T443 [M]	Joe "Fingers" Carr and His Ragtime Band	1954	30.00
❑ T1217 [M]	Joe "Fingers" Carr and His Swingin' String Band	1959	25.00
❑ ST1217 [S]	Joe "Fingers" Carr and His Swingin' String Band	1959	30.00
❑ T345 [M]	Roughhouse Piano	1953	30.00

WARNER BROS.
| ❑ W1386 [M] | The World's Greatest Ragtime Piano Player | 1960 | 18.00 |
| ❑ WS1386 [S] | The World's Greatest Ragtime Piano Player | 1960 | 25.00 |

CARR, JOYCE

AUDIOPHILE
| ❑ AP-148 | Joyce Carr | 198? | 15.00 |

SEECO
| ❑ 440 [M] | Make The Man Love Me | 1960 | 325.00 |

CARR, LEROY

COLUMBIA
| ❑ CL1911 [M] | Blues Before Sunrise | 1962 | 30.00 |
| ❑ CS8511 [R] | Blues Before Sunrise | 1962 | 25.00 |

CARR, LODI

LAURIE
| ❑ LLP-1007 [M] | Lady Bird | 1960 | 30.00 |

CARR, VIKKI

COLUMBIA
❑ KC31470	Canta En Espanol	1972	12.00
❑ PC33340	Hoy (Today)	1975	12.00
❑ KG32526	Live at the Greek Theatre	1973	15.00
❑ CG33609	Love Story/The First Time Ever	1976	15.00
❑ KC32251	Ms. America	1973	12.00
❑ KC32860	One Hell of a Woman	1974	12.00
❑ C31040	Superstar	1971	12.00
❑ KC31453	The First Time Ever (I Saw Your Face)	1972	12.00
❑ C30662	Vikki Carr's Love Story	1971	12.00

LIBERTY
❑ LRP-3314 [M]	Color Her Great	1963	18.00
❑ LST-7314 [S]	Color Her Great	1963	25.00
❑ LRP-3354 [M]	Discovery!	1964	18.00
❑ LST-7354 [S]	Discovery!	1964	25.00
❑ LRP-3383 [M]	Discovery! Volume Two	1964	18.00
❑ LST-7383 [S]	Discovery! Volume Two	1964	25.00
❑ LST-7565	Don't Break My Pretty Balloon	1969	18.00
❑ LST-7604	For Once in My Life	1969	18.00
❑ LRP-3506 [M]	Intimate Excitement	1967	25.00
❑ LST-7506 [S]	Intimate Excitement	1967	18.00
❑ LRP-3533 [M]	It Must Be Him	1967	25.00
❑ LST-7533 [S]	It Must Be Him	1967	18.00
❑ LST-11001	Nashville by Carr	1970	18.00
❑ LRP-3420 [M]	The Anatomy of Love	1965	18.00
❑ LST-7420 [S]	The Anatomy of Love	1965	25.00
❑ LN-10108	The Best of Vikki Carr	1981	10.00
❑ LRP-3456 [M]	The Way of Today	1966	18.00
❑ LST-7456 [S]	The Way of Today	1966	25.00
❑ LST-7548 [S]	Vikki	1968	18.00
❑ LRP-3548 [M]	Vikki	1968	30.00

—Mono stock copy inside stereo cover with "Audition Mono LP Not for Sale" sticker

PAIR
| ❑ PDL2-1082 | From the Heart | 1986 | 15.00 |

PICKWICK
| ❑ SPC-3587 | Intimate | 1978 | 10.00 |
| ❑ SPC-3613 | Unforgettable | 1978 | 10.00 |

SUNSET
| ❑ SUS-5228 | That's All | 1969 | 12.00 |
| ❑ SUS-5293 | Unforgettable | 1971 | 12.00 |

UNITED ARTISTS
| ❑ LM-1006 | It Must Be Him | 1980 | 12.00 |

—Abridged reissue of Liberty 7533

| ❑ UAS-5581 | The Best of Vikki Carr | 1972 | 15.00 |
| ❑ UA-LA244-G | The Very Best of Vikki Carr | 1974 | 12.00 |

Number	Title	Yr	NM
❏ UAS-6813	The Ways to Love a Man	1972	12.00
❏ UA-LA089-G	Vikki Carr's Golden Songbook/Superpak	1973	15.00

CARRACK, PAUL

CHRYSALIS
❏ F1-21709	Groove Approved	1989	15.00
❏ BFV41578	One Good Reason	1987	10.00
❏ 6V41663	The Carrack Collection	1988	12.00

EPIC
| ❏ ARE38161 | Suburban Voodoo | 1982 | 10.00 |

CARRASCO, JOE "KING", AND THE CROWNS

HANNIBAL
| ❏ HNBL-1308 | Joe "King" Carrasco and the Crowns | 1980 | 18.00 |
| ❏ HNEP-3301 [EP] | Party Safari | 1981 | 18.00 |

MCA
| ❏ 5404 | Party Weekend | 1983 | 15.00 |
| ❏ 5308 | Synapse Gap | 1982 | 18.00 |

ROUNDER
| ❏ 9012 | Bandido Rock | 1987 | 12.00 |

CARRINGTON, TERRI LYNN

VERVE
| ❏ 837697-1 | Real Life Story | 1989 | 18.00 |

CARROLL, ANDREA /BEVERLY WARREN

B.T. PUPPY
| ❏ BTS-1017 | Andrea Carroll and Beverly Warren Side By Side | 1971 | 150.00 |

CARROLL, BAIKIDA

HAT HUT
| ❏ 0M/N | The Spoken Word | 197? | 25.00 |

SOUL NOTE
| ❏ SN-1023 | Shadows & Reflections | 198? | 15.00 |

CARROLL, BARBARA

ATLANTIC
| ❏ ALR-132 [10] | Piano Panorama | 195? | 80.00 |

BLUE NOTE
| ❏ BN-LA645-G | Barbara Carroll | 1976 | 18.00 |

DISCOVERY
| ❏ DS-847 | Barbara Carrol at the Piano | 1980 | 18.00 |

KAPP
❏ KL-1113 [M]	Flower Drum Song	1958	30.00
❏ KS-(# unk) [S]	Flower Drum Song	1958	30.00
❏ KL-1193 [M]	Satin Doll	1959	30.00

LIVINGSTON
| ❏ 1081 [10] | Barbara Carroll Trio | 1953 | 100.00 |

RCA VICTOR
❏ LJM-1001 [M]	Barbara Carroll Trio	1954	50.00
❏ LPM-1137 [M]	Have You Met Miss Carroll?	1956	50.00
❏ LPM-1396 [M]	It's a Wonderful World	1957	50.00
❏ LJM-1023 [M]	Lullabies in Rhythm	1955	50.00
❏ LPM-1296 [M]	We Just Couldn't Say Goodbye	1956	50.00

SESAC
| ❏ N-3201 [M] | Why Not? | 1959 | 30.00 |
| ❏ SN-3201 [S] | Why Not? | 1959 | 40.00 |

UNITED ARTISTS
| ❏ UA-LA778-H | From the Beginning | 1978 | 18.00 |

VERVE
❏ MGV-2095 [M]	Barbara	1958	40.00
❏ V-2095 [M]	Barbara	1961	25.00
❏ MGV-2063 [M]	Funny Face	1957	60.00
—Orange label			
❏ MGV-2063 [M]	Funny Face	1957	50.00
—Black label			
❏ MGV-2092 [M]	The Best of George and Ira Gershwin	1958	40.00
❏ V-2092 [M]	The Best of George and Ira Gershwin	1961	25.00

WARNER BROS.
❏ W1710 [M]	Barbara Carroll Live! Her Piano and Trio	1967	25.00
❏ WS1710 [S]	Barbara Carroll Live! Her Piano and Trio	1967	25.00
❏ W1543 [M]	Hello Dolly" and "What Makes Sammy Run	1964	18.00
❏ WS1543 [S]	Hello Dolly" and "What Makes Sammy Run	1964	25.00

CARROLL, BARBARA/MARY LOU WILLIAMS

ATLANTIC
❏ 1271 [M]	Ladies in Jazz	1958	50.00
—Black label			
❏ 1271 [M]	Ladies in Jazz	1961	25.00
—Multi-color label, white "fan" logo			

CARROLL, CORKY

CASUAL TUNA
| ❏ 0(# unknown) | A Surfer for President | 1979 | 40.00 |

RURAL
| ❏ RR-001 | Laid Back | 1971 | 75.00 |

CARROLL, DAVID

AMBASSADOR
| ❏ S-98051 | All Time Great Hits | 196? | 12.00 |

MERCURY
❏ PPS-2022 [M]	All the World Dances	196?	18.00
❏ PPS-6022 [S]	All the World Dances	196?	25.00
❏ SR-60873 [S]	All the World Dances	196?	25.00
❏ MG-20873 [M]	All the World Dances	196?	18.00
❏ MG-20351 [M]	Dance and Stay Young	195?	18.00
❏ SR-60027 [S]	Dance and Stay Young	1959	25.00
❏ MG-20109 [M]	Dancer's Delight	195?	25.00
❏ SR-60690 [S]	David Carroll Galaxy	196?	25.00
❏ MG-20690 [M]	David Carroll Galaxy	196?	18.00
❏ MG-20301 [M]	Dreams	195?	25.00
❏ MG-20286 [M]	Feathery Feeling	195?	25.00
❏ SR-60026 [S]	Feathery Feeling	1959	25.00
❏ MG-20935 [M]	Golden Oldies for Today's Teens	196?	15.00
❏ SR-60935 [S]	Golden Oldies for Today's Teens	196?	18.00
❏ MG-20846 [M]	Happy Feet	196?	18.00
❏ SR-60846 [S]	Happy Feet	196?	25.00
❏ MG-20962 [M]	House Party Discotheque	196?	15.00
❏ SR-60962 [S]	House Party Discotheque	196?	18.00
❏ PPS-2000 [M]	Latin Percussion	196?	18.00
❏ PPS-6000 [S]	Latin Percussion	196?	25.00
❏ MG-20281 [M]	Let's Dance	195?	18.00
❏ SR-60001 [S]	Let's Dance	1959	25.00
❏ MG-20470 [M]	Let's Dance Again	195?	18.00
❏ SR-60152 [S]	Let's Dance Again	1959	25.00
❏ MG-20649 [M]	Let's Dance Dance Dance	196?	18.00
❏ SR-60649 [S]	Let's Dance Dance Dance	196?	25.00
❏ MG-20739 [M]	Let's Dance to America's Waltz Favorites	196?	18.00
❏ SR-60739 [S]	Let's Dance to America's Waltz Favorites	196?	25.00
❏ MG-20688 [M]	Let's Dance to the Movie Themes	196?	18.00
❏ MG-60688 [S]	Let's Dance to the Movie Themes	196?	25.00
❏ MG-20660 [M]	Mexico and 11 Other Great Hits	196?	18.00
❏ SR-60660 [S]	Mexico and 11 Other Great Hits	196?	25.00
❏ MG-20926 [M]	Music Makes Me Want to Dance!	196?	15.00
❏ SR-60926 [S]	Music Makes Me Want to Dance!	196?	18.00
❏ MG-20166 [M]	Percussion in Hi-Fi	195?	18.00
❏ SR-60003 [S]	Percussion in Hi-Fi	1959	25.00
❏ MG-20867 [M]	Percussion Orientale	196?	18.00
❏ SR-60867 [S]	Percussion Orientale	196?	25.00
❏ PPS-2008 [M]	Percussion Parisienne	196?	18.00
❏ PPS-6008 [S]	Percussion Parisienne	196?	25.00
❏ MG-20955 [M]	Percussion Parisienne	196?	15.00
❏ SR-60955 [S]	Percussion Parisienne	196?	18.00
❏ MG-20389 [M]	RePercussion	195?	18.00
❏ SR-60029 [S]	RePercussion	1959	25.00
❏ MG-20156 [M]	Serenade to a Princess	195?	25.00
❏ MG-20154 [M]	Shimmering Strings	195?	25.00
❏ MG-20411 [M]	Show Stoppers from the Fabulous Fifties	195?	18.00
❏ SR-60060 [S]	Show Stoppers from the Fabulous Fifties	1959	25.00
❏ MG-20503 [M]	Solo Encores	196?	18.00
❏ SR-60180 [S]	Solo Encores	195?	25.00
❏ SR-60786 [S]	Today's Top Hits	196?	25.00
❏ MG-20786 [M]	Today's Top Hits	196?	18.00
❏ MG-20064 [M]	Toe-Tappers	195?	25.00
❏ MG-20086 [M]	Waltzes, Wine and Candlelight	195?	25.00

WING
❏ MGW-12146 [M]	Contrasts	195?	18.00
❏ SRW-12508 [S]	Contrasts	195?	18.00
❏ MGW-12106 [M]	Dance Date	195?	18.00
❏ SRW-16106 [S]	Dance Date	195?	18.00
❏ SRW-16367	Let's Dance	196?	15.00
❏ MGW-12256 [M]	Waltzes	196?	15.00
❏ SRW-16256 [S]	Waltzes	196?	15.00

CARROLL, DIAHANN, AND ANDRE PREVIN

UNITED ARTISTS
❏ UAL3069 [M]	Diahann Carroll and Andre Previn	1960	25.00
❏ UAS6069 [S]	Diahann Carroll and Andre Previn	1960	30.00
❏ UAL4021 [M]	Porgy and Bess	1959	25.00
❏ UAS5021 [S]	Porgy and Bess	1959	30.00

CARROLL, DIAHANN

ATLANTIC
| ❏ 8048 [M] | Fun Life | 1961 | 25.00 |
| ❏ SD8048 [S] | Fun Life | 1961 | 30.00 |

RCA CAMDEN
| ❏ CAL-695 [M] | Show-Stoppers (She's Diahann Carroll) | 1961 | 15.00 |

RCA VICTOR
| ❏ LPM-1467 [M] | Diahann Carroll Sings Harold Arlen | 1957 | 40.00 |

UNITED ARTISTS
| ❏ UAL3080 [M] | Diahann Carroll at the Persian Room | 1960 | 25.00 |
| ❏ UAS6080 [S] | Diahann Carroll at the Persian Room | 1960 | 30.00 |

VIK
| ❏ LXA-1131 [M] | Best Beat Forward | 1958 | 30.00 |

CARROLL, JIM, BAND

ATCO
| ❏ SD 38-132 | Catholic Boy | 1980 | 25.00 |
| ❏ SD 38-145 | Dry Dreams | 1982 | 16.00 |

ATLANTIC
| ❏ 80123 | I Write Your Name | 1984 | 18.00 |

CARROLL, JIM

A&M
| ❏ SP-4323 | Jim Carroll | 1971 | 15.00 |

CARROLL, JOE

CHARLIE PARKER
| ❏ PLP-802 [M] | The Man with the Happy Sound | 1962 | 30.00 |
| ❏ PLP-802S [S] | The Man with the Happy Sound | 1962 | 30.00 |

EPIC
| ❏ LN3272 [M] | Joe Carroll | 1956 | 50.00 |

CARROLL BROTHERS, THE

CAMEO
| ❏ C-1015 [M] | College Twist Party | 1962 | 30.00 |
| ❏ SC-1015 [S] | College Twist Party | 1962 | 40.00 |

CARS, THE

DCC COMPACT CLASSICS
| ❏ LPZ-2056 | The Cars Greatest Hits | 1998 | 30.00 |
| —Audiophile vinyl | | | |

ELEKTRA
❏ 5E-507	Candy-O	1979	12.00
—No title and artist listed on front cover (information was on a sticker on the shrink wrap)			
❏ R123334	Candy-O	1979	15.00
—RCA Music Service edition has "The Cars Candy-O" printed on upper left front cover			
❏ R161593	Door to Door	1987	12.00
—BMG Direct Marketing edition			
❏ 60747	Door to Door	1987	10.00
❏ R153702	Greatest Hits	1985	15.00
—RCA Music Service edition			
❏ 60464	Greatest Hits	1985	12.00
❏ R143650	Heartbeat City	1984	12.00
—RCA Music Service edition			
❏ 60296	Heartbeat City	1984	10.00
❏ 60296 [DJ]	Heartbeat City	1984	18.00
—Promo-only audiophile pressing on Qulex II vinyl			
❏ 5E-514	Panorama	1980	12.00
❏ 5E-567	Shake It Up	1981	12.00
❏ 5E-567 [PD]	Shake It Up	1981	40.00
—Promo-only picture disc with blank back			
❏ 5E-567 [PD]	Shake It Up	1981	50.00
—Promo-only picture disc with "KMET FM" imprinted on back			
❏ R144033	The Cars	1978	15.00
—RCA Music Service edition			
❏ 6E-135	The Cars	1978	12.00

NAUTILUS
❏ NR-49	Candy-O	1982	30.00
—Audiophile "Super Disc			
❏ NR-14	The Cars	1981	30.00
—Audiophile "Super Disc			

CARSON, MARTHA

CAPITOL
❏ T1607 [M]	A Talk with the Lord	1961	30.00
❏ ST1607 [S]	A Talk with the Lord	1961	30.00
❏ T1507 [M]	Satisfied	1960	30.00
❏ ST1507 [S]	Satisfied	1960	30.00

RCA VICTOR
| ❏ LPM-1145 [M] | Journey to the Sky | 1955 | 40.00 |
| ❏ LPM-1490 [M] | Rock-a My Soul | 1957 | 50.00 |

SIMS
| ❏ LP-100 [M] | Martha Carson | 196? | 30.00 |

CARSON, WAYNE

MONUMENT
| ❏ Z30906 | Life Lines | 1972 | 18.00 |

CARTER, ANITA

CAPITOL
| ❏ ST-11085 | So Much Love | 1972 | 18.00 |

MERCURY
❏ MG-20847 [M]	Anita of the Carter Family	1964	30.00
❏ SR-60847 [S]	Anita of the Carter Family	1964	30.00
❏ MG-20770 [M]	Folk Songs Old and New	1963	30.00
❏ SR-60770 [S]	Folk Songs Old and New	1963	30.00

CARTER, BENNY; BEN WEBSTER; BARNEY BIGARD

SWINGVILLE
| ❏ SVLP-2032 [M] | B.B.B. & Co. | 1962 | 40.00 |
| —Purple label | | | |

Number	Title	Yr	NM
❏ SVST-2032 [S]	B.B.B. & Co.	1962	50.00
— Red label			
❏ SVLP-2032 [M]	B.B.B. & Co.	1965	25.00
— Blue label, trident logo at right			
❏ SVST-2032 [S]	B.B.B. & Co.	1965	30.00
— Blue label, trident logo at right			

CARTER, BENNY

20TH CENTURY-FOX

Number	Title	Yr	NM
❏ TFM-3134 [M]	Benny Carter in Paris	1963	25.00
❏ TFS-4134 [S]	Benny Carter in Paris	1963	30.00

ABC IMPULSE!

❏ AS-9116 [S]	Additions to Further Definitions	1968	15.00
❏ AS-12 [S]	Further Definitions	1968	15.00

ANALOGUE PRODUCTIONS

❏ AP-13	Jazz Giant	199?	30.00
— Audiophile reissue			

AUDIO LAB

❏ AL-1505 [M]	The Fabulous Benny Carter	1959	150.00

CLEF

❏ MGC-141 [10]	Cosmopolite	1953	250.00

CONCORD JAZZ

❏ CJ-285	A Gentleman and His Music	1985	12.00

CONTEMPORARY

❏ C-3555 [M]	Jazz Giant	1958	50.00
❏ S-7028 [S]	Jazz Giant	1960	30.00
— Reissue of Stereo Records 7028			
❏ S-7555 [S]	Jazz Giant	197?	15.00
— Reissue of 7028			
❏ M-3561 [M]	Swingin' the Twenties	1959	40.00
❏ S-7561 [S]	Swingin' the Twenties	1959	40.00

FANTASY

❏ OJC-167	Jazz Giant	198?	12.00
— Reissue of Contemporary 7555			
❏ OJC-374	Montreux '77	1988	12.00
— Reissue of Pablo Live 2308 204			
❏ OJC-339	Swingin' the Twenties	198?	12.00
— Reissue of Contemporary 7561			

HINDSIGHT

❏ HSR-218	Benny Carter and His Orchestra 1944	1985	12.00

IMPULSE!

❏ A-9116 [M]	Additions to Further Definitions	1966	30.00
❏ AS-9116 [S]	Additions to Further Definitions	1966	40.00
❏ A-12 [M]	Further Definitions	1962	30.00
❏ AS-12 [S]	Further Definitions	1962	30.00

MCA

❏ 29066	Additions to Further Definitions	198?	10.00
❏ 29006	Further Definitions	198?	10.00

MCA IMPULSE!

❏ MCA-5651	Further Definitions	1986	12.00

MOVIETONE

❏ 1020 [M]	Autumn Leaves	1967	25.00
❏ 72020 [S]	Autumn Leaves	1967	18.00

MUSICAL HERITAGE SOCIETY

❏ MHS912375Z	In the Mood for Swing	1989	15.00

NORGRAN

❏ MGN-1058 [M]	Alone Together	1956	120.00
— With Oscar Peterson			
❏ MGN-1015 [M]	Benny Carter Plays Pretty	1955	200.00
❏ MGN-1070 [M]	Cosmopolite	1956	120.00
❏ MGN-1044 [M]	New Jazz Sounds	1955	120.00
— With Dizzy Gillespie, Bill Harris			
❏ MGN-21 [10]	The Formidable Benny Carter	1954	150.00
❏ MGN-10 [10]	The Urbane Mr. Carter	1954	150.00

PABLO

❏ 2310926	Benny Carter Meets Oscar Peterson	1987	12.00
❏ 2310781	Cater, Gillespie, Inc.	1976	15.00
— With Dizzy Gillespie			
❏ 2310935	My Kind of Trouble	1989	15.00
❏ 2405409	The Best of Benny Carter	198?	12.00
❏ 2310768	The King	1975	15.00
❏ 2310922	Wonderland	1987	12.00

PABLO LIVE

❏ 2308216	Live and Well in Japan	1979	15.00
❏ 2308204	Montreux '77	1978	15.00

PRESTIGE

❏ PR-7643	Benny Carter 1933	1969	18.00
❏ 2513	Opening Blues	198?	12.00

STEREO RECORDS

❏ S-7028 [S]	Jazz Giant	1959	40.00

STORYVILLE

❏ 4047	Summer Serenade	1981	12.00

SWING

❏ SW-8403	Benny Carter and His Orchestra 1938 and 1946	1985	12.00

TIME-LIFE

❏ STL-J-10	Giants of Jazz	1980	25.00

UNITED ARTISTS

Number	Title	Yr	NM
❏ UAL-4017 [M]	Aspects	1960	30.00
❏ UAS-5017 [S]	Aspects	1960	40.00
❏ UAL-3055 [M]	Can Can" and "Anything Goes	1959	30.00
❏ UAS-6055 [S]	Can Can" and "Anything Goes	1959	40.00
❏ UAL-4073 [M]	Can Can" and "Anything Goes	1960	25.00
❏ UAS-5073 [S]	Can Can" and "Anything Goes	1960	30.00
❏ UAL-4080 [M]	Jazz Calendar	1960	25.00
❏ UAS-5080 [S]	Jazz Calendar	1960	30.00
❏ UAL-4094 [M]	Sax A La Carter	1961	25.00
❏ UAS-5094 [S]	Sax A La Carter	1961	30.00

VERVE

❏ MGV-8148 [M]	Alone Together	1957	60.00
— Reissue of Norgran 1058			
❏ V-8148 [M]	Alone Together	1961	25.00
❏ MGV-8160 [M]	Cosmopolite	1957	60.00
— Reissue of Norgran 1070			
❏ V-8160 [M]	Cosmopolite	1961	25.00
❏ MGV-2025 [M]	Moonglow -- Love Songs by Benny Carter	1957	60.00
— Reissue of Norgran 1015			
❏ V-2025 [M]	Moonglow -- Love Songs by Benny Carter	1961	25.00
❏ MGV-8135 [M]	New Jazz Sounds	1957	60.00
— Reissue of Norgran 1044			
❏ V-8135 [M]	New Jazz Sounds	1961	25.00

CARTER, BETTY

ABC IMPULSE!

❏ AS-9321	What a Little Moonlight	197?	25.00

ABC-PARAMOUNT

❏ ABC-363 [M]	The Modern Sound of Betty Carter	1960	60.00
❏ ABCS-363 [S]	The Modern Sound of Betty Carter	1960	80.00

ATCO

❏ 33-152 [M]	'Round Midnight	1963	50.00
❏ SD 33-152 [S]	'Round Midnight	1963	60.00

BET-CAR

❏ 1001	Betty Carter	1970	30.00
❏ MK1003	The Audience with Betty Carter	1980	25.00
❏ 1002	The Betty Carter Album	197?	30.00

PEACOCK

❏ PLP-90 [M]	Out There with Betty Carter	1958	120.00

ROULETTE

❏ SR-5000	Finally	1969	30.00
❏ SR-5005	Now It's My Turn	1976	25.00
❏ SR-5001 [B]	'Round Midnight	1975	25.00

UNITED ARTISTS

❏ UAL3379 [M]	Inside Betty Carter	1964	50.00
❏ UAS6379 [S]	Inside Betty Carter	1964	60.00
❏ UAS-5639	Inside Betty Carter	1971	25.00
— Reissue of 6379			

VERVE

❏ 843991-1	Droppin' Things	1990	18.00
❏ 835661-1	Look What I Got	1988	15.00
❏ 835684-1	The Audience with Betty Carter	1988	18.00
— Reissue of Bet-Car 1003			
❏ 835682-1	The Betty Carter Album	1988	15.00
— Reissue of Bet-Car 1002			

CARTER, CALVIN

VEE JAY

❏ LP-1041 [M]	Twist with Calvin Carter	1962	100.00
❏ SR-1041 [S]	Twist with Calvin Carter	1962	150.00

CARTER, CLARENCE

ABC

❏ X-943	A Heart Full of Song	1976	18.00
❏ X-896	Loneliness & Temptation	1975	18.00
❏ X-833	Real	1974	18.00

ATLANTIC

❏ 8267 [M]	Patches	1970	60.00
— Mono is white label promo only; "d/j copy monaural" sticker on stereo cover			
❏ SD8267 [S]	Patches	1970	30.00
❏ SD8238	Testifyin'	1969	30.00
❏ SD8282	The Best of Clarence Carter	1971	25.00
❏ SD8199	The Dynamic Clarence Carter	1969	30.00
❏ SD8192	This Is Clarence Carter	1968	30.00

FAME

❏ FM-LA186-F	Sixty Minutes	1973	18.00

ICHIBAN

❏ ICH-1068	Between a Rock and a Hard Place	1989	15.00
❏ ICH-1003	Dr. C.C.	1986	15.00
❏ ICH-1016	Hooked on Love	1987	15.00
❏ ICH-1001	Messin' with My Mind	1986	15.00
❏ ICH-1116	The Best of Clarence Carter: The Dr.'s Greatest Presciptions	1991	15.00
❏ ICH-1032	Touch of Blues	1988	15.00

VENTURE

Number	Title	Yr	NM
❏ VL1005	Let's Burn	1980	12.00
❏ VL1009	Mr. Clarence Carter In Person	1981	12.00

CARTER, JACK

AAMCO

❏ ALP-316 [M]	Broadway A La Carter	1958	30.00

CARTER, JOHN, AND BOBBY BRADFORD

FLYING DUTCHMAN

❏ FDS-108	Flight for Four	1969	25.00
❏ FD-10108	Flight for Four	1971	18.00
— Reissue of 108			
❏ FDS-128	Self Determination Music	1970	25.00
❏ FD-10128	Self Determination Music	1971	18.00
— Reissue of 128			

REVELATION

❏ 18	Secrets	1978	18.00
❏ 9	The New Art Ensemble	1977	18.00

CARTER, JOHN

BLACK SAINT

❏ BSR-0057	Dauwhe	1983	15.00
❏ BSR-0047	Night Fire	1982	15.00

FLYING DUTCHMAN

❏ FDS-109	John Carter	1969	25.00

GRAMAVISION

❏ 18-8603	Castles of Ghana	1986	15.00
❏ 18-8704	Dance of the Love Ghosts	1987	15.00
❏ 18-8809	Ghosts	1988	15.00
❏ 79422	Shadows on the Wall	1989	15.00

CARTER, JUNE

COLUMBIA

❏ KC33686	Appalachian Pride	1975	18.00
— As "June Carter Cash			

CARTER, LYNDA

EPIC

❏ JE35308	Portrait	1978	18.00
❏ 35308 [PD]	Portrait	1978	60.00
— Picture disc version			

CARTER, MEL

AMOS

❏ 7010	This Is My Life	1971	15.00

DERBY

❏ LPM-702 [M]	When a Boy Falls in Love	1963	300.00

IMPERIAL

❏ LP-9300 [M]	All of a Sudden My Heart Sings	1966	18.00
❏ LP-12300 [S]	All of a Sudden My Heart Sings	1966	25.00
❏ LP-9319 [M]	Easy Listening	1966	18.00
❏ LP-12319 [S]	Easy Listening	1966	25.00
❏ LP-9289 [M]	Hold Me, Thrill Me, Kiss Me	1965	18.00
❏ LP-12289 [S]	Hold Me, Thrill Me, Kiss Me	1965	25.00

SUNSET

❏ SUS-5295	Easy Goin'	1970	12.00
❏ SUS-5227	Mel Carter	1968	12.00

CARTER, MOTHER MAYBELLE

AMBASSADOR

❏ 98069 [M]	Mother Maybelle Carter	195?	150.00

COLUMBIA

❏ CL2475 [M]	A Living Legend	1965	25.00
❏ CS9275 [S]	A Living Legend	1965	30.00
❏ KG32436	Mother Maybelle Carter	1973	30.00

KAPP

❏ KL-1413 [M]	Queen of the Autoharp	1964	25.00
❏ KS-3413 [S]	Queen of the Autoharp	1964	30.00

SMASH

❏ MGS-27025 [M]	Mother Maybelle Carter and Her Autoharp	1963	25.00
❏ SRS-67025 [S]	Mother Maybelle Carter and Her Autoharp	1963	30.00
❏ MGS-27041 [M]	Pickin' and Singin'	1963	25.00
❏ SRS-67041 [S]	Pickin' and Singin'	1963	30.00

CARTER, RON, AND JIM HALL

CONCORD JAZZ

❏ CJ-245	Live at Village West	1983	18.00
❏ CJ-270	Telephone	1985	18.00

CARTER, RON; HERBIE HANCOCK; TONY WILLIAMS

MILESTONE

❏ M-9105	Third Plane	1981	15.00

CARTER, RON

CTI

❏ 6037	All Blues	1974	25.00
❏ 6027	Blues Farm	1973	25.00
❏ 8001	Blues Farm	1979	18.00

Number	Title	Yr	NM
—Reissue of 6027			
❏ 6051	Spanish Blue	1975	25.00
❏ 6064	Yellow and Green	1976	25.00

ELEKTRA/MUSICIAN

Number	Title	Yr	NM
❏ 60214	Etudes	1984	15.00

EMARCY

❏ 836366-1	All Alone	1988	15.00

EMBRYO

❏ SD521	Uptown Conversation	1970	25.00

FANTASY

❏ OJC-432	Where?	1990	15.00

KUDU

❏ 25	Anything Goes	1976	18.00

MILESTONE

❏ M-9086	A Song for You	1978	15.00
❏ M-9096	New York Slick	1979	18.00
❏ M-9088	Parade	1978	15.00
❏ M-9107	Parfait	1981	15.00
❏ M-9073	Pastels	1976	15.00
❏ M-9099	Patrao	1980	18.00
❏ M-9082	Peg Leg	1977	15.00
❏ M-55004	Piccolo	1977	25.00
❏ M-9092	Pick 'Em	1979	15.00
❏ M-9100	Super Strings	1981	15.00

NEW JAZZ

❏ NJLP-8265 [M]	Where?	1961	80.00
—With Eric Dolphy and Mal Waldron; purple label			
❏ NJLP-8265 [M]	Where?	1965	30.00
—With Eric Dolphy and Mal Waldron;; blue label, trident logo at right			

RSO

❏ RS-1-3085	Empire Jazz	1980	25.00

CARTER FAMILY, THE

ACME

❏ LP-1 [M]	All Time Favorites	1960	200.00
❏ LP-2 [M]	In Memory of A.P. Carter	1960	200.00

COLUMBIA

❏ CL2617 [M]	Country Album	1967	30.00
❏ CS9417 [S]	Country Album	1967	25.00
❏ KC34266	Country's First Family	1976	25.00
❏ CL2319 [M]	The Best of the Carter Family	1965	18.00
❏ CS9119 [S]	The Best of the Carter Family	1965	25.00
❏ KC33084	Three Generations	1974	25.00
❏ KC31454	Travelin' Minstrel Band	1972	25.00

DECCA

❏ DL4404 [M]	A Collection of Favorites by the Carter Family	1963	30.00
❏ DL4557 [M]	More Favorites by the Carter Family	1964	30.00

LIBERTY

❏ LRP-3230 [M]	The Carter Family Album	1962	30.00
❏ LST-7230 [S]	The Carter Family Album	1962	40.00

RCA CAMDEN

❏ CAL-2473 [M]	Lonesome Pine Special	1971	15.00
❏ CAS-2554(e) [R]	More Golden Gems from the Original Carter Family	1972	12.00
❏ ACL1-0047 [R]	My Old Cottage Home	1973	12.00
❏ CAL-586 [M]	The Original and Great Carter Family	1960	18.00
—Two-tone blue label with "RCA Camden" at top			
❏ CAL-586 [M]	The Original and Great Carter Family	1969	12.00
—All-blue label with "RCA" on its side at left and "Camden" straight at right (reissue)			

RCA VICTOR

❏ LPM-2772 [M]	'Mid the Green Fields of Virginia	1963	40.00
❏ LSP-2772 [R]	'Mid the Green Fields of Virginia	1963	25.00

STARDAY

❏ SLP-248 [M]	Echoes of the Carter Family	1963	40.00

CARTWRIGHT, ANGELA

STAR-BRIGHT

❏ HLP-102 [M]	Angela Cartwright Sings	1959	50.00

CARVER, JOHNNY

ABC

❏ ABCX-812	Double Exposure	1974	15.00
❏ ABCD-843	Please Don't Tell (That Sweet Ole Lady of Mine)	1974	15.00
❏ ABCD-864	Strings	1975	15.00
❏ ABCX-792	Tie a Yellow Ribbon Around the Ole Oak Tree	1973	15.00

ABC DOT

❏ DO-2042	Afternoon Delight	1976	15.00
❏ DO-2083	The Best of Johnny Carver	1977	15.00

HARMONY

❏ KH32476	I Start Thinking About You	1973	15.00

IMPERIAL

❏ LP-12412	Leaving Again	1968	25.00
❏ LP-12347 [S]	Really Country	1967	25.00
❏ LP-9347 [M]	Really Country	1967	30.00
❏ LP-12380	You're in Good Hands with Johnny Carver	1968	25.00

CARY, DICK

BELL

❏ BLP-44 [M]	Hot and Cool	1961	30.00

CIRCLE

❏ CLP-018	The Amazing Dick Cary	198?	12.00

FAMOUS DOOR

❏ HL-140	California Doings	1980	15.00

GOLDEN CREST

❏ GC-3024 [M]	Dixieland Goes Progressive	1958	50.00

STEREOCRAFT

❏ RTN-106 [S]	Hot and Cool	196?	30.00
—riginal with "shaded dog" label			

CASCADES, THE

UNI

❏ 73069	Maybe the Rain Will Fall	1969	30.00

VALIANT

❏ W405 [M]	Rhythm of the Rain	1963	150.00
❏ WS405 [S]	Rhythm of the Rain	1963	300.00

CASEY, AL

STACY

❏ STM-100 [M]	Surfin' Hootenanny	1963	300.00
❏ STS-100 [S]	Surfin' Hootenanny	1963	400.00

SUNDAZED

❏ LP-5026	Surfin' Hootenanny	1996	12.00

CASEY, AL (2)

MOODSVILLE

❏ MVLP-12 [M]	The Al Casey Quartet	1960	50.00
—Green label			
❏ MVLP-12 [M]	The Al Casey Quartet	1965	30.00
—Blue label, trident logo at right			

SWINGVILLE

❏ SVLP-2007 [M]	Buck Jumpin'	1960	50.00
—Purple label			
❏ SVLP-2007 [M]	Buck Jumpin'	1965	30.00
—Blue label, trident logo at right			

CASH, ALVIN

MAR-V-LUS

❏ 1827 [M]	Twine Time	1965	30.00

CASH, JOHNNY, AND JUNE CARTER

COLUMBIA

❏ CL2728 [M]	Carryin' On with Johnny Cash and June Carter	1967	25.00
❏ CS9528 [S]	Carryin' On with Johnny Cash and June Carter	1967	25.00
❏ KC32443	Johnny Cash and His Woman	1973	18.00

CASH, JOHNNY

ACCORD

❏ SN-7134	I Walk the Line	1983	12.00
❏ SN-7208	Years Gone By	1983	12.00

ALLEGIANCE

❏ AV-5017	The First Years	1986	12.00

AMERICAN

❏ C69691 [B]	American III: Solitary Man	2000	75.00
❏ 440-063336-1	American IV: The Man Comes Around	2002	25.00
❏ B0019507-01 [B]	American IV: The Man Comes Around	2014	35.00
❏ 45520 [B]	American Recordings	1994	100.00
❏ B0002769-01	American V: A Hundred Highways	2006	15.00
❏ 43097	Unchained	1996	120.00

ARCHIVE OF FOLK MUSIC

❏ 278	Johnny Cash	198?	15.00

CACHET

❏ 9001	A Believer Sings the Truth	1979	18.00

CLEOPATRA

❏ 1996 [B]	Hayride Anthology		30.00
—picture disc			

COLUMBIA

❏ PC38074	A Believer Sings the Truth	1985	10.00
—Reissue of Priority 38074			
❏ KC32091	Any Old Wind That Blows	1973	15.00
❏ KC31332	A Thing Called Love	1972	15.00
❏ C2L38 [M]	Ballads of the True West	1965	30.00
❏ C2S838 [S]	Ballads of the True West	1965	30.00
❏ CL2248 [M]	Bitter Tears (Ballads of the American Indian)	1964	18.00
❏ CS9048 [S]	Bitter Tears (Ballads of the American Indian)	1964	25.00
❏ CL1930 [M]	Blood, Sweat & Tears	1963	25.00
❏ CS8730 [S]	Blood, Sweat & Tears	1963	30.00
❏ KC32898	Children's Album	1974	15.00
❏ JC36866	Classic Christmas	1980	15.00
❏ FC37355	Encore	1981	12.00
❏ CL2492 [M]	Everybody Loves a Nut	1966	18.00
❏ CS9292 [S]	Everybody Loves a Nut	1966	25.00
❏ C32951	Five Feet High and Rising	1974	15.00
❏ CL2647 [M]	From Sea to Shining Sea	1967	25.00

Number	Title	Yr	NM
❏ CS9447 [S]	From Sea to Shining Sea	1967	25.00
❏ KC31256	Give My Love to Rose	1972	15.00
❏ KC35646	Gone Girl	1978	15.00
❏ KCS9943	Hello, I'm Johnny Cash	1970	15.00
❏ FC40056	Highwayman	1985	12.00
—Waylon Jennings/Willie Nelson/Johnny Cash/Kris Kristofferson			
❏ C45240	Highwayman 2	1990	18.00
—Waylon Jennings/Willie Nelson/Johnny Cash/Kris Kristofferson			
❏ CL1284 [M]	Hymns by Johnny Cash	1959	30.00
❏ CS8125 [S]	Hymns by Johnny Cash	1959	40.00
❏ CL1722 [M]	Hymns from the Heart	1962	25.00
❏ CS8522 [S]	Hymns from the Heart	1962	30.00
❏ CL2190 [M]	I Walk the Line	1964	18.00
❏ CS8990 [S]	I Walk the Line	1964	25.00
❏ S30397	I Walk the Line	1970	15.00
—Soundtrack from movie			
❏ KC35313	I Would Like to See You Again	1978	12.00
❏ FC38696	Johnny 99	1983	12.00
❏ PC38696	Johnny 99	1986	10.00
—Budget-line reissue			
❏ KC31645	Johnny Cash: America (A 200-Year Salute in Story and Song)	1972	15.00
❏ CS9639 [M]	Johnny Cash at Folsom Prison	1968	50.00
—White label promo with stereo number; "Special Mono Radio Station Copy" sticker on cover			
❏ CS9639 [S]	Johnny Cash at Folsom Prison	1968	25.00
—Red label with "360 Sound Stereo" at bottom			
❏ CL2839 [M]	Johnny Cash at Folsom Prison	1968	150.00
—Red label with "Mono" at bottom; this is a stock copy			
❏ CG33639	Johnny Cash at Folsom Prison/Johnny Cash at San Quentin	1974	18.00
❏ CS9827	Johnny Cash at San Quentin	1969	15.00
❏ CQ30961 [Q]	Johnny Cash at San Quentin	1971	25.00
❏ FC38317	Johnny Cash's Biggest Hits	1982	12.00
❏ CL2678 [M]	Johnny Cash's Greatest Hits, Volume 1	1967	25.00
❏ CS9478 [S]	Johnny Cash's Greatest Hits, Volume 1	1967	25.00
❏ JC35637	Johnny Cash's Greatest Hits, Volume 3	1978	15.00
❏ C33087	Johnny Cash Sings Precious Memories	1974	15.00
❏ KC33370	John R. Cash	1975	15.00
❏ KC33814	Look at Them Beans	1975	15.00
❏ KC30550	Man in Black	1971	15.00
❏ CL2446 [M]	Mean as Hell	1965	18.00
❏ CS9246 [S]	Mean as Hell	1965	25.00
❏ CL1463 [M]	Now, There Was a Song!	1960	30.00
❏ CS8254 [S]	Now, There Was a Song!	1960	40.00
❏ KC34193	One Piece at a Time	1976	15.00
❏ CL2309 [M]	Orange Blossom Special	1965	18.00
❏ CS9109 [S]	Orange Blossom Special	1965	25.00
❏ FC39951	Rainbow	1985	12.00
❏ CL1464 [M]	Ride This Train	1960	30.00
❏ CS8255 [S]	Ride This Train	1960	40.00
❏ CS8255 [S]	Ride This Train	197?	12.00
—Reissue on orange label			
❏ CL2052 [M]	Ring of Fire (The Best of Johnny Cash)	1963	25.00

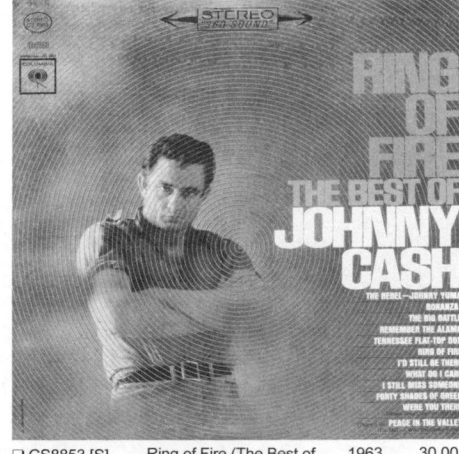

❏ CS8853 [S]	Ring of Fire (The Best of Johnny Cash)	1963	30.00
❏ JC36779	Rockabilly Blues	1980	12.00
❏ JC36086	Silver	1979	15.00
❏ CL1339 [M]	Songs of Our Soil	1959	30.00
❏ CS8148 [S]	Songs of Our Soil	1959	40.00
❏ KC34088	Strawberry Cake	1976	15.00
❏ C32240	Sunday Morning Coming Down	1973	15.00
❏ CL2537 [M]	That's What You Get for Lovin' Me	1966	18.00
❏ CS9337 [S]	That's What You Get for Lovin' Me	1966	25.00
❏ FC38094	The Adventures of Johnny Cash	1982	12.00

Number	Title	Yr	NM
❑ FC37179	The Baron	1981	12.00
❑ CL2117 [M]	The Christmas Spirit	1963	30.00
❑ CS8917 [S]	The Christmas Spirit	1963	30.00
❑ CL1253 [M]	The Fabulous Johnny Cash	1958	25.00
❑ CS8122 [S]	The Fabulous Johnny Cash	1959	40.00
❑ C32253	The Gospel Road	1973	15.00
❑ CG32253	The Gospel Road	1973	30.00
❑ STS2004	The Heart of Johnny Cash	196?	25.00
— *Columbia Star Series" release; has "360 Sound" labels*			
❑ KCS9726	The Holy Land	1969	18.00
❑ KC30887	The Johnny Cash Collection (His Greatest Hits, Volume II)	1971	15.00
❑ C30100	The Johnny Cash Show	1970	15.00
❑ KC33086	The Junkie and the Juicehead	1974	15.00
❑ JC34314	The Last Gunfighter Ballad	1977	15.00
❑ CL1622 [M]	The Lure of the Grand Canyon	1961	40.00
— *Cash narrates; with Andre Kostelanetz and His Orchestra*			
❑ CS8422 [S]	The Lure of the Grand Canyon	1961	50.00
— *Cash narrates; with Andre Kostelanetz and His Orchestra*			
❑ C32917	The Ragged Old Flag	1974	15.00
❑ JC34833	The Rambler	1977	15.00
❑ CL1802 [M]	The Sound of Johnny Cash	1962	25.00
❑ CS8602 [S]	The Sound of Johnny Cash	1962	30.00
❑ GP29	The World of Johnny Cash	1970	18.00

COLUMBIA LIMITED EDITION

❑ LE10063 [S]	The Fabulous Johnny Cash	197?	18.00
— *Reissue of 8122*			

COLUMBIA SPECIAL PRODUCTS

❑ P13043	Destination Victoria Station	1977	40.00
— *Alternate number is "VS 150*			
❑ P13832	Hello, I'm Johnny Cash	1977	15.00
❑ 363	Legends and Love Songs	196?	25.00

DORAL/CSP

❑ (# unknown)0	Doral Presents Johnny Cash	1972	40.00
— *Mail-order offer from Doral cigarettes*			

EVEREST

❑ 276	Johnny Cash	19??	15.00

HARMONY

❑ KH32388	Ballads of the American Indian	1973	15.00
❑ HS11249	Golden Sounds of Country Music	1968	15.00
❑ HS11342	Johnny Cash	1969	15.00
❑ KH31602	The Johnny Cash Songbook	1972	15.00
❑ KH30138	The Walls of a Prison	1970	15.00
❑ KH30916	Understand Your Man	1971	15.00

MERCURY

❑ 832031-1	Johnny Cash Is Coming to Town	1987	12.00
❑ 834778-1	Water from the Wells of Home	1988	12.00

MUSIC WORLD ENTERTAINMENT

❑ CR9295121	Johnny Cash Remixed	2008	30.00

PAIR

❑ PDL2-1107	Classic Cash	1986	18.00

POWER PAK

❑ 246	Country Gold	198?	12.00

PRIORITY

❑ PU38074	A Believer Sings the Truth	1982	15.00
— *Reissue of Cachet album*			
❑ PU33087	Johnny Cash Sings Precious Memories	1982	15.00
— *Reissue of Columbia album of the same name*			
❑ UG32253	The Gospel Road	1981	18.00
— *Reissue of Columbia album of the same name*			

RHINO

❑ RNLP70229	The Vintage Years	1987	15.00

SHARE

❑ 5001	Folsom Prison Blues	197?	15.00
❑ 5000	I Walk the Line	197?	15.00
❑ 5003	Johnny Cash Sings the Greatest Hits	197?	15.00
❑ 5002	The Blue Train	197?	15.00

SUN

❑ SLP-1270 [M]	All Aboard the Blue Train	1963	50.00
❑ DT-91458 [R]	All Aboard the Blue Train	196?	30.00
— *Capitol Record Club edition*			
❑ LP-140	Folsom Prison Blues	1979	12.00
❑ LP-105	Get Rhythm	1969	15.00
❑ LP-139	I Walk the Line	1979	12.00
❑ LP-126	Johnny Cash: The Man, The World, His Music	1971	25.00
❑ SLP-1240 [M]	Johnny Cash's Greatest!	1959	50.00
❑ SLP-1245 [M]	Johnny Cash Sings Hank Williams	1960	50.00
❑ SLP-1245 [R]	Johnny Cash Sings Hank Williams	196?	25.00
— *Reissue in rechanneled stereo; front cover says "STEREO*			
❑ DT-91284 [R]	Johnny Cash Sings Hank Williams	196?	30.00
— *Capitol Record Club edition*			
❑ T-91284 [M]	Johnny Cash Sings Hank Williams	196?	40.00
— *Capitol Record Club edition*			
❑ LP-142	Johnny Cash Sings the Greatest Hits	1979	12.00
❑ LP-118	Johnny Cash – The Legend	1970	25.00

Number	Title	Yr	NM
❑ SLP-1220 [M]	Johnny Cash with His Hot and Blue Guitar	1956	100.00
❑ SLP-1220 [R]	Johnny Cash with His Hot and Blue Guitar	196?	25.00
— *Reissue in rechanneled stereo; front cover says "STEREO*			
❑ SLP-1255 [M]	Now Here's Johnny Cash	1961	50.00
❑ SLP-1255 [R]	Now Here's Johnny Cash	196?	25.00
— *Reissue in rechanneled stereo; front cover says "STEREO*			
❑ DT-90678 [R]	Now Here's Johnny Cash	1966	25.00
— *Capitol Record Club edition*			
❑ LP-100	Original Golden Hits, Volume I	1969	15.00
❑ ST-92085	Original Golden Hits, Volume I	1969	25.00
— *Capitol Record Club edition; uses older Sun label*			
❑ LP-101	Original Golden Hits, Volume II	1969	15.00
❑ ST-92086	Original Golden Hits, Volume II	1969	25.00
— *Capitol Record Club edition; uses older Sun label*			
❑ LP-127	Original Golden Hits, Volume III	1972	15.00
❑ LP-106	Showtime	1969	15.00
❑ LP-104	Story Songs of the Trains and Rivers	1969	15.00
❑ 1002	Superbilly (1955-58)	198?	12.00
❑ LP-141	The Blue Train	1979	12.00
❑ SQBO-93213	The Greatness of Johnny Cash	197?	25.00
— *Capitol Record Club exclusive*			
❑ 1006	The Original Johnny Cash	1980	12.00
❑ SLP-1275 [M]	The Original Sun Sound of Johnny Cash	1965	50.00
❑ LP-122	The Rough Cut King of Country Music	1971	15.00
❑ LP-115	The Singing Story Teller	1970	15.00
❑ SLP-1235 [M]	The Songs That Made Him Famous	1958	100.00
❑ SLP-1235 [R]	The Songs That Made Him Famous	196?	25.00
— *Reissue in rechanneled stereo; front cover says "STEREO*			
❑ DT-90668 [R]	The Songs That Made Him Famous	1966	30.00
— *Capitol Record Club edition*			
❑ T-90668 [M]	The Songs That Made Him Famous	1966	40.00
— *Capitol Record Club edition*			
❑ LP1220 [B]	With His Hot And Blue Guitar	2014	30.00

SUNDAZED

❑ LP-5176	Blood, Sweat & Tears	2003	18.00
— *Reissue on 180-gram vinyl*			
❑ LP-5170	Town Hall Party Live! 1958	2003	18.00
— *Reissue on 180-gram vinyl*			
❑ LP-5171	Town Hall Party Live! 1959	2003	18.00
— *Reissue on 180-gram vinyl*			

TIME-LIFE

❑ TLCS-3	Country & Western Classics	1982	25.00
❑ STW-108	Country Music	1981	15.00

WORD

❑ WR-8333	Believe in Him	1986	15.00

CASH, JOHNNY/TAMMY WYNETTE

COLUMBIA MUSICAL TREASURIES

❑ P4S5376	The King/The Queen	1969	30.00
— *Box set; two records by Johnny Cash, two records by Tammy Wynette; records are individually numbered from DS 562 through DS 565*			
❑ DS608	The King/The Queen	1969	18.00
— *One record by Johnny Cash, the other by Tammy Wynette*			

CASH, ROSEANNE

COLUMBIA

❑ OC45054	Hits 1979-1989	1989	15.00
❑ AS1527 [DJ]	Interview with Martha Hume	1982	30.00
— *Generic cover with sticker*			
❑ FC40777	King's Record Shop	1987	12.00
❑ FC39463	Rhythm and Romance	1985	12.00
❑ JC36155	Right or Wrong	1980	12.00
❑ PC36155	Right or Wrong	1984	10.00
— *Budget-line reissue with new prefix and "02" added to bar code*			
❑ JC36965	Seven Year Ache	1981	12.00
❑ HC46965	Seven Year Ache	1981	50.00
— *Half-speed mastered edition*			
❑ PC36965	Seven Year Ache	1984	10.00
— *Budget-line reissue with new prefix and "02" added to bar code*			
❑ FC37570	Somewhere in the Stars	1982	12.00
❑ PC37570	Somewhere in the Stars	1984	10.00
— *Budget-line reissue with new prefix and "02" added to bar code*			

CASH, TOMMY

ELEKTRA

❑ CM-5	Only a Stone	1975	18.00

EPIC

❑ E30860	American Way of Life	1971	18.00
❑ E30556	Cash Country	1971	18.00
❑ E30107	Rise and Shine	1970	18.00
❑ BN26535	Six White Horses	1970	18.00
❑ KE31747	That Certain One	1972	18.00

Number	Title	Yr	NM
❑ KE31995	The Best of Tommy Cash, Volume I	1972	18.00
❑ BN26484	Your Lovin' Takes the Leavin' Out of Me	1969	25.00

MONUMENT

❑ 7619	The New Spirit	1978	15.00

UNITED ARTISTS

❑ UAS-6628	Here Comes Tommy Cash	1968	25.00

CASHMAN, PISTILLI AND WEST

ABC

❑ ABCS-629	Bound to Happen	1968	25.00

CAPITOL

❑ ST-211	Cashman, Pistilli, and West	1969	18.00

CASHMAN, TERRY

LIFESONG

❑ LS8137	Talkin' Baseball	1981	18.00
❑ LS6006	Terry Cashman	1976	15.00
❑ PZ34999	Terry Cashman	1977	12.00
— *Reissue of 6006*			

CASHMAN AND WEST

ABC DUNHILL

❑ DSX-50126	A Song or Two	1972	15.00
❑ DSX-50179	Lifesong	1974	15.00
❑ DSX-50141	Moondog Serenade	1973	15.00

CASIMIR, JOHN

JAZZOLOGY

❑ JCE-5	Casimir's Paragon Jazz Band	1967	18.00
❑ JCE-21	Tomorrow Tomorrow	1967	18.00

CASINOS, THE (1)

FRATERNITY

❑ LP-1019 [M]	Then You Can Tell Me Goodbye	1967	40.00
❑ LPS-1019 [S]	Then You Can Tell Me Goodbye	1967	60.00

CASIOPEA

ALFA

❑ AAA10002	Eyes of the Mind	1981	18.00

MILESTONE

❑ M-9133	Zoom	1985	15.00

CASSELL, PETE

HILLTOP

❑ 6023	The Legend of Pete Cassell	1965	30.00

CASSIDY, DAVID

BELL

❑ 1312	Cassidy Live	1974	30.00
❑ 6070	Cherish	1972	25.00
❑ 1321	David Cassidy's Greatest Hits	1974	18.00
❑ 1132 [B]	Dreams Are Nothing More Than Wishes	1973	25.00
❑ 1109	Rock Me Baby	1972	25.00

RCA VICTOR

❑ APL1-1852	Gettin' It in the Street	1976	40.00
❑ APL1-1309	Home Is Where the Heart Is	1976	18.00
❑ APL1-1066	The Higher They Climb…	1975	18.00
— *Black vinyl*			
❑ APL1-1066	The Higher They Climb…	1975	100.00
— *Blue vinyl*			

CASSIDY, EVA

S&P

❑ 501	Songbird	2004	30.00
— *180-gram edition*			

CASTELLES, THE

COLLECTABLES

❑ COL-5002	The Sweet Sounds of the Castelles	198?	15.00

CASTELLS, THE

ERA

❑ EL-109 [M]	So This Is Love	1962	120.00
❑ ES-109 [S]	So This Is Love	1962	400.00

CASTLE, LEE

CELEBRITY

❑ CEL-203 [M]	World Famous Dixieland Favorites	1952	40.00

DAVIS

❑ JD-105 [M]	Dixieland Heaven	1951	60.00

CASTLE, PAULA

BETHLEHEM

❑ BCP-1036 [10]	Paula Castle	1955	500.00

Number	Title	Yr	NM

CASTOR, JIMMY, BUNCH

ATLANTIC
☐ SD18124	Butt Of Course	1975	12.00
☐ SD18186	E-Man Groovin'	1976	12.00
☐ SD19111	Maximum Stimulation	1977	12.00
☐ SD18150	Supersound	1975	12.00
☐ SD7305	The Everything Man	1974	12.00

COTILLION
| ☐ SD5215 | The Jimmy Castor Bunch | 1979 | 15.00 |

DRIVE
| ☐ 407 | Let It Out | 1978 | 15.00 |

LONG DISTANCE
| ☐ 1201 | C | 1980 | 15.00 |

RCA VICTOR
| ☐ APD1-0103 [Q] | Dimension III | 1973 | 25.00 |
— All copies are quadraphonic
☐ LSP-4640	It's Just Begun	1972	18.00
☐ LSP-4783	Phase Two	1972	18.00
☐ APL1-0313	The Everything Man	1974	18.00

SMASH
| ☐ MGS-27091 [M] | Hey Leroy! | 1967 | 40.00 |
| ☐ SRS-67091 [S] | Hey Leroy! | 1967 | 40.00 |

CASTRO, JOE

ATLANTIC
| ☐ 1324 [M] | Groove Funk Soul | 1960 | 40.00 |
— Black label
| ☐ SD1324 [S] | Groove Funk Soul | 1960 | 50.00 |
— Green label
| ☐ 1264 [M] | Mood Jazz | 1957 | 50.00 |
— Black label
| ☐ 1264 [M] | Mood Jazz | 1961 | 25.00 |
— Multicolor label with white "fan" logo
| ☐ SD1264 [S] | Mood Jazz | 1959 | 40.00 |
— Green label
| ☐ SD1264 [S] | Mood Jazz | 1961 | 18.00 |
— Multicolor label with white "fan" logo

CAT MOTHER AND THE ALL NIGHT NEWS BOYS

POLYDOR
☐ 24-4023	Albion Doo-Wah	1970	18.00
☐ PD-5017	Cat Mother	1972	18.00
☐ PD-5042	Last Chance Dance	1972	18.00
☐ 24-4001 [B]	The Street Giveth…And the Street Taketh Away	1969	35.00
— Produced by Jimi Hendrix

CATALINAS, THE (1)

RIC
| ☐ M-1006 [M] | Fun, Fun, Fun | 1964 | 100.00 |
| ☐ S-1006 [S] | Fun, Fun, Fun | 1964 | 150.00 |

CATALYST

COBBLESTONE
| ☐ 9018 | Catalyst | 1972 | 25.00 |

MUSE
☐ MR-5069	A Tear and a Smile	1975	18.00
☐ MR-5170	Catalyst	198?	15.00
☐ MR-5025	Perception	1973	18.00
☐ MR-5042	Unity	1974	18.00

CATANOOGA CATS, THE

FORWARD
| ☐ ST-F-1018 | The Catanooga Cats | 1969 | 40.00 |

CATAPILLA

VERTIGO
| ☐ 1006 [B] | Catapilla | 1971 | 100.00 |

CATES, GEORGE

CORAL
| ☐ CRL57220 [M] | Exciting | 1958 | 30.00 |
| ☐ CRL57126 [M] | Under European Skies | 1957 | 40.00 |

DOT
☐ DLP-3564 [M]	Hit Songs -- Hit Sounds	1964	15.00
☐ DLP-25564 [S]	Hit Songs -- Hit Sounds	1964	18.00
☐ DLP-3355 [M]	Polynesian Percussion	1961	15.00
☐ DLP-25355 [S]	Polynesian Percussion	1961	25.00
☐ DLP-3400 [M]	Take Five	1961	15.00
☐ DLP-25400 [S]	Take Five	1961	25.00
☐ DLP-3464 [M]	Third Man Theme	1962	18.00
☐ DLP-25464 [S]	Third Man Theme	1962	15.00
☐ DLP-25422 [S]	Twistin' 12 Great Hits	1962	25.00
☐ DLP-3422 [M]	Twistin' 12 Great Hits	1962	18.00

HAMILTON
☐ HLP-161 [M]	1965's Great Hits	1966	18.00
☐ HLP-12161 [S]	1965's Great Hits	1966	25.00
☐ HLP-127 [M]	The Great Hit Sounds of George Cates	1964	12.00
☐ HLP-12127 [S]	The Great Hit Sounds of George Cates	1964	15.00

RANWOOD
| ☐ 8039 | Hawaii | 1969 | 15.00 |

Number	Title	Yr	NM

CATHCART, DICK

WARNER BROS.
| ☐ W1275 [M] | Bix/MCMLIX | 1959 | 30.00 |
| ☐ WS1275 [S] | Bix/MCMLIX | 1959 | 30.00 |

CATHERINE, PHILIP

WARNER BROS.
| ☐ BS2950 | Nairam | 1977 | 18.00 |

CATHERINE WHEEL, THE

MERCURY
| ☐ 526850-1 [B] | Happy Days | 1995 | 30.00 |
— Clear vinyl

CATHY JEAN AND THE ROOMATES

VALMOR
| ☐ 789 [M] | At the Hop! | 1961 | 900.00 |
| ☐ 78 [M] | Great Oldies | 1962 | 800.00 |
— Reissue of 789 with titles on cover and no group shot

CAUTHEN, STEVE

BAREBACK
| ☐ BB3334 | …And Steve Cauthen Sings Too! | 1977 | 25.00 |

CAVALIERE, FELIX

BEARSVILLE
| ☐ BR6958 | Destiny | 1975 | 15.00 |
| ☐ BR6955 | Felix Cavaliere | 1974 | 15.00 |

EPIC
| ☐ JE35990 | Castles in the Air | 1979 | 12.00 |

CAVANAUGH, PAGE

CAPITOL
| ☐ T879 [M] | Fats Sent Me | 1957 | 40.00 |
| ☐ T1001 [M] | Swingin' Down the Road from Paris to Rome | 1958 | 40.00 |

X
| ☐ LX-3027 [10] | Page Cavanaugh Trio | 1954 | 50.00 |

CAVE, NICK, AND THE BAD SEEDS

ANTI
| ☐ 86668 | Nocturama | 2003 | 18.00 |
— Actually contains two records, but the second record is a single-sided disc with one song

ENIGMA
| ☐ 775401-1 | Tender Prey | 1988 | 30.00 |

HOMESTEAD
☐ HMS 065 [B]	Kicking Against the Pricks	1986	40.00
☐ HMS 026 [B]	The Firstborn is Dead	1985	40.00
☐ HMS 073	Your Funeral, My Trial	1986	40.00

CELEBRATION FEATURING MIKE LOVE

PACIFIC ARTS
| ☐ 122 | Celebration | 1978 | 18.00 |

CELESTIN, OSCAR

FOLKLYRIC
| ☐ 9030 | Oscar "Papa" Celestin and His New Orleans Jazz Band | 198? | 12.00 |

IMPERIAL
☐ LP-9149 [M]	Birth of the Blues	1961	25.00
☐ LP-9125 [M]	Dixieland King	1961	25.00
☐ LP-12062 [S]	Dixieland King	1961	18.00
☐ LP-9199 [M]	Oscar "Papa" Celestin's New Orleans Jazz Band	1962	25.00
☐ LP-12199 [S]	Oscar "Papa" Celestin's New Orleans Jazz Band	1962	18.00

JAZZOLOGY
| ☐ JCE-28 | Ragtime Band | 1968 | 12.00 |

SOUTHLAND
| ☐ SLP-206 [10] | Papa's Golden Wedding | 1955 | 50.00 |

CELL BLOCK SEVEN

DIXIELAND JUBILEE
| ☐ DJ-506 [M] | A Dixieland Riot | 195? | 50.00 |
| ☐ DJS-506 [R] | A Dixieland Riot | 196? | 15.00 |

CENTAURUS

AZRA
| ☐ 61549 | Centaurus | 1978 | 50.00 |
— Issued on clear vinyl

CENTIPEDE

RCA VICTOR
| ☐ CPL2-5042 | Septober Energy | 1974 | 40.00 |

CENTRAL NERVOUS SYSTEM

MUSIC FACTORY
| ☐ MFS-12003 [S] | I Could Have Danced All Night | 1968 | 25.00 |
| ☐ MF-12003 [M] | I Could Have Danced All Night | 1968 | 35.00 |
— White label promo only (no stock copies were issued in mono)

Number	Title	Yr	NM

CENTURIONS, THE

DEL-FI
| ☐ DFLP-1228 [M] | Surfer's Pajama Party | 1963 | 100.00 |
| ☐ DFST-1228 [S] | Surfer's Pajama Party | 1963 | 200.00 |
— Above has the same title and number, and almost the same cover, as the album of the same name by Bruce Johnston, but the contents are different

CERRONE

ATLANTIC
| ☐ SD19250 | Cerrone V -- Angelina | 1979 | 12.00 |

COTILLION
☐ SD5202	Cerrone 3 -- Supernature	1977	15.00
☐ SD5208	Cerrone IV -- The Golden Touch	1978	15.00
☐ SD9917	Cerrone's Paradise	1977	15.00
☐ SD9913	Love in C Minor	1977	15.00

PAVILLION
| ☐ FZ38159 | Back Track | 1982 | 15.00 |

PURE
| ☐ PE2250-1 | Best of Cerrone Remixes | 1995 | 18.00 |

CESANA

MODERN
| ☐ M-100 [M] | Tender Emotions | 1964 | 25.00 |

CETERA, PETER

FULL MOON
| ☐ FMH3624 | Peter Cetera | 1981 | 12.00 |

WARNER BROS.
| ☐ 25704 | One More Story | 1988 | 10.00 |
| ☐ 25474 | Solitude/Solitaire | 1986 | 10.00 |

CEYLEIB PEOPLE, THE

VAULT
| ☐ LP-117 [M] | Tanyet | 1968 | 200.00 |
— With Ry Cooder
| ☐ LP-117 [S] | Tanyet | 1968 | 150.00 |
— with Ry Cooder

CHACKSFIELD, FRANK

COMPLEAT
| ☐ 671020-1 | TV's Golden Hits | 198? | 15.00 |

EXCELSIOR
☐ XRP-7005	After the Lovin'	1980	15.00
☐ XRP-7008	Dust in the Wind	1980	15.00
☐ XRP-7001	Great Film Music	1980	12.00
☐ XRP-7004	In the Country	1980	15.00
☐ XRP-7009	Love Is in the Air	1980	15.00
☐ XRP-7006	Sunflower	1980	15.00
☐ XRP-7007	Weekend in New England	1980	15.00

LONDON
☐ CHA-S-1	Academy Award Hit Songs 1934-1967	1969	15.00
☐ LL3347 [M]	Best of the New Film Themes	196?	12.00
☐ PS347 [S]	Best of the New Film Themes	196?	16.00
☐ LL1509 [M]	Broadway Melodies	195?	15.00
☐ LL3322 [M]	Ebb Tide	196?	12.00
☐ PS322 [S]	Ebb Tide	196?	15.00
☐ LL3038 [M]	Evening in London	195?	15.00
☐ PS135 [S]	Evening in London	195?	18.00
☐ LL997 [M]	Evening in Paris	195?	18.00
☐ LL1205 [M]	Evening in Rome	195?	18.00
☐ PS126 [S]	Evening in Rome, Evening in Paris	195?	18.00
☐ LL1041 [M]	Frank Chacksfield and His Orchestra, Vol. 1	195?	18.00
☐ PS436 [S]	Great Country and Western Hits	1965	15.00
☐ LL3436 [M]	Great Country and Western Hits	1965	12.00
☐ LL3330 [M]	Here's Love	196?	12.00
☐ PS330 [S]	Here's Love	196?	15.00
☐ LL3102/3 [M]	Hollywood Almanac -- Award Winners 1934-1957	195?	18.00
☐ PS320/1 [S]	Hollywood Almanac -- Award Winners 1934-1957	195?	25.00
☐ PS122 [S]	Immortal Serenades	195?	18.00
☐ LL3061 [M]	Immortal Serenades	195?	15.00
☐ LL3257 [M]	King of Kings and Other Film Spectaculars	196?	12.00
☐ PS246 [S]	King of Kings and Other Film Spectaculars	196?	15.00
☐ LL3298 [M]	Lawrence of Arabia and Other Themes	196?	12.00
☐ PS298 [S]	Lawrence of Arabia and Other Themes	196?	15.00
☐ PS145 [S]	Love Letters in the Sand	195?	18.00
☐ LL3027 [M]	Love Letters in the Sand	195?	15.00
☐ LL1614 [M]	Lovely Lady -- The Music of Jimmy McHugh	195?	15.00
☐ PS304 [S]	Magic Strings	196?	15.00
☐ LL3304 [M]	Magic Strings	196?	12.00
☐ LL1440 [M]	Mean to Me	195?	18.00
☐ LL1588 [M]	Mediterranean Moonlight	195?	15.00
☐ PS316 [S]	Music from "She Loves Me	196?	15.00
☐ LL3316 [M]	Music from "She Loves Me	196?	12.00
☐ LL1203 [M]	Music of George Gershwin	195?	18.00
☐ PS120 [S]	Music of George Gershwin	195?	18.00
☐ LL1062 [M]	Music of Noel Coward	195?	18.00

Number	Title	Yr	NM
❑ LL3158 [M]	On the Beach	1960	15.00
❑ PS203 [S]	On the Beach	1960	18.00
❑ SPC21092	Opera's Golden Moments	197?	12.00
❑ LL1538 [M]	South Sea Island Magic	195?	15.00
❑ PS416 [S]	The First Hits of 1965	1965	15.00
❑ LL3416 [M]	The First Hits of 1965	1965	12.00
❑ LL3431 [M]	The New Limelight	1965	12.00
❑ LL1440 [M]	Velvet	195?	18.00
❑ LL1603 [M]	Waltzes to Remember	195?	15.00
❑ LL1355 [M]	You	195?	18.00

LONDON PHASE 4

Number	Title	Yr	NM
❑ SP-44158	Chacksfield Plays Bacharach	197?	18.00
❑ SP-44151	Chacksfield Plays Simon and Garfunkel and Jim Webb	1970	18.00
❑ SP-44142	Chacksfield Plays the Beatles' Songbook	1970	18.00
❑ SP-44112	Foreign Film Festival	196?	18.00
❑ SP-44090	France	196?	18.00
❑ SP-44275	Frank Chacksfield Plays Hoagy Carmichael	197?	18.00
❑ SP-44254	Frank Chacksfield Plays Irving Berlin	197?	18.00
❑ SP-44249	Frank Chacksfield Plays Lerner and Loewe	197?	18.00
❑ SP-44223	Frank Chacksfield Plays Rodgers and Hart	1975	18.00
❑ SP-44059	Globetrotting	196?	18.00
❑ SP-44087	Hawaii	196?	18.00
❑ SP-44102	Music from Doctor Dolittle	196?	18.00
❑ SP-44141	New York	196?	18.00
❑ SP-44194	The Glory That Was ... Gershwin	1973	15.00
❑ SW-95146	The Glory That Was ... Gershwin	1973	18.00
— Longines Symphonette Record Club edition			
❑ SP-44077	The Great TV Themes	196?	18.00
❑ SP-44213	The Incomparable Jerome Kern	1974	18.00
❑ SP-44185	The Music of Cole Porter	1972	18.00
❑ SP-44053	The New Ebb Tide	1964	18.00
❑ SP-44066 [S]	The New Limelight	1965	18.00
❑ SP-44289	Vintage '52	1977	18.00

MCA

Number	Title	Yr	NM
❑ 5239	Love Songs	1981	15.00

PHOENIX 20

Number	Title	Yr	NM
❑ P20-604	How Deep Is Your Love	1980	10.00

PICKWICK

Number	Title	Yr	NM
❑ SPC-3231	Ebb Tide	197?	10.00

RICHMOND

Number	Title	Yr	NM
❑ S30078 [S]	Ebb Tide	1960	15.00
❑ B20078 [M]	Ebb Tide	1960	12.00
❑ B20073 [M]	Great Strauss Waltzes	1960	12.00
❑ S30073 [S]	Great Strauss Waltzes	1960	15.00
❑ S30087 [S]	Love Themes from Great Operas	196?	15.00
❑ B20087 [M]	Love Themes from Great Operas	196?	12.00
❑ S30045 [S]	Million Sellers	195?	15.00
❑ B20045 [M]	Million Sellers	195?	12.00
❑ S30095 [S]	Movie Themes	196?	15.00
❑ B20095 [M]	Movie Themes	196?	12.00
❑ B20056 [M]	Music for a Merry Christmas	1959	12.00
❑ S30056 [S]	Music for a Merry Christmas	1959	15.00
❑ S30093 [S]	My Gypsy Love	196?	15.00
❑ B20093 [M]	My Gypsy Love	196?	12.00
❑ B20059 [M]	Porgy and Bess/Show Boat	1960	12.00
❑ S30059 [S]	Porgy and Bess/Show Boat	1960	15.00
❑ B20080 [M]	Songs of Sunny Italy	196?	12.00
❑ S30080 [S]	Songs of Sunny Italy	196?	15.00
❑ B20046 [M]	South Pacific	195?	12.00
❑ S30046 [S]	South Pacific	195?	15.00
❑ B20086 [M]	The Best of Herbert and Romberg	196?	12.00
❑ S30086 [S]	The Best of Herbert and Romberg	196?	15.00

STARBORNE

Number	Title	Yr	NM
❑ SB-9002	Mirrors	1980	30.00
❑ SB-9003	People in Love	1980	30.00

CHAD AND JEREMY

CAPITOL

Number	Title	Yr	NM
❑ TT2546 [M]	More Chad and Jeremy	1966	12.00
❑ STT2546 [P]	More Chad and Jeremy	1966	15.00
❑ T2470 [M]	The Best of Chad and Jeremy	1966	12.00
— Black label with colorband			
❑ ST2470 [P]	The Best of Chad and Jeremy	1966	15.00
— Black label with colorband			
❑ T2470 [M]	The Best of Chad and Jeremy	1967	10.00
— Starline" label			
❑ ST2470 [P]	The Best of Chad and Jeremy	1967	12.00
— Starline" label			
❑ SN-16135 [P]	The Best of Chad and Jeremy	1980	10.00
— Budget-line reissue			

COLUMBIA

Number	Title	Yr	NM
❑ CL2374 [M]	Before and After	1965	25.00
❑ CS9174 [S]	Before and After	1965	30.00
❑ CL2564 [M]	Distant Shores	1966	25.00
❑ CS9364 [P]	Distant Shores	1966	30.00
— Distant Shores" is rechanneled			
❑ CL2398 [M]	I Don't Want to Lose You Baby	1966	30.00
❑ CS9198 [S]	I Don't Want to Lose You Baby	1966	40.00
❑ CL2671 [M]	Of Cabbages and Kings	1967	40.00
❑ CS9471 [S]	Of Cabbages and Kings	1967	30.00
❑ CS9699 [S]	The Arc	1968	30.00
— Some copies spell the LP title this way on the cover			
❑ CL2899 [M]	The Ark	1968	30.00
❑ CS9699 [S]	The Ark	1968	30.00
— Correct spelling of LP title on cover			

FIDU

Number	Title	Yr	NM
❑ FM-101 [M]	5 + 10 = 15 Fabulous Hits	1966	12.00
❑ FS-101 [P]	5 + 10 = 15 Fabulous Hits	1966	15.00

HARMONY

Number	Title	Yr	NM
❑ HS11357 [S]	Chad and Jeremy	1973	10.00

ROCSHIRE

Number	Title	Yr	NM
❑ XR-22018 [B]	Chad Stuart and Jeremy Clyde	1983	12.00

WORLD ARTISTS

Number	Title	Yr	NM
❑ WAM-2005 [M]	Chad and Jeremy Sing for You	1965	15.00
❑ WAS-3005 [S]	Chad and Jeremy Sing for You	1965	18.00
❑ WAM-2002 [M]	Yesterday's Gone	1964	15.00
❑ WAS-3002 [P]	Yesterday's Gone	1964	18.00
— Yesterday's Gone" is rechanneled.			

CHAIRMEN OF THE BOARD

INVICTUS

Number	Title	Yr	NM
❑ ST-9801	Bittersweet	1972	40.00
❑ ST-7300 [B]	Chairmen of the Board (Featuring "Give Me Just a Little More Time")	1970	50.00
❑ SKAO-7304	In Session	1970	40.00
❑ KZ32526 [B]	The Skin I'm In	1974	50.00

CHAKIRIS, GEORGE

CAPITOL

Number	Title	Yr	NM
❑ T1750 [M]	George Chakiris	1962	18.00
❑ ST1750 [S]	George Chakiris	1962	25.00
❑ T2391 [M]	It's Been a Swingin' Summer	1965	15.00
❑ ST2391 [S]	It's Been a Swingin' Summer	1965	18.00
❑ T1813 [M]	Memories Are Made of These	1963	18.00
❑ ST1813 [S]	Memories Are Made of These	1963	25.00

HORIZON

Number	Title	Yr	NM
❑ WP-1610 [M]	The Gershwin Songbook	1962	18.00
❑ ST-1610 [S]	The Gershwin Songbook	1962	25.00

CHALKER, CURLY

COLUMBIA

Number	Title	Yr	NM
❑ CL2596 [M]	Big Hits on Big Steel	1965	25.00
❑ CS9396 [S]	Big Hits on Big Steel	1965	30.00

CHALLENGERS, THE (1)

FANTASY

Number	Title	Yr	NM
❑ F-9443	Where Were You in the Summer of '62	1973	15.00

GNP CRESCENDO

Number	Title	Yr	NM
❑ GNP-609 [M]	25 Great Instrumental Hits	1967	30.00
❑ GNPS-609 [S]	25 Great Instrumental Hits	1967	25.00
❑ GNP-2030 [M]	Billy Strange and the Challengers	1966	25.00
❑ GNPS-2030 [S]	Billy Strange and the Challengers	1966	30.00
❑ GNP-2025 [M]	California Kicks	1966	25.00
❑ GNPS-2025 [S]	California Kicks	1966	30.00
❑ GNPS-2045	Light My Fire with Classical Gas	1968	25.00
❑ GNPS-2093	Sidewalk Surfing	1975	15.00
❑ GNP-2010 [M]	The Challengers at the Teenage Fair	1965	25.00
❑ GNPS-2010 [S]	The Challengers at the Teenage Fair	1965	30.00
❑ GNP-2018 [M]	The Man from U.N.C.L.E.	1965	30.00
❑ GNPS-2018 [S]	The Man from U.N.C.L.E.	1965	30.00
❑ GNPS-2056 [B]	Vanilla Funk	1970	25.00
❑ GNP-2031 [M]	Wipe Out	1966	25.00
❑ GNPS-2031 [S]	Wipe Out	1966	30.00

RHINO

Number	Title	Yr	NM
❑ RNLP-053	Best of the Challengers	1982	12.00

TRIUMPH

Number	Title	Yr	NM
❑ TR-100 [M]	The Challengers Go Sidewalk Surfing	1965	25.00
❑ TRS-100 [S]	The Challengers Go Sidewalk Surfing	1965	30.00

VAULT

Number	Title	Yr	NM
❑ LP-107 [M]	K-39	1964	80.00
❑ VS-101 [S]	(Lloyd Thaxton Goes) Surfin' with the Challengers	1963	250.00
— Either title; orange vinyl			
❑ LP-101 [M]	Lloyd Thaxton Goes Surfin' with the Challengers	1963	60.00
— Original title			
❑ VS-101 [S]	(Lloyd Thaxton Goes) Surfin' with the Challengers	1963	250.00
— Either title; red vinyl			
❑ VS-101 [S]	Lloyd Thaxton Goes Surfin' with the Challengers	1963	100.00
— Original title; black vinyl			
❑ VS-101 [S]	(Lloyd Thaxton Goes) Surfin' with the Challengers	1963	250.00
— Either title; yellow vinyl			
❑ VS-101 [S]	(Lloyd Thaxton Goes) Surfin' with the Challengers	1963	250.00
— Either title; blue vinyl			
❑ LP-100 [M]	Surfbeat	1963	50.00
❑ VS-100 [S]	Surfbeat	1963	80.00
— Black vinyl			
❑ VS-100 [S]	Surfbeat	1963	250.00
— Orange vinyl			
❑ VS-100 [S]	Surfbeat	1963	250.00
— Red vinyl			
❑ VS-100 [S]	Surfbeat	1963	250.00
— Yellow vinyl			
❑ LP-101 [M]	Surfin' with the Challengers	1963	50.00
— Altered title			
❑ VS-101 [S]	Surfin' with the Challengers	1963	80.00
— Altered title; black vinyl			
❑ LP-110 [M]	The Challengers A-Go-Go	1966	30.00
❑ VS-110 [S]	The Challengers A-Go-Go	1966	40.00
❑ LP-111 [M]	The Challengers' Greatest Hits	1967	30.00
❑ VS-111 [S]	The Challengers' Greatest Hits	1967	30.00
❑ LP-102 [M]	The Challengers On The Move	1963	40.00
❑ VS-102 [S]	The Challengers On The Move	1963	60.00
❑ LP-109 [M]	The Surf's Up	1965	40.00
❑ VS-109 [S]	The Surf's Up	1965	60.00

CHALOFF, SERGE

CAPITOL

Number	Title	Yr	NM
❑ M-11032	Blue Serge	1972	18.00
— Capitol Jazz Classics, Vol. 7			
❑ T742 [M]	Blue Serge	1956	350.00
— Turquoise label			
❑ T742 [M]	Blue Serge	1959	60.00
— Black colorband label, logo at left			
❑ T6510 [M]	Boston Blow-Up	1955	150.00

MOSAIC

Number	Title	Yr	NM
❑ MQ5-147	The Complete Serge Chaloff Sessions	1993	120.00

STORYVILLE

Number	Title	Yr	NM
❑ STLP-350 [10]	Serge & Boots	1955	300.00
❑ STLP-317 [10]	The Fable of Mable	1954	300.00

CHALOFF, SERGE/OSCAR PETTIFORD

MERCER

Number	Title	Yr	NM
❑ LP-1003 [10]	New Stars, New Sounds, Volume 2	1951	300.00

CHAMAELEON CHURCH

MGM

Number	Title	Yr	NM
❑ SE-4574 [B]	Chamaeleon Church	1968	25.00

CHAMBERLAIN, RICHARD

METRO

Number	Title	Yr	NM
❑ M-564 [M]	Richard Chamberlain Sings	1966	15.00
❑ MS-564 [S]	Richard Chamberlain Sings	1966	15.00

MGM

Number	Title	Yr	NM
❑ E-4287 [M]	Joy in the Morning	1965	18.00
❑ SE-4287 [S]	Joy in the Morning	1965	25.00
❑ T90512 [M]	Richard Chamberlain Sings	1965	30.00
— Capitol Record Club edition			
❑ ST90512 [S]	Richard Chamberlain Sings	1965	30.00
— Capitol Record Club edition			
❑ E-4088 [M]	Richard Chamberlain Sings	1962	18.00
❑ SE-4088 [S]	Richard Chamberlain Sings	1962	25.00
❑ E-4185 [M]	Twilight of Honor	1963	18.00
❑ SE-4185 [S]	Twilight of Honor	1963	25.00

CHAMBERS, PAUL, AND JOHN COLTRANE

BLUE NOTE

Number	Title	Yr	NM
❑ BN-LA451-H2	High Step	1975	30.00
— Reissue of Blue Note 1534 plus other material			

CHAMBERS, PAUL

BLUE NOTE

Number	Title	Yr	NM
❑ BLP-1569 [M]	Bass on Top	1957	500.00
— Deep groove" version; W. 63rd St. address on label			
❑ BLP-1569 [M]	Bass on Top	1957	120.00
— Regular version, W. 63rd St. address on label			
❑ BLP-1569 [M]	Bass on Top	1963	40.00
— New York, USA" address on label			
❑ BST-1569 [S]	Bass on Top	1959	700.00
— Deep groove" version, W. 63rd St. address on label			
❑ BST-1569 [S]	Bass on Top	1959	120.00
— Regular version, W. 63rd St. address on label			
❑ BST-1569 [S]	Bass on Top	1963	30.00
— New York, USA" address on label			
❑ BST-81569 [S]	Bass on Top	196?	25.00
— A Division of Liberty Records" on label			
❑ BLP-1564 [M]	Paul Chambers Quintet	1957	400.00
— Deep groove" version, W. 63rd St. address on label			
❑ BLP-1564 [M]	Paul Chambers Quintet	1957	200.00
— Regular version, W. 63rd St. address on label			

Number	Title	Yr	NM
❏ BLP-1564 [M]	Paul Chambers Quintet	1963	40.00
— "New York, USA" address on label			
❏ BST-1564 [S]	Paul Chambers Quintet	1959	250.00
— "Deep groove" version, W. 63rd St. address on label			
❏ BST-1564 [S]	Paul Chambers Quintet	1959	150.00
— Regular version, W. 63rd St. address on label			
❏ BST-1564 [S]	Paul Chambers Quintet	1963	30.00
— "New York, USA" address on label			
❏ BST-81564 [S]	Paul Chambers Quintet	196?	25.00
— "A Division of Liberty Records" on label			
❏ BLP-1534 [M]	Whims of Chambers	1956	700.00
— "Deep groove" version, Lexington Ave. address on label			
❏ BLP-1534 [M]	Whims of Chambers	1958	250.00
— "Deep groove" version, W, 63rd St. address on label			
❏ BLP-1534 [M]	Whims of Chambers	1963	40.00
— "New York, USA" address on label			
❏ BST-81534 [R]	Whims of Chambers	196?	25.00
— "A Division of Liberty Records" on label			
EPITAPH			
❏ E-4001	Paul Chambers 1935-1969	1975	25.00
IMPERIAL			
❏ LP-9182 [M]	A Jazz Delegation from the East: Chambers' Music	1961	40.00
❏ LP-12182 [S]	A Jazz Delegation from the East: Chambers' Music	1961	30.00
JAZZ WEST			
❏ JWLP-7 [M]	A Jazz Delegation from the East: Chambers' Music	1956	600.00
SCORE			
❏ SLP-4033 [M]	A Jazz Delegation from the East: Chambers' Music	1958	80.00
TRIP			
❏ 5026	Just Friends	197?	18.00
VEE JAY			
❏ LP-3012 [M]	First Bassman	1960	50.00
❏ SR-3012 [S]	First Bassman	1960	80.00
❏ VJS-3012 [S]	First Bassman	198?	18.00
— Reissue on thinner vinyl			
❏ LP-1014 [M]	Go	1959	250.00
❏ SR-1014 [S]	Go	1959	100.00
❏ VJS-1014 [S]	Go	198?	18.00
— Reissue on thinner vinyl			

CHAMBERS BROTHERS, THE

Number	Title	Yr	NM
AVCO			
❏ 69003	Night Move	1975	25.00
❏ 11013	Unbonded	1974	15.00
COLUMBIA			
❏ CS9671	A New Time -- A New Day	1968	25.00
❏ KGP20	Love, Peace and Happiness	1969	30.00
❏ C30032	New Generation	1970	18.00
❏ C30871	The Chambers Brothers' Greatest Hits	1971	18.00
❏ PC30871	The Chambers Brothers' Greatest Hits	198?	10.00
— Reissue with new prefix			
❏ CL2722 [M]	The Time Has Come	1967	30.00
❏ CS9522 [S]	The Time Has Come	1967	25.00
— Red "360 Sound" label			
❏ CS9522	The Time Has Come	1971	15.00
— Orange label			
❏ PC9522	The Time Has Come	198?	10.00
— Reissue with new prefix			
❏ CG33642	The Time Has Come/A New Time -- A New Day	1975	18.00
FANTASY			
❏ 24718	The Best of the Chambers Brothers	1973	18.00
FOLKWAYS			
❏ 31008	Groovin' Time	1968	18.00
ROXBURY			
❏ RLX-106	Live In Concert on Mars	1976	30.00
VAULT			
❏ VS-128	Feelin' the Blues	1969	18.00
❏ LP-9003 [M]	People Get Ready	1966	25.00
❏ LPS-9003 [S]	People Get Ready	1966	30.00
❏ VS-135 [B]	The Chambers Brothers Greatest Hits	1970	25.00
❏ LP-115 [M]	The Chambers Brothers Now	1967	18.00
❏ VS-115 [S]	The Chambers Brothers Now	1967	18.00
❏ VS-120	The Chambers Brothers Shout	1968	18.00

CHAMBLEE, EDDIE

Number	Title	Yr	NM
EMARCY			
❏ MG-36124 [M]	Chamblee Music	1958	50.00
❏ MG-36131 [M]	Doodlin'	1958	50.00
❏ SR-80007 [S]	Doodlin'	1959	40.00
MERCURY			
❏ SR-60127 [S]	Chamblee Music	1960	30.00
PRESTIGE			
❏ PRLP-7321 [M]	The Rocking Tenor Sax of Eddie Chamblee	1964	30.00
— Yellow label			
❏ PRST-7321 [S]	The Rocking Tenor Sax of Eddie Chamblee	1964	30.00
— Silver label			

CHAMPLIN, BILL

Number	Title	Yr	NM
ELEKTRA			
❏ 5E-563	Runaway	1981	12.00
FULL MOON/EPIC			
❏ JE35367	Single	1978	18.00

CHAMPS, THE

Number	Title	Yr	NM
CHALLENGE			
❏ CHL-614 [M]	All American Music from the Champs	1962	120.00
❏ CHS-2514 [S]	All American Music from the Champs	1962	200.00
❏ CHL-605 [M]	Everybody's Rockin' with the Champs	1959	200.00
❏ CHS-2500 [S]	Everybody's Rockin' with the Champs	1959	300.00
❏ CHL-601 [M]	Go Champs Go	1958	2400.00
— Blue vinyl; VG value 800; VG+ value 1600			
❏ CHL-601 [M]	Go Champs Go	1958	250.00
❏ CHL-613 [M]	Great Dance Hits	1962	120.00
❏ CHS-2513 [S]	Great Dance Hits	1962	200.00

CHANDLER, GENE, AND JERRY BUTLER

Number	Title	Yr	NM
MERCURY			
❏ SR-61330	Gene & Jerry -- One & One	1971	18.00

CHANDLER, GENE

Number	Title	Yr	NM
20TH CENTURY			
❏ T-625	Ear Candy	1980	12.00
❏ T-605	Gene Chandler '80	1980	12.00
❏ T-629	Here's to Love	1981	12.00
❏ T-598	When You're #1	1979	12.00
BRUNSWICK			
❏ BL54124 [M]	The Girl Don't Care	1967	30.00
❏ BL754124 [S]	The Girl Don't Care	1967	25.00
❏ BL754131	There Was a Time	1968	25.00
❏ BL754149	The Two Sides of Gene Chandler	1969	25.00
CHECKER			
❏ LP-3003 [M]	The Duke of Soul	1967	50.00
❏ LPS-3003 [S]	The Duke of Soul	1967	30.00
CHI-SOUND			
❏ T-578	Get Down	1978	12.00
CONSTELLATION			
❏ LP1425 [M]	Gene Chandler -- Live On Stage in '65	1965	50.00
❏ LP1421 [M]	Greatest Hits by Gene Chandler	1964	50.00
❏ LP1423 [M]	Just Be True	1964	50.00
MERCURY			
❏ SR-61304	The Gene Chandler Situation	1970	18.00
SOLID SMOKE			
❏ SS-8027	Stroll On with the Duke	198?	12.00
UPFRONT			
❏ UPF105	Duke of Earl	197?	12.00
VEE JAY			
❏ LP-1040 [M]	The Duke of Earl	1962	120.00
❏ SR-1040 [S]	The Duke of Earl	1962	800.00
— Stereophonic" on front cover; top back cover contains note that begins: "Important Notice...This Is a Stereophonic Record"; "Stereo" on record labels			
❏ SR-1040 [S]	The Duke of Earl	1962	250.00
— "Stereo" sticker on mono cover; "Stereo" on record labels			
❏ SR-1040 [M]	The Duke of Earl	196?	50.00
— "Stereophonic" on front; no "Important Notice..." on back; record plays mono. Most labels are all-black with "VJ" in brackets. This was a semi-authorized reissue after ex-Vee Jay executives bought the company's remnants in bankruptcy court in 1966.			
❏ VJLP-1040	The Duke of Earl	198?	12.00
— Mid-1980s authorized reissue			

CHANDLER, JEFF

Number	Title	Yr	NM
LIBERTY			
❏ LRP-3067 [M]	Jeff Chandler Sings to You	1957	40.00
❏ LRP-3074 [M]	Warm and Easy	1958	40.00
SUNSET			
❏ SUS-5127	Sincerely Yours	1969	15.00

CHANNEL, BRUCE

Number	Title	Yr	NM
SMASH			
❏ MGS-27008 [M]	Hey! Baby (And 11 Other Songs About Your Baby)	1962	100.00
❏ SRS-67008 [R]	Hey! Baby (And 11 Other Songs About Your Baby)	1962	60.00

CHANNING, CAROL

Number	Title	Yr	NM
CAEDMON			
❏ TC1303	The Year Without a Santa Claus and Other Stories for Christmas	1969	15.00
— Spoken-word recordings			
COMMAND			
❏ 33-880 [M]	Carol Channing Entertains	1966	18.00
❏ 880SD [S]	Carol Channing Entertains	1966	25.00

Number	Title	Yr	NM
PLANTATION			
❏ PLP-527	Carol Channing With the Original Country Cast	1978	25.00
VANGUARD			
❏ VRS-9056 [M]	Carol Channing	1959	30.00
❏ VSD-2041 [S]	Carol Channing	1959	40.00

CHANTAYS

Number	Title	Yr	NM
DOT			
❏ DLP3516 [M]	Pipeline	1963	50.00
❏ DLP25516 [S]	Pipeline	1963	80.00
❏ DLP3771 [M]	Two Sides of the Chantays	1966	50.00
❏ DLP25771 [S]	Two Sides of the Chantays	1966	80.00
DOWNEY			
❏ DLP-1002 [M]	Pipeline	1963	220.00
❏ DLPS-1002 [S]	Pipeline	1963	350.00

CHANTELS, THE

Number	Title	Yr	NM
CARLTON			
❏ LP-144 [M]	The Chantels On Tour/Look in My Eyes	1962	200.00
❏ STLP-144 [P]	The Chantels On Tour/Look in My Eyes	1962	400.00
— Eight tracks are true stereo, two are mono, two are rechanneled			
END			
❏ LP-312 [M]	There's Our Song Again	1962	120.00
❏ LP-301 [M]	We Are the Chantels	1958	1500.00
— Group photo on front cover; gray label with "11-17-58" in trail-off wax; VG value 500; VG+ value 1000			
❏ LP-301 [M]	We Are the Chantels	1959	400.00
— Jukebox on front cover; gray label, "11-17-58" in trail-off wax			
❏ LP-301 [M]	We Are the Chantels	1962	200.00
— Jukebox on front cover; gray label, "1962" in trail-off wax			
❏ LP-301 [M]	We Are the Chantels	1965	100.00
— Jukebox on front cover; gray label, "8-65" in trail-off wax			
❏ LP-301 [M]	We Are the Chantels	1965	80.00
— Jukebox on front cover; multicolor label, "8-65" in trail-off wax			
❏ END-301 [R]	We Are the Chantels	197?	30.00
— Reissue in rechanneled stereo; orange bar through center hole and "END" on both sides of center hole			
FORUM			
❏ F-9104 [M]	The Chantels Sing Their Favorites	1964	50.00
❏ FS-9104 [R]	The Chantels Sing Their Favorites	1964	30.00

CHAPARRAL BROTHERS, THE

Number	Title	Yr	NM
CAPITOL			
❏ ST2922	Introducing the Chaparral Brothers	1968	25.00
❏ ST-551	Just for the Record	1970	18.00

CHAPIN, HARRY

Number	Title	Yr	NM
BOARDWALK			
❏ FW36872	Sequel	1980	12.00
ELEKTRA			
❏ 60413	Anthology of Harry Chapin	1985	12.00
❏ 9E-301	Dance Band on the Titanic	1977	15.00
❏ 7E-2009	Greatest Stories Live	1976	15.00
❏ 8E-6003	Greatest Stories Live	1978	12.00
— Reissue of 7E-2009			
❏ EKS-75023	Heads and Tales	1972	12.00
❏ BB-703	Legends of the Lost and Found -- New Greatest Stories Live	1979	15.00
❏ 6E-142	Living Room Suite	1978	12.00
❏ 7E-1082	On the Road to Kingdom Come	1976	12.00
❏ 7E-1041	Portrait Gallery	1975	12.00
❏ EKS-75065	Short Stories	1973	12.00
❏ EKS-75042	Sniper and Other Love Songs	1972	12.00
❏ 7E-1012	Verities & Balderdash	1974	12.00

CHAPIN, JIM

Number	Title	Yr	NM
CLASSIC JAZZ			
❏ 6 [M]	Jim Chapin Sextet	197?	12.00
❏ 7 [M]	Skin Tight	197?	12.00
PRESTIGE			
❏ PRLP-213 [10]	Jim Chapin Sextet	1955	250.00

CHAPINS, THE

Number	Title	Yr	NM
ROCK-LAND			
❏ RR-66 [M]	Chapin Music	1966	75.00
— As "The Chapin Brothers"; both mono and stereo, same price			

CHAPMAN, BETH NIELSEN

Number	Title	Yr	NM
CAPITOL			
❏ ST-12050	Hearing It First	1980	50.00

CHAPMAN, MARSHALL

Number	Title	Yr	NM
EPIC			
❏ JE35341	Jaded Virgin	1978	12.00
❏ JE36192	Marshall	1979	12.00
❏ PE34422	Me, I'm Feelin' Free	1977	12.00

Number	Title	Yr	NM

ROUNDER

| ❏ 3069 | Take It On Home | 1982 | 15.00 |

CHAPMAN, TRACY

ELEKTRA

❏ 60888	Crossroads	1989	15.00
❏ R142496	Crossroads	1989	15.00
—BMG Direct Marketing edition			
❏ R153582	Tracy Chapman	1988	15.00
—BMG Direct Marketing edition			
❏ 60774	Tracy Chapman	1988	12.00

CHARIOT

NATIONAL GENERAL

| ❏ NG-2003 [B] | Chariot | 1971 | 85.00 |

CHARIOTEERS, THE

COLUMBIA

| ❏ CL6014 [10] | Sweet and Low | 1949 | 300.00 |

HARMONY

| ❏ HL7089 [M] | The Charioteers with Billy Williams | 1957 | 100.00 |

CHARISMA

ROULETTE

| ❏ SR-42037 [B] | Charisma | 1970 | 30.00 |

CHARITY

UNI

| ❏ 73061 | Charity Now | 1969 | 30.00 |

CHARLATANS, THE

PHILIPS

| ❏ PHS600309 | The Charlatans | 1969 | 100.00 |

CHARLEE

AMERAMA

| ❏ 1005 | Standing in Your Shoes | 1977 | 18.00 |

CHARLENE

MOTOWN

❏ 6007ML	Charlene	1981	12.00
❏ 6090ML	Hit and Run Lover	1985	12.00
❏ 6027ML	Used to Be	1982	12.00

PRODIGAL

| ❏ P6-10015 | Charlene | 1976 | 25.00 |
| ❏ P6-10018 | Songs of Love | 1977 | 25.00 |

CHARLES, RAY, AND BETTY CARTER

ABC

| ❏ S-385 [S] | Ray Charles and Betty Carter | 1967 | 25.00 |
| *—Reissue of ABC-Paramount ABCS-385* | | | |

ABC-PARAMOUNT

| ❏ ABC-385 [M] | Ray Charles and Betty Carter | 1961 | 60.00 |
| ❏ ABCS-385 [S] | Ray Charles and Betty Carter | 1961 | 80.00 |

DCC COMPACT CLASSICS

| ❏ LPZ-2005 | Ray Charles and Betty Carter | 1995 | 150.00 |
| *—Audiophile vinyl* | | | |

DUNHILL COMPACT CLASSICS

| ❏ DZL-039 | Ray Charles and Betty Carter | 1988 | 18.00 |
| *—Clear vinyl reissue* | | | |

CHARLES, RAY, AND CLEO LAINE

RCA VICTOR

❏ CPL2-1831	Porgy & Bess	1976	18.00
❏ DJL1-2163	Porgy & Bess	1976	25.00
—Promo-only excerpts from 2-record set			

CHARLES, RAY, AND MILT JACKSON

ATLANTIC

❏ 1279 [M]	Soul Brothers	1958	50.00
—Black label			
❏ 1279 [M]	Soul Brothers	1960	30.00
—Red and white label, white fan logo on right			
❏ 1279 [M]	Soul Brothers	1962	25.00
—Red and white label, black fan logo on right			
❏ SD1279 [S]	Soul Brothers	1959	50.00
—Green label			
❏ SD1279 [S]	Soul Brothers	1960	30.00
—Blue and green label, white fan logo on right			
❏ SD1279 [S]	Soul Brothers	1962	25.00
—Blue and green label, black fan logo on right			
❏ 1360 [M]	Soul Meeting	1961	30.00
—Red and white label, white fan logo on right			
❏ 1360 [M]	Soul Meeting	1962	25.00
—Red and white label, black fan logo on right			
❏ SD1360 [S]	Soul Meeting	1961	30.00
—Blue and green label, white fan logo on right			
❏ SD1360 [S]	Soul Meeting	1962	30.00
—Blue and green label, black fan logo on right			

Number	Title	Yr	NM

CHARLES, RAY, SINGERS

ABC

| ❏ X-772 | Moods of Love | 1973 | 12.00 |

ATCO

| ❏ SD 33-263 | Memories of a Middle-Aged Movie Fan | 1970 | 12.00 |

COMMAND

❏ 33-870 [M]	Al-Di-La and Other Extra Special Songs for Young Lovers	1964	12.00
❏ SD870 [S]	Al-Di-La and Other Extra Special Songs for Young Lovers	1964	15.00
❏ SD923	At the Movies	1968	12.00
❏ 33-876 [M]	Command Performances	1965	12.00
❏ SD876 [S]	Command Performances	1965	15.00
❏ 33-896 [M]	Command Performances Vol. 2	1966	12.00
❏ SD896 [S]	Command Performances Vol. 2	1966	15.00
❏ CQ-40005 [Q]	Love Me with All of Your Heart	1972	18.00
❏ SD936	MacArthur Park	1969	12.00
❏ SD949	Move Me, O Wondrous Music	1969	12.00
❏ 33-898 [M]	One of Those Songs	1966	12.00
❏ SD898 [S]	One of Those Songs	1966	15.00
❏ 33-845 [M]	Paradise Islands	1962	12.00
❏ SD845 [S]	Paradise Islands	1962	15.00
❏ 33-839 [M]	Rome Revisited	1962	12.00
❏ SD839 [S]	Rome Revisited	1962	15.00
❏ 33-866 [M]	Something Special for Young Lovers	1964	12.00
❏ SD866 [S]	Something Special for Young Lovers	1964	15.00
❏ 33-827 [M]	Something Wonderful	1961	12.00
❏ SD827 [S]	Something Wonderful	1961	15.00
❏ 33-886 [M]	Songs for Latin Lovers	1965	12.00
❏ SD886 [S]	Songs for Latin Lovers	1965	15.00
❏ 33-874 [M]	Songs for Lonesome Lovers	1964	12.00
❏ SD874 [S]	Songs for Lonesome Lovers	1964	15.00
❏ 33-914 [M]	Special Something	1967	15.00
❏ SD914 [S]	Special Something	1967	12.00
❏ SD926	Take Me Along	1968	12.00
❏ 33-903 [M]	What the World Needs Now Is Love	1966	12.00
❏ SD903 [S]	What the World Needs Now Is Love	1966	15.00
❏ 33-890 [M]	Young Lovers on Broadway	1965	12.00
❏ SD890 [S]	Young Lovers on Broadway	1965	15.00

DECCA

❏ DL8988 [M]	Deep Night	1960	15.00
❏ DL78988 [S]	Deep Night	1960	18.00
❏ DL8787 [M]	Highest Fidelity -- Love and Marriage	1958	15.00
❏ DL78787 [S]	Highest Fidelity -- Love and Marriage	1958	18.00
❏ DL8874 [M]	In the Evening by the Moonlight	1959	15.00
❏ DL78874 [S]	In the Evening by the Moonlight	1959	18.00
❏ DL8838 [M]	Sunrise Serenade	1958	15.00
❏ DL78838 [S]	Sunrise Serenade	1958	18.00
❏ DL8940 [M]	We Gather Together -- Beloved Hymns	1959	15.00
❏ DL78940 [S]	We Gather Together -- Beloved Hymns	1959	18.00

MCA

| ❏ 4162 | The Best of the Ray Charles Singers | 1980 | 12.00 |

METRO

| ❏ M-507 [M] | Spring, Spring, Spring | 1965 | 12.00 |
| ❏ MS-507 [S] | Spring, Spring, Spring | 1965 | 12.00 |

MGM

❏ E-4163 [M]	Autumn Moods	1963	15.00
❏ SE-4163 [S]	Autumn Moods	1963	15.00
❏ E-4166 [M]	Christmas at Home	1963	15.00
❏ SE-4166 [S]	Christmas at Home	1963	15.00
❏ E-3568 [M]	Here's to My Lady	1957	18.00
—Yellow label			
❏ E-3568 [M]	Here's to My Lady	1960	15.00
—Black label			
❏ E-4164 [M]	Songs for a Lazy Summer Afternoon	1963	15.00
❏ SE-4164 [S]	Songs for a Lazy Summer Afternoon	1963	15.00
❏ E-4257 [M]	The Very Best of the Ray Charles Singers	1964	15.00
❏ SE-4257 [S]	The Very Best of the Ray Charles Singers	1964	15.00
❏ E-4165 [M]	We Love Paris	1963	15.00
❏ SE-4165 [S]	We Love Paris	1963	15.00
❏ E-3387 [M]	Winter Wonderland	1956	18.00
—Yellow label			
❏ E-3387 [M]	Winter Wonderland	1960	15.00
—Black label			

SOMERSET

❏ P-21400 [M]	Quiet Moments for Young Lovers	196?	12.00
❏ SF-21400 [S]	Quiet Moments for Young Lovers	196?	12.00
❏ P-21500 [M]	Young Lovers in Far Away Places	196?	12.00
❏ SF-21500 [S]	Young Lovers in Far Away Places	196?	12.00

Number	Title	Yr	NM

VOCALION

| ❏ VL3784 [M] | Love Is a Many-Splendored Thing | 196? | 12.00 |
| ❏ VL73784 [S] | Love Is a Many-Splendored Thing | 196? | 12.00 |

CHARLES, RAY

ABC

❏ H-731	A 25th Anniversary in Show Business Salute to Ray Charles	1971	18.00
❏ X-781/2	All-Time Great Country & Western Hits	1973	18.00
❏ 590X [M]	A Man and His Soul	1967	18.00
❏ S-590X [S]	A Man and His Soul	1967	25.00
❏ X-755	A Message from the People	1972	15.00
❏ S-625	A Portrait of Ray	1968	15.00
❏ S-544 [S]	Crying Time	1967	15.00
❏ S-355 [S]	Dedicated to You	1967	15.00
❏ S-695	Doing His Thing	1969	15.00
❏ S-495 [S]	Have a Smile with Me	1967	15.00
❏ S-675	I'm All Yours -- Baby!	1969	15.00
❏ S-465 [S]	Ingredients in a Recipe for Soul	1967	15.00
❏ S-707	Love Country Style	1971	15.00
❏ S-410 [S]	Modern Sounds in Country and Western Music	1967	15.00
❏ S-435 [S]	Modern Sounds in Country and Western Music (Volume Two)	1967	15.00
❏ S-415 [S]	Ray Charles' Greatest Hits	1967	15.00
❏ 595 [M]	Ray Charles Invites You to Listen	1967	25.00
❏ S-595 [S]	Ray Charles Invites You to Listen	1967	18.00
❏ ST-91233 [S]	Ray Charles Invites You to Listen	1967	18.00
—Capitol Record Club edition			
❏ S-500 [S]	Ray Charles Live in Concert	1967	15.00
❏ S-550 [S]	Ray's Moods	1967	15.00
❏ S-480 [S]	Sweet & Sour Tears	1967	15.00
❏ S-335 [S]	The Genius Hits the Road	1967	15.00
❏ QBO-91036 [M]	The Ray Charles Story	1967	30.00
—Capitol Record Club exclusive			
❏ SQBO-91036 [S]	The Ray Charles Story	1967	30.00
—Capitol Record Club exclusive			
❏ X-765	Through the Eyes of Love	1972	15.00
❏ S-520 [S]	Together Again	1967	15.00
❏ S-726	Volcanic Action of My Soul	1971	15.00

ABC IMPULSE!

| ❏ AS-2 [S] | Genius + Soul = Jazz | 1968 | 15.00 |

ABC-PARAMOUNT

❏ 520 [M]	Country & Western Meets Rhythm & Blues	1965	18.00
❏ S-520 [S]	Country & Western Meets Rhythm & Blues	1965	25.00
❏ 544 [M]	Crying Time	1966	18.00
❏ S-544 [S]	Crying Time	1966	25.00
❏ T-90625 [M]	Crying Time	1966	25.00
—Capitol Record Club edition			
❏ ST-90625 [S]	Crying Time	1966	25.00
—Capitol Record Club edition			
❏ 355 [M]	Dedicated to You	1961	25.00
❏ S-355 [S]	Dedicated to You	1961	30.00
❏ 495 [M]	Have a Smile with Me	1964	25.00
❏ S-495 [S]	Have a Smile with Me	1964	30.00
❏ 465 [M]	Ingredients in a Recipe for Soul	1963	25.00
❏ S-465 [S]	Ingredients in a Recipe for Soul	1963	30.00
❏ 410 [M]	Modern Sounds in Country and Western Music	1962	30.00
❏ S-410 [S]	Modern Sounds in Country and Western Music	1962	30.00
❏ 435 [M]	Modern Sounds in Country and Western Music (Volume Two)	1962	25.00
❏ S-435 [S]	Modern Sounds in Country and Western Music (Volume Two)	1962	30.00
❏ 415 [M]	Ray Charles' Greatest Hits	1962	25.00
❏ S-415 [S]	Ray Charles' Greatest Hits	1962	30.00
❏ 500 [M]	Ray Charles Live in Concert	1965	18.00
❏ S-500 [S]	Ray Charles Live in Concert	1965	25.00
❏ T-90144 [M]	Ray Charles Live in Concert	1965	25.00
—Capitol Record Club edition			
❏ ST-90144 [S]	Ray Charles Live in Concert	1965	25.00
—Capitol Record Club edition			
❏ 550 [M]	Ray's Moods	1966	18.00
❏ S-550 [S]	Ray's Moods	1966	25.00
❏ ST-90929 [S]	Ray's Moods	1966	30.00
—Capitol Record Club edition			
❏ 480 [M]	Sweet & Sour Tears	1964	25.00
❏ S-480 [S]	Sweet & Sour Tears	1964	30.00
❏ 335 [M]	The Genius Hits the Road	1960	25.00
❏ S-335 [S]	The Genius Hits the Road	1960	30.00
❏ 520 [M]	Together Again	196?	18.00
—Retitled version of "Country and Western Meets Rhythm and Blues			
❏ S-520 [S]	Together Again	196?	25.00
—Retitled version of "Country and Western Meets Rhythm and Blues			
❏ ST-90847 [S]	Together Again	1966	30.00
—Capitol Record Club edition			

ATLANTIC

| ❏ SD19251 | Ain't It So | 1979 | 15.00 |

Number	Title	Yr	NM
❏ SD19281	Brother Ray Is At It Again	1980	15.00
❏ 8054 [M]	Do the Twist!	1961	30.00
—Red and white label, white fan logo on right			
❏ 8054 [M]	Do the Twist!	1962	25.00
—Red and white label, black fan logo on right			
❏ 8006 [M]	Hallelujah! I Love Her So	1962	25.00
—Red and white label, black fan logo on right; retitled version			
❏ SD19199	Love and Peace	1978	15.00
❏ 3700	Ray Charles: A Life in Music	198?	50.00
❏ 1289 [M]	Ray Charles at Newport	1958	50.00
—Black label			
❏ 1289 [M]	Ray Charles at Newport	1960	30.00
—Red and white label, black fan logo on right			
❏ 1289 [M]	Ray Charles at Newport	1962	25.00
—Red and white label, black fan logo on right			
❏ SD1289 [S]	Ray Charles at Newport	1959	50.00
—Green label			
❏ SD1289 [S]	Ray Charles at Newport	1960	30.00
—Blue and green label, white fan logo on right			
❏ SD1289 [S]	Ray Charles at Newport	1962	25.00
—Blue and green label, black fan logo on right			
❏ 8039 [M]	Ray Charles In Person	1960	40.00
—Black label			
❏ 8039 [M]	Ray Charles In Person	1960	30.00
—Red and white label, white fan logo on right			
❏ 8039 [M]	Ray Charles In Person	1962	25.00
—Red and white label, black fan logo on right			
❏ SD 2-503	Ray Charles Live	1973	18.00
❏ 8006 [M]	Ray Charles (Rock and Roll)	1957	90.00
—Black label			
❏ 8006 [M]	Ray Charles (Rock and Roll)	1960	30.00
—Red and white label, white fan logo on right			
❏ SD1543	The Best of Ray Charles	1970	15.00
❏ 1369 [M]	The Genius After Hours	1961	30.00
—Red and white label, white fan logo on right			
❏ 1369 [M]	The Genius After Hours	1962	25.00
—Red and white label, black fan logo on right			
❏ SD1369 [S]	The Genius After Hours	1961	30.00
—Blue and green label, white fan logo on right			
❏ SD1369 [S]	The Genius After Hours	1962	30.00
—Blue and green label, black fan logo on right			
❏ 90464	The Genius After Hours	1986	12.00
—Reissue			
❏ 1312 [M]	The Genius of Ray Charles	1960	40.00
—Black label			
❏ 1312 [M]	The Genius of Ray Charles	1960	40.00
—White "bullseye" label			
❏ 1312 [M]	The Genius of Ray Charles	1960	30.00
—Red and white label, white fan logo on right			
❏ 1312 [M]	The Genius of Ray Charles	1962	25.00
—Red and white label, black fan logo on right			
❏ SD1312 [S]	The Genius of Ray Charles	1960	50.00
—Green label			
❏ SD1312 [S]	The Genius of Ray Charles	1960	50.00
—White "bullseye" label			
❏ SD1312 [S]	The Genius of Ray Charles	1960	30.00
—Blue and green label, white fan logo on right			
❏ SD1312 [S]	The Genius of Ray Charles	1962	25.00
—Blue and green label, black fan logo on right			
❏ SD1312 [S]	The Genius of Ray Charles	1968	25.00
—Brown and purple label			
❏ 8052 [M]	The Genius Sings the Blues	1961	30.00
—Red and white label, white fan logo on right			
❏ 8052 [M]	The Genius Sings the Blues	1962	25.00
—Red and white label, black fan logo on right			
❏ SD7101 [S]	The Great Hits of Ray Charles Recorded on 8-Track Stereo	1966	30.00
❏ 1259 [M]	The Great Ray Charles	1957	50.00
—Black label			
❏ 1259 [M]	The Great Ray Charles	1960	30.00
—Red and white label, white fan logo on right			
❏ 1259 [M]	The Great Ray Charles	1962	25.00
—Red and white label, black fan logo on right			
❏ SD1259 [S]	The Great Ray Charles	1959	50.00
—Green label			
❏ SD1259 [S]	The Great Ray Charles	1960	30.00
—Blue and green label, white fan logo on right			
❏ SD1259 [S]	The Great Ray Charles	1962	25.00
—Blue and green label, black fan logo on right			
❏ 2-900 [M]	The Ray Charles Story	1962	40.00
❏ 8063 [M]	The Ray Charles Story, Volume 1	1962	25.00
❏ 8064 [M]	The Ray Charles Story, Volume 2	1962	25.00
❏ 8083 [M]	The Ray Charles Story, Volume 3	1963	25.00
❏ 8094 [M]	The Ray Charles Story, Volume 4	1964	25.00
❏ SD8094 [S]	The Ray Charles Story, Volume 4	1964	30.00
❏ SD19142	True to Life	1977	15.00
❏ 8029 [M]	What'd I Say	1959	50.00
—Black label			
❏ 8029 [M]	What'd I Say	1960	40.00
—White "bullseye" label			
❏ 8029 [M]	What'd I Say	1960	30.00
—Red and white label, white fan logo on right			
❏ 8029 [M]	What'd I Say	1962	25.00
—Red and white label, black fan logo on right			
❏ 8025 [M]	Yes, Indeed!	1958	50.00

Number	Title	Yr	NM
—Black label; cover has screaming girls			
❏ 8025 [M]	Yes, Indeed!	1960	30.00
—Red and white label, white fan logo on right; cover has screaming girls			
❏ 8025 [M]	Yes, Indeed!	1962	25.00
—Red and white label, black fan logo on right; cover has Ray on it			

BARONET
❏ B-111 [M]	The Artistry of Ray Charles	196?	15.00
❏ BS-111 [R]	The Artistry of Ray Charles	196?	12.00
❏ B-117 [M]	The Great Ray Charles	196?	15.00
❏ BS-117 [R]	The Great Ray Charles	196?	12.00

BLUESWAY
❏ 6053	The Genius Live	1973	15.00

COLUMBIA
❏ FC38990	Do I Ever Cross Your Mind	1984	12.00
❏ FC39415	Friendship	1985	12.00
❏ AS1920 [DJ]	Friendship Radio Show	1984	25.00
❏ FC40338	From the Pages of My Mind	1986	12.00
❏ FC45062	Seven Spanish Angels and Other Hits (1982-1986)	1989	15.00
❏ FC40125	The Spirit of Christmas	1985	12.00
❏ FC38293	Wish You Were Here Tonight	1983	12.00
❏ PC38293	Wish You Were Here Tonight	1985	10.00
—Budget-line reissue			

CORONET
❏ CX-173 [M]	Ray Charles	196?	15.00
❏ CXS-173 [R]	Ray Charles	196?	12.00

CROSSOVER
❏ 9000	Come Live with Me	1974	15.00
❏ 9007	My Kind of Jazz, Part 3	1976	15.00
❏ 9005	Renaissance	1975	15.00

DCC COMPACT CLASSICS
❏ LPZ-2012	Greatest Country and Western Hits	1995	100.00
—Audiophile vinyl			

DUNHILL COMPACT CLASSICS
❏ DZL-038	Genius + Soul = Jazz	1988	18.00
—Clear vinyl reissue			

EVEREST ARCHIVE OF FOLK & JAZZ
❏ 244	Ray Charles	1970	15.00
❏ 292	Ray Charles, Vol. 2	197?	12.00
❏ 358	Rockin' with Ray	1979	12.00

HOLLYWOOD
❏ 505 [M]	The Fabulous Ray Charles	1959	150.00
❏ 504 [M]	The Original Ray Charles	1959	150.00

IMPULSE!
❏ A-2 [M]	Genius + Soul = Jazz	1961	30.00
❏ AS-2 [S]	Genius + Soul = Jazz	1961	30.00

INTERMEDIA
❏ QS-5013	Goin' Down Slow	198?	12.00

LONGINES SYMPHONETTE
❏ 95647	The Greatest Hits of Ray Charles	1974	40.00

PAIR
❏ PDL2-1139	The Real Ray Charles	1986	15.00

PREMIER
❏ PS-6001 [R]	Fantastic Ray Charles	196?	12.00
❏ PM2004 [M]	The Great Ray Charles	196?	15.00
❏ PS2004 [R]	The Great Ray Charles	196?	12.00

RHINO
❏ R1-70097	Greatest Hits, Volume 1	1988	12.00
❏ R1-70098	Greatest Hits, Volume 2	1988	12.00
❏ R1-70099	Modern Sounds in Country and Western Music	1988	12.00

TANGERINE
❏ 1512	My Kind of Jazz	1970	15.00
❏ 1516	My Kind of Jazz No. II	1973	15.00

WARNER BROS.
❏ 26343	Would You Believe?	1990	18.00

CHARLES, RAY / HARRY BELAFONTE

CORONET
❏ CX-203 [M]	The Greatest Ever	196?	15.00
❏ CXS-203 [R]	The Greatest Ever	196?	12.00

CHARLES, RAY/IVORY JOE HUNTER/JIMMY RUSHING

DESIGN
❏ DLP-909 [M]	Three of a Kind	196?	15.00
❏ DLS-909 [R]	Three of a Kind	196?	12.00

CHARLES, TEDDY

ATLANTIC
❏ 1229 [M]	The Teddy Charles Tentet	1956	80.00
—Black label			
❏ 1229 [M]	The Teddy Charles Tentet	1961	30.00
—Multicolor label with white "fan" logo			
❏ 1274 [M]	Word from Bird	1956	80.00
—Black label			
❏ 1274 [M]	Word from Bird	1961	30.00
—Multicolor label with white "fan" logo			

BETHLEHEM
❏ BCP-6044 [M]	On Campus -- Ivy League Jazz Concert	1960	50.00

Number	Title	Yr	NM
❏ BCP-6032 [M]	Salute to Hamp	1959	50.00

ELEKTRA
❏ EKL-136 [M]	Vibe-Rant	1957	250.00

FANTASY
❏ OJC-122	Collaboration: West	198?	12.00
—Reissue of Prestige 7028			

JOSIE
❏ JOZ-3505 [M]	Teddy Charles Trio Plays Duke Ellington	1963	30.00
❏ JJS-3505 [S]	Teddy Charles Trio Plays Duke Ellington	1963	30.00

JUBILEE
❏ JLP-1047 [M]	Three for Duke	1957	50.00
❏ JGS-1047 [S]	Three for Duke	1959	40.00

NEW JAZZ
❏ NJLP-1106 [10]	Teddy Charles New Directions Quartet	1955	600.00

PRESTIGE
❏ PRLP-7028 [M]	Collaboration: West	1956	100.00
—Yellow label with 446 W. 50th St. address			
❏ PRLP-7028 [M]	Collaboration: West	196?	30.00
—Blue label, trident logo on right			
❏ PRLP-7078 [M]	Evolution	1957	100.00
—Yellow label			
❏ PRLP-7078 [M]	Evolution	196?	30.00
—Blue label, trident logo on right			
❏ PRLP-143 [10]	New Directions Vol. 1	1953	300.00
❏ PRLP-150 [10]	New Directions Vol. 2	1953	300.00
❏ PRLP-164 [10]	New Directions Vol. 3	1953	300.00
❏ PRLP-169 [10]	New Directions Vol. 4	1954	300.00
❏ PRLP-178 [10]	New Directions Vol. 5	1954	300.00
—With Bob Brookmeyer			
❏ PRLP-132 [10]	Teddy Charles and His Trio	1952	400.00
❏ PRLP-206 [10]	Teddy Charles New Directions Quartet	1955	300.00
—Reissue of New Jazz 1106			

SAVOY
❏ MG-12174 [M]	The Vibe-Rant Quintet	1961	30.00
—Reissue of Elektra LP			

SOUL NOTE
❏ 121183	Live at the Verona Jazz Festival, 1988	1990	15.00

UNITED ARTISTS
❏ UAL-3365 [M]	Russia Goes Jazz	1964	30.00
❏ UAS-6365 [S]	Russia Goes Jazz	1964	30.00

WARWICK
❏ W-2033 [M]	Jazz in the Garden of the Museum of Modern Art	1960	50.00

CHARLES RIVER VALLEY BOYS, THE

ELEKTRA
❏ EKL-4006 [M]	Beatle Country	1967	25.00
❏ EKS-74006 [S]	Beatle Country	1967	30.00

CHARLESTON CITY ALL-STARS

ABC WESTMINSTER GOLD
❏ WGAS-68004	The Roaring 20's, Volume 2	197?	15.00

GRAND AWARD
❏ GA 33-411 [M]	Dixieland	1959	15.00
❏ GA243SD [S]	Dixieland	1959	18.00
❏ GA 33-327 [M]	The Roaring 20's	1957	18.00
❏ GA201SD [S]	The Roaring 20's	1958	25.00
❏ GA 33-340 [M]	The Roaring 20's, Volume 2	1957	18.00
❏ CA211SD [S]	The Roaring 20's, Volume 2	1958	25.00
❏ GA 33-353 [M]	The Roaring 20's, Volume 3	1957	18.00
❏ GA229SD [S]	The Roaring 20's, Volume 3	1958	25.00
❏ GA 33-370 [M]	The Roaring 20's, Volume 4	1958	18.00

WALDORF MUSIC HALL
❏ MH 33-142 [M]	The Roaring Twenties	195?	25.00

-CHARTERS, ANN

GNP CRESCENDO
❏ GNPS-9021	A Joplin Bouquet	197?	12.00
❏ GNPS-9032	The Genius of Scott Joplin	197?	12.00

KICKING MULE
❏ 101	Scott Joplin and His Friends	198?	12.00

CHARTS, THE

COLLECTABLES
❏ COL-5029	Greatest Hits	1986	15.00

LOST-NITE
❏ LLP-10 [10]	The Charts	1981	15.00
—Red vinyl			

CHASE, CAROL

CASABLANCA
❏ NBLP-7237	Chase Is On	1980	15.00
❏ CAC-6001	Sexy Songs	1980	15.00

CHASE, LINCOLN

LIBERTY
❏ LRP-3076 [M]	The Explosive Lincoln Chase	1958	50.00

CHASE

EPIC

Number	Title	Yr	NM
❑ E30472	Chase	1971	15.00
❑ EQ30472 [Q]	Chase	1973	25.00
❑ EG33737	Chase/Ennea	1976	18.00
❑ KE31097	Ennea	1972	15.00
❑ KE32572	Pure Music	1974	15.00
❑ EQ32572 [Q]	Pure Music	1974	25.00

CHEAP TRICK

EPIC

Number	Title	Yr	NM
❑ FE36498	All Shook Up	1980	12.00
❑ PE36498	All Shook Up	1984	10.00
❑ E46013	Busted	1990	15.00
❑ PE34400 [B]	Cheap Trick	1976	18.00
—Originals have orange labels			
❑ PE34400	Cheap Trick	1979	10.00
—Later editions have dark blue labels; may or may not have bar code on back			
❑ FE35795 [B]	Cheap Trick at Budokan	1979	15.00
—Orange label; came with gold-colored obi (add 5/6 if there) and booklet (deduct 1/6 if missing)			
❑ FE35795 [B]	Cheap Trick at Budokan	1979	18.00
—Dark blue label; some copies came with gold-colored obi (add 100% if there) and all came with booklet (deduct 20% if missing)			
❑ FE35795 [DJ]	Cheap Trick at Budokan	1979	25.00
—White label promo			
❑ PE35795	Cheap Trick at Budokan	1984	10.00
❑ FE35773	Dream Police	1979	12.00
—Despite lower number, this came out after Epic 35795			
❑ PE35773	Dream Police	1984	10.00
❑ PE38541 [EP]	Found All the Parts	1983	10.00
—Six-song reissue of Epic/Nu-Disk release on 12-inch LP			
❑ AS518 [DJ]	From Tokyo to You	1979	50.00
—Promo-only sampler from Cheap Trick at Budokan			
❑ JE35312	Heaven Tonight	1978	15.00
—Originals have orange labels			
❑ PE35312	Heaven Tonight	1979	10.00
—Later editions have dark blue labels; may or may not have bar code			
❑ JE34884	In Color	1977	15.00
—Originals have orange labels			
❑ PE34884	In Color	1979	10.00
—Later editions have dark blue labels; may or may not have bar code on back			
❑ OE40922	Lap of Luxury	1988	12.00
❑ FE38794	Next Position Please	1983	12.00
❑ PE38794	Next Position Please	1985	10.00
❑ FE38021	One on One	1982	12.00
❑ PE38021	One on One	1984	10.00
❑ FE39592	Standing on the Edge	1985	12.00
❑ PE39592	Standing on the Edge	1987	10.00
❑ FE40405	The Doctor	1986	12.00
❑ PE40405	The Doctor	1987	10.00
—Reissue with new prefix on cover			

EPIC/NU-DISK

Number	Title	Yr	NM
❑ 4E36453 [10]	Found All the Parts	1980	30.00
—10-inch, four-track EP with bonus 45, "Everything Works If You Let It" (AE7 1206)			

CHEATHAM, DOC, AND SAMMY PRICE

SACKVILLE

Number	Title	Yr	NM
❑ 3029	Black Beauty	198?	15.00
❑ 3013	Doc & Sammy	198?	15.00
❑ 3024	Sweet Substitute	198?	15.00

CHEATHAM, DOC

CLASSIC JAZZ

Number	Title	Yr	NM
❑ 113	Good for What Ails Ya	1977	15.00

CHEATHAM, JEANNIE AND JIMMY

CONCORD JAZZ

Number	Title	Yr	NM
❑ CJ-373	Back to the Neighborhood	1989	15.00
❑ CJ-321	Homeward Bound	1987	12.00
❑ CJ-297	Midnight Mama	1986	12.00
❑ CJ-258	Sweet Baby Blues	1985	12.00

CHECKER, CHUBBY

ABKCO

Number	Title	Yr	NM
❑ 4219	Chubby Checker's Greatest Hits	1972	25.00

EVEREST

Number	Title	Yr	NM
❑ 4111	Chubby Checker's Greatest Hits	1981	15.00

MCA

Number	Title	Yr	NM
❑ 5291	The Change Has Come	1982	12.00

PARKWAY

Number	Title	Yr	NM
❑ P7014 [M]	All the Hits (For Your Dancin' Party)	1962	30.00
❑ P7030 [M]	Beach Party	1963	30.00
❑ SP7030 [S]	Beach Party	1963	40.00
❑ P7026 [M]	Chubby Checker In Person	1963	30.00
❑ SP7026 [S]	Chubby Checker In Person	1963	40.00
—The above record is labeled "Twist It Up			
❑ P7022 [M]	Chubby Checker's Biggest Hits	1962	30.00
❑ SP7022 [R]	Chubby Checker's Biggest Hits	1962	30.00
❑ P7048 [M]	Chubby Checker's Eighteen Golden Hits	1966	30.00
❑ SP7048 [P]	Chubby Checker's Eighteen Golden Hits	1966	40.00
❑ P7036 [M]	Chubby Checker With Sy Oliver and His Orchestra	1964	30.00
❑ SP7036 [S]	Chubby Checker With Sy Oliver and His Orchestra	1964	40.00
❑ P7045 [M]	Discotheque	1965	30.00
❑ SP7045 [S]	Discotheque	1965	40.00
❑ P7040 [M]	Folk Album	1964	30.00
❑ SP7040 [S]	Folk Album	1964	40.00
❑ P7009 [M]	For Teen Twisters Only	1962	30.00
❑ SP7009 [S]	For Teen Twisters Only	1962	40.00
❑ P7002 [M]	For Twisters Only	1960	40.00
—All-orange label			
❑ P7002 [M]	For Twisters Only	1962	30.00
—Orange and yellow label			
❑ P7003 [M]	It's Pony Time	1961	40.00
—All-orange label			
❑ P7003 [M]	It's Pony Time	1962	30.00
—Orange and yellow label			
❑ P7027 [M]	Let's Limbo Some More	1963	30.00
❑ SP7027 [S]	Let's Limbo Some More	1963	40.00
❑ P7004 [M]	Let's Twist Again	1961	40.00
—All-orange label			
❑ P7004 [M]	Let's Twist Again	1962	30.00
—Orange and yellow label			
❑ P7020 [M]	Limbo Party	1962	30.00
❑ SP7020 [S]	Limbo Party	1962	40.00
❑ P7008 [M]	Twistin' Round the World	1962	30.00
❑ SP7008 [B]	Twistin' Round the World	1962	40.00
❑ P7001 [M]	Twist with Chubby Checker	1962	30.00
—Orange and yellow label			
❑ P7001 [M]	Twist with Chubby Checker	1960	40.00
—All-orange label			
❑ P7007 [M]	Your Twist Party	1961	40.00
—All-orange label			
❑ P7007 [M]	Your Twist Party	1962	30.00
—Orange and yellow label			

CHECKMATES, THE

JUSTICE

Number	Title	Yr	NM
❑ JLP-149	The Checkmates	1966	400.00

CHECKMATES LTD., THE

A&M

Number	Title	Yr	NM
❑ SP-4183	Love Is All I Have to Give	1969	30.00

CAPITOL

Number	Title	Yr	NM
❑ T2840 [M]	Live at Caesar's Palace	1968	30.00
❑ ST2840 [S]	Live at Caesar's Palace	1968	25.00

FANTASY

Number	Title	Yr	NM
❑ 9541	We Got the Moves	1978	18.00

CHEECH AND CHONG

MCA

Number	Title	Yr	NM
❑ 5640	Get Out of My Room	1985	10.00

ODE

Number	Title	Yr	NM
❑ SP-77014 [B]	Big Bambu	1972	18.00
—Add 50% if rolling paper is still enclosed			
❑ SP-77010	Cheech and Chong	1971	15.00
❑ PE34947	Cheech and Chong	1977	12.00
—Reissue of 77010			
❑ SP-77025 [B]	Cheech and Chong's Wedding Album	1974	18.00
❑ PE34954	Cheech and Chong's Wedding Album	1977	12.00
—Reissue of 77025			
❑ SP-77019 [B]	Los Cochinos	1973	18.00
❑ PE34951	Los Cochinos	1977	12.00
—Reissue of 77019			
❑ SP-77040 [B]	Sleeping Beauty	1976	18.00
❑ PE34960	Sleeping Beauty	1977	12.00
—Reissue of 77040			

WARNER BROS.

Number	Title	Yr	NM
❑ BSK3251	Big Bambu	1978	10.00
❑ BSK3250	Cheech and Chong	1978	10.00
❑ BSK3614	Cheech and Chong's Greatest Hit	1982	10.00
❑ BSK3253	Cheech and Chong's Wedding Album	1978	10.00
❑ HS3391	Let's Make a New Dope Deal	1980	12.00
❑ BSK3252	Los Cochinos	1978	10.00
❑ BSK3254	Sleeping Beauty	1978	10.00
❑ BSK3249	Up in Smoke	1978	12.00

CHELSEA

DECCA

Number	Title	Yr	NM
❑ DL75262	The Chelsea Album	1972	100.00

CHEMICAL BROTHERS, THE

ASTRALWERKS

Number	Title	Yr	NM
❑ ASW6180	Dig Your Own Hole	1997	18.00
❑ ASW6157 [B]	Exit Planet Dust	1995	30.00
❑ ASW47610	Surrender	1999	18.00

CHER

ATCO

Number	Title	Yr	NM
❑ SD 33-298 [S]	3614 Jackson Highway	1969	25.00
❑ 33-298 [M]	3614 Jackson Highway	1969	30.00
—White label promo only (no stock copies issued in mono)			

CASABLANCA

Number	Title	Yr	NM
❑ NBLP-7184	Prisoner	1980	12.00
❑ NBLP-7133	Take Me Home	1979	12.00
❑ NBPIX-7133 [PD]	Take Me Home	1979	50.00

COLUMBIA

Number	Title	Yr	NM
❑ FC38096	I Paralyze	1982	12.00

GEFFEN

Number	Title	Yr	NM
❑ GHS24164	Cher	1987	12.00
❑ GHS24239	Heart of Stone	1989	18.00
—Original cover with Cher in heart-shaped pose next to "skeleton rock			
❑ GHS24239	Heart of Stone	1989	12.00
—Later cover with larger picture of Cher and no rock			

IMPERIAL

Number	Title	Yr	NM
❑ LP-9292 [M]	All I Really Want to Do	1965	25.00
❑ LP-12292 [S]	All I Really Want to Do	1965	30.00
❑ LP-12373 [M]	Backstage	1968	40.00
—Stereo cover with designate mono sticker attached; label is stock			
❑ LP-12373 [S]	Backstage	1968	25.00
❑ LP-9320 [M]	Cher	1966	18.00
❑ LP-12320 [S]	Cher	1966	25.00
❑ LP-12406	Cher's Golden Greats	1968	25.00
❑ LP-9301 [M]	The Sonny Side of Cher	1966	25.00
❑ LP-12301 [S]	The Sonny Side of Cher	1966	30.00
❑ LP-9358 [M]	With Love -- Cher	1967	18.00
❑ LP-12358 [S]	With Love -- Cher	1967	25.00

KAPP

Number	Title	Yr	NM
❑ KS-3649	Cher	1971	25.00
—Original title of LP (without "Gypsys, Tramps & Thieves" title on front cover)			
❑ KRS-5514	Foxy Lady	1972	18.00
❑ SW-94485	Foxy Lady	1972	25.00
—Capitol Record Club edition			
❑ KS-3649	Gypsys, Tramps & Thieves	1971	18.00
—Retitled version of above LP; red and orange swirl label			
❑ KRS-5549	Gypsys, Tramps & Thieves	1972	18.00
—Reissue of 3649; black label			

LIBERTY

Number	Title	Yr	NM
❑ LN-10110	The Very Best of Cher, Vol. 1	1981	10.00
❑ LN-10111	The Very Best of Cher, Vol. 2	1981	10.00

MCA

Number	Title	Yr	NM
❑ 2101	Bittersweet White Light	1973	15.00
❑ 624	Cher	197?	12.00
❑ 2113	Dark Lady	1974	15.00
❑ 2127	Greatest Hits	1974	15.00
❑ 37028	Greatest Hits	1981	10.00
—Reissue of MCA 2127			
❑ 2104	Half-Breed	1973	15.00

PICKWICK

Number	Title	Yr	NM
❑ SPC-3619	This Is Cher	1978	12.00

SPRINGBOARD

Number	Title	Yr	NM
❑ SPB-4028	Cher's Greatest Hits	197?	12.00
❑ SPB-4029	Cher Sings the Hits	197?	12.00

SUNSET

Number	Title	Yr	NM
❑ SUS-5276	This Is Cher	1970	18.00

UNITED ARTISTS

Number	Title	Yr	NM
❑ UXS-88	Cher Superpak	1971	25.00
❑ UXS-89	Cher Superpak, Vol. II	1972	25.00
—The above are reissues of Imperial recordings			
❑ UA-LA237-G	The Very Best of Cher	1974	15.00
❑ UA-LA377-E	The Very Best of Cher	1975	12.00
❑ UA-LA435-E	The Very Best of Cher, Vol. 2	1975	15.00

WARNER BROS.

Number	Title	Yr	NM
❑ BS3046	Cherished	1977	15.00
❑ BS2898	I'd Rather Believe in You	1976	15.00
❑ BS2850	Stars	1975	15.00

CHEROKEE

ABC

Number	Title	Yr	NM
❑ ABCS-719	Cherokee	1970	25.00

CHERRY, DON

COLUMBIA

Number	Title	Yr	NM
❑ CL893 [M]	Swingin' for Two	1956	30.00

MONUMENT

Number	Title	Yr	NM
❑ SLP-18124	Don Cherry	1970	15.00
❑ MLP-8049 [M]	Don Cherry Smashes	1966	15.00
❑ SLP-18049 [S]	Don Cherry Smashes	1966	18.00
❑ SLP-18088	Let It Be Me	1968	15.00
❑ SLP-18109	Take a Message to Mary	1969	15.00
❑ MLP-8075 [M]	There Goes My Everything	1967	18.00
❑ SLP-18075 [S]	There Goes My Everything	1967	15.00
❑ KZG32334 [B]	The World of Don Cherry	1972	18.00
❑ 8601	The World of Don Cherry	197?	15.00
—Reissue of 32334			

CHERRY, DON (2)

A&M

Number	Title	Yr	NM
❑ SP-5258	Art Deco	1989	25.00

ANTILLES

Number	Title	Yr	NM
❑ AN7034	The Eternal Now	197?	50.00

Number	Title	Yr	NM
ATLANTIC			
❑ SD18217	Hear and Now	1977	50.00
BASF			
❑ 20680	Eternal Rhythm	1972	30.00
BLUE NOTE			
❑ BLP-4226 [M]	Complete Communion	1966	50.00
— *New York, USA" address on label*			
❑ BST-84226 [S]	Complete Communion	1966	60.00
— *New York, USA" address on label*			
❑ BST-84226 [S]	Complete Communion	1968	40.00
— *A Division of Liberty Records" on label*			
❑ BLP-4247 [M]	Symphony for Improvisers	1966	50.00
— *New York, USA" address on label*			
❑ BST-84247 [S]	Symphony for Improvisers	1966	60.00
— *New York, USA" address on label*			
❑ BST-84247 [S]	Symphony for Improvisers	1968	40.00
— *A Division of Liberty Records" on label*			
❑ BST-84311	Where Is Brooklyn?	1969	60.00
— *A Division of Liberty Records" on label*			
ECM			
❑ ECM1-1230	El Corazon	1982	18.00
— *With Ed Blackwell; distributed by Warner Bros.*			
HORIZON			
❑ SP-717	Don Cherry	1976	30.00
INNER CITY			
❑ IC1009	Togetherness	197?	25.00
JCOA			
❑ 1006	Relativity Suite	1974	50.00
MOSAIC			
❑ MQ3-145	The Complete Blue Note Recordings of Don Cherry	199?	60.00
PICCADILLY			
❑ PIC-3515	Tibet	1981	30.00
CHERRY, NENEH			
VIRGIN			
❑ R174031	Raw Like Sushi	1989	15.00
— *BMG Direct Marketing edition*			
❑ 91252	Raw Like Sushi	1989	12.00
CHERRY PEOPLE, THE			
HERITAGE			
❑ HT35000 [M]	The Cherry People	1968	50.00
— *Stereo cover with "Mono" and "DJ" stickers attached; all records appear to be white label promos*			
❑ HTS35000 [S]	The Cherry People	1968	25.00
CHESS, TUBBY, AND HIS CANDY STRIPE TWISTERS			
GRAND PRIX			
❑ K-187 [M]	Do the Twist	1962	25.00
❑ KS-187 [S]	Do the Twist	1962	30.00
CHESTER, BOB			
CIRCLE			
❑ 44	Bob Chester and His Orchestra: 1940-41	198?	12.00
❑ 74	Bob Chester and His Orchestra: More 1940-41	198?	12.00
CHESTER, GARY			
DCP			
❑ DCL3803 [M]	Yeah, Yeah, Yeah	1964	25.00
❑ DCS6803 [S]	Yeah, Yeah, Yeah	1964	30.00
CHEVALIER, MAURICE			
CAPITOL			
❑ T10360 [M]	The Young Chevalier	196?	25.00
EPIC			
❑ FXS15117	Maurice Chevalier at 80	1968	25.00
LONDON			
❑ GH46001/4 [M]	60 Years of Song	1966	40.00
❑ GHS56001/4 [S]	60 Years of Song	1966	50.00
MGM			
❑ E-3773 [M]	A Tribute to Al Jolson	1959	30.00
— *Yellow label original*			
❑ SE-3773 [S]	A Tribute to Al Jolson	1959	30.00
— *Yellow label original*			
❑ E-3801 [M]	Life Is Just a Bowl of Cherries	1960	25.00
❑ SE-3801 [S]	Life Is Just a Bowl of Cherries	1960	30.00
❑ E-3738 [M]	Maurice Chevalier Sings Broadway	1959	30.00
— *Yellow label original*			
❑ SE-3738 [S]	Maurice Chevalier Sings Broadway	1959	30.00
— *Yellow label original*			
❑ E-4015 [M]	Maurice Chevalier Sings Lerner, Loewe & Chevalier	1962	25.00
❑ SE-4015 [S]	Maurice Chevalier Sings Lerner, Loewe & Chevalier	1962	30.00
❑ E-4120 [M]	Paris to Broadway	1963	25.00
❑ SE-4120 [S]	Paris to Broadway	1963	30.00
❑ E-3835 [M]	Thank Heaven for Little Girls	1960	25.00
❑ SE-3835 [S]	Thank Heaven for Little Girls	1960	30.00

Number	Title	Yr	NM
❑ E-4205 [M]	The Very Best of Maurice Chevalier	1964	18.00
❑ SE-4205 [S]	The Very Best of Maurice Chevalier	1964	25.00
❑ E-3703 [M]	Today	1958	30.00
— *Yellow label original*			
❑ SE-3703 [S]	Today	1958	30.00
— *Yellow label original*			
❑ E-3702 [M]	Yesterday	1958	30.00
— *Yellow label original*			
❑ SE-3702 [S]	Yesterday	1958	30.00
— *Yellow label original*			
❑ 2E-5 [M]	Yesterday…Today	1958	40.00
— *Yellow label original; also released separately as 3702 and 3703*			
❑ 2SE-5 [S]	Yesterday…Today	1958	60.00
— *Yellow label original; also released separately as 3702 and 3703*			
RCA VICTOR			
❑ LPM-2076 [M]	Thank Heaven for Maurice Chevalier	1960	30.00
❑ LSP-2076 [S]	Thank Heaven for Maurice Chevalier	1960	30.00
TIME			
❑ 52072 [M]	Maurice Chevalier	1963	25.00
❑ S-2072 [S]	Maurice Chevalier	1963	30.00
CHEVRONS, THE			
TIME			
❑ T-10008 [M]	Sing-a-Long Rock & Roll	1961	80.00
CHI-LITES, THE			
BRUNSWICK			
❑ BL754188	A Letter to Myself	1973	30.00
❑ BL754179 [B]	A Lonely Man	1972	30.00
❑ BL754197	Chi-Lites	1973	30.00
❑ BL754170	(For God's Sake) Give More Power to the People	1971	30.00
❑ BL754152	Give It Away	1969	30.00
❑ BL754204	Half a Love	1975	30.00
❑ BL754165	I Like Your Lovin', Do You Like Mine?	1970	30.00
❑ BL754184	The Chi-Lites Greatest Hits	1972	30.00
❑ BL754208	The Chi-Lites Greatest Hits, Volume 2	1976	30.00
❑ BL754200	Toby	1974	30.00
CHI-SOUND			
❑ T-619	Heavenly Body	1980	18.00
❑ T-635	Me and You	1982	18.00
EPIC			
❑ PE38627	Greatest Hits	1983	12.00
ICHIBAN			
❑ ICH-1057	Just Say You Love Me	198?	12.00
LARC			
❑ 8103	Bottom's Up	1983	15.00
MERCURY			
❑ SRM-1-1147	Fantastic	1977	18.00
❑ SRM-1-1118	Happy Being Lonely	1976	18.00
PRIVATE I			
❑ FZ39316	Steppin' Out	1984	12.00
❑ PZ39316	Steppin' Out	1985	10.00
— *Budget-line reissue*			
CHICAGO			
ACCORD			
❑ SN-7140	Toronto Rock 'n Roll Revival, 1982 Part I		15.00
— *Reissue of Magnum LP*			
COLUMBIA			
❑ KGP24	Chicago	1970	40.00
— *Red labels with "360 Sound" at bottom; label and spine call the album "Chicago*			
❑ (no #)	Chicago	1976	250.00
— *Promo-only set: The first 10 Chicago LPs with gold stamps on covers, box, side panel and wraparound*			
❑ FC36105	Chicago 13	1979	15.00
❑ C4X30865	Chicago at Carnegie Hall	1971	30.00
— *With box, 4 posters and program; deduct for missing items*			
❑ KG30863	Chicago at Carnegie Hall, Vol. 1 & 2	1971	18.00
— *First half of the 4-LP box, possibly for Columbia Record Club only*			
❑ KG30864	Chicago at Carnegie Hall, Vol. 3 & 4	1971	18.00
— *Second half of the 4-LP box, possibly for Columbia Record Club only*			
❑ FC37682	Chicago -- Greatest Hits, Volume II	1981	15.00
❑ KGP24	Chicago II	1970	18.00
— *Orange labels*			
❑ GQ33258 [Q]	Chicago II	1975	30.00
❑ KGP24	Chicago II	1970	30.00
— *Red labels with "360 Sound" at bottom; label and spine call the album "Chicago II*			
❑ C230110	Chicago III	1971	18.00
❑ C2Q30110 [Q]	Chicago III	1974	30.00
❑ PC33900	Chicago IX -- Chicago's Greatest Hits	1975	12.00
❑ PCQ33900 [Q]	Chicago IX -- Chicago's Greatest Hits	1975	30.00

Number	Title	Yr	NM
❑ HC43900	Chicago IX -- Chicago's Greatest Hits	1982	30.00
— *Half-speed mastered edition*			
❑ GP8	Chicago Transit Authority	1969	30.00
— *Red labels with "360 Sound" at bottom*			
❑ GP8	Chicago Transit Authority	1970	18.00
— *Orange labels; most copies add a Roman numeral "I" to the title on spine*			
❑ GQ33255 [Q]	Chicago Transit Authority	1975	30.00
❑ KC31102	Chicago V	1972	18.00
❑ CQ31102 [Q]	Chicago V	1974	30.00
❑ KC32400	Chicago VI	1973	15.00
❑ CQ32400 [Q]	Chicago VI	1974	30.00
❑ C232810	Chicago VII	1974	18.00
❑ C2Q32810 [Q]	Chicago VII	1974	30.00
❑ PC33100	Chicago VIII	1975	15.00
❑ PCQ33100 [Q]	Chicago VIII	1975	30.00
❑ PC34200	Chicago X	1976	12.00
❑ PCQ34200 [Q]	Chicago X	1976	30.00
❑ HC44200	Chicago X	1982	40.00
— *Half-speed mastered edition*			
❑ JC34860	Chicago XI	1977	12.00
❑ FC36517	Chicago XIV	1980	15.00
❑ FC35512	Hot Streets	1978	12.00
❑ PC38590	If You Leave Me Now	1982	15.00
❑ PC39579	Take Me Back to Chicago	1983	15.00
FULL MOON			
❑ 23689	Chicago 16	1982	10.00
MAGNUM			
❑ MR604	Chicago Transit Authority Live in Concert	1978	25.00
— *Taken from their 1969 Toronto Rock 'n Roll Revival performance*			
MOBILE FIDELITY			
❑ 2-128	Chicago Transit Authority	1983	80.00
— *Audiophile vinyl*			
REPRISE			
❑ 25714	Chicago 19	1988	10.00
❑ 26080	Greatest Hits 1982-1989	1989	12.00
❑ R110533	Twenty 1	1991	25.00
— *BMG Direct Marketing version*			
WARNER BROS.			
❑ 25060	Chicago 17	1984	10.00
❑ 25060 [DJ]	Chicago 17	1984	25.00
— *Promo pressing on Quiex II vinyl*			
❑ 25509	Chicago 18	1986	10.00
CHICAGO HOT SIX			
GHB			
❑ 176	Stompin' at the Good Time	1982	12.00
CHICKEN SHACK			
BLUE HORIZON			
❑ BH7706	100-Ton Chicken	1969	30.00
❑ BH4809	Accept Chicken Shack	1970	30.00
❑ BH7705	O.K. Ken?	1969	30.00
DERAM			
❑ DES18063	Imagination Lady	1972	25.00
EPIC			
❑ LN24414 [M]	Forty Blue Fingers, Freshly Packed and Ready to Serve	1968	150.00
❑ BN26414 [S]	Forty Blue Fingers, Freshly Packed and Ready to Serve	1968	30.00
LONDON			
❑ XPS632	Unlucky Boy	1973	25.00
CHICKENFOOT			
REDLINE ENTERTAINMENT			
❑ 20092	Chickenfoot	2009	30.00
CHIEFTAINS, THE			
COLUMBIA			
❑ JC36401	Boil the Breakfast Early	1981	15.00
❑ PC36401	Boil the Breakfast Early	198?	10.00
— *Budget-line reissue*			
❑ JC35612	The Chieftains 7	1979	15.00
❑ PC35612	The Chieftains 7	198?	10.00
— *Budget-line reissue*			
❑ JC35726	The Chieftains 8	1980	15.00
ISLAND			
❑ ILPS9432	Bonaparte's Retreat	1977	15.00
❑ ILPS9364	The Chieftains 1	1976	15.00
— *Black label original; first US issue*			
❑ ILPS9365	The Chieftains 2	1976	15.00
— *Black label original; first US issue*			
❑ ILPS9379	The Chieftains 3	1976	15.00
— *Black label original; first US issue*			
❑ ILPS9380	The Chieftains 4	1976	15.00
— *Black label original; first US issue*			
❑ ILP39334	The Chieftains 5	1975	15.00
— *Black label original*			
❑ ILPS9501	The Chieftains Live	1978	15.00
RCA			
❑ 7858-1-R	A Chieftains Celebration	1989	15.00
❑ 6358-1-R	Celtic Wedding	1987	12.00

Number	Title	Yr	NM
SHANACHIE			
❏ 79026	Bonaparte's Retreat	198?	12.00
— Reissue of Island 9432			
❏ 79019	Cotton-Eyed Joe	198?	12.00
❏ 79051	The Ballad of Iron Horse	198?	12.00
❏ 79021	The Chieftains 1	1982	12.00
— Reissue of Island 9364			
❏ 79022	The Chieftains 2	198?	12.00
— Reissue of Island 9365			
❏ 79023	The Chieftains 3	198?	12.00
— Reissue of Island 9379			
❏ 79024	The Chieftains 4	198?	12.00
— Reissue of Island 9380			
❏ 79025	The Chieftains 5	198?	12.00
— Reissue of Island 9334			
❏ 79050	The Chieftains in China	198?	12.00
❏ 79036	Year of the French	1983	12.00
CHIFFONS, THE			
B.T. PUPPY			
❏ S-1011	My Secret Love	1970	400.00
COLLECTABLES			
❏ COL-5042	Golden Classics	198?	15.00
LAURIE			
❏ 4001	Everything You Always Wanted to Hear by the Chiffons	1975	25.00
❏ LLP-2018 [M]	He's So Fine	1963	120.00
❏ DT-90075 [R]	He's So Fine	1965	200.00
— Capitol Record Club edition			
❏ LLP-2020 [M]	One Fine Day	1963	200.00
❏ LLP-2036 [M]	Sweet Talkin' Guy	1966	100.00
❏ SLP-2036 [S]	Sweet Talkin' Guy	1966	150.00
❏ ST-90779 [S]	Sweet Talkin' Guy	1966	200.00
— Capitol Record Club edition			
CHILDERS, BUDDY			
LIBERTY			
❏ LJH-6013 [M]	Buddy Childers Quartet	1957	100.00
❏ LJH-6009 [M]	Sam Songs	1956	100.00
TREND			
❏ TR-539	Just Buddy's	1986	25.00
CHILDRE, LEW			
STARDAY			
❏ SLP-153 [M]	Old Time Get Together	1961	30.00
CHILDREN, THE			
ATCO			
❏ SD 33-271	Rebirth	1968	30.00
CINEMA			
❏ CLP-1	Rebirth	1968	200.00
CHILDS, SUE			
STUDIO 4			
❏ 200 [M]	Sue Childs	195?	250.00
CHILES AND PETTIFORD			
ATLANTIC			
❏ 8111 [M]	Live at Jilly's	1965	40.00
❏ SD8111 [S]	Live at Jilly's	1965	50.00
CHILLIWACK			
A&M			
❏ SP-4375 [B]	All Over You	1972	30.00
❏ SP-3509	Chilliwack	1971	30.00
MILLENNIUM			
❏ BXL1-7766	Opus X	1982	12.00
❏ BXL1-7759	Wanna Be a Star	1981	12.00
MUSHROOM			
❏ MRS-5015	Breakdown in Paradise	1980	15.00
❏ MRS-5006	Dreams, Dreams, Dreams	1977	15.00
❏ MRS-5011	Lights from the Valley	1978	15.00
PARROT			
❏ PAS71040	Chilliwack	1970	30.00
SIRE			
❏ SASD-7506	Chilliwack	1975	18.00
❏ SASD-7511	Rockerbox	1976	18.00
CHIPMUNKS, THE, DAVID SEVILLE AND			
LIBERTY			
❏ LRP-3170 [M]	Around the World with the Chipmunks	1960	40.00
— Original cover features "realistic" chipmunks on and near a plane			
❏ LRP-3170 [M]	Around the World with the Chipmunks	1961	25.00
— Second cover features the "cartoon" Chipmunks on and near a camel			
❏ LST-7170 [S]	Around the World with the Chipmunks	1960	50.00
— Original covers have "realistic" chipmunks on and near a plane.			
❏ LST-7170 [S]	Around the World with the Chipmunks	1960	30.00
— Second cover features the "cartoon" Chipmunks on and near a camel			

Number	Title	Yr	NM
❏ LRP-3256 [M]	Christmas with the Chipmunks	1962	30.00
❏ LST-7256 [S]	Christmas with the Chipmunks	1962	30.00
❏ LM-1070	Christmas with the Chipmunks	1980	10.00
— Reissue with two tracks omitted			
❏ LRP-3334 [M]	Christmas with the Chipmunks, Vol. 2	1963	30.00
❏ LST-7334 [S]	Christmas with the Chipmunks, Vol. 2	1963	30.00
❏ LRP-3132 [M]	Let's All Sing with the Chipmunks	1959	60.00
— Red vinyl			
❏ LRP-3132 [M]	Let's All Sing with the Chipmunks	1959	30.00
— Black vinyl; original cover features "realistic" chipmunks and no reference to "The Alvin Show"			
❏ LRP-3132 [M]	Let's All Sing with the Chipmunks	1961	25.00
— Second cover features the "cartoon" Chipmunks and a reference to "The Alvin Show"			
❏ LST-7132 [S]	Let's All Sing with the Chipmunks	1959	80.00
— Red vinyl			
❏ LST-7132 [S]	Let's All Sing with the Chipmunks	1959	40.00
— Black vinyl; original cover features "realistic" chipmunks and no reference to "The Alvin Show"			
❏ LST-7132 [S]	Let's All Sing with the Chipmunks	1961	30.00
— Second cover features the "cartoon" Chipmunks and a reference to "The Alvin Show"			
❏ LRP-3159 [M]	Sing Again with the Chipmunks	1960	40.00
— Original cover features "realistic" chipmunks			
❏ LRP-3159 [M]	Sing Again with the Chipmunks	1961	25.00
— Second cover features the "cartoon" Chipmunks			
❏ LST-7159 [S]	Sing Again with the Chipmunks	1960	50.00
— Original cover features "realistic" chipmunks			
❏ LST-7159 [S]	Sing Again with the Chipmunks	1961	30.00
— Second cover features the "cartoon" Chipmunks			
❏ LRP-3209 [M]	The Alvin Show	1961	30.00
❏ LST-7209 [S]	The Alvin Show	1961	30.00
❏ LRP-3424 [M]	The Chipmunks A-Go-Go	1965	25.00
❏ LST-7424 [S]	The Chipmunks A-Go-Go	1965	30.00
❏ LRP-3388 [M]	The Chipmunks Sing the Beatles Hits	1964	30.00
❏ LST-7388 [S]	The Chipmunks Sing the Beatles Hits	1964	40.00
❏ LRP-3405 [M]	The Chipmunks Sing with Children	1965	25.00
❏ LST-7405 [S]	The Chipmunks Sing with Children	1965	30.00
❏ LRP-3229 [M]	The Chipmunks Songbook	1962	30.00
❏ LST-7229 [S]	The Chipmunks Songbook	1962	30.00
MISTLETOE			
❏ MLP-1216	Christmas with the Chipmunks	197?	10.00
— Reissue of Liberty LST-7256			
❏ MLP-1217	Christmas with the Chipmunks, Vol. 2	197?	10.00
— Reissue of Liberty LST-7334			
PICKWICK			
❏ SPC-1034	Christmas with the Chipmunks	1980	12.00
❏ SPC-1035	The Twelve Days of Christmas with The Chipmunks	1980	12.00
— Reissue of "Christmas with the Chipmunks, Vol. 2"			
SUNSET			
❏ LST-7334 [S]	Christmas with the Chipmunks, Vol. 2	1968	25.00
— Budget-line reissue of Liberty LST-7334			
❏ LST-7424 [S]	The Chipmunks A-Go-Go	196?	18.00
— Same cover as Liberty 7424, but with "SUNSET" sticker at upper right			
UNITED ARTISTS			
❏ UA-LA352-E2	Christmas with the Chipmunks	1974	25.00
— Entire contents of both original Liberty LPs			
CHIPMUNKS, THE			
EXCELSIOR			
❏ X-6008	Chipmunk Punk	1980	18.00
RCA VICTOR			
❏ AQL1-4041	A Chipmunk Christmas	1981	18.00
— With booklet			
❏ AFL1-4304	Chipmunk Rock	1982	12.00
❏ AFL1-4376	The Chipmunks Go Hollywood	1983	12.00
❏ AFL1-4027	Urban Chipmunk	1981	12.00
CHITTISON, HERMAN			
AUDIOPHILE			
❏ AP-39 [M]	The Melody Lingers On	1986	12.00
COLUMBIA			
❏ CL6134 [10]	Herman Chittison	1950	50.00
❏ CL6182 [10]	Herman Chittison Trio	1951	50.00

Number	Title	Yr	NM
ROYALE			
❏ 1824 [10]	Cocktail Time	195?	40.00
CHOATES, HARRY			
D			
❏ 7000 [M]	Jole Blon	196?	40.00
CHOCO AND HIS MALIMBA DRUM RHYTHMS			
AUDIO FIDELITY			
❏ AFLP-2102 [M]	African Latin Voodoo Drums	1962	30.00
❏ AFSD-6102 [S]	African Latin Voodoo Drums	1962	35.00
CHOCOLATE WATCH BAND, THE			
RHINO			
❏ RNLP-108	The Best of the Chocolate Watch Band	1983	15.00
TOWER			
❏ T5096 [M]	No Way Out	1967	500.00
❏ ST5096 [S]	No Way Out	1967	500.00
❏ ST5153	One Step Beyond	1969	250.00
❏ T5106 [M]	The Inner Mystique	1968	500.00
❏ ST5106 [S]	The Inner Mystique	1968	500.00
CHORDETTES, THE			
BARNABY			
❏ BR-4003	All the Very Best of the Chordettes	1976	15.00
CADENCE			
❏ CLP-3020 [M]	Barbershop Harmony	1958	40.00
❏ CLP-1002 [10]	Close Harmony	1955	50.00
❏ CLP-3056 [M]	Never on Sunday	1962	25.00
❏ CLP-25056 [S]	Never on Sunday	1962	30.00
❏ CLP-3001 [M]	The Chordettes	1957	40.00
COLUMBIA			
❏ CL6218 [10]	Harmony Encores	1952	50.00
❏ CL6111 [10]	Harmony Time	1950	50.00
❏ CL6170 [10]	Harmony Time, Vol. 2	1951	50.00
❏ CL956 [M]	Listen	1955	50.00
❏ CL2519 [10]	The Chordettes	1955	40.00
❏ CL6285 [10]	Your Requests	1953	50.00
HARMONY			
❏ HL7164 [M]	The Chordettes	196?	18.00
RHINO			
❏ R1-70849	The Best of the Chordettes	1989	15.00
CHOSEN FEW, THE			
MAPLE			
❏ 6000	Takin' All the Love I Can	196?	25.00
RCA VICTOR			
❏ LSP-4242	The Chosen Few	1969	25.00
CHRISTIAN, CHARLIE			
COLUMBIA			
❏ G30779	Solo Flight -- The Genius of Charlie Christian	1972	25.00
COLUMBIA JAZZ MASTERPIECES			
❏ CJ40846	Charlie Christian -- The Genius of the Electric Guitar	1986	18.00
COUNTERPOINT			
❏ 548 [M]	The Harlem Jazz Scene 1941	195?	60.00
ESOTERIC			
❏ ESJ-1 [10]	Jazz Immortal	1951	200.00
— Red vinyl			
❏ ES-548 [M]	The Harlem Jazz Scene 1941	1956	80.00
EVEREST ARCHIVE OF FOLK & JAZZ			
❏ 219	Charlie Christian	197?	12.00
CHRISTIAN DEATH			
CLEOPATRA			
❏ 3296 [B]	Sleepless Nights Live 1990		25.00
EPITAPH			
❏ 80103-1LP [B]	Only Theatre of Pain	1997	25.00
FRONTIER			
❏ FLP1007 [B]	Only Theatre of Pain	1982	100.00
— with double sided insert			
FUTURE			
❏ FL2LP [B]	Only Theatre of Pain	1983	80.00
— with double sided black insert			
IMPORTANT			
❏ IRD014 [B]	Ashes	1985	50.00
— includes 16 page booklet			
LSR			
❏ NOS1055-1LP [B]	Ashes	1989	30.00
❏ NOS1054-1LP [B]	Catastrophe Ballet	1989	30.00
— includes eight page booklet			
NORMAL			
❏ 15 [B]	Ashes	1986	40.00
— includes 12 page booklet			
❏ 15 [B]	Ashes	1988	40.00

Number	Title	Yr	NM
—gatefold sleeve			
❏ 84 [B]	Deathwish	1990	30.00
❏ 56 [B]	Only Theatre of Pain	1987	30.00

CHRISTIE, LOU

51 WEST

❏ P18260	Lou Christie Does Detroit	1983	18.00

BUDDAH

❏ BDS-5052	I'm Gonna Make You Mine	1969	18.00
❏ BDS-5073	Paint America Love	1971	18.00

CO & CE

❏ LP-1231 [M]	Lou Christie Strikes Back	1966	40.00
—The front cover and spine use this title, but the back cover and label use "Lou Christie Strikes Again			

COLPIX

❏ CP-4001 [M]	Lou Christie Strikes Again	1966	30.00
❏ SCP-4001 [S]	Lou Christie Strikes Again	1966	50.00

MGM

❏ E-4360 [M]	Lightnin' Strikes	1966	18.00
❏ SE-4360 [S]	Lightnin' Strikes	1966	25.00
❏ E-4394 [M]	Painter of Hits	1966	18.00
❏ SE-4394 [S]	Painter of Hits	1966	25.00

RHINO

❏ R1-70246	EnLightnin'Ment: The Best of Lou Christie	1988	15.00

ROULETTE

❏ R25208 [M]	Lou Christie	1963	50.00
—Blue background on front cover			
❏ R25208 [M]	Lou Christie	1963	40.00
—White wall in background on front cover			
❏ SR25208 [S]	Lou Christie	1963	80.00
—Blue background on front cover			
❏ SR25208 [S]	Lou Christie	1963	60.00
—White wall in background on front cover			
❏ R25332 [M]	Lou Christie Strikes Again	1966	30.00
❏ SR25332 [S]	Lou Christie Strikes Again	1966	30.00

SPIN-O-RAMA

❏ M-173 [M]	Starring Lou Christie and the Classics	1966	25.00
❏ S-173 [R]	Starring Lou Christie and the Classics	1966	15.00
— The above LP also includes other artists			

THREE BROTHERS

❏ THB-2000	Lou Christie	1973	25.00

CHRISTMAS REVELS, THE

REVELS

❏ RC1087	Christmas Day in the Morning: A Revels Celebration of the Winter Solstice	1987	15.00
❏ RC1078	The Christmas Revels	1978	15.00
—Various spoken and musical bits by a collection of artists under one umbrella			
❏ RC1082	Wassail! Wassail!	1982	15.00

CHRISTOPHER, JORDAN

UNITED ARTISTS

❏ UAL3479 [M]	Jordan Christopher Has the Knack	1966	25.00
❏ UAS6479 [S]	Jordan Christopher Has the Knack	1966	30.00

CHRISTOPHER (1)

BELL

❏ 1203	R.P.M.	1970	25.00

CHRISTOPHER (2)

CHRIS-TEE

❏ 12411	What'cha Gonna Do	1969	3000.00
—100 copies were pressed; VG value 1500; VG+ value 2250			

CHRISTOPHER (3)

METROMEDIA

❏ 1024	Christopher	1970	400.00

CHRISTY, JUNE

CAPITOL

❏ T1308 [M]	Ballads for Night People	1959	30.00
—Black label with colorband, Capitol logo at left			
❏ ST1308 [S]	Ballads for Night People	1959	40.00
—Black label with colorband, Capitol logo at left			
❏ T1845 [M]	Big Band Specials	1962	25.00
❏ ST1845 [S]	Big Band Specials	1962	30.00
❏ T1586 [M]	Do-Re-Mi	1961	40.00
—Black label with colorband, Capitol logo at left			
❏ ST1586 [S]	Do-Re-Mi	1961	50.00
—Black label with colorband, Capitol logo at left			
❏ T656 [M]	Duets	1955	40.00
—Turquoise label			
❏ T902 [M]	Gone for the Day	1957	40.00
—Turquoise label			
❏ T1202 [M]	June Christy Recalls Those Kenton Days	1959	30.00
—Black label with colorband, Capitol logo at left			

Number	Title	Yr	NM
❏ ST1202 [S]	June Christy Recalls Those Kenton Days	1959	40.00
—Black label with colorband, Capitol logo at left			
❏ T833 [M]	June -- Fair and Warmer!	1957	40.00
—Turquoise label			
❏ T1076 [M]	June's Got Rhythm	1958	30.00
—Black label with colorband, Capitol logo at left			
❏ ST1076 [S]	June's Got Rhythm	1958	40.00
—Black label with colorband, Capitol logo at left			
❏ T1498 [M]	Off Beat	1961	40.00
—Black label with colorband, Capitol logo at left			
❏ ST1498 [S]	Off Beat	1961	50.00
—Black label with colorband, Capitol logo at left			
❏ TBO1327 [M]	Road Show	1960	30.00
—Black label with colorband, Capitol logo at left			
❏ STBO1327 [S]	Road Show	1960	40.00
—Black label with colorband, Capitol logo at left			
❏ T2410 [M]	Something Broadway, Something Latin	1965	30.00
❏ ST2410 [S]	Something Broadway, Something Latin	1965	30.00
❏ H516 [10]	Something Cool	1954	80.00
❏ T516 [M]	Something Cool	1955	50.00
—Turquoise label; blue-green cover with June's eyes closed			
❏ T516 [M]	Something Cool	1959	30.00
—Black label with colorband, logo at left; with original blue-green cover with June's eyes closed			
❏ SM-516 [S]	Something Cool	197?	12.00
❏ ST516 [S]	Something Cool	1960	18.00
—Re-recording of the original mono LP; issued with different cover than original mono LP, in color with June's eyes open; black label, Capitol logo at left			
❏ T516 [M]	Something Cool	1962	18.00
—Black label with colorband, logo at top; issued with different cover than original mono LP, in color with June's eyes open			
❏ T1605 [M]	That Time of Year	1961	40.00
❏ ST1605 [S]	That Time of Year	1961	50.00
—Black label with colorband, Capitol logo at left			
❏ T1693 [M]	The Best of June Christy	1962	30.00
—Black label with colorband			
❏ ST1693 [S]	The Best of June Christy	1962	30.00
—Black logo with colorband			
❏ SM-11961	The Best of June Christy	1979	12.00
❏ T1398 [M]	The Cool School	1960	30.00
—Black label with colorband, Capitol logo at left			
❏ ST1398 [S]	The Cool School	1960	40.00
—Black label with colorband, Capitol logo at left			
❏ T1953 [M]	The Intimate June Christy	1963	25.00
❏ ST1953 [S]	The Intimate June Christy	1963	30.00
❏ T725 [M]	The Misty Miss Christy	1956	40.00
—Turquoise label			
❏ T1114 [M]	The Song Is June!	1959	30.00
—Black label with colorband, Capitol logo at left			
❏ ST1114 [S]	The Song Is June!	1959	40.00
—Black label with colorband, Capitol logo at left			
❏ T1006 [M]	This Is June Christy!	1958	40.00
—Turquoise label			

DISCOVERY

❏ DS-836	Impromptu	1982	15.00
❏ DS-911	Interlude	1986	12.00
❏ DS-919	The Misty Miss Christy	1986	12.00

HINDSIGHT

❏ HSR-219	June Christy, Vol. 1	1986	12.00
❏ HSR-235	June Christy, Vol. 2	1988	12.00

PAUSA

❏ 9039	Big Band Specials	198?	12.00

CHROME

CLEOPATRA

❏ 7287 [B]	3rd From The Sun		25.00
❏ 2075 [B]	Alien Soundtracks		25.00
❏ CLP3239 [B]	Blood on the Moon	2008	40.00
—US release of 1981 UK LP			
❏ 7286 [B]	Half Machine Lip Moves		25.00
❏ CLP1310 [B]	Read Only Memory	2014	25.00
❏ CLP3026 [B]	Red Exposure	2008	40.00
—US reissue of 1980 UK release on Beggars Banquet			
❏ CLP1000 [B]	The Visitation	2013	30.00

SIREN RECORDS

❏ DE777 [B]	3rd from The Sun	1982	80.00
❏ DE21-22SEC-L [B]	Alien Soundtracks	1977	100.00
❏ DE333SEC [B]	Half Machine Lip Moves	1979	100.00
❏ DE444 [B]	Read Only Memory	1979	100.00
❏ DE1000 [B]	The Visitation	1976	100.00

TOUCH & GO

❏ T&G057 [B]	Alien Soundtracks	1990	30.00
❏ TG058 [B]	Half Machine Lip Moves	1991	25.00

CHRYSALIS

MGM

❏ SE-4547	Definition	1968	30.00
❏ SE-4547 [Mono]	Definition	1968	75.00

CHURCH, THE

ARISTA

❏ AL8579	Gold Afternoon Fix	1990	12.00
❏ R171667	Gold Afternoon Fix	1990	15.00
—BMG Direct Marketing edition			

Number	Title	Yr	NM
❏ AL8567	Heyday	1988	12.00
—Reissue of Warner Bros. 25370			
❏ AL8563	Of Skins and Heart	1988	12.00
—First U.S. issue of first Australian album			
❏ AL8566	Remote Luxury	1988	12.00
—Reissue of Warner Bros. 25152			
❏ AL8565	Seance	1988	12.00
—First U.S. issue of third Australian album			
❏ 18727-1	Sometime Anywhere	1994	18.00
❏ R173703	Starfish	1988	15.00
—BMG Direct Marketing edition			
❏ AL8521	Starfish	1988	12.00
❏ ADP9713 [DJ]	Sum of the Parts	1988	40.00
—Interviews and live acoustic tracks			
❏ ADP9713 [DJ]	Sum of the Parts	1988	40.00
—Interviews and live acoustic tracks			
❏ AL8564	The Blurred Crusade	1988	12.00
—First U.S. issue of second Australian album			

CAPITOL

❏ ST-12193	The Church	1982	18.00

WARNER BROS.

❏ 25370	Heyday	1985	18.00
❏ 25152	Remote Luxury	1984	18.00

CINDERELLA

MERCURY

❏ 848018-1	Heartbreak Station	1990	15.00
❏ 834612-1	Long Cold Winter	1988	10.00
❏ 830076-1	Night Songs	1986	10.00
❏ 832255-1 [PD]	Night Songs	1987	25.00
—Picture disc in plastic sleeve with sticker			
❏ 522947-1	Still Climbing	1995	15.00
—Numbered limited edition on clear vinyl; CD version issued in late 1994			

CIRCLE

ECM

❏ 1018/19 ST	Paris Concert	197?	25.00
—Original issue, made in Germany?			
❏ ECM2-1018	Paris Concert	1972	18.00
—Distributed by Polydor			

CIRCUS

METROMEDIA

❏ 7401	Circus	1973	75.00

CIRCUS MAXIMUS

VANGUARD

❏ VRS-9260 [M]	Circus Maximus	1967	30.00
❏ VSD-79260 [S]	Circus Maximus	1967	30.00
❏ VSD-79274	Neverland Revisited	1968	30.00

CIRILLO, WALLY/BOBBY SCOTT

SAVOY

❏ MG-15055 [10]	Cirillo and Scott	1955	80.00

CISSEL, CHUCK

ARISTA

❏ AL9581	If I Had the Chance	1982	30.00
❏ AB4257	Just for You	1979	18.00

CITIZEN KING

WARNER BROS.

❏ PRO-A-9653 [DJ]	Mobile Estates	1999	15.00
—Promo version in generic white sleeve with sticker			
❏ 47023	Mobile Estates	1999	15.00
—Stock version in full-color jacket			

CITY, THE

ODE

❏ Z1244012	Now That Everything's Been Said	1968	80.00
—Color front cover			
❏ Z1244012	Now That Everything's Been Said	1971	15.00
—Black & white front cover			

CITY BOY

ATLANTIC

❏ SD19285	Heads Are Rolling	1980	12.00
❏ SD19249	The Day the Earth Caught Fire	1979	12.00

MERCURY

❏ SRM-1-3737	Book Early	1978	12.00
❏ SRM-1-1098	City Boy	1976	15.00
❏ SRM-1-1121	Dinner at the Ritz	1977	15.00
❏ SRM-1-1182 [B]	Young Men Gone West	1977	15.00

CIVIL WARS, THE

COLUMBIA

❏ C-375352 [B]	Barton Hollow	2013	40.00
❏ 88843 04141 [B]	Live at Eddie's Attic	2014	30.00
❏ 88883 738501 [B]	The Civil Wars	2013	40.00

Number	Title	Yr	NM

SENSIBILITY

	A Place at the Table (with T-Bone Burnett)	2012	40.00
796745099323 [B]			
[B]	Barton Hollow	2011	60.00
001 [B]	Unplugged on VH1	2013	40.00

CLANTON, JIMMY

ACE

1008 [M]	Jimmy's Blue	1960	40.00
1007 [M]	Jimmy's Happy	1960	40.00
DLP-100 [M]	Jimmy's Happy/Jimmy's Blue	1960	400.00

— *The "Happy" album is red vinyl, the "Blue" album is blue*

| DLP-100 [M] | Jimmy's Happy/Jimmy's Blue | 1960 | 150.00 |

— *Black vinyl; also released as two separate albums, 1007 and 1008*

DLP-100	Jimmy's Happy/Jimmy's Blue Poster	1960	80.00
1001 [M]	Just a Dream	1959	120.00
1011 [M]	My Best to You	1960	100.00
1014 [M]	Teenage Millionaire	1961	100.00
1026 [M]	Venus in Blue Jeans	1962	100.00

PHILIPS

| PHM200154 [M] | The Best of Jimmy Clanton | 1964 | 30.00 |
| PHS600154 [S] | The Best of Jimmy Clanton | 1964 | 30.00 |

CLANTON, JIMMY/BRISTOW HOOPER

DESIGN

| DLP-176 [M] | Jimmy Clanton and Bristow Hooper | 196? | 18.00 |
| DLS-176 [R] | Jimmy Clanton and Bristow Hooper | 196? | 12.00 |

CLAP

NOVA SOL

| 1001 | Have You Reached Yet? | 1972 | 1000.00 |

CLAPTON, ERIC

ATCO

| -0 [DJ] | Eric Clapton | 1970 | 100.00 |

— *Mono pressing is promo only*

| 33-329 [DJ] | Eric Clapton | 1970 | 100.00 |

— *Mono pressing is promo only*

| SD 33-329 | Eric Clapton | 1970 | 25.00 |
| SD 33-329 | Eric Clapton | 1970 | 200.00 |

— *Odd pressing with alternate takes of "After Midnight" and "Blues Power" plus remixes of other tracks. Look for "CTH" in trail-off area.*

| SD 2-803 | History of Eric Clapton | 1972 | 25.00 |

— *Contains tracks from the Yardbirds, John Mayall's Bluesbreakers, Cream, Blind Faith, and solo records*

DUCK

25476	August	1986	12.00
25166	Behind the Sun	1985	12.00
23773	Money and Cigarettes	1983	12.00

MOBILE FIDELITY

| 1-220 | Eric Clapton | 1995 | 30.00 |

— *Audiophile vinyl*

NAUTILUS

| NR-32 | Just One Night | 1981 | 150.00 |

— *Audiophile vinyl*

POLYDOR

| 1775318 | 461 Ocean Boulevard | 2008 | 25.00 |
| 24-5526 | Clapton | 1973 | 18.00 |

— *Compiles tracks from his first solo album plus Derek and the Dominos*

| 835261-1 | Crossroads | 1988 | 50.00 |

— *Box set; contains material from all phases of his career*

| PD3503 | Eric Clapton at His Best | 1972 | 25.00 |

— *Compiles tracks from his first solo album plus Derek and the Dominos*

| SKBO-94837 | Eric Clapton at His Best | 1972 | 30.00 |

— *Capitol Record Club edition*

| 8171881 | Slowhand | 2008 | 25.00 |

— *Audiophile vinyl*

REPRISE

| W1-26420 | 24 Nights | 1991 | 30.00 |

— *Vinyl copies released only through Columbia House*

45735-1 [B]	From the Cradle		30.00
26074	Journeyman	1989	15.00
48423-1	Me and Mr. Johnson	2004	25.00

— *Regular edition on 140-gram vinyl; distributed by Classic Records*

| 48423-1 SV | Me and Mr. Johnson | 2004 | 30.00 |

— *200-gram vinyl edition, distributed by Classic Records*

RHINO

| R1537929 [B] | Crossroads Guitar Festival 2013 | 2014 | 30.00 |

RSO

| SO4801 | 461 Ocean Boulevard | 1974 | 18.00 |

— *With "Give Me Strength"*

| SO4801 [B] | 461 Ocean Boulevard | 1974 | 30.00 |

— *With "Better Make It Through the Day*

| QD4801 [Q] | 461 Ocean Boulevard | 1974 | 40.00 |
| RS-1-3023 | 461 Ocean Boulevard | 1977 | 15.00 |

— *Reissue of RSO 4801*

Number	Title	Yr	NM

| 811697-1 | 461 Ocean Boulevard | 198? | 10.00 |

— *Reissue of RSO 3023*

| RX-1-3095 | Another Ticket | 1981 | 12.00 |
| 827579-1 | Another Ticket | 1985 | 10.00 |

— *Reissue of RSO 3095*

RS-1-3039	Backless	1978	15.00
SO4809	E.C. Was Here	1975	15.00
RS-1-3008	Eric Clapton	1977	15.00

— *Reissue of Atco LP of the same name*

| 825093-1 | Eric Clapton | 1984 | 10.00 |

— *Reissue of RSO 3008*

SO877	Eric Clapton's Rainbow Concert	1973	18.00
RS-2-4202	Just One Night	1980	18.00
825391-1	Just One Night	1984	12.00

— *Reissue of RSO 4202*

| 1009 [DJ] | Limited Backless | 1978 | 40.00 |

— *White vinyl promo*

| RPO-1009 [DJ] | Limited Backless | 1978 | 50.00 |

— *White vinyl promo*

| RS-1-3004 | No Reason to Cry | 1976 | 15.00 |
| 35 [DJ] | Slowhand | 1977 | 30.00 |

— *White vinyl promo*

| RS-1-3030 [B] | Slowhand | 1977 | 15.00 |
| PRO 035 [DJ] | Slowhand | 1977 | 40.00 |

— *White vinyl promo sampler*

| 823276-1 | Slowhand | 1983 | 10.00 |

— *Reissue of RSO 3030*

SO4806	There's One in Every Crowd	1975	15.00
QD4806 [Q]	There's One in Every Crowd	1975	35.00
RS-1-3099	Time Pieces/The Best of Eric Clapton	1982	12.00
825382-1	Time Pieces/The Best of Eric Clapton	1984	10.00

— *Reissue of RSO 3099*

CLARINET SUMMIT

INDIA NAVIGATION

| IN-1062 | In Concert at the Public Theater, Vol. 1 | 1985 | 15.00 |
| IN-1067 | In Concert at the Public Theater, Vol. 2 | 1985 | 15.00 |

CLARK, ALICE

MAINSTREAM

| MRL-362 | Alice Clark | 1972 | 25.00 |

CLARK, CHRIS

MOTOWN

| M-664 [M] | Soul Sounds | 1967 | 50.00 |
| MS-664 [S] | Soul Sounds | 1967 | 60.00 |

WEED

| 801 | C.C. Rides Again | 1969 | 80.00 |

CLARK, CLAUDINE

CHANCELLOR

| CHL-5029 [M] | Party Lights | 1962 | 250.00 |

CLARK, DAVE, FIVE

CORTLEIGH

| C-1073 [M] | The Dave Clark Five with Ricky Astor | 1964 | 30.00 |

— *With two early DC5 tracks and assorted other stuff by other artists*

| CS-1073 [R] | The Dave Clark Five with Ricky Astor | 1964 | 18.00 |

— *With two early DC5 tracks and assorted other stuff by other artists*

CROWN

| CLP-5473 [M] | Chaquita/In Your Heart | 1964 | 30.00 |

— *With two early DC5 tracks and assorted other stuff by other artists*

| CST-473 [R] | Chaquita/In Your Heart | 1964 | 18.00 |

— *With two early DC5 tracks and assorted other stuff by other artists*

| CLP-5400 [M] | The Dave Clark Five with the Playbacks | 1964 | 30.00 |

— *With two early DC5 tracks and assorted other stuff by other artists*

| CST-400 [R] | The Dave Clark Five with the Playbacks | 1964 | 18.00 |

— *With two early DC5 tracks and assorted other stuff by other artists*

| CST-644 [R] | The Dave Clark Five with the Playbacks | 196? | 15.00 |

— *Reissue*

CUSTOM

| CS1098 [R] | The Dave Clark Five with the Playbacks | 196? | 15.00 |

— *Reissue*

EPIC

LN24236 [M]	5 by 5	1967	30.00
BN26236 [S]	5 by 5	1967	40.00
LN24117 [M]	American Tour	1964	40.00
BN26117 [R]	American Tour	1964	30.00
LN24128 [M]	Coast to Coast	1965	40.00
BN26128 [R]	Coast to Coast	1965	30.00
LN24354 [M]	Everybody Knows	1968	30.00
BN26354 [S]	Everybody Knows	1968	40.00

Number	Title	Yr	NM

| LN24093 [M] | Glad All Over | 1964 | 80.00 |

— *Group photo, no instruments*

| BN26093 [R] | Glad All Over | 1964 | 50.00 |

— *Group photo, no instruments*

| LN24093 [M] | Glad All Over | 1964 | 40.00 |

— *Group photo with instruments*

| BN26093 [R] | Glad All Over | 1964 | 30.00 |

— *Group photo with instruments*

KEG33459 [M]	Glad All Over Again	1975	50.00
LN24162 [M]	Having a Wild Weekend	1965	40.00
BN26162 [R]	Having a Wild Weekend	1965	30.00
LN24178 [M]	I Like It Like That	1965	40.00
BN26178 [R]	I Like It Like That	1965	30.00
LN24221 [M]	More Greatest Hits	1966	30.00
BN26221 [R]	More Greatest Hits	1966	25.00
LN24212 [M]	Satisfied with You	1966	30.00
BN26212 [R]	Satisfied with You	1966	30.00
EG30434 [S]	The Dave Clark Five	1971	100.00

— *Twenty hits and near-hits, all in true stereo! Yellow label.*

| EG30434 [S] | The Dave Clark Five | 1973 | 80.00 |

— *Twenty hits and near-hits, all in true stereo! Orange label.*

XEM0 [DJ]	The Dave Clark Five Interview	1964	600.00
	The Dave Clark Five Interview	1964	600.00
XEM77238/9 [DJ]			
LN24104 [M]	The Dave Clark Five Return	1964	40.00
BN26104 [R]	The Dave Clark Five Return	1964	30.00
LN24185 [M]	The Dave Clark Five's Greatest Hits	1966	30.00
BN26185 [R]	The Dave Clark Five's Greatest Hits	1966	25.00

— *Yellow label*

| BN26185 [R] | The Dave Clark Five's Greatest Hits | 1973 | 40.00 |

— *Orange label*

LN24198 [M]	Try Too Hard	1966	30.00
BN26198 [R]	Try Too Hard	1966	30.00
LN24139 [M]	Weekend in London	1965	40.00
BN26139 [R]	Weekend in London	1965	30.00
LN24312 [M]	You Got What It Takes	1967	30.00
BN26312 [S]	You Got What It Takes	1967	40.00

CLARK, DEE

ABNER

LP-2000 [M]	Dee Clark	1959	120.00
SR-2000 [S]	Dee Clark	1959	350.00
LP-2002 [M]	How About That	1960	80.00
SR-2002 [S]	How About That	1960	120.00

SOLID SMOKE

| 8026 | His Best Recordings | 1983 | 12.00 |

SUNSET

| SUS-5217 | Wondering | 1968 | 15.00 |

VEE JAY

LP-1037 [M]	Hold On, It's Dee Clark	1961	50.00
SR-1037 [S]	Hold On, It's Dee Clark	1961	100.00
LP-1047 [M]	The Best of Dee Clark	1964	50.00
SR-1047 [S]	The Best of Dee Clark	1964	100.00
VJLP-1047	The Best of Dee Clark	1986	15.00

— *Authorized reissue*

| LP-1019 [M] | You're Looking Good | 1960 | 50.00 |

CLARK, DOTTIE

MAINSTREAM

| 56006 [M] | I'm Lost | 1966 | 25.00 |
| S-6006 [S] | I'm Lost | 1966 | 30.00 |

CLARK, DOUG, AND THE HOT NUTS

GROSS

108	Freak Out	196?	30.00
107	Hell Night	196?	30.00
103	Homecoming	196?	30.00
101	Nuts to You	196?	30.00
102	On Campus	196?	30.00
105	Panty Raid	196?	30.00
104	Rush Week	1967	30.00
106	Summer Session	196?	30.00
109	With a Hat On	196?	30.00

CLARK, GENE

4 MEN WITH BEARDS

| 4M116LP [B] | Gene Clark (White Light) | | 25.00 |
| 4M200LP [B] | No Other | | 25.00 |

A&M

| SP-4292 | White Light | 1971 | 18.00 |

ASYLUM

| 7E-1016 | No Other | 1974 | 40.00 |

COLUMBIA

KC31123	Early L.A. Sessions	1972	18.00
CL2618 [M]	Gene Clark with the Gosdin Brothers	1967	30.00
CS9418 [S]	Gene Clark with the Gosdin Brothers	1967	50.00

RSO

| RS-1-3011 | Two Sides to Every Story | 1976 | 25.00 |

SUNDAZED

| LP5062 | Gene Clark with the Gosdin Brothers | 2000 | 18.00 |

— *Reissue of Columbia LP*

TAKOMA

| TAK-7112 | Firebyrd | 1984 | 12.00 |

Number	Title	Yr	NM

CLARK, GUY

4 MEN WITH BEARDS

Number	Title	Yr	NM
❏ 4M236 [B]	Old No. 1	2014	30.00

RCA VICTOR

❏ APL1-1303	Old No. 1	1976	25.00
❏ AHL1-1303	Old No. 1	198?	12.00

— *Reissue with new prefix*

❏ APL1-1944	Texas Cookin'	1976	25.00

SUGAR HILL

❏ SH-1025	Old Friends	198?	15.00

WARNER BROS.

❏ 23880	Better Days	1983	15.00
❏ BSK3241	Guy Clark	1978	18.00
❏ WBMS-105 [DJ]	On the Road, Live!	198?	60.00

— *Part of "The Warner Bros. Music Show" series; promo only*

❏ BSK3381	South Coast of Texas	1981	18.00

CLARK, KEN, AND DON ANTHONY

STARDAY

❏ SLP-114 [M]	Fiddlin' Country Style	1959	40.00

CLARK, PETULA

COCA-COLA

❏ 103 [DJ]	Petula Clark Swings the Jingle	1966	150.00
❏ 103 [DJ]	Petula Clark Swings the Jingle	1966	150.00

GNP CRESCENDO

❏ 2069	Live at the Royal Albert Hall	1972	12.00
❏ 2170	The Greatest Hits of Petula Clark	1984	10.00

IMPERIAL

❏ LP-9079 [M]	Pet Clark	1959	50.00
❏ LP-12027 [S]	Pet Clark	1959	80.00
❏ LP-9281 [M]	Uptown with Petula Clark	1965	25.00

— *Reissue of Imperial 9079*

❏ LP-12281 [S]	Uptown with Petula Clark	1965	30.00

— *Reissue of Imperial 12079*

JANGO

❏ 779	Give It a Try	1986	12.00

LAURIE

❏ LLP-2032 [M]	In Love!	1965	18.00
❏ ST-90497 [S]	In Love!	1965	25.00

— *Capitol Record Club edition*

❏ SLP-2032 [S]	In Love!	1965	18.00
❏ T-90497 [M]	In Love!	1965	25.00

— *Capitol Record Club edition*

MGM

❏ SE-4859	Pet Clark Now	1972	12.00

PREMIER

❏ PM-9016 [M]	The English Sound Starring Petula Clark	1965	15.00
❏ PS-9016 [S]	The English Sound Starring Petula Clark	1965	18.00

ROULETTE

❏ 1	Petula	1975	25.00

SUNSET

❏ SUM-1101 [M]	This Is Petula Clark	1965	15.00
❏ SUS-5101 [S]	This Is Petula Clark	1965	18.00

WARNER BROS.

❏ W1673 [M]	Color My World/Who Am I	1967	12.00
❏ WS1673 [S]	Color My World/Who Am I	1967	15.00
❏ W1590 [M]	Downtown	1965	18.00

— *Originals have gray labels*

❏ W1590 [M]	Downtown	1966	15.00

— *Reissues have gold labels*

❏ WS1590 [S]	Downtown	1965	25.00

— *Originals have gray labels*

❏ WS1765	Greatest Hits, Volume I	1968	12.00
❏ ST-91598	Greatest Hits, Volume I	1968	18.00

— *Capitol Record Club edition*

❏ SQBO-93215 [P]	Hits...My Way	1969	30.00

— *Capitol Record Club exclusive; "The Other Man's Grass Is Always Greener" is rechanneled.*

❏ W1645 [M]	I Couldn't Live Without Your Love	1966	12.00
❏ WS1645 [S]	I Couldn't Live Without Your Love	1966	15.00
❏ W1598 [M]	I Know a Place	1965	18.00

— *Originals have gray labels*

❏ W1598 [M]	I Know a Place	1966	15.00

— *Reissues have gold labels*

❏ WS1598 [S]	I Know a Place	1965	25.00

— *Originals have gold labels*

❏ WS1598 [S]	I Know a Place	1968	15.00

— *Green label with "W7" logo in box at top*

❏ WS1823	Just Pet	1969	12.00
❏ WS1862	Memphis	1970	12.00
❏ W1630 [M]	My Love	1966	12.00
❏ WS1630 [S]	My Love	1966	15.00
❏ W1743 [M]	Petula	1968	15.00
❏ WS1743 [S]	Petula	1968	15.00
❏ WS1789	Portrait of Petula	1969	12.00
❏ W1719 [M]	The Other Man's Grass Is Always Greener	1968	15.00

❏ WS1719 [P]	The Other Man's Grass Is Always Greener	1968	15.00

— *The Other Man's Grass Is Always Greener" is rechanneled.*

❏ W1698 [M]	These Are My Songs	1967	12.00
❏ WS1698 [S]	These Are My Songs	1967	15.00
❏ ST-91348 [S]	These Are My Songs	1967	18.00

— *Capitol Record Club edition*

❏ W1608 [M]	The World's Greatest International Hits	1965	18.00

— *Originals have gray labels*

❏ W1608 [M]	The World's Greatest International Hits	1965	15.00

— *Reissues have gold labels*

❏ WS1608 [S]	The World's Greatest International Hits	1965	25.00

— *Originals have gold labels*

❏ WS1865	Warm and Tender (The Song of My Life)	1971	12.00

CLARK, ROY, AND BUCK TRENT

ABC

❏ AY-1084	Banjo Bandits	1978	12.00

ABC DOT

❏ 2015	A Pair of Fives (Banjos, That Is)	1975	12.00

CLARK, ROY

ABC

❏ AB-1053	Labor of Love	1978	12.00

ABC DOT

❏ DOSD-2010	Classic Clark	1974	12.00
❏ DOSD-2041	Heart to Heart	1975	12.00
❏ DO-2099	Hookin' It	1977	12.00

— *Reissue of Record 2 of 2072*

❏ DO-2072	My Music and Me/Vocal & Instrumental	1977	15.00
❏ DOSD-2005	Roy Clark, Family & Friends	1974	12.00
❏ DOSD-2054	Roy Clark In Concert	1976	12.00
❏ DOSD-2030	Roy Clark's Greatest Hits -- Volume 1	1975	12.00
❏ DOSD-2001	Roy Clark/The Entertainer	1974	12.00

CAPITOL

❏ T2031 [M]	Happy to Be Unhappy	1964	25.00
❏ ST2031 [3]	Happy to Be Unhappy	1964	30.00
❏ T2452 [M]	Roy Clark Sings Lonesome Love Ballads	1966	25.00
❏ ST2452 [S]	Roy Clark Sings Lonesome Love Ballads	1966	30.00
❏ SM-11412	So Much to Remember	1975	12.00
❏ T2535 [M]	Stringing Along with the Blues	1966	25.00
❏ ST2535 [S]	Stringing Along with the Blues	1966	30.00
❏ SABB-11264	The Entertainer of the Year	1974	18.00
❏ SKAO-369	The Greatest!	1969	15.00
❏ SM-369	The Greatest!	197?	12.00

— *Reissue with new prefix*

❏ SN-16161	The Greatest!	198?	10.00
❏ T1780 [M]	The Lightning Fingers of Roy Clark	1962	25.00
❏ ST1780 [S]	The Lightning Fingers of Roy Clark	1962	30.00
❏ SN-16227	The Lightning Fingers of Roy Clark	198?	10.00
❏ T2425 [M]	The Roy Clark Guitar Spectacular	1965	25.00
❏ ST2425 [S]	The Roy Clark Guitar Spectacular	1965	30.00
❏ SM-2425	The Roy Clark Guitar Spectacular	197?	12.00

— *Reissue with new prefix*

❏ T1972 [M]	The Tip of My Fingers	1963	25.00
❏ ST1972 [S]	The Tip of My Fingers	1963	30.00
❏ SM-12032	The Tip of My Fingers	1980	10.00

CHURCHILL

❏ 9421	The Roy Clark Show Live from Austin City Limits	1982	12.00
❏ 9425	Turned Loose	1982	12.00

DOT

❏ DOS-26010	Come Live with Me	1973	15.00
❏ DLP-25895	Do You Believe This Roy Clark	1968	15.00
❏ DLP-25980	I Never Picked Cotton	1970	15.00
❏ DOS-25997	Roy Clark Country!	1972	15.00
❏ ST-94463	Roy Clark Country!	1972	18.00

— *Capitol Record Club edition*

❏ DOS-26005	Roy Clark Live!	1972	15.00
❏ DOS-26018	Roy Clark's Family Album	1973	15.00
❏ DOS-26008	Roy Clark/Superpicker	1973	15.00
❏ DOS-25986	The Best of Roy Clark	1971	15.00
❏ DLP-25972	The Everlovin' Soul of Roy Clark	1969	15.00
❏ ST-93117	The Everlovin' Soul of Roy Clark	1969	18.00

— *Capitol Record Club edition with old-style black Dot label with multi-color logo*

❏ DOS-26090	The Incredible Roy Clark	1971	15.00
❏ DOS-25993	The Magnificent Sanctuary Band	1971	15.00
❏ DLP-25977	The Other Side of Roy Clark	1970	15.00
❏ DOS-000112	The Special Talents of Roy Clark	1973	15.00
❏ DLP-25863	Urban, Suburban	1968	15.00
❏ DLP-25953	Yesterday, When I Was Young	1969	15.00

HILLTOP

❏ 6094	He'll Have to Go	1970	12.00
❏ 6154	Honky Tonk	197?	12.00
❏ 6046	Roy Clartk	196?	18.00
❏ 6080	Silver Threads and Golden Needles	1970	12.00
❏ 6135	Take Me As I Am	197?	12.00

MCA

❏ 37131	A Pair of Fives (Banjos, That Is)	198?	10.00
❏ 811	Back to the Country	198?	10.00
❏ 37130	Banjo Bandits	198?	10.00

— *With Buck Trent*

❏ 676	Heart to Heart	1980	10.00
❏ 677	Hookin' It	1980	10.00
❏ 675	Labor of Love	1980	10.00
❏ 3161	Makin' Music	1980	12.00

— *With Gatemouth Brown*

❏ 37142	My Music	198?	10.00
❏ 3189	My Music	1980	12.00
❏ 37132	Roy Clark In Concert	198?	10.00
❏ 37134	Roy Clark Live!	198?	10.00
❏ 27050	Roy Clark's Greatest Hits -- Volume 1	198?	10.00
❏ 679	Roy Clark/Superpicker	198?	10.00
❏ 27015	The Best of Roy Clark	198?	10.00
❏ 678	Yesterday, When I Was Young	198?	10.00

PAIR

❏ PDL2-1088	Country Standard Time	1986	15.00

PICKWICK

❏ PTP-2043	Roy Clark	1973	15.00
❏ PTP-2093	The Entertainer of the Year	1978	15.00

SONGBIRD

❏ 5260	The Last Word in Jesus Is Us	1981	12.00

TOWER

❏ DT5118 [R]	In the Mood	1968	18.00
❏ T5055 [M]	Roy Clark Live	1967	18.00
❏ ST5055 [S]	Roy Clark Live	1967	25.00

WORD

❏ 8654	Roy Clark Sings Gospel	1975	15.00

CLARK, SANFORD

LHI

❏ 12003	Return of the Fool	1968	60.00

CLARK, SONNY

BLUE NOTE

❏ BLP-1588 [M]	Cool Struttin'	1958	3000.00

— *Deep groove" version (deep indentation under label on both sides)*

❏ BLP-1588 [M]	Cool Struttin'	1958	800.00

— *Regular version, W. 63rd St. address on label*

❏ BLP-1588 [M]	Cool Struttin'	1963	100.00

— *New York, USA" address on label*

❏ BST-1588 [S]	Cool Struttin'	1959	1000.00

— *Deep groove" version (deep indentation under label on both sides)*

❏ BST-1588 [S]	Cool Struttin'	1959	60.00

— *Regular version, W. 63rd St. address on label*

❏ BST-1588 [S]	Cool Struttin'	1963	25.00

— *New York, USA" address on label*

❏ BST-81588 [S]	Cool Struttin'	1967	30.00

— *A Division of Liberty Records" on label*

❏ BST-81588 [S]	Cool Struttin'	1970	25.00

— *Mostly black label, "Liberty/UA" at bottom*

❏ BLJ-81588	Cool Struttin'	1987	15.00

— *The Finest in Jazz Since 1939" reissue*

❏ BST-1588-45 [S]	Cool Struttin'	200?	150.00

— *Classic Records box set of four 45 rpm 12-inch records*

❏ BST-1588 [S]	Cool Struttin'	1997	30.00

— *180-gram reissue; distributed by Classic Records*

❏ BLP-1570 [M]	Dial "S" for Sonny	1957	400.00

— *Deep groove" version; W. 63rd St. address on label*

❏ BLP-1570 [M]	Dial "S" for Sonny	1957	200.00

— *Regular version, W. 63rd St. address on label*

❏ BLP-1570 [M]	Dial "S" for Sonny	1963	50.00

— *New York, USA" address on label*

❏ BST-1570 [S]	Dial "S" for Sonny	1959	350.00

— *Deep groove" version; W. 63rd St. address on label*

❏ BST-1570 [S]	Dial "S" for Sonny	1959	120.00

— *Regular version, W. 63rd St. address on label*

❏ BST-1570 [S]	Dial "S" for Sonny	1963	40.00

— *New York, USA" address on label*

❏ BST-81570 [S]	Dial "S" for Sonny	1967	30.00

— *A Division of Liberty Records" on label*

❏ BLP-4091 [M]	Leapin' and Lopin'	1961	200.00

— *W. 63rd St. address on label*

❏ BLP-4091 [M]	Leapin' and Lopin'	1963	100.00

— *New York, USA" address on label*

❏ BST-84091 [S]	Leapin' and Lopin'	1961	150.00

— *W. 63rd St. address on label*

❏ BST-84091 [S]	Leapin' and Lopin'	1963	50.00

— *New York, USA" address on label*

❏ BST-84091 [S]	Leapin' and Lopin'	1967	30.00

— *A Division of Liberty Records" on label*

❏ BLP-1579 [M]	Sonny Clark Trio	1958	800.00

— *Deep groove" version; W. 63rd St. address on label*

Number	Title	Yr	NM
❏ BLP-1579 [M]	Sonny Clark Trio	1958	150.00
—Regular version, W. 63rd St. address on label			
❏ BLP-1579 [M]	Sonny Clark Trio	1963	40.00
—New York, USA" address on label			
❏ BST-1579 [S]	Sonny Clark Trio	1959	250.00
—Deep groove" version; W. 63rd St. address on label			
❏ BST-1579 [S]	Sonny Clark Trio	1959	120.00
—Regular version, W. 63rd St. address on label			
❏ BST-1579 [S]	Sonny Clark Trio	1963	30.00
—New York, USA" address on label			
❏ BST-81579 [S]	Sonny Clark Trio	1967	30.00
—A Division of Liberty Records" on label			
❏ BLP-1576 [M]	Sonny's Crib	1957	3000.00
—Deep groove" version; W. 63rd St. address on label			
❏ BLP-1576 [M]	Sonny's Crib	1957	200.00
—Regular version, W. 63rd St. address on label			
❏ BLP-1576 [M]	Sonny's Crib	1963	50.00
—New York, USA" address on label			
❏ BST-1576 [S]	Sonny's Crib	1959	250.00
—Deep groove" version; W. 63rd St. address on label			
❏ BST-1576 [S]	Sonny's Crib	1959	120.00
—Regular version, W. 63rd St. address on label			
❏ BST-1576 [S]	Sonny's Crib	1963	40.00
—New York, USA" address on label			
❏ BST-81576 [S]	Sonny's Crib	1967	30.00
—A Division of Liberty Records" on label			
TIME			
❏ T-70010 [M]	Sonny Clark Trio	1960	750.00
❏ ST-70010 [S]	Sonny Clark Trio	1960	500.00
❏ 52101 [M]	Sonny Clark Trio	1962	30.00
❏ S-2101 [S]	Sonny Clark Trio	1962	30.00
XANADU			
❏ 121	Memorial Album	1975	18.00

CLARK, YODELING SLIM

Number	Title	Yr	NM
CONTINENTAL			
❏ C-1505 [M]	Cowboy and Yodel Songs	1962	40.00
MASTERSEAL			
❏ MS-57 [M]	Cowboy Songs	1963	30.00
❏ MS-135 [M]	Cowboy Songs Vol. 2	1964	30.00
❏ MS-112 [M]	Songs by Yodeling Slim Clark	1964	30.00
PALOMINO			
❏ 306 [M]	I Feel a Trip Coming On	1966	40.00
❏ 307 [M]	Old Chestnuts	1967	40.00
❏ 311 [M]	The Ballad of Billy Venero	1968	40.00
❏ 310 [M]	Yodeling Slim Clark Happens Again	1967	40.00
❏ 314 [M]	Yodeling Slim Clark's 50th Anniversary Album	1968	50.00
—Gold vinyl			
❏ 301 [M]	Yodeling Slim Clark Sings and Yodels Favorite Montana Slim Songs of the Mountains and Plains, Vol. 1	1966	60.00
❏ 303 [M]	Yodeling Slim Clark Sings and Yodels Favorite Montana Slim Songs of the Mountains and Plains, Vol. 2	1966	40.00
❏ 300 [M]	Yodeling Slim Clark Sings the Legendary Jimmie Rodgers Songs	1966	60.00
PLAYHOUSE			
❏ 2017 [10]	Western Songs and Dances	1954	50.00

CLARK SISTERS, THE

Number	Title	Yr	NM
CORAL			
❏ CRL57290 [M]	Beauty Shop Beat	1960	25.00
❏ CRL757290 [S]	Beauty Shop Beat	1960	30.00
DOT			
❏ DLP-3104 [M]	Sing, Sing, Sing	1957	30.00
❏ DLP-3137 [M]	The Clark Sisters Swing Again	1958	30.00
❏ DLP-25137 [S]	The Clark Sisters Swing Again	1958	30.00

CLARKE, ALLAN

Number	Title	Yr	NM
ASYLUM			
❏ 7E-1056	I've Got Time	1976	12.00
ATLANTIC			
❏ SD19175	I Wasn't Born Yesterday	1978	12.00
ELEKTRA			
❏ 6E-267	Legendary Heroes	1980	12.00
EPIC			
❏ KE31757	My Real Name Is 'Arold	1972	18.00

CLARKE, BUCK

Number	Title	Yr	NM
ARGO			
❏ LP-4007 [M]	Drum Sum	1961	30.00
❏ LPS-4007 [S]	Drum Sum	1961	30.00
❏ LP-4021 [M]	The Buck Clarke Sound	1963	30.00
❏ LPS-4021 [S]	The Buck Clarke Sound	1963	30.00
OFFBEAT			
❏ OLP-3003 [M]	Cool Hands	1960	30.00
❏ OS-93003 [S]	Cool Hands	1960	40.00

CLARKE, KEN

Number	Title	Yr	NM
MGM			
❏ E-205 [10]	Jazz Piano	1953	50.00

CLARKE, KENNY, AND ERNIE WILKINS

Number	Title	Yr	NM
SAVOY			
❏ MG-12007 [M]	Plenty for Kenny	1955	80.00

CLARKE, KENNY

Number	Title	Yr	NM
BLUE NOTE			
❏ BLP4092 [B]	The Golden Eight	1961	125.00
EPIC			
❏ LN3376 [M]	Kenny Clarke Plays Andre Hodeir	1957	40.00
PRESTIGE			
❏ PRST-7605	Paris Bebop Sessions	1969	18.00
SAVOY			
❏ MG-12017 [M]	Bohemia After Dark	1955	80.00
❏ MG-15051 [10]	Kenny Clarke, Vol. 1	195?	200.00
❏ MG-15053 [10]	Kenny Clarke, Vol. 2	195?	200.00
❏ MG-12065 [M]	Klook's Clique	1956	100.00
❏ MG-12006 [M]	Telefunken Blues	1955	80.00
SAVOY JAZZ			
❏ SJL-1111	Kenny Clarke Meets the Detroit Jazzmen	198?	12.00
SOUL NOTE			
❏ SN-1078	Pieces of Time	1983	15.00
SWING			
❏ SW-8411	Kenny Clarke in Paris Vol. 1	1986	12.00

CLARKE, STANLEY, AND GEORGE DUKE

Number	Title	Yr	NM
EPIC			
❏ FE36918	The Clarke/Duke Project	1981	15.00
❏ PE36918	The Clarke/Duke Project	198?	10.00
—Budget-line reissue			
❏ FE38934	The Clarke/Duke Project II	1983	12.00

CLARKE, STANLEY

Number	Title	Yr	NM
EPIC			
❏ FE40040	Find Out!	1985	12.00
❏ FE40275	Hideaway	1986	12.00
❏ PE36974	Journey to Love	1981	10.00
—Reissue of Nemperor 433			
❏ FE38086	Let Me Know You	1982	15.00
❏ JE36506	Rocks, Pebbles and Sand	1980	12.00
❏ PE36975	School Days	1981	10.00
—Reissue of Nemperor 900			
❏ PE36973	Stanley Clarke	1981	10.00
—Reissue of Nemperor 431			
❏ FE38688	Time Exposure	1984	12.00
NEMPEROR			
❏ KZ235680	I Wanna Play for You	1979	18.00
❏ NE433	Journey to Love	1975	15.00
❏ JZ35303	Modern Man	1978	12.00
—Original issue			
❏ PZ35303	Modern Man	1985	10.00
—Reissue with new prefix and bar code			
❏ NE439	School Days	1976	15.00
❏ SD900	School Days	1978	12.00
—Reissue of 439			
❏ NE431	Stanley Clarke	1974	15.00
POLYDOR			
❏ PD-5531	Children of Forever	1973	18.00
❏ 827559-1	Children of Forever	1985	10.00
—Reissue			
PORTRAIT			
❏ FR40923	If This Bass Could Only Talk	1988	12.00

CLARKE-BOLAND BIG BAND, THE

Number	Title	Yr	NM
ATLANTIC			
❏ 1401 [M]	Jazz Is Universal	1963	30.00
❏ SD1401 [S]	Jazz Is Universal	1963	40.00
❏ 1404 [M]	The Clarke-Boland Big Band	1963	30.00
❏ SD1404 [S]	The Clarke-Boland Big Band	1963	40.00
BASF			
❏ 29686	All Smiles	1972	18.00
❏ 25102	The Big Band Sound	1971	25.00
BLACK LION			
❏ 131	At Her Majesty's Pleasure	1974	18.00
BLUE NOTE			
❏ BLP-4092 [M]	The Golden Eight	1961	200.00
—As "Kenny Clarke-Francy Boland & Co."; W. 63rd St. address on label			
❏ BLP-4092 [M]	The Golden Eight	1963	100.00
—As "Kenny Clarke-Francy Boland & Co."; "New York, USA" address on label			
❏ BST-84092 [S]	The Golden Eight	1961	150.00
—As "Kenny Clarke-Francy Boland & Co."; W. 63rd St. address on label			
❏ BST-84092 [S]	The Golden Eight	1963	80.00
—As "Kenny Clarke-Francy Boland & Co."; "New York, USA" address on label			
❏ BST-84092 [S]	The Golden Eight	1967	30.00
—As "Kenny Clarke-Francy Boland & Co."; "A Division of Liberty Records" on label			
COLUMBIA			
❏ CL2314 [M]	Now Hear Our Meanin'	1965	18.00
❏ CS9114 [S]	Now Hear Our Meanin'	1965	25.00

Number	Title	Yr	NM
MUSE			
❏ MR-5056	Open Door	197?	15.00
PAUSA			
❏ 7097	Sax No End	198?	12.00
POLYDOR			
❏ 24-4501	Volcano	1970	18.00
PRESTIGE			
❏ PRST-7634	Fire, Heat, Soul and Guts	1969	18.00
❏ PRST-7760	Latin Kaleidoscope	1970	18.00
❏ PRST-7699	Let's Face the Music	1969	18.00

CLARY, ROBERT

Number	Title	Yr	NM
ATLANTIC			
❏ 8053 [M]	Livin' It Up at the Playboy Club	1961	30.00
❏ SD8053 [S]	Livin' It Up at the Playboy Club	1961	40.00
EPIC			
❏ LN3281 [M]	Hooray for Love	1956	30.00
❏ LN3171 [M]	Meet Robert Clary	1955	30.00
MERCURY			
❏ MG-20367 [M]	Gigi Sung by Robert Clary	1958	25.00
❏ SR-60042 [S]	Gigi Sung by Robert Clary	1958	30.00

CLASH, THE

Number	Title	Yr	NM
EPIC			
❏ PE38540	Black Market Clash	1982	12.00
—12-inch version of 10-inch record			
❏ -0 [DJ]	Combat Rock	1982	40.00
—Camouflage green vinyl promo			
❏ FE37689	Combat Rock	1982	18.00
—First pressings (with custom labels) contain a commercial in the middle of the song "Inoculated City			
❏ AS 99-1592 [PD]	Combat Rock	1982	40.00
—Promo-only picture disc			
❏ AS 99-1595 [DJ]	Combat Rock	1982	30.00
—Camouflage green vinyl promo			
❏ FE37689	Combat Rock	1982	12.00
—Second and later pressings (with standard dark blue labels) delete commercial during "Inoculated City			
❏ FE40017 [B]	Cut the Crap	1985	12.00
❏ JE35543 [DJ]	Give 'Em Enough Rope	1978	30.00
—White label promo; timing strip; back cover has one incorrect song title			
❏ JE35543	Give 'Em Enough Rope	1978	18.00
—Script cover; orange label			
❏ JE35543 [DJ]	Give 'Em Enough Rope	1978	30.00
—White label promo; timing strip; back cover has one incorrect song title			
❏ JE35543	Give 'Em Enough Rope	1978	18.00
—Block letters on cover; orange label			
❏ AS952 [DJ]	If Music Could Talk (Interchords)	1981	30.00
—Promo-only interview record			
❏ AS952 [DJ]	If Music Could Talk (Interchords)	1981	40.00
—Promo-only interview record			
❏ E236238 [DJ]	London Calling	1980	30.00
—White label promo			
❏ E236329 [B]	London Calling	1979	30.00
❏ E236238 [DJ]	London Calling	1980	30.00
—White label promo			
❏ E3X37037	Sandinista!	1981	30.00
❏ AS913 [DJ]	Sandinista Now!	1981	25.00
—Promo-only sampler			
❏ AS913 [DJ]	Sandinista Now!	1981	45.00
—Promo-only sampler			
❏ JE36060	The Clash	1979	18.00
❏ PE36060	The Clash	1979	10.00
—Budget-line reissue; no bonus single			
❏ E244025	The Story of the Clash, Vol. 1	1988	18.00
❏ AS1594 [DJ]	The World According to the Clash	1982	40.00
—Promo-only sampler			
❏ AS1594 [DJ]	The World According to the Clash	1982	40.00
—Promo-only sampler			
EPIC LEGACY			
❏ E353191 [10]	Super Black Market Clash	1993	30.00
EPIC NU-DISK			
❏ 4E36846 [10]	Black Market Clash	1980	30.00

CLASS-AIRES, THE

Number	Title	Yr	NM
HONEY BEE			
❏ (# unknown)0	Tears Start to Fall	195?	300.00

CLASSIC JAZZ ENSEMBLE

Number	Title	Yr	NM
DELMARK			
❏ DE-221	Classic Blues	1989	12.00

CLASSIC JAZZ QUARTET, THE

Number	Title	Yr	NM
JAZZOLOGY			
❏ J-139	The Classic Jazz Quartet	1985	12.00
STOMP OFF			
❏ SOS-1125	MCMLXXXVI	1986	12.00

Number	Title	Yr	NM

CLASSICS IV

ACCORD
| ❑ SN-7107 | Stormy | 1981 | 12.00 |

IMPERIAL
❑ LP-16000	Dennis Yost & the Classics IV/Golden Greats - Volume I	1969	25.00
❑ LP-12407	Mamas and Papas/Soul Train	1969	25.00
❑ LP-12371 [S]	Spooky	1968	25.00
❑ LP-9371 [M]	Spooky	1968	40.00
—Mono has stock copy label inside stereo cover with white "Monaural" sticker			
❑ LP-12429	Traces	1969	25.00

LIBERTY
| ❑ LST-11003 | Song | 1970 | 18.00 |
| ❑ LN-10109 | The Very Best of the Classics IV | 198? | 10.00 |

MGM SOUTH
| ❑ 702 | Dennis Yost and the Classics IV | 1973 | 18.00 |

UNITED ARTISTS
| ❑ UA-LA446-E | The Very Best of the Classics IV | 1975 | 15.00 |

CLAUSON, WILLIAM

CAPITOL
| ❑ T10158 [M] | Concert | 195? | 30.00 |
| ❑ T10176 [M] | Scandinavia | 195? | 30.00 |

RCA VICTOR
| ❑ LPM-1286 [M] | Folk Songs | 1956 | 30.00 |

CLAY, CASSIUS

COLUMBIA
| ❑ CL2093 [M] | I Am the Greatest! | 1963 | 60.00 |
| ❑ CS8893 [S] | I Am the Greatest! | 1963 | 80.00 |

CLAY, JAMES, AND DAVID "FATHEAD" NEWMAN

FANTASY
| ❑ OJC-257 | The Sound of the Wide Open Spaces!!! | 1987 | 15.00 |

RIVERSIDE
❑ RLP 12-327 [M]	The Sound of the Wide Open Spaces!!!	1960	80.00
—Blue label			
❑ RLP-1178 [S]	The Sound of the Wide Open Spaces!!!	1960	80.00
—Black label			

CLAY, JAMES

RIVERSIDE
❑ RLP-349 [M]	A Double Dose of Soul	1961	120.00
—Blue label			
❑ RS-9349 [S]	A Double Dose of Soul	1961	40.00
—Black label			

CLAY, TOM

MOWEST
| ❑ 103 | What the World Needs Now Is Love | 1971 | 18.00 |

CLAYTON, BUCK, AND BUDDY TATE

PRESTIGE
| ❑ 24040 | Kansas City Nights | 1974 | 18.00 |

SWINGVILLE
❑ SVLP-2017 [M]	Buck and Buddy	1961	50.00
—Purple label			
❑ SVLP-2017 [M]	Buck and Buddy	1965	30.00
—Blue label, trident logo at right			
❑ SVLP-2030 [M]	Buck and Buddy Blow the Blues	1962	40.00
—Purple label			
❑ SVLP-2030 [M]	Buck and Buddy Blow the Blues	1965	25.00
—Blue label, trident logo at right			
❑ SVST-2030 [S]	Buck and Buddy Blow the Blues	1962	50.00
—Red label			
❑ SVST-2030 [S]	Buck and Buddy Blow the Blues	1965	30.00
—Blue label, trident logo at right			

CLAYTON, BUCK; RUBY BRAFF; MEL POWELL

VANGUARD
❑ VRS-8514 [M]	Buckin' the Blues	1957	40.00
❑ VRS-8008 [10]	Buck Meets Ruby	1954	50.00
❑ VRS-8517 [M]	Buck Meets Ruby and Mel	1957	40.00

CLAYTON, BUCK

ALLEGRO ELITE
| ❑ 4121 [10] | Buck Clayton All Stars | 195? | 40.00 |

CHIAROSCURO
❑ 132	A Buck Clayton Jam Session	1974	15.00
❑ 143	A Buck Clayton Jam Session, Vol. II	1975	15.00
❑ 152	A Buck Clayton Jam Session, Vol. III: Jazz Party Time	1976	15.00

| ❑ 163 | A Buck Clayton Jam Session, Vol. IV: Jay Hawk | 1977 | 15.00 |

COLUMBIA
❑ CL882 [M]	All the Cats Join In	1956	40.00
—Red and black label with six "eye" logos			
❑ CL614 [M]	Buck Clayton Jams Benny Goodman	1955	50.00
—Maroon label, gold print			
❑ CL614 [M]	Buck Clayton Jams Benny Goodman	1955	30.00
—Red and black label with six "eye" logos			
❑ CL567 [M]	How Hi the Fi: A Jam Session	1954	50.00
—Maroon label, gold print			
❑ CL6326 [10]	How Hi the Fi: A Jam Session	1954	60.00
❑ CL567 [M]	How Hi the Fi: A Jam Session	1955	30.00
—Red and black label with six "eye" logos			
❑ CL808 [M]	Jazz Spectacular	1956	40.00
—Red and black label with six "eye" logos			
❑ CL701 [M]	Jumpin' at the Woodside	1955	40.00
—Red and black label with six "eye" logos			
❑ CL6325 [10]	Moten Swing -- Sentimental Journey	1954	60.00
❑ CL1320 [M]	Songs for Swingers	1959	30.00
—Red and black label with six "eye" logos			
❑ CS8123 [S]	Songs for Swingers	1959	30.00
—Red and black label with six "eye" logos			
❑ CL548 [M]	The Huckle-Buck and Robbins' Nest: A Jam Session	1954	50.00
—Maroon label, gold print			
❑ CL548 [M]	The Huckle-Buck and Robbins' Nest: A Jam Session	1955	30.00
—Red and black label with six "eye" logos			

COLUMBIA JAZZ MASTERPIECES
| ❑ CJ44291 | Jam Sessions from the Vaults | 1988 | 15.00 |

FANTASY
| ❑ OJC-1709 | The Classic Swing of Buck Clayton | 1985 | 15.00 |

INNER CITY
| ❑ 7009 | Passport to Paradise | 1980 | 12.00 |

JAZZTONE
| ❑ J-1225 [M] | Meet Buck Clayton | 1956 | 40.00 |

STASH
| ❑ ST-281 | A Swingin' Dream | 1989 | 15.00 |

STEEPLECHASE
| ❑ SCC-6006/7 | Copenhagen Concert | 198? | 18.00 |

VANGUARD
| ❑ 103/104 | Essential Buck Clayton | 197? | 18.00 |

CLAYTON, BUCK/WILD BILL DAVISON

JAZZTONE
| ❑ J-1267 [M] | Singing Trumpets | 1957 | 40.00 |

CLAYTON, KID

FOLKWAYS
| ❑ FJ-2859 | The First Kid Clayton Session (1952) | 1983 | 15.00 |

JAZZOLOGY
| ❑ JCE-22 | Exit Stares | 1967 | 15.00 |

CLAYTON, MERRY

MCA
| ❑ 3200 | Emotion | 1980 | 12.00 |

ODE
❑ SP-77001	Gimme Shelter	1970	18.00
❑ SP-77030	Keep Your Eye on the Sparrow	1975	15.00
❑ PE34957	Keep Your Eye on the Sparrow	1977	10.00
❑ SP-77012	Merry Clayton	1971	15.00
❑ PE34948	Merry Clayton	1977	10.00

CLAYTON, PAUL

ELEKTRA
| ❑ EKL-155 [M] | Bobby Burns' Merry Muses | 1958 | 30.00 |
| ❑ EKL-147 [M] | Unholy Matrimony | 1958 | 30.00 |

FOLKWAYS
❑ FA-2106 [M]	Bay State Ballads	1956	60.00
❑ FW-8708 [M]	British Broadside Ballads in Popular Tradition	1957	40.00
❑ FA-2007 [M]	Cumberland Mountain Folksongs	1957	60.00
❑ FA-2429 [M]	Foc'sle Songs and Shanties	1959	30.00
❑ FA-2310 [M]	Folk Ballads of the English-Speaking World	1956	60.00
❑ FA-2110 [M]	Folksongs and Ballads of Virginia	1956	60.00

MONUMENT
| ❑ MLP-8017 [M] | Folk Singer | 1965 | 25.00 |
| ❑ SLP-18017 [S] | Folk Singer | 1965 | 30.00 |

RIVERSIDE
| ❑ RLP 12-615 [M] | Bloody Ballads | 1957 | 30.00 |
| ❑ RLP 12-648 [M] | Timber-r-r! -- Folk Songs and Ballads of the Lumberjack | 1958 | 30.00 |

| ❑ RLP 12-640 [M] | Wanted for Murder -- American Folksongs of Outlaws and Desperadoes | 1958 | 30.00 |

STINSON
| ❑ SLP-70 [10] | Waters of Tyme -- English North Country Songs | 1958 | 40.00 |
| ❑ SLP-69 [10] | Whaling Songs and Ballads | 1958 | 40.00 |

TRADITION
| ❑ TLP-1005 [M] | Whaling and Sailing Songs from the Days of Moby Dick | 1956 | 30.00 |

CLAYTON, STEVE

SOVEREIGN
| ❑ SOV-501 | All Aglow Again | 1986 | 12.00 |
| ❑ SOV-500 | Inner Spark | 1985 | 12.00 |

CLAYTON-THOMAS, DAVID

ABC
| ❑ AA-1104 | Clayton | 1978 | 12.00 |

COLUMBIA
| ❑ KC31000 | David Clayton-Thomas | 1972 | 18.00 |
| ❑ KC31700 | Tequila Sunrise | 1972 | 18.00 |

DECCA
| ❑ DL75146 | David Clayton-Thomas! | 1969 | 25.00 |

RCA VICTOR
| ❑ APL1-0173 | David Clayton-Thomas | 1973 | 15.00 |
| ❑ APD1-0173 [Q] | David Clayton-Thomas | 1973 | 25.00 |

CLAYTON BROTHERS, THE

CONCORD JAZZ
| ❑ CJ-138 | It's All in the Family | 1980 | 12.00 |
| ❑ CJ-89 | The Clayton Brothers | 1978 | 12.00 |

CLEAN LIVING

VANGUARD
| ❑ VSD-79318 [B] | Clean Living | 1972 | 15.00 |
| ❑ VSD-79334 [B] | Meadow Muffin | 1973 | 15.00 |

CLEANLINESS AND GODLINESS SKIFFLE BAND, THE

VANGUARD
| ❑ VSD-79285 | Greatest Hits | 1968 | 30.00 |

CLEAR LIGHT

ELEKTRA
| ❑ EKL-4011 [M] | Clear Light | 1967 | 40.00 |
| ❑ EKS-74011 [S] | Clear Light | 1967 | 35.00 |

SUNDAZED
| ❑ LP5125 | Clear Light | 2002 | 15.00 |
| *—Reissue on 180-gram vinyl* | | | |

CLEARY, DON

PALOMINO
| ❑ 302 [M] | Don Cleary Sings Traditional Cowboy Songs | 1966 | 50.00 |

CLEAVER, ELDRIDGE

MORE
| ❑ 4000 [M] | Soul On Wax | 1968 | 30.00 |

CLEFTONES, THE

GEE
❑ GLP-707 [M]	For Sentimental Reasons	1961	250.00
❑ SGLP-707 [S]	For Sentimental Reasons	1961	1200.00
❑ GLP-705 [M]	Heart and Soul	1961	200.00
❑ SGLP-705 [S]	Heart and Soul	1961	500.00

CLEMENT, JACK

ELEKTRA
| ❑ 6E-122 | All I Want to Do in Life | 1978 | 15.00 |

CLEMENTS, BOOTS

WEST
| ❑ WLP1005 | Walkin' Proud | 1986 | 12.00 |

CLEMENTS, VASSAR

FLYING FISH
❑ 038	Bluegrass Session	197?	12.00
❑ 101	Hillbilly Jazz	197?	18.00
❑ 385	Hillbilly Jazz Rides Again	1986	12.00
❑ 073	Nashville Jam	197?	15.00
❑ 232	Vassar	1980	12.00

MCA
❑ 2270	Vassar Clements Band	1977	18.00
❑ 695	Vassar Clements Band	198?	10.00
—Budget-line reissue of 2270			

MERCURY
| ❑ SRM-1-1058 | Superbow | 1975 | 15.00 |
| ❑ SRM-1-1022 | Vassar Clements | 1975 | 15.00 |

MIND DUST
| ❑ MDM1002 | Westport Drive | 1984 | 15.00 |

ROUNDER
| ❑ 0016 | Crossing the Catskills | 198? | 15.00 |

CLEMONS, CLARENCE

COLUMBIA

Number	Title	Yr	NM
❑ FC40917	A Night with Mr. C.	1989	15.00
❑ FC40010	Hero	1985	12.00
❑ BFC38933	Rescue	1983	12.00

CLEVELAND, JAMES (REV.)

APOLLO

Number	Title	Yr	NM
❑ LP-509	In the Beginning	197?	18.00

HOB

Number	Title	Yr	NM
❑ 239	Give Glory to God	197?	18.00
❑ 233	Love of God	197?	18.00
—With the Voices of Tabernacle			
❑ 253	The Best of James Cleveland	197?	18.00

KENWOOD

Number	Title	Yr	NM
❑ LP-509	In the Beginning	197?	18.00

SAVOY

Number	Title	Yr	NM
❑ MG-14260	Amazing Grace	197?	25.00
—With the Southern California Community Choir			
❑ MG-14311	Down Memory Lane	197?	18.00
❑ SL14412	Give It To Me	197?	15.00
❑ MG-14352	God Has Smiled on Me	1975	15.00
❑ MG-14131	He Leadeth Me	196?	30.00
❑ MG-14282	I'll Do His Will	197?	18.00
—With the Southern California Community Choir			
❑ SGL-7035	It's a New Day	1979	18.00
—With the Southern California Community Choir			
❑ SGL-7071	I Want to Be Ready When You Come	1981	25.00
—With the Los Angeles Chapter of the GMWA			
❑ MG-14159	Jame Cleveland in Hollywood	196?	30.00
❑ MG-14211	James Cleveland and the Cleveland Singers	196?	25.00
❑ MG-14265	James Cleveland and the Cleveland Singers	197?	25.00
❑ SGL-7046	James Cleveland and the Voices of Cornerstone	1979	18.00
❑ MG-14226	James Cleveland and the Voices of Tabernacle	196?	25.00
❑ SGL-7059	James Cleveland Sings with the World's Greatest Choirs	1980	18.00
❑ DBL-7014	Live at Carnegie Hall	1977	18.00
❑ SGL-7038	Lord Let Me Be an Instrument	1979	18.00
—With the Charles Fold Singers			
❑ MG-14195	Merry Christmas from James Cleveland and the Angelic Choir	196?	30.00
❑ MG-14076	Peace Be Still	1964	30.00
—With the Angelic Choir			
❑ MG-14269	Somehow I Can Sing	197?	18.00
❑ MG-14176	Songs My Mother Taught Me	196?	30.00
❑ SGL-7103	The Last Live Recording of the King of Gospel Music	1991	18.00
—With the L.A. Gospel Messengers			
❑ SL14425	The Lord Is My Life	197?	15.00
❑ MG-14252	The One and Only	197?	25.00
❑ MG-14068	The Soul of James Cleveland	196?	30.00
❑ MG-14085	The Sun Will Shine After Awhile	196?	30.00
❑ SL14438	Think of His Goodness to You	197?	15.00
❑ SGL-7072	This, Too, Will Pass	1981	25.00
—With the Charles Fold Singers			
❑ MG-14360	To the Glory of God	1975	15.00
—With the Southern California Community Choir			
❑ SL14541	Victory Shall Be Mine	197?	15.00
—With the Salem Inspirational Choir			
❑ DBL-7020	Volume 3/Recorded Live in Cincinnati, Ohio/(Is There Any Hope for) Tomorrow	1978	18.00
—With the Charles Fold Singers			
❑ MG-14096	Volume 4	196?	30.00
❑ MG-14205	Volume 8 -- Part 1	196?	30.00
—With the Angelic Choir			
❑ SGL-7066	Where Is Your Faith	1981	18.00
—With the Southern California Community Choir			

UPFRONT

Number	Title	Yr	NM
❑ UPF-163	I Walk with God	197?	15.00
❑ UPF-190	Rev. James Cleveland	197?	15.00

CLEVELAND, JIMMY

EMARCY

Number	Title	Yr	NM
❑ MG-36126 [M]	Cleveland Style	1958	50.00
❑ MG-36066 [M]	Introducing Jimmy Cleveland and His All Stars	1956	75.00
❑ MG-26003 [M]	Rhythm Crazy	1964	30.00

MERCURY

Number	Title	Yr	NM
❑ MG-20442 [M]	A Map of Jimmy Cleveland	1959	40.00
❑ SR-60117 [S]	A Map of Jimmy Cleveland	1959	30.00
❑ MG-20553 [M]	Cleveland Style	1960	40.00
❑ SR-60121 [S]	Cleveland Style	1959	30.00

CLIBURN, VAN

RCA VICTOR RED SEAL

Number	Title	Yr	NM
❑ LM-2680 [M]	Beethoven: Piano Concerto No. 4	1963	15.00
❑ LSC-2680 [S]	Beethoven: Piano Concerto No. 4	1963	18.00
—Shaded dog" pressing ("Living Stereo" on label)			
❑ LSC-2680 [S]	Beethoven: Piano Concerto No. 4	1965	15.00
—White dog" pressing ("Stereo" on label)			
❑ LSC-2680 [S]	Beethoven: Piano Concerto No. 4	1969	12.00
—No dog" pressing ("RCA" sideways at left)			
❑ LM-2562 [M]	Beethoven: Piano Concerto No. 5 (Emperor Concerto)	1961	18.00
❑ LSC-2562 [S]	Beethoven: Piano Concerto No. 5 (Emperor Concerto)	1961	25.00
—Shaded dog" pressing ("Living Stereo" on label)			
❑ LSC-2562 [S]	Beethoven: Piano Concerto No. 5 (Emperor Concerto)	1964	25.00
—White dog" pressing ("Stereo" on label)			
❑ LSC-2562 [S]	Beethoven: Piano Concerto No. 5 (Emperor Concerto)	1969	15.00
—No dog" pressing ("RCA" sideways at left)			
❑ LM-2581 [M]	Brahms: Piano Concerto No. 2	1962	18.00
❑ LSC-2581 [S]	Brahms: Piano Concerto No. 2	1962	25.00
—Shaded dog" pressing ("Living Stereo" on label)			
❑ LSC-2581 [S]	Brahms: Piano Concerto No. 2	1965	18.00
—White dog" pressing ("Stereo" on label)			
❑ LSC-2581 [S]	Brahms: Piano Concerto No. 2	1969	15.00
—No dog" pressing ("RCA" sideways at left)			
❑ LSC-2581 [S]	Brahms: Piano Concerto No. 2	1976	10.00
—Late dog" pressing (dog near top)			
❑ LM-2576 [M]	My Favorite Chopin	1962	18.00
❑ LSC-2576 [S]	My Favorite Chopin	1962	25.00
—Shaded dog" pressing ("Living Stereo" on label)			
❑ LSC-2576 [S]	My Favorite Chopin	1965	18.00
—White dog" pressing ("Stereo" on label)			
❑ LSC-2576 [S]	My Favorite Chopin	1969	15.00
—No dog" pressing ("RCA" sideways at left)			
❑ LSC-2576 [S]	My Favorite Chopin	1976	10.00
—Late dog" pressing (dog near top)			
❑ LM-2507 [M]	Prokofiev: Piano Concerto No. 3; MacDowell: Piano Concerto No. 2	1961	18.00
❑ LSC-2507 [S]	Prokofiev: Piano Concerto No. 3; MacDowell: Piano Concerto No. 2	1961	30.00
—Shaded dog" pressing ("Living Stereo" on label)			
❑ LSC-2507 [S]	Prokofiev: Piano Concerto No. 3; MacDowell: Piano Concerto No. 2	1965	30.00
—White dog" pressing ("Stereo" on label)			
❑ LSC-2507 [S]	Prokofiev: Piano Concerto No. 3; MacDowell: Piano Concerto No. 2	1969	15.00
—No dog" pressing ("RCA" sideways at left)			
❑ LM-2601 [M]	Rachmaninoff: Piano Concerto No. 2	1962	18.00
❑ LSC-2601 [S]	Rachmaninoff: Piano Concerto No. 2	1962	25.00
—Shaded dog" pressing ("Living Stereo" on label)			
❑ LSC-2601 [S]	Rachmaninoff: Piano Concerto No. 2	1962	18.00
—White dog" pressing ("Stereo" on label)			
❑ LSC-2601 [S]	Rachmaninoff: Piano Concerto No. 2	1969	15.00
—No dog" pressing ("RCA" sideways at left)			
❑ LM-2355 [M]	Rachmaninoff: Piano Concerto No. 3	1959	25.00
❑ LSC-2355 [S]	Rachmaninoff: Piano Concerto No. 3	1959	30.00
—Shaded dog" pressing ("Living Stereo" on label)			
❑ LSC-2355 [S]	Rachmaninoff: Piano Concerto No. 3	1965	18.00
—White dog" pressing ("Stereo" on label)			
❑ LSC-2355 [S]	Rachmaninoff: Piano Concerto No. 3	1969	15.00
—No dog" pressing ("RCA" sideways at left)			
❑ ARP1-4688	Rachmaninoff: Piano Concerto No. 3	198?	12.00
—Half-speed mastered reissue			
❑ LM-2455 [M]	Schumann: Piano Concerto in A Minor	1960	18.00
❑ LSC-2455 [S]	Schumann: Piano Concerto in A Minor	1960	25.00
—Shaded dog" pressing ("Living Stereo" on label)			
❑ LSC-2455 [S]	Schumann: Piano Concerto in A Minor	1965	18.00
—White dog" pressing ("Stereo" on label)			
❑ LSC-2455 [S]	Schumann: Piano Concerto in A Minor	1969	15.00
—No dog" pressing ("RCA" sideways at left)			
❑ LM-2252 [M]	Tchaikovsky: Piano Concerto No. 1	1958	25.00
❑ LSC-2252 [S]	Tchaikovsky: Piano Concerto No. 1	1958	30.00
—Shaded dog" pressing ("Living Stereo" on label)			
❑ LSC-2252 [S]	Tchaikovsky: Piano Concerto No. 1	1965	18.00
—White dog" pressing ("Stereo" on label)			
❑ LSC-2252 [S]	Tchaikovsky: Piano Concerto No. 1	1969	15.00
—No dog" pressing ("RCA" sideways at left)			
❑ LSC-2252 [S]	Tchaikovsky: Piano Concerto No. 1	1976	10.00
—Late dog" pressing (dog near top)			
❑ ARP1-4441	Tchaikovsky: Piano Concerto No. 1	198?	12.00
—Half-speed mastered reissue			
❑ LSC-3323	The World's Favorite Piano Music	196?	15.00

CLIFF, JIMMY

A&M

Number	Title	Yr	NM
❑ SP-4251	Wonderful World, Beautiful People	1970	30.00
❑ SP-3189	Wonderful World, Beautiful People	198?	10.00
—Reissue of 4251			

COLUMBIA

Number	Title	Yr	NM
❑ FC40002	Cliff Hanger	1985	12.00
❑ FC40845	Hanging Fire	1988	12.00
❑ FC38099	Special	1982	12.00
❑ PC38099	Special	198?	10.00
—Budget-line reissue			
❑ FC38986	The Power and the Glory	1983	12.00
❑ PC38996	The Power and the Glory	1985	10.00
—Budget-line reissue			

ISLAND

Number	Title	Yr	NM
❑ SW-9343	Struggling Man	1973	25.00

MANGO

Number	Title	Yr	NM
❑ ILPS9235	Struggling Man	197?	15.00
—Reissue of Island SW-9343			

MCA

Number	Title	Yr	NM
❑ 5217	Give the People What They Want	1981	15.00
❑ 820	Give the People What They Want	198?	10.00
—Reissue of 5217			
❑ 5153	I Am the Living	1980	15.00
❑ 813	I Am the Living	198?	10.00
—Reissue of 5153			

REPRISE

Number	Title	Yr	NM
❑ MS2218 [B]	Follow My Mind	1975	18.00
❑ MS2256	In Concert: The Best of Jimmy Cliff	1976	18.00
❑ MS2188	Music Maker	1974	18.00
❑ MS2147	Unlimited	1973	18.00

VEEP

Number	Title	Yr	NM
❑ VPS-16536	Can't Get Enough of It	1969	40.00

WARNER BROS.

Number	Title	Yr	NM
❑ BSK3240	Give Thankx	1978	15.00

CLIFFORD, BUZZ

COLUMBIA

Number	Title	Yr	NM
❑ CL1616 [M]	Baby Sittin' with Buzz	1961	100.00
❑ CS8416 [S]	Baby Sittin' with Buzz	1961	150.00

DOT

Number	Title	Yr	NM
❑ DLP-25965	See Your Way Clear	1969	30.00

CLIFFORD, DOUG

FANTASY

Number	Title	Yr	NM
❑ 9411	Cosmo	1972	18.00

CLIFFORD, MIKE

UNITED ARTISTS

Number	Title	Yr	NM
❑ UAL-3409 [M]	For the Love of Mike	1965	25.00
❑ UAS-6409 [S]	For the Love of Mike	1965	30.00

CLIFTON, BILL, AND THE DIXIE MOUNTAIN BOYS

STARDAY

Number	Title	Yr	NM
❑ SLP-271 [M]	Code of the Mountains	1965	30.00
❑ SLP-111 [M]	Mountain Folk Songs	1959	40.00
❑ SLP-213 [M]	Soldier, Sing Me a Song	1963	30.00
❑ SLP-159 [M]	The Bluegrass Sound of Bill Clifton	1961	30.00
❑ SLP-146 [M]	The Carter Family Memorial Album	1961	30.00

CLIFTON, BILL

COLUMBIA

Number	Title	Yr	NM
❑ CL6166 [10]	Piano Moods	1951	50.00

CLIMAX

ROCKY ROAD

Number	Title	Yr	NM
❑ 3506	Climax	1972	18.00

CLIMAX BLUES BAND

SIRE

Number	Title	Yr	NM
❑ SES-4901	#3	1971	18.00
❑ SAS-2-7411	FM/Live	1973	18.00
❑ 2XS6013	FM/Live	1977	15.00
❑ SASD-7523	Gold Plated	1976	15.00
❑ SR6004	Lot of Bottle	1977	12.00
❑ SRK3334	Real to Reel	1979	12.00
❑ SES-7402	Rich Man	1972	18.00
❑ SAS-7501	Sense of Direction	1974	15.00
❑ SRK6056	Shine On	1978	12.00
❑ SASD-7507	Stamp Album	1975	15.00
❑ SR6016	Stamp Album	1977	12.00
❑ SES-97013	The Climax Chicago Blues Band	1969	18.00

Number	Title	Yr	NM
❑ SR6003	The Climax Chicago Blues Band	1978	12.00
❑ SES-97023	The Climax Chicago Blues Band Plays On	1970	18.00
❑ SR6033	The Climax Chicago Blues Band Plays On	1978	12.00
❑ SES-5903	Tightly Knit	1972	18.00
❑ SR6008	Tightly Knit	1977	12.00
VIRGIN/EPIC			
❑ FE38631	Sample and Hold	1983	12.00
WARNER BROS.			
❑ BSK3493	Flying the Flag	1981	15.00
❑ BSK3623	Lucky for Some	1982	12.00
CLINE, PATSY			
ACCORD			
❑ SN-7153	Let the Teardrops Fall	1981	12.00
ALLEGIANCE			
❑ AV-5021	Stop, Look and Listen	198?	12.00
CLEOPATRA			
❑ 8726 [B]	Walkin' After Midnight		30.00
—picture disc			
DECCA			
❑ DL4508 [M]	A Portrait of Patsy Cline	1964	30.00
❑ DL74508 [S]	A Portrait of Patsy Cline	1964	40.00
❑ DL8611 [M]	Patsy Cline	1957	100.00
—Black label with silver print			
❑ DL8611 [M]	Patsy Cline	1960	50.00
—Black label with color bars			
❑ DL4854 [M]	Patsy Cline's Greatest Hits	1967	25.00
❑ DL74854 [S]	Patsy Cline's Greatest Hits	1967	30.00
❑ DL4202 [M]	Patsy Cline Showcase	1961	40.00
❑ DL74202 [S]	Patsy Cline Showcase	1961	50.00
❑ DL4282 [M]	Sentimentally Yours	1962	30.00
❑ DL74282 [S]	Sentimentally Yours	1962	40.00
❑ DL4586 [M]	That's How a Heartache Begins	1964	30.00
❑ DL74586 [S]	That's How a Heartache Begins	1964	40.00
❑ DXB176 [M]	The Patsy Cline Story	1963	40.00
❑ DXSB7176 [S]	The Patsy Cline Story	1963	50.00
EVEREST			
❑ 5204 [M]	Encores	1962	25.00
❑ 1204 [R]	Encores	1962	15.00
❑ 5200 [M]	Golden Hits	1962	25.00
❑ 1200 [R]	Golden Hits	1962	15.00
❑ ST 90070 [R]	Golden Hits	1962	18.00
—Capitol Record Club edition			
❑ 5217 [M]	In Memoriam	1963	25.00
❑ 1217 [R]	In Memoriam	1963	15.00
❑ 5223 [M]	Legend	1963	25.00
❑ 5229 [M]	Reflections	1964	25.00
❑ 1229 [R]	Reflections	1964	15.00
HILLTOP			
❑ 6148	Country Music Hall of Fame	197?	12.00
❑ 6016 [M]	I Can't Forget You	1966	15.00
❑ S-6016 [R]	I Can't Forget You	1966	12.00
❑ JS-6072	In Care of the Blues	1969	12.00
❑ S-6039	Stop the World	1968	12.00
❑ 6001 [M]	Today, Tomorrow, Forever	1965	15.00
❑ S-6001 [R]	Today, Tomorrow, Forever	1965	12.00
MCA			
❑ 3263	Always	1980	18.00
❑ 27069	Always	198?	10.00
❑ 224	A Portrait of Patsy Cline	1973	15.00
—Reissue of Decca 74508; black label with rainbow			
❑ 738	Here's Patsy Cline	198?	12.00
—Reissue of Vocalion 73753			
❑ 42142	Live at the Opry	1988	12.00
❑ 42284	Live Volume 2	1989	15.00
❑ 12	Patsy Cline's Greatest Hits	1973	15.00
—Reissue of Decca 74854; black label with rainbow			
❑ 12	Patsy Cline's Greatest Hits	1977	12.00
—Tan label			
❑ 12	Patsy Cline's Greatest Hits	1980	10.00
—Blue label with rainbow			
❑ 87	Patsy Cline Showcase	1973	15.00
—Reissue of Decca 74202; black label with rainbow			
❑ 90	Sentimentally Yours	1973	15.00
—Reissue of Decca 74282; black label with rainbow			
❑ 1440	Stop, Look and Listen	198?	10.00
❑ 6149	Sweet Dreams -- The Life and Times of Patsy Cline	1985	12.00
❑ 736	The Great Patsy Cline	198?	12.00
—Reissue of Vocalion 73872			
❑ 4038	The Patsy Cline Story	1974	18.00
—Reissue of Decca 7176; black labels with rainbow			
❑ 1463	Today, Tomorrow and Forever	198?	10.00
METRO			
❑ M-540 [M]	Gotta Lot of Rhythm in My Soul	1965	15.00
❑ MS-540 [R]	Gotta Lot of Rhythm in My Soul	1965	12.00
RHINO			
❑ R1-70048	Her First Recordings, Vol. 1: Walkin' Dreams	1989	15.00
❑ R1-70049	Her First Recordings, Vol. 2: Hungry for Love	1989	15.00
❑ R1-70050	Her First Recordings, Vol. 3: The Rockin' Side	1989	15.00

Number	Title	Yr	NM
SEARS			
❑ SPS-112	I Can't Forget You	1968	30.00
❑ SPS-127	In Care of the Blues	1968	30.00
❑ SP-102 [M]	Walkin' After Midnight	196?	30.00
❑ SPS-102 [R]	Walkin' After Midnight	196?	25.00
VOCALION			
❑ VL73872	Country Great!	1969	12.00
❑ VL3753 [M]	Here's Patsy Cline	1965	15.00
❑ VL73753 [R]	Here's Patsy Cline	1965	12.00
CLINTON, GEORGE			
550 MUSIC			
❑ B267144	T.A.P.O.A.F.O.M. -- The Awesome Power of a Fully Operational Mothership	1996	18.00
—Red vinyl			
ABC			
❑ D-831	The George Clinton Band Arrives	1974	18.00
CAPITOL			
❑ ST-12246	Computer Games	1982	12.00
❑ C1-33911	Greatest Funkin' Hits	1996	15.00
—Red vinyl			
❑ ST-12481	R&B Skeletons in the Closet	1986	12.00
❑ ST-12417	Some of My Best Jokes Are Friends	1985	12.00
❑ CJ-48424	The Best of George Clinton	1987	12.00
❑ MLP-15021 [EP]	The Mothership Connection Live from Houston, Texas	1986	18.00
❑ ST-12308	You Shouldn't-Nuf Bit Fish	1984	12.00
INVICTUS			
❑ ST-9815	Black Vampire	1973	25.00
PAISLEY PARK			
❑ PRO-A-6537 [DJ]	Hey Man... Smell My Finger	1993	30.00
—Promo-only vinyl issue			
❑ 25994	The Cinderella Theory	1989	15.00
WARNER BROS.			
❑ 25887	George Clinton Presents Our Gang Funky	1988	12.00
❑ 25991	Under a Nouveau Groove	1989	12.00
CLINTON, LARRY			
CIRCLE			
❑ 58	Larry Clinton and His Orchestra 1941 and 1949	198?	12.00
EVEREST			
❑ LPBR-5096 [M]	My Million Sellers	196?	25.00
❑ SDBR-1096 [S]	My Million Sellers	196?	30.00
HINDSIGHT			
❑ HSR-109	Larry Clinton and His Orchestra 1937-38	198?	12.00
RCA CAMDEN			
❑ CAL-434 [M]	Dance Date	1958	25.00
SUNBEAM			
❑ 208	Larry Clinton and His Orchestra 1937-41	198?	12.00
CLIQUE, THE (1)			
WHITE WHALE			
❑ WWS-7126	The Clique	1969	25.00
CLOONEY, ROSEMARY, AND BING CROSBY			
CAPITOL			
❑ T2300 [M]	That Travelin' Two-Beat	1965	25.00
❑ ST2300 [S]	That Travelin' Two-Beat	1965	30.00
RCA CAMDEN			
❑ CAS-2330	Rendezvous	1968	18.00
RCA VICTOR			
❑ LPM-1854 [M]	Fancy Meeting You Here	1958	25.00
❑ LSP-1854 [S]	Fancy Meeting You Here	1958	30.00
CLOONEY, ROSEMARY			
COLUMBIA			
❑ CL2572 [10]	A Date with the King	1956	50.00
❑ CL872 [M]	Blue Rose	1956	40.00
❑ CL2569 [10]	Children's Favorites	1955	50.00
❑ CL969 [M]	Clooney Tunes	1957	80.00
❑ CL6224 [10]	Hollywood's Best	1952	60.00
❑ CL585 [M]	Hollywood's Best	1955	50.00
❑ CL2597 [10]	My Fair Lady	1956	50.00
❑ CL2581 [10]	On Stage	1956	50.00
❑ CL1006 [M]	Ring Around the Rosie	1957	40.00
—With the Hi-Lo's			
❑ CL6297 [10]	Rosemary Clooney (While We're Young)	1954	60.00
❑ CL1230 [M]	Rosie's Greatest Hits	1958	40.00
—Six "eye" logos on label			
❑ CL1230 [M]	Rosie's Greatest Hits	1962	30.00
—Guaranteed High Fidelity" on label			
❑ CL1230 [M]	Rosie's Greatest Hits	1965	18.00
—360 Sound Mono" on label			
❑ CL2525 [10]	Tenderly	1955	50.00
❑ CL6338 [10]	White Christmas	1954	60.00
COLUMBIA SPECIAL PRODUCTS			
❑ P13085	Blue Rose	197?	15.00
❑ P14382	Come On-a My House	197?	15.00
❑ P13083	Hollywood's Best	197?	15.00

Number	Title	Yr	NM
CONCORD JAZZ			
❑ CJ-47	Everything's Coming Up Rosie	1978	15.00
❑ CJ-81	Here's to My Lady	1979	15.00
❑ CJ-226	My Buddy	1984	15.00
—With Woody Herman			
❑ CJ-282	Rosemary Clooney Sings Ballads	1985	15.00
❑ CJ-185	Rosemary Clooney Sings Cole Porter	1982	15.00
❑ CJ-210	Rosemary Clooney Sings Harold Arlen	1983	15.00
❑ CJ-112	Rosemary Clooney Sings Ira Gershwin	1980	15.00
❑ CJ-333	Rosemary Clooney Sings the Lyrics of Johnny Mercer	1988	15.00
❑ CJ-255	Rosemary Clooney Sings the Music of Irving Berlin	1985	15.00
❑ CJ-308	Rosemary Clooney Sings the Music of Jimmy Van Heusen	1987	15.00
❑ CJ-60	Rosie Sings Bing	1979	15.00
❑ CJ-364	Show Tunes	1989	15.00
❑ CJ-144	With Love	1981	15.00
CORAL			
❑ CRL57266 [M]	Swing Around Rosie	1959	30.00
❑ CRL757266 [S]	Swing Around Rosie	1959	40.00
HARMONY			
❑ HL7213 [M]	Hollywood Hits	195?	30.00
❑ HL7454 [M]	Mixed Emotions	1968	25.00
❑ HS11254 [R]	Mixed Emotions	1968	15.00
❑ HL7123 [M]	Rosemary Clooney in High Fidelity	195?	30.00
❑ HL9501 [M]	Rosemary Clooney Sings for Children	196?	25.00
HINDSIGHT			
❑ HSR-234	Rosemary Clooney 1951-1952	1988	12.00
HOLIDAY			
❑ 1946	Christmas with Rosemary Clooney	1981	12.00
MGM			
❑ E-3782 [M]	Hymns from the Heart	1959	30.00
❑ SE-3782 [S]	Hymns from the Heart	1959	40.00
❑ E-3687 [M]	Oh, Captain!	1958	40.00
❑ E-3834 [M]	Rosie Clooney Swings Softly	1960	30.00
❑ SE-3834 [S]	Rosie Clooney Swings Softly	1960	40.00
MISTLETOE			
❑ MLP-1234	Christmas with Rosemary Clooney	1978	15.00
RCA VICTOR			
❑ LPM-2133 [M]	A Touch of Tabasco	1960	25.00
❑ LSP-2133 [S]	A Touch of Tabasco	1960	30.00
❑ LPM-2212 [M]	Clap Hands, Here Comes Rosie	1960	25.00
❑ LSP-2212 [S]	Clap Hands, Here Comes Rosie	1960	30.00
❑ LPM-2565 [M]	Country Hits from the Heart	1963	25.00
❑ LSP-2565 [S]	Country Hits from the Heart	1963	30.00
❑ LPM-2265 [M]	Rosie Solves the Swingin' Riddle	1961	25.00
❑ LSP-2265 [S]	Rosie Solves the Swingin' Riddle	1961	30.00
REPRISE			
❑ R-6088 [M]	Love	1963	30.00
❑ R9-6088 [S]	Love	1963	40.00
❑ R-6108 [M]	Thanks for Nothing	1964	30.00
❑ RS-6108 [S]	Thanks for Nothing	1964	40.00
TIME-LIFE			
❑ SLGD-16	Legendary Singers: Rosemary Clooney	1986	18.00
CLOONEY SISTERS, THE			
EPIC			
❑ LN3160 [M]	The Clooney Sisters with Tony Pastor	1956	60.00
CLOUD, BRUCE			
CAPITOL			
❑ ST-343	California Soul	1969	25.00
CLOVER, TIMOTHY			
TOWER			
❑ ST5114	A Harvard Square Affair	1968	25.00
CLOVER			
FANTASY			
❑ 8395	Clover	1969	30.00
❑ 8405	Forty-Niner	1970	30.00
CLOVERS, THE			
ATCO			
❑ SD 33-374	Their Greatest Recordings/ The Early Years	1971	15.00
ATLANTIC			
❑ 8034 [M]	Dance Party	1959	400.00
—Black label			
❑ 8034 [M]	Dance Party	1960	300.00
—White "bullseye" label			
❑ 8034 [M]	Dance Party	1961	200.00
—Red and white label			

Number	Title	Yr	NM
❑ 1248 [M]	The Clovers	1956	600.00
❑ 8009 [M]	The Clovers	1957	400.00
—Reissue of 1248 on the "pop" series; black label			
❑ 8009 [M]	The Clovers	1960	300.00
—White "bullseye" label			
❑ 8009 [M]	The Clovers	1961	200.00
—Red and white label			

GRAND PRIX

Number	Title	Yr	NM
❑ K-428 [M]	The Original Love Potion Number Nine	1964	30.00
❑ KS-428 [R]	The Original Love Potion Number Nine	1964	15.00

POPLAR

Number	Title	Yr	NM
❑ 1001 [M]	The Clovers In Clover	1958	400.00

UNITED ARTISTS

Number	Title	Yr	NM
❑ UAL-3099 [M]	Love Potion Number Nine	1959	250.00
❑ UAS-6099 [S]	Love Potion Number Nine	1959	500.00
❑ UAL-3033 [M]	The Clovers In Clover	1959	300.00
❑ UAS-6033 [R]	The Clovers In Clover	196?	200.00

CLOWER, JERRY

DECCA

Number	Title	Yr	NM
❑ DL75286	From Yazoo City, Mississippi Talkin'	1971	15.00
❑ DL75342	Mouth of Mississippi	1972	15.00

MCA

Number	Title	Yr	NM
❑ 5602	An Officer and a Ledbetter	1985	12.00
❑ 42178	Classic Clower	1988	12.00
❑ 317	Clower Power	1973	12.00
❑ 417	Country Ham	1974	12.00
❑ 5321	Dogs I Have Known	1982	12.00
❑ 33	From Yazoo City, Mississippi Talkin'	1973	12.00
—Reissue of Decca 75286			
❑ 3152	Greatest Hits	1979	12.00
❑ 5422	Live at Cleburne, Texas	1983	12.00
❑ 3062	Live from the Stage of the Grand Ole Opry!	1979	12.00
❑ 486	Live in Picayune	1975	12.00
❑ 5215	More Good 'Uns	1981	12.00
❑ 47	Mouth of Mississippi	1973	12.00
—Reissue of Decca 75342			
❑ 2281	On the Road	1978	12.00
❑ 5773	Runaway Truck	1986	12.00
❑ 5491	Starke Raving	1984	12.00
❑ 2205	The Ambassador of Goodwill	1976	12.00
❑ 3247	The Ledbetter Olympics	1980	12.00
❑ 42034	Top Gum	1987	12.00

WORD

Number	Title	Yr	NM
❑ WSB-8737	Ain't God Good!	197?	15.00

CLUB NOUVEAU

RIP-IT

Number	Title	Yr	NM
❑ 9004	Everything Is Black	1995	18.00

WARNER BROS.

Number	Title	Yr	NM
❑ 25531	Life, Love & Pain	1986	10.00
❑ 25687	Listen to the Message	1988	10.00
❑ 25991	Under a Nouveau Groove	1989	12.00

CLUSTER & ENO

4 MEN WITH BEARDS

Number	Title	Yr	NM
❑ 4M141LP [B]	Cluster & Eno		25.00

CLUSTER

4 MEN WITH BEARDS

Number	Title	Yr	NM
❑ 4M140LP [B]	Cluster '71		25.00
❑ 4M162LP [B]	Sowiesoso		25.00

COASTERS, THE

ATCO

Number	Title	Yr	NM
❑ 33-135 [M]	Coast Along with the Coasters	1962	100.00
—Gold and gray label			
❑ SD 33-135 [P]	Coast Along with the Coasters	1962	150.00
—Purple and brown label; "Wait a Minute" is rechanneled			
❑ 33-123 [M]	One By One	1960	150.00
—Yellow "harp" label			
❑ SD 33-123 [S]	One By One	1960	400.00
—Yellow "harp" label			
❑ 33-123 [M]	One By One	196?	60.00
—Gold and gray label			
❑ SD 33-123 [S]	One By One	196?	150.00
—Purple and brown label			
❑ 33-101 [M]	The Coasters	1958	300.00
—Yellow "harp" label			
❑ 33-101 [M]	The Coasters	196?	60.00
—Gold and dark blue label			
❑ 33-111 [M]	The Coasters' Greatest Hits	1959	150.00
—Yellow "harp" label			
❑ 33-111 [M]	The Coasters' Greatest Hits	196?	60.00
—Gold and gray label			
❑ SD 33-371	Their Greatest Recordings/ The Early Years	1971	25.00

CLARION

Number	Title	Yr	NM
❑ 605 [M]	That Is Rock and Roll	1965	40.00
❑ SD605 [S]	That Is Rock and Roll	1965	50.00

KING

Number	Title	Yr	NM
❑ KS-1146	The Coasters On Broadway	1971	30.00

POWER PAK

Number	Title	Yr	NM
❑ 310	Greatest Hits	198?	12.00

TRIP

Number	Title	Yr	NM
❑ 8028	It Ain't Sanitary	197?	15.00

COATES, JOHN, JR.

OMNISOUND

Number	Title	Yr	NM
❑ 1021	After the Before	1978	15.00
❑ 1015	Alone and Live at the Deer Head	1977	15.00
❑ 1022	In the Open Space	1979	18.00
❑ 1038	Pocono Friends	1981	18.00
❑ 1045	Pocono Friends Encore	1982	15.00
❑ 1024	Rainbow Road	1979	15.00
❑ 1004	The Jazz Piano of John Coates, Jr.	197?	15.00
❑ 1032	Tokyo Concert	1980	15.00

SAVOY

Number	Title	Yr	NM
❑ MG-12082 [M]	Portrait	1956	40.00

COBB, ARNETT; DIZZY GILLESPIE; JEWEL BROWN

FANTASY

Number	Title	Yr	NM
❑ F-9659	Show Time	1987	15.00

COBB, ARNETT

APOLLO

Number	Title	Yr	NM
❑ LAP-105 [10]	Swingin' with Arnett Cobb	1952	250.00

BEE HIVE

Number	Title	Yr	NM
❑ BH-7017	Keep On Pushin'	1985	15.00

CLASSIC JAZZ

Number	Title	Yr	NM
❑ 102	The Wild Man from Texas	1976	18.00

FANTASY

Number	Title	Yr	NM
❑ OJC-219	Party Time	198?	12.00
❑ OJC-323	Smooth Sailing	1988	12.00

HOME COOKING

Number	Title	Yr	NM
❑ HCS-114	The Wild Man from Texas	1990	15.00
—Reissue of Classic Jazz 102			

MOODSVILLE

Number	Title	Yr	NM
❑ MVLP-14 [M]	Ballads by Cobb	1961	50.00
—Green label			
❑ MVLP-14 [M]	Ballads by Cobb	1965	30.00
—Blue label, trident logo at right			

MUSE

Number	Title	Yr	NM
❑ MR-5191	Live at Sandy's	1977	15.00
❑ MR-5236	More Live at Sandy's	1979	15.00

PRESTIGE

Number	Title	Yr	NM
❑ PRLP-7151 [M]	Blow, Arnett, Blow	1959	50.00
—Yellow label			
❑ PRLP-7151 [M]	Blow, Arnett, Blow	1963	30.00
—Blue label, trident logo at right			
❑ PRST-7151 [R]	Blow, Arnett, Blow	196?	15.00
❑ PRST-7835	Go Power!	1970	18.00
❑ PRLP-7175 [M]	More Party Time	1960	50.00
—Yellow label			
❑ PRLP-7175 [M]	More Party Time	1963	30.00
—Blue label, trident logo at right			
❑ PRLP-7216 [M]	Movin' Right Along	1961	100.00
—Yellow label			
❑ PRLP-7216 [M]	Movin' Right Along	1963	30.00
—Blue label, trident logo at right			
❑ PRLP-7165 [M]	Party Time	1959	50.00
—Yellow label			
❑ PRLP-7165 [M]	Party Time	1963	30.00
—Blue label, trident logo at right			
❑ PRLP-7227 [M]	Sizzlin'	1962	40.00
—Yellow label			
❑ PRLP-7227 [M]	Sizzlin'	1963	25.00
—Blue label, trident logo at right			
❑ PRST-7227 [S]	Sizzlin'	1962	50.00
—Silver label			
❑ PRST-7227 [S]	Sizzlin'	1963	30.00
—Blue label, trident logo at right			
❑ PRLP-7184 [M]	Smooth Sailing	1960	50.00
—Yellow label			
❑ PRLP-7184 [M]	Smooth Sailing	1963	30.00
—Blue label, trident logo at right			
❑ PRST-7711	The Best of Arnett Cobb	1969	18.00

PROGRESSIVE

Number	Title	Yr	NM
❑ 7037	Arnett Cobb Is Back!	1978	15.00
❑ 7054	Funky Butt	1981	15.00

COBB, JUNIE C.

RIVERSIDE

Number	Title	Yr	NM
❑ RLP-415 [M]	Junie C. Cobb and His New Hometown Band	1962	25.00
❑ RS-9415 [S]	Junie C. Cobb and His New Hometown Band	1962	30.00

COBHAM, BILLY, AND GEORGE DUKE

ATLANTIC

Number	Title	Yr	NM
❑ SD18194	Live On Tour in Europe	1976	12.00

COBHAM, BILLY

ATLANTIC

Number	Title	Yr	NM
❑ SD18149	A Funky Thide of Sings	1975	15.00
❑ SD7300	Crosswinds	1974	18.00
—Original pressings have "1841 Broadway" address on label			
❑ SD19174	Inner Conflicts	1978	15.00
❑ SD18166	Life & Times	1976	15.00
❑ SD18139	Shabazz (Recorded Live in Europe)	1975	18.00
❑ SD7268	Spectrum	1973	18.00
—Original pressings have "1841 Broadway" address on label			
❑ SD19238	The Best of Billy Cobham	1979	15.00
❑ SD18121	Total Eclipse	1974	18.00

COLUMBIA

Number	Title	Yr	NM
❑ JC35993	B.C.	1979	15.00
❑ JC34939	Magic	1977	15.00
❑ JC35457	Simplicity of Expression -- Depth of Thought	1978	15.00
❑ JC36400	The Best of Billy Cobham	1980	15.00

ELEKTRA/MUSICIAN

Number	Title	Yr	NM
❑ 60123	Observations &	1982	18.00
❑ 60233	Smokin'	1983	18.00

GRP

Number	Title	Yr	NM
❑ GR-9575	Billy's Best Hits	1988	12.00
❑ GR-1040	Picture This	1987	12.00
❑ GR-1027	Power Play	1986	12.00
❑ GR-1020	Warning	1986	15.00

COCHRAN, CHARLES

AUDIOPHILE

Number	Title	Yr	NM
❑ AP-177	Haunted Heart	1982	15.00

COCHRAN, EDDIE

EMI AMERICA

Number	Title	Yr	NM
❑ SQ17245	On the Air	1987	18.00

LIBERTY

Number	Title	Yr	NM
❑ LRP-3172 [M]	Eddie Cochran (12 of His Biggest Hits)	1960	120.00
❑ LN-10204	Great Hits	198?	10.00
❑ LRP-3220 [M]	Never to Be Forgotten	1962	100.00
❑ LRP-3061 [M]	Singin' to My Baby	1957	800.00
—Green label			
❑ LRP-3061 [M]	Singin' to My Baby	1960	300.00
—Black label			
❑ LN-10137	Singin' to My Baby	198?	15.00
—Budget-line reissue			

SUNSET

Number	Title	Yr	NM
❑ SUM-1123 [M]	Summertime Blues	1966	40.00
❑ SUS-5123 [R]	Summertime Blues	1966	30.00

UNITED ARTISTS

Number	Title	Yr	NM
❑ UAS-9959 [B]	Legendary Masters Series #4	1972	30.00
❑ UA-LA428-E	The Very Best of Eddie Cochran	1975	15.00

COCHRAN, HANK

CAPITOL

Number	Title	Yr	NM
❑ ST-11807	With a Little Help from His Friends	1978	15.00

ELEKTRA

Number	Title	Yr	NM
❑ 6E-277	Make the World Go Away	1980	12.00

MONUMENT

Number	Title	Yr	NM
❑ SLP-18089	The Heart of Hank	1968	25.00

RCA VICTOR

Number	Title	Yr	NM
❑ LPM-3431 [M]	Going in Training	1965	25.00
❑ LSP-3431 [S]	Going in Training	1965	30.00
❑ LPM-3303 [M]	Hits from the Heart	1965	25.00
❑ LSP-3303 [S]	Hits from the Heart	1965	30.00

COCHRAN, TODD

VITAL

Number	Title	Yr	NM
❑ VTL-001	Todd	1991	25.00

COCHRAN, WAYNE

BETHLEHEM

Number	Title	Yr	NM
❑ 10002	High and Ridin'	1970	18.00

CHESS

Number	Title	Yr	NM
❑ LPS-1519	Wayne Cochran!	1968	40.00

EPIC

Number	Title	Yr	NM
❑ KE30889	Cochran	1972	18.00

KING

Number	Title	Yr	NM
❑ KS-1116	Alive and Well	1970	25.00

COCHRANE, MICHAEL

SOUL NOTE

Number	Title	Yr	NM
❑ SN-1151	Elements	198?	15.00

COCK ROBIN

COLUMBIA

Number	Title	Yr	NM
❑ BFC40375	After Here Through Midland	1987	10.00
❑ BFC39582	Cock Robin	1985	10.00

COCKBURN, BRUCE

EPIC

Number	Title	Yr	NM
❑ KE31768	Sunwheel Dance	1972	25.00
❑ E30812	True North	1971	25.00

GOLD CASTLE

Number	Title	Yr	NM
❑ D1-71320	Big Circumstance	1988	10.00

Number	Title	Yr	NM
❑ 171009-1	Dancing in the Dragon's Jaws	1987	10.00
—Reissue of Gold Mountain GM-3276			
❑ 171010-1	Stealing Fire	1987	10.00
—Reissue of Gold Mountain GM-80012			
❑ 171008-1	The Trouble with Normal	1987	10.00
—Reissue of Gold Mountain GM-3283			
❑ 171005-1	Waiting for a Miracle	1987	15.00

GOLD MOUNTAIN

Number	Title	Yr	NM
❑ GM-3276	Dancing in the Dragon's Jaws	1985	10.00
—Reissue of Millennium BXL1-7747			
❑ GM-80012	Stealing Fire	1984	10.00
❑ GM-3283	The Trouble with Normal	1985	10.00

ISLAND

Number	Title	Yr	NM
❑ ILTA9475	Circles in the Stream	1977	18.00
❑ ILSP9528	Furhter Adventures of	1978	15.00
❑ ILTN9463	In the Falling Dark	1976	15.00

MCA

Number	Title	Yr	NM
❑ 5772	World of Wonders	1986	10.00

MILLENNIUM

Number	Title	Yr	NM
❑ BXL1-7747 [B]	Dancing in the Dragon's Jaws	1979	12.00
❑ BXL1-7752	Humans	1980	12.00
❑ BXL1-7761	Inner City Front	1981	12.00
❑ DJL1-3830 [DJ]	RCA College Radio Series, Vol. II	1980	25.00
—Promo-only music and interview			
❑ DJL1-3583 [DJ]	RCA Special Radio Series	1980	25.00
—Promo-only music and interview			
❑ BXL1-7757	Resume	1981	12.00
❑ DJL1-0(# unknown) [DJ]	Selected Cuts from 1980 U.S. Tour	1980	50.00
—Promo-only four-song live EP			

COCKER, JOE

A&M

Number	Title	Yr	NM
❑ SP-3633	I Can Stand a Little Rain	1974	12.00
❑ SP-3175	I Can Stand a Little Rain	1980	10.00
❑ SP-4529	Jamaica Say You Will	1975	12.00
❑ SP-4368	Joe Cocker	1972	15.00
—Brown label			
❑ SP-4368	Joe Cocker	1974	12.00
—Silver label			
❑ SP-4224	Joe Cocker!	1969	15.00
—Brown label			
❑ SP-4224	Joe Cocker!	1974	12.00
—Silver label			
❑ SP-4670	Joe Cocker's Greatest Hits	1977	12.00
❑ SP-3257	Joe Cocker's Greatest Hits	1982	10.00
❑ SP-6002	Mad Dogs and Englishmen	1970	18.00
—Brown labels			
❑ SP-6002	Mad Dogs and Englishmen	1974	15.00
—Silver labels			
❑ SP-4574	Stingray	1976	12.00
❑ SP-4182	With a Little Help from My Friends	1969	15.00
—Brown label			
❑ SP-4182	With a Little Help from My Friends	1974	12.00
—Silver label			
❑ SP-3106	With a Little Help from My Friends	1980	10.00

ASYLUM

Number	Title	Yr	NM
❑ DP-400 [PD]	Luxury You Can Afford	1978	18.00
❑ 6E-145	Luxury You Can Afford	1978	12.00

CAPITOL

Number	Title	Yr	NM
❑ ST-12335	Civilized Man	1984	12.00
❑ ST-12394	Cocker	1986	12.00
❑ C1-92861	One Night of Sin	1989	15.00
❑ CLT-48285	Unchain My Heart	1988	12.00

ISLAND

Number	Title	Yr	NM
❑ 90096	One More Time	1983	12.00
❑ IL9750	Sheffield Steel	1982	12.00

MOBILE FIDELITY

Number	Title	Yr	NM
❑ 1-223	Sheffield Steel	1995	40.00
—Audiophile vinyl			

COCTEAU TWINS

CAPITOL

Number	Title	Yr	NM
❑ C1-90892	Blue Bell Knoll	1988	15.00
❑ SPRO79066/7 [DJ]	Cocteau Twins	1991	60.00
—Promo-only 10-song collection			
❑ C1-93669	Heaven Or Las Vegas	1990	18.00

RELATIVITY/4AD

Number	Title	Yr	NM
❑ 88561-8141-1 [EP]	Love's Easy Tears	1986	15.00
❑ 88561-8143-1	The Moon and the Melodies	1987	15.00
—With Harold Budd			
❑ EMC8040	The Pink Opaque	1986	15.00

CODONA

ECM

Number	Title	Yr	NM
❑ 1132	Codona	1979	15.00
❑ 1177	Codona 2	1980	15.00
❑ 23785	Codona 3	1983	15.00

COE, DAVID ALLAN

COLUMBIA

Number	Title	Yr	NM
❑ FC40571	A Matter of Life... And Death	1987	12.00
❑ FC38318	Biggest Hits	1982	12.00
❑ FC38535	Castles in the Sand	1983	12.00
❑ PC38535	Castles in the Sand	1985	10.00
—Budget-line reissue with new prefix			
❑ JC36277	Compass Point	1980	12.00
❑ PC36277	Compass Point	198?	10.00
—Budget-line reissue with new prefix			
❑ FC45057	Crazy Daddy	1989	12.00
❑ FC38093	D.A.C.	1982	12.00
❑ FC39617	Darlin', Darlin'	1985	12.00
❑ PC34310	David Allan Coe Rides Again	1977	12.00
❑ FC37352	Encore	1981	12.00
❑ PC37352	Encore	198?	10.00
—Budget-line reissue with new prefix			
❑ KC35306	Family Album	1978	12.00
❑ KC239585	For the Record -- The First 10 Years	1984	15.00
❑ KC35627	Greatest Hits	1978	12.00
❑ PC35627	Greatest Hits	198?	10.00
—Budget-line reissue			
❑ FC38926	Hello In There	1983	12.00
❑ KC35535	Human Emotions -- Happy Side/Su-I-Side	1978	12.00
❑ JC36970	Invictus (Means) Unconquered	1981	12.00
❑ PC36970	Invictus (Means) Unconquered	198?	10.00
—Budget-line reissue with new prefix			
❑ JC36489	I've Got Something to Say	1980	12.00
❑ PC36489	I've Got Something to Say	198?	10.00
—Budget-line reissue with new prefix			
❑ FC39269	Just Divorced	1984	12.00
❑ PC39269	Just Divorced	1986	10.00
—Budget-line reissue with new prefix			
❑ PC33916	Longhaired Redneck	1976	12.00
❑ KC32942	Mysterious Rhinestone Cowboy	1974	15.00
❑ PC32942	Mysterious Rhinestone Cowboy	197?	12.00
—Early reissue with new prefix and no bar code			
❑ KC33085	Once Upon a Rhyme	1975	15.00
❑ PC33085	Once Upon a Rhyme	197?	12.00
—Early reissue with new prefix and no bar code			
❑ FC37736	Rough Rider	1982	12.00
❑ PC37736	Rough Rider	198?	10.00
—Budget-line reissue with new prefix			
❑ FC40346	Son of the South	1986	12.00
❑ KC35789	Spectrum, VII	1979	12.00
❑ PC34780	Tattoo	1977	12.00
❑ FC37454	Tennessee Whiskey	1981	12.00
❑ PC37454	Tennessee Whiskey	198?	10.00
—Budget-line reissue with new prefix			
❑ FC40195	Unchained	1985	12.00

PAIR

Number	Title	Yr	NM
❑ PDL2-1075	Best of David Allan Coe	1986	15.00

PLANTATION

Number	Title	Yr	NM
❑ 507	Texas Moon	197?	18.00

SSS INTERNATIONAL

Number	Title	Yr	NM
❑ 9 [B]	Penitentiary Blues	1968	75.00
❑ SSS31	Requiem for a Harlequin	1973	320.00

COE, JIMMY

DELMARK

Number	Title	Yr	NM
❑ DL-443	After Hours Joint	1989	12.00

COFFEY, DENNIS

ORPHEUS

Number	Title	Yr	NM
❑ D1-75617	Under the Moonlight	1989	15.00

SUSSEX

Number	Title	Yr	NM
❑ SUX-7021	Electric Coffey	1972	15.00
❑ SUX-7004	Evolution	1971	15.00
❑ SUX-7010	Goin' for Myself	1972	15.00
❑ SUX-8031	Instant Coffey	1974	15.00

WESTBOUND

Number	Title	Yr	NM
❑ W-212	Finger Lickin' Good	1975	12.00
❑ WD300	Home	1977	12.00
❑ 6105	The Sweet Taste of Sin	1978	12.00

COHEN, LEONARD

COLUMBIA

Number	Title	Yr	NM
❑ FC44191	I'm Your Man	1988	12.00
❑ CL2733 [M]	Leonard Cohen	1967	60.00
❑ CS9533 [S]	Leonard Cohen	1967	15.00
—Red "360 Sound" label			
❑ CS9533 [S]	Leonard Cohen	1970	12.00
—Orange label			
❑ PC9533	Leonard Cohen	198?	10.00
—Reissue with new prefix			
❑ KC31724	Leonard Cohen: Live Songs	1973	15.00
❑ KC33167	New Skin for the Old Ceremony	1974	15.00
❑ JC36264	Recent Songs	1979	12.00
❑ PC36264	Recent Songs	198?	10.00
—Budget-line reissue			
❑ CS9767	Songs From a Room	1969	15.00
—Red "360 Sound" label			
❑ CS9767	Songs From a Room	1970	12.00
—Orange label			
❑ PC9767	Songs From a Room	198?	10.00
—Reissue with new prefix			
❑ C30103	Songs of Love and Hate	1971	15.00
❑ PC30103	Songs of Love and Hate	198?	10.00
—Budget-line reissue			
❑ C85953	Ten New Songs	2001	25.00
❑ PC34077	The Best of Leonard Cohen	1975	12.00
—No bar code			
❑ PC34077	The Best of Leonard Cohen	198?	10.00
—Reissue with bar code			

PASSPORT

Number	Title	Yr	NM
❑ PB-6045	Various Positions	1985	12.00

WARNER BROS.

Number	Title	Yr	NM
❑ BSK3125	Death of a Ladies' Man	1977	12.00

COHEN, MYRON

AUDIO FIDELITY

Number	Title	Yr	NM
❑ 701 [M]	Myron Cohen	196?	25.00

RCA VICTOR

Number	Title	Yr	NM
❑ LPM-3534 [M]	Everybody Gotta Be Someplace	1966	15.00
❑ LSP-3534 [S]	Everybody Gotta Be Someplace	1966	18.00
❑ LPM-3791 [M]	It's Not a Question	1967	15.00
❑ LSP-3791 [S]	It's Not a Question	1967	18.00
❑ VPS-6052	This Is Myron Cohen	1972	18.00

COHN, AL, AND BILLY MITCHELL

XANADU

Number	Title	Yr	NM
❑ 185	Night Flight to Dakar	1980	12.00
❑ 180	Xanadu in Africa	1979	12.00

COHN, AL, AND JIMMY ROWLES

XANADU

Number	Title	Yr	NM
❑ 145	Heavy Love	1978	12.00

COHN, AL, AND ZOOT SIMS

ABUNDANT SOUNDS

Number	Title	Yr	NM
❑ 1 [M]	Either Way	1960	100.00

CORAL

Number	Title	Yr	NM
❑ CRL57171 [M]	Al and Zoot	1958	100.00

MCA

Number	Title	Yr	NM
❑ 1377	Al Cohn Quintet Featuring Zoot Sims	198?	15.00

MERCURY

Number	Title	Yr	NM
❑ MG-20606 [M]	You 'n Me	1960	40.00
❑ SR 60606 [S]	You 'n Me	1960	50.00

MUSE

Number	Title	Yr	NM
❑ MR-5016	Body and Soul	1974	18.00
❑ MR-5356	Body and Soul	1988	12.00
—Reissue of 5016			

RCA VICTOR

Number	Title	Yr	NM
❑ LPM-1282 [M]	From A to Z	1956	80.00

SONET

Number	Title	Yr	NM
❑ 684	Motoring Along	197?	15.00

TRIP

Number	Title	Yr	NM
❑ 5548	You 'n Me	197?	12.00

ZIM

Number	Title	Yr	NM
❑ 2002	Either Way	197?	15.00

COHN, AL; RICH KAMUCA; BILL PERKINS

RCA VICTOR

Number	Title	Yr	NM
❑ LPM-1162 [M]	The Brothers	1955	80.00

COHN, AL; SCOTT HAMILTON; BUDDY TATE

CONCORD JAZZ

Number	Title	Yr	NM
❑ CJ-172	Tour de Force	198?	12.00

COHN, AL

BIOGRAPH

Number	Title	Yr	NM
❑ 12063	Be Loose	197?	12.00

CONCORD JAZZ

Number	Title	Yr	NM
❑ CJ-155	Nonpareil	1981	12.00
❑ CJ-194	Overtures	1982	12.00
❑ CJ-241	Standards of Excellence	1983	12.00

CORAL

Number	Title	Yr	NM
❑ CRL57118 [M]	Al Cohn Quintet	1957	50.00

DAWN

Number	Title	Yr	NM
❑ DLP-1110 [M]	Cohn on the Saxophone	1956	120.00

PRESTIGE

Number	Title	Yr	NM
❑ PRST-7819	Broadway 1954	1970	15.00

PROGRESSIVE

Number	Title	Yr	NM
❑ PLP-3002 [10]	Al Cohn Quartet	1953	300.00
❑ PLP-3004 [10]	Al Cohn Quintet	1953	300.00

RCA VICTOR

Number	Title	Yr	NM
❑ LPM-1161 [M]	Four Brass, One Tenor	1956	80.00
❑ LJM-1024 [M]	Mr. Music	1955	80.00
❑ LPM-2312 [M]	Son of Drum Suite	1960	40.00
❑ LSP-2312 [S]	Son of Drum Suite	1960	50.00
❑ LPM-1207 [M]	That Old Feeling	1956	80.00
❑ LPM-1116 [M]	The Natural Seven	1955	80.00

SAVOY

Number	Title	Yr	NM
❑ MG-12048 [M]	Cohn's Tones	1956	80.00

Number	Title	Yr	NM

SAVOY JAZZ
- ❏ SJL-1126 — The Progressive — 197? — 12.00

TIMELESS
- ❏ LPSJP-259 — Rifftide — 1990 — 15.00

XANADU
- ❏ 138 — America — 1976 — 12.00
- ❏ 179 — No Problem — 1979 — 12.00
- ❏ 110 — Play It Now — 1975 — 12.00

COHN, AL/SHORTY ROGERS

RCA VICTOR
- ❏ LJM-1020 [M] — East Coast -- West Coast Scene — 1954 — 150.00

COHN, STEVE

CADENCE JAZZ
- ❏ CJ-1020 — Shapes Sounds Theories — 198? — 10.00

COIL, PAT

SHEFFIELD LABS
- ❏ TLP-34 — Just Ahead — 1993 — 30.00
- —Audiophile vinyl
- ❏ TLP-31 — Steps — 1991 — 40.00
- —Audiophile vinyl

COKER, DOLO

XANADU
- ❏ 178 — All Alone — 1979 — 12.00
- ❏ 142 — California Hard — 1976 — 12.00
- ❏ 139 — Dolo! — 1976 — 12.00
- ❏ 153 — Third Down — 1977 — 12.00

COKER, JERRY

FANTASY
- ❏ 3214 [M] — Modern Music from Indiana University — 1956 — 60.00
- —Red vinyl
- ❏ 3214 [M] — Modern Music from Indiana University — 1957 — 40.00
- —Black vinyl

REVELATION
- ❏ 45 — A Re-Emergence — 1983 — 15.00
- ❏ 47 — Rebirth — 1984 — 15.00

COLA, GEORGE "KID SHEIK"

GHB
- ❏ GHB-187 — Kid Sheik in England — 1986 — 12.00
- ❏ GHB-47 — Kid Sheik Plays Blues and Standards — 197? — 12.00
- ❏ GHB-76 — Stompers — 197? — 12.00

JAZZOLOGY
- ❏ JCE-31 — Kid Sheik and Sheik's Swingers — 1967 — 15.00

COLBY, MARK

COLUMBIA
- ❏ JC35725 — One Good Turn — 1979 — 12.00
- ❏ JC35298 — Serpentine Fire — 1978 — 12.00

COLD BLOOD

ABC
- ❏ D-917 — Lydia Pense and Cold Blood — 1976 — 12.00

REPRISE
- ❏ MS2074 — First Taste of Sin — 1972 — 15.00
- ❏ MS2130 — Thriller! — 1973 — 15.00

SAN FRANCISCO
- ❏ SD200 — Cold Blood — 1969 — 25.00
- ❏ SD205 — Sisyphus — 1970 — 25.00

WARNER BROS.
- ❏ BS2806 — Lydia — 1974 — 12.00

COLD SWEAT

JMT
- ❏ 834426-1 — Cold Sweat Plays J.B. — 1989 — 18.00

COLDCUT

TOMMY BOY
- ❏ 25974 — What's That Noise? — 1989 — 15.00

COLE, BUDDY

COLUMBIA
- ❏ CL1224 [M] — Pipes & Chimes of Christmas — 1958 — 25.00
- —Red label with six "eye" logos
- ❏ CS8032 [S] — Pipes & Chimes of Christmas — 1958 — 30.00
- —Red and black label with six "eye" logos

PICKWICK
- ❏ SPCX-1001 — Christmas Organ and Chimes — 196? — 15.00

COLE, COZY

AUDITION
- ❏ 33-5943 [M] — Cozy Cole — 1955 — 50.00

Number	Title	Yr	NM

BETHLEHEM
- ❏ BCP-21 [M] — Jazz at the Metropole Café — 1955 — 50.00

CHARLIE PARKER
- ❏ PLP-403 [M] — A Cozy Conaption of Carmen — 1962 — 25.00
- ❏ PLP-403S [S] — A Cozy Conaption of Carmen — 1962 — 30.00

COLUMBIA
- ❏ CL2553 [M] — It's a Rockin' Thing — 1965 — 18.00
- ❏ CS9353 [S] — It's a Rockin' Thing — 1965 — 25.00

CORAL
- ❏ CRL57423 [M] — Drum Beat Dancing Feet — 1962 — 18.00
- ❏ CRL757423 [S] — Drum Beat Dancing Feet — 1962 — 25.00
- ❏ CRL57457 [M] — It's a Cozy World — 1964 — 18.00
- ❏ CRL757457 [S] — It's a Cozy World — 1964 — 25.00

FELSTED
- ❏ 7002 [M] — Cozy's Caravan/Earl's Backroom — 1958 — 50.00
- ❏ 2002 [S] — Cozy's Caravan/Earl's Backroom — 1958 — 40.00

GRAND AWARD
- ❏ GA 33-334 [M] — After Hours — 1956 — 40.00

KING
- ❏ 673 [M] — Cozy Cole — 1959 — 60.00
- ❏ KS-673 [S] — Cozy Cole — 1959 — 150.00

LOVE
- ❏ 500M [M] — Topsy — 1959 — 100.00
- ❏ 500S [S] — Topsy — 1959 — 200.00

PARIS
- ❏ 122 [M] — Cozy Cole and His All-Stars — 1958 — 50.00

PLYMOUTH
- ❏ P 12-155 [M] — Cozy Cole and His All Stars — 195? — 30.00

SAVOY
- ❏ MG-12197 [M] — Concerto for Cozy — 196? — 25.00

WHO'S WHO IN JAZZ
- ❏ 21003 — Lionel Hampton Presents Cozy Cole & Marty Napoleon — 1977 — 12.00

COLE, COZY/JIMMY MCPARTLAND

WALDORF MUSIC HALL
- ❏ MH 33-162 [10] — After Hours — 195? — 50.00

COLE, HOLLY

BLUE NOTE JAZZ
- ❏ JP-5003 — Temptation — 2001 — 40.00
- —Audiophile edition issued by Classic Records (CD was issued in 1995)

COLE, IKE

DEE GEE
- ❏ LPM-4001 [M] — Ike Cole's Tribute to His Brother Nat — 1966 — 40.00
- ❏ ST-4001 [S] — Ike Cole's Tribute to His Brother Nat — 1966 — 50.00

DOT
- ❏ DLP-25943 — Picture This! — 1969 — 30.00

GUEST STAR
- ❏ G-1502 [M] — Ike Cole -- The Brother of Nat King Cole — 196? — 18.00
- ❏ GS-1502 [S] — Ike Cole -- The Brother of Nat King Cole — 196? — 18.00

PROMENADE
- ❏ 2099 [M] — Ike Cole Sings — 196? — 18.00

UNITED ARTISTS
- ❏ UAL-3569 [M] — Same Old You — 1967 — 30.00
- ❏ UAS-6569 [S] — Same Old You — 1967 — 30.00

COLE, JERRY

BEAT ROCKET
- ❏ BR117 — Guitars A-Go-Go! — 2000 — 15.00
- ❏ BR118 — Wild Strings! — 2001 — 15.00

CAPITOL
- ❏ T2061 [M] — Hot Rod Dance Party — 1964 — 80.00
- ❏ ST2061 [S] — Hot Rod Dance Party — 1964 — 100.00
- ❏ (S)T2061 — Hot Rod Dance Party Bonus Photo — 1964 — 30.00
- ❏ T2044 [M] — Outer Limits — 1963 — 50.00
- ❏ ST2044 [S] — Outer Limits — 1963 — 80.00
- ❏ T2112 [M] — Surf Age — 1964 — 100.00
- —With bonus single by Dick Dale, "Thunder Wave"/"Spanish Kiss
- ❏ ST2112 [S] — Surf Age — 1964 — 120.00
- —With bonus single by Dick Dale, "Thunder Wave"/"Spanish Kiss
- ❏ T2112 [M] — Surf Age — 1964 — 80.00
- —With bonus single missing
- ❏ ST2112 [S] — Surf Age — 1964 — 100.00
- —With bonus single missing

LIBERTY
- ❏ LRP-3362 [M] — Sounds of the Big Irons — 1964 — 50.00
- ❏ LST-7362 [S] — Sounds of the Big Irons — 1964 — 60.00

COLE, JOHNNY

CROWN
- ❏ CMX100 — Famous Christmas Carols — 196? — 15.00

Number	Title	Yr	NM

- ❏ CLP5081 [M] — Famous Christmas Carols — 196? — 15.00
- —Same as Crown CMX 100
- ❏ CLP5132 [M] — Wishing You a Merry Christmas — 196? — 15.00
- —Same as Crown 165, but in mono
- ❏ 165 [S] — Wishing You a Merry Christmas — 196? — 18.00

CUSTOM
- ❏ CS6 [S] — 12 Days of Christmas — 196? — 15.00
- —Reissue of Crown 165 with new title

YULETIDE SERIES
- ❏ YS-216 — 12 Days of Christmas — 197? — 12.00
- —Reissue of Custom album of the same name
- ❏ YS-211 — Famous Christmas Carols — 197? — 12.00
- —Reissue of Crown LP of the same name
- ❏ YS-213 — Rudolph the Red-Nosed Reindeer — 197? — 12.00

COLE, MARIA

KAPP
- ❏ 102 [10] — Maria Cole — 1954 — 50.00

COLE, NAT KING

CAMAY
- ❏ CA-3004 — Nat King Cole — 196? — 15.00

CAPITOL
- ❏ ST-12219 — 16 Grandes Exitos — 1982 — 12.00
- ❏ DN-16165 — A Blossom Fell — 1981 — 10.00
- ❏ W782 [M] — After Midnight — 1956 — 40.00
- —Turquoise label
- ❏ W782 [M] — After Midnight — 1958 — 30.00
- —Black label with colorband, "Capitol" at left
- ❏ W782 [M] — After Midnight — 1962 — 25.00
- —Black label with colorband, "Capitol" at top
- ❏ SM-11796 — After Midnight — 1978 — 12.00
- ❏ W1220 [M] — A Mis Amigos — 1959 — 30.00
- —Black label with colorband, "Capitol" at left
- ❏ W1220 [M] — A Mis Amigos — 1962 — 25.00
- —Black label with colorband, "Capitol" at top
- ❏ SW1220 [S] — A Mis Amigos — 1959 — 40.00
- —Black label with colorband, "Capitol" at left
- ❏ SW1220 [S] — A Mis Amigos — 1962 — 30.00
- —Black label with colorband, "Capitol" at top
- ❏ SN-16136 — A Mis Amigos — 1980 — 10.00
- ❏ T680 [M] — Ballads of the Day — 1956 — 40.00
- —Turquoise label
- ❏ T680 [M] — Ballads of the Day — 1958 — 30.00
- —Black label with colorband, "Capitol" at left
- ❏ T680 [M] — Ballads of the Day — 1962 — 25.00
- —Black label with colorband, "Capitol" at top
- ❏ DT680 [R] — Ballads of the Day — 1963 — 18.00
- —Black label with colorband
- ❏ T2820 [M] — Beautiful Ballads — 1967 — 18.00
- ❏ ST2820 [S] — Beautiful Ballads — 1967 — 15.00
- ❏ DWBB-252 — Close-Up — 1969 — 18.00
- —Reissue of 680 and 1891
- ❏ W1031 [M] — Cole Espanol — 1958 — 30.00
- —Black label with colorband, "Capitol" at left
- ❏ W1031 [M] — Cole Espanol — 1962 — 25.00
- —Black label with colorband, "Capitol" at top
- ❏ DW1031 [R] — Cole Espanol — 196? — 18.00
- —Black label with colorband
- ❏ SM-1031 — Cole Espanol — 197? — 10.00
- —Reissue with new prefix
- ❏ N-16166 — Cole Espanol — 1981 — 10.00
- ❏ T1838 [M] — Dear Lonely Hearts — 1962 — 18.00
- ❏ ST1838 [S] — Dear Lonely Hearts — 1962 — 25.00
- ❏ H9110 [10] — Eight Top Pops — 1954 — 50.00
- ❏ W1249 [M] — Every Time I Feel the Spirit — 1960 — 30.00
- —Black label with colorband, "Capitol" at left
- ❏ SW1249 [S] — Every Time I Feel the Spirit — 1960 — 30.00
- —Black label with colorband, "Capitol" at left
- ❏ H213 [10] — Harvest of Hits — 1950 — 70.00
- —Original; purple label
- ❏ L213 [10] — Harvest of Hits — 195? — 60.00
- —Reissue; maroon label, "H" mechanically crossed out on back cover with "L" stamped next to it
- ❏ T2454 [M] — Hymns and Spirituals — 1966 — 15.00
- ❏ ST2454 [S] — Hymns and Spirituals — 1966 — 18.00
- ❏ T2118 [M] — I Don't Want to Be Hurt Anymore — 1964 — 18.00
- ❏ ST2118 [S] — I Don't Want to Be Hurt Anymore — 1964 — 25.00
- ❏ T592 [M] — Instrumental Classics — 1955 — 40.00
- ❏ W903 [M] — Just One of Those Things — 1957 — 40.00
- —Turquoise or gray label
- ❏ W903 [M] — Just One of Those Things — 1958 — 30.00
- —Black label with colorband, "Capitol" at left
- ❏ W903 [M] — Just One of Those Things — 1962 — 25.00
- —Black label with colorband, "Capitol" at top
- ❏ SW903 [S] — Just One of Those Things — 1959 — 30.00
- —Black label with colorband, "Capitol" at left
- ❏ SW903 [S] — Just One of Those Things — 1962 — 25.00
- —Black label with colorband, "Capitol" at top
- ❏ W2008 [M] — Let's Face the Music — 1963 — 18.00
- ❏ SW2008 [S] — Let's Face the Music — 1963 — 25.00
- ❏ T2361 [M] — Looking Back — 1965 — 15.00
- ❏ ST2361 [S] — Looking Back — 1965 — 18.00
- ❏ SM-11882 — Looking Back — 1979 — 12.00
- ❏ T2195 [M] — L-O-V-E — 1965 — 18.00

Number	Title	Yr	NM
❑ ST2195 [S]	L-O-V-E	1965	25.00
❑ SWAK-11355	Love Is Here to Stay	1974	15.00
❑ W824 [M]	Love Is the Thing	1957	40.00
— Turquoise or gray label			
❑ W824 [M]	Love Is the Thing	1958	30.00
— Black label with colorband, "Capitol" at left			

Number	Title	Yr	NM
❑ W824 [M]	Love Is the Thing	1962	25.00
— Black label with colorband, "Capitol" at top			
❑ SW824 [S]	Love Is the Thing	1959	30.00
— Black label with colorband, "Capitol" at left			
❑ SW824 [S]	Love Is the Thing	1962	25.00
— Black label with colorband, "Capitol" at top			
❑ SW824 [S]	Love Is the Thing	1969	15.00
— Lime green label			
❑ SM-824	Love Is the Thing	197?	10.00
— Reissue with new prefix			
❑ SN-16163	Love Is the Thing	1981	10.00
❑ W1749 [M]	More Cole Espanol	1962	30.00
— Black label with colorband, "Capitol" at left			
❑ W1749 [M]	More Cole Espanol	1963	18.00
— Black label with colorband, "Capitol" at top			
❑ SW1749 [S]	More Cole Espanol	1962	30.00
— Black label with colorband, "Capitol" at left			
❑ SW1749 [S]	More Cole Espanol	1963	25.00
— Black label with colorband, "Capitol" at top			
❑ SM-1749	More Cole Espanol	197?	10.00
— Reissue with new prefix			
❑ SN-16167	More Cole Espanol	1981	10.00
❑ W2117 [M]	My Fair Lady	1964	18.00
❑ SW2117 [S]	My Fair Lady	1964	25.00
— Black label with colorband			
❑ SW2117 [S]	My Fair Lady	1969	15.00
— Lime green label			
❑ SM-2117	My Fair Lady	197?	10.00
— Reissue with new prefix			
❑ H156 [10]	Nat King Cole at the Piano	1950	100.00
❑ MAS2434 [M]	Nat King Cole at the Sands	1966	15.00
❑ SMAS2434 [S]	Nat King Cole at the Sands	1966	18.00
❑ SM-2434	Nat King Cole at the Sands	197?	10.00
— Reissue with new prefix			
❑ SKAO-373	Nat King Cole's Greatest	1969	15.00
❑ H420 [10]	Nat King Cole Sings for Two in Love	1953	50.00
— Original; purple label			
❑ T420 [M]	Nat King Cole Sings for Two in Love	1955	40.00
— Turquoise label			
❑ T420 [M]	Nat King Cole Sings for Two in Love	1958	30.00
— Black label with colorband, "Capitol" at left			
❑ T420 [M]	Nat King Cole Sings for Two in Love	1962	25.00
— Black label with colorband, "Capitol" at top			
❑ DT420 [R]	Nat King Cole Sings for Two in Love	1963	18.00
❑ L420 [10]	Nat King Cole Sings for Two in Love	195?	50.00
— Reissue; maroon label, back cover probably has "H" mechanically crossed out with "L" stamped next to it			
❑ W1675 [M]	Nat King Cole Sings/George Shearing Plays	1962	30.00
— Black label with colorband, "Capitol" at left			
❑ W1675 [M]	Nat King Cole Sings/George Shearing Plays	1963	18.00
— Black label with colorband, "Capitol" at top			
❑ SW1675 [S]	Nat King Cole Sings/George Shearing Plays	1962	30.00
— Black label with colorband, "Capitol" at left			
❑ SW1675 [S]	Nat King Cole Sings/George Shearing Plays	1963	25.00
— Black label with colorband, "Capitol" at top			
❑ SM-1675	Nat King Cole Sings/George Shearing Plays	197?	10.00
— Reissue with new prefix			
❑ W1713 [M]	Nat King Cole Sings the Blues	1962	25.00
— Black label with colorband, "Capitol" at left			
❑ SW1713 [S]	Nat King Cole Sings the Blues	1962	30.00
— Black label with colorband, "Capitol" at left			
❑ W1929 [M]	Nat King Cole Sings the Blues, Volume 2	1963	18.00
❑ SW1929 [S]	Nat King Cole Sings the Blues, Volume 2	1963	25.00
❑ T1891 [M]	Nat King Cole's Top Pops	1963	18.00
❑ DT1891 [R]	Nat King Cole's Top Pops	1963	15.00
❑ T2348 [M]	Nature Boy	1965	18.00
❑ DT2348 [R]	Nature Boy	1965	15.00
❑ H332 [10]	Penthouse Serenade	1951	60.00
— Original; purple label			
❑ T332 [M]	Penthouse Serenade	1955	40.00
❑ L332 [10]	Penthouse Serenade	195?	50.00
— Reissue; maroon label, "H" mechanically crossed out on back cover with "L" stamped next to it			
❑ T1793 [M]	Ramblin' Rose	1962	18.00
❑ ST1793 [S]	Ramblin' Rose	1962	25.00
❑ SN-16032	Ramblin' Rose	1980	10.00
❑ T2680 [M]	Sincerely, Nat King Cole	1967	18.00
❑ ST2680 [S]	Sincerely, Nat King Cole	1967	15.00
❑ T2340 [M]	Songs from "Cat Ballou" and Other Motion Pictures	1965	15.00
❑ ST2340 [S]	Songs from "Cat Ballou" and Other Motion Pictures	1965	18.00
❑ SM-11804	Songs from "Cat Ballou" and Other Motion Pictures	1978	12.00
❑ W993 [M]	St. Louis Blues	1958	50.00
— Turquoise or gray label			
❑ W993 [M]	St. Louis Blues	1962	40.00
— Black label with colorband, "Capitol" at left			
❑ SW993 [S]	St. Louis Blues	1959	50.00
— Black label with colorband, "Capitol" at left			
❑ SN-16137	St. Louis Blues	1980	10.00
❑ W1331 [M]	Tell Me About Yourself	1960	30.00
— Black label with colorband, "Capitol" at left			
❑ SW1331 [S]	Tell Me About Yourself	1960	30.00
— Black label with colorband, "Capitol" at left			
❑ W514 [M]	Tenth Anniversary Album	1955	40.00
— Gray label; released simultaneously with H1-514 and H2-514			
❑ H1-514 [10]	Tenth Anniversary Album, Part 1	1954	50.00
— Contains Side 1 of W 514			
❑ H2-514 [10]	Tenth Anniversary Album, Part 2	1954	50.00
— Contains Side 2 of W 514			
❑ T2759 [M]	Thank You Pretty Baby	1967	18.00
❑ ST2759 [S]	Thank You Pretty Baby	1967	15.00
❑ SKAO2944	The Best of Nat King Cole	1968	15.00
❑ SN-16036	The Best of Nat King Cole	1980	10.00
❑ N-16260	The Best of the King Cole Trio -- Volume 1	1982	10.00
❑ N-16281	The Best of the King Cole Trio -- Volume 2	1982	10.00
❑ W1967 [M]	The Christmas Song	1962	18.00
— Reissue of W 1444 with title song added and another deleted			
❑ SW1967 [S]	The Christmas Song	1962	18.00
— Black label with colorband			
❑ SW1967 [S]	The Christmas Song	1969	15.00
— Lime-green label			
❑ SW1967 [S]	The Christmas Song	1971	15.00
— Red label			
❑ SW1967 [S]	The Christmas Song	1973	12.00
— Orange label, "Capitol" at bottom			
❑ SM-1967 [S]	The Christmas Song	197?	10.00
— Budget-line reissue			
❑ T2558 [M]	The Great Songs!	1966	15.00
❑ ST2558 [S]	The Great Songs!	1966	18.00
❑ H8 [10]	The King Cole Trio	1950	100.00
❑ H29 [10]	The King Cole Trio, Volume 2	1950	100.00
❑ H59 [10]	The King Cole Trio, Volume 3	1950	100.00
❑ H177 [10]	The King Cole Trio, Volume 4	1950	70.00
❑ W1444 [M]	The Magic of Christmas	1960	25.00
❑ SW1444 [S]	The Magic of Christmas	1960	25.00
❑ SQBO-93741	The Man and His Music	197?	25.00
— Capitol Record Club exclusive; with booklet			
❑ TCL2873 [M]	The Nat King Cole Deluxe Set	1968	30.00
❑ STCL2873 [P]	The Nat King Cole Deluxe Set	1968	30.00
❑ WCL1613 [M]	The Nat King Cole Story	1961	30.00
❑ SWCL1613 [S]	The Nat King Cole Story	1961	30.00
❑ W1926 [M]	The Nat King Cole Story, Volume 1	1962	15.00
❑ SW1926 [S]	The Nat King Cole Story, Volume 1	1962	18.00
❑ SN-16033	The Nat King Cole Story, Volume 1	1980	10.00
❑ W1927 [M]	The Nat King Cole Story, Volume 2	1963	15.00
❑ SW1927 [S]	The Nat King Cole Story, Volume 2	1963	18.00
❑ SN-16034	The Nat King Cole Story, Volume 2	1980	10.00
❑ W1928 [M]	The Nat King Cole Story, Volume 3	1963	15.00
❑ SW1928 [S]	The Nat King Cole Story, Volume 3	1963	18.00
❑ SN-16035	The Nat King Cole Story, Volume 3	1980	10.00
❑ H220 [10]	The Nat King Cole Trio	1950	60.00
❑ T2311 [M]	The Nat King Cole Trio	1965	15.00
❑ W689 [M]	The Piano Style of Nat King Cole	1956	40.00
— Turquoise label			
❑ W689 [M]	The Piano Style of Nat King Cole	1958	30.00
— Black label with colorband, "Capitol" at left			
❑ W689 [M]	The Piano Style of Nat King Cole	1962	25.00
— Black label with colorband, "Capitol" at top			
❑ ST-310	There! I've Said It Again	1969	15.00
❑ SQBO91278	The Swingin' Moods of Nat King Cole	1967	30.00
— Capitol Record Club exclusive			
❑ W1574 [M]	The Touch of Your Lips	1961	25.00
— Black label with colorband, "Capitol" at left			
❑ W1574 [M]	The Touch of Your Lips	1962	18.00
— Black label with colorband, "Capitol" at top			
❑ SW1574 [S]	The Touch of Your Lips	1961	30.00
— Black label with colorband, "Capitol" at left			
❑ SW1574 [S]	The Touch of Your Lips	1962	25.00
— Black label with colorband, "Capitol" at top			
❑ SQBO90938	The Velvet Moods of Nat King Cole	1967	30.00
— Capitol Record Club exclusive			
❑ W1084 [M]	The Very Thought of You	1958	30.00
— Black label with colorband, "Capitol" at left			
❑ W1084 [M]	The Very Thought of You	1962	25.00
— Black label with colorband, "Capitol" at top			
❑ SW1084 [S]	The Very Thought of You	1959	30.00
— Black label with colorband, "Capitol" at left			
❑ SW1084 [S]	The Very Thought of You	1962	25.00
— Black label with colorband, "Capitol" at top			
❑ T2529 [M]	The Vintage Years	1966	15.00
❑ T870 [M]	This Is Nat "King" Cole	1957	40.00
— Turquoise or gray label			
❑ T870 [M]	This Is Nat "King" Cole	1958	30.00
— Black label with colorband, "Capitol" at left			
❑ T870 [M]	This Is Nat "King" Cole	1962	25.00
— Black label with colorband, "Capitol" at top			
❑ DT870 [R]	This Is Nat "King" Cole	1963	18.00
— Black label with colorband			
❑ T1932 [M]	Those Lazy-Hazy-Crazy Days of Summer	1963	18.00
❑ ST1932 [S]	Those Lazy-Hazy-Crazy Days of Summer	1963	25.00
❑ W1190 [M]	To Whom It May Concern	1959	30.00
— Black label with colorband, "Capitol" at left			
❑ SW1190 [S]	To Whom It May Concern	1959	40.00
— Black label with colorband, "Capitol" at left			
❑ M-11033 [M]	Trio Days	1972	18.00
❑ H357 [10]	Unforgettable	1952	60.00
❑ T357 [M]	Unforgettable	1955	40.00
— Turquoise label			
❑ T357 [M]	Unforgettable	1958	30.00
— Black label with colorband, "Capitol" at left			
❑ T357 [M]	Unforgettable	1962	25.00
— Black label with colorband, "Capitol" at top			
❑ DT357 [R]	Unforgettable	1965	15.00
❑ SM-357	Unforgettable	197?	10.00
— Reissue with new prefix			
❑ SN-16162	Unforgettable	1981	10.00
❑ T591 [M]	Vocal Classics	1955	40.00
❑ DN-16164	Walkin' My Baby Back Home	1981	10.00
❑ STBB-503	Walkin' My Baby Back Home/A Blossom Fell	1970	18.00
❑ W1120 [M]	Welcome to the Club	1959	30.00
— Black label with colorband, "Capitol" at left			
❑ SW1120 [S]	Welcome to the Club	1959	40.00
— Black label with colorband, "Capitol" at left			
❑ W1859 [M]	Where Did Everyone Go?	1963	18.00
❑ SW1859 [S]	Where Did Everyone Go?	1963	25.00
❑ WAK1392 [M]	Wild Is Love	1960	30.00
— Black label with colorband, "Capitol" at left			
❑ SWAK1392 [S]	Wild Is Love	1960	30.00
— Black label with colorband, "Capitol" at left			
❑ SN-16037	Wild Is Love	1980	10.00

DCC COMPACT CLASSICS

Number	Title	Yr	NM
❑ LPZ-2029	Love Is the Thing	1997	120.00
— Audiophile vinyl			
❑ LPZ-2061	The Greatest Hits	1998	120.00
— Audiophile vinyl			
❑ LPZ-2047	The Very Thought of You	1998	100.00
— Audiophile vinyl			

DECCA

Number	Title	Yr	NM
❑ DL8260 [M]	In the Beginning	1956	40.00
— Black label, silver print			
❑ DL8260 [M]	In the Beginning	1960	30.00
— Black label with color bars			

EVEREST ARCHIVE OF FOLK & JAZZ

Number	Title	Yr	NM
❑ 290	Nature Boy	197?	12.00

MARK 56

Number	Title	Yr	NM
❑ 739	Early 1940s	197?	18.00

MCA

Number	Title	Yr	NM
❑ 4020	From the Very Beginning	1973	15.00

MOBILE FIDELITY

Number	Title	Yr	NM
❑ 1-081	Nat King Cole Sings/George Shearing Plays	1981	40.00
— Audiophile vinyl			

Number	Title	Yr	NM
MOSAIC			
❑ MR27-138	The Complete Capitol Recordings of the Nat King Cole Trio	1991	800.00
PAIR			
❑ PDL2-1026	Love Moods	1986	15.00
❑ PDL2-1128	Tenderly	1986	15.00
❑ PDL2-1025	Weaver of Dreams	1986	15.00
PICKWICK			
❑ SPC-3046 [B]	Love Is a Many Splendored Thing	196?	12.00
❑ SPC-3249	Nature Boy	197?	12.00
❑ PTP-2058	Nature Boy	1973	15.00
❑ SPC-3105	Stay As Sweet As You Are	196?	12.00
❑ SPC-3071	When You're Smiling	196?	12.00
❑ SPC-3154	You're My Everything	197?	12.00
SAVOY JAZZ			
❑ SJL-1205	Nat King Cole & The King Cole Trio	1989	15.00
SCORE			
❑ SLP-4019 [M]	The King Cole Trio and Lester Young	1957	80.00
TIME-LIFE			
❑ SLGD-01	Legendary Singers: Nat King Cole	1985	18.00
❑ SLGD-15	Legendary Singers: Nat King Cole: Take Two	1986	18.00
TRIP			
❑ 7	The Nat "King" Cole Trio	197?	15.00
VERVE			
❑ VSP-14 [M]	Nat Cole at JATP	1966	18.00
❑ VSPS-14 [R]	Nat Cole at JATP	1966	15.00
❑ VSP-25 [M]	Nat Cole at JATP 2	1966	18.00
❑ VSPS-25 [R]	Nat Cole at JATP 2	1966	15.00

COLE, NATALIE, AND PEABO BRYSON

Number	Title	Yr	NM
CAPITOL			
❑ SOO-12025	We're the Best of Friends	1979	12.00

COLE, NATALIE

Number	Title	Yr	NM
CAPITOL			
❑ ST-12242	A Collection	1982	12.00
❑ SN-16310	A Collection	1985	10.00
—Budget-line reissue			
❑ ST-12079	Don't Look Back	1980	12.00
❑ ST-12165	Happy Love	1981	12.00
❑ SO-11928	I Love You So	1979	12.00
❑ ST-11429	Inseparable	1975	12.00
❑ SN-16038	Inseparable	198?	10.00
—Budget-line reissue			
❑ ST-11517	Natalie	1976	12.00
❑ SKBL-11709	Natalie..Live!	1978	15.00
❑ SW-11708	Thankful	1978	12.00
❑ SO-11600	Unpredictable	1977	12.00
ELEKTRA			
❑ 61049	Unforgettable	1991	25.00
EMI			
❑ E1-48902	Good to Be Back	1989	12.00
EPIC			
❑ FE38280	I'm Ready	1983	12.00
MANHATTAN			
❑ 53051	Everlasting	1987	12.00
MOBILE FIDELITY			
❑ 1-032 [B]	Thankful	1980	25.00
—Audiophile vinyl			
MODERN			
❑ 90270	Dangerous	1985	12.00

COLE, RICHIE, AND BOOTS RANDOLPH

Number	Title	Yr	NM
PALO ALTO			
❑ PA-8041	Yakety Madness	1983	12.00

COLE, RICHIE, AND ERIC KLOSS

Number	Title	Yr	NM
MUSE			
❑ MR-5082	Battle of the Saxes	1976	12.00

COLE, RICHIE, AND HANK CRAWFORD

Number	Title	Yr	NM
MILESTONE			
❑ M-9180	Bossa International	1990	15.00

COLE, RICHIE, AND PHIL WOODS

Number	Title	Yr	NM
MUSE			
❑ MR-5237	Side by Side	1980	12.00

COLE, RICHIE

Number	Title	Yr	NM
ADELPHI			
❑ AD5001	Starburst	1976	25.00
CONCORD JAZZ			
❑ CJ-314	Pure Imagination	1987	12.00
MILESTONE			
❑ M-9152	Popbop	1987	12.00
❑ M-9162	Signature	1988	12.00
MUSE			
❑ MR-5270	Alive at the Village Vanguard	1981	12.00
❑ MR-5155	Alto Madness	1977	12.00

Number	Title	Yr	NM
❑ MR-5245	Cool "C"	1981	12.00
❑ MR-5207	Hollywood Madness	1979	12.00
❑ MR-5192	Keeper of the Flame	1978	12.00
❑ MR-5119	New York Afternoon	1976	12.00
❑ MR-5295	Some Things Speak for Themselves	1982	12.00
PALO ALTO			
❑ PA-8036	Alto Annie's Theme	1983	12.00
❑ PA-8070	Bossa Nova Eyes	1985	12.00
❑ PA-8023	Return to Alto Acres	1982	12.00

COLE, TONY

Number	Title	Yr	NM
20TH CENTURY			
❑ T-403	If the Music Stops	1972	15.00
❑ T-416	Magnificently Mad	1973	15.00

COLEMAN, ALBERT, 'S ATLANTA POPS

Number	Title	Yr	NM
EPIC			
❑ FE38630	Classic Country	1983	10.00
❑ FE38154	Just Hooked on Country	1982	10.00

COLEMAN, BILL

Number	Title	Yr	NM
BLACK LION			
❑ 128	London!	197?	15.00
❑ 212	Mainstream at Montreux	1974	15.00
DRG			
❑ SL-5200	Blowing for the Cats: The Final Big Band Sessions	198?	12.00
SWING			
❑ SW-8410	Bill Coleman with George Duvivier & Co.	198?	12.00
❑ SW-8402	Paris 1936-38	198?	12.00

COLEMAN, CY

Number	Title	Yr	NM
BENIDA			
❑ LP-1023A [10]	Cy Coleman	1955	50.00
CAPITOL			
❑ T1952 [M]	Piano Witchcraft	1963	25.00
❑ ST1952 [S]	Piano Witchcraft	1963	30.00
❑ T2355 [M]	The Art of Love	1965	18.00
❑ ST2355 [S]	The Art of Love	1965	25.00
COLUMBIA			
❑ C32804	Broadway Tunesmith	1973	12.00
❑ CL2578 [M]	If My Friends Could See Me Now	1966	15.00
❑ CS9378 [S]	If My Friends Could See Me Now	1966	18.00
DRG			
❑ SL-5205	Comin' Home	1988	12.00
EVEREST			
❑ LPBR-5092 [M]	Playboy's Penthouse	196?	30.00
❑ SDBR-1092 [S]	Playboy's Penthouse	196?	30.00
MGM			
❑ SE-4501	Ages of Rock	1968	30.00
WESTMINSTER			
❑ WLP-15001 [M]	Cool Coleman	195?	40.00

COLEMAN, EARL

Number	Title	Yr	NM
ATLANTIC			
❑ SD8172	Love Songs	1968	18.00
FANTASY			
❑ OJC-187	Earl Coleman Returns	1986	12.00
PRESTIGE			
❑ PRLP-7045 [M]	Earl Coleman Returns	1956	50.00
—Yellow label			
❑ PRLP-7045 [M]	Earl Coleman Returns	196?	30.00
—Blue label, trident logo at right			
STASH			
❑ 243	Stardust	1984	12.00
XANADU			
❑ 147	A Song for You	1978	15.00
❑ 175	There's Something About an Old Love	1979	15.00

COLEMAN, ERNIE

Number	Title	Yr	NM
WARNER BROS.			
❑ W1261 [M]	Be Gentle, Please	1959	30.00
❑ WS1261 [S]	Be Gentle, Please	1959	30.00

COLEMAN, GEORGE

Number	Title	Yr	NM
THERESA			
❑ TR-126	George Coleman at Yoshi's	1989	15.00
❑ TR-120	Manhattan Panorama	1986	12.00
TIMELESS			
❑ 312	Meditation	197?	15.00

COLEMAN, GLORIA

Number	Title	Yr	NM
ABC IMPULSE!			
❑ AS-47	Soul Sisters	1968	15.00
IMPULSE!			
❑ A-47 [M]	Soul Sisters	1963	30.00
❑ AS-47 [S]	Soul Sisters	1963	30.00
MAINSTREAM			
❑ MRL-322	Gloria Coleman Sings and Swings -- Organ	1972	15.00

COLEMAN, ORNETTE

Number	Title	Yr	NM
ABC IMPULSE!			
❑ AS-9187	Crisis	1969	30.00
❑ AS-9178	Ornette at 12	1968	30.00
ANTILLES			
❑ AN-2001	Of Human Feelings	198?	18.00
ARISTA FREEDOM			
❑ AL1900	The Great London Concert	1978	25.00
ARTISTS HOUSE			
❑ 1	Body Meta	1977	25.00
❑ 6	Soapsuds	1978	25.00
ATLANTIC			
❑ 1327 [M]	Change of the Century	1960	30.00
—Multicolor label, white "fan" logo			
❑ 1327 [M]	Change of the Century	1963	18.00
—Multicolor label, black "fan" logo			
❑ SD1327 [S]	Change of the Century	1960	40.00
—Multicolor label, white "fan" logo			
❑ SD1327 [S]	Change of the Century	1963	25.00
—Multicolor label, black "fan" logo			
❑ SD1327 [S]	Change of the Century	1060	15.00
—Red and green label, "1841 Broadway" on label			
❑ 1327 [M]	Change of the Century	1960	50.00
—Black label			
❑ SD1327 [S]	Change of the Century	1960	60.00
—Green label			
❑ SD1327 [S]	Change of the Century	1976	12.00
❑ 1364 [M]	Free Jazz	1961	40.00
—Multicolor label, white "fan" logo			
❑ 1364 [M]	Free Jazz	1963	25.00
—Multicolor label, black "fan" logo			
❑ SD1364 [S]	Free Jazz	1961	50.00
—Multicolor label, white "fan" logo			
❑ SD1364 [S]	Free Jazz	1963	30.00
—Multicolor label, black "fan" logo			
❑ SD1364 [S]	Free Jazz	1969	15.00
—Red and green label			
❑ 1378 [M]	Ornette	1961	30.00
—Multicolor label, white "fan" logo			
❑ 1378 [M]	Ornette	1963	18.00
—Multicolor label, black "fan" logo			
❑ SD1378 [S]	Ornette	1961	40.00
—Multicolor label, white "fan" logo			
❑ SD1378 [S]	Ornette	1963	25.00
—Multicolor label, black "fan" logo			
❑ SD1378 [S]	Ornette	1969	15.00
—Red and green label			
❑ 90530	Ornette	198?	12.00
—Reissue of 1378			
❑ 1394 [M]	Ornette on Tenor	1962	25.00
—Multicolor label, black "fan" logo			
❑ SD1394 [S]	Ornette on Tenor	1962	30.00
—Multicolor label, black "fan" logo			
❑ SD1394 [S]	Ornette on Tenor	1969	15.00
—Red and green label			
❑ SD1572	The Art of Improvisors	1971	18.00
❑ SD1558	The Best of Ornette Coleman	1970	18.00
❑ 1317 [M]	The Shape of Jazz to Come	1959	80.00
—"Bullseye" label			
❑ 1317 [M]	The Shape of Jazz to Come	1960	30.00
—Multicolor label, white "fan" logo			
❑ 1317 [M]	The Shape of Jazz to Come	1963	18.00
—Multicolor label, black "fan" logo			
❑ SD1317 [S]	The Shape of Jazz to Come	1959	50.00
—"Bullseye" label			
❑ SD1317 [S]	The Shape of Jazz to Come	1960	30.00
—Multicolor label, white "fan" logo			
❑ SD1317 [S]	The Shape of Jazz to Come	1963	25.00
—Multicolor label, black "fan" logo			
❑ SD1317 [S]	The Shape of Jazz to Come	1969	15.00
—Red and green label			
❑ 1353 [M]	This Is Our Music	1960	30.00
—Multicolor label, white "fan" logo			
❑ 1353 [M]	This Is Our Music	1963	18.00
—Multicolor label, black "fan" logo			
❑ SD1353 [S]	This Is Our Music	1960	40.00
—Multicolor label, white "fan" logo			
❑ SD1353 [S]	This Is Our Music	1963	25.00
—Multicolor label, black "fan" logo			
❑ SD1353 [S]	This Is Our Music	1969	15.00
—Red and green label			
❑ SD1588	Twins	1972	18.00
❑ SD8810	Twins	198?	15.00
BLUE NOTE			
❑ BST-84356	Love Call	1970	25.00
❑ BST-84287	New York Is Now!	1968	30.00
❑ BLP-4224 [M]	Ornette Coleman at the Golden Circle, Stockholm, Volume 1	1965	30.00
❑ BST-84224 [S]	Ornette Coleman at the Golden Circle, Stockholm, Volume 1	1965	40.00
—New York, USA" on label			
❑ BST-84224 [S]	Ornette Coleman at the Golden Circle, Stockholm, Volume 1	1967	18.00
—A Division of Liberty Records" on label			

Number	Title	Yr	NM
❑ BLP-4225 [M]	Ornette Coleman at the Golden Circle, Stockholm, Volume 2	1965	30.00
❑ BST-84225 [S]	Ornette Coleman at the Golden Circle, Stockholm, Volume 2	1965	40.00
—New York, USA" on label			
❑ BST-84225 [S]	Ornette Coleman at the Golden Circle, Stockholm, Volume 2	1967	18.00
—A Division of Liberty Records" on label			
❑ BLP-4246 [M]	The Empty Foxhole	1966	30.00
❑ BST-84246 [S]	The Empty Foxhole	1966	40.00
—New York, USA" on label			
❑ BST-84246 [S]	The Empty Foxhole	1967	30.00
—A Division of Liberty Records" on label			
❑ B1-28982	The Empty Foxhole	1994	18.00

COLUMBIA

Number	Title	Yr	NM
❑ FC38029	Broken Shadows	198?	15.00
❑ KC31061	Science Fiction	1972	25.00
❑ CG33669	Science Fiction/Skies of America	1976	25.00
❑ KC31562	Skies of America	1972	25.00

CONTEMPORARY

Number	Title	Yr	NM
❑ C-3551 [M]	The Music of Ornette Coleman -- Something Else!	1958	120.00
❑ S-7551 [S]	The Music of Ornette Coleman -- Something Else!	1959	80.00
❑ M-3569 [M]	Tomorrow Is the Question	1959	80.00
❑ S-7569 [S]	Tomorrow Is the Question	1959	60.00

ESP-DISK'

Number	Title	Yr	NM
❑ 1006 [M]	Town Hall Concert, December 1962	1965	100.00
❑ S-1006 [S]	Town Hall Concert, December 1962	1965	80.00
❑ S1006 [B]	Town Hall Concert, December 1962	1965	800.00

—Promo with blank white labels. Includes ESP press release and original inner sleeve with essay "The New Music" by Robert Ostermann and ESP catalogue. Cover is silkscreened. Back cover is blank.

FANTASY

Number	Title	Yr	NM
❑ OJC-163	The Music of Ornette Coleman -- Something Else!	198?	15.00
—Reissue of Contemporary 7551			
❑ OJC-342	Tomorrow Is the Question	198?	15.00
—Reissue of Contemporary 7569			

FLYING DUTCHMAN

Number	Title	Yr	NM
❑ 123	Friends and Neighbors	1970	25.00
❑ FD-10123	Friends and Neighbors	1972	18.00
—Reissue of 123			

HORIZON

Number	Title	Yr	NM
❑ 722	Dancing in Your Head	1977	18.00

IAI

Number	Title	Yr	NM
❑ 373852	Classics, Volume 1	197?	25.00

INNER CITY

Number	Title	Yr	NM
❑ 1001	Live at the Hillcrest Club 1958	197?	25.00

MOON

Number	Title	Yr	NM
❑ MLP-022	Broken Shadows	1992	18.00

PORTRAIT

Number	Title	Yr	NM
❑ OR44301	Virgin Beauty	1988	18.00

RCA VICTOR

Number	Title	Yr	NM
❑ LPM-2982 [M]	The Music of Ornette Coleman	1964	30.00
❑ LSP-2982 [S]	The Music of Ornette Coleman	1964	30.00

COLEMAN, STEVE

JMT

Number	Title	Yr	NM
❑ 850001	Motherland Pulse	1985	18.00
❑ 860005	On the Edge of Tomorrow	1986	18.00
❑ 834425-1	Strata Institute Cipher Syntax	1988	15.00
❑ 870010	World Expansion	1987	18.00

NOVUS

Number	Title	Yr	NM
❑ 63180-1 [EP]	A Tale of 3 Cities The EP	1995	15.00

COLES, JOHNNY

BLUE NOTE

Number	Title	Yr	NM
❑ BLP-4144 [M]	Little Johnny C	1963	150.00
—New York, USA" on label			
❑ BST-84144 [S]	Little Johnny C	1963	50.00
—New York, USA" on label			
❑ BST-84144 [S]	Little Johnny C	1967	18.00
—A Division of Liberty Records" on label			

EPIC

Number	Title	Yr	NM
❑ LA16015 [M]	The Warm Sound	1961	1000.00
—deep groove			
❑ BA17015 [S]	The Warm Sound	1961	150.00

MAINSTREAM

Number	Title	Yr	NM
❑ MRL-346	Katumbo (Dance)	1972	25.00

COLIANNI, JOHN

CONCORD JAZZ

Number	Title	Yr	NM
❑ CJ-367	Blues-O-Matic	1989	15.00
❑ CJ-309	John Colianni	1987	12.00

COLINA, MICHAEL

PRIVATE MUSIC

Number	Title	Yr	NM
❑ 2041-1-P	The Shadow of Urbano	1988	12.00

COLLAGE, THE

SMASH

Number	Title	Yr	NM
❑ SRS-67101	The Collage	1968	25.00

COLLECTIVE SOUL

ATLANTIC

Number	Title	Yr	NM
❑ 82984-1	Disciplined Breakdown	1997	15.00

COLLECTORS, THE

WARNER BROS.

Number	Title	Yr	NM
❑ WS1774	Grass and Wild Strawberries	1969	30.00
❑ W1746 [M]	The Collectors	1968	50.00
—May be white label promo only			
❑ WS1746 [S]	The Collectors	1968	30.00

COLLEGIANS, THE (1)

LOST-NITE

Number	Title	Yr	NM
❑ LLP-5 [10]	The Best of the Collegians	1981	12.00
—Red vinyl			

WINLEY

Number	Title	Yr	NM
❑ LP-6004 [M]	Sing Along with the Collegians	195?	400.00

COLLETTE, BUDDY

ABC-PARAMOUNT

Number	Title	Yr	NM
❑ ABC-179 [M]	Calm, Cool and Collette	1957	60.00

CHALLENGE

Number	Title	Yr	NM
❑ CHL-603 [M]	Everybody's Buddy	1958	50.00

CONTEMPORARY

Number	Title	Yr	NM
❑ C-3522 [M]	Man of Many Parts	1956	50.00
❑ S-7522 [S]	Man of Many Parts	1959	40.00
❑ C-3531 [M]	Nice Day with Buddy Collette	1957	50.00
❑ S-7531 [S]	Nice Day with Buddy Collette	1959	40.00

CROWN

Number	Title	Yr	NM
❑ CLP-5019 [M]	Bongo Madness	195?	30.00

DIG

Number	Title	Yr	NM
❑ LP-101 [M]	Tanganyika	1956	100.00

DOOTO

Number	Title	Yr	NM
❑ DTL-245 [M]	Buddy's Best	1957	100.00
—Red vinyl			
❑ DTL-245 [M]	Buddy's Best	1957	60.00
—Black vinyl			

EMARCY

Number	Title	Yr	NM
❑ MG-36133 [M]	Swingin' Shepherds	1958	50.00
❑ SR-80005 [S]	Swingin' Shepherds	1959	40.00

FANTASY

Number	Title	Yr	NM
❑ OJC-239	Man of Many Parts	198?	12.00

INTERLUDE

Number	Title	Yr	NM
❑ MO-505 [M]	Modern Interpretations of Porgy & Bess	196?	30.00
❑ ST-1005 [S]	Modern Interpretations of Porgy & Bess	196?	40.00

LEGEND

Number	Title	Yr	NM
❑ 1004	Now and Then	1974	15.00

MERCURY

Number	Title	Yr	NM
❑ MG-20447 [M]	At the Cinema	1959	40.00
❑ SR-60132 [S]	At the Cinema	1959	40.00

MUSIC & SOUND

Number	Title	Yr	NM
❑ 1001 [M]	Polynesia	196?	30.00
❑ S-1001 [S]	Polynesia	196?	40.00

RGB

Number	Title	Yr	NM
❑ 2001	Block Buster	1975	15.00

SOUL NOTE

Number	Title	Yr	NM
❑ 121165	Flute Talk	1990	18.00

SPECIALTY

Number	Title	Yr	NM
❑ SP-5002 [M]	Jazz Loves Paris	1960	50.00

SURREY

Number	Title	Yr	NM
❑ S-1009 [M]	Buddy Collette on Broadway	1965	18.00
❑ SS-1009 [S]	Buddy Collette on Broadway	1965	25.00

TAMPA

Number	Title	Yr	NM
❑ TP-34 [M]	Star Studded Cast	1959	80.00

WORLD PACIFIC

Number	Title	Yr	NM
❑ WP-1823 [M]	Warm Winds	1964	25.00
❑ ST-1823 [S]	Warm Winds	1964	30.00

COLLIE, MAX, AND HIS RHYTHM ACES

GHB

Number	Title	Yr	NM
❑ GHB-63	On Tour in the U.S.A.	198?	12.00

COLLIER, MITTY

CHESS

Number	Title	Yr	NM
❑ LP-1492 [M]	Shades of a Genius	1965	80.00
❑ LPS-1492 [S]	Shades of a Genius	1965	120.00

COLLINS, AARON

CROWN

Number	Title	Yr	NM
❑ CLP-5028 [M]	Calypso U.S.A.	1958	600.00

COLLINS, AL "JAZZBO

ABC IMPULSE!

Number	Title	Yr	NM
❑ AS-9150 [S]	A Lovely Bunch of Al "Jazzbo" Collins	1968	18.00

CORAL

Number	Title	Yr	NM
❑ CRL57035 [M]	East Coast Jazz Scene	1956	80.00

EVEREST

Number	Title	Yr	NM
❑ LPBR-5097 [M]	Swingin' at the Opera	1960	30.00
❑ SDBR-1097 [S]	Swingin' at the Opera	1960	40.00

IMPULSE!

Number	Title	Yr	NM
❑ A-9150 [M]	A Lovely Bunch of Al "Jazzbo" Collins	1967	40.00
❑ AS-9150 [S]	A Lovely Bunch of Al "Jazzbo" Collins	1967	30.00

OLD TOWN

Number	Title	Yr	NM
❑ LP-2001 [M]	In the Purple Grotto	1961	30.00

COLLINS, ALBERT

ALLIGATOR

Number	Title	Yr	NM
❑ AL-4752	Cold Snap	1986	12.00
❑ AL-4730	Don't Lose Your Cool	1983	12.00
❑ AL-4719	Frostbite	1980	12.00
❑ AL-4725	Frozen Alive!	1981	12.00
❑ AL-4713	Ice Pickin'	1978	12.00
❑ AL-4733	Live in Japan	1984	12.00
❑ AL-4743	Showdown!	1985	12.00
—With Robert Cray and Johnny Copeland			

BLUE THUMB

Number	Title	Yr	NM
❑ BTS8	Truckin' with Albert Collins	1969	30.00
—Reissue of TCF Hall LP			

IMPERIAL

Number	Title	Yr	NM
❑ LP-12428	Love Can Be Found Anywhere	1968	30.00
❑ LP-12449	The Compleat Albert Collins	1970	30.00
❑ LP-12438	Trash Talkin'	1969	30.00

MOBILE FIDELITY

Number	Title	Yr	NM
❑ 1-226	Cold Snap	1995	25.00
—Audiophile vinyl			
❑ 1-217	Showdown!	1995	30.00
—With Robert Cray and Johnny Copeland; audiophile vinyl			

TCF HALL

Number	Title	Yr	NM
❑ 8002 [M]	The Cool Sound of Albert Collins	1965	300.00

TUMBLEWEED

Number	Title	Yr	NM
❑ TWS-103	There's Gotta Be a Change	1971	18.00

COLLINS, BOOTSY

COLUMBIA

Number	Title	Yr	NM
❑ FC44107	What's Bootsy Doin'?	1988	12.00

WARNER BROS.

Number	Title	Yr	NM
❑ BSK3667	The One Giveth, The Count Taketh Away	1982	12.00

COLLINS, BRIAN

ABC

Number	Title	Yr	NM
❑ AC-1029	The ABC Collection	1977	18.00

ABC DOT

Number	Title	Yr	NM
❑ DOSD-2008	That's the Way Love Should Be	1974	18.00

DOT

Number	Title	Yr	NM
❑ DLP-26017	This Is Brian Collins	1973	18.00

COLLINS, DAVE AND ANSIL

BIG TREE

Number	Title	Yr	NM
❑ 2005 [B]	Double Barrel	1971	60.00

COLLINS, DICK

RCA VICTOR

Number	Title	Yr	NM
❑ LJM-1019 [M]	Horn of Plenty	1955	100.00
❑ LJM-1027 [M]	King Richard the Swing Hearted	1955	100.00

COLLINS, DOROTHY

CORAL

Number	Title	Yr	NM
❑ CRL57105 [M]	Dorothy Collins at Home	1957	30.00
❑ CRL57150 [M]	Picnic	1958	30.00
❑ CRL57106 [M]	Songs by Dorothy Collins	1957	30.00

EVEREST

Number	Title	Yr	NM
❑ LPBR-5026 [M]	Singing and Swinging	196?	25.00
❑ SDBR-1026 [S]	Singing and Swinging	196?	30.00

TOP RANK

Number	Title	Yr	NM
❑ TM-340 [M]	A New Way to Travel	1959	30.00

COLLINS, JOYCE

DISCOVERY

Number	Title	Yr	NM
❑ 828	Moment to Moment	198?	12.00

JAZZLAND

Number	Title	Yr	NM
❑ JLP-24 [M]	The Girl Here Plays Mean Piano	1960	30.00
❑ JLP-924 [S]	The Girl Here Plays Mean Piano	1960	30.00

Number	Title	Yr	NM

COLLINS, JUDY

DCC COMPACT CLASSICS

Number	Title	Yr	NM
❑ LPZ-2067	Colors of the Day/The Best of Judy Collins	1998	30.00

—*Audiophile vinyl*

DIRECT DISK

| ❑ SD-16607 | Judith | 1980 | 40.00 |

—*Audiophile vinyl*

ELEKTRA

| ❑ 7E-1076 | Bread and Roses | 1976 | 12.00 |
| ❑ EKS-75030 | Colors of the Day/The Best of Judy Collins | 1972 | 15.00 |

—*Butterfly label, no Warner Communications logo*

| ❑ EKS-75030 | Colors of the Day/The Best of Judy Collins | 1975 | 10.00 |

—*Any label with Warner Communications logo*

| ❑ EQ-5030 [Q] | Colors of the Day/The Best of Judy Collins | 1973 | 30.00 |
| ❑ EKL-222 [M] | Golden Apples of the Sun | 1962 | 30.00 |

—*Guitar player" label*

| ❑ EKL-222 [M] | Golden Apples of the Sun | 1966 | 25.00 |

—*Gold/tan label*

| ❑ EKS-7222 [R] | Golden Apples of the Sun | 196? | 15.00 |

—*Gold/tan label or red label with large stylized "E*

| ❑ EKS-7222 [R] | Golden Apples of the Sun | 1971 | 12.00 |

—*Butterfly label, no Warner Communications logo*

| ❑ EKS-7222 [R] | Golden Apples of the Sun | 1975 | 10.00 |

—*Any label with Warner Communications logo*

❑ 6E-171	Hard Times for Lovers	1979	12.00
❑ 60304	Home Again	1985	12.00
❑ EKL-320 [M]	In My Life	1966	25.00
❑ EKS-7320 [S]	In My Life	1966	30.00
❑ EKS-74027	In My Life	1968	25.00

—*Reissue of 7320; gold/tan label*

| ❑ EKS-74027 | In My Life | 1969 | 18.00 |

—*Red label with large stylized "E*

| ❑ EKS-74027 | In My Life | 1971 | 15.00 |

—*Butterfly label, no Warner Communications logo*

| ❑ EKS-74027 | In My Life | 1975 | 10.00 |

—*Any label with Warner Communications logo*

❑ 7E-1032	Judith	1975	15.00
❑ EQ-1032 [Q]	Judith	1975	30.00
❑ 6E-111	Judith	1977	10.00

—*Reissue of 7E-1032*

| ❑ DS500 | Judy | 1969 | 18.00 |

—*Columbia Record Club exclusive; red label with large stylized "E*

| ❑ EKL-243 [M] | Judy Collins #3 | 1963 | 30.00 |

—*Guitar player" label*

| ❑ EKL-243 [M] | Judy Collins #3 | 1966 | 25.00 |

—*Gold/tan label*

| ❑ EKS-7243 [S] | Judy Collins #3 | 1963 | 40.00 |

—*Guitar player" label*

| ❑ EKS-7243 [S] | Judy Collins #3 | 1966 | 30.00 |

—*Gold/tan label*

| ❑ EKS-7243 [S] | Judy Collins #3 | 1969 | 18.00 |

—*Red label with large stylized "E*

| ❑ EKS-7243 [S] | Judy Collins #3 | 1971 | 12.00 |

—*Butterfly label, no Warner Communications logo*

| ❑ EKS-7243 [S] | Judy Collins #3 | 1975 | 10.00 |

—*Any label with Warner Communications logo*

| ❑ JC-1 [DJ] | Judy Collins | 1967 | 18.00 |

—*Promo-only compilation of six songs, each in mono on one side, stereo on the other*

| ❑ EKL-280 [M] | Judy Collins' Concert | 1964 | 30.00 |

—*Guitar player" label*

| ❑ EKL-280 [M] | Judy Collins' Concert | 1966 | 25.00 |

—*Gold/tan label*

| ❑ EKS-7280 [S] | Judy Collins' Concert | 1964 | 40.00 |

—*Guitar player" label*

| ❑ EKS-7280 [S] | Judy Collins' Concert | 1966 | 30.00 |

—*Gold/tan label*

| ❑ EKS-7280 [S] | Judy Collins' Concert | 1969 | 18.00 |

—*Red label with large stylized "E*

| ❑ EKS-7280 [S] | Judy Collins' Concert | 1971 | 15.00 |

—*Butterfly label, no Warner Communications logo*

| ❑ EKS-7280 [S] | Judy Collins' Concert | 1975 | 10.00 |

—*Any label with Warner Communications logo*

| ❑ EKL-300 [M] | Judy Collins' Fifth Album | 1965 | 30.00 |

—*Guitar player" label*

| ❑ EKL-300 [M] | Judy Collins' Fifth Album | 1966 | 25.00 |

—*Gold/tan label*

| ❑ EKS-7300 [S] | Judy Collins' Fifth Album | 1965 | 40.00 |

—*Guitar player" label*

| ❑ EKS-7300 [S] | Judy Collins' Fifth Album | 1966 | 30.00 |

—*Gold/tan label*

| ❑ EKS-7300 [S] | Judy Collins' Fifth Album | 1969 | 18.00 |

—*Red label with large stylized "E*

| ❑ EKS-7300 [S] | Judy Collins' Fifth Album | 1971 | 15.00 |

—*Butterfly label, no Warner Communications logo*

| ❑ EKS-7300 [S] | Judy Collins' Fifth Album | 1975 | 10.00 |

—*Any label with Warner Communications logo*

| ❑ EKS-75014 | Living | 1971 | 15.00 |

—*Butterfly label, no Warner Communications logo*

| ❑ EKS-75014 | Living | 1975 | 10.00 |

—*Any label with Warner Communications logo*

| ❑ EKL-209 [M] | Maid of Constant Sorrow | 1961 | 40.00 |

—*Guitar player" label*

| ❑ EKL-209 [M] | Maid of Constant Sorrow | 1966 | 25.00 |

—*Gold/tan label*

| ❑ EKS-7209 [R] | Maid of Constant Sorrow | 1966 | 15.00 |

—*Gold/tan label or red label with large stylized "E*

| ❑ EKS-7209 [R] | Maid of Constant Sorrow | 1971 | 12.00 |

—*Butterfly label, no Warner Communications logo*

| ❑ EKS-7209 [R] | Maid of Constant Sorrow | 1975 | 10.00 |

—*Any label with Warner Communications logo*

| ❑ EKS-7209 [R] | Maid of Constant Sorrow | 1964 | 25.00 |

—*Guitar player" label (first edition)*

| ❑ EKS-74055 | Recollections | 1969 | 18.00 |

—*Red label with large stylized "E*

| ❑ EKS-74055 | Recollections | 1971 | 15.00 |

—*Butterfly label, no Warner Communications logo*

| ❑ EKS-74055 | Recollections | 1975 | 10.00 |

—*Any label with Warner Communications logo*

❑ 6E-253	Running for My Life	1980	12.00
❑ 8E-6002	So Early in the Spring: The First 15 Years	1977	15.00
❑ 60001	Times of Our Lives	1982	12.00
❑ EKS-75053	True Stories and Other Dreams	1973	15.00

—*Butterfly label*

| ❑ EKS-75053 | True Stories and Other Dreams | 1980 | 10.00 |

—*Red or red/black label*

| ❑ EKS-75010 | Whales & Nightingales | 1970 | 15.00 |

—*Butterfly label, no Warner Communications logo*

| ❑ EKS-75010 | Whales & Nightingales | 1975 | 10.00 |

—*Any label with Warner Communications logo*

| ❑ EKS-74033 | Who Knows Where the Time Goes | 1968 | 25.00 |

—*Gold/tan label*

| ❑ EKS-74033 | Who Knows Where the Time Goes | 1969 | 18.00 |

—*Red label with large stylized "E*

| ❑ EKS-74033 | Who Knows Where the Time Goes | 1971 | 15.00 |

—*Butterfly label, no Warner Communications logo*

| ❑ EKS-74033 | Who Knows Where the Time Goes | 1975 | 10.00 |

—*Any label with Warner Communications logo*

| ❑ EKL-4012 [M] | Wildflowers | 1967 | 30.00 |
| ❑ EKS-74012 [S] | Wildflowers | 1967 | 25.00 |

—*Gold/tan label*

| ❑ EKS-74012 [S] | Wildflowers | 1969 | 18.00 |

—*Red label with large stylized "E*

| ❑ EKS-74012 [S] | Wildflowers | 1971 | 15.00 |

—*Butterfly label, no Warner Communications logo*

| ❑ EKS-74012 [S] | Wildflowers | 1975 | 10.00 |

—*Any label with Warner Communications logo*

GOLD CASTLE

❑ D1-71318	Sanity and Grace	1989	15.00
❑ 171002	Trust Your Heart	1988	15.00
❑ D1-71302	Trust Your Heart	1989	15.00

—*Reissue of 171002*

PAIR

| ❑ PDL2-1141 | Her Finest Hour | 1986 | 15.00 |

WARNER SPECIAL PRODUCTS

| ❑ 61-6462 | Judy Collins | 1981 | 80.00 |

—*Book-of-the-Month Club exclusive*

COLLINS, LYN

PEOPLE

| ❑ PE-6605 | Check Me Out | 1975 | 100.00 |

—*This album has been "reissued"; be careful of sealed copies*

| ❑ PE-5602 | Think (About It) | 1972 | 150.00 |

—*This album has been "reissued"; be careful of sealed copies*

COLLINS, PHIL

ATLANTIC

| ❑ 82050 | ... But Seriously | 1989 | 15.00 |
| ❑ PR759 [DJ] | Collins on Collins: Exclusive Candid Interview | 1985 | 30.00 |

—*Promo-only interview album with cue sheets*

❑ SD16029	Face Value	1981	10.00
❑ 80035	Hello, I Must Be Going!	1982	10.00
❑ 81240	No Jacket Required	1985	10.00
❑ 82157	Serious Hits... Live!	1990	25.00

COLLINS, SHIRLEY AND DOROTHY

HARVEST

| ❑ SKAO-370 | Anthems in Eden | 1969 | 50.00 |

COLLINS, TOMMY

CAPITOL

❑ T1125 [M]	Light of the Lord	1959	100.00
❑ T1436 [M]	Songs I Love to Sing	1961	50.00
❑ ST1436 [S]	Songs I Love to Sing	1961	60.00
❑ T1196 [M]	This Is Tommy Collins	1959	60.00
❑ T776 [M]	Words and Music Country Style	1957	100.00

COLUMBIA

❑ CL2510 [M]	The Dynamic Tommy Collins	1966	30.00
❑ CS9310 [S]	The Dynamic Tommy Collins	1966	40.00
❑ CL2778 [M]	Tommy Collins On Tour -- His Most Requested Songs	1968	60.00
❑ CS9578 [S]	Tommy Collins On Tour -- His Most Requested Songs	1968	30.00

STARDAY

| ❑ SLP-474 | Tommy Collins Callin' | 1972 | 25.00 |

TOWER

❑ T5021 [M]	Let's Live a Little	1966	30.00
❑ DT5021 [R]	Let's Live a Little	1966	25.00
❑ T5107 [M]	Shindig	1967	40.00
❑ DT5107 [R]	Shindig	1967	25.00

COLMAN, RONALD

DECCA

| ❑ DLP8010 [M] | A Christmas Carol/Mr. Pickwick's Christmas | 1949 | 25.00 |

—*Side 2 read by Charles Laughton*

MCA

| ❑ 15010 | A Christmas Carol/Mr. Pickwick's Christmas | 1973 | 12.00 |

—*Side 2 read by Charles Laughton; reissue of Decca LP*

COLONNA, JERRY

DECCA

| ❑ DL5540 [10] | Music? For Screaming!!! | 1955 | 60.00 |

LIBERTY

| ❑ SL-9004 [M] | Along the Dixieland Hi-Fi Way | 1957 | 40.00 |
| ❑ LRP-3046 [M] | Let's All Sing with Jerry Colonna | 1957 | 40.00 |

COLOSSEUM

ABC DUNHILL

❑ DSX-50101 [B]	Daughter of Time	1971	30.00
❑ DS-50079 [B]	The Grass Is Green	1970	30.00
❑ DS-50062 [B]	Those Who Are About to Die Salute You	1969	30.00

WARNER BROS.

| ❑ 2WS1942 [B] | Colosseum Live | 1972 | 30.00 |
| ❑ PRO500 [DJ] | Colosseum Live | 1972 | 30.00 |

—*Highlights for radio*

COLOURS

DOT

| ❑ DLP-25935 | Atmosphere | 1969 | 30.00 |
| ❑ DLP-3854 [M] | Colours | 1968 | 50.00 |

—*Record has a black label, resembling a stock copy, but it is in a stereo cover with "Monaural" and "Promotional Copy Not for Sale" stickers on front*

| ❑ DLP-25854 [S] | Colours | 1968 | 30.00 |

COLTER, JESSI

CAPITOL

❑ ST-11543	Diamond in the Rough	1976	12.00
❑ ST-11363	I'm Jessi Colter	1975	12.00
❑ ST-11477	Jessi	1976	12.00
❑ ST-11583	Mirriam	1977	12.00
❑ ST-12185	Ridin' Shotgun	1981	12.00
❑ ST-11863	That's the Way a Cowboy Rocks and Rolls	1978	12.00
❑ ST-511863	That's the Way a Cowboy Rocks and Rolls	1978	15.00

—*Columbia House edition*

RCA VICTOR

| ❑ LSP-4333 | Country Star | 1970 | 25.00 |

COLTRANE, ALICE, AND CARLOS SANTANA

COLUMBIA

| ❑ PC32900 | Illuminations | 1974 | 25.00 |

—*No bar code on cover*

COLTRANE, ALICE

ABC IMPULSE!

❑ AS-9156	A Monastic Trio	1968	80.00
❑ AS-9185	Huntington Ashram Monastery	1969	60.00
❑ AS-9203	Journey in Satchidananda	1970	50.00
❑ AS-9224	Lord of Lords	1972	40.00
❑ AS-9196	Ptah the El Daoud	1969	50.00
❑ AS-9232	Reflection On Creation and Space	1973	30.00
❑ AS-9210	Universal Consciousness	1971	60.00
❑ AS-9218	World Galaxy	1972	40.00

GRP/IMPULSE!

| ❑ IMP-228 | Journey in Satchidanada | 1997 | 18.00 |

—*180-gram reissue*

WARNER BROS.

❑ BS2916	Eternity	1975	25.00
❑ BS2986	Radha-Krsna Nama Sankirtana	1976	30.00
❑ BS3077	Transcendence	1977	25.00
❑ 2WB3218	Transfiguration	1978	40.00

COLTRANE, CHI

COLUMBIA

| ❑ KC31275 | Chi Coltrane | 1972 | 15.00 |
| ❑ KC32463 | Let It Ride | 1973 | 15.00 |

COLTRANE, JOHN

ABC IMPULSE!

| ❑ AS-6 [S] | Africa/Brass | 1968 | 30.00 |

Number	Title	Yr	NM
❑ AS-9273	Africa/Brass, Volume 2	1974	40.00
❑ AS-77 [S]	A Love Supreme	1968	30.00
—Black label with red border			
❑ AS-77 [S]	A Love Supreme	1978	15.00
—abc" musical note at top of yellow, red, purple "target" label			
❑ AS-77 [S]	A Love Supreme	1974	18.00
—Green, blue, purple "target" label			
❑ AS-95 [S]	Ascension	1968	30.00
—With "Edition II" in dead wax; black label with red ring			
❑ AS-95 [S]	Ascension	1978	15.00
—abc" musical note at top of yellow, red, purple "target" label			
❑ AS-32 [S]	Ballads	1968	30.00
—Black label with red ring			
❑ AS-32 [S]	Ballads	1973	25.00
—All-black label			
❑ AS-21 [S]	Coltrane	1968	30.00
—Black label with red ring			
❑ AS-50 [S]	Coltrane Live at Birdland	1968	30.00
—Black label with red ring			
❑ AS-50 [S]	Coltrane Live at Birdland	1975	18.00
—Green blue, purple "target" label			
❑ IA-9246	Concert Japan	1973	18.00
❑ AS-9148 [B]	Cosmic Music	1969	25.00
—Credited to "Alice and John Coltrane"; reissue of Coltrane LP			
❑ AS-66 [S]	Crescent	1968	30.00
—Black label with red ring			
❑ AS-30 [S]	Duke Ellington and John Coltrane	1968	50.00
—Black label with red ring			
❑ AS-30 [S]	Duke Ellington and John Coltrane	1973	30.00
—All-black label			
❑ AS-9120 [S]	Expression	1968	30.00
—Black label with red ring			
❑ IA-9332	First Meditations	1978	15.00
❑ AS-9200	Greatest Years	1971	25.00
❑ AS-9223	Greatest Years, Volume 2	1973	18.00
❑ IA-9278	Greatest Years, Volume 3	1974	18.00
❑ AS-42 [S]	Impressions	1968	30.00
—Black label with red ring			
❑ AS-9225	Infinity	1973	15.00
❑ IA-9277	Interstellar Space	1974	15.00
❑ AS-40 [S]	John Coltrane + Johnny Hartman	1968	30.00
—Black label with red ring			
❑ AS-40 [S]	John Coltrane + Johnny Hartman	1975	18.00
—Green blue, purple "target" label			
❑ AS-9106 [S]	Kulu Se Mama	1968	30.00
—Black label with red ring			
❑ AS-10 [S]	Live at the Village Vanguard	1968	18.00
❑ AS-9124 [S]	Live at the Village Vanguard Again!	1968	30.00
—Black label with red ring			
❑ AS-9124 [S]	Live at the Village Vanguard Again!	1975	18.00
—Green, blue and purple "target" label			
❑ AS-9202	Live in Seattle	1971	25.00
❑ AS-9110 [S]	Meditations	1968	30.00
—Black label with red ring			
❑ AS-9110 [S]	Meditations	1975	18.00
—Green, blue and purple "target" label			
❑ AS-9110 [S]	Meditations	1978	15.00
—abc" musical note at top of yellow, red, purple "target" label			
❑ AS-94 [S]	New Thing at Newport	1968	30.00
—Black label with red ring			
❑ AS-9140 [S]	Om	1968	30.00
—Black label with red ring			
❑ AS-9161	Selflessness	1969	25.00
❑ AS-9211	Sun Ship	1971	25.00
❑ IA-9306	The Gentle Side of John Coltrane	1976	18.00
❑ AS-85 [S]	The John Coltrane Quartet Plays	1968	30.00
—Black label with red ring			
❑ IZ-9345	The Mastery of John Coltrane Vol. 1: Feelin' Good	1978	15.00
❑ IZ-9346	The Mastery of John Coltrane Vol. 2: Different Drum	1978	15.00
❑ IA-9360	The Mastery of John Coltrane Vol. 3: Jupiter Variation	1978	15.00
❑ IZ-9361	The Mastery of John Coltrane Vol. 4: Trane's Moods	1978	15.00
❑ IA-9325	The Other Village Vanguard Tapes	1977	18.00
❑ AS-9195	Transition	1969	25.00

ATLANTIC

Number	Title	Yr	NM
❑ 1354 [M]	Coltrane Jazz	1960	300.00
—Orange and purple label, white fan logo			
❑ 1354 [M]	Coltrane Jazz	1962	100.00
—Orange and purple label, black fan logo			
❑ SD1354 [S]	Coltrane Jazz	1960	400.00
—Green and blue label, white fan logo			
❑ SD1354 [S]	Coltrane Jazz	1962	80.00
—Green and blue label, black fan logo			
❑ SD1354 [S]	Coltrane Jazz	1969	40.00
—Red and green label			
❑ 1382 [M]	Coltrane Plays the Blues	1962	200.00
❑ SD1382 [S]	Coltrane Plays the Blues	1962	300.00
—Green and blue label, black fan logo			
❑ SD1382 [S]	Coltrane Plays the Blues	1969	60.00
—Red and green label			
❑ 1419 [M]	Coltrane's Sound	1964	80.00
❑ SD1419 [S]	Coltrane's Sound	1964	100.00
—Green and blue label, black fan logo			
❑ SD1419 [S]	Coltrane's Sound	1969	30.00
—Red and green label			
❑ 90462	Countdown	1986	12.00
❑ 1311 [M]	Giant Steps	1959	1000.00
—Black label			
❑ 1311 [M]	Giant Steps	1960	250.00
—Orange and purple label, white fan logo			
❑ 1311 [M]	Giant Steps	1962	80.00
—Orange and purple label, black fan logo			
❑ SD1311 [S]	Giant Steps	1959	60.00
—Green label			
❑ SD1311 [S]	Giant Steps	1960	30.00
—Green and blue label, white fan logo			
❑ SD1311 [S]	Giant Steps	1962	100.00
—Green and blue label, black fan logo			
❑ SD1311 [S]	Giant Steps	1969	30.00
—Red and green label			
❑ SD1311 [S]	Giant Steps	1959	70.00
—Bullseye" label			
❑ 1361 [M]	My Favorite Things	1961	300.00
—Orange and purple label, white fan logo			
❑ 1361 [M]	My Favorite Things	1962	18.00
—Orange and purple label, black fan logo			
❑ SD1361 [S]	My Favorite Things	1961	30.00
—Green and blue label, white fan logo			
❑ SD1361 [S]	My Favorite Things	1962	150.00
—Green and blue label, black fan logo			
❑ SD1361 [S]	My Favorite Things	1969	30.00
—Red and green label			
❑ 1373 [M]	Ole' Coltrane	1961	300.00
—Orange and purple label, white fan logo			
❑ 1373 [M]	Ole' Coltrane	1962	150.00
—Orange and purple label, black fan logo			
❑ SD1373 [S]	Ole' Coltrane	1961	300.00
—Green and blue label, white fan logo			
❑ SD1373 [S]	Ole' Coltrane	1962	150.00
—Green and blue label, black fan logo			
❑ SD1373 [S]	Ole' Coltrane	1969	30.00
—Red and green label			
❑ SD 2-313	The Art of John Coltrane	1973	18.00
❑ 1451 [M]	The Avant Garde	1966	150.00
❑ SD1451 [S]	The Avant Garde	1966	150.00
—Green and blue label, black fan logo			
❑ SD1451 [S]	The Avant Garde	1969	25.00
—Red and green label			
❑ 90041	The Avant-Garde	1983	12.00
❑ SD1541	The Best of John Coltrane	1970	15.00
❑ SD1553	The Coltrane Legacy	1971	15.00

ATLANTIC/RHINO

Number	Title	Yr	NM
❑ R1-71984	The Heavyweight Champion: The Complete Atlantic Recordings	1995	250.00
—Box set with liner notes; albums pressed on 150-gram vinyl			

ATLANTIC/RHINO HANDMADE

Number	Title	Yr	NM
❑ RHM1-7784	The Heavyweight Champion: The Complete Atlantic Recordings (Year 2000 Second Edition)	2000	200.00
—Year 2000 Second Edition" at lower right back cover; limited, numbered edition of 1,500 copies on 180-gram vinyl			
❑ RHM1-7784	The Heavyweight Champion: The Complete Atlantic Recordings (Year 2000 Second Edition)	2000	200.00
—Year 2000 Second Edition" on lower left back cover; limited edition of 1,500, un-numbered, on 180-gram vinyl; pressed in the U.S. for export			

BLUE NOTE

Number	Title	Yr	NM
❑ BLP-1577 [M]	Blue Train	1957	1500.00
—Deep groove" version; W. 63rd St., NYC address on label			
❑ BLP-1577 [M]	Blue Train	1957	250.00
—Regular version, W. 63rd St., NYC address on label			
❑ BST-1577 [S]	Blue Train	1959	800.00
—Deep groove" version; W. 63rd St., NYC address on label			
❑ BST-1577 [S]	Blue Train	1959	200.00
—Regular version, W. 63rd St., NYC address on label			
❑ BLP-1577 [M]	Blue Train	1965	60.00
—New York, USA" address on label			
❑ BST-1577 [S]	Blue Train	1965	50.00
—New York, USA" address on label			
❑ BST-81577	Blue Train	1967	30.00
—A Division of Liberty Records" on label			
❑ BST-81577	Blue Train	198?	15.00
—The Finest in Jazz Since 1939" reissue			
❑ B1 81577	Blue Train	1988	15.00
—Reissue with new prefix			
❑ B1-46095	Blue Train	1997	18.00
—180-gram reissue			

COLTRANE

Number	Title	Yr	NM
❑ AU-4950	Cosmic Music	1966	300.00
❑ AU-5000	Cosmic Music	1966	200.00

DCC COMPACT CLASSICS

Number	Title	Yr	NM
❑ LPZ-2032	Lush Life	1997	60.00
—Audiophile vinyl			

FANTASY

Number	Title	Yr	NM
❑ OJC-415	Bahia	1990	15.00
❑ OJC-352	Black Pearls	1989	12.00
❑ OJC-460	Cattin' with Coltrane and Quinichette	1990	15.00
❑ OJC-020	Coltrane	198?	12.00
❑ OJC-393	Dakar	1989	12.00
❑ OJC-394	Last Trane	1989	12.00
❑ OJC-131	Lush Life	198?	12.00
❑ OJC-078	Settin' the Pace	198?	12.00
❑ OJC-021	Soultrane	198?	12.00
❑ OJC-246	Standard Coltrane	1987	12.00
❑ OJC-127	Tenor Conclave	1991	15.00
❑ OJC-189	Traneing In	1986	12.00

GRP/IMPULSE!

Number	Title	Yr	NM
❑ GR-155	A Love Supreme	1995	18.00
❑ GR-156	Ballads	1995	18.00
❑ IMP-215	Coltrane	1997	18.00
❑ IMP-198	Coltrane Live at Birdland	1997	18.00
❑ IMP-200	Crescent	1997	18.00
❑ IMP-166	Duke Ellington and John Coltrane	1997	18.00
❑ GR-157	John Coltrane + Johnny Hartman	1995	18.00
❑ IMP-213	Live at the Village Vanguard Again!	1997	18.00
❑ IMP-169	Stellar Regions	1995	18.00
❑ IMP-167	Sun Ship	1997	18.00
❑ IMP-214	The John Coltrane Quartet Plays	1997	18.00

IMPULSE!

Number	Title	Yr	NM
❑ A-6 [M]	Africa/Brass	1961	80.00
❑ AS-6 [S]	Africa/Brass	1961	100.00
❑ A-77 [M]	A Love Supreme	1965	120.00
❑ AS-77 [S]	A Love Supreme	1965	150.00
❑ A-95 [M]	Ascension	1965	150.00
—Without "Edition II" in dead wax			
❑ A-95 [M]	Ascension	1966	100.00
—With "Edition II" in dead wax			
❑ AS-95 [S]	Ascension	1965	180.00
—Without "Edition II" in dead wax			
❑ AS 95 [S]	Ascension	1966	120.00
—With "Edition II" in dead wax			
❑ A-32 [M]	Ballads	1963	80.00
❑ AS-32 [S]	Ballads	1963	100.00
❑ A-21 [M]	Coltrane	1962	80.00
❑ AS-21 [S]	Coltrane	1962	100.00
❑ A-50 [M]	Coltrane Live at Birdland	1963	80.00
❑ AS-50 [S]	Coltrane Live at Birdland	1963	100.00
❑ SMAS-90232 [S]	Coltrane Live at Birdland	1964	80.00
—Capitol Record Club edition			
❑ A-66 [M]	Crescent	1964	80.00
❑ AS-66 [S]	Crescent	1964	100.00
❑ A-30 [M]	Duke Ellington and John Coltrane	1963	100.00
❑ AS-30 [S]	Duke Ellington and John Coltrane	1963	350.00
❑ A-9120 [M]	Expression	1967	100.00
❑ AS-9120 [S]	Expression	1967	80.00
❑ SMAS-91288 [S]	Expression	1967	60.00
—Capitol Record Club edition			
❑ A-42 [M]	Impressions	1963	60.00
❑ AS-42 [S]	Impressions	1963	80.00
❑ A-40 [M]	John Coltrane + Johnny Hartman	1963	100.00
❑ AS 40 [S]	John Coltrane + Johnny Hartman	1963	120.00
❑ A-9106 [M]	Kulu Se Mama	1966	100.00
❑ AS-9106 [S]	Kulu Se Mama	1966	120.00
❑ A-10 [M]	Live at the Village Vanguard	1962	60.00
❑ AS-10 [S]	Live at the Village Vanguard	1962	80.00
❑ A-9124 [M]	Live at the Village Vanguard Again!	1967	100.00
❑ AS-9124 [S]	Live at the Village Vanguard Again!	1967	80.00
❑ A-9110 [M]	Meditations	1966	80.00
❑ AS-9110 [S]	Meditations	1966	100.00
❑ A-94 [M]	New Thing at Newport	1965	60.00
❑ AS-94 [S]	New Thing at Newport	1965	80.00
❑ A-9140 [M]	Om	1967	150.00
❑ AS-9140 [S]	Om	1967	80.00
❑ A-85 [M]	The John Coltrane Quartet Plays	1965	60.00
❑ AS-85 [S]	The John Coltrane Quartet Plays	1965	80.00

MCA

Number	Title	Yr	NM
❑ 29007	Africa/Brass	1981	10.00
❑ 29008	Africa/Brass, Volume 2	1981	10.00
❑ 29017	A Love Supreme	1981	10.00
❑ 29020	Ascension	1981	10.00
❑ 29012	Ballads	1981	10.00
❑ 29011	Coltrane	1981	10.00
❑ 29015	Coltrane Live at Birdland	1981	10.00
❑ 4135	Concert Japan	1981	12.00
❑ 29025	Cosmic Music	1981	10.00
❑ 29016	Crescent	1981	10.00
❑ 29032	Duke Ellington and John Coltrane	1981	10.00
❑ 29023	Expression	1981	10.00
❑ 29030	First Meditations	1981	10.00
❑ 4131	Greatest Years	1981	12.00

Number	Title	Yr	NM
❑ 4132	Greatest Years, Volume 2	1981	12.00
❑ 4133	Greatest Years, Volume 3	1981	12.00
❑ 29014	Impressions	1981	10.00
❑ 29029	Interstellar Space	1981	10.00
❑ 29013	John Coltrane + Johnny Hartman	1981	10.00
❑ 29021	Kulu Se Mama	1981	10.00
❑ 29009	Live at the Village Vanguard	1981	10.00
❑ 29010	Live at the Village Vanguard Again!	1981	10.00
❑ 4134	Live in Seattle	1981	12.00
❑ 29022	Meditations	1981	10.00
❑ 29019	New Thing at Newport	1981	10.00
❑ 29024	Om	1981	10.00
❑ 29026	Selflessness	1981	10.00
❑ 29028	Sun Ship	1981	10.00
❑ 4136	The Gentle Side of John Coltrane	1981	12.00
❑ 29018	The John Coltrane Quartet Plays	1981	10.00
❑ 4138	The Mastery of John Coltrane Vol. 1: Feelin' Good	1981	12.00
❑ 4139	The Mastery of John Coltrane Vol. 2: Different Drum	1981	12.00
❑ 29031	The Mastery of John Coltrane Vol. 3: Jupiter Variation	1981	10.00
❑ 4140	The Mastery of John Coltrane Vol. 4: Trane's Moods	1981	12.00
❑ 4137	The Other Village Vanguard Tapes	1981	12.00
❑ 29027	Transition	1981	10.00

MCA/IMPULSE!

Number	Title	Yr	NM
❑ 42231	Africa/Brass	1988	12.00
❑ 42232	Africa/Brass, Volume 2	1988	12.00
❑ 5660	A Love Supreme	1986	12.00
❑ 5885	Ballads	1987	12.00
❑ 5883	Coltrane	1987	12.00
❑ 33109	Coltrane Live at Birdland	198?	12.00
❑ 5889	Crescent	1987	12.00
❑ 39103	Duke Ellington and John Coltrane	1988	12.00
❑ 5887	Impressions	1987	12.00
❑ 5661	John Coltrane + Johnny Hartman	1986	12.00
❑ 39136	Live at the Village Vanguard	1988	12.00
❑ 39118	Om	1988	12.00
❑ 33110	The John Coltrane Quartet Plays	198?	12.00

PABLO

Number	Title	Yr	NM
❑ 2405417	The Best of John Coltrane	198?	12.00

PABLO LIVE

Number	Title	Yr	NM
❑ 2620101	Afro Blue Impressions	198?	15.00
❑ 2308227	Bye Bye Blackbird	1981	15.00
❑ 2308222	European Tour	1981	15.00
❑ 2308217	The Paris Concert	1980	15.00

PRESTIGE

Number	Title	Yr	NM
❑ PRLP-7353 [M]	Bahia	1965	30.00
❑ PRST-7353 [S]	Bahia	1965	30.00
❑ 24110	Bahia	198?	15.00
❑ PRLP-7316 [M]	Black Pearls	1964	40.00
— Yellow label			
❑ PRST-7316 [S]	Black Pearls	1964	40.00
— Silver label			
❑ PRLP-7316 [M]	Black Pearls	1964	30.00
— Blue label with trident logo			
❑ PRST-7316 [S]	Black Pearls	1964	30.00
— Blue label with trident logo			
❑ 24037	Black Pearls	1974	18.00
❑ PRLP-7158 [M]	Cattin' with Coltrane and Quinichette	1959	80.00
— Yellow label			
❑ PRLP-7158 [M]	Cattin' with Coltrane and Quinichette	1964	30.00
— Blue label with trident logo			
❑ PRLP-7105 [M]	Coltrane	1957	100.00
— Yellow label			
❑ PRLP-7105 [M]	Coltrane	1964	30.00
— Blue label with trident logo			
❑ PRLP-7280 [M]	Dakar	1963	40.00
— Yellow label			
❑ PRST-7280 [S]	Dakar	1963	40.00
— Silver label			
❑ PRLP-7280 [M]	Dakar	1964	30.00
— Blue label with trident logo			
❑ PRST-7280 [S]	Dakar	1964	30.00
— Blue label with trident logo			
❑ 24104	Dakar	198?	15.00
❑ 24003	John Coltrane	1972	18.00
❑ PRLP-7123 [M]	John Coltrane and the Red Garland Trio	1957	100.00
— Yellow label			
❑ PRLP-7426 [M]	John Coltrane Plays for Lovers	1966	30.00
❑ PRST-7426 [S]	John Coltrane Plays for Lovers	1966	30.00
❑ PRLP-7188 [M]	Lush Life	1960	80.00
— Yellow label			
❑ PRLP-7188 [M]	Lush Life	1964	30.00
— Blue label with trident logo			
❑ PRST-7581 [R]	Lush Life	1968	15.00
❑ PRLP-7247 [M]	Mating Call	1962	40.00
— Yellow label			
❑ PRST-7247 [R]	Mating Call	196?	30.00
— Silver label			
❑ PRLP-7247 [M]	Mating Call	1964	30.00
— Blue label with trident logo			
❑ PRST-7247 [R]	Mating Call	1964	25.00
— Blue label with trident logo			
❑ PRST-7725	Mating Call	1970	15.00
❑ 24014	More Lasting Than Bronze	1973	18.00
❑ 24084	On a Misty Night	198?	15.00
❑ 24094	Rain or Shine	198?	15.00
❑ PRLP-7213 [M]	Settin' the Pace	1961	80.00
— Yellow label			
❑ PRLP-7213 [M]	Settin' the Pace	1964	30.00
— Blue label with trident logo			
❑ PRLP-7142 [M]	Soultrane	1958	80.00
— Yellow label			
❑ PRLP-7531 [M]	Soultrane	1967	30.00
❑ PRLP-7142 [M]	Soultrane	1964	30.00
— Blue label with trident logo			
❑ PRST-7531 [R]	Soultrane	1967	15.00
❑ PRLP-7243 [M]	Standard Coltrane	1962	40.00
— Yellow label			
❑ PRST-7243 [S]	Standard Coltrane	1962	50.00
— Silver label			
❑ PRLP-7243 [M]	Standard Coltrane	1964	30.00
— Blue label with trident logo			
❑ PRST-7243 [S]	Standard Coltrane	1964	30.00
— Blue label with trident logo			
❑ PRLP-7268 [M]	Stardust	1963	40.00
— Yellow label			
❑ PRST-7268 [S]	Stardust	1963	40.00
— Silver label			
❑ PRLP-7268 [M]	Stardust	1964	30.00
— Blue label with trident logo			
❑ PRST-7268 [S]	Stardust	1964	30.00
— Blue label with trident logo			
❑ PRLP-7249 [M]	Tenor Conclave	1962	40.00
— Yellow label			
❑ PRST-7249 [R]	Tenor Conclave	196?	30.00
— Silver label			
❑ PRLP-7249 [M]	Tenor Conclave	1964	30.00
— Blue label with trident logo			
❑ PRST-7249 [R]	Tenor Conclave	1964	25.00
— Blue label with trident logo			
❑ PRLP-7292 [M]	The Believer	1964	40.00
— Yellow label			
❑ PRST-7292 [S]	The Believer	1964	40.00
— Silver label			
❑ PRLP-7292 [M]	The Believer	1964	30.00
— Blue label with trident logo			
❑ PRST-7292 [S]	The Believer	1964	30.00
— Blue label with trident logo			
❑ PRST-7609 [R]	The First Trane	1969	15.00
❑ PRLP-7378 [M]	The Last Trane	1965	30.00
❑ PRST-7378 [S]	The Last Trane	1965	30.00
❑ PRST-7825	The Master	1971	15.00
❑ 24056	The Stardust Session	197?	18.00
❑ PRLP-7123 [M]	Traneing In	1964	30.00
— Blue label with trident logo; reissue with new title			
❑ PRST-7651 [R]	Traneing In	1969	15.00
❑ PRST-7746	Trane's Reign	1970	15.00
❑ PRST-7670 [R]	Two Tenors	1969	15.00
❑ 24069	Wheelin'	197?	15.00

RHINO

Number	Title	Yr	NM
❑ R1-75203	Giant Steps	2003	18.00
— Reissue on 180-gram vinyl			

SOLID STATE

Number	Title	Yr	NM
❑ SM-17025 [M]	Coltrane Time	1968	30.00
❑ SS-18025 [S]	Coltrane Time	1968	18.00

TRIP

Number	Title	Yr	NM
❑ 5001	Trane Tracks	1974	18.00

UNITED ARTISTS

Number	Title	Yr	NM
❑ UAJ-14001 [M]	Coltrane Time	1962	40.00
❑ UAJS-15001 [S]	Coltrane Time	1962	50.00
❑ UAS-5638	Coltrane Time	1972	15.00
— Reissue of 15001			

COLUMBIA CHOIR, THE

COLUMBIA

Number	Title	Yr	NM
❑ CL1051 [M]	The Christmas Mood	1957	30.00
— Expanded version of 10-inch LP with B-side instrumentals			
❑ CL(# unk) [10]	The Christmas Mood	1954	50.00
— First appearance of the "Albert Burt Carols" on record			
❑ CL2546 [10]	The Christmas Mood	1955	40.00
— House Party Series" reissue			

COLUMBO, CHRIS

STRAND

Number	Title	Yr	NM
❑ SL-1044 [M]	Jazz Rediscovered	1962	30.00
❑ SLS-1044 [S]	Jazz Rediscovered	1962	40.00
❑ SL-1095 [M]	Summertime	1963	30.00
❑ SLS-1095 [S]	Summertime	1963	40.00

COLVIN, SHAWN

COLUMBIA

Number	Title	Yr	NM
❑ FC45209	Steady On	1989	15.00

COLWELL-WINFIELD BLUES BAND, THE

VERVE FORECAST

Number	Title	Yr	NM
❑ FTS-3056	Cold Wind Blues	1968	25.00

ZA-ZOO

Number	Title	Yr	NM
❑ 1	Live Bust	1971	200.00

COLYER, KEN

GHB

Number	Title	Yr	NM
❑ 161	Live at the 100 Club	198?	12.00

LONDON

Number	Title	Yr	NM
❑ LL1340 [M]	Back to the Delta	1956	40.00
❑ LL1618 [M]	Club Session with Colyer	1957	40.00
❑ PB904 [10]	New Orleans to London	1954	50.00

STORYVILLE

Number	Title	Yr	NM
❑ SLP-144	Ken's Early Days	197?	15.00

COMBUSTIBLE EDISON

SUB POP

Number	Title	Yr	NM
❑ SP244	I, Swinger	1994	12.00
❑ SP313	Schizophonic	1996	12.00
❑ SP431	The Impossible World	1998	15.00

COMFORTABLE CHAIR, THE

ODE

Number	Title	Yr	NM
❑ Z1244005	The Comfortable Chair	1968	25.00

COMMANDER CODY AND HIS LOST PLANET AIRMEN

ARISTA

Number	Title	Yr	NM
❑ AB4183	Flying Dreams	1978	18.00
❑ AL4125	Rock 'N' Roll Again	1977	12.00

BLIND PIG

Number	Title	Yr	NM
❑ BP-2086	Let's Rock	1986	12.00

MCA

Number	Title	Yr	NM
❑ 660	Country Casanova	1980	10.00
— Reissue of Paramount 6054			
❑ 661	Hot Licks, Cold Steel & Truckers Favorites	1980	10.00
— Reissue of Paramount 6031			
❑ 659	Live from Deep in the Heart of Texas	1980	10.00
— Reissue of Paramount 1017			
❑ 37101	Lost in the Ozone	1980	10.00
— Reissue of Paramount 6017			

PARAMOUNT

Number	Title	Yr	NM
❑ PAS-6054	Country Casanova	1973	15.00
❑ PAS-6031	Hot Licks, Cold Steel & Truckers Favorites	1972	15.00
❑ PAS-1017	Live from Deep in the Heart of Texas	1974	15.00
❑ PAS-6017	Lost in the Ozone	1971	18.00

WARNER BROS.

Number	Title	Yr	NM
❑ BS2847	Commander Cody and His Lost Planet Airmen	1975	12.00
❑ BS2883	Tales from the Ozone	1975	12.00
❑ 2LS2939	We've Got a Live One Here!	1976	15.00

COMMANDERS, THE

DECCA

Number	Title	Yr	NM
❑ DL8117 [M]	Dance Party	1955	40.00
— Led by Eddie Grady			

COMMODORES

MOTOWN

Number	Title	Yr	NM
❑ PR39 [DJ]	1978 Platinum Tour	1978	25.00
— Promo-only compilation			
❑ 6028ML	All the Great Hits	1982	12.00
❑ 6044ML2	Anthology	1983	15.00
❑ M6-820	Caught in the Act	1975	12.00
❑ M5-240V1	Caught in the Act	1982	10.00
❑ M7-884	Commodores	1977	12.00
❑ M5-222V1	Commodores	1982	10.00
❑ 6054ML	Commodores 13	1983	12.00
❑ M7-912	Commodores' Greatest Hits	1978	12.00
❑ M9-894	Commodores Live!	1977	15.00
❑ M8-939	Heroes	1980	12.00
❑ M6-867	Hot on the Tracks	1976	12.00
❑ 5257ML	Hot on the Tracks	1983	10.00
❑ M8-955	In the Pocket	1981	12.00
❑ M5-121V1	Machine Gun	1981	12.00
— Reissue			
❑ M6-798	Machine Gun	1974	18.00
❑ M8-926	Midnight Magic	1979	12.00
❑ M6-848	Movin' On	1975	12.00
❑ M5-179V1	Movin' On	1981	10.00
❑ M7-902	Natural High	1978	12.00
❑ 5293ML [B]	Natural High	1983	10.00
❑ 6124ML	Nightshift	1985	12.00

POLYDOR

Number	Title	Yr	NM
❑ 835369-1	Rock Solid	1988	12.00
❑ 831194-1	United	1986	12.00

COMMON PEOPLE, THE

CAPITOL

Number	Title	Yr	NM
❑ ST-266	Of the People/By the People/For the People/From the Common People	1969	200.00

COMO, PERRY

PAIR

Number	Title	Yr	NM
❑ PDL2-1112	Blue Skies	1986	15.00
❑ PDL2-1001	Easy Listening	1986	15.00
❑ PDL2-1038	Love Moods	1986	15.00

PICKWICK

Number	Title	Yr	NM
❑ CAS-660 [R]	Perry Como Sings Merry Christmas Music	1977	10.00
—Reissue of RCA Camden CAS-660 with another new cover			

RCA

Number	Title	Yr	NM
❑ 6368-1-R	Perry Como Today	1988	12.00

RCA CAMDEN

Number	Title	Yr	NM
❑ CAL-742 [M]	An Evening with Perry Como	196?	18.00
❑ CAL-511 [M]	Como's Wednesday Night Music Hall	1959	25.00
❑ CAS-2482	Door of Dreams	1971	12.00
❑ CAL-403 [M]	Dream Along with Me	1957	25.00
❑ CAS-403(e) [R]	Dream Along with Me	1962	12.00
❑ CAL-582 [M]	Dreamer's Holiday	1960	18.00
❑ CAS-2609	Dream On Little Dreamer	1972	12.00
❑ CXS-9002	Easy Listening	1972	15.00
❑ CAL-2122 [M]	Hello Young Lovers	1967	18.00
❑ CAS-2122 [R]	Hello Young Lovers	1967	12.00
❑ CAL-805 [M]	Love Makes the World Go 'Round	1964	15.00
❑ CAS-805 [S]	Love Makes the World Go 'Round	1964	12.00
❑ CAL-694 [M]	Make Someone Happy	1962	15.00
❑ CAL-941 [M]	No Other Love	1966	15.00
❑ CAS-941 [S]	No Other Love	1966	12.00
❑ CAL-440 [M]	Perry Como Sings Just for You	1958	18.00
❑ CAS-440(e) [R]	Perry Como Sings Just for You	1962	12.00
❑ CAL-660 [M]	Perry Como Sings Merry Christmas Music	1961	15.00
—Reissue of RCA Victor LPM-1243 with new cover			
❑ CAS-660(e) [R]	Perry Como Sings Merry Christmas Music	1961	12.00
❑ CAL-858 [M]	Somebody Loves Me	1965	15.00
❑ CAS-858 [S]	Somebody Loves Me	1965	12.00
❑ CAS-2299	The Lord's Prayer	1968	12.00
❑ CAS-2547	The Shadow of Your Smile	1972	12.00
❑ CAL-2201 [M]	You Are Never Far Away	1968	18.00
❑ CAS-2201 [S]	You Are Never Far Away	1968	12.00

RCA CUSTOM EDITION

Number	Title	Yr	NM
❑ DRL1-0010	Seattle	1973	15.00

RCA SPECIAL PRODUCTS

Number	Title	Yr	NM
❑ DPL1-0193	By Special Request	1974	15.00
—Sold only at Sylvania dealers			

RCA VICTOR

Number	Title	Yr	NM
❑ CPL1-1752	A Legendary Performer	1976	12.00
❑ APL1-0100	And I Love You So	1973	12.00
❑ APD1-0100 [Q]	And I Love You So	1974	18.00
❑ AYL1-3672	And I Love You So	1980	10.00
—Reissue			
❑ LPM-3133 [10]	Around the Christmas Tree	1953	40.00
❑ LPM-3035 [10]	A Sentimental Date with Perry Como	1952	40.00
❑ LPM-1177 [M]	A Sentimental Date with Perry Como	1956	30.00
❑ LPM-2567 [M]	By Request	1962	18.00
❑ LSP-2567 [S]	By Request	1962	25.00
❑ LPM-3224 [10]	Como's Golden Records	1954	40.00
❑ LOP-1007 [M]	Como's Golden Records	1958	30.00
❑ LPM-1981 [M]	Como's Golden Records	1959	25.00
—Reissue of LOP-1007			
❑ LSP-1981(e) [R]	Como's Golden Records	1962	15.00
❑ AFL1-1981	Como's Golden Records	1977	12.00
—Reissue with new prefix			
❑ AYL1-3802	Como's Golden Records	1981	10.00
—Reissue			
❑ LPM-2010 [M]	Como Swings	1959	25.00
❑ LSP-2010 [S]	Como Swings	1959	30.00
❑ ANL1-2485	Especially for You	1977	12.00
❑ LPM-2343 [M]	For the Young at Heart	1960	18.00
❑ LSP-2343 [S]	For the Young at Heart	1960	25.00
❑ LPM-3124 [10]	Hits from Broadway Shows	1953	40.00
❑ LPM-1191 [M]	Hits from Broadway Shows	1956	30.00
❑ LPM-3188 [10]	I Believe	1954	40.00
❑ LPM-1172 [M]	I Believe	1956	30.00
❑ LSP-1172(e) [R]	I Believe	1962	15.00
❑ LSP-4539	I Think of You	1971	18.00
❑ AFL1-4539	I Think of You	1977	12.00
—Reissue with new prefix			
❑ LSP-4473	It's Impossible	1970	18.00
❑ AFL1-4473	It's Impossible	1977	12.00
—Reissue with new prefix			
❑ AYL1-3804	It's Impossible	1981	10.00
—Reissue			
❑ AYL1-4526	I Wish It Could Be Christmas Forever	1982	12.00
❑ APL1-0863	Just Out of Reach	1975	12.00
❑ APD1-0863 [Q]	Just Out of Reach	1975	18.00
❑ LPM-3552 [M]	Lightly Latin	1966	15.00
❑ LSP-3552 [S]	Lightly Latin	1966	18.00
❑ LSP-4052	Look to Your Heart	1968	18.00
❑ LPM-51 [10]	Merry Christmas	1951	40.00
❑ ANL1-2969(e)	Over the Rainbow	1976	12.00
❑ CPL1-0585	Perry	1974	12.00
❑ APD1-0585 [Q]	Perry	1974	18.00
❑ AFL1-3629	Perry Como	1980	12.00
❑ LSPX-1001	Perry Como at the International Hotel, Las Vegas	1970	18.00
❑ LPM-3608 [M]	Perry Como in Italy	1966	15.00
❑ LSP-3608 [S]	Perry Como in Italy	1966	18.00
❑ LPM-1243 [M]	Perry Como Sings Merry Christmas Music	1956	30.00
❑ ANL1-0972	Pure Gold	1975	12.00
❑ LPM-1176 [M]	Relaxing with Perry Como	1956	30.00
❑ LOP-1004 [M]	Saturday Night with Mr. C.	1958	30.00
❑ LPM-1971 [M]	Saturday Night with Mr. C.	1959	25.00
—Reissue of LOP-1004			
❑ LSP-1971 [S]	Saturday Night with Mr. C.	1958	30.00
❑ LPM-2066 [M]	Season's Greetings from Perry Como	1959	25.00
—Later front covers have "LPM-2066" in upper right, inside RCA Victor box			
❑ LSP-2066 [S]	Season's Greetings from Perry Como	1959	30.00
❑ LPM-2066 [M]	Season's Greetings from Perry Como	1959	30.00
—Original front covers have "LPM-2066" in lower left corner			
❑ LSP-4183	Seattle	1969	18.00
❑ LPM-2390 [M]	Sing to Me, Mr. C.	1961	18.00
❑ LSP-2390 [S]	Sing to Me, Mr. C.	1961	25.00
❑ AFL1-4272	So It Goes	1983	12.00
❑ LPM-1085 [M]	So Smooth	1955	30.00
❑ LPM-3044 [10]	Supper Club Favorites	1952	40.00
❑ LPM-2630 [M]	The Best of Irving Berlin's Songs from "Mr. President	1962	18.00
❑ LSP-2630 [S]	The Best of Irving Berlin's Songs from "Mr. President	1962	25.00
❑ LSP-4016	The Perry Como Christmas Album	1968	15.00
❑ ANL1-1929	The Perry Como Christmas Album	1976	10.00
—Budget-line reissue of LSP-4016			
❑ LPM-3396 [M]	The Scene Changes	1965	15.00
❑ LSP-3396 [S]	The Scene Changes	1965	18.00
❑ LPM-2708 [M]	The Songs I Love	1963	18.00
❑ LSP-2708 [S]	The Songs I Love	1963	25.00
❑ ACL1-0444	The Sweetest Sounds	1974	12.00
❑ VPS-6026	This Is Perry Como	1970	18.00
❑ VPS-6067	This Is Perry Como, Volume 2	1972	18.00
❑ LPM-3013 [10]	TV Favorites	1952	40.00
❑ LPM-1463 [M]	We Get Letters	1957	30.00
❑ LPM-1885 [M]	When You Come to the End of the Day	1958	25.00
❑ LSP-1885 [S]	When You Come to the End of the Day	1958	30.00
❑ AFL1-2641	Where You're Concerned	1978	12.00
❑ AYL1-3803	Where You're Concerned	1981	10.00
—Reissue			

READER'S DIGEST

Number	Title	Yr	NM
❑ RDA-144/D	Christmas with Perry Como	1983	12.00

TIME-LIFE

Number	Title	Yr	NM
❑ SLGD-04	Legendary Singers: Perry Como	1985	18.00

COMPETITORS, THE

DOT

Number	Title	Yr	NM
❑ DLP-3542 [M]	Hits of the Street and Strip	1963	150.00
❑ DLP-25542 [S]	Hits of the Street and Strip	1963	200.00

COMPOSER'S WORKSHOP ENSEMBLE, THE

STRATA-EAST

Number	Title	Yr	NM
❑ 1972-3	The Composer's Workshop Ensemble	197?	30.00
❑ 7422	(We've Been) Around	1974	30.00

COMPTON BROTHERS, THE

DOT

Number	Title	Yr	NM
❑ DLP-25974	Haunted House/Charlie Brown	1970	25.00
❑ DLP-25867	Off the Top of...	1968	25.00
❑ DLP-25998	Yellow River	1972	25.00

COMSTOCK, BOBBY

ASCOT

Number	Title	Yr	NM
❑ AM-13026 [M]	Out of Sight	1966	30.00
❑ AS-16026 [S]	Out of Sight	1966	30.00

CON BRIO

PLUG

Number	Title	Yr	NM
❑ PLUG-4	Con Brio	1986	15.00

CONCORD ALL STARS, THE

CONCORD JAZZ

Number	Title	Yr	NM
❑ CJ-348	Ow!	1988	12.00
❑ CJ-347	Take 8	1988	12.00

CONCORD FESTIVAL ALL STARS, THE

CONCORD JAZZ

Number	Title	Yr	NM
❑ CJ-366	20th Anniversary	1989	15.00

CONCORD JAZZ ALL STARS, THE

CONCORD JAZZ

Number	Title	Yr	NM
❑ CJ-182	The Concord Jazz All Stars at Northsea Jazz Festival	1982	15.00
❑ CJ-205	The Concord Jazz All Stars at Northsea Jazz Festival, Vol. 2	1982	15.00

CONCORD SUPER BAND, THE

CONCORD JAZZ

Number	Title	Yr	NM
❑ CJ-120	CSB II	1980	18.00
❑ CJ-80	The Concord Super Band in Tokyo	1979	18.00

CONCRETE BLONDE

I.R.S.

Number	Title	Yr	NM
❑ X1-13037	Bloodletting	1990	40.00
—Stock copy; red vinyl			
❑ 82037 [DJ]	Bloodletting	1990	30.00
—Promo only, sticker on generic cover, black vinyl			
❑ 5835	Concrete Blonde	1987	15.00
❑ 82001	Free	1989	15.00

CONCRETE COWBOY BAND

EXCELSIOR

Number	Title	Yr	NM
❑ 88007	Concrete Cowboys	1981	15.00

CONDELLO

SCEPTER

Number	Title	Yr	NM
❑ SPS-542	Phase 1	1968	75.00
—Avaliable in mono and stereo; both same price			

CONDON, EDDIE

ATLANTIC

Number	Title	Yr	NM
❑ 90461	That Toddlin' Town: Chicago Jazz Revisited	1986	12.00

CHIAROSCURO

Number	Title	Yr	NM
❑ 154	Eddie Condon in Japan	1978	15.00
❑ 108	Town Hall Concerts, Volume 1	197?	15.00
❑ 113	Town Hall Concerts, Volume 2	197?	15.00

COLUMBIA

Number	Title	Yr	NM
❑ CL719 [M]	Dixieland	1955	40.00
—Red and black label with six "eye" logos			
❑ CL632 [M]	Chicago Style Jazz	1955	40.00
—Red and black label with six "eye" logos			
❑ CL881 [M]	Eddie Condon's Treasury of Jazz	1956	40.00
—Red and black label with six "eye" logos			
❑ CL616 [M]	Jammin' at Condon's	1955	50.00
—Maroon label, gold print			
❑ CL616 [M]	Jammin' at Condon's	1955	40.00
—Red and black label with six "eye" logos			
❑ CL1089 [M]	The Roaring Twenties	1958	40.00
—Red and black label with six "eye" logos			
❑ KG31564	The World of Eddie Condon	1972	25.00
❑ PG31564	The World of Eddie Condon	197?	18.00
—Reissue with new prefix			

COMMODORE

Number	Title	Yr	NM
❑ XFL-16568	A Good Band Is Hard to Find	198?	12.00
❑ FL20022 [M]	Ballin' the Jack	195?	50.00
❑ FL30010 [M]	Condon A La Carte	195?	60.00
❑ XFL-15355	The Liederkranz Sessions	198?	12.00
❑ XFL-14427	Windy City Seven/Jam Sessions at Commodore	198?	12.00

DECCA

Number	Title	Yr	NM
❑ DL8281 [M]	A Night at Eddie Condon's	1956	40.00
❑ DL5137 [10]	George Gershwin Jazz Concert	1950	50.00
❑ DL9234 [M]	Gershwin Program (1941-1945)	1968	30.00
❑ DL79234 [R]	Gershwin Program (1941-1945)	1968	15.00
❑ DL8282 [M]	Ivy League Jazz	195?	40.00
❑ DL5195 [10]	Jazz Band Ball (Volume 1)	1951	50.00
❑ DL5203 [10]	Jazz Concert at Eddie Condon's	1951	50.00
❑ DL5218 [10]	Jazz Concert at Eddie Condon's	1950	50.00
❑ DL5246 [10]	We Call It Music	1951	50.00

DESIGN

Number	Title	Yr	NM
❑ DLP-47 [M]	Confidentially…It's Condon	196?	15.00
❑ DLP-148 [M]	Eddie Condon & Dixieland All Stars	196?	15.00

DOT

Number	Title	Yr	NM
❑ DLP-3141 [M]	Dixieland Dance Party	1958	40.00

EPIC

Number	Title	Yr	NM
❑ LA16024 [M]	Midnight in Moscow	1962	18.00
❑ BA17024 [S]	Midnight in Moscow	1962	25.00

JAZZOLOGY

Number	Title	Yr	NM
❑ J-101/2	1944 Jam Sessions	198?	18.00
❑ JCE-10	Eddie Condon Concert	196?	18.00
❑ J-50	Eddie Condon Jazz	197?	18.00
❑ J-73	The Spirit of Condon	1979	15.00
❑ JCE-1001/2	Town Hall Concerts, Volume 1	1988	18.00
❑ JCE-1003/4	Town Hall Concerts, Volume 2	1988	18.00
❑ JCE-1005/6	Town Hall Concerts, Volume 3	1988	18.00
❑ JCE-1007/8	Town Hall Concerts, Volume 4	1990	18.00
❑ JCE-1009/10	Town Hall Concerts, Volume 5	1990	18.00

Number	Title	Yr	NM
❑ JCE-1011/12	Town Hall Concerts, Volume 6	1990	18.00
❑ JCE-1013/14	Town Hall Concerts, Volume 7	1992	18.00

JAZZ PANORAMA

Number	Title	Yr	NM
❑ 1805 [10]	Eddie Condon	1951	40.00

JOLLY ROGER

Number	Title	Yr	NM
❑ 5025 [10]	Eddie Condon	1954	40.00
❑ 5018 [10]	Eddie Condon and His Orchestra Featuring Pee Wee Russell	1954	40.00

MAINSTREAM

Number	Title	Yr	NM
❑ 56024 [M]	Eddie Condon: A Legend	1965	30.00
❑ S-6024 [R]	Eddie Condon: A Legend	1965	18.00

MCA

Number	Title	Yr	NM
❑ 4071	The Best of Eddie Condon	197?	18.00

—Black rainbow labels

MCA CORAL

Number	Title	Yr	NM
❑ 20013	Sunny Day	198?	12.00

MGM

Number	Title	Yr	NM
❑ E-3651 [M]	Eddie Condon Is Uptown Now	1960	30.00
❑ SE-3651 [S]	Eddie Condon Is Uptown Now	1960	30.00

MOSAIC

Number	Title	Yr	NM
❑ MQ7-152	The Complete CBS Recordings of Eddie Condon and His All-Stars	199?	120.00

SAVOY

Number	Title	Yr	NM
❑ MG-12055 [M]	Ringside at Condon's	1956	40.00

TRIP

Number	Title	Yr	NM
❑ 5800	Eddie Condon and His Jazz Concert Orchestra	197?	18.00

WARNER BROS.

Number	Title	Yr	NM
❑ W1315 [M]	That Toddlin' Town	1959	30.00
❑ WS1315 [S]	That Toddlin' Town	1959	40.00

X

Number	Title	Yr	NM
❑ LX-3005 [M]	Eddie Condon's Hot Shots	1954	50.00

CONLEE, JOHN

16TH AVENUE

Number	Title	Yr	NM
❑ D1-70555	Fellow Travelers	1989	12.00

ABC

Number	Title	Yr	NM
❑ AY-1105	Rose Colored Glasses	1978	15.00

COLUMBIA

Number	Title	Yr	NM
❑ FC40442	American Travelers	1987	10.00
❑ FC40257	Harmony	1986	10.00

MCA

Number	Title	Yr	NM
❑ 5521	Blue Highway	1984	10.00
❑ 5310	Busted	1982	12.00
❑ 5818	Conlee Country	1986	10.00
❑ 3174	Forever	1979	12.00
❑ 3246	Friday Night Blues	1980	12.00
❑ 27029	Friday Night Blues	198?	10.00

—Budget-line reissue

Number	Title	Yr	NM
❑ 5642	Greatest Hits Volume 2	1985	10.00
❑ 5434	In My Eyes	1983	10.00
❑ 5405	John Conlee's Greatest Hits	1983	12.00
❑ AY-1105	Rose Colored Glasses	1979	12.00

—Reissue of ABC 1105

Number	Title	Yr	NM
❑ 3281	Rose Colored Glasses	1980	10.00

—Reissue of 1105

Number	Title	Yr	NM
❑ 5699	Songs for the Working Man	1986	10.00
❑ 5213	With Love...	1981	12.00

CONLEY, ARTHUR

ATCO

Number	Title	Yr	NM
❑ SD 33-276 [S]	More Sweet Soul	1969	30.00
❑ 33-276 [M]	More Sweet Soul	1969	70.00

—Mono is white label promo only; "d/j copy monaural" sticker on stereo cover

Number	Title	Yr	NM
❑ 33-220 [M]	Shake, Rattle & Roll	1967	40.00
❑ SD 33-220 [S]	Shake, Rattle & Roll	1967	30.00
❑ SD 33-243 [S]	Soul Directions	1968	30.00
❑ 33-243 [M]	Soul Directions	1968	60.00

—Mono is white label promo only; "Mono" sticker over the word "Stereo" on front cover

Number	Title	Yr	NM
❑ 33-215 [M]	Sweet Soul Music	1967	40.00
❑ SD 33-215 [S]	Sweet Soul Music	1967	30.00

CONLEY, EARL THOMAS

RCA

Number	Title	Yr	NM
❑ 6824-1-R	The Heart of It All	1988	10.00
❑ 5619-1-R	Too Many Times	1986	10.00

RCA VICTOR

Number	Title	Yr	NM
❑ AHL1-4713	Don't Make It Easy for Me	1983	10.00
❑ AHL1-4135	Fire & Smoke	1981	10.00
❑ AHL1-7032	Greatest Hits	1985	10.00
❑ AHL1-4348	Somewhere Between Right and Wrong	1982	10.00
❑ AHL1-5175	Treadin' Water	1984	10.00

SUNBIRD

Number	Title	Yr	NM
❑ 50105	Blue Pearl	1980	18.00

CONNELLY, PEGGY

BETHLEHEM

Number	Title	Yr	NM
❑ BCP-53 [M]	That Old Black Magic	1957	120.00

CONNICK, HARRY, JR.

COLUMBIA

Number	Title	Yr	NM
❑ FC44369	20	1988	15.00
❑ C269794	30	2001	18.00
❑ BFC40702	Harry Connick, Jr.	1987	15.00
❑ C46223	Lofty's Roach Souffle	1990	18.00
❑ C86077	Songs I Heard	2001	18.00
❑ C46146	We Are in Love	1990	18.00
❑ SC45319	When Harry Met Sally... (soundtrack)	1989	15.00
❑ 474551-1	When My Heart Finds Christmas	1993	18.00

—Vinyl version is European import only

CONNIFF, RAY

COLUMBIA

Number	Title	Yr	NM
❑ PC34477	After the Lovin'	1977	12.00
❑ KC31629	Alone Again (Naturally)	1972	12.00
❑ CQ31629 [Q]	Alone Again (Naturally)	1972	18.00
❑ FC44152	Always in My Heart	1988	12.00
❑ KC33564	Another Somebody Done Somebody Wrong Song	1975	12.00
❑ CQ33564 [Q]	Another Somebody Done Somebody Wrong Song	1975	18.00
❑ CS1022	Bridge Over Troubled Water	1970	12.00
❑ CL1252 [M]	Broadway in Rhythm	1959	18.00
❑ CS8064 [S]	Broadway in Rhythm	1959	25.00

—Red and black label with six "eye" logos

Number	Title	Yr	NM
❑ C32413	Charlotte's Web	1973	12.00
❑ PC38300	Christmas Album	1982	12.00
❑ PC39470	Christmas Caroling	1984	12.00
❑ CL1390 [M]	Christmas with Conniff	1959	18.00
❑ CS8185 [S]	Christmas with Conniff	1959	15.00
❑ CL1163 [M]	Concert in Rhythm	1958	18.00
❑ CS8022 [S]	Concert in Rhythm	1958	25.00

—Red and black label with six "eye" logos

Number	Title	Yr	NM
❑ CL1415 [M]	Concert in Rhythm -- Volume II	1960	15.00
❑ CS8212 [S]	Concert in Rhythm -- Volume II	1960	18.00
❑ G30122	Concert in Stereo/Live at the Sahara/Tahoe	1970	18.00
❑ CS8155 [S]	Conniff Meets Butterfield	1959	30.00

—Red and black label with six "eye" logos

Number	Title	Yr	NM
❑ CL1004 [M]	Dance the Bop	1957	30.00

—Red and black label with six "eye" logos; includes instruction booklet

Number	Title	Yr	NM
❑ CL2608 [M]	En Espanol	1967	15.00
❑ CS9408 [S]	En Espanol	1967	12.00
❑ CL2210 [M]	Friendly Persuasion	1964	12.00
❑ CS9110 [S]	Friendly Persuasion	1964	15.00
❑ C30755	Great Contemporary Instrumental Hits	1971	12.00
❑ CL2461 [M]	Happiness Is	1966	12.00
❑ CS9261 [S]	Happiness Is	1966	15.00
❑ KC32553	Harmony	1973	12.00
❑ CQ32553 [Q]	Harmony	1973	18.00
❑ CL2747 [M]	Hawaiian Album	1967	15.00
❑ CS9547 [S]	Hawaiian Album	1967	12.00
❑ CL2406 [M]	Here We Come a-Caroling	1965	15.00
❑ CS9206 [S]	Here We Come a-Caroling	1965	12.00
❑ GP3	Here We Come a-Caroling/ Ray Conniff's World of Hits	1968	18.00
❑ CL1310 [M]	Hollywood in Rhythm	1959	18.00
❑ CS8117 [S]	Hollywood in Rhythm	1959	25.00

—Red and black label with six "eye" logos

Number	Title	Yr	NM
❑ CS9661	Honey	1968	12.00
❑ KC32090	I Can See Clearly Now	1973	12.00
❑ KC31220	I'd Like to Teach the World to Sing	1972	12.00
❑ CS9777	I Love How You Love Me	1969	12.00
❑ CL2264 [M]	Invisible Tears	1964	12.00
❑ CS9064 [S]	Invisible Tears	1964	15.00
❑ CL2795 [M]	It Must Be Him	1968	18.00
❑ CS9595 [S]	It Must Be Him	1968	12.00
❑ CL1334 [M]	It's the Talk of the Town	1959	15.00
❑ CS8143 [S]	It's the Talk of the Town	1959	18.00
❑ PC36255	I Will Survive	1979	12.00
❑ KC34040	I Write the Songs	1976	12.00
❑ CQ34040 [Q]	I Write the Songs	1976	18.00
❑ CS9920	Jean	1969	12.00
❑ CL2022 [M]	Just Kiddin' Around	1963	15.00
❑ CS8822 [S]	Just Kiddin' Around	1963	18.00
❑ CQ33332 [Q]	Laughter in the Rain	1975	18.00
❑ CL2352 [M]	Love Affair	1965	12.00
❑ CS9152 [S]	Love Affair	1965	15.00
❑ C30498	Love Story	1971	12.00
❑ CQ30498 [Q]	Love Story	1972	18.00
❑ KC31473	Love Theme from "The Godfather	1972	12.00
❑ CQ31473 [Q]	Love Theme from "The Godfather	1972	18.00
❑ KC33884	Love Will Keep Us Together	1975	12.00
❑ CQ33884 [Q]	Love Will Keep Us Together	1975	18.00
❑ CL1574 [M]	Memories Are Made of This	1961	15.00
❑ CS8374 [S]	Memories Are Made of This	1961	18.00
❑ CL2366 [M]	Music from Mary Poppins, The Sound of Music, My Fair Lady & Other Great Movie Themes	1965	12.00
❑ CS9166 [S]	Music from Mary Poppins, The Sound of Music, My Fair Lady & Other Great Movie Themes	1965	15.00
❑ JC36749	Perfect "10" Classics	1980	12.00
❑ JC35659	Ray Conniff Plays the Bee Gees and Other Hits	1978	12.00
❑ CS9839	Ray Conniff's Greatest Hits	1969	12.00
❑ CL2500 [M]	Ray Conniff's World of Hits	1966	15.00
❑ CS9300 [S]	Ray Conniff's World of Hits	1966	12.00
❑ CL1878 [M]	Rhapsody in Rhythm	1962	15.00
❑ CS8678 [S]	Rhapsody in Rhythm	1962	18.00
❑ CL1137 [M]	'S Awful Nice	1958	18.00
❑ CS8001 [S]	'S Awful Nice	1958	25.00

—Red and black label with six "eye" logos

Number	Title	Yr	NM
❑ CL1490 [M]	Say It With Music (A Touch of Latin)	1960	15.00
❑ CS8282 [S]	Say It With Music (A Touch of Latin)	1960	18.00
❑ FC40384	Say You, Say Me	1986	12.00
❑ CL1776 [M]	'S Continental	1962	15.00
❑ CS8576 [S]	'S Continental	1962	18.00
❑ KC34170	Send In the Clowns	1976	12.00
❑ CQ34170 [Q]	Send In the Clowns	1976	18.00
❑ CL1074 [M]	'S Marvelous	1957	18.00
❑ CS8037 [S]	'S Marvelous	1958	25.00

—Red and black label with six "eye" logos

Number	Title	Yr	NM
❑ CL1642 [M]	Somebody Loves Me	1961	15.00
❑ CS8442 [S]	Somebody Loves Me	1961	18.00
❑ CL2519 [M]	Somewhere My Love	1966	15.00
❑ CS9319 [S]	Somewhere My Love	1966	12.00
❑ CG33603	Somewhere My Love/Bridge Over Troubled Water	1975	15.00
❑ CL1720 [M]	So Much in Love	1962	15.00
❑ CS8520 [S]	So Much in Love	1962	18.00
❑ CL2150 [M]	Speak to Me of Love	1964	12.00
❑ CS8950 [S]	Speak to Me of Love	1964	15.00
❑ KC34312	S.W.A.T.	1976	12.00
❑ CQ34312 [Q]	S.W.A.T.	1976	18.00
❑ CL925 [M]	'S Wonderful!	1956	25.00

—Red and black label with six "eye" logos

Number	Title	Yr	NM
❑ CL1949 [M]	The Happy Beat	1963	15.00
❑ CS8749 [S]	The Happy Beat	1963	18.00
❑ KC33139	The Happy Sound	1974	12.00
❑ CQ33139 [Q]	The Happy Sound	1974	18.00
❑ FC38072	The Nashville Connection	1981	12.00
❑ KC32802	The Way We Were	1974	12.00
❑ CQ32802 [Q]	The Way We Were	1974	18.00
❑ CL2676 [M]	This Is My Song	1967	15.00
❑ CS9476 [S]	This Is My Song	1967	12.00
❑ CS9712	Turn Around Look at Me	1968	12.00
❑ C30410	We've Only Just Begun	1970	12.00
❑ CL1892 [M]	We Wish You a Merry Christmas	1962	18.00
❑ CS8692 [S]	We Wish You a Merry Christmas	1962	15.00
❑ KC32376	You Are the Sunshine of My Life	1973	12.00
❑ CL2118 [M]	You Make Me Feel So Young	1964	15.00
❑ CS8918 [S]	You Make Me Feel So Young	1964	18.00
❑ CL1489 [M]	Young at Heart	1960	15.00
❑ CS8281 [S]	Young at Heart	1960	18.00

COLUMBIA RECORD CLUB

Number	Title	Yr	NM
❑ D267 [M]	Ray Conniff's World of Favorites	196?	15.00
❑ DS267 [S]	Ray Conniff's World of Favorites	196?	18.00

HARMONY

Number	Title	Yr	NM
❑ HS11346 [B]	Love Is a Many-Splendored Thing	1969	12.00
❑ KH30134	The Impossible Dream	1970	12.00

CONNOR, CHRIS, AND MAYNARD FERGUSON

ATLANTIC

Number	Title	Yr	NM
❑ 8049 [M]	Double Exposure	1961	30.00

—Multi-color label, white "fan" logo

Number	Title	Yr	NM
❑ 8049 [M]	Double Exposure	196?	15.00

—Multi-color label, black "fan" logo

Number	Title	Yr	NM
❑ SD8049 [S]	Double Exposure	1961	40.00

—Multi-color label, white "fan" logo

Number	Title	Yr	NM
❑ SD8049 [S]	Double Exposure	196?	18.00

—Multi-color label, black "fan" logo

Number	Title	Yr	NM
❑ 90143	Double Exposure	198?	12.00

—Reissue

ROULETTE

Number	Title	Yr	NM
❑ R52068 [M]	Two's Company	1961	30.00

—White label with colored spokes

Number	Title	Yr	NM
❑ SR52068 [S]	Two's Company	1961	40.00

—White label with colored spokes

CONNOR, CHRIS

ABC

Number	Title	Yr	NM
❑ ABC-585 [M]	Chris Connor Now	1966	25.00
❑ ABCS-585 [S]	Chris Connor Now	1966	30.00

ABC-PARAMOUNT

Number	Title	Yr	NM
❑ ABC-529 [M]	Gentle Bossa Nova	1965	25.00
❑ ABCS-529 [S]	Gentle Bossa Nova	1965	30.00

APPLAUSE

Number	Title	Yr	NM
❑ APLP-1020	Chris Connor Live	1982	18.00

ATLANTIC

Number	Title	Yr	NM
❑ 1286 [M]	A Jazz Date with Chris Connor	1958	50.00

—Black label

Number	Title	Yr	NM
❑ 1286 [M]	A Jazz Date with Chris Connor	196?	25.00

—Multi-color label, white "fan" logo

Number	Title	Yr	NM
❑ 1286 [M]	A Jazz Date with Chris Connor	196?	15.00

—Multi-color label, black "fan" logo

Number	Title	Yr	NM
❏ 8046 [M]	A Portrait of Chris	1960	40.00
—Multi-color label, white "fan" logo			
❏ 8046 [M]	A Portrait of Chris	196?	15.00
—Multi-color label, black "fan" logo			
❏ SD8046 [S]	A Portrait of Chris	1960	50.00
—Multi-color label, white "fan" logo			
❏ SD8046 [S]	A Portrait of Chris	196?	18.00
—Multi-color label, black "fan" logo			
❏ 1307 [M]	Ballads of the Sad Café	1959	50.00
—Black label			
❏ 1307 [M]	Ballads of the Sad Café	196?	25.00
—Multi-color label, white "fan" logo			
❏ 1307 [M]	Ballads of the Sad Café	196?	15.00
—Multi-color label, black "fan" logo			
❏ SD1307 [S]	Ballads of the Sad Café	1959	60.00
—Green label			
❏ SD1307 [S]	Ballads of the Sad Café	196?	30.00
—Multi-color label, white "fan" logo			
❏ SD1307 [S]	Ballads of the Sad Café	196?	18.00
—Multi-color label, black "fan" logo			
❏ 1228 [M]	Chris Connor	1956	50.00
—Black label			
❏ 1228 [M]	Chris Connor	196?	25.00
—Multi-color label, white "fan" logo			
❏ 1228 [M]	Chris Connor	196?	15.00
—Multi-color label, black "fan" logo			
❏ SD1228 [S]	Chris Connor	1958	60.00
—Green label			
❏ SD1228 [S]	Chris Connor	196?	30.00
—Multi-color label, white "fan" logo			
❏ SD1228 [S]	Chris Connor	196?	18.00
—Multi-color label, black "fan" logo			
❏ 2-601 [M]	Chris Connor Sings the George Gershwin Almanac of Song	1957	100.00
—Black label			
❏ 2-601 [M]	Chris Connor Sings the George Gershwin Almanac of Song	196?	40.00
—Multi-color label, white "fan" logo			
❏ 2-601 [M]	Chris Connor Sings the George Gershwin Almanac of Song	196?	25.00
—Multi-color label, black "fan" logo			
❏ 1309 [M]	Chris Connor Sings the George Gershwin Almanac of Song, Vol. 1	1959	40.00
—Black label			
❏ 1309 [M]	Chris Connor Sings the George Gershwin Almanac of Song, Vol. 1	196?	25.00
—Multi-color label, white "fan" logo			
❏ 1309 [M]	Chris Connor Sings the George Gershwin Almanac of Song, Vol. 1	196?	15.00
—Multi-color label, black "fan" logo			
❏ 1310 [M]	Chris Connor Sings the George Gershwin Almanac of Song, Vol. 2	1959	40.00
—Black label			
❏ 1310 [M]	Chris Connor Sings the George Gershwin Almanac of Song, Vol. 2	196?	25.00
—Multi-color label, white "fan" logo			
❏ 1310 [M]	Chris Connor Sings the George Gershwin Almanac of Song, Vol. 2	196?	15.00
—Multi-color label, black "fan" logo			
❏ 1290 [M]	Chris Craft	1958	50.00
—Black label			
❏ 1290 [M]	Chris Craft	196?	25.00
—Multi-color label, white "fan" logo			
❏ 1290 [M]	Chris Craft	196?	15.00
—Multi-color label, black "fan" logo			
❏ 8040 [M]	Chris In Person	1959	50.00
—Black label			
❏ 8040 [M]	Chris In Person	196?	25.00
—Multi-color label, white "fan" logo			
❏ 8040 [M]	Chris In Person	196?	15.00
—Multi-color label, black "fan" logo			
❏ SD8040 [S]	Chris In Person	1959	60.00
—Green label			
❏ SD8040 [S]	Chris In Person	196?	30.00
—Multi-color label, white "fan" logo			
❏ SD8040 [S]	Chris In Person	196?	18.00
—Multi-color label, black "fan" logo			
❏ 8061 [M]	Free Spirits	1962	30.00
—Multi-color label, black "fan" logo			
❏ SD8061 [S]	Free Spirits	1962	40.00
—Multi-color label, black "fan" logo			
❏ 1240 [M]	He Loves Me, He Loves Me Not	1956	50.00
—Black label			
❏ 1240 [M]	He Loves Me, He Loves Me Not	196?	25.00
—Multi-color label, white "fan" logo			
❏ 1240 [M]	He Loves Me, He Loves Me Not	196?	15.00
—Multi-color label, black "fan" logo			
❏ SD1240 [S]	He Loves Me, He Loves Me Not	1958	60.00
—Green label			

Number	Title	Yr	NM
❏ SD1240 [S]	He Loves Me, He Loves Me Not	196?	30.00
—Multi-color label, white "fan" logo			
❏ SD1240 [S]	He Loves Me, He Loves Me Not	196?	18.00
—Multi-color label, black "fan" logo			
❏ 1240 [M]	He Loves Me, He Loves Me Not	1960	40.00
—White "bullseye" label			
❏ SD1240 [S]	He Loves Me, He Loves Me Not	1960	50.00
—White "bullseye" label			
❏ 8014 [M]	I Miss You So	1957	50.00
—Black label			
❏ 8014 [M]	I Miss You So	196?	25.00
—Multi-color label, white "fan" logo			
❏ 8014 [M]	I Miss You So	196?	15.00
—Multi-color label, black "fan" logo			
❏ 8014 [M]	I Miss You So	1960	40.00
—White "bullseye" label			
❏ 8032 [M]	Witchcraft	1959	50.00
—Black label			
❏ 8032 [M]	Witchcraft	196?	25.00
—Multi-color label, white "fan" logo			
❏ 8032 [M]	Witchcraft	196?	15.00
❏ SD8032 [S]	Witchcraft	1959	60.00
—Green label			
❏ SD8032 [S]	Witchcraft	196?	30.00
—Multi-color label, white "fan" logo			
❏ SD8032 [S]	Witchcraft	196?	18.00
—Multi-color label, black "fan" logo			
❏ 8032 [M]	Witchcraft	1960	40.00
—White "bullseye" label			

AUDIOPHILE

Number	Title	Yr	NM
❏ AP-208	Sweet and Swinging	199?	18.00

BAINBRIDGE

Number	Title	Yr	NM
❏ 6230	Sketches	198?	12.00
—Reissue of Stanyan 10029			

BETHLEHEM

Number	Title	Yr	NM
❏ BCP-56 [M]	Chris	1957	60.00
❏ BCP-1002 [10]	Chris Connor Sings Lullabys for Lovers	1954	80.00
❏ BCP-1001 [10]	Chris Connor Sings Lullabys of Birdland	1954	80.00
❏ BCP-6004 [M]	Chris Connor Sings Lullabys of Birdland	1955	50.00
❏ BCP-6004 [M]	Chris Connor Sings Lullabys of Birdland	1984	15.00
—Reissue			
❏ BCP-6010	Cocktails and Dusk	197?	15.00
❏ 2BP-1001	The Finest	197?	18.00
❏ BCP-20 [M]	This Is Chris	1955	60.00

CLARION

Number	Title	Yr	NM
❏ 611 [M]	Chris Connor Sings George Gershwin	1966	18.00
—Abbreviated version of Atlantic 2-601			
❏ SD611 [R]	Chris Connor Sings George Gershwin	1966	12.00

CONTEMPORARY

Number	Title	Yr	NM
❏ C-14023	Classic	1987	15.00
❏ C-14038	New Again	1988	15.00

FM

Number	Title	Yr	NM
❏ 312 [M]	A Weekend in Paris	1964	50.00
❏ S-312 [S]	A Weekend in Paris	1964	60.00
❏ 300 [M]	Chris Connor at the Village Gate	1963	50.00
❏ S-300 [S]	Chris Connor at the Village Gate	1963	60.00

PROGRESSIVE

Number	Title	Yr	NM
❏ 7028	Sweet and Singing	1979	15.00

STANYAN

Number	Title	Yr	NM
❏ 10029	Sketches	1972	18.00

STASH

Number	Title	Yr	NM
❏ 232	Love Being Here with You	1984	15.00

CONNORS, BILL

ECM

Number	Title	Yr	NM
❏ 1120	Of Mist and Melting	1977	18.00
❏ 1158	Swimming with a Hole in My Body	1979	15.00
❏ 1057	Theme to the Gaurdian	197?	18.00

PATHFINDER

Number	Title	Yr	NM
❏ PTF-8707	Assembler	1987	12.00
❏ PTF-8620	Double Up	1986	12.00
❏ PTF-8503	Step It	1985	12.00

CONNORS, NORMAN

ACCORD

Number	Title	Yr	NM
❏ SN-7210	Just Imagine	1982	10.00

ARISTA

Number	Title	Yr	NM
❏ AB4216	Invitation	1979	12.00
❏ AL9575	Mr. C.	1981	12.00
❏ AL9534	Take It to the Limit	1980	12.00
❏ AB4177	This Is Your Life	1978	12.00

BUDDAH

Number	Title	Yr	NM
❏ BDS-5674	Dance of Magic	1977	25.00
—Reissue of Cobblestone 9024			
❏ BDS-5675	Dark of Light	1977	25.00

Number	Title	Yr	NM
—Reissue of Cobblestone 9035			
❏ BDS-5142	Love from the Sun	1973	15.00
❏ BDS-5682	Romantic Journey	1977	12.00
❏ BDS-5643	Saturday Night Special	1975	12.00
❏ BDS-5611	Slewfoot	1974	15.00
❏ BDS-5716	The Best of Norman Connors & Friends	1978	12.00
❏ BDS-5655	You Are My Starship	1976	12.00

CAPITOL

Number	Title	Yr	NM
❏ C1-48515	Passion	1988	12.00

COBBLESTONE

Number	Title	Yr	NM
❏ 9024	Dance of Magic	1972	30.00
❏ 9035	Dark of Light	1973	30.00

CONSTANTINE, EDDIE

KAPP

Number	Title	Yr	NM
❏ KL-1018 [M]	La Grande Sensation de la Paris	1957	30.00

MERCURY

Number	Title	Yr	NM
❏ MG-20339 [M]	The Rage of Paris	1958	30.00

CONTEMPORARY JAZZ ENSEMBLE, THE

PRESTIGE

Number	Title	Yr	NM
❏ PRLP-163 [10]	New Sounds from Rochester	1953	100.00

CONTI, ROBERT

DISCOVERY

Number	Title	Yr	NM
❏ 834	Robert Conti Jazz Quintet	1981	15.00

TREND

Number	Title	Yr	NM
❏ TR-540	Laura	1986	15.00
❏ TR-519	Solo Guitar	198?	25.00
—Direct-to-disc recording			

CONTI, TOM

CAEDMON

Number	Title	Yr	NM
❏ TC1657	Charles Dickens' "A Christmas Carol"	1980	15.00
—Spoken-word recording			

CONTINENTAL OCTETTE, THE

CROWN

Number	Title	Yr	NM
❏ CLP-5220 [M]	Modern Jazz Greats	196?	25.00

CONTOURS, THE

GORDY

Number	Title	Yr	NM
❏ G901 [M]	Do You Love Me?	1962	500.00

MOTOWN

Number	Title	Yr	NM
❏ M5-188V1	Do You Love Me?	1981	12.00

CONWAY, JULIE

HARMONY

Number	Title	Yr	NM
❏ HL7143 [M]	Good Housekeeping's Plan for Reducing Off-the-Record	1960	25.00

COODER, RY

MOBILE FIDELITY

Number	Title	Yr	NM
❏ 1-085	Jazz	198?	400.00
—Audiophile vinyl			

REPRISE

Number	Title	Yr	NM
❏ MS2117	Boomer's Story	1973	15.00
❏ MS2254	Chicken Skin Music	1976	15.00
❏ MS2052	Into the Purple Valley	1972	15.00
❏ MS2179 [B]	Paradise and Lunch	1974	15.00
❏ RS-6402	Ry Cooder	1969	18.00
—Two-tone orange label with "r:" and "W7" logos			
❏ RS-6402 [B]	Ry Cooder	1970	15.00
—No "W7" on label; one-tone orange (almost tan) label			
❏ PRO588 [DJ]	The Ry Cooder Radio Show	1976	125.00

WARNER BROS.

Number	Title	Yr	NM
❏ BSK3358	Bop Till You Drop	1979	12.00
❏ BSK3489	Borderline	1980	12.00
❏ 25399	Crossroads	1986	12.00
❏ 25639	Get Rhythm	1987	12.00
❏ BSK3197	Jazz	1978	12.00
❏ 25996	Johnny Handsome	1989	12.00
❏ 25270	Paris, Texas	1984	12.00
❏ BS3059	Show Time	1977	12.00
❏ HS3448	The Long Riders	1980	12.00
❏ BSK3651	The Slide Area	1982	12.00

COOK, JUNIOR

JAZZLAND

Number	Title	Yr	NM
❏ JLP-58 [M]	Junior's Cookin'	1961	250.00
❏ JLP-958 [S]	Junior's Cookin'	1961	150.00

MUSE

Number	Title	Yr	NM
❏ MR-5159	Good Cookin'	1979	15.00
❏ MR-5218	Something's Cookin'	1981	15.00

COOKE, ALISTAIR

COLUMBIA MASTERWORKS

Number	Title	Yr	NM
❏ ML4970 [M]	An Evening with Alistair Cooke	1955	40.00

COOKE, SAM

51 WEST

Number	Title	Yr	NM
❑ Q16032	My Foolish Heart	198?	15.00

ABKCO

Number	Title	Yr	NM
❑ 9899-1 [B]	Ain't That Good News	2014	40.00
❑ 2970-1	Sam Cooke at the Copa	1988	15.00
—Reissue			
❑ 1124-1	Sam Cooke's Night Beat	1995	15.00
—Reissue			

FAMOUS

Number	Title	Yr	NM
❑ 512	Cha-Cha-Cha	1969	40.00
❑ 505	Only Sixteen	1969	40.00
❑ 502	Sam's Songs	1969	40.00
❑ 508	So Wonderful	1969	40.00
❑ 509	You Send Me	1969	40.00

KEEN

Number	Title	Yr	NM
❑ A-2003 [M]	Encore	1958	200.00
❑ 86101 [M]	Hit Kit	1959	250.00
❑ 86103 [M]	I Thank God	1960	400.00
❑ A-2001 [M]	Sam Cooke	1958	200.00
❑ 86106 [M]	The Wonderful World of Sam Cooke	1960	350.00
❑ A-2004 [M]	Tribute to the Lady	1959	150.00
❑ AS-2004 [S]	Tribute to the Lady	1959	200.00

PAIR

Number	Title	Yr	NM
❑ PDL2-1006	You Send Me	1986	18.00

RCA CAMDEN

Number	Title	Yr	NM
❑ CAS-2433	Sam Cooke	1970	15.00
❑ CAL-2264 [M]	The One and Only Sam Cooke	1967	25.00
❑ CAS-2264 [R]	The One and Only Sam Cooke	1967	15.00
❑ CAS-2610	The Unforgettable Sam Cooke	1972	15.00
❑ ACS1-0445	You Send Me	1974	15.00

RCA VICTOR

Number	Title	Yr	NM
❑ LPM-2899 [M]	Ain't That Good News	1964	30.00
❑ LSP-2899 [S]	Ain't That Good News	1964	40.00
❑ LPM-2221 [M]	Cooke's Tour	1960	40.00
❑ LSP-2221 [S]	Cooke's Tour	1960	50.00
❑ LPM-2236 [M]	Hits of the 50's	1960	40.00
❑ LSP-2236 [S]	Hits of the 50's	1960	50.00
❑ AFL1-5181	Live at the Harlem Square Club, 1963	1985	15.00
❑ LPM-2673 [M]	Mr. Soul	1963	30.00
❑ LSP-2673 [S]	Mr. Soul	1963	40.00
❑ LPM-2392 [M]	My Kind of Blues	1961	40.00
❑ LSP-2392 [S]	My Kind of Blues	1961	50.00
❑ LPM-2709 [M]	Night Beat	1963	30.00
❑ LSP-2709 [S]	Night Beat	1963	40.00
❑ LPM-2970 [M]	Sam Cooke at the Copa	1964	30.00
❑ LSP-2970 [S]	Sam Cooke at the Copa	1964	40.00
❑ ANL1-2658	Sam Cooke at the Copa	1977	15.00
—Reissue of LSP-2970			
❑ LPM-3367 [M]	Shake	1965	30.00
❑ LSP-3367 [S]	Shake	1965	30.00
❑ LPM-2293 [M]	Swing Low	1960	40.00
❑ LSP-2293 [S]	Swing Low	1960	50.00
❑ LPM-2625 [M]	The Best of Sam Cooke	1962	30.00
❑ LSP-2625 [R]	The Best of Sam Cooke	1962	25.00
❑ AFL1-2625	The Best of Sam Cooke	1977	15.00
—Reissue with new prefix			
❑ AYL1-3863	The Best of Sam Cooke	1981	10.00
—Budget-line reissue			
❑ LPM-3373 [M]	The Best of Sam Cooke, Volume 2	1965	30.00
❑ LSP-3373 [S]	The Best of Sam Cooke, Volume 2	1965	30.00
❑ CPL2-7127	The Man and His Music	1986	18.00
❑ LPM-3991 [M]	The Man Who Invented Soul	1968	50.00
❑ LSP-3991 [S]	The Man Who Invented Soul	1968	30.00
❑ LPM-3517 [M]	The Unforgettable Sam Cooke	1966	25.00
❑ LSP-3517 [S]	The Unforgettable Sam Cooke	1966	30.00
❑ VPS-6027	This Is Sam Cooke	1970	25.00
❑ LPM-3435 [M]	Try a Little Love	1965	30.00
❑ LSP-3435 [S]	Try a Little Love	1965	30.00
❑ LPM-2555 [M]	Twistin' the Night Away	1962	40.00
❑ LSP 2555 [S]	Twistin' the Night Away	1962	50.00

SPECIALTY

Number	Title	Yr	NM
❑ SPS-2106	Sam Cooke and the Soul Stirrers	1970	18.00
❑ SPS-2146	That's Heaven to Me	197?	18.00
❑ SPS-2116	The Gospel Soul of Sam Cooke, Vol. 1	1970	18.00
❑ SPS-2128	The Gospel Soul of Sam Cooke, Vol. 2	197?	18.00
❑ SPS-2119	Two Sides of Sam Cooke	1970	18.00

TRIP

Number	Title	Yr	NM
❑ 8030	The Golden Sound of Sam Cooke	1972	18.00

UPFRONT

Number	Title	Yr	NM
❑ 160	The Billie Holiday Story	1973	18.00

COOKIES, THE/LITTLE EVA/CAROLE KING

DIMENSION

Number	Title	Yr	NM
❑ DLP-6001 [M]	The Dimension Dolls, Vol. 1	1964	350.00

COOL, CALVIN, AND THE SURF KNOBS

CHARTER

Number	Title	Yr	NM
❑ CLP-103 [M]	The Surfer's Beat	1963	40.00
❑ CLS-103 [S]	The Surfer's Beat	1963	50.00

COOL BRITONS, THE

BLUE NOTE

Number	Title	Yr	NM
❑ BLP-5052 [10]	New Sounds from Olde England	1954	300.00

COOLEY, SPADE

COLUMBIA

Number	Title	Yr	NM
❑ CL9007 [10]	Sagebrush Swing	1949	200.00

DECCA

Number	Title	Yr	NM
❑ DL5563 [10]	Dance-O-Rama	1955	300.00

RAYNOTE

Number	Title	Yr	NM
❑ R-5007 [M]	Fidoolin'	1959	40.00
❑ RS-5007 [S]	Fidoolin'	1959	50.00

ROULETTE

Number	Title	Yr	NM
❑ R25145 [M]	Fidoolin'	1961	30.00
❑ SR25145 [S]	Fidoolin'	1961	40.00

COOLIDGE, RITA

A&M

Number	Title	Yr	NM
❑ SP-4616 [B]	Anytime...Anywhere	1977	12.00
❑ SP-3163	Anytime...Anywhere	198?	10.00
—Budget-line reissue			
❑ SP-3627	Fall Into Spring	1974	12.00
❑ SP-3238	Greatest Hits	198?	10.00
—Budget-line reissue			
❑ SP-4836	Greatest Hits	1981	12.00
❑ SP-3727	Heartbreak Radio	1981	12.00
❑ SP-5003	Inside the Fire	1984	12.00
❑ SP-4531	It's Only Love	1975	12.00
❑ SP-4669	Love Me Again	1978	12.00
❑ SP-4914	Never Let You Go	1983	12.00
❑ SP-4325	Nice Feelin'	1971	12.00
❑ SP-3130	Nice Feelin'	198?	10.00
—Budget-line reissue			
❑ SP-4291	Rita Coolidge	1971	12.00
❑ SP-3107	Rita Coolidge	198?	10.00
—Budget-line reissue			
❑ SP-4701	Satisfied	1979	12.00
❑ SP-4370	The Lady's Not for Sale	1972	12.00

NAUTILUS

Number	Title	Yr	NM
❑ NR-16	Anytime...Anywhere	1981	30.00
—Audiophile vinyl			

COON, JACKIE

SEA BREEZE

Number	Title	Yr	NM
❑ SB-1009	Jazzin' Around	1987	12.00

COOPER, ALICE

ACCORD

Number	Title	Yr	NM
❑ SN-7162	Toronto Rock 'n' Roll Revival 1969	1981	15.00

ATLANTIC

Number	Title	Yr	NM
❑ SD18130	Welcome to My Nightmare	1975	12.00
❑ SD19157	Welcome to My Nightmare	1978	10.00
—Reissue of 18130			

EPIC

Number	Title	Yr	NM
❑ E46786 [B]	Hey Stoopid	1991	30.00
❑ OE45137	Trash	1989	15.00

FRIDAY MUSIC

Number	Title	Yr	NM
❑ FRM2803 [B]	Greatest Hits	2013	30.00
❑ FRM2567 [B]	Killer	2012	25.00

MCA

Number	Title	Yr	NM
❑ 5761	Constrictor	1986	10.00
❑ 42091	Raise Your Fist and Yell	1987	10.00

MOBILE FIDELITY

Number	Title	Yr	NM
❑ 1-063	Welcome to My Nightmare	1980	50.00
—Audiophile vinyl			

PAIR

Number	Title	Yr	NM
❑ PDL2-1163	A Man Called Alice	1987	18.00

STRAIGHT

Number	Title	Yr	NM
❑ WS1845 [DJ]	Easy Action	1970	100.00
—White label promo			
❑ WS1845	Easy Action	1970	50.00
—Pink label stock copy; "Alice Cooper" in black on cover			
❑ WS1845	Easy Action	1970	30.00
—Pink label stock copy; "Alice Cooper" in white on cover			
❑ WS1883 [DJ]	Love It to Death	1971	100.00
—White label promo			
❑ WS1883	Love It to Death	1971	50.00
—Pink label stock copy			
❑ STS-1051 [DJ]	Pretties for You	1969	200.00
—White label promo			
❑ STS-1051	Pretties for You	1969	150.00
—Yellow label stock copy			
❑ WS1840 [B]	Pretties for You	1970	75.00
—Pink label stock copy			

TPM/RHINO EXCLUSIVE

Number	Title	Yr	NM
❑ 1845	Easy Action	2008	12.00
❑ 1883	Love It to Death	2008	12.00
❑ 1840	Pretties for You	2008	12.00

WARNER BROS.

Number	Title	Yr	NM
❑ BS2896	Alice Cooper Goes to Hell	1976	12.00
❑ W2803	Alice Cooper's Greatest Hits	1974	12.00
❑ BSK3107	Alice Cooper's Greatest Hits	1977	10.00
—Reissue of BS 2803			
❑ BS2685	Billion Dollar Babies	1973	15.00
—Green "WB" label			
❑ BS42685 [Q]	Billion Dollar Babies	1974	50.00
❑ 23969	Da Da	1983	12.00
❑ BSK3436	Flush the Fashion	1980	12.00
❑ BSK3263	From the Inside	1978	12.00
❑ BS2567	Killer	1971	30.00
—Early copies have an attached 1972 calendar/poster			
❑ BS2567	Killer	1972	15.00
—Later copies no longer have the calendar/poster			
❑ BSK3027	Lace and Whiskey	1977	12.00
❑ WS1883 [B]	Love It To Death	2010	30.00
❑ WS1883 [B]	Love It to Death	1971	50.00
—Version 1: Green "WB" label; cover has Alice's thumb sticking out in such a way that it appears to be another part of the body			
❑ WS1883	Love It to Death	1971	25.00
—Version 2: Green "WB" label; same as above, but has a white box reading "Contains the Hit 'I'm Eighteen'			
❑ WS1883	Love It to Death	1971	25.00
—Version 3: Green "WB" label; cover has large white areas at top and bottom with lower half of the photo cropped out			
❑ WS1883	Love It to Death	1971	15.00
—Version 4: Green "WB" label; with "I'm Eighteen" box and Alice's protruding thumb airbrushed off the cover			
❑ BS2748	Muscle of Love	1973	12.00
❑ BS42748 [Q]	Muscle of Love	1974	60.00
❑ WS1840	Pretties for You	1973	25.00
—Burbank" palm trees label; comes in Straight cover			
❑ WS1840	Pretties for You	1971	30.00
—Green label; comes in "Straight" cover			
❑ BS2623	School's Out	1972	40.00
—With paper panties intact; back cover does not list song titles			
❑ BS2623	School's Out	1972	25.00
—Back cover does not list song titles, but panties are missing			
❑ BS2623	School's Out	1972	30.00
—With paper panties intact; back cover lists song titles			
❑ BS2623	School's Out	1972	15.00
—No panties, with song titles listed			
❑ BSK3581	Special Forces	1981	12.00
❑ PRO789 [DJ]	The Alice Cooper Radio Show	1978	30.00
❑ BSK3138	The Alice Cooper Show	1977	12.00
❑ 23719 [B]	Zipper Catches Skin	1982	12.00

COOPER, BOB

CAPITOL

Number	Title	Yr	NM
❑ H6501 [10]	Bob Cooper	1954	80.00
❑ T6501 [M]	Bob Cooper	1955	50.00
❑ T1586 [M]	Do Re Mi	1961	30.00
❑ ST1586 [S]	Do Re Mi	1961	30.00
❑ H6513 [10]	Shifting Winds	1955	60.00
❑ T6513 [M]	Shifting Winds	1955	50.00

CONTEMPORARY

Number	Title	Yr	NM
❑ C-3544 [M]	Coop!	1958	50.00
❑ S-7012 [S]	Coop!	1959	40.00
—Reissue of Stereo Records 7012			
❑ C-14017	In a Mellotone	1986	12.00

DISCOVERY

Number	Title	Yr	NM
❑ 822	Bob Cooper Plays the Music of Michel Legrand	1981	15.00

FANTASY

Number	Title	Yr	NM
❑ OJC-161	Coop!	198?	12.00

STEREO RECORDS

Number	Title	Yr	NM
❑ S-7012 [S]	Coop!	1958	50.00

TREND

Number	Title	Yr	NM
❑ TR-518	Tenor Sax Impressions	198?	25.00
—Direct-to-disc recording			

WORLD PACIFIC

Number	Title	Yr	NM
❑ WPM-411 [M]	Bob Cooper Swings TV	1958	50.00

COOPER, JACKIE

DOT

Number	Title	Yr	NM
❑ DLP-3146 [M]	The Movies Swing!	1958	30.00

COOPER, JEROME

ABOUT TIME

Number	Title	Yr	NM
❑ 1008	Outer and Interactions	1988	12.00
❑ 1002	The Unpredictability of Predictability	1979	12.00

HAT HUT

Number	Title	Yr	NM
❑ 07	For the People	1980	15.00

COOPER, LES, AND THE SOUL ROCKERS

EVERLAST

Number	Title	Yr	NM
❑ ELP-202 [M]	Wiggle Wobble	1963	50.00

COOPER, PAT

UNITED ARTISTS

Number	Title	Yr	NM
❑ UAS6690	More Saucy Stories from... Pat Cooper	1969	15.00
❑ UAL3446 [M]	Our Hero...Pat Cooper	1966	15.00
❑ UAS6446 [S]	Our Hero...Pat Cooper	1966	18.00
❑ UAL3548 [M]	Spaghetti Sauce & Other Delights	1966	15.00

Number	Title	Yr	NM
❏ UAS6548 [S]	Spaghetti Sauce & Other Delights	1966	18.00
❏ UAS6600	You Don't Have to Be Italian To Like Pat Cooper	1968	15.00

COOPER, WILMA LEE AND STONEY

DECCA
❏ DL4784 [M]	Wilma Lee and Stoney Cooper Sing	1966	25.00
❏ DL74784 [S]	Wilma Lee and Stoney Cooper Sing	1966	30.00

HARMONY
❏ HL7233 [M]	Sacred Songs	1960	30.00

HICKORY
❏ LP-106 [M]	Family Favorites	1962	40.00
❏ LP-112 [M]	New Songs of Inspiration	1962	40.00
❏ LP-100 [M]	There's a Big Wheel	1960	50.00

COPAS, COWBOY, AND HAWKSHAW HAWKINS

KING
❏ 984 [M]	24 Great Hits	1968	30.00
❏ 835 [M]	In Memory	1963	40.00
❏ 850 [M]	The Legend of Cowboy Copas and Hawkshaw Hawkins	1964	40.00

COPAS, COWBOY

KING
❏ 824 [M]	As You Remember Cowboy Copas	1963	40.00
❏ 720 [M]	Broken Hearted Melodies	1960	80.00
❏ 817 [M]	Country Gentleman of Song	1963	40.00
❏ 894 [M]	Cowboy Copas Hymns	1964	40.00
❏ 553 [M]	Cowboy Copas Sings His All-Time Hits	1957	100.00
❏ 556 [M]	Favorite Sacred Songs	1957	80.00
❏ 619 [M]	Sacred Songs by Cowboy Copas	1959	80.00
❏ 714 [M]	Tragic Tales of Love and Life	1960	80.00

STARDAY
❏ SLP-118 [M]	All Time Country Music Great	1960	40.00
❏ SLP-212 [M]	Beyond the Sunset	1963	40.00
❏ SLP-208 [M]	Country Music Entertainer #1	1963	40.00
❏ SLP-144 [M]	Cowboy Copas	1961	40.00
❏ SLP-268 [M]	Cowboy Copas and His Friends	1964	40.00
❏ SLP-133 [M]	Inspirational Songs	1961	40.00
❏ SLP-175 [M]	Mister Country Music	1962	40.00
❏ SLP-157 [M]	Opry Star Spotlight on Cowboy Copas	1962	40.00
❏ SLP-184 [M]	Songs That Made Him Famous	1962	40.00
❏ SLP-247 [M]	Star of the Grand Ole Opry	1963	40.00
❏ SLP-458	The Best of Cowboy Copas	1970	18.00
❏ SLP-347 [M]	The Cowboy Copas Story	1965	30.00
❏ SLP (9)-347 [R]	The Cowboy Copas Story	1965	30.00
❏ SLP-317 [M]	The Legend Lives On	1965	30.00
❏ SLP-234 [M]	The Unforgettable Cowboy Copas	1963	40.00

COPAS, COWBOY/HAWKSHAW HAWKINS/PATSY CLINE

STARDAY
❏ SLP-346 [M]	Gone But Not Forgotten	1965	30.00

COPE, JULIAN

ISLAND
❏ 91025	My Nation Underground	1988	12.00
❏ PR126667 [EP]	Peggy Suicide (Sampler)	1991	18.00
—Promo only; 6 tracks			
❏ 90571	Saint Julian	1987	12.00
❏ 90560 [EP]	World Shut Your Mouth (Julian Cope)	1987	10.00

COPELAND, STEWART

A&M
❏ SP-6-4983	Rumble Fish	1983	15.00
❏ SP-5084	The Rhythmatist	1985	12.00

I.R.S.
❏ 42099	The Equalizer and Other Cliffhangers	1988	12.00

COPPER PLATED INTEGRATED CIRCUIT, THE

COMMAND
❏ RS-945SD	Plugged In Pop	1969	30.00

COPPERPENNY

RCA VICTOR
❏ LSP-4291 [B]	Copperpenny	1970	25.00

CORBIN, HAROLD

ROULETTE
❏ R-52079 [M]	Soul Brother	1961	30.00
❏ SR-52079 [S]	Soul Brother	1961	30.00
—and			

CORCORAN, CORKY

C.C. PRODUCTION
❏ 4012 [M]	Corky Corcoran Plays Everywhere	1974	15.00

Number	Title	Yr	NM
CELESTIAL			
❏ Vol.1 [M]	Sounds of Jazz	1958	300.00
—Red vinyl			
❏ Vol.1 [M]	Sounds of Jazz	1958	200.00
—Black vinyl			
EPIC			
❏ LN3319 [M]	The Sound of Love	1956	80.00
RCS			
❏ 2555 [M]	Corky Corcoran Plays Something	197?	30.00

CORDIALS, THE

CATAMOUNT
❏ 902	Blue Eyed Soul	1967	30.00

COREA, CHICK, AND LIONEL HAMPTON

WHO'S WHO IN JAZZ
❏ WWLP21016	Live at Midem	1980	18.00

COREA, CHICK; HERBIE HANCOCK; KEITH JARRETT; MCCOY TYNER

ATLANTIC
❏ SD1696	Corea/Hancock/Jarrett/Tyner	1976	15.00

COREA, CHICK

51 WEST
❏ Q16078	Jazzman	1979	18.00

ATLANTIC
❏ SD 2-305	Inner Space	1973	18.00

BLUE NOTE
❏ BN-LA395-H2	Chick Corea	1975	18.00
—The Blue Note Reissue Series" labels			
❏ LWB-395	Chick Corea	1981	12.00
—Reissue with new prefix			
❏ BN-LA472-H2	Circling In	1976	25.00
—The Blue Note Reissue Series" labels			
❏ BN-LA882-J2	Circulus	1978	25.00
❏ B1-90055	Now He Sings, Now He Sobs	1988	15.00
—Reissue; "The Finest in Jazz Since 1939" on label			
❏ BST-84353	Song of Singing	1970	40.00
—A Division of Liberty Records" on label			
❏ BST-84353	Song of Singing	1984	25.00
—Reissue, "The Finest in Jazz Since 1939" on label			

ECM
❏ 1009ST	A.R.C.	197?	18.00
—Original issue, made in Germany?			
❏ ECM1-1009	A.R.C.	1977	15.00
—Distributed by Polydor			
❏ 25005	Children's Songs	1984	12.00
—Distributed by Warner Bros.			
❏ 1267	Children's Songs	1984	16.00
—Made in Germany			
❏ 1014ST	Piano Improvisations, Vol. 1	1974	18.00
—Original edition, made in Germany?			
❏ ECM-1-1014	Piano Improvisations, Vol. 1	1977	15.00
—Distributed by Polydor			
❏ 1020ST	Piano Improvisations, Vol. 2	197?	18.00
—Original edition; made in Germany?			
❏ ECM1-1020	Piano Improvisations, Vol. 2	1977	15.00
—Distributed by Polydor			
❏ 25035	Septet	1985	12.00
—Distributed by Warner Bros.			
❏ 1297	Septet	1985	15.00
—Made in Germany			
❏ 1232	Trio Music	198?	15.00
❏ 25013	Voyage	1985	12.00
—Distributed by Warner Bros.			
❏ 1282	Voyage	1985	15.00
—Made in Germany			

ELEKTRA/MUSICIAN
❏ 60167	Again & Again	1984	12.00

GROOVE MERCHANT
❏ 4406	Piano Giants	197?	25.00
❏ 2202	Sundance	1972	30.00
❏ GM530	Sundance	1974	18.00
—Reissue of 2202			

GRP
❏ GR-1053	Eye of the Beholder	1988	12.00
❏ GR-9601	Inside Out	1991	18.00
❏ GR-1036	Light Years	1987	12.00
❏ GR-9582	The Chick Corea Akoustic Band	1989	15.00
❏ GRP-A-1026	The Chick Corea Elektric Band	1987	12.00

MUSE
❏ MR5011	Bliss!	1973	25.00

PACIFIC JAZZ
❏ LN-10057	Now He Sings, Now He Sobs	1981	12.00
—Reissue of Solid State 18039			

POLYDOR
❏ PD-1-6208	Delphi I	1979	12.00
❏ PD-2-6334	Delphi II & III	1982	18.00

Number	Title	Yr	NM
❏ PD-1-6160	Friends	1978	12.00
❏ PD-2-9003	My Spanish Heart	1976	18.00
❏ PD-1-6176	Secret Agent	1979	12.00
❏ PD-6062	The Leprechaun	1976	12.00
❏ PD-1-6130	The Mad Hatter	1978	12.00
QUINTESSENCE			
❏ QJ-25011	Before Forever	1978	15.00
SOLID STATE			
❏ SS-18055	Chick Corea "Is	1969	25.00
❏ SS-18039	Now He Sings, Now He Sobs	1969	25.00
VORTEX			
❏ 2004	Tones for Joan's Bones	1971	30.00
WARNER BROS.			
❏ BSK3425	Tap Step	1980	12.00
❏ BSK3552	Three Quartets	1981	12.00
❏ 23699	Touchstone	1983	12.00

COREY, JILL

COLUMBIA
❏ CL1095 [M]	Sometimes I'm Happy, Sometimes I'm Blue	1957	30.00

CORNELIUS, HELEN

MCA DOT
❏ 39034	Helen Cornelius	198?	10.00

CORNELIUS BROTHERS AND SISTER ROSE

UNITED ARTISTS
❏ UAS-5568	Cornelius Brothers and Sister Rose	1972	18.00
❏ UA-LA593-G	Greatest Hits	1976	15.00

CORNELL, DON

ABC-PARAMOUNT
❏ ABC-537 [M]	Incomparable	1966	15.00
❏ ABCS-537 [S]	Incomparable	1966	18.00

CORAL
❏ CRL57055 [M]	Don	1955	30.00
❏ CRL57133 [M]	For Teenagers Only	1957	30.00

DOT
❏ DLP-3160 [M]	Don Cornell's Great Hits	1959	30.00
❏ DLP-25160 [S]	Don Cornell's Great Hits	1959	30.00

MOVIETONE
❏ 71013 [M]	I Wish You Love	1966	15.00
❏ S-72013 [S]	I Wish You Love	1966	18.00

SIGNATURE
❏ SM-1001 [M]	Don Cornell Sings Love Songs	1960	25.00
❏ SS-1001 [S]	Don Cornell Sings Love Songs	1960	30.00

VOCALION
❏ VL3657 [M]	Don Cornell	196?	15.00

CORNELLS, THE

GAREX
❏ LPGA-100 [M]	Beach Bound	1963	500.00

SUNDAZED
❏ LP-5013	Surf Fever!	199?	12.00

CORPORATION, THE

AGE OF AQUARIUS
❏ 4150	Get On Our Swing	1968	30.00
❏ 4250	Hassles in My Mind	1969	30.00

CAPITOL
❏ ST-175	The Corporation	1969	50.00

CORPUS

ACORN
❏ 1001 [B]	Creation: A Child	1971	600.00
—Banded tracks			
❏ 1001 [B]	Creation: A Child	1971	250.00
—Second pressing, green/pink label, unbanded			

CORPUS CHRISTI CATHEDRAL CHORALE AND YOUTH CHOIR

(NO LABEL)
❏ NR17261	A Cathedral Christmas	1987	12.00

CORTEZ, DAVE "BABY

CHESS
❏ LP-1473 [M]	Rinky Dink	1962	50.00

CLOCK
❏ C-331 [M]	Dave "Baby" Cortez	1960	40.00
❏ CS-331 [S]	Dave "Baby" Cortez	1960	50.00
❏ MGC-20647 [M]	Dave "Baby" Cortez	1961	30.00
❏ SRC-60647 [S]	Dave "Baby" Cortez	1961	40.00

CORONET
❏ CX-201 [M]	The Whistling Organ	196?	18.00

DESIGN
❏ DLP-163 [R]	The Happy Organ	1962	15.00

METRO
❏ M-550 [M]	The Fabulous Organ of Dave "Baby" Cortez	1965	18.00

Number	Title	Yr	NM

❑ MS-550 [R] | The Fabulous Organ of Dave "Baby" Cortez | 1965 | 15.00

RCA VICTOR
❑ LPM-2099 [M] | The Happy Organ | 1959 | 80.00
❑ LSP-2099 [S] | The Happy Organ | 1959 | 100.00

ROULETTE
❑ R-25328 [M] | In Orbit with Dave "Baby" Cortez | 1966 | 25.00
❑ SR-25328 [S] | In Orbit with Dave "Baby" Cortez | 1966 | 30.00
❑ R-25298 [M] | Organ Shindig | 1965 | 25.00
❑ SR-25298 [S] | Organ Shindig | 1965 | 30.00
❑ R-25315 [M] | Tweety Pie | 1966 | 25.00
❑ SR-25315 [S] | Tweety Pie | 1966 | 30.00

T-NECK
❑ TNS-3005 | The Isley Brothers Way | 1970 | 25.00

CORWIN, BOB

RIVERSIDE
❑ RLP 12-220 [M] | Bob Corwin Quartet with Don Elliott | 1956 | 80.00
— White label, blue print
❑ RLP 12-220 [M] | Bob Corwin Quartet with Don Elliott | 1957 | 40.00
— Blue label with microphone logo

CORYELL, LARRY, AND ALPHONSE MOUZON

ATLANTIC
❑ SD18220 | Back Together Again | 1977 | 15.00

CORYELL, LARRY, AND BRIAN KEANE

FLYING FISH
❑ FF-337 | Just Like Being Born | 1985 | 15.00

CORYELL, LARRY, AND PHILIP CATHERINE

ELEKTRA
❑ 6E-153 | Splendid | 1978 | 15.00
❑ 6E-123 | Twin House | 1977 | 15.00

CORYELL, LARRY, AND STEVE KAHN

ARISTA
❑ AB4156 | Two for the Road | 1978 | 15.00

CORYELL, LARRY

ARISTA
❑ AL4077 | Aspects | 1976 | 18.00
❑ AL4052 | Level One | 1975 | 18.00
❑ AL4108 | The Lion and the Ram | 1977 | 18.00

ARISTA/NOVUS
❑ AN3005 | European Imperssions | 1978 | 15.00
❑ AN3017 | Tributaries | 1979 | 15.00

CONCORD JAZZ
❑ CJ-289 | Together | 1986 | 12.00

FLYING DUTCHMAN
❑ FD-10139 | Barefoot Boy | 1971 | 18.00
❑ 51-1000 | Fairyland | 1971 | 25.00

MEGA
❑ 607 | Fairyland | 197? | 18.00
— Reissue of Flying Dutchman 51-1000

MUSE
❑ MR-5303 | Comin' Home | 1985 | 12.00
❑ MR-5319 | Equipoise | 1986 | 12.00
❑ MR-5350 | Toku Do | 1988 | 15.00

RCA VICTOR
❑ AYL-3961 | Barefoot Boy | 198? | 10.00
— Reissue of Flying Dutchman 10139

SHANACHIE
❑ 97005 | The Dragon Gate | 1990 | 18.00

STEEPLECHASE
❑ SCS-1187 | A Quiet Day in Spring | 1983 | 12.00

VANGUARD
❑ VSD-79360 | Another Side of Larry Coryell | 1975 | 18.00
❑ VSD-79375 | Basics | 1976 | 15.00
❑ VSD-6547 | Coryell | 1969 | 18.00
❑ VSD-79342 | Introducing the Eleventh House | 1974 | 18.00
❑ VSQ-40036 [Q] | Introducing the Eleventh House | 1974 | 25.00
❑ VSD-6509 | Lady Coryell | 1969 | 18.00
❑ VSD-79410 | Larry Coryell and the Eleventh House at Montreux | 1978 | 15.00
❑ VSD-6573 | Larry Coryell at the Village Gate | 1971 | 18.00
❑ VSQ-40006 [Q] | Larry Coryell at the Village Gate | 197? | 25.00
❑ VSD-79319 | Offering | 1972 | 18.00
❑ VSQ-40013 [Q] | Offering | 197? | 25.00
❑ VSD-79367 | Planet End | 1975 | 15.00
❑ VSD-79426 | Return | 1979 | 15.00
❑ VSD-6558 | Spaces | 1970 | 18.00
❑ VSD-79345 | Spaces | 1974 | 15.00
— Reissue of 6558 with new cover
❑ VSD-75/76 | The Essential Larry Coryell | 1975 | 18.00
❑ VSD-79329 | The Real Great Escape | 1973 | 18.00
❑ VSQ-40023 [Q] | The Real Great Escape | 197? | 25.00
❑ VSD-79353 | The Restful Mind | 1975 | 15.00

COSBY, BILL

CAPITOL
❑ ST-11530 | Bill Cosby Is Not Himself These Days, Rat Own, Rat Own, Rat Own | 1976 | 12.00
❑ ST-11731 | Bill's Best Friend | 1978 | 12.00
❑ ST-11683 | Let's Boogie (Disco Bill) | 1977 | 12.00
❑ ST-11590 | My Father Confused Me… What Must I Do? What Must I Do? | 1977 | 12.00

GEFFEN
❑ GHS24104 | Those of You With or Without Children, You'll Understand | 1986 | 12.00

MCA
❑ 8005 | Bill | 197? | 15.00
❑ 333 | Fat Albert | 1973 | 12.00
❑ 553 | For Adults Only | 197? | 10.00
— Reissue of Uni 73112
❑ 554 | Inside the Mind of Bill Cosby | 197? | 10.00
— Reissue of Uni 73139
❑ 169 | When I Was a Kid | 197? | 10.00
— Reissue of Uni 73100

MOTOWN
❑ 6026ML | Bill Cosby "Himself | 1982 | 12.00
❑ 5364ML | Bill Cosby "Himself | 198? | 12.00
— Reissue of 6026 with new cover

TETRAGRAMMATON
❑ TD-5100 | 8:15 12:15 | 1969 | 25.00

UNI
❑ 73066 | Bill Cosby | 1969 | 12.00
❑ 73101 | Bill Cosby Talks to Kids About Drugs | 1971 | 18.00
❑ 73112 | For Adults Only | 1971 | 12.00
❑ 73139 | Inside the Mind of Bill Cosby | 1972 | 12.00
❑ 73082 | Live" Madison Square Garden Center | 1970 | 12.00
❑ 73100 | When I Was a Kid | 1971 | 12.00

WARNER BROS.
❑ WS1757 | 200 M.P.H. | 1968 | 15.00
❑ W1518 [M] | Bill Cosby Is a Very Funny Fellow Right! | 1964 | 18.00
❑ W1728 [M] | Bill Cosby Sings/Hooray for the Salvation Army Band | 1968 | 18.00
❑ WS1728 [S] | Bill Cosby Sings/Hooray for the Salvation Army Band | 1968 | 15.00
❑ W1709 [M] | Bill Cosby Sings/Silver Throat | 1967 | 18.00
❑ WS1709 [S] | Bill Cosby Sings/Silver Throat | 1967 | 15.00
❑ W1567 [M] | I Started Out as a Child | 1964 | 18.00
❑ WS1567 [S] | I Started Out as a Child | 1964 | 25.00
— Gold label
❑ WS1770 [B] | It's True! It's True! | 1969 | 15.00
❑ WS1836 | More of the Best of Bill Cosby | 1970 | 15.00
❑ PRO249 [DJ] | Radio Sampler Album -- The Best of Bill Cosby | 1969 | 25.00
— Promo LP with edits of 12 tracks for radio use
❑ PRO249 [DJ] | Radio Sampler Album -- The Best of Bill Cosby | 1969 | 25.00
— Promo LP with edits of 12 tracks for radio use
❑ W1691 [M] | Revenge | 1967 | 18.00
❑ WS1798 [B] | The Best of Bill Cosby | 1969 | 15.00
❑ W1734 [M] | To Russell, My Brother, Whom I Slept With | 1968 | 18.00
❑ WS1734 [S] | To Russell, My Brother, Whom I Slept With | 1968 | 15.00
❑ W1606 [M] | Why Is There Air? | 1965 | 18.00
❑ WS1606 [S] | Why Is There Air? | 1965 | 25.00
— Gold label
❑ W1634 [M] | Wonderfulness | 1966 | 18.00
❑ WS1634 [S] | Wonderfulness | 1966 | 18.00
— Gold label

COSMIC TWINS, THE

STRATA-EAST
❑ SES-7410 | The Waterbearers | 1974 | 30.00

COSTA, DON

ABC-PARAMOUNT
❑ ABC-362 [M] | Don Costa Conducts His 15 Hits | 1961 | 30.00
❑ ABC-107 [M] | Music to Break a Lease | 1956 | 30.00
❑ ABC-212 [M] | Music to Break a Sub-Lease | 1958 | 30.00

COLUMBIA
❑ CL2041 [M] | Hits! Hits! Hits! | 1963 | 18.00
❑ CS8841 [S] | Hits! Hits! Hits! | 1963 | 30.00
❑ CS8680 [S] | Hollywood Premiere | 1962 | 30.00
❑ CL1880 [M] | Hollywood Premiere | 1962 | 18.00

DCP INTERNATIONAL
❑ DCL3806 [M] | Don Costa Plays Music from Umbrellas of Cherbourg and Other Film Music | 1965 | 15.00
❑ DCS6806 [S] | Don Costa Plays Music from Umbrellas of Cherbourg and Other Film Music | 1965 | 18.00
❑ DCL3802 [M] | The Golden Touch | 1964 | 15.00
❑ DCS6802 [S] | The Golden Touch | 1964 | 18.00

HARMONY
❑ HL7347 [M] | Days of Wine and Roses and Other Great Hits | 1965 | 15.00
❑ HS11147 [S] | Days of Wine and Roses and Other Great Hits | 1965 | 18.00

MERCURY
❑ SR61177 | Instrumental Versions of Simon and Garfunkel | 1968 | 25.00
❑ SR61216 | The Don Costa Concept | 1969 | 25.00

UNITED ARTISTS
❑ WW7501 [M] | Echoing Voices and Trombones | 1960 | 25.00
❑ WWS8501 [S] | Echoing Voices and Trombones | 1960 | 30.00
❑ UAL3134 [M] | Magnificent Motion Picture Music | 1960 | 18.00
❑ UAS6134 [S] | Magnificent Motion Picture Music | 1960 | 25.00
❑ WW3513 [M] | The Sound of the Million Sellers | 1960 | 18.00
❑ WWS8513 [S] | The Sound of the Million Sellers | 1960 | 30.00
❑ UAL3119 [M] | The Unforgiven | 1960 | 25.00

VERVE
❑ V-8702 [M] | Modern Delights | 1967 | 25.00
❑ V6-8702 [S] | Modern Delights | 1967 | 18.00

COSTA, EDDIE, AND ART FARMER

PREMIER
❑ PM-2002 [M] | In Their Own Sweet Way | 1962 | 25.00
❑ PMS-2002 [R] | In Their Own Sweet Way | 196? | 15.00

COSTA, EDDIE

CORAL
❑ CRL57230 [M] | Guys and Dolls Like Vibes | 1958 | 200.00

DOT
❑ DLP-3206 [M] | The House of Blue Lights | 1959 | 600.00
❑ DLP-25206 [S] | The House of Blue Lights | 1959 | 500.00

INTERLUDE
❑ MO-508 [M] | Eddie Costa Quintet | 1959 | 100.00
— Reissue of Mode 118
❑ ST-1008 [S] | Eddie Costa Quintet | 1959 | 60.00

JOSIE
❑ JOZ-3509 [M] | Eddie Costa with the Burke Trio | 1963 | 25.00
❑ JSS-2509 [S] | Eddie Costa with the Burke Trio | 1963 | 30.00

JUBILEE
❑ JLP-1025 [M] | Eddie Costa Quintet with the Vinnie Burke Trio | 1956 | 60.00

MODE
❑ LP-118 [M] | Eddie Costa Quintet | 1957 | 250.00

COSTA, EDDIE/MAT MATTHEWS AND DON ELLIOTT

VERVE
❑ MGV-8237 [M] | Eddie Costa with Rolf Kuhn and Dick Johnson/Mat Matthews and Don Elliott at Newport | 1958 | 60.00
❑ V-8237 [M] | Eddie Costa with Rolf Kuhn and Dick Johnson/Mat Matthews and Don Elliott at Newport | 1961 | 30.00

COSTA, JOHNNY

CORAL
❑ CRL57117 [M] | The Most Beautiful Girl in the World | 1957 | 30.00

SAVOY
❑ MG-15056 [10] | Johnny Costa | 1955 | 80.00
❑ MG-12052 [M] | The Amazing Johnny Costa | 1956 | 50.00

SAVOY JAZZ
❑ SJL-1190 | Neighborhood | 198? | 12.00

COSTANZO, JACK

GENE NORMAN
❑ GNP-19 [M] | Mr. Bongo | 1955 | 50.00

LIBERTY
❑ LRP-3137 [M] | Afro Can-Can | 1960 | 30.00
❑ LST-7137 [S] | Afro Can-Can | 1960 | 30.00
❑ LRP-3109 [M] | Bongo Fever | 1959 | 30.00
❑ LST-7109 [S] | Bongo Fever | 1959 | 30.00
❑ LRP-3093 [M] | Latin Fever | 1958 | 30.00
❑ LST-7020 [S] | Latin Fever | 1958 | 30.00
❑ LRP-3177 [M] | Learn-Play Bongos | 1960 | 30.00
❑ LRP-3195 [M] | Naked City | 1961 | 30.00
❑ LST-7195 [S] | Naked City | 1961 | 30.00

NORGRAN
❑ MGN-32 [10] | Afro-Cubano | 1954 | 150.00

SUNSET
❑ SUM-1134 [M] | Bongo Fever | 196? | 15.00
❑ SUS-5134 [S] | Bongo Fever | 196? | 15.00

COSTANZO, JACK/ANDRE'S CUBAN ALL STARS

NORGRAN
❑ MGN-1067 [M] | Afro-Cubano | 1956 | 100.00
— Combined reissue of Norgran 32 (by the former) and Clef 515 (by the latter)

Number	Title	Yr	NM

VERVE

| ❑ MGV-8157 [M] | Afro-Cubano | 1957 | 50.00 |
| ❑ V-8157 [M] | Afro-Cubano | 1961 | 30.00 |

COSTELLO, ELVIS

COLUMBIA

| ❑ AS1318 [DJ] | Almost Blue | 1981 | 60.00 |

—*Radio sampler with introductions by Elvis before each track*

| ❑ FC37562 | Almost Blue | 1981 | 12.00 |
| ❑ PC37562 | Almost Blue | 1984 | 10.00 |

—*Budget-line reissue with new prefix*

| ❑ AS1318 [DJ] | Almost Blue: Elvis Introduces His Favorite Country Songs | 1981 | 60.00 |

—*Radio sampler with introductions by Elvis before each track*

| ❑ JC35709 [DJ] | Armed Forces | 1979 | 18.00 |

—*White label promo, includes bonus 7" single*

| ❑ JC35709 [DJ] | Armed Forces | 1979 | 18.00 |

—*White label promo; add 20 percent if bonus 7-inch single is there; add another 33 percent if the 7-inch's picture sleeve is there*

| ❑ JC35709 | Armed Forces | 1979 | 12.00 |

—*Stock copy; add 30 percent if bonus 7-inch single is there; add another 50 percent if the 7-inch's picture sleeve is there*

| ❑ PC35709 | Armed Forces | 1984 | 10.00 |

—*Budget-line reissue with new prefix; not issued with bonus single*

❑ FC40518	Blood & Chocolate	1986	12.00
❑ JC36347	Get Happy!!	1980	12.00
❑ PC36347	Get Happy!!	1984	10.00

—*Budget-line reissue with new prefix*

| ❑ FC39429 | Goodbye Cruel World | 1984 | 12.00 |
| ❑ PC39429 | Goodbye Cruel World | 198? | 10.00 |

—*Budget-line reissue with new prefix*

| ❑ FC38157 | Imperial Bedroom | 1982 | 12.00 |
| ❑ HC48157 | Imperial Bedroom | 1982 | 50.00 |

—*Half-speed mastered edition*

| ❑ PC38157 | Imperial Bedroom | 1984 | 10.00 |

—*Budget-line reissue with new prefix*

| ❑ FC40173 | King of America | 1986 | 12.00 |

—*By "The Costello Show Featuring Elvis Costello"*

| ❑ PC40173 | King of America | 198? | 10.00 |

—*By "The Costello Show Featuring Elvis Costello"; budget-line reissue with new prefix*

| ❑ AS529 [EP] | Live at Hollywood High | 1978 | 25.00 |

—*Promo-only 12-inch version of 7-inch single*

| ❑ JC35037 | My Aim Is True | 1977 | 18.00 |

—*First pressings have yellow back covers*

| ❑ JC35037 [B] | My Aim Is True | 1978 | 12.00 |

—*Second pressings have a white back cover and no bar code*

| ❑ PC35037 | My Aim Is True | 1984 | 10.00 |

—*Budget-line reissue with new prefix*

| ❑ (no #)0 [PD] | My Aim Is True/This Year's Model | 1978 | 100.00 |

—*Promo-only picture disc; contains six songs from one album and six from the other*

| ❑ FC38897 | Punch the Clock | 1983 | 12.00 |
| ❑ JC36839 | Taking Liberties | 1980 | 12.00 |

—*With custom old style Columbia label*

| ❑ JC36839 | Taking Liberties | 1980 | 10.00 |
| ❑ PC36839 | Taking Liberties | 1984 | 10.00 |

—*Budget-line reissue with new prefix*

❑ FC40101	The Best of Elvis Costello	1985	15.00
❑ AS958 [DJ]	The Elvis Costello Interview with Tom Snyder	1981	30.00
❑ JC35331	This Year's Model	1978	15.00

—*With "Costello" replacing "Columbia" on labels*

| ❑ JC35331 | This Year's Model | 1978 | 12.00 |

—*With standard Columbia label*

| ❑ PC35331 | This Year's Model | 1984 | 10.00 |

—*Budget-line reissue with new prefix*

❑ AS958 [DJ]	Tom Snyder Interview	1981	25.00
❑ JC37051	Trust	1981	12.00
❑ PC37051	Trust	1984	10.00

—*Budget-line reissue with new prefix*

COSTELLO

| ❑ AS847 [EP] | Taking Liberties | 1980 | 18.00 |

—*Promo-only four-song sampler' "Costello" is where "Columbia" would normally be on the 78-rpm-style label*

LOST HIGHWAY

| ❑ B0003905-01 [10] | Delta-Verite: The Clarksdale Sessions | 2005 | 12.00 |
| ❑ B0003905-01 [10] | Delta-Verite: The Clarksdale Sessions | 2005 | 12.00 |

—*Black vinyl; this album has been counterfeited; originals have a white border around all four sides of the front cover and the words "The Round-Up Factor" at the bottom of the back cover, and counterfeits do not; also, counterfeits use the catalog number "CN-005" and have white labels*

| ❑ B0002593-01 | The Delivery Man | 2004 | 25.00 |

MOBILE FIDELITY

❑ MFSL1-355 [B]	Almost Blue	2012	30.00
❑ MFSL1-353 [B]	Imperial Bedroom	2012	30.00
❑ MFSL1-389 [B]	Punch The Clock	2013	40.00

RHINO

| ❑ R1-74285 | My Aim Is True | 2003 | 18.00 |

—*180-gram vinyl; first U.S. issue of British track lineup*

WARNER BROS.

| ❑ 46198 | All This Useless Beauty | 1996 | 100.00 |
| ❑ R100841 | Spike | 1989 | 15.00 |

—*BMG Direct Marketing edition*

| ❑ 25848 | Spike | 1989 | 12.00 |
| ❑ -03488 [DJ] | Spike -- The Elvis Costello Hour | 1989 | 30.00 |

—*Music and conversation; generic gatefold sleeve with sticker on cover*

| ❑ PRO-A-3488 [DJ] | The Elvis Costello Hour | 1989 | 40.00 |

—*Music and interview; generic gatefold sleeve with sticker on cover*

COTTON, GENE

ABC

| ❑ D-933 | For All the Young Writers | 1975 | 12.00 |
| ❑ D-983 | Rain On | 1977 | 12.00 |

ARIOLA AMERICA

| ❑ SW-50070 | No Strings Attached | 1979 | 12.00 |
| ❑ SW-50031 | Save the Dancer | 1978 | 12.00 |

KNOLL

| ❑ 1001 | Eclipse of the Blue Moon | 1981 | 12.00 |

MYRRH

| ❑ MSB-6517 | In the Gray of the Morning | 1973 | 15.00 |
| ❑ MSB-6524 | Liberty | 1974 | 15.00 |

COTTON, JAMES

ALLIGATOR

| ❑ AL-4737 | High Compression | 1984 | 12.00 |
| ❑ AL-4746 | Live from Chicago | 1986 | 12.00 |

ANTONE'S

| ❑ ANT-0007 | James Cotton Live | 1988 | 15.00 |

BLIND PIG

| ❑ BP-2587 | Take Me Back | 1987 | 12.00 |

BUDDAH

❑ BDS-5620	100% Cotton	1974	15.00
❑ BDS-5650	High Energy	1975	15.00
❑ BDS-5661	Live & On the Move!	1976	18.00

CAPITOL

| ❑ ST-814 | Taking Care of Business | 1971 | 18.00 |
| ❑ SM-814 | Taking Care of Business | 197? | 12.00 |

—*Reissue with new prefix*

INTERMEDIA

| ❑ QS-5006 | Dealing with the Devil | 198? | 12.00 |
| ❑ QS-5011 | Two Sides of the Blues | 198? | 12.00 |

VANGUARD

| ❑ VSD-79283 | Cut You Loose! | 1969 | 18.00 |

VERVE FORECAST

❑ FTS-3038 [B]	Pure Cotton	1968	25.00
❑ FT-3023 [M]	The James Cotton Blues Band	1967	30.00
❑ FTS-3023 [S]	The James Cotton Blues Band	1967	25.00

COTTON PICKERS, THE

PHILIPS

| ❑ PHM200025 [M] | Country Guitar | 1962 | 25.00 |
| ❑ PHS600025 [S] | Country Guitar | 1962 | 30.00 |

COTTRELL, LOUIS

NOBILITY

| ❑ LP-703 | Dixieland Hall Presents Louis Cottrell and His New Orleans Jazz | 197? | 18.00 |

RIVERSIDE

| ❑ RLP-385 [M] | Bourbon Street | 1961 | 25.00 |
| ❑ RS-9385 [S] | Bourbon Street | 1961 | 30.00 |

COUCH, ORVILLE

VEE JAY

| ❑ VJLP-1087 [M] | Hello Trouble | 1964 | 25.00 |
| ❑ VJS-1087 [S] | Hello Trouble | 1964 | 40.00 |

COULSON, DEAN, MCGUINNESS, FLINT

SIRE

| ❑ SAS-7405 [B] | Lo and Behold | 1972 | 30.00 |

COULTER, CLIFF

ABC IMPULSE!

| ❑ AS-9216 | Do It Now! | 1972 | 25.00 |
| ❑ AS-9197 | Eastside San Jose | 1971 | 25.00 |

COULTER, PHIL

SHANACHIE

| ❑ 53005 | Phil Coulter's Christmas | 1983 | 12.00 |

COUNCE, CURTIS

ANALOGUE PRODUCTIONS

| ❑ AP-3006 | You Get More Bounce with Curtis Counce | 199? | 18.00 |

BOPLICITY

| ❑ BOP-7 | Exploring the Future | 198? | 15.00 |

—*Reissue of Dooto LP*

CONTEMPORARY

| ❑ M-3574 [M] | Carl's Blues | 1960 | 100.00 |
| ❑ S-7574 [S] | Carl's Blues | 1960 | 120.00 |

| ❑ C-7539 | Counceltation | 197? | 25.00 |

—*Retitled version of "You Get More Bounce with Curtis Counce*

❑ C-3526 [M]	Curtis Counce Group	1957	100.00
❑ S-7526 [S]	Curtis Counce Group	1959	60.00
❑ S-7526 [S]	Landslide	196?	30.00

—*Retitled version of "Curtis Counce Group*

❑ C-7655	Sonority	198?	25.00
❑ M-3539 [M]	You Get More Bounce with Curtis Counce	1957	100.00
❑ S-7539 [S]	You Get More Bounce with Curtis Counce	1959	60.00

DOOTO

| ❑ DTL-247 [M] | Exploring the Future | 1958 | 50.00 |

FANTASY

| ❑ OJC-423 | Carl's Blues | 1990 | 15.00 |

—*Reissue of Contemporary 7574*

| ❑ OJC-159 | You Get More Bounce with Curtis Counce | 198? | 12.00 |

—*Reissue of Contemporary 7539*

COUNT FIVE, THE

DOUBLE SHOT

| ❑ DSM-1001 [M] | Psychotic Reaction | 1966 | 60.00 |
| ❑ DSS-5001 [R] | Psychotic Reaction | 1966 | 30.00 |

COUNTING CROWS

DGC

❑ 24975	Recovering the Satellites	1996	18.00
❑ DGC2-24975	Recovering the Satellites	1996	50.00
❑ 069490415-1	This Desert Life	1999	50.00

—*Side 2 of the second record is blank*

COUNTRY ALL-STARS, THE

RCA VICTOR

| ❑ LPM-3167 [10] | String Dustin' | 1953 | 150.00 |

COUNTRY CUT-UPS, THE

TOWN HOUSE

| ❑ 1000 [M] | The Country Cut-Ups Go to College | 195? | 80.00 |

COUNTRY GENTLEMEN, THE

CIMARRON

| ❑ 2001 [M] | Songs of the Pioneers | 1962 | 40.00 |

MERCURY

| ❑ MG-20858 [M] | Folk Session Inside | 1963 | 25.00 |
| ❑ SR-60858 [S] | Folk Session Inside | 1963 | 30.00 |

STARDAY

❑ SLP-174 [M]	Bluegrass at Carnegie Hall	1962	40.00
❑ SLP-311 [M]	Songs of the Pioneers	1965	30.00
❑ SLP-109 [M]	Traveling Dobro Blues	1959	50.00

COUNTRY GOSPELAIRES, THE

STARDAY

| ❑ SLP-105 [M] | The Church Back Home | 1959 | 30.00 |

COUNTRY JOE AND THE FISH

CUSTOM FIDELITY

| ❑ CFS-2348 | Joe McDonald | 1968 | 1000.00 |

—*Recorded in 1964, 200 copies were pressed for Joe McDonald; VG value 500; VG+ value 750*

FANTASY

❑ 9525	Goodbye Blues	1977	12.00
❑ 9586	Leisure Suite	1980	12.00
❑ 9511	Love Is a Fire	1976	12.00
❑ 9495	Paradise with an Ocean View	1975	12.00
❑ 9530	Reunion	1977	15.00
❑ 9544	Rock and Roll Music From the Planet Earth	1978	12.00

FIRST AMERICAN

| ❑ PIC-3309 | The Early Years | 1979 | 12.00 |

MOBLIE FIDELITY

| ❑ 1-056 | Paradise with an Ocean View | 1981 | 30.00 |

—*Audiophile vinyl*

VANGUARD

❑ VSD-6555	C.J. Fish	1970	25.00
❑ VSD-6545	Country Joe & The Fish/ Greatest Hits	1969	25.00
❑ VSD-79348	Country Joe	1974	15.00
❑ VRS-9244 [M]	Electric Music for the Mind and Body	1967	100.00

—*Black label (unverified)*

| ❑ VRS-9244 [M] | Electric Music for the Mind and Body | 1967 | 80.00 |

—*Gold label*

| ❑ VSD-79244 [S] | Electric Music for the Mind and Body | 1967 | 50.00 |

—*Black label (unverified)*

| ❑ VSD-79244 [S] | Electric Music for the Mind and Body | 1967 | 40.00 |

—*Gold label*

❑ VSD-79299	Here We Are Again	1969	25.00
❑ VSD-79304	Hold On It's Coming	1971	18.00
❑ 9266/79266 [B]	I-Feel-Like-I'm-Fixin'-to-Die "Fish Game" Poster	1967	18.00

Number	Title	Yr	NM
❏ VSD79266 [B]	I-Feel-Like-I'm-Fixin'-To-Die	2013	30.00
❏ VRS-9266 [M]	I-Feel-Like-I'm-Fixin'-to-Die	1967	35.00
❏ VSD-79266 [S]	I-Feel-Like-I'm-Fixin'-to-Die	1967	25.00
❏ VSD-79316	Incredible! Live!	1972	15.00
❏ VSD-79328	Paris Sessions	1973	15.00
❏ VSD-85/86	The Essential Country Joe	1977	15.00
❏ VSD-27/28	The Life and Times of Country Joe & the Fish From Haight-Ashbury to Woodstock	1971	25.00
❏ VSQ-40004/5 [Q]	The Life and Times of Country Joe & the Fish From Haight-Ashbury to Woodstock	197?	40.00
❏ VSD-6546	Thinking of Woody	1969	18.00
❏ VSD-79277	Together	1968	25.00
❏ VSD-6557	Tonight I'm Singing Just for You	1970	18.00
❏ VSD-79315	War, War, War	1971	18.00

COUNTRY MIKE

GRAND ROYAL
| ❏ CM-1 | Country Mike's Greatest Hits 2000 | | 200.00 |
| | | | |

— Black vinyl; this album has been counterfeited; originals have a white border around all four sides of the front cover and the words "The Round-Up Factor" at the bottom of the back cover, and counterfeits do not; also, counterfeits use the catalog number "CN-005" and have white labels

| ❏ CM-1 | Country Mike's Greatest Hits 2000 | | 300.00 |

— Red vinyl

COUNTS, THE (2)

AWARE
| ❏ 2006 | Funk Pump | 1975 | 25.00 |
| ❏ 2002 | Love Sign | 1973 | 30.00 |

WESTBOUND
| ❏ 2011 | What's Up Front That Counts | 1972 | 30.00 |

COURTLAND, JEROME

JUBILEE
| ❏ LP22 [10] | Through a Long and Sleepless Night | 1955 | 40.00 |

COURTNEY, LOU

EPIC
| ❏ KE33011 | I'm in Need of Love | 1974 | 15.00 |

RCA VICTOR
| ❏ APL1-1969 | Buffalo Smoke | 1976 | 15.00 |

RIVERSIDE
| ❏ 92000 | Skate Now (Shing-a-Ling) | 1967 | 30.00 |

COUSIN WILBUR

C.W.
| ❏ 100 [M] | The Cousin Wilbur Show | 195? | 50.00 |

COUSINS, THE (2)

PARKWAY
| ❏ P-7005 [M] | Music of the Strip | 1961 | 25.00 |
| ❏ SP-7005 [S] | Music of the Strip | 1961 | 30.00 |

COVAY, DON

ATLANTIC
❏ 8104 [M]	Mercy	1965	40.00
❏ SD8104 [S]	Mercy	1965	50.00
❏ 8120 [M]	See Saw	1966	40.00
❏ SD8120 [S]	See Saw	1966	50.00
❏ SD8237	The House of Blue Lights	1969	30.00

JANUS
| ❏ 3038 | Different Strokes for Different Folks | 1972 | 18.00 |

MERCURY
❏ 835030-1	Checkin' In with Don Covay	1988	12.00
❏ SRM-1-1020	Hot Blood	1974	15.00
❏ SRM-1-653	Super Dude I	1973	15.00

PHILADELPHIA INT'L.
| ❏ PZ33958 | Travelin' In Heavy Traffic | 1977 | 12.00 |

COVEN

BUDDAH
| ❏ BDS-5614 | Blood on the Snow | 1974 | 30.00 |

MERCURY
| ❏ SR61239 [B] | Witchcraft Destroys Minds and Reaps Souls | 1969 | 150.00 |

MGM
| ❏ SE-4801 [B] | Coven | 1971 | 60.00 |

COWARD, NOEL, AND GERTRUDE LAWRENCE

RCA VICTOR
| ❏ LPM-1156 [M] | Noel and Gertie | 1955 | 30.00 |

COWARD, NOEL

COLUMBIA MASTERWORKS
| ❏ ML5063 [M] | Noel Coward at Las Vegas | 1955 | 30.00 |

COWBOY JUNKIES

LATENT RECORDINGS
| ❏ LATEX4 | Whites Off Earth Now!! | 1986 | 30.00 |

— Canada-only release

RCA
| ❏ 8568-1-R | The Trinity Session | 1988 | 18.00 |
| ❏ 8568-1-R | The Trinity Session | 1997 | 40.00 |

— Classic Records reissue on audiophile vinyl

COWELL, STANLEY

ARISTA FREEDOM
| ❏ AL1009 | Beautiful Circles | 197? | 15.00 |
| ❏ AL1032 | Blues for the Viet Cong | 197? | 15.00 |

ECM
| ❏ 1026 | Illusion Suite | 1973 | 30.00 |

GALAXY
❏ 5125	Equipoise	1979	15.00
❏ 5131	New World	1979	15.00
❏ 5111	Talkin' 'Bout Love	1978	15.00
❏ 5104	Waiting for ...	1977	15.00

STRATA-EAST
| ❏ SES-19743 | Musa-Ancestral Streams | 1974 | 25.00 |
| ❏ SES-19765 | Regeneration | 1976 | 25.00 |

COWSILL, BILL

MGM
| ❏ SE-4706 | Nervous Breakthrough | 1970 | 18.00 |

COWSILLS, THE

LONDON
| ❏ PS587 [B] | On My Side | 1971 | 30.00 |

MGM
| ❏ E-4554 [M] | Captain Sad and His Ship of Fools | 1968 | 40.00 |

— Mono appears to be yellow label promo only

❏ SE-4554 [S]	Captain Sad and His Ship of Fools	1968	18.00
❏ SE-4639	II X II	1969	25.00
❏ SE-4597	The Best of the Cowsills	1968	18.00
❏ E-4498 [M]	The Cowsills	1967	25.00
❏ SE-4498 [S]	The Cowsills	1967	18.00
❏ GAS-103	The Cowsills (Golden Archive Series)	1970	18.00
❏ SE-4619	The Cowsills in Concert	1969	18.00
❏ E-4534 [M]	We Can Fly	1968	30.00

— Appears to exist only as a yellow label promo

| ❏ SE-4534 [S] | We Can Fly | 1968 | 18.00 |

WING
| ❏ SRW-16354 | The Cowsills Plus the Lincoln Park Zoo | 1968 | 15.00 |

COX, DANNY

PIONEER
| ❏ 2125 | Sunny | 1968 | 30.00 |

TOGETHER
| ❏ 1011 | Birth Announcement | 1969 | 30.00 |

COX, IDA

FANTASY
| ❏ OJC-1758 | Blues for Rampart Street | 198? | 18.00 |

— Reissue of Riverside 9374

RIVERSIDE
| ❏ RLP-374 [M] | Blues for Rampart Street | 1961 | 30.00 |
| ❏ RS-9374 [S] | Blues for Rampart Street | 1961 | 40.00 |

COX, KENNY, CONTEMPORARY JAZZ QUINTET

BLUE NOTE
| ❏ BST-84302 | Introducing Kenny Cox | 1969 | 25.00 |
| ❏ BST-84339 | Multidirection | 1970 | 25.00 |

COX, SONNY

CADET
| ❏ LP-765 [M] | The Wailer | 1966 | 18.00 |
| ❏ LPS-765 [S] | The Wailer | 1966 | 25.00 |

COXON'S ARMY

SAM MILLER EXCHANGE
| ❏ (no cat #)0 | Live from Sam Miller's Exchange Cafe | 1974 | 250.00 |

— Original is on Sam Miller Exchange purple label

TRACE
| ❏ (no cat #)0 | Live from Sam Miller's Exchange Cafe | 1975 | 250.00 |

— Reprint is on black Trace label

CRACK THE SKY

GRUDGE
| ❏ 4500-1-F | From the Greenhouse | 1989 | 12.00 |

LIFESONG
| ❏ LS6005 | Animal Notes | 1976 | 18.00 |
| ❏ PZ34998 | Animal Notes | 1977 | 12.00 |

— Reissue of 6004

| ❏ LS6000 | Crack the Sky | 1975 | 18.00 |
| ❏ PZ34994 | Crack the Sky | 1977 | 12.00 |

— Reissue of 6000

❏ PZ35620	Live Sky	1978	15.00
❏ LS8133	Photoflamingo	1981	12.00
❏ LS6015	Safety in Numbers	1978	18.00
❏ PZ35041	Safety in Numbers	1978	12.00

— Reissue of 6015

CRACKER

VIRGIN
| ❏ 39012 | Kerosene Hat | 1993 | 18.00 |
| ❏ 41498 | The Golden Age | 1996 | 25.00 |

— Classic Records/Rock the House edition on audiophile vinyl

CRACKERBASH

EMPTY
| ❏ MT-179 | Crackerbash | 1992 | 15.00 |
| ❏ MT-239 [10] | Tin Toy | 1993 | 15.00 |

CRADDOCK, BILLY "CRASH"

ABC
❏ X-777	Afraid I'll Want to Love Her One More Time	1973	30.00
❏ AB-1078	Billy "Crash" Craddock Sings His Greatest Hits	1978	12.00
❏ X-850	Greatest Hits -- Volume One	1975	15.00
❏ X-788	Mr. Country Rock	1973	18.00
❏ X-817	Rub It In	1974	18.00

— Black label

| ❏ X-817 | Rub It In | 1974 | 15.00 |

— Multicolor label

| ❏ ABCD-875 | Still Thinkin' Bout You | 1975 | 15.00 |
| ❏ X-777 | Two Sides of "Crash" | 1973 | 18.00 |

— Retitled version of above

ABC DOT
❏ 2063	Crash	1976	15.00
❏ DOSD-2040	Easy As Pie	1976	15.00
❏ 2082	Live!	1977	15.00

ATLANTIC
| ❏ 82012 | Back on Track | 1989 | 15.00 |

CAPITOL
❏ ST-11758	Billy "Crash" Craddock	1978	12.00
❏ ST-12054	Changes	1980	12.00
❏ ST-12304	Greatest Hits	1983	12.00
❏ ST-11946	Laughing and Crying, Living and Dying	1979	12.00
❏ ST-12249	The New Will Never Wear Off	1981	12.00
❏ SW-11853	Turning Up and Turning On	1978	12.00

CARTWHEEL
| ❏ 193 | Knock Three Times | 1971 | 25.00 |
| ❏ 05001 | You Better Move On | 1972 | 25.00 |

CHART
| ❏ 1053 | The Best of Billy Crash Craddock | 1973 | 18.00 |

HARMONY
| ❏ KH32186 | Billy "Crash" Craddock | 1973 | 15.00 |

KING
| ❏ 912 [M] | I'm Tore Up | 1964 | 100.00 |

MCA
| ❏ 663 | Billy "Crash" Craddock Sings His Greatest Hits | 1981 | 10.00 |

— Reissue of ABC 1078

| ❏ 664 | Easy As Pie | 1981 | 10.00 |

— Reissue of ABC Dot 2040

| ❏ 662 | Greatest Hits -- Volume One | 1981 | 10.00 |

— Reissue of ABC 850

| ❏ 665 | Live! | 1981 | 10.00 |

— Reissue of ABC Dot 2082

| ❏ 4165 | The Best of Billy "Crash" Craddock | 198? | 15.00 |
| ❏ 666 | The First Time | 1981 | 10.00 |

MCA DOT
| ❏ 39054 | Crash Craddock | 1986 | 12.00 |

STARDAY
| ❏ 3005 | 16 Favorite Hits | 1978 | 12.00 |

CRAM, PAUL

ONARI/A&M
| ❏ 006 | Blue Tales in Time | 1982 | 15.00 |

CRAMER, FLOYD

MGM
❏ E-4223 [M]	Floyd Cramer Goes Honky Tonkin'	1964	18.00
❏ SE-4223 [R]	Floyd Cramer Goes Honky Tonkin'	1964	15.00
❏ SE-4666	Floyd Cramer Goes Honky Tonkin'	1970	15.00

— Reissue of 4223

| ❏ E-3502 [M] | That Honky-Tonk Piano | 1957 | 40.00 |

PAIR
| ❏ PDL2-1049 | Country Classics | 1986 | 15.00 |

RCA
| ❏ 5621-1-R | Our Class Reunion | 1987 | 12.00 |

RCA CAMDEN
❏ CXS-9016	A Date with Floyd Cramer	1972	18.00
❏ CAS-2508	Almost Persuaded	1971	15.00
❏ CAL-2104 [M]	Distinctive Piano Styling	196?	15.00
❏ CAS-2104 [S]	Distinctive Piano Styling	196?	15.00
❏ ACL2-0128	Floyd Cramer Plays the Big Hits	1973	15.00
❏ CAL-2152 [M]	Night Train	1967	15.00
❏ CAS-2152 [S]	Night Train	1967	15.00
❏ ACL1-0563	Spotlight On Floyd Cramer	1974	12.00

Number	Title	Yr	NM
❑ CAL-874 [M]	The Magic Touch	1965	15.00
❑ CAS-874(e) [P]	The Magic Touch	1965	15.00

—*Even though this album is labeled "Stereo Electronically Reprocessed," nine of the 10 tracks are in true stereo*

RCA VICTOR

Number	Title	Yr	NM
❑ LPM-2466 [M]	America's Biggest Selling Pianist	1962	18.00
❑ LSP-2466 [S]	America's Biggest Selling Pianist	1962	25.00
❑ LSP-4821	Best of the Class of…	1973	18.00
❑ AHL1-4119	Best of the West	1982	12.00
❑ LPM-3405 [M]	Class of '65	1965	15.00
❑ LSP-3405 [S]	Class of '65	1965	18.00
❑ LPM-3650 [M]	Class of '66	1966	15.00
❑ LSP-3650 [S]	Class of '66	1966	18.00
❑ LPM-3827 [M]	Class of '67	1967	18.00
❑ LSP-3827 [S]	Class of '67	1967	18.00
❑ LPM-4025 [M]	Class of '68	1968	50.00
❑ LSP-4025 [S]	Class of '68	1968	18.00
❑ LSP-4162	Class of '69	1969	18.00
❑ LSP-4437	Class of '70	1970	18.00
❑ LSP-4590	Class of '71	1971	18.00
❑ LSP-4772	Class of '72	1972	18.00
❑ APL1-0299	Class of '73	1973	15.00
❑ APD1-0299 [Q]	Class of '73	1973	18.00
❑ APL1-1191	Class of '74 and '75	1975	12.00
❑ APD1-1191 [Q]	Class of '74 and '75	1975	18.00
❑ AHL1-5452	Collector's Series	1985	12.00
❑ LPM-2701 [M]	Comin' On	1963	18.00
❑ LSP-2701 [S]	Comin' On	1963	25.00
❑ LPM-2800 [M]	Country Piano -- City Strings	1964	18.00
❑ LSP-2800 [S]	Country Piano -- City Strings	1964	25.00
❑ LPM-2883 [M]	Cramer at the Console	1964	18.00
❑ LSP-2883 [S]	Cramer at the Console	1964	25.00
❑ AHL1-3613	Dallas	1980	12.00
❑ LSP-4676	Detours	1972	18.00
❑ APL1-2278	Floyd Cramer & the Keyboard Kick Band	1977	12.00
❑ APL1-1541	Floyd Cramer Country	1976	12.00
❑ APD1-1541 [Q]	Floyd Cramer Country	1976	18.00
❑ LPM-2428 [M]	Floyd Cramer Gets Organized	1962	18.00
❑ LSP-2428 [S]	Floyd Cramer Gets Organized	1962	25.00
❑ APL1-0661	Floyd Cramer In Concert	1974	15.00
❑ ANL1-3469	Floyd Cramer In Concert	1979	10.00
❑ LPM-3925 [M]	Floyd Cramer Plays Country Classics	1968	25.00
❑ LSP-3925 [S]	Floyd Cramer Plays Country Classics	1968	18.00
❑ LSP-4220	Floyd Cramer Plays More Country Classics	1969	18.00
❑ LPM-3811 [M]	Floyd Cramer Plays the Monkees	1967	18.00
❑ LSP-3811 [S]	Floyd Cramer Plays the Monkees	1967	18.00
❑ LSP-4367	Floyd Cramer with the Music City Pops	1970	18.00
❑ AYL1-4008	Great Country Hits	1981	10.00
❑ LPM-2151 [M]	Hello Blues	1960	18.00
❑ LSP-2151 [S]	Hello Blues	1960	25.00
❑ LPM-3746 [M]	Here's What's Happening!	1967	18.00
❑ LSP-3746 [S]	Here's What's Happening!	1967	18.00
❑ ANL1-2344	Hits from Country Hall	1977	12.00
❑ LPM-3318 [M]	Hits from the Country Hall of Fame	1965	18.00
❑ LSP-3318 [S]	Hits from the Country Hall of Fame	1965	25.00
❑ LPM-2544 [M]	I Remember Hank Williams	1962	18.00
❑ LSP-2544 [S]	I Remember Hank Williams	1962	25.00
❑ LPM-2350 [M]	Last Date	1961	25.00
❑ LSP-2350 [S]	Last Date	1961	30.00
❑ AHL1-3487	Last Date	1979	12.00
❑ AHL1-2644	Looking for Mr. Goodbar	1978	12.00
❑ LSP-4070	MacArthur Park	1968	18.00
❑ LPM-2359 [M]	On the Rebound	1961	18.00
❑ LSP-2359 [S]	On the Rebound	1961	25.00
❑ APL1-0893	Piano Masterpieces (1900-75)	1975	12.00
❑ APD1-0893 [Q]	Piano Masterpieces (1900-75)	1975	18.00
❑ AYL1-3745	Piano Masterpieces (1900-75)	1980	10.00
❑ LSP-4500	Sounds of Sunday	1971	18.00
❑ APD1-0155 [Q]	Super Country Hits	1973	18.00

—*All copies are in quadraphonic*

Number	Title	Yr	NM
❑ AHL1-3209	Super Hits	1979	12.00
❑ LPM-2642 [M]	Swing Along	1963	18.00
❑ LSP-2642 [S]	Swing Along	1963	25.00
❑ LPM-2888 [M]	The Best of Floyd Cramer	1964	15.00
❑ LSP-2888 [S]	The Best of Floyd Cramer	1964	18.00
❑ AYL1-3900	The Best of Floyd Cramer	1981	10.00
❑ LSP-4091	The Best of Floyd Cramer, Volume 2	1969	18.00
❑ LPM-3533 [M]	The Big Ones	1966	15.00
❑ LSP-3533 [S]	The Big Ones	1966	18.00
❑ LSP-4312	The Big Ones, Volume II	1970	18.00
❑ APL1-0469	The Young and the Restless	1974	15.00
❑ APD1-0469 [Q]	The Young and the Restless	1974	18.00
❑ VPS-6031	This Is Floyd Cramer	1970	25.00
❑ LPM-3828 [M]	We Wish You a Merry Christmas	1967	30.00
❑ LSP-3828 [S]	We Wish You a Merry Christmas	1967	15.00

CRAMPS, THE

ENIGMA

Number	Title	Yr	NM
❑ 21	Smell of Female	1983	18.00
❑ 268 [DJ]	Stay Sick!	1990	25.00

—*Promo-only version*

Number	Title	Yr	NM
❑ 73543	Stay Sick!	1990	18.00
❑ EPRO268 [DJ]	Stay Sick!	1990	30.00

—*Promo-only version*

EPITAPH

Number	Title	Yr	NM
❑ 86516	Big Beat from Badsville	1997	15.00
❑ 86449	Flamejob	199?	15.00

—*Reissue of Medicine Label 24592*

I.R.S.

Number	Title	Yr	NM
❑ SP-70042	Bad Music for Bad People	1984	18.00
❑ SP-70501 [EP]	Gravest Hits	198?	12.00

—*Reissue of 501*

Number	Title	Yr	NM
❑ SP-501 [EP]	Gravest Hits	1979	35.00
❑ SP-70016	Psychedelic Jungle	1981	25.00
❑ SP-007 [B]	Songs the Lord Taught Us	1980	35.00
❑ SP-70007	Songs the Lord Taught Us	198?	15.00

—*Reissue of 007*

MEDICINE LABEL

Number	Title	Yr	NM
❑ 24592 [B]	Flamejob	1994	30.00

CRANBERRIES, THE

ISLAND

Number	Title	Yr	NM
❑ 524234-1	To the Faithful Departed	1996	15.00

— *Yellow vinyl, fold-open poster-bag cover; British import for distribution in U.S. (no "Made in England" stickers)*

CRANE, BOB

EPIC

Number	Title	Yr	NM
❑ LN24224 [M]	The Funny Side of TV	1966	30.00
❑ BN26224 [S]	The Funny Side of TV	1966	30.00

CRANE, LES

WARNER BROS.

Number	Title	Yr	NM
❑ BS2570	Desiderata	1971	12.00
❑ SW-94266	Desiderata	1972	15.00

—*Capitol Record Club edition*

CRAWFORD, HANK, AND JIMMY McGRIFF

MILESTONE

Number	Title	Yr	NM
❑ M-9177	On the Blue Side	1990	15.00
❑ M-9142	Soul Survivors	1986	12.00
❑ M-9153	Steppin' Up	1988	12.00

CRAWFORD, HANK

ATLANTIC

Number	Title	Yr	NM
❑ 1455 [M]	After Hours	1966	18.00
❑ SD1455 [S]	After Hours	1966	25.00
❑ 1436 [M]	Dig These Blues	1965	18.00
❑ SD1436 [S]	Dig These Blues	1965	25.00
❑ SD1503	Double Cross	1968	30.00
❑ 1387 [M]	From the Heart	1962	18.00
❑ SD1387 [S]	From the Heart	1962	25.00
❑ 1356 [M]	More Soul	1960	25.00

—*Purple and red label, white fan logo*

Number	Title	Yr	NM
❑ SD1356 [S]	More Soul	1960	30.00

—*Green and blue label, white fan logo*

Number	Title	Yr	NM
❑ 1356 [M]	More Soul	1962	15.00

—*Purple and red label, black fan logo*

Number	Title	Yr	NM
❑ SD1356 [S]	More Soul	1962	18.00

—*Green and blue label, black fan logo*

Number	Title	Yr	NM
❑ 1470 [M]	Mr. Blues	1967	25.00
❑ SD1470 [S]	Mr. Blues	1967	18.00
❑ SD1523	Mr. Blues Plays Lady Soul	1969	18.00
❑ 1405 [M]	Soul of the Ballad	1963	18.00
❑ SD1405 [S]	Soul of the Ballad	1963	25.00
❑ SD 2-315	The Art of Hank Crawford	1973	18.00
❑ SD1557	The Best of Hank Crawford	1970	18.00
❑ 1372 [M]	The Soul Clinic	1961	25.00

—*Purple and red label, white fan logo*

Number	Title	Yr	NM
❑ SD1372 [S]	The Soul Clinic	1961	30.00

—*Green and blue label, white fan logo*

Number	Title	Yr	NM
❑ 1372 [M]	The Soul Clinic	1962	15.00

—*Purple and red label, black fan logo*

Number	Title	Yr	NM
❑ SD1372 [S]	The Soul Clinic	1962	18.00

—*Green and blue label, black fan logo*

Number	Title	Yr	NM
❑ 1423 [M]	True Blue	1964	18.00
❑ SD1423 [S]	True Blue	1964	25.00

COTILLION

Number	Title	Yr	NM
❑ SD18003	It's a Funky Thing to Do	1971	25.00

KUDU

Number	Title	Yr	NM
❑ KU-39	Cajun Sunrise	1979	18.00
❑ KU-19	Don't You Worry 'Bout a Thing	1975	25.00
❑ KU-33	Hank Crawford's Back	1977	18.00
❑ KU-06	Help Me Make It Through the Night	1972	25.00
❑ KU-26	I Hear a Symphony	1976	25.00
❑ KU-35	Tico Rico	1977	18.00
❑ KU-08	We've Got a Good Thing	1973	25.00
❑ KU-15	Wildflower	1974	25.00

MILESTONE

Number	Title	Yr	NM
❑ M-9129	Down on the Deuce	1985	12.00
❑ M-9182	Groove Master	1990	15.00
❑ M-9119	Indigo Blue	1984	12.00
❑ M-9112	Midnight Ramble	1983	12.00
❑ M-9149	Mr. Chips	1987	12.00
❑ M-9168	Night Beat	1988	12.00
❑ M-9140	Roadhouse Symphony	1986	12.00

MOBILE FIDELITY

Number	Title	Yr	NM
❑ 1-224	Soul of the Ballad	1995	30.00

—*Audiophile vinyl*

CRAWFORD, JESSE

DECCA

Number	Title	Yr	NM
❑ DL8794 [M]	Christmas	1958	15.00
❑ DL78794 [S]	Christmas	1958	18.00

DESIGN

Number	Title	Yr	NM
❑ DLPX-7 [M]	Organ and Chimes for Christmas	196?	15.00

—*Same recordings as Promenade LP, but in slightly different order*

Number	Title	Yr	NM
❑ SDLPX-7 [S]	Organ and Chimes for Christmas	196?	18.00

—*Same as above, but in stereo*

DIPLOMAT

Number	Title	Yr	NM
❑ SX1010 [S]	Organ and Chimes	196?	18.00

—*Textured cover; same order and contents as Promenade LP*

PROMENADE

Number	Title	Yr	NM
❑ CH-1000 [M]	Organ and Chimes for Christmas	196?	15.00

CRAWFORD, JOHNNY

DEL-FI

Number	Title	Yr	NM
❑ DFLP-1223 [M]	A Young Man's Fancy	1962	30.00
❑ DFST-1223 [S]	A Young Man's Fancy	1962	40.00
❑ DFLP-1248 [M]	Greatest Hits, Volume 2	1964	25.00
❑ DFST-1248 [S]	Greatest Hits, Volume 2	1964	30.00
❑ DFLP-1229 [M]	His Greatest Hits	1963	30.00
❑ DFST-1229 [S]	His Greatest Hits	1963	40.00
❑ DFLP-1224 [M]	Rumors	1963	30.00
❑ DFST-1224 [S]	Rumors	1963	40.00
❑ DFLP-1220 [M]	The Captivating Johnny Crawford	1962	40.00

GUEST STAR

Number	Title	Yr	NM
❑ GS-1470 [M]	Johnny Crawford	196?	25.00
❑ GSS-1470 [S]	Johnny Crawford	196?	30.00

RHINO

Number	Title	Yr	NM
❑ RNDF-202	The Best of Johnny Crawford	1982	15.00

SUPREME

Number	Title	Yr	NM
❑ M-110 [M]	Songs from "The Restless Ones	1965	25.00
❑ MS-210 [S]	Songs from "The Restless Ones	1965	30.00

CRAYTON, PEE WEE

CROWN

Number	Title	Yr	NM
❑ CLP-5175 [M]	Pee Wee Crayton	1959	100.00

—*Black label*

Number	Title	Yr	NM
❑ CLP-5175 [M]	Pee Wee Crayton	196?	25.00

—*Gray label*

VANGUARD

Number	Title	Yr	NM
❑ VSD-6566 [B]	The Things I Used to Do	1971	18.00

CRAZY ELEPHANT

BELL

Number	Title	Yr	NM
❑ 6034	Crazy Elephant	1969	25.00

CRAZY HORSE

EPIC

Number	Title	Yr	NM
❑ KE31710	Crazy Horse at Crooked Lake	1972	18.00

— *Yellow label*

Number	Title	Yr	NM
❑ KE31710	Crazy Horse at Crooked Lake	1973	15.00

— *Orange label*

RCA VICTOR

Number	Title	Yr	NM
❑ AFL1-3054	Crazy Moon	1978	15.00

REPRISE

Number	Title	Yr	NM
❑ RS6438	Crazy Horse	1971	18.00
❑ MS2059	Loose	1972	18.00

CRAZY JOE AND THE VARIABLE SPEED BAND

CASABLANCA

Number	Title	Yr	NM
❑ NBLP7254	Crazy Joe and the Variable Speed Band	1980	18.00

CRAZY OTTO

DECCA

Number	Title	Yr	NM
❑ DL8113 [M]	Crazy Otto	1955	25.00

—*Black label, silver print*

Number	Title	Yr	NM
❑ DL8113 [M]	Crazy Otto	1960	15.00

—*Black label with color bars*

Number	Title	Yr	NM
❑ DL8163 [M]	Crazy Otto Rides Again	1956	25.00
❑ DL8627 [M]	Crazy Otto's Back in Town	1957	18.00
❑ DL8919 [M]	Golden Award Songs	1960	18.00
❑ DL78919 [S]	Golden Award Songs	1960	25.00
❑ DL4157 [M]	Have Piano, Will Travel	1961	18.00
❑ DL74157 [S]	Have Piano, Will Travel	1961	25.00
❑ DL8737 [M]	Honky Tonk Piano	1958	18.00
❑ DL8367 [M]	Not So Crazy	1956	25.00

MGM

Number	Title	Yr	NM
❑ E-4150 [M]	Crazy Otto Plays Crazy Tunes	1963	15.00

Number	Title	Yr	NM
❏ SE-4150 [S]	Crazy Otto Plays Crazy Tunes	1963	18.00

VOCALION

Number	Title	Yr	NM
❏ VL3663 [M]	Crazy Otto Goes Sentimental	196?	15.00

CREACH, PAPA JOHN

BUDDAH

Number	Title	Yr	NM
❏ BDS-5649	I'm the Fiddle Man	1975	15.00
❏ BDS-5660	Rock Father	1977	15.00

DJM

| ❏ 11 | Cat & Fiddle | 1977 | 15.00 |
| ❏ 18 | Inphasion | 1978 | 15.00 |

GRUNT

| ❏ FTR-1009 | Filthy! | 1972 | 18.00 |
| ❏ BXL1-1009 | Filthy! | 197? | 15.00 |

— *Reissue with new prefix*

| ❏ FTR-1003 | Papa John Creach | 1971 | 18.00 |
| ❏ BXL1-1003 | Papa John Creach | 197? | 15.00 |

— *Reissue with new prefix*

| ❏ BFL1-0418 | Playing My Fiddle for You | 1974 | 18.00 |

CREAM

ATCO

Number	Title	Yr	NM
❏ SD 33-291	Best of Cream	1969	30.00
❏ 33-232 [M]	Disraeli Gears	1967	80.00
❏ SD 33-232 [S]	Disraeli Gears	1967	30.00

— *Purple and brown labels*

| ❏ SD 33-232 [S] | Disraeli Gears | 1969 | 18.00 |

— *Yellow labels*

| ❏ 33-206 [M] | Fresh Cream | 1967 | 50.00 |
| ❏ SD 33-206 [S] | Fresh Cream | 1967 | 30.00 |

— *Purple and brown labels*

| ❏ SD 33-206 [S] | Fresh Cream | 1969 | 18.00 |

— *Yellow labels*

| ❏ SD7001 | Goodbye | 1969 | 30.00 |

— *Purple and brown labels; deduct 33% if poster is missing*

| ❏ SD7001 | Goodbye | 1969 | 18.00 |

— *Yellow labels*

❏ SD 33-328 [B]	Live Cream	1970	30.00
❏ SD7005	Live Cream -- Volume II	1972	30.00
❏ 2-700 [M]	Wheels of Fire	1968	200.00

— *White label promo; no stock copies are mono*

| ❏ SD 2-700 [S] | Wheels of Fire | 1968 | 50.00 |

— *Purple and brown labels; foil-like cover*

| ❏ SD 2-700 [S] | Wheels of Fire | 1969 | 25.00 |

— *Yellow labels; dull gray cover*

DCC COMPACT CLASSICS

| ❏ LPZ-2015 | Fresh Cream | 1996 | 100.00 |

— *Audiophile vinyl*

| ❏ 2-066 | Wheels of Fire | 1980 | 90.00 |

— *Audiophile vinyl*

POLYDOR

❏ 1775315 [S]	Disraeli Gears	2008	25.00
❏ 24-3502	Heavy Cream	1972	18.00
❏ 24-5529	Off the Top	1973	18.00
❏ 8275781 [S]	Wheels of Fire	2009	30.00

REPRISE

| ❏ 494616-1 [B] | Royal Albert Hall - London - May 2-3-5-6 05 | 2013 | 80.00 |
| ❏ 49416-1 | Royal Albert Hall London May 2-3-5-6 2005 | 2005 | 50.00 |

— *Box set; contains three 180-gram LPs, each in its own cardboard cover, plus a 12x12 cardboard poster and bubble padding*

RSO

| ❏ RS-1-3012 | Best of Cream | 1977 | 15.00 |
| ❏ 15 [DJ] | Classic Cuts | 1978 | 40.00 |

— *Promo-only compilation*

| ❏ 015 [DJ] | Classic Cuts | 1978 | 40.00 |

— *Promo-only compilation*

❏ RS-1-3010	Disraeli Gears	1977	15.00
❏ RS-1-3009	Fresh Cream	1977	15.00
❏ RS-1-3013	Goodbye	1977	15.00
❏ RS-1-3014	Live Cream	1977	15.00
❏ RS-1-3015	Live Cream -- Volume 2	1977	15.00
❏ RS-2-3802	Wheels of Fire	1977	18.00

SPRINGBOARD

| ❏ SPB4037 | Early Cream | 1972 | 18.00 |

CREATION OF SUNLIGHT

WINDI

| ❏ 1001 | Creation of Sunlight | 1968 | 600.00 |

CREEDENCE CLEARWATER REVIVAL

4 MEN WITH BEARDS

❏ 4M224LP [B]	Live In Europe		30.00
❏ 4M224 [B]	Live in Europe	2014	30.00
❏ 4M225LP [M]	The Concert		25.00

ANALOGUE PRODUCTIONS

| ❏ AAPP-8387 | Bayou Country | 2002 | 30.00 |

— *Audiophile edition on heavy vinyl*

| ❏ AAPP-8402 | Cosmo's Factory | 2002 | 30.00 |

— *Audiophile edition on heavy vinyl*

| ❏ AAPP-8382 | Creedence Clearwater Revival | 2002 | 30.00 |

— *Audiophile edition on heavy vinyl*

| ❏ AAPP-8393 | Green River | 2002 | 30.00 |

— *Audiophile edition on heavy vinyl*

| ❏ AAPP-9404 | Mardi Gras | 2002 | 30.00 |

— *Audiophile edition on heavy vinyl*

| ❏ AAPP-8397 | Willie and the Poor Boys | 2002 | 30.00 |

— *Audiophile edition on heavy vinyl*

DCC COMPACT CLASSICS

| ❏ LPZ-2019 | Willie and the Poor Boys | 1996 | 50.00 |

— *Audiophile vinyl*

FANTASY

| ❏ -0 [DJ] | Bayou Country | 1969 | 80.00 |

— *White label promo*

| ❏ F-8387 [DJ] | Bayou Country | 1969 | 80.00 |

— *White label promo*

| ❏ F-8387 | Bayou Country | 1969 | 18.00 |

— *Dark blue label*

| ❏ F-8387 | Bayou Country | 1973 | 12.00 |

— *Brown label*

| ❏ ORC-4513 | Bayou Country | 1981 | 10.00 |

— *Reissue of 8387*

❏ F-9621	Chooglin'	1982	10.00
❏ CCR-3	Chronicle, Volume 2	1987	18.00
❏ CCR-2	Chronicle (The 20 Greatest Hits)	1976	18.00

— *Brown labels*

| ❏ CCR-2 | Chronicle (The 20 Greatest Hits) | 1979 | 15.00 |

— *Whitish or light blue labels*

| ❏ -0 [DJ] | Cosmo's Factory | 1970 | 80.00 |

— *White label promo*

| ❏ F-8402 [DJ] | Cosmo's Factory | 1970 | 80.00 |

— *White label promo*

| ❏ F-8402 | Cosmo's Factory | 1970 | 18.00 |

— *Dark blue label*

| ❏ F-8402 | Cosmo's Factory | 1973 | 12.00 |

— *Brown label*

| ❏ ORC-4516 | Cosmo's Factory | 1981 | 10.00 |

— *Reissue of 8402*

| ❏ -0 [DJ] | Creedence Clearwater Revival | 1968 | 80.00 |

White label promo

| ❏ F-8382 [DJ] | Creedence Clearwater Revival | 1968 | 80.00 |

— *White label promo*

| ❏ F-8382 | Creedence Clearwater Revival | 1968 | 30.00 |

— *With no reference to "Susie Q" on the front cover*

| ❏ F-8382 | Creedence Clearwater Revival | 1968 | 18.00 |

— *With "Susie Q" mentioned on the front cover; dark blue label*

| ❏ F-8382 | Creedence Clearwater Revival | 1973 | 12.00 |

— *Brown label*

| ❏ ORC-4512 | Creedence Clearwater Revival | 1981 | 10.00 |

— *Reissue of 8382*

| ❏ CCR-68 | Creedence Clearwater Revival 1968/69 | 1981 | 15.00 |
| ❏ CCR-69 | Creedence Clearwater Revival 1969 | 1981 | 15.00 |

— *Compilation of 8382 and 8387*

| ❏ CCR-70 | Creedence Clearwater Revival 1970 | 1981 | 15.00 |

— *Compilation of 8393 and 8397*

| | | | |

— *Compilation of 8402 and 8410*

❏ MPF-4509	Creedence Country	1981	12.00
❏ F-9418	Creedence Gold	1972	12.00
❏ FPM-4001 [Q]	Creedence Gold	1975	50.00
❏ -0 [DJ]	Green River	1969	80.00

— *White label promo*

| ❏ F-8393 [DJ] | Green River | 1969 | 80.00 |

— *White label promo*

| ❏ F-8393 | Green River | 1969 | 18.00 |

— *Dark blue label*

| ❏ F-8393 | Green River | 1973 | 12.00 |

— *Brown label*

| ❏ ORC-4514 | Green River | 1981 | 10.00 |

— *Reissue of 8393*

❏ CCR-1	Live in Europe	1973	15.00
❏ ORC-4526	Live in Europe	1986	12.00
❏ F-9404	Mardi Gras	1972	18.00

— *Dark blue label*

| ❏ F-9404 | Mardi Gras | 1973 | 12.00 |

— *Brown label*

| ❏ ORC-4518 | Mardi Gras | 1981 | 10.00 |

— *Reissue of 9404*

| ❏ F-9430 | More Creedence Gold | 1973 | 12.00 |
| ❏ F-8410 | Pendulum | 1970 | 18.00 |

— *Dark blue label*

| ❏ F-8410 | Pendulum | 1973 | 12.00 |

— *Brown label*

| ❏ ORC-4517 | Pendulum | 1981 | 10.00 |

— *Reissue of 8410*

| ❏ MPF-4501 | The Concert | 1981 | 12.00 |

— *Retitled version*

| ❏ MPF-4522 | The Movie Album | 1985 | 10.00 |
| ❏ MPF-4501 | The Royal Albert Hall Concert | 1980 | 18.00 |

— *Album withdrawn and changed when it was discovered this didn't come from the Royal Albert Hall*

❏ -0 [DJ]	Willy and the Poor Boys	1969	80.00
— *White label promo*			
❏ F-8397 [DJ]	Willy and the Poor Boys	1969	80.00

— *White label promo*

| ❏ F-8397 | Willy and the Poor Boys | 1969 | 18.00 |

— *Dark blue label*

| ❏ F-8397 | Willy and the Poor Boys | 1973 | 12.00 |

— *Brown label*

| ❏ ORC-4515 | Willy and the Poor Boys | 1981 | 10.00 |

— *Reissue of 8397*

HEARTLAND

| ❏ HR2039 | Creedence Clearwater Revival | 1990 | 18.00 |

K-TEL

| ❏ NU9360 | The Best of Creedence Clearwater Revival -- 20 Super Hits | 1978 | 18.00 |

MOBILE FIDELITY

| ❏ 1-037 | Cosmo's Factory | 1979 | 70.00 |

— *Audiophile vinyl*

TIME-LIFE

| ❏ SCLR-18 | Classic Rock: Creedence Clearwater Revival | 1989 | 18.00 |

CREEKMORE, TOM

DISCOVERY

| ❏ DS-791 | She Is It | 198? | 12.00 |

CREME SODA

TRINITY

| ❏ CST-11 | Tricky Zingers | 1977 | 200.00 |

— *With white cover*

| ❏ CST-11 | Tricky Zingers | 1975 | 400.00 |

— *With photo of group on cover*

CRENSHAW, MARSHALL

WARNER BROS.

❏ 25319	Downtown	1985	12.00
❏ 23873	Field Day	1983	12.00
❏ 25908	Good Evening	1989	12.00
❏ BSK3673	Marshall Crenshaw	1982	12.00
❏ 25583	Mary Jean and 9 Others	1987	12.00

CRESCENDOS, THE (1)

GUEST STAR

| ❏ G-1453 [M] | Oh Julie | 1962 | 50.00 |
| ❏ GS-1453 [R] | Oh Julie | 1962 | 25.00 |

CRESTS, THE

COED

| ❏ LPC-904 [M] | The Best of the Crests/16 Fabulous Hits | 1961 | 400.00 |

— *Label simply calls this "16 Fabulous Hits"*

| ❏ LPC-901 [M] | The Crests Sing All Biggies | 1960 | 400.00 |

— *Yellow label, black print*

| ❏ LPC-901 [M] | The Crests Sing All Biggies | 1960 | 200.00 |

— *Red label*

COLLECTABLES

| ❏ COL-5009 | Greatest Hits | 1982 | 15.00 |

POST

| ❏ 3000 | The Crests Sing | 196? | 40.00 |

RHINO

| ❏ R1-70948 | The Best of the Crests | 1989 | 15.00 |

CREVELING, CAROLE

EUTERPE

| ❏ ETP-101 [M] | Carole Creveling | 1955 | 50.00 |

CREW CUTS, THE

CAMAY

| ❏ CA-1002 [M] | The Great New Sound of the Crew Cuts | 196? | 25.00 |
| ❏ CA-3002 [S] | The Great New Sound of the Crew Cuts | 196? | 30.00 |

MERCURY

❏ MG-20143 [M]	Crew Cut Capers	1956	50.00
❏ MG-20199 [M]	Music A La Carte	1957	50.00
❏ MG-20144 [M]	Rock and Roll Bash	1956	80.00
❏ MG-20067 [M]	The Crew Cuts Go Longhair	1955	50.00
❏ MG-25200 [10]	The Crew Cuts On Campus	1956	80.00
❏ MG-20140 [M]	The Crew Cuts On Campus	1956	50.00

PICADILLY

| ❏ PIC-3560 | The Wonderful Happy Crazy Innocent World | 1980 | 12.00 |

RCA VICTOR

❏ LPM-1933 [M]	Surprise Package	1958	30.00
❏ LSP-1933 [S]	Surprise Package	1959	40.00
❏ PR-129 [M]	The Crew Cuts Have a Ball	1960	

— *Produced for Ebonite bowling balls; Side 2 has "Bowling Tips by Top Stars"*

❏ LPM-2037 [M]	The Crew Cuts Sing	1959	30.00
❏ LSP-2037 [S]	The Crew Cuts Sing	1959	40.00
❏ PR-102 [M]	The Crew Cuts Sing Out!	1960	30.00
❏ LPM-2067 [M]	You Must Have Been a Beautiful Baby	1960	30.00
❏ LSP-2067 [S]	You Must Have Been a Beautiful Baby	1960	40.00

Number	Title	Yr	NM
WING			
❑ MGW-12180 [M]	High School Favorites	196?	25.00
❑ MGW-12125 [M]	Rock and Roll Bash	196?	30.00
❑ MGW-12177 [M]	The Crew Cuts	196?	25.00
❑ MGW-12145 [M]	The Crew Cuts On Campus	196?	25.00
❑ MGW-12195 [M]	The Crew Cuts Sing the Masters	196?	25.00
CREWE, BOB			
CGC			
❑ 1000	Let Me Touch You	1970	15.00
DYNO VOICE			
❑ DV-1902 [M]	Music to Watch Birds By	1967	18.00
❑ DV-31902 [S]	Music to Watch Birds By	1967	15.00
❑ DV-9003 [M]	Music to Watch Girls By	1967	18.00
❑ DVS-9003 [S]	Music to Watch Girls By	1967	15.00
❑ DV-1906 [M]	The Bob Crewe Generation In Classic Form	1968	18.00
❑ DV-31906 [S]	The Bob Crewe Generation In Classic Form	1968	15.00
ELEKTRA			
❑ 7E-1103	Motivation	1977	15.00
❑ 7E-1083	Street Talk	1976	15.00
PHILIPS			
❑ PHM200150 [M]	All the Song Hits of the Four Seasons	1964	30.00
❑ PHS600150 [S]	All the Song Hits of the Four Seasons	1964	30.00
❑ PHM200238 [M]	Bob Crewe Plays the Four Seasons' Hits	1967	25.00
❑ PHS600238 [S]	Bob Crewe Plays the Four Seasons' Hits	1967	18.00
WARWICK			
❑ W-2034 [M]	Crazy in the Heart	1961	30.00
❑ WST-2034 [S]	Crazy in the Heart	1961	50.00
❑ W-2009 [M]	Kicks	1960	30.00
❑ WST-2009 [S]	Kicks	1960	50.00
CRICKETS, THE (1)			
BARNABY			
❑ Z30268	Rockin' 50's Rock 'N' Roll	1970	30.00
BRUNSWICK			
❑ BL54038 [M]	The "Chirping" Crickets	1957	800.00
— Textured cover			
❑ BL54038 [M]	The "Chirping" Crickets	1958	600.00
— Regular cover			
CORAL			
❑ CRL57320 [M]	In Style with the Crickets	1960	200.00
❑ CRL757320 [S]	In Style with the Crickets	1960	400.00
EPIC			
❑ FE44446	T-Shirt	1988	18.00
LIBERTY			
❑ LRP-3351 [M]	California Sun/She Loves You	1964	100.00
❑ LST-7351 [S]	California Sun/She Loves You	1964	150.00
❑ LRP-3272 [M]	Something Old, Something New, Something Blue, Somethin' Else	1962	150.00
❑ LST-7272 [S]	Something Old, Something New, Something Blue, Somethin' Else	1962	200.00
VERTIGO			
❑ VEL-1020	Remnants	1973	25.00
CRICKETS, THE (2)			
RELIC			
❑ LP-5040	The Crickets Featuring Dean Barlow	1987	12.00
CRISS, GARY			
SALSOUL			
❑ SA8504	Rio de Janeiro	1978	25.00
CRISS, PETER			
CASABLANCA			
❑ NBLP-7240	Out of Control	1980	30.00
❑ NBLP-7122	Peter Criss	1978	25.00
❑ NBPIX-7122 [PD]	Peter Criss	1978	50.00
CRISS, SONNY			
ABC IMPULSE!			
❑ AS-9326	The Joy of Sax	197?	18.00
❑ AS-9312	Warm and Sonny	197?	18.00
CLEF			
❑ MGC-122 [10]	Sonny Criss Collates	1953	250.00
FANTASY			
❑ OJC-655	Portrait of Sonny Criss	1991	15.00
— Reissue of Prestige 7526			
❑ OJC-430	This Is Sonny Criss!	1990	15.00
— Reissue of Prestige 7511			
IMPERIAL			
❑ LP-9205 [M]	Criss Cross	1963	100.00
❑ LP-12205 [R]	Criss Cross	1963	25.00
❑ LP-9020 [M]	Go Man: It's Sonny Criss & Modern Jazz	1956	600.00
❑ LP-9006 [M]	Jazz U.S.A.	1956	200.00

Number	Title	Yr	NM
❑ LP-9024 [M]	Sonny Criss Plays Cole Porter	1956	500.00
MUSE			
❑ MR-5068	Crisscraft	1975	18.00
❑ MR-5089	Out of Nowhere	1976	18.00
PABLO			
❑ 2310929	Intermission Riff	1988	12.00
PEACOCK			
❑ PLP-91 [M]	At the Crossroads	1959	350.00
PRESTIGE			
❑ PRST-7742	Hits of the 60s	1970	18.00
❑ PRST-7628	I'll Catch the Sun	1969	25.00
❑ PRLP-7526 [M]	Portrait of Sonny Criss	1967	30.00
❑ PRST-7526 [S]	Portrait of Sonny Criss	1967	30.00
❑ PRST-7610	Rockin' in Rhythm	1969	25.00
❑ PRST-7576	Sonny's Dream	1968	25.00
❑ PRST-7558	The Beat Goes On	1968	25.00
❑ PRLP-7511 [M]	This Is Sonny Criss!	1966	30.00
❑ PRST-7511 [S]	This Is Sonny Criss!	1966	30.00
❑ PRLP-7530 [M]	Up, Up and Away	1967	40.00
❑ PRST-7530 [S]	Up, Up and Away	1967	30.00
XANADU			
❑ 200	Memorial Album	198?	12.00
❑ 105	Saturday Morning	197?	18.00
CRITTERS, THE			
KAPP			
❑ KL-1485 [M]	Younger Girl	1966	30.00
❑ KS-3485 [S]	Younger Girl	1966	40.00
PROJECT 3			
❑ PR4002SD	The Critters	1969	30.00
❑ PR4001SD	Touch 'n Go with the Critters	1968	30.00
CRITTERS, THE /THE YOUNG RASCALS/LOU CHRISTIE			
BOUTIQUE			
❑ CA-1079 [M]	A Taste of the Critters & The Young Rascals & Lou Christie	1966	40.00
CROCE, JIM			
21 RECORDS			
❑ 90469	Down the Highway	1985	12.00
❑ 90467	Photographs & Memories/ His Greatest Hits	1985	10.00
❑ 90468	Time In a Bottle -- Jim Croce's Greatest Love Songs	1985	10.00
ABC			
❑ ABCX-797	I Got a Name	1973	18.00
❑ ABCX-769	Life and Times	1973	18.00
❑ ABCD-835	Photographs & Memories/ His Greatest Hits	1974	18.00
❑ ABCX-756	You Don't Mess Around with Jim	1972	25.00
— Original covers have no green box advertising "Time in a Bottle"			
❑ ABCX-756	You Don't Mess Around with Jim	1973	18.00
— Posthumous covers have a green box advertising "Time in a Bottle"			
CAPITOL			
❑ SMAS-315	Jim and Ingrid Croce	1970	30.00
COMMAND			
❑ QD-40008 [Q]	I Got a Name	1974	30.00
❑ QD-40007 [Q]	Life and Times	1974	30.00
❑ QD-40020 [Q]	Photographs & Memories/ His Greatest Hits	1974	30.00
❑ QD-40006 [Q]	You Don't Mess Around with Jim	1974	30.00
— Without border around outside of front cover			
❑ QD-40006 [Q]	You Don't Mess Around with Jim	1974	30.00
— With wide border around the outside of front cover			
CROCE			
❑ 101	Facets	1966	300.00
DCC COMPACT CLASSICS			
❑ LPZ-2054	His Greatest Recordings	1998	40.00
— Audiophile vinyl			
LIFESONG			
❑ JZ35571	Bad, Bad Leroy Brown: Jim Croce's Greatest Character Songs	1978	12.00
❑ JZ35009	I Got a Name	1978	12.00
❑ JZ35008	Life and Times	1978	12.00
❑ JZ35010	Photographs & Memories/ His Greatest Hits	1978	12.00
❑ LS900	The Faces I've Been	1975	18.00
❑ LS6007	Time in a Bottle -- Jim Croce's Greatest Love Songs	1976	15.00
❑ JZ35000	Time in a Bottle -- Jim Croce's Greatest Love Songs	1978	12.00
❑ JZ34993	You Don't Mess Around with Jim	1978	12.00
MOBILE FIDELITY			
❑ 1-079	You Don't Mess Around with Jim	1981	40.00
— Audiophile vinyl			

Number	Title	Yr	NM
PICKWICK			
❑ SPC-3332	Another Day, Another Town	1973	12.00
— Reissue of Capitol LP			
CROME SYRCUS, THE			
COMMAND			
❑ RS925SD	The Love Cycle	1968	75.00
CRONHAM, CHARLES R.			
WING			
❑ MGW12173 [M]	Christmas Carols with Organ and Chimes	195?	18.00
CROOKS, RICHARD			
CATHEDRAL			
❑ ARC012-20-43	The Voice of Firestone -- Christmas 1943 Radio Broadcast	1978	18.00
CROPPER, STEVE			
MCA			
❑ 5340	Night After Night	1982	12.00
❑ 5171	Playin' My Thang	1980	12.00
VOLT			
❑ VOS-6006 [B]	With a Little Help from My Friends	1970	30.00
CROSBY, BING, AND FRED ASTAIRE			
UNITED ARTISTS			
❑ UA-LA588-G	A Couple of Song and Dance Men	1976	15.00
CROSBY, BING, AND LOUIS ARMSTRONG			
CAPITOL			
❑ SM-11735	Bing Crosby and Louis Armstrong	1977	12.00
MGM			
❑ E-3882 [M]	Bing and Satchmo	1960	18.00
❑ SE-3882 [S]	Bing and Satchmo	1960	25.00
CROSBY, BING			
20TH CENTURY			
❑ T-551	A Holiday Toast	1977	15.00
AMOS			
❑ AAS-7001	Hey Jude/Hey Bing!	1969	15.00
BIOGRAPH			
❑ C-13	Bing Crosby 1929-33	1973	15.00
❑ M 1	When the Blue of the Night Meets the Gold of the Day	197?	12.00
BRUNSWICK			
❑ BL58000 [10]	Bing Crosby, Volume 1	1950	50.00
❑ BL58001 [10]	Bing Crosby, Volume 2	1950	50.00
❑ BL54005 [M]	The Voice of Bing in the 1930s	1957	30.00
CAPITOL			
❑ SM-11738	Bing Crosby Classics, Vol. 1	1977	12.00
❑ SM-11739	Bing Crosby Classics, Vol. 2	1977	12.00
❑ SM-11740	Bing Crosby Classics, Vol. 3	1977	12.00
❑ SM-11732	Bing Crosby's Christmas Classics	1977	12.00
— "A Capitol Re-Issue"; same recordings as on Warner Bros. 1484			
❑ T2346 [M]	Great Country Hits	1965	18.00
❑ ST2346 [S]	Great Country Hits	1965	25.00
❑ SM-11737	Great Country Hits	1977	12.00
❑ T2300 [M]	That Travelin' Two-Beat	1965	18.00
❑ ST2300 [S]	That Travelin' Two-Beat	1965	25.00
❑ SM-11736	That Travelin' Two-Beat	1977	12.00
COLUMBIA			
❑ C35093	Bing Crosby Collection, Vol. 1	1977	12.00
❑ C35094	Bing Crosby Collection, Vol. 2	1977	12.00
❑ C2L43	Bing in Hollywood 1930-1934	196?	18.00
— Red "360 Sound" labels			
❑ C2L43	Bing in Hollywood 1930-1934	1971	15.00
— Orange labels			
❑ CL6027 [10]	Crosby Classics	1949	50.00
❑ CL6105 [10]	Crosby Classics, Volume 2	1950	50.00
❑ CL2502 [10]	Der Bingle	1955	40.00
❑ C4X44229	The Crooner: The Columbia Years	1988	40.00
COLUMBIA SPECIAL PRODUCTS			
❑ P14369	Bing	197?	12.00
❑ CE2E-201	The Bing Crosby Story, Volume 1	1974	15.00
— Reissue of Encore E2E-201			
DAYBREAK			
❑ 2006	A Time to Be Jolly	1971	15.00
❑ 2014	Bing and Basie	1972	15.00
DECCA			
❑ DL8419 [M]	A Christmas Sing with Bing Around the World	1957	40.00
❑ DL78419 [R]	A Christmas Sing with Bing Around the World	196?	12.00
❑ DL8318 [M]	Anything Goes	1956	50.00
❑ DL8687 [M]	Around the World	1958	40.00

Number	Title	Yr	NM
☐ DL5028 [10]	Auld Lang Syne	1950	50.00
☐ DL5351 [10]	Beloved Hymns	1951	50.00
☐ DX151 [M]	Bing: A Musical Autobiography	195?	150.00
☐ DL9054 [M]	Bing: A Musical Autobiography 1927-1934	1961	40.00
☐ DL9064 [M]	Bing: A Musical Autobiography 1934-1941	1961	40.00
☐ DL9067 [M]	Bing: A Musical Autobiography 1941-44	1961	40.00
☐ DL9077 [M]	Bing: A Musical Autobiography 1944-47	1961	40.00
☐ DL9078 [M]	Bing: A Musical Autobiography 1947-1953	1961	40.00
☐ DL5390 [10]	Bing and Connee	1953	50.00
— With Connee Boswell			
☐ DL5323 [10]	Bing and the Dixieland Bands	1951	50.00
☐ DL8493 [M]	Bing and the Dixieland Bands	1957	40.00
☐ DL8780 [M]	Bing in Paris	1958	40.00
☐ DL4258 [M]	Bing's Hollywood: Accentuate the Positive	1962	30.00
☐ DL4264 [M]	Bing's Hollywood: Anything Goes	1962	30.00
☐ DL4259 [M]	Bing's Hollywood: Blue Skies	1962	30.00
☐ DL4260 [M]	Bing's Hollywood: But Beautiful	1962	30.00
☐ DL4262 [M]	Bing's Hollywood: Cool of the Evening	1962	30.00
☐ DL4253 [M]	Bing's Hollywood: East Side of Heaven	1962	30.00
☐ DL4250 [M]	Bing's Hollywood: Easy to Remember	1962	30.00
☐ DL4256 [M]	Bing's Hollywood: Holiday Inn	1962	30.00
☐ DL4255 [M]	Bing's Hollywood: Only Forever	1962	30.00
☐ DL4251 [M]	Bing's Hollywood: Pennies from Heaven	1962	30.00
☐ DL4252 [M]	Bing's Hollywood: Pocket Full of Dreams	1962	30.00
☐ DL4261 [M]	Bing's Hollywood: Sunshine Cake	1962	30.00
☐ DL4257 [M]	Bing's Hollywood: Swinging on a Star	1962	30.00
☐ DL4254 [M]	Bing's Hollywood: The Road Begins	1962	30.00
☐ DL4263 [M]	Bing's Hollywood: Zing a Little Zong	1962	30.00
☐ DL5220 [10]	Bing Sings Hits	1950	50.00
☐ DL5520 [10]	Bing Sings the Hits	1954	50.00
☐ DL5355 [10]	Bing Sings Victor Herbert	1951	50.00
☐ DL8269 [M]	Blue Hawaii	1956	40.00
☐ DL5102 [10]	Blue of the Night	1950	50.00
☐ DL5042 [10]	Blue Skies	1950	50.00
☐ DLP5020 [10]	Christmas Greetings	1949	60.00
☐ DL5064 [10]	Cole Porter Songs	1950	50.00
☐ DL6009 [10]	Collector's Classics: Anything Goes/Two for Tonight	1951	60.00
☐ DL6014 [10]	Collector's Classics: Big Broadcast of 1936	1951	60.00
☐ DL6008 [10]	Collector's Classics: Mississippi/Here Is My Heart	1951	60.00
☐ DL6012 [10]	Collector's Classics: Paris Honeymoon	1951	60.00
☐ DL6010 [10]	Collector's Classics: Rhythm on the Range/Pennies from Heaven	1951	60.00
☐ DL6015 [10]	Collector's Classics: The Road to Singapore/If I Had My Way	1951	60.00
☐ DL6013 [10]	Collector's Classics: The Star Maker/Doctor Rhythm	1951	60.00
☐ DL6011 [10]	Collector's Classics: Waikiki Wedding	1951	60.00
☐ DL5556 [10]	Country Girl/Little Boy Lost/ Anything Goes	1954	50.00
☐ DL5331 [10]	Country Style	1951	50.00
☐ DL5107 [10]	Cowboy Songs	1950	50.00
☐ DL5129 [10]	Cowboy Songs, Volume 2	1950	50.00
☐ DL5063 [10]	Don't Fence Me In	1950	50.00
☐ DL5340 [10]	Down Memory Lane	1951	50.00
☐ DL5343 [10]	Down Memory Lane, Volume 2	1951	50.00
☐ DL5119 [10]	Drifting and Dreaming	1950	50.00
☐ DL8268 [M]	Drifting and Dreaming	1956	40.00
☐ DLP5011 [10]	El Bingo	1949	50.00
☐ DL5299 [10]	Favorite Hawaiian Songs	1951	50.00
☐ DL34522	Favorite Songs of Christmas	1968	18.00
— Decca Records Custom Division pressing			
☐ DL5052 [10]	Going My Way/The Bells of St. Mary's	1950	60.00
☐ DL5302 [10]	Go West, Young Man	1951	50.00
☐ DL5122 [10]	Hawaiian Songs	1950	50.00
☐ DL8272 [M]	High Tor	1956	400.00
☐ DL5298 [10]	Hits from Broadway Shows	1951	50.00
☐ DLP5000 [10]	Hits from Musical Comedies	1949	50.00
☐ DL4281 [M]	Holiday in Europe	1962	30.00
☐ DL74281 [R]	Holiday in Europe	1962	18.00
☐ DL8210 [M]	Home on the Range	1956	40.00
☐ DL6001 [10]	Ichabod/Rip Van Winkle	1950	50.00
☐ DL9106 [M]	Ichabod/Rip Van Winkle	1962	30.00
☐ DL79106 [R]	Ichabod/Rip Van Winkle	1962	12.00
☐ DL8846 [M]	In a Little Spanish Town	1959	30.00
☐ DLP5001 [10]	Jerome Kern Songs	1949	50.00
☐ DL5417 [10]	Just for You	1952	50.00
☐ DL8110 [M]	Lullaby Time	1955	40.00
☐ DLP5019 [10]	Merry Christmas	1949	60.00
— Original editions have a light blue-green cover and "DLP" prefix			

Number	Title	Yr	NM
☐ DL8128 [M]	Merry Christmas	1955	40.00
— Expanded version of 10-inch LP; all-black label			
☐ DL78128 [R]	Merry Christmas	196?	12.00
☐ DL8128 [M]	Merry Christmas	1960	30.00
— Reissue on black label with color bars			
☐ DL8178 [M]	Merry Christmas	196?	60.00
— Black label with color bars; at least one copy is known to exist on red vinyl			
☐ DL5019 [10]	Merry Christmas	1950	50.00
— Second editions have a blue-green cover, but a "DL" prefix on the record, though not necessarily on the cover			
☐ DL5019 [10]	Merry Christmas	1951	40.00
— Third editions have a brand-new red and green cover			
☐ DL5284 [10]	Mr. Music	1950	50.00
☐ DL4086 [M]	My Golden Favorites	1961	30.00
☐ DL8575 [M]	New Tricks	1957	40.00
☐ DX152 [M]	Old Masters	195?	150.00
☐ DL8207 [M]	Shillelaghs and Shamrocks	1956	40.00
☐ DL78207 [R]	Shillelaghs and Shamrocks	196?	12.00
☐ DL5508 [10]	Some Fine Old Chestnuts	1953	50.00
☐ DL8374 [M]	Some Fine Old Chestnuts	1957	40.00
☐ DL5499 [10]	Song Hits of Paris/Le Bing	1953	50.00
☐ DL8352 [M]	Song I Wish I Had Sung… The First Time Around	1956	40.00
☐ DL5081 [10]	Songs by Gershwin	1950	50.00
☐ DL4415 [M]	Songs Everybody Knows	1964	30.00
☐ DL74415 [R]	Songs Everybody Knows	1964	18.00
☐ DL78352 [R]	Songs I Wish I Had Sung… The First Time Around	196?	12.00
☐ DL5126 [10]	Stardust	1950	50.00
☐ DLP5010 [10]	Stephen Foster Songs	1949	50.00
☐ DL5037 [10]	St. Patrick's Day	1950	50.00
☐ DL5039 [10]	St. Valentine's Day	1950	50.00
☐ DL8781 [M]	That Christmas Feeling	1958	30.00
— Expanded version of DL 5020; all-black label, textured cover			
☐ DL78781 [R]	That Christmas Feeling	196?	12.00
☐ DL8781 [M]	That Christmas Feeling	196?	25.00
— Reissue on black label with color bars, smooth cover			
☐ DXB184 [M]	The Best of Bing	1965	30.00
☐ DXSB7184 [R]	The Best of Bing	1965	18.00
☐ DL8020 [M]	The Man Without a Country/ What So Proudly We Hail	1950	40.00
☐ DL5444 [10]	The Road to Bali	1952	60.00
☐ DL74283 [R]	The Small One	1962	12.00
☐ DL5272 [10]	Top o' the Morning/The Emperor Waltz	1950	50.00
☐ DL8365 [M]	Twilight on the Trail	1957	40.00
☐ DL4283	Two Favorite Stories by Bing Crosby	1962	30.00
☐ DL6000 [10]	Two Favorite Stories by Bing Crosby	1950	60.00
☐ DL5310 [10]	Way Back Home	1951	50.00
☐ DL5403 [10]	When Irish Eyes Are Smiling	1952	50.00
☐ DL8262 [M]	When Irish Eyes Are Smiling	1956	40.00
☐ DL78262 [R]	When Irish Eyes Are Smiling	196?	12.00
☐ DL5326 [10]	Yours Is My Heart Alone	1951	50.00

ENCORE

Number	Title	Yr	NM
☐ E2E-201	The Bing Crosby Story, Volume 1	1968	18.00
☐ E2E-202	The Bing Crosby Story, Volume 2	1968	18.00

FOX AMERICAN

Number	Title	Yr	NM
☐ SMF210	Bing Crosby Sings Christmas	1978	12.00
— Side 1 from radio show Dec. 19, 1951; Side 2 from radio show Dec. 14, 1949			

GNP CRESCENDO

Number	Title	Yr	NM
☐ GNP-9044	The Radio Years, Vol. 1	1985	10.00
☐ GNP-9046	The Radio Years, Vol. 2	1986	10.00
☐ GNP-9047	The Radio Years, Vol. 3	1986	10.00
☐ GNP-9048	The Radio Years, Vol. 4	1986	10.00

GOLDEN

Number	Title	Yr	NM
☐ A298:20 [M]	Ali Baba and the 40 Thieves	1957	30.00
☐ A298:21 [M]	How Lovely Is Christmas/A Christmas Story	195?	30.00

HARMONY

Number	Title	Yr	NM
☐ HL7094 [M]	Crosby Classics	1958	18.00
☐ HS11313 [R]	Crosby Classics	196?	12.00

LONDON

Number	Title	Yr	NM
☐ PS679	Feels Good	1977	15.00

MARK 56

Number	Title	Yr	NM
☐ 762	Original Radio Broadcasts	197?	12.00

MCA

Number	Title	Yr	NM
☐ 15018 [R]	A Christmas Sing with Bing Around the World	197?	10.00
— Reissue of Decca DL7-8419			
☐ 3031	Bing Crosby's Greatest Hits	1977	12.00
☐ 37076	Bing Crosby's Greatest Hits	198?	10.00
☐ 915	Hey Bing!	198?	12.00
☐ 15024 [R]	Merry Christmas	197?	10.00
— Reissue of Decca DL7-8128			
☐ 1502	Rare 1930-31 Brunswick Recordings	198?	12.00
☐ 177	Shillelaghs and Shamrocks	1973	12.00
☐ 15019 [R]	That Christmas Feeling	1973	10.00
— Reissue of Decca DL7-8781			
☐ 2-4045	The Best of Bing	197?	15.00
— Black labels with rainbow; gatefold cover			
☐ 2-4045	The Best of Bing	197?	12.00
— Blue labels with rainbow; regular cover			
☐ 15017	Two Favorite Stories by Bing Crosby	197?	12.00
— Reissue of Decca DL 4283			

Number	Title	Yr	NM
☐ 519	When Irish Eyes Are Smiling	197?	12.00

METRO

Number	Title	Yr	NM
☐ M-523 [M]	Bing Crosby	1965	15.00
☐ MS-523 [S]	Bing Crosby	1965	18.00

MGM

Number	Title	Yr	NM
☐ E-3890 [M]	Senor Bing	1961	18.00
☐ SE-3890 [S]	Senor Bing	1961	25.00
☐ E-4129 [M]	The Great Standards	1963	18.00
☐ SE-4129 [S]	The Great Standards	1963	25.00
☐ E-4203 [M]	The Very Best of Bing Crosby	1964	18.00
☐ SE-4203 [S]	The Very Best of Bing Crosby	1964	25.00

MOBILE FIDELITY

Number	Title	Yr	NM
☐ 1-260	Bing Sings Whilst Bregman Swings	1996	25.00
— Audiophile vinyl			

MURRAY HILL

Number	Title	Yr	NM
☐ 894637	Bing Crosby and His Friends	197?	30.00

PHILCO

Number	Title	Yr	NM
☐ LP436 [10]	Crosby Classics	195?	40.00
— Custom item for Philco (front cover has "Philco: Famous for Quality the World Over")			

PICKWICK

Number	Title	Yr	NM
☐ SPC-3583	Thoroughly Modern Bing	1978	10.00

P.I.P.

Number	Title	Yr	NM
☐ 6802	Thoroughly Modern Bing	1971	15.00

POLYDOR

Number	Title	Yr	NM
☐ PD-1-6128	Seasons: The Closing Chapter	1978	15.00

RCA VICTOR

Number	Title	Yr	NM
☐ CPL1-2086(e)	A Legendary Performer	1976	12.00
☐ LPM-1473 [M]	Bing with a Beat	1957	30.00
☐ LPM-1854 [M]	Fancy Meeting You Here	1958	25.00
☐ LSP-1854 [S]	Fancy Meeting You Here	1958	30.00
☐ AFL1-1854	Fancy Meeting You Here	1977	12.00
☐ LPM-2071 [M]	Young Bing Crosby	1959	25.00

READER'S DIGEST

Number	Title	Yr	NM
☐ RDA-175	Christmas with Bing	1980	12.00
— Repackage of Warner Bros. and Capitol recordings			

REPRISE

Number	Title	Yr	NM
☐ R-6106 [M]	Return to Paradise Islands	1964	18.00
☐ R9-6106 [S]	Return to Paradise Islands	1964	25.00

SPOKANE

Number	Title	Yr	NM
☐ 21	Bing Crosby & the Music Maids	197?	12.00
☐ 1	Bing Crosby On the Air, 1934 and 1938	197?	12.00
☐ 12	Bing in the 30's	197?	12.00
☐ 14	Bing in the 30s, Vol. 2	197?	12.00
☐ 24	Bing in the 30s, Vol. 3	1986	10.00
☐ 25	Bing in the 30s, Vol. 4	1986	10.00
☐ 26	Bing in the 30s, Vol. 5	1986	10.00
☐ 27	Bing in the 30s, Vol. 6	1986	10.00
☐ 5	Der Bingle, Vol. 1	197?	12.00
☐ 10	Der Bingle, Vol. 2	197?	12.00
☐ 20	Der Bingle, Vol. 3	197?	12.00
☐ 15	Holiday Inn/The Bells of St. Mary's	197?	12.00
☐ 16	Kraft Music Hall Highlights	197?	12.00
☐ 19	Kraft Music Hall Highlights, Vol. 2	197?	12.00

SUNBEAM

Number	Title	Yr	NM
☐ 502	Distinctively Bing, Vol. 1	197?	12.00
☐ 504	Distinctively Bing, Vol. 2	197?	12.00

TIME-LIFE

Number	Title	Yr	NM
☐ SLGD-06	Legendary Singers: Bing Crosby	1985	18.00

UNITED ARTISTS

Number	Title	Yr	NM
☐ UA-LA554-G	That's What Life Is All About	1976	15.00

VERVE

Number	Title	Yr	NM
☐ MGV2020 [M]	Bing Sings Whilst Bregman Swings	1956	50.00
☐ V-2020 [M]	Bing Sings Whilst Bregman Swings	1961	30.00

VOCALION

Number	Title	Yr	NM
☐ VL3603 [M]	Bing Crosby Sings	195?	18.00
☐ VL73603 [R]	Bing Crosby Sings	196?	12.00

WARNER BROS.

Number	Title	Yr	NM
☐ 2W1401 [M]	101 Gang Songs	1961	25.00
☐ 2WS1401 [S]	101 Gang Songs	1961	30.00
☐ W1484 [M]	I Wish You a Merry Christmas	1962	18.00
☐ WS1484 [S]	I Wish You a Merry Christmas	1962	25.00
☐ W1435 [M]	Join Bing and Sing Along	1962	18.00
☐ WS1435 [S]	Join Bing and Sing Along	1962	25.00
☐ W1422 [M]	Join Bing in a Gang Song Sing-Along	1961	18.00
☐ WS1422 [S]	Join Bing in a Gang Song Sing-Along	1961	25.00
☐ W1363 [M]	Join with Bing and Sing Along	1960	18.00
☐ WS1363 [S]	Join with Bing and Sing Along	1960	25.00
☐ W1482 [M]	On the Happy Side	1962	18.00
☐ WS1482 [S]	On the Happy Side	1962	25.00

X

Number	Title	Yr	NM
☐ XLVA-4250 [M]	Young Bing Crosby	1955	50.00

Number	Title	Yr	NM

CROSBY, BOB

AIRCHECK
| ❏ 17 | Bob Crosby and His Orchestra 1940 | 197? | 12.00 |

CAPITOL
❏ H293 [10]	Bob Crosby and His Bobcats	1952	50.00
❏ T293 [M]	Bob Crosby and His Bobcats	1955	40.00
❏ T1556 [M]	The Hits of Bob Crosby's Bobcats	1961	25.00

CIRCLE
| ❏ 1 | Bob Crosby and His Orchestra 1938 | 198? | 12.00 |
| ❏ 34 | Bob Crosby and His Orchestra 1938-39 | 198? | 12.00 |

COLUMBIA
| ❏ CL766 [M] | The Bob Crosby Show | 1956 | 30.00 |

CORAL
❏ CRL57060 [M]	Bobcats' Blues	1956	40.00
❏ CRL57061 [M]	Bobcats On Parade	1956	40.00
❏ CRL57089 [M]	Bob Crosby 1936-1956	1957	40.00
❏ CRL57062 [M]	Bob Crosby in Hi-Fi	1956	40.00
❏ CRL56003 [10]	Dixieland Jazz 1	1950	50.00
❏ CRL56018 [10]	Marches in Dixieland Style	1950	50.00
❏ CRL56039 [10]	St. Louis Blues	1950	50.00
❏ CRL56000 [10]	Swinging at the Sugar Bowl	1950	50.00
❏ CRL57005 [M]	The Bobcats' Ball	1955	40.00
❏ CRL57170 [M]	The Bobcats in Hi-Fi	1958	40.00

DECCA
❏ DL8061 [M]	Bob Crosby's Bobcats	1954	40.00
❏ DL4856 [M]	Bob Crosby's Bobcats -- Their Greatest Hits	1967	25.00
❏ DL74856 [R]	Bob Crosby's Bobcats -- Their Greatest Hits	1967	15.00
❏ DL8042 [M]	Five Feet of Swing	1954	40.00

DOT
❏ DLP-3278 [M]	Bob Crosby's Great Hits	196?	25.00
❏ DLP-25278 [S]	Bob Crosby's Great Hits	196?	30.00
❏ DLP-3382 [M]	C'est Si Bon	196?	25.00
❏ DLP-25382 [S]	C'est Si Bon	196?	30.00
❏ DLP-3170 [M]	Petite Fleur	1959	25.00
❏ DLP-25170 [S]	Petite Fleur	1959	30.00
❏ DLP-3136 [M]	South Pacific Blows Warm	1958	25.00
❏ DLP-25136 [S]	South Pacific Blows Warm	1959	30.00

HINDSIGHT
| ❏ HSR-192 | Bob Crosby and His Orchestra 1941-42 | 198? | 10.00 |
| ❏ HSR-209 | Bob Crosby and His Orchestra 1952-53 | 1985 | 10.00 |

MCA
| ❏ 253 | Bob Crosby's Bobcats -- Their Greatest Hits | 1974 | 12.00 |
| ❏ 4083 | The Best of Bob Crosby | 1974 | 15.00 |

MONMOUTH-EVERGREEN
| ❏ 7026 | Mardi Gras Parade | 1970 | 18.00 |
| ❏ 6815 | The Bob Crosby Orchestra Live | 1968 | 18.00 |

PAUSA
| ❏ 9034 | This Hits of Bob Crosby's Bobcats | 198? | 12.00 |
— Reissue of Capitol 1556

SUNBEAM
| ❏ 216 | The Bob Crosby Orchestra 1938-39 | 197? | 12.00 |

TIME-LIFE
| ❏ STBB-14 | Big Bands: Bob Crosby | 1984 | 18.00 |

CROSBY, DAVID

A&M
| ❏ SP-5232 | Oh Yes I Can | 1989 | 12.00 |

ATLANTIC
| ❏ SD7203 | If I Could Only Remember My Name... | 2000 | 30.00 |
— Classic Records reissue on audiophile vinyl
| ❏ SD7203 | If I Could Only Remember My Name… | 1971 | 18.00 |

CROSBY, GARY

VERVE
| ❏ MGV-2112 [M] | Gary Crosby Belts the Blues | 1959 | 100.00 |

CROSBY, STILLS, NASH & YOUNG

ATLANTIC
| ❏ -0 [DJ] | 4 Way Street | 1971 | 50.00 |
— White label stereo promo
| ❏ PR18102 [DJ] | A Rap with C, S, N & Y | 1974 | 50.00 |
— Promo-only interview album
| ❏ PR165 [M] | Celebration/CSNY Month | 1974 | 100.00 |
— Promo-only LP in mono
| ❏ PR165 [S-DJ] | Celebration/CSNY Month | 1974 | 50.00 |
— Promo-only LP in stereo
| ❏ SD7200 [DJ] | Deja Vu | 1970 | 60.00 |
— White label stereo promo

CROSBY, STILLS, NASH & YOUNG

ATLANTIC
| ❏ SD 2-902 | 4 Way Street | 1971 | 25.00 |
| ❏ 2-902 [M] | 4 Way Street | 1971 | 100.00 |
— White label promo; no stock copies are mono

| ❏ SD 2-902 [DJ] | 4 Way Street | 1971 | 50.00 |
— White label stereo promo
| ❏ 81888 | American Dream | 1988 | 12.00 |
| ❏ PR18102 [DJ] | A Rap with C, S, N & Y | 1974 | 50.00 |
— Promo-only interview album
| ❏ PR165 [M] | Celebration/CSNY Month | 1974 | 100.00 |
— Promo-only LP in mono
| ❏ PR165 [S] | Celebration/CSNY Month | 1974 | 50.00 |
— Promo-only LP in stereo
| ❏ 7200 [M] | Deja Vu | 1970 | 150.00 |
— White label promo; no stock copies are mono
| ❏ SD7200 [DJ] | Deja Vu | 1970 | 60.00 |
— White label stereo promo
| ❏ SD7200 | Deja Vu | 1970 | 18.00 |
— Pasted-on front cover photo must still be intact
| ❏ SD19118 | Deja Vu | 1977 | 12.00 |
— Reissue of 7200, this time with photo as part of the cover rather than as a paste-on
| ❏ SD18100 | So Far | 1974 | 15.00 |
| ❏ SD19119 | So Far | 1977 | 12.00 |
— Reissue of 18100

MOBILE FIDELITY
| ❏ 1-088 | Deja Vu | 198? | 200.00 |
— Audiophile vinyl

CROSBY, STILLS AND NASH

ATLANTIC
❏ 80075	Allies	1983	15.00
❏ SD8229	Crosby, Stills & Nash	1969	25.00
❏ SD19117	Crosby, Stills & Nash	1977	12.00
— Reissue of 8229
| ❏ SD8229 | Crosby, Stills & Nash | 2000 | 30.00 |
— Classic Records reissue on 180-gram vinyl
❏ SD19104	CSN	1977	15.00
❏ SD19360	Daylight Again	1982	15.00
❏ 82107	Live It Up	1990	18.00
❏ SD16026	Replay	1980	15.00
— Also has solo cuts by Stephen Stills

NAUTILUS
| ❏ NR-48 | Crosby, Stills and Nash | 1982 | 150.00 |
— Audiophile vinyl

CROSS, CHRISTOPHER

REPRISE
| ❏ 25685 | Back of My Mind | 1988 | 12.00 |

WARNER BROS.
❏ 23757	Another Page	1983	10.00
❏ BSK3383	Christopher Cross	1979	10.00
❏ 25341	Every Turn of the World	1985	10.00

CROSS COUNTRY

ATCO
| ❏ SD7024 [S] | Cross Country | 1973 | 18.00 |
| ❏ 7024 [M] | Cross Country | 1973 | 40.00 |
— Mono is white label promo only; "d/j copy monaural" sticker on cover

CROTHERS, SCATMAN

CRAFTSMAN
| ❏ 8036 [M] | Gone with the Scat Man | 1960 | 30.00 |

DOOTO
| ❏ DTL814 [M] | Comedy Sweepstakes | 1961 | 30.00 |

MOTOWN
| ❏ M777L | Big Ben Sings | 1973 | 25.00 |

TOPS
| ❏ 1511 [M] | Rock and Roll with Scat Man | 1956 | 80.00 |

CROW

AMARET
❏ AST-5012	Best of Crow	1972	18.00
❏ ST-5006	Crow By Crow	1970	25.00
❏ ST-5002 [B]	Crow Music	1969	30.00
❏ ST-5013	David Crow d/b/a Crow	1973	18.00
❏ ST-5009	Mosaic	1971	25.00

CROWDED HOUSE

CAPITOL
| ❏ R133277 | Crowded House | 1987 | 15.00 |
— BMG Direct Marketing edition
| ❏ ST-12485 | Crowded House | 1987 | 12.00 |
| ❏ R114827 | Temple of Low Men | 1988 | 15.00 |
— BMG Direct Marketing edition
| ❏ C1-48763 | Temple of Low Men | 1988 | 15.00 |
| ❏ C1-93559 | Woodface | 1991 | 18.00 |

CROWELL, RODNEY

COLUMBIA
| ❏ CAS2001 [DJ] | Dialog with T-Bone Burnett | 1989 | 30.00 |
— Promo-only interview record
❏ FC44076	Diamonds and Dirt	1988	12.00
❏ FC45242	Keys to the Highway	1989	15.00
❏ FC40116	Street Language	1986	10.00
❏ CAS2456 [DJ]	Street Language Interchords	1986	30.00
— Promo-only interview record

WARNER BROS.
❏ BSK3228	Ain't Living Long Like This	1978	18.00
❏ BSK3407	But What Will the Neighbors Think	1980	12.00
❏ BSK3587	Rodney Crowell	1981	12.00

CROWS, THE / THE HARPTONES

ROULETTE
| ❏ RE-114 | Echoes of a Rock Era: The Groups | 1973 | 25.00 |

CRUCIFIX

UNIVERSAL
| ❏ RON2 [EP] | Crucifix | 1982 | 40.00 |

CRUDUP, ARTHUR

COLLECTABLES
| ❏ COL-5130 | Mean Ol' Frisco | 1988 | 12.00 |

DELMARK
| ❏ DS-621 | Crudup's Mood | 1969 | 40.00 |
| ❏ DS-614 | Look on Yonder's Wall | 1969 | 40.00 |

FIRE
| ❏ 103 [M] | Mean Ol' Frisco | 1960 | 900.00 |

RCA VICTOR
| ❏ LVP-573 | Father of Rock and Roll | 1971 | 25.00 |

TRIP
| ❏ 7501 | Mean Ol' Frisco | 1975 | 18.00 |

CRUSADERS, THE (1)

ABC BLUE THUMB
❏ 6022	Chain Reaction	1975	12.00
❏ BT-6001	Crusaders 1	1975	15.00
❏ SPMK-42 [DJ]	Crusaders In-Store Sampler Album	1978	25.00
— Promo-only issue
❏ 6029	Free As the Wind	1977	12.00
❏ BA-6030	Images	1978	12.00
❏ BT-6010	Scratch	1975	12.00
— Reissue
❏ BTSY-9002	Southern Comfort	1974	15.00
❏ 6027	The Best of the Crusaders	1976	15.00
❏ 6024	Those Southern Knights	1976	12.00

APPLAUSE
| ❏ APRI -2313 | Powerhouse | 197? | 15.00 |
— Reissue of Pacific Jazz 20136

BLUE NOTE
❏ LT-1046	Live Sides	1980	12.00
❏ BN-LA170-G	Tough Talk	1974	15.00
❏ BN-LA530-H2	Young Rabbits	1977	15.00
❏ LWB-530	Young Rabbits	1981	12.00
— Reissue of BN-LA530-H2

BLUE THUMB
❏ BT-6001	Crusaders 1	1972	18.00
❏ BT-6010	Scratch	1974	15.00
❏ BT-7000	The 2nd Crusade	1973	18.00
❏ BTSA1 [DJ]	The Crusaders Promotional Album	1973	25.00
— Promo-only album contains one side of material from "Crusaders 1" and one side from "The 2nd Crusade"
| ❏ BT-6007 | Unsung Heroes | 1973 | 15.00 |

CHISA
| ❏ 804 | Old Socks, New Shoes… New Socks, Old Shoes | 1970 | 15.00 |
— As "Jazz Crusaders"
| ❏ 807 | Pass the Plate | 1971 | 15.00 |

CRUSADERS
| ❏ 16002 | Ongaku-Kai: Live in Japan | 1982 | 30.00 |
— Audiophile vinyl
| ❏ 16000 | Street Life | 1982 | 30.00 |
— Audiophile vinyl

LIBERTY
| ❏ LST-11005 | Give Peace a Chance | 1970 | 18.00 |
— As "Jazz Crusaders"

MCA
| ❏ 6015 | 2nd Crusade | 198? | 12.00 |
— Reissue of Blue Thumb 7000
| ❏ 37146 | Chain Reaction | 198? | 10.00 |
— Reissue of Blue Thumb 6022
| ❏ 6014 | Crusaders 1 | 198? | 12.00 |
— Reissue of Blue Thumb 6001
| ❏ 37073 | Free As the Wind | 198? | 10.00 |
— Reissue of Blue Thumb 6029
| ❏ 5429 | Ghetto Blaster | 1984 | 12.00 |
| ❏ 37074 | Images | 198? | 10.00 |
— Reissue of Blue Thumb 6030
❏ 42168	Life in the Modern World	1988	12.00
❏ 5124	Rhapsody and Blues	1980	12.00
❏ 37174	Rhapsody and Blues	198?	10.00
— Reissue of 5124
| ❏ 8017 | Royal Jam | 1982 | 15.00 |
| ❏ 37072 | Scratch | 198? | 10.00 |
— Reissue of Blue Thumb 6010
| ❏ 6016 | Southern Comfort | 198? | 12.00 |
— Reissue of Blue Thumb 9002
| ❏ 5254 | Standing Tall | 1981 | 12.00 |
| ❏ 37240 | Standing Tall | 1985 | 10.00 |

Number	Title	Yr	NM
—Reissue of 5254			
❑ 3094	Street Life	1979	12.00
❑ 6006	The Best of the Crusaders	1980	12.00
—Reissue of Blue Thumb 6027			
❑ 5781	The Good and Bad Times	1987	12.00
❑ 42087	The Vocal Album	1988	12.00
❑ 37147	Those Southern Knights	198?	10.00
—Reissue of Blue Thumb 6024			

MOBILE FIDELITY

Number	Title	Yr	NM
❑ 1-010	Chain Reaction	1979	25.00
—Audiophile vinyl			

MOTOWN

Number	Title	Yr	NM
❑ M796	The Crusaders At Their Best	1973	15.00
❑ M5-195V1	The Crusaders At Their Best	1981	12.00

MOWEST

Number	Title	Yr	NM
❑ 118	Hollywood	1972	15.00

PACIFIC JAZZ

Number	Title	Yr	NM
❑ PJ-10092 [M]	Chili Con Soul	1965	25.00
❑ ST-20092 [S]	Chili Con Soul	1965	30.00
❑ T-90598 [M]	Chili Con Soul	1965	30.00
—Capitol Record Club edition			
❑ PJ-27 [M]	Freedom Sound	1961	30.00
❑ ST-27 [S]	Freedom Sound	1961	30.00
❑ PJ-76 [M]	Heat Wave	1963	30.00
❑ ST-76 [S]	Heat Wave	1963	30.00
❑ ST-20131	Lighthouse '68	1968	25.00
❑ PJ-10098 [M]	Live at the Lighthouse '66	1966	25.00
❑ ST-20098 [S]	Live at the Lighthouse '66	1966	30.00
❑ PJ-43 [M]	Lookin' Ahead	1962	30.00
❑ ST-43 [S]	Lookin' Ahead	1962	30.00
—Black vinyl			
❑ ST-43 [S]	Lookin' Ahead	1962	60.00
—Yellow vinyl			
❑ ST-20136	Powerhouse	1968	25.00
❑ PJ-83 [M]	Stretchin' Out	1964	30.00
❑ ST-83 [S]	Stretchin' Out	1964	30.00
❑ PJ-10106 [M]	Talk That Talk	1966	25.00
❑ ST-20106 [S]	Talk That Talk	1966	30.00
❑ ST-20175	The Best of the Jazz Crusaders	1969	25.00
❑ PJ-10115 [M]	The Festival Album	1967	30.00
❑ ST-20115 [S]	The Festival Album	1967	25.00
❑ PJ-57 [M]	The Jazz Crusaders at the Lighthouse	1962	30.00
❑ ST-57 [S]	The Jazz Crusaders at the Lighthouse	1962	30.00
❑ ST-90481 [S]	The Jazz Crusaders at the Lighthouse	1965	30.00
—Capitol Record Club edition			
❑ ST-20165	The Jazz Crusaders at the Lighthouse '69	1969	25.00
❑ PJ-87 [M]	The Thing	1964	30.00
❑ ST-87 [S]	The Thing	1964	30.00
❑ PJ-68 [M]	Tough Talk	1963	30.00
❑ ST-68 [S]	Tough Talk	1963	30.00
❑ PJ-10124	Uh Huh	1967	30.00
❑ ST-20124	Uh Huh	1967	25.00

PAUSA

Number	Title	Yr	NM
❑ 9005	The Best of the Jazz Crusaders	1979	12.00
—As "Jazz Crusaders			

WORLD PACIFIC JAZZ

Number	Title	Yr	NM
❑ ST-20098 [S]	Live at the Lighthouse '66	1970	18.00
—Reissue with "Liberty/UA" on label			

CRYAN' SHAMES, THE

COLUMBIA

Number	Title	Yr	NM
❑ CL2786 [M]	A Scratch in the Sky	1967	30.00
❑ CS9586 [S]	A Scratch in the Sky	1967	25.00
❑ CL2589 [M]	Sugar & Spice	1967	35.00
❑ CS9389 [S]	Sugar & Spice	1967	25.00
❑ CS9719	Synthesis	1969	25.00

CRYSTALS, THE (1)

PHILLES

Number	Title	Yr	NM
❑ PHLP-4001 [M]	He's a Rebel	1963	600.00
❑ PHLP-4003 [M]	The Crystals Sing the Greatest Hits, Vol. 1	1963	600.00
❑ PHLP-4000 [M]	Twist Uptown	1962	600.00
❑ T-90722 [M]	Twist Uptown	1965	600.00
—Capitol Record Club edition			
❑ DT-90722 [R]	Twist Uptown	1965	1200.00
—Capitol Record Club edition			

CUBY AND THE BLIZZARDS

PHILIPS

Number	Title	Yr	NM
❑ PHS600307	Cuby and the Blizzards Live	1969	25.00
❑ PHS600331	King of the World	1970	25.00

CUFF LINKS, THE (1)

DECCA

Number	Title	Yr	NM
❑ DL75235	The Cuff Links	1970	25.00
❑ DL75160	Tracy	1969	25.00

CUGAT, XAVIER

COLUMBIA

Number	Title	Yr	NM
❑ CL1016 [M]	Bread, Love and Cha Cha Cha	1957	15.00
❑ CL718 [M]	Cha Cha Cha	1956	30.00
—Red and black label with six "eye" logos			
❑ CL6077 [10]	Conga with Cugat	1949	50.00
❑ CL1094 [M]	Cugat Cavalcade	1958	30.00
—Red and black label with six "eye" logos			
❑ CS8055 [S]	Cugat Cavalcade	1959	30.00
—Red and black label with six "eye" logos			
❑ CL6021 [10]	Cugat's Favopite Rhumbas	1949	50.00
❑ CL6005 [10]	Cugat's Rhumba	1948	50.00
❑ CL6121 [10]	Dance Date	1950	50.00
❑ CL537 [M]	Dance with Cugat	1953	40.00
—Maroon label, gold print			
❑ CL537 [M]	Dance with Cugat	1955	30.00
—Red and black label with six "eye" logos			
❑ CL579 [M]	Favorite Rhumbas	1954	40.00
—Maroon label, gold print			
❑ CL579 [M]	Favorite Rhumbas	1955	30.00
—Red and black label with six "eye" logos			
❑ CL579 [M]	Favorite Rhumbas	1962	18.00
—Red "Guaranteed High Fidelity" label			
❑ CL579 [M]	Favorite Rhumbas	1965	15.00
—Red "Mono 360 Sound" label			
❑ CL2506 [10]	Mambo!	1955	50.00
❑ CL6213 [10]	Mambo at the Waldorf	1951	50.00
❑ CL732 [M]	Mambo at the Waldorf	1956	30.00
—Red and black label with six "eye" logos			
❑ CL733 [M]	Merengue by Cugat	1956	30.00
—Red and black label with six "eye" logos			
❑ CL733 [M]	Merengue by Cugat	1962	18.00
—Red "Guaranteed High Fidelity" label			
❑ CL733 [M]	Merengue by Cugat	1965	15.00
—Red "Mono 360 Sound" label			
❑ CS8646 [R]	Merengue by Cugat	1963	15.00
❑ CL626 [M]	Mucho Mucho Mambo	1955	40.00
—Maroon label, gold print			
❑ CL626 [M]	Mucho Mucho Mambo	1955	30.00
—Red and black label with six "eye" logos			
❑ CL610 [M]	Ole	1955	40.00
—Maroon label, gold print			
❑ CL610 [M]	Ole	1955	30.00
—Red and black label with six "eye" logos			
❑ CL515 [M]	Relaxing with Cugat (Quiet Music, Volume VI)	1952	50.00
—Original copies have black label, silver print and a "GL" prefix			
❑ CL515 [M]	Relaxing with Cugat (Quiet Music, Volume VI)	1953	40.00
—Second editions have maroon label, gold print and a "CL" prefix			
❑ CL6036 [10]	Rhumba with Cugat	1949	50.00
❑ CL6236 [10]	Samba with Cugat	1951	50.00
❑ CL6234 [10]	Tango with Cugat	1951	50.00
❑ CL6086 [10]	Tropical Bouquet	1950	50.00
❑ CL1143 [M]	Waltzes! But By Cugat	1959	30.00
—Red and black label with six "eye" logos			
❑ CS8059 [S]	Waltzes! But By Cugat	1959	30.00
—Red and black label with six "eye" logos			

DECCA

Number	Title	Yr	NM
❑ DL4799 [M]	Bang Bang	1966	18.00
❑ DL74799 [S]	Bang Bang	1966	25.00
❑ DL4740 [M]	Dance Party	1966	18.00
❑ DL74740 [S]	Dance Party	1966	25.00
❑ DL4672 [M]	Feeling Good	1965	18.00
❑ DL74672 [S]	Feeling Good	1965	25.00
❑ DL4851 [M]	Xavier Cugat Today	1967	18.00
❑ DL74851 [S]	Xavier Cugat Today	1967	25.00

MERCURY

Number	Title	Yr	NM
❑ MG-20888 [M]	Cugat Caricatures	1964	18.00
❑ SR-60888 [S]	Cugat Caricatures	1964	25.00
❑ PPS-2021 [M]	Cugat Plays Continental Favorites	1961	25.00
❑ PPS-6021 [S]	Cugat Plays Continental Favorites	1961	30.00
❑ MG20065 [M]	Cugat's Favorites	1955	30.00
❑ MG-20798 [M]	Cugat's Golden Goodies	1963	25.00
❑ SR-60798 [S]	Cugat's Golden Goodies	1963	30.00
❑ MG-20832 [M]	Cugi's Cocktails	1963	25.00
❑ SR-60832 [S]	Cugi's Cocktails	1963	30.00
❑ MG25149 [10]	Dance with Cugat/The Great Latin-American Rhythms of Xavier Cugat	195?	40.00
❑ MG25120 [10]	Here's Cugat	195?	40.00
❑ MG20108 [M]	Mambo!/Music for Latin Lovers	1957	30.00
❑ MG25168 [10]	Mambos by Cugat	195?	40.00
❑ PPS-2015 [M]	The Best of Cugat	1961	25.00
❑ PPS-6015 [S]	The Best of Cugat	1961	30.00
❑ MG-20870 [M]	The Best of Cugat	1964	18.00
—Reissue of 2015			
❑ SR-60870 [S]	The Best of Cugat	1964	25.00
—Reissue of 6015			
❑ MG-20745 [M]	The Most Popular Movie Themes As Styled by Cugat	1961	25.00
❑ SR-60745 [S]	The Most Popular Movie Themes As Styled by Cugat	1961	30.00
❑ MG-20705 [M]	Twist with Cugat	1962	25.00
❑ SR-60705 [S]	Twist with Cugat	1962	30.00
❑ PPS-2003 [M]	Viva Cugat!	1961	25.00
❑ PPS-6003 [S]	Viva Cugat!	1961	30.00
❑ MG-20868 [M]	Viva Cugat!	1964	18.00
—Reissue of 2003			
❑ SR-60868 [S]	Viva Cugat!	1964	25.00
—Reissue of 6003			

RCA VICTOR

Number	Title	Yr	NM
❑ LPM-1987 [M]	Chili Con Cugie	1959	25.00
❑ LSP-1987 [S]	Chili Con Cugie	1959	30.00
❑ LPM-2173 [M]	Cugat in France, Spain and Italy	1960	25.00
❑ LSP-2173 [S]	Cugat in France, Spain and Italy	1960	30.00
❑ LPM-1894 [M]	Cugat in Spain	1959	25.00
❑ LSP-1894 [S]	Cugat in Spain	1959	30.00
❑ ANL1-1310	Pure Gold	1976	10.00
❑ LPT-11 [10]	Tangos	195?	40.00
❑ LPM-1882 [M]	The King Plays Some Aces	1958	25.00
❑ LSP-1882 [S]	The King Plays Some Aces	1958	30.00

CULLEY, FRANK "FLOORSHOW

BATON

Number	Title	Yr	NM
❑ BL1201 [M]	Rock 'n Roll: Instrumentals for Dancing the Lindy Hop	1955	600.00
—B-side tracks by Buddy Tate Orchestra			

CULT, THE

SIRE

Number	Title	Yr	NM
❑ R184083	Electric	1987	15.00
—RCA Music Service edition			
❑ 25555	Electric	1987	12.00
❑ R134608	Love	1985	15.00
—RCA Music Service edition			
❑ 25259	Love	1985	12.00
❑ R101015	Sonic Temple	1989	15.00
—BMG Direct Marketing edition			
❑ 25871 [B]	Sonic Temple	1989	12.00

WARNER BROS.

Number	Title	Yr	NM
❑ -0 [DJ]	Electric Interview	1987	40.00
❑ WBMS-147 [DJ]	Electric Interview	1987	50.00
—Part of "The Warner Bros. Music Show" series			

CULTURE CLUB

VIRGIN/EPIC

Number	Title	Yr	NM
❑ QE39107	Colour by Numbers	1983	12.00
❑ 9E9-39237 [PD]	Colour by Numbers	1983	30.00
—Picture disc in plastic sleeve			
❑ OE40345	From Luxury to Heartache	1986	12.00
❑ ARE38398	Kissing to Be Clever	1982	15.00
—First pressings have nine tracks and do not contain "Time (Clock of the Heart)			
❑ FE38398	Kissing to Be Clever	1983	12.00
—This version has 10 tracks with the addition of "Time (Clock of the Heart)" as the first song on side 2			
❑ FE40913	This Time: The First Four Years	1987	15.00
❑ OE39881	Waking Up with the House on Fire	1984	12.00
❑ 9E9-40005 [PD]	Waking Up with the House on Fire	1984	30.00

CUMBERLAND THREE, THE

ROULETTE

Number	Title	Yr	NM
❑ R25132 [M]	Civil War Almanac, Volume 1: The Yankees	1960	25.00
❑ SR25132 [S]	Civil War Almanac, Volume 1: The Yankees	1960	30.00
❑ R25133 [M]	Civil War Almanac, Volume 2: The Rebels	1960	25.00
❑ SR25133 [S]	Civil War Almanac, Volume 2: The Rebels	1960	30.00
❑ R25121 [M]	Folk Scene U.S.A.	1960	25.00
❑ SR25121 [S]	Folk Scene U.S.A.	1960	30.00

CUMMINGS, BURTON

ALFA

Number	Title	Yr	NM
❑ AAB-11007	Sweet Sweet	1981	12.00

PORTRAIT

Number	Title	Yr	NM
❑ PR34261	Burton Cummings	1976	12.00
❑ PRQ34261 [Q]	Burton Cummings	1976	40.00
❑ JR35481	Dream of a Child	1978	12.00
❑ PR34698	My Own Way to Rock	1977	12.00

CUOZZO, MIKE

JUBILEE

Number	Title	Yr	NM
❑ JLP-1027 [M]	Mike Cuozzo	1957	100.00

SAVOY

Number	Title	Yr	NM
❑ MG-12051 [M]	Mighty Mike	1956	100.00

CURE, THE

A&M

Number	Title	Yr	NM
❑ SP-6020 [B]	Happily Ever After	1981	40.00
❑ SP-4902	Pornography	1982	25.00

ELEKTRA

Number	Title	Yr	NM
❑ 62236 [B]	Bloodflowers	2000	50.00
❑ 60786	Boys Don't Cry	1988	12.00
—Reissue of PVC 7916			
❑ R101109	Disintegration	1989	15.00
—BMG Direct Marketing edition			
❑ 60855	Disintegration	1989	12.00
❑ 60783 [B]	Faith	1988	18.00
—Reissue of third U.K. album			
❑ 62117	Galore: The Singles 1987-1997	1997	80.00
❑ 60737 [DJ]	Kiss Me, Kiss Me, Kiss Me	1987	30.00
—Promo-only audiophile pressing			

Number	Title	Yr	NM
❏ R242404	Kiss Me, Kiss Me, Kiss Me	1987	25.00
— *BMG Direct Marketing edition*			
❏ 60737	Kiss Me, Kiss Me, Kiss Me	1987	18.00
❏ 60737 [DJ]	Kiss Me, Kiss Me, Kiss Me	1987	40.00
— *Promo-only audiophile pressing*			
❏ 60978	Mixed Up	1990	40.00
— *LP version has one extra track not on CD or cassette*			
❏ R274190	Mixed Up	1990	30.00
— *BMG Direct Marketing edition*			
❏ 60785	Pornography	1988	12.00
— *Reissue of A&M SP-4902*			
❏ 60784	Seventeen Seconds	1988	12.00
— *Reissue of second U.K. album*			
❏ R150024	Standing on a Beach -- The Singles	1986	15.00
— *BMG Direct Marketing edition*			
❏ 60477	Standing on a Beach -- The Singles	1986	12.00
❏ 60435	The Head on the Door	1985	15.00
❏ 61744	Wild Mood Swings	1996	30.00
GEFFEN			
❏ B0002870-01	The Cure	2004	18.00
PVC			
❏ 7916 [B]	Boys Don't Cry	1980	30.00
— *revised version of first U.K. album*			
RHINO			
❏ R160737 [B]	Kiss Me Kiss Me Miss Me	2013	40.00
SIRE			
❏ 25076	Japanese Whispers	1983	18.00
❏ 25086	The Top	1984	18.00
❏ 23928 [EP]	The Walk	1983	15.00

CURIOSITY KILLED THE CAT

MERCURY

Number	Title	Yr	NM
❏ 842010-1	Get Ahead	1989	15.00
❏ 832025-1	Keep Your Distance	1987	12.00

CURLESS, DICK, AND KAY ADAMS

TOWER

Number	Title	Yr	NM
❏ T5025 [M]	A Devil Like Me Needs an Angel Like You	1966	30.00
❏ DT5025 [R]	A Devil Like Me Needs an Angel Like You	1966	25.00

CURLESS, DICK

CAPITOL

Number	Title	Yr	NM
❏ ST-792	Comin' On Country	1971	25.00
❏ ST-689	Doggin' It	1971	25.00
❏ ST-552	Hard, Hard Travelin' Man	1970	25.00
❏ ST-11119	Live at the Wheeling Truck Driver's Jamboree	1973	25.00
❏ ST-11087	Stonin' Around	1972	25.00
❏ ST-11211	The Last Blues Song	1973	30.00
— *First cover shows Dick Curless with an eye patch*			
❏ ST-11211	The Last Blues Song	1973	25.00
— *Second cover shows Dick Curless with no eye patch*			
❏ ST-11011	Tombstone Every Mile	1972	18.00
— *Reissue of Tower DT 5005*			
TIFFANY			
❏ 1016 [M]	Dick Curless Sings Songs of the Open Country	1958	100.00
❏ 1033 [M]	I Love to Tell a Story	1960	100.00
❏ 1028 [M]	Singing Just for Fun	1959	100.00
TOWER			
❏ T5066 [M]	All of Me Belongs to You	1967	30.00
❏ ST5066 [S]	All of Me Belongs to You	1967	30.00
❏ T5016 [M]	At Home with Dick Curless	1966	30.00
❏ DT5016 [R]	At Home with Dick Curless	1966	25.00
❏ T5012 [M]	Hymns	1965	30.00
❏ DT5012 [R]	Hymns	1965	25.00
❏ ST5089 [S]	Ramblin' Country	1967	30.00
❏ T5089 [M]	Ramblin' Country	1967	30.00
❏ ST5108	The Long Lonesome Road	1968	30.00
❏ T5013 [M]	The Soul of Dick Curless	1966	30.00
❏ DT5013 [R]	The Soul of Dick Curless	1966	25.00
❏ ST5139	The Wild Side of Town	1969	30.00
❏ T5005 [M]	Tombstone Every Mile	1965	30.00
❏ DT5005 [R]	Tombstone Every Mile	1965	25.00
❏ T5015 [M]	Travelin' Man	1966	30.00
❏ DT5015 [R]	Travelin' Man	1966	25.00

CURSON, TED

ARISTA FREEDOM

Number	Title	Yr	NM
❏ AL1030	Flip Top	197?	18.00
❏ AL1021	Tears	197?	18.00
ATLANTIC			
❏ 1441 [M]	The New Thing and the Blue Thing	1965	25.00
❏ SD1441 [S]	The New Thing and the Blue Thing	1965	30.00
AUDIO FIDELITY			
❏ AFLP-2123 [M]	Now Hear This	1964	25.00
❏ AFSD-6123 [S]	Now Hear This	1964	30.00
FANTASY			
❏ OJC-1744	Fire Down Below	1990	15.00
INDIA NAVIGATION			
❏ IN-1054	Blue Piccolo	1976	18.00

INNER CITY

Number	Title	Yr	NM
❏ IC1017	Jubilant Power	1976	15.00
INTERPLAY			
❏ 7716	Blowin' Away	1978	15.00
❏ 7726	I Heard Mingus	1980	15.00
❏ 7722	The Trio	1979	15.00
OLD TOWN			
❏ LP-2003 [M]	Plenty of Horn	1961	700.00
PRESTIGE			
❏ PRLP-7263 [M]	Fire Down Below	1963	30.00
— *Yellow label, Bergenfield, N.J. address*			
❏ PRLP-7263 [M]	Fire Down Below	1965	25.00
— *Blue label with trident logo at right*			
❏ PRST-7263 [S]	Fire Down Below	1963	40.00
— *Silver label, Bergenfield, N.J. address*			
❏ PRST-7263 [S]	Fire Down Below	1965	30.00
— *Blue label with trident logo at right*			

CURTIS, KEN

CAPITOL

Number	Title	Yr	NM
❏ T2418 [M]	Gunsmoke's Festus	1965	30.00
❏ ST2418 [S]	Gunsmoke's Festus	1965	40.00
DOT			
❏ DLP-25859	Gunsmoke's Festus Calls Out Ken Curtis	1968	30.00

CURTIS, MAC

EPIC

Number	Title	Yr	NM
❏ BN26419	The Sunshine Man	1969	25.00
HMG/HIGHTONE			
❏ HT6601	Rockabilly Uprising: The Best of Mac Curtis	1997	12.00
ROLLIN' ROCK			
❏ LP-007	Good Rockin' Tomorrow	1975	40.00
❏ LP-002	Ruffabilly	1975	40.00
❏ LP-002	Ruffabilly	1977	25.00
— *Reissue*			

CURTIS, SONNY

ELEKTRA

Number	Title	Yr	NM
❏ 6E-283	Love Is All Around	1980	12.00
❏ 6E-349	Rollin'	1981	12.00
❏ 6E-227	Sonny Curtis	1979	12.00
IMPERIAL			
❏ LP-9276 [M]	Beatle Hits Flamenco Style	1964	40.00
❏ LP-12276 [S]	Beatle Hits Flamenco Style	1964	50.00
VIVA			
❏ V-36012	The First of Sonny Curtis	1968	30.00
❏ V-36021	The Sonny Curtis Style	1969	30.00

CUTTING CREW

VIRGIN

Number	Title	Yr	NM
❏ R163456	Broadcast	1987	12.00
— *BMG Direct Marketing edition*			
❏ 90573	Broadcast	1987	10.00
❏ R101103	The Scattering	1989	15.00
— *BMG Direct Marketing edition*			
❏ 91239	The Scattering	1989	12.00

CYKLE, THE

LABEL

Number	Title	Yr	NM
❏ 9-261	The Cykle	1969	500.00

CYMBAL, JOHNNY

KAPP

Number	Title	Yr	NM
❏ KL-1324 [M]	Mr. Bass Man	1963	50.00
❏ KS-3324 [S]	Mr. Bass Man	1963	70.00

CYMBAL & CLINGER

CHELSEA

Number	Title	Yr	NM
❏ 1002	Cymbal & Clinger	1972	15.00

CYRILLE, ANDREW, AND MILFORD GRAVES

IPS

Number	Title	Yr	NM
❏ 001	Dialogue of the Drums	1974	25.00

CYRKLE, THE

COLUMBIA

Number	Title	Yr	NM
❏ CL2632 [M]	Neon	1967	18.00
❏ CS9432 [S]	Neon	1967	25.00
❏ CL2544 [M]	Red Rubber Ball	1966	25.00
❏ CS9344 [S]	Red Rubber Ball	1966	30.00

CYRUS, BILLY RAY

MERCURY

Number	Title	Yr	NM
❏ 1P-8218	Some Gave All	1992	30.00
— *Only released on vinyl through Columbia House*			

D

DA COSTA, PAULINHO

FANTASY

Number	Title	Yr	NM
❏ OJC-630	Agora	1991	15.00
PABLO			
❏ 2310785	Agora	1976	18.00
PABLO TODAY			
❏ 2312102	Happy People	1979	15.00

D'ABO, MIKE

A&M

Number	Title	Yr	NM
❏ SP-3634 [B]	Broken Rainbows	1974	18.00
❏ SP-4346 [B]	Down at Rachel's Place	1972	18.00

DADDY COOL

REPRISE

Number	Title	Yr	NM
❏ RS6471	Daddy Who? Daddy Cool!	1971	18.00
❏ MS2088	Teenage Heaven	1972	25.00

DADDY DEWDROP

SUNFLOWER

Number	Title	Yr	NM
❏ SNF-5006	Daddy Dewdrop	1971	25.00

DAFT PUNK

VIRGIN

Number	Title	Yr	NM
❏ 49606 [B]	Discovery	2001	25.00
❏ 42609	Homework	1997	18.00

DAGRADI, TONY

GRAMAVISION

Number	Title	Yr	NM
❏ 8103	Lunar Eclipse	1982	15.00
❏ 8001	Oasis	1981	15.00
ROUNDER			
❏ 2071	Dreams of Love	1988	12.00

DAHL, STEVE

HILARIA

Number	Title	Yr	NM
❏ SD1983 [EP]	Pet Fishsticks	1983	15.00

DAHLANDER, NILS-BERTIL "BERT"

EVERYDAY

Number	Title	Yr	NM
❏ EDLP528	Talkin' Jazz: Untitled #1	1990	18.00
— *As "Bert Dahlander*			
VERVE			
❏ MGV-8253 [M]	Skol	1958	50.00
❏ V-8253 [M]	Skol	1961	25.00

DAILEY, ALBERT

COLUMBIA

Number	Title	Yr	NM
❏ KC31278	Day After the Dawn	1973	18.00
MUSE			
❏ MR-5256	Textures	198?	12.00
STEEPLECHASE			
❏ SCS-1107	That Old Feeling	198?	12.00

DAILEY, DON

CROWN

Number	Title	Yr	NM
❏ CLP-5314 [M]	Surf Stompin'	1963	30.00
❏ CST-314 [R]	Surf Stompin'	1963	18.00

DAILY, PETE

CAPITOL

Number	Title	Yr	NM
❏ H385 [10]	Dixie by Daily	1953	50.00
❏ T385 [M]	Dixie by Daily	1954	40.00
❏ H183 [10]	Dixieland Band	1950	50.00
❏ T183 [M]	Dixieland Band	1954	40.00

DAILY, PETE/PHIL NAPOLEON

DECCA

Number	Title	Yr	NM
❏ DL5261 [10]	Pete Daily/Phil Napoleon	195?	50.00

DAKUS, WES

KAPP

Number	Title	Yr	NM
❏ KL-1536 [M]	Wes Dakus' Rebels	1967	30.00
❏ KS-3536 [S]	Wes Dakus' Rebels	1967	30.00

DALE, DICK, AND THE DEL-TONES

CAPITOL

Number	Title	Yr	NM
❏ T2002 [M]	Checkered Flag	1963	60.00
❏ ST2002 [S]	Checkered Flag	1963	80.00
❏ T1930 [M]	King of the Surf Guitar	1963	80.00
❏ ST1930 [S]	King of the Surf Guitar	1963	120.00
❏ T2053 [M]	Mr. Eliminator	1964	60.00
❏ ST2053 [S]	Mr. Eliminator	1964	100.00
❏ T2293 [M]	Rock Out -- Live at Ciro's	1965	100.00
❏ ST2293 [S]	Rock Out -- Live at Ciro's	1965	150.00
❏ T2111 [M]	Summer Surf	1964	100.00
— *With bonus single by Jerry Cole, "Racing Waves"/"Movin' Surf," in front cover pocket*			
❏ T2111 [M]	Summer Surf	1964	50.00
— *Without bonus single*			

Number	Title	Yr	NM
❑ ST2111 [S]	Summer Surf	1964	120.00

— With bonus single by Jerry Cole, "Racing Waves"/"Movin' Surf," in front cover pocket

❑ ST2111 [S]	Summer Surf	1964	70.00

— Without bonus single

CLOISTER

❑ CLP-6301 [M]	Silver Sounds of the Surf	1963	200.00

— With tracks by the Stompers

DELTONE

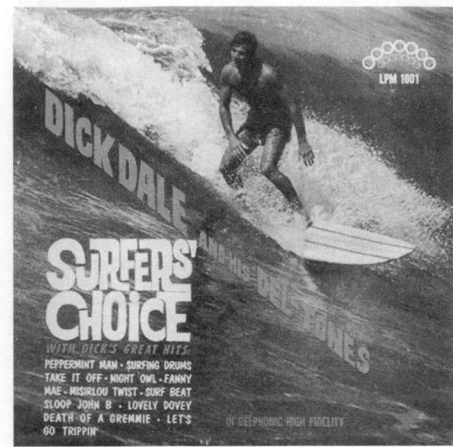

❑ LPM-1001 [M]	Surfer's Choice	1962	150.00
❑ T1886 [M]	Surfer's Choice	1962	60.00
❑ DT1886 [R]	Surfer's Choice	1962	40.00

DUB TONE

❑ LP-1246 [M]	The Surf Family	1964	30.00

— With tracks by the Hollywood Surfers

GNP CRESCENDO

❑ GNPS-2095	Greatest Hits	1975	15.00

RHINO

❑ RNLP-70074 [B]	King of the Surf Guitar: The Best of Dick Dale and the Del-Tones, 1961-1964	1986	18.00

DALE AND GRACE

MICHELLE

❑ 100 [M]	I'm Leaving It Up to You	1964	150.00

MONTEL

❑ 100 [M]	I'm Leaving It Up to You	1964	150.00

DALEY, JOE

RCA VICTOR

❑ LPM-2763 [M]	Joe Daley at Newport '63	1963	25.00
❑ LSP-2763 [S]	Joe Daley at Newport '63	1963	30.00

DALLAS, DEAN, AND THE DOUGHBOYS

CUMBERLAND

❑ MGC-29516 [M]	Golden Country Hits	1965	25.00
❑ SRC-69516 [S]	Golden Country Hits	1965	30.00

DALLAS, MARIA

RCA VICTOR

❑ LPM-3950 [M]	Tumblin' Down	1968	40.00
❑ LSP-3950 [S]	Tumblin' Down	1968	25.00

DALTO, JORGE

CONCORD PICANTE

❑ CJP-275	Urban Oasis	1985	12.00

DALTON, KAREN

CAPITOL

❑ ST271	It's So Hard to Tell	1969	100.00

JUST SUNSHINE/PARAMOUNT

❑ PAS6008	In My Own Time	1972	50.00

DALTON, KATHY

DISCREET

❑ MS2168	Amazing	1973	25.00
❑ DS2208	Boogie Bands and One Night Stands	1974	15.00

DALTREY, ROGER

ATLANTIC

❑ 81759	Can't Wait to See the Movie	1987	12.00
❑ 80128	Parting Should Be Painless	1984	12.00
❑ 81269	Under a Raging Moon	1985	12.00

MCA

❑ 5301	Best Bits	1982	12.00
❑ 2349	Daltrey	1977	12.00

— Reissue of Track 328

❑ 37032	Daltrey	1980	10.00

— Budget-line reissue

❑ 2271 [B]	One of the Boys	1977	18.00
❑ 37031	One of the Boys	1980	10.00

— Budget-line reissue

❑ 2147 [B]	Ride a Rock Horse	1975	18.00
❑ 37030	Ride a Rock Horse	1980	10.00

— Budget-line reissue

POLYDOR

❑ PD-1-6284	McVicar	1980	12.00

TRACK

❑ 328	Daltrey	1973	15.00

D'AMBROSIO, MEREDITH

PALO ALTO

❑ 8019	Little Jazz Bird	1982	15.00

SHIAH

❑ SR-109	Another Time	198?	18.00

SPRING INC.

❑ 0SPR	Lost in His Arms	1978	18.00

SUNNYSIDE

❑ SSC-1017	Another Time	1987	12.00
❑ SSC-1011	It's Your Dance	1985	12.00
❑ SSC-1018	Lost in His Arms	1987	12.00
❑ SSC-1039	South to a Warmer Place	1989	15.00
❑ SSC-1028	The Cove	1988	12.00

DAMERON, TADD

FANTASY

❑ OJC-055	Fontainebleu	198?	15.00

— Reissue of Prestige 7037

❑ OJC-212	Mating Call	198?	15.00

— Reissue of Prestige 7070

❑ OJC-143	The Magic Touch of Tadd Dameron	198?	15.00

— Reissue of Riverside 9419

JAZZLAND

❑ JLP-50 [M]	Fats Navarro Featured with the Tadd Dameron Quintet	1962	150.00
❑ JLP-68 [M]	The Tadd Dameron Band	1962	150.00

MILESTONE

❑ M-47041	Fats Navarro Featured with the Tadd Dameron Band	1977	25.00

PRESTIGE

❑ PRLP-159 [10]	A Study in Dameronia	1953	600.00
❑ PRLP-16007 [M]	Dameronia	1964	100.00
❑ PRLP-7037 [M]	Fontainebleu	1956	250.00
❑ PRLP-7070 [M]	Mating Call	1956	200.00

— Reissued as 7247 and 7725 as a John Coltrane LP; see his listings

❑ PRST-7842	Memorial Album	1970	18.00

RIVERSIDE

❑ RS-3019	Good Bait	1968	30.00
❑ RLP-419 [M]	The Magic Touch of Tadd Dameron	1962	80.00
❑ RS-9419 [S]	The Magic Touch of Tadd Dameron	1962	80.00

DAMIAN, MICHAEL

CYPRESS

❑ YL9-0130	Where Do We Go from Here	1989	15.00

D'AMICO, HANK

BETHLEHEM

❑ BCP-1006 [10]	Hank's Holiday	1954	120.00

DAMIN EIH, A.L.K. AND BROTHER CLARK

DEMELOT

❑ 7310	Never Mind	1973	150.00

DAMITA JO

ABC-PARAMOUNT

❑ 378 [M]	The Big Fifteen	1961	80.00
❑ S-378 [S]	The Big Fifteen	1961	100.00

EPIC

❑ LN24244 [M]	If You Go Away	1967	25.00
❑ BN26244 [S]	If You Go Away	1967	18.00
❑ LN24202 [M]	Midnight Session	1966	18.00
❑ BN26202 [S]	Midnight Session	1966	25.00
❑ LN24164 [M]	One More Time with Feeling	1965	18.00
❑ BN26164 [S]	One More Time with Feeling	1965	25.00
❑ LN24131 [M]	This Is Damita Jo	1965	18.00
❑ BN26131 [S]	This Is Damita Jo	1965	25.00

MERCURY

❑ MG-20703 [M]	Damita Jo Live at the Diplomat	1962	30.00
❑ SR-60703 [S]	Damita Jo Live at the Diplomat	1962	30.00
❑ MG-20642 [M]	I'll Save the Last Dance for You	1961	30.00
❑ SR-60642 [S]	I'll Save the Last Dance for You	1961	40.00
❑ MG-20734 [M]	Sing a Country Song	1962	30.00
❑ SR-60734 [S]	Sing a Country Song	1962	30.00
❑ MG-20818 [M]	This One's for Me	1963	25.00
❑ SR-60818 [S]	This One's for Me	1963	30.00

RANWOOD

❑ RLP.8037	Miss Damita Jo	1968	18.00

RCA CAMDEN

❑ CAL-900 [M]	Go Go with Damita Jo	196?	18.00
❑ CAS-900(e) [R]	Go Go with Damita Jo	196?	15.00

SUNSET

❑ SUS-5198	The Irresistible Damita Jo	1968	15.00

VEE JAY

❑ LP-1137 [M]	Damita Jo Sings	1965	30.00
❑ LPS-1137 [S]	Damita Jo Sings	1965	50.00

WING

❑ WC-16333	This One's for Me	196?	15.00

DAMNATION OF ADAM BLESSING, THE

UNITED ARTISTS

❑ UAS-6738 [B]	The Damnation of Adam Blessing	1970	35.00
❑ UAS-6773 [B]	The Second Damnation	1970	35.00
❑ UAS-5533 [B]	Which Is the Justice, Which Is the Thief	1971	35.00

DAMNED, THE

CLEOPATRA

❑ 8110 [B]	Punk & Nasty		25.00
❑ CLP8360 [B]	Punk Oddities & Rare Tracks 1977-1982	2014	25.00
❑ 8360 [B]	Pure Punk 1977-1982		30.00

— picture disc

❑ 2021 [B]	Recorded Live At Woolwich Coronet - Thursday 11 July 1985		25.00
❑ 8119 [B]	The Chaos Years - Live & Studio Demos 1977-1982		25.00

FRONTIER

❑ 1003	Damned Damned Damned	1987	18.00

— Reissue of 1976-77 material

I.R.S.

❑ SP-70012	The Black Album	1980	15.00

MCA

❑ 5966 [B]	Anything	1987	18.00
❑ 2-8024	Light at the End of the Tunnel	1988	18.00
❑ 39039 [B]	Phantasmagoria	1986	25.00

DAMON

ANKH

❑ 968	Song of a Gypsy	1969	1500.00

— Gatefold cover

❑ 968	Song of a Gypsy	1969	1500.00

— Regular cover

DAMONE, VIC

APPLAUSE

❑ 1018	Over the Rainbow	197?	12.00

CAPITOL

❑ T1646 [M]	Linger Awhile with Vic Damone	1962	15.00
❑ ST1646 [S]	Linger Awhile with Vic Damone	1962	18.00
❑ T1811 [M]	My Baby Loves to Swing	1963	15.00
❑ ST1811 [S]	My Baby Loves to Swing	1963	18.00
❑ T2123 [M]	On the Street Where You Live	1964	15.00
❑ ST2123 [S]	On the Street Where You Live	1964	18.00
❑ T1691 [M]	Strange Enchantment	1962	15.00
❑ ST1691 [S]	Strange Enchantment	1962	18.00
❑ T1944 [M]	The Liveliest	1963	15.00
❑ ST1944 [S]	The Liveliest	1963	18.00
❑ T1748 [M]	The Lively Ones	1962	15.00
❑ ST1748 [S]	The Lively Ones	1962	18.00

COLUMBIA

❑ CL1088 [M]	Angela Mia	1957	25.00
❑ CS8046 [S]	Angela Mia	1959	30.00
❑ CL1174 [M]	Closer Than a Kiss	195?	25.00
❑ CS8019 [S]	Closer Than a Kiss	1959	30.00
❑ CL1573 [M]	On the Swingin' Side	1961	18.00
❑ CS8373 [S]	On the Swingin' Side	1961	25.00
❑ CL900 [M]	That Towering Feeling!	1956	30.00
❑ CL1368 [M]	This Game of Love	1960	18.00
❑ CS8169 [S]	This Game of Love	1960	25.00

HARMONY

❑ HL7328 [M]	The Best of Vic Damone	196?	15.00
❑ HS11128 [S]	The Best of Vic Damone	196?	15.00
❑ HL7431 [M]	Vic Damone Sings	196?	15.00
❑ HS11231 [S]	Vic Damone Sings	196?	15.00

HOLIDAY

❑ HDY1936	Christmas with Vic Damone	1981	12.00

MERCURY

❑ MG-25133 [10]	April in Paris	1952	40.00
❑ MG-25092 [10]	Christmas Favorites	1951	40.00
❑ MG-20193 [M]	My Favorites	1957	30.00
❑ MG-25054 [10]	Song Hits	1950	40.00
❑ MG-25131 [10]	The Night Has a Thousand Eyes	1952	40.00
❑ MG-25028 [10]	Vic Damone	1950	40.00
❑ MG-25029 [10]	Vic Damone	1950	40.00
❑ MG-25045 [10]	Vic Damone	1950	40.00
❑ MG-25156 [10]	Vic Damone	1952	40.00
❑ MG-25100 [10]	Vic Damone and Others	1952	40.00
❑ MG-25132 [10]	Vocals by Vic	1952	40.00

Number	Title	Yr	NM
❑ MG-20163 [M]	Yours for a Song	1957	30.00
RANWOOD			
❑ 8204	The Best of Vic Damone – Live	198?	12.00
RCA VICTOR			
❑ LPM-3916 [M]	A Damone Type of Thing	1968	18.00
❑ LSP-3916 [S]	A Damone Type of Thing	1968	18.00
❑ LPM-3765 [M]	On the South Side of Chicago	1967	15.00
❑ LSP-3765 [S]	On the South Side of Chicago	1967	18.00
❑ LPM-3671 [M]	Stay with Me	1966	15.00
❑ LSP-3671 [S]	Stay with Me	1966	18.00
❑ ANL1-2462	The Best of Vic Damone	1977	12.00
❑ LSP-3984	Why Can't I Walk Away	1968	18.00
REBECCA			
❑ 1212	Feelings	1976	12.00
❑ 1213	Inspiration	19??	12.00
❑ 100	Let's Fall in Love Again	1981	15.00
UNITED TALENT			
❑ 4501	Don't Let Me Go	1969	15.00
WARNER BROS.			
❑ W1607 [M]	Country Love Songs	1965	15.00
❑ WS1607 [S]	Country Love Songs	1965	18.00
❑ W1602 [M]	You Were Only Fooling	1965	15.00
❑ WS1602 [S]	You Were Only Fooling	1965	18.00
WING			
❑ MGW12113 [M]	I'll Sing for You	196?	15.00
❑ SRW16113 [R]	I'll Sing for You	196?	15.00
❑ MGW12157 [M]	Tenderly	196?	15.00
❑ SRW16157 [R]	Tenderly	196?	15.00
❑ MGW12182 [M]	Yours for a Song	196?	15.00
❑ SRW16182 [R]	Yours for a Song	196?	15.00

DAN AND DALE

Number	Title	Yr	NM
DIPLOMAT			
❑ D-2364 [M]	Country & Western Hits	196?	12.00
❑ DS-2364 [S]	Country & Western Hits	196?	15.00
❑ D-2361 [M]	Country and Western Waltzes	196?	12.00
❑ DS-2361 [S]	Country and Western Waltzes	196?	15.00
❑ D-2340 [M]	Dear Heart, Willow Weep for Me and Other Love Songs	196?	12.00
❑ DS-2340 [S]	Dear Heart, Willow Weep for Me and Other Love Songs	196?	15.00
❑ DS-2343 [S]	Themes from Goldfinger and Zorba the Greek	196?	15.00
❑ D-2343 [M]	Themes from Goldfinger and Zorba the Greek	196?	12.00
❑ D-2390 [M]	The Nearness of You	196?	12.00
❑ DS-2390 [S]	The Nearness of You	196?	15.00
TIFTON			
❑ M-8002 [M]	Batman and Robin	1966	30.00
❑ S-78002 [S]	Batman and Robin	1966	40.00

DANA, VIC

Number	Title	Yr	NM
DOLTON			
❑ BLP-2041 [M]	Crystal Chandelier	1966	18.00
❑ BST-8041 [S]	Crystal Chandelier	1966	25.00
❑ BLP-2048 [M]	Golden Greats	1966	18.00
❑ BST-8048 [S]	Golden Greats	1966	25.00
❑ BLP-2049 [M]	Little Altar Boy and Other Christmas Songs	1966	18.00
❑ BST-8049 [S]	Little Altar Boy and Other Christmas Songs	1966	25.00
❑ BLP-2036 [M]	Moonlight and Roses	1965	18.00
❑ BST-8036 [S]	Moonlight and Roses	1965	25.00
❑ BLP-2026 [M]	More	1963	18.00
❑ BST-8026 [S]	More	1963	25.00
❑ BLP-2032 [M]	Now	1964	18.00
❑ BST-8032 [S]	Now	1964	25.00
❑ BLP-2034 [M]	Red Roses for a Blue Lady	1965	18.00
❑ BST-8034 [S]	Red Roses for a Blue Lady	1965	25.00
❑ BLP-2028 [M]	Shangri-La	1964	18.00
❑ BST-8028 [S]	Shangri-La	1964	25.00
❑ BLP-2013 [M]	This Is Vic Dana	1961	25.00
❑ BST-8013 [S]	This Is Vic Dana	1961	30.00
❑ BLP-2046 [M]	Town and Country	1966	18.00
❑ BST-8046 [S]	Town and Country	1966	25.00
❑ BLP-2015 [M]	Warm and Wild	1962	18.00
❑ BST-8015 [S]	Warm and Wild	1962	25.00
LIBERTY			
❑ LST-8063	If I Never Knew Your Name	1969	15.00
❑ BST-8049 [S]	Little Altar Boy and Other Christmas Songs	1967	15.00
—Liberty record in Dolton cover			
SUNSET			
❑ SUM-1182 [M]	On the Country Side	1967	12.00
❑ SUS-5182 [S]	On the Country Side	1967	15.00
❑ SUM-1130 [M]	Warm and Wonderful	196?	12.00
❑ SUS-5130 [S]	Warm and Wonderful	196?	15.00

DANCY, MEL

Number	Title	Yr	NM
MAINSTREAM			
❑ MRL-378	A Little Lovin'	1972	15.00

D'ANDREA, FRANCO

Number	Title	Yr	NM
RED			
❑ NS-201	My One and Only Love	198?	15.00
❑ NS-202	No Idea of Time	1985	15.00

DANE, BARBARA

Number	Title	Yr	NM
BARBARY COAST			
❑ 33014 [M]	Trouble in Mind	1959	40.00
—Reissue of San Francisco LP			
CAPITOL			
❑ T1758 [M]	On My Way	1962	30.00
❑ ST1758 [S]	On My Way	1962	40.00
DOT			
❑ DLP-3177 [M]	Living with the Blues	1959	30.00
❑ DLP-25177 [S]	Living with the Blues	1959	40.00
FOLKWAYS			
❑ FA-2468	Barbara Dane and the Chambers Brothers	1966	50.00
❑ FA-2471	Folk Songs	1966	30.00
HORIZON			
❑ WP-1602 [M]	When I Was a Young Girl	1962	30.00
❑ WPS-1602 [S]	When I Was a Young Girl	1962	40.00
—Black vinyl			
❑ WPS-1602 [S]	When I Was a Young Girl	1962	60.00
—Gold vinyl			
PAREDON			
❑ 1003	FTA! Songs of the GI Resistance	1970	18.00
❑ 1014	I Hate the Capitalist System	1973	18.00
❑ 1046	When We Make It Through	1982	18.00
SAN FRANCISCO			
❑ 33014 [M]	Trouble in Mind	1957	60.00

D'ANGELO

Number	Title	Yr	NM
VIRGIN			
❑ 48499	Voodoo	2000	18.00
❑ SPRO14969 [DJ]	Voodoo DJ Soul Essentials	2000	25.00
—Six-song promo-only sampler			

DANIEL, TED

Number	Title	Yr	NM
UJAMAA			
❑ 1001	Ted Daniel	197?	15.00

DANIELS, CHARLIE, BAND

Number	Title	Yr	NM
CAPITOL			
❑ ST-790	Charlie Daniels	1971	30.00
❑ SN-16039	Charlie Daniels	1979	10.00
—Budget-line reissue			
❑ ST-11414	Charlie Daniels	1975	15.00
—Reissue of ST-790			
EPIC			
❑ FE38795	A Decade of Hits	1983	12.00
❑ JE34365	Fire on the Mountain	1976	12.00
—Reissue of Kama Sutra 2603 without bonus EP; orange label, no bar code on cover			
❑ PE34365	Fire on the Mountain	198?	10.00
—Budget-line reissue			
❑ HE44365	Fire on the Mountain	1982	40.00
Half-speed mastered edition			
❑ FE36571 [B]	Full Moon	1980	12.00
❑ PE36571	Full Moon	198?	10.00
—Budget-line reissue			
❑ JE34377	High Lonesome	1976	12.00
—Orange label, no bar code on cover			
❑ PE34377	High Lonesome	198?	10.00
—Budget-line reissue			
❑ FE44324	Homesick Man	1988	12.00
❑ AS586 [DJ]	Interchords	1979	18.00
—Music and interviews; promo only			
❑ FE39878	Me and the Boys	1985	12.00
❑ PE39878	Me and the Boys	198?	10.00
—Budget-line reissue			
❑ JE34970	Midnight Wind	1977	12.00
—Orange label, no bar code on cover			
❑ PE34970	Midnight Wind	198?	10.00
—Budget-line reissue			
❑ JE35751	Million Mile Reflections	1979	12.00
❑ PE35751	Million Mile Reflections	198?	10.00
—Budget-line reissue			
❑ HE45751	Million Mile Reflections	1982	40.00
—Half-speed mastered edition			
❑ JE34402	Nightrider	1977	12.00
—Reissue of Kama Sutra 2607; orange label, no bar code on cover			
❑ PE34402	Nightrider	198?	10.00
—Budget-line reissue			
❑ FE40760	Powder Keg	1987	10.00
❑ JE34150	Saddle Tramp	1976	12.00
—Orange label, no bar code on cover			
❑ PE34150	Saddle Tramp	198?	10.00
—With bar code on cover			
❑ FE45316	Simple Man	1989	15.00
❑ JE34665	Te John, Grease and Wolfman	1977	12.00
—Reissue of Kama Sutra 2060; orange label, no bar code on cover			
❑ PE34665	Te John, Grease and Wolfman	198?	10.00
—Budget-line reissue			
❑ EAS1780 [DJ]	The Charlie Daniels Story	1990	18.00

Number	Title	Yr	NM
—Promo-only interview/radio show			
❑ JE34369	Uneasy Rider	1976	12.00
—Reissue of Kama Sutra 2071 with new name; orange label, no bar code on cover			
❑ PE34369	Uneasy Rider	198?	10.00
—Budget-line reissue			
❑ JE34664	Whiskey	1977	12.00
—Reissue of Kama Sutra 2076 with new name; orange label, no bar code on cover			
❑ PE34664	Whiskey	198?	10.00
—Budget-line reissue			
❑ FE37694	Windows	1982	12.00
❑ PE37694	Windows	198?	10.00
—Budget-line reissue			
KAMA SUTRA			
❑ KSBS2603	Fire on the Mountain	1974	18.00
—Includes bonus EP, "Volunteer Jam" (deduct 20% if missing)			
❑ KSBS2071	Honey in the Rock	1973	18.00
❑ KSBS2607	Nightrider	1975	18.00
❑ KSBS2060	Te John, Grease and Wolfman	1972	18.00
❑ KSBS2076	Way Down Yonder	1974	18.00
MOBILE FIDELITY			
❑ 1-176	Million Mile Reflections	1984	30.00
—Audiophile vinyl			

DANIELS, EDDIE

Number	Title	Yr	NM
CHOICE			
❑ 1002	A Flower for All Seasons	1974	15.00
COLUMBIA			
❑ JC36290	Morning Thunder	1980	12.00
GRP			
❑ GR-9584	Blackwood	1989	15.00
❑ GR-1024	Breakthrough	198?	12.00
❑ GR-1050	Memos from Paradise: The Music of Roger Kellaway	1988	12.00
❑ GR-1034	To Bird with Love	1987	12.00
MUSE			
❑ MR-5154	Brief Encounter	1978	15.00
PRESTIGE			
❑ PRLP-7506 [M]	First Prize	1967	40.00
❑ PRST-7506 [S]	First Prize	1967	30.00

DANIELS, HALL

Number	Title	Yr	NM
JUMP			
❑ JL-9 [10]	Hall Daniels Septet	1955	80.00
—Issued on blue vinyl			

DANIELS, MIKE, AND HIS DELTA JAZZMEN

Number	Title	Yr	NM
STOMP OFF			
❑ SOS-1203	Together Again -- Thirty Years On!	1991	15.00

DANKO, RICK

Number	Title	Yr	NM
ARISTA			
❑ AB4141	Rick Danko	1977	15.00

DANKWORTH, JOHN

Number	Title	Yr	NM
DRG			
❑ MRS-507	Movies 'N' Me	198?	12.00
FONTANA			
❑ SRF-67603	The Sophisticated Johnnie Dankworth	1969	25.00
❑ MGF-27543 [M]	Zodiac Variations	1966	18.00
❑ SRF-67543 [S]	Zodiac Variations	1966	25.00
IAJRC			
❑ LP39	Johnny Dankworth's Big Band In the Fifties	198?	12.00
MCA CLASSICS			
❑ 25932	Crossing Over the Bridge	1987	12.00
ROULETTE			
❑ R-52059 [M]	Collaboration	1961	25.00
❑ SR-52059 [S]	Collaboration	1961	30.00
❑ R-52040 [M]	England's Ambassador of Jazz	1960	25.00
❑ SR-52040 [S]	England's Ambassador of Jazz	1960	30.00
❑ R-52096 [M]	Jazz from Abroad	1963	25.00
❑ SR-52096 [S]	Jazz from Abroad	1963	30.00
VERVE			
❑ MG V-20006 [M]	5 Steps to Dankworth	1957	40.00
—Also contains several tracks by others who are performing songs Dankworth wrote			

DANKWORTH, JOHN/BILLY STRAYHORN

Number	Title	Yr	NM
ROULETTE			
❑ RE-121	Echoes of an Era	1973	18.00

DANNY AND THE JUNIORS

Number	Title	Yr	NM
MCA			
❑ 1555	Rockin' with Danny and the Juniors	1987	12.00

DANTE, RON

Number	Title	Yr	NM
HANDSHAKE			
❑ JW37341	Street Angel	1981	15.00

Number	Title	Yr	NM

KIRSHNER
| ❑ KES-106 | Ron Dante Brings You Up | 1970 | 25.00 |

DANTE

MADISON
| ❑ MA-LP1002 [M] | Dante and the Evergreens | 1961 | 550.00 |

DANZIG, GLENN

PLAN 9
| ❑ PL9-11 [B] | Black Aria | 1992 | 35.00 |

DANZIG

AMERICAN
| ❑ 45647 [B] | 4 | 1994 | 30.00 |
DEF AMERICAN
| ❑ DEF24208 [B] | Danzig | 1988 | 40.00 |
| ❑ DEF24281 [B] | Lucifuge | 1990 | 40.00 |

D'ARBY, TERENCE TRENT

COLUMBIA
| ❑ BFC40964 | Introducing the Hardline According to Terence Trent D'Arby | 1987 | 15.00 |
| ❑ C45351 | Neither Fish Nor Flesh | 1989 | 12.00 |

DARCEL, DENISE

CAMEO
| ❑ C-1002 [M] | Banned in Boston | 1958 | 40.00 |

DARCH, BOB

UNITED ARTISTS
| ❑ UAL-3120 [M] | Ragtime Piano | 1960 | 25.00 |
| ❑ UAS-6120 [S] | Ragtime Piano | 1960 | 30.00 |

DARDANELLE AND VIVIAN LORD

STASH
| ❑ ST-231 | The Two of Us | 1983 | 12.00 |

DARENSBOURG, JOE

GHB
| ❑ 90 | Barrelhousin' with Joe | 197? | 12.00 |
GNP CRESCENDO
| ❑ GNP-515 | Petite Fleur | 197? | 12.00 |
| ❑ GNP-514 | Yellow Dog Blues | 197? | 12.00 |

DARIN, BOBBY

ATCO
❑ 33-102 [M]	Bobby Darin	1958	100.00
— Yellow "harp" label			
❑ 33-102 [M]	Bobby Darin	1962	30.00
— Gold and dark blue label			
❑ 33-140 [M]	Bobby Darin Sings Ray Charles	1962	30.00
❑ SD 33-140 [S]	Bobby Darin Sings Ray Charles	1962	30.00
❑ 33-122 [M]	Darin at the Copa	1960	40.00
— Yellow "harp" label			
❑ 33-122 [M]	Darin at the Copa	1962	25.00
— Gold and dark blue label			
❑ SD 33-122 [S]	Darin at the Copa	1960	80.00
— Yellow "harp" label			
❑ SD 33-122 [S]	Darin at the Copa	1962	30.00
— Purple and brown label			
❑ SP1001 [M]	For Teenagers Only	1960	150.00
— Gatefold with fold-open poster and paper insert			
❑ SP1001 [M]	For Teenagers Only	1960	75.00
— With extras missing			
❑ 33-124 [M]	It's You or No One	1960	40.00
— Yellow "harp" label			
❑ 33-124 [M]	It's You or No One	1962	25.00
— Gold and dark blue label			
❑ SD 33-124 [S]	It's You or No One	1960	80.00
— Yellow "harp" label			
❑ SD 33-124 [S]	It's You or No One	1962	30.00
Purple and brown label			
❑ 33-134 [M]	Love Swings	1961	40.00
— Yellow "harp" label			
❑ 33-134 [M]	Love Swings	1962	25.00
— Gold and dark blue label			
❑ SD 33-134 [S]	Love Swings	1961	50.00
— Yellow "harp" label			
❑ SD 33-134 [S]	Love Swings	1962	30.00
— Purple and brown label			
❑ 33-104 [M]	That's All	1959	40.00
— Yellow "harp" label			
❑ 33-104 [M]	That's All	1962	25.00
— Gold and dark blue label			
❑ SD 33-104 [S]	That's All	1959	100.00
— Yellow "harp" label			
❑ SD 33-104 [S]	That's All	1962	30.00
— Purple and brown label			
❑ 33-125 [M]	The 25th Day of December	1960	50.00
— Yellow "harp" label			
❑ SD 33-125 [S]	The 25th Day of December	1960	60.00
— Yellow "harp" label			
❑ 33-125 [M]	The 25th Day of December	1962	25.00
— Gold and dark blue label			

Number	Title	Yr	NM

❑ SD 33-125 [S]	The 25th Day of December	1962	30.00
— Gold and dark blue label			
❑ 33-131 [M]	The Bobby Darin Story	1961	40.00
— Yellow "harp" label; white cover			
❑ 33-131 [M]	The Bobby Darin Story	1962	25.00
— Gold and dark blue label; black cover			
❑ SD 33-131 [S]	The Bobby Darin Story	1961	50.00
— Yellow "harp" label; white cover			
❑ SD 33-131 [S]	The Bobby Darin Story	1962	30.00
— Purple and brown label; black cover			
❑ SD 33-131	The Bobby Darin Story	1969	15.00
— Yellow label, "Atco" on left			
❑ SD 33-131	The Bobby Darin Story	1978	10.00
— Any later Atco label			
❑ 33-146 [M]	Things & Other Things	1962	30.00
❑ SD 33-146 [S]	Things & Other Things	1962	30.00
❑ 33-115 [M]	This Is Darin	1960	40.00
— Yellow "harp" label			
❑ 33-115 [M]	This Is Darin	1962	25.00
— Gold and dark blue label			
❑ SD 33-115 [S]	This Is Darin	1960	80.00
— Yellow "harp" label			
❑ SD 33-115 [S]	This Is Darin	1960	30.00
— Purple and brown label			
❑ 33-138 [M]	Twist with Bobby Darin	1961	40.00
— Yellow "harp" label			
❑ 33-138 [M]	Twist with Bobby Darin	1962	25.00
— Gold and dark blue label			
❑ SD 33-138 [S]	Twist with Bobby Darin	1961	50.00
— Yellow "harp" label			
❑ SD 33-138 [S]	Twist with Bobby Darin	1962	30.00
— Purple and brown label			
❑ 33-126 [M]	Two of a Kind	1961	40.00
— Yellow "harp" label			
❑ 33-126 [M]	Two of a Kind	1962	25.00
— Gold and dark blue label			
❑ SD 33-126 [S]	Two of a Kind	1961	50.00
— Yellow "harp" label			
❑ SD 33-126 [S]	Two of a Kind	1962	30.00
— Purple and brown label			
❑ 90484	Two of a Kind	1986	12.00
❑ 33-167 [M]	Winners	1964	30.00
❑ SD 33-167 [S]	Winners	1964	30.00
ATLANTIC
❑ 8154 [M]	Bobby Darin Sings Doctor Dolittle	1967	18.00
❑ SD8154 [S]	Bobby Darin Sings Doctor Dolittle	1967	18.00
❑ 8135 [M]	If I Were a Carpenter	1967	18.00
❑ SD8135 [S]	If I Were a Carpenter	1967	50.00
— Inexplicably rare in stereo			
❑ 8126 [M]	In a Broadway Bag	1966	18.00
❑ SD8126 [S]	In a Broadway Bag	1966	25.00
❑ 8142 [M]	Inside Out	1967	18.00
❑ SD8142 [S]	Inside Out	1967	30.00
❑ 8121 [M]	The Shadow of Your Smile	1966	18.00
❑ SD8121 [S]	The Shadow of Your Smile	1966	25.00
BAINBRIDGE
| ❑ 6220 | Bobby Darin at the Copa | 1981 | 12.00 |
CAPITOL
❑ T1942 [M]	18 Yellow Roses	1963	18.00
❑ ST1942 [S]	18 Yellow Roses	1963	25.00
❑ ST2084 [S]	As Long As I'm Singing	1964	200.00
— Canceled; price is for an acetate, which is known to exist			
❑ T1826 [M]	Earthy	1963	18.00
❑ ST1826 [S]	Earthy	1963	25.00
❑ T2194 [M]	From Hello Dolly to Goodbye Charlie	1964	18.00
❑ ST2194 [S]	From Hello Dolly to Goodbye Charlie	1964	25.00
❑ T2007 [M]	Golden Folk Hits	1963	18.00
❑ ST2007 [S]	Golden Folk Hits	1963	25.00
❑ W1791 [M]	Oh! Look at Me Now	1962	25.00
❑ SW1791 [S]	Oh! Look at Me Now	1962	30.00
❑ T1791 [M]	Oh! Look at Me Now	1962	18.00
❑ ST1791 [S]	Oh! Look at Me Now	1962	25.00
❑ T2571 [M]	The Best of Bobby Darin	1966	18.00
❑ ST2571 [S]	The Best of Bobby Darin	1966	18.00
❑ T2322 [M]	Venice Blue	1965	18.00
❑ ST2322 [S]	Venice Blue	1965	25.00
❑ T1866 [M]	You're the Reason I'm Living	1963	18.00
❑ ST1866 [S]	You're the Reason I'm Living	1963	25.00
CLARION
| ❑ 603 [M] | Clementine | 1966 | 25.00 |
| ❑ SD603 [S] | Clementine | 1966 | 30.00 |
DIRECTION
| ❑ 1936 | Born Walden Robert Cassotto | 1968 | 30.00 |
| ❑ 1937 | Commitment | 1969 | 30.00 |
MOTOWN
❑ M753L	Bobby Darin	1972	25.00
❑ M6-813L	Darin 1936-1973	1974	18.00
❑ M5-185V1	Darin 1936-1973	1981	15.00
— Reissue			
❑ MS-739	Finally	1972	500.00
— Unreleased; value is for RCA test pressing			

DARIUS

CHARTMAKER
| ❑ 1102 | Darius | 1968 | 500.00 |

Number	Title	Yr	NM

DARLING, DENVER

AUDIO LAB
| ❑ AL-1507 [M] | Songs of the Trail | 1958 | 100.00 |

DARNEL, BILL

X
| ❑ LVA-(# unk) [10] | Bill Darnel Sings | 1955 | 40.00 |

DARR, ALICE

CHARLIE PARKER
| ❑ PLP-611 [M] | I Only Know How to Cry | 1962 | 30.00 |
| ❑ PLP-611S [S] | I Only Know How to Cry | 1962 | 40.00 |

DARRELL, JOHNNY

CAPRICORN
| ❑ CP 0154 | Water Glass Full of Whiskey | 1975 | 12.00 |
SUNSET
| ❑ SUS-5232 | The Johnny Darrell Sound | 1969 | 12.00 |
UNITED ARTISTS
❑ UAS6752	California Stop-Over	1970	25.00
❑ UAS6594 [S]	Ruby, Don't Take Your Love to Town	1967	25.00
❑ UAL3594 [M]	Ruby, Don't Take Your Love to Town	1967	30.00
❑ UAS6759	The Best of Johnny Darrell, Volume 1	1970	18.00
❑ UAS6634	The Son of Hickory Holler's Tramp	1968	25.00
❑ UAS6707	Why You Been Gone So Long	1969	25.00
❑ UAS6660	With Pen in Hand	1968	25.00

DARREN, JAMES

COLPIX
❑ CP-418 [M]	Gidget Goes Hawaiian (James Darren Sings the Movies)	1961	30.00
❑ SCP-418 [S]	Gidget Goes Hawaiian (James Darren Sings the Movies)	1961	40.00
❑ CP-406 [M]	James Darren (Album No. 1)	1960	50.00
— Black vinyl			
❑ CP-406 [M]	James Darren (Album No. 1)	1960	150.00
— Green vinyl			
❑ CP-424 [M]	James Darren Sings for All Sizes	1962	30.00
❑ SCP-424 [S]	James Darren Sings for All Sizes	1962	40.00
❑ CP-428 [M]	Love Among the Young	1962	30.00
❑ SCP-428 [S]	Love Among the Young	1962	40.00
KIRSHNER
| ❑ KES-116 | Love Songs from the Movies | 1972 | 18.00 |
| ❑ KES-115 | Mammy Blue | 1971 | 18.00 |
WARNER BROS.
| ❑ W1668 [M] | James Darren/All | 1967 | 18.00 |
| ❑ WS1668 [S] | James Darren/All | 1967 | 25.00 |

DARREN, JAMES/ SHELLEY FABARES/PAUL PETERSEN

COLPIX
❑ CP-468 [M]	More Teenage Triangle	1964	40.00
❑ SCP-468 [P]	More Teenage Triangle	1964	60.00
❑ CP-444 [M]	Teenage Triangle	1963	40.00
❑ SCP-444 [R]	Teenage Triangle	1963	40.00

DARRIEU, DANIELLE

LONDON
| ❑ LB-616 [10] | Le Voix de France | 1954 | 50.00 |

DARRIEUX, DANIELLE

CAPITOL
| ❑ T10319 [M] | Incomparable Danielle Darrieux | 1963 | 25.00 |
| ❑ ST10319 [S] | Incomparable Danielle Darrieux | 1963 | 30.00 |

DARTELLS, THE

DOT
| ❑ DLP-3522 [M] | Hot Pastrami | 1963 | 30.00 |
| ❑ DLP-25522 [S] | Hot Pastrami | 1963 | 40.00 |

DARTMOUTH INDIAN CHIEFS

TRANSITION
| ❑ TRLP-23 [M] | Chiefly Jazz | 1956 | 120.00 |

DARTS, THE

DEL-FI
| ❑ DFLP-1244 [M] | Hollywood Drag | 1963 | 60.00 |
| ❑ DFST-1244 [S] | Hollywood Drag | 1963 | 80.00 |

DASH, JULIAN

MASTER JAZZ
| ❑ 8106 | Portrait | 1970 | 25.00 |

DASHIEL, BUD, AND THE KINSMEN

WARNER BROS.
| ❑ W1429 [M] | Folk Music in a Contemporary Manner | 1961 | 30.00 |

Number	Title	Yr	NM
❏ WS1429 [S]	Folk Music in a Contemporary Manner	1961	30.00
❏ W1432 [M]	Live Concert Extraordinaire -- Bud Dashiel and the Kinsmen Sing Everybody's Hits	1961	30.00
❏ WS1432 [S]	Live Concert Extraordinaire -- Bud Dashiel and the Kinsmen Sing Everybody's Hits	1961	30.00

DAUGHERTY, JACK

A&M

| ❏ SP-3038 | Jack Daugherty and the Class of '71 | 1971 | 25.00 |

MONTEREY

| ❏ 100 | Carmel by the Sea | 1976 | 18.00 |

DAUGHTERS OF ALBION, THE

FONTANA

| ❏ SRF-67586 | The Daughters of Albion | 1968 | 40.00 |

DAVE & SUGAR

RCA VICTOR

❏ APL1-1818	Dave & Sugar	1976	12.00
❏ AHL1-3915	Dave & Sugar/Greatest Hits	1981	12.00
❏ AHL1-3823	New York Wine Tennessee Shine	1980	12.00
❏ AHL1-3360	Stay with Me/Golden Tears	1979	12.00
❏ APL1-2861	Tear Time	1978	12.00
❏ APL1-2477	That's the Way Love Should Be	1976	12.00

DAVE DEE, DOZY, BEAKY, MICK & TICH

FONTANA

❏ MGF-27567 [M]	Greatest Hits	1967	40.00
❏ SRF-67567 [P]	Greatest Hits	1967	40.00
—Bend It" and "Hold Tight" are rechanneled.			

IMPERIAL

| ❏ LP-12402 [P] | Time to Take Off | 1968 | 60.00 |
| —Zabadak" is rechanneled. | | | |

DAVEY AND THE BADMEN

GOTHIC

| ❏ KRW-054 | Wanted | 1963 | 200.00 |

DAVID, THE

V.M.C.

| ❏ 124 | Another Day, Another Lifetime | 1968 | 200.00 |
| —Mono and stereo versions same price | | | |

DAVID AND DAVID

A&M

❏ R183799	Boomtown	1987	15.00
—RCA Music Service edition			
❏ SP5134	Boomtown	1986	12.00

DAVID AND JONATHAN

CAPITOL

| ❏ T2473 [M] | Michelle | 1966 | 18.00 |
| ❏ ST2473 [S] | Michelle | 1966 | 25.00 |

DAVIDSON, JOHN

20TH CENTURY

| ❏ T-512 | Every Time I Sing | 1976 | 12.00 |
| ❏ T-429 | Touch Me | 1974 | 12.00 |

ACCORD

| ❏ SN-7202 | Closeup | 1981 | 10.00 |

COLPIX

| ❏ CP-485 [M] | The Young Warm Sound of John Davidson | 1964 | 18.00 |
| ❏ SCP-485 [S] | The Young Warm Sound of John Davidson | 1964 | 25.00 |

COLUMBIA

❏ CL2734 [M]	A Kind of Hush	1967	12.00
❏ CS9534 [S]	A Kind of Hush	1967	15.00
❏ C30098	Everything Is Beautiful	1970	12.00
❏ CS9654	Goin' Places	1968	12.00
❏ PC36956	Incredible	1981	10.00
❏ CS9795	John Davidson	1969	12.00
❏ CL2648 [M]	My Best to You	1967	12.00
❏ CS9448 [S]	My Best to You	1967	15.00
❏ CS9859	My Cherie Amour	1969	12.00
❏ CS9864	My Christmas Favorites	1969	15.00
❏ CL2580 [M]	The Time of My Life	1966	12.00
❏ CS9380 [S]	The Time of My Life	1966	15.00

MERCURY

| ❏ SRM-1-658 | Well, Here I Am | 1973 | 12.00 |

DAVIDSON, LOWELL

ESP-DISK'

| ❏ 1012 [M] | Lowell Davidson Trio | 1965 | 18.00 |
| ❏ S-1012 [S] | Lowell Davidson Trio | 1965 | 25.00 |

DAVIE, HUTCH

ATCO

| ❏ 33-105 [M] | Much Hutch | 1958 | 60.00 |

DAVIES, DAVE

RCA VICTOR

| ❏ AFL1-3603 | AFL1-3603 | 1980 | 12.00 |
| ❏ AFL1-4036 | Glamour | 1981 | 12.00 |

WARNER BROS.

| ❏ 23917 | Chosen People | 1983 | 12.00 |

DAVIS, ANTHONY

GRAMAVISION

❏ 8101	Episteme	1981	15.00
❏ 8303	Hemispheres	1983	15.00
❏ 8201	I've Known Rivers	1982	15.00
❏ 8401	Middle Passage	1984	15.00
❏ R1-79441	Trio Squared	1989	15.00
❏ 8612	Undine	1986	15.00

INDIA NAVIGATION

❏ IN-1041	Hidden Voices	1979	18.00
❏ IN-1047	Lady in the Mirror	1980	18.00
❏ IN-1036	Songs for the Old World	1978	18.00
❏ IN-1056	Variations in Dream-Time	1981	18.00

PAUSA

| ❏ 7120 | Under the Double Moon | 198? | 12.00 |

SACKVILLE

| ❏ 3020 | Of Blues and Dreams | 198? | 12.00 |

DAVIS, ART

INTERPLAY

| ❏ 7728 | Reemergence | 197? | 15.00 |

SOUL NOTE

| ❏ 121143 | Life | 198? | 15.00 |

DAVIS, BOB

STEPHENY

| ❏ MF-4000 [M] | Jazz in Orbit | 1958 | 60.00 |
| ❏ MFS-8003 [S] | Jazz in Orbit | 1960 | 50.00 |

ZEPHYR

| ❏ 12001 [M] | Jazz from the North Coast | 1959 | 50.00 |

DAVIS, CHARLES

STRATA-EAST

| ❏ 7425 | Ingia! | 1974 | 18.00 |

WEST 54

| ❏ 8006 | Dedicated to Tadd | 1979 | 15.00 |

DAVIS, DANNY, AND THE NASHVILLE BRASS

PICKWICK

| ❏ ACL-7034 | Down Yonder | 197? | 10.00 |
| ❏ ACL-7048 | Super Country | 1977 | 10.00 |

RCA SPECIAL PRODUCTS

| ❏ DPL1-0176 | America 200 Years Young | 1976 | 18.00 |
| —Available only at Amana dealers | | | |

RCA VICTOR

❏ APL1-0565	Bluegrass Country	1974	12.00
❏ APD1-0565 [Q]	Bluegrass Country	1974	18.00
❏ APL1-0232	Cairbbean Cruise	1973	12.00
❏ APD1-0232 [Q]	Cairbbean Cruise	1973	18.00
❏ LSP-4377	Christmas with Danny Davis and the Nashville Brass	1970	12.00
❏ ANL1-1930	Christmas with Danny Davis and the Nashville Brass	1976	10.00
—Reissue of LSP-4377			
❏ APL1-2980	Cookin' Country	1978	12.00
❏ AHL1-4022	Cotton Eyed Joe	1981	12.00
❏ LSP-4424	Down Homers	1970	12.00
❏ APL1-1043	Dream Country	1975	12.00
❏ APD1-1043 [Q]	Dream Country	1975	15.00
❏ APL1-1240	Gold	1975	12.00
❏ APD1-1240 [Q]	Gold	1975	15.00
❏ AHL1-3415	Great Songs of the Big Band Era	1979	12.00
❏ APL1-2721	How I Love Them Ol' Songs	1977	12.00
❏ LSP-4720	Live -- In Person	1972	12.00
❏ APL1-2310	Live Vegas	1977	12.00
❏ LSP-4176	More Nashville Sounds	1969	12.00
❏ LSP-4232	Movin' On	1969	12.00
❏ ANL1-0902	Orange Blossom Special	1974	12.00
❏ LSP-4475	Somethin' Else	1971	12.00
❏ APL1-1986	Super	1976	12.00
❏ LSP-4571	Super Country	1971	12.00
❏ APL1-1578	Texas	1976	12.00
❏ APD1-1578 [Q]	Texas	1976	15.00
❏ APL1-0425	The Best of Danny Davis and the Nashville Brass	1973	12.00
❏ APL1-0774	The Latest and Greatest	1974	12.00
❏ APD1-0774 [Q]	The Latest and Greatest	1974	18.00
❏ LSP-4059	The Nashville Sound	1969	12.00
❏ APD1-0034 [Q]	Travelin'	1973	15.00
❏ LSP-4803	Turn On Some Happy!	1972	12.00
❏ LSP-4627	Turns to Gold	1972	12.00
❏ LSP-4334	You Ain't Heard Nothin' Yet	1970	12.00

DAVIS, EDDIE "LOCKJAW", AND HARRY "SWEETS" EDISON

PABLO

| ❏ 2310882 | Jazz at the Philharmonic 1983 | 1983 | 15.00 |

STORYVILLE

| ❏ 4004 | Eddie "Lockjaw" Davis and Harry "Sweets" Edison | 197? | 15.00 |

DAVIS, EDDIE "LOCKJAW", AND JOHNNY GRIFFIN

FANTASY

| ❏ OJC-264 | Griff & Lock | 1987 | 12.00 |

JAZZLAND

❏ JLP-60 [M]	Blues Up and Down	1961	40.00
❏ JLP-960 [S]	Blues Up and Down	1961	50.00
❏ JLP-42 [M]	Griff & Lock	1961	40.00
❏ JLP-942 [S]	Griff & Lock	1961	50.00
❏ JLP-39 [M]	Lookin' at Monk	1961	40.00
❏ JLP-939 [S]	Lookin' at Monk	1961	50.00
❏ JLP-76 [M]	Tough Tenor Favorites	1962	40.00
❏ JLP-976 [S]	Tough Tenor Favorites	1962	50.00
❏ JLP-31 [M]	Tough Tenors	1960	40.00
❏ JLP-931 [S]	Tough Tenors	1960	50.00

MILESTONE

| ❏ 47035 | The Toughest Tenors | 198? | 18.00 |

PAUSA

| ❏ 7062 | The Tough Tenors Again 'n' Again | 197? | 12.00 |

PRESTIGE

❏ PRLP-7282 [M]	Battle Stations	1963	30.00
❏ PRST-7282 [S]	Battle Stations	1963	40.00
❏ 24009	Live at Minton's	197?	18.00
❏ PRLP-7407	The Breakfast Show	1965	30.00
—Reissue of 7191			
❏ PRST-7407 [S]	The Breakfast Show	1965	30.00
❏ PRLP-7309 [M]	The First Set -- Recorded Live at Minton's	1964	30.00
❏ PRST-7309 [S]	The First Set -- Recorded Live at Minton's	1964	40.00
❏ PRLP-7357 [M]	The Late Show -- Recorded Live!	1965	30.00
❏ PRST-7357 [S]	The Late Show -- Recorded Live!	1965	30.00
❏ PRLP-7330 [M]	The Midnight Show at Minton's Playhouse	1964	30.00
❏ PRST-7330 [S]	The Midnight Show at Minton's Playhouse	1964	30.00
❏ PRLP-7191	The Tenor Scene	1961	50.00

DAVIS, EDDIE "LOCKJAW", AND SHIRLEY SCOTT

FANTASY

| ❏ OJC-216 | Jaws | 198? | 12.00 |
| ❏ OJC-322 | Jaws in Orbit | 1988 | 12.00 |

MOODSVILLE

❏ MVLP-4 [M]	Eddie "Lockjaw" Davis with Shirley Scott	1960	50.00
—Green label			
❏ MVLP-4 [M]	Eddie "Lockjaw" Davis with Shirley Scott	1965	30.00
—Blue label, trident logo on right			
❏ MVLP-30 [M]	Misty	1963	50.00
—Green label			
❏ MVLP-30 [M]	Misty	1965	30.00
—Blue label, trident logo on right			
❏ MVST-30 [S]	Misty	1963	50.00
—Green label			
❏ MVST-30 [S]	Misty	1965	30.00
Blue label, trident logo on right			

PRESTIGE

❏ PRLP-7178 [M]	Bacalao	1960	80.00
❏ PRLP-7154 [M]	Jaws	1959	50.00
❏ PRLP-7171 [M]	Jaws in Orbit	1959	50.00
❏ PRLP-7301 [M]	Smokin'	1964	40.00
❏ PRST-7301 [S]	Smokin'	1964	30.00
❏ PRST-7710	The Best of Eddie "Lockjaw" Davis with Shirley Scott	1970	18.00

DAVIS, EDDIE "LOCKJAW

BETHLEHEM

❏ BCP-6035 [M]	Eddie's Function	197?	18.00
—Reissue material, distributed by RCA Victor			
❏ BCP-6069 [M]	The Best of Eddie "Lockjaw" Davis	1963	40.00
❏ BCPS-6069 [R]	The Best of Eddie "Lockjaw" Davis	196?	25.00

CLASSIC JAZZ

| ❏ 116 | Sweet and Lovely | 197? | 15.00 |

ENJA

| ❏ 3097 | Jaws' Blues | 1981 | 15.00 |

FANTASY

❏ OJC-403	Afro-Jaws	1989	15.00
❏ OJC-384	Montreux '77	1989	15.00
❏ OJC-629	Straight Ahead	1991	15.00
❏ OJC-652	The Eddie "Lockjaw" Davis Cookbook, Vol. 1	1991	15.00
❏ OJC-653	The Eddie "Lockjaw" Davis Cookbook, Vol. 2	1991	15.00
❏ OJC-429	Trane Whistle	1990	15.00

INNER CITY

| ❏ IC-2058 | Swingin' Till the Girls Come Home | 1976 | 18.00 |

JAZZLAND

| ❏ JLP-97 [M] | Alma Alegre | 1962 | 30.00 |
| ❏ JLP-997 [S] | Alma Alegre | 1962 | 30.00 |

KING

❏ 599 [M]	Big Beat Jazz	1958	100.00
❏ 566 [M]	Jazz with a Beat	1957	100.00
❏ 395-526 [M]	Jazz with a Horn	1957	100.00

Number	Title	Yr	NM
❏ 395-506 [M]	Modern Jazz Expression	1956	100.00
❏ 637 [M]	This and That	1959	100.00
❏ 606 [M]	Uptown	1958	100.00

MUSE

❏ MR-5202	Heavy Hitter	1979	15.00

PABLO

❏ 2310778	Straight Ahead	197?	18.00
❏ 2405414	The Best of Eddie "Lockjaw" Davis	198?	12.00

PABLO LIVE

❏ 2308214	Montreux '77	1978	15.00

PRESTIGE

❏ PRLP-7242 [M]	Goin' to the Meeting	1962	40.00
❏ PRST-7242 [S]	Goin' to the Meeting	1962	50.00
❏ PRST-7660	In the Kitchen	1969	18.00
— Reissue of 7141 in (rechanneled?) stereo			
❏ PRLP-7261 [M]	I Only Have Eyes for You	1963	40.00
❏ PRST-7261 [S]	I Only Have Eyes for You	1963	50.00
❏ PRST-7834	Stolen Moments	197?	18.00
— Reissue of 7206 in (rechanneled?) stereo			
❏ PRLP-7141 [M]	The Eddie "Lockjaw" Davis Cookbook	1958	80.00
— Cover photo features Davis with no hat			
❏ PRLP-7141 [M]	The Eddie "Lockjaw" Davis Cookbook	1959	50.00
— Cover photo features Davis with hat			
❏ 24039	The Eddie "Lockjaw" Davis Cookbook	197?	25.00
❏ PRLP-7161 [M]	The Eddie "Lockjaw" Davis Cookbook, Vol. 2	1959	100.00
❏ PRLP-7219 [M]	The Eddie "Lockjaw" Davis Cookbook, Vol. 3	1961	50.00
❏ PRST-7219 [S]	The Eddie "Lockjaw" Davis Cookbook, Vol. 3	1961	40.00
❏ PRST-7782	The Rev.	197?	18.00
— Reissue of 7161 in (rechanneled?) stereo			
❏ PRLP-7271 [M]	Trackin'	1963	40.00
❏ PRST-7271 [S]	Trackin'	1963	50.00
❏ PRLP-7206 [M]	Trane Whistle	1961	50.00

RCA VICTOR

❏ LPM-3652 [M]	Lock the Fox	1966	25.00
❏ LSP-3652 [S]	Lock the Fox	1966	30.00
❏ LPM-3882 [M]	Love Calls	1967	30.00
❏ LSP-3882 [S]	Love Calls	1967	25.00
❏ LPM-3741 [M]	The Fox and the Hounds	1967	30.00
❏ LSP-3741 [S]	The Fox and the Hounds	1967	25.00

RIVERSIDE

❏ RLP-373 [M]	Afro-Jaws	1961	30.00
❏ RS-9373 [S]	Afro-Jaws	1961	40.00
❏ RLP-430 [M]	Jawbreakers	1962	30.00
❏ RS-9430 [S]	Jawbreakers	1962	40.00

ROOST

❏ RST-2227 [M]	Eddie Davis Trio	1957	100.00
❏ LP-422 [10]	Goodies	1954	150.00

ROULETTE

❏ R-52007 [M]	Count Basie Presents Eddie Davis	1958	60.00
— White label with color spokes			
❏ R-52007 [M]	Count Basie Presents Eddie Davis	1963	30.00
— Orange and yellow "roulette wheel" label			
❏ SR-52007 [S]	Count Basie Presents Eddie Davis	1959	50.00
— White label with color spokes			
❏ SR-52007 [S]	Count Basie Presents Eddie Davis	1963	25.00
— Orange and yellow "roulette wheel" label			
❏ R-52019 [M]	Eddie Davis Trio	1959	60.00
— White label with color spokes			
❏ R-52019 [M]	Eddie Davis Trio	1963	30.00
— Orange and yellow "roulette wheel" label			
❏ SR-52019 [S]	Eddie Davis Trio	1959	50.00
— White label with color spokes			
❏ SR-52019 [S]	Eddie Davis Trio	1963	25.00
— Orange and yellow "roulette wheel" label			

STEEPLECHASE

❏ SCS-1181	All of Me	198?	12.00
❏ SCS-1058	Swingin' Till the Girls Come Home	198?	12.00

DAVIS, JACKIE

CAPITOL

❏ T815 [M]	Chasing Shadows	1957	40.00
— Turquoise or gray label			
❏ T1180 [M]	Jackie Davis Meets the Trombones	1959	30.00
— Black colorband label, logo at left			

DAVIS, JESSE ED

ATCO

❏ SD 33-346	Jesse Ed Davis	1970	18.00
❏ SD 33-382	Ululu	1972	18.00

EPIC

❏ KE32133	Keep On Comin'	1973	15.00

DAVIS, JIMMIE

DECCA

❏ DL4868 [M]	Going Home for Christmas	1967	15.00
❏ DL74868 [S]	Going Home for Christmas	1967	15.00

Number	Title	Yr	NM
❏ DL8786 [M]	Hail Him with a Song	1958	30.00
❏ DL8572 [M]	Hymn Time	1957	30.00
❏ DL4587 [M]	It's Christmas Time Again	1964	15.00
❏ DL74587 [S]	It's Christmas Time Again	1964	18.00
❏ DL8174 [M]	Near the Cross	1955	30.00
❏ DL8953 [M]	Suppertime	1960	25.00
❏ DL78953 [S]	Suppertime	1960	30.00
❏ DL8729 [M]	The Door Is Always Open	1958	30.00
❏ DL8896 [M]	You Are My Sunshine	1959	25.00
❏ DL78896 [S]	You Are My Sunshine	1959	30.00

DAVIS, JOHNNY "SCAT

KING

❏ 626 [M]	Here's Lookin' Atcha	1959	80.00

DAVIS, LINK

MERCURY

❏ SR-61243	Cajun Crawdaddy	1969	25.00

DAVIS, MAC

ACCORD

❏ SN-7165	Little Touch of Love	1981	10.00
❏ SN-7189	With Love	1981	10.00

ALLEGIANCE

❏ AV-5031	Losers	198?	10.00
❏ AV-5019	Volume XC	198?	10.00

CASABLANCA

❏ NBLP7207	It's Hard to Be Humble	1980	10.00
❏ NBLP7257	Midnight Crazy	1981	10.00
❏ NBLP7239	Texas in My Rear View Mirror	1980	10.00
❏ 822638-1	The Very Best and More	1984	10.00

COLUMBIA

❏ PC32927	All the Love in the World	1975	12.00
❏ PCQ32927 [Q]	All the Love in the World	1975	18.00
❏ KC31770	Baby Don't Get Hooked on Me	1972	12.00
❏ CQ31770 [Q]	Baby Don't Get Hooked on Me	1972	18.00
❏ PC33551	Burnin' Thing	1975	12.00
❏ JC35284	Fantasy	1978	12.00
❏ PC34105	Forever Lovers	1976	12.00
❏ JC36317	Greatest Hits	1979	12.00
❏ C30926	I Believe in Music	1971	12.00
❏ KC32206	Mac Davis	1973	12.00
❏ CS9969	Song Painter	1970	18.00
— Red "360 Sound" label			
❏ CS9969	Song Painter	1974	12.00
— Orange label			
❏ KC32582	Stop and Smell the Roses	1974	12.00
❏ CQ32582 [Q]	Stop and Smell the Roses	1974	18.00
❏ PC34313	Thunder in the Afternoon	1976	12.00
❏ PCQ34313 [Q]	Thunder in the Afternoon	1976	18.00
❏ FC38950	Who's Lovin' You	1983	10.00

MCA

❏ 5718	Somewhere in America	1986	10.00
❏ 5590	Till I Made It with You	1985	10.00

SPRINGBOARD

❏ SPB-4024	Mac Davis	197?	10.00

TRIP

❏ 9502	Mac Davis	1973	10.00

DAVIS, MARTHA

CAPITOL

❏ CLT-48054	Policy	1988	15.00
❏ CLT-79197/8 [DJ]	Policy (Radio Cue Card)	1987	30.00

DAVIS, MAXWELL

ALADDIN

❏ LP-709 [10]	Maxwell Davis	1955	400.00
❏ LP-804 [M]	Maxwell Davis	1956	200.00

SCORE

❏ SLP-4106 [M]	Blue Tango	1957	200.00

DAVIS, MEL

EPIC

❏ LN3268 [M]	Trumpet with a Soul	1956	40.00

RCA CAMDEN

❏ CAL-2127 [M]	The Big Ones of '66	1966	15.00
❏ CAS-2127 [S]	The Big Ones of '66	1966	18.00

TIME

❏ 52087 [M]	Shoot the Trumpet Player	1962	25.00
❏ S-2087 [S]	Shoot the Trumpet Player	1962	30.00
❏ 52117 [M]	We Like Broadway	1963	25.00
❏ S-2117 [S]	We Like Broadway	1963	30.00

DAVIS, MILES, AND JOHN COLTRANE

MOODSVILLE

❏ MVLP-32 [M]	Miles Davis and John Coltrane Play Richard Rodgers	1963	50.00
— Green label			
❏ MVLP-32 [M]	Miles Davis and John Coltrane Play Richard Rodgers	1965	30.00
— Blue label, trident logo at right			

Number	Title	Yr	NM

PRESTIGE

❏ PRLP-7322 [M]	Miles Davis and John Coltrane Play Rodgers and Hart	1964	40.00
❏ PRST-7322 [R]	Miles Davis and John Coltrane Play Rodgers and Hart	1964	25.00

DAVIS, MILES, AND MARCUS MILLER

WARNER BROS.

❏ 25655	Music from Siesta	1987	18.00

DAVIS, MILES, AND TADD DAMERON

COLUMBIA

❏ JC34804	Paris Festival International, May 1949	1978	25.00

DAVIS, MILES, AND THELONIOUS MONK

COLUMBIA

❏ CL2178 [M]	Miles and Monk at Newport	1964	40.00
— "Guaranteed High Fidelity" on label			
❏ CL2178 [M]	Miles and Monk at Newport	1965	30.00
— "360 Sound Mono" on label			
❏ CS8978 [S]	Miles and Monk at Newport	1964	60.00
— "360 Sound Stereo" in black on label			
❏ CS8978 [S]	Miles and Monk at Newport	1965	30.00
— "360 Sound Stereo" in white on label			
❏ KCS8978	Miles and Monk at Newport	1974	12.00
— Orange label, new prefix			
❏ PC8978	Miles and Monk at Newport	1977	10.00
— Orange label, new prefix; some have bar codes			
❏ PC8978	Miles and Monk at Newport	199?	15.00
— 180-gram reissue			

DAVIS, MILES

ALA

❏ AJ-503	Archives of Jazz, Vol. 3	198?	15.00

BLUE NOTE

❏ BLP-5022 [10]	Miles Davis, Vol. 2	1953	1000.00
❏ BLP-5040 [10]	Miles Davis, Vol. 3	1954	1000.00
❏ BLP-1501 [M]	Miles Davis, Volume 1	1955	500.00
— Deep groove" version; Lexington Ave. address on label			
❏ BLP-1501 [M]	Miles Davis, Volume 1	1958	250.00
— Deep groove" version, W. 63rd St. address on label			
❏ BLP-1501 [M]	Miles Davis, Volume 1	1958	100.00
— Regular version, W. 63rd St. address on label			
❏ BLP-1501 [M]	Miles Davis, Volume 1	1963	40.00
— New York, USA" address on label			
❏ BLP-1501 [M]	Miles Davis, Volume 1	1966	25.00
— With "A Division of Liberty Records" on label			
❏ BLP-81501	Miles Davis, Volume 1	1968	18.00
— Rechanneled stereo version of 1501			
❏ BST-81501	Miles Davis, Volume 1	1985	15.00
— The Finest in Jazz Since 1939" reissue label			
❏ BLP-1502 [M]	Miles Davis, Volume 2	1955	500.00
— Deep groove" version; Lexington Ave. address on label			
❏ BLP-1502 [M]	Miles Davis, Volume 2	1955	250.00
— Deep groove" version; W. 63rd St. address on label			
❏ BLP-1502 [M]	Miles Davis, Volume 2	1958	100.00
— Regular version, W. 63rd St. address on label			
❏ BLP-1502 [M]	Miles Davis, Volume 2	1963	40.00
— With New York, USA address on label			
❏ BLP-1502 [M]	Miles Davis, Volume 2	1966	30.00
— With "A Division of Liberty Records" on label			
❏ BLP-81502	Miles Davis, Volume 2	1968	18.00
— Rechanneled stereo version of 1502			
❏ BST-81502	Miles Davis, Volume 2	1985	15.00
— The Finest in Jazz Since 1939" reissue label			
❏ BLP-5013 [10]	Miles Davis (Young Man with a Horn)	1952	1000.00

BOOK-OF-THE-MONTH CLUB

❏ 91-7725	Master of Styles	198?	40.00

CAPITOL

❏ T762 [M]	Birth of the Cool	1956	200.00
— Turquoise label			
❏ T1974 [M]	Birth of the Cool	1963	40.00
— Reissue of 762; black label with rainbow ring, Capitol logo at top			
❏ DT1974 [R]	Birth of the Cool	1963	18.00
❏ T762 [M]	Birth of the Cool	1958	100.00
— Black label wirh rainbow ring, Capitol logo at left			
❏ T762 [M]	Birth of the Cool	2003	40.00
— Classic Records reissue on 200-gram vinyl			
❏ H459 [10]	Classics in Jazz	1954	250.00
— First 33 1/3 rpm issue of some of the "Birth of the Cool" sessions			
❏ M-11026 [M]	The Complete Birth of the Cool	1972	25.00
❏ N-16168 [M]	The Complete Birth of the Cool	198?	12.00
— Budget-line reissue			

CHARLIE PARKER

❏ PLP-824	Many Miles of Davis	196?	50.00

COLUMBIA

❏ PG33967	Agharta	1976	40.00
❏ KC30455	A Tribute to Jack Johnson	1971	25.00
— Original issue			

Number	Title	Yr	NM
❑ PC30455	A Tribute to Jack Johnson	1977	10.00
—Orange label, new prefix; some with bar codes			
❑ PC30455	A Tribute to Jack Johnson	199?	15.00
—180-gram reissue			
❑ C2X45332	Aura	1989	30.00
❑ C32025	Basic Miles -- The Classic Performances of Miles Davis	1973	25.00
—Original prefix			
❑ PC32025	Basic Miles -- The Classic Performances of Miles Davis	198?	10.00
—Budget-line reissue; bar code on cover			
❑ PC32025	Basic Miles -- The Classic Performances of Miles Davis	199?	15.00
—180-gram reissue			
❑ CG32866	Big Fun	1974	30.00
—Original prefix			
❑ PG32866	Big Fun	1977	18.00
—Orange labels, new prefix			
❑ GP26	Bitches Brew	1970	60.00
—360 Sound Stereo" on red labels			
❑ GP26	Bitches Brew	1970	30.00
—Orange labels; no bar code on cover			
❑ GQ30997 [Q]	Bitches Brew	1972	60.00
❑ PG26	Bitches Brew	1977	18.00
—Orange labels, new prefix; some have bar code on cover			
❑ KC236278	Circle in the Round	1980	25.00
❑ FC38991	Decoy	1984	15.00
—Original issue			
❑ FC38991	Decoy	199?	15.00
—180-gram reissue			
❑ KC236472	Directions	1981	25.00
❑ CL2350 [M]	E.S.P.	1965	30.00
—Guaranteed High Fidelity" on label			
❑ CL2350 [M]	E.S.P.	1965	25.00
—360 Sound Mono" on label			
❑ CS9150 [S]	E.S.P.	1965	60.00
—360 Sound Stereo" in black on label			
❑ CS9150 [S]	E.S.P.	1965	50.00
—360 Sound Stereo" in white on label			
❑ CS9150	E.S.P.	1971	25.00
—Orange label			
❑ KCS9150	E.S.P.	1974	18.00
—Orange label, new prefix			
❑ PC9150	E.S.P.	1977	10.00
—Orange label, new prefix; some have bar code on back			
❑ PC9150	E.S.P.	199?	15.00
—180-gram reissue			
❑ J1	Facets	1973	15.00
❑ CS9750	Filles de Kilimanjaro	1969	25.00
—360 Sound Stereo" on red label			
❑ CS9750	Filles de Kilimanjaro	1971	15.00
—Orange label			
❑ KCS9750	Filles de Kilimanjaro	1974	12.00
—Orange label, new prefix			
❑ PC9750	Filles de Kilimanjaro	1977	10.00
—Orange label, new prefix; some have bar codes			
❑ PC9750	Filles de Kilimanjaro	199?	15.00
—180-gram reissue			
❑ CL2453 [M]	Four" & More -- Recorded Live in Concert	1966	30.00
❑ CS9253 [S]	Four" & More -- Recorded Live in Concert	1966	30.00
—360 Sound Stereo" on red label			
❑ CS9253	Four" & More -- Recorded Live in Concert	1971	18.00
—Orange label			
❑ KCS9253	Four" & More -- Recorded Live in Concert	1974	15.00
—Orange label, new prefix			
❑ PC9253	Four" & More -- Recorded Live in Concert	1977	10.00
—Orange label, new prefix; some have bar codes			
❑ PC9253	Four" & More -- Recorded Live in Concert	199?	15.00
—180-gram reissue			
❑ KG33236	Get Up With It	1974	30.00
—Original prefix			
❑ PG33236	Get Up With It	1977	25.00
—Orange labels, new prefix			
❑ C238506	Heard 'Round the World	1983	25.00
❑ CS9875	In a Silent Way	1969	40.00
—360 Sound Stereo" on red label			
❑ CS9875	In a Silent Way	1971	25.00
—Orange label			
❑ KCS9875	In a Silent Way	1974	15.00
—Orange label, new prefix			
❑ PC9875	In a Silent Way	1977	10.00
—Orange label, new prefix; some have bar codes			
❑ KG32092	In Concert	1973	30.00
❑ PG32092	In Concert	1977	18.00
—Orange labels, new prefix			
❑ S30455	Jack Johnson	1971	50.00
—Original issue on gray "Masterworks" label			
❑ C32470	Jazz at the Plaza, Vol. 1	1973	25.00
—Original prefix			
❑ PC32470	Jazz at the Plaza, Vol. 1	1977	10.00
—Reissue with new prefix; some have bar codes			
❑ PC32470	Jazz at the Plaza, Vol. 1	199?	15.00
—180-gram reissue			
❑ CL1268 [M]	Jazz Track	1958	100.00
—Red and black label with six "eye" logos; with abstract			

Number	Title	Yr	NM
drawing on cover			
❑ CL1268 [M]	Jazz Track	1958	70.00
—Red and black label with six "eye" logos; with Miles and a woman on cover			
❑ CL1355 [M]	Kind of Blue	1959	100.00
—Red and black label with six "eye" logos			
❑ CL1355 [M]	Kind of Blue	1963	50.00
—Guaranteed High Fidelity" on label			
❑ CL1355 [M]	Kind of Blue	1965	30.00
—360 Sound Mono" on label			
❑ CS8163 [S]	Kind of Blue	1959	250.00
—Black and red label with "Stereo Fidelity" at top and "Columbia" in white at bottom; six white "eye" logos on label			
❑ CS8163 [S]	Kind of Blue	1963	60.00
—360 Sound Stereo" in black on label			
❑ CS8163 [S]	Kind of Blue	1965	40.00
—360 Sound Stereo" in white on label			
❑ CS8163	Kind of Blue	1971	25.00
—Orange label			
❑ KCS8163	Kind of Blue	1974	15.00
—Orange label, new prefix			
❑ PC8163	Kind of Blue	1977	10.00
—Orange label, new prefix; some have bar codes			
❑ CS8163	Kind of Blue	1997	150.00
—Contains both the original Side 1, which was mastered slightly fast, and the "correct" Side 1 (as Side 3), with an alternate take of "Flamenco Sketches" on Side 4 (at 45 rpm); distributed by Classic Records			
❑ CS8163	Kind of Blue	2002	300.00
—Blue vinyl; 200-gram edition; distributed by Classic Records; approximately 100 copies were pressed			
❑ CS8163	Kind of Blue	2002	200.00
—Blue vinyl; 180-gram edition; distributed by Classic Records; 500 copies were pressed			
❑ CS8163-45	Kind of Blue	1999	100.00
—Distributed by Classic Records; pressed on four single-sided 12-inch 45 rpm records			
❑ CS8163	Kind of Blue	2001	30.00
—200-gram pressing; distributed by Classic Records; contains Side 1 at its "correct" speed			
❑ C238266	Live at the Plugged Nickel	1982	25.00
❑ C30954	Live-Evil	1971	30.00
—Original edition			
❑ GQ30954 [Q]	Live-Evil	1973	60.00
❑ CL1041 [M]	Miles Ahead	1957	200.00
—Red and black label with six "eye" logos; cover has a white woman and her child on a sailboat			
❑ CL1041 [M]	Miles Ahead	1957	100.00
—Red and black label with six "eye" logos; cover has Miles Davis blowing his trumpet			
❑ CL1041 [M]	Miles Ahead	1963	40.00
—Guaranteed High Fidelity" on label			
❑ CL1041 [M]	Miles Ahead	1965	30.00
—360 Sound Mono" on label			
❑ CS8633 [R]	Miles Ahead	1963	25.00
—Rechanneled stereo version of 1041; "360 Sound Stereo" in black on label			
❑ CS8633	Miles Ahead	1971	15.00
—Orange label			
❑ KCS8633	Miles Ahead	1974	12.00
—Orange label, new prefix			
❑ PC8633	Miles Ahead	1977	10.00
—Orange label, new prefix; some have bar codes			
❑ CS8633 [R]	Miles Ahead	1963	18.00
—360 Sound Stereo" in white on label			
❑ CL1812 [M]	Miles Davis at Carnegie Hall	1962	50.00
—Red and black label with six "eye" logos			
❑ CL1812 [M]	Miles Davis at Carnegie Hall	1963	30.00
—Guaranteed High Fidelity" on label			
❑ CL1812 [M]	Miles Davis at Carnegie Hall	1965	25.00
—Mono" on label			
❑ CS8612 [S]	Miles Davis at Carnegie Hall	1962	60.00
—Red and black label with six "eye" logos			
❑ CS8612 [S]	Miles Davis at Carnegie Hall	1962	30.00
—360 Sound Stereo" in black on label			
❑ CS8612 [S]	Miles Davis at Carnegie Hall	1965	30.00
—360 Sound Stereo" in white on label			
❑ CS8612	Miles Davis at Carnegie Hall	1971	18.00
—Orange label			
❑ KCS8612	Miles Davis at Carnegie Hall	1974	15.00
—Orange label, new prefix			
❑ PC8612	Miles Davis at Carnegie Hall	1977	10.00
—Orange label, new prefix; may have bar code on back cover			
❑ PC8612	Miles Davis at Carnegie Hall	199?	15.00
—180-gram vinyl reissue			
❑ G30038	Miles Davis at Fillmore	1970	30.00
—Original prefix			
❑ CG30038	Miles Davis at Fillmore	197?	18.00
—Later prefix			
❑ J17	Miles Davis at Newport	1973	15.00
❑ CS9808	Miles Davis' Greatest Hits	1969	25.00
—360 Sound Stereo" on red label			
❑ CS9808	Miles Davis' Greatest Hits	1971	15.00
—Orange label			
❑ KCS9808	Miles Davis' Greatest Hits	1974	12.00
—Orange label, new prefix			
❑ PC9808	Miles Davis' Greatest Hits	1977	10.00
—Orange label, new prefix; some have bar codes			
❑ PC9808	Miles Davis' Greatest Hits	199?	15.00
—180-gram reissue			

Number	Title	Yr	NM
❑ CL2183 [M]	Miles Davis in Europe	1964	40.00
—Guaranteed High Fidelity" on label			
❑ CL2183 [M]	Miles Davis in Europe	1965	30.00
—360 Sound Mono" on label			
❑ CS8983 [S]	Miles Davis in Europe	1964	40.00
—360 Sound Stereo" in black on label			
❑ CS8983 [S]	Miles Davis in Europe	1965	30.00
—360 Sound Stereo" in white on label			
❑ CS8983	Miles Davis in Europe	1971	18.00
—Orange label			
❑ KCS8983	Miles Davis in Europe	1974	15.00
—Orange label, new prefix			
❑ PC8983	Miles Davis in Europe	1977	10.00
—Orange label, new prefix; some have bar codes			
❑ PC8983	Miles Davis in Europe	199?	15.00
—180-gram reissue			
❑ CL1669 [M]	Miles Davis in Person, Vol. 1 (Friday Nights at the Blackhawk, San Francisco)	1961	30.00
—Red and black label with six "eye" logos; later pressings may exist			
❑ CS8469 [S]	Miles Davis in Person, Vol. 1 (Friday Nights at the Blackhawk, San Francisco)	1961	30.00
—Red and black label with six "eye" logos; later pressings may exist			
❑ CL1670 [M]	Miles Davis in Person, Vol. 2 (Saturday Nights at the Blackhawk, San Francisco)	1961	30.00
—Six "eye" logos on label; later pressings may exist			
❑ CS8470 [S]	Miles Davis in Person, Vol. 2 (Saturday Nights at the Blackhawk, San Francisco)	1961	30.00
—Six "eye" logos on label; later pressings may exist			
❑ C2L20 [M]	Miles Davis in Person (Friday & Saturday Nights at the Blackhawk, San Francisco)	1961	50.00
—Six "eye" logos on label			
❑ C2L20 [M]	Miles Davis in Person (Friday & Saturday Nights at the Blackhawk, San Francisco)	1963	30.00
—Guaranteed High Fidelity" on label			
❑ C2L20 [M]	Miles Davis in Person (Friday & Saturday Nights at the Blackhawk, San Francisco)	1965	30.00
Mono" on label			
❑ C2S820 [S]	Miles Davis in Person (Friday & Saturday Nights at the Blackhawk, San Francisco)	1961	60.00
—Red and black label with six "eye" logos			
❑ C2S820 [S]	Miles Davis in Person (Friday & Saturday Nights at the Blackhawk, San Francisco)	1963	30.00
—360 Sound Stereo" in black on label			
❑ C2S820 [S]	Miles Davis in Person (Friday & Saturday Nights at the Blackhawk, San Francisco)	1965	30.00
—360 Sound Stereo" in white on label			
❑ C2S820	Miles Davis in Person (Friday & Saturday Nights at the Blackhawk, San Francisco)	1971	10.00
—Orange labels			
❑ CL2828 [M]	Miles in the Sky	1968	150.00
❑ CS9628 [S]	Miles in the Sky	1968	30.00
—360 Sound Stereo" on red label			
❑ CS9628	Miles in the Sky	1971	18.00
—Orange label			
❑ KCS9628	Miles in the Sky	1974	15.00
—Orange label, new prefix			
❑ PC9628	Miles in the Sky	1977	10.00
—Orange label, new prefix; some have bar codes			
❑ PC9628	Miles in the Sky	199?	15.00
—180-gram reissue			
❑ CL2601 [M]	Miles Smiles	1966	40.00
❑ CS9401 [S]	Miles Smiles	1966	30.00
—360 Sound Stereo" on red label			
❑ CS9401	Miles Smiles	1971	18.00
—Orange label			
❑ KCS9401	Miles Smiles	1974	15.00
—Orange label, new prefix			
❑ PC9401	Miles Smiles	1977	10.00
—Orange label, new prefix; some have bar codes			
❑ PC9401	Miles Smiles	199?	15.00
—180-gram reissue			
❑ A2S1374 [DJ]	Miles to Go	1982	40.00
—Promo-only compilation			
❑ CL1193 [M]	Milestones	1958	80.00
—Red and black label with six "eye" logos			
❑ CL1193 [M]	Milestones	1963	40.00
—Guaranteed High Fidelity" on label			
❑ CL1193 [M]	Milestones	1965	30.00
—360 Sound Mono" on label			
❑ CL2628 [M]	Milestones	1967	30.00
—Reissue of 1193?			
❑ CS8021 [S]	Milestones	1959	200.00
—Red and black label with six "eye" logos			
❑ CS8021 [S]	Milestones	1963	100.00

Number	Title	Yr	NM
—360 Sound Stereo" in black on label			
❑ CS8021 [S]	Milestones	1965	60.00
—360 Sound Stereo" in white on label			
❑ CS9428 [R]	Milestones	1967	30.00
—360 Sound Stereo" on red label; reissue of 8021			
❑ KCS9428	Milestones	1974	15.00
—Orange label, new prefix			
❑ PC9428	Milestones	1977	10.00
—Orange label, new prefix; some have bar codes			
❑ CS9428	Milestones	1971	18.00
—Orange label			
❑ CL2306 [M]	My Funny Valentine	1965	30.00
—Guaranteed High Fidelity" on label			
❑ CL2306 [M]	My Funny Valentine	1965	25.00
—Mono" on label			
❑ CS9106 [S]	My Funny Valentine	1965	30.00
—360 Sound Stereo" in black on label			
❑ CS9106 [S]	My Funny Valentine	1965	25.00
—360 Sound Stereo" in white on label			
❑ CS9106	My Funny Valentine	1971	15.00
—Orange label			
❑ KCS9106	My Funny Valentine	1974	12.00
—Orange label, new prefix			
❑ PC9106	My Funny Valentine	1977	10.00
—Orange label, new prefix			
❑ CL2794 [M]	Nefertiti	1968	50.00
❑ CS9594 [S]	Nefertiti	1968	25.00
—360 Sound Stereo" on red label			
❑ CS9594	Nefertiti	1971	15.00
—Orange label			
❑ KCS9594	Nefertiti	1974	12.00
—Orange label, new prefix			
❑ PC9594	Nefertiti	1977	10.00
—Orange label, new prefix			
❑ KC31906	On the Corner	1972	15.00
❑ PC31906	On the Corner	1977	10.00
—Orange label, new prefix			
❑ CL1274 [M]	Porgy and Bess	1958	50.00
—Six "eye" logos on label			
❑ CL1274 [M]	Porgy and Bess	1963	30.00
—Guaranteed High Fidelity" on label			
❑ CL1274 [M]	Porgy and Bess	1965	25.00
—Mono" on label			
❑ CS8085 [S]	Porgy and Bess	1959	50.00
—Six "eye" logos on label			
❑ CS8085 [S]	Porgy and Bess	1963	30.00
—360 Sound Stereo" in black on label			
❑ CS8085 [S]	Porgy and Bess	1965	25.00
—360 Sound Stereo" in white on label			
❑ CS8085	Porgy and Bess	1971	15.00
—Orange label			
❑ KCS8085	Porgy and Bess	1974	12.00
—Orange label, new prefix			
❑ PC8085	Porgy and Bess	1977	10.00
—Orange label, new prefix			
❑ CL2106 [M]	Quiet Nights	1964	30.00
—Guaranteed High Fidelity" on label			
❑ CL2106 [M]	Quiet Nights	1965	25.00
—Mono" on label			
❑ CS8906 [S]	Quiet Nights	1964	30.00
—360 Sound Stereo" in black on label			
❑ CS8906 [S]	Quiet Nights	1965	25.00
—360 Sound Stereo" in white on label			
❑ CS8906	Quiet Nights	1971	15.00
—Orange label			
❑ KCS8906	Quiet Nights	1974	12.00
—Orange label, new prefix			
❑ PC8906	Quiet Nights	1977	10.00
—Orange label, new prefix			
❑ CL949 [M]	'Round About Midnight	1957	50.00
—Six "eye" logos on label			
❑ CL949 [M]	'Round About Midnight	1963	30.00
—Guaranteed High Fidelity" on label			
❑ CL949 [M]	'Round About Midnight	1965	25.00
—Mono" on label			
❑ CS8649 [R]	'Round About Midnight	1963	15.00
—Rechanneled stereo version of 949			
❑ CS8649	'Round About Midnight	1971	15.00
—Orange label			
❑ KCS8649	'Round About Midnight	1974	12.00
—Orange label, new prefix			
❑ PC8649	'Round About Midnight	1977	10.00
—Orange label, new prefix			
❑ CL2051 [M]	Seven Steps to Heaven	1963	30.00
—Guaranteed High Fidelity" on label			
❑ CL2051 [M]	Seven Steps to Heaven	1965	25.00
—Mono" on label			
❑ CS8851 [S]	Seven Steps to Heaven	1963	30.00
—360 Sound Stereo" in black on label			
❑ CS8851 [S]	Seven Steps to Heaven	1965	25.00
—360 Sound Stereo" in white on label			
❑ CS8851	Seven Steps to Heaven	1971	15.00
—Orange label			
❑ KCS8851	Seven Steps to Heaven	1974	12.00
—Orange label, new prefix			
❑ PC8851	Seven Steps to Heaven	1977	10.00
—Orange label, new prefix			
❑ CL1480 [M]	Sketches of Spain	1960	50.00

Number	Title	Yr	NM
—Six "eye" logos on label			
❑ CL1480 [M]	Sketches of Spain	1963	30.00
—Guaranteed High Fidelity" on label			
❑ CL1480 [M]	Sketches of Spain	1965	25.00
—Mono" on label			
❑ CS8271 [S]	Sketches of Spain	1960	80.00
—Red and black label with six "eye" logos			
❑ CS8271 [S]	Sketches of Spain	1963	30.00
—360 Sound Stereo" in black on label			
❑ CS8271 [S]	Sketches of Spain	1965	25.00
—360 Sound Stereo" in white on label			
❑ CS8271	Sketches of Spain	1971	15.00
—Orange label			
❑ KCS8271	Sketches of Spain	1974	12.00
—Orange label, new prefix			
❑ PC8271	Sketches of Spain	1977	10.00
—Orange label, new prefix			
❑ CS8271 [S]	Sketckes of Spain	1999	30.00
—Audiophile reissue; distributed by Classic Records			
❑ CL1656 [M]	Someday My Prince Will Come	1961	40.00
—Six "eye" logos on label			
❑ CL1656 [M]	Someday My Prince Will Come	1963	30.00
—Guaranteed High Fidelity" on label			
❑ CL1656 [M]	Someday My Prince Will Come	1965	25.00
—Mono" on label			
❑ CS8456 [S]	Someday My Prince Will Come	1961	40.00
—Six "eye" logos on label			
❑ CS8456 [S]	Someday My Prince Will Come	1963	30.00
—360 Sound Stereo" in black on label			
❑ CS8456 [S]	Someday My Prince Will Come	1965	25.00
—360 Sound Stereo" in white on label			
❑ CS8456 [B]	Someday My Prince Will Come	1971	15.00
—Orange label			
❑ KCS8456	Someday My Prince Will Come	1974	12.00
—Orange label, new prefix			
❑ PC8456	Someday My Prince Will Come	1977	10.00
—Orange label, new prefix			
❑ CL2732 [M]	Sorcerer	1967	30.00
❑ CS9532 [S]	Sorcerer	1967	25.00
—360 Sound Stereo" on red label			
❑ CS9532	Sorcerer	1971	15.00
—Orange label			
❑ KCS9532	Sorcerer	1974	12.00
—Orange label, new prefix			
❑ PC9532	Sorcerer	1977	10.00
—Orange label, new prefix			
❑ FC38657	Star People	1983	12.00
❑ C5X45000	The Columbia Years 1955-1985	1988	60.00
❑ FC36790	The Man with the Horn	1981	15.00
—Original edition			
❑ HC46790	The Man with the Horn	1982	50.00
—Half-Speed Mastered" on cover			
❑ PC36790	The Man with the Horn	198?	10.00
—Budget-line reissue with new prefix			
❑ PC36790	The Man with the Horn	199?	15.00
—180-gram reissue			
❑ C6X36976	The Miles Davis Collection Vol. 1: 12 Sides of Miles	1980	100.00
❑ PC34396	Water Babies	1977	15.00
—Original has no bar code			
❑ PC34396	Water Babies	198?	10.00
—Reissue with bar code			
❑ C238005	We Want Miles	1982	15.00
❑ FC40023	You're Under Arrest	1985	12.00

COLUMBIA JAZZ MASTERPIECES

Number	Title	Yr	NM
❑ CJ44151	Ballads	1988	12.00
❑ CJ44151	Ballads	199?	15.00
—180-gram reissue			
❑ C2J40577	Bitches Brew	1987	18.00
❑ CJ40645	Cookin' at the Plugged Nickel	1987	18.00
❑ CJ40580	In a Silent Way	1987	12.00
❑ CJ40580	In a Silent Way	199?	15.00
—180-gram reissue			
❑ CJ40579	Kind of Blue	1987	18.00
—Reissue; when this version of the album was prepared, Columbia discovered that all of Side 1 on the original LP was mastered at the wrong speed; this album was the first time it was mastered "correctly			
❑ CJ40609	Live Miles: More Music from the Legendary Carnegie Hall Concert	1987	12.00
❑ CJ40609	Live Miles: More Music from the Legendary Carnegie Hall Concert	199?	15.00
—180-gram reissue			
❑ CJ40784	Miles Ahead	1987	12.00
❑ CJ40784	Miles Ahead	199?	15.00
—180-gram reissue			
❑ CJ44052	Miles and Coltrane	1988	12.00
❑ CJ44052	Miles and Coltrane	199?	15.00
—180-gram reissue			
❑ CJ44257	Miles Davis in Person, Vol. 1 (Friday Nights at the Blackhawk, San Francisco)	1988	12.00
❑ CJ44257	Miles Davis in Person, Vol. 1 (Friday Nights at the Blackhawk, San Francisco)	199?	15.00
—180-gram reissue			
❑ CJ44425	Miles Davis in Person, Vol. 2 (Saturday Nights at the Blackhawk, San Francisco)	1989	12.00
❑ CJ40837	Milestones	1987	12.00
❑ CJ40837	Milestones	199?	15.00
—180-gram reissue			
❑ CJ40647	Porgy and Bess	1987	12.00
❑ CJ40610	'Round About Midnight	1987	12.00
❑ CJ40578	Sketches of Spain	1987	12.00
❑ CJ40947	Someday My Prince Will Come	1987	12.00

COLUMBIA LIMITED EDITION

Number	Title	Yr	NM
❑ LE10018	Miles Davis in Person, Vol. 1 (Friday Nights at the Blackhawk, San Francisco)	197?	18.00
❑ LE10076	Miles Davis in Person, Vol. 2 (Saturday Nights at the Blackhawk, San Francisco)	197?	18.00

COLUMBIA SPECIAL PRODUCTS

Number	Title	Yr	NM
❑ P13811	Facets	1977	15.00

CONTEMPORARY

Number	Title	Yr	NM
❑ C-7645	Miles Davis and the Lighthouse All-Stars At Last!	1985	18.00

DEBUT

Number	Title	Yr	NM
❑ DEB120 [M]	Blue Moods	1955	400.00

EVEREST ARCHIVE OF FOLK & JAZZ

Number	Title	Yr	NM
❑ FS-283	Miles Davis	197?	12.00

FANTASY

Number	Title	Yr	NM
❑ OJC-245	Bags Groove	1987	15.00
—Reissue of Prestige 7109			
❑ OJC-093	Blue Haze	198?	15.00
—Reissue of Prestige 7054			
❑ 6001 [M]	Blue Moods	1962	150.00
—Reissue of Debut album; red vinyl			
❑ 6001 [M]	Blue Moods	1963	70.00
—Black vinyl, red label			
❑ 86001 [R]	Blue Moods	1962	60.00
—Blue vinyl			
❑ 86001 [R]	Blue Moods	1963	30.00
—Black vinyl, blue label			
❑ OJC-043	Blue Moods	198?	15.00
—Reissue of Fantasy 6001			
❑ OJC-071	Collectors' Item	198?	15.00
—Reissue of Prestige 7044			
❑ OJC-128	Cookin' with the Miles Davis Quintet	198?	15.00
—Reissue of Prestige 7094			
❑ OJC-005	Dig Miles Davis/Sonny Rollins	198?	15.00
—Reissue of Prestige 7012			
❑ OJC-053	Miles Davis and Horns	198?	15.00
—Reissue of Prestige 7025			
❑ OJC-480	Miles Davis and the Lighthouse All-Stars At Last!	1991	15.00
—Reissue of Contemporary 7645			
❑ OJC-012	Miles Davis and the Milt Jackson Quintet/Sextet	198?	12.00
—Reissue of Prestige 7034			
❑ OJC-347	Miles Davis and the Modern Jazz Giants	198?	15.00
—Reissue of Prestige 7150			
❑ OJC-006	Miles -- The New Miles Davis Quintet	198?	15.00
—Reissue of Prestige 7014			
❑ OJC-190	Relaxin' with the Miles Davis Quintet	1985	12.00
—Reissue of Prestige 7129			
❑ OJC-391	Steamin' with the Miles Davis Quintet	1989	12.00
—Reissue of Prestige 7200			
❑ OJC-004	The Musings of Miles	198?	15.00
—Reissue of Prestige 7007			
❑ OJC-213	Walkin'	1987	12.00
—Reissue of Prestige 7076			
❑ OJC-296	Workin' with the Miles Davis Quintet	1987	12.00
—Reissue of Prestige 7166			

FONTANA

Number	Title	Yr	NM
❑ MGF-27532 [M]	Jazz on the Screen	1965	40.00
—With Art Blakey and the Jazz Messengers			
❑ SRF-67532 [S]	Jazz on the Screen	1965	40.00

JAZZ HERITAGE

Number	Title	Yr	NM
❑ 913427F [M]	Dig Miles Davis/Sonny Rollins	198?	18.00
—Mail-order reissue			

MOBILE FIDELITY

Number	Title	Yr	NM
❑ MFSL1-376 [B]	Four & More - Recorded Live In Concert	2013	40.00
❑ MFSL1-377 [B]	In A Silent Way	2013	35.00
❑ MFSL1-374 [B]	Milestones	2013	35.00
❑ MFSL1-373 [B]	Round About Midnight	2013	30.00
❑ MFSL1-375 [B]	Sketches of Spain	2013	35.00
❑ 1-177	Someday My Prince Will Come	1985	80.00
—Audiophile vinyl			

Number	Title	Yr	NM
MOSAIC			
❑ MQ11-164	Miles Davis & Gil Evans: The Complete Columbia Studio Recordings	1996	400.00
❑ MQ6-183	The Complete Bitches Brew Sessions	1999	100.00
❑ MQ6-220	The Complete Blackhawk Sessions	2003	100.00
❑ MQ9-191	The Complete Columbia Recordings of Miles Davis with John Coltrane	2000	170.00
❑ MQ5-209	The Complete In a Silent Way Sessions (September 1968-February 1969)	2002	80.00
❑ MQ10-158	The Complete Plugged Nickel Sessions	1995	300.00
❑ MQ10-177	The Complete Studio Recordings of the Miles Davis Quintet 1965-June 1968	1998	150.00
PAIR			
❑ PDL2-1095	Best of Miles Davis	1986	15.00
PHILIPS			
❑ 836305-1	Elevator to the Scaffold (L'Ancenseur Pour L'Echafaud)	198?	15.00
—Reissue of Columbia 1268			
PRESTIGE			
❑ PRLP-7076 [M]	All Stars	1957	200.00
—With W. 50th St. address on yellow label			
❑ PRLP-7076 [M]	All Stars	196?	40.00
—With trident on blue label			
❑ PRLP-7076 [M]	All Stars	1958	100.00
—With Bergenfield, N.J. address on yellow label			
❑ PRLP-7109 [M]	Bags Groove	1957	200.00
—With W. 50th St. address on yellow label			
❑ PRLP-7109 [M]	Bags Groove	196?	40.00
—With trident on blue label			
❑ PRLP-7109 [M]	Bags Groove	1958	100.00
—With Bergenfield, N.J. address on yellow label			
❑ PRLP-7054 [M]	Blue Haze	1956	200.00
—With W. 50th St. address on yellow label			
❑ PRLP-7054 [M]	Blue Haze	196?	40.00
—With trident on blue label			
❑ PRLP-140 [10]	Blue Period	1953	250.00
❑ P-12	Chronicle: The Complete Prestige Recordings	1980	150.00
❑ PRLP-7044 [M]	Collectors' Item	1956	200.00
—With W. 50th St. address on yellow label			
❑ PRLP-7044 [M]	Collectors' Item	196?	40.00
—With trident on blue label			
❑ P-24022	Collector's Items	1973	25.00
❑ PRST-7744 [R]	Conception	1970	25.00
❑ PRLP-7094 [M]	Cookin' with the Miles Davis Quintet	1957	300.00
—With W. 50th St. address on yellow label			
❑ PRLP-7094 [M]	Cookin' with the Miles Davis Quintet	196?	40.00
—With trident on blue label			
❑ PRLP-7094 [M]	Cookin' with the Miles Davis Quintet	1958	120.00
—With Bergenfield, N.J. address on yellow label			
❑ P-24054	Dig	197?	18.00
❑ PRLP-7281 [M]	Diggin'	1963	100.00
—Reissue of 7012; with Bergenfield, NJ address on yellow label			
❑ PRLP-7281 [M]	Diggin'	196?	40.00
—With trident on blue label			
❑ PRST-7281 [R]	Diggin'	1963	30.00
❑ PRLP-7012 [M]	Dig Miles Davis/Sonny Rollins	1956	250.00
—Gray cover			
❑ PRLP-7012 [M]	Dig Miles Davis/Sonny Rollins	1957	200.00
—Color cover; yellow label with W. 50th St. address			
❑ PRLP-7168 [M]	Early Miles	1959	150.00
—Reissue of 7025; with Bergenfield, NJ address on yellow label			
❑ PRLP-7168 [M]	Early Miles	196?	40.00
—With trident on blue label			
❑ PRST-7674 [R]	Early Miles	1969	18.00
—Reissue of 7168			
❑ P-24064	Green Haze	1976	25.00
❑ PRLP-7373 [M]	Jazz Classics	1965	30.00
❑ PRST-7373 [R]	Jazz Classics	1965	25.00
❑ PRST-7822 [R]	Miles Ahead!	1971	18.00
❑ PR-24001	Miles Davis	1972	25.00
❑ PRLP-196 [10]	Miles Davis All Stars, Volume 1	1955	250.00
❑ PRLP-200 [10]	Miles Davis All Stars, Volume 2	1955	250.00
❑ PRLP-7025 [M]	Miles Davis and Horns	1956	400.00
—Yellow label with W. 50th St. address			
❑ PRLP-7025 [M]	Miles Davis and Horns	1958	250.00
—Yellow label, Bergenfield, N.J. address			
❑ PRLP-7034 [M]	Miles Davis and the Milt Jackson Quintet/Sextet	1956	400.00
—With W. 50th St. address on yellow label			
❑ PRLP-7034 [M]	Miles Davis and the Milt Jackson Quintet/Sextet	196?	40.00
—With trident on blue label			
❑ PRLP-7034 [M]	Miles Davis and the Milt Jackson Quintet/Sextet	1958	250.00
—Yellow label with Bergenfield, N.J. address			

Number	Title	Yr	NM
❑ PRLP-7150 [M]	Miles Davis and the Modern Jazz Giants	1958	250.00
—With Bergenfield, NJ address on yellow label			
❑ PRLP-7150 [M]	Miles Davis and the Modern Jazz Giants	196?	40.00
—With trident on blue label			
❑ PRST-7650 [R]	Miles Davis and the Modern Jazz Giants	1969	25.00
—Reissue of 7150			
❑ 16-3 [M]	Miles Davis and the Modern Jazz Giants	1957	1000.00
—This album plays at 16 2/3 rpm and is marked as such; white label			
❑ PRLP-161 [10]	Miles Davis Featuring Sonny Rollins	1953	250.00
❑ PRLP-7457 [M]	Miles Davis' Greatest Hits	1967	30.00
❑ PRST-7457 [R]	Miles Davis' Greatest Hits	1967	18.00
❑ PRLP-154 [10]	Miles Davis Plays Al Cohn Compositions	1953	250.00
❑ PRLP-7352 [M]	Miles Davis Plays for Lovers	1965	30.00
❑ PRST-7352 [R]	Miles Davis Plays for Lovers	1965	25.00
❑ PRLP-7322 [M]	Miles Davis Plays Richard Rodgers	1964	30.00
❑ PRST-7322 [R]	Miles Davis Plays Richard Rodgers	1964	25.00
❑ PRLP-185 [10]	Miles Davis Quintet	1954	250.00
❑ PRLP-187 [10]	Miles Davis Quintet Featuring Sonny Rollins	1954	250.00
❑ PRLP-182 [10]	Miles Davis Sextet	1954	250.00
❑ PRLP-7014 [M]	Miles -- The New Miles Davis Quintet	1956	300.00
—Yellow label with W. 50th St. address			
❑ PRST-7540 [R]	Odyssey	1968	15.00
—Reissue of 7034			
❑ PRST-7847	Oleo	1972	15.00
❑ PRLP-7129 [M]	Relaxin' with the Miles Davis Quintet	1957	300.00
—With W. 50th St. address on yellow label			
❑ PRLP-7129 [M]	Relaxin' with the Miles Davis Quintet	196?	40.00
—With trident on blue label			
❑ PRLP-7129 [M]	Relaxin' with the Miles Davis Quintet	1957	120.00
—With Bergenfield, NJ address on yellow label			
❑ PRST 7580 [R]	Steamin'	1968	15.00
—Reissue of 7200			
❑ PRLP-7200 [M]	Steamin' with the Miles Davis Quintet	1961	80.00
—With Bergenfield, NJ address on yellow label			
❑ PRLP-7200 [M]	Steamin' with the Miles Davis Quintet	196?	30.00
—With trident on blue label			
❑ PRLP-7221 [M]	The Beginning	1962	50.00
—Reissue of 7007; with Bergenfield, NJ address on yellow label			
❑ PRLP-7221 [M]	The Beginning	196?	30.00
—With trident on blue label			
❑ PRLP-7007 [M]	The Musings of Miles	1955	400.00
—Yellow label with W. 50th St. address			
❑ PRLP-124 [10]	The New Sounds of Miles Davis	195?	250.00
❑ PRLP-7254 [M]	The Original Quintet	1963	50.00
—Reissue of 7014; with Bergenfield, NJ address on yellow label			
❑ PRLP-7254 [M]	The Original Quintet	196?	30.00
—With trident on blue label			
❑ PRST-7254 [R]	The Original Quintet	1963	25.00
❑ 24012	The Tallest Trees	1972	18.00
❑ 24077	Tune Up	197?	15.00
❑ PRST-7608 [R]	Walkin'	1969	15.00
—Reissue of 7076			
❑ 24034	Workin' and Steamin'	1973	18.00
❑ PRLP-7166 [M]	Workin' with the Miles Davis Quintet	1959	80.00
—With Bergenfield, NJ address on yellow label			
❑ PRLP-7166 [M]	Workin' with the Miles Davis Quintet	196?	30.00
—With trident on blue label			
SAVOY JAZZ			
❑ SJL-1196	First Miles	1989	15.00
TRIP			
❑ 5015	Miles of Jazz	1974	12.00
UNITED ARTISTS			
❑ UAS-9952	Miles Davis	1972	25.00
—Reissue of Blue Note material			
WARNER BROS.			
❑ 25873	Amandla	1989	25.00
❑ 26938	Doo-Bop	1992	18.00
❑ 25490	Tutu	1986	12.00

DAVIS, PAUL

Number	Title	Yr	NM
ARISTA			
❑ AL9578	Cool Night	1981	12.00
❑ AL8376	Cool Night	198?	10.00
—Reissue of 9578			
BANG			
❑ BLPS-223	A Little Bit of Paul Davis	1970	40.00
❑ JZ36094	Paul Davis	1980	12.00
❑ 401	Ride 'Em Cowboy	1974	15.00
❑ 410	Singer of Songs -- Teller of Tales	1977	15.00
❑ 405	Southern Tracks and Fantasies	1976	15.00
❑ PZ37973	The Best of Paul Davis	1982	12.00

DAVIS, REVEREND GARY

Number	Title	Yr	NM
BLUESVILLE			
❑ BVLP-1032 [M]	A Little More Faith	1961	100.00
—Blue label, silver print			
❑ BVLP-1032 [M]	A Little More Faith	1964	30.00
—Blue label with trident logo			
❑ BVLP-1015 [M]	Harlem Street Singer	1961	100.00
—Blue label, silver print			
❑ BVLP-1015 [M]	Harlem Street Singer	1964	30.00
—Blue label with trident logo			
❑ BVLP-1049 [M]	Say No to the Devil	1962	100.00
—Blue label, silver print			
❑ BVLP-1049 [M]	Say No to the Devil	1964	30.00
—Blue label with trident logo			
FOLKLORE			
❑ F-14033 [M]	Guitar and Banjo	196?	40.00
❑ F-14028 [M]	Pure Religion	196?	40.00
STINSON			
❑ SLP-56 [10]	The Singing Reverend	195?	100.00

DAVIS, SAMMY, JR., AND CARMEN MCRAE

Number	Title	Yr	NM
DECCA			
❑ DL8490 [M]	Boy Meets Girl	1957	30.00

DAVIS, SAMMY, JR., AND COUNT BASIE

Number	Title	Yr	NM
MGM			
❑ SE-4825	Sammy Davis Jr. and Count Basie	1972	12.00
—Reissue of Verve LP?			
VERVE			
❑ V-8605 [M]	Our Shining Hour	1965	15.00
❑ V6-8605 [S]	Our Shining Hour	1965	18.00

DAVIS, SAMMY, JR.

Number	Title	Yr	NM
DECCA			
❑ DL8779 [M]	All the Way And Then Some	1958	30.00
❑ DL4381 [M]	Forget-Me-Nots for First Nighters	1963	18.00
❑ DL74381 [S]	Forget-Me-Nots for First Nighters	1963	25.00
❑ DL8351 [M]	Here's Looking at You	1956	30.00
❑ DL8981 [M]	I Got a Right to Swing	1960	25.00
❑ DL78981 [S]	I Got a Right to Swing	1960	30.00
❑ DL8641 [M]	It's All Over But the Swingin'	1957	30.00
❑ DL8170 [M]	Just for Lovers	1955	30.00
❑ DL8676 [M]	Mood to Be Wooed	1958	30.00
❑ DL4153 [M]	Mr. Entertainment	1961	18.00
❑ DL74153 [S]	Mr. Entertainment	1961	25.00
❑ DL8854 [M]	Porgy and Bess	1959	25.00
❑ DL78854 [S]	Porgy and Bess	1959	30.00
❑ DL8841 [M]	Sammy Davis, Jr., at Town Hall	1959	25.00
❑ DL78841 [S]	Sammy Davis, Jr., at Town Hall	1959	30.00
❑ DL8486 [M]	Sammy Swings	1957	30.00
❑ DL8118 [M]	Starring Sammy Davis, Jr.	1955	30.00
❑ DXB192 [M]	The Best of Sammy Davis, Jr.	1966	18.00
❑ DXSB7192 [S]	The Best of Sammy Davis, Jr.	1966	25.00
❑ DL8921 [M]	The Sammy Awards	1960	25.00
❑ DL78921 [S]	The Sammy Awards	1960	30.00
❑ DL4582 [M]	Try a Little Tenderness	1965	15.00
❑ DL74582 [S]	Try a Little Tenderness	1965	18.00
HARMONY			
❑ HS11305	Let There Be Love	1970	12.00
❑ HS11299	The Great Sammy Davis, Jr.	196?	15.00
❑ H30568	What Kind of Fool Am I	1971	12.00
MCA			
❑ 4109	Sammy Davis Jr. At His Greatest	1975	15.00
MGM			
❑ SE-4852	Portrait of Sammy Davis, Jr.	1972	12.00
❑ SE-4832	Sammy Davis Jr. Now	1972	12.00
❑ M3G-4965	That's Entertainment!	1974	12.00
MOTOWN			
❑ 4519ML	Hello Detroit!	1984	12.00
❑ MS710	Something for Everyone	1970	15.00
PICKWICK			
❑ SPC-3002	The Many Faces of Sammy Davis, Jr.	196?	12.00
REPRISE			
❑ R-6033 [M]	All Star Spectacular	1962	18.00
❑ R9-6033 [S]	All Star Spectacular	1962	25.00
❑ R-6082 [M]	As Long As She Needs Me	1963	18.00
❑ R9-6082 [S]	As Long As She Needs Me	1963	25.00
❑ R-6126 [M]	California Suite	1964	18.00
❑ RS-6126 [S]	California Suite	1964	25.00
❑ R-6159 [M]	If I Ruled the World	1965	15.00
❑ RS-6159 [S]	If I Ruled the World	1965	18.00
❑ RS-6324	I've Gotta Be Me	1969	15.00
❑ RS-6308	Lonely Is the Name	1968	15.00
❑ R-2010 [M]	Sammy Davis, Jr., Belts the Best of Broadway	1962	18.00
❑ R9-2010 [S]	Sammy Davis, Jr., Belts the Best of Broadway	1962	25.00
❑ RS-6410	Sammy Davis, Jr., Steps Out	1970	15.00
❑ RS-6291	Sammy Davis, Jr.'s Greatest Hits	1968	15.00

Number	Title	Yr	NM
❏ R-6236 [M]	Sammy Davis. Jr., Sings/ Laurindo Almeida Plays	1966	15.00
❏ RS-6236 [S]	Sammy Davis. Jr., Sings/ Laurindo Almeida Plays	1966	18.00
❏ R-6063 [M]	Sammy Davis Jr. at the Cocoanut Grove	1963	25.00
❏ R9-6063 [S]	Sammy Davis Jr. at the Cocoanut Grove	1963	30.00
❏ R-6095 [M]	Sammy Davis Jr. Salutes the Stars of the London Palladium	1964	18.00
❏ RS-6095 [S]	Sammy Davis Jr. Salutes the Stars of the London Palladium	1964	25.00
❏ R-6131 [M]	Sammy Davis Jr. Sings the Big Ones for Young Lovers	1964	15.00
❏ RS-6131 [S]	Sammy Davis Jr. Sings the Big Ones for Young Lovers	1964	18.00
❏ R-6264 [M]	Sammy Davis Jr. Sings the Complete Dr. Dolittle	1967	25.00
❏ RS-6264 [S]	Sammy Davis Jr. Sings the Complete Dr. Dolittle	1967	15.00
❏ R-6169 [M]	Sammy's Back on Broadway	1965	15.00
❏ RS-6169 [S]	Sammy's Back on Broadway	1965	18.00
❏ R-6237 [M]	That's All	1967	18.00
❏ RS-6237 [S]	That's All	1967	25.00
❏ RS-6339	The Goin's Great	1969	15.00
❏ R-6164 [M]	The Nat Cole Song Book	1965	15.00
❏ RS-6164 [S]	The Nat Cole Song Book	1965	18.00
❏ R-6188 [M]	The Sammy Davis, Jr., Show	1965	15.00
❏ RS-6188 [S]	The Sammy Davis, Jr., Show	1965	18.00
❏ R-6114 [M]	The Shelter of Your Arms	1964	18.00
❏ RS-6114 [S]	The Shelter of Your Arms	1964	25.00
❏ R-6214 [M]	The Sounds of '66	1966	15.00
❏ RS-6214 [S]	The Sounds of '66	1966	18.00
❏ R-2003 [M]	The Wham of Sam	1961	18.00
❏ R9-2003 [S]	The Wham of Sam	1961	25.00
❏ R-6096 [M]	Treasury of Golden Hits	1964	18.00
❏ RS-6096 [S]	Treasury of Golden Hits	1964	25.00
❏ R-6051 [M]	What Kind of Fool Am I and Other Show-Stoppers	1962	18.00
❏ R9-6051 [S]	What Kind of Fool Am I and Other Show-Stoppers	1962	25.00
❏ R-6144 [M]	When the Feeling Hits You	1965	15.00
❏ RS-6144 [S]	When the Feeling Hits You	1965	18.00

WARNER BROS.

Number	Title	Yr	NM
❏ BSK3128	Live Performance	1977	12.00

WARNER SPECIAL PRODUCTS

Number	Title	Yr	NM
❏ OP-1501	The Sound of Sammy	1978	12.00
—Special item for Alka-Seltzer			

DAVIS, SKEETER, AND NRBQ

ROUNDER

Number	Title	Yr	NM
❏ 3092	She Sings, They Play	1986	15.00

DAVIS, SKEETER

GUSTO

Number	Title	Yr	NM
❏ 0014	Best of the Best	1978	12.00

RCA CAMDEN

Number	Title	Yr	NM
❏ CAL-899 [M]	Blueberry Hill and Other Favorites	1965	15.00
❏ CAS-899 [S]	Blueberry Hill and Other Favorites	1965	18.00
❏ CAS-2367	Easy to Love	1970	15.00
❏ CAS-2517	Foggy Mountain Top	1971	15.00
❏ ACL1-0622	He Wakes Me with a Kiss	1974	12.00
❏ CAL-818 [M]	I Forgot More Than You'll Ever Know	196?	15.00
❏ CAS-818(e) [R]	I Forgot More Than You'll Ever Know	196?	18.00
❏ CAS-2607	The End of the World	1972	12.00

RCA VICTOR

Number	Title	Yr	NM
❏ LSP-4310	A Place in the Country	1970	18.00
❏ LSP-4642	Bring It on Home	1972	18.00
❏ LPM-2736 [M]	Cloudy, With Occasional Tears	1963	30.00
❏ LSP-2736 [S]	Cloudy, With Occasional Tears	1963	30.00
❏ LPM-3763 [M]	Hand in Hand with Jesus	1967	30.00
❏ LSP-3763 [S]	Hand in Hand with Jesus	1967	25.00
❏ LPM-2327 [M]	Here's the Answer	1961	30.00
❏ LSP-2327 [S]	Here's the Answer	1961	30.00
❏ LSP-4818	Hillbilly Singer	1972	18.00
❏ APL1-0322	I Can't Believe That It's All Over	1974	15.00
❏ LPM-2197 [M]	I'll Sing You a Song and Harmonize, Too	1960	30.00
❏ LSP-2197 [S]	I'll Sing You a Song and Harmonize, Too	1960	30.00
❏ LSP-4055	I Love Flatt & Scruggs	1968	25.00
❏ LSP-4382	It's Hard to Be a Woman	1970	18.00
❏ LPM-2980 [M]	Let Me Get Close to You	1964	25.00
❏ LSP-2980 [S]	Let Me Get Close to You	1964	30.00
❏ LSP-4557	Love Takes a Lot	1971	18.00
❏ LSP-4200	Maryfrances	1969	25.00
❏ LPM-3667 [M]	My Heart's in the Country	1966	25.00
❏ LSP-3667 [S]	My Heart's in the Country	1966	30.00
❏ LPM-3567 [M]	Singin' in the Summer Sun	1966	25.00
❏ LSP-3567 [S]	Singin' in the Summer Sun	1966	30.00
❏ LSP-4486	Skeeter	1971	18.00
❏ LPM-3790 [M]	Skeeter Davis Sings Buddy Holly	1967	50.00
❏ LSP-3790 [S]	Skeeter Davis Sings Buddy Holly	1967	40.00
❏ LSP-4732	Skeeter Sings Dolly	1972	18.00
❏ LPM-3463 [M]	Skeeter Sings Standards	1965	25.00
❏ LSP-3463 [S]	Skeeter Sings Standards	1965	30.00
❏ LPM-3374 [M]	The Best of Skeeter Davis	1965	25.00
❏ LSP-3374 [S]	The Best of Skeeter Davis	1965	30.00
❏ APL1-0190	The Best of Skeeter Davis, Volume 2	1973	15.00
❏ LSP-4124	The Closest Thing to Love	1969	25.00
❏ LPM-2699 [M]	The End of the World	1963	30.00
❏ LSP-2699 [S]	The End of the World	1963	30.00
❏ LPM-3876 [M]	What Does It Take (To Keep a Man Like You Satisfied)	1967	30.00
❏ LSP-3876 [S]	What Does It Take (To Keep a Man Like You Satisfied)	1967	25.00
❏ LPM-3960 [M]	Why So Lonely?	1968	50.00
❏ LSP-3960 [S]	Why So Lonely?	1968	25.00
❏ LPM-3382 [M]	Written by the Stars	1965	25.00
❏ LSP-3382 [S]	Written by the Stars	1965	30.00

DAVIS, SPENCER, GROUP

ALLEGIANCE

Number	Title	Yr	NM
❏ AV-442	Crossfire	1983	12.00

DATE

Number	Title	Yr	NM
❏ TES-4021 [B]	Funky	1971	250.00
—Deleted almost immediately upon release			

MEDIARTS

Number	Title	Yr	NM
❏ 41-11	It's Been So Long	1971	15.00

RHINO

Number	Title	Yr	NM
❏ RNLP117	The Best of the Spencer Davis Group	1983	10.00
❏ RNLP70172	The Best of the Spencer Davis Group (Golden Archive Series)	1987	15.00

UNITED ARTISTS

Number	Title	Yr	NM
❏ UAL3578 [M]	Gimme Some Lovin'	1967	50.00
❏ UAS6578 [R]	Gimme Some Lovin'	1967	40.00
❏ ST-91127 [R]	Gimme Some Lovin'	1967	50.00
—Capitol Record Club edition			
❏ UAS6691	Heavies	1969	25.00
❏ UAL3589 [M]	I'm a Man	1967	40.00
❏ UAS6589 [S]	I'm a Man	1967	50.00
❏ UAS6641 [P]	The Spencer Davis Group's Greatest Hits	1968	30.00
❏ UA-LA433-E	The Very Best of the Spencer Davis Group	1975	12.00
❏ UAS6652	With Their New Face On	1968	25.00

VERTIGO

Number	Title	Yr	NM
❏ VEL-1015 [B]	Gluggo	1973	25.00
❏ VEL-1021 [B]	Living in a Back Street	1974	25.00

DAVIS, TYRONE

COLUMBIA

Number	Title	Yr	NM
❏ JC36230	Can't You Tell It's Me	1979	15.00
❏ FC37366	Everything in Place	1981	15.00
❏ JC35305	I Can't Go On This Way	1978	15.00
❏ JC36598	I Just Can't Keep On Going	1980	15.00
❏ JC35723	In the Mood with Tyrone Davis	1979	15.00
❏ PC34654	Let's Be Closer Together	1977	15.00
❏ PC34268	Love and Touch	1976	15.00
❏ PC37979	The Best of Tyrone Davis	1982	12.00

DAKAR

Number	Title	Yr	NM
❏ DK-9005	Can I Change My Mind	1969	30.00
❏ DK-76915	Homewrecker	1975	25.00
❏ DK-76901	I Had It All the Time	1972	30.00
❏ DK-76909	It's All in the Game	1974	25.00
❏ DK-9027	Turn Back the Hands of Time	1970	30.00
❏ DK-76918	Turning Point	1976	25.00
❏ DK-76902	Tyrone Davis' Greatest Hits	1972	30.00
❏ DK-76904	Without You in My Life	1973	30.00

EPIC

Number	Title	Yr	NM
❏ PE38626	Tyrone Davis' Greatest Hits	1983	10.00

HIGHRISE

Number	Title	Yr	NM
❏ 103	Tyrone Davis	1982	12.00

ICHIBAN

Number	Title	Yr	NM
❏ ICH1103	I'll Always Love You	1991	15.00

DAVIS, WALTER, JR.

BLUE NOTE

Number	Title	Yr	NM
❏ BLP-4018 [M]	Davis Cup	1959	750.00
—"Deep groove" version (deep indentation under label on both sides)			
❏ BLP-4018 [M]	Davis Cup	1959	80.00
—Regular version with W. 63rd St. address on label			
❏ BLP-4018 [M]	Davis Cup	1964	30.00
—With New York, USA address on label			
❏ BST-84018 [S]	Davis Cup	1959	60.00
—Regular version with W. 63rd St. address on label			
❏ BST-84018 [S]	Davis Cup	1964	25.00
—With New York, USA address on label			
❏ BST-84018 [S]	Davis Cup	1967	18.00
—With "A Division of Liberty Records" on label			
❏ B1-32098	Davis Cup	1995	18.00

RED

Number	Title	Yr	NM
❏ VPA-150	A Being Such As You	198?	15.00
❏ VPA-153	Blues Walk	198?	15.00

DAVIS, WILD BILL

CORAL

Number	Title	Yr	NM
❏ CRL57427 [M]	Lover	1962	25.00
❏ CRL757427 [S]	Lover	1962	30.00
❏ CRL57417 [M]	One More Time	1962	25.00
❏ CRL757417 [S]	One More Time	1962	30.00

EPIC

Number	Title	Yr	NM
❏ LN3308 [M]	Evening Concerto	1956	60.00
❏ LN1004 [10]	Here's Wild Bill Davis	1954	100.00
❏ LN1121 [M]	On the Loose	1955	60.00
❏ LN3118 [M]	Wild Bill Davis at Birdland	1955	60.00

EVEREST

Number	Title	Yr	NM
❏ LPBR-5094 [M]	Dance the Madison	1960	30.00
❏ SDBR-1094 [S]	Dance the Madison	1960	30.00
❏ LPBR-5125 [M]	Dis Heah	1961	30.00
❏ SDBR-1125 [S]	Dis Heah	1961	30.00
❏ LPBR-5052 [M]	Flying High	1959	30.00
❏ SDBR-1052 [S]	Flying High	1959	30.00
❏ LPBR-5014 [M]	My Fair Lady	1958	30.00
❏ SDBR-1014 [S]	My Fair Lady	1959	30.00
❏ LPBR-5116 [M]	Organ Grinder's Swing	1960	30.00
❏ SDBR-1116 [S]	Organ Grinder's Swing	1960	30.00
❏ LPBR-5133 [M]	The Music from "Milk and Honey	1961	30.00
❏ SDBR-1133 [S]	The Music from "Milk and Honey	1961	30.00

IMPERIAL

Number	Title	Yr	NM
❏ LP-9015 [M]	Wild Bill Davis in Hollywood	1956	50.00
❏ LP-9010 [M]	Wild Bill Davis on Broadway	1956	50.00
❏ LP-9201 [M]	Wild Wild Wild Wild Wild Wild Wild Wild	1963	40.00
❏ LP-12201 [R]	Wild Wild Wild Wild Wild Wild Wild Wild	1963	25.00

RCA VICTOR

Number	Title	Yr	NM
❏ LSP-4139	Doin' His Thing	1969	18.00
❏ LPM-3314 [M]	Free, Frantic and Funky	1965	18.00
❏ LSP-3314 [S]	Free, Frantic and Funky	1965	25.00
❏ LPM-3578 [M]	Live at Count Basie's	1966	18.00
❏ LSP-3578 [S]	Live at Count Basie's	1966	25.00
❏ LPM-3799 [M]	Midnight to Dawn	1967	25.00
❏ LSP-3799 [S]	Midnight to Dawn	1967	18.00

SUNSET

Number	Title	Yr	NM
❏ SUS-5191	Flying Home	196?	18.00

TANGERINE

Number	Title	Yr	NM
❏ 1509	Wonderful World	197?	18.00

DAVISON, WILD BILL

AIRCHECK

Number	Title	Yr	NM
❏ 31	Wild Bill Davison	198?	12.00

AUDIOPHILE

Number	Title	Yr	NM
❏ AP-149	Beautifully Wild	197?	15.00

CHIAROSCURO

Number	Title	Yr	NM
❏ 124	Live at the Rainbow Room	197?	18.00

CIRCLE

Number	Title	Yr	NM
❏ LP-405 [10]	Showcase	1951	80.00

COLUMBIA

Number	Title	Yr	NM
❏ CL871 [M]	Pretty Wild: Wild Bill Davison with Strings	1956	40.00
❏ CL983 [M]	Wild Bill Davison with Strings Attached	1957	40.00

COMMODORE

Number	Title	Yr	NM
❏ FL-20000 [10]	Dixieland Jazz Jamboree	1950	100.00
❏ FL-30009 [M]	Mild and Wild	1959	60.00
❏ XFL-14939	That's a-Plenty	198?	12.00

DIXIELAND JUBILEE

Number	Title	Yr	NM
❏ DJ-508 [M]	Greatest of the Greats	1958	30.00
❏ DJS-508 [S]	Greatest of the Greats	1958	25.00

JAZZOLOGY

Number	Title	Yr	NM
❏ J-22	After Hours	196?	18.00
❏ J-18	Blowin' Wild	1966	18.00
❏ J-37	Jazz on a Saturday Afternoon, Vol. 1	197?	15.00
❏ J-38	Jazz on a Saturday Afternoon, Vol. 2	197?	15.00
❏ J-39	Jazz on a Saturday Afternoon, Vol. 3	197?	15.00
❏ J-128	Lady of the Evening	1986	12.00
❏ J-133	Live in Memphis	1986	12.00
❏ J-14 [M]	Rompin' and Stompin'	196?	25.00
❏ JCE-14 [S]	Rompin' and Stompin'	196?	15.00
❏ J-25	Surfside Jazz	196?	18.00
❏ J-151	Wild Bill Davison and His 75th Anniversary Jazz Band	1986	12.00
❏ J-103	Wild Bill Davison and His Jazz Band	198?	12.00
❏ J-70	Wild Bill Davison and the Classic Jazz Collegium	197?	15.00
❏ J-30	Wild Bill Davison at Bull Run	1968	18.00
❏ J-121	Wild Bill Davison In London	1987	12.00
❏ J-2 [M]	Wild Bill Davison's Jazzologists	1962	25.00
❏ JCE-2 [S]	Wild Bill Davison's Jazzologists	1962	15.00
❏ J-160	Wild Bill Davison with Freddy Randall and His Band	198?	12.00

REGENT

Number	Title	Yr	NM
❏ MG-6026 [M]	When the Saints Go Marching In	196?	25.00

RIVERSIDE

Number	Title	Yr	NM
❏ RLP 12-211 [M]	Sweet and Hot	1956	60.00
—White label, blue print			
❏ RLP 12-211 [M]	Sweet and Hot	195?	30.00
—Blue label, microphone logo at top			

SACKVILLE

Number	Title	Yr	NM
❏ 3002	The Jazz Giants	198?	12.00

Number	Title	Yr	NM
SAVOY			
❏ MG-12214 [M]	Dixieland	1969	18.00
❏ MG-12035 [M]	Jazz at Storyville	1955	60.00
❏ MG-12055 [M]	Ringside at Condon's	1955	60.00
—Reissue of two 10-inch LPs (15029 and 15030) that are listed in the Various Artists Collection area			
SAVOY JAZZ			
❏ SJL-2229	Individualism	198?	18.00
❏ SJC-403	Ringside at Condon's	198?	12.00
STORYVILLE			
❏ 4048	But Beautiful	197?	12.00
❏ 4029	Papa Bue's Viking Jazz Band	197?	12.00
❏ 4005	Wild Bill Davison with Eddie Condon's All Stars	197?	12.00
DAWE, TIM			
STRAIGHT			
❏ STS-1058 [B]	Penrod	1969	100.00
WARNER BROS.			
❏ WS1841	Penrod	1970	18.00
DAWN (1)			
ARISTA			
❏ AL4045	Greatest Hits	1975	12.00
❏ AQ4045 [Q]	Greatest Hits	1975	18.00
❏ AL4059	Skybird	1975	12.00
❏ A2L9006	The World of Tony Orlando and Dawn	1977	15.00
BELL			
❏ 1320	Candida & Knock Three Times	1974	12.00
—Reissue of 6052			
❏ 6052	Candida	1970	15.00
❏ 6069	Dawn Featuring Tony Orlando	1971	15.00
❏ 1130	Dawn's New Ragtime Follies	1973	12.00
❏ 1317	Prime Time	1974	12.00
❏ 1322	Tony Orlando & Dawn II	1974	12.00
—Reissue of 6069			
❏ 1112	Tuneweaving	1973	12.00
ELEKTRA			
❏ 7E-1034	He Don't Love You (Like I Love You)	1975	12.00
❏ EQ-1034 [Q]	He Don't Love You (Like I Love You)	1975	18.00
❏ 7E-1049	To Be with You	1976	12.00
❏ EQ-1049 [Q]	To Be with You	1976	18.00
DAWSON, SID			
DELMAR			
❏ DL-109 [10]	Sid Dawson's Riverboat Gamblers	195?	60.00
DAY, BOBBY			
CLASS			
❏ LP-5002 [M]	Rockin' with Robin	1959	400.00
COLLECTABLES			
❏ COL-5074	Golden Classics	198?	12.00
RENDEZVOUS			
❏ M-1312 [M]	Rockin' with Robin	196?	100.00
RHINO			
❏ RNDF-208	The Best of Bobby Day	1984	15.00
DAY, CORA LEE			
ROULETTE			
❏ R-52048 [M]	My Crying Hour	1960	30.00
❏ SR-52048 [S]	My Crying Hour	1960	40.00
DAY, DENNIS			
DESIGN			
❏ DLPX-1 [M]	Dennis Day Sings "Christmas Is for the Family	195?	25.00
—Cover features Jack Benny as Santa; he also appears briefly on the LP			
❏ DLP-X-17 [M]	White Christmas	1965	15.00
❏ SDLP-X-17 [S]	White Christmas	1965	18.00
GLENDALE			
❏ 6029	Christmas Winterland	19??	12.00
STEREO-SPECTRUM			
❏ SDLPX-1 [S]	Dennis Day Sings "Christmas Is for the Family	195?	30.00
—Same as Design 1			
DAY, DORIS			
COLUMBIA			
❏ CL1614 [M]	Bright and Shiny	1960	25.00
❏ CS8414 [S]	Bright and Shiny	1960	30.00
❏ CL6248 [10]	By the Light of the Silvery Moon	1953	60.00
❏ CL6273 [10]	Calamity Jane	1953	60.00
❏ CL1232 [M]	Cuttin' Capers	1959	25.00
❏ CS8078 [S]	Cuttin' Capers	1959	30.00

Number	Title	Yr	NM
❏ CL942 [M]	Day By Day	1957	30.00
❏ CL1053 [M]	Day By Night	1958	25.00
❏ CS8089 [S]	Day By Night	1959	30.00
❏ CL624 [M]	Day Dreams	1955	40.00
—Red label, gold print			
❏ CL624 [M]	Day Dreams	1956	30.00
—Six "eye" logos on label			
❏ CL749 [M]	Day in Hollywood	1956	30.00
❏ CL1210 [M]	Doris Day's Greatest Hits	1958	30.00
—Six "eye" logos on label			
❏ CS8635 [P]	Doris Day's Greatest Hits	1962	18.00
—"360 Sound Stereo" in black at bottom			
❏ CL1210 [M]	Doris Day's Greatest Hits	1962	15.00
—"Guaranteed High Fidelity" or "Mono" on label			
❏ PC8635	Doris Day's Greatest Hits	198?	10.00
—Budget-line reissue			
❏ CL1752 [M]	Duet	1962	25.00
—With Andre Previn			
❏ CS8552 [S]	Duet	1962	30.00
—With Andre Previn			
❏ C2L5 [M]	Hooray for Hollywood	1959	40.00
❏ C2S805 [S]	Hooray for Hollywood	1959	50.00
❏ CL1366 [M]	Hooray for Hollywood, Volume 1	1959	25.00
❏ CS8066 [S]	Hooray for Hollywood, Volume 1	1959	30.00
❏ CL1367 [M]	Hooray for Hollywood, Volume 2	1959	25.00
❏ CS8067 [S]	Hooray for Hollywood, Volume 2	1959	30.00
❏ CL1660 [M]	I Have Dreamed	1961	25.00
❏ CS8460 [S]	I Have Dreamed	1961	30.00
❏ CL6198 [10]	I'll See You in My Dreams	1951	60.00
❏ CL2310 [M]	Latin for Lovers	1965	15.00
❏ CS9110 [S]	Latin for Lovers	1965	18.00
❏ CL2518 [10]	Lights, Camera, Action	1955	50.00
❏ DD1 [M]	Listen to Day	1960	25.00
❏ DDS1 [S]	Listen to Day	1960	30.00
❏ CL2131 [M]	Love Him!	1964	18.00
❏ CS8931 [S]	Love Him!	1964	25.00
❏ CL710 [M]	Love Me or Leave Me	1955	50.00
Red label, gold print			
❏ CL710 [M]	Love Me or Leave Me	1956	30.00
—Six "eye" logos on label			
❏ CL710 [M]	Love Me or Leave Me	1962	18.00
—"Guaranteed High Fidelity" or "Mono" on label			
❏ CS8773 [R]	Love Me or Leave Me	1963	15.00
❏ CL6168 [10]	Lullaby of Broadway	1951	60.00
❏ CL6186 [10]	On Moonlight Bay	1951	60.00
❏ CL2360 [M]	Sentimental Journey	1965	15.00
❏ CS9160 [S]	Sentimental Journey	1965	18.00
❏ CL1470 [M]	Show Time	1960	25.00
❏ CS8261 [S]	Show Time	1960	25.00
❏ CL6149 [10]	Tea for Two	1950	60.00
❏ CL2226 [M]	The Doris Day Christmas Album	1964	15.00
❏ CS9026 [S]	The Doris Day Christmas Album	1964	18.00
❏ CL1438 [M]	What Every Girl Should Know	1960	25.00
❏ CS8234 [S]	What Every Girl Should Know	1960	30.00
❏ CL2266 [M]	With a Smile and a Song	1965	15.00
❏ CS9066 [S]	With a Smile and a Song	1965	18.00
❏ CL1904 [M]	You'll Never Walk Alone	1962	18.00
❏ CS8704 [S]	You'll Never Walk Alone	1962	25.00
❏ CL6339 [10]	Young at Heart	1954	60.00
—Six songs by Doris Day, two by Frank Sinatra			
❏ CL6106 [10]	Young Man with a Horn	1950	100.00
❏ CL582 [M]	Young Man with a Horn	1954	40.00
—Reissue of 6106; red label, gold print			
❏ CL6071 [10]	You're My Thrill	1949	60.00
COLUMBIA LIMITED EDITION			
❏ LE10197	The Doris Day Christmas Album	197?	12.00
COLUMBIA SPECIAL PRODUCTS			
❏ P13346	The Doris Day Christmas Album	197?	12.00
—Reissue of CS 9026			

Number	Title	Yr	NM
❏ C10988	The Doris Day Christmas Album	197?	12.00
—Reissue of CS 9026			
❏ P213231	The Magic of Doris Day	1976	18.00
❏ XTV82021/2 [M]	Wonderful Day	1961	40.00
HARMONY			
❏ HL9559 [M]	Do Re Mi (And Other Children's Favorites)	196?	15.00
❏ HS14559 [S]	Do Re Mi (And Other Children's Favorites)	196?	15.00
❏ HL7392 [M]	Great Movie Hits	1966	15.00
❏ HS11192 [R]	Great Movie Hits	1966	15.00
❏ KH31498	Softly, As I Leave You	1972	12.00
❏ HS11382	The Magic of Doris Day	1970	15.00
❏ HS11282	Whatever Will Be, Will Be (Que Sera, Sera)	1968	15.00
HEARTLAND			
❏ HL1102/3	The Best of Doris Day	1990	18.00
—Mail-order offer; alternate number is CBS Special Products P2 22031			
HINDSIGHT			
❏ HSR-200	Doris Day with Van Alexander's Orchestra	198?	12.00
DAY, JIMMY			
PHILIPS			
❏ PHM200016 [M]	Golden Steel Guitar Hits	1962	30.00
❏ PHS600016 [S]	Golden Steel Guitar Hits	1962	30.00
❏ PHM200075 [M]	Steel and Strings	1963	30.00
❏ PHS600075 [S]	Steel and Strings	1963	30.00
DAY BLINDNESS			
STUDIO 10			
❏ DBX-101	Day Blindness	1969	60.00
DAYNE, TAYLOR			
ARISTA			
❏ AL-8581	Can't Fight Fate	1989	12.00
❏ AL-8529	Tell It to My Heart	1987	12.00
—ue of Bearsville LP			
DE-FENDERS, THE			
DEL-FI			
❏ DFLP-1242 [M]	Drag Beat	1963	50.00
❏ DFST-1242 [S]	Drag Beat	1963	60.00
WORLD PACIFIC			
❏ WP-1810 [M]	The De-Fenders Play the Big Ones	1963	50.00
❏ ST-1810 [S]	The De-Fenders Play the Big Ones	1963	150.00
—Red vinyl			
❏ ST 1810 [S]	The De-Fenders Play the Big Ones	1963	150.00
—Green vinyl			
❏ ST-1810 [S]	The De-Fenders Play the Big Ones	1963	70.00
—Black vinyl			
DE LA SOUL			
TOMMY BOY			
❏ TB1019	3 Feet High and Rising	1989	25.00
—Original edition			
❏ TB1019	3 Feet High and Rising	2001	18.00
—Reissue, expanded to a two-disc set			
❏ TB1362	AOI: Bionix	2001	18.00
❏ TB1443 [DJ]	AOI: Bionix//Edited	2001	18.00
—Promo-only "clean" version			
❏ TB1546	AOI: Bionix Instrumentals	2002	18.00
❏ TB1361	Art Official Intelligence: Mosaic Thump	2000	18.00
❏ TB1437	Art Official Intelligence: Mosaic Thump Instrumentals	2000	18.00
❏ TB1063 [DJ]	Buhloone Mindstate	1993	30.00
—Vinyl appears to be promo only			
❏ TB1093 [DJ]	Clear Lake Auditorium	1994	30.00
—Promo-only on clear vinyl (black vinyl editions are counterfeits)			
❏ TB1029 [B]	De La Soul Is Dead	1991	30.00
❏ TB1041 [B]	De La Soul Is Dead	1991	35.00
—Promo-only two-record set			
❏ TB1149	Stakes Is High	1996	18.00
❏ TB1175 [DJ]	Stakes Is High Sampler	1996	30.00
—Promo only; contains eight songs from the full-length edition			
DEAD BOYS			
BOMP!			
❏ 4017	Night of the Living Dead Boys	1981	18.00
SIRE			
❏ SRK-6054	We Have Come for Your Children	1978	30.00
❏ SRK-6054	We Have Come for Your Children	1978	50.00
—With original title Down To Kill on label			
❏ SR-6038 [B]	Young, Loud & Snotty	1977	35.00

DEAD KENNEDYS

ALTERNATIVE TENTACLES

Number	Title	Yr	NM
❑ VIRUS50 [B]	Bedtime for Democracy	1986	35.00

—Originals have a newspaper insert

Number	Title	Yr	NM
❑ VIRUS45 [B]	Frankenchrist	1985	60.00

—Originals have a poster of H.R. Giger's painting Landscape #20, which was involved in an obscenity trial. The poster is still available, but only by mailing in a coupon inside the LP.

Number	Title	Yr	NM
❑ VIRUS1	Fresh Fruit for Rotting Vegetables	1988	25.00

—Reissue of I.R.S. album

Number	Title	Yr	NM
❑ VIRUS57	Give Me Convenience or Give Me Death	1987	18.00
❑ VIRUS5 [EP]	In God We Trust, Inc.	1981	50.00
❑ VIRUS27 [B]	Plastic Surgery Disasters	1982	40.00

FAULTY

Number	Title	Yr	NM
❑ 70014	Fresh Fruit for Rotting Vegetables	1982	40.00

—With nursing home photo on back cover, no reference to I.R.S. on label or cover

I.R.S./FAULTY PRODUCTS

Number	Title	Yr	NM
❑ SP-70014 [B]	Fresh Fruit for Rotting Vegetables	1980	60.00

—Originals have an orange cover "to distinguish it from imports

Number	Title	Yr	NM
❑ SP-70014	Fresh Fruit for Rotting Vegetables	1980	25.00

—Reissues have a black front cover, same as imports; it was changed at the insistence of band member Jello Biafra

DEAD MILKMEN, THE

ENIGMA

Number	Title	Yr	NM
❑ 73351	Beelzebubba	1988	18.00
❑ D1-73260	Bucky Fellini	1988	18.00

FEVER/ENIGMA

Number	Title	Yr	NM
❑ 72054	Big Lizard in My Backyard	1985	25.00

RESTLESS

Number	Title	Yr	NM
❑ 72131	Eat Your Paisley	1988	18.00

DEAD OR ALIVE

EPIC

Number	Title	Yr	NM
❑ FE40572	Mad, Bad and Dangerous to Know	1986	15.00
❑ OE45224	Nude	1989	15.00
❑ EAS2668 [DJ]	Radio Special with Pete Burns	1986	70.00

—Promo-only music and interviews

Number	Title	Yr	NM
❑ OE44255	Rip It Up	1988	15.00
❑ BFE39274	Sophisticated Boom Boom	1984	15.00
❑ FE39274	Sophisticated Boom Boom	1985	10.00

—Reissue with new prefix

Number	Title	Yr	NM
❑ BFE40119	Youthquake	1985	12.00
❑ FE40119	Youthquake	1985	10.00

—Reissue with new prefix

DEADLY ONES, THE

VEE JAY

Number	Title	Yr	NM
❑ LP-1090 [M]	It's Monster Surfing Time	1964	100.00
❑ LPS-1090 [S]	It's Monster Surfing Time	1964	120.00

DEAN, ALAN

DESIGN

Number	Title	Yr	NM
❑ DLP-102 [M]	Songs of Faith	1959	15.00
❑ SDLP-300 [S]	The Lord's Prayer	1969	12.00

GRAND PRIX

Number	Title	Yr	NM
❑ K-184 [M]	Songs of Faith	196?	12.00
❑ KS-184 [S]	Songs of Faith	196?	15.00

INTERNATIONAL AWARD SERIES

Number	Title	Yr	NM
❑ AKS-184 [S]	Songs of Faith	196?	15.00
❑ AK-184 [M]	Songs of Faith	196?	12.00

MGM

Number	Title	Yr	NM
❑ E-3461 [M]	Heart and Soul	1956	30.00

STEREO-SPECTRUM

Number	Title	Yr	NM
❑ SS-45 [S]	Songs of Faith	1959	18.00

DEAN, EDDIE

SAGE AND SAND

Number	Title	Yr	NM
❑ C-1 [M]	Greatest Westerns	1956	50.00
❑ C-5 [M]	Hi-Country	1957	50.00
❑ C-16 [M]	Hillbilly Heaven	1961	30.00

SOUND

Number	Title	Yr	NM
❑ LP-603 [M]	Greatest Westerns	1957	30.00

DEAN, JIMMY

COLUMBIA

Number	Title	Yr	NM
❑ CL1735 [M]	Big Bad John and Other Fabulous Songs and Tales	1961	25.00

—With the version of "Big Bad John" containing the lyric "At the bottom of this mine lies a big, big man"; confirmed copies have trail-off numbers of "XLP-54925-1F" and "XLP-54925-1J

Number	Title	Yr	NM
❑ CS8535 [S]	Big Bad John and Other Fabulous Songs and Tales	1961	30.00

—It's possible that two different editions exist, one with the "hell of a man" lyrics of "Big Bad John" and the other with the "big, big man" lyrics, but this has not been confirmed.

Number	Title	Yr	NM
❑ CL1735 [M]	Big Bad John and Other Fabulous Songs and Tales	1961	30.00

—With the version of "Big Bad John" containing the lyric "At the bottom of this mine lies one hell of a man"; confirmed copies have a trail-off number of "XLP-54925-2A" and "XLP-54925-2B

Number	Title	Yr	NM
❑ CS9677 [M]	Dean's List	1968	30.00

—White label promo; "Special Mono Radio Station Copy" sticker on cover

Number	Title	Yr	NM
❑ CS9677 [S]	Dean's List	1968	18.00
❑ CL2027 [M]	Everybody's Favorite	1963	18.00
❑ CS8827 [S]	Everybody's Favorite	1963	25.00
❑ CL2404 [M]	Jimmy Dean's Christmas Card	1965	18.00
❑ CS9204 [S]	Jimmy Dean's Christmas Card	1965	15.00
❑ CL2485 [M]	Jimmy Dean's Greatest Hits	1966	18.00
❑ CS9285 [S]	Jimmy Dean's Greatest Hits	1966	18.00
❑ PC9285	Jimmy Dean's Greatest Hits	198?	10.00

—Budget-line reissue

Number	Title	Yr	NM
❑ CL1025 [M]	Jimmy Dean's Hour of Prayer	1957	40.00
❑ CS9424 [R]	Jimmy Dean's Hour of Prayer	1966	15.00
❑ CL1894 [M]	Portrait of Jimmy Dean	1962	25.00
❑ CS8694 [S]	Portrait of Jimmy Dean	1962	30.00
❑ CL2188 [M]	Songs We All Love Best	1964	18.00
❑ CS8988 [S]	Songs We All Love Best	1964	25.00
❑ CL2538 [M]	The Big Ones	1966	18.00
❑ CS9338 [S]	The Big Ones	1966	18.00
❑ CL2401 [M]	The First Thing Every Morning	1965	18.00
❑ CS9201 [S]	The First Thing Every Morning	1965	25.00

CROWN

Number	Title	Yr	NM
❑ 291	Jimmy Dean and the Western Gentlemen	196?	15.00

GRT

Number	Title	Yr	NM
❑ 8014	I.O.U.	1977	12.00

HARMONY

Number	Title	Yr	NM
❑ HL7268 [M]	Hymns	1960	18.00
❑ HS11042 [R]	Hymns	1960	15.00
❑ HL7408 [M]	Mr. Country Music	1967	15.00
❑ HS11208 [S]	Mr. Country Music	1967	15.00
❑ HS11270	The Country's Favorite Son	1968	15.00

HILLTOP

Number	Title	Yr	NM
❑ 6004	Golden Favorites	196?	15.00

KING

Number	Title	Yr	NM
❑ 686 [M]	Favorites of Jimmy Dean	1961	60.00

MERCURY

Number	Title	Yr	NM
❑ MG-20319 [M]	Jimmy Dean Sings His Television Favorites	1957	40.00

RCA VICTOR

Number	Title	Yr	NM
❑ LPM-3999 [M]	A Thing Called Love	1968	30.00
❑ LSP-3999 [S]	A Thing Called Love	1968	18.00
❑ LSP-4434	Country Boy and Country Girl	1970	18.00
❑ LSP-4323	Dean of Country	1970	18.00
❑ LSP-4511	Everybody Knows	1971	18.00
❑ LPM-3727 [M]	Jimmy Dean Is Here	1967	18.00
❑ LSP-3727 [S]	Jimmy Dean Is Here	1967	18.00
❑ LPM-3824 [M]	Most Richly Blesed	1967	25.00
❑ LSP-3824 [S]	Most Richly Blesed	1967	18.00
❑ LSP-4035	Speaker of the House	1968	18.00
❑ LPM-3890 [M]	The Jimmy Dean Show	1967	25.00
❑ LSP-3890 [S]	The Jimmy Dean Show	1967	18.00
❑ LSP-4618	These Hands	1972	18.00

SEARS

Number	Title	Yr	NM
❑ 105	Jimmy Dean's Golden Favorites	196?	18.00

SPIN-O-RAMA

Number	Title	Yr	NM
❑ 137	Coutnry Round-Up Featuring Jimmy Dean	196?	15.00
❑ 108	Featuring the Coutnry Singing of Jimmy Dean	196?	15.00

WING

Number	Title	Yr	NM
❑ MGW-12292 [M]	Jimmy Dean Sings His Television Favorites	196?	18.00
❑ SRW-16292 [R]	Jimmy Dean Sings His Television Favorites	196?	15.00

WYNCOTE

Number	Title	Yr	NM
❑ 9032	Country Favorites	196?	15.00

DEAN, JIMMY / JOHNNY HORTON

LA BREA

Number	Title	Yr	NM
❑ L8014 [M]	Bummin' Around with Jimmy Dean and Johnny Horton	1961	80.00

STARDAY

Number	Title	Yr	NM
❑ SLP-325 [M]	Bummin' Around with Jimmy Dean and Johnny Horton	1965	30.00

DEAN, PETER

AUDIO FIDELITY

Number	Title	Yr	NM
❑ AFSD-6280	Peter Dean in Fun City	197?	18.00

BUDDAH

Number	Title	Yr	NM
❑ BDS-5613	Four or Five Times	1974	18.00

INNER CITY

Number	Title	Yr	NM
❑ IC-4002	Only Time Will Tell	1979	15.00

MONMOUTH-EVERGREEN

Number	Title	Yr	NM
❑ 7092	Where Did the Magic Go	198?	15.00

PROJECT 3

Number	Title	Yr	NM
❑ PR5075SD	Ding Dong Daddy!	196?	18.00

DEAN, SUZANNE

NOVA

Number	Title	Yr	NM
❑ 8808-1	Dreams Come True	198?	12.00
❑ 9028-1	I Wonder	1988	12.00

DEARANGO, BILL

EMARCY

Number	Title	Yr	NM
❑ MG-26020 [10]	Bill DeArango	1954	50.00

DEARIE, BLOSSOM

CAPITOL

Number	Title	Yr	NM
❑ T2086 [M]	May I Come In	1964	18.00
❑ ST2086 [S]	May I Come In	1964	25.00
❑ SM-2086	May I Come In	1976	12.00

—Reissue with new prefix

DAFFODIL

Number	Title	Yr	NM
❑ BMD-102	1975	1975	18.00
❑ BMD-101	Blossom Dearie Sings	197?	18.00
❑ BMD-109	Chez Wahlberg, Part I	198?	15.00
❑ BMD-108	Et Tu Bruce (Volume VIII)	198?	12.00
❑ BMD-103	My New Celebrity Is You	197?	25.00
❑ BMD-105	Needlepoint Magic	198?	15.00
❑ BMD-107	Positively Volume VII	198?	12.00
❑ BMD-106	Simply Volume VI	1983	12.00
❑ BMD-110	Songs of Chelsea	1987	12.00
❑ BMD-104	Winchester in Apple Blossom Time	197?	25.00

DRG

Number	Title	Yr	NM
❑ DARC-1105	Blossom Dearie On Broadway	1980	18.00

FONTANA

Number	Title	Yr	NM
❑ MGF-27562 [M]	Blossom Time	1966	18.00
❑ SRF-67562 [S]	Blossom Time	1966	25.00

VERVE

Number	Title	Yr	NM
❑ MGV-2037 [M]	Blossom Dearie	1957	60.00
❑ V-2037 [M]	Blossom Dearie	1961	25.00
❑ UMV-2639	Blossom Dearie	198?	12.00
❑ MGV-2109 [M]	Blossom Dearie Sings Comden & Green	1959	60.00
❑ MGVS-6050 [S]	Blossom Dearie Sings Comden & Green	1960	50.00
❑ V-2109 [M]	Blossom Dearie Sings Comden & Green	1961	25.00
❑ V6-2109 [S]	Blossom Dearie Sings Comden & Green	1961	30.00
❑ MGV-2133 [M]	Broadway Song Hits	1960	50.00
❑ MGVS-6139 [S]	Broadway Song Hits	1960	60.00
❑ V-2133 [M]	Broadway Song Hits	1961	25.00
❑ V6-2133 [S]	Broadway Song Hits	1961	30.00
❑ MGV-2081 [M]	Give Him the Ooh-La-La	1958	60.00
❑ V-2081 [M]	Give Him the Ooh-La-La	1961	25.00
❑ MGV-2125 [M]	My Gentleman Friend	1959	60.00
❑ MGVS-6112 [S]	My Gentleman Friend	1960	50.00
❑ V-2125 [M]	My Gentleman Friend	1961	25.00
❑ V6-2125 [S]	My Gentleman Friend	1961	30.00
❑ MGV-2111 [M]	Once Upon a Summertime	1958	60.00
❑ MGVS-6020 [S]	Once Upon a Summertime	1960	50.00
❑ V-2111 [M]	Once Upon a Summertime	1961	25.00
❑ V6-2111 [S]	Once Upon a Summertime	1961	30.00
❑ 827757-1	Once Upon a Summertime	1986	12.00

DEATH CAB FOR CUTIE

BARSUK

Number	Title	Yr	NM
❑ BARK47	Plans	2005	30.00
❑ BARK21	The Photo Album	2001	50.00
❑ BARK11 [B]	We Have the Facts and We're Voting Yes	2000	50.00

SONIC BOOM

Number	Title	Yr	NM
❑ SBR 002	Something About Airplanes	1998	50.00

—Blue marbled vinyl

Number	Title	Yr	NM
❑ SBR 012	Transatlanticism	2004	25.00

DEAUVILLE, RONNIE

ERA

Number	Title	Yr	NM
❑ 20002 [M]	Smoke Dreams	1957	40.00

IMPERIAL

Number	Title	Yr	NM
❑ LP-9060 [M]	Romance	1959	30.00
❑ LP-12009 [S]	Romance	1959	30.00

DEBARGE, EL

GORDY

Number	Title	Yr	NM
❑ 6181GL	El DeBarge	1986	10.00

MOTOWN

Number	Title	Yr	NM
❑ PR-189 [DJ]	El Elaborates!	1986	30.00

—Promo-only interview and music album

Number	Title	Yr	NM
❑ MOT-6264	Gemini	1989	12.00

DEBARGE

GORDY

Number	Title	Yr	NM
❑ 6012GL	All This Love	1982	10.00
❑ 6061GL	In a Special Way	1983	10.00
❑ 6123GL	Rhythm of the Night	1985	10.00
❑ G8-1003M1	The DeBarges	1981	15.00

MOTOWN

Number	Title	Yr	NM
❑ 5335ML	The DeBarges	1985	10.00

—Reissue of Gordy 1003

STRIPED HORSE

Number	Title	Yr	NM
❑ SHL2004	Bad Boys	1987	12.00

Number	Title	Yr	NM

DEBRIS

STATIC DISPOSAL
| ☐ 00000 [B] | Debris | 1976 | 120.00 |

DECARLO, YVONNE

MASTERSEAL
| ☐ MS33-1869/70 [M] | Yvonne DeCarlo Sings | 1957 | 80.00 |

DECASTRO SISTERS, THE

ABBOTT
| ☐ 5002 [M] | The DeCastro Sisters | 1956 | 60.00 |

CAPITOL
☐ T1402 [M]	The DeCastros Sing	1960	30.00
☐ ST1402 [S]	The DeCastros Sing	1960	30.00
☐ T1501 [M]	The Rockin' Beat	1961	30.00
☐ ST1501 [S]	The Rockin' Beat	1961	30.00

DECEMBER'S CHILDREN

MAINSTREAM
| ☐ S-6128 | December's Children | 1970 | 150.00 |

DEDRICK, RUSTY

4 CORNERS OF THE WORLD
| ☐ FC-4207 [M] | The Big Band Sound | 1964 | 18.00 |
| ☐ FCS-4207 [S] | The Big Band Sound | 1964 | 25.00 |

COUNTERPOINT
| ☐ 552 [M] | Salute to Bunny | 1957 | 50.00 |

ESOTERIC
| ☐ ESJ-9 [10] | Rhythm and Winds | 1955 | 100.00 |

KEYNOTE
| ☐ 1103 | Rusty Dedrick | 1955 | 60.00 |

MONMOUTH-EVERGREEN
| ☐ 6918 | Harold Arlen in Hollywood | 1969 | 18.00 |
| ☐ 7035 | Many Facets, Many Friends | 1970 | 18.00 |

MONUMENT
| ☐ MLP-6502 [M] | A Jazz Journey | 1965 | 18.00 |
| ☐ SLP-16502 [S] | A Jazz Journey | 1965 | 25.00 |

DEE, DUANE

CAPITOL
| ☐ ST2931 | My Shining Hour | 1968 | 18.00 |

DEE, JOEY, AND THE STARLITERS

FORUM
| ☐ FC9099 [M] | Joey Dee and the Starliters | 1963 | 15.00 |
| ☐ FCS9099 [S] | Joey Dee and the Starliters | 1963 | 15.00 |

JUBILEE
| ☐ JGM-8000 [M] | Hitsville | 1966 | 30.00 |
| ☐ JGS-8000 [S] | Hitsville | 1966 | 30.00 |

ROULETTE
☐ R-25171 [M]	All the World Is Twistin'	1962	30.00
☐ SR 25171 [S]	All the World Is Twistin'	1962	40.00
☐ R-25173 [M]	Back at the Peppermint Lounge -- Twistin'	1962	30.00
☐ SR-25173 [S]	Back at the Peppermint Lounge -- Twistin'	1962	40.00
☐ R-25221 [M]	Dance, Dance, Dance	1963	30.00
☐ SR-25221 [S]	Dance, Dance, Dance	1963	30.00
☐ R-25166 [M]	Doin' the Twist at the Peppermint Lounge	1961	40.00
☐ SR-25166 [S]	Doin' the Twist at the Peppermint Lounge	1961	50.00
☐ R-25197 [M]	Joey Dee	1963	30.00
☐ SR-25197 [S]	Joey Dee	1963	30.00

SCEPTER
| ☐ S503 [M] | The Peppermint Twisters | 1962 | 30.00 |
| ☐ SS503 [S] | The Peppermint Twisters | 1962 | 35.00 |

DEE, KATHY

GUEST STAR
| ☐ G-1445 [M] | Teardrops in My Heart | 1964 | 18.00 |
| ☐ GS-1445 [S] | Teardrops in My Heart | 1964 | 18.00 |

DEE, KIKI

LIBERTY
☐ LST-7613	Patterns	1969	18.00
☐ LN-10148	Patterns	1981	10.00
—Budget-line reissue			

RCA VICTOR
| ☐ AFL1-4180 | Perfect Timing | 1981 | 12.00 |

ROCKET
☐ PIG-458	I've Got the Music In Me	1974	15.00
☐ BXL1-2257	Kiki Dee	1977	12.00
☐ PIG-395	Loving and Free	1973	12.00
☐ BXL1-3011	Stay with Me	1979	12.00

TAMLA
| ☐ TS303 [B] | Great Expectations | 1970 | 30.00 |

DEE, LENNY

DECCA
☐ DL4429 [M]	By Popular Dee-Mand	1963	12.00
☐ DL74429 [S]	By Popular Dee-Mand	1963	15.00
☐ DL8628 [M]	Dee-Day	1957	15.00
☐ DL8718 [M]	Dee-Latin Hi-Fi Organ	1958	15.00

Number	Title	Yr	NM
☐ DL8275 [M]	Dee-Licious	1956	15.00
☐ DL8114 [M]	Dee-Lightful	1955	18.00
☐ DL8165 [M]	Dee-Lirious	1956	15.00
☐ DL8308 [M]	Dee-Most	1956	15.00
☐ DL75196	Easy Come, Easy Go	1970	12.00
☐ DL75320	Easy Lovin'	1972	12.00
☐ DL4994 [M]	Gentle on My Mind	1968	15.00
☐ DL74994 [S]	Gentle on My Mind	1968	15.00
☐ DL4112 [M]	Golden Organ Favorites	1961	12.00
☐ DL74112 [S]	Golden Organ Favorites	1961	15.00
☐ DL4146 [M]	Happy Holi-Dee	1961	12.00
☐ DL74146 [S]	Happy Holi-Dee	1961	15.00
☐ DL8406 [M]	Hi-Dee-Fi	1957	15.00
☐ DL4818 [M]	In the Mood	1967	12.00
☐ DL74818 [S]	In the Mood	1967	15.00
☐ DL4365 [M]	Lenny Dee Down South	1963	12.00
☐ DL74365 [S]	Lenny Dee Down South	1963	15.00
☐ DL4315 [M]	Lenny Dee In Hollywood	1962	12.00
☐ DL74315 [S]	Lenny Dee In Hollywood	1962	15.00
☐ DL8857 [M]	Lenny Dee Plays the Hits	1959	15.00
☐ DL78857 [S]	Lenny Dee Plays the Hits	1959	18.00
☐ DL75112	Little Green Apples	1969	12.00
☐ DL8796 [M]	Mellow-Dee	1959	15.00
☐ DL78796 [S]	Mellow-Dee	1959	18.00
☐ DL4572 [M]	Most Requested	1964	12.00
☐ DL74572 [S]	Most Requested	1964	15.00
☐ DL4880 [M]	Moving On	1967	15.00
☐ DL78880 [S]	Moving On	1967	12.00
☐ DL8497 [M]	Mr. Dee Goes to Town	1957	15.00
☐ DL4706 [M]	My Favorite Things	1966	15.00
☐ DL74706 [S]	My Favorite Things	1966	15.00
☐ DL4946 [M]	Relaxin'	1968	15.00
☐ DL74946 [S]	Relaxin'	1968	12.00
☐ DL75255	Remember Me	1971	12.00
☐ DL4498 [M]	Something Special	1964	12.00
☐ DL74498 [S]	Something Special	1964	15.00
☐ DL8978 [M]	Songs Everybody Knows	1960	12.00
☐ DL78978 [S]	Songs Everybody Knows	1960	15.00
☐ DL75152	Spinning Wheel	1969	12.00
☐ DL4632 [M]	Sweethearts on Parade	1965	12.00
☐ DL74632 [S]	Sweethearts on Parade	1965	15.00
☐ DXS7199	The Best of Lenny Dee	1968	15.00
☐ DL8913 [M]	The Lenny Dee Show	1960	12.00
☐ DL78913 [S]	The Lenny Dee Show	1960	15.00
☐ DL4654 [M]	The Lenny Dee Tour	1965	12.00
☐ DL74654 [S]	The Lenny Dee Tour	1965	15.00
☐ DL75073	Turn Around, Look at Me	1969	12.00
☐ DL75366	Where Is the Love	1972	12.00

MCA
☐ 476	City Lights	1974	10.00
☐ 290	Easy Come, Easy Go	1973	10.00
—Reissue of Decca 75196			
☐ 297	Easy Lovin'	1973	10.00
—Reissue of Decca 75320			
☐ 271	Gentle on My Mind	1973	10.00
—Reissue of Decca 74994			
☐ 182	Golden Organ Favorites	1973	10.00
—Reissue of Decca 74112			
☐ 2162	I'll Play for You	1975	10.00
☐ 172	In the Mood	1973	10.00
—Reissue of Decca 74818			
☐ 379	Lenny	1973	10.00
☐ 334	Lenny Dee	1973	10.00
☐ 279	Little Green Apples	1973	10.00
—Reissue of Decca 75112			
☐ 2236	Misty Blue	1976	10.00
☐ 231	Most Requested	1973	10.00
—Reissue of Decca 74572			
☐ 241	My Favorite Things	1973	10.00
—Reissue of Decca 74706			
☐ 2370	Organ Celebration	1978	10.00
☐ 2301	Organ Magic	1977	10.00
☐ 26	Remember Me	1971	10.00
—Reissue of Decca 75255			
☐ 334	Sing" and Others	1973	10.00
☐ 221	Something Special	1973	10.00
—Reissue of Decca 74498			
☐ 533	Songs Everybody Knows	1975	10.00
—Reissue of Decca 78978			
☐ 455	Steppin' Out with Lenny Dee	1974	10.00
☐ 2200	Take It to the Limit	1976	10.00
☐ 4042	The Best of Lenny Dee	197?	12.00
—Reissue of Decca 7179			
☐ 4084	The Best of Lenny Dee, Volume II	1977	12.00
☐ 504	Where Is the Love	1974	10.00
—Reissue of Decca 75366			

VOCALION
☐ VL3782 [M]	Here's Lenny Dee at the Organ	1967	12.00
☐ VL73782 [S]	Here's Lenny Dee at the Organ	1967	12.00
☐ VL73817	Organ Special	1968	12.00
☐ VL73819	Varieties	1969	12.00

DEEP, THE

PARKWAY
| ☐ P7051 [M] | Psychedelic Moods | 1966 | 300.00 |
| ☐ SP7051 [S] | Psychedelic Moods | 1966 | 500.00 |

DEEP PURPLE

DCC COMPACT CLASSICS
| ☐ LPZ-2052 | Made in Japan | 1998 | 40.00 |
| —Audiophile vinyl | | | |

Number	Title	Yr	NM

EAGLE ROCK
| ☐ ER20083-1 | Rapture of the Deep | 2005 | 25.00 |

FRIDAY MUSIC
| ☐ FRM10370 [B] | Last Concert in Japan | 2012 | 30.00 |

MERCURY
☐ 835897-1	Nobody's Perfect	1988	12.00
☐ 824003-1	Perfect Strangers	1984	12.00
☐ 831318-1	The House of Blue Light	1987	10.00

PARLOPHONE
| ☐ 2564633757 [B] | Shades of Deep Purple | 2014 | 35.00 |

RCA
| ☐ 2421-1-R | Slaves and Masters | 1990 | 18.00 |

RHINO
| ☐ R1-75622 | Machine Head | 2003 | 18.00 |
| —180-gram reissue | | | |

SCEPTER CITATION
| ☐ CTN-18010 | The Best of Deep Purple | 1972 | 25.00 |

TETRAGRAMMATON
☐ T-131 [B]	Concerto for Group and Orchestra	1970	250.00
☐ T-119	Deep Purple	1969	30.00
☐ T-102	Shades of Deep Purple	1968	30.00
☐ T-107	The Book of Taliesyn	1968	30.00

WARNER BROS.
☐ W2766	Burn	1974	12.00
☐ WS1860 [B]	Concerto for Group and Orchestra	1970	18.00
☐ WS1877 [B]	Deep Purple in Rock	1970	18.00
☐ BS2564 [B]	Fireball	1971	18.00
☐ BS2607 [B]	Machine Head	1972	18.00
☐ BS2607	Machine Head	1973	12.00
—Burbank" labels			
☐ BS42607 [Q]	Machine Head	1974	60.00
☐ BSK3100	Machine Head	1976	10.00
☐ 2WS2701 [B]	Made in Japan	1973	30.00
☐ 2WS2701 [B]	Made in Japan	1979	18.00
—White labels			
☐ 2LS2644	(Purple Passages)	1972	18.00
☐ BS2678	Who Do We Think We Are!	1973	15.00
—Original copies have green "WB" labels			
☐ BS2678	Who Do We Think We Are!	1973	12.00
—Burbank" labels			

WARNER BROS./PURPLE
☐ PR2895	Come Taste the Band	1975	12.00
☐ PRK3486	Deepest Purple: The Best of Deep Purple	1980	12.00
☐ PR2995	Made in Europe	1976	12.00
☐ PR2832	Stormbringer	1974	12.00
☐ PR42832 [Q]	Stormbringer	1974	50.00
☐ PRK3223	When We Rock, We Rock, and When We Roll, We Roll	1978	12.00

DEEP RIVER BOYS, THE

QUE
| ☐ FLS-104 [M] | Midnight Magic | 1957 | 150.00 |

RCA CAMDEN
| ☐ CAL-303 [M] | Presenting the Deep River Boys | 1957 | 60.00 |
| —Reissue of "X" album | | | |

WALDORF MUSIC HALL
☐ MH 33-108 [10]	The Deep River Boys Sing Songs of Jubilee	1954	300.00
—Photo of group on cover			
☐ MH 33-108 [10]	The Deep River Boys Sing Songs of Jubilee	195?	150.00
—Cartoon on cover			

X
| ☐ LXA-1019 [M] | Presenting the Deep River Boys | 1956 | 120.00 |

DEERFIELD

FLAT ROCK
| ☐ FRS-1 | Nil Desperandum | 1971 | 200.00 |

DEES, RICK

ATLANTIC
| ☐ 81288 | I'm Not Crazy | 1985 | 15.00 |
| ☐ 81231 | Put It Where the Moon Don't Shine | 1984 | 15.00 |

NO BUDGET
| ☐ NBR102 | Hurt Me Baby -- Make Me Write Bad Checks! | 1983 | 18.00 |

RSO
| ☐ RS-1-3017 [B] | The Original Disco Duck | 1976 | 30.00 |

DEES, SAM

ATLANTIC
| ☐ SD18134 | The Show Must Go On | 1975 | 150.00 |

DEF LEPPARD

MERCURY
☐ SRM-1-4021	High 'n' Dry	1981	15.00
—Chicago skyline label			
☐ 818836-1	High 'n' Dry	1984	10.00
—Altered version of 4021; "Bringin' on the Heartbreak" is			

Number	Title	Yr	NM
remixed, and "Me & My Wine" is added		1987	10.00
❏ 830675-1	Hysteria	1987	10.00
❏ 832962-1 [PD]	Hysteria	1987	40.00
—Limited-edition picture disc in plastic sleeve			
❏ 1775319	Hysteria	2008	25.00
❏ SRM-1-3828	On Through the Night	1980	15.00
—Chicago skyline label			
❏ 822533-1	On Through the Night	198?	10.00
—Reissue of 3828			
❏ 810308-1	Pyromania	1983	10.00
❏ 810308-1	Pyromania	2008	25.00

DEFRANCO, BUDDY, AND TOMMY GUMINA

MERCURY
Number	Title	Yr	NM
❏ MG-20743 [M]	Kaleidoscope	1962	25.00
❏ SR-60743 [S]	Kaleidoscope	1962	30.00
❏ MG-20833 [M]	Polytones	1963	25.00
❏ SR-60833 [S]	Polytones	1963	30.00
❏ MG-20685 [M]	Presenting the Buddy DeFranco-Tommy Gumina Quintet	1962	25.00
❏ SR-60685 [S]	Presenting the Buddy DeFranco-Tommy Gumina Quintet	1962	30.00
❏ MG-20900 [M]	The Girl from Ipanema	1964	25.00
❏ SR-60900 [S]	The Girl from Ipanema	1964	30.00

DEFRANCO, BUDDY

CHOICE
Number	Title	Yr	NM
❏ 1008	Free Sail	1974	18.00
❏ 1017	Waterbed	1977	15.00

CLASSIC JAZZ
| ❏ 33 | Buddy DeFranco and Jim Gillis | 1978 | 15.00 |

DECCA
| ❏ DL4031 [M] | Pacific Standard Swingin' Time | 1961 | 25.00 |
| ❏ DL74031 [S] | Pacific Standard Swingin' Time | 1961 | 30.00 |

DOT
| ❏ DLP-9006 [M] | Cross-Country Suite | 1958 | 40.00 |

GENE NORMAN
| ❏ GNP-2 [10] | Buddy DeFranco Takes You to the Stars | 1954 | 120.00 |

HAMILTON
| ❏ HL-133 [M] | Cross-Country Suite | 1964 | 25.00 |
| ❏ HS-12133 [R] | Cross-Country Suite | 1964 | 15.00 |

MGM
❏ E-3396 [M]	Buddy DeFranco	1956	80.00
❏ E-253 [10]	Buddy DeFranco with Strings	1954	100.00
❏ E-177 [10]	King of the Clarinet	1952	120.00

MOSAIC
| ❏ MR5-117 | The Complete Recordings of the Buddy DeFranco Quartet/Quintet with Sonny Clark | 199? | 100.00 |

NORGRAN
❏ MGN-1096 [M]	Autumn Leaves	1956	80.00
❏ MGN-1012 [M]	Buddy DeFranco and His Clarinet	1954	100.00
❏ MGN-1016 [M]	Buddy DeFranco and Oscar Peterson Play George Gershwin	1955	100.00
❏ MGN-1026 [M]	Buddy DeFranco Quartet	1955	100.00
❏ MGN-1079 [M]	In a Mellow Mood	1956	80.00
❏ MGN-1068 [M]	Jazz Tones	1956	80.00
❏ MGN-1069 [M]	Mr. Clarinet	1956	80.00
❏ MGN-1094 [M]	Odalisque	1956	80.00
❏ MGN-16 [10]	Pretty Moods by Buddy DeFranco	1954	150.00
❏ MGN-3 [10]	The Buddy DeFranco Quartet	1954	150.00
❏ MGN-1085 [M]	The Buddy DeFranco Wailers	1956	80.00
❏ MGN-1006 [M]	The Progressive Mr. DeFranco	1954	120.00

PABLO
| ❏ 2310906 | Mr. Lucky | 198? | 15.00 |

PROGRESSIVE
| ❏ 7014 | Like Someone in Love | 1979 | 15.00 |

SONET
| ❏ 724 | Boronquin | 197? | 15.00 |

VERVE
❏ MGV-8183 [M]	Autumn Leaves	1957	50.00
—Reissue of Norgran 1096			
❏ V-8183 [M]	Autumn Leaves	1961	25.00
❏ MGV-8315 [M]	Bravura	1959	50.00
❏ MGVS-6051 [S]	Bravura	1960	40.00
❏ V-8315 [M]	Bravura	1961	25.00
❏ V6-8315 [S]	Bravura	1961	25.00
❏ MGV-2033 [M]	Broadway Showcase	1957	50.00
❏ V-2033 [M]	Broadway Showcase	1961	25.00
❏ MGV-8210 [M]	Buddy DeFranco and the Oscar Peterson Quartet	1958	50.00
❏ V-8210 [M]	Buddy DeFranco and the Oscar Peterson Quartet	1961	25.00
❏ MGV-2090 [M]	Buddy DeFranco Plays Artie Shaw	1958	50.00
❏ V-2090 [M]	Buddy DeFranco Plays Artie Shaw	1961	25.00
❏ MGV-2089 [M]	Buddy DeFranco Plays Benny Goodman	1958	50.00

Number	Title	Yr	NM
❏ V-2089 [M]	Buddy DeFranco Plays Benny Goodman	1961	25.00
❏ MGV-8382 [M]	Closed Session	1960	40.00
❏ MGVS-6165 [S]	Closed Session	1960	40.00
❏ V-8382 [M]	Closed Session	1961	25.00
❏ V6-8382 [S]	Closed Session	1961	25.00
❏ UMV-2632	Closed Session	198?	12.00
❏ MGV-8221 [M]	Cooking the Blues	1958	80.00
❏ V-8221 [M]	Cooking the Blues	1961	25.00
❏ MGV-8363 [M]	Generalissimo	1960	50.00
❏ MGVS-6132 [S]	Generalissimo	1960	40.00
❏ V-8363 [M]	Generalissimo	1961	25.00
❏ V6-8363 [S]	Generalissimo	1961	25.00
❏ MGV-2108 [M]	I Hear Benny Goodman and Artie Shaw	1958	50.00
❏ MGVS-6032 [S]	I Hear Benny Goodman and Artie Shaw	1960	40.00
❏ V-2108 [M]	I Hear Benny Goodman and Artie Shaw	1961	25.00
❏ V6-2108 [S]	I Hear Benny Goodman and Artie Shaw	1961	25.00
❏ MGV-8169 [M]	In a Mellow Mood	1957	50.00
—Reissue of Norgran 1079			
❏ V-8169 [M]	In a Mellow Mood	1961	25.00
❏ MGV-8158 [M]	Jazz Tones	1957	50.00
—Reissue of Norgran 1068			
❏ V-8158 [M]	Jazz Tones	1961	25.00
❏ MGV-8383 [M]	Live Date!	1960	40.00
❏ MGVS-6166 [S]	Live Date!	1960	40.00
❏ V-8383 [M]	Live Date!	1961	25.00
❏ V6-8383 [S]	Live Date!	1961	25.00
❏ MGV-8159 [M]	Mr. Clarinet	1957	50.00
—Reissue of Norgran 1069			
❏ V-8159 [M]	Mr. Clarinet	1961	25.00
❏ MGV-8182 [M]	Odalisque	1957	50.00
—Reissue of Norgran 1094			
❏ V-8182 [M]	Odalisque	1961	25.00
❏ MGV-8224 [M]	Sweet and Lovely	1958	50.00
❏ V-8224 [M]	Sweet and Lovely	1961	25.00
❏ MGV-8175 [M]	The Buddy DeFranco Wailers	1957	50.00
—Reissue of Norgran 1085			
❏ V-8175 [M]	The Buddy DeFranco Wailers	1961	25.00
❏ MGV-2022 [M]	The George Gershwin Songbook	1956	50.00
—Reissue of Norgran 1016			
❏ MGV-8375 [M]	Wholly Cats	1960	40.00
❏ MGVS-6150 [S]	Wholly Cats	1960	40.00
❏ V-8375 [M]	Wholly Cats	1961	25.00
❏ V6-8375 [S]	Wholly Cats	1961	25.00

DEFRANCO FAMILY, THE

20TH CENTURY
Number	Title	Yr	NM
❏ T-422	Heartbeat, It's a Lovebeat	1973	12.00
❏ T-441	Save the Last Dance for Me	1974	12.00

DEHAVEN, DOC

CUCA
❏ K-3000 [M]	Dixieland Treasure	1962	25.00
❏ K-3100 [M]	Doc DeHaven On Location	1963	25.00
❏ K-3200 [M]	Doc Swings a Little	1964	25.00
❏ K-3400 [M]	Erle of Madison	1967	25.00
❏ K-3300 [M]	Just Off State Street	1966	25.00
❏ KS-3300 [S]	Just Off State Street	1966	30.00

DEHAVEN, PENNY

MAIN STREET
| ❏ 9310 | Penny DeHaven | 1984 | 12.00 |

UNITED ARTISTS
| ❏ UAS-6821 | Penny DeHaven | 1972 | 18.00 |

DEJOHN SISTERS, THE

EPIC
| ❏ LN1116 [M] | The DeJohn Sisters | 195? | 30.00 |

UNITED ARTISTS
| ❏ UAL-3103 [M] | Yes Indeed | 1960 | 25.00 |
| ❏ UAS-6103 [M] | Yes Indeed | 1960 | 30.00 |

DEJOHNETTE, JACK

COLUMBIA
| ❏ C31176 | Compost (Take Off Your Body) | 1971 | 25.00 |

ECM
❏ 25010	Album Album	1984	12.00
❏ 23790	Inflation Blues	1983	12.00
❏ 1128	New Directions	1978	15.00
❏ 1157	New Directions in Europe	1980	15.00
❏ 1103	New Rags	1977	15.00
❏ 1079	Pictures	1976	15.00
❏ 1152	Special Edition	1980	15.00
❏ 1189	Tin Can Alley	1981	15.00
❏ 1074	Untitled	1976	15.00

IMPULSE!/MCA
| ❏ 5992 | Irresistible Force | 1987 | 12.00 |

LANDMARK
| ❏ LLP-1504 | The Piano Album | 1985 | 12.00 |

MCA
| ❏ 42313 | Parallel Realities | 1990 | 18.00 |
| ❏ 42160 | Zebra | 1986 | 12.00 |

MILESTONE
Number	Title	Yr	NM
❏ MSP-9029	Have You Heard?	1970	18.00
❏ MSP-9022	The DeJohnette Complex	1969	25.00

PRESTIGE
| ❏ 10094 | Cosmic Chicken | 1975 | 18.00 |
| ❏ 10081 | Sorcery | 1974 | 18.00 |

DEKKER, DESMOND, AND THE ACES

BULLDOG
| ❏ 1037 | The Israelites | 198? | 12.00 |

UNI
| ❏ 73059 | Israelites | 1969 | 30.00 |

DEL AMITRI

A&M
| ❏ SP-5287 | Waking Hours | 1990 | 15.00 |

CHRYSALIS
| ❏ BFV41499 | Del Amitri | 1985 | 15.00 |

DEL FUEGOS, THE

RCA
| ❏ 9860 | Smoking in the Fields | 1989 | 12.00 |

SLASH
❏ 25339	Boston, Mass.	1985	12.00
❏ 25540	Stand Up	1987	12.00
❏ 25174	The Longest Day	1984	12.00

DEL LORDS, THE

EMI AMERICA
| ❏ ST-17183 | Johnny Comes Marching Home | 1986 | 15.00 |

ENIGMA
| ❏ D1-73326 | Based on a True Story | 1988 | 12.00 |

DEL SATINS

B.T. PUPPY
| ❏ BTS-1019 | Out to Lunch | 1972 | 300.00 |

DEL VIKINGS, THE

COLLECTABLES
| ❏ COL-5010 | The Best of the Dell-Vikings | 198? | 15.00 |

DOT
| ❏ DLP-3685 [M] | Come Go with Me | 1966 | 200.00 |
| ❏ DLP-25685 [R] | Come Go with Me | 1966 | 150.00 |

LUNIVERSE
| ❏ LP-1000 [M] | Come Go with the Del Vikings | 1957 | 500.00 |
| *—Eight tracks, cover is composed of slicks. Counterfeits have more tracks and a preprinted cover (not slicks)* | | | |

MERCURY
| ❏ MG-20353 [M] | A Swinging, Singing Record Session | 1958 | 200.00 |
| ❏ MG-20314 [M] | They Sing -- They Swing | 1957 | 300.00 |

DEL VIKINGS, THE / THE SONNETS

CROWN
| ❏ CLP-5368 [M] | The Del Vikings and the Sonnets | 1963 | 40.00 |

DELANEY, JACK

SOUTHLAND
❏ LP-201 [10]	Jack Delaney and George Girard in New Orleans	1954	50.00
❏ LP-214 [M]	Jack Delaney and the New Orleans Jazz Babies	195?	40.00
❏ LP-214 [10]	Jack Delaney with Lee Collins	1954	50.00

DELANEY AND BONNIE

ATCO
❏ SD 33-383	Country Life	1972	25.00
❏ SD 33-326	Delaney & Bonnie & Friends On Tour with Eric Clapton	1970	30.00
—Yellow label original			
❏ SD 33-326	Delaney & Bonnie & Friends On Tour with Eric Clapton	197?	12.00
—Later pressings on other labels			
❏ SD 33-358	Motel Shot	1971	30.00
❏ SD7014 [B]	The Best of Delaney and Bonnie	1972	25.00
❏ SD 33-341 [S]	To Bonnie from Delaney	1970	30.00
❏ 33-341 [M]	To Bonnie from Delaney	1970	40.00
—White label promo; no stock copies were issued in mono			

COLUMBIA
| ❏ KC31377 | D&B Together | 1972 | 25.00 |

ELEKTRA
| ❏ EKS-74039 | Accept No Substitute -- The Original Delaney & Bonnie & Friends | 1969 | 30.00 |

GNP CRESCENDO
| ❏ GNPS-2054 | Genesis | 1970 | 25.00 |

STAX
| ❏ STS-2026 | Home | 1969 | 30.00 |

Number	Title	Yr	NM
DELEGATES, THE (1)			
MAINSTREAM			
❏ 100	The Delegates	1973	25.00
DELFONICS, THE			
ARISTA			
❏ AL8333	The Best of the Delfonics	198?	12.00
COLLECTABLES			
❏ COL-5109	Golden Classics	198?	12.00
KORY			
❏ 1002	The Best of the Delfonics	1977	15.00
PHILLY GROOVE			
❏ 1501	Alive & Kicking	1974	50.00
❏ 1150	La La Means I Love You	1968	80.00
❏ 1154	Tell Me This Is a Dream	1972	50.00
❏ 1153	The Delfonics	1970	50.00
❏ 1152	The Delfonics Super Hits	1969	50.00
❏ 1151	The Sexy Sound of Soul	1969	80.00
POOGIE			
❏ 121680	The Delfonics Return	1981	15.00
DELLER, ALFRED			
VANGUARD			
❏ VRS-499 [M]	The Holly and the Ivy – Christmas Songs of Old England	1956	40.00
❏ VRS-479 [M]	The Three Ravens	195?	40.00
DELLS, THE, AND THE DRAMATICS			
CADET			
❏ 60027	The Dells Vs. the Dramatics	1974	30.00
DELLS, THE			
20TH CENTURY			
❏ T-618	I Touched a Dream	1980	15.00
❏ T-633	Whatever Turns You On	1981	15.00
ABC			
❏ AA-1113	Face to Face	1978	15.00
❏ AA-1100	New Beginnings	1978	15.00
BUDDAH			
❏ BDS-5053	The Dells	1969	18.00
CADET			
❏ 50004	Freedom Means	1971	30.00
❏ 50037	Give Your Baby a Standing Ovation	1973	30.00
❏ LPS-837	Like It Is, Like It Was	1970	50.00
❏ LPS-829	Love Is Blue	1969	50.00
❏ 50021	Sweet As Funk Can Be	1972	30.00
❏ 50046	The Dells	1973	30.00
❏ LPS-824	The Dells Greatest Hits	1969	50.00
❏ 60036	The Dells' Greatest Hits, Vol. 2	1975	25.00
❏ LPS-822	The Dells Musical Menu/ Always Together	1969	50.00
❏ 50017	The Dells Sing Dionne Warwicke's Greatest Hits	1972	30.00
❏ 60030	The Mighty Mighty Dells	1974	30.00
❏ LPS-804	There Is	1968	50.00
CHESS			
❏ CH-9103	The Dells	198?	12.00
—Reissue			
❏ CH-9288	There Is	1989	12.00
—Reissue of Cadet 804			
LOST-NITE			
❏ LLP-21 [10]	The Dells	1981	18.00
—Red vinyl, generic red cover			
MERCURY			
❏ SRM-1-3711	Love Connection	1977	18.00
❏ SRM-1-1084	No Way Back	1976	18.00
❏ SRM-1-1145	They Said It Couldn't Be Done	1977	18.00
❏ SRM-1-1059	We Got to Get Our Thing Together	1975	18.00
PRIVATE I			
❏ BFZ39309	One Step Closer	1984	12.00
SOLID SMOKE			
❏ 8029	Breezy Ballads and Tender Tunes: The Best of the Early Years (1955-65)	1984	12.00
UPFRONT			
❏ UPF-105	Stay In My Corner	1968	18.00
URGENT			
❏ URG-4108	The Second Time	1991	15.00
VEE JAY			
❏ LP1141 [M]	It's Not Unusual	1965	100.00
❏ LPS1141 [S]	It's Not Unusual	1965	150.00
❏ LP1010 [M]	Oh What a Nite	1959	800.00
—Maroon label			
❏ LP1010 [M]	Oh What a Nite	1961	300.00
—Black label with colorband			
❏ VJLP-1010	Oh What a Nite	198?	12.00
—Late-80s reissue on reactivated Vee Jay label. "Trade Mark Reg." on label.			
VJ INTERNATIONAL			
❏ 7305	The Dells In Concert	197?	15.00

Number	Title	Yr	NM
ZOO			
❏ 11023	I Salute You	1992	18.00
DELMORE BROTHERS, THE			
KING			
❏ 983 [M]	24 Great Country Songs	1966	30.00
❏ KS-983 [R]	24 Great Country Songs	1966	25.00
❏ 785 [M]	30th Anniversary Album	1962	80.00
❏ 910 [M]	In Memory	1964	40.00
❏ 920 [M]	In Memory, Volume 2	1964	40.00
❏ 589 [M]	Songs by the Delmore Brothers	1958	150.00
DEMANO, HANK			
FREEWAY			
❏ FLJP-1 [M]	Hank DeMano Quartet	1955	50.00
DEMENSIONS, THE			
CORAL			
❏ CRL57430 [M]	My Foolish Heart	1963	150.00
❏ CRL757430 [S]	My Foolish Heart	1963	300.00
DEMERLE, LES			
DOBRE			
❏ 1020	Transfusion	1978	15.00
PALO ALTO			
❏ 8008	On Fire	1981	15.00
DEMIAN			
ABC			
❏ ABCS-718	Demian	1970	100.00
DENNIS, JOHN			
DEBUT			
❏ DEB-121 [M]	New Piano Expressions	1955	120.00
DENNIS, MATT			
JUBILEE			
❏ JLP-1105 [M]	Welcome Matt Dennis	1959	25.00
❏ JGS-1105 [S]	Welcome Matt Dennis	1959	30.00
KAPP			
❏ KL-1024 [M]	Matt Dennis Plays and Sings Matt Dennis	1956	30.00
MCA			
❏ 1547	Matt Dennis Plays and Sings Matt Dennis	198?	15.00
RCA VICTOR			
❏ LPM-1134 [M]	Dennis, Anyone?	1955	40.00
❏ LPM-1322 [M]	Play Melancholy Baby	1956	30.00
❏ LPM-1065 [M]	She Danced Overhead	1954	40.00
DENNY, DOTTY			
A440			
❏ AJ-506 [M]	Dotty Digs Duke	1954	70.00
❏ AJ-505 [M]	Tribute to Edgar Sampson	1954	70.00
DENNY, MARTIN			
FIRST AMERICAN			
❏ 7743	From Hawaii With Love	1981	12.00
LIBERTY			
❏ LRP-3415 [M]	20 Golden Hawaiian Hits	1965	18.00
❏ LST-7415 [S]	20 Golden Hawaiian Hits	1965	18.00
❏ LRP-3111 [M]	Afro-Desia	1959	30.00
—Turquoise label			
❏ LRP-3111 [M]	Afro-Desia	1960	25.00
—Black rainbow label			
❏ LST-7111 [S]	Afro-Desia	1959	40.00
—All-black label			
❏ LST-7111 [S]	Afro-Desia	1960	30.00
—Black rainbow label			
❏ LRP-3277 [M]	Another Taste of Honey	1963	18.00
❏ LST-7277 [S]	Another Taste of Honey	1963	25.00
❏ LRP-3328 [M]	A Taste of Hits	1964	15.00
❏ LST-7328 [S]	A Taste of Hits	1964	18.00
❏ LRP-3237 [M]	A Taste of Honey	1962	18.00
❏ LST-7237 [S]	A Taste of Honey	1962	25.00
❏ LRP-3034 [M]	Exotica	1957	40.00
—Turquoise label			
❏ LRP-3034 [M]	Exotica	1960	30.00
—Black rainbow label			
❏ LST-7034 [R]	Exotica	1958	30.00
—All-black label			
❏ LST-7034 [R]	Exotica	1960	25.00
—Black rainbow label			
❏ LRP-3116 [M]	Exotica, Vol. III	1959	30.00
—Turquoise label			
❏ LRP-3116 [M]	Exotica, Vol. III	1960	25.00
—Black rainbow label			
❏ LST-7116 [S]	Exotica, Vol. III	1959	40.00
—All-black label			
❏ LST-7116 [S]	Exotica, Vol. III	1960	30.00
❏ LRP-3077 [M]	Exotica, Volume II	1957	30.00
—Turquoise label			
❏ LRP-3077 [M]	Exotica, Volume II	1960	25.00
—Black rainbow label			
❏ LST-7006 [S]	Exotica, Volume II	1958	40.00

Number	Title	Yr	NM
—All-black label			
❏ LST-7006 [S]	Exotica, Volume II	1960	30.00
—Black rainbow label			
❏ LRP-3513 [M]	Exotica Classica	1967	15.00
❏ LST-7513 [S]	Exotica Classica	1967	18.00
❏ LM-1009	Exotica Vol. 1	1982	10.00
—Reissue of United Artists 1009			
❏ LST-7621	Exotic Moog	1969	40.00
❏ LRP-3168 [M]	Exotic Percussion	1961	25.00
❏ LST-7168 [S]	Exotic Percussion	1961	30.00
❏ LRP-3158 [M]	Exotic Sounds from the Silver Screen	1960	25.00
❏ LST-7158 [S]	Exotic Sounds from the Silver Screen	1960	30.00
❏ LRP-3163 [M]	Exotic Sounds Visit Broadway	1960	25.00
❏ LST-7163 [S]	Exotic Sounds Visit Broadway	1960	30.00
❏ LRP-3081 [M]	Forbidden Island	1958	30.00
—Turquoise label; woman in jungle on cover			
❏ LRP-3081 [M]	Forbidden Island	1960	25.00
—Black rainbow label; white foil on cover			
❏ LST-7001 [S]	Forbidden Island	1958	40.00
—All-black label; woman in jungle on cover			
❏ LST-7001 [S]	Forbidden Island	1960	30.00
—Black rainbow label; white foil on cover			
❏ LRP-3467 [M]	Golden Greats	1966	15.00
❏ LST-7467 [S]	Golden Greats	1966	18.00
❏ LRP-3488 [M]	Hawaii	1967	15.00
❏ LST-7488 [S]	Hawaii	1967	18.00
❏ LRP-3445 [M]	Hawaiian A-Go-Go	1966	15.00
❏ LST-7445 [S]	Hawaiian A-Go-Go	1966	18.00
❏ LRP-3394 [M]	Hawaii Tattoo	1964	15.00
❏ LST-7394 [S]	Hawaii Tattoo	1964	18.00
❏ LRP-3102 [M]	Hypnotique	1958	30.00
—Turquoise label			
❏ LRP-3102 [M]	Hypnotique	1960	25.00
—Black rainbow label			
❏ LST-7102 [S]	Hypnotique	1958	40.00
—All-black label			
❏ LST-7102 [S]	Hypnotique	1960	30.00
—Black rainbow label			
❏ LRP-3378 [M]	Latin Village	1964	15.00
❏ LST-7378 [S]	Latin Village	1964	18.00
❏ LRP-3438 [M]	Martin Denny	1965	15.00
❏ LST-7438 [S]	Martin Denny	1965	18.00
❏ LRP-3087 [M]	Primitiva	1958	30.00
—Turquoise label			
❏ LRP-3087 [M]	Primitiva	1960	25.00
—Black rainbow label			
❏ LST-7023 [S]	Primitiva	1958	40.00
—All-black label			
❏ LST-7023 [S]	Primitiva	1960	30.00
—Black rainbow label			
❏ LRP-3122 [M]	Quiet Village	1959	30.00
—Turquoise label			
❏ LRP-3122 [M]	Quiet Village	1960	25.00
—Black rainbow label			
❏ LST-7122 [S]	Quiet Village	1959	40.00
—All-black label			
❏ LST-7122 [S]	Quiet Village	1960	30.00
—Black rainbow label			
❏ L-5502 [M]	The Best of Martin Denny	1962	18.00
❏ S-6602 [S]	The Best of Martin Denny	1962	25.00
❏ LRP-3141 [M]	The Enchanted Sea	1959	30.00
—Turquoise label			
❏ LRP-3141 [M]	The Enchanted Sea	1960	25.00
—Black rainbow label			
❏ LST-7141 [S]	The Enchanted Sea	1959	40.00
—All-black label			
❏ LST-7141 [S]	The Enchanted Sea	1960	30.00
—Black rainbow label			
❏ LRP-3224 [M]	The Exotic Sounds of Martin Denny In Person	1962	18.00
❏ LST-7224 [S]	The Exotic Sounds of Martin Denny In Person	1962	25.00
❏ LRP-3307 [M]	The Versatile Martin Denny	1963	18.00
❏ LST-7307 [S]	The Versatile Martin Denny	1963	25.00
SUNSET			
❏ SUS-5199	Exotic Night	1969	15.00
❏ SUM-1102 [M]	Paradise Moods	196?	15.00
❏ SUS-5102 [S]	Paradise Moods	196?	15.00
❏ SUM-1169 [M]	Sayonara	1967	15.00
❏ SUS-5169 [S]	Sayonara	1967	15.00
UNITED ARTISTS			
❏ LM-1009	Exotica Vol. 1	1980	12.00
—Reissue of Liberty 7034			
❏ UA-LA234-G	The Very Best of Martin Denny	1974	12.00
❏ UA-LA383-E	The Very Best of Martin Denny	1975	12.00
DENNY, SANDY			
A&M			
❏ SP-4371	Sandy	1972	18.00
❏ SP-4317	The Northstar Grassman and the Ravens	1971	18.00
CARTHAGE			
❏ CGLP-4425	Like an Old Fashioned Waltz	1985	12.00
—Reissue of Island 9340			
❏ CGLP-4423	Rendezvous	1985	12.00
—Reissue of Island 9433			

Number	Title	Yr	NM
❑ CGLP-4429	The Northstar Grassman and the Ravens	1985	12.00
— Reissue of A&M 4317			

HANNIBAL

Number	Title	Yr	NM
❑ HNBX-5301	Who Knows Where the Time Goes	198?	25.00

ISLAND

Number	Title	Yr	NM
❑ SW-9340	Like an Old Fashioned Waltz	1974	18.00
❑ ILPS9433	Rendezvous	1977	18.00

DENVER, JOHN, AND THE MUPPETS

RCA VICTOR

Number	Title	Yr	NM
❑ AFL1-3451	A Christmas Together	1979	15.00

DENVER, JOHN

HJD

Number	Title	Yr	NM
❑ 66 [B]	John Denver Sings	1966	1000.00
— Private issue of 300 or so, made by JD as Christmas gifts to friends.			

MERCURY

Number	Title	Yr	NM
❑ SRM-1-704	Beginnings	1972	25.00
— With illustration on cover			
❑ SRM-1-704	Beginnings	1974	15.00
— With mountain scene on cover			

RCA

Number	Title	Yr	NM
❑ 7624-1-R	Back Home Again	1988	12.00
— Last vinyl reissue			
❑ 7631-1-R	Poems, Prayers and Promises	1988	12.00
— Last vinyl reissue			
❑ 7632-1-R	Rocky Mountain High	1988	12.00
— Last vinyl reissue			

RCA VICTOR

Number	Title	Yr	NM
❑ LSP-4607	Aerie	1971	15.00
— Orange label			
❑ LSP-4607	Aerie	1975	12.00
— Tan label or black label, dog near top			
❑ AFL1-4607	Aerie	197?	10.00
— Reissue			
❑ CPL2-0764	An Evening with John Denver	1975	15.00
— Orange or tan labels			
❑ CPL2-0764	An Evening with John Denver	1976	12.00
— Black label, dog near top			
❑ AQL1-3449	Autograph	1980	10.00
❑ CPL1-0548	Back Home Again	1974	12.00
— Orange or tan label			
❑ CPL1-0548	Back Home Again	1976	10.00
— Black label, dog near top			
❑ AFL1-0548	Back Home Again	197?	10.00
— Reissue			
❑ AQL1-0548	Back Home Again	197?	10.00
— Later reissue			
❑ AFL1-5458	Dreamland Express	1985	10.00
❑ APL1-0101	Farewell Andromeda	1973	15.00
— Orange label			
❑ APL1-0101	Farewell Andromeda	1975	12.00
— Tan label or black label, dog near top			
❑ AFL1-4683	It's About Time	1983	10.00
❑ AFL1-2521	I Want to Live	1977	10.00
❑ AQL1-3075	John Denver	1979	10.00
❑ CPL1-0374	John Denver's Greatest Hits	1974	12.00
— Orange label			
❑ CPL1-0374	John Denver's Greatest Hits	1975	10.00
— Tan label or black label, dog near top			
❑ APL1-0374	John Denver's Greatest Hits	197?	10.00
— Reissue			
❑ AQL1-0374	John Denver's Greatest Hits	197?	10.00
— Later reissue			
❑ CPL1-2195	John Denver's Greatest Hits, Volume 2	1977	12.00
❑ AQL1-2195	John Denver's Greatest Hits, Volume 2	197?	10.00
— Reissue			
❑ AJL1-5313	John Denver's Greatest Hits, Volume 3	1984	10.00
❑ AFL1-5811	One World	1986	10.00
❑ LSP-4499	Poems, Prayers and Promises	1971	15.00
— Orange label			
❑ LSP-4499	Poems, Prayers and Promises	1975	12.00
— Tan label or black label, dog near top			
❑ AFL1-4499	Poems, Prayers and Promises	197?	10.00
— Reissue			
❑ LSP-4207	Rhymes & Reasons	1969	18.00
— Orange label, non-flexible vinyl			
❑ APL1-1201	Rocky Mountain Christmas	1975	12.00
— Tan label			
❑ AFL1-1201	Rocky Mountain Christmas	197?	10.00
— Reissue			
❑ APL1-1201	Rocky Mountain Christmas	1976	10.00
— Black label, dog near top			
❑ LSP-4731	Rocky Mountain High	1972	15.00
— Orange label			
❑ LSP-4731	Rocky Mountain High	1975	12.00

Number	Title	Yr	NM
— Tan label or black label, dog near top			
❑ AFL1-4731	Rocky Mountain High	197?	10.00
— Reissue			
❑ AQL1-4731	Rocky Mountain High	197?	10.00
— Later reissue			
❑ AFL1-4256	Seasons of the Heart	1982	10.00
❑ AFL1-4055	Some Days Are Diamonds	1981	10.00
❑ APL1-1694	Spirit	1976	12.00
— Originals are black label, dog near top			
❑ AFL1-1694	Spirit	197?	10.00
— Reissue			
❑ LSP-4278	Take Me to Tomorrow	1970	18.00
— Orange label, non-flexible vinyl			
❑ APL2-1263	The John Denver Gift Pak	1974	30.00
— Contains "Rocky Mountain Christmas" and "Windsong" in a special Christmas sleeve.			
❑ DJL1-5398 [DJ]	The John Denver Holiday Radio Show	1984	25.00
❑ DJL1-0075 [DJ]	The John Denver Radio Show	1973	30.00
❑ DJL1-0683 [DJ]	The Second John Denver Radio Show	1974	30.00
❑ LSP-4414	Whose Garden Was This?	1970	18.00
— Orange label, non-flexible vinyl			
❑ APL1-1183	Windsong	1975	12.00
— Tan label			
❑ APL1-1183	Windsong	1976	10.00
— Black label, dog near top			
❑ AFL1-1183	Windsong	197?	10.00
— Reissue			
❑ AQL1-1183	Windsong	197?	10.00
— Later reissue			

DEODATO

ATLANTIC

Number	Title	Yr	NM
❑ 82048	Somewhere Out There	1989	15.00

CTI

Number	Title	Yr	NM
❑ 7081	2001	1977	12.00
❑ CTS-6029	Deodato 2	1973	15.00
❑ CTSQ-6029 [Q]	Deodato 2	1973	25.00
❑ CTS-6021	Prelude	1972	15.00
❑ CTSQ-6021 [Q]	Prelude	1973	25.00
❑ 0021	Prelude	198?	10.00
— Reissue of 6021			

MCA

Number	Title	Yr	NM
❑ 457	Artistry	1974	12.00
❑ 491	First Cuckoo	1975	12.00
❑ 2219	Very Together	1976	12.00
❑ 697	Very Together	198?	10.00
— Reissue of 2219			
❑ 410	Whirlwinds	1974	12.00

WARNER BROS.

Number	Title	Yr	NM
❑ BSK3649	Happy Hour	1981	12.00
❑ BSK3321	Knights of Fantasy	1979	12.00
❑ BSK3132	Love Island	1978	12.00
❑ 25175	Motion	1984	12.00
❑ BSK3467	Night Cruiser	1980	15.00

DEODATO/AIRTO

CTI

Number	Title	Yr	NM
❑ CTS-6041	In Concert	1974	15.00
❑ CTSQ-6041 [Q]	In Concert	1974	25.00

DEPARIS, SIDNEY

BLUE NOTE

Number	Title	Yr	NM
❑ B-6501	DeParis Dixie	1969	25.00
❑ BLP-7016 [10]	Sidney DeParis' Blue Note Stompers	1951	300.00

DEPARIS, SIDNEY/JAMES P. JOHNSON

BLUE NOTE

Number	Title	Yr	NM
❑ B-6506	Original Blue Note Jazz, Volume 3	1969	25.00

DEPARIS, WILBUR, AND JIMMY WITHERSPOON

ATLANTIC

Number	Title	Yr	NM
❑ 1266 [M]	New Orleans Blues	1957	70.00
— Black label			
❑ 1266 [M]	New Orleans Blues	1961	30.00
— Multicolor label, white "fan" logo			
❑ 1266 [M]	New Orleans Blues	1964	30.00
— Multicolor label, black "fan" logo			

DEPARIS, WILBUR

A440

Number	Title	Yr	NM
❑ AJ-503 [10]	New New Orleans Jazz	1954	60.00

ATLANTIC

Number	Title	Yr	NM
❑ 1233 [M]	Marchin' and Swingin'	1956	50.00
— Black label			
❑ 1233 [M]	Marchin' and Swingin'	1961	25.00
— Multicolor label, white "fan" logo			
❑ 1233 [M]	Marchin' and Swingin'	1964	18.00
— Multicolor label, black "fan" logo			
❑ SD1233 [S]	Marchin' and Swingin'	1958	40.00
— Green label			
❑ SD1233 [S]	Marchin' and Swingin'	1961	25.00
— Multicolor label, white "fan" logo			

Number	Title	Yr	NM
❑ SD1233 [S]	Marchin' and Swingin'	1964	18.00
— Multicolor label, black "fan" logo			
❑ 1219 [M]	New New Orleans Jazz	1956	50.00
— Black label			
❑ 1219 [M]	New New Orleans Jazz	1961	25.00
— Multicolor label, white "fan" logo			
❑ 1219 [M]	New New Orleans Jazz	1964	18.00
— Multicolor label, black "fan" logo			
❑ SD1219 [S]	New New Orleans Jazz	1958	40.00
— Green label			
❑ SD1219 [S]	New New Orleans Jazz	1961	25.00
— Multicolor label, white "fan" logo			
❑ SD1219 [S]	New New Orleans Jazz	1964	18.00
— Multicolor label, black "fan" logo			
❑ SD1552	Over and Over Again	1970	18.00
❑ 1300 [M]	Something Old, New, Gay, Blue	1958	50.00
— Black label			
❑ 1300 [M]	Something Old, New, Gay, Blue	1961	25.00
— Multicolor label, white "fan" logo			
❑ 1300 [M]	Something Old, New, Gay, Blue	1964	18.00
— Multicolor label, black "fan" logo			
❑ SD1300 [S]	Something Old, New, Gay, Blue	1958	40.00
— Green label			
❑ SD1300 [S]	Something Old, New, Gay, Blue	1961	25.00
— Multicolor label, white "fan" logo			
❑ SD1300 [S]	Something Old, New, Gay, Blue	1964	18.00
— Multicolor label, black "fan" logo			
❑ 1318 [M]	That's a-Plenty	1959	50.00
— Black label			
❑ 1318 [M]	That's a-Plenty	1961	25.00
— Multicolor label, white "fan" logo			
❑ 1318 [M]	That's a-Plenty	1964	18.00
— Multicolor label, black "fan" logo			
❑ SD1318 [S]	That's a-Plenty	1959	40.00
— Green label			
❑ SD1318 [S]	That's a-Plenty	1961	25.00
— Multicolor label, white "fan" logo			
❑ SD1318 [S]	That's a-Plenty	1964	18.00
— Multicolor label, black "fan" logo			
❑ 1336 [M]	The Wild Jazz Age	1960	30.00
— Multicolor label, white "fan" logo			
❑ 1336 [M]	The Wild Jazz Age	1964	18.00
— Multicolor label, black "fan" logo			
❑ SD1336 [S]	The Wild Jazz Age	1960	30.00
— Multicolor label, white "fan" logo			
❑ SD1336 [S]	The Wild Jazz Age	1964	25.00
— Multicolor label, black "fan" logo			
❑ ALS-143 [10]	Wilbur DeParis, Volume 2	1953	100.00
❑ ALS-141 [10]	Wilbur DeParis and His Rampart Street Ramblers	1952	100.00
❑ 1253 [M]	Wilbur DeParis at Symphony Hall	1957	50.00
— Black label			
❑ 1253 [M]	Wilbur DeParis at Symphony Hall	1961	25.00
— Multicolor label, white "fan" logo			
❑ 1253 [M]	Wilbur DeParis at Symphony Hall	1964	18.00
— Multicolor label, black "fan" logo			
❑ SD1253 [S]	Wilbur DeParis at Symphony Hall	1958	40.00
— Green label			
❑ SD1253 [S]	Wilbur DeParis at Symphony Hall	1961	25.00
— Multicolor label, white "fan" logo			
❑ SD1253 [S]	Wilbur DeParis at Symphony Hall	1964	18.00
— Multicolor label, black "fan" logo			
❑ 1363 [M]	Wilbur DeParis on the Riviera	1961	30.00
— Multicolor label, white "fan" logo			
❑ 1363 [M]	Wilbur DeParis on the Riviera	1964	18.00
— Multicolor label, black "fan" logo			
❑ SD1363 [S]	Wilbur DeParis on the Riviera	1961	30.00
— Multicolor label, white "fan" logo			
❑ SD1363 [S]	Wilbur DeParis on the Riviera	1964	25.00
— Multicolor label, black "fan" logo			
❑ 1288 [M]	Wilbur DeParis Plays Cole Porter	1958	50.00
— Black label			
❑ 1288 [M]	Wilbur DeParis Plays Cole Porter	1961	25.00
— Multicolor label, white "fan" logo			
❑ 1288 [M]	Wilbur DeParis Plays Cole Porter	1964	18.00
— Multicolor label, black "fan" logo			

HERITAGE

Number	Title	Yr	NM
❑ SS-1207 [M]	Wilbur DeParis	1956	50.00

DEPAUR CHORUS, THE

COLUMBIA

Number	Title	Yr	NM
❑ CL923 [M]	Calypso Christmas	1956	40.00
❑ CL725 [M]	The Spirit of Christmas/God Is With Us	1955	30.00

Number	Title	Yr	NM

COLUMBIA MASTERWORKS

❏ AL45 [10]	Swing Low	1953	60.00
❏ ML2119 [10]	Work Songs and Spirituals	195?	60.00

MERCURY LIVING PRESENCE

❏ SR90418 [S]	Danse Calinda! Creole Songs, Work Songs and Spirituals	196?	50.00

—*Maroon label, no "Vendor: Mercury Record Corporation*

❏ SR90418 [S]	Danse Calinda! Creole Songs, Work Songs and Spirituals	196?	30.00

—*Maroon label, with "Vendor: Mercury Record Corporation*

❏ SR90382 [S]	Songs of New Nations	196?	60.00

—*Maroon label, no "Vendor: Mercury Record Corporation*

❏ SR90382 [S]	Songs of New Nations	196?	40.00

—*Maroon label, with "Vendor: Mercury Record Corporation*

DEPECHE MODE

MUTE

❏ WBA1234300 [B]	Exciter	2014	30.00
❏ MUTEL5	The Singles 86-98	1998	30.00

—*Numbered, limited box set pressed in England with U.S. bar code sticker*

SIRE

❏ 25853	101	1989	18.00
❏ 23751	A Broken Frame	1982	15.00
❏ 25429	Black Celebration	1986	12.00
❏ R143674	Catching Up with Depeche Mode	1985	15.00

—*RCA Music Service edition*

❏ 25346	Catching Up with Depeche Mode	1985	12.00
❏ R100560	Catching Up with Depeche Mode	1990	15.00

—*BMG Direct Marketing edition; reissue*

❏ 23900	Construction Time Again	1983	15.00
❏ R100598	Music for the Masses	1988	15.00

—*BMG Direct Marketing edition*

❏ 25614	Music for the Masses	1987	12.00
❏ 25124	People Are People	1984	12.00
❏ PRO-A-5192 [DJ]	Selections from the Commercially Available Limited Edition Box Sets One and Two	1991	40.00

—*Promo-only sampler*

❏ PRO-A-5242 [DJ]	Selections from the Commercially Available Limited Edition Box Set Three	1991	40.00
❏ 25194	Some Great Reward	1984	15.00
❏ SRK3042	Speak & Spell	1981	18.00
❏ WBA1234364 [B]	Ultra	2014	35.00
❏ 26081	Violator	1990	18.00
❏ R173408	Violator	1990	18.00

—*BMG Direct Marketing edition*

❏ WBA1233980 [B]	Violator	2014	35.00

DEPENDABLES, THE

UNITED ARTISTS

❏ UAS-6799	Klaatu Berrada Niktu	1971	25.00

DEPUTIES, THE

FARON YOUNG

❏ 002 [M]	Sounds of the Deputies	1965	30.00

DEREK AND THE DOMINOS

ATCO

❏ 2-704 [M]	Layla and Other Assorted Love Songs	1970	300.00

—*White label promo only*

❏ SD 2-704 [DJ]	Layla and Other Assorted Love Songs	1970	200.00

—*White label promo*

❏ SD 2-704 [S]	Layla and Other Assorted Love Songs	1970	30.00

DIRECT DISK

❏ SD-16629	Layla and Other Assorted Love Songs	1981	150.00

—*Audiophile vinyl*

MOBILE FIDELITY

❏ 2-239	Derek and the Dominos in Concert	1996	50.00

—*Audiophile vinyl*

MOTOWN

❏ 5310373	Layla and Other Assorted Love Songs	2008	30.00

POLYDOR

❏ PD2-3501	Layla and Other Assorted Love Songs	1972	25.00

RSO

❏ SO 2-8800	Derek and the Dominos in Concert	1973	25.00
❏ RS-2-3801	Layla and Other Assorted Love Songs	1977	18.00

DERISE, JOE

AUDIOPHILE

❏ AP-153	House of Flowers	1981	15.00

❏ AP-231	Joe DeRise Sings and Plays the Jimmy Van Heusen Anthology, Vol. 1	1989	12.00
❏ AP-232	Joe DeRise Sings and Plays the Jimmy Van Heusen Anthology, Vol. 2	1989	12.00
❏ AP-233	Joe DeRise Sings and Plays the Jimmy Van Heusen Anthology, Vol. 3	1989	12.00
❏ AP-174	The Blues Are Out of Town	1982	15.00
❏ AP-215	The Joe DeRise Tentette Is Mad About You	1986	12.00

BETHLEHEM

❏ BCP-1039 [10]	Joe DeRise Sings	1955	100.00
❏ BCP-51 [M]	Joe DeRise with the Australian Jazz Quintet	1956	50.00

INNER CITY

❏ IC-4003	I'll Remember Suzanne	1979	15.00

DERRINGER, RICK

BLUE SKY

❏ KZ32481	All American Boy	1973	18.00
❏ ZQ32481 [Q]	All American Boy	1974	30.00
❏ PZ32481	All American Boy	197?	10.00

—*Reissue with new prefix*

❏ PZ34181	Derringer	1976	15.00
❏ PZ34848	Derringer Live	1977	15.00

—*Without bar code*

❏ PZ34848	Derringer Live	198?	10.00

—*Reissue with bar code*

❏ JZ36551	Face to Face	1980	12.00
❏ JZ36092	Guitars and Women	1979	12.00
❏ JZ35075	If I Weren't So Romantic I'd Shoot You	1978	12.00
❏ PRO265	Live in Cleveland	1977	24.00

—*Promo*

❏ PZ33423	Spring Fever	1975	15.00
❏ PZQ33423 [Q]	Spring Fever	1975	30.00
❏ PZ34470	Sweet Evil	1977	18.00

PASSPORT

❏ PB-6025	Good Dirty Fun	1983	12.00

DESANTO, SUGAR PIE

CHECKER

❏ LP 2979 [M]	Sugar Pie DeSanto	1961	200.00

DESARIO, TERI

CASABLANCA

❏ NBLP-7231	Caught	1980	15.00
❏ NBLP-7178	Moonlight Madness	1979	12.00
❏ NBLP-7115	Pleasure Train	1978	15.00

DAYSPRING

❏ 701-411301-1	Call to Us All	1983	15.00
❏ 701-413101-X	Voices in the Wind	1985	15.00

DESCENDANTS OF MIKE & PHOEBE, THE

STRATA-EAST

❏ SES-19744	A Spirit Speaks	1973	60.00

DESCENDENTS

EPITAPH

❏ 86481 [B]	Everything Sucks	1996	18.00

FAT WRECK CHORDS

❏ FAT673	Cool to Be You	2004	15.00

NEW ALLIANCE

❏ NAR-025	Bonus Fat	1985	18.00
❏ NAR-029	Enjoy!	1986	18.00
❏ NAR-026	I Don't Want to Grow Up	1985	18.00
❏ NAR-012	Milo Goes to College	1982	18.00

SST

❏ 112	All	1987	15.00
❏ 144	Bonus Fat	198?	15.00
❏ 242	Enjoy!	1989	15.00
❏ 205	Hallraker Live!	1988	15.00
❏ 143	I Don't Want to Grow Up	198?	15.00
❏ 163	Liveage!	1988	15.00
❏ 142	Milo Goes to College	198?	15.00
❏ 259	Somery	1991	18.00

DESERT ROSE BAND, THE

MCA

❏ 42169	Running	1988	10.00
❏ 5991	The Desert Rose Band	1987	10.00

DESHANNON, JACKIE

AMHERST

❏ AMH1016	Quick Touches	1978	15.00
❏ AMX1010	You're the Only Dancer	1977	15.00

ATLANTIC

❏ SD7231	Jackie	1972	15.00
❏ SD7303	Your Baby Is a Lady	1974	15.00

CAPITOL

❏ ST-772	Songs	1971	15.00

COLUMBIA

❏ PC33500	New Arrangement	1975	15.00

IMPERIAL

❏ LP-9328 [M]	Are You Ready for This?	1966	18.00
❏ LP-12328 [S]	Are You Ready for This?	1966	25.00

❏ LP-9352 [M]	For You	1967	18.00
❏ LP-12352 [S]	For You	1967	25.00
❏ LP-9296 [M]	In the Wind	1965	25.00

—*Black and pink label*

❏ LP-9296 [M]	In the Wind	1966	18.00

—*Black and green label*

❏ LP-12296 [S]	In the Wind	1965	30.00

—*Black and pink label*

❏ LP-12296 [S]	In the Wind	1966	25.00

—*Black and green label*

❏ LP-12415	Laurel Canyon	1969	18.00
❏ LP-12386	Me About You	1968	18.00
❏ LP-9344 [M]	New Image	1967	18.00
❏ LP-12344 [S]	New Image	1967	25.00
❏ LP-12442	Put a Little Love in Your Heart	1969	18.00
❏ LP-9286 [M]	This Is Jackie DeShannon	1965	25.00

—*Black and pink label*

❏ LP-9286 [M]	This Is Jackie DeShannon	1966	18.00

—*Black and green label*

❏ LP-12286 [S]	This Is Jackie DeShannon	1965	30.00

—*Black and pink label*

❏ LP-12286 [S]	This Is Jackie DeShannon	1966	25.00

—*Black and green label*

❏ LP-12453	To Be Free	1970	18.00
❏ LP-12404	What the World Needs Now Is Love	1968	18.00
❏ LP-9294 [M]	You Won't Forget Me	1965	25.00

—*Black and pink label*

❏ LP-9294 [M]	You Won't Forget Me	1966	18.00

—*Black and green label*

❏ LP-12294 [S]	You Won't Forget Me	1965	30.00

—*Black and pink label*

❏ LP-12294 [S]	You Won't Forget Me	1966	25.00

—*Black and green label*

LIBERTY

❏ LRP-3390 [M]	Breakin' It Up on the Beatles Tour!	1964	40.00
❏ LST-7390 [S]	Breakin' It Up on the Beatles Tour!	1964	50.00
❏ LRP-3320 [M]	Jackie DeShannon	1963	40.00
❏ LST-7320 [S]	Jackie DeShannon	1963	50.00
❏ LN-10265	Jackie DeShannon	1985	10.00
❏ LN-10179	The Very Best of Jackie DeShannon	1983	10.00

—*Reissue of United Artists 434*

SUNSET

❏ SUS-5322	Jackie DeShannon	1970	15.00
❏ SUS-5225	Lonely Girl	1968	15.00

UNITED ARTISTS

❏ UA-LA434-E	The Very Best of Jackie DeShannon	1975	15.00

DESMARAIS, LORRAINE

JAZZIMAGE

❏ JZ-106	Andiamo	1985	15.00
❏ JZ 100	Lorraine Desmarais Trio	1984	15.00

DESMOND, JOHNNY

COLUMBIA

❏ CL1477 [M]	Blue Smoke	1960	18.00
❏ CS8268 [S]	Blue Smoke	1960	25.00
❏ CL1399 [M]	Once Upon a Time	1959	25.00
❏ CS8194 [S]	Once Upon a Time	1959	30.00

CORAL

❏ CRL57073 [M]	Desmo Sings Desmond	195?	50.00
❏ CRL57130 [M]	Easy Come Easy Go	195?	40.00
❏ CRL56124 [10]	Hearts and Flowers	1955	60.00
❏ CRL57079 [M]	Souvenir d'Italie	195?	40.00

CORONET

❏ CXS-236 [S]	Johnny Desmond In Las Vegas!	196?	12.00

CRAFTSMEN

❏ C-8019 [M]	Hymns	196?	12.00
❏ C-8030 [M]	Johnny Desmond Sings for Dancing	196?	12.00

EVON

❏ 343 [M]	Johnny Desmond Sings Hymns for You	196?	12.00

GOLDEN TONE

❏ C-4045 [M]	Dance Party Featuring Johnny Desmond	196?	12.00
❏ 14045 [S]	Dance Party Featuring Johnny Desmond	196?	15.00
❏ 9628S [S]	Hymns	196?	15.00
❏ C-4031 [M]	Hymns	196?	12.00

LION

❏ L-70061 [M]	Dreams of Paris	1958	18.00

MAYFAIR

❏ 9628S [S]	Hymns	1958	18.00

—*Yellow vinyl*

❏ 9635S [S]	Johnny Desmond Swings	1958	18.00

—*Yellow vinyl*

MGM

❏ E-186 [10]	Hands Across the Table	1952	40.00
❏ E-3561 [M]	Hands Across the Table	1957	30.00

MOVIETONE

❏ 71011 [M]	Johnny Desmond On Location	1966	15.00

Number	Title	Yr	NM
❑ S-72011 [S]	Johnny Desmond On Location	1966	18.00
PICKWICK			
❑ SPC-3558	Hymns for the Family	197?	12.00
RONDO			
❑ 9762 [S]	Dance Party Featuring Johnny Desmond	196?	15.00
❑ 1762 [M]	Dance Party Featuring Johnny Desmond	196?	12.00
TOPS			
❑ 1762 [M]	Dance Party Featuring Johnny Desmond	196?	12.00
❑ 9762 [S]	Dance Party Featuring Johnny Desmond	196?	15.00
❑ L1628 [M]	Hymns	1958	12.00
❑ L1635 [S]	Johnny Desmond Swings	1958	15.00
VENISE			
❑ 7013 [M]	So Nice!	196?	12.00
❑ 10013 [S]	So Nice!	196?	18.00
— Yellow vinyl			
VOCALION			
❑ VL3773 [M]	Johnny Desmond	1966	15.00
❑ VL73773 [R]	Johnny Desmond	1966	12.00

DESMOND, JOHNNY/JOHNNY KAY

Number	Title	Yr	NM
CORONET			
❑ CX-193 [M]	Johnny Desmond Sings	196?	15.00
❑ CXS-193 [R]	Johnny Desmond Sings	196?	12.00

DESMOND, PAUL

Number	Title	Yr	NM
A&M			
❑ SP-3032	Bridge Over Troubled Water	1970	25.00
❑ SP-3024	From the Hot Afternoon	1969	18.00
❑ SP9-3024	From the Hot Afternoon	198?	25.00
— Audio Master Plus" reissue			
❑ SP-3015	Summertime	1969	18.00
ARTISTS HOUSE			
❑ AH2	Paul Desmond	1978	12.00
CTI			
❑ CTS-6059	Pure Desmond	1975	12.00
❑ CTS-6039	Skylark	1974	12.00
CTI/CBS ASSOCIATED			
❑ FZ40806	Pure Desmond	1987	12.00
— Reissue of CTI 6059			
❑ FZ44170	Skylark	1988	12.00
— Reissue of CTI 6039			
DISCOVERY			
❑ 840	East of the Sun	198?	12.00
FANTASY			
❑ 3-21 [10]	Paul Desmond	1955	100.00
❑ 3235 [M]	Paul Desmond Quartet Featuring Don Elliott	1956	80.00
— Red vinyl			
❑ 3235 [M]	Paul Desmond Quartet Featuring Don Elliott	1957	40.00
— Black vinyl, red label, non-flexible vinyl			
❑ 3235 [M]	Paul Desmond Quartet Featuring Don Elliott	1962	25.00
— Black vinyl, red label, flexible vinyl			
❑ OJC-119	Paul Desmond Quartet Featuring Don Elliott	198?	12.00
— Reissue of Fantasy 3235			
FINESSE			
❑ FW37487	Paul Desmond and the Modern Jazz Quartet	1981	12.00
HORIZON			
❑ 850	Paul Desmond Live	1976	18.00
MOSAIC			
❑ MR6-120	The Complete Recordings of the Paul Desmond Quartet with Jim Hall	199?	300.00
RCA CAMDEN			
❑ ACL1-0201	Samba de Orfeo	1973	12.00
RCA VICTOR			
❑ LPM-3320 [M]	Boss Antigua	1965	25.00
❑ LSP-3320 [S]	Boss Antigua	1965	30.00
❑ LPM-2438 [M]	Desmond Blue	1961	30.00
❑ LSP-2438 [S]	Desmond Blue	1961	30.00
❑ LPM-3480 [M]	Easy Living	1965	25.00
❑ LSP-3480 [S]	Easy Living	1965	30.00
❑ LPM-3407 [M]	Glad to Be Unhappy	1965	25.00
❑ LSP-3407 [S]	Glad to Be Unhappy	1965	30.00
❑ ANL1-2807	Pure Gold	1978	12.00
❑ LPM-2569 [M]	Take Ten	1962	30.00
❑ LSP-2569 [S]	Take Ten	1962	30.00
❑ LPM-2654 [M]	Two of a Mind	1963	30.00
❑ LSP-2654 [S]	Two of a Mind	1963	30.00
WARNER BROS.			
❑ W1356 [M]	First Place Again	1960	30.00
❑ WS1356 [S]	First Place Again	1960	30.00

DESOUZA, RAUL

Number	Title	Yr	NM
CAPITOL			
❑ SW-11774	Don't Ask My Neighbors	1978	15.00
❑ ST-11648	Sweet Lucy	1977	15.00
❑ ST-11918	'Til Tomorrow Comes	1979	15.00

Number	Title	Yr	NM
MILESTONE			
❑ 9061	Colors	1975	18.00

DESPAIR [AKA THE VIBRATORS]

Number	Title	Yr	NM
CLEOPATRA			
❑ 6613 [B]	The Birth Of The Vibrators 1973-1975		25.00

DESTINY'S CHILD

Number	Title	Yr	NM
COLUMBIA			
❑ CAS56652 [DJ]	Holiday Sampler	2001	18.00
— Contains 8 tracks -- 3 versions of "Emotion," 3 versions of "8 Days of Christmas" and 2 versions of "Sexy Daddy"			
❑ C261063	Survivor	2001	18.00
❑ C269870	The Writing's on the Wall	1999	18.00
❑ C286431	This Is the Remix	2002	18.00
❑ DES-01 [DJ]	This Is the Remix Sampler	2002	18.00
— Five-song sampler			

DETERGENTS, THE

Number	Title	Yr	NM
ROULETTE			
❑ R25308 [M]	The Many Faces of the Detergents	1965	120.00
❑ SR25308 [R]	The Many Faces of the Detergents	1965	100.00

DEUCE COUPES, THE

Number	Title	Yr	NM
CROWN			
❑ CLP-5393 [M]	The Shut Downs	1963	25.00
❑ CST-393 [S]	The Shut Downs	1963	30.00
DEL-FI			
❑ DFLP-1243 [M]	Hotrodder's Choice	1963	50.00
❑ DFST-1243 [S]	Hotrodder's Choice	1963	60.00

DEUCHAR, JIMMY

Number	Title	Yr	NM
CONTEMPORARY			
❑ C-3529 [M]	Pub Crawling	1957	50.00
DISCOVERY			
❑ DL-2004 [10]	New Sounds from England	1953	80.00

DEVIANTS, THE

Number	Title	Yr	NM
CLEOPATRA			
❑ CLP1803 [B]	Ptooff!	2014	25.00
SIRE			
❑ SES-97005 [B]	Disposable	1969	200.00
❑ SES-97016 [B]	No. 3	1969	200.00
❑ SES-97001 [B]	Ptoof!	1968	250.00

DEVILED HAM

Number	Title	Yr	NM
SUPER K			
❑ SKS-6003	I Had Too Much to Dream Last Night	1968	30.00

DEVIL'S ANVIL, THE

Number	Title	Yr	NM
COLUMBIA			
❑ CL2664 [M]	Hard Rock from the Middle East	1967	100.00
❑ CS9464 [S]	Hard Rock from the Middle East	1967	100.00

DEVO

Number	Title	Yr	NM
DUTCH EAST INDIA			
❑ DE-112008-1	Smooth Noodle Maps	1991	30.00
— Red vinyl, 1,000 copies pressed			
ENIGMA			
❑ 73514	Now It Can Be Told!	1989	15.00
❑ EPRO326 [DJ]	Smooth Noodle Maps	1990	25.00
— Promo only, no picture cover			
❑ 73303	Total Devo	1988	15.00
JACKPOT			
❑ JPR028 [B]	Live At Max's Kansas City - November 15, 1977	2014	30.00
WARNER BROS.			
❑ MINI3548 [EP]	Dev-O Live	1981	12.00
— All copies came in plastic sleeve			
❑ BSK3337	Duty Now for the Future	1979	15.00
❑ BSK3435	Freedom of Choice	1980	12.00
❑ PRO-A-928 [EP]	Freedom of Choice/Whip It/ Be Still/Gates of Steel	1980	16.00
— Promo version of "Dev-O Live"			
❑ BSK3595	New Traditionalists	1981	25.00
— First pressings include bonus 45 (EP 3595) and poster; deduct 1/3 if missing			
❑ 23741 [B]	Oh No! It's Devo	1982	12.00
❑ W1-23741	Oh No! It's Devo	1982	15.00
— Columbia House version, no easel cutout on back cover			
❑ BSK3239	Q: Are We Not Men? A: We Are Devo!	1978	18.00
❑ 25097	Shout	1984	15.00

DEVOL, FRANK

Number	Title	Yr	NM
ABC-PARAMOUNT			
❑ 534 [M]	Italian Romance American Style	1966	15.00
❑ S-534 [S]	Italian Romance American Style	1966	18.00

Number	Title	Yr	NM
❑ 513 [M]	Theme from "Peyton Place" and 11 Other Great Themes	1965	15.00
❑ S-513 [S]	Theme from "Peyton Place" and 11 Other Great Themes	1965	18.00
COLUMBIA			
❑ CL1371 [M]	Fabulous Hollywood	1959	18.00
❑ CS8172 [S]	Fabulous Hollywood	1959	25.00
❑ CL1451 [M]	Four Seasons of Love	1960	18.00
❑ CS0(# unk) [S]	Four Seasons of Love	1960	25.00
❑ CL1482 [M]	More Old Sweet Songs	1960	18.00
❑ CS8273 [S]	More Old Sweet Songs	1960	25.00
❑ CL1108 [M]	Portraits	1957	18.00
❑ C2L12 [M]	The Columbia Album of Irving Berlin	1958	30.00
❑ C2S812 [S]	The Columbia Album of Irving Berlin	1958	40.00
❑ CL1260 [M]	The Columbia Album of Irving Berlin, Volume 1	1958	18.00
❑ CS8044 [S]	The Columbia Album of Irving Berlin, Volume 1	1958	25.00
❑ CL1261 [M]	The Columbia Album of Irving Berlin, Volume 2	1958	18.00
❑ CS8045 [S]	The Columbia Album of Irving Berlin, Volume 2	1958	25.00
❑ CL1413 [M]	The Old Sweet Songs	1960	18.00
❑ CS8209 [S]	The Old Sweet Songs	1960	25.00
❑ CL1543 [M]	The Old Sweet Songs of Christmas	1960	18.00
❑ CS8343 [S]	The Old Sweet Songs of Christmas	1960	18.00
COLUMBIA SPECIAL PRODUCTS			
❑ EN216437	The Columbia Album of Irving Berlin	1983	15.00
HARMONY			
❑ HL7356 [M]	The Old Sweet Songs of Christmas	196?	15.00
❑ HS11156 [S]	The Old Sweet Songs of Christmas	196?	18.00

DEVROE, BILLY, AND THE DEVILAIRES

Number	Title	Yr	NM
TAMPA			
❑ TP-31 [M]	Billy Devroe and the Devilaires, Vol. 1	1957	40.00
❑ TP-39 [M]	Billy Devroe and the Devilaires, Vol. 2	1958	40.00

DEWITT, GEORGE

Number	Title	Yr	NM
EPIC			
❑ LN3562 [M]	George DeWitt Sings That Tune	1959	25.00
❑ BN531 [S]	George DeWitt Sings That Tune	1959	30.00

DEXTER, AL

Number	Title	Yr	NM
CAPITOL			
❑ T1701 [M]	Al Dexter Sings and Plays His Greatest Hits	1962	30.00
❑ ST1701 [S]	Al Dexter Sings and Plays His Greatest Hits	1962	40.00
COLUMBIA			
❑ CL9005 [10]	Songs of the Southwest	195?	50.00
HARMONY			
❑ HL7293 [M]	Pistol Packin' Mama	1961	25.00

DEXY'S MIDNIGHT RUNNERS

Number	Title	Yr	NM
CAPITOL			
❑ SN-16288	Searching for the Young Soul Rebels	1983	12.00
— Budget-line reissue			
EMI AMERICA			
❑ SW-17042	Searching for the Young Soul Rebels	1980	18.00
MERCURY			
❑ 822989-1	Don't Stand Me Down	1985	12.00
❑ SRM-1-4069	Too-Rye-Ay	1982	12.00
PARLOPHONE			
❑ 2564629701 [B]	Searching For The Young Soul Rebels	2014	25.00

DEYOUNG, CLIFF

Number	Title	Yr	NM
MCA			
❑ 432	Cliff DeYoung	1974	12.00
❑ 387	Sunshine	1973	18.00

DEYOUNG, DENNIS

Number	Title	Yr	NM
A&M			
❑ SP-5109	Back to the World	1986	10.00
❑ SP-5006	Desert Moon	1984	10.00

DIALOGUE

Number	Title	Yr	NM
COLD			
❑ (no #)0	Dialogue	1974	150.00
— White cover with insert			
❑ (no #)0	Dialogue	1972	150.00
— Orange cover with insert			

DIALS, THE

Number	Title	Yr	NM
TIME			
❑ 52100 [M]	It's Monkey Time	1964	30.00
❑ S-2100 [S]	It's Monkey Time	1964	30.00

Number	Title	Yr	NM

DIAMOND, GREGG

MARLIN
❑ 2217	Star Cruiser	1978	18.00

MERCURY
| ❑ SRM-1-3757 | Hardware | 1979 | 15.00 |

POLYDOR
❑ PD-1-6123	Bionic Boogie	1978	15.00
— As "Bionic Boogie"			
❑ PD-1-6162	Hot Butterfly	1978	18.00
— As "Gregg Diamond Bionic Boogie"			
❑ PD-1-6237	Tiger Tiger	1979	15.00

DIAMOND, LEO

ABC-PARAMOUNT
| ❑ ABC-303 [M] | Subliminal Sounds | 1960 | 30.00 |
| ❑ ABCS-303 [S] | Subliminal Sounds | 1960 | 40.00 |

RCA VICTOR
| ❑ LPM-1165 [M] | Skin Diver Suite and Other Selections | 1955 | 60.00 |

REPRISE
❑ R-6002 [M]	Exciting Sounds of the South Seas	1961	30.00
❑ R9-6002 [S]	Exciting Sounds of the South Seas	1961	30.00
❑ R-6024 [M]	Off Shore	1962	30.00
❑ R9-6024 [S]	Off Shore	1962	30.00
❑ R-6009 [M]	Themes from Great Foreign Films	1961	30.00
❑ R9-6009 [S]	Themes from Great Foreign Films	1961	30.00

DIAMOND, NEIL

BANG
❑ BLPS224 [P]	Do It!	1971	30.00
❑ BLPS224	Do It!	1974	15.00
— Later pressing on blue "clouds" label			
❑ BLPS-227 [S]	Double Gold	1973	40.00
❑ BLPS227	Double Gold	1974	18.00
— Later pressing on blue "clouds" label			
❑ BLP217 [M]	Just for You	1967	40.00
— With blurb for "Thank the Lord for the Night Time" on cover			
❑ BLPS217 [P]	Just for You	1967	50.00
— With blurb for "Thank the Lord for the Night Time" on cover			
❑ BLPS217 [P]	Just for You	1968	40.00
— With blurb for "Shilo" pasted over "Thank the Lord for the Night Time" blurb			
❑ BLPS217 [P]	Just for You	1970	25.00
— With blurb for "Shilo" imprinted on cover			
❑ BLPS217	Just for You	1974	15.00
— Later pressing on blue "clouds" label			
❑ BLPS219 [P]	Neil Diamond's Greatest Hits	1968	40.00
— First editions have the single version of "Solitary Man" in rechanneled stereo			
❑ BLPS219 [P]	Neil Diamond's Greatest Hits	196?	25.00
— Later editions have an alternate take of "Solitary Man" in true stereo			
❑ BLPS219	Neil Diamond's Greatest Hits	1974	15.00
— Later pressing on blue "clouds" label			
❑ BLPS221 [S]	Shilo	1970	40.00
❑ BLPS221	Shilo	1974	15.00
— Later pressing on blue "clouds" label			
❑ BLP214 [M]	The Feel of Neil Diamond	1966	60.00
— All tracks play mono			
❑ BLP214 [P]	The Feel of Neil Diamond	1966	80.00
— Album is labeled mono, but plays in stereo			
❑ BLPS214 [P]	The Feel of Neil Diamond	1966	100.00
— Album is labeled stereo and plays in stereo (except "Solitary Man," "Do It," "I'll Come Running" are rechanneled)			
❑ BLPS214	The Feel of Neil Diamond	1974	15.00
— Later pressing on blue "clouds" label			

CAPITOL
| ❑ SWAV-12120 | The Jazz Singer | 1980 | 12.00 |

COLUMBIA
❑ TC38068	12 Greatest Hits, Vol. II	1982	12.00
❑ HC48068	12 Greatest Hits, Vol. II	1982	100.00
— Half-speed mastered edition			
❑ 8-2876-77507-1	12 Songs	2006	25.00
❑ PC33965	Beautiful Noise	1976	15.00
— Originals have no bar code			
❑ PC38792	Classics -- The Early Years	1983	12.00
— Possibly a reissue of Frog King 1			
❑ OC40368	Headed for the Future	1986	10.00
❑ TC38359	Heartlight	1982	12.00
❑ HC48359	Heartlight	1982	40.00
— Half-speed mastered edition			
❑ AS 99-1586 [DJ]	Heartlight	1982	30.00
— Promo-only picture disc			
❑ CG240990	Hot August Night II	1987	15.00
❑ JC34990	I'm Glad You're Here with Me Tonight	1977	15.00
❑ KS32550	Jonathan Livingston Seagull	1973	15.00
— With booklet			
❑ HC42550	Jonathan Livingston Seagull	1982	50.00
— Half-speed mastered edition			
❑ KC234404	Love at the Greek	1977	18.00
❑ C48610	Lovescape	1991	30.00
❑ TC37628	On the Way to the Sky	1981	12.00
❑ HC47628	On the Way to the Sky	1982	30.00
— Half-speed mastered edition			

Number	Title	Yr	NM
❑ QC39199	Primitive	1984	12.00
❑ 9C939915 [PD]	Primitive	1984	25.00
❑ FC36121	September Morn	1979	15.00
❑ PC32919	Serenade	1974	15.00
❑ PCQ32919 [Q]	Serenade	1974	30.00
❑ OC45025	The Best Years of Our Lives	1988	10.00
❑ FC35625	You Don't Bring Me Flowers	1978	15.00
❑ HC45625	You Don't Bring Me Flowers	1982	40.00
— Half-speed mastered edition			

DIRECT DISK
| ❑ SD16612 | His 12 Greatest Hits | 1982 | 50.00 |
| — Audiophile vinyl | | | |

FROG KING
| ❑ AAR-1 | Early Classics | 1972 | 40.00 |
| — Compilation of Bang material for Columbia Record Club; includes songbook (deduct 25% if missing) | | | |

MCA
❑ 2227	And the Singer Sings His Song	1976	18.00
❑ 37060	And the Singer Sings His Song	1980	10.00
❑ 37209	Gold	1981	10.00
❑ 8000	Hot August Night	1972	25.00
❑ 6896	Hot August Night	1980	15.00
— Reissue of MCA 2-8000			
❑ 5239	Love Songs	1981	12.00
❑ 2005	Moods	1973	12.00
❑ 37194	Moods	1981	10.00
❑ 2007	Neil Diamond/Gold	1973	12.00
❑ 2106	Neil Diamond/His 12 Greatest Hits	1974	18.00
❑ 5219	Neil Diamond/His 12 Greatest Hits	1981	12.00
— Reissue of MCA 2106			
❑ 1489	Neil Diamond/His 12 Greatest Hits	1987	10.00
— Reissue of MCA 5219			
❑ 37252	Neil Diamond/His 12 Greatest Hits	198?	10.00
— Reissue of MCA 5219			
❑ 2103	Rainbow	1973	18.00
— Compilation of Uni tracks			
❑ 37059	Rainbow	1980	10.00
❑ 2008	Stones	1973	12.00
❑ 37195	Stones	1981	10.00
❑ 2011	Sweet Caroline (Brother Love's Travelling Salvation Show)	1973	12.00
❑ 37057	Sweet Caroline/Brother Love's Travelling Salvation Show	1980	10.00
❑ 2013	Tap Root Manuscript	1973	12.00
❑ 37196	Tap Root Manuscript	1981	10.00
❑ 2006	Touching You Touching Me	1973	12.00
❑ 37058	Touching You Touching Me	1980	10.00
❑ 37056	Velvet Gloves and Spit	1980	10.00

MOBILE FIDELITY
❑ 2-024 [B]	Hot August Night	1979	60.00
— Audiophile vinyl			
❑ 1-071	The Jazz Singer	1981	30.00
— Audiophile vinyl			

SILVER EAGLE
| ❑ MSM-35151 | The Neil Diamond Collection | 1988 | 30.00 |
| — Mail-order offer; contains material from his Uni period | | | |

UNI
❑ 73047	Brother Love's Travelling Salvation Show	1969	30.00
— First editions do not include "Sweet Caroline"			
❑ 73047	Brother Love's Travelling Salvation Show	1969	25.00
— Later editions add "Sweet Caroline"			
❑ 93047	Brother Love's Travelling Salvation Show	1971	18.00
— Reissue of the version with "Sweet Caroline," with new number			
❑ 93136	Moods	1972	25.00
❑ ND-11 [DJ]	Neil Diamond DJ Sampler	1970	250.00
❑ 73084	Neil Diamond/Gold	1970	25.00
❑ 1913 [DJ]	Open-End Interview with Neil Diamond	1971	300.00
❑ 93106	Stones	1971	25.00
❑ 73092	Tap Root Manuscript	1970	25.00
❑ ST-93501	Tap Root Manuscript	1970	30.00
— Capitol Record Club issue			
❑ 73071	Touching You Touching Me	1969	25.00
❑ 93071	Touching You Touching Me	1971	18.00
— Reissue of 73071			
❑ 73030	Velvet Gloves and Spit	1968	30.00
— First editions do not include "Shilo"			
❑ 73030-N	Velvet Gloves and Spit	1970	25.00
— Later editions add a new recording of "Shilo"			
❑ 93030-N	Velvet Gloves and Spit	1971	18.00
— Reissue of the version with "Shilo" added, with new number			

DIAMONDS, THE (1)

MERCURY
❑ MG-20213 [M]	Collection of Golden Hits	1956	120.00
❑ MG-20480 [M]	Songs from the Old West	1959	80.00
❑ SR-60159 [S]	Songs from the Old West	1959	120.00
❑ MG-20309 [M]	The Diamonds	1957	120.00

Number	Title	Yr	NM
❑ MG-20368 [M]	The Diamonds Meet Pete Rugolo	1958	80.00
❑ SR-60076 [S]	The Diamonds Meet Pete Rugolo	1959	120.00

RHINO
| ❑ RNDF-209 | The Best of the Diamonds | 1984 | 15.00 |

WING
| ❑ MGW-12178 [M] | Pop Hits by the Diamonds | 1962 | 30.00 |
| ❑ MGW-12114 [M] | The Diamonds: America's Famous Song Stylists | 1959 | 30.00 |

DICK AND DEEDEE

LIBERTY
| ❑ LRP-3236 [M] | Tell Me/The Mountain's High | 1962 | 50.00 |
| ❑ LST-7236 [R] | Tell Me/The Mountain's High | 1962 | 40.00 |

WARNER BROS.
❑ W1623 [M]	Song We've Sung on "Shindig	1966	30.00
❑ WS1623 [S]	Song We've Sung on "Shindig	1966	30.00
❑ W1586 [M]	Thou Shalt Not Steal	1965	30.00
❑ WS1586 [S]	Thou Shalt Not Steal	1965	30.00
❑ W1538 [M]	Turn Around	1964	30.00
❑ WS1538 [S]	Turn Around	1964	30.00
❑ W1500 [M]	Young and In Love	1963	30.00
❑ WS1500 [S]	Young and In Love	1963	30.00

DICKENS, JIMMY

COLUMBIA
❑ CS9648 [S]	Big Man in Country Music	1968	30.00
❑ CS9648 [M]	Big Man in Country Music	1968	50.00
— White label promo with stereo number and "Mono" on label; "Special Mono Radio Station Copy" sticker and timing strip on front cover			
❑ CL1545 [M]	Big Songs by Little Jimmy Dickens	1960	30.00
❑ CS8345 [S]	Big Songs by Little Jimmy Dickens	1960	40.00
❑ CL2288 [M]	Handle with Care	1964	30.00
❑ CS9088 [S]	Handle with Care	1964	30.00
❑ CL2551 [M]	Little Jimmy Dickens' Greatest Hits	1966	30.00
❑ CS9351 [S]	Little Jimmy Dickens' Greatest Hits	1966	30.00
❑ CL1887 [M]	Little Jimmy Dickens Sings Out Behind the Barn	1962	30.00
❑ CS8687 [S]	Little Jimmy Dickens Sings Out Behind the Barn	1962	40.00
❑ CL2442 [M]	May the Bird of Paradise Fly Up Your Nose	1965	30.00
❑ CS9242 [S]	May the Bird of Paradise Fly Up Your Nose	1965	30.00
❑ CL1047 [M]	Raisin' the Dickens	1957	80.00
❑ CL9053 [10]	The Old Country Church	1954	120.00

DECCA
❑ DL75091	Jimmy Dickens Comes Callin'	1968	25.00
❑ DL75133	Jimmy Dickens' Greatest Hits	1969	25.00
❑ DL4967 [M]	Jimmy Dickens Sings	1967	30.00
❑ DL74967 [S]	Jimmy Dickens Sings	1967	25.00

DICKENSON, VIC, AND JOE THOMAS

ATLANTIC
❑ 1303 [M]	Mainstream	1958	50.00
— Black label			
❑ 1303 [M]	Mainstream	1961	25.00
— Multicolor label, white "fan" logo			
❑ SD1303 [S]	Mainstream	1958	40.00
— Green label			
❑ SD1303 [S]	Mainstream	1961	25.00
— Multicolor label, white "fan" logo			

DICKENSON, VIC

JAZZTONE
| ❑ J-1259 [M] | Slidin' Swing | 1956 | 40.00 |

SACKVILLE
| ❑ 2015 | Just Friends | 198? | 15.00 |

SONET
| ❑ 720 | Trombone Cholly | 197? | 12.00 |

STORYVILLE
| ❑ STLP-920 [M] | Vic's Boston Story | 1957 | 40.00 |

VANGUARD
❑ VRS-99/100	The Essential Vic Dickenson	197?	18.00
❑ VRS-8001 [10]	Vic Dickenson Septet, Volume 1	1953	50.00
❑ VRS-8002 [10]	Vic Dickenson Septet, Volume 2	1953	50.00
❑ VRS-8012 [10]	Vic Dickenson Septet, Volume 3	1954	50.00
❑ VRS-8013 [10]	Vic Dickenson Septet, Volume 4	1954	50.00
❑ VRS-8520 [M]	Vic Dickenson Showcase, Volume 1	1958	40.00
❑ VRS-8521 [M]	Vic Dickenson Showcase, Volume 2	1958	40.00

DICKERSON, DWIGHT

DISCOVERY
| ❑ DS-792 | Sooner or Later | 1978 | 15.00 |

Number	Title	Yr	NM

DICKERSON, WALT

AUDIO FIDELITY
❏ AFLP-2131 [M]	Unity	1963	25.00
❏ AFSD-6131 [S]	Unity	1963	30.00
❏ AFLP-2217 [M]	Vibes in Motion	1968	30.00
—Reissue of Dauntless 4313			
❏ AFSD-6217 [S]	Vibes in Motion	1968	18.00
—Reissue of Dauntless 6313			

DAUNTLESS
❏ DM-4313 [M]	Jazz Impressions of "Lawrence of Arabia"	1963	30.00
❏ DS-6313 [S]	Jazz Impressions of "Lawrence of Arabia"	1963	30.00

INNER CITY
❏ IC-2042	Peace	1976	18.00

MGM
❏ E-4358 [M]	Impressions of "A Patch of Blue	1965	25.00
❏ SE-4358 [S]	Impressions of "A Patch of Blue	1965	30.00

NEW JAZZ
❏ NJLP-8268 [M]	A Sense of Direction	1962	50.00
—Purple label			
❏ NJLP-8268 [M]	A Sense of Direction	1965	30.00
—Blue label, trident logo at right			
❏ NJLP-8275 [M]	Relativity	1962	50.00
—Purple label			
❏ NJLP-8275 [M]	Relativity	1965	30.00
—Blue label, trident logo at right			
❏ NJLP-8254 [M]	This Is Walt Dickerson	1961	300.00
—Purple label			
❏ NJLP-8254 [M]	This Is Walt Dickerson	1965	30.00
—Blue label, trident logo at right			
❏ NJLP-8283 [M]	To My Queen	1962	50.00
—Purple label			
❏ NJLP-8283 [M]	To My Queen	1965	30.00
—Blue label, trident logo at right			

SOUL NOTE
❏ SN-1028	Life Rays	1982	15.00

STEEPLECHASE
❏ SCG-1089	Divine Gemini	197?	15.00
❏ SCS-1146	I Hear You John	198?	15.00
❏ SCS-1115	Landscape with Open Door	1978	15.00
❏ SCS-1042	Peace	197?	12.00
—Reissue of Inner City 2042			
❏ SCS-1070	Serendipity	197?	15.00
❏ SCD-17002	Shades of Love	198?	30.00
—Direct-to-disc recording			
❏ SCS-1213	Tenderness	198?	15.00
❏ SCS-1112	To My Queen Revisited	1978	15.00
❏ SCS-1130	To My Son	1979	15.00
❏ SCS-1126	Visions	1979	15.00

DICKIES, THE

A&M
❏ SP-4796	Dawn of the Dickies	1979	18.00
❏ SP-4742	The Incredible Shrinking Dickies	1979	25.00
—First pressing on yellow vinyl			
❏ SP-4742	The Incredible Shrinking Dickies	1979	18.00

ENIGMA
❏ D1-73322 [EP]	Killer Klowns (From Outer Space)	1988	10.00
❏ D1-73289	Second Coming	1989	10.00

PVC
❏ 6903	Stukas Over Disneyland	1983	15.00

TAANG!
❏ 56 [B]	Locked and Loaded	1991	25.00

TRIPLE X
❏ 51168	Idjit Savant	1994	18.00

DICKS, THE

ALTERNATIVE TENTACLES
❏ VIRUS43	These People	1985	18.00

RADICAL
❏ RRR80351	Recorded Live at Raul's	1980	60.00
—One side features the Big Boys; the other side, the Dicks			

SST
❏ 017	Kill from the Heart	1983	30.00

DICKY DOO AND THE DON'TS

UNITED ARTISTS
❏ UAL-3097 [M]	Teen Scene	1959	40.00
❏ UAS-6097 [S]	Teen Scene	1959	50.00
❏ UAL-3094 [M]	The Madison and Other Dances	1959	40.00
❏ UAS-6094 [S]	The Madison and Other Dances	1959	50.00

DICTATORS, THE

ASYLUM
❏ 6E-147	Bloodbrothers	1978	18.00
❏ 7E-1109	Manifest Destiny	1977	16.00

EPIC
❏ KE33348	The Dictators Go Girl Crazy	1975	25.00

DIDDLEY, BO

ACCORD
❏ SN-7182	Toronto Rock and Roll Revival, Vol. 5	1982	25.00

CHECKER
❏ LP2989 [M]	16 All Time Greatest Hits	1964	50.00
❏ LPS2989 [R]	16 All Time Greatest Hits	1964	30.00
❏ LP2996 [M]	500% More Man	1965	60.00
❏ LPS2996 [R]	500% More Man	1965	30.00
❏ LP2984 [M]	Bo Diddley	1962	100.00
❏ LP1431 [M]	Bo Diddley	1958	200.00
❏ LP2985 [M]	Bo Diddley and Company	1963	120.00
❏ LP2977 [M]	Bo Diddley Is a Gunslinger	1961	200.00
❏ LP2980 [M]	Bo Diddley Is a Lover	1961	200.00
❏ LP2982 [M]	Bo Diddley's a Twister	1962	150.00
❏ LP2988 [M]	Bo Diddley's Beach Party	1963	100.00
❏ LP3007 [M]	Boss Man	1967	80.00
—Reissue of Chess 1431			
❏ LPS3007 [R]	Boss Man	1967	50.00
❏ LP1436 [M]	Go Bo Diddley	1959	200.00
❏ LP3006 [M]	Go Bo Diddley	1967	50.00
—Reissue of 1436			
❏ LPS3006 [R]	Go Bo Diddley	1967	40.00
❏ LP2974 [M]	Have Guitar, Will Travel	1960	200.00
❏ LP2992 [M]	Hey! Good Lookin'	1965	80.00
❏ LPS2992 [R]	Hey! Good Lookin'	1965	30.00
❏ LP2982 [M]	Road Runner	1967	100.00
—Reissue of "Bo Diddley's a Twister"			
❏ LPS-2982 [R]	Road Runner	1967	50.00
❏ LP2976 [M]	Spotlight on Bo Diddley	1960	200.00
❏ LP2987 [M]	Surfin' with Bo Diddley	1964	120.00
❏ LPS2987 [R]	Surfin' with Bo Diddley	1964	30.00
❏ LPS3013	The Black Gladiator	1968	30.00
❏ LP3001 [M]	The Originator	1966	30.00
❏ LPS3001 [S]	The Originator	1966	40.00

CHESS
❏ CH50001	Another Dimension	1971	40.00
❏ CH50047	Big Bad Bo	1974	30.00
❏ LP1431 [M]	Bo Diddley	1958	250.00
❏ CH-9194	Bo Diddley	1986	12.00
—Reissue of 1431			
❏ CH-9285	Bo Diddley Is a Gunslinger	1989	12.00
—Reissue of Checker 2977			
❏ CH-9196	Go Bo Diddley	1986	12.00
—Reissue of Checker 1436			
❏ 2CH60005	Got My Own Bag of Tricks	1972	30.00
❏ CH-9187	Have Guitar, Will Travel	1985	12.00
—Reissue of Checker 2974			
❏ CH-9106	His Greatest Sides, Vol. 1	1984	12.00
❏ CH-9264	Spotlight on Bo Diddley	1987	12.00
—Reissue of Checker 2976			
❏ CH3-19502	The Chess Box	1990	40.00
❏ CH50029	The London Bo Diddley Sessions	1973	30.00
❏ CH-9296	The London Bo Diddley Sessions	1989	12.00
—Reissue of 50029			
❏ CH50016	Where It All Began	1972	40.00

CLEOPATRA
❏ 8837 [B]	I'm A Man - Live '84		25.00
—picture disc			

RCA VICTOR
❏ APL1-1229	The 20th Anniversary of Rock and Roll	1976	25.00

SUNDAZED
❏ LP5443 [B]	Bo Diddley	2014	30.00
❏ LP [B]	Bo Diddley's Beach Party	2014	30.00

DIDDLEY, BO/CHUCK BERRY

CHECKER
❏ LP2991 [M]	Two Great Guitars	1964	60.00
❏ LPS2991 [R]	Two Great Guitars	1964	40.00

CHESS
❏ CH-9170	Two Great Guitars	1985	12.00
—Reissue of Checker 2991			

DIDDLEY, BO/MUDDY WATERS/HOWLIN' WOLF

CHECKER
❏ LP3010 [M]	Super, Super Blues Band	1968	50.00
❏ LPS3010 [S]	Super, Super Blues Band	1968	40.00

CHESS
❏ CH-9169	Super, Super Blues Band	1985	12.00
—Reissue of Checker 3010			

DIDDLEY, BO/MUDDY WATERS/LITTLE WALTER

CHECKER
❏ LP3008 [M]	Super Blues Band	1968	50.00
❏ LPS3008 [S]	Super Blues Band	1968	40.00

CHESS
❏ CH-9168	Super Blues Band	1985	12.00
—Reissue of Checker 3008			

DIDO

ARISTA
❏ RTH-2015	Life for Rent	2004	30.00
—Audiophile edition on 200-gram vinyl			
❏ RTH-2003	No Angel	2001	30.00
—Audiophile edition on 200-gram vinyl			

DIESEL

REGENCY
❏ SD19315	Watts in a Tank	1981	12.00
—Reissue, distributed by Atlantic			
❏ 9603	Watts in a Tank	1981	15.00
—Original release, distributed by JEM			

DIETRICH, MARLENE

CAPITOL
❏ T10443 [M]	Marlene Dietrich's Berlin	1966	25.00
❏ ST10443 [S]	Marlene Dietrich's Berlin	1966	30.00
❏ T10397 [M]	Marlene (Songs in German by the Inimitable Dietrich)	1965	25.00
❏ ST10397 [S]	Marlene (Songs in German by the Inimitable Dietrich)	1965	30.00
❏ STCR-300	The Magic of Marlene	1969	40.00
—All three of her Capitol LPs in one box			
❏ T10282 [M]	Wiedersehn Mit Marlene	1961	25.00
❏ ST10282 [S]	Wiedersehn Mit Marlene	1961	30.00

CLEOPATRA
❏ 3671 [B]	Lili Marlene		25.00
❏ 8142 [B]	Lili Marlene		30.00
—picture disc			

COLUMBIA
❏ CL1275 [M]	Lili Marlene	1959	50.00
❏ CL105 [10]	Overseas -- Songs for the O.S.S.	1953	100.00
❏ C32245	The Best of Marlene Dietrich	1973	15.00

COLUMBIA MASTERWORKS
❏ ML4975 [M]	At the Café de Paris	1955	50.00
❏ OL6430 [M]	Dietrich in London	1966	30.00
❏ OS2830 [S]	Dietrich in London	1966	30.00
❏ WL164 [M]	Dietrich in Rio	195?	40.00
❏ WS316 [S]	Dietrich in Rio	195?	50.00

DECCA
❏ DL8465 [M]	Marlene Dietrich	1957	40.00
—Black label, silver print			
❏ DL8465 [M]	Marlene Dietrich	196?	30.00
—Black label with color bars			
❏ DL78465 [R]	Marlene Dietrich	196?	25.00
❏ DL5100 [10]	Souvenir Album	1950	80.00

MURRAY HILL/CSP
❏ P314689	The Legendary Marlene Dietrich	1978	30.00

VOX
❏ VS-3040 [10]	Marlene Dietrich Sings	1950	80.00

DIGA RHYTHM BAND, THE

ROUND
❏ RX-110	The Diga Rhythm Band	1976	30.00

DIGGS, DAVID

INSTANT JOY
❏ 1002	Supercook!	198?	12.00

PALO ALTO
❏ 8037	Realworld	198?	12.00

PBR
❏ 12	Elusion	1979	15.00
❏ 9	Out on a Limb	197?	15.00

TBA
❏ TB-213	Right Before Your Eyes	1986	12.00
❏ TB-207	Streetshadows	1985	12.00

DIGITAL UNDERGROUND

CRITIQUE
❏ 15452	Future Rhythm	1996	15.00

JAKE
❏ INT2-92061	Who Got the Gravy?	1998	18.00

TOMMY BOY
❏ TB1470	No Nose Job: The Legend of Digital Underground	2001	18.00
❏ TB1026 [B]	Sex Packets	1990	18.00
❏ TB1045	Sons of the P.	1991	15.00
❏ TB964 [EP]	This Is an E.P. Release	1991	18.00

DILCHER, CHERYL

A&M
❏ SP-4394	Butterfly	1973	30.00
❏ SP-3640	Magic	1974	25.00

AMPEX
❏ A-10109	Special Songs	1970	50.00

BUTTERFLY
❏ FLY 003	Blue Sailor	1977	25.00
—Clear vinyl			
❏ FLY 003	Blue Sailor	1977	15.00
—Black vinyl			

DILL, DANNY

LIBERTY
❏ LRP-3301 [M]	Folk Songs from the Country	1963	25.00
❏ LST-7301 [S]	Folk Songs from the Country	1963	30.00

Number	Title	Yr	NM
MGM			
❏ E-3819 [M]	Folk Songs from the Wild West	1960	25.00
❏ SE-3819 [S]	Folk Songs from the Wild West	1960	30.00

DILLARD, DOUG
TOGETHER

| ❏ STT-1003 | The Banjo Album | 1970 | 80.00 |

DILLARD, VARETTA
SAVOY JAZZ

| ❏ SJL-1203 | Mercy, Mr. Percy, Volume 1 | 1989 | 15.00 |

DILLARD AND CLARK
A&M

| ❏ SP-4158 | The Fantastic Expedition of Dillard and Clark | 1968 | 25.00 |
| —Brown label | | | |

DILLARDS, THE
ANTHEM

| ❏ ANS-5901 | Roots and Branches | 1972 | 18.00 |

CRYSTAL CLEAR

| ❏ CCS-5007 | Mountain Rock | 1979 | 30.00 |
| —Direct-to-disc recording | | | |

ELEKTRA

❏ EKL-232 [M]	Back Porch Bluegrass	1963	30.00
❏ EKS-7232 [S]	Back Porch Bluegrass	1963	30.00
—Mandolin-player label			
❏ EKS-74054	Copperfields	1969	25.00
—Red label with large stylized "E" on top			
❏ EKL-285 [M]	Pickin' and Fiddlin'	1965	25.00
❏ EKS-7285 [S]	Pickin' and Fiddlin'	1965	30.00
—Mandolin-player label			
❏ EKL-265 [M]	The Dillards, Live!!! Almost!!!	1964	25.00
❏ EKS-7265 [S]	The Dillards, Live!!! Almost!!!	1964	30.00
—Mandolin-player label			
❏ EKS-74035	Wheatstraw Suite	1968	25.00
—Tan label with large stylized "E" on top			
❏ EKS-74035	Wheatstraw Suite	1969	18.00
—Red label with large stylized "E" on top			

FLYING FISH

❏ FF 082	Decade Waltz	1979	15.00
❏ FF215	Homecoming and Family Reunion	1979	15.00
❏ FF 040	The Dillards Vs. the Incredible L.A. Time Machine	1977	15.00

POPPY

| ❏ PP-LA175-F | Tribute to the American Duck | 1973 | 18.00 |

DILS, THE
LOST

| ❏ 001 | The Dils | 1990 | 15.00 |

TRIPLE X

| ❏ 51003 | The Dils Live | 1987 | 18.00 |
| —White vinyl | | | |

DIMENSIONS, THE
(NO LABEL)

| ❏ (# unknown)0 | From All Dimensions | 1966 | 800.00 |

DIMEOLA, AL
COLUMBIA

❏ JC35277	Casino	1978	12.00
❏ PC35277	Casino	1980	10.00
—Budget-line reissue			
❏ HC46454	Electric Rendezvous	198?	50.00
—Half-speed mastered edition			
❏ FC37654	Electric Rendezvous	1982	12.00
❏ PC37654	Electric Rendezvous	198?	10.00
—Budget-line reissue			
❏ HC44461	Elegant Gypsy	198?	40.00
—Half-speed mastered edition			
❏ PC34461	Elegant Gypsy	1976	12.00
—Original issue with no bar code			
❏ JC35561	Elegant Gypsy	197?	10.00
—Reissue with new prefix			
❏ PC35561	Elegant Gypsy	198?	10.00
—Budget-line reissue with bar code			
❏ HC47152	Friday Night in San Francisco	198?	50.00
—Half-speed mastered edition			
❏ PC34074	Land of the Midnight Sun	1976	12.00
—Original issue with no bar code			
❏ PC34074	Land of the Midnight Sun	1980	10.00
—Budget-line reissue with bar code			
❏ FC38944	Scenario	1983	12.00
❏ C2X36270	Splendido Hotel	1980	15.00
❏ FC38373	Tour de Force -- "Live	1982	12.00

EMI-MANHATTAN

| ❏ MLT-46995 | Tirami Su | 1987 | 12.00 |

Number	Title	Yr	NM
MANHATTAN			
❏ ST-53002	Cielo E Terra	1985	12.00
❏ ST-53011	Soaring Through a Dream	1987	12.00

DINNING, MARK
MGM

❏ E-3828 [M]	Teen Angel	1960	80.00
❏ SE-3828 [S]	Teen Angel	1960	150.00
❏ E-3855 [M]	Wanderin'	1960	80.00
❏ SE-3855 [S]	Wanderin'	1960	120.00

DINNING SISTERS, THE
CAPITOL

| ❏ H318 [10] | The Dinning Sisters | 195? | 50.00 |

DINO, DESI AND BILLY
REPRISE

❏ R6176 [M]	I'm a Fool	1965	25.00
❏ RS6176 [S]	I'm a Fool	1965	30.00
❏ R6198 [M]	Memories Are Made of This	1966	25.00
❏ RS6198 [S]	Memories Are Made of This	1966	30.00
❏ R6194 [M]	Our Time's Coming	1966	25.00
❏ RS6194 [S]	Our Time's Coming	1966	30.00
❏ R6224 [M]	Souvenir	1966	25.00
❏ RS6224 [S]	Souvenir	1966	30.00

DINOSAUR JR
HOMESTEAD

| ❏ 015-2 | Dinosaur | 1985 | 50.00 |
| —Released under the name "Dinosaur | | | |

RHINO VINYL

❏ 77630	Green Mind	2006	18.00
—Reissue on 180-gram vinyl			
❏ 77631	Where You Been	2006	18.00
—Reissue of Sire 45108 on 180-gram vinyl			

SIRE

❏ 26479 [B]	Green Mind	1991	50.00
❏ 45108 [B]	Where You Been	1993	25.00
❏ 45719 [B]	Without a Sound	1994	25.00

SST

❏ 216	Bug	1988	12.00
❏ 152 [EP]	Dinosaur Jr	1987	15.00
—Originals on purple swirl vinyl			
❏ 910 [10]	Dinosaur Jr	1987	10.00
❏ 275 [EP]	Fossils	1991	18.00
❏ 925 [10]	Fossils	1991	18.00
❏ 244 [EP]	Just Like Heaven	1989	10.00
❏ 914 [10]	Just Like Heaven	1989	10.00
❏ 130	You're Living All Over Me	1987	25.00
—First released under the name "Dinosaur			
❏ 130	You're Living All Over Me	1987	18.00
—As "Dinosaur Jr", purple swirl vinyl			
❏ 130	You're Living All Over Me	1987	12.00
—As "Dinosaur Jr"; black vinyl			

DIO, RONNIE
JOVE

| ❏ J-108 | Dio at Domino's | 1963 | 200.00 |

DIO
WARNER BROS.

❏ WB25612	Dream Evil	1987	10.00
❏ WB23836	Holy Diver	1983	12.00
❏ WB25443	Intermission	1986	10.00
❏ W1262121	Lock Up The Wolves	1990	14.00
❏ WB25292	Sacred Heart	1985	10.00
❏ WB25100	The Last in Line	1984	12.00

DION
ARISTA

| ❏ AL8549 | Yo Frankie | 1989 | 12.00 |

COLLECTABLES

| ❏ 5027 | Runaround Sue | 198? | 12.00 |

COLUMBIA

❏ KC31942	Dion's Greatest Hits	1973	25.00
❏ PC31942	Dion's Greatest Hits	198?	10.00
—Budget-line reissue			
❏ CL2107 [M]	Donna the Prima Donna	1963	30.00
❏ CS8907 [S]	Donna the Prima Donna	1963	40.00
❏ CL2010 [M]	Ruby Baby	1963	30.00
❏ CS8810 [S]	Ruby Baby	1963	40.00
❏ CS9773	Wonder Where I'm Bound	1969	25.00

DAYSPRING

❏ DST-4022	Inside Job	1980	15.00
❏ WR-8111	I Put Away My Idols	198?	15.00
❏ DST-4027	Only Jesus	198?	15.00
❏ 7-01-412901-5	Seasons	1984	15.00
❏ WR-8112	Seasons (The Best of Dion)	198?	15.00

LAURIE

❏ LES-4004	Abraham, Martin and John	197?	15.00
—Reissue of SLP-2047			
❏ LLP2004 [M]	Alone with Dion	1960	200.00
—With three wallet-size photos on inside strip (deduct 50% if missing)			
❏ SLP2047 [B]	Dion	1968	25.00
❏ ST-91577	Dion	1968	30.00
—Capitol Record Club edition			

Number	Title	Yr	NM
❏ LLP2013 [M]	Dion Sings His Greatest Hits	1962	70.00
❏ SLP2013 [R]	Dion Sings His Greatest Hits	196?	50.00
❏ T-90366 [M]	Dion Sings His Greatest Hits	1965	120.00
—Capitol Record Club edition			
❏ DT-90366 [R]	Dion Sings His Greatest Hits	1965	120.00
—Capitol Record Club edition			
❏ LLP2019 [M]	Dion Sings the 15 Million Sellers	1963	50.00
❏ SLP2019 [R]	Dion Sings the 15 Million Sellers	196?	30.00
❏ LES-4013	Dion Sings the Hits of the 50's and 60's	1978	15.00
❏ LLP2017 [M]	Dion Sings to Sandy (And All His Other Girls)	1963	50.00
❏ LLP2015 [M]	Love Came to Me	1963	70.00
❏ LLP2012 [M]	Lovers Who Wander	1962	70.00
❏ LLP2022 [M]	More of Dion's Greatest Hits	1964	50.00
❏ SLP2022 [R]	More of Dion's Greatest Hits	196?	30.00
❏ T-91128 [M]	More of Dion's Greatest Hits	196?	120.00
—Capitol Record Club edition			
❏ DT-91128 [R]	More of Dion's Greatest Hits	196?	120.00
—Capitol Record Club edition			
❏ LLP2009 [M]	Runaround Sue	1961	800.00
—Colored vinyl (gold, green or blue)			
❏ LLP2009 [M]	Runaround Sue	1961	100.00
—Black vinyl			
❏ T-91027 [M]	Runaround Sue	196?	120.00
—Capitol Record Club edition			
❏ DT-91027 [R]	Runaround Sue	196?	120.00
—Capitol Record Club edition			
❏ LLP2009 [M]	Runaround Sue	1962	80.00
—Black vinyl; with sticker on front cover: "Includes the Hit Singles 'The Majestic'/'The Wanderer'			

LIFESONG

| ❏ JZ35356 | Return of the Wanderer | 1978 | 15.00 |

WARNER BROS.

❏ WS1945	Sanctuary	1971	18.00
❏ WS1826	Sit Down, Old Friend	1969	25.00
❏ BS2954	Streetheart	1976	18.00
❏ BS2642	Suite for Late Summer	1972	18.00
❏ WS1872	You're Not Alone	1971	18.00

WORD

| ❏ WR-8285 | Kingdom in the Streets | 1985 | 15.00 |

DION AND THE BELMONTS
ABC

| ❏ 599 [M] | Together Again | 1967 | 30.00 |
| ❏ S-599 [S] | Together Again | 1967 | 40.00 |

ARISTA

| ❏ A2L8206 | 24 Original Classics | 1984 | 15.00 |

COLLECTABLES

❏ 5041	20 Golden Classics	198?	12.00
❏ 5025	Presenting Dion & The Belmonts	198?	12.00
❏ 5026	Wish Upon a Star	198?	12.00

LAURIE

❏ SLP6000	60 Greatest Hits	197?	30.00
—In box			
❏ SLP6000	60 Greatest Hits	197?	25.00
—In regular cover			
❏ LES4002	Everything You Always Wanted to Hear by Dion and the Belmonts	197?	18.00
❏ LLP1002 [M]	Presenting Dion & The Belmonts	1959	250.00
❏ LLP2002 [M]	Presenting Dion & The Belmonts	1960	150.00
❏ SLP2002 [R]	Presenting Dion & The Belmonts	196?	900.00
—Despite its rechanneled stereo sound, this record is collectible because of its utter rarity			
❏ LLP2016 [M]	Together" On Records -- By Special Request	1963	50.00
❏ LLP2006 [M]	Wish Upon a Star	1960	150.00

PAIR

| ❏ PDL2-1142 | The Best of Dion and the Belmonts | 1986 | 15.00 |

PICKWICK

| ❏ SPC-3521 | Doo Wop | 1975 | 12.00 |
| —Reissue of ABC tracks | | | |

RHINO

| ❏ RNLP70228 | Reunion -- Live at Madison Square Garden -- 1972 | 1987 | 12.00 |
| —Reissue of ABC tracks | | | |

WARNER BROS.

| ❏ BS2664 | Reunion -- Live at Madison Square Garden -- 1972 | 1973 | 18.00 |

DIRE STRAITS
WARNER BROS.

❏ 25264 [DJ]	Brothers in Arms	1985	80.00
—Promo on Quiex II vinyl			
❏ 25264	Brothers in Arms	1985	12.00
❏ 49377-1	Brothers in Arms	2006	30.00
—Remastered reissue; contains the full-length version of the album as it appears on the CD version, with longer versions of five songs			
❏ HS3330	Communique	1979	12.00
❏ BSK3266	Dire Straits	1979	12.00
❏ WBMS-109 [DJ]	Dire Straits Live	1980	100.00

Number	Title	Yr	NM

— The Warner Bros. Music Show" promo
| ☐ 25085 [DJ] | Dire Straits Live -- Alchemy | 1984 | 60.00 |

— Promo on Quiex II vinyl
| ☐ 25085 | Dire Straits Live -- Alchemy | 1984 | 15.00 |
| ☐ 23728 [DJ] | Love Over Gold | 1982 | 60.00 |

— Promo on Quiex II vinyl; the times of the songs are listed differently than on stock copies, for they are not rounded to the nearest 0 or 5
| ☐ 23728 | Love Over Gold | 1982 | 12.00 |

— On U.S. stock copies, the times of the songs as listed on the labels are rounded to the nearest 0 or 5
☐ BSK3480	Making Movies	1980	12.00
☐ 25794 [B]	Money for Nothing	1989	18.00
☐ 26680	On Every Street	1991	30.00
☐	Selectins from Dire Straits	1984	18.00
PRO-A-2149 [EP]	Live -- Alchemy		

— Three-song promo-only sampler

DIRECT FLIGHT

DIRECT DISC
| ☐ DD-104 | Spectrum | 1980 | 30.00 |

— Direct-to-disc recording

DIRTY BLUES BAND, THE

BLUESWAY
| ☐ BLS-6020 | Stone Dirt | 1968 | 25.00 |
| ☐ BLS-6010 | The Dirty Blues Band | 1968 | 25.00 |

DIRTY DOZEN JAZZ BAND, THE

COLUMBIA
| ☐ FC45042 | Voodoo | 1989 | 18.00 |

GEORGE WEIN COLLECTION
| ☐ GW-3005 | My Feet Can't Fail Me Now | 1984 | 15.00 |

ROUNDER
| ☐ 2052 | Live: Mardi Gras in Montreux | 1986 | 15.00 |

DISCO-TEX AND THE SEX-O-LETTES

CHELSEA
☐ CHL555	A Piece of the Rock	1977	12.00
☐ CHL505	Disco-Tex and His Sex-O-lettes	1975	12.00
☐ CHL516	Manhattan Millionaire	1976	12.00

DITMARS, IVAN

CROWN
| ☐ 5049 [M] | Joy to the World | 196? | 15.00 |

— Same as Crown CST 8, but in mono
| ☐ CST8 [S] | Joy to the World | 196? | 18.00 |
| ☐ CMX800 [M] | Joy to the World | 196? | 15.00 |

YULETIDE SERIES
| ☐ YS-218 [S] | Joy to the World | 197? | 12.00 |

— Same as Crown CST 8

DITMAS, BRUCE

CHIAROSCURO
| ☐ 195 | Aeray Dust | 1977 | 18.00 |

DIVINYLS

CHRYSALIS
☐ BFV41404	Desperate	1983	12.00
☐ BFV41627	Temperamental	1989	15.00
☐ BFV41511	What a Life!	1985	15.00

DIXIE CHICKS

COLUMBIA
| ☐ C286840 | Home | 2002 | 18.00 |

DIXIE CUPS, THE

ABC-PARAMOUNT
| ☐ 525 [M] | Riding High | 1965 | 60.00 |
| ☐ S-525 [S] | Riding High | 1965 | 80.00 |

RED BIRD
☐ RB 20-100 [M]	Chapel of Love	1964	60.00
☐ RBS 20-100 [S]	Chapel of Love	1964	80.00
☐ RB 20-103 [M]	Iko Iko	1965	150.00

DIXIE DREGS, THE

DIRECT DISK
| ☐ SD-16620 | Dregs of the Earth | 1980 | 40.00 |

— Audiophile vinyl

(NO LABEL)
| ☐ 0 | The Great Spectacular Dixie Dregs | 1975 | 200.00 |

DIXIE SMALL FRY, THE

LIBERTY
| ☐ LRP-3057 [M] | The Dixie Small Fry in Hi-Fi | 1957 | 40.00 |
| ☐ LST-7010 [S] | The Dixie Small Fry in Hi-Fi | 1958 | 40.00 |

DIXIE STOMPERS, THE

DELMAR
| ☐ DL-204 [M] | Jazz at Westminster College | 195? | 60.00 |

— Blue vinyl; label says "DL-201" though cover says "204

Number	Title	Yr	NM
☐ DL-112 [10]	The Dixie Stompers Play New Orleans Jazz	195?	80.00
☐ DL-113 [10]	Wake the Levee	195?	80.00

RCA VICTOR
| ☐ LPM-1212 [M] | New York Land Dixie | 1956 | 80.00 |

DIXIEBELLES, THE

SOUND STAGE 7
| ☐ SSM-5000 [M] | Down at Papa Joe's | 1963 | 40.00 |
| ☐ SSS-15000 [R] | Down at Papa Joe's | 1963 | 30.00 |

DIXIELAND RHYTHM KINGS, THE

BLACKBIRD
| ☐ 12006 | A Trip to Waukesha | 197? | 18.00 |

EMPIRICAL
| ☐ LP-102 [10] | The Dixieland Rhythm Kings | 1954 | 80.00 |

GHB
| ☐ GHB-7 | The Dixieland Rhythm Kings | 1963 | 18.00 |

RIVERSIDE
| ☐ RLP 12-210 [M] | Dixieland in Hi-Fi | 1956 | 60.00 |

— White label, blue print
| ☐ RLP 12-210 [M] | Dixieland in Hi-Fi | 1957 | 50.00 |

— Blue label, microphone logo
☐ RLP 12-289 [M]	Jazz in Retrospect	1959	40.00
☐ RLP-2505 [10]	New Orleans Jazz Party	1954	80.00
☐ RLP 12-259 [M]	The Dixieland Rhythm Kings at the Hi-Fi Jazz Band Ball	1958	40.00

DIXON, BILL

CADENCE JAZZ
| ☐ CJ-1024/25 | Collection | 1985 | 25.00 |

RCA VICTOR
| ☐ LPM-3844 [M] | Intents and Purposes | 1967 | 30.00 |
| ☐ LSP-3844 [S] | Intents and Purposes | 1967 | 25.00 |

SAVOY
| ☐ MG-12184 | The Bill Dixon 7-Tette | 1964 | 25.00 |

SOUL NOTE
☐ SN-1008	Bill Dixon in Italy, Volume 1	1980	15.00
☐ SN-1011	Bill Dixon in Italy, Volume 2	1981	15.00
☐ SN-1037/38	Nov-81	1982	18.00
☐ 121138	Son of Sisyphus	1990	18.00
☐ 121111	Thoughts	1987	15.00

DIXON, ERIC

MASTER JAZZ
| ☐ 8124 | Eric's Edge | 197? | 18.00 |

DIXON, WILLIE, AND MEMPHIS SLIM

BATTLE
| ☐ BV-6122 [M] | In Paris | 1963 | 30.00 |
| ☐ BVS-6122 [S] | In Paris | 1963 | 40.00 |

VERVE
| ☐ MGV-3007 [M] | Blues Every Which Way | 1961 | 120.00 |

DIXON, WILLIE

BLUESVILLE
| ☐ BVLP-1003 [M] | Willie's Blues | 1960 | 150.00 |

— Blue and silver label
| ☐ BVLP-1003 [M] | Willie's Blues | 1964 | 40.00 |

— Blue label, trident logo at right

CHESS
| ☐ CH3-16500 | The Chess Box: Willie Dixon | 1988 | 30.00 |

COLUMBIA
| ☐ CS9987 [B] | I Am the Blues | 1970 | 30.00 |

— Red label, "360 Sound

DMZ

4 MEN WITH BEARDS
| ☐ 4M528LP [B] | DMZ | | 25.00 |

BOMP
| ☐ VXS200004 | Relics | 1981 | 30.00 |

SIRE
| ☐ SRK6051 | DMZ | 1978 | 35.00 |

DOBBINS, BILL

ADVENT
| ☐ 5003 | Textures | 1974 | 18.00 |

OMNISOUND
| ☐ 1036 | Dedications | 1980 | 12.00 |
| ☐ 1041 | Where One Relaxes | 1981 | 12.00 |

TELARC
| ☐ 5003 | Textures | 198? | 12.00 |

— Reissue of Advent LP

DOBKINS, CARL, JR.

DECCA
| ☐ DL8938 [M] | Carl Dobkins, Jr. | 1959 | 100.00 |
| ☐ DL78938 [S] | Carl Dobkins, Jr. | 1959 | 150.00 |

DOC HOLLIDAY

METROMEDIA
| ☐ 1017 | Doc Holliday | 1973 | 25.00 |

Number	Title	Yr	NM

DOCTOR ROSS

FORTUNE
| ☐ F-3011 [M] | Doctor Ross, The Harmonica Boss | 1962 | 50.00 |
| ☐ FS-3011 [S] | Doctor Ross, The Harmonica Boss | 1962 | 100.00 |

TESTAMENT
| ☐ 2206 [M] | Doctor Ross | 196? | 25.00 |

DOCTORS OF MADNESS, THE

UNITED ARTISTS
| ☐ UA-LA871J2 [B] | Doctors of Madness | 1978 | 40.00 |

— 2LP compilation of first 2 UK LPs

DODD, BILLY

JAZZOLOGY
☐ J-161	Billy Dodd's Swing All-Stars, Volume One	198?	12.00
☐ J-162	Billy Dodd's Swing All-Stars, Volume Two	198?	12.00
☐ J-130	Doctor Billy Dodd and Friends	1985	12.00

DODD, DICK

TOWER
| ☐ ST5142 | The First Evolution of Dick Dodd | 1968 | 50.00 |

DODD, JIMMIE

DISNEYLAND
| ☐ DQ-1302 [M] | Favorite Hymns for Family Singing | 1967 | 18.00 |

— Reissue of 1014
| ☐ WDL-1014 [M] | Jimmie Dodd Sings His Favorite Hymns | 1959 | 30.00 |

— Reissue of 3014 with new number
| ☐ WDL-3014 [M] | Jimmie Dodd Sings His Favorite Hymns | 1958 | 30.00 |
| ☐ DQ-1235 [M] | Sing Along with Jimmie Dodd | 1963 | 30.00 |

IMPERIAL
☐ LP-9089 [M]	Lonely Guitar	1959	40.00
☐ LP-9121 [M]	Swing-A-Spell	1960	40.00
☐ LP-12058 [S]	Swing-A-Spell	1960	50.00

DODD, KEN

LIBERTY
| ☐ LRP-3442 [M] | Tears and The River | 1966 | 18.00 |
| ☐ LST-7442 [S] | Tears and The River | 1966 | 25.00 |

DODDS, BABY

AMERICAN MUSIC
☐ 1 [M]	Baby Dodds No. 1	1951	50.00
☐ 2 [M]	Baby Dodds No. 2	1951	50.00
☐ 3 [M]	Baby Dodds No. 3	1951	50.00

FOLKWAYS
| ☐ FP-30 [10] | Footnotes to Jazz, Vol. 1 -- Baby Dodds' Drum Solos | 1951 | 60.00 |

GHB
| ☐ GHB-50 | Jazz A La Creole | 1969 | 18.00 |

DODDS, JOHNNY, AND KID ORY

EPIC
| ☐ LN3207 [M] | Johnny Dodds and Kid Ory | 1956 | 50.00 |
| ☐ LA16004 [M] | Johnny Dodds and Kid Ory | 1960 | 30.00 |

DODDS, JOHNNY

BIOGRAPH
| ☐ 12024 | Johnny Dodds and Tommy Ladner, 1923-28 | 198? | 12.00 |

BRUNSWICK
| ☐ BL58016 [10] | The King of New Orleans Clarinets | 1951 | 100.00 |

HERWIN
| ☐ 115 | Paramount Recordings Vol. 1: 1926-1929 | 198? | 15.00 |

JOLLY ROGER
| ☐ 5012 [10] | Johnny Dodds | 1954 | 50.00 |

MCA
| ☐ 42326 | South Side Chicago Jazz | 1990 | 18.00 |
| ☐ 1328 | Spirit of New Orleans | 198? | 12.00 |

MILESTONE
| ☐ M-2011 | Chicago Mess Around | 1968 | 25.00 |
| ☐ M-2002 [M] | The Immortal Johnny Dodds | 1967 | 25.00 |

RCA VICTOR
| ☐ LPV-558 [M] | Sixteen Rare Recordings | 1965 | 30.00 |

RIVERSIDE
☐ RLP 12-135 [M]	In the Alley: Johnny Dodds, Volume 2	1961	40.00
☐ RLP-1002 [10]	Johnny Dodds, Volume 1	1953	80.00
☐ RLP-1015 [10]	Johnny Dodds, Volume 2	1953	80.00
☐ RLP 12-104 [M]	Johnny Dodds' New Orleans Clarinet	1956	60.00

— White label, blue print
| ☐ RLP 12-104 [M] | Johnny Dodds' New Orleans Clarinet | 195? | 40.00 |

— Blue label with microphone logo

Number	Title	Yr	NM
TIME-LIFE			
☐ STL-J-26	Giants of Jazz	1982	25.00
X			
☐ LX-3006 [10]	Johnny Dodds' Washboard Band	1954	60.00
DODDS, JOHNNY/JIMMY NOONE			
BRUNSWICK			
☐ BL58046 [10]	Battle of Jazz, Volume 8	1953	80.00
DODDS, MALCOLM			
RCA CAMDEN			
☐ CAL-873 [M]	Happiness Is a Thing Called Love	196?	18.00
☐ CAS-873 [S]	Happiness Is a Thing Called Love	196?	15.00
DODSON, MARGE			
COLUMBIA			
☐ CL1309 [M]	In the Still of the Night	1959	30.00
☐ CL1458 [M]	New Voice in Town	1960	30.00
☐ CS8258 [S]	New Voice in Town	1960	40.00
DOGGETT, BILL			
ABC-PARAMOUNT			
☐ 507 [M]	Wow!	1965	25.00
☐ S-507 [S]	Wow!	1965	30.00
AFTER HOURS			
☐ AFT-4112	The Right Choice	1991	18.00
COLUMBIA			
☐ CL2082 [M]	Fingertips	1963	25.00
☐ CS8882 [S]	Fingertips	1963	30.00
☐ CL1814 [M]	Oops!	1962	25.00
☐ CS8614 [S]	Oops!	1962	30.00
☐ CL1942 [M]	Prelude to the Blues	1963	25.00
☐ CS8742 [S]	Prelude to the Blues	1963	30.00
KING			
☐ K-5009	14 Original Greatest Hits	1977	12.00
☐ 395-600 [M]	A Bill Doggett Christmas	1959	40.00
☐ 295-89 [10]	All-Time Christmas Favorites	1955	200.00
☐ 830 [M]	American Songs in the Bossa Nova Style	1963	40.00
☐ 395-533 [M]	A Salute to Ellington	1958	60.00
☐ 395-523 [M]	As You Desire	1957	60.00
☐ KLP-523 [M]	As You Desire	1987	12.00
—Reissue with "Highland Records" on label			
☐ 723 [M]	Back Again with More	1960	50.00
☐ 611 [M]	Big City Dance Party	1959	50.00
☐ 295-82 [10]	Bill Doggett -- His Organ and Combo	1955	150.00
☐ 295-83 [10]	Bill Doggett -- His Organ and Combo, Volume 2	1955	150.00
☐ 667 [M]	Bill Doggett On Tour	1959	50.00
☐ 959 [M]	Bonanza of 24 Hit Songs	1966	30.00
☐ 759 [M]	Bonanza of 24 Songs	1960	50.00
☐ 395-563 [M]	Candle Glow	1958	60.00
☐ 395-532 [M]	Dame Dreaming	1958	60.00
☐ KLP-532 [M]	Dame Dreaming	1987	12.00
—Reissue with "Highland Records" on label			
☐ 395-585 [M]	Dance Awhile	1959	60.00
☐ KLP-585 [M]	Dance Awhile	1987	12.00
—Reissue with "Highland Records" on label			
☐ 395-531 [M]	Everybody Dance to the Honky Tonk	1958	60.00
☐ 706 [M]	For Reminiscent Lovers, Romantic Songs	1960	50.00
☐ 633 [M]	High and Wide	1959	50.00
☐ 395-609 [M]	Hold It	1959	60.00
☐ KS-1078	Honky Tonk Popcorn	1969	50.00
☐ 395-514 [M]	Hot Doggett	1957	60.00
☐ 868 [M]	Impressions	1964	40.00
☐ 395-502 [M]	Moondust	1957	60.00
☐ KS-1101	Ram-Bunk-Shush	1970	30.00
☐ KS-1104	Sentimental Journey	1970	30.00
☐ 295-102 [10]	Sentimentally Yours	1956	150.00
☐ KS-1108	Soft	1970	30.00
☐ 395-582 [M]	Swingin' Easy	1959	60.00
☐ 908 [M]	The Best of Bill Doggett	1964	40.00
☐ 395-557 [M]	The Doggett Beat for Dancing Feet	1958	60.00
☐ KLP-557 [M]	The Doggett Beat for Dancing Feet	1987	12.00
—Reissue with "Highland Records" on label			
☐ 778 [M]	The Many Moods of Bill Doggett	1960	50.00
☐ KLP-778 [M]	The Many Moods of Bill Doggett	1987	12.00
—Reissue with "Highland Records" on label			
☐ KS-1097	The Nearness of You	1970	30.00
POWER PAK			
☐ 269	Hold It!	197?	12.00
ROULETTE			
☐ R25330 [M]	Honky Tonk A La Mod	1966	25.00
☐ SR25330 [S]	Honky Tonk A La Mod	1966	30.00
STARDAY			
☐ 3023	16 Bandstand Favorites	197?	12.00
WARNER BROS.			
☐ W1404 [M]	3,046 People Danced 'Til 4 AM	1960	25.00
☐ WS1404 [S]	3,046 People Danced 'Til 4 AM	1960	30.00
☐ W1452 [M]	Bill Doggett Swings	1962	25.00

Number	Title	Yr	NM
☐ WS1452 [S]	Bill Doggett Swings	1962	30.00
☐ W1421 [M]	The Band with the Beat	1961	25.00
☐ WS1421 [S]	The Band with the Beat	1961	30.00
WHO'S WHO IN JAZZ			
☐ 21002	Lionel Hampton Presents Bill Doggett	1977	15.00
DOGGY STYLE			
CLEOPATRA			
☐ 6537 [B]	Punkers Anthem		25.00
DOHENY, NED			
ASYLUM			
☐ SD5059	Ned Doheny	1973	25.00
COLUMBIA			
☐ PC34259	Hard Candy	1976	18.00
DOHERTY, DENNY			
ABC DUNHILL			
☐ DS-50096	Watcha' Gonna Do?	1970	18.00
EMBER			
☐ EMS-1036	Waiting for a Song	1975	15.00
DOJO			
ECLIPSE			
☐ ES-7309	Down for the Last Time	1971	30.00
DOKY, NIELS LAN			
MILESTONE			
☐ M-9178	Dreams	1990	18.00
STORYVILLE			
☐ SLP-4160	Daybreak	1989	15.00
☐ SLP-4117	Here or There	1986	12.00
☐ SLP-4140	The Target	1987	12.00
☐ SLP-4144	The Truth	1988	12.00
DOLBY, THOMAS			
CAPITOL			
☐ ST-12309	The Flat Earth	1984	12.00
☐ ST12271 [B]	The Golden Age of Wireless	1983	12.00
EMI MANHATTAN			
☐ E1-48075	Aliens Ate My Buick	1988	12.00
HARVEST			
☐ MLP15007 [EP]	Blinded by Science	1983	15.00
☐ ST12271	The Golden Age of Wireless	1982	15.00
DOLDINGER, KLAUS			
PHILIPS			
☐ PHM200125 [M]	Dig Doldinger	1966	25.00
☐ PHS600125 [S]	Dig Doldinger	1966	30.00
WORLD PACIFIC			
☐ WPS-20176	Blues Happening	1969	25.00
DOLENZ, JONES, BOYCE & HART			
CAPITOL			
☐ ST-11513	Dolenz, Jones, Boyce & Hart	1976	18.00
DOLLAR, JOHNNY			
DATE			
☐ TEM3009 [M]	Johnny Dollar	1967	30.00
☐ TES4009 [S]	Johnny Dollar	1967	25.00
DOLPHY, ERIC			
BLUE NOTE			
☐ BT-85131	Other Aspects	1987	25.00
☐ BLP-4163 [M]	Out to Lunch!	1964	80.00
☐ BST-84163 [S]	Out to Lunch!	1964	80.00
—New York, USA" on label			
☐ BST-84163 [S]	Out to Lunch!	1966	30.00
— A Division of Liberty Records" on label			
☐ BST-84163 [S]	Out to Lunch!	1970	25.00
—Mostly black label with "Liberty/UA" at bottom			
☐ BST-84163 [S]	Out to Lunch!	1971	18.00
—A Division of United Artists" on label			
☐ BST-84163 [S]	Out to Lunch!	1985	15.00
—The Finest in Jazz Since 1939" reissue			
☐ B1-46524	Out to Lunch!	199?	18.00
—Reissue of 84163			
☐ BST-84163 [S]	Out to Lunch!	1973	15.00
—Dark blue label with black stylized "b" at upper right			
CELLULOID			
☐ CELL-5014	Conversations	198?	12.00
☐ CELL-5015	Iron Man	198?	12.00
DOUGLAS			
☐ SD785	Iron Man	1969	30.00
☐ KZ30873	Iron Man	1971	25.00
☐ 6002	Jitterbug Waltz	197?	18.00
EPITAPH			
☐ E-4010	Eric Dolphy 1928-1964	1975	18.00
EVEREST ARCHIVE OF FOLK & JAZZ			
☐ FS-227	Eric Dolphy and Cannonball Adderley	1968	15.00
EXODUS			
☐ EX-6005 [M]	The Memorial Album	1966	25.00

Number	Title	Yr	NM
—Reissue of Vee Jay LP-2503			
☐ EXS-6005 [S]	The Memorial Album	1966	25.00
—Reissue of Vee Jay LPS-2503			
FANTASY			
☐ OJC-133	Eric Dolphy at the Five Spot	198?	12.00
—Reissue of New Jazz 8260			
☐ OJC-247	Eric Dolphy at the Five Spot Volume 2	198?	12.00
—Reissue of Prestige 7294			
☐ OJC-413	Eric Dolphy in Europe, Volume 1	1990	15.00
—Reissue of Prestige 7304			
☐ OJC-414	Eric Dolphy in Europe, Volume 2	1990	15.00
—Reissue of Prestige 7350			
☐ OJC-415	Eric Dolphy in Europe, Volume 3	1990	15.00
—Reissue of Prestige 7366			
☐ OJC-353	Eric Dolphy Memorial Album	198?	12.00
—Reissue of Prestige 7334			
☐ OJC-400	Far Cry	1989	15.00
—Reissue of New Jazz 8270			
☐ OJC-023	Out There	198?	12.00
—Reissue of New Jazz 8252			
☐ OJC-022	Outward Bound	198?	12.00
—Reissue of New Jazz 8236			
FM			
☐ 308 [M]	Conversations	1963	40.00
☐ S-308 [S]	Conversations	1963	50.00
FONTANA			
☐ 822226-1	Last Date	1986	12.00
GM			
☐ GM-3005	Vintage Dolphy	1986	18.00
INNER CITY			
☐ IC-3017	The Berlin Concerts	1978	18.00
LIMELIGHT			
☐ LM-82013 [M]	Last Date	1964	30.00
☐ LS-86013 [S]	Last Date	1964	40.00
NEW JAZZ			
☐ NJLP-8260 [M]	Eric Dolphy at the Five Spot	1961	200.00
—Purple label			
☐ NJLP-8260 [M]	Eric Dolphy at the Five Spot	1965	60.00
—Blue label, trident logo at right			
☐ NJLP-8270 [M]	Far Cry	1962	200.00
—Purple label			
☐ NJLP-8270 [M]	Far Cry	1965	60.00
—Blue label, trident logo at right			
☐ NJLP-8252 [M]	Out There	1960	200.00
—Purple label			
☐ NJLP-8252 [M]	Out There	1965	50.00
—Blue label, trident logo at right			
☐ NJLP-8236 [M]	Outward Bound	1960	250.00
PRESTIGE			
☐ MPP-2503	Caribe	198?	12.00
☐ 24027	Copenhagen Concert	197?	25.00
☐ MPP-2517	Dash One	198?	12.00
☐ 24008	Eric Dolphy	197?	25.00
☐ PRLP-7294 [M]	Eric Dolphy at the Five Spot, Volume 2	1964	40.00
— Yellow label			
☐ PRLP-7294 [M]	Eric Dolphy at the Five Spot, Volume 2	1965	25.00
—Blue label, trident logo at right			
☐ PRST-7294 [S]	Eric Dolphy at the Five Spot, Volume 2	1964	50.00
— Silver label			
☐ PRST-7294 [S]	Eric Dolphy at the Five Spot, Volume 2	1965	30.00
—Blue label, trident logo at right			
☐ PRLP-7304 [M]	Eric Dolphy in Europe, Volume 1	1964	40.00
— Yellow label			
☐ PRLP-7304 [M]	Eric Dolphy in Europe, Volume 1	1965	25.00
—Blue label, trident logo at right			
☐ PRST-7304 [S]	Eric Dolphy in Europe, Volume 1	1964	50.00
— Silver label			
☐ PRST-7304 [S]	Eric Dolphy in Europe, Volume 1	1965	30.00
—Blue label, trident logo at right			
☐ PRLP-7350 [M]	Eric Dolphy in Europe, Volume 2	1965	25.00
☐ PRST-7350 [S]	Eric Dolphy in Europe, Volume 2	1965	30.00
☐ PRLP-7366 [M]	Eric Dolphy in Europe, Volume 3	1965	25.00
☐ PRST-7366 [S]	Eric Dolphy in Europe, Volume 3	1965	30.00
☐ PRLP-7334 [M]	Eric Dolphy Memorial Album	1964	25.00
☐ PRST-7334 [S]	Eric Dolphy Memorial Album	1964	30.00
☐ PRST-7747	Far Cry	1970	18.00
☐ 34002	Great Concert	1974	30.00
☐ PRLP-7382 [M]	Here and There	1965	25.00
☐ PRST-7382 [S]	Here and There	1965	30.00
☐ PRST-7611	Live at the Five Spot, Volume 1	1969	18.00
☐ PRST-7826	Live at the Five Spot, Volume 2	1971	18.00
☐ 24053	Magic	197?	18.00
☐ PRST-7652	Out There	1969	18.00

Number	Title	Yr	NM
❑ PRLP-7311 [M]	Outward Bound	1964	50.00
—Yellow label			
❑ PRLP-7311 [M]	Outward Bound	1965	30.00
—Blue label, trident logo at right			
❑ PRST-7311 [S]	Outward Bound	1964	40.00
—Silver label			
❑ PRST-7311 [S]	Outward Bound	1965	25.00
—Blue label, trident logo at right			
❑ P-24070	Status	1977	18.00
❑ PRST-7843	Where?	1971	18.00

TRIP

Number	Title	Yr	NM
❑ 5506	Last Date	197?	15.00
❑ 5012	The Greatness of Eric Dolphy	197?	15.00

VEE JAY

Number	Title	Yr	NM
❑ LP-2503 [M]	The Memorial Album	1964	30.00
❑ LPS-2503 [S]	The Memorial Album	1964	40.00

DOMINGO, PLACIDO, AND THE VIENNA CHOIR BOYS

RCA RED SEAL

Number	Title	Yr	NM
❑ ARL1-3835	Placido Domingo and the Vienna Choir Boys	1980	12.00

DOMINGO, PLACIDO

CBS

Number	Title	Yr	NM
❑ FM37245	Christmas with Placido Domingo	1981	15.00
—dark front cover			
❑ FM37245	Christmas with Placido Domingo	1982	12.00
—white front cover			

CBS MASTERWORKS

Number	Title	Yr	NM
❑ HM47243	Perhaps Love	1982	25.00
—Half-speed mastered edition			

DOMINO, FATS

ABC

Number	Title	Yr	NM
❑ S-479 [S]	Fats on Fire	1967	18.00
❑ S-510 [S]	Get Away with Fats Domino	1967	18.00
❑ ST-90167 [S]	Get Away with Fats Domino	1969	30.00
—Capitol Record Club edition; reissue			
❑ S-455 [S]	Here Comes... Fats Domino	1967	18.00

ABC-PARAMOUNT

Number	Title	Yr	NM
❑ 479 [M]	Fats on Fire	1964	25.00
❑ S-479 [S]	Fats on Fire	1964	30.00
❑ 510 [M]	Get Away with Fats Domino	1965	25.00
❑ S-510 [S]	Get Away with Fats Domino	1965	30.00
❑ T-90167 [M]	Get Away with Fats Domino	1965	30.00
—Capitol Record Club edition			
❑ ST-90167 [S]	Get Away with Fats Domino	1965	30.00
—Capitol Record Club edition			
❑ 455 [M]	Here Comes... Fats Domino	1963	25.00
❑ S-455 [S]	Here Comes... Fats Domino	1963	30.00

ATLANTIC

Number	Title	Yr	NM
❑ 81751	Live in Montreux	1987	15.00

COLUMBIA

Number	Title	Yr	NM
❑ C35996	When I'm Walking	1979	12.00
—Reissue of Harmony LP			
❑ PC35996	When I'm Walking	1986	10.00
—Budget-line reissue			

COLUMBIA SPECIAL PRODUCTS

Number	Title	Yr	NM
❑ P213197	The Legendary Music Man	1976	18.00
—Candelite Music TV offer			

EVEREST ARCHIVE OF FOLK & JAZZ

Number	Title	Yr	NM
❑ 280	Fats Domino	1974	12.00
❑ 330	Fats Domino, Vol. II	1975	12.00

GRAND AWARD

Number	Title	Yr	NM
❑ 267 [M]	Fats Domino	196?	25.00
❑ S-267 [R]	Fats Domino	196?	12.00

HARLEM HIT PARADE

Number	Title	Yr	NM
❑ 5005	Fats' Hits	197?	12.00

HARMONY

Number	Title	Yr	NM
❑ HS11343	When I'm Walking	1969	15.00

IMPERIAL

Number	Title	Yr	NM
❑ LP-9127 [M]	A Lot of Dominos	1960	100.00
—Black label with stars on top			
❑ LP-9127 [M]	A Lot of Dominos	1964	30.00
—Black and pink label			
❑ LP-9127 [M]	A Lot of Dominos	1967	25.00
—Black and green label			
❑ LP-12066 [S]	A Lot of Dominos	1961	150.00
—Black label with silver top			
❑ LP-12066 [S]	A Lot of Dominos	1964	40.00
—Black and pink label			
❑ LP-12066 [S]	A Lot of Dominos	1967	30.00
—Black and green label			
❑ LP-9009 [M]	Fats Domino Rock and Rollin'	1956	150.00
—Maroon label			
❑ LP-9009 [M]	Fats Domino Rock and Rollin'	1958	80.00
—Black label with stars on top			
❑ LP-9009 [M]	Fats Domino Rock and Rollin'	1964	30.00
—Black and pink label			
❑ LP-9009 [M]	Fats Domino Rock and Rollin'	1967	25.00
—Black and green label			
❑ LP-12388 [R]	Fats Domino Rock and Rollin'	1968	15.00
—Rechanneled reissue of 9009			
❑ LP-9062 [M]	Fats Domino Swings	1959	100.00
—Black label with stars on top			
❑ LP-9062 [M]	Fats Domino Swings	1964	30.00
—Black and pink label			
❑ LP-9062 [M]	Fats Domino Swings	1967	25.00
—Black and green label			
❑ LP-12091 [R]	Fats Domino Swings	1964	25.00
—Black and pink label			
❑ LP-12091 [R]	Fats Domino Swings	1967	18.00
—Black and green label			
❑ LP-9248 [M]	Here He Comes Again	1963	50.00
—Black label with stars on top			
❑ LP-9248 [M]	Here He Comes Again	1964	30.00
—Black and pink label			
❑ LP-9248 [M]	Here He Comes Again	1967	25.00
—Black and green label			
❑ LP-12248 [R]	Here He Comes Again	1964	25.00
—Black and pink label			
❑ LP-12248 [R]	Here He Comes Again	1967	18.00
—Black and green label			
❑ LP-9038 [M]	Here Stands Fats Domino	1957	150.00
—Maroon label			
❑ LP-9038 [M]	Here Stands Fats Domino	1958	80.00
—Black label with stars on top			
❑ LP-9038 [M]	Here Stands Fats Domino	1964	30.00
—Black and pink label			
❑ LP-9038 [M]	Here Stands Fats Domino	1967	25.00
—Black and green label			
❑ LP-12390 [R]	Here Stands Fats Domino	1968	15.00
—Rechanneled reissue of 9038			
❑ LP-9138 [M]	I Miss You So	1961	100.00
—Black label with stars on top			
❑ LP-9138 [M]	I Miss You So	1964	30.00
—Black and pink label			
❑ LP-9138 [M]	I Miss You So	1967	25.00
—Black and green label			
❑ LP-12398 [R]	I Miss You So	1968	15.00
—Rechanneled reissue of 9138			
❑ LP-9208 [M]	Just Domino	1962	50.00
—Black label with stars on top			
❑ LP-9208 [M]	Just Domino	1964	30.00
—Black and pink label			
❑ LP-9208 [M]	Just Domino	1967	25.00
—Black and green label			
❑ LP-9239 [M]	Let's Dance with Domino	1963	50.00
—Black label with stars on top			
❑ LP-9239 [M]	Let's Dance with Domino	1964	30.00
—Black and pink label			
❑ LP-9239 [M]	Let's Dance with Domino	1967	25.00
—Black and green label			
❑ LP-9065 [M]	Let's Play Fats Domino	1959	100.00
—Black label with stars on top			
❑ LP-9065 [M]	Let's Play Fats Domino	1964	30.00
—Black and pink label			
❑ LP-9065 [M]	Let's Play Fats Domino	1967	25.00
—Black and green label			
❑ LP-12395 [R]	Let's Play Fats Domino	1968	15.00
—Rechanneled reissue of 9065			
❑ LP-9153 [M]	Let the Four Winds Blow	1961	100.00
—Black label with stars on top			
❑ LP-9153 [M]	Let the Four Winds Blow	1964	30.00
—Black and pink label			
❑ LP-9153 [M]	Let the Four Winds Blow	1967	25.00
—Black and green label			
❑ LP-12073 [S]	Let the Four Winds Blow	1961	150.00
—Black label with silver top			
❑ LP-12073 [S]	Let the Four Winds Blow	1964	40.00
—Black and pink label			
❑ LP-12073 [S]	Let the Four Winds Blow	1967	30.00
—Black and green label			
❑ LP-9103 [M]	Million Record Hits	1960	100.00
—Black label with stars on top			
❑ LP-9103 [M]	Million Record Hits	1964	30.00
—Black and pink label			
❑ LP-9103 [M]	Million Record Hits	1967	25.00
—Black and green label			
❑ LP-12103 [R]	Million Record Hits	1964	25.00
—Black and pink label			
❑ LP-12103 [R]	Million Record Hits	1967	18.00
—Black and green label			
❑ LP-9195 [M]	Million Sellers by Fats	1962	50.00
—Black label with stars on top			
❑ LP-9195 [M]	Million Sellers by Fats	1964	30.00
—Black and pink label			
❑ LP-9195 [M]	Million Sellers by Fats	1967	25.00
—Black and green label			
❑ LP-12195 [R]	Million Sellers by Fats	1964	25.00
—Black and pink label			
❑ LP-12195 [R]	Million Sellers by Fats	1967	18.00
—Black and green label			
❑ LP-9004 [M]	Rock and Rollin' with Fats Domino	1956	150.00
—Maroon label			
❑ LP-9004 [M]	Rock and Rollin' with Fats Domino	1958	80.00
—Black label with stars on top			
❑ LP-9004 [M]	Rock and Rollin' with Fats Domino	1964	30.00
—Black and pink label			
❑ LP-9004 [M]	Rock and Rollin' with Fats Domino	1967	25.00
—Black and green label			
❑ LP-12387 [R]	Rock and Rollin' with Fats Domino	1968	15.00
—Rechanneled reissue of 9004			
❑ LP-9055 [M]	The Fabulous Mr. D.	1958	100.00
—Black label with stars on top			
❑ LP-9055 [M]	The Fabulous Mr. D.	1964	30.00
—Black and pink label			
❑ LP-9055 [M]	The Fabulous Mr. D.	1967	25.00
—Black and green label			
❑ LP-12394 [R]	The Fabulous Mr. D.	1968	15.00
—Rechanneled reissue of 9055			
❑ LP-9040 [M]	This Is Fats	1957	150.00
—Maroon label			
❑ LP-9040 [M]	This Is Fats	1958	80.00
—Black label with stars on top			
❑ LP-9040 [M]	This Is Fats	1964	30.00
—Black and pink label			
❑ LP-9040 [M]	This Is Fats	1967	25.00
—Black and green label			
❑ LP-12391 [R]	This Is Fats	1968	15.00
—Rechanneled reissue of 9040			
❑ LP-9028 [M]	This Is Fats Domino!	1957	150.00
—Maroon label			
❑ LP-9028 [M]	This Is Fats Domino!	1958	80.00
—Black label with stars on top			
❑ LP-9028 [M]	This Is Fats Domino!	1964	30.00
—Black and pink label			
❑ LP-9028 [M]	This Is Fats Domino!	1967	25.00
—Black and green label			
❑ LP-12389 [R]	This Is Fats Domino!	1968	15.00
—Rechanneled reissue of 9028			
❑ LP-9170 [M]	Twistin' the Stomp	1962	60.00
—Black label with stars on top			
❑ LP-9170 [M]	Twistin' the Stomp	1964	30.00
—Black and pink label			
❑ LP-9170 [M]	Twistin' the Stomp	1967	25.00
—Black and green label			
❑ LP-9227 [M]	Walking to New Orleans	1963	50.00
—Black label with stars on top			
❑ LP-9227 [M]	Walking to New Orleans	1964	30.00
—Black and pink label			
❑ LP-9227 [M]	Walking to New Orleans	1967	25.00
—Black and green label			
❑ LP-12227 [R]	Walking to New Orleans	1964	25.00
—Black and pink label			
❑ LP-12227 [R]	Walking to New Orleans	1967	18.00
—Black and green label			
❑ LP-9164 [M]	What a Party	1962	60.00
—Black label with stars on top			
❑ LP-9164 [M]	What a Party	1964	30.00
—Black and pink label			
❑ LP-9164 [M]	What a Party	1967	25.00
—Black and green label			

LIBERTY

Number	Title	Yr	NM
❑ LWB-122	Cookin' with Fats (Superpak)	1981	15.00
—Budget-line reissue of UA 122			
❑ LWB-9958	Legendary Masters	1981	12.00
—Budget-line reissue of UA 9958			
❑ LN-10135	Let's Play Fats Domino	1981	10.00
—Budget-line reissue			
❑ LM-1027	Million Sellers by Fats	1981	10.00
—Budget-line reissue of UA 1027			
❑ LN-10136	The Fabulous Mr. D.	1981	10.00
—Budget-line reissue			

MCA/SILVER EAGLE

Number	Title	Yr	NM
❑ 6170	Greatest Hits	198?	12.00

MERCURY

Number	Title	Yr	NM
❑ MG-21039 [M]	Fats Domino '65	1965	30.00
❑ SR-61039 [S]	Fats Domino '65	1965	40.00

PICKWICK

Number	Title	Yr	NM
❑ SPC-3111	Blueberry Hill	197?	12.00
❑ SPC-3295 [B]	My Blue Heaven	1971	12.00
❑ SPC-3165	When My Dreamboat Comes Home	197?	12.00

QUICKSILVER

Number	Title	Yr	NM
❑ QS-1016	Live Hits	198?	12.00

REPRISE

Number	Title	Yr	NM
❑ RS6439	Fats	1970	500.00
—Officially unreleased, test pressings and coverless stock copies are known to exist			
❑ RS6304	Fats Is Back	1968	30.00

SEARS

Number	Title	Yr	NM
❑ SPS-473	Blueberry Hill!	1970	30.00

SUNSET

Number	Title	Yr	NM
❑ SUS-5299 [R]	Ain't That a Shame	1970	15.00
❑ SUM-1103 [M]	Fats Domino	1966	15.00
❑ SUS-5103 [R]	Fats Domino	1966	15.00

Number	Title	Yr	NM
❏ SUM-1158 [M]	Stompin' Fats Domino	1967	15.00
❏ SUS-5158 [R]	Stompin' Fats Domino	1967	15.00
❏ SUS-5200 [P]	Trouble in Mind	1968	25.00
UNITED ARTISTS			
❏ UA-LA122-F2	Cookin' with Fats (Superpak)	1974	30.00
❏ UA-LA122-F2 [DJ]	Cookin' with Fats (Superpak)	1974	300.00

— Promo with one black vinyl record and one colored vinyl record

❏ UAS-9958	Legendary Masters	1972	18.00
❏ LM-1027	Million Sellers by Fats	1980	12.00
❏ UAMG-104 [DJ]	The Fats Domino Sound	1973	40.00

— Promo compilation of 30 excerpts of Fats hits

❏ UA-LA233-G	The Very Best of Fats Domino	1974	15.00

DOMNERUS, ARNE

PRESTIGE

❏ PRLP-134 [10]	New Sounds from Sweden, Volume 4	1952	250.00

RCA CAMDEN

❏ CAL-417 [M]	Swedish Modern Jazz	1958	30.00

RCA VICTOR

❏ LPT-3032 [10]	Around the World in Jazz	1953	250.00

DOMNERUS, ARNE/LARS GULLIN

PRESTIGE

❏ PRLP-133 [10]	New Sounds from Sweden, Volume 3	1952	250.00

DON, DICK & JIMMY

CROWN

❏ CLP-5005 [M]	Spring Fever	1958	40.00

DOT

❏ DLP-3152 [M]	Don, Dick & Jimmy	1959	30.00

MODERN

❏ MLP-1205 [M]	Spring Fever	1957	120.00

VERVE

❏ MGV-2084 [M]	Medium Rare	1958	40.00
❏ MGV-2107 [M]	Songs for the Hearth	1959	40.00

DON AND THE GOODTIMES

BEAT ROCKET

❏ BR-130	The Original Northwest Sound of Don and the Goodtimes	2000	15.00

BURDETTE

❏ 300 [M]	Don and the Goodtimes' Greatest Hits	1966	150.00
❏ 300S [S]	Don and the Goodtimes' Greatest Hits	1966	300.00

— LP plays true stereo

❏ 300S [R]	Don and the Goodtimes' Greatest Hits	1966	100.00

— LP plays rechanneled stereo

EPIC

❏ LN24311 [M]	So Good	1967	30.00
❏ BN26311 [S]	So Good	1967	40.00

PICCADILLY

❏ 3394	Goodtime Rock 'n' Roll	1980	30.00

WAND

❏ WDS-679	Where the Action Is	1969	30.00

DON ARMANDO'S SECOND AVENUE RHUMBA BAND

ZE

❏ 33-005	Don Armando's Second Avenue Rhumba Band	1979	25.00

DONAHUE, SAM

CAPITOL

❏ H626 [10]	Classics in Jazz	1955	50.00
❏ H613 [10]	For Young Moderns in Love	1955	60.00
❏ T613 [M]	For Young Moderns in Love	1956	40.00

DONALDSON, BO, AND THE HEYWOODS

ABC

❏ D-824	Bo Donaldson and the Heywoods	1974	12.00

CAPITOL

❏ ST-11501	Farther On	1976	18.00

FAMILY PRODUCTIONS

❏ FPS-2711	Special Someone	1972	18.00

DONALDSON, BOBBY

GOLDEN CREST

❏ GC-1003	Unlimited	196?	25.00

SAVOY

❏ MG-12128 [M]	Dixieland Jazz Party	1958	40.00
❏ SST-13003 [S]	Dixieland Jazz Party	1959	30.00

WORLD WIDE

❏ 20005	Bobby Donaldson and the 7th Avenue Stompers	196?	25.00

DONALDSON, LOU

ARGO

❏ LP-747 [M]	Cole Slaw	1965	30.00

Number	Title	Yr	NM
❏ LPS-747 [S]	Cole Slaw	1965	30.00
❏ LP-734 [M]	Possum Head	1964	30.00
❏ LPS-734 [S]	Possum Head	1964	30.00
❏ LP-724 [M]	Signifyin'	1963	30.00
❏ LPS-724 [S]	Signifyin'	1963	30.00

BLUE NOTE

❏ BLP-4263 [M]	Alligator Boogaloo	1967	80.00
❏ BST-84263 [S]	Alligator Boogaloo	1967	50.00

— With "A Division of Liberty Records" on label

❏ BLP-1593 [M]	Blues Walk	1958	350.00

—Deep groove" version; W. 63rd St. address on label

❏ BLP-1593 [M]	Blues Walk	1958	150.00

— Regular version with W. 63rd St. address on label

❏ BLP-1593 [M]	Blues Walk	1963	40.00

— With New York, USA address on label

❏ BST-1593 [S]	Blues Walk	1959	500.00

—Deep groove" version (deep indentation under label on both sides)

❏ BST-1593 [S]	Blues Walk	1959	50.00

— Regular version with W. 63rd St. address on label

❏ BST-1593 [S]	Blues Walk	1963	25.00

— With New York, USA address on label

❏ BST-81593 [S]	Blues Walk	1967	15.00

— With "A Division of Liberty Records" on label

❏ BST-81593	Blues Walk	1985	15.00

— The Finest in Jazz Since 1939" reissue

❏ BST-84370	Cosmos	1971	18.00
❏ BST-84337	Everything I Play Is Funky	1970	50.00

— With "A Division of Liberty Records" on label

❏ B1-31248	Everything I Play Is Funky	1995	18.00

— Reissue of 84337

❏ BLP-4125 [M]	Good Gracious	1963	80.00
❏ BST-84125 [S]	Good Gracious	1963	50.00

— With "New York, USA" on label

❏ BST-84125 [S]	Good Gracious	1967	25.00

— With "A Division of Liberty Records" on label

❏ BLP-4079 [M]	Gravy Train	1962	200.00

— With W. 63rd St. address on label

❏ BLP-4079 [M]	Gravy Train	1963	100.00

— With New York, USA address on label

❏ BST-84079 [S]	Gravy Train	1962	100.00

— With W. 63rd St. address on label

❏ BST-84079 [S]	Gravy Train	1963	50.00

— With New York, USA address on label

❏ BST-84079 [S]	Gravy Train	1967	30.00

— With "A Division of Liberty Records" on label

❏ BLP-4066 [M]	Here 'Tis	1961	200.00

— With W. 63rd St. address on label

❏ BLP-4066 [M]	Here 'Tis	1963	80.00

— With New York, USA address on label

❏ BST-84066 [S]	Here 'Tis	1961	100.00

— With W. 63rd St. address on label

❏ BST-84066 [S]	Here 'Tis	1963	50.00

— With New York, USA address on label

❏ BST-84066 [S]	Here 'Tis	1967	25.00

— With "A Division of Liberty Records" on label

❏ BST-84318	Hot Dog	1969	50.00

— With "A Division of Liberty Records" on label

❏ B1-20267	Hot Dog	1994	18.00

— Reissue of 84318

❏ BLP-4012 [M]	LD + 3	1959	400.00

—Deep groove" version; W. 63rd St. address on label

❏ BLP-4012 [M]	LD + 3	1959	120.00

— Regular version with W. 63rd St. address on label

❏ BLP-4012 [M]	LD + 3	1963	40.00

— With New York, USA address on label

❏ BST-4012 [S]	LD + 3	1960	300.00

—Deep groove" version; W. 63rd St. address on label

❏ BST-4012 [S]	LD + 3	1960	80.00

— Regular version with W. 63rd St. address on label

❏ BST-4012 [S]	LD + 3	1963	30.00

— With New York, USA address on label

❏ BLP-4053 [M]	Light Foot	1960	120.00

— With W. 63rd St. address on label

❏ BLP-4053 [M]	Light Foot	1963	50.00

— With New York, USA address on label

❏ BST-84053 [S]	Light Foot	1960	100.00

— With W. 63rd St. address on label

❏ BST-84053 [S]	Light Foot	1963	50.00

— With New York, USA address on label

❏ BLP-5030 [10]	Lou Donaldson-Clifford Brown	1954	500.00
❏ BLP-1537 [M]	Lou Donaldson Quartet/Quintet/Sextet	1957	400.00

—Deep groove" version; Lexington Ave. address on label

❏ BLP-1537 [M]	Lou Donaldson Quartet/Quintet/Sextet	1958	300.00

—Deep groove" version; W. 63rd St. address on label

❏ BLP-1537 [M]	Lou Donaldson Quartet/Quintet/Sextet	1958	100.00

— Regular version with W. 63rd St. address on label

❏ BLP-1537 [M]	Lou Donaldson Quartet/Quintet/Sextet	1963	40.00

— With New York, USA address on label

❏ B1-81537	Lou Donaldson Quartet/Quintet/Sextet	1989	15.00

— Reissue of 1537

❏ BLP-5021 [10]	Lou Donaldson Quintet/Quartet	1953	500.00
❏ BLP-5055 [10]	Lou Donaldson Sextet, Volume 2	1955	500.00

Number	Title	Yr	NM
❏ BLP-1591 [M]	Lou Takes Off	1958	250.00

—Deep groove" version; W. 63rd St. address on label

❏ BLP-1591 [M]	Lou Takes Off	1958	150.00

— Regular version with W. 63rd St. address on label

❏ BLP-1591 [M]	Lou Takes Off	1963	40.00

— With New York, USA address on label

❏ BST-1591 [S]	Lou Takes Off	1959	300.00

—Deep groove" version; W. 63rd St. address on label

❏ BST-1591 [S]	Lou Takes Off	1959	100.00

— Regular version with W. 63rd St. address on label

❏ BST-1591 [S]	Lou Takes Off	1963	30.00

— With New York, USA address on label

❏ BST-81591 [S]	Lou Takes Off	1966	25.00

— With "A Division of Liberty Records" on label

❏ BST-84254	Lush Life	1986	18.00

— The Finest in Jazz Since 1939" label; first issue of this LP

❏ BST-84280	Midnight Creeper	1968	60.00

— A Division of Liberty Records" on label

❏ LT-1028	Midnight Sun	1980	30.00
❏ BLP-4271 [M]	Mr. Shing-a-Ling	1968	120.00
❏ BST-84271 [S]	Mr. Shing-a-Ling	1968	50.00

— With "A Division of Liberty Records" on label

❏ B1-89794	Pretty Thing	1993	18.00

— Reissue of 84359

❏ BST-84359	Pretty Things	1970	18.00
❏ BN-LA109-F	Sassy Soul Strut	1973	30.00
❏ BST-84299	Say It Loud!	1969	50.00

— With "A Division of Liberty Records" on label

❏ BN-LA024-F	Sophisticated Lou	1972	30.00
❏ BLP-4036 [M]	Sunny Side Up	1960	200.00

—Deep groove" version; W. 63rd St. address on label

❏ BLP-4036 [M]	Sunny Side Up	1960	120.00

— Regular version with W. 63rd St. address on label

❏ BLP-4036 [M]	Sunny Side Up	1963	40.00

— With New York, USA address on label

❏ BST-84036 [S]	Sunny Side Up	1960	100.00

— With W. 63rd St. address on label

❏ BST-84036 [S]	Sunny Side Up	1963	50.00

— With New York, USA address on label

❏ B1-32095	Sunny Side Up	1995	18.00

— Reissue of 84036

❏ BN-LA259-G	Sweet Lou	1974	30.00
❏ BLP-1566 [M]	Swing and Soul	1957	250.00

—Deep groove" version; W. 63rd St. address on label

❏ BLP-1566 [M]	Swing and Soul	1957	150.00

— Regular version with W. 63rd St. address on label

❏ BLP-1566 [M]	Swing and Soul	1963	40.00

— With New York, USA address on label

❏ BST-1566 [S]	Swing and Soul	1959	150.00

—Deep groove" version; W. 63rd St. address on label

❏ BST-1566 [S]	Swing and Soul	1959	100.00

— Regular version with W. 63rd St. address on label

❏ BST-1566 [S]	Swing and Soul	1963	30.00

— With New York, USA address on label

❏ BLP-4108 [M]	The Natural Soul	1963	150.00
❏ BST-84108 [S]	The Natural Soul	1963	60.00

— With "New York, USA" on label

❏ BST-84108 [S]	The Natural Soul	1967	25.00

— With "A Division of Liberty Records" on label

❏ BST-84108	The Natural Soul	1987	15.00

— The Finest in Jazz Since 1939" reissue

❏ B1-31876	The Scorpion: Live at the Cadillac Club	1995	18.00
❏ BLP-4025 [M]	The Time Is Right	1960	120.00

—Deep groove" version (deep indentation under label on both sides)

❏ BLP-4025 [M]	The Time Is Right	1960	80.00

— Regular version with W. 63rd St. address on label

❏ BLP-4025 [M]	The Time Is Right	1963	30.00

— With New York, USA address on label

❏ BST-84025 [S]	The Time Is Right	1960	100.00

— With W. 63rd St. address on label

❏ BST-84025 [S]	The Time Is Right	1963	50.00

— With New York, USA address on label

❏ BLP-1545 [M]	Wailing with Lou	1957	250.00

—Deep groove" version; W. 63rd St. address on label

❏ BLP-1545 [M]	Wailing with Lou	1957	150.00

— Regular version with W. 63rd St. address on label

❏ BLP-1545 [M]	Wailing with Lou	1963	40.00

— With New York, USA address on label

CADET

❏ LP-789 [M]	Blowin' in the Wind	1967	30.00
❏ LPS-789 [S]	Blowin' in the Wind	1967	25.00
❏ LP-747 [M]	Cole Slaw	1966	25.00

— Reissue of Argo 747

❏ LPS-747 [S]	Cole Slaw	1966	18.00

— Reissue of Argo 747

❏ LPS-842	Fried Buzzard -- Lou Donaldson Live	1970	25.00
❏ LPS-815	Lou Donaldson At His Best	1969	25.00
❏ LP-759 [M]	Musty Rusty	1966	30.00
❏ LPS-759 [S]	Musty Rusty	1966	30.00
❏ LP-734 [M]	Possum Head	1966	25.00

— Reissue of Argo 734

❏ LPS-734 [S]	Possum Head	1966	18.00

— Reissue of Argo 734

❏ LP-768 [M]	Rough House Blues	1966	30.00
❏ LPS-768 [S]	Rough House Blues	1966	30.00
❏ LP-724 [M]	Signifyin'	1966	25.00

— Reissue of Argo 724

Number	Title	Yr	NM
❏ LPS-724 [S]	Signifyin'	1966	18.00
—Reissue of Argo 724			

CHESS
Number	Title	Yr	NM
❏ 2CA60007	Ha' Mercy	1972	15.00

COTILLION
Number	Title	Yr	NM
❏ SD9905	A Different Scene	1976	18.00
❏ SD9915	Color As a Way of Life	1977	18.00

MUSE
Number	Title	Yr	NM
❏ MR-5292	Back Street	1983	15.00
❏ MR-5247	Sweet Poppa Lou	1982	15.00

SUNSET
Number	Title	Yr	NM
❏ SUS-5258	Down Home	1969	15.00
❏ SUS-5318	I Won't Cry Anymore	1970	15.00

TIMELESS
Number	Title	Yr	NM
❏ SJP-153	Forgotten Man	198?	12.00

DONEGAN, DOROTHY

AUDIOPHILE
Number	Title	Yr	NM
❏ AP-209	The Explosive Dorothy Donegan	198?	12.00

CAPITOL
Number	Title	Yr	NM
❏ T1226 [M]	Donnybrook with Dorothy	1960	30.00
❏ ST1226 [S]	Donnybrook with Dorothy	1960	40.00
❏ T1135 [M]	Dorothy Donegan Live!	1959	30.00
❏ ST1135 [S]	Dorothy Donegan Live!	1959	40.00

FORUM
Number	Title	Yr	NM
❏ F-9003 [M]	Dorothy Donegan at the Embers	196?	18.00
—Reissue of Roulette R-25010			
❏ SF-9003 [R]	Dorothy Donegan at the Embers	196?	15.00

JUBILEE
Number	Title	Yr	NM
❏ LP-11 [10]	Dorothy Donegan Trio	1955	80.00
❏ JLP-1013 [M]	September Song	1956	60.00

MGM
Number	Title	Yr	NM
❏ E-278 [10]	Dorothy Donegan Piano	1954	80.00

PROGRESSIVE
Number	Title	Yr	NM
❏ PRO-7056	The Explosive Dorothy Donegan	198?	15.00

ROULETTE
Number	Title	Yr	NM
❏ R-25010 [M]	Dorothy Donegan at the Embers	1957	50.00
❏ R-25154 [M]	It Happened One Night	1961	30.00
❏ SR-25154 [S]	It Happened One Night	1961	40.00

DONEGAN, LONNIE

ABC-PARAMOUNT
Number	Title	Yr	NM
❏ 433 [M]	Sing Hallelujah	1963	25.00
❏ S-433 [S]	Sing Hallelujah	1963	30.00

ATLANTIC
Number	Title	Yr	NM
❏ 8038 [M]	Skiffle Folk Songs	1960	40.00
❏ SD8038 [S]	Skiffle Folk Songs	1960	50.00

DOT
Number	Title	Yr	NM
❏ DLP-3159 [M]	Lonnie Donegan	1959	40.00

MERCURY
Number	Title	Yr	NM
❏ MG-20229 [M]	An Englishman Sings American Folk Songs	1957	50.00

UNITED ARTISTS
Number	Title	Yr	NM
❏ UA-LA827-?	Puttin' On the Style	1977	12.00

DONNAS, THE

LOOKOUT!
Number	Title	Yr	NM
❏ LK-191	American Teenage Rock 'n' Roll Machine	1998	12.00
❏ LK-225	Get Skintight	1999	12.00
❏ LK-288 [B]	Spend the Night	2002	12.00
❏ LK-255	Turn 21	2001	12.00

SUPER*TEEM
Number	Title	Yr	NM
❏ SUP3301	The Donnas	1996	40.00

DONNER, RAL

GONE
Number	Title	Yr	NM
❏ LP-5012 [M]	Takin' Care of Business	1961	300.00

STARFIRE
Number	Title	Yr	NM
❏ 1004	An Evening with Ral Donner	1982	18.00
—All copies on multi-color vinyl			

DONNER, RAL/RAY SMITH/BOBBY DALE

CROWN
Number	Title	Yr	NM
❏ CLP-5335 [M]	Ral Donner, Ray Smith and Bobby Dale	1963	40.00
❏ CST-335 [R]	Ral Donner, Ray Smith and Bobby Dale	1963	25.00

DONNIE AND THE DELCHORDS

TAURUS
Number	Title	Yr	NM
❏ 1000	Sing with Triple Stereo	1967	300.00

DONOVAN

ALLEGIANCE
Number	Title	Yr	NM
❏ AV-437	Lady of the Stars	1983	12.00

ARISTA
Number	Title	Yr	NM
❏ AB4143	Donovan	1980	12.00

BELL
Number	Title	Yr	NM
❏ 1135	Early Treasures	1973	12.00

COLUMBIA LIMITED EDITION
Number	Title	Yr	NM
❏ LE10184	Mellow Yellow	197?	12.00

EPIC
Number	Title	Yr	NM
❏ PE33245	7-Tease	1974	15.00
❏ L2N6071 [M]	A Gift from a Flower to a Garden	1967	50.00
—Boxed set of two LPs with portfolio of lyrics and drawings. The two records also were issued separately as Epic 24349 and 24350.			
❏ B2N171 [S]	A Gift from a Flower to a Garden	1967	30.00
—Boxed set of two LPs with portfolio of lyrics and drawings. The two records also were issued separately as Epic 26349 and 26350.			
❏ E2171	A Gift from a Flower to a Garden	1979	18.00
—Blue label			
❏ BN26481 [B]	Barabajagal	1969	30.00
❏ PE26481	Barabajagal	1987	10.00
—Blue label, new prefix			
❏ KE32156	Cosmic Wheels	1973	18.00
—With enclosed poster			
❏ BN26386 [B]	Donovan in Concert	1968	25.00
❏ EG33734	Donovan in Concert/Sunshine Superman	1975	18.00
❏ BXN26439 [P]	Donovan's Greatest Hits	1969	15.00
—Yellow label; "Mellow Yellow" is rechanneled; "Sunshine Superman" is the full-length version in stereo; "Catch the Wind" and "Colours" were re-recorded			
❏ BXN26439 [P]	Donovan's Greatest Hits	1973	12.00
—Orange label			
❏ PE26439	Donovan's Greatest Hits	1979	10.00
—Blue label			
❏ KE32800	Essence to Essence	1974	15.00
❏ LN24350 [M]	For Little Ones	1967	18.00
—Part of Epic 6071, issued simultaneously			
❏ BN26350 [S]	For Little Ones	1967	18.00
—Part of Epic 171, issued simultaneously			
❏ BN26420 [S]	Hurdy Gurdy Man	1968	15.00
❏ PE26420	Hurdy Gurdy Man	1986	10.00
—Blue label, new prefix			
❏ BN26420 [M]	Hurdy Gurdy Man	1968	70.00
—Mono is white label promo only; "Mono" sticker on stereo front cover			
❏ EG33731	Hurdy Gurdy Man/Barabajagal	1975	18.00
❏ LN24239 [M]	Mellow Yellow	1967	30.00
❏ BN26239 [R]	Mellow Yellow	1967	18.00
❏ E30125	Open Road	1970	15.00
❏ PE33945	Slow Down World	1976	15.00
❏ LN24217 [M]	Sunshine Superman	1966	30.00
—Contains the single version of "Sunshine Superman"			
❏ BN26217 [R]	Sunshine Superman	1966	18.00
—Contains the single version of "Sunshine Superman" (rechanneled)			
❏ KEG31210	The World of Donovan	1972	15.00
❏ LN24349 [M]	Wear Your Love Like Heaven	1967	18.00
—Part of Epic 6071, issued simultaneously			
❏ BN26349 [S]	Wear Your Love Like Heaven	1967	18.00
—Part of Epic 171, issued simultaneously			

HICKORY
Number	Title	Yr	NM
❏ LPM-123 [M]	Catch the Wind	1965	30.00
—Most pressings have Donovan facing left, so he is correctly strumming his guitar with his right hand			
❏ LPS-123 [R]	Catch the Wind	1965	30.00
❏ LPM-123 [M]	Catch the Wind	1965	40.00
—First pressings have Donovan facing right, so it appears as if he's strumming his guitar with his left hand			
❏ LPM-127 [M]	Fairy Tale	1965	25.00
❏ LPS-127 [R]	Fairy Tale	1965	30.00
—Colours" is rechanneled			
❏ LPS-143 [P]	Like It Is, Was and Evermore Shall Be	1968	25.00
❏ LPS-149 [P]	The Best of Donovan	1969	25.00
❏ LPM-135 [M]	The Real Donovan	1966	25.00
❏ LPS-135 [P]	The Real Donovan	1966	30.00
—Half stereo, including "Colours," the rest rechanneled.			

JANUS
Number	Title	Yr	NM
❏ 3022	Donovan P. Leitch	1970	12.00
❏ 3025	Hear Me Now	1971	12.00

KORY
Number	Title	Yr	NM
❏ 3012	Early Treasures	1977	10.00

PYE
Number	Title	Yr	NM
❏ 502	Donovan	1975	12.00

SUNDAZED
Number	Title	Yr	NM
❏ LP5430 [B]	Mellow Yellow	2013	30.00
❏ LP5432 [B]	The Hurdy Gurdy Man	2013	30.00
❏ LP5431 [B]	Wear Your Love Like Heaven	2013	30.00

DOOBIE BROTHERS, THE

CAPITOL
Number	Title	Yr	NM
❏ C1-594623	Brotherhood	1991	25.00
—U.S. vinyl version available only through Columbia House			
❏ C1-90371	Cycles	1989	15.00

DCC COMPACT CLASSICS
Number	Title	Yr	NM
❏ LPZ-2053	Best of the Doobies	1998	40.00
—Audiophile vinyl			

MOBILE FIDELITY
Number	Title	Yr	NM
❏ 1-122	Takin' It to the Streets	1983	40.00
—Audiophile vinyl			

NAUTILUS
Number	Title	Yr	NM
❏ NR-18	Minute by Minute	1981	30.00
—Audiophile vinyl			
❏ NR-5	The Captain and Me	1980	40.00
—Audiophile vinyl			

PICKWICK
Number	Title	Yr	NM
❏ SPC-3721	Introducing the Doobie Brothers	1980	40.00
—Pre-Warner Bros. recordings; withdrawn shortly after release			

TPM/RHINO EXCLUSIVE
Number	Title	Yr	NM
❏ 9000	Minute by Minute	2008	25.00

WARNER BROS.
Number	Title	Yr	NM
❏ BS2978	Best of the Doobies	1976	15.00
❏ BSK3112	Best of the Doobies	1978	12.00
—Burbank" label			
❏ BSK3112	Best of the Doobies	1979	10.00
—Cream label			
❏ BSK3612	Best of the Doobies, Volume 2	1981	12.00
❏ 23772	Farewell Tour	1983	18.00
❏ BSK3045	Livin' on the Fault Line	1977	12.00
—Burbank" label			
❏ BSK3045	Livin' on the Fault Line	1977	10.00
—Cream label			
❏ BSK3193	Minute by Minute	1978	12.00
❏ HS3452	One Step Closer	1980	12.00
❏ BS2835	Stampede	1975	12.00
—Burbank" label			
❏ BS2835	Stampede	1979	10.00
—Cream label			
❏ BS42835 [Q]	Stampede	1975	30.00
❏ BS2899	Takin' It to the Streets	1076	12.00
—Burbank" label			
❏ BS2899	Takin' It to the Streets	1979	10.00
—Cream label			
❏ BS2694	The Captain and Me	1973	15.00
—Burbank" label			
❏ BS42694 [Q]	The Captain and Me	1974	30.00
❏ BS2694 [B]	The Captain and Me	1979	10.00
—Cream label			
❏ BS2694	The Captain and Me	1973	25.00
—Green label			
❏ WS1919	The Doobie Brothers	1971	18.00
—Green label original			
❏ WS1919	The Doobie Brothers	1973	12.00
—Burbank" label			
❏ BS2634	Toulouse Street	1972	18.00
—Green label original			
❏ BS2634	Toulouse Street	1973	12.00
—Burbank" label			
❏ BS42634 [Q]	Toulouse Street	1975	30.00
❏ W2750	What Were Once Vices Are Now Habits	1974	12.00
—Burbank" label			
❏ W2750	What Were Once Vices Are Now Habits	1979	10.00
—Cream label			
❏ W42750 [Q]	What Were Once Vices Are Now Habits	1974	30.00

DOONICAN, VAL

DECCA
Number	Title	Yr	NM
❏ DL4962 [M]	If the Whole World Stopped Lovin'	1968	18.00
❏ DL74962 [S]	If the Whole World Stopped Lovin'	1968	15.00

LONDON
Number	Title	Yr	NM
❏ LL3515 [M]	The Many Shades of Val Doonican	1967	15.00
❏ PS515 [S]	The Many Shades of Val Doonican	1967	18.00

DOORS, THE

DCC COMPACT CLASSICS
Number	Title	Yr	NM
❏ LPZ-2050	L.A. Woman	1998	150.00
—Audiophile vinyl			
❏ LPZ-2045	Strange Days	1997	80.00
—Audiophile vinyl			
❏ LPZ-2046	The Doors	1997	150.00
—Audiophile vinyl			
❏ LPZ-2049	Waiting for the Sun	1998	120.00
—Audiophile vinyl			

ELEKTRA
Number	Title	Yr	NM
❏ EKS-74079 [DJ]	13	1970	40.00
—White label promo			
❏ EKS-74079	13	1970	18.00
—Butterfly labels			
❏ EKS-74079	13	1980	12.00
—Red labels with Warner Communications logo in lower right			
❏ EKS-74079	13	1983	10.00

Number	Title	Yr	NM
— Red and black labels			
❑ EKS-9002 [DJ]	Absolutely Live	1970	80.00
— White label promo			
❑ EKS-9002	Absolutely Live	1970	30.00
— Butterfly labels			
❑ EKS-9002	Absolutely Live	1980	18.00
— Red labels with Warner Communications logo in lower right			
❑ EKS-9002	Absolutely Live	1983	15.00
— Red and black labels			
❑ 60269	Alive, She Cried	1984	15.00
❑ 5E-502	An American Prayer	1978	15.00
— Butterfly labels			
❑ 5E-502	An American Prayer	1980	12.00
— Red labels with Warner Communications logo in lower right			
❑ 5E-502	An American Prayer	1983	10.00
— Red and black labels			
❑ 61812	An American Prayer	1995	18.00
— Remastered and lengthened version of 5E-502			
❑ 5E-502SP DJ [DJ]	An American Prayer	1978	60.00
— White label; with sticker on cover "This album has been edited for broadcast from..."; only six tracks are on Side One rather than the eight on stock copies			
❑ EQ-5035 [Q]	Best of the Doors	1973	30.00
— Butterfly labels			
❑ EQ-5035 [Q]	Best of the Doors	1980	18.00
— Red labels with Warner Communications logo in lower right			
❑ EQ-5035 [Q]	Best of the Doors	1983	12.00
— Red and black labels			
❑ 6E-5035 [S]	Best of the Doors	1977	25.00
— Columbia Record Club edition in stereo with the quad markings blacked out on the cover; note different prefix			
❑ 60417	Classics	1986	15.00
❑ EKS-75038	Full Circle	1972	18.00
❑ 5E-515	Greatest Hits	1980	12.00
— Red labels with Warner Communications logo in lower right			
❑ 5E-515	Greatest Hits	1983	10.00
— Red and black labels			
❑ EKS-75011 [DJ]	L.A. Woman	1971	100.00
— White label promo			
❑ EKS-75011	L.A. Woman	1971	50.00
— With see-through window on cover and yellow innersleeve with photo of Jim Morrison on a cross			
❑ EKS-75011	L.A. Woman	197?	15.00
— Butterfly label, standard cover			
❑ EKS-75011	L.A. Woman	1980	12.00
— Red labels with Warner Communications logo in lower right			
❑ EKS-75011	L.A. Woman	1983	10.00
— Red and black labels			
❑ R1528723 [B]	L.A. Woman: The Workshop Sessions	2012	40.00
❑ R1532513 [B]	Live at the Bowl '68	2012	40.00
❑ 60741 [EP]	Live at the Hollywood Bowl	1988	15.00
❑ EKS-75007	Morrison Hotel	1970	30.00
— Red labels with large stylized "E			
❑ EKS-75007 [DJ]	Morrison Hotel	1970	100.00
— White label promo			
❑ EKS-75007	Morrison Hotel	1971	15.00
— Butterfly labels			
❑ EKS-75007	Morrison Hotel	1980	12.00
— Red labels with Warner Communications logo in lower right			
❑ EKS-75007	Morrison Hotel	1983	10.00
— Red and black labels			
❑ EKS-75007	Morrison Hotel	1970	60.00
— Brown or tan labels			
❑ EKS-75017	Other Voices	1971	18.00
❑ EKL-4014 [M]	Strange Days	1967	600.00
— Value assumes the record is mono. There are two different covers for this; some copies have mono numbers on the two covers and the stereo number on the spine, and others have the mono number on the spine and stereo number on front and back covers.			
❑ EKS-74014 [S]	Strange Days	1967	40.00
— Brown labels			
❑ EKS-74014 [S]	Strange Days	1969	18.00
— Red labels with large stylized "E			
❑ EKS-74014 [S]	Strange Days	1971	15.00
— Butterfly labels			
❑ EKS-74014 [S]	Strange Days	1980	12.00
— Red labels with Warner Communications logo in lower right			
❑ EKS-74014 [S]	Strange Days	1983	10.00
— Red and black labels			
❑ 60345	The Best of the Doors	1985	18.00
❑ 60345	The Best of the Doors	1985	40.00
— White label promo on audiophile vinyl			
❑ EKL-4007 [M]	The Doors	1967	200.00
❑ EKS-74007 [S]	The Doors	1967	50.00
— Brown labels			
❑ EKS-74007 [S]	The Doors	1969	18.00
— Red labels with large stylized "E			
❑ EKS-74007 [S]	The Doors	1971	15.00
— Butterfly labels			
❑ EKS-74007 [S]	The Doors	1980	12.00
— Red labels with Warner Communications logo in lower right			
❑ EKS-74007 [S]	The Doors	1983	10.00
— Red and black labels			
❑ E1-61047	The Doors	1991	100.00
— Soundtrack from the movie; only available on US vinyl from Columbia House			
❑ EKS-75005	The Soft Parade	1969	50.00
— Brown or tan labels			
❑ EKS-75005	The Soft Parade	1969	25.00
— Red labels with large stylized "E			
❑ EKS-75005	The Soft Parade	1971	15.00
— Butterfly labels			
❑ EKS-75005	The Soft Parade	1980	12.00
— Red labels with Warner Communications logo in lower right			
❑ EKS-75005	The Soft Parade	1983	10.00
— Red and black labels			
❑ EKL-4024 [M]	Waiting for the Sun	1968	1000.00
❑ EKS-74024 [S]	Waiting for the Sun	1968	150.00
— White label promo			
❑ EKS-74024 [S]	Waiting for the Sun	1968	30.00
— Brown labels			
❑ EKS-74024 [S]	Waiting for the Sun	1969	18.00
— Red labels with large stylized "E			
❑ EKS-74024 [S]	Waiting for the Sun	1971	15.00
— Butterfly labels			
❑ EKS-74024 [S]	Waiting for the Sun	1980	12.00
— Red labels with Warner Communications logo in lower right			
❑ EKS-74024 [S]	Waiting for the Sun	1983	10.00
— Red and black labels			
❑ 8E-6001	Weird Scenes Inside the Gold Mine	1972	25.00
— Butterfly labels			
❑ 8E-6001	Weird Scenes Inside the Gold Mine	1980	15.00
— Red labels with Warner Communications logo in lower right			
❑ 8E-6001	Weird Scenes Inside the Gold Mine	1983	12.00
— Red and black labels			

MOBILE FIDELITY

Number	Title	Yr	NM
❑ 1-051	The Doors	1980	80.00
— Audiophile vinyl			

RHINO

Number	Title	Yr	NM
❑ R1537456 [B]	Curated By Record Store Day	2013	50.00
❑ R16001 [B]	Weird Scenes Inside The Gold Mine	2014	75.00

DORFMAN, ANIA

RCA VICTOR RED SEAL

Number	Title	Yr	NM
❑ LSC 2207 [S]	Schumann: Carnaval	1959	30.00
— Original with "shaded dog" label			

DORHAM, KENNY

ABC-PARAMOUNT

Number	Title	Yr	NM
❑ ABC-122 [M]	Kenny Dorham and the Jazz Prophets	1956	80.00

BAINBRIDGE

Number	Title	Yr	NM
❑ 1048	Kenny Dorham	198?	12.00
❑ 1043	Show Boat	198?	12.00

BLUE NOTE

Number	Title	Yr	NM
❑ BLP-5055 [10]	Afro Cuban Holiday	1955	300.00
❑ BLP-1535 [M]	Kenny Dorham Octet/Sextet	1956	300.00
— Deep groove" version (deep indentation under label on both sides)			
❑ BLP-1535 [M]	Kenny Dorham Octet/Sextet	1956	150.00
— Regular version with Lexington Ave. address on label			
❑ BLP-1535 [M]	Kenny Dorham Octet/Sextet	1963	30.00
— New York, USA" address on label			
❑ BLP-1524 [M]	'Round About Midnight at the Café Bohemia	1956	200.00
— Deep groove" version (deep indentation under label on both sides)			
❑ BLP-1524 [M]	'Round About Midnight at the Café Bohemia	1956	150.00
— Regular version with Lexington Ave. address on label			
❑ BLP-1524 [M]	'Round About Midnight at the Café Bohemia	1963	30.00
— New York, USA" address on label			
❑ BLP-4181 [M]	Trompeta Toccata	1964	30.00
— New York, USA" address on label			
❑ BST-84181 [S]	Trompeta Toccata	1964	40.00
— New York, USA" address on label			
❑ BST-84181 [S]	Trompeta Toccata	1966	18.00
— A Division of Liberty Records" on label			
❑ BST-84181	Trompeta Toccata	1985	12.00
— The Finest in Jazz Since 1939" reissue			
❑ BLP-4127 [M]	Una Mas	1963	30.00
— New York, USA" address on label			
❑ BST-84127 [S]	Una Mas	1963	40.00
— New York, USA" address on label			
❑ BST-84127 [S]	Una Mas	1966	18.00
— A Division of Liberty Records" on label			
❑ BST-84127 [S]	Una Mas	197?	15.00
— United Artists" on label			
❑ BLP-4063 [M]	Whistle Stop	1961	80.00
— W. 63rd St. address on label			
❑ BLP-4063 [M]	Whistle Stop	1963	30.00
— New York, USA" address on label			
❑ BST-84063 [S]	Whistle Stop	1961	60.00
— W. 63rd St. address on label			
❑ BST-84063 [S]	Whistle Stop	1963	30.00
— New York, USA" address on label			
❑ BST-84063 [S]	Whistle Stop	1966	18.00
— A Division of Liberty Records" on label			
❑ BST-84063 [S]	Whistle Stop	197?	15.00
— United Artists" on label			
❑ B1-28978	Whistle Stop	1994	18.00

DEBUT

Number	Title	Yr	NM
❑ DLP-9 [10]	Kenny Dorham Quintet	1954	300.00

FANTASY

Number	Title	Yr	NM
❑ OJC-463	2 Horns 2 Rhythm	1990	15.00
— Reissue of Riverside 255			
❑ OJC-134	Blue Spring	198?	12.00
❑ OJC-028	Jazz Contrasts	198?	12.00
❑ OJC-113	Kenny Dorham Quintet	198?	12.00
— Reissue of Debut 9			
❑ OJC-250	Quiet Kenny	1987	12.00
— Reissue of New Jazz 8225			

JARO

Number	Title	Yr	NM
❑ JAM-5007 [M]	The Arrival of Kenny Dorham	1960	400.00
❑ JAS-8007 [S]	The Arrival of Kenny Dorham	1960	400.00

JAZZLAND

Number	Title	Yr	NM
❑ JLP-14 [M]	Kenny Dorham and Friends	1960	40.00
❑ JLP-914 [S]	Kenny Dorham and Friends	1960	50.00
❑ JLP-82 [M]	Kenny Dorham and Friends	1962	25.00
❑ JLP-982 [S]	Kenny Dorham and Friends	1962	30.00
❑ JLP-3 [M]	The Swingers	1960	40.00
❑ JLP-903 [S]	The Swingers	1960	50.00

MILESTONE

Number	Title	Yr	NM
❑ 47036	But Beautiful	197?	18.00

MUSE

Number	Title	Yr	NM
❑ MR-5053	Ease It	1974	18.00

NEW JAZZ

Number	Title	Yr	NM
❑ NJLP-8225 [M]	Quiet Kenny	1959	2000.00
— Purple label			
❑ NJLP-8225 [M]	Quiet Kenny	1965	30.00
— Blue label, trident logo at right			

PACIFIC JAZZ

Number	Title	Yr	NM
❑ PJ-41 [M]	Inta Somethin' -- Recorded Live at the Jazz Workshop	1962	30.00
❑ ST-41 [S]	Inta Somethin' -- Recorded Live at the Jazz Workshop	1962	40.00

PRESTIGE

Number	Title	Yr	NM
❑ PRST-7754	Kenny Dorham 1959	1970	25.00

RIVERSIDE

Number	Title	Yr	NM
❑ RLP 12-255 [M]	2 Horns 2 Rhythm	1957	50.00
❑ RLP 12-297 [M]	Blue Spring	1959	50.00
❑ RLP-1139 [S]	Blue Spring	1959	40.00
❑ RLP 12-239 [M]	Jazz Contrasts	1957	80.00
— White label, blue print			
❑ RLP 12-239 [M]	Jazz Contrasts	1959	40.00
— Blue label, microphone logo			
❑ RLP-1105 [S]	Jazz Contrasts	1959	30.00
— Black label, microphone logo			
❑ 6075	Jazz Contrasts	197?	18.00
❑ RLP 12-275 [M]	This Is the Moment!	1958	50.00

STEEPLECHASE

Number	Title	Yr	NM
❑ SCC-6011	Scandia Skies	198?	15.00
❑ SCC-6010	Short Story	198?	15.00

TIME

Number	Title	Yr	NM
❑ 52004 [M]	Jazz Contemporary	1960	40.00
❑ S-2004 [S]	Jazz Contemporary	1960	50.00
❑ 52024 [M]	Show Boat	1960	40.00
❑ S-2024 [S]	Show Boat	1960	50.00

UNITED ARTISTS

Number	Title	Yr	NM
❑ UAJ-14007 [M]	Matador	1962	30.00
❑ UAJS-15007 [S]	Matador	1962	40.00
❑ UAS-5631	Matador	1971	25.00
— Reissue of 15007			

XANADU

Number	Title	Yr	NM
❑ 125	Memorial Album	197?	18.00

DORHAM, KENNY/CLARK TERRY

JAZZLAND

Number	Title	Yr	NM
❑ JLP-10 [M]	Top Trumpets	1960	40.00
❑ JLP-910 [S]	Top Trumpets	1960	50.00

DOROUGH, BOB

BETHLEHEM

Number	Title	Yr	NM
❑ BCP-11 [M]	Devil May Care	1955	120.00
❑ BCP-6023	Yardbird Suite	197?	25.00
— Reissue of 11, distributed by RCA Victor			

CLASSIC JAZZ

Number	Title	Yr	NM
❑ 18	An Excursion Through Oliver	197?	18.00
❑ 19	The Medieval Jazz Quartet Plus 3	197?	18.00

FOCUS

Number	Title	Yr	NM
❑ FL-336 [M]	Better Than Anything	1967	30.00
❑ FS-336 [S]	Better Than Anything	1967	25.00

INNER CITY

Number	Title	Yr	NM
❑ IC-1023	Just About Everything	197?	18.00

LAISSEZ-FAIRE

Number	Title	Yr	NM
❑ 02	Beginning to See the Light	1976	25.00

MUSIC MINUS ONE

Number	Title	Yr	NM
❑ 225 [M]	Oliver	1963	30.00

DORS, DIANA

COLUMBIA

Number	Title	Yr	NM
❑ CL1436 [M]	Swingin' Dors	1960	80.00
❑ CS8232 [S]	Swingin' Dors	1960	100.00

Number	Title	Yr	NM

DORSEY, JIMMY

ATLANTIC
| ❑ 81801 | Dorsey, Then and Now | 1988 | 12.00 |

CIRCLE
| ❑ 30 | Jimmy Dorsey and His Orchestra 1939-40 | 198? | 12.00 |
| ❑ 46 | Jimmy Dorsey and His Orchestra Mostly 1940 | 198? | 12.00 |

COLUMBIA
❑ CL6095 [10]	Dixie by Dorsey	1950	50.00
❑ CL608 [M]	Dixie by Dorsey	1955	40.00
—Maroon label with gold print			
❑ CL608 [M]	Dixie by Dorsey	1955	30.00
—Red and black label with six "eye" logos			
❑ CL6114 [10]	Dorseyland Band	1950	50.00

CORAL
❑ CRL56004 [10]	Contrasting Music, Volume 1	1950	50.00
❑ CRL56008 [10]	Contrasting Music, Volume 2	1950	50.00
❑ CRL56033 [10]	Gershwin Music	1950	50.00

DECCA
❑ DL4853 [M]	Jimmy Dorsey's Greatest Hits	1967	25.00
❑ DL74853 [R]	Jimmy Dorsey's Greatest Hits	1967	15.00
❑ DL5091 [10]	Latin American Favorites	1950	50.00
❑ DL8153 [M]	Latin American Favorites	1955	30.00
—Black label, silver print			
❑ DL8609 [M]	The Great Jimmy Dorsey	1957	30.00
—Black label, silver print			

DOT
❑ DLP-3437 [M]	So Rare	1962	25.00
—Reissue of Fraternity LP			
❑ DLP-25437 [R]	So Rare	196?	15.00

FRATERNITY
| ❑ F-1008 [M] | Fabulous Jimmy Dorsey | 1957 | 30.00 |

HINDSIGHT
❑ HSR-101	Jimmy Dorsey and His Orchestra 1939-40	198?	12.00
❑ HSR-153	Jimmy Dorsey and His Orchestra 1942-44	198?	12.00
❑ HSR-203	Jimmy Dorsey and His Orchestra 1948	198?	12.00
❑ HSR-165	Jimmy Dorsey and His Orchestra 1949, 1951	198?	12.00
❑ HSR-178	Jimmy Dorsey and His Orchestra 1950	198?	12.00

INSIGHT
| ❑ 210 | Jimmy Dorsey and His Orchestra 1939-42 | 198? | 12.00 |

LION
| ❑ L-70063 [M] | Jimmy Dorsey and His Orchestra | 1958 | 25.00 |

MCA
❑ 252	Jimmy Dorsey's Greatest Hits	197?	15.00
—Reissue of Decca 74853; black label with rainbow			
❑ 252	Jimmy Dorsey's Greatest Hits	198?	10.00
—Reissue; blue label with rainbow			
❑ 4073	The Best of Jimmy Dorsey	1975	15.00
—Original edition has a gatefold cover and black labels with rainbow			

POWER PAK
| ❑ 244 | Jimmy Dorsey Plays His Biggest Hits | 197? | 12.00 |

TIME-LIFE
| ❑ STBB-10 | Big Bands: Jimmy Dorsey | 1984 | 18.00 |

TRIP
| ❑ 5815 | So Rare! | 197? | 12.00 |

DORSEY, LEE

AMY
❑ 8010 [M]	Ride Your Pony	1966	30.00
❑ 8010-S [S]	Ride Your Pony	1966	40.00
❑ 8011 [M]	The New Lee Dorsey/ Working in the Coal Mine-Holy Cow	1966	30.00
❑ 8011-S [S]	The New Lee Dorsey/ Working in the Coal Mine-Holy Cow	1966	30.00

ARISTA
| ❑ AL8387 | Holy Cow! The Best of Lee Dorsey | 1985 | 12.00 |

FURY
| ❑ 1002 [M] | Ya Ya | 1962 | 300.00 |

POLYDOR
| ❑ 24-4024 | Yes We Can | 1970 | 15.00 |

SPHERE SOUND
❑ SR-7003 [M]	Ya Ya	196?	100.00
—Reissue of Fury 1002			
❑ SSR-7003 [R]	Ya Ya	196?	50.00
—Rechanneled reissue of Fury 1002			

DORSEY, TOMMY, ORCHESTRA (WARREN COVINGTON, DIRECTOR)

DECCA
| ❑ DL8904 [M] | Dance and Romance | 1959 | 18.00 |
| ❑ DL78904 [S] | Dance and Romance | 1959 | 25.00 |

Number	Title	Yr	NM

❑ DL4120 [M]	Dance to the Songs Everybody Knows	1960	18.00
❑ DL74120 [S]	Dance to the Songs Everybody Knows	1960	25.00
❑ DL8996 [M]	It Takes Two to Bunny Hop..	1960	18.00
❑ DL78996 [S]	It Takes Two to Bunny Hop..	1960	25.00
❑ DL8980 [M]	It Takes Two to Cha-Cha...	1959	18.00
❑ DL78980 [S]	It Takes Two to Cha-Cha...	1959	25.00
❑ DL8943 [M]	More Tea for Two Cha Chas	1959	18.00
❑ DL78943 [S]	More Tea for Two Cha Chas	1959	25.00
❑ DL8842 [M]	Tea for Two Cha Chas	1958	18.00
❑ DL78842 [S]	Tea for Two Cha Chas	1958	25.00
❑ DL8802 [M]	The Fabulous Arrangements of Tommy Dorsey	1958	18.00
❑ DL78802 [S]	The Fabulous Arrangements of Tommy Dorsey	1958	25.00
❑ DL4130 [M]	Tricky Trombones	1961	18.00
❑ DL74130 [S]	Tricky Trombones	1961	25.00

MCA
❑ 185	It Takes Two to Bunny Hop..	197?	12.00
❑ 534	It Takes Two to Cha-Cha…	197?	12.00
—Reissue of Decca 78996			
❑ 180	More Tea for Two Cha Chas	197?	12.00
—Reissue of Decca 78943			
❑ 178	Tea for Two Cha Chas	197?	12.00
—Reissue of Decca 78842			

DORSEY, TOMMY

20TH CENTURY FOX
❑ TFM-3157 [M]	This Is Tommy Dorsey and His Greatest Band, Vol. 1	196?	25.00
❑ TFS-4157 [R]	This Is Tommy Dorsey and His Greatest Band, Vol. 1	196?	15.00
❑ TFM-3158 [M]	This Is Tommy Dorsey and His Greatest Band, Vol. 2	196?	25.00
❑ TFS-4158 [R]	This Is Tommy Dorsey and His Greatest Band, Vol. 2	196?	15.00
❑ FOX1005 [M]	Tommy Dorsey and His Orchestra: His Greatest Arrangements -- His Greatest Band	196?	18.00
—Million Seller Hits" reissue series			
❑ TCF101/102 [M]	Tommy Dorsey's Greatest Band	1959	30.00

BLUEBIRD
❑ AXM2-5521	The Complete Tommy Dorsey, Volume 1	197?	18.00
❑ AXM2-5549	The Complete Tommy Dorsey, Volume 2	197?	18.00
❑ AXM2-5560	The Complete Tommy Dorsey, Volume 3	197?	18.00
❑ AXM2-5564	The Complete Tommy Dorsey, Volume 4	197?	18.00
❑ AXM2-5573	The Complete Tommy Dorsey, Volume 5	197?	18.00
❑ AXM2-5578	The Complete Tommy Dorsey, Volume 6	197?	18.00
❑ AXM2-5582	The Complete Tommy Dorsey, Volume 7	197?	18.00
❑ AXM2-5586	The Complete Tommy Dorsey, Volume 8	197?	18.00
❑ 9987-1-RB	Yes, Indeed!	1990	18.00

COLPIX
❑ CP401 [M]	The Great T.D.	1958	25.00
❑ CP436 [M]	Tommy Dorsey & His Orchestra Volume 4	1962	25.00
❑ CP498 [M]	Tommy Dorsey -- A Man and His Trombone	196?	25.00

DECCA
❑ DL5448 [10]	In a Sentimental Mood	1952	50.00
❑ DL5449 [10]	Tenderly	1952	50.00
❑ DL5317 [10]	Tommy Dorsey Plays Howard Dietz	1951	50.00
❑ DL5452 [10]	Your Invitation to Dance	1952	50.00

HARMONY
| ❑ HL7334 [M] | On the Sentimental Side | 196? | 18.00 |
| ❑ KH32014 | The Beat of the Big Bands | 1972 | 12.00 |

MCA
| ❑ 732 | Sentimental | 198? | 10.00 |
| ❑ 4074 | The Best of Tommy Dorsey | 197? | 15.00 |

MOVIETONE
❑ MTM-1019 [M]	The Tommy Dorsey Years	1967	18.00
❑ MTS-72019 [R]	The Tommy Dorsey Years	1967	15.00
❑ MTM-1004 [M]	Tommy Dorsey's Hullaballoo	196?	18.00
❑ MTS-72004 [R]	Tommy Dorsey's Hullaballoo	196?	15.00

PICKWICK
| ❑ PTP-2035 | I'm Getting Sentimental* | 197? | 15.00 |

RCA CAMDEN
❑ CAL-800 [M]	Dedicated to You*	1964	18.00
❑ CAS-800(e) [R]	Dedicated to You*	1964	12.00
❑ ADL2-0178	I'll See You in My Dreams*	1973	18.00
❑ CXS-9027	I'm Getting Sentimental*	1972	18.00
❑ CAL-650 [M]	The One and Only Tommy Dorsey*	1961	18.00
❑ CAS-650(e) [R]	The One and Only Tommy Dorsey*	196?	12.00

RCA VICTOR
❑ ALPT-15 [M]	All Time Hits*	1951	80.00
❑ LPT-10 [M]	Getting Sentimental with Tommy Dorsey*	1951	80.00
❑ LPM-1643 [M]	Having a Wonderful Time*	1958	40.00
❑ ANL1-2162(e)	On the Sunny Side of the Street	1977	12.00
❑ ANL1-1586	Pure Gold*	1976	12.00

Number	Title	Yr	NM

❑ LPM-6003 [M]	That Sentimental Gentleman*	1957	80.00
—Box set			
❑ LPM-3674 [M]	The Best of Tommy Dorsey*	1966	25.00
❑ LSP-3674 [R]	The Best of Tommy Dorsey*	1966	15.00
❑ ANL1-1087	The Best of Tommy Dorsey	1976	12.00
❑ LPT-3005 [M]	This Is Tommy Dorsey*	1952	50.00
❑ VPM-6038	This Is Tommy Dorsey*	1971	30.00
❑ LPT-3018 [10]	This Is Tommy Dorsey*	1952	50.00
❑ VPM-6064	This Is Tommy Dorsey, Volume 2*	197?	30.00
❑ VPM-6087	This Is Tommy Dorsey and His Clambake Seven	1973	25.00
—Orange labels			
❑ VPM-6087	This Is Tommy Dorsey and His Clambake Seven	1977	18.00
—Black labels, dog near top			
❑ LPM-1425 [M]	Tommy Dorsey Plays Cole Porter and Jerome Kern	1956	30.00
❑ LPM-22 [10]	Tommy Dorsey Plays Cole Porter for Dancing	1951	50.00
❑ LPM-1432 [M]	Tribute to Dorsey, Volume 1*	1956	40.00
❑ LPM-1433 [M]	Tribute to Dorsey, Volume 2*	1956	40.00
❑ LPM-1229 [M]	Yes Indeed*	1956	50.00

SUNBEAM
| ❑ 201 | Tommy Dorsey and His Orchestra 1935-39 | 197? | 12.00 |
| ❑ 220 | Tommy Dorsey and His Orchestra 1944-46 | 197? | 12.00 |

TIME-LIFE
| ❑ STBB-19 | Big Bands: Sentimental Genrtleman* | 1985 | 25.00 |
| ❑ STBB-02 | Big Bands: Tommy Dorsey* | 1983 | 25.00 |

VOCALION
| ❑ VL3613 [M] | Dance Party | 196? | 18.00 |
| ❑ VL73613 [R] | Dance Party | 196? | 12.00 |

DORSEY BROTHERS, THE

CIRCLE
| ❑ 20 | The Dorsey Brothers Orchestra 1935 | 198? | 12.00 |

COLUMBIA
❑ CL1240 [M]	Sentimental and Swinging	1958	30.00
—Red and black label with six "eye" logos			
❑ C2L8	The Fabulous Dorseys in Hi-Fi	1958	40.00
—Red and black labels with six "eye" logos			
❑ CL1190 [M]	The Fabulous Dorseys in Hi Fi, Volume I	1957	30.00
—Red and black labels with six "eye" logos			

DECCA
❑ DL8631 [M]	Dixieland Jazz	1958	30.00
—Black label, silver print			
❑ DL8631 [M]	Dixieland Jazz	1961	18.00
—Black label with color bars			
❑ DL8654 [M]	The Swinging Dorseys	1958	30.00
—Black label, silver print			
❑ DL8654 [M]	The Swinging Dorseys	1961	18.00
—Black label with color bars			

DESIGN
| ❑ DLP-20 [M] | Their Shining Hour | 196? | 15.00 |
| ❑ DLPS-20 [R] | Their Shining Hour | 196? | 12.00 |

MCA
| ❑ 1505 | The 1934-35 Decca Sessions | 198? | 12.00 |

RIVERSIDE
❑ RLP 12-811 [M]	A Backward Glance	1958	60.00
❑ RLP-1008 [10]	Jazz of the Roaring Twenties	1953	80.00
❑ RLP-1051 [10]	The Dorsey Brothers with the California Ramblers	1955	80.00

SUNBEAM
❑ 301	The Dorsey Brothers 1934	197?	12.00
❑ 210	The Fabulous Dorsey Brothers	197?	12.00
❑ 224	The Fabulous Dorsey Brothers, Volume 2	197?	12.00

DOTTSY

RCA VICTOR
| ❑ APL1-1358 | The Sweetest Thing | 1976 | 15.00 |
| ❑ AHL1-3380 | Tryin' to Satisfy You | 1979 | 15.00 |

DOUBLE IMAGE

CELESTIAL HARMONIES
| ❑ CEL-015 | In Lands I Never Saw | 1986 | 12.00 |

ECM
| ❑ 1146 | Dawn | 1978 | 15.00 |

ENJA
| ❑ 2096 | Double Image | 198? | 15.00 |

INNER CITY
| ❑ IC-3013 | Double Image | 1978 | 18.00 |

DOUBLE SIX OF PARIS, THE

CAPITOL
| ❑ T10259 [M] | The Double Six of Paris | 1961 | 80.00 |
| ❑ ST10259 [S] | The Double Six of Paris | 1961 | 100.00 |

PHILIPS
| ❑ PHM200026 [M] | Swingin' Singin' | 1962 | 40.00 |

Number	Title	Yr	NM
❑ PHS600026 [S]	Swingin' Singin'	1962	60.00
❑ PHM200141 [M]	The Double Six of Paris Sings Ray Charles	1964	100.00
❑ PHS600141 [S]	The Double Six of Paris Sings Ray Charles	1964	150.00

DOUG AND THE SLUGS

AVION

Number	Title	Yr	NM
❑ AVF4603	Doug and the Slugs	1987	15.00

RCA VICTOR

Number	Title	Yr	NM
❑ AFL1-3887	Cognac and Bologna	1981	14.00
❑ AFL1-4432	Music for the Hard of Thinking	1983	14.00
❑ AFL1-4261	Wrap It	1982	14.00

DOUGLAS, CARL

20TH CENTURY

Number	Title	Yr	NM
❑ T-464	Kung Fu Fighting and Other Great Love Songs	1974	15.00

DOUGLAS, GLENN

DECCA

Number	Title	Yr	NM
❑ DL8748 [M]	Heartbreak Alley	1958	50.00

DOUGLAS, K.C.

BLUESVILLE

Number	Title	Yr	NM
❑ BVLP-1050 [M]	Big Road Blues	1962	80.00
—Blue label, silver print			
❑ BVLP-1050 [M]	Big Road Blues	1964	30.00
—Blue label, trident logo at right			
❑ BVLP-1023 [M]	K.C.'s Blues	1961	80.00
—Blue label, silver print			
❑ BVLP-1023 [M]	K.C.'s Blues	1964	30.00
—Blue label, trident logo at right			

COOK ROAD

Number	Title	Yr	NM
❑ 5002 [M]	A Dead Beat Guitar and the Mississippi Blues	1956	500.00

DOUGLAS, LEW

CARLTON

Number	Title	Yr	NM
❑ LP 12-126 [M]	Themes from Motion Pictures and TV	1960	30.00

DOUGLAS, MIKE

ATLANTIC

Number	Title	Yr	NM
❑ SD18168	Mike Douglas Sings It All	1976	12.00

EPIC

Number	Title	Yr	NM
❑ LN24205 [M]	Dear Mike, Please Sing	1966	15.00
❑ BN26205 [S]	Dear Mike, Please Sing	1966	18.00
❑ LN24169 [M]	It's Time for Mike Douglas	1965	15.00
❑ BN26169 [S]	It's Time for Mike Douglas	1965	18.00
❑ LN24322 [M]	My Kind of Christmas	1967	15.00
❑ BN26322 [S]	My Kind of Christmas	1967	15.00
❑ LN24186 [M]	The Men in My Little Girl's Life	1966	15.00
❑ BN26186 [S]	The Men in My Little Girl's Life	1966	18.00
❑ LN24179 [M]	You Don't Have to Be Irish	1965	15.00
❑ BN26179 [S]	You Don't Have to Be Irish	1965	18.00

HARMONY

Number	Title	Yr	NM
❑ HS11263	Young at Heart	1968	15.00

WORD

Number	Title	Yr	NM
❑ 8815	Christmas Album	198?	12.00
❑ WR-8791	I'll Sing This Song for You	197?	12.00

DOUGLAS, STEVE

CROWN

Number	Title	Yr	NM
❑ CLP-5251 [M]	Twist with Steve Douglas and the Rebel Rousers	1962	25.00

MERCURY

Number	Title	Yr	NM
❑ SR-61217	Reflections in a Golden Horn	1969	30.00

DOUGLAS, TONY

DOT

Number	Title	Yr	NM
❑ DLP-26009	Thank You for Touching My Life	1973	18.00

PAULA

Number	Title	Yr	NM
❑ LP2198	Heart	1967	25.00

DOVAL, JIM, AND THE GAUCHOS

ABC-PARAMOUNT

Number	Title	Yr	NM
❑ ABC-506 [M]	The Gauchos Featuring Jim Doval	1965	30.00
❑ ABCS-506 [S]	The Gauchos Featuring Jim Doval	1965	40.00

DOVE, RONNIE

DIAMOND

Number	Title	Yr	NM
❑ D5007 [M]	Cry	1967	18.00
❑ DS5007 [S]	Cry	1967	25.00
❑ D5004 [M]	I'll Make All Your Dreams Come True	1965	25.00
❑ DS5004 [S]	I'll Make All Your Dreams Come True	1965	30.00
❑ D5003 [M]	One Kiss for Old Times' Sake	1965	25.00
❑ DS5003 [S]	One Kiss for Old Times' Sake	1965	30.00
❑ D5002 [M]	Right or Wrong	1964	25.00
❑ DS5002 [S]	Right or Wrong	1964	30.00
❑ D5006 [M]	Ronnie Dove Sings the Hits for You	1966	18.00
❑ DS5006 [S]	Ronnie Dove Sings the Hits for You	1966	25.00
❑ D5005 [M]	The Best of Ronnie Dove	1966	18.00
❑ DS5005 [S]	The Best of Ronnie Dove	1966	25.00
❑ D-5008 [M]	The Best of Ronnie Dove -- Vol. 2	1968	30.00
❑ SD-5008 [S]	The Best of Ronnie Dove -- Vol. 2	1968	18.00

POWER PAK

Number	Title	Yr	NM
❑ 286	Greatest Hits	1975	15.00

DOVELLS, THE

CAMEO

Number	Title	Yr	NM
❑ C-1082 [M]	Len Barry Sings with the Dovells	1965	30.00
❑ SC-1082 [S]	Len Barry Sings with the Dovells	1965	50.00

PARKWAY

Number	Title	Yr	NM
❑ P7010 [M]	All the Hits of the Teen Groups	1962	80.00
❑ P7021 [M]	For Your Hully Gully Party	1962	50.00
❑ P7006 [M]	The Bristol Stomp	1961	100.00
—Light orange label			
❑ P7006 [M]	The Bristol Stomp	1962	50.00
—Dark orange and yellow label			
❑ P7025 [M]	You Can't Sit Down	1963	50.00

WYNCOTE

Number	Title	Yr	NM
❑ W9052 [M]	Discotheque	1965	25.00
❑ SW9052 [R]	Discotheque	1965	18.00
❑ W9114 [M]	The Dovells' Biggest Hits	1965	25.00
❑ SW9114 [R]	The Dovells' Biggest Hits	1965	18.00

DOWELL, JOE

SMASH

Number	Title	Yr	NM
❑ MGS-27011 [M]	German American Hits	1962	30.00
❑ SRS-67011 [S]	German American Hits	1962	30.00
❑ MGS-27000 [M]	Wooden Heart	1961	40.00
❑ SRS-67000 [S]	Wooden Heart	1961	50.00

WING

Number	Title	Yr	NM
❑ MGW-12328 [M]	Wooden Heart	196?	25.00
❑ SRW-16328 [S]	Wooden Heart	196?	25.00

DOWLING, CHET, AND BILL MINKIN

COLUMBIA

Number	Title	Yr	NM
❑ CL2776 [M]	Senator Bobby's Christmas Party	1967	25.00
❑ CS9576 [S]	Senator Bobby's Christmas Party	1967	25.00

DOWNS, HUGH

EPIC

Number	Title	Yr	NM
❑ LN3597 [M]	An Evening with Hugh Downs	1961	30.00
❑ BN541 [S]	An Evening with Hugh Downs	1961	30.00

DOYLE, BOBBY, THREE

COLUMBIA

Number	Title	Yr	NM
❑ CL1858 [M]	In a Most Unusual Way	1962	40.00
❑ CS8658 [S]	In a Most Unusual Way	1962	50.00

DOYLE, MIKE

FLEETWOOD

Number	Title	Yr	NM
❑ FLP-3018 [M]	The Secrets of Surfing	1963	120.00

DOZIER, GENE, AND THE BROTHERHOOD

MINIT

Number	Title	Yr	NM
❑ 40010 [M]	Blues Power	1967	30.00
❑ 24010 [S]	Blues Power	1967	30.00

DR. BUZZARD'S ORIGINAL SAVANNAH BAND

ELEKTRA

Number	Title	Yr	NM
❑ 6E-218	James Monroe H.S. Presents Dr. Buzzard's Original Savannah Band Goes to Washington	1979	12.00

PASSPORT

Number	Title	Yr	NM
❑ 6013	Calling All Beatniks	1986	12.00

RCA VICTOR

Number	Title	Yr	NM
❑ APL1-1504	Dr. Buzzard's Original Savannah Band	1976	18.00
—Original copies have tan labels			
❑ AYL1-3767	Dr. Buzzard's Original Savannah Band	1980	10.00
—Reissue			
❑ APL1-1504	Dr. Buzzard's Original Savannah Band	1976	12.00
—Reissue on black label with "Nipper" logo			
❑ AFL1-2402	Dr. Buzzard's Original Savannah Band Meets King Pennet	1978	15.00

DR. DRE

AFTERMATH

Number	Title	Yr	NM
❑ 490486	2001	1999	18.00
❑ 490571	2001: Instrumentals	2000	25.00

DEATH ROW

Number	Title	Yr	NM
❑ P1-50611	The Chronic	1993	18.00

DR. FEELGOOD AND THE INTERNS

OKEH

Number	Title	Yr	NM
❑ OKM12101 [M]	Dr. Feelgood and the Interns	1962	100.00
❑ OKS14101 [S]	Dr. Feelgood and the Interns	1962	200.00

DR. HOOK

CAPITOL

Number	Title	Yr	NM
❑ ST-11522	A Little Bit More	1976	12.00
❑ SN-16180	A Little Bit More	198?	10.00
—Budget-line reissue			
❑ ST-11397	Bankrupt	1975	12.00
❑ SN-16179	Bankrupt	198?	10.00
—Budget-line reissue			
❑ SOO-12122	Dr. Hook/Greatest Hits	1980	12.00
❑ SN-16325	Dr. Hook/Greatest Hits	198?	10.00
—Budget-line reissue			
❑ ST-12114	Live	1981	12.00
❑ ST-11632	Makin' Love and Music	1977	12.00
❑ SN-16228	Makin' Love and Music	198?	10.00
—Budget-line reissue			
❑ SW-11859	Pleasure and Pain	1978	12.00
❑ SN-16181	Pleasure and Pain	198?	10.00
—Budget-line reissue			
❑ ST-12018	Sometimes You Win...	1979	12.00
❑ SN-16229	Sometimes You Win...	198?	10.00
—Budget-line reissue			
❑ SOO-12023	Sometimes You Win...	1979	12.00
—Other than the prefix and the number, we don't know if there are any differences between this and 12018, but both do exist			
❑ ST-12325	The Rest of Dr. Hook	1984	10.00

CASABLANCA

Number	Title	Yr	NM
❑ NBLP-7264	Players in the Dark	1982	12.00
❑ NBLP-7251	Rising	1980	12.00

COLUMBIA

Number	Title	Yr	NM
❑ KC32270	Belly Up!	1973	18.00
❑ KC30898	Dr. Hook & The Medicine Show	1972	18.00
❑ PC30898	Dr. Hook & The Medicine Show	198?	10.00
—Budget-line reissue			
❑ C34147	Dr. Hook and the Medicine Show Revisited	1976	12.00
❑ PC34147	Dr. Hook and the Medicine Show Revisited	198?	10.00
—Budget-line reissue			
❑ KC31622	Sloppy Seconds	1972	18.00
❑ PC31622	Sloppy Seconds	198?	10.00
—Budget-line reissue			

MERCURY

Number	Title	Yr	NM
❑ 000061 1	Players in the Dark	1983	10.00
—Reissue of Casablanca 7264			

DR. JOHN

ACCORD

Number	Title	Yr	NM
❑ SN-7118	Love Potion	1982	12.00

ALLIGATOR

Number	Title	Yr	NM
❑ AL-3901	Dr. John's Gumbo	1980	12.00
—Reissue of Atco 7006			
❑ AL-3904	Gris-Gris	1987	12.00
—Reissue of Atco 33-234			

ATCO

Number	Title	Yr	NM
❑ SD 33-270	Babylon	1969	18.00
❑ SD7043	Desitively Bonaroo	1974	15.00
❑ SD 33-362 [B]	Dr. John, The Night Tripper (The Sun, Moon & Herbs)	1971	18.00
❑ SD7006	Dr. John's Gumbo	1972	15.00
❑ SD 33-234	Gris-Gris	1968	30.00
—Purple and brown label			
❑ SD 33-234	Gris-Gris	1968	18.00
—Yellow label			
❑ SD7018	In the Right Place	1973	15.00
❑ SD 33-316	Remedies	1970	18.00

CLEAN CUTS

Number	Title	Yr	NM
❑ 705	Dr. John Plays Mac Rebennack	1982	12.00
❑ 707	The Brightest Smile in Town	1984	12.00

HORIZON

Number	Title	Yr	NM
❑ SP-732	City Lights	1978	12.00
❑ SP-740	Tango Palace	1979	12.00

KARATE

Number	Title	Yr	NM
❑ 5404	One Night Late	1978	12.00

TRIP

Number	Title	Yr	NM
❑ TLX-350	Superpak	1975	15.00

UNITED ARTISTS

Number	Title	Yr	NM
❑ UA-LA552-G	Hollywood Be Thy Name	1975	15.00

WARNER BROS.

Number	Title	Yr	NM
❑ 25889	In a Sentimental Mood	1989	15.00

DR. JOHN AND CHRIS BARBER

GREAT SOUTHERN

Number	Title	Yr	NM
❑ GS-11024	On a Mardi Gras Day	1991	15.00

Number	Title	Yr	NM

DR. WEST'S MEDICINE SHOW AND JUG BAND

GO GO
❑ 22-17-002 [S]	The Eggplant That Ate Chicago	1967	30.00
❑ 22-17-001 [M]	The Eggplant That Ate Chicago	1967	50.00

GREGAR
❑ GG-101	Norman Greenbaum with Dr. West's Medicine Show and Jug Band	1970	25.00

DRAGONFLY

MEGAPHONE
❑ MS-1202	Dragonfly	1970	300.00

DRAGSTERS, THE

WING
❑ MGW-12269 [M]	Hey Little Cobra/Drag City	1964	80.00
❑ SRW-16269 [S]	Hey Little Cobra/Drag City	1964	100.00

DRAKE, DONNA

LUXOR
❑ LP-1 [M]	The Wynton Kelly Trio Introduces Donna Drake -- Donna Sings Dinah	1968	30.00
❑ LPS-1 [S]	The Wynton Kelly Trio Introduces Donna Drake -- Donna Sings Dinah	1968	25.00

DRAKE, GUY

ROYAL AMERICAN
❑ 1001	Welfare Cadillac	1970	30.00

DRAKE, NICK

ANTILLES
❑ AN-7028	Bryter Layter	1977	80.00
—Released in England in 1970			
❑ AN-7010	Five Leaves Left	1976	85.00
—Released in England in 1969			

HANNIBAL
❑ HNBX-5302 [B]	Fruit Tree	1986	200.00
❑ HNBL-1318	Time of No Reply	1987	55.00

ISLAND
❑ SMAS-9307 [B]	Nick Drake	1971	100.00
—U.S.-only compilation of selected songs from his first two British LPs			
❑ SMAS-9318	Pink Moon	1972	125.00

UNIVERSAL
❑ 3732604 [B]	Nick Drake	2013	40.00

DRAKE, PETE

CANAAN
❑ 4640 [M]	Steel Away	1967	18.00
❑ 9640 [S]	Steel Away	1967	25.00

CUMBERLAND
❑ MGC-29053 [M]	Country Steel Guitar	1963	25.00
❑ SRC-69053 [S]	Country Steel Guitar	1963	30.00

HILLTOP
❑ 6052 [M]	Are You Sincere	1967	15.00
❑ S-6052 [S]	Are You Sincere	1967	15.00

SMASH
❑ MGS-27053 [M]	Forever	1964	18.00
❑ SRS-67053 [S]	Forever	1964	25.00
❑ MGS-27064 [M]	Talking Steel and Singing Strings	1965	18.00
❑ SRS-67064 [S]	Talking Steel and Singing Strings	1965	25.00
❑ MGS-27060 [M]	Talking Steel Guitar	1965	18.00
❑ SRS-67060 [S]	Talking Steel Guitar	1965	25.00

STARDAY
❑ SLP-319 [M]	The Amazing Incredible Pete Drake	1964	30.00
❑ SLP-180 [M]	The Fabulous Steel Guitar of Pete Drake	1962	40.00

STOP
❑ 1011	The Pete Drake Show	1970	15.00

DRAMATICS, THE

ABC
❑ AA-1125	Anytime, Anyplace	1979	18.00
❑ AA-1072	Do What You Wanna Do	1978	18.00
❑ D-916	Drama V	1975	18.00
❑ D-955	Joy Ride	1976	18.00
❑ AB-1010	Shake It Well	1977	18.00
❑ D-867	The Dramatic Jackpot	1975	18.00

CAPITOL
❑ ST-12205	New Dimension	1982	12.00

FANTASY
❑ 9642	Somewhere in Time: A Dramatic Reunion	1986	15.00

MCA
❑ 3196	10 1/2	1980	12.00
❑ 762	10 1/2	198?	10.00
—Reissue of 3196			
❑ AA-1125	Anytime, Anyplace	1979	15.00
—Reissue of ABC 1125			
❑ 5149	Dramatic Way	1981	12.00

❑ 761	Dramatic Way	198?	10.00
—Reissue of 5149			

STAX
❑ STX-4131	A Dramatic Experience	1979	15.00
—Reissue of Volt 6019			
❑ MPS-8523	Dramatically Yours	198?	10.00
—Reissue of Volt 9501			
❑ MPS-8526	The Best of the Dramatics	198?	12.00
❑ MPS-8545	The Dramatics Live	1988	12.00
❑ STX-4111	Whatcha See Is Whatcha Get	1978	15.00
—Reissue of Volt 6018			

VOLT
❑ VOS-6019	A Dramatic Experience	1973	30.00
❑ VOS-9501	Dramatically Yours	1974	30.00
❑ V-3402	Positive State of Mind	1989	12.00
❑ V-3407	Stone Cold	1990	12.00
❑ VOS-6018	Whatcha See Is Whatcha Get	1972	30.00

DRAPER, RAY

JOSIE
❑ JOZ-3004 [M]	Tuba Jazz	1963	30.00
❑ JLPS-3004 [S]	Tuba Jazz	1963	25.00

JUBILEE
❑ JLP-1090 [M]	Tuba Jazz	1959	50.00

NEW JAZZ
❑ NJLP-8228 [M]	Ray Draper Quintet Featuring John Coltrane	1958	100.00
—Purple label			
❑ NJLP-8228 [M]	Ray Draper Quintet Featuring John Coltrane	1965	30.00
—Blue label, trident logo at right			

PRESTIGE
❑ PRLP-7096 [M]	Tuba Sounds	1957	200.00

DRAPER, RUSTY

GOLDEN CREST
❑ 31029	The Rusty Draper Show	1973	15.00
❑ 31030	Tour the USA	1973	15.00

MERCURY
❑ MG-20657 [M]	Country and Western Golden Greats	1961	30.00
❑ SR-60657 [S]	Country and Western Golden Greats	1961	40.00
❑ MG-20117 [M]	Encores	1957	30.00
❑ MG-20499 [M]	Hits That Sold a Million	1960	30.00
❑ SR-60176 [S]	Hits That Sold a Million	1960	40.00
❑ MG-20068 [M]	Music for a Rainy Night	1956	30.00
❑ MG-20118 [M]	Rusty Draper Sings	1957	30.00
❑ MG-20173 [M]	Rusty Meets Hoagy	1957	30.00

MONUMENT
❑ MLP-8005 [M]	Greatest Hits	1964	18.00
❑ SLP-18005 [S]	Greatest Hits	1964	25.00
❑ 6638	Greatest Hits	1977	15.00
❑ MLP-8018 [M]	Night Life	1964	18.00
❑ SLP-18018 [S]	Night Life	1964	25.00
❑ MLP-8026 [M]	Rusty Draper Plays Guitar	1965	18.00
❑ SLP-18026 [S]	Rusty Draper Plays Guitar	1965	25.00
❑ SLP-18105	Something Old, Something New	1969	18.00
❑ ZG33870	Swingin' Country/Something Old, Something New	1976	18.00

PLAYCRAFT
❑ PLP-1302 [M]	Sing-a-Long with Rusty Draper	1958	30.00

WING
❑ MGW-12274 [M]	Country Classics	196?	18.00
❑ SRW-16274 [S]	Country Classics	196?	18.00
❑ MGW-12243 [M]	Hits That Sold a Million	196?	18.00
❑ SRW-16243 [S]	Hits That Sold a Million	196?	18.00

DREAD ZEPPELIN

I.R.S.
❑ X1-13048	Un-Led-Ed	1990	25.00
—All copies on gold vinyl			

DREAM 6

HAPPY HERMIT
❑ 1983 [EP]	Dream 6	1983	40.00

DREAM ACADEMY, THE

REPRISE
❑ 25625	Remembrance Days	1987	10.00

WARNER BROS.
❑ R154271	The Dream Academy	1986	12.00
—RCA Music Service edition			
❑ 25265	The Dream Academy	1985	10.00
❑ WBMS-133 [DJ]	The Warner Bros. Music Show	1986	18.00
—Promo-only interview; one side is the Dream Academy, one side is Lloyd Cole and the Commotions			

DREAM SYNDICATE, THE

4 MEN WITH BEARDS
❑ 4M520LP [B]	The Days of Wine and Roses		25.00

A&M
❑ SP-12511	This Is Not the New Dream Syndicate Album...Live	1984	15.00

BIG TIME
❑ 10022	Out of the Grey	1985	12.00

DOWN THERE
❑ 2 [EP]	Sure Thing + 3	1982	25.00

ENIGMA
❑ 73341	Ghost Stories	1988	10.00

RUBY
❑ 807 [B]	The Days of Wine and Roses	1982	30.00

SLASH
❑ 23844 [B]	The Days of Wine and Roses	1982	25.00

DREAMLOVERS, THE

COLLECTABLES
❑ COL-5004	The Best of the Dreamlovers	198?	15.00
❑ COL-5005	The Best of the Dreamlovers, Volume Two	198?	15.00

COLUMBIA
❑ CL2020 [M]	The Bird and Other Golden Dancing Grooves	1963	40.00
❑ CS8820 [S]	The Bird and Other Golden Dancing Grooves	1963	50.00

DREW, KENNY; DONALD BYRD; HANK MOBLEY

JAZZLAND
❑ JLP-6 [M]	Hard Bop	1960	50.00
—Reissue of Riverside 236			
❑ JLP-906 [S]	Hard Bop	1960	40.00

DREW, KENNY; PAUL CHAMBERS; PHILLY JOE JONES

JAZZLAND
❑ JLP-909 [S]	The Tough Piano Trio	1960	40.00
❑ JLP-9 [M]	The Tough Piano Trio	1960	50.00
—Reissue of Riverside 224			

DREW, KENNY

BLUE NOTE
❑ BLP-5023 [10]	Introducing the Kenny Drew Trio	1953	400.00
❑ BLP-4059 [M]	Undercurrent	1961	400.00
—W. 63rd St." address on label			
❑ BLP-4059 [M]	Undercurrent	1964	30.00
—New York, USA" address on label			
❑ BST-84059 [S]	Undercurrent	1961	80.00
—W. 63rd St." address on label			
❑ BST-84059 [S]	Undercurrent	1964	30.00
—New York, USA" address on label			
❑ BST-84059 [S]	Undercurrent	1966	18.00
—A Division of Liberty Records" on label			

FANTASY
❑ OJC-065	Kenny Drew Trio	198?	12.00
❑ OJC-6007	Kenny Drew Trio/Quartet/Quintet	198?	15.00
❑ OJC-483	This Is New	1991	15.00

INNER CITY
❑ IC-2007	Everything I Love	1973	18.00
❑ IC-2034	If You Could See Me Now	1974	18.00
❑ IC-2048	Morning	1975	18.00

JAZZ WEST
❑ JWLP-4 [M]	Talkin' and Walkin' with the Kenny Drew Quartet	1955	700.00

JUDSON
❑ L-3005 [M]	Harold Arlen Showcase	1957	50.00
❑ L-3004 [M]	Harry Warren Showcase	1957	50.00

NORGRAN
❑ MGN-1002 [M]	Progressive Piano	1954	200.00
❑ MGN-29 [10]	The Ideation of Kenny Drew	1954	250.00
❑ MGN-1066 [M]	The Modernity of Kenny Drew	1956	200.00

RIVERSIDE
❑ RLP 12-811 [M]	I Love Jerome Kern	1956	150.00
❑ RLP 12-224 [M]	Kenny Drew Trio	1956	150.00
—White label, blue print			
❑ RLP 12-224 [M]	Kenny Drew Trio	195?	50.00
—Blue labe, microphone logo at top			
❑ 6037	Kenny Drew Trio	197?	15.00
❑ RLP 12-249 [M]	Pal Joey	1957	50.00
❑ RLP-1112 [S]	Pal Joey	1959	40.00
❑ 6106	Pal Joey	197?	15.00
❑ RLP 12-236 [M]	This Is New	1957	150.00
—White label, blue print			
❑ RLP 12-236 [M]	This Is New	195?	50.00
—Blue labe, microphone logo at top			
❑ 6066	This Is New	197?	15.00

SOUL NOTE
❑ SN-1040	It Might As Well Be Spring	1981	15.00
❑ SN-1081	Kenny Drew and Far Away	1983	15.00
❑ 121081	Kenny Drew and Far Away	198?	12.00
—Reissue of 1081			
❑ SN-1031	Your Soft Eyes	1980	15.00
❑ 121031	Your Soft Eyes	198?	12.00
—Reissue of 1031			

Number	Title	Yr	NM

STEEPLECHASE

Number	Title	Yr	NM
❑ SCS-1016	Dark Beauty	198?	15.00
❑ SCS-1007	Everything I Love	198?	15.00
— Reissue of Inner City 2007			
❑ SCS-1034	If You Could See Me Now	198?	15.00
— Reissue of Inner City 2034			
❑ SCS-1106	In Concert	198?	15.00
❑ SCS-1077	Lite Flite	198?	15.00
❑ SCS-1048	Morning	198?	15.00
❑ SCS-1129	Ruby, My Dear	1977	15.00

XANADU

Number	Title	Yr	NM
❑ 167	For Sure	197?	15.00
❑ 166	Home Is Where the Soul Is	197?	15.00

DREW, PATTI

CAPITOL

Number	Title	Yr	NM
❑ ST-156	I've Been Here All the Time	1969	25.00
❑ T2804 [M]	Tell Him	1968	30.00
❑ ST2804 [S]	Tell Him	1968	30.00
❑ ST-408	Wild Is Love	1970	25.00

DRIFTERS, THE

ARISTA

Number	Title	Yr	NM
❑ AB4140	Every Night Is Saturday Night	1976	15.00

ATCO

Number	Title	Yr	NM
❑ SD 33-375 [R]	Their Greatest Recordings -- The Early Years	1971	15.00

ATLANTIC

Number	Title	Yr	NM
❑ 81931	All-Time Greatest Hits and More: 1959-1965	1989	18.00
❑ 8003 [M]	Clyde McPhatter and the Drifters	1956	500.00
— Black label			
❑ 8003 [M]	Clyde McPhatter and the Drifters	1959	60.00
— Red and purple label, white "fan" logo at right			
❑ 8003 [M]	Clyde McPhatter and the Drifters	1963	40.00
— Red and purple label, black "fan" logo at right			
❑ 8113 [M]	I'll Take You Where the Music's Playing	1965	40.00
❑ SD8113 [S]	I'll Take You Where the Music's Playing	1965	50.00
❑ 81927	Let the Boogie-Woogie Roll: Greatest Hits 1953-1958	1989	18.00
❑ 8093 [M]	Our Biggest Hits	1964	60.00
— Red and purple label, white "fan" logo at right			
❑ SD8093 [S]	Our Biggest Hits	1964	80.00
— Mostly red label, black "fan" logo			
❑ 8022 [M]	Rockin' and Driftin'	1958	600.00
— Black label			
❑ 8022 [M]	Rockin' and Driftin'	1958	500.00
— White "bullseye" label			
❑ 8022 [M]	Rockin' and Driftin'	1959	60.00
— Red and purple label, white "fan" logo at right			
❑ 8022 [M]	Rockin' and Driftin'	1963	40.00
— Red and purple label, black "fan" logo at right			
❑ 8059 [M]	Save the Last Dance for Me	1962	120.00
— Red and purple label, white "fan" logo at right			
❑ SD8059 [S]	Save the Last Dance for Me	1962	200.00
— Green and blue label, white "fan" logo at right			
❑ 8059 [M]	Save the Last Dance for Me	1963	60.00
— Red and purple label, black "fan" logo at right			
❑ SD8059 [S]	Save the Last Dance for Me	1963	100.00
— Green and blue label, black "fan" logo at right			
❑ SD8059 [S]	Save the Last Dance for Me	1969	30.00
— Red and green label, white horizontal stripe through center hole			
❑ 8153 [M]	The Drifters' Golden Hits	1968	30.00
❑ SD8153 [P]	The Drifters' Golden Hits	1968	30.00
— Green and blue label			
❑ SD8153 [P]	The Drifters' Golden Hits	1969	18.00
— Red and green label			
❑ 8041 [M]	The Drifters' Greatest Hits	1960	600.00
— Black label			
❑ 8041 [M]	The Drifters' Greatest Hits	1960	100.00
— Red and purple label, white "fan" logo at right			
❑ 8041 [M]	The Drifters' Greatest Hits	1963	50.00
— Red and purple label, black "fan" logo at right			
❑ 8103 [M]	The Good Life with the Drifters	1965	40.00
❑ SD8103 [S]	The Good Life with the Drifters	1965	50.00
❑ 8099 [M]	Under the Boardwalk	1964	80.00
— Black and white photo of group on cover			
❑ 8099 [M]	Under the Boardwalk	1964	50.00
— Color photo of group on cover			
❑ SD8099 [S]	Under the Boardwalk	1964	120.00
— Black and white photo of group on cover			
❑ SD8099 [S]	Under the Boardwalk	1964	60.00
— Color photo of group on cover			
❑ 8073 [M]	Up on the Roof -- The Best of the Drifters	1963	100.00
— Red and purple label, black "fan" logo at right			
❑ SD8073 [S]	Up on the Roof -- The Best of the Drifters	1963	150.00
— Green and blue label, black "fan" logo at right			

CLARION

Number	Title	Yr	NM
❑ 608 [M]	The Drifters	1964	25.00
❑ SD608 [P]	The Drifters	1964	30.00

GUSTO

Number	Title	Yr	NM
❑ 0063	Greatest Hits -- The Drifters	1980	12.00

TRIP

Number	Title	Yr	NM
❑ TOP-16-6	16 Greatest Hits -- The Drifters	1976	12.00

DRIFTIN' SLIM

MILESTONE

Number	Title	Yr	NM
❑ MLS-93004	Driftin' Slim and His Blues Band	1968	30.00

DRIFTING COWBOYS, THE

MGM

Number	Title	Yr	NM
❑ SE-4626	We Remember Hank Williams	1968	25.00

DRIFTWOOD, JIMMIE

MONUMENT

Number	Title	Yr	NM
❑ MLP-8019 [M]	Down in the Arkansas	1965	25.00
❑ SLP-18019 [S]	Down in the Arkansas	1965	30.00
❑ MLP-8006 [M]	Voice of the People	1963	25.00
❑ SLP-18006 [S]	Voice of the People	1963	30.00

RCA VICTOR

Number	Title	Yr	NM
❑ LPM-2443 [M]	Driftwood at Sea	1962	30.00
❑ LSP-2443 [S]	Driftwood at Sea	1962	40.00
❑ LPM-1994 [M]	Jimmie Driftwood and the Wilderness Road	1959	30.00
❑ LSP-1994 [S]	Jimmie Driftwood and the Wilderness Road	1959	40.00
❑ LPM-1635 [M]	Newly Discovered Early American Folk Songs	1958	50.00
❑ LPM-2316 [M]	Songs of Billy Yank and Johnny Reb	1961	30.00
❑ LSP-2316 [S]	Songs of Billy Yank and Johnny Reb	1961	40.00
❑ LPM-2228 [M]	Tall Tales in Song	1960	30.00
❑ LSP-2228 [S]	Tall Tales in Song	1960	40.00
❑ LPM-2171 [M]	The Westward Movement	1960	30.00
❑ LSP-2171 [S]	The Westward Movement	1960	40.00

DRISCOLL, JULIE, BRIAN AUGER & THE TRINITY

ATCO

Number	Title	Yr	NM
❑ SD 33-258 [S]	Open	1968	30.00
❑ 33-258 [M]	Open	1968	150.00
— White label promo; no stock copies were issued in mono			
❑ SD 2-701 [B]	Streetnoise	1969	80.00

CAPITOL

Number	Title	Yr	NM
❑ DT-136 [R]	Jools & Brian	1969	15.00
— American issue of pre-Atco material			

DRISCOLL, JULIE

SPRINGBOARD

Number	Title	Yr	NM
❑ SPB4043 [B]	Julie Driscoll		25.00

DRIVE-BY TRUCKERS

LOST HIGHWAY

Number	Title	Yr	NM
❑ 088170308-1	Southern Rock Opera	2003	25.00

D'RONE, FRANK

CADET

Number	Title	Yr	NM
❑ LPS-806	Brand New Morning	1968	18.00

MERCURY

Number	Title	Yr	NM
❑ MG-20586 [M]	After the Ball	1960	30.00
❑ SR-60246 [S]	After the Ball	1960	40.00
❑ SR-60721 [S]	Frank D'Rone In Person	196?	30.00
❑ MG-20721 [M]	Frank D'Rone In Person	196?	30.00
❑ MG-20418 [M]	Frank D'Rone Sings	1959	30.00
❑ SR-90064 [S]	Frank D'Rone Sings	1959	40.00

DRU HILL

ISLAND BLACK MUSIC

Number	Title	Yr	NM
❑ PRLP-7317 [DJ]	97 -- The Year of the Dru	1997	18.00
— Promo-only edition of their debut album, "Dru Hill"			

DRUIDS OF STONEHENGE, THE

UNI

Number	Title	Yr	NM
❑ 3004 [M]	Creation	1967	100.00
❑ 73004 [S]	Creation	1967	150.00

DRUSKY, ROY, AND PRISCILLA MITCHELL

MERCURY

Number	Title	Yr	NM
❑ MG-21078 [M]	Together Again	1966	25.00
❑ SR-61078 [S]	Together Again	1966	30.00

DRUSKY, ROY

DECCA

Number	Title	Yr	NM
❑ DL4160 [M]	Anymore with Roy Drusky	1961	30.00
❑ DL74160 [S]	Anymore with Roy Drusky	1961	30.00
❑ DL4340 [M]	It's My Way	1962	25.00
❑ DL74340 [S]	It's My Way	1962	30.00

MERCURY

Number	Title	Yr	NM
❑ SR-61306	All My Hard Times	1970	25.00
❑ MG-21006 [M]	Country Music All Around the World	1965	25.00
❑ SR-61006 [S]	Country Music All Around the World	1965	30.00
❑ MG-21097 [M]	If the Whole World Stopped Lovin'	1966	25.00
❑ SR-61097 [S]	If the Whole World Stopped Lovin'	1966	30.00
❑ SR-61260	I'll Make Amends	1970	25.00
❑ SR-61336	I Love the Way That You've Been Lovin' Me	1971	25.00
❑ MG-21083 [M]	In a New Dimension	1966	25.00
❑ SR-61083 [S]	In a New Dimension	1966	30.00
❑ SR-61173	Jody and the Kid	1968	25.00
❑ SR-61233	My Grass Is Green	1969	25.00
❑ MG-21118 [M]	Now Is a Lonely Time	1967	30.00
❑ SR-61118 [S]	Now Is a Lonely Time	1967	25.00
❑ SR-61206	Portrait of Roy Drusky	1969	25.00
❑ MG-21052 [M]	Roy Drusky's Greatest Hits	1965	25.00
❑ SR-61052 [S]	Roy Drusky's Greatest Hits	1965	30.00
❑ SR-61145 [S]	Roy Drusky's Greatest Hits Vol. 2	1968	25.00
❑ MG-21145 [M]	Roy Drusky's Greatest Hits Vol. 2	1968	40.00
— Mono is white label promo only			
❑ MG-20883 [M]	Songs of the Cities	1963	25.00
❑ SR-60883 [S]	Songs of the Cities	1963	30.00
❑ SR-61266	The Best of Roy Drusky	1970	25.00
❑ MG-20973 [M]	The Pick of the Country	1964	25.00
❑ SR-60973 [S]	The Pick of the Country	1964	30.00
❑ MG-20919 [M]	Yesterday's Gone	1964	25.00
❑ SR-60919 [S]	Yesterday's Gone	1964	30.00

DRY CITY SCAT BAND, THE

ELEKTRA

Number	Title	Yr	NM
❑ EKL-292 [M]	The Dry City Scat Band	1965	30.00
❑ EKS-7292 [M]	The Dry City Scat Band	1965	30.00

DRY JACK

INNER CITY

Number	Title	Yr	NM
❑ IC-1063	Magical Elements	1978	18.00
❑ IC-1075	Whale City	1979	18.00

DRY THROAT FIVE, THE

STOMP OFF

Number	Title	Yr	NM
❑ SOS-1151	My Melancholy Baby	1989	12.00
❑ SOS-1114	Who's Blue?	1986	12.00

DUALS, THE

SUE

Number	Title	Yr	NM
❑ LP-2002 [M]	Stick Shift	1961	400.00
— Cartoon cover			
❑ LP-2002 [M]	Stick Shift	1964	200.00
— Photo cover			

DUBS, THE / THE SHELLS

JOSIE

Number	Title	Yr	NM
❑ JM-4001 [M]	The Dubs Meet the Shells	1962	300.00
❑ JES-4001 [S]	The Dubs Meet the Shells	1962	600.00

DUCKS DELUXE

RCA VICTOR

Number	Title	Yr	NM
❑ AFL1-3025	Don't Mind Rockin' Tonight	1978	12.00
❑ LPL1-5008	Ducks Deluxe	1973	18.00

DUDLEY, DAVE

GOLDEN RING

Number	Title	Yr	NM
❑ GR110 [M]	Dave Dudley Sings Six Days on the Road	1963	80.00

MERCURY

Number	Title	Yr	NM
❑ MG-21133 [M]	Dave Dudley Country	1967	30.00
❑ SR-61133 [S]	Dave Dudley Country	1967	25.00
❑ MG-21046 [M]	Dave Dudley's Greatest Hits	1965	25.00
❑ SR-61046 [S]	Dave Dudley's Greatest Hits	1965	30.00
❑ SR-61315	Dave Dudley Sings "Listen Betty, I'm Singing Your Song	1971	18.00
❑ MG-21098 [M]	Free and Easy	1966	25.00
❑ SR-61098 [S]	Free and Easy	1966	25.00
❑ MG-21144 [M]	Greatest Hits Vol. 2	1968	30.00
❑ SR-61144 [S]	Greatest Hits Vol. 2	1968	25.00
❑ SRM-1-669	Keep On Truckin'	1973	18.00
❑ MG-21074 [M]	Lonelyville	1966	25.00
❑ SR-61074 [S]	Lonelyville	1966	30.00
❑ SR-61215	One More Mile	1969	25.00
❑ MG-20999 [M]	Rural Route #1	1965	25.00
❑ SR-60999 [S]	Rural Route #1	1965	30.00
❑ MG-20899 [M]	Songs About the Working Man	1964	25.00
❑ SR-60899 [S]	Songs About the Working Man	1964	30.00
❑ MG-20970 [M]	Talk of the Town	1964	25.00
❑ SR-60970 [S]	Talk of the Town	1964	30.00
❑ SR-61172	Thanks for All the Miles	1968	25.00
❑ SR-61268	The Best of Dave Dudley	1970	18.00
❑ SR-61365	The Original Traveling Man	1972	18.00
❑ SR-61276	The Pool Shark	1970	18.00
❑ MG-21057 [M]	There's a Star Spangled Banner Waving Somewhere	1966	25.00
❑ SR-61057 [S]	There's a Star Spangled Banner Waving Somewhere	1966	30.00
❑ MG-20927 [M]	Travelin' with Dave Dudley	1964	25.00
❑ SR-60927 [S]	Travelin' with Dave Dudley	1964	30.00
❑ MG-21028 [M]	Truck Drivin' Son-of-a-Gun	1965	25.00
❑ SR-61028 [S]	Truck Drivin' Son-of-a-Gun	1965	30.00
❑ SR-61351	Will the Real Dave Dudley Please Sing	1971	18.00

UNITED ARTISTS

Number	Title	Yr	NM
❑ UA-LA512-G	Uncommonly Good Country	1975	15.00

Number	Title	Yr	NM

DUDZIAK, URSZULA

ARISTA
| AL4132 | Midnight Rain | 1976 | 18.00 |
| AL4065 | Urszula | 1975 | 18.00 |

COLUMBIA
| KC32902 | Newborn Light | 1972 | 25.00 |

INNER CITY
| IC-1066 | Future Talk | 1979 | 18.00 |

DUFFY

MERCURY
| 1082201 | Rockferry | 2008 | 25.00 |

DUKE, DOUGLAS

HERALD
| HLP-0102 [M] | Sounds Impossible | 1956 | 50.00 |

REGENT
| MG-6013 [M] | Jazz Organist | 196? | 30.00 |

DUKE, GEORGE

ELEKTRA
60480	George Duke	1986	15.00
60778	Night After Night	1989	15.00
60398	Thief in the Night	1985	18.00

EPIC
FE38208	1976 Solo Keyboard Album	1983	25.00
FE36483	A Brazilian Love Affair	1980	18.00
JE35366	Don't Let Go	1978	15.00
PE35366	Don't Let Go	198?	10.00
—Budget-line reissue with new prefix and bar code			
FE37532	Dream On	1982	15.00
JE35701	Follow the Rainbow	1979	18.00
PE34469	From Me to You	1977	15.00
—Orange label, no bar code on cover			
PE34469	From Me to You	198?	10.00
—Budget-line reissue; dark blue label, bar code on cover			
FE38513	Guardian of the Light	1983	15.00
JE36263	Master of the Game	1979	18.00
PE36263	Master of the Game	198?	12.00
—Budget-line reissue with new prefix			
JE34883	Reach For It	1977	18.00
—Orange label; no bar code on cover			
PE34883	Reach For It	198?	10.00
—Budget-line reissue; dark blue label, bar code on back			
FE39262	Rendezvous	1984	18.00

LIBERTY
| ST-11004 | Save the Country | 1970 | 30.00 |
| —Original issue | | | |

MPS/BASF
22018	Faces in Reflection	1974	18.00
25355	Feel	1974	25.00
25671	I Love the Blues, She Heard My Cry	1975	25.00
22835	Liberated Fantasies	1976	18.00
25613	The Aura Will Prevail	1975	25.00

PACIFIC JAZZ
PJ-LA891-H	George Duke	1978	18.00
LN-10127	Save the Country	198?	15.00
—Reissue			

PAUSA
PR7070	I Love the Blues	1980	12.00
PR7042	The Aura Will Prevail	198?	12.00
—Reissue of MPS/BASF 25613			

PICKWICK
| SPC-3588 | Save the Country | 1978 | 18.00 |
| —Reissue of Liberty 11004 | | | |

VERVE/MPS
821665-1	Feel	1984	12.00
—Reissue of MPS/BASF 25355			
821837-1	The Aura Will Prevail	1984	12.00
—Reissue of Pausa 7042			

DUKE, KENO

STRATA-EAST
| SES-7416 | Sense of Values | 1974 | 30.00 |

TRIDENT
| 501 | Crest of the Wave | 197? | 25.00 |

DUKE, PATTY, WITH NORMAN VINCENT PEALE

GUIDEPOSTS
| GP-101 [M] | Guideposts for Christmas | 1963 | 80.00 |

DUKE, PATTY

UNART
| 20005 [M] | TV's Teen Star | 1967 | 15.00 |
| S20005 [S] | TV's Teen Star | 1967 | 18.00 |

UNITED ARTISTS
UAL-3452 [M]	Don't Just Stand There	1965	30.00
UAS-6452 [S]	Don't Just Stand There	1965	30.00
UAL-3492 [M]	Patty	1966	30.00
UAS-6492 [S]	Patty	1966	30.00
UAL-3535 [M]	Patty Duke's Greatest Hits	1966	18.00
UAS-6535 [S]	Patty Duke's Greatest Hits	1966	30.00

Number	Title	Yr	NM

| UAS-6623 | Songs from the Valley of the Dolls | 1968 | 30.00 |

DUKE, VERNON

ATLANTIC
| 407 [10] | Vernon Duke Plays Vernon Duke | 1954 | 100.00 |

DUKE OF IRON, THE

PRESTIGE
| PRLP-13068 [M] | Limbo, Limbo, Limbo | 1963 | 30.00 |

DUKE OF PADUCAH, THE

STARDAY
| SLP-148 [M] | Button Shoes, Belly Laughs and Monkey Business | 1961 | 40.00 |

DUKES, JOE, AND JACK McDUFF

PRESTIGE
| PRLP-7324 [M] | Soulful Drums | 1964 | 30.00 |
| PRST-7324 [S] | Soulful Drums | 1964 | 30.00 |

DUKE'S MEN, THE

EPIC
| LN3237 [M] | Ellington's Sidekicks | 1956 | 50.00 |
| LG3108 [M] | The Duke's Men | 1955 | 50.00 |

DUKES OF DIXIELAND, THE

AUDIO FIDELITY
AFLP-1918 [M]	Carnegie Hall Concert	1959	18.00
AFSD-5918 [S]	Carnegie Hall Concert	1959	18.00
AFLP-1924 [M]	Louie and the Dukes of Dixieland	1960	18.00
AFSD-5924 [S]	Louie and the Dukes of Dixieland	1960	18.00
AFLP-1851 [M]	Marching Along with the Dukes of Dixieland, Vol. 3	1957	18.00
AFSD-5851 [S]	Marching Along with the Dukes of Dixieland, Vol. 3	1958	25.00
AFLP-1862 [M]	Mardi Gras Time	1958	18.00
AFSD-5862 [S]	Mardi Gras Time	1958	25.00
AFLP-1861 [M]	Minstrel Time with the Phenomenal Dukes of Dixieland, Volume 5	1957	18.00
AFSD-5861 [S]	Minstrel Time with the Phenomenal Dukes of Dixieland, Volume 5	1958	25.00
AFLP-1976 [M]	More of the Best of the Dukes of Dixieland	1962	18.00
AFSD-5976 [S]	More of the Best of the Dukes of Dixieland	1962	18.00
AFLP-1928 [M]	Piano Ragtime (Vol. 11)	1960	18.00
AFSD-5928 [S]	Piano Ragtime (Vol. 11)	1960	18.00
AFSD-6172	Tailgating	1967	15.00
AFLP-1956 [M]	The Best of the Dukes of Dixieland	1961	18.00
AFSD-5956 [S]	The Best of the Dukes of Dixieland	1961	18.00
AFLP-1860 [M]	The Dukes of Dixieland On Bourbon Street, Vol. 4	1958	18.00
AFSD-5860 [S]	The Dukes of Dixieland On Bourbon Street, Vol. 4	1958	25.00
AFLP-1891 [M]	The Dukes of Dixieland On Campus	1959	18.00
AFSD-5891 [S]	The Dukes of Dixieland On Campus	1959	25.00
AFSD-6174	The Dukes of Dixieland On Parade	1967	15.00
AFLP-1892 [M]	Up the Mississippi	1959	18.00
AFSD-5892 [S]	Up the Mississippi	1959	25.00
AFLP-1823 [M]	You Have to Hear It to Believe It -- The Dukes of Dixieland, Vol. 1	1956	18.00
AFSD-5823 [S]	You Have to Hear It to Believe It -- The Dukes of Dixieland, Vol. 1	196?	25.00
AFLP-1840 [M]	You Have to Hear It to Believe It -- The Dukes of Dixieland, Vol. 2	1957	18.00
AFSD-5840 [S]	You Have to Hear It to Believe It -- The Dukes of Dixieland, Vol. 2	196?	25.00

COLUMBIA
CL1728 [M]	Breakin' It Up on Broadway	1962	15.00
CS8528 [S]	Breakin' It Up on Broadway	1962	18.00
CL1871 [M]	Dixieland Hootenanny!	1963	15.00
CS8671 [S]	Dixieland Hootenanny!	1963	18.00
CL2194 [M]	Struttin' at the World's Fair	1964	15.00
CS8994 [S]	Struttin' at the World's Fair	1964	18.00
CL1966 [M]	The Dukes at Disneyland, Volume 1	1963	15.00
CS8766 [S]	The Dukes at Disneyland, Volume 1	1963	18.00

DECCA
DL4708 [M]	Come On and Hear	1966	15.00
DL74708 [S]	Come On and Hear	1966	18.00
DL4863 [M]	Come to the Cabaret	1967	18.00
DL74863 [S]	Come to the Cabaret	1967	15.00
DL74975	Dixieland's Greatest Hits	1968	15.00
DL4653 [M]	Live" At Bourbon Street, Chicago	1965	15.00
DL74653 [S]	Live" At Bourbon Street, Chicago	1965	18.00
DL4807 [M]	Sunrise, Sunset	1966	15.00
DL74807 [S]	Sunrise, Sunset	1966	18.00
DL4864 [M]	Thoroughly Modern Millie	1967	18.00
DL74864 [S]	Thoroughly Modern Millie	1967	15.00

Number	Title	Yr	NM

HARMONY
| HL7349 [M] | Best of the Dukes of Dixieland | 1965 | 15.00 |
| HS11149 [S] | Best of the Dukes of Dixieland | 1965 | 15.00 |

MCA
| 268 | Dixieland's Greatest Hits | 1973 | 12.00 |
| —Reissue of Decca 74975 | | | |

RCA VICTOR
| LPM-2097 [M] | The Dukes of Dixieland at the Jazz Band Ball | 1960 | 15.00 |
| LSP-2097(e) [R] | The Dukes of Dixieland at the Jazz Band Ball | 1960 | 18.00 |

ROULETTE
| R-25029 [M] | Curtain Going Up | 1958 | 25.00 |

VIK
| LX-1025 [M] | The Dukes of Dixieland at the Jazz Band Ball | 1956 | 30.00 |

VOCALION
| VL73846 | Hello, Dolly! | 1968 | 12.00 |

DUNBAR, AYNSLEY

BLUE THUMB
BTS-6 [B]	Doctor Dunbar's Prescription	1969	35.00
BTS-4 [B]	The Aynsley Dunbar Retaliation	1968	40.00
BTS-16 [B]	To Mum From Aynsley and the Boys	1970	30.00

DUNBAR, TED

XANADU
196	Jazz Guitarist	1982	15.00
155	Opening Remarks	1978	18.00
181	Secundum Artem	1980	15.00

DUNCAN, BILL

KING
| 825 [M] | A Scene Near My Country Home | 1962 | 30.00 |

DUNCAN, DANNY

X
| LVA-3040 [10] | Ragtime Jamboree | 1955 | 50.00 |

DUNCAN, JOHNNY

COLUMBIA
KC35039	Come a Little Bit Closer	1977	15.00
KC35628	Greatest Hits	1978	15.00
JC36508	In My Dreams	1980	12.00
PC34442	Johnny Duncan	1977	15.00
CS9824	Johnny One Time	1969	25.00
KC35775	See You When the Sun Goes Down	1979	15.00
JC36260	Straight from Texas	1980	12.00
KC32440	Sweet Country Woman	1973	18.00
KC35451	The Best Is Yet to Come	1978	15.00
KC34243	The Best of Johnny Duncan	1976	15.00
C30618	There's Something About a Lady	1971	18.00
JC36829	You're On My Mind	1981	12.00

HARMONY
| KH32477 | You're Gonna Need a Man | 1973 | 15.00 |

DUNHAM, KATHERINE

AUDIO FIDELITY
| AFLP-1803 [M] | The Singing Gods-Drum Rhythms of Cuba, Haiti, Brazil | 1957 | 40.00 |

DECCA
| DL5251 [10] | Afro-Caribbean Songs and Rhythms | 1951 | 60.00 |

DUNN, HOLLY

MTM
ST-71070	Across the Rio Grande	1988	15.00
ST-71063	Cornerstone	1987	15.00
ST-71052	Holly Dunn	1986	15.00

WARNER BROS.
PRO-A-3692 [DJ]	Blue Rose of Texas Radio Special	1989	30.00
—Promo-only interview record			
25939	The Blue Rose of Texas	1989	12.00

DUNSTEDTER, EDDIE

CAPITOL
T2395 [M]	Christmas Candy	1965	15.00
ST2395 [S]	Christmas Candy	1965	18.00
T1264 [M]	The Bells of Christmas	1959	15.00
ST1264 [S]	The Bells of Christmas	1959	18.00
T1968 [M]	The Bells of Christmas Chime Again	1963	15.00
ST1968 [S]	The Bells of Christmas Chime Again	1963	18.00

DUPRE, MARCEL

MERCURY LIVING PRESENCE
| SR90227 [S] | Dupre at Saint-Sulpice, Vol. 1 | 196? | 40.00 |
| —Maroon label, no "Vendor: Mercury Record Corporation" | | | |

Number	Title	Yr	NM
❏ SR90229 [S]	Dupre at Saint-Sulpice, Vol. 2	196?	80.00
— Maroon label, no "Vendor: Mercury Record Corporation			
❏ SR90229 [S]	Dupre at Saint-Sulpice, Vol. 2	196?	50.00
— Maroon label, with "Vendor: Mercury Record Corporation			
❏ SR90228 [S]	Dupre at Saint-Sulpice, Vol. 3	196?	40.00
— Maroon label, no "Vendor: Mercury Record Corporation			
❏ SR90228 [S]	Dupre at Saint-Sulpice, Vol. 3	196?	25.00
— Maroon label, with "Vendor: Mercury Record Corporation			
❏ SR90230 [S]	Dupre at Saint-Sulpice, Vol. 4	196?	80.00
— Maroon label, no "Vendor: Mercury Record Corporation			
❏ SR90230 [S]	Dupre at Saint-Sulpice, Vol. 4	196?	25.00
— Maroon label, with "Vendor: Mercury Record Corporation			
❏ SR90231 [S]	Dupre at Saint-Sulpice, Vol. 5	196?	60.00
— Maroon label, no "Vendor: Mercury Record Corporation			
❏ SR90231 [S]	Dupre at Saint-Sulpice, Vol. 5	196?	30.00
— Maroon label, with "Vendor: Mercury Record Corporation			
❏ SR90168 [S]	Franck: Piece Heroique; 3 Chorales	196?	50.00
— Maroon label, no "Vendor: Mercury Record Corporation			
❏ SR90168 [S]	Franck: Piece Heroique; 3 Chorales	196?	30.00
— Maroon label, with "Vendor: Mercury Record Corporation			
❏ SR90168 [S]	Franck: Piece Heroique; 3 Chorales	196?	25.00
— Third edition: Dark red (not maroon) label			
❏ SR90169 [S]	Organ Recital	196?	200.00
— Maroon label, no "Vendor: Mercury Record Corporation			
❏ SR90169 [S]	Organ Recital	196?	200.00
— Maroon label, with "Vendor: Mercury Record Corporation			

DUPREE, CHAMPION JACK, AND JIMMY RUSHING

AUDIO LAB
| ❏ AL-1512 [M] | Two Shades of Blue | 1958 | 200.00 |

DUPREE, CHAMPION JACK, AND MICKEY BAKER

SIRE
| ❏ SES-97010 | In Heavy Blues | 1969 | 30.00 |

DUPREE, CHAMPION JACK

ATLANTIC
❏ 8019 [M]	Blues from the Gutter	1959	150.00
— Black label			
❏ 8019 [M]	Blues from the Gutter	1960	50.00
— White 'fan' logo at left of label			
❏ 8019 [M]	Blues from the Gutter	1963	25.00
— Black 'fan' logo at right of label			
❏ SD8019 [S]	Blues from the Gutter	1959	200.00
— Green label			
❏ SD8019 [S]	Blues from the Gutter	1960	60.00
— Green and blue label, white 'fan' logo at right of label			
❏ SD8019 [S]	Blues from the Gutter	1963	30.00
— Green and blue label, black 'fan' logo at right of label			
❏ SD8255	Blues from the Gutter	1970	18.00
❏ 8056 [M]	Champion of the Blues	1961	50.00
— White 'fan' logo at right of label			
❏ 8056 [M]	Champion of the Blues	1963	25.00
— Black 'fan' logo at right of label			
❏ SD8056 [R]	Champion of the Blues	196?	18.00
❏ 8045 [M]	Natural and Soulful Blues	1961	50.00
— White 'fan' logo at right of label			
❏ 8045 [M]	Natural and Soulful Blues	1963	25.00
— Black 'fan' logo at right of label			
❏ SD8045 [S]	Natural and Soulful Blues	1961	60.00
— Green and blue label, white 'fan' logo at right of label			
❏ SD8045 [S]	Natural and Soulful Blues	1963	30.00
— Green and blue label, black 'fan' logo at right of label			

BLUE HORIZON
| ❏ 7702 | When You Feel the Feeling | 1969 | 30.00 |

BULLSEYE
| ❏ BB-9502 | Back Home In New Orleans | 1990 | 15.00 |

CONTINENTAL
| ❏ CLP-16002 [M] | Low Down Blues | 1961 | 250.00 |

EVEREST ARCHIVE OF FOLK & JAZZ
| ❏ 217 | Champion Jack Dupree | 197? | 12.00 |

FOLKWAYS
| ❏ FS-3825 [M] | Women Blues of Champion Jack Dupree | 1961 | 30.00 |

GNP CRESCENDO
❏ GNPS-10005	Happy to Be Free	1974	15.00
❏ GNPS-10013	Legacy of Blues 3	197?	15.00
❏ GNPS-10001	Tricks	1974	15.00

JAZZ MAN
| ❏ BLZ-5501 | Champion Jack Dupree | 1982 | 12.00 |

KING
| ❏ 735 [M] | Champion Jack Dupree Sings the Blues | 1961 | 300.00 |
| ❏ KS-1084 | Walking the Blues | 1970 | 18.00 |

LONDON
| ❏ PS553 | From New Orleans to Chicago | 1969 | 25.00 |

OKEH
| ❏ OKM12103 [M] | Cabbage Greens | 1963 | 30.00 |

STORYVILLE
| ❏ 4010 | Best of the Blues | 1982 | 12.00 |
| ❏ 4040 | I'm Growing Older Every Day | 198? | 12.00 |

DUPREE, SIMON, AND THE BIG SOUND

TOWER
| ❏ ST-5097 [S] | Without Reservations | 1968 | 40.00 |
| ❏ T-5097 [M] | Without Reservations | 1968 | 100.00 |

DUPREES, THE

COED
| ❏ LPC-906 [M] | Have You Heard | 1963 | 200.00 |
| ❏ LPC-905 [M] | You Belong to Me | 1962 | 300.00 |

COLLECTABLES
| ❏ COL-5008 | The Best of the Duprees | 198? | 15.00 |

COLOSSUS
| ❏ 5000 | Duprees Gold | 1970 | 30.00 |
| *— As "The Italian Asphalt & Pavement Co.* | | | |

HERITAGE
❏ HT-35002 [M]	Total Recall	1968	80.00
— Mono is promo only; in stereo cover with "DJ Monaural" sticker on front			
❏ HTS-35002 [S]	Total Recall	1968	30.00

POST
| ❏ 1000 | The Duprees Sing | 196? | 30.00 |

DURAN, EDDIE

CONCORD JAZZ
| ❏ CJ-94 | Ginza | 1979 | 15.00 |
| ❏ CJ-271 | One By One | 1985 | 12.00 |

FANTASY
❏ 3247 [M]	Jazz Guitarist	1957	80.00
— Red vinyl			
❏ 3247 [M]	Jazz Guitarist	195?	40.00
— Black vinyl			
❏ OJC-120	Jazz Guitarist	198?	12.00

DURAN DURAN

CAPITOL
❏ R140395	Arena	1984	15.00
— RCA Music Service edition			
❏ SWAV-12374	Arena	1984	12.00
— With booklet (deduct 25% if cut out or if booklet is missing)			
❏ R100682	Big Thing	1988	15.00
— BMG Direct Marketing edition			
❏ C1-90958	Big Thing	1988	12.00
— Deduct 25% for cut-outs			
❏ R173573	Decade	1989	15.00
— BMG Direct Marketing edition			
❏ C1-93178	Decade	1989	15.00
❏ R134452	Duran Duran	1983	15.00
— RCA Music Service edition; with "Is There Something I Should Know?			
❏ ST-12158	Duran Duran	1983	12.00
— Reissue of Harvest 12158 with new cover and 9 tracks, adding "Is There Something I Should Know			
❏ SPRO-79097/8 [EP]	Duran Goes Dutch	1987	80.00
— Promo-only five-song EP recorded live in Rotterdam			
❏ R163458	Liberty	1990	18.00
— BMG Direct Marketing edition			
❏ C1-94292	Liberty	1990	18.00
❏ R114794	Notorious	1987	15.00
— RCA Music Service edition			
❏ PJ-12540	Notorious	1986	10.00
❏ R163452	Rio	1983	18.00
— RCA Music Service edition; contains Harvest Version 1 of the album			
❏ ST-12211	Rio	1983	18.00
— Version 4: Capitol logo replaces Harvest logo on back cover, otherwise it's the same as Harvest Version 3, with the same trail-off markings			
❏ ST-512211 [B]	Rio	1983	12.00
— Columbia House edition; otherwise the same as Version 4			
❏ ST-12310 [B]	Seven and the Ragged Tiger	1983	10.00

EPIC
| ❏ E292900 | Astronaut | 2004 | 18.00 |

HARVEST
❏ MLP-15006 [EP]	Carnival	1982	25.00
❏ ST-12158	Duran Duran	1981	18.00
— Original US issue with yellow label and 8 songs			
❏ ST-12211	Rio	1982	25.00
— Version 1: Harvest logo on lower back cover, contains the same versions of the songs as the original UK release; trail-off wax number on Side 1 is "ST-1-12211 Z1			
❏ ST-12211	Rio	1982	18.00
— Version 2: Harvest logo on lower back cover, with five songs remixed by David Kershenbaum; Side 1 trail-off wax number is "ST-1-12211-Z13-RE1 #1			
❏ ST-12211	Rio	1982	15.00
— Version 3: Harvest logo on lower back cover, with five songs			

remixed by David Kershenbaum, but with a different mix of "Hungry Like the Wolf" than Version 2; Side 1 trail-off wax number is "ST-1-12211-Z18

MOBILE FIDELITY
| ❏ 1-182 | Seven and the Ragged Tiger | 1985 | 25.00 |
| *— Audiophile vinyl* | | | |

DURANTE, JIMMY

DECCA
❏ DL9049 [M]	Club Durant	195?	30.00
❏ DL5116 [10]	Jimmy Durante	195?	50.00
❏ DL8884 [M]	Jimmy Durante at the Piano	1959	18.00
❏ DL78884 [S]	Jimmy Durante at the Piano	1959	25.00

LION
| ❏ L-70053 [M] | Jimmy Durante in Person | 195? | 30.00 |

MGM
❏ E-3242 [M]	Jimmy Durante in Person	1955	30.00
❏ E-4207 [M]	The Very Best of Jimmy Durante	1964	15.00
❏ SE-4207 [S]	The Very Best of Jimmy Durante	1964	18.00

ROULETTE
| ❏ R-25123 [M] | Jimmy Durante at the Copacabana | 1961 | 25.00 |
| ❏ SR-25123 [S] | Jimmy Durante at the Copacabana | 1961 | 30.00 |

WARNER BROS.
❏ W1531 [M]	Hello Young Lovers	1964	18.00
❏ WS1531 [S]	Hello Young Lovers	1964	25.00
❏ W1577 [M]	Jimmy Durante's Way of Life	1965	18.00
❏ WS1577 [S]	Jimmy Durante's Way of Life	1965	25.00
❏ W1655 [M]	One of Those Songs	1966	18.00
❏ WS1655 [S]	One of Those Songs	1966	25.00
❏ W1506 [M]	September Song	1963	18.00
❏ WS1506 [S]	September Song	1963	25.00
❏ W1713 [M]	Songs for Sunday	1967	18.00
❏ WS1713 [S]	Songs for Sunday	1967	25.00

DURBIN, DEANNA

DECCA
| ❏ DL8785 [M] | Deanna Durbin | 1958 | 50.00 |

DURUTTI COLUMN

4 MEN WITH BEARDS
| ❏ 4M522LP [B] | LC | | 25.00 |
| ❏ 4M521LP [B] | The Return of the Durutti Column | | 25.00 |

DURY, IAN, AND THE BLOCKHEADS

POLYDOR
| ❏ PD1-6337 [B] | Lord Upminster | 1981 | 18.00 |

STIFF
| ❏ STF 0002 [B] | New Boots and Panties | 1978 | 25.00 |

STIFF AMERICA
❏ USE17	Juke Box Dury	1981	15.00
❏ USE 02 [B]	New Boots and Panties	1980	18.00
— Reissue of Stiff 0002			

STIFF/EPIC
| ❏ JE36104 [B] | Do It Yourself | 1979 | 18.00 |
| ❏ JE36998 [B] | Laughter | 1980 | 18.00 |

DUSHON, JEAN

ARGO
| ❏ LP-4039 [M] | Make Way for Jean DuShon | 1964 | 30.00 |
| ❏ LPS-4039 [S] | Make Way for Jean DuShon | 1964 | 30.00 |

DUVAL, DENISE / GEORGES PRETRE

RCA VICTOR RED SEAL
| ❏ LDS-2385 [S] | Poulenc: La Voix Humana | 1960 | 60.00 |
| *— Original with "shaded dog" label; also includes booklet* | | | |

DWARVES

SUB POP
❏ 67	Blood, Guts and Pussy	1990	25.00
— First 1,000 on red vinyl			
❏ 67 [B]	Blood, Guts and Pussy	1990	35.00
❏ 197 [B]	Sugar Fix	1993	35.00
❏ 126 [B]	Thank Heaven for Little Girls	1991	30.00

DYANI, JOHNNY; OKAY TEMIZ; MONGEZI FEZA

ANTILLES
| ❏ AN-7035 | Music for Xaba | 197? | 30.00 |

DYKE AND THE BLAZERS

ORIGINAL SOUND
❏ LPS8877	Dyke's Greatest Hits	1968	75.00
❏ LP8876 [M]	The Funky Broadway	1967	50.00
❏ LPS8876 [S]	The Funky Broadway	1967	75.00

DYLAN, BOB, AND ALAN J. WEBERMAN

FOLKWAYS
| ❏ FB-5322 [M] | Bob Dylan Vs. A.J. Weberman | 1977 | 300.00 |
| *— A tape-recorded phone conversation; quickly withdrawn from the market* | | | |

DYLAN, BOB

ASYLUM

Number	Title	Yr	NM
❑ AB-201 [DJ]	Before the Flood	1974	50.00
—White label promo			
❑ AB-201	Before the Flood	1974	25.00
❑ 7E-1003 [DJ]	Ceremonies of the Horsemen	1974	3000.00
—Original title of "Planet Waves"; no records were pressed with this title, but never-glued covers exist, of which 3 or 4 are known. Value is for one of these covers; VG value 1500; VG+ value 2250			
❑ 7E-1003	Planet Waves	1974	18.00
—Without wraparound (olive green) second cover			
❑ 7E-1003	Planet Waves	1974	25.00
—With wraparound (olive green) second cover			
❑ 7E-1003 [DJ]	Planet Waves	1974	50.00
—White label promo			
❑ EQ-1003 [Q]	Planet Waves	1974	70.00

COLUMBIA

Number	Title	Yr	NM
❑ 88883 73489 1 [B]	Another Self Portrait	2013	50.00
❑ CL2193 [M]	Another Side of Bob Dylan	1964	400.00
—White label promo			
❑ CL2193 [M]	Another Side of Bob Dylan	1964	40.00
—Guaranteed High Fidelity" on label			
❑ CL2193 [M]	Another Side of Bob Dylan	1965	30.00
—Mono" on label			
❑ CS8993 [S]	Another Side of Bob Dylan	1964	40.00
—360 Sound Stereo" in black on label			
❑ CS8993 [S]	Another Side of Bob Dylan	1965	30.00
—360 Sound Stereo" in white on label			
❑ CS8993 [S]	Another Side of Bob Dylan	1970	15.00
—Orange label			
❑ KCS8993 [S]	Another Side of Bob Dylan	197?	12.00
❑ PC8993 [S]	Another Side of Bob Dylan	198?	10.00
—Budget-line reissue			
❑ PC8993 [S]	Another Side of Bob Dylan	2001	15.00
—Reissue on 180-gram vinyl (sealed copies have a sticker indicating this)			
❑ CG37661	Before the Flood	1983	15.00
—Reissue of Asylum AB-201			
❑ C5X38830	Biograph	1985	30.00
❑ C2L41 [M]	Blonde on Blonde	1966	1000.00
—White label promo			
❑ C2L41 [M]	Blonde on Blonde	1966	100.00
—Female photos" inner gatefold with two women pictured			
❑ C2L41 [M]	Blonde on Blonde	1968	300.00
—No photos of women inside gatefold			
❑ C2S841 [S]	Blonde on Blonde	1966	60.00
—Female photos" inner gatefold with two women pictured			
❑ C2S841 [S]	Blonde on Blonde	1968	30.00
—No photos of women inside gatefold; "360 Sound Stereo" on label			
❑ C2S841 [S]	Blonde on Blonde	1970	18.00
—Orange label			
❑ CG841 [S]	Blonde on Blonde	198?	15.00
❑ PC33235 [DJ]	Blood on the Tracks	1975	5000.00
—Test pressing with radically different versions of five songs including "Idiot Wind" and "Tangled Up in Blue"; VG value 2500; VG+ value 3750			
❑ PC33235 [DJ]	Blood on the Tracks	1975	30.00
—Regular white label promo			
❑ PC33235	Blood on the Tracks	1979	10.00
—With bar code on back cover			
❑ PC33235	Blood on the Tracks	1975	15.00
—First editions have liner notes on the back cover in black print			
❑ PC33235	Blood on the Tracks	1975	18.00
—With drawing on back cover and no liner notes. Actually a second pressing, but available only for a short time			
❑ HC43235	Blood on the Tracks	198?	50.00
—Half-speed mastered edition			
❑ PC33235	Blood on the Tracks	2001	15.00
—Reissue on 180-gram vinyl (sealed copies have a sticker indicating this)			
❑ PC33235	Blood on the Tracks	1975	12.00
—Third editions have liner notes restored (after they won a Grammy), but in white print			
❑ PC33235	Blood on the Tracks	1975	2000.00
—First edition cover; with the original rejected version of Side 2, though Side 1 is the standard version; the master number in the trail-off wax on Side 2 is "-1A"; one copy known, but others may exist			
❑ CL1779 [M]	Bob Dylan	1962	500.00
—Six "eye" logos on label; "A New Star on Columbia" sticker on cover and promo stamp on label			
❑ CL1779 [M]	Bob Dylan	1962	250.00
—Black and red (not orange) label with six white "eye" logos, three at 9 o'clock, three at 3 o'clock; stock copy			
❑ CL1779 [M]	Bob Dylan	1963	40.00
—Guaranteed High Fidelity" on label			
❑ CL1779 [M]	Bob Dylan	1966	30.00
—Mono" on label			
❑ CS8579 [S]	Bob Dylan	1962	600.00
—Six "eye" logos on label; "A New Star on Columbia" sticker on cover and promo stamp on label			
❑ CS8579 [S]	Bob Dylan	1962	400.00
—Red and black label with six white "eye" logos, three together at the left, three together at the right, with "Stereo Fidelity" at the top of the label and "Columbia" at the bottom; stock copy			
❑ CS8579 [S]	Bob Dylan	1963	40.00
—360 Sound Stereo" in black on label			
❑ CS8579 [S]	Bob Dylan	1965	30.00
—360 Sound Stereo" in white on label			
❑ CS8579 [S]	Bob Dylan	1970	15.00
—Orange label			
❑ KCS8579 [S]	Bob Dylan	197?	12.00
❑ PC8579 [S]	Bob Dylan	198?	10.00
—Budget-line reissue			
❑ JC8579 [S]	Bob Dylan	197?	10.00
—Some copies of this pressing of the above album may have the song "You're No Good" listed on the label as "She's No Good." No extra premium has been attached to this error as yet.			
❑ PC8579 [S]	Bob Dylan	2001	15.00
—Reissue on 180-gram vinyl (sealed copies have a sticker indicating this)			
❑ PC236067	Bob Dylan at Budokan	1979	18.00
❑ PC236067 [DJ]	Bob Dylan at Budokan	1979	30.00
—White label promo			
❑ CG36067	Bob Dylan at Budokan	198?	15.00
❑ CL2302/CS 9102	Bob Dylan In Concert	1965	4000.00
—Never pressed; value is for a cover slick, some of which were printed; VG value 2000; VG+ value 3000			
❑ KCL2663 [M]	Bob Dylan's Greatest Hits	1967	50.00
❑ KCS9463 [S]	Bob Dylan's Greatest Hits	1967	18.00
—360 Sound Stereo" label			
❑ KCS9463 [S]	Bob Dylan's Greatest Hits	1970	15.00
—Orange label			
❑ JC9463 [S]	Bob Dylan's Greatest Hits	197?	12.00
❑ JC9463 [S]	Bob Dylan's Greatest Hits	2001	15.00
—Reissue on 180-gram vinyl (sealed copies have a sticker indicating this)			
❑ KG31120	Bob Dylan's Greatest Hits, Vol. II	1971	18.00
❑ PG31120	Bob Dylan's Greatest Hits, Vol. II	197?	15.00
❑ CG31120	Bob Dylan's Greatest Hits, Vol. II	198?	12.00
❑ 474000 [B]	Bob Dylan -- The 30th Anniversary Concert Celebration	1993	40.00
—Albums pressed in US for export to Europe; some stayed here			
❑ CL2328 [M]	Bringing It All Back Home	1965	300.00
—White label promo			
❑ CL2328 [M]	Bringing It All Back Home	1965	50.00
—Guaranteed High Fidelity" on label			
❑ CL2328 [M]	Bringing It All Back Home	1965	30.00
—Mono" on label			
❑ CS9128 [S]	Bringing It All Back Home	1965	40.00
—360 Sound Stereo" in black on label			
❑ CS9128 [S]	Bringing It All Back Home	1965	30.00
—360 Sound Stereo" in white on label			
❑ CS9128 [S]	Bringing It All Back Home	1970	15.00
—Orange label			
❑ KCS9128 [S]	Bringing It All Back Home	197?	12.00
❑ JC9128 [S]	Bringing It All Back Home	197?	12.00
❑ PC9128 [S]	Bringing It All Back Home	198?	10.00
—Budget-line reissue			
❑ PC9128 [S]	Bringing It All Back Home	2001	15.00
—Reissue on 180-gram vinyl (sealed copies have a sticker indicating this)			
❑ PC33893	Desire	1976	15.00
❑ PC33893 [DJ]	Desire	1976	30.00
—White label promo			
❑ PCQ33893 [Q]	Desire	1976	50.00
❑ JC33893	Desire	1977	12.00
—No bar code on back cover			
❑ JC33893	Desire	1979	10.00
—With bar code on back cover			
❑ OC40957	Down in the Groove	1988	12.00
❑ PC32747	Dylan	1973	18.00
—No bar code on cover			
❑ PC32747	Dylan	1979	10.00
—With bar code on back cover			
❑ OC45056	Dylan and the Dead	1989	15.00
—With backing by The Grateful Dead			
❑ AS1471 [DJ]	Electric Lunch	1982	30.00
—Promo-only sampler			
❑ FC40110	Empire Burlesque	1985	12.00
❑ C53200 [B]	Good As I Been to You	1992	70.00
❑ PC34349	Hard Rain	1976	15.00
—No bar code on back cover			
❑ PC34349 [DJ]	Hard Rain	1976	30.00
—White label promo			
❑ JC34349	Hard Rain	1977	12.00
❑ PC34349	Hard Rain	198?	10.00
—With bar code on back cover			
❑ CL2389 [M]	Highway 61 Revisited	1965	400.00
—White label promo			
❑ CL2389 [M]	Highway 61 Revisited	1965	80.00
❑ CS9189 [S]	Highway 61 Revisited	1965	250.00
—With alternate take of "From a Buick 6." Matrix number on Side 1 will end in "--1" plus a letter			
❑ CS9189 [S]	Highway 61 Revisited	1965	30.00
—With "regular" take of "From a Buick 6." Matrix number on Side 1 will end in "--2" or higher, plus a letter; "360 Sound Stereo" on label			
❑ CS9189 [S]	Highway 61 Revisited	1970	15.00
—Orange label			
❑ KCS9189 [S]	Highway 61 Revisited	197?	12.00
❑ JC9189 [S]	Highway 61 Revisited	197?	12.00
❑ PC9189 [S]	Highway 61 Revisited	198?	10.00
—Budget-line reissue			
❑ PC9189 [S]	Highway 61 Revisited	2001	15.00
—Reissue on 180-gram vinyl (sealed copies have a sticker indicating this)			
❑ AS1770 [DJ]	Infidels	1983	25.00
—Promo-only sampler			
❑ QC38819	Infidels	1983	12.00
❑ PC38819	Infidels	1986	10.00
—Budget-line reissue			
❑ CL2804 [M]	John Wesley Harding	1968	150.00
❑ CS9604 [S]	John Wesley Harding	1968	25.00
—360 Sound Stereo" label			
❑ CS9604 [S]	John Wesley Harding	1970	15.00
—Orange label			
❑ KCS9604 [S]	John Wesley Harding	197?	12.00
❑ JC9604 [S]	John Wesley Harding	197?	12.00
❑ PC9604 [S]	John Wesley Harding	198?	10.00
—Budget-line reissue			
❑ PC9604 [S]	John Wesley Harding	2001	15.00
—Reissue on 180-gram vinyl (sealed copies have a sticker indicating this)			
❑ OC40439	Knocked Out Loaded	1986	12.00
❑ C285975	Love and Theft	2001	18.00
❑ 82876-87606-1	Modern Times	2006	18.00
❑ C267000 [B]	MTV Unplugged	1995	30.00
❑ KCS9825	Nashville Skyline	1969	30.00
—360 Sound Stereo" label			
❑ KCS9825	Nashville Skyline	1970	15.00
—Orange label			
❑ JC9825	Nashville Skyline	197?	12.00
❑ PC9825	Nashville Skyline	198?	10.00
—Budget-line reissue			
❑ KCQ32825 [Q]	Nashville Skyline	1973	35.00
❑ HC49825	Nashville Skyline	198?	60.00
—Half-speed mastered edition			
❑ KC30290	New Morning	1970	18.00
❑ PC30290	New Morning	197?	10.00
❑ PC30290	New Morning	2001	15.00
—Reissue on 180-gram vinyl (sealed copies have a sticker indicating this)			
❑ OC45281	Oh Mercy	1989	15.00
❑ KC32460	Pat Garrett and Billy the Kid	1973	18.00
❑ PC32460	Pat Garrett and Billy the Kid	197?	10.00
❑ PC37637	Planet Waves	1981	12.00
—Reissue of Asylum 7E-1003			
❑ FC39944	Real Live	1984	12.00
❑ AS422 [DJ]	Renaldo and Clara	1976	50.00
—Promo-only sampler from the movie. Authentic copies have a sticker on a white cover; counterfeits have the title printed on the cover			
❑ FC36553	Saved	1980	12.00
❑ AS798 [DJ]	Saved	1980	30.00
—Promo sampler from LP			
❑ PC36553	Saved	198?	10.00
—Budget-line reissue with new cover			
❑ C2X30050	Self Portrait	1970	150.00
—360 Sound Stereo" labels			
❑ C2X30050	Self Portrait	1970	25.00
—Orange labels			
❑ P2X30050	Self Portrait	197?	18.00
❑ CG30050	Self Portrait	198?	15.00
❑ TC37496	Shot of Love	1981	12.00
❑ PC37496	Shot of Love	198?	10.00
—Budget-line reissue			
❑ 88883772551 [B]	Side Tracks	2013	40.00
❑ FC36120	Slow Train Coming	1979	12.00
❑ FC36120 [DJ]	Slow Train Coming	1979	30.00
—White label promo			
❑ PC36120	Slow Train Coming	198?	10.00
—Budget-line reissue			
❑ JC35453	Street Legal	1978	15.00
❑ JC35453 [DJ]	Street Legal	1978	30.00
—White label promo			
❑ PC35453	Street Legal	198?	10.00
❑ 88725457601 [B]	Tempest	2012	40.00
❑ PC233682 [DJ]	The Basement Tapes	1975	40.00
—White label promo			
❑ PC233682	The Basement Tapes	1975	25.00
❑ CG33682	The Basement Tapes	198?	15.00
❑ CK2-65759-1 [B]	The Bootleg Series Vol. 4: Bob Dylan Live 1966, The "Royal Albert Hall" Concert	1999	120.00
—Classic Records box set with 12x12 booklet and two records individually packaged in cardboard jackets and sleeves			
❑ C2K-87047-1	The Bootleg Series Vol. 5: Rolling Thunder Revue Starring Bob Dylan	2003	100.00
—Classic Records box set with 12x12 booklet, three 200-gram 12-inch records individually packaged in cardboard jackets and sleeves, a blue vinyl 7-inch single in a picture sleeve, a poster, a souvenir handbill and facsimile tickets to the show			
❑ C2K-87047-1	The Bootleg Series Vol. 5: Rolling Thunder Revue Starring Bob Dylan	2003	50.00
—Similar to the other package, but records are pressed on 140-gram vinyl and come in plain paper (rather than lined) sleeves			

Number	Title	Yr	NM
❑ AS1259 [DJ]	The Dylan London Interview, 1981 July 1981		30.00
❑ CL1986 [M]	The Freewheelin' Bob Dylan 1963		12000.00

— *"Guaranteed High Fidelity" on label; plays "Let Me Die in My Footsteps," "Rocks and Gravel," "Talkin' John Birch Blues" and "Gamblin' Willie's Dead Man's Hand." Label does NOT list these. In dead wax, matrix number ends in "--1" followed by a letter; VG value 4000; VG+ value 8000*

| ❑ CL1986 [M] | The Freewheelin' Bob Dylan 1963 | | 3000.00 |

— *White label promo; label and timing strip list the deleted tracks but record plays the "correct" tracks; VG value 1000; VG+ value 2000*

| ❑ CL1986 [M] | The Freewheelin' Bob Dylan 1963 | | 2000.00 |

— *White label promo; label lists deleted tracks; timing strip lists, and record plays, "correct" tracks*

| ❑ CL1986 [M] | The Freewheelin' Bob Dylan 1966 | | 30.00 |

— *"Mono" on label*

| ❑ CS8786 [S] | The Freewheelin' Bob Dylan 1963 | | 50.00 |

— *"360 Sound Stereo" in black on label (no arrows)*

| ❑ CL1986 [M] | The Freewheelin' Bob Dylan 1963 | | 800.00 |

— *White label promo; timing strip lists deleted tracks; label lists, and record plays, "correct" tracks*

| ❑ CL1986 [M] | The Freewheelin' Bob Dylan 1963 | | 500.00 |

— *White label promo; label AND timing strip list, and record plays, "correct" tracks*

| ❑ CL1986 [M] | The Freewheelin' Bob Dylan 1963 | | 40.00 |

— *"Guaranteed High Fidelity" on label; corrected version (record plays what label says)*

| ❑ CS8786 [S] | The Freewheelin' Bob Dylan 1963 | | 30000.00 |

— *"360 Sound Stereo" in black on label (no arrows); record plays, and label lists, "Let Me Die in My Footsteps," "Rocks and Gravel," "Talkin' John Birch Blues" and "Gamblin' Willie's Dead Man's Hand." No known stereo copies play these without listing them, but just in case, check the trail-off for the numbers "XSM-58719-1A" and "XSM-58720-1A." If the number after the dash is "2" or higher, it's the standard version; VG value 15000; VG+ value 22500*

| ❑ CS8786 [S] | The Freewheelin' Bob Dylan 1964 | | 40.00 |

— *360 Sound Stereo" in black on label (with arrows)*

| ❑ CS8786 [S] | The Freewheelin' Bob Dylan 1965 | | 30.00 |

— *360 Sound Stereo" in white on label*

| ❑ CS8786 [S] | The Freewheelin' Bob Dylan 1970 | | 15.00 |

— *Orange label*

| ❑ KCS8786 [S] | The Freewheelin' Bob Dylan 197? | | 12.00 |
| ❑ PC8786 [S] | The Freewheelin' Bob Dylan 198? | | 10.00 |

— *Budget-line reissue*

| ❑ CS8786 [S] | The Freewheelin' Bob Dylan 197? | | 1000.00 |

— *Orange label; unauthorized red vinyl pressing*

| ❑ CS8786 [S] | The Freewheelin' Bob Dylan 1963 | | 400.00 |

— *Canadian pressing with the deleted tracks listed on the front cover. The label lists, and the record plays, the "correct" tracks.*

| ❑ PC8786 [S] | The Freewheelin' Bob Dylan 2001 | | 15.00 |

— *Reissue on 180-gram vinyl (sealed copies have a sticker indicating this)*

| ❑ CL2105 [M] | The Times They Are a-Changin' | 1964 | 400.00 |

— *White label promo*

| ❑ CL2105 [M] | The Times They Are a-Changin' | 1964 | 40.00 |

— *Guaranteed High Fidelity" on label*

| ❑ CL2105 [M] | The Times They Are a-Changin' | 1965 | 30.00 |

— *Mono" on label*

| ❑ C30005 [S] | The Times They Are a-Changin' | 1964 | 40.00 |

— *360 Sound Stereo" in black on label*

| ❑ CS8905 [S] | The Times They Are a-Changin' | 1965 | 30.00 |

— *360 Sound Stereo" in white on label*

| ❑ CS8905 [S] | The Times They Are a-Changin' | 1970 | 15.00 |

— *Orange label*

| ❑ KCS8905 [S] | The Times They Are a-Changin' | 197? | 12.00 |
| ❑ PC8905 [S] | The Times They Are a-Changin' | 198? | 10.00 |

— *Budget-line reissue*

| ❑ PC8905 [S] | The Times They Are a-Changin' | 2001 | 15.00 |

— *Reissue on 180-gram vinyl (sealed copies have a sticker indicating this)*

| ❑ C268556 | Time Out of Mind | 1998 | 18.00 |
| ❑ CAS2222 [DJ] | Time Passes Slowly | 1985 | 30.00 |

— *Promo-only sampler from Biograph box set*

| ❑ C46794 | Under the Red Sky | 1990 | 15.00 |

ISLAND

| ❑ AB-201 | Before the Flood | 1974 | 40.00 |

— *Error pressing with wrong labels (should be Asylum)*

MOBILE FIDELITY

❑ MFSL2-379 [B]	Another Side Of Bob Dylan	2012	40.00
❑ MFSL2-426 [B]	Before the Flood	2014	40.00
❑ MFSL3-45009 [B]	Blonde On Blonde	2013	90.00
❑ MFSL1-381 [B]	Blood On The Tracks	2013	40.00
❑ MFSL2-380 [B]	Bringing It All Back Home	2012	40.00
❑ MFSL2-416 [B]	Desire	2014	50.00
❑ MFSL2-422 [B]	Highway 61 Revisited	2014	50.00
❑ MFSL1-425 [B]	New Morning	2014	30.00
❑ MFSL2-382 [B]	The Basement Tapes	2014	40.00
❑ MFSL2-378 [B]	The Freewheelin' Bob Dylan	2012	40.00
❑ MFSL2-421 [B]	The Times They Are A-Changin'	2014	50.00
❑ 1-114	The Times They Are a-Changin'	1982	75.00

— *Audiophile vinyl*

SUNDAZED

| ❑ LP5121 [M] | Another Side of Bob Dylan | 2002 | 18.00 |

— *180-gram reissue of the original mono mix*

| ❑ LP5110 [M] | Blonde on Blonde | 2002 | 30.00 |

— *180-gram reissue of the original mono mix*

| ❑ LP5120 [M] | Bob Dylan | 2004 | 18.00 |

— *180-gram reissue of the original mono mix*

| ❑ LP5156 [M] | Bob Dylan's Greatest Hits | 2003 | 18.00 |

— *180-gram reissue of the original mono mix*

| ❑ LP5070 [M] | Bringing It All Back Home | 2001 | 18.00 |

— *180-gram reissue of the original mono mix*

| ❑ LP5071 [M] | Highway 61 Revisited | 2001 | 18.00 |

— *180-gram reissue of the original mono mix*

| ❑ LP5123 [M] | John Wesley Harding | 2003 | 18.00 |

— *180-gram reissue of the original mono mix*

| ❑ LP5115 [M] | The Freewheelin' Bob Dylan | 2001 | 18.00 |

— *180-gram reissue of the original mono mix*

| ❑ LP5108 [M] | The Times They Are a-Changin' | 2001 | 18.00 |

— *180-gram reissue of the original mono mix*

WARNER BROS./7 ARTS MUSIC

| ❑ XTV221567 [DJ] | Bob Dylan | 1969 | 1500.00 |

— *One-sided publisher's demo with 8 Dylan performances of then-unreleased songs from the "Basement Tapes" era; add $500 if includes sheet music.*

E

EAGER, ALLAN

SAVOY

| ❑ MG-9015 [10] | New Trends in Modern Music, Volume 2 | 1952 | 250.00 |
| ❑ MG-15044 [10] | Tenor Sax | 1954 | 200.00 |

EAGLE

JANUS

| ❑ JLS-3011 | Come Under Nancy's Tent | 1970 | 60.00 |

EAGLE BRASS BAND, THE

GHB

| ❑ GHB-60 | The Eagle Brass Band | 1978 | 12.00 |
| ❑ GHB-170 | The Last of the Line | 1986 | 12.00 |

EAGLES

ASYLUM

| ❑ SD5068 | Desperado | 1973 | 15.00 |

— *Clouds label*

| ❑ SD5054 | Eagles | 1972 | 18.00 |

— *Gatefold cover; white label with door-in-a-circle logo at top*

| ❑ SD5054 | Eagles | 1973 | 15.00 |

— *Regular cover; clouds label*

| ❑ 5054 [M] | Eagles | 1972 | 50.00 |

— *Promo only; white label with "d/j copy monaural" sticker on cover*

❑ 60205	Eagles Greatest Hits, Volume 2	1982	12.00
❑ BB-705	Eagles Live	1980	15.00
❑ 7E-1052	Eagles -- Their Greatest Hits 1971-1975	1976	12.00
❑ 6E-105	Eagles -- Their Greatest Hits 1971-1975	1977	10.00
❑ 7E-1084	Hotel California	1976	12.00

| ❑ 6E-103 [B] | Hotel California | 1977 | 10.00 |
| ❑ 7E-1039 | One of These Nights | 1975 | 12.00 |

— *Clouds label*

| ❑ EQ1039 [Q] | One of These Nights | 1975 | 30.00 |
| ❑ 7E-1004 | On the Border | 1974 | 15.00 |

— *Clouds label*

| ❑ EQ1004 [Q] | On the Border | 1974 | 30.00 |
| ❑ 5E-508 | The Long Run | 1979 | 10.00 |

DCC COMPACT CLASSICS

| ❑ LPZ-2051 | Eagles -- Their Greatest Hits 1971-1975 | 1998 | 100.00 |

— *Audiophile vinyl*

| ❑ LPZ-2043 | Hotel California | 1997 | 120.00 |

— *Audiophile vinyl*

MOBILE FIDELITY

| ❑ 1-126 | Hotel California | 1984 | 100.00 |

— *Audiophile vinyl*

RHINO

| ❑ RRM1536271 [B] | The Studio Albums 1972-1979 | 2013 | 120.00 |

EAGLES OF DEATH METAL

IPECAC

| ❑ IPC111 | Heart On | 2009 | 25.00 |

EAGLIN, SNOOKS

ARHOOLIE

| ❑ 2014 | Possum Up a Simmon Tree | 198? | 12.00 |

BLACK TOP

| ❑ BT-1037 | Baby, You Can Get Your Gun | 1987 | 12.00 |
| ❑ BT-1046 | Out of Nowhere | 198? | 12.00 |

BLUESVILLE

| ❑ BVLP-1046 [M] | That's All Right | 1962 | 60.00 |

— *Blue label, silver print*

| ❑ BVLP-1046 [M] | That's All Right | 1964 | 30.00 |

— *Blue label, trident logo at right*

FOLKWAYS

| ❑ FA-2476 [M] | New Orleans Street Singer | 1959 | 40.00 |

GNP CRECENDO

| ❑ 10023 | Down Yonder | 1979 | 12.00 |

EANES, JIM

JESSUP

| ❑ 152 | Statesman of Bluegrass Music | 1977 | 18.00 |

LEATHER

| ❑ 7703 | Where the Cool Waters Flow | 1978 | 25.00 |

REBEL

❑ 1643	Bluegrass Ballads	198?	18.00
❑ 1673	Let Him Lead You	1989	18.00
❑ 1653	Reminiscing	1987	18.00

ROUNDER

| ❑ 1016 | The Early Days of Bluegrass, Volume 4 | 1978 | 18.00 |

RURAL RHYTHM

| ❑ 221 | Jim Eanes | 1969 | 18.00 |
| ❑ 197 | Jim Eanes with Red Smiley and the Bluegrass Cutups | 1968 | 18.00 |

WEBCO

| ❑ WLPS 0110 | Shenandoah Grass, Yesterday and Today | 1983 | 18.00 |

EARDLEY, JON

FANTASY

| ❑ OJC-1746 | From Hollywood to New York | 1988 | 12.00 |
| ❑ OJC-123 | Jon Eardley Seven | 198? | 12.00 |

NEW JAZZ

| ❑ NJLP-1105 [10] | Jon Eardley in Hollywood | 1954 | 200.00 |

PRESTIGE

❑ PRLP-207 [10]	Hey There	1955	200.00
❑ PRLP-205 [10]	Jon Eardley in Hollywood	1955	150.00
❑ PRLP-7033 [M]	Jon Eardley Seven	1956	400.00

EARLAND, CHARLES

COLUMBIA

❑ JC36449	Coming to You Live	1980	12.00
❑ FC37573	Earland's Jam	1982	12.00
❑ FC38547	Earland's Street Themes	1983	12.00

FANTASY

| ❑ OJC-335 | Black Talk! | 1988 | 12.00 |

— *Reissue of Prestige 7758*

MERCURY

❑ SRM-1-1049	Odyssey	1976	12.00
❑ SRM-1-3720	Perception	1978	12.00
❑ SRM-1-1149	Revelation	1977	12.00
❑ SRM-1-1139	The Great Pyramid	1976	12.00

MILESTONE

| ❑ M-9165 | Front Burner | 1988 | 12.00 |
| ❑ M-9175 | Third Degree Burn | 1989 | 12.00 |

MUSE

❑ MR-5181	Infant Eyes	1980	12.00
❑ MR-5240	In the Pocket	1984	12.00
❑ MR-5156	Mama Roots	1979	12.00
❑ MR-5201	Pleasant Afternoon	1981	12.00
❑ MR-5126	Smokin'	1978	12.00

PRESTIGE

| ❑ PRST-7815 | Black Drops | 1970 | 18.00 |
| ❑ 10029 | Black Drops | 1971 | 12.00 |

— *Reissue of 7815*

| ❑ PRST-7758 | Black Talk! | 1970 | 25.00 |

Number	Title	Yr	NM
❏ 10024	Black Talk!	1971	12.00
— Reissue of 7758			
❏ 2501	Burners	1982	12.00
❏ 10061	Charles III	1973	15.00
❏ 10041	Intensity	1972	15.00
❏ 10095	Kharma	1975	15.00
❏ 66002	Leaving This Planet	1974	18.00
❏ 10051	Live at the Lighthouse	1972	15.00
❏ 10009	Living Black!	1971	15.00
❏ 10018	Soul Story	1971	15.00

TRIP

Number	Title	Yr	NM
❏ 5004	Charles Earland	1974	12.00

EARLE, STEVE

EPIC

Number	Title	Yr	NM
❏ FE39226	Early Tracks	1987	14.00

MCA

Number	Title	Yr	NM
❏ R143506	Exit 0	1987	15.00
— BMG Direct Marketing edition			
❏ 5998	Exit 0	1987	12.00
❏ R154072	Guitar Town	1986	15.00
— RCA Music Service edition			
❏ 5713	Guitar Town	1986	12.00

UNI

Number	Title	Yr	NM
❏ R100679	Copperhead Road	1988	15.00
— BMG Direct Marketing edition			
❏ 7	Copperhead Road	1988	12.00

EARLS, THE (1)

CHANCE

Number	Title	Yr	NM
❏ 1001	The Earls Today	1983	15.00

OLD TOWN

Number	Title	Yr	NM
❏ LP-104 [M]	Remember Me Baby	1963	500.00
— Counterfeit identification: Counterfeits have more than 1-inch trailoffs or as little as 1/2 inch trailoffs; legitimate copies have 5/8- to 3/4-inch trailoff			

WOODBURY

Number	Title	Yr	NM
❏ 104	Remember Me Baby	1976	18.00

EARTH, WIND, AND FIRE

ARC

Number	Title	Yr	NM
❏ KC236705	Faces	1980	15.00
❏ FC35730	I Am	1979	12.00
❏ HC45730	I Am	1981	30.00
— Half-speed mastered edition			
❏ PC35730	I Am	1984	10.00
— Budget-line reissue			
❏ TC37548	Raise!	1981	12.00
❏ HC47548	Raise!	1982	30.00
— Half-speed mastered edition			
❏ PC37548	Raise!	1984	10.00
— Budget-line reissue			
❏ FC35647	The Best of Earth, Wind & Fire, Vol. 1	1978	12.00
❏ HC45647	The Best of Earth, Wind & Fire, Vol. 1	1981	30.00
— Half-speed mastered edition			

COLUMBIA

Number	Title	Yr	NM
❏ JC34905	All 'N All	1977	15.00
❏ PC34905	All 'N All	198?	10.00
— Budget-line reissue			
❏ QC38980	Electric Universe	1983	12.00
❏ PG33694	Gratitude	1975	18.00
— No bar code			
❏ PG33694	Gratitude	198?	12.00
— Budget-line reissue with bar code			
❏ KC32194	Head to the Sky	1973	15.00
❏ CQ32194 [Q]	Head to the Sky	1973	25.00
❏ PC32194	Head to the Sky	197?	10.00
— Reissue			
❏ C45268	Heritage	1990	18.00
❏ KC31702	Last Days and Time	1972	18.00
❏ PC31702	Last Days and Time	197?	10.00
— Reissue			
❏ KC32712	Open Our Eyes	1974	15.00
❏ CQ32712 [Q]	Open Our Eyes	1974	25.00
❏ PC32712 [B]	Open Our Eyes	197?	10.00
— Reissue			
❏ TC38367	Powerlight	1983	12.00
❏ HC48367	Powerlight	1983	40.00
— Half-speed mastered edition			
❏ PC38367	Powerlight	1984	10.00
— Budget-line reissue			
❏ PC34241	Spirit	1976	15.00
— No bar code			
❏ PCQ34241 [Q]	Spirit	1976	30.00
❏ PC34241	Spirit	198?	10.00
— Budget-line reissue with bar code			
❏ PC33280	That's the Way of the World	1975	15.00
— No bar code			
❏ PC33280	That's the Way of the World	198?	10.00
— Budget-line reissue with bar code			
❏ PCQ33280 [Q]	That's the Way of the World	1975	25.00
❏ OC45013	The Best of Earth, Wind & Fire, Vol. 1	1988	12.00
❏ FC40596	Touch the World	1987	12.00

MOBILE FIDELITY

Number	Title	Yr	NM
❏ 1-159	That's the Way of the World	198?	30.00
— Audiophile vinyl			

PAIR

Number	Title	Yr	NM
❏ PDL2-1064	Beat It to Life	1986	15.00

WARNER BROS.

Number	Title	Yr	NM
❏ 2WS2798	Another Time	1974	25.00
— Burbank" palm trees labels			
❏ WS1905	Earth, Wind, and Fire	1971	25.00
— Green label			
❏ WS1958	The Need of Love	1971	25.00
— Green label			

EARTH AND FIRE

RED BULLET

Number	Title	Yr	NM
❏ RBLP-3000	Earth and Fire	197?	18.00

EARTH ISLAND

PHILPS

Number	Title	Yr	NM
❏ PHS600340	We Must Survive	1970	30.00

EARTH OPERA

ELEKTRA

Number	Title	Yr	NM
❏ EKS-74016 [B]	Earth Opera	1968	30.00
❏ EKS-74038	The Great American Eagle Tragedy	1969	25.00

EARTH QUAKE

A&M

Number	Title	Yr	NM
❏ SP-4308	Earth Quake	1971	18.00
❏ SP-4337	Why Don't You Try Me?	1972	18.00

BESERKLEY

Number	Title	Yr	NM
❏ 0047	8.5	1976	15.00
❏ PZ34754	8.5	1977	12.00
— Reissue of 0047			
❏ 0054	Leveled	1977	15.00
❏ PZ34801	Leveled	1977	12.00
— Reissue of 0054			
❏ 0045	Rockin' the World	1975	15.00
❏ PZ34752	Rockin' the World	1977	12.00
— Reissue of 0045			
❏ BZ-10065	Two Years in a Padded Cell	1979	12.00

EARWOOD, MUNDO

EXCELSIOR

Number	Title	Yr	NM
❏ 88006	Mundo Earwood	1981	12.00

EASLEY, BILL

SUNNYSIDE

Number	Title	Yr	NM
❏ SSC-1022	Wind Inventions	1988	12.00

EASON, GERALD, AND ROBERT KNOTT

BARONET

Number	Title	Yr	NM
❏ BS1003 [S]	Organ and Chimes for Christmas	1961	18.00
— Textured silvery cover			

EAST

CAPITOL

Number	Title	Yr	NM
❏ ST-11083	East	1972	30.00

EAST NEW YORK ENSEMBLE DE PARIS, THE

FOLKWAYS

Number	Title	Yr	NM
❏ F-33867	At the Helm	1974	18.00

EAST OF EDEN

DERAM

Number	Title	Yr	NM
❏ DES18023	Mercator Projected	1969	25.00
❏ DES18043	Snafu	1970	25.00

HARVEST

Number	Title	Yr	NM
❏ SW-806	East of Eden	1971	25.00

EAST SIDE KIDS, THE

UNI

Number	Title	Yr	NM
❏ 73032	The Tiger and the Lamb	1968	30.00

EASTERN REBELLION

TIMELESS

Number	Title	Yr	NM
❏ 306	Eastern Rebellion	1976	18.00
❏ 318	Eastern Rebellion II	1977	18.00

EASTMAN FRENCH HORN AND TROMBONE

EASTON, ELLIOT

ELEKTRA

Number	Title	Yr	NM
❏ 60393	Change No Change	1985	12.00

EASTON, SHEENA

EMI

Number	Title	Yr	NM
❏ E1-593338	The Sheena Easton Collection	1989	18.00
— Columbia House edition			

EMI AMERICA

Number	Title	Yr	NM
❏ ST-17132	A Private Heaven	1984	10.00
❏ R144428	A Private Heaven	1984	12.00
— RCA Music Service edition			
❏ ST-517132	A Private Heaven	1984	12.00
— Columbia House edition			
❏ ST-17101	Best Kept Secret	1983	10.00
❏ ST-517101	Best Kept Secret	1983	12.00
— Columbia House edition			
❏ R163514	Best Kept Secret	1983	12.00
— RCA Music Service edition			
❏ SJ-17173	Do You	1985	10.00
❏ ST-17080	Madness, Money and Music	1982	10.00
❏ R114422	Madness, Money and Music	1982	12.00
— RCA Music Service edition			
❏ ST-17049	Sheena Easton	1981	10.00
❏ ST-517049	Sheena Easton	1981	12.00
— Columbia House edition			
❏ R133902	Sheena Easton	1981	12.00
— RCA Music Service edition			
❏ SW-17061	You Could Have Been with Me	1981	10.00
❏ SW-517061	You Could Have Been with Me	1981	12.00
— Columbia House version			

MCA

Number	Title	Yr	NM
❏ 42249	The Lover in Me	1988	12.00
❏ 10131	What Comes Naturally	1991	15.00

EASTON, TED

CIRCLE

Number	Title	Yr	NM
❏ 12	A Salute to Satchmo	198?	12.00

EASTWOOD, CLINT

CAMEO

Number	Title	Yr	NM
❏ C-1056 [M]	Clint Eastwood Sings Cowboy Favorites	1963	100.00
❏ SC-1056 [S]	Clint Eastwood Sings Cowboy Favorites	1963	150.00

EASY RIDERS JAZZ BAND, THE

JAZZ CRUSADE

Number	Title	Yr	NM
❏ 1002	My Life Will Be Sweeter Someday	1963	40.00

EASYBEATS, THE

RHINO

Number	Title	Yr	NM
❏ RNLP-124	The Best of the Easybeats	1985	10.00

UNITED ARTISTS

Number	Title	Yr	NM
❏ UAS6667 [P]	Falling Off the Edge of the World	1968	40.00
— Women" is rechanneled.			
❏ UAL3588 [M]	Friday on My Mind	1967	40.00
❏ UAS6588 [P]	Friday on My Mind	1967	50.00
— Make You Feel Alright" is rechanneled.			

EATON, CLEVELAND

OVATION

Number	Title	Yr	NM
❏ OV-1703	Instant Hip	1974	25.00
❏ OV-1742	Keep Love Alive	197?	18.00

EATON, CONNIE, AND DAVE PEEL

CHART

Number	Title	Yr	NM
❏ 1034	Hit the Road Jack	1970	18.00

EATON, JOHN

CHIAROSCURO

Number	Title	Yr	NM
❏ CH-174	Like Old Times	1977	15.00
❏ CH-137	Solo Piano	1975	15.00

EATON, JOHNNY

COLUMBIA

Number	Title	Yr	NM
❏ CL737 [M]	College Jazz: Modern	1956	40.00
❏ CL996 [M]	Far Out, Far In	1957	40.00

EAVES, HUBERT

INNER CITY

Number	Title	Yr	NM
❏ IC-6012	Esteric Funk	1976	25.00

EBON-KNIGHTS, THE

STEPHENY

Number	Title	Yr	NM
❏ 4001 [M]	First Date	1959	1500.00

EBONYS, THE

BUDDAH

Number	Title	Yr	NM
❏ BDS5679	Sing About Life	1976	40.00

PHILADELPHIA INT'L.

Number	Title	Yr	NM
❏ KZ32419	The Ebonys	1973	15.00

EBSEN, BUDDY

REPRISE

Number	Title	Yr	NM
❏ R-6174 [M]	Buddy Ebsen Sings Howdy!	1965	30.00
❏ RS-6174 [S]	Buddy Ebsen Sings Howdy!	1965	40.00

ECHO AND THE BUNNYMEN

SIRE

Number	Title	Yr	NM
❏ SRK6096 [B]	Crocodiles	1980	18.00
❏ 25597 [B]	Echo and the Bunnymen	1987	15.00
❏ SRK3569 [B]	Heaven Up Here	1981	18.00
❏ 25084 [B]	Ocean Rain	1984	18.00
❏ 23770 [B]	Porcupine	1983	18.00

Number	Title	Yr	NM
❑ 25360	Songs to Learn and Sing	1986	15.00
❑ 23987 [EP]	The Echo	1983	12.00
ECHOES OF HARLEM			
ROYALE			
❑ LP-18128 [10]	Echoes of Harlem	195?	80.00
ECKSTINE, BILLY			
AUDIO LAB			
❑ AL-1549 [M]	Mr. B	1960	120.00
DELUXE			
❑ FA-2010 [M]	Billy Eckstine and His Orchestra	195?	80.00
EMARCY			
❑ MG-36129 [M]	Billy Eckstine's Imagination	1958	60.00
❑ MG-26025 [10]	Blues for Sale	1954	120.00
❑ MG-36029 [M]	Blues for Sale	1955	80.00
❑ MG-36010 [M]	I Surrender, Dear	1955	80.00
❑ MG-26027 [10]	The Love Songs of Mr. B	1954	120.00
❑ MG-36030 [M]	The Love Songs of Mr. B	1955	80.00
ENTERPRISE			
❑ ENS-1017	Feel the Warm	1971	18.00
❑ ENS-5004	Senior Soul	1972	18.00
❑ ENS-1013	Stormy	1971	18.00
FORUM			
❑ F-9027 [M]	Once More with Feeling	196?	18.00
❑ SF-9027 [S]	Once More with Feeling	196?	18.00
KING			
❑ 295-12 [10]	The Great Mr. B	1953	300.00
LION			
❑ L-70057 [M]	The Best of Billy Eckstine	1958	30.00
MERCURY			
❑ MG-20674 [M]	Billy Eckstine and Quincy Jones at Basin St. East	1962	30.00
❑ SR-60674 [S]	Billy Eckstine and Quincy Jones at Basin St. East	1962	30.00
❑ MG-20333 [M]	Billy's Best	1958	40.00
❑ SR-60086 [S]	Billy's Best	1958	50.00
❑ MG-20637 [M]	Broadway, Bongos and Mr. B	1961	30.00
❑ SR-60637 [S]	Broadway, Bongos and Mr. B	1961	30.00
❑ MG-20736 [M]	Don't Worry 'Bout Me	1962	30.00
❑ SR-60736 [S]	Don't Worry 'Bout Me	1962	30.00
❑ MG-20796 [M]	The Golden Hits of Billy Eckstine	1963	18.00
❑ SR-60796 [S]	The Golden Hits of Billy Eckstine	1963	25.00
METRO			
❑ M-537 [M]	Everything I Have Is Yours	1965	18.00
❑ MS-537 [R]	Everything I Have Is Yours	1965	15.00
MGM			
❑ E-153 [10]	Billy Eckstine Sings Rodgers & Hammerstein	1952	150.00
❑ E-548 [10]	Favorites	1951	160.00
❑ E-257 [10]	I Let a Song Go Out of My Heart	1954	150.00
❑ E-3176 [M]	Mr. B with a Beat	1955	50.00
❑ E-3209 [M]	Rendezvous	1955	50.00
❑ E-523 [10]	Songs by Billy Eckstine	1951	160.00
❑ E-219 [10]	Tenderly	1953	150.00
❑ E-3275 [M]	That Old Feeling	1956	50.00
MOTOWN			
❑ MS677	For Love of Ivy	1969	30.00
❑ M646 [M]	My Way	1966	25.00
❑ MS646 [S]	My Way	1966	30.00
❑ M632 [M]	Prime of My Life	1965	25.00
❑ MS632 [S]	Prime of My Life	1965	30.00
NATIONAL			
❑ NLP-2001 [10]	Billy Eckstine Sings	1949	200.00
REGENT			
❑ MG-6054 [M]	My Deep Blue Dream	1957	50.00
❑ MG-6052 [M]	Prisoner of Love	1957	50.00
❑ MG-6053 [M]	The Duke, the Blues and Me	1957	50.00
❑ MG-6058 [M]	You Call It Madness	1957	50.00
ROULETTE			
❑ R-25052 [M]	No Cover, No Minimum	1961	30.00
❑ SR-25052 [S]	No Cover, No Minimum	1961	30.00
❑ R-25104 [M]	Once More with Feeling	1962	30.00
❑ SR-25104 [S]	Once More with Feeling	1962	30.00
SAVOY			
❑ 1127	Billy Eckstine Sings	1979	15.00
❑ SJL-2214	Mr. B and the Band/The Savoy Sessions	1976	18.00
TRIP			
❑ 5567	The Modern Sound of Mr. B	197?	12.00
VERVE			
❑ 819442-1	Everything I Have Is Yours: The MGM Years	1986	18.00
XANADU			
❑ 207	I Want to Talk About You	1987	12.00
ECLECTION			
ELEKTRA			
❑ EKS-74023	Eclection	1968	18.00
ECSTASY, PASSION AND PAIN			
ROULETTE			
❑ SR-3013	Ecstasy, Passion and Pain	1974	18.00
EDDIE AND BETTY			
WARNER BROS.			
❑ W1350 [M]	Nightlife for Daydreamers	1959	30.00
❑ WS1350 [S]	Nightlife for Daydreamers	1959	30.00
EDDIE AND THE SUBTITLES			
13TH STORY			
❑ MR3301	Dead Drunks Don't Dance	1983	30.00
(NO LABEL)			
❑ (no #)0	Skeletons in the Closet	1981	40.00
EDDY, DUANE			
CAPITOL			
❑ ST-12567	Duane Eddy	1987	15.00
COLPIX			
❑ CP-490 [M]	Duane A-Go-Go	1965	30.00
❑ CPS-490 [S]	Duane A-Go-Go	1965	40.00
❑ CPL-494 [M]	Duane Eddy Does Bob Dylan	1965	30.00
❑ SCP-494 [S]	Duane Eddy Does Bob Dylan	1965	40.00
JAMIE			
❑ JLPM-3014 [M]	$1,000,000.00 Worth of Twang	1960	40.00
❑ JLPS-3014 [S]	$1,000,000.00 Worth of Twang	1960	70.00
—All but one song -- "Up and Down" -- is in true stereo			
❑ JLPM-3021 [M]	$1,000,000.00 Worth of Twang, Volume 2	1962	40.00
❑ JLPS-3021 [R]	$1,000,000.00 Worth of Twang, Volume 2	1962	30.00
❑ JLPM-3026 [M]	16 Greatest Hits	1964	40.00
❑ JLPS-3026 [R]	16 Greatest Hits	1964	30.00
❑ JLPM-3025 [M]	Duane Eddy & The Rebels -- In Person	1963	30.00
❑ JLPS-3025 [S]	Duane Eddy & The Rebels -- In Person	1963	40.00
❑ T-90663 [M]	Duane Eddy & The Rebels -- In Person	1965	40.00
—Capitol Record Club edition			
❑ ST-90663 [S]	Duane Eddy & The Rebels -- In Person	1965	50.00
—Capitol Record Club edition			
❑ JLPM-3006 [M]	Especially for You...	1959	60.00
❑ JLPS-3006 [S]	Especially for You...	1959	80.00
❑ JLPM-3019 [M]	Girls! Girls! Girls!	1961	40.00
❑ JLPS-3019 [R]	Girls! Girls! Girls!	1961	30.00
❑ JLP-3000 [M]	Have "Twangy" Guitar -- Will Travel	1958	160.00
—Duane sitting with guitar case, title on cover in white (1st)			
❑ JLP-3000 [M]	Have "Twangy" Guitar -- Will Travel	1959	100.00
—Duane sitting with guitar case, title on cover in green and red (2nd)			
❑ JLP-3000 [M]	Have "Twangy" Guitar -- Will Travel	1959	50.00
—Duane standing with guitar (3rd)			
❑ JLPS-3000 [S]	Have "Twangy" Guitar -- Will Travel	1958	400.00
—Duane sitting with guitar case, title on cover in white (1st)			
❑ JLPS-3000 [S]	Have "Twangy" Guitar -- Will Travel	1959	300.00
—Duane sitting with guitar case, title on cover in green and red (2nd)			
❑ JLPS-3000 [S]	Have "Twangy" Guitar -- Will Travel	1959	100.00
—Duane standing with guitar (3rd), album plays true stereo			
❑ JLPS-3000 [R]	Have "Twangy" Guitar -- Will Travel	196?	50.00
—Duane standing with guitar (3rd), album plays fake stereo			
❑ T-90682 [M]	Have "Twangy" Guitar -- Will Travel	1965	60.00
—Capitol Record Club edition			
❑ ST-90682 [S]	Have "Twangy" Guitar -- Will Travel	1965	80.00
—Capitol Record Club edition			
❑ JLPM-3011 [M]	Songs of Our Heritage	1960	80.00
—Gatefold cover			
❑ JLPM-3011 [M]	Songs of Our Heritage	196?	30.00
—Regular cover			
❑ JLPS-3011 [S]	Songs of Our Heritage	1960	100.00
—Gatefold cover			
❑ JLPS-3011 [S]	Songs of Our Heritage	1960	500.00
—Gatefold cover, red vinyl			
❑ JLPS-3011 [S]	Songs of Our Heritage	1960	500.00
—Gatefold cover, blue vinyl			
❑ JLPS-3011 [S]	Songs of Our Heritage	196?	40.00
—Regular cover			
❑ JLPM-3024 [M]	Surfin'	1963	50.00
❑ JLPS-3024 [S]	Surfin'	1963	80.00
❑ JLPM-3009 [M]	The "Twangs" The "Thang	1959	40.00
❑ JLPS-3009 [S]	The "Twangs" The "Thang	1959	60.00
❑ T-91301 [M]	The "Twangs" The "Thang	1966	60.00
—Capitol Record Club edition			
❑ ST-91301 [S]	The "Twangs" The "Thang	1966	60.00
—Capitol Record Club edition			
❑ JLPM-3022 [M]	Twistin' with Duane Eddy	1962	40.00
❑ JLPS-3022 [P]	Twistin' with Duane Eddy	1962	40.00
RCA VICTOR			
❑ LPM-2648 [M]	Dance with the Guitar Man	1962	30.00
❑ LSP-2648 [S]	Dance with the Guitar Man	1962	40.00
❑ LPM-2798 [M]	Lonely Guitar	1964	25.00
❑ LSP-2798 [S]	Lonely Guitar	1964	30.00
❑ ANL1-2671	Pure Gold	1978	12.00
❑ LPM-3477 [M]	The Best of Duane Eddy	1965	25.00
❑ LSP-3477 [P]	The Best of Duane Eddy	1965	30.00
—Black "Stereo" label			
❑ LSP-3477 [P]	The Best of Duane Eddy	1969	18.00
—Orange label			
❑ LPM-2681 [M]	Twang a Country Song	1963	30.00
❑ LSP-2681 [S]	Twang a Country Song	1963	40.00
❑ LPM-2700 [M]	Twangin' " Up a Storm!	1963	30.00
❑ LSP-2700 [S]	Twangin' " Up a Storm!	1963	40.00
❑ LPM-2993 [M]	Twangin' the Golden Hits	1965	25.00
❑ LSP-2993 [S]	Twangin' the Golden Hits	1965	30.00
❑ LPM-3432 [M]	Twangsville	1965	25.00
❑ LSP-3432 [S]	Twangsville	1965	30.00
❑ LPM-2576 [M]	Twangy Guitar -- Silky Strings	1962	30.00
❑ LSP-2576 [S]	Twangy Guitar -- Silky Strings	1962	40.00
❑ LPM-2525 [M]	Twistin' 'N' Twangin'	1962	30.00
❑ LSP-2525 [S]	Twistin' 'N' Twangin'	1962	40.00
❑ LPM-2918 [M]	Water Skiing	1964	25.00
❑ LSP-2918 [S]	Water Skiing	1964	30.00
REPRISE			
❑ R-6218 [M]	The Biggest Twang of Them All	1966	30.00
❑ RS-6218 [S]	The Biggest Twang of Them All	1966	40.00
❑ R-6240 [M]	The Roaring Twangies	1967	30.00
❑ RS-6240 [S]	The Roaring Twangies	1967	40.00
SIRE			
❑ SASH-3707-2	The Vintage Years	1975	30.00
EDDY, NELSON			
COLUMBIA MASTERWORKS			
❑ ML4442 [M]	Songs for Christmas	195?	40.00
HARMONY			
❑ HL7201 [M]	Nelson Eddy Sings the Best Loved Carols of Christmas	195?	25.00
EDELMAN, RANDY			
20TH CENTURY			
❑ T-494	Farewell Fairbanks	1975	15.00
❑ T-443	Prime Cuts	1974	18.00
ARISTA			
❑ AB4139	If Love Is Real	1977	15.00
❑ AB4210	You're the One	1979	15.00
LION			
❑ LN-1013	The Laughter and the Tears	1972	18.00
SUNFLOWER			
❑ SNF-5005	Randy Edelman	1971	18.00
EDEN, BARBARA			
DOT			
❑ DLP-3795 [M]	Miss Barbara Eden	1967	40.00
❑ DLP-25795 [S]	Miss Barbara Eden	1967	50.00
EDEN'S CHILDREN			
ABC			
❑ 624 [M]	Eden's Children	1968	40.00
❑ S-624 [S]	Eden's Children	1968	30.00
❑ S-652	Sure Looks Real	1968	25.00
EDGE, GRAEME			
LONDON			
❑ PS686	Paradise Ballroom	1977	15.00
THRESHOLD			
❑ THS15	Kick Off Your Muddy Boots	1975	18.00
EDGE, THE			
NOSE			
❑ NRS-48003 [B]	The Edge	1970	50.00
EDISON, HARRY "SWEETS			
AMERICAN RECORDING SOCIETY			
❑ G-430 [M]	Sweets	1957	40.00
CLEF			
❑ MGC-717 [M]	Sweets	1956	250.00
LIBERTY			
❑ LRP-3484 [M]	When Lights Are Low	1966	25.00
❑ LST-7484 [S]	When Lights Are Low	1966	30.00
PABLO			
❑ 2310934	For My Pals	198?	15.00
❑ 2310780	Lights	1976	18.00
❑ 2310806	Simply Sweets	1977	18.00
PABLO LIVE			
❑ 2308237	'S Wonderful	198?	15.00
PACIFIC JAZZ			
❑ PJLP-4 [10]	Harry Edison Quartet	1953	150.00
❑ PJ-11 [M]	The Inventive Harry Edison	1960	50.00
ROULETTE			
❑ R-52041 [M]	Patented by Edison	1960	30.00
❑ SR-52041 [S]	Patented by Edison	1960	40.00
❑ R-52023 [M]	Sweetenings	1960	40.00
❑ SR-52023 [S]	Sweetenings	1960	40.00
SUE			
❑ LP-1030 [M]	Sweets for the Sweet	1964	40.00
❑ STLP-1030 [S]	Sweets for the Sweet	1964	50.00

Number	Title	Yr	NM

VEE JAY
- LP-1104 [M] — For the Sweet Taste of Love — 1964 — 30.00
- LPS-1104 [S] — For the Sweet Taste of Love — 1964 — 40.00
- VJS-3065 — Home with Sweets — 1975 — 25.00

VERVE
- MGV-8211 [M] — Gee Baby, Ain't I Good to You? — 1958 — 50.00
- V-8211 [M] — Gee Baby, Ain't I Good to You? — 1961 — 25.00
- MGV-8293 [M] — Harry Edison Swings Buck Clayton, And Vice Versa — 1958 — 50.00
- V-8293 [M] — Harry Edison Swings Buck Clayton, And Vice Versa — 1961 — 25.00
- MGVS-6016 [S] — Harry Edison Swings Buck Clayton, And Vice Versa — 1959 — 40.00
- V6-8293 [S] — Harry Edison Swings Buck Clayton, And Vice Versa — 1961 — 25.00
- MGV-8353 [M] — Mr. Swing — 1959 — 50.00
- V-8353 [M] — Mr. Swing — 1961 — 25.00
- MGVS-6118 [S] — Mr. Swing — 1960 — 40.00
- V6-8358 [S] — Mr. Swing — 1961 — 25.00
- MGV-8097 [M] — Sweets — 1957 — 50.00
- V-8097 [M] — Sweets — 1961 — 25.00
- MGV-8295 [M] — The Swinger — 1959 — 50.00
- V-8295 [M] — The Swinger — 1961 — 25.00
- MGVS-6037 [S] — The Swinger — 1960 — 40.00
- V6-8295 [S] — The Swinger — 1961 — 25.00

EDISON ELECTRIC BAND, THE

COTILLION
- SD9022 — Bless You, Dr. Woodward — 1970 — 25.00

EDMONSON, TRAVIS

HORIZON
- WP-1606 [M] — Travis On Cue — 1962 — 25.00
- WPS-1606 [S] — Travis On Cue — 1962 — 30.00

REPRISE
- R-6035 [M] — Travis On His Own — 1962 — 30.00
- R9-6035 [S] — Travis On His Own — 1962 — 30.00

EDMUNDS, DAVE

ATLANTIC
- PR320 [DJ] — College Network — 1978 — 50.00
- *— Promo-only interview album*

CAPITOL
- C1-90372 — Closer to the Flame — 1990 — 18.00

COLUMBIA
- FC37930 — D.E. 7th — 1982 — 15.00
- PC37930 — D.E. 7th — 198? — 10.00
- *— Budget-line reissue ("02" added to bar code on back cover)*
- FC40603 — I Hear You Rockin' — 1987 — 12.00
- PC40603 — I Hear You Rockin' — 198? — 10.00
- *— Budget-line reissue ("02" added to bar code on back cover)*
- FC38651 — Information — 1983 — 15.00
- PC38651 — Information — 198? — 10.00
- *— Budget-line reissue ("02" added to bar code on back cover)*
- FC39273 — Riff Raff — 1984 — 12.00

MAM
- 3 [B] — Rockpile — 1972 — 50.00

RCA VICTOR
- LPL1-5003 [B] — Subtle as a Flying Mallet — 1975 — 25.00
- AYL1-4238 — Subtle as a Flying Mallet — 1982 — 12.00
- *— Reissue (black label, dog near top)*

SWAN SONG
- SS8418 — Get It — 1977 — 18.00
- SS8507 — Repeat When Necessary — 1979 — 18.00
- SS8510 — The Best of Dave Edmunds — 1981 — 15.00
- SS8505 — Trax on Wax 4 — 1978 — 18.00
- SD16034 — Twangin' — 1981 — 15.00

EDWARD BEAR

CAPITOL
- SKAO-426 [B] — Bearings — 1970 — 25.00
- ST-11192 [M] — Close Your Eyes — 1973 — 18.00
- ST-580 [B] — Eclipse — 1971 — 25.00
- ST-11157 [B] — Edward Bear — 1972 — 18.00

EDWARDS, EDDIE

COMMODORE
- FL-20003 [10] — Eddie Edwards' Original Dixieland Jazz Band — 1950 — 60.00

EDWARDS, JONATHAN

ATCO
- SD7036 — Have a Good Time for Me — 1973 — 15.00
- 7015 [M] — Honky-Tonk Stardust Cowboy — 1972 — 30.00
- *— Mono is promo only; white label, "dj copy monaural" sticker on stereo cover*
- SD7015 [S] — Honky-Tonk Stardust Cowboy — 1972 — 15.00
- SD 36-104 — Lucky Day — 1974 — 15.00

CAPRICORN
- SD862 — Jonathan Edwards — 1971 — 15.00
- *— Original has green label*
- SD862 — Jonathan Edwards — 198? — 10.00
- *— Reissue with tan label*

CHRONIC
- 1001 — Live! — 1982 — 15.00

MCA CURB
- 42256 — The Natural Thing — 1989 — 12.00

REPRISE
- MS2238 — Rockin' Chair — 1976 — 12.00

SUGAR HILL
- SH-3747 — Blue Ridge — 1985 — 12.00
- *— With the Seldom Scene*

WARNER BROS.
- BS3020 — Sailboat — 1977 — 12.00

EDWARDS, JONATHAN AND DARLENE

COLUMBIA
- CL1513 [M] — Jonathan and Darlene Edwards In Paris — 1960 — 30.00
- CS8313 [S] — Jonathan and Darlene Edwards In Paris — 1960 — 30.00
- CL1024 [M] — The Piano Artistry of Jonathan Edwards — 1955 — 50.00

CORINTHIAN
- 103 — Jonathan and Darlene Edwards In Paris — 198? — 12.00
- 120 — Sing Along with Jonathan and Darlene — 198? — 12.00
- 122 — Songs for Sheiks and Flappers — 1986 — 12.00
- 104 — The Original Piano Artistry of Jonathan Edwards — 198? — 12.00

DOT
- DLP-3792 [M] — Songs for Sheiks and Flappers — 1967 — 18.00
- DLP-25792 [S] — Songs for Sheiks and Flappers — 1967 — 25.00

RCA VICTOR
- LPM-2495 [M] — Sing Along with Jonathan and Darlene — 1962 — 25.00
- LSP-2495 [S] — Sing Along with Jonathan and Darlene — 1962 — 30.00

EDWARDS, KATHLEEN

ROUNDER
- 1431151 — Asking for Flowers — 2008 — 25.00

EDWARDS, STONEY

CAPITOL
- ST-11499 [M] — Blackbird — 1976 — 25.00
- ST-741 — Country Singer — 1970 — 30.00
- ST-834 — Down Home in the Country — 1971 — 25.00
- ST-11401 — Mississippi on My Mind — 1975 — 25.00
- ST-11173 — She's My Rock — 1973 — 25.00
- ST-11090 — Stoney Edwards — 1972 — 25.00

EDWARDS, TEDDY

CONTEMPORARY
- M-3592 [M] — Good Gravy — 1961 — 250.00
- S-7592 [S] — Good Gravy — 1961 — 30.00
- M-3606 [M] — Heart and Soul — 1962 — 50.00
- S-7606 [S] — Heart and Soul — 1962 — 30.00
- M-3583 [M] — Teddy's Ready — 1960 — 30.00
- S-7583 [S] — Teddy's Ready — 1960 — 30.00
- M-3588 [M] — Together Again — 1961 — 70.00
- S-7588 [S] — Together Again — 1961 — 40.00

FANTASY
- OJC-177 — Heart and Soul — 198? — 12.00
- OJC-424 — Together Again — 1990 — 15.00

MUSE
- MR-5045 — Feelin's — 1974 — 15.00

PACIFIC JAZZ
- PJ-6 [M] — It's About Time — 1960 — 50.00
- ST-6 [S] — It's About Time — 1960 — 40.00
- PJ-14 [M] — Sunset Eyes — 1961 — 200.00

PRESTIGE
- PRLP-7522 [M] — It's Alright — 1967 — 30.00
- PRST-7522 [S] — It's Alright — 1967 — 30.00
- PRLP-7518 [M] — Nothin' But the Truth — 1967 — 30.00
- PRST-7518 [S] — Nothin' But the Truth — 1967 — 30.00

STEEPLECHASE
- SCS-1147 — Out of This World — 1980 — 15.00

XANADU
- 134 — Inimitable — 1976 — 15.00

EDWARDS, TOMMY

LION
- L-70120 [M] — Tommy Edwards — 1959 — 30.00

METRO
- M-511 [M] — Tommy Edwards — 1965 — 15.00
- MS-511 [S] — Tommy Edwards — 1965 — 18.00

MGM
- E-3760 [M] — For Young Lovers — 1959 — 30.00
- *— Yellow label*
- SE-3760 [S] — For Young Lovers — 1959 — 40.00
- *— Yellow label*
- E-3760 [M] — For Young Lovers — 1960 — 25.00
- *— Black label*
- SE-3760 [S] — For Young Lovers — 1960 — 30.00
- *— Black label*
- E-3959 [M] — Golden Coutnry Hits — 1961 — 25.00
- SE-3959 [S] — Golden Coutnry Hits — 1961 — 30.00
- E-3732 [M] — It's All in the Game — 1958 — 30.00
- *— Yellow label*
- SE-3732 [S] — It's All in the Game — 1959 — 40.00
- *— Yellow label*
- E-3732 [M] — It's All in the Game — 1960 — 25.00
- *— Black label*
- SE-3732 [S] — It's All in the Game — 1960 — 30.00
- *— Black label*
- E-4060 [M] — Soft Strings and Two Guitars — 1962 — 25.00
- SE-4060 [S] — Soft Strings and Two Guitars — 1962 — 30.00
- E-4020 [M] — Stardust — 1962 — 25.00
- SE-4020 [S] — Stardust — 1962 — 30.00
- E-3822 [M] — Step Out Singing — 1960 — 25.00
- SE-3822 [S] — Step Out Singing — 1960 — 30.00
- E-4141 [M] — The Very Best of Tommy Edwards — 1963 — 18.00
- SE-4141 [S] — The Very Best of Tommy Edwards — 1963 — 25.00
- GAS-123 — Tommy Edwards (Golden Archive Series) — 1970 — 18.00
- E-3884 [M] — Tommy Edwards' Greatest Hits — 1961 — 25.00
- SE-3884 [S] — Tommy Edwards' Greatest Hits — 1961 — 30.00
- E-3838 [M] — Tommy Edwards in Hawaii — 1960 — 25.00
- SE-3838 [S] — Tommy Edwards in Hawaii — 1960 — 30.00
- E-3805 [M] — You Started Me Dreaming — 1960 — 25.00
- SE-3805 [S] — You Started Me Dreaming — 1960 — 30.00

REGENT
- MG-6096 [M] — Tommy Edwards Sings — 1958 — 60.00

EDWARDS, VINCENT

DECCA
- DL4399 [M] — In Person at the Riviera — 1963 — 25.00
- DL74399 [S] — In Person at the Riviera — 1963 — 30.00
- DL4336 [M] — Sometimes I'm Happy... Sometimes I'm Blue — 1962 — 25.00
- DL74336 [S] — Sometimes I'm Happy... Sometimes I'm Blue — 1962 — 30.00
- DL4311 [M] — Vincent Edwards Sings — 1962 — 25.00
- DL74311 [S] — Vincent Edwards Sings — 1962 — 30.00

VOCALION
- VL3852 [M] — Here's Vincent Edwards — 1967 — 15.00
- VL73852 [S] — Here's Vincent Edwards — 1967 — 15.00

EELS

BONG LOAD
- BL47 — Daisies of the Galaxy — 2000 — 100.00

DREAMWORKS
- DRM2-50052 [10] — Electro-shock Blues — 1998 — 50.00

SPINART
- 128 — Shootenanny! — 2003 — 30.00

EGAN, MARK

GRP
- GR-9572 — A Touch of Light — 1988 — 12.00

HIPPOCKET
- HP-104 — Mosaic — 1985 — 12.00

WINDHAM HILL
- WH-0104 — Mosaic — 1987 — 12.00
- *— Reissue of HipPocket 104*

EGAN, WALTER

BACKSTREET
- 5400 — Wild Exhibitions — 1983 — 10.00

COLUMBIA
- PC34679 — Fundamental Roll — 1977 — 12.00
- JC35796 — Hi Fi — 1979 — 12.00
- JC35077 — Not Shy — 1978 — 12.00
- JC36513 — The Last Stroll — 1981 — 12.00

EGILSSON, ARNI

INNER CITY
- IC-1103 — Bassus Erectus — 1981 — 15.00

EIGHT MINUTES, THE

PERCEPTION
- 27 — An American Family — 1973 — 50.00

8TH DAY, THE

A&M
- SP-4942 — The 8th Day — 1983 — 12.00

INVICTUS
- ST-9809 — I Gotta Get Home — 1973 — 15.00
- ST-7306 — The 8th Day — 1971 — 15.00

KAPP
- KS3554 — On the Eighth Day — 1968 — 18.00

EIRE APPARENT, THE

BUDDAH
- BDS-5031 [B] — Sunrise — 1969 — 50.00

EITHER/ORCHESTRA, THE

ACCURATE
- AC-2222 — Dial "E" for Either/Orchestra — 1987 — 15.00
- AC-3232 — Radium — 1989 — 15.00

Number	Title	Yr	NM

EL CAMPO JADES, THE

GOLD EAGLE
| LP-101 [M] | The El Campo Jades | 1966 | 50.00 |

EL CHICANO

KAPP
KS-3663	Celebration	1972	15.00
KS-3640	Revolucion	1971	15.00
KS-3632	Viva Tirado	1970	15.00

MCA
401	Cinco	1974	12.00
312	El Chicano	1973	12.00
2150	Pyramid of Love	1975	12.00
69	Revolucion	1973	12.00

—Reissue of Kapp 3640
| 437 | The Best of Everything | 1975 | 12.00 |
| 548 | Viva Tirado | 197? | 12.00 |

—Reissue of Kapp 3632

SHADY BROOK
| SB 33-005 | This Is El Chicano | 1977 | 18.00 |

EL DORADOS

LOST-NITE
| LLP-20 [10] | The El Dorados | 1981 | 15.00 |

—Red vinyl

SOLID SMOKE
| 8025 | Low Mileage/High Octane | 1984 | 12.00 |

VEE JAY
| LP-1001 [M] | Crazy Little Mama | 1959 | 800.00 |

—Maroon label, thick silver band
| LP-1001 [M] | Crazy Little Mama | 1960 | 400.00 |

—Maroon label, thin silver band
| LP-1001 [M] | Crazy Little Mama | 1962 | 250.00 |

—Black label with colorband
| VJLP-1001 [M] | Crazy Little Mama | 198? | 12.00 |

—Authorized reissue

ELASTICA

DGC
| 24728 | Elastica | 1995 | 12.00 |

GEFFEN
| B0020112-01 [B] | Elastica | 2014 | 30.00 |

ELBERT, DONNIE

ALL PLATINUM
| 3019 | Dancin' the Night Away | 1977 | 30.00 |
| 3007 | Where Did Our Love Go | 1971 | 30.00 |

DELUXE
| 12003 | Have I Sinned | 1971 | 30.00 |

KING
| 629 [M] | The Sensational Donnie Elbert Sings | 1959 | 400.00 |

SUGAR HILL
| 256 | From the Git Go | 1981 | 15.00 |

TRIP
| 9514 | Donnie Elbert Sings | 197? | 18.00 |
| 9524 | Stop in the Name of Love | 197? | 18.00 |

ELDRIDGE, ROY, AND BENNY CARTER

AMERICAN RECORDING SOCIETY
| G-413 [M] | The Urbane Jazz of Roy Eldridge and Benny Carter | 1957 | 40.00 |

VERVE
| MGV-8202 [M] | The Urbane Jazz of Roy Eldridge and Benny Carter | 1957 | 50.00 |
| V-8202 [M] | The Urbane Jazz of Roy Eldridge and Benny Carter | 1961 | 25.00 |

ELDRIDGE, ROY, AND DIZZY GILLESPIE

CLEF
MGC-641 [M]	Roy and Diz	1955	150.00
MGC-671 [M]	Roy and Diz, Volume 2	1955	150.00
MGC-731 [M]	The Trumpet Kings	1956	100.00
MGC-730 [M]	Trumpet Battle	1956	100.00

PABLO
| 2310816 | Jazz Maturity | 1977 | 18.00 |

VERVE
VSP-28 [M]	Soul Mates	1966	18.00
VSPS-28 [R]	Soul Mates	1966	15.00
MGV-8110 [M]	The Trumpet Kings	1957	50.00
V-8110 [M]	The Trumpet Kings	1961	25.00
MGV-8109 [M]	Trumpet Battle	1957	50.00
V-8109 [M]	Trumpet Battle	1961	25.00

ELDRIDGE, ROY; DIZZY GILLESPIE; HARRY "SWEETS" EDISON

VERVE
| MGV-8212 [M] | Tour de Force | 1958 | 50.00 |
| V-8212 [M] | Tour de Force | 1961 | 25.00 |

ELDRIDGE, ROY

AMERICAN RECORDING SOCIETY
| G-420 [M] | Swing Goes Dixie | 1956 | 40.00 |

CLEF
MGC-705 [M]	Dale's Wail	1956	100.00
MGC-683 [M]	Little Jazz	1956	100.00
MGC-704 [M]	Rockin' Chair	1956	100.00
MGC-113 [10]	Roy Eldridge Collates	1953	150.00
MGC-150 [10]	The Roy Eldridge Quintet	1954	150.00
MGC-162 [10]	The Strolling Mr. Eldridge	1954	150.00

COLUMBIA
| C238033 | Early Years | 1983 | 15.00 |

DIAL
| LP-304 [10] | Little Jazz Four: Trumpet Fantasy | 1953 | 400.00 |

DISCOVERY
| DL-2009 [10] | Roy Eldridge with Zoot Sims | 1954 | 120.00 |

EMARCY
| MG-36084 [M] | Roy's Got Rhythm | 1956 | 80.00 |

FANTASY
| OJC-628 | Happy Time | 1991 | 15.00 |
| OJC-373 | Montreux '77 | 1989 | 15.00 |

GNP CRESCENDO
| GNP-9009 | Roy Eldridge | 197? | 15.00 |

JAZZ ARCHIVES
| JA-14 | Arcadia Shuffle | 198? | 12.00 |

LONDON
| PB375 [10] | Roy Eldridge Quartet | 1954 | 120.00 |

MASTER JAZZ
| 8110 | The Nifty Cat | 1970 | 25.00 |
| 8121 | The Nifty Cat Strikes West | 197? | 25.00 |

MCA
| 1355 | All the Cats Join In | 198? | 12.00 |

MERCURY
| MGC-113 [10] | Roy Eldridge Collates | 1952 | 200.00 |

METRO
| M-513 [M] | Roy Eldridge | 1965 | 15.00 |
| MS-513 [R] | Roy Eldridge | 1965 | 12.00 |

PABLO
2310746	Happy Time	1975	18.00
2310869	Little Jazz	198?	15.00
2310928	Loose Walk	198?	12.00
2405413	The Best of Roy Eldridge	198?	12.00
2310766	What It's All About	1976	18.00

PABLO LIVE
| 2308203 | Montreux '77 | 1978 | 15.00 |

PRESTIGE
| PRLP-114 [10] | Roy Eldridge in Sweden | 1951 | 250.00 |

VERVE
| MGV-8089 [M] | Dale's Wail | 1957 | 50.00 |

—Reissue of Clef 705
V-8089 [M]	Dale's Wail	1961	25.00
VE-2-2531	Dale's Wail	198?	18.00
MGV-8068 [M]	Little Jazz	1957	50.00

—Reissue of Clef 683
| V-8068 [M] | Little Jazz | 1961 | 25.00 |
| MGV-8088 [M] | Rockin' Chair | 1957 | 50.00 |

—Reissue of Clef 704
| V-8088 [M] | Rockin' Chair | 1961 | 25.00 |
| UMV-2686 | Rockin' Chair | 198? | 12.00 |

MGV-1010 [M]	Swing Goes Dixie	1957	50.00
V-1010 [M]	Swing Goes Dixie	1961	25.00
MGV-8389 [M]	Swingin' on the Town	1960	50.00
V-8389 [M]	Swingin' on the Town	1961	25.00

XANADU
| 140 | Roy Eldridge at Jerry Newman's | 198? | 12.00 |

ELDRIDGE, ROY/SAMMY PRICE

BRUNSWICK
| BL58045 [10] | Battle of Jazz, Volume 7 | 1953 | 60.00 |

ELECTRAS, THE

ELECTRA
| ELT-201 | The Electras | 1961 | 450.00 |

ELECTRIC FLAG, THE

ATLANTIC
| SD18112 | The Band Kept Playing | 1974 | 12.00 |

COLUMBIA
| CS9597 [B] | A Long Time Comin' | 1968 | 25.00 |

—360 Sound" label
| CS9597 | A Long Time Comin' | 1970 | 12.00 |

—Orange label
| PC9597 | A Long Time Comin' | 198? | 10.00 |

—Budget-line reissue
| C30422 | The Best of the Electric Flag | 1971 | 12.00 |
| CS9714 | The Electric Flag | 1968 | 18.00 |

—360 Sound" label
| CS9714 | The Electric Flag | 1970 | 12.00 |

—Orange label

ELECTRIC INDIAN, THE

UNITED ARTISTS
| UAS6728 | Keem-O-Sabe | 1969 | 18.00 |

ELECTRIC LIGHT ORCHESTRA

CBS ASSOCIATED
| FZ40048 | Balance of Power | 1986 | 12.00 |

JET
Z4X36966	A Box of Their Best	1980	30.00
JZ35529	A New World Record	1978	12.00
PZ35529	A New World Record	1981	10.00
FZ35769	Discovery	1979	12.00
HZ45789	Discovery	1980	30.00

—Half-speed mastered edition
PZ35769	Discovery	1987	10.00
JZ35526	Eldorado	1978	12.00
PZ35526	Eldorado	198?	10.00
JZ35533	Electric Light Orchestra II	1978	12.00
PZ35533	Electric Light Orchestra II	1981	10.00
FZ36310	ELO's Greatest Hits	1979	12.00
PZ36310	ELO's Greatest Hits	1987	10.00
HZ36310	ELO's Greatest Hits	1981	40.00

—Half-speed mastered edition
JZ35527	Face the Music	1978	12.00
PZ35527 [B]	Face the Music	1981	10.00
JZ35524	No Answer	1978	12.00
PZ35524	No Answer	1981	10.00
JZ35528	Ole Elo	1978	12.00
PZ35528 [B]	Ole Elo	1981	10.00
JZ35525	On the Third Day	1978	12.00
PZ35525	On the Third Day	1981	10.00
JT-LA823-L2 [DJ]	Out of the Blue	1977	30.00

—Promo only on blue vinyl
| JT-LA823-L2 | Out of the Blue | 1977 | 18.00 |

—Originals include poster and die-cut cardboard "spaceship
KZ235530	Out of the Blue	1978	15.00
QZ38490	Secret Messages	1983	12.00
HZ48490	Secret Messages	1983	30.00

—Half-speed mastered edition
PZ38490	Secret Messages	1987	10.00
FZ37371	Time	1981	12.00
H747371	Time	1982	30.00

—Half-speed mastered edition
| PZ37371 | Time | 1987 | 10.00 |

UNITED ARTISTS
| UA-LA679-G | A New World Record | 1976 | 15.00 |

—All copies have custom labels
| UA-LA339-G | Eldorado | 1974 | 15.00 |

—Tan label
| UA-LA339-G | Eldorado | 1977 | 12.00 |

—Sunrise label
| UA-LA040-F | Electric Light Orchestra II | 1973 | 18.00 |

—Tan label
| UA-LA040-F | Electric Light Orchestra II | 1978 | 12.00 |

—Sunrise label
| UA-LA546-G | Face the Music | 1975 | 15.00 |

—Tan label
| UA-LA546-G | Face the Music | 1978 | 12.00 |

—Sunrise label
| UA-LA546-DJ [DJ] | Face the Music | 1975 | 30.00 |

—Promo only, banded for airplay
| UAS-5573 | No Answer | 1972 | 18.00 |

—Tan label
| UAS-5573 | No Answer | 1978 | 12.00 |

—Sunrise label
| SP-123 [DJ] | Ole Elo | 1976 | 100.00 |

—Gold vinyl, cover similar to the released version except for the single line "Ole Elo" (no "Electric Light Orchestra" underneath) at the top of the front cover
| SP-123 [DJ] | Ole Elo | 1976 | 80.00 |

—Red, blue or white vinyl promos with generic cover
| SP-123 [DJ] | Ole Elo | 1976 | 50.00 |

—Gold vinyl promo with generic cover
| UA-LA630-G | Ole Elo | 1976 | 15.00 |

—Tan label
| UA-LA630-G | Ole Elo | 1978 | 12.00 |

—Sunrise label
| UA-LA188-F | On the Third Day | 1973 | 18.00 |

—Tan label
| UA-LA188-F | On the Third Day | 1978 | 12.00 |

—Sunrise label

Number	Title	Yr	NM

WARNER BROS.

| ❏ K56058 | The Night the Light Went On in Long Beach | 1974 | 30.00 |

— Import otherwise unavailable in U.S.

ELECTRIC PRUNES, THE

REPRISE

❏ RS-6342	Just Good Rock 'n Roll	1969	30.00
❏ R-6275 [M]	Mass in F Minor	1967	100.00
❏ RS-6275 [S]	Mass in F Minor	1967	60.00
❏ RS-6316	Release of an Oath	1968	30.00
❏ R-6248 [M]	The Electric Prunes	1967	80.00
❏ RS-6248 [S]	The Electric Prunes	1967	60.00
❏ R-6262 [M]	Underground	1967	80.00
❏ RS-6262 [S]	Underground	1967	60.00

ELECTRIC TOILET, THE

NASCO

| ❏ 9004 | In the Hands of Karma | 1968 | 400.00 |

ELECTRIC UNDERGROUND, THE

PREMIER

| ❏ P-9060 [M] | Guitar Explosion | 1967 | 70.00 |
| ❏ PS-9060 [S] | Guitar Explosion | 1967 | 50.00 |

ELECTRONIC CONCEPT ORCHESTRA

LIMELIGHT

| ❏ 86072 | Electric Love | 1969 | 12.00 |
| ❏ 86070 | Moog Groove | 1969 | 12.00 |

MERCURY

| ❏ SR-61279 | Cinemoog | 1970 | 12.00 |

ELECTROSONICS, THE

PHILIPS

| ❏ PHM200047 [M] | Electronic Music | 1962 | 70.00 |
| ❏ PHS600047 [S] | Electronic Music | 1962 | 90.00 |

ELEGANTS, THE

MURRAY HILL

| ❏ 210 | Little Star | 1986 | 12.00 |

ELEMENTS

ANTILLES

| ❏ AN-1021 | Forward Motion | 198? | 12.00 |
| ❏ AN-1017 | The Elements | 198? | 12.00 |

— Reissue of Philo album

NOVUS

| ❏ 3031-1-N | Illumination | 1988 | 12.00 |
| ❏ 3058-1-N | Liberal Arts | 1989 | 15.00 |

PHILO

| ❏ 9011 | The Elements | 198? | 18.00 |

ELEPHANTS MEMORY

APPLE

| ❏ SMAS-3389 [B] | Elephants Memory | 1972 | 35.00 |

BUDDAH

| ❏ BDS-5033 | Elephants Memory | 1969 | 18.00 |
| ❏ BDS-5038 | Songs from Midnight Cowboy | 1970 | 18.00 |

METROMEDIA

| ❏ MD-1035 | Take It to the Streets | 1970 | 25.00 |

RCA VICTOR

| ❏ APL1-0569 | Angela Forever | 1974 | 18.00 |

ELEVENTH HOUR, THE

20TH CENTURY

| ❏ T-435 | Greatest Hits | 1974 | 15.00 |
| ❏ T-511 | Hollywood Hot | 1975 | 18.00 |

ELEVENTH HOUSE, THE (WITH LARRY CORYELL)

ARISTA

| ❏ AL4077 | Aspects | 1976 | 12.00 |
| ❏ AL4052 | Level One | 1975 | 12.00 |

VANGUARD

| ❏ VSQ-40036 [Q] | Introducing the Eleventh House with Larry Coryell | 1974 | 30.00 |
| ❏ VSD-79342 | Introducing the Eleventh House with Larry Coryell | 1974 | 15.00 |

ELF

EPIC

| ❏ KE31789 | Elf | 1972 | 30.00 |

— Yellow label

| ❏ KE31789 | Elf | 1973 | 25.00 |

— Orange label

MGM

| ❏ M3G4974 | L.A. 59 | 1974 | 25.00 |
| ❏ M3G4994 | Trying to Burn the Sun | 1975 | 25.00 |

ELFMAN, DANNY

MCA

| ❏ 5535 | So-Lo | 1984 | 12.00 |

Number	Title	Yr	NM

ELGART, BILL

MARK LEVINSON

| ❏ 3 | A Life | 1980 | 30.00 |

ELGART, CHARLIE

NOVUS

| ❏ 3068-1-N | Balance | 1989 | 15.00 |
| ❏ 3045-1-N | Signs of Life | 1988 | 12.00 |

ELGART, LARRY

BRUNSWICK

| ❏ BL58054 [10] | Impressions of Outer Space | 1954 | 60.00 |

DECCA

| ❏ DL8034 [M] | Music for Barefoot Ballerinas | 1955 | 40.00 |
| ❏ DL5526 [10] | The Larry Elgart Band with Strings | 1954 | 100.00 |

MGM

❏ E-4080 [M]	More Music in Motion!	1962	18.00
❏ SE-4080 [S]	More Music in Motion!	1962	25.00
❏ E-4028 [M]	Music in Motion!	1962	18.00
❏ SE-4028 [S]	Music in Motion!	1962	25.00
❏ E-3891 [M]	Sophisticated Sixties	1960	18.00
❏ SE-3891 [S]	Sophisticated Sixties	1960	25.00
❏ E-4007 [M]	The City	1961	18.00
❏ SE-4007 [S]	The City	1961	25.00
❏ E-3896 [M]	The Shape of Sounds to Come	1961	18.00
❏ SE-3896 [S]	The Shape of Sounds to Come	1961	25.00
❏ E-3961 [M]	Visions	1961	18.00
❏ SE-3961 [S]	Visions	1961	25.00

PROJECT 3

| ❏ PR5102 | The Larry Elgart Dance Band | 1979 | 12.00 |

RCA CAMDEN

❏ CAL-575 [M]	Easy Goin' Swing	1960	15.00
❏ CAS-575 [S]	Easy Goin' Swing	1960	18.00
❏ CXS-9036	That Old Feeling	1972	15.00

RCA VICTOR

❏ AFL1-4095	Flight of the Condor	1981	12.00
❏ AFL1-4343	Hooked on Swing	1982	12.00
❏ AYL1-5025	Hooked on Swing	1984	10.00

— Budget-line reissue

| ❏ AFL1-4589 | Hooked on Swing, Volume 2 | 1983 | 12.00 |
| ❏ AYL1-5026 | Hooked on Swing, Volume 2 | 1984 | 10.00 |

— Budget-line reissue

❏ AFL1-4850	Larry Elgart and His Manhattan Swing Orchestra	1984	12.00
❏ LPM-1961 [M]	Larry Elgart and His Orchestra	1959	18.00
❏ LSP-1961 [S]	Larry Elgart and His Orchestra	1959	25.00
❏ LPM-2045 [M]	New Sounds at the Roosevelt	1959	18.00
❏ LSP-2045 [S]	New Sounds at the Roosevelt	1959	25.00
❏ LPM-2166 [M]	Saratoga	1960	18.00
❏ LSP-2166 [S]	Saratoga	1960	25.00
❏ AYL1-7178	(The Theme from) La Cage Aux Folles	1986	10.00

ELGART, LES

CIRCLE

| ❏ CLP-126 | Les Elgart and His Orchestra | 198? | 12.00 |

COLUMBIA

❏ CS8690 [S]	Best Band on Campus	1963	30.00
❏ CL1890 [M]	Best Band on Campus	1963	25.00
❏ CL2578 [10]	Campus Hop	1955	40.00
❏ CL1500 [M]	Designs for Dancing	1960	25.00
❏ CS8291 [S]	Designs for Dancing	1960	30.00
❏ CL1008 [M]	For Dancers Also	1957	30.00
❏ CL803 [M]	For Dancers Only	1956	30.00
❏ CL1567 [M]	Half Satin - Half Latin	1961	25.00
❏ CS8367 [S]	Half Satin - Half Latin	1961	30.00
❏ CL1659 [M]	It's De-Lovely	1961	25.00
❏ CS8459 [S]	It's De-Lovely	1961	30.00
❏ CL6287 [10]	Just One More Dance	195?	40.00
❏ CL594 [M]	Just One More Dance	1954	30.00

— Maroon label, gold print

| ❏ CL594 [M] | Just One More Dance | 1955 | 25.00 |

— Red and black label with six "eye" logos

❏ CL1052 [M]	Les and Larry Elgart and Their Orchestra	1957	25.00
❏ CS8092 [S]	Les and Larry Elgart and Their Orchestra	1959	30.00
❏ CL1291 [M]	Les Elgart On Tour	1959	25.00
❏ CS8103 [S]	Les Elgart On Tour	1959	30.00
❏ CL2590 [10]	More of Les	1955	40.00
❏ CL2503 [10]	Prom Date	1954	40.00
❏ CL536 [M]	Sophisticated Swing	1953	30.00

— Maroon label, gold print

| ❏ CS8002 [S] | Sound Ideas | 1958 | 30.00 |
| ❏ CL619 [M] | The Band of the Year | 1955 | 40.00 |

— Maroon label, gold print; first LP appearance of "Bandstand Boogie"

❏ CS8245 [S]	The Band with That Sound	1960	30.00
❏ CL1450 [M]	The Band with That Sound	1960	25.00
❏ CL684 [M]	The Dancing Sound	1955	30.00
❏ CL875 [M]	The Elgart Touch	1956	30.00

— Red and black label, six "eye" logos

| ❏ CL1350 [M] | The Great Sound of Les Elgart | 1959 | 25.00 |

Number	Title	Yr	NM

❏ CS8159 [S]	The Great Sound of Les Elgart	1959	30.00
❏ CS8585 [S]	The Twist Goes to College	1962	30.00
❏ CL1785 [M]	The Twist Goes to College	1962	25.00

COLUMBIA SPECIAL PRODUCTS

| ❏ P13168 | The Greatest Dance Band in the Land | 197? | 12.00 |

HARMONY

| ❏ HL7374 [M] | The Greatest Dance Band in the Land | 196? | 15.00 |
| ❏ HS11174 [R] | The Greatest Dance Band in the Land | 196? | 12.00 |

SUTTON

| ❏ SU283 [M] | Les Elgart and Blazing Brass | 196? | 12.00 |

ELGART, LES AND LARRY

COLUMBIA

❏ CL2112 [M]	Big Band Hootenanny	1963	18.00
❏ CS8912 [S]	Big Band Hootenanny	1963	25.00
❏ CL2221 [M]	Command Performance! Les & Larry Elgart Play the Great Dance Hits	1964	18.00
❏ CS9021 [S]	Command Performance! Les & Larry Elgart Play the Great Dance Hits	1964	25.00
❏ CL2355 [M]	Elgart Au-Go-Go	1965	18.00
❏ CS9155 [S]	Elgart Au-Go-Go	1965	25.00
❏ CL2633 [M]	Girl Watchers	1967	25.00
❏ CS9433 [S]	Girl Watchers	1967	18.00
❏ CS9722	Les & Larry Elgart's Greatest Hits	1968	18.00
❏ CL1123 [M]	Sound Ideas	1958	25.00
❏ CL2511 [M]	Sound of the Times	1966	18.00
❏ CS9311 [S]	Sound of the Times	1966	25.00
❏ PC38341	Swingtime	1982	12.00
❏ CL2301 [M]	The New Elgart Touch	1965	18.00
❏ CS9101 [S]	The New Elgart Touch	1965	25.00
❏ CL2780 [M]	The Wonderful World of Today's Hits	1968	30.00
❏ CS9580 [S]	The Wonderful World of Today's Hits	1968	18.00
❏ CL2591 [M]	Warm and Sensuous	1966	18.00
❏ CS9391 [S]	Warm and Sensuous	1966	25.00

HARMONY

| ❏ KH32053 | Wonderful World | 1972 | 12.00 |

SWAMPFIRE

❏ 207	Bridge Over Troubled Water	1971	15.00
❏ 202	Nashville Country Brass	196?	15.00
❏ 203	Nashville Country Guitars	196?	15.00
❏ 201	Nashville Country Piano	196?	15.00

ELGINS, THE (1)

V.I.P.

| ❏ 400 [M] | Darling Baby | 1966 | 70.00 |
| ❏ S-400 [S] | Darling Baby | 1966 | 100.00 |

ELIAS, ELIANE

BLUE NOTE

❏ B1-48785	Cross Currents	1988	12.00
❏ BST-46994	Illusions	1987	12.00
❏ B1-91411	So Far So Close	1989	15.00

ELIAS, ROSALIND, AND GIORGIO TOZZI

RCA VICTOR RED SEAL

| ❏ LSC-2350 [S] | A Yuletide Song Fest | 1959 | 40.00 |

— Original with "shaded dog" label

ELIGIBLES, THE

CAPITOL

❏ T1310 [M]	Along the Trail	1960	30.00
❏ ST1310 [S]	Along the Trail	1960	30.00
❏ T1411 [M]	Love Is a Gamble	1960	30.00
❏ ST1411 [S]	Love Is a Gamble	1960	30.00

ELIMINATORS, THE

LIBERTY

| ❏ LRP-3365 [M] | Liverpool! Dragsters! Cycles! Surfing! | 1964 | 80.00 |
| ❏ LST-7365 [S] | Liverpool! Dragsters! Cycles! Surfing! | 1964 | 100.00 |

ELIOVSON, STEVE

ECM

| ❏ 1198 | Dawn Dance | 198? | 12.00 |

ELIZABETH

VANGUARD

| ❏ VSD-6501 | Elizabeth | 1968 | 75.00 |

— Gold label

ELLIAS, RODDY

INNER CITY

| ❏ IC-1081 | A Night for Stars | 1980 | 12.00 |

ELLIE POP

MAINSTREAM

| ❏ S-6115 | Ellie Pop | 1968 | 125.00 |

Number	Title	Yr	NM

ELLIMAN, YVONNE

DECCA
| ☐ DL75341 | Yvonne Elliman | 1972 | 18.00 |

MCA
| ☐ 356 | Food of Love | 1973 | 15.00 |

RSO
☐ RS-1-3018	Love Me	1977	12.00
☐ RS-1-3031	Night Flight	1978	12.00
☐ RS-1-3038	Yvonne	1979	12.00

ELLINGSON, PAUL

IVY JAZZ
| ☐ IJ-1-E-1-2 | Solo Piano Jazz | 198? | 18.00 |

ELLINGTON, DUKE, ORCHESTRA (MERCER ELLINGTON, DIRECTOR)

DOCTOR JAZZ
| ☐ FW40029 | Hot and Bothered: A Re-Creation | 1986 | 12.00 |
| ☐ FW40359 | New Mood Indigo | 1987 | 12.00 |

FANTASY
| ☐ F-9481 | Continuum | 1975 | 15.00 |

GRP
| ☐ GR-1038 | Digital Duke | 1987 | 12.00 |

HOLIDAY
| ☐ HDY1916 | Take the Holiday Train | 1980 | 10.00 |

ELLINGTON, DUKE

AAMCO
☐ ALP-301 [M]	The Royal Concert of Duke Ellington, Vol. 1	196?	30.00
— Reissue of Bethlehem material			
☐ ALP-313 [M]	The Royal Concert of Duke Ellington, Vol. 2	196?	30.00
— Reissue of Bethlehem material			

ABC IMPULSE!
☐ 9285	Ellingtonia, Volume 2	1974	18.00
☐ 9256	Ellingtonia: Reevaluations, The Impulse Years	1973	18.00
☐ IA-9350	Great Tenor Encounters	1978	18.00

AIRCHECK
| ☐ 4 | Duke on the Air | 197? | 12.00 |
| ☐ 29 | Duke on the Air, Vol. 2 | 198? | 12.00 |

ALLEGRO
☐ 3082 [M]	Duke Ellington	1953	50.00
☐ 1591 [M]	Duke Ellington and His Orchestra Play	1955	50.00
☐ 4014 [10]	Duke Ellington and His Orchestra Play	1954	100.00
☐ 4038 [10]	Duke Ellington and His Orchestra Play	1954	100.00

ATLANTIC
☐ SD1688	Jazz Violin Session	1976	15.00
☐ SD1500	New Orleans Suite	1971	15.00
☐ QD1580 [Q]	New Orleans Suite	1974	30.00
☐ SD1665	Recollections of the Big Band Era	1974	15.00
☐ 90043	Recollections of the Big Band Era	1982	12.00
☐ SD 2-304	The Great Paris Concert	1972	18.00

BASF
| ☐ 21704 | Collages | 1973 | 15.00 |

BETHLEHEM
☐ BCP-6005 [M]	Duke Ellington Presents	1956	60.00
☐ BCP-60 [M]	Historically Speaking, The Duke	1956	60.00
☐ 6013	The Bethlehem Years, Vol. 1	197?	12.00

BIOGRAPH
| ☐ M-2 | Band Shorts (1929-1935) | 1978 | 12.00 |

BLUEBIRD
☐ 6287-1-RB	And His Mother Called Him Bill	1987	10.00
— Reissue of RCA Victor 3906			
☐ 6641-1-RB	Black, Brown and Beige	1988	30.00
☐ 5659-1-RB	Duke Ellington: The Blanton-Webster Band	1986	30.00
☐ 6852-1-RB	Early Ellington	1989	12.00

BLUE NOTE
| ☐ BT-85129 | Money Jungle | 1986 | 12.00 |
| — Reissue of United Artists 15017 | | | |

BOOK-OF-THE-MONTH
| ☐ 30-5622 | At Fargo, 1940 | 1978 | 25.00 |

BRIGHT ORANGE
| ☐ 709 | The Stereophonic Sound of Duke Ellington | 1973 | 15.00 |

BRUNSWICK
☐ BL54007 [M]	Early Ellington	1954	50.00
☐ BL58002 [10]	Ellingtonia, Volume 1	1950	100.00
☐ BL58012 [10]	Ellingtonia, Volume 2	1950	100.00

BULLDOG
| ☐ BDL-2021 | 20 Golden Pieces of Duke Ellington | 198? | 12.00 |

CAPITOL
☐ T637 [M]	Dance to the Duke	1955	40.00
— Turquoise label			
☐ T637 [M]	Dance to the Duke	1958	25.00

Number	Title	Yr	NM
— Black label with colorband, logo at left			
☐ T521 [M]	Ellington '55	1955	40.00
— Turquoise label			
☐ T521 [M]	Ellington '55	1958	25.00
— Black label with colorband, logo at left			
☐ M-11674	Ellington '55	1977	12.00
☐ T679 [M]	Ellington Showcase	1956	40.00
— Turquoise label			
☐ T679 [M]	Ellington Showcase	1958	25.00
— Black label with colorband, logo at left			
☐ M-11058	Piano Reflections	1972	15.00
☐ H440 [10]	Premiered by Ellington	1953	100.00
☐ T1602 [M]	The Best of Duke Ellington	1961	25.00
☐ DT1602 [R]	The Best of Duke Ellington	1961	15.00
☐ SM-1602	The Best of Duke Ellington	197?	12.00
— Reissue with new prefix			
☐ N-16172	The Best of Duke Ellington	198?	10.00
— Budget-line reissue			
☐ H477 [10]	The Duke Plays Ellington	1954	100.00
☐ T477 [M]	The Duke Plays Ellington	1954	40.00
— Turquoise label			
☐ T477 [M]	The Duke Plays Ellington	1958	25.00
— Black label with colorband, logo at left			

CIRCLE
☐ CLP-101	Duke Ellington World Broadcasting Series, Vol. 1	1986	12.00
☐ CLP-102	Duke Ellington World Broadcasting Series, Vol. 2	1986	12.00
☐ CLP-103	Duke Ellington World Broadcasting Series, Vol. 3	1986	12.00
☐ CLP-104	Duke Ellington World Broadcasting Series, Vol. 4	199?	12.00
☐ CLP-105	Duke Ellington World Broadcasting Series, Vol. 5 (1943)	199?	12.00
☐ CLP-106	Duke Ellington World Broadcasting Series, Vol. 6 (1945)	1988	12.00
☐ CLP-108	Duke Ellington World Broadcasting Series, Vol. 8 (1945)	1988	12.00
☐ CLP-109	Duke Ellington World Broadcasting Series, Vol. 9 (1945)	1988	12.00

COLUMBIA
☐ CL951 [M]	A Drum Is a Woman	1957	40.00
☐ CL2593 [10]	Al Hibbler with the Duke	1956	80.00
☐ CL1790 [M]	All American	1962	25.00
☐ CS8590 [S]	All American	1962	30.00
☐ CL663 [M]	Blue Light	1955	40.00
☐ CL1445 [M]	Blues in Orbit	1960	30.00
☐ CS8241 [S]	Blues in Orbit	1960	30.00
☐ CL1162 [M]	Brown, Black and Beige	1958	30.00
☐ CS8015 [S]	Brown, Black and Beige	1958	30.00
☐ CL1282 [M]	Duke Ellington at the Bal Masque	1959	30.00
☐ CS8098 [S]	Duke Ellington at the Bal Masque	1959	30.00
☐ CL1323 [M]	Duke Ellington Jazz Party	1959	30.00
☐ CS8127 [S]	Duke Ellington Jazz Party	1959	30.00
☐ KC32064	Duke Ellington Presents Ivie Anderson	1973	18.00
☐ CS9629	Duke Ellington's Greatest Hits	1960	18.00
☐ CL2522 [10]	Duke's Mixture	1955	80.00
☐ CS8648 [R]	Ellington at Newport	1963	15.00
☐ PC8648	Ellington at Newport	198?	10.00
— Budget-line reissue			
☐ CL934 [M]	Ellington at Newport '56	1957	40.00
— Red and black label with six "eye" logos			
☐ CL934 [M]	Ellington at Newport '56	1963	18.00
— Red label with "Guaranteed High Fidelity" or "360 Sound Mono"			
☐ CL1085 [M]	Ellington Indigos	1958	30.00
☐ CS8053 [S]	Ellington Indigos	1958	30.00
— Red and black label with six "eye" logos			
☐ CL1085 [M]	Ellington Indigos	1963	18.00
— Red label with "Guaranteed High Fidelity" or "360 Sound Mono"			
☐ CS8053 [S]	Ellington Indigos	1963	18.00
— Red label with "360 Sound Stereo"			
☐ PC8053	Ellington Indigos	198?	10.00
— Budget-line reissue			
☐ CL1400 [M]	Festival Session	1960	30.00
☐ CL1715 [M]	First Time	1962	30.00
☐ CS8515 [S]	First Time	1962	30.00
☐ CL2562 [10]	Here's the Duke	1955	80.00
☐ CL830 [M]	Hi-Fi Ellington Uptown	1956	40.00
☐ CL830 [M]	Hi-Fi Ellington Uptown	1963	18.00
— Red label with "Guaranteed High Fidelity" or "360 Sound Mono"			
☐ PC37340	It Don't Mean a Thing	1981	10.00
— Reissue			
☐ C32471	Jazz at the Plaza -- Vol. II	1973	15.00
☐ CL6073 [10]	Liberian Suite	1949	100.00
☐ CL848 [M]	Liberian Suite	1956	40.00
— Reissue of Columbia 6073			
☐ CL825 [M]	Masterpieces by Ellington	1956	40.00
— Reissue of Columbia Masterworks 4418			
☐ CL825 [M]	Masterpieces by Ellington	1963	18.00
— Red label with "Guaranteed High Fidelity" or "360 Sound Mono"			
☐ CL1907 [M]	Midnight in Paris	1963	25.00
☐ CS8829 [S]	Midnight in Paris	1963	30.00
☐ CL6024 [10]	Mood Ellington	1949	100.00

Number	Title	Yr	NM
☐ CL1245 [M]	Newport 1958	1959	30.00
☐ CS8072 [S]	Newport 1958	1959	30.00
☐ CL1597 [M]	Peer Gynt Suite/Suite Thursday	1961	30.00
☐ CS8397 [S]	Peer Gynt Suite/Suite Thursday	1961	30.00
☐ CL1546 [M]	Piano in the Background	1960	30.00
☐ CS8346 [S]	Piano in the Background	1960	40.00
☐ CL1546 [M]	Piano in the Background	1963	18.00
— Red label with "Guaranteed High Fidelity" or "360 Sound Mono"			
☐ CS8346 [S]	Piano in the Background	1963	18.00
— Red label with "360 Sound Stereo"			
☐ CL1033 [M]	Such Sweet Thunder	1957	40.00
☐ CL1198 [M]	The Cosmic Scene	1959	80.00
☐ C3L27 [M]	The Ellington Era, Vol. 1	1963	40.00
☐ C3L39 [M]	The Ellington Era, Vol. 2	1964	40.00
☐ FC38028	The Girl's Suite & Perfume Suite	1982	12.00
☐ CL558 [M]	The Music of Duke Ellington	1954	50.00
— Maroon label with gold print			
☐ CL558 [M]	The Music of Duke Ellington	1956	40.00
— Red and black label with six "eye" logos			
☐ CL558 [M]	The Music of Duke Ellington	1963	18.00
— Red label with "Guaranteed High Fidelity" or "360 Sound Mono"			
☐ CL1541 [M]	The Nutcracker Suite	1960	30.00
☐ CS8341 [S]	The Nutcracker Suite	1960	40.00
☐ G32564	The World of Duke Ellington	1974	18.00
☐ KG33341	The World of Duke Ellington, Volume 2	1975	18.00
☐ CG33961	The World of Duke Ellington, Volume 3	1975	18.00

COLUMBIA JAZZ MASTERPIECES
☐ CJ44051	Blues in Orbit	1988	12.00
— Reissue of Columbia 8241			
☐ CJ40712	Duke Ellington Jazz Party	1987	12.00
— Reissue of Columbia 8127			
☐ CJ40587	Ellington at Newport	1987	12.00
— Reissue of Columbia 934			
☐ CJ44444	Ellington Indigos	1989	12.00
— Reissue of Columbia 8053			
☐ CJ40586	First Time	1987	12.00
— Reissue of Columbia 8515			
☐ CJ40836	Uptown	1987	12.00

COLUMBIA JAZZ ODYSSEY
| ☐ PC36979 | The Festival Session | 1981 | 12.00 |

COLUMBIA MASTERWORKS
☐ ML4639 [M]	Ellington Uptown	1951	100.00
— Blue or green label, gold print			
☐ ML4639 [M]	Ellington Uptown	195?	50.00
— Oddly, this exists as a reissue on the red and black "6 eye" label			
☐ ML4418 [M]	Masterpieces by Ellington	1951	100.00

COLUMBIA SPECIAL PRODUCTS
☐ P13291	Duke Ellington's Greatest Hits (Recorded Live in Concert)	1976	12.00
☐ P13500	Festival Session	1976	12.00
☐ P14359	Suite Thursday/Controversial Suite/Harlem Suite	198?	12.00

DAYBREAK
| ☐ DR2017 | The Symphonic Ellington | 1973 | 15.00 |

DECCA
☐ DL9224 [M]	Duke Ellington, Volume 1 -- In the Beginning	1958	40.00
— Black label, silver print			
☐ DL9224 [M]	Duke Ellington, Volume 1 -- In the Beginning	1961	30.00
— Black label with color bars			
☐ DL79224 [R]	Duke Ellington, Volume 1 -- In the Beginning	1958	30.00
— Black label, silver print			
☐ DL79224 [R]	Duke Ellington, Volume 1 -- In the Beginning	1961	18.00
— Black label with color bars			
☐ DL9241 [M]	Duke Ellington, Volume 2 -- Hot in Harlem	1959	40.00
— Black label, silver print			
☐ DL9241 [M]	Duke Ellington, Volume 2 -- Hot in Harlem	1961	30.00
— Black label with color bars			
☐ DL79241 [R]	Duke Ellington, Volume 2 -- Hot in Harlem	1959	30.00
— Black label, silver print			
☐ DL79241 [R]	Duke Ellington, Volume 2 -- Hot in Harlem	1961	18.00
— Black label with color bars			
☐ DL9247 [M]	Duke Ellington, Volume 3 -- Rockin' in Rhythm	1959	40.00
— Black label, silver print			
☐ DL9247 [M]	Duke Ellington, Volume 3 -- Rockin' in Rhythm	1961	30.00
— Black label with color bars			
☐ DL79247 [R]	Duke Ellington, Volume 3 -- Rockin' in Rhythm	1959	30.00
— Black label, silver print			
☐ DL79247 [R]	Duke Ellington, Volume 3 -- Rockin' in Rhythm	1961	18.00
— Black label with color bars			
☐ DL75069	Duke Ellington in Canada	1969	18.00

Number	Title	Yr	NM
DISCOVERY			
❏ 871	Afro Bossa	198?	12.00
— Reissue of Reprise 6069			
❏ 841	Concert in the Virgin Islands	198?	12.00
— Reissue of Reprise 6185			
DOCTOR JAZZ			
❏ W2X39137	All-Star Road Band	1984	15.00
❏ W2X40012	All-Star Road Band, Vol. 2	1985	15.00
❏ FW40030	Happy Reunion	1985	12.00
❏ FW40359	New Mood Indigo	1986	12.00
DO YOU LIKE JAZZ			
❏ P13293	Monologue	1973	15.00
EVEREST ARCHIVE OF FOLK & JAZZ			
❏ 327	Duke Ellington at Carnegie Hall	197?	15.00
❏ 221	Early Duke Ellington	1968	15.00
❏ 249	Early Duke Ellington Vol. 2	1970	15.00
❏ 266	Early Duke Ellington Vol. 3	1972	15.00
FANTASY			
❏ F-9498	Afro-American Eclipse	1976	15.00
❏ F-9636	Duke Ellington Featuring Paul Gonsalves	198?	12.00
❏ OJC-623	Duke Ellington Featuring Paul Gonsalves	1991	15.00
— Reissue of 9636			
❏ F-8407/8	Duke Ellington's Second Sacred Concert	1971	18.00
❏ OJC-108	Great Times!	198?	12.00
— Reissue of Riverside 9475			
❏ F-8419	Latin American Suite	1971	15.00
❏ OJC-469	Latin American Suite	1990	12.00
— Reissue of 8419			
❏ OJC-645	The Afro-Eurasian Eclipse	1991	15.00
— Reissue of 9498			
❏ OJC-446	The Ellington Suites	1990	12.00
— Reissue of Pablo 2310 762			
❏ F-9640	The Intimacy of the Blues	1986	12.00
❏ OJC-624	The Intimacy of the Blues	1991	15.00
— Reissue of 9640			
❏ F-9462	The Pianist	1974	15.00
❏ OJC-633	Up in Duke's Workshop	1991	15.00
— Reissue of Pablo 2310 815			
❏ F-9433	Yale Concert	1974	15.00
FLYING DUTCHMAN			
❏ 10166	It Don't Mean a Thing	1973	15.00
❏ BXL1-2832	It Don't Mean a Thing	1978	12.00
— Reissue			
❏ 10112	My People	1969	18.00
FOLKWAYS			
❏ FJ-2968	First Annual Tourn of the Pacific Northwest, Spring, 1952	198?	12.00
GALAXY			
❏ 4807	Duke Ellington and His Famous Orchestra and Soloists	197?	18.00
GNP CRESCENDO			
❏ GNP-9045	The 1953 Pasadena Concert	1986	12.00
❏ GNP-9049	The 1954 Los Angeles Concert	1987	12.00
HALL OF FAME			
❏ 625/6/7	The Immortal Duke Ellington	197?	25.00
HARMONY			
❏ H30566	Duke Ellington's Greatest Hits Live	1971	15.00
❏ HL7436 [M]	Fantasies	1967	18.00
❏ HS11236 [R]	Fantasies	1967	15.00
❏ HS11323	In My Solitude	1969	15.00
HINDSIGHT			
❏ HSR-125	Duke Ellington 1946	198?	12.00
❏ HSR-126	Duke Ellington 1946, Volume 2	198?	12.00
❏ HSR-127	Duke Ellington 1946, Volume 3	198?	12.00
❏ HSR-128	Duke Ellington 1947	198?	12.00
❏ HSR-129	Duke Ellington 1947, Volume 2	198?	12.00
IAJRC			
❏ LP-45	Fairfield, Connecticut Jazz Fest 1956	198?	10.00
INTERMEDIA			
❏ QS-5021	Do Nothin' Till You Hear from Me	198?	12.00
❏ QS-5020	Lullaby of Birdland	198?	12.00
❏ QS-5063	Satin Doll	198?	12.00
❏ QS-5002	Sophisticated Duke	198?	12.00
JAZZBIRD			
❏ 2009	Meadowbrook to Manhattan	1980	12.00
JAZZ ODYSSEY			
❏ 32160252	Nutcracker and Peer Gynt Suites	196?	15.00
JAZZ PANORAMA			
❏ 1802 [10]	Duke Ellington -- Vol. 1	1951	100.00
❏ 1811 [10]	Duke Ellington -- Vol. 2	1951	100.00
❏ 1816 [10]	Duke Ellington -- Vol. 3	1951	100.00
LONDON			
❏ AL-3551 [10]	The Duke -- 1926	195?	100.00

Number	Title	Yr	NM
MCA			
❏ 1374	Brunswick-Vocalion Rarities	198?	12.00
❏ 2075	Duke Ellington, Volume 1 -- In the Beginning	197?	12.00
— Reissue of Decca 79224			
❏ 1358	Duke Ellington, Volume 1 -- In the Beginning	198?	10.00
— Reissue of 2075			
❏ 2076	Duke Ellington, Volume 2 -- Hot in Harlem	197?	12.00
— Reissue of Decca 79241			
❏ 1359	Duke Ellington, Volume 2 -- Hot in Harlem	198?	10.00
— Reissue of 2076			
❏ 2077	Duke Ellington, Volume 3 -- Rockin' in Rhythm	197?	12.00
— Reissue of Decca 79247			
❏ 1360	Duke Ellington, Volume 3 -- Rockin' in Rhythm	198?	10.00
— Reissue of 2077			
❏ 4142	Great Tenor Encounters	198?	15.00
— Reissue of Impulse! 9350			
❏ 42325	The Brunswick Era, Vol. 1	1990	15.00
MOBILE FIDELITY			
❏ 1-214	Anatomy of a Murder	1995	40.00
— Audiophile vinyl			
MOSAIC			
❏ MQ8-160	The Complete Capitol Recordings of Duke Ellington	199?	150.00
MUSICRAFT			
❏ 2002	Carnegie Hall Concert	1986	12.00
PABLO			
❏ 2310703	Duke's Big 4	1974	15.00
❏ 2310787	Intimate	197?	15.00
❏ 2405401	The Best of Duke Ellington	198?	12.00
❏ 2310762	The Ellington Suites	197?	15.00
❏ 2310721	This One's for Blanton	197?	15.00
❏ 2310815	Up in Duke's Workshop	1980	12.00
PABLO LIVE			
❏ 2308245	Harlem	198?	12.00
❏ 2308247	In the Uncommon Market	198?	12.00
PAIR			
❏ PDL2-1011	Original Recordings by Duke Ellington	1986	15.00
PICCADILLY			
❏ 3524	Classic Ellington	198?	12.00
PICKWICK			
❏ SPC-3390	We Love You Madly	197?	12.00
PRESTIGE			
❏ 24045	Duke Ellington's Second Sacred Concert	1974	15.00
— Reissue of Fantasy 8407/8			
❏ 24073	The Carnegie Hall Concerts: December 1944	1977	18.00
❏ 24075	The Carnegie Hall Concerts: December 1947	1977	18.00
❏ 34003	The Carnegie Hall Concerts: January 1943	197?	25.00
❏ 24074	The Carnegie Hall Concerts: January 1946	1977	18.00
❏ 24029	The Golden Duke	1973	18.00
RCA CAMDEN			
❏ CAL-394 [M]	Duke Ellington at Tanglewood	1958	25.00
❏ CAL-459 [M]	Duke Ellington at the Cotton Club	1959	25.00
❏ ACL2-0152	Mood Indigo	1973	18.00
❏ ACL-7052	The Duke at Tanglewood	197?	12.00
— Reissue of RCA Red Seal LSC-2857			
RCA VICTOR			
❏ LPM-3906 [M]	And His Mother Called Him Bill	1968	50.00
❏ LSP-3906 [S]	And His Mother Called Him Bill	1968	18.00
❏ LPM-3582 [M]	Concert of Sacred Music	1966	18.00
❏ LSP-3582 [S]	Concert of Sacred Music	1966	25.00
❏ LPV-506 [M]	Daybreak Express	1964	25.00
❏ LPM-1092 [M]	Duke and His Men	1955	40.00
❏ WPT-11 [10]	Duke Ellington	1951	100.00
❏ LPM-1715 [M]	Duke Ellington at His Very Best	1958	40.00
❏ LPT-3067 [10]	Duke Ellington Plays the Blues	1952	100.00
❏ APL1-1023	Eastbourne Performance	1974	15.00
❏ LPT-1004 [M]	Ellington's Greatest	1954	40.00
❏ LPM-3782 [M]	Far East Suite	1967	30.00
❏ LSP-3782 [S]	Far East Suite	1967	18.00
❏ LPV-568 [M]	Flaming Youth	1969	25.00
❏ LPM-1364 [M]	In a Mellotone	1957	40.00
— Black label, dog at top, "Long Play" at bottom			
❏ LPM-1364 [M]	In a Mellotone	196?	30.00
— Black label, dog at top, "Mono" at bottom			
❏ LPM-1364 [M]	In a Mellotone	1969	25.00
— Orange label			
❏ LPV-541 [M]	Johnny Come Lately	1967	25.00
❏ LPV-517 [M]	Jumpin' Punkins	1965	25.00
❏ LPV-553 [M]	Pretty Woman	1968	25.00
❏ ANL1-2811	Pure Gold	1978	12.00
❏ LJM-1002 [M]	Seattle Concert	1954	50.00
❏ CPL2-4098	Sophisticated Ellington	1983	15.00
❏ SP-33-394 [M]	The Duke at Tanglewood	1966	30.00

Number	Title	Yr	NM
— Special Interview Recording for Radio Station Programming			
❏ LPM-6009 [M]	The Indispensible Duke Ellington	1961	50.00
❏ LPM-3576 [M]	The Popular Duke Ellington	1966	18.00
❏ LSP-3576 [S]	The Popular Duke Ellington	1966	25.00
❏ VPM-6042	This Is Duke Ellington	1972	18.00
❏ LPT-3017 [10]	This Is Duke Ellington and His Orchestra	1952	100.00
RCA VICTOR RED SEAL			
❏ LM-2857 [M]	The Duke at Tanglewood	1966	18.00
❏ LSC-2857 [S]	The Duke at Tanglewood	1966	25.00
REPRISE			
❏ R-6069 [M]	Afro-Bossa	1962	25.00
❏ R9-6069 [S]	Afro-Bossa	1962	25.00
❏ R-6185 [M]	Concert in the Virgin Islands	1965	25.00
❏ RS-6185 [S]	Concert in the Virgin Islands	1965	18.00
❏ R-6234 [M]	Duke Ellington's Greatest Hits	1967	25.00
❏ RS-6234 [S]	Duke Ellington's Greatest Hits	1967	18.00
❏ R-6122 [M]	Ellington '65: Hits of the '60s/ This Time by Ellington	1964	25.00
❏ RS-6122 [S]	Ellington '65: Hits of the '60s/ This Time by Ellington	1964	25.00
❏ R-6154 [M]	Ellington '66	1965	25.00
❏ RS-6154 [S]	Ellington '66	1965	18.00
❏ R-6141 [M]	Mary Poppins	1964	25.00
❏ RS-6141 [S]	Mary Poppins	1964	25.00
❏ R-6097 [M]	The Symphonic Ellington	1963	25.00
❏ R9-6097 [S]	The Symphonic Ellington	1963	25.00
❏ R-6168 [M]	Will Big Bands Ever Come Back?	1965	25.00
❏ RS-6168 [S]	Will Big Bands Ever Come Back?	1965	18.00
RIVERSIDE			
❏ RLP 12-129 [M]	Birth of Big Band Jazz	1956	60.00
— White label, blue print			
❏ RLP 12-129 [M]	Birth of Big Band Jazz	195?	30.00
— Blue label with mike logo			
❏ RLP-475 [M]	Great Times!	1963	30.00
❏ RS-9475 [S]	Great Times!	1963	30.00
RONDO-I FTTE			
❏ A-7 [M]	Duke Ellington and Orchestra	1958	30.00
ROULETTE			
❏ 108	Echoes of an Era	1971	18.00
ROYALE			
❏ 18143 [10]	Duke Ellington and His Orchestra	195?	50.00
❏ 18152 [10]	Duke Ellington Plays Ellington	195?	50.00
SMITHSONIAN COLLECTION			
❏ P6-15079	An Explosion of Genius 1938-1940	1976	50.00
— Produced in association with Columbia Special Products			
SOLID STATE			
❏ SS-19000	75th Birthday	1970	25.00
❏ SM-18022	Money Jungle	1968	18.00
— Reissue of United Artists 15017			
STANYAN			
❏ 10105	For Always	197?	15.00
STARDUST			
❏ SD-124 [M]	Duke	196?	15.00
❏ SDS-124 [R]	Duke	196?	15.00
STORYVILLE			
❏ SLP-4003	Duke Ellington and His Orchestra	198?	12.00
SUPER MAJESTIC			
❏ 2000	Duke Ellington	197?	15.00
SUTTON			
❏ SU-276 [M]	Duke Meets Leonard Feather	196?	15.00
TIME-LIFE			
❏ STBB-16	Big Bands: Cotton Club Nights	1983	18.00
❏ STBB-05	Big Bands: Duke Ellington	1983	18.00
❏ STL-J-02	Giants of Jazz	1978	25.00
TREND			
❏ 2004	Carnegie Hall Concert	198?	12.00
❏ 529	The Symphonic Ellington	1982	25.00
UNITED ARTISTS			
❏ UAJ-14017 [M]	Money Jungle	1962	40.00
❏ UAJS-15017 [S]	Money Jungle	1962	40.00
❏ UAS-5632	Money Jungle	1972	15.00
— Reissue			
❏ UXS-92	Togo Bravo Suite	1972	18.00
VEE JAY			
❏ VJS-3061	Love You Madly	198?	12.00
VERVE			
❏ V-8701 [M]	Soul Call	1967	18.00
❏ V6-8701 [S]	Soul Call	1967	15.00
X			
❏ LVA-3037 [10]	Duke Ellington Plays	1955	100.00

ELLINGTON, HARVEY

STEPHENY

❏ MF-4010 [M]	I Can't Hide the Blues	1959	100.00

Number	Title	Yr	NM

ELLINGTON, MERCER

CORAL
CRL0(# unk) [M]	Black and Tan Fantasy	1958	30.00
CRL0(# unk) [S]	Black and Tan Fantasy	1958	40.00
CRL57293 [M]	Colors in Rhythm	1959	30.00
CRL757293 [S]	Colors in Rhythm	1959	40.00
CRL57225 [M]	Stepping Into Swing Society	1958	30.00
CRL757225 [S]	Stepping Into Swing Society	1958	40.00

MCA
| 349 | Black and Tan Fantasy | 197? | 15.00 |

ELLINGTONIANS, THE

MERCER
| LP-1004 [10] | The Ellingtonians with Al Hibbler | 1951 | 250.00 |

ELLIOT, CASS

ABC DUNHILL
DS-50055 [B]	Bubble Gum, Lemonade &... Something for Mama	1969	25.00
DS-50040	Dream a Little Dream	1968	25.00
DS-50071	Make Your Own Kind of Music	1969	18.00
— Reissue of 50055 with new title and one added song
| DS-50093 | Mama's Big Ones | 1970 | 18.00 |

MCA
| 719 | Mama's Big Ones | 1980 | 10.00 |

RCA VICTOR
LSP-4619	Cass Elliot	1971	18.00
APL1-0303	Don't Call Me Mama Anymore	1973	18.00
LSP-4753	The Road Is No Place for a Lady	1972	18.00

ELLIOT, MIKE

ASI
5003	Atrio	197?	12.00
5007	City Traffic	197?	12.00
5001	Natural Life	197?	12.00

PAUSA
| 7139 | Diffusion | 1981 | 12.00 |

ELLIOT, RICHARD

INTIMA
| SJE-73283 | Initial Approach | 1987 | 12.00 |
— Reissue of ITI album
D1-73348	Take to the Skies	1989	15.00
D1-73321	The Power of Suggestion	1988	15.00
SJ-73233	Trolltown	1987	15.00

ITI
| JL-030 | Initial Approach | 198? | 18.00 |

ELLIOTT, DEAN

CAPITOL
T1864 [M]	Heartstrings	1962	25.00
ST1864 [S]	Heartstrings	1962	30.00
T1834 [M]	Zounds! What Sounds!	1962	40.00
ST1834 [S]	Zounds! What Sounds!	1962	50.00

ELLIOTT, DON

ABC-PARAMOUNT
ABC-142 [M]	Don Elliott at the Modern Jazz Room	1956	40.00
ABC-228 [M]	Jamaica Jazz	1958	40.00
ABCS-228 [S]	Jamaica Jazz	1959	30.00
ABC-106 [M]	Musical Offering	1956	40.00
ABC-190 [M]	The Voices of Don Elliott	1957	50.00

BETHLEHEM
| BCP-15 [M] | Don Elliott Sings | 1955 | 50.00 |
| BCP-12 [M] | Mellophone | 1955 | 50.00 |

COLUMBIA
| PC33799 | Rejuvenation | 1975 | 15.00 |

DECCA
| DL9208 [M] | The Mello Sound | 1958 | 40.00 |
| DL79208 [S] | The Mello Sound | 1958 | 50.00 |

DESIGN
| DLP-69 [M] | Music for the Sensational 60's | 196? | 18.00 |
| DLPS-69 [S] | Music for the Sensational 60's | 196? | 15.00 |

HALLMARK
| 317 [M] | Pal Joey | 1957 | 50.00 |

JAZZLAND
| JLP-15 [M] | Double Trumpet Doings | 1960 | 40.00 |
| JLP-915 [S] | Double Trumpet Doings | 1960 | 30.00 |

RCA VICTOR
| LJM-1007 [M] | Don Elliott Quintet | 1954 | 60.00 |

RIVERSIDE
| RLP 12-218 [M] | Counterpoint for Six Valves | 1956 | 100.00 |
— White label, blue print
| RLP 12-218 [M] | Counterpoint for Six Valves | 195? | 40.00 |
— Blue label, microphone logo
| RLP-2517 [10] | Six Valves | 1955 | 120.00 |

SAVOY
| MG-9033 [10] | The Versatile Don Elliott | 1953 | 120.00 |

VANGUARD
| VRS-8016 [10] | Doubles in Brass | 1954 | 100.00 |

ELLIOTT, DON/SAM MOST

JAZZTONE
| J-1256 [M] | Doubles in Jazz | 1957 | 40.00 |

VANGUARD
| VRS-8522 [M] | Doubles in Jazz | 1957 | 60.00 |
— Partial reissue of 8016 and 8014

ELLIOTT, RAMBLIN' JACK

FOLKLORE
FL14029 [M]	Country Style	1964	25.00
FL14019 [M]	Hootenanny with Jack Elliott	1964	25.00
FL14014 [M]	Ramblin'	1964	25.00
FL14011 [M]	The Songs of Woody Guthrie	1964	25.00

MONITOR
MF-380 [M]	Jack Elliott Sings Woody Guthrie and Jimmie Rodgers	1962	30.00
MS-380 [S]	Jack Elliott Sings Woody Guthrie and Jimmie Rodgers	1962	30.00
MF-379 [M]	Ramblin' Cowboy	1962	30.00

PRESTIGE
PRLP-13045 [M]	Country Style	1962	30.00
PRLP-13065 [M]	Jack Elliott at the Second Fret	1962	30.00
PRLP-13033 [M]	Ramblin'	1961	30.00
PRLP-13016 [M]	The Songs of Woody Guthrie	1961	30.00

TOPIC
| T-15 [10] | Jack Takes the Floor | 195? | 40.00 |

VANGUARD
| VRS-9151 [M] | Jack Elliott | 1964 | 25.00 |
| VSD-79151 [S] | Jack Elliott | 1964 | 30.00 |

ELLIOTT, RON

WARNER BROS.
| WS1833 | Candlestickmaker | 1969 | 18.00 |

ELLIOTT, WALTER & BENNETT

JAM
| 104/105 | Elliott, Walter & Bennett | 197? | 25.00 |
| (# unknown) | Save a Piece of the World | 1975 | 50.00 |
— As "Elliott and Walter
| 106 | Zeti Reticuli | 197? | 80.00 |

ELLIS, ANITA

ELEKTRA
| EKL-179 [M] | The World in My Arms | 1959 | 40.00 |

EPIC
| LN3419 [M] | Him | 1958 | 40.00 |
| LN3280 [M] | I Wonder What Became of Me | 1956 | 40.00 |

ELLIS, DON

ATLANTIC
| SD19178 | Live at Montreux | 1977 | 15.00 |
| SD18227 | Survival/Music from Other Galaxies and Planets | 1977 | 15.00 |

BARNABY
| BR-5020 | How Time Passes | 197? | 15.00 |
— Reissue of Candid LP

BASF
| 25341 | Haiku | 1974 | 18.00 |
| 25123 | Soaring | 1973 | 18.00 |

CANDID
| CJM-8004 [M] | How Time Passes | 1961 | 50.00 |
| CJS-9004 [S] | How Time Passes | 1961 | 60.00 |

COLUMBIA
CS9721	Autumn	1969	18.00
KC31766	Connection	1972	18.00
G30243	Don Ellis at the Fillmore	1970	25.00
CG30243	Don Ellis at the Fillmore	197?	18.00
— Reissue with new prefix
CL2785 [M]	Electric Bath	1968	30.00
CS9585 [S]	Electric Bath	1968	18.00
CS9668	Shock Treatment	1968	18.00
G30927	Tears of Joy	1971	25.00
CG30927	Tears of Joy	197?	18.00
— Reissue with new prefix
| CS9889 | The New Don Ellis Band Goes Underground | 1969 | 25.00 |

FANTASY
| OJC-431 | New Ideas | 1990 | 15.00 |

NEW JAZZ
| NJLP-8257 [M] | New Ideas | 1961 | 50.00 |
— Purple label
| NJLP-8257 [M] | New Ideas | 1965 | 30.00 |
— Blue label, trident logo at right

PACIFIC JAZZ
PJ-10112 [M]	Don Ellis "Live" At Monterey	1967	25.00
ST-20112 [S]	Don Ellis "Live" At Monterey	1967	18.00
PJ-55 [M]	Essence	1962	30.00
ST-55 [S]	Essence	1962	40.00
PJ-10123 [M]	Live in 3/2 3/4 Time	1967	25.00
ST-20123 [S]	Live in 3/2 3/4 Time	1967	18.00

PAUSA
| 7028 | Soaring | 1979 | 12.00 |
— Reissue of BASF 25123

PRESTIGE
| PRST-7607 | New Ideas | 1969 | 18.00 |

ELLIS, HERB, AND JOE PASS

CONCORD JAZZ
| CJ-1 | Jazz/Concord | 197? | 18.00 |
| CJ-2 | Seven Come Eleven | 197? | 18.00 |

PABLO
| 2310714 | Two for the Road | 1974 | 18.00 |

ELLIS, HERB, AND RAY BROWN

CONCORD JAZZ
CJ-6	After You've Gone	197?	15.00
CJ-12	Hot Tracks	1977	15.00
CJ-10	Rhythm Willie	197?	15.00
CJ-3	Soft Shoe	197?	15.00

ELLIS, HERB, AND RED MITCHELL

CONCORD JAZZ
| CJ-372 | Doggin' Around | 1989 | 15.00 |

ELLIS, HERB, AND REMO PALMIER

CONCORD JAZZ
| CJ-56 | Windflower | 1978 | 15.00 |

ELLIS, HERB, AND ROSS TOMPKINS

CONCORD JAZZ
| CJ-17 | A Pair to Draw On | 1977 | 15.00 |

ELLIS, HERB

COLUMBIA
| CL2330 [M] | Herb Ellis Guitar | 1965 | 18.00 |
| CS9130 [S] | Herb Ellis Guitar | 1965 | 25.00 |

CONCORD JAZZ
CJ-116	Herb Ellis at Montreux, Summer 1979	1980	12.00
CJ-181	Herb Mix	1982	12.00
CJ-77	Soft and Mellow	1979	12.00

DOT
| DLP-3678 [M] | The Man with the Guitar | 1965 | 18.00 |
| DLP-25678 [S] | The Man with the Guitar | 1965 | 25.00 |

EPIC
LA16030 [M]	Herb Ellis and "Stuff" Smith Together	1963	25.00
BA17039 [S]	Herb Ellis and "Stuff" Smith Together	1963	30.00
LA16034 [M]	The Midnight Roll	1962	30.00
BA17034 [S]	The Midnight Roll	1962	30.00
LA16036 [M]	Three Guitars in Bossa Nova Time	1963	25.00
BA17036 [S]	Three Guitars in Bossa Nova Time	1963	30.00

NORGRAN
| MGN-1081 [M] | Ellis in Wonderland | 1956 | 100.00 |

VERVE
| MGV-8171 [M] | Ellis in Wonderland | 1957 | 50.00 |
— Reissue of Norgran 1081
V-8171 [M]	Ellis in Wonderland	1961	25.00
MGV-8311 [M]	Herb Ellis Meets Jimmy Giuffre	1959	80.00
MGVS-6045 [S]	Herb Ellis Meets Jimmy Giuffre	1960	40.00
V-8311 [M]	Herb Ellis Meets Jimmy Giuffre	1961	25.00
V6-8311 [S]	Herb Ellis Meets Jimmy Giuffre	1961	25.00
MGV-8252 [M]	Nothing But the Blues	1958	80.00
V-8252 [M]	Nothing But the Blues	1961	25.00
V-8448 [M]	Softly...But With That Feeling	1962	25.00
V6-8448 [M]	Softly...But With That Feeling	1962	30.00
MGV-8381 [M]	Thank You, Charlie Christian	1960	50.00
MGVS-6164 [S]	Thank You, Charlie Christian	1960	40.00
V-8381 [M]	Thank You, Charlie Christian	1961	25.00
V6-8381 [S]	Thank You, Charlie Christian	1961	25.00

ELLIS, JIMMY

BOBLO
| 78-829 | By Request Jimmy Sings Elvis | 1978 | 100.00 |

ELLIS, LLOYD

CARLTON
| LP 12-104 [M] | Fastest Guitar in the World | 1958 | 50.00 |

FAMOUS DOOR
| HL-100 | Las Vegas 3 AM | 197? | 15.00 |

TREY
| TLP-902 [M] | So Tall, So Cool, So There! | 1960 | 30.00 |

ELLIS, MATTHEW

WARNER BROS.
| BS2610 | Matthew Ellis | 1972 | 18.00 |

Number	Title	Yr	NM

ELLIS, PEE WEE

SAVOY
| ❏ SJL-3301 | Home in the Country | 1976 | 25.00 |

ELLIS, RAY

ATCO
| ❏ 33-187 [M] | Big Hits for Swingers | 1966 | 15.00 |
| ❏ SD 33-187 [S] | Big Hits for Swingers | 1966 | 18.00 |

COLUMBIA
❏ CL1122 [M]	Dancing with Gigi	1958	18.00
❏ CL993 [M]	Ellis in Wonderland	1957	18.00
❏ CL1097 [M]	Let's Get Away from It All	1957	18.00

HARMONY
❏ HS11003 [S]	Gigi	1959	18.00
❏ HL7183 [M]	Gigi	1959	15.00
❏ E-3779 [M]	I'm in the Mood for Strings	1959	15.00
❏ SE-3779 [S]	I'm in the Mood for Strings	1959	18.00
❏ E-3820 [M]	I'm in the Mood to Swing	1960	15.00
❏ SE-3820 [S]	I'm in the Mood to Swing	1960	18.00
❏ E-3813 [M]	The Best of Peter Gunn	1960	15.00
❏ E-3842 [M]	The Big Voices, The Big Bands, The Big Songs, The Big Sounds	1960	15.00
❏ SE-3842 [S]	The Big Voices, The Big Bands, The Big Songs, The Big Sounds	1960	18.00

RCA VICTOR
❏ LPM-2493 [M]	How to Succeed in Business Without Really Trying	1961	15.00
❏ LSP-2493 [S]	How to Succeed in Business Without Really Trying	1961	18.00
❏ LPM-2410 [M]	La Dolce Vita	1961	15.00
❏ LSP-2410 [S]	La Dolce Vita	1961	18.00
❏ LPM-2615 [M]	Our Man on Broadway	1963	15.00
❏ LSP-2615 [S]	Our Man on Broadway	1963	18.00
❏ LPM-2400 [M]	Ray Ellis Plays the Top 20	1961	15.00
❏ LSP-2400 [S]	Ray Ellis Plays the Top 20	1961	18.00

ELLIS, RED

STARDAY
❏ SLP-168 [M]	Holy Cry from the Cross	1962	30.00
❏ SLP-273 [M]	Old Time Religion Bluegrass Style	1963	30.00
❏ SLP-203 [M]	The Sacred Sound of Bluegrass Music	1962	30.00

ELLIS, SHIRLEY

COLUMBIA
| ❏ CL2679 [M] | Sugar, Let's Shing-a-Ling | 1967 | 25.00 |
| ❏ CS9479 [S] | Sugar, Let's Shing-a-Ling | 1967 | 30.00 |

CONGRESS
❏ CGL-3002 [M]	Shirley Ellis In Action	1964	30.00
❏ CGS-3002 [S]	Shirley Ellis In Action	1964	30.00
❏ CGL-3003 [M]	The Name Game	1965	30.00
❏ CGS-3003 [S]	The Name Game	1965	30.00

ELLIS, STEVE, AND THE STARFIRES

I.G.L.
| ❏ 105 | The Steve Ellis Songbook | 1967 | 500.00 |

ELLISON, LORRAINE

WARNER BROS.
❏ W1674 [M]	Heart and Soul	1967	40.00
❏ WS1674 [S]	Heart and Soul	1967	30.00
❏ BS2780 [S]	Lorraine Ellison	1974	18.00
❏ WS1821	Stay with Me	1969	40.00

ELMAN, ZIGGY

CIRCLE
| ❏ 70 | Ziggy Elman and His Orchestra 1947 | 198? | 12.00 |

MGM
❏ E-163 [10]	Dancing with Zig	1952	50.00
❏ E-3389 [M]	Sentimental Trumpet	1956	40.00
❏ E-535 [10]	Ziggy Elman and His Orchestra	195?	50.00

SUNBEAM
| ❏ 202 | Angels Sing 1938-39 | 198? | 12.00 |

ELMER GANTRY'S VELVET OPERA

EPIC
| ❏ BN26415 | Elmer Gantry's Velvet Opera | 1968 | 75.00 |

ELMO AND PATSY

EPIC
❏ PE39931	Grandma Got Run Over by a Reindeer	1985	10.00
—reissue of 5E 39931			
❏ 5E39931	Grandma Got Run Over by a Reindeer	1984	12.00

ELMORE, ROBERT

MERCURY LIVING PRESENCE
❏ SR90127 [S]	Bach on the Biggest	1960	30.00
—Maroon label, no "Vendor: Mercury Record Corporation			
❏ SR90109 [S]	Boardwalk Pipes	196?	100.00
—Maroon label, no "Vendor: Mercury Record Corporation			

ELSTAK, NEDLEY

ESP-DISK'
| ❏ 1076 | The Machine | 1969 | 25.00 |

ELVIS BROTHERS, THE

PORTRAIT
| ❏ BFR38865 | Movin' Up | 1983 | 15.00 |

ELY, CHET

GHB
| ❏ 67 | Til Times Get Better | 197? | 12.00 |

ELY, JOE

HIGHTONE
| ❏ 8015 | Dig All Night | 1988 | 12.00 |
| ❏ 8008 | Lord of the Highway | 1987 | 12.00 |

MCA
❏ 3080	Down on the Drag	1979	16.00
—Originals have a gatefold sleeve			
❏ 5480	Hi-Res	1984	15.00
❏ 2333	Honky Tonk Masquerade	1978	16.00
❏ 2242	Joe Ely	1977	16.00
❏ R124826	Live at Liberty Lunch	1990	18.00
—BMG Music Service edition			
❏ 5262	Live Shots	1981	15.00

SOUTHCOAST
| ❏ 5183 | Musta Notta Gotta Lotta | 1981 | 15.00 |

EMANUELE, VITTORIO

RCA VICTOR RED SEAL
| ❏ LSC-2424 [S] | Vivaldi: The Four Seasons | 1960 | 25.00 |
| —With the Societa Corelli; original with "shaded dog" label | | | |

EMBERS, THE

EEE
| ❏ 1069 [M] | Burn You a New One | 1967 | 200.00 |

JCP
| ❏ 2009 [M] | Just for the Birds | 1966 | 200.00 |
| ❏ 2006 [M] | The Embers Roll Eleven | 1965 | 200.00 |

EMERSON, KEITH

EMERSON
| ❏ KEITH LP-1 | The Christmas Album | 1993 | 25.00 |
| —British import only | | | |

EMERSON, LAKE AND PALMER

RAZOR & TIE
| ❏ 7930183398-1 [B] | The First Five: Picture Disc Collection | 2013 | 100.00 |

EMERSON, LAKE AND PALMER

ATLANTIC
❏ SD19124	Brain Salad Surgery	1977	10.00
❏ SD19120	Emerson, Lake and Palmer	1977	10.00
❏ SD19255	Emerson, Lake and Palmer In Concert	1979	12.00
❏ SD19211	Love Beach	1978	12.00
❏ PR281 [DJ]	On Tour with Emerson, Lake and Palmer	1977	40.00
❏ SD19122	Pictures at an Exhibition	1977	10.00
❏ SD19121	Tarkus	1977	10.00
❏ SD19283	The Best of Emerson, Lake and Palmer	1980	12.00
❏ SD19123	Trilogy	1977	10.00
❏ SD7000	Works Volume 1	1977	18.00
❏ PR277 [DJ]	Works Volume 1	1977	18.00
—Promo-only sampler			
❏ SD19147	Works Volume 2	1977	12.00

COTILLION
❏ SD9040	Emerson, Lake and Palmer	1971	15.00
❏ ELP66666	Pictures at an Exhibition	1971	15.00
❏ SD9900	Tarkus	1971	15.00
❏ SD9903	Trilogy	1972	15.00
❏ SMAS-94773	Trilogy	1972	18.00
—Capitol Record Club edition			

MANTICORE
| ❏ ELP66669 | Brain Salad Surgery | 1973 | 15.00 |
| ❏ SD 3-200 | Welcome Back, My Friends, to the Show That Never Ends, Ladies and Gentlemen | 1974 | 25.00 |

MOBILE FIDELITY
❏ 1-031	Pictures at an Exhibition	1980	55.00
—Audiophile vinyl			
❏ 1-203	Tarkus	1994	40.00
—Audiophile vinyl			
❏ 1-218	Trilogy	1994	60.00
—Audiophile vinyl			

EMERSON, LAKE AND POWELL

POLYDOR
| ❏ 829297-1 | Emerson, Lake and Powell | 1986 | 12.00 |

EMERSON'S OLD-TIMEY CUSTARD-SUCKIN' BAND

ESP-DISK'
| ❏ 2006 | Emerson's Old-Timey Custard-Suckin' Band | 1970 | 30.00 |

EMF

EMI
| ❏ E1-96238 | Schubert Dip | 1991 | 30.00 |

EMINEM

AFTERMATH
❏ 1286301 [B]	Relapse	2008	30.00
❏ 493290-1	The Eminem Show	2002	25.00
❏ 490629-1	The Marshall Mathers LP	2000	25.00
❏ 4906291	The Marshall Mathers LP	2008	30.00
❏ 90287 [B]	The Slim Shady LP	1999	30.00

EMMONS, BOBBY

HI
| ❏ HL-32024 [M] | Blues with a Beat | 1965 | 30.00 |
| ❏ SHL-32024 [S] | Blues with a Beat | 1965 | 30.00 |

EMMONS, BUDDY, AND SHOT JACKSON

STARDAY
| ❏ SLP-230 [M] | Singing Strings of Steel and Dobro | 196? | 40.00 |

EMMONS, BUDDY

MERCURY
| ❏ MG-20843 [M] | Steel Guitar Jazz | 1963 | 80.00 |
| ❏ SR-60843 [S] | Steel Guitar Jazz | 1963 | 100.00 |

STEP ONE
| ❏ SOR-0024 | Christmas Sounds of the Steel Guitar | 198? | 15.00 |

EMOTIONS, THE (1)

ARC
| ❏ JC36149 | Come Into Our World | 1979 | 12.00 |
| ❏ FC37456 | New Affair | 1981 | 12.00 |

COLUMBIA
❏ PC34163	Flowers	1976	12.00
—No bar code on cover			
❏ PC34163	Flowers	198?	10.00
—With bar code on cover			
❏ PC34762	Rejoice	1977	12.00
—No bar code on cover			
❏ PC34762	Rejoice	198?	10.00
—With bar code on cover			
❏ JC35385	Sunbeam	1978	12.00

MOTOWN
| ❏ 6136ML | If I Only Knew | 1985 | 10.00 |

RED LABEL
| ❏ 001 | Sincerely | 1984 | 12.00 |

STAX
❏ STX-4121	Chronicle	1979	12.00
❏ STX-4110	So I Can Love You	1978	12.00
—Reissue of Volt 6008			
❏ STX-4100	Sunshine	1977	12.00
❏ STX-4112	Untouched	1978	12.00
—Reissue of Volt 6015			

VOLT
| ❏ VOS-6008 | So I Can Love You | 1971 | 30.00 |
| ❏ VOS-6015 | Untouched | 1972 | 30.00 |

EN VOGUE

ATLANTIC
| ❏ 82084 [B] | Born to Sing | 1990 | 25.00 |

END, THE

LONDON
| ❏ PS560 | Introspection | 1969 | 50.00 |

ENESCU, GEORGE

CONTINENTAL
❏ CLP104 [M]	Bach: Six Sonatas and Partitas for Unaccompanied Violin	1949	10000.00
—In original box			
❏ CLP106 [M]	Bach: Sonatas 5 and 6	1949	4000.00

ENEVOLDSEN, BOB

LIBERTY
| ❏ LJH-6008 [M] | Smorgasbord | 1956 | 50.00 |

NOCTURNE
| ❏ NLP-6 [M] | Bob Enevoldsen Quintet | 1954 | 150.00 |

TAMPA
❏ TP-14 [M]	Reflections in Jazz	1957	100.00
—Colored vinyl			
❏ TP-14 [M]	Reflections in Jazz	1958	50.00
—Black vinyl			

Number	Title	Yr	NM
ENGLAND DAN AND JOHN FORD COLEY			
A&M			
❏ SP-4305	England Dan and John Ford Coley	1971	18.00
❏ SP-4350	Fables	1972	18.00
❏ SP-4613	I Hear Music	1976	15.00
BIG TREE			
❏ BT76018	Best of England Dan & John Ford Coley	1980	12.00
❏ BT76000	Dowdy Ferry Road	1977	12.00
❏ BT76015	Dr. Heckle & Mr. Jive	1979	12.00
❏ BT89517	Nights Are Forever	1976	12.00
❏ BT76006	Some Things Don't Come Easy	1978	12.00

ENGLE, BUTCH, AND THE STYX

BEAT ROCKET

| ❏ BR106 | The Best of Butch Engle and the Styx: No Matter What You Say | 2000 | 15.00 |

ENGLISH BEAT, THE

I.R.S.

| ❏ SP-70606 | I Just Can't Stop It | 1983 | 12.00 |

—Reissue of Sire album of the same name

| ❏ SP-70032 | Special Beat Service | 1982 | 12.00 |
| ❏ SP-70607 | Wha'ppen? | 1983 | 12.00 |

—Reissue of Sire album of the same name

| ❏ SP-70040 | What Is Beat? | 1983 | 12.00 |

SIRE

| ❏ SRK-6091 | I Just Can't Stop It | 1980 | 18.00 |
| ❏ SRK-3567 | Wha'ppen | 1981 | 18.00 |

ENGLISH CONGREGATION, THE

SIGNPOST

| ❏ SP8405 | Jesahel | 1972 | 15.00 |
| ❏ SP7217 | Softly Whispering I Love You | 1972 | 15.00 |

ENNIS, ETHEL

BASF

| ❏ 25121 | 10 Sides of Ethel Ennis | 1973 | 18.00 |

CAPITOL

| ❏ T941 | Change of Scenery | 1957 | 40.00 |
| ❏ T1078 [M] | Have You Forgotten? | 1959 | 40.00 |

JUBILEE

❏ JLP-5024 [M]	Ethel Ennis Sings	1963	25.00
❏ SJLP-5024 [S]	Ethel Ennis Sings	1963	30.00
❏ JLP-1021 [M]	Lullabies for Losers	1956	50.00

PICKWICK

| ❏ PC-3021 [M] | Ethel Ennis | 196? | 15.00 |
| ❏ SPC-3021 [S] | Ethel Ennis | 196? | 15.00 |

RCA CAMDEN

| ❏ ACL1-0157 | God Bless the Child | 1973 | 12.00 |

RCA VICTOR

❏ LPM-2984 [M]	Eyes for You	1964	25.00
❏ LSP-2984 [S]	Eyes for You	1964	30.00
❏ LSP-2862 [S]	Once Again, Ethel Ennis	1964	30.00
❏ LPM-2862 [M]	Once Again, Ethel Ennis	1964	25.00
❏ LPM-2786 [M]	This Is Ethel Ennis	1964	25.00
❏ LSP-2786 [S]	This Is Ethel Ennis	1964	30.00

ENNIS, SKINNAY

HINDSIGHT

| ❏ HSR-164 | Skinnay Ennis 1947-48 | 198? | 12.00 |

ENO, BRIAN

ANTILLES

| ❏ AN-7030 | Discreet Music | 1975 | 15.00 |
| ❏ AN-7018 [B] | Evening Star | 1975 | 18.00 |

—By Robert Fripp and Eno

| ❏ AN-7070 | Music for Films | 1978 | 18.00 |
| ❏ AN-7001 [B] | No Pussyfooting | 1973 | 30.00 |

—By Robert Fripp and Eno

EDITIONS EG

| ❏ EGS-201 | Ambient #1 -- Music for Airports | 1982 | 15.00 |

—Reissue

| ❏ EGS-202 [B] | Ambient 2 -- The Plateaux of Mirrors | 1982 | 18.00 |

—By Harold Budd and Brian Eno

| ❏ EGED-20 [B] | Ambient 4 -- On Land | 1982 | 18.00 |
| ❏ ENO-3 | Another Green World | 1982 | 12.00 |

—Reissue

| ❏ ENO-5 [B] | Apollo: Atmospheres and Soundtracks | 1983 | 25.00 |
| ❏ ENO-4 | Before and After Science | 1982 | 12.00 |

—Reissue

| ❏ EGS-303 | Discreet Music | 1983 | 15.00 |

—Reissue

| ❏ EGS-103 | Evening Star | 1982 | 12.00 |

—By Robert Fripp and Eno; reissue

| ❏ EGS-107 | Fourth World Volume 1: Possible Musics | 1980 | 15.00 |

—With Jon Hassell

| ❏ ENO-1 | Here Come the Warm Jets | 1982 | 12.00 |
| ❏ EGS-105 | Music for Films | 1982 | 12.00 |

—Reissue

Number	Title	Yr	NM
❏ EGS-102 [B]	No Pussyfooting	1982	12.00

—By Robert Fripp and Eno; reissue

| ❏ EGS-301 | Pavilion of Dreams | 1982 | 15.00 |

—By Harold Budd and Brian Eno

| ❏ ENO-2 | Taking Tiger Mountain (By Strategy) | 1982 | 12.00 |

—Reissue

| ❏ EGED-37 | The Pearl | 1984 | 15.00 |

—By Harold Budd and Brian Eno

| ❏ EGBS-2 | Working Backwards: 1983-1973 | 1984 | 100.00 |

—Boxed set of nine albums plus Music For Films II and Rarities 12

ISLAND

| ❏ ILPS9351 [B] | Another Green World | 1975 | 30.00 |
| ❏ ILPS9478 [B] | Before and After Science | 1977 | 30.00 |

—Double the value if four lithographs are included with the package.

| ❏ ILPS9268 [B] | Here Come the Warm Jets | 1973 | 35.00 |
| ❏ ILPS9309 [B] | Taking Tiger Mountain (By Strategy) | 1974 | 35.00 |

JEM

| ❏ ENO DJ [DJ] | Music for Airplay | 1981 | 50.00 |

—Promo-only 10-track sampler

OPAL/WARNER BROS.

| ❏ 25769 | Music for Films, Vol. III | 1988 | 12.00 |
| ❏ 26421 | Wrong Way Up | 1990 | 12.00 |

—With John Cale

PVC

| ❏ 7908 [B] | Ambient #1 -- Music for Airports | 1979 | 30.00 |

ENO/MOEBIUS/ROEDELIUS

4 MEN WITH BEARDS

| ❏ 4M163LP [B] | After The Heat | | 25.00 |

ENRIQUEZ, BOBBY

GNP CRESCENDO

❏ GNPS-2155	Espana	1983	12.00
❏ GNPS-2179	Live at Concerts by the Sea	1985	10.00
❏ GNPS-2183	Live at Concerts by the Sea, Volume II	1986	10.00
❏ GNPS-2161	Live in Tokyo	198?	10.00
❏ GNPS-2168	Live in Tokyo, Volume II	198?	10.00
❏ GNPS-2151	Prodigious Piano	198?	10.00
❏ GNPS-2144	The Wildman	198?	10.00
❏ GNPS-2148	The Wildman Meets the Madman	198?	10.00

PORTRAIT

| ❏ FR44160 | Wild Piano | 1988 | 15.00 |

ENSEMBLE AL-SALAAM, THE

STRATA-EAST

| ❏ SES-7418 | The Sojourner | 1974 | 40.00 |

ENSEMBLE FOR EARLY MUSIC

NONESUCH

| ❏ H-71315 | Christmas in Anglia: Early English Music for Christmastide | 1979 | 15.00 |

—Frederick Renz, director

ENTWISTLE, JOHN

ATCO

| ❏ SD 38-142 | Too Late the Hero | 1981 | 12.00 |

DECCA

| ❏ DL79183 [B] | Smash Your Head Against the Wall | 1971 | 30.00 |

MCA

| ❏ 2024 | Smash Your Head Against the Wall | 1973 | 15.00 |

—Reissue of Decca 79183

TRACK

❏ MCA-2129	Mad Dog	1975	18.00
❏ MCA-321 [B]	Rigor Mortis Sets In	1973	30.00
❏ DL79190	Whistle Rymes	1972	30.00
❏ L33-1926 [DJ]	Who's Ox	1975	100.00

—Promo-only sampler

ENYA

GEFFEN

| ❏ GHS24233 | Watermark | 1988 | 18.00 |

ENYARD, RON, AND PAULA OWEN

CADENCE JAZZ

| ❏ CJR-1031 | Red, Green and Blues (In Living Black and White) | 1987 | 12.00 |

EPIC CHOIR, THE

EPIC

| ❏ LC3144 [M] | The Story of Christmas | 1954 | 30.00 |

—Gatefold cover with bound-in booklet

EPPS, PRESTON

ORIGINAL SOUND

| ❏ LPM-5002 [M] | Bongo, Bongo, Bongo | 1960 | 50.00 |

Number	Title	Yr	NM
❏ LPS-8851 [S]	Bongo, Bongo, Bongo	1960	80.00
❏ LPM-5009 [M]	Surfin' Bongos	1963	40.00
❏ LPS-8872 [S]	Surfin' Bongos	1963	50.00
TOP RANK			
❏ RM-349 [M]	Bongola	1961	40.00
❏ RS-349 [S]	Bongola	1961	50.00

EQUALS, THE

LAURIE

| ❏ LLP-2045 [M] | Unequalled | 1967 | 30.00 |
| ❏ SLP-2045 [S] | Unequalled | 1967 | 30.00 |

PRESIDENT

❏ PTL-1015	Equal Sensation	1968	30.00
❏ PTL-1025	Equals Supreme	1968	30.00
❏ PTL-1030	Strikeback	1969	30.00
❏ PTL-1020	The Sensational Equals	1968	30.00

RCA VICTOR

| ❏ LSP-4078 | Baby Come Back | 1968 | 30.00 |

EQUITABLE CHIMES, THE

(NO LABEL)

| ❏ CTV-84282/3 [10] | The Equitable Chimes Play Ten of the World's Best-Loved Christmas Carols | 1962 | 18.00 |

ERASURE

MUTE

| ❏ 9198 | Other People's Songs | 2003 | 15.00 |

MUTE/ELEKTRA

| ❏ ED5621 [EP] | Abba-esque | 1992 | 30.00 |

—Promo-only vinyl; remixes of 4-song EP; no special jacket

SIRE

❏ 25904 [EP]	Crackers International	1989	10.00
❏ 25554	The Circus	1987	12.00
❏ R101009	The Innocents	1988	15.00

—BMG Music Service edition

❏ 25730	The Innocents	1988	12.00
❏ 25667	The Two Ring Circus	1988	18.00
❏ 26026	Wild!	1989	15.00
❏ 25354	Wonderland	1987	12.00

ERICA

ESP-DISK'

| ❏ 1099 | You Used to Think | 1968 | 200.00 |

ERICKSON, ROKY

LIGHT IN THE ATTIC

❏ LITA098 [B]	Don't Slander Me	2013	35.00
❏ LITA099 [B]	Gremlins Have Pictures	2013	30.00
❏ LITA097 [B]	The Evil One	2013	30.00

ERICSON, ROLF

EMARCY

| ❏ MG-36106 [M] | Rolf Ericson and His All American Stars | 1957 | 50.00 |

ERIK

VANGUARD

| ❏ VRS-9267 [M] | Look Where I Am | 1967 | 25.00 |
| ❏ VSD-79267 [S] | Look Where I Am | 1967 | 25.00 |

ERIK AND THE VIKINGS

KARATE

| ❏ KLP-1401 [M] | Sing A-Long Rock 'n Roll | 1965 | 200.00 |

ERNEY, DEWEY

DISCOVERY

| ❏ DS-881 | A Beautiful Friendship | 1982 | 12.00 |

ERSKINE, PETER

CONTEMPORARY

| ❏ C-14010 | Peter Erskine | 1983 | 15.00 |

FANTASY

| ❏ OJC-610 | Peter Erskine | 1991 | 15.00 |

PASSPORT

| ❏ 88032 | Transition | 198? | 12.00 |

ERVIN, BOOKER

BARNABY

| ❏ Z30560 | That's It! | 1971 | 18.00 |

—Reissue of Candid 9014

BETHLEHEM

| ❏ BCP-6048 [M] | The Book Cooks | 1961 | 40.00 |
| ❏ BCP-6025 | The Book Cooks | 197? | 18.00 |

—Reissue with RCA Victor distrbution

| ❏ BN-LA488-H2 | Back from the Gig | 1975 | 25.00 |
| ❏ BST-84283 | The In Between | 1969 | 30.00 |

CANDID

| ❏ CJM-8014 [M] | That's It! | 1961 | 150.00 |
| ❏ CJS-9014 [S] | That's It! | 1961 | 50.00 |

PACIFIC JAZZ

| ❏ PJ-10199 [M] | Structurally Sound | 1968 | 40.00 |
| ❏ ST-20199 [S] | Structurally Sound | 1968 | 25.00 |

PRESTIGE

Number	Title	Yr	NM
❏ PRLP-7293 [M]	Exultation!	1964	125.00
❏ PRST-7293 [S]	Exultation!	1964	30.00
❏ PRST-7844	Exultation!	197?	18.00
—Reissue of 7293			
❏ 24091	Freedom and the Space Sessions	1979	18.00
❏ PRLP-7417 [M]	Groovin' High	1966	35.00
❏ PRST-7417 [S]	Groovin' High	1966	30.00
❏ PRLP-7499 [M]	Heavy!	1968	50.00
❏ PRST-7499 [S]	Heavy!	1968	25.00
❏ PRLP-7435 [M]	Settin' the Pace	1967	30.00
❏ PRST-7435 [S]	Settin' the Pace	1967	25.00
❏ PRLP-7340 [M]	The Blues Book	1965	100.00
❏ PRST-7340 [S]	The Blues Book	1965	30.00
❏ PRLP-7295 [M]	The Freedom Book	1964	75.00
❏ PRST-7295 [S]	The Freedom Book	1964	30.00
❏ PRLP-7318 [M]	The Song Book	1964	200.00
❏ PRST-7318 [S]	The Song Book	1964	30.00
❏ PRLP-7386 [M]	The Space Book	1965	30.00
❏ PRST-7386 [S]	The Space Book	1965	30.00
❏ PRLP-7462 [M]	The Trance	1967	50.00
❏ PRST-7462 [S]	The Trance	1967	25.00

SAVOY

Number	Title	Yr	NM
❏ MG-12154 [M]	Cookin'	1960	50.00

SAVOY JAZZ

Number	Title	Yr	NM
❏ SJL-1119	Down in the Dumps	198?	12.00

ERVIN, BOOKER/HORACE PARLAN

INNER CITY

Number	Title	Yr	NM
❏ IC-3006	Lament	1977	18.00

ERVIN, SENATOR SAM

COLUMBIA

Number	Title	Yr	NM
❏ KC32756	Senator Sam at Home	1973	30.00

ERWIN, PEE WEE

BRUNSWICK

Number	Title	Yr	NM
❏ BL54011 [M]	The Land of Dixie	1956	40.00

CADENCE

Number	Title	Yr	NM
❏ CLP-1011 [M]	Dixieland at Grandview Inn	1956	40.00

JAZZOLOGY

Number	Title	Yr	NM
❏ J-80	Swingin' That Music	1981	12.00

STRAND

Number	Title	Yr	NM
❏ SL-1001 [M]	Peter Meets the Wolf in Dixieland	1959	50.00
❏ SLS-1001 [S]	Peter Meets the Wolf in Dixieland	1959	60.00

URANIA

Number	Title	Yr	NM
❏ UJLP-1202 [M]	Accent on Dixieland	1955	40.00

ESCAPE CLUB, THE

ATLANTIC

Number	Title	Yr	NM
❏ 81871	Wild, Wild West	1988	10.00

EMI AMERICA

Number	Title	Yr	NM
❏ ST-17215	White Fields	1986	12.00

ESCHETE, RON

BAINBRIDGE

Number	Title	Yr	NM
❏ BT-6267	Christmas Impressions	1986	12.00
❏ BT-6264	Stump Jumper	1986	12.00

MUSE

Number	Title	Yr	NM
❏ MR-5246	Line-Up	1980	15.00
❏ MR-5186	To Let You Know I Care	1979	15.00

MUSIC IS MEDICINE

Number	Title	Yr	NM
❏ 9055	Christmas Impressions	1982	18.00

ESCORTS, THE (1)

ALITHIA

Number	Title	Yr	NM
❏ 9104	All We Need Is One More Chance	1973	18.00
❏ 9106	Three Down and Four to Go	1974	18.00

ESCORTS, THE (4)

TEO

Number	Title	Yr	NM
❏ LPM-5000 [M]	The Escorts Bring Down the House	1966	200.00

ESCOVEDO, PETE

CROSSOVER

Number	Title	Yr	NM
❏ CR-5005	Mister E.	1988	15.00
❏ CR-5002	Yesterday's Memories, Tomorrow's Dreams	1987	15.00

ESCOVEDO, PETE AND SHEILA

FANTASY

Number	Title	Yr	NM
❏ F-9545	Happy Together	1977	18.00
❏ F-9524	Solo Two	1976	18.00

ESHELMAN, DAVE, JAZZ GARDEN BIG BAND

SEA BREEZE

Number	Title	Yr	NM
❏ SB-2039	Deep Voices	1989	15.00

ESP

DREAM

Number	Title	Yr	NM
❏ DRE187301	The Future Is Now	1986	50.00

ESQUERITA

CAPITOL

Number	Title	Yr	NM
❏ T1186 [M]	Esquerita	1959	1000.00

ESQUIRES, THE (1)

BUNKY

Number	Title	Yr	NM
❏ 300	Get On Up and Get Away	1968	35.00

ESQUIVEL

BAR NONE

Number	Title	Yr	NM
❏ LP-056	Music for a Sparkling Planet	1995	15.00
❏ LP-043	Space Age Bachelor Pad Music	1994	15.00

RCA VICTOR

Number	Title	Yr	NM
❏ LPM-1978 [M]	Exploring New Sounds in Hi-Fi	1959	30.00
❏ LSP-1978 [S]	Exploring New Sounds in Hi-Fi	1959	60.00
❏ LPM-1749 [M]	Four Corners of the World	1958	30.00
❏ LSP-1749 [S]	Four Corners of the World	1958	50.00
❏ LPM-2225 [M]	Infinity in Sound	1960	30.00
❏ LSP-2225 [S]	Infinity in Sound	1960	60.00
❏ LPM-2296 [M]	Infinity in Sound, Vol. 2	1961	30.00
❏ LSP-2296 [S]	Infinity in Sound, Vol. 2	1961	60.00
❏ LPM-2418 [M]	Latin-esque	1962	25.00
❏ LSP-2418 [S]	Latin-esque	1962	60.00
—Die-cut cover that reveals inner sleeve			
❏ LSP-2418 [S]	Latin-esque	1962	40.00
—Standard cover			
❏ LPM-1753 [M]	Other Worlds, Other Sounds	1959	30.00
❏ LSP-1753 [S]	Other Worlds, Other Sounds	1959	50.00
❏ LPM-1988 [M]	Strings Aflame	1959	30.00
❏ LSP-1988 [S]	Strings Aflame	1959	50.00
❏ LPM-3502 [M]	The Best of Esquivel	1966	25.00
❏ LSP-3502 [S]	The Best of Esquivel	1966	30.00
❏ LPM-3607 [M]	The Genius of Esquivel	1967	25.00
❏ LSP-3697 [S]	The Genius of Esquivel	1967	30.00
❏ LPM-1345 [M]	To Love Again	1957	50.00

REPRISE

Number	Title	Yr	NM
❏ R-6046 [M]	More of Other World, Other Sounds	1962	30.00
❏ P9-6046 [S]	More of Other World, Other Sounds	1962	30.00

ESSEX, DAVID

COLUMBIA

Number	Title	Yr	NM
❏ PC33813	All the Fun of the Fair	1975	18.00
❏ KC33289	David Essex	1974	18.00
❏ KC32560	Rock On	1974	25.00
❏ CQ32560 [Q]	Rock On	1974	35.00

MERCURY

Number	Title	Yr	NM
❏ 812936-1	David Essex	1983	18.00

ESSEX, THE

ROULETTE

Number	Title	Yr	NM
❏ R-25235 [M]	A Walkin' Miracle	1963	40.00
❏ SR-25235 [S]	A Walkin' Miracle	1963	50.00
❏ R-25234 [M]	Easier Said Than Done	1963	40.00
❏ SR-25234 [S]	Easier Said Than Done	1963	50.00
❏ R-25246 [M]	Young and Lively	1964	40.00
❏ SR-25246 [S]	Young and Lively	1964	50.00

ESTABLISHMENT, THE

KING

Number	Title	Yr	NM
❏ KS-1123	The Establishment	1971	15.00

ESTEFAN, GLORIA

CBS INTERNATIONAL

Number	Title	Yr	NM
❏ DFL80432	Exitos De Gloria Estefan	1990	30.00

EPIC

Number	Title	Yr	NM
❏ OE45217	Cuts Both Ways	1989	12.00
❏ E69200	Gloria!	1998	25.00
❏ E46988	Into the Light	1991	15.00
❏ OE40769	Let It Loose	1987	10.00

ETC.

WINDI

Number	Title	Yr	NM
❏ WLPS-1011	Etc. Is the Name of the Band!	1976	30.00

ETERNITY'S CHILDREN

TOWER

Number	Title	Yr	NM
❏ ST-5123 [S]	Eternity's Children	1968	100.00
❏ T-5123 [M]	Eternity's Children	1968	150.00
❏ ST-5144	Timeless	1969	400.00
—Canada only release, but sold into the US.			

ETHEL AND THE SHAMELESS HUSSIES

MCA

Number	Title	Yr	NM
❏ 42191	Born to Burn	1988	12.00

ETHERIDGE, MELISSA

ISLAND

Number	Title	Yr	NM
❏ 91285	Brave and Crazy	1989	15.00
❏ 546591	Breakdown	1999	18.00
—With bonus 7-inch single			
❏ 90875	Melissa Etheridge	1988	12.00

ETHNIC HERITAGE ENSEMBLE, THE

RED

Number	Title	Yr	NM
❏ VPA-156	Impressions	198?	18.00

SILKHEART

Number	Title	Yr	NM
❏ SH-108	Ancestral Song	198?	15.00

ETHRIDGE, KELLIS

INNER CITY

Number	Title	Yr	NM
❏ IC-1109	Tomorrow Sky	1980	12.00

ETZEL, ROY

MGM

Number	Title	Yr	NM
❏ E-4330 [M]	The Silence (Il Silenzio)	1965	15.00
❏ SE-4330 [S]	The Silence (Il Silenzio)	1965	18.00

EUBANKS, JACK

MONUMENT

Number	Title	Yr	NM
❏ LP-8044 [M]	Guitar Sounds of the South	1966	18.00
❏ SLP-18044 [S]	Guitar Sounds of the South	1966	25.00

EUBANKS, KEVIN

ELEKTRA/MUSICIAN

Number	Title	Yr	NM
❏ 60213	Guitarist	1983	18.00

GRP

Number	Title	Yr	NM
❏ GR-1029	Face to Face	1985	12.00
❏ GR-1041	Heat of Heat	1986	12.00
❏ GR-1031	Opening Night	1985	12.00
❏ GR-1054	Shadow Prophets	1988	12.00
❏ GR-1008	Sundance	1984	12.00
❏ GR-9580	The Searcher	1989	15.00

EUBANKS, ROBIN

JMT

Number	Title	Yr	NM
❏ 834433-1	Dedication	1989	15.00
❏ 834424-1	Different Perspectives	1988	12.00

EUPHONIOUS WAIL

KAPP

Number	Title	Yr	NM
❏ KS-3668	Euphonious Wail	1973	40.00

EUPHORIA (2)

HERITAGE

Number	Title	Yr	NM
❏ HTS35005	Euphoria	1971	30.00

EUPHORIA (3)

CAPITOL

Number	Title	Yr	NM
❏ SKAO-363	A Gift from Euphoria	1969	200.00

EUPHORIA (4)

RAINBOW

Number	Title	Yr	NM
❏ 1003	Lost in a Trance	1973	300.00

EUREKA BRASS BAND, THE

ATLANTIC

Number	Title	Yr	NM
❏ 1408 [M]	The Eureka Brass Band	1963	18.00
❏ SD1408 [S]	The Eureka Brass Band	1963	25.00
—Multicolor label with black "fan" logo at right			
❏ SD1408 [S]	The Eureka Brass Band	1969	12.00
—Red and green label with "1841 Broadway" address			
❏ SD1408 [S]	The Eureka Brass Band	1975	10.00
—Red and green label with "75 Rockefeller Plaza" address and "W" logo in perimeter print			

FOLKWAYS

Number	Title	Yr	NM
❏ FA-2642 [M]	Music of New Orleans	195?	50.00

PAX

Number	Title	Yr	NM
❏ LP-9001 [10]	New Orleans Parade	1954	60.00

EUROGLIDERS

COLUMBIA

Number	Title	Yr	NM
❏ BFC40269	Absolutely	1986	12.00
❏ BFC39588	This Island	1984	12.00

EURYTHMICS

ARISTA

Number	Title	Yr	NM
❏ AL8606	We Too Are One	1989	15.00

RCA

Number	Title	Yr	NM
❏ 5707-1-RDAA [EP]	Rough and Tough at the Roxy	1986	35.00
—Promo-only 4-song live album			
❏ 6794-1-R	Savage	1987	15.00

RCA VICTOR

Number	Title	Yr	NM
❏ ABL1-5371	1984 (For the Love of Big Brother)	1984	15.00
❏ AJL1-5429	Be Yourself Tonight	1985	15.00
❏ AJL1-5847	Revenge	1986	15.00
❏ AFL1-4681	Sweet Dreams (Are Made of This)	1983	12.00

Number	Title	Yr	NM

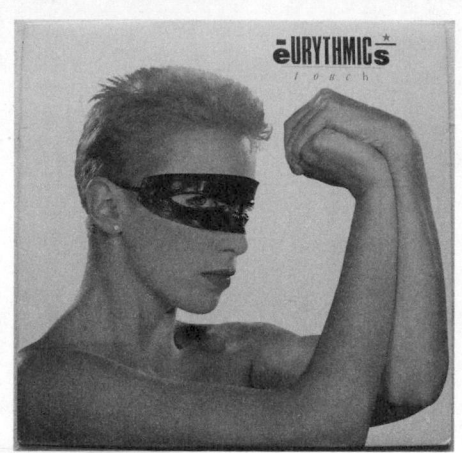

❏ AFL1-4917 [B]	Touch	1984	15.00
❏ CPL1-5086 [EP]	Touch Dance	1983	15.00

EVANS, BILL (1), AND JIM HALL

BLUE NOTE
❏ B1-90583	Undercurrent	1988	12.00

SOLID STATE
❏ SS-18018	Undercurrent	1968	25.00

UNITED ARTISTS
❏ UAJ-14003 [M]	Undercurrent	1962	40.00
❏ UAJS-15003 [S]	Undercurrent	1962	50.00
❏ UAS-5640	Undercurrent	197?	18.00

EVANS, BILL (1)

COLUMBIA
❏ KC31490	Living Time: Events I-VIII	1972	18.00
❏ C30855	The Bill Evans Album	1971	18.00
❏ PC30855	The Bill Evans Album	198?	10.00
—Budget-line reissue			
❏ CG33672	The Bill Evans Album/Living Time	1976	18.00

CTI
❏ 6004	Montreux II	1971	18.00

ELEKTRA/MUSICIAN
❏ 60164	The Paris Concert, Volume 1	1984	16.00
❏ 60311	The Paris Concert, Volume 2	1986	15.00

FANTASY
❏ F-9542	Alone (Again)	1977	15.00
❏ OJC-263	Bill Evans at Shelly's Manne-Hole	1987	12.00
❏ F-9568	Crosscurrents	1978	15.00
❏ F-9618	Eloquence	1982	12.00
❏ OJC-068	Everybody Digs Bill Evans	198?	12.00
❏ OJC-037	Explorations	198?	12.00
❏ F-9630	From the 70s	198?	12.00
❏ OJC-369	How My Heart Sings	198?	12.00
❏ OJC-308	Interplay	198?	12.00
❏ F-9475	Intuition	1975	15.00
❏ OJC-470	Intuition	1990	15.00
❏ F-9593	I Will Say Goodbye	1980	15.00
❏ F-9510	Montreux III	1976	15.00
❏ OJC-434	Moonbeams	1990	15.00
❏ OJC-025	New Jazz Conceptions	1982	12.00
❏ OJC-088	Portrait in Jazz	198?	12.00
❏ F-9529	Quintessence	1976	15.00
❏ F-9608	Re: The Person I Knew	198?	12.00
❏ F-9501	Since We Met	1975	15.00
❏ OJC-622	Since We Met	1991	15.00
❏ OJC-140	Sunday at the Village Vanguard	198?	12.00
❏ F-9457	The Tokyo Concert	1974	15.00
❏ OJC-345	The Tokyo Concert	1990	15.00
❏ OJC-210	Waltz for Debby	198?	12.00

MGM
❏ SE-4723	From Left to Right	1970	18.00

MILESTONE
❏ 47063	Conception	198?	18.00
❏ 9151	Jazzhouse	1988	12.00
❏ 9125	More from the Vanguard	198?	12.00
❏ 47024	Peace Piece & Others	197?	18.00
❏ 47034	Spring Leaves	197?	18.00
❏ 47066	The Interplay Sessions	198?	15.00
❏ 47046	The Second Trio	197?	18.00
❏ 9170	The Solo Sessions, Volume 1	1989	15.00
❏ 47002	The Village Vanguard Sessions	197?	18.00
❏ 47068	Time Remembered	198?	15.00
❏ 9164	You're Gonna Hear from Me	198?	12.00

MOSAIC
❏ MQ10-171	The Final Village Vanguard Sessions – June 1980	1996	200.00

PAUSA
❏ 7050	Symbiosis	1979	12.00

RIVERSIDE
❏ 6197	Bill Evans at Shelly's Manne-Hole	198?	12.00

Number	Title	Yr	NM
❏ RLP-487 [M]	Bill Evans at Shelly's Manne- Hole, Hollywood, California	1965	25.00
❏ RS-9487 [S]	Bill Evans at Shelly's Manne- Hole, Hollywood, California	1965	30.00
❏ RLP 12-291 [M]	Everybody Digs Bill Evans	1958	150.00
—blue label			
❏ RLP1129 [S]	Everybody Digs Bill Evans	1959	30.00
❏ 6090	Everybody Digs Bill Evans	197?	15.00
❏ RLP-351 [M]	Explorations	1960	250.00
—blue label			
❏ RS-9351 [S]	Explorations	1960	250.00
—black label			
❏ 6038	Explorations	197?	15.00
❏ RLP-473 [M]	How My Heart Sings!	1964	30.00
❏ RS-9473 [S]	How My Heart Sings!	1964	30.00
❏ RLP-445 [M]	Interplay	1963	100.00
❏ RS-9445 [S]	Interplay	1963	30.00
❏ RS-3013	Live at Shelly's Manne-Hole	1968	15.00
❏ RM-3006 [M]	Live at the Village Vanguard	1967	18.00
❏ RS-3006 [S]	Live at the Village Vanguard	1967	15.00
❏ RLP-428 [M]	Moonbeams	1962	150.00
❏ RS-9428 [S]	Moonbeams	1962	30.00
❏ 6175	Moonbeams	198?	12.00
❏ RLP 12-223 [M]	New Jazz Conceptions	1956	500.00
—Photo on cover, label is white with blue print			
❏ RLP 12-223 [M]	New Jazz Conceptions	1958	30.00
—New cover, label is blue with microphone logo at top			
❏ RS-3042	Peace Pieces	1969	15.00
❏ RM-3001 [M]	Polka Dots and Moonbeams	1967	18.00
❏ RS-3001 [S]	Polka Dots and Moonbeams	1967	15.00
❏ RLP 12-315 [M]	Portrait in Jazz	1959	400.00
—deep groove pressing with small reel logos on the label			
❏ RLP1162 [S]	Portrait in Jazz	1959	30.00
❏ RLP-376 [M]	Sunday at the Village Vanguard	1961	50.00
❏ RS-9376 [S]	Sunday at the Village Vanguard	1961	30.00
❏ R-018	The Complete Riverside Recordings	1985	200.00
❏ RLP-399 [M]	Waltz for Debby	1961	150.00
—blue label			
❏ RS-9399 [S]	Waltz for Debby	1961	200.00
—black label			
❏ 6118	Waltz for Debby	197?	15.00

TIMELESS
❏ LPSJP-331	Consecration I	1990	18.00
❏ LPSJP-332	Consecration II	1990	18.00

VERVE
❏ V-8675 [M]	A Simple Matter of Conviction	1966	18.00
❏ V6-8675 [S]	A Simple Matter of Conviction	1966	25.00
❏ UMV-2107	A Simple Matter of Conviction	198?	12.00
❏ V6-8792	Bill Evans Alone	1969	18.00
❏ V6-8762	Bill Evans at the Montreux Jazz Festival	1968	18.00
❏ 827844-1	Bill Evans at the Montreux Jazz Festival	1986	12.00
❏ V6-8762	Bill Evans at the Montreux Jazz Festival	199?	30.00
—Classic Records reissue on audiophile vinyl			
❏ V-0683 [M]	Bill Evans at Town Hall	1966	18.00
❏ V6-8683 [S]	Bill Evans at Town Hall	1966	25.00
❏ V-8578 [M]	Bill Evans Trio '64	1964	18.00
❏ V6-8578 [S]	Bill Evans Trio '64	1964	25.00
❏ V-8613 [M]	Bill Evans Trio '65	1965	18.00
❏ V6-8613 [S]	Bill Evans Trio '65	1965	25.00
❏ V-8640 [M]	Bill Evans Trio with Symphony Orchestra	1965	18.00
❏ V6-8640 [S]	Bill Evans Trio with Symphony Orchestra	1965	25.00
❏ VE-2-2545	California Here I Come	198?	15.00
❏ V-8526 [M]	Conversations with Myself	1963	25.00
❏ V6-8526 [S]	Conversations with Myself	1963	30.00
❏ V-8497 [M]	Empathy	1962	30.00
❏ V6-8497 [S]	Empathy	1962	30.00
❏ V-8727 [M]	Further Conversations with Myself	1967	25.00
❏ V6-8727 [S]	Further Conversations with Myself	1967	18.00
❏ V-8655 [M]	Intermodulation	1966	100.00
❏ V6-8655 [S]	Intermodulation	1966	25.00
❏ UMV-2106	Intermodulation	198?	12.00
❏ V3HB-8841	Return Engagement	1973	25.00
❏ V-8747 [M]	The Best of Bill Evans	1967	25.00
❏ V6-8747 [S]	The Best of Bill Evans	1967	18.00
❏ UMV-2053	The Bill Evans Trio at Town Hall	198?	12.00
❏ VE-2-2509	Trios and Duos	197?	18.00
❏ V6-8777	What's New	1968	18.00

WARNER BROS.
❏ BSK3293	Affinity	1978	15.00
❏ BSK3177	New Conversations	1977	15.00
❏ HS3411	We Will Meet Again	1979	15.00
❏ HS3504	You Must Believe in Spring	1981	15.00

EVANS, BILL (2)

BLUE NOTE
❏ BT-05111	The Alternative Man	1985	12.00

ELEKTRA/MUSICIAN
❏ 60349	Living in the Crest of a Wave	1986	12.00

EVANS, DALE

ALLEGRO ELITE
❏ 4116 [10]	Dale Evans Sings	195?	40.00

Number	Title	Yr	NM
CAPITOL			
❏ ST-399	Get to Know the Lord	1970	18.00
❏ T2772 [M]	It's Real	1967	30.00
❏ ST2772 [S]	It's Real	1967	30.00

EVON
❏ 336 [M]	Dale Evans Sings Western Favorites/Johnny 'O Calls Western Dances	195?	30.00
—Only Side 1 is by Dale Evans			

MANNA
❏ MS-2075	Reflections of Life	1981	15.00

SACRED
❏ LPS-4507	Favorite Gospel Songs	197?	15.00
—Reissue of Word WST-8546			

WORD
❏ WST-8661	Country Dale	1976	15.00
❏ WST-8566	Faith, Hope and Charity	1972	18.00
❏ WST-8658 [B]	Heart of the Country	1975	18.00
❏ WST-8546	It's Real	1971	18.00
❏ WST-8803	Totally Free	1979	15.00

EVANS, DAME EDITH

GOLDEN
❏ GW245 [M]	The First Christmas	196?	15.00

EVANS, DOC

AUDIOPHILE
❏ AP-50 [M]	Classics of the 20's	195?	40.00
—Red vinyl			
❏ AP-29 [M]	Dixieland Session	195?	40.00
❏ AP-11 [M]	Doc Evans and His Band, Volume 1	195?	40.00
❏ AP-12 [M]	Doc Evans and His Band, Volume 2	195?	40.00
❏ AP-95	Doc Evans at the Gas Light	1989	12.00
—Reissue with same number			
❏ AP-95 [M]	Doc Evans at the Gas Light	196?	25.00
❏ AS-95 [S]	Doc Evans at the Gas Light	196?	30.00
❏ AP-4	Down in Jungle Town	1987	12.00
❏ APS-5968	Reminiscing in Dixieland	196?	30.00
—Red vinyl			
❏ AP-31 [M]	The Cornet Artistry of Doc Evans	195?	40.00
❏ AP-34 [M]	Traditional Jazz	195?	40.00
—Red vinyl			
❏ AP-44 [M]	Traditional Jazz	195?	40.00
—Red vinyl			
❏ AP-45 [M]	Traditional Jazz	195?	40.00
—Red vinyl			
❏ AP-33 [M]	Traditional Jazz	195?	40.00
—Red vinyl			
❏ XL-328 [M]	Traditional Jazz	195?	40.00
❏ XL-329 [M]	Traditional Jazz	195?	40.00

CONCERT DISC
❏ CS-47	Doc Evans + 4 = Dixie	1961	30.00
❏ CS-48	Muskrat Ramble	196?	30.00

FOLKWAYS
❏ FA-2855	Doc Evans and His Dixieland Jazz Band	195?	25.00

JAZZOLOGY
❏ J-86	Blues in Dixieland	197?	12.00
❏ J-87	Command Performance	197?	12.00
❏ J-85	Jazz Heritage, Volume 1	197?	12.00

SOMA
❏ MG-1201 [M]	Classic Jazz at Carleton	1954	40.00
❏ MG-100 [M]	Dixieland Concert	1953	50.00
❏ MG-101 [10]	Dixieland Concert	1953	50.00

EVANS, GIL

ABC IMPULSE!
❏ AS-9 [S]	Into the Hot	1968	18.00
❏ AS-4 [S]	Out of the Cool	1968	18.00
❏ IA-9340	The Great Arrangers	1978	18.00

AMPEX
❏ A-10102	Gil Evans	1971	18.00

ANTILLES
❏ AN-1010	Priestess	198?	12.00

ARTISTS HOUSE
❏ 14	Where Flamingoes Fly	198?	12.00

ATLANTIC
❏ SD1643	Svengali	1973	15.00
❏ QD1643 [Q]	Svengali	1973	25.00
❏ 90048	Svengali	1983	10.00

BLUE NOTE
❏ BN-LA461-H2	Pacific Standard Time	1975	18.00

EMARCY
❏ 836401-1	Rhythm-A-Ning	1989	15.00

FANTASY
❏ OJC-346	Gil Evans Plus Ten	198?	12.00

IMPULSE!
❏ A-9 [M]	Into the Hot	1962	30.00
❏ AS-9 [S]	Into the Hot	1962	30.00
❏ A-4 [M]	Out of the Cool	1961	30.00
❏ AS-4 [S]	Out of the Cool	1961	30.00

Number	Title	Yr	NM
INNER CITY			
❏ IC-1110	Little Wing	198?	15.00
MCA			
❏ 29034	Into the Hot	198?	10.00
❏ 29033	Out of the Cool	198?	10.00
❏ 4143	The Great Arrangers	198?	12.00
MCA IMPULSE!			
❏ 5653	Out of the Cool	1986	12.00
NEW JAZZ			
❏ NJLP-8215 [M]	Big Stuff	1959	50.00
—Purple label			
❏ NJLP-8215 [M]	Big Stuff	1965	30.00
—Blue label, trident logo at right			
PACIFIC JAZZ			
❏ PJ-28 [M]	America's #1 Arranger	1961	30.00
❏ PJ-40 [M]	Cannonball Adderley/Gil Evans	1962	30.00
❏ ST-40 [S]	Cannonball Adderley/Gil Evans	1962	30.00
PRESTIGE			
❏ 24049	An Arranger's Touch	197?	18.00
❏ PRST-7756	Big Stuff	1970	18.00
❏ PRLP-7120 [M]	Gil Evans Plus Ten	1957	150.00
RCA VICTOR			
❏ CPL1-0667	Gil Evans Plays Jimi Hendrix	1974	25.00
❏ LPM-1057 [M]	There Comes a Time	1955	80.00
❏ APL1-1057	There Comes a Time	1976	15.00
VERVE			
❏ V6-8838	Previously Unreleased Recordings	1974	15.00
❏ V-8555 [M]	The Individualism of Gil Evans	1963	25.00
❏ V6-8555 [S]	The Individualism of Gil Evans	1963	30.00
WORLD PACIFIC			
❏ WP-1270 [M]	Great Jazz Standards	1959	50.00
❏ ST-1027 [S]	Great Jazz Standards	1959	40.00
❏ WP-1246 [M]	New Bottle, Old Wine	1958	50.00
❏ ST-1011 [S]	New Bottle, Old Wine	1959	40.00
EVANS, JOHN			
OMEGA			
❏ OL-49 [M]	Mainstream Jazz Piano	1960	25.00
❏ OSL-49 [S]	Mainstream Jazz Piano	1960	25.00
EVANS, LEE			
CAPITOL			
❏ T1625 [M]	Big Piano/Big Band/Big Sound	1962	18.00
❏ ST1625 [S]	Big Piano/Big Band/Big Sound	1962	25.00
❏ T1847 [M]	The Lee Evans Trio	1963	18.00
❏ ST1847 [S]	The Lee Evans Trio	1963	25.00
EVANS, PAUL			
CARLTON			
❏ TLP-130 [M]	Folk Songs of Many Lands	1961	40.00
❏ STLP-130 [S]	Folk Songs of Many Lands	1961	60.00
❏ TLP-129 [M]	Hear Paul Evans in Your Home Tonight	1961	40.00
❏ STLP-129 [S]	Hear Paul Evans in Your Home Tonight	1961	60.00
GUARANTEED			
❏ GUL-1000 [M]	Fabulous Teens	1960	70.00
❏ GUS-1000 [S]	Fabulous Teens	1960	80.00
KAPP			
❏ KL-1346 [M]	21 Years in a Tennessee Jail	1964	30.00
❏ KS-3346 [S]	21 Years in a Tennessee Jail	1964	40.00
❏ KL-1475 [M]	Another Town, Another Jail	1966	30.00
❏ KS-3475 [S]	Another Town, Another Jail	1966	30.00
EVANS, RICHARD			
ARGO			
❏ LP-675 [M]	Home Cookin'	1961	30.00
❏ LPS-675 [S]	Home Cookin'	1961	30.00
❏ LP-658 [M]	Richard's Almanac	1960	30.00
❏ LPS-658 [S]	Richard's Almanac	1960	40.00
EVANS, ROBERT			
CUSTOM			
❏ CS2	O Come All Ye Faithful	196?	15.00
YULETIDE SERIES			
❏ YS-212	O Come All Ye Faithful	197?	12.00
—Reissue of Custom LP			
EVANS, SARA			
RCA			
❏ 66995-1 [DJ]	Three Chords and the Truth	1997	18.00
—Vinyl is promo only			
EVANS QUARTET, THE			
DECCA			
❏ DL4162 [M]	Merry Christmas -- Barbershop Style	1961	15.00
❏ DL74162 [S]	Merry Christmas -- Barbershop Style	1961	18.00

Number	Title	Yr	NM
EVEN DOZEN JUG BAND, THE			
ELEKTRA			
❏ EKL-246 [M]	The Even Dozen Jug Band	1964	30.00
❏ EKS-7246 [S]	The Even Dozen Jug Band	1964	50.00
EVERCLEAR			
CAPITOL			
❏ C1-36503	So Much for the Afterglow	1997	25.00
—Blue vinyl			
CAPITOL/TIMKERR			
❏ C130929	Sparkle and Fade	1995	40.00
—Price includes bonus 45 "Live on the Radio"; deduct 25 percent if missing			
EVERETT, BETTY, AND JERRY BUTLER			
BUDDAH			
❏ BDS-7505	Together	1969	18.00
❏ BDS-7505	Together	1969	18.00
TRADITION			
❏ 2073	Starring Betty Everett with Jerry Butler	197?	15.00
VEE JAY			
❏ LP-1099 [M]	Delicious Together	1964	25.00
❏ VJS-1099 [S]	Delicious Together	1964	30.00
❏ VJLP-1099	Delicious Together	198?	12.00
—Reissue of original 1099; has softer vinyl			
❏ LP1099 [M]	Delicious Together	1964	25.00
❏ VJS1099 [S]	Delicious Together	1964	30.00
❏ VJLP1099	Delicious Together	198?	15.00
—Authorized reissue			
EVERETT, BETTY			
FANTASY			
❏ 9480	Happy Endings	1975	15.00
❏ 9447	Love Rhymes	1974	15.00
SUNSET			
❏ SUS-5220	I Need You So	1968	18.00
UNI			
❏ 73048	There'll Come a Time	1969	30.00
VEE JAY			
❏ LP1077 [M]	It's In His Kiss	1964	30.00
❏ SR1077 [S]	It's In His Kiss	1964	50.00
❏ LP1122 [M]	The Very Best of Betty Everett	1965	40.00
❏ VJS1122 [S]	The Very Best of Betty Everett	1965	50.00
❏ VJLP1122	The Very Best of Betty Everett	198?	12.00
—Authorized reissue			
❏ LP1077 [M]	You're No Good	1964	40.00
❏ SR1077 [S]	You're No Good	1964	70.00
EVERETTE, LEON			
MERCURY			
❏ 824309-1	Where's the Fire	1985	10.00
ORLANDO			
❏ 1101	I Don't Want to Lose	1980	15.00
RCA VICTOR			
❏ MHL1-8513 [EP]	Doin' What I Feel	1984	10.00
❏ AHL1-4152	Hurricane	1981	12.00
❏ AHL1-3916	If I Keep On Going Crazy	1981	12.00
❏ MHL1-8600 [EP]	Leon Everette	1983	10.00
TRUE			
❏ 1002	Goodbye King of Rock and Roll	1977	30.00
—Deduct 40% if poster of Elvis Presley is missing			
EVERGREEN BLUES, THE			
ABC			
❏ S-669	Comin' On	1969	18.00
MERCURY			
❏ SR-61157 [S]	7 Do 11	1968	25.00
❏ MG-21157 [M]	7 Do 11	1968	50.00
—Mono is white label promo only			
EVERGREEN CLASSIC JAZZ BAND			
STOMP OFF			
❏ SOS-1202	Trust Me… I'm a Musician	1991	12.00
EVERLAST			
TOMMY BOY			
❏ TBLP1411	Eat at Whitey's	2000	25.00
WARNER BROS.			
❏ 26007	Forever Everlasting	1990	25.00
EVERLY, DON			
ABC HICKORY			
❏ AH-44003	Brother Juke-Box	1977	15.00
ODE			
❏ SP-77005	Don Everly	1970	18.00
❏ SP-77023	Sunset Towers	1974	18.00

Number	Title	Yr	NM
EVERLY, PHIL			
ELEKTRA			
❏ 6E-213	Living Alone	1979	12.00
PYE			
❏ 12121	Mystic Line	1976	15.00
❏ 12104	Phil's Diner	1975	15.00
RCA VICTOR			
❏ APL1-0092	Star Spangled Springer	1973	18.00
EVERLY BROTHERS, THE			
ARISTA			
❏ AL9-8207	24 Original Classics	1985	18.00
BARNABY			
❏ ZG30260	End of an Era	1971	18.00
❏ 4004	Greatest Hits, Vol. 1	1977	12.00
❏ 4005	Greatest Hits, Vol. 2	1977	12.00
❏ 4006	Greatest Hits, Vol. 3	1977	12.00
❏ BR-15008	History of the Everly Brothers	1973	18.00
❏ BR-6006	The Everly Brothers' Greatest Hits	1974	18.00
❏ BGP-350	The Everly Brothers' Original Golden Hits	1970	25.00
CADENCE			
❏ CLP-3062 [M]	15 Everly Hits 15	1963	40.00
❏ CLP-25062 [P]	15 Everly Hits 15	1963	50.00
❏ CLP-3059 [M]	Folk Songs of the Everly Brothers	1963	50.00
—Reissue of 3016			
❏ CLP-25059 [R]	Folk Songs of the Everly Brothers	1963	40.00
❏ CLP-3016 [M]	Songs Our Daddy Taught Us	1958	100.00
—Maroon label with metronome logo			
❏ CLP-3016 [M]	Songs Our Daddy Taught Us	1962	60.00
—Red label with black border			
❏ CLP-3003 [M]	The Everly Brothers	1958	100.00
—Maroon label with metronome logo			
❏ CLP-3003 [M]	The Everly Brothers	1962	60.00
—Red label with black border			
❏ CLP-3025 [M]	The Everly Brothers' Best	1959	90.00
—Maroon label with metronome logo			
❏ CLP-3025 [M]	The Everly Brothers' Best	1962	60.00
—Red label with black border			
❏ CLP-3040 [M]	The Fabulous Style of the Everly Brothers	1960	80.00
—Maroon label with metronome logo			
❏ CLP-25040 [P]	The Fabulous Style of the Everly Brothers	1960	120.00
—Maroon label with metronome logo			
❏ CLP-3040 [M]	The Fabulous Style of the Everly Brothers	1962	50.00
—Red label with black border			
❏ CLP-25040 [P]	The Fabulous Style of the Everly Brothers	1962	60.00
—Red label with black border			
HARMONY			
❏ KH11388	Chained to a Memory	1970	15.00
❏ HS11350	Christmas with the Everly Brothers and the Boys Town Choir	1969	25.00
❏ HS11304	Wake Up Little Susie	1969	15.00
MERCURY			
❏ 826142-1	Born Yesterday	1986	12.00
❏ 822431-1	EB 84	1984	12.00
❏ 832520-1	Some Hearts	1989	15.00
PAIR			
❏ PDL1-1063	Living Legends	1986	15.00
PASSPORT			
❏ 11001	The Everly Brothers Reunion Concert	1984	18.00
RCA VICTOR			
❏ AFL1-5401	Home Again	1985	12.00
❏ LSP-4781	Pass the Chicken and Listen	1972	18.00
❏ LSP-4620	Stories We Could Tell	1972	18.00
RHINO			
❏ RNLP-214	All They Had to Do Was Dream	1985	12.00
❏ RNDF-258 [PD]	Heartaches and Harmonies	1985	25.00
❏ R11752 [B]	Roots	2014	25.00
❏ RNLP-212	Songs Our Daddy Taught Us	1985	12.00
❏ RNLP-70173	The Best of the Everly Brothers (Golden Archive Series)	1987	12.00
❏ RNLP-211	The Everly Brothers	1985	12.00
❏ RNLP-213	The Fabulous Style of the Everly Brothers	1985	12.00
TIME-LIFE			
❏ SRNR-09	The Everly Brothers: 1957-1962	1986	25.00
—Part of "The Rock 'n' Roll Era" series; box set with insert			
WARNER BROS.			
❏ W1395 [M]	A Date with the Everly Brothers	1960	50.00
—Gatefold edition with poster and wallet-size photos			
❏ WS1395 [S]	A Date with the Everly Brothers	1960	75.00
—Gatefold edition with poster and wallet-size photos			
❏ W1395 [M]	A Date with the Everly Brothers	1960	40.00
—Gatefold edition without poster or photos			

Number	Title	Yr	NM
❑ WS1395 [S]	A Date with the Everly Brothers	1960	50.00
— Gatefold edition without poster or photos			
❑ W1395 [M]	A Date with the Everly Brothers	1961	30.00
— Regular edition			
❑ WS1395 [S]	A Date with the Everly Brothers	1961	40.00
— Regular edition			
❑ W1605 [M]	Beat & Soul	1965	40.00
❑ WS1605 [S]	Beat & Soul	1965	50.00
❑ W1418 [M]	Both Sides of an Evening	1961	30.00
❑ WS1418 [S]	Both Sides of an Evening	1961	40.00
❑ W1483 [M]	Christmas with the Everly Brothers and the Boys Town Choir	1962	40.00
❑ WS1483 [S]	Christmas with the Everly Brothers and the Boys Town Choir	1962	50.00
❑ W1585 [M]	Gone, Gone, Gone	1965	40.00
❑ WS1585 [S]	Gone, Gone, Gone	1965	50.00
❑ W1513 [M]	Great Country Hits	1963	40.00
❑ WS1513 [S]	Great Country Hits	1963	50.00
❑ W1620 [M]	In Our Image	1966	40.00
❑ WS1620 [S]	In Our Image	1966	50.00
❑ W1430 [M]	Instant Party!	1962	30.00
❑ WS1430 [S]	Instant Party!	1962	40.00
❑ PRO134 [10]	It's Everly Time!	1960	600.00
— Promo "souvenir sampler" from their debut on WB			
❑ W1381 [M]	It's Everly Time!	1960	30.00
❑ WS1381 [S]	It's Everly Time!	1960	40.00
❑ W1578 [M]	Rock & Soul	1964	40.00
❑ WS1578 [S]	Rock & Soul	1964	50.00
❑ WS1752	Roots	1968	40.00
❑ ST-91601	Roots	1968	50.00
— Capitol Record Club edition			
❑ WS1858	The Everly Brothers Show	1970	30.00
❑ STAO-93286	The Everly Brothers Show	1970	40.00
— Capitol Record Club edition			
❑ W1708 [M]	The Everly Brothers Sing	1967	50.00
❑ WS1708 [S]	The Everly Brothers Sing	1967	40.00
❑ W1471 [M]	The Golden Hits of the Everly Brothers	1962	30.00
❑ WS1471 [S]	The Golden Hits of the Everly Brothers	1962	40.00
— Gold label			
❑ WS1471	The Golden Hits of the Everly Brothers	1967	25.00
— Green "W7" label			
❑ WS1471	The Golden Hits of the Everly Brothers	1970	18.00
— Green "WB" label			
❑ WS1471	The Golden Hits of the Everly Brothers	1973	15.00
— Burbank" palm-tree label			

Number	Title	Yr	NM
❑ WS1471 [B]	The Golden Hits of the Everly Brothers	1979	12.00
— White or tan label			
❑ W1676 [M]	The Hit Sound of the Everly Brothers	1967	50.00
❑ WS1676 [S]	The Hit Sound of the Everly Brothers	1967	40.00
❑ W1554 [M]	The Very Best of the Everly Brothers	1964	30.00
— Originals have yellow covers			
❑ W1554 [M]	The Very Best of the Everly Brothers	1965	25.00
— Later pressings have white covers			
❑ WS1554 [S]	The Very Best of the Everly Brothers	1964	40.00
— Originals have yellow covers			
❑ WS1554 [S]	The Very Best of the Everly Brothers	1965	30.00
— White cover, gold label			
❑ ST-91343 [S]	The Very Best of the Everly Brothers	1967	40.00
— Capitol Record Club edition			
❑ WS1554	The Very Best of the Everly Brothers	1967	25.00
— Green "W7" label			

Number	Title	Yr	NM
❑ WS1554	The Very Best of the Everly Brothers	1970	18.00
— Green "WB" label			
❑ WS1554	The Very Best of the Everly Brothers	1973	15.00
— Burbank" palm-tree label			
❑ WS1554	The Very Best of the Everly Brothers	1979	12.00
— White or tan label			
❑ W1646 [M]	Two Yanks in England	1966	40.00
❑ WS1646 [S]	Two Yanks in England	1966	50.00

EVERPRESENT FULLNESS, THE

WHITE WHALE
| ❑ 7132 | The Everpresent Fullness | 1970 | 75.00 |

EVERY MOTHERS' SON

MGM
❑ E-4471 [M]	Every Mothers' Son	1967	25.00
❑ SE-4471 [S]	Every Mothers' Son	1967	25.00
❑ E-4504 [M]	Every Mothers' Son's Back	1967	25.00
❑ SE-4504 [S]	Every Mothers' Son's Back	1967	25.00

EVERYMAN BAND

ECM
| ❑ 1234 | Everyman Band | 1983 | 15.00 |
| ❑ 1290 | Without Warning | 1985 | 12.00 |

EVERYTHING BUT THE GIRL

ATLANTIC
| ❑ 83214 | Temperamental | 1999 | 18.00 |
| ❑ 82057 | The Language of Life | 1990 | 15.00 |
SIRE
❑ 25494	Baby, the Stars Shine Bright	1986	12.00
❑ 25214	Everything But The Girl	1984	12.00
❑ 25721	Idlewild	1988	12.00
❑ 25274	Love Not Money	1985	12.00

EVERYTHING IS EVERYTHING

VANGUARD
| ❑ VSD-6512 | Everything Is Everything | 1969 | 30.00 |

EVIE

WORD
| ❑ 7-01-895210-7 | Christmas, A Happy Time | 1984 | 12.00 |
| ❑ 8770 | Come On, Ring Those Bells | 1977 | 15.00 |

EWELL, DON

ANALOGUE PRODUCTIONS
| ❑ APJ-19 | Yellow Dog Blues | 199? | 30.00 |
| *— Audiophile reissue on red vinyl* | | | |
AUDIOPHILE
| ❑ APS-5966 | Yellow Dog Blues | 196? | 25.00 |
CHIAROSCURO
❑ 130	Don Ewell	1974	18.00
❑ 106	Jazz Portrait of the Artist	1972	18.00
❑ 127	Take It in Stride	1973	18.00
GHB
❑ 30	Don Ewell in New Orleans	196?	25.00
GOOD TIME JAZZ
❑ L-12046 [M]	Free 'N Easy	1956	40.00
❑ S-10046 [S]	Free 'N Easy	1960	30.00
❑ L-12021 [M]	Music to Listen to Don Ewell By	1955	40.00
❑ L-12043 [M]	The Man Here Plays Fine Piano	1956	40.00
❑ S-10043 [S]	The Man Here Plays Fine Piano	1960	30.00
JAZZOLOGY
❑ JCE-84	Don Ewell and Bob Greene Together!	198?	12.00
❑ J-29	Don Ewell and the All-Stars	197?	12.00
❑ J-69	Don Ewell Quintet	198?	12.00
NEW ORLEANS
❑ NOR-7209	Don Ewell and Herb Hall in New Orleans	198?	12.00
STOMP OFF
❑ SOS-1077	Chicago '57	198?	12.00
WINDIN' BALL
❑ LP-101 [10]	Don Ewell	1953	50.00
❑ LP-102 [10]	Don Ewell and Mama Yancey	1953	50.00
❑ LP-103 [10]	Don Ewell Plays Tunes Played by the King Oliver Band	1953	50.00
❑ LP-103 [M]	Don Ewell Plays Tunes Played by the King Oliver Band	195?	30.00

EWING, SKIP

MCA
| ❑ 42128 | The Coast of Colorado | 1988 | 12.00 |
| ❑ 42301 | The Will to Love | 1989 | 12.00 |

EXCITERS, THE

RCA VICTOR
| ❑ LSP-4211 | Caviar and Chitlins | 1969 | 30.00 |

ROULETTE
| ❑ R25326 [M] | The Exciters | 1966 | 30.00 |
| ❑ SR25326 [S] | The Exciters | 1966 | 40.00 |
TODAY
| ❑ 1001 [B] | Black Beauty | 1971 | 25.00 |
UNITED ARTISTS
| ❑ UAL-3264 [M] | Tell Him | 1963 | 70.00 |
| ❑ UAS-6264 [S] | Tell Him | 1963 | 150.00 |

EXILE

ARISTA
| ❑ AL-9624 | Still Standing | 1990 | 18.00 |
EPIC
❑ B6E39154	Exile	1983	10.00
❑ FE40401	Greatest Hits	1986	10.00
❑ BFE40000	Hang On to Your Heart	1985	10.00
❑ FE39424	Kentucky Hearts	1984	10.00
❑ FE40901	Shelter from the Night	1987	10.00
MCA CURB
❑ 946	All There Is	1986	10.00
❑ 5581	Best of Exile	1985	10.00
❑ 964	Don't Leave Me This Way	1986	10.00
❑ 947	Heart and Soul	1986	10.00
❑ 963	Mixed Emotions	1986	10.00
❑ 1456	More of the Best of Exile	1986	10.00
RCA VICTOR
❑ AFL1-3086	Exile	1978	15.00
❑ AFL1-3087	Stage Pass	1978	15.00
WARNER BROS.
❑ BSK3323	All There Is	1979	12.00
❑ BSK3437	Don't Leave Me This Way	1980	12.00
❑ BSK3588	Heart and Soul	1981	12.00
❑ BSK3205	Mixed Emotions	1978	12.00
WOODEN NICKEL
❑ BWL1-0120	Exile	1973	18.00

EXOTIC GUITARS

RANWOOD
❑ 8171	300 Watt Music Box	1975	12.00
❑ 8090	All the Guitar Hits	1971	12.00
❑ 8080	Country Music	1970	12.00
❑ 8061	Everybody's Talkin'	1970	12.00
❑ 8073	Holly Holy	1970	12.00
❑ 8085	I Can't Stop Loving You	1971	12.00
❑ 8051	Indian Love Call	1969	15.00
❑ 8002	The Exotic Guitars	1968	15.00
❑ 8040	Those Were the Days	1968	15.00

EXPLOITED, THE

CLEOPATRA
| ❑ 7318 [B] | Punk At Leeds '83 | | 26.00 |

EXPOSE

ARISTA
| ❑ AL-8441 | Exposure | 1987 | 10.00 |
| ❑ AL-8532 | What You Don't Know | 1989 | 12.00 |

EYEBALL

CMP
| ❑ CMP-11-ST | Eyeball | 198? | 15.00 |

EYERMANN, TIM, AND EAST COAST OFFERING

BLUEMOON
| ❑ R1-79151 | Jazz on L | 1989 | 15.00 |
| ❑ R1-79163 | Outside/Inside | 1990 | 15.00 |
INNER CITY
| ❑ IC-1095 | Aloha | 198? | 15.00 |
MCA
| ❑ 5494 | East Coast Offering | 1985 | 12.00 |
| ❑ 5589 | Walkin' With You | 1986 | 12.00 |

EYES OF BLUE

MERCURY
| ❑ SR-61184 | Crossroads of Time | 1968 | 30.00 |
| ❑ SR-61220 | In Fields of Ardath | 1969 | 30.00 |

EYGES, DAVID

MUSIC UNLIMITED
| ❑ 7432 | Crossroads | 1982 | 15.00 |
| ❑ 7431 | The Arrow | 1981 | 15.00 |

EZELL, WILLIAM

RIVERSIDE
| ❑ RLP-1043 [10] | Gin Mill Jazz | 1954 | 80.00 |

F

Number	Title	Yr	NM

FABARES, SHELLEY

COLPIX
❑ CP-426 [M]	Shelley!	1962	150.00
❑ SCP-426 [S]	Shelley!	1962	600.00

❑ CP-431 [M]	The Things We Did Last Summer	1962	100.00
❑ SCP-431 [S]	The Things We Did Last Summer	1962	400.00

FABIAN

ABC
❑ X-806	16 Greatest Hits	1973	15.00

CHANCELLOR
❑ OI IL-5024 [M]	Fabian's 16 Fabulous Hits	1962	75.00
❑ CHL-5005 [M]	Fabulous Fabian	1959	50.00
❑ CHLS-5005 [S]	Fabulous Fabian	1959	75.00
❑ CHL-5003 [M]	Hold That Tiger!	1959	100.00
—Pink label			
❑ CHL-5003 [M]	Hold That Tiger!	1959	50.00
—Black label			
❑ CHLS-5003 [S]	Hold That Tiger!	1959	150.00
—Pink label			
❑ CHLS-5003 [S]	Hold That Tiger!	1959	75.00
—Black label			
❑ CHL-5019 [M]	Rockin' Hot	1961	75.00
❑ CHL-69802 [M]	The Fabian Facade: Young and Wonderful	1960	80.00
—Felt gatefold cover with die-cut window			
❑ CHL-5012 [M]	The Good Old Summertime	1960	50.00
❑ CHLS-5012 [S]	The Good Old Summertime	1960	75.00

MCA
❑ 27095	The Best of Fabian	1985	10.00

UNITED ARTISTS
❑ UA-LA449-E	The Very Best of Fabian	1975	15.00

FABIAN / FRANKIE AVALON

CHANCELLOR
❑ CHL-5009 [M]	The Hit Makers	1960	100.00

FABRIC, BENT

ATCO
❑ 33-148 [M]	Alley Cat	1962	18.00
❑ SD 33-148 [S]	Alley Cat	1962	25.00
❑ 33-185 [M]	Never Tease Tigers	1966	15.00
❑ SD 33-185 [S]	Never Tease Tigers	1966	18.00
❑ 33-202 [M]	Operation Lovebirds	1967	15.00
❑ SD 33-202 [S]	Operation Lovebirds	1967	18.00
❑ 33-164 [M]	Organ Grinder's Swing	1964	15.00
❑ SD 33-164 [S]	Organ Grinder's Swing	1964	18.00
❑ 33-221 [M]	Relax	1967	18.00
❑ SD 33-221 [S]	Relax	1967	15.00
❑ 33-173 [M]	The Drunken Penguin	1965	15.00
❑ SD 33-173 [S]	The Drunken Penguin	1965	18.00
❑ 33-155 [M]	The Happy Puppy	1963	15.00
❑ SD 33-155 [S]	The Happy Puppy	1963	18.00

FABULOUS COUNTS, THE

COTILLION
❑ SD9011	Jan Jan	1969	100.00
❑ SD9011	Jan Jan	199?	15.00
—Reissue; superficially almost identical to original			

FABULOUS FLIPPERS, THE

VERITAS
❑ VS-2570	Something Tangible	1970	30.00

FABULOUS JOKERS, THE

MONUMENT
❑ MLP-8059 [M]	Guitars Extraordinaire	1966	100.00
❑ SLP-18059 [S]	Guitars Extraordinaire	1966	150.00

FABULOUS POODLES

EPIC
❑ JE35666 [B]	Mirror Stars	1978	15.00
❑ JE35666 [DJ]	Mirror Stars	1978	25.00
—White label promo on pink vinyl			
❑ JE36256	Think Pink	1979	12.00

FABULOUS RHINESTONES, THE

JUST SUNSHINE
❑ 9	Freewheelin'	1973	15.00
❑ 1	The Fabulous Rhinestones	1972	15.00

FABULOUS THUNDERBIRDS, THE

CBS ASSOCIATED
❑ FZ40818	Hot Number	1987	10.00
❑ OZ45094	Powerful Stuff	1989	12.00
❑ BFZ40304	Tuff Enuff	1986	12.00
❑ FZ40304 [B]	Tuff Enuff	1986	10.00
—Reissue with new prefix			

CHRYSALIS
❑ CHR1319	Butt Rockin'	1981	15.00
❑ PV41319	Butt Rockin'	198?	10.00
—Reissue of 1319			
❑ CHR1395	T-Bird Rhythm	1982	15.00
❑ FV41395	T-Bird Rhythm	1983	12.00
—Reissue of 1395			
❑ PV41395	T-Bird Rhythm	198?	10.00
—Reissue with new prefix			
❑ PV41250	The Fabulous Thunderbirds	198?	10.00
—Reissue of Takoma 7068			
❑ CHR1287	What's the Word	1980	15.00
❑ PV41287	What's the Word	198?	10.00
—Reissue of 1287			

TAKOMA
❑ TAK7068	The Fabulous Thunderbirds	1979	15.00

FACES

4 MEN WITH BEARDS
❑ 4M215LP [B]	First Step		25.00

WARNER BROS.
❑ BS2574	A Nod Is As Good As a Wink...To a Blind Horse	1971	18.00
—Green label			
❑ BS2574	A Nod Is As Good As a Wink...To a Blind Horse	1973	15.00
—Burbank" palm trees label			
❑ WS1851	First Step	1970	25.00
—First pressings have "small faces." on front cover			
❑ WS1851 [B]	First Step	1970	15.00
—Later pressings have "faces." on front cover			
❑ WS1892	Long Player	1971	18.00
❑ ST-93718	Long Player	1971	25.00
—Capitol Record Club edition			
❑ BS2665	Ooh La La	1973	18.00
—Green label			
❑ BS2665	Ooh La La	1973	15.00
—Burbank" palm trees label			
❑ BS2897	Snakes and Ladders: The Best of Faces	1976	15.00

FACHIN, ERIA

CRITIQUE
❑ 90936	My Name Is Eria Fachin	1988	10.00

FACTS OF LIFE

KAYVETTE
❑ KAY-803	Matter of Fact	1978	18.00
❑ LPK-802	Sometimes	1977	18.00

FADDIS, JON

BUDDAH
❑ BDS-5727	Good and Plenty	1979	15.00

CONCORD JAZZ
❑ CJ-291	Legacy	1986	12.00

EPIC
❑ OE45266	Into the FaddisPhere	1989	18.00

PABLO
❑ 2310765	Youngblood	1977	18.00

FAGAN, SCOTT

ATCO
❑ SD 33-267	South Atlantic Blues	1968	25.00

RCA VICTOR
❑ APL1-1185	Many Sunny Places	1976	18.00

FAGEN, DONALD

MOBILE FIDELITY
❑ 1-120	The Nightfly	1982	40.00
—Audiophile vinyl			

WARNER BROS.
❑ 23696 [B]	The Nightfly	1982	10.00

FAGERQUIST, DON

MODE
❑ LP-124 [M]	Music to Fill a Void	1957	100.00

FAHEY, JOHN

4 MEN WITH BEARDS
❑ 4M117LP [B]	America		30.00
❑ 4M600LP [B]	The Transcendental Waterfall: Guitar Excursions 1962-1967		120.00
—The Transcendental Waterfall: Guitar Excursions 1962-1967 is a 6-LP box set drawing from John Fahey's best, and most influential, period. Included in the set are Blind Joe Death, Death Chants, Breakdowns, And Military Waltzes, The Dance Of Death And Other Plantation Favorites, The Great San Bernardino Birthday Party, The Transfiguration Of Blind Joe Death, and Days Have Gone By, all reissued on 180 gram vinyl with deluxe tip-on jackets. Also included are a t-shirt (size L only), a poster, and a postcard, all of which are housed in a deluxe box. An amazing package featuring some of the most important guitar solo recordings of the 20th century. Limited to 2,000 numbered copies.			
❑ 4M219LP [B]	The Voice of the Turtle		30.00
❑ 4M205 [B]	Volume 5 - The Transfiguration Of Blind Joe Death	2013	25.00

REPRISE
❑ MS2145	After the Ball	1973	25.00
❑ MS2089	Of Rivers and Religions	1972	25.00

RIVERBOAT
❑ RB-1 [M]	The Transfiguration of Blind Joe Death	1967	60.00
—Green cover with booklet; "Volume 5" added to back cover			
❑ RB-1 [M]	The Transfiguration of Blind Joe Death	1965	200.00
—Original issue of 50 copies with booklet, hand-written labels and no "Volume 5" anywhere on the cover			

SHANACHIE
❑ 97006	God, Time and Causality	1990	18.00

TABLE OF THE ELEMENTS
❑ 38	Georgia Stomps, Atlanta Struts, and Other Contemporary Dance Favorites	1999	25.00

TAKOMA
❑ C-1030	America	1972	30.00
—With gatefold jacket and booklet			
❑ C-1030	America	197?	18.00
—Later pressings with no gatefold			
❑ C-1002	Blind Joe Death	1964	50.00
—White cover, similar to first edition, except it has a Berkeley, California address on cover; six tracks were re-recorded for this edition			
❑ TAK-7002	Blind Joe Death	1979	15.00
—Reissue of 1002			
❑ 0(# unknown) [B]	Blind Joe Death	1959	350.00
—Original edition of 1,000 has a white cover with "Blind Joe Death" on one side and "John Fahey" on the other; possibly pressed by RCA Victor Custom Division; no Berkeley, California address on cover			
❑ C-1045	Christmas with John Fahey, Vol. 2	1975	18.00
❑ TAK-7045	Christmas with John Fahey, Vol. 2	198?	15.00
—Reissue of 1045			
❑ C-1004	Dance of Death & Other Plantation Favorites/John Fahey Vol. 3	1964	60.00
—White cover with block lettering			
❑ TAK-7004	Dance of Death and Other Plantation Favorites	198?	15.00
—Reissue of 1004			
❑ C-1014	Days Have Gone By Volume 6	1967	30.00
—With booklet			
❑ C-1014	Days Have Gone By Volume 6	1968	15.00
—Without booklet			
❑ C-1003	Death Chants, Break Downs & Military Waltzes	1964	60.00
—First cover is white with block print with title on cover as above			
❑ TAK-7003	Death Chants, Breakdowns and Military Waltzes	198?	15.00
—Reissue of 1003			
❑ C-1003 [B]	Death Chants, Breakdowns and Military Waltzes Vol. II	1965	60.00
—Second cover is white with what looks like handwritten print; title is as listed above and "Vol. II" is added to the lower left corner			
❑ C-1035	Fare Forward Voyagers	1973	25.00
❑ TAK-7035	Fare Forward Voyagers	198?	15.00
—Reissue of 1035			
❑ TAK-7069	John Fahey Visits Washington, D.C.	1979	15.00
❑ TAK-7089	Live in Tasmania	198?	15.00
❑ C-1043	Old Fashioned Love	1975	18.00
❑ TAK-7043	Old Fashioned Love	198?	15.00
—Reissue of 1043			
❑ TAK-7102	Railroads I	1981	15.00
❑ C-1058	The Best of John Fahey 1959-1977	1977	18.00
❑ TAK-7058	The Best of John Fahey 1959-1977	198?	15.00
—Reissue of 1058			
❑ C-1020	The New Possibility: John Fahey's Guitar Soli Christmas Album	1968	30.00

Number	Title	Yr	NM
— Originals with back cover liner notes			
❏ C-1020	The New Possibility: John Fahey's Guitar Soli Christmas Album	197?	18.00
— Later pressings with no liner notes			
❏ TAK-7020	The New Possibility: John Fahey's Guitar Soli Christmas Album	198?	15.00
— Reissue of 1020			
❏ R-9015	The Transfiguration of Blind Joe Death	1969	25.00
— Reissue of Riverboat RB-1; logo added to lower right front cover, and the drawing in the center is much more green than on 1967 Riverboat covers			
❏ TAK-7015	The Transfiguration of Blind Joe Death	198?	15.00
— Reissue of 9015			
❏ C-1019	The Voice of the Turtle	1971	30.00
— With gatefold jacket and booklet			
❏ C-1019	The Voice of the Turtle	197?	18.00
— Later pressings with no gatefold			
❏ C-1008	Vol. 4: The Great San Bernardino Birthday Party	1966	30.00
— First pressings have a discography on the back cover			
❏ C-1008	Vol. 4: The Great San Bernardino Birthday Party	1968	15.00
— Without discography on back cover			
❏ C-1002	Volume 1: Blind Joe Death	1967	40.00
— Psychedelic gold and blue cover; the entire album was re-recorded for this edition, including the six songs re-recorded for the first Berkeley edition and one song not on the white-cover editions, "I'm Gonna Do All I Can For My Lord"			
❏ C-1002	Volume 1: Blind Joe Death	1968	18.00
— Blue and white cover with "Stereo" added to upper left			
❏ C-1003	Volume 2: Death Chants, Breakdowns & Military Waltzes	1967	40.00
— Psychedelic gold and orange cover; most of the album was re-recorded for this edition			
❏ C-1003	Volume 2: Death Chants, Breakdowns & Military Waltzes	1968	18.00
— Orange and white cover with orange lettering			
❏ C-1004	Volume 3: The Dance of Death & Other Plantation Favorites	1967	40.00
— Psychedelic gold and brown cover			
❏ C-1004	Volume 3: The Dance of Death & Other Plantation Favorites	1968	18.00
— Brown and white cover			
❏ TAK-7085	Yes! Jesus Loves Me	1980	15.00
TERRA			
❏ T-2	Requia	1985	12.00
— Reissue of Vanguard 79259			
VANGUARD			
❏ VSD55/56	Essential John Fahey	1974	25.00
❏ VRS-9259 [M]	Requia	1968	30.00
❏ VSD-79259 [S]	Requia	1968	25.00
❏ VSD-79293	The Yellow Princess	1969	25.00
VARRICK			
❏ VR-028	I Remember Blind Joe Death	1987	15.00
❏ VR-002	John Fahey Christmas Guitar, Volume 1	1982	18.00
❏ VR-008	Let Go	1983	18.00
❏ VR-012	Popular Songs of Christmas and New Year's	1983	18.00
❏ VR-019	Rain Forests, Oceans & Other Themes	1985	15.00

FAIR, YVONNE

MOTOWN

Number	Title	Yr	NM
❏ M6-832S1 [B]	The Bitch Is Black	1975	35.00

FAIRCHILD, BARBARA

COLUMBIA

Number	Title	Yr	NM
❏ KC31720	A Sweeter Love	1973	15.00
❏ PC34868	Free & Easy	1977	15.00
❏ KC35311	Greatest Hits	1978	15.00
❏ KC32711	Kid Stuff	1974	15.00
❏ KC32960	Love Is a Gentle Thing	1974	15.00
❏ C31092	Love's Old Song	1971	15.00
❏ PC34307	Mississippi	1976	15.00
❏ C30123	Someone Special	1970	18.00
❏ KC33058	Standing in Your Line	1974	15.00
❏ KC35536	This Is Me	1978	15.00

FAIRGROUND ATTRACTION

RCA

Number	Title	Yr	NM
❏ 8596-1-R	The First of a Million Kisses	1988	12.00

FAIRPORT CONVENTION

4 MEN WITH BEARDS

Number	Title	Yr	NM
❏ 4M159LP [B]	Liege & Lief		25.00
❏ 4M158LP [B]	Unhalfbricking		25.00
❏ 4M157LP [B]	What We Did On Our Holidays		25.00

A&M

Number	Title	Yr	NM
❏ SP-4316 [B]	Angel Delight	1971	30.00
❏ SP-4333 [B]	Babbacombe" Lee	1972	30.00
❏ SP-4185 [B]	Fairport Convention	1969	25.00
— Not a reissue of Cotillion LP, but the US issue of the second			

Number	Title	Yr	NM
UK LP "What We Did On Our Holidays			
❏ SP-4407	Fairport Nine	1973	18.00
❏ SP-3603 [B]	Fairport Nine	1974	15.00
— Early reissue of 4407			
❏ SP-4265 [B]	Full House	1970	30.00
❏ SP-4257 [B]	Liege and Lief	1970	30.00
❏ SP-4383	Rosie	1973	18.00
❏ SP-3530	The Fairport Chronicles	1976	18.00
❏ SP-6016	The Fairport Chronicles	198?	15.00
— Reissue of 3530			
❏ SP-4206 [B]	Unhalfbricking	1969	25.00
ANTILLES			
❏ 7054	Gottle O' Geer	1976	15.00
CARTHAGE			
❏ CGLP-4417	Full House	198?	12.00
— Reissue of A&M 4265			
❏ CGLP-4418	Unhalfbricking	198?	12.00
— Reissue of A&M 4206			
❏ CGLP-4430	What We Did on Our Holidays	198?	12.00
— Reissue of A&M 4185 with UK title restored			
COTILLION			
❏ 9024 [M]	Fairport Convention	1968	100.00
— Mono is white label promo only; "DJ Copy Monaural" sticker on front cover			
❏ SD9024 [S]	Fairport Convention	1968	30.00
HANNIBAL			
❏ HNBL-1329	Heyday	1987	12.00
❏ HNBL-1319	House Full	1986	12.00
ISLAND			
❏ ILPS-9285	Fairport Live/A Movable Feast	1974	15.00
❏ 90678	In Real Time – Live '87	1987	12.00
❏ ILPS-9313	Rising for the Moon	1975	15.00
VARRICK			
❏ VR-029 [B]	Expletive Delighted!	1987	15.00
❏ VR-023	Gladys' Leap	1986	12.00

FAITH, ADAM

AMY

Number	Title	Yr	NM
❏ 8005 [M]	Adam Faith	1965	30.00
❏ S-8005 [S]	Adam Faith	1965	30.00
MGM			
❏ E-3951 [M]	England's Top Singer	1961	40.00
❏ SE-3951 [S]	England's Top Singer	1961	50.00

FAITH, PERCY

COLUMBIA

Number	Title	Yr	NM
❏ CL1010 [M]	Adventure in the Sun	1957	25.00
❏ KG31588	All-Time Greatest Hits	1972	15.00
❏ PG31588	All-Time Greatest Hits	198?	12.00
— Budget-line reissue			
❏ CL1957 [M]	American Serenade	1963	15.00
❏ CS8757 [S]	American Serenade	1963	15.00
❏ KC32803	A New Thing	1974	12.00
❏ CQ32803 [Q]	A New Thing	1974	18.00
❏ CL2906 [M]	Angel of the Morning (Hit Themes for Young Lovers)	1968	25.00
❏ CS9706 [S]	Angel of the Morning (Hit Themes for Young Lovers)	1968	15.00
❏ CL1386 [M]	A Night with Jerome Kern	1959	18.00
❏ CS8181 [S]	A Night with Jerome Kern	1959	25.00
❏ CL1302 [M]	A Night with Sigmund Romberg	1959	18.00
❏ CS8108 [S]	A Night with Sigmund Romberg	1959	25.00
❏ G30330	A Time for Love	1971	18.00
❏ CL2529 [M]	Bim Bam Boom	1966	15.00
❏ CS9329 [S]	Bim Bam Boom	1966	15.00
❏ C30800	Black Magic Woman	1971	12.00
❏ CL1417 [M]	Bon Voyage!	1960	18.00
❏ CS8214 [S]	Bon Voyage!	1960	18.00
❏ CL1322 [M]	Bouquet	1959	18.00
❏ CS8124 [S]	Bouquet	1959	18.00
❏ CL1681 [M]	Bouquet of Love	1962	15.00
❏ CS8481 [S]	Bouquet of Love	1962	18.00
❏ CL2356 [M]	Broadway Bouquet	1965	15.00
❏ CS9156 [S]	Broadway Bouquet	1965	15.00
❏ CL1570 [M]	Camelot	1960	15.00
❏ CS8370 [S]	Camelot	1960	18.00
❏ KC33244	Chinatown (Featuring "The Entertainer")	1974	12.00
❏ CQ33244 [Q]	Chinatown (Featuring "The Entertainer")	1974	18.00
❏ CS9377 [S]	Christmas Is…	1966	15.00
❏ CL2577 [M]	Christmas Is…	1966	15.00
❏ 3C9377	Christmas Is…	198?	10.00
— Budget-line reissue			
❏ PC39471	Christmas Melodies	1984	10.00
— Repackage of previously released material			
❏ KC32164	Clair	1973	12.00
❏ CQ32164 [Q]	Clair	1973	18.00
❏ CL525 [M]	Continental Music	1955	25.00
❏ KC32714	Corazon	1974	12.00
❏ KC33142	Country Bouquet	1975	12.00
❏ KC31627	Day By Day	1972	12.00
❏ CQ31627 [Q]	Day By Day	1972	10.00
❏ CL681 [M]	Delicado	1956	25.00
❏ KC33549	Disco Party	1975	12.00
❏ CL2317 [M]	Do I Hear a Waltz	1965	15.00
❏ CS9117 [S]	Do I Hear a Waltz	1965	15.00
❏ CL1902 [M]	Exotic Strings	1963	15.00
❏ CS8702 [S]	Exotic Strings	1963	15.00

Number	Title	Yr	NM
❏ CL6148 [10]	Football Songs	1950	40.00
❏ GP1	Forever Young	1968	18.00
❏ CL2810 [M]	For Those in Love	1968	25.00
❏ CS9610 [S]	For Those in Love	1968	15.00
❏ CL2108 [M]	Great Folk Themes	1964	15.00
❏ CS8908 [S]	Great Folk Themes	1964	15.00
❏ CG33895	Great Moments of Percy Faith	1976	15.00
❏ CL1187 [M]	Hallelujah!	1957	25.00
❏ CS8033 [S]	Hallelujah!	1958	30.00
❏ CS1019	Held Over! Today's Great Movie Themes	1970	15.00
❏ CL1783 [M]	Hollywood's Great Themes	1962	15.00
❏ CS8583 [S]	Hollywood's Great Themes	1962	18.00
❏ CL640 [M]	House of Flowers	1956	25.00
❏ C30502	I Think I Love You	1971	12.00
❏ CQ30502 [Q]	I Think I Love You	1971	18.00
❏ CL1501 [M]	Jealousy	1960	15.00
❏ CS8292 [S]	Jealousy	1960	18.00
❏ C31042	Jesus Christ Superstar	1971	12.00
❏ C31301	Joy	1972	12.00
❏ CQ31301 [Q]	Joy	1972	18.00
❏ CL1188 [M]	Jubilation!	1957	25.00
❏ CL550 [M]	Kismet	1955	25.00
❏ CS8642 [R]	Kismet	1963	12.00
❏ CL2279 [M]	Latin Themes for Young Lovers	1966	15.00
❏ CS9079 [S]	Latin Themes for Young Lovers	1965	15.00
❏ CS9983	Leaving on a Jet Plane	1970	15.00
❏ CL955 [M]	L'il Abner	1957	25.00
❏ CL2209 [M]	Love Goddess	1966	15.00
❏ CS9009 [S]	Love Goddess	1964	15.00
❏ CS9906	Love Theme from "Romeo & Juliet"	1969	15.00
❏ CQ31004 [Q]	Love Theme from "Romeo & Juliet"	1971	18.00
❏ CL1267 [M]	Malaguena	1958	25.00
❏ CS8081 [S]	Malaguena	1958	30.00
❏ CL2167 [M]	More Themes for Young Lovers	1964	15.00
❏ CS8967 [S]	More Themes for Young Lovers	1964	15.00
❏ CL1639 [M]	Mucho Gusto! More Music of Brazil	1961	15.00
❏ CS8439 [S]	Mucho Gusto! More Music of Brazil	1961	18.00
❏ CL705 [M]	Music for Her	1956	25.00
❏ CL577 [M]	Music from Hollywood	1955	25.00
❏ CL1381 [M]	Music of Christmas	1959	25.00
— Re-recorded version of CL 588 with same track order			
❏ CS8176 [S]	Music of Christmas	1959	18.00
❏ PC38302	Music of Christmas	1983	10.00
❏ CL588 [M]	Music of Christmas	1955	30.00
❏ CL2405 [M]	Music of Christmas, Volume 2	1965	15.00
❏ CS9206 [S]	Music of Christmas, Volume 2	1965	15.00
❏ CS9004 [R]	My Fair Lady	1964	15.00
❏ CL895 [M]	My Fair Lady	1957	25.00
❏ KC32380	My Love	1973	12.00
❏ CL880 [M]	Passport to Romance	1956	25.00
❏ CL1493 [M]	Percy Faith's Greatest Hits	1960	18.00
❏ CS8637 [S]	Percy Faith's Greatest Hits	1963	12.00
❏ PC8637 [R]	Percy Faith's Greatest Hits	198?	10.00
— Budget-line reissue			
❏ C38105 [S]	Porgy and Bess	1958	25.00
❏ CL1298 [M]	Porgy and Bess	1958	18.00
❏ C32585	Remembering the Hits of the 60's	1973	12.00
❏ CL2024 [M]	Shangri-La!	1963	15.00
❏ CS8824 [S]	Shangri-La!	1963	15.00
❏ CL1105 [M]	South Pacific	1957	18.00
❏ CS8005 [S]	South Pacific	1958	30.00
❏ KC33915	Summer of '76	1976	12.00
❏ CL1627 [M]	Tara's Theme from "Gone with the Wind" and Other Themes	1961	15.00
❏ CS8427 [S]	Tara's Theme from "Gone with the Wind" and Other Themes	1961	18.00
❏ CL2650 [M]	The Academy Award Winner and Other Great Movie Themes	1967	18.00
❏ CS9450 [S]	The Academy Award Winner and Other Great Movie Themes	1967	15.00
❏ C30097	The Beatles Album	1970	15.00
❏ C2L15 [M]	The Columbia Album of Christmas Music	1958	30.00
— Combines CL 588 and CL 1187 into one gatefold package			
❏ PCQ33006 [Q]	The Entertainer	1974	18.00
❏ CL2441 [M]	Themes for the "In" Crowd	1966	15.00
❏ CS9241 [S]	Themes for the "In" Crowd	1966	15.00
❏ CL2023 [M]	Themes for Young Lovers	1963	15.00
❏ CS8823 [S]	Themes for Young Lovers	1963	15.00
❏ CL1822 [M]	The Music of Brazil!	1962	15.00
❏ CS8622 [S]	The Music of Brazil!	1962	15.00
❏ CL1418 [M]	The Sound of Music	1960	18.00
❏ CS8215 [S]	The Sound of Music	1960	18.00
❏ CS9762	Those Were the Days	1969	15.00
❏ CL2704 [M]	Today's Themes for Young Lovers	1967	18.00
❏ CS9504 [S]	Today's Themes for Young Lovers	1967	15.00
❏ CL1182 [M]	Touchdown!	1957	25.00
❏ CL1075 [M]	Viva!	1957	25.00
❏ CS8038 [S]	Viva!	1958	30.00
❏ CG33606	Viva!/Mucho Gusto!	1975	15.00
❏ CS9835	Windmills of Your Mind	1969	15.00

Number	Title	Yr	NM

COLUMBIA LIMITED EDITION
❏ LE10042	Bouquet	197?	12.00
❏ LE10095	Great Folk Themes	197?	12.00
❏ LE10350	Hallelujah!	197?	12.00
❏ LE10131	Jealousy	197?	12.00
❏ LE10082	Music of Christmas	197?	12.00

— Brown label "Limited Edition" series; same contents as CS 8176

❏ LE10088	Music of Christmas, Volume 2	197?	12.00
❏ LE10004	Tara's Theme from "Gone with the Wind" and Other Themes	197?	12.00
❏ LE10041	Themes for the "In" Crowd	197?	12.00
❏ LE10185	Those Were the Days	197?	12.00
❏ LE10015	Windmills of Your Mind	197?	12.00

COLUMBIA SPECIAL PRODUCTS
❏ P13827	American Serenade	197?	10.00
❏ P13091	Broadway Bouquet	197?	10.00
❏ P13277	Leaving on a Jet Plane	197?	10.00
❏ P213719	The Columbia Album of George Gershwin	197?	15.00

HARMONY
❏ KH30607	A Summer Place	1971	12.00
❏ KH31777	Every Night at the Movies	1972	12.00
❏ KH30977	Raindrops Keep Fallin'	1971	12.00
❏ HS11348	Sounds of Music	1969	12.00
❏ H30020	Younger Than Springtime	1970	12.00

VOCALION
| ❏ VL3600 [M] | North and South of the Border | 1958 | 18.00 |

FAITH BAND
MERCURY
❏ SRM-1-3770	Face to Face	1979	15.00
❏ SRM-1-3759	Rock'n Romance	1978	15.00
❏ SRM-1-3807	Vital Signs	1979	12.00

VILLAGE
| ❏ VR7703 | Excuse Me ... I Just Cut an Album | 1977 | 25.00 |
| ❏ VR7805 | Rock'n Romance | 1978 | 25.00 |

FAITH NO MORE
MORDAM
| ❏ FNM1 | We Care a Lot | 1985 | 30.00 |
SLASH
❏ 25559	Introduce Yourself	1987	18.00
❏ 45723	King for a Day/Fool for a Lifetime	1995	30.00
❏ 25878	The Real Thing	1989	25.00
TPM/RHINO EXCLUSIVE
| ❏ 2310 | Angel Dust | 2008 | 40.00 |

FAITHFULL, MARIANNE
ABKCO
| ❏ 75471 | Greatest Hits | 1988 | 12.00 |
— Reissue of London PS 547

ISLAND
| ❏ 90066 | A Child's Adventure | 1983 | 12.00 |
| ❏ 90066 [DJ] | A Child's Adventure | 1983 | 35.00 |
— Promo-only Quiex II audiophile pressing
| ❏ PRO794 [EP] | Blazing Away Sampler | 1990 | 25.00 |
— Promo-only sampler for radio
| ❏ ILPS9570 | Broken English | 1979 | 12.00 |
| ❏ 90039 | Broken English | 1983 | 10.00 |
— Reissue
❏ ILPS9570 [B]	Broken English	1979	18.00
❏ ILPS9648	Dangerous Acquaintances	1981	12.00
❏ 90613	Strange Weather	1987	12.00
LONDON
❏ LL3482 [M]	Faithfull Forever	1966	18.00
❏ PS482 [S]	Faithfull Forever	1966	25.00
❏ LL3482 [B]	Faithfull Forever	1966	18.00
❏ LL3452 [M]	Go Away from My World	1965	30.00
— No Oldham credit.
| ❏ PS452 [S] | Go Away from My World | 1965 | 25.00 |
| ❏ LL3452 [M] | Go Away from My World | 1965 | 30.00 |
— With Oldham credit.
❏ PS547	Greatest Hits	1969	18.00
❏ LL3423 [M]	Marianne Faithfull	1965	25.00
❏ PS423 [R]	Marianne Faithfull	1965	18.00
❏ LL3423 [B]	Marianne Faithfull	1965	25.00
❏ PS547 [B]	Marianne Faithfull's Greatest Hits		18.00
MOBILE FIDELITY
| ❏ 1-235 | Broken English | 1995 | 45.00 |
— Audiophile vinyl

FALCO
A&M
❏ SP-6-4951	Einzelhaft	1982	12.00
❏ SP-5105	Falco 3	1985	10.00
❏ SP-4993	Junge Roemer	1985	12.00
SIRE
| ❏ 25522 | Emotional | 1986 | 12.00 |
| ❏ 25690 | Wiener Blut | 1988 | 12.00 |

FALL, THE
BEGGARS BANQUET
| ❏ 2430-1-H | 458489 | 1990 | 12.00 |

Number	Title	Yr	NM
❏ 9582-1-H	I Am Kurious Oranj	1988	12.00
❏ 9807-1-H	Seminal Live	1989	12.00
❏ 6897-1-H	The Frenz Experiment	1988	12.00

I.R.S.
| ❏ SP-003 | Live at the Witch Trials | 1979 | 25.00 |
I.R.S./FAULTY
| ❏ COPE-2 | Early Years 77-79 | 1981 | 18.00 |
MATADOR
| ❏ OLE95-1 | Middle Class Revolt | 1994 | 12.00 |
| ❏ OLE55-1 | The Infotainment Scan | 1993 | 12.00 |
PVC
| ❏ 8932 | The Wonderful and Frightening World of The Fall | 1984 | 16.00 |
| ❏ 8940 | This Nation's Saving Grace | 1985 | 18.00 |
ROUGH TRADE
| ❏ ROUGH US-8 | Grotesque (After the Gramme) | 1981 | 18.00 |
| ❏ TRADE3/10 [10] | Slates | 1981 | 15.00 |
— 10-inch EP

FALL OUT BOY
ISLAND
| ❏ 1219601 | Folie a Deux | 2008 | 30.00 |

FALLEN ANGELS, THE
ROULETTE
❏ SR42011	It's a Long Way Down	1968	400.00
❏ R25358 [M]	The Fallen Angels	1967	30.00
❏ SR25358 [S]	The Fallen Angels	1967	40.00

FALLENROCK
CAPRICORN
| ❏ CP 0143 | Watch for Fallenrock | 1974 | 12.00 |

FALTERMEYER, HAROLD
MCA
| ❏ 42165 | Harold F | 1988 | 12.00 |

FALTSKOG, AGNETHA
ATLANTIC
| ❏ 81820 | I Stand Alone | 1988 | 18.00 |
POLYDOR
| ❏ 813242-1 | Wrap Your Arms Around Me | 1983 | 12.00 |

FAME, GEORGIE, AND ANNIE ROSS
DRG
| ❏ 5197 | Georgie Fame and Annie Ross in Hoagland | 198? | 15.00 |

FAME, GEORGIE
EPIC
| ❏ BN26563 | Shorty Featuring Georgie Fame | 1968 | 30.00 |
| ❏ BN26368 | The Ballad of Bonnie and Clyde | 1968 | 30.00 |
IMPERIAL
❏ LP-9331 [M]	Get Away	1966	30.00
❏ LP-12331 [R]	Get Away	1966	25.00
❏ LP-9282 [M]	Yeh, Yeh	1965	30.00
❏ LP-12282 [P]	Yeh, Yeh	1965	30.00
— Entire album is stereo except "Yeh, Yeh" (rechanneled)
ISLAND
| ❏ ILPS9293 | Georgie Fame | 1975 | 12.00 |

FAME GANG, THE
FAME
| ❏ SKAO-4200 | Solid Gold from Muscle Shoals | 1969 | 30.00 |

FAMILY, THE
PAISLEY PARK
| ❏ 25322 | The Family | 1985 | 12.00 |

FAMILY
REPRISE
❏ RS-6384	A Song for Me	1970	18.00
❏ RS-6340	Family Entertainment	1969	18.00
❏ RS-6313 [B]	Music in a Doll's House	1968	30.00
UNITED ARTISTS
❏ UAS-5527	Anyway	1971	18.00
❏ UAS-5644	Bandstand	1972	18.00
❏ UAS-5562	Fearless	1972	18.00
❏ UA-LA181-F	It's Only a Movie	1974	15.00

FAMILY BROWN
UNITED ARTISTS
| ❏ UA-LA828-G | Imaginary World | 1978 | 15.00 |

FAMILY DOGG
BUDDAH
| ❏ BDS-5100 | The View from Rowland's Head | 1972 | 30.00 |

Number	Title	Yr	NM

FAMILY TREE, THE
RCA VICTOR
| ❏ LSP-3955 | Miss Butters | 1968 | 18.00 |

FAMOUS CASTLE JAZZ BAND, THE
GOOD TIME JAZZ
❏ L-12030 [M]	The Famous Castle Jazz Band in Hi-Fi	1957	40.00
❏ S-7021 [S]	The Famous Castle Jazz Band in Stereo	1959	30.00
❏ S-10030 [S]	The Famous Castle Jazz Band in Stereo	197?	12.00
❏ L-12037 [M]	The Famous Castle Jazz Band Plays the Five Pennies	1959	40.00
❏ S-10037 [S]	The Famous Castle Jazz Band Plays the Five Pennies	1959	30.00
STEREO RECORDS
| ❏ S-7021 [S] | The Famous Castle Jazz Band in Stereo | 1958 | 40.00 |

FANCY (1)
BIG TREE
| ❏ BT89502 | Wild Thing | 1974 | 15.00 |
RCA VICTOR
| ❏ APL1-1482 | Fancy Turns You On | 1976 | 15.00 |

FANCY (2)
POISON RING
| ❏ PRR-2238 | Meeting You Here | 1971 | 80.00 |

FANKHAUSER, MERRILL
MAUI
| ❏ 101 | Merrill Fankhauser | 1976 | 125.00 |
SHAMLEY
| ❏ SS-701 | Things Going Round in My Mind | 1968 | 100.00 |

FANNY
CASABLANCA
| ❏ NBLP7007 | Rock & Roll Survivors | 1974 | 15.00 |
REPRISE
❏ RS-6456	Charity Ball	1971	18.00
❏ RS-6416	Fanny	1970	18.00
❏ MS-2058	Fanny Hill	1972	18.00
❏ MS-2137	Mother's Pride	1973	18.00

FANTASTIC BAGGYS, THE
IMPERIAL
| ❏ LP-9270 [M] | Tell 'Em I'm Surfin' | 1964 | 150.00 |
| ❏ LP-12270 [S] | Tell 'Em I'm Surfin' | 1964 | 300.00 |
LIBERTY
| ❏ LN-10192 | Tell 'Em I'm Surfin' | 1982 | 12.00 |

FANTASTIC DEE JAYS, THE
STONE
| ❏ SLP-4003 | The Fantastic Dee Jays | 1966 | 1000.00 |

FANTASTIC FOUR, THE
| ❏ SS-717 | The Best of the Fantastic Four | 1969 | 40.00 |
WESTBOUND
❏ W201	Alvin Stone (The Birth and Death of a Gangster)	1975	18.00
❏ WT6108	BYOF (Bring Your Own Funk)	1978	18.00
❏ WT306	Got to Have Your Love	1977	18.00
❏ W226	Night People	1976	18.00

FANTASTIC JOHNNY C, THE
PHIL-LA OF SOUL
| ❏ 4000 | Boogaloo Down Broadway | 1968 | 80.00 |

FANTASY
LIBERTY
| ❏ LSP-7643 | Fantasy | 1970 | 25.00 |

FAPARDOKLY
U.I.P.
| ❏ 2250 | Fapardokly | 1967 | 500.00 |

FAR CRY
VANGUARD APOSTOLIC
| ❏ VSD-6510 | Far Cry | 1968 | 75.00 |

FARAGHER BROTHERS, THE
ABC
| ❏ AB-1009 | Family Ties | 1977 | 12.00 |
| ❏ ABCD-941 | The Faragher Brothers | 1976 | 12.00 |
POLYDOR
| ❏ PD-1-6167 | Open Your Eyes | 1979 | 12.00 |
| ❏ PD-1-6232 | The Faraghers | 1980 | 12.00 |

FARDON, DON
DECCA
| ❏ DL75225 | I've Paid My Dues | 1970 | 18.00 |

Number	Title	Yr	NM
GNP CRESCENDO			
❑ GNPS-2044	Indian Reservation	1968	25.00
FARGO, DONNA			
ABC/DOT			
❑ DOSD-2002	Miss Donna Fargo	1974	15.00
❑ DO-2075	The Best of Donna Fargo	1977	15.00
❑ DOSD-2029	Whatever I Say Means I Love You	1975	15.00
DOT			
❑ DOS-26019	All About a Feeling	1973	15.00
❑ DOS-26006	My Second Album	1973	15.00
❑ DOS-26000	The Happiest Girl in the Whole U.S.A.	1972	15.00
MCA			
❑ 37108	The Best of Donna Fargo	198?	10.00
— Budget-line reissue			
❑ 667	The Happiest Girl in the Whole U.S.A.	198?	10.00
— Budget-line reissue			
MERCURY			
❑ 830236-1	Winners	1986	15.00
❑ 832507-1	Winners	1987	10.00
— Reissue with two songs deleted and one added from above			
PICKWICK			
❑ SPC-6187	Superman	197?	10.00
SONGBIRD			
❑ 5203	Brotherly Love	1982	12.00
WARNER BROS.			
❑ BSK3191	Dark Eyed Lady	1978	12.00
❑ BS2996	Donna Fargo Country	1977	12.00
❑ BSK3470	Fargo	1980	12.00
❑ BSK3377	Just for You	1979	12.00
❑ BS2926	On the Move	1976	12.00
❑ BS3099	Shame on Me	1977	12.00
FARLOW, TAL			
AMERICAN RECORDING SOCIETY			
❑ G-418 [M]	The Swinging Guitar of Tal Farlow	1957	40.00
BLUE NOTE			
❑ BLP-5042 [10]	Tal Farlow Quartet	1954	300.00
CONCORD JAZZ			
❑ CJ-154	Chromatic Palette	1981	15.00
❑ CJ-204	Cookin' on All Burners	1982	15.00
❑ CJ-26	Sign of the Times	1976	15.00
❑ CJ-57	Tal Farlow '78	1978	15.00
❑ CJ-266	The Legendary Tal Farlow	1986	12.00
FANTASY			
❑ OJC-356	The Return of Tal Farlow/1969	198?	12.00
INNER CITY			
❑ IC-1099	Trilogy	197?	15.00
NORGRAN			
❑ MGN-1030 [M]	A Recital by Tal Farlow	1955	600.00
❑ MGN 1097 [M]	Autumn in New York	1956	100.00
❑ MGN-1101 [M]	Fascinating Rhythm	1956	100.00
❑ MGN-1102 [M]	Tal	1956	100.00
❑ MGN-1014 [M]	The Artistry of Tal Farlow	1955	120.00
❑ MGN-1027 [M]	The Interpretations of Tal Farlow	1955	500.00
❑ MGN-19 [10]	The Tal Farlow Album	1954	150.00
❑ MGN-1047 [M]	The Tal Farlow Album	1955	100.00
PRESTIGE			
❑ 24042	Guitar Player	197?	25.00
❑ PRST-7732	The Return of Tal Farlow/1969	1969	25.00
VERVE			
❑ MGV-8123 [M]	A Recital by Tal Farlow	1957	50.00
— Reissue of Norgran 1030			
❑ V-8123 [M]	A Recital by Tal Farlow	1961	25.00
❑ MGV-8184 [M]	Autumn in New York	1957	50.00
— Reissue of Norgran 1097			
❑ V-8184 [M]	Autumn in New York	1961	25.00
❑ 815236-1	Poppin' and Burnin'	198?	15.00
❑ MGV-8021 [M]	Tal	1957	50.00
— Reissue of Norgran 1102			
❑ V-8021 [M]	Tal	1961	25.00
❑ UMV-2565	Tal	198?	12.00
❑ MGV-8371 [M]	Tal Farlow Plays the Music of Harold Arlen	1960	50.00
❑ V-8371 [M]	Tal Farlow Plays the Music of Harold Arlen	1961	25.00
❑ MGV-8370 [M]	The Guitar Artistry of Tal Farlow	1960	50.00
❑ MGVS-6143 [S]	The Guitar Artistry of Tal Farlow	1960	40.00
❑ V-8370 [M]	The Guitar Artistry of Tal Farlow	1961	25.00
❑ V6-8370 [S]	The Guitar Artistry of Tal Farlow	1961	18.00
❑ MGV-8011 [M]	The Interpretations of Tal Farlow	1957	50.00
— Reissue of Norgran 1027			
❑ V-8011 [M]	The Interpretations of Tal Farlow	1961	25.00
❑ MGV-8201 [M]	The Swinging Guitar of Tal Farlow	1957	100.00
❑ V-8201 [M]	The Swinging Guitar of Tal Farlow	1961	25.00

Number	Title	Yr	NM
❑ MGV-8138 [M]	The Tal Farlow Album	1957	50.00
— Reissue of Norgran 1047			
❑ V-8138 [M]	The Tal Farlow Album	1961	25.00
❑ UMV-2584	The Tal Farlow Album	198?	12.00
❑ MGV-8289 [M]	This is Tal Farlow	1958	50.00
❑ V-8289 [M]	This Is Tal Farlow	1961	25.00
XANADU			
❑ 109	The Fuerst Set	197?	15.00
❑ 119	The Second Set	197?	15.00
FARLOWE, CHRIS			
COLUMBIA			
❑ CL2593 [M]	The Fabulous Chris Farlowe	1966	40.00
❑ CS9393 [R]	The Fabulous Chris Farlowe	1966	30.00
IMMEDIATE			
❑ Z1252010 [B]	Paint It Farlowe	1968	30.00
POLYDOR			
❑ 24-4041	From Here to Mama Rosa with the Hill	1970	15.00
FARM BAND, THE			
MANTRA			
❑ 777	The Farm Band	1972	75.00
— With poster			
FARMER, ART			
ABC-PARAMOUNT			
❑ ABC-200 [M]	Last Night When We Were Young	1958	60.00
ARGO			
❑ LP-678 [M]	Art	1961	30.00
❑ LPS-678 [S]	Art	1961	30.00
❑ LP-738 [M]	Perception	1964	30.00
❑ LPS-738 [S]	Perception	1964	30.00
ATLANTIC			
❑ 1412 [M]	Interaction	1963	30.00
❑ SD1412 [S]	Interaction	1963	30.00
❑ 1421 [M]	Live at the Half Note	1964	30.00
❑ SD1421 [S]	Live at the Half Note	1964	30.00
❑ 1442 [M]	Sing Me Softly of the Blues	1965	25.00
❑ SD1442 [S]	Sing Me Softly of the Blues	1965	30.00
❑ 1430 [M]	To Sweden with Love	1964	25.00
❑ SD1430 [S]	To Sweden with Love	1964	30.00
COLUMBIA			
❑ CL2746 [M]	Art Farmer Plays the Great Jazz Hits	1967	30.00
❑ CS9546 [S]	Art Farmer Plays the Great Jazz Hits	1967	25.00
❑ CL2588 [M]	Baroque Sketches	1966	25.00
❑ CS9388 [S]	Baroque Sketches	1966	25.00
❑ CL2649 [M]	The Time and the Place	1967	30.00
❑ CS9449 [S]	The Time and the Place	1967	25.00
❑ C238232	Time and Place	198?	15.00
COLUMBIA JAZZ ODYSSEY			
❑ PC36826	Art Farmer Plays the Great Jazz Hits	1980	12.00
CONCORD JAZZ			
❑ CJ-212	Warm Valley	1982	15.00
❑ CJ-179	Work of Art	198?	15.00
CONTEMPORARY			
❑ C-14042	Blame It on My Youth	198?	12.00
❑ S-7636	On the Road	197?	18.00
❑ C-14055	Ph. D.	1989	15.00
❑ C-3554 [M]	Portrait of Art Farmer	1958	50.00
❑ S-7027 [S]	Portrait of Art Farmer	1959	30.00
❑ S-7554	Portrait of Art Farmer	197?	18.00
❑ C-14029	Something to Live For: The Music of Billy Strayhorn	1987	12.00
CTI			
❑ 7083	Big Blues	1978	18.00
❑ 7073	Crawl	1977	18.00
❑ 7080	Something You Got	1977	18.00
❑ 9000	Yama	198?	15.00
FANTASY			
❑ OJC-241	Art Farmer Quintet	1987	12.00
❑ OJC-398	Farmer's Market	1989	15.00
❑ OJC-478	On the Road	1990	15.00
❑ OJC-166	Portrait of Art	198?	12.00
❑ OJC-054	The Art Farmer Septet	198?	12.00
❑ OJC-018	Two Trumpets	198?	12.00
❑ OJC-072	When Farmer Met Gryce	198?	12.00
INNER CITY			
❑ IC-6024	Live at Boomer's	197?	18.00
❑ IC-6004	The Summer Knows	197?	18.00
❑ IC-6014	To Duke with Love	197?	18.00
MAINSTREAM			
❑ MRL-371	Gentle Eyes	1972	25.00
❑ MRL-332	Homecoming	1971	25.00
MERCURY			
❑ MG-20786 [M]	Listen to Art Farmer and the Orchestra	1963	25.00
❑ SR-60786 [S]	Listen to Art Farmer and the Orchestra	1963	30.00
MOON			
❑ MLP-014	Art Worker	199?	18.00
NEW JAZZ			
❑ NJLP-8258 [M]	Early Art	1961	40.00
— Purple label			

Number	Title	Yr	NM
❑ NJLP-8258 [M]	Early Art	1965	30.00
— Blue label, trident logo at right			
❑ NJLP-8289 [M]	Evening in Casablanca	1962	40.00
— Purple label			
❑ NJLP-8289 [M]	Evening in Casablanca	1965	30.00
— Blue label, trident logo at right			
❑ NJLP-8203 [M]	Farmer's Market	1958	150.00
— Yellow label			
❑ NJLP-8203 [M]	Farmer's Market	1958	50.00
— Purple label			
❑ NJLP-8203 [M]	Farmer's Market	1965	30.00
— Blue label, trident logo at right			
❑ NJLP-8278 [M]	Work of Art	1962	40.00
— Purple label			
❑ NJLP-8278 [M]	Work of Art	1965	30.00
— Blue label, trident logo at right			
PAUSA			
❑ 7133	From Vienna with Art	198?	15.00
❑ 9025	Modern Art	198?	12.00
PRESTIGE			
❑ PRLP-193 [10]	Art Farmer Quartet	1954	300.00
❑ PRLP-181 [10]	Art Farmer Quintet	1954	300.00
❑ PRLP-209 [10]	Art Farmer Quintet	1955	300.00
❑ PRLP-7017 [M]	Art Farmer Quintet Featuring Gigi Gryce	1956	150.00
— Yellow label with W. 50th St. address			
❑ PRLP-177 [10]	Art Farmer Quintet Featuring Sonny Rollins	1954	400.00
❑ PRLP-162 [10]	Art Farmer Septet	1953	300.00
❑ PRLP-7031 [M]	Art Farmer Septet	1956	150.00
— Yellow label with W. 50th St. address			
❑ PRST-7665	Early Art	1969	18.00
❑ 24032	Farmer's Market	197?	18.00
❑ PRLP-7092 [M]	Three Trumpets	1957	250.00
❑ PRLP-7344 [M]	Trumpets All Out	1964	50.00
❑ PRST-7344 [R]	Trumpets All Out	1964	30.00
❑ PRLP-7062 [M]	Two Trumpets	1956	200.00
❑ PRLP-7085 [M]	When Farmer Met Gryce	1957	500.00
SCEPTER			
❑ S-521 [M]	The Many Faces of Art Farmer	1964	25.00
❑ SS-521 [S]	The Many Faces of Art Farmer	1964	30.00
SOUL NOTE			
❑ SN-1026	I'll Take Manhattan	198?	15.00
❑ SN-1046	Mirage	1983	15.00
❑ SN-1076	You Make Me Smile	1985	15.00
STEREO RECORDS			
❑ S-7027 [S]	Portrait of Art Farmer	1958	40.00
UNITED ARTISTS			
❑ UAL-4062 [M]	Aztec Suite	1959	50.00
❑ UAS-5062 [S]	Aztec Suite	1959	40.00
❑ UAL-4047 [M]	Brass Shout	1959	50.00
❑ UAS-5047 [S]	Brass Shout	1959	40.00
❑ UAL-4007 [M]	Modern Art	1958	50.00
❑ UAS-5007 [S]	Modern Art	1959	40.00
FARMER, ART/ART TAYLOR			
PRESTIGE			
❑ PRLP-7342 [M]	Hard Cookin'	1964	50.00
❑ PRST-7342 [R]	Hard Cookin'	1964	30.00
FARNER, MARK, AND DON BREWER			
QUADICO			
❑ 7401	Monumental Funk	1977	12.00
❑ 7401 [PD]	Monumental Funk	1977	25.00
— Picture disc			
FARNER, MARK			
ATLANTIC			
❑ SD18232	Mark Farner	1977	12.00
❑ SD19196	No Frills	1978	12.00
FARQUAHR			
ELEKTRA			
❑ EKS-74083	Farquhr	1970	15.00
VERVE FORECAST			
❑ FTS-3053	Fabulous Farquahr	1969	15.00
FARR, JIMMY			
CIRCLE			
❑ CLP-26	Best by Farr	197?	12.00
FARRAH, SHAMEK			
STRATA-EAST			
❑ SES-7412	First Impressions	1974	40.00
FARRELL, JOE; FLORA PURIM; AIRTO MOREIRA			
REFERENCE RECORDINGS			
❑ RR-24	Three-Way Mirror	1989	25.00
FARRELL, JOE			
CONTEMPORARY			
❑ C-14002	Sonic Text	1980	15.00
CTI			
❑ 6053	Canned Funk	1975	18.00

Number	Title	Yr	NM
❑ 6003	Joe Farrell Quartet	1970	25.00
❑ 6023	Moon Germs	1972	25.00
❑ 8003	Moon Germs	197?	12.00
— Reissue of 6023			
❑ 6014	Outback	1971	25.00
❑ 8005	Outback	197?	12.00
— Reissue of 6014			
❑ 6034	Penny Arcade	1973	18.00
❑ 6065	Song of the Wind	1976	18.00
❑ 6042	Upon This Rock	1974	18.00

JAZZ A LA CARTE

❑ 4	Farrell's Inferno	1979	18.00

WARNER BROS.

❑ BS3121	La Cathedral y El Toro	1977	15.00
❑ BSK3225	Night Dancing	1978	15.00

XANADU

❑ 174	Skateboard Park	1979	18.00

FARRELL, RICHARD

MERCURY LIVING PRESENCE

❑ SR90126 [S]	Lizst: Piano Concerto No. 1; Grieg: Piano Concerto in A	1960	30.00
— Maroon label, no "Vendor: Mercury Record Corporation			

FARROW, CEE

ROCSHIRE

❑ 22006	Red and Blue	1983	18.00

FASCIANI, GUY

INNER CITY

❑ IC-1161	The Stairway Caper	198?	18.00

FASOLI, CLAUDIO

SOUL NOTE

❑ SN-1071	Lido	1983	18.00

FASTER PUSSYCAT

ELEKTRA

❑ 60730	Faster Pussycat	1987	10.00
❑ 60883	Wake Me When It's Over	1989	12.00

FAT BOYS

SUTRA

❑ SUS1017	Big and Beautiful	1986	12.00
❑ SUS1015	Fat Boys	1984	12.00
❑ SUS1018	The Best Part of the Fat Boys	1987	18.00
❑ SUS1016	The Fat Boys Are Back	1985	12.00

TIN PAN APPLE

❑ 835809-1	Coming Back Hard Again	1988	10.00
❑ 831948-1	Crushin'	1987	10.00
❑ 838867-1	On and On	1989	12.00

FAT CITY

ABC PROBE

❑ 4508	Reincarnation	1969	25.00

PARAMOUNT

❑ PAS-6028	Welcome to Fat City	1972	18.00

FAT JOE

ATLANTIC

❑ 83472	J.O.S.E. (Jealous Ones Still Envy)	2001	18.00

BIG BEAT

❑ 92805	Don Cartagena	1998	18.00

RELATIVITY

❑ 1239	Jealous One's Envy	1995	15.00
❑ 1175	Represent	1993	15.00

FAT MATTRESS

ATCO

❑ 33-309 [M]	Fat Mattress	1969	40.00
— White label promo only; "DJ Copy Monaural" sticker on cover			
❑ SD 33-309 [S]	Fat Mattress	1969	25.00
❑ SD 33-347 [S]	Fat Mattress II	1970	18.00
❑ 33-347 [M]	Fat Mattress II	1970	40.00
— White label promo only; "DJ Copy Monaural" sticker on cover			

FATBACK

COTILLION

❑ 90168	Phoenix	1984	10.00
❑ 90253	So Delicious	1985	10.00

EVENT

❑ 6902	Keep On Steppin'	1974	18.00
— As "The Fatback Band			
❑ 6905	Raising Hell	1976	18.00
— As "The Fatback Band			
❑ 6904	Yum Yum	1975	18.00
— As "The Fatback Band			

SPRING

❑ 6729	14 Karat	1980	12.00
❑ 6721	Bright Lites, Big City	1979	12.00

Number	Title	Yr	NM
❑ 6723	Fatback XII	1979	12.00
❑ 6718	Fired Up 'N' Kickin'	1978	12.00
❑ 6734	Gigolo	1981	12.00
❑ 6726	Hot Box	1980	12.00
❑ 6717	Man with a Plan	1978	15.00
— As "The Fatback Band			
❑ 6711	Night Fever	1976	15.00
— As "The Fatback Band			
❑ 6714	NYCNYUSA	1977	15.00
— As "The Fatback Band			
❑ 6736	On the Floor	1982	12.00
❑ 6731	Tasty Jam	1981	12.00

FATBOY SLIM

ASTRALWERKS

❑ ASW6203 [B]	Better Living Through Chemistry	1997	25.00
❑ 50460 [B]	Halfway Between the Gutter and the Stars	2000	25.00
❑ ASW6221 [EP]	The Beat Burger	1997	10.00
❑ ASW6247 [B]	You've Come a Long Way, Baby	1998	25.00

FATHER M.C.

UPTOWN

❑ 10542	Close to You	1992	25.00
❑ 10061	Father's Day	1990	18.00
❑ 10937	Sex Is Law	1993	25.00
— As "Father			

FATOOL, NICK

JAZZOLOGY

❑ J-158	Nick Fatool's Jazz Band — Spring of '87	1987	12.00

FATTBURGER

INTIMA

❑ SJ-73287	Good News	1987	12.00
❑ D1-73334	Living in Paradise	1988	12.00
❑ D1-73503	Time Will Tell	1989	15.00

OPTIMISM

❑ OP-2001	One of a Kind	198?	15.00

FAUN

GREGAR

❑ 7000	Faun	1969	100.00

FAUST

4 MEN WITH BEARDS

❑ 4M174LP [B]	So Far		25.00

FAY, FRANK

BALLY

❑ BAL-10215 [M]	Be Frank with Fay	1957	40.00

FAYE, FRANCES

BETHLEHEM

❑ BCP-6006	Bad, Bad, Frances Faye	1976	18.00
— Reissue of 23, distributed by RCA Victor			
❑ BCP-6017 [M]	Frances Faye Sings Folk Songs	1957	40.00
❑ BCP-23 [M]	I'm Wild Again	1955	50.00
❑ BCP-62 [M]	Relaxin' with Frances Faye	1957	40.00

CAPITOL

❑ H512 [10]	No Reservations	1954	80.00
❑ T512 [M]	No Reservations	1955	50.00
— Turquoise or gray label			
❑ T512 [M]	No Reservations	1958	30.00
— Black label with colorband, logo at left			

GENE NORMAN

❑ GNP-41 [M]	Caught in the Act	1958	40.00
❑ GNP-92 [M]	Caught in the Act, Volume 2	1959	40.00

GNP CRESCENDO

❑ GNP-41 [M]	Caught in the Act	196?	18.00
❑ GNPS-41 [S]	Caught in the Act	196?	15.00
❑ GNP-92 [M]	Caught in the Act, Volume 2	196?	18.00
❑ GNPS-92 [S]	Caught in the Act, Volume 2	196?	15.00
❑ LP-9158 [M]	Frances Faye Sings the Blues	1961	40.00
❑ LP-9059 [M]	Frances Faye Swings Fats Domino	1958	40.00
❑ LP-12007 [S]	Frances Faye Swings Fats Domino	1959	50.00

REGINA

❑ R-315 [M]	You Gotta Go! Go! Go!	1964	30.00
❑ RS-315 [S]	You Gotta Go! Go! Go!	1964	30.00

VERVE

❑ MGV-2147 [M]	Frances Faye in Frenzy	1961	40.00
❑ V-2147 [M]	Frances Faye in Frenzy	1961	25.00
❑ V-8434 [M]	Swinging All the Way with Frances Faye	1962	25.00
❑ V6-8434 [S]	Swinging All the Way with Frances Faye	1962	30.00

FAZOLA, IRVING

MERCURY

❑ MG-25016 [10]	Irving Fazola and His Dixielanders	1950	50.00

Number	Title	Yr	NM

FAZOLA, IRVING/GEORGE HARTMANN

EMARCY

❑ MG-36022 [M]	New Orleans Express	1954	40.00

FEAR

RESTLESS

❑ 72039	More Beer	1985	18.00

SLASH

❑ SR111 [B]	The Record	1982	40.00
❑ 23933 [B]	The Record	1982	30.00

FEAR ITSELF

DOT

❑ DLP-25942	Fear Itself	1969	30.00

FEATHER, LEONARD

ABC-PARAMOUNT

❑ ABC-110 [M]	Swingin' on the Vibories	1956	60.00

INTERLUDE

❑ MO-511 [M]	Leonard Feather Presents 52nd Street	1959	40.00
❑ ST-1011 [S]	Leonard Feather Presents 52nd Street	1959	30.00

MAINSTREAM

❑ MRL-388	Freedom Jazz Dance	1974	25.00
❑ MRL-348	Night Blooming Jazzmen	1972	25.00

MGM

❑ E-3494 [M]	Hi-Fi Suite	1957	50.00
❑ E-3650 [M]	Oh, Captain!	1958	50.00
❑ E-270 [10]	Winter Sequence	1954	120.00

MODE

❑ LP-127 [M]	Leonard Feather Presents Bop	1957	60.00

FEDERAL DUCK

MUSICOR

❑ MS-3162	Federal Duck	1968	50.00

FEELIES, THE

A&M

❑ SP-5214	Only Life	1988	18.00
❑ 750217403-1 [DJ]	Paint It Black + 5	1990	25.00
— Promo-only 6-song sampler			
❑ 750215344-1	Time for a Witness	1991	18.00

COYOTE/TWINTONE

❑ TTC8673	The Good Earth	1986	18.00

STIFF

❑ USE-4	Crazy Rhythms	1980	40.00
— Price is for an actual U.S. pressing. Most copies sold in U.S. were U.K. copies with stickers.			

FELDER, DON

ASYLUM

❑ 60295	Airborne	1983	12.00

FELDER, WILTON

ABC

❑ AA-1109	We All Have a Star	1978	18.00

MCA

❑ 5406	Gentle Fire	1983	12.00
❑ 5144	Inherit the Wind	1980	12.00
❑ 27031	Inherit the Wind	198?	10.00
— Reissue			
❑ 42096	Love Is a Rush	1987	12.00
❑ 5510	Secrets	1985	12.00
❑ AA-1109	We All Have a Star	1979	12.00
— Reissue of ABC 1109			
❑ 700	We All Have a Star	198?	10.00
— Budget-line reissue of MCA 1109			

WORLD PACIFIC

❑ ST-20152	Bullitt	196?	25.00

FELDMAN, VICTOR

AVA

❑ A-19 [M]	Soviet Jazz Themes	1963	30.00
❑ AS-19 [S]	Soviet Jazz Themes	1963	30.00

CHOICE

❑ CRS1005 [M]	Your Smile	1974	18.00

COHEARANT

❑ CSR1001	In My Pocket	1977	40.00

CONCORD JAZZ

❑ CJ-38	The Artful Dodger	1977	15.00

CONTEMPORARY

❑ M-5005 [M]	Latinsville	1960	150.00
❑ S-9005 [S]	Latinsville	1960	100.00
❑ C-3541 [M]	Suite Sixteen	1957	40.00
❑ S-7541 [S]	Suite Sixteen	1959	30.00
❑ C-3549 [M]	The Arrival of Victor Feldman	1958	40.00
❑ S-7549 [S]	The Arrival of Victor Feldman	1959	30.00

Number	Title	Yr	NM
FANTASY			
❑ OJC-402	Merry Olde Soul	1989	15.00
❑ OJC-268	The Arrival of Victor Feldman	1987	12.00
INFINITY			
❑ 5000 [M]	A Taste of Honey and a Taste of Bossa Nova	1962	30.00
INTERLUDE			
❑ MO-510 [M]	With Mallets Aforethought	1959	40.00
— Reissue of Mode LP			
MODE			
❑ LP-120 [M]	Victor Feldman on Vibes	1957	60.00
NAUTILUS			
❑ NR-50	The Secret of the Andes	1982	25.00
— Audiophile vinyl			
PACIFIC JAZZ			
❑ ST-20128 [S]	Venezuela Joropo	196?	30.00
❑ PJ-20128 [M]	Venezuela Joropo	196?	30.00
❑ PJ-10121 [M]	Victor Feldman Plays Everything in Sight	196?	25.00
❑ ST-20121 [S]	Victor Feldman Plays Everything in Sight	196?	30.00
PALO ALTO			
❑ PA-8066	Fiesta	1984	12.00
❑ PA-8053	The Secret of the Andes	1982	12.00
❑ PA-8056	To Chopin with Love	1983	12.00
RIVERSIDE			
❑ RLP-366 [M]	Merry Ole Soul	1961	30.00
❑ RS-9366 [S]	Merry Ole Soul	1961	30.00
VEE JAY			
❑ LP-2507 [M]	It's a Wonderful World	1965	25.00
❑ LP-1096 [M]	Love Me with All Your Heart	1964	30.00
WORLD PACIFIC			
❑ WP-1807 [M]	Stop the World, I Want to Get Off	1962	30.00
❑ ST-1807 [S]	Stop the World, I Want to Get Off	1962	25.00
— Black vinyl			
❑ ST-1807 [S]	Stop the World, I Want to Get Off	1962	50.00
— Yellow vinyl			

FELICE, DEE

Number	Title	Yr	NM
BETHLEHEM			
❑ B-10000	In Heat	1969	50.00
— Produced by JAMES BROWN.			

FELICE, ERNIE

Number	Title	Yr	NM
CAPITOL			
❑ H192 [10]	Ernie Felice Quartet	1950	60.00

FELICIANO, JOSE

Number	Title	Yr	NM
MOTOWN			
❑ 6018ML	Escenas de Amor	1982	12.00
❑ M8-953	Jose Feliciano	1981	12.00
❑ 6035ML	Romance in the Night	1983	12.00
PAIR			
❑ PDL2-1091	His Hits and Other Classics	1986	15.00
PRIVATE STOCK			
❑ PS-2010	Angela	1976	12.00
❑ PS-2022	Sweet Soul	1977	12.00
RCA CAMDEN			
❑ CAS-2563	Jose Feliciano Sings	1972	12.00
RCA VICTOR			
❑ LSP-6021	Alive Alive-O!	1969	18.00
❑ CPL1-0407	And the Feeling's Good	1974	12.00
❑ AFL1-0407	And the Feeling's Good	1977	10.00
— Reissue with new prefix			
❑ LPM-3503 [M]	Bag Full of Soul (Folk, Rock and Blues)	1966	18.00
❑ LSP-3503 [S]	Bag Full of Soul (Folk, Rock and Blues)	1966	25.00
❑ APD1-0141 [Q]	Compartments	1973	30.00
— All copies are quadraphonic			
❑ LSPX-1005	Encore! Jose Feliciano's Finest Performances	1971	15.00
❑ AFL1-2824	Encore! Jose Feliciano's Finest Performances	1978	12.00
— Reissue of LSPX-1005			
❑ FSP-277	En Mi Soledad	1971	25.00
❑ LPM-3581 [M]	Fantastic Feliciano	1966	18.00
❑ LSP-3581 [S]	Fantastic Feliciano	1966	25.00
❑ FSP-253	Fantastico	1970	25.00
❑ LPM-3957 [M]	Feliciano!	1968	30.00
❑ LSP-3957 [S]	Feliciano!	1968	18.00
❑ AFL1-3957	Feliciano!	1977	10.00
— Reissue with new prefix			
❑ LSP-4185	Feliciano/10 to 23	1969	18.00
❑ AFL1-4185	Feliciano/10 to 23	1977	10.00
— Reissue with new prefix			
❑ LSP-4370	Fireworks	1970	15.00
❑ AFL1-4370	Fireworks	1977	10.00
— Reissue with new prefix			
❑ APL1-0266	For My Love...Mother Music	1974	12.00
❑ AFL1-0266	For My Love...Mother Music	1977	10.00
— Reissue with new prefix			
❑ LSP-4421	Jose Feliciano	1970	18.00

Number	Title	Yr	NM
❑ APL1-1005	Just Wanna Rock 'n' Roll	1975	12.00
❑ AFL1-1005	Just Wanna Rock 'n' Roll	1977	10.00
— Reissue with new prefix			
❑ LSP-4656	Memphis Menu	1972	15.00
❑ LSP-4045	Souled	1968	18.00
❑ LSP-4573	That the Spirit Needs	1971	15.00
❑ LPM-3358 [M]	The Voice and Guitar of Jose Feliciano	1965	18.00
❑ LSP-3358 [S]	The Voice and Guitar of Jose Feliciano	1965	25.00

FELT

Number	Title	Yr	NM
NASCO			
❑ 9006	Felt	1971	500.00

FELTS, NARVEL

Number	Title	Yr	NM
ABC			
❑ 1080	Inside Love	1978	12.00
❑ 1115	One Run for the Roses	1979	12.00
ABC DOT			
❑ DO-2065	Doin' What I Feel	1976	15.00
❑ 2036	Greatest Hits Vol. 1	1975	15.00
❑ DO-2095	Narvel	1977	15.00
❑ DOSD-2025	Narvel Felts	1975	15.00
❑ 2033	Narvel the Marvel	1976	15.00
❑ DO-2070	The Touch of Felts	1977	15.00
CINNAMON			
❑ 5000	Drift Away	1973	18.00
❑ 5002	When Your Good Love Was Mine	1974	18.00
HI			
❑ 32098	This Time	1976	15.00
MCA			
❑ 699	Inside Love	198?	10.00
— Reissue of ABC 1080			
❑ 635	Narvel	198?	10.00
— Reissue of ABC Dot 2095			
❑ 799	One Run for the Roses	198?	10.00
— Reissue of ABC 1115			
❑ 634	The Touch of Felts	198?	10.00
— Reissue of ABC Dot 2070			
❑ 27020	The Very Best of Narvel Felts	198?	10.00
POWER PAK			
❑ PO-237	Live!	197?	12.00

FEMININE COMPLEX, THE

Number	Title	Yr	NM
ATHENA			
❑ 6001	Livin' Love	1969	75.00

FENDER, FREDDY

Number	Title	Yr	NM
ABC			
❑ AA-1062	Swamp Gold	1978	12.00
❑ AA-1132	Tex-Mex	1979	15.00
ABC/DOT			
❑ DOSD-2044	Are You Ready for Freddy	1975	15.00
❑ DOSD-2020	Before the Next Teardrop Falls	1975	15.00
❑ DP-2090	If You Don't Love Me	1977	15.00
❑ DOSD-2061	If You're Ever in Texas	1976	15.00
❑ DO-2101	Merry Christmas -- Feliz Navidad	1977	15.00
❑ DOSD-2050	Rock 'n' Country	1976	15.00
❑ DO-2079	The Best of Freddy Fender	1977	15.00
ACCORD			
❑ SN-7121	Since I Met You Baby	1981	12.00
GRT			
❑ 8005	Since I Met You Baby	1975	15.00
INTERMEDIA			
❑ QS-5035	Before the Next Teardrop Falls	198?	10.00
MCA			
❑ 639	Are You Ready for Freddy	1980	10.00
— Reissue of ABC/Dot 2044			
❑ 37110	Before the Next Teardrop Falls	1980	10.00
— Reissue of ABC/Dot 2020			
❑ 15037	Christmas Time in the Valley	198?	12.00
❑ 669	If You Don't Love Me	1980	10.00
— Reissue of ABC/Dot 2090			
❑ 15025	Merry Christmas	198?	10.00
❑ 668	Swamp Gold	1980	10.00
— Reissue of ABC 1062			
❑ AA-1132	Tex-Mex	1979	12.00
— Reissue of ABC 1132			
❑ 37109	Tex-Mex	1980	10.00
— Reissue of MCA 1132			
❑ 835	The Best of Freddy Fender	198?	10.00
— Reissue of MCA 3285			
❑ 3285	The Best of Freddy Fender	1979	12.00
— Reissue of ABC/Dot 2079			
PICCADILLY			
❑ 3589	Enter My Heart	1981	12.00
PICKWICK			
❑ JS-6178	Freddy Fender	1975	12.00
POWER PAK			
❑ PO-280	Recorded Inside Louisiana State Prison	1975	12.00

Number	Title	Yr	NM
STARFLITE			
❑ JZ36073	Balladeer	1980	12.00
❑ JZ36284	Together We Drifted Apart	1980	12.00

FENDERMEN, THE

Number	Title	Yr	NM
BEAT ROCKET			
❑ BR116	Mule Skinner Blues	2000	18.00
KOALA			
❑ 14565	Poison Ivy	1980	50.00
SOMA			
❑ MG-1240 [M]	Mule Skinner Blues	1960	4000.00
— Blue vinyl; VG value 2000; VG+ value 3000			

Number	Title	Yr	NM
❑ MG-1240 [M]	Mule Skinner Blues	1960	1200.00
— Black vinyl			

FENIX JAZZ BAND OF ARGENTINA, THE

Number	Title	Yr	NM
STOMP OFF			
❑ SOS-1129	Grandpa's Spells	1987	12.00

FERGUSON, ALLYN

Number	Title	Yr	NM
AVA			
❑ A-32 [M]	Pictures at an Exhibition Framed in Jazz	1963	30.00
❑ AS-32 [S]	Pictures at an Exhibition Framed in Jazz	1963	30.00
DISCOVERY			
❑ DS-810	Pictures at an Exhibition Framed in Jazz	1980	15.00
— Reissue of AS-32			

FERGUSON, JAY

Number	Title	Yr	NM
ASYLUM			
❑ 7E-1063	All Alone in the End Zone	1976	12.00
❑ 6E-158	Real Life Ain't This Way	1979	12.00
❑ 7E-1115	Thunder Island	1978	12.00
CAPITOL			
❑ ST-12083	Terms and Conditions	1980	12.00
❑ ST-12196	White Noise	1982	12.00

FERGUSON, MAYNARD

Number	Title	Yr	NM
BASF			
❑ 20662	Trumpet Rhapsody	1973	15.00
BLACK HAWK			
❑ BKH-50101	Body and Soul	1986	12.00
BLUEBIRD			
❑ 6455-1-RB	The Bluebird Dreamband	1987	12.00
CAMEO			
❑ C-1066 [M]	Come Blow Your Horn	1964	25.00
❑ SC-1066 [S]	Come Blow Your Horn	1964	30.00
❑ C-1046 [M]	The New Sounds of Maynard Ferguson	1963	25.00
❑ SC-1046 [S]	The New Sounds of Maynard Ferguson	1963	30.00
COLUMBIA			
❑ C31117	Alive and Well in London	1972	15.00
❑ PC31117	Alive and Well in London	198?	10.00
— Budget-line reissue			
❑ JC35480	Carnival	1978	12.00
❑ PC35480	Carnival	1980	10.00
— Budget-line reissue			
❑ KC33007	Chameleon	1974	15.00
❑ PC33007	Chameleon	1975	12.00
— Early reissue of KC 33007; no bar code			
❑ PC33007	Chameleon	1980	10.00
— Budget-line reissue with bar code			
❑ PC34457	Conquistador	1977	12.00
— No bar code			
❑ PCQ34457 [Q]	Conquistador	1977	25.00
❑ PC34457	Conquistador	1980	10.00
— Budget-line reissue with bar code			
❑ HC44457	Conquistador	1982	50.00
— Half-speed mastered edition			

Number	Title	Yr	NM
FC37713	Hollywood	1982	12.00
JC36124	Hot	1979	12.00
JC36766	It's My Time	1980	12.00
PC36978	Maynard Ferguson	1981	12.00
C30466	M.F. Horn	1971	15.00
PC30466	M.F. Horn	198?	10.00
—Budget-line reissue			
KC32403	M.F. Horn/3	1973	15.00
PC32403	M.F. Horn/3	198?	10.00
—Budget-line reissue			
KG32732	M.F. Horn 4 & 5/Live at Jimmy's	1973	18.00
PG32732	M.F. Horn 4 & 5/Live at Jimmy's	198?	12.00
—Budget-line reissue			
CG33660	M.F. Horn/M.F. Horn Two	1975	18.00
KC31709	M.F. Horn Two	1972	15.00
PC31709	M.F. Horn Two	198?	10.00
—Budget-line reissue			
JC34971	New Vintage	1977	12.00
PC33953	Primal Scream	1976	12.00
—No bar code			
JC36361	The Best of Maynard Ferguson	1980	12.00
PC36361	The Best of Maynard Ferguson	1986	10.00
—Budget-line reissue			

EMARCY

Number	Title	Yr	NM
MG-36076 [M]	Around the Horn with Maynard Ferguson	1956	50.00
MG-36114 [M]	Boy with Lots of Brass	1957	50.00
MG-26024 [10]	Dimensions	1954	100.00
MG-36044 [M]	Dimensions	1956	50.00
MG-36009 [M]	Jam Session Featuring Maynard Ferguson	1955	50.00
MG-36021 [M]	Maynard Ferguson Octet	1955	60.00
MG-26017 [10]	Maynard Ferguson's Hollywood Party	1954	100.00
MG-36046 [M]	Maynard Ferguson's Hollywood Party	1956	50.00
EMS-2-406	Stratospheric	1976	15.00

EMUS

Number	Title	Yr	NM
ES-12024 [S]	Maynard	197?	12.00
—Reissue of Roulette material			

ENTERPRISE

Number	Title	Yr	NM
S-13-101	Ridin' High	1968	18.00

FORUM

Number	Title	Yr	NM
F-9035 [M]	Jazz for Dancing	196?	15.00
SF-9035 [S]	Jazz for Dancing	196?	18.00

INTIMA

Number	Title	Yr	NM
D1-73390	Big Bop Nouveau	1990	15.00
SJ-73279	High Voltage	1987	15.00

MAINSTREAM

Number	Title	Yr	NM
MRL-372	6 By 6	1973	15.00
805	Big "F"	1974	18.00
56031 [M]	Color Him Wild	1965	18.00
S-6031 [S]	Color Him Wild	1965	25.00
MRL-359	Dues	1972	15.00
56060 [M]	Maynard Ferguson Sextet	1966	18.00
S-6060 [S]	Maynard Ferguson Sextet	1966	25.00
MRL-316	Screamin' Blue	1971	15.00
56045 [M]	The Blues Roar	1965	18.00
S-6045 [S]	The Blues Roar	1965	25.00

MERCURY

Number	Title	Yr	NM
MG-20556 [M]	Boy with Lots of Brass	1960	30.00
SR-60124 [S]	Boy with Lots of Brass	1960	30.00

MOSAIC

Number	Title	Yr	NM
MQ14-156	The Complete Roulette Recordings of the Maynard Ferguson Orchestra	1994	250.00

NAUTILUS

Number	Title	Yr	NM
NR-57	Storm	1983	40.00
—Audiophile vinyl			

PALO ALTO

Number	Title	Yr	NM
PA-8077	Live from San Francisco	1985	12.00
PA-8052	Storm	1983	12.00

PAUSA

Number	Title	Yr	NM
7037	Trumpet Rhapsody	1980	12.00
—Reissue of BASF LP			

PRESTIGE

Number	Title	Yr	NM
PRLP-7636	Maynard Ferguson 1969	1969	18.00

ROULETTE

Number	Title	Yr	NM
R52027 [M]	A Message from Birdland	1959	30.00
SR52027 [S]	A Message from Birdland	1959	30.00
R52012 [M]	A Message from Newport	1958	30.00
SR52012 [S]	A Message from Newport	1958	30.00
RE-116	A Message from Newport/Newport Suite	1972	18.00
—Reissue of 52012 and 52047 in one package			
R52055 [M]	Let's Face the Music and Dance	1960	30.00
SR52055 [S]	Let's Face the Music and Dance	1960	30.00
R52064 [M]	Maynard '61	1961	30.00
SR52064 [S]	Maynard '61	1961	30.00
RE-122	Maynard '61/Si! Si! M.F.	1973	18.00
—Reissue of 52064 and 52084 in one package			
R52083 [M]	Maynard '62	1962	18.00
SR52083 [S]	Maynard '62	1962	25.00
R52097 [M]	Maynard '63	1963	18.00
SR52097 [S]	Maynard '63	1963	25.00
R52107 [M]	Maynard '64	1964	18.00
SR52107 [S]	Maynard '64	1964	25.00
R52038 [M]	Maynard Ferguson Plays Jazz for Dancing	1959	30.00
SR52038 [S]	Maynard Ferguson Plays Jazz for Dancing	1959	30.00
R52047 [M]	Newport Suite	1960	30.00
SR52047 [S]	Newport Suite	1960	30.00
R52084 [M]	Si! Si! M.F.	1962	18.00
SR52084 [S]	Si! Si! M.F.	1962	25.00
R52058 [M]	Swingin' My Way Through College	1960	30.00
SR52058 [S]	Swingin' My Way Through College	1960	30.00
SK-101	The Ferguson Years	197?	18.00
R52110 [M]	The World of Maynard Ferguson	1964	18.00
SR52110 [S]	The World of Maynard Ferguson	1964	25.00

TRIP

Number	Title	Yr	NM
5558	Around the Horn with Maynard Ferguson	197?	10.00
5507	Dimensions	197?	10.00
5525	Jam Session Featuring Maynard Ferguson	197?	10.00

VIK

Number	Title	Yr	NM
LX-1070 [M]	Birdland Dream Band, Vol. 1	1957	40.00
LX-1077 [M]	Birdland Dream Band, Vol. 2	1957	40.00

FERLINGHETTI, LAWRENCE

FANTASY

Number	Title	Yr	NM
7004 [M]	The Impeachment of Eisenhower	1958	200.00
—Red vinyl			
7004 [M]	The Impeachment of Eisenhower	1958	150.00
—Black vinyl			

FERRANTE AND TEICHER

ABC

Number	Title	Yr	NM
558 [M]	Autumn Leaves	1966	12.00
S-558 [S]	Autumn Leaves	1966	15.00
560 [M]	Bolero	1966	12.00
S 560 [S]	Bolero	1966	15.00
555 [M]	Heaven Sounds	1966	12.00
S-555 [S]	Heaven Sounds	1966	15.00
554 [M]	Memories	1966	12.00
S-554 [S]	Memories	1966	15.00
561 [M]	Temptation	1966	12.00
S-561 [S]	Temptation	1966	15.00
557 [M]	Twin Piano Magic, Vol. 1	1966	12.00
S-557 [S]	Twin Piano Magic, Vol. 1	1966	15.00
559 [M]	Twin Piano Magic, Vol. 2	1966	12.00
S-559 [S]	Twin Piano Magic, Vol. 2	1966	15.00
556 [M]	We've Got Rhythm	1966	12.00
S-556 [S]	We've Got Rhythm	1966	15.00
553 [M]	World's Greatest Semi-Classical Favorites	1966	12.00
S-553 [S]	World's Greatest Semi-Classical Favorites	1966	15.00

ABC-PARAMOUNT

Number	Title	Yr	NM
285 [M]	Ferrante and Teicher Blast Off	1959	18.00
S-285 [S]	Ferrante and Teicher Blast Off	1959	25.00
313 [M]	Ferrante and Teicher Play Light Classics	1960	18.00
S-313 [S]	Ferrante and Teicher Play Light Classics	1960	25.00
248 [M]	Ferrante and Teicher with Percussion	1958	18.00
S-248 [S]	Ferrante and Teicher with Percussion	1958	25.00
221 [M]	Heavenly Sounds in Hi-Fi	1958	18.00
S-221 [S]	Heavenly Sounds in Hi-Fi	1958	25.00
437 [M]	Popular Classics	1962	15.00
S-437 [S]	Popular Classics	1962	18.00
430 [M]	Postcards from Paris	1962	15.00
S-430 [S]	Postcards from Paris	1962	18.00
ST-90467 [S]	Postcards from Paris	196?	18.00
—Capitol Record Club edition			
454 [M]	The Artistry of Ferrante and Teicher	1963	15.00
S-454 [S]	The Artistry of Ferrante and Teicher	1963	18.00
336 [M]	Themes from Broadway Shows	1960	18.00
S-336 [S]	Themes from Broadway Shows	1960	25.00

BAINBRIDGE

Number	Title	Yr	NM
BT-6263	A Few of Our Favorites on Stage	1986	12.00
BT-6266	American Fantasy	1987	12.00

COLUMBIA

Number	Title	Yr	NM
CL573 [M]	Hi-Fire Works	1955	30.00

GRAND AWARD

Number	Title	Yr	NM
GA-263	Themes from Broadway Shows	1962	15.00

HARMONY

Number	Title	Yr	NM
HS11411	Encore	1970	12.00
HL7427 [M]	Fireworks	1967	15.00
HS11227 [R]	Fireworks	1967	12.00
HL7325 [M]	Twin Piano Magic	1965	15.00
HS11125 [R]	Twin Piano Magic	1965	12.00

LIBERTY

Number	Title	Yr	NM
LWB-70	10th Anniversary -- Golden Piano Hits	198?	12.00
—Reissue of United Artists 70			
LT-980	Classical Disco	198?	10.00
—Reissue of United Artists 980			
LN-10198	Classic Lites	1983	10.00
LN-10158	Concert for Lovers	1981	10.00
—Budget-line reissue of United Artists 6315			
LW-662	Feelings	198?	10.00
—Reissue of United Artists 662			
LN-10242	Ferrante and Teicher Superpak	1984	12.00
LKDL-831	For You with Love	198?	25.00
—Reissue of United Artists 831			
LM-1016	Midnight Cowboy	1981	10.00
—Reissue of United Artists 1016			
LT-782	Rocky and Other Knockouts	198?	10.00
—Reissue of United Artists 782			
LN-10175	Showstoppers	1983	10.00
LN-10142	Snowbound	1981	10.00
—Budget-line reissue of United Artists 6233			
LN-10113	Star Wars	198?	10.00
—Reissue of United Artists 855			
LN-10112	Supermen	198?	10.00
—Reissue of United Artists 941			
LWB-73	The Best of Ferrante and Teicher	198?	12.00
—Reissue of United Artists 73			
LN-10176	The Movie Theme Team	1983	10.00
LN-10210	The Movie Theme Team II	1984	10.00
LN-10141	The People's Choice	1981	10.00
—Budget-line reissue of United Artists 6385			
LT-908	You Light Up My Life	198?	10.00
—Reissue of United Artists 908			

PICKWICK

Number	Title	Yr	NM
PC-3003 [M]	Excitement	196?	12.00
SPC-3003 [S]	Excitement	196?	12.00
SPC-3612	Fabulous Favorites	197?	10.00
SPC-3586	Getting Together	1978	10.00
SPC-3397	How High the Moon	197?	10.00
PC-3077 [M]	In Love	196?	12.00
SPC-3077 [S]	In Love	196?	12.00

SUNSET

Number	Title	Yr	NM
SUS-5235	Incomparable Piano	1969	10.00
SUS-5313	Love Is a Rainbow	1971	10.00
SUS-5277	Midnight Memories	1970	10.00

UNITED ARTISTS

Number	Title	Yr	NM
UXS-70	10th Anniversary -- Golden Piano Hits	1969	15.00
UAL3343 [M]	50 Fabulous Piano Favorites	1964	15.00
UAS6343 [S]	50 Fabulous Piano Favorites	1964	18.00
UAS6659	A Bouquet of Hits	1968	12.00
UAL3572 [M]	A Man and a Woman & Other Motion Picture Themes	1967	12.00
UAS6572 [S]	A Man and a Woman & Other Motion Picture Themes	1967	15.00
UA-LA681-G	Around	1977	12.00
UAL3416 [M]	By Popular Demand	1965	12.00
UAS6416 [S]	By Popular Demand	1965	15.00
LT-980	Classical Disco	1979	12.00
UAL3315 [M]	Concert for Lovers	1964	15.00
UAS6315 [S]	Concert for Lovers	1964	18.00
UA-LA195-G	Dial M for Music	1974	12.00
WW7504 [M]	Dynamic Twin Pianos	1961	15.00
UAL3340 [M]	Exotic Love Themes	1964	15.00
UAS6340 [S]	Exotic Love Themes	1964	18.00
UA-LA662-G	Feelings	1976	12.00
UAS5588	Ferrante and Teicher Play Hit Themes	1972	12.00
UAS5645	Ferrante and Teicher Salute Nashville	1972	12.00
UXS-77	Ferrante and Teicher Superpak	1972	15.00
UAS5552	Fiddler on the Roof	1971	12.00
UAL3483 [M]	For Lovers of All Ages	1966	12.00
UAS6483 [S]	For Lovers of All Ages	1966	15.00
UA-LA831-P	For You with Love	1978	25.00
UAS5501	Getting Together	1970	12.00
WW7505 [M]	Golden Piano Hits	1961	15.00
WWS8505 [S]	Golden Piano Hits	1961	18.00
UAL3269 [M]	Golden Piano Hits	1963	12.00
—Reissue of 7505			
UAS6269 [S]	Golden Piano Hits	1963	15.00
—Reissue of 8505			
UAL3210 [M]	Golden Themes from Motion Pictures	1962	15.00
UAS6210 [S]	Golden Themes from Motion Pictures	1962	18.00
UA-LA101-G2	Greatest Love Themes of the Twentieth Century	1973	15.00
UA-LA018-F	Hear & Now	1972	12.00
UAL3298 [M]	Holiday for Pianos	1963	12.00
UAS6298 [S]	Holiday for Pianos	1963	15.00
UA-LA227-G	In a Soulful Mood	1974	12.00
UAS5531	It's Too Late	1971	12.00
UAL3284 [M]	Keyboard Kapers	1963	12.00
UAS6284 [S]	Keyboard Kapers	1963	15.00
UAL3247 [M]	Keys to Her Apartment	1963	15.00
UAS6247 [S]	Keys to Her Apartment	1963	18.00
UA-LA118-G	Killing Me Softly	1973	12.00
UAL3135 [M]	Latin Pianos	1960	15.00
UAS6135 [S]	Latin Pianos	1960	18.00

Number	Title	Yr	NM
❑ UAS6701	Listen to the Movies	1969	12.00
❑ UAS6771	Love Is a Soft Touch	1970	12.00
❑ WW7514 [M]	Love Themes	1961	15.00
❑ WWS8514 [S]	Love Themes	1961	18.00
❑ UAL3282 [M]	Love Themes	1963	12.00
—Reissue of 7514			
❑ UAS6282 [S]	Love Themes	1963	15.00
—Reissue of 8514			
❑ UAL3290 [M]	Love Themes from Cleopatra	1963	15.00
❑ UAS6290 [S]	Love Themes from Cleopatra	1963	18.00
❑ UAS6725	Midnight Cowboy	1969	12.00
❑ LM-1016	Midnight Cowboy	1980	10.00
—Reissue of 6725			
❑ UAL3361 [M]	My Fair Lady	1964	12.00
❑ UAS6361 [S]	My Fair Lady	1964	15.00
❑ UAL3434 [M]	Only the Best	1965	12.00
❑ UAS6434 [S]	Only the Best	1965	15.00
❑ UAL3556 [M]	Our Golden Favorites	1967	15.00
❑ UAS6556 [S]	Our Golden Favorites	1967	12.00
❑ UA-LA585-G	Piano Portraits	1976	12.00
❑ UAL3230 [M]	Pianos in Paradise	1962	15.00
❑ UAS6230 [S]	Pianos in Paradise	1962	18.00
❑ UA-LA782-G	Rocky and Other Knockouts	1977	12.00
❑ UAL3233 [M]	Snowbound	1962	15.00
❑ UAS6233 [S]	Snowbound	1962	18.00
❑ UA-LA573-G	Spirit of 1976	1975	12.00
❑ UAL3406 [M]	Springtime	1965	12.00
❑ UAS6406 [S]	Springtime	1965	15.00
❑ UA-LA855-G	Star Wars	1978	15.00
❑ UA-LA941-H	Supermen	1979	12.00
❑ UXS-73	The Best of Ferrante and Teicher	1971	15.00
❑ UA-LA490-G	The Carpenters Songbook	1975	12.00
❑ UAL3375 [M]	The Enchanted World of Ferrante and Teicher	1964	15.00
❑ UAS6375 [S]	The Enchanted World of Ferrante and Teicher	1964	18.00
❑ UAL3444 [M]	The Ferrante and Teicher Concert	1965	12.00
❑ UAS6444 [S]	The Ferrante and Teicher Concert	1965	15.00
❑ UAL3475 [M]	The Ferrante and Teicher Concert, Part 2	1966	12.00
❑ UAS6475 [S]	The Ferrante and Teicher Concert, Part 2	1966	15.00
❑ UAL3211 [M]	The Many Moods of Ferrante & Teicher	1962	15.00
❑ UAS6211 [S]	The Many Moods of Ferrante & Teicher	1962	18.00
❑ UAS6792	The Music Lovers	1971	12.00
❑ UAL3385 [M]	The People's Choice	1964	12.00
❑ UAS6385 [S]	The People's Choice	1964	15.00
❑ UA-LA072-G	The Roaring 20's	1973	12.00
❑ UA-LA236-G	The Very Best of Ferrante and Teicher	1974	12.00
❑ UAL3121 [M]	The World's Greatest Themes	1960	15.00
❑ UAS6121 [S]	The World's Greatest Themes	1960	18.00
❑ UAL3171 [M]	Tonight	1962	15.00
❑ UAS6171 [S]	Tonight	1962	18.00
❑ UAL3166 [M]	West Side Story & Other Motion Picture & Broadway Hits	1961	15.00
❑ UAS6166 [S]	West Side Story & Other Motion Picture & Broadway Hits	1961	18.00
❑ UAL3536 [M]	We Wish You a Merry Christmas	1966	18.00
❑ UAS6536 [S]	We Wish You a Merry Christmas	1966	15.00
❑ UAS6536 [S]	We Wish You a Merry Christmas	1972	10.00
—Tan label (may also exist on late-1960s UA labels)			
❑ UAL3526 [M]	You Asked For It!	1966	12.00
❑ UAS6526 [S]	You Asked For It!	1966	15.00
❑ ST-90931 [S]	You Asked For It!	1966	18.00
—Capitol Record Club edition			
❑ UA-LA908-H	You Light Up My Life	1978	12.00

URANIA

| ❑ 8011 | Rhapsody | 196? | 15.00 |

WESTMINSTER

❑ WP6021 [M]	Adventure in Carols	195?	25.00
❑ WL3044 [M]	Christmas Hi-Fi Favorites	195?	25.00
❑ SW1048 [S]	Latin American Adventure	195?	30.00
❑ WP6001 [M]	Postcards from Paris	195?	25.00
❑ SW1045 [S]	Soundproof	195?	30.00

FERRARI, LARRY

SURE

❑ SM703 [M]	I Wish You the Merriest	1966	12.00
❑ SS703 [S]	I Wish You the Merriest	1966	15.00
❑ SM701 [M]	Merry Christmas Carols	196?	12.00
❑ SS701 [S]	Merry Christmas Carols	196?	15.00

FERRY, BRYAN

ATLANTIC

❑ SD18113	Another Time, Another Place	1974	10.00
❑ SD18216	In Your Mind	1977	15.00
❑ SD18187	Let's Stick Together	1976	15.00
❑ SD19205	The Bride Stripped Bare	1978	15.00
❑ SD7304 [B]	These Foolish Things	1973	18.00

REPRISE

| ❑ 25598 | Bete Noire | 1988 | 15.00 |

WARNER BROS.

| ❑ 25082 | Boys and Girls | 1985 | 15.00 |
| —bel, with "Vendor: Mercury Record Corporation" | | | |

FESTIVAL QUARTET

RCA VICTOR RED SEAL

❑ LSC-2517 [S]	Brahms: Piano Quartet in A	1961	200.00
—Originals with "shaded dog" label			
❑ LSC-2330 [S]	Brahms: Piano Quartet in C	1959	200.00
—Original with "shaded dog" label			
❑ LM-2473 [M]	Brahms: Piano Quartet in G	1961	80.00
—Originals with "shaded dog" label; a rare instance when even the mono version is sought after			
❑ LSC-2473 [S]	Brahms: Piano Quartet in G	1961	120.00
—Originals with "shaded dog" label			
❑ LSC-2735 [S]	Faure: Piano Quartet in G	1963	60.00
—Original with "shaded dog" label			
❑ LSC-2147 [S]	Schubert: Trout Quintet	1958	180.00
—Original with "shaded dog" label			
❑ LSC-2147 [S]	Schubert: Trout Quintet	1964	120.00
—Second edition with "white dog" label			

FEVER TREE

AMPEX

| ❑ A-10113 | For Sale | 1970 | 30.00 |

MCA

| ❑ 551 | Fever Tree | 197? | 12.00 |

UNI

❑ 73040	Another Time, Another Place	1968	30.00
❑ 73067	Creation	1970	30.00
❑ 73024	Fever Tree	1968	30.00

FIELD, SALLY

COLGEMS

| ❑ COM-106 [M] | The Flying Nun | 1967 | 30.00 |
| ❑ COS-106 [S] | The Flying Nun | 1967 | 30.00 |

FIELDING, JANE

JAZZ WEST

| ❑ LP-5 [M] | Embers Glow | 1956 | 300.00 |
| ❑ LP-3 [M] | Jazz Trio for Voice, Piano and Bass | 1955 | 300.00 |

FIELDING, JERRY

ABC-PARAMOUNT

| ❑ ABC-542 [M] | Hollywood Brass | 1966 | 18.00 |
| ❑ ABCS-542 [S] | Hollywood Brass | 1966 | 25.00 |

COMMAND

| ❑ RS 33-921 [M] | Near East Brass | 1967 | 30.00 |
| ❑ RS921SD [S] | Near East Brass | 1967 | 10.00 |

DECCA

❑ DL8450 [M]	Fielding's Formula	1957	30.00
❑ DL8669 [M]	Hollywood Wind Jazztet	1958	30.00
❑ DL8100 [M]	Sweet with a Beat	1955	30.00
❑ DL8371 [M]	Swingin' in Hi-Fi	1956	30.00

KAPP

| ❑ KL-1026 [M] | Dance Concert | 1956 | 50.00 |

SIGNATURE

| ❑ SM-1028 [M] | Favorite Christmas Music | 1960 | 25.00 |
| ❑ SS-1028 [S] | Favorite Christmas Music | 1960 | 30.00 |

TIME

❑ 52059 [M]	A Bit of Ireland	196?	18.00
❑ S-2059 [S]	A Bit of Ireland	196?	25.00
❑ 52042 [M]	Magnificence in Brass	196?	18.00
❑ S-2042 [S]	Magnificence in Brass	196?	25.00
❑ 52119 [M]	We Like Brass	196?	18.00
❑ S-2119 [S]	We Like Brass	196?	25.00

TREND

| ❑ TL-1000 [10] | Jerry Fielding and His Great New Orchestra | 1953 | 120.00 |
| ❑ TL-1004 [10] | Jerry Fielding Plays a Dance Concert | 1954 | 100.00 |

FIELDS, BRANDON

NOVA

| ❑ 8602 | The Other Side of the Story | 1986 | 12.00 |
| ❑ 8811 | The Traveler | 1988 | 12.00 |

FIELDS, ERNIE

RENDEZVOUS

| ❑ 1309 [M] | In the Mood | 1960 | 60.00 |

FIELDS, GRACIE

LIBERTY

| ❑ LRP-3059 [M] | Our Gracie | 1957 | 40.00 |

FIELDS, HERBIE

DECCA

| ❑ DL8130 [M] | Blow Hot Blow Cool | 1956 | 40.00 |

FRATERNITY

| ❑ F-1011 [M] | Fields in Clover | 1959 | 60.00 |

RKO UNIQUE

| ❑ ULP-146 [M] | A Night at Kitty's | 1957 | 50.00 |

FIELDS, IRVING

ABC-PARAMOUNT

| ❑ ABC-187 [M] | Irving Fields at the St. Moritz | 1956 | 30.00 |

DECCA

❑ DL8901 [M]	At the Emerald Room, Hotel Astor	1959	25.00
❑ DL78901 [S]	At the Emerald Room, Hotel Astor	1959	30.00
❑ DL8856 [M]	Bagels and Bongos	1959	25.00
❑ DL78856 [S]	Bagels and Bongos	1959	30.00
❑ DL4323 [M]	Bikinis and Bongos	1962	25.00
❑ DL74323 [S]	Bikinis and Bongos	1962	30.00
❑ DL4238 [M]	Champagne and Bongos	1962	25.00
❑ DL74238 [S]	Champagne and Bongos	1962	30.00
❑ DL4114 [M]	More Bagels and Bongos	1961	25.00
❑ DL74114 [S]	More Bagels and Bongos	1961	30.00
❑ DL4174 [M]	Pizzas and Bongos	1961	25.00
❑ DL74174 [S]	Pizzas and Bongos	1961	30.00

EVEREST

| ❑ LPBR-5134 [M] | Twisting | 1962 | 25.00 |
| ❑ SDBR-1134 [S] | Twisting | 1962 | 30.00 |

FIESTA

| ❑ FLP-1228 [M] | Fabulous Fingers | 195? | 30.00 |

GONE

| ❑ LP-5003 [M] | Fabulous Touch | 1959 | 30.00 |

KING

❑ 724 [M]	Classics Go Latin	1960	30.00
❑ 724-S [S]	Classics Go Latin	1960	30.00
❑ 703 [M]	Irving Fields Favorites	1960	30.00
❑ 709 [M]	Live It Up	1960	30.00
❑ 742 [M]	Lox, Latin and Bongos	1960	25.00
❑ 742-S [S]	Lox, Latin and Bongos	1960	30.00

RCA VICTOR

| ❑ LPT-38 [10] | Fields Favorites | 195? | 50.00 |

TOPS

| ❑ L-1562 [M] | Irving Fields Plays Irving Berlin | 1957 | 30.00 |

FIELDS, THE

UNI

| ❑ 73050 | Fields | 1969 | 50.00 |

FIFTH DIMENSION, THE

ABC

| ❑ D-897 | Earthbound | 1975 | 12.00 |

ARISTA

❑ ABM-1106	Greatest Hits on Earth	1975	10.00
—Reissue of Bell 1106			
❑ AL8335	Greatest Hits on Earth	198?	10.00
—Reissue of Arista 1106			

BELL

❑ 1106	Greatest Hits on Earth	1972	12.00
❑ 6073	Individually & Collectively	1972	12.00
❑ 1116 [B]	Living Together, Growing Together	1973	12.00
❑ 6060	Love's Lines, Angles and Rhymes	1971	15.00
❑ 6045	Portrait	1970	15.00
❑ 6065	Reflections	1971	12.00
❑ 1315	Soul and Inspiration	1974	12.00
❑ 9000	The 5th Dimension/Live!!	1971	15.00

MOTOWN

| ❑ M7-896 | Star | 1978 | 12.00 |

PAIR

| ❑ PDL2-1108 | The Glory Days | 1986 | 15.00 |

RHINO

| ❑ RNDA-71104 | The 5th Dimension Anthology | 1986 | 15.00 |

SOUL CITY

❑ SCS-92002	Stoned Soul Picnic	1968	18.00
❑ SCS-33900	The 5th Dimension/Greatest Hits	1970	15.00
❑ SCS-92005 [B]	The Age of Aquarius	1969	18.00
❑ SCS-33901	The July 5th Album	1970	15.00
❑ SCM-91001 [M]	The Magic Garden	1967	25.00
❑ SCS-92005 [S]	The Magic Garden	1967	18.00
❑ SCM-91000 [M]	Up, Up and Away	1967	25.00
❑ SCS-92000 [S]	Up, Up and Away	1967	18.00

FIFTH ESTATE, THE

JUBILEE

| ❑ JGM-8005 [M] | Ding Dong! The Witch Is Dead | 1967 | 40.00 |
| ❑ JGS-8005 [S] | Ding Dong! The Witch Is Dead | 1967 | 50.00 |

FIFTY FOOT HOSE

LIMELIGHT

| ❑ 86062 | Cauldron | 1968 | 200.00 |

50 GUITARS, THE

MISTLETOE

| ❑ MLP-1229 | Christmas with the 50 Guitars | 1977 | 12.00 |

Number	Title	Yr	NM

FIGURES ON A BEACH

METRO AMERICA
| ❏ MA-1002 [EP] | Swimming | 1983 | 25.00 |

SIRE
| ❏ 25804 | Figures on a Beach | 1989 | 12.00 |
| ❏ 25596 | Standing on Ceremony | 1987 | 12.00 |

FILETS OF SOUL

SQUID
| ❏ 4857 | Freedom | 1968 | 200.00 |

FILTER

REPRISE
| ❏ 45864 | Short Bus | 1995 | 18.00 |

FINCHLEY BOYS, THE

GOLDEN THROAT
| ❏ 200-19 | Everlasting Tribute | 1972 | 100.00 |

FINE YOUNG CANNIBALS

I.R.S.
❏ R143927	Fine Young Cannibals	1986	15.00
—BMG Direct Marketing edition			
❏ 5683	Fine Young Cannibals	1986	12.00
❏ R101068	The Raw and the Cooked	1989	12.00
—BMG Direct Marketing edition			
❏ 6273	The Raw and the Cooked	1989	12.00
❏ 10125	The Raw and the Remix	1990	15.00

FINN, TIM

A&M
| ❏ SP-4972 | Escapade | 1983 | 12.00 |

CAPITOL
| ❏ C1-48735 | Tim Finn | 1989 | 12.00 |

VIRGIN
| ❏ 90879 | Big Canoe | 1988 | 12.00 |

FINNEY, ALBERT

MOTOWN
| ❏ M6-889 | The Albert Finney Album | 1977 | 25.00 |

FINNEY, MAURY

SOUNDWAVES
| ❏ 3301 | Sax Life in Nashville | 1976 | 18.00 |

FIONA

ATLANTIC
❏ 81639	Beyond the Pale	1986	12.00
❏ 81242	Fiona	1985	12.00
❏ 81903	Heart Like a Gun	1989	15.00

FIORILLO, ELISA

CHRYSALIS
| ❏ BFV41608 | Elisa Fiorillo | 1987 | 12.00 |
| ❏ F1-21678 | I Am | 1990 | 15.00 |

FIRE & ICE LTD.

CAPITOL
| ❏ T2577 [M] | The Happening | 1966 | 30.00 |
| ❏ ST2577 [S] | The Happening | 1966 | 40.00 |

FIRE

ABC
| ❏ ABCS-661 [B] | Fire | 1969 | 30.00 |

FIRE AND RAIN

MERCURY
| ❏ SRM-1-654 | Fire and Rain | 1973 | 18.00 |

FIRE ESCAPE, THE

GNP CRESCENDO
❏ GNP-2034 [M]	Psychotic Reaction	1967	40.00
—Mono pressings are all original first pressings.			
❏ GNPS-2034 [S]	Psychotic Reaction	1967	30.00
—Stereo pressings in circulation are various re-pressings.			

FIREBALLET

PASSPORT
| ❏ 98010 | Night on Bald Mountain | 1975 | 15.00 |
| ❏ 98016 | Two, Too… | 1976 | 15.00 |

FIREBALLS, THE

ATCO
❏ SD 33-239 [S]	Bottle of Wine	1968	30.00
❏ 33-239 [M]	Bottle of Wine	1968	40.00
❏ SD 33-275	Come On, React!	1969	30.00

CROWN
| ❏ CLP-5376 [M] | Jimmy Gilmer and the Fireballs & The Sugar Shackers | 1963 | 30.00 |
| ❏ CST-376 [R] | Jimmy Gilmer and the Fireballs & The Sugar Shackers | 1963 | 30.00 |

| ❏ CLP-5387 [M] | The Sensational Jimmy Gilmer & The Fireballs | 1964 | 30.00 |
| ❏ CST-387 [R] | The Sensational Jimmy Gilmer & The Fireballs | 1964 | 30.00 |

DOT
❏ DLP-3577 [M]	Buddy's Buddy	1964	50.00
—Jimmy Gilmer and the Fireballs			
❏ DLP-25577 [S]	Buddy's Buddy	1964	80.00
—Jimmy Gilmer and the Fireballs			
❏ DLP-3709 [M]	Campusology	1966	30.00
❏ DLP-25709 [S]	Campusology	1966	40.00
❏ DLP-25856 [S]	Firewater	1968	30.00
❏ DLP-3856 [M]	Firewater	1968	50.00
—Stereo cover with "Monaural" and "Promotional Copy Not for Sale" stickers, but the record is stock mono			
❏ DLP-3668 [M]	Folkbeat	1965	30.00
❏ DLP-25668 [S]	Folkbeat	1965	40.00
❏ DLP-3643 [M]	Lucky 'Leven	1965	30.00
❏ DLP-25643 [S]	Lucky 'Leven	1965	40.00
❏ DLP-3545 [M]	Sugar Shack	1963	40.00
—Jimmy Gilmer and the Fireballs			
❏ DLP-25545 [S]	Sugar Shack	1963	60.00
—Jimmy Gilmer and the Fireballs			
❏ DLP-3512 [M]	Torquay	1963	50.00
❏ DLP-25512 [S]	Torquay	1963	80.00

SUNDAZED
❏ LP-5018	Gunshot!	1995	12.00
❏ LP-5016	The Fireballs	1995	12.00
❏ LP-5017	Torquay	1995	12.00

TOP RANK
❏ RM-324 [M]	The Fireballs	1960	150.00
❏ RM-343 [M]	Vaquero	1960	150.00
❏ RS-643 [S]	Vaquero	1960	200.00

WARWICK
| ❏ W-2042 [M] | Here Are the Fireballs | 1961 | 150.00 |
| ❏ WST-2042 [S] | Here Are the Fireballs | 1961 | 250.00 |

FIREBIRDS, THE

CROWN
| ❏ CST-589 | Light My Fire | 1968 | 70.00 |

FIREFALL

ATLANTIC
❏ 80017	Break of Dawn	1983	12.00
❏ SD16024	Clouds Across the Sun	1980	12.00
❏ SD19183	Elan	1978	12.00
❏ SD18174	Firefall	1976	12.00
❏ SD19125	Firefall	1977	10.00
—Reissue of 18174			
❏ SD19101	Luna Sea	1977	12.00
❏ 80120	Mirror of the World	1983	12.00
❏ SD19316	The Best of Firefall	1981	12.00
❏ SD16006	Undertow	1980	12.00

FIREFLIES, THE

TAURUS
| ❏ 1002 [M] | You Were Mine | 196? | 100.00 |
| ❏ S-1002 [S] | You Were Mine | 196? | 300.00 |

FIREHOSE

COLUMBIA
| ❏ C47839 | Flyin' the Flannel | 1991 | 15.00 |

SST
❏ 235	fROMOHIO	1989	15.00
❏ 115	If'n	1987	15.00
❏ 079	Ragin' Full-On	1986	15.00

FIREHOUSE FIVE PLUS TWO, THE

GOOD TIME JAZZ
❏ L-12044 [M]	Around the World	1961	30.00
❏ S-10044 [S]	Around the World	1961	30.00
❏ L-12040 [M]	Dixieland Favorites	1960	30.00
❏ S-10040 [S]	Dixieland Favorites	1960	30.00
❏ L-1 [10]	The Firehouse Five Plus Two, Volume 1	1953	50.00
❏ L-2 [10]	The Firehouse Five Plus Two, Volume 2	1953	50.00
❏ L-6 [10]	The Firehouse Five Plus Two, Volume 3	1953	50.00
❏ L-16 [10]	The Firehouse Five Plus Two, Volume 4	1953	50.00
❏ L-12049 [M]	The Firehouse Five Plus Two at Disneyland	1962	30.00
❏ S-10049 [S]	The Firehouse Five Plus Two at Disneyland	1962	30.00
❏ L-12038 [M]	The Firehouse Five Plus Two Crashes a Party	1960	30.00
❏ S-10038 [S]	The Firehouse Five Plus Two Crashes a Party	1960	30.00
❏ L-12018 [M]	The Firehouse Five Plus Two Goes South!	1955	30.00
❏ L-23 [10]	The Firehouse Five Plus Two Goes South!, Volume 5	1954	60.00
❏ L-12052 [M]	The Firehouse Five Plus Two Goes to a Fire	1964	30.00
❏ S-10052 [S]	The Firehouse Five Plus Two Goes to a Fire	1964	30.00
❏ L-12028 [M]	The Firehouse Five Plus Two Goes to Sea	1957	30.00
❏ S-10028 [S]	The Firehouse Five Plus Two Goes to Sea	1960	30.00
❏ L-12014 [M]	The Firehouse Five Plus Two Plays for Lovers	1955	30.00

❏ L-12010 [M]	The Firehouse Five Story, Volume 1	1955	30.00
❏ L-12011 [M]	The Firehouse Five Story, Volume 2	1955	30.00
❏ L-12012 [M]	The Firehouse Five Story, Volume 3	1955	30.00
❏ L-12054 [M]	Twenty Years Later	196?	30.00
❏ S-10054 [S]	Twenty Years Later	1969	30.00

STEREO RECORDS
| ❏ S-7005 [S] | The Firehouse Five Plus Two Goes to Sea | 1959 | 40.00 |

FIRESIGN THEATRE, THE

BUTTERFLY
| ❏ 001 | Jost Folks...A Firesign Chat | 1977 | 12.00 |

COLUMBIA
❏ KC32411	David Ossman's How Time Flys	1973	15.00
❏ KG31099 [B]	Dear Friends	1972	25.00
❏ C30102 [B]	Don't Crush That Dwarf, Hand Me the Pliers	1970	18.00
❏ KC33141	Everything You Know Is Wrong	1974	15.00
❏ CQ33141 [Q]	Everything You Know Is Wrong	1974	25.00
❏ PG34391	Forward Into the Past (An Anthology)	1977	18.00
❏ CS9884	How Can You Be in Two Places at Once When You're Not Anywhere at All	1969	18.00
—360 Sound" label			
❏ PC33475	In the Next World You're On Your Own	1975	15.00
❏ C30737	I Think We're All Bozos on This Bus	1971	18.00
❏ CQ30737 [Q]	I Think We're All Bozos on This Bus	1972	25.00
❏ KC31585	Not Insane or Anything You Want To	1972	18.00
❏ KC32730	The Tale of the Giant Rat of Sumatra	1974	15.00
❏ CL2718 [M]	Waiting for the Electrician or Someone Like Him	1968	30.00
❏ CS9518 [S]	Waiting for the Electrician or Someone Like Him	1968	18.00
—360 Sound" label			

MERCURY
| ❏ 826452-1 | Eat or Be Eaten | 1985 | 12.00 |

RHINO
❏ RNLP-018	Fighting Clowns	1979	15.00
❏ RNLP-806	Lawyer's Hospital	1981	15.00
❏ RNEP-506 [EP]	Nick Danger, Third Eye	1983	12.00
❏ RNLP-812	Nick Danger In: The Three Faces of Al	1984	15.00
❏ RNLP-904	Reagan/Carter	1980	15.00
❏ RNLP-807	Shakespeare's Lost Comedie	1982	15.00

FIRM, THE

ATLANTIC
❏ 81628	Mean Business	1986	10.00
❏ PR883 [DJ]	Talks Business	1985	25.00
—Promo-only music and interview album			
❏ 81239	The Firm	1985	10.00

FIRST CHOICE

GOLD MIND
❏ GA9505	Breakaway	1980	30.00
❏ 7501	Delusions	1977	18.00
❏ GA9502	Hold Your Horses	1979	25.00

PHILLY GROOVE
| ❏ 1400 | Armed and Extremely Dangerous | 1973 | 18.00 |
| ❏ 1502 | The Player | 1974 | 25.00 |

WARNER BROS.
| ❏ BS2934 | So Let Us Entertain You | 1976 | 18.00 |

FIRST CLASS (1)

UK
| ❏ 53108 | The First Class | 1974 | 18.00 |

FIRST EDITION, THE

JOLLY ROGERS
❏ 5001	Backroads	1973	18.00
❏ 5004	Monumental	1974	18.00
—All the above as "Kenny Rogers and the First Edition			
❏ 5003	Rollin'	1974	18.00

MCA
❏ 913	Country Songs	1984	10.00
❏ 1460	Greatest Hits	1985	10.00
—Reissue of Reprise 6437			
❏ 942	Hits and Pieces	1985	10.00
❏ 912	Love Songs	1984	10.00
❏ 944	Pieces of Calico Silver	1985	10.00
❏ 943	The 60's Revisited	1985	10.00

REPRISE
❏ RS-6437	Greatest Hits	1971	25.00
❏ RS-6352	Ruby, Don't Take Your Love to Town	1969	25.00
—Starting above, as "Kenny Rogers and the First Edition			
❏ ST-92060	Ruby, Don't Take Your Love to Town	1969	30.00

Number	Title	Yr	NM
—Capitol Record Club edition			
❑ RS-6385	Something's Burning	1970	25.00
❑ RS-6412	Tell It All Brother	1970	25.00
❑ 2XS6476	The Ballad of Calico	1972	30.00
❑ R-6276 [M]	The First Edition	1967	30.00
❑ R-6276 [S]	The First Edition	1967	30.00
❑ RS-6328	The First Edition '69	1969	30.00
❑ RS-6302	The First Edition's Second	1968	30.00
❑ MS2039	Transition	1971	25.00
—As "Kenny Rogers and the First Edition			
WARNER SPECIAL PRODUCTS			
❑ OP-2514	Kenny Rogers and the First Edition	1979	18.00
—Manufactured for Lakeshore Music			

FIRST HOUSE

Number	Title	Yr	NM
ECM			
❑ 1393	Cantilena	1990	15.00
❑ 1307	Erendira	1987	12.00

FIRST JAZZ PIANO QUARTET, THE

Number	Title	Yr	NM
WARNER BROS.			
❑ W1274 [M]	The First Jazz Piano Quartet	1959	30.00
❑ WS1274 [S]	The First Jazz Piano Quartet	1959	30.00

FISCHER, CLARE

Number	Title	Yr	NM
ATLANTIC			
❑ SD1520	Thesaurus	1969	18.00
COLUMBIA			
❑ CL2691 [M]	Songs for Rainy Day Lovers	1967	30.00
❑ CS9491 [S]	Songs for Rainy Day Lovers	1967	18.00
DISCOVERY			
❑ DS-820	Alone Together	198?	12.00
❑ DS-786	America	1978	15.00
❑ DS-934	By and With Himself	1987	12.00
❑ DS-852	Clare Fischer and the Sometimes Voices	1982	12.00
❑ DS-914	Crazy Bird	1984	12.00
❑ DS-807	Duality	1979	15.00
❑ DS-921	Free Fall	1986	12.00
❑ DS-835	Machacha	198?	12.00
❑ DS-817	Salsa Picante	1979	15.00
❑ DS-798	'Twas Only Yesterday	1978	15.00
LIGHT			
❑ 5544	Love Is Surrender	197?	15.00
PACIFIC JAZZ			
❑ PJ-77 [M]	Extension	1963	30.00
❑ ST-77 [S]	Extension	1963	30.00
❑ PJ-52 [M]	First Time Out	1962	30.00
❑ ST-52 [S]	First Time Out	1962	30.00
❑ PJ-10096 [M]	Manteca	1966	10.00
❑ ST-20096 [S]	Manteca	1966	25.00
❑ PJ-67 [M]	Surging Ahead	1963	30.00
❑ ST-67 [S]	Surging Ahead	1963	30.00
PAUSA			
❑ 7086	2 Plus 2	198?	12.00
REVELATION			
❑ REV-2	Easy Living	1968	18.00
❑ REV-37	Head, Heart and Hands	198?	12.00
❑ REV-31	Jazz Song	1979	15.00
❑ REV-6	One to Get Ready, Four to Go	1968	18.00
❑ REV-15	Reclamation Act of 1972	1972	18.00
❑ REV-23	T'Da-a-a!	1976	18.00
❑ REV-13	The Great White Hope	1969	18.00
❑ REV-26	The State of His Art	1976	15.00
WORLD PACIFIC			
❑ WP-1830 [M]	So Danco Samba	1964	25.00
❑ ST-21830 [S]	So Danco Samba	1964	30.00

FISCHER, LOU

Number	Title	Yr	NM
SEA BREEZE			
❑ SB-2012	Royal St.	198?	12.00

FISCHER, WILD MAN

Number	Title	Yr	NM
REPRISE			
❑ 2XS6332 [B]	An Evening with Wild Man Fischer	1969	80.00
RHINO			
❑ RNLP-022	Nothing Scary	1981	15.00
❑ RNLP-021	Pronounced Normal	1981	12.00
❑ RNLP-001	Wildmania	1978	18.00

FISCHER, WILLIAM S.

Number	Title	Yr	NM
EMBRYO			
❑ 529	Circles	1970	15.00

FISCHOFF, GEORGE

Number	Title	Yr	NM
MMG			
❑ 1140	Pretty Kitty: The Piano Magic of George Fischoff	1982	25.00

FISELE, JERRY

Number	Title	Yr	NM
DELMAR			
❑ DL-101 [10]	Jerry Fisele and the Fabulous Windy City Six	1954	50.00

FISHBONE

Number	Title	Yr	NM
COLUMBIA			
❑ B6C40032 [EP]	Fishbone	1985	15.00
❑ CAS1416 [DJ]	Interchords	198?	30.00
—Promo-only music and interviews			
❑ BFC40333	In Your Face	1986	15.00
❑ 4C44097 [EP]	It's a Wonderful Life (Gonna Have a Good Time)	1987	12.00
❑ CAS2235 [EP]	New and Improved Bonin'	1990	15.00
—Promo-only five-song sampler			
❑ C46142	The Reality of My Surroundings	1991	18.00
❑ FC40891	Truth and Soul	1988	15.00

FISHER, AL, AND LOU MARKS

Number	Title	Yr	NM
CAMEO			
❑ C-1081 [M]	Rome on the Range	1964	25.00
SWAN			
❑ SLP-514 [M]	It's a Beatle (Coo-Coo) World	1964	40.00

FISHER, CHIP

Number	Title	Yr	NM
RCA VICTOR			
❑ LPM-1797 [M]	Chipper at the Sugar Bowl	1958	40.00
❑ LSP-1797 [S]	Chipper at the Sugar Bowl	1958	50.00

FISHER, EDDIE, QUINTET

Number	Title	Yr	NM
CADET			
❑ CA-848	The Next Hundred Years	1971	18.00
❑ LPS-828	The Third Cup	1969	18.00
STANG			
❑ 1032	Hot Lunch	1977	18.00

FISHER, EDDIE

Number	Title	Yr	NM
DOT			
❑ DLP-3631 [M]	Eddie Fisher Today!	1965	15.00
❑ DLP-25361 [S]	Eddie Fisher Today!	1965	18.00
❑ DLP-3785 [M]	His Greatest Hits	1967	15.00
❑ DLP-25785 [S]	His Greatest Hits	1967	18.00
❑ DLP-3658 [M]	Mary Christmas	1965	18.00
❑ DLP-25658 [S]	Mary Christmas	1965	25.00
❑ DLP-3648 [M]	When I Was Young	1965	15.00
❑ DLP-25648 [S]	When I Was Young	1965	18.00
❑ DLP-3670 [M]	Young and Foolish	1966	15.00
❑ DLP-25670 [S]	Young and Foolish	1966	18.00
MCA			
❑ 1549	The Best of Eddie Fisher	1983	10.00
PICKWICK			
❑ SPC-3141	Oh My Papa	196?	15.00
RAMROD			
❑ RR-1 [M]	Eddie Fisher at the Winter Garden	1963	18.00
❑ RRS-1 [S]	Eddie Fisher at the Winter Garden	1963	25.00
RCA CAMDEN			
❑ CAL-789 [M]	Bring Back the Thrill	196?	15.00
❑ CAS-789 [R]	Bring Back the Thrill	196?	12.00
RCA VICTOR			
❑ LOC-1024 [M]	Academy Award Winners	1955	40.00
❑ LPM-1647 [M]	As Long As There's Music	1958	30.00
❑ LSP-1647 [S]	As Long As There's Music	1958	50.00
❑ LPM-1399 [M]	Bundle of Joy	1957	30.00
❑ LPM-3065 [10]	Christmas with Eddie Fisher	1952	50.00
❑ LPM-2504 [M]	Eddie Fisher's Greatest Hits	1962	18.00
❑ LSP-2504 [S]	Eddie Fisher's Greatest Hits	1962	25.00
❑ ANL1-1138	Eddie Fisher's Greatest Hits	1975	10.00
❑ LPM-3025 [10]	Fisher Sings	1952	50.00
❑ LPM-3726 [M]	Games That Lovers Play	1966	18.00
❑ LSP-3726 [S]	Games That Lovers Play	1966	18.00
❑ LPM-1097 [M]	I Love You	1955	30.00
❑ LPM-3058 [10]	I'm in the Mood for Love	1952	50.00
❑ LPM-1180 [M]	I'm in the Mood for Love	1955	30.00
❑ LPM-3122 [10]	Irving Berlin Favorites	1953	50.00
❑ LPM-3185 [10]	May I Sing to You?	1953	50.00
❑ LPM-1181 [M]	May I Sing to You?	1955	30.00
❑ LPM-3820 [M]	People Like You	1967	25.00
❑ LSP-3820 [S]	People Like You	1967	15.00
❑ LPM-3375 [M]	The Best of Eddie Fisher	1965	18.00
❑ LSP-3375 [R]	The Best of Eddie Fisher	1965	15.00
❑ LPM-1548 [M]	Thinking of You	1957	30.00
❑ LSP-3914	You Ain't Heard Nothin' Yet	1968	15.00

FISHER, ELLIOT

Number	Title	Yr	NM
DOBRE			
❑ 1003	In the Land of Make Believe	1976	25.00

FISHER, KING

Number	Title	Yr	NM
JAZZOLOGY			
❑ J-13	King Fisher and His All Stars	196?	15.00

FISHER, TONI

Number	Title	Yr	NM
SIGNET			
❑ WP-509 [S]	The Big Hurt	1960	50.00
—Issued in "Stereomonic			

FITCH, MAL

Number	Title	Yr	NM
EMARCY			
❑ MG-36041 [M]	Mal Fitch	1956	50.00

FITE, BUDDY

Number	Title	Yr	NM
BELL			
❑ 6058	Buddy Fite and Friend	1970	18.00
CYCLONE			
❑ CY4100	Buddy Fite	1971	15.00
❑ CY4110	Changes	1972	15.00
DIFFERENT DRUMMER			
❑ 1001	Buddy Fite Plays for Satin Dolls	1975	18.00

FITZGERALD, ELLA, AND BILLIE HOLIDAY

Number	Title	Yr	NM
AMERICAN RECORDING SOCIETY			
❑ G-433 [M]	Ella Fitzgerald and Billie Holiday at Newport	1957	40.00
VERVE			
❑ MGV-8234 [M]	Ella Fitzgerald and Billie Holiday at Newport	1958	50.00
❑ MGVS-6022 [S]	Ella Fitzgerald and Billie Holiday at Newport	1960	40.00
❑ V-8234 [M]	Ella Fitzgerald and Billie Holiday at Newport	1961	25.00
❑ V6-8234 [S]	Ella Fitzgerald and Billie Holiday at Newport	1961	25.00
❑ V-8826	Newport Years	1973	15.00

FITZGERALD, ELLA, AND COUNT BASIE

Number	Title	Yr	NM
PABLO TODAY			
❑ 2312110	A Perfect Match	1980	15.00
—Red vinyl			
VERVE			
❑ V-4061 [M]	Ella and Basie!	1963	30.00
❑ V6-4061 [S]	Ella and Basie!	1963	30.00
❑ ST-90028 [S]	Ella and Basie!	1964	30.00
—Capitol Record Club edition			
❑ T-90028 [M]	Ella and Basie!	1964	30.00
—Capitol Record Club edition			

FITZGERALD, ELLA, AND DUKE ELLINGTON

Number	Title	Yr	NM
PABLO LIVE			
❑ 2308242	The Stockholm Concert 1966	1984	12.00

FITZGERALD, ELLA, AND LOUIS ARMSTRONG

Number	Title	Yr	NM
METRO			
❑ M-601 [M]	Louis and Ella	1967	15.00
❑ MS-601 [S]	Louis and Ella	1967	15.00
MOBILE FIDELITY			
❑ 2-248	Ella and Louis Again	1996	150.00
—Audiophile vinyl			
VERVE			
❑ MGV-4003 [M]	Ella and Louis	1956	150.00
—orange label			
❑ V-4003 [M]	Ella and Louis	1961	25.00
❑ V6-8811	Ella and Louis	1972	18.00
❑ MGV-4006-2 [M]	Ella and Louis Again	1956	80.00
❑ V-4006-2 [M]	Ella and Louis Again	1961	30.00
❑ MGV-4017 [M]	Ella and Louis Again, Vol. 1	1958	50.00
❑ V-4017 [M]	Ella and Louis Again, Vol. 1	1961	25.00
❑ MGV-4018 [M]	Ella and Louis Again, Vol. 2	1958	50.00
❑ V-4018 [M]	Ella and Louis Again, Vol. 2	1961	25.00
❑ MGV-4011-2 [M]	Porgy and Bess	1957	80.00
❑ MGVS-6040-2 [S]	Porgy and Bess	1960	60.00
❑ V-4011-2 [M]	Porgy and Bess	1961	30.00
❑ V6-4011-2 [S]	Porgy and Bess	1961	30.00
❑ VE-1-2507	Porgy and Bess	197?	12.00
❑ 827475-1	Porgy and Bess	198?	15.00

FITZGERALD, ELLA

Number	Title	Yr	NM
AMERICAN RECORDING SOCIETY			
❑ G-433 [M]	Ella Fitzgerald At Newport	195?	40.00
ATLANTIC			
❑ SD1631	Ella Loves Cole	1972	15.00
BAINBRIDGE			
❑ 6223	Things Ain't What They Used to Be	1982	12.00
—Reissue of Reprise 6432			
BASF			
❑ 20712	Watch What Happens	1972	15.00
CAPITOL			
❑ T2685 [M]	Brighten the Corner	1967	25.00
❑ ST2685 [S]	Brighten the Corner	1967	18.00
❑ SM-11793	Brighten the Corner	1978	12.00
❑ T2805 [M]	Ella Fitzgerald's Christmas	1967	25.00
❑ ST2805 [S]	Ella Fitzgerald's Christmas	1967	15.00
—Same as above, but in stereo			
❑ ST2888	Misty Blue	1968	18.00
❑ ST2960	Thirty by Ella	1968	18.00
❑ SN-16276	Thirty by Ella	1983	12.00
—Budget-line reissue			
CLASSICS RECORD LIBRARY/VERVE			
❑ 80-55713	Ella Fitzgerald Sings the George and Ira Gershwin Songbook	1978	40.00
—Reissue of the entire set for Book-of-the-Month Club			

Number	Title	Yr	NM
COLUMBIA			
❑ KG32557	Carnegie Hall & Newport Jazz Festival 1973	1973	18.00
DECCA			
❑ DL4447 [M]	Early Ella	1964	18.00
❑ DL74447 [R]	Early Ella	1964	15.00
❑ DL8477 [M]	Ella and Her Fellas	1957	40.00
❑ DL5300 [10]	Ella Fitzgerald Sings Gershwin Songs	1951	120.00
❑ DL8378 [M]	Ella Sings Gershwin	1957	40.00
❑ DL4451 [M]	Ella Sings Gershwin	1964	18.00
❑ DL74451 [R]	Ella Sings Gershwin	1964	15.00
❑ DL8832 [M]	For Sentimental Reasons	1958	40.00
❑ DL4129 [M]	Golden Favorites	1961	25.00
❑ DL74129 [R]	Golden Favorites	1961	15.00
❑ DL8149 [M]	Lullabies of Birdland	1955	50.00
❑ DL8696 [M]	Miss Ella Fitzgerald and Mr. Nelson Riddle Invite You to Listen and Relax	1958	40.00
❑ DL4887 [M]	Smooth Sailing	1967	18.00
❑ DL74887 [R]	Smooth Sailing	1967	15.00
❑ DL8068 [M]	Songs in a Mellow Mood	1954	50.00
❑ DL5084 [10]	Souvenir Album	1950	120.00
❑ DL4446 [M]	Stairway to the Stars	1964	18.00
❑ DL74446 [R]	Stairway to the Stars	1964	15.00
❑ DL8155 [M]	Sweet and Hot	1955	50.00
❑ DXB156 [M]	The Best of Ella	1959	40.00
—Black labels, silver print			
❑ DXB156 [M]	The Best of Ella	1961	30.00
—Black labels with color bars			
❑ DXSB7156 [R]	The Best of Ella	196?	25.00
❑ DL8695 [M]	The First Lady of Song	1958	40.00
EVEREST ARCHIVE OF FOLK & JAZZ			
❑ 276	Ella Fitzgerald	1973	15.00
FANTASY			
❑ OJC-442	Ella & Nice	1990	15.00
—Reissue of Pablo Live 2308 234			
❑ OJC-376	Montreux '77	1989	15.00
—Reissue of Pablo Live 2308 206			
INTERMEDIA			
❑ QS-5049	Ella by Starlight	198?	12.00
MCA			
❑ 215	Ella Sings Gershwin	1973	12.00
❑ 734	Memories	198?	12.00
❑ 4047	The Best of Ella	197?	18.00
❑ 4016	The Best of Ella Fitzgerald, Vol. II	1973	18.00
METRO			
❑ M-500 [M]	Ella Fitzgerald	1965	15.00
❑ MS-500 [S]	Ella Fitzgerald	1965	15.00
❑ M-567 [M]	The World of Ella Fitzgerald	1966	15.00
❑ MS-567 [S]	The World of Ella Fitzgerald	1966	15.00
MGM			
❑ GAS-130	Ella Fitzgerald (Golden Archive Series)	1970	18.00
PABLO			
❑ 2310772	Again	1977	15.00
❑ 2310938	All That Jazz	1990	15.00
❑ 2310814	Dream Dancing	1978	15.00
❑ 2310921	Easy Living	1987	12.00
❑ 2310759	Ella and Oscar	1976	15.00
❑ 2310711	Ella in London	1974	15.00
❑ 2310829	Fine and Mellow	1979	15.00
❑ 2310825	Lady Time	1978	15.00
❑ 2310751	Montreux '75	1976	15.00
❑ 2310888	Speak Love	1983	12.00
❑ 2310702	Take Love Easy	1974	15.00
❑ 2405421	The Best of Ella Fitzgerald	198?	12.00
PABLO LIVE			
❑ 2308234	Ella & Nice	197?	18.00
❑ 2308206	Montreux '77	1978	15.00
PABLO TODAY			
❑ 2312132	A Classy Pair	1983	12.00
❑ 2630201	Ella Abraca Jobim: Ella Fitzgerald Sings the Antonio Carlos Jobim Song Book	1981	18.00
❑ 2312140	Nice Work If You Can Get It	198?	12.00
❑ 2312138	The Best Is Yet to Come	1982	12.00
PAUSA			
❑ 7130	Love You Madly	198?	12.00
PICKWICK			
❑ SPC-3259	Misty Blues	1974	12.00
PRESTIGE			
❑ PRLP-7685	Sunshine of Your Love	1970	18.00
REPRISE			
❑ RS-6354	Ella	1969	18.00
❑ RS-6432	Things Ain't What They Used to Be	1971	15.00
SUNBEAM			
❑ 205	Ella Fitzgerald and Her Orchestra, 1940	197?	12.00
TIME-LIFE			
❑ SLGD-03	Legendary Singers: Ella Fitzgerald	1985	18.00
VERVE			
❑ V-4066 [M]	A Tribute to Cole Porter	1964	30.00
❑ V6-4066 [S]	A Tribute to Cole Porter	1964	30.00
❑ V-4053 [M]	Clap Hands, Here Comes Charley	1962	40.00

Number	Title	Yr	NM
❑ V6-4053 [S]	Clap Hands, Here Comes Charley	1962	150.00
❑ V-8745 [M]	Ella "Live	1968	30.00
❑ V6-8745 [S]	Ella "Live	1968	18.00
❑ V-4072 [M]	Ella & Duke at Cote d'Azur	1967	40.00
❑ V6-4072 [S]	Ella & Duke at Cote d'Azur	1967	30.00
❑ V-4070 [M]	Ella at Duke's Place	1966	25.00
❑ V6-4070 [S]	Ella at Duke's Place	1966	25.00
❑ SMAS-90644 [S]	Ella at Duke's Place	1966	30.00
—Capitol Record Club edition			
❑ V-4065 [M]	Ella at Juan Les Pins	1964	30.00
❑ V6-4065 [S]	Ella at Juan Les Pins	1964	30.00
❑ MGV-8264 [M]	Ella Fitzgerald at the Opera House	1958	50.00
❑ MGVS-6026 [S]	Ella Fitzgerald at the Opera House	1960	40.00
❑ V-8264 [M]	Ella Fitzgerald at the Opera House	1961	25.00
❑ V6-8264 [S]	Ella Fitzgerald at the Opera House	1961	25.00
❑ MGV-4049 [M]	Ella Fitzgerald Sings Cole Porter	1961	40.00
❑ V-4049 [M]	Ella Fitzgerald Sings Cole Porter	1961	25.00
❑ MGV-4050 [M]	Ella Fitzgerald Sings More Cole Porter	1961	40.00
❑ V-4050 [M]	Ella Fitzgerald Sings More Cole Porter	1961	25.00
❑ MGV-4001-2 [M]	Ella Fitzgerald Sings the Cole Porter Song Book	1956	80.00
❑ V-4001-2 [M]	Ella Fitzgerald Sings the Cole Porter Song Book	1961	30.00
❑ MGV-4010-4 [M]	Ella Fitzgerald Sings the Duke Ellington Song Book	1957	150.00
—Combines 4008 and 4009 into one package			
❑ V-10-4 [M]	Ella Fitzgerald Sings the Duke Ellington Song Book	196?	50.00
❑ MGV-4008-2 [M]	Ella Fitzgerald Sings the Duke Ellington Song Book, Vol. 1	1957	80.00
❑ V-4008-2 [M]	Ella Fitzgerald Sings the Duke Ellington Song Book, Vol. 1	1961	30.00
❑ MGV-4009-2 [M]	Ella Fitzgerald Sings the Duke Ellington Song Book, Vol. 2	1957	80.00
❑ V-4009-2 [M]	Ella Fitzgerald Sings the Duke Ellington Song Book, Vol. 2	1961	30.00
❑ MGV-4029-5 [M]	Ella Fitzgerald Sings the George and Ira Gershwin Song Book	1959	250.00
—Box set with 4024 through 4028 plus bonus 10-inch LP			
❑ MGV-4029-5 [M]	Ella Fitzgerald Sings the George and Ira Gershwin Song Book	1959	500.00
—Box set with 4024 through 4028 plus bonus 10-inch LP, all in walnut box with leather pockets			
❑ MGVS-6082-5 [S]	Ella Fitzgerald Sings the George and Ira Gershwin Song Book	1960	200.00
—Box set with 6077 through 6081 plus bonus 10-inch LP			
❑ V-29-5 [M]	Ella Fitzgerald Sings the George and Ira Gershwin Song Book	196?	100.00
—Reissue of MGV-4029			
❑ V6-29-5 [S]	Ella Fitzgerald Sings the George and Ira Gershwin Song Book	196?	100.00
—Reissue of MGVS-6082			
❑ MGV-4024 [M]	Ella Fitzgerald Sings the George and Ira Gershwin Song Book, Vol. 1	1959	50.00
❑ MGVS-6077 [S]	Ella Fitzgerald Sings the George and Ira Gershwin Song Book, Vol. 1	1960	40.00
❑ V-4024 [M]	Ella Fitzgerald Sings the George and Ira Gershwin Song Book, Vol. 1	1961	25.00
❑ V6-4024 [S]	Ella Fitzgerald Sings the George and Ira Gershwin Song Book, Vol. 1	1961	25.00
❑ MGV-4025 [M]	Ella Fitzgerald Sings the George and Ira Gershwin Song Book, Vol. 2	1959	50.00
❑ MGVS-6078 [S]	Ella Fitzgerald Sings the George and Ira Gershwin Song Book, Vol. 2	1960	40.00
❑ V-4025 [M]	Ella Fitzgerald Sings the George and Ira Gershwin Song Book, Vol. 2	1961	25.00
❑ V6-4025 [S]	Ella Fitzgerald Sings the George and Ira Gershwin Song Book, Vol. 2	1961	25.00
❑ MGV-4026 [M]	Ella Fitzgerald Sings the George and Ira Gershwin Song Book, Vol. 3	1959	50.00
❑ MGVS-6079 [S]	Ella Fitzgerald Sings the George and Ira Gershwin Song Book, Vol. 3	1960	40.00
❑ V-4026 [M]	Ella Fitzgerald Sings the George and Ira Gershwin Song Book, Vol. 3	1961	25.00
❑ V6-4026 [S]	Ella Fitzgerald Sings the George and Ira Gershwin Song Book, Vol. 3	1961	25.00
❑ MGV-4027 [M]	Ella Fitzgerald Sings the George and Ira Gershwin Song Book, Vol. 4	1959	50.00
❑ MGVS-6080 [S]	Ella Fitzgerald Sings the George and Ira Gershwin Song Book, Vol. 4	1960	40.00

Number	Title	Yr	NM
❑ V-4027 [M]	Ella Fitzgerald Sings the George and Ira Gershwin Song Book, Vol. 4	1961	25.00
❑ V6-4027 [S]	Ella Fitzgerald Sings the George and Ira Gershwin Song Book, Vol. 4	1961	25.00
❑ MGV-4028 [M]	Ella Fitzgerald Sings the George and Ira Gershwin Song Book, Vol. 5	1959	50.00
❑ MGVS-6081 [S]	Ella Fitzgerald Sings the George and Ira Gershwin Song Book, Vol. 5	1960	40.00
❑ V-4028 [M]	Ella Fitzgerald Sings the George and Ira Gershwin Song Book, Vol. 5	1961	25.00
❑ V6-4028 [S]	Ella Fitzgerald Sings the George and Ira Gershwin Song Book, Vol. 5	1961	25.00
❑ MGV-4013 [M]	Ella Fitzgerald Sings the Gershwin Song Book	1957	50.00
❑ MGVS-7000 [S]	Ella Fitzgerald Sings the Gershwin Song Book	1959	50.00
❑ MGV-4046-2 [M]	Ella Fitzgerald Sings the Harold Arlen Song Book	1961	60.00
❑ V-4057 [M]	Ella Fitzgerald Sings the Harold Arlen Song Book, Vol. 1	1962	30.00
❑ V6-4057 [S]	Ella Fitzgerald Sings the Harold Arlen Song Book, Vol. 1	1962	30.00
❑ V-4058 [M]	Ella Fitzgerald Sings the Harold Arlen Song Book, Vol. 2	1962	30.00
❑ V6-4058 [S]	Ella Fitzgerald Sings the Harold Arlen Song Book, Vol. 2	1962	30.00
❑ MGV-4019-2 [M]	Ella Fitzgerald Sings the Irving Berlin Song Book	1958	80.00
❑ MGVS-6005-2 [S]	Ella Fitzgerald Sings the Irving Berlin Song Book	1960	60.00
❑ V-4019-2 [M]	Ella Fitzgerald Sings the Irving Berlin Song Book	1961	30.00
❑ V6-4019-2 [S]	Ella Fitzgerald Sings the Irving Berlin Song Book	1961	30.00
❑ MGV-4030 [M]	Ella Fitzgerald Sings the Irving Berlin Song Book, Vol. 1	1959	50.00
❑ MGVS-6052 [S]	Ella Fitzgerald Sings the Irving Berlin Song Book, Vol. 1	1960	40.00
❑ V-4030 [M]	Ella Fitzgerald Sings the Irving Berlin Song Book, Vol. 1	1961	25.00
❑ V6-4030 [S]	Ella Fitzgerald Sings the Irving Berlin Song Book, Vol. 1	1961	25.00
❑ MGV-4031 [M]	Ella Fitzgerald Sings the Irving Berlin Song Book, Vol. 2	1959	50.00
❑ MGVS-6053 [S]	Ella Fitzgerald Sings the Irving Berlin Song Book, Vol. 2	1960	40.00
❑ V-4031 [M]	Ella Fitzgerald Sings the Irving Berlin Song Book, Vol. 2	1961	25.00
❑ V6-4031 [S]	Ella Fitzgerald Sings the Irving Berlin Song Book, Vol. 2	1961	25.00
❑ V-4060 [M]	Ella Fitzgerald Sings the Jerome Kern Song Book	1963	30.00
❑ V6-4060 [S]	Ella Fitzgerald Sings the Jerome Kern Song Book	1963	30.00
❑ V-4067 [M]	Ella Fitzgerald Sings the Johnny Mercer Song Book	1965	25.00
❑ V6-4067 [S]	Ella Fitzgerald Sings the Johnny Mercer Song Book	1965	25.00
❑ MGV-4002-2 [M]	Ella Fitzgerald Sings the Rodgers & Hart Song Book	1956	80.00
❑ MGV-4022 [M]	Ella Fitzgerald Sings the Rodgers & Hart Song Book, Vol. 1	1959	50.00
❑ MGVS-6009 [S]	Ella Fitzgerald Sings the Rodgers & Hart Song Book, Vol. 1	1960	40.00
❑ V-4022 [M]	Ella Fitzgerald Sings the Rodgers & Hart Song Book, Vol. 1	1961	25.00
❑ V6-4022 [S]	Ella Fitzgerald Sings the Rodgers & Hart Song Book, Vol. 1	1961	25.00
❑ MGV-4023 [M]	Ella Fitzgerald Sings the Rodgers & Hart Song Book, Vol. 2	1959	50.00
❑ MGVS-6010 [S]	Ella Fitzgerald Sings the Rodgers & Hart Song Book, Vol. 2	1960	40.00
❑ V-4023 [M]	Ella Fitzgerald Sings the Rodgers & Hart Song Book, Vol. 2	1961	25.00
❑ V6-4023 [S]	Ella Fitzgerald Sings the Rodgers & Hart Song Book, Vol. 2	1961	25.00
❑ V-4002-2 [M]	Ella Fitzgerald Sings the Rodgers and Hart Song Book	1961	30.00
❑ V-4069 [M]	Ella in Hamburg	1966	25.00
❑ V6-4069 [S]	Ella in Hamburg	1966	25.00
❑ MGV-4052 [M]	Ella in Hollywood	1961	40.00
❑ V-4052 [M]	Ella in Hollywood	1961	25.00
❑ 835454-1	Ella in Rome: The Birthday Concert	1988	12.00
❑ V-4059 [M]	Ella Sings Broadway	1963	30.00
❑ V6-4059 [S]	Ella Sings Broadway	1963	30.00
❑ V-4054 [M]	Ella Swings Brightly with Nelson	1962	30.00

Number	Title	Yr	NM
❏ V6-4054 [S]	Ella Swings Brightly with Nelson	1962	30.00
❏ V-4055 [M]	Ella Swings Gently with Nelson	1962	30.00
❏ V6-4055 [S]	Ella Swings Gently with Nelson	1962	30.00
❏ MGV-4021 [M]	Ella Swings Lightly	1958	50.00
❏ MGVS-6019 [S]	Ella Swings Lightly	1960	40.00
❏ V-4021 [M]	Ella Swings Lightly	1961	25.00
❏ V6-4021 [S]	Ella Swings Lightly	1961	25.00
❏ MGV-4042 [M]	Ella Wishes You a Swinging Christmas	1960	50.00
❏ MGVS-64042 [S]	Ella Wishes You a Swinging Christmas	1960	60.00
❏ V-4042 [M]	Ella Wishes You a Swinging Christmas	1961	40.00
❏ V6-4042 [S]	Ella Wishes You a Swinging Christmas	1961	50.00
❏ VE-1-2539	Ella Wishes You a Swinging Christmas	198?	15.00
— Reissue			
❏ 827150-1	Ella Wishes You a Swinging Christmas	198?	12.00
❏ MGV-4036 [M]	Get Happy!	1960	40.00
❏ MGVS-6102 [S]	Get Happy!	1960	40.00

GET HAPPY • ELLA FITZGERALD — mono — ELLA FITZGERALD — get happy!

Number	Title	Yr	NM
❏ V-4036 [M]	Get Happy!	1961	25.00
❏ V6-4036 [S]	Get Happy!	1961	25.00
❏ V-4064 [M]	Hello, Dolly!	1964	30.00
❏ V6-4064 [S]	Hello, Dolly!	1964	30.00
❏ MGV-4034 [M]	Hello, Love	1959	50.00
❏ MGVS-6100 [S]	Hello, Love	1960	40.00
❏ V-4034 [M]	Hello, Love	1961	25.00
❏ V6-4034 [S]	Hello, Love	1961	25.00
❏ V6-8817	History	1973	18.00
❏ 825098-1	Lady Be Good	1985	12.00
❏ MGV-4043 [M]	Let No Man Write My Epitaph	1961	40.00
❏ V-4043 [M]	Let No Man Write My Epitaph	1961	25.00
❏ V6-4043 [S]	Let No Man Write My Epitaph	1961	25.00
❏ MGV-4004 [M]	Like Someone in Love	1957	50.00
❏ MGVS-6000 [S]	Like Someone in Love	1960	40.00
❏ V-4004 [M]	Like Someone in Love	1961	25.00
❏ V6-4004 [S]	Like Someone in Love	1961	25.00
❏ MGV-4041 [M]	Mack the Knife -- Ella in Berlin	1960	40.00
❏ MGVS-6163 [S]	Mack the Knife -- Ella in Berlin	1960	40.00
❏ V-4041 [M]	Mack the Knife -- Ella in Berlin	1961	25.00
❏ V6-4041 [S]	Mack the Knife -- Ella in Berlin	1961	25.00
❏ 825670-1	Mack the Knife -- Ella in Berlin	1985	12.00
❏ MGVS-64041 [S]	Mack the Knife -- Ella in Berlin	1960	50.00
❏ MGV-8288 [M]	One O'Clock Jump	1958	50.00
❏ V-8288 [M]	One O'Clock Jump	1961	25.00
❏ V-4068 [M]	Porgy & Bess	1965	25.00
❏ V6-4068 [S]	Porgy & Bess	1965	25.00
❏ V-4056 [M]	Rhythm Is My Business	1962	30.00
❏ V6-4056 [S]	Rhythm Is My Business	1962	30.00
❏ MGV-4032 [M]	Sweet Songs for Swingers	1959	50.00
❏ MGVS-6072 [S]	Sweet Songs for Swingers	1960	40.00
❏ V-4032 [M]	Sweet Songs for Swingers	1961	25.00
❏ V6-4032 [S]	Sweet Songs for Swingers	1961	25.00
❏ V-4063 [M]	The Best of Ella Fitzgerald	1964	18.00
❏ V6-4063 [S]	The Best of Ella Fitzgerald	1964	18.00
❏ V-8720 [M]	The Best of Ella Fitzgerald	1967	18.00
❏ V6-8720 [S]	The Best of Ella Fitzgerald	1967	15.00
❏ V6-8795	The Best of Ella Fitzgerald, Vol. 2	1969	15.00
❏ VE-2-2511	The Cole Porter Song Book	197?	18.00
❏ 823278-1	The Cole Porter Song Book	198?	15.00
❏ VE-2-2535	The Duke Ellington Song Book	1979	18.00
❏ 827163-1	The Duke Ellington Song Book, Vol. 1	198?	15.00
❏ VE-2-2540	The Duke Ellington Song Book, Vol. 2	1982	18.00
❏ 827169-1	The Duke Ellington Song Book, Vol. 2	198?	15.00
❏ 825024-1	The George and Ira Gershwin Songbook (Complete)	198?	30.00

Number	Title	Yr	NM
❏ 823279-1	The George and Ira Gershwin Songbook (Highlights)	198?	15.00
❏ VE-2-2525	The George Gershwin Song Book	1978	18.00
❏ 817526-1	The Harold Arlen Song Book	1984	18.00
❏ 829533-1	The Irving Berlin Song Book	1988	15.00
❏ 825669-1	The Jerome Kern Song Book	1985	12.00
❏ 823247-1	The Johnny Mercer Song Book	1985	12.00
❏ VE-2-2519	The Rodgers and Hart Song Book	197?	18.00
❏ 821693-1	The Rodgers and Hart Song Book	198?	15.00
❏ V-4062 [M]	These Are the Blues	1963	30.00
❏ V6-4062 [S]	These Are the Blues	1963	30.00
❏ V-4071 [M]	Whisper Not	1966	25.00
❏ V6-4071 [S]	Whisper Not	1966	25.00

VOCALION

❏ VL3797 [M]	Ella Fitzgerald	1967	15.00
❏ VL73797 [R]	Ella Fitzgerald	1967	15.00

FIVE, THE

RCA VICTOR

❏ LPM-1121 [M]	The Five	1955	80.00

FIVE-A-SLIDE

AUDIOPHILE

❏ AP-180	Five-a-Slide	198?	15.00

FIVE AMERICANS, THE

ABNAK

❏ ABST-2071	Now and Then	1968	30.00
❏ AB-1969 [M]	Progressions	1967	40.00
❏ ABST-2069 [S]	Progressions	1967	60.00
❏ AB-1967 [M]	Western Union/Sound of Love	1967	30.00
❏ ABST-2067 [S]	Western Union/Sound of Love	1967	30.00

HANNA-BARBERA

❏ HST-9503 [S]	I See the Light	1966	75.00
❏ HLP-8503 [M]	I See the Light	1966	40.00

FIVE BROTHERS

TAMPA

❏ TP-25 [M]	Five Brothers	1957	150.00
— Red vinyl			
❏ TP-25 [M]	Five Brothers	1958	80.00
— Black vinyl			

FIVE BY FIVE

PAULA

❏ LPS-2202	Next Exit	1969	40.00

FIVE DISCS, THE

CRYSTAL BALL

❏ 119	Unchained	1978	18.00

MAGIC CARPET

❏ 1002	The Five Discs Sing Again	1991	25.00
— Dark blue cover			

FIVE EMPREES, THE

FREEPORT

❏ 4001	Little Miss Sad	1966	100.00
— Same LP, new title			
❏ 3001 [M]	Little Miss Sad	1966	150.00
— Same LP, new title			
❏ 3001 [M]	The Five Emprees	1965	150.00
❏ 3001 [S]	The Five Emprees	1965	100.00

FIVE KEYS, THE

ALADDIN

❏ LP-806 [M]	The Best of the Five Keys	1956	2000.00
— Copies of Aladdin 806 entitled "On the Town" are bootlegs made in the 1970s; VG value 1000; VG+ value 1500			

CAPITOL

❏ T1769 [M]	The Fantastic Five Keys	1962	300.00
❏ M-1769	The Fantastic Five Keys	1977	25.00
— Reissue with new prefix			
❏ T828 [M]	The Five Keys On Stage!	1957	500.00
— On cover, the far left singer's "offending" thumb is airbrushed out			
❏ T828 [M]	The Five Keys On Stage!	1957	300.00
— On cover, the far left singer has his thumb sticking out (inadvertently?) in a phallic way			

HARLEM HIT PARADE

❏ 5004	The Five Keys	1972	18.00

KING

❏ 5013	14 Hits	1978	15.00
❏ 692 [M]	Rhythm and Blues Hits, Past and Present	1960	600.00
❏ 688 [M]	The Five Keys	1960	800.00

SCORE

❏ LP-4003 [M]	The Five Keys On the Town	1957	800.00
— Reissue of Aladdin 806.			

FIVE MAN ELECTRICAL BAND

CAPITOL

❏ ST-165	Five Man Electrical Band	1969	25.00

LION

❏ LN-1009 [B]	Sweet Paradise	1973	25.00

LIONEL

❏ LRS-1101	Coming of Age	1971	25.00
❏ LRS-1100	Good-Byes & Butterflies	1970	30.00

MGM

❏ SE-4725	Good-Byes & Butterflies	1970	50.00

PICKWICK

❏ SPC-3289	Five Man Electrical Band	1973	12.00
— Reissue of Capitol material			

FIVE ROYALES, THE

APOLLO

❏ LP-488 [M]	The Rockin' 5 Royales	1956	4000.00
— Purple label; VG value 2000; VG+ value 3000			
❏ LP-488 [M]	The Rockin' 5 Royales	1956	2000.00
— Green label; VG value 1000; VG+ value 1500			
❏ LP-488 [M]	The Rockin' 5 Royales	1956	1000.00
— Yellow label			

KING

❏ 5014	17 Hits	197?	15.00
❏ 955 [M]	24 All Time Hits	1966	100.00
❏ 580 [M]	Dedicated to You	1957	500.00
❏ 616 [M]	The 5 Royales Sing for You	1959	400.00
❏ 678 [M]	The Five Royales	1960	250.00

FIVE SATINS, THE

BUDDAH

❏ BDS-5654	Black Satin	1976	18.00
— As "Black Satin			

CELEBRITY SHOWCASE

❏ JB-7671	The Best of the Five Satins	1970	25.00

COLLECTABLES

❏ COL-5017	The Five Satins Sing Their Greatest Hits	198?	12.00

ELEKTRA

❏ 60152	Fred Parris and the Satins	1982	25.00

FMBER

❏ ELP-401 [M]	The Five Satins Encore	1960	200.00
— Mostly white "logs" label			
❏ ELP-401 [M]	The Five Satins Encore	1961	100.00
— Black label			
❏ ELP-100 [M]	The Five Satins Sing	1957	2000.00
— Red label; group pictured on front cover; blue vinyl; VG value 1000; VG+ value 1500			
❏ ELP-100 [M]	The Five Satins Sing	1957	600.00
— Red label; group pictured on front cover; black vinyl			
❏ ELP-100 [M]	The Five Satins Sing	1959	300.00
— Mostly white "logs" label; group pictured on front cover			
❏ ELP-100 [M]	The Five Satins Sing	1959	200.00
— Mostly white "logs" label; no picture on cover			
❏ ELP-100 [M]	The Five Satins Sing	1961	100.00
— Black label; no picture on cover			

LOST-NITE

❏ LLP-8 [10]	The Five Satins	1981	12.00
— Red vinyl			
❏ LLP-9 [10]	The Five Satins	1981	12.00
— Red vinyl			

MOUNT VERNON

❏ 108	The Five Satins Sing	196?	30.00

RELIC

❏ 5008	The Five Satins' Greatest Hits (1956-1959), Volume 1	198?	12.00
❏ 5013	The Five Satins' Greatest Hits (1956-1959), Volume 2	198?	12.00
❏ 5024	The Five Satins' Greatest Hits (1956-1959), Volume 3	198?	12.00

FIVE SPECIAL

ELEKTRA

❏ 6E-206	Five Special	1979	18.00
❏ 6E-270	Something Special	1980	18.00
❏ 5E-553	Trak'n	1981	25.00

FIVE STAIRSTEPS, THE

BUDDAH

❏ BDS-5008	Our Family Portrait	1967	25.00
❏ BDS-5061	Stairsteps	1970	18.00
— As "Stairsteps			
❏ BDS-5068	Step by Step by Step	1970	18.00
— As "Stairsteps			

COLLECTABLES

❏ COL-5023	Greatest Hits	1985	12.00

CURTOM

❏ 8002	Love's Happening	1969	25.00

WINDY C

❏ 6000 [M]	The Five Stairsteps	1967	30.00
❏ S-6000 [S]	The Five Stairsteps	1967	30.00

Number	Title	Yr	NM

FIVE STAR
EPIC
| ❑ E46768 | Five Star | 1990 | 15.00 |
RCA
| ❑ 6635-1-R | Between the Lines | 1987 | 12.00 |
| ❑ NFL1-8052 | Luxury of Life | 1985 | 12.00 |

— Original issue

| ❑ AFL1-9506 | Luxury of Life | 1986 | 10.00 |

— Reissue

| ❑ AFL1-5901 | Silk and Steel | 1986 | 12.00 |

FIXX, THE
IMPACT
| ❑ 10205 | Ink | 1991 | 15.00 |
MCA
| ❑ 42316 | Greatest Hits | 1989 | 18.00 |
| ❑ R153353 | Phantoms | 1984 | 12.00 |

— RCA Music Service edition

| ❑ 5507 | Phantoms | 1984 | 10.00 |
| ❑ L33-1213 [DJ] | Phantoms | 1984 | 15.00 |

— Advance version; no interviews

| ❑ L33-1212 [DJ] | Phantoms | 1984 | 18.00 |

— Promo sampler; contains three complete songs, "Are We Ourselves?", "Sunshine in the Shade" and "Less Cities, More Morving People," plus spoken introductions for all the songs on the album

| ❑ 39001 [B] | Reach the Beach | 1983 | 15.00 |

— Original issue

| ❑ 5417 | Reach the Beach | 1983 | 10.00 |

— Reissue

| ❑ R164166 | React | 1987 | 12.00 |

— BMG Direct Marketing edition

❑ 42008	React	1987	12.00
❑ 5345	Shuttered Room	1982	12.00
❑ R164360	Walkabout	1986	12.00

— RCA Music Service edition

| ❑ 5705 | Walkabout | 1986 | 10.00 |
RCA
| ❑ 8566-1-R | Calm Animals | 1989 | 12.00 |

FLACK, ROBERTA, AND DONNY HATHAWAY
ATLANTIC
| ❑ SD7216 | Roberta Flack and Donny Hathaway | 1972 | 12.00 |

FLACK, ROBERTA
ATLANTIC
❑ SD19149	Blue Lights in the Basement	1977	12.00
❑ SD1569	Chapter Two	1970	12.00
❑ SD18131	Feel Like Makin' Love	1974	12.00
❑ SD8230	First Take	1969	12.00

— Red and green label (second edition)

| ❑ SW-94346 | First Take | 1972 | 18.00 |

— Capitol Record Club edition

| ❑ SD8230 | First Take | 1969 | 25.00 |

— Brown and purple label (first edition)

❑ SD19354	I'm the One	1982	12.00
❑ SD7271	Killing Me Softly	1973	12.00
❑ SD19154	Killing Me Softly	1978	10.00

— Reissue of 7271

❑ QD7271 [Q]	Killing Me Softly	1973	25.00
❑ 81916	Oasis	1988	12.00
❑ SD1594	Quiet Fire	1971	12.00
❑ SD19186	Roberta Flack	1978	12.00
❑ SD16013	Roberta Flack Featuring Donny Hathaway	1980	12.00

— Only two tracks feature Mr. Hathaway

| ❑ SD19317 | The Best of Roberta Flack | 1981 | 12.00 |
MCA
| ❑ 5141 | Bustin' Loose | 1981 | 12.00 |

FLAGG, FANNIE
RCA VICTOR
| ❑ LPM-3856 [M] | Rally 'Round the Flagg | 1967 | 25.00 |
| ❑ LSP-3856 [S] | Rally 'Round the Flagg | 1967 | 18.00 |

FLAHIVE, LARRY
SEA BREEZE
| ❑ SB-2020 | Standard Flay | 1983 | 12.00 |

FLAIRS, THE (1)
CROWN
| ❑ CLP-5356 [M] | The Flairs | 1963 | 100.00 |

FLAME, THE
BROTHER
| ❑ BR-2500 | The Flame | 1970 | 30.00 |

— Deduct 1/3 if poster is missing

FLAMIN' GROOVIES, THE
4 MEN WITH BEARDS
❑ 4M537 [B]	Jumpin' In The Night	2014	25.00
❑ 4M536 [B]	Now!	2013	25.00
❑ 4M535 [B]	Shake Some Action	2013	25.00
BUDDAH
| ❑ BDS-5683 | Shill Shakin' | 1977 | 18.00 |
EPIC
| ❑ BN26487 | Supersnazz | 1969 | 50.00 |
KAMA SUTRA
| ❑ KSBS-2021 [B] | Flamingo | 1970 | 40.00 |

— Pink label

| ❑ KSBS-2021 [B] | Flamingo | 1972 | 25.00 |

— Blue label

| ❑ KSBS-2031 [B] | Teenage Head | 1971 | 40.00 |

— Pink label

| ❑ KSBS-2031 [B] | Teenage Head | 1972 | 25.00 |

— Blue label

SIRE
❑ SRK6067	Jumpin' in the Night	1979	15.00
❑ SASD-7521	Shake Some Action	1976	18.00
❑ SRK6059	The Flamin' Groovies Now	1978	18.00

— Originals have 12 tracks

| ❑ SRK6059 | The Flamin' Groovies Now | 1978 | 15.00 |

— Reissues have 14 tracks

SNAZZ
| ❑ R-2371 [10] | Sneekers | 1969 | 300.00 |

— Beware - this album has been counterfeited.

FLAMING EMBER, THE
HOT WAX
| ❑ HA-705 | Sunshine | 1971 | 18.00 |
| ❑ HA-702 | Westbound #9 | 1970 | 18.00 |

FLAMING LIPS, THE
ATAVISTIC
| ❑ ALP-04 [EP] | Unconsciously Screamin' | 1991 | 35.00 |
LOVELY SORTS OF DEATH
| ❑ (# unknown)0 [EP] | The Flaming Lips (Bag Full of Thoughts) | 1984 | 120.00 |

— Green vinyl; dark brown background on jacket

| ❑ (# unknown)0 [EP] | The Flaming Lips (Bag Full of Thoughts) | 1984 | 80.00 |

— Red vinyl; black background on jacket

PINK DUST
| ❑ 72173 | Hear It Is | 1986 | 40.00 |

— Originals on white vinyl

| ❑ 72188 [EP] | The Flaming Lips | 1985 | 40.00 |

— Originals on lavender vinyl; reissue of Lovely Sorts of Death EP

PLAIN
| ❑ 111 | Hear It Is | 2006 | 18.00 |

— Reissue on white vinyl

| ❑ 114 | In a Priest Driven Ambulance | 2006 | 18.00 |

— Reissue on pink vinyl

| ❑ 112 | Oh My Gawd!!!... The Flaming Lips | 2006 | 18.00 |

— Reissue on clear vinyl

| ❑ 113 | Telepathic Surgery | 2006 | 18.00 |

— Reissue on blue vinyl

RESTLESS
| ❑ 72359 | In a Priest Driven Ambulance | 1990 | 30.00 |

— Pink vinyl

| ❑ 72207 | Oh My Gawd, The Flaming Lips | 1987 | 40.00 |

— Clear vinyl

| ❑ 72350 | Telepathic Surgery | 1989 | 30.00 |
WARNER BROS.
| ❑ 542236-1 [B] | 7 Skies H3 | 2014 | 30.00 |
| ❑ 1-44250 | At War with the Mystics | 2006 | 30.00 |

— 180-gram edition on black vinyl

| ❑ 1-49966 | At War with the Mystics | 2006 | 30.00 |

— 150-gram edition; one record is on orange vinyl, the other is on turquoise vinyl

❑ 45911	Clouds Taste Metallic	1995	18.00
❑ 45334	Transmissions from the Satellite Heart	1993	25.00
❑ 48141	Yoshimi Battles the Pink Robots	2002	25.00

FLAMING YOUTH
UNI
| ❑ 73075 [B] | Ark 2 | 1969 | 60.00 |

FLAMINGO, JOHNNY
DIADON
| ❑ 201 [M] | Johnny Flamingo Sings In the Wee Small Hours | 1961 | 100.00 |

FLAMINGOS, THE, AND THE MOONGLOWS
VEE JAY
| ❑ LP-1052 [M] | The Flamingos Meet the Moonglows on the Dusty Road of Hits | 1962 | 150.00 |
| ❑ VJLP-1052 [M] | The Flamingos Meet the Moonglows on the Dusty Road of Hits | 198? | 18.00 |

— Authorized reissue

FLAMINGOS, THE
CHECKER
| ❑ LP-1433 [M] | The Flamingos | 1959 | 400.00 |

— Black label

| ❑ LP-1433 [M] | The Flamingos | 196? | 150.00 |

— Blue label

| ❑ LPS-3005 [R] | The Flamingos | 1966 | 30.00 |

— Rechanneled reissue of 1433

CONSTELLATION
| ❑ CS-3 [M] | Collectors Showcase: The Flamingos | 1964 | 100.00 |

— With hot pink lettering on cover

| ❑ CS-3 [M] | Collectors Showcase: The Flamingos | 1964 | 50.00 |

— With more restrained pink lettering on cover

END
❑ LP-307 [M]	Flamingo Favorites	1960	100.00
❑ LPS-307 [R]	Flamingo Favorites	1960	70.00
❑ LP-304 [M]	Flamingo Serenade	1959	200.00

— Gray label with dog

| ❑ LPS-304 [S] | Flamingo Serenade | 1959 | 500.00 |

— Cover says "Stereo

| ❑ LPS-304 [S] | Flamingo Serenade | 196? | 200.00 |

— Cover says "Rechanneled Stereo" (only one track is)

| ❑ LP-304 [M] | Flamingo Serenade | 1959 | 400.00 |

— Black label with shadow print logo

❑ LP-308 [M]	Requestfully Yours	1960	100.00
❑ LPS-308 [R]	Requestfully Yours	1960	70.00
❑ LP-316 [M]	The Sound of the Flamingos	1962	100.00
❑ LPS-316 [S]	The Sound of the Flamingos	1962	200.00

— Stereo" at upper right corner of front cover

| ❑ LPS-316 [S] | The Sound of the Flamingos | 1962 | 70.00 |

LOST-NITE
| ❑ LLP-7 [10] | The Flamingos | 1981 | 12.00 |

— Red vinyl

PHILIPS
| ❑ PHM200206 [M] | Their Hits -- Then and Now | 1966 | 30.00 |
| ❑ PHS600206 [S] | Their Hits -- Then and Now | 1966 | 30.00 |
RONZE
| ❑ RLP-1001 | The Flamingos Today | 1972 | 18.00 |
SOLID SMOKE
| ❑ 8018 | Golden Teardrops | 198? | 12.00 |

FLANAGAN, TOMMY, AND HANK JONES
GALAXY
| ❑ 5152 | More Delights | 1985 | 12.00 |
| ❑ 5113 | Our Delights | 1978 | 15.00 |

FLANAGAN, TOMMY
ENJA
| ❑ 4014 | Confirmation | 1982 | 15.00 |
| ❑ 4022 | Giant Steps | 1983 | 15.00 |
FANTASY
❑ OJC-372	Montreux '77	1989	15.00
❑ OJC-473	Something Borrowed, Something Blue	1990	15.00
❑ OJC-182	The Tommy Flanagan Trio	198?	12.00
GALAXY
| ❑ 5110 | Something Borrowed, Something Blue | 1978 | 15.00 |
INNER CITY
❑ IC-3029	Ballads and Blues	1979	18.00
❑ IC-3009	Eclypso	1977	18.00
❑ IC-1071	Tommy Flanagan Plays the Music of Harold Arlen	1980	15.00
❑ IC-1084	Trinity	198?	12.00
MOODSVILLE
| ❑ MVLP-9 [M] | The Tommy Flanagan Trio | 1960 | 50.00 |

— Green label

| ❑ MVLP-9 [M] | The Tommy Flanagan Trio | 1965 | 30.00 |

— Blue label, trident logo at right

NEW JAZZ
| ❑ 8217 [B] | The Cats | 1959 | 250.00 |

— purple label

ONYX
| ❑ 206 | The Tommy Flanagan Trio and Sextet | 197? | 18.00 |

Number	Title	Yr	NM
PABLO			
2405410	The Best of Tommy Flanagan	198?	12.00
2310724	Tokyo Recital	1975	18.00
PABLO LIVE			
2308202	Montreux '77	1978	18.00
PRESTIGE			
PRLP-7134 [M]	Overseas	1958	1000.00
PRST-7632	Overseas	1969	18.00
REGENT			
MG-6055 [M]	Jazz... It's Magic	1958	80.00
SAVOY JAZZ			
SJL-1158	Jazz... It's Magic	1986	12.00
STATIRAS			
SLP-8073	The Magnificent	1985	12.00
TIMELESS			
SJP-301	Jazz Poet	1990	15.00

FLANDERS, TOMMY

Number	Title	Yr	NM
VERVE FORECAST			
FTS-3075	Moonstone	1969	25.00

FLANDERS AND SWANN

Number	Title	Yr	NM
ANGEL			
65042 [M]	At the Drop of a Hat	1959	30.00
— Original issue			
35797 [M]	At the Drop of a Hat	196?	25.00
S35797 [S]	At the Drop of a Hat	196?	30.00
36388 [M]	At the Drop of Another Hat	1966	25.00
S36388 [S]	At the Drop of Another Hat	1966	30.00
36112 [M]	The Bestiary of Flanders and Swann	196?	25.00
S36112 [S]	The Bestiary of Flanders and Swann	196?	30.00

FLARES, THE

Number	Title	Yr	NM
PRESS			
PR73001 [M]	Encore of Foot Stompin' Hits	196?	80.00
PRS83001 [S]	Encore of Foot Stompin' Hits	196?	120.00

FLASH

Number	Title	Yr	NM
SOVEREIGN/CAPITOL			
SMAS-11040	Flash	1972	15.00
SMAS-11115	Flash in the Can	1972	15.00
SMAS-11218	Out of Our Hands	1973	15.00

FLASH AND THE PAN

Number	Title	Yr	NM
EPIC			
BFE39618	Early Morning Wake-Up Call	1984	12.00
JE36018	Flash And The Pan	1979	12.00
ARE37725	Headlines	1982	15.00
JE36432	Lights in the Night	1980	12.00

FLASH CADILLAC AND THE CONTINENTAL KIDS

Number	Title	Yr	NM
EPIC			
KE31787	Flash Cadillac and the Continental Kids	1972	18.00
— Yellow label			
KE31787	Flash Cadillac and the Continental Kids	1973	15.00
— Orange label			
KE32488	There's No Face Like Chrome	1974	15.00
PRIVATE STOCK			
PS2003 [B]	Sons of Beaches	1975	18.00

FLAT EARTH SOCIETY, THE

Number	Title	Yr	NM
FLEETWOOD			
3027	Waleeco	1968	400.00

FLATT, LESTER, AND MAC WISEMAN

Number	Title	Yr	NM
RCA VICTOR			
LSP-4547	Lester 'n' Mac	1971	25.00
LSP-4688	On the South Bound	1972	25.00

FLATT, LESTER

Number	Title	Yr	NM
COLUMBIA			
CS1006	Flatt Out	1970	25.00
NUGGET			
104	The One and Only	1971	25.00
RCA VICTOR			
APL1-0131	Country Boy	1973	18.00
LSP-4789	Foggy Mountain Breakdown	1972	25.00
LSP-4633	Kentucky Ridgerunner	1972	25.00
LSP-4495	Lester Flatt on Victor	1971	25.00

FLATT AND SCRUGGS

Number	Title	Yr	NM
COLUMBIA			
GP30	20 All-Time Great Recordings	1970	25.00
C32244	A Boy Named Sue	1973	15.00
C30347	Breaking Out	1971	15.00
CS9596 [S]	Changin' Times Featuring Foggy Mountain Breakdown	1968	25.00
— Red "360 Sound" label			
CS9596	Changin' Times Featuring Foggy Mountain Breakdown	1970	15.00

Number	Title	Yr	NM
— Orange label with six "Columbia"s along edge			
CL2796 [M]	Changin' Times Featuring Foggy Mountain Breakdown	1968	40.00
CS9945	Final Fling	1970	18.00
CL2045 [M]	Flatt and Scruggs at Carnegie Hall	1963	25.00
CS8845 [S]	Flatt and Scruggs at Carnegie Hall	1963	30.00
PC8845	Flatt and Scruggs at Carnegie Hall	198?	10.00
— Budget-line reissue			
CL2570 [M]	Flatt and Scruggs' Greatest Hits	1966	18.00
CS9370 [S]	Flatt and Scruggs' Greatest Hits	1966	25.00
PC9370	Flatt and Scruggs' Greatest Hits	198?	10.00
— Budget-line reissue			
CL1564 [M]	Foggy Mountain Banjo	1961	25.00
CS8364 [S]	Foggy Mountain Banjo	1961	30.00
CL1019 [M]	Foggy Mountain Jamboree	1957	50.00
CL1830 [M]	Folk Songs of Our Land	1962	25.00
CS8630 [S]	Folk Songs of Our Land	1962	30.00
CL1951 [M]	Hard Travelin' Featuring The Ballad of Jed Clampett	1963	25.00
CS8751 [S]	Hard Travelin' Featuring The Ballad of Jed Clampett	1963	30.00
CL2686 [M]	Hear the Whistle Blow	1967	25.00
CS9486 [S]	Hear the Whistle Blow	1967	25.00
FC37469	Lester Flatt & Earl Scruggs	1981	12.00
CS9741	Nashville Airplane	1969	25.00
CL2354 [M]	Pickin' Strummin' and Singin'	1965	18.00
CS9154 [S]	Pickin' Strummin' and Singin'	1965	25.00
CL2134 [M]	Recorded Live at Vanderbilt University	1964	25.00
CS8934 [S]	Recorded Live at Vanderbilt University	1964	30.00
CL1424 [M]	Songs of Glory	1960	25.00
CS8221 [S]	Songs of Glory	1960	30.00
CL1664 [M]	Songs of the Famous Carter Family	1961	25.00
CS8464 [S]	Songs of the Famous Carter Family	1961	30.00
CL2643 [M]	Strictly Instrumental	1967	25.00
CS9443 [S]	Strictly Instrumental	1967	25.00
CL2255 [M]	The Fabulous Sound of Flatt & Scruggs	1964	25.00
CS9055 [S]	The Fabulous Sound of Flatt & Scruggs	1964	30.00
CS9649 [M]	The Story of Bonnie & Clyde	1968	25.00
CS9649 [M]	The Story of Bonnie & Clyde	1968	40.00
— White label promo with "Special Mono Radio Station Copy" sticker and timing strip on front cover			
CG31964	The World of Flatt and Scruggs	1972	18.00
CL2443 [M]	Town and Country	1966	18.00
CS9243 [S]	Town and Country	1966	25.00
CL2513 [M]	When the Saints Go Marching In	1966	18.00
CS9313 [S]	When the Saints Go Marching In	1966	25.00
COLUMBIA LIMITED EDITION			
LE10149	Breaking Out	197?	12.00
COLUMBIA MUSICAL TREASURY			
DS493	Detroit City	1969	18.00
COUNTY			
CCS-111	You Can Feel It in Your Soul	1988	12.00
EVEREST ARCHIVE OF FOLK & JAZZ			
259	Lester Flatt & Earl Scruggs	197?	12.00
HARMONY			
HS11401	Foggy Mountain Chimes	1970	15.00
HL7340 [M]	Great Original Recordings	1965	18.00
HL7250 [M]	Lester Flatt & Earl Scruggs	1960	18.00
HL7402 [M]	Sacred Songs	1967	18.00
HS11202 [S]	Sacred Songs	1967	15.00
HL7465 [M]	Songs to Cherish	1968	18.00
HS11265 [S]	Songs to Cherish	1968	15.00
H30932	Wabash Cannonball	197?	12.00
MERCURY			
MG-20358 [M]	Country Music	1958	40.00
MG-20542 [M]	Lester Flatt & Earl Scruggs	1959	40.00
SR-61162	Original Theme from Bonnie & Clyde	1968	25.00
MG-20773 [M]	The Original Sound of Flatt & Scruggs	1963	30.00
SR-60773 [R]	The Original Sound of Flatt & Scruggs	1963	18.00
NASHVILLE			
2087	The Best of Flatt and Scruggs	1970	15.00
PICKWICK			
6140	Blue Grass Banjos	197?	12.00
6093	Foggy Mountain Breakdown	197?	15.00
POWER PAK			
297	Golden Hits	197?	12.00
ROUNDER			
SS-08	Don't Get Above Your Raisin'	198?	12.00
SS-05	The Golden Era	198?	12.00
SS-18	The Mercury Sessions, Volume 1	1985	12.00
SS-19	The Mercury Sessions, Volume 2	1985	12.00
STARDAY			
SLP-365 [M]	Stars of the Grand Ol' Opry	1966	30.00
— With Jim and Jesse			

Number	Title	Yr	NM
WING			
SRW-16376	The Original Foggy Mountain Breakdown	1968	15.00

FLAVOR

Number	Title	Yr	NM
JU-PAR			
JP6-1002S1	In Good Taste	1976	25.00

FLEETWOOD, MICK

Number	Title	Yr	NM
RCA VICTOR			
AFL1-4652	I'm Not Me	1983	10.00
AFL1-4080	The Visitor	1981	10.00
DJL1-4106 [EP]	The Visitor	1981	10.00
— Four-song promo sampler from LP			

FLEETWOOD MAC

Number	Title	Yr	NM
BLUE HORIZON			
BH-4802	Blues Jam in Chicago, Vol. 1	1970	18.00
BH-4803	Blues Jam in Chicago, Vol. 2	1970	18.00
BH-3801	Fleetwood Mac in Chicago	1970	30.00
EPIC			
KE30632	Black Magic Woman	1971	25.00
LN24446 [M]	English Rose	1969	100.00
— White label promo only			
BN26446 [S]	English Rose	1969	30.00
LN24402 [M]	Fleetwood Mac	1968	100.00
— White label promo only			
BN26402 [S]	Fleetwood Mac	1968	30.00
KE33740	Fleetwood Mac/English Rose	1974	18.00
MOBILE FIDELITY			
1-012 [B]	Fleetwood Mac	1980	75.00
— Audiophile vinyl			
1-119 [B]	Mirage	1984	50.00
— Audiophile vinyl			
NAUTILUS			
NR-8 [B]	Rumours	1980	60.00
— Audiophile vinyl			
REPRISE			
MS2080	Bare Trees	1972	15.00
— With brown line near all four edges of the front cover			
MSK2278	Bare Trees	1977	10.00
— Reissue; no brown line on the front cover			
MS2080	Bare Trees	197?	18.00
— Without brown line on front cover; uncommon with the MS 2080 number			
MS2225	Fleetwood Mac	1975	12.00
MSK2281	Fleetwood Mac	1977	10.00
RS6465	Future Games	1971	30.00
— Originals have a pale yellow cover			
RS6465	Future Games	1972	18.00
— Later pressings have a pale green cover			
MS2196	Heroes Are Hard to Find	1974	15.00
RS6408	Kiln House	1970	18.00
MS2158	Mystery to Me	1973	25.00
— With "Good Things (Come to Those Who Wait)" listed on the album cover; it was replaced at the last minute by "For Your Love"			
MS2158	Mystery to Me	1973	15.00
— With "For Your Love" listed correctly on the back cover			
MSK2279	Mystery to Me	1977	10.00
MS2138 [B]	Penguin	1973	18.00
RS6368	Then Play On	1969	30.00
— First pressings include "When You Say" and "My Dream"			
RS6368	Then Play On	1970	18.00
— Later pressings replace above two tracks with "Oh Well (Parts 1 and 2)."			
SIRE			
SASH-3715	Fleetwood Mac in Chicago	1975	18.00
— Reissue of Blue Horizon 3801			
2XS-6009	Fleetwood Mac in Chicago	1977	15.00
2XS-6045	The Original Fleetwood Mac	1977	15.00
SASH-3706	Vintage Years	1975	18.00
2XS-6006	Vintage Years	1977	15.00
VARRICK			
VR-020	Jumping at Shadows	1985	15.00
WARNER BROS.			
26111	Behind the Mask	1990	18.00
2WB3500	Fleetwood Mac Live	1980	15.00
R125801 [B]	Greatest Hits	2014	25.00
25801	Greatest Hits	1989	12.00
23607 [DJ]	Mirage	1982	40.00
— Promo on Quiex II vinyl			
23607	Mirage	1982	12.00
BSK3010	Rumours	1977	12.00
— With short version (2:02) of "Never Going Back Again"; we do not yet know how to identify these without playing them			
BSK3010	Rumours	1977	10.00
— With long version (2:16) of "Never Going Back Again"; we do not yet know how to identify these without playing them			
25471	Tango in the Night	1987	12.00
2HS3350	Tusk	1979	18.00
PRO-A-866 [DJ]	Tusk Remix	1979	25.00
— Promo-only EP			

Number	Title	Yr	NM

FLEETWOODS, THE

DOLTON

Number	Title	Yr	NM
BLP-2030 [M]	Before and After	1965	30.00
BST-8030 [S]	Before and After	1965	40.00
BLP-2007 [M]	Deep in a Dream	1961	40.00
—Pale blue label with dolphins on top			
BST-8007 [S]	Deep in a Dream	1961	50.00
—Pale blue label with dolphins on top			
BLP-2007 [M]	Deep in a Dream	1963	25.00
—Dark label, logo on left			
BST-8007 [S]	Deep in a Dream	1963	30.00
—Dark label, logo on left			
BLP-2039 [M]	Folk Rock	1965	30.00
BST-8039 [S]	Folk Rock	1965	40.00
BLP-2025 [M]	Goodnight My Love	1963	30.00
BST-8025 [S]	Goodnight My Love	1963	40.00
BLP-2001 [M]	Mr. Blue	1959	80.00
—Pale blue label with dolphins on top			
BST-8001 [S]	Mr. Blue	1959	100.00
—Pale blue label with dolphins on top			
BLP-2001 [M]	Mr. Blue	1963	25.00
—Dark label, logo on left			
BST-8001 [S]	Mr. Blue	1963	30.00
—Dark label, logo on left			
BLP-2005 [M]	Softly	1961	50.00
—Pale blue label with dolphins on top			
BST-8005 [S]	Softly	1961	70.00
—Pale blue label with dolphins on top			
BLP-2005 [M]	Softly	1963	25.00
—Dark label, logo on left			
BST-8005 [S]	Softly	1963	30.00
—Dark label, logo on left			
BLP-2011 [M]	The Best of the Oldies	1962	40.00
—Pale blue label with dolphins on top			
BST-8011 [S]	The Best of the Oldies	1962	50.00
—Pale blue label with dolphins on top			
BLP-2011 [M]	The Best of the Oldies	1963	25.00
—Dark label, logo on left			
BST-8011 [S]	The Best of the Oldies	1963	30.00
—Dark label, logo on left			
BLP-2002 [M]	The Fleetwoods	1960	50.00
—Pale blue label with dolphins on top			
BST-8002 [S]	The Fleetwoods	1960	70.00
—Pale blue label with dolphins on top			
BLP-2002 [M]	The Fleetwoods	1963	25.00
—Dark label, logo on left			
BST-8002 [S]	The Fleetwoods	1963	30.00
—Dark label, logo on left			
BLP-2018 [M]	The Fleetwoods' Greatest Hits	1962	30.00
BST-8018 [S]	The Fleetwoods' Greatest Hits	1962	30.00
BLP-2020 [M]	The Fleetwoods Sings for Lovers by Night	1963	30.00
BST-8020 [S]	The Fleetwoods Sings for Lovers by Night	1963	40.00

LIBERTY

Number	Title	Yr	NM
LN-10199	Buried Treasure	1983	10.00
LN-10160	The Best Goodies of the Oldies	1982	10.00
LN-10159	The Fleetwoods' Greatest Hits	1982	10.00

SUNSET

Number	Title	Yr	NM
SUM-1131 [M]	In a Mellow Mood	1966	15.00
SUS-5131 [S]	In a Mellow Mood	1966	18.00

UNITED ARTISTS

Number	Title	Yr	NM
UA-LA334-E	The Very Best of the Fleetwoods	1975	15.00

FLEMING, KING

ARGO

Number	Title	Yr	NM
LP-4004 [M]	Misty Night	1961	30.00
LPS-4004 [S]	Misty Night	1961	30.00
LP-4019 [M]	Stand By!	1962	30.00
LPS-4019 [S]	Stand By!	1962	30.00

CADET

Number	Title	Yr	NM
LP-4053 [M]	Weary Traveler	1966	18.00
LPS-4053 [S]	Weary Traveler	1966	25.00

FLEMING, RHONDA

COLUMBIA

Number	Title	Yr	NM
CL1080 [M]	Rhonda	1958	60.00

FLEMONS, WADE

VEE JAY

Number	Title	Yr	NM
LP-1011 [M]	Wade Flemons	1959	150.00
—Maroon label			
LP-1011 [M]	Wade Flemons	196?	80.00
—Black label			

FLESH FOR LULU

CAPITOL

Number	Title	Yr	NM
SPRO79992/3 [DJ]	Final Vinyl (And Live Flesh)	1990	25.00
—Red vinyl; sticker on generic cover			
CLT-48217	Long Live the New Flesh	1987	15.00
C1-90232	Plastic Fantastic	1989	15.00

FLESHEATERS

HOMESTEAD

Number	Title	Yr	NM
124-1	Live	1988	12.00
(# unknown)0	Prehistoric Hits Vol. 1	198?	15.00

RUBY

Number	Title	Yr	NM
JRR-101	A Minute to Pray, a Second to Die	1981	25.00
JRR805	Forever Came Today	1982	25.00

SST

Number	Title	Yr	NM
094	Destroyed by Fire/Greatest Hits	1991	12.00
—Reissue with new name			
273	Dragstrip Riot	1991	15.00
094	Greatest Hits	1986	15.00
264	Prehistoric Fits	1990	15.00

UPSETTER

Number	Title	Yr	NM
UP56	A Hard Road to Follow	1983	30.00
UPCJ-34	No Questions Asked	1980	40.00

FLETCHER, SAM

VAULT

Number	Title	Yr	NM
LP-116 [M]	The Look of Love, the Sound of Soul	1967	30.00
VS-116 [S]	The Look of Love, the Sound of Soul	1967	30.00

VEE JAY

Number	Title	Yr	NM
LP-1094 [M]	Sam Fletcher Sings	1964	40.00

FLINT, SHELBY

MAD SATYR

Number	Title	Yr	NM
MSR-101	You've Been On My Mind	1982	30.00

VALIANT

Number	Title	Yr	NM
VL-5003 [M]	Cast Your Fate to the Wind	1966	30.00
VLS-25003 [S]	Cast Your Fate to the Wind	1966	30.00
LP-403 [M]	Shelby Flint Sings Folk	1962	50.00
LPS-403 [S]	Shelby Flint Sings Folk	1962	50.00
LP-401 [M]	Shelby Flint -- The Quiet Girl	1961	50.00

FLIPPER

4 MEN WITH BEARDS

Number	Title	Yr	NM
4M513LP [B]	Generic Flipper		25.00
4M514LP [B]	Gone Fishin'		25.00
4M515LP [B]	Public Flipper Limited: Live 1980-1985		30.00
4M516LP [B]	Sex Bomb Baby!		25.00

SUBTERRANEAN

Number	Title	Yr	NM
SUB25 [B]	Generic Flipper	1981	35.00
SUB42 [B]	Gone Fishin'	1982	35.00
SUB53 [B]	Public Flipper Ltd.	1985	35.00

FLIRTATIONS, THE (1)

DERAM

Number	Title	Yr	NM
DES-18028	Nothing But a Heartache	1969	25.00

FLIRTS, THE

CBS ASSOCIATED

Number	Title	Yr	NM
BFZ40197	Blondes, Brunettes and Redheads	1985	12.00
BFZ40419	Questions of the Heart	1986	12.00

O

Number	Title	Yr	NM
1	10 Cents a Dance	1982	18.00

PREPPY

Number	Title	Yr	NM
1217 [EP]	Heartbreak USA	1984	15.00

TELEFON

Number	Title	Yr	NM
8001	Made in America	1984	15.00

FLO AND EDDIE

COLUMBIA

Number	Title	Yr	NM
PC33554 [B]	Illegal, Immoral and Fattening	1975	18.00
PC34262 [B]	Moving Targets	1976	18.00

EPIPHANY

Number	Title	Yr	NM
ELP-4010 [B]	Rock Steady with Flo & Eddie	1981	30.00

REPRISE

Number	Title	Yr	NM
MS2141 [B]	Flo and Eddie	1973	30.00
MS2099 [B]	The Phlorescent Leech and Eddie	1972	30.00

RHINO

Number	Title	Yr	NM
RNTA-1999 [B]	History of Flo & Eddie	198?	40.00

FLOATERS, THE

ABC

Number	Title	Yr	NM
AB-1030	Floaters	1977	12.00
AA-1047	Magic	1978	12.00

FEE

Number	Title	Yr	NM
WW-711	Get Ready for the Floaters and Shu-Ga	1981	30.00

MCA

Number	Title	Yr	NM
3093	Into the Future	1979	12.00

FLOATING BRIDGE, THE

VAULT

Number	Title	Yr	NM
VS-124	The Floating Bridge	1969	100.00

FLOCK, THE

COLUMBIA

Number	Title	Yr	NM
C30007	Dinosaur Swamps	1970	25.00
—360 Sound" label			
C30007	Dinosaur Swamps	1970	18.00
—Orange label			
CS9911	The Flock	1969	25.00
—360 Sound" label			
CS9911	The Flock	1970	18.00
—Orange label			

MERCURY

Number	Title	Yr	NM
SRM-1-1035	Inside Out	1975	18.00

FLOCK OF SEAGULLS, A

JIVE

Number	Title	Yr	NM
1009-1-J	A Dream Come True	1986	10.00
—Reissue			
JL8-8411	A Dream Come True	1986	12.00
VA66000	A Flock of Seagulls	1982	15.00
—Original issue			
1007-1-J	A Flock of Seagulls	1986	10.00
—Reissue			
VA33003	A Flock of Seagulls	1983	12.00
—Second edition			
JL8-8013	Listen	1983	12.00
—Early reissue of 33004			
1008-1-J	Listen	1986	10.00
—Reissue			
VA33004	Listen	1983	18.00
—Original issue			
1034-1-J	The Best of A Flock of Seagulls	1987	15.00
JL8-8250	The Story of a Young Heart	1984	12.00

FLORENCE, BOB

CARLTON

Number	Title	Yr	NM
LP 12-115 [M]	Name Band: 1959	1959	40.00
STLP 12-115 [S]	Name Band: 1959	1959	60.00

DISCOVERY

Number	Title	Yr	NM
DS-832	Westlake	1982	12.00

ERA

Number	Title	Yr	NM
EL-20003 [M]	Bob Florence and Trio	1956	100.00

TREND

Number	Title	Yr	NM
TR-523	Live at Concerts by the Sea	1980	12.00
TR-536	Magic Time	1984	12.00
TR-545	Trash Can City	1987	12.00

WORLD PACIFIC

Number	Title	Yr	NM
WPS-21860 [S]	Pet Project: The Bob Florence Big Band Plays Petula Clark Hits	196?	30.00
WP-1860 [M]	Pet Project: The Bob Florence Big Band Plays Petula Clark Hits	196?	25.00

FLORES, CHUCK

CONCORD JAZZ

Number	Title	Yr	NM
CJ-49	Drum Flower	1978	15.00

DONRE

Number	Title	Yr	NM
1001	Flores Azules	1976	15.00

FLORES, ROSIE

REPRISE

Number	Title	Yr	NM
25626	Rosie Flores	1987	10.00

FLORY, MED

JOSIE

Number	Title	Yr	NM
JOZ-3506 [M]	Med Flory Big Band	1963	30.00
JJS-3506 [S]	Med Flory Big Band	1963	25.00

JUBILEE

Number	Title	Yr	NM
JLP-1066 [M]	Jazzwave	1958	50.00
SDJLP-1066 [S]	Jazzwave	1959	40.00

FLOW

CTI

Number	Title	Yr	NM
1003 [B]	Flow	1970	30.00

FLOWERS, PHIL

GUEST STAR

Number	Title	Yr	NM
G-1456 [M]	I Am the Greatest	1964	30.00
GS-1456 [S]	I Am the Greatest	1964	40.00
G-1457 [M]	Phil Flowers Sings a Tribute	1964	30.00
GS-1457 [S]	Phil Flowers Sings a Tribute	1964	40.00

MOUNT VERNON

Number	Title	Yr	NM
154 [M]	Rhythm and Blues	196?	30.00

FLOYD, EDDIE

MALACO

Number	Title	Yr	NM
6352	Experience	1977	15.00

STAX

Number	Title	Yr	NM
STS-3016	Baby Lay Your Head Down	1973	30.00
STS-2029	California Girl	1970	30.00
STX-4122	Chronicle	1979	15.00
STS-2041 [B]	Down to Earth	1971	30.00
STS-2002	I've Never Found a Girl	1968	30.00
714 [M]	Knock on Wood	1967	100.00

Number	Title	Yr	NM
❑ ST714 [S]	Knock on Wood	1967	70.00
❑ STS-2011	Rare Stamps	1969	30.00
❑ STS-5512	Soul Street	1974	30.00
❑ MPS-8527	Soul Street	198?	12.00
❑ STS-2017	You've Got to Have Eddie	1969	30.00

FLOYD, KING

CHIMNEYVILLE
❑ SD9047	King Floyd	1971	18.00

PULSAR
❑ 10602	A Man in Love	1969	25.00

V.I.P.
❑ 407	The Heart of the Matter	1970	40.00

FLYING BURRITO BROTHERS, THE

4 MEN WITH BEARDS
❑ 4M153LP [B]	Burrito Deluxe		25.00
❑ 4M135LP [B]	The Gilded Palace of Sin		25.00

A&M
❑ SP-4258	Burrito Deluxe	1970	18.00
— Brown label			
❑ SP-4258	Burrito Deluxe	1974	15.00
— Silvery label			
❑ SP-3631 [B]	Close Up the Honky-Tonks	1974	30.00
❑ SP-6510	Close Up the Honky-Tonks	198?	15.00
— Reissue of 3631			
❑ SP-8070 [DJ]	Hot Burrito	1975	40.00
— Promo-only issue with poster			
❑ SP-4343	Last of the Red Hot Burritos	1972	18.00
— Brown label			
❑ SP-4343	Last of the Red Hot Burritos	1974	15.00
— Silvery label			
❑ SP-4578	Sleepless Nights	1976	15.00
— As "Gram Parsons/The Flying Burrito Bros."			
❑ SP-4295	The Flying Burrito Bros.	1971	18.00
— Brown label			
❑ SP-4295	The Flying Burrito Bros.	1974	15.00
— Silvery label			
❑ SP-4175	The Gilded Palace of Sin	1969	25.00
— Brown label			
❑ SP-4175	The Gilded Palace of Sin	1974	15.00
— Silvery label			
❑ SP-3122	The Gilded Palace of Sin	198?	10.00
— Budget-line reissue			

COLUMBIA
❑ PC34222	Airborne	1976	15.00
❑ PC33817	Flying Again	1976	15.00

CURB
❑ JZ37004	Hearts on the Line	1981	12.00
— As "Burrito Brothers"			
❑ FZ37705	Sunset Sundown	1982	12.00
— As "Burrito Brothers"			

REGENCY
❑ REG-79001	Live from Tokyo	1980	12.00

FLYING ISLAND

VANGUARD
❑ VSD-79368	Another Kind of Space	197?	18.00
❑ VSD-79359	Flying Island	197?	18.00

FLYING LIZARDS, THE

VIRGIN
❑ VA13137	The Flying Lizards	1980	15.00

FLYING MACHINE, THE

JANUS
❑ JLS-3007	The Flying Machine	1969	25.00

FOCUS

ATCO
❑ SD 36-100	Hamburger Concerto	1974	15.00
❑ SD 36-117	Mother Focus	1975	15.00

HARVEST
❑ ST-11721	Focus Con Proby	1978	15.00
— With P.J. Proby			

MERCURY
❑ 824524-1	Focus: Jan Akkerman and Thijs Van Leer	1986	15.00

SIRE
❑ SASD-7505	Dutch Masters -- A Selection of Their Finest Recordings 1969-1973	1975	15.00
❑ SAS-3901	Focus 3	1973	18.00
❑ SES-97027	In and Out of Focus	1970	25.00
— Original issue			
❑ SAS-7404	In and Out of Focus	1973	15.00
— Reissue of 97027			
❑ SAS-7408	Live at the Rainbow	1973	15.00
❑ SAS-7401	Moving Waves	1972	15.00
❑ SASD-7531	Ship of Memories	1977	15.00

FOGEL, MARTY

CMP
❑ CMP-37-ST	Many Bobbing Heads, At Last	1990	15.00

FOGELBERG, DAN, AND TIM WEISBERG

FULL MOON/EPIC
❑ JE35339	Twin Sons of Different Mothers	1978	12.00
❑ PE35339	Twin Sons of Different Mothers	198?	10.00
— Budget-line reissue			
❑ HE45339	Twin Sons of Different Mothers	198?	30.00
— Half-speed mastered edition			

FOGELBERG, DAN

COLUMBIA
❑ KC31751	Home Free	1972	15.00
❑ PC31751	Home Free	197?	10.00
— Reissue with new prefix			

FULL MOON/EPIC
❑ PE33499	Captured Angel	1975	12.00
— No bar code on cover			
❑ PE33499	Captured Angel	198?	10.00
— With bar code on cover			
❑ PEQ33499 [Q]	Captured Angel	1975	25.00
❑ QE38308	Dan Fogelberg/Greatest Hits	1982	12.00
❑ HE48308	Dan Fogelberg/Greatest Hits	1983	30.00
— Half-speed mastered edition			
❑ OE40271	Exiles	1987	12.00
❑ FE39616	High Country Snows	1985	12.00
❑ A2S1335 [DJ]	Interchords	1982	30.00
— Promo-only release			
❑ PE34185	Nether Lands	1977	12.00
— No bar code on cover			
❑ PE34185	Nether Lands	198?	10.00
— With bar code on cover			
❑ FE35634	Phoenix	1979	12.00
❑ HE45634	Phoenix	1981	30.00
— Half-speed mastered edition			
❑ PE35364	Phoenix	198?	10.00
— Budget-line reissue			
❑ KE33137	Souvenirs	1974	15.00
— First pressings have orange Epic label with small Full Moon logo			
❑ KE33137	Souvenirs	1975	15.00
— Second pressings have dark blue/black Full Moon label			
❑ PE33137	Souvenirs	197?	10.00
— Reissue with new prefix			
❑ KE237393	The Innocent Age	1981	15.00
❑ AS1284 [DJ]	The Innocent Age Sampler	1982	15.00
— Promo only; 6 songs			
❑ QE39004	Windows and Walls	1984	12.00

FOGERTY, JOHN

❑ 7E-1046	John Fogerty	1975	15.00

FANTASY
❑ MPF-4502	John Fogerty: The Blue Ridge Rangers	1981	12.00
— Reissues prominently place John Fogerty's name on the cover			
❑ FLP-30523	Revival	2007	18.00
❑ F-9415	The Blue Ridge Rangers	1973	18.00
— As "The Blue Ridge Rangers"			

WARNER BROS.
❑ 25203	Centerfield	1985	18.00
— Originals have the last song on side 2 as "Zanz Kant Danz"			
❑ 25203	Centerfield	1986	12.00
— Later editions have the last song on side 2 re-recorded and listed as "Vanz Kant Danz"			
❑ 25203 [DJ]	Centerfield	1985	30.00
— Promo versions on Quiex II audiophile vinyl			
❑ 25449	Eye of the Zombie	1986	12.00

FOGERTY, TOM

FANTASY
❑ 9611	Deal It Out	1981	12.00
❑ 9413	Excalibur	1972	18.00
❑ 9469	Myopia	1974	15.00
❑ 9407	Tom Fogerty	1972	18.00
❑ 9448	Zephyr National	1974	15.00

FOGHAT

BEARSVILLE
❑ BHS6990	Boogie Motel	1979	12.00
❑ BR6950	Energized	1974	12.00
❑ BR2077	Foghat	1972	15.00
❑ BR2136	Foghat	1973	15.00
❑ BRK6971	Foghat Live	1977	12.00
❑ BR6959	Fool for the City	1975	12.00
❑ BRK6980	Fool for the City	1978	10.00
— Reissue of 6959			
❑ BRK3578	Girls to Chat & Boys to Bounce	1981	12.00
❑ 23747	In the Mood for Something Rude	1982	12.00
❑ BR6962	Night Shift	1976	12.00
❑ BR6956	Rock and Roll Outlaws	1974	12.00
❑ BRK6977	Stone Blue	1978	12.00
❑ BHS6999	Tight Shoes	1980	12.00
❑ 23888	Zig-Zag Walk	1983	12.00

RHINO
❑ RNLP-70883	Energized	1988	10.00
— Reissue of Bearsville 6950			
❑ RNLP-70887	Foghat	1988	10.00
— Reissue of Bearsville 2077			
❑ R1-70890	Foghat	1988	10.00
— Reissue of Bearsville 2136			
❑ RNLP-70884	Foghat Live	1988	10.00
— Reissue of Bearsville 6971			
❑ RNLP-70882	Fool for the City	1987	10.00
— Reissue of Bearsville 6980			
❑ RNLP-70888	Night Shift	1988	10.00
— Reissue of Bearsville 6962			
❑ R1-70889	Rock and Roll Outlaws	1988	10.00
— Reissue of Bearsville 6956			
❑ RNLP-70881	Stone Blue	1987	10.00
— Reissue of Bearsville 6977			
❑ R1-70088	The Best of Foghat	1989	12.00

TPM/RHINO EXCLUSIVE
❑ 295	Fool for the City	2008	25.00

FOL, RAYMOND

PHILIPS
❑ PHM200198 [M]	Vivaldi's Four Seasons in Jazz	1966	15.00
❑ PHS600198 [S]	Vivaldi's Four Seasons in Jazz	1966	18.00

FOLDS, BEN, FIVE

550 MUSIC
❑ B68809	Fear of Pop Volume 1	1998	18.00
— By Ben Folds with numerous guests			
❑ B69808	The Unauthorized Biography of Reinhold Messner	1999	18.00
❑ B67762	Whatever and Ever, Amen	1997	40.00

EPIC
❑ E261610	Rockin' the Suburbs	2001	30.00

SUNDAZED
❑ LP5164	Ben Folds Live	2003	25.00

FOLEY, LORD ADRIAN

MGM
❑ E-3358 [M]	Lord Adrian Foley at the Piano	1955	40.00

FOLEY, RED

DECCA
❑ DL8296 [M]	Beyond the Sunset	1956	50.00
❑ DL4140 [M]	Company's Comin'	1961	25.00
❑ DL74140 [S]	Company's Comin'	1961	30.00
❑ DL4290 [M]	Dear Hearts and Gentle People	1962	25.00
❑ DL74290 [S]	Dear Hearts and Gentle People	1962	30.00
❑ DL38068 [M]	Gratefully	1958	100.00
— Special-products issue for Dickies clothing			
❑ DL8767 [M]	He Walks with Thee	1958	50.00
❑ DL8903 [M]	Let's All Sing to Him	1959	40.00
❑ DL78903 [S]	Let's All Sing to Him	1959	50.00
❑ DL8847 [M]	Let's All Sing with Red Foley	1959	40.00
❑ DL78847 [S]	Let's All Sing with Red Foley	1959	50.00
❑ DL5338 [10]	Lift Up Your Voice	1952	80.00
❑ DL8806 [M]	My Keepsake Album	1958	50.00
❑ DL4107 [M]	Red Foley's Golden Favorites	1961	25.00
❑ DL74107 [S]	Red Foley's Golden Favorites	1961	30.00
❑ DL5003 [M]	Red Foley's Greatest Hits	1968	50.00
— White label promo; mono copies may only exist as promos			
❑ DL75003 [S]	Red Foley's Greatest Hits	1968	18.00
❑ DL5303 [10]	Red Foley Souvenir Album	1951	80.00
❑ DL8294 [M]	Red Foley Souvenir Album	1956	50.00
❑ DL4603 [M]	Songs Everybody Knows	1965	25.00
❑ DL74603 [S]	Songs Everybody Knows	1965	30.00
❑ DL4849 [M]	Songs for the Soul	1967	30.00
❑ DL74849 [S]	Songs for the Soul	1967	25.00
❑ DL4198 [M]	Songs of Devotion	1961	25.00
❑ DL74198 [S]	Songs of Devotion	1961	30.00
❑ DL4341 [M]	The Red Foley Show	1963	25.00
❑ DL74341 [S]	The Red Foley Show	1963	30.00
❑ DXB177 [M]	The Red Foley Story	1964	30.00
❑ DXSB7177 [S]	The Red Foley Story	1964	30.00

FOLK SINGERS, THE

ELEKTRA
❑ EKL-157 [M]	The Folk Singers	1958	30.00

FOLKNIKS, THE

HIFI-LIFE SERIES
❑ L-1017 [M]	The Sound of Twelve-String Guitar and Banjo	1964	25.00
❑ SL-1017 [S]	The Sound of Twelve-String Guitar and Banjo	1964	30.00

FOLKSWINGERS, THE

WORLD PACIFIC
❑ WP-1812 [M]	12 String Guitar!	1963	30.00
❑ ST-1812 [S]	12 String Guitar!	1963	30.00
— Black vinyl			
❑ ST-1812 [S]	12 String Guitar!	1963	60.00
— Red vinyl			
❑ WP-1814 [M]	12 String Guitar, Volume 2	1963	30.00

Number	Title	Yr	NM
❑ ST-1814 [S]	12 String Guitar, Volume 2	1963	30.00
❑ WP-1846 [M]	Raga Rock	1966	75.00
❑ ST-1846 [S]	Raga Rock	1966	75.00

FONDA, HENRY

CORAL

Number	Title	Yr	NM
❑ CRL57308 [M]	Voices of the 20th Century	1958	60.00

FONTAINE, FRANK

ABC-PARAMOUNT

Number	Title	Yr	NM
❑ 541 [M]	All Time Great Hits	1966	18.00
❑ S-541 [S]	All Time Great Hits	1966	25.00
❑ 470 [M]	How Sweet It Is	1964	18.00
❑ S-470 [S]	How Sweet It Is	1964	25.00
❑ 514 [M]	I'm Counting on You	1965	18.00
❑ S-514 [S]	I'm Counting on You	1965	25.00
❑ 490 [M]	More Songs I Sing on the Jackie Gleason Show	1964	18.00
❑ S-490 [S]	More Songs I Sing on the Jackie Gleason Show	1964	25.00
❑ 460 [M]	Sings Like Crazy	1963	18.00
❑ S-460 [S]	Sings Like Crazy	1963	25.00
❑ 442 [M]	Songs I Sing on the Jackie Gleason Show	1963	18.00
❑ S-442 [S]	Songs I Sing on the Jackie Gleason Show	1963	25.00
❑ T-90121 [M]	Songs I Sing on the Jackie Gleason Show	1964	25.00

—Capitol Record Club edition

MGM

Number	Title	Yr	NM
❑ E-4470 [M]	Frank Fontaine's Ireland	1967	15.00
❑ SE-4470 [S]	Frank Fontaine's Ireland	1967	18.00

FONTANA, WAYNE, AND THE MINDBENDERS

FONTANA

Number	Title	Yr	NM
❑ MGF-27542 [M]	The Game of Love	1965	30.00
❑ SRF-67542 [R]	The Game of Love	1965	30.00

FONTANA, WAYNE

MGM

Number	Title	Yr	NM
❑ E-4459 [M]	Wayne Fontana	1967	35.00
❑ SE-4459 [S]	Wayne Fontana	1967	30.00

FONTANE SISTERS, THE

DOT

Number	Title	Yr	NM
❑ DLP-3042 [M]	A Visit with the Fontane Sisters	1957	30.00
❑ DLP-104 [10]	The Fontane Sisters	1955	50.00
❑ DLP-3004 [M]	The Fontanes Sing	1956	40.00

—Maroon label

Number	Title	Yr	NM
❑ DLP-3004 [M]	The Fontanes Sing	1957	30.00

—Black label

Number	Title	Yr	NM
❑ DLP-3531 [M]	The Tips of My Fingers	1963	18.00
❑ DLP-25531 [S]	The Tips of My Fingers	1963	25.00

FOO FIGHTERS

ROSWELL/CAPITOL

Number	Title	Yr	NM
❑ C1-34027	Foo Fighters	1995	30.00
❑ 55832	The Colour and the Shape	1997	60.00

ROSWELL/RCA

Number	Title	Yr	NM
❑ 82876-68038-1	In Your Honor	2005	40.00

—Box set; all four records play at 45 rpm

Number	Title	Yr	NM
❑ 07863-68008-1 [10]	One By One	2002	25.00
❑ 07863-67892-1 [B]	There Is Nothing Left to Lose	1999	30.00

FOOD

CAPITOL

Number	Title	Yr	NM
❑ ST-304	Forever Is a Dream	1969	140.00

FOOL, THE

MERCURY

Number	Title	Yr	NM
❑ SR-61178	The Fool	1968	30.00

FOOLS, THE

EMI AMERICA

Number	Title	Yr	NM
❑ SW-17046	Heavy Mental	1981	15.00
❑ SW-17024	Sold Out	1980	15.00
❑ SPRO-9393/4 [DJ]	The First Annual Official Unofficial April Fools Day Live Bootleg...	1980	25.00

PVC

Number	Title	Yr	NM
❑ 8962	Wake Up... It's Alive	1987	18.00
❑ 8962	Wake Up ... It's Alive!!!	1987	18.00
❑ 8930	World Dance Party	1985	18.00

FOOLS GOLD

COLUMBIA

Number	Title	Yr	NM
❑ PC34828	Mr. Lucky	1977	15.00

MORNING SKY

Number	Title	Yr	NM
❑ ML5500	Fools Gold	1976	15.00

FORBERT, STEVE

GEFFEN

Number	Title	Yr	NM
❑ GHS24194	Streets of This Town	1988	12.00

NEMPEROR

Number	Title	Yr	NM
❑ JZ35538	Alive on Arrival	1978	12.00

—Original prefix

Number	Title	Yr	NM
❑ PZ35538	Alive on Arrival	1980	10.00

—Budget-line reissue with new prefix

Number	Title	Yr	NM
❑ JZ36191	Jackrabbit Slim	1979	12.00
❑ JZ36595	Little Stevie Orbit	1980	12.00
❑ ARZ37434	Steve Forbert	1982	12.00

FORBES, GRAHAM

PHILLIPS INTERNATIONAL

Number	Title	Yr	NM
❑ PLP-1955 [M]	The Martini Set	1959	800.00

FORCE M.D.'S

TOMMY BOY

Number	Title	Yr	NM
❑ TBLP1010	Chillin'	1985	12.00
❑ TBLP1003	Love Letters	1984	15.00
❑ 25893	Step to Me	1990	18.00
❑ 25631	Touch and Go	1987	12.00

FORCE OF NATURE

PHILADELPHIA INT'L.

Number	Title	Yr	NM
❑ PZ34123 [B]	Unemployment Blues	1976	30.00

FORD, FRANKIE

ACE

Number	Title	Yr	NM
❑ LP1005 [M]	Let's Take a Sea Cruise	1959	300.00

BRIARMEADE

Number	Title	Yr	NM
❑ BR-5002	Frankie Ford	1976	15.00

FORD, LITA

MERCURY

Number	Title	Yr	NM
❑ 818864-1	Dancin' on the Edge	1984	12.00
❑ 810331-1	Out for Blood	1984	30.00

—Original cover has Lita holding a bloody, gored guitar

Number	Title	Yr	NM
❑ 810331-1	Out for Blood	1984	10.00

—Reissue cover has a different photo of Lita holding a non-bloody guitar

RCA

Number	Title	Yr	NM
❑ 6397-1-R [B]	Lita	1988	12.00
❑ 2090-1-R	Stiletto	1990	12.00

FORD, MARY

CHALLENGE

Number	Title	Yr	NM
❑ CHL-623 [M]	A Brand New Ford	1966	30.00
❑ CHS-2623 [S]	A Brand New Ford	1966	30.00

FORD, NEAL, AND THE FANATICS

HICKORY

Number	Title	Yr	NM
❑ LPS-141	Neal Ford and the Fanatics	1968	35.00

FORD, RICKY

MUSE

Number	Title	Yr	NM
❑ MR-5227	Flying Colors	1981	12.00
❑ MR-5296	Future's Gold	198?	12.00
❑ MR-5275	Interpretations	198?	12.00
❑ MR-5322	Looking Ahead	1987	12.00
❑ MR-5188	Manhattan Plaza	1979	15.00
❑ MR-5349	Saxotic Stomp	1988	12.00
❑ MR-5314	Shorter Ideas	1985	12.00
❑ MR-5250	Tenor for the Times	1982	12.00

NEW WORLD

Number	Title	Yr	NM
❑ 204	Loxodonta Africana	1977	18.00

FORD, RITA

COLUMBIA

Number	Title	Yr	NM
❑ CL1698 [M]	A Music Box Christmas	1961	25.00

—Black and red label with six "eye" logos

Number	Title	Yr	NM
❑ CS8498 [R]	A Music Box Christmas	1961	18.00
❑ CS9738	The Story of Christmas	1968	15.00

EPIC

Number	Title	Yr	NM
❑ LN24022 [M]	Music Box Wonderland Christmas with Rita Ford's Music Boxes	1962	25.00
❑ BN26022 [R]	Music Box Wonderland Christmas with Rita Ford's Music Boxes	1962	18.00

HARMONY

Number	Title	Yr	NM
❑ KH31577	Christmas with Rita Ford's Music Boxes	1972	15.00

—Reissue of Epic BN 26022

FORD, ROCKY BILLY

AUDIO LAB

Number	Title	Yr	NM
❑ AL-1561 [M]	A New Singing Star	1960	150.00

FORD, TENNESSEE ERNIE

CAPITOL

Number	Title	Yr	NM
❑ SVBB-11326	25th Anniversary/Hymns & Gospel	1974	15.00
❑ SVBB-11325	25th Anniversary/Yesterday and Today	1974	15.00
❑ ST-730	Abide with Me	1971	15.00
❑ T1272 [M]	A Friend We Have	1959	18.00
❑ ST1272 [S]	A Friend We Have	1959	25.00
❑ T2681 [M]	Aloha from Tennessee Ernie Ford	1967	18.00
❑ ST2681 [S]	Aloha from Tennessee Ernie Ford	1967	15.00
❑ STAO-412	America the Beautiful	1970	15.00
❑ SM-412	America the Beautiful	197?	10.00

—Reissue with new prefix

Number	Title	Yr	NM
❑ SKAO2949	Best Hymns	1968	15.00
❑ T1794 [M]	Book of Favorite Hymns	1962	18.00
❑ ST1794 [S]	Book of Favorite Hymns	1962	25.00
❑ SM-12033	Book of Favorite Hymns	1980	12.00
❑ ST-831 [S]	C-H-R-I-S-T-M-A-S	1971	15.00
❑ STBB-485	Christmas Special	1970	18.00
❑ T1539 [M]	Civil War Songs of the North	1961	18.00
❑ ST1539 [S]	Civil War Songs of the North	1961	25.00
❑ T1540 [M]	Civil War Songs of the South	1961	18.00
❑ ST1540 [S]	Civil War Songs of the South	1961	25.00
❑ T2097 [M]	Country Hits…Feelin' Blue	1964	15.00
❑ ST2097 [S]	Country Hits…Feelin' Blue	1964	18.00
❑ SM-2097	Country Hits…Feelin' Blue	197?	10.00

—Reissue with new prefix

Number	Title	Yr	NM
❑ ST-583	Everything Is Beautiful	1971	15.00
❑ T2761 [M]	Faith of Our Fathers	1967	18.00
❑ ST2761 [S]	Faith of Our Fathers	1967	15.00
❑ SM-2761	Faith of Our Fathers	197?	10.00

—Reissue with new prefix

Number	Title	Yr	NM
❑ T1227 [M]	Gather 'Round	1959	18.00
❑ ST1227 [S]	Gather 'Round	1959	25.00
❑ T2618 [M]	God Lives	1966	15.00
❑ ST2618 [S]	God Lives	1966	18.00
❑ SN-16042	Gospel	1981	10.00
❑ T2026 [M]	Great Gospel Songs	1964	15.00
❑ ST2026 [S]	Great Gospel Songs	1964	18.00
❑ SM-2026	Great Gospel Songs	197?	10.00

—Reissue with new prefix

Number	Title	Yr	NM
❑ T1684 [M]	Here Comes the Mississippi Showboat	1962	15.00
❑ ST1684 [S]	Here Comes the Mississippi Showboat	1962	18.00
❑ ST-334	Holy, Holy, Holy	1969	15.00
❑ T756 [M]	Hymns	1956	30.00

—Turquoise label

Number	Title	Yr	NM
❑ T756 [M]	Hymns	1959	25.00

—Black label with colorband, logo at left

Number	Title	Yr	NM
❑ T756 [M]	Hymns	1962	18.00

—Black label with colorband, logo at top

Number	Title	Yr	NM
❑ ST756 [S]	Hymns	1962	18.00

—Re-recording of the original mono LP

Number	Title	Yr	NM
❑ SN-16043	Hymns	1981	10.00
❑ SN-16173	Hymns	1981	10.00
❑ T1694 [M]	Hymns at Home	1962	15.00
❑ ST1694 [S]	Hymns at Home	1962	18.00
❑ T1751 [M]	I Love to Tell the Story	1962	15.00
❑ ST1751 [S]	I Love to Tell the Story	1962	18.00
❑ ST-11092	It's Tennessee Ernie Ford	1973	12.00
❑ T2296 [M]	Let Me Walk with Thee	1965	15.00
❑ ST2296 [S]	Let Me Walk with Thee	1965	18.00
❑ SF-8-0508	Let Me Walk with Thee	1970	18.00

—Capitol Record Club edition

Number	Title	Yr	NM
❑ T1875 [M]	Long Long Ago	1963	15.00
❑ ST1875 [S]	Long Long Ago	1963	18.00
❑ ST-11290	Make a Joyful Noise	1974	12.00
❑ ST-11001	Mr. Words and Music	1972	12.00
❑ T2444 [M]	My Favorite Things	1966	15.00
❑ ST2444 [S]	My Favorite Things	1966	18.00
❑ T1005 [M]	Nearer the Cross	1958	25.00

—Black label with colorband, logo at left

Number	Title	Yr	NM
❑ T1005 [M]	Nearer the Cross	1962	18.00

—Black label with colorband, logo at top

Number	Title	Yr	NM
❑ ST1005 [S]	Nearer the Cross	1959	30.00

—Black label with colorband, logo at left

Number	Title	Yr	NM
❑ ST1005 [S]	Nearer the Cross	1962	25.00

—Black label with colorband, logo at top

Number	Title	Yr	NM
❑ ST2968	O Come All Ye Faithful	1968	15.00
❑ T888 [M]	Ol' Rockin' Ern	1957	50.00

—Turquoise or gray label

Number	Title	Yr	NM
❑ T2845 [M]	Our Garden of Hymns	1968	25.00
❑ ST2845 [S]	Our Garden of Hymns	1968	15.00
❑ SVBB-11382	Precious Memories	1975	15.00
❑ TAO1332 [M]	Sing a Hymn with Me	1960	25.00

—With hymnal

Number	Title	Yr	NM
❑ STAO1332 [S]	Sing a Hymn with Me	1960	30.00

—With hymnal

Number	Title	Yr	NM
❑ T1679 [M]	Sing a Hymn with Me	1962	15.00

—Reissue of 1332 with standard cover?

Number	Title	Yr	NM
❑ ST1679 [S]	Sing a Hymn with Me	1962	18.00

—Reissue of 1332 with standard cover?

Number	Title	Yr	NM
❑ T1680 [M]	Sing a Spiritual with Me	1962	15.00
❑ ST1680 [S]	Sing a Spiritual with Me	1962	18.00
❑ T2394 [M]	Sing We Now of Christmas	1965	15.00
❑ ST2394 [S]	Sing We Now of Christmas	1965	18.00

—Same as above, but in stereo

Number	Title	Yr	NM
❑ T1380 [M]	Sixteen Tons	1960	18.00
❑ DT1380 [R]	Sixteen Tons	196?	15.00
❑ ST-127	Songs I Like to Sing	1969	15.00
❑ T818 [M]	Spirituals	1957	30.00

—Turquoise label

Number	Title	Yr	NM
❑ T818 [M]	Spirituals	1959	25.00

—Black label with colorband, logo at left

Number	Title	Yr	NM
❑ T818 [M]	Spirituals	1962	18.00

—Black label with colorband, logo at top

Number	Title	Yr	NM
❑ ST818 [S]	Spirituals	1962	18.00

—Re-recording of the original mono LP

Number	Title	Yr	NM
❑ SN-16174	Spirituals	1981	10.00
❑ SF-8-0507	Sweet Hour of Prayer	1970	18.00

—Capitol Record Club edition

Number	Title	Yr	NM
❑ STBB-506	Sweet Hour of Prayer/Let Me Walk with Thee	1971	18.00

Number	Title	Yr	NM
❏ T841 [M]	Tennessee Ernie Ford Favorites	1958	25.00

— *Black label with colorband, logo at left*

❏ T841 [M]	Tennessee Ernie Ford Favorites	1962	18.00

— *Black label with colorband, logo at top*

❏ DT841 [R]	Tennessee Ernie Ford Favorites	196?	15.00
❏ T841 [M]	Tennessee Ernie Ford Favorites	1957	30.00

— *Turquoise label*

❏ ST-11232	Tennessee Ernie Ford Sings About Jesus	1973	12.00
❏ ST-11495	Tennessee Ernie Ford Sings His Great Love Songs	1975	12.00
❏ ST-833	The Folk Album	1971	15.00
❏ T1071 [M]	The Star Carol	1958	30.00

— *Black labels with colorband, "Capitol" logo on left*

❏ ST1071 [S]	The Star Carol	1958	30.00

— *Black labels with colorband, Capitol logo on left*

❏ T1071 [M]	The Star Carol	1962	18.00

— *Black label with colorband, logo on top*

❏ ST1071 [S]	The Star Carol	1962	25.00

— *Black label with colorband, "Capitol" logo on top. This was also reissued on later Capitol labels into the 1970s with values no more than half the above.*

❏ SN-16289	The Star Carol	1982	10.00

— *Budget-line reissue*

❏ T1994 [M]	The Story of Christmas	1963	18.00

— *With the Roger Wagner Chorale*

❏ ST1994 [S]	The Story of Christmas	1963	25.00
❏ STCL2942	The Tennessee Ernie Ford Deluxe Set	1968	25.00
❏ ST2896	The World of Pop and Country Hits	1968	15.00
❏ TBL2183 [M]	The World's Best Loved Hymns	1964	25.00
❏ STBL2183 [S]	The World's Best Loved Hymns	1964	30.00
❏ T700 [M]	This Lusty Land	1956	30.00

— *Turquoise label*

❏ T700 [M]	This Lusty Land	1959	25.00

— *Black label with colorband, logo at left*

❏ T700 [M]	This Lusty Land!	1963	18.00

— *Black label with colorband, logo at top*

❏ DT700 [R]	This Lusty Land!	196?	15.00
❏ T1937 [M]	We Gather Together	1963	15.00
❏ ST1937 [S]	We Gather Together	1963	18.00
❏ T2557 [M]	Wonderful Peace	1966	15.00
❏ ST2557 [S]	Wonderful Peace	1966	18.00
❏ SN-16040	Yesterday	1981	10.00

EVEREST ARCHIVE OF FOLK & JAZZ

❏ 279	Tennessee Ernie Ford	197?	12.00

PICKWICK

❏ SPC-3308	Amazing Grace	197?	12.00
❏ SPC-3047	Bless Your Pea-Pickin' Heart	196?	15.00
❏ PTP-2050	Hymns	197?	15.00
❏ SPC-3066	I Love You So Much	196?	15.00
❏ SPC-3273	Jesus Loves Me	197?	12.00
❏ SPC-3353	Rock of Ages	197?	12.00
❏ SPC-3268	Sixteen Tons	197?	12.00
❏ PTP-2016	Tennessee Ernie Ford	197?	15.00
❏ SPC-3222	The Need for Prayer	197?	12.00

RANWOOD

❏ RLP 7026	Tennessee Ernie Ford Sings 22 Favorite Hymns	198?	15.00

WORD

❏ 8764	He Touched Me	1978	12.00
❏ 8798	Swing Wide Your Golden Gate	198?	12.00
❏ 8841	Tell Me the Old Story	1979	12.00
❏ 8841	Tell Me the Old Story	198?	12.00
❏ 8858	There's a Song in My Heart	198?	12.00

FORD THEATRE, THE

ABC

❏ S-681	Time Changes	1969	25.00
❏ S-658	Trilogy	1968	75.00

FORDHAM, JULIA

VIRGIN

❏ 90955	Julia Fordham	1988	12.00
❏ 91325	Porcelain	1989	15.00

FOREFRONT, THE

AFI

❏ 21557	Incantation	197?	25.00

FOREIGNER

ATLANTIC

❏ SD16999	4	1981	12.00

— *First pressings have a hologram sticker on the upper back cover*

❏ SD16999 [B]	4	1982	10.00

— *No hologram sticker on back cover*

❏ 81999	Agent Provocateur	1984	10.00
❏ SD19999	Double Vision	1978	15.00

— *Original cover is mostly brown with the words "Double Vision" barely visible along the bottom edge of front cover*

❏ SD19999	Double Vision	1979	10.00

— *Third cover is the same as the second cover, but has a red tint*

❏ SD19999	Double Vision	1978	12.00

— *Second cover has a blue tint with the words "Double Vision" right under the band name*

❏ SD19109 [B]	Foreigner	1977	10.00

— *Reissue of 18215*

❏ SD18215	Foreigner	1977	12.00
❏ SD29999	Head Games	1979	12.00
❏ 81808	Inside Information	1988	10.00
❏ 80999	Records	1982	12.00
❏ A1-82299	Unusual Heat	1990	30.00

— *U.S. vinyl available only through Columbia House*

MOBILE FIDELITY

❏ 1-052	Double Vision	1981	50.00

— *Audiophile vinyl*

FOREST

HARVEST

❏ SKAO-419 [B]	Forest	1970	80.00

FORETICH, HERMAN

AUDIOPHILE

❏ AP-124	Herman Foretich and His Atlanta Swing Quartet	196?	18.00

JAZZOLOGY

❏ J-144	The Foretich Four	1987	12.00

FOREVER MORE

RCA VICTOR

❏ LSP-4425	Words on Black Plastic	1971	18.00
❏ LSP-4272	Yours Forever More	1970	18.00

FORGOTTEN CHILD

BLUE LAMPION

❏ BLM10001	Forgotten Child	1986	60.00

FORMAN, BRUCE, AND GEORGE CABLES

CONCORD JAZZ

❏ CJ-279	Dynamics	1985	12.00

FORMAN, BRUCE

CHOICE

❏ 1026	Coast to Coast	1980	15.00

CONCORD JAZZ

❏ CJ-251	Full Circle	1984	12.00
❏ CJ-368	Pardon Me!	1989	15.00
❏ CJ-332	There Are Times	1988	12.00

MUSE

❏ MR-5273	20/20	1982	12.00
❏ MR-5299	In Transit	1982	12.00
❏ MR-5251	River Journey	1981	12.00
❏ MR-5315	The Bash	1985	12.00

FORMAN, MITCHELL

MAGENTA

❏ MA-0201	Train of Thought	198?	15.00

SOUL NOTE

❏ SN 1050	Childhood Dreams	198?	15.00
❏ SN-1070	Only a Memory	198?	15.00

FORMULA V

BURLINGUEN

❏ (# unknown)0	Formula V	197?	30.00

MIAMI

❏ 6076	Formula V	197?	30.00

FORREST, EUGENE "FLIP"

SAVOY

❏ MG-14392	I Heard It on the Radio	197?	25.00

FORREST, HELEN, AND DICK HAYMES

MCA

❏ 1546	Long Ago and Far Away	198?	15.00

FORREST, HELEN

AUDIOPHILE

❏ AP-47	On the Sunny Side of the Street	1958	60.00

CAPITOL

❏ T704 [M]	Voice of the Name Bands	1956	50.00

— *Turquoise label*

JOYCE

❏ 6008	Big Bands' Greatest Vocalists, Vol. 2	197?	18.00
❏ 6012	Big Bands' Greatest Vocalists, Vol. 4	197?	18.00
❏ 6019	Big Bands' Greatest Vocalists, Vol. 7	197?	18.00
❏ 6021	Big Bands' Greatest Vocalists, Vol. 8	197?	18.00

STASH

❏ ST-225	Now and Forever	198?	18.00

FORREST, JIMMY, AND MILES DAVIS

PRESTIGE

❏ PRST-7858	Live at the Barrel	197?	18.00
❏ PRST-7860	Live at the Barrel, Volume 2	197?	18.00

FORREST, JIMMY

DELMARK

❏ DL-404	All the Gin Is Gone	196?	25.00
❏ DL-427	Black Forrest	1972	18.00
❏ DL-435	Night Train	197?	18.00

FANTASY

❏ OJC-199	Forrest Fire	1985	15.00
❏ OJC-350	Most Much!	198?	15.00
❏ OJC-097	Out of the Forrest	198?	15.00

NEW JAZZ

❏ NJLP-8250 [M]	Forrest Fire	1960	100.00

— *Purple label*

❏ NJLP-8250 [M]	Forrest Fire	1965	50.00

— *Blue label with trident logo at right*

❏ NJLP-8293 [M]	Soul Street	1962	100.00

— *Purple label*

❏ NJLP-8293 [M]	Soul Street	1965	50.00

— *Blue label with trident logo at right*

PALO ALTO

❏ 8021	Heart of the Forrest	1982	15.00

PRESTIGE

❏ PRLP-7218 [M]	Most Much!	1961	80.00

— *Yellow label*

❏ PRLP-7218 [M]	Most Much!	1965	40.00

— *Blue label with trident logo at right*

❏ PRLP-7202 [M]	Out of the Forrest	1961	80.00

— *Yellow label*

❏ PRLP-7202 [M]	Out of the Forrest	1965	40.00

— *Blue label with trident logo at right*

❏ PRLP-7235 [M]	Sit Down and Relax with Jimmy Forrest	1962	80.00

— *Yellow label*

❏ PRLP-7235 [M]	Sit Down and Relax with Jimmy Forrest	1965	40.00

— *Blue label with trident logo at right*

❏ PRST-7235 [S]	Sit Down and Relax with Jimmy Forrest	1962	100.00

— *Silver label*

❏ PRST-7235 [S]	Sit Down and Relax with Jimmy Forrest	1965	50.00

— *Blue label with trident logo at right*

❏ PRST-7235 [S]	Sit Down and Relax with Jimmy Forrest	1973	30.00

— *Green label reissue*

❏ PRST-7712	The Best of Jimmy Forrest	196?	15.00

UNITED

❏ 002 [10]	Night Train	1955	120.00

FORRESTER, BOBBY

DOBRE

❏ 1012	Organist	197?	15.00

FORRESTER, HOWDY

CUB

❏ 8008 [M]	Fancy Fiddlin' Country Style	1960	40.00

MGM

❏ E-4035 [M]	Fancy Fiddlin' Country Style	1962	30.00

— *Reissue of Cub LP*

UNITED ARTISTS

❏ UAL-3295 [M]	Fiddlin' Country Style	1963	25.00
❏ UAS-6295 [S]	Fiddlin' Country Style	1963	30.00

FORRESTER, MAUREEN

RCA VICTOR RED SEAL

❏ LSC-2275 [S]	Brahms, Schumann: Lieder	1959	25.00

— *Original with "shaded dog" label*

FORT MUDGE MEMORIAL DUMP, THE

MERCURY

❏ SR-61256	The Fort Mudge Memorial Dump	1970	50.00

FORTE, JOHN

RUFFHOUSE

❏ C268639	Poly Sci	1998	15.00
❏ C2S41073 [DJ]	Poly Sci	1998	18.00

— *Promo version of LP*

FORTUNE, JOHNNY

PARK AVENUE

❏ P-1301 [M]	Soul Surfer	1963	200.00
❏ S-401 [S]	Soul Surfer	1963	300.00

FORTUNE, SONNY

ATLANTIC

❏ SD19187	Infinity Is	1978	15.00
❏ SD18225	Serengeti Minstrel	1977	15.00
❏ SD19239	With Sound Reason	1979	15.00

HORIZON

❏ 704	Awakening	1975	10.00
❏ 711	Waves	1976	18.00

STRATA-EAST

❏ SES-7423	Long Before Our Mothers Cried	1974	25.00

Number	Title	Yr	NM

FORTUNE (1)

MCA CAMEL

Number	Title	Yr	NM
❏ 5673	Fortune	1985	12.00

FORTUNE (2)

WARNER BROS.

❏ BSK3246	Fortune	1978	12.00

FORTUNES, THE (1)

❏ ST-809	Here Comes That Rainy Day Feeling Again	1971	25.00
❏ ST-11041	Storm in a Teacup	1972	18.00

— Contains the canceled "Freedom" LP with one track deleted, plus the title song added

COCA-COLA

❏ (no #)0 [DJ]	It's the Real Thing	1969	60.00

PRESS

❏ PR73002 [M]	The Fortunes	1965	35.00
❏ PRS83002 [S]	The Fortunes	1965	50.00

WORLD PACIFIC

❏ WPS-21904	That Same Old Feeling	1970	18.00

49ERS

4TH & B'WAY

❏ 444021-1	49ers	1990	15.00

49TH PARALLEL, THE

MAVERICK

❏ MAS-7001	The 49th Parallel	1969	250.00

FORUM, THE

MIRA

❏ MLP-301 [M]	The River Is Wide	1967	18.00
❏ MLPS-301 [S]	The River Is Wide	1967	25.00

FOSTER, BRUCE

MILLENNIUM

❏ MNLP8000	After the Show	1977	15.00

FOSTER, CHUCK

CIRCLE

❏ 68	Chuck Foster and His Orchestra 1945-46	198?	12.00

HINDSIGHT

❏ HSR-171	Chuck Foster and His Orchestra 1938-39	198?	12.00
❏ HSR-115	Chuck Foster and His Orchestra 1940	198?	12.00

PHILLIPS INTERNATIONAL

❏ PLP-1965 [M]	Chuck Foster at the Hotel Peabody	1961	200.00

SEA BREEZE

❏ SB-2023	Long Overdue	1985	12.00

FOSTER, DAVID

ATLANTIC

❏ 81642	David Foster	1986	10.00
❏ 81799	The Symphony Sessions	1988	10.00

MOBILE FIDELITY

❏ 1-123	The Best of Me	1982	30.00

— Audiophile vinyl

FOSTER, FRANK, AND FRANK WESS

CONCORD JAZZ

❏ CJ-276	Frankly Speaking	1986	12.00

PABLO

❏ 2310905	Two for the Blues	198?	15.00

SAVOY JAZZ

❏ SJL-2249	Two Franks Please!	198?	15.00

FOSTER, FRANK

ARGO

❏ LP-717 [M]	Basie Is Our Boss	1963	30.00
❏ LPS-717 [S]	Basie Is Our Boss	1963	30.00
❏ BLP-5043 [10]	Frank Foster Quintet	1954	400.00
❏ BST-84278	Manhattan Fever	1968	30.00

MAINSTREAM

❏ MRL-349	The Loud Minority	1972	25.00

PRESTIGE

❏ PRLP-7461 [M]	Fearless	1966	30.00
❏ PRST-7461 [S]	Fearless	1966	30.00
❏ PRLP-7479 [M]	Soul Outing!	1967	30.00
❏ PRST-7479 [S]	Soul Outing!	1967	30.00

STEEPLECHASE

❏ SCS-1170	A House That Love Built	1982	15.00

FOSTER, GARY

REVELATION

❏ REV-19	Grand Clu Classe	197?	25.00
❏ REV-5	Subconsciously	1968	25.00

FOSTER, HERMAN

ARGO

❏ LP-727 [M]	Ready and Willing	1964	50.00
❏ LPS-727 [S]	Ready and Willing	1964	30.00

EPIC

Number	Title	Yr	NM
❏ LA16010 [M]	Have You Heard?	1960	25.00
❏ BA17010 [S]	Have You Heard?	1960	30.00
❏ LA16016 [M]	The Explosive Piano of Herman Foster	1961	200.00
❏ BA17016 [S]	The Explosive Piano of Herman Foster	1961	30.00

FOSTER, PAT

COUNTERPOINT

❏ CPT-560 [M]	Documentary Talking Blues	195?	40.00

RIVERSIDE

❏ RLP-12-654 [M]	Gold Rush Songs	195?	40.00

FOSTER, RONNIE

BLUE NOTE

❏ BN-LA425-G	Cheshire Cat	1975	18.00
❏ BN-LA261-G	On the Avenue	1974	18.00
❏ BN-LA098-G	Sweet Revival	1973	18.00
❏ BST-84382	Two Headed Freap	1972	25.00
❏ B1-32082	Two Headed Freap	1995	18.00

— Reissue of 84382

COLUMBIA

❏ JC36019	Delight	1979	15.00
❏ JC35373	Love Satellite	1978	15.00

FOUL DOGS, THE

RHYTHM SOUND

❏ GA-481	No. 1	1966	400.00

FOUNDATIONS, THE

UNI

❏ 73016	Baby Now That I've Found You	1968	30.00
❏ 73043	Build Me Up Buttercup	1969	30.00
❏ 73058	Digging the Foundations	1969	30.00

FOUNTAIN, PETE, AND "BIG" TINY LITTLE

CORAL

❏ CRL57334 [M]	Mr. New Orleans Meets Mr. Honky Tonk	1961	18.00
❏ CRL757334 [S]	Mr. New Orleans Meets Mr. Honky Tonk	1961	25.00

FOUNTAIN, PETE, AND AL HIRT

CORAL

❏ CRL57389 [M]	Bourbon Street	1962	18.00
❏ CRL757389 [S]	Bourbon Street	1962	25.00

MGM

❏ E-4216 [M]	The Very Best of Al Hirt and Pete Fountain	1964	15.00
❏ SE-4216 [S]	The Very Best of Al Hirt and Pete Fountain	1964	18.00

MONUMENT

❏ 8602	Super I	1975	12.00

FOUNTAIN, PETE

CAPITOL

❏ SN-16224	Pete Fountain and Friends	1982	10.00
❏ SN-16225	Way Down Yonder in New Orleans	1982	10.00

CORAL

❏ CRL57486 [M]	A Taste of Honey	1966	15.00
❏ CRL757486 [S]	A Taste of Honey	1966	18.00
❏ CRL757507	Both Sides Now	1969	15.00
❏ CRL57487 [M]	Candy Clarinet -- Merry Christmas from Pete Fountain	1966	15.00
❏ CRL757487 [S]	Candy Clarinet -- Merry Christmas from Pete Fountain	1966	18.00
❏ CRL757513	Dr. Fountain's Magical Licorice Stick	1971	15.00
❏ CRL757511	Golden Favorites	1970	15.00
❏ CRL57378 [M]	I Love Paris	1961	18.00
❏ CRL757378 [S]	I Love Paris	1961	25.00
❏ CRL57488 [M]	I've Got You Under My Skin	1967	15.00
❏ CRL757488 [S]	I've Got You Under My Skin	1967	18.00
❏ CRL57200 [M]	Lawrence Welk Presents Pete Fountain	1958	25.00
❏ CRL57460 [M]	Licorice Stick	1964	15.00
❏ CRL757460 [S]	Licorice Stick	1964	18.00
❏ CRL757510	Make Your Own Kind of Music	1970	15.00
❏ CRL57484 [M]	Mood Indigo	1966	15.00
❏ CRL757484 [S]	Mood Indigo	1966	18.00
❏ CRL57473 [M]	Mr. Stick Man	1965	15.00
❏ CRL757473 [S]	Mr. Stick Man	1965	18.00
❏ CRL57496 [M]	Music to Turn You On	1967	18.00
❏ CRL757496 [S]	Music to Turn You On	1967	15.00
❏ CRL57429 [M]	New Orleans at Midnight	1964	15.00
❏ CRL757429 [S]	New Orleans at Midnight	1964	18.00
❏ CRL57419 [M]	New Orleans Scene	1963	18.00
❏ CRL757419 [S]	New Orleans Scene	1963	25.00
❏ CRL757517	New Orleans Tennessee	1971	15.00
❏ CRL57314 [M]	Pete Fountain at the Bateau Lounge	1960	18.00
❏ CRL757314 [S]	Pete Fountain at the Bateau Lounge	1960	25.00
❏ CRL57313 [M]	Pete Fountain Day	1960	18.00
❏ CRL757313 [S]	Pete Fountain Day	1960	25.00
❏ CRL57357 [M]	Pete Fountain On Tour	1961	18.00

Number	Title	Yr	NM
❏ CRL757357 [S]	Pete Fountain On Tour	1961	25.00
❏ CRL57499 [M]	Pete Fountain Plays Bert Kaempfert	1968	18.00
❏ CRL757499 [S]	Pete Fountain Plays Bert Kaempfert	1968	15.00
❏ CRL57333 [M]	Pete Fountain Salutes the Great Clarinetists	1960	18.00
❏ CRL757333 [S]	Pete Fountain Salutes the Great Clarinetists	1960	25.00
❏ CRL57359 [M]	Pete Fountain's French Quarter	1961	18.00
❏ CRL757359 [S]	Pete Fountain's French Quarter	1961	25.00
❏ CRL57401 [M]	Pete Fountain's Music from Dixie	1962	18.00
❏ CRL757401 [S]	Pete Fountain's Music from Dixie	1962	25.00
❏ CRL57282 [M]	Pete Fountain's New Orleans	1959	18.00
❏ CRL757282 [S]	Pete Fountain's New Orleans	1959	25.00
❏ CRL57453 [M]	Pete's Place	1964	15.00
❏ CRL757453 [S]	Pete's Place	1964	18.00
❏ CRL57424 [M]	Plenty of Pete	1963	15.00
❏ CRL757424 [S]	Plenty of Pete	1963	18.00
❏ CRL757516	Something/Misty	1971	15.00
❏ CRL57440 [M]	South Rampart Street Parade	1963	15.00
❏ CRL757440 [S]	South Rampart Street Parade	1963	18.00
❏ CRL57474 [M]	Standing Room Only	1965	15.00
❏ CRL757474 [S]	Standing Room Only	1965	18.00
❏ CRL57394 [M]	Swing Low Sweet Chariot	1962	18.00
❏ CRL757394 [S]	Swing Low Sweet Chariot	1962	25.00
❏ CXS-710	The Best of Pete Fountain	1969	18.00
❏ CRL57284 [M]	The Blues	1959	18.00
❏ CRL757284 [S]	The Blues	1959	25.00
❏ CRL757505	Those Were the Days	1969	15.00
❏ CRL757503	Walking Through New Orleans	1968	15.00

DECCA

❏ DL75378	Dr. Fountain's Magical Licorice Stick	1972	12.00

— Reissue of Coral 757513

❏ DL75377	Mr. New Orleans	1972	15.00
❏ DL75380	New Orleans Tennessee	1972	15.00

— Reissue of Coral 757517

❏ DL75374	Pete Fountain's New Orleans	1972	15.00

— Reissue of Coral 757282

❏ DL75379	Something/Misty	1972	12.00

— Reissue of Coral 757516

❏ DL75375	The Blues	1972	15.00

— Reissue of Coral 757284

EVEREST ARCHIVE OF FOLK & JAZZ

❏ 257	New Orleans All-Stars	197?	12.00

FIRST AMERICAN

❏ 7706	New Orleans Jazz	1978	12.00

INTERMEDIA

❏ QS-5038	Down on Rampart Street	198?	10.00

JUCU

❏ JMK-12S	Pete Fountain's Jazz Reunion	1976	15.00

MCA

❏ 336	Crescent City	1974	12.00
❏ 507	Dr. Fountain's Magical Licorice Stick	1974	12.00

— Reissue of Decca 75378

❏ 165	Mr. New Orleans	1973	12.00

— Reissue of Decca 75377

❏ 508	New Orleans Tennessee	1974	12.00

— Reissue of Decca 75380

❏ 505	Pete Fountain's New Orleans	1974	12.00

— Reissue of Decca 75374

❏ 176	Something/Misty	1973	12.00

— Reissue of Decca 75379

❏ 2-4032	The Best of Pete Fountain	1974	15.00

— Reissue of Coral 710

❏ 2-4095	The Best of Pete Fountain, Vol. 2	1976	15.00

— Black labels with rainbow

❏ 2-4095	The Best of Pete Fountain, Vol. 2	1977	15.00

— Tan labels

❏ 506	The Blues	1974	12.00

— Reissue of Decca 75375

PICKWICK

❏ SPC-3201	High Society	1971	12.00
❏ SPC-3024	Pete Fountain	196?	15.00

RCA CAMDEN

❏ CAL-727 [M]	Dixieland	1962	15.00
❏ CAS-727 [R]	Dixieland	1962	12.00

RCA VICTOR

❏ LPM-2097 [M]	Pete Fountain at the Jazz Band Ball	1960	18.00
❏ LSP-2097 [S]	Pete Fountain at the Jazz Band Ball	1960	25.00

VOCALION

❏ VL3803 [M]	And the Angels Sing	1967	15.00
❏ VL73803 [S]	And the Angels Sing	1967	15.00

FOUR ACES

DECCA

Number	Title	Yr	NM
❑ DL8944 [M]	Beyond the Blue Horizon	1959	40.00
—All-black label, silver print			
❑ DL78944 [S]	Beyond the Blue Horizon	1959	50.00
—All-black label, silver print			
❑ DL8944 [M]	Beyond the Blue Horizon	196?	25.00
—Black label with color bars			
❑ DL78944 [S]	Beyond the Blue Horizon	196?	30.00
—Black label with color bars			
❑ DL8228 [M]	Heart and Soul	1956	50.00
—All-black label, silver print			
❑ DL8228 [M]	Heart and Soul	196?	25.00
—Black label with color bars			
❑ DL8855 [M]	Hits from Broadway	1959	40.00
—All-black label, silver print			
❑ DL78855 [S]	Hits from Broadway	1959	50.00
—All-black label, silver print			
❑ DL8855 [M]	Hits from Broadway	196?	25.00
—Black label with color bars			
❑ DL78855 [S]	Hits from Broadway	196?	30.00
—Black label with color bars			
❑ DL8693 [M]	Hits from Hollywood	1958	50.00
—All-black label, silver print			
❑ DL8693 [M]	Hits from Hollywood	196?	25.00
—Black label with color bars			
❑ DL8191 [M]	Merry Christmas	1956	50.00
❑ DL8227 [M]	Sentimental Souvenirs	1956	50.00
—All-black label, silver print			
❑ DL8227 [M]	Sentimental Souvenirs	196?	25.00
—Black label with color bars			
❑ DL8312 [M]	She Sees All the Hollywood Hits	1957	50.00
❑ DL8567 [M]	Shuffling Along	1957	50.00
—All-black label, silver print			
❑ DL8567 [M]	Shuffling Along	196?	25.00
—Black label with color bars			
❑ DL5429 [10]	The Four Aces	1952	80.00
❑ DL4013 [M]	The Golden Hits of the Four Aces	1960	25.00
❑ DL74013 [S]	The Golden Hits of the Four Aces	1960	30.00
❑ DL8122 [M]	The Mood for Love	1955	50.00
—All-black label, silver print			
❑ DL8122 [M]	The Mood for Love	196?	25.00
—Black label with color bars			
❑ DL8766 [M]	The Swingin' Aces	1958	40.00
—All-black label, silver print			
❑ DL78766 [S]	The Swingin' Aces	1958	50.00
—All-black label, silver print			
❑ DL8766 [M]	The Swingin' Aces	196?	25.00
—Black label with color bars			
❑ DL78766 [S]	The Swingin' Aces	196?	30.00
—Black label with color bars			

MCA

Number	Title	Yr	NM
❑ 4033	The Best of the Four Aces	197?	18.00

PICKWICK

Number	Title	Yr	NM
❑ SPC-3527	Love Is a Many-Splendored Thing	197?	12.00

UNITED ARTISTS

Number	Title	Yr	NM
❑ UAL-3337 [M]	Record Oldies	1963	25.00
❑ UAS-6337 [S]	Record Oldies	1963	30.00

VOCALION

Number	Title	Yr	NM
❑ VL3604 [M]	The Four Aces Sing	196?	18.00
❑ VL73881	There Goes My Heart	1969	15.00
❑ VL73902	Written on the Wind	1970	15.00

FOUR BROTHERS, THE

VIK

Number	Title	Yr	NM
❑ LX-1096 [M]	The Four Brothers -- Together Again	1957	80.00

FOUR COINS, THE

EPIC

Number	Title	Yr	NM
❑ LN1104 [M]	The Four Coins	1955	50.00
❑ LN3445 [M]	The Four Coins in Shangri-La	1958	30.00

MGM

Number	Title	Yr	NM
❑ E-3944 [M]	Greek Songs	1961	18.00
❑ SE-3944 [S]	Greek Songs	1961	25.00

ROULETTE

Number	Title	Yr	NM
❑ R-25288 [M]	Greek Songs Mama Never Taught Me	1965	18.00
❑ SR-25288 [S]	Greek Songs Mama Never Taught Me	1965	25.00

FOUR FRESHMEN, THE

CAPITOL

Number	Title	Yr	NM
❑ T763 [M]	4 Freshmen and 5 Trumpets	1957	40.00
❑ SM-11965	Best of the Four Freshmen	1978	12.00
❑ T1378 [M]	First Affair	1960	25.00
❑ ST1378 [S]	First Affair	1960	30.00
❑ T844 [M]	Four Freshmen and Five Saxes	1957	40.00
❑ T683 [M]	Four Freshmen and Five Trombones	1956	40.00
❑ SM-11639	Four Freshmen and Five Trombones	1977	12.00
❑ T743 [M]	Freshmen Favorites	1956	40.00
❑ DT743 [R]	Freshmen Favorites	196?	15.00
❑ SM-743	Freshmen Favorites	197?	12.00
❑ T1103 [M]	Freshmen Favorites, Vol. 2	1959	25.00
❑ ST1103 [S]	Freshmen Favorites, Vol. 2	1959	30.00
❑ T1485 [M]	Freshmen Year	1961	25.00
❑ ST1485 [S]	Freshmen Year	1961	30.00
❑ T2067 [M]	Funny How Time Slips Away	1964	18.00
❑ ST2067 [S]	Funny How Time Slips Away	1964	25.00
❑ T1950 [M]	Got That Feelin'	1963	18.00
❑ ST1950 [S]	Got That Feelin'	1963	25.00
❑ T1189 [M]	Love Lost	1959	25.00
❑ ST1189 [S]	Love Lost	1959	30.00
❑ T2168 [M]	More Four Freshmen and Five Trombones	1964	18.00
❑ ST2168 [S]	More Four Freshmen and Five Trombones	1964	25.00
❑ T1682 [M]	Stars in Our Eyes	1962	25.00
❑ ST1682 [S]	Stars in Our Eyes	1962	30.00
❑ T1753 [M]	Swingers	1963	18.00
❑ ST1753 [S]	Swingers	1963	25.00
❑ T1640 [M]	The Best of the Four Freshmen	1962	25.00
❑ ST1640 [S]	The Best of the Four Freshmen	1962	30.00
❑ T1255 [M]	The Four Freshmen and Five Guitars	1959	25.00
❑ ST1255 [S]	The Four Freshmen and Five Guitars	1959	30.00
❑ T1008 [M]	The Four Freshmen In Person	1958	30.00
❑ ST1008 [S]	The Four Freshmen In Person	1958	40.00
❑ T1860 [M]	The Four Freshmen In Person, Volume 2	1963	18.00
❑ ST1860 [S]	The Four Freshmen In Person, Volume 2	1963	25.00
❑ T1295 [M]	Voices and Brass	1960	25.00
❑ ST1295 [S]	Voices and Brass	1960	30.00
❑ T1543 [M]	Voices in Fun	1961	25.00
❑ ST1543 [S]	Voices in Fun	1961	30.00
❑ T992 [M]	Voices in Latin	1958	30.00
❑ T1074 [M]	Voices in Love	1958	25.00
❑ ST1074 [S]	Voices in Love	1958	30.00
❑ H522 [10]	Voices in Modern	1955	50.00
❑ T522 [M]	Voices in Modern	1955	40.00

CREATIVE WORLD

Number	Title	Yr	NM
❑ ST-1059	Stan Kenton and the Four Freshmen at Butler University	1972	25.00

LIBERTY

Number	Title	Yr	NM
❑ LST-7630	Different Strokes	1969	18.00
❑ LST-7590	In a Class By Themselves	1969	18.00
❑ LN-10181	In a Class By Themselves	198?	10.00
❑ LST-7563	Today Is Tomorrow	1968	18.00

PAUSA

Number	Title	Yr	NM
❑ PR-9040	4 Freshmen and 5 Trumpets	1985	12.00
❑ PR-7193	Fresh!	1986	12.00
❑ PR-9029	The Four Freshmen and Five Guitars	198?	12.00

PICKWICK

Number	Title	Yr	NM
❑ SPC-3563	A Taste of Honey	1977	12.00
❑ SPC-3080	The Fabulous Four Freshmen	196?	15.00

SUNSET

Number	Title	Yr	NM
❑ SUS-5289	My Special Angel	1970	15.00

FOUR GIRLS, THE

CORAL

Number	Title	Yr	NM
❑ CRL57158 [M]	Make a Joyful Noise Unto the Lord	1957	60.00

FOUR JACKS AND A JILL (1)

RCA VICTOR

Number	Title	Yr	NM
❑ LSP-4103	Fables	1968	18.00
❑ LPM-4019 [M]	Master Jack	1968	30.00
❑ LSP-4019 [S]	Master Jack	1968	18.00

FOUR KNIGHTS, THE

CAPITOL

Number	Title	Yr	NM
❑ H346 [10]	Spotlight Songs	1953	200.00
❑ T346 [M]	Spotlight Songs	1956	150.00

CORAL

Number	Title	Yr	NM
❑ CRL57309 [M]	Million Dollar Baby	1960	60.00
❑ CRL757309 [S]	Million Dollar Baby	1960	80.00
❑ CRL57221 [M]	The Four Knights	1959	100.00

FOUR LADS, THE

COLUMBIA

Number	Title	Yr	NM
❑ CL1223 [M]	Breezin' Along	1958	30.00
❑ CS8035 [S]	Breezin' Along	1958	30.00
❑ CL1550 [M]	Everything Goes	1960	18.00
❑ CS8350 [S]	Everything Goes	1960	25.00
❑ CL1111 [M]	Four on the Aisle	1958	30.00
❑ CS8047 [S]	Four on the Aisle	1958	30.00
❑ CL1407 [M]	High Spirits!	1959	30.00
❑ CS8203 [S]	High Spirits!	1959	30.00
❑ CL1602 [M]	Love Affair	1960	18.00
❑ CS8293 [S]	Love Affair	1960	25.00
❑ CL912 [M]	On the Sunny Side	1956	40.00
❑ CL6329 [10]	Stage Show	1954	50.00
❑ CL2577 [10]	Stage Show	1956	50.00
❑ CL1235 [M]	The Four Lads' Greatest Hits	1958	30.00
❑ CL2545 [10]	The Four Lads Sing Frank Loesser	1956	50.00
❑ CL1045 [M]	The Four Lads Sing Frank Loesser	1957	40.00
❑ CL1299 [M]	The Four Lads Swing Along	1959	30.00
❑ CS8106 [S]	The Four Lads Swing Along	1959	30.00
❑ CL861 [M]	The Four Lads with Frankie Laine	1956	40.00

DOT

Number	Title	Yr	NM
❑ DLP-3438 [M]	Hits of the 60's	1962	18.00
❑ DLP-25438 [S]	Hits of the 60's	1962	25.00
❑ DLP-3533 [M]	Oh Happy Day	1963	18.00
❑ DLP-25533 [S]	Oh Happy Day	1963	25.00

HARMONY

Number	Title	Yr	NM
❑ HS11369	Moments to Remember	1970	15.00

KAPP

Number	Title	Yr	NM
❑ KL-1254 [M]	Dixieland Doin's	1961	18.00
❑ KS-3254 [S]	Dixieland Doin's	1961	25.00
❑ KL-1224 [M]	Twelve Hits	1961	18.00
❑ KS-3224 [S]	Twelve Hits	1961	25.00

UNITED ARTISTS

Number	Title	Yr	NM
❑ UAL-3399 [M]	Songs of World War I	1964	18.00
❑ UAS-6399 [S]	Songs of World War I	1964	25.00
❑ UAL-3356 [M]	This Year's Top Movie Hits	1964	18.00
❑ UAS-6356 [S]	This Year's Top Movie Hits	1964	25.00

FOUR LOVERS, THE

RCA VICTOR

Number	Title	Yr	NM
❑ LPM-1317 [M]	Joyride	1956	700.00

FOUR MOST, THE

DAWN

Number	Title	Yr	NM
❑ DLP-1111 [M]	The Four Most	1956	80.00

4 OUT OF 5 DOCTORS

NEMPEROR

Number	Title	Yr	NM
❑ JZ36575	4 Out of 5 Doctors	1981	15.00
❑ ARZ37700	Second Opinion	1982	12.00

FOUR PREPS, THE

CAPITOL

Number	Title	Yr	NM
❑ T1814 [M]	Campus Confidential	1963	18.00
❑ ST1814 [S]	Campus Confidential	1963	25.00
❑ T1647 [M]	Campus Encore	1962	25.00
❑ ST1647 [S]	Campus Encore	1962	30.00
❑ T1216 [M]	Dancing and Dreaming	1959	25.00
❑ ST1216 [S]	Dancing and Dreaming	1959	30.00
❑ T1291 [M]	Early in the Morning	1960	30.00
❑ DT1291 [R]	Early in the Morning	1960	15.00
❑ T2169 [M]	How to Succeed in Love	1964	18.00
❑ ST2169 [S]	How to Succeed in Love	1964	25.00
❑ T1976 [M]	Songs for a Campus Party	1963	18.00
❑ ST1976 [S]	Songs for a Campus Party	1963	25.00
❑ T2708 [M]	The Best of the Four Preps	1967	18.00
❑ ST2708 [S]	The Best of the Four Preps	1967	15.00
❑ T994 [M]	The Four Preps	1958	30.00
❑ T1566 [M]	The Four Preps on Campus	1961	25.00
❑ ST1566 [S]	The Four Preps on Campus	1961	30.00
❑ T1090 [M]	The Things We Did Last Summer	1958	30.00

FOUR SEASONS, THE

MCA/CURB

Number	Title	Yr	NM
❑ 5632	Starfighter	1985	12.00

MOWEST

Number	Title	Yr	NM
❑ MW108L	Chameleon	1972	15.00

PHILIPS

Number	Title	Yr	NM
❑ PHM200221 [M]	2nd Vault of Golden Hits	1966	18.00
❑ PHS600221 [S]	2nd Vault of Golden Hits	1966	25.00
❑ PHM200150 [M]	All the Song Hits of the Four Seasons	1964	25.00
❑ PHS600150 [S]	All the Song Hits of the Four Seasons	1964	30.00
❑ PHM200193 [M]	Big Hits by Burt Bacharach... Hal David...Bob Dylan	1965	25.00
—"Open book" cover			
❑ PHM200193 [M]	Big Hits by Burt Bacharach... Hal David...Bob Dylan	1966	30.00
—Group photos on cover			
❑ PHS600193 [S]	Big Hits by Burt Bacharach... Hal David...Bob Dylan	1965	30.00
—"Open book" cover			
❑ PHS600193 [S]	Big Hits by Burt Bacharach... Hal David...Bob Dylan	1966	40.00
—Group photos on cover			
❑ PHM200129 [M]	Born to Wander	1964	25.00
❑ PHS600129 [S]	Born to Wander	1964	30.00
❑ PHM200124 [M]	Dawn (Go Away) and 11 Other Great Songs	1964	25.00
❑ PHS600124 [S]	Dawn (Go Away) and 11 Other Great Songs	1964	30.00
❑ PHS-2-6501	Edizione d'Oro	1968	30.00
—Number "4" on cover is red on gold foil			
❑ PHS-2-6501	Edizione d'Oro	1968	30.00
—Number "4" on cover is white on gold foil			
❑ PHS-2-6501	Edizione d'Oro	1969	30.00
—Number "4" on cover is white on gold board			
❑ PHS600341	Half & Half	1970	25.00
❑ PHM200222 [M]	Lookin' Back	1966	25.00
❑ PHS600222 [S]	Lookin' Back	1966	30.00
❑ PHM200243 [M]	New Gold Hits	1967	25.00
❑ PHS600243 [S]	New Gold Hits	1967	30.00
❑ PHM200146 [M]	Rag Doll	1964	25.00
—Without yellow seal noting presence of "Save It For Me			

Number	Title	Yr	NM
❏ PHM200146 [M] Rag Doll		1964	25.00
— With yellow seal noting presence of "Save It For Me"			
❏ PHS600146 [S] Rag Doll		1964	30.00
— Without yellow seal noting presence of "Save It For Me"			
❏ PHS600146 [S] Rag Doll		1964	25.00
— With yellow seal noting presence of "Save It For Me"			
❏ PHM200164 [M] The 4 Seasons Entertain You		1965	25.00
— With orange seal noting presence of "Bye Bye Baby"			
❏ PHM200164 [M] The 4 Seasons Entertain You		1965	25.00
— With orange seal noting presence of "Bye Bye Baby" and "Toy Soldier"			
❏ PHM200164 [M] The 4 Seasons Entertain You		1965	18.00
— With blue seal noting presence of "Bye Bye Baby" and "Toy Soldier"			
❏ PHS600164 [S] The 4 Seasons Entertain You		1965	30.00
— With orange seal noting presence of "Bye Bye Baby"			
❏ PHS600164 [S] The 4 Seasons Entertain You		1965	25.00
— With blue seal noting presence of "Bye Bye Baby" and "Toy Soldier"			
❏ PHS600164 [S] The 4 Seasons Entertain You		1965	30.00
— With orange seal noting presence of "Bye Bye Baby" and "Toy Soldier"			
❏ PHM200196 [M] The 4 Seasons' Gold Vault of Hits		1965	25.00
— Title in red print with no border			
❏ PHM200196 [M] The 4 Seasons' Gold Vault of Hits		1965	18.00
— Title in red print with black border			
❏ PHM200196 [M] The 4 Seasons' Gold Vault of Hits		196?	15.00
— Title in all-black print			
❏ PHS600196 [S] The 4 Seasons' Gold Vault of Hits		1965	30.00
— Title in red print with no border			
❏ PHS600196 [S] The 4 Seasons' Gold Vault of Hits		1965	25.00
— Title in red print with black border			
❏ PHS600196 [S] The 4 Seasons' Gold Vault of Hits		196?	18.00
— Title in all-black print			
❏ PHM200223 [M] The Four Seasons' Christmas Album		1966	30.00
— Reissue of Vee Jay album (same contents and order) with new cover			
❏ PHS600223 [S] The Four Seasons' Christmas Album		1966	30.00
❏ PHS600290 The Genuine Imitation Life Gazette		1969	30.00
— Yellow newspaper			
❏ PHS600290 The Genuine Imitation Life Gazette		1969	18.00
— White newspaper			
❏ PHM200201 [M] Working My Way Back to You		1966	25.00
❏ PHS600201 [S] Working My Way Back to You		1966	30.00
PICKWICK			
❏ SPC-3223	Brotherhood of Man	1970	15.00
— Mass-market version of Sears 609			
PRIVATE STOCK			
❏ PS-7000	The Four Seasons Story	1975	18.00
RHINO			
❏ RNRP-72998	25th Anniversary Collection	1987	30.00
❏ R1-71490	Anthology	1988	15.00
❏ R1-71248	Big Hits by Burt Bacharach... Hal David...Bob Dylan	1988	12.00
— Reissue of Philips 600-193			
❏ RNLP70234	The Four Seasons' Christmas Album	1987	15.00
— Reissue of Philips album (same contents and order)			
❏ R1-70249	The Genuine Imitation Life Gazette	1988	12.00
— Reissue of Philips 600-290			
❏ R1-70247	Working My Way Back to You	1988	12.00
— Reissue of Philips 600-201			
SEARS			
❏ SPS-609	Brotherhood of Man	1970	30.00
VEE JAY			
❏ LP-1059 [M]	Ain't That a Shame and 11 Others	1963	30.00
❏ SR-1059 [S]	Ain't That a Shame and 11 Others	1963	40.00
❏ LP-1056 [M]	Big Girls Don't Cry and Twelve Others	1963	30.00
❏ SR-1056 [S]	Big Girls Don't Cry and Twelve Others	1963	40.00
❏ LP-1082 [M]	Folk-Nanny	1964	30.00
❏ SR-1082 [S]	Folk-Nanny	1964	40.00
❏ LP-1065 [M]	Golden Hits of the Four Seasons	1963	30.00
❏ SR-1065 [S]	Golden Hits of the Four Seasons	1963	40.00
❏ LP-1088 [M]	More Golden Hits by the Four Seasons	1964	30.00
— With "Long Lonely Nights" on record			
❏ LP-1088 [M]	More Golden Hits by the Four Seasons	1964	25.00
— With "Apple of My Eye" on record			

Number	Title	Yr	NM
❏ SR-1088 [S]	More Golden Hits by the Four Seasons	1964	40.00
— With "Long Lonely Nights" on record			
❏ SR-1088 [S]	More Golden Hits by the Four Seasons	1964	30.00
— With "Apple of My Eye" on record			
❏ LP-1154 [M]	Recorded Live on Stage	1965	30.00
❏ LPS-1154 [S]	Recorded Live on Stage	1965	40.00
❏ LP-1053 [M]	Sherry & 11 Others	1962	40.00
❏ SR-1053 [S]	Sherry & 11 Others	1962	60.00
❏ LP-1082 [M]	Stay & Other Great Hits	1964	30.00
— Retitled version of Folk-Nanny			
❏ SR-1082 [S]	Stay & Other Great Hits	1964	30.00
— Retitled version of Folk-Nanny			
❏ LP1055 [M]	The Four Seasons Greetings	1962	30.00
❏ SR1055 [S]	The Four Seasons Greetings	1962	40.00
❏ LP-1121 [M]	We Love Girls	1965	30.00
❏ LPS-1121 [S]	We Love Girls	1965	40.00
WARNER BROS.			
❏ BS3016	Helicon	1977	15.00
❏ 2WB3497	Reunited Live	1980	18.00
❏ BS2900	Who Loves You	1975	15.00

FOUR TOPS, THE

Number	Title	Yr	NM
ABC			
❏ AA-1092	At the Top	1978	15.00
❏ D-968	Catfish	1976	15.00
❏ D-862	Night Lights Harmony	1975	15.00
❏ D-1014	The Show Must Go On	1977	15.00
ABC DUNHILL			
❏ DSX-50129	Keeper of the Castle	1972	15.00
❏ DSX-50188	Live & In Concert	1974	15.00
❏ DSX-50144	Main Street People	1973	15.00
❏ DSX-50166	Meeting of the Minds	1974	15.00
ARISTA			
❏ AL-8492	Indestructible	1988	10.00
CASABLANCA			
❏ NBLP7266	One More Mountain	1982	12.00
❏ NBLP7258	Tonight!	1981	12.00
COMMAND			
❏ CQD-40011 [Q]	Keeper of the Castle	1974	25.00
❏ CQD-40012 [Q]	Main Street People	1974	25.00
MCA			
❏ 27019	Greatest Hits	198?	12.00
MOTOWN			
❏ 657 [M]	4 Tops on Broadway	1967	30.00
❏ MS-657 [S]	4 Tops on Broadway	1967	30.00
❏ 647 [M]	4 Tops On Top	1966	30.00
❏ MS-647 [S]	4 Tops On Top	1966	30.00
❏ M9-809A3	Anthology	1974	25.00
❏ 6066ML	Back Where I Belong	1983	12.00
❏ MS-721	Changing Times	1970	25.00
❏ 622 [M]	Four Tops	1964	30.00
❏ MS-622 [S]	Four Tops	1964	40.00
❏ M5-122V1	Four Tops	1981	10.00
— Reissue of 622			
❏ M-740L	Four Tops Greatest Hits, Vol. 2	1971	25.00
❏ 654 [M]	Four Tops Live!	1966	30.00
❏ MS-654 [S]	Four Tops Live!	1966	30.00
❏ 5258ML	Four Tops Live!	1983	10.00
— Reissue of 654			
❏ MS-675	Four Tops Now!	1969	25.00
❏ 660 [M]	Four Tops Reach Out	1967	30.00
❏ MS-660 [S]	Four Tops Reach Out	1967	30.00
❏ M5-149V1	Four Tops Reach Out	1981	10.00
— Reissue of 660			
❏ 634 [M]	Four Tops Second Album	1965	30.00
❏ MS-634 [S]	Four Tops Second Album	1965	30.00
❏ 5314ML	Great Songs	1983	12.00
❏ 6130ML	Magic	1985	12.00
❏ M-748L	Nature Planned It	1972	25.00
❏ MS-695	Soul Spin	1969	25.00
❏ MS-704	Still Waters Run Deep	1970	25.00
❏ 5224ML	Still Waters Run Deep	1982	10.00
— Reissue of 704			
❏ M5-114V1	Superstar Series, Vol. 14	1981	12.00
❏ M-764D	The Best of the 4 Tops	1973	18.00
❏ 662 [M]	The Four Tops Greatest Hits	1967	30.00
❏ MS-662 [S]	The Four Tops Greatest Hits	1967	25.00
❏ M5-209V1	The Four Tops' Greatest Hits	1981	10.00
— Reissue of 662			
❏ 669 [M]	Yesterday's Dreams	1968	30.00
❏ MS-669 [S]	Yesterday's Dreams	1968	25.00
UNIVERSAL MOTOWN			
❏ 5315998 [S]	Four Tops Reach Out	2009	25.00

FOUR TUNES, THE

Number	Title	Yr	NM
JUBILEE			
❏ LP-1039 [M]	12 x 4	1957	250.00

FOURTH CEKCION, THE

Number	Title	Yr	NM
SOLAR			
❏ 110	The Fourth Cekcion	1970	60.00

FOURTH WAY, THE

Number	Title	Yr	NM
CAPITOL			
❏ ST-317	The Fourth Way	1969	30.00

Number	Title	Yr	NM
HARVEST			
❏ SKAO-423	The Sun and Moon Have Come Together	1970	25.00
❏ ST-666	Werewolf	1971	25.00

FOWLER, WALLY

Number	Title	Yr	NM
DECCA			
❏ DL8560 [M]	Call of the Cross	1958	40.00
DOVE			
❏ 1000	A Tribute to Elvis Presley	1977	25.00
KING			
❏ 702 [M]	Gospel Song Festival	1960	100.00
STARDAY			
❏ SLP-301 [M]	All Nite Singing Concert	1964	30.00
❏ SLP-112 [M]	All Nite Singing Gospel Concert	1960	40.00

FOWLEY, KIM

Number	Title	Yr	NM
ANTILLES			
❏ AN-7075	Snake Document Masquerade	1979	15.00
CAPITOL			
❏ ST-11248	Automatic	1974	25.00
❏ ST-11075	I'm Bad	1972	25.00
❏ ST-11159	International Heroes	1973	25.00
GNP CRESCENDO			
❏ GNPS-2132 [B]	Hollywood Confidential	197?	25.00
IMPERIAL			
❏ LP-12413	Born to Be Wild	1968	40.00
❏ LP-12443	Good Clean Fun	1969	40.00
❏ LP-12423	Outrageous	1969	40.00
PVC			
❏ 7906 [B]	Sunset Boulevard	1978	25.00
TOWER			
❏ T5080 [M]	Love Is Alive and Well	1967	30.00
❏ ST5080 [S]	Love Is Alive and Well	1967	40.00

FOX, CURLY

Number	Title	Yr	NM
HARMONY			
❏ HL7302 [M]	Traveling Blues	1963	25.00
STARDAY			
❏ SLP-235 [M]	Curly Fox and Texas Ruby	1963	30.00

FOX, SAMANTHA

Number	Title	Yr	NM
JIVE			
❏ 1150-1-J	I Wanna Have Some Fun	1988	12.00
❏ 1357-1-J	Just One Night	1991	15.00
❏ 1061-1-J	Samantha Fox	1987	12.00
❏ 1012-1-J	Touch Me	1986	12.00

FOXX, INEZ (AND CHARLIE)

Number	Title	Yr	NM
DYNAMO			
❏ DM-7000 [M]	Come By Here	1967	30.00
❏ DS-8000 [S]	Come By Here	1967	40.00
❏ DM-7002 [M]	Inez and Charlie Foxx's Greatest Hits	1967	30.00
❏ DS-8002 [S]	Inez and Charlie Foxx's Greatest Hits	1967	40.00
❏ DS-8003	Swingin' Mockin' Band	1968	30.00
SUE			
❏ LP-1027 [M]	Mockingbird	1966	100.00
SYMBOL			
❏ SYM-4400 [M]	Mockingbird	1963	150.00
VOLT			
❏ VOS-6022	Inez Foxx at Memphis	1973	18.00

FOXY

Number	Title	Yr	NM
DASH			
❏ D30001	Foxy	1976	15.00
❏ D30005	Get Off	1978	12.00
❏ D30010	Hot Number	1979	12.00
❏ D30016	Live	1980	15.00
❏ D30015	Party Boys	1980	15.00

FRACTION

Number	Title	Yr	NM
ANGELUS			
❏ 571	Moon Blood	1971	2000.00
— VG value 1000; VG+ value 1500			

FRAGER, MALCOLM

Number	Title	Yr	NM
RCA VICTOR RED SEAL			
❏ LSC-2465 [S]	Prokofiev: Piano Concerto No. 2	1961	100.00
— Originals with "shaded dog" label			

FRAMPTON, PETER

Number	Title	Yr	NM
A&M			
❏ SP-3722	Breaking All the Rules	1981	12.00
❏ SP-4512	Frampton	1975	12.00
❏ SP-3703	Frampton Comes Alive!	1976	15.00
❏ SP-6505	Frampton Comes Alive!	198?	12.00
— Budget-line reissue			
❏ PR-3703 [B]	Frampton Comes Alive!	1976	35.00
— Single-record picture disc of highlights			
❏ SP-4389	Frampton's Camel	1973	15.00

Number	Title	Yr	NM
—Brown label			
❑ SP-4389	Frampton's Camel	1974	12.00
—Silvery label			
❑ SP-4704	I'm In You	1977	12.00
❑ SP-4704 [DJ]	I'm In You	1977	40.00
—Promo-only picture disc			
❑ SP-17100 [DJ]	Peter Frampton Radio Special	1979	25.00
—Promo-only interview record			
❑ SP-3619	Somethin's Happening	1974	15.00
❑ SP-4905	The Art of Control	1982	12.00
❑ SP-3710	Where I Should Be	1979	12.00
❑ SP-4348	Wind of Change	1972	15.00
—Brown label			
❑ SP-4348	Wind of Change	1974	12.00
—Silvery label			
❑ SP-3133	Wind of Change	198?	10.00
—Budget-line reissue			

ATLANTIC

Number	Title	Yr	NM
❑ PR848 [DJ]	Frampton Is Alive!	1986	25.00
—Promo-only interview record			
❑ PR3093 [DJ]	Perfect Fit: A Candid Interview	1989	25.00
—Promo-only album			
❑ 81290 [B]	Premonition	1986	10.00
❑ 82030	Where All the Pieces Fit	1989	10.00

MOBILE FIDELITY

Number	Title	Yr	NM
❑ 2-262	Frampton Comes Alive!	1996	40.00
—Audiophile vinyl			

SWEET THUNDER

Number	Title	Yr	NM
❑ 6	Frampton Comes Alive!	198?	100.00
—Audiophile edition			

FRANCIS, CONNIE, AND HANK WILLIAMS, JR.

MGM

Number	Title	Yr	NM
❑ E-4251 [M]	Connie Francis & Hank Williams, Jr. Sing Great Country Favorites	1964	30.00
❑ SE-4251 [S]	Connie Francis & Hank Williams, Jr. Sing Great Country Favorites	1964	40.00

FRANCIS, CONNIE

LEO

Number	Title	Yr	NM
❑ LE-903 [M]	Connie Francis and the Kids Next Door	1967	50.00
❑ LES-903 [S]	Connie Francis and the Kids Next Door	1967	60.00

MATI-MOR

Number	Title	Yr	NM
❑ 8002 [M]	Sing Along wth Connie Francis	1961	40.00
—Made for Brylcreem			

METRO

Number	Title	Yr	NM
❑ M-519 [M]	Connie Francis	1964	25.00
❑ MS-519 [S]	Connie Francis	1964	30.00
❑ M-538 [M]	Folk Favorites	1965	25.00
❑ MS-538 [S]	Folk Favorites	1965	30.00
❑ M-571 [M]	Songs of Love	1966	25.00
❑ MS-571 [S]	Songs of Love	1966	30.00
❑ M-603 [M]	The Incomparable Connie Francis	1967	25.00
❑ MS-603 [S]	The Incomparable Connie Francis	1967	30.00

MGM

Number	Title	Yr	NM
❑ E-4298 [M]	All Time International Hits	1965	30.00
❑ SE-4298 [S]	All Time International Hits	1965	30.00
❑ E-4253 [M]	A New Kind of Connie	1964	30.00
❑ SE-4253 [S]	A New Kind of Connie	1964	30.00
❑ T-90068 [M]	A New Kind of Connie	1964	30.00
—Capitol Record Club issue			
❑ ST-90068 [S]	A New Kind of Connie	1964	35.00
—Capitol Record Club issue			
❑ E-4048 [M]	Award Winning Motion Picture Hits	1963	30.00
❑ SE-4048 [S]	Award Winning Motion Picture Hits	1963	30.00
❑ T-90027 [M]	Award Winning Motion Picture Hits	196?	30.00
—Capitol Record Club edition			
❑ ST-90027 [S]	Award Winning Motion Picture Hits	196?	30.00
—Capitol Record Club edition			
❑ E-3792 [M]	Christmas in My Heart	1959	30.00
❑ SE-3792 [S]	Christmas in My Heart	1959	40.00
—Same as above, but in stereo			
❑ SE-4573 [S]	Connie & Clyde	1968	30.00
❑ E-4573 [M]	Connie & Clyde	1968	150.00
—Yellow label "Special Disc Jockey Record" in stereo cover with "Mono" sticker			
❑ E-3913 [M]	Connie Francis at the Copa	1961	30.00
❑ SE-3913 [S]	Connie Francis at the Copa	1961	40.00
❑ E-4472 [M]	Connie Francis On Broadway Today	1967	30.00
❑ SE-4472 [S]	Connie Francis On Broadway Today	1967	30.00
❑ SE-4585	Connie Francis Sings Bacharach & David	1968	30.00
❑ E-4294 [M]	Connie Francis Sings For Mama	1965	30.00
❑ SE-4294 [S]	Connie Francis Sings For Mama	1965	30.00
❑ E-4049 [M]	Connie Francis Sings Second Hand Love and Other Hits	1962	30.00
❑ SE-4049 [S]	Connie Francis Sings Second Hand Love and Other Hits	1962	30.00
❑ E-4399 [M]	Connie's Christmas	1966	30.00
❑ SE-4399 [S]	Connie's Christmas	1966	30.00
❑ E-3793 [M]	Connie's Greatest Hits	1960	30.00
❑ E-3795 [M]	Country and Western Golden Hits	1960	30.00
❑ SE-3795 [S]	Country and Western Golden Hits	1960	40.00
❑ E-4079 [M]	Country Music Connie Style	1962	30.00
❑ SE-4079 [S]	Country Music Connie Style	1962	30.00
❑ E-4022 [M]	Dance Party	196?	30.00
—Retitled version of "Do the Twist			
❑ SE-4022 [S]	Dance Party	196?	30.00
—Retitled version of "Do the Twist			
❑ E-4022 [M]	Do the Twist	1962	30.00
❑ SE-4022 [S]	Do the Twist	1962	40.00
❑ E-3969 [M]	Folk Song Favorites	1961	30.00
❑ SE-3969 [S]	Folk Song Favorites	1961	40.00
❑ E-4123 [M]	Follow the Boys	1963	30.00
❑ SE-4123 [S]	Follow the Boys	1963	30.00
❑ E-4023 [M]	Fun Songs for Children	1962	50.00
❑ E-4124 [M]	German Favorites	1963	30.00
❑ SE-4124 [S]	German Favorites	1963	30.00
❑ E-4474 [M]	Grandes Exitos del Cine de los Anos 60	1967	30.00
❑ SE-4474 [S]	Grandes Exitos del Cine de los Anos 60	1967	30.00
❑ E-4145 [M]	Greatest American Waltzes	1963	30.00
❑ SE-4145 [S]	Greatest American Waltzes	1963	30.00
❑ GAS-109	Greatest Golden Groovie Goodies (Golden Archive Series)	1970	30.00
❑ MG-1-5410	Greatest Hits	198?	15.00
❑ MG-1-5411	Greatest Jewish Hits	198?	15.00
❑ E-4522 [M]	Hawaii: Connie	1968	100.00
❑ SE-4522 [S]	Hawaii: Connie	1968	30.00
❑ MG-1-5406	I'm Me Again	198?	15.00
❑ E-4210 [M]	In the Summer of His Years	1964	30.00
❑ SE-4210 [S]	In the Summer of His Years	1964	30.00
❑ E-4013 [M]	Irish Favorites	1962	30.00
❑ SE-4013 [S]	Irish Favorites	1962	40.00
❑ E-3791 [M]	Italian Favorites	1959	30.00
❑ SE-3791 [S]	Italian Favorites	1959	40.00
❑ E-4355 [M]	Jealous Heart	1966	30.00
❑ SE-4355 [S]	Jealous Heart	1966	30.00
❑ E-3869 [M]	Jewish Favorites	1961	30.00
❑ SE-3869 [S]	Jewish Favorites	1961	40.00
❑ E-4411 [M]	Live at the Sahara in Las Vegas	1967	30.00
❑ SE-4411 [S]	Live at the Sahara in Las Vegas	1967	30.00
❑ E-4229 [M]	Looking for Love	1964	30.00
❑ SE-4229 [S]	Looking for Love	1964	30.00
❑ E-4448 [M]	Love, Italian Style	1967	30.00
❑ SE-4448 [S]	Love, Italian Style	1967	30.00
❑ E-4161 [M]	Mala Femmena & Connie's Big Hits from Italy	1963	30.00
❑ SE-4161 [S]	Mala Femmena & Connie's Big Hits from Italy	1963	30.00
❑ E-4102 [M]	Modern Italian Hits	1963	30.00
❑ SE-4102 [S]	Modern Italian Hits	1963	30.00
❑ E-3942 [M]	More Greatest Hits	1961	30.00
❑ SE-3942 [S]	More Greatest Hits	1961	40.00
❑ E-3871 [M]	More Italian Favorites	1960	30.00
❑ SE-3871 [S]	More Italian Favorites	1960	40.00
❑ E-4382 [M]	Movie Greats of the 60's	1966	30.00
❑ SE-4382 [S]	Movie Greats of the 60's	1966	30.00
❑ ST-91145	My Best to You	1968	30.00
—Capitol Record Club			
❑ E-4487 [M]	My Heart Cries for You	1967	30.00
❑ SE-4487 [S]	My Heart Cries for You	1967	30.00
❑ E-3776 [M]	My Thanks to You	1959	30.00
❑ SE-3776 [S]	My Thanks to You	1959	40.00
❑ E-3965 [M]	Never on Sunday and Other Title Songs from Motion Pictures	1961	30.00
❑ SE-3965 [S]	Never on Sunday and Other Title Songs from Motion Pictures	1961	40.00
❑ ST-90592 [S]	Never on Sunday and Other Title Songs from Motion Pictures	1965	30.00
—Capitol Record Club edition			
❑ E-3794 [M]	Rock 'N' Roll Million Sellers	1960	30.00
❑ SE-3794 [S]	Rock 'N' Roll Million Sellers	1960	40.00
❑ E-3893 [M]	Songs to a Swinging Band	1961	30.00
❑ SE-3893 [S]	Songs to a Swinging Band	1961	40.00
❑ E-3853 [M]	Spanish and Latin American Favorites	1960	30.00
❑ SE-3853 [S]	Spanish and Latin American Favorites	1960	40.00
❑ E-3761 [M]	The Exciting Connie Francis	1959	80.00
—Yellow label			
❑ SE-3761 [S]	The Exciting Connie Francis	1959	100.00
—Yellow label			
❑ E-3761 [M]	The Exciting Connie Francis	1959	30.00
—Black label			
❑ SE-3761 [S]	The Exciting Connie Francis	1959	40.00
—Black label			
❑ SE-4655	The Songs of Les Reed	1969	30.00
❑ T90510 [M]	The Very Best of Connie Francis	1965	40.00
—Capitol Record Club edition			
❑ ST90510 [S]	The Very Best of Connie Francis	1965	40.00
—Capitol Record Club edition			
❑ E-4167 [M]	The Very Best of Connie Francis	1963	30.00
❑ SE-4167 [S]	The Very Best of Connie Francis	1963	30.00
❑ SE-4637	The Wedding Cake	1969	30.00
❑ E-3686 [M]	Who's Sorry Now?	1958	100.00
—Yellow label			
❑ E-3686 [M]	Who's Sorry Now?	1960	40.00
—Black label			

POLYDOR

Number	Title	Yr	NM
❑ 839923-1	12 Exitos De Connie Francis	198?	12.00
❑ 827582-1	Greatest Hits	1985	12.00
❑ 827584-1	Greatest Jewish Hits	1985	12.00
❑ 839922-1	Lo Mejor De Su Repertorio	198?	12.00
❑ 827569-1	The Very Best of Connie Francis	1985	12.00

FRANCIS, PANAMA

20TH CENTURY FOX

Number	Title	Yr	NM
❑ TFS-6101 [S]	Tough Talk	196?	30.00
❑ TFM-6101 [M]	Tough Talk	196?	30.00

CLASSIC JAZZ

Number	Title	Yr	NM
❑ 149	Panama Francis and His Savoy Sultans, Volume 1	197?	12.00
❑ 150	Panama Francis and His Savoy Sultans, Volume 2	197?	12.00

EPIC

Number	Title	Yr	NM
❑ LN3839 [M]	Exploding Drums	1959	30.00
❑ BN629 [S]	Exploding Drums	1959	30.00

STASH

Number	Title	Yr	NM
❑ ST-223	Everything Swings	198?	12.00
❑ ST-218	Grooving	198?	12.00

FRANKE AND THE KNOCKOUTS

MCA

Number	Title	Yr	NM
❑ 5473	Makin' the Point	1984	12.00

MILLENNIUM

Number	Title	Yr	NM
❑ BXL1-7763	Below the Belt	1982	10.00
❑ DJL1-7764 [EP]	Below the Belt Sampler	1982	25.00
—Promo-only three-song sampler; contains live version of "I Need Love (The Knockout Shuffle)" that was not issued on LP			
❑ BXL1-7755	Franke and the Knockouts	1981	10.00
❑ DJL1-4015 [DJ]	Special Radio Series Volume X	1981	25.00
—Promo-only music and interview disc			

FRANKIE AND JOHNNY

WARNER BROS.

Number	Title	Yr	NM
❑ BS2675	The Sweetheart Sampler	1973	25.00

FRANKIE GOES TO HOLLYWOOD

ATLANTIC

Number	Title	Yr	NM
❑ 82587	Bang...The Greatest Hits of Frankie Goes to Hollywood	1994	18.00

ISLAND

Number	Title	Yr	NM
❑ R120202	Liverpool	1986	12.00
—RCA Music Service edition			
❑ 90546	Liverpool	1986	10.00
❑ 90232	Welcome to the Pleasuredome	1985	18.00

FRANKLIN, ALAN, EXPLOSION

ALADDIN

Number	Title	Yr	NM
❑ 104049	Come Home Baby	1969	80.00

HORNE

Number	Title	Yr	NM
❑ 0	Climax	1970	250.00
—Pre-release or demo versions of tracks from The Blues Climax.			
❑ JC-888	The Blues Climax	1970	100.00

FRANKLIN, ARETHA

4 MEN WITH BEARDS

Number	Title	Yr	NM
❑ 4M115	Aretha Live at Fillmore West	2003	18.00
—Reissue on 180-gram vinyl			
❑ 4M131	Aretha Now	2006	18.00
—Reissue on 180-gram vinyl			
❑ 4M101	I Never Loved a Man the Way I Love You	2001	18.00
—Reissue on 180-gram vinyl			
❑ 4M130	Lady Soul	2006	18.00
—Reissue on 180-gram vinyl			
❑ 4M111	Soul '69	2002	18.00
—Reissue on 180-gram vinyl			
❑ 4M114	Spirit in the Dark	2003	18.00
—Reissue on 180-gram vinyl			

ARISTA

Number	Title	Yr	NM
❑ AL-9538	Aretha	1980	12.00
❑ AL-8442	Aretha	1986	12.00
—Different album than 9538			
❑ AL8-8019	Get It Right	1983	12.00
❑ AL-9602	Jump To It	1982	12.00
❑ AL-8344	Jump To It	1985	10.00
—Budget-line reissue			
❑ AL-9552	Love All the Hurt Away	1981	12.00
❑ AL-8368	Love All the Hurt Away	1985	10.00
—Budget-line reissue			

Number	Title	Yr	NM
❑ A2L-8497	One Lord, One Faith, One Baptism	1987	25.00
❑ AL-8572	Through the Storm	1989	12.00
❑ AL8-8286	Who's Zoomin' Who	1985	12.00

ATLANTIC

Number	Title	Yr	NM
❑ 81668	30 Greatest Hits	1986	18.00
❑ SD19161	Almighty Fire	1978	15.00
❑ SD 2-906	Amazing Grace	1972	25.00
❑ 8176 [M]	Aretha: Lady Soul	1968	30.00
❑ SD8176 [S]	Aretha: Lady Soul	1968	25.00
—Green and blue label			
❑ SD8176	Aretha: Lady Soul	1969	15.00
—Green and red label			
❑ 8150 [M]	Aretha Arrives	1967	30.00
❑ SD8150 [S]	Aretha Arrives	1967	25.00
—Green and blue label			
❑ SD8150	Aretha Arrives	1969	15.00
—Green and red label			
❑ 8212 [M]	Aretha Franklin: Soul '69	1969	50.00
—White label promo; no stock copies in mono			
❑ SD8212 [S]	Aretha Franklin: Soul '69	1969	18.00
❑ SD8207	Aretha in Paris	1968	18.00
❑ QD7205 [Q]	Aretha Live at Fillmore West	1973	30.00
❑ SD7205 [S]	Aretha Live at Fillmore West	1971	18.00
❑ 7205 [M]	Aretha Live at Fillmore West	1971	40.00
—Mono is white label promo only with "d/j copy monaural" sticker on front cover			
❑ SD8186	Aretha Now	1968	25.00
—Green and blue label			
❑ SD8186	Aretha Now	1969	15.00
—Green and red label			
❑ SD8227	Aretha's Gold	1969	18.00
❑ SD8295 [S]	Aretha's Greatest Hits	1971	18.00
❑ 8295 [M]	Aretha's Greatest Hits	1971	40.00
—Mono is white label promo only in stereo cover with "d/j monaural" sticker			
❑ 81230	Aretha's Jazz	1984	12.00
❑ SD7265	Hey Now Hey (The Other Side of the Sky)	1973	15.00
❑ STAO-95151	Hey Now Hey (The Other Side of the Sky)	1973	18.00
—Capitol Record Club edition			
❑ 8139 [M]	I Never Loved a Man the Way I Love You	1967	30.00
❑ SD8139 [S]	I Never Loved a Man the Way I Love You	1967	25.00
—Green and blue label			
❑ SD8139	I Never Loved a Man the Way I Love You	1969	15.00
—Green and red label			
❑ SD19248	La Diva	1979	15.00
❑ SD7292	Let Me in Your Life	1974	15.00
❑ SD18176	Sparkle	1976	15.00
❑ SD8265 [S]	Spirit in the Dark	1970	18.00
❑ 8265 [M]	Spirit in the Dark	1970	40.00
—Mono is white label promo only in stereo cover with "d/j monaural" sticker			
❑ SD19102	Sweet Passion	1977	15.00
❑ SD18204	Ten Years of Gold	1976	15.00
❑ QD8305 [Q]	The Best of Aretha Franklin	1974	25.00
❑ 81280	The Best of Aretha Franklin	1985	12.00
❑ SD8248 [S]	This Girl's in Love with You	1970	18.00
❑ 8248 [M]	This Girl's in Love with You	1970	40.00
—Mono is white label promo only; cover has "d/j copy monaural" sticker on front			
❑ SD18116	With Everything I Feel in Me	1974	15.00
❑ SD18151	You	1975	15.00
❑ SD7213 [S]	Young, Gifted & Black	1972	18.00
❑ 7213 [M]	Young, Gifted & Black	1972	40.00
—Mono is promo only; "d/j copy monaural" sticker on front cover			

CHECKER

Number	Title	Yr	NM
❑ 10009 [M]	Gospel Soul	1967	25.00
—Reissue with new title and cover			
❑ 10009 [M]	Songs of Faith	1965	500.00
—Original issue of this album; cover has Aretha sitting at a piano			

COLUMBIA

Number	Title	Yr	NM
❑ CL1612 [M]	Aretha	1961	50.00
—Red and black label with six "eye" logos			
❑ CL1612 [M]	Aretha	1963	25.00
—Guaranteed High Fidelity" on label			
❑ CL1612 [M]	Aretha	1965	18.00
—360 Sound Mono" on label			
❑ CS8412 [S]	Aretha	1961	80.00
—Red and black label with six "eye" logos			
❑ CS8412 [S]	Aretha	1963	30.00
—360 Sound Stereo" on label			
❑ FC40708	Aretha After Hours	1987	12.00
❑ CL2673 [M]	Aretha Franklin's Greatest Hits	1967	30.00
❑ CS9473 [S]	Aretha Franklin's Greatest Hits	1967	25.00
—360 Sound Stereo" on label			
❑ CS9601	Aretha Franklin's Greatest Hits, Volume 2	1968	25.00
—360 Sound Stereo" on label			
❑ FC40105	Aretha Franklin Sings the Blues	1985	12.00
❑ KG31355	In the Beginning/The World of Aretha Franklin 1960-1967	1972	25.00
❑ CL2079 [M]	Laughing on the Outside	1963	25.00
—Guaranteed High Fidelity" on label			
❑ CL2079 [M]	Laughing on the Outside	1965	18.00
—360 Sound Mono" on label			
❑ CS8879 [S]	Laughing on the Outside	1963	30.00
—360 Sound Stereo" on label			
❑ CL2281 [M]	Runnin' Out of Fools	1964	25.00
—Guaranteed High Fidelity" on label			
❑ CL2281 [M]	Runnin' Out of Fools	1965	18.00
—360 Sound Mono" on label			
❑ CS9081 [S]	Runnin' Out of Fools	1964	30.00
—360 Sound Stereo" on label			
❑ CS9776	Soft and Beautiful	1969	25.00
—360 Sound Stereo" on label			
❑ CL2521 [M]	Soul Sister	1966	25.00
❑ CS9321 [S]	Soul Sister	1966	30.00
—360 Sound Stereo" on label			
❑ PC38042	Sweet Bitter Love	1982	12.00
❑ CL2754 [M]	Take a Look	1967	30.00
❑ CS9554 [S]	Take a Look	1967	25.00
—360 Sound Stereo" on label			
❑ CL2629 [M]	Take It Like You Give It	1967	30.00
❑ CS9429 [S]	Take It Like You Give It	1967	25.00
—360 Sound Stereo" on label			
❑ CL1761 [M]	The Electrifying Aretha Franklin	1962	40.00
—Red and black label with six "eye" logos			
❑ CL1761 [M]	The Electrifying Aretha Franklin	1963	25.00
—Guaranteed High Fidelity" on label			
❑ CL1761 [M]	The Electrifying Aretha Franklin	1965	18.00
—360 Sound Mono" on label			
❑ CS8561 [S]	The Electrifying Aretha Franklin	1962	50.00
—Red and black label with six "eye" logos			
❑ CS8561 [S]	The Electrifying Aretha Franklin	1963	30.00
—360 Sound Stereo" on label			
❑ KC31953	The First 12 Sides	1973	15.00
❑ C237377	The Legendary Queen of Soul	1981	15.00
❑ CL1876 [M]	The Tender, The Moving, The Swinging Aretha Franklin	1962	40.00
—Red and black label with six "eye" logos			
❑ CL1876 [M]	The Tender, The Moving, The Swinging Aretha Franklin	1963	25.00
—Guaranteed High Fidelity" on label			
❑ CL1876 [M]	The Tender, The Moving, The Swinging Aretha Franklin	1965	18.00
—360 Sound Mono" on label			
❑ CS8676 [S]	The Tender, The Moving, The Swinging Aretha Franklin	1963	30.00
—360 Sound Stereo" on label			
❑ CS8676 [S]	The Tender, The Moving, The Swinging Aretha Franklin	1962	50.00
—Red and black label with six "eye" logos			
❑ CS9956	Today I Sing the Blues	1970	18.00
—360 Sound Stereo" on label			
❑ GP4	Two All-Time Great Albums in One Great Package	196?	30.00
—Contains CS 9081 and CS 9429			
❑ CL2163 [M]	Unforgettable	1964	25.00
—Guaranteed High Fidelity" on label			
❑ CL2163 [M]	Unforgettable	1965	18.00
—360 Sound Mono" on label			
❑ CS8963 [S]	Unforgettable	1964	30.00
—360 Sound Stereo" on label			
❑ CL2351 [M]	Yeah!!!	1965	25.00
—Guaranteed High Fidelity" on label			
❑ CL2351 [M]	Yeah!!!	1966	18.00
—360 Sound Mono" on label			
❑ CS9151 [S]	Yeah!!!	1965	30.00
—360 Sound Stereo" on label			

COLUMBIA SPECIAL PRODUCTS

Number	Title	Yr	NM
❑ C11282	Runnin' Out of Fools	1972	15.00
❑ C10589	Take a Look	1971	15.00

HARMONY

Number	Title	Yr	NM
❑ KH30606	Greatest Hits 1960-1965	1971	15.00
❑ KH30606	Greatest Hits 1960-1966	1972	15.00
❑ HS11349	Once in a Lifetime	1969	15.00
❑ HS11418	Two Sides of Love	1970	15.00

FRANTIC

LIZARD

Number	Title	Yr	NM
❑ 20103	Conception	1971	30.00

FRATERNITY OF MAN, THE

ABC

Number	Title	Yr	NM
❑ S-647	The Fraternity of Man	1968	30.00

DOT

Number	Title	Yr	NM
❑ DLP-25955	Get It On	1969	30.00

FRAWLEY, WILLIAM

DOT

Number	Title	Yr	NM
❑ DLP-3061 [M]	William Frawley Sings the Old Ones	1958	40.00

FRAZIER, CAESAR

EASTBOUND

Number	Title	Yr	NM
❑ 9009	Caesar Frazier '74	1974	40.00
❑ 9002	Hail Caesar!	1973	50.00

WESTBOUND

Number	Title	Yr	NM
❑ WT6103	Another Life	1978	30.00
❑ 206	Caesar Frazier '75	1975	30.00

FRAZIER, DALLAS

CAPITOL

Number	Title	Yr	NM
❑ T2552 [M]	Elvira	1966	25.00
❑ ST2552 [S]	Elvira	1966	30.00
❑ T2764 [M]	Tell It Like It Is	1967	30.00
❑ ST2764 [S]	Tell It Like It Is	1967	25.00

FREAK SCENE, THE

COLUMBIA

Number	Title	Yr	NM
❑ CL2656 [M]	Psychedelic Psoul	1967	70.00
❑ CS9456 [S]	Psychedelic Psoul	1967	100.00

FREBERG, STAN

CAPITOL

Number	Title	Yr	NM
❑ T777 [M]	A Child's Garden of Freberg	1957	50.00
—Turquoise label			
❑ T1694 [M]	Face the Funnies	1962	30.00
❑ T1816 [M]	Madison Ave. Werewolf	1962	30.00
❑ W1573 [M]	Stan Freberg Presents the United States of America	1961	30.00
❑ SW1573 [S]	Stan Freberg Presents the United States of America	1961	30.00
❑ T1242 [M]	Stan Freberg with the Original Cast	1959	30.00
❑ SM-1242 [R]	Stan Freberg with the Original Cast	197?	12.00
❑ T2020 [M]	The Best of Stan Freberg	1964	30.00
❑ SM-2020 [R]	The Best of Stan Freberg	197?	12.00
❑ WBO1035 [M]	The Best of the Stan Freberg Shows	1958	60.00
❑ SM-11765	The Best of the Stan Freberg Shows	197?	15.00
❑ T2551 [M]	The Stan Freberg Underground Show #1	1966	25.00
❑ ST2551 [S]	The Stan Freberg Underground Show #1	1966	30.00
❑ SM-2551 [S]	The Stan Freberg Underground Show #1	197?	12.00

FRED, JOHN, AND HIS PLAYBOY BAND

GUINNESS

Number	Title	Yr	NM
❑ GNS36022	Juke Box	1977	40.00

JIN

Number	Title	Yr	NM
❑ 9027	The Best of John Fred and His Playboys	198?	12.00

PAULA

Number	Title	Yr	NM
❑ LP-2193 [M]	34:40 of John Fred and His Playboys	1967	25.00
❑ LPS-2193 [S]	34:40 of John Fred and His Playboys	1967	35.00
❑ LP-2197 [M]	Agnes English	1967	30.00
❑ LPS-2197 [S]	Agnes English	1967	35.00
❑ LP-2191 [M]	John Fred and His Playboys	1966	25.00
❑ LPS-2191 [S]	John Fred and His Playboys	1966	35.00
❑ LPS-2197 [S]	Judy in Disguise with Glasses	1968	25.00
—Retitled version of "Agnes English			
❑ LPS-2201	Permanently Stated	1969	35.00

UNI

Number	Title	Yr	NM
❑ 73077	Love in My Soul	1970	30.00

FREDDIE AND THE DREAMERS

CAPITOL

Number	Title	Yr	NM
❑ SM-11896 [B]	The Best of Freddie and the Dreamers	1976	12.00
—I'm Telling You Now," "You Were Made for Me," "I Just Don't Understand," "A Little You" and "Over You" are in stereo, the rest are mono.			

MERCURY

Number	Title	Yr	NM
❑ MG-21026 [M]	Do the Freddie	1965	25.00
❑ SR-61026 [S]	Do the Freddie	1965	30.00
❑ MG-21053 [M]	Frantic Freddie	1965	18.00
❑ SR-61053 [S]	Frantic Freddie	1965	25.00
❑ MG-21017 [M]	Freddie and the Dreamers	1965	30.00
❑ SR-61017 [R]	Freddie and the Dreamers	1965	25.00
❑ MG-21061 [M]	Fun Lovin' Freddie	1966	18.00
❑ SR-61061 [S]	Fun Lovin' Freddie	1966	25.00
❑ MG-21031 [M]	Seaside Swingers	1965	25.00
❑ SR-61031 [S]	Seaside Swingers	1965	30.00

TOWER

Number	Title	Yr	NM
❑ T5003 [M]	I'm Telling You Now	1965	30.00
—Contains only two Freddie and the Dreamers songs, but the group's picture is on the cover. Also includes Four Just Men (2), Heinz (2), Linda Laine and the Sinners (2), Mike Rabin and the Demons (2) and The Toggery Five (2)			
❑ DT5003 [R]	I'm Telling You Now	1965	25.00
—Contains only two Freddie and the Dreamers songs, but the group's picture is on the cover. Also includes Four Just Men (2), Heinz (2), Linda Laine and the Sinners (2), Mike Rabin and the Demons (2) and The Toggery Five (2)			

FREDRIC

FORTE

Number	Title	Yr	NM
❑ 80461	Phases and Faces	1968	800.00

Number	Title	Yr	NM

FREE

A&M
SP-3663	Best of Free	1975	15.00
SP-4268	Fire and Water	1970	18.00
SP-3126	Fire and Water	198?	10.00
—Budget-line reissue
5318185	Fire and Water	2009	25.00
SP-4204	Free	1969	18.00
SP-4349	Free at Last	1972	18.00
SP-4306	Free Live!	1971	18.00
SP-4287	Highway	1971	18.00
SP-4198	Tons of Sobs	1969	18.00

ISLAND
| SW-9324 | Heartbreaker | 1973 | 15.00 |
—Original U.S. number, distributed by Capitol
| ILPS9217 | Heartbreaker | 1975 | 12.00 |
—U.S. reissue with same number as original U.K. issue
| ILSD4 [B] | The Free Story | 1975 | 30.00 |

PICKWICK
| SPC-3706 | Free at Last | 197? | 12.00 |

FREE BAND, THE

VANGUARD
| VSD-6507 | The Free Band | 1969 | 25.00 |

FREE DESIGN, THE

AMBROTYPE
| 1016 | There Is a Song | 1972 | 150.00 |

PROJECT 3
PR-5037SD	Heaven/Earth	1969	30.00
PR-5019SD	Kites Are Fun	1967	30.00
PR-5019QD [Q]	Kites Are Fun	197?	40.00
PR-5061SD	One By One	1971	30.00
PR-5045SD	Stars/Times/Bubbles/Love	1971	30.00
PR4006SD	The Free Design Sing for Very Important People	1970	30.00
PR-5031SD	You Could Be Born Again	1968	30.00

FREE FLIGHT

ARABESQUE
| 8130 | Free Flight | 1981 | 15.00 |

CBS
| RFM42143 | Illumination | 1986 | 12.00 |

PALO ALTO
PA-8075	Beyond the Clouds	1984	12.00
PA-8050	Soaring	1983	12.00
PA-8024	The Jazz/Classical Union	1982	12.00

VOSS
| VLP1-42932 | Free Flight | 1988 | 12.00 |
—Reissue of Arabesque LP

FREE MOVEMENT, THE

COLUMBIA
| KC31136 | I've Found Someone of My Own | 1972 | 18.00 |

FREE MUSIC QUARTET, THE

ESP-DISK'
| 1083 | Free Music One and Two | 1969 | 25.00 |

FREEBORNE

MONITOR
| MPS-607 | Peak Impressions | 1967 | 150.00 |

FREED, ALAN

BRUNSWICK
| BL54043 [M] | The Alan Freed Rock 'n' Roll Show | 1959 | 150.00 |

CORAL
CRL57216 [M]	Alan Freed Presents the King's Henchmen	1958	150.00
CRL57063 [M]	Alan Freed's Rock 'n' Roll Dance Party, Vol. 1	1956	150.00
CRL57115 [M]	Alan Freed's Rock 'n' Roll Dance Party, Vol. 2	1957	150.00
CRL57177 [M]	Go Go Go -- Alan Freed's TV Record Hop	1957	150.00
CRL57213 [M]	Rock Around the Block	1958	150.00

MGM
| E-293 [10] | The Big Beat | 195? | 200.00 |

FREEDMAN, BOB

COBBLESTONE
| 9009 | Journeys of Odysseus | 1972 | 25.00 |

SAVOY
| MG-15040 [10] | Piano Moods | 1954 | 50.00 |

FREEMAN, BOBBY

AUTUMN
| LP102 [M] | C'mon and S-W-I-M | 1964 | 50.00 |

JOSIE
| JM-4007 [M] | Get In the Swim with Bobby Freeman | 1965 | 30.00 |
| JS-4007 [R] | Get In the Swim with Bobby Freeman | 1965 | 30.00 |

JUBILEE
JLP-1086 [M]	Do You Wanna Dance?	1959	140.00
JLPS-1086 [S]	Do You Wanna Dance?	1959	200.00
JGM-5010 [M]	Twist with Bobby Freeman	1962	100.00

KING
| 930 [M] | The Lovable Style of Bobby Freeman | 1965 | 250.00 |

FREEMAN, BUD, AND BUDDY TATE

CIRCLE
| 69 | Two Beautiful | 198? | 12.00 |

FREEMAN, BUD

BETHLEHEM
| BCP-29 [M] | Newport News | 1955 | 80.00 |
| BCP-6033 | Test of Time | 197? | 15.00 |
—Reissue, distributed by RCA Victor

CAPITOL
| H625 [10] | Classics in Jazz | 1955 | 80.00 |
| T625 [M] | Classics in Jazz | 1955 | 50.00 |

CHIAROSCURO
| 135 | The Joy of Sax | 1975 | 18.00 |

CIRCLE
| 10 | Bud Freeman and Jimmy McPartland Meet the Ted Easton Jazz Band | 198? | 12.00 |

COLUMBIA
| CL6107 [10] | Comes Jazz | 1950 | 100.00 |
| CL2558 [10] | Jazz -- Chicago Style | 1955 | 80.00 |

COMMODORE
| XFL-14941 | Three's No Crowd | 198? | 15.00 |

DECCA
| DL5213 [10] | Wolverine Jazz | 1950 | 100.00 |

DOT
DLP-3166 [M]	Bud Freeman and His Summa Cum Laude Trio	1959	40.00
DLP-25166 [S]	Bud Freeman and His Summa Cum Laude Trio	1959	30.00
DLP-3254 [M]	Midnight Session	1960	30.00
DLP-25254 [S]	Midnight Session	1960	40.00

EMARCY
| MG-36013 [M] | Midnight at Eddie Condon's | 1955 | 60.00 |

FANTASY
| OJC-183 | Bud Freeman All Stars | 198? | 12.00 |
—Reissue of Swingville 2012

HALO
| 50275 [M] | Bud Freeman | 195? | 18.00 |

HARMONY
| HL7046 [M] | Bud Freeman and His All-Star Jazz | 1957 | 30.00 |

IAJRC
| LP-53 | See What the Boys in the Back Room Will Have | 198? | 12.00 |

JAZZ ARCHIVES
| JA-38 | Summer Concert 1960 | 198? | 12.00 |

JAZZOLOGY
| J-165 | The Compleat Bud Freeman | 198? | 12.00 |

MONMOUTH-EVERGREEN
| 7022 | The Compleat Bud Freeman | 1970 | 25.00 |

PARAMOUNT
| CJS-105 [10] | Bud Freeman and the Chicagoans | 195? | 80.00 |

PROMENADE
| 2134 [M] | Dixieland U.S.A. | 196? | 15.00 |

RCA VICTOR
| LPM-1508 [M] | Chicago Austin High School Jazz in Hi-Fi | 1957 | 50.00 |

SWINGVILLE
| SVLP-2012 [M] | Bud Freeman All Stars | 1960 | 50.00 |
—Purple label
| SVLP-2012 [M] | Bud Freeman All Stars | 1965 | 30.00 |
—Blue label with trident logo at right

TRIP
| 5529 | Midnight at Eddie Condon's | 197? | 12.00 |

UNITED ARTISTS
| UAJ-14033 [M] | Something Tender -- Bud Freeman and Two Guitars | 1963 | 40.00 |
| UAJS-15033 [S] | Something Tender -- Bud Freeman and Two Guitars | 1963 | 50.00 |

FREEMAN, CHICO

BLACKHAWK
| BKH-50801 | The Pied Piper | 1986 | 12.00 |

BLACK SAINT
| BSR-0036 | No Time Left | 1977 | 15.00 |

CONTEMPORARY
C-7640	Beyond the Rain	1978	15.00
C-14008	Destiny's Dance	1981	15.00
C-14005	Peaceful Heart, Gentle Spirit	1980	15.00

ELEKTRA/MUSICIAN
| 60361 | Tangents | 1984 | 12.00 |
| 60163 | Tradition in Transition | 1983 | 12.00 |

FANTASY
| OJC-479 | Beyond the Rain | 1991 | 12.00 |

INDIA NAVIGATION
IN-1031	Chico	1977	18.00
IN-1035	Kings of Mali	1978	18.00
IN-1063	Morning Prayer	198?	15.00
IN-1045	Spirit Sensitive	1979	18.00
IN-1042	The Outside Within	1981	15.00
IN-1059	The Search	1981	15.00

FREEMAN, ERNIE

DUNHILL
| D50026 [M] | Hitmaker | 1967 | 15.00 |
| DS50026 [S] | Hitmaker | 1967 | 18.00 |

IMPERIAL
LP-9133 [M]	Dark at the Top of the Stairs	1959	30.00
LP-12067 [S]	Dark at the Top of the Stairs	1959	40.00
LP-9057 [M]	Ernie Freeman	1958	50.00
LP-9022 [M]	Ernie Freeman Plays Irving Berlin	1957	50.00
LP-9030 [M]	Jivin' Around	1957	50.00
LP-9148 [M]	Raunchy	1960	50.00
LP-9193 [M]	The Stripper	1962	25.00
LP-12193 [S]	The Stripper	1962	30.00
LP-9157 [M]	Twistin' Time	1961	30.00
LP-12081 [S]	Twistin' Time	1961	40.00

LIBERTY
LRP-3331 [M]	Comin' Home Baby	1963	25.00
LST-7331 [S]	Comin' Home Baby	1963	30.00
LRP-3264 [M]	Ernie Freeman's Soulful Sounds of Country Classics	1962	25.00
LST-7264 [S]	Ernie Freeman's Soulful Sounds of Country Classics	1962	30.00
LRP-3283 [M]	Limbo Dance Party	1962	25.00
LST-7283 [S]	Limbo Dance Party	1962	30.00

FREEMAN, EVELYN

IMPERIAL
| LP-9101 [M] | Sky High | 1960 | 25.00 |
| LP-12043 [S] | Sky High | 1960 | 30.00 |

UNITED ARTISTS
| UAL-3178 [M] | Didn't It Rain | 1962 | 25.00 |
| UAS-6178 [S] | Didn't It Rain | 1962 | 30.00 |

FREEMAN, GEORGE

DELMARK
| DS-424 | Birth Sign | 197? | 15.00 |

GROOVE MERCHANT
| 3305 | Man and Woman | 1975 | 18.00 |
| 519 | New Improved Funk | 1973 | 18.00 |

FREEMAN, RUSS

PACIFIC JAZZ
| PJ-1232 [M] | Quartet: Russ Freeman/ Chet Baker | 1957 | 100.00 |
—Label says Pacific Jazz, but cover is on World Pacific
| PJLP-8 [10] | The Russ Freeman Trio | 1953 | 120.00 |
| PJ-1212 [M] | Trio: Russ Freeman/Richard Twardzik | 1956 | 100.00 |

WORLD PACIFIC
| WP 1232 [M] | Quartet: Russ Freeman/ Chet Baker | 1958 | 50.00 |
—Both label and cover are on World Pacific
| WP-1212 [M] | Trio: Russ Freeman/Richard Twardzik | 1958 | 50.00 |

FREEMAN, STAN

AUDIOPHILE
| AP-202 | Not a Care in the World | 1986 | 12.00 |

COLUMBIA
CL6193 [10]	Come On-a Stan's House	1951	60.00
CL6158 [10]	Piano Moods	1951	50.00
CL1120 [M]	Stan Freeman Swings "The Music Man"	1958	30.00

HARMONY
| HL7067 [M] | Stan Freeman Plays 30 All-Time Hits | 195? | 25.00 |

FREEMAN, VON

ATLANTIC
| SD1628 | Doin' It Right Now | 1972 | 15.00 |

NESSA
| 6 | Have No Fear | 1975 | 18.00 |
| 11 | Serenade and Blues | 197? | 18.00 |

FREEPORT

MAINSTREAM
| S-6130 | Freeport | 1970 | 50.00 |

FREES, PAUL

MGM
| SE-4735 | Paul Frees and the Poster People | 1969 | 30.00 |

FREHLEY, ACE

CASABLANCA
	Ace Frehley	1978	50.00
NBPIX-7121 [PD]			
NBLP-7121 [B]	Ace Frehley	1978	25.00

Number	Title	Yr	NM
MEGAFORCE/ATLANTIC			
❏ 81749 [B]	Frehley's Comet	1987	10.00
❏ 81826	Live + 1	1988	10.00
❏ 81862	Second Sighting	1988	10.00
❏ 82042	Trouble Walkin'	1989	14.00

FRENCH, ALBERT "PAPA

Number	Title	Yr	NM
NOBILITY			
❏ LP-702 [M]	A Night at Dixieland Hall	195?	40.00

FRESH, DOUG E., AND THE GET FRESH CREW

Number	Title	Yr	NM
GEE STREET			
❏ 444069-1	Play	1993	18.00
REALITY			
❏ 9649	Oh, My God!	1986	40.00
❏ 9658	The World's Greatest Entertainer	1988	30.00

FREY, GLENN

Number	Title	Yr	NM
ASYLUM			
❏ E1-60129	No Fun Aloud	1982	12.00
MCA			
❏ 6239	Soul Searchin'	1988	12.00
❏ 5501 [B]	The Allnighter	1984	18.00
— Quiex II vinyl promo			

FRIAR TUCK

Number	Title	Yr	NM
MERCURY			
❏ MG-21111 [M]	Friar Tuck and His Psychedelic Guitar	1967	40.00
❏ SR-61111 [S]	Friar Tuck and His Psychedelic Guitar	1967	50.00

FRICKE, JANIE

Number	Title	Yr	NM
COLUMBIA			
❏ FC40666	After Midnight	1987	12.00
❏ FC40383	Black & White	1986	12.00
❏ C240684	Celebration	1987	15.00
❏ JC36268	From the Heart	1980	15.00
❏ FC38310	Greatest Hits	1982	12.00
❏ JC36820	I'll Need Someone to Hold Me When I Cry	1980	12.00
❏ PC36820	I'll Need Someone to Hold Me When I Cry	198?	10.00
— Budget-line reissue with new prefix			
❏ FC38214	It Ain't Easy	1982	12.00
❏ AS991535 [DJ]	Janie Fricke On Tour	1982	60.00
— Promo-only picture disc			
❏ FC45087	Labor of Love	1989	15.00
❏ FC38730	Love Lies	1983	12.00
❏ PC38730	Love Lies	1985	10.00
— Budget-line reissue with new prefix			
❏ KC35774	Love Notes	1979	15.00
❏ PC35774	Love Notes	198?	10.00
— Budget-line reissue with new prefix			
❏ FC44143	Saddle the Wind	1988	12.00
❏ KC35315	Singer of Songs	1978	15.00
❏ PC35315	Singer of Songs	198?	10.00
— Budget-line reissue with new prefix			
❏ FC37535	Sleeping with Your Memory	1981	12.00
❏ PC37535	Sleeping with Your Memory	198?	10.00
— Budget-line reissue with new prefix			
❏ FC39975	Somebody Else's Fire	1985	12.00
❏ FC39338	The First Word in Memory	1984	12.00
❏ FC40165	The Very Best of Janie	1985	12.00

FRIEDMAN, DAVID

Number	Title	Yr	NM
ENJA			
❏ 3089	Of the Wind's Eye	1982	15.00
INNER CITY			
❏ IC-3004	Futures Passed	1976	15.00
❏ IC-6005	Winter Love April Joy	1979	15.00

FRIEDMAN, DEAN

Number	Title	Yr	NM
LIFESONG			
❏ LS6008	Dean Friedman	1977	15.00
❏ JZ35361	Well, Well, Said the Rocking Chair	1978	18.00

FRIEDMAN, DON

Number	Title	Yr	NM
PRESTIGE			
❏ PRLP-7488 [M]	Metamorphosis	1966	30.00
❏ PRST-7488 [S]	Metamorphosis	1966	30.00
PROGRESSIVE			
❏ PRO-7036	Hot Knepper and Pepper	198?	15.00
RIVERSIDE			
❏ RLP-384 [M]	A Day in the City	1961	40.00
❏ RS-9384 [S]	A Day in the City	1961	50.00
❏ RLP-431 [M]	Circle Waltz	1962	200.00
❏ RS-9431 [S]	Circle Waltz	1962	40.00
❏ 6082	Circle Waltz	197?	18.00
— Reissue of 9431			
❏ RLP-485 [M]	Dreams and Explorations	1965	25.00
❏ RS-9485 [S]	Dreams and Explorations	1965	30.00
❏ RLP-463 [M]	Flashback	1963	30.00
❏ RS-9463 [S]	Flashback	1963	40.00
❏ 6094	Flashback	197?	18.00
— Reissue of 9463			

FRIEDMAN, ERICK

Number	Title	Yr	NM
RCA VICTOR RED SEAL			
❏ LSC-2610 [S]	Paganini: Violin Concerto No. 1; Saint-Saens: Intro and Rondo Capriccioso	1962	40.00
— Original with "shaded dog" label			
❏ LSC-2610 [S]	Paganini: Violin Concerto No. 1; Saint-Saens: Intro and Rondo Capriccioso	1964	25.00
— Second edition with "white dog" label			

FRIEDMAN, KINKY

Number	Title	Yr	NM
ABC			
❏ X-829	Kinky Friedman	1974	12.00
EPIC			
❏ PE34304	Lasso from El Paso	1976	12.00
VANGUARD			
❏ VSD-79333	Sold American	1973	15.00

FRIEND AND LOVER

Number	Title	Yr	NM
VERVE FORECAST			
❏ FTS-3055	Reach Out of the Darkness	1968	25.00

FRIENDS, THE

Number	Title	Yr	NM
MGM			
❏ SE-4901	The Friends	1973	15.00

FRIENDS

Number	Title	Yr	NM
OBLIVION			
❏ OD-3	Friends	1974	25.00
— Jazz-rock band with John Abercrombie and Marc Cohen			

FRIENDS OF DISTINCTION, THE

Number	Title	Yr	NM
RCA VICTOR			
❏ LSP-4492	Friends & People	1971	18.00
❏ LSP-4149	Grazin'	1969	18.00
❏ LSP-4819	Greatest Hits	1972	15.00
❏ APD1-0276 [Q]	Greatest Hits	1973	30.00
❏ LSP-4212	Highly Distinct	1969	18.00
❏ LSP-4829	Love Can Make It Easier	1973	15.00
❏ LSP-4313	Real Friends	1970	18.00
❏ LSP-4408	Whatever	1970	18.00

FRIESEN, DAVID

Number	Title	Yr	NM
GLOBAL PACIFIC			
❏ OW40718	Inner Voices	1987	12.00
INNER CITY			
❏ IC-1086	Other Mansions	1980	15.00
❏ IC-1019	Star Dance	1977	15.00
❏ IC-1027	Waterfall Rainbow	1978	15.00
MUSE			
❏ MR-5109	Color Pool	197?	15.00
❏ MR-5255	Storyteller	1981	12.00
STEEPLECHASE			
❏ SCS-1138	Paths Beyond Tracing	1980	15.00

FRIGO, JOHNNY

Number	Title	Yr	NM
MERCURY			
❏ MG-20285 [M]	I Love Johnny Frigo, He Swings	1957	30.00

FRIJID PINK

Number	Title	Yr	NM
FANTASY			
❏ 9464	All Pink Inside	1974	18.00
LION			
❏ LN-1004	Earth Omen	1972	25.00
PARROT			
❏ PAS71041	Defrosted	1970	30.00
❏ PAS71033	Frijid Pink	1970	30.00

FRIPP AND ENO

Number	Title	Yr	NM
❏ AN-7001 [B]	No Pussyfooting	1976	35.00

FRISELL, BILL, AND VERNON REID

Number	Title	Yr	NM
MINOR MUSIC			
❏ MM-005	Smash and Scatteration	1984	18.00

FRISELL, BILL

Number	Title	Yr	NM
ECM			
❏ 1241	In Line	198?	12.00
❏ 25026	Rambler	1985	12.00
ELEKTRA/MUSICIAN			
❏ 60843	Before We Were Born	1988	12.00

FRITH, FRED & KAISER, HENRY

Number	Title	Yr	NM
METALANGUAGE			
❏ ML123 [B]	Who Needs Enemies	1983	25.00
❏ ML107 [B]	With Friends Like These	1979	30.00

FRITH, FRED

Number	Title	Yr	NM
RALPH			
❏ FF8057L [B]	Gravity	1980	25.00
❏ FF8106 [B]	Speechless	1981	18.00

Number	Title	Yr	NM
T.E.C. TONES			
❏ FF8057 [B]	Gravity	1990	18.00
❏ FF8106 [B]	Speechless	1990	18.00

FRIZZELL, DAVID, AND SHELLY WEST

Number	Title	Yr	NM
VIVA			
❏ 25148	Golden Duets (The Best of Frizzell & West)	1984	10.00
❏ 23907	In Session	1984	10.00
WARNER BROS.			
❏ BSK3555	Carryin' On the Family Names	1981	12.00
❏ 23754	Our Best to You	1983	12.00
❏ BSK3643	The David Frizzell & Shelly West Album	1982	12.00

FRIZZELL, DAVID

Number	Title	Yr	NM
MCA			
❏ 27093	David Frizzell	1983	10.00
VIVA			
❏ 23907	On My Own Again	1983	10.00
❏ 25112	Solo	1984	10.00
WARNER BROS.			
❏ 23688	The Family's Fine, But This One's All Mine	1982	10.00

FRIZZELL, LEFTY

Number	Title	Yr	NM
ABC			
❏ ABCX-799	Lefty	1974	30.00
— Original title			
❏ AC-30035	The ABC Collection	1976	25.00
❏ ABCX-799	The Legendary Lefty Frizzell	1974	25.00
— Revised title			
COLUMBIA			
❏ CL2488 [M]	Lefty Frizzell's Greatest Hits	1966	30.00
❏ CS9288 [S]	Lefty Frizzell's Greatest Hits	1966	40.00
— Red label, "360 Sound Stereo" at bottom			
❏ CL9019 [10]	Lefty Frizzell Sings the Songs of Jimmie Rodgers	1951	250.00
❏ C32249	Lefty Frizzell Sings the Songs of Jimmie Rodgers	1973	25.00
❏ CL9021 [10]	Listen to Lefty	1952	250.00
❏ CL2772 [M]	Puttin' On	1967	50.00
❏ CS9572 [S]	Puttin' On	1967	40.00
❏ PC33882	Remembering…The Greatest Hits of Lefty Frizzell	1975	25.00
❏ CL2169 [M]	Saginaw, Michigan	1964	30.00
❏ CS8969 [S]	Saginaw, Michigan	1964	40.00
❏ CL1342 [M]	The One and Only Lefty Frizzell	1959	120.00
❏ CL2386 [M]	The Sad Side of Love	1965	30.00
❏ CS9186 [S]	The Sad Side of Love	1965	40.00
COLUMBIA LIMITED EDITION			
❏ LE10027	Saginaw, Michigan	197?	12.00
HARMONY			
❏ HL7241 [M]	Lefty Frizzell Sings the Songs of Jimmie Rodgers	1960	30.00
❏ HS11186 [R]	The Great Sound of "Lefty" Frizzell	196?	25.00

FROEBA, FRANK

Number	Title	Yr	NM
DECCA			
❏ DL5043 [10]	Back Room Piano	1950	50.00
❏ DL5048 [10]	Old Time Piano	1950	50.00
ROYALE			
❏ 1818 [10]	Old Time Piano	1954	40.00
VARSITY			
❏ 6031 [10]	Boys in the Backroom	1950	50.00

FROGGIE BEAVER

Number	Title	Yr	NM
FROGGIE BEAVER			
❏ 7301 [B]	From the Pond	1973	60.00

FROLK HAVEN

Number	Title	Yr	NM
LRS			
❏ RT-6023	At the Apex of High	1972	180.00

FROM THE OTHER SIDE JAZZ BAND

Number	Title	Yr	NM
SOUL NOTE			
❏ 121106	From the Other Side	1990	15.00

FROMAN, JANE

Number	Title	Yr	NM
CAPITOL			
❏ T726 [M]	Faith	1956	30.00
❏ T889 [M]	Songs at Sunset	1957	30.00
❏ H354 [10]	Yours Alone	1952	40.00
DECCA			
❏ DL6021 [10]	Souvenirs	1952	40.00
RCA VICTOR			
❏ LPT-3055 [10]	Gems from Gershwin	1952	40.00

FRONTIERE, DOMINIC

Number	Title	Yr	NM
COLUMBIA			
❏ CL1427 [M]	Love Eyes: The Moods of Romance	1960	30.00
❏ CS8224 [S]	Love Eyes: The Moods of Romance	1960	40.00
❏ CL1273 [M]	Pagan Festival	1958	40.00

Number	Title	Yr	NM
LIBERTY			
❏ LRP-3032 [M]	Dom Frontiere Plays the Classics	1957	40.00
❏ LRP-3015 [M]	Fabulous!	1956	40.00
❏ LST-7008 [S]	Mr. Accordion	1958	40.00
—Evidently not issued in mono			
❏ LJH-6002 [M]	The Dom Frontiere Sextet	1956	50.00
FROST, FRANK			
EARWIG			
❏ 4914	Midnight Prowler	1990	12.00
❏ 4901	Rockin' the Juke Joint Down	1986	12.00
JEWEL			
❏ LPS-5013	Frank Frost	1973	18.00
PHILLIPS INTERNATIONAL			
❏ PLP-1975 [M]	Hey Boss Man!	1962	3000.00
—VG value 1500; VG+ value 2250			
FROST, MAX, AND THE TROOPERS			
TOWER			
❏ ST-5147	Shape of Things to Come	1968	50.00
FROST, THE			
VANGUARD			
❏ VSD-79392	Early Frost	1978	18.00
❏ VSD-6520	Frost Music	1969	25.00
❏ VSD-6541	Rock and Roll Music	1969	25.00
❏ VSD-6556	Through the Eyes of Love	1970	25.00
FROST, THOMAS AND RICHARD			
UNI			
❏ 73124	Thomas and Richard Frost	1972	18.00
FRUSCELLA, TONY			
ATLANTIC			
❏ 1220 [M]	Tony Fruscella	1955	500.00
FRUT			
TRASH			
❏ (# unknown)0	Keep On Truckin'	1971	80.00
—Originals on yellow vinyl			
WESTBOUND			
❏ WB-2005	Keep On Truckin'	1971	30.00
—Reissue of Trash LP			
❏ WB-2008	Spoiled Rotten	1972	30.00
FRYE, DAVID			
BUDDAH			
❏ 1600	Richard Nixon: A Fantasy	1973	15.00
❏ BDS-5097	Richard Nixon: Superstar	1971	15.00
ELEKTRA			
❏ EKS-75006	I Am the President	1969	15.00
❏ EKS-74085	Radio Free Nixon	1971	15.00
FRYE			
❏ DFP-80	The Great Debate	1980	18.00
FU-SCHNICKENS			
JIVE			
❏ 41519	Nervous Breakdown	1994	18.00
FUEL			
550 MUSIC			
❏ D68554	Sunburn	1998	15.00
FUGAZI			
DISCHORD			
❏ 30 [EP]	Fugazi	1988	40.00
❏ 70 [B]	In On the Kill Taker	1993	30.00
❏ 35 [EP]	Margin Walker	1989	40.00
❏ 90-V [B]	Red Medicine	1995	30.00
❏ 44 [B]	Repeater	1990	30.00
❏ 60 [B]	Steady Diet of Nothing	1991	30.00
FUGEES			
RUFFHOUSE			
❏ C67904	Bootleg Versions	1996	18.00
❏ C267147	The Score	1995	18.00
FUGITIVES, THE, AND OTHERS			
WESTCHESTER			
❏ 1005 [M]	Friday at the Cage A-Go-Go	1965	1500.00
FUGITIVES, THE			
HIDEOUT			
❏ 1001 [M]	The Fugitives at Dave's Hideout	1965	1200.00
JUSTICE			
❏ JLP-141	The Fugitives On the Run	1967	300.00
—Different group from "Hideout" FUGITIVES.			
FUGS, THE			
4 MEN WITH BEARDS			
❏ 4M148LP [B]	It Crawled Into My Hand, Honest		25.00

Number	Title	Yr	NM
❏ 4M147LP [B]	Tenderness Junction		25.00
BROADSIDE			
❏ 304 [M]	The Village Fugs Sing Ballads of Contemporary Protest, Point of View, and General Dissatisfaction	1965	500.00
—With insert			
❏ 304 [M]	The Village Fugs Sing Ballads of Contemporary Protest, Point of View, and General Dissatisfaction	1965	400.00
—Without insert			
ESP-DISK			
❏ 2018	Fugs 4, Rounders Score	196?	80.00
❏ 1028 [S]	The Fugs	1966	50.00
—Black and white cover, back cover photos staggered			
❏ 1028 [S]	The Fugs	1966	30.00
—Black and white cover, back cover photos aligned			
❏ 1028 [S]	The Fugs	1966	80.00
—Psychedelic color shield on cover			
❏ 1018 [M]	The Fugs First Album	1966	40.00
—Reissue of Broadside 304" on cover			
❏ 1018 [M]	The Fugs First Album	1966	200.00
—Turquoise and black cover, different from all other versions			
❏ 1018 [M]	The Fugs First Album	1967	30.00
—No reference to reissue on cover			
❏ 1038 [S]	Virgin Fugs	1967	150.00
—For Adult Minds" sticker on cover; with poster, book and stickers			
❏ 1038 [S]	Virgin Fugs	1967	50.00
—For Adult Minds" sticker, no inserts			
❏ 1038 [S]	Virgin Fugs	1967	50.00
—For Adult Minds" stamped on cover			
❏ 1038 [S]	Virgin Fugs	1967	50.00
—For Adult Minds" printed on cover			
PVC			
❏ 8914	Proto Punk: The Fugs Greatest Hits, Vol. 1	1982	18.00
REPRISE			
❏ RS-6359 [B]	Belle of Avenue A	1969	35.00
❏ RS-6396	Golden Fifth	1970	30.00
❏ RS-6305 [B]	It Crawled Into My Hand, Honest	1968	40.00
❏ R-6280 [M]	Tenderness Junction	1968	50.00
❏ RS-6280 [S]	Tenderness Junction	1968	30.00
FULL MOON			
DOUGLAS			
❏ KZ31904	Full Moon	1972	18.00
FULL SWING			
CYPRESS			
❏ YL 0109	In Full Swing	1988	12.00
❏ YL 0128	The End of the Sky	1989	15.00
PLANET			
❏ BXL1-4426	Good Times Are Back!	1982	12.00
FULLER, BOBBY, FOUR			
MUSTANG			
❏ M-901 [M]	I Fought the Law	1966	100.00
❏ MS-901 [S]	I Fought the Law	1966	200.00
❏ M-900 [M]	KRLA King of the Wheels	1965	200.00
❏ MS-900 [S]	KRLA King of the Wheels	1965	250.00
RHINO			
❏ RNDF-201	The Best of the Bobby Fuller Four	1981	15.00
❏ RNLP70174	The Best of the Bobby Fuller Four (Golden Archive Series)	1987	12.00
❏ RNLP-057 [B]	The Bobby Fuller Tapes, Vol. 1	1983	15.00
VOXX			
❏ VXS200028 [B]	The Bobby Fuller Tapes, Vol. 2	1984	18.00
FULLER, CURTIS			
ABC IMPULSE!			
❏ AS-22 [S]	Cabin in the Sky	1968	15.00
BEE HIVE			
❏ BH-7007	Fire and Filigree	197?	15.00
BLUE NOTE			
❏ BLP-1572 [M]	Bone and Bari	1957	350.00
—Deep groove" version (deep indentation under label on both sides)			
❏ BLP-1572 [M]	Bone and Bari	1957	80.00
—Regular version with W. 63rd St. address on label			
❏ BLP-1572 [M]	Bone and Bari	1963	30.00
—New York, USA" address on label			
❏ BST-1572 [S]	Bone and Bari	1959	500.00
—Deep groove" version (deep indentation under label on both sides)			
❏ BST-1572 [S]	Bone and Bari	1959	50.00
—Regular version with W. 63rd St. address on label			
❏ BST-1572 [S]	Bone and Bari	1963	25.00
—New York, USA" address on label			
❏ BST-81572 [S]	Bone and Bari	1967	18.00
—A Division of Liberty Records" on label			
❏ BLP-1583 [M]	Curtis Fuller, Volume 3	1958	900.00

Number	Title	Yr	NM
—Deep groove" version (deep indentation under label on both sides)			
❏ BLP-1583 [M]	Curtis Fuller, Volume 3	1958	80.00
—Regular version with W. 63rd St. address on label			
❏ BLP-1583 [M]	Curtis Fuller, Volume 3	1963	30.00
—New York, USA" address on label			
❏ BST-1583 [S]	Curtis Fuller, Volume 3	1959	250.00
—Deep groove" version (deep indentation under label on both sides)			
❏ BST-1583 [S]	Curtis Fuller, Volume 3	1959	50.00
—Regular version with W. 63rd St. address on label			
❏ BST-1583 [S]	Curtis Fuller, Volume 3	1963	25.00
—New York, USA" address on label			
❏ BST-81583 [S]	Curtis Fuller, Volume 3	1967	18.00
—A Division of Liberty Records" on label			
❏ BLP-1567 [M]	The Opener	1957	120.00
—Deep groove" version (deep indentation under label on both sides)			
❏ BLP-1567 [M]	The Opener	1957	80.00
—Regular version with W. 63rd St. address on label			
❏ BLP-1567 [M]	The Opener	1963	30.00
—New York, USA" address on label			
❏ BST-1567 [S]	The Opener	1959	500.00
—Deep groove" version (deep indentation under label on both sides)			
❏ BST-1567 [S]	The Opener	1959	50.00
—Regular version with W. 63rd St. address on label			
❏ BST-1567 [S]	The Opener	1963	25.00
—New York, USA" address on label			
❏ BST-81567 [S]	The Opener	1967	18.00
—A Division of Liberty Records" on label			
EPIC			
❏ LA16020 [M]	South American Cookin'	1961	300.00
❏ BA17020 [S]	South American Cookin'	1961	50.00
❏ LA16013 [M]	The Magnificent Trombone	1961	30.00
❏ BA17013 [S]	The Magnificent Trombone	1961	40.00
FANTASY			
❏ OJC-077	New Trombone	198?	12.00
IMPULSE!			
❏ A-22 [M]	Cabin in the Sky	1962	30.00
❏ AS-22 [S]	Cabin in the Sky	1962	30.00
❏ A-13 [M]	Soul Trombone	1962	30.00
❏ AS-13 [S]	Soul Trombone	1962	30.00
MAINSTREAM			
❏ MRL-333	Crankin'	1971	25.00
❏ MRL-370	Smokin'	1972	25.00
❏ NJLP 8277 [M]	Curtis Fuller with Red Garland	1962	50.00
—Purple label			
❏ NJLP-8277 [M]	Curtis Fuller with Red Garland	1965	30.00
—Blue label, trident logo at right			
PRESTIGE			
❏ PRLP-7107 [M]	New Trombone	1957	300.00
REGENT			
❏ MG-6055 [M]	Jazz...It's Magic	1957	80.00
SAVOY			
❏ MG 12141 [M]	Blues-Ette	1959	50.00
❏ ST-13006 [S]	Blues-Ette	1959	40.00
❏ MG-12151 [M]	Curtis Fuller	1960	40.00
❏ MG-12164 [M]	Images of Curts Fuller	1960	40.00
❏ MG-12144 [M]	Imagination	1959	40.00
❏ MG-12209 [M]	Jazz...It's Magic	196?	25.00
❏ MG-12143 [M]	The Curtis Fuller Jazztet with Benny Golson	1959	40.00
SAVOY JAZZ			
❏ SJL 2239	All-Star Sextets	197?	15.00
❏ SJL-1135	Blues-Ette	198?	12.00
SMASH			
❏ MGS-27034 [M]	Jazz Conference Abroad	1962	30.00
❏ SRS-67034 [S]	Jazz Conference Abroad	1962	30.00
STATUS			
❏ ST-8305 [M]	Curtis Fuller and Hampton Hawes with French Horns	1965	40.00
UNITED ARTISTS			
❏ UAL-4051 [M]	Sliding Easy	1959	300.00
❏ UAS-5051 [S]	Sliding Easy	1959	40.00
WARWICK			
❏ W-2038 [M]	Boss of the Soul Stream Trombone	1961	50.00
❏ W-2038ST [S]	Boss of the Soul Stream Trombone	1961	50.00
FULLER, GIL			
PACIFIC JAZZ			
❏ PJ-93 [M]	Gil Fuller and the Monterey Jazz Orchestra with Dizzy Gillespie	1965	30.00
❏ ST-93 [S]	Gil Fuller and the Monterey Jazz Orchestra with Dizzy Gillespie	1965	30.00
❏ LN-10060	Gil Fuller and the Monterey Jazz Orchestra with Dizzy Gillespie	198?	10.00
—Budget-line reissue			
❏ PJ-10101 [M]	Night Flight	1966	25.00
❏ ST-20101 [S]	Night Flight	1966	30.00
❏ LN-10128	Night Flight	198?	10.00
—Budget-line reissue			

Number	Title	Yr	NM

FULLER, JERRY

LIN
❑ 100 [M]	Teenage Love	1960	250.00

MCA
❑ 3170	My Turn Now	1979	15.00

FULLER, JERRY (2)

ANDEX
❑ A-3008 [M]	Clarinet Portrait	1958	40.00
❑ AS-3008 [S]	Clarinet Portrait	1959	30.00

FULSON, LOWELL

ARHOOLIE
❑ R-2003	Early Recordings	1962	30.00

BIG TOWN
❑ 1008	Lovemaker	1978	15.00

CHESS
❑ 408	Hung Down Head	197?	18.00

GRANITE
❑ 1006	Ol' Blues Singer	1976	18.00

JEWEL
❑ LPS-5003	In a Heavy Bag	1970	18.00
❑ LPS-5009	I've Got the Blues	1973	18.00

KENT
❑ KLP-5016 [M]	Lowell Fulsom	1965	30.00
❑ KST-516 [S]	Lowell Fulsom	1965	40.00
❑ KST-531	Lowell Fulsom Now	1969	30.00
❑ KLP-5020 [M]	Tramp	1967	30.00
❑ KST-520 [S]	Tramp	1967	40.00

ROUNDER
❑ 2088	It's a Good Day	198?	15.00

FUN AND GAMES

UNI
❑ 73042	Elephant Candy	1968	30.00

FUNK INC.

PRESTIGE
❑ 10043	Chicken Lickin'	1972	18.00
❑ 10031	Funk Inc.	1971	18.00
❑ 10059	Hangin' Out	1973	18.00
❑ 10087	Priced to Sell	1974	18.00
❑ 10071	Superfunk	1973	18.00

FUNKADELIC

4 MEN WITH BEARDS
❑ 4M179LP [B]	America Eats Its Young		25.00
❑ 4M173LP [B]	Cosmic Slop		25.00
❑ 4M172LP [B]	Free Your Mind... And Your Ass Will Follow		25.00
❑ 4M160LP [B]	Funkadelic		25.00
❑ 4M160 [B]	Funkadelic	2014	30.00
❑ 4M207LP [B]	Let's Take It To The Stage		25.00
❑ 4M161LP [B]	Maggot Brain		25.00
❑ 4M180LP [B]	Standing On The Verge Of Getting It On		25.00
❑ 4M208LP [B]	Tales Of Kidd Funkadelic		25.00

SCARFACE/PRIORITY
❑ 53873	Hardcore Jollies	1993	18.00
—Limited-edition reissue of Warner Bros. 2973			
❑ 53872	One Nation Under a Groove	1993	18.00
—Limited-edition reissue of Warner Bros. 3209			
❑ 53874	The Electric Spanking of War Babies	1993	18.00
—Limited-edition reissue of Warner Bros. 3482			
❑ 53875	Uncle Jam Wants You	1993	18.00
—Limited-edition reissue of Warner Bros. 3371			

WARNER BROS.
❑ BS2973	Hardcore Jollies	1976	30.00
❑ BS3209 [B]	One Nation Under a Groove	1978	30.00
—Includes bonus 7-inch single with small hole (deduct 20% if missing)			
❑ BSK3482	The Electric Spanking of War Babies	1981	30.00
❑ BSK3371	Uncle Jam Wants You	1979	30.00

WESTBOUND
❑ 2020	America Eats Its Young	1972	60.00
❑ 221	America Eats Its Young	1976	30.00
—Reissue of Westbound 2020			
❑ 2020	America Eats Its Young	1991	25.00
—Reissue with bar code			
❑ 303	Best of the Early Years	197?	40.00
❑ 2022	Cosmic Slop	1973	50.00
❑ 223	Cosmic Slop	1976	30.00
—Reissue of Westbound 2022			
❑ 2022	Cosmic Slop	1991	18.00
—Reissue with bar code			
❑ 2001	Free Your Mind...And Your Ass Will Follow	1970	50.00
❑ 2001	Free Your Mind...And Your Ass Will Follow	1990	18.00
—Reissue with bar code			
❑ 217	Free Your Mind...And Your Ass Will Follow	1975	30.00
—Reissue of Westbound 2001			
❑ 2000	Funkadelic	1970	50.00
❑ 216	Funkadelic	1975	30.00

Number	Title	Yr	NM
—Reissue of Westbound 2000			
❑ 2000	Funkadelic	1990	18.00
—Reissue with bar code			
❑ 1004	Funkadelic's Greatest Hits	1975	50.00
❑ 215	Let's Take It to the Stage	1975	50.00
❑ 215	Let's Take It to the Stage	1992	18.00
—Reissue with bar code			
❑ 2007	Maggot Brain	1971	50.00
❑ 218	Maggot Brain	1975	30.00
—Reissue of Westbound 2007			
❑ 2007 [B]	Maggot Brain	1990	18.00
—Reissue with bar code			
❑ 1001	Standing on the Verge of Getting It On	1974	50.00
❑ 208	Standing on the Verge of Getting It On	1975	30.00
—Reissue of Westbound 1001			
❑ 1001	Standing on the Verge of Getting It On	1991	18.00
—Reissue with bar code			
❑ 227	Tales of Kidd Funkadelic	1976	50.00
❑ 227	Tales of Kidd Funkadelic	1992	18.00
—Reissue with bar code			

FUNKADELIC (2)

LAX
❑ FW37087	Connections and Disconnections	1981	12.00

FUNKDOOBIEST

IMMORTAL
❑ E64195	Brothas Doobie	1995	15.00

FUNKMASTER FLEX

DEF JAM
❑ 538258-1	The Tunnel	1999	18.00
—With Big Kap			

LOUD
❑ 1961-1	60 Minutes of Funk, Volume IV: The Mixtape	2000	18.00
❑ 67472	Funkmaster Flex: The Mix Tape Volume II	1997	18.00
❑ 67647	Funkmaster Flex: The Mix Tape Volume III	1998	18.00
❑ 66805	Funkmaster Flex Presents the Mix Tape Volume 1	1995	18.00

FUNKY COMMUNICATIONS COMMITTEE

FREE FLIGHT
❑ AHL1-3406	Baby I Want You	1979	18.00

RCA VICTOR
❑ AHL1-3583	Do You Believe in Magic	1980	18.00

FUNKY GREEN DOGS

TWISTED
❑ 11511	Get Fired Up!	1997	18.00

FUNKY KINGS

ARISTA
❑ AL4078	Funky Kings	1976	15.00

FUNT, ALLEN

BLOOPERS
❑ CM 0001 [M]	The Best of Allen Funt's Candid Mike	196?	25.00

COLUMBIA MASTERWORKS
❑ ML4344 [M]	Allen Funt's Candid Microphone	1950	40.00
—Green label			
❑ ML4449 [M]	Allen Funt's Candid Microphone, Vol. 2	1951	40.00
—Green label			
❑ ML4450 [M]	Allen Funt's Candid Microphone, Vol. 3	1951	40.00

HARMONY
❑ HL7243 [M]	Allen Funt's Candid Microphone	195?	25.00

JUBILEE
❑ KS-2 [M]	Candid Camera	196?	25.00

RCA VICTOR
❑ LPM-3679 [M]	Allen Funt and Candid Kids	1967	40.00
❑ LSP-3679 [S]	Allen Funt and Candid Kids	1967	30.00

FURAY, RICHIE

ASYLUM
❑ 6E-115	Dance a Little Light	1978	12.00
❑ 6E-231	I Still Have Dreams	1979	12.00
❑ 7E-1067	I've Got a Reason	1976	18.00

MYRRH
❑ MSB-6672	I've Got a Reason	1981	25.00
—Christian-market reissue of Asylum 7E-1067			
❑ MSB-6695	Seasons of Change	1982	12.00

FUSE

EPIC
❑ BN26502	Fuse	1970	80.00

Number	Title	Yr	NM

FUTURE, THE

SHAMLEY
❑ 703	Down the Country Road	1969	25.00

FUTURES, THE

BUDDAH
❑ BDS-5630	Castles in the Sky	1975	100.00

PHILADELPHIA INT'L.
❑ JZ36414	Greetings of Peace	1980	60.00
❑ JZ35458	Past, Present and the Futures	1979	50.00

FUZZ, THE

CALLA
❑ SD2001	The Fuzz	1971	18.00

FUZZTONES, THE

CLEOPATRA
❑ 3746 [B]	Lysergic Legacy		25.00

SUNDAZED
❑ LP5044	Flashbacks	199?	18.00

G

G.B.H.

CLEOPATRA
❑ 7926 [B]	Punked In The O.C. - Live At The Celebrity Theater 1988		25.00

G.T.O.'S, THE (2)

REPRISE
❑ RS6390 [B]	Permanent Damage	1970	70.00
—Without booklet			
❑ RS6390	Permanent Damage	1970	70.00
With booklet			

STRAIGHT
❑ STS-1059 [B]	Permanent Damage	1969	100.00
—Without booklet			
❑ STS-1059 [B]	Permanent Damage	1969	150.00
—With booklet			

GABRIEL, PETER

ATCO

❑ SD 36-147 [B]	Peter Gabriel	1977	18.00
—The "Solsbury Hill" album -- Original pressing has yellow labels			
❑ SD 36-147	Peter Gabriel	1980	12.00
—The "Solsbury Hill" album -- Other than yellow labels			

ATLANTIC
❑ SD-19181	Peter Gabriel	1978	18.00
—The "D.I.Y." album			

DIRECT DISK
❑ SD-16615	Peter Gabriel	1980	80.00
—The "Solsbury Hill" album; contains a long version of "Slowburn" not available elsewhere			

GEFFEN
❑ GHS24070	Birdy (Soundtrack)	1985	12.00
❑ GHS24206	Passion: Music for "The Last Temptation of Christ	1989	18.00
❑ GHSP2035	Peter Gabriel	1983	12.00
—Reissue of Mercury album			
❑ R153801	Peter Gabriel (Security)	1982	15.00
—RCA Music Service edition			
❑ GHS2011	Peter Gabriel (Security)	1982	12.00

Number	Title	Yr	NM
❏ GHS2011 [DJ]	Peter Gabriel (Security)	1982	40.00
—Promo-only Quiex II audiophile pressing			
❏ R243372	Plays Live	1983	25.00
—RCA Music Service edition			
❏ 2GHS4012	Plays Live	1983	18.00
❏ R114764	So	1986	15.00
—BMG Direct Marketing edition			
❏ GHS24088	So	1986	12.00
MERCURY			
❏ SRM-1-3848	Peter Gabriel	1980	15.00
—(The "Games Without Frontiers" album)			
REAL WORLD			
❏ PGDLP-6	Birdy (Soundtrack)	2004	30.00
—Classic Records reissue on 200-gram vinyl			
❏ PGDLP-8	Passion: Music for "The Last Temptation of Christ	2004	30.00
—Classic Records reissue on 200-gram vinyl			
❏ PGDLP-1	Peter Gabriel	2002	30.00
—(The "Solsbury Hill" album) -- Classic Records audiophile issue			
❏ PGDLP-2	Peter Gabriel	2002	30.00
—(The "D.I.Y." album) -- Classic Records audiophile issue			
❏ PGDLP-3	Peter Gabriel	2003	30.00
—(The "Games Without Frontiers" album) -- Classic Records audiophile issue			
❏ PGDLP-4	Peter Gabriel (Security)	2003	30.00
—Classic Records audiophile edition			
❏ PGDLP5	Plays Live	2004	40.00
—Classic Records audiophile issue			
❏ PGDLP-7	So	2003	30.00
—Classic Records audiophile edition			
❏ PGDLP11	Up	2002	40.00
—Classic Records audiophile issue; includes bonus 45 in picture sleeve			
❏ PGDLP-9	Us	2004	40.00
—Classic Records edition on 200-gram vinyl			

GABRIEL BONDAGE

DHARMA

❏ D-804 [B]	Angel Dust	1975	50.00
❏ D-808	Another Trip to Earth	1977	25.00
—Exists on white, red, or blue vinyl; each of similar value			

GAILLARD, SLIM

ALLEGRO ELITE

❏ 4050 [10]	Slim Gaillard Plays	195?	30.00
CLEF			
❏ MGC-126 [10]	Mish Mash	1953	100.00
❏ MGC-138 [10]	Slim Cavorts	1953	100.00
DISC			
❏ DLP-505 [10]	Opera in Vout	195?	200.00
DOT			
❏ DLP-25190 [S]	Slim Gaillard Rides Again	1959	40.00
❏ DLP-3190 [M]	Slim Gaillard Rides Again	1959	30.00
KING			
❏ 295-80 [10]	Slim Gaillard/Boogie	195?	100.00
MCA			
❏ 1508	The Dot Sessions	198?	12.00
NORGRAN			
❏ MGN-13 [10]	Slim Gaillard and His Musical Aggregation Wherever They May Be	1954	100.00
VERVE			
❏ MGV-2013 [M]	Smorgasbord, Help Yourself	1956	50.00
❏ V-2013 [M]	Smorgasbord, Help Yourself	1961	25.00

GAILLARD, SLIM/DIZZY GILLESPIE

ULTRAPHONIC

❏ ULP-50273 [M]	Gaillard and Gillespie	1958	40.00

GAILLARD, SLIM/MEADE LUX LEWIS

CLEF

❏ MGC-506 [10]	Boogie Woogie at the Philharmonic	1954	150.00
MERCURY			
❏ MGC-506 [10]	Boogie Woogie at the Philharmonic	1951	250.00

GAINSBOURG, SERGE

4 MEN WITH BEARDS

❏ 4M171LP [B]	Aux Armes Et Caetera		25.00
❏ 4M195LP [B]	Gainsbourg Percussions		25.00
❏ 4M196LP [B]	Initials B.B.		25.00
❏ 4M170LP [B]	L'Homme A Tete De Chou		25.00

GALAHADS, THE

LIBERTY

❏ LRP-3371 [M]	Hello, Galahads	1964	30.00
❏ LST-7371 [S]	Hello, Galahads	1964	35.00

GALASSO, MICHAEL

ECM

❏ 1245	Scenes	198?	15.00

GALAXY ALL-STARS, THE

GALAXY

❏ GXY-95001	Live Under the Sky	1979	18.00

GALBRAITH, BARRY

DECCA

❏ DL9200 [M]	Guitar and the Wind	1958	50.00
❏ DL79200 [S]	Guitar and the Wind	1959	40.00

GALBRAITH, ROB

COLUMBIA

❏ CS1057	Nashville Dirt	1970	25.00

GALE, EDDIE

BLUE NOTE

❏ BST-84320	Black Rhythm Happening	1969	30.00
❏ BST-84294	Eddie Gale's Ghetto Music	1968	30.00

GALE, ERIC

COLUMBIA

❏ PC34421	Ginseng	1977	12.00
—Original edition with no bar code			
❏ JC34938	Multiplication	1978	12.00
❏ JC35715	Part of You	1979	12.00
❏ JC36363	The Best of Eric Gale	1980	12.00
❏ JC36570	Touch of Silk	1981	12.00
ELEKTRA/MUSICIAN			
❏ 60022	Blue Horizon	1982	12.00
❏ 60198	Island Breeze	1984	12.00
EMARCY			
❏ 836369-1	In a Jazz Tradition	1989	15.00
KUDU			
❏ 11	Forecast	1973	18.00

GALE, SUNNY

CANADIAN AMERICAN

❏ CALP-1015 [M]	Goldies by the Girls	1964	30.00
RCA VICTOR			
❏ LPM-1277 [M]	Sunny and Blue	1956	40.00
ROYALE			
❏ 18123 [10]	Sunny Gale and Jazz Orchestra	1954	50.00
THIMBLE			
❏ TLP-10 [B]	Sunny Sings Dixieland and Blues	1974	25.00
WARWICK			
❏ W-2018 [M]	Sunny	1960	30.00

GALLAGHER, BRIAN

CYPRESS

❏ 0126	Coming Home	1989	15.00

GALLAGHER, RORY

ATCO

❏ SD7004 [B]	Deuce	1971	25.00
❏ SD 33-368 [B]	Rory Gallagher	1971	25.00
CHRYSALIS			
❏ CHR1098 [B]	Against the Grain	1975	18.00
❏ CHR1124 [B]	Calling Card	1976	18.00
❏ CHR1170 [B]	Photo-Finish	1978	18.00
❏ CHR1280 [B]	Stage Struck	1980	18.00
❏ CHR1235 [B]	Top Priority	1979	18.00
MERCURY			
❏ SRM-1-4051 [B]	Jinx	1982	18.00
POLYDOR			
❏ PD-5522 [B]	Blueprint	1973	25.00
❏ PD-9501 [B]	Irish Tour '74	1974	30.00
❏ PD-5513 [B]	Rory Gallagher/Live!	1972	25.00
❏ PD-1-6510 [B]	Sinner...And Saint	1975	25.00
❏ PD-5539 [B]	Tattoo	1973	25.00
❏ PD-1-6519 [B]	The Story So Far	1975	25.00
SPRINGBOARD			
❏ SPB-4056 [B]	Take It Easy Baby	1976	18.00

GALLERY

SUSSEX

❏ SUX-7026	Jim Gold and Gallery	1973	15.00
❏ SUX-7017	Nice to Be with You	1972	15.00

GALLERY (2)

ECM

❏ 1206	Gallery	1982	15.00

GALLODORO, AL

ARCO

❏ AL-3 [10]	Al Gallodoro Concert	1950	50.00
COLUMBIA			
❏ CL6188 [10]	Al Gallodoro	1951	50.00

GALLOP, FRANK

MUSICOR

❏ MM-2110 [M]	Frank Gallop Sings	1966	18.00
❏ MS-3110 [S]	Frank Gallop Sings	1966	25.00

GALLOWAY, JIM

SACKVILLE

❏ 4002	The Metro Stompers	198?	12.00
❏ 4011	Thou Swell	198?	12.00
❏ 2007	Three Is Company	198?	12.00

GALPER, HAL

BLACKHAWK

❏ BKH529	Naturally	1987	18.00
CENTURY			
❏ 1120	Speak with a Single Voice	1978	18.00
CONCORD JAZZ			
❏ CJ-383	Portrait	1988	12.00
ENJA			
❏ 4006	Speak with a Single Voice	198?	15.00
INNER CITY			
❏ IC-3012	Now Hear This	1977	18.00
❏ IC-2067	Reach Out	1978	18.00
MAINSTREAM			
❏ MRL-398 [B]	Inner Journey	1974	25.00
❏ MRL-337	The Guerrilla Band	1971	25.00
❏ MRL-354	Wild Bird	1972	25.00
STEEPLECHASE			
❏ SCS-1067	Reach Out	198?	15.00
—Reissue of Inner City 2067			

GALS & PALS

FONTANA

❏ MGF-27557 [M]	Gals & Pals Sing Something for Everybody	1966	18.00
❏ SRF-67557 [S]	Gals & Pals Sing Something for Everybody	1966	25.00
❏ MGF-27538 [M]	Gals & Pals (The Exciting Vocal Sounds of Europe's Newest "In" Group)	1965	18.00
❏ SRF-67538 [S]	Gals & Pals (The Exciting Vocal Sounds of Europe's Newest "In" Group)	1965	25.00

GAMBRELL, FREDDIE, AND PAUL HORN

WORLD PACIFIC

❏ WP-1262 [M]	Mikado	1959	40.00
❏ ST-1023 [S]	Mikado	1959	30.00

GAMBRELL, FREDDIE

WORLD PACIFIC

❏ WP-1256 [M]	Freddie Gambrell	1959	50.00

GAME

EVOLUTION

❏ 2021	Game	1970	15.00
❏ 3008	Long Hot Summer	1971	15.00
FAITHFUL VIRTUE			
❏ 2003	Game	1969	25.00

GANDALF

CAPITOL

❏ ST-121 [B]	Gandalf	1969	300.00

GANDALF THE GREY

G.W.R.

❏ 7 [B]	The Grey Wizard Am I	1972	700.00

GANDELMAN, LEO

VERVE FORECAST

❏ 836424-1	Western World	1989	15.00

GANELIN TRIO, THE

HAT ART

❏ 2027	Non Troppo	1986	18.00

GANG OF FOUR

WARNER BROS.

❏ MINI3646 [EP]	Another Day, Another Dollar	1982	12.00
❏ BSK3446	Entertainment!	1980	14.00
❏ BSK3494	Gang of Four	1980	12.00
❏ 23936	Hard	1983	12.00
❏ BSK3565	Solid Gold	1981	12.00
❏ 23683	Songs of the Free	1982	12.00

GANG STARR

CHRYSALIS

❏ F1-21910	Daily Operation	1992	18.00
❏ F1-28435	Hard to Earn	1994	18.00
❏ F1-21798	Step In the Arena	1991	18.00
VIRGIN			
❏ 47279	Full Clip -- A Decade of Gang Starr	1999	25.00
❏ 45585	Moment of Truth	1998	18.00
WILD PITCH			
❏ E1-98709	No More Mr. Nice Guy	1992	15.00
❏ 2001	No More Mr. Nice Guy	1989	18.00

GANNON, JIM

CATALYST

❏ 7605	Gannon's Back in Town	1976	18.00

Number	Title	Yr	NM

GANT, CECIL

KING
❏ 671 [M]	Cecil Gant	1960	80.00

RED MILL
❏ (no #)0 [M]	Cecil Gant	1956	500.00
—Red vinyl			

SOUND
❏ 601 [M]	The Incomparable Cecil Gant	1958	100.00

GANTS, THE

LIBERTY
❏ LRP-3432 [M]	Road Runner	1965	40.00
❏ LST-7432 [S]	Road Runner	1965	40.00
❏ LRP-3473 [M]	The Gants Again	1966	40.00
❏ LST-7473 [S]	The Gants Again	1966	40.00
❏ LRP-3455 [M]	The Gants Galore	1966	40.00
❏ LST-7455 [S]	The Gants Galore	1966	40.00

GAP BAND, THE

CAPITOL
❏ C1-90799	Round Trip	1989	12.00

MERCURY
❏ 826808-1	The 12" Collection	1986	10.00
❏ SRM-1-3758	The Gap Band	1979	12.00
❏ SRM-1-3804	The Gap Band II	1979	12.00
❏ SRM-1-4003	The Gap Band III	1980	12.00
❏ 822788-1	The Gap Band III	198?	10.00
—Reissue			

PASSPORT
❏ PB-6026	Strike a Groove	1983	12.00

SHELTER
❏ 2111	Magicians' Holiday	1974	18.00

TATTOO
❏ BJL1-2168	The Gap Band	1977	18.00

TOTAL EXPERIENCE
❏ 2700-1-T	Gap Band 8	1986	10.00
❏ TE-1-3001	Gap Band IV	1982	10.00
❏ TEL8-5705	Gap Band VI	1984	10.00
❏ TEL8-5714	Gap Band VII	1986	10.00
❏ TE-1-3004	Gap Band V -- Jammin'	1983	10.00
❏ 824343-1	Gap Gold/Best of the Gap Band	1985	10.00
❏ 2710-1-T	Straight from the Heart	1987	10.00

GARAGIOLA, JOE

UNITED ARTISTS
❏ UAL-3032 [M]	That Holler Guy!	1959	40.00
❏ UAS-6032 [S]	That Holler Guy!	1959	50.00

GARBAGE

ALMO SOUNDS
❏ 80004 [B]	Garbage	1995	25.00

GARBAREK, JAN, AND BOBO STENSON

ECM
❏ 1075	Dansere	1976	15.00
❏ 1041	Witchi-Tai-To	1973	15.00

GARBAREK, JAN, AND KJELL JOHNSEN

ECM
❏ 1169	Aftenland	1980	12.00

GARBAREK, JAN

ECM
❏ 1093	Dis	1977	15.00
❏ 1200	Eventyr	1981	12.00
❏ 25033	It's OK to Listen to the Gray Voice	1985	12.00
❏ 1151	Magico	1979	12.00
❏ 1223	Paths, Prints	1982	12.00
❏ 1135	Photo With…	1978	12.00
❏ 1118	Places	1978	12.00
❏ 23798	Wayfarer	1984	12.00

FLYING DUTCHMAN
❏ FD-10125	The Esoteric Circle	1971	25.00

GARBER, JAN

DECCA
❏ DL8932 [M]	Christmas Dance Party	1959	18.00
—Black label, silver print			
❏ DL78932 [S]	Christmas Dance Party	1959	25.00
—Black label, silver print			
❏ DL8482 [M]	Dance at Home	195?	25.00
—Black label, silver print			
❏ DL8484 [M]	Designed for Dancing	195?	25.00
—Black label, silver print			
❏ DL8483 [M]	In a Dancing Mood	195?	25.00
—Black label, silver print			
❏ DL8867 [M]	Jan Garber in Danceland	195?	18.00
—Black label, silver print			
❏ DL78867 [S]	Jan Garber in Danceland	195?	25.00
—Black label, silver print			
❏ DL8793 [M]	Music from the Blue Room, Roosevelt Hotel, New Orleans	195?	18.00
—Black label, silver print			
❏ DL78793 [S]	Music from the Blue Room, Roosevelt Hotel, New Orleans	195?	25.00
—Black label, silver print			
❏ DL8824 [M]	Waltzes	195?	18.00
—Black label, silver print			
❏ DL78824 [S]	Waltzes	195?	25.00
—Black label, silver print			

GARBO, GRETA

MGM
❏ E-4201 [M]	Garbo	1964	40.00

GARCIA, DICK

DAWN
❏ DLP-1106 [M]	A Message from Dick Garcia	1956	100.00

SEECO
❏ SLP-428 [M]	A Message from Dick Garcia	1958	40.00

GARCIA, JERRY

ARISTA
❏ AB4160	Cats Under the Stars	1978	16.00
❏ AL9603	Run for the Roses	1982	15.00
❏ AL8364	Run for the Roses	198?	10.00
—Reissue of 9603			

MOBILE FIDELITY
❏ MFSL2-430 [B]	Jerry Garcia / David Grisman	2014	60.00

ROUND
❏ RX-102	Garcia	1974	30.00
❏ JGFRR1005 [B]	Garcia	2014	30.00
❏ RX-107	Reflections	1975	30.00
❏ RN-LA565-G	Reflections	1976	25.00
—Reissue of Round 107 with United Artists distribution			

WARNER BROS.
❏ BS2582	Garcia	1972	40.00
—Green label with "WB" logo			

GARCIA, RUSS, AND MARTY PAICH

BETHLEHEM
❏ BCP-6039 [M]	Jazz Music for Birds and Hep Cats	1960	50.00
❏ SBCP-6039 [S]	Jazz Music for Birds and Hep Cats	1960	50.00

GARCIA, RUSS

ABC-PARAMOUNT
❏ ABC-147 [M]	The Johnny Evergreens	1956	50.00

BETHLEHEM
❏ BCP-46 [M]	Four Horns and a Lush Life	1956	50.00
❏ BCP-6044	I'll Never Forget What's Her Name	1978	15.00
—Reissue, distributed by RCA Victor			
❏ BCP-1040 [10]	Wigville	1955	200.00

DISCOVERY
❏ DS-814	I Lead a Charmed Life	1980	15.00

KAPP
❏ KL-1050 [M]	Listen to the Music of Russell Garcia	1957	50.00

LIBERTY
❏ LRP-3062 [M]	Enchantment (The Music of Joe Greene)	1958	30.00
❏ LRP-3084 [M]	Fantastica	1958	30.00
❏ LST-7005 [S]	Fantastica	1958	40.00

VERVE
❏ MGV-2088 [M]	The Warm Feeling	1957	50.00
❏ V-2088 [M]	The Warm Feeling	1961	25.00

GARDNER, BROTHER DAVE

4 STAR
❏ 4S75003	Brother Dave Gardner's New Comedy Album	1976	25.00

CAPITOL
❏ T1867 [M]	It Don't Make No Difference	1963	25.00
❏ ST1867 [S]	It Don't Make No Difference	1963	30.00
❏ T2055 [M]	It's All in How You Look at It	1964	25.00
❏ ST2055 [S]	It's All in How You Look at It	1964	30.00

RCA VICTOR
❏ LPM-2335 [M]	Ain't That Weird?	1961	25.00
❏ LSP-2335 [S]	Ain't That Weird?	1961	30.00
❏ LPM-2628 [M]	All Seriousness Aside	1963	25.00
❏ LSP-2628 [S]	All Seriousness Aside	1963	30.00
❏ LPM-2852 [M]	Best of Dave Gardner	1964	25.00
❏ LSP-2852 [S]	Best of Dave Gardner	1964	30.00
❏ LPM-2498 [M]	Did You Ever?	1962	25.00
❏ LSP-2498 [S]	Did You Ever?	1962	30.00
❏ LPM-2761 [M]	It's Bigger Than Both of Us	1963	25.00
❏ LSP-2761 [S]	It's Bigger Than Both of Us	1963	30.00
❏ LPM-2239 [M]	Kick Thy Own Self	1960	25.00
❏ LSP-2239(e) [S]	Kick Thy Own Self	196?	30.00
❏ LPM-2083 [M]	Rejoice, Dear Hearts!	1960	25.00
❏ LSP-2083(e) [S]	Rejoice, Dear Hearts!	196?	30.00

TONKA
❏ TLP713	Out Front	1969	25.00

TOWER
❏ T5050 [M]	Hip-ocracy	1966	18.00
❏ ST5050 [S]	Hip-ocracy	1966	25.00
❏ T5075 [M]	It Don't Make No Difference	1967	30.00
❏ ST5075 [S]	It Don't Make No Difference	1967	25.00

GARDNER, DON, AND DEE DEE FORD

COLLECTABLES
❏ COL-5155	Golden Classics: Need Your Lovin'	198?	15.00

FIRE
❏ LP-105 [M]	Need Your Lovin'	1962	400.00

SUE
❏ LP-1044 [M]	Don Gardner and Dee Dee Ford In Sweden	1965	120.00

GARFUNKEL, ART

COLUMBIA
❏ KC31474	Angel Clare	1973	15.00
❏ CQ31474 [Q]	Angel Clare	1973	40.00
❏ PC31474	Angel Clare	197?	10.00
—Reissue			
❏ PC33700 [B]	Breakaway	1975	15.00
—Originals have no bar code			
❏ PCQ33700 [Q]	Breakaway	1975	50.00
❏ PC33700	Breakaway	197?	10.00
—With bar code on cover			
❏ JC35780	Fate for Breakfast	1979	15.00
—With six different covers, each illustrating Art Garfunkel at a different stage of eating breakfast. No difference in value.			
❏ OC45008	Garfunkel	1989	12.00
❏ FC40942	Lefty	1988	10.00
❏ FC37392	Scissors Cut	1981	12.00
❏ FC40212	The Animals' Christmas By Jimmy Webb	1986	12.00
—With Amy Grant			
❏ JC34975 [DJ]	Watermark	1978	60.00
—Test pressing or white label promo with "Fingerpaint" on side 2			
❏ JC34975	Watermark	1978	100.00
—Stock copy with "Fingerpaint" on side 2			
❏ JC34975	Watermark	1978	15.00
—Stock copy with "(What a) Wonderful World" on side 2			
❏ PC34975	Watermark	198?	10.00
—Reissue			

GARI, RALPH

EMARCY
❏ MG-36019 [M]	Ralph Gari	1955	50.00

GARLAND, HANK

COLUMBIA
❏ CL1572 [M]	Jazz Winds from a New Direction	1961	30.00
❏ CS8372 [S]	Jazz Winds from a New Direction	1961	40.00
❏ CL1913 [M]	The Unforgettable Guitar of Hank Garland	1962	30.00
❏ CS8713 [S]	The Unforgettable Guitar of Hank Garland	1962	40.00

HARMONY
❏ HL7231 [M]	Velvet Guitar	196?	25.00
❏ HS11028 [S]	Velvet Guitar	196?	30.00

SESAC
❏ SN-2301/2 [M]	Subtle Swing	196?	100.00

GARLAND, JUDY, AND LIZA MINNELLI

CAPITOL
❏ WBO2295 [M]	Live" at the London Palladium	1965	30.00
❏ SWBO2295 [S]	Live" at the London Palladium	1965	30.00
❏ ST-11191	Live" at the London Palladium	1973	15.00
—Condensation of above 2-record set			

MOBILE FIDELITY
❏ 1-048	Live" at the London Palladium	1981	30.00
—Audiophile vinyl			

GARLAND, JUDY

ABC
❏ 620 [M]	Judy Garland At Home at the Palace -- Opening Night	1967	25.00
❏ S-620 [S]	Judy Garland At Home at the Palace -- Opening Night	1967	30.00
❏ AC-30007	The ABC Collection	1976	18.00

A.E.I.
❏ 2108	Judy Garland Vol. 1: Born in a Trunk	198?	12.00
❏ 2109 [M]	Judy Garland Vol. 2: Stardom 1940-45	1980	12.00
❏ 2110	Judy Garland Vol. 3: Superstar 1945-50	198?	12.00

CAPITOL
❏ T835 [M]	Alone	1957	40.00
❏ DT835 [R]	Alone	1963	18.00
❏ SM-11763	Alone	1978	12.00
—Edited reissue of 835			

Number	Title	Yr	NM
❑ T1118 [M]	Garland at the Grove	1959	30.00
❑ ST1118 [S]	Garland at the Grove	1959	40.00
❑ W1861 [M]	I Could Go On Singing	1963	40.00
❑ SW1861 [P]	I Could Go On Singing	1963	60.00
—"I Am the Monarch of the Sea" and "It Never Was You" are rechanneled			
❑ T734 [M]	Judy	1956	40.00
❑ DT734 [R]	Judy	1963	18.00
❑ WBO1569 [M]	Judy at Carnegie Hall	1961	40.00
❑ SWBO1569 [S]	Judy at Carnegie Hall	1961	50.00
❑ T1036 [M]	Judy in Love	1958	30.00
❑ ST1036 [S]	Judy in Love	1959	40.00
❑ T1467 [M]	Judy -- That's Entertainment	1960	30.00
—Black rainbow label, Capitol logo at left			
❑ ST1467 [S]	Judy -- That's Entertainment	1960	40.00
—Black rainbow label, Capitol logo at left			
❑ SM-11876	Judy -- That's Entertainment	1978	12.00
—Edited reissue			
❑ T1467 [M]	Judy -- That's Entertainment	196?	18.00
—Black rainbow label, Capitol logo at top			
❑ ST1467 [S]	Judy -- That's Entertainment	196?	25.00
—Black rainbow label, Capitol logo at top			
❑ W2062 [M]	Just for Openers	1964	25.00
❑ DW2062 [R]	Just for Openers	1964	18.00
❑ M-12034	Just for Openers	1979	12.00
—Edited reissue			
❑ W676 [M]	Miss Show Business	1955	40.00
❑ DW676 [R]	Miss Show Business	1963	15.00
❑ T1941 [M]	Our Love Letter	1963	25.00
—Reissue of T 1188			
❑ ST1941 [S]	Our Love Letter	1963	30.00
—Reissue of ST 1188			
❑ W1710 [M]	The Garland Touch	1962	25.00
❑ SW1710 [S]	The Garland Touch	1962	30.00
❑ T1999 [M]	The Hits of Judy Garland	1964	25.00
❑ ST1999 [P]	The Hits of Judy Garland	1964	30.00
—Over the Rainbow," "Come Rain or Come Shine" and "April Showers" are rechanneled			
❑ SM-1999	The Hits of Judy Garland	197?	12.00
—Reissue			
❑ SN-16175	The Hits of Judy Garland	198?	10.00
—Budget-line reissue			
❑ STCL2988	The Judy Garland Deluxe Set	1968	40.00
❑ T1188 [M]	The Letter	1959	30.00
—Add 80% if letter is on cover			
❑ ST1188 [S]	The Letter	1959	40.00
—Add 80% if letter is on cover			
❑ DNFR-7632	The Magic of Judy Garland	196?	40.00
—Box set with 4-page insert; 20 of the 60 tracks are rechanneled			

DECCA

Number	Title	Yr	NM
❑ DL6020 [10]	Judy at the Palace	1952	100.00
❑ DL75150 [R]	Judy Garland's Greatest Hits	1969	15.00
❑ DL8190 [M]	Judy Garland's Greatest Performances	1955	40.00
—Black label, silver print			
❑ DL8190 [M]	Judy Garland's Greatest Performances	196?	30.00
—Black label with color bars			
❑ DXB172 [M]	The Best of Judy Garland	1963	25.00
❑ DXSB7172 [R]	The Best of Judy Garland	1963	25.00
❑ DL4199 [M]	The Magic of Judy Garland	1961	30.00

DRG

Number	Title	Yr	NM
❑ SL-5187	The Beginning	1979	18.00
❑ SL5179	The Wit and the Wonder of Judy Garland	1977	18.00

LONGINES SYMPHONETTE

Number	Title	Yr	NM
❑ SY5217	The Magic of Judy Garland	197?	30.00

MARK 56

Number	Title	Yr	NM
❑ 632 [PD]	In Concert: San Francisco	1978	60.00

MCA

Number	Title	Yr	NM
❑ 4046	Collector's Items (1936-45)	197?	15.00
❑ 907	From the Decca Vaults	1984	12.00
❑ 4003	The Best of Judy Garland	1973	18.00
—Black label with rainbow			
❑ 4003	The Best of Judy Garland	1980	12.00
—Blue label with rainbow			
❑ 25165	The Best of Judy Garland from MGM Classic Films	1988	15.00

METRO

Number	Title	Yr	NM
❑ M-505 [M]	Judy Garland	1965	18.00
❑ MS-505 [S]	Judy Garland	1965	25.00
❑ M-581 [M]	Judy Garland in Song	1966	18.00
❑ MS-581 [S]	Judy Garland in Song	1966	25.00

MGM

Number	Title	Yr	NM
❑ PX102	Forever Judy	1969	30.00
—White label "Limited Edition" with poster			
❑ SDP-1	Golden Years at MGM	1969	30.00
❑ E-3149 [M]	If You Feel Like Singing, Sing	1955	60.00
❑ E-82 [10]	Judy Garland Sings	1951	100.00
❑ E-3989 [M]	The Judy Garland Story Vol. 1: The Star Years	1961	30.00
❑ E-4005 [M]	The Judy Garland Story Vol. 2: The Hollywood Years	1962	30.00
❑ E-4204 [M]	The Very Best of Judy Garland	1964	30.00
❑ SE-4204 [R]	The Very Best of Judy Garland	1964	18.00
—Black label			
❑ SE-4204 [R]	The Very Best of Judy Garland	1964	12.00
—Blue and gold label			

MINERVA

Number	Title	Yr	NM
❑ LP-6JG-FNJ	Judy Garland and Friends	1982	12.00
❑ LP-6JG-FST	The Judy Garland Show: Mutual Admiration Society	1982	12.00

PAIR

Number	Title	Yr	NM
❑ PDL2-1030	Golden Memories	1986	15.00
❑ PDL2-1127	The Legendary Judy Garland	1986	15.00

PICKWICK

Number	Title	Yr	NM
❑ PTP-2010	Her Greatest Hits	197?	15.00
❑ SPC-3053	I Feel a Song Coming On	197?	15.00

SPRINGBOARD

Number	Title	Yr	NM
❑ SPB-4054	Over the Rainbow	197?	10.00

STANYAN

Number	Title	Yr	NM
❑ 10095	More Than a Memory	1974	12.00
❑ POW-3001	More Than a Memory	198?	12.00
—Reissue of 10095			

TIME-LIFE

Number	Title	Yr	NM
❑ SLGD-12	Legendary Singers: Judy Garland	1986	25.00

TROPHY

Number	Title	Yr	NM
❑ TR-7-2145	Judy Garland Concert	1974	18.00

GARLAND, RED

FANTASY

Number	Title	Yr	NM
❑ OJC-126	A Garland of Red	198?	12.00
—Reissue of Prestige 7064			
❑ OJC-193	All Kinds of Weather	1985	12.00
—Reissue of Prestige 7148			
❑ OJC-293	All Morning Long	1988	12.00
—Reissue of Prestige 7130			
❑ OJC-265	Bright and Breezy	1987	12.00
—Reissue of Jazzland 948			
❑ OJC-472	Crossings	1990	15.00
—Reissue of Galaxy 5106			
❑ OJC-392	Dig It!	1989	15.00
—Reissue of Prestige 7229			
❑ OJC-061	Groovy	198?	12.00
—Reissue of Prestige 7113			
❑ OJC-349	High Pressure	198?	12.00
—Reissue of Prestige 7209			
❑ OJC-428	Manteca	1990	15.00
—Reissue of Prestige 7139			
❑ OJC-647	Red Alert	1991	15.00
—Reissue of Galaxy 5109			
❑ OJC-360	Red Garland & Eddie "Lockjaw" Davis	198?	12.00
—Reissue of Moodsville 1			
❑ OJC-073	Red Garland's Piano	198?	12.00
—Reissue of Prestige 7086			
❑ OJC-295	Red in Bluesville	198?	12.00
—Reissue of Prestige 7157			
❑ OJC-481	Soul Junction	1991	15.00
—Reissue of Prestige 7181			
❑ OJC-224	The Red Garland Trio	198?	12.00
—Reissue of Moodsville 6			

GALAXY

Number	Title	Yr	NM
❑ 5106	Crossings	1978	15.00
❑ 5115	Equinox	1979	15.00
❑ 5109	Red Alert	1978	15.00
❑ 5129	Stepping Out	198?	12.00
❑ 5135	Strike Up the Band	198?	12.00

JAZZLAND

Number	Title	Yr	NM
❑ JLP-48 [M]	Bright and Breezy	1961	100.00
❑ JLP-948 [S]	Bright and Breezy	1961	120.00
❑ JLP-87 [M]	Red's Good Groove!	1963	120.00
❑ JLP-987 [S]	Red's Good Groove!	1963	120.00
❑ JLP-73 [M]	Solar	1962	100.00
❑ JLP-973 [S]	Solar	1962	120.00
❑ JLP-62 [M]	The Nearness of You -- Ballads Played by Red Garland	1962	100.00
❑ JLP-962 [S]	The Nearness of You -- Ballads Played by Red Garland	1962	120.00

MOODSVILLE

Number	Title	Yr	NM
❑ MVLP-10 [M]	Alone with the Blues	1960	100.00
—Green label			
❑ MVLP-10 [M]	Alone with the Blues	1965	50.00
—Blue label, trident logo at right			
❑ MVLP-3 [M]	Red Alone -- Vol. 3	1960	100.00
—Green label			
❑ MVLP-3 [M]	Red Alone -- Vol. 3	1965	50.00
—Blue label, trident logo at right			
❑ MVLP-1 [M]	Red Garland & Eddie "Lockjaw" Davis	1960	100.00
—Green label			
❑ MVLP-1 [M]	Red Garland & Eddie "Lockjaw" Davis	1965	50.00
—Blue label, trident logo at right			
❑ MVLP-6 [M]	The Red Garland Trio	1960	100.00
—Green label			
❑ MVLP-6 [M]	The Red Garland Trio	1965	50.00
—Blue label, trident logo at right			

MUSE

Number	Title	Yr	NM
❑ MR-5130	Feelin' Red	1980	15.00
❑ MR-5311	I Left My Heart	1985	12.00

PRESTIGE

Number	Title	Yr	NM
❑ PRLP-7064 [M]	A Garland of Red	1956	300.00
—Yellow label, W. 50th St., New York address on label			
❑ PRLP-7064 [M]	A Garland of Red	1958	120.00
—Yellow label with Bergenfield, N.J. address			
❑ PRLP-7148 [M]	All Kinds of Weather	1958	250.00
—Yellow label with Bergenfield, N.J. address			
❑ PRLP-7130 [M]	All Morning Long	1958	300.00
—Yellow label, W. 50th St., New York address on label			
❑ PRLP-7130 [M]	All Morning Long	1958	120.00
—Yellow label with Bergenfield, N.J. address			
❑ PRLP-7276 [M]	Can't See for Lookin'	1963	60.00
❑ PRST-7276 [S]	Can't See for Lookin'	1963	60.00
❑ PRLP-7229 [M]	Dig It!	1962	80.00
❑ PRST-7229 [S]	Dig It!	1962	80.00
❑ PRLP-7113 [M]	Groovy	1957	500.00
—Yellow label, W. 50th St., New York address on label			
❑ PRLP-7113 [M]	Groovy	1958	120.00
—Yellow label with Bergenfield, N.J. address			
❑ PRLP-7288 [M]	Halleloo-Y'all	1964	60.00
❑ PRST-7288 [S]	Halleloo-Y'all	1964	80.00
❑ PRLP-7209 [M]	High Pressure	1961	200.00
—Yellow label with Bergenfield, N.J. address			
❑ PRST-7838	It's a Blue World	1971	25.00
❑ 24023	Jazz Junction	1972	18.00
❑ PRLP-7139 [M]	Manteca	1958	120.00
—Yellow label with Bergenfield, N.J. address			
❑ PRLP-7139 [M]	Manteca	1958	200.00
—Yellow label, W. 50th St. NYC address on label			
❑ PRST-7752	P.C. Blues	1970	25.00
❑ PRLP-7170 [M]	Red Garland at the Prelude	1959	100.00
—Yellow label with Bergenfield, N.J. address			
❑ PRST-7658	Red Garland Revisited!	1969	25.00
❑ PRLP-7086 [M]	Red Garland's Piano	1957	200.00
—Yellow label, W. 50th St., New York address on label			
❑ PRLP-7086 [M]	Red Garland's Piano	1958	120.00
—Yellow label with Bergenfield, N.J. address			
❑ PRLP-7157 [M]	Red in Bluesville	1959	100.00
—Yellow label with Bergenfield, N.J. address			
❑ 24078	Rediscovered Masters	1979	18.00
❑ PRLP-7193 [M]	Rojo	1961	80.00
—Yellow label with Bergenfield, N.J. address			
❑ 24090	Saying Something	1980	18.00
❑ PRLP-7307 [M]	Soul Burnin'	1964	50.00
❑ PRST-7307 [S]	Soul Burnin'	1964	60.00
❑ PRLP-7181 [M]	Soul Junction	1960	100.00
—Yellow label with Bergenfield, N.J. address			
❑ PRLP-7258 [M]	When There Are Grey Skies	1963	250.00
❑ PRST-7258 [S]	When There Are Grey Skies	1963	60.00

RIVERSIDE

Number	Title	Yr	NM
❑ 6099	Bright and Breezy	197?	18.00

STATUS

Number	Title	Yr	NM
❑ ST-8325 [M]	High Pressure	1965	60.00
❑ ST-8314 [M]	Li'l Darlin'	1965	60.00
❑ ST-8326 [M]	Red Garland Live!	1965	60.00

GARNER, ERROLL

ABC-PARAMOUNT

Number	Title	Yr	NM
❑ 395 [M]	Closeup in Swing	1961	25.00
❑ S-395 [S]	Closeup in Swing	1961	30.00
❑ 365 [M]	Dreamstreet	1961	25.00
❑ S-365 [S]	Dreamstreet	1961	30.00

ATLANTIC

Number	Title	Yr	NM
❑ ALR-112 [10]	Erroll Garner at the Piano	1951	200.00
❑ ALR-128 [10]	Passport to Fame	1952	200.00
❑ 1315 [M]	Perpetual Motion	1959	40.00
—Black label			
❑ ALR-135 [10]	Piano Solos, Volume 2	1952	200.00
❑ ALR-109 [10]	Rhapsody	1950	200.00
❑ 1227 [M]	The Greatest Garner	1956	40.00
—Black label			
❑ 1227 [M]	The Greatest Garner	1961	18.00
—Multi-color label with white "fan" logo			
❑ 1227 [M]	The Greatest Garner	196?	15.00
—Multi-color label with black "fan" logo			

BARONET

Number	Title	Yr	NM
❑ B-109 [M]	Informal Piano Improvisations	1962	15.00
❑ BS-109 [R]	Informal Piano Improvisations	1962	12.00

BLUE NOTE

Number	Title	Yr	NM
❑ BLP-5007 [10]	Overture to Dawn, Volume 1	1952	500.00
❑ BLP-5008 [10]	Overture to Dawn, Volume 2	1952	500.00
❑ BLP-5014 [10]	Overture to Dawn, Volume 3	1953	500.00
❑ BLP-5015 [10]	Overture to Dawn, Volume 4	1953	500.00
❑ BLP-5016 [10]	Overture to Dawn, Volume 5	1953	500.00

CLARION

Number	Title	Yr	NM
❑ 610 [M]	Serenade in Blue	1966	15.00
❑ SD610 [S]	Serenade in Blue	1966	15.00

COLUMBIA

Number	Title	Yr	NM
❑ CL883 [M]	Concert by the Sea	1956	30.00
❑ CS9821 [R]	Concert by the Sea	1970	15.00
❑ CL1141 [M]	Encores in Hi-Fi	1958	30.00
❑ CL535 [M]	Erroll Garner	1953	60.00
—Red label with gold print			
❑ CL535 [M]	Erroll Garner	1956	30.00

Number	Title	Yr	NM
— Red and black label with six "eye" logos			
❑ CL6259 [10]	Erroll Garner Plays for Dancing	1953	80.00
❑ CL667 [M]	Erroll Garner Plays for Dancing	1956	30.00
❑ CL2540 [10]	Garnerland	1955	60.00
❑ CL6173 [10]	Gems	1951	80.00
❑ CL583 [M]	Gems	1954	60.00
— Red label with gold print			
❑ CL583 [M]	Gems	1956	30.00
— Red and black label with six "eye" logos			
❑ CL617 [M]	Gone Garner Gonest	1955	60.00
— Red label with gold print			
❑ CL617 [M]	Gone Garner Gonest	1956	30.00
— Red and black label with six "eye" logos			
❑ CL2606 [10]	He's Here! He's Gone! He's Garner!	1956	60.00
❑ CL1014 [M]	Other Voices	1957	30.00
— Red and black label wirh six "eye" logos			
❑ CS9820 [R]	Other Voices	1970	15.00
❑ C2L9 [M]	Paris Impressions	1958	40.00
❑ CL1216 [M]	Paris Impressions, Volume 1	1958	25.00
❑ CS8131 [S]	Paris Impressions, Volume 1	1958	30.00
❑ CL1217 [M]	Paris Impressions, Volume 2	1958	25.00
❑ CL6139 [10]	Piano Moods	1950	80.00
❑ PG33424	Play It Again, Erroll!	1975	15.00
❑ CL1060 [M]	Soliloquy	1957	30.00
❑ CL6209 [10]	Solo Flight	1952	80.00
❑ CL1512 [M]	Swinging Solos	1960	25.00
❑ CS8312 [S]	Swinging Solos	1960	30.00
❑ CL939 [M]	The Most Happy Piano	1957	30.00
❑ CL1452 [M]	The One and Only Erroll Garner	1960	25.00
❑ CS8252 [S]	The One and Only Erroll Garner	1960	30.00
❑ CL1587 [M]	The Provocative Erroll Garner	1961	25.00
❑ CS8387 [S]	The Provocative Erroll Garner	1961	30.00

COLUMBIA JAZZ MASTERPIECES

Number	Title	Yr	NM
❑ CJ40863	Long Ago and Far Away	1987	15.00

COLUMBIA SPECIAL PRODUCTS

Number	Title	Yr	NM
❑ P14386	Dreamy	1978	12.00

DIAL

Number	Title	Yr	NM
❑ LP-205 [10]	Erroll Garner, Volume 1	1950	200.00
❑ LP-902 [M]	Free Piano Improvisations Recorded by Baron Timme Rosenkranz at One of His Famous Gaslight Jazz Sessions	1949	300.00

EMARCY

Number	Title	Yr	NM
❑ MG-36001 [M]	Contrasts	1955	30.00
❑ MG-36069 [M]	Erroll!	1956	30.00
❑ 826224-1	Erroll Garner Plays Gershwin and Kern	1986	12.00
❑ MG-26016 [10]	Garnering	1954	80.00
❑ MG-36026 [M]	Garnering	1955	30.00
❑ MG-26042 [10]	Gone with Garner	1954	80.00
❑ 832994-1	The Erroll Garner Collection Vol. 1: Easy to Love	1988	12.00
❑ 834935-1	The Erroll Garner Collection Vol. 2: Dancing on the Ceiling	1989	12.00

EVEREST ARCHIVE OF FOLK & JAZZ

Number	Title	Yr	NM
❑ 245	Erroll Garner	1970	12.00

GUEST STAR

Number	Title	Yr	NM
❑ G1403 [M]	Piano Greats	196?	15.00
— With tracks by Art Tatum and Mike Di Napoli			
❑ GS1403 [S]	Piano Greats	196?	12.00
— With tracks by Art Tatum and Mike Di Napoli			

HALL OF FAME

Number	Title	Yr	NM
❑ 610	Early Erroll	198?	12.00

HARMONY

Number	Title	Yr	NM
❑ HS11268	One More Time	1968	15.00

JAZZTONE

Number	Title	Yr	NM
❑ J-1269 [M]	Early Erroll	1957	40.00

KING

Number	Title	Yr	NM
❑ 295-17 [10]	Piano Stylist	1952	80.00
❑ 395-540 [M]	Piano Variations	1958	150.00

LONDON

Number	Title	Yr	NM
❑ XPS617	Gemini	1972	15.00
❑ APS640	Magician	1973	15.00

MERCURY

Number	Title	Yr	NM
❑ MG-20090 [M]	Afternoon of an Elf	1955	50.00
❑ 826457-1	Afternoon of an Elf	1986	12.00
— Reissue			
❑ MG-25117 [10]	Erroll Garner at the Piano	1951	80.00
❑ MG-20009 [M]	Erroll Garner at the Piano	1953	50.00
❑ MG-20662 [M]	Erroll Garner Plays Misty	1962	18.00
❑ SR-60662 [S]	Erroll Garner Plays Misty	1962	25.00
— Black label, all-silver print			
❑ SR-60662 [S]	Erroll Garner Plays Misty	1965	15.00
— Red label, "MERCURY" in all caps at top			
❑ SR-60662	Erroll Garner Plays Misty	1975	12.00
— Chicago skyline label			
❑ SR-60662	Erroll Garner Plays Misty	1983	10.00
— Black label, neon-style "mercury" logo			
❑ MG-21308 [M]	Feeling Is Believing	1964	18.00
❑ SR-61308 [S]	Feeling Is Believing	1964	25.00
❑ SR-61308 [S]	Feeling Is Believing	1970	15.00
— Newer Mercury logo on cover			
❑ MG-25157 [10]	Gone with Garner	1951	80.00
❑ MG-20055 [M]	Mambo Moves Garner	1954	50.00
❑ MG-20859 [M]	New Kind of Love	1963	18.00
❑ SR-60859 [S]	New Kind of Love	1963	25.00
❑ MG-20063 [M]	Solitaire	1954	50.00
❑ MG-20803 [M]	The Best of Erroll Garner	1963	18.00
❑ SR-60803 [S]	The Best of Erroll Garner	1963	25.00

MGM

Number	Title	Yr	NM
❑ E-4361 [M]	Campus Concert	1966	15.00
❑ SE-4361 [S]	Campus Concert	1966	18.00
❑ E-4335 [M]	Now Playing: Erroll Garner	1966	15.00
❑ SE-4335 [S]	Now Playing: Erroll Garner	1966	18.00
❑ E-4463 [M]	That's My Kick	1967	18.00
❑ SE-4463 [S]	That's My Kick	1967	15.00
❑ E-4520 [M]	Up in Erroll's Room	1967	18.00
❑ SE-4520 [S]	Up in Erroll's Room	1967	15.00

PICKWICK

Number	Title	Yr	NM
❑ SPC-3254	Deep Purple	197?	12.00

REPRISE

Number	Title	Yr	NM
❑ R6080 [M]	One World Concert	1963	25.00
❑ RS6080 [S]	One World Concert	1963	30.00
❑ R6080 [DJ]	One World Concert	1963	40.00
— Six-song sampler -- three on each side -- on a 12-inch record that plays at 45 rpm. This comes in a different cover than the stock copy; this is clearly marked "Special 45 RPM Preview Record" on the top front.			

RONDO-LETTE

Number	Title	Yr	NM
❑ A-15 [M]	Erroll Garner	1958	30.00

SAVOY

Number	Title	Yr	NM
❑ SJL-2207	Elf	198?	15.00
❑ MG-15026 [10]	Erroll Garner at the Piano	1953	80.00
❑ MG-15000 [10]	Erroll Garner Plays Piano Solos	1950	80.00
❑ MG-15001 [10]	Erroll Garner Plays Piano Solos, Volume 2	1950	80.00
❑ MG-15002 [10]	Erroll Garner Plays Piano Solos, Volume 3	1950	80.00
❑ MG-15003 [10]	Erroll Garner Plays Piano Solos, Volume 4	1950	80.00
❑ MG-12002 [M]	Penthouse Serenade	1955	30.00
❑ SJC-411	Penthouse Serenade	1985	12.00
❑ MG-12003 [M]	Serenade to "Laura	1955	30.00
❑ SJL-1118	Yesterdays	198?	12.00

TRIP

Number	Title	Yr	NM
❑ 5519	Garnering	197?	12.00

WING

Number	Title	Yr	NM
❑ MGW12134	Erroll Garner Moods	196?	15.00

GARNER, ERROLL/BILLY TAYLOR

SAVOY

Number	Title	Yr	NM
❑ MG-12008 [M]	Erroll Garner/Billy Taylor	1955	50.00

GARNER, ERROLL/OSCAR PETERSON/ART TATUM

RCA CAMDEN

Number	Title	Yr	NM
❑ CAL-882 [M]	Great Jazz Pianists of Our Time	196?	18.00
❑ CAS-882 [R]	Great Jazz Pianists of Our Time	196?	15.00

GARNER, ERROLL/PETE JOHNSON

GRAND AWARD

Number	Title	Yr	NM
❑ GA 33-321 [M]	Jazz Piano	1956	100.00
— With removable David Stone Martin cover still attached			
❑ GA 33-321 [M]	Jazz Piano	1956	30.00
— Without removable cover			

GARNER, MORRIS

THUNDERBIRD

Number	Title	Yr	NM
❑ TH-1958 [M]	The Worst of Morris Garner	196?	30.00

GARNETT, CARLOS

MUSE

Number	Title	Yr	NM
❑ MR-5040	Black Love	1973	18.00
❑ MR-5104	Cosmos Nucleus	1976	40.00
❑ MR-5057	Journey to Enlightenment	1974	25.00
❑ MR-5079	Let the Melody Ring On	1975	30.00
❑ MR-5133	New Love	1977	40.00

GARNETT, GALE

COLUMBIA

Number	Title	Yr	NM
❑ CL2825 [M]	An Audience with the King of Wands	1968	30.00
❑ CS9625 [S]	An Audience with the King of Wands	1968	18.00
❑ CS9625 [M]	An Audience with the King of Wands	1968	30.00
— White label promo with stereo number and "Mono" on label; "Special Mono Radio Station Copy" sticker and timing strip on front cover			
❑ CS9760	Sausalito Heliport	1969	18.00

RCA VICTOR

Number	Title	Yr	NM
❑ LPM-3747 [M]	Gale Garnett Sings About Flying & Rainbows & Love & Other Groovy Things	1967	30.00
❑ LSP-3747 [S]	Gale Garnett Sings About Flying & Rainbows & Love & Other Groovy Things	1967	25.00
❑ LPM-3305 [M]	Lovin' Place	1965	18.00
❑ LSP-3305 [S]	Lovin' Place	1965	25.00
❑ LPM-2833 [M]	My Kind of Folk Songs	1964	40.00
— Black and white/blueish cover			
❑ LPM-2833 [M]	My Kind of Folk Songs	1965	18.00
— Color photo on cover			
❑ LSP-2833 [S]	My Kind of Folk Songs	1964	50.00
— Black and white/blueish cover			
❑ LSP-2833 [S]	My Kind of Folk Songs	1965	25.00
— Color photo on cover			
❑ LPM-3586 [M]	New Adventures	1966	18.00
❑ LSP-3586 [S]	New Adventures	1966	25.00
❑ LPM-3325 [M]	The Many Faces of Gale Garnett	1965	18.00
❑ LSP-3325 [S]	The Many Faces of Gale Garnett	1965	25.00
❑ LPM-3493 [M]	Variety Is the Spice of Gale Garnett	1966	18.00
❑ LSP-3493 [S]	Variety Is the Spice of Gale Garnett	1966	25.00

GARRETT, KENNY

ATLANTIC

Number	Title	Yr	NM
❑ 82046	Prisoner of Love	1989	15.00

GARRETT, LEIF

ATLANTIC

Number	Title	Yr	NM
❑ SD19152	Leif Garrett	1977	15.00
— With poster			

SCOTTI BROTHERS

Number	Title	Yr	NM
❑ SB7111	Can't Explain	1980	15.00
❑ SB7100	Feel the Need	1978	15.00
— With photo insert			
❑ FZ37625	My Movie of You	1981	12.00
❑ SB16008	Same Goes for You	1979	15.00

GARRETT, SNUFF, 'S TEXAS OPERA COMPANY

RANWOOD

Number	Title	Yr	NM
❑ 8158	Classical Country	1976	12.00

GARRETT, TOMMY, 50 GUITARS OF

LIBERTY

Number	Title	Yr	NM
❑ LMM-13025 [M]	50 Guitars Go Country	1963	15.00
❑ LSS-14025 [S]	50 Guitars Go Country	1963	18.00
❑ LMM-13028 [M]	50 Guitars Go Italiano	1964	15.00
❑ LSS-14028 [S]	50 Guitars Go Italiano	1964	18.00
❑ LMM-13005 [M]	50 Guitars Go South of the Border	1961	15.00
❑ LSS-14005 [S]	50 Guitars Go South of the Border	1961	18.00
❑ LMM-13016 [M]	50 Guitars Go South of the Border, Volume 2	1962	15.00
❑ LSS-14016 [S]	50 Guitars Go South of the Border, Volume 2	1962	18.00
❑ LMM-13037 [M]	50 Guitars in Love	1966	15.00
❑ LSS-14037 [S]	50 Guitars in Love	1966	18.00
❑ LMM-13022 [M]	50 Guitars Visit Hawaii	1962	15.00
❑ LSS-14022 [S]	50 Guitars Visit Hawaii	1962	18.00
❑ LMM-13031 [M]	Bordertown Bandito	1964	15.00
❑ LSS-14031 [S]	Bordertown Bandito	1964	18.00
❑ LMM-13032 [M]	Espana	1964	15.00
❑ LSS-14032 [S]	Espana	1964	18.00
❑ LSS-14047	For Midnight Lovers	1970	15.00
❑ L-5507 [M]	Limited Edition	196?	15.00
❑ S-6607 [S]	Limited Edition	196?	18.00
❑ LMM-13035 [M]	Love Songs from South of the Border	1965	15.00
❑ LSS-14035 [S]	Love Songs from South of the Border	1965	18.00
❑ LMM-13030 [M]	Maria Elena	1963	15.00
❑ LSS-14030 [S]	Maria Elena	1963	18.00
❑ LSS-14046	Mexican Leather	1969	15.00
❑ LMM-13039 [M]	More 50 Guitars in Love	1967	15.00
❑ LSS-14039 [S]	More 50 Guitars in Love	1967	15.00
❑ LMM-13033 [M]	Return to Paradise	1965	15.00
❑ LSS-14033 [S]	Return to Paradise	1965	18.00
❑ LSS-14045	The Best of the 50 Guitars of Tommy Garrett	1969	15.00
❑ LSS-35001	The Best of the 50 Guitars of Tommy Garrett, Volumes 2 & 3	1970	18.00
❑ LMM-13036 [M]	Viva Mexico	1966	15.00
❑ LSS-14036 [S]	Viva Mexico	1966	18.00

MUSICOR

Number	Title	Yr	NM
❑ 4606	The Best of the 50 Guitars of Tommy Garrett	1976	15.00

PICKWICK

Number	Title	Yr	NM
❑ SPC-3615	Brazilian Mood	197?	10.00
❑ SPC-3585	In Love	197?	10.00

SUNSET

Number	Title	Yr	NM
❑ SUS-5282	The Fabulous 50 Guitars of Tommy Garrett	197?	12.00

UNITED ARTISTS

Number	Title	Yr	NM
❑ UAS-5528	50 Guitars Go South of the Border, Volume 3	1971	12.00
❑ UAS-5569	The Way of Love	1972	12.00
❑ UXS-79	Tommy Garrett Superpak	1972	15.00
❑ UA-LA039-F	You're a Lady	1973	12.00

GARRISON, GLEN

IMPERIAL

Number	Title	Yr	NM
❑ LP-9346 [M]	Country Country	1967	18.00
❑ LP-12346 [S]	Country Country	1967	18.00
❑ LP-12378	If I Lived Here	1968	18.00

Number	Title	Yr	NM

GARROWAY, DAVE

CAMEO

❑ C-1001 [M]	An Adventure in Hi-Fi Music	1958	40.00

—*Black label, brown print, cameo figure at top*

GARSON, GREER

LION

❑ L-70102 [M]	Greer Garson Babysits with Stories and Songs	1958	30.00

GARSON, MIKE, AND JIM WALKER

REFERENCE RECORDINGS

❑ RR-18	Reflections	1987	18.00

GARSON, MIKE

CONTEMPORARY

❑ C-14003 [B]	Avant Garson	1979	18.00

JAZZ HOUNDS

❑ 0005	Jazzical	1982	15.00

REFERENCE RECORDINGS

❑ RR-20	Serendipity	1987	18.00
❑ RR-37	The Oxnard Sessions	1991	25.00
❑ RR-53	The Oxnard Sessions, Volume Two	1993	30.00

GARVIN, REX, AND THE MIGHTY CRAVERS

TOWER

❑ ST5130	Raw Funky Earth	1968	30.00

GARY, JOHN

CHURCHILL

❑ 67236	In a Class By Himself	1977	12.00

LA BREA

❑ 8010 [M]	John Gary	1961	30.00
❑ S-8010 [S]	John Gary	1961	30.00

METRO

❑ M-522 [M]	John Gary	1966	12.00
❑ MS-522 [S]	John Gary	1966	15.00

PICKWICK

❑ SPC-3025	John Gary	197?	12.00

RCA CAMDEN

❑ CAL-983 [M]	The One and Only John Gary	1966	12.00
❑ CAS-983 [S]	The One and Only John Gary	1966	15.00

RCA VICTOR

❑ LPM-3666 [M]	A Heart Filled with Song	1966	15.00
❑ LSP-3666 [S]	A Heart Filled with Song	1966	18.00
❑ LPM-2994 [M]	A Little Bit of Heaven	1965	15.00
❑ LSP-2994 [S]	A Little Bit of Heaven	1965	18.00
❑ ANL1-2672	A Little Bit of Heaven	1978	12.00
—*Reissue of LSP-2994*			
❑ LPM-2745 [M]	Catch a Rising Star	1963	18.00
❑ LSP-2745 [S]	Catch a Rising Star	1963	25.00
❑ LPM-3501 [M]	Choice	1966	15.00
❑ LSP-3501 [S]	Choice	1966	18.00
❑ LPM-2804 [M]	Encore	1964	18.00
❑ LSP-2804 [S]	Encore	1964	25.00
❑ LPM-3695 [M]	Especially for You	1967	18.00
❑ LSP-3695 [S]	Especially for You	1967	15.00
❑ LSP-4075	Holding Your Mind	1969	15.00
❑ LPM-3928 [M]	John Gary On Broadway	1968	25.00
❑ LSP-3928 [S]	John Gary On Broadway	1968	15.00
❑ LPM-3992 [M]	John Gary Sings/John Gary Swings	1968	25.00
❑ LSP-3992 [S]	John Gary Sings/John Gary Swings	1968	15.00
❑ LSP-4134	Love of a Gentle Woman	1970	15.00
❑ ANL1-2342	Pure Gold	1977	12.00
❑ LPM-2922 [M]	So Tenderly	1964	18.00
❑ LSP-2922 [S]	So Tenderly	1964	25.00
❑ LPM-3785 [M]	Spanish Moonlight	1967	18.00
❑ LSP-3785 [S]	Spanish Moonlight	1967	15.00
❑ LSP-4233	That's the Way It Was	1971	15.00
❑ LPM-3730 [M]	The Best of John Gary	1967	18.00
❑ LSP-3730 [S]	The Best of John Gary	1967	15.00
❑ LOC-1139 [M]	The John Gary Carnegie Hall Concert	1967	25.00
❑ LSO-1139 [S]	The John Gary Carnegie Hall Concert	1967	15.00
❑ LPM-2940 [M]	The John Gary Christmas Album	1964	18.00
❑ LSP-2940 [S]	The John Gary Christmas Album	1964	25.00
❑ LPM-3349 [M]	The Nearness of You	1965	15.00
❑ LSP-3349 [S]	The Nearness of You	1965	18.00
❑ VPS-6041	This Is John Gary	1971	18.00
❑ LPM-3570 [M]	Your All-Time Country Favorites	1966	15.00
❑ LSP-3570 [S]	Your All-Time Country Favorites	1966	18.00
❑ LPM-3411 [M]	Your All-Time Favorite Songs	1965	15.00
❑ LSP-3411 [S]	Your All-Time Favorite Songs	1965	18.00

GARY, SAM

TRANSITION

❑ TRLP-F-1 [M]	Spirituals and Work Songs	1958	30.00

GAS MASK

TONSIL

❑ 4001 [B]	Gas Mask	1970	30.00

GASCA, LUIS

ATLANTIC

❑ SD1527	Little Giants	1970	30.00

BLUE THUMB

❑ BTS-37	Luis Gasca	1972	30.00

FANTASY

❑ F-9461	Born to Love You	1974	30.00
❑ F-9504	Collage	1976	30.00

—*Brown label (original)*

GASKIN, LEONARD

SWINGVILLE

❑ SVLP-2033 [M]	At the Darktown Strutters' Ball	1962	40.00
—*Purple label*			
❑ SVLP-2033 [M]	At the Darktown Strutters' Ball	1965	25.00
—*Blue label, trident logo at right*			
❑ SVST-2033 [S]	At the Darktown Strutters' Ball	1962	50.00
—*Red label*			
❑ SVST-2033 [S]	At the Darktown Strutters' Ball	1965	30.00
—*Blue label, trident logo at right*			
❑ SVLP-2031 [M]	At the Jazz Band Ball	1962	40.00
—*Purple label*			
❑ SVLP-2031 [M]	At the Jazz Band Ball	1965	25.00
—*Blue label, trident logo at right*			
❑ SVST-2031 [S]	At the Jazz Band Ball	1962	50.00
—*Red label*			
❑ SVST-2031 [S]	At the Jazz Band Ball	1965	30.00
—*Blue label, trident logo at right*			

GASLINI, GIORGIO

SOUL NOTE

❑ 121270	Ayler's Wings	1991	15.00
❑ SN-1020	Gaslini Plays Monk	1981	15.00
❑ 121020	Gaslini Plays Monk	199?	12.00
—*Reissue of 1020*			
❑ 121220	Multipli	199?	15.00
❑ SN-1120	Schumann Reflections	1984	15.00
❑ 121120	Schumann Reflections	199?	12.00
—*Reissue of 1120*			

GATES, DAVID

ARISTA

❑ AL9563	Take Me Now	1981	12.00

ELEKTRA

❑ 6E-251	Falling in Love Again	1980	12.00
❑ EKS-75066	First	1973	15.00
❑ EQ-5066 [Q]	First	1973	25.00
❑ 6E-148	Goodbye Girl	1978	15.00
❑ 7E-1028	Never Let Her Go	1975	15.00
❑ EQ-1028 [Q]	Never Let Her Go	1975	25.00

GATES, HEN

MASTERSEAL

❑ MLP-700 [M]	Let's All Dance to Rock and Roll	1956	100.00

PALACE

❑ P-700 [M]	Let's All Dance to Rock and Roll	1958	60.00
—*Reissue of Masterseal 700*			
❑ PST-700 [S]	Let's All Dance to Rock and Roll	1958	80.00
—*Labeled stereo, but plays in mono*			

PARIS

❑ 101 [M]	Rock and Roll Festival	1957	60.00

PLYMOUTH

❑ R12-144 [M]	Rock and Roll	1956	60.00
❑ R12-149 [M]	Rock and Roll, No. 2	1957	60.00

GATEWAY SINGERS, THE

DECCA

❑ DL8413 [M]	Puttin' On the Style	1956	40.00
❑ DL8671 [M]	The Gateway Singers at the Hungry I	1958	30.00
❑ DL8742 [M]	The Gateway Singers in Hi-Fi	1958	30.00

MGM

❑ E-3905 [M]	Down in the Valley	1961	25.00
❑ SE-3905 [S]	Down in the Valley	1961	30.00
❑ E-4154 [M]	Hootenanny	1963	25.00
❑ SE-4154 [S]	Hootenanny	1963	30.00

WARNER BROS.

❑ W1295 [M]	The Gateway Singers on the Lot	1959	30.00
❑ WS1295 [S]	The Gateway Singers on the Lot	1959	30.00
❑ W1334 [M]	Wagons West	1960	30.00
❑ WS1334 [S]	Wagons West	1960	30.00

GATEWAY TRIO, THE

CAPITOL

❑ T2184 [M]	The Gateway Trio	1964	18.00
❑ ST2184 [S]	The Gateway Trio	1964	30.00
❑ T1868 [M]	The Mad, Mad, Mad Gateway Trio	1963	18.00
❑ ST1868 [S]	The Mad, Mad, Mad Gateway Trio	1963	30.00

GATLIN, LARRY, AND THE GATLIN BROTHERS BAND

COLUMBIA

❑ FC38183	A Gatlin Family Christmas	1982	15.00
❑ PC38183	A Gatlin Family Christmas	198?	10.00
—*Budget-line reissue*			
❑ FC40905	Alive and Well...Living in the Land of Dreams	1988	12.00
❑ JC36582	Help Yourself	1980	12.00
❑ PC36582	Help Yourself	198?	10.00
—*Budget-line reissue*			
❑ PC36582	Help Yourself	198?	10.00
—*Budget-line reissue*			
❑ PC38338	High Time	1982	10.00
—*Reissue of Monument 6644*			
❑ FC39291	Houston to Denver	1984	12.00
❑ JC36488	Larry Gatlin's Greatest Hits, Volume 1	1980	10.00
—*Reissue of Monument 7628*			
❑ FC38923	Larry Gatlin's Greatest Hits, Volume 2	1983	12.00
❑ PC38337	Larry Gatlin with Family and Friends	1982	10.00
—*Reissue of Monument 6634*			
❑ PC38336	Love Is Just a Game	1982	10.00
—*Reissue of Monument 7616*			
❑ FC37464	Not Guilty	1981	12.00
❑ PC37464	Not Guilty	198?	10.00
—*Budget-line reissue*			
❑ PC38340	Oh! Brother	1982	10.00
—*Reissue of Monmunet 7626*			
❑ FC40431	Partners	1986	12.00
❑ PC38339	Rain-Rainbow	1982	10.00
—*Reissue of Monmunet 6633*			
❑ FC40068	Smile!	1985	12.00
❑ JC36250	Straight Ahead	1979	12.00
❑ FC38135	Sure Feels Like Love	1982	12.00
❑ PC38135	Sure Feels Like Love	198?	10.00
—*Budget-line reissue*			
❑ HC48135	Sure Feels Like Love	1982	250.00
—*Half-speed mastered edition*			
❑ FC44471	The Gatlin Brothers' Biggest Hits (1984-88)	1989	12.00
❑ PC36541	The Pilgrim	1980	10.00
—*Reissue of Monument 6632*			

MONUMENT

❑ 6644	High Time	1977	15.00
❑ MG7628	Larry Gatlin's Greatest Hits	1978	15.00
❑ KZ34042	Larry Gatlin with Family & Friends	1975	18.00
❑ 6634	Larry Gatlin with Family and Friends	1976	15.00
—*Reissue of KZ 34042*			
❑ MG7616	Love Is Just a Game	1978	15.00
❑ MG7626	Oh! Brother	1978	15.00
❑ KZ33069	Rain-Rainbow	1974	18.00
❑ 6633	Rain-Rainbow	1976	15.00
—*Reissue of KZ 33069*			
❑ KZ32571	The Pilgrim	1974	18.00
❑ 6632	The Pilgrim	1976	15.00
—*Reissue of KZ 32571*			

SWORD & SHIELD

❑ 9009 [M]	The Old Country Church	1961	100.00

—*As "The Gatlin Quartet" (with sister La Donna joining Larry, Rudy and Steve)*

GAVIN, KEVIN

CHARLIE PARKER

❑ PLP-810 [M]	Hey! This Is Kevin Gavin	1962	30.00
❑ PLP-810S [S]	Hey! This Is Kevin Gavin	1962	40.00

GAYE, MARVIN, AND KIM WESTON

❑ T270 [M]	Take Two	1966	30.00
❑ TS270 [S]	Take Two	1966	40.00

GAYE, MARVIN, AND MARY WELLS

MOTOWN

❑ M613 [M]	Together	1964	50.00
❑ 5260ML	Together	1982	12.00

GAYE, MARVIN, AND TAMMI TERRELL

MOTOWN

❑ M5-102V1	Motown Superstar Series, Vol. 2	1981	12.00
❑ M5-200V1	United	1981	12.00
—*Reissue of Tamla 277*			
❑ M5-142V1	You're All I Need	1981	12.00
—*Reissue of Tamla 284*			

TAMLA

❑ TS294	Easy	1969	25.00

Number	Title	Yr	NM
❑ TS302	Marvin Gaye & Tammi Terrell/Greatest Hits	1970	25.00
❑ T277 [M]	United	1967	40.00
❑ TS277 [S]	United	1967	30.00
❑ T284 [M]	You're All I Need	1968	50.00
❑ TS284 [S]	You're All I Need	1968	25.00

GAYE, MARVIN

CLEOPATRA

Number	Title	Yr	NM
❑ 8222 [B]	Live		30.00

—picture disc

COLUMBIA

Number	Title	Yr	NM
❑ FC39916	Dream of a Lifetime	1985	12.00
❑ 9C940133 [PD]	Dream of a Lifetime	1985	25.00
❑ FC38197	Midnight Love	1982	12.00
❑ HC48197	Midnight Love	1984	40.00

—Half-speed mastered edition

Number	Title	Yr	NM
❑ PC38197	Midnight Love	1986	10.00

—Budget-line reissue

Number	Title	Yr	NM
❑ FC40208	Romantically Yours	1986	12.00

MOTOWN

Number	Title	Yr	NM
❑ 6255ML	A Musical Testament 1964-1984	1988	15.00
❑ M9-791A3	Anthology	1974	25.00
❑ M5-216V1	A Tribute to the Great Nat King Cole	1981	12.00

—Reissue of Tamla 261

Number	Title	Yr	NM
❑ 6058ML	Every Great Motown Hit of Marvin Gaye	1983	12.00
❑ 952921	I Want You	2008	25.00
❑ M5-192V1	Let's Get It On	1981	12.00

—Reissue of Tamla 329

Number	Title	Yr	NM
❑ M5-181V1	Marvin Gaye Live!	1981	12.00

—Reissue of Tamla 333

Number	Title	Yr	NM
❑ 5259ML	Marvin Gaye Live at the London Palladium	1983	15.00

—Reissue of Tamla 352

Number	Title	Yr	NM
❑ M5-191V1	Marvin Gaye's Greatest Hits	1981	12.00

—Reissue of Tamla 348

Number	Title	Yr	NM
❑ M5-115V1	Motown Superstar Series, Vol. 15	1981	12.00
❑ M5-125V1	M.P.G.	1981	12.00

—Reissue of Tamla 292

Number	Title	Yr	NM
❑ 5306ML	Super Hits	198?	12.00
❑ M5-218V1	That Stubborn Kinda' Fellow	1981	12.00

—Reissue of Tamla 239

Number	Title	Yr	NM
❑ 374631296-1 [DJ]	The Master 1961-1984	1995	25.00

—Vinyl is promo only; 8-song sampler from box set

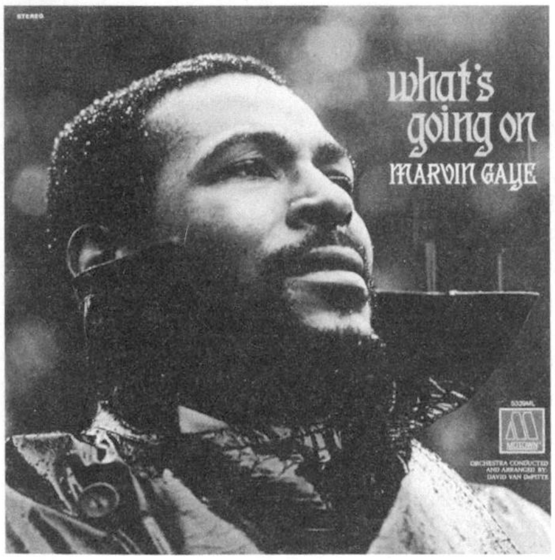

Number	Title	Yr	NM
❑ 5339ML [B]	What's Going On	198?	12.00

—Reissue of Tamla 322

NATURAL RESOURCES

Number	Title	Yr	NM
❑ NR4007T1	The Soulful Moods of Marvin Gaye	1978	15.00

—Reissue of Tamla 221

TAMLA

Number	Title	Yr	NM
❑ T261 [M]	A Tribute to the Great Nat King Cole	1965	50.00
❑ TS261 [S]	A Tribute to the Great Nat King Cole	1965	50.00
❑ T259 [M]	Hello Broadway, This Is Marvin	1965	50.00
❑ TS259 [S]	Hello Broadway, This Is Marvin	1965	50.00
❑ T13-364	Here, My Dear	1978	18.00
❑ T258 [M]	How Sweet It Is to Be Loved by You	1965	50.00
❑ TS258 [S]	How Sweet It Is to Be Loved by You	1965	50.00
❑ TS285 [S]	I Heard It Through the Grapevine	1969	25.00

—Retitled version of "In the Groove

Number	Title	Yr	NM
❑ T8-374	In Our Lifetime	1981	12.00
❑ T285 [M]	In the Groove	1968	50.00
❑ TS285 [S]	In the Groove	1968	30.00
❑ T6-342	I Want You	1976	18.00
❑ T6-329	Let's Get It On	1973	18.00
❑ TS293	Marvin Gaye and His Girls	1969	25.00

—Includes duets with Tammi Terrell, Mary Wells, Kim Weston

Number	Title	Yr	NM
❑ T252 [M]	Marvin Gaye/Greatest Hits	1964	50.00
❑ TS252 [S]	Marvin Gaye/Greatest Hits	1964	40.00
❑ T278 [M]	Marvin Gaye/Greatest Hits, Vol. 2	1967	30.00
❑ TS278 [S]	Marvin Gaye/Greatest Hits, Vol. 2	1967	25.00
❑ T6-333	Marvin Gaye Live!	1974	18.00
❑ T7-352	Marvin Gaye Live at the London Palladium	1977	18.00
❑ T6-348	Marvin Gaye's Greatest Hits	1976	18.00
❑ TS300	Marvin Gaye Super Hits	1970	25.00
❑ T266 [M]	Moods of Marvin Gaye	1966	40.00
❑ TS266 [S]	Moods of Marvin Gaye	1966	50.00
❑ 6172TL	Motown Remembers Marvin Gaye	1986	12.00
❑ TS292	M.P.G.	1969	25.00
❑ T242 [M]	Recorded Live -- Marvin Gaye on Stage	1963	300.00
❑ TS299	That's the Way Love Is	1969	25.00
❑ T239 [M]	That Stubborn Kinda' Fella	1963	600.00
❑ TM221 [M]	The Soulful Moods of Marvin Gaye	1961	1000.00
❑ T5-322	Trouble Man	1972	18.00
❑ T5-310	What's Going On	1971	18.00
❑ T251 [M]	When I'm Alone I Cry	1964	250.00

UNIVERSAL MOTOWN

Number	Title	Yr	NM
❑ 5300221	What's Going On	2008	25.00

GAYLE, CHARLES

SILKHEART

Number	Title	Yr	NM
❑ SH-115	Always Born	1988	12.00
❑ SH-116	Homeless	1988	12.00
❑ SH-117	Spirits Before	1988	12.00

GAYLE, CRYSTAL, AND GARY MORRIS

WARNER BROS.

Number	Title	Yr	NM
❑ 25507	What If We Fell in Love?	1987	12.00

GAYLE, CRYSTAL

COLUMBIA

Number	Title	Yr	NM
❑ FC38803	Crystal Gayle's Greatest Hits	1983	12.00
❑ FC37438	Hollywood, Tennessee	1981	12.00
❑ PC37438	Hollywood, Tennessee	198?	10.00

—Budget-line reissue

Number	Title	Yr	NM
❑ JC36203	Miss the Mississippi	1979	12.00
❑ PC36203	Miss the Mississippi	198?	10.00

—Budget-line reissue

Number	Title	Yr	NM
❑ JC36512	These Days	1980	12.00
❑ PC36512	These Days	198?	10.00

—Budget-line reissue

ELEKTRA

Number	Title	Yr	NM
❑ 60200	True Love	1982	12.00

LIBERTY

Number	Title	Yr	NM
❑ LOO-1080	A Woman's Heart	1981	12.00
❑ LN-10150	Classic Crystal	1982	10.00

—Budget-line reissue of UA 982

Number	Title	Yr	NM
❑ LN-10004	Crystal	1981	10.00

—Budget-line reissue of UA 614

Number	Title	Yr	NM
❑ LN-10002	Crystal Gayle	1981	10.00
❑ LOO-1034	Favorites	1981	10.00

—Reissue of UA 1034

Number	Title	Yr	NM
❑ LN-10229	Favorites	1984	10.00

—Budget-line reissue

Number	Title	Yr	NM
❑ LN-10003	Somebody Loves You	1981	10.00

—Budget-line reissue of UA 543

Number	Title	Yr	NM
❑ LN-10005	We Must Believe in Magic	1981	10.00

—Budget-line reissue of UA 771

Number	Title	Yr	NM
❑ LN-10006	We Should Be Together	1980	10.00

—Budget-line reissue

Number	Title	Yr	NM
❑ LMAS-858	When I Dream	1981	10.00

—Reissue of UA 858

Number	Title	Yr	NM
❑ LN-10227	When I Dream	1984	10.00

—Budget-line reissue

MCA

Number	Title	Yr	NM
❑ 2334	I've Cried the Blue Right Out of My Eyes	1977	12.00

—Reissue of Decca material

Number	Title	Yr	NM
❑ 37077	I've Cried the Blue Right Out of My Eyes	198?	10.00

—Budget-line reissue

MOBILE FIDELITY

Number	Title	Yr	NM
❑ 1-043	We Must Believe in Magic	1981	25.00

—Audiophile vinyl

NAUTILUS

Number	Title	Yr	NM
❑ NR-36	When I Dream	198?	30.00

—Audiophile vinyl

PAIR

Number	Title	Yr	NM
❑ PDL2-1083	Country Pure	1986	15.00
❑ PDL2-1126	Musical Jewels	1986	15.00

UNITED ARTISTS

Number	Title	Yr	NM
❑ LOO-982	Classic Crystal	1979	12.00
❑ UA-LA614-G	Crystal	1976	15.00
❑ LOO-1034	Favorites	1980	12.00
❑ UA-LA543-G	Somebody Loves You	1975	15.00
❑ UA-LA771-G	We Must Believe in Magic	1977	12.00
❑ UA-LA969-H	We Should Be Together	1979	12.00
❑ UA-LA858-H	When I Dream	1978	12.00

WARNER BROS.

Number	Title	Yr	NM
❑ 25508	A Crystal Christmas	1986	18.00

—Original cover has decorated Christmas tree on front

Number	Title	Yr	NM
❑ 25508	A Crystal Christmas	1987	12.00

—Reissue cover has photo of Crystal Gayle on front

Number	Title	Yr	NM
❑ 23958	Cage the Songbird	1983	12.00
❑ 25706	Nobody's Angel	1988	12.00
❑ 25154	Nobody Wants to Be Alone	1984	12.00
❑ 25405	Straight to the Heart	1986	12.00
❑ 25622	The Best of Crystal Gayle	1987	12.00
❑ 60200	True Love	1983	10.00

—Reissue of Elektra 60200

GAYLE, ROZELLE

MERCURY

Number	Title	Yr	NM
❑ MG-20374 [M]	Like, Be My Guest	1958	40.00

GAYLORDS, THE

MERCURY

Number	Title	Yr	NM
❑ MG-20620 [M]	American Hits in Italian	1961	25.00
❑ SR-60620 [S]	American Hits in Italian	1961	30.00
❑ MG-25198 [10]	By Request	1955	50.00
❑ MG-20213 [M]	Collection of Golden Hits	1957	30.00
❑ MG-20186 [M]	Italia	1957	30.00
❑ MG-20356 [M]	Let's Have a Pizza Party	1958	25.00
❑ SR-60075 [S]	Let's Have a Pizza Party	1959	30.00
❑ MG-20742 [M]	Party Style	1963	25.00
❑ SR-60742 [S]	Party Style	1963	30.00
❑ MG-20430 [M]	That's Amore	1959	25.00
❑ SR-60102 [S]	That's Amore	1959	30.00
❑ MG-20695 [M]	The Gaylords at the Shamrock	1962	25.00
❑ SR-60695 [S]	The Gaylords at the Shamrock	1962	30.00

TIME

Number	Title	Yr	NM
❑ 52127 [M]	Bella Italia	196?	18.00
❑ S-2127 [S]	Bella Italia	196?	25.00
❑ 52109 [M]	Live at Lake Tahoe	196?	18.00
❑ S-2109 [S]	Live at Lake Tahoe	196?	25.00

WING

Number	Title	Yr	NM
❑ MGW-12139 [M]	Italiano Favorites	196?	15.00
❑ SRW-16139 [S]	Italiano Favorites	196?	15.00
❑ MGW-12278 [M]	Let's Have a Pizza Party	196?	15.00
❑ SRW-16278 [S]	Let's Have a Pizza Party	196?	15.00

GAYNOR, GLORIA

ATLANTIC

Number	Title	Yr	NM
❑ 80033	Gloria Gaynor	1982	12.00

MGM

Number	Title	Yr	NM
❑ M3G-4997	Experience Gloria Gaynor	1975	12.00
❑ M3G-4982	Never Can Say Goodbye	1975	12.00

POLYDOR

Number	Title	Yr	NM
❑ PD-1-6139	Gloria Gaynor's Park Avenue Sound	1978	12.00
❑ PD-1-6095	Glorious	1977	12.00
❑ PD-1-6231	I Have a Right	1979	12.00
❑ PD-1-6063	I've Got You	1976	12.00
❑ PD-1-6184	Love Tracks	1978	12.00
❑ PD-1-6274	Stories	1980	12.00

GAYNOR, MITZI

VERVE

Number	Title	Yr	NM
❑ MGV-2110 [M]	Mitzi	1959	30.00
❑ MGVS-6014 [S]	Mitzi	1959	40.00
❑ MGV-2115 [M]	Mitzi Gaynor Sings the Lyrics of Ira Gershwin	1959	30.00
❑ MGVS-6049 [S]	Mitzi Gaynor Sings the Lyrics of Ira Gershwin	1959	40.00

GEARS, THE

PLAYGEMS

Number	Title	Yr	NM
❑ GS6471	Rockin' at Ground Zero	1980	30.00

GEDDES, DAVID

BIG TREE

Number	Title	Yr	NM
❑ BT89511	Run Joey Run	1975	15.00

GEE, MATTHEW

RIVERSIDE

Number	Title	Yr	NM
❑ RLP 12-221 [M]	Jazz by Gee!	1956	80.00

—White label, blue print

Number	Title	Yr	NM
❑ RLP 12-221 [M]	Jazz by Gee!	1958	40.00

—Blue label, microphone logo at top

GEEZINSLAW BROTHERS, THE

CAPITOL

Number	Title	Yr	NM
❑ T2570 [M]	Can You Believe...The Geezinslaw Brothers!	1966	25.00
❑ ST2570 [S]	Can You Believe...The Geezinslaw Brothers!	1966	30.00
❑ T2771 [M]	My Dirty, Lowdown, Rotten, Cotton-Pickin' Little Darlin'	1967	25.00
❑ ST2771 [S]	My Dirty, Lowdown, Rotten, Cotton-Pickin' Little Darlin'	1967	30.00
❑ ST2885 [S]	The Geezinslaw Brothers & "Chubby	1968	30.00
❑ T2885 [M]	The Geezinslaw Brothers & "Chubby	1968	40.00

Number	Title	Yr	NM
❑ ST-130	The Geezinslaw Brothers Are Alive	1969	25.00

COLUMBIA

Number	Title	Yr	NM
❑ CL2100 [M]	The Kooky World of the Geezinslaw Brothers	1963	30.00
❑ CS8900 [S]	The Kooky World of the Geezinslaw Brothers	1963	30.00

GEILS, J., BAND

ATLANTIC

Number	Title	Yr	NM
❑ SD19234	Best of the J. Geils Band	1979	12.00
❑ SD19284	Best of the J. Geils Band -- 2	1980	12.00
❑ SD7260	Bloodshot	1973	25.00
—Red vinyl			
❑ SD7260	Bloodshot	1973	15.00
—Black vinyl			
❑ QD7260 [Q]	Bloodshot	1973	40.00
❑ SD18147	Hotline	1975	15.00
❑ SD7286	Ladies Invited	1973	15.00
❑ SD7241	Live" -- Full House	1972	15.00
❑ SD 2-507	Live -- Blow Your Face Out	1976	18.00
❑ SD19103	Monkey Island	1977	15.00
—As "Geils			
❑ SD18107	Nightmares and Other Tales from the Vinyl Jungle	1974	15.00
❑ QD18107 [Q]	Nightmares and Other Tales from the Vinyl Jungle	1974	40.00
❑ 8275 [M]	The J. Geils Band	1970	40.00
— Mono is white label promo only; stereo cover with "dj copy monaural" sticker			
❑ SD8275 [S]	The J. Geils Band	1970	18.00
❑ SD8297 [S]	The Morning After	1971	15.00
❑ 8297 [M]	The Morning After	1971	40.00
—Mono version is white label promo only with "d/j copy monaural" stucker on front cover			

EMI AMERICA

Number	Title	Yr	NM
❑ ST-17174	Flashback -- The Best of the J. Geils Band	1985	10.00
❑ SOO-17062	Freeze-Frame	1981	12.00
❑ SN-16374	Freeze-Frame	1986	10.00
—Reissue			
❑ SOO-17016	Love Stinks	1980	12.00
❑ SN-16375	Love Stinks	1986	10.00
—Reissue			
❑ SO-17006	Sanctuary	1978	12.00
❑ SN-16316	Sanctuary	1985	10.00
—Reissue			
❑ SO-17087	Showtime!	1982	12.00
❑ SN-16373	Showtime!	1986	10.00
—Reissue			
❑ SJ-17137	You're Gettin' Even While I'm Gettin' Odd	1984	10.00

NAUTILUS

Number	Title	Yr	NM
❑ NR-25	Love Stinks	1982	25.00
—Audiophile vinyl			

GELDOF, BOB

ATLANTIC

Number	Title	Yr	NM
❑ 81687	Deep in the Heart of Nowhere	1986	12.00
❑ 1010 [DJ]	Questions and Answers (Interview)	1987	12.00
❑ 1010 [DJ]	Questions and Answers (Interview)	1987	12.00

GELLER, HERB

ATCO

Number	Title	Yr	NM
❑ 33-109 [M]	Gypsy	1959	40.00

ATLANTIC

Number	Title	Yr	NM
❑ SD1681	Rhyme and Reason	1975	15.00

EMARCY

Number	Title	Yr	NM
❑ MG-26045 [10]	Herb Geller Plays	1954	120.00
❑ MG-36045 [M]	Herb Geller Plays	1955	80.00
❑ MG-36024 [M]	The Gellers	1955	100.00
❑ MG-36040 [M]	The Herb Geller Sextette	1955	80.00

JOSIE

Number	Title	Yr	NM
❑ JOZ-3502 [M]	Alto Saxophone	1962	30.00
❑ JLPS-3502 [S]	Alto Saxophone	1962	25.00

JUBILEE

Number	Title	Yr	NM
❑ JLP-1044 [M]	Fire in the West	1957	50.00
❑ SDJLP-1044 [S]	Fire in the West	1959	40.00
❑ JG-1094 [M]	Stax of Sax	1959	50.00

GELLER, LORRAINE

DOT

Number	Title	Yr	NM
❑ DLP-3174 [M]	Lorraine Geller at the Piano	1959	500.00

GENE AND DEBBE

TRX

Number	Title	Yr	NM
❑ 1001	Here and Now	1968	30.00

GENE LOVES JEZEBEL

GEFFEN

Number	Title	Yr	NM
❑ GHS24118	Discover	1986	12.00
❑ 141 [DJ]	Discover Interview	1986	30.00
❑ GHS24260	Kiss of Life	1990	15.00
❑ GHS24165	Promise	1988	12.00
—First American issue of 1983 U.K. debut			
❑ 4192 [EP]	Remix Sampler	1990	25.00
—Promo-only collection			
❑ GHS24171	The House of Dolls	1988	12.00

RELATIVITY

Number	Title	Yr	NM
❑ EMC8075 [EP]	Desire	1985	10.00
❑ EMC8036 [B]	Immigrant	1985	15.00

WARNER BROS.

Number	Title	Yr	NM
❑ WBMS-141 [DJ]	Discover Interview	1986	25.00
—Part of "The Warner Bros. Music Show" series; in die-cut cover			

GENERAL PUBLIC

I.R.S.

Number	Title	Yr	NM
❑ SP70046	...All the Rage	1984	12.00
❑ R142295	Hand to Mouth	1986	15.00
—RCA Music Service edition			
❑ 5782	Hand to Mouth	1986	12.00

GENERATION BAND, THE

NAUTILUS

Number	Title	Yr	NM
❑ NR-62	Soft Shoulder	198?	40.00
—Audiophile vinyl			

PALO ALTO

Number	Title	Yr	NM
❑ PA-8054	Soft Shoulder	198?	15.00

TBA

Number	Title	Yr	NM
❑ TB-202	Call of the Wild	198?	12.00
❑ TB-208	High Visibility	1985	12.00

GENERATION X

CHRYSALIS

Number	Title	Yr	NM
❑ CHR1169	Generation X	1978	30.00
❑ PV41169	Generation X	1984	18.00
—Reissue			
❑ CHR1327	Kiss Me Deadly	1981	30.00
❑ PV41327	Kiss Me Deadly	1985	18.00
—Reissue			
❑ CHR1193	Valley of the Dolls	1979	30.00
❑ PV41193	Valley of the Dolls	1984	25.00
—Reissue			

GENESIS

ABC

Number	Title	Yr	NM
❑ ABCX-816	Trespass	1971	18.00
—Reissue of Impulse album; black label			
❑ ABCX-816	Trespass	1974	15.00
—Reissue; concentric yellow/orange/purple "target" label			

ABC IMPULSE!

Number	Title	Yr	NM
❑ ASD-9205	Trespass	1971	30.00

ATCO

Number	Title	Yr	NM
❑ SD 36-129	A Trick of the Tail	1976	15.00
❑ SD 38-101	A Trick of the Tail	1978	12.00
—Reissue of SD 36-129			
❑ SD 2-401	The Lamb Lies Down on Broadway	1974	18.00
—Originals have yellow labels (other labels worth less)			
❑ SD 36-144	Wind & Wuthering	1977	15.00
❑ SD 38-100	Wind & Wuthering	1978	12.00
—Reissue of SD 36-144			

ATLANTIC

Number	Title	Yr	NM
❑ SD19313	Abacab	1981	12.00
—Released with four different covers, lettered "A" through "D" on the upper part of the spine; no difference in value			
❑ SD19173	...And Then There Were Three	1978	12.00
❑ SD16014	Duke	1980	12.00
❑ 81848	Foxtrot	1988	12.00
—Reissue of Charisma LP of the same name			
❑ 80116	Genesis	1983	10.00
❑ 81855	Genesis Live	1988	12.00
—Reissue of Charisma LP of the same name			
❑ 81641	Invisible Touch	1986	10.00
❑ 80030	Nursery Cryme	1982	10.00
—Reissue of Charisma LP of same name			
❑ SD 2-9002	Seconds Out	1977	15.00
❑ SD19277	Selling England by the Pound	1981	10.00
—Reissue of Charisma LP of same name			
❑ SD 2-2000	Three Sides Live	1982	15.00
❑ PR965 [DJ]	Tonight, Tonight, Tonight -- Exclusive Candid Interview	1986	30.00
—Promo-only music and interviews; came with cover letter and cue sheet (deduct 1/3 if missing)			

BUDDAH

Number	Title	Yr	NM
❑ BDS-5659	The Best ... Genesis	1976	25.00
—Reissue of "Nursery Cryme" and "Foxtrot" in one set			

CHARISMA

Number	Title	Yr	NM
❑ CAS-1058 [B]	Foxtrot	1972	30.00
❑ CAS-1058	Foxtrot	2001	30.00
—Classic Records reissue on 180-gram vinyl			
❑ CAS-1666 [B]	Genesis Live	1974	30.00
❑ CAS-1666	Genesis Live	2001	30.00
—Classic Records reissue on 180-gram vinyl			
❑ CAS-1052 [B]	Nursery Cryme	1971	30.00
❑ CAS-1052	Nursery Cryme	2000	30.00
—Classic Records reissue on 180-gram vinyl			
❑ CA2-2701 [B]	Nursery Cryme/Foxtrot	1976	35.00
—Repackage of the individual albums of these names			
❑ FC-6060	Selling England by the Pound	1973	18.00
❑ FC-6060	Selling England by the Pound	2001	30.00
—Classic Records reissue on 180-gram vinyl			

LONDON

Number	Title	Yr	NM
❑ PS643	From Genesis to Revelation	1974	30.00
—First US release of debut album			
❑ LC-50006	In the Beginning	1977	15.00
❑ 820322-1	In the Beginning	198?	12.00
—Reissue of London 50006			

MCA

Number	Title	Yr	NM
❑ ABCX-816	Trespass	1979	12.00
—Reissue of ABC ABCX-816			
❑ 37151	Trespass	198?	10.00
—Reissue of MCA 816			

MOBILE FIDELITY

Number	Title	Yr	NM
❑ 1-062 [B]	A Trick of the Tail	1981	50.00
—Audiophile vinyl			

GENESIS (3)

MERCURY

Number	Title	Yr	NM
❑ SR61175	In the Beginning	1968	100.00
—First pressing is textured cover, red label.			
❑ SR61175	In the Beginning	197?	25.00
—Second pressing is non-textured cover, skyline label.			

GENTLE GIANT

CAPITOL

Number	Title	Yr	NM
❑ ST-11428	Free Hand	1975	12.00
❑ SN-16048	Free Hand	1980	10.00
—Budget-line reissue			
❑ SW-11813	Giant for a Day	1978	12.00
❑ SN-16045	Giant for a Day	1980	10.00
—Budget-line reissue			
❑ ST-11532	Interview	1976	12.00
❑ SN-16047	Interview	1980	10.00
—Budget-line reissue			
❑ ST-11696	The Missing Piece	1977	12.00
❑ SN-16046	The Missing Piece	1980	10.00
—Budget-line reissue			
❑ SKBB-11592	The Official "Live" Gentle Giant -- Playing the Fool	1977	15.00
❑ ST-11337	The Power and the Glory	1974	12.00
❑ SN-16044	The Power and the Glory	1980	10.00
—Budget-line reissue			

COLUMBIA

Number	Title	Yr	NM
❑ JC36341	Civilian	1980	12.00
❑ KC32022	Octopus	1973	15.00
❑ PC32022	Octopus	197?	10.00
—Reissue			
❑ KC31649	Three Friends	1972	15.00
❑ PC31649	Three Friends	197?	10.00
—Reissue			

VERTIGO

Number	Title	Yr	NM
❑ VE-1005	Acquiring the Taste	1971	18.00

GENTLE SOUL, THE

EPIC

Number	Title	Yr	NM
❑ BN26374	The Gentle Soul	1969	200.00
—Reproductions exist			

GENTRY, BOBBIE

CAPITOL

Number	Title	Yr	NM
❑ SKAO-381	Bobbie Gentry's Greatest!	1969	18.00
❑ SM-381	Bobbie Gentry's Greatest!	197?	10.00
❑ ST-428	Fancy	1970	18.00
❑ T2830 [M]	Ode to Billie Joe	1967	25.00
❑ ST2830 [S]	Ode to Billie Joe	1967	18.00
❑ SM-2830	Ode to Billie Joe	197?	10.00
❑ ST-494	Patchwork	1970	18.00
❑ STBB-704	Sittin' Pretty/Tobacco Road	1971	18.00
❑ ST2842 [S]	The Delta Sweete	1968	18.00
❑ T2842 [M]	The Delta Sweete	1968	30.00
❑ ST2964	The Local Gentry	1968	18.00
❑ ST-155	Touch 'Em with Love	1969	18.00

GENTRYS, THE

MGM

Number	Title	Yr	NM
❑ E-4346 [M]	Gentry Time	1966	25.00
❑ SE-4346 [S]	Gentry Time	1966	30.00
❑ E-4336 [M]	Keep On Dancing	1965	30.00
❑ SE-4336 [P]	Keep On Dancing	1965	30.00
❑ GAS-127	The Gentrys (Golden Archive Series)	1970	25.00

SUN

Number	Title	Yr	NM
❑ LP-117	The Gentrys	1970	30.00

GEORDIE

MGM

Number	Title	Yr	NM
❑ SE-4903	Hope You Like It	1973	30.00

GEORGE, BARBARA

A.F.O.

Number	Title	Yr	NM
❑ LP5001 [M]	I Know (You Don't Love Me No More)	1962	250.00

GEORGE, LOWELL

WARNER BROS.

Number	Title	Yr	NM
❏ 3194	Thanks I'll Eat it Here	1979	18.00

GEORGIA GRINDERS, THE

STOMP OFF

Number	Title	Yr	NM
❏ SOS-1068	A Tribute to Roy Palmer	1984	12.00

GEORGIA SATELLITES, THE

ELEKTRA

Number	Title	Yr	NM
❏ 60496	Georgia Satellites	1986	12.00
❏ 60887	In the Land of Salvation and Sin	1989	15.00
❏ 60793	Open All Night	1988	12.00

GERARD, DANYEL

MGM VERVE

Number	Title	Yr	NM
❏ MV5081	Danyel Gerard	1972	15.00

GERHARD, RAMONA

SOMA

Number	Title	Yr	NM
❏ MG1202	Christmas in Hi-Fi with Ramona Gerhard	195?	25.00

—*Red vinyl*

GERMS, THE

CLEOPATRA

Number	Title	Yr	NM
❏ 8088 [B]	I Fu*#ed Your Mom - Live '78-'79		25.00
❏ 2908 [B]	The Whisky / The Hong Kong Cafe		25.00

MOHAWK

Number	Title	Yr	NM
❏ SCALP-001	Recorded Live at the Whiskey, June, 1977	1981	25.00

—*Second edition: Un-numbered edition, with sticker*

❏ SCALP-001 [B]	Recorded Live at the Whiskey, June, 1977	1981	60.00

—*First edition: Numbered edition, with sticker*

RHINO

Number	Title	Yr	NM
❏ R1-78602	(GI)	2005	18.00

—*Reissue on 180 gram vinyl*

SLASH

Number	Title	Yr	NM
❏ 23932 [B]	(GI)	1983	15.00
—*Reissue*			
❏ SR-103 [B]	(GI)	1981	30.00
❏ SREP108	What We Do Is Secret	1981	18.00

GERONIMO BLACK

UNI

Number	Title	Yr	NM
❏ 73132	Geronimo Black	1972	30.00

GERRY AND THE PACEMAKERS

CAPITOL

Number	Title	Yr	NM
❏ SM-11898 [B]	The Best of Gerry and the Pacemakers	1979	10.00

—*All stereo except "I Like It," "Away from You" and "I'm the One," which are mono.*

LAURIE

Number	Title	Yr	NM
❏ LLP-2024 [M]	Don't Let the Sun Catch You Crying	1964	30.00
❏ SLP-2024 [R]	Don't Let the Sun Catch You Crying	1964	30.00
❏ T90555 [M]	Don't Let the Sun Catch You Crying	1964	40.00
—*Capitol Record Club edition*			
❏ DT90555 [R]	Don't Let the Sun Catch You Crying	1964	30.00
—*Capitol Record Club edition*			
❏ LLP-2027 [M]	Gerry and the Pacemakers' Second Album	1964	30.00
❏ SLP-2027 [R]	Gerry and the Pacemakers' Second Album	1964	30.00
❏ LLP-2037 [M]	Girl on a Swing	1966	30.00
❏ SLP-2037 [S]	Girl on a Swing	1966	25.00
❏ LLP-2031 [M]	Greatest Hits	1965	30.00
❏ SLP-2031 [R]	Greatest Hits	1965	18.00
❏ T90384 [M]	Greatest Hits	1965	30.00
—*Capitol Record Club edition*			
❏ DT90384 [R]	Greatest Hits	1965	30.00
—*Capitol Record Club edition*			
❏ LLP-2030 [M]	I'll Be There	1964	30.00
❏ SLP-2030 [R]	I'll Be There	1964	30.00

UNITED ARTISTS

Number	Title	Yr	NM
❏ UAL3387 [M]	Ferry Cross the Mersey	1965	30.00
—*Also contains incidental music by George Martin*			
❏ UAS6387 [S]	Ferry Cross the Mersey	1965	40.00
❏ T90812 [M]	Ferry Cross the Mersey	1965	40.00
—*Capitol Record Club edition*			
❏ ST90812 [S]	Ferry Cross the Mersey	1965	50.00
—*Capitol Record Club edition*			

GESTURES, THE

SUNDAZED

Number	Title	Yr	NM
❏ LP-5021	The Gestures	199?	12.00

GETZ, EDDIE

MGM

Number	Title	Yr	NM
❏ E-3462 [M]	The Eddie Getz Quintette	1957	50.00

GETZ, STAN, AND ALBERT DAILEY

ELEKTRA/MUSICIAN

Number	Title	Yr	NM
❏ 60370	Poetry	1985	12.00

GETZ, STAN, AND BILL EVANS

VERVE

Number	Title	Yr	NM
❏ V3G-8833	Previously Unreleased Recordings	1974	15.00

GETZ, STAN, AND BOB BROOKMEYER

VERVE

Number	Title	Yr	NM
❏ V-8418 [M]	Stan Getz and Bob Brookmeyer (Recorded Fall 1961)	1961	25.00
❏ V6-8418 [S]	Stan Getz and Bob Brookmeyer (Recorded Fall 1961)	1961	25.00

GETZ, STAN, AND CHARLIE BYRD

DCC COMPACT CLASSICS

Number	Title	Yr	NM
❏ LPZ-2011	Jazz Samba	1995	30.00
—*Audiophile vinyl*			

VERVE

Number	Title	Yr	NM
❏ V-8432 [M]	Jazz Samba	1962	25.00
❏ V6-8432 [S]	Jazz Samba	1962	30.00
—*With "MGM Records" on label print*			
❏ UMJ-3158	Jazz Samba	198?	12.00
❏ 810061-1	Jazz Samba	198?	12.00
—*Reissue*			
❏ V6-8432 [S]	Jazz Samba	1976	15.00

—*"Manufactured and Marketed by Polydor Incorporated" on label*

GETZ, STAN, AND CHET BAKER

STORYVILLE

Number	Title	Yr	NM
❏ 4090	Line for Lyons	1984	12.00

GETZ, STAN, AND GERRY MULLIGAN

MAINSTREAM

Number	Title	Yr	NM
❏ MRL364	Yesterday	1972	18.00

GETZ, STAN, AND HORACE SILVER

BARONET

Number	Title	Yr	NM
❏ B-102 [M]	A Pair of Kings	1962	18.00
❏ BS-102 [R]	A Pair of Kings	196?	12.00

GETZ, STAN, AND J.J. JOHNSON

Number	Title	Yr	NM
❏ MGV-8265 [M]	Stan Getz and J.J. Johnson at the Opera House	1958	50.00
❏ MGVS-6027 [S]	Stan Getz and J.J. Johnson at the Opera House	1960	40.00
❏ V-8265 [M]	Stan Getz and J.J. Johnson at the Opera House	1961	25.00
❏ V6-8265 [S]	Stan Getz and J.J. Johnson at the Opera House	1961	18.00
❏ V6-8490 [S]	Stan Getz and J.J. Johnson at the Opera House	1962	18.00
❏ V-8490 [M]	Stan Getz and J.J. Johnson at the Opera House	1962	18.00

GETZ, STAN, AND JOAO GILBERTO

MOBILE FIDELITY

Number	Title	Yr	NM
❏ 1-208	Getz/Gilberto	1994	50.00
—*Audiophile vinyl*			

VERVE

Number	Title	Yr	NM
❏ V-8623 [M]	Getz/Gilberto #2	1965	18.00
❏ V6-8623 [S]	Getz/Gilberto #2	1965	25.00
❏ V-8545 [M]	Getz/Gilberto	1964	18.00
❏ V6-8545 [S]	Getz/Gilberto	1964	25.00
❏ UMV-2099	Getz/Gilberto	198?	12.00
—*Reissue*			
❏ 810048-1	Getz/Gilberto	198?	12.00
—*Reissue*			

GETZ, STAN, AND LAURINDO ALMEIDA

VERVE

Number	Title	Yr	NM
❏ V-8665 [M]	Stan Getz with Guest Artist Laurindo Almeida	1965	18.00
❏ V6-8665 [S]	Stan Getz with Guest Artist Laurindo Almeida	1965	25.00

GETZ, STAN, AND OSCAR PETERSON

VERVE

Number	Title	Yr	NM
❏ MGV-8251 [M]	Stan Getz and the Oscar Peterson Trio	1958	50.00
❏ V-8251 [M]	Stan Getz and the Oscar Peterson Trio	1961	25.00
—*Reissue of MGV-8251*			
❏ V6-8251 [R]	Stan Getz and the Oscar Peterson Trio	196?	15.00
❏ UMV-2665	Stan Getz and the Oscar Peterson Trio	198?	12.00
—*Reissue*			

Number	Title	Yr	NM
❏ MGV-8348 [M]	Stan Getz with Gerry Mulligan and the Oscar Peterson Trio	1959	50.00
❏ V-8348 [M]	Stan Getz with Gerry Mulligan and the Oscar Peterson Trio	1961	25.00
—*Reissue of MGV-8348*			
❏ V6-8348 [R]	Stan Getz with Gerry Mulligan and the Oscar Peterson Trio	1961	15.00

GETZ, STAN, AND WARDELL GRAY

DAWN

Number	Title	Yr	NM
❏ DLP-1126 [M]	Tenors Anyone?	1958	120.00

SEECO

Number	Title	Yr	NM
❏ SLP-7 [10]	Highlights in Modern Jazz	1954	200.00

GETZ, STAN, AND ZOOT SIMS

FANTASY

Number	Title	Yr	NM
❏ OJC-008	The Brothers	1982	15.00

PRESTIGE

Number	Title	Yr	NM
❏ PRLP-7022 [M]	The Brothers	1956	400.00
—*Yellow label with W. 50th St. address*			
❏ PRLP-7252 [M]	The Brothers	1963	100.00
—*Yellow label with Bergenfield, N.J. address*			

GETZ, STAN; DIZZY GILLESPIE; SONNY STITT

VERVE

Number	Title	Yr	NM
❏ MGV-8198 [M]	For Musicians Only	1958	80.00
❏ V-8198 [M]	For Musicians Only	1961	30.00

GETZ, STAN

A&M

Number	Title	Yr	NM
❏ SP-5297	Apasionado	1990	18.00

AMERICAN RECORDING SOCIETY

Number	Title	Yr	NM
❏ G-407 [M]	Cool Jazz of Stan Getz	1956	40.00
❏ G-428 [M]	Intimate Portrait	1957	40.00
❏ G-443 [M]	Stan Getz '57	1957	40.00

BLACKHAWK

Number	Title	Yr	NM
❏ BKH-51101	Voyage	1986	12.00

BLUE RIBBON

Number	Title	Yr	NM
❏ BR-8012 [M]	Rhythms	1961	25.00
❏ BS-8012 [R]	Rhythms	1961	12.00

CLEF

Number	Title	Yr	NM
❏ MGC-137 [10]	Stan Getz Plays	1953	200.00
❏ MGC-143 [10]	The Artistry of Stan Getz	1953	200.00

COLUMBIA

Number	Title	Yr	NM
❏ PC33703	Best of Two Worlds	1975	18.00
❏ PC32706	Captain Marvel	1974	18.00
❏ JC35992	Children of the World	1979	15.00
❏ JC36403	The Best of Stan Getz	1980	15.00
❏ CJ44047	The Lyrical Stan Getz	1988	15.00
❏ FC38272	The Master	1983	12.00
❏ JC34873	The Peacocks	1977	15.00

CONCORD JAZZ

Number	Title	Yr	NM
❏ CJ-188	Pure Getz	1983	15.00
❏ CJ-158	The Dolphin	198?	15.00

CROWN

Number	Title	Yr	NM
❏ CLP-5002 [M]	Groovin' High	1957	40.00
—*Reissue of Modern 1202*			
❏ CLP-5284 [M]	Groovin' High	196?	25.00
—*Reissue of 5002*			

DALE

Number	Title	Yr	NM
❏ 21 [10]	In Retrospect	1951	300.00

EMARCY

Number	Title	Yr	NM
❏ 838771-1	Billy Highstreet Samba	1990	15.00

FANTASY

Number	Title	Yr	NM
❏ OJC-121	Stan Getz Quartets	198?	12.00
—*Reissue of Prestige 7002*			

HALL OF FAME

Number	Title	Yr	NM
❏ 606	Stan Getz and His Tenor Sax	197?	15.00

INNER CITY

Number	Title	Yr	NM
❏ 1040	Gold	1977	15.00

INTERMEDIA

Number	Title	Yr	NM
❏ QS-5057	Stella by Starlight	198?	12.00

JAZZ MAN

Number	Title	Yr	NM
❏ 5014	Forrest Eyes	1982	15.00

JAZZTONE

Number	Title	Yr	NM
❏ J-1230 [M]	Stan Getz	1956	40.00
❏ J-1240 [M]	Stan Getz '57	1957	40.00

METRO

Number	Title	Yr	NM
❏ M-501 [M]	The Melodic Stan Getz	1965	15.00
❏ MS-501 [S]	The Melodic Stan Getz	1965	18.00

METRONOME

Number	Title	Yr	NM
❏ BLP-6 [M]	The Sound	1956	50.00

MGM

Number	Title	Yr	NM
❏ SE-4696	Marrakesh Express	1970	18.00

MODERN

Number	Title	Yr	NM
❏ MLP-1202 [M]	Groovin' High	1956	150.00

MOSAIC

Number	Title	Yr	NM
❏ MR4-131	The Complete Recordings of the Stan Getz Quintet with Jimmy Raney	199?	60.00

Number	Title	Yr	NM

NEW JAZZ

Number	Title	Yr	NM
❑ NJLP-8214 [M]	Long Island Sound	1959	60.00

— Reissue of Prestige 7002; purple label

| ❑ NJLP-8214 [M] | Long Island Sound | 1965 | 30.00 |

— Blue label with trident logo on right

NORGRAN

❑ MGN-1008 [M]	Interpretations by the Stan Getz Quintet #2	1954	120.00
❑ MGN-1029 [M]	Interpretations by the Stan Getz Quintet #3	1955	150.00
❑ MGN-1000 [M]	Interpretations by the Stan Getz Quintet	1954	120.00
❑ MGN-1088 [M]	More West Coast Jazz with Stan Getz	1956	100.00
❑ MGN-1087 [M]	Stan Getz '56	1956	100.00
❑ MGN-2000-2 [M]	Stan Getz at the Shrine	1955	200.00

— Boxed set with booklet

| ❑ MGN-1042 [M] | Stan Getz Plays | 1955 | 100.00 |

— Reissue of Clef 137 and 143 on one 12-inch LP

| ❑ MGN-1032 [M] | West Coast Jazz | 1955 | 150.00 |

PICKWICK

| ❑ SPC-3031 | Stan Getz In Concert | 197? | 12.00 |

PRESTIGE

❑ 24088	Early Getz	197?	15.00
❑ PRLP-7255 [M]	Early Stan	1963	40.00
❑ PRST-7255 [R]	Early Stan	1963	25.00
❑ PRLP-7434 [M]	Getz Plays Jazz Classics	1967	30.00

— Reissue of PRLP 7255

| ❑ PRST-7434 [R] | Getz Plays Jazz Classics | 1967 | 18.00 |

— Reissue of PRST 7255

❑ PRLP-7516 [M]	Preservation	1967	30.00
❑ PRST-7516 [R]	Preservation	1967	18.00
❑ 24019	Stan Getz	197?	18.00
❑ PRLP-104 [10]	Stan Getz, Volume 2	1951	200.00
❑ PRLP-102 [10]	Stan Getz and the Tenor Sax Stars	1951	200.00
❑ PRLP-7256 [M]	Stan Getz' Greatest Hits	1963	40.00
❑ PRST-7256 [R]	Stan Getz' Greatest Hits	1963	25.00
❑ PRLP-7337 [M]	Stan Getz' Greatest Hits	1967	30.00

— Reissue of PRLP 7256

| ❑ PRST-7337 [R] | Stan Getz' Greatest Hits | 1967 | 18.00 |

— Reissue of PRST 7256

| ❑ PRLP-108 [10] | Stan Getz-Lee Konitz | 1951 | 200.00 |
| ❑ PRLP-7002 [M] | Stan Getz Quartets | 1955 | 100.00 |

ROOST

❑ R-417 [10]	Chamber Music	1953	150.00
❑ LP-2258 [M]	Getz Age	1963	30.00
❑ SLP-2258 [R]	Getz Age	1963	18.00
❑ R-407 [10]	Jazz at Storyville	1952	150.00
❑ R-411 [10]	Jazz at Storyville, Volume 2	1952	150.00
❑ R-420 [10]	Jazz at Storyville, Volume 3	1954	150.00
❑ LP-2255 [M]	Modern World	1963	30.00
❑ SLP-2255 [R]	Modern World	1963	18.00
❑ LP-2251 [M]	Moonlight in Vermont	1963	30.00
❑ SLP-2251 [R]	Moonlight in Vermont	1963	18.00
❑ R-423 [10]	Split Kick	1954	150.00
❑ R-402 [10]	Stan Getz	1950	200.00
❑ R-404 [10]	Stan Getz and the Swedish All Stars	1951	200.00
❑ LP-2209 [M]	Storyville	1956	80.00

— Reissue of R-407 and half of R-411

| ❑ LP-2225 [M] | Storyville, Volume 2 | 1957 | 80.00 |

— Reissue of R-423 and the other half of R-411

❑ LP-2249 [M]	The Greatest of Stan Getz	1963	30.00
❑ SLP-2249 [R]	The Greatest of Stan Getz	1963	18.00
❑ LP-2207 [M]	The Sounds of Stan Getz	1956	80.00

— Reissue of R-402

| ❑ RK-103 [M] | The Stan Getz Years | 1964 | 40.00 |
| ❑ SRK-103 [R] | The Stan Getz Years | 1964 | 30.00 |

ROULETTE

| ❑ RE-123 | Stan Getz/Sonny Stitt | 1973 | 18.00 |
| ❑ RE-119 | The Best of Stan Getz | 1972 | 18.00 |

SAVOY

| ❑ MG-9004 [10] | New Sounds in Modern Music | 1951 | 300.00 |
| ❑ SJL-1105 | Opus de Bop | 1977 | 15.00 |

STEEPLECHASE

| ❑ SCS-1073/4 | Live at Montmartre | 1986 | 15.00 |

VERVE

| ❑ VS-200 [M] | An Introduction to the World of Stan Getz | 1964 | 18.00 |
| ❑ V6S-200 [S] | An Introduction to the World of Stan Getz | 1964 | 25.00 |

— Sampler of material from five LPs plus one single-only track

❑ VSP-22 [M]	Another Time, Another Place	1966	18.00
❑ VSPS-22 [R]	Another Time, Another Place	1966	12.00
❑ MGV-8296 [M]	Award Winner	1959	50.00
❑ V-8296 [M]	Award Winner	1961	25.00

— Reissue of MGV-8296

❑ V6-8296 [R]	Award Winner	196?	15.00
❑ V-8494 [M]	Big Band Bossa Nova	1962	25.00
❑ V6-8494 [S]	Big Band Bossa Nova	1962	30.00
❑ V6-8807	Communications '72	1972	18.00
❑ MGV-8379 [M]	Cool Velvet -- Stan Getz and Strings	1960	50.00
❑ V-8379 [M]	Cool Velvet -- Stan Getz and Strings	1961	25.00

— Reissue of MGV-8379

| ❑ V6-8379 [S] | Cool Velvet -- Stan Getz and Strings | 1961 | 25.00 |
| ❑ MGVS-68379 [S] | Cool Velvet -- Stan Getz and Strings | 1960 | 50.00 |

Number	Title	Yr	NM
❑ V6-8780	Didn't We	1969	18.00
❑ V6-8802-2	Dynasty	1971	25.00
❑ VSP-2 [M]	Eloquence	1966	18.00
❑ VSPS-2 [R]	Eloquence	1966	12.00
❑ V-8412 [M]	Focus	1961	30.00
❑ V6-8412 [S]	Focus	1961	25.00
❑ VR-1-2528	Focus	1977	12.00

— Reissue of 8412

| ❑ UMV-2071 | Focus | 198? | 12.00 |

— Reissue

❑ V-8600 [M]	Getz Au Go Go	1964	18.00
❑ V6-8600 [S]	Getz Au Go Go	1964	25.00
❑ UMV-2075	Getz Au Go Go	198?	12.00

— Reissue

| ❑ 821725-1 | Getz Au Go Go | 198? | 12.00 |

— Reissue

❑ V6-8815-2	History of Stan Getz	1973	18.00
❑ MGV-8331 [M]	Imported from Europe	1959	50.00
❑ V-8331 [M]	Imported from Europe	1961	25.00

— Reissue of MGV-8331

| ❑ V6-8331 [R] | Imported from Europe | 196? | 15.00 |
| ❑ MGV-8122 [M] | Interpretations by the Stan Getz Quintet #3 | 1957 | 50.00 |

— Reissue of Norgran 1029

| ❑ V-8122 [M] | Interpretations by the Stan Getz Quintet #3 | 1961 | 25.00 |

— Reissue of MGV-8122

| ❑ UMV-2100 | Jazz Samba Encore | 198? | 12.00 |

— Reissue

| ❑ 823613-1 | Jazz Samba Encore | 198? | 12.00 |

— Reissue

| ❑ V-8523 [M] | Jazz Samba Encore! | 1963 | 18.00 |

— With Luiz Bonfa

| ❑ V6-8523 [S] | Jazz Samba Encore! | 1963 | 30.00 |

— With Luiz Bonfa

| ❑ MGV-8177 [M] | More West Coast Jazz with Stan Getz | 1957 | 50.00 |

— Reissue of Norgran 1088

| ❑ V-8177 [M] | More West Coast Jazz with Stan Getz | 1961 | 25.00 |

— Reissue of MGV-8177

❑ V6-8177 [R]	More West Coast Jazz with Stan Getz	196?	15.00
❑ V-8554 [M]	Reflections	1964	18.00
❑ V6-8554 [S]	Reflections	1964	25.00
❑ V3HB-8844	Return Engagement	1974	18.00
❑ MGV-8029 [M]	Stan Getz '57	1957	50.00

— Reissue of Norgran 1087 with revised title

| ❑ V-8029 [M] | Stan Getz '57 | 1961 | 25.00 |

— Reissue of MGV-8029

| ❑ MGV-8200 [M] | Stan Getz and the Cool Sounds | 1957 | 50.00 |

— Reissue of American Recording Society 407 with new name

| ❑ V-8200 [M] | Stan Getz and the Cool Sounds | 1961 | 25.00 |

— Reissue of MGV-8200

❑ V6-8200 [R]	Stan Getz and the Cool Sounds	196?	15.00
❑ MGV-8393-2 [M]	Stan Getz At Large	1960	60.00
❑ V-8393-2 [M]	Stan Getz At Large	1961	30.00

— Reissue of MGV-8393-2

| ❑ V6-8393-2 [R] | Stan Getz At Large | 1961 | 18.00 |
| ❑ MGV-8188-2 [M] | Stan Getz at the Shrine | 1957 | 100.00 |

— Reissue of Norgran 2000-2

| ❑ V-8188-2 [M] | Stan Getz at the Shrine | 1961 | 30.00 |

— Reissue of MGV-8188-2

| ❑ V6-8188-2 [R] | Stan Getz at the Shrine | 196? | 18.00 |
| ❑ MGV-8213 [M] | Stan Getz in Stockholm | 1958 | 50.00 |

— Reissue of American Recording Society 428 with new name

| ❑ V-8213 [M] | Stan Getz in Stockholm | 1961 | 25.00 |

— Reissue of MGV-8213

| ❑ V6-8213 [R] | Stan Getz in Stockholm | 196? | 15.00 |
| ❑ UMV-2614 | Stan Getz in Stockholm | 198? | 12.00 |

— Reissue

| ❑ MGV-8133 [M] | Stan Getz Plays | 1957 | 50.00 |

— Reissue of Norgran 1042

| ❑ V-8133 [M] | Stan Getz Plays | 1961 | 25.00 |

— Reissue of MGV-8133

❑ V6-8133 [R]	Stan Getz Plays	196?	15.00
❑ VSP-31 [M]	Stan Getz Plays Blues	1966	18.00
❑ VSPS-31 [R]	Stan Getz Plays Blues	1966	12.00
❑ MGV-8263 [M]	Stan Meets Chet	1958	60.00

— With Chet Baker

| ❑ V-8263 [M] | Stan Meets Chet | 1961 | 25.00 |

— Reissue of MGV-8263

❑ V6-8263 [R]	Stan Meets Chet	196?	15.00
❑ 815239-1	Stan the Man	1983	12.00
❑ V-8693 [M]	Sweet Rain	1967	30.00
❑ V6-8693 [S]	Sweet Rain	1967	18.00
❑ V-8719 [M]	The Best of Stan Getz	1967	30.00
❑ V6-8719 [S]	The Best of Stan Getz	1967	18.00
❑ VE-2-2510	The Corea/Evans Sessions	1976	18.00
❑ 823242-1	The Corea/Evans Sessions	198?	15.00

— Reissue

❑ 823611-1	The Girl from Ipanema: The Bossa Nova Years	1984	50.00
❑ MGV-8321 [M]	The Soft Swing	1959	50.00
❑ V-8321 [M]	The Soft Swing	1961	25.00

— Reissue of MGV-8321

❑ V6-8321 [R]	The Soft Swing	196?	15.00
❑ MGV-8294 [M]	The Steamer	1959	50.00
❑ V-8294 [M]	The Steamer	1961	25.00

— Reissue of MGV-8294

Number	Title	Yr	NM
❑ V6-8294 [R]	The Steamer	196?	15.00
❑ V-8707 [M]	Voices	1967	30.00
❑ V6-8707 [S]	Voices	1967	18.00
❑ MGV-8028 [M]	West Coast Jazz	1957	50.00

— Reissue of Norgran 1032

| ❑ V-8028 [M] | West Coast Jazz | 1961 | 25.00 |

— Reissue of MGV-8028

❑ V6-8028 [R]	West Coast Jazz	196?	15.00
❑ V-8752 [M]	What the World Needs Now -- Stan Getz Plays Bacharach and David	1968	30.00
❑ V6-8752 [S]	What the World Needs Now -- Stan Getz Plays Bacharach and David	1968	18.00

GHOULS, THE

CAPITOL

| ❑ T2215 [M] | Dracula's Deuce | 1965 | 120.00 |
| ❑ ST2215 [S] | Dracula's Deuce | 1965 | 150.00 |

GIANT CRAB, THE

UNI

| ❑ 73037 | A Giant Crab Comes Forth | 1968 | 30.00 |
| ❑ 73057 | Cool It, Helios | 1969 | 30.00 |

GIBB, ANDY

RSO

❑ RS-1-3069	After Dark	1980	12.00
❑ RS-1-3091	Andy Gibb's Greatest Hits	1980	12.00
❑ RS-1-3019	Flowing Rivers	1977	12.00
❑ RS-1-3034	Shadow Dancing	1978	12.00

GIBB, BARRY

MCA

| ❑ 5506 | Now Voyager | 1984 | 12.00 |

GIBB, ROBIN

ATCO

| ❑ SD 33-323 | Robin's Reign | 1969 | 40.00 |

MIRAGE

| ❑ 90170 | Secret Agent | 1984 | 10.00 |

POLYDOR

| ❑ 810896-1 | How Old Are You? | 1983 | 12.00 |

GIBBS, GEORGIA

BELL

| ❑ 6000 [M] | Call Me Georgia Gibbs | 1966 | 18.00 |
| ❑ 6000S [S] | Call Me Georgia Gibbs | 1966 | 25.00 |

CORAL

| ❑ CRL56037 [10] | Ballin' the Jack | 1951 | 50.00 |
| ❑ CRL57183 [M] | Her Nibs | 1957 | 40.00 |

EMARCY

| ❑ MG-36103 [M] | Swingin' with Gibbs | 1957 | 30.00 |

EPIC

| ❑ LN24059 [M] | Georgia Gibbs' Greatest Hits | 1963 | 18.00 |
| ❑ BN26059 [S] | Georgia Gibbs' Greatest Hits | 1963 | 25.00 |

GOLDEN TONE

| ❑ 14003 [R] | Her Nibs!! Miss Georgia Gibbs | 1962 | 12.00 |

— Cover misspells it "Nibbs

| ❑ 4093 [M] | Her Nibs!! Miss Georgia Gibbs | 1962 | 15.00 |

IMPERIAL

| ❑ LP-9107 [M] | Something's Gotta Give | 1960 | 25.00 |
| ❑ LP-12064 [S] | Something's Gotta Give | 1960 | 30.00 |

MERCURY

❑ MG-25175 [10]	Georgia Gibbs Sings Oldies	1953	50.00
❑ MG-20071 [M]	Music and Memories	1955	40.00
❑ MG-20114 [M]	Song Favorites	1956	40.00
❑ MG-20170 [M]	Swingin' with Her Nibs	1956	40.00
❑ MG-25199 [10]	The Man That Got Away	1954	50.00

ROYALE

| ❑ 18126 [10] | Georgia Gibbs and Orchestra | 195? | 40.00 |

SUNSET

| ❑ SUM-1113 [M] | Her Nibs, Miss Georgia Gibbs | 196? | 18.00 |
| ❑ SUS-5113 [S] | Her Nibs, Miss Georgia Gibbs | 196? | 18.00 |

GIBBS, MICHAEL, AND GARY BURTON

POLYDOR

| ❑ PD-6503 | In the Public Interest | 197? | 18.00 |

GIBBS, MICHAEL

DERAM

| ❑ DES18048 | Michael Gibbs | 1970 | 25.00 |

GIBBS, TERRI

CANAAN

| ❑ 80398 | Comfort the People | 198? | 15.00 |

HORIZON

| ❑ SP759 | Turn Around | 1987 | 12.00 |

MCA

| ❑ 5255 | I'm a Lady | 1981 | 12.00 |
| ❑ 5443 | Over Easy | 1983 | 10.00 |

Number	Title	Yr	NM
❑ 5173	Somebody's Knockin'	1981	12.00
❑ 37178	Somebody's Knockin'	198?	10.00

— Budget-line reissue of 5173

Number	Title	Yr	NM
❑ 5315	Some Days It Rains All Night Long	1982	10.00
❑ 1575	The Best of Terri Gibbs	198?	10.00

WARNER BROS.

Number	Title	Yr	NM
❑ 25309	Old Friends	1985	10.00

GIBBS, TERRY, AND BILL HARRIS

MODE

Number	Title	Yr	NM
❑ LP-129 [M]	The Ex-Hermanites	1957	80.00

PREMIER

Number	Title	Yr	NM
❑ PM-2006 [M]	Woodchoppers' Ball	1963	18.00
❑ PS-2006 [R]	Woodchoppers' Ball	1963	12.00

GIBBS, TERRY, AND BUDDY DEFRANCO

CONTEMPORARY

Number	Title	Yr	NM
❑ C-14056	Air Mail Special	1990	15.00
❑ C-14036	Chicago Fire	1987	12.00

PALO ALTO

Number	Title	Yr	NM
❑ PA-8011	Jazz Party -- First Time Together	1982	12.00

GIBBS, TERRY

ABC IMPULSE!

Number	Title	Yr	NM
❑ AS-58 [S]	Take It from Me	1968	18.00

BRUNSWICK

Number	Title	Yr	NM
❑ BL54009 [M]	Terry	1955	50.00
❑ BL56055 [10]	Terry Gibbs Quartet	1954	100.00

CONTEMPORARY

Number	Title	Yr	NM
❑ C-7647	Dream Band	1986	12.00
❑ C-14022	The Latin Connection	1986	12.00
❑ C-7652	Volume 2: The Sundown Sessions	1987	12.00
❑ C-7654	Volume 3: Flying Home	1988	12.00
❑ C-7656	Volume 4: Main Stem	1990	15.00

DOT

Number	Title	Yr	NM
❑ DLP-3726 [M]	Reza	1966	18.00
❑ DLP-25726 [S]	Reza	1966	25.00

EMARCY

Number	Title	Yr	NM
❑ MG-36075 [M]	Mallets A-Plenty	1956	50.00
❑ MG-36148 [M]	More Vibes on Velvet	1959	50.00
❑ MG-36138 [M]	Steve Allen's All Stars	1958	50.00
❑ SR-80004 [S]	Steve Allen's All Stars	1959	40.00
❑ MG-36103 [M]	Swingin' Terry Gibbs	1957	50.00
❑ MG-36047 [M]	Terry Gibbs	1956	50.00
❑ MG-36128 [M]	Terry Plays the Duke	1958	50.00
❑ MG-36064 [M]	Vibes on Velvet	1956	50.00

IMPULSE!

Number	Title	Yr	NM
❑ A-58 [M]	Take It from Me	1964	30.00
❑ AS-58 [S]	Take It from Me	1964	30.00

INTERLUDE

Number	Title	Yr	NM
❑ MO-506 [M]	Vibrations	1959	40.00
❑ ST-1006 [S]	Vibrations	1959	30.00

JAZZ A LA CARTE

Number	Title	Yr	NM
❑ 1	Live at the Lord	1978	18.00
❑ 2	Smoke 'Em Up	1978	15.00

LIMELIGHT

Number	Title	Yr	NM
❑ LM-82005 [M]	El Nutto	1964	25.00
❑ LS-86005 [S]	El Nutto	1964	30.00

MAINSTREAM

Number	Title	Yr	NM
❑ 56048 [M]	It's Time We Met	1965	18.00
❑ S-6048 [S]	It's Time We Met	1965	25.00

MCA

Number	Title	Yr	NM
❑ 29035	Take It from Me	198?	10.00

MERCURY

Number	Title	Yr	NM
❑ MG-20704 [M]	Explosion!	1962	18.00
❑ SR-60704 [S]	Explosion!	1962	25.00
❑ MG-20812 [M]	Jewish Melodies in Jazztime	1963	18.00
❑ SR-60812 [S]	Jewish Melodies in Jazztime	1963	25.00
❑ MG-20440 [M]	Launching a New Sound in Music	1959	40.00
❑ SR-60112 [S]	Launching a New Sound in Music	1959	30.00
❑ MG-20518 [M]	Steve Allen's All Stars	1960	30.00
❑ SR-60195 [S]	Steve Allen's All Stars	1960	30.00

MODE

Number	Title	Yr	NM
❑ LP-123 [M]	A Jazz Band Ball	1957	80.00

ROOST

Number	Title	Yr	NM
❑ LP-2260 [M]	El Latino	1965	18.00
❑ RS-2260 [S]	Latino	1965	25.00

TIME

Number	Title	Yr	NM
❑ 52105 [M]	Hootenanny My Way	1963	30.00
❑ S-2105 [S]	Hootenanny My Way	1963	30.00
❑ 52120 [M]	Terry Gibbs with Sal Nistico	196?	25.00
❑ S-2120 [S]	Terry Gibbs with Sal Nistico	196?	30.00

TRIP

Number	Title	Yr	NM
❑ 5545	Launching a New Band	197?	12.00

VERVE

Number	Title	Yr	NM
❑ MGV-2136 [M]	Music from Cole Porter's "Can-Can	1960	40.00
❑ V-2136 [M]	Music from Cole Porter's "Can-Can	1961	25.00
❑ MGVS-6145 [S]	Music from Cole Porter's "Can-Can	1960	40.00
❑ V6-2136 [S]	Music from Cole Porter's "Can-Can	1961	25.00
❑ V-8496 [M]	Straight Ahead	1962	25.00
❑ V6-8496 [S]	Straight Ahead	1962	30.00
❑ MGV-2134 [M]	Swing Is Here!	1960	40.00
❑ V-2134 [M]	Swing Is Here!	1961	25.00
❑ MGVS-6140 [S]	Swing Is Here!	1960	40.00
❑ V6-2134 [S]	Swing Is Here!	1961	25.00
❑ V-8447 [M]	That Swing Thing	1962	25.00
❑ V6-8447 [S]	That Swing Thing	1962	30.00
❑ MGV-2151 [M]	The Exciting Terry Gibbs Big Band	1960	40.00
❑ V-2151 [M]	The Exciting Terry Gibbs Big Band	1961	25.00
❑ V6-2151 [S]	The Exciting Terry Gibbs Big Band	1961	30.00

WING

Number	Title	Yr	NM
❑ MGW-12255 [M]	Terry Plays the Duke	196?	18.00
❑ SRW-16255 [R]	Terry Plays the Duke	196?	12.00

XANADU

Number	Title	Yr	NM
❑ 210	Bopstacle Course	198?	12.00

— ut numbers on records are DS 346 and DS 347

GIBSON, ALTHEA

DOT

Number	Title	Yr	NM
❑ DLP-3105 [M]	Althea Gibson Sings	1959	40.00
❑ DLP-25105 [S]	Althea Gibson Sings	1959	50.00

GIBSON, BOB, AND BOB CAMP

ELEKTRA

Number	Title	Yr	NM
❑ EKL-207 [M]	Gibson and Camp at the Gate of Horn	1961	40.00
❑ EKS-7207 [S]	Gibson and Camp at the Gate of Horn	1961	50.00

MOUNTAIN RAILROAD

Number	Title	Yr	NM
❑ 52781 [S]	Homemade Music	1978	18.00

GIBSON, BOB

ELEKTRA

Number	Title	Yr	NM
❑ EKL-177 [M]	Ski Songs	1959	30.00
❑ EKS-7177 [S]	Ski Songs	1959	30.00
❑ EKL-239 [M]	Where I'm Bound	1964	25.00
❑ EKS-7239 [S]	Where I'm Bound	1964	30.00
❑ EKL-197 [M]	Yes I See	1961	25.00
❑ EKS-7197 [S]	Yes I See	1961	30.00

RIVERSIDE

Number	Title	Yr	NM
❑ RLP 12-816 [M]	Carnegie Concert	1958	40.00
❑ RM7542 [M]	Hootenanny at Carnegie	1963	25.00

— Reissue of 12-816 with slightly altered lineup

Number	Title	Yr	NM
❑ RLP 12-806 [M]	I Come For to Sing	1957	40.00
❑ RLP 12-802 [M]	Offbeat Folk Songs	1956	40.00
❑ RLP 12-830 [M]	There's a Meetin' Here Tonight	1958	40.00
❑ RLP-1111 [S]	There's a Meetin' Here Tonight	1959	50.00

STINSON

Number	Title	Yr	NM
❑ SLP-76 [10]	Folksongs of Ohio	1954	50.00

GIBSON, DEBBIE

ATLANTIC

Number	Title	Yr	NM
❑ 81932	Electric Youth	1989	12.00
❑ 81780	Out of the Blue	1987	12.00

GIBSON, DON, AND SUE THOMPSON

HICKORY/MGM

Number	Title	Yr	NM
❑ H3G-4520	Oh How Love Changes	1975	15.00

GIBSON, DON

ABC HICKORY

Number	Title	Yr	NM
❑ AH-44007	If You Ever	1977	15.00
❑ AH-44001	I'm All Wrapped Up in You	1976	15.00
❑ AH-44014	Look Who's Blue	1978	15.00
❑ AH-44010	Starting All Over	1978	15.00

HARMONY

Number	Title	Yr	NM
❑ KH31765	Sample Kisses	1972	12.00
❑ HL7358 [M]	The Fabulous Don Gibson Sings	196?	18.00
❑ HS11158 [R]	The Fabulous Don Gibson Sings	196?	15.00

HICKORY

Number	Title	Yr	NM
❑ LPS-160	Country Green	1971	18.00
❑ LPS-157	Don Gibson Sings Hank Williams	1971	18.00
❑ LPS-153	Hits, The Don Gibson Way	1970	18.00
❑ LPS-155	Perfect Mountain	1971	18.00
❑ LPS-166	Woman (Sensuous Woman)	1972	18.00
❑ ST-94817	Woman (Sensuous Woman)	1972	25.00

— Capitol Record Club edition

HICKORY/MGM

Number	Title	Yr	NM
❑ H3G-4516	Bring Back Your Love to Me	1974	15.00
❑ H3G-4519	I'm the Loneliest Man	1975	15.00
❑ H3F-4509	Snap Your Fingers	1974	18.00
❑ H3G-4502	The Very Best of Don Gibson	1974	18.00
❑ HR-4501	Touch the Morning/That's What I'll Do	1973	18.00

LION

Number	Title	Yr	NM
❑ L-70069 [M]	Songs by Don Gibson	1958	80.00

METRO

Number	Title	Yr	NM
❑ M-529 [M]	Don Gibson	1965	15.00
❑ MS-529 [R]	Don Gibson	1965	12.00

MGM

Number	Title	Yr	NM
❑ GAS-138	Don Gibson (Golden Archive Series)	1970	18.00

RCA CAMDEN

Number	Title	Yr	NM
❑ CAL-852 [M]	A Blue Million Tears	196?	15.00
❑ CAS-852 [P]	A Blue Million Tears	196?	15.00

— All tracks are rechanneled except "I Let Her Get Lonely" and "I May Never Get to Heaven," which are true stereo

Number	Title	Yr	NM
❑ CAS-2592	Am I That Easy to Forget	1972	15.00
❑ CAL-2101 [M]	Hurtin' Inside	1966	15.00
❑ CAS-2101 [S]	Hurtin' Inside	1966	18.00
❑ CAS-2246	I Love You So Much	1968	15.00
❑ CAS-2502	I Walk Alone	1971	15.00
❑ ACL1-0328	Just Call Me Lonesome	1973	12.00
❑ ACL1-0758	Just One Time	1974	12.00
❑ CAS-2392	Lovin' Lies	1970	15.00
❑ CAS-2317	My God Is Real	1969	15.00

RCA VICTOR

Number	Title	Yr	NM
❑ LPM-3843 [M]	All My Love	1967	25.00
❑ LSP-3843 [S]	All My Love	1967	30.00
❑ LSP-4169	All-Time Country Gold	1969	18.00
❑ CPL1-7052	Collector's Series	1985	12.00
❑ LPM-3594 [M]	Don Gibson with Spanish Guitars	1966	25.00
❑ LSP-3594 [S]	Don Gibson with Spanish Guitars	1966	30.00
❑ LPM-2361 [M]	Girls, Guitars and Gibson	1961	30.00
❑ LSP-2361 [S]	Girls, Guitars and Gibson	1961	40.00
❑ LPM-2878 [M]	God Walks These Hills	1964	25.00
❑ LSP-2878 [S]	God Walks These Hills	1964	30.00
❑ LPM-3680 [M]	Great Country Songs	1966	25.00
❑ LSP-3680 [S]	Great Country Songs	1966	30.00
❑ LPM-2702 [M]	I Wrote a Song	1963	30.00
❑ LSP-2702 [S]	I Wrote a Song	1963	40.00
❑ LPM-2184 [M]	Look Who's Blue	1960	30.00
❑ LSP-2184 [S]	Look Who's Blue	1960	40.00
❑ LSP-4053	More Country Soul	1968	25.00
❑ LPM-1918 [M]	No One Stands Alone	1959	30.00
❑ LSP-1918 [S]	No One Stands Alone	1959	40.00
❑ LPM-1743 [M]	Oh Lonesome Me	1958	50.00
❑ LPM-2448 [M]	Some Favorites of Mine	1962	30.00
❑ LSP-2448 [S]	Some Favorites of Mine	1962	40.00
❑ LPM-2269 [M]	Sweet Dreams	1960	30.00
❑ LSP-2269 [S]	Sweet Dreams	1960	40.00
❑ LPM-2038 [M]	That Gibson Boy	1959	30.00
❑ LSP-2038 [S]	That Gibson Boy	1959	40.00
❑ LPM-3376 [M]	The Best of Don Gibson	1965	25.00
❑ LSP-3376 [S]	The Best of Don Gibson	1965	30.00
❑ LSP-4281	The Best of Don Gibson, Vol. 2	1970	18.00
❑ LPM-3974 [M]	The King of Country Soul	1968	50.00
❑ LSP-3974 [S]	The King of Country Soul	1968	25.00
❑ LPM-3470 [M]	Too Much Hurt	1965	25.00
❑ LSP-3470 [S]	Too Much Hurt	1965	30.00

GIBSON, DON (2)

JAZZOLOGY

Number	Title	Yr	NM
❑ J-40	The Al Capone Memorial Jazz Band	197?	15.00

GIBSON, GERALD, AND HIS SING-A-LONGERS

INTERNATIONAL AWARD SERIES

Number	Title	Yr	NM
❑ AK-0	Christmas Sing-a-Long	196?	15.00

GIBSON, STEVE, AND THE RED CAPS

MERCURY

Number	Title	Yr	NM
❑ MG-25116 [10]	Blueberry Hill (Singing & Swinging)	1952	400.00
❑ MG-25115 [10]	You're Driving Me Crazy (Harmony Time)	1952	400.00

GIFFORD, KATHIE LEE

HEARTLAND

Number	Title	Yr	NM
❑ HL-3046	Christmas with Kathie Lee Gifford	1993	25.00

GILBERT, ANN

GROOVE

Number	Title	Yr	NM
❑ LG-1004 [M]	The Many Moods of Ann	1956	50.00

GILBERT, RONNIE

MERCURY

Number	Title	Yr	NM
❑ MG-20917 [M]	Alone with Ronnie Gilbert	1964	25.00
❑ SR-60917 [S]	Alone with Ronnie Gilbert	1964	30.00

RCA VICTOR

Number	Title	Yr	NM
❑ LPM-1591 [M]	In Hi-Fi, The Legend of Bessie Smith	1958	40.00

GILBERT & SULLIVAN JAZZ WORKSHOP, THE

ANDEX

Number	Title	Yr	NM
❑ A-27101 [M]	The Coolest Mikado	1961	25.00
❑ AS-27101 [S]	The Coolest Mikado	1961	30.00

GILBERTO, ASTRUD

CTI

Number	Title	Yr	NM
❑ CTS-6008	Astrud Gilberto with Stanley Turrentine	1970	15.00

Number	Title	Yr	NM
ELEKTRA/MUSICIAN			
❏ 60760	Live in Montreux	1988	12.00
PERCEPTION			
❏ 29	Now	1973	12.00
VERVE			
❏ V6-8793	17-Sep-69	1969	15.00
❏ V-8673 [M]	A Certain Smile, A Certain Sadness	1966	15.00
❏ V6-8673 [S]	A Certain Smile, A Certain Sadness	1966	18.00
❏ V-8708 [M]	Beach Samba	1967	15.00
❏ V6-8708 [S]	Beach Samba	1967	18.00
❏ V6-8776	I Haven't Got Anything Better to Do	1969	15.00
❏ V-8643 [M]	Look to the Rainbow	1966	15.00
❏ V6-8643 [S]	Look to the Rainbow	1966	18.00
❏ 821566-1	Look to the Rainbow	1986	12.00
— Reissue of V6-8643			
❏ V-8608 [M]	The Astrud Gilberto Album	1965	15.00
❏ V6-8608 [S]	The Astrud Gilberto Album	1965	18.00
❏ V-8629 [M]	The Shadow of Your Smile	1965	15.00
❏ V6-8629 [S]	The Shadow of Your Smile	1965	18.00
❏ SW-90649 [S]	The Shadow of Your Smile	1965	25.00
— Capitol Record Club edition			
❏ V6-8754	Windy	1968	15.00

GILBERTO, JOAO

Number	Title	Yr	NM
ATLANTIC			
❏ 8070 [M]	The Boss of the Bossa Nova	1963	18.00
❏ SD8070 [S]	The Boss of the Bossa Nova	1963	25.00
❏ 8076 [M]	The Warm World of Joao Gilberto	1964	18.00
❏ SD8076 [S]	The Warm World of Joao Gilberto	1964	25.00
CAPITOL			
❏ T2160 [M]	Joao Gilberto and Antonio Carlos Jobim	1964	18.00
❏ ST2160 [S]	Joao Gilberto and Antonio Carlos Jobim	1964	25.00
❏ ST2160 [S]	Joao Gilberto and Antonio Carlos Jobim	1978	12.00
— Purple label, large Capitol logo			
❏ T10280 [M]	Pops in Portuguese	196?	25.00
❏ ST10280 [S]	Pops in Portuguese	196?	30.00
WARNER BROS.			
❏ BS3053	Amoroso	1978	12.00
❏ BSK3613	Brasel	1981	12.00

GILDER, NICK

Number	Title	Yr	NM
CASABLANCA			
❏ NBLP7259	Body Talk Muzik	1982	18.00
❏ NBLP7243	Rock America	1980	12.00
CHRYSALIS			
❏ CHR1202	City Nights	1978	12.00
❏ CHR1219	Frequency	1979	12.00
❏ CHR1147	You Know Who You Are	1977	15.00
RCA VICTOR			
❏ NFL1-8051	Nick Gilder	1985	12.00

GILELS, EMIL

Number	Title	Yr	NM
RCA VICTOR RED SEAL			
❏ LSC-2219 [S]	Brahms: Piano Concerto No. 2	1959	80.00
— With Fritz Reiner/Chicago Symphony Orchestra; original with "shaded dog" label			
❏ LSC-2493 [S]	Schubert: Piano Sonata, op. 53	1961	50.00
— Original with "shaded dog" label			

GILES, GILES & FRIPP

Number	Title	Yr	NM
DERAM			
❏ DES18019 [B]	The Cheerful Insanity of Giles, Giles & Fripp	1968	400.00

GILKYSON, TERRY

Number	Title	Yr	NM
COLUMBIA			
❏ CL1103 [M]	Blue Mountain	1958	40.00
❏ CL990 [M]	Marianne and Other Songs	1957	50.00
❏ CL1302 [M]	Wanderin' Folk Songs	1959	30.00
DECCA			
❏ DL5263 [10]	Folk Songs	1950	50.00
❏ DL5457 [10]	Golden Minutes of Folk Music	1952	50.00
KAPP			
❏ KL1196 [M]	Rollin'	1960	18.00
❏ KS3196 [S]	Rollin'	1960	25.00
❏ KL1327 [M]	The Cry of the Wild Goose	1963	18.00
❏ KS3327 [S]	The Cry of the Wild Goose	1963	25.00

GILL, VINCE

Number	Title	Yr	NM
MCA			
❏ R173590	Pocket Full of Gold	1991	25.00
— Only released on vinyl through BMG Direct Marketing			
❏ 42321	When I Call Your Name	1989	25.00
RCA			
❏ 5923-1-R	The Way Back Home	1987	18.00
RCA VICTOR			
❏ CPL1-5348	The Things That Matter	1985	18.00
❏ MHL1-8517 [EP]	Turn Me Loose	1984	12.00

Number	Title	Yr	NM
GILLAN, IAN, & ROGER GLOVER			
VIRGIN			
❏ 90953	Accidentally on Purpose	1988	15.00

GILLAN

Number	Title	Yr	NM
VIRGIN			
❏ 2196 [B]	Future Shock	1981	18.00
❏ 13146 [B]	Glory Road	1980	18.00

GILLAN BAND, IAN

Number	Title	Yr	NM
ISLAND			
❏ ILPS9500 [B]	Clear Air Turbulence	1977	25.00
❏ ILPS9511	Scarabus	1978	18.00
— Different cover from UK issue			
OYSTER			
❏ OY11602 [B]	Child In Time	1976	30.00

GILLEN, THEODORE

Number	Title	Yr	NM
THE LITURGICAL PRESS			
❏ 8146-7131-4	The Nativity of the Lord	1980	12.00

GILLESPIE, DARLENE

Number	Title	Yr	NM
DISNEYLAND			
❏ WDL-3010 [M]	Darlene of the Teens	1957	80.00
❏ DQ-1228 [M]	Sleeping Beauty	1962	25.00
— Cover is black and white; later pressings, which go for less, are shaded blue on the back			
❏ WDL-3010 [M]	Top Tunes of the '50's -- Darlene Gillespie Sings TV Favorites	1958	50.00
— Reissue with new title and cover			
❏ WDL-1010 [M]	Top Tunes of the '50's -- Darlene Gillespie Sings TV Favorites	1959	40.00
— Reissue of 3010			
MICKEY MOUSE CLUB			
❏ MM-32 [M]	Sleeping Beauty	1959	40.00

GILLESPIE, DIZZY, AND CHARLIE PARKER

Number	Title	Yr	NM
ROOST			
❏ LP-2234 [M]	Diz 'n' Bird In Concert	1959	80.00
❏ SK-106 [M]	The Beginning: Diz and Bird	1960	100.00

GILLESPIE, DIZZY, AND DJANGO REINHARDT

Number	Title	Yr	NM
VERVE			
❏ MGV-8015 [M]	Jazz from Paris	1957	60.00
❏ V-8015 [M]	Jazz from Paris	1961	30.00

GILLESPIE, DIZZY, AND STAN GETZ

Number	Title	Yr	NM
NORGRAN			
❏ MGN-1050 [M]	Diz and Getz	1956	120.00
❏ MGN-2 [10]	The Dizzy Gillespie-Stan Getz Sextet #1	1954	300.00
❏ MGN-18 [10]	The Dizzy Gillespie-Stan Getz Sextet #2	1954	300.00
VERVE			
❏ MGV-8141 [M]	Diz and Getz	1957	80.00
— Reissue of Norgran 1050			
❏ V-8141 [M]	Diz and Getz	1961	30.00
❏ VE-2-2521	Diz and Getz	197?	18.00

GILLESPIE, DIZZY

Number	Title	Yr	NM
ALLEGRO			
❏ 3083 [M]	Dizzy Gillespie	195?	120.00
❏ 4023 [10]	Dizzy Gillespie	195?	200.00
❏ 3017 [M]	Dizzy Gillespie Plays	195?	120.00
❏ 4108 [10]	Dizzy Gillespie Plays	195?	200.00
AMERICAN RECORDING SOCIETY			
❏ G-423 [M]	Big Band Jazz	1955	100.00
❏ G-405 [M]	Jazz Creations/Dizzy Gillespie	1955	100.00
ATLANTIC			
❏ 81646	Closer to the Source	1986	12.00
❏ 1257 [M]	Dizzy at Home and Abroad	1957	100.00
— Black label			
❏ 1257 [M]	Dizzy at Home and Abroad	1961	30.00
— Multi-color label with white "fan" logo			
❏ ALR-138 [10]	Dizzy Gillespie	1952	400.00
❏ ALR-142 [10]	Dizzy Gillespie, Vol. 2	1952	400.00
BANDSTAND			
❏ BDLP-1513	Groovin' High	1992	18.00
BARONET			
❏ 105 [M]	A Handful of Modern Jazz	1961	40.00
BLUEBIRD			
❏ 5785-1-RB	Dizziest	1987	18.00
BLUE NOTE			
❏ BLP-5017 [10]	Horn of Plenty	1953	300.00
BULLDOG			
❏ BDL-2006	20 Golden Pieces of Dizzy Gillespie	198?	12.00
CLEF			
❏ MGC-136 [10]	Dizzy Gillespie with Strings	1953	200.00
CONTEMPORARY			
❏ C-2504 [10]	Dizzy in Paris	1953	200.00

Number	Title	Yr	NM
COUNTERPOINT			
❏ C-5548	Dizzy Gillespie, 1941	197?	15.00
DEE GEE			
❏ LP-1000 [10]	Dizzy Gillespie	1950	300.00
DIAL			
❏ 212 [10]	Modern Trumpets	1952	400.00
DISCOVERY			
❏ DL-3013 [10]	Dizzy Gillespie Plays, Johnny Richards Conducts	1950	300.00
ELEKTRA/MUSICIAN			
❏ 60300	One Night in Washington	1984	12.00
EMARCY			
❏ EMS-2-410	Composer's Concepts	197?	18.00
EVEREST ARCHIVE OF FOLK & JAZZ			
❏ 237	Dizzy Gillespie	1970	12.00
❏ 272	Dizzy Gillespie, Volume 2	197?	12.00
❏ 301	Dizzy Gillespie, Volume 3	197?	12.00
❏ 346	The King of Bop	198?	12.00
FANTASY			
❏ OJC-447	Afro-Cuban Jazz Moods	1990	15.00
❏ OJC-381	Dizzy Gillespie Jam: Montreux '77	1989	12.00
❏ OJC-443	Dizzy's Big Four	1990	12.00
GATEWAY			
❏ 7025	Sweet Soul	198?	15.00
GENE NORMAN			
❏ GNP-23 [M]	Dizzy Gillespie and His Big Band	1957	80.00
❏ GNP-4 [10]	Dizzy Gillespie with His Original Big Band	195?	200.00
GNP CRESCENDO			
❏ GNP-9028	Dizzy!	197?	12.00
❏ GNP-23 [M]	Dizzy Gillespie and His Big Band	196?	25.00
❏ GNPS-23 [R]	Dizzy Gillespie and His Big Band	196?	15.00
❏ GNP-9006	Paris Concert	197?	12.00
GRP			
❏ GR-1012	New Faces	198?	12.00
GWP			
❏ 2023	Souled Out	197?	18.00
IMPULSE!			
❏ AS-9149	Swing Low, Sweet Cadillac!	1967	25.00
INTERMEDIA			
❏ QS-5033	Body & Soul Featuring Sarah Vaughan	198?	12.00
JAZZ MAN			
❏ 5017	The Giant	198?	15.00
❏ 5021	The Source	198?	15.00
LIMELIGHT			
❏ LM-82007 [M]	Jambo Caribe	1964	25.00
❏ LS-86007 [S]	Jambo Caribe	1964	30.00
❏ LM-82042 [M]	The Melody Lingers On	1967	25.00
❏ LS-86042 [S]	The Melody Lingers On	1967	30.00
❏ LM-82022 [M]	The New Continent	1965	25.00
❏ LS-86022 [S]	The New Continent	1965	30.00
MAINSTREAM			
❏ MRL 325	Dizzy Gillespie with the Mitchell-Ruff Duo	1972	18.00
MCA			
❏ 29036	Swing Low, Sweet Cadillac	198?	10.00
MOON			
❏ MLP-035	Angel City	1992	18.00
MUSICRAFT			
❏ MVS-2009	Groovin' High	1986	12.00
❏ MVS-2010	One Bass Hit	1986	12.00
NORGRAN			
❏ MGN-1003 [M]	Afro Dizzy	1954	120.00
❏ MGN-1090 [M]	Diz Big Band	1956	120.00
❏ MGN-1023 [M]	Dizzy and Strings	1955	120.00
❏ MGN-1083 [M]	Jazz Recital	1956	120.00
❏ MGN-1084 [M]	World Statesman	1956	120.00
PABLO			
❏ 2310771	Afro-Cuban Jazz Moods	1976	15.00
❏ 2625708	Bahiana	1976	18.00
❏ 2310719	Dizzy's Big Four	1975	15.00
❏ 2310749	Dizzy's Big Seven: Montreux '75	1976	15.00
❏ 2310794	Free Ride	1977	15.00
❏ 2310889	In Helsinki: To a Finland Station	198?	12.00
❏ 2310784	Party	1977	15.00
❏ 2312136	The Alternate Blues	198?	12.00
❏ 2310885	The Best of Dizzy Gillespie	198?	12.00
❏ 2405411	The Best of Dizzy Gillespie	198?	12.00
PABLO LIVE			
❏ 2308226	Digital Dizzy at Montreux 1980	1980	15.00
❏ 2308211	Dizzy Gillespie Jam: Montreux '77	1977	15.00
❏ 2308229	Sumemrtime	1980	15.00
PERCEPTION			
❏ 13	Portrait of Jenny	1971	18.00
❏ 2	The Real Thing	197?	18.00
PHILIPS			
❏ PHM200048 [M]	Dizzy at the French Riviera	1962	25.00
❏ PHS600048 [S]	Dizzy at the French Riviera	1962	30.00

Number	Title	Yr	NM
❑ PHM200106 [M]	Dizzy Gillespie and the Double Six of Paris	1963	100.00
❑ PHS600106 [S]	Dizzy Gillespie and the Double Six of Paris	1963	150.00
❑ PHM200123 [M]	Dizzy Gillespie Goes Hollywood	1964	25.00
❑ PHS600123 [S]	Dizzy Gillespie Goes Hollywood	1964	30.00
❑ 822897-1	Dizzy Gillespie on the France Riviera	1986	12.00
❑ PHM200070 [M]	New Wave!	1962	25.00
❑ PHS600070 [S]	New Wave!	1962	30.00
❑ PHM200091 [M]	Something Old, Something New	1963	25.00
❑ PHS600091 [S]	Something Old, Something New	1963	30.00
❑ PHM200138 [M]	The Cool World	1964	50.00
❑ PHS600138 [S]	The Cool World	1964	80.00

PHOENIX

| ❑ 4 | The Big Bands | 197? | 12.00 |
| ❑ 2 | The Small Groups | 197? | 12.00 |

PRESTIGE

❑ PRST-7818	Dizzy Gillespie at Salle Plevel '48	1970	15.00
❑ 24030	In the Beginning	197?	18.00
❑ P-24047	The Giant	1975	18.00

RCA VICTOR

❑ LJM-1009 [M]	Dizzier and Dizzier	1954	120.00
❑ LPV-530 [M]	Dizzy Gillespie	1966	30.00
❑ LPM-2398 [M]	The Greatest of Dizzy Gillespie	1961	50.00
— Long Play" on label			

REGENT

| ❑ MG-6043 [M] | School Days | 1957 | 100.00 |

REPRISE

| ❑ R-6072 [M] | Dateline: Europe | 1963 | 25.00 |
| ❑ R9-6072 [S] | Dateline: Europe | 1963 | 30.00 |

RONDO-LETTE

| ❑ A-11 [M] | Dizzy Gillespie | 195? | 30.00 |

ROOST

| ❑ LP-2214 [M] | Concert in Paris | 1957 | 120.00 |
| ❑ R-414 [10] | Dizzy Over Paris | 1953 | 250.00 |

SAVOY

❑ MG-12020 [M]	Groovin' High	1955	60.00
❑ MG-12047 [M]	The Champ	1956	60.00
❑ MG-12110 [M]	The Dizzy Gillespie Story	1957	60.00

SAVOY JAZZ

| ❑ SJL-2209 | Dee Gee Days | 197? | 18.00 |
| ❑ SJC-402 | The Dizzy Gillespie Story | 1985 | 12.00 |

SOLID STATE

❑ SS-18061	Cornucopia	1969	25.00
❑ SS-18034	Live at the Village Vanguard	1968	25.00
❑ SS-18054	My Way	1969	25.00

SUTTON

| ❑ SU-287 [M] | Featuring Dizzy Gillespie | 196? | 18.00 |
| ❑ SSU-287 [S] | Featuring Dizzy Gillespie | 196? | 15.00 |

TIMELESS

| ❑ LPSJP-250 | Dizzy Gillespie Meets the Phil Woods Quintet | 1990 | 15.00 |

TRIP

| ❑ 5566 | Something Old, Something New | 197? | 12.00 |

VERNON

| ❑ 506 [M] | The Everlivin' "Diz | 196? | 18.00 |
| ❑ 506 [S] | The Everlivin' "Diz | 196? | 15.00 |

VERVE

❑ MGV-8191 [M]	Afro Dizzy	1957	60.00
❑ V-8401 [M]	An Electrifying Evening with the Dizzy Gillespie Quintet	1961	25.00
❑ V6-8401 [S]	An Electrifying Evening with the Dizzy Gillespie Quintet	1961	30.00
❑ UMV-2605	An Electrifying Evening with the Dizzy Gillespie Quintet	198?	12.00
❑ V-8423 [M]	Carnegie Hall Concert	1962	25.00
❑ V6-8423 [S]	Carnegie Hall Concert	1962	30.00
❑ VE-2-2524	Diz and Roy	197?	18.00
❑ MGV-8178 [M]	Diz Big Band	1957	70.00
❑ V-8178 [M]	Diz Big Band	1961	30.00
❑ V-8477 [M]	Dizzy, Rollins & Stitt	1962	25.00
— Reissue of MGV-8260			
❑ V6-8477 [S]	Dizzy, Rollins & Stitt	1962	30.00
❑ V-8560 [M]	Dizzy at Newport	1964	25.00
❑ V6-8560 [S]	Dizzy at Newport	1964	30.00
❑ MGV-8214 [M]	Dizzy Gillespie and Stuff Smith	1958	60.00
❑ V-8214 [M]	Dizzy Gillespie and Stuff Smith	1961	30.00
❑ MGV-8242 [M]	Dizzy Gillespie at Newport	1958	60.00
❑ V-8242 [M]	Dizzy Gillespie at Newport	1961	30.00
❑ MGVS-6023 [S]	Dizzy Gillespie at Newport	1960	60.00
❑ V6-8242 [S]	Dizzy Gillespie at Newport	1961	30.00
❑ MGV-8017 [M]	Dizzy in Greece	1957	60.00
❑ V-8017 [M]	Dizzy in Greece	1961	30.00
❑ MGV-8260 [M]	Duets	1958	60.00
— With Sonny Rollins and Sonny Stitt			
❑ MGV-8394 [M]	Gillespiana	1960	60.00
❑ V-8394 [M]	Gillespiana	1961	30.00
❑ V6-8394 [S]	Gillespiana	1961	30.00
❑ MGV-8352 [M]	Greatest Trumpet of Them All	1959	60.00
❑ V6-8352 [S]	Greatest Trumpet of Them All	1961	30.00

Number	Title	Yr	NM
❑ V-8352 [M]	Greatest Trumpet of Them All	1961	30.00
❑ MGVS-6117 [S]	Greatest Trumpet of Them All	1960	60.00
❑ MGV-8313 [M]	Have Trumpet, Will Excite	1959	60.00
❑ V-8313 [M]	Have Trumpet, Will Excite	1961	30.00
❑ MGVS-6047 [S]	Have Trumpet, Will Excite	1960	60.00
❑ V6-8313 [S]	Have Trumpet, Will Excite	1961	30.00
❑ UMV-2692	Have Trumpet, Will Excite	198?	12.00
❑ MGV-8173 [M]	Jazz Recital	1957	60.00
❑ V-8173 [M]	Jazz Recital	1961	30.00
❑ MGV-8208 [M]	Manteca	1958	60.00
❑ V-8208 [M]	Manteca	1961	30.00
❑ VSP-7 [M]	Night in Tunisia	1966	18.00
❑ VSPS-7 [S]	Night in Tunisia	1966	18.00
❑ V-8411 [M]	Perceptions	1961	25.00
❑ V6-8411 [S]	Perceptions	1961	30.00
❑ MGV-8386 [M]	Portrait of Duke	1960	60.00
❑ V-8386 [M]	Portrait of Duke	1961	30.00
❑ MGV-8328 [M]	The Ebullient Mr. Gillespie	1959	60.00
❑ V6-8328 [M]	The Ebullient Mr. Gillespie	1961	30.00
❑ V-8328 [M]	The Ebullient Mr. Gillespie	1961	30.00
❑ MGVS-6068 [S]	The Ebullient Mr. Gillespie	1960	60.00
❑ V-8566 [M]	The Essential Dizzy Gillespie	1964	25.00
❑ V6-8566 [S]	The Essential Dizzy Gillespie	1964	30.00
❑ V6-8830	The Newport Years	197?	15.00
❑ 821662-1	The Reunion Big Band	198?	12.00
❑ VE-2-2505	The Sonny Rollins/Sonny Stitt Sessions	1976	18.00
❑ MGV-8174 [M]	World Statesman	1957	60.00
❑ V-8174 [M]	World Statesman	1961	30.00

WING

| ❑ MGW-12318 [M] | The New Wave! | 1966 | 15.00 |
| ❑ SRW-16318 [S] | The New Wave! | 1966 | 15.00 |

GILLESPIE, DIZZY/JIMMY MCPARTLAND

MGM

| ❑ E-3286 [M] | Hot vs. Cool | 1955 | 80.00 |

GILLEY, MICKEY

ACCORD

| ❑ SN-7151 | Suburban Cowboy | 1981 | 12.00 |

ASTRO

| ❑ 101 [M] | Lonely Wine | 1964 | 300.00 |

COLUMBIA SPECIAL PRODUCTS

| ❑ P16198 | All My Best | 1982 | 12.00 |

EPIC

❑ PE37595	Christmas at Gilley's	1981	12.00
— Some labels have "FE" prefix			
❑ JE36851	Encore	1981	12.00
❑ PE34776	First Class	198?	10.00
— Budget-line reissue			
❑ FE38583	Fool for Your Love	1983	12.00
❑ PE38583	Fool for Your Love	1985	10.00
— Budget-line reissue			
❑ FE40115	I Feel Good (About Lovin' You)	1985	12.00
❑ FE39900	Live at Gilley's	1984	12.00
❑ JE36201	Mickey Gilley	1980	12.00
❑ FE38320	Mickey Gilley's Biggest Hits	1982	12.00
❑ FE38082	Put Your Dreams Away	1982	12.00
❑ PE38082	Put Your Dreams Away	198?	10.00
— Budget-line reissue			
❑ PE34736	Room Full of Roses	198?	10.00
— Budget-line reissue			
❑ PE34749	Smokin'	198?	10.00
— Budget-line reissue			
❑ KE35174	Songs We Made Love To	1979	12.00
❑ KE239867	Ten Years of Hits	1984	15.00
❑ JE36492	That's All That Matters to Me	1980	12.00
❑ PE36492	That's All That Matters to Me	198?	10.00
— Budget-line reissue			
❑ FE40353	The One and Only	1986	12.00
❑ FE39324	Too Good to Stop Now	1983	12.00
❑ FE37416	You Don't Know Me	1981	12.00
❑ PE37416	You Don't Know Me	198?	10.00
— Budget-line reissue			
❑ FE39000	You've Really Got a Hold on Me	1983	12.00

INTERMEDIA

| ❑ QS-5024 | With Love from Pasadena, Texas | 198? | 12.00 |

J.M.

| ❑ 8127 | Norwegian Wood | 1981 | 15.00 |

PAIR

| ❑ PDL2-1072 | The Best of Mickey Gilley | 1986 | 15.00 |

PAULA

❑ LP-2195 [M]	Down the Line	1967	40.00
❑ LPS-2195 [S]	Down the Line	1967	40.00
❑ LPS-2234	Mickey Gilley	1978	15.00
❑ LPS-2224	Mickey Gilley at His Best	1974	18.00

PICKWICK

| ❑ SPC-6180 | Wild Side of Life | 1975 | 12.00 |

PLAYBOY

❑ PB-403	City Lights	1974	25.00
❑ PZ34776	First Class	1977	15.00
❑ KZ35099	Flyin' High	1978	15.00
❑ KZ34881	Gilley's Greatest Hits, Vol. 2	1977	15.00
❑ PB-409	Gilley's Greatest Hits Vol. 1	1976	18.00

Number	Title	Yr	NM
❑ PZ34743	Gilley's Greatest Hits Vol. 1	1977	12.00
— Reissue of 409			
❑ PZ34749	Gilley's Smokin'	1977	15.00
— Reissue of 415			
❑ PB-415	Gilley's Smokin'	1976	18.00
❑ PB-405 [B]	Mickey's Movin' On	1975	18.00
❑ PB-408	Overnight Sensation	1976	18.00
❑ PZ34742	Overnight Sensation	1977	12.00
— Reissue of 408			
❑ PB-128	Room Full of Roses	1974	25.00
❑ PZ34736	Room Full of Roses	1977	12.00
— Reissue of 128			

GILMER, JULIA ANN

ABC-PARAMOUNT

| ❑ ABC-168 [M] | Cads, Blackguards and False True-Loves | 1956 | 30.00 |

GILMORE, JIMMIE DALE

HIGHTONE

| ❑ HT-8011 | Fair and Square | 1988 | 12.00 |
| ❑ HT-8018 | Jimmie Dale Gilmore | 1989 | 12.00 |

GILSTRAP, JIM

ROXBURY

| ❑ 105 | Love Talk | 1976 | 12.00 |
| ❑ 102 | Swing Your Daddy | 1975 | 12.00 |

GIN BLOSSOMS

A&M

| ❑ 7502153691 [EP] | Up and Crumbling | 1991 | 18.00 |

SAN JACINTO

| ❑ DRAM 019 | Dusted | 1989 | 25.00 |
| — With picture insert and biographical material | | | |

GINGOLD, HERMIONE

DOLPHIN

| ❑ D-7 [M] | La Gingold | 195? | 18.00 |

DRG

| ❑ MRS-902 | La Gingold | 197? | 12.00 |

GINNY AND THE GALLIONS

DOWNEY

| ❑ D-1003 [M] | Two Sides of Ginny and the Gallions | 1964 | 30.00 |
| ❑ DS-1003 [S] | Two Sides of Ginny and the Gallions | 1964 | 40.00 |

GINSBERG, ALLEN

ATLANTIC

| ❑ 4001 [M] | Allen Ginsburg Reads Kaddish | 1966 | 30.00 |

FANTASY

❑ F-7006 [M]	Howl and Other Poems	1959	500.00
— Red vinyl			
❑ F-7006 [M]	Howl and Other Poems	1959	300.00
— Black non-flexible vinyl			

GIOVANNI, NIKKI

NIKTOM

| ❑ NK4200 | Like a Ripple on a Pond | 1973 | 12.00 |
| ❑ NK4201 | The Way I Feel | 1975 | 12.00 |

RIGHT-ON

| ❑ 5001 | Truth Is On Its Way | 1971 | 12.00 |

GIRARD, GEORGE

VIK

| ❑ LX-1058 [M] | Jam Session on Bourbon Street | 1957 | 40.00 |
| ❑ LX-1063 [M] | Stompin' at the Famous Door | 1957 | 40.00 |

GIRLS NEXT DOOR

| ❑ ST-71053 | The Girls Next Door | 1986 | 12.00 |
| ❑ ST-71062 | What a Girl Next Door Could Do | 1987 | 12.00 |

GITS, THE

BROKEN REKIDS

| ❑ SKIP44 [B] | Kings & Queens | 1995 | 30.00 |
| ❑ SKIP87 | Seafish Louisville | 2000 | 18.00 |

C/Z

| ❑ 051 [B] | Frenching the Bully | 1992 | 40.00 |
| — Originals on red vinyl | | | |

GIUFFRE, JIMMY, AND MARTY PAICH

GNP CRESCENDO

| ❑ GNPS-9040 | Tenors West | 197? | 15.00 |

GIUFFRE, JIMMY

ATLANTIC

❑ 1295 [M]	Four Brothers Sound	1959	50.00
— Black label			
❑ 1295 [M]	Four Brothers Sound	1960	25.00

Number	Title	Yr	NM
— Multicolor label, white "fan" logo at right			
❑ SD1295 [S]	Four Brothers Sound	1959	50.00
— Green label			
❑ SD1295 [S]	Four Brothers Sound	1960	25.00
— Multicolor label, white "fan" logo at right			
❑ 90144	Jimmy Giuffre Clarinet	198?	12.00
❑ 1276 [M]	Music Man	1958	50.00
— Black label			
❑ 1276 [M]	Music Man	1960	25.00
— Multicolor label, white "fan" logo at right			
❑ 1276 [M]	Music Man	1963	18.00
— Multicolor label, black "fan" logo at right			
❑ SD1276 [S]	Music Man	1959	50.00
— Green label			
❑ SD1276 [S]	Music Man	1960	25.00
— Multicolor label, white "fan" logo at right			
❑ SD1276 [S]	Music Man	1963	18.00
— Multicolor label, black "fan" logo at right			
❑ 1238 [M]	The Jimmy Giuffre Clarinet	1956	50.00
— Black label			
❑ 1238 [M]	The Jimmy Giuffre Clarinet	1960	25.00
— Multicolor label, white "fan" logo at right			
❑ 1238 [M]	The Jimmy Giuffre Clarinet	1963	18.00
— Multicolor label, black "fan" logo at right			
❑ 1254 [M]	The Jimmy Giuffre Three	1957	50.00
— Black label			
❑ 1254 [M]	The Jimmy Giuffre Three	1960	25.00
— Multicolor label, white "fan" logo at right			
❑ 1254 [M]	The Jimmy Giuffre Three	1963	18.00
— Multicolor label, black "fan" logo at right			
❑ 1282 [M]	Trav'lin' Light	1958	50.00
— Black label			
❑ 1282 [M]	Trav'lin' Light	1960	25.00
— Multicolor label, white "fan" logo at right			
❑ 1282 [M]	Trav'lin' Light	1963	18.00
— Multicolor label, black "fan" logo at right			
❑ SD1282 [S]	Trav'lin' Light	1959	50.00
— Green label			
❑ SD1282 [S]	Trav'lin' Light	1960	25.00
— Multicolor label, white "fan" logo at right			
❑ SD1282 [S]	Trav'lin' Light	1963	18.00
— Multicolor label, black "fan" logo at right			
❑ 1330 [M]	Western Suite	1960	50.00
— Multicolor label, white "fan" logo at right			
❑ 1330 [M]	Western Suite	1963	18.00
— Multicolor label, black "fan" logo at right			
❑ SD1330 [S]	Western Suite	1960	50.00
— Multicolor label, white "fan" logo at right			
❑ SD1330 [S]	Western Suite	1963	18.00
— Multicolor label, black "fan" logo at right			

CAPITOL

Number	Title	Yr	NM
❑ H549 [10]	Jimmy Giuffre	1954	250.00
❑ T549 [M]	Jimmy Giuffre	1955	120.00
❑ T634 [M]	Tangents in Jazz	1955	120.00

CHOICE

Number	Title	Yr	NM
❑ 1001	Music for People, Birds, Butterflies and Mosquitos	1974	25.00
❑ 1011	River Chant	1975	25.00

COLUMBIA

Number	Title	Yr	NM
❑ CL1964 [M]	Free Fall	1963	18.00
❑ CS8764 [S]	Free Fall	1963	25.00

IAI

Number	Title	Yr	NM
❑ 373859	Jimmy Giuffre at the IAI Festival	1978	15.00

MOSAIC

Number	Title	Yr	NM
❑ MQ10-176	The Complete Capitol & Atlantic Recordings of Jimmy Giuffre	1998	200.00
— Limited edition of 5,000			

SOUL NOTE

Number	Title	Yr	NM
❑ SN-1058	Dragonfly	1983	18.00
❑ 121058	Dragonfly	199?	15.00
❑ 121158	Liquid Dancers	1991	18.00
❑ SN-1108	Quasar	1986	25.00
❑ 121108	Quasar	199?	15.00

VERVE

Number	Title	Yr	NM
❑ MGV-8361 [M]	Ad Lib	1960	40.00
❑ V-8361 [M]	Ad Lib	1961	25.00
❑ MGVS-6130 [S]	Ad Lib	1960	30.00
❑ V6-8361 [S]	Ad Lib	1961	18.00
❑ MGV-8397 [M]	Fusion	1961	40.00
❑ V-8397 [M]	Fusion	1961	25.00
❑ V6-8397 [S]	Fusion	1961	30.00
❑ MGV-8395 [M]	Piece for Clarinet and String Orchestra	1961	40.00
❑ V-8395 [M]	Piece for Clarinet and String Orchestra	1961	25.00
❑ V6-8395 [S]	Piece for Clarinet and String Orchestra	1961	30.00
❑ MGV-8307 [M]	Seven Pieces	1959	40.00
❑ V-8307 [M]	Seven Pieces	1961	25.00
❑ MGVS-6039 [S]	Seven Pieces	1960	30.00
❑ V6-8307 [S]	Seven Pieces	1961	18.00
❑ MGV-8337 [M]	The Easy Way	1960	40.00
❑ V-8337 [M]	The Easy Way	1961	25.00
❑ MGVS-6095 [S]	The Easy Way	1960	30.00
❑ V6-8337 [S]	The Easy Way	1961	18.00
❑ MGV-8387 [M]	The Jimmy Giuffre Quartet In Person	1961	40.00
❑ V-8387 [M]	The Jimmy Giuffre Quartet In Person	1961	25.00
❑ V6-8387 [S]	The Jimmy Giuffre Quartet In Person	1961	30.00
❑ MGV-8402 [M]	Thesis	1961	40.00
❑ V-8402 [M]	Thesis	1961	25.00
❑ V6-8402 [S]	Thesis	1961	30.00

GLACIERS, THE

MERCURY

Number	Title	Yr	NM
❑ MG-20895 [M]	From Sea to Ski	1964	50.00
❑ SR-60895 [S]	From Sea to Ski	1964	60.00

GLAD, THE

ABC

Number	Title	Yr	NM
❑ S-655	Feelin' Glad	1969	30.00

GLADSTONE

ABC

Number	Title	Yr	NM
❑ ABCX-751	From Down Home in Tyler, Texas, U.S.A.	1972	15.00
❑ ABCX-778	Lookin' for a Smile	1973	15.00

GLASEL, JOHN

ABC-PARAMOUNT

Number	Title	Yr	NM
❑ ABC-165 [M]	Jazz Session	1957	50.00

GOLDEN CREST

Number	Title	Yr	NM
❑ 1002 [M]	Jazz Unlimited	1960	30.00

GLASER, JIM

MCA

Number	Title	Yr	NM
❑ 5723	Everybody Knows I'm Yours	1986	10.00
❑ 5612	Past the Point of No Return	1985	10.00

NOBLE VISION

Number	Title	Yr	NM
❑ 2001	The Man in the Mirror	1983	12.00

STARDAY

Number	Title	Yr	NM
❑ SLP-158 [M]	Just Looking for a Home	1961	60.00
❑ SLP-149 [M]	Old Time Christmas Singing	1960	70.00

GLASER, TOMPALL

ABC

Number	Title	Yr	NM
❑ AB-1036	The Wonder of It All	1977	12.00
❑ AB-978	Tompall Glaser and His Outlaw Band	1977	12.00

MGM

Number	Title	Yr	NM
❑ M3G-5014	The Great Tompall and His Outlaw Band	1976	15.00
❑ M3G-4977	Tompall	1974	15.00

GLASS HARP

DECCA

Number	Title	Yr	NM
❑ DL75261	Glass Harp	1971	30.00
❑ DL75358	It Makes Me Glad	1972	30.00
❑ DL75306	Synergy	1971	30.00

MCA

Number	Title	Yr	NM
❑ 293	Glass Harp	1974	12.00
— Reissue of Decca 75261			

GLASS HOUSE, THE

INVICTUS

Number	Title	Yr	NM
❑ ST-7305	Inside the Glass House	1971	15.00
❑ ST-9810	Thanks I Needed That	1972	15.00

GLASS PRISM, THE

RCA VICTOR

Number	Title	Yr	NM
❑ LSP-4270 [B]	On Joy and Sorrow	1970	18.00
❑ LSP-4201 [B]	Poe Through the Glass Prism	1969	18.00

GLAZER, TOM

KAPP

Number	Title	Yr	NM
❑ KL1331 [M]	On Top of Spaghetti	1963	15.00
❑ KS3331 [S]	On Top of Spaghetti	1963	18.00

UNITED ARTISTS

Number	Title	Yr	NM
❑ UAL3540 [M]	Tom Glazer Sings the Ballad of Namu the Killer Whale and Other Ballads of Adventure	1966	30.00
❑ UAS6540 [S]	Tom Glazer Sings the Ballad of Namu the Killer Whale and Other Ballads of Adventure	1966	30.00

WASHINGTON

Number	Title	Yr	NM
❑ WC-301 [M]	The Tom Glazer Concert For and With Children	1959	30.00

GLEASON, JACKIE

CAPITOL

Number	Title	Yr	NM
❑ STBB-346	All I Want for Christmas	1969	18.00
❑ WBO1619 [M]	A Lover's Portfolio	1962	25.00
❑ SWBO1619 [S]	A Lover's Portfolio	1962	30.00
❑ W1979 [M]	A Lover's Portfolio, Vol. 1 (Music for Sippin' and Dancin')	1963	15.00
❑ SW1979 [S]	A Lover's Portfolio, Vol. 1 (Music for Sippin' and Dancin')	1963	18.00
❑ W1980 [M]	A Lover's Portfolio, Vol. 2 (Music for Listenin' and Lovin')	1963	15.00
❑ SW1980 [S]	A Lover's Portfolio, Vol. 2 (Music for Listenin' and Lovin')	1963	18.00
❑ H511 [10]	And Awaaay We Go!	1954	80.00
❑ W511 [M]	And Awaaay We Go!	1955	40.00
❑ W1250 [M]	Aphrodisia	1960	25.00
❑ SW1250 [S]	Aphrodisia	1960	30.00
❑ W2684 [M]	A Taste of Brass For Lovers Only	1967	15.00
❑ SW2684 [S]	A Taste of Brass For Lovers Only	1967	18.00
❑ W1830 [M]	Champagne, Candlelight & Kisses	1963	15.00
❑ SW1830 [S]	Champagne, Candlelight & Kisses	1963	18.00
❑ SWBB-256	Close-Up	1969	18.00
— Reissue of Capitol DW 352 and DW 509 in one package			
❑ ST-480	Come Saturday Morning	1970	15.00
❑ SW2880	Doublin' in Brass	1968	18.00
❑ W2582 [M]	How Sweet It Is For Lovers Only	1966	15.00
❑ SW2582 [S]	How Sweet It Is For Lovers Only	1966	18.00
❑ SW-106	Irving Berlin's Music	1968	15.00
❑ W568 [M]	Jackie Gleason Plays Romantic Jazz	1955	30.00
❑ W905 [M]	Jackie Gleason Presents "Oooo!	1957	30.00
❑ SW905 [S]	Jackie Gleason Presents "Oooo!	1959	30.00
— We haven't confirmed if this is in true stereo or not.			
❑ W2144 [M]	Last Dance For Lovers Only	1964	15.00
❑ SW2144 [S]	Last Dance For Lovers Only	1964	18.00
❑ W1439 [M]	Lazy Lively Love	1961	25.00
❑ SW1439 [S]	Lazy Lively Love	1961	30.00
❑ H627 [10]	Lonesome Echo	1955	30.00
❑ W627 [M]	Lonesome Echo	1955	30.00
❑ DW627 [R]	Lonesome Echo	196?	12.00
❑ W1689 [M]	Love, Embers and Flame	1962	18.00
❑ SW1689 [S]	Love, Embers and Flame	1962	25.00
❑ H366 [10]	Lover's Rhapsody	1953	30.00
❑ W758 [M]	Merry Christmas	1956	30.00
❑ DW758 [R]	Merry Christmas	196?	12.00
❑ W1877 [M]	Movie Themes -- For Lovers Only	1963	15.00
❑ SW1877 [S]	Movie Themes -- For Lovers Only	1963	18.00
❑ W509 [M]	Music, Martini and Memories	1954	30.00
❑ SW509 [S]	Music, Martini and Memories	196?	18.00
— Re-recorded for stereo			
❑ SM-509	Music, Martini and Memories	197?	12.00
— Reissue			
❑ H1-509 [10]	Music, Martini and Memories Part 1	1954	30.00
❑ H2-509 [10]	Music, Martini and Memories Part 2	1954	30.00
❑ W2471 [M]	Music Around the World -- For Lovers Only	1966	15.00
❑ SW2471 [S]	Music Around the World -- For Lovers Only	1966	18.00
❑ H352 [10]	Music for Lovers Only	1952	30.00
❑ W352 [M]	Music for Lovers Only	1953	30.00
❑ SW352 [S]	Music for Lovers Only	1963	12.00
— Re-recorded version; black rainbow label, Capitol logo at top			
❑ SM-352	Music for Lovers Only	197?	12.00
— Reissue			
❑ SW352 [S]	Music for Lovers Only	1959	18.00
— Re-recorded version of W 352; black rainbow label, Capitol logo at left			
❑ WAO475 [M]	Music for Lovers Only/Music to Make You Misty	1954	40.00
❑ W816 [M]	Music for the Love Hours	1957	30.00
❑ DW816 [R]	Music for the Love Hours	196?	12.00
❑ W632 [M]	Music to Change Her Mind	1956	30.00
❑ DW632 [R]	Music to Change Her Mind	196?	12.00
❑ H455 [10]	Music to Make You Misty	1954	30.00
❑ W455 [M]	Music to Make You Misty	1954	30.00
❑ DW455 [R]	Music to Make You Misty	196?	12.00
❑ SM-455	Music to Make You Misty	197?	12.00
— Reissue			
❑ W570 [M]	Music to Remember Her	1955	30.00
❑ DW570 [R]	Music to Remember Her	196?	12.00
❑ W717 [M]	Night Winds	1956	30.00
❑ DW717 [R]	Night Winds	196?	12.00
❑ W1315 [M]	Opiate D'Amour	1960	18.00
❑ SW1315 [S]	Opiate D'Amour	1960	25.00
❑ W1075 [M]	Rebound	1959	25.00
❑ SW1075 [S]	Rebound	1959	30.00
❑ W1020 [M]	Riff Jazz	1958	25.00
❑ SW1020 [S]	Riff Jazz	1959	30.00
❑ ST-398	Romeo and Juliet	1970	15.00
❑ W2409 [M]	Silk 'N' Brass	1966	15.00
❑ SW2409 [S]	Silk 'N' Brass	1966	18.00
❑ L471 [10]	Tawny	1954	30.00
❑ W471 [M]	Tawny	1954	30.00
❑ STBB-510	Tenderly/Laura	1971	18.00
❑ W1147 [M]	That Moment	1959	25.00
❑ SW1147 [S]	That Moment	1959	30.00
❑ W2796 [M]	The Best of Jackie Gleason	1967	18.00
❑ SW2796 [S]	The Best of Jackie Gleason	1967	18.00
❑ SM-2796	The Best of Jackie Gleason	197?	12.00
— Reissue			
❑ SKAO-146	The Best of Jackie Gleason (Vol. 2)	1968	15.00
❑ W1519 [M]	The Gentle Touch	1961	25.00

Number	Title	Yr	NM
❑ SW1519 [S]	The Gentle Touch	1961	30.00
❑ TCL2816 [M]	The Jackie Gleason Deluxe Set	1968	30.00
❑ STCL2816 [S]	The Jackie Gleason Deluxe Set	1968	30.00
—Reissue of three complete LPs (titles unknown)			
❑ SW2935	The Now Sound ... For Today's Lovers	1968	18.00
❑ W961 [M]	The Torch with Blue Flame	1958	25.00
❑ SW961 [S]	The Torch with Blue Flame	1959	30.00
❑ ST2791 [S]	'Tis the Season	1967	18.00
❑ T2791 [M]	'Tis the Season	1967	25.00
❑ W1978 [M]	Today's Romantic Hits/For Lovers Only	1963	15.00
❑ SW1978 [S]	Today's Romantic Hits/For Lovers Only	1963	18.00
❑ W2056 [M]	Today's Romantic Hits/For Lovers Only, Vol. 2	1964	15.00
❑ SW2056 [S]	Today's Romantic Hits/For Lovers Only, Vol. 2	1964	18.00
❑ SQBO91546	Velvet & Gold: For Lovers Only	196?	25.00
—Capitol Record Club exclusive			
❑ W859 [M]	Velvet Brass	1957	30.00
❑ SW859 [S]	Velvet Brass	1959	30.00
—We haven't confirmed if this is in true stereo or not.			
❑ SM-859	Velvet Brass	197?	12.00
—Reissue			
❑ ST-693	Words of Love	1971	15.00
PAIR			
❑ PDL2-1069	Lush Moods	1986	15.00
PICKWICK			
❑ SPC-3064	Plays Pretty for the People	196?	12.00
❑ SPC-2004	Romantic Moods	197?	12.00
❑ SPC-3218	Shangri-La	197?	12.00
❑ SPC-2029	The More I See You	197?	12.00
❑ SPC-1008	White Christmas	197?	12.00
—Abridged version of Capitol ST 2791			

GLENN, DARRELL

NRC
| ❑ LPA-5 [M] | Crying in the Chapel | 1959 | 30.00 |
| ❑ SLPA-5 [S] | Crying in the Chapel | 1959 | 30.00 |

GLENN, LLOYD

ALADDIN
❑ LP-808 [M]	Chica-Boo	1956	2000.00
—Red vinyl; VG value 1000; VG+ value 1500			
❑ LP-808 [M]	Chica-Boo	1956	1000.00
—Black vinyl			
BLACK & BLUE			
❑ 33077	Old Time Shuffle	1977	15.00
IMPERIAL			
❑ LP-9175 [M]	After Hours	1962	150.00
❑ LP-12175 [S]	After Hours	1962	200.00
❑ LP-9174 [M]	Chica-Boo	1962	150.00
❑ LP-12174 [S]	Chica-Boo	1962	200.00
SCORE			
❑ SLP-4020 [M]	After Hours	1958	1000.00
❑ SLP-4006 [M]	Lloyd Glenn	1957	1000.00
SWING TIME			
❑ 1901 [10]	Lloyd Glenn Presents All Time Favorites	1954	3000.00
—VG value 1500; VG+ value 2250			

GLENN, ROGER

FANTASY
| ❑ F-9516 | Reachin' | 197? | 15.00 |

GLENN, TYREE

ROULETTE
❑ R-25115 [M]	Let's Have a Ball	1960	30.00
❑ SR-25115 [S]	Let's Have a Ball	1960	30.00
❑ R-25184 [M]	The Trombone Artistry of Tyree Glenn	1962	25.00
❑ SR-25184 [S]	The Trombone Artistry of Tyree Glenn	1962	30.00
❑ R-25075 [M]	Try a Little Tenderness	1959	40.00
❑ SR-25075 [S]	Try a Little Tenderness	1959	30.00
❑ R-25138 [M]	Tyree Glenn at London House in Chicago	1961	25.00
❑ SR-25138 [S]	Tyree Glenn at London House in Chicago	1961	30.00
❑ R-25009 [M]	Tyree Glenn at the Embers	1957	40.00
❑ R-25050 [M]	Tyree Glenn at the Roundtable	1959	40.00
❑ SR-25050 [S]	Tyree Glenn at the Roundtable	1959	30.00

GLITTER, GARY

BELL
❑ 6082	Gary Glitter	1973	18.00
❑ 1108	Glitter	1972	18.00
EPIC			
❑ PE39299	The Leader	1984	18.00
EPIC/NU-DISK			
❑ 3E36848 [10]	Glitter & Gold	1981	18.00

GLITTERHOUSE

DYNOVOICE
| ❑ 31905 | Color Blind | 1968 | 25.00 |

GLOBETROTTERS, THE

KIRSHNER
| ❑ KES-108 | The Globetrotters | 1970 | 25.00 |

GLORY (1)

AVALANCHE
| ❑ AV-LA148-F | Glory | 1973 | 18.00 |

GLORY (2)

TEXAS REVOLUTION
| ❑ CFS-2531 | A Meat Music Sampler | 1969 | 100.00 |

GO-GO'S, THE

RCA VICTOR
| ❑ LPM-2930 [M] | Swim with the Go-Go's | 1964 | 30.00 |
| ❑ LSP-2930 [S] | Swim with the Go-Go's | 1964 | 30.00 |

GO-GO'S

I.R.S.
❑ SP70021	Beauty and the Beat	1981	15.00
—First pressings with peach-colored cover and light label			
❑ SP70021	Beauty and the Beat	1981	10.00
—Second pressings with dark blue cover and darker label			
❑ R151667	Talk Show	1984	12.00
—RCA Music Service edition			
❑ SP70041	Talk Show	1984	10.00
❑ SP70031	Vacation	1982	10.00

GO WEST

CHRYSALIS
❑ BFV41550	Dancing on the Couch	1987	12.00
❑ BFV41495	Go West	1985	15.00
❑ FV41495	Go West	1987	10.00
—Reissue with new prefix			

GODLEY AND CREME

MERCURY
❑ SRM-31700 [B]	Consequences	1977	60.00
—with booklet. LP credit to Lol Creme/Kevin Godley			
MIRAGE			
❑ WTG19341	Snack Attack	1981	15.00
POLYDOR			
❑ PD-1-6257	Freeze Frame	1979	15.00
❑ 835348-1	Goodbye Blue Sky	1988	12.00
❑ PD-1-6177	L	1978	15.00
❑ 825981-1 [B]	The History Mix Volume 1	1985	15.00

GODZ, THE

ESP-DISK'
❑ 1037 [M]	Contact High with the Godz	1967	60.00
❑ S-1037 [S]	Contact High with the Godz	1967	50.00
❑ 1047	Godz 2	1968	50.00
❑ 2017	Godzundheit	1970	50.00
❑ 1077	Third Testament	1969	50.00

GOGGLES, THE

AUDIO FIDELITY
| ❑ AFSD-6244 | The Goggles | 1971 | 18.00 |

GOLD, ANDREW

ASYLUM
❑ 6E-116 [B]	All This and Heaven Too	1978	15.00
❑ 7E-1047 [B]	Andrew Gold	1975	15.00
❑ 7E-1086 [B]	What's Wrong with This Picture?	1977	15.00
❑ 6E-264 [B]	Whirlwind	1979	15.00

GOLD, MARTY

KAPP
❑ KL-1125 [M]	By the Waters of the Minnetonka	1959	18.00
PICKWICK			
❑ ACL-9003	Songs from "How the Grinch Stole Christmas" and Other Children's Christmas Songs	197?	10.00
RCA VICTOR			
❑ LSP-2290 [S]	It's Magic	1961	18.00
❑ LPM-2290 [M]	It's Magic	1961	15.00
❑ LSP-3599 [S]	Soundaroundus	1966	15.00
❑ LPM-2620 [M]	Soundpower!	1963	15.00
❑ LSP-2620 [S]	Soundpower!	1963	18.00
❑ LSP-2381 [S]	Stereo Action Goes Hollywood	1962	15.00
VIK			
❑ LX-1069 [M]	Organized for Hi-Fi	1957	18.00

GOLD, SANFORD

PRESTIGE
| ❑ PRLP-7019 [M] | Piano d'Or | 1956 | 60.00 |

GOLDBERG, BARRY

ATCO
| ❑ SD7040 | Barry Goldberg | 1974 | 15.00 |

BUDDAH
❑ BDS-5081	Blast from My Past	1974	18.00
❑ BDS-5051	Street Man	1970	18.00
❑ BDM-1012 [M]	The Barry Goldberg Reunion	1968	50.00
—White-label promo in stereo cover with "mono" sticker			
❑ BDS-5012 [S]	The Barry Goldberg Reunion	1968	30.00
❑ BDS-5029	Two Jews Blues	1969	30.00
EPIC			
❑ LN24199 [M]	Blowing My Mind	1966	30.00
❑ BN26199 [S]	Blowing My Mind	1966	40.00
RECORD MAN			
❑ CR5015	Barry Goldberg and Friends	1972	18.00

GOLDEBRIARS, THE

EPIC
❑ LN24114 [M]	Straight Ahead	1964	18.00
❑ BN26114 [S]	Straight Ahead	1964	25.00
❑ LN24087 [M]	The Goldebriars	1964	18.00
❑ BN26087 [S]	The Goldebriars	1964	25.00

GOLDEN AGE JAZZ BAND

ARHOOLIE
| ❑ 4007 | Golden Age Jazz Band | 197? | 18.00 |

GOLDEN DAWN

INTERNATIONAL ARTISTS
❑ 4	Power Plant	1968	300.00
❑ 4	Power Plant	1979	18.00
—Reissue with "Masterfonics" in trail-off wax			

GOLDEN EARRING

21 RECORDS
❑ T1-1-9004	Cut	1982	12.00
❑ 817585-1	Cut	1985	10.00
—Reissue			
❑ T1-1-9008	N.E.W.S.	1984	12.00
❑ 823717-1 [B]	Something Heavy Going Down -- Live from the Twilight Zone	1984	18.00
❑ 90514	The Hole	1986	12.00
ATLANTIC			
❑ SD8244 [B]	Eight Miles High	1970	40.00
CAPITOL			
❑ ST-164 [B]	Miracle Mirror	1969	60.00
❑ ST-11315	The Golden Earring	1974	15.00
❑ T2823 [M]	Winter Harvest	1967	250.00
❑ ST2823 [S]	Winter Harvest	1967	150.00
DWARF			
❑ 2000 [B]	Golden Earring	1971	40.00
MCA			
❑ 8009	Golden Earring Live!	1977	18.00
❑ 6004	Golden Earring Live!	198?	12.00
—Reissue of 8009			
❑ 3057	Grab It For a Second	1978	15.00
❑ 703	Grab It For a Second	198?	10.00
—Reissue of 3057			
❑ 2254	Mad Love	1977	15.00
❑ 2352	Moontan	1978	12.00
—Reissue of Track 396			
❑ 37172	Moontan	198?	10.00
—Reissue of 2352			
❑ 2139 [B]	Switch	197?	12.00
—Reissue of Track 2139			
❑ 827	Switch	198?	10.00
—Reissue of 2139			
❑ 2183	To the Hilt	1976	15.00
POLYDOR			
❑ PD-1-6303	Long Blond Animal	1980	15.00
❑ PD-1-6223	No Promises...No Debts	1979	15.00
TRACK			
❑ 396 [B]	Moontan	1974	30.00
—Original cover with nude dancer			
❑ 396	Moontan	1974	18.00
—Reissue cover with close-up of earring in ear			
❑ 2139 [B]	Switch	1975	25.00

GOLDEN GATE QUARTET, THE

COLUMBIA
❑ CL6102 [10]	Golden Gate Spirituals	1950	150.00
HARMONY			
❑ HL7018 [M]	The Golden Chariot	1957	80.00
—Original pressing has maroon labels			
❑ HL7018 [M]	The Golden Chariot	195?	30.00
—Second pressing has black labels			
MERCURY			
❑ MG-25063 [10]	Spirituals	1951	150.00
RCA CAMDEN			
❑ CAL-308 [M]	The Golden Gate Quartet	1956	80.00

GOLDEN GATE STRINGS, THE

EPIC
❑ LN24160 [M]	A String of Hits	1965	15.00
❑ BN26160 [S]	A String of Hits	1965	18.00
❑ LN24158 [M]	The Bob Dylan Song Book	1965	15.00
❑ BN26158 [S]	The Bob Dylan Song Book	1965	18.00

Number	Title	Yr	NM
❏ LN24248 [M]	The Monkees Song Book	1967	15.00
❏ BN26248 [S]	The Monkees Song Book	1967	18.00

GOLDEN STATE JAZZ BAND

STOMP OFF
❏ SOS-1006	Alive and At Bay	1983	12.00

GOLDEN STRINGS

SOUND 80
❏ S80-173-1812S	Holiday Request Album	1974	12.00
—Jacket has Side 1 and Side 2 reversed; this is as they appear on the record			

GOLDENROD

CHARTMAKER
❏ CSG-1101	Goldenrod	1968	400.00

GOLDIE, DON

ARGO
❏ LP-4010 [M]	Brilliant!	1961	30.00
❏ LPS-4010 [S]	Brilliant!	1961	30.00
❏ LP-708 [M]	Trumpet Caliente	1963	30.00
❏ LPS-708 [S]	Trumpet Caliente	1963	30.00

JAZZOLOGY
❏ J-135	Don Goldie's Jazz Express	1986	12.00

VERVE
❏ V-8475 [M]	Trumpet Exodus	1962	30.00
❏ V6-8475 [S]	Trumpet Exodus	1962	30.00

GOLDKETTE, JEAN

X
❏ LVA-3017 [10]	Jean Goldkette and His Orchestra Featuring Bix Beiderbecke	1954	60.00

GOLDSBORO, BOBBY

CURB
❏ JZ36822	Bobby Goldsboro	1980	15.00
❏ FZ37734	Round-Up Saloon	1982	12.00

EPIC
❏ PE34703	Goldsboro	1977	15.00

LIBERTY
❏ LN-10007	Bobby Goldsboro's 10th Anniversary Album, Volume 1	1981	10.00
❏ LN-10047	Bobby Goldsboro's 10th Anniversary Album, Volume 2	1981	10.00
❏ LMAS-5502	Bobby Goldsboro's Greatest Hits	1981	10.00
—Reissue of United Artists 5502			
❏ LN-10114	The Best of Bobby Goldsboro	1981	10.00

SUNSET
❏ SUS-5313	Autumn of My Life	1971	15.00
❏ SUS-5284	Pledge of Love	1970	15.00
❏ SUS-5236	This Is Bobby Goldsboro	1969	15.00

UNITED ARTISTS
❏ UAL3552 [M]	Blue Autumn	1967	25.00
❏ UAS6552 [S]	Blue Autumn	1967	30.00
❏ UA-LA311-H2	Bobby Goldsboro's 10th Anniversary Album	1974	25.00
❏ UAS5502	Bobby Goldsboro's Greatest Hits	1970	25.00
❏ UA-LA019-F	Brand New Kind of Love	1972	18.00
❏ UAL3471 [M]	Broomstick Cowboy	1966	25.00
❏ UAS6471 [S]	Broomstick Cowboy	1966	30.00
❏ UA-LA639-G	Butterfly for Bucky	1976	15.00
❏ UAS-5578	California Wine	1972	18.00
❏ UAS5516	Come Back Home	1971	18.00
❏ UAS6642 [S]	Honey	1968	25.00
—Later copies have the correct title "Honey" on the label			
❏ ST-91460	Honey	1968	30.00
—Capitol Record Club edition			
❏ UAL3642 [M]	Honey	1968	40.00
—Some, if not all, copies of this have the title "Pledge of Love" on the label			
❏ UAL6642 [S]	Honey	1968	30.00
—Early copies of this have the title "Pledge of Love" on the label			
❏ UAL3381 [M]	I Can't Stop Loving You	1964	25.00
❏ UAS6358 [S]	I Can't Stop Loving You	1964	30.00
❏ UAL3486 [M]	It's Too Late	1966	25.00
❏ UAS6486 [S]	It's Too Late	1966	30.00
❏ UAL3425 [M]	Little Things	1965	25.00
❏ UAS6425 [S]	Little Things	1965	30.00
❏ UAS6735	Muddy Mississippi Line	1969	25.00
❏ UAL3599 [M]	Romantic, Soulful, Wacky	1967	25.00
❏ UAS6599 [S]	Romantic, Soulful, Wacky	1967	25.00
❏ UAL3561 [M]	Sold Goldsboro/Bobby Goldsboro's Greatest Hits	1967	25.00
❏ UAS6561 [S]	Sold Goldsboro/Bobby Goldsboro's Greatest Hits	1967	25.00
❏ UA-LA124-F	Summer (The First Time)	1973	18.00
❏ UAL3358 [M]	The Bobby Goldsboro Album	1964	25.00
❏ UAS6358 [S]	The Bobby Goldsboro Album	1964	30.00
❏ SP-58 [DJ]	The Bobby Goldsboro Family Album	1971	50.00
—Promo-only compilation			
❏ UA-LA424-G	Through the Eyes of a Man	1975	15.00
❏ UAS6704	Today	1969	25.00

Number	Title	Yr	NM
❏ UAS6777 [B]	Watching Scotty Grow	1971	18.00
—Retitled version of above			
❏ UAS6777	We Gotta Start Lovin'	1970	25.00
❏ UAS6657	Word Pictures Featuring Autumn of My Life	1968	25.00
❏ SKAO-91543 [B]	Word Pictures Featuring Autumn of My Life	1968	30.00
—Capitol Record Club edition			

GOLDTONES, THE

LABREA
❏ L-8011 [M]	The Goldtones	1961	40.00
❏ LS-8011 [S]	The Goldtones	1961	50.00

GOLIA, VINNY

NINE WINDS
❏ NW 0110	Compositions for Large Ensemble	1984	25.00
❏ NW 0120	Facts of Their Own Lives	1986	18.00
❏ NW 0117	Goin' Ahead	1985	15.00
❏ NW 0103	... In the Right Order ...	1979	18.00
❏ NW 0102	Openhearted	1978	15.00
❏ NW 0127	Out for Blood	1989	15.00
❏ NW 0108	Slice of Life	1981	15.00
❏ NW 0104	Solo	1980	15.00
❏ NW 0101	Spirits in Fellowship	1977	15.00
❏ NW 0109	The Gift of Fury	1982	15.00

GOLLIWOGS, THE

FANTASY
❏ F-9474	Pre-Creedence	1975	30.00
—Reissue of Fantasy and Scorpio sides			

GOLSON, BENNY

ARGO
❏ LP-716 [M]	Free	1963	50.00
❏ LPS-716 [S]	Free	1963	60.00
❏ LP-681 [M]	Take a Number from 1 to 10	1961	30.00
❏ LPS-681 [S]	Take a Number from 1 to 10	1961	40.00

AUDIO FIDELITY
❏ AFLP-2150 [M]	Just Jazz	1966	30.00
❏ AFSD-6150 [S]	Just Jazz	1966	40.00
❏ AFLP-1978 [M]	Pop + Jazz = Swing	1962	30.00
❏ AFSD-5978 [S]	Pop + Jazz = Swing	1962	40.00

COLUMBIA
❏ JC35359	I'm Always Dancin' to the Music	1978	25.00
❏ PC34678	Killer Joe	1977	25.00

CONTEMPORARY
❏ C-3552 [M]	Benny Golson's New York Scene	1958	80.00

FANTASY
❏ OJC-164	Benny Golson's New York Scene	198?	15.00
—Reissue of Contemporary 3552			
❏ OJC-226	Groovin' with Golson	198?	15.00
—Reissue of New Jazz 8220			
❏ OJC-1750	The Other Side of Benny Golson	1990	18.00
—Reissue of Riverside 290			

JAZZLAND
❏ JLP-85 [M]	Reunion	1962	60.00
❏ JLP-985 [S]	Reunion	1962	50.00

MERCURY
❏ MG-20801 [M]	Turning Point	1963	30.00
❏ SR-60801 [S]	Turning Point	1963	40.00

MILESTONE
❏ M-47048	Blues On Down	1978	25.00

NEW JAZZ
❏ NJLP-8248 [M]	Gettin' With It	1960	120.00
—Purple label			
❏ NJLP-8248 [M]	Gettin' With It	1965	40.00
—Blue label, trident logo at right			
❏ NJLP-8235 [M]	Gone with Golson	1960	400.00
—Purple label			
❏ NJLP-8235 [M]	Gone with Golson	1965	40.00
—Blue label, trident logo at right			
❏ NJLP-8220 [M]	Groovin' with Golson	1959	120.00
—Purple label			
❏ NJLP-8220 [M]	Groovin' with Golson	1965	40.00
—Blue label, trident logo at right			

PRESTIGE
❏ PRLP-7361 [M]	Stockholm Sojourn	1965	30.00
❏ PRST-7361 [S]	Stockholm Sojourn	1965	40.00

RIVERSIDE
❏ 6070	The Modern Touch	197?	15.00
❏ RLP 12-256 [M]	The Modern Touch of Benny Golson	1957	100.00
❏ RLP 12-290 [M]	The Other Side of Benny Golson	1958	100.00

SWING
❏ SW-8418	Benny Golson in Paris	1987	15.00

TIMELESS
❏ LPSJP-177	California Message	1980	18.00
❏ LPSJP-235	This Is for You, John	1983	18.00

Number	Title	Yr	NM
UNITED ARTISTS			
❏ UAL-4020 [M]	Benny Golson and the Philadelphians	1959	100.00
❏ UAS-5020 [S]	Benny Golson and the Philadelphians	1959	80.00

VERVE
❏ V-8710 [M]	Tune In, Turn On	1967	40.00
❏ V6-8710 [S]	Tune In, Turn On	1967	30.00

GONN

BEAT ROCKET
❏ BR108	The Loudest Band in Town	1999	15.00

GONSALVES, PAUL, AND ROY ELDREDGE

FANTASY
❏ F-9646	Mexican Bandit Meets Pittsburgh Pirate	1986	12.00

GONSALVES, PAUL

ABC IMPULSE!
❏ AS-41 [S]	Cleopatra Feelin' Jazzy	1967	18.00
❏ AS-52 [S]	Salt and Pepper	1967	18.00
❏ AS-55 [S]	Tell It the Way It Is	1967	18.00

ARGO
❏ LP-626 [M]	Cookin'	1958	250.00
❏ LPS-626 [S]	Cookin'	1959	40.00

BLACK LION
❏ 191	Just a Sittin' and a Rockin'	197?	18.00

CATALYST
❏ 7913	Buenos Aires	197?	18.00

FANTASY
❏ OJC-203	Gettin' Together	198?	12.00

IMPULSE!
❏ A-41 [M]	Cleopatra Feelin' Jazzy	1963	30.00
❏ AS-41 [S]	Cleopatra Feelin' Jazzy	1963	30.00
❏ A-52 [M]	Salt and Pepper	1963	30.00
❏ AS-52 [S]	Salt and Pepper	1963	30.00
❏ A-55 [M]	Tell It the Way It Is	1963	30.00
❏ AS-55 [S]	Tell It the Way It Is	1963	30.00

JAZZLAND
❏ JLP-36 [M]	Gettin' Together	1961	120.00
❏ JLP-936 [S]	Gettin' Together	1961	60.00

GONSALVES, VIRGIL

LIBERTY
❏ LJH-6010 [M]	Jazz San Francisco Style	1956	50.00

NOCTURNE
❏ NLP-8 [10]	Virgil Gonsalves	1954	80.00

OMEGA
❏ OML-1047 [M]	Jazz at Monterey	1959	40.00

GONZALES, BABS

CHIAROSCURO
❏ 2025	Live at Small's Paradise	197?	18.00

DAUNTLESS
❏ DM-4311 [M]	Sunday Afternoon at Small's Paradise	1963	40.00
❏ DS-6311 [S]	Sunday Afternoon at Small's Paradise	1963	50.00

HOPE
❏ 001	Voila!	1958	150.00

JARO
❏ JAM-5000 [M]	Cool Philosophy	1959	150.00
❏ JAS-8000 [S]	Cool Philosophy	1959	100.00

GOO GOO DOLLS

ENIGMA
❏ 773406-1	JED	1989	25.00

MERCENARY
❏ MER-2102	Goo Goo Dolls	1987	75.00

GOOD AND PLENTY

SENATE
❏ LP-21001 [M]	The World of Good and Plenty	1967	30.00
❏ LPS-21001 [S]	The World of Good and Plenty	1967	30.00

GOOD GUYS, THE

GNP CRESCENDO
❏ GNP-2001 [M]	Sidewalk Surfing	1964	30.00
❏ GNPS-2001 [S]	Sidewalk Surfing	1964	40.00

UNITED ARTISTS
❏ UAL-3370 [M]	The Good Guys Sing	1964	18.00
❏ UAS-6370 [S]	The Good Guys Sing	1964	25.00

GOOD RATS, THE

KAPP
❏ KS-3580	The Good Rats	1969	40.00

PASSPORT
❏ PB-9830	Birth Comes to Us All	1978	15.00
❏ PB-9825	From Rats to Riches	1978	15.00
❏ SP-20 [DJ]	Rats the Way You Like It (Live)	1978	45.00

Number	Title	Yr	NM

RAT CITY

RCR-8003	Great American Music	1981	15.00
998	Live at Last	1979	18.00
RCR-8001	Rat City in Blue	1975	25.00
RCR-8002	Tasty	1978	15.00

RAT CITY/GEMM

| RCR-8004 | Rat City in Blue | 1976 | 25.00 |

— *Reissue with extra track*

WARNER BROS.

| BS2813 | Tasty | 1974 | 30.00 |

GOOD TIMES, THE

KAMA SUTRA

| KLP-8052 [M] | The Good Times | 1966 | 18.00 |
| KSLP-8052 [S] | The Good Times | 1966 | 25.00 |

GOODEES, THE

HIP

| HIS-7002 | Candy Coated Goodees | 1969 | 30.00 |

GOODMAN, BENNY

ABC

| AC-30014 | The ABC Collection | 1976 | 15.00 |

AIRCHECK

| 16 | Benny Goodman and His Orchestra | 197? | 15.00 |
| 16 | Benny Goodman and His Orchestra On the Air, Vol. 1 | 1986 | 12.00 |

— *Reissue of above with revised title*

| 32 | Benny Goodman and His Orchestra On the Air, Vol. 2 | 1986 | 12.00 |
| 34 | Benny Goodman and His Orchestra On the Air, Vol. 3 | 1986 | 12.00 |

BIOGRAPH

| C-1 | Great Soloists 1929-33 | 1972 | 12.00 |

BLUEBIRD

AXM2-5505	The Complete Benny Goodman, Vol. 1 (1935)	197?	15.00
AXM2-5515	The Complete Benny Goodman, Vol. 2 (1935-36)	197?	15.00
AXM2-5532	The Complete Benny Goodman, Vol. 3 (1936)	197?	15.00
AXM2-5537	The Complete Benny Goodman, Vol. 4 (1936-37)	197?	15.00
AXM2-5557	The Complete Benny Goodman, Vol. 5 (1937-38)	197?	15.00
AXM2-5566	The Complete Benny Goodman, Vol. 6 (1938)	197?	15.00
AXM2-5567	The Complete Benny Goodman, Vol. 7 (1938-39)	197?	15.00
AXM2-5568	The Complete Benny Goodman, Vol. 8 (1936-39)	197?	15.00

BRUNSWICK

| BL54010 [M] | Benny Goodman 1927-34 | 1954 | 30.00 |
| BL58015 [10] | Chicago Jazz Classics | 1950 | 50.00 |

CAPITOL

| T669 [M] | Benny Goodman Combos | 1956 | 30.00 |

— *Turquoise label*

| T669 [M] | Benny Goodman Combos | 1958 | 25.00 |

— *Black label with colorband, Capitol logo on left*

| W565 [M] | B.G. in Hi-Fi | 1955 | 40.00 |

— *Gray label*

| W565 [M] | B.G. in Hi-Fi | 1958 | 25.00 |

— *Black label with colorband, Capitol logo on left*

H1-565 [10]	B.G. in Hi-Fi (Volume 1)	1955	30.00
H2-565 [10]	B.G. in Hi-Fi (Volume 2)	1955	30.00
H295 [10]	Easy Does It	1952	50.00
T2157 [M]	Hello Benny!	1964	15.00
ST2157 [S]	Hello Benny!	1964	18.00
T2282 [M]	Made in Japan	1965	15.00
ST2282 [S]	Made in Japan	1965	18.00
T668 [M]	Mostly Sextets	1956	30.00

— *Turquoise label*

| T668 [M] | Mostly Sextets | 1958 | 25.00 |

— *Black label with colorband, Capitol logo on left*

| S706 [M] | Selections Featured in "The Benny Goodman Story | 1956 | 30.00 |

— *Turquoise label*

| S706 [M] | Selections Featured in "The Benny Goodman Story | 1958 | 25.00 |

— *Black label with colorband, Capitol logo on left*

| SM-706 | Selections Featured in "The Benny Goodman Story | 197? | 12.00 |

— *Reissue of S 706*

| H202 [10] | Session for Six | 1950 | 50.00 |
| T395 [10] | Session for Six | 1953 | 40.00 |

— *Turquoise label*

| T395 [M] | Session for Six | 1958 | 25.00 |

— *Black label with colorband, Capitol logo on left*

H479 [10]	Small Combo 1947	1954	50.00
H409 [10]	The Benny Goodman Band	1953	50.00
T409 [M]	The Benny Goodman Band	1953	40.00

— *Turquoise label*

| T409 [M] | The Benny Goodman Band | 1958 | 25.00 |

— *Black label with colorband, Capitol logo on left*

H343 [10]	The Benny Goodman Trio	1952	50.00
H441 [10]	The Goodman Touch	1953	50.00
T441 [M]	The Goodman Touch	1953	40.00

— *Turquoise label*

| T441 [M] | The Goodman Touch | 1958 | 25.00 |

— *Black label with colorband, Capitol logo on left*

| T1514 [M] | The Hits of Benny Goodman | 1961 | 25.00 |

— *Black label with colorband, Capitol logo on left*

| T1514 [M] | The Hits of Benny Goodman | 1963 | 18.00 |

— *Black label with colorband, Capitol logo on top*

| DT1514 [R] | The Hits of Benny Goodman | 1961 | 15.00 |
| SM-1514 | The Hits of Benny Goodman | 197? | 12.00 |

— *Reissue of DT 1514*

CBS MASTERWORKS

| OSL160 [M] | The Famous 1938 Carnegie Hall Jazz Concert | 198? | 18.00 |

— *Late reissue; grayish labels with "CBS Masterworks" circling the edge*

CENTURY

| 1150 | The King of Swing Direct to Disc | 1979 | 30.00 |

— *Direct-to-disc audiophile recording*

CHESS

| LP-1440 [DJ] | Benny Rides Again | 1960 | 100.00 |

— *Multi-color swirl vinyl*

LP-1440 [M]	Benny Rides Again	1960	50.00
LPS-1440 [S]	Benny Rides Again	1960	30.00
CH-9161	Benny Rides Again	1984	12.00

— *Reissue*

CLASSICS RECORD LIBRARY

| RL-7673 [M] | An Album of Swing Classics | 1967 | 50.00 |
| SRL-7673 [S] | An Album of Swing Classics | 1967 | 40.00 |

— *Above two were compiled for Book-of-the-Month Club*

COLUMBIA

| CL2533 [10] | Benny at the Ballroom | 1955 | 40.00 |

— *Retitled reissue of 6100*

| CL534 [M] | Benny Goodman and His Orchestra | 1953 | 40.00 |

— *Maroon label with gold print*

| CL534 [M] | Benny Goodman and His Orchestra | 1955 | 30.00 |

— *Red and black label with six "eye" logos*

| CL6033 [10] | Benny Goodman and Peggy Lee | 1949 | 80.00 |
| CL523 [M] | Benny Goodman Presents Eddie Sauter Arrangements | 1953 | 40.00 |

— *Maroon label with gold print*

| CL523 [M] | Benny Goodman Presents Eddie Sauter Arrangements | 1955 | 30.00 |

— *Red and black label with six "eye" logos*

| GL523 [M] | Benny Goodman Presents Eddie Sauter Arrangements | 1953 | 50.00 |

— *Black label, silver print*

| CL524 [M] | Benny Goodman Presents Fletcher Henderson Arrangements | 1954 | 40.00 |

— *Maroon label with gold print*

| CL524 [M] | Benny Goodman Presents Fletcher Henderson Arrangements | 1953 | 30.00 |

— *Red and black label with six "eye" logos*

| GL524 [M] | Benny Goodman Presents Fletcher Henderson Arrangements | 1953 | 50.00 |

— *Black label, silver print*

| CL2483 [M] | Benny Goodman's Greatest Hits | 1966 | 18.00 |
| CS9283 [S] | Benny Goodman's Greatest Hits | 1966 | 15.00 |

— *360 Sound Stereo" on label*

| PC9283 | Benny Goodman's Greatest Hits | 198? | 10.00 |

— *Reissue*

CL1579 [M]	Benny Goodman Swings Again	1960	30.00
CS8379 [S]	Benny Goodman Swings Again	1960	30.00
C2L16 [M]	Benny in Brussels	195?	40.00

— *Red and black label with six white "eye" logos*

CL1247 [M]	Benny in Brussels, Vol. I	1958	30.00
CS8075 [S]	Benny in Brussels, Vol. I	1959	40.00
CL1248 [M]	Benny in Brussels, Vol. II	1958	30.00
CS8076 [S]	Benny in Brussels, Vol. II	1959	40.00
CL814 [M]	Carnegie Hall Jazz Concert, Volume 1	1956	30.00

— *Red and black label with six "eye" logos*

| CL814 [M] | Carnegie Hall Jazz Concert, Volume 1 | 1963 | 25.00 |

— *Red label with "Guaranteed High Fidelity" or "Mono" at bottom*

| CL815 [M] | Carnegie Hall Jazz Concert, Volume 2 | 1956 | 30.00 |

— *Red and black label with six "eye" logos*

| CL815 [M] | Carnegie Hall Jazz Concert, Volume 2 | 1963 | 25.00 |

— *Red label with "Guaranteed High Fidelity" or "Mono" at bottom*

| CL815 [M] | Carnegie Hall Jazz Concert, Volume 2 | 197? | 15.00 |

— *Orange label with "Mono" under "CL 815" at left*

| CL816 [M] | Carnegie Hall Jazz Concert, Volume 3 | 1956 | 30.00 |

— *Red and black label with six "eye" logos*

| CL816 [M] | Carnegie Hall Jazz Concert, Volume 3 | 1963 | 25.00 |

— *Red label with "Guaranteed High Fidelity" or "Mono" at bottom*

| CL500 [M] | Combos | 1952 | 40.00 |

— *Maroon label with gold print*

| CL500 [M] | Combos | 1955 | 30.00 |

— *Red and black label with six "eye" logos*

| GL500 [M] | Combos | 1951 | 50.00 |

— *Black label, silver print*

CL6048 [10]	Dance Parade	1949	50.00
CL6100 [10]	Dance Parade, Volume 2	1950	50.00
CL6052 [10]	Goodman Sextet Session	1949	50.00
GL102 [10]	Let's Hear the Melody	1950	60.00
CL6302 [10]	Let's Hear the Melody	1951	50.00

— *Reissue of GL 102*

FC38265	Seven Come Eleven	1983	12.00
PG33405	Solid Gold Instrumental Hits	1975	15.00
XTV28995/6 [M]	Swing Into Spring	1959	25.00

— *Special item made for Texaco service stations*

| KG31547 | The All-Time Greatest Hits of Benny Goodman | 1972 | 18.00 |
| PG31547 | The All-Time Greatest Hits of Benny Goodman | 197? | 15.00 |

— *Reissue*

| CL652 [M] | The Benny Goodman Sextet and Orchestra with Charlie Christian | 1955 | 30.00 |

— *Red and black label with six "eye" logos*

| CL652 [M] | The Benny Goodman Sextet and Orchestra with Charlie Christian | 1963 | 25.00 |

— *Red label with "Guaranteed High Fidelity" or "Mono" at bottom*

| CL516 [M] | The Benny Goodman Trio Plays for the Fletcher Henderson Fund | 1953 | 40.00 |

— *Maroon label with gold print*

| CL516 [M] | The Benny Goodman Trio Plays for the Fletcher Henderson Fund | 1955 | 30.00 |

— *Red and black label with six "eye" logos*

| GL516 [M] | The Benny Goodman Trio Plays for the Fletcher Henderson Fund | 1952 | 50.00 |

— *Reissue of Martin Block 1000; black label, silver print*

| CL2564 [10] | The B.G. Six | 1955 | 40.00 |

— *Retitled reissue of 6052*

| CL501 [M] | The Golden Era Series Presents Benny Goodman and His Orchestra | 1952 | 40.00 |

— *Maroon label with gold print*

| CL501 [M] | The Golden Era Series Presents Benny Goodman and His Orchestra | 1955 | 30.00 |

— *Red and black label with six "eye" logos*

| GL501 [M] | The Golden Era Series Presents Benny Goodman and His Orchestra | 1951 | 50.00 |

— *Black label, silver print*

| CL820 [M] | The Great Benny Goodman | 1956 | 30.00 |

— *Red and black label with six "eye" logos*

| CL820 [M] | The Great Benny Goodman | 1963 | 25.00 |

— *Red label with "Guaranteed High Fidelity" or "Mono" at bottom*

| CS8643 [R] | The Great Benny Goodman | 1962 | 15.00 |

— *Red label, "360 Sound Stereo" at bottom*

| PC8643 | The Great Benny Goodman | 198? | 10.00 |

— *Reissue*

| CS8643 [R] | The Great Benny Goodman | 1970 | 12.00 |

— *Orange label*

CL1324 [M]	The Happy Session	1959	30.00
CS8129 [S]	The Happy Session	1959	30.00
CL817 [M]	The King of Swing, Volume 1	1956	30.00
CL818 [M]	The King of Swing, Volume 2	1956	30.00
CL819 [M]	The King of Swing, Volume 3	1956	30.00
CL552 [M]	The New Benny Goodman Sextet	1954	40.00

— *Maroon label with gold print*

| CL552 [M] | The New Benny Goodman Sextet | 1955 | 30.00 |

— *Red and black label with six "eye" logos*

| CL821 [M] | Vintage Goodman | 1956 | 30.00 |

COLUMBIA JAZZ MASTERPIECES

| CJ44292 | Slipped Disc, 1945-1946 | 1988 | 12.00 |

COLUMBIA MASTERWORKS

SL180 [M]	1937-38 Jazz Concert No. 2	1950	75.00
ML4590 [M]	1937-38 Jazz Concert No. 2, Volume 1	1950	40.00
ML4591 [M]	1937-38 Jazz Concert No. 2, Volume 2	1950	40.00
ML4358 [M]	Carnegie Hall Jazz Concert, Volume 1	1950	40.00
ML4359 [M]	Carnegie Hall Jazz Concert, Volume 2	1950	40.00
SL176 [M]	King of Swing	1950	150.00
ML4613 [M]	King of Swing, Volume 1	1950	40.00
ML4614 [M]	King of Swing, Volume 2	1950	40.00
ML6205 [M]	Meeting at the Summit	1961	18.00

— *With the Columbia Jazz Combo and the Columbia Orchestra*

| MS6805 [S] | Meeting at the Summit | 1961 | 25.00 |

— *With the Columbia Jazz Combo and the Columbia Orchestra*

| SL160 [M] | The Famous 1938 Carnegie Hall Jazz Concert | 1950 | 100.00 |

— *Green labels*

| OSL160 [M] | The Famous 1938 Carnegie Hall Jazz Concert | 1963 | 40.00 |

Number	Title	Yr	NM
—Gray labels with "Columbia" at top			
❑ OSL160 [M]	The Famous 1938 Carnegie Hall Jazz Concert	1956	75.00
—Gray and black labels with six "eye" logos			
❑ OSL160 [M]	The Famous 1938 Carnegie Hall Jazz Concert	1970	25.00
—Olive labels with "Columbia" circling edge			
❑ OSL180 [M]	The King of Swing	1956	75.00
—Gray and black labels with six "eye" logos			
❑ OSL180 [M]	The King of Swing	1963	40.00
—Gray labels with "Columbia" at top			

COLUMBIA MUSICAL TREASURY

Number	Title	Yr	NM
❑ P4M5678	The Best of Benny Goodman	197?	30.00
—Issued by Columbia House			

COMMAND

Number	Title	Yr	NM
❑ RS-921	Benny Goodman & Paris: Listen to the Magic	1967	18.00

DECCA

Number	Title	Yr	NM
❑ DXB188 [M]	The Benny Goodman Story	1956	60.00
—Black label, silver print			
❑ DXB188 [M]	The Benny Goodman Story	1961	40.00
—Black label with color bars			
❑ DXSB7188 [R]	The Benny Goodman Story	196?	18.00
❑ DL8252 [M]	The Benny Goodman Story, Volume 1	1956	30.00
—Black label, silver print			
❑ DL8252 [M]	The Benny Goodman Story, Volume 1	1961	25.00
—Black label with color bars			
❑ DL78252 [R]	The Benny Goodman Story, Volume 1	1961	12.00
❑ DL8253 [M]	The Benny Goodman Story, Volume 2	1956	30.00
—Black label, silver print			
❑ DL8253 [M]	The Benny Goodman Story, Volume 2	1961	25.00
—Black label with color bars			
❑ DL78253 [R]	The Benny Goodman Story, Volume 2	1961	12.00

DOCTOR JAZZ

Number	Title	Yr	NM
❑ W2X40350	Airplay	1986	15.00

EVEREST ARCHIVE OF FOLK & JAZZ

Number	Title	Yr	NM
❑ 277	Benny Goodman	1973	15.00

GIANTS OF JAZZ

Number	Title	Yr	NM
❑ 1030	The Benny Goodman Caravans -- Big Band Broadcasts Vol. 1: Ciribiribin	1983	12.00
❑ 1033	The Benny Goodman Caravans -- Big Band Broadcasts Vol. 2: Swingin' Down the Lane	1985	12.00
❑ 1036	The Benny Goodman Caravans -- Big Band Broadcasts Vol. 3: One O'Clock Jump	1985	12.00
❑ 1039	The Benny Goodman Caravans -- Big Band Broadcasts Vol. 4: Sing, Sing, Sing	1985	12.00
❑ 1034	The Benny Goodman Caravans -- The Small Groups, Vol. 1	1985	12.00

HARMONY

Number	Title	Yr	NM
❑ HL7005 [M]	Peggy Lee Sings with Benny Goodman	1957	25.00
❑ HS11271 [R]	Sing, Sing, Sing	1968	12.00
❑ HL7278 [M]	Swingin' Benny Goodman Sextet	196?	18.00
❑ HL7225 [M]	Swing Time	196?	18.00
❑ HL7190 [M]	Swing with Benny Goodman in High Fidelity	196?	18.00
❑ HS11090 [R]	Swing with Benny Goodman in High Fidelity	196?	12.00

INTERMEDIA

Number	Title	Yr	NM
❑ QS-5046	All the Cats Join In	198?	12.00

LONDON

Number	Title	Yr	NM
❑ PS918/9	Live at Carnegie Hall 1978	1979	18.00

LONDON PHASE 4

Number	Title	Yr	NM
❑ SP-44182/83	Benny Goodman On Stage	1972	18.00
❑ SPB-21	Benny Goodman Today	1971	18.00

MARTIN BLOCK

Number	Title	Yr	NM
❑ MB-1000 [M]	The Benny Goodman Trio Plays for the Fletcher Henderson Fund	1951	60.00

MCA

Number	Title	Yr	NM
❑ 4018	Jazz Holiday	197?	15.00

MEGA

Number	Title	Yr	NM
❑ 51-5002	Let's Dance Again	1971	15.00
❑ 606	Let's Dance Again	1974	12.00
—Reissue of 51-5002			

MGM

Number	Title	Yr	NM
❑ E-3788 [M]	Performance Recordings, Volume 1	1959	30.00
❑ E-3789 [M]	Performance Recordings, Volume 2	1959	30.00
❑ E-3790 [M]	Performance Recordings, Volume 3	1959	30.00
❑ 3E-9 [M]	The Benny Goodman Treasure Chest	1959	150.00
❑ E-3788 [M]	The Benny Goodman Treasure Chest, Volume 1	198?	10.00
—Reissue on blue and gold label			
❑ E-3789 [M]	The Benny Goodman Treasure Chest, Volume 2	198?	10.00
—Reissue on blue and gold label			
❑ E-3790 [M]	The Benny Goodman Treasure Chest, Volume 3	198?	10.00
—Reissue on blue and gold label			
❑ E-3810 [M]	The Sound of Music	1960	25.00
❑ SE-3810 [S]	The Sound of Music	1960	30.00

MOSAIC

Number	Title	Yr	NM
❑ MQ6-148	The Complete Capitol Small Group Recordings of Benny Goodman 1944-1955	199?	100.00

MUSICMASTERS

Number	Title	Yr	NM
❑ MM-20112Z	Let's Dance	1986	12.00
—From the PBS TV special of 1985			

PAIR

Number	Title	Yr	NM
❑ PDL2-1014	Original Recordings by Benny Goodman	1986	15.00
❑ PDL2-1054	Original Recordings by Benny Goodman, Volume 2	1986	15.00
❑ PDL2-1093	Original Recordings by Benny Goodman, Volume 3	1986	15.00

PAUSA

Number	Title	Yr	NM
❑ 9031	The Benny Goodman Trios (and One Duet)	198?	12.00

PICKWICK

Number	Title	Yr	NM
❑ SPC-3529	Francaise	197?	12.00
❑ SPC-3270	Let's Dance	197?	12.00

PRESTIGE

Number	Title	Yr	NM
❑ PRST-7644	Benny Goodman and the Giants of Swing	1969	18.00

RCA CAMDEN

Number	Title	Yr	NM
❑ CAL-872 [M]	Benny Goodman and His Orchestra Featuring Great Vocalists of Our Times	1965	18.00
❑ CAS-872 [S]	Benny Goodman and His Orchestra Featuring Great Vocalists of Our Times	1965	15.00
❑ CAL-624 [M]	Swing, Swing, Swing	1960	18.00
❑ CAS-624(e) [R]	Swing, Swing, Swing	1960	12.00

RCA VICTOR

Number	Title	Yr	NM
❑ CPL1-2470	A Legendary Performer	1977	12.00
❑ LPT-17 [10]	A Treasury of Immortal Performances	1951	50.00
❑ WPT12 [10]	Benny Goodman	1951	50.00
❑ LPT-1005 [M]	Benny Goodman	1954	40.00
❑ LOC-6008 [M]	Benny Goodman In Moscow	1962	25.00
❑ LSO-6008 [S]	Benny Goodman In Moscow	1962	30.00
❑ LPT-3004 [10]	Benny Goodman Quartet	1952	50.00
❑ LPV-521 [M]	B.G. The Small Groups	1965	18.00
❑ WPT26 [10]	Immortal Performances	1952	50.00
❑ ANL1-0973(e)	Pure Gold	1974	12.00
—Reissue of LSP-4005(e)			
❑ LPM-1226 [M]	The Benny Goodman Trio/Quartet/Quintet	1956	40.00
❑ LSP-4005(e)	The Best of Benny Goodman	1968	18.00
❑ AFL1-4005(e)	The Best of Benny Goodman	1977	12.00
—Reissue of LSP-4005			
❑ LPM-1099 [M]	The Golden Age of Benny Goodman	1956	40.00
❑ LPT-6703 [M]	The Golden Age of Swing	1956	600.00
—Five-record set in white vinyl binder with bound-in booklet			
❑ LPM-2247 [M]	The Kingdom of Swing	1960	25.00
❑ LSP-2247 [S]	The Kingdom of Swing	1960	30.00
❑ LPM-1239 [M]	This Is Benny Goodman	1956	40.00
❑ VPM-6040 [PS]	This Is Benny Goodman	1971	18.00
❑ VPM-6063	This Is Benny Goodman, Vol. 2	1972	18.00
❑ LPT-3056 [10]	This Is Benny Goodman and His Orchestra	1954	50.00
❑ LPM-2698 [M]	Together Again	1964	18.00
❑ LSP-2698 [S]	Together Again	1964	25.00

SUNBEAM

Number	Title	Yr	NM
❑ 126	At the Madhattan Room Dec. 18, 1937	197?	15.00
❑ 123	At the Madhattan Room Nov. 4, 1937	197?	15.00
❑ 116	At the Madhattan Room Oct. 13, 1937	197?	15.00
❑ 117	At the Madhattan Room Oct. 16, 1937	197?	15.00
❑ 118	At the Madhattan Room Oct. 20, 1937	197?	15.00
❑ 133	Benny Goodman 1933	197?	12.00
❑ 148	Benny Goodman 1934	197?	12.00
❑ 158	Benny Goodman 1941-42	1984	12.00
❑ 154	Benny Goodman 1946	197?	12.00
❑ 111	Benny Goodman Accompanies Girls 1931-33	197?	12.00
❑ 138	Benny Goodman and His Orchestra 1931-33, Volume 1	197?	12.00
❑ 139	Benny Goodman and His Orchestra 1931-33, Volume 2	197?	12.00
❑ 140	Benny Goodman and His Orchestra 1931-33, Volume 3	197?	12.00
❑ 152	Benny Goodman and His Orchestra 1937-38	197?	15.00
❑ 135	Benny Goodman and the Modernists 1934-35	197?	12.00
❑ 106	Benny Goodman In a Mellotone Manner 1930-31	197?	12.00
❑ 105	Benny Goodman On the Air 1935-36, Volume 1	197?	12.00
❑ 153	Benny Goodman On the Air 1935-36, Volume 2	197?	12.00
❑ 107	Benny Goodman On the Side 1929-31	197?	12.00
❑ 142	Benny Goodman On V-Disc 1939-48, Volume 1	197?	12.00
❑ 143	Benny Goodman On V-Disc 1939-48, Volume 2	197?	12.00
❑ 144	Benny Goodman On V-Disc 1939-48, Volume 3	197?	12.00
❑ 156	Broadcasts from Hollywood 1946-47	197?	12.00
❑ 146	Camel Caravan 1937, Volume 1	197?	12.00
❑ 147	Camel Caravan 1937, Volume 2	197?	12.00
❑ 145	Fitch Bandwagon 1945	197?	12.00
❑ 128/32	From the Congress Hotel, Chicago, 1935-36	197?	30.00
❑ 149	Jam Session 1935-37	197?	12.00
❑ 112	Rare Benny Goodman 1927-29	197?	12.00
❑ 141	The Benny Goodman Boys 1928-29	197?	12.00
❑ 151	The Benny Goodman Show 1946	197?	12.00
❑ 113	The Hotsy Totsy Gang 1928-29	197?	12.00
❑ 100	The Let's Dance Broadcasts 1934-35, Volume 1	197?	12.00
❑ 104	The Let's Dance Broadcasts 1934-35, Volume 2	197?	12.00
❑ 150	The Let's Dance Broadcasts 1934-35, Volume 3	197?	12.00
❑ 114	Whoopee Makers 1928-29	197?	12.00

TIME-LIFE

Number	Title	Yr	NM
❑ STBB-03	Big Bands: Benny Goodman	1983	18.00
❑ STBB-23	Big Bands: King of Swing	1986	18.00
❑ STL-J-05	Giants of Jazz	1979	25.00

VERVE

Number	Title	Yr	NM
❑ V-8582 [M]	The Essential Benny Goodman	1964	18.00
❑ V6-8582 [S]	The Essential Benny Goodman	1964	18.00

WESTINGHOUSE

Number	Title	Yr	NM
❑ XTV27713/4 [M]	Benny Goodman Plays World Favorites in High Fidelity	1958	30.00
—No number on cover or label; these numbers come from the trail-off wax			
❑ (no #)0 [M]	Benny in Brussels	1958	100.00

GOODMAN, BENNY/CHARLIE BARNET

CAPITOL

Number	Title	Yr	NM
❑ M-11061	BeBop Spoken Here	197?	15.00

GOODMAN, DICKIE

CASH

Number	Title	Yr	NM
❑ CR6000	Mr. Jaws and Other Fables	1975	30.00

COMET

Number	Title	Yr	NM
❑ 69	My Son, the Joke	1963	40.00

IX CHAINS

Number	Title	Yr	NM
❑ NCS9000	The Original Flying Saucers	1973	40.00

RHINO

Number	Title	Yr	NM
❑ RNLP-811	Dickie Goodman's Greatest Hits	1983	18.00

RORI

Number	Title	Yr	NM
❑ 3301	The Many Heads of Dickie Goodman	1962	80.00

GOODMAN, STEVE

ASYLUM

Number	Title	Yr	NM
❑ 6E-174	High and Outside	1979	15.00
❑ 6E-297	Hot Spot	1980	15.00
❑ 7E-1037	Jessie's Jig & Other Favorites	1975	15.00
❑ 7E-1118	Say It in Private	1977	15.00
❑ 7E-1061	Words We Can Dance To	1976	15.00

BUDDAH

Number	Title	Yr	NM
❑ BDS5121	Somebody Else's Troubles	1972	18.00
❑ BDS5096	Steve Goodman	1971	18.00
❑ BDS5665	The Essential Steve Goodman	1976	18.00

RED PAJAMAS

Number	Title	Yr	NM
❑ RPJ-002	Affordable Art	1983	15.00
❑ RPJ-001	Artistic Hair	1982	15.00
❑ RPJ-006	Best of the Asylum Years, Vol. 1	198?	15.00
❑ RPJ-007	Best of the Asylum Years, Vol. 2	198?	15.00
❑ RPJ-003	Santa Ana Winds	1984	15.00
❑ RPJ-005	Unfinished Business	1985	15.00

GOODWIN, RON

CAPITOL

Number	Title	Yr	NM
❑ T10078 [M]	It Can't Be Wrong	1957	25.00
❑ SP-10560	Jet Flight to Beirut	196?	25.00
❑ T10251 [M]	Music for an Arabian Night	1959	30.00
❑ ST10251 [S]	Music for an Arabian Night	1959	30.00
❑ T10188 [M]	Music in Orbit	1958	30.00
❑ ST10188 [S]	Music in Orbit	1958	40.00

Number	Title	Yr	NM
❑ ST-11012	Ron Goodwin Plays Someone Named Burt Bacharach	1972	12.00
❑ T10177 [M]	Swinging Sweethearts	1958	25.00

GOOSE CREEK SYMPHONY

CAPITOL

Number	Title	Yr	NM
❑ SM-444	Goose Creek Symphony	197?	12.00
— Reissue			
❑ ST-444	Goose Creek Symphony	1970	18.00
❑ ST-690 [B]	Welcome to Goose Creek	1971	18.00
❑ ST-11044	Words of Earnest	1972	18.00

COLUMBIA

Number	Title	Yr	NM
❑ KC32918	Do Your Thing But Don't Touch Mine	1974	15.00

GORDIAN KNOT, THE

VERVE

Number	Title	Yr	NM
❑ V-5062 [M]	Tones	1968	30.00
— White label promo only (no stock copies were issued in mono)			
❑ V6-5062 [S]	Tones	1968	18.00

GORDON, BARRY

CAPITOL

Number	Title	Yr	NM
❑ ST-805	Pieces of Time	1971	15.00

UNITED ARTISTS

Number	Title	Yr	NM
❑ UAL3491 [M]	Yes Sir, That's My Baby	1966	18.00
❑ UAS6491 [S]	Yes Sir, That's My Baby	1966	25.00

GORDON, BOB

PACIFIC JAZZ

Number	Title	Yr	NM
❑ PJLP-12 [10]	Meet Mr. Gordon	1954	200.00

TAMPA

Number	Title	Yr	NM
❑ TP-26 [M]	Jazz Impressions	1957	120.00
— Red vinyl			
❑ TP-26 [M]	Jazz Impressions	1958	60.00
— Black vinyl			

GORDON, BOBBY

DECCA

Number	Title	Yr	NM
❑ DL4726 [M]	The Lamp Is Low	1966	15.00
❑ DL74726 [S]	The Lamp Is Low	1966	18.00
❑ DL4394 [M]	Warm and Sentimental	1963	15.00
❑ DL74394 [S]	Warm and Sentimental	1963	18.00
❑ DL4507 [M]	Young Man's Fancy	1964	15.00
❑ DL74507 [S]	Young Man's Fancy	1964	18.00

GORDON, BOB/CLIFFORD BROWN

PACIFIC JAZZ

Number	Title	Yr	NM
❑ PJ-3 [M]	Jazz Immortal	1960	50.00
❑ PJ-1214 [M]	The Bob Gordon Quintet/ The Clifford Brown Ensemble	1956	100.00

GORDON, DEXTER

BASF

Number	Title	Yr	NM
❑ 20698	A Day in Copenhagen	197?	18.00

BETHLEHEM

Number	Title	Yr	NM
❑ BCP-36 [M]	Daddy Plays the Horn	1956	120.00
❑ BCP-6008	The Bethlehem Years	197?	15.00
— Reissue, distributed by RCA Victor			

BLACK LION

Number	Title	Yr	NM
❑ 108	The Montmartre Collection	197?	18.00

BLUE NOTE

Number	Title	Yr	NM
❑ BLP-4133 [M]	A Swingin' Affair	1963	120.00
— With "New York, USA" address on label			
❑ BST-84133 [S]	A Swingin' Affair	1963	150.00
— With "New York, USA" address on label			
❑ BST-84133 [S]	A Swingin' Affair	1967	40.00
— With "A Division of Liberty Records" on label			
❑ BST-84133	A Swingin' Affair	199?	30.00
— Classic Records 180-gram audiophile reissue			
❑ LT-989	Clubhouse	1980	15.00
❑ BLP-4083 [M]	Dexter Calling	1961	200.00
— With W. 63rd St. address on label			
❑ BLP-4083 [M]	Dexter Calling	1963	150.00
— With "New York, USA" address on label			
❑ BST-84083 [S]	Dexter Calling	1961	200.00
— With W. 63rd St. address on label			
❑ BST-84083 [S]	Dexter Calling	1963	150.00
— With "New York, USA" address on label			
❑ BST-84083 [S]	Dexter Calling	1967	40.00
— With "A Division of Liberty Records" on label			
❑ BN-LA393-H2	Dexter Gordon	1975	30.00
❑ BLP-4077 [M]	Doin' Allright	1961	250.00
— With W. 63rd St. addresss on label			
❑ BLP-4077 [M]	Doin' Allright	1963	150.00
— With "New York, USA" address on label			
❑ BST-84077 [S]	Doin' Allright	1961	300.00
— With W. 63rd St. addresss on label			
❑ BST-84077 [S]	Doin' Allright	1963	200.00
— With "New York, USA" address on label			
❑ BST-84077 [S]	Doin' Allright	1967	40.00
— With "A Division of Liberty Records" on label			
❑ BST-84077	Doin' Allright	1985	15.00
— The Finest in Jazz Since 1939" reissue			
❑ BST-84077 [S]	Doin' Allright	1970	30.00
— Mostly black label with "Liberty/UA" at bottom			
❑ BLP-4204 [M]	Gettin' Around	1965	80.00
— With "New York, USA" address on label			
❑ BST-84204 [S]	Gettin' Around	1965	80.00
— With "New York, USA" address on label			
❑ BST-84204 [S]	Gettin' Around	1967	30.00
— With "A Division of Liberty Records" on label			
❑ BLP-4112 [M]	Go	1962	150.00
— With "New York, USA" address on label			
❑ BST-84112 [S]	Go	1962	120.00
— With "New York, USA" address on label			
❑ BST-84112 [S]	Go	1967	40.00
— With "A Division of Liberty Records" on label			
❑ BST-84112 [B]	Go	1985	15.00
— The Finest in Jazz Since 1939" reissue			
❑ LT-1051	Landslide	1980	15.00
❑ BABB-85112	Nights at the Keystone	198?	15.00
❑ BLP-4176 [M]	One Flight Up	1964	80.00
— With "New York, USA" address on label			
❑ BST-84176 [S]	One Flight Up	1964	80.00
— With "New York, USA" address on label			
❑ BST-84176 [S]	One Flight Up	1967	30.00
— With "A Division of Liberty Records" on label			
❑ BST-84176	One Flight Up	1986	15.00
— The Finest in Jazz Since 1939" reissue			
❑ BLP-4146 [M]	Our Man in Paris	1963	80.00
— With "New York, USA" address on label			
❑ BST-84146 [S]	Our Man in Paris	1963	100.00
— With "New York, USA" address on label			
❑ BST-84146 [S]	Our Man in Paris	1967	30.00
— With "A Division of Liberty Records" on label			
❑ BST-84146	Our Man in Paris	1987	15.00
— The Finest in Jazz Since 1939" reissue			
❑ B1-91139	The Best of Dexter Gordon	1988	15.00
❑ BT-85135	The Other Side of 'Round Midnight	1986	15.00

BOPLICITY

Number	Title	Yr	NM
❑ BOP-6	Dexter Blows Hot and Cool	198?	12.00

COLUMBIA

Number	Title	Yr	NM
❑ JC36853	Gotham City	1981	12.00
❑ JC36853	Gotham City	2000	15.00
— 180-gram reissue			
❑ JC35987	Great Encounters	1979	12.00
❑ PG34650	Homecoming	1977	18.00
❑ JC35608	Manhattan Symphonie	1978	15.00
❑ PC35608	Manhattan Symphonie	198?	10.00
— Budget-line reissue			
❑ JC34989	Sophisticated Giant	1977	15.00
❑ JC36356	The Best of Dexter Gordon	1979	12.00

DIAL

Number	Title	Yr	NM
❑ LP-204 [10]	Dexter Gordon Quintet	1950	400.00

DISCOVERY

Number	Title	Yr	NM
❑ 79005	American Classic	1995	18.00

DOOTO

Number	Title	Yr	NM
❑ DL-207 [M]	Dexter Blows Hot and Cool	196?	400.00
— Maroon label with "Dooto			

DOOTONE

Number	Title	Yr	NM
❑ DL-207 [M]	Dexter Blows Hot and Cool	1956	2000.00
— Red vinyl			
❑ DL-207 [M]	Dexter Blows Hot and Cool	1957	1200.00
— Black vinyl; "Dootone" label with no zip code			
❑ DL-207 [M]	Dexter Blows Hot and Cool	197?	100.00
— Maroon label with zip code			

ELEKTRA/MUSICIAN

Number	Title	Yr	NM
❑ 60126	American Classic	1983	12.00

FANTASY

Number	Title	Yr	NM
❑ OJC-299	Tower of Power	198?	12.00

INNER CITY

Number	Title	Yr	NM
❑ IC-2080	Biting the Apple	1977	15.00
❑ IC-2060	Bouncin'	197?	18.00
❑ IC-2030	More Than You Know	197?	18.00
❑ IC-2040	Stable Mable	1975	18.00
❑ IC-2050	Swiss Nights	1975	18.00
❑ IC-2025	The Apartment	197?	18.00
❑ IC-2006	The Meeting	1973	18.00
❑ IC-2020	The Source	1973	18.00

JAZZLAND

Number	Title	Yr	NM
❑ JLP-29 [M]	The Resurgence of Dexter Gordon	1960	50.00
❑ JLP-929 [S]	The Resurgence of Dexter Gordon	1960	60.00

JAZZ MAN

Number	Title	Yr	NM
❑ 5023	Dexter Gordon at Montmartre	198?	12.00

PAUSA

Number	Title	Yr	NM
❑ 7058	A Day in Copenhagen	1980	12.00

PRESTIGE

Number	Title	Yr	NM
❑ PRST-7763	A Day in Copenhagen	1970	25.00
❑ 10079	Blues A La Suisse	1973	18.00
❑ 10051	Ca' Purange	197?	18.00
❑ 10069	Generation	197?	18.00
❑ 10020	Jumpin' Blues	197?	18.00
❑ PRST-7680	More Power	1969	25.00
❑ PRST-7829	Panther!	1971	25.00
❑ 2511	Resurgence	198?	12.00
❑ 10091	Tangerine	197?	18.00
❑ 2502	The Ballad Album	198?	12.00
❑ PRST-7623	The Tower of Power	1969	25.00

SAVOY

Number	Title	Yr	NM
❑ MG-9003 [10]	All Star Series -- Dexter Gordon	1951	250.00
❑ MG-12130 [M]	Dexter Rides Again	1958	100.00
❑ MG-9016 [10]	New Trends in Modern Jazz, Volume 3	1952	250.00

SAVOY JAZZ

Number	Title	Yr	NM
❑ SJC-407	Jazz Concert, West Coast	1985	12.00
❑ SJL-2211	Long Tall Dexter	197?	18.00
❑ SJL-1154	Master Takes: The Savoy Recordings	198?	12.00
❑ SJL-2222	The Hunt	197?	18.00

STEEPLECHASE

Number	Title	Yr	NM
❑ SCC-6028	Billie's Bounce	198?	15.00
❑ SCC-1080	Biting the Apple	198?	12.00
❑ SCS-1060	Bouncin'	198?	12.00
❑ SCC-6008	Cheese Cake	198?	15.00
❑ SCC-6004	Cry Me a River	198?	15.00
❑ SCC-6022	It's You or No One	198?	15.00
❑ SCC-6015	I Want More	198?	15.00
❑ SCS-1156	Lullaby for a Monster	198?	12.00
❑ SCS-1030	More Than You Know	198?	12.00
❑ SCS-1136	Something Different	1980	15.00
❑ SCS-1040	Stable Mable	198?	12.00
❑ SCS-1145	Strings & Things	198?	15.00
❑ SCS-1050	Swiss Nights, Volume 1	198?	18.00
❑ SCS-1090	Swiss Nights, Volume 2	198?	12.00
❑ SCS-1110	Swiss Nights, Volume 3	198?	12.00
❑ SCS-1025	The Apartment	198?	12.00
❑ SCS-1206	The Shadow of Your Smile	198?	15.00

WHO'S WHO IN JAZZ

Number	Title	Yr	NM
❑ 21011	Who's Who Presents Dexter Gordon and Lionel Hampton	1977	15.00

GORDON, DEXTER/HOWARD MCGHEE

JAZZTONE

Number	Title	Yr	NM
❑ J-1235 [M]	The Chase	1956	40.00

GORDON, HONI

PRESTIGE

Number	Title	Yr	NM
❑ PRLP-7230 [M]	Honi Gordon Sings	1962	40.00
❑ PRST-7230 [S]	Honi Gordon Sings	1962	50.00

GORDON, JOE

CONTEMPORARY

Number	Title	Yr	NM
❑ M-3597 [M]	Lookin' Good	1961	30.00
❑ S-7597 [S]	Lookin' Good	1961	40.00

EMARCY

Number	Title	Yr	NM
❑ MG-26046 [10]	Introducing Joe Gordon	1954	150.00
❑ MG-36025 [M]	Introducing Joe Gordon	1955	100.00

FANTASY

Number	Title	Yr	NM
❑ OJC-174	Lookin' Good	198?	12.00

TRIP

Number	Title	Yr	NM
❑ 5535	Introducing Joe Gordon	197?	12.00

GORDON, JOHN

STRATA-EAST

Number	Title	Yr	NM
❑ SES-19760	Step by Step	197?	25.00

GORDON, JON

GEMINI TAURUS

Number	Title	Yr	NM
❑ TRLP-827	Beginning and Endings	1989	15.00

GORDON, JUSTIN

DOT

Number	Title	Yr	NM
❑ DLP-3214 [M]	Justin Gordon Swings	1959	40.00

GORDON, KELLY

CAPITOL

Number	Title	Yr	NM
❑ ST-201	Defunked	1969	25.00

GORDON, ROBERT

PRIVATE STOCK

Number	Title	Yr	NM
❑ PS-7008 [B]	Fresh Fish Special	1978	16.00
❑ PS-2030 [B]	Robert Gordon with Link Wray	1977	25.00
— Formerly with Tuff Darts			

RCA VICTOR

Number	Title	Yr	NM
❑ AFL1-3773	Are You Gonna Be the One	1981	15.00
❑ AFL1-3523	Bad Boy	1980	15.00
❑ DJL1-3411 [DJ]	Essential Robert Gordon	1979	30.00
— Promo-only live album with tracks from Tuff Darts			
❑ DJL1-3411 [DJ]	Essential Robert Gordon	1979	30.00
— Promo-only live album with tracks from Tuff Darts			
❑ AFL1-3299	Fresh Fish Special	1979	15.00
— Reissue			
❑ AFL1-3296	Robert Gordon with Link Wray	1979	15.00
— Reissue			
❑ AFL1-3294	Rock Billy Boogie	1979	25.00
— Original pressing on white vinyl			
❑ AFL1-3294	Rock Billy Boogie	1979	15.00
❑ AFL1-4380	Too Fast to Live, Too Young to Die	1982	15.00

Number	Title	Yr	NM

GORDON 'N ROGERS' INTER-URBAN ELECTRIC A&E PIT CREW & RHYTHM BAND

CAPITOL
| ☐ STAO-276 | Bug In! | 1969 | 25.00 |

GORE, CHARLIE

AUDIO LAB
| ☐ AL-1526 [M] | The Country Gentleman | 1959 | 200.00 |

GORE, LESLEY

A&M
| ☐ SP-4564 | Love Me by Name | 1975 | 18.00 |

MERCURY
| ☐ MG21066 [M] | All About Love | 1966 | 30.00 |
| ☐ SR61066 [S] | All About Love | 1966 | 40.00 |
— Stereo version has a different cover and liner notes than the mono version
☐ MG20901 [M]	Boys, Boys, Boys	1964	30.00
☐ SR60901 [S]	Boys, Boys, Boys	1964	40.00
☐ MG21120 [M]	California Nights	1967	30.00
☐ SR61120 [S]	California Nights	1967	40.00
☐ MG20943 [M]	Girl Talk	1964	30.00
☐ SR60943 [S]	Girl Talk	1964	40.00
☐ SR61185	Golden Hits Vol. 2	1968	40.00
☐ MG20805 [M]	I'll Cry If I Want To	1963	30.00
— With no blurb for "It's My Party"
| ☐ MG20805 [M] | I'll Cry If I Want To | 1964 | 25.00 |
— With blurb for "It's My Party"
| ☐ SR60805 [S] | I'll Cry If I Want To | 1963 | 40.00 |
— With no blurb for "It's My Party"
| ☐ SR60805 [S] | I'll Cry If I Want To | 1964 | 30.00 |
— With blurb for "It's My Party"
| ☐ ML-8016 | I'll Cry If I Want To | 1980 | 12.00 |
— Reissue of 60805
☐ MG20849 [M]	Lesley Gore Sings of Mixed-Up Hearts	1963	30.00
☐ SR60849 [S]	Lesley Gore Sings of Mixed-Up Hearts	1963	40.00
☐ MG21042 [M]	My Town, My Guy & Me	1965	30.00
☐ SR61042 [S]	My Town, My Guy & Me	1965	40.00
☐ MG21024 [M]	The Golden Hits of Lesley Gore	1965	30.00
☐ SR61024 [S]	The Golden Hits of Lesley Gore	1965	40.00
— Originals have 12 tracks
| ☐ SR61024 [S] | The Golden Hits of Lesley Gore | 196? | 18.00 |
— Reissues have 10 tracks
| ☐ 810370-1 | The Golden Hits of Lesley Gore | 1983 | 12.00 |
— Reissue of 61024

MOWEST
| ☐ MW117L | Someplace Else Now | 1972 | 18.00 |

RHINO
| ☐ RNFP-71496 | The Lesley Gore Anthology (1963-1968) | 1986 | 18.00 |

WING
☐ SRW-16350	Girl Talk	1968	18.00
☐ SRW-16382	Love, Love, Love	1968	18.00
☐ PRW-2-119	The Sound of Young Love	1969	25.00

GORME, EYDIE

ABC-PARAMOUNT
☐ 150 [M]	Eydie Gorme	1957	30.00
☐ 218 [M]	Eydie Gorme Vamps the Roaring 20's	1958	30.00
☐ S-218 [S]	Eydie Gorme Vamps the Roaring 20's	196?	15.00
☐ 343 [M]	Eydie in Dixieland	1960	30.00
☐ S-343 [S]	Eydie in Dixieland	1960	30.00
☐ 246 [M]	Eydie in Love	1958	30.00
☐ S-246 [S]	Eydie in Love	196?	15.00
☐ 192 [M]	Eydie Swings the Blues	1957	30.00
☐ 273 [M]	Love Is a Season	1959	30.00
☐ S-273 [S]	Love Is a Season	1959	30.00
☐ 307 [M]	On Stage	1959	30.00
☐ S-307 [S]	On Stage	1959	30.00
☐ 254 [M]	Show Stoppers	1959	30.00
☐ S-254 [S]	Show Stoppers	1959	30.00
☐ 512 [M]	The Best of Romance, Ballads, Blues, Dixieland, Roaring 20's, Showstoppers	1965	18.00
☐ S-512 [S]	The Best of Romance, Ballads, Blues, Dixieland, Roaring 20's, Showstoppers	1965	25.00

COLUMBIA
☐ CL2203 [M]	Amor	1964	18.00
☐ CS9003 [S]	Amor	1964	25.00
☐ PC9003	Amor	198?	10.00
— Budget-line reissue
☐ CL2012 [M]	Blame It on the Bossa Nova	1963	18.00
☐ CS8812 [S]	Blame It on the Bossa Nova	1963	25.00
☐ CL2476 [M]	Don't Go to Strangers	1966	18.00
☐ CS9276 [S]	Don't Go to Strangers	1966	25.00
☐ CL2764 [M]	Eydie Gorme's Greatest Hits	1967	25.00
☐ CS9564 [S]	Eydie Gorme's Greatest Hits	1967	25.00
☐ PC9564	Eydie Gorme's Greatest Hits	198?	10.00
— Budget-line reissue
☐ CL2120 [M]	Gorme Country Style	1964	18.00
☐ CS8920 [S]	Gorme Country Style	1964	25.00
☐ CL2065 [M]	Let the Good Times Roll	1963	18.00
☐ CS8865 [S]	Let the Good Times Roll	1963	25.00
☐ CL2376 [M]	More Amor	1965	18.00
☐ CS9176 [S]	More Amor	1965	25.00
☐ CL2557 [M]	Navidad Means Christmas	1966	18.00
— With Trio Los Panchos
| ☐ CS9357 [S] | Navidad Means Christmas | 1966 | 25.00 |
— With Trio Los Panchos
☐ CL2594 [M]	Softly, As I Leave You	1967	18.00
☐ CS9394 [S]	Softly, As I Leave You	1967	25.00
☐ CS9652 [M]	The Look of Love	1968	30.00
— White label promo; "Special Mono Radio Station Copy" sticker on front of stereo jacket
☐ CS9652 [S]	The Look of Love	1968	18.00
☐ CL2300 [M]	The Sound of Music (And Other Broadway Hits)	1965	18.00
☐ CS9100 [S]	The Sound of Music (And Other Broadway Hits)	1965	25.00

CORAL
| ☐ CRL57109 [M] | Delight | 1957 | 40.00 |

HARMONY
| ☐ KH30319 | If He Walked Into My Life | 1971 | 12.00 |
| ☐ HS11361 | Yes Indeed! | 1970 | 12.00 |

MGM
| ☐ SE-4780 | It Was a Good Time | 1971 | 15.00 |

RCA VICTOR
| ☐ LSP-4093 | Eydie | 1968 | 15.00 |
| ☐ LSP-4303 | Tonight I'll Say a Prayer | 1970 | 15.00 |

UNITED ARTISTS
☐ UAL3143 [M]	Come Sing with Me	1961	25.00
☐ UAS6143 [S]	Come Sing with Me	1961	30.00
☐ UAL3152 [M]	I Feel So Spanish	1961	25.00
☐ UAS6152 [S]	I Feel So Spanish	1961	30.00
☐ UAL3189 [M]	The Very Best of Eydie	1962	25.00
☐ UAS6189 [S]	The Very Best of Eydie	1962	30.00

VOCALION
| ☐ VL3708 [M] | Here's Eydie Gorme | 196? | 18.00 |
| ☐ VL73708 [R] | Here's Eydie Gorme | 196? | 15.00 |

GORRILL, LIZ, AND ANDY FITE

NEW ARTISTS
| ☐ NA-1004 | Phantasmagoria | 1988 | 12.00 |

GORRILL, LIZ

JAZZ RECORDS
| ☐ JR-2 | I Feel Like I'm Home | 198? | 18.00 |
| ☐ JR 7 | True Fun | 198? | 15.00 |

GOSPEL STARS, THE

TAMLA
| ☐ M-222 [M] | The Great Gospel Stars | 1961 | 3000.00 |
— VG value 1000; VG+ value 2000

GOSSETT, LOU

B.T. PUPPY
| ☐ BTS-1013 | From Me to You | 1970 | 40.00 |

GOSSEZ, PIERRE

VANGUARD CARDINAL
| ☐ C-10061 | Bach Takes a Trip | 1969 | 25.00 |

GOULD, CHUCK

VIK
| ☐ LX-1123 [M] | Chuck Gould Plays A La Fletcher Henderson | 1957 | 50.00 |

GOULD, MORTON

COLUMBIA MASTERWORKS
| ☐ ML2065 [10] | Christmas Music for Orchestra | 1949 | 40.00 |

RCA VICTOR RED SEAL
| ☐ LSC-2217 [S] | Baton and Bows | 1959 | 30.00 |
— Original with "shaded dog" label
| ☐ LSC-2437 [S] | Bizet: Carmen for Orchestra | 1960 | 40.00 |
— Original with "shaded dog" label
| ☐ LSC-2104 [S] | Blues in the Night | 1958 | 30.00 |
— Original with "shaded dog" label
| ☐ LSC-2080 [S] | Brass and Percussion | 1958 | 25.00 |
— Original with "shaded dog" label
| ☐ LSC-2195 [S] | Copland: Billy the Kid; Rodeo | 1959 | 40.00 |
— Original with "shaded dog" label
| ☐ LSC-2195 [S] | Copland: Billy the Kid; Rodeo | 1964 | 30.00 |
— Second edition with "white dog" label
| ☐ LSC-2308 [S] | Doubling in Brass | 1959 | 50.00 |
— Original with "shaded dog" label
| ☐ LSC-2532 [S] | Fall River Legend | 1961 | 30.00 |
— Original with "shaded dog" label
| ☐ LSC-2559 [S] | Jerome Kern and Cole Porter Favorites | 1961 | 25.00 |
— Original with "shaded dog" label
| ☐ LSC-1994 [S] | Jungle Drums | 1958 | 30.00 |
— Original with "shaded dog" label
| ☐ LSC-2317 [S] | Living Strings | 1959 | 30.00 |
— Original with "shaded dog" label
| ☐ LSC-2232 [S] | Moon, Wind and Stars | 1959 | 25.00 |
— Original with "shaded dog" label
| ☐ LSC-2579 [S] | Piano Favorites | 1962 | 50.00 |
— Original with "shaded dog" label
| ☐ LSC-2686 [S] | Spirituals for Strings | 1962 | 30.00 |
— Original with "shaded dog" label
| ☐ LSC-2345 [S] | Tchaikovsky: 1812 Overture; Ravel: Bolero | 1960 | 25.00 |
— Original with "shaded dog" label
| ☐ LSC-2224 [S] | Where's the Melody? | 1959 | 25.00 |
— Original with "shaded dog" label

GOULDMAN, GRAHAM

RCA VICTOR
| ☐ LPM-3954 [M] | The Graham Gouldman Thing | 1968 | 100.00 |
| ☐ LSP-3954 [S] | The Graham Gouldman Thing | 1968 | 60.00 |

GOULET, ROBERT

COLUMBIA
☐ CL1676 [M]	Always You	1962	15.00
☐ CS8476 [S]	Always You	1962	18.00
☐ CL2342 [M]	Begin to Love	1965	15.00
☐ CS9142 [S]	Begin to Love	1965	18.00
☐ CS9763	Both Sides Now	1969	15.00
☐ CL2727 [M]	Hollywood Mon Amour (Great Songs from the Movies)	1967	18.00
☐ CS9527 [S]	Hollywood Mon Amour (Great Songs from the Movies)	1967	15.00
☐ CL2482 [M]	I Remember You	1966	15.00
☐ CS9282 [S]	I Remember You	1966	18.00
☐ CG30011	I Wish You Love	1970	18.00
☐ CS9096 [S]	My Love, Forgive Me	1964	18.00
☐ CL2296 [M]	My Love Forgive Me	1964	15.00
☐ CL2088 [M]	Robert Goulet in Person	1963	15.00
☐ CS8888 [S]	Robert Goulet in Person	1963	18.00
☐ CL2418 [M]	Robert Goulet on Broadway	1965	15.00
☐ CS9218 [S]	Robert Goulet on Broadway	1965	18.00
☐ CL2586 [M]	Robert Goulet on Broadway, Volume 2	1967	15.00
☐ CS9386 [S]	Robert Goulet on Broadway, Volume 2	1967	18.00
☐ CS9815	Robert Goulet's Greatest Hits	1969	15.00
☐ PC9815	Robert Goulet's Greatest Hits	197?	10.00
— Reissue with new prefix
☐ CS9734	Robert Goulet's Wonderful World of Christmas	1968	15.00
☐ CL1931 [M]	Sincerely Yours	1962	15.00
☐ CS8731 [S]	Sincerely Yours	1962	18.00
☐ CS9874	Souvenir d'Italie	1969	15.00
☐ CL2380 [M]	Summer Sounds	1965	15.00
☐ CS9180 [S]	Summer Sounds	1965	18.00
☐ CL1993 [M]	The Wonderful World of Love	1963	15.00
☐ CS8793 [S]	The Wonderful World of Love	1963	18.00
☐ CL2076 [M]	This Christmas I Spend with You	1963	15.00
☐ CS8876 [S]	This Christmas I Spend with You	1963	18.00
☐ C1051	Today's Greatest Hits	1970	15.00
☐ CS1051	Today's Greatest Hits	1970	15.00
☐ PC1051	Today's Greatest Hits	198?	10.00
— Budget-line reissue
☐ CL2541 [M]	Traveling On	1966	15.00
☐ CS9341 [S]	Traveling On	1966	18.00
☐ CL1826 [M]	Two of Us	1962	15.00
☐ CS8626 [S]	Two of Us	1962	18.00
☐ CL2200 [M]	Without You	1964	15.00
☐ CS9000 [S]	Without You	1964	18.00
☐ CS9695	Woman, Woman	1968	15.00

COLUMBIA SPECIAL PRODUCTS
| ☐ P13345 | Robert Goulet's Wonderful World of Christmas | 1976 | 15.00 |
— Same as CS 9734, but "Exclusively distributed by Sutton Distributors, Inc.

HARMONY
| ☐ KH31107 | Bridge Over Troubled Water | 1972 | 12.00 |
| ☐ KH30507 | Raindrops Keep Fallin' on My Head | 1971 | 12.00 |

MERLIN
| ☐ 2001 | I Never Did As I Was Told | 1971 | 15.00 |

GOWANS, BRAD

RCA VICTOR
| ☐ LJM-3000 [10] | Brad Gowans' New York Nine | 1954 | 50.00 |

GOYKOVICH, DUSKO

ENJA
| ☐ 2020 | After Hours | 197? | 15.00 |

GOZZO, CONRAD

RCA VICTOR
| ☐ LPM-1124 [M] | Goz the Great | 1955 | 50.00 |

GRAAS, JOHN

ANDEX
| ☐ A-3003 [M] | Premiere in Jazz | 1958 | 50.00 |
| ☐ AS-3003 [S] | Premiere in Jazz | 1959 | 40.00 |

Number	Title	Yr	NM
DECCA			
❑ DL8343 [M]	Jazz Lab 1	1956	50.00
❑ DL8478 [M]	Jazz Lab 2	1957	50.00
❑ DL8677 [M]	Jazzmantics	1958	50.00
❑ DL8079 [M]	Jazz Studio 2	1954	50.00
❑ DL8104 [M]	Jazz Studio 3	1955	50.00
EMARCY			
❑ MG-36117 [M]	Coup de Graas	1958	50.00
KAPP			
❑ KL-1046 [M]	French Horn Jazz	1957	50.00
MERCURY			
❑ SR-80020 [S]	Coup de Graas	1959	40.00
TREND			
❑ TL-1005 [10]	French Horn Jazz	1954	120.00

GRACEN, THELMA

Number	Title	Yr	NM
EMARCY			
❑ MG-36096 [M]	Thelma Gracen	1956	200.00
WING			
❑ MGW-60005 [M]	Thelma Gracen	1956	150.00

GRACIOUS

Number	Title	Yr	NM
CAPITOL			
❑ ST-602	Gracious	1970	40.00

GRADY, DON

Number	Title	Yr	NM
ELEKTRA			
❑ EKS-75057	Homegrown	1973	18.00
— As "Don Agrati			

GRAFFITI

Number	Title	Yr	NM
ABC			
❑ S-663	Graffiti	1968	60.00

GRAFFMAN, GARY

Number	Title	Yr	NM
RCA VICTOR RED SEAL			
❑ LSC-2396 [S]	Beethoven: Piano Concerto No. 3	1960	300.00
— Original with "shaded dog" label			
❑ LSC-2274 [S]	Brahms: Piano Concerto No. 1	1959	30.00
— With Charles Munch/Boston Symphony Orchestra; original with "shaded dog" label			
❑ LSC-2304 [S]	Chopin: Ballades	1959	25.00
— Original with "shaded dog" label			
❑ LSC-2468 [S]	Chopin: Concerto No. 1; Mendelssohn: Capriccio Brilliant	1961	100.00
— Original with "shaded dog" label			

GRAHAM, DAVY

Number	Title	Yr	NM
LONDON			
❑ PS552 [B]	Large As Life and Twice As Natural	1968	30.00

GRAHAM, ED

Number	Title	Yr	NM
M&K REALTIME			
❑ 106	Hot Stix	1980	40.00
— Direct-to-disc recording; plays at 45 rpm			

GRAMMER, BILLY

Number	Title	Yr	NM
DECCA			
❑ DL4642 [M]	Country Guitar	1965	15.00
❑ DL74642 [S]	Country Guitar	1965	18.00
❑ DL4460 [M]	Golden Gospel Favorites	1964	15.00
❑ DL74460 [S]	Golden Gospel Favorites	1964	18.00
❑ DL4212 [M]	Gospel Guitar	1962	18.00
❑ DL74212 [S]	Gospel Guitar	1962	25.00
❑ DL4542 [M]	Gotta Travel On	1965	15.00
❑ DL74542 [S]	Gotta Travel On	1965	18.00
EPIC			
❑ LN24233 [M]	Sunday Guitar	1967	18.00
❑ BN26233 [S]	Sunday Guitar	1967	18.00
MONUMENT			
❑ MLP-4000 [M]	Travelin' On	1959	40.00
❑ MLP-8039 [M]	Travelin' On	1965	30.00
❑ SLP-18039 [P]	Travelin' On	1965	30.00
VOCALION			
❑ VL73826	Favorites	1968	15.00

GRANATA, ROCCO

Number	Title	Yr	NM
LAURIE			
❑ LLP-2003 [M]	Marina and Other Italian Favorites	1960	30.00

GRAND DOMINION JAZZ BAND

Number	Title	Yr	NM
GHB			
❑ GHB-174	Grand Dominion Jazz Band	1984	12.00
STOMP OFF			
❑ SOS-1189	Ain't Nobody Got the Blues Like Me	1988	12.00
❑ SOS-1139	Don't Give Up the Ship	1987	12.00

GRAND FUNK RAILROAD

Number	Title	Yr	NM
CAPITOL			
❑ SO-11356	All the Girls in the World Beware!!!	1974	18.00
— With poster (deduct 33% if missing)			
❑ ST-11482	Born to Die	1976	12.00
❑ SABB-11445	Caught in the Act	1975	12.00
❑ SKAO-471	Closer to Home	1970	18.00
❑ SN-16176	Closer to Home	1981	10.00
❑ SW-853 [B]	E Pluribus Funk	1971	50.00
— Round cover designed like a coin; price reflects rarity in NM condition			
❑ SKAO-406	Grand Funk	1970	18.00
❑ SN-16177	Grand Funk	1981	10.00
❑ ST-11579	Grand Funk Hits	1976	12.00
❑ SN-16138	Grand Funk Hits	1981	10.00
❑ SWBB-633	Live Album	1970	18.00
— Includes poster			
❑ SABB-11042 [B]	Mark, Don and Mel 1969-71	1972	25.00
❑ ST-307 [B]	On Time	1969	30.00
❑ SN-16178	On Time	1981	10.00
❑ SMAS-11099	Phoenix	1972	15.00
❑ SWAE-11278	Shinin' On	1974	30.00
— With 3-D glasses attached to cover and with 3-D poster			
❑ SWAE-11278	Shinin' On	1974	10.00
— With 3-D glasses missing and no poster			
❑ SW-764	Survival	1971	18.00
— Lime-green label; add $5 if individual photos of the band members are included			
❑ SW-764 [B]	Survival	1971	18.00
— Red "target" label; add $5 if individual photos of the band members are included			
❑ SW-764	Survival	1973	12.00
— Orange label, "Capitol" at bottom			
❑ SMAS-11207	We're An American Band	1973	30.00
— Gold vinyl with sheet of four stickers			
❑ SMAS-11207	We're An American Band	1973	12.00
— Black vinyl			
❑ SMAS-11207	We're An American Band	1973	25.00
— Gold vinyl without sheet of four stickers			
❑ 21692	We're An American Band	1999	30.00
— Limited-edition reissue on 180-gram gold vinyl with original 1973 packaging			
FULL MOON			
❑ HS3625	Grand Funk Lives	1981	12.00
❑ 23750	What's Funk	1983	12.00
MCA			
❑ 2216	Good Singin' Good Playin'	1976	15.00
— Produced by Frank Zappa			

GRANDMA'S ROCKERS

Number	Title	Yr	NM
FREDLO			
❑ 6727	Homemade Apple Pie	1967	1500.00
— VG value 500; VG+ value 1000			

GRANDMASTER FLASH

Number	Title	Yr	NM
ELEKTRA			
❑ 60723	Ba-Dop-Boom-Bang	1987	12.00
❑ 60769	On the Strength	1988	15.00
❑ 60389	They Said It Couldn't Be Done	1985	15.00
SUGAR HILL			
❑ SH9121	Greatest Messages	1984	25.00
❑ SH268 [B]	The Message	1982	25.00
— Note: This album has been reissued to look like the original			

GRANT, AMY

Number	Title	Yr	NM
A&M			
❑ SP-5057	A Christmas Album	1985	12.00
— Reissue of Myrrh 6768			
❑ SP-5056	Age to Age	1985	10.00
— Reissue of Myrrh 6697			
❑ SP-5051	Amy Grant	1985	10.00
— Reissue of Myrrh 6586 with new cover			
❑ SP-5054	Amy Grant In Concert	1985	10.00
— Reissue of Myrrh 6668			
❑ SP-5055	Amy Grant In Concert, Volume Two	1985	10.00
— Reissue of Myrrh 6677			
❑ 7502153211	Heart in Motion	1991	18.00
❑ SP-5199	Lead Me On	1988	10.00
— Issued simultaneously with Myrrh 687106			
❑ SP-5052	My Father's Eyes	1985	10.00
— Reissue of Myrrh 6625			
❑ SP-5053	Never Alone	1985	10.00
— Reissue of Myrrh 6645			
❑ SP-5058	Straight Ahead	1985	10.00
— Reissue of Myrrh 675706			
❑ SP-3900	The Collection	1986	10.00
— Issued simultaneously with Myrrh 684306			
❑ SP-5060	Unguarded	1985	10.00
— Issued simultaneously with Myrrh 680606, and with four different covers; "W" on spine			
❑ SP-5060	Unguarded	1985	10.00
— Issued simultaneously with Myrrh 680606, and with four different covers; "O" on spine			
❑ SP-5060	Unguarded	1985	10.00
— Issued simultaneously with Myrrh 680606, and with four different covers; "R" on spine			
❑ SP-5060	Unguarded	1985	10.00
— Issued simultaneously with Myrrh 680606, and with four different covers; "D" on spine			
MYRRH			
❑ MSB-6768	A Christmas Album	1983	15.00
❑ 901-611135-2 [DJ]	A Christmas Album	1983	80.00
— Promo-only picture disc in die-cut sleeve			
❑ MSB-6697	Age to Age	1982	15.00
❑ MSB-6586 [B]	Amy Grant	1977	25.00
— With colorized "ugly cover" of Amy's head and shoulders; "Amy Grant" at upper left			
❑ MSB-6586	Amy Grant	198?	12.00
— With new cover of Amy in natural color; "Amy Grant" at upper right			
❑ MSB-6668	Amy Grant In Concert	1981	15.00
❑ MSB-6677	Amy Grant In Concert, Volume Two	1981	15.00
❑ 701-687106-1	Lead Me On	1988	12.00
— Issued simultaneously with A&M 5199			
❑ MSB-6625	My Father's Eyes	1979	15.00
❑ MSB-6645	Never Alone	1980	15.00
❑ 701-675706-4	Straight Ahead	1984	12.00
❑ 901-622335-5 [DJ]	Straight Ahead	1984	100.00
— Promo-only music and interview album for Christian radio stations			
❑ 701-684306-8	The Collection	1986	12.00
— Issued simultaneously with A&M 3900			
❑ 701-680606-5	Unguarded	1985	12.00
— Issued simultaneously with A&M 5060, and with four different covers; "W" on spine			
❑ 701-680606-5	Unguarded	1985	12.00
— Issued simultaneously with A&M 5060, and with four different covers; "O" on spine			
❑ 701-680606-5	Unguarded	1985	12.00
— Issued simultaneously with A&M 5060, and with four different covers; "R" on spine			
❑ 701-680606-5	Unguarded	1985	12.00
— Issued simultaneously with A&M 5060, and with four different covers; "D" on spine			

GRANT, EARL

Number	Title	Yr	NM
DECCA			
❑ DL75158	A Time for Us	1970	15.00
❑ DL4806 [M]	Bali Ha'I	1967	15.00
❑ DL74806 [S]	Bali Ha'I	1967	18.00
❑ DL4231 [M]	Beyond the Reef	1962	15.00
❑ DL74231 [S]	Beyond the Reef	1962	18.00
❑ DL4188 [M]	Earl After Dark	1961	15.00
❑ DL74188 [S]	Earl After Dark	1961	18.00
❑ DL75223	Earl Grant	1970	15.00
❑ DL4299 [M]	Earl Grant at Basin Street East	1962	15.00
❑ DL74299 [S]	Earl Grant at Basin Street East	1962	18.00
❑ DL4813 [M]	Earl Grant's Greatest Hits	1967	18.00
❑ DL74813 [S]	Earl Grant's Greatest Hits	1967	18.00
❑ DL4165 [M]	Ebb Tide	1961	15.00
❑ DL74165 [S]	Ebb Tide	1961	18.00
❑ DL4454 [M]	Fly Me to the Moon	1963	15.00
❑ DL74454 [S]	Fly Me to the Moon	1963	18.00
❑ DL4937 [M]	Gently Swingin'	1968	25.00
❑ DL74937 [S]	Gently Swingin'	1968	18.00
❑ DL8905 [M]	Grant Takes Rhythm	1959	18.00
❑ DL78905 [S]	Grant Takes Rhythm	1959	25.00
❑ DL75052	In Motion	1969	18.00
❑ DL4811 [M]	Just a Closer Walk with Thee	1967	18.00
❑ DL74811 [S]	Just a Closer Walk with Thee	1967	18.00
❑ DL4506 [M]	Just for a Thrill	1964	15.00
❑ DL74506 [S]	Just for a Thrill	1964	18.00
❑ DL4576 [M]	Just One More Time	1964	15.00
❑ DL74576 [S]	Just One More Time	1964	18.00
❑ DL4338 [M]	Midnight Sun	1963	15.00
❑ DL74338 [S]	Midnight Sun	1963	18.00
❑ DL8916 [M]	Nothing But the Blues	1960	18.00
❑ DL78916 [S]	Nothing But the Blues	1960	25.00
❑ DL8935 [M]	Paris Is My Beat	1960	18.00
❑ DL78935 [S]	Paris Is My Beat	1960	25.00
❑ DL4729 [M]	Songs Made Famous by Nat Cole	1966	15.00
❑ DL74729 [S]	Songs Made Famous by Nat Cole	1966	18.00
❑ DL4974 [M]	Spanish Eyes	1968	30.00
❑ DL74974 [S]	Spanish Eyes	1968	18.00
❑ DL4624 [M]	Spotlight on Earl Grant	1965	15.00
❑ DL74624 [S]	Spotlight on Earl Grant	1965	18.00
❑ DL4738 [M]	Stand By Me	1966	15.00
❑ DL74738 [S]	Stand By Me	1966	18.00
❑ DXS7204	The Best of Earl Grant	1969	25.00
❑ DL8830 [M]	The End	1959	18.00
❑ DL78830 [S]	The End	1959	25.00
❑ DL4044 [M]	The Magic of Earl Grant	1960	15.00
❑ DL74044 [S]	The Magic of Earl Grant	1960	18.00
❑ DL8672 [M]	The Versatile Earl Grant	1958	25.00
❑ DL75108	This Magic Moment	1970	18.00
❑ DL4623 [M]	Trade Winds	1965	15.00
❑ DL74623 [S]	Trade Winds	1965	18.00
❑ DL4677 [M]	Winter Wonderland	1965	15.00
❑ DL74677 [S]	Winter Wonderland	1965	18.00
❑ DL4405 [M]	Yes Sirree	1963	15.00
❑ DL74405 [S]	Yes Sirree	1963	18.00

Number	Title	Yr	NM

VOCALION

Number	Title	Yr	NM
❑ VL3793 [M]	It's So Good	1967	15.00
❑ VL73793 [S]	It's So Good	1967	15.00
❑ VL73893	One for My Baby	1969	15.00
❑ VL73860	Send for Me	1969	15.00

GRANT, EDDY

EPIC

❑ JE36522	My Turn to Love You	1980	15.00
❑ JE36244	Walking on Sunshine	1979	15.00

PORTRAIT

❑ BFR40284	Born Tuff	1986	12.00
❑ FR39261	Going for Broke	1984	12.00
❑ B6R38554	Killer on the Rampage	1983	12.00
— Original prefix			
❑ FR38554	Killer on the Rampage	1983	10.00
— Reissue prefix after LP became popular			

GRANT, GOGI

ERA

❑ 20001 [M]	Suddenly There's Gogi Grant	1956	100.00
— Red vinyl			
❑ 20001 [M]	Suddenly There's Gogi Grant	1956	60.00
— Black vinyl			
❑ EL-106 [M]	The Wayward Wind	196?	30.00

LIBERTY

❑ LRP-3144 [M]	If You Want to Get to Heaven, Shout	1960	30.00
❑ LST-7144 [S]	If You Want to Get to Heaven, Shout	1960	40.00

PETE

❑ S-1101	Gogi Grant	1968	18.00
❑ S-1111	The Way a Woman Feels	1970	18.00

RCA VICTOR

❑ LPM-2000 [M]	Granted… It's Gogi	1960	30.00
❑ LSP-2000 [S]	Granted… It's Gogi	1960	40.00
❑ LOC-1030 [M]	The Helen Morgan Story	1957	60.00
❑ LPM-1940 [M]	Torch Time	1959	30.00
❑ LSP-1940 [S]	Torch Time	1959	40.00
❑ LPM-1717 [M]	Welcome to My Heart	1958	40.00

GRANT, TOM

CMG

❑ CML-0007	Heart of the City	198?	10.00
❑ CML-8009	Just the Right Moment	198?	10.00
❑ CML-8010	Take Me to Your Dream	198?	10.00
❑ CML-8008	Tom Grant	198?	10.00

PAUSA

❑ 7174	Just the Right Moment	1985	12.00
❑ 7199	Take Me to Your Dream	1986	12.00
❑ 7145	Tom Grant	198?	12.00

GRAPEFRUIT

ABC DUNHILL

❑ DS-50050 [B]	Around Grapefruit	1968	60.00

RCA VICTOR

❑ LSP-4215	Deep Water	1969	30.00

GRAPPELLI, STEPHANE, AND BARNEY KESSEL

BLACK LION

❑ 105	I Remember Django	197?	18.00

JAZZ MAN

❑ 5008	I Remember Django	198?	12.00

MOBILE FIDELITY

❑ 1-111	I Remember Django	1984	50.00
— Audiophile vinyl			

GRAPPELLI, STEPHANE, AND DAVID GRISMAN

WARNER BROS.

❑ BSK3550	Live	1981	12.00

GRAPPELLI, STEPHANE, AND GEORGE SHEARING

VERVE

❑ 821868-1	The Reunion	1985	12.00

GRAPPELLI, STEPHANE, AND HANK JONES

MUSE

❑ MR-5287	A Two-fer	198?	12.00

GRAPPELLI, STEPHANE, AND JEAN-LUC PONTY

EVEREST ARCHIVE OF FOLK & JAZZ

❑ FS-355	Violin Summit	1979	12.00

PAUSA

❑ 7074	Giants	1979	12.00

GRAPPELLI, STEPHANE, AND MCCOY TYNER

MILESTONE

❑ M-9181	One on One	1990	15.00

GRAPPELLI, STEPHANE, AND TERESA BREWER

DOCTOR JAZZ

❑ FW38448	On the Road Again	1983	12.00

GRAPPELLI, STEPHANE, AND VASSAR CLEMENTS

FLYING FISH

❑ FF-421	Together at Last	1987	12.00

GRAPPELLI, STEPHANE, AND YO-YO MA

CBS

❑ FM45574	Anything Goes: The Music of Cole Porter	1989	15.00

GRAPPELLI, STEPHANE

ANGEL

❑ DS-37790	Brandenberg Boogie (Music of Bach)	1980	15.00
❑ DS-38063	Just One of Those Things	198?	15.00
❑ DS-37886	We've Got the World on a String	198?	15.00

ARSITA FREEDOM

❑ AL1033	The Parisian	197?	15.00

ATLANTIC

❑ 1391 [M]	Feeling + Finesse = Jazz	1962	18.00
❑ SD1391 [S]	Feeling + Finesse = Jazz	1962	25.00
❑ 90140	Feeling + Finesse = Jazz	198?	12.00
❑ 82095	Olympia '88	1990	15.00

BARCLAY

❑ 820007	Music to Pass the Time	196?	25.00

BASF

❑ 20876	Afternoon in Paris	1972	18.00

BLACK LION

❑ 047	I Got Rhythm	1974	25.00
❑ 211	Just One of the Things	1974	18.00
❑ 313	Talk of the Town	1975	15.00

CLASSIC JAZZ

❑ 23	Homage to Django	197?	25.00
❑ 24	Stephane Grappelli and Bill Coleman	197?	18.00

COLUMBIA

❑ JC35415	Uptown Dance	1978	12.00

CONCORD JAZZ

❑ CJ 139	Stephane Grappelli at the Winery	1980	12.00
❑ CJ-225	Stephanova	1983	12.00
❑ CJ-169	Vintage 1981	1981	12.00

DOCTOR JAZZ

❑ FW38727	Live at Carnegie Hall	1983	12.00

EMARCY

❑ MG-36120 [M]	Improvisations	1957	60.00

EVEREST ARCHIVE OF FOLK & JAZZ

❑ 311	Stephane Grappelli	197?	15.00

FANTASY

❑ OJC-441	Tivoli Gardens	1990	12.00

GRP

❑ GR-1032	Stephane Grappelli Plays Jerome Kern	1987	12.00

PABLO LIVE

❑ 2308220	Tivoli Gardens	1979	15.00

PAUSA

❑ 7071	Afternoon in Paris	1979	12.00
❑ 7098	Violinspiration	198?	12.00
❑ 7041	Young Django	1979	12.00

VANGUARD

❑ VSD-81/82	Satin Doll	197?	18.00
❑ VMS-73130	Satin Doll, Volume 1	198?	12.00

VERVE

❑ MGV-20001 [M]	Musique Pour Arreter Le Temps (Music to Stop the Clock By)	195?	30.00
— As "Stephane Grappelly			
❑ 815672-1	Young Django	198?	12.00

GRASS ROOTS, THE

ABC

❑ AC-30003	The ABC Collection	1976	18.00

ABC DUNHILL

❑ DSX-50137	A Lotta Mileage	1973	18.00
❑ DS-50027	Feelings	1968	18.00
— Reissue with ABC logo			
❑ DS-50047	Golden Grass	1968	25.00
❑ DS-50067	Leaving It All Behind	1969	25.00
❑ DS-50052	Lovin' Things	1969	25.00
❑ DS-50087	More Golden Grass	1970	25.00
❑ DSX-50112	Move Along	1972	18.00
❑ DSX-50107	Their 16 Greatest Hits	1971	25.00

COMMAND

❑ QD-40013 [Q]	Their 16 Greatest Hits	1974	30.00

DUNHILL

❑ D-50027 [M]	Feelings	1968	30.00
❑ DS-50027 [S]	Feelings	1968	25.00
❑ D-50020 [M]	Let's Live for Today	1967	30.00
❑ DS-50020 [S]	Let's Live for Today	1967	30.00
❑ D-50011 [M]	Where Were You When I Needed You	1966	75.00
❑ DS-50011 [S]	Where Were You When I Needed You	1966	100.00

HAVEN

❑ ST-9204	The Grass Roots	1975	18.00

MCA

❑ 5331	Powers of the Night	1982	15.00
❑ 37154	Their 16 Greatest Hits	198?	10.00
— Budget-line reissue of ABC Dunhill 50107			

GRATEFUL DEAD, THE

ARISTA

❑ AL8575	Built to Last	1989	18.00
❑ A2L8606	Dead Set	1981	18.00
❑ AL8112	Dead Set	198?	25.00
— Budget-line reissue of 8606			
❑ AL9508	Go to Heaven	1980	15.00
❑ AL8332	Go to Heaven	198?	12.00
— Budget-line reissue of 9508			
❑ SP-35 [DJ]	Grateful Dead Sampler	1978	50.00
❑ AL8452	In the Dark	1987	18.00
❑ A2L8604	Reckoning	1981	18.00
❑ AB4198 [B]	Shakedown Street	1978	18.00
❑ AL8321	Shakedown Street	198?	12.00
— Budget-line reissue of 4198			
❑ AL7001	Terrapin Station	1977	18.00
❑ AL7001 [DJ]	Terrapin Station	1977	50.00
— Radio station promos are banded for airplay			
❑ AL8329	Terrapin Station	198?	12.00
— Budget-line reissue of 7001			
❑ AL38634	Without a Net	1990	30.00

DIRECT DISK

❑ SD-16619	Terrapin Station	1980	100.00
— Audiophile vinyl			

GRATEFUL DEAD

❑ GD-LA494-G [B]	Blues for Allah	1975	30.00
❑ GD-102	Grateful Dead from the Mars Hotel	1974	25.00
— Without United Artists distribution			
❑ GD-102	Grateful Dead from the Mars Hotel	1975	18.00
— With United Artists distribution and "Grateful Dead" label			
❑ GD-LA620-J2 [B]	Steal Your Face	1976	30.00
❑ GD-01 [DJ]	Wake of the Flood	1973	400.00
— Green vinyl meant for fan-club members; ironically, most copies were damaged in a flood before distribution			
❑ GD-01 [B]	Wake of the Flood	1973	30.00
— With no contributing artists on back cover			
❑ GD-01	Wake of the Flood	1975	18.00
— With contributing artists on back cover and United Artists distribution			

MOBILE FIDELITY

❑ 1-014	American Beauty	1980	80.00
— Audiophile vinyl			
❑ 1-172 [B]	Grateful Dead from the Mars Hotel	1984	76.00
— Audiophile vinyl			

PAIR

❑ PDL2-1053	For the Faithful...	1986	15.00

PRIDE

❑ PRD 0016	The History of the Grateful Dead	1972	30.00
— Reissue of material from Sunflower LPs			

RHINO

❑ R1-74397	American Beauty	2003	25.00
— Reissue on 180-gram vinyl			
❑ R1537164 [B]	Family Dog At The Great Highway, San Francisco, CA, April 18, 1970	2013	35.00
❑ R1541159 [B]	Hampton '79	2014	45.00
❑ R1-74395	Live/Dead	2003	30.00
— Reissue on 180-gram vinyl			
❑ R1534703 [B]	Rare Cuts & Oddities 1966	2013	40.00
❑ R1536031 [B]	Veneta, Oregon 8/27/72 (Sunshine Daydream)	2013	100.00
❑ R1-74396	Workingman's Dead	2003	25.00
— Reissue on 180-gram vinyl			

SUNFLOWER

❑ SNF-5004	Historic Dead	1971	40.00
❑ SUN-5001	Vintage Dead	1970	40.00
— Album has been counterfeited, but bogus covers are 1/4" shorter than normal LP cover			

UNITED ARTISTS

❑ GD-102	Grateful Dead from the Mars Hotel	1978	18.00
— With United Artists "sunrise" label			

WARNER BROS.

❑ WS1893	American Beauty	1970	30.00
— Green label with "WB" logo			
❑ WS1893	American Beauty	1973	15.00
— "Burbank" palm-trees label			
❑ WS1893	American Beauty	1979	10.00
— White or tan label			
❑ ST-93416	American Beauty	1970	50.00
— Capitol Record Club edition; green label with "W7" logo			
❑ WS1749	Anthem of the Sun	1968	30.00
— Green label with "W7" logo			
❑ WS1749	Anthem of the Sun	1970	18.00
— Green label with "WB" logo, purple cover			

Number	Title	Yr	NM
❏ WS1749	Anthem of the Sun	197?	50.00
— Green label with "WB" logo, white background on cover with radically remixed version of LP			
❏ WS1749	Anthem of the Sun	1973	15.00
— Burbank" palm-trees label			
❏ WS1749	Anthem of the Sun	1979	10.00
— White or tan label			
❏ WS1790	Aoxomoxoa	1969	30.00
— Green label with "W7" logo			
❏ WS1790	Aoxomoxoa	1970	18.00
— Green label with "WB" logo			
❏ WS1790	Aoxomoxoa	1973	15.00
— Burbank" palm-trees label			
❏ WS1790	Aoxomoxoa	1979	10.00
— White or tan label			
❏ 3WX2668	Europe '72	1972	40.00
— Green labels with "WB" logo			
❏ 3WX2668	Europe '72	1973	25.00
— Burbank" palm-trees labels			
❏ 3WX2668	Europe '72	1979	15.00
— White or tan labels			
❏ 2WS1935	Grateful Dead	1971	30.00
— Green labels with "WB" logo			
❏ 2WS1935	Grateful Dead	1973	18.00
— Burbank" palm-trees labels			
❏ 2WS1935	Grateful Dead	1979	12.00
— White or tan labels			
❏ BS2721	History of the Grateful Dead, Vol. 1 (Bear's Choice)	1973	25.00
— Burbank" palm-trees labels			
❏ BS2721	History of the Grateful Dead, Vol. 1 (Bear's Choice)	1978	10.00
— White or tan labels			
❏ 2WS1830	Live/Dead	1969	40.00
— Green labels with "W7" logo			
❏ 2WS1830	Live/Dead	1970	25.00
— Green labels with "WB" logo			
❏ 2WS1830	Live/Dead	1973	18.00
— Burbank" palm-trees labels			
❏ 2WS1830	Live/Dead	1979	12.00
— White or tan labels			
❏ W2764	The Best of/Skeletons from the Closet	1974	25.00
— Burbank" palm-trees labels			
❏ W2764	The Best of/Skeletons from the Closet	1979	10.00
— White or tan labels			
❏ W1689 [M]	The Grateful Dead	1967	200.00
❏ WS1689 [S]	The Grateful Dead	1967	80.00
— Gold label			
❏ WS1689 [S]	The Grateful Dead	1968	30.00
— Green label with "W7" logo			
❏ WS1689 [S]	The Grateful Dead	1970	18.00
— Green label with "WB" logo			
❏ WS1689 [S]	The Grateful Dead	1973	15.00
— Burbank" palm-trees label			
❏ WS1689 [S]	The Grateful Dead	1979	10.00
— White or tan label			
❏ 2WS3091	What a Long Strange Trip It's Been: The Best of the Grateful Dead	1977	25.00
— Burbank" palm-trees labels			
❏ 2WS3091	What a Long Strange Trip It's Been: The Best of the Grateful Dead	1979	12.00
— White or tan labels			
❏ WS1869	Workingman's Dead	1970	30.00
— Green label with "WB" logo; textured cover with back cover slick upside down			
❏ WS1869	Workingman's Dead	1973	15.00
— Burbank" palm-trees label; standard cover with back cover right side up			
❏ WS1869	Workingman's Dead	1979	10.00
— White or tan label			

GRAVEDIGGAZ

GEE STREET
❏ 32501-1	The Pick, the Sickle and the Shovel	1997	15.00

GRAVENITES, NICK

COLUMBIA
❏ CS9899 [B]	My Labors	1969	25.00

GRAVES, CONLEY

DECCA
❏ DL8220 [M]	Genius at Work	1956	40.00
❏ DL8412 [M]	Piano Dynamics	1957	40.00
❏ DL8475 [M]	Rendezvous in Paris	1957	40.00

LIBERTY
❏ LRP-3007 [M]	V.I.P. (Very Important Pianist)	1956	40.00

NOCTURNE
❏ NLP-4 [10]	Piano Artistry	1954	100.00

GRAVES, JOE

CAPITOL
❏ T1977 [M]	The Great New Swingers	1963	30.00
❏ ST1977 [S]	The Great New Swingers	1963	30.00

GRAVES, MILFORD

ESP-DISK'
❏ 1015 [M]	Milford Graves Percussion Ensemble	1966	25.00
❏ S-1015 [S]	Milford Graves Percussion Ensemble	1966	30.00

IPS
❏ 004	Babi	197?	18.00
❏ 290	Nommo	197?	18.00

GRAVES, TERESA

KIRSHNER
❏ KOS-104	Teresa Graves	1970	30.00

GRAVINE, ANITA

STASH
❏ ST-256	I Always Knew	1985	12.00

GRAVITY ADJUSTERS EXPANSION BAND

NOCTURNE
❏ NRS-302	One	1973	300.00

GRAY, BILLY

DECCA
❏ DL5567 [10]	Dance-O-Rama	1956	200.00

GRAY, CLAUDE

DECCA
❏ DL4882 [M]	Claude Gray Sings	1967	30.00
❏ DL74882 [S]	Claude Gray Sings	1967	25.00
❏ DL74963	The Easy Way of Claude Gray	1968	25.00

HILLTOP
❏ JM-6051 [M]	Treasure of Love	1967	18.00
❏ JS-6051 [S]	Treasure of Love	1967	15.00

MERCURY
❏ MG-20718 [M]	Country Goes to Town	1962	25.00
❏ SR-60718 [S]	Country Goes to Town	1962	30.00
❏ SR-60658 [S]	Songs of Broken Love Affairs	1962	30.00
❏ MG 20658 [M]	Songs of Broken Love Affairs	1962	25.00

GRAY, DOBIE

CAPITOL
❏ ST-12489	From Where I Stand	1986	12.00

CAPRICORN
❏ CP 0163	New Ray of Sunshine	1976	12.00

CHARGER
❏ CHR-M-2002 [M]	Dobie Gray Sings for "In" Crowders That Go "Go Go"	1965	40.00
❏ CHR-S-2002 [S]	Dobie Gray Sings for "In" Crowders That Go "Go Go"	1965	120.00

DECCA
❏ DL75397	Drift Away	1973	15.00

INFINITY
❏ INF-9001	Midnight Diamond	1979	12.00

MCA
❏ 515	Drift Away	1974	12.00
— Reissue of Decca 75397			
❏ 449	Hey Dixie	1974	12.00
❏ 371	Loving Arms	1973	12.00

ROBOX
❏ RBX8102	Welcome Home	1981	12.00

STRIPE
❏ LPM2001 [M]	Look -- Dobie Gray	1963	100.00

GRAY, DOLORES

CAPITOL
❏ T897 [M]	Warm Brandy	1957	30.00

GRAY, GLEN

CAPITOL
❏ T856 [M]	Casa Loma Caravan	1957	25.00
— Turquoise label			
❏ W747 [M]	Casa Loma in Hi-Fi!	1956	30.00
❏ T1506 [M]	Please Mr. Gray…More Sounds of the Great Bands	1961	15.00
❏ ST1506 [S]	Please Mr. Gray…More Sounds of the Great Bands	1961	18.00
❏ T1615 [M]	Shall We Swing?	1961	15.00
❏ ST1615 [S]	Shall We Swing?	1961	18.00
❏ T1234 [M]	Solo Spotlight	1960	15.00
❏ ST1234 [S]	Solo Spotlight	1960	18.00
❏ W1022 [M]	Sounds of the Great Bands!	1959	15.00
❏ SW1022 [S]	Sounds of the Great Bands!	1959	18.00
❏ SM-1022	Sounds of the Great Bands!	197?	12.00
— Reissue			
❏ T2131 [M]	Sounds of the Great Bands in Latin	1964	12.00
❏ ST2131 [S]	Sounds of the Great Bands in Latin	1964	15.00
❏ T1067 [M]	Sounds of the Great Bands Volume 2	1959	15.00
❏ ST1067 [S]	Sounds of the Great Bands Volume 2	1959	18.00
❏ SM-1067	Sounds of the Great Bands Volume 2	197?	12.00

Number	Title	Yr	NM
— Reissue			
❏ T1739 [M]	Sounds of the Great Bands Volume 5: They All Swung the Blues	1962	15.00
❏ ST1739 [S]	Sounds of the Great Bands Volume 5: They All Swung the Blues	1962	18.00
❏ T1938 [M]	Sounds of the Great Bands Volume 7: Today's Best	1963	12.00
❏ ST1938 [S]	Sounds of the Great Bands Volume 7: Today's Best	1963	15.00
❏ T2014 [M]	Sounds of the Great Bands Volume 8: More of Today's Best	1964	12.00
❏ ST2014 [S]	Sounds of the Great Bands Volume 8: More of Today's Best	1964	15.00
❏ T1588 [M]	Sounds of the Great Casa Loma Band	1961	18.00
❏ DT1588 [R]	Sounds of the Great Casa Loma Band	1961	15.00
❏ SM-1588	Sounds of the Great Casa Loma Band	197?	12.00
— Reissue			
❏ T1289 [M]	Swingin' Decade	1960	15.00
❏ ST1289 [S]	Swingin' Decade	1960	18.00
❏ T1400 [M]	Swingin' Southern Style	1961	15.00
❏ ST1400 [S]	Swingin' Southern Style	1961	18.00
❏ T1812 [M]	Themes of the Great Bands	1963	15.00
❏ ST1812 [S]	Themes of the Great Bands	1963	18.00
❏ SM-1812	Themes of the Great Bands	197?	12.00
— Reissue			

CIRCLE
❏ 16	Glen Gray and the Casa Loma Orchestra	198?	12.00

CORAL
❏ CRL56009 [10]	Glen Gray Souvenirs	1950	50.00
❏ CRL56006 [10]	Hoagy Carmichael Songs	1950	50.00

CREATIVE WORLD
❏ ST-1055	Shall We Swing?	197?	12.00

DECCA
❏ DL75016 [R]	Greatest Hits	1968	15.00
❏ DL5089 [10]	Musical Smoke Rings	1950	50.00
❏ DL5397 [10]	No-Name Jive	1953	50.00
❏ DL8570 [M]	Smoke Rings	1957	25.00

HARMONY
❏ HL7045 [M]	The Great Recordings of Glen Gray	1957	25.00

HINDSIGHT
❏ HSR-104	Glen Gray and the Casa Loma Orchestra, 1939-1940	198?	12.00
❏ HSR-120	Glen Gray and the Casa Loma Orchestra, 1943-1946	198?	12.00

INSIGHT
❏ 214	Glen Gray and the Casa Loma Orchestra, 1939-1940	198?	12.00

MCA
❏ 122	Greatest Hits	1973	12.00
— Reissue of Decca 75016			
❏ 20199	Smoke Rings	198?	10.00
❏ 4076	The Best of Glen Gray	197?	15.00

GRAY, JERRY

CRAFTSMAN
❏ 8035 [M]	More Miller Hits	195?	25.00

DECCA
❏ DL5375 [10]	A Tribute to Glenn Miller	1951	50.00
❏ DL5478 [10]	Dance Time	1952	50.00
❏ DL5266 [10]	Dance to the Music of Gray	1950	50.00
❏ DL5312 [10]	In the Mood ...	1951	50.00
❏ DL8101 [M]	Jerry Gray and His Orchestra	1955	40.00

DOT
❏ DLP-3741 [M]	This Is Jerry Gray	1966	15.00
❏ DLP-25741 [S]	This Is Jerry Gray	1966	18.00

GOLDEN TONE
❏ C-4005 [M]	Glenn Miller Favorites	196?	15.00

HINDSIGHT
❏ HSR-212	Jerry Gray and His Orchestra 1952	198?	12.00

LIBERTY
❏ LRP-3038 [M]	Hi-Fi Shades of Gray	1956	40.00
❏ LST-7002 [S]	Hi-Fi Shades of Gray	1958	40.00
❏ LRP-3089 [M]	Jerry Gray at the Hollywood Palladium	1958	40.00
❏ LST-7013 [S]	Jerry Gray at the Hollywood Palladium	1958	40.00

TOPS
❏ L-1627 [M]	A Salute to Glenn Miller	1958	25.00
❏ L-1640 [M]	Glenn Miller Greats	1958	25.00

VOCALION
❏ VL3602 [M]	A Tribute to Glenn Miller	196?	25.00

WARNER BROS.
❏ W1446 [M]	Singin' and Swingin'	1962	25.00
❏ WS1446 [S]	Singin' and Swingin'	1962	30.00

GRAY, MACY

EPIC
❏ E69490	On How Life Is	1999	15.00
❏ E85200	The Id	2001	15.00

Number	Title	Yr	NM

GRAY, MARK

COLUMBIA
❏ FC39143	Magic	1984	10.00
❏ FC40126	That Feeling Inside	1986	10.00
❏ FC39518	This Ol' Piano	1984	10.00

GRAY, WARDELL, AND DEXTER GORDON

DECCA
❏ DL7025 [10]	The Chase and the Steeple Chase	1952	250.00

JAZZTONE
❏ J-1235 [M]	The Chase and the Steeple Chase	1956	50.00

MCA
❏ 1336	The Chase and the Steeple Chase	198?	12.00

GRAY, WARDELL

CROWN
❏ CLP-5293 [M]	Wardell Gray	196?	18.00
— Gray label			
❏ CST-293 [R]	Wardell Gray	196?	15.00
❏ CLP-5004 [M]	Way Out Wardell	1957	40.00
— Originals have a black label with the word "crown" in small letters at top			
❏ CLP-5278 [M]	Way Out Wardell	1962	25.00
❏ CST-278 [R]	Way Out Wardell	1962	15.00

CUSTOM
❏ CS-1060 [R]	Shades of Gray	196?	15.00
❏ CM-2060 [M]	Shades of Gray	196?	18.00

FANTASY
❏ OJC-050	Wardell Gray Memorial, Volume 1	1982	12.00
— Reissue of Prestige 7008			
❏ OJC-051	Wardell Gray Memorial, Volume 2	1982	12.00
— Reissue of Prestige 7009			

MODERN
❏ MLP-1204 [M]	Way Out Wardell	1956	300.00

PHILOLOGY/SPHERE
❏ W-14	Light Gray, Vol. 1	198?	12.00
❏ W-36	Light Gray, Vol. 2	198?	12.00

PRESTIGE
❏ P-24062	Central Ave.	1976	25.00
❏ PRLP-128 [10]	Jazz Concert	1952	250.00
❏ PRLP-7008 [M]	Wardell Gray Memorial, Volume 1	1955	100.00
❏ PRLP-7009 [M]	Wardell Gray Memorial, Volume 2	1955	100.00
❏ PRLP-7343 [M]	Wardell Gray Memorial Album	1964	50.00
❏ PRST-7343 [R]	Wardell Gray Memorial Album	1964	30.00
❏ PRLP-147 [10]	Wardell Gray's Los Angeles Stars	1953	250.00
❏ PRLP-115 [10]	Wardell Gray Tenor Sax	1951	250.00

UNITED
❏ US-7722 [R]	Shades of Gray	197?	15.00

XANADU
❏ 146	Live in Hollywood	197?	18.00

GRAYE, TONY

FUTURA
❏ 55514	Let's Swing Away	197?	18.00
❏ 55515	The Blue Horn of Tony Graye	197?	18.00

ZIM
❏ ZMS-2001	Oh Gee!	1975	18.00

GREAT SCOTS, THE

BEAT ROCKET
❏ BR101	The Great Scots ... Arrive!	199?	12.00

SUNDAZED
❏ LP5052	The Great Lost Great Scots Album!	199?	12.00

GREAT SOCIETY, THE

COLUMBIA
❏ CS9627 [M]	Conspicuous Only In Its Absence	1968	50.00
— White label promo only; "Special Mono Radio Station Copy" sticker on front; same number as stereo version			
❏ CS9627 [S]	Conspicuous Only In Its Absence	1968	30.00
— Red label, "360 Sound Stereo			
❏ CS9702 [B]	How It Was	1968	30.00
— Red label, "360 Sound Stereo			
❏ G30459	The Great Society Collectors Item	1971	18.00

HARMONY
❏ KH30391	Somebody to Love	1970	15.00

GREAT SPECKLED BIRD

AMPEX
❏ A-10103 [B]	Great Speckled Bird	1970	30.00

GREAVES, R.B.

ATCO
❏ SD 33-311	R.B. Greaves	1969	25.00

INTERMEDIA
❏ QS-5032	Rock and Roll	198?	12.00

GRECH, RIC

RSO
❏ SO876 [B]	The Last Five Years	1973	18.00
— Compiles his work with such groups as Family, Traffic, Blind Faith, Ginger Baker's Air Force and KGB			

GRECO, BUDDY

APPLAUSE
❏ APLP-1004	Hot Nights	1982	12.00

BAINBRIDGE
❏ 8004	Greatest Hits	198?	18.00

CORAL
❏ CRL57022 [M]	Buddy Greco at Mister Kelly's	1956	30.00

EPIC
❏ LN24010 [M]	Buddy and Soul	1962	15.00
❏ BN26010 [S]	Buddy and Soul	1962	18.00
❏ LN24043 [M]	Buddy Greco's Greatest Hits	1963	15.00
❏ BN26043 [S]	Buddy Greco's Greatest Hits	1963	18.00
❏ LN24057 [M]	Buddy Greco Sings for Intimate Moments	1963	15.00
❏ BN26057 [S]	Buddy Greco Sings for Intimate Moments	1963	18.00
❏ LN3771 [M]	Buddy's Back in Town	1961	15.00
❏ BN593 [S]	Buddy's Back in Town	1961	18.00
❏ LN24181 [M]	From the Wrists Down	1965	15.00
❏ BN26181 [S]	From the Wrists Down	1965	18.00
❏ LN3793 [M]	I Like It Swinging	1961	15.00
❏ BN602 [S]	I Like It Swinging	1961	18.00
❏ LN3820 [M]	Let's Love	1961	15.00
❏ BN615 [S]	Let's Love	1961	18.00
❏ LN24130 [M]	Modern Sounds of Hank Williams	1965	15.00
❏ BN26130 [S]	Modern Sounds of Hank Williams	1965	18.00
❏ LN3660 [M]	My Buddy	1960	15.00
❏ BN557 [S]	My Buddy	1960	18.00
❏ LN24088 [M]	My Last Night in Rome	1964	15.00
❏ BN26088 [S]	My Last Night in Rome	1964	18.00
❏ LN24116 [M]	On Stage	1964	15.00
❏ BN26116 [S]	On Stage	1964	18.00
❏ LN24032 [M]	Soft and Gentle	1962	15.00
❏ BN26032 [S]	Soft and Gentle	1962	18.00
❏ LN3746 [M]	Songs for Swinging Losers	1960	15.00
❏ BN585 [S]	Songs for Swinging Losers	1960	18.00

HARMONY
❏ HL7440 [M]	You're Something Else	196?	12.00
❏ HS11248 [S]	You're Something Else	196?	15.00

KAPP
❏ KL-1033 [M]	Broadway Melodies	1956	25.00
❏ KL-1107 [M]	Buddy	1958	25.00
❏ KL-1231 [M]	The Best of Buddy Greco	1961	18.00

PROJECT 3
❏ PR5105	For Once In My Life, In Concert	1900	12.00

REPRISE
❏ RS-6256 [S]	Away We Go!	1967	15.00
❏ R-6256 [M]	Away We Go!	1967	18.00
❏ R-6220 [M]	Big Band and Ballads	1966	15.00
❏ RS-6220 [S]	Big Band and Ballads	1966	18.00
❏ RS-6230 [S]	Buddy's in a Brand New Bag	1966	18.00
❏ R-6230 [M]	Buddy's in a Brand New Bag	1966	15.00

SCEPTER
❏ SPS-579	Let the Sunshine In	1969	15.00

SUTTON
❏ SSU282 [M]	All Time Favorites Featuring Buddy Greco	196?	12.00

VOCALION
❏ VL3706 [M]	Here's Buddy Greco	1964	15.00
❏ VL73706 [R]	Here's Buddy Greco	1964	12.00

GRECO, JULIETTE

COLUMBIA
❏ CL569 [M]	St. Germain-des-Pres	1954	30.00
— Maroon label, gold print			

GREEK FOUNTAIN RIVER FRONT BAND, THE

MONTEL
❏ 110 [M]	The Greek Fountain River Band Takes Requests	1965	120.00

GREELEY, GEORGE

CAPITOL
❏ H438 [10]	Piano Demitasse	1954	30.00

REPRISE
❏ R6092 [M]	Piano Rhapsodies of Love	1964	12.00
❏ RS6092 [S]	Piano Rhapsodies of Love	1964	15.00

WARNER BROS.
❏ WS1338 [S]	22 Best Loved Christmas Piano Concertos	1959	25.00
❏ W1503 [M]	A Classic Affair	1963	15.00
❏ WS1503 [S]	A Classic Affair	1963	18.00
❏ W1560 [M]	Best Loved Christmas Piano Concertos	1965	15.00
❏ WS1560 [S]	Best Loved Christmas Piano Concertos	1965	18.00
❏ W1427 [M]	Famous Film Themes	1961	15.00
❏ WS1427 [S]	Famous Film Themes	1961	18.00
❏ W1451 [M]	George Greeley Plays George Gershwin	1962	15.00
❏ WS1451 [S]	George Greeley Plays George Gershwin	1962	18.00
❏ W1415 [M]	Great Broadway Musicals	1961	15.00
❏ WS1415 [S]	Great Broadway Musicals	1961	18.00
❏ W1402 [M]	Piano Italiano	1961	15.00
❏ WS1402 [S]	Piano Italiano	1961	18.00
❏ W1410 [M]	The Best of the Popular Piano Concertos	1961	15.00
❏ WS1410 [S]	The Best of the Popular Piano Concertos	1961	18.00
❏ W1319 [M]	The Greatest Motion Picture Piano Concertos	1959	18.00
❏ WS1319 [S]	The Greatest Motion Picture Piano Concertos	1959	25.00
❏ W1476 [M]	Themes from Mutiny on the Bounty and Other Great Films	1962	15.00
❏ WS1476 [S]	Themes from Mutiny on the Bounty and Other Great Films	1962	18.00
❏ W1366 [M]	The Most Beautiful Music of Hawaii	1960	15.00
❏ WS1366 [S]	The Most Beautiful Music of Hawaii	1960	18.00
❏ W1387 [M]	The World's Greatest Love Themes	1960	15.00
❏ WS1387 [S]	The World's Greatest Love Themes	1960	18.00
❏ W1249 [M]	The World's Greatest Popular Piano Concertos	1958	18.00
❏ WS1249 [S]	The World's Greatest Popular Piano Concertos	1959	25.00
❏ W1291 [M]	World Renowned Popular Piano Concertos	1959	18.00
❏ WS1291 [S]	World Renowned Popular Piano Concertos	1959	25.00

GREEN, AL

A&M
❏ SP-5228	I Get Joy	1989	12.00
❏ SP-5150	Soul Survivor	1987	12.00

BELL
❏ 6076	Al Green	1972	25.00
— Reissue of Hot Line LP			

BLUE NOTE
❏ BTE74584	Everything's OK	2005	18.00
❏ 93556	I Can't Stop	2003	18.00

DCC COMPACT CLASSICS
❏ LPZ-2058	Greatest Hits	1998	30.00
— Audiophile vinyl			

HI
❏ SHL-32087	Al Green Explores Your Mind	1974	18.00
❏ SHL-32062	Al Green Gets Next to You	1971	10.00
❏ 8001	Al Green Gets Next to You	1977	15.00
❏ SHL-32089	Al Green/Greatest Hits	1975	18.00
❏ SHL-32092	Al Green Is Love	1975	18.00
❏ SHL-32105	Al Green's Greatest Hits, Volume 2	1977	18.00
❏ SHL-32077	Call Me	1973	18.00
❏ SHL-32097	Full of Fire	1976	18.00
❏ SHL-32055	Green Is Blues	1969	18.00
❏ SHL-32103	Have a Good Time	1976	18.00
❏ SHL-32074	I'm Still in Love with You	1972	18.00
❏ SHL-32070	Let's Stay Together	1972	18.00
❏ 8007	Let's Stay Together	1977	15.00
❏ SHL-32082	Livin' for You	1973	10.00
❏ 6004	The Belle Album	1977	15.00
❏ 8000	Tired of Being Alone	1977	15.00
❏ 6009	Truth 'N' Time	1978	15.00

HOT LINE
❏ 1500 [M]	Back Up Train	1967	50.00
— As "Al Greene"			
❏ S-1500 [S]	Back Up Train	1967	80.00
— As "Al Greene"			

KORY
❏ 1005	Al Green	1977	12.00
— Reissue of Bell LP			

MCA
❏ 42308	Love Ritual	1988	12.00

MOTOWN
❏ 5283ML	Al Green/Greatest Hits	198?	12.00
— Reissue of Hi 32089			
❏ 5291ML	Al Green's Greatest Hits, Volume II	198?	12.00
— Reissue of Hi 32105			
❏ 5284ML	I'm Still in Love with You	198?	12.00
— Reissue of Hi 32074			
❏ 5290ML	Let's Stay Together	198?	12.00
— Reissue of Hi 32070			
❏ 5317ML	Truth N' Time	198?	12.00

MYRRH
❏ MSB-6774	Al Green and the Full Gospel Tabernacle Choir	1984	12.00

Number	Title	Yr	NM
❑ WR-8209	Al Green and the Full Gospel Tabernacle Choir	1986	10.00
—Reissue with new number and A&M logo			
❑ MSB-6671	Higher Plane	1981	12.00
❑ WR-8114	Higher Plane	1985	10.00
—Reissue with new number and A&M logo			
❑ MSB-6747	I'll Rise Again	1982	12.00
❑ WR-8116	I'll Rise Again	1985	10.00
—Reissue with new number and A&M logo			
❑ MSB-6702	Precious Lord	1981	12.00
❑ WR-8115	Precious Lord	1985	10.00
—Reissue with new number and A&M logo			
❑ MSB-6661	The Lord Will Make a Way	1980	12.00
❑ WR-8113	The Lord Will Make a Way	1985	10.00
—Reissue with new number and A&M logo			
❑ WR-8118	Trust in God	1985	10.00
—Reissue with new number and A&M logo			
❑ 7-01-678306-?	Trust in God	1984	12.00
❑ WR-8117	White Christmas	1985	12.00
—Reissue with new number and A&M logo			
❑ 7-01-678006-6	White Christmas	1984	15.00

THE RIGHT STUFF

Number	Title	Yr	NM
❑ T1-27627	I'm Still in Love with You	1995	18.00
—Green vinyl reissue			
❑ T1-27121	Let's Stay Together	1995	18.00
—Green vinyl reissue			

WORD

Number	Title	Yr	NM
❑ E77000	One in a Million	1991	15.00

GREEN, BENNIE

BAINBRIDGE

Number	Title	Yr	NM
❑ 1048	Bennie Green	198?	12.00

BARBARY

Number	Title	Yr	NM
❑ M33015 [M]	Play More Than You Can Stand	196?	30.00

BETHLEHEM

Number	Title	Yr	NM
❑ BCP-6018	Cat Walk	197?	18.00
—Reissue of 6054, distributed by RCA Victor			
❑ BCP-6054 [M]	Hornful of Soul	1961	30.00
❑ BCP-4019 [M]	Hornful of Soul	196?	25.00
—Reissue of 6054			

BLUE NOTE

Number	Title	Yr	NM
❑ BLP-1587 [M]	Back on the Scene	1958	300.00
—Deep groove" version (deep indentation under label on both sides)			
❑ BLP-1587 [M]	Back on the Scene	1958	80.00
—Regular version with W. 63rd St. addresss on label			
❑ BLP-1587 [M]	Back on the Scene	1963	30.00
—With "New York, USA" address on label			
❑ BST-1587 [S]	Back on the Scene	1959	350.00
—Deep groove" version (deep indentation under label on both sides)			
❑ BST-1587 [S]	Back on the Scene	1959	60.00
—Regular version with W. 63rd St. addresss on label			
❑ BST-81587 [S]	Back on the Scene	1963	25.00
—With "New York, USA" address on label			
❑ BST-81587 [S]	Back on the Scene	1967	18.00
—With "A Division of Liberty Records" on label			
❑ BLP-1599 [M]	Soul Stirrin'	1958	120.00
—Deep groove" version (deep indentation under label on both sides)			
❑ BLP-1599 [M]	Soul Stirrin'	1958	80.00
—Regular version with W. 63rd St. address on label			
❑ BLP-1599 [M]	Soul Stirrin'	1963	30.00
—With "New York, USA" address on label			
❑ BST-1599 [S]	Soul Stirrin'	1959	80.00
—Deep groove" version (deep indentation under label on both sides)			
❑ BST-1599 [S]	Soul Stirrin'	1959	60.00
—Regular version with W. 63rd St. address on label			
❑ BST-81599 [S]	Soul Stirrin'	1963	25.00
—With "New York, USA" address on label			
❑ BST-81599 [S]	Soul Stirrin'	1967	18.00
—With "A Division of Liberty Records" on label			
❑ BLP-4010 [M]	Walkin' and Talkin'	1959	120.00
—Deep groove" version (deep indentation under label on both sides)			
❑ BLP-4010 [M]	Walkin' and Talkin'	1959	80.00
—Regular version with W. 63rd St. addresss on label			
❑ BLP-4010 [M]	Walkin' and Talkin'	1963	30.00
—With "New York, USA" address on label			
❑ BST-4010 [S]	Walkin' and Talkin'	1959	80.00
—Deep groove" version (deep indentation under label on both sides)			
❑ BST-4010 [S]	Walkin' and Talkin'	1959	60.00
—Regular version with W. 63rd St. addresss on label			
❑ BST-84010 [S]	Walkin' and Talkin'	1963	25.00
—With "New York, USA" address on label			
❑ BST-84010 [S]	Walkin' and Talkin'	1967	18.00
—With "A Division of Liberty Records" on label			

ENRICA

Number	Title	Yr	NM
❑ 2002 [M]	Bennie Green Swings the Blues	1960	30.00
❑ S-2002 [S]	Bennie Green Swings the Blues	1960	40.00

FANTASY

Number	Title	Yr	NM
❑ OJC-1728	Bennie Green Blows His Horn	198?	12.00
❑ OJC-1752	Walkin' Down	198?	12.00

JAZZLAND

Number	Title	Yr	NM
❑ JLP-43 [M]	Glidin' Along	1961	30.00
❑ JLP-943 [S]	Glidin' Along	1961	30.00

PRESTIGE

Number	Title	Yr	NM
❑ PRLP-210 [10]	Bennie Blows His Horn	1955	150.00
❑ PRLP-7041 [M]	Bennie Green and Art Farmer	1956	100.00
❑ PRLP-7052 [M]	Bennie Green Blows His Horn	1956	100.00
❑ PRLP-7160 [M]	Bennie Green Blows His Horn	1959	80.00
❑ PRST-7776	The Best of Bennie Green	1970	18.00
❑ PRLP-7049 [M]	Walking Down	1956	100.00

RCA VICTOR

Number	Title	Yr	NM
❑ LPM-2376 [M]	Futura	1961	30.00
❑ LSP-2376 [S]	Futura	1961	30.00

TIME

Number	Title	Yr	NM
❑ 52021 [M]	Bennie Green	1960	40.00
❑ S-2021 [S]	Bennie Green	1960	50.00

VEE JAY

Number	Title	Yr	NM
❑ LP-1005 [M]	The Swingin'est	1959	50.00
❑ SR-1005 [S]	The Swingin'est	1959	50.00
—This LP was reissued as "Juggin' Around" by GENE AMMONS on Vee Jay 3024			
❑ VJS-1005 [S]	The Swingin'est	198?	12.00
—Reissue on thinner vinyl			

GREEN, BENNIE/PAUL QUINICHETTE

DECCA

Number	Title	Yr	NM
❑ DL8176 [M]	Blow Your Horn	1955	50.00

GREEN, BERNIE

BARBARY COAST

Number	Title	Yr	NM
❑ 33015-S [S]	Bernie Green Plays More Than You Can Stand in Hi-Fi	1958	50.00

RCA VICTOR

Number	Title	Yr	NM
❑ LSA-2376 [S]	Futura	1961	50.00
❑ LPM-1929 [M]	Musically Mad	1959	60.00
❑ LSP-1929 [S]	Musically Mad	1959	100.00

SAN FRANCISCO

Number	Title	Yr	NM
❑ M-33015 [M]	Bernie Green Plays More Than You Can Stand in Hi-Fi	1957	50.00

GREEN, BUNKY

ARGO

Number	Title	Yr	NM
❑ LP-753 [M]	Testifyin' Time	1965	30.00
❑ LPS-753 [S]	Testifyin' Time	1965	30.00

CADET

Number	Title	Yr	NM
❑ LP-766 [M]	Playin' for Keeps	1966	30.00
❑ LPS-766 [S]	Playin' for Keeps	1966	30.00
❑ LP-753 [M]	Testifyin' Time	1966	18.00
❑ LPS-753 [S]	Testifyin' Time	1966	25.00
❑ LP-780 [M]	The Latinization of Bunky Green	1967	30.00
❑ LPS-780 [S]	The Latinization of Bunky Green	1967	30.00

VANGUARD

Number	Title	Yr	NM
❑ VSD-79425	Places We've Never Been	1979	15.00
❑ VSD-79387	Transformations	197?	15.00
❑ VSD-79413	Visions	1978	15.00

GREEN, BYRDIE

PRESTIGE

Number	Title	Yr	NM
❑ PRLP-7509 [M]	I Got It Bad	1967	25.00
❑ PRST-7509 [S]	I Got It Bad	1967	18.00
❑ PRST-7574	Sister Byrdie	1968	18.00
❑ PRLP-7503 [M]	The Golden Thrush Speaks	1967	25.00
❑ PRST-7503 [S]	The Golden Thrush Speaks	1967	18.00

GREEN, FREDDIE

RCA VICTOR

Number	Title	Yr	NM
❑ LPM-1210 [M]	Mr. Rhythm	1956	50.00

GREEN, GARLAND

RCA VICTOR

Number	Title	Yr	NM
❑ APL1-2351	Love Is What We Came Here For	1977	15.00

UNI

Number	Title	Yr	NM
❑ 73073	Jealous Kind of Fellow	1969	25.00

GREEN, GRANT

BLUE NOTE

Number	Title	Yr	NM
❑ BLP-84360	Alive!	1970	60.00
—We're not sure what the original label is; it could be the blue and white label with "A Division of Liberty Records," the mostly black label with "Liberty/UA," or the blue and white label with "A Division of United Artists Records			
❑ BLP-84360	Alive!	1973	30.00
—Dark blue label with black stylized "b" at upper right			
❑ BLP-4139 [M]	Am I Blue	1963	100.00
—With "New York, USA" on label			
❑ BLP-84139 [S]	Am I Blue	1963	100.00
—With New York, USA address on label			
❑ BLP-84139 [S]	Am I Blue	1968	30.00
—With "A Division of Liberty Records" on label			
❑ BLP-84432	Born to Be Blue	1985	50.00
❑ BLP-84327	Carryin' On	1969	100.00
—A Division of Liberty Records" on label			
❑ BLP-4132 [M]	Feelin' the Spirit	1963	40.00
❑ BLP-84132 [S]	Feelin' the Spirit	1963	100.00
—With New York, USA address on label			
❑ BLP-84132 [S]	Feelin' the Spirit	1968	30.00
—With "A Division of Liberty Records" on label			
❑ BLP-84310	Goin' West	1969	100.00
—A Division of Liberty Records" on label			
❑ BLP-4064 [M]	Grant's First Stand	1961	200.00
—With W. 63rd St. addresss on label			
❑ BLP-4064 [M]	Grant's First Stand	1963	50.00
—With New York, USA address on label			
❑ BLP-84064 [S]	Grant's First Stand	1961	150.00
—With W. 63rd St. addresss on label			
❑ BLP-84064 [S]	Grant's First Stand	1963	80.00
—With New York, USA address on label			
❑ BLP-84064 [S]	Grant's First Stand	1968	30.00
—With "A Division of Liberty Records" on label			
❑ BLP-4086 [M]	Grant Stand	1962	200.00
—With W. 63rd St. address on label			
❑ BLP-4086 [M]	Grant Stand	1963	100.00
—With New York, USA address on label			
❑ BLP-84086 [S]	Grant Stand	1962	150.00
—With W. 63rd St. address on label			
❑ BLP-84086 [S]	Grant Stand	1963	100.00
—With New York, USA address on label			
❑ BLP-84086 [S]	Grant Stand	1968	30.00
—With "A Division of Liberty Records" on label			
❑ BLP-84086 [S]	Grant Stand	197?	25.00
—Dark blue label with white stylized "b" at upper right			
❑ BLP-84342	Green Is Beautiful	1970	60.00
—A Division of Liberty Records" on label			
❑ BLP-4071 [M]	Green Street	1961	200.00
—With W. 63rd St. address on label			
❑ BLP-4071 [M]	Green Street	1963	60.00
—With New York, USA address on label			
❑ BLP-84071 [S]	Green Street	1961	150.00
—With W. 63rd St. address on label			
❑ BLP-84071 [S]	Green Street	1963	60.00
—With New York, USA address on label			
❑ BLP-84071 [S]	Green Street	1968	30.00
—With "A Division of Liberty Records" on label			
❑ BLP-4154 [M]	Idle Moments	1964	40.00
❑ BLP-84154 [S]	Idle Moments	1964	100.00
—With New York, USA address on label			
❑ BLP-84154 [S]	Idle Moments	1968	30.00
—With "A Division of Liberty Records" on label			
❑ BLP-4202 [M]	I Want to Hold Your Hand	1964	40.00
❑ BLP-84202 [S]	I Want to Hold Your Hand	1964	100.00
—With New York, USA address on label			
❑ BLP-84202 [S]	I Want to Hold Your Hand	1968	30.00
—With "A Division of Liberty Records" on label			
❑ BN-LA037-G2	Live at the Lighthouse	1973	50.00
❑ LT-1032	Nigeria	1980	50.00
❑ BLP-84413	Shades of Green	1972	80.00
—A Division of United Artists Records" on blue and white label			
❑ LT-990	Solid	1980	40.00
❑ BLP-4253 [M]	Street of Dreams	1967	100.00
—A Division of Liberty Records" on label			
❑ BLP-84253 [S]	Street of Dreams	1967	80.00
—A Division of Liberty Records" on label			
❑ BLP-4099 [M]	Sunday Mornin'	1962	200.00
—With W. 63rd St. address on label			
❑ BLP-4099 [M]	Sunday Mornin'	1963	150.00
—With New York, USA address on label			
❑ BLP-84099 [S]	Sunday Mornin'	1962	150.00
—With W. 63rd St. address on label			
❑ BLP-84099 [S]	Sunday Mornin'	1963	120.00
—With New York, USA address on label			
❑ BLP-84099 [S]	Sunday Mornin'	1968	25.00
—With "A Division of Liberty Records" on label			
❑ BLP-4183 [M]	Talkin' About!	1964	40.00
❑ BLP-84183 [S]	Talkin' About!	1964	100.00
—With New York, USA address on label			
❑ BLP-84183 [S]	Talkin' About!	1968	30.00
—With "A Division of Liberty Records" on label			
❑ BLP-84415	The Final Comedown	1972	80.00
—A Division of United Artists Records" on blue and white label			
❑ BLP-4111 [M]	The Latin Bit	1962	100.00
—With "New York, USA" on label			
❑ BLP-84111 [S]	The Latin Bit	1962	100.00
—With New York, USA address on label; reproductions exist			
❑ BLP-84111 [S]	The Latin Bit	1968	30.00
—With "A Division of Liberty Records" on label			
❑ BLP-84373	Visions	1971	80.00

COBBLESTONE

Number	Title	Yr	NM
❑ CST-9002	Iron City	1972	100.00
—Reproductions exist			

DELMARK

Number	Title	Yr	NM
❑ DL-404 [M]	All the Gin Is Gone	1966	30.00
❑ DS-404 [S]	All the Gin Is Gone	1966	30.00
❑ DL-427 [M]	Black Forrest	1966	30.00
❑ DS-427 [S]	Black Forrest	1966	30.00

KUDU

Number	Title	Yr	NM
❑ KU-29	The Main Attraction	1976	30.00

Number	Title	Yr	NM
MOSAIC			
❏ MR5-133	The Complete Blue Note Recordings of Grant Green with Sonny Clark	199?	300.00
MUSE			
❏ MR-5014	Green Blues	1973	30.00
❏ MR-5120	Iron City	197?	30.00
VERSATILE			
❏ MSG-6002	Easy	1978	25.00
VERVE			
❏ V-8627 [M]	His Majesty, King Funk	1965	100.00
❏ V6-8627 [S]	His Majesty, King Funk	1965	120.00

GREEN, LLOYD

Number	Title	Yr	NM
CHART			
❏ CHS-1010	Cool Steel Man	1969	30.00
❏ 1024	Moody River	1970	30.00
❏ CHM-1006 [M]	Mr. Nashville Sound	1968	50.00
❏ CHS-1006 [S]	Mr. Nashville Sound	1968	30.00
GRT			
❏ 8018	Feelings	1977	15.00
LITTLE DARLIN'			
❏ LD-4002	Day for Decision	196?	30.00
❏ LD4005	The Hit Sounds of Lloyd Green	196?	30.00
MONUMENT			
❏ KZ32532	Shades of Steel	1973	18.00
❏ KZ33368	Steel Rides	1975	18.00
TIME			
❏ T-2152 [M]	Big Steel Guitar	1964	30.00
❏ ST-2152 [S]	Big Steel Guitar	1964	40.00

GREEN, PETER

Number	Title	Yr	NM
REPRISE			
❏ RS6436 [B]	The End of the Game	1970	30.00
SAIL			
❏ 0110 [B]	In the Skies	1979	15.00
❏ 0112 [B]	Little Dreamer	1980	15.00

GREEN, PHIL

Number	Title	Yr	NM
LONDON			
❏ LPB-17 [10]	Rhythm on Reeds	1950	50.00

GREEN, URBIE

Number	Title	Yr	NM
ABC-PARAMOUNT			
❏ ABC-137 [M]	All About Urbie Green	1956	50.00
❏ ABC-101 [M]	Blues and Other Shades of Green	1955	60.00
BETHLEHEM			
❏ BCP-14 [M]	East Coast Jazz, Volume 6	1955	80.00
❏ BCP-6041	The Lyrical Language of Urbie Green	197?	15.00
—Reissue of 14, distributed by RCA Victor			
BLUE NOTE			
❏ BLP-5036 [10]	Urbie Green Septet	1954	250.00
COMMAND			
❏ RS 33-815 [M]	The Persuasive Trombone of Urbie Green	1960	15.00
❏ RS815SD [S]	The Persuasive Trombone of Urbie Green	1960	18.00
❏ RS 33-838 [M]	The Persuasive Trombone of Urbie Green, Volume 2	1962	15.00
❏ RS838SD [S]	The Persuasive Trombone of Urbie Green, Volume 2	1962	18.00
❏ RS 33-857 [M]	Urbie Green and His 6-Tet	1963	15.00
❏ RS857SD [S]	Urbie Green and His 6-Tet	1963	18.00
CTI			
❏ 7079	Senor Blues	1977	15.00
❏ 7070	The Fox	1976	15.00
PROJECT 3			
❏ PR5014SD	21 Trombones	1967	15.00
❏ PR5024SD	21 Trombones, Volume 2	1968	15.00
❏ PR5066SD	Bein' Green	1972	15.00
❏ PR5087SD	Big Beautiful Band	1974	12.00
❏ PR5052SD	Green Power	1970	15.00
RCA VICTOR			
❏ LPM-1969 [M]	Best of the New Broadway Show Hits	1959	40.00
❏ LSP-1969 [S]	Best of the New Broadway Show Hits	1959	40.00
❏ LPM-1741 [M]	Jimmy McHugh in Hi-Fi	1958	50.00
❏ LSP-1741 [S]	Jimmy McHugh in Hi-Fi	1958	60.00
❏ LPM-1667 [M]	Let's Face the Music and Dance	1958	40.00
❏ LSP-1667 [S]	Let's Face the Music and Dance	1958	40.00
VANGUARD			
❏ VRS-8010 [10]	Urbie Green and His Band	1954	120.00
X			
❏ LXA-3026 [10]	A Cool Yuletide	1954	120.00

GREEN, URBIE/VIC DICKENSON

Number	Title	Yr	NM
JAZZTONE			
❏ J-1259 [M]	Urbie Green Octet/Slidin' Swing	1957	40.00

GREEN, WILLIAM

Number	Title	Yr	NM
EVEREST			
❏ LPBR-5213 [M]	Shades of Green	1963	18.00
❏ SDBR-1213 [S]	Shades of Green	1963	25.00

GREEN

Number	Title	Yr	NM
ATCO			
❏ SD 33-282	Green	1969	18.00
❏ SD 33-366	To Help Somebody	1971	15.00

GREEN BULLFROG

Number	Title	Yr	NM
DECCA			
❏ DL75269 [B]	Green Bullfrog	1971	40.00

GREEN DAY

Number	Title	Yr	NM
ADELINE			
❏ AR033-1	American Idiot	2006	30.00
❏ 012-1	Warning:	2000	25.00
LOOKOUT!			
❏ 22 [B]	39/Smooth	1990	30.00
❏ 46 [B]	Kerplunk	1992	30.00
REPRISE			
❏ 541860-1 [B]	Demolicious	2014	30.00
❏ 45529	Dookie	1994	25.00
—Original stock issue on black vinyl			
❏ 45529 [B]	Dookie	1995	30.00
—Reissue on pink vinyl			
❏ 45529 [DJ]	Dookie	1994	35.00
—Promo version on clear green vinyl in plain white cover			
❏ 45529 [DJ]	Dookie	1994	30.00
—Promo version on milky pale-green vinyl			
❏ 46046 [B]	Insomniac	1995	30.00
❏ 47613-1 [B]	Warning	2014	25.00

GREEN RIVER

Number	Title	Yr	NM
HOMESTEAD			
❏ 031 [B]	Come On Down	1985	50.00
—Originals do not have a UPC code (deduct 25% if UPC is there)			
SUB POP			
❏ 11 [EP]	Dry as a Bone	1987	80.00
—First 2,000 copies have yellow inserts			
❏ 11 [EP]	Dry as a Bone	1987	50.00
—Later copies have pink inserts			
❏ 15 [EP]	Rehab Doll	1988	50.00
—First 1,000 copies on green vinyl			
❏ 15 [EP]	Rehab Doll	1988	35.00

GREENBAUM, NORMAN

Number	Title	Yr	NM
REPRISE			
❏ RS6422	Back Home Again	1970	18.00
❏ MS2048	Petaluma	1972	30.00
❏ RS6365	Spirit in the Sky	1969	18.00
VARESE SARABANDE			
❏ 3020662291 [B]	Spirit in the Sky	2014	30.00

GREENBRIAR BOYS, THE

Number	Title	Yr	NM
ELEKTRA			
❏ EKL-233 [M]	Dian and the Greenbriar Boys	1963	30.00
❏ EKS-7233 [S]	Dian and the Greenbriar Boys	1963	30.00
VANGUARD			
❏ VRS-9233 [M]	Better Late Than Never	1966	25.00
❏ VSD 79233 [S]	Better Late Than Never	1966	30.00
❏ VRS-9159 [M]	Ragged But Right	1964	25.00
❏ VSD-79159 [S]	Ragged But Right	1964	30.00
❏ VRS-9104 [M]	The Greenbriar Boys	1962	30.00

GREENE, BOB

Number	Title	Yr	NM
RCA VICTOR			
❏ ARL1-0504	The World of Jelly Roll Morton	1974	15.00

GREENE, BURTON, AND ALAN SILVA

Number	Title	Yr	NM
HAT HUT			
❏ 15	Ongoing Strings	198?	18.00

GREENE, BURTON

Number	Title	Yr	NM
COLUMBIA			
❏ CS9784	Presenting Burton Greene	1969	18.00
ESP-DISK'			
❏ 1024 [M]	Burton Greene	1966	30.00
❏ S-1024 [S]	Burton Greene	1966	25.00
❏ S-1074	Burton Greene Concert Tour	1968	30.00

GREENE, DODO

Number	Title	Yr	NM
BLUE NOTE			
❏ BLP-9001 [M]	My Hour of Need	1962	50.00
—With W. 63rd St. addresss on label			
❏ BLP-9001 [M]	My Hour of Need	1963	30.00
—With "New York, USA" address on label			
❏ BST-89001 [S]	My Hour of Need	1967	25.00
—With "A Division of Liberty Records" on label			

GREENE, JACK, AND JEANNIE SEELY

Number	Title	Yr	NM
DECCA			
❏ DL75171	Jack Greene and Jeannie Seely	1970	18.00
❏ DL75392	Two for the Show	1972	18.00
MCA			
❏ 77	Two for the Show	1973	15.00
—Reissue of Decca 75392			

GREENE, JACK

Number	Title	Yr	NM
DECCA			
❏ DL4904 [M]	All the Time	1967	25.00
❏ DL74904 [S]	All the Time	1967	18.00
❏ DL75156	Back in the Arms of Love	1969	18.00
❏ DL75208	Greatest Hits	1970	18.00
❏ DL75308	Greene Country	1972	18.00
❏ DL75080	I Am Not Alone	1969	18.00
❏ DL75188	Lord Is That Me	1970	18.00
❏ DL75124	Statue of a Fool	1969	18.00
❏ DL4845 [M]	There Goes My Everything	1967	25.00
❏ DL74845 [S]	There Goes My Everything	1967	18.00
❏ DL75283	There's a Whole Lot About a Woman	1971	18.00
❏ DL4939 [M]	What Locks the Door	1968	30.00
❏ DL74939 [S]	What Locks the Door	1968	18.00
❏ T-91433 [M]	What Locks the Door	1968	40.00
—Capitol Record Club edition			
❏ ST-91433 [S]	What Locks the Door	1968	25.00
—Capitol Record Club edition			
❏ DL4079 [M]	You Are My Treasure	1968	30.00
❏ DL74979 [S]	You Are My Treasure	1968	18.00
MCA			
❏ 291	Greatest Hits	1973	15.00
—Reissue of Decca 75208			
❏ 295	Greene Country	1973	15.00
—Reissue of Decca 75308			
PICKWICK			
❏ SPC-6173	I Never Had It So Good	197?	12.00

GREENE, LORNE; MICHAEL LANDON; DAN BLOCKER

Number	Title	Yr	NM
RCA VICTOR			
❏ LPM-2583 [M]	Bonanza -- Ponderosa Party Time!	1962	30.00
❏ LSP-2583 [S]	Bonanza -- Ponderosa Party Time!	1962	40.00
❏ LPM-2757 [M]	Christmas on the Ponderosa	1963	30.00
❏ LSP-2757 [S]	Christmas on the Ponderosa	1963	30.00

GREENE, LORNE

Number	Title	Yr	NM
RCA CAMDEN			
❏ CAS-2391	Five Card Stud	1970	30.00
RCA VICTOR			
❏ LPM-3410 [M]	Have a Happy Holiday	1965	30.00
❏ LSP-3410 [S]	Have a Happy Holiday	1965	30.00
❏ LPM-3409 [M]	Lorne Greene's American West	1965	30.00
❏ LSP 3409 [S]	Lorne Greene's American West	1965	30.00
❏ SP0327 [DJ]	Palaver with The Man	1965	50.00
—Promo-only interview record with script			
❏ SP-33-327 [DJ]	Palaver with The Man	1965	50.00
—Promo-only interview record with script			
❏ LPM-3678 [M]	Portrait of the West	1966	30.00
❏ LSP-3678 [S]	Portrait of the West	1966	30.00
❏ LPM-3302 [M]	The Man	1965	30.00
❏ LSP-3302 [S]	The Man	1965	30.00
❏ LPM-2843 [M]	Welcome to the Ponderosa	1964	30.00
❏ LSP-2843 [S]	Welcome to the Ponderosa	1964	30.00
❏ LPM-2661 [M]	Young at Heart	1963	30.00
❏ LSP-2661 [S]	Young at Heart	1963	30.00
RCA VICTOR RED SEAL			
❏ LM-2783 [M]	Peter and the Wolf	1964	30.00
❏ LSC-2783 [S]	Peter and the Wolf	1964	30.00
—Above with the London Symphony Orchestra			

GREENSLEEVES, EDDIE

Number	Title	Yr	NM
CAMEO			
❏ C-1031 [M]	Humorous Folk Songs	1963	25.00
❏ SC-1031 [S]	Humorous Folk Songs	1963	30.00

GREENWICH, ELLIE

Number	Title	Yr	NM
UNITED ARTISTS			
❏ UAS-6648	Ellie Greenwich Composes, Produces and Sings	1968	50.00
VERVE			
❏ V6-5091	Let It Be Written, Let It Be Sung	1973	30.00

GREENWICH, SONNY

Number	Title	Yr	NM
PM			
❏ PMR-016	Evol-ution: Love's Opposite	1978	18.00

GREENWOOD, LEE

Number	Title	Yr	NM
MCA			
❏ 5623	Christmas to Christmas	1985	12.00
❏ 5582	Greatest Hits	1985	10.00
❏ 42219	Greatest Hits -- Volume Two	1988	10.00

Number	Title	Yr	NM
❏ 42300	If Only for One Night	1989	12.00
❏ 5999	If There's Any Justice	1987	10.00
❏ 5305	Inside and Out	1982	15.00
— Original title			
❏ 5305	Inside Out	1982	10.00
— Corrected title			
❏ 5770	Love Will Find Its Way to You	1986	10.00
❏ 5403	Somebody's Gonna Love You	1983	10.00
❏ 5622	Streamline	1985	10.00
❏ 42167	This Is My Country	1988	10.00
❏ 5488	You've Got a Good Love Comin'	1984	10.00

GREENWOOD COUNTY SINGERS, THE

KAPP

❏ KL1448 [M]	Ballad of Cat Ballou	1965	15.00
❏ KS3448 [S]	Ballad of Cat Ballou	1965	18.00
❏ KL1422 [M]	Have You Heard	1965	15.00
❏ KS3422 [S]	Have You Heard	1965	18.00
❏ KL1487 [M]	Tear Down the Walls	1966	15.00
— As "The Greenwood Singers"			
❏ KS3487 [S]	Tear Down the Walls	1966	18.00
— As "The Greenwood Singers"			
❏ KL1362 [M]	The First Recordings by the Joyful Greenwood County Singers	1964	18.00
— Original title			
❏ KS3362 [S]	The First Recordings by the Joyful Greenwood County Singers	1964	25.00
— Original title			
❏ KL1362 [M]	The New Frankie and Johnny Song	1964	15.00
❏ KS3362 [S]	The New Frankie and Johnny Song	1964	18.00

RCA VICTOR

❏ LSP-4384	Return to Greenwood County	1970	18.00

GREER, PAULA

WORKSHOP JAZZ

❏ WSJ203 [M]	Introducing Miss Paula Greer	1963	250.00

GREGG, BOBBY

EPIC

❏ LN24051 [M]	Let's Stomp and Wild Weekend	1963	30.00
❏ BN26051 [S]	Let's Stomp and Wild Weekend	1963	40.00

GREGORY, DICK

COLPIX

❏ CP420 [M]	East and West	1961	30.00
❏ CP417 [M]	In Living Black and White	1961	30.00
❏ CP480 [M]	We All Have Problems	1964	30.00

GATEWAY

❏ GLP9007 [M]	My Brother's Keeper	1963	40.00

POPPY

❏ PP-LA176-G2	Caught in the Act	1973	18.00
❏ PYS60005	Dick Gregory at Kent State	1971	18.00
❏ PYS40011	Dick Gregory at the Village Gate	1972	18.00
❏ PYS40008	Dick Gregory On...	1970	18.00
❏ PYS60004	Frankenstein	1970	18.00
❏ PYS60001	The Light Side: The Dark Side	1969	25.00

TOMATO

❏ 9001	The Best of Dick Gregory	1978	25.00

VEE JAY

❏ LP4001 [M]	Dick Gregory Talks Turkey	1962	30.00
❏ LP1093 [M]	Running for President	1964	30.00
❏ LP4005 [M]	Two Sides of Dick Gregory	1963	30.00

GRENFELL, JOYCE

ELEKTRA

❏ EKL-184 [M]	Presenting Joyce Grenfell	1960	35.00

GREY, AL, AND WILD BILL DAVIS

CLASSIC JAZZ

❏ 103	Keybone	197?	18.00

GREY, AL

ARGO

❏ LP-689 [M]	Al Grey and the Billy Mitchell Sextet	1962	25.00
❏ LPS-689 [S]	Al Grey and the Billy Mitchell Sextet	1962	30.00
❏ LP-731 [M]	Boss Bones	1964	25.00
❏ LPS-731 [S]	Boss Bones	1964	30.00
❏ LP-718 [M]	Having a Ball	1963	25.00
❏ LPS-718 [S]	Having a Ball	1963	30.00
❏ LP-711 [M]	Night Song	1963	25.00
❏ LPS-711 [S]	Night Song	1963	30.00
❏ LP-700 [M]	Snap Your Fingers	1962	25.00
❏ LPS-700 [S]	Snap Your Fingers	1962	30.00
❏ LP-653 [M]	The Last of the Big Plungers	1960	30.00
❏ LPS-653 [S]	The Last of the Big Plungers	1960	30.00
❏ LP-677 [M]	The Thinking Man's Trombone	1961	25.00

Number	Title	Yr	NM
❏ LPS-677 [S]	The Thinking Man's Trombone	1961	30.00

CHESS

❏ 2-ACMJ-409	Basic Grey	1976	18.00

CLASSIC JAZZ

❏ 118	Grey's Mood	197?	18.00

COLUMBIA

❏ FC38505	Struttin' and Shoutin'	1983	12.00

TANGERINE

❏ TRC-1504 [M]	Shades of Grey	1965	18.00
❏ TRCS-1504 [S]	Shades of Grey	1965	25.00

GRIER, ROOSEVELT

RIC

❏ M-1008 [M]	Soul City	1964	25.00
❏ S-1008 [S]	Soul City	1964	30.00

WORD

❏ WR-8342	Committed	1986	15.00

GRIFF, RAY

ABC DOT

❏ DOSD-2011	Expressions	1974	15.00

CAPITOL

❏ ST-11486	Ray Griff	1976	12.00
❏ ST-11718	Raymond's Place	1977	12.00
❏ ST-11566	The Last of the Winfield Amateurs	1976	12.00

DOT

❏ DLP-25868	A Ray of Sunshine	1968	25.00
❏ DOS-26013	Songs for Everyone	1973	18.00

ROYAL AMERICAN

❏ RAS1007	Ray Griff Sings	1972	18.00

GRIFFIN, DELLA

DOBRE

❏ 1009	Della Griffin Sings	1978	15.00

GRIFFIN, DICK

STRATA-EAST

❏ SES-19747	The Eighth Wonder	1975	25.00

GRIFFIN, JIMMY

POLYDOR

❏ PD6018	James Griffin and Co.	1973	18.00

REPRISE

❏ R-6091 [M]	Summer Holiday	1963	50.00
❏ R9-6091 [S]	Summer Holiday	1963	60.00

GRIFFIN, JOHNNY, AND MATTHEW GEE

ATLANTIC

❏ 1431 [M]	Soul Groove	1965	25.00
❏ SD1431 [S]	Soul Groove	1965	30.00

GRIFFIN, JOHNNY

ARGO

❏ LP-624 [M]	Johnny Griffin Quartet	1958	50.00

BLACK LION

❏ 304	You Leave Me Breathless	197?	18.00

BLUE NOTE

❏ BLP-1559 [M]	A Blowing Session	1957	250.00
— Deep groove" version (deep indentation under label on both sides)			
❏ BLP-1559 [M]	A Blowing Session	1957	100.00
— Regular version, "W. 63rd St." address on label			
❏ BLP-1559 [M]	A Blowing Session	1963	30.00
— With "New York, USA" address on label			
❏ BST-85133	Introducing Johnny Griffin	1985	12.00
— The Finest in Jazz Since 1939" reissue			
❏ BT-46536	Introducing Johnny Griffin	198?	12.00
— Another "The Finest in Jazz Since 1939" reissue			
❏ BLP-1533 [M]	Introducing Johnny Griffin	1956	1000.00
— Deep groove" version (deep indentation under label on both sides)			
❏ BLP-1533 [M]	Introducing Johnny Griffin	1956	500.00
— Regular version, Lexington Ave. address on label			
❏ BLP-1533 [M]	Introducing Johnny Griffin	1957	200.00
— With "W. 63rd St." address on label			
❏ BLP-1533 [M]	Introducing Johnny Griffin	1963	100.00
— With "New York, USA" address on label			
❏ BST-81580 [S]	The Congregation	1967	18.00
— With "A Division of Liberty Records" on label			
❏ B1-89383	The Congregation	1994	18.00
— The Finest in Jazz Since 1939" reissue			
❏ BLP-1580 [M]	The Congregation	1958	1000.00
— Deep groove" version (deep indentation under label on both sides). Andy Warhol cover			
❏ BLP-1580 [M]	The Congregation	1958	500.00
— Regular version, "W. 63rd St." address on label. Andy Warhol cover			
❏ BLP-1580 [M]	The Congregation	1963	125.00
— With "New York, USA" address on label. Andy Warhol cover			
❏ BST-1580 [S]	The Congregation	1959	600.00
— Deep groove" version (deep indentation under label on both sides). Andy Warhol cover			
❏ BST-1580 [S]	The Congregation	1959	300.00

Number	Title	Yr	NM
— Regular version, "W. 63rd St." address on label. Andy Warhol cover			
❏ BST-1580 [S]	The Congregation	1963	100.00
— With "New York, USA" address on label. Andy Warhol cover			

EMARCY

❏ MG-26001 [M]	Night Lady	1967	40.00
❏ SR-66001 [S]	Night Lady	1967	30.00

FANTASY

❏ OJC-485	The Big Soul-Band	1990	15.00
❏ OJC-136	The Little Giant	198?	12.00

GALAXY

❏ 5126	Bush Dance	1979	15.00
❏ 5146	Call It Whatchawaana	1984	15.00
❏ 5132	NYC Underground	1980	15.00
❏ 5117	Return of the Griffin	1979	15.00
❏ 5139	To the Ladies	1981	15.00

INNER CITY

❏ IC-2004	Blues for Harvey	1973	18.00
❏ IC-6042	Live Tokyo	197?	25.00

JAZZLAND

❏ JLP-93 [M]	The Little Giant	1961	40.00
❏ JLP-993 [S]	The Little Giant	1961	30.00

MILESTONE

❏ 47014	Big Soul	197?	25.00
❏ 47054	Little Giant	197?	18.00

MOON

❏ MLP-004	Body and Soul	1992	18.00

RIVERSIDE

❏ RLP-368 [M]	Change of Pace	1961	30.00
❏ RS-9368 [S]	Change of Pace	1961	30.00
❏ RLP-462 [M]	Do Nothing 'Til You Hear from Me	1963	30.00
❏ RS-9462 [S]	Do Nothing 'Til You Hear from Me	1963	30.00
❏ RLP-437 [M]	Grab This!	1962	30.00
❏ RS-9437 [S]	Grab This!	1962	30.00
❏ RLP 12-264 [M]	Johnny Griffin Sextet	1958	350.00
❏ 6145	Studio Jazz Party	198?	15.00
❏ RLP-338 [M]	Studio Jazz Party	1960	40.00
❏ RS-9338 [S]	Studio Jazz Party	1960	30.00
❏ RLP 12-331 [M]	The Big Soul-Band	1960	40.00
❏ RLP-1171 [3]	The Big Soul-Band	1960	30.00
❏ RLP-420 [M]	The Kerry Dancers	1962	30.00
❏ RS-9420 [S]	The Kerry Dancers	1962	30.00
❏ RLP 12-304 [M]	The Little Giant	1959	50.00
❏ RLP-1149 [S]	The Little Giant	1959	40.00
❏ RLP-479 [M]	Wade in the Water	1964	25.00
❏ RS-9479 [S]	Wade in the Water	1964	30.00
❏ RLP 12-274 [M]	Way Out!	1958	50.00
❏ RLP-387 [M]	White Gardenia	1961	30.00
❏ RS-9387 [S]	White Gardenia	1961	30.00

STEEPLECHASE

❏ SCS-1004	Blues for Harvey	198?	15.00

TIMELESS

❏ 311	The Jamfs Are Coming	198?	15.00
❏ LPSJP-121	The Jamfs Are Coming	1990	12.00
— Reissue of 311			

GRIFFIN, KEN

COLUMBIA

❏ CL6130 [10]	Christmas Carols by Ken Griffin	1950	30.00
❏ CS8760 [S]	The Organ Plays at Christmas	1963	15.00
❏ CL692 [M]	The Organ Plays at Christmas	1955	30.00
— Red and black label with six "eye" logos			

GRIFFIN, MERV

51 WEST

❏ Q16281	P.S. I Love You	198?	10.00

CAMEO

❏ C-1060 [M]	My Favorite Songs	1964	25.00
❏ SC-1060 [S]	My Favorite Songs	1964	30.00

CARLTON

❏ LP-12-134 [M]	Merv Griffin's Dance Party	1961	30.00
❏ STLP-12-134 [S]	Merv Griffin's Dance Party	1961	40.00

GRIFFIN

❏ G3G-1501	As Time Goes By	1973	15.00

METROMEDIA

❏ MD1023	Appearing Nightly	1969	15.00

MGM

❏ E-4381 [M]	'Alf and 'Alf: Songs of the British Music Hall	1966	18.00
— With Arthur Treacher			
❏ SE-4381 [S]	'Alf and 'Alf: Songs of the British Music Hall	1966	25.00
— With Arthur Treacher			
❏ E-4401 [M]	And a Sled .... And a Catcher's Mitt ... And a Puppy ... And a Popgun ... And a Big Christmas Album from Merv Griffin and His TV Family	1966	25.00

Number	Title	Yr	NM
❑ SE-4401 [S]	And a Sled .... And a Catcher's Mitt ... And a Puppy ... And a Popgun ... And a Big Christmas Album from Merv Griffin and His TV Family	1966	30.00
❑ E-4326 [M]	A Tinkling Piano in the Next Apartment	1965	15.00
❑ SE-4326 [S]	A Tinkling Piano in the Next Apartment	1965	18.00

GRIFFITH, ANDY

CAPITOL

❑ T2066 [M]	Andy and Cleopatra	1964	25.00
❑ ST2066 [S]	Andy and Cleopatra	1964	30.00
❑ T1105 [M]	Andy Griffith Shouts the Blues and Old Timey Songs	1959	40.00
❑ ST1105 [S]	Andy Griffith Shouts the Blues and Old Timey Songs	1959	50.00
❑ T962 [M]	Just for Laughs	1958	40.00
❑ T1611 [M]	Songs, Themes and Laughs from The Andy Griffith Show	1961	80.00
❑ ST1611 [S]	Songs, Themes and Laughs from The Andy Griffith Show	1961	120.00
❑ T1215 [M]	This Here Andy Griffith	1959	30.00
❑ ST1215 [S]	This Here Andy Griffith	1959	40.00

GRIFFITH, JOHNNY, TRIO

WORKSHOP JAZZ

❑ WSJ205 [M]	Jazz	1963	200.00

GRIFFITH, NANCI

B.F. DEAL

❑ BFD9	There's a Light Beyond These Woods	1978	50.00

ELEKTRA

❑ 62015	Blue Roses from the Moons	1997	15.00

FEATHERBED

❑ FB902	Poet in My Window	1982	25.00
❑ FB903	There's a Light Beyond These Woods	1982	25.00

MCA

❑ 42102	Little Love Affairs	1988	10.00
❑ 5927	Lone Star State of Mind	1987	10.00
❑ 42255	One Fair Summer Evening	1988	10.00
❑ 6319	Storms	1989	12.00

PHILO

❑ PH-1109	Last of the True Believers	1986	15.00
❑ PH-1096	Once in a Very Blue Moon	1984	15.00
❑ PH-1098	Poet in My Window	1986	15.00
❑ PH-1097	There's a Light Beyond These Woods	1986	15.00

GRIFFITH, SHIRLEY

BLUESVILLE

❑ BVLP-1087 [M]	The Blues of Shirley Griffith	1964	50.00
— Blue label, silver print			
❑ BVLP-1087 [M]	The Blues of Shirley Griffith	1964	30.00
— Blue label, trident logo at right			

GRIMES, GARY

DIRECT DISK

❑ SD-16630	Starhand Visions	198?	30.00
— Audiophile vinyl			

GRIMES, HENRY

FSP-DISK'

❑ 1027 [M]	Henry Grimes Trio	1966	25.00
❑ S-1027 [S]	Henry Grimes Trio	1966	30.00

GRIMES, TINY

CLASSIC JAZZ

❑ 114	Some Groovy Fours	197?	15.00

COLLECTABLES

❑ COL-5321	Tiny Grimes and Friends	198?	12.00
❑ COL-5317	Tiny Grimes and His Rocking Highlanders, Volume 2	198?	12.00
❑ COL-5304	Tiny Grimes Featuring Screamin' Jay Hawkins	198?	12.00

FANTASY

❑ OJC-191	Callin' the Blues	1985	12.00

MUSE

❑ MR-5012	Profoundly Blue	1974	15.00

PRESTIGE

❑ PRLP-7138 [M]	Blues Grooves	1958	100.00
— Yellow label			
❑ PRLP-7144 [M]	Callin' the Blues	1958	200.00

SWINGVILLE

❑ SVLP-2004 [M]	Callin' the Blues	1960	50.00
— Purple label			
❑ SVLP-2004 [M]	Callin' the Blues	1965	30.00
— Blue label, trident logo at right			
❑ SVLP-2002 [M]	Tiny in Swingville	1960	50.00
— Purple label			
❑ SVLP-2002 [M]	Tiny in Swingville	1965	30.00
— Blue label, trident logo at right			

Number	Title	Yr	NM
UNITED ARTISTS			
❑ UAL-3232 [M]	Big Time Guitar	1962	30.00
❑ UAS-6232 [S]	Big Time Guitar	1962	30.00

GRIN

A&M

❑ SP-4415	Gone Crazy	1973	12.00

COLUMBIA LIMITED EDITION

❑ LE10265	All Out	197?	12.00
— Remixed version on Columbia's brown-label "Limited Edition" series			

EPIC

❑ PE34247	The Best of Grin	1976	12.00
— Without bar code on back			
❑ PE34247	The Best of Grin	198?	10.00
— With bar code on back			

SPINDIZZY

❑ Z31038	1 + 1	1972	15.00
❑ KZ31701	All Out	1973	15.00
❑ Z30321 [B]	Grin	1971	15.00

GRISMAN, DAVID

HORIZON

❑ SP-731	Hot Dawg	1979	16.00

ROUNDER

❑ 0190	Acoustic Christmas	1983	15.00
❑ 0169	Here Today	198?	12.00
❑ 0251/2	Home Is Where the Heart Is	1988	15.00
❑ 0069	The Rounder Album	1976	16.00

SUGAR HILL

❑ SH-3713	Early Dawg	1980	12.00

WARNER BROS.

❑ BSK3469	David Grisman Quintet '80	1980	12.00
❑ 23804	Dawg Jazz	1983	12.00
❑ BSK3618	Mondo Mando	1982	12.00

ZEBRA/ACOUSTIC

❑ ZEA-6153	Acousticity	1986	12.00

GRISMAN QUINTET, DAVID

KALEIDOSCOPE

❑ 5	David Grisman Quintet	1977	25.00

GRISSOM, JIMMY

ARGO

❑ LP-729 [M]	World of Trouble	1963	30.00
❑ LPS-729 [S]	World of Trouble	1963	30.00

GROCE, LARRY

DAYBREAK

❑ 2010	Crescentville	1972	15.00
❑ 2000	The Wheat Lies Low	1971	15.00

DISNEYLAND

❑ 1V-8120	Disney's Children's Favorites Volume I	1979	18.00
— Part of Realm Records numbering system; probably Columbia House record club edition			
❑ 2505	Disney's Children's Favorites Volume I	1979	18.00
❑ 1V-8121	Disney's Children's Favorites Volume II	1979	18.00
— Part of Realm Records numbering system; probably Columbia House record club edition			
❑ 2508	Disney's Children's Favorites Volume II	1979	18.00
❑ 2525	Disney's Children's Favorites Volume III	1986	18.00

WARNER BROS.

❑ BS2933	Junkfood Junkie	1976	12.00

GRODECK WHIPPERJENNY

PEOPLE

❑ 3000	Grodeck Whipperjenny	1969	200.00

GROLNICK, DON, AND MICHAEL BRECKER

HIPPOCKET

❑ HP-106	Hearts and Numbers	1985	15.00

WINDHAM HILL

❑ WH-0106	Hearts and Numbers	1987	12.00
— Reissue of HipPocket 106			

GROOTNA

COLUMBIA

❑ C31033	Grootna	1971	25.00

GROOV-U

GATEWAY

❑ GLP-3010	Groov-U On Campus	196?	40.00

GROOVE COLLECTIVE, THE

REPRISE

❑ 45541	The Groove Collective	1994	25.00

Number	Title	Yr	NM
GROOVIE GOOLIES, THE			

RCA VICTOR

❑ LSP-4420	The Groovie Goolies	1970	30.00

GROSS, HENRY

A&M

❑ SP-4416	Henry Gross	1973	15.00
❑ SP-4502	Plug Me Into Something	1974	15.00

ABC

❑ X-747	Henry Gross	1971	18.00

CAPITOL

❑ ST12113	What's in a Name	1980	12.00

LIFESONG

❑ JZ35280	Love Is the Stuff	1978	12.00
❑ LS6002	Release	1976	12.00
❑ PZ34995	Release	1978	10.00
— Reissue of 6002			
❑ LS6010	Show Me to the Stage	1977	12.00
❑ PZ35002	Show Me to the Stage	1978	10.00
— Reissue of 6010			

GROSZ, MARTY

RIVERSIDE

❑ RLP 12-268 [M]	Hurrah for Bix	1958	40.00
❑ RLP-1109 [S]	Hurrah for Bix	1959	30.00

STOMP OFF

❑ SOS-1158	Marty Grosz and the Keepers of the Flame	1988	12.00
❑ SOS-1214	Unsaturated Fats	1991	12.00

GROUNDHOGS, THE

CLEVE

❑ CH-82871	The Groundhogs with John Lee Hooker and John Mayall	196?	100.00

IMPERIAL

❑ LP-12452	Blues Obituary	1969	40.00

LIBERTY

❑ LST-7644 [B]	Thank Christ for the Bomb	1970	30.00

UNITED ARTISTS

❑ UA-LA680-G	Black Diamond	1976	25.00
❑ UA-LA603-G	Crosscut Saw	1976	25.00
❑ UA-LA008-F	Hogwash	1973	25.00
❑ UAS-5513	The Groundhogs Split	1971	25.00
❑ UAS-5570	Who Will Save the World	1972	25.00

WORLD PACIFIC

❑ WPS-21892	Scratching the Surface	1968	40.00

GROUP, THE

BELL

❑ 6038	The Group	1970	25.00

RCA VICTOR

❑ LPM-2663 [M]	The Group	1963	25.00
❑ LSP-2663 [S]	The Group	1963	30.00

GROWING CONCERN, THE

MAINSTREAM

❑ 56108 [M]	The Growing Concern	1968	80.00
❑ S-6108 [S]	The Growing Concern	1968	250.00

GROWL

DISCREET

❑ DS2209	Growl	1974	200.00

GRUNING, TOM

INNER CITY

❑ IC-1119	Midnight Lullaby	198?	15.00

GRUNTZ, GEORGE

PHILIPS

❑ PHM200162 [M]	Bach Humbug	1964	18.00
❑ PHS600162 [S]	Bach Humbug	1964	25.00

GRUSIN, DAVE, AND LEE RITENOUR

GRP

❑ GRPA-1015	Harlequin	1985	12.00

GRUSIN, DAVE

COLUMBIA

❑ CL2344 [M]	Kaleidoscope	1965	25.00
❑ CS9144 [S]	Kaleidoscope	1965	30.00

EPIC

❑ LN24023 [M]	Piano Strings and Moonlight	1962	40.00
❑ BN26023 [S]	Piano Strings and Moonlight	1962	50.00
❑ LN3829 [M]	Subways Are for Sleeping	1962	40.00
❑ BN622 [S]	Subways Are for Sleeping	1962	50.00

GRP

❑ GR-1037	Cinemagic	1987	12.00
❑ GRP-A-1001	Dave Grusin and the NY/LA Dream Band	1982	12.00
❑ GR-9592	Migration	1989	15.00
❑ GRP-A-1018	Mountain Dance	198?	10.00
— Another reissue of GRP/Arista 5010			
❑ GRP-A-1006	Night-Lines	1984	12.00
❑ GR-1011	One of a Kind	198?	12.00

Number	Title	Yr	NM
❏ GR-1051	Sticks and Stones	1988	12.00
❏ GR-9579	The Dave Grusin Collection	1989	15.00
GRP/ARISTA			
❏ GL5506	Live in Japan	1981	12.00
❏ GRP-5010	Mountain Dance	1980	12.00
❏ GL8-8058	Mountain Dance	198?	10.00
—Budget-line reissue			
❏ GRP-5900	Mountain Dance	1981	12.00
—Limiteed edition special pressing			
❏ GRP-5510	Out of the Shadows	1982	12.00
❏ GL8-8139	Out of the Shadows	198?	10.00
—Budget-line reissue			
POLYDOR			
❏ PD-1-6118	One of a Kind	1977	18.00
SHEFFIELD LABS			
❏ SL-5	Discovered Again!	1976	30.00
—Direct-to-disc recording			
SHEFFIELD TREASURY			
❏ ST-500	Discovered Again!	198?	25.00
—Reissue of Sheffield Labs 5			
VERSATILE			
❏ NED1135	Don't Touch	1977	25.00

GRYCE, GIGI, AND CLIFFORD BROWN

BLUE NOTE			
❏ BLP-5048 [10]	Gigi Gryce-Clifford Brown Sextet	1954	400.00

GRYCE, GIGI

BLUE NOTE			
❏ BLP-5050 [10]	Gigi Gryce and His Little Band, Volume 2	1954	300.00
❏ BLP-5051 [10]	Gigi Gryce Quintet/Sextet, Volume 3	1954	300.00
❏ BLP-5049 [10]	Gigi Gryce's Jazztime Paris	1954	300.00
FANTASY			
❏ OJC-081	The Rat Race Blues	198?	12.00
MERCURY			
❏ MG-20628 [M]	Reminiscin'	1961	30.00
❏ SR-60628 [S]	Reminiscin'	1961	40.00
METROJAZZ			
❏ E-1006 [M]	Gigi Gryce	1958	350.00
❏ SE-1006 [S]	Gigi Gryce	1959	60.00
NEW JAZZ			
❏ NJLP-8230 [M]	Sayin' Somethin'!	1959	150.00
—Purple label			
❏ NJLP-8230 [M]	Sayin' Somethin'!	1965	30.00
—Blue label, trident logo at right			
❏ NJLP-8246 [M]	The Hap'nin's	1960	100.00
—Purple label			
❏ NJLP-8246 [M]	The Hap'nin's	1965	30.00
—Blue label, trident logo at right			
❏ NJLP-8262 [M]	The Rat Race Blues	1961	50.00
—Purple label			
❏ NJLP-8262 [M]	The Rat Race Blues	1965	30.00
—Blue label, trident logo at right			
SAVOY			
❏ MG-12137 [M]	Nica's Tempo	1958	80.00
SIGNAL			
❏ S-1201 [M]	Gigi Gryce Quartet	1955	300.00

GRYPHON

BELL			
❏ 1316	Red Queen to Gryphon Three	1974	25.00
(NO LABEL)			
❏ 12497	Gryphon	1973	80.00

GUADALCANAL DIARY

DB			
❏ 73	Walking in the Shadow of the Big Man	1984	18.00
ELEKTRA			
❏ 60752	2X4	1987	12.00
❏ 60848 [DJ]	Flip-Flop	1989	12.00
—Promo-only white label audiophile vinyl			
❏ 60848	Flip-Flop	1989	12.00
❏ 60848 [DJ]	Flip-Flop	1989	15.00
—Promo-only white label audiophile vinyl			
❏ 60478	Jamboree	1986	12.00
❏ 60429 [B]	Walking in the Shadow of the Big Man	1985	12.00
ENTERTAINMENT ON DISC			
❏ EOD102 [EP]	Watusi Rodeo	1983	30.00

GUARALDI, VINCE

FANTASY			
❏ 85017 [B]	A Boy Named Charlie Brown – Jazz Impressions	196?	30.00
❏ 8430 [B]	A Boy Named Charlie Brown – Jazz Impressions	1971	25.00
—Reissue of 85017			
❏ 8431	A Charlie Brown Christmas	1971	30.00
—Reissue of 85019; dark blue label			

Number	Title	Yr	NM
❏ 8431	A Charlie Brown Christmas	1988	18.00
—Remastered version with "1988" on back cover. Lighter blue label. Also has a bonus track!			
❏ 5019 [M]	A Charlie Brown Christmas	1964	30.00

STEREO
"A CHARLIE BROWN CHRISTMAS"
featuring the famous **PEANUTS** characters
ORIGINAL SOUND TRACK **Vince Guaraldi** HIGH FIDELITY

Number	Title	Yr	NM
❏ 85019 [S]	A Charlie Brown Christmas	1964	40.00
❏ 3257 [M]	A Flower Is a Lovesome Thing	1958	40.00
—Red vinyl			
❏ 3257 [M]	A Flower Is a Lovesome Thing	195?	30.00
—Black vinyl, red label, non-flexible vinyl			
❏ 3257 [M]	A Flower Is a Lovesome Thing	196?	18.00
—Black vinyl, red label, flexible vinyl			
❏ OJC-235	A Flower Is a Lovesome Thing	198?	12.00
—Reissue of 3257			
❏ 3362 [M]	From All Sides	1966	25.00
❏ 8362 [S]	From All Sides	1966	25.00
❏ 3359 [M]	Jazz Impressions	1965	30.00
❏ 8359 [S]	Jazz Impressions	1965	30.00
❏ OJC-287	Jazz Impressions	1987	12.00
—Reissue of 8359			
❏ 3337 [M]	Jazz Impressions of Black Orpheus (Cast Your Fate to the Wind)	1962	40.00
—Red vinyl			
❏ 3337 [M]	Jazz Impressions of Black Orpheus (Cast Your Fate to the Wind)	1962	30.00
—Black vinyl, red label, non-flexible vinyl			
❏ 3337 [M]	Jazz Impressions of Black Orpheus (Cast Your Fate to the Wind)	1962	18.00
—Black vinyl, red label, flexible vinyl			
❏ 8089 [S]	Jazz Impressions of Black Orpheus (Cast Your Fate to the Wind)	1962	40.00
—Blue vinyl			
❏ 8089 [S]	Jazz Impressions of Black Orpheus (Cast Your Fate to the Wind)	1962	18.00
—Black vinyl, blue label, flexible vinyl			
❏ 8089 [S]	Jazz Impressions of Black Orpheus (Cast Your Fate to the Wind)	1962	30.00
—Black vinyl, blue label, non-flexible vinyl			
❏ OJC-437	Jazz Impressions of Black Orpheus (Cast Your Fate to the Wind)	198?	12.00
—Reissue of 8089			
❏ 3371 [M]	Live at the El Matador	1967	25.00
❏ 8371 [S]	Live at the El Matador	1967	25.00
❏ OJC-289	Live at the El Matador	1987	12.00
—Reissue of 8371			
❏ 8377	Live-Live-Live	1968	25.00
❏ 3213 [M]	Modern Music from San Francisco	1956	50.00
—Red vinyl			
❏ 3213 [M]	Modern Music from San Francisco	195?	30.00
—Black vinyl, red label, non-flexible vinyl			
❏ OJC-272	Modern Music from San Francisco	1987	12.00
—Reissue of 3213			
❏ 3360 [M]	The Latin Side of Vince Guaraldi	1965	30.00
❏ 8360 [S]	The Latin Side of Vince Guaraldi	1965	30.00
❏ 3358 [M]	Tour de Force	1964	30.00
❏ 8358 [S]	Tour de Force	1964	30.00
❏ 3356 [M]	Vince Guaraldi and Bola Sete and Friends	1964	30.00
❏ 8356 [S]	Vince Guaraldi and Bola Sete and Friends	1964	30.00
❏ 3367 [M]	Vince Guaraldi at Grace Cathedral	1967	25.00
❏ 8367 [S]	Vince Guaraldi at Grace Cathedral	1967	25.00
❏ 3352 [M]	Vince Guaraldi in Person	1963	30.00
❏ 8352 [S]	Vince Guaraldi in Person	1963	30.00

Number	Title	Yr	NM
❏ MPF-4505 ♦	Vince Guaraldi's Greatest Hits	1981	15.00
❏ 3225 [M]	Vince Guaraldi Trio	1956	50.00
—Red vinyl			
❏ 3225 [M]	Vince Guaraldi Trio	195?	30.00
—Black vinyl, red label, non-flexible vinyl			
❏ 3225 [M]	Vince Guaraldi Trio	196?	18.00
—Black vinyl, red label, flexible vinyl			
❏ OJC-149	Vince Guaraldi Trio	198?	12.00
—Reissue of 3225			
MOBILE FIDELITY			
❏ 1-112	Jazz Impressions of Black Orpheus (Cast Your Fate to the Wind)	1983	50.00
—Audiophile vinyl			
WARNER BROS.			
❏ WS1828	Alma-Ville	1970	18.00
❏ WS1775	Eclectic	1969	18.00
❏ WS1747	Oh Good Grief!	1968	25.00

GUARALDI, VINCE/CONTE CANDOLI

CROWN			
❏ CLP-5417 [M]	Vince Guaraldi and the Conte Candoli All Stars	1963	15.00
❏ CST-417 [R]	Vince Guaraldi and the Conte Candoli All Stars	1963	12.00
PREMIER			
❏ PM-2009 [M]	Vince Guaraldi-Conte Candoli Quartet	1963	15.00
❏ PS-2009 [R]	Vince Guaraldi-Conte Candoli Quartet	1963	12.00

GUARALDI, VINCE/FRANK ROSOLINO

PREMIER			
❏ PM-2014 [M]	Vince Guaraldi-Frank Rosolino Quintet	1963	15.00
❏ PS-2014 [R]	Vince Guaraldi-Frank Rosolino Quintet	1963	12.00

GUARD, DAVE, AND THE WHISKEYHILL SINGERS

CAPITOL			
❏ T1728 [M]	Dave Guard and the Whiskeyhill Singers	1962	25.00
❏ ST1728 [S]	Dave Guard and the Whiskeyhill Singers	1962	30.00

GUARNIERI, JOHNNY

CLASSIC JAZZ			
❏ 105	Gliss Me Again	197?	15.00
CORAL			
❏ CRL57085 [M]	Songs of Hudson and DeLange	1957	40.00
❏ CRL57086 [M]	The Duke Again	1957	40.00
DOBRE			
❏ 1017	Johnny Guarnieri Plays Walter Donaldson	197?	15.00
DOT			
❏ DLP-3647 [M]	Piano Dimensions	1965	15.00
❏ DLP-25647 [S]	Piano Dimensions	1965	18.00
GOLDEN CREST			
❏ GC-3020 [M]	Johnny Guarnieri Plays Johnny Guarnieri	1958	40.00
JIM TAYLOR PRESENTS			
❏ 102	Johnny Guarnieri Plays Harry Warren	197?	15.00
RCA CAMDEN			
❏ CAL-345 [M]	Cheerful Little Earful	1958	18.00
❏ CAL-391 [M]	Side by Side	1958	18.00
ROYALE			
❏ 1296 [M]	An Hour of Modern Music	1952	40.00
❏ VLP6047 [10]	Johnny Guarnieri/Tony Mottola/Bob Haggart/Cozy Cole	195?	50.00
SAVOY			
❏ MG-15007 [10]	Hot Piano	1951	80.00
SOUNDS GREAT			
❏ SG-5001	Echoes of Ellington	198?	12.00
TAZ-JAZ			
❏ 1002	Stealin' Apples	1977	15.00
❏ 1001	Superstride	1976	15.00

GUESS WHO, THE

COMPLEAT			
❏ 672012-1	The Best of the Guess Who, Live	1986	25.00
HILLTAK			
❏ HT19227	All This for a Song	1979	15.00
MGM			
❏ SE-4645	The Guess Who	1969	18.00
—Compilation of pre-RCA Victor recordings			
PICKWICK			
❏ SPC-3246	Wild One	1970	15.00
—Available in two different covers - "bike" cover and "girl on car" cover; both same price			
P.I.P.			
❏ 6806	The Guess Who Play Pure Guess Who	197?	15.00

Number	Title	Yr	NM
PRIDE			
❑ PRD 0012	The History of the Guess Who	197?	15.00
RCA			
❑ 7622-1-R	The Greatest of the Guess Who	1987	12.00
—Late reissue			
RCA VICTOR			
❑ APL1-0130	#10	1973	18.00
❑ APD1-0130 [Q]	#10	1974	30.00
❑ LSP-4266	American Woman	1970	25.00
—Orange label, non-flexible vinyl			
❑ LSP-4266	American Woman	1971	15.00
—Orange label, flexible vinyl			
❑ AFL1-4266	American Woman	1977	12.00
—Reissue with new prefix			
❑ AYL1-3673	American Woman	1979	10.00
—Best Buy Series" reissue			
❑ LSP-4830	Artificial Paradise	1973	18.00
—Add 1/3 if paper bag is with package			
❑ LSP-4157	Canned Wheat Packed By the Guess Who	1969	25.00
—Orange label, non-flexible vinyl			
❑ LSP-4157	Canned Wheat Packed By the Guess Who	1971	15.00
—Orange label, flexible vinyl			
❑ ANL1-0983	Canned Wheat Packed By the Guess Who	1975	12.00
—Reissue of LSP-4157			
❑ CPL1-0636	Flavours	1975	18.00
❑ CPD1-0636 [Q]	Flavours	1975	30.00
❑ LSP-4779	Live at the Paramount (Seattle)	1972	30.00
❑ APL1-0995	Power in the Music	1975	18.00
❑ APD1-0995 [Q]	Power in the Music	1975	30.00
❑ APL1-0405	Road Food	1974	18.00
❑ APD1-0405 [Q]	Road Food	1974	30.00
❑ LSP-4602	Rockin'	1972	18.00
❑ LSP-4359	Share the Land	1970	25.00
—Orange label, non-flexible vinyl			
❑ LSP-4359	Share the Land	1971	15.00
—Orange label, flexible vinyl			
❑ LSP-4574	So Long, Bannatyne	1971	18.00
❑ LSPX-1004	The Best of the Guess Who	1971	18.00
❑ AYL1-3662	The Best of the Guess Who	1979	10.00
—Best Buy Series" reissue			
❑ AFL1-2594	The Best of the Guess Who	1978	12.00
—Reissue of LSPX-1004			
❑ APL1-0269	The Best of the Guess Who, Volume II	1973	18.00
❑ APD1-0269 [Q]	The Best of the Guess Who, Volume II	1974	30.00
❑ AFL1-0269	The Best of the Guess Who, Volume II	1977	12.00
—Reissue with new prefix			
❑ APL1-2253	The Greatest of the Guess Who	1977	18.00
❑ AYL1-3746	The Greatest of the Guess Who	1980	10.00
—Best Buy Series" reissue			
❑ APL1-1778	The Way They Were	1976	18.00
❑ LSP-4141	Wheatfield Soul	1969	25.00
—Orange label, non-flexible vinyl			
❑ LSP-4141	Wheatfield Soul	1971	15.00
—Orange label, flexible vinyl			
❑ ANL1-1117	Wheatfield Soul	1975	12.00
—Reissue of LSP-4141			
SCEPTER			
❑ SP-533 [M]	Shakin' All Over	1966	40.00
❑ SPS-533 [P]	Shakin' All Over	1966	30.00
—The above lists the artist as "The Guess Who's Chad Allan & The Expressions" on the cover			
SPRINGBOARD			
❑ SPB-4022	Shakin' All Over	1972	12.00
SUNDAZED			
❑ LP5113	Shakin' All Over	2001	18.00
WAND			
❑ WDS-691 [P]	Born in Canada	1969	18.00
—Reissue of Scepter LP; three tracks are rechanneled			

GUIDED BY VOICES

Number	Title	Yr	NM
E RECORDS			
❑ GBV 0001	Devil Between My Toes	1987	300.00
HALO			
❑ 1 [B]	Sandbox	1987	100.00
❑ 2	Self Inflicted Aerial Nostalgia	1989	150.00
I WANNA			
❑ (no #)0 [EP]	Forever Since Breakfast	1986	150.00
MATADOR			
❑ OLE-123 [B]	Alien Lanes	1995	18.00
❑ OLE-241	Mag Earwhig!	1997	12.00
❑ OLE-185 [EP]	Sunfish Holy Breakfast	1996	12.00
❑ OLE-161	Under the Bushes, Under the Stars	1996	15.00
—One side of Record 2 is blank			
ROCKATHON			
❑ (no #)0	Propeller	1992	1000.00
—Hand-colored cover with nature-book paste-on; signed and numbered			
❑ 02	Tonics & Twisted Chasers	1997	15.00
—1,000 copies were pressed on various colors of vinyl			
ROCKATHON/FADING CAPTAIN SERIES			
❑ 10	Daredevil Stamp Collector: Do the Collapse B-Sides	2001	15.00
—1,000 copies were pressed			
❑ 7	Suitcase Abridged: Drinks and Deliveries	2000	15.00
—500 copies were pressed			
ROCKET #9			
❑ (no #)0 [B]	Same Place the Fly Got Smashed	1990	60.00
SCAT			
❑ 35 [B]	Bee Thousand	1994	18.00
❑ 40	Box	1994	60.00
❑ 31 [B]	Vampire on Titus	1993	30.00
TVT			
❑ 1980	Do the Collapse	1999	12.00
❑ 2160	Isolation Drills	2001	12.00

GUITAR, BONNIE

Number	Title	Yr	NM
DOT			
❑ DLP-25947	Affair!	1969	25.00
❑ DLP-3793 [M]	Award Winner	1967	25.00
❑ DLP-25793 [S]	Award Winner	1967	25.00
❑ DLP-25840	Bonnie Guitar	1968	25.00
❑ DLP-3335 [M]	Dark Moon	1961	30.00
❑ DLP-25335 [R]	Dark Moon	196?	18.00
❑ DLP-25892	Leaves Are the Tears of Autumn	1968	25.00
❑ DLP-3746 [M]	Merry Christmas from Bonnie Guitar	1966	25.00
❑ DLP-25746 [S]	Merry Christmas from Bonnie Guitar	1966	30.00
❑ DLP-3737 [M]	Miss Bonnie Guitar	1966	25.00
❑ DLP-25737 [S]	Miss Bonnie Guitar	1966	30.00
❑ DLP-3069 [M]	Moonlight and Shadows	1957	50.00
❑ DLP-25069 [R]	Moonlight and Shadows	196?	18.00
❑ DLP-3696 [M]	Two Worlds	1966	25.00
❑ DLP-25696 [S]	Two Worlds	1966	30.00
❑ DLP-3151 [M]	Whispering Hope	1958	40.00
❑ DLP-25151 [S]	Whispering Hope	1958	50.00
PARAMOUNT			
❑ PAS-5018	Allegheny	1970	18.00
PICKWICK			
❑ SPC-3086	Favorite Lady of Song	196?	15.00
❑ SPC-3144	Green, Green Grass of Home	196?	15.00
RCA CAMDEN			
❑ CAS-2339	Night Train to Memphis	1969	18.00

GUITAR RAMBLERS, THE

Number	Title	Yr	NM
COLUMBIA			
❑ CL2067 [M]	The Happy, Youthful New Sounds of the Guitar Ramblers	1964	30.00
❑ CS8867 [S]	The Happy, Youthful New Sounds of the Guitar Ramblers	1964	30.00

GUITAR SLIM

Number	Title	Yr	NM
ATLANTIC			
❑ 81760	The Atco Sessions	1987	12.00
SPECIALTY			
❑ SP-2130	Things That I Used to Do	1969	25.00

GULLIN, LARS

Number	Title	Yr	NM
ATLANTIC			
❑ 1246 [M]	Baritone Sax	1956	120.00
—Black label			
❑ 1246 [M]	Baritone Sax	1960	50.00
—Multicolor label, white "fan" logo at right			
CONTEMPORARY			
❑ C-2505 [10]	Modern Sounds	1953	250.00
EASTWEST			
❑ 4003 [M]	Lars Gullin Swings	196?	60.00
EMARCY			
❑ MG-26044 [10]	Gullin's Garden	1954	200.00
❑ MG-36012 [M]	Lars Gullin	1955	120.00
❑ MG-26041 [10]	Lars Gullin Quartet	1954	200.00
❑ MG-36059 [M]	Lars Gullin with the Moretone Singers	1955	120.00
PRESTIGE			
❑ PRLP-144 [10]	New Sounds from Sweden, Volume 5	1953	200.00
❑ PRLP-151 [10]	New Sounds from Sweden, Volume 7	1953	200.00

GULLIVER

Number	Title	Yr	NM
ELEKTRA			
❑ EKS-74070	Gulliver	1970	25.00

GUN

Number	Title	Yr	NM
EPIC			
❑ BN26468 [B]	Gun	1969	30.00
❑ BN26551	Gunsight	1970	30.00

GUNS N' ROSES

Number	Title	Yr	NM
GEFFEN			
❑ R170348	Appetite for Destruction	1987	15.00
—BMG Direct Marketing edition			
❑ GHS24148	Appetite for Destruction	1987	18.00
❑ XXXG24148 [B]	Appetite for Destruction	1987	60.00
—Original "rape cover"; the XXXG prefix is on the cover only; all copies of the record use the GHS prefix			
❑ GHS24148	Appetite for Destruction	2008	25.00
❑ R100805	G N' R Lies	1988	15.00
—BMG Direct Marketing edition			
❑ GHS24198	G N' R Lies	1988	15.00
❑ 490514-1	Live Era '87-'93	1999	120.00
❑ GEF24617 [B]	The Spaghetti Incident?	1993	40.00
—Orange vinyl			
❑ GEF24415	Use Your Illusion I	1991	30.00
❑ GEF24420	Use Your Illusion II	1991	30.00
UZI SUICIDE			
❑ USR 001 [EP]	Live ?!*@ Like a Suicide	1986	300.00

GUNTER, ARTHUR

Number	Title	Yr	NM
EXCELLO			
❑ LPS-8017	Black and Blues	1971	30.00

GURU

Number	Title	Yr	NM
CHRYSALIS			
❑ F1-21998	Jazzmatazz Vol. 1	1993	25.00
❑ F1-34290	Jazzmatazz Vol. 2: The New Reality	1995	18.00
VIRGIN			
❑ 50188	Jazzmatazz Vol. 3: Streetsoul	2000	18.00

GUTHRIE, ARLO

Number	Title	Yr	NM
REPRISE			
❑ R6267 [M]	Alice's Restaurant	1967	25.00
❑ RS6267 [S]	Alice's Restaurant	1967	18.00
—Pink, green and gold label			
❑ RS6267 [S]	Alice's Restaurant	1968	15.00
—With "W7" and "r:" logos on two-tone orange label			
❑ RS6267 [S]	Alice's Restaurant	1970	12.00
—With only "r:" logo on all-orange (tan) label			
❑ MS2239	Amigo	1976	15.00
❑ RS6299	Arlo	1968	18.00
—With "W7" and "r:" logos on two-tone orange label			
❑ RS6299	Arlo	1970	12.00
—With only "r:" logo on all-orange (tan) label			
❑ MS2183	Arlo Guthrie	1974	15.00
❑ MS2060	Hobo's Lullabye	1972	15.00
❑ MS2142	Last of the Brooklyn Cowboys	1973	15.00
❑ MS42142 [Q]	Last of the Brooklyn Cowboys	1973	25.00
❑ RS6346	Running Down the Road	1969	18.00
—With "W7" and "r:" logos on two-tone orange label			
❑ RS6346	Running Down the Road	1970	12.00
—With only "r:" logo on all-orange (tan) label			
❑ RS6411	Washington County	1970	15.00
WARNER BROS.			
❑ BSK3232	One Night	1978	12.00
❑ BSK3336	Outlasting the Blues	1979	12.00
❑ BSK3558	Power of Love	1981	12.00
❑ BSK3117	The Best of Arlo Guthrie	1977	12.00
—Burbank" palm trees label			
❑ BSK3117	The Best of Arlo Guthrie	1979	10.00
—White or tan label			

GUTHRIE, JACK

Number	Title	Yr	NM
CAPITOL			
❑ T2456 [M]	Jack Guthrie's Greatest Songs	1966	30.00

GUTHRIE, WOODY, AND CISCO HOUSTON

Number	Title	Yr	NM
STINSON			
❑ SLP-32 [10]	Cowboy Songs	1951	250.00
❑ SLP-44 [10]	Folk Songs, Vol. 1	1952	200.00
—Red vinyl			
❑ SLP-53 [10]	More Songs	1953	200.00

GUTHRIE, WOODY; SONNY TERRY; ALEX STEWART

Number	Title	Yr	NM
STINSON			
❑ SLP-7 [10]	Chain Gang, Vol. 1	1950	350.00
❑ SLP-8 [10]	Chain Gang, Vol. 2	1950	350.00

GUTHRIE, WOODY

Number	Title	Yr	NM
COLLECTABLES			
❑ COL-5095	Golden Classics Vol. 1: Worried Man Blues	198?	15.00
❑ COL-5098	Golden Classics Vol. 2: Immortal	198?	15.00
ELEKTRA			
❑ EKL-271/2 [M]	The Library of Congress Recordings	1964	40.00
—Original pressing has "guitar player" labels			
EVEREST ARCHIVE OF FOLK & JAZZ			
❑ 204	Woody Guthrie	1966	15.00

Number	Title	Yr	NM

FOLKWAYS

Number	Title	Yr	NM
❏ FH-5485 [M]	Ballads of Sacco and Vanzetti	196?	35.00
❏ FA-2481 [M]	Bound for Glory: Songs and Stories of Woody Guthrie	1956	60.00
❏ FP-11 [10]	Dust Bowl Ballads	1950	150.00
❏ FA-2011 [10]	Dust Bowl Ballads	195?	75.00
—Reissue of FP-11			
❏ FH-5212 [M]	Dust Bowl Ballads	1964	30.00
❏ FC-7005 [10]	Songs to Grow On	1950	500.00
❏ FP-715 [10]	Songs to Grow On For Mother and Child	195?	150.00
❏ FC-7015 [10]	Songs to Grow On For Mother and Child	1953	150.00
—Reissue of FP-715			
❏ FC-7027 [10]	Songs to Grow On Vol. 3	1951	150.00
❏ FA-2485 [M]	Struggle	1964	50.00
❏ 31001 [R]	This Land Is Your Land	196?	15.00
❏ FA-2483 [M]	Woody Guthrie Sings Folk Songs	1964	50.00
❏ FA-2484 [M]	Woody Guthrie Sings Folk Songs, Vol. 2	1964	50.00

RCA VICTOR

Number	Title	Yr	NM
❏ LPV-502 [M]	Dust Bowl Ballads	1964	30.00

ROUNDER

Number	Title	Yr	NM
❏ 1036	Columbia River Collection	1987	12.00
❏ 1040	Dust Bowl Ballads	1988	12.00
❏ 1041/2/3	The Library of Congress Recordings	1988	25.00

SMITHSONIAN FOLKWAYS

Number	Title	Yr	NM
❏ SF-40025	Struggle	1989	15.00
❏ SF-40007	Woody Guthrie Sings Folk Songs	1989	15.00

VERVE FOLKWAYS

Number	Title	Yr	NM
❏ FV-9007 [M]	Bed on the Floor	1965	35.00
❏ FVS-9007 [R]	Bed on the Floor	1965	25.00
❏ FV-9036 [M]	Bonneville Dam & Other Columbia River Songs	1965	35.00
❏ FVS-9036 [R]	Bonneville Dam & Other Columbia River Songs	1965	25.00

GUY, BUDDY

BLUE THUMB

Number	Title	Yr	NM
❏ BTS20	Buddy and the Juniors	1970	30.00

CHESS

Number	Title	Yr	NM
❏ CH-9115	Buddy Guy	1984	10.00
❏ LP-1527 [M]	I Left My Blues in San Francisco	1968	30.00
❏ LP-409	I Was Walking Through the Woods	1970	25.00

MCA

Number	Title	Yr	NM
❏ 11165	I Was Walking Through the Woods	1995	30.00
—Heavy Vinyl" audiophile reissue			

VANGUARD

Number	Title	Yr	NM
❏ VSD-79272	A Man and the Blues	1968	30.00
❏ VSD-79323	Hold That Plane!	1972	25.00
❏ VSD-79290 [B]	This Is Buddy Guy	1969	30.00

GUY, CHARLES

CAPITOL

Number	Title	Yr	NM
❏ T1920 [M]	Prisoner's Dream	1963	25.00
❏ ST1920 [S]	Prisoner's Dream	1963	30.00

GWALTNEY, TOMMY

RIVERSIDE

Number	Title	Yr	NM
❏ RLP-353 [M]	Goin' to Kansas City	1960	30.00
❏ RS-9353 [S]	Goin' to Kansas City	1960	40.00

GYPSY

METROMEDIA

Number	Title	Yr	NM
❏ MD-1031 [B]	Gypsy	1970	30.00
❏ MD1044 [B]	In the Garden	1971	25.00

RCA VICTOR

Number	Title	Yr	NM
❏ LSP-4775	Antithesis	1972	18.00
❏ APL1-0093	Unlock the Gates	1973	18.00

H

H.P. LOVECRAFT

MERCURY

Number	Title	Yr	NM
❏ SRM-1-1041	We Love You	1975	25.00

PHILIPS

Number	Title	Yr	NM
❏ PHM200252 [M]	H.P. Lovecraft	1967	60.00

Number	Title	Yr	NM
❏ PHS600252 [S]	H.P. Lovecraft	1967	30.00
❏ PHS600279	Lovecraft II	1968	30.00

REPRISE

Number	Title	Yr	NM
❏ RS6419	Valley of the Moon	1970	30.00

SUNDAZED

Number	Title	Yr	NM
❏ LP-5004 [B]	Live May 11, 1968	1991	25.00

HACKETT, BOBBY, AND BILLY BUTTERFIELD

VERVE

Number	Title	Yr	NM
❏ V-8723 [M]	Bobby/Billy/Brazil	1967	18.00
❏ V6-8723 [S]	Bobby/Billy/Brazil	1967	15.00

HACKETT, BOBBY

BRUNSWICK

Number	Title	Yr	NM
❏ BL56014 [10]	Trumpet Solos	1950	50.00

CAPITOL

Number	Title	Yr	NM
❏ T1172 [M]	Blues with a Kick	1959	30.00
❏ ST1172 [S]	Blues with a Kick	1959	30.00
❏ T1077 [M]	Bobby Hackett at the Embers	1958	30.00
—Black colorband label, logo at left			
❏ ST1077 [S]	Bobby Hackett at the Embers	1958	30.00
—Black colorband label, logo at left			
❏ T1077 [M]	Bobby Hackett at the Embers	1962	18.00
—Black colorband label, logo at top			
❏ ST1077 [S]	Bobby Hackett at the Embers	1962	25.00
—Black colorband label, logo at top			
❏ T1235 [M]	Bobby Hackett Quartet	1959	30.00
❏ ST1235 [S]	Bobby Hackett Quartet	1959	30.00
❏ T692 [M]	Coast Concert	1956	40.00
—Turquoise or gray label			
❏ T692 [M]	Coast Concert	1956	30.00
—Black colorband label, logo at left			
❏ T1002 [M]	Don't Take Your Love from Me	1958	40.00
—Turquoise or gray label			
❏ T1002 [M]	Don't Take Your Love from Me	1958	30.00
—Black colorband label, logo at left			
❏ T1413 [M]	Easy Beat	1960	25.00
❏ ST1413 [S]	Easy Beat	1960	30.00
❏ T857 [M]	Gotham Jazz Scene	1957	40.00
—Turquoise or gray label			
❏ T857 [M]	Gotham Jazz Scene	1957	30.00
—Black colorband label, logo at left			
❏ T575 [M]	In a Mellow Mood	1955	40.00
—Turquoise or gray label			
❏ T575 [M]	In a Mellow Mood	1955	30.00
—Black colorband label, logo at left			
❏ T933 [M]	Jazz Ultimate	1958	40.00
—Turquoise or gray label			
❏ T933 [M]	Jazz Ultimate	1958	30.00
—Black colorband label, logo at left			
❏ ST933 [S]	Jazz Ultimate	1959	30.00
—Black colorband label, logo at left			
❏ SM-933	Jazz Ultimate	1976	12.00
—Reissue with new prefix			
❏ T719 [M]	Rendezvous	1956	40.00
—Turquoise or gray label			
❏ T719 [M]	Rendezvous	1956	30.00
—Black colorband label, logo at left			
❏ H458 [10]	Soft Lights	1954	50.00
❏ T458 [M]	Soft Lights	1955	40.00
—Turquoise or gray label			
❏ T458 [M]	Soft Lights	1955	30.00
—Black colorband label, logo at left			

CHIAROSCURO

Number	Title	Yr	NM
❏ 105	Live at Roosevelt Grill	1972	15.00
❏ 138	Live at Roosevelt Grill, Volume 2	197?	15.00
❏ 161	Live at Roosevelt Grill, Volume 3	197?	15.00

COLUMBIA

Number	Title	Yr	NM
❏ CL1602 [M]	Dream Awhile	1961	25.00
❏ CS8402 [S]	Dream Awhile	1961	30.00
❏ CL6156 [10]	Jazz Session	1951	50.00
❏ CL1895 [M]	Night Love	1962	18.00
❏ CS8695 [S]	Night Love	1962	25.00
❏ CL2566 [10]	The Bobby Hackett Horn	1955	50.00
❏ CL1729 [M]	The Most Beautiful Horn in the World	1962	25.00
❏ CS8529 [S]	The Most Beautiful Horn in the World	1962	30.00

COMMODORE

Number	Title	Yr	NM
❏ FL-20016 [10]	Horn A Plenty	1951	50.00

DOBRE

Number	Title	Yr	NM
❏ 1004	Thanks Bobby	197?	12.00

ENCORE

Number	Title	Yr	NM
❏ EE22003 [M]	The Bobby Hackett Horn	1968	15.00

EPIC

Number	Title	Yr	NM
❏ LN24174 [M]	A String of Pearls	1966	15.00
❏ BN26174 [S]	A String of Pearls	1966	18.00
❏ LN24099 [M]	Hello, Louis!	1964	15.00
❏ BN26099 [S]	Hello, Louis!	1964	18.00
❏ LA16037 [M]	Oliver!	1963	15.00
❏ BA17037 [S]	Oliver!	1963	18.00
❏ LN3106 [M]	The Hackett Horn	1956	40.00
❏ LN24080 [M]	The Music of Bert Kaempfert	1964	15.00
❏ BN26080 [S]	The Music of Bert Kaempfert	1964	18.00
❏ LN24061 [M]	The Music of Mancini	1963	15.00
❏ BN26061 [S]	The Music of Mancini	1963	18.00
❏ FLM13107 [M]	The Swingin'est Gals in Town	196?	18.00
❏ FLS15107 [S]	The Swingin'est Gals in Town	196?	25.00
❏ LN24155 [M]	The Trumpet's Greatest Hits	1965	15.00
❏ BN26155 [S]	The Trumpet's Greatest Hits	1965	18.00
❏ LN24220 [M]	Tony Bennett's Greatest Hits	1966	15.00
❏ BN26220 [S]	Tony Bennett's Greatest Hits	1966	18.00

FLYING DUTCHMAN

Number	Title	Yr	NM
❏ BDL1-0829	Strike Up the Band	1975	15.00
❏ FD-10159	What a Wonderful World	1973	15.00

JAZZOLOGY

Number	Title	Yr	NM
❏ J-111	Bobby Hackett and His Orchestra, 1943	198?	12.00
❏ JCE-76	Live from Manassas	1979	12.00

PAUSA

Number	Title	Yr	NM
❏ 9038	Coast Concert	198?	12.00

PICKWICK

Number	Title	Yr	NM
❏ PC-3012 [M]	Bobby Hackett with Strings	1966	15.00
❏ SPC-3012 [S]	Bobby Hackett with Strings	1966	12.00

PROJECT 3

Number	Title	Yr	NM
❏ PR5016SD	A Time for Love	1968	15.00
❏ PR26033	Memorable and Mellow	1979	15.00
❏ PR5006SD	That Midnight Touch	1967	15.00
❏ PR5034SD	This Is My Bag	1969	15.00

SEAGULL

Number	Title	Yr	NM
❏ LG-8201	Goodnight My Love	198?	12.00

SESAC

Number	Title	Yr	NM
❏ N-4105 [M]	Candlelight and Romance	1960	30.00
❏ SN-4105 [S]	Candlelight and Romance	1960	30.00
❏ N-4101 [M]	The Spirit Swings Me	1960	30.00
❏ SN-4101 [S]	The Spirit Swings Me	1960	30.00

STORYVILLE

Number	Title	Yr	NM
❏ 4059	Sextet Recordings	198?	12.00

VERVE

Number	Title	Yr	NM
❏ V-8698 [M]	Creole Cookin'	1967	18.00
❏ V6-8698 [S]	Creole Cookin'	1967	15.00

HACKETT, BOBBY/MAX KAMINSKY

BRUNSWICK

Number	Title	Yr	NM
❏ BL58043 [10]	Battle of Jazz, Vol. 5	1953	50.00

HADAWAY, HENRY, ORCHESTRA AND CHORUS

RCA VICTOR

Number	Title	Yr	NM
❏ AFL1-4454	Turned On Christmas	1982	12.00

HADEN, CHARLIE, AND HAMPTON HAWES

ARTISTS HOUSE

Number	Title	Yr	NM
❏ 4	As Long As There's Music	1979	15.00

HADEN, CHARLIE; JAN GARBAREK; EGBERTO GISMONTI

ECM

Number	Title	Yr	NM
❏ 1170	Folk Songs	1979	15.00

HADEN, CHARLIE

ABC IMPULSE!

Number	Title	Yr	NM
❏ AS-9183	Liberation Music Orchestra	1973	25.00

ECM

Number	Title	Yr	NM
❏ 23794	Ballad of the Fallen	1982	12.00

HORIZON

Number	Title	Yr	NM
❏ SP-710	Closeness	197?	18.00
❏ SP-727	The Golden Number	1978	18.00

SOUL NOTE

Number	Title	Yr	NM
❏ 121172	Silence	1990	15.00

VERVE

Number	Title	Yr	NM
❏ 831673-1	Quartet West	1987	12.00
❏ 837031-1	Quartet West in Angel City	1988	12.00

HAGAR, ERNIE

SAGE AND SAND

Number	Title	Yr	NM
❑ C-42 [M]	Swinging Steel Guitar	1965	30.00

HAGAR, SAMMY

CAPITOL

Number	Title	Yr	NM
❑ SMAS-11812	All Night Long	1978	15.00
❑ SN-16326	All Night Long	198?	10.00
—Budget-line reissue of 11812			
❑ ST-12069	Danger Zone	1980	15.00
—With poster (deduct if missing)			
❑ SK-12299	Live 1980	1983	12.00
❑ SN-16376	Live 1980	1986	10.00
—Budget-line reissue of 12299			
❑ ST-11706	Musical Chairs	1977	15.00
❑ SN-16051	Musical Chairs	1979	10.00
—Budget-line reissue of 11706			
❑ ST-11489 [B]	Nine on a Ten Scale	1976	15.00
❑ SN-16049	Nine on a Ten Scale	1979	10.00
—Budget-line reissue of 11489			
❑ ST-12238	Rematch	1982	12.00
❑ SN-16336	Rematch	198?	10.00
—Budget-line reissue of 12238			
❑ ST-11599	Sammy Hagar	1977	15.00
❑ SN-16050	Sammy Hagar	1979	10.00
—Budget-line reissue of 11599			
❑ ST-11983	Street Machine	1979	15.00
❑ SN-16340	Street Machine	198?	10.00
—Budget-line reissue of 11983			

GEFFEN

Number	Title	Yr	NM
❑ GHS24144	Sammy Hagar	1987	12.00
❑ GHS2006	Standing Hampton	1982	12.00
❑ GHS2021	Three Lock Box	1982	12.00
❑ GHS24043	VOA	1984	12.00

HAGEN, NINA

COLUMBIA

Number	Title	Yr	NM
❑ ARC38008	Nunsexmonkrock	1982	15.00
❑ PC38008	Nunsexmonkrock	198?	12.00
—Reissue with new prefix			
❑ 3C36817 [10]	TV Glotzer	1980	15.00

HAGERS, THE

BARNABY

Number	Title	Yr	NM
❑ BR15002	Music on the Countryside	1972	18.00

CAPITOL

Number	Title	Yr	NM
❑ ST-783	Apple Pie, Motherhood and the Flag	1971	18.00
❑ ST-438	The Hagers	1970	18.00
❑ ST-553	Two Hagers Are Better Than One	1970	18.00

ELEKTRA

Number	Title	Yr	NM
❑ 7E-1021	The Hagers	1974	15.00

HAGGARD, MERLE, AND BONNIE OWENS

CAPITOL

Number	Title	Yr	NM
❑ T2453 [M]	Just Between the Two of Us	1966	30.00
❑ ST2453 [S]	Just Between the Two of Us	1966	30.00

HAGGARD, MERLE, AND GEORGE JONES

EPIC

Number	Title	Yr	NM
❑ FE38203	A Taste of Yesterday's Wine	1982	12.00

HAGGARD, MERLE, AND LEONA WILLIAMS

MERCURY

Number	Title	Yr	NM
❑ 812183-1	Heart to Heart	1983	12.00

HAGGARD, MERLE, AND WILLIE NELSON

EPIC

Number	Title	Yr	NM
❑ FE37958	Pancho and Lefty	1983	12.00
—Reissue corrects spelling of LP title			
❑ FE37958	Poncho and Lefty	1983	18.00
—Note misspelled LP title			
❑ FE40293	Seashores of Old Mexico	1987	12.00

HAGGARD, MERLE

CAPITOL

Number	Title	Yr	NM
❑ ST-319	A Portrait of Merle Haggard	1969	25.00
❑ ST-638	A Tribute to the Best Damn Fiddle Player in the World (Or, My Salute to Bob Wills)	1970	30.00
❑ SN-16279	A Tribute to the Best Damn Fiddle Player in the World (Or, My Salute to Bob Wills)	1982	10.00
—Budget-line reissue			
❑ ST-11693	A Working Man Can't Get Nowhere Today	1977	15.00
❑ T2789 [M]	Branded Man	1967	30.00
❑ ST2789 [S]	Branded Man	1967	30.00
❑ SWBB-259	Close-Up	1969	30.00
—Reissue in one package of "Strangers" and "Swinging Doors			
❑ ST-11745	Eleven Winners	1977	15.00
❑ SN-16303	Eleven Winners	1984	10.00
—Budget-line reissue			
❑ ST-735	Hag	1971	18.00
❑ SN-16053	High on a Hilltop	1979	10.00
—Budget-line reissue			
❑ ST-11276	If We Make It Through December	1974	15.00
❑ ST-11200	I Love Dixie Blues...So I Recorded "Live" in New Orleans	1973	15.00
❑ T2702 [M]	I'm a Lonesome Fugitive	1967	30.00
❑ ST2702 [S]	I'm a Lonesome Fugitive	1967	30.00
❑ SM-2702	I'm a Lonesome Fugitive	197?	12.00
—Reissue with new prefix			
❑ SM-12036	It's All in the Movies	1979	12.00
—Reissue			
❑ ST-11483	It's All in the Movies	1975	15.00
❑ ST-11127	It's Not Love	1972	15.00
❑ ST-11365	Keep Movin' On	1975	15.00
❑ ST-882	Let Me Tell You About a Song	1972	25.00
❑ ST2972	Mama Tried	1968	30.00
❑ ST-11331	Merle Haggard Presents His 30th Album	1974	15.00
❑ ST-11230	Merle Haggard's Christmas Present (Something Old, Something New)	1973	15.00
❑ SM-11823	My Love Affair with Trains	1978	12.00
—Reissue			
❑ ST-11544	My Love Affair with Trains	1976	15.00
❑ ST-384	Okie from Muskogee	1970	25.00
❑ SN-16277	Okie from Muskogee	1982	10.00
—Budget-line reissue			
❑ SKAO-168	Pride In What I Am	1969	30.00
❑ SM-168	Pride In What I Am	197?	12.00
—Reissue with new prefix			
❑ SWBB-223	Same Train, A Different Time	1969	30.00
❑ SN-16052	Sing a Sad Song	1979	10.00
—Budget-line reissue			
❑ STBB-707	Sing a Sad Song/High on a Hilltop	1971	30.00
❑ T2848 [M]	Sing Me Back Home	1968	30.00
❑ ST2848 [S]	Sing Me Back Home	1968	30.00
❑ ST-835	Someday We'll Look Back	1971	25.00
❑ SABB-11531	Songs I'll Always Sing	1976	18.00
❑ T2373 [M]	Strangers	1965	30.00
❑ ST2373 [S]	Strangers	1965	30.00
❑ T2585 [M]	Swinging Doors	1966	30.00
❑ ST2585 [S]	Swinging Doors	1966	30.00
❑ SM-2585	Swinging Doors	197?	12.00
—Reissue with new prefix			
❑ SKAO2951	The Best of Merle Haggard	1968	30.00
❑ SN-16054	The Best of Merle Haggard	1979	10.00
—Budget-line reissue			
❑ ST-11082	The Best of the Best of Merle Haggard	1972	18.00
❑ ST-451	The Fightin' Side of Me	1970	25.00
❑ SN-16278	The Fightin' Side of Me	1982	10.00
—Budget-line reissue			
❑ SWBO-803	The Land of Many Churches	1971	60.00
❑ ST2912	The Legend of Bonnie and Clyde	1968	30.00
❑ ST-11586	The Roots of My Raising	1976	15.00
❑ SW-11839	The Way It Was	1978	15.00
❑ ST-11141	Totally Instrumental with One Exception	1973	18.00
❑ ST-823	Truly the Best of Merle Haggard	1971	40.00

CAPITOL SPECIAL MARKETS

Number	Title	Yr	NM
❑ SLB-8137	Merle Haggard Salutes the Greats	1980	18.00
❑ SL-8086	Songs I'll Always Sing	1977	25.00

EPIC

Number	Title	Yr	NM
❑ FE44283	5:01 Blues	1989	12.00
❑ FE40286	A Friend in California	1986	12.00
❑ FE40224	Amber Waves of Grain	1985	12.00
❑ FE37593	Big City	1981	12.00
❑ PE37593	Big City	1985	10.00
—Budget-line reissue			
❑ FE40986	Chill Factor	1988	12.00
❑ FE38092	Going Where the Lonely Go	1982	12.00
❑ PE38092	Going Where the Lonely Go	1985	10.00
—Budget-line reissue			
❑ PE38307	Goin' Home for Christmas	1982	12.00
❑ FE39545	His Epic Hits: The First 11	1985	12.00
❑ FE39364	It's All in the Game	1984	12.00
❑ FE39602	Kern River	1985	12.00
❑ FE40107	Out Among the Stars	1986	12.00
❑ PE40107	Out Among the Stars	1986	10.00
—Budget-line reissue			
❑ FE38815	That's the Way Love Goes	1983	12.00
❑ FE39159	The Epic Collection	1983	12.00
❑ PE39159	The Epic Collection	1985	10.00
—Budget-line reissue			

MCA

Number	Title	Yr	NM
❑ 5139	Back to the Barrooms	1980	15.00
❑ 5386	Greatest Hits	1982	15.00
❑ 5573	His Best	1985	12.00
❑ 2375	I'm Always on a Mountain	1978	15.00
❑ 37140	I'm Always on a Mountain	1980	10.00
—Budget-line reissue			
❑ 2314	My Farewell to Elvis	1977	18.00
❑ 37139	My Farewell to Elvis	1980	10.00
—Budget-line reissue			
❑ 37138	Ramblin' Fever	1980	10.00
—Budget-line reissue			
❑ 2267	Ramblin' Fever	1977	15.00
❑ 3089	Serving 190 Proof	1979	15.00
❑ 37141	Serving 190 Proof	1980	10.00
—Budget-line reissue			
❑ 5250 [B]	Songs for the Mamma That Tried	1981	15.00
❑ 3229	The Way I Am	1980	15.00
❑ 37207	The Way I Am	1982	10.00
—Budget-line reissue			

HAHN, JERRY

ARHOOLIE

Number	Title	Yr	NM
❑ 8006	Jerry Hahn Quintet	197?	18.00

CHANGES

Number	Title	Yr	NM
❑ LP-7001	Arabein	1968	25.00

FANTASY

Number	Title	Yr	NM
❑ F-9426	Moses	1974	18.00

HAIG, AL, AND JIMMY RANEY

CHOICE

Number	Title	Yr	NM
❑ 1010	Strings Attached	197?	15.00

HAIG, AL

COUNTERPOINT

Number	Title	Yr	NM
❑ C-551 [M]	Jazz Will o' the Wisp	1957	100.00

ESOTERIC

Number	Title	Yr	NM
❑ ESJ-7 [10]	Al Haig Trio	1954	200.00

EVEREST ARCHIVE OF FOLK & JAZZ

Number	Title	Yr	NM
❑ 293	Jazz Will o' the Wisp	197?	12.00

INNER CITY

Number	Title	Yr	NM
❑ IC-1073	Al Haig Plays Music of Jerome Kern	197?	15.00

INTERPLAY

Number	Title	Yr	NM
❑ 7707	Portrait of Bud Powell	1978	15.00
❑ 7713	Serendipity	1978	15.00

MINT

Number	Title	Yr	NM
❑ AL-711 [M]	Al Haig Today	1964	150.00

PACIFIC JAZZ

Number	Title	Yr	NM
❑ PJLP-18 [10]	Al Haig Trio	1955	150.00

PERIOD

Number	Title	Yr	NM
❑ SPL-1104 [10]	Al Haig Quartet	1954	150.00

PRESTIGE

Number	Title	Yr	NM
❑ PRST-7841	Al Haig Trio and Quartet	1970	18.00

SEABREEZE

Number	Title	Yr	NM
❑ 1005	Interplay	1977	15.00
❑ 1008	Manhattan Memories	1978	15.00
❑ 1001	Piano Interpretation	1976	15.00
❑ 1006	Piano Time	1977	15.00

SEECO

Number	Title	Yr	NM
❑ SLP-7 [10]	Highlights in Modern Jazz	195?	120.00

XANADU

Number	Title	Yr	NM
❑ 206	Live in Hollywood	198?	12.00

HAIG, AL/MARY LOU WILLIAMS

PRESTIGE

Number	Title	Yr	NM
❑ PRLP-175 [10]	Piano Moderns	1953	200.00

HAINES, CONNIE

CORAL

Number	Title	Yr	NM
❑ CRL56055 [10]	Connie Haines Sings	1955	120.00

RCA VICTOR

Number	Title	Yr	NM
❑ LPM-2264 [M]	Faith, Hope and Charity	1961	25.00
❑ LSP-2264 [S]	Faith, Hope and Charity	1961	30.00

TOPS

Number	Title	Yr	NM
❑ L-1606 [M]	Connie Haines Sings Helen Morgan	1959	30.00

HAIRCUT ONE HUNDRED

ARISTA

Number	Title	Yr	NM
❑ AL6600	Pelican West	1982	18.00
❑ ALB6-8330	Pelican West	198?	15.00
—Reissue			

HAISLEY, LINDSAY

ARMADILLO

Number	Title	Yr	NM
❑ ARLP82-1	Christmas on the Autoharp	1982	12.00

HAKIM, OMAR

GRP

Number	Title	Yr	NM
❑ GR-9585	Rhythm Deep	1989	15.00

HAKIM, SADIK

STEEPLECHASE

Number	Title	Yr	NM
❑ SCS-1091	Witches, Goblins	198?	15.00

HALE, CORKY

GENE NORMAN

Number	Title	Yr	NM
❑ GNP-17 [M]	Corky Hale	1956	50.00

GNP CRESCENDO

Number	Title	Yr	NM
❑ GNP-17 [M]	Corky Hale	196?	18.00
❑ GNP-9035	Corky Hale Plays Gershwin and Duke	197?	15.00

STASH

Number	Title	Yr	NM
❑ ST-245	Harp Beat	198?	15.00

Number Title Yr NM

HALEN, CARL

EMPIRICAL
❑ LP-101 [10] Gin Bottle Seven 1957 50.00

RIVERSIDE
❑ RLP 12-231 [M] Gin Bottle Jazz 1958 60.00
—White label, blue print
❑ RLP 12-231 [M] Gin Bottle Jazz 1959 30.00
—Blue label, microphone logo at top
❑ RLP 12-261 [M] Whoopee Makers' Jazz 1958 40.00
❑ RLP-1103 [S] Whoopee Makers' Jazz 1958 30.00

HALEY, BILL, AND HIS COMETS

51 WEST
❑ Q16120 Live in New York/Greatest Hits 1981 12.00
—All selections under license from Buddah Records

ACCORD
❑ SN-7125 Rockin' and Rollin' 1981 12.00

DECCA
❑ DL8821 [M] Bill Haley's Chicks 1959 100.00
❑ DL78821 [S] Bill Haley's Chicks 1959 200.00
❑ DXSE-7211 Bill Haley's Golden Hits 1972 18.00
❑ DL75027 Bill Haley's Greatest Hits 1968 18.00
❑ DL8315 [M] Music for the Boyfriend 1956 150.00
❑ DL8225 [M] Rock Around the Clock 1955 250.00
—All-black label with silver print
❑ DL8225 [M] Rock Around the Clock 1960 50.00
—Black label with colorband, no mention of MCA on label
❑ DL8225 [M] Rock Around the Clock 1967 30.00
—Black label with colorband, "A Division of MCA" on label
❑ DL78225 [R] Rock Around the Clock 1959 100.00
—All-black label with silver print
❑ DL78225 [R] Rock Around the Clock 1960 30.00
—Black label with colorband, no mention of MCA on label
❑ DL78225 [R] Rock Around the Clock 1967 18.00
—Black label with colorband, "A Division of MCA" on label
❑ DL8692 [M] Rockin' Around the World 1958 150.00
❑ DL8775 [M] Rockin' the Joint 1958 150.00
❑ DL8569 [M] Rockin' the Oldies 1957 150.00
❑ DL8345 [M] Rock 'n Roll Stage Show 1956 150.00
❑ DL5560 [10] Shake, Rattle and Roll 1955 1000.00
❑ DL8964 [M] Strictly Instrumental 1960 100.00
❑ DL78964 [S] Strictly Instrumental 1960 150.00

ESSEX
❑ LP202 [M] Rock with Bill Haley and the Comets 1955 500.00

GNP CRESCENDO
❑ GNPS-2097 Rock Around the Country 1976 15.00
❑ GNPS-2077 Rock 'N' Roll 1973 15.00

GREAT NORTHWEST
❑ GNW4015 Interviewed by Red Robinson 1981 15.00

JANUS
❑ 7003 Razzle-Dazzle 1972 18.00
❑ 3035 Travelin' Band 1972 30.00

KAMA SUTRA
❑ KLPS-2014 Scrapbook 1970 30.00

MCA
❑ 4010 Bill Haley's Golden Hits 1973 15.00
—Reissue of Decca 7211
❑ 161 Bill Haley's Greatest Hits 1973 12.00
—Reissue of Decca 75027
❑ 5539 From the Original Master Tapes 1987 15.00

PAIR
❑ MSM2-35069 Rock and Roll Giant 1986 15.00

PICCADILLY
❑ PIC-3408 Greatest Hits 1980 12.00

PICKWICK
❑ SPC-3256 Bill Haley and the Comets 1970 12.00
❑ PTP-2077 Rock 'N' Roll 197? 15.00
❑ SPC-3280 Rock 'N' Roll Revival 197? 12.00

ROULETTE
❑ R25174 [M] Twistin' Knights at the Roundtable 1962 80.00
❑ SR25174 [S] Twistin' Knights at the Roundtable 1962 100.00

SOMERSET
❑ P-4600 [M] Rock with Bill Haley and the Comets 1958 150.00

TRANS WORLD
❑ LP202 [M] Rock with Bill Haley and the Comets 1956 300.00

VOCALION
❑ VL3696 [M] Bill Haley and the Comets 1963 30.00

WARNER BROS.
❑ W1378 [M] Bill Haley and His Comets 1959 50.00
❑ WS1378 [S] Bill Haley and His Comets 1959 70.00
❑ W1391 [M] Bill Haley's Jukebox 1960 50.00
❑ WS1391 [S] Bill Haley's Jukebox 1960 70.00
❑ WS1831 Rock 'N' Roll Revival 1970 18.00
❑ ST-93103 Rock 'N' Roll Revival 1970 30.00
—Capitol Record Club edition

Number Title Yr NM

HALIFAX THREE, THE

COLUMBIA SPECIAL PRODUCTS
❑ CSRP26038 [S] The Halifax Three 196? 12.00
—Special Archive Series" sticker on cover

EPIC
❑ LN24060 [M] San Francisco Bay Blues 1963 15.00
❑ BN26060 [S] San Francisco Bay Blues 1963 18.00
❑ LN24038 [M] The Halifax Three 1962 15.00
❑ BN26038 [S] The Halifax Three 1962 18.00

HALL, ADELAIDE

MONMOUTH-EVERGREEN
❑ 7080 That Wonderful... 1970 25.00

HALL, BECKY

AAMCO
❑ ALP-324 [M] A Tribute to Bessie Smith 1958 30.00

HALL, CONNIE

DECCA
❑ DL4217 [M] Connie Hall 1962 30.00
❑ DL74217 [S] Connie Hall 1962 30.00

VOCALION
❑ VL73752 [S] Country Songs 1965 30.00
❑ VL3752 [M] Country Songs 1965 25.00
❑ VL3801 [M] Country Style 1968 25.00
❑ VL73801 [S] Country Style 1968 25.00

HALL, DARYL, AND JOHN OATES

ALLEGIANCE
❑ AV-5014 Nucleus 198? 10.00

ARISTA
❑ AL-8614 Change of Season 1989 15.00
❑ AL-8539 Ooh Yeah! 1988 12.00

ATLANTIC
❑ SD7269 [B] Abandoned Luncheonette 1973 15.00
❑ SD19139 Abandoned Luncheonette 1977 10.00
❑ SD18213 No Goodbyes 1977 12.00
❑ SD18109 War Babies 1974 15.00
❑ SD7242 Whole Oats 1972 15.00
❑ 7242 [M] Whole Oats 1972 60.00
—White label promo only with "d/j copy monaural" sticker on cover

CHELSEA
❑ CHL-547 Past Times Behind 1976 15.00

INTERMEDIA
❑ QS-5040 The Early Years 198? 10.00

JEM
❑ 55002 Early Years 198? 10.00

MOBILE FIDELITY
❑ 1-069 [B] Abandoned Luncheonette 1982 40.00
—Audiophile vinyl
❑ MFSL1-413 [B] H20 2014 35.00
❑ MFSL1-412 [B] Private Eyes 2014 35.00
❑ MFSL1-411 [B] Voices 2014 35.00

RCA VICTOR
❑ AFL1-2804 Along the Red Ledge 1978 12.00
❑ AYL1-4231 Along the Red Ledge 1981 10.00
❑ AFL1-2804 Along the Red Ledge 1978 18.00
—Red vinyl
❑ AFL1-2300 Beauty on a Back Street 1977 12.00
❑ AYL1-4230 Beauty on a Back Street 1981 10.00
❑ AJL1-5336 Big Bam Boom 1984 12.00
❑ AFL1-5309 Big Bam Boom 1984 15.00
❑ APL1-1467 [B] Bigger Than Both of Us 1976 12.00
❑ AYL1-3866 Bigger Than Both of Us 1980 10.00
❑ APL1-1144 Daryl Hall & John Oates 1976 12.00
❑ ANL1-3463 Daryl Hall & John Oates 1979 10.00
❑ AYL1-3836 Daryl Hall & John Oates 1980 10.00
❑ AFL1-4383 H2O 1982 12.00
❑ AFL1-7035 Live at the Apollo 1985 12.00
❑ AFL1-2802 Livetime! 1978 12.00
❑ AYL1-4722 Livetime! 1983 10.00
❑ DJL1-3512 [DJ] Post Static 1979 25.00
—Promo-only one-sided 4-song sampler
❑ AFL1-4028 Private Eyes 1981 12.00
❑ DJL1-3832 [B] RCA Radio Special Interview Series 1980 30.00
❑ CPL1-4858 Rock 'n Soul Part 1 1983 15.00
—Original cover: back cover says "Plus Two New Songs (Recorded September 1983)" WITHOUT mentioning what the songs are
❑ CPL1-4858 Rock 'n Soul Part 1 1983 12.00
—RE" on lower left back: back cover says "Plus Two New Songs (Recorded September 1983)," then mentions "Say It Isn't So" and "Adult Education
❑ CPL1-4858 Rock 'n Soul Part 1 1983 10.00
—RE 2" on lower left back: Variation unknown
❑ DJL1-4179 Special Radio Series 1981 18.00
❑ AQL1-3646 Voices 1980 15.00
—No "RE" of any type on back cover: Embossed lettering and sound waves, Hall's head almost touches the word "Voices" on front
❑ AQL1-3646 Voices 1980 15.00
—RE" on back cover: Variation unknown
❑ AQL1-3646 Voices 1980 15.00
—RE 3" on back cover: Cover lettering in black

Number Title Yr NM

❑ AQL1-3646 Voices 1980 12.00
—RE 2" on back cover: Cover not embossed; Hall's head 3 inches-plus below "Voices" on front cover
❑ AQL1-3646 Voices 1980 10.00
—RE 4" on back cover: Color photo of Hall and Oates on each side
❑ AQL1-3646 Voices 1981 10.00
—RE 5" on back cover: Variation unknown
❑ AQL1-3646 Voices 1981 10.00
—RE 6" on back cover: Bar code on upper left back cover
❑ AFL1-3494 X-Static 1979 12.00
❑ AYL1-4303 X-Static 1982 10.00

HALL, DARYL

RCA VICTOR
❑ AFL1-3573 Sacred Songs 1980 12.00
❑ AJL1-7196 Three Hearts in the Happy Ending Machine 1986 10.00

HALL, DICKSON

EPIC
❑ LN3427 [M] 25 All-Time Country and Western Hits 1958 30.00

KAPP
❑ KS-3464 [S] 24 Fabulous Country Hits 1966 30.00
❑ KL-1464 [M] 24 Fabulous Country Hits 1966 25.00
❑ KL-1067 [M] Fabulous Country Hits Way Out West 1957 30.00

MGM
❑ E-329 [10] Outlaws of the Old West 1954 60.00
❑ E-3263 [M] Outlaws of the Old West 1956 40.00

PERFECT
❑ P-14016 [M] Country & Western Million Sellers 1960 25.00
❑ PS-14016 [S] Country & Western Million Sellers 1960 30.00

HALL, EDMOND

BLUE NOTE
❑ B-6505 [M] Celestial Express 1969 25.00

CIRCLE
❑ C-52 Rompin' in '44 198? 12.00

MOSAIC
❑ MR6-109 The Complete Edmond Hall/James P. Johnson/Sidney De Paris/Vic Dickenson Blue Note Sessions 199? 100.00

MOUNT VERNON
❑ MVM-124 Rumpus on Rampart St. 197? 15.00

STORYVILLE
❑ 4009 Live at Club Hangover, Volume 4 198? 12.00

UNITED ARTISTS
❑ UAL-4028 [M] Petite Fleur 1959 40.00
❑ UAS-5028 [S] Petite Fleur 1959 30.00

HALL, EDMOND/ART HODES

BLUE NOTE
❑ B-6504 [M] Original Blue Note Jazz, Volume 1 1969 25.00

HALL, EDMOND/SIDNEY DEPARIS

BLUE NOTE
❑ BLP-7007 [10] Jamming in Jazz Hall 1951 200.00

HALL, GEORGE

BLUEBIRD
❑ AXM2-5504 George Hall and His Taft Hotel Orchestra (1933-1937) 1975 18.00

HINDSIGHT
❑ HSR-144 George Hall and His Orchestra 1937 198? 12.00

HALL, HERB

BIOGRAPH
❑ 3003 Herb Hall Quartet 196? 18.00

HALL, JIM, AND RED MITCHELL

ARTISTS HOUSE
❑ 5 Jim Hall and Red Mitchell 1979 15.00

HALL, JIM, AND RON CARTER

FANTASY
❑ OJC-467 Alone Together 1990 15.00

MILESTONE
❑ 9045 Alone Together 1974 18.00

HALL, JIM

BASF
❑ 20708 It's Nice to Be with You 1972 18.00

CONCORD JAZZ
❑ CJ-384 All Across the City 1989 15.00
❑ CJ-161 Circles 1982 12.00
❑ CJ-298 Jim Hall's Three 1986 12.00

CTI
❑ 6060 Concierto 1977 15.00

Number	Title	Yr	NM
FANTASY			
❏ OJC-649	Where Would I Be	1991	15.00
HORIZON			
❏ SP-715	Commitment	1976	15.00
❏ SP-705	Live	1975	15.00
MILESTONE			
❏ 9037	Where Would I Be	1973	18.00
PACIFIC JAZZ			
❏ PJ-10 [M]	Good Friday Blues	1960	40.00
❏ PJ-1227 [M]	Jazz Guitar	1957	250.00
❏ PJ-79 [M]	Jazz Guitar	1963	30.00
❏ ST-79 [S]	Jazz Guitar	1963	30.00
PAUSA			
❏ 7112	In a Sentimental Mood	198?	12.00
WORLD PACIFIC			
❏ WP-1227 [M]	Jazz Guitar	1958	50.00

HALL, JOANIE

Number	Title	Yr	NM
SAGE AND SAND			
❏ C-34 [M]	Western Meets Country	1962	12.00

HALL, JUANITA

Number	Title	Yr	NM
COUNTERPOINT			
❏ 558 [S]	Juanita Hall Sings the Blues	1959	150.00

HALL, LARRY

Number	Title	Yr	NM
STRAND			
❏ SL-1005 [M]	Sandy	1960	150.00
❏ SLS-1005 [S]	Sandy	1960	200.00

HALL, TOM T., AND EARL SCRUGGS

Number	Title	Yr	NM
COLUMBIA			
❏ FC37953	Storyteller and Banjo Man	1982	12.00

HALL, TOM T.

Number	Title	Yr	NM
MERCURY			
❏ SR-61307	100 Children	1970	16.00
❏ SRM-1-1139	About Love	1977	10.00
❏ SR-61211	Ballad of Forty Dollars and His Other Great Songs	1969	16.00
❏ SRM-1-1009	Country Is	1974	10.00
❏ 834779-1	Country Songs for Children	1988	10.00
—Reissue			
❏ SRM-1-1076	Faster Horses	1976	10.00
❏ SRM-1-687	For the People in the Last Hard Town	1974	10.00
❏ SR-61369	Greatest Hits	1972	12.00
❏ 824143-1	Greatest Hits	1985	10.00
—Reissue			
❏ SRM-1-1044	Greatest Hits, Volume 2	1975	10.00
❏ 824144-1	Greatest Hits, Volume 2	1985	10.00
—Reissue			
❏ SRM-1-5008	Greatest Hits, Volume 3	1978	10.00
❏ 824145-1	Greatest Hits, Volume 3	1985	10.00
—Reissue			
❏ SR-61247	Homecoming	1969	16.00
❏ SR-61350	In Search of a Song	1971	12.00
❏ 822500-1	In Search of a Song	1987	10.00
❏ SRM-1-1033 [B]	I Wrote A Song About It	1975	10.00
❏ 814025-1	Jesus to Jack Daniels	1983	10.00
❏ SRM-1-1111	Magnificent Music	1977	10.00
❏ 822425-1	Natural Dreams	1984	10.00
❏ 824150-1	Song in a Seashell	1985	10.00
❏ SRM-1-500	Songs of Fox Hollow	1975	10.00
❏ 832350-1	Songs of Fox Hollow	1987	10.00
—Reissue			
❏ SRM-1-668	The Rhymer and Other Five and Dimers	1973	10.00
❏ SR-61362	We All Got Together And…	1972	12.00
❏ SR-61277	Witness Life	1970	16.00
PICCADILLY			
❏ 3558	I Like Beer	198?	10.00
RCA VICTOR			
❏ AHL1-4749	In Concert: Recorded Live at the Grand Ole Opry	1983	12.00
❏ AYL1-5432	In Concert: Recorded Live at the Grand Ole Opry	1985	10.00
—Best Buy Series" reissue			
❏ AHL1-2622	New Train	1978	12.00
❏ AHL1-3018	Places I've Been	1979	12.00
❏ AHL1-3685	Soldier of Fortune	1980	12.00
❏ AHL1-3495	T's in Town	1979	12.00

HALL BROTHERS JAZZ BAND, THE

Number	Title	Yr	NM
GHB			
❏ GHBS-11 [S]	Hall Brothers Jazz Band	1964	18.00
❏ GHB-11 [M]	Hall Brothers Jazz Band	1964	15.00
❏ GHBS-46 [S]	Sweet Like This	196?	18.00
❏ GHB-46 [M]	Sweet Like This	196?	15.00
STOMP OFF			
❏ SOS-1062	Fizz Water	198?	12.00
❏ SOS-1013	Waiting at the End of the Road	198?	12.00

HALLBERG, BENGT

Number	Title	Yr	NM
EPIC			
❏ LN3375 [M]	Bengt Hallberg	1957	120.00

Number	Title	Yr	NM
PRESTIGE			
❏ PRLP-176 [10]	Bengt Hallberg's Swedish All-Stars	1953	350.00

HALLBERG, BENGT/ARNE DOMNERUS

Number	Title	Yr	NM
PRESTIGE			
❏ PRLP-145 [10]	New Sounds from Sweden, Volume 6	1953	400.00

HALLBERG, BENGT/LARS GULLIN

Number	Title	Yr	NM
PRESTIGE			
❏ PRLP-121 [10]	New Sounds from Sweden, Volume 2	1952	400.00

HALLE ORCHESTRA (GEORGE WELDON, CONDUCTOR)

Number	Title	Yr	NM
MERCURY LIVING PRESENCE			
❏ SR90137 [S]	Khachaturian: Gayne Ballet Suite; Mussorgsky: Night on Bare Mountain	196?	30.00
—Maroon label, no "Vendor: Mercury Record Corporation			

HALLE ORCHESTRA (JOHN BARBIROLLI, CONDUCTOR)

Number	Title	Yr	NM
MERCURY LIVING PRESENCE			
❏ SR90125 [S]	Elgar: Enigma Variations; Purcell: Suite for Strings	1960	25.00
—Maroon label, no "Vendor: Mercury Record Corporation			
❏ SR90161 [S]	Encore Please, Sir John!	196?	200.00
—Maroon label, no "Vendor: Mercury Record Corporation			
❏ SR90164 [S]	Grieg: Peer Gynt Suite; Symphonic Dances; Elegiac Melodies	196?	80.00
—Maroon label, no "Vendor: Mercury Record Corporation			
❏ SR90160 [S]	Suppe: Overtures	196?	50.00
—Maroon label, no "Vendor: Mercury Record Corporation			
❏ SR90124 [S]	Viennese Night at the Proms	1960	30.00
—Maroon label, no "Vendor: Mercury Record Corporation			
❏ SR90115 [S]	Williams, Vaughan: Symphony No. 8; Bax: Garden of Fand; Butterworth: Shropshire Lad	1960	30.00
—Maroon label, no "Vendor: Mercury Record Corporation			

HALLEY, PAUL

Number	Title	Yr	NM
GRAMAVISION			
❏ 7704	Nightwatch	198?	12.00
LIVING MUSIC			
❏ LM-0009	Pianosong	1986	12.00

HALLYDAY, JOHNNY

Number	Title	Yr	NM
PHILIPS			
❏ PHM200019 [M]	America's Rockin' Hits	1962	100.00
❏ PHS600019 [S]	America's Rockin' Hits	1962	120.00

HALOS, THE

Number	Title	Yr	NM
WARWICK			
❏ W-2046 [M]	The Halos	1962	400.00

HAMBLEN, STUART

Number	Title	Yr	NM
COLUMBIA			
❏ CL1769 [M]	Of God I Sing	1962	25.00
❏ CS8569 [S]	Of God I Sing	1962	30.00
❏ CL1588 [M]	The Spell of the Yukon	1961	25.00
❏ CS8388 [S]	The Spell of the Yukon	1961	30.00
CORAL			
❏ CRL57254 [M]	Remember Me	1960	30.00
HARMONY			
❏ HL7009 [M]	Hymns	1957	30.00
RCA CAMDEN			
❏ CAL-537 [M]	Beyond the Sun	1959	30.00
RCA VICTOR			
❏ LPM-1436 [M]	Grand Old Hymns	1957	40.00
❏ LPM-3265 [10]	It Is No Secret	1954	60.00
❏ LPM-1253 [M]	It Is No Secret	1956	40.00

HAMBRO, LENNY

Number	Title	Yr	NM
COLUMBIA			
❏ CL757 [M]	Message from Hambro	1956	40.00
EPIC			
❏ LN3361 [M]	The Nature of Things	1956	40.00
SAVOY			
❏ MG-15031 [10]	Mambo Hambro	1954	50.00

HAMILTON, CHICO

Number	Title	Yr	NM
ABC IMPULSE!			
❏ AS-82 [S]	Chi Chi Chico	1968	18.00
❏ AS-9102 [S]	El Chico	1968	18.00
❏ AS-9213	His Great Hits	1971	25.00
❏ AS-59 [S]	Man from Two Worlds	1968	18.00
❏ AS-29 [S]	Passin' Thru	1968	18.00
❏ AS-9174	The Best of Chico Hamilton	1969	18.00
❏ AS-9130 [S]	The Dealer	1968	18.00
❏ AS-9114 [S]	The Further Adventures of El Chico	1968	18.00

Number	Title	Yr	NM
BLUE NOTE			
❏ BN-LA622-G	Chico Hamilton & Players	1976	15.00
❏ BN-LA520-G	Peregrinations	1975	15.00
COLUMBIA			
❏ CL1619 [M]	Chico Hamilton Special	1961	30.00
❏ CS8419 [S]	Chico Hamilton Special	1961	30.00
❏ CL1807 [M]	Drumfusion	1962	30.00
❏ CS8607 [S]	Drumfusion	1962	30.00
❏ CL1590 [M]	Selections from "Bye Bye Birdie	1961	30.00
❏ CS8390 [S]	Selections from "Bye Bye Birdie	1961	30.00
DECCA			
❏ DL8614 [M]	Jazz from the Sweet Smell of Success	1957	50.00
DISCOVERY			
❏ 831	Gongs East	1981	12.00
—Reissue of Warner Bros. 1271			
ELEKTRA			
❏ 6E-257	Nomad	1980	12.00
ENTERPRISE			
❏ SD7501	The Master	1974	15.00
FLYING DUTCHMAN			
❏ 10135	Exigente	1971	18.00
IMPULSE!			
❏ A-82 [M]	Chi Chi Chico	1965	25.00
❏ AS-82 [S]	Chi Chi Chico	1965	30.00
❏ A-9102 [M]	El Chico	1965	25.00
❏ AS-9102 [S]	El Chico	1965	30.00
❏ A-59 [M]	Man from Two Worlds	1964	30.00
❏ AS-59 [S]	Man from Two Worlds	1964	30.00
❏ A-29 [M]	Passin' Thru	1963	30.00
❏ AS-29 [S]	Passin' Thru	1963	30.00
❏ A-9130 [M]	The Dealer	1966	25.00
❏ SMAS-91138 [S]	The Dealer	1966	30.00
—Capitol Record Club edition			
❏ A-9114 [M]	The Further Adventures of El Chico	1966	25.00
❏ AS-9114 [S]	The Further Adventures of El Chico	1966	30.00
JAZZTONE			
❏ J-1264 [M]	Delightfully Modern	1957	40.00
MCA			
❏ 638	El Chico	198?	10.00
—Reissue of Impulse! 9102			
❏ 637	Man from Two Worlds	198?	10.00
—Reissue of Impulse! 59			
❏ 29037	Passin' Thru	198?	12.00
—Reissue of Impulse! 29			
❏ 29038	The Best of Chico Hamilton	198?	12.00
Reissue of Impulse! 9174			
MERCURY			
❏ SRM-1-1163	Catwalk	1977	15.00
NAUTILUS			
❏ NR-13	Reaching for the Top	1981	30.00
—Audiophile vinyl			
PACIFIC JAZZ			
❏ PJ-1231 [M]	Chico Hamilton Plays the Music of Fred Katz	1957	75.00
❏ PJ-1209 [M]	Chico Hamilton Quintet	1955	75.00
❏ PJ-1225 [M]	Chico Hamilton Quintet	1957	75.00
❏ PJ-1216 [M]	Chico Hamilton Quintet In Hi-Fi	1956	75.00
❏ PJLP-17 [10]	Chico Hamilton Trio	1955	100.00
❏ PJ-1220 [M]	Chico Hamilton Trio	1956	75.00
❏ PJ-39 [M]	Spectacular	1962	30.00
—Reissue of 1209			
REPRISE			
❏ R-6078 [M]	A Different Journey	1963	30.00
❏ R9-6078 [S]	A Different Journey	1963	40.00
SOLID STATE			
❏ SS-18050	Headhunters	1969	18.00
❏ SS-18043	The Gamut	1969	18.00
SOUL NOTE			
❏ 121191	Reunion	1989	15.00
SUNSET			
❏ SUS-5215	Easy Livin'	196?	15.00
WARNER BROS.			
❏ W1245 [M]	Chico Hamilton Quintet with Strings Attached	1958	50.00
❏ WS1245 [S]	Chico Hamilton Quintet with Strings Attached	1958	60.00
❏ W1271 [M]	Gongs East	1958	50.00
❏ WS1271 [S]	Gongs East	1958	60.00
❏ W1344 [M]	The Three Faces of Chico	1959	150.00
❏ WS1344 [S]	The Three Faces of Chico	1959	80.00
WORLD PACIFIC			
❏ WP-1231 [M]	Chico Hamilton Plays the Music of Fred Katz	1958	50.00
❏ WP-1225 [M]	Chico Hamilton Quintet	1958	50.00
❏ ST-1005 [S]	Chico Hamilton Quintet	1958	40.00
❏ WP-1216 [M]	Chico Hamilton Quintet In Hi-Fi	1958	50.00
❏ WP-1258 [M]	Ellington Suite	1959	50.00
❏ ST-1016 [S]	Ellington Suite	1959	40.00
❏ PJ-1238 [M]	South Pacific in Hi-Fi	1957	50.00
❏ WP-1238 [M]	South Pacific in Hi-Fi	1958	40.00

HAMILTON, CHICO

Number	Title	Yr	NM
ST-1003 [S]	South Pacific in Hi-Fi	1958	40.00
PJ-1242 [M]	The Chico Hamilton Trio Featuring Freddie Gambrell	1957	50.00
WP-1242 [M]	The Chico Hamilton Trio Featuring Freddie Gambrell	1958	40.00
ST-1008 [S]	The Chico Hamilton Trio Featuring Freddie Gambrell	1958	40.00
WP-1287 [M]	The Original Hamilton Quintet	1960	50.00

HAMILTON, DAVE
WORKSHOP JAZZ

Number	Title	Yr	NM
WSJ-206 [M]	Blue Vibrations	1963	80.00

HAMILTON, GEORGE, IV
ABC

Number	Title	Yr	NM
X-750	16 Greatest Hits	1972	12.00
AC-30032	The ABC Collection	1975	15.00

ABC/DOT

DO-2081	Fine Lace	1977	12.00

ABC-PARAMOUNT

461 [M]	George Hamilton IV's Big 15	1963	30.00
S-461 [P]	George Hamilton IV's Big 15	1963	40.00
220 [M]	On Campus	1958	40.00
S-220 [S]	On Campus	1958	50.00
251 [M]	Sing Me a Sad Song (A Tribute to Hank Williams)	1958	40.00
S-251 [S]	Sing Me a Sad Song (A Tribute to Hank Williams)	1958	50.00

DOT

39033	George Hamilton IV	1985	12.00

HARMONY

HS11379	Your Cheatin' Heart	1970	12.00

LAMB AND LION

1015	Bluegrass Gospel	1974	15.00

MCA

3206	Forever Young	1980	12.00
705	Forever Young	198?	10.00

—Reissue of 3206

RCA CAMDEN

CAL-2200 [M]	A Rose and a Baby Ruth	1907	18.00
CAS-2200 [S]	A Rose and a Baby Ruth	1967	12.00
CAS-2468	Early Morning Rain	1971	12.00
ACL1-0242	Singin' on the Mountains	1973	12.00

RCA VICTOR

LPM-2778 [M]	Abilene	1963	30.00
LSP-2778 [S]	Abilene	1963	30.00
LSP-4342	Back Where It's At	1970	18.00
LSP-4164	Canadian Pacific	1969	18.00
LPM-3510 [M]	Coast Country	1966	30.00
LSP-3510 [S]	Coast Country	1966	30.00
LSP-4700	Country Music in My Soul	1972	15.00
LSP-4435	Down Home in the Country	1971	18.00
LPM-3752 [M]	Folk Country Classics	1967	30.00
LSP-3752 [S]	Folk Country Classics	1967	25.00
LPM-3854 [M]	Folksy	1967	30.00
LSP-3854 [S]	Folksy	1967	25.00
LPM-2972 [M]	Fort Worth, Dallas or Houston	1964	30.00
LSP-2972 [S]	Fort Worth, Dallas or Houston	1964	30.00
APL1-0455	Greatest Hits	1974	15.00
LSP-4826	International Ambassador	1973	15.00
LSP-4066	In the 4th Dimension	1968	25.00
LPM-3371 [M]	Mister Sincerity... A Tribute to Ernest Tubb	1965	30.00
LSP-3371 [S]	Mister Sincerity... A Tribute to Ernest Tubb	1965	30.00
LSP-4517	North Country	1971	18.00
LPM-3601 [M]	Steel Rail Blues	1966	25.00
LSP-3601 [S]	Steel Rail Blues	1966	25.00
LSP-4265	The Best of George Hamilton IV	1970	18.00
LPM-3962 [M]	The Gentle Country Sound of George Hamilton IV	1968	40.00
LSP-3962 [S]	The Gentle Country Sound of George Hamilton IV	1968	25.00
LPM-2373 [M]	To You and Yours from Me and Mine	1961	30.00
LSP-2373 [S]	To You and Yours from Me and Mine	1961	30.00
LSP-4772	Travelin' Light	1972	15.00
LSP-4609	West Texas Highway	1971	18.00

HAMILTON, GEORGE, V
MTM

ST-71061	House of Tears	1987	12.00

—As "Hege V"

HAMILTON, GEORGE
ABC-PARAMOUNT

535 [M]	By George	1966	12.00
S-535 [S]	By George	1966	15.00

HAMILTON, JEFF
CONCORD JAZZ

CJ-187	Indiana	1982	12.00

HAMILTON, JIMMY
EVEREST

LPBR-5100 [M]	Swing Low, Sweet Chariot	1960	30.00

SDBR-1100 [S]	Swing Low, Sweet Chariot	1960	30.00

SWINGVILLE

SVLP-2028 [M]	Can't Help Swingin'	1961	50.00

—Purple label

SVLP-2028 [M]	Can't Help Swingin'	1965	30.00

—Blue label, trident logo at right

SVLP-2022 [M]	It's About Time	1961	60.00

—Purple label

SVLP-2022 [M]	It's About Time	1965	35.00

—Blue label, trident logo at right

URANIA

UJLP-1204 [M]	Accent on Clarinet	1955	50.00
UJLP-1003 [10]	Clarinet in Hi-Fi	1954	120.00
UJLP-1208 [M]	Clarinet in Hi-Fi	1955	50.00

HAMILTON, JOE FRANK & REYNOLDS
ABC DUNHILL

DSX-50113	Hallway Symphony	1972	12.00
DS-50103	Hamilton, Joe Frank & Reynolds	1971	12.00
SKAO-93823	Hamilton, Joe Frank & Reynolds	1971	18.00

—Capitol Record Club edition; label has the old-style "Dunhill" label without the "ABC" in the logo

PLAYBOY

PB-407	Fallin' in Love	1975	12.00
PZ34741	Fallin' in Love	1977	10.00

—Reissue of 107

HAMILTON, ROY
EPIC

LN3561 [M]	Come Out Swingin'	1959	30.00
BN530 [S]	Come Out Swingin'	1959	30.00
LN3364 [M]	Golden Boy	1957	50.00
LN3580 [M]	Have Blues, Must Travel	1959	30.00
BN535 [S]	Have Blues, Must Travel	1959	30.00
LN24000 [M]	Mr. Rock and Soul	1962	30.00
BN26000 [S]	Mr. Rock and Soul	1962	30.00
LN3807 [M]	Only You	1961	30.00
BN610 [S]	Only You	1961	30.00
LN3176 [M]	Roy Hamilton	1955	60.00
LN3628 [M]	Roy Hamilton At His Best	1960	40.00
LN24009 [M]	Roy Hamilton's Greatest Hits	1962	25.00
BN26009 [S]	Roy Hamilton's Greatest Hits	1962	30.00
LN24316 [M]	Roy Hamilton's Greatest Hits, Vol. 2	1967	25.00
BN26316 [S]	Roy Hamilton's Greatest Hits, Vol. 2	1967	30.00
LN3717 [M]	Soft 'n Warm	1960	30.00
BN578 [S]	Soft 'n Warm	1960	30.00
LN3654 [M]	Spirituals	1960	30.00
BN551 [S]	Spirituals	1960	30.00
LN1103 [10]	The Voice of Roy Hamilton	1954	200.00
LN3545 [M]	Why Fight The Feeling?	1959	30.00
BN525 [S]	Why Fight The Feeling?	1959	30.00
LN3519 [M]	With All My Love	1958	30.00
BN518 [S]	With All My Love	1958	40.00
LN3775 [M]	You Can Have Her	1961	30.00
BN595 [S]	You Can Have Her	1961	40.00
LN1023 [10]	You'll Never Walk Alone	1954	200.00
LN3294 [M]	You'll Never Walk Alone	1956	70.00
BN632 [R]	You'll Never Walk Alone	1962	25.00

MGM

E-4233 [M]	Sentimental, Lonely & Blue	1964	18.00
SE-4233 [S]	Sentimental, Lonely & Blue	1964	25.00
E-4139 [M]	Warm and Soul	1963	18.00
SE-4139 [S]	Warm and Soul	1963	25.00

RCA VICTOR

LPM-3552 [M]	The Impossible Dream	1966	18.00
LSP-3552 [S]	The Impossible Dream	1966	25.00

HAMILTON, RUSS
KAPP

KL-1076 [M]	Rainbow	1957	80.00

HAMILTON, SCOTT, AND BUDDY TATE
CONCORD JAZZ

CJ-85	Back to Back	1979	15.00
CJ-148	Scott's Buddy	1981	12.00

HAMILTON, SCOTT, AND WARREN VACHE
CONCORD JAZZ

CJ-111	Skyscrapers	1980	12.00
CJ-70	With Scott's Band in New York	1978	15.00

HAMILTON, SCOTT; JAKE HANNA; DAVE MCKENNA
CONCORD JAZZ

CJ-305	Major League	1986	12.00

HAMILTON, SCOTT
CONCORD JAZZ

CJ-165	Apples and Oranges	1981	12.00
CJ-197	Close Up	1982	12.00
CJ-233	In Concert	1984	12.00
CJ-61	Scott Hamilton 2	1978	15.00
CJ-42	Scott Hamilton Is a Good Wind Who Is Blowing Us No lll	1977	15.00

CJ-127	Tenorshoes	1980	12.00
CJ-311	The Right Time	1987	12.00
CJ-254	The Second Set	1984	12.00

FAMOUS DOOR

119	The Swinging Young Scott	197?	25.00

PROGRESSIVE

7026	Grand Appearance	1979	12.00

HAMLIN, JOHNNY
ARGO

LP-4001 [M]	Johnny Hamiln Quintet	1961	30.00
LPS-4001 [S]	Johnny Hamiln Quintet	1961	30.00

HAMLISCH, MARVIN
MCA

2115	The Entertainer	1974	12.00
390 [B]	The Sting	1973	15.00
37091	The Sting	198?	10.00

—Budget-line reissue

HAMMACK, BOBBY
LIBERTY

LRP-3016 [M]	Power House	1956	40.00

HAMMER, ATLE
GEMINI TAURUS

GMLP-65	Arizona Blue	1991	18.00

HAMMER, BOB
ABC-PARAMOUNT

ABC-497 [M]	Beatle Jazz	1964	30.00
ABCS-497 [S]	Beatle Jazz	1964	40.00

HAMMER, JACK
WARWICK

W-2014 [M]	Rebellion: Jack Hammer Sings and Reads Songs and Poems of the Beat Generation	1960	80.00

HAMMER, JAN
ASYLUM

6E-173	Black Sheep	1979	12.00
6E-232	Hammer	1979	12.00

BASF

MC20688	Make Love	1976	15.00

—Recorded in 1968

MCA

42103	Escape from Television	1988	12.00

NEMPEROR

JZ35003	Melodies	1977	12.00
PZ35003	Melodies	198?	10.00

—Budget-line reissue

NE437	Oh, Yeah?	1976	18.00
BZ40382	The Early Years (1974-1977)	1986	12.00
NE432	The First Seven Days	1975	15.00
AS424 [DJ]	The Jan Hammer Group Live	1978	30.00

—Promo-only album

PASSPORT

PB6051	City Slicker	1985	15.00

—With James Young

HAMMER, MC
BUSTIN'

BR-LP-001	Feel My Power	1987	30.00

CAPITOL

SPRO-79080 [EP]	A Bit Legit	1991	10.00

—Promo-only three-track sampler

C1-90924	Let's Get It Started	1988	12.00
C1-92857	Please Hammer Don't Hurt 'Em	1990	18.00
C1-98151	Too Legit to Quit	1991	18.00

GIANT

PRO-A-6798 [DJ]	The Funky Headhunter	1994	25.00

—Vinyl version is promo only

HAMMER
SAN FRANCISCO

SD203	Hammer	1970	18.00

HAMMILL, PETER
CHARISMA

CAS-1037 [B]	Fool's Mate	1972	30.00
CH-1-2205 [B]	PH 7	1979	18.00
CH-1-2202 [B]	The Future Now	1978	18.00

ENIGMA

ST-73205 [B]	And Close As This	1987	18.00
ST-73206 [B]	Skin	1986	15.00

PVC

8902	Sitting Targets	1981	15.00

Number	Title	Yr	NM
RESTLESS			
❑ 772337-1 [B]	In A Foreign Town	1988	15.00
VISA			
❑ IMP016 [B]	Vision	1978	18.00

HAMMOND, ALBERT

Number	Title	Yr	NM
COLUMBIA			
❑ FC38181	Somewhere in America	1982	12.00
❑ JC36964	Your World and My World	1981	12.00
EPIC			
❑ JE35049	When I Need You	1977	12.00
MUMS			
❑ KZ32834	Albert Hammond	1974	12.00
❑ KZ31905	It Never Rains in Southern California	1972	12.00
❑ KZ32267	The Free Electric Band	1973	12.00

HAMMOND, JOHN

Number	Title	Yr	NM
ATLANTIC			
❑ 8152 [M]	I Can Tell	1967	25.00
❑ SD8152 [S]	I Can Tell	1967	25.00
❑ SD8206	Sooner or Later	1968	18.00
❑ SD8251	Southern Fried	1969	18.00
CAPRICORN			
❑ CP 0153	Can't Beat the Kid	1975	15.00
COLUMBIA			
❑ KC31318	I'm Satisfied	1972	15.00
❑ C30458	Source Point	1971	15.00
FLYING FISH			
❑ FF-502	Nobody But You	1988	12.00
ROUNDER			
❑ 3060	Frogs for Snakes	1982	12.00
❑ 3074	John Hammond Live	1984	12.00
❑ 3042	Mileage	1980	12.00
VANGUARD			
❑ VRS-9153 [M]	Big City Blues	1964	30.00
❑ VSD-79153 [S]	Big City Blues	1964	30.00
❑ VRS-9198 [M]	Country Blues	1966	30.00
❑ VSD-79198 [S]	Country Blues	1966	30.00
❑ VSD-79400	Footwork	1978	12.00
❑ VSD-79424	Hot Tracks	1979	12.00
❑ VRS-9132 [M]	John Hammond	1964	30.00
❑ VSD-2148 [S]	John Hammond	1964	30.00
❑ VRS-9245 [M]	Mirrors	1967	30.00
❑ VSD-79245 [S]	Mirrors	1967	30.00
❑ VSD-79380 [B]	Solo	1976	12.00
❑ VRS-9178 [M]	So Many Roads	1965	30.00
❑ VSD-79178 [S]	So Many Roads	1965	30.00
❑ VSD11/12 [B]	The Best of John Hammond	1970	25.00

HAMMOND, JOHNNY

Number	Title	Yr	NM
KUDU			
❑ 01	Breakout	1971	15.00
❑ 16	Higher Ground	1974	15.00
❑ KSQX-16 [Q]	Higher Ground	1974	25.00
❑ 10	The Prophet	1973	15.00
❑ 04	Wild Horses/Rock Steady	1972	15.00
MILESTONE			
❑ 9083	Don't Let the System Get You	1978	18.00
❑ 9068	Forever Taurus	1976	18.00
❑ 9062	Gears	1975	18.00
❑ 9076	Storm Warning	1977	18.00
NEW JAZZ			
❑ NJLP-8221 [M]	All Soul	1959	50.00
— Purple label			
❑ NJLP-8221 [M]	All Soul	1965	30.00
— Blue label with trident logo			
❑ NJLP-8288 [M]	Look Out!	1962	50.00
— Purple label			
❑ NJLP-8288 [M]	Look Out!	1965	30.00
— Blue label with trident logo			
❑ NJLP-8241 [M]	Talk That Talk	1960	50.00
— Purple label			
❑ NJLP-8241 [M]	Talk That Talk	1965	30.00
— Blue label with trident logo			
❑ NJLP-8229 [M]	That Good Feelin'	1959	50.00
— Purple label			
❑ NJLP-8229 [M]	That Good Feelin'	1965	30.00
— Blue label with trident logo			
PRESTIGE			
❑ PRST-7777	Best for Lovers	1970	18.00
❑ PRST-7736	Black Feeling	1969	18.00
❑ PRST-7564	Dirty Grape	1968	25.00
❑ PRLP-7494 [M]	Ebb Tide	1967	30.00
❑ PRST-7494 [S]	Ebb Tide	1967	25.00
❑ PRLP-7217 [M]	Gettin' the Message	1961	40.00
— Yellow label			
❑ PRLP-7217 [M]	Gettin' the Message	1965	30.00
— Blue label with trident logo			
❑ PRST-7846	Good 'Nuff	1970	18.00
❑ 10002	Here It 'Tis	1971	18.00
❑ PRLP-7482 [M]	Love Potion #9	1967	30.00
❑ PRST-7482 [S]	Love Potion #9	1967	25.00
❑ PRST-7588	Nasty	1968	25.00
❑ PRLP-7420 [M]	Opus de Funk	1966	25.00
❑ PRST-7420 [S]	Opus de Funk	1966	30.00
❑ PRST-7549	Soul Flowers	1968	25.00

Number	Title	Yr	NM
❑ PRST-7681	Soul Talk	1969	25.00
❑ PRLP-7203 [M]	Stimulation	1961	50.00
— Yellow label			
❑ PRLP-7203 [M]	Stimulation	1965	30.00
— Blue label with trident logo			
❑ PRST-7786	Stimulation	1970	18.00
❑ PRST-7705	The Best of Johnny "Hammond" Smith	1969	18.00
❑ PRLP-7408 [M]	The Stinger	1965	25.00
❑ PRST-7408 [S]	The Stinger	1965	30.00
❑ PRLP-7464 [M]	The Stinger Meets the Golden Thrush	1966	25.00
❑ PRST-7464 [S]	The Stinger Meets the Golden Thrush	1966	30.00
❑ 10015	What's Going On	1971	18.00
RIVERSIDE			
❑ RLP-496 [M]	A Little Taste	1965	25.00
❑ RS-9496 [S]	A Little Taste	1965	30.00
❑ RLP-442 [M]	Black Coffee	1963	30.00
❑ RS-9442 [S]	Black Coffee	1963	30.00
❑ RLP-466 [M]	Mr. Wonderful	1963	30.00
❑ RS-9466 [S]	Mr. Wonderful	1963	30.00
❑ RLP-482 [M]	Open House!	1965	25.00
❑ RS-9482 [S]	Open House!	1965	30.00
SALVATION			
❑ 702	A Gambler's Life	1974	15.00

HAMPEL, GUNTER, AND BOULOU FERRE

Number	Title	Yr	NM
BIRTH			
❑ 006	Espace	1970	30.00

HAMPEL, GUNTER

Number	Title	Yr	NM
BIRTH			
❑ 0028	All Is Real	1978	25.00
❑ 0031	All the Things You Could Be If Charles Mingus Was Your Daddy	1980	25.00
❑ 009	Angel	1972	25.00
❑ 0032	A Place to Be with Us	1981	25.00
❑ 0011	Broadway/Folksong	1972	25.00
❑ 0034	Cavana	1982	25.00
❑ 0021/0022	Celebrations	1974	30.00
❑ 0036	Companion	1983	25.00
❑ 0024	Cosmic Dancer	1975	25.00
❑ 002	Dances	1970	30.00
❑ 0025	Entant Terrible	1976	25.00
❑ 008	Familie	1972	25.00
❑ 0030	Freedom of the Universe	1978	25.00
❑ 0039	Fresh Heat	1985	25.00
❑ 0035	Generator	1982	25.00
❑ 0012	I Love Being with You	1972	25.00
❑ 0017	Journey to the Song Within	1974	25.00
❑ 0038	Jubilation	1984	25.00
❑ 0033	Life on This Planet 1981	1981	25.00
❑ 0016	Out from Under	1974	25.00
❑ 005	People Symphony	1970	30.00
❑ 0023	Ruomi	1975	25.00
❑ 007	Spirits	1971	25.00
❑ 003	Symphony No. 5 and 6	1970	30.00
❑ 0027	That Came Down on Me	1978	25.00
❑ 001	The 8th of July, 1969	1969	40.00
❑ 0026	Transformation	1976	25.00
❑ 0013	Unity Dance	1973	25.00
❑ 0029	Vogelfrei	1978	25.00
❑ 0010	Waltz for 3 Universes in a Corridor	1972	25.00
ESP-DISK'			
❑ 1042 [M]	Music from Europe	1967	30.00
❑ S-1042 [S]	Music from Europe	1967	25.00
FLYING DUTCHMAN			
❑ 126	The 8th of July, 1969	1970	40.00
❑ FD-10126	The 8th of July, 1969	1971	25.00
FMP			
❑ 0770	Wellen/Waves	1980	18.00
HORO			
❑ 33/34	Oasis	1978	30.00
KHARMA			
❑ PK8	Flying Carpet	1978	15.00

HAMPTON, LIONEL, AND CHARLIE TEAGARDEN

Number	Title	Yr	NM
CORAL			
❑ CRL57438 [M]	The Great Hamp and Little T.	1963	15.00
❑ CRL757438 [S]	The Great Hamp and Little T.	1963	18.00

HAMPTON, LIONEL, AND STAN GETZ

Number	Title	Yr	NM
NORGRAN			
❑ MGN-1037 [M]	Hamp and Getz	1955	100.00
VERVE			
❑ MGV-8128 [M]	Hamp and Getz	1957	50.00
❑ V-8128 [M]	Hamp and Getz	1961	25.00

HAMPTON, LIONEL, AND SVEND ASMUSSEN

Number	Title	Yr	NM
SONET			
❑ 770	As Time Goes By	1979	15.00

HAMPTON, LIONEL; ART TATUM; BUDDY RICH

Number	Title	Yr	NM
CLEF			
❑ MGC-709 [M]	The Hampton-Tatum-Rich Trio	1956	80.00

Number	Title	Yr	NM
VERVE			
❑ MGV-8093 [M]	The Hampton-Tatum-Rich Trio	1957	50.00
❑ V-8093 [M]	The Hampton-Tatum-Rich Trio	1961	25.00

HAMPTON, LIONEL

Number	Title	Yr	NM
ABC IMPULSE!			
❑ AS-78 [S]	You Better Know It	1968	18.00
AMERICAN RECORDING SOCIETY			
❑ G-403 [M]	The Swinging Jazz of Lionel Hampton	1956	40.00
ATLANTIC			
❑ 81644	Sentimental Journey	1986	12.00
AUDIO FIDELITY			
❑ AFLP-1913 [M]	Hamp's Big Band	1958	30.00
❑ AFSD-5913 [S]	Hamp's Big Band	1958	40.00

Number	Title	Yr	NM
❑ AFLP-1849 [M]	Lionel	1957	30.00
❑ AFSD-5849 [S]	Lionel	1958	40.00
BLUEBIRD			
❑ 6458-1-RB	Hot Mallets	1987	12.00
❑ AXM6 5536	The Complete Lionel Hampton 1937-1941	1976	50.00
BLUE NOTE			
❑ BLP-5046 [10]	Rockin' and Groovin'	1954	300.00
BRUNSWICK			
❑ BL754213	Off Into a Black Thing	1977	15.00
❑ BL754190	Please Sunrise	1973	18.00
❑ BL754203	Stop! I Don't Need No Sympathy	1974	18.00
❑ BL754182	Them Changes	1972	18.00
❑ BL754198	There It Is!	1974	18.00
CLASSIC JAZZ			
❑ 136	Jazz Giants '77	198?	12.00
CLEF			
❑ MGC-727 [M]	Air Mail Special	1956	70.00
❑ MGC-735 [M]	Flying Home	1956	70.00
❑ MGC-738 [M]	Hamp!	1956	70.00
❑ MGC-744 [M]	Hamp's Big Four	1956	70.00
❑ MGC-726 [M]	King of the Vibes	1956	70.00
❑ MGC-670 [M]	Lionel Hampton Big Band	1955	100.00
❑ MGC-714 [M]	Lionel Hampton Plays Love Songs	1956	70.00
❑ MGC-736 [M]	Swingin' with Hamp	1956	70.00
❑ MGC-142 [10]	The Lionel Hampton Quartet	1953	120.00
❑ MGC-611 [M]	The Lionel Hampton Quartet	1954	80.00
❑ MGC-673 [M]	The Lionel Hampton Quartet	1955	80.00
❑ MGC-667 [M]	The Lionel Hampton Quartet and Quintet	1955	100.00
❑ MGC-628 [M]	The Lionel Hampton Quintet	1954	80.00
❑ MGC-642 [M]	The Lionel Hampton Quintet, Volume 2	1955	100.00
COLUMBIA			
❑ CL1304 [M]	Golden Vibes	1959	30.00
❑ CS8110 [S]	Golden Vibes	1959	25.00
❑ CL1486 [M]	Silver Vibes	1960	30.00
❑ CS8277 [S]	Silver Vibes	1960	25.00
❑ CL1661 [M]	Soft Vibes	1961	25.00
❑ CS8461 [S]	Soft Vibes	1961	25.00
❑ CL711 [M]	Wailin' at the Trianon	1956	40.00
CONTEMPORARY			
❑ C-3502 [M]	Hampton in Paris	1955	50.00
CORONET			
❑ CX-159 [M]	Lionel Hampton	196?	15.00
❑ CXS-159 [S]	Lionel Hampton	196?	15.00
DECCA			
❑ DL8088 [M]	All American Award Concert at Carnegie Hall	1955	50.00
— Black label, silver print			
❑ DL0088 [M]	All American Award Concert at Carnegie Hall	196?	25.00
— Black label with color bars			
❑ DL5230 [10]	Boogie Woogie	1950	80.00
❑ DL4296 [M]	Hamp's Golden Favorites	1962	18.00
❑ DL74296 [M]	Hamp's Golden Favorites	1962	25.00
❑ DL7013 [10]	Just Jazz	1962	80.00

Number	Title	Yr	NM
❑ DL9055 [M]	Just Jazz	1958	50.00
❑ DL5297 [10]	Moonglow	1951	80.00
❑ DL8230 [M]	Moonglow	1956	50.00
—Black label, silver print			
❑ DL8230 [M]	Moonglow	196?	25.00
—Black label with color bars			
❑ DL79244 [R]	Stepping Out Volume 1 1942-1945	197?	15.00
❑ DL4194 [M]	The Original Star Dust	1962	18.00
❑ DL74194 [S]	The Original Star Dust	1962	25.00

EMARCY

Number	Title	Yr	NM
❑ MG-27538 [10]	Crazy Hamp	1954	100.00
❑ MG-36034 [M]	Crazy Rhythm	1955	50.00
❑ MG-27537 [10]	Hamp in Paris	1954	100.00
❑ MG-36032 [M]	Hamp in Paris	1955	50.00
❑ MG-36035 [M]	Jam Session in Paris	1955	50.00

EPIC

Number	Title	Yr	NM
❑ LN3190 [M]	Apollo Hall Concert 1954	1955	50.00
❑ LA16027 [M]	Many Splendored Vibes	1962	25.00
❑ BA17027 [S]	Many Splendored Vibes	1962	30.00

EVEREST ARCHIVE OF FOLK & JAZZ

Number	Title	Yr	NM
❑ 348	Hamp in Paris	197?	12.00

FOLKWAYS

Number	Title	Yr	NM
❑ FJ-2871	A Jazz Man for All Seasons	196?	18.00

GATEWAY

Number	Title	Yr	NM
❑ 7020	Jazz Showcase	197?	15.00

GENE NORMAN

Number	Title	Yr	NM
❑ GNP-15 [M]	Lionel Hampton with the Just Jazz All-Stars	1956	50.00

GLAD HAMP

Number	Title	Yr	NM
❑ GH-3050 [M]	All That Twistin' Jazz	1962	30.00
❑ GHS-3050 [S]	All That Twistin' Jazz	1962	30.00
❑ GH-1024	Ambassador at Large	198?	12.00
❑ GH-1009 [M]	A Taste of Hamp	1965	25.00
❑ GHS-1009 [S]	A Taste of Hamp	1965	25.00
❑ GH-1004 [M]	Bossa Nova Jazz	1963	25.00
❑ GHS-1004 [S]	Bossa Nova Jazz	1963	25.00
❑ GH-1021	Chameleon	198?	12.00
❑ GH-1007 [M]	East Meets West	1965	25.00
❑ GHS-1007 [S]	East Meets West	1965	25.00
❑ GH-1006 [M]	Hamp in Japan	1964	25.00
❑ GHS-1006 [S]	Hamp in Japan	1964	25.00
❑ GHS-1011	Hamp Stamps	196?	18.00
❑ GH-1005 [M]	Lionel Hampton on Tour	1963	25.00
❑ GHS-1005 [S]	Lionel Hampton on Tour	1963	25.00
❑ GH-1020	Lionel Hampton's Big Band Live	198?	12.00
❑ GH-1023	Made in Japan	198?	12.00
❑ GH-1026	One of a Kind	1988	12.00
❑ GH-1022	Outrageous	198?	12.00
❑ GH-1003 [M]	The Exciting Hamp in Europe	1962	25.00
❑ GHS-1003 [S]	The Exciting Hamp in Europe	1962	25.00
❑ GH-1001 [M]	The Many Sides of Lionel Hampton	1961	25.00
❑ GHS-1001 [S]	The Many Sides of Lionel Hampton	1961	25.00

GNP CRESCENDO

Number	Title	Yr	NM
❑ GNP-15 [M]	Lionel Hampton with the Just Jazz All-Stars	196?	25.00
❑ GNPS-15 [R]	Lionel Hampton with the Just Jazz All-Stars	196?	15.00

GROOVE MERCHANT

Number	Title	Yr	NM
❑ 4400	The Works!	197?	18.00

HARMONY

Number	Title	Yr	NM
❑ KH32165	Good Vibes	1972	12.00
❑ HL7115 [M]	Hamp in Hi-Fi	1958	25.00
❑ HL7281 [M]	The One and Only Lionel Hampton	1961	25.00

HINDSIGHT

Number	Title	Yr	NM
❑ HSR-237	Lionel Hampton Septet 1962	1988	12.00

IMPULSE!

Number	Title	Yr	NM
❑ A-78 [M]	You Better Know It	1965	30.00
❑ AS-78 [S]	You Better Know It	1965	30.00

JAZZ MAN

Number	Title	Yr	NM
❑ 5011	Lionel Hampton and His Giants	198?	12.00

JAZZTONE

Number	Title	Yr	NM
❑ J-1246 [M]	Lionel Hampton's All Star Groups	1957	40.00
❑ J-1238 [M]	The Fabulous Lionel Hampton and His All-Stars	1957	40.00
❑ J-1040 [10]	Visit on a Skyscraper	195?	50.00

LION

Number	Title	Yr	NM
❑ L-70064 [M]	Lionel Hampton and His Orchestra	1958	25.00

MCA

Number	Title	Yr	NM
❑ 42329	Gene Norman Presents Just Jazz	1990	15.00
❑ 204	Golden Favorites	197?	12.00
❑ 1351	Rarities	198?	12.00
❑ 1315	Steppin' Out	198?	12.00
❑ 1331	Sweatin' with Hamp	198?	12.00
❑ 4057	The Best of Lionel Hampton	197?	15.00

MGM

Number	Title	Yr	NM
❑ E-285 [10]	Oh, Rock	1954	120.00
❑ E-3386 [M]	Oh, Rock	1956	50.00

NORGRAN

Number	Title	Yr	NM
❑ MGN-1080 [M]	Lionel Hampton and His Giants	1956	100.00

PERFECT

Number	Title	Yr	NM
❑ 12002 [M]	Lionel Hampton Swings	1959	30.00
❑ 14002 [S]	Lionel Hampton Swings	1959	40.00

QUINTESSENCE

Number	Title	Yr	NM
❑ 25031	Flyin'	197?	15.00

RCA CAMDEN

Number	Title	Yr	NM
❑ CAL-402 [M]	Jivin' the Vibes	1958	25.00
❑ CAL-317 [M]	Open House	1957	25.00

RCA VICTOR

Number	Title	Yr	NM
❑ LPT-18 [10]	A Treasury of Immortal Performances	1951	100.00
❑ LJM-1000 [M]	Hot Mallets	1954	50.00
❑ LPM-1422 [M]	Jazz Flamenco	1957	50.00
❑ LPM-3917 [M]	Lionel Hampton Plays Bert Kaempfert	1968	30.00
❑ LSP-3917 [S]	Lionel Hampton Plays Bert Kaempfert	1968	18.00
❑ LPM-2318 [M]	Swing Classics	1961	30.00
❑ LSP-2318 [R]	Swing Classics	196?	18.00

SPIN-O-RAMA

Number	Title	Yr	NM
❑ M-3077 [M]	Lionel Hampton at the Vibes	196?	15.00

SWING

Number	Title	Yr	NM
❑ SW-8415	Lionel Hampton in Paris	1987	12.00

TIMELESS

Number	Title	Yr	NM
❑ LPSJP-142	Lionel Hampton's All Star Band at Newport '78	1990	15.00
❑ 303	Live in Emmen, Holland	197?	15.00

TIME-LIFE

Number	Title	Yr	NM
❑ STBB-24	Big Bands: Lionel Hampton	1986	18.00

UPFRONT

Number	Title	Yr	NM
❑ UPF-153	Jammin'	197?	15.00

VERVE

Number	Title	Yr	NM
❑ MGV-8106 [M]	Air Mail Special	1957	30.00
❑ V-8106 [M]	Air Mail Special	1961	25.00
❑ MGV-8112 [M]	Flying Home	1957	30.00
❑ V-8112 [M]	Flying Home	1961	25.00
❑ MGV-8226 [M]	Hallelujah Hamp	1958	30.00
❑ V-8226 [M]	Hallelujah Hamp	1961	25.00
❑ MGV-8114 [M]	Hamp!	1957	30.00
❑ V-8114 [M]	Hamp!	1961	25.00
❑ MGV-8117 [M]	Hamp's Big Four	1957	30.00
❑ V-8117 [M]	Hamp's Big Four	1961	25.00
❑ MGV-8105 [M]	King of the Vibes	1957	30.00
❑ V-8105 [M]	King of the Vibes	1961	25.00
❑ MGV-8223 [M]	Lionel Hampton '58	1958	30.00
❑ V-8223 [M]	Lionel Hampton '58	1961	25.00
❑ MGV-8170 [M]	Lionel Hampton and His Giants	1957	30.00
❑ V-8170 [M]	Lionel Hampton and His Giants	1961	25.00
❑ MGV-2018 [M]	Lionel Hampton Plays Love Songs	1957	30.00
❑ V-2018 [M]	Lionel Hampton Plays Love Songs	1961	25.00
❑ MGV-8113 [M]	Swingin' with Hamp	1957	30.00
❑ V-8113 [M]	Swingin' with Hamp	1961	25.00
❑ VE-2-2543	The Blues Ain't News to Me	1982	18.00
❑ MGV-8215 [M]	The Genius of Lionel Hampton	1958	30.00
❑ V-8215 [M]	The Genius of Lionel Hampton	1961	25.00
❑ MGV-8228 [M]	The High and the Mighty	1958	30.00
❑ V-8228 [M]	The High and the Mighty	1961	25.00
❑ MGV-8019 [M]	Travelin' Band	1957	30.00
❑ V-8019 [M]	Travelin' Band	1961	25.00

WHO'S WHO IN JAZZ

Number	Title	Yr	NM
❑ 21017	Blackout	1978	15.00
❑ 21008	Who's Who Presents Lionel Hampton	1977	15.00

HAMPTON, SLIDE

ATLANTIC

Number	Title	Yr	NM
❑ 1396 [M]	Explosion!	1962	25.00
❑ SD1396 [S]	Explosion!	1962	30.00
❑ 1379 [M]	Jazz with a Twist	1962	30.00
❑ SD1379 [S]	Jazz with a Twist	1962	30.00
❑ 1339 [M]	Sister Salvation	1960	30.00
—Multicolor label, white "fan" logo at right			
❑ 1339 [M]	Sister Salvation	1962	18.00
—Multicolor label, black "fan" logo at right			
❑ SD1339 [S]	Sister Salvation	1960	40.00
—Multicolor label, white "fan" logo at right			
❑ SD1339 [S]	Sister Salvation	1962	25.00
—Multicolor label, black "fan" logo at right			
❑ 1362 [M]	Somethin' Sanctified	1961	30.00
—Multicolor label, white "fan" logo at right			
❑ 1362 [M]	Somethin' Sanctified	1962	18.00
—Multicolor label, black "fan" logo at right			
❑ SD1362 [S]	Somethin' Sanctified	1961	40.00
—Multicolor label, white "fan" logo at right			
❑ SD1362 [S]	Somethin' Sanctified	1962	25.00
—Multicolor label, black "fan" logo at right			

CHARLIE PARKER

Number	Title	Yr	NM
❑ PLP-803 [M]	Two Sides of Slide	1962	30.00
❑ PLP-803S [S]	Two Sides of Slide	1962	30.00

EPIC

Number	Title	Yr	NM
❑ LA16030 [M]	Drum Suite	1963	25.00
❑ BA17030 [S]	Drum Suite	1963	30.00

STRAND

Number	Title	Yr	NM
❑ SL-1006 [M]	Slide Hampton and His Horn of Plenty	1959	40.00
❑ SLS-1006 [S]	Slide Hampton and His Horn of Plenty	1959	40.00

HAMPTON STRING QUARTET

RCA RED SEAL

Number	Title	Yr	NM
❑ 5621-1-RC	What If Mozart Wrote "Have Yourself a Merry Little Christmas	1986	12.00

HANCOCK, HERBIE, AND CHICK COREA

COLUMBIA

Number	Title	Yr	NM
❑ PC235663	An Evening with Herbie Hancock and Chick Corea	1979	15.00

POLYDOR

Number	Title	Yr	NM
❑ PD-2-6238	An Evening with Chick Corea and Herbie Hancock	1979	18.00

HANCOCK, HERBIE

BLUE NOTE

Number	Title	Yr	NM
❑ BLP-4175 [M]	Empyrean Isles	1964	75.00
❑ BST-84175 [S]	Empyrean Isles	1964	100.00
—With New York, USA address on label			
❑ BST-84175 [S]	Empyrean Isles	1967	18.00
—With "A Division of Liberty Records" on label			
❑ BST-84175	Empyrean Isles	1985	12.00
—The Finest in Jazz Since 1939" reissue			
❑ BN-LA399-H2	Herbie Hancock	1975	18.00
❑ BLP-4147 [M]	Inventions and Dimensions	1963	35.00
❑ BST-84147 [S]	Inventions and Dimensions	1963	50.00
—With New York, USA address on label			
❑ BST-84147 [S]	Inventions and Dimensions	1967	18.00
—With "A Division of Liberty Records" on label			
❑ BST-84147	Inventions and Dimensions	1987	12.00
—The Finest in Jazz Since 1939" reissue			
❑ BLP-4195 [M]	Maiden Voyage	1965	35.00
❑ BST-84195 [S]	Maiden Voyage	1965	300.00
—With New York, USA address on label			
❑ BST-84195 [S]	Maiden Voyage	1967	18.00
—With "A Division of Liberty Records" on label			
❑ BST-84195 [S]	Maiden Voyage	197?	15.00
—A Division of United Artists" on label			
❑ B1-46339	Maiden Voyage	1997	25.00
—Audiophile reissue			
❑ BST-84195 [S]	Maiden Voyage	1985	12.00
—The Finest in Jazz Since 1939" reissue			
❑ BLP-4126 [M]	My Point of View	1963	50.00
❑ BST-84126 [S]	My Point of View	1963	100.00
—With New York, USA address on label			
❑ BST-84126 [S]	My Point of View	1967	18.00
—With "A Division of Liberty Records" on label			
❑ BST-84126	My Point of View	1987	12.00
—The Finest in Jazz Since 1939" reissue			
❑ BST-84279	Speak Like a Child	1968	18.00
❑ BST-84279	Speak Like a Child	1986	12.00
—The Finest in Jazz Since 1939" reissue			
❑ BN-LA152-F	Succotash	1974	15.00
❑ BLP-4109 [M]	Takin' Off	1962	50.00
❑ BST-84109 [S]	Takin' Off	1962	150.00
—With New York, USA address on label			
❑ BST-84109 [S]	Takin' Off	1967	18.00
—With "A Division of Liberty Records" on label			
❑ BST-84109	Takin' Off	1987	12.00
—The Finest in Jazz Since 1939" reissue			
❑ BST-84407	The Best of Herbie Hancock	1971	18.00
❑ B1-91142	The Best of Herbie Hancock	1988	12.00
❑ BST-84321	The Prisoner	1969	18.00
❑ BST-84321	The Prisoner	1987	12.00
—The Finest in Jazz Since 1939" reissue			

COLUMBIA

Number	Title	Yr	NM
❑ JC35764	Feets Don't Fail Me Now	1979	15.00
❑ PC35764	Feets Don't Fail Me Now	198?	10.00
—Budget-line reissue			
❑ FC38814	Future Shock	1983	12.00
❑ 8C839913 [EP]	Hardrock	1984	15.00
—Picture disc			
❑ KC32371	Head Hunters	1973	15.00
❑ CQ32371 [Q]	Head Hunters	1973	30.00
❑ PC32371	Head Hunters	197?	10.00
—Reissue (with or without bar code)			
❑ FC37928	Lite Me Up	1982	12.00
❑ PC37928	Lite Me Up	198?	10.00
—Budget-line reissue			
❑ FC37387	Magic Windows	1981	12.00
❑ PC37387	Magic Windows	198?	10.00
—Budget-line reissue			
❑ PC33812	Man-Child	1975	15.00
—No bar code on cover			
❑ PC33812	Man-Child	198?	10.00
—Budget-line reissue with bar code			
❑ JC36415	Monster	1980	12.00
❑ PC36415	Monster	198?	10.00
—Budget-line reissue			
❑ JC36578	Mr. Hands	1980	12.00
❑ PC36578	Mr. Hands	198?	10.00
—Budget-line reissue			
❑ FC40025	Perfect Machine	1988	12.00

Number	Title	Yr	NM
❑ SC40464	'Round Midnight	1986	12.00
❑ PC34280	Secrets	1976	15.00
— No bar code on cover			
❑ PCQ34280 [Q]	Secrets	1976	30.00
❑ PC34280	Secrets	198?	10.00
— Budget-line reissue with bar code			
❑ KC32212	Sextant	1973	15.00
❑ PC32212	Sextant	198?	10.00
— Budget-line reissue			
❑ PCQ32212 [Q]	Sextant	197?	25.00
❑ FC39478	Sound-System	1984	12.00
❑ PC39478	Sound-System	1985	10.00
— Budget-line reissue			
❑ JC34907	Sunlight	1978	15.00
❑ JC36309	The Best of Herbie Hancock	1979	15.00
❑ PC32965	Thrust	1974	15.00
— No bar code on cover			
❑ PCQ32965 [Q]	Thrust	1974	30.00
❑ PC32965	Thrust	198?	10.00
— Budget-line reissue with bar code			
❑ FC39870	Village Life	1985	12.00
❑ PG34688	V.S.O.P.	1977	18.00
❑ C234976	V.S.O.P. Quintet	1978	18.00
MGM			
❑ E-4447 [M]	Blow-Up	1967	40.00
❑ SE-4447 [S]	Blow-Up	1967	50.00
— Also includes one track by the Yardbirds			
PAUSA			
❑ 9002	Succotash	198?	12.00
TRIP			
❑ UPF-194	Traces	197?	15.00
WARNER BROS.			
❑ BS2617	Crossings	1972	18.00
❑ WS1834	Fat Albert Rotunda	1970	18.00
❑ WS1898	Mwandishi	1971	18.00
❑ 2WS2807	Treasure Chest	1974	18.00

HANDSOME BOY MODELING SCHOOL

ELEKTRA

❑ 62941	White People	2004	18.00
TOMMY BOY			
❑ TB1258	So...How's Your Girl?	1999	30.00

HANDY, CAP'N JOHN

GHB

❑ GHBS-41	All Aboard, Volume 1	1967	25.00
❑ GHBS-42	All Aboard, Volume 2	1967	25.00
❑ GHBS-43	All Aboard, Volume 3	1967	25.00
❑ GHB-100	Cap'n John Handy with Geoff Bull and Bary Martyn's Band	1986	12.00
❑ GHB-38	Everybody's Talking	1967	25.00
RCA VICTOR			
❑ LPM-3762 [M]	Introducing Cap'n John Handy	1967	30.00
❑ LSP-3762 [S]	Introducing Cap'n John Handy	1967	18.00
❑ LSP-3929	New Orleans and the Blues	1968	25.00

HANDY, GEORGE

X

❑ LXA-1032 [M]	By George! Handy, Of Course	1954	80.00
❑ LXA-1004 [M]	Handyland, U.S.A.	1954	100.00

HANDY, JOHN

ABC IMPULSE!

❑ AS-9324	Carnival	1977	12.00
❑ ASD-9314	Hard Work	1976	18.00
COLUMBIA			
❑ CL2697 [M]	New View	1967	30.00
❑ CS9497 [S]	New View	1967	30.00
❑ CS9689	Projections	1968	30.00
❑ CL2462 [M]	Recorded Live at the Monterey Jazz Festival	1966	18.00
❑ CS9262 [S]	Recorded Live at the Monterey Jazz Festival	1966	25.00
❑ CL2567 [M]	The Second John Handy Album	1966	25.00
❑ CS9367 [S]	The Second John Handy Album	1966	30.00
MILESTONE			
❑ M-9173	Centerpiece: John Handy with Class	1989	15.00
QUARTET			
❑ Q-1005	Excursion in Blue	1988	30.00
ROULETTE			
❑ RE-132	In the Vernacular	197?	25.00
— Compilation of earlier material			
❑ R52042 [M]	In the Ver-nac'-u-lar	1960	25.00
❑ SR52042 [S]	In the Ver-nac'-u-lar	1960	25.00
❑ R52121 [M]	John Handy Jazz	1964	24.00
❑ SR52121 [3]	John Handy Jazz	1964	30.00
❑ R52088 [M]	No Coast Jazz	1962	24.00
❑ SR52088 [S]	No Coast Jazz	1962	30.00
❑ R52124 [M]	Quote, Unquote	1964	24.00
❑ SR52124 [S]	Quote, Unquote	1964	30.00
WARNER BROS.			
❑ BSK3242	Handy Dandy Man	1978	15.00

Number	Title	Yr	NM
❑ BSK3170	Where Go the Boats	1978	15.00

HANDY, W.C.

DRG

❑ SL-5192	Father of the Blues	1980	12.00
HERITAGE			
❑ 0052 [10]	Blues Revisited	195?	120.00

HANGMEN, THE

MONUMENT

❑ MLP-8077 [M]	Bitter Sweet	1967	70.00
❑ SLP-18077 [S]	Bitter Sweet	1967	40.00

HANKINS, ESCO

AUDIO LAB

❑ AL-1547 [M]	Country Style	1961	200.00

HANNA, JAKE

CONCORD JAZZ

❑ CJ-11	Jake Hanna and Carl Fontana Live	1975	15.00
❑ CJ-35	Jake Hanna Takes Manhattan	1977	15.00
❑ CJ-22	Kansas City Express	1976	15.00

HANNA, KEN

CAPITOL

❑ T6512 [M]	Jazz for Dancers	1955	40.00

HANNA, ROLAND, AND GEORGE MRAZ

CHOICE

❑ 1018	Sir Elf Plus One	1978	18.00

HANNA, ROLAND

ARISTA FREEDOM

❑ AL1010	Perugia	1975	15.00
ATCO			
❑ 33-108 [M]	Destry Rides Again	1959	40.00
❑ SD 33-108 [S]	Destry Rides Again	1959	40.00
❑ 33-121 [M]	Easy to Love	1960	30.00
❑ SD 33-121 [S]	Easy to Love	1960	40.00
AUDIOPHILE			
❑ AP-157	This Must Be Love	198?	12.00
BASF			
❑ 20875	Child of Gemini	1972	30.00
BEE HIVE			
❑ BH-7013	Roland Hanna and the New York Jazz Quartet in Chicago	198?	12.00
CHOICE			
❑ 1003	Sir Elf	1974	18.00
INNER CITY			
❑ IC-1072	Roland Hanna Plays Music of Alec Wilder	197?	15.00
PROGRESSIVE			
❑ 7012	Time for the Dancers	1978	15.00
STORYVILLE			
❑ 4018	Swing Me No Waltzes	198?	12.00
WEST 54TH			
❑ 8003	A Gift from the Magi	1979	15.00

HANNIBAL

ATLANTIC

❑ 81973	Visions of a New World	1989	15.00

HANRAHAN, KIP

AMERICAN CLAVE

❑ 1011 [EP]	A Few Short Notes at the End of the Run	1987	15.00
❑ 1007	Coup De Tete	198?	15.00
❑ 1008/9	Desire Develops an Edge	1984	18.00
❑ 1010	Vertical's Currency	1985	15.00
PANGAEA			
❑ 42137	Days & Nights of Blue Luck Inverted	1988	12.00

HANSON

MANTICORE

❑ MC66672 [B]	Magic Dragon	1974	15.00
❑ MC66670	Now Hear This	1973	15.00

HANSSON, BO

CHARISMA

❑ CAS-1059	Lord of the Rings	1973	15.00
❑ FC6062	Magician's Hat	1974	15.00
SIRE			
❑ SASD-7525	Attic Thoughts	1976	12.00
❑ SR6044	Music Inspired by Watership Down	1977	12.00

HA'PENNYS, THE

FERSCH

❑ FL-1110	Love Is Not the Same	1968	200.00

Number	Title	Yr	NM

HAPPENINGS, THE

B.T. PUPPY

❑ BTP-1003 [M]	Psycle	1967	30.00
❑ BTPS-1003 [S]	Psycle	1967	30.00
❑ BTP-1001 [M]	The Happenings (Bye-Bye, So Long, Farewell...See You in September)	1966	40.00
❑ BTS-1001 [S]	The Happenings (Bye-Bye, So Long, Farewell...See You in September)	1966	30.00
❑ BTS-1004	The Happenings Golden Hits!	1968	40.00
JUBILEE			
❑ JGS-8028	Piece of Mind	1969	30.00
❑ JGS-8030	The Happenings' Greatest Hits	1969	30.00

HAPPY CHIPMUNKS, THE

HOLIDAY

❑ HDY-1950	Merry Christmas from the Happy Chipmunks	1982	30.00
— Record quickly pulled from market because of unauthorized use of the name "Chipmunks"			

HAPPY CRICKETS, THE

GRAND PRIX

❑ KX-9	Christmas with the Happy Crickets	1959	18.00

HAPPY DRAGON BAND, THE

FIDDLER'S MUSIC

❑ 1157	The Happy Dragon Band	1977	80.00

HAPPY JAZZ BAND, THE

AUDIOPHILE

❑ AP-114	College Street Caper	196?	15.00
❑ AP-96 [M]	Goose Pimples	196?	15.00
❑ APS-96 [S]	Goose Pimples	196?	18.00
❑ AP-200	High Society	196?	15.00
❑ AP-86 [M]	Jazz from the San Antonio River	196?	15.00
❑ APS-86 [S]	Jazz from the San Antonio River	196?	18.00
❑ AP-93 [M]	Jim Cullum's Happy Jazz Band	196?	15.00
❑ APS-93 [S]	Jim Cullum's Happy Jazz Band	196?	18.00
❑ AP 87 [M]	Real Stuff	196?	15.00
❑ APS-87 [S]	Real Stuff	196?	18.00
HAPPY JAZZ			
❑ HJ-202	We've Had Mighty Good Weather	1970	15.00
❑ HJ-201	Zacatecas	1969	15.00
— Cliff Brewton, piano; Benny Valfre, banjo; Harvey Kindervater, drums; Willson Davis, sousaphone; Gene McKinney, trombone; Jim Cullum Jr., cornet; Jim Cullum Sr., clarinet.			

HAPPY MONDAYS

ELEKTRA

❑ 60854	Bummed	1980	12.00

HAPSHASH AND THE COLOURED COAT

IMPERIAL

❑ LP-9377 [M]	Hapshash and the Coloured Coat	1968	100.00
❑ LP-12377 [S]	Hapshash and the Coloured Coat	1968	40.00
❑ LP-12430	Western Flyer	1969	40.00

HAQUE, FAREED

PANGAEA

❑ 82012	Manresa	1989	15.00
❑ 42156	Voices Rising	1988	12.00

HARD MEAT

WARNER BROS.

❑ WS1852	Hard Meat	1969	18.00
❑ WS1879	Through a Window	1970	18.00

HARD TIMES, THE

WORLD PACIFIC

❑ WP-1867 [M]	Blew Mind	1968	30.00
❑ WPS-21867 [S]	Blew Mind	1968	30.00

HARDAWAY, BOB

BETHLEHEM

❑ BCP-1028 [10]	Bob Hardaway	1955	200.00

HARDEN, ARLENE

COLUMBIA

❑ CS9633 [S]	Sing Me Back Home	1967	25.00
❑ CL2833 [M]	Sing Me Back Home	1967	30.00
❑ CS9674	What Can I Say	1968	25.00

HARDEN, BOBBY

STARDAY

❑ SLP-443	Nashville Sensation	1969	18.00

Number	Title	Yr	NM

HARDEN, WILBUR

SAVOY
❏ MG-12131 [M]	Jazz Way Out	1958	50.00
❏ SST-13004 [S]	Jazz Way Out	1959	40.00
❏ MG-12127 [M]	Mainstream 1958/The East Coast Jazz Scene Featuring John Coltrane	1958	60.00
❏ MG-12136 [M]	Tanganyika Suite	1958	50.00
❏ SST-13005 [S]	Tanganyika Suite	1959	40.00
❏ MG-12134 [M]	The King and I	1958	50.00
❏ SST-13002 [S]	The King and I	1959	40.00

HARDEN TRIO, THE

COLUMBIA
❏ CL2506 [M]	Tippy Toeing	1966	25.00
❏ CS9306 [S]	Tippy Toeing	1966	30.00

HARDIMAN, DAVID

THERESA
❏ 104	It'll Be Alright	197?	12.00

HARDIN, GUS

RCA VICTOR
❏ CPL1-4937	Fallen Angel	1984	10.00
❏ CPL1-5358	Wall of Tears	1985	10.00
❏ CPL1-7033	Wall of Tears	1985	10.00

HARDIN, TIM

ANTILLES
❏ 7023	Nine	1974	12.00

ATCO
❏ 33-210 [M]	This Is Tim Hardin	1967	60.00
❏ SD 33-210 [R]	This Is Tim Hardin	1967	18.00

COLUMBIA
❏ C30551	Bird on a Wire	1971	25.00
❏ KC31764	Painted Head	1972	25.00
❏ CS9787 [B]	Suite for Susan Moore and Damion -- We Are -- One, One, All in One	1969	30.00
— 360 Sound" label			
❏ PC37164	The Shock of Grace	1981	15.00

MGM
❏ M3G-4952	Archetypes	1974	12.00
❏ GAS-104	Tim Hardin (Golden Archive Series)	1970	15.00

POLYDOR
❏ PD-1-6333	Memorial Album	1981	15.00

VERVE FOLKWAYS
❏ FT-3004 [M]	Tim Hardin/1	1966	60.00
❏ FTS-3004 [S]	Tim Hardin/1	1966	30.00

VERVE FORECAST
❏ FTS-3078	The Best of Tim Hardin	1970	25.00
❏ FT-3004 [M]	Tim Hardin/1	1967	70.00
❏ FTS-3004 [S]	Tim Hardin/1	1967	25.00
❏ FTS-3022	Tim Hardin/2	1967	30.00
❏ FTS-3049	Tim Hardin/3 -- Live in Concert	1968	30.00
❏ FTS-3064	Tim Hardin/4	1969	30.00

HARDING, ELLERINE

MAINSTREAM
❏ MRL-377	Ellerine Harding	1972	12.00

HARDMAN, BILL

MUSE
❏ MR-5259	Focus	198?	12.00
❏ MR-5152	Home	1978	15.00
❏ MR-5184	Politely	1981	15.00

SAVOY
❏ MG-12170 [M]	Bill Hardman Quintet	1961	150.00

SAVOY JAZZ
❏ SJL-1164	Saying Something	1986	12.00

HARDWATER

CAPITOL
❏ ST-2954	Hardwater	1968	40.00

HARDY, FRANCOISE

4 CORNERS OF THE WORLD
❏ FCL-4231 [M]	Francoise...	1968	60.00
❏ FCS-4231 [S]	Francoise...	1968	35.00
❏ FCL-4238 [M]	Je Vous Aime	1969	60.00
❏ FCS-4238 [S]	Je Vous Aime	1969	35.00
❏ FCL-4219 [M]	Maid in Paris	1967	60.00
❏ FCS-4219 [S]	Maid in Paris	1967	50.00
❏ FCL-4208 [M]	The "Yeh Yeh" Girl from Paris!	1965	60.00
❏ FCS-4208 [S]	The "Yeh Yeh" Girl from Paris!	1965	50.00
❏ FCS-4255 [S]	The Best of Francoise Hardy	1969	30.00

REPRISE
❏ RS6290	Francoise Hardy	1968	30.00
❏ RS6318	Loving	1969	30.00
❏ RS6345	Mon Amour, Adieu	1969	30.00

HARDY, HAGOOD

CAPITOL
❏ ST-11552	Maybe Tomorrow	1976	12.00
❏ ST-11488	The Homecoming	1975	12.00
❏ SN-16300	The Homecoming	198?	10.00
— Budget-line reissue			

HARDY BOYS, THE

RCA VICTOR
❏ LSP-4217	Here Come the Hardy Boys	1969	25.00
❏ LSP-4315	Wheels	1970	25.00

HARGROVE, LINDA

CAPITOL
❏ ST-11685	Impressions	1977	15.00
❏ ST-11564	Just Like You	1976	15.00
❏ ST-11463	Love, You're the Teacher	1975	15.00

ELEKTRA
❏ 7E-1013	Blue Jean Country Queen	1974	15.00
❏ EKS-75063	Music Is Your Mistress	1973	18.00

HARGROVE, ROY

NOVUS
❏ 3082-1-N	Diamond in the Rough	1990	15.00

HARIAN, KENT

CARAVAN
❏ LP-15611 [M]	Echoes of Joy	1956	250.00

HARLEY, RUFUS

ATLANTIC
❏ SD3001 [S]	Bagpipe Blues	1967	18.00
❏ 3001 [M]	Bagpipe Blues	1967	25.00
❏ SD1539	King/Queens	1970	18.00
❏ SD3006	Scotch & Soul	1968	18.00
❏ SD1504	Tribute to Courage	1969	18.00

HARMONAIRES MALE QUINTET, THE

VARSITY
❏ 6015 [10]	Spirituals	195?	80.00

HARMONY BLAZERS, THE

HARMONY
❏ HL7126 [M]	Rock & Roll Vol. II	1959	40.00
❏ HL7103 [M]	Ten Big Hits	1959	40.00
❏ HL7200 [M]	The Big Ten	1959	40.00

HARMONY CHORISTERS, THE

HARMONY
❏ HL7073 [M]	Christmas Hymns and Carols	195?	18.00

HARNELL, JOE

CAPITOL
❏ ST-11657	Harnell	1977	15.00

COLUMBIA
❏ CL2699 [M]	Bossa Now	1967	18.00
❏ CS9499 [S]	Bossa Now	1967	15.00
❏ CL2466 [M]	Golden Piano Hits	1966	15.00
❏ CS9266 [S]	Golden Piano Hits	1966	18.00

EPIC
❏ BN573 [S]	I Want to Be Happy	1960	25.00
❏ LN0(# unknown) [M]	I Want to Be Happy	1960	18.00

JUBILEE
❏ JGM-5020 [M]	Joe Harnell and His Trio	1963	18.00
— Reissue of 1015			
❏ JLP-1015 [M]	Piano Inventions of Jo Harnell	1956	50.00

KAPP
❏ KL1318 [M]	Fly Me to the Moon and the Bossa Nova Pops	1962	18.00
❏ KS3318 [S]	Fly Me to the Moon and the Bossa Nova Pops	1962	25.00
❏ KL1339 [M]	Joe Harnell	1963	18.00
❏ KS3339 [S]	Joe Harnell	1963	25.00
❏ KL1325 [M]	More Joe Harnell, More Bossa Nova Pops	1963	18.00
❏ KS3325 [S]	More Joe Harnell, More Bossa Nova Pops	1963	25.00
❏ KL1480 [M]	The Best of Joe Harnell	1966	15.00
❏ KS3480 [S]	The Best of Joe Harnell	1966	18.00
❏ KL1416 [M]	The Rhythm and the Fire	1965	15.00
❏ KS3416 [S]	The Rhythm and the Fire	1965	18.00

MOTOWN
❏ MS-698	Moving On!!	1969	40.00

HARPER, BEN

CARDAS
❏ CR5818	Pleasure and Pain	1992	500.00
— With Tom Freund			

VIRGIN
❏ 48151	Burn to Shine	1999	50.00
— As "Ben Harper and the Innocent Criminals			
❏ 83003	Diamonds on the Inside	2003	25.00
❏ 10079	Live from Mars	2001	100.00

— As "Ben Harper and the Innocent Criminals			
❏ 71206	There Will Be a Light	2005	25.00
— With the Blind Boys of Alabama			

HARPER, BILLY

BLACK SAINT
❏ BSR-0001	Black Saint	198?	18.00

SOUL NOTE
❏ SN-1001	Billy Harper In Europe	198?	18.00

STRATA-EAST
❏ SES-19739	Capra Black	1973	40.00

HARPER, HERBIE

BETHLEHEM
❏ BCP-1025 [10]	Herbie Harper	1955	120.00

LIBERTY
❏ LRP-6003 [M]	Herbie Harper	1956	80.00

MODE
❏ LP-100 [M]	Herbie Harper Sextet	1957	100.00

NOCTURNE
❏ NLP-7 [10]	Herbie Harper	1954	150.00
❏ NLP-1 [10]	Herbie Harper Quintet	1954	150.00

SEABREEZE
❏ SBD-101	Herbie Harper Revisited	1981	15.00

TAMPA
❏ TP-11 [M]	Herbie Harper Quintet	1957	100.00
— Red vinyl			
❏ TP-11 [M]	Herbie Harper Quintet	1958	50.00
— Black vinyl			

HARPER, JANICE

CAPITOL
❏ T1337 [M]	Embers of Love	1960	25.00
❏ ST1337 [S]	Embers of Love	1960	30.00

HARPER, ROY

CHRYSALIS
❏ CH21164	Flashes from the Archives of Oblivion	1978	18.00
— Released in the UK in 1974			
❏ CHR1160	Flat Baroque and Berserk	1978	18.00
— Reissue of Harvest LP			
❏ PRO-620 [DJ]	Introduction to Roy Harper	1976	40.00
❏ PRO-620 [DJ]	Introduction to Roy Harper	1976	30.00
❏ CHR1162	Lifemask	1978	15.00
— Released in the UK in 1973			
❏ CHR1139	One of Those Days in England	1977	18.00
❏ CHR1161	Stormcock	1978	15.00
— Released in the UK in 1971			
❏ CHR1163	Valentine	1978	15.00
— Released in the UK in 1974			
❏ CHR1105	When An Old Cricketer Leaves the Crease	1976	18.00

HARVEST
❏ SKAO-418	Flat Baroque and Berserk	1970	30.00

PVC
❏ 8937 [B]	Whatever Happened to Jugula	198?	15.00
— featuring Jimmy Page			

WORLD PACIFIC
❏ WPS-21888	Folkjokeopus	1969	30.00

HARPER, TONI

RCA VICTOR
❏ LPM-2092 [M]	Lady Lonely	1960	30.00
❏ LSP-2092 [S]	Lady Lonely	1960	40.00
❏ LPM-2253 [M]	Night Mood	1960	30.00
❏ LSP-2253 [S]	Night Mood	1960	40.00

VERVE
❏ MGV-2001 [M]	Toni Harper Sings	1956	150.00
❏ V-2001 [M]	Toni Harper Sings	1961	50.00

HARPER, WALT

GATEWAY
❏ 7005 [M]	Harper's Ferry	1964	18.00
❏ 7016 [M]	On the Road	1966	25.00
❏ S-7016 [S]	On the Road	1966	18.00

HARPER BROTHERS, THE

VERVE
❏ 837033-1	The Harper Brothers	1988	12.00

HARPERS BIZARRE

FOREST BAY
❏ 7545	As Time Goes By	1976	18.00

WARNER BROS.
❏ WS1716	Anything Goes	1967	25.00
❏ ST-91351	Anything Goes	1968	25.00
— Capitol Record Club edition			
❏ W1693 [M]	Feelin' Groovy	1967	25.00
❏ WS1693 [S]	Feelin' Groovy	1967	14.00
— Gold label			

Number	Title	Yr	NM
❑ WS1693 [S]	Feelin' Groovy	1968	18.00
— Green "W7" label			
❑ WS1784	Harpers Bizarre Four	1969	16.00
❑ WS1739	The Secret Life of Harpers Bizarre	1968	16.00

HARPO, SLIM

EXCELLO

Number	Title	Yr	NM
❑ LP-8005 [M]	Baby Scratch My Back	1966	200.00
— Orange and blue label			
❑ LPS-8005 [M]	Baby Scratch My Back	196?	100.00
— All-blue label			
❑ LP-8003 [M]	Raining in My Heart	1961	250.00
— Orange and blue label			
❑ LPS-8003 [M]	Raining in My Heart	196?	100.00
— All-blue label			
❑ LPS-8013 [M]	Slim Harpo Knew the Blues	1970	50.00
❑ LPS-8010 [M]	The Best of Slim Harpo	1969	50.00
❑ LPS-8008 [M]	Tip On In	1968	50.00

RHINO

Number	Title	Yr	NM
❑ R1-70169	Scratch My Back: The Best of Slim Harpo	1989	15.00
❑ RNLP-106	The Best of Slim Harpo	198?	18.00

HARPTONES, THE

AMBIENT SOUND

Number	Title	Yr	NM
❑ FZ37718	Love Needs	1982	15.00

HARLEM HIT PARADE

Number	Title	Yr	NM
❑ 5006	The Harptones	197?	18.00

RELIC

Number	Title	Yr	NM
❑ LP-5001	The Greatest Hits of the Harptones, Vol. 1	197?	15.00
❑ LP-5003	The Greatest Hits of the Harptones, Vol. 2	197?	15.00

HARRELL, TOM

BLACKHAWK

Number	Title	Yr	NM
❑ BKH-50901	The Play of Light	1986	12.00

CONTEMPORARY

Number	Title	Yr	NM
❑ C-14059	Form	1990	15.00
❑ C-14054	Sail Away	1989	15.00
❑ C-14043	Stories	1988	12.00

HARRIOTT, JOE

ATLANTIC

Number	Title	Yr	NM
❑ 1482 [M]	Indo-Jazz Fusions	1967	18.00
❑ SD1482 [S]	Indo-Jazz Fusions	1967	15.00
❑ 1465 [M]	Indo-Jazz Suite	1966	15.00
❑ SD1465 [S]	Indo-Jazz Suite	1966	18.00

CAPITOL

Number	Title	Yr	NM
❑ T10351 [M]	Abstract	1962	30.00
❑ DT10351 [R]	Abstract	1962	15.00

JAZZLAND

Number	Title	Yr	NM
❑ JLP-49 [M]	Free Form	1961	30.00
❑ JLP 949 [S]	Free Form	1961	30.00
❑ JLP-37 [M]	Southern Horizons	1961	30.00
❑ JLP-937 [S]	Southern Horizons	1961	30.00

HARRIS, ART, AND MITCH LEIGH

EPIC

Number	Title	Yr	NM
❑ LG1010 [10]	Modern Woodwind Expressions	1954	50.00
❑ LN3200 [M]	New Jazz in Hi-Fi	1956	40.00

KAPP

Number	Title	Yr	NM
❑ KL-1011 [M]	Baroque Band and Brass Choir -- Jazz 1775	1956	40.00

HARRIS, ART

KAPP

Number	Title	Yr	NM
❑ KL-1015 [M]	Jazz Goes to Post-Graduate School	1956	40.00

HARRIS, BARRY

ARGO

Number	Title	Yr	NM
❑ LP-644 [M]	Breakin' It Up	1959	40.00
❑ LPS-644 [S]	Breakin' It Up	1959	30.00

CADET

Number	Title	Yr	NM
❑ LP-644 [M]	Breakin' It Up	1966	25.00
❑ LPS-644 [S]	Breakin' It Up	1966	18.00

FANTASY

Number	Title	Yr	NM
❑ OJC-208	Barry Harris at the Jazz Workshop	1986	12.00
❑ OJC-486	Preminado	1991	15.00

MILESTONE

Number	Title	Yr	NM
❑ 47050	Stay Right With It	197?	18.00

PRESTIGE

Number	Title	Yr	NM
❑ PRST-7600	Bull's Eye	1969	25.00
❑ PRLP-7498 [M]	Luminescence	1967	30.00
❑ PRST-7498 [S]	Luminescence	1967	25.00
❑ PRST 7733	Magnificent!	1970	25.00

RIVERSIDE

Number	Title	Yr	NM
❑ RLP 12-326 [M]	Barry Harris at the Jazz Workshop	1960	300.00
❑ RLP-1177 [S]	Barry Harris at the Jazz Workshop	1960	200.00
❑ 6123	Barry Harris at the Jazz Workshop	197?	15.00
❑ RLP-435 [M]	Chasin' the Bird	1962	30.00
❑ RS-9435 [S]	Chasin' the Bird	1962	30.00
❑ RLP-392 [M]	Listen to Barry Harris	1961	30.00
❑ RS-9392 [S]	Listen to Barry Harris	1961	40.00
❑ RLP-413 [M]	Newer Than New	1962	30.00
❑ RS-9413 [S]	Newer Than New	1962	30.00
❑ RLP-354 [M]	Preminado	1961	140.00
❑ RS-9354 [S]	Preminado	1961	40.00
❑ 6047	Preminado	197?	15.00

XANADU

Number	Title	Yr	NM
❑ 154	Barry Harris Plays Barry Harris	1978	15.00
❑ 113	Barry Harris Plays Tadd Dameron	1975	15.00
❑ 130	Live in Tokyo	1976	15.00
❑ 213	The Bird of Red and Gold	1990	18.00
❑ 177	Tokyo: 1976	1980	15.00

HARRIS, BEAVER, AND DON PULLEN

HANNIBAL

Number	Title	Yr	NM
❑ HNBL-2701	A Well Kept Secret	198?	12.00

HARRIS, BEAVER

BLACK SAINT

Number	Title	Yr	NM
❑ BSR-0006/7	In-Sanity	198?	25.00

CADENCE JAZZ

Number	Title	Yr	NM
❑ 1002	Live at Nyon	198?	15.00
❑ 1003	Negcaumongus	198?	12.00

RED

Number	Title	Yr	NM
❑ VPA-146	360 Degree Aeutopia	198?	15.00
❑ VPA-151	Safe	198?	15.00

SOUL NOTE

Number	Title	Yr	NM
❑ SN-1002	Beautiful Africa	198?	18.00

HARRIS, BILL (1), AND CHARLIE VENTURA

PHOENIX

Number	Title	Yr	NM
❑ 14	Aces	197?	12.00
❑ 11	Live at the Three Deuces	197?	12.00

HARRIS, BILL (1)

CLEF

Number	Title	Yr	NM
❑ MGC-125 [10]	Bill Harris Collates	1953	150.00

FANTASY

Number	Title	Yr	NM
❑ 3263 [M]	Bill Harris and Friends	1958	40.00
— Red vinyl			
❑ 3263 [M]	Bill Harris and Friends	1959	30.00
— Black vinyl			
❑ OJC-083	Bill Harris and Friends	198?	12.00

NORGRAN

Number	Title	Yr	NM
❑ MGN-1062 [M]	The Bill Harris Herd	1956	120.00

VERVE

Number	Title	Yr	NM
❑ MGV-8152 [M]	The Bill Harris Herd	1957	60.00

XANADU

Number	Title	Yr	NM
❑ 191	Memorial Album	198?	15.00

HARRIS, BILL (2)

EMARCY

Number	Title	Yr	NM
❑ MG-36097 [M]	Bill Harris	1950	40.00
❑ MG-36113 [M]	The Harris Touch	1957	40.00

MERCURY

Number	Title	Yr	NM
❑ MG-20552 [M]	The Harris Touch	1960	30.00
❑ SR-60552 [S]	The Harris Touch	1960	30.00

WING

Number	Title	Yr	NM
❑ MGW-12220 [M]	Great Guitar Sounds	1963	25.00
❑ SRW-16220 [S]	Great Guitar Sounds	1963	18.00

HARRIS, DAVE

DECCA

Number	Title	Yr	NM
❑ DL4113 [M]	Dinner Music for a Pack of Hungry Cannibals	1961	25.00
❑ DL74113 [S]	Dinner Music for a Pack of Hungry Cannibals	1961	30.00

HARRIS, EDDIE

ANGELACO

Number	Title	Yr	NM
❑ AN3002	Sounds Incredible	1980	15.00

ATLANTIC

Number	Title	Yr	NM
❑ SD1675	Bad Luck Is All I Have	1975	15.00
❑ SD1554	Come On Down!	1970	18.00
❑ SD1595	Eddie Harris Live at Newport	1971	15.00
❑ SD1625	Eddie Harris Sings the Blues	1973	15.00
❑ SD1647	E.H. in the U.K.	1974	15.00
❑ SD 2-311	Excursions	1973	18.00
❑ SD1573	Free Speech	1971	18.00
❑ SD1529	High Voltage	1969	18.00
❑ SD1698	How Can You Live Like That	1977	15.00
❑ SD1669	I Need Some Money	1975	15.00
❑ SD1611	Instant Death	1972	15.00
❑ SW-94771	Instant Death	1972	18.00
— Capitol Record Club edition			
❑ SD1659	Is It In	1974	15.00
❑ 1453 [M]	Mean Greens	1966	15.00
❑ SD1453 [S]	Mean Greens	1966	18.00
❑ SD1506	Plug Me In	1968	18.00
❑ SD1517	Silver Cycles	1969	18.00
❑ SD1545	The Best of Eddie Harris	1970	18.00
❑ 1545 [M]	The Best of Eddie Harris	1970	30.00
— Promo-only white label mono pressing			
❑ SD1495	The Electrifying Eddie Harris	1968	18.00
❑ 1448 [M]	The In Sound	1966	15.00
❑ SD1448 [S]	The In Sound	1966	18.00
❑ 1478 [M]	The Tender Storm	1967	18.00
❑ SD1478 [S]	The Tender Storm	1967	18.00
❑ SD8807	The Versatile Eddie Harris	1982	12.00
❑ SD1683	Why You're Overweight	1976	15.00

BUDDAH

Number	Title	Yr	NM
❑ BDS4004	Sculpture	1969	15.00

COLUMBIA

Number	Title	Yr	NM
❑ CL2168 [M]	Cool Sax, Warm Heart	1964	18.00
❑ CS8968 [S]	Cool Sax, Warm Heart	1964	25.00
❑ CL2295 [M]	Cool Sax from Hollywood to Broadway	1965	18.00
❑ CS9095 [S]	Cool Sax from Hollywood to Broadway	1965	25.00
❑ CS9681 [S]	Here Comes the Judge	1968	18.00
❑ CS9681 [M]	Here Comes the Judge	1968	30.00
— Mono copies are promo only			

EXODUS

Number	Title	Yr	NM
❑ EX-6002 [M]	For Bird and Bags	1966	18.00

GNP CRESCENDO

Number	Title	Yr	NM
❑ GNPS-2073	Black Sax	1973	18.00

JANUS

Number	Title	Yr	NM
❑ 3020	Smokin'	1970	15.00

MUTT & JEFF

Number	Title	Yr	NM
❑ 5018	The Real Electrifying Eddie Harris	1982	15.00

RCA VICTOR

Number	Title	Yr	NM
❑ APL1-2942	I'm Tired	1978	12.00
❑ AFL1-3402	Playin' With Myself	1980	12.00

STEEPLECHASE

Number	Title	Yr	NM
❑ 1151	Eddie Harris Steps Up	1981	12.00

SUNSET

Number	Title	Yr	NM
❑ SUS-5234	The Explosive Eddie Harris	1969	15.00

TRADITION

Number	Title	Yr	NM
❑ 2067	Genius	1969	15.00

TRIP

Number	Title	Yr	NM
❑ 5005	Shades of Eddie Harris	1974	15.00

UPFRONT

Number	Title	Yr	NM
❑ UPF-106	The Soul of Eddie Harris	197?	12.00

VEE JAY

Number	Title	Yr	NM
❑ LP3028 [M]	A Study in Jazz	1962	25.00
❑ SR3028 [S]	A Study in Jazz	1962	30.00
❑ LP3034 [M]	Bossa Nova	1963	25.00
❑ SR3034 [S]	Bossa Nova	1963	30.00
❑ LP3031 [M]	Eddie Harris Goes to the Movies	1962	25.00
❑ SR3031 [S]	Eddie Harris Goes to the Movies	1962	30.00
❑ LP3016 [M]	Exodus to Jazz	1961	30.00
❑ SR3016 [S]	Exodus to Jazz	1961	40.00
❑ VJS-3016	Exodus to Jazz	198?	12.00
— Reissue with thinner vinyl			
❑ VJO-3068	For Bird and Bags	198?	12.00
❑ LP3037 [M]	Half and Half	1963	30.00
❑ SR3037 [S]	Half and Half	1963	30.00
❑ LP3027 [M]	Jazz for "Breakfast at Tiffany's	1961	30.00
❑ SR3027 [S]	Jazz for "Breakfast at Tiffany's	1961	40.00
❑ LP3025 [M]	Mighty Like a Rose	1961	30.00
❑ SR3025 [S]	Mighty Like a Rose	1961	40.00
❑ VJLP1081 [M]	The Theme from Exodus and Other Film Spectaculars	1964	18.00
❑ VJLPS1081 [S]	The Theme from Exodus and Other Film Spectaculars	1964	25.00

HARRIS, EMMYLOU

JUBILEE

Number	Title	Yr	NM
❑ JGS-8031 [B]	Gliding Bird	1969	200.00
— Originals have color covers; counterfeit covers are black and white			

MOBILE FIDELITY

Number	Title	Yr	NM
❑ 1-015	Quarter Moon in a Ten Cent Town	1979	40.00
— Audiophile vinyl			

REPRISE

Number	Title	Yr	NM
❑ 25776	Bluebird	1989	15.00
❑ MS2236	Elite Hotel	1976	12.00
❑ MSK2286 [B]	Elite Hotel	1977	10.00
— Reissue of 2236			
❑ MS2213	Pieces of the Sky	1975	12.00
❑ MSK2284	Pieces of the Sky	1977	10.00
— Reissue of 2213			

WARNER BROS.

Number	Title	Yr	NM
❑ 25585	Angel Band	1987	12.00
❑ BSK3318	Blue Kentucky Girl	1979	12.00
❑ BSK3603	Cimarron	1981	12.00
❑ BSK3508	Evangeline	1981	12.00
❑ 23740	Last Date	1982	12.00
❑ BSK3484	Light of the Stable: The Christmas Album	1980	12.00
❑ BSK3115	Luxury Liner	1977	12.00
— Reissue of 2998			
❑ BS2998	Luxury Liner	1977	15.00
❑ BSK3258	Profile/Best of Emmylou Harris	1978	12.00

Number	Title	Yr	NM
❑ 25161	Profile II -- The Best of Emmylou Harris	1984	12.00
❑ BSK3141	Quarter Moon in a Ten Cent Town	1978	12.00
❑ BSK3422	Roses in the Snow	1980	12.00
❑ 25205	The Ballad of Sally Rose	1985	12.00
❑ 25352	Thirteen	1986	12.00
❑ 23961	White Shoes	1983	12.00

HARRIS, GENE

BLUE NOTE

Number	Title	Yr	NM
❑ BN-LA313-G	Astral Signal	1974	25.00
❑ BST-84423	Gene Harris of the Three Sounds	1972	25.00
❑ BN-LA519-G	Nexus	1975	18.00
❑ BN-LA634-G	Special Way	1976	18.00
❑ BST-84378	The Three Sounds	1971	25.00
❑ BN-LA760-H	Tone Tantrum	1977	18.00
❑ BN-LA141-G	Yesterday, Today and Tomorrow	1973	30.00

CONCORD JAZZ

Number	Title	Yr	NM
❑ CJ-303	The Gene Harris Trio Plus One	1986	12.00

JAM

Number	Title	Yr	NM
❑ 008	Hot Lips	198?	15.00

JUBILEE

Number	Title	Yr	NM
❑ JGM-1115 [M]	Genie in My Soul	1959	40.00
❑ JLP-1005 [M]	Our Love Is Here to Stay	1955	50.00

HARRIS, HAROLD

VEE JAY

Number	Title	Yr	NM
❑ LP-3036 [M]	Harold Harris at the Playboy Club	1963	30.00
❑ SR-3036 [S]	Harold Harris at the Playboy Club	1963	30.00
❑ LP-3018 [M]	Here's Harold	1962	30.00
❑ SR-3018 [S]	Here's Harold	1962	30.00

HARRIS, MAJOR

ATLANTIC

Number	Title	Yr	NM
❑ SD18160	Jealousy	1976	18.00
❑ SD18119	My Way	1974	18.00

RCA VICTOR

Number	Title	Yr	NM
❑ APL1-2803	How Do You Take Your Love	1978	15.00

WMOT

Number	Title	Yr	NM
❑ 627	Mellow Major	1977	15.00
❑ PW37067	The Best of Major Harris, Now and Then	1981	12.00

HARRIS, PEPPERMINT

TIME

Number	Title	Yr	NM
❑ 5 [M]	Peppermint Harris	1962	200.00

HARRIS, PHIL

MEGA

Number	Title	Yr	NM
❑ MLPS-608	Southern Comfort ... The Best of Phil Harris	1974	18.00

RCA CAMDEN

Number	Title	Yr	NM
❑ CAL-456 [M]	That's What I Like About the South	1963	18.00
❑ CAS-456(e) [R]	That's What I Like About the South	1963	12.00

RCA VICTOR

Number	Title	Yr	NM
❑ LPM-3037 [10]	Phil Harris On the Record	1952	40.00
❑ LPM-1985 [M]	The South Shall Rise Again	1959	30.00
❑ LSP-1985 [S]	The South Shall Rise Again	1959	30.00

SUNBEAM

Number	Title	Yr	NM
❑ HB302	Broadcasts from the Cocoanut Grove, L.A., 1932	198?	12.00

HARRIS, RICHARD

ABC DUNHILL

Number	Title	Yr	NM
❑ DS-50032 [B]	A Tramp Shining	1968	25.00
❑ DSX-50159	I, In the Membership	1974	10.00
❑ DSX-50160	Jonathan Livingston Seagull	1973	10.00
—Spoken-word recording			
❑ DSX-50116	My Boy	1971	10.00
❑ DSX-50133	Slides	1972	10.00
❑ DSX-50139	The Great Performances	1973	10.00
❑ DS-50074 [B]	The Love Album	1970	15.00
❑ DS-50042 [B]	The Yard Went On Forever	1968	25.00

ATLANTIC

Number	Title	Yr	NM
❑ SD18120	The Prophet by Kahlil Gibran	1974	10.00
—Spoken-word recording			
❑ QD18120 [Q]	The Prophet by Kahlil Gibran	1974	30.00
—Spoken-word recording			

MCA

Number	Title	Yr	NM
❑ 27016	A Tramp Shining	198?	10.00
—Budget-line reissue			

PICKWICK

Number	Title	Yr	NM
❑ SPC-3626	A Tramp Shining	1978	12.00

HARRIS, ROLF

EPIC

Number	Title	Yr	NM
❑ LN24110 [M]	Join Rolf Harris Singing The Count of King Caractacus (And Other Fun Songs)	1964	18.00
❑ BN26110 [S]	Join Rolf Harris Singing The Count of King Caractacus (And Other Fun Songs)	1964	15.00
❑ LN24053 [M]	Tie Me Kangaroo Down, Sport & Sun Arise	1963	18.00
❑ BN26053 [S]	Tie Me Kangaroo Down, Sport & Sun Arise	1963	15.00

HARRIS, SHAUN

CAPITOL

Number	Title	Yr	NM
❑ ST-11168	Shaun Harris	1973	30.00

HARRIS, WYNONIE

KING

Number	Title	Yr	NM
❑ KS-1086	Good Rockin' Blues	1970	30.00

HARRISON, CASS

MGM

Number	Title	Yr	NM
❑ E-3388 [M]	The Duke and I	1956	40.00
❑ E-3495 [M]	Wrappin' It Up	1957	40.00

HARRISON, GEORGE, AND FRIENDS

APPLE

Number	Title	Yr	NM
❑ STCX-3385	The Concert for Bangla Desh	1971	40.00
—With 64-page booklet and custom innersleeves			
❑ STCX-3385	The Concert for Bangla Desh	1975	50.00
—As above, but with "All Rights Reserved" on labels			

CAPITOL

Number	Title	Yr	NM
❑ SABB-12248	The Concert for Bangla Desh	1982	300.00
—Scheduled reissue that was never officially released, though a few copies got out by mistake			

HARRISON, GEORGE

APPLE

Number	Title	Yr	NM
❑ STCH-639 [B]	All Things Must Pass	1970	60.00
—Apple labels on first two records and "Apple Jam" labels on third; includes poster and lyric innersleeves			
❑ SMAS-3418	Dark Horse	1974	10.00
❑ SW-3420	Extra Texture (Read All About It)	1975	18.00
❑ SMAS-3410	Living in the Material World	1973	18.00
❑ ST-3350	Wonderwall Music	1968	30.00
—With "Mfd. by Apple" on label			
❑ ST-3350	Wonderwall Music	1968	150.00
—With Capitol logo on Side 2 bottom			

CAPITOL

Number	Title	Yr	NM
❑ STCH-639	All Things Must Pass	1976	30.00
—Orange labels with poster and lyric innersleeves			
❑ STCH-639 [B]	All Things Must Pass	1978	30.00
—Purple labels with poster and lyric innersleeves			
❑ STCH-639	All Things Must Pass	1983	100.00
—Black labels, print in colorband, with poster and lyric innersleeves			
❑ SN-16055	Dark Horse	1980	18.00
—Budget-line reissue; reverses front and back covers			
❑ SN-16217	Extra Texture (Read All About It)	1980	30.00
—Budget-line reissue			
❑ SN-16216	Living in the Material World	1980	25.00
—Budget-line reissue			
❑ ST-11578	The Best of George Harrison	1976	18.00
—Custom label, no bar code on back			
❑ ST-11578	The Best of George Harrison	1976	180.00
—Orange label			
❑ ST-11578	The Best of George Harrison	1978	12.00
—Purple label, large Capitol logo			
❑ ST-11578	The Best of George Harrison	1983	30.00
—Black label, print in colorband			
❑ ST-11578	The Best of George Harrison	1988	30.00
—Odd reissue with custom label; large stand-alone "S" in trail-off area; bar code on cover			
❑ ST-11578	The Best of George Harrison	1989	80.00
—Purple label, small Capitol logo			

CAPITOL/APPLE

Number	Title	Yr	NM
❑ STCH-639	All Things Must Pass	1988	80.00
—Odd pressing with Apple labels and Capitol cover (look for stand-alone "S" in trail-off wax); with large sticker on back cover			

DARK HORSE

Number	Title	Yr	NM
❑ PRO649 [DJ]	A Personal Music Dialogue at Thirty Three and 1/3	1976	50.00
❑ PRO649 [DJ]	A Personal Music Dialogue at Thirty Three and 1/3	1976	40.00
❑ 25726	Best of Dark Horse 1976-1989	1989	30.00
❑ W1-25726	Best of Dark Horse 1976-1989	1989	18.00
—Columbia House edition			
❑ R180307	Best of Dark Horse 1976-1989	1989	18.00
—BMG Direct Marketing edition			
❑ 25643	Cloud Nine	1987	12.00
❑ W1-25643	Cloud Nine	1987	15.00
—Columbia House edition			
❑ R174328	Cloud Nine	1987	18.00
—BMG Direct Marketing edition			
❑ (no0 [DJ]	Dark Horse Radio Special	1974	400.00
—Promo-only; George Harrison introduces his new record label and artists			
❑ (no #)0 [DJ]	Dark Horse Radio Special	1974	400.00
—Promo-only; George Harrison introduces his new record label and artists			
❑ DHK3255	George Harrison	1979	12.00
—Deduct 30% for cut-outs			
❑ DHK3255	George Harrison	1979	40.00
—Columbia House edition (back cover says "Manufactured by Columbia House Under License			
❑ 23724 [DJ]	Gone Troppo	1982	30.00
—Promo on Quiex II vinyl			
❑ 23724 [B]	Gone Troppo	1982	12.00
—Deduct 30% for cut-outs			
❑ 23724 [DJ]	Gone Troppo	1982	30.00
—Promo on Quiex II vinyl			
❑ DHK3492	Somewhere in England	1981	12.00
—Deduct 30% for cut-outs			
❑ DH3005	Thirty Three and 1/3	1976	12.00
—Deduct 30% for cut-outs			

ZAPPLE

Number	Title	Yr	NM
❑ ST-3358 [B]	Electronic Sound	1969	80.00

HARRISON, JERRY

SIRE

Number	Title	Yr	NM
❑ 25663	Casual Gods	1988	12.00
❑ SRK3631	The Red and the Black	1981	12.00
❑ 25943	Walk on Water	1990	12.00

HARRISON, NOEL

LONDON

Number	Title	Yr	NM
❑ LL3459 [M]	Noel Harrison	1966	25.00
❑ PS459 [S]	Noel Harrison	1966	30.00

REPRISE

Number	Title	Yr	NM
❑ R-6263 [M]	Collage	1967	18.00
❑ RS-6263 [S]	Collage	1967	25.00
❑ RS-6295 [S]	Santa Monica Pier	1968	18.00
❑ R-6295 [M]	Santa Monica Pier	1968	40.00
—White label promo only			
❑ RS-6321	The Great Electric Experiment Is Over	1969	18.00

HARRISON, WENDELL

REBIRTH

Number	Title	Yr	NM
❑ WHR-140	Birth of a Fossil	1986	12.00
❑ WHR-160	Carnivorous Lady	1988	15.00
❑ WHR-015	Dreams of a Love Supreme	1985	12.00
❑ WHR-016	Organic Dream	1985	12.00
❑ WHR-040	Reawakening	1985	12.00
❑ WHR-150	Wait' Broke the Wagon Down	1987	12.00

TRIBE

Number	Title	Yr	NM
❑ PRSD-2212	Evening with the Devil	197?	100.00
❑ PRSD-4002	Message from the Tribe, Vol. 3	197?	100.00

WENHA

Number	Title	Yr	NM
❑ 015	Dreams of a Love Supreme	198?	50.00
❑ 2212	Evening with the Devil	198?	25.00
—Reissue of Tribe 2212			
❑ 4002	Message from the Tribe	198?	25.00
—Reissue of Tribe 4002			
❑ 016	Organic Dream	198?	40.00

HARRISON, WES

PHILIPS

Number	Title	Yr	NM
❑ PHM200103 [M]	You Won't Believe Your Ears	1963	25.00
❑ PHS600103 [S]	You Won't Believe Your Ears	1963	30.00

HARRISON, WILBERT

BUDDAH

Number	Title	Yr	NM
❑ BDS-5002	Wilbert Harrison	1971	30.00

CHELSEA

Number	Title	Yr	NM
❑ CH523	Wilbert Harrison	1977	25.00

JUGGERNAUT

Number	Title	Yr	NM
❑ ST-8803 [B]	Shoot You Full of Love	1971	50.00

SAVOY JAZZ

Number	Title	Yr	NM
❑ SJL-1182	Listen to My Song	1987	15.00

SPHERE SOUND

Number	Title	Yr	NM
❑ SSR-7000 [M]	Kansas City	1965	250.00
❑ SSSR-7000 [R]	Kansas City	1965	200.00

SUE

Number	Title	Yr	NM
❑ SSLP-8801	Let's Work Together	1970	50.00

WET SOUL

Number	Title	Yr	NM
❑ 1001	Anything You Want	197?	50.00

HARROW, NANCY

ATLANTIC

Number	Title	Yr	NM
❑ 8075 [M]	You Never Know	1963	30.00
❑ SD8075 [S]	You Never Know	1963	30.00

AUDIOPHILE

Number	Title	Yr	NM
❑ AP-142	Anything Goes	1979	15.00

CANDID

Number	Title	Yr	NM
❑ CD-8008 [M]	Wild Women Don't Have the Blues	1962	30.00

Number	Title	Yr	NM
❑ CD-9008 [S]	Wild Women Don't Have the Blues	1962	40.00

HARRY, DEBBIE

CHRYSALIS

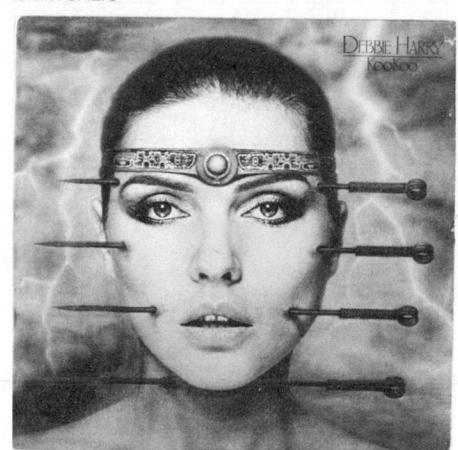

Number	Title	Yr	NM
❑ FV41347 [B]	Koo Koo	1983	12.00
—Reissue			
❑ CHR1347	Koo Koo	1981	12.00
GEFFEN			
❑ R124347	Rockbird	1986	15.00
—RCA Music Service edition			
❑ GHS24123	Rockbird	1986	12.00
SIRE			
❑ 25938	Def, Dumb & Blonde	1989	15.00

HART, BILLY

GRAMAVISION

❑ 18-8502	Oshumare	1986	15.00
HORIZON			
❑ SP-725	Enchance	1978	15.00

HART, CLAY

METROMEDIA

❑ 1008	Spring	1969	18.00
RANWOOD			
❑ 8122	Most Requested Country Favorites	1973	12.00
❑ 8135	Travelin' Minstrel Man	1974	12.00

HART, FREDDIE

CAPITOL

❑ ST-11073	Bless Your Heart	1972	15.00
❑ ST-593	California Grapevine	1970	15.00
❑ ST-11353	Country Heart 'N' Soul	1975	15.00
❑ ST-838	Easy Loving	1971	15.00
❑ ST-11107	Got the All-Overs	1972	15.00
❑ ST-11374	Greatest Hits	1975	15.00
❑ ST-11296	Hang In There Girl	1974	15.00
❑ ST-11252	If You Can't Feel It	1974	15.00
❑ ST-11014	My Hang-Up Is You	1972	15.00
❑ ST-469	New Sounds	1970	15.00
❑ ST-11724	Only You	1978	12.00
❑ ST-11504	People Put to Music	1976	12.00
❑ ST-11156	Super Kind of Woman	1973	15.00
❑ ST-11568	That Look in Her Eyes	1976	12.00
❑ ST-11449	The First Time	1975	12.00
❑ ST-11626	The Pleasure's Been All Mine	1977	12.00
❑ ST-11197	Trip to Heaven	1973	15.00
COLUMBIA			
❑ CL1792 [M]	The Spirited Freddie Hart	1962	40.00
❑ G31550	The World of Freddie Hart	1972	18.00
HARMONY			
❑ KH31165	Lonesome Love	1972	12.00
❑ HL7412 [M]	The Best of Freddie Hart	1967	15.00
❑ HS11212 [S]	The Best of Freddie Hart	1967	15.00
❑ KH32467	You Are My World	1973	12.00
HILLTOP			
❑ 6117	From Canada to Tennessee	1972	12.00
KAPP			
❑ KS-3568	Born a Fool	1968	25.00
❑ KS-3592	Greatest Hits	1969	18.00
❑ KL-1513 [M]	Hurtin' Man	1967	25.00
❑ KS-3513 [S]	Hurtin' Man	1967	25.00
❑ KL-1492 [M]	Straight from the Heart	1966	18.00
❑ KS-3492 [S]	Straight from the Heart	1966	25.00
❑ KL-1456 [M]	The Hart of Country Music	1966	18.00
❑ KS-3456 [S]	The Hart of Country Music	1966	25.00
❑ KL-1539 [M]	The Neon and the Rain	1967	25.00
❑ KS-3539 [S]	The Neon and the Rain	1967	25.00
❑ KS-3546	Togetherness	1968	25.00
MCA			
❑ 4088	The Best of Freddie Hart	1975	18.00

Number	Title	Yr	NM
SUNBIRD			
❑ ST-50100	Sure Thing	1980	15.00

HART, JOHN

BLUE NOTE

❑ B1-93476	One Down	1990	18.00

HART, MICKEY, AIRTO, FLORA PURIM, BATUCAJE

REFERENCE RECORDINGS

❑ RR-12	Dafos	1985	18.00

HART, MICKEY

RELIX

❑ 2026 [B]	Rolling Thunder	1987	15.00
WARNER BROS.			
❑ BS2635	Rolling Thunder	1972	25.00

HARTFORD, JOHN

FLYING FISH

❑ FF-044	All in the Name of Love	1983	12.00
❑ FF-259	Catalogue	1982	12.00
❑ FF-289	Gum Tree Canoe	1984	12.00
❑ FF-063	Headin' Down Into the Mystery Below	1978	12.00
❑ FF-020	Mark Twang	1976	12.00
❑ FF-440	Me Oh My, How Time Flies	1987	12.00
❑ FF-028	Nobody Knows What You Do	1977	12.00
❑ FF-095	Slumberin' on the Cumberland	1979	12.00
—With Pat Burton and Benny Martin			
❑ FF-228	You and Me at Home	1980	12.00
MCA			
❑ 5861	Annual Waltz	1987	10.00
RCA VICTOR			
❑ LPM-3796 [M]	Earthwords and Music	1967	30.00
❑ LSP-3796 [S]	Earthwords and Music	1967	18.00
❑ LSP-4068	Gentle on My Mind and Other Originals	1968	18.00
❑ LPM-3998 [M]	Housing Project	1968	50.00
❑ LSP-3998 [S]	Housing Project	1968	18.00
❑ LSP-4337	Iron Mountain Depot	1970	18.00
❑ LSP-4156	John Hartford	1969	18.00
❑ LPM-3687 [M]	John Hartford Looks at Life	1966	25.00
❑ LSP-3687 [S]	John Hartford Looks at Life	1966	18.00
❑ LPM-3884 [M]	The Love Album	1967	30.00
❑ LSP-3884 [S]	The Love Album	1967	18.00
WARNER BROS.			
❑ WS1916	Aereo-Plain	1971	15.00
❑ BS2651	Morning Bugle	1972	15.00

HARTH, ALFRED

ECM

❑ 1264	This Earth	198?	12.00

HARTLEY, KEEF

DERAM

❑ DES18024 [B]	Halfbreed	1969	25.00
❑ XDES18070	Lancashire Hustler	1973	18.00
❑ DES18057	Overdog	1971	18.00
❑ XDES18065	The 72nd Brave	1972	18.00
❑ DES18035	The Battle of North West Six	1970	18.00
❑ DES18047	The Time Is Near	1970	18.00

HARTMAN, DAN

BLUE SKY

❑ JZ35641	Instant Replay	1978	15.00
❑ JZ36302	Relight My Fire	1980	15.00
MCA			
❑ 5525	I Can Dream About You	1984	12.00

HARTMAN, JOHNNY

ABC IMPULSE!

❑ AS-57 [S]	I Just Dropped By to Say Hello	1968	15.00
❑ AS-74 [S]	The Voice That Is	1968	15.00
ABC-PARAMOUNT			
❑ ABC-574 [M]	The Unforgettable Johnny Hartman	1966	30.00
❑ ABCS-574 [S]	The Unforgettable Johnny Hartman	1966	40.00
AUDIOPHILE			
❑ AP-181	This One's for Tedi	1981	15.00
BEE HIVE			
❑ BH-7012	Once in Every Life	198?	12.00
BETHLEHEM			
❑ BCP-6045	All of Me	197?	15.00
—Reissue, distributed by RCA Victor			
❑ BCP-6014 [M]	All of Me: The Debonair Mr. Hartman	1957	80.00
❑ BCP-43 [M]	Songs from the Heart	1956	80.00
IMPULSE!			
❑ A-57 [M]	I Just Dropped By to Say Hello	1964	25.00
❑ AS-57 [S]	I Just Dropped By to Say Hello	1964	25.00
❑ A-74 [M]	The Voice That Is	1965	25.00

Number	Title	Yr	NM
❑ AS-74 [S]	The Voice That Is	1965	25.00
MCA			
❑ 29039	I Just Dropped By to Say Hello	1980	12.00
❑ 29040	The Voice That Is	1980	12.00
MUSICOR			
❑ 2502	Johnny Hartman, Johnny Hartman	1976	15.00
PERCEPTION			
❑ PLP-41	I've Been There	1973	18.00
REGENT			
❑ MG-6014 [M]	Just You, Just Me	1956	80.00
SAVOY JAZZ			
❑ SJL-1134	First, Lasting and Always	198?	12.00

HARTMAN, LISA

KIRSHNER

❑ JZ35609	Hold On	1978	30.00
❑ PZ34109	Lisa Hartman	1976	30.00

HARUMI

VERVE FORECAST

❑ FTS-3030 [B]	Harumi	1968	30.00

HARVEY, ALEX (1)

ATLANTIC

❑ SD18248 [B]	Live	1975	18.00
VERTIGO			
❑ VEL-1017 [B]	Next	1973	18.00
❑ VEL-2000 [B]	The Impossible Dream	1974	18.00
❑ VEL-2004 [B]	Tomorrow Belongs to Me	1975	18.00

HARVEY, ALEX (2)

CAPITOL

❑ ST-789	Alex Harvey	1972	15.00
❑ ST-11128	Souvenirs	1973	15.00

HARVEY, LAURENCE

ATLANTIC

❑ 1367 [M]	This Is My Beloved	1962	40.00
❑ SD1367 [S]	This Is My Beloved	1962	50.00

HARVEY, PJ

ISLAND

❑ 524085-1	To Bring You My Love	1995	18.00

HASHIM, MICHAEL

STASH

❑ 227	Peacocks	1983	12.00

HASKELL, JACK

STRAND

❑ SL-1020 [M]	Jack Haskell Swings for Jack Paar	1961	25.00
❑ SLS-1020 [S]	Jack Haskell Swings for Jack Paar	1961	30.00

HASKELL, JIMMIE

IMPERIAL

❑ LP-9068 [M]	Countdown	1959	30.00
❑ LP-12015 [S]	Countdown	1959	50.00

HASKILL, CLARA

MERCURY LIVING PRESENCE

❑ SR90413 [S]	Mozart: Piano Concertos No. 20 and 23; Rondo in A	196?	30.00
—Maroon label, no "Vendor: Mercury Record Corporation"			
❑ SR90413 [S]	Mozart: Piano Concertos No. 20 and 23; Rondo in A	196?	80.00
—Maroon label, with "Vendor: Mercury Record Corporation" (second edition is more sought after than the first)			

HASSELBACH, MARK

JAZZIMAGE

❑ JZ-104	Hasselblast	198?	15.00

HASSELL, JON

ECM

❑ 1327	Power Spot	1987	15.00
INTUITION			
❑ C1-91186	Flash of the Spirit	1989	15.00
❑ C1-46880	The Surgeon of the Nightsky Restores Dead Things by the Power of Sound	1988	15.00
LOVELY			
❑ 1021	Vernal Equinox	1978	18.00
OPAL/WARNER BROS.			
❑ 26153	City: Works of Fiction	1990	18.00
TOMATO			
❑ TOM-7019	Earthquake Island	1979	18.00

HASSLES, THE

LIBERTY

❑ LN-10139	Hour of the Wolf	1981	15.00

Number	Title	Yr	NM
❑ LN-10138	The Hassles	1981	15.00

UNITED ARTISTS

Number	Title	Yr	NM
❑ UAS-6699	Hour of the Wolf	1969	30.00
❑ UAS-6631 [B]	The Hassles	1968	30.00

HATFIELD, BOBBY

MGM

Number	Title	Yr	NM
❑ SE-4727	Messin' in Muscle Shoals	1971	15.00

HATHAWAY, DONNY

ATCO

Number	Title	Yr	NM
❑ SD 33-360	Donny Hathaway	1971	15.00
❑ SD 33-386	Donny Hathaway Live	1972	15.00
❑ SD 33-332	Everything Is Everything	1970	15.00
❑ SD7029	Extension of a Man	1973	12.00
❑ QD7029 [Q]	Extension of a Man	1974	25.00
❑ SD 38-107	The Best of Donny Hathaway	1978	12.00

ATLANTIC

Number	Title	Yr	NM
❑ SD19278	In Performance	1980	12.00

RHINO

Number	Title	Yr	NM
❑ R1541097 [B]	Live at the Bitter End, 1971	2014	30.00

HATZA, GREG

CORAL

Number	Title	Yr	NM
❑ CRL57495 [M]	Organized Jazz	1963	18.00
❑ CRL757495 [S]	Organized Jazz	1963	25.00
❑ CRL57493 [M]	The Wizardry of Greg Hatza	1962	15.00
❑ CRL757493 [S]	The Wizardry of Greg Hatza	1962	18.00

HAUSER, FRITZ

HAT ART

Number	Title	Yr	NM
❑ 2023	Solodrumming	1986	18.00

HAVENS, BOB

GHB

Number	Title	Yr	NM
❑ GHB-143 [M]	Bob Havens' New Orleans All-Stars	1969	15.00

SOUTHLAND

Number	Title	Yr	NM
❑ 226 [M]	Bob Havens in New Orleans	1961	18.00
❑ 213 [M]	Bob Havens' New Orleans All-Stars	1966	15.00

HAVENS, RICHIE

A&M

Number	Title	Yr	NM
❑ SP-4641	Mirage	1977	12.00
❑ SP-4598	The End of the Beginning	1976	12.00

DOUGLAS

Number	Title	Yr	NM
❑ D-780 [M]	Electric Havens	1966	25.00
❑ SD-780 [S]	Electric Havens	1966	18.00
❑ D-779 [M]	Richie Havens' Record	1966	25.00
❑ SD-779 [S]	Richie Havens' Record	1966	16.00

ELEKTRA

Number	Title	Yr	NM
❑ 6E-242	Connections	1980	12.00

MGM

Number	Title	Yr	NM
❑ SE-4698	Mixed Bag	1970	18.00
— Reissue of Verve Forecast 3006			
❑ SE-4700	Richard P. Havens, 1963	1970	25.00
— Reissue of Verve Forecast 3047			
❑ SE-4699	Something Else Again	1970	18.00
— Reissue of Verve Forecast 3034			

RBI

Number	Title	Yr	NM
❑ 400	Simple Things	1987	12.00

STORMY FOREST

Number	Title	Yr	NM
❑ SFS-6005	Alarm Clock	1970	15.00
❑ SFS-6201	Mixed Bag II	1974	15.00
❑ SFS-6013	Portfolio	1973	15.00
❑ SFS-6012 [B]	Richie Havens On Stage	1972	25.00
❑ SFS-6001	Stonehenge	1969	18.00
❑ SFS-6010	The Great Blind Degree	1971	15.00

VERVE FOLKWAYS

Number	Title	Yr	NM
❑ FT-3006 [M]	Mixed Bag	1967	30.00
❑ FTS-3006 [S]	Mixed Bag	1967	25.00

VERVE FORECAST

Number	Title	Yr	NM
❑ FTS-3006	Mixed Bag	1968	18.00
❑ FTS-3047	Richard P. Havens, 1983	1968	30.00
❑ FT-3034 [M]	Something Else Again	1968	40.00
❑ FTS-3034 [S]	Something Else Again	1968	25.00

HAWES, HAMPTON

ARISTA FREEDOM

Number	Title	Yr	NM
❑ AL1043	Copenhagen Night Music	1977	25.00
❑ AL1020	Live at the Montmartre	1976	25.00

BLACK LION

Number	Title	Yr	NM
❑ 122	Spanish Steps	197?	25.00

CONCORD JAZZ

Number	Title	Yr	NM
❑ CJ-222	Recorded Live at the Great American Music Hall	198?	18.00

CONTEMPORARY

Number	Title	Yr	NM
❑ C-3545 [M]	All Night Session! Volume 1	1958	80.00
❑ S-7545 [S]	All Night Session! Volume 1	1960	70.00
❑ C-3546 [M]	All Night Session! Volume 2	1958	80.00
❑ S-7546 [S]	All Night Session! Volume 2	1960	70.00
❑ C-3547 [M]	All Night Session! Volume 3	1958	80.00
❑ S-7547 [S]	All Night Session! Volume 3	1960	70.00
❑ C-3523 [M]	Everybody Likes Hampton Hawes	1956	80.00
❑ M-3589 [M]	For Real!	1959	60.00
❑ S-7589 [S]	For Real!	1959	50.00
❑ C-3553 [M]	Four! Hampton Hawes!!!	1958	80.00
❑ S-7553 [S]	Four! Hampton Hawes!!!	1960	70.00
❑ C-3505 [M]	Hampton Hawes	1955	100.00
❑ M-3616 [M]	Here and Now	1965	50.00
❑ S-7616 [S]	Here and Now	1965	40.00
❑ M-3631 [M]	I'm All Smiles	1967	60.00
❑ S-7631 [S]	I'm All Smiles	1967	30.00
❑ M-3614 [M]	The Green Leaves of Summer	1964	50.00
❑ S-7614 [S]	The Green Leaves of Summer	1964	50.00
❑ M-3621 [M]	The Seance	1966	40.00
❑ S-7621 [S]	The Seance	1966	40.00
❑ C-3515 [M]	This Is Hampton Hawes	1956	100.00

ENJA

Number	Title	Yr	NM
❑ 3099	Live at Jazz Showcase in Chicago, Vol. 1	198?	18.00

FANTASY

Number	Title	Yr	NM
❑ OJC-638	All Night Session! Volume 1	1991	18.00
❑ OJC-639	All Night Session! Volume 2	1991	18.00
❑ OJC-640	All Night Session! Volume 3	1991	18.00
❑ OJC-421	Everybody Likes Hampton Hawes	1990	18.00
❑ OJC-165	Four! Hampton Hawes!!!	198?	15.00
❑ OJC-316	Hampton Hawes	198?	15.00
❑ OJC-178	I'm All Smiles	198?	15.00
❑ OJC-455	Seance	1990	18.00
❑ OJC-476	The Green Leaves of Summer	1991	18.00
❑ OJC-318	This Is Hampton Hawes	198?	15.00

JAS

Number	Title	Yr	NM
❑ JAS-4002	Hampton Hawes Trio at Montreux	1976	18.00
❑ JAS-4004	The Two Sides of Hampton Hawes	1977	25.00

JAZZ MAN

Number	Title	Yr	NM
❑ 5022	Spanish Steps	198?	12.00

MOON

Number	Title	Yr	NM
❑ MLP-005	Autumn Leaves in Paris	1990	30.00

PRESTIGE

Number	Title	Yr	NM
❑ PR-10000	Blues for Walls	1973	30.00
❑ PRST-7695	Hampton Hawes in Europe	1969	30.00
❑ PRLP-212 [10]	Hampton Hawes Quartet	1955	200.00
❑ 10088	Northern Windows	1974	40.00
❑ P-10077	Playin' in the Yard	1974	30.00
❑ PR-10046	The Universe	1972	30.00

RCA VICTOR

Number	Title	Yr	NM
❑ JPL1-1508	Challenge	1976	25.00

STEREO RECORDS

Number	Title	Yr	NM
❑ S-7026 [S]	Four! Hampton Hawes!!!	1959	100.00

VANTAGE

Number	Title	Yr	NM
❑ VLP-1 [10]	Hamp Hawes	1954	300.00

VAULT

Number	Title	Yr	NM
❑ LPS-9009	Hampton Hawes Plays Movie Musicals	1969	25.00
❑ LPS-9010	High in the Sky	1970	30.00

XANADU

Number	Title	Yr	NM
❑ 161	Memorial Album	198?	18.00

HAWES, HAMPTON/PAUL CHAMBERS

XANADU

Number	Title	Yr	NM
❑ 104	The East/West Controversy	1975	30.00

HAWKINS, COLEMAN, AND BENNY CARTER

MOON

Number	Title	Yr	NM
❑ MLP-001	Jammin' the Blues	199?	18.00

SWING

Number	Title	Yr	NM
❑ 8403	Coleman Hawkins and Benny Carter	1985	12.00

HAWKINS, COLEMAN, AND BUD POWELL

BLACK LION

Number	Title	Yr	NM
❑ 159	Hawk in Germany	197?	15.00

HAWKINS, COLEMAN, AND CLARK TERRY

COLUMBIA

Number	Title	Yr	NM
❑ CL1991 [M]	Back in Bean's Bag	1963	18.00
❑ CS8791 [S]	Back in Bean's Bag	1963	25.00
❑ CS8791 [S]	Back in Bean's Bag	1999	30.00
— Classic Records reissue on audiophile vinyl			

HAWKINS, COLEMAN, AND FRANK HUNTER

MIRA

Number	Title	Yr	NM
❑ M-3003 [M]	The Hawk and the Hunter	1965	25.00
❑ MS-3003 [S]	The Hawk and the Hunter	1965	30.00

HAWKINS, COLEMAN, AND LESTER YOUNG

DOCTOR JAZZ

Number	Title	Yr	NM
❑ FW38446	Classic Tenors	1983	12.00

FLYING DUTCHMAN

Number	Title	Yr	NM
❑ BXM1-2823	Classic Tenors	1978	15.00

ZIM

Number	Title	Yr	NM
❑ 1000	Coleman Hawkins and Lester Young	197?	12.00

HAWKINS, COLEMAN, AND PEE WEE RUSSELL

CANDID

Number	Title	Yr	NM
❑ CD-8020 [M]	Jazz Reunion	1960	40.00
❑ CS-9020 [S]	Jazz Reunion	1960	40.00

HAWKINS, COLEMAN, AND ROY ELDREDGE

PHOENIX

Number	Title	Yr	NM
❑ 3	Coleman Hawkins and Roy Eldredge 1939	197?	12.00

VERVE

Number	Title	Yr	NM
❑ MGV-8266 [M]	At the Opera House	1958	50.00
❑ V-8266 [M]	At the Opera House	1961	30.00
❑ MGVS-6028 [S]	At the Opera House	1960	40.00
❑ V6-8266 [S]	At the Opera House	1961	25.00

HAWKINS, COLEMAN; ROY ELDREDGE; JOHNNY HODGES

VERVE

Number	Title	Yr	NM
❑ V-8509 [M]	Alive at the Village Gate	1963	25.00
❑ V6-8509 [S]	Alive at the Village Gate	1963	30.00
❑ V6-8509 [S]	Alive at the Village Gate	199?	30.00
— Classic Records reissue on audiophile vinyl			

HAWKINS, COLEMAN; ROY ELDREDGE; PETE BROWN; JO JONES

VERVE

Number	Title	Yr	NM
❑ MGV-8240 [M]	All Stars at Newport	1958	50.00
❑ V-8240 [M]	All Stars at Newport	1961	25.00

HAWKINS, COLEMAN

ABC IMPULSE!

Number	Title	Yr	NM
❑ AS-28 [S]	Desafinado	1968	18.00
❑ AS-26 [S]	Duke Ellington Meets Coleman Hawkins	1968	18.00
❑ AS-9258	Reevaluations: The Impulse Years	197?	18.00
❑ AS-34 [S]	Today and Now	1968	18.00
❑ AS-87 [S]	Wrapped Tight	1968	18.00

ADVANCE

Number	Title	Yr	NM
❑ LSP-9 [10]	Coleman Hawkins Favorites	1951	300.00

AMERICAN RECORDING SOCIETY

Number	Title	Yr	NM
❑ G-316 [M]	Coleman Hawkins and His Orchestra	1956	50.00

APOLLO

Number	Title	Yr	NM
❑ LAP-101 [10]	Coleman Hawkins All Stars	1951	300.00

BLUEBIRD

Number	Title	Yr	NM
❑ 5658-1-RB	Body and Soul	1986	18.00

BRUNSWICK

Number	Title	Yr	NM
❑ BL58030 [10]	Tenor Sax	1952	200.00

CAPITOL

Number	Title	Yr	NM
❑ H327 [10]	Classics in Jazz	1952	250.00
❑ T819 [M]	Gilded Hawk	1957	80.00
❑ M-11030	Hollywood Stampede	1973	18.00

COMMODORE

Number	Title	Yr	NM
❑ XFL-14936	Coleman Hawkins	198?	12.00
❑ FL-20025 [10]	King of the Tenor Sax	1952	300.00

CONCERT HALL JAZZ

Number	Title	Yr	NM
❑ J-1201 [M]	Improvisations Unlimited	1955	60.00

CONTINENTAL

Number	Title	Yr	NM
❑ 16006 [M]	On the Bean	1962	30.00
❑ S-16006 [S]	On the Bean	1962	30.00

CROWN

Number	Title	Yr	NM
❑ CLP-5181 [M]	Coleman Hawkins and His Orchestra	1960	25.00
❑ CST-206 [R]	Coleman Hawkins and His Orchestra	196?	12.00
❑ CLP-5207 [M]	The Hawk Swing	1961	25.00
❑ CST-224 [R]	The Hawk Swing	196?	12.00

DECCA

Number	Title	Yr	NM
❑ DL4081 [M]	The Hawk Blows at Midnight	1961	30.00
❑ DL74081 [S]	The Hawk Blows at Midnight	1961	40.00
❑ DL8127 [M]	The Hawk Talks	1955	80.00

EMARCY

Number	Title	Yr	NM
❑ MG-26013 [10]	The Bean	1954	200.00

EVEREST ARCHIVE OF FOLK & JAZZ

Number	Title	Yr	NM
❑ 252	Coleman Hawkins	197?	12.00

FANTASY

Number	Title	Yr	NM
❑ OJC-181	At Ease with Coleman Hawkins	1985	12.00
❑ OJC-418	Coleman Hawkins Plus the Red Garland Trio	1990	15.00
❑ OJC-294	Hawk Eyes	1988	12.00
❑ OJC-6001	In a Mellow Tone	1988	12.00
❑ OJC-420	Night Hawk	1990	15.00
❑ OJC-096	Soul	198?	12.00
❑ OJC-225	The Coleman Hawkins All Stars	198?	12.00
❑ OJC-027	The Hawk Flies High	1982	12.00

FELSTED

Number	Title	Yr	NM
❑ FAJ-7005 [M]	The High and Mighty Hawk	1959	60.00
❑ SJA-2005 [S]	The High and Mighty Hawk	1959	80.00

GNP CRESCENDO

Number	Title	Yr	NM
❑ GNP-9003	Coleman Hawkins in Holland	197?	12.00

GRP IMPULSE!

Number	Title	Yr	NM
❑ 227 [S]	Desafinado	199?	18.00
— Reissue on audiophile vinyl			

Number	Title	Yr	NM
IMPULSE!			
❏ A-28 [M]	Desafinado	1963	30.00
❏ AS-28 [S]	Desafinado	1963	30.00
❏ A-26 [M]	Duke Ellington Meets Coleman Hawkins	1962	30.00
❏ AS-26 [S]	Duke Ellington Meets Coleman Hawkins	1962	30.00
❏ A-34 [M]	Today and Now	1963	30.00
❏ AS-34 [S]	Today and Now	1963	30.00
❏ A-87 [M]	Wrapped Tight	1965	30.00
❏ AS-87 [S]	Wrapped Tight	1965	30.00
JAZZ MAN			
❏ 5042	Jazz Reunion	198?	12.00
JAZZTONE			
❏ J-1201 [M]	Timeless Jazz	1955	50.00
— Reissue of Concert Hall Jazz 1201			
MAINSTREAM			
❏ 56037 [M]	Meditations	1965	30.00
❏ S-6037 [R]	Meditations	1965	18.00
MASTER JAZZ			
❏ 8115	The High and Mighty Hawk	197?	15.00
MILESTONE			
❏ M-47015	The Hawk Flies	1973	18.00
MOODSVILLE			
❏ MVLP-7 [M]	At Ease with Coleman Hawkins	1960	50.00
— Green label			
❏ MVLP-7 [M]	At Ease with Coleman Hawkins	1965	30.00
— Blue label, trident logo at right			
❏ MVLP-23 [M]	Good Old Broadway	1962	40.00
— Gren label			
❏ MVLP-23 [M]	Good Old Broadway	1965	25.00
— Blue label, trident logo at right			
❏ MVST-23 [S]	Good Old Broadway	1962	50.00
— Green label			
❏ MVST-23 [S]	Good Old Broadway	1965	30.00
— Blue label, trident logo at right			
❏ MVLP-31 [M]	Make Someone Happy	1963	40.00
— Green label			
❏ MVLP-31 [M]	Make Someone Happy	1965	25.00
— Blue label, trident logo at right			
❏ MVST-31 [S]	Make Someone Happy	1963	50.00
— Green label			
❏ MVST 31 [S]	Make Someone Happy	1965	30.00
— Blue label, trident logo at right			
❏ MVLP-15 [M]	The Hawk Relaxes	1961	50.00
— Green label			
❏ MVLP 16 [M]	The Hawk Relaxes	1965	30.00
— Blue label, trident logo at right			
❏ MVLP-25 [M]	The Jazz Version of No Strings	1962	40.00
— Green label			
❏ MVLP-25 [M]	The Jazz Version of No Strings	1965	25.00
— Blue label, trident logo at right			
❏ MVST-25 [S]	The Jazz Version of No Strings	1962	50.00
— Green label			
❏ MVST-25 [S]	The Jazz Version of No Strings	1965	30.00
— Blue label, trident logo at right			
MOON			
❏ MLP-018	Coleman Hawkins Vs. Oscar Peterson	199?	18.00
PABLO			
❏ 2310933	Bean Stalkin'	198?	15.00
❏ 2310707	Sirius	197?	18.00
PHILIPS			
❏ PHM200022 [M]	Jazz at the Metropole	1962	25.00
❏ PHS600022 [S]	Jazz at the Metropole	1962	30.00
PHOENIX			
❏ 13	Centerpiece	197?	12.00
❏ 8	In Concert	197?	12.00
PRESTIGE			
❏ PRST-7824	Bean and the Boys	1970	18.00
❏ PRST-7753	Blues Groove	1970	18.00
❏ PRST-7824	Coleman Hawkins and the Boys	1971	15.00
❏ PRLP-7156 [M]	Hawk Eyes	1958	80.00
❏ PRST-7857	Hawk Eyes!	1971	18.00
❏ 24051	Jam Session in Swingville	198?	15.00
❏ P-24106	Moonglow	1981	15.00
❏ PRST-7671	Night Hawk	1969	18.00
❏ PRST-7647	Pioneers	1969	18.00
❏ PRLP-7149 [M]	Soul	1958	80.00
❏ 24083	The Real Thing	198?	15.00
QUINTESSENCE			
❏ 25371	Golden Hawk	1979	12.00
RCA VICTOR			
❏ LPV-501 [M]	Body and Soul	1965	25.00
❏ LJM-1017 [M]	Hawk In Flight	1955	80.00

THE HAWK IN HI FI
COLEMAN HAWKINS WITH BILLY BYERS AND HIS ORCHESTRA
RCA VICTOR
LPM-1281

Number	Title	Yr	NM
❏ LPM-1281 [M]	Hawk in Hi-Fi	1956	80.00
RIVERSIDE			
❏ RLP 12-117/8 [M]	Coleman Hawkins: A Documentary	1956	200.00
❏ RLP 12-233 [M]	The Hawk Flies High	1957	200.00
— White label, blue print			
❏ RLP 12-233 [M]	The Hawk Flies High	1959	50.00
— Blue label, microphone logo at top			
❏ 3049	Think Deep	1970	18.00
SAVOY			
❏ MG-12013 [M]	The Hawk Returns	1955	120.00
❏ MG-15039 [10]	The Hawk Talks	1954	200.00
SAVOY JAZZ			
❏ SJL-1123	Coleman Hawkins Meets the Big Sax Section	1979	12.00
STINSON			
❏ SLP-22 [10]	Originals with Hawkins	1950	300.00
❏ SLP-22 [M]	Originals with Hawkins	195?	40.00
SUNBEAM			
❏ 204	Coleman Hawkins at the Savoy 1940	197?	12.00
SWINGVILLE			
❏ SVLP-2035 [M]	Blues Groove	1962	50.00
— Purple label			
❏ SVLP-2035 [M]	Blues Groove	1965	30.00
— Blue label, trident logo at right			
❏ SVST-2035 [S]	Blues Groove	1962	40.00
— Red label			
❏ SVST-2035 [S]	Blues Groove	1965	25.00
— Blue label, trident logo at right			
❏ SVLP-2001 [M]	Coleman Hawkins Plus the Red Garland Trio	1960	50.00
— Purple label			
❏ SVLP-2001 [M]	Coleman Hawkins Plus the Red Garland Trio	1965	30.00
— Blue label, trident logo at right			
❏ SVLP-2039 [M]	Hawk Eyes	1962	50.00
— Purple label			
❏ SVLP-2039 [M]	Hawk Eyes	1965	30.00
— Blue label, trident logo at right			
❏ SVST-2039 [S]	Hawk Eyes	1962	40.00
— Red label			
❏ SVST-2039 [S]	Hawk Eyes	1965	25.00
— Blue label, trident logo at right			
❏ SVLP-2016 [M]	Night Hawk	1961	50.00
— Purple label			
❏ SVLP-2016 [M]	Night Hawk	1965	30.00
— Blue label, trident logo at right			
❏ SVLP-2038 [M]	Soul	1962	50.00
— Purple label			
❏ SVLP-2038 [M]	Soul	1965	30.00
— Blue label, trident logo at right			
❏ SVST-2038 [S]	Soul	1962	40.00
— Red label			
❏ SVST-2038 [S]	Soul	1965	25.00
— Blue label, trident logo at right			
❏ SVLP-2005 [M]	The Coleman Hawkins All Stars	1960	50.00
— Purple label			
❏ SVLP-2005 [M]	The Coleman Hawkins All Stars	1965	30.00
— Blue label, trident logo at right			
❏ SVLP-2024 [M]	Things Ain't What They Used to Be	1961	40.00
— Purple label			
❏ SVLP-2024 [M]	Things Ain't What They Used to Be	1965	25.00
— Blue label, trident logo at right			
❏ SVST-2024 [S]	Things Ain't What They Used to Be	1961	50.00
— Red label			
❏ SVST-2024 [S]	Things Ain't What They Used to Be	1965	30.00
— Blue label, trident logo at right			

Number	Title	Yr	NM
❏ SVLP-2025 [M]	Years Ago	1961	40.00
— Purple label			
❏ SVLP-2025 [M]	Years Ago	1965	25.00
— Blue label, trident logo at right			
❏ SVST-2025 [S]	Years Ago	1961	50.00
— Red label			
❏ SVST-2025 [S]	Years Ago	1965	30.00
— Blue label, trident logo at right			
TIME-LIFE			
❏ STL-J-06	Giants of Jazz	1979	25.00
TRIP			
❏ 5515	Coleman Hawkins and the Trumpet Kings	197?	12.00
URANIA			
❏ UJLP-1201 [M]	Accent on Tenor Sax	1955	100.00
❏ UJLP-41201 [R]	Accent on Tenor Sax	196?	25.00
VERVE			
❏ MGV-8346 [M]	Coleman Hawkins and His Confreres with the Oscar Peterson Trio	1959	50.00
❏ MGVS-6110 [S]	Coleman Hawkins and His Confreres with the Oscar Peterson Trio	1960	40.00
❏ V-8346 [M]	Coleman Hawkins and His Confreres with the Oscar Peterson Trio	1961	30.00
❏ V6-8346 [S]	Coleman Hawkins and His Confreres with the Oscar Peterson Trio	1961	25.00
❏ UMV-2623	Coleman Hawkins at Newport	198?	12.00
❏ MGV-8327 [M]	Coleman Hawkins Encounters Ben Webster	1959	50.00
❏ MGVS-6066 [S]	Coleman Hawkins Encounters Ben Webster	1960	40.00
❏ V-8327 [M]	Coleman Hawkins Encounters Ben Webster	1961	30.00
❏ V6-8327 [S]	Coleman Hawkins Encounters Ben Webster	1961	25.00
❏ UMV-2532	Coleman Hawkins Encounters Ben Webster	198?	12.00
❏ MGVS-6066 [S]	Coleman Hawkins Encounters Ben Webster	199?	30.00
— Classic Records reissue on audiophile vinyl			
❏ V-8509 [M]	Hawkins! Alive! At the Village Gate	1963	30.00
❏ V6-8509 [S]	Hawkins! Alive! At the Village Gate	1963	30.00
❏ V 8568 [M]	The Essential Coleman Hawkins	1964	25.00
❏ V6-8568 [S]	The Essential Coleman Hawkins	1964	30.00
❏ MGV-8261 [M]	The Genius of Coleman Hawkins	1958	50.00
❏ MGVS-6033 [S]	The Genius of Coleman Hawkins	1960	40.00
❏ V-8261 [M]	The Genius of Coleman Hawkins	1961	30.00
❏ V6-8261 [S]	The Genius of Coleman Hawkins	1961	25.00
❏ 825673-1	The Genius of Coleman Hawkins	1986	12.00
❏ V6-8829	The Newport Years	197?	18.00
VIK			
❏ LX-1059 [M]	The Hawk in Paris	1957	80.00
WORLD WIDE			
❏ MGS-20001 [S]	Coleman Hawkins with the Basie Saxophone Section	1958	50.00
XANADU			
❏ 189	Dutch Treat	198?	12.00
❏ 195	Jazz Tones	198?	12.00
❏ 111	Thanks for the Memory	198?	12.00

HAWKINS, COLEMAN/BEN WEBSTER

Number	Title	Yr	NM
BRUNSWICK			
❏ BL54016 [M]	The Big Sounds of Coleman Hawkins and Ben Webster	1956	80.00

HAWKINS, COLEMAN/GEORGIE AULD

Number	Title	Yr	NM
GRAND AWARD			
❏ GA 33-316 [M]	Jazz Concert	1955	100.00
— With wrap-around cover intact			
❏ GA 33-316 [M]	Jazz Concert	1955	50.00
— Without wrap-around cover			

HAWKINS, DALE

Number	Title	Yr	NM
BELL			
❏ 6036	L.A., Memphis and Tyler, Texas	1969	40.00
CHESS			
❏ ACRR-706	Dale Hawkins	1976	18.00
❏ LP-1429 [M]	Oh! Susie-Q	1958	1500.00
— VG value 500; VG+ value 1000			
ROULETTE			
❏ R25175 [M]	Let's All Twist at the Miami Beach Peppermint Lounge	1962	200.00
❏ SR25175 [S]	Let's All Twist at the Miami Beach Poppermint Lounge	1962	300.00

HAWKINS, DOLORES

Number	Title	Yr	NM
EPIC			
❏ LN3250 [M]	Dolores	1957	40.00

Number	Title	Yr	NM
❑ LN1119 [M]	Meet Dolores Hawkins	1955	40.00

HAWKINS, EDWIN

ACCORD
❑ SN-7120	The Genius of Edwin Hawkins	1981	12.00

BIRTHRIGHT
❑ ST-70202	Angels Will Be Singing	1987	10.00
❑ WR-8119	Edwin Hawkins Live	198?	12.00
❑ ST-70300	Give Us Peace	1987	10.00
❑ ST-70201	Have Mercy	1987	10.00
❑ D1-70208	Live with the Oakland Symphony, Vol. 1	1988	10.00
— Reissue of Myrrh 6691			
❑ D1-70210	Live with the Oakland Symphony, Vol. 2	1988	10.00
— Reissue of Myrrh 6700			
❑ 4020	The Comforter	197?	15.00
❑ LS5904	The Edwin Hawkins Christmas Album	1985	18.00
❑ ST-70200	The Edwin Hawkins Christmas Album	1987	10.00
— Reissue			
❑ D1-70315	The Name	1988	12.00

BUDDAH
❑ BDS-5086	Children (Get Together)	1971	18.00
❑ BDS-5101	I'd Like to Teach the World to Sing	1972	18.00
❑ BDS-5064	More Happy Days	1970	18.00
❑ BDS-5070	Oh Happy Day	1970	15.00
— Reissue of Pavilion LP			
❑ BDS-5054	Peace Is Blowin' in the Wind	1969	18.00
❑ BDS-5606	The Edwin Hawkins Singers -- Live	1974	18.00

LECTION
❑ 501	Imagine Heaven	1982	12.00
❑ 810639-1	The Edwin Hawkins Mass Choir	198?	12.00

MYRRH
❑ 6691	Live with the Oakland Symphony, Vol. 1	198?	12.00
❑ 6700	Live with the Oakland Symphony, Vol. 2	198?	12.00

PAVILION
❑ DP3-10002	He's a Friend of Mine	1969	18.00
❑ BPS-10001	Let Us Go Into the House of the Lord	1969	18.00

SAVOY
❑ 7077	The Best of the Edwin Hawkins Singers	198?	15.00

HAWKINS, ERSKINE

CORAL
❑ CRL56051 [10]	After Hours	1954	120.00

DECCA
❑ DL4081 [M]	The Hawk Blows at Midnight	1960	30.00
❑ DL74081 [S]	The Hawk Blows at Midnight	1960	40.00

IMPERIAL
❑ LP-9191 [M]	25 Golden Years of Jazz, Volume 1	1962	30.00
❑ LP-12191 [S]	25 Golden Years of Jazz, Volume 1	1962	30.00
❑ LP-9197 [M]	25 Golden Years of Jazz, Volume 2	1962	30.00
❑ LP-12197 [S]	25 Golden Years of Jazz, Volume 2	1962	30.00

MCA
❑ 1361	Tuxedo Junction	198?	12.00

RCA VICTOR
❑ LPM-2227 [M]	After Hours	1960	40.00

HAWKINS, HAWKSHAW

GLADWYNNE
❑ G-2006 [M]	Country Western Cavalcade with Hawkshaw Hawkins	195?	120.00

HARMONY
❑ HL7301 [M]	The Great Hawkshaw Hawkins	1963	25.00
❑ HS11044 [R]	The Great Hawkshaw Hawkins	1963	18.00

KING
❑ 592 [M]	Grand Ole Opry Favorites	1958	100.00
❑ 587 [M]	Hawkshaw Hawkins	1958	100.00
❑ 599 [M]	Hawkshaw Hawkins	1959	100.00
❑ 858 [M]	Taken From Our Vaults, Volume 1	1963	40.00
❑ 870 [M]	Taken From Our Vaults, Volume 2	1963	40.00
❑ 873 [M]	Taken From Our Vaults, Volume 3	1964	40.00
❑ 808 [M]	The All New Hawkshaw Hawkins	1963	80.00
❑ KS-808 [S]	The All New Hawkshaw Hawkins	1963	100.00

LABREA
❑ 8020 [M]	Hawkshaw Hawkins	195?	100.00

Number	Title	Yr	NM

RCA CAMDEN
❑ CAL-808 [M]	Hawkshaw Hawkins Sings	1964	25.00
❑ CAS-808 [R]	Hawkshaw Hawkins Sings	1964	18.00
❑ CAL-931 [M]	The Country Gentleman	1966	25.00
❑ CAS-931 [R]	The Country Gentleman	1966	18.00

HAWKINS, JENNELL

AMAZON
❑ 1002 [M]	Moments to Remember	1962	150.00
❑ 1001 [M]	The Many Moods of Jenny	1961	150.00

HAWKINS, RONNIE

ACCORD
❑ SN-7213	Premonition	1983	12.00

COTILLION
❑ SD9019	Ronnie Hawkins	1970	18.00
❑ SD9039	The Hawk	1971	18.00

MONUMENT
❑ KZ31330	Rock and Roll Resurrection	1972	15.00
❑ ZG33855	Rock and Roll Resurrection/ The Ghost of Rock and Roll	1976	18.00
❑ KZ32940	The Giant of Rock 'n' Roll	1974	15.00

ROULETTE
❑ R25102 [M]	Mr. Dynamo	1960	150.00
❑ SR25102 [S]	Mr. Dynamo	1960	200.00
— Black vinyl			
❑ SR25102 [S]	Mr. Dynamo	1960	600.00
— Red vinyl			
❑ R25078 [M]	Ronnie Hawkins	1959	150.00
— White label with spokes			
❑ SR25078 [S]	Ronnie Hawkins	1959	200.00
— White label with spokes; black vinyl			
❑ SR25078 [S]	Ronnie Hawkins	1959	600.00
— White label with spokes; red vinyl			
❑ R25078 [M]	Ronnie Hawkins	1964	70.00
— Orange/yellow label			
❑ SR25078 [S]	Ronnie Hawkins	1964	60.00
— Orange/yellow label			
❑ R25137 [M]	Ronnie Hawkins Sings the Songs of Hank Williams	1960	100.00
❑ SR25137 [S]	Ronnie Hawkins Sings the Songs of Hank Williams	1960	150.00
❑ SR42045	The Best of Ronnie Hawkins and His Band	1970	30.00
❑ R25120 [M]	The Folk Ballads of Ronnie Hawkins	1960	100.00
❑ SR25120 [S]	The Folk Ballads of Ronnie Hawkins	1960	150.00

UNITED ARTISTS
❑ UA-LA968-H	The Hawk	1979	12.00

HAWKINS, SCREAMIN' JAY

EPIC
❑ LN3448 [M]	At Home with Screamin' Jay Hawkins	1958	800.00
❑ LN3457 [M]	I Put a Spell on You	1958	800.00
❑ BN26457 [R]	I Put a Spell on You	1969	100.00

PHILIPS
❑ PHS600336	Screamin' Jay Hawkins	1970	40.00
❑ PHS600319	What That Is	1969	40.00

SOUNDS OF HAWAII
❑ 5015	A Night at Forbidden City	196?	50.00

HAWKS, BILLY

PRESTIGE
❑ PRST-7556	More Heavy Soul	1968	25.00
❑ PRLP-7501 [M]	New Genius of the Blues	1967	30.00
❑ PRST-7501 [S]	New Genius of the Blues	1967	25.00

HAWKWIND

4 MEN WITH BEARDS
❑ 4M185LP [B]	Hawkwind		25.00

ATCO
❑ SD 36-115 [B]	Warrior on the Edge of Time	1975	30.00

GWR
❑ 1237 [B]	Live Chronicles	1986	18.00

LIBERTY
❑ LW-5567 [B]	In Search of Space	1981	25.00
— Reissue of United Artists 5567			
❑ LWB-120 [B]	Space Ritual/Alive in Liverpool and London	1981	30.00
— Reissue of United Artists 120			

SIRE
❑ SRK6047 [B]	Quark Strangeness and Charm	1978	30.00

UNITED ARTISTS
❑ UA-LA001-F [B]	Doremi Fasol Latido	1973	45.00
❑ UA-LA328-G [B]	Hall of the Mountain Grill	1974	35.00
❑ UAS-5519 [B]	Hawkwind	1971	35.00
❑ UAS-5567 [B]	In Search of Space	1972	50.00
❑ UA-LA120-H [B]	Space Ritual/Alive in Liverpool and London	1973	60.00

Number	Title	Yr	NM

HAWN, GOLDIE

REPRISE

❑ MS2061 [B]	Goldie	1972	18.00

HAY, COLIN JAMES

COLUMBIA
❑ FC40611	Looking for Jack	1987	12.00

MCA
❑ 6346	Wayfaring Sons	1990	12.00
— As "Colin Hay Band			

HAYDEN, WILLIE

DOOTO
❑ DTL-293 [M]	Blame It on the Blues	1960	500.00
— Maroon label			
❑ DTL-293 [M]	Blame It on the Blues	196?	200.00
— Multi-color label			

HAYES, ALVIN

PALO AITO/TBA
❑ TBA-221	Star Gaze	1987	12.00

HAYES, BILL

ABC-PARAMOUNT
❑ 194 [M]	Bill Hayes Sings the Best of Disney	1957	40.00

DAYBREAK
❑ DR-2020	The Look of Love	1972	30.00

KAPP
❑ KL-1106 [M]	Jimmy Crack Corn	1958	30.00

HAYES, CLANCY

DELMARK
❑ DS-210 [M]	Oh By Jingo	1965	25.00
❑ DS-9210 [S]	Oh By Jingo	1965	30.00

DOWN HOME
❑ MGD-3 [M]	Clancy Hayes Sings	1956	60.00

GOOD TIME JAZZ
❑ L-12050 [M]	Swingin' Minstrel	1963	25.00
❑ S-10050 [S]	Swingin' Minstrel	1963	30.00

VERVE
❑ MGV-1003 [M]	Clancy Hayes Sings	1957	40.00

HAYES, ISAAC, AND DIONNE WARWICK

ABC/HBS
❑ D-996	A Man and a Woman	1977	18.00

MCA
❑ 10012	A Man and a Woman	198?	15.00
— Reissue of ABC/HBS 996			

HAYES, ISAAC

ABC/HBS
❑ D-874 [B]	Chocolate Chip	1975	18.00
❑ D-923	Disco Connection	1975	15.00
❑ D-925	Groove-a-Thon	1976	15.00
❑ D-953 [B]	Juicy Fruit (Disco Freak)	1976	15.00

ATLANTIC
❑ SD1599	In the Beginning	1972	18.00
— Reissue of Enterprise 100			

COLUMBIA
❑ FC40941	Love Attack	1988	12.00
❑ FC40316	U-Turn	1986	12.00

ENTERPRISE
❑ ENS-5003	Black Moses	1971	25.00
❑ ENS-1001	Hot Buttered Soul	1969	25.00

Number	Title	Yr	NM

Number	Title	Yr	NM
❏ ENS-5007 [B]	Joy	1973	15.00
❏ EQS-5007 [Q]	Joy	1973	40.00
❏ ENS-5005	Live at the Sahara Tahoe	1973	18.00
❏ XQS-5005 [Q]	Live at the Sahara Tahoe	1973	60.00
❏ E-100 [M]	Presenting Isaac Hayes	1968	100.00
❏ ES-100 [S]	Presenting Isaac Hayes	1968	40.00
❏ ENS-5002	Shaft	1971	25.00
❏ EQS-2-5002 [Q]	Shaft	1971	80.00
❏ ENS-7510	The Best of Isaac Hayes	1975	15.00
❏ ENS-1010	The Isaac Hayes Movement	1970	25.00
❏ ENS-1014	To Be Continued	1970	25.00
❏ ENS-7504	Tough Guys	1974	15.00
❏ EQS-7504 [Q]	Tough Guys	1974	40.00
❏ ENS-7507	Truck Turner	1974	18.00

MOBILE FIDELITY

Number	Title	Yr	NM
❏ MFSL 1-273	Hot Buttered Soul	2003	50.00

— *Original Master Recording" at top of front cover*

POINTBLANK

Number	Title	Yr	NM
❏ SPRO-12787 [DJ]	Funky Junky	1995	18.00

— *Vinyl is promo only*

POLYDOR

Number	Title	Yr	NM
❏ PD-1-6269	And Once Again	1980	12.00
❏ PD-1-6224	Don't Let Go	1979	12.00
❏ PD-1-6164	For the Sake of Love	1978	12.00
❏ PD-1-6120	New Horizon	1977	12.00

STAX

Number	Title	Yr	NM
❏ STX-88003	Enterprise: His Greatest Hits	1980	15.00
❏ MPS-8509	Excerpts from Black Moses	1981	12.00
❏ MPS-8515	His Greatest Hit Singles	1982	12.00
❏ STX-4102 [B]	Hotbed	197?	15.00
❏ STX-4114 [B]	Hot Buttered Soul	1978	15.00

— *Reissue of Enterprise 1001*

| ❏ MPS-8530 | Joy | 1984 | 12.00 |

— *Reissue of Enterprise 5007*

| ❏ STX-88004 | Live at the Sahara Tahoe | 198? | 15.00 |

— *Reissue of Enterprise 5005*

| ❏ STX-88002 | Shaft | 1979 | 15.00 |

— *Reissue of Enterprise 5002*

| ❏ STX-4129 | The Isaac Hayes Movement | 197? | 12.00 |

— *Reissue of Enterprise 1010*

| ❏ STX-4133 | To Be Continued | 197? | 12.00 |

— *Reissue of Enterprise 1014*

HAYES, LOUIS, AND JUNIOR COOK

TIMELESS

Number	Title	Yr	NM
❏ 307	Ichi-Ban	1979	25.00

HAYES, LOUIS

GRYPHON

Number	Title	Yr	NM
❏ G-787	Variety Is the Spice of Life	1979	25.00

MUSE

| ❏ MR-5052 | Breath of Life | 1974 | 30.00 |
| ❏ MR-5125 | Real Thing | 1977 | 18.00 |

VEE JAY

| ❏ LP-3010 [M] | Louis Hayes | 1960 | 80.00 |
| ❏ SR-3010 [S] | Louis Hayes | 1960 | 150.00 |

HAYES, MARTHA

JUBILEE

Number	Title	Yr	NM
❏ JLP-1023 [M]	A Hayes Named Martha	1956	50.00

HAYES, RICHARD

ABC-PARAMOUNT

Number	Title	Yr	NM
❏ ABC-131 [M]	Richard Hayes	1956	40.00

MALA

| ❏ MLP-25 [M] | Love on the Rocks | 1969 | 30.00 |

HAYES, ROLAND

VANGUARD

Number	Title	Yr	NM
❏ VRS-7016 [10]	Christmas Carols of the Nations	195?	50.00

Number	Title	Yr	NM
❏ VRS-494 [M]	My Songs, Aframerican Religious Folk Songs	1955	30.00
❏ VRS-462 [M]	The Life of Christ in Folk Song	1954	30.00

HAYES, TUBBY

EPIC

Number	Title	Yr	NM
❏ LA16019 [M]	Introducing Tubby	1961	40.00
❏ BA17019 [S]	Introducing Tubby	1961	50.00
❏ LA16023 [M]	Tubby the Tenor	1962	40.00
❏ BA17023 [S]	Tubby the Tenor	1962	50.00
❏ BA17023 [S]	Tubby the Tenor	199?	30.00

— *Classic Records reissue on audiophile vinyl*

IMPERIAL

| ❏ LP-9046 [M] | Little Giant of Jazz | 1957 | 80.00 |

SMASH

| ❏ MGS-27026 [M] | Tubby's Back in Town | 1963 | 40.00 |
| ❏ SRS-67026 [S] | Tubby's Back in Town | 1963 | 50.00 |

HAYMARKET SQUARE

CHAPARRAL

Number	Title	Yr	NM
❏ 201	Magic Lantern	1968	1500.00

HAYMES, DICK

AUDIOPHILE

Number	Title	Yr	NM
❏ AP-130	For You, For Me, Forevermore	197?	15.00
❏ AP-79	Imagination	1978	15.00
❏ AP-200	Keep It Simple	198?	15.00

BALLAD

❏ DHS-6	As Time Goes By	1978	18.00
❏ DHS-7	Last Goodbye	1980	18.00
❏ DHS-8	Rare Dick Haymes	198?	18.00

CAPITOL

| ❏ T787 [M] | Moondreams | 1956 | 30.00 |

— *Turquoise label*

| ❏ T713 [M] | Rain or Shine | 1956 | 30.00 |

— *Turquoise label*

DAYBREAK

| ❏ DR2016 | Dick Haymes Comes Home | 1973 | 18.00 |

DECCA

❏ DL5022 [10]	Christmas Songs	1949	50.00
❏ DL5023 [10]	Dick Haymes Sings Irving Berlin	1949	50.00
❏ DL5243 [10]	Dick Haymes Sings with Helen Forrest, Volume 1	195?	50.00
❏ DL5038 [10]	Little Shamrocks	1950	50.00
❏ DL8773 [M]	Little White Lies	1959	40.00
❏ DL5291 [10]	Sentimental Songs	195?	50.00
❏ DL5012 [10]	Souvenir Album	1949	50.00
❏ DL5335 [10]	Sweethearts	195?	50.00

MCA

| ❏ 2-4097 | The Best of Dick Haymes | 1976 | 18.00 |

— *Black labels with rainbow*

MCA CORAL

| ❏ CB-20016 | Easy | 1973 | 12.00 |

VOCALION

| ❏ VL3616 [M] | Dick Haymes | 196? | 18.00 |

WARWICK

| ❏ W-2023 [M] | Richard the Lion-Hearted | 1960 | 30.00 |

HAYNES, GRAHAM

MUSE

Number	Title	Yr	NM
❏ MR-5402	What Time It Be!	1991	15.00

HAYNES, ROY; PHINEAS NEWBORN; PAUL CHAMBERS

FANTASY

Number	Title	Yr	NM
❏ OJC-196	We Three	1986	12.00

NEW JAZZ

| ❏ NJLP-8210 [M] | We Three | 1958 | 100.00 |

HAYNES, ROY

ABC IMPULSE!

Number	Title	Yr	NM
❏ AS-23	Out of the Afternoon	1968	25.00

— *Black label with red ring*

EMARCY

| ❏ MG-26048 [10] | Bushman's Holiday | 1954 | 150.00 |

GALAXY

| ❏ 5103 | Thank You | 1978 | 15.00 |
| ❏ 5116 | Vistalite | 1979 | 15.00 |

IMPULSE!

| ❏ A-23 [M] | Out of the Afternoon | 1962 | 60.00 |
| ❏ AS-23 [S] | Out of the Afternoon | 1962 | 80.00 |

MAINSTREAM

| ❏ MRL-313 | Hip Ensemble | 1971 | 25.00 |
| ❏ MRL-351 | Senyah | 1972 | 25.00 |

MCA

| ❏ 639 | Out of the Afternoon | 1980 | 12.00 |

NEW JAZZ

| ❏ NJLP-8286 [M] | Cracklin' | 1962 | 80.00 |

— *Purple label*

| ❏ NJLP-8286 [M] | Cracklin' | 1965 | 30.00 |

— *Blue label, trident logo at right*

Number	Title	Yr	NM
❏ NJLP-8287 [M]	Cymbalism	1962	80.00

— *Purple label*

| ❏ NJLP-8287 [M] | Cymbalism | 1965 | 30.00 |

— *Blue label, trident logo at right*

| ❏ NJLP-8245 [M] | Just Us | 1960 | 200.00 |

— *Purple label*

| ❏ NJLP-8245 [M] | Just Us | 1965 | 30.00 |

— *Blue label, trident logo at right*

PACIFIC JAZZ

| ❏ PJ-82 [M] | People | 1964 | 30.00 |
| ❏ ST-82 [S] | People | 1964 | 40.00 |

PRESTIGE

| ❏ 2504 | Bad News | 198? | 15.00 |

HAYNES, ROY/QUINCY JONES

EMARCY

Number	Title	Yr	NM
❏ MG-36083 [M]	Jazz Abroad	1956	100.00

HAYWARD, JUSTIN, AND JOHN LODGE

THRESHOLD

Number	Title	Yr	NM
❏ THS14 [B]	Blue Jays	1975	18.00
❏ THSX101 [DJ]	Blue Jays	1975	30.00

— *Open-end interview with script; used to promote the LP of the same name*

HAYWARD, JUSTIN

DERAM

Number	Title	Yr	NM
❏ DRL4801	Night Flight	1980	15.00
❏ DES18073	Songwriter	1977	18.00

HAYWOOD, LEON

20TH CENTURY

Number	Title	Yr	NM
❏ T-411 [B]	Back to Stay	1973	15.00
❏ T-476	Come and Get Yourself Some	1975	12.00
❏ T-440 [B]	Keep It in the Family	1974	15.00
❏ T-613	Naturally	1980	12.00

COLUMBIA

| ❏ PC34363 | Intimate | 1976 | 12.00 |

DECCA

| ❏ DL74949 | It's Got to Be Mellow | 1969 | 25.00 |

FAT FISH

| ❏ LP2525 | Soul Cargo | 1966 | 60.00 |

GALAXY

| ❏ 8206 | Mellow, Mellow | 196? | 25.00 |

MCA

| ❏ 2322 | Double My Pleasure | 1978 | 12.00 |
| ❏ 3000 | Energy | 1979 | 12.00 |

HAYZI FANTAYZEE

RCA

Number	Title	Yr	NM
❏ AFL1-4823 [B]	Battle Hymns for Children Singing	1983	18.00

HAZARD, DONNA

EXCELSIOR

Number	Title	Yr	NM
❏ 88008	My Turn	1981	12.00

HAZEL, EDDIE

WARNER BROS.

Number	Title	Yr	NM
❏ BSK3058	Games, Dames and Guitar Thangs	1977	50.00

HAZEL, MONK

SOUTHLAND

Number	Title	Yr	NM
❏ SLP-217 [M]	Monk Hazel	1956	40.00

HAZELL, EDDIE

AUDIOPHILE

Number	Title	Yr	NM
❏ AP-179	Live at Gulliver's -- I Go for That!	1984	12.00
❏ AP-137	Sugar, Don't You Know	1979	15.00

MONMOUTH-EVERGREEN

| ❏ 7075 | Take Your Shoes Off, Baby | 197? | 15.00 |

HAZILLA, JON

CADENCE JAZZ

Number	Title	Yr	NM
❏ CJR-1035	Chicplacity	1988	12.00

HAZLEWOOD, LEE

CAPITOL

Number	Title	Yr	NM
❏ ST-11171	Poet, Fool or Bum	1973	40.00

HARMONY

| ❏ HS11290 [S] | Houston | 196? | 25.00 |

— *Reissue of Reprise 6163*

LHI

| ❏ S-12009 | Forty | 1969 | 40.00 |
| ❏ S 12006 | Trouble Is a Lonesome Town | 1969 | 25.00 |

— *Reissue of Mercury 60860*

LIGHT IN THE ATTIC

| ❏ LITA096 [B] | Trouble is a Lonesome Town | 2013 | 30.00 |

Number	Title	Yr	NM

MERCURY
| ❑ MG-20860 [M] | Trouble Is a Lonesome Town | 1964 | 40.00 |
| ❑ SR-60860 [S] | Trouble Is a Lonesome Town | 1964 | 40.00 |

MGM
❑ E-4403 [M]	Lee Hazlewoodism - Its Cause and Cure	1966	30.00
❑ SE-4403 [S]	Lee Hazlewoodism - Its Cause and Cure	1966	40.00
❑ E-4362 [M]	The Very Special World of Lee Hazlewood	1966	30.00
❑ SE-4362 [S]	The Very Special World of Lee Hazlewood	1966	30.00

REPRISE
❑ RS-6163 [S]	Friday's Child	1965	40.00
❑ R-6163 [M]	Friday's Child	1965	40.00
❑ RS-6297 [B]	Love and Other Crimes	1968	40.00
❑ R-6133 [M]	The N.S.V.I.P.'s	1965	30.00
❑ RS-6133 [S]	The N.S.V.I.P.'s	1965	40.00

SMELLS LIKE
❑ SLR-40	13	2000	18.00
❑ SLR-30	Cowboy in Sweden	1999	18.00
❑ SLR-38	Requiem for an Almost Lady	1999	18.00
❑ SLR-37	Trouble Is a Lonesome Town	1999	18.00

HEAD, JIM, AND HIS DEL RAYS

HP
| ❑ 22893 [M] | Jim Head and His Del Rays | 1963 | 300.00 |

HEAD, MURRAY

A&M
| ❑ SP-4558 | Say It Ain't So | 1976 | 15.00 |

HEAD, ROY

ABC
| ❑ AB-1054 | Tonight's the Night | 1978 | 12.00 |

ABC DOT
| ❑ DO-2066 | A Head of His Time | 1977 | 15.00 |
| ❑ DO-2051 | Head First | 1976 | 15.00 |

ABC DUNHILL
| ❑ DS-50080 [B] | Same People | 1970 | 25.00 |

ELEKTRA
| ❑ 6E-234 | In Our Room | 1979 | 12.00 |
| ❑ 6E-298 | The Many Sides of Roy Head | 1980 | 12.00 |

MCA
| ❑ 796 | Tonight's the Night | 1980 | 10.00 |
| —Reissue of ABC album | | | |

SCEPTER
| ❑ S-532 [M] | Treat Me Right | 1965 | 30.00 |
| ❑ SS-532 [S] | Treat Me Right | 1965 | 40.00 |

TMI
| ❑ 1000 | Dismal Prisoner | 1972 | 18.00 |

TNT
| ❑ 101 [M] | Roy Head and the Traits | 1965 | 150.00 |
| —Counterfeit alert: Authentics do NOT contain the hit "Treat Her Right." | | | |

HEAD EAST

A&M
| ❑ SP-4795 | A Different Kind of Crazy | 1979 | 12.00 |

❑ SP-4537 [B]	Flat as a Pancake	1975	12.00
❑ SP-3196 [B]	Flat as a Pancake	198?	10.00
—Budget-line reissue			
❑ SP-4624	Gettin' Lucky	1977	12.00
❑ SP-4579	Get Yourself Up	1976	12.00
❑ SP-3162	Get Yourself Up	198?	10.00
—Budget-line reissue			
❑ SP-4680	Head East	1978	12.00
❑ SP-6007	Head East Live!	1979	15.00
❑ SP-4826	U.S. 1	1980	12.00

ALLEGIANCE
| ❑ AV-432 | Onward and Upward | 1986 | 10.00 |

PYRAMID
| ❑ 0(no #) | Flat as a Pancake | 1974 | 200.00 |
| —Original issue; 5,000 were pressed; has a different cover than the A&M version of the same album, plus the A and B sides are opposite the reissue | | | |

HEAD OVER HEELS

CAPITOL
| ❑ ST-797 | Head Over Heels | 1971 | 30.00 |

HEAD SHOP, THE

EPIC
| ❑ BN26476 [B] | The Head Shop | 1969 | 80.00 |

HEADHUNTERS

ARISTA
❑ AB4146	Straight from the Gate	1978	40.00
❑ AL4038	Survival of the Fittest	1975	60.00
—Reproductions exist			

HEADS, HANDS AND FEET

ATCO
| ❑ SD7025 | Old Soldiers Never Die | 1973 | 18.00 |

CAPITOL
| ❑ SVBB-680 | Heads, Hands and Feet | 1971 | 25.00 |
| ❑ ST-11051 | Tracks | 1972 | 18.00 |

HEADS, THE

LIBERTY
| ❑ LST-7581 | Heads Up | 1968 | 30.00 |

HEADSTONE

STARR
| ❑ (# unknown)0 | Still Looking | 1974 | 150.00 |

HEALY, PAT

WORLD PACIFIC
| ❑ WP-409 [M] | Just Before Dawn | 1958 | 80.00 |

HEARD, J.C.

ARGO
| ❑ LP-633 [M] | This Is Me, J.C. | 1958 | 40.00 |
| ❑ LPS-633 [S] | This Is Me, J.C. | 1959 | 30.00 |

HEART

CAPITOL
❑ PJ-12546	Bad Animals	1987	10.00
❑ PJ-512546	Bad Animals	1987	12.00
—Columbia House edition			
❑ R153552	Bad Animals	1987	12.00
—BMG Direct Marketing edition			
❑ C1-91820	Brigade	1990	15.00
❑ C1-591820	Brigade	1990	15.00
—Columbia House edition			
❑ SQ-12500	Dreamboat Annie	1986	10.00
❑ 72435-21184-1	Dreamboat Annie	1999	18.00
—180-gram audiophile reissue			
❑ ST-12410	Heart	1985	18.00
—With original mix of "Never"			
❑ ST-12410	Heart	1985	12.00
—With remix of "Never." Side one trail-off wax has an "RE-1			
❑ ST-512410	Heart	1985	18.00
—Columbia House edition; has original mix of "Never			
❑ SQ-12501	Magazine	1986	10.00

EPIC
❑ FE36371	Bebe Le Strange	1980	12.00
❑ KE236888	Greatest Hits/Live	1980	15.00
❑ AS884 [DJ]	Heart	1980	25.00
—Promo-only sampler from "Greatest Hits/Live			
❑ AS884 [DJ]	Heart	1980	25.00
—Promo-only sampler from "Greatest Hits/Live			
❑ QE38800	Passionworks	1983	12.00
❑ PE38800	Passionworks	1985	10.00
❑ FE38049	Private Audition	1982	12.00
❑ PE38049 [B]	Private Audition	1985	10.00

MUSHROOM
❑ MRS-5005 [B]	Dreamboat Annie	1976	12.00
❑ MRS-2-SP [PD]	Dreamboat Annie	1978	30.00
❑ MRS-5008 [B]	Magazine	1977	80.00
—Original issue, quickly recalled; "Magazine" is the last song on side 1; Side 2, Track 3 is "Blues Medley (Mother Earth) (You Shook Me Babe)"; at the bottom of the back cover is "Mushroom Records regrets that a contractual dispute has made it necessary to complete this record without the cooperation or endorsement of the group Heart, who have expressly disclaimed artistic involvement in completing this record.			
❑ MRS-5008	Magazine	1978	12.00
—Authorized edition; Side 2, Track 3 is "Mother Earth Blues"			
❑ MRS-1-SP [PD]	Magazine	1978	25.00

NAUTILUS
| ❑ NR-3 [B] | Dreamboat Annie | 1980 | 50.00 |
| —Audiophile pressing | | | |

PORTRAIT
❑ FR35555	Dog and Butterfly	1978	12.00
❑ PR35555	Dog and Butterfly	1981	10.00
❑ JR34799	Little Queen	1977	12.00
❑ HR44799	Little Queen	1981	50.00
—Half-speed mastered edition			
❑ PR34799 [B]	Little Queen	1984	10.00

HEART (3)

LOOK
| ❑ LLP-11000 | Heart | 1969 | 15.00 |

HEART (U)

KING
| ❑ KS-1119 | Have a Heart | 1970 | 15.00 |

NATURAL RESOURCES
| ❑ NR-102 | Heart | 1972 | 15.00 |

HEARTBEATS, THE

EMUS
| ❑ ES-12033 | A Thousand Miles Away | 1979 | 30.00 |

ROULETTE
| ❑ R25107 [M] | A Thousand Miles Away | 1960 | 400.00 |

HEARTBEATS, THE /SHEP AND THE LIMELITES

ROULETTE
| ❑ RE-115 [B] | Echoes of a Rock Era: The Groups | 1972 | 25.00 |

HEARTS, THE

ZELLA
| ❑ 337 [M] | I Feel Good | 1963 | 400.00 |

HEARTS AND FLOWERS

CAPITOL
❑ T2762 [M]	Now Is the Time for Hearts and Flowers	1967	40.00
❑ ST2762 [S]	Now Is the Time for Hearts and Flowers	1967	40.00
❑ ST2868 [B]	Of Horses, Kids and Forgotten Women	1968	50.00

HEARTS OF STONE

V.I.P.
| ❑ VIPS-404 | Stop the World... We Wanna Get On | 1970 | 40.00 |

HEARTSFIELD

COLUMBIA
| ❑ PC34456 | Collector's Item | 1976 | 12.00 |

MERCURY
❑ SRM-1-1034	Foolish Pleasures	1975	12.00
❑ SRM-1-688	Heartsfield	1973	12.00
❑ SRM-1-1003	The Wonder of It All	1974	12.00

HEATH, ALBERT

MUSE
| ❑ MR-5031 | Kwanza (The First) | 1974 | 25.00 |

O'BE
| ❑ LP-301 | Kawaida | 1969 | 40.00 |

TRIP
| ❑ 5032 | Kawaida | 1974 | 30.00 |
| —As "Kuumba Toudie Heath" | | | |

HEATH, JIMMY

COBBLESTONE
| ❑ CST-9012 | The Gap Sealer | 197? | 18.00 |

FANTASY
| ❑ OJC-6006 | Nice People | 198? | 12.00 |

LANDMARK
| ❑ LLP-1506 | New Picture | 1986 | 12.00 |
| ❑ LLP-1514 | Peer Pleasure | 1987 | 12.00 |

MILESTONE
| ❑ 47025 | Fast Company | 197? | 18.00 |

MUSE
| ❑ MR-5138 | Jimmy | 197? | 18.00 |
| ❑ MR-5028 | Love and Understanding | 1974 | 18.00 |

RIVERSIDE
❑ RLP-486 [M]	On the Trail	1965	25.00
❑ RS-9486 [S]	On the Trail	1965	30.00
❑ RLP 12-333 [M]	Really Big	1960	30.00
❑ RLP-1188 [S]	Really Big	1960	40.00
❑ 6060	Swamp Seed	197?	15.00
❑ RLP-465 [M]	Swamp Soul	1963	30.00
❑ RS-9465 [S]	Swamp Soul	1963	40.00
❑ RLP-372 [M]	The Quota	1961	30.00
❑ RS-9372 [S]	The Quota	1961	40.00
❑ RLP 12-314 [M]	The Thumper	1960	40.00
❑ RLP-1160 [S]	The Thumper	1960	40.00
❑ RLP-400 [M]	Triple Threat	1962	30.00
❑ RS-9400 [S]	Triple Threat	1962	40.00

XANADU
| ❑ 118 | Picture of Heath | 1976 | 15.00 |

Number	Title	Yr	NM

HEATH, TED, BAND

LONDON PHASE 4

❑ SP44186	A Salute to Glenn Miller	1972	12.00
❑ SP44148	Beatles, Bach and Bacharach	1971	18.00
❑ SP44177	Big Band Themes Revisited	197?	12.00
❑ SP44178	Big Band Themes Revisited, Volume 2	197?	12.00
❑ SP44140	Big Ones	1970	15.00
❑ SP44284	Coast to Coast	1977	12.00
❑ SP44104	Swing Is King	1968	15.00
❑ SP44113	Swing Is King, Volume 2	1969	15.00
❑ SP44220	The Ted Heath Band Salutes the Duke	197?	12.00
❑ SP44228	The Ted Heath Band Salutes Tommy Dorsey	197?	12.00
❑ SP44164	Those Were the Days	1971	15.00

HEATH, TED

EVEREST ARCHIVE OF FOLK & JAZZ

❑ 215	Ted Heath's Big Band	1970	12.00

LONDON

❑ PS535	21st Anniversary Album	1968	15.00
❑ LL1716 [M]	All Time Top Twelve	1957	25.00
❑ PS117 [S]	All Time Top Twelve	1958	30.00
—Re-recorded version of LL 1716			
❑ LL1676 [M]	A Yank in Europe	1956	25.00
❑ LL3125 [M]	Big Band Blues	1959	25.00
❑ PS172 [S]	Big Band Blues	1959	30.00
❑ LL3325 [M]	Big Band Spirituals	1963	15.00
❑ LB-732 [10]	Black and White Magic	195?	40.00
❑ LL1217 [M]	Gershwin for Moderns	1956	25.00
❑ LL3106 [M]	Great Film Hits	1959	25.00
❑ PS159 [S]	Great Film Hits	1959	30.00
❑ LL3057 [M]	Hits I Missed	1958	25.00
❑ PS116 [S]	Hits I Missed	1958	30.00
❑ LL1211 [M]	Jazz Concert at the London Palladium, Vol. 3	1955	25.00
❑ LL1379 [M]	Jazz Concert at the London Palladium, Vol. 4	1956	25.00
❑ LL1279 [M]	Kern for Moderns	1956	25.00
❑ LL3195 [M]	Latin Swingers	1961	18.00

❑ PS219 [S]	Latin Swingers	1961	25.00
❑ LB-511 [10]	Listen to My Music	195?	40.00
❑ LL3127 [M]	My Very Good Friends The Bandleaders	1959	25.00
❑ PS174 [S]	My Very Good Friends The Bandleaders	1959	30.00
❑ LL3367 [M]	New Palladium Performances	1964	15.00
❑ LL3058 [M]	Old English	1958	25.00
❑ LL3124 [M]	Pop Hits from the Classics	1959	25.00
❑ PS171 [S]	Pop Hits from the Classics	1959	30.00
❑ LL1749 [M]	Rhapsody in Blue	1957	25.00
❑ LL1500 [M]	Rodgers for Moderns	1956	25.00
❑ LL3062 [M]	Shall We Dance	1959	25.00
❑ PS148 [S]	Shall We Dance	1959	30.00
❑ LL1737 [M]	Showcase	1957	25.00
❑ LL3146 [M]	Songs for the Young at Heart	1960	18.00
❑ PS190 [S]	Songs for the Young at Heart	1960	25.00
❑ LL1721 [M]	Spotlight on Sidemen	1957	25.00
❑ PS138 [S]	Swing Session	1958	30.00
—New stereo recordings of the same material as appears on LL 802			
❑ LPB-374 [10]	Ted Heath and His Orchestra	195?	40.00
❑ LL1566 [M]	Ted Heath at Carnegie Hall	1956	25.00
❑ LL802 [M]	Ted Heath at the London Palladium	1953	25.00
❑ LL3143 [M]	Ted Heath in Concert	1960	18.00
❑ PS187 [S]	Ted Heath in Concert	1960	25.00
❑ LL978 [M]	Ted Heath Plays the Music of Fats Waller	1954	25.00
❑ LL1564 [M]	Ted Heath's First American Tour	1956	25.00
❑ LL750 [M]	Ted Heath Strikes Up the Band	1953	25.00
❑ LL1475 [M]	Ted Heath Swings in Hi-Fi	1956	25.00

❑ PS140 [S]	Ted Heath Swings in High Stereo	1958	30.00
❑ LPB-340 [10]	Tempo for Dancing	195?	40.00
❑ LL1000 [M]	The 100th London Palladium Concert	1955	25.00
❑ LL3138 [M]	The Big Band Dixie Sound	1960	18.00
❑ PS184 [S]	The Big Band Dixie Sound	1960	25.00
❑ LL3192 [M]	The Hits of the Thirties	1961	18.00
❑ PS216 [S]	The Hits of the Thirties	1961	25.00
❑ LL3128 [M]	The Hits of the Twenties	1960	18.00
❑ PS175 [S]	The Hits of the Twenties	1960	25.00
❑ LL3047 [M]	Things to Come	1958	25.00
❑ LL1743 [M]	Tribute to the Fabulous Dorseys	1957	25.00

LONDON PHASE 4

❑ SP44017	Big Band Bash	1962	18.00
❑ P54002 [M]	Big Band Percussion	1961	15.00
❑ SP44002 [S]	Big Band Percussion	1961	18.00
❑ SP44036 [S]	Big Band Spirituals	1963	18.00
❑ SP44074	Chartbusters	1966	15.00
❑ SP44046 [S]	New Palladium Performances	1964	15.00
❑ SP44079	Pow!	1966	15.00
❑ SP44023	Satin Strings and Bouncing Brass	1963	18.00
❑ SP44038	Swing vs. Latin	1964	18.00
❑ SP44063	The Sound of Music	1965	15.00

RICHMOND

❑ B20034 [M]	Big Band Beat	196?	15.00
❑ B20096 [M]	Big Band Gershwin	196?	15.00
❑ B20097 [M]	Big Band Kern	196?	15.00
❑ B20098 [M]	Big Band Rodgers	196?	15.00
❑ B20037 [M]	Ted Heath Plays Gershwin	196?	15.00
❑ B20082 [M]	Ted Heath Plays the Music of Fats Waller	196?	15.00

HEATH BROTHERS, THE

ANTILLES

❑ AN-1003	Brotherly Love	1982	15.00
❑ AN-1016	Brothers and Others	198?	15.00

COLUMBIA

❑ FC37126	Expressions of Life	1981	15.00
❑ JC35816	In Motion: The Heath Brothers and Brass Choir	1979	15.00
❑ FC36374	Live at the Public Theatre	1980	15.00
❑ JC35573	Passin' Thru	1978	15.00

STRATA-EAST

❑ SES-19766 [B]	Marchin' On	1975	80.00

HEATHER BLACK

AMERICAN PLAYBOY

❑ 1001	Heather Black Live	197?	60.00
❑ 1001	Heather Black Live	197?	150.00
—Evidently, some copies of this were 2-record sets			

DOUBLE BAYOU

❑ 2000	Heather Black	197?	30.00

HEATHERTON, JOEY

MGM

❑ SE-4868	The Joey Heatherton Album	1972	18.00

HEATS, THE

ALBATROSS

❑ 1001	The Heats	1980	30.00

HEATWAVE

EPIC

❑ FE36873	Candles	1980	12.00
❑ JE35260	Central Heating	1978	12.00
—Originals have orange labels			
❑ FE38065	Current	1982	12.00
❑ FE39279	Greatest Hits	1984	12.00
❑ PE39279	Greatest Hits	198?	10.00
—Budget-line reissue			
❑ FE35970	Hot Property	1979	12.00
❑ PE34761 [B]	Too Hot to Handle	1977	15.00
—Originals have orange labels			

HEAVEN & HELL

WARNER BROS./RHINO

❑ 519252 [B]	The Devil You Know	2009	25.00

HEAVEN 17

ARISTA

❑ AL6606	Heaven 17	1982	15.00
❑ AL8-8007	Heaven 17	1983	12.00
—Reissue			
❑ AL8-8259	How Men Are	198?	12.00
❑ AL8-8020	Luxury Gap	1983	12.00

CAROLINE

❑ 1393	Teddy Bear Duke & Psycho	1988	12.00

VIRGIN

❑ 90569	Pleasure One	1986	12.00

HEAVY BALLOON, THE

ELEPHANT

❑ EVS-104 [B]	32,000 Lbs.	1969	100.00

HEBB, BOBBY

EPIC

❑ BN26523 [B]	Love Games	1970	15.00

PHILIPS

❑ PHM200212 [M]	Sunny	1966	30.00
—With "200-212" in trail-off; this record is mono			
❑ PHS600212 [S]	Sunny	1966	30.00
❑ PHM200212 [S]	Sunny	1966	30.00
—With "2/600-212" in trail-off; this record plays stereo, though labeled mono			

HECKMAN, DON

ICTUS

❑ 101	Summerlin Improvisational Jazz Workshop	1967	60.00

HEDGE & DONNA

CAPITOL

❑ ST-107	2	1969	18.00
—Black label with rainbow ring			
❑ ST-279	All the Friendly Colours	1969	18.00
—Lime green label			
❑ ST-2869	Hedge & Donna	1968	18.00
—The label calls this LP "Love"			
❑ ST-447	Special Circumstances	1970	18.00

JANUS

❑ JLS-3045	Capers & Carson	1973	15.00

POLYDOR

❑ 24-4063	Revolution	1971	15.00

HEE

BUDDAH

❑ BDS-5062	Head	1970	30.00
—With coloring book (deduct 1/3 if missing)			

HEFTI, NEAL

COLUMBIA

❑ CL1516 [M]	Light and Right	1960	25.00
❑ CS8316 [S]	Light and Right	1960	30.00

CORAL

❑ CX2 [M]	Hollywood Song Book	1959	40.00
❑ 7CX2 [S]	Hollywood Song Book	1959	60.00
❑ CRL57241 [M]	Hollywood Song Book, Volume 1	1958	25.00
❑ CRL757241 [S]	Hollywood Song Book, Volume 1	1959	30.00
❑ CRL57242 [M]	Hollywood Song Book, Volume 2	1958	25.00
❑ CRL757242 [S]	Hollywood Song Book, Volume 2	1959	30.00
❑ CRL57256 [M]	Music U.S.A.	1959	25.00
❑ CRL757256 [S]	Music U.S.A.	1959	30.00
❑ CRL56083 [10]	Swingin' on a Coral Reef	1953	50.00

EPIC

❑ LN3481 [M]	Pardon My Do-Wah	1958	30.00
❑ LN3113 [M]	Singing Instrumentals	1956	50.00
❑ LN3440 [M]	Singing Instrumentals	1958	30.00
❑ LG1013 [10]	Singing Instrumentals	1955	60.00

RCA VICTOR

❑ LPM-3573 [M]	Batman Theme (and 11 Other Bat-Songs)	1966	50.00
❑ LSP-3573 [S]	Batman Theme (and 11 Other Bat-Songs)	1966	60.00
❑ LPM-3621 [M]	Hefti in Gotham City	1966	50.00
❑ LSP-3621 [S]	Hefti in Gotham City	1966	60.00

REPRISE

❑ R-6039 [M]	Jazz Pops	1962	25.00
❑ R9-6039 [S]	Jazz Pops	1962	30.00
❑ R-6018 [M]	Themes from TV's Top 12	1962	30.00
❑ R9-6018 [S]	Themes from TV's Top 12	1962	30.00

VIK

❑ LX-1092 [M]	Concert Miniatures	1957	60.00

X

❑ LXA-3021 [10]	Music of Rudolf Frimi	1954	50.00

HEIFETZ, JASCHA, AND GREGOR PIATIGORSKI

RCA VICTOR RED SEAL

❑ LDS-2513 [S]	Brahms: Double Concerto	1961	40.00
—Originals with "shaded dog" label			

HEIFETZ, JASCHA; WILLIAM PRIMROSE; GREGOR PIATIGORSKI

RCA VICTOR RED SEAL

❑ LSC-2550 [S]	Beethoven: Serenade, op. 8; Kodaly: Duo	1961	40.00
—Originals with "shaded dog" label			
❑ LSC-2563 [S]	Beethoven: Trio in D; Bach: Three Sinfonias; Schubert: Trio No. 2	1961	40.00
—Original with "shaded dog" label			

HEIFETZ, JASCHA

RCA VICTOR RED SEAL

❑ LSC-2577 [S]	Bach: Concerto for Two Violins; Beethoven: Kreutzer Sonata	1962	70.00

Number	Title	Yr	NM
— Original with "shaded dog" label			
❏ LSC-1992 [S]	Beethoven: Violin Concerto in D	1958	50.00
— With Charles Munch/Boston Symphony Orchestra			
❏ LSC-1903 [S]	Brahms: Violin Concerto	1958	50.00
— With Fritz Reiner/Chicago Symphony Orchestra; original with "shaded dog" label			
❏ LSC-2603 [S]	Bruch: Scottish Fantasy; Vieuxtemps; Violin Concerto No. 5	1962	50.00
— Original with "shaded dog" label			
❏ LSC-2652 [S]	Bruch: Violin Concerto No. 1 in G; Mozart: Violin Concerto No. 4 in D	1962	60.00
— Original with "shaded dog" label			
❏ LSC-2734 [S]	Glazunov: Violin Concerto; Mozart: Sinfonia Concertante	1963	100.00
— Original with "shaded dog" label			
❏ LSC-2314 [S]	Mendelssohn: Violin Concerto in E; Prokofiev: Violin Concerton in G	1959	30.00
— With Charles Munch/Boston Symphony Orchestra			
❏ LSC-2435 [S]	Sibelius: Violin Concerto	1960	40.00
— Originals with "shaded dog" label			
❏ LSC-2129 [S]	Tchaikovsky: Violin Concerto	1958	40.00
— With Fritz Reiner/Chicago Symphony Orchestra; original with "shaded dog" label			
❏ LSC-2129 [S]	Tchaikovsky: Violin Concerto	1999	30.00
— Classic Records reissue			

HEINDORF, RAY

DCC COMPACT CLASSICS
| ❏ LPZ-2023 | For Whom the Bell Tolls | 1996 | 30.00 |
| — Audiophile vinyl | | | |

WARNER BROS.
❏ B1201 [M]	For Whom the Bell Tolls	1958	30.00
— Re-recording of 1943 movie score; the first LP on Warner Bros. Records			
❏ BS1201 [S]	For Whom the Bell Tolls	1959	40.00
— Gold label			
❏ W1213 [M]	Spellbound	1958	30.00
— Re-recording of 1945 movie score			
❏ WS1213 [3]	Spellbound	1959	40.00
— Gold label			

HEINTJE

MGM
| ❏ SE-4772 | Best of All | 1971 | 15.00 |
| ❏ SE-4739 | Mama | 1970 | 15.00 |

HELIOCENTRIC

DISCOVERY
| ❏ 806 | Heliocentric | 1979 | 15.00 |

HELL, RICHARD, AND THE VOIDOIDS

RED STAR
| ❏ RED801 | Destiny Street | 1982 | 25.00 |
| — Richard Hell solo | | | |

SIRE
| ❏ SRK6037 | Blank Generation | 1977 | 30.00 |

HELLBORG, JONAS

DAY EIGHT
❏ DEM 002	All Our Steps	1983	18.00
❏ DEM 006	Axis	1986	15.00
❏ DEM 009	Bass	1988	15.00
❏ DEM 004	Elegant Punk	1984	15.00
❏ DEM0(# unknown)	Jonas Hellborg Group	1988	15.00
❏ DEM 001	The Bassic Thing	1982	25.00

HELLERS, THE

COMMAND
| ❏ RS934SD | Singers, Talkers, Players, Swingers and Doers | 1968 | 25.00 |

HELLO PEOPLE, THE

ABC
| ❏ D-882 | Bricks | 1975 | 12.00 |
ABC DUNHILL
| ❏ DS-50184 | The Handsome Devils | 1974 | 12.00 |
MEDIARTS
| ❏ 41-8 | Have You Seen the Light | 1970 | 15.00 |
PHILIPS
❏ PHS600276	Fusion	1969	18.00
❏ PHS600265 [S]	The Hello People	1968	18.00
❏ PHS200265 [M]	The Hello People	1968	18.00
— Possibly white label promo only			
UNITED ARTISTS
| ❏ UAS5524 | Have You Seen the Light | 1971 | 12.00 |
| — Reissue of Mediarts LP | | | |

HELM, BOB

RIVERSIDE
| ❏ RLP-2510 [10] | Bob Helm | 1954 | 80.00 |

HELM, BOB/LU WATTERS

RIVERSIDE
| ❏ RLP 12-213 [M] | San Francisco Style | 1956 | 60.00 |

HELMS, BOBBY

COLUMBIA
| ❏ CL2060 [M] | The Best of Bobby Helms | 1963 | 30.00 |
| ❏ CS8860 [S] | The Best of Bobby Helms | 1963 | 30.00 |
DECCA
| ❏ DL8638 [M] | Bobby Helms Sings to My Special Angel | 1957 | 120.00 |
HARMONY
| ❏ HL7409 [M] | Fraulein | 1967 | 25.00 |
| ❏ HS11209 [S] | Fraulein | 1967 | 18.00 |
KAPP
❏ KL1463 [M]	I'm the Man	1966	18.00
❏ KS3463 [S]	I'm the Man	1966	25.00
❏ KL1505 [M]	Sorry My Name Isn't Fred	1966	18.00
❏ KS3505 [S]	Sorry My Name Isn't Fred	1966	25.00
LITTLE DARLIN'
| ❏ 8088 | All New Just for You | 1968 | 30.00 |
MISTLETOE
| ❏ MLP-1206 [B] | Jingle Bell Rock | 197? | 15.00 |
POWER PAK
| ❏ 283 | Greatest Hits | 197? | 12.00 |
VOCALION
❏ VL73874	My Special Angel	1969	15.00
❏ VL3743 [M]	Someone Already There	1965	18.00
❏ VL73743 [R]	Someone Already There	1965	15.00

HELMS, DON

SMASH
❏ MGS-27019 [M]	Don Helms' Steel Guitar	1962	25.00
❏ SRS-67019 [S]	Don Helms' Steel Guitar	1962	30.00
❏ MGS-27001 [M]	The Steel Guitar Sounds of Hank Williams	1962	25.00
❏ SRS-67001 [S]	The Steel Guitar Sounds of Hank Williams	1962	30.00

HELP

DECCA
| ❏ DL75257 | Help | 1970 | 30.00 |
| ❏ DL75304 | Second Coming | 1971 | 30.00 |

HEMPHILL, JULIUS

ARISTA FREEDOM
| ❏ AL1012 [B] | 'Coon Bid'ness | 1975 | 25.00 |
| ❏ AL1028 [B] | Dogon A.D. | 1976 | 30.00 |
BLACK SAINT
| ❏ BSR-0040 | Flat-Out Jump Suite | 198? | 18.00 |
| ❏ BSR-0015 | Raw Material and Residuals | 197? | 18.00 |
ELEKTRA/MUSICIAN
| ❏ 60831 | Julius Hemphill's Big Band | 1988 | 12.00 |
MBARI
❏ (# unknown)0	Blue Boye	1977	60.00
❏ (# unknown)0	'Coon Bid'ness	1974	40.00
❏ 5001	Dogon A.D.	1972	50.00
MINOR MUSIC
| ❏ MM-003 | Georgia Blue | 1985 | 15.00 |
RED
| ❏ VPA-138 | Live in New York | 1976 | 18.00 |
SACKVILLE
| ❏ 3018 | Buster Bee | 198? | 15.00 |

HENDERSON, BILL

DISCOVERY
❏ 779	Live at the Times	1978	15.00
❏ 802	Street of Dreams	1979	15.00
❏ 846	Tribute to Johnny Mercer	1982	15.00
MGM
| ❏ E-4128 [M] | Bill Henderson with the Oscar Peterson Trio | 1963 | 30.00 |
| ❏ SE-4128 [S] | Bill Henderson with the Oscar Peterson Trio | 1963 | 30.00 |
VEE JAY
❏ LP-1031 [M]	Bill Henderson	1961	30.00
❏ SR-1031 [S]	Bill Henderson	1961	40.00
❏ LP-1015 [M]	Bill Henderson Sings	1959	30.00
❏ SR-1015 [S]	Bill Henderson Sings	1959	40.00
VERVE
| ❏ V-8619 [M] | When My Dreamboat Comes Home | 1965 | 25.00 |
| ❏ V6-8619 [S] | When My Dreamboat Comes Home | 1965 | 30.00 |

HENDERSON, BOBBY

CHIAROSCURO
❏ 102 [B]	Home in the Clouds	1971	18.00
— Reissue of Halcyon 102			
❏ 122	Last Recordings	1973	18.00
HALCYON
| ❏ 102 | Home in the Clouds | 1970 | 25.00 |
VANGUARD
| ❏ VRS-8511 [M] | Handful of Keys | 1955 | 40.00 |

HENDERSON, BUGS

ARMADILLO
| ❏ LP-78-1 [B] | The Bugs Henderson Group At Last | 1978 | 40.00 |

HENDERSON, EDDIE

BLUE NOTE
| ❏ BN-LA636-G | Heritage | 1976 | 25.00 |
| ❏ BN-LA464-G | Sunburst | 1975 | 25.00 |
CAPITOL
❏ ST-11761	Comin' Through	1977	18.00
❏ SW-11846	Mahal	1978	15.00
❏ ST-11984	Runnin' To Your Love	1979	15.00
CAPRICORN
| ❏ CP 0122 | Inside Out | 1974 | 18.00 |
| ❏ CP 0118 | Realization | 1973 | 18.00 |

HENDERSON, FLETCHER

BIOGRAPH
| ❏ 12039 | Fletcher Henderson 1923-27 | 197? | 15.00 |
| ❏ C-12 | Fletcher Henderson 1924-41 | 197? | 15.00 |
BLUEBIRD
| ❏ AXM2-5507 | The Complete Fletcher Henderson | 197? | 18.00 |
COLUMBIA
❏ C4L19 [M]	The Fletcher Henderson Story	1961	100.00
— Box set with booklet; red and black labels with six "eye" logos			
❏ C4L19 [M]	The Fletcher Henderson Story	1963	50.00
— Red "Guaranteed High Fidelity" labels			
❏ C4L19 [M]	The Fletcher Henderson Story	1966	30.00
— Red "360 Sound Mono" labels			
DECCA
❏ DL9227 [M]	Fletcher Henderson: First Impression (Vol. 1 1924-1931)	1958	50.00
— Black label, silver print			
❏ DL9227 [M]	Fletcher Henderson: First Impression (Vol. 1 1924-1931)	1961	30.00
— Black label with color bars			
❏ DL79227 [R]	Fletcher Henderson: First Impression (Vol. 1 1924-1931)	196?	18.00
❏ DL9228 [M]	Fletcher Henderson: The Swing's the Thing (Vol. 2 1931-1934)	1958	50.00
— Black label, silver print			
❏ DL9228 [M]	Fletcher Henderson: The Swing's the Thing (Vol. 2 1931-1934)	1961	30.00
— Black label with color bars			
❏ DL79228 [R]	Fletcher Henderson: The Swing's the Thing (Vol. 2 1931-1934)	196?	18.00
❏ DL6025 [10]	Fletcher Henderson Memorial Album	1952	150.00
HISTORICAL
| ❏ 13 | Fletcher Henderson 1923-24 | 1967 | 25.00 |
| ❏ 18 | Fletcher Henderson Volume 2: 1923-25 | 1967 | 25.00 |
JAZZTONE
| ❏ J-1285 [M] | The Big Reunion | 1958 | 30.00 |
MCA
❏ 1310	First Impressions	198?	12.00
❏ 1346	The Rarest Fletcher	198?	12.00
❏ 1318	The Swing's the Thing	198?	12.00
MILESTONE
| ❏ M-2005 | The Immortal Fletcher Henderson | 196? | 30.00 |
RIVERSIDE
| ❏ RLP-1055 [10] | Fletcher Henderson | 1954 | 150.00 |
SAVOY JAZZ
| ❏ SJL-1152 | The Crown King of Swing | 198? | 12.00 |
SUTTON
| ❏ SSL-286 [M] | Fletcher Henderson with Slam Stewart | 195? | 30.00 |
SWING
| ❏ SW-8445/6 | Fletcher Henderson and His Dixie Stompers 1925-1928 | 198? | 18.00 |
X
| ❏ LVA-3013 [10] | Fletcher Henderson and His Connie's Inn Orchestra | 1954 | 150.00 |

HENDERSON, JOE

BLUE NOTE
❏ BLP-4189 [M]	Inner Urge	1965	150.00
❏ BST-84189 [S]	Inner Urge	1965	200.00
— New York, USA address on label			
❏ BST-84189 [S]	Inner Urge	1967	18.00
— A Division of Liberty Records on label			
❏ BLP-4166 [M]	In 'n Out	1964	250.00
❏ BST-84166 [S]	In 'n Out	1964	100.00
— New York, USA address on label			
❏ BST-84166 [S]	In 'n Out	1967	18.00
— A Division of Liberty Records" on label			

Number	Title	Yr	NM
❏ BLP-4227 [M]	Mode for Joe	1966	100.00
❏ BST-84227 [S]	Mode for Joe	1966	80.00
—New York, USA" address on label			
❏ BST-84227 [S]	Mode for Joe	1967	18.00
—A Division of Liberty Records" on label			
❏ BLP-4152 [M]	Our Thing	1963	125.00
❏ BST-84152 [S]	Our Thing	1963	100.00
—New York, USA" address on label			
❏ BST-84152 [S]	Our Thing	1967	18.00
—A Division of Liberty Records" on label			
❏ BLP-4140 [M]	Page One	1963	200.00
❏ BST-84140 [S]	Page One	1963	100.00
—New York, USA" address on label			
❏ BST-84140 [S]	Page One	1967	18.00
—A Division of Liberty Records" on label			
❏ BT-85123	State of the Tenor	1987	12.00
❏ BT-85126	State of the Tenor Vol. 2: Live at the Village Vanguard	1987	12.00

CONTEMPORARY

| ❏ C-14006 | Relaxin' at Camarillo | 198? | 15.00 |

FANTASY

| ❏ OJC-465 | The Kicker | 1990 | 15.00 |

FONTANA

| ❏ SRF-67590 | Hits, Hits, Hits! | 1969 | 30.00 |

MILESTONE

❏ M-9040	Black Is the Color	1972	25.00
❏ M-9066	Black Miracle	1976	18.00
❏ M-9071	Black Narcissus	1976	18.00
❏ M-9057	Canyon Lady	1974	18.00
❏ M-9053	Elements	1974	18.00
❏ 47058	Foresight	198?	18.00
❏ M-9028	If You're Not Part	1970	25.00
❏ M-9034	In Pursuit of Blackness	1971	25.00
❏ M-9047	Joe Henderson In Japan	1972	25.00
❏ M-9050	Multiple	1973	18.00
❏ M-9024 [B]	Power to the People	1970	25.00
❏ M-9017 [B]	Tetragon	1969	25.00
❏ M-9008	The Kicker	1968	25.00

PAUSA

| ❏ 7075 | Mirror, Mirror | 1980 | 12.00 |

TODD

| ❏ MT-2701 [M] | Snap Your Fingers | 1962 | 50.00 |
| ❏ ST-2701 [S] | Snap Your Fingers | 1962 | 70.00 |

HENDERSON, MICHAEL

BUDDAH

❏ BDS5719	Do It All	1979	18.00
❏ BDS6004	Fickle	1983	18.00
❏ BDS5693	Goin' Places	1977	15.00
❏ BDS5712	In the Night-Time	1978	18.00
❏ BDS6002	Slingshot	1981	15.00
❏ BDS5662	Solid	1976	18.00
❏ BDS6001	Wide Receiver	1980	15.00

EMI AMERICA

| ❏ ST-17181 | Bedtime Stories | 1986 | 12.00 |

HENDERSON, SKITCH

CAPITOL

| ❏ H110 [10] | Keyboard Sketches | 1950 | 50.00 |

HENDERSON, WAYNE

ABC

| ❏ AB-1020 | Big Daddy's Place | 1977 | 12.00 |

POLYDOR

| ❏ PD-1-6227 | Emphasized | 1980 | 12.00 |
| ❏ PD-1-6145 | Living on a Dream | 1978 | 12.00 |

HENDRICKS, JON

COLUMBIA

❏ CL1583 [M]	Evolution of the Blues	1961	30.00
❏ CS8383 [S]	Evolution of the Blues	1961	40.00
❏ CL1805 [M]	Fast Livin' Blues	1962	30.00
❏ CS8605 [S]	Fast Livin' Blues	1962	40.00

ENJA

| ❏ 4032 | Cloudburst | 198? | 15.00 |

MUSE

| ❏ MR-5258 | Love | 1982 | 12.00 |

REPRISE

| ❏ R-6089 [M] | Salud! | 1964 | 30.00 |
| ❏ R9-6089 [S] | Salud! | 1964 | 30.00 |

SMASH

| ❏ MGS-27069 [M] | Recorded In Person at the Trident | 1963 | 30.00 |
| ❏ SRS-67069 [S] | Recorded In Person at the Trident | 1963 | 30.00 |

STANYAN

| ❏ 10132 | September Songs | 197? | 15.00 |

WORLD PACIFIC

| ❏ WP-1283 [M] | A Good Git-Together | 1959 | 80.00 |

HENDRICKS, MICHELE

MUSE

| ❏ MR-5336 | Carryin' On | 1988 | 12.00 |
| ❏ MR-5363 | Keepin' Me Satisfied | 1989 | 15.00 |

Number	Title	Yr	NM

HENDRIX, JIMI, AND LITTLE RICHARD

EVEREST ARCHIVE OF FOLK & JAZZ

| ❏ 296 | Roots of Rock | 1974 | 15.00 |

PICKWICK

| ❏ SPC-3347 | Jimi Hendrix and Little Richard Together | 1973 | 15.00 |

HENDRIX, JIMI, AND LONNIE YOUNGBLOOD

MAPLE

| ❏ 6004 | Two Great Experiences Together | 1971 | 50.00 |

HENDRIX, JIMI

ACCORD

❏ SN-7112	Before London	1981	12.00
❏ SN-7139	Cosmic Feeling	1981	12.00
❏ SN-7101	Kaleidoscope	1981	12.00

CAPITOL

❏ STAO-472	Band of Gypsys	1970	25.00
❏ SN-16319	Band of Gypsys	1985	12.00
—Budget-line reissue			
❏ C1-96414 [B]	Band of Gypsys	1995	25.00
—Numbered reissue			
❏ SJ-12416	Band of Gypsys 2	1986	12.00
—Side 2 lists, and plays, three songs			
❏ SJ-12416	Band of Gypsys 2	1986	150.00
—Side 2 lists three songs, but plays four completely different songs. Four bands are visible on the record.			
❏ T2894 [M]	Flashing	1968	100.00
❏ ST2894 [S]	Flashing	1968	40.00
❏ T2856 [M]	Get That Feeling	1967	80.00
❏ ST2856 [S]	Get That Feeling	1967	40.00
❏ SWBB-659	Get That Feeling/Flashing	1971	30.00
❏ MLP-15022 [EP]	Johnny B. Goode	1986	10.00

EXPERIENCE HENDRIX

| ❏ 88843042031 [B] | Live at Monterey | 2014 | 40.00 |

EXPERIENCE HENDRIX/CAPITOL

| ❏ ST-472 | Band of Gypsys | 1997 | 30.00 |
| —Limited edition on "heavy vinyl" with booklet; distributed by Classic Records | | | |

EXPERIENCE HENDRIX/CLASSIC

❏ RTH2006	Blues	2002	60.00
—Limited edition on 200-gram blue vinyl			
❏ RTH2006	Blues	2003	40.00
—Limited edition on 200-gram black vinyl			
❏ B0000698-01	Martin Scorsese Presents the Blues: Jimi Hendrix	2004	50.00
—Limited edition of 1,000 on blue vinyl			
❏ B0000698-01	Martin Scorsese Presents the Blues: Jimi Hendrix	2004	40.00
—Regular edition on black vinyl			
❏ RTH-2016	Voodoo Child: The Jimi Hendrix Collection	2005	40.00
—Box set; red vinyl			
❏ RTH-2016	Voodoo Child: The Jimi Hendrix Collection	2005	80.00
—Black 200-gram vinyl			

EXPERIENCE HENDRIX/MCA

❏ 11602	Are You Experienced?	1997	50.00
—Limited edition on "heavy vinyl" with booklet			
❏ 11608	Are You Experienced?	1997	40.00
—Limited edition on "heavy vinyl" with booklet; pressed in U.S. for export to Europe; has different cover than US version			
❏ 11601	Axis: Bold As Love	1997	50.00
—Limited edition on "heavy vinyl" with booklet			
❏ 11607	Band of Gypsys	1997	30.00
—Limited edition on "heavy vinyl" with booklet; pressed in U.S. for export to Europe			
❏ 11742 [M]	BBC Sessions	1998	35.00
❏ 113086-1	Blue Wild Angel: Jimi Hendrix Live at the Isle of Wight	2002	40.00
❏ 11600	Electric Ladyland	1997	40.00
—Limited edition on "heavy vinyl" with booklet			
❏ 11671	Experience Hendrix: The Best of Jimi Hendrix	1998	30.00
—Despite lower number, was released after South Saturn Delta			
❏ 11599 [B]	First Rays of the New Rising Sun	1997	60.00
—Limited edition on "heavy vinyl" with booklet			
❏ B0001159-01	Live at Berkeley	2003	30.00
❏ 11931	Live at the Fillmore East	1999	30.00
❏ 11987	Live at Woodstock	1999	40.00
❏ 311987	Live at Woodstock	2009	40.00
❏ 311987	Live at Woodstock	2009	40.00
❏ 112984	Smash Hits	2002	18.00
—Limited edition on "heavy vinyl"			
❏ 11684 [B]	South Saturn Delta	1997	35.00
—Numbered, limited edition on "heavy vinyl"			
❏ 112316	The Jimi Hendrix Experience	2000	100.00
—Limited edition of 5,000 in purple felt box			

EXPERIENCE HENDRIX/UME

| ❏ B0009845-01 | The Jimi Hendrix Experience Live at Monterey | 2007 | 18.00 |

NUTMEG

| ❏ 1002 | Cosmic Turnaround | 1981 | 15.00 |

Number	Title	Yr	NM
❏ 1001	High, Live 'N' Dirty	1978	30.00
—Red vinyl			
❏ 1001	High, Live 'N' Dirty	1978	30.00
—Black vinyl			

PHOENIX 10

| ❏ PHX320 | Rare Hendrix | 1981 | 10.00 |
| ❏ PHX324 | Roots of Hendrix | 1981 | 10.00 |

PICKWICK

| ❏ SPC-3528 | Jimi | 197? | 12.00 |

REPRISE

❏ R6261 [M]	Are You Experienced?	1967	250.00
❏ RS6261 [S]	Are You Experienced?	1967	80.00
—Pink, gold and green label			
❏ RS6261 [S]	Are You Experienced?	1968	30.00
—With "W7" and "r." logos on two-tone orange label			
❏ RS6261 [S]	Are You Experienced?	1970	15.00
—With only "r." logo on all-orange (tan) label			
❏ RS6261 [S]	Are You Experienced?	198?	10.00
—Red and black label or gold and light blue label			
❏ R6281 [M]	Axis: Bold As Love	1968	2500.00
❏ RS6281 [S]	Axis: Bold As Love	1968	80.00
—Pink, gold and green label			
❏ RS6281 [S]	Axis: Bold As Love	1968	30.00
—With "W7" and "r." logos on two-tone orange label			
❏ RS6281 [S]	Axis: Bold As Love	1970	15.00
—With only "r." logo on all-orange (tan) label			
❏ RS6281 [S]	Axis: Bold As Love	198?	10.00
—Red and black label or gold and light blue label			
❏ SKAO-91441	Axis: Bold As Love	1968	40.00
—Capitol Record Club edition; two-tone orange label with "W7" and "r." at top			
❏ MS2204	Crash Landing	1975	18.00
❏ 2R6307 [M]	Electric Ladyland	1968	4000.00
—Mono is promo only; VG value 2000; VG+ value 3000			
❏ 2RS6307 [S]	Electric Ladyland	1968	100.00
—With "W7" and "r." logos on two-tone orange label			
❏ 2RS6307 [S]	Electric Ladyland	1970	18.00
—With only "r." logo on all-orange (tan) label			
❏ 2RS6307 [S]	Electric Ladyland	198?	15.00
—Red and black label or gold and light blue label			
❏ STBO-91568	Electric Ladyland	1968	150.00
—Capitol Record Club edition			
❏ MS2049 [B]	Hendrix in the West	1972	30.00
❏ MS2029	Historic Performances As Recorded at the Monterey International Pop Festival	1970	25.00
—Side 1: Jimi Hendrix; Side 2: Otis Redding; with only "r." logo on all-orange (tan) label			
❏ MS2029	Historic Performances As Recorded at the Monterey International Pop Festival	1970	200.00
—Side 1: Jimi Hendrix; Side 2: Otis Redding; with "W7" and "r." logos on two-tone orange label			
❏ 25358	Jimi Plays Monterey	1986	12.00
❏ 25119	Kiss the Sky	1984	12.00
❏ MS2229	Midnight Lightning	1975	18.00
❏ HS2299	Nine to the Universe	1980	12.00
❏ MS2040	Rainbow Bridge	1971	25.00
❏ SMAS-93972	Rainbow Bridge	1971	50.00
—Capitol Record Club edition			
❏ MS2025	Smash Hits	1969	40.00
—With "W7" and "r." logos on two-tone orange label			
❏ MS2025	Smash Hits	1970	15.00
—With only "r." logo on all-orange (tan) label			
❏ MS2025	Smash Hits	198?	10.00
—Red and black label or gold and light blue label			
❏ MSK2276	Smash Hits	1977	12.00
—Reissue			
❏ MS2025	Smash Hits Bonus Poster	1969	40.00
❏ 2RS6481	Soundtrack Recordings from the Film Jimi Hendrix	1973	30.00
❏ MS2034	The Cry of Love	1971	500.00
—With "W7" and "r." logos on two-tone orange label			
❏ MS2034	The Cry of Love	1971	18.00
—With only "r." logo on all-orange (tan) label			
❏ SMAS-93467	The Cry of Love	1971	60.00
—Capitol Record Club edition			
❏ 2RS2245	The Essential Jimi Hendrix	1978	25.00
❏ HS2293	The Essential Jimi Hendrix Volume Two	1979	18.00
—Add 100% if bonus single of "Gloria" with picture sleeve is enclosed			
❏ 22306	The Jimi Hendrix Concerts	1982	15.00
❏ MS2103	War Heroes	1972	25.00

RHINO

| ❏ RNDF-254 [PD] | The Jimi Hendrix Interview | 1982 | 30.00 |

RYKO ANALOGUE

❏ RALP-0038 [B]	Live at Winterland	1988	60.00
❏ RALP-0078 [B]	Radio One	1988	75.00
—Clear vinyl			

SPRINGBOARD

| ❏ SPB-4010 | Jimi Hendrix | 197? | 12.00 |

TRACK

| ❏ 612003 [M] | Axis: Bold As Love | 2000 | 30.00 |
| —Classic Records issue of the original U.K. mono mix, on a reproduction of the original British label | | | |

TRIP

| ❏ TLP-9512 | Moods | 1973 | 15.00 |

Number	Title	Yr	NM
❑ TLP-9500	Rare Hendrix	1972	18.00
❑ TLP-9501	Roots of Hendrix	1972	15.00
❑ 3509	Superpak	197?	18.00
❑ TLP-9523	The Genius of Jimi Hendrix	1973	15.00

UNITED ARTISTS

❑ UA-LA505-E	The Very Best of Jimi Hendrix	1975	15.00

WARNER BROS.

❑ HS2299	Nine to the Universe	1980	18.00

— *Reprise cover, Warner Bros. tan "pinstripe" label; possibly Columbia House edition?*

HENKE, MEL

CONTEMPORARY

❑ C-5001 [M]	Dig Mel Henke	1955	50.00
❑ C-5003 [M]	Now Spin This	1956	50.00

DOBRE

❑ 1031	Love Touch	197?	15.00

WARNER BROS.

❑ WS1472 [S]	La Dolce Henke	1962	50.00
❑ W1472 [M]	La Dolce Henke	1962	40.00

HENLEY, DON

ASYLUM

❑ E1-60048 [B]	I Can't Stand Still	1982	12.00

GEFFEN

❑ GHS24026	Building the Perfect Beast	1984	12.00
❑ GHS24217	The End of the Innocence	1989	15.00

HENRIQUE, LUIZ

FONTANA

❑ MGF-27553 [M]	Listen to Me	1966	25.00
❑ SRF-67553 [S]	Listen to Me	1966	30.00

VERVE

❑ V-8697 [M]	Barra Limpa	1967	30.00
❑ V6-8697 [S]	Barra Limpa	1967	25.00

HENRY, CLARENCE

ARGO

❑ LP-4009 [M]	You Always Hurt the One You Love	1961	150.00

CADET

❑ LP-4009 [M]	You Always Hurt the One You Love	1966	50.00

— *Includes copies of Cadet LP in Argo sleeves*

ROULETTE

❑ SR42039	Alive and Well and Living in New Orleans	1969	30.00

HENRY, ERNIE

FANTASY

❑ OJC-086	Last Chorus	198?	12.00
❑ OJC-102	Presenting Ernie Henry	198?	15.00
❑ OJC-1722	Seven Standards and a Blues	198?	15.00

RIVERSIDE

❑ RLP 12-266 [M]	Last Chorus	1958	150.00
❑ RLP 12-222 [M]	Presenting Ernie Henry	1956	500.00
❑ 6040	Presenting Ernie Henry	197?	30.00
❑ RLP 12-248 [M]	Seven Standards and a Blues	1957	150.00

HENRY COW

INTERZONE

❑ IZ1001 [B]	Western Culture	1980	30.00

RED

❑ RED003 [B]	In Praise Of Learning	1979	30.00
❑ RED001 [B]	The Henry Cow Legend	1973	40.00
❑ RED002 [B]	Unrest	1979	30.00

HENRY TREE

MAINSTREAM

❑ S-6129	Electric Holy Man	1968	30.00

HENSKE, JUDY, AND JERRY YESTER

REPRISE

❑ RS-6388	Farewell Aldebaran	1969	25.00

STRAIGHT

❑ STS-1052	Farewell Aldebaran	1968	50.00

HENSKE, JUDY

ELEKTRA

❑ EKL-241 [M]	High Flying Bird	1964	25.00
❑ EKL-7241 [S]	High Flying Bird	1964	30.00
❑ EKL-231 [M]	Judy Henske	1963	25.00
❑ EKS-7231 [S]	Judy Henske	1963	30.00

MERCURY

❑ MG-21010 [M]	Little Bit of Sunshine…Little Bit of Rain	1965	25.00
❑ SR-61010 [S]	Little Bit of Sunshine…Little Bit of Rain	1965	30.00

REPRISE

❑ R-6203 [M]	The Death Defying Judy Henske: The First Concert Album	1966	25.00

Number	Title	Yr	NM
❑ RS-6203 [S]	The Death Defying Judy Henske: The First Concert Album	1966	30.00

HENSLEY, WALTER

CAPITOL

❑ T2149 [M]	The Five-String Banjo Today	1964	18.00
❑ ST2149 [S]	The Five-String Banjo Today	1964	25.00

HENSON-CONANT, DEBORAH

GRP

❑ GR-9578	On the Rise	1989	18.00

HERBERT, MORT

SAVOY

❑ MG-12073 [M]	Night People	1956	40.00

HERBIG, GARY

HEADFIRST

❑ A-723	Gary Herbig	198?	12.00

HERD, THE

FONTANA

❑ SRF-67579	Lookin' Thru You	1968	30.00

HERDSMEN, THE

FANTASY

❑ 3201 [M]	The Herdsmen Play Paris	1955	80.00

— *Green vinyl*

❑ 3201 [M]	The Herdsmen Play Paris	1955	40.00

— *Black vinyl*

HERMAN, JERRY

UNITED ARTISTS

❑ UAL-3432 [M]	Hello, Jerry!	1965	25.00
❑ UAS-6432 [S]	Hello, Jerry!	1965	30.00

HERMAN, WOODY

ACCORD

❑ SN-7185	All Star Session	1981	12.00

AMERICAN RECORDING SOCIETY

❑ G-410 [M]	The Progressive Big Band Sound	1956	40.00

ATLANTIC

❑ 1328 [M]	Woody Herman at the Monterey Jazz Festival	1960	40.00
❑ SD1328 [S]	Woody Herman at the Monterey Jazz Festival	1960	30.00
❑ 90044	Woody Herman at the Monterey Jazz Festival	1982	12.00

— *Reissue of 1328*

BRUNSWICK

❑ BL54024 [M]	The Swinging Herman Herd	1957	40.00

BULLDOG

❑ 2005	20 Golden Pieces of Woody Herman	198?	12.00

CADET

❑ LPS-835	Heavy Exposure	1969	15.00
❑ LPS-819	Light My Fire	1969	15.00
❑ LPS-845	Woody	1970	15.00

CAPITOL

❑ T784 [M]	Blues Groove	1956	40.00
❑ H324 [10]	Classics in Jazz	1952	70.00
❑ T324 [M]	Classics in Jazz	1955	40.00
❑ M-11034	Early Autumn	1972	12.00
❑ T748 [M]	Jackpot!	1956	40.00
❑ T658 [M]	Road Band	1955	40.00
❑ T1554 [M]	The Hits of Woody Herman	1961	25.00
❑ DT1554 [R]	The Hits of Woody Herman	1961	15.00
❑ SM-1554	The Hits of Woody Herman	197?	10.00
❑ T560 [M]	The Woody Herman Band	1955	40.00

CENTURY

❑ CR-1110	Chick, Donald, Walter and Woodrow	1978	15.00
❑ CRDD-1080	Road Father	1979	30.00

— *Direct-to-disc recording*

CHESS

❑ 402	Double Exposure	197?	18.00

CLEF

❑ MGC-745 [M]	Jazz, the Utmost!	1956	80.00

COLUMBIA

❑ CL6049 [10]	Dance Parade	1949	70.00
❑ C32530	Jazz Hoot	1974	15.00
❑ CL651 [M]	Music for Tired Lovers	1955	40.00
❑ CL2357 [M]	My Kind of Broadway	1965	15.00
❑ CS9157 [S]	My Kind of Broadway	1965	18.00
❑ CL2509 [10]	Ridin' Herd	1955	60.00
❑ CL6026 [10]	Sequence in Jazz	1949	70.00
❑ CL2552 [M]	The Jazz S(w)inger	1966	15.00
❑ CS9352 [S]	The Jazz S(w)inger	1966	18.00
❑ CL592 [M]	The Three Herds	1955	50.00

— *Maroon label with gold print*

❑ CL592 [M]	The Three Herds	1956	30.00

— *Red and black label with six "eye" logos*

❑ C3L25 [M]	The Thundering Herds	1963	50.00
❑ CL683 [M]	Twelve Shades of Blue	1956	30.00

Number	Title	Yr	NM
❑ CL2563 [10]	Woody!	1955	60.00
❑ CL6092 [10]	Woody Herman and His Woodchoppers	1950	70.00
❑ CL2491 [M]	Woody Herman's Greatest Hits	1966	15.00
❑ CS9291 [S]	Woody Herman's Greatest Hits	1966	18.00
❑ PC9291	Woody Herman's Greatest Hits	1987?	10.00

— *Reissue with new prefix*

❑ CL2693 [M]	Woody Live -- East & West	1967	18.00
❑ CS9493 [S]	Woody Live -- East & West	1967	15.00
❑ CL2436 [M]	Woody's Winners	1965	15.00
❑ CS9236 [S]	Woody's Winners	1965	18.00

CONCORD JAZZ

❑ CJ-302	50th Anniversary Tour	1986	15.00
❑ CJ-191	Live at the Concord Jazz Festival	1982	15.00
❑ CJ-170	Woody Herman and Friends at the Monterey Jazz Festival 1979	198?	15.00
❑ CJ-330	Woody's Gold Star	1987	15.00
❑ CJ-240	World Class	1983	15.00

CORAL

❑ CRL56005 [10]	Blue Prelude	1950	70.00
❑ CRL56010 [10]	Woody Herman Souvenirs	1950	70.00
❑ CRL56090 [10]	Woody's Best	1953	70.00

CROWN

❑ CLP5180 [M]	The New Swingin' Herman Band	1960	25.00
❑ CST205 [S]	The New Swingin' Herman Herd	1960	25.00

DECCA

❑ DL9229 [M]	The Turning Point -- 1943-44	1967	18.00
❑ DL79229 [R]	The Turning Point -- 1943-44	1967	12.00
❑ DL8133 [M]	Woodchopper's Ball	1955	40.00
❑ DL4484 [M]	Woody Herman's Golden Hits	1964	18.00
❑ DL74484 [R]	Woody Herman's Golden Hits	1964	12.00

DIAL

❑ LP-210 [10]	Swinging with the Woodchoppers	1950	150.00

DISCOVERY

❑ 015	The Third Herd	198?	12.00
❑ 845	The Third Herd, Volume 2	198?	12.00

EVEREST

❑ SDBR-1032 [S]	Moody Woody	1958	40.00
❑ LPBR-5032 [M]	Moody Woody	1958	30.00
❑ EV-1222 [M]	The Best of Woody Herman	1963	18.00
❑ EV-5222 [S]	The Best of Woody Herman	1963	25.00
❑ LPBR-5003 [M]	The Herd Rides Again	1958	30.00
❑ SDBR-1003 [S]	The Herd Rides Again… In Stereo	1958	40.00

EVEREST ARCHIVE OF FOLK & JAZZ

❑ 281	Woody Herman	197?	12.00
❑ 316	Woody Herman, Vol. 2	197?	12.00
❑ 338	Woody Herman, Vol. 3	197?	12.00

FANTASY

❑ 8414	Brand New	1971	15.00
❑ F-9477	Children of Lima	1975	15.00
❑ FPM-4003 [Q]	Children of Lima	1975	25.00
❑ F-9609	Feelin' So Blue	1982	12.00
❑ F-9432	Giant Steps	1973	15.00
❑ OJC-344	Giant Steps	198?	12.00

— *Reissue of 9432*

❑ F-9499	King Cobra	1976	15.00
❑ F-9470	The Herd at Montreux	1974	15.00
❑ 9416	The Raven Speaks	1972	15.00
❑ F-9452	The Thundering Herd	1973	15.00

FORUM

❑ F-9016 [M]	Woody Herman Sextet at the Round Table	196?	25.00
❑ FS-9016 [S]	Woody Herman Sextet at the Round Table	196?	30.00

HARMONY

❑ HL7013 [M]	Bijou	1957	25.00
❑ HL7093 [M]	Summer Sequence	1957	25.00

HINDSIGHT

❑ HSR-116	Woody Herman and His Orchestra 1937	198?	12.00
❑ HSR-134	Woody Herman and His Orchestra 1944	198?	12.00

INSIGHT

❑ 208	Woody Herman and His Orchestra 1937-44	198?	12.00

JAZZLAND

❑ JLP-17 [M]	The Fourth Herd	1960	30.00
❑ JLP-917 [S]	The Fourth Herd	1960	30.00

LION

❑ L-70059 [M]	The Herman Herd at Carnegie Hall	1958	30.00

MARS

❑ MRX-1 [10]	Dance Date on Mars	1952	250.00
❑ MRX-2 [10]	Woody Herman Goes Native	1953	250.00

MCA

❑ 219	Golden Favorites	1973	12.00
❑ 4077	The Best of Woody Herman	197?	18.00

METRO

❑ M-514 [M]	Woody Herman	1966	18.00
❑ MS-514 [R]	Woody Herman	1966	12.00

Number	Title	Yr	NM
MGM			
❏ E-284 [10]	Blue Flame	1955	70.00
❏ E-3043 [M]	Carnegie Hall 1946	1953	50.00
— Compiles 158 and 159 on one 12-inch LP			
❏ E-3385 [M]	Hi-Fi-ing Herd	1956	45.00
❏ E-192 [10]	The Third Herd	1953	70.00
❏ E-158 [10]	Woody Herman at Carnegie Hall	1952	70.00
❏ E-159 [10]	Woody Herman at Carnegie Hall, 1946, Vol. 1	1952	70.00
	Woody Herman at Carnegie Hall, 1946, Vol. 2		
MOBILE FIDELITY			
❏ 1-219	The Fourth Herd	1994	30.00
— Audiophile vinyl			
PHILIPS			
❏ PHM200092 [M]	Encore: Woody Herman 1963	1963	18.00
❏ PHS600092 [S]	Encore: Woody Herman 1963	1963	25.00
❏ PHM200004 [M]	Swing Low, Sweet Chariot	1962	18.00
❏ PHS600004 [S]	Swing Low, Sweet Chariot	1962	25.00
❏ PHM200131 [M]	The Swinging Herman Herd Recorded Live	1964	18.00
❏ PHS600131 [S]	The Swinging Herman Herd Recorded Live	1964	25.00
❏ PHM200118 [M]	Woody Herman: 1964	1964	18.00
❏ PHS600118 [S]	Woody Herman: 1964	1964	25.00
❏ PHM200065 [M]	Woody Herman 1963	1963	18.00
❏ PHS600065 [S]	Woody Herman 1963	1963	25.00
❏ PHM200171 [M]	Woody's Big Band Goodies	1965	18.00
❏ PHS600171 [S]	Woody's Big Band Goodies	1965	25.00
PICCADILLY			
❏ 3333	It's Coolin' Time	198?	12.00
PICKWICK			
❏ SPC-3591	Blowin' Up a Storm	1978	12.00
RCA VICTOR			
❏ BGL2-2203	40th Anniversary Carnegie Hall Concert	1977	18.00
ROULETTE			
❏ R25067 [M]	Woody Herman Sextet at the Round Table	1959	30.00
❏ SR25067 [S]	Woody Herman Sextet at the Round Table	1959	40.00
SUNBEAM			
❏ 206	Woody Herman and His Orchestra 1938	198?	12.00
SUNSET			
❏ SUM-1139 [M]	Blowin' Up a Storm	1966	12.00
❏ SUS-5139 [S]	Blowin' Up a Storm	1966	15.00
TIME-LIFE			
❏ STBB-09	Big Bands: Woody Herman	1984	18.00
TRIP			
❏ 5547	Woody 1963	1974	12.00
VERVE			
❏ V6-8764	Concerto for Herd	1968	25.00
❏ MGV-2030 [M]	Early Autumn	1957	40.00
❏ V-2030 [M]	Early Autumn	1963	18.00
❏ V-8558 [M]	Hey! Heard the Herd?	1963	25.00
— Reissue of Verve 8216			
❏ V6-8558 [S]	Hey! Heard the Herd?	1963	18.00
❏ MGV-8014 [M]	Jazz, the Utmost!	1957	40.00
— Reissue of Clef LP			
❏ V-8014 [M]	Jazz, the Utmost!	1963	18.00
❏ MGV-2096 [M]	Love Is the Sweetest Thing -- Sometimes	1958	40.00
❏ V-2096 [M]	Love Is the Sweetest Thing -- Sometimes	1963	18.00
❏ MGV-8216 [M]	Men from Mars	1958	40.00
❏ MGV-2069 [M]	Songs for Hip Lovers	1957	40.00
❏ V-2069 [M]	Songs for Hip Lovers	1963	18.00
❏ VSP-1 [M]	The First Herd at Carnegie Hall	1966	18.00
❏ VSPS-1 [R]	The First Herd at Carnegie Hall	1966	12.00
❏ MGV-8255 [M]	Woody Herman '58	1958	40.00
❏ V-8255 [M]	Woody Herman '58	1963	18.00
❏ VSP-26 [M]	Woody Herman's Woodchoppers & The First Herd Live at Carnegie Hall	1966	18.00
❏ VSPS-26 [R]	Woody Herman's Woodchoppers & The First Herd Live at Carnegie Hall	1966	12.00
WHO'S WHO IN JAZZ			
❏ 21013	Lionel Hampton Presents Woody Herman	1979	15.00
WING			
❏ MGW-12329 [M]	Woody's Big Band Goodies	1966	12.00
❏ SRW-16329 [S]	Woody's Big Band Goodies	1966	15.00

HERMAN, WOODY/TITO PUENTE

Number	Title	Yr	NM
EVEREST			
❏ LPBR-5010 [M]	Herman's Beat of Puente	1958	40.00
❏ SDBR-1010 [S]	Herman's Beat of Puente	1958	40.00

HERMAN'S HERMITS

Number	Title	Yr	NM
ABKCO			
❏ 4227-1	Their Greatest Hits	1988	10.00
— Abridged version of AB 4227			
❏ AB-4227	XX (Greatest Hits)	1973	15.00
MGM			
❏ E-4478 [M]	Blaze	1967	30.00
❏ SE-4478 [S]	Blaze	1967	12.00

Number	Title	Yr	NM
❏ T-91286 [M]	Blaze	1967	30.00
— Capitol Record Club edition			
❏ ST-91286 [S]	Blaze	1967	25.00
— Capitol Record Club edition			

Number	Title	Yr	NM
❏ E-4386 [M]	Both Sides of Herman's Hermits	1966	12.00
❏ SE-4386 [R]	Both Sides of Herman's Hermits	1966	10.00
❏ E-4295 [M]	Herman's Hermits On Tour	1965	15.00
❏ SE-4295 [R]	Herman's Hermits On Tour	1965	12.00
❏ ST-90421 [R]	Herman's Hermits On Tour	1965	25.00
— Capitol Record Club edition			
❏ T-90421 [M]	Herman's Hermits On Tour	1965	30.00
— Capitol Record Club edition			
❏ E-4342 [M]	Hold On!	1966	18.00
❏ SE-4342 [P]	Hold On!	1966	15.00
❏ T-90646 [M]	Hold On!	1966	30.00
— Capitol Record Club edition			
❏ ST-90646 [R]	Hold On!	1966	25.00
— Capitol Record Club edition			
❏ E-4282 [M]	Introducing Herman's Hermits	1965	30.00
— Version 1: With "Including Their Hit Single 'I'm Into Something Good' " on front cover			
❏ SE-4282 [R]	Introducing Herman's Hermits	1965	25.00
— Version 1: With "Including Their Hit Single 'I'm Into Something Good' " on front cover			
❏ E-4282 [M]	Introducing Herman's Hermits	1965	25.00
— Version 2: Same as above, but with a sticker that says "Featuring "Mrs. Brown You Have a Lovely Daughter".			
❏ SE-4282 [R]	Introducing Herman's Hermits	1965	18.00
— Version 2: Same as above, but with a sticker that says "Featuring "Mrs. Brown You Have a Lovely Daughter".			
❏ E-4282 [M]	Introducing Herman's Hermits	1965	18.00
— Version 3: With "Including 'Mrs. Brown You've Got a Lovely Daughter' " on front cover			
❏ SE-4282 [R]	Introducing Herman's Hermits	1965	12.00
— Version 3: With "Including 'Mrs. Brown You've Got a Lovely Daughter' " on front cover			
❏ T-90416 [M]	Introducing Herman's Hermits	1965	30.00
— Capitol Record Club edition			
❏ ST-90416 [R]	Introducing Herman's Hermits	1965	25.00
— Capitol Record Club edition			
❏ SE-4548 [P]	Mrs. Brown You've Got a Lovely Daughter	1968	12.00
— "Mrs. Brown You've Got a Lovely Daughter" and "There's a Kind of Hush" are rechanneled			
❏ E-4315 [M]	The Best of Herman's Hermits	1965	15.00
❏ SE-4315 [R]	The Best of Herman's Hermits	1965	12.00
❏ KAO-90613 [M]	The Best of Herman's Hermits	1966	18.00
— Capitol Record Club edition			
❏ E-4416 [M]	The Best of Herman's Hermits, Volume 2	1966	15.00
— Add 50% if bonus photo of Herman is included			
❏ SE-4416 [P]	The Best of Herman's Hermits, Volume 2	1966	12.00
— Add 50% if bonus photo of Herman is included. "Hold On" and "Leaning on the Lamp Post" are in true stereo.			
❏ E-4505 [M]	The Best of Herman's Hermits, Volume 3	1967	15.00
❏ SE-4505 [P]	The Best of Herman's Hermits, Volume 3	1967	12.00
— Don't Go Out Into the Rain," "Museum," "Last Bus Home" and "Mum and Dad" are in true stereo.			
❏ E-4438 [M]	There's a Kind of Hush All Over the World	1967	25.00
❏ SE-4438 [R]	There's a Kind of Hush All Over the World	1967	10.00

Number	Title	Yr	NM
### HERMETO			
MUSE			
❏ MR-5086	Hermeto	197?	15.00
WARNER BROS.			
❏ BS2980	Slaves Mass	1976	18.00
### HERNANDEZ, PATRICK			
COLUMBIA			
❏ JC36100	Born to Be Alive	1979	15.00
### HERON, MIKE			
ELEKTRA			
❏ EKS-74093 [B]	Smiling Men with Bad Reputations	1971	30.00
### HERRICK, CHRISTOPHER			
MUSICAL HERITAGE SOCIETY			
❏ MHS7005	Christmas Organ Music from Westminster Abbey	1984	12.00
— Recorded in 1979			
### HERRMANN, BERNARD			
MOBILE FIDELITY			
❏ 1-240	The Fantasy Film World of Bernard Herrmann	1996	30.00
— Audiophile vinyl			
❏ 1-255	The Four Faces of Jazz	1996	30.00
— Audiophile vinyl			
### HERSCH, FRED			
CHESKY			
❏ 90	Dancing in the Dark	1993	25.00
CONCORD JAZZ			
❏ CJ-267	Horizons	1985	12.00
### HESITATIONS, THE			
KAPP			
❏ KS-3574	Solid Gold	1969	30.00
❏ KL-1525 [M]	Soul Superman	1967	30.00
❏ KS-3525 [S]	Soul Superman	1967	30.00
❏ KS-3548	The New Born Free	1968	30.00
❏ KS-3561	Where We're At	1968	30.00
### HESS, CHUCK			
STRAND			
❏ SL-1084 [M]	Country & Western Favorites	1960	25.00
❏ SLS-1084 [S]	Country & Western Favorites	1960	30.00
### HESTER, CAROLYN			
COLUMBIA			
❏ CL1796 [M]	Carolyn Hester	1962	80.00
— With Bob Dylan on harmonica on three tracks; black and red label with six "eye" logos			
❏ CC8506 [S]	Carolyn Hester	1962	80.00
— With Bob Dylan on harmonica on three tracks; black and red label with six "eye" logos			
❏ CL1796 [M]	Carolyn Hester	1963	60.00
— Red label with "Guaranteed High Fidelity"			
❏ CS8596 [S]	Carolyn Hester	1963	50.00
— Red label, "360 Sound Stereo" in black			
❏ CL2032 [M]	This Life I'm Living	1963	40.00
❏ CS8832 [S]	This Life I'm Living	1963	50.00
CORAL			
❏ CRL57143 [M]	Scarlet Ribbons	1957	50.00
DOT			
❏ DLP-3638 [M]	Carolyn Hester at Town Hall One	1965	18.00
❏ DLP-25638 [S]	Carolyn Hester at Town Hall One	1965	25.00
❏ DLP-3649 [M]	Carolyn Hester at Town Hall Two	1965	18.00
❏ DLP-25649 [S]	Carolyn Hester at Town Hall Two	1965	25.00
❏ DLP-3604 [M]	That's My Song	1964	18.00
❏ DLP-25604 [S]	That's My Song	1964	25.00
FOLK ODYSSEY			
❏ 32160264	Simply Carolyn Hester	196?	25.00
METROMEDIA			
❏ MD-1022	Magazine	1970	60.00
❏ MD-1001	The Carolyn Hester Coalition	1969	25.00
RCA VICTOR			
❏ APD1-0086 [Q]	Carolyn Hester	1973	25.00
— Only released in quadraphonic			
TRADITION			
❏ TLP-1043 [M]	Carolyn Hester	1961	40.00
### HEYWARD, NICK			
ARISTA			
❏ AL8-8106	North of a Miracle	1983	12.00
REPRISE			
❏ 25758	I Love You Avenue	1988	12.00

Number	Title	Yr	NM
☐ PRO-A-3384 [DJ]	Words and Music	1988	25.00
—Promo-only interview record			

HEYWOOD, EDDIE

BRUNSWICK
☐ BL58036 [10]	Eddie Heywood '45	1953	50.00

CAPITOL
☐ ST-163	Soft Summer Breeze	1969	15.00
☐ ST2833	With Love and Strings	1968	15.00

COLUMBIA
☐ CL6157 [10]	Piano Moods	1951	50.00

COMMODORE
☐ FL-20007 [10]	Eight Selections	1950	75.00
☐ XFL-15876	The Biggest Little Band of the Forties	198?	15.00

CORAL
☐ CRL57095 [M]	Featuring Eddie Heywood	1957	40.00

DECCA
☐ DL8202 [M]	Lightly and Politely	1956	30.00
☐ DL8270 [M]	Swing Low Sweet Heywood	1956	30.00

EMARCY
☐ MG-36042 [M]	Eddie Heywood	1955	40.00

EPIC
☐ LN3327 [M]	Eddie Heywood at Twilight	1956	30.00

LIBERTY
☐ LRP-3313 [M]	Canadian Sunset Bossa Nova	1963	15.00
☐ LST-7313 [S]	Canadian Sunset Bossa Nova	1963	18.00
☐ LRP-3250 [M]	Eddie Heywood's Golden Encores	1962	15.00
☐ LST-7250 [S]	Eddie Heywood's Golden Encores	1962	18.00
☐ LST-7279 [S]	Manhattan Beat	1963	18.00
☐ LRP-3279 [M]	Manhattan Beat	1963	15.00

MAINSTREAM
☐ S-6001 [S]	Begin the Beguine	1964	18.00
☐ 96001 [M]	Begin the Beguine	1964	15.00

MERCURY
☐ MG-20445 [M]	Broozin' Along with the Breeze	1959	25.00
☐ SR-60115 [S]	Breezin' Along with the Breeze	1959	30.00
☐ MG-20590 [M]	Eddie Heywood at the Piano	1960	25.00
☐ SR-60248 [S]	Eddie Heywood at the Piano	1960	30.00
☐ MG-20632 [M]	One for My Baby	1960	25.00
☐ SR-60632 [S]	One for My Baby	1960	30.00

MGM
☐ E-3260 [M]	Eddie Heywood	1956	40.00
☐ E-135 [10]	It's Easy to Remember	1952	50.00
☐ E-3093 [M]	Pianorama	1955	40.00

RCA VICTOR
☐ LPM-1529 [M]	Canadian Sunset	1957	30.00
☐ LSP-1529 [S]	Canadian Sunset	1958	40.00
☐ LPM-1900 [M]	The Keys and I	1958	30.00
☐ LPM-1466 [M]	The Touch of Eddie Heywood	1957	30.00

SUNSET
☐ SUM-1121 [M]	An Affair to Remember	196?	15.00
☐ SUS-5121 [S]	An Affair to Remember	196?	15.00

VOCALION
☐ VL3748 [M]	The Piano Stylings of Eddie Heywood	1966	18.00
☐ VL73748 [R]	The Piano Stylings of Eddie Heywood	1966	15.00

WING
☐ MGW-12287 [M]	Breezin' Along	196?	18.00
☐ SRW-16287 [S]	Breezin' Along	196?	15.00
☐ MGW-12137 [M]	Eddie Heywood	196?	18.00
☐ SRW-16137 [S]	Eddie Heywood	196?	15.00

HI-LITES, THE (2)

DANDEE
☐ DLP-206 [M]	For Your Precious Love	1961	2000.00

HI-LO'S, THE

COLUMBIA
☐ CL1509 [M]	All Over the Place	1960	30.00
☐ CS8300 [S]	All Over the Place	1960	30.00
☐ CL1416 [M]	Broadway Playbill	1959	30.00
☐ CS8213 [S]	Broadway Playbill	1959	40.00
☐ CS8057 [S]	Love Nest	1958	40.00
☐ CL1023 [M]	Now Hear This	1957	30.00
☐ CL952 [M]	Suddenly It's the Hi-Lo's	1957	30.00
☐ CL1259 [M]	The Hi-Lo's and All That Jazz	1958	30.00
☐ CS8077 [S]	The Hi-Lo's and All That Jazz	1958	40.00
☐ CL1723 [M]	This Time It's Love	1962	30.00
☐ CS8523 [S]	This Time It's Love	1962	30.00

COLUMBIA SPECIAL PRODUCTS
☐ P14387	Harmony in Jazz	1978	15.00

DRG
☐ SL5184	Clap Yo' Hands	198?	15.00

KAPP
☐ KL1194 [M]	On Hand	1960	30.00
—Reissue of Starlite 7008			

☐ KL1027 [M]	The Hi-Lo's and the Jerry Fielding Band	1956	30.00
☐ KL1184 [M]	Under Glass	1959	30.00
—Reissue of Starlite 7005			

MCA
☐ 4171	The Hi-Lo's Collection	197?	18.00

OMEGA
☐ OSL-11 [S]	The Hi-Lo's in Stereo	195?	30.00

PAUSA
☐ 7040	Back Again	198?	15.00
☐ 7093	Now	198?	15.00

REPRISE
☐ R-6066 [M]	The Hi-Lo's Happen to Bossa Nova	1963	25.00
☐ R9-6066 [S]	The Hi-Lo's Happen to Bossa Nova	1963	30.00

STARLITE
☐ 6004 [10]	Listen!	1955	60.00
☐ 7006 [M]	Listen!	1956	40.00
—Reissue of 6004			
☐ 7008 [M]	On Hand	1956	40.00
☐ 6005 [10]	The Hi-Lo's, I Presume	1955	60.00
☐ 7007 [M]	The Hi-Lo's. I Presume	1956	40.00
—Reissue of 6005			
☐ 7005 [M]	Under Glass	1956	40.00

HI-TONES, THE

HI
☐ HL-31011 [M]	Raunchy Sounds	1963	25.00
☐ SHL-32011 [S]	Raunchy Sounds	1963	30.00

L&M
☐ 223	I'm So Sorry	196?	200.00

HIATT, JOHN

A&M
☐ SP-5158	Bring the Family	1987	12.00
☐ SP-5206	Slow Turning	1988	12.00
☐ 7502153101	Stolen Moments	1990	15.00

EPIC
☐ KF32688	Hangin' Around the Observatory	1974	12.00
☐ KE33190	Overcoats	1975	12.00
☐ PE33190	Overcoats	198?	10.00
—Budget-line reissue			

GEFFEN
☐ GHS2009	All of a Sudden	1982	12.00
☐ GHS4017	Riding with the King	1983	12.00
☐ GHS24055	Warming Up to the Ice Age	1984	12.00

MCA
☐ 3088	Slug Line	1979	15.00
☐ 747	Slug Line	198?	10.00
—Reissue			
☐ 5123	Two-Bit Monster	1980	15.00
☐ 741	Two-Bit Monster	198?	10.00
—Reissue			

MOBILE FIDELITY
☐ 1-210	Bring the Family	1994	50.00
—Audiophile vinyl			

HIBBLER, AL

ARGO
☐ LP-601 [M]	Melodies by Al Hibbler	1956	40.00
—Reissue of Marterry LP			

ATLANTIC
☐ 1251 [M]	After the Lights Go Down Low	1957	50.00
—Black label			
☐ 1251 [M]	After the Lights Go Down Low	1961	30.00
—Mostly red label, white fan logo			
☐ 1251 [M]	After the Lights Go Down Low	1963	25.00
—Mostly red label, black fan logo			

BRUNSWICK
☐ BL54036 [M]	Al Hibbler with the Ellingtonians	1957	50.00

DECCA
☐ DL8862 [M]	Al Hibbler Remembers the Big Songs of the Big Bands	1959	30.00
☐ DL78862 [S]	Al Hibbler Remembers the Big Songs of the Big Bands	1959	40.00
☐ DL8420 [M]	Here's Hibbler	1957	30.00
☐ DL8757 [M]	Hits by Hibbler	1958	30.00
☐ DL8328 [M]	Starring Al Hibbler	1956	30.00
☐ DL8697 [M]	Torchy and Blue	1958	30.00

DISCOVERY
☐ 842	It's Monday Every Day	198?	15.00
—Reissue of Reprise LP			

LMI
☐ 10001 [M]	Early One Morning	1964	30.00

MARTERRY
☐ LP-601 [M]	Melodies by Al Hibbler	1956	100.00

MCA
☐ 4098	The Best of Al Hibbler	197?	18.00

NORGRAN
☐ MGN-4 [10]	Al Hibbler Favorites	1954	150.00
☐ MGN-15 [10]	Al Hibbler Sings Duke Ellington	1954	150.00

OPEN SKY
☐ OSR-3126	For Sentimental Reasons	1986	15.00

REPRISE
☐ R-2005 [M]	It's Monday Every Day	1961	30.00
☐ R9-2005 [S]	It's Monday Every Day	1961	40.00

SCORE
☐ SLP-4013 [M]	I Surrender, Dear	1957	100.00

VERVE
☐ MGV-4000 [M]	Al Hibbler Sings Love Songs	1956	60.00
☐ V-4000 [M]	Al Hibbler Sings Love Songs	1961	25.00

HICKEY, ERSEL

BACK-TRAC
☐ P18750	The Rockin' Bluebird	1985	60.00
—Allegedly, only 200 copies of this were pressed			

HICKMAN, DWAYNE

CAPITOL
☐ T1441 [M]	Dobie!	1960	40.00
☐ ST1441 [S]	Dobie!	1960	50.00

HICKS, DAN, AND HIS HOT LICKS

BLUE THUMB
☐ BTS-51	Last Train to Hicksville…The Home of Happy Feet	1973	15.00
☐ BTS-36	Striking It Rich!	1972	15.00
☐ BTS-29	Where's the Money?	1971	15.00

EPIC
☐ BN26464	Original Recordings	1969	18.00
—Yellow label			
☐ BN26464	Original Recordings	1973	12.00
—Orange label			
☐ PE26464	Original Recordings	198?	10.00
—Reissue with new prefix			

MCA
☐ 671	Last Train to Hicksville…The Home of Happy Feet	198?	10.00
—Reissue			
☐ 670	Striking It Rich!	198?	10.00
—Reissue			

WARNER BROS.
☐ BSK3158	It Happened One Bite	1978	12.00

HICKS, JOHN

STRATA-EAST
☐ SES-8002	Hells Bells	1979	18.00

THERESA
☐ TR-119	John Hicks	1986	15.00
☐ TR-123	John Hicks In Concert	1987	15.00
☐ TR-115	Some Other Time	1983	15.00

WEST 54TH
☐ 8004	After the Morning	1980	15.00

HIGGINS, CHUCK

COMBO
☐ LP-300 [M]	Pachuko Hop	195?	800.00
—Naked woman" cover (well, she's wearing a scarf)			
☐ LP-300 [M]	Pachuko Hop	195?	40.00
—Chuck Higgins on cover, fully clothed			

HIGGINS, EDDIE

ATLANTIC
☐ 1446 [M]	Soulero	1966	18.00
☐ SD1446 [S]	Soulero	1966	25.00

VEE JAY
☐ LP-3017 [M]	Eddie Higgins	1961	30.00
☐ SR-3017 [S]	Eddie Higgins	1961	40.00

HIGH TIDE

LIBERTY
☐ LST-7638 [B]	Sea Shanties	1969	80.00

HIGH TREASON

ABBOTT
☐ ABS-1209 [B]	High Treason	1968	80.00

HIGHER PRIMATES

GM
☐ 3003	Environmental Impressions	1985	12.00

HIGHFILL, GEORGE

WARNER BROS.
☐ 25618	Waitin' Up	1987	15.00

HIGHTOWER, DEAN

ABC-PARAMOUNT
☐ ABC-312 [M]	Twangy Guitar with a Beat	1959	30.00
☐ ABCS-312 [S]	Twangy Guitar with a Beat	1959	30.00

Number	Title	Yr	NM

HIGHTOWER, DONNA

CAPITOL
❏ T1273 [M]	Gee Baby…Ain't I Good to You	1959	40.00
❏ ST1273 [S]	Gee Baby…Ain't I Good to You	1959	50.00
❏ T1133 [M]	Take One	1959	40.00
❏ ST1133 [S]	Take One	1959	50.00

HIGHTOWER, WILLIE

CAPITOL
| ❏ ST-367 | If I Had a Hammer | 1969 | 100.00 |

COLLECTABLES
| ❏ COL-5170 | Golden Classics | 198? | 12.00 |

HIGHWAY 101

WARNER BROS.
| ❏ 25742 | 101 (2) | 1988 | 10.00 |
| ❏ 1P8076 | Greatest Hits | 1990 | 18.00 |
— *Columbia House edition (no regular vinyl version)*
| ❏ R183480 | Greatest Hits | 1990 | 25.00 |
— *BMG Direct Marketing edition (no regular vinyl version)*
| ❏ 25608 | Highway 101 | 1987 | 10.00 |
| ❏ 25992 | Paint the Town | 1989 | 12.00 |

HIGHWAYMEN, THE

ABC-PARAMOUNT
| ❏ 522 [M] | On a New Road | 1965 | 12.00 |
| ❏ S-522 [S] | On a New Road | 1965 | 15.00 |

UNITED ARTISTS

❏ UAL3225 [M]	Encore!	1962	15.00
❏ UAS6225 [S]	Encore!	1962	18.00
❏ UAL3348 [M]	Homecoming	1964	15.00
❏ UAS6348 [S]	Homecoming	1964	10.00
❏ UAL3294 [M]	Hootenanny with the Highwaymen	1963	15.00
❏ UAS6294 [S]	Hootenanny with the Highwaymen	1963	18.00
❏ UAL3245 [M]	March On, Brothers	1963	15.00
❏ UAS6245 [S]	March On, Brothers	1963	18.00
❏ UAL3323 [M]	One More Time	1964	12.00
❏ UAS6323 [S]	One More Time	1964	18.00
❏ UAL3168 [M]	Standing Room Only!	1962	15.00
❏ UAS6168 [S]	Standing Room Only!	1962	18.00
❏ UAL3125 [M]	The Highwaymen	1961	12.00
❏ UAS6125 [S]	The Highwaymen	1961	18.00

HILDEBRAND, RAY

WORD
| ❏ WST-8411 | He's Everything to Me | 196? | 15.00 |
| ❏ WST-8465 | I Need You Every Hour | 1971 | 15.00 |

HILDEGARDE

DECCA
| ❏ DL8656 [M] | Souvenir Album | 1958 | 30.00 |
— *Black label, silver print*

HILDINGER, DAVE

BATON
| ❏ 1204 [M] | The Young Moderns | 1957 | 40.00 |

HILL, ANDREW

ARISTA FREEDOM
| ❏ AL1023 | Montreux | 1976 | 18.00 |
| ❏ AL1007 | Spiral | 1975 | 18.00 |

ARTISTS HOUSE
| ❏ 9 | From California with Love | 1979 | 15.00 |
| ❏ BST-84203 [S] | Andrew!!! -- The Music of Andrew Hill | 1967 | 75.00 |
— *With "A Division of Liberty Records" on label; version with "New York, USA" on label not known to exist*
| ❏ BLP-4151 [M] | Black Fire | 1963 | 300.00 |
| ❏ BST-84151 [S] | Black Fire | 1963 | 100.00 |

— *With "New York, USA" address on label*
| ❏ BST-84151 [S] | Black Fire | 1967 | 18.00 |
— *With "A Division of Liberty Records" on label*
| ❏ BLP-4217 [M] | Compulsion | 1965 | 30.00 |
| ❏ BST-84217 [S] | Compulsion | 1965 | 30.00 |
— *With "New York, USA" address on label*
| ❏ BST-84217 [S] | Compulsion | 1967 | 18.00 |
— *With "A Division of Liberty Records" on label*
❏ LN-1030	Dance with Andrew Hill	1980	15.00
❏ BST-84303	Grass Roots	1968	25.00
❏ B1-92051	Internal Spirit	198?	12.00
❏ BLP-4159 [M]	Judgment!	1964	100.00
❏ BST-84159 [S]	Judgment!	1964	40.00
— *With "New York, USA" address on label*
| ❏ BST-84159 [S] | Judgment! | 1967 | 18.00 |
— *With "A Division of Liberty Records" on label*
❏ B1-28981	Judgment!	1994	18.00
❏ BST-84330	Lift Every Voice	1969	25.00
❏ BN-LA459-H2	One for One	1975	25.00
❏ BLP-4167 [M]	Point of Departure	1964	30.00
❏ BST-84167 [S]	Point of Departure	1964	40.00
— *With "New York, USA" address on label*
| ❏ BST-84167 [S] | Point of Departure | 1967 | 18.00 |
— *With "A Division of Liberty Records" on label*
❏ B1-32097	Smokestack	1995	18.00
❏ BLP-4160 [M]	Smoke Stack	1964	100.00
❏ BST-84160 [S]	Smoke Stack	1964	40.00
— *With "New York, USA" address on label*
| ❏ BST-84160 [S] | Smoke Stack | 1967 | 18.00 |
— *With "A Division of Liberty Records" on label*

INNER CITY
❏ IC-2044	Divine Revelation	1976	18.00
❏ IC-2026	Invitation	1975	18.00
❏ IC-6022	Nefertiti	1977	18.00

MOSAIC
| ❏ MQ10-161 [B] | The Complete Andrew Hill Blue Note Sessions | 199? | 400.00 |

SOUL NOTE
❏ SN-1010	Faces of Hope	198?	15.00
❏ 121113	Shades	199?	15.00
❏ SN-1013	Strange Serenade	198?	15.00
❏ 121110	Verona Rag	199?	15.00

STEEPLECHASE
| ❏ SCS-1044 | Divine Revelation | 198? | 15.00 |
| ❏ SCS-1026 | Invitation | 198? | 15.00 |

WARWICK
| ❏ W-2002 [M] | So in Love | 1960 | 60.00 |
| ❏ W-2002ST [S] | So in Love | 1960 | 80.00 |

HILL, BENNY

CAPITOL
| ❏ SN-12049 | Words and Music | 1979 | 18.00 |

HILL, GOLDIE

DECCA
❏ DL4219 [M]	According to My Heart	1962	25.00
❏ DL74219 [S]	According to My Heart	1962	30.00
❏ DL4492 [M]	Country Hit Parade	1964	25.00
❏ DL74492 [S]	Country Hit Parade	1964	30.00
❏ DL4034 [M]	Goldie Hill	1960	30.00
❏ DL74034 [S]	Goldie Hill	1960	30.00
❏ DL4148 [M]	Lonely Heartaches	1961	25.00
❏ DL74148 [S]	Lonely Heartaches	1961	30.00

VOCALION
| ❏ VL73800 | Country Songs | 196? | 15.00 |

HILL, LAURYN

RUFFHOUSE
| ❏ C269035 | The Miseducation of Lauryn Hill | 1998 | 18.00 |

HILL, TINY

HINDSIGHT
| ❏ HSR-159 | The Uncollected Tiny Hill and His Orchestra, 1944 | 1980 | 12.00 |

MERCURY
❏ MG-20630 [M]	Dancin' and Singin' with Tiny Hill	195?	30.00
❏ MG-20631 [M]	Golden Hits	195?	30.00
❏ SR-60631 [R]	Golden Hits	196?	18.00
❏ MG-25126 [10]	Tiny Hill	1952	50.00

HILL, VINCE

TOWER
| ❏ T5064 [M] | At the Club | 1966 | 30.00 |

HILL, VINSON

SAVOY
| ❏ MG-12187 [M] | The Vinson Hill Trio | 1966 | 30.00 |

HILL, Z.Z.

COLUMBIA
| ❏ JC35030 | Let's Make a Deal | 1978 | 15.00 |
| ❏ JC36125 | The Mark of Z.Z. | 1979 | 15.00 |

KENT
| ❏ KST-528 | A Whole Lot of Soul | 1969 | 18.00 |
| ❏ KST-560 | Dues Paid in Full | 1971 | 18.00 |

MALACO
| ❏ 7415 | I'm a Blues Man | 1984 | 12.00 |
| ❏ 7411 | The Rhyhtm & The Blues | 1983 | 12.00 |

MANKIND
| ❏ 201 | The Brand New Z.Z. Hill | 1971 | 18.00 |

UNITED ARTISTS
| ❏ UA-LA417-G | Keep On Lovin' You | 1975 | 15.00 |
| ❏ UAS5589 | The Best Thing That's Ever Happened to Me | 1972 | 15.00 |

HILLAGE, STEVE

ATLANTIC
| ❏ SD18205 [B] | L | 1976 | 18.00 |
| ❏ SD19144 [B] | Motivation Radio | 1977 | 18.00 |

VIRGIN
| ❏ VR13-118 [B] | Fish Rising | 1975 | 25.00 |

HILLMAN, CHRIS

ASYLUM
| ❏ 7E-1104 | Clear Sailin' | 1977 | 15.00 |
| ❏ 7E-1062 | Slippin' Away | 1976 | 15.00 |

SUGAR HILL
| ❏ SH3743 | Desert Rose | 1984 | 15.00 |
| ❏ SH3729 | Morning Sky | 1982 | 15.00 |

HILLMEN, THE

TOGETHER
| ❏ STT-1012 | The Hillmen | 1970 | 80.00 |

HILLOW HAMMET

HOUSE OF FOX
| ❏ 2 | Hammer | 1968 | 150.00 |

HILLSIDE SINGERS, THE

METROMEDIA
| ❏ MD1051 | I'd Like to Teach the World to Sing | 1971 | 15.00 |

HILLTOPPERS, THE

DOT
❏ DLP-3073 [M]	Love in Bloom	1958	30.00
❏ DLP-105 [10]	The Hilltoppers	1954	60.00
❏ DLP-106 [10]	The Hilltoppers	1954	60.00
❏ DLP-3003 [M]	The Hilltoppers Present Tops in Pops	1955	50.00
— *Cartoon of female fan on cover*
| ❏ DLP-3003 [M] | The Hilltoppers Present Tops in Pops | 1956 | 30.00 |
— *Four caps with "W" on them on cover*
| ❏ DLP-3029 [M] | The Towering Hilltoppers | 1957 | 30.00 |

HINES, EARL "FATHA," AND COLEMAN HAWKINS

LIMELIGHT
| ❏ LM-82020 [M] | The Grand Reunion | 1965 | 25.00 |
| ❏ LS-86020 [S] | The Grand Reunion | 1965 | 30.00 |

TRIP
| ❏ 5557 | The Grand Reunion | 197? | 12.00 |

HINES, EARL "FATHA," AND JAKI BYARD

VERVE/MPS
| ❏ 825195-1 | Duet | 1985 | 12.00 |

HINES, EARL "FATHA," AND MARVA JOSIE

CATALYST
| ❏ 7622 | His Old Lady and Me | 197? | 15.00 |

HINES, EARL "FATHA," AND MAXINE SULLIVAN

CHIAROSCURO
| ❏ 107 | Live at the Overseas Press Club | 1971 | 18.00 |

HINES, EARL "FATHA," AND PAUL GONSALVES

BLACK LION
| ❏ 306 | It Don't Mean a Thing | 197? | 15.00 |

HINES, EARL "FATHA," AND ROY ELDRIDGE

LIMELIGHT
| ❏ LM-82028 [M] | The Grand Reunion, Volume 2 | 1965 | 25.00 |
| ❏ LS-86028 [S] | The Grand Reunion, Volume 2 | 1965 | 30.00 |

XANADU
| ❏ 106 | At the Village Vanguard | 197? | 15.00 |

HINES, EARL "FATHA," AND TERESA BREWER

DOCTOR JAZZ
| ❏ FW38810 | We Love You Fats | 1983 | 12.00 |

HINES, EARL "FATHA

ABC IMPULSE!
| ❏ AS-9108 [S] | Once Upon a Time | 1968 | 18.00 |

ADVANCE
| ❏ 4 [10] | Fats Waller Memorial Set | 1951 | 150.00 |

Number	Title	Yr	NM
ATLANTIC			
❏ ALS-120 [10]	Earl Hines: QRS Solos	1952	200.00
AUDIOPHILE			
❏ APS-112	Earl Hines Comes In Handy	197?	18.00
❏ APS-113	Hines Does Hoagy	197?	18.00
❏ APS-111	My Tribute to Louis	1971	18.00
BASF			
❏ 20749	Fatha and His Flock On Tour	1972	18.00
BIOGRAPH			
❏ 12056	Earl Hines in New Orleans	197?	12.00
❏ 12055	Solo Walk in Tokyo	197?	12.00
BLACK LION			
❏ 112	Tea for Two	1973	15.00
❏ 200	Tour de Force	1974	15.00
BLUEBIRD			
❏ AXM2-5508	Fatha Jumps	197?	18.00
BRAVO			
❏ K-134	Earl Fatha Hines and His Orchestra	196?	12.00
BRUNSWICK			
❏ BL58035 [10]	Earl Hines Plays Fats Waller	1953	120.00
CAPITOL			
❏ T1971 [M]	Earl "Fatha" Hines	1963	30.00
❏ ST1971 [S]	Earl "Fatha" Hines	1963	30.00
CHIAROSCURO			
❏ 116	An Evening with Hines	1972	25.00
❏ 200	Earl Hines in New Orleans	1978	15.00
❏ 157	Live at the New School	1974	15.00
❏ 180	Live at the New School, Volume 2	1977	15.00
❏ 131	Quintessential 1974	1974	18.00
❏ 120	Quintessential Continued	1973	18.00
❏ 101	Quintessential Recording Session	1971	18.00
—Reissue of Halcyon 101			
CLASSIC JAZZ			
❏ 144	Earl Hines at Sundown	198?	15.00
❏ 31	Earl Hines Plays Gershwin	1974	18.00
COLUMBIA			
❏ CL6171 [10]	Piano Moods	1951	120.00
❏ CL2320 [M]	The New Earl Hines Trio	1965	25.00
❏ CS9120 [S]	The New Earl Hines Trio	1965	30.00
COLUMBIA JAZZ MASTERPIECES			
❏ CJ44197	Live at the Village Vanguard	1988	12.00
CONTACT			
❏ 2 [M]	Spontaneous Explorations	1964	30.00
❏ S-2 [S]	Spontaneous Explorations	1964	30.00
CRAFTSMEN			
❏ 8041 [M]	Swingin' and Singin'	1960	30.00
DECCA			
❏ DL79235 [R]	Earl Hines at the Apex Club	1968	15.00
❏ DL9235 [M]	Earl Hines at the Apex Club	1968	30.00
❏ DL75048	Fatha Blows Best	1969	18.00
❏ DL9221 [M]	Southside Swing (1934-35)	1967	30.00
❏ DL79221 [R]	Southside Swing (1934-35)	1967	15.00
DELMARK			
❏ DS-212	Earl Hines At Home	1969	15.00
DIAL			
❏ LP-306 [10]	Earl Hines All Stars	1953	250.00
❏ LP-303 [10]	Earl Hines Trio	1952	250.00
ENSIGN			
❏ 22021	Earl Hines Rhythm	1969	25.00
EPIC			
❏ LN3501 [M]	Earl "Fatha" Hines	1958	50.00
❏ LN3223 [M]	Oh, Fatha!	1956	50.00
EVEREST ARCHIVE OF FOLK & JAZZ			
❏ 246	Earl "Fatha" Hines	1970	15.00
❏ 322	Earl "Fatha" Hines, Volume 2	197?	12.00
FANTASY			
❏ OJC-1740	A Monday Date	198?	12.00
❏ 3238 [M]	Earl "Fatha" Hines Solo	1956	100.00
—Red vinyl			
❏ 3238 [M]	Earl "Fatha" Hines Solo	195?	50.00
—Black vinyl			
❏ 3217 [M]	Fatha" Plays "Fats	1956	100.00
—Red vinyl			
❏ 3217 [M]	Fatha" Plays "Fats	195?	50.00
—Black vinyl			
❏ 8381	Incomparable	1968	15.00
FLYING DUTCHMAN			
❏ FD-10147	The Mighty Fatha	1973	18.00
FOCUS			
❏ FM-335 [M]	The Real Earl Hines In Concert	1965	30.00
❏ FS-335 [S]	The Real Earl Hines In Concert	1965	30.00
GNP CRESCENDO			
❏ GNP-9042	Earl "Fatha" Hines All-Stars	197?	12.00
❏ GNP-9043	Earl "Fatha" Hines All-Stars, Vol. 2	197?	12.00
❏ GNP-9010	Earl "Fatha" Hines in Paris	197?	12.00
❏ GNPS-9054	Live at the Crescendo	1992	15.00

Number	Title	Yr	NM
HALCYON			
❏ 101	The Quintessential Recording Session	196?	25.00
HALL OF FAME			
❏ 609	Earl "Fatha" Hines All-Stars	197?	12.00
IMPROV			
❏ 7114	Live at the Downtown Club	1976	15.00
IMPULSE!			
❏ A-9108 [M]	Once Upon a Time	1966	30.00
❏ AS-9108 [S]	Once Upon a Time	1966	30.00
INNER CITY			
❏ IC-1142	Paris Session	198?	15.00
JAZZ PANORAMA			
❏ 7 [M]	All Stars	1961	40.00
M&K			
❏ 105	Fatha	1979	30.00
—Direct-to-disc recording			
MASTER JAZZ			
❏ 8101	Blues and Things	1970	18.00
❏ 8114	Earl Hines Plays Duke Ellington	1971	18.00
❏ 8132	Earl Hines Plays Duke Ellington, Volume 4	1975	15.00
❏ 8126	Earl Hines Plays Duke Ellington, Volumes 2 and 3	1973	25.00
❏ 8109	Hines '65	1971	18.00
MCA			
❏ 29070	Once Upon a Time	198?	12.00
❏ 1373	Rhythm Sundae	198?	12.00
❏ 1311	South Side Swing	198?	12.00
MERCURY			
❏ MG-25018 [10]	Earl Hines and the All Stars	1950	250.00
MGM			
❏ E-3832 [M]	Earl's Pearls	1960	30.00
❏ SE-3832 [S]	Earl's Pearls	1960	30.00
MILESTONE			
❏ 2012	Monday Date 1928	197?	15.00
MUSE			
❏ MR-2001/2	The Legendary Little Theatre Concert of 1964	198?	18.00
❏ DE-602	The Legendary Little Theatre Concert of 1964, Volume 1	198?	12.00
NOCTURNE			
❏ NLP-5 [10]	Earl "Fatha" Hines	1954	150.00
PRESTIGE			
❏ 24043	Another Monday Date	197?	18.00
❏ 2515	Boogie Woogie on St. Louis Blues	198?	15.00
QUICKSILVER			
❏ QS-9001	Fatha	198?	12.00
❏ QS-9000	Live and in Living Jazz	198?	12.00
RCA VICTOR			
❏ LPT-20 [10]	Earl Hines with Billy Eckstine	1953	120.00
❏ LPV-512 [M]	The Grand Terrace Band	1965	30.00
❏ LPM-3380 [M]	Up to Date	1965	25.00
❏ LSP-3380 [S]	Up to Date	1965	30.00
RIVERSIDE			
❏ RLP-398 [M]	A Monday Date	1961	30.00
❏ RS-9398 [R]	A Monday Date	196?	25.00
ROYALE			
❏ 18166 [10]	Eal "Fatha" Hines -- Great Piano Solos	195?	120.00
STORYVILLE			
❏ 4063	Earl Hines at the Club Hangover	198?	12.00
TIARA			
❏ TMT-7524 [M]	Earl "Fatha" Hines with Buck Clayton	195?	25.00
TIME-LIFE			
❏ STL-J-11	Giants of Jazz	1980	30.00
TOPS			
❏ L-1599 [M]	Fatha	195?	30.00
TRIP			
❏ J-3	All-Star Session	1970	15.00
VERVE			
❏ VSP-35 [M]	Life with Fatha	1966	25.00
❏ VSPS-35 [R]	Life with Fatha	1966	15.00
WHO'S WHO IN JAZZ			
❏ 21004	Lionel Hampton Presents Earl Hines	1978	15.00
X			
❏ LVA-3023 [10]	Piano Solos	1954	120.00
XANADU			
❏ 203	Varieties!	1985	12.00
HINES, ERNIE			
WE PRODUCE			
❏ 1902	Electrified	1972	50.00
HINES, HINES & DAD			
COLUMBIA			
❏ CS9679	Pandemonium	1968	25.00

Number	Title	Yr	NM
HINES, MIMI			
DECCA			
❏ DL4834 [M]	Mimi Hines Is a Happening	1967	30.00
❏ DL74834 [S]	Mimi Hines Is a Happening	1967	25.00
❏ DL4709 [M]	Mimi Hines Sings	1966	25.00
❏ DL74709 [S]	Mimi Hines Sings	1966	30.00
HINSON, DON, AND THE RIGAMORTICIANS			
CAPITOL			
❏ T2219 [M]	Monster Dance Party	1964	50.00
❏ ST2219 [S]	Monster Dance Party	1964	50.00
HINTON, JOE			
BACK BEAT			
❏ B-60 [M]	Funny (How Time Slips Away)	1965	50.00
❏ BS-60 [S]	Funny (How Time Slips Away)	1965	70.00
DUKE			
❏ DLPS-91	Duke-Peacock Remembers Joe Hinton	1969	25.00
HINTON, MILT; WENDELL MARSHALL; BULL RUTHER			
RCA VICTOR			
❏ LPM-1107 [M]	Basses Loaded!	1955	80.00
HINTON, MILT			
BETHLEHEM			
❏ BCP-10 [M]	East Coast Jazz Series #5	1957	50.00
❏ BCP-1020 [10]	Milt Hinton Quartet	1955	80.00
CHIAROSCURO			
❏ 188	Trio	1978	15.00
EPIC			
❏ LN3271 [M]	The Rhythm Section	1956	50.00
EXPOSURE			
❏ 6231910	The Judge's Decision	198?	15.00
FAMOUS DOOR			
❏ 104	Here Swings The Judge	197?	18.00
HINTON, SAM			
DECCA			
❏ DL8418 [M]	A Family Tree of Folk Songs	1957	30.00
❏ DL8108 [M]	Singing Across the Land	1955	40.00
HINZE, CHRIS			
ATLANTIC			
❏ SD19185	Bamboo	1978	15.00
COLUMBIA			
❏ KC33363	Sister Slick	1975	15.00
HIPP, JUTTA			
BLUE NOTE			
❏ BLP-1515 [M]	Jutta Hipp at the Hickory House, Volume 1	1956	600.00
—Deep groove" version, Lexington Ave. address on label			
❏ BLP-1515 [M]	Jutta Hipp at the Hickory House, Volume 1	1956	400.00
—Deep groove" version, W. 63rd St. address on label			
❏ BLP-1515 [M]	Jutta Hipp at the Hickory House, Volume 1	1963	50.00
—With "New York, USA" address on label			
❏ BLP-1516 [M]	Jutta Hipp at the Hickory House, Volume 2	1956	1500.00
—Deep groove" version, Lexington Ave. address on label			
❏ BLP-1516 [M]	Jutta Hipp at the Hickory House, Volume 2	1956	800.00
—Deep groove" version, W. 63rd St. address on label			
❏ BLP-1516 [M]	Jutta Hipp at the Hickory House, Volume 2	1963	150.00
—With "New York, USA" address on label			
❏ BLP-1530 [M]	Jutta Hipp with Zoot Sims	1956	600.00
—Deep groove" version; Lexington Ave. address on label			
❏ BLP-1530 [M]	Jutta Hipp with Zoot Sims	1956	400.00
—Deep groove" version, W. 63sr St. address on label			
❏ BLP-1530 [M]	Jutta Hipp with Zoot Sims	1963	40.00
—With "New York, USA" address on label			
❏ BLP-1530 [M]	Jutta Hipp with Zoot Sims	1971	25.00
—A Division of United Artists" on label			
❏ BLP-1530 [M]	Jutta Hipp with Zoot Sims	2003	30.00
—200-gram reissue; distributed by Classic Records			
❏ BLP-5056 [10]	Jutta -- New Faces, New Sounds from Germany	1955	800.00
MGM			
❏ E-3157 [M]	Cool Europe	1955	150.00
HIRT, AL, AND ANN-MARGRET			
RCA VICTOR			
❏ LPM-2690 [M]	Beauty and the Beard	1964	25.00
❏ LSP-2690 [S]	Beauty and the Beard	1964	25.00
HIRT, AL			
ACCORD			
❏ SN-7187	Java	1981	10.00
ALLEGIANCE			
❏ AV-5032	Blues Line	1986	10.00

Number	Title	Yr	NM
❑ AV-5018	Showtime	1985	10.00
AUDIO FIDELITY			
❑ AF-6282	Hirt…So Good!	1978	12.00
❑ AFLP-1878 [M]	Swingin' Dixie	1959	18.00
❑ AFSD-5878 [S]	Swingin' Dixie	1959	18.00
❑ AFLP-1877 [M]	Swingin' Dixie (At Dan's Pier 600 in New Orleans)	1959	18.00
❑ AFSD-5877 [S]	Swingin' Dixie (At Dan's Pier 600 in New Orleans)	1959	18.00
❑ AFLP-1926 [M]	Swingin' Dixie (Vol. 3)	1961	18.00
❑ AFSD-5926 [S]	Swingin' Dixie (Vol. 3)	1961	18.00
❑ T-90284 [M]	Swingin' Dixie (Vol. 3)	196?	25.00
— Capitol Record Club edition			
❑ ST-90284 [S]	Swingin' Dixie (Vol. 3)	196?	25.00
— Capitol Record Club edition			
❑ AFLP-1927 [M]	Swingin' Dixie (Vol. 4)	1961	18.00
❑ AFSD-5927 [S]	Swingin' Dixie (Vol. 4)	1961	18.00
CORAL			
❑ CRL57402 [M]	Al Hirt in New Orleans	1962	15.00
❑ CRL757402 [S]	Al Hirt in New Orleans	1962	18.00
CROWN			
❑ CLP-5457 [M]	The Dawn Busters	196?	15.00
❑ CST-457 [S]	The Dawn Busters	196?	15.00
GHB			
❑ 107	Mardi Gras Parade Music	197?	12.00
GWP			
❑ 2005	Al Hirt Country	1971	12.00
❑ 2004	Al Hirt Gold	1971	12.00
❑ 2002	Paint Your Wagon	1970	12.00
LONGINES SYMPHONETTE			
❑ LWCP1	The Best of Dixieland Jazz	196?	15.00
METRO			
❑ M-517 [M]	Al Hirt	1965	12.00
❑ MS-517 [S]	Al Hirt	1965	15.00
MONUMENT			
❑ 7603	Jumbo's Gumbo	1977	10.00
— Reissue of 33885			
❑ PZ33885	Jumbo's Gumbo	1975	12.00
❑ KZ32913	Raw Sugar/Sweet Sauce/ Banana Puddin'	1974	12.00
❑ 6642	Raw Sugar/Sweet Sauce/ Banana Puddin'	1976	10.00
— Reissue of 32913			
PAIR			
❑ PDL2-1048	New Orleans By Night	1986	15.00
RCA CAMDEN			
❑ CXS-9015	Al Hirt Blows His Own Horn	1972	15.00
❑ CAS-2316	Al's Place	1970	12.00
❑ CAS-2573	Have a Merry Little	1971	12.00
❑ CAL-2138 [M]	Struttin' Down Royal Street	1967	15.00
❑ CAS-2138 [S]	Struttin' Down Royal Street	1967	12.00
RCA VICTOR			
❑ LPM-2354 [M]	Al (He's the King) Hirt and His Band	1961	15.00
❑ LSP-2354 [S]	Al (He's the King) Hirt and His Band	1961	18.00
❑ LSP-4247	Al Hirt	1970	15.00
❑ LPM-2497 [M]	Al Hirt at the Mardi Gras	1962	15.00
❑ LSP-2497 [S]	Al Hirt at the Mardi Gras	1962	18.00
❑ LSP-4101	Al Hirt Now	1969	15.00
❑ LPM-3917 [M]	Al Hirt Plays Bert Kaempfert	1968	18.00
❑ LSP-3917 [S]	Al Hirt Plays Bert Kaempfert	1968	18.00
❑ LPM-2917 [M]	Cotton Candy	1964	15.00
❑ LSP-2917 [S]	Cotton Candy	1964	18.00
❑ LSP-4161	Here in My Heart	1969	15.00
❑ LPM-2733 [M]	Honey in the Horn	1963	15.00
❑ LSP-2733 [S]	Honey in the Horn	1963	18.00
❑ LPM-2446 [M]	Horn A-Plenty	1962	15.00
❑ LSP-2446 [S]	Horn A-Plenty	1962	18.00
❑ LSP-4020	In Love with You	1968	15.00
❑ LPM-3653 [M]	Latin in the Horn	1966	15.00
❑ LSP-3653 [S]	Latin in the Horn	1966	18.00
❑ LPM-3416 [M]	Live at Carnegie Hall	1965	15.00
❑ LSP-3416 [S]	Live at Carnegie Hall	1965	18.00
❑ LPM-3773 [M]	Music to Watch Girls By	1967	15.00
❑ LSP-3773 [S]	Music to Watch Girls By	1967	18.00
❑ LPM-2607 [M]	Our Man in New Orleans	1963	15.00
❑ LSP-2607 [S]	Our Man in New Orleans	1963	18.00
❑ LM-2729 [M]	Pops" Goes the Trumpet	1964	18.00
❑ LSC-2729 [S]	Pops" Goes the Trumpet	1964	18.00
— With the Boston Pops Orchestra conducted by Arthur Fiedler			
❑ LPM-3878 [M]	Soul in the Horn	1967	18.00
❑ LSP-3878 [S]	Soul in the Horn	1967	18.00
❑ LPM-2965 [M]	Sugar Lips	1964	15.00
❑ LSP-2965 [S]	Sugar Lips	1964	18.00
❑ LPM-3337 [M]	That Honey Horn Sound	1965	15.00
❑ LSP-3337 [S]	That Honey Horn Sound	1965	18.00
❑ LPM-3309 [M]	The Best of Al Hirt	1965	15.00
❑ LSP-3309 [S]	The Best of Al Hirt	1965	18.00
❑ ANL1-1034	The Best of Al Hirt	1975	12.00
❑ LPM-3556 [M]	The Best of Al Hirt, Volume 2	1966	15.00
❑ LSP-3556 [S]	The Best of Al Hirt, Volume 2	1966	18.00
❑ LPM-2366 [M]	The Greatest Horn in the World	1961	15.00
❑ LSP-2366 [S]	The Greatest Horn in the World	1961	18.00
❑ LPM-3579 [M]	The Happy Trumpet	1966	15.00
❑ LSP-3579 [S]	The Happy Trumpet	1966	18.00
❑ LPM-3716 [M]	The Horn Meets the Hornet	1967	15.00
❑ LSP-3716 [S]	The Horn Meets the Hornet	1967	18.00
❑ LPM-3417 [M]	The Sound of Christmas	1965	12.00
❑ LSP-3417 [S]	The Sound of Christmas	1965	15.00

Number	Title	Yr	NM
❑ LPM-3492 [M]	They're Playing Our Song	1966	15.00
❑ LSP-3492 [S]	They're Playing Our Song	1966	18.00
❑ VPS-6025	This Is Al Hirt	1970	18.00
❑ VPS-6057	This Is Al Hirt, Volume 2	1972	18.00
❑ LPM-2584 [M]	Trumpet and Strings	1962	15.00
❑ LSP-2584 [S]	Trumpet and Strings	1962	18.00
❑ LPM-3979 [M]	Unforgettable	1968	18.00
❑ LSP-3979 [S]	Unforgettable	1968	15.00
VERVE			
❑ MGV-1027 [M]	Blockbustin' Dixie!	195?	25.00
❑ V-1027 [M]	Blockbustin' Dixie!	1961	18.00
❑ MGV-1012 [M]	Swinging Dixie from Dan's Pier 600	1957	30.00
VOCALION			
❑ VL73907	Floatin' Down to Cotton Town	1970	12.00
WYNCOTE			
❑ 9089	The Dawn Busters	196?	12.00

HITCHCOCK, ROBYN, AND THE EGYPTIANS

Number	Title	Yr	NM
A&M			
❑ SP-5182 [B]	Globe of Frogs	1988	15.00
❑ 7502153681 [B]	Perspex Island	1991	30.00
❑ SP-5241	Queen Elvis	1989	15.00
RELATIVITY			
❑ 88561-8088-1	Black Snake Diamond Role	1986	15.00
— First U.S. issue of U.K. album			
❑ 88561-8130-1	Element of Light	1987	15.00
❑ 8074 [EP]	Exploding in Silence	1986	30.00
— Picture disc			
❑ EMC8056	Gotta Let This Hen Out	1985	15.00
❑ 88561-8083-1	Groovy Decoy	1986	15.00
— First U.S. issue of U.K. album			
❑ 88561-8089-1	Invisible Hitchcock	1986	15.00
❑ 88561-8082-1	I Often Dream of Trains	1986	15.00
— First U.S. issue of U.K. album			
SLASH			
❑ 25316	Fegmania!	1985	15.00
TWIN/TONE			
❑ TTR89175	Eye	1990	15.00
WARNER BROS.			
❑ 46399	Mossy Liquor	1996	30.00
— Collection of demos; released only on vinyl			
❑ 47147	Storefront Hitchcock	1998	25.00

HITCHCOCK, STAN

Number	Title	Yr	NM
AUDIOGRAPH			
❑ 6004	Stan Hitchcock	1982	12.00
CINNAMON			
❑ CIN5001	Stan Hitchcock Country	1973	18.00
EPIC			
❑ BN26530	Honey, I'm Home	1969	18.00
❑ BN26408 [M]	I'm Easy to Love	1968	40.00
— White label promo with stereo number; "Epic Mono" sticker on front cover			
❑ BN26408 [S]	I'm Easy to Love	1968	25.00
❑ LN24138 [M]	Just Call Me Lonesome	1965	25.00
❑ BN26138 [S]	Just Call Me Lonesome	1965	30.00
❑ BN26438	Softly and Tenderly	1969	25.00
GRT			
❑ 20001	Dixie Belle	1970	18.00

HIVES, THE

Number	Title	Yr	NM
GEARHEAD			
❑ RPM30	Barely Legal	2000	18.00
❑ RPM40	Veni Vidi Vicious	2001	15.00
INTERSCOPE			
❑ B0002756-01	Tyrannosaurus Hives	2004	25.00

HO, DON

Number	Title	Yr	NM
REPRISE			
❑ R-6186 [M]	Don Ho…Again!	1966	12.00
❑ RS-6186 [S]	Don Ho…Again!	1966	15.00
❑ RS-6461	Don Ho at the Polynesian Palace	1970	12.00
❑ RS-6357	Don Ho -- Greatest Hits!	1969	15.00
❑ R-6244 [M]	East Coast/West Coast	1967	15.00
❑ RS-6244 [S]	East Coast/West Coast	1967	15.00
❑ RS-6303	Hawaii-Ho!	1968	15.00
❑ RS-6418	Hawaii's Greatest Hits	1970	12.00
❑ RS-6283	Instant Happy	1968	15.00
❑ RS-6331	Suck 'Em Up	1969	15.00
❑ R-6161 [M]	The Don Ho Show	1965	15.00
❑ RS-6161 [S]	The Don Ho Show	1965	18.00
❑ RS-6367	The Don Ho TV Show	1969	15.00
❑ R-6232 [M]	Tiny Bubbles	1966	12.00
❑ RS-6232 [S]	Tiny Bubbles	1966	15.00
❑ R-6219 [M]	You're Gonna Hear From Me	1966	12.00
❑ RS-6219 [S]	You're Gonna Hear From Me	1966	15.00

HOBBITS, THE

Number	Title	Yr	NM
DECCA			
❑ DL4920 [M]	Down to Middle-Earth	1967	80.00
❑ DL74920 [S]	Down to Middle-Earth	1967	50.00
❑ DL75009 [S]	Men and Doors	1968	30.00
❑ DL5009 [M]	Men and Doors	1968	100.00

HOBBS, BECKY

Number	Title	Yr	NM
MCA			
❑ 434	Becky Hobbs	1974	18.00
MTM			
❑ D1-71067	All Keyed Up	1988	12.00
TATTOO			
❑ BJL1-2169	Everyday	1977	15.00
❑ BJL1-1673	Heartland	1976	15.00

HODEIR, ANDRE

Number	Title	Yr	NM
EMARCY			
❑ SR-66005	Plain Old Blues	1967	18.00
JAZZOLOGY			
❑ J-7	Summit Meeting	1965	18.00
PHILIPS			
❑ PHM200073 [M]	Jazz Et Al	1963	30.00
❑ PHS600073 [S]	Jazz Et Al	1963	30.00
SAVOY			
❑ MG-12104 [M]	American Jazzmen Play Andre Hodeir	1957	40.00
❑ MG-12113 [M]	Andre Hodeir Presents the Paris Scene	1957	40.00
SAVOY JAZZ			
❑ SJL-1194	Essais	198?	12.00

HODES, ART

Number	Title	Yr	NM
AUDIOPHILE			
❑ AP-54	Mostly Blues	196?	18.00
❑ AP-54	Some Legendary Art	1986	12.00
— Retitled reissue			
BLUE NOTE			
❑ BLP-7005 [10]	Art Hodes' Hot Five	1950	500.00
❑ BLP-7015 [10]	Dixieland Clambake	1951	500.00
❑ BLP-7006 [10]	Dixieland Jubilee	1950	500.00
❑ BLP-7021 [10]	Out of the Backroom	1952	500.00
❑ B-6508 [M]	Sittin' In	1969	30.00
❑ BLP-7004 [10]	The Best in Two-Beat	1950	500.00
❑ B-6502 [M]	The Funky Piano of Art Hodes	1969	30.00
— A Division of Liberty Records" on label			
CAPITOL			
❑ M-11030	Hollywood Stampede	1973	25.00
DELMARK			
❑ DS-215	Friar's Inn Revisited	197?	18.00
❑ DS-213	Hodes' Art	197?	18.00
❑ DS-211	My Bucket's Got a Hole In It	1969	25.00
DOTTED EIGHTH			
❑ 1000 [M]	Art for Art's Sake	195?	50.00
EMARCY			
❑ MG-26104 [10]	Jazz Chicago Style	1954	150.00
❑ SRE-66005	Plain Old Blues	196?	25.00
EUPHONIC			
❑ 1213	I Remember Bessie	198?	12.00
❑ 1207	The Art of Hodes	198?	12.00
❑ 1218	When Music Was Music	198?	12.00
GHB			
❑ 171	Art Hodes and the Magolia Jazz Band, Vol. 1	1984	18.00
❑ 172	Art Hodes and the Magolia Jazz Band, Vol. 2	1984	18.00
JAZZOLOGY			
❑ J-20	Andre Hodeir with the All-Star Stompers	1966	25.00
❑ J-104	Apex Blues	198?	15.00
❑ J-155	Art Hodes and His Blues Six-Blues Groove	198?	15.00
❑ J-74	Down Home Blues	197?	15.00
❑ J-79	Echoes of Chicago	1979	18.00
❑ J-46 [M]	For Art's Sake	196?	25.00
❑ J-58	Home Cookin'	1974	18.00
❑ J-83	The Jazz Record Story, Vol. 2	1979	15.00
❑ J-113	The Trios	198?	15.00
MERCURY			
❑ MG-20185 [M]	Chicago Style Jazz	1957	60.00
MOSAIC			
❑ MR5-114	The Complete Art Hodes Blue Note Sessions	199?	200.00
— Limited edition of 7,500			
MUSE			
❑ MR-5279	Just the Two of Us	1982	12.00
❑ MR-5252	Someone to Watch Over Me	1981	12.00
PARAMOUNT			
❑ LP-113 [M]	The Trios	1955	150.00
PRESTIGE			
❑ 24083	The Real Thing	198?	18.00
RIVERSIDE			
❑ RLP-1012 [10]	Chicago Rhythm Kings	1953	150.00
SACKVILLE			
❑ 3039	Blues in the Night	198?	12.00
STOMP OFF			
❑ SOS-1184	The Music of Lovie Austin	1988	12.00
STORYVILLE			
❑ 4057	Selections from the Gutter	198?	12.00

HODGES, JOHNNY, AND EARL "FATHA" HINES

VERVE

Number	Title	Yr	NM
❑ V-8647 [M]	Stride Right	1966	25.00
❑ V6-8647 [S]	Stride Right	1966	30.00
❑ V-8732 [M]	Swing's Our Thing	1967	30.00
❑ V6-8732 [S]	Swing's Our Thing	1967	18.00

HODGES, JOHNNY, AND WILD BILL DAVIS

RCA VICTOR

Number	Title	Yr	NM
❑ LPM-3393 [M]	Con-Soul and Sax	1965	25.00
❑ LSP-3393 [S]	Con-Soul and Sax	1965	30.00
❑ LPM-3706 [M]	Eddie Hodges and Wild Bill Davis In Atlantic City	1966	18.00
❑ LSP-3706 [S]	Eddie Hodges and Wild Bill Davis In Atlantic City	1966	25.00

VERVE

Number	Title	Yr	NM
❑ V-8570 [M]	A Mess of Blues	1964	25.00
❑ V6-8570 [S]	A Mess of Blues	1964	30.00
❑ V-8406 [M]	Blue Hodges	1961	25.00
❑ V6-8406 [S]	Blue Hodges	1961	30.00
❑ V-8635 [M]	Blue Pyramid	1965	25.00
❑ V6-8635 [S]	Blue Pyramid	1965	30.00
❑ V-8599 [M]	Blue Rabbit	1964	25.00
❑ V6-8599 [S]	Blue Rabbit	1964	30.00
❑ V-8617 [M]	Joe's Blues	1965	25.00
❑ V6-8617 [S]	Joe's Blues	1965	30.00
❑ V-8630 [M]	Wings and Things	1965	25.00
❑ V6-8630 [S]	Wings and Things	1965	30.00

HODGES, JOHNNY

ABC IMPULSE!

Number	Title	Yr	NM
❑ AS-61 [S]	Everybody Knows	1968	18.00

AMERICAN RECORDING SOCIETY

Number	Title	Yr	NM
❑ G-421 [M]	Johnny Hodges and the Ellington All-Stars	195?	40.00

BLUEBIRD

Number	Title	Yr	NM
❑ 5903-1-RB	Triple Play	1987	12.00

CLEF

Number	Title	Yr	NM
❑ MGC-128 [10]	Johnny Hodges Collates #2	1953	200.00
❑ MGC-111 [10]	Johnny Hodges Collates	1953	150.00

DOT

Number	Title	Yr	NM
❑ DLP-3682 [M]	Johnny Hodges with Lawrence Welk's Orchestra	1966	18.00
❑ DLP-25682 [S]	Johnny Hodges with Lawrence Welk's Orchestra	1966	25.00

ENCORE

Number	Title	Yr	NM
❑ EE-22001 [M]	Hodge Podge	1968	18.00

EPIC

Number	Title	Yr	NM
❑ LN3105 [M]	Hodge Podge	1955	60.00

FLYING DUTCHMAN

Number	Title	Yr	NM
❑ FD-10120	Three Shades of Blue	1972	18.00
❑ 120	Three Shades of Blue	1971	25.00

IMPULSE!

Number	Title	Yr	NM
❑ A-61 [M]	Everybody Knows	1964	30.00
❑ AS-61 [S]	Everybody Knows	1964	30.00

JAZZ PANORAMA

Number	Title	Yr	NM
❑ 1806 [10]	Johnny Hodges	1951	150.00

MASTER JAZZ

Number	Title	Yr	NM
❑ 8107	Memory	1970	18.00

MCA

Number	Title	Yr	NM
❑ 29071	Everybody Knows	198?	12.00

MERCER

Number	Title	Yr	NM
❑ LP-1000 [10]	Johnny Hodges, Vol. 1	1951	150.00
❑ LP-1006 [10]	Johnny Hodges, Vol. 2	1951	150.00
❑ MGC-111 [10]	Johnny Hodges Collates	1952	250.00

MGM

Number	Title	Yr	NM
❑ SE-4715	Tribute	1970	18.00

MOSAIC

Number	Title	Yr	NM
❑ MR6-126	The Complete Johnny Hodges Sessions 1951-1955	199?	150.00

NORGRAN

Number	Title	Yr	NM
❑ MGN-1048 [M]	Castle Rock	1955	120.00
❑ MGN-1045 [M]	Creamy	1955	150.00
❑ MGN-1055 [M]	Ellingtonia '56	1956	100.00
❑ MGN-1092 [M]	In a Mellow Tone	1956	100.00
❑ MGN-1059 [M]	In a Tender Mood	1956	100.00
❑ MGN-1024 [M]	Johnny Hodges Dance Bash	1955	150.00
❑ MGN-1004 [M]	Memories of Ellington	1954	150.00
❑ MGN-1009 [M]	More of Johnny Hodges	1954	150.00
❑ MGN-1091 [M]	Perdido	1956	100.00
❑ MGN-1 [10]	Swing with Johnny Hodges	1954	200.00
❑ MGN-1061 [M]	The Blues	1956	100.00
❑ MGN-1060 [M]	Used to Be Duke	1956	100.00

ONYX

Number	Title	Yr	NM
❑ 216	Ellingtonia	197?	15.00

PABLO LIVE

Number	Title	Yr	NM
❑ 2620102	Sportpalast, Berlin	1978	18.00

PRESTIGE

Number	Title	Yr	NM
❑ 24103	Caravan	198?	18.00

RCA VICTOR

Number	Title	Yr	NM
❑ LPT-3000 [10]	Alto Sax	1952	150.00
❑ LPV-533 [M]	Things Ain't What They Used to Be	1966	25.00
❑ LPM-3867 [M]	Triple Play	1967	30.00
❑ LSP-3867 [S]	Triple Play	1967	25.00

STORYVILLE

Number	Title	Yr	NM
❑ 4073	A Man and His Music	198?	15.00

TIME-LIFE

Number	Title	Yr	NM
❑ STL-J-19	Giants of Jazz	1981	25.00

VERVE

Number	Title	Yr	NM
❑ VSP-20 [M]	Alto Blues	1966	15.00
❑ VSPS-20 [R]	Alto Blues	1966	12.00
❑ MGV-8317 [M]	Back to Back -- Duke Ellington and Johnny Hodges Play the Blues	1959	50.00
❑ MGVS-6055 [S]	Back to Back -- Duke Ellington and Johnny Hodges Play the Blues	1960	40.00
❑ V-8317 [M]	Back to Back -- Duke Ellington and Johnny Hodges Play the Blues	1961	25.00
❑ V6-8317 [S]	Back to Back -- Duke Ellington and Johnny Hodges Play the Blues	1961	25.00
❑ V-8680 [M]	Blue Notes	1966	18.00
❑ V6-8680 [S]	Blue Notes	1966	25.00
❑ MGV-8358 [M]	Blues-a-Plenty	1960	50.00
❑ V-8358 [M]	Blues-a-Plenty	1961	25.00
❑ V6-8358 [S]	Blues-a-Plenty	1961	25.00
❑ V6-8358 [S]	Blues-a-Plenty	199?	30.00
—Classic Records reissue on audiophile vinyl			
❑ MGV-8139 [M]	Castle Rock	1957	50.00
—Reissue of Norgran 1048			
❑ V-8139 [M]	Castle Rock	1961	25.00
❑ 827758-1	Castle Rock	1986	12.00
❑ MGV-8136 [M]	Creamy	1957	50.00
—Reissue of Norgran 1045			
❑ V-8136 [M]	Creamy	1961	25.00
❑ V-8726 [M]	Don't Sleep in the Subway	1967	25.00
❑ V6-8726 [S]	Don't Sleep in the Subway	1967	18.00
❑ MGV-8203 [M]	Duke's in Bed	1957	50.00
❑ V-8203 [M]	Duke's in Bed	1961	25.00
❑ MGV-8145 [M]	Ellingtonia '56	1957	50.00
—Reissue of Norgran 1055			
❑ V-8145 [M]	Ellingtonia '56	1961	25.00
❑ MGV-8180 [M]	In a Mellow Tone	1957	50.00
—Reissue of Norgran 1092			
❑ V-8180 [M]	In a Mellow Tone	1961	25.00
❑ MGV-8149 [M]	In a Tender Mood	1957	50.00
—Reissue of Norgran 1059			
❑ V-8149 [M]	In a Tender Mood	1961	25.00
❑ VSP-3 [M]	Johnny Hodges and All the Duke's Men	1966	15.00
❑ VSPS-3 [R]	Johnny Hodges and All the Duke's Men	1966	12.00
❑ V-8452 [M]	Johnny Hodges with Billy Strayhorn	1962	30.00
❑ V6-8452 [S]	Johnny Hodges with Billy Strayhorn	1962	30.00
❑ MGV-8355 [M]	Not So Dukish	1960	50.00
❑ V-8355 [M]	Not So Dukish	1961	25.00
❑ MGV-8179 [M]	Perdido	1957	50.00
—Reissue of Norgran 1091			
❑ V-8179 [M]	Perdido	1961	25.00
❑ V6-8834	Previously Unreleased Recordings	1973	18.00
❑ V6-8753	Rippin' and Runnin'	1968	18.00
❑ V-8561 [M]	Sandy's Gone	1963	30.00
❑ V6-8561 [S]	Sandy's Gone	1963	30.00
❑ MGV-8345 [M]	Side by Side	1959	50.00
❑ MGVS-6109 [S]	Side by Side	1960	40.00
❑ V-8345 [M]	Side by Side	1961	25.00
❑ V6-8345 [S]	Side by Side	1961	25.00
❑ MGVS-6109 [S]	Side by Side	199?	30.00
—Classic Records reissue on audiophile vinyl			
❑ MGV-8271 [M]	The Big Sound	1958	50.00
❑ MGVS-6017 [S]	The Big Sound	1960	40.00
❑ V-8271 [M]	The Big Sound	1961	25.00
❑ V6-8271 [S]	The Big Sound	1961	25.00
❑ UMV-2525	The Big Sound	198?	12.00
❑ MGV-8151 [M]	The Blues	1957	50.00
—Reissue of Norgran 1061			
❑ V-8151 [M]	The Blues	1961	25.00
❑ V-8492 [M]	The Eleventh Hour	1962	30.00
❑ V6-8492 [S]	The Eleventh Hour	1962	30.00
❑ MGV-8314 [M]	The Prettiest Gershwin	1959	50.00
❑ MGVS-6048 [S]	The Prettiest Gershwin	1960	40.00
❑ V 8314 [M]	The Prettiest Gershwin	1961	25.00
❑ V6-8314 [S]	The Prettiest Gershwin	1961	25.00
❑ VE2-2532	The Smooth One	1979	18.00
❑ MGV-8150 [M]	Used to Be Duke	1957	50.00
—Reissue of Norgran 1060			
❑ V-8150 [M]	Used to Be Duke	1961	25.00

HOFFMAN, ABBIE

BIG TOE

Number	Title	Yr	NM
❑ 1 [B]	Wake Up, America!	196?	60.00

HOFNER, ADOLPH

COLUMBIA

Number	Title	Yr	NM
❑ CL9017 [10]	Dude Ranch Dances	1951	200.00

DECCA

Number	Title	Yr	NM
❑ DL5564 [10]	Dance-O-Rama	1955	400.00

HOG HEAVEN

ROULETTE

Number	Title	Yr	NM
❑ SR42057	Hog Heaven	1971	25.00

HOGAN, CLAIRE

MGM

Number	Title	Yr	NM
❑ E-4501 [M]	Boozers and Losers	1967	25.00
❑ SE-4501 [S]	Boozers and Losers	1967	30.00

HOGAN, SILAS

EXCELLO

Number	Title	Yr	NM
❑ LPS-8019	Trouble at Home	1972	25.00

HOGG, SMOKEY

CROWN

Number	Title	Yr	NM
❑ CLP-5226 [M]	Smokey Hogg Sings the Blues	1962	50.00

TIME

Number	Title	Yr	NM
❑ 6 [M]	Smokey Hogg	1962	80.00

UNITED

Number	Title	Yr	NM
❑ US-7745	Smokey Hogg	1970	15.00

HOLDEN, RANDY

HOBBIT

Number	Title	Yr	NM
❑ 5002	Population II	1968	200.00

HOLDEN, RON

DONNA

Number	Title	Yr	NM
❑ DLP-2111 [M]	I Love You So	1960	250.00
❑ DLPS-2111 [M]	I Love You So	1960	300.00
—Stereo records not known to exist; this is for a mono record in a stereo cover			

HOLDSWORTH, ALLAN

CTI

Number	Title	Yr	NM
❑ 6068	Velvet	197?	18.00

ENIGMA

Number	Title	Yr	NM
❑ ST-73203	Atavachron	1986	15.00
❑ 72031-1	I.O.U.	1985	18.00
—Reissue			

LUNA CRACK

Number	Title	Yr	NM
❑ AH-100	I.O.U.	1982	25.00

HOLIDAY, BILLIE, AND STAN GETZ

DALE

Number	Title	Yr	NM
❑ 25 [10]	Billie and Stan	1951	400.00

HOLIDAY, BILLIE

AMERICAN RECORDING SOCIETY

Number	Title	Yr	NM
❑ G-409 [M]	Billie Holiday Sings	1956	60.00
—Reissue of Clef 713			
❑ G-431 [M]	Lady Sings the Blues	1957	60.00
—Reissue of Clef 721			

ATLANTIC

Number	Title	Yr	NM
❑ 1614	Strange Fruit	1972	18.00

BLACKHAWK

Number	Title	Yr	NM
❑ BKH-50701	Billie Holiday at Monterey	1986	12.00

BOOK-OF-THE-MONTH CLUB

Number	Title	Yr	NM
❑ 90-5652	Ain't Nobody's Business If I Do	1975	30.00
—Box set with booklet; pressed on CSP labels; alternate number is "P4 12969			

BULLDOG

Number	Title	Yr	NM
❑ 1007	Billie's Blues	198?	12.00

CLEF

Number	Title	Yr	NM
❑ MGC-144 [10]	An Evening with Billie Holiday	1954	200.00
❑ MGC-686 [M]	A Recital by Billie Holiday	1956	120.00
—Reissue of 144 and 161 as one 12-inch LP			
❑ MGC-169 [10]	Billie Holiday at Jazz at the Philharmonic	1955	180.00
❑ MGC-161 [10]	Billie Holiday Favorites	1954	180.00
❑ MGC-118 [10]	Billie Holiday Sings	1953	200.00
❑ MGC-721 [M]	Lady Sings the Blues	1956	120.00
❑ MGC-669 [M]	Music for Torching	1955	150.00
❑ MGC-690 [M]	Solitude -- Songs by Billie Holiday	1956	120.00
—Reissue of 118			
❑ MGC-713 [M]	Velvet Mood	1956	120.00

CLEOPATRA

Number	Title	Yr	NM
❑ 8768 [B]	Lady Day - The Ultimate Collection		30.00
—picture disc			
❑ 5365 [B]	The Essential Rare Collection		25.00

COLLECTABLES

Number	Title	Yr	NM
❑ COL-5142	Fine and Mellow	198?	15.00

COLUMBIA

Number	Title	Yr	NM
❑ CL6163 [10]	Billie Holiday Favorites	1951	200.00
❑ CL2666 [M]	Billie Holiday's Greatest Hits	1967	18.00
❑ CL6129 [10]	Billie Holiday Sings	1950	200.00
❑ C32080	Billie's Blues/The Original Recordings by Billie Holiday	1973	18.00
❑ PC32080	Billie's Blues/The Original Recordings by Billie Holiday	198?	10.00
—Reissue of Harmony LP			
❑ G30782	God Bless the Child	1972	25.00
❑ CL637 [M]	Lady Day	1954	70.00
—Maroon label, gold print			

Number	Title	Yr	NM
❑ CL637 [M]	Lady Day	1956	40.00
—Red and black label with six "eye" logos			
❑ CL637 [M]	Lady Day	1962	18.00
—Red "Guaranteed High Fidelity" or "360 Sound" label			
❑ CL637 [M]	Lady Day	197?	15.00
—Orange label			
❑ CL1157 [M]	Lady in Satin	1958	40.00
—Red and black label with six "eye" logos			
❑ CS8048 [S]	Lady in Satin	1958	40.00
—Red and black label with six "eye" logos			
❑ CL1157 [M]	Lady in Satin	1962	18.00
—Red "Guaranteed High Fidelity" or "360 Sound" label			
❑ CS8048 [S]	Lady in Satin	1962	18.00
—Red "Guaranteed High Fidelity" or "360 Sound" label			
❑ CS8048 [S]	Lady in Satin	1999	30.00
—Classic Records reissue on audiophile vinyl			
❑ CG32121	The Billie Holiday Story, Volume 1	1973	18.00
❑ CG32124	The Billie Holiday Story, Volume 2	1973	18.00
❑ CG32127	The Billie Holiday Story, Volume 3	1973	18.00
❑ C3L21 [M]	The Golden Years	1962	50.00
—Red and black label with six "eye" logos			
❑ C3L21 [M]	The Golden Years	1963	30.00
—Red "Guaranteed High Fidelity" or "360 Sound" label			
❑ C3L40 [M]	The Golden Years, Volume 2	1966	30.00
—Red label, "Mono" at bottom			
❑ C3L40 [M]	The Golden Years, Volume 2	197?	25.00
—Orange labels			

COLUMBIA JAZZ MASTERPIECES

Number	Title	Yr	NM
❑ CJ40247	Lady in Satin	1987	12.00
❑ CJ40646	The Quintessential Billie Holiday, Vol. 1	1987	12.00
❑ CJ40790	The Quintessential Billie Holiday, Vol. 2	1987	12.00
❑ CJ44048	The Quintessential Billie Holiday, Vol. 3	1988	12.00
❑ CJ44252	The Quintessential Billie Holiday, Vol. 4	1988	12.00
❑ CJ44423	The Quintessential Billie Holiday, Vol. 5	1989	12.00
❑ C45449	The Quintessential Billie Holiday, Vol. 6	1990	12.00
❑ C46180	The Quintessential Billie Holiday, Vol. 7	1990	12.00

COLUMBIA MUSICAL TREASURY

Number	Title	Yr	NM
❑ P3M5869	The Golden Years	197?	25.00

COLUMBIA SPECIAL PRODUCTS

Number	Title	Yr	NM
❑ P14338	Swing, Brother, Swing	198?	12.00

COMMODORE

Number	Title	Yr	NM
❑ FL-30008 [M]	Billie Holiday	1959	50.00
—Reissue of 20006			
❑ FL-20005 [10]	Billie Holiday, Volume 1	1950	300.00
❑ FL-20006 [10]	Billie Holiday, Volume 2	1950	300.00
❑ FL-30011 [M]	Billie Holiday with Eddie Heywood and His Orchestra	1959	50.00
—Reissue of 20005			

CROWN

Number	Title	Yr	NM
❑ CLP-5380 [M]	Billie Holliday & Vivian Fears	196?	25.00
❑ CST-380 [R]	Billie Holiday & Vivian Fears	196?	15.00

DECCA

Number	Title	Yr	NM
❑ DL75040 [R]	Billie Holiday's Greatest Hits	1968	15.00
❑ DL5040 [M]	Billie Holiday's Greatest Hits	1968	30.00
—Mono is white label promo only; "Monaural" sticker covers the word "Stereo" on cover			
❑ DL5345 [10]	Lover Man	1951	200.00
❑ DL8702 [M]	Lover Man	1958	60.00
❑ DXB-161 [M]	The Billie Holiday Story	1959	25.00
❑ DXSB-7161 [R]	The Billie Holiday Story	1959	18.00
❑ DL8701 [M]	The Blues Are Brewin'	1958	60.00
❑ DL8215 [M]	The Lady Sings	1956	60.00

ESP-DISK'

Number	Title	Yr	NM
❑ 3002	The Lady Lives, Vol. 1	1973	15.00
❑ 3003	The Lady Lives, Vol. 2	1973	15.00

EVEREST ARCHIVE OF FOLK & JAZZ

Number	Title	Yr	NM
❑ 265	Billie Holiday	197?	15.00
❑ FS-310	Billie Holiday, Vol. 2	1976	15.00

HALL

Number	Title	Yr	NM
❑ 622	I've Gotta Right to Sing	197?	15.00

HARMONY

Number	Title	Yr	NM
❑ KH32080	Billie's Blues	1973	12.00

INTERMEDIA

Number	Title	Yr	NM
❑ QS-5076	Billie Holiday Talks and Sings	198?	12.00

JAZZ MAN

Number	Title	Yr	NM
❑ 5005	Billie Holiday at Storyville	198?	12.00

JAZZTONE

Number	Title	Yr	NM
❑ J-1209 [M]	Billie Holiday Sings	1955	50.00
—Reissue of Commodore 20005			

JOLLY ROGER

Number	Title	Yr	NM
❑ 5020 [10]	Billie Holiday, Volume 1	1954	100.00
❑ 5021 [10]	Billie Holiday, Volume 2	1954	100.00
❑ 5022 [10]	Billie Holiday, Volume 3	1954	100.00

KENT GOSPEL

Number	Title	Yr	NM
❑ KST600	Billie Holiday Sings	197?	18.00

MAINSTREAM

Number	Title	Yr	NM
❑ 56022 [M]	Once Upon a Time	1965	30.00
❑ S-6022 [R]	Once Upon a Time	1965	15.00
❑ 56000 [M]	The Commodore Recordings	1965	30.00
❑ S-6000 [R]	The Commodore Recordings	1965	15.00

MCA

Number	Title	Yr	NM
❑ 275	Billie Holiday's Greatest Hits	1973	12.00
—Reissue of Decca 75040			
❑ 4006	The Billie Holiday Story	1973	15.00
—Reissue of Decca 7161			

METRO

Number	Title	Yr	NM
❑ M-515 [M]	Billie Holiday	1965	18.00
❑ MS-515 [R]	Billie Holiday	1965	15.00

MGM

Number	Title	Yr	NM
❑ M3G-4948	Archetypes	1974	15.00
❑ E-3764 [M]	Billie Holiday	1959	40.00
❑ SE-3764 [S]	Billie Holiday	1959	50.00
❑ GAS-122	Billie Holiday (Golden Archive Series)	1970	15.00

MOBILE FIDELITY

Number	Title	Yr	NM
❑ 1-247	Body and Soul	1996	120.00
—Audiophile vinyl			

MONMOUTH/EVERGREEN

Number	Title	Yr	NM
❑ 7046	Gallant Lady	1973	15.00

PARAMOUNT

Number	Title	Yr	NM
❑ PA-6059	Songs and Conversations	1973	15.00

PHOENIX 10

Number	Title	Yr	NM
❑ PHX-312	Billie Holiday Live	1981	10.00

PICKWICK

Number	Title	Yr	NM
❑ PC-3335	Billie Holiday Sings the Blues	197?	12.00

RIC

Number	Title	Yr	NM
❑ M-2001 [M]	Rare Live Recording	1964	30.00

SCORE

Number	Title	Yr	NM
❑ SLP-4014 [M]	Billie Holiday Sings the Blues	1957	120.00

SOLID STATE

Number	Title	Yr	NM
❑ SS-18040	Lady Love	1969	15.00

SUNSET

Number	Title	Yr	NM
❑ SUM-1147 [M]	Shades of Blue	1967	15.00
❑ SUS-5147 [R]	Shades of Blue	1967	12.00

TIME-LIFE

Number	Title	Yr	NM
❑ STL-J-03	Giants of Jazz	1979	30.00
—Alternate number is Columbia Special Products P3 14786			

TOTEM

Number	Title	Yr	NM
❑ 1037	Billie Holiday On the Air	198?	12.00

TRIP

Number	Title	Yr	NM
❑ 5024	Billie Holiday Live	1974	12.00

UNITED ARTISTS

Number	Title	Yr	NM
❑ UAJ-14014 [M]	Lady Love	1962	40.00
❑ UASJ-15014 [S]	Lady Love	1962	50.00
❑ UAS-5625	Lady Love	1972	12.00
—Reissue of 15014			

VERVE

Number	Title	Yr	NM
❑ MGV-8329 [M]	All or Nothing at All	1959	50.00
❑ V-8329 [M]	All or Nothing at All	1959	25.00
❑ V6-8329 [R]	All or Nothing at All	196?	15.00
❑ VE-2-2529	All or Nothing at All	198?	18.00
❑ 827160-1	All or Nothing at All	1987	12.00
❑ MGV-8027 [M]	A Recital by Billie Holiday	1957	40.00
—Reissue of Clef 686			
❑ V-8027 [M]	A Recital by Billie Holiday	1961	25.00
❑ MGV-8197 [M]	Body and Soul	1957	60.00
❑ V-8197 [M]	Body and Soul	1961	25.00
❑ 817359-1	Embraceable You	198?	15.00
❑ 2V6S-8816	History of the Real Billie Holiday	1973	18.00
❑ 823233-1	History of the Real Billie Holiday	198?	15.00
❑ VSP-5 [M]	Lady	1966	18.00
❑ VSPS-5 [R]	Lady	1966	15.00
❑ MGV-8099 [M]	Lady Sings the Blues	1957	40.00
—Reissue of Clef 721			
❑ V-8099 [M]	Lady Sings the Blues	1957	50.00
❑ MGV-8026 [M]	Music for Torching	1957	40.00
—Reissue of Clef 669			
❑ V-8026 [M]	Music for Torching	1961	25.00
❑ MGV-8074 [M]	Solitude -- Songs by Billie Holiday	1957	40.00
—Reissue of Clef 690			
❑ V-8074 [M]	Solitude -- Songs by Billie Holiday	1961	25.00
❑ V6-8074 [R]	Solitude -- Songs by Billie Holiday	196?	15.00
❑ MGV-8257 [M]	Songs for Distingue Lovers	1958	60.00
❑ MGVS-6021 [S]	Songs for Distingue Lovers	1960	60.00
❑ V-8257 [M]	Songs for Distingue Lovers	1961	25.00
❑ V6-8257 [S]	Songs for Distingue Lovers	1961	30.00
❑ MGVS-6021-45 [S]	Songs for Distingue Lovers	1999	25.00
—Classic Records reissue on two 12-inch 45-rpm records			
❑ MGVS-6021 [S]	Songs for Distingue Lovers	199?	30.00
—Classic Records reissue on audiophile vinyl			
❑ MGV-8302 [M]	Stay with Me	1959	50.00
❑ V-8302 [M]	Stay with Me	1961	25.00
❑ VE-2-2515	Stormy Blues	1976	18.00
❑ 823230-1	Stormy Blues	198?	15.00
❑ V6-8808 [R]	The Best of Billie Holiday	1973	12.00
❑ 823246-1	The Billie Holiday Songbook	198?	12.00
❑ V-8410 [M]	The Essential Billie Holiday	1961	25.00
❑ V6-8410 [R]	The Essential Billie Holiday	1961	15.00
❑ V-8505 [M]	The Essential Jazz Vocals	1963	25.00
❑ V6-8505 [R]	The Essential Jazz Vocals	1963	15.00
❑ VE-2-2503	The First Verve Sessions	1976	18.00
❑ MGV-8338-2 [M]	The Unforgettable Lady Day	1959	80.00
❑ V-8338-2 [M]	The Unforgettable Lady Day	1961	30.00
❑ MGV-8096 [M]	Velvet Mood	1957	40.00
—Reissue of Clef 713			
❑ V-8096 [M]	Velvet Mood	1961	25.00

HOLIDAY, BILLIE/AL HIBBLER

IMPERIAL

Number	Title	Yr	NM
❑ LP-9185 [M]	Billie Holiday, Al Hibbler and the Blues	1962	50.00
❑ LP-12185 [R]	Billie Holiday, Al Hibbler and the Blues	196?	30.00

HOLIDAY, JIMMY

MINIT

Number	Title	Yr	NM
❑ LP-24005 [M]	Turning Point	1966	30.00
❑ LP-40005 [S]	Turning Point	1966	40.00

HOLIDAY, JOE

DECCA

Number	Title	Yr	NM
❑ DL8487 [M]	Holiday for Jazz	1957	60.00

PRESTIGE

Number	Title	Yr	NM
❑ PRLP-131 [10]	Joe Holiday	1952	200.00

HOLIDAY, JOE/BILLY TAYLOR

PRESTIGE

Number	Title	Yr	NM
❑ PRLP-171 [10]	Mambo Jazz	1953	150.00

HOLIDAY BELLS, THE

KAPP

Number	Title	Yr	NM
❑ KL-1155 [M]	Ring the Bells on Christmas Day	1959	18.00

HOLLAND, DAVE

ECM

Number	Title	Yr	NM
❑ 1027	Conference of the Birds	1974	18.00
—As "David Holland			
❑ 1109	Emerald Tears	1978	15.00
❑ 25001	Jumpin' In	1984	12.00
❑ 23787	Life Cycle	1983	12.00
❑ 25032	Seeds of Time	1985	12.00

HOLLAND, EDDIE

MOTOWN

Number	Title	Yr	NM
❑ 604 [M]	Eddie Holland	1963	400.00

HOLLIDAY, JUDY, AND GERRY MULLIGAN

DRG

Number	Title	Yr	NM
❑ SL-5191	Holliday with Mulligan	1979	15.00

HOLLIDAY, JUDY

COLUMBIA

Number	Title	Yr	NM
❑ CL1153 [M]	Trouble Is a Man	1958	30.00
❑ CS8041 [S]	Trouble Is a Man	1959	40.00

DRG

Number	Title	Yr	NM
❑ MRS-602	Trouble Is a Man	198?	12.00

HOLLIES, THE

ATLANTIC

Number	Title	Yr	NM
❑ 80076	What Goes Around	1983	12.00

CAPITOL

Number	Title	Yr	NM
❑ N-16056	Hollies' Greatest	1980	10.00

COLUMBIA LIMITED EDITION

Number	Title	Yr	NM
❑ LE10178	He Ain't Heavy, He's My Brother	1976	15.00

EMI AMERICA

Number	Title	Yr	NM
❑ SN-16397	More Great Hits (1963-1968)	1986	10.00

EPIC

Number	Title	Yr	NM
❑ JE35334	A Crazy Steal	1978	12.00
❑ PE33387	Another Night	1975	12.00
❑ PE34714	Clarke, Hicks, Sylvester, Calvert & Elliot	1977	12.00
❑ LN24344 [M]	Dear Eloise/King Midas in Reverse	1967	30.00
❑ BN26344 [S]	Dear Eloise/King Midas in Reverse	1967	30.00
❑ KE30958	Distant Light	1972	18.00
—Yellow label			
❑ KE30958	Distant Light	1974	12.00
—Orange label			
❑ PE30958	Distant Light	1986	10.00
—Blue label			
❑ AS138 [DJ]	Everything You Always Wanted to Hear by the Hollies But Were Afraid to Ask For	1976	25.00
—Promo-only sampler album			
❑ LN24315 [M]	Evolution	1967	30.00
❑ BN26315 [S]	Evolution	1967	30.00
❑ BN26538	He Ain't Heavy, He's My Brother	1970	25.00
❑ KE32574	Hollies	1974	12.00

Number	Title	Yr	NM
❑ E30255	Moving Finger	1971	25.00
❑ KE31992	Romany	1972	15.00
— Yellow label			
❑ KE31992	Romany	1974	12.00
— Orange label			
❑ KE32061	The Hollies' Greatest Hits	1973	15.00
— Yellow label			
❑ KE32061	The Hollies' Greatest Hits	1974	12.00
— Orange label			
❑ PE32061	The Hollies' Greatest Hits	1979	10.00
— Blue label			
❑ BN26447	Words and Music by Bob Dylan	1969	18.00
— Yellow label			
❑ BN26447	Words and Music by Bob Dylan	1973	12.00
— Orange label			

IMPERIAL

Number	Title	Yr	NM
❑ LP-9330 [M]	Bus Stop	1966	30.00
— Black and pink label			
❑ LP-9330 [M]	Bus Stop	1966	30.00
— Black and green label			
❑ LP-12330 [R]	Bus Stop	1966	30.00
— Black and pink label			
❑ LP-12330 [R]	Bus Stop	1966	25.00
— Black and green label			
❑ LP-9299 [M]	Hear! Here!	1965	50.00
❑ LP-12299 [R]	Hear! Here!	1965	30.00
❑ LP-9265 [M]	Here I Go Again	1964	150.00
— Black label with stars			
❑ LP-9265 [M]	Here I Go Again	1964	50.00
— Black and pink label			
❑ LP-12265 [R]	Here I Go Again	1964	100.00
— Black label with silver print			
❑ LP-12265 [R]	Here I Go Again	1964	30.00
— Black and pink label			
❑ LP-9339 [M]	Stop! Stop! Stop!	1966	30.00
❑ LP-12339 [S]	Stop! Stop! Stop!	1966	30.00
❑ LP-9312 [M]	The Hollies -- Beat Group	1966	30.00
❑ LP-12312 [R]	The Hollies -- Beat Group	1966	40.00
❑ LP-9350 [M]	The Hollies' Greatest Hits	1967	25.00
❑ LP-12350 [P]	The Hollies' Greatest Hits	1967	30.00

LIBERTY

Number	Title	Yr	NM
❑ LN-10216	Pay You Back with Interest	1982	10.00

PAIR

| ❑ PDL2-1041 | Hottest Hits | 1986 | 18.00 |

REALM

❑ 2V-8026	The Hollies, Volume 1	1976	18.00
— Two-record TV package			
❑ 1V-8027	The Hollies, Volume 2	1976	15.00
— TV package sold with Realm 8026			

UNITED ARTISTS

| ❑ UA-LA329-E | The Very Best of the Hollies | 1975 | 12.00 |

HOLLOWAY, BRENDA

MOTOWN

| ❑ 5242ML | Every Little Bit Hurts | 1982 | 15.00 |

TAMLA

| ❑ T257 [M] | Every Little Bit Hurts | 1964 | 200.00 |
| ❑ TS257 [R] | Every Little Bit Hurts | 1964 | 150.00 |

HOLLOWAY, LOLEATTA

GOLD MIND

❑ 7500	Loleatta	1977	25.00
❑ GA-9506	Love Sensation	1979	25.00
❑ A-9501 [B]	Queen of the Night	1978	25.00

HOLLOWAY, RED

CONCORD JAZZ

| ❑ CJ-322 | Red Holloway & Company | 1987 | 12.00 |

FANTASY

| ❑ OJC-327 | Cookin' Together | 1988 | 12.00 |

JAM

| ❑ 014 | Hittin' the Road Again | 198? | 15.00 |

PRESTIGE

❑ PRST-7778	Best of the Soul Organ Giants	1970	18.00
❑ PRLP-7299 [M]	Burner	1964	50.00
— Yellow label, Bergenfield, N.J. address			
❑ PRLP-7299 [M]	Burner	1965	30.00
— Blue label, trident logo at right			
❑ PRST-7299 [S]	Burner	1964	50.00
— Yellow label, Bergenfield, N.J. address			
❑ PRST-7299 [S]	Burner	1965	30.00
— Blue label, trident logo at right			
❑ PRLP-7325 [M]	Cookin' Together	1964	30.00
❑ PRST-7325 [S]	Cookin' Together	1964	40.00
❑ PRLP-7473 [M]	Red Soul	1966	25.00
❑ PRST-7473 [S]	Red Soul	1966	30.00
❑ PRLP-7390 [M]	Sax, Strings and Soul	1965	25.00
❑ PRST-7390 [S]	Sax, Strings and Soul	1965	30.00

STEEPLECHASE

| ❑ SCS-1192 | Nica's Dream | 198? | 15.00 |

Number	Title	Yr	NM

HOLLY, BUDDY

CORAL

Number	Title	Yr	NM
❑ CRL57210 [M]	Buddy Holly	1958	400.00
— Maroon label			
❑ CRL57210 [M]	Buddy Holly	1964	100.00
— Black label with color bars			
❑ CRL57405 [M]	Buddy Holly and the Crickets	1962	150.00
— Reissue of the Crickets LP on Brunswick 54038			
❑ CRL757405 [R]	Buddy Holly and the Crickets	1963	40.00
❑ CRL57492 [M]	Buddy Holly's Greatest Hits	1967	80.00
❑ CRL757492 [P]	Buddy Holly's Greatest Hits	1967	50.00
❑ CRL57450 [M]	Buddy Holly Showcase	1964	100.00
❑ CRL757450 [R]	Buddy Holly Showcase	1964	80.00
❑ CRL757504 [S]	Giant	1969	50.00
❑ CRL57463 [M]	Holly in the Hills	1965	120.00
❑ CRL757463 [R]	Holly in the Hills	1965	100.00
❑ CRL57426 [M]	Reminiscing	1963	200.00
— Maroon label			
❑ CRL57426 [M]	Reminiscing	1964	80.00
— Black label with color bars			
❑ CRL757426 [R]	Reminiscing	1964	40.00
❑ CXB8 [M]	The Best of Buddy Holly	1966	80.00
❑ CXSB8 [R]	The Best of Buddy Holly	1966	50.00
❑ CRL57279 [M]	The Buddy Holly Story	1959	300.00
— Maroon label; back color print in black and red			
❑ CRL57279 [M]	The Buddy Holly Story	1959	150.00
— Maroon label; back color print in all black			
❑ CRL57279 [M]	The Buddy Holly Story	1963	80.00
— Black label with color bars			
❑ CRL757279 [R]	The Buddy Holly Story	1963	40.00
❑ CRL57326 [M]	The Buddy Holly Story, Vol. 2	1959	200.00
— Maroon label			
❑ CRL57326 [M]	The Buddy Holly Story, Vol. 2	1963	80.00
— Black label with color bars			
❑ CRL757326 [R]	The Buddy Holly Story, Vol. 2	1963	40.00

CRICKET

| ❑ C001000 | Buddy Holly Live -- Volume 1 | 197? | 25.00 |
| ❑ C001001 | Buddy Holly Live -- Volume 1 | 197? | 25.00 |

DECCA

❑ DXSE7207	A Rock 'n' Roll Collection	1972	40.00
❑ DL8707 [M]	That'll Be the Day	1958	1500.00
— Black label with silver print			
❑ DL8707 [M]	That'll Be the Day	1961	300.00
— Black label with color bars			

GREAT NORTHWEST

| ❑ GNW-4014 | Visions of Buddy | 197? | 12.00 |
| — Interview album | | | |

MCA

❑ 4009	A Rock 'n' Roll Collection	1973	25.00
— Black labels with rainbow			
❑ 4009	A Rock 'n' Roll Collection	1978	15.00
— Later pressings on tan or blue/rainbow labels			
❑ 25239	Buddy Holly	1989	15.00
— Reissue of Coral 57210			
❑ 11161	Buddy Holly	1995	40.00
— Audiophile "Heavy Vinyl" reissue with gatefold cover			
❑ 3040	Buddy Holly/The Crickets 20 Golden Greats	1978	18.00
❑ 1484	Buddy Holly/The Crickets 20 Golden Greats	198?	10.00
— Reissue of 3040			
❑ 27059	For the First Time Anywhere	1983	12.00
❑ 5540	From the Original Master Tapes	1986	30.00
❑ 4184	Legend	1985	25.00
❑ 80000	The Complete Buddy Holly	1981	80.00
— Box set with booklet and custom innersleeves			
❑ 737	The Great Buddy Holly	197?	12.00
— Reissue of MCA Coral LP			

MCA CORAL

| ❑ CD-20101 | The Great Buddy Holly | 1973 | 15.00 |

VOCALION

❑ VL73923	Good Rockin'	1971	120.00
❑ VL3811 [M]	The Great Buddy Holly	1967	80.00
❑ VL73811 [R]	The Great Buddy Holly	1967	50.00

HOLLY, DOYLE

BARNABY

| ❑ BR-15010 | Doyle Holly | 1973 | 18.00 |
| ❑ BR-15011 | Just Another Cowboy Song | 1973 | 18.00 |

HOLLY AND THE ITALIANS

VIRGIN

| ❑ ARE38287 | Holly and the Italians | 1982 | 12.00 |
| ❑ NFE37359 | The Right to Be Italian | 1981 | 12.00 |

HOLLYDAY, CHRISTOPHER

JAZZ BEAT

| ❑ 102 | Oh Brother! | 198? | 18.00 |

NOVUS

| ❑ 3055-1-N | Christopher Hollyday | 1989 | 15.00 |

Number	Title	Yr	NM
❑ 3087-1-N	On Course	1990	18.00

RBI

| ❑ 402 | Reverence | 1988 | 18.00 |

HOLLYRIDGE STRINGS, THE

CAPITOL

Number	Title	Yr	NM
❑ T2404 [M]	Christmas Favorites by the Hollyridge Strings	1965	15.00
❑ ST2404 [S]	Christmas Favorites by the Hollyridge Strings	1965	18.00
❑ SM-11830	Christmas Favorites by the Hollyridge Strings	1978	12.00
— Abridged reissue of ST 2404			
❑ T2221 [M]	Hits Made Famous by Elvis Presley	1965	18.00
❑ ST2221 [S]	Hits Made Famous by Elvis Presley	1965	25.00
❑ ST2998	Hits Made Famous by Simon and Garfunkel	1968	18.00
❑ T2199 [M]	Hits Made Famous by the Four Seasons	1965	18.00
❑ ST2199 [S]	Hits Made Famous by the Four Seasons	1965	25.00
❑ ST-883 [B]	Hits of the 70's	1971	15.00
❑ T2564 [M]	Oldies But Goldies	1966	18.00
❑ ST2564 [S]	Oldies But Goldies	1966	25.00
❑ T2611 [M]	Skyscraper	1966	18.00
❑ ST2611 [S]	Skyscraper	1966	25.00
❑ T2156 [M]	The Beach Boys Song Book	1964	18.00
❑ ST2156 [S]	The Beach Boys Song Book	1964	25.00
❑ SM-2156	The Beach Boys Song Book	197?	12.00
❑ T2749 [M]	The Beach Boys Song Book, Vol. 2	1967	25.00
❑ ST2749 [S]	The Beach Boys Song Book, Vol. 2	1967	18.00
❑ T2116 [M]	The Beatles Song Book	1964	18.00
❑ ST2116 [S]	The Beatles Song Book	1964	25.00
❑ SM-2116	The Beatles Song Book	197?	12.00
❑ T2202 [M]	The Beatles Song Book, Vol. 2	1965	18.00
❑ ST2202 [S]	The Beatles Song Book, Vol. 2	1965	25.00
❑ T2656 [M]	The Beatles Song Book, Vol. 4	1967	25.00
❑ ST2656 [S]	The Beatles Song Book, Vol. 4	1967	18.00
❑ T2310 [M]	The Nat King Cole Song Book	1965	18.00
❑ ST2310 [S]	The Nat King Cole Song Book	1965	25.00
❑ T2429 [M]	The New Beatles Song Book	1966	18.00
❑ ST2429 [S]	The New Beatles Song Book	1966	25.00
❑ SM-2429	The New Beatles Song Book	197?	12.00

HOLLYWOOD ARGYLES, THE

LUTE

| ❑ L-9001 [M] | The Hollywood Argyles (Alley Oop) | 1960 | 700.00 |

HOLLYWOOD PERSUADERS, THE

ORIGINAL SOUND

| ❑ LPM-5013 [M] | Drums a-Go-Go | 1965 | 50.00 |
| ❑ LPS-8874 [S] | Drums a-Go-Go | 1965 | 60.00 |

HOLLYWOOD ROSE

CLEOPATRA

| ❑ 8144 [B] | The Roots Of Guns N' Roses | | 30.00 |
| — picture disc | | | |

HOLLYWOOD SAXOPHONE QUARTET, THE

LIBERTY

❑ LRP-3047 [M]	Gold Rush Suite	1957	40.00
❑ LRP-3080 [M]	Sax Appeal	1958	30.00
❑ LRP-6005 [M]	The Hollywood Saxophone Quartet	1955	40.00

HOLMAN, BILL

ANDEX

❑ A-3004 [M]	In a Jazz Orbit	1958	40.00
❑ AS-3004 [S]	In a Jazz Orbit	1959	30.00
❑ A-3005 [M]	Jive for Five	1958	40.00
❑ AS-3005 [S]	Jive for Five	1959	30.00

CAPITOL

❑ T1464 [M]	Great Big Band	1960	30.00
❑ ST1464 [S]	Great Big Band	1960	30.00
❑ H6500 [10]	The Bill Holman Octet	1954	120.00

CORAL

| ❑ CRL57188 [M] | The Fabulous Bill Holman | 1958 | 80.00 |

CREATIVE WORLD

| ❑ ST-1053 | Great Big Band | 197? | 18.00 |

HOLMAN, EDDIE

ABC

| ❑ S-701 | I Love You | 1970 | 30.00 |

SALSOUL

| ❑ 5511 | A Night to Remember | 1977 | 12.00 |

Number	Title	Yr	NM

HOLMBERG, JIM

ESP-DISK'
| ☐ 1098 | MIJ | 196? | 25.00 |

HOLMES, CARL, AND THE COMMANDERS

ATLANTIC
| ☐ 8060 [M] | Twist Party at the Roundtable | 1962 | 40.00 |
| ☐ SD8060 [S] | Twist Party at the Roundtable | 1962 | 50.00 |

HOLMES, JAKE

COLUMBIA
| ☐ C30996 | Jake Holmes | 1972 | 15.00 |
POLYDOR
| ☐ 24-4007 | Jake Holmes | 1969 | 15.00 |
| ☐ 24-4034 | So Close, So Very Far to Go | 1970 | 15.00 |
TOWER
☐ T5079 [M]	Above Ground	1967	25.00
☐ DT5079 [R]	Above Ground	1967	18.00
☐ ST5127	Letter to Katherine December	1968	18.00

HOLMES, MARVIN

BROWN DOOR
| ☐ MH-6581 | Honor Thy Father | 1975 | 50.00 |
| ☐ MH-6573 | Summer of '73 | 1973 | 50.00 |
UNI
| ☐ 73046 | Ooh, Ooh, The Dragon And Other Monsters | 1969 | 100.00 |
— *Reproductions exist*

HOLMES, RICHARD "GROOVE

BLUE NOTE
| ☐ BST-84372 | Comin' On Home | 1971 | 15.00 |
FANTASY
| ☐ OJC-329 | Soul Message | 1988 | 12.00 |
— *Reissue of Prestige 7435*
FLYING DUTCHMAN
| ☐ BDL1-1537 | I'm in the Mood for Love | 1976 | 15.00 |
GROOVE MERCHANT
☐ 505	American Pie	1972	15.00
☐ 4402 [B]	Hunk-A-Funk	1975	25.00
☐ 527	New Groove	1973	15.00
☐ 512	Night Glider	1972	15.00
MUSE
☐ 5358	Blues All Day Long	1989	12.00
☐ 5239	Broadway	1981	12.00
☐ 5167	Good Vibrations	1979	12.00
☐ 5134	Shippin' Out	1978	12.00
PACIFIC JAZZ
☐ PJ-59 [M]	After Hours	1962	25.00
☐ ST-59 [S]	After Hours	1962	30.00
☐ ST-20171	Come Together	1970	18.00
☐ PJ-32 [M]	Groovin' with Jug	1961	30.00
☐ ST-32 [S]	Groovin' with Jug	1961	40.00
☐ LN-10130	Groovin' with Jug	198?	10.00
— *Budget-line reissue*
☐ PJ-23 [M]	Richard "Groove" Holmes	1961	30.00
☐ ST-23 [S]	Richard "Groove" Holmes	1961	30.00
☐ PJ-51 [M]	Somethin' Special	1962	25.00
☐ ST-51 [S]	Somethin' Special	1962	30.00
☐ PJ-10105 [M]	Tell It Like It Tis	1966	18.00
☐ ST-20105 [S]	Tell It Like It Tis	1966	25.00
☐ ST-20153	Workin' on a Groovy Thing	1969	18.00
☐ ST-20163	X-77	1969	18.00
PRESTIGE
☐ PRLP-7514 [M]	Get Up and Get It	1967	30.00
☐ PRST-7514 [S]	Get Up and Get It	1967	18.00
☐ PRLP-7468 [M]	Living Soul	1966	18.00
☐ PRST-7468 [S]	Living Soul	1966	25.00
☐ PRLP-7485 [M]	Misty	1966	18.00
☐ PRST-7485 [S]	Misty	1966	25.00
☐ PRLP-7435 [M]	Soul Message	1966	18.00
☐ PRST-7435 [S]	Soul Message	1966	25.00
☐ PRST-7741	Soul Mist	1970	18.00
☐ PRST-7543	Soul Power	1968	18.00
☐ PRLP-7493 [M]	Spicy	1967	25.00
☐ PRST-7493 [S]	Spicy	1967	18.00
☐ PRLP-7497 [M]	Super Cool	1967	25.00
☐ PRST-7497 [S]	Super Cool	1967	18.00
☐ PRST-7601	That Healin' Feelin'	1969	18.00
☐ PRST-7768	The Best for Beautiful People	1971	18.00
☐ PRST-7700	The Best of Richard "Groove" Holmes	1969	18.00
☐ PRST-7778	The Best of Soul Organ Giants	1972	15.00
☐ PRST-7570	The Groover	1968	18.00
VERSATILE
| ☐ MSG6003 | Dancing in the Sun | 1977 | 18.00 |
WARNER BROS.
| ☐ W1553 [M] | Book of the Blues | 1964 | 25.00 |
| ☐ WS1553 [S] | Book of the Blues | 1964 | 30.00 |
WORLD PACIFIC
| ☐ ST-20147 | Welcome Home | 1968 | 25.00 |

HOLMES, RUPERT

ELEKTRA
| ☐ 5E-560 | Full Circle | 1982 | 12.00 |
EPIC
☐ KE33443	Rupert Holmes	1975	15.00
☐ PE34288	Singles	1976	15.00
☐ KE32864	Widescreen	1974	15.00
EXCELSIOR
| ☐ XMP-6000 | Rupert Holmes | 1980 | 12.00 |
| ☐ XMP-6022 | She Lets Her Hair Down | 1981 | 12.00 |
INFINITY
| ☐ 9020 | Partners in Crime | 1979 | 12.00 |
MCA
| ☐ 5129 | Adventure | 1980 | 12.00 |
| ☐ 9020 | Partners in Crime | 1980 | 10.00 |
— *Reissue of Infinity LP*
| ☐ 37166 | Pursuit of Happiness | 198? | 10.00 |
— *Reissue of Private Stock LP*
PRIVATE STOCK
| ☐ PS-7006 | Pursuit of Happiness | 1978 | 15.00 |

HOLT, RED

ARGO
| ☐ LP-696 [M] | Look Out! Look Out! | 1962 | 25.00 |
| ☐ LPS-696 [S] | Look Out! Look Out! | 1962 | 30.00 |
PAULA
| ☐ 4006 | Isaac, Isaac, Isaac | 197? | 18.00 |
| ☐ 4007 | The Other Side of the Moon | 197? | 18.00 |

HOLY MACKEREL, THE

REPRISE
| ☐ RS-6311 | The Holy Mackerel | 1968 | 30.00 |

HOLY MODAL ROUNDERS, THE

4 MEN WITH BEARDS
| ☐ 4M184LP [B] | 2 | | 25.00 |
| ☐ 4M183LP [B] | The Holy Modal Rounders | | 25.00 |
ADELPHIA
| ☐ 1030 | Last Round | 198? | 12.00 |
ELEKTRA
| ☐ EKS-74026 [B] | The Moray Eels Eat the Holy Modal Rounders | 1968 | 30.00 |
ESP-DISK'
| ☐ 1068 [M] | Indian War Whoop | 1967 | 70.00 |
| ☐ 1068-S [S] | Indian War Whoop | 1967 | 40.00 |
FANTASY
| ☐ F-24711 | Stampfel and Weber | 1972 | 25.00 |
FOLKLORE
| ☐ FRLP-14031 [M] | The Holy Modal Rounders | 1964 | 80.00 |
METROMEDIA
| ☐ MD-1000 | Good Taste Is Timeless | 1970 | 30.00 |
PRESTIGE
| ☐ PRLP-7451 [M] | The Holy Modal Rounders | 1966 | 40.00 |
— *Reissue of Folklore LP*
| ☐ PR-7720 | The Holy Modal Rounders | 1969 | 30.00 |
| ☐ PRLP-7410 [M] | The Holy Modal Rounders 2 | 1965 | 40.00 |
ROUNDER
| ☐ 3004 | Alleged In Their Own Time | 198? | 12.00 |
SUNDAZED
| ☐ LP5126 | The Moray Eels Eat the Holy Modal Rounders | 2002 | 15.00 |
— *Reissue on 180-gram vinyl*

HOMBRES, THE

VERVE FORECAST
| ☐ FT-3036 [M] | Let It Out (Let It All Hang Out) | 1967 | 30.00 |
| ☐ FTS-3036 [S] | Let It Out (Let It All Hang Out) | 1967 | 30.00 |

HOMER

UNITED
| ☐ HS-101 | Grown in U.S.A. | 1970 | 250.00 |

HOMER AND JETHRO

AUDIO LAB
| ☐ AL-1513 [M] | Musical Madness | 1958 | 100.00 |
KING
☐ KS-1005	24 Great Songs in the Homer & Jethro Style	1967	25.00
☐ 848 [M]	Cornier Than Corn	1963	70.00
☐ 639 [M]	They Sure Are Corny	1959	100.00
RCA CAMDEN
| ☐ CAL-707 [M] | Homer and Jethro Strike Back | 1961 | 18.00 |
RCA VICTOR
☐ LPM-3538 [M]	Any News from Nashville?	1966	30.00
☐ LSP-3538 [S]	Any News from Nashville?	1966	30.00
☐ LPM-1412 [M]	Barefoot Ballads	1957	50.00
☐ LSP-4001	Cool, Crazy Christmas	1968	25.00
☐ LPM-2928 [M]	Cornfucius Say	1964	30.00
☐ LSP-2928 [S]	Cornfucius Say	1964	30.00
☐ LPM-2954 [M]	Fractured Folk Songs	1964	30.00
☐ LSP-2954 [S]	Fractured Folk Songs	1964	30.00
☐ LPM-3112 [10]	Homer & Jethro Fracture Frank Loesser	1953	150.00
☐ LPM-2492 [M]	Homer and Jethro at the Convention	1962	30.00
☐ LSP-2492 [S]	Homer and Jethro at the Convention	1962	30.00
☐ LPM-2181 [M]	Homer and Jethro at the Country Club	1960	30.00
☐ LSP-2181 [S]	Homer and Jethro at the Country Club	1960	40.00
☐ LSP-4024	Homer and Jethro at Vanderbilt U.	1969	25.00
☐ LPM-2674 [M]	Homer and Jethro Go West	1963	30.00
☐ LSP-2674 [S]	Homer and Jethro Go West	1963	30.00
☐ LPM-3357 [M]	Homer and Jethro Sing Tenderly	1965	30.00
☐ LSP-3357 [S]	Homer and Jethro Sing Tenderly	1965	30.00
☐ LSP-4148	Homer and Jethro's Next Album	1969	25.00
☐ LPM-3701 [M]	It Ain't Necessarily Square	1967	30.00
☐ LSP-3701 [S]	It Ain't Necessarily Square	1967	30.00
☐ LPM-1880 [M]	Life Can Be Miserable	1958	30.00
☐ LSP-1880 [S]	Life Can Be Miserable	1958	50.00
☐ LPM-3822 [M]	Nashville Cats	1967	40.00
☐ LSP-3822 [S]	Nashville Cats	1967	30.00
☐ LPM-2743 [M]	Ooh, That's Corny	1963	30.00
☐ LSP-2743 [S]	Ooh, That's Corny	1963	30.00
☐ LPM-2459 [M]	Playing It Straight	1962	30.00
☐ LSP-2459 [M]	Playing It Straight	1962	30.00
☐ LPM-3877 [M]	Somethin' Stupid	1967	50.00
☐ LSP-3877 [S]	Somethin' Stupid	1967	30.00
☐ LPM-2286 [M]	Songs My Mother Never Sang	1961	30.00
☐ LSP-2286 [S]	Songs My Mother Never Sang	1961	30.00
☐ LPM-3474 [M]	The Best of Homer and Jethro	1966	30.00
☐ LSP-3474 [S]	The Best of Homer and Jethro	1966	30.00
☐ LPM-3462 [M]	The Old Crusty Minstrels	1965	30.00
☐ LSP-3462 [S]	The Old Crusty Minstrels	1965	30.00
☐ LPM-3973 [M]	There's Nothing Like an Old Hippie	1968	100.00
☐ LSP-3973 [S]	There's Nothing Like an Old Hippie	1968	30.00
☐ LPM-1560 [M]	The Worst of Homer & Jethro	1958	50.00
☐ LPM-3673 [M]	Wanted for Murder	1966	30.00
☐ LSP-3673 [S]	Wanted for Murder	1966	30.00
☐ LPM-2455 [M]	Zany Songs of the '30s	1962	30.00
☐ LSP-2455 [S]	Zany Songs of the '30s	1962	30.00

HOMESICK JAMES

PRESTIGE
| ☐ PRLP-7388 [M] | Homesick James | 1965 | 30.00 |

HONDELLS, THE

MERCURY
☐ MG-20940 [M]	Go Little Honda	1964	40.00
☐ SR-60940 [S]	Go Little Honda	1964	60.00
☐ MG-20982 [M]	The Hondells	1965	50.00
☐ SR-60982 [S]	The Hondells	1965	80.00

HONEY AND THE BEES

JOSIE
| ☐ JOS-4013 | Love | 1970 | 25.00 |

HONEY CONE, THE

HOT WAX
☐ HA-713	Love, Peace & Soul	1972	15.00
☐ HA-707	Soulful Tapestry	1971	15.00
☐ HA-706	Sweet Replies	1971	15.00
☐ HA-701	Take Me With You	1970	15.00

HONEY DREAMERS, THE

FANTASY
| ☐ 3207 [M] | The Honey Dreamers Sing Gershwin | 1956 | 80.00 |
— *Red vinyl*
| ☐ 3207 [M] | The Honey Dreamers Sing Gershwin | 195? | 40.00 |
— *Black vinyl*

HONEY LTD

LIGHT IN THE ATTIC
| ☐ LITA102 [M] | The Complete LHI Recordings | 2013 | 30.00 |

HONEYCOMBS, THE

INTERPHON
| ☐ IN-88001 [M] | Here Are the Honeycombs | 1964 | 50.00 |
| ☐ IN-88001 [R] | Here Are the Honeycombs | 1964 | 50.00 |
VEE JAY
| ☐ IN-88001 [M] | Here Are the Honeycombs | 1964 | 60.00 |
| ☐ IN-88001 [R] | Here Are the Honeycombs | 1964 | 60.00 |

HONEYMOON SUITE

WARNER BROS.
| ☐ 25098 | Honeymoon Suite | 1984 | 12.00 |
| ☐ R162140 | Racing After Midnight | 1988 | 15.00 |
— *BMG Direct Marketing edition*
| ☐ 25652 | Racing After Midnight | 1988 | 12.00 |

Number	Title	Yr	NM
❑ R144489	The Big Prize	1986	15.00
—RCA Music Service edition			
❑ 25293	The Big Prize	1986	12.00

HOODOO GURUS

A&M

❑ SP5012	Stone Age Romeos	1983	15.00

BIG TIME

❑ 009 [B]	Mars Needs Guitars	1985	18.00

ELEKTRA

❑ 60728	Blow Your Cool	1987	12.00
❑ 60485	Mars Needs Guitars	1986	12.00
—Reissue of Big Time LP			

RCA

❑ 9781-1-R	Magnum Cum Louder	1989	12.00

HOODOO RHYTHM DEVILS, THE

CAPITOL

❑ ST-842	The Hoodoo Rhythm Devils	1971	25.00

HOOK, THE

UNI

❑ 73038	Hooked	1969	18.00
❑ 73023	The Hook Will Grab You	1968	18.00

HOOKER, EARL

ARHOOLIE

❑ LP1044	2 Bugs and a Roach	1968	30.00
❑ LP1066	His First and Last Recordings	1970	30.00
❑ LP1051	Hooker and Steve	1969	30.00

BLUES ON BLUES

❑ 10002	The Last of the Great Earl Hooker	197?	25.00

BLUESWAY

❑ BLS-6032	Don't Have to Worry	1969	30.00
❑ BLS-6072	Do You Remember the Great Earl Hooker	1973	18.00
❑ BLS-6038	If You Miss Him	1970	30.00

BLUE THUMB

❑ BTS12	Sweet Black Angel	1969	30.00

CUCA

❑ 3400 [M]	The Genius of Earl Hooker	1965	250.00

HOOKER, JOHN LEE, AND CANNED HEAT

LIBERTY

❑ 35002	Hooker 'n' Heat	1971	25.00

RHINO

❑ RNDA-71105	Infinite Boogie	1987	15.00
❑ RNLP-801	Recorded Live at the Fox Venice Theatre	1985	15.00

HOOKER, JOHN LEE

ABC

❑ X-768	Born in Mississippi, Raised Up in Tennessee	1973	25.00
❑ XQ-768 [Q]	Born in Mississippi, Raised Up in Tennessee	1974	30.00
❑ S-720	Endless Boogie	1971	25.00
❑ X-838	Free Beer and Chicken	1974	18.00
❑ XQ-838 [Q]	Free Beer and Chicken	1974	30.00
❑ X-761	Live at Soledad Prison	1972	25.00
❑ XQ-761 [Q]	Live at Soledad Prison	1974	30.00
❑ X-736	Never Get Out of These Blues Alive	1972	25.00
❑ XQ-736 [Q]	Never Get Out of These Blues Alive	1974	30.00

ATCO

❑ 33-151 [M]	Don't Turn Me From Your Door	1963	100.00
❑ SD 33-151 [R]	Don't Turn Me From Your Door	1967	50.00

ATLANTIC

❑ SD7228	Detroit Special	1972	25.00

BATTLE

❑ Bl P-6114 [M]	How Long Blues	196?	150.00
❑ BLP-6113 [M]	John Lee Hooker	196?	150.00

BLUESWAY

❑ BLS-6038	If You Miss 'Em	1969	25.00
❑ BL-6002 [M]	Live at Café A-Go-Go	1967	30.00
❑ BLS-6002 [S]	Live at Café A-Go-Go	1967	25.00
❑ BLS-6052	Live at Kabuki-Wuki	1973	18.00
❑ BLQ-6052 [Q]	Live at Kabuki-Wuki	1974	30.00
❑ BLS-6023	Simply the Truth	1968	25.00
❑ BL-6012 [M]	Urban Blues	1967	30.00
❑ BLS-6012 [S]	Urban Blues	1967	25.00

BUDDAH

❑ BDS-7506	Big Band Blues	1970	18.00
❑ BDS-4002	The Very Best of John Lee Hooker	1970	18.00

CHAMELEON

❑ D1-74808	The Healer	1989	12.00
❑ D1-74794	The Hook	1989	12.00

CHESS

❑ LP-1438 [M]	House of the Blues	1960	300.00
—Black label			
❑ LP-1438 [M]	House of the Blues	1966	50.00

—Blue and white label			
❑ CH-9258	House of the Blues	1987	10.00
❑ LP-1454 [M]	John Lee Hooker Plays and Sings the Blues	1961	300.00
—Black label			
❑ LP-1454 [M]	John Lee Hooker Plays and Sings the Blues	1966	50.00
—Blue and white label			
❑ CH-9199	John Lee Hooker Plays and Sings the Blues	1986	10.00
—Reissue			
❑ 60011	Mad Man Blues	1973	25.00
❑ CH2-92507	Mad Man Blues	198?	15.00
❑ LP-1508 [M]	Real Folk Blues	1966	50.00
❑ LPS-1508 [R]	Real Folk Blues	1966	30.00
❑ CH-9271	The Real Folk Blues	1988	10.00

CLEOPATRA

❑ 3479 [B]	Blues On Fire		25.00
❑ 8836 [B]	Electric Blues		40.00
—picture disc			

COLLECTABLES

❑ COL-5151	Golden Classics	198?	15.00

CROWN

❑ CLP-5295 [M]	Folk Blues	1962	30.00
—Gray label			
❑ CLP-5295 [M]	Folk Blues	1962	15.00
—Black label with multi-color "Crown"			
❑ CLP-5232 [M]	John Lee Hooker Sings the Blues	1962	100.00
—Black label with silver "Crown"			
❑ CLP-5232 [M]	John Lee Hooker Sings the Blues	1962	30.00
—Gray label			
❑ CLP-5232 [M]	John Lee Hooker Sings the Blues	196?	15.00
—Black label with multi-color "Crown"			
❑ CLP-5157 [M]	The Blues	1960	100.00
—Black label with silver "Crown"			
❑ CLP-5157 [M]	The Blues	1962	30.00
—Gray label			
❑ CLP-5157 [M]	The Blues	196?	15.00
—Black label with multi-color "Crown"			
❑ CLP-5353 [M]	The Great John Lee Hooker	1963	30.00
—Gray label			
❑ CLP-5353 [M]	The Great John Lee Hooker	1963	15.00
—Black label with multi-color "Crown"			

EVEREST ARCHIVE OF FOLK & JAZZ

❑ 347	Hooked On Blues	1980	15.00
❑ 222	John Lee Hooker	1968	15.00

EXODUS

❑ 325 [M]	Is He the World's Greatest Blues Singer?	1966	30.00

FANTASY

❑ 24722	Black Snake	197?	18.00
❑ 24706	Boogie Chillun	1972	18.00

GALAXY

❑ 201 [M]	I'm John Lee Hooker	1961	250.00
❑ 205 [M]	Live at Sugar Hill	1962	250.00
❑ 8205 [S]	Live at Sugar Hill	1962	250.00

GNP CRESCENDO

❑ GNPS-10007	The Best of John Lee Hooker	1974	18.00

GREENE BOTTLE

❑ 3130	Johnny Lee	1972	18.00

IMPULSE!

❑ A-9103 [M]	It Serves You Right to Suffer	1966	30.00
❑ AS-9103 [S]	It Serves You Right to Suffer	1966	40.00

JEWEL

❑ 5005	I Feel Good	1971	18.00

KING

❑ 727 [M]	John Lee Hooker Sings the Blues	1960	500.00
❑ KLP-727	John Lee Hooker Sings the Blues	1988	10.00
—Reissue of earlier 727			
❑ KS-1085	Moanin' and Stompin' Blues	1970	30.00

LABOR

❑ 4	Alone	1982	12.00

MUSE

❑ 5205	Sittin' Here Thinkin'	1980	15.00

PAUSA

❑ PR-7197	Jealous	1986	12.00

RIVERSIDE

❑ RLP 12-321 [M]	That's My Story	1960	100.00
❑ RLP 12-838 [M]	The Country Blues of John Lee Hooker	1959	100.00

SPECIALTY

❑ SPS-2125	Alone	1970	30.00
❑ SPS-2127	Going Down Highway 51	1970	30.00

STAX

❑ STS-2013	That's Where It's At	1970	18.00
❑ STX-4134	That's Where It's At	1979	12.00
—Reissue of 2013			

TOMATO

❑ 7009	The Cream	1978	18.00

TRADITION

❑ 2089	Real Blues	1970	18.00

UNITED ARTISTS

❑ UAS-5512	Coast to Coast Blues Band	1971	18.00
❑ UA-LA127-J	John Lee Hooker's Detroit	1974	30.00

VEE JAY

❑ LP-1043 [M]	Burnin'	1962	50.00
❑ SR-1043 [S]	Burnin'	1962	150.00
❑ LP-1078 [M]	Concert at Newport	1964	50.00
❑ SR-1078 [S]	Concert at Newport	1964	150.00
❑ VJLP-1078 [B]	Concert at Newport	1986	10.00
—Reissue of original on flimsier vinyl			
❑ LP-1007 [M]	I'm John Lee Hooker	1959	300.00
—Maroon label			
❑ LP-1007 [M]	I'm John Lee Hooker	1960	80.00
—Black label with colorband			
❑ VJLP-1007	I'm John Lee Hooker	1986	10.00
—Reissue of original on flimsier vinyl			
❑ LP-8502 [M]	Is He the World's Greatest Blues Singer?	1965	40.00
—This is the title on the cover; the label calls it "Is He Really the World's Greatest Blues Singer?"			
❑ VJLP-8502	Is He the World's Greatest Blues Singer?	1986	10.00
—Reissue of original on flimsier vinyl; this is the title on the cover; the label calls it "Is He Really the World's Greatest Blues Singer?"			
❑ DY-7301	John Lee Hooker In Person	198?	10.00
❑ LP-1066 [M]	John Lee Hooker On Campus	1963	50.00
❑ SR-1066 [S]	John Lee Hooker On Campus	1963	150.00
❑ LP-1049 [M]	The Best of John Lee Hooker	1962	50.00
❑ SR-1049 [P]	The Best of John Lee Hooker	1962	80.00
❑ VJLP-1049	The Best of John Lee Hooker	1986	10.00
—Reissue of original on flimsier vinyl			
❑ LP-1058 [M]	The Big Soul of John Lee Hooker	1963	50.00
❑ SR-1058 [S]	The Big Soul of John Lee Hooker	1963	150.00
❑ VJLP-1058	The Big Soul of John Lee Hooker	1986	10.00
—Reissue of original on flimsier vinyl			
❑ LP-1033 [M]	The Folk Lore of John Lee Hooker	1961	50.00
❑ SR-1033 [S]	The Folk Lore of John Lee Hooker	1961	80.00
❑ LP-1023 [M]	Travelin'	1960	80.00

VERVE FOLKWAYS

❑ FT-3003 [M]	John Lee Hooker and Seven Nights	1965	30.00
❑ FTS-3003 [S]	John Lee Hooker and Seven Nights	1965	40.00

WAND

❑ WDS-689	On the Waterfront	1972	18.00

HOOPER, LES

CHURCHILL

❑ 67234	Dorian Blue	1977	15.00
❑ 67235	Hoopla	1978	15.00

CREATIVE WORLD

❑ ST-3002	Look What They've Done	197?	18.00

JAZZ HOUNDS

❑ 0004	Raisin' the Roof	1982	15.00

PAUSA

❑ 7185	Hoopla	1986	12.00

HOOPES, RONNIE

REVELATION

❑ 21	Respect for a Great Tradition	197?	18.00

HOOTCH

PROGRESS

❑ PRS-4844	Hootch	1974	600.00

HOOTERS

ANTENNA

❑ HOO83	Amore	1983	25.00

COLUMBIA

❑ BFC39912	Nervous Night	1985	15.00
❑ FC39912	Nervous Night	1985	12.00
—Reissue with new prefix			
❑ OC40659	One Way Home	1987	12.00
❑ C45058	Zig Zag	1989	12.00

HOOTIE & THE BLOWFISH

ATLANTIC

❑ 82613	Cracked Rear View	1995	60.00
—Red vinyl			
❑ 82886	Fairweather Johnson	1996	25.00
❑ 83136	Musical Chairs	1998	18.00

HOPE, BOB

CADET

❑ LP-4046 [B]	On the Road to Vietnam	1965	18.00

Number	Title	Yr	NM
CAPITOL			
❏ ST-11538 [B]	America Is 200 Years Old ... And There's Still Hope!	1976	15.00
DECCA			
❏ DL4396 [M]	Hope in Russia and One Other Place	1963	25.00
❏ DL74396 [S]	Hope in Russia and One Other Place	1963	30.00
MCA			
❏ 906	Bob Hope in Hollywood	1984	15.00
RADIOLA			
❏ MR-1060	The Bob Hope Radio Show	197?	12.00
—Includes two radio shows: October 23, 1945 and December 18, 1945			
RCA VICTOR			
❏ LOC-1055 [M]	Not So Long Ago: NBC Project Twenty	1960	25.00
❏ LSO-1055 [S]	Not So Long Ago: NBC Project Twenty	1960	30.00
SPEAR			
❏ 4700	Holidays	1973	18.00

HOPE, ELMO

Number	Title	Yr	NM
AUDIO FIDELITY			
❏ AFLP-2119 [M]	Sounds from Riker's Island	1963	100.00
❏ AFSD-6119 [S]	Sounds from Riker's Island	1963	80.00
BEACON			
❏ B-401 [M]	High Hopes	1961	300.00
❏ BS-401 [S]	High Hopes	1961	40.00
BLUE NOTE			
❏ BLP-5044 [10]	Elmo Hope Quintet	1954	300.00
❏ BLP-5029 [10]	Elmo Hope Trio	1953	300.00
CELEBRITY			
❏ 209 [M]	Elmo Hope Trio	1962	30.00
❏ S-209 [S]	Elmo Hope Trio	1962	30.00
CONTEMPORARY			
❏ M-3620 [M]	The Elmo Hope Trio	1966	30.00
❏ S-7620 [S]	The Elmo Hope Trio	1966	30.00
FANTASY			
❏ OJC-477	Elmo Hope Trio	1991	15.00
❏ OJC-1703	Hope Meets Foster	1985	12.00
❏ OJC-1751	Meditations	198?	12.00
HIFI			
❏ J-616 [M]	Elmo Hope	1960	40.00
❏ JS-616 [S]	Elmo Hope	1960	50.00
INNER CITY			
❏ IC-1018	Last Sessions	197?	18.00
❏ IC-1037	Last Sessions, Volume 2	1978	18.00
MILESTONE			
❏ 47037	All Star Sessions	197?	18.00
PRESTIGE			
❏ PRST-7675	Elmo Hope Memorial Album	1969	18.00
❏ PRLP-7021 [M]	Hope Meets Foster	1956	120.00
❏ PRLP-7043 [M]	Informal Jazz	1956	150.00
❏ PRLP-7010 [M]	Meditations	1956	600.00
❏ PRLP-7021 [M]	Wail, Frank, Wail	1957	80.00
—Retitled reissue of above album			
RIVERSIDE			
❏ RLP-381 [M]	Homecoming!	1961	40.00
❏ RS-9381 [S]	Homecoming!	1961	50.00
❏ 6161	Homecoming!	198?	15.00
❏ RLP-408 [M]	Hope-Full	1962	30.00
❏ RS-9408 [S]	Hope-Full	1962	30.00

HOPE, LYNN

Number	Title	Yr	NM
ALADDIN			
❏ LP-707 [10]	Lynn Hope and His Tenor Sax	1953	600.00
❏ LP-805 [M]	Lynn Hope and His Tenor Sax	1955	500.00
IMPERIAL			
❏ LP-9177-A [M]	Tenderly	1962	40.00
❏ LP-12177-A [S]	Tenderly	1962	60.00
KING			
❏ 717 [M]	Maharajah of the Saxophone	1961	120.00
SCORE			
❏ SLP-4015 [M]	Tenderly	1957	200.00

HOPKIN, MARY

Number	Title	Yr	NM
APPLE			
❏ SMAS-3381	Earth Song/Ocean Song	1970	18.00
❏ ST-3351 [B]	Post Card	1969	18.00
❏ ST-5-3351	Post Card	1969	25.00
—Capitol Record Club edition			
❏ SW-3395 [B]	Those Were the Days	1972	30.00

HOPKINS, CLAUDE

Number	Title	Yr	NM
CHIAROSCURO			
❏ 114	Crazy Fingers	1972	18.00
DESIGN			
❏ DLP-30 [M]	Golden Era of Dixieland Jazz 1887-1937	1957	30.00
JAZZ ARCHIVES			
❏ JA-27	Singin' in the Rain	198?	12.00

Number	Title	Yr	NM
SWINGVILLE			
❏ SVLP-2020 [M]	Let's Jam	1961	50.00
—Purple label			
❏ SVLP-2020 [M]	Let's Jam	1965	30.00
—Blue label, trident logo at right			
❏ SVLP-2041 [M]	Swing Time	1962	50.00
—Purple label			
❏ SVLP-2041 [M]	Swing Time	1965	30.00
—Blue label, trident logo at right			
❏ SVLP-2009 [M]	Yes Indeed	1960	50.00
—Purple label			
❏ SVLP-2009 [M]	Yes Indeed	1965	30.00
—Blue label, trident logo at right			

HOPKINS, KENYON

Number	Title	Yr	NM
VERVE			
❏ V-8694 [M]	Dream Songs	1967	25.00
❏ V6-8694 [S]	Dream Songs	1967	15.00

HOPKINS, LIGHTNIN'

Number	Title	Yr	NM
ANALOGUE PRODUCTIONS			
❏ AAPB-014	Goin' Away	199?	40.00
—Audiophile reissue			
ARHOOLIE			
❏ 1030	Blues Festival	196?	18.00
❏ 2007	Early Recordings	197?	18.00
❏ 2010	Early Recordings Volume 2	197?	18.00
❏ 1022	Lightnin' Hopkins, His Brother and Barbara Dane	196?	25.00
❏ 1011	Lightnin' Hopkins and His Guitar	196?	25.00
❏ 1063	Lightnin' Hopkins in Berkeley	1969	18.00
❏ 1087	Poor Lightnin'	1970	18.00
❏ 1034	Texas Blues Man	1968	18.00
BARNABY			
❏ Z30247	Lightnin' Hopkins in New York	1970	18.00
BLUES CLASSICS			
❏ 30	Historic Recordings 1952-1953	1986	15.00
BLUESVILLE			
❏ BVLP-1045 [M]	Blues in My Bottle	1962	100.00
—Blue label, silver print			
❏ BVLP-1045 [M]	Blues in My Bottle	1964	30.00
—Blue label, trident logo on right			
❏ BVLP-1086 [M]	Down Home Blues	1964	30.00
❏ BVLP-1073 [M]	Goin' Away	1963	100.00
—Blue label, silver print			
❏ BVLP-1073 [M]	Goin' Away	1964	30.00
—Blue label, trident logo on right			
❏ BVLP-1081 [M]	Gotta Move Your Baby	1964	30.00
—Blue label, trident logo on right			
❏ BVLP-1029 [M]	Last Night Blues	1961	100.00
—Blue label, silver print			
❏ BVLP-1061 [M]	Lightnin' & Co.	1963	100.00
—Blue label, silver print			
❏ BVLP-1061 [M]	Lightnin' & Co.	1964	30.00
—Blue label, trident logo on right			
❏ BVLP-1019 [M]	Lightnin'	1961	100.00
—Blue label, silver print			
❏ BVLP-1019 [M]	Lightnin'	1964	30.00
—Blue label, trident logo on right			
❏ BVLP-1084 [M]	Lightnin' Hopkins' Greatest Hits	1964	40.00
❏ BVLP-1070 [M]	Smokes Like Lightnin'	1963	100.00
—Blue label, silver print			
❏ BVLP-1070 [M]	Smokes Like Lightnin'	1964	30.00
—Blue label, trident logo on right			
❏ BVLP-1057 [M]	Walkin' This Street	1962	100.00
—Blue label, silver print			
❏ BVLP-1057 [M]	Walkin' This Street	1964	30.00
—Blue label, trident logo on right			
BLUESWAY			
❏ S-6039	If You Miss 'Im	1969	25.00
BULLDOG			
❏ 1010	The Texas Bluesman	1965	18.00
CANDID			
❏ CM-8010 [M]	Lightnin' in New York	1961	120.00
❏ CS-9010 [S]	Lightnin' in New York	1961	150.00
COLLECTABLES			
❏ COL-5143	Golden Classics, Part 1: Drinkin' the Blues	198?	12.00
❏ COL-5144	Golden Classics, Part 2: Prison Blues	198?	12.00
❏ COL-5145	Golden Classics, Part 3: Mama and Papa Hopkins	198?	12.00
❏ COL-5146	Golden Classics, Part 4: Nothin' But the Blues	198?	12.00
❏ COL-5111	Golden Classics -- Mojo Hand	198?	12.00
❏ COL-5121	The Herald Recordings/1954	198?	12.00
❏ COL-5203	The Lost Texas Tapes, Vol. 1	198?	12.00
❏ COL-5204	The Lost Texas Tapes, Vol. 2	198?	12.00
❏ COL-5205	The Lost Texas Tapes, Vol. 3	198?	12.00
❏ COL-5206	The Lost Texas Tapes, Vol. 4	198?	12.00
❏ COL-5207	The Lost Texas Tapes, Vol. 5	198?	12.00
CROWN			
❏ CLP-5224 [M]	Lightnin' Hopkins Sings the Blues	1962	100.00

Number	Title	Yr	NM
—Black label, silver "Crown"			
❏ CLP-5224 [M]	Lightnin' Hopkins Sings the Blues	1962	50.00
—Gray label			
❏ CLP-5224 [M]	Lightnin' Hopkins Sings the Blues	196?	30.00
—Black label, multi-color logo			
DART			
❏ D-8000 [M]	Blues Underground	196?	200.00
—Retitled version of above			
❏ D-8000 [M]	Lightning Strikes Again	1960	400.00
DCC COMPACT CLASSICS			
❏ LPZ-2007	Blues Hoot	1996	50.00
—Audiophile vinyl			
EVEREST ARCHIVE OF FOLK & JAZZ			
❏ 342	Autobiography in Blues	1979	15.00
❏ 241	Lightnin' Hopkins	1969	18.00
❏ 313	Lightnin' Hopkins, Vol. 2	197?	18.00
FANTASY			
❏ OBC-506	Blues in My Bottle	198?	15.00
❏ 24702	Double Blues	1972	25.00
❏ OBC-522	Goin' Away	1988	15.00
❏ 24725	How Many More Years	1981	18.00
❏ OBC-532	Lightnin'	1990	15.00
FIRE			
❏ FLP104 [M]	Mojo Hand	1960	1500.00
FOLKLORE			
❏ FRLP-14021 [M]	Hootin' the Blues	1964	60.00
❏ FRST-14021 [S]	Hootin' the Blues	1964	70.00
FOLKWAYS			
❏ FS-3822 [M]	Lightnin' Hopkins	1962	40.00
❏ 31011	Roots	196?	18.00
GNP CRESCENDO			
❏ 10022	Legacy of the Blues, Volume 12	1978	15.00
GUEST STAR			
❏ G-1459 [M]	Live" at the Bird Lounge, Houston, Texas	1964	30.00
❏ GS-1459 [R]	Live" at the Bird Lounge, Houston, Texas	1964	25.00
HERALD			
❏ LP1012 [M]	Lightnin' and the Blues	1959	1500.00
—Black label; VG value 750; VG+ value 1125			
❏ LP1012 [M]	Lightnin' and the Blues	1959	800.00
—Yellow label			

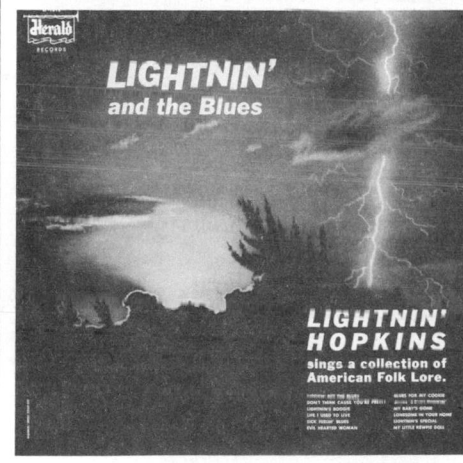

Number	Title	Yr	NM
❏ LP1012 [M]	Lightnin' and the Blues	196?	500.00
—Multi-color label			
IMPERIAL			
❏ LP-9211 [M]	Lightnin' Hopkins and the Blues	1963	200.00
❏ LP-12211 [R]	Lightnin' Hopkins and the Blues	1963	100.00
❏ LP-9180 [M]	Lightnin' Hopkins On Stage	1962	300.00
❏ LP-9186 [M]	Lightnin' Hopkins Sings the Blues	1962	300.00
INTERNATIONAL ARTISTS			
❏ IA-6	Free Form Patterns	1968	200.00
— With photo on cover			
❏ IA-6	Free Form Patterns	1968	50.00
— With psychedelic art on cover			
JAZZ MAN			
❏ BLZ-5502	Lightnin' in New York	1982	12.00
JEWEL			
❏ 5000	Blue Lightnin'	1967	18.00
❏ 5015	Great Electric Show and Dance	1970	18.00
❏ 5001	Talkin' Some Sense	1968	18.00
KING			
❏ KS-1085	Moanin' Blues	1969	18.00
MAINSTREAM			
❏ S-6040 [S]	Blues	196?	30.00

Number	Title	Yr	NM
56040 [M]	Blues	196?	30.00
326	Dirty Blues	197?	18.00
405	Low Down Dirty Blues	1974	18.00
311	The Blues	1971	18.00
MOUNT VERNON			
104 [M]	Nothin' But the Blues	196?	30.00
OLYMPIC GOLD MEDAL			
7110	Blues Giant	1974	15.00
POPPY			
60002	Lightnin'!	1969	30.00
PRESTIGE			
PRST-7831	Gotta Move Your Baby	1970	18.00
PRST-7806	Hootin' the Blues	1969	18.00
PRST-7592	Lightnin' Hopkins' Greatest Hits	1969	18.00
PRLPT-7370 [M]	My Life with the Blues	1965	60.00
PRST-7370 [S]	My Life with the Blues	1965	70.00
PRLP-7377 [M]	Soul Blues	1966	50.00
PRST-7377 [S]	Soul Blues	1966	60.00
PRST-7714	The Best of Lightnin' Hopkins & His Texas Blues Band	1969	18.00
PRST-7811	The Blues of Lightnin' Hopkins	1969	18.00
RHINO			
RNLP103	Los Angeles Blues	1982	12.00
SCORE			
SLP-4022 [M]	Lightnin' Hopkins Strums the Blues	1958	1200.00
SMITHSONIAN FOLKWAYS			
SF-40019	Lightnin' Hopkins	1990	15.00
SPHERE SOUND			
SSR-7001 [M]	Lightnin' Hopkins	1964	400.00
SSSR-7001 [R]	Lightnin' Hopkins	1964	300.00
TIME			
1 [M]	Blues/Folk	1960	120.00
2 [M]	Blues/Folk Volume 2	1960	120.00
T-70004 [M]	Last of the Great Blues Singers	1962	120.00
ST-70004 [S]	Last of the Great Blues Singers	1962	120.00
TOMATO			
7004	Lightnin'!	1977	18.00
TRADITION			
TLP-1040 [M]	Autobiography in Blues	1961	30.00
TLP-1035 [M]	Country Blues	1960	30.00
TLP-2103 [M]	Lightnin' Strikes	1972	18.00
TLP-2056 [M]	The Best of Lightnin' Hopkins	1967	25.00
TRIP			
TLP-8015	Lightnin' Hopkins	1971	15.00
UNITED			
US-7785	A Legend in His Time	196?	18.00
US-7713	Lightnin' Hopkins Sings the Blues	196?	18.00
US-7744	Original Folk Blues	196?	18.00
UNITED ARTISTS			
UAS-5512	Coast to Coast Blues Band	197?	18.00
UP FRONT			
158	Lightnin' Blues	1973	15.00
VAULT			
129	California Mudslide	1969	30.00
VEE JAY			
LP1044 [M]	Lightnin' Strikes	1962	50.00
VERVE			
V-8453 [M]	Fast Life Woman	1962	40.00
VERVE FOLKWAYS			
FV-9022 [M]	Lightnin' Strikes	1965	30.00
FVS-9022 [S]	Lightnin' Strikes	1965	30.00
FV-9000 [M]	The Roots of Lightnin' Hopkins	1965	30.00
FVS-9000 [S]	The Roots of Lightnin' Hopkins	1965	30.00
VERVE FORECAST			
FTS-3031	Lightnin' Strikes	1968	25.00
FT-3013 [M]	Something Blue	1967	25.00
FTS-3013 [S]	Something Blue	1967	30.00
WORLD PACIFIC			
WP-1817 [M]	First Meetin'	1963	30.00
ST-1817 [S]	First Meetin'	1963	80.00
— Red vinyl			
ST-1817 [S]	First Meetin'	1963	40.00
— Black vinyl			

HOPKINS, NICKY

Number	Title	Yr	NM
COLUMBIA			
KC32074 [B]	The Tin Man Was a Dreamer	1973	30.00
MERCURY			
SRM-1-1028 [B]	No More Changes	1975	30.00

HOPNEY

Number	Title	Yr	NM
ILLUSION			
CM-1034	Cosmic Rockout	1977	500.00
CM-1032	Ends and Means	1979	250.00
CM-1033	Perils of Love	1978	250.00

HORN, PAUL

Number	Title	Yr	NM
ABC IMPULSE!			
IA-9356	Plenty of Horn	1978	18.00
BLUE NOTE			
BN-LA529-H2	Paul Horn in India	1975	18.00
COLUMBIA			
CL2050 [M]	Impressions of "Cleopatra	1963	18.00
CS8850 [S]	Impressions of "Cleopatra	1963	15.00
CL1922 [M]	Profile of a Jazz Musician	1962	15.00
CS8722 [S]	Profile of a Jazz Musician	1962	15.00
CL1677 [M]	The Sound of Paul Horn	1961	12.00
CS8477 [S]	The Sound of Paul Horn	1961	30.00
DOT			
DLP-3091 [M]	House of Horn	1957	50.00
DLP-9002 [M]	Plenty of Horn	1958	50.00
DLP-29002 [S]	Plenty of Horn	1959	40.00
EPIC			
PE34231	Altura do Sol	1976	15.00
BXN26466	Inside	1969	18.00
PE26466	Inside	198?	10.00
— Budget-line reissue with new prefix			
KE31600	Inside II	1971	18.00
KE33561	Paul Horn + Nexus	1975	15.00
KE32837	Visions	1973	15.00
EVEREST ARCHIVE OF FOLK & JAZZ			
308	Paul Horn	197?	12.00
HIFI			
J-615 [M]	Something Blue	1960	30.00
JS-615 [S]	Something Blue	1960	40.00
ISLAND			
ILSD6	Special Edition	197?	15.00
KUCKUCK			
11075	Inside the Cathedral	198?	15.00
KU-060/061	Inside the Great Pyramid	198?	25.00
12060	Inside the Great Pyramid	198?	18.00
— Reissue with new number			
11062	Inside the Taj Mahal	198?	15.00
11083	The Peace Album	1988	15.00
LOST LAKE			
LL-0091	Sketches: A Collection	1986	15.00
MCA			
4144	Plenty of Horn	198?	15.00
OVATION			
OV-1405	Concert Ensemble	1970	18.00
RCA VICTOR			
LPM-3386 [M]	Cycle	1965	12.00
LSP-3386 [S]	Cycle	1965	12.00
LPM-3519 [M]	Here's That Rainy Day	1966	18.00
LSP-3519 [S]	Here's That Rainy Day	1966	25.00
LPM-3414 [M]	Jazz Suite on the Mass Texts	1965	12.00
LSP-3414 [S]	Jazz Suite on the Mass Texts	1965	12.00
LPM-3613 [M]	Monday, Monday	1966	12.00
LSP-3613 [S]	Monday, Monday	1966	25.00
WORLD PACIFIC			
WP-1266 [M]	Impressions	1959	50.00

HORN, SHIRLEY

Number	Title	Yr	NM
ABC-PARAMOUNT			
ABC-538 [M]	Travelin' Light	1965	40.00
ABCS-538 [S]	Travelin' Light	1965	50.00
MERCURY			
MG-20761 [M]	Loads of Love	1963	50.00
SR-60761 [S]	Loads of Love	1963	60.00
MG-20835 [M]	Shirley Horn with Horns	1963	50.00
SR-60835 [S]	Shirley Horn with Horns	1963	60.00
SR-60835 [S]	Shirley Horn with Horns	199?	30.00
— Classic Records reissue on audiophile vinyl			
STEEPLECHASE			
SCS-1111	A Lazy Afternoon	1979	15.00
SCS-1157	All Night Long	1981	15.00
SCS-1023	Garden of the Blues	198?	15.00
SCS-1164	Violets for Your Furs	1982	15.00
STEREO-CRAFT			
RTN-16 [M]	Embers and Ashes	1961	60.00
RTS-16 [S]	Embers and Ashes	1961	80.00
VERVE			
837933-1	Close Enough for Love	1989	15.00
832235-1	I Thought About You	1987	12.00

HORNE, JIMMY "BO

Number	Title	Yr	NM
SUNSHINE SOUND			
SSE-7801	Dance Across the Floor	1978	25.00
SSE-7805	Goin' Home for Love	1979	18.00

HORNE, LENA, AND HARRY BELAFONTE

Number	Title	Yr	NM
RCA VICTOR			
LOC-1507 [M]	Porgy and Bess	1959	30.00
LSO-1507 [S]	Porgy and Bess	1959	40.00

HORNE, LENA

Number	Title	Yr	NM
20TH CENTURY FOX			
TF-4115 [M]	Here's Lena Now	1964	18.00
TFS-4115 [S]	Here's Lena Now	1964	25.00
ACCORD			
SN-7190	Standing Room Only	198?	12.00
BLUEBIRD			
9985-1-RB	Stormy Weather: The Legendary Lena	1990	15.00
BUDDAH			
BDS-5084	Nature's Baby	1971	15.00
BDS-5669	The Essential Lena Horne	197?	15.00
BULLDOG			
BDL-2000	20 Golden Pieces of Lena Horne	198?	12.00
CHARTER			
CLP-101 [M]	Lena Sings Your Requests	1963	18.00
CLS-101 [S]	Lena Sings Your Requests	1963	25.00
CLP-106 [M]	Like Latin	1964	18.00
CLS-106 [S]	Like Latin	1964	25.00
DRG			
MRS-510	Lena Goes Latin	1986	12.00
MRS-501	Lena Horne With Lennie Hayton & the Marty Paich Orchestra	1985	12.00
JAZZTONE			
J-1262 [M]	Lena and Ivie	1957	50.00
LIBERTY			
LN-10194	Lena in Hollywood	198?	10.00
LION			
L-70050 [M]	I Feel So Smoochie	1959	25.00
MGM			
E-545 [10]	Lena Horne Sings	1952	50.00
M3G-5409	The One and Only	197?	12.00
MOBILE FIDELITY			
2-094	Lena Horne: The Lady and Her Music	1982	40.00
— Audiophile vinyl			
MOVIETONE			
MTM71005 [M]	Once in a Lifetime	196?	18.00
MTS72005 [S]	Once in a Lifetime	196?	25.00
PAIR			
PDL2-1055	Lena	1986	15.00
QWEST			
2QW3597	Lena Horne: The Lady and Her Music	1981	15.00
RCA VICTOR			
LPM-1879 [M]	Give the Lady What She Wants	1958	30.00
LSP-1879 [S]	Give the Lady What She Wants	1958	40.00
LPM-1148 [M]	It's Love	1955	50.00
BGL1-1799	Lena	1976	15.00
AYL1-4389	Lena, A New Album	1983	10.00
— Best Buy Series" reissue			
BGL1-1026	Lena and Michel	1975	15.00
— With Michel Legrand			
LPM-2364 [M]	Lena Horne at the Sands	1961	30.00
LSP-2364 [S]	Lena Horne at the Sands	1961	30.00
LOC-1028 [M]	Lena Horne at the Waldorf Astoria	1957	30.00
LSO-1028 [S]	Lena Horne at the Waldorf Astoria	1957	40.00
LPM-2587 [M]	Lena…Lovely and Alive	1963	30.00
LSP-2587 [S]	Lena…Lovely and Alive	1963	30.00
LPM-2465 [M]	Lena on the Blue Side	1962	30.00
LSP-2465 [S]	Lena on the Blue Side	1962	30.00
LPM-1895 [M]	Songs of Burke and Van Heusen	1959	30.00
LSP-1895 [S]	Songs of Burke and Van Heusen	1959	40.00
LPM-1375 [M]	Stormy Weather	1956	50.00
LPT-3061 [10]	This Is Lena Horne	1952	50.00
SKYE			
15	Lena & Gabor	1970	18.00
— With Gabor Szabo			
STANYAN			
POW-3006	Stormy Weather	198?	12.00
— Reissue of 10126			
10126	Stormy Weather	197?	15.00
SUNBEAM			
212	A Date with Lena Horne	198?	12.00
— With Fletcher Henderson and His Orchestra			
THREE CHERRIES			
TC-44411	The Men in My Life	1989	12.00
TIME-LIFE			
SLGD-05	Legendary Singers: Lena Horne	1985	18.00
TOPS			
L-1502 [M]	Lena Horne	1958	25.00
L-931 [10]	Lena Horne Sings	195?	40.00
L-910 [10]	Moanin' Low	195?	40.00
UNITED ARTISTS			
UAL3433 [M]	Feelin' Good	1965	18.00
UAS6433 [S]	Feelin' Good	1965	25.00
UAL3470 [M]	Lena in Hollywood	1966	18.00
UAS6470 [S]	Lena in Hollywood	1966	25.00
UAL3546 [M]	Merry from Lena	1966	18.00
UAS6546 [S]	Merry from Lena	1966	25.00
— Black label, "United Artists" in rounded box at top			
UAS6546 [S]	Merry from Lena	1972	15.00

Number	Title	Yr	NM
— Tan label			
❏ UAL3496 [M]	Soul	1966	18.00
❏ UAS6496 [S]	Soul	1966	25.00

HORNETS, THE

LIBERTY

Number	Title	Yr	NM
❏ LRP-3364 [M]	Big Drag Boats U.S.A.	1964	50.00
❏ LST-7364 [S]	Big Drag Boats U.S.A.	1964	60.00
❏ LRP-3348 [M]	Motorcycles U.S.A.	1963	40.00
❏ LST-7348 [S]	Motorcycles U.S.A.	1963	50.00

HORNSBY, BRUCE, AND THE RANGE

RCA

Number	Title	Yr	NM
❏ 2041-1-R	A Night on the Town	1990	15.00
❏ 6275-1-R [DJ]	Live The Way It Is Tour 1986-87	1987	50.00
— Promo-only release			
❏ 6686-1-R	Scenes from the Southside	1988	10.00

RCA VICTOR

Number	Title	Yr	NM
❏ NFL1-8058	The Way It Is	1986	18.00
— Original edition; cover is light brown with blurry picture of Hornsby in the middle			
❏ 5904-1-RX	The Way It Is	1986	10.00
— Revised cover and altered catalog number			
❏ AFL1-5904	The Way It Is	1986	12.00
— Revised edition; cover is dark with a photo of the whole band; "AFL1" prefix			

HOROWITZ, VLADIMIR

RCA VICTOR RED SEAL

Number	Title	Yr	NM
❏ LSC-2366 [S]	Beethoven: Piano Sonata in D "Appassionata"	1960	25.00
— Originals with "shaded dog" label			

HORSES

WHITE WHALE

Number	Title	Yr	NM
❏ WWS-7121	Horses	1970	40.00

HORSLIPS

ATCO

Number	Title	Yr	NM
❏ SD7030	Happy to Meet, Sorry to Part	1973	15.00
❏ SD7039	The Taln	1974	15.00

DJM

Number	Title	Yr	NM
❏ 16	Aliens	1978	12.00
❏ 10	Book of Invasions	1977	12.00
❏ 20	The Man Who Built America	1979	12.00

HORSLIPS

Number	Title	Yr	NM
❏ M 009	Drive the Cold Winter Away	1975	25.00
— U.K./Ireland import			

MERCURY

Number	Title	Yr	NM
❏ SRM-1-3842	Belfast Gigs	1980	12.00
❏ SRM-1-3809	Short Stories/Tall Tales	1979	12.00

RCA VICTOR

Number	Title	Yr	NM
❏ CPL1-0709	Dancehall Sweethearts	1974	15.00

HORTA, TONINHO

VERVE FORECAST

Number	Title	Yr	NM
❏ 835183-1	Diamond Land	1988	12.00
❏ 839734-1	Moonstone	1989	15.00

HORTON, JOHNNY

BRIAR

Number	Title	Yr	NM
❏ 104 [M]	Done Rovin'	196?	150.00

COLUMBIA

Number	Title	Yr	NM
❏ CL1721 [M]	Honky-Tonk Man	1962	30.00
❏ CS8779 [R]	Honky-Tonk Man	1962	18.00
❏ CL2299 [M]	I Can't Forget You	1965	30.00
❏ CS9099 [R]	I Can't Forget You	1965	18.00
❏ CL1478 [M]	Johnny Horton Makes History	1960	30.00
❏ CS8269 [S]	Johnny Horton Makes History	1960	40.00
❏ CL2566 [M]	Johnny Horton on Stage at the Louisiana Hayride	1966	25.00
❏ CS9366 [S]	Johnny Horton on Stage at the Louisiana Hayride	1966	30.00
❏ CS9940	Johnny Horton On the Road	1969	18.00
❏ CL1596 [M]	Johnny Horton's Greatest Hits	1961	30.00
❏ CS8396 [S]	Johnny Horton's Greatest Hits	1961	30.00
❏ PC8396	Johnny Horton's Greatest Hits	198?	10.00
— Budget-line reissue			
❏ 1596/8396	Johnny Horton's Greatest Hits Bonus Photo	1961	12.00
❏ CL1362 [M]	The Spectacular Johnny Horton	1959	30.00
❏ CS8167 [S]	The Spectacular Johnny Horton	1959	40.00
❏ G30884	The World of Johnny Horton	1971	18.00

DOT

Number	Title	Yr	NM
❏ DLP3221 [M]	Johnny Horton	1962	30.00
❏ DLP25221 [R]	Johnny Horton	1962	18.00

HARMONY

Number	Title	Yr	NM
❏ KH30394	The Battle of New Orleans	1971	15.00
❏ HS11384	The Legendary Johnny Horton	1970	15.00

Number	Title	Yr	NM
❏ HS11291 [R]	The Unforgettable Johnny Horton	196?	15.00

HILLTOP

Number	Title	Yr	NM
❏ JS-6060	All for the Love of a Girl	196?	15.00
❏ 6012	The Voice of Johnny Horton	196?	15.00

MERCURY

Number	Title	Yr	NM
❏ MG-20478 [M]	The Fantastic Johnny Horton	1959	50.00

SESAC

Number	Title	Yr	NM
❏ 1201 [M]	Free and Easy Songs	1959	150.00

HORTON, ROBERT

COLUMBIA

Number	Title	Yr	NM
❏ CL2408 [M]	A Man Called Shenandoah	1966	30.00
❏ CS9208 [S]	A Man Called Shenandoah	1966	30.00
❏ CL2202 [M]	The Very Thought of You	1964	30.00
❏ CS9002 [S]	The Very Thought of You	1964	30.00

HORTON, STEVEN WAYNE

CAPITOL

Number	Title	Yr	NM
❏ C1-91983	Steven Wayne Horton	1989	15.00

HORTON, WALTER "SHAKEY"

ARGO

Number	Title	Yr	NM
❏ LP-4037 [M]	The Soul of Blues Harmonica	1964	150.00
❏ I PS-4037 [S]	The Soul of Blues Harmonica	1964	250.00

HOT BUTTER

MUSICOR

Number	Title	Yr	NM
❏ MS-3242	Popcorn	1972	25.00
— Die-cut cover			
❏ MS-3242	Popcorn	1972	15.00
— Regular cover			

HOT CHOCOLATE

BIG TREE

Number	Title	Yr	NM
❏ BT76002	10 Greatest Hits	1977	12.00
❏ BT89503	Cicero Park	1975	12.00
❏ BT89512	Hot Chocolate	1975	12.00
❏ B189519	Man to Man	1976	12.00

EMI AMERICA

Number	Title	Yr	NM
❏ S1-17077	Mystery	1982	12.00

INFINITY

Number	Title	Yr	NM
❏ INF-9002	Every 1's a Winner	1978	12.00
❏ INF-9010	Going Through the Motions	1979	12.00

HOT DOGGERS, THE

EPIC

Number	Title	Yr	NM
❏ LN24054 [M]	Surfin' U.S.A.	1963	150.00
❏ BN26054 [S]	Surfin' U.S.A.	1963	200.00

HOT JAZZ ORCHESTRA

REVELATION

Number	Title	Yr	NM
❏ 28	Hot Jazz Orchestra	1979	12.00

HOT POOP

HOT POOP

Number	Title	Yr	NM
❏ 3072	Hot Poop Does Their Own Thing	1971	300.00

HOT RODDERS, THE

CROWN

Number	Title	Yr	NM
❏ CLP-5378 [M]	Big Hot Rod	1963	25.00
❏ CST-378 [S]	Big Hot Rod	1963	30.00

HOT TUNA

GRUNT

Number	Title	Yr	NM
❏ BFL1-0820	America's Choice	1975	18.00
❏ BFD1-0820 [Q]	America's Choice	1975	30.00
❏ FTR-1004	Burgers	1972	18.00
❏ BXL1-2591	Burgers	1978	15.00
— Reissue of 1004			
❏ CYL2-2545	Double Dose	1978	25.00
❏ BXL1-3357	Final Vinyl	1979	15.00
❏ BFL1-1920	Hoppkorv	1976	18.00
❏ DJL1-2852 [DJ]	The Last Interview? A Live Hot Tuna Radio Classic	1978	30.00
❏ BFL1-0348	The Phosphorescent Rat	1974	18.00
❏ BFL1-1238	Yellow Fever	1975	18.00
❏ BFD1-1238 [Q]	Yellow Fever	1975	30.00

RCA VICTOR

Number	Title	Yr	NM
❏ AYL1-3951	Burgers	1981	10.00
— Best Buy Series" reissue			
❏ LSP-4550	First Pull Up Then Pull Down	1971	18.00
❏ AYL1-3865	First Pull Up Then Pull Down	1981	10.00
— Best Buy Series" reissue			
❏ LSP-4353	Hot Tuna	1970	18.00
❏ AYL1-3064	Hot Tuna	1981	10.00
— Best Buy Series" reissue			

HOTHOUSE FLOWERS

LONDON

Number	Title	Yr	NM
❏ 85 [DJ]	Conversation and Music with Hothouse Flowers	1988	18.00
❏ 085 [DJ]	Conversation and Music with Hothouse Flowers	1988	18.00
❏ PRO884-1 [DJ]	Live	1990	30.00
— Six-song promo-only live EP			
❏ 828101-1	People	1988	15.00

HOTLEGS

CAPITOL

Number	Title	Yr	NM
❏ ST-587 [B]	Hotlegs Thinks: School Stinks	1970	40.00

HOUK, RALPH

CARLTON

Number	Title	Yr	NM
❏ HH-16 [M]	Hear How to Play Better Baseball	1961	40.00

HOUR GLASS, THE

LIBERTY

Number	Title	Yr	NM
❏ LRP-3536 [M]	The Hour Glass	1967	60.00
❏ LST-7536 [S]	The Hour Glass	1967	30.00
❏ LST-7555	The Power of Love	1968	30.00

SPRINGBOARD

Number	Title	Yr	NM
❏ SPB-4016	Duane and Gregg Allman with the Hour Glass	1976	12.00

UNITED ARTISTS

Number	Title	Yr	NM
❏ UA-LA013-G2 [B]	The Hour Glass	1973	18.00

HOUSE, SON, AND J.D. SHORT

VERVE FOLKWAYS

Number	Title	Yr	NM
❏ FV-9035 [M]	Blues from the Mississippi Delta	1966	40.00
❏ FVS-9035 [R]	Blues from the Mississippi Delta	1966	25.00

HOUSE, SON

COLUMBIA

Number	Title	Yr	NM
❏ CL2417 [M]	Father of the Folk Blues	1965	25.00
❏ CS9217 [S]	Father of the Folk Blues	1965	30.00
— Red "360 Sound" label			

HOUSE OF PAIN

TOMMY BOY

Number	Title	Yr	NM
❏ TB1056	House of Pain (Fine Malt Lyrics)	1992	40.00
❏ TB1161	Truth Crushed to Earth Shall Rise Again	1996	30.00

HOUSEMARTINS, THE

ELEKTRA

Number	Title	Yr	NM
❏ 60501	London 0 Hull 4	1986	12.00
❏ 60761 [DJ]	The People Who Grinned Themselves to Death	1987	15.00
— Promo-only audiophile pressing			
❏ 60761	The People Who Grinned Themselves to Death	1987	12.00
❏ 60761 [DJ]	The People Who Grinned Themselves to Death	1987	18.00
— Promo-only white label audiophile pressing			

HOUSTON, DAVID, AND BARBARA MANDRELL

EPIC

Number	Title	Yr	NM
❏ KE31705	A Perfect Match	1972	15.00
❏ KE32915	The Best of David Houston and Barbara Mandrell	1974	15.00

HOUSTON, DAVID, AND TAMMY WYNETTE

EPIC

Number	Title	Yr	NM
❏ LN24325 [M]	My Elusive Dreams	1967	25.00
❏ BN26325 [S]	My Elusive Dreams	1967	18.00

HOUSTON, DAVID

EPIC

Number	Title	Yr	NM
❏ LN24156 [M]	12 Great Country Hits	1965	18.00
❏ BN26156 [S]	12 Great Country Hits	1965	25.00
❏ LN24213 [M]	Almost Persuaded	1966	18.00
❏ BN26213 [S]	Almost Persuaded	1966	25.00
❏ LN24303 [M]	A Loser's Cathedral	1967	25.00
❏ BN26303 [S]	A Loser's Cathedral	1967	18.00
❏ BN26391	Already It's Heaven	1968	18.00
❏ KE33350	A Man Needs Love	1975	15.00
❏ E30657	A Woman Always Knows	1971	18.00
❏ BN26539	Baby, Baby	1970	18.00
❏ BN26482	David	1969	18.00
❏ LN24342 [M]	David Houston's Greatest Hits	1968	30.00
❏ BN26342 [S]	David Houston's Greatest Hits	1968	18.00
❏ E30602	David Houston's Greatest Hits, Volume 2	1971	18.00
❏ LN24320 [M]	Golden Hymns	1967	25.00
❏ BN26320 [S]	Golden Hymns	1967	18.00
❏ KE32189	Good Things	1973	15.00
❏ LN24112 [M]	New Voice from Nashville	1964	18.00
❏ BN26112 [S]	New Voice from Nashville	1964	25.00
❏ E30437	Sweet Lovin'	1971	18.00
❏ KE31385	The Day Love Walked In	1972	15.00
❏ EGP502	The World of David Houston	1970	25.00
❏ KE33948	What a Night	1976	15.00
❏ BN26432	Where Love Used to Live	1969	18.00
❏ E30108	Wonders of the Wine	1970	18.00

Number	Title	Yr	NM
❏ LN24338 [M]	You Mean the World to Me	1967	25.00
❏ BN26338 [S]	You Mean the World to Me	1967	18.00
GUSTO			
❏ 0012	The Best of David Houston	1978	12.00
HARMONY			
❏ HS11412	David Houston	1970	12.00
❏ KH32287	Old Time Religion	1973	12.00
❏ KH31778	The Many Sides of David Houston	1972	12.00
RCA CAMDEN			
❏ CAL-2126 [M]	David Houston Sings	1966	18.00
❏ CAS-2126 [R]	David Houston Sings	1966	12.00
STARDAY			
❏ 990	David Houston	1978	12.00

HOUSTON, JOE

Number	Title	Yr	NM
COMBO			
❏ LP-100 [M]	Joe Houston	195?	400.00
— Color photo of Joe Houston on cover			
❏ LP-100 [M]	Joe Houston	195?	400.00
— Silver cover with "J" in the shape of a saxophone			
❏ LP-400 [M]	Rockin' at the Drive In	195?	300.00
— Black ink on front and back covers			
❏ LP-400 [M]	Rockin' at the Drive In	195?	200.00
— Blue ink on front and back covers			
CROWN			
❏ CLP-5246 [M]	Doin' the Twist	1962	40.00
❏ CLP-5006 [M]	Joe Houston Rock and Rolls All Night Long	195?	100.00
— Black label, gold print			
❏ CLP-5006 [M]	Joe Houston Rock and Rolls All Night Long	196?	40.00
— Gray label, black print			
❏ CLP-5319 [M]	Limbo	1963	40.00
❏ CST-319 [R]	Limbo	1963	30.00
❏ CLP-5313 [M]	Surf Rockin'	1963	40.00
❏ CST-313 [R]	Surf Rockin'	1963	30.00
❏ CLP-5203 [M]	Wild Man of the Tenor Sax	1962	40.00
MODERN			
❏ LMP-1206 [M]	Joe Houston Blows All Night Long	1956	300.00
TOPS			
❏ L-1518 [M]	Rock and Roll	195?	80.00

HOUSTON, THELMA, AND JERRY BUTLER

Number	Title	Yr	NM
MOTOWN			
❏ M6-887	Thelma and Jerry	1977	12.00
❏ M7-903	Two to One	1978	12.00

HOUSTON, THELMA

Number	Title	Yr	NM
ABC DUNHILL			
❏ DS-50054	Sun Shower	1969	30.00
MCA			
❏ 5527	Qualifying Heat	1984	12.00
❏ 5395	Thelma Houston	1983	12.00
MOTOWN			
❏ M5-226V1 [B]	Any Way You Like It	1982	12.00
❏ M5-127V1	Sunshower	1981	10.00
❏ M5-120V1	Superstar Series, Vol. 20	1981	12.00
MOWEST			
❏ MW-102	Thelma Houston	1972	25.00
RCA VICTOR			
❏ AFL1-3500	Breakwater Cat	1980	12.00
❏ AFL1-3842	Never Gonna Be Another One	1981	12.00
REPRISE			
❏ 26234	Throw You Down	1990	18.00
SHEFFIELD LABS			
❏ 2	I've Got the Music In Me	1975	40.00
SHEFFIELD TREASURY			
❏ ST-200	I've Got the Music In Me	1983	25.00
— Reissue of Sheffield Labs 2			
TAMLA			
❏ T6-345R1	Any Way You Like It	1976	15.00
❏ T7-361R1	Ready to Roll	1978	12.00
❏ T7-358R1	The Devil in Me	1977	12.00

HOUSTON, WHITNEY

Number	Title	Yr	NM
ARISTA			
❏ AL18616 [B]	I'm Your Baby Tonight	1990	18.00
❏ 19037	My Love Is Your Love	1998	15.00
❏ 14652	The Unreleased Mixes	2000	25.00
— Box set of 12-inch single remixes			
❏ AL8405 [B]	Whitney	1987	15.00
❏ AL8212 [B]	Whitney Houston	1985	15.00

HOUSTON FEARLESS

Number	Title	Yr	NM
IMPERIAL			
❏ LP-12421	Houston Fearless	1969	25.00

HOWARD, CHUCK

Number	Title	Yr	NM
BRYLEN			
❏ BN4478	The Fire Behind His Eyes	198?	12.00

HOWARD, DAVE

Number	Title	Yr	NM
CHOREO			
❏ C-5 [M]	I Love Everybody	1961	30.00
❏ CS-5 [S]	I Love Everybody	1961	30.00

HOWARD, EDDY

Number	Title	Yr	NM
CIRCLE			
❏ 29 [B]	Eddy Howard 1949-1952	198?	18.00
❏ 79 [B]	Eddy Howard 1949-1953	1985	18.00
COLUMBIA			
❏ CL6067 [10]	Eddy Howard	1949	60.00
HINDSIGHT			
❏ HSR-156	Eddy Howard 1945-1948	198?	12.00
❏ HSR-119	Eddy Howard 1946-1951	198?	12.00
❏ HSR-405	Eddy Howard and His Orchestra Play 22 Original Big Band Favorites	198?	15.00
INSIGHT			
❏ 205	Eddy Howard and His Orchestra 1945-1951	198?	12.00
MERCURY			
❏ MG-20562 [M]	Eddy Howard's Golden Hits	1961	18.00
❏ SR-60562 [S]	Eddy Howard's Golden Hits	1961	25.00
❏ MG-20817 [M]	Eddy Howard Sings and Plays the Great Band Hits	196?	18.00
❏ SR-60817 [S]	Eddy Howard Sings and Plays the Great Band Hits	196?	25.00
❏ MG-20665 [M]	Eddy Howard Sings and Plays the Great Old Waltzes	1962	18.00
❏ SR-60665 [S]	Eddy Howard Sings and Plays the Great Old Waltzes	1962	25.00
❏ MG-20432 [M]	Great for Dancing	1958	25.00
❏ SR-60104 [S]	Great for Dancing	1959	30.00
❏ MG-20910 [M]	Intimately Yours	1965	18.00
❏ SR-60910 [S]	Intimately Yours	1965	25.00
❏ MG-20593 [M]	More Eddy Howard's Golden Hits	1962	18.00
❏ SR-60593 [S]	More Eddy Howard's Golden Hits	1962	25.00
❏ MG-20312 [M]	Paradise Isle	195?	30.00
❏ MG-25011 [10]	Selected Song Favorites	1949	50.00
— Title appears only on label; cover simply states "Eddy Howard and His Orchestra"			
❏ MG-20112 [M]	Singing in the Rain	195?	30.00
❏ MG-21014 [M]	Softly and Sincerely	196?	18.00
❏ SR-61014 [S]	Softly and Sincerely	196?	25.00
WING			
❏ MGW-12171 [M]	Eddy Howard Sings Words of Love	196?	15.00
❏ SRW-16171 [S]	Eddy Howard Sings Words of Love	196?	15.00
❏ MGW-12104 [M]	Saturday Night Dance Date	196?	15.00
❏ SRW-16104 [S]	Saturday Night Dance Date	196?	15.00
❏ MGW-12194 [M]	Sleepy Serenade	196?	15.00
❏ SRW-16194 [S]	Sleepy Serenade	196?	15.00
❏ MGW-12249 [M]	The Velvet Voice	196?	15.00
❏ SRW-16249 [S]	The Velvet Voice	196?	15.00
❏ MGW-12171 [M]	Words of Love	196?	15.00
❏ SRW-16171 [S]	Words of Love	196?	15.00

HOWARD, HARLAN

Number	Title	Yr	NM
CAPITOL			
❏ T1631 [M]	Harlan Howard Sings Harlan Howard	1961	30.00
❏ ST1631 [S]	Harlan Howard Sings Harlan Howard	1961	40.00
MONUMENT			
❏ MLP-8038 [M]	All-Time Favorite Country Songwriter	1965	30.00
❏ SLP-18038 [S]	All-Time Favorite Country Songwriter	1965	30.00
RCA VICTOR			
❏ LPM-3886 [M]	Down to Earth	1968	50.00
❏ LSP-3886 [S]	Down to Earth	1968	25.00
❏ LPM-3729 [M]	Mr. Songwriter	1967	30.00
❏ LSP-3729 [S]	Mr. Songwriter	1967	25.00

HOWARD, JAN

Number	Title	Yr	NM
CAPITOL			
❏ T1779 [M]	Sweet and Sentimental	1962	25.00
❏ ST1779 [S]	Sweet and Sentimental	1962	30.00
DECCA			
❏ DL4832 [M]	Bad Seed	1966	18.00
❏ DL74832 [S]	Bad Seed	1966	25.00
❏ DL5012 [M]	Count Your Blessings, Woman	1968	40.00
— White label promo only			
❏ DL75012 [S]	Count Your Blessings, Woman	1968	25.00
❏ DL75166	For God and Country	1969	30.00
❏ DL75130	Jan Howard	1969	25.00
❏ DL4793 [M]	Jan Howard Sings Evil on Your Mind	1966	18.00
❏ DL74793 [S]	Jan Howard Sings Evil on Your Mind	1966	25.00
❏ DL75293	Love Is Like a Spinning Wheel	1972	25.00
❏ DL75207	Rock Me Back to Little Rock	1970	25.00
❏ DL4931 [M]	This Is Jan Howard Country	1967	30.00
❏ DL74931 [S]	This Is Jan Howard Country	1967	25.00
PICKWICK			
❏ JS6174	Rock Me Back to Little Rock!	197?	12.00

Number	Title	Yr	NM
TOWER			
❏ T5068 [M]	Lonely Country	1967	25.00
❏ ST5068 [S]	Lonely Country	1967	25.00
❏ DT5119 [R]	The Real Me	1968	18.00
WRANGLER			
❏ 1005 [M]	Jan Howard	1962	30.00
❏ S-1005 [S]	Jan Howard	1962	30.00

HOWARD, JOE

Number	Title	Yr	NM
KING			
❏ 661 [M]	The Golden Sound	1959	50.00
SUNSET			
❏ SU-3001 [M]	Patterns for Trombone	1955	40.00

HOWARD, NOAH

Number	Title	Yr	NM
ALTOSAX			
❏ 1001	Patterns	197?	18.00
❏ 25055	Quartetto	197?	18.00
CHIAROSCURO			
❏ 2016	Oie	1979	15.00
ESP-DISK'			
❏ S-1064 [S]	Live at Judson Hall	1969	25.00
❏ 1031 [M]	Noah Howard Quartet	1966	25.00
❏ S-1031 [S]	Noah Howard Quartet	1966	30.00

HOWE, STEVE

Number	Title	Yr	NM
ATLANTIC			
❏ SD18154	Beginnings	1975	15.00
❏ SD19243	The Steve Howe Album	1980	15.00

HOWELL, REUBEN

Number	Title	Yr	NM
MOTOWN			
❏ M771L	Reuben Howell	1973	25.00
❏ M6-799S1	Rings	1974	18.00

HOWL THE GOOD

Number	Title	Yr	NM
RARE EARTH			
❏ RS-537 [B]	Howl the Good	1972	35.00

HOWLIN' WOLF

Number	Title	Yr	NM
CADET			
❏ LPS-319	This Is Howlin' Wolf's New Album	1969	30.00
CHESS			
❏ CH-50045	Back Door Wolf	1974	25.00
❏ CH-93001	Change My Way	198?	12.00
❏ CH-9182	Chicago -- 26 Golden Years	1985	12.00
❏ LP-1540	Evil	1969	30.00
❏ CH-9107	His Greatest Sides, Vol. 1	1985	12.00
❏ LP-1469 [M]	Howlin' Wolf	1962	600.00
❏ 201	Howlin' Wolf	1976	18.00
❏ CH-60016	Howlin' Wolf, AKA Chester Burnett	1972	30.00
❏ CH-50015	Live and Cookin'	1972	25.00
❏ CH-50002	Message to the Young	1971	25.00
❏ LP-1434 [M]	Moanin' in the Moonlight	1958	600.00
❏ CH-9195	Moanin' in the Moonlight	1986	10.00
— Reissue of 1434			
❏ LP-1512 [M]	More Real Folk Blues	1966	150.00
❏ CH-9279	More Real Folk Blues	1988	12.00
— Reissue of 1512			
❏ CH5-9332	The Chess Box	1991	40.00
❏ CH-60008	The London Howlin' Wolf Sessions	1971	25.00
❏ CH-9297	The London Howlin' Wolf Sessions	1989	12.00
— Reissue of 60008			
❏ LP-1502 [M]	The Real Folk Blues	1966	150.00
❏ CH-9273	The Real Folk Blues	1988	12.00
— Reissue of 1502			
CLEOPATRA			
❏ 6796 [B]	Killing Floor - Blues Essentials		25.00
CROWN			
❏ CLP-5240 [M]	Howlin' Wolf Sings the Blues	1962	30.00
CUSTOM			
❏ CM-2055 [M]	Big City Blues	196?	40.00
❏ CS-2055 [R]	Big City Blues	196?	25.00
KENT			
❏ KST-527	Howlin' Wolf's 20 Greatest R&B Hits	1968	15.00
❏ KLP-526 [M]	Original Folk Blues	1967	18.00
❏ KST-526 [R]	Original Folk Blues	1967	15.00
❏ KST-535	Underground Blues	1968	15.00
ROUNDER			
❏ SS-28	Cadillac Daddy: Memphis Recordings, 1952	1989	15.00

HUBBARD, DAVE

Number	Title	Yr	NM
MAINSTREAM			
❏ MRL-317	Dave Hubbard	1971	18.00

HUBBARD, FREDDIE, AND OSCAR PETERSON

Number	Title	Yr	NM
PABLO			
❏ 2310876	Face to Face	198?	12.00

Number	Title	Yr	NM

HUBBARD, FREDDIE, AND STANLEY TURRENTINE

CTI

Number	Title	Yr	NM
❑ CTS-6044	In Concert, Volume 1	1974	12.00
❑ CTS-6049	In Concert, Volume 2	1975	12.00

HUBBARD, FREDDIE

ABC IMPULSE!

❑ AS-9237	Re-Evaluation: The Impulse Years	1973	18.00
❑ AS-27 [S]	The Artistry of Freddie Hubbard	1968	15.00
❑ AS-38 [S]	The Body and Soul of Freddie Hubbard	1968	15.00

ATLANTIC

❑ 1477 [M]	Backlash	1967	30.00
❑ SD1477 [S]	Backlash	1967	18.00
❑ 90466	Backlash	1986	10.00
— Reissue of SD 1477			
❑ SD1549	Black Angel	1971	15.00
❑ SD1501	High Pressure Blues	1969	18.00
❑ SD1526	Soul Experiment	1970	15.00
❑ 80108	Sweet Return	1983	12.00
❑ SD 2-314	The Art of Freddie Hubbard	1974	18.00

BASF

| ❑ 10726 | The Hub of Hubbard | 1972 | 15.00 |

BLUE NOTE

❑ BLP-4196 [M]	Blue Spirits	1965	125.00
❑ BST-84196 [S]	Blue Spirits	1965	80.00
— With New York, USA address on label			
❑ BST-84196 [S]	Blue Spirits	1967	18.00
— With "A Division of Liberty Records" on label			
❑ BST-84196	Blue Spirits	1987	12.00
— The Finest in Jazz Since 1939" reissue			
❑ BLP-4172 [M]	Breaking Point	1964	125.00
❑ BST-84172 [S]	Breaking Point	1964	80.00
— With New York, USA address on label			
❑ BST-84172 [S]	Breaking Point	1967	18.00
— With "A Division of Liberty Records" on label			
❑ B1-85121	Doubletake	1987	12.00
❑ BN-LA356-H	Freddie Hubbard	1975	18.00
❑ BLP-4056 [M]	Goin' Up	1960	300.00
— With W. 63rd St. address on label			
❑ BLP-4056 [M]	Goin' Up	1963	25.00
— With New York, USA address on label			
❑ BST-84056 [S]	Goin' Up	1960	150.00
— With W. 63rd St. addresss on label			
❑ BST-84056 [S]	Goin' Up	1963	30.00
— With New York, USA address on label			
❑ BST-84056 [S]	Goin' Up	1967	18.00
— With "A Division of Liberty Records" on label			
❑ BST-84135	Here to Stay	1985	15.00
❑ BLP-4073 [M]	Hub Cap	1961	200.00
— With W. 63rd St. address on label			
❑ BLP-4073 [M]	Hub Cap	1963	25.00
— With New York, USA address on label			
❑ BST-84073 [S]	Hub Cap	1961	100.00
— With W. 63rd St. address on label			
❑ BST-84073 [S]	Hub Cap	1963	30.00
— With New York, USA address on label			
❑ BST-84073 [S]	Hub Cap	1967	18.00
— With "A Division of Liberty Records" on label			
❑ BST-84073	Hub Cap	198?	12.00
— The Finest in Jazz Since 1939" reissue			
❑ BLP-4115 [M]	Hub Tones	1962	150.00
❑ BST-84115 [S]	Hub-Tones	1962	30.00
— With New York, USA address on label			
❑ BST-84115 [S]	Hub-Tones	1967	18.00
— With "A Division of Liberty Records" on label			
❑ BST-84115	Hub-Tones	1985	12.00
— The Finest in Jazz Since 1939" reissue			
❑ B1-85139	Life-Flight	1987	12.00
❑ BLP-4040 [M]	Open Sesame	1960	500.00
— Deep groove" version (deep indentation under label on both sides)			
❑ BLP-4040 [M]	Open Sesame	1960	300.00
— Regular version with W. 63rd St. address on label			
❑ BLP-4040 [M]	Open Sesame	1963	25.00
— With New York, USA address on label			
❑ BST-84040 [S]	Open Sesame	1960	60.00
— With W. 63rd St. addresss on label			
❑ BST-84040 [S]	Open Sesame	1963	30.00
— With New York, USA address on label			
❑ BST-84040 [S]	Open Sesame	1967	18.00
— With "A Division of Liberty Records" on label			
❑ BST-84040	Open Sesame	1989	12.00
— The Finest in Jazz Since 1939" reissue			
❑ BST-84040 [S]	Open Sesame	199?	30.00
— Classic Records reissue on audiophile vinyl			
❑ BLP-4085 [M]	Ready for Freddie	1961	150.00
— With 61st St. address on label			
❑ BLP-4085 [M]	Ready for Freddie	1963	25.00
— With New York, USA address on label			
❑ BST-84085 [S]	Ready for Freddie	1961	100.00
— With 61st St. addresss on label			
❑ BST-84085 [S]	Ready for Freddie	1963	30.00
— With New York, USA address on label			
❑ BST-84085 [S]	Ready for Freddie	1967	18.00
— With "A Division of Liberty Records" on label			

❑ B1-32094	Ready for Freddie	1995	15.00
— The Finest in Jazz Since 1939" reissue			
❑ B1-93202	The Best of Freddie Hubbard	1989	15.00
❑ BJT-48017	The Eternal Triangle	1988	15.00
❑ BLP-4207 [M]	The Night of the Cookers -- Live at Club Le Marchal, Vol. 1	1965	30.00
❑ BST-84207 [S]	The Night of the Cookers -- Live at Club Le Marchal, Vol. 1	1965	30.00
— With New York, USA address on label			
❑ BST-84207 [S]	The Night of the Cookers -- Live at Club Le Marchal, Vol. 1	1967	18.00
— With "A Division of Liberty Records" on label			
❑ BLP-4208 [M]	The Night of the Cookers -- Live at Club Le Marchal, Vol. 2	1965	30.00
❑ BST-84208 [S]	The Night of the Cookers -- Live at Club Le Marchal, Vol. 2	1965	30.00
— With New York, USA address on label			
❑ BST-84208 [S]	The Night of the Cookers -- Live at Club Le Marchal, Vol. 2	1967	18.00
— With "A Division of Liberty Records" on label			
❑ B1-90905	Times 'R Changin'	1989	15.00

COLUMBIA

❑ PC34902	Bundle of Joy	1977	12.00
❑ KC33048	High Energy	1974	12.00
❑ PC33556	Liquid Love	1975	12.00
❑ JC36015	Love Connection	1979	12.00
❑ FC36418	Skagly	1980	12.00
❑ JC35386	Super Blue	1978	12.00
❑ JC36358	The Best of Freddie Hubbard	1979	12.00
❑ PC34166	Windjammer	1976	12.00

CTI

❑ CTS-6013	First Light	1972	15.00
❑ 8017	First Light	198?	10.00
— Reissue of 6013			
❑ CTS-6044	Freddie Hubbard In Concert	1974	12.00
❑ CTS-6036	Keep Your Soul Together	1974	12.00
❑ CTS-6056	Polar AC	1975	12.00
❑ CTS-6001	Red Clay	1970	15.00
❑ 8016	Red Clay	198?	10.00
— Reissue of 6001			
❑ CTS-6018	Sky Dive	1973	12.00
❑ CTS-6047	The Baddest Hubbard	1974	12.00
❑ CTS-6007	The Straight Life	1971	15.00
❑ 8022	The Straight Life	198?	10.00
— Reissue of 6007			

CTI/CBS ASSOCIATED

| ❑ FZ40687 | First Light | 1987 | 12.00 |

ELEKTRA/MUSICIAN

| ❑ 60029 | Ride Like the Wind | 1982 | 12.00 |

ENJA

| ❑ 3095 | Outpost | 1981 | 12.00 |

FANTASY

❑ 9626	A Little Night Music	1983	12.00
❑ 9635	Classics	1984	12.00
❑ 9615	Keystone Bop	1982	12.00
❑ 9610	Splash	1981	12.00

IMPULSE!

❑ A-27 [M]	The Artistry of Freddie Hubbard	1962	30.00
❑ AS-27 [S]	The Artistry of Freddie Hubbard	1962	30.00
❑ A-38 [M]	The Body and Soul of Freddie Hubbard	1963	30.00
❑ AS-38 [S]	The Body and Soul of Freddie Hubbard	1963	30.00

LIBERTY

| ❑ LT-1110 | Mistral | 1981 | 12.00 |

PABLO

| ❑ 2312134 | Born to Be Blue | 1982 | 12.00 |
| ❑ 2310884 | The Best of Freddie Hubbard | 1983 | 12.00 |

PABLO LIVE

| ❑ 2620113 | Live at the Northsea Jazz Festival, The Hague, 1980 | 1983 | 15.00 |

PABLO TODAY

| ❑ 2312134 | Born to Be Blue | 198? | 12.00 |

PAUSA

| ❑ 7122 | Rollin' | 1982 | 12.00 |

PHOENIX 10

| ❑ PHX318 | Extended | 1981 | 10.00 |

PICCADILLY

| ❑ 3467 | Intrepid Fox | 198? | 12.00 |

QUINTESSENCE

| ❑ 25161 | Skylark | 1978 | 12.00 |

REAL TIME

| ❑ 305 | Back to Birdland | 198? | 12.00 |

HUBBELL, FRANK

PHILIPS

| ❑ PHS600293 | Frank Hubbell and the Stompers | 1969 | 18.00 |

HUBNER, ABBI, AND HIS LOW DOWN WIZARDS

STOMP OFF

| ❑ SOS-1093 | Twenty Years, Live in Concert | 1986 | 12.00 |

HUCKO, PEANUTS, AND RALPH SUTTON

CHIAROSCURO

| ❑ 167 | Live at Condon's | 1978 | 15.00 |

HUCKO, PEANUTS

CIRCLE

| ❑ C-21 | Peanuts | 198? | 12.00 |

GRAND AWARD

| ❑ GA 33-331 [M] | Tribute to Benny Goodman | 1956 | 40.00 |

WALDORF MUSIC HALL

| ❑ MH 33-153 [10] | A Tribute to Benny Goodman | 1956 | 30.00 |

HUCKO, PEANUTS/RAY MCKINLEY

GRAND AWARD

| ❑ GA 33-333 [M] | The Swingin' 30s | 1956 | 40.00 |

HUDSON, ROCK

STANYAN

| ❑ SR-10014 [B] | Rock Gently | 1971 | 30.00 |

HUDSON BROTHERS, THE

ARISTA

| ❑ AB4199 | The Truth About Us | 1978 | 12.00 |

CASABLANCA

| ❑ NBLP-7004 | Hollywood Situation | 1974 | 12.00 |

ELEKTRA

| ❑ 6E-299 | Damn Those Kids | 1980 | 12.00 |
| — As "Hudson | | | |

FIRST AMERICAN

| ❑ 7708 | The Hudson Brothers | 1980 | 12.00 |

PLAYBOY

| ❑ 102 | Hudson | 1972 | 18.00 |

ROCKET

| ❑ PIG-2169 | Ba-Fa | 1975 | 12.00 |
| ❑ PIG-460 | Totally Out of Control | 1974 | 12.00 |

HUEBNER, LOUISE

HI HORSE

| ❑ 18190 [B] | Seduction Through Witchcraft | 2009 | 35.00 |
| — reissue | | | |

WARNER BROS./7 ARTS MUSIC

| ❑ WS1819 [B] | Seduction Through Witchcraft | 1969 | 150.00 |

HUES CORPORATION, THE

RCA VICTOR

❑ APL1-0323	Freedom for the Stallion	1973	12.00
❑ APL1-0938	Love Corporation	1975	12.00
❑ APD1-0938 [Q]	Love Corporation	1975	18.00
❑ APL1-0755	Rockin' Soul	1974	12.00
❑ APD1-0755 [Q]	Rockin' Soul	1974	18.00
❑ ANL1-2147	Rock the Boat	1976	10.00
❑ APL1-2408	The Best of the Hues Corporation	1977	12.00

WARNER BROS.

| ❑ BS3043 | I Caught Your Act | 1977 | 12.00 |
| ❑ BSK3196 | Your Place or Mine | 1978 | 12.00 |

HUGHES, FRED

BRUNSWICK

| ❑ BL754147 [B] | Baby Boy | 1970 | 25.00 |

HUGHES, FREDDIE

WAND

| ❑ WDS-664 | Send My Baby Back | 1968 | 30.00 |
| — The numbering system suggests this would have been issued in 1965, but the singles from this LP were issued in 1968, thus we use the later date. | | | |

HUGHES, JIMMY

ATCO

| ❑ 33-209 [M] | Why Not Tonight | 1967 | 25.00 |
| ❑ SD 33-209 [S] | Why Not Tonight | 1967 | 25.00 |

VEE JAY

| ❑ VJ-1102 [M] | Steal Away | 1965 | 30.00 |
| ❑ VJS-1102 [R] | Steal Away | 1965 | 30.00 |

VOLT

| ❑ VOS-6003 | Something Special | 1969 | 25.00 |

HUGHES, LANGSTON

FOLKWAYS

| ❑ FA-7312 [10] | The Story of Jazz for Children | 1954 | 100.00 |
| — With booklet | | | |

Number	Title	Yr	NM

MGM

Number	Title	Yr	NM
❏ E-3697 [M]	The Weary Blues	1958	150.00
— Yellow label			

VERVE

| ❏ VSP-36 [M] | The Weary Blues | 1966 | 25.00 |
| ❏ VSPS-36 [R] | The Weary Blues | 1966 | 15.00 |

HUGHES, RHETA

COLUMBIA

| ❏ CL2385 [M] | Introducing An Electrifying New Star | 1965 | 30.00 |
| ❏ CS9185 [S] | Introducing An Electrifying New Star | 1965 | 40.00 |

HULLABALLOOS, THE

ROULETTE

❏ R-25297 [M]	England's Newest Singing Sensations	1965	50.00
❏ SR-25297 [P]	England's Newest Singing Sensations	1965	75.00
❏ R-25310 [M]	The Hullabaloos on Hullabaloo	1965	50.00
❏ SR-25310 [P]	The Hullabaloos on Hullabaloo	1965	75.00

HULLABALOO SINGERS AND ORCHESTRA, THE

COLUMBIA

| ❏ CL2410 [M] | The Hullabaloo Show | 1965 | 30.00 |
| ❏ CS9210 [S] | The Hullabaloo Show | 1965 | 35.00 |

HUMAN BEINZ, THE

CAPITOL

| ❏ ST2926 | Evolutions | 1968 | 40.00 |
| ❏ ST2906 | Nobody But Me | 1968 | 30.00 |

GATEWAY

| ❏ GLP-3012 | Nobody But Me | 1968 | 40.00 |
| — With added tracks by The Mammals | | | |

HUMAN LEAGUE

A&M

❏ R162455	Crash	1986	15.00
— RCA Music Service edition			
❏ SP-5129	Crash	1986	12.00
❏ SP-6-4892	Dare	1981	12.00
❏ SP-12501 [EP]	Fascination!	1983	12.00
❏ R100837	Greatest Hits	1989	18.00
— BMG Direct Marketing edition			
❏ SP-5227	Greatest Hits	1989	18.00
❏ SP-4923	Hysteria	1984	12.00
❏ SP-3209	Love and Dancing	1982	12.00
— As "The League Unlimited Orchestra"; instrumental versions			
❏ 7502153061	Romantic?	1990	15.00

VIRGIN

❏ 90881	Reproduction	1988	12.00
— First issue of early U.K. album			
❏ 90880	Travelogue	1988	12.00
— Reissue of early U.K. album			

VIRGIN INTERNATIONAL

| ❏ VI2160 | Travelogue | 1980 | 18.00 |
| — U.S. pressings have "VI" prefix; imports, which go for less, have simply a "V" prefix | | | |

HUMBLE PIE

A&M

❏ SP-3701 [B]	Eat It	1973	25.00
❏ SP-6503	Eat It	1981	12.00
— Budget-line reissue			
❏ SP-4270	Humble Pie	1970	15.00
❏ SP-3127	Humble Pie	1981	10.00
— Budget-line reissue			
❏ SP-3513 [B]	Lost and Found	1972	25.00
❏ SP-6009	Lost and Found	1981	12.00
— Budget-line reissue			
❏ SP-3506 [B]	Performance -- Rockin' the Fillmore	1971	25.00
❏ SP-6008	Performance -- Rockin' the Fillmore	1981	12.00
— Budget-line reissue			
❏ SP-4301	Rock On	1971	15.00
❏ SP-4342	Smokin'	1972	15.00
❏ SP-3132	Smokin'	1981	10.00
— Budget-line reissue			
❏ SP-4514	Street Rats	1975	15.00
❏ SP-3208	The Best of Humble Pie	1982	12.00
❏ SP-3611 [B]	Thunderbox	1974	15.00

ACCORD

| ❏ SN-7192 | Recaptured | 1981 | 12.00 |

ATCO

| ❏ SD 38-131 | Go for the Throat | 1981 | 12.00 |
| ❏ SD 38-122 | On to Victory | 1980 | 12.00 |

CLEOPATRA

| ❏ 7546 [B] | California '81 | | 25.00 |
| ❏ 5128 [B] | Live At Winterland | | 40.00 |

COMPLEAT

| ❏ 672009-1 | A Slice of Humble Pie | 1985 | 15.00 |

IMMEDIATE

| ❏ IMOCS-101 | As Safe As Yesterday Is | 1969 | 30.00 |

Number	Title	Yr	NM

HUMBLEBUMS, THE

LIBERTY

| ❏ LST-7656 | Open Up the Door | 1970 | 30.00 |
| ❏ LST-7636 | The Humblebums | 1969 | 25.00 |

HUMES, HELEN

AUDIOPHILE

| ❏ AP-107 | Helen Humes | 1980 | 25.00 |

CLASSIC JAZZ

| ❏ 120 | Let the Good Times Roll | 197? | 15.00 |
| ❏ 110 | Sneakin' Around | 197? | 15.00 |

COLUMBIA

| ❏ PC33488 | The Talk of the Town | 1975 | 18.00 |

CONTEMPORARY

❏ M-3582 [M]	Songs I Like to Sing	1960	50.00
❏ S-7582 [S]	Songs I Like to Sing	1960	50.00
❏ M-3598 [M]	Swingin' with Humes	1961	40.00
❏ S-7598 [S]	Swingin' with Humes	1961	50.00
❏ M-3571 [M]	'Tain't Nobody's Biz-Ness If I Do	1960	50.00
❏ S-7571 [S]	'Tain't Nobody's Biz-Ness If I Do	1960	50.00

FANTASY

❏ OJC-171	Songs I Like to Sing	198?	15.00
❏ OJC-608	Swingin' with Humes	1991	18.00
❏ OJC-453	'Tain't Nobody's Biz-Ness If I Do	1990	18.00

JAZZ MAN

| ❏ 5003 | On the Sunny Side of the Street | 1981 | 18.00 |

JAZZOLOGY

| ❏ J-55 | Incomparable | 197? | 15.00 |

MUSE

| ❏ MR-5233 | Helen | 1980 | 15.00 |
| ❏ MR-5217 | Helen Humes with the Muse All Stars | 197? | 15.00 |

SAVOY JAZZ

| ❏ SJL-1159 | E-Baba-Le-Ba": The Rhythm & Blues Years | 1986 | 15.00 |

HUMPERDINCK, ENGELBERT

EPIC

❏ PE34381	After the Lovin'	1976	12.00
— Orange label			
❏ PE34381	After the Lovin'	1979	10.00
— Dark blue label; back cover does not yet have bar code			
❏ E2X36782	All of Me/Live in Concert	1980	15.00
❏ PE36765	A Merry Christmas with Engelbert Humperdinck	1980	12.00
— Some copies of the record have a "JE" prefix			
❏ PE35031	Christmas Tyme	1977	15.00
❏ FE37128	Don't You Love Me Anymore	1981	12.00
❏ PE37128	Don't You Love Me Anymore	1983	10.00
— Budget-line reissue			
❏ E34719	Golden Love Songs	1977	12.00
— Orange label			
❏ PE34719	Golden Love Songs	198?	10.00
— Reissue with bar code; dark blue label			
❏ JE35020	Last of the Romantics	1978	12.00
— Orange label			
❏ (no #) [PD]	Last of the Romantics	1978	30.00
❏ PE35020	Last of the Romantics	198?	10.00
— Reissue with bar code; dark blue label			
❏ JE36431	Love's Only Love	1980	12.00
❏ PE34730	Miracles	1977	12.00
— Orange label			
❏ PE34730	Miracles	198?	10.00
— Reissue with bar code; dark blue label			
❏ E34436	The Ultimate	1977	12.00
— Orange label			
❏ PE34436	The Ultimate	198?	10.00
— Reissue with bar code; dark blue label			
❏ JE35791	This Moment in Time	1979	12.00
❏ PE35791	This Moment in Time	198?	10.00
— Budget-line reissue			
❏ PE39469	White Christmas	1984	12.00
❏ FE38087	You and Your Lover	1983	12.00

LONDON

| ❏ BP688/9 | Engelbert Humperdinck Sings for You | 1977 | 18.00 |
| ❏ PS709 | Love Letters | 1978 | 12.00 |

PARROT

❏ PAS71022	A Man Without Love	1968	18.00
❏ XPAS71048	Another Time, Another Place	1971	18.00
❏ PAS71026	Engelbert	1969	18.00
❏ XPAS71030	Engelbert Humperdinck	1969	18.00
❏ PAS71067	His Greatest Hits	1974	18.00
❏ XPAS71056	In Time	1972	18.00
❏ XPAS71061	King of Hearts	1973	18.00
❏ XPAS71051	Live at the Riviera, Las Vegas	1971	18.00
❏ APAS71065	My Love	1974	18.00
❏ PA61012 [M]	Release Me	1967	25.00
❏ PAS71012 [S]	Release Me	1967	18.00
❏ XPAS71043	Sweetheart	1971	18.00
❏ PA61015 [M]	The Last Waltz	1967	25.00
❏ PAS71015 [S]	The Last Waltz	1967	18.00
❏ XPAS71038	We Made It Happen	1970	18.00
❏ SW-93216	We Made It Happen	1970	25.00
— Capitol Record Club edition			

Number	Title	Yr	NM

SILVER EAGLE

| ❏ SE1034 | A Lovely Way to Spend an Evening | 1985 | 18.00 |
| — Mail-order offer | | | |

HUMPHREY, BOBBI

BLUE NOTE

❏ BN-LA142-G	Blacks and Blues	1974	12.00
❏ BST-84421	Dig This	1972	15.00
❏ BN-LA550-G	Fancy Dancer	1975	12.00
❏ BST-84379	Flute-In	1971	15.00
❏ BN-LA344-G	Satin Doll	1974	12.00
❏ BN-LA699-G	The Best of Bobbi Humphrey	1976	12.00

EPIC

❏ JE35338	Freestyle	1978	12.00
❏ PE34704	Tailor Made	1977	12.00
❏ JE36368	The Best of Bobbi Humphrey	1980	12.00
❏ JE35607	The Good Life	1979	12.00

HUMPHREY, EARL

BIOGRAPH

| ❏ CEN-11 | Earl Humphrey and His Footwarmers | 197? | 15.00 |

HUMPHREY, PAUL

BLUE THUMB

| ❏ BTS66 | America, Wake Up! | 1974 | 15.00 |
| ❏ BTS47 | Supermellow | 1973 | 15.00 |

DISCOVERY

| ❏ DS-850 | Paul Humphrey Sextet | 1981 | 12.00 |

LIZARD

| ❏ 20106 | Paul Humphrey & the Cool Aid Chemists | 1971 | 18.00 |

HUMPHREY, PERCY

BIOGRAPH

| ❏ CEN-13 | Percy Humphrey at Manny's Tavern | 197? | 15.00 |

GHB

| ❏ 85 | Percy Humphrey and the Crescent City Joymakers | 197? | 12.00 |

JAZZOLOGY

| ❏ JCE-26 | Percy Humphrey and the Crescent City Joymakers | 197? | 15.00 |

PEARL

| ❏ PS-3 | Climax Rag | 197? | 18.00 |

RIVERSIDE

| ❏ RLP-378 [M] | Percy Humphrey's Crescent City Joymakers | 1961 | 30.00 |
| ❏ RS-9378 [R] | Percy Humphrey's Crescent City Joymakers | 196? | 18.00 |

HUMPHREY, WILLIE

GHB

| ❏ 248 | New Orleans Jazz from Willie Humphrey | 198? | 12.00 |

HUNDLEY, CRAIG

WORLD PACIFIC

❏ WPS-21880	Arrival of a Young Giant	1968	18.00
❏ WPS-21900	Rhapsody in Blue	1970	18.00
❏ WPS-21896	The Craig Hundley Trio Plays with the Big Boys	1969	18.00

HUNGER

PUBLIC

| ❏ 1006 | Strictly from Hunger | 1969 | 600.00 |

HUNLEY, CON

MCA

| ❏ 5423 | Once You Get the Feel of It | 1983 | 18.00 |

WARNER BROS.

❏ BSK3617	Ask Any Woman	1981	12.00
❏ BSK3285	Con Hunley	1979	12.00
— With this title on both cover and label			
❏ BSK3474	Don't It Break Your Heart	1980	12.00
❏ BSK3378	I Don't Want to Lose You	1980	12.00
❏ BSK3285	No Limit	1979	18.00
— Same cover as "Con Hunley," but the above title is on the label			
❏ BSK3693	Oh Girl	1982	12.00

HUNT, PEE WEE

ALLEGRO

| ❏ 1633 [M] | Dixieland | 1956 | 30.00 |

CAPITOL

❏ T984 [M]	Cole Porter Ala Dixie	1957	30.00
— Turquoise label			
❏ T573 [M]	Dixieland Classics	1955	30.00
❏ H312 [10]	Dixieland Detour	1952	50.00
❏ T1265 [M]	Dixieland Kickoff	1959	30.00
❏ ST1265 [S]	Dixieland Kickoff	1959	30.00
❏ T783 [M]	Pee Wee and Fingers	1956	30.00
❏ T1362 [M]	Pee Wee Hunt's Dance Party	1960	18.00

Number	Title	Yr	NM
❑ ST1362 [S]	Pee Wee Hunt's Dance Party	1960	25.00
❑ H203 [10]	Straight from Dixie	1950	40.00
❑ T203 [M]	Straight from Dixie	195?	30.00
❑ H492 [10]	Swingin' Around	1954	40.00
❑ T1853 [M]	The Best of Pee Wee Hunt	1962	18.00
❑ DT1853 [R]	The Best of Pee Wee Hunt	1962	15.00
❑ T1144 [M]	The Blues A La Dixie	1958	30.00

ROYALE

❑ 18153 [10]	Pee Wee Hunt and His Dixieland Band	195?	40.00

SOLITAIRE

❑ 507 [10]	Dixieland Capers	195?	30.00

HUNT, PEE WEE/PEE WEE RUSSELL

RONDO-LETTE

❑ A2 [M]	Dixieland: Pee Wee Hunt and Pee Wee Russell	195?	30.00

HUNT, TOMMY

DYNAMO

❑ D-7001 [M]	Tommy Hunt's Greatest Hits	1967	25.00
❑ DS-8001 [S]	Tommy Hunt's Greatest Hits	1967	30.00

SCEPTER

❑ 506 [M]	I Just Don't Know What to Do with Myself	1962	50.00
❑ SS-506 [S]	I Just Don't Know What to Do with Myself	1962	60.00

HUNTER, FRANK

JUBILEE

❑ JLP-1020 [M]	Sounds of Hunter	1956	50.00

HUNTER, IAN, AND MICK RONSON

MERCURY

❑ 838973-1	Y U I Orta	1989	15.00

HUNTER, IAN

CHRYSALIS

❑ 2CHS1269 [B]	Ian Hunter Live/Welcome to the Club	1980	25.00
❑ CHS1326	Short Back N' Sides	1981	12.00
❑ PV41326	Short Back N' Sides	1982	10.00
— Budget-line reissue			
❑ CHR1214 [B]	You're Never Alone with a Schizophrenic	1979	18.00
❑ PV41214 [B]	You're Never Alone with a Schizophrenic	1982	10.00
— Budget-line reissue			

COLUMBIA

❑ PC34142 [B]	All American Alien Boy	1976	18.00
— No bar code on cover			
❑ PC34142	All American Alien Boy	198?	10.00
— Budget-line reissue with bar code			
❑ FC38628	All of the Good Ones Are Taken	1983	12.00
❑ PC33480	Ian Hunter	1975	18.00
— No bar code on cover			
❑ PC33480	Ian Hunter	198?	10.00
— Budget-line reissue with bar code			
❑ PC34721 [B]	Overnight Angels	1977	25.00
— No bar code on cover			
❑ C236251 [B]	Shades of Ian Hunter	1980	18.00

HUNTER, IVORY JOE

ATLANTIC

❑ 8008 [M]	Ivory Joe Hunter	1957	200.00
— Black label			
❑ 8008 [M]	Ivory Joe Hunter	1960	100.00
— Purple and red label			
❑ 8015 [M]	The Old and the New	1958	200.00
— Black label			
❑ 8015 [M]	The Old and the New	1960	100.00
— Purple and red label			

DOT

❑ DLP-3569 [M]	This Is Ivory Joe Hunter	1964	40.00
❑ DLP-25569 [S]	This Is Ivory Joe Hunter	1964	50.00

EPIC

❑ E30348	The Return of Ivory Joe Hunter	1971	25.00

EVEREST ARCHIVE OF FOLK & JAZZ

❑ 289	Ivory Joe Hunter	1974	15.00

GOLDISC

❑ 403 [M]	The Fabulous Ivory Joe Hunter	1961	60.00

HOME COOKING

❑ 112	I'm Coming Down with the Blues	1989	15.00

KING

❑ 605 [M]	16 of His Greatest Hits	1958	400.00

LION

❑ L-70068 [M]	I Need You So	1959	60.00

MGM

❑ E-3488 [M]	I Get That Lonesome Feeling	1957	300.00

PARAMOUNT

❑ PAS-6080	I've Always Been Country	1974	15.00

POLYDOR

❑ 830897-1	Since I Met You Baby	1987	15.00

SMASH

❑ MGS-27037 [M]	Ivory Joe Hunter's Golden Hits	1963	40.00
❑ SRS-67037 [S]	Ivory Joe Hunter's Golden Hits	1963	50.00

SOUND

❑ M-603 [M]	Ivory Joe Hunter	1959	150.00

STRAND

❑ SL-1123 [M]	The Artistry of Ivory Joe Hunter	196?	40.00
❑ SLS-1123 [S]	The Artistry of Ivory Joe Hunter	196?	50.00

HUNTER, LURLEAN

ATLANTIC

❑ 1344 [M]	Blue and Sentimental	1960	50.00
❑ SD1344 [S]	Blue and Sentimental	1960	60.00

RCA VICTOR

❑ LPM-1151 [M]	Lonesome Gal	1955	100.00

VIK

❑ LX-1061 [M]	Night Life	1956	80.00
❑ LX-1116 [M]	Stepping Out	1957	80.00

HUNTER, ROBERT

RELIX

❑ 2002 [PD]	Promontory Rider	1982	25.00
— Limited edition of 1,000 picture discs			

ROUND

❑ RX-101	Tales of the Great Rum Runners	1974	25.00
❑ RX-105	Tiger Rose	1975	25.00

HUNTER, STAN, AND SONNY FORTUNE

PRESTIGE

❑ PRLP-7458 [M]	Trip on the Strip	1967	30.00
❑ PRST-7458 [S]	Trip on the Strip	1967	25.00

HUNTER, TAB

DOT

❑ DLP-3370 [M]	Young Love	1961	25.00
❑ DLP-25370 [S]	Young Love	1961	25.00

WARNER BROS.

❑ W1367 [M]	R.F.D. Tab Hunter	1960	25.00
❑ WS1367 [S]	R.F.D. Tab Hunter	1960	30.00
❑ W1221 [M]	Tab Hunter	1958	25.00
❑ WS1221 [S]	Tab Hunter	1958	30.00
❑ W1292 [M]	When I Fall In Love	1959	25.00
❑ WS1292 [S]	When I Fall in Love	1959	30.00

HUNTER MUSKETT

BRADLEY

❑ 1003	Hunter Muskett	1973	80.00

HURT, MISSISSIPPI JOHN

BIOGRAPH

❑ C-4 [M]	1928: His First Recordings	1972	25.00

PIEDMONT

❑ PLP-13157 [M]	Folk Songs and Blues	1963	80.00
❑ PLP-13181 [M]	Worried Blues	1964	80.00

VANGUARD

❑ VRS-9145 [M]	Blues at Newport	1965	30.00
❑ VSD-79145 [S]	Blues at Newport	1965	30.00
❑ VRS-9220 [M]	Mississippi John Hurt/Today	1966	30.00
❑ VSD-79220 [S]	Mississippi John Hurt/Today	1966	30.00
❑ VSD-19/20	The Best of Mississippi John Hurt	197?	30.00
❑ VRS-9248 [M]	The Immortal Mississippi John Hurt	1967	30.00
❑ VSD-79248 [S]	The Immortal Mississippi John Hurt	1967	30.00
❑ VSD-79327	The Last Session	1972	25.00

HURVITZ, SANDY

VERVE

❑ V6-5064	Sandy's Album Is Here at Last	1968	30.00
— Produced by FRANK ZAPPA			

HUSKER DU

NEW ALLIANCE

❑ 007 [B]	Land Speed Record	1982	30.00
— No reference to SST on cover			
❑ 007	Land Speed Record	1982	15.00
— Second pressing, "Marketed by SST" on cover			

REFLEX

❑ #D0	Everything Falls Apart	1982	40.00

RHINO

❑ R125385 [B]	Candy Apple Grey	2014	30.00

SST

❑ PSST E-27 [DJ]	Eight Miles High/6 from Zen Arcade	1984	30.00
— Promo sampler, etched design on side 1, sticker cover			

❑ 915 [10]	Eight Miles High/Makes No Sense at All	199?	12.00
❑ 055	Flip Your Wig	1985	18.00
❑ 195	Land Speed Record	198?	15.00
— Reissue of New Alliance 007			
❑ 020 [EP]	Metal Circus	1983	15.00
❑ 908 [10]	Metal Circus	199?	10.00
❑ 031	New Day Rising	1985	18.00
❑ 027 [B]	Zen Arcade	1984	18.00

WARNER BROS.

❑ 25385	Candy Apple Grey	1986	15.00
❑ WBMS-145 [DJ]	The Warehouse Interview	1987	15.00
— Promo only, part of the Warner Bros. Music Show series			
❑ PRO02719 [DJ]	Warehouse: Songs and Stories	1987	10.00
— Promo-only four-song sampler			
❑ 25544	Warehouse: Songs and Stories	1987	18.00
❑ PRO-A-2719 [DJ]	Warehouse: Songs and Stories	1987	18.00
— Promo-only four-song sampler			

HUSKY, FERLIN

ABC

❑ X-849	Champagne Ladies and Blue Ribbon Babies	1974	15.00
❑ X-818	Freckles and Polliwog Days	1974	15.00
❑ X-803	Sweet Honky Tonk	1974	15.00
❑ X-884	The Foster-Rice Songbook	1975	15.00
❑ X-776	True True Lovin'	1973	15.00

CAPITOL

❑ T1204 [M]	Born to Lose	1959	40.00
— Black colorband label, Capitol logo at left			
❑ T1204 [M]	Born to Lose	1962	30.00
— Black colorband label, Capitol logo at top			
❑ T880 [M]	Boulevard of Broken Dreams	1957	60.00
— Turquoise label			
❑ T880 [M]	Boulevard of Broken Dreams	1958	40.00
— Black colorband label, Capitol logo at left			
❑ T2101 [M]	By Request	1964	18.00
❑ ST2101 [S]	By Request	1964	25.00
❑ T2793 [M]	Christmas All Year Long	1967	18.00
❑ ST2793 [S]	Christmas All Year Long	1967	18.00
❑ T2439 [M]	Ferlin Husky Sings the Songs of Music City, U.S.A.	1966	18.00
❑ ST2439 [S]	Ferlin Husky Sings the Songs of Music City, U.S.A.	1966	25.00
❑ T1280 [M]	Ferlin's Favorites	1960	40.00
— Black colorband label, Capitol logo at left			
❑ T1280 [M]	Ferlin's Favorites	1962	30.00
— Black colorband label, Capitol logo at top			
❑ T1383 [M]	Gone	1960	40.00
— Black colorband label, Capitol logo at left			
❑ T1383 [M]	Gone	1962	30.00
— Black colorband label, Capitol logo at top			
❑ DT1383 [R]	Gone	196?	15.00
❑ T1383 [M]	Gone	196?	25.00
— Gold "The Star Line" label; "The Star Line" logo on cover			
❑ T2548 [M]	I Could Sing All Night	1966	18.00
❑ ST2548 [S]	I Could Sing All Night	1966	25.00
❑ T2870 [M]	Just for You	1968	30.00
❑ ST2870 [S]	Just for You	1968	18.00
❑ ST-11069	Just Plain Lonely	1972	18.00
❑ T1633 [M]	Memories of Home	1961	30.00
— Black colorband label, Capitol logo at left			
❑ T1633 [M]	Memories of Home	1962	18.00
— Black colorband label, Capitol logo at top			
❑ ST1633 [S]	Memories of Home	1961	30.00
— Black colorband label, Capitol logo at left			
❑ ST1633 [S]	Memories of Home	1962	25.00
— Black colorband label, Capitol logo at top			
❑ ST-768	One More Time	1971	18.00
❑ T976 [M]	Sittin' On a Rainbow	1958	60.00
— Turquoise label			
❑ T1720 [M]	Some of My Favorites	1962	18.00
❑ ST1720 [S]	Some of My Favorites	1962	25.00
❑ T718 [M]	Songs of the Home and Heart	1956	60.00
— Turquoise label			
❑ T718 [M]	Songs of the Home and Heart	1959	40.00
— Black colorband label, Capitol logo at left			
❑ T718 [M]	Songs of the Home and Heart	1962	30.00
— Black colorband label, Capitol logo at top			
❑ ST-239	That's Why I Love You So Much	1969	18.00
❑ SKAO-143	The Best of Ferlin Husky	1969	18.00
❑ SM-143	The Best of Ferlin Husky	197?	12.00
— Reissue with new prefix			
❑ T1885 [M]	The Heart and Soul of Ferlin Husky	1963	18.00
❑ ST1885 [S]	The Heart and Soul of Ferlin Husky	1963	25.00
❑ T1991 [M]	The Hits of Ferlin Husky	1963	18.00
❑ DT1991 [R]	The Hits of Ferlin Husky	1963	15.00
❑ T2305 [M]	True, True Lovin'	1965	18.00
❑ ST2305 [S]	True, True Lovin'	1965	25.00
❑ T1546 [M]	Walkin' and Hummin'	1961	30.00
— Black colorband label, Capitol logo at left			
❑ T1546 [M]	Walkin' and Hummin'	1962	18.00

Number	Title	Yr	NM
— Black colorband label, Capitol logo at top			
❏ ST1546 [S]	Walkin' and Hummin'	1961	30.00
— Black colorband label, Capitol logo at left			
❏ ST1546 [S]	Walkin' and Hummin'	1962	25.00
— Black colorband label, Capitol logo at top			
❏ T2705 [M]	What Am I Gonna Do Now?	1967	25.00
❏ ST2705 [S]	What Am I Gonna Do Now?	1967	18.00
❏ ST2913	Where No One Stands Alone	1968	18.00
❏ ST-115	White Fences and Evergreen Trees	1968	18.00
❏ ST-433	Your Love Is Heavenly Sunshine	1970	18.00
❏ ST-591	Your Sweet Love Lifted Me	1970	18.00
HILLTOP			
❏ 6086	Green, Green Grass of Home	1970	15.00
❏ 6005	Ole Opry Favorites	196?	15.00
❏ 6099	Wings of a Dove	197?	15.00
KING			
❏ 647 [M]	Country Tunes Sung from the Heart	1959	70.00
❏ 728 [M]	Easy Livin'	1960	70.00
STARDAY			
❏ 3018	Greatest Hits	197?	15.00

HUSTAD, DON, AND TEDD SMITH

WORD

Number	Title	Yr	NM
❏ WST-8319	Christmastime with Don Hustad and Tedd Smith	196?	15.00

HUSTLER

A&M

Number	Title	Yr	NM
❏ SP4504	High Street	1974	18.00
❏ SP4556	Play Loud	1975	18.00

HUTCHERSON, BOBBY

BLUE NOTE

Number	Title	Yr	NM
❏ BST-84333	Bobby Hutcherson Now	1969	25.00
— With "A Division of Liberty Records" on label			
❏ BN-LA257-G	Cirrus	1973	15.00
❏ BLP-4213 [M]	Components	1966	125.00
❏ BST-84213 [S]	Components	1966	60.00
— With "New York, USA" address on label			
❏ BST-84213 [S]	Components	1967	18.00
— With "A Division of Liberty Records" on label			
❏ B1-29027	Components	1994	18.00
— Reissue			
❏ BLP-4198 [M]	Dialogue	1965	125.00
❏ BST-84198 [S]	Dialogue	1965	70.00
— With "New York, USA" address on label			
❏ BST-84198 [S]	Dialogue	1967	18.00
— With "A Division of Liberty Records" on label			
❏ BST-84198	Dialogue	198?	12.00
— The Finest in Jazz Since 1939" reissue			
❏ BLP-4231 [M]	Happenings	1967	100.00
❏ BST-84231 [S]	Happenings	1967	80.00
— With "New York, USA" address on label			
❏ BST-84231 [S]	Happenings	1967	30.00
— With "A Division of Liberty Records" on label			
❏ BST-84376	Head On	1971	18.00
❏ BN-LA789-H	Knucklebean	1977	15.00
❏ BN-LA396-G	Linger Lane	1974	15.00
❏ LT-1086	Medina	1980	12.00
❏ BN-LA551-G	Montara	1975	15.00
❏ BST-84416	Natural Illusions	1972	18.00
❏ LT-1044	Patterns	1980	12.00
❏ B1-33583	Patterns	1995	18.00
— Reissue			
❏ BST-84362	San Francisco	1970	25.00
❏ B1-28268	San Francisco	1994	18.00
— Reissue			
❏ LT-996	Spiral	1979	12.00
❏ BST-84244 [S]	Stick-Up!	1968	25.00
— With "A Division of Liberty Records" on label			
❏ BST-84291	Total Eclipse	1969	25.00
— With "A Division of Liberty Records" on label			
❏ BST-84291	Total Eclipse	1985	12.00
— The Finest in Jazz Since 1939" reissue			
❏ BN-LA710-G	View from Inside	1977	15.00
❏ BN-LA615-G	Waiting	1976	15.00
COLUMBIA			
❏ JC35814	Conception: The Gift of Love	1979	12.00
❏ JC35550	Highway 1	1978	12.00
❏ FC36402	Un Poco Loco	1980	12.00
CONTEMPORARY			
❏ C-14009	Solo/Quartet	1982	15.00
FANTASY			
❏ OJC-425	Solo/Quartet	1990	15.00
LANDMARK			
❏ LLP-1522	Ambos Mundos	1989	18.00
❏ LLP-1508	Color Schemes	1986	15.00
❏ LLP-1517	Cruisin' the 'Bird	1988	15.00
❏ LLP-501	Good Bait	1985	15.00
❏ LLP-1513	In the Vanguard	1987	15.00
THERESA			
❏ TR-124	Farewell Keystone	1989	15.00

HUTTON, BETTY

CAPITOL

Number	Title	Yr	NM
❏ H256 [10]	Square in the Social Circle	1950	60.00

WARNER BROS.

Number	Title	Yr	NM
❏ W1267 [M]	Betty Hutton at the Saints and Sinners Ball	1959	25.00
❏ WS1267 [S]	Betty Hutton at the Saints and Sinners Ball	1959	30.00

HUTTON, DANNY

MGM

Number	Title	Yr	NM
❏ SE-4664	Pre-Dog Night	1970	25.00

HYLAND, BRIAN

ABC-PARAMOUNT

Number	Title	Yr	NM
❏ 463 [M]	Country Meets Folk	1964	30.00
❏ S-463 [S]	Country Meets Folk	1964	40.00
❏ 400 [M]	Let Me Belong to You	1961	30.00
❏ S-400 [S]	Let Me Belong to You	1961	40.00
❏ 431 [M]	Sealed with a Kiss	1962	30.00
❏ S-431 [S]	Sealed with a Kiss	1962	40.00
DOT			
❏ DLP25954	Stay and Love Me All Summer	1969	18.00
❏ DLP25926	Tragedy/A Million to One	1969	18.00
KAPP			
❏ KL1202 [M]	The Bashful Blonde	1960	50.00
❏ KS3202 [S]	The Bashful Blonde	1960	80.00
PHILIPS			
❏ PHM200136 [M]	Here's to Our Love	1964	25.00
❏ PHS600136 [S]	Here's to Our Love	1964	30.00
❏ PHM200158 [M]	Rockin' Folk	1965	25.00
❏ PHS600158 [S]	Rockin' Folk	1965	30.00
❏ PHM200217 [M]	Run, Run, Look and See/The Joker Went Wild	1966	25.00
— With "200-217" in trail-off; this record plays mono			
❏ PHS600217 [S]	Run, Run, Look and See/The Joker Went Wild	1966	30.00
❏ PHM200217 [S]	Run, Run, Look and See/The Joker Went Wild	1966	25.00
— With "2/600-217" in trail-off; this record plays stereo, though labeled mono			
PICKWICK			
❏ SPC-3261	Young Years	197?	12.00
PRIVATE STOCK			
❏ PS-7003	In a State of Bayou	1977	15.00
RHINO			
❏ RNLP-70226	Greatest Hits	1987	12.00
UNI			
❏ 73097	Brian Hyland	1970	18.00
— The album is listed as "stereo," but "Gypsy Woman" is rechanneled			
WING			
❏ MGW-12341 [M]	Here's to Our Love	1967	15.00
❏ SRW-16341 [S]	Here's to Our Love	1967	15.00

HYMAN, DICK

ATLANTIC

Number	Title	Yr	NM
❏ SD1671	Satchmo Remembered	1975	12.00
CHIAROSCURO			
❏ 198	Themes and Variations on "A Child Is Born"	1978	12.00
COLUMBIA MASTERWORKS			
❏ M32587	Ferdinand "Jelly Roll" Morton -- Transcriptions for Orchestra	1974	15.00
COMMAND			
❏ RS 33-911 [M]	Brazilian Impressions	1966	18.00
❏ RS911SD [S]	Brazilian Impressions	1966	25.00
❏ RS951SD	Concerto Electro	1970	30.00
❏ RS 33-856 [M]	Electrodynamics	1963	18.00
❏ RS856SD [S]	Electrodynamics	1963	25.00
❏ RS 33-862 [M]	Fabulous	1963	18.00
❏ RS862SD [S]	Fabulous	1963	25.00
❏ RS 33-899 [M]	Happening!	1966	18.00
❏ RS899SD [S]	Happening!	1966	25.00
❏ RS 33-875 [M]	Keyboard Kaleidoscope	1964	18.00
❏ RS875SD [S]	Keyboard Kaleidoscope	1964	25.00
❏ RS924SD	Mirrors	1967	25.00
❏ RS938SD	Moog -- The Electric Eclectics of Dick Hyman	1968	30.00
❏ RSSD980/2	Organ Antics	1974	25.00
❏ RS 33-811 [M]	Provocative Piano	1960	18.00
❏ RS811SD [S]	Provocative Piano	1960	25.00
❏ RS 33-824 [M]	Provocative Piano Volume 2	1961	18.00
❏ RS824SD [S]	Provocative Piano Volume 2	1961	25.00
❏ RS933SD	Sweet Sweet Soul	1968	30.00
❏ RS946SD [B]	The Age of Electronicus	1969	40.00
❏ RS 33-832 [M]	The Dick Hyman Trio	1961	18.00
❏ RS832SD [S]	The Dick Hyman Trio	1961	25.00
❏ RSSD973/2	The Kaleidoscopic Keyboard	1974	25.00
❏ RS 33-891 [M]	The Man from O.R.G.A.N.	1965	40.00
❏ RS891SD [S]	The Man from O.R.G.A.N.	1965	50.00
❏ RSSD968/2	The Synthesizer	1973	25.00
— Reissue of "Electric Eclectics" and "Age of Electronicus"			
GRAPEVINE			
❏ 3309	Waltz Dressed in Blue	1978	15.00

Number	Title	Yr	NM
LION			
❏ L-70067 [M]	Swingin' Double Date	1958	18.00
MGM			
❏ E-3535 [M]	60 Great All-Time Songs, Vol. 1	1957	25.00
— Yellow label			
❏ E-3536 [M]	60 Great All-Time Songs, Vol. 2	1957	25.00
— Yellow label			
❏ E-3537 [M]	60 Great All-Time Songs, Vol. 3	1957	25.00
— Yellow label			
❏ E-3586 [M]	60 Great All-Time Songs, Vol. 4	1958	25.00
— Yellow label			
❏ E-3587 [M]	60 Great All-Time Songs, Vol. 5	1958	25.00
— Yellow label			
❏ E-3588 [M]	60 Great All-Time Songs, Vol. 6	1958	25.00
— Yellow label			
❏ E-3726 [M]	60 Great Continental and Classical Favorites	1959	25.00
❏ E-3725 [M]	60 Great Songs from Broadway Musicals	1959	25.00
— Yellow label			
❏ E-3724 [M]	60 Great Songs That Say "I Love You	1959	25.00
— Yellow label			
❏ E-3821 [M]	After Six	1960	25.00
❏ SE-3821 [S]	After Six	1960	30.00
❏ E-3379 [M]	Behind a Shady Nook	1956	30.00
— Yellow label			
❏ E-3606 [M]	Dick Hyman and Harpsichord in Hi-Fi	1958	25.00
— Yellow label			
❏ E-3642 [M]	Gigi	1958	25.00
— Yellow label			
❏ E-3494 [M]	Hi-Fi Suite	1957	30.00
— Yellow label			
❏ E-4119 [M]	Moon Gas	1963	25.00
❏ SE-4119 [S]	Moon Gas	1963	30.00
❏ E-3483 [M]	Red Sails in the Sunset	1957	30.00
— Yellow label			
❏ E-3553 [M]	Rockin' Sax and Rollin' Organ	1958	30.00
— Yellow label			
❏ SE-4649	Space Reflex	1969	18.00
❏ E-3808 [M]	Strictly Organic	1960	25.00
❏ SE-3808 [S]	Strictly Organic	1960	30.00
❏ E-3329 [M]	The "Unforgettable" Sound of the Dick Hyman Trio	1955	30.00
— Yellow label			
❏ E-289 [10]	The "Unforgettable" Sound of the Dick Hyman Trio	1955	40.00
❏ E-3280 [M]	The Dick Hyman Trio Swings	1954	30.00
— Yellow label			
❏ E-3747 [M]	Whoop-Up!	1959	25.00
— Yellow label			
❏ SE-3747 [S]	Whoop-Up!	1959	30.00
MONMOUTH-EVERGREEN			
❏ MES7065	Genius at Play	1974	18.00
MUSICAL HERITAGE SOCIETY			
❏ MHS912213K	Face the Music: Irving Berlin	198?	12.00
PROJECT 3			
❏ PR5057SD	Fantomfingers	1971	30.00
❏ PR5070SD	Piano Solos	1972	18.00
❏ PR5054SD	The Sensuous Piano of "D	1970	18.00
❏ PR5080SD	Traditional Jazz Piano	1973	18.00
RCA VICTOR GOLD SEAL			
❏ AGL1-3651	Scott Joplin: 16 Classic Rags	1980	10.00
— Reissue			
RCA VICTOR RED SEAL			
❏ XRL1-4746	Kitten on the Keys: Music of Zez Confrey	1983	12.00
❏ ARL1-1257	Scott Joplin: 16 Classic Rags	1976	12.00
REFERENCE RECORDINGS			
❏ RR-33	Dick Hyman Plays Fats Waller	1991	30.00
SEAGULL			
❏ LG-8209	Love Story	198?	12.00
STOMP OFF			
❏ SOS-1141	Gulf Coast Blues: The Music of Clarence Williams	1987	12.00
SUNSET			
❏ SUM-1140 [M]	I'll Never Be the Same	1966	15.00
❏ SUS-5140 [S]	I'll Never Be the Same	1966	18.00

HYMAN, PHYLLIS

ARISTA

Number	Title	Yr	NM
❏ AL9544	Can't We Fall in Love Again	1981	15.00
❏ AL8-8021	Goddess of Love	1983	15.00
❏ AB4202	Somewhere in My Lifetime	1979	15.00
❏ AL9509	You Know How to Love Me	1979	15.00
BUDDAH			
❏ BDS-5681	Phyllis Hyman	1977	18.00
PHILADELPHIA INT'L.			
❏ ST-53029	Living All Alone	1986	10.00

Number	Title	Yr	NM

I

IAN, JANIS

ANALOGUE PRODUCTIONS
Number	Title	Yr	NM
☐ AAP 027	Breaking Silence	1995	30.00

—Audiophile vinyl

CAPITOL
☐ SKAO-683	Present Company	1971	18.00
☐ SN-683	Present Company	1975	12.00

COLUMBIA
☐ PC33919	Aftertones	1976	12.00

—No bar code on cover
☐ PCQ33919 [Q]	Aftertones	1976	18.00
☐ PC33919	Aftertones	1979	10.00

—With bar code on cover
☐ PC33394	Between the Lines	1975	12.00

—No bar code on cover
☐ PCQ33394 [Q]	Between the Lines	1975	18.00
☐ PC33394 [B]	Between the Lines	1979	10.00

—With bar code on cover
☐ JC35325	Janis Ian	1978	12.00
☐ JC34440	Miracle Row	1977	12.00
☐ JC36139	Night Rains	1979	12.00
☐ PC36139	Night Rains	198?	10.00
☐ FC37360	Restless Eyes	1981	12.00
☐ KC32857	Stars	1974	12.00
☐ PC32857 [B]	Stars	197?	10.00

MGM
☐ GAS-121	Janis Ian (Golden Archive Series)	1970	30.00

POLYDOR
☐ PD-6058	Janis Ian	1976	12.00

VERVE FOLKWAYS
☐ FT-3017 [M]	Janis Ian	1967	25.00
☐ FTS-3017 [S]	Janis Ian	1967	25.00

VERVE FORECAST
☐ FT-3024 [M]	For All the Seasons of Your Mind	1967	25.00
☐ FTS-3024 [S]	For All the Seasons of Your Mind	1967	18.00
☐ FT-3017 [M]	Janis Ian	1967	25.00
☐ FTS-3017 [S]	Janis Ian	1967	18.00
☐ FTS-3048	The Secret Life of J. Eddy Fink	1968	18.00
☐ FTS 3063	Who Really Cares?	1969	18.00

IAN AND SYLVIA

AMPEX
☐ A-10103	Great Speckled Bird	1970	25.00

COLUMBIA
☐ C30736	Ian and Sylvia	1971	15.00
☐ G32516	The Best of Ian and Sylvia	1973	18.00
☐ KC31337	You Were On My Mind	1972	15.00

MGM
☐ SE-4550 [S]	Full Circle	1968	25.00
☐ E-4550 [M]	Full Circle	1968	50.00

—Mono is yellow label promo only; cover has "DJ Monaural" sticker on front
☐ GAS-115	Ian and Sylvia (Golden Archive Series)	1970	18.00
☐ E-4388 [M]	Lovin' Sound	1967	30.00
☐ SE-4388 [S]	Lovin' Sound	1967	18.00

VANGUARD
☐ VRS-9175 [M]	Early Morning Rain	1965	25.00
☐ VSD-79175 [S]	Early Morning Rain	1965	30.00
☐ VRS-9133 [M]	Four Strong Winds	1963	25.00
☐ VSD-2149 [S]	Four Strong Winds	1963	30.00
☐ VSD-73114	Greatest Hits	1985	12.00
☐ VRS-9109 [M]	Ian and Sylvia	1963	30.00
☐ VSD-2113 [S]	Ian and Sylvia	1963	30.00
☐ VSD-5/6	Ian and Sylvia's Greatest Hits	1969	18.00
☐ VSD-23/24	Ian and Sylvia's Greatest Hits, Vol. 2	1970	18.00
☐ VSD-79284	Nashville	1968	18.00
☐ VRS-9154 [M]	Northern Journey	1964	25.00
☐ VSD-79154 [S]	Northern Journey	1964	30.00
☐ VRS-9215 [M]	Play One More	1966	25.00
☐ VSD-79215 [S]	Play One More	1966	30.00
☐ VRS-9241 [M]	So Much for Dreaming	1967	25.00
☐ VSD-79241 [S]	So Much for Dreaming	1967	30.00
☐ VSD-79269	The Best of Ian & Sylvia	1968	18.00

IAN AND THE ZODIACS

PHILIPS
☐ PHM200176 [M]	Ian and the Zodiacs	1965	40.00
☐ PHS600176 [S]	Ian and the Zodiacs	1965	50.00

ICE-T

ATOMIC POP
☐ AP 0011	Greatest Hits: The Evidence	2000	25.00

Number	Title	Yr	NM

RHYME SYNDICATE

☐ 53858 [B]	Home Invasion	1993	25.00

SIRE
☐ PRO-A-4959 [DJ]	O.G. Original Gangster	1991	30.00

—Promo-only radio-ready version of album otherwise unavailable on U.S. vinyl
☐ 25765	Power	1988	18.00
☐ 25602	Rhyme Pays	1987	18.00
☐ 26028	The Iceberg/Freedom of Speech...Just Watch What You Say	1989	18.00

ICE CUBE

BEST SIDE
☐ 50700	War & Peace Vol. 1 (The War Disc)	1998	18.00
☐ 50015	War & Peace Vol. 2 (The Peace Disc)	2000	18.00

PRIORITY
☐ 57120	AmeriKKKa's Most Wanted	1990	18.00
☐ P1-53921	Bootlegs & B-Sides	1994	18.00
☐ 57155	Death Certificate	1991	18.00
☐ 29091	Greatest Hits	2001	18.00
☐ 7230 [FP]	Kill at Will	1990	15.00
☐ P1-53876	Lethal Injection	1993	18.00
☐ 57185	The Predator	1992	18.00

ICEHOUSE

CHRYSALIS
☐ BV41436 [FP]	Fresco	1983	12.00

—Five-track LP, with same songs on both sides
☐ R100935	Great Southern Land	1989	18.00

—BMG Direct Marketing edition
☐ F1-21680	Great Southern Land	1989	18.00
☐ CHR1350	Icehouse	1981	15.00
☐ FV41350	Icehouse	1983	10.00

—Reissue of CHS 1350
☐ R143633	Man of Colours	1987	15.00

—BMG Direct Marketing edition
☐ OV41592	Man of Colours	1987	12.00
☐ R144571	Measure for Measure	1986	15.00

—RCA Music Service edition
☐ BFV41527	Measure for Measure	1986	12.00
☐ CHR1390	Primitive Man	1982	15.00
☐ FV41390	Primitive Man	1983	12.00

—Reissue of CHR 1390
☐ PV41390	Primitive Man	198?	10.00

—Reissue with new prefix
☐ FV41458	Sidewalk	1983	12.00

ICICLE WORKS

ARISTA
☐ AL6-8202	Icicle Works	1984	12.00

BEGGARS BANQUET
☐ 6447-1-H	If You Want to Defeat Your Enemy, Sing His Song	1987	15.00

ID, THE

AURA
☐ 1000	Where Are We Going?	1976	50.00

RCA VICTOR
☐ LPM-3805 [M]	The Inner Sounds of the Id	1967	60.00
☐ LSP-3805 [S]	The Inner Sounds of the Id	1967	40.00

IDES OF MARCH, THE

RCA VICTOR
☐ APL1-0143	Midnight Oil	1973	18.00
☐ LSP-4812 [B]	World Woven	1972	18.00

SUNDAZED
☐ LP-5032	Ideology	199?	15.00

Number	Title	Yr	NM

WARNER BROS.
☐ WS1896	Common Bond	1971	18.00
☐ WS1863	Vehicle	1970	25.00

—Green "W7" label
☐ WS1863 [B]	Vehicle	1970	25.00

—Green "WB" label

IDLE RACE, THE

LIBERTY
☐ LST-7603 [B]	Birthday Party	1969	50.00
☐ LST7603 [B]	Birthday Party	1969	60.00

PARLOPHONE
☐ 825646335374 [B]	The Birthday Party	2014	40.00

IDOL, BILLY

CHRYSALIS
☐ R104806	Billy Idol	1982	15.00

—RCA Music Service edition
☐ CHR1377	Billy Idol	1982	15.00
☐ FV41377	Billy Idol	1983	12.00

—Reissue of Chrysalis CHR 1377
☐ VAS2610 [DJ]	Billy Idol Interview	1983	30.00
☐ R162264	Charmed Life	1990	14.00

—BMG Direct Marketing edition
☐ F1-21735 [B]	Charmed Life	1990	15.00
☐ R153899 [EP]	Don't Stop	1981	15.00

—RCA Music Service edition
☐ CEP4000 [EP]	Don't Stop	1981	15.00
☐ 5V44000 [EP]	Don't Stop	1983	10.00

—Reissue of CEP 4000
☐ R124674	Rebel Yell	1984	15.00

—RCA Music Service edition
☐ FV41450	Rebel Yell	1983	12.00
☐ R154038	Vital Idol	1987	15.00

—BMG Direct Marketing edition
☐ OV41620	Vital Idol	1987	12.00
☐ R154108	Whiplash Smile	1986	15.00

—RCA Music Service edition
☐ OV41514	Whiplash Smile	1986	12.00

IF

CAPITOL
☐ ST-539 [B]	If	1970	18.00
☐ SW-676	If2	1971	18.00
☐ SMAS-820	If3	1971	18.00
☐ ST-11299 [B]	Not Just Another Bunch of Pretty Faces	1974	18.00
☐ ST-11344	Tea Break Over -- Back On Your 'Eads!	1974	15.00

METROMEDIA
☐ BML1-0174	Double Diamond	1973	15.00
☐ KMD-1057	Waterfall	1972	16.00

IGGY AND THE STOOGES

BOMP!
☐ 1018 [B]	Kill City	1978	30.00

—By "Iggy Pop and James Williamson"

CLEOPATRA
☐ 8614 [B]	I Wanna Be Your Dog		30.00

—picture disc
☐ 4588 [B]	I Wanna be Your Dog		25.00
☐ 9051 [B]	Jesus Loves The Stooges		25.00
☐ 3687 [B]	More Power		25.00

COLUMBIA
☐ KC32111 [B]	Raw Power	1973	60.00
☐ 88691959351 [B]	Raw Power	2012	40.00

—double album includes original mix and later Iggy remix

ELEKTRA
☐ EKS74101 [B]	Fun House	1970	80.00

—By "The Stooges"; red label with large stylized "E" (butterfly label, deduct 60%)
☐ EKS74051 [B]	The Stooges	1969	80.00

—By "The Stooges"; red label with large stylized "E" (butterfly label, deduct 60%)

IMPORT/BOMP!
☐ 1018 [B]	Kill City	1978	40.00

—By "Iggy Pop and James Williamson"; original issue on green vinyl
☐ 1015	Metallic K.O.	1977	25.00

SUNDAZED
☐ LP5150 [B]	Fun House	2002	18.00

—By "The Stooges"; reissue on 180-gram vinyl
☐ LP5149 [B]	The Stooges	2002	18.00

—By "The Stooges"; reissue on 180-gram vinyl

IGGY POP

4 MEN WITH BEARDS
☐ 4M525LP [B]	Lust For Life		25.00
☐ 4M524LP [B]	The Idiot		25.00

A&M
☐ R134099	Blah Blah Blah	1986	15.00

—RCA Music Service edition

Number	Title	Yr	NM

Number	Title	Yr	NM
❑ SP-5145 [B]	Blah Blah Blah	1986	12.00
❑ SP-5198	Instinct	1988	12.00
❑ SP-17641 [DJ]	Live at the Channel 7/19/88	1988	40.00
— Numbered, rubber-stamped promo-only edition			

ANIMAL
❑ 6000 [B]	Zombie Birdhouse	1982	18.00
❑ FV41399	Zombie Birdhouse	1983	10.00
— Reissue			

ARISTA
❑ AL4237 [B]	New Values	1979	30.00
❑ AL9572 [B]	Party	1981	18.00
❑ AL5-8189	Party	198?	10.00
— Reissue			
❑ AB4259 [B]	Soldier	1980	25.00
❑ AL5-8172	Soldier	198?	10.00
— Reissue			
❑ SP-115 [EP]	Special Rock Club Versions	1981	26.00
— Promo-only remixes of 4 songs from the "Party" LP			

CLEOPATRA
| ❑ 3738 [B] | Iggy & Ziggy - Cleveland '77 | | 25.00 |

PAIR
| ❑ PDL2-1051 | Iggy Pop | 1986 | 15.00 |
| *— Compilation of RCA Victor material* | | | |

RCA VICTOR
❑ AFL1-4957	Choice Cuts	1984	18.00
❑ AFL1-2488 [B]	Lust for Life	1977	30.00
❑ APL1-2275 [B]	The Idiot	1977	30.00
❑ AFL1-2796 [B]	TV Eye -- 1977 Live	1978	35.00

SUNDAZED
❑ LP5039	New Values	200?	15.00
— Reissue on 180-gram vinyl			
❑ LP5041	Soldier	200?	15.00
— Reissue on 180-gram vinyl			

VIRGIN
| ❑ 91381 | Brick by Brick | 1990 | 14.00 |

IGLESIAS, JULIO

COLUMBIA
| ❑ FC38640 | Julio | 1984 | 10.00 |

IKETTES, THE

MODERN
| ❑ M-102 [M] | Soul Hits | 1965 | 50.00 |
| ❑ MST-102 [S] | Soul Hits | 1965 | 40.00 |

UNITED ARTISTS
| ❑ UA-LA190-F [B] | (G)Old and New | 1973 | 15.00 |

ILL WIND, THE

ABC
| ❑ S-641 [B] | Flashes | 1968 | 100.00 |

ILLINOIS SPEED PRESS, THE

COLUMBIA
| ❑ CS9976 | Duet | 1970 | 18.00 |
| ❑ CS9792 | The Illinois Speed Press | 1969 | 18.00 |

ILLUSION, THE

STEED
❑ ST-37006	If It's So	1970	18.00
❑ ST-37003	The Illusion	1969	25.00
❑ ST-37005	Together (As a Way of Life)	1969	18.00

ILLUSTRATION

JANUS
| ❑ JLP-3010 [B] | Illustration | 1969 | 30.00 |

ILMO SMOKEHOUSE

BEAUTIFUL SOUND
| ❑ 3002 [B] | Ilmo Smokehouse | 1971 | 50.00 |

ROULETTE
| ❑ RS-3002 | Ilmo Smokehouse | 1971 | 25.00 |

ILORI, SOLOMON

BLUE NOTE
❑ BLP-4136 [M]	African High Life	1963	60.00
❑ BST-84136 [S]	African High Life	1963	80.00
— With "New York, USA" address on label			
❑ BST-84136 [S]	African High Life	1967	30.00
— With "A Division of Liberty Records" on label			

IMPACS, THE

KING
❑ 916 [M]	A Weekend with the Impacs	1964	200.00
❑ KS-916 [S]	A Weekend with the Impacs	1964	300.00
❑ 886 [M]	Impact!	1964	200.00
❑ KS-886 [S]	Impact!	1964	300.00

IMPACTS, THE

DEL-FI
❑ DFLP-1234 [M]	Wipe Out	1963	60.00
❑ DFS-1234 [S]	Wipe Out	1963	80.00
❑ DLF-1234 [B]	Wipe Out	199?	15.00
— Reissue with bar code			

IMPALA SYNDROME, THE

PARALLAX
| ❑ 4002 [B] | The Impala Syndrome | 1970 | 150.00 |

IMPALAS, THE

CUB
❑ 8003 [M]	Sorry (I Ran All the Way Home)	1959	400.00
❑ S-8003 [S]	Sorry (I Ran All the Way Home)	1959	600.00
— ssue of Dayspring LP			

IMPRESSIONS, THE

ABC
❑ S-727	16 Greatest Hits	1971	15.00
❑ D-780	Curtis Mayfield/His Early Years with the Impressions	1973	25.00
❑ S-654	The Best of the Impressions	1968	18.00
❑ ST-91540	The Best of the Impressions	1968	25.00
— Capitol Record Club edition			
❑ 606 [M]	The Fabulous Impressions	1967	40.00
❑ S-606 [S]	The Fabulous Impressions	1967	30.00
❑ S-668 [B]	The Versatile Impressions	1969	18.00
❑ S-635	We're a Winner	1968	18.00

ABC-PARAMOUNT
❑ 493 [M]	Keep On Pushing	1964	30.00
❑ S-493 [S]	Keep On Pushing	1964	40.00
❑ ST-90106 [S]	Keep On Pushing	1965	50.00
— Capitol Record Club edition			
❑ 523 [M]	One By One	1965	25.00
❑ S-523 [S]	One By One	1965	30.00
❑ T-90520 [M]	One By One	1965	30.00
— Capitol Record Club edition			
❑ ST-90520 [S]	One By One	1965	30.00
— Capitol Record Club edition			
❑ 505 [M]	People Get Ready	1965	30.00
❑ S-505 [S]	People Get Ready	1965	40.00
❑ ST-90097 [S]	People Get Ready	1965	50.00
— Capitol Record Club edition			
❑ 545 [M]	Ridin' High	1966	25.00
❑ S-545 [S]	Ridin' High	1966	30.00
❑ 450 [M]	The Impressions	1963	30.00
❑ S-450 [S]	The Impressions	1963	40.00
❑ T-90472 [M]	The Impressions	1965	40.00
— Capitol Record Club edition			
❑ 515 [M]	The Impressions' Greatest Hits	1965	25.00
❑ S-515 [S]	The Impressions' Greatest Hits	1965	30.00
❑ 468 [M]	The Never Ending Impressions	1964	30.00
❑ S-468 [S]	The Never Ending Impressions	1964	40.00
❑ ST-90492 [S]	The Never Ending Impressions	1965	50.00
— Capitol Record Club edition			

CHI-SOUND
| ❑ T-596 | Come to My Party | 1979 | 12.00 |
| ❑ T-624 | Fan the Fire | 1981 | 12.00 |

COTILLION
| ❑ SD9912 | It's About Time | 1976 | 15.00 |

CURTOM
❑ CRS-8004	Best Impressions -- Curtis, Sam, Dave	1969	18.00
❑ CRS-8006	Check Out Your Mind	1970	18.00
❑ CRS-8019	Finally Got Myself Together	1974	18.00
❑ CU5003	First Impressions	1975	15.00
❑ CUR-2006	Lasting Impressions	198?	12.00
❑ CU5009	Loving Power	1976	15.00
❑ CRS-8016	Preacher Man	1973	18.00
❑ CRS-8003	The Young Mods' Forgotten Story	1969	18.00
❑ CRS-8001	This Is My Country	1968	18.00
❑ CRS-8012	Times Have Changed	1972	18.00

LOST-NITE
| ❑ LLP-22 [10] | Jerry Butler and the Impressions | 1981 | 18.00 |
| *— Red vinyl* | | | |

MCA
| ❑ 5373 | In the Heat of the Night | 1982 | 12.00 |
| ❑ 1500 | The Impressions Greatest Hits | 1982 | 10.00 |

PICKWICK
| ❑ SPC-3602 | The Impressions | 1978 | 10.00 |

SCEPTER CITATION
| ❑ CTN-18018 | The Best of Curtis Mayfield and the Impressions | 1972 | 12.00 |

SIRE
| ❑ SASH-3717 | The Vintage Years | 1977 | 18.00 |
| *— Includes solo hits by Jerry Butler and Curtis Mayfield* | | | |

IMUS, DON

BANG
| ❑ 407 | This Honky's Nuts | 1974 | 30.00 |

RCA VICTOR
❑ LSP-4699	1200 Hamburgers to Go	1972	30.00
— As "Imus in the Morning			
❑ LSP-4819	One Sacred Chicken to Go	1973	30.00

IN-SECT, THE

RCA CAMDEN
| ❑ CAL-909 [M] | Introducing the In-Sect Direct from England | 1964 | 40.00 |
| ❑ CAS-909 [S] | Introducing the In-Sect Direct from England | 1964 | 50.00 |

IN GROUP, THE

IN
| ❑ I-1002 [M] | Swinging 12 String | 1964 | 25.00 |
| ❑ IS-1002 [S] | Swinging 12 String | 1964 | 30.00 |

IN PURSUIT

MTM
| ❑ ST-71057 | Standing in Your Shadow | 1986 | 12.00 |
| ❑ MLP-72150 [EP] | When Darkness Falls | 1986 | 10.00 |

INCREDIBLE BONGO BAND, THE

PRIDE
❑ 0028	Bongo Rock	1973	80.00
— Note: This album has been reissued to look like the original			
❑ 6010	The Return of the Incredible Bongo Band	1974	25.00

INCREDIBLE STRING BAND, THE

4 MEN WITH BEARDS
| ❑ 4M210LP [B] | The Big Huge | | 25.00 |
| ❑ 4M209LP [B] | Wee Tam | | 25.00 |

CARTHAGE
| ❑ CGLP-4421 | The Hangman's Beautiful Daughter | 198? | 15.00 |

ELEKTRA
❑ EKS-74057 [B]	Changing Horses	1969	30.00
— Red label, large stylized "E			
❑ EKS-74057	Changing Horses	1971	15.00
— Butterfly label			
❑ EKS-74061 [B]	I Looked Up	1970	30.00
— Red label, large stylized "E			
❑ EKS-74061	I Looked Up	1971	15.00
— Butterfly label			
❑ EKS-74112 [B]	Liquid Acrobat As Regards the Air	1972	30.00
— Butterfly label			
❑ 7E-2004 [B]	Relics of the Incredible String Band	1971	30.00
— Butterfly label			
❑ EKM-4010 [M]	The 5,000 Spirits	1967	70.00
❑ EKS-74010 [S]	The 5,000 Spirits	1967	30.00
— Brown label			
❑ EKS-74010	The 5,000 Spirits	1969	18.00
— Red label, large stylized "E			
❑ EKS-74010 [B]	The 5,000 Spirits	1971	18.00
— Butterfly label			
❑ EKS-74037 [B]	The Big Huge	1969	30.00
— Brown label			
❑ EKS-74037	The Big Huge	1969	18.00
— Red label, large stylized "E			
❑ EKS-74037	The Big Huge	1971	15.00
— Butterfly label			
❑ EKS-74021 [B]	The Hangman's Beautiful Daughter	1968	30.00
— Brown label			
❑ EKS-74021	The Hangman's Beautiful Daughter	1969	18.00
— Red label, large stylized "E			
❑ EKS-74021	The Hangman's Beautiful Daughter	1971	15.00
— Butterfly label			
❑ EKM-322 [M]	The Incredible String Band	1967	30.00
❑ EKS-7322 [S]	The Incredible String Band	1967	25.00
— Brown label			
❑ EKS-7322	The Incredible String Band	1969	18.00

Number	Title	Yr	NM

—Red label, large stylized "E
| ❑ EKS-7322 | The Incredible String Band | 1971 | 15.00 |

—Butterfly label
| ❑ 7E-2002 | 'U' | 1971 | 30.00 |

—Butterfly label
| ❑ EKS-74036 [B] | Wee Tam | 1969 | 30.00 |

—Brown label
| ❑ EKS-74036 | Wee Tam | 1969 | 18.00 |

—Red label, large stylized "E
| ❑ EKS-74036 | Wee Tam | 1971 | 15.00 |

—Butterfly label

REPRISE
❑ MS2122 [B]	Earthspan	1973	18.00
❑ MS2198 [B]	Hard Rope and Silver Twine	1974	18.00
❑ MS2139 [B]	No Ruinous Feud	1973	18.00

SUNDAZED
| ❑ LP5128 [S] | The 5,000 Spirits | 2003 | 15.00 |

—Reissue on 180-gram vinyl
| ❑ LP5129 [S] | The Hangman's Beautiful Daughter | 2003 | 15.00 |

—Reissue on 180-gram vinyl
| ❑ LP5127 [S] | The Incredible String Band | 2003 | 15.00 |

—Reissue on 180-gram vinyl

INCREDIBLES, THE

AUDIO ARTS
| ❑ AAS-7000 | Heart and Soul | 1970 | 25.00 |

IND, PETER

WAVE
| ❑ W-1 [M] | Looking Out | 1961 | 30.00 |
| ❑ WS-1 [S] | Looking Out | 1961 | 30.00 |

INDEPENDENTS, THE

WAND
❑ WDS-699	Discs of Gold	1974	25.00
❑ WDS-694	The First Time We Met	1973	25.00
❑ WDS-696	The Independents	1973	25.00

INDEX

DC
| ❑ 71 | The Index | 1968 | 3000.00 |

—Black label; issued with black and white jacket; number is from deal wax; VG value 1500; VG+ value 2250
| ❑ 4736 | The Index | 1968 | 2000.00 |

- Red label; issued with generic white jacket, though sometimes found in first LP's jacket; number in dead wax; VG value 1000; VG+ value 1500

INDIA.ARIE

MOTOWN
| ❑ 440 013770-1 | Acoustic Soul | 2001 | 18.00 |

INDIAN SUMMER

RCA/NEON
| ❑ NE-3 | Indian Summer | 1971 | 30.00 |

INDIGO GIRLS

DRAGON PATH
| ❑ 0LMM-I [EP] | Indigo Girls | 1986 | 200.00 |

—Blue or clear vinyl (each of equal value)
| ❑ 0LMM-I [EP] | Indigo Girls | 1986 | 150.00 |

—Black vinyl

EPIC
| ❑ FE45044 | Indigo Girls | 1989 | 18.00 |
| ❑ EAS4020 [DJ] | Indigo Girls Live | 1991 | 40.00 |

—Promo-only version of "Back on the Bus Y'All
| ❑ EAS1481 [EP] | Indigo Girls Sampler | 1989 | 18.00 |

—Promo-only with tour-dates sticker on white cardboard cover; includes Kid Fears/Closer to Fine/Center Stage/Prince of Darkness
| ❑ EAS1861 [EP] | Land of Canaan Plus Five Live | 1989 | 30.00 |

—Promo-only item with five live tracks on B-side
❑ E46820	Nomads*Indians*Saints	1990	25.00
❑ EAS2201 [DJ]	Shades of Indigo: An Interview by Shawn Colvin	1990	70.00
❑ FE45427	Strange Fire	1989	18.00

—Reissue of Indigo release
| ❑ E57621 | Swamp Ophelia | 1994 | 40.00 |

—Black vinyl; all copies autographed on the label by the Indigo Girls
| ❑ E57621 | Swamp Ophelia | 1994 | 40.00 |

—Green vinyl; all copies autographed on the label by the Indigo Girls

INDIGO
| ❑ 0LMM-II | Strange Fire | 1987 | 150.00 |

—Black vinyl
| ❑ 0LMM-II | Strange Fire | 1987 | 200.00 |

—Blue, clear or red vinyl (each of equal value)

INFLUENCE

ABC
| ❑ ABCS-630 | Influence | 1968 | 30.00 |

INGMANN, JORGEN

ATCO
| ❑ 33-130 [M] | Apache | 1961 | 40.00 |
| ❑ 33-139 [M] | The Many Guitars of Jorgen Ingmann | 1962 | 40.00 |

MERCURY
| ❑ MG-20200 [M] | Swinging Guitar | 1956 | 60.00 |
| ❑ MG-20292 [M] | Swing Softly | 1956 | 60.00 |

UNITED ARTISTS
| ❑ UAS-6785 | El Condor Pasa | 1970 | 25.00 |

INGRAM, JAMES

QWEST
| ❑ 23970 | It's Your Night | 1983 | 10.00 |
| ❑ 23970 [DJ] | It's Your Night | 1983 | 18.00 |

— Promo version on "Quiex II" vinyl
| ❑ 25424 | Never Felt So Good | 1986 | 10.00 |

WARNER BROS.
| ❑ 25924 | It's Real | 1989 | 15.00 |

INGRAM, LUTHER

KOKO
| ❑ KOS-2202 | If Loving You Is Wrong I Don't Want to Be Right | 1972 | 18.00 |
| ❑ KOS-2201 | I've Been Here All the Time | 1971 | 18.00 |

INK SPOTS

COLORTONE
| ❑ 4901 [M] | The Ink Spots | 1958 | 60.00 |
| ❑ 4947 [M] | The Ink Spots, Vol. 2 | 1959 | 60.00 |

CROWN
❑ CLP5221 [M]	More Ink Spots	196?	18.00
❑ CLP-5142 [M]	The Ink Spots	1961	25.00
❑ CST-175 [S]	The Ink Spots	1961	30.00

—Black vinyl
| ❑ CST-175 [S] | The Ink Spots | 1961 | 50.00 |

—Red vinyl
| ❑ CLP-5112 [M] | The Ink Spots' Greatest Hits | 1959 | 25.00 |
| ❑ CST-144 [S] | The Ink Spots' Greatest Hits | 1959 | 30.00 |

—Black vinyl
| ❑ CST-144 [S] | The Ink Spots' Greatest Hits | 1959 | 50.00 |

—Red vinyl
| ❑ CLP-5187 [M] | The Sensational Ink Spots | 1962 | 25.00 |
| ❑ CST-217 [S] | The Sensational Ink Spots | 1962 | 30.00 |

—Black vinyl
| ❑ CST-217 [S] | The Sensational Ink Spots | 1962 | 50.00 |

—Red vinyl

DECCA
❑ DL4297 [M]	Our Golden Favorites	1962	30.00
❑ DL74297 [S]	Our Golden Favorites	1962	25.00
❑ DL5333 [10]	Precious Memories	1951	50.00
❑ DL5541 [10]	Street of Dreams	1954	50.00
❑ DL8154 [M]	The Best of the Ink Spots	1955	40.00

—Black label, silver print
❑ DXB182 [M]	The Best of the Ink Spots	1965	30.00
❑ DXSB7182 [P]	The Best of the Ink Spots	1965	25.00
❑ DL5056 [10]	The Ink Spots	1950	50.00
❑ DL5071 [10]	The Ink Spots, Vol. 2	1950	50.00
❑ DL8232 [M]	Time Out for Tears	1956	40.00

—Black label, silver print
| ❑ DL8768 [M] | Torch Time | 1958 | 40.00 |

—Black label, silver print

EVEREST ARCHIVE OF FOLK & JAZZ
| ❑ 350 | The Ink Spots in London | 197? | 12.00 |

GOLDEN TONE
| ❑ C4037 | Ink Spots Vol. II | 195? | 15.00 |
| ❑ C4024 | The Fabulous Ink Spots | 195? | 15.00 |

GRAND AWARD
❑ GA 33-328 [M]	The Ink Spots' Greatest, Volume 1	1958	30.00
❑ GA 33-354 [M]	The Ink Spots' Greatest, Volume 2	1958	30.00
❑ GA 33-396 [M]	The Ink Spots' Greatest, Volume 3	1959	30.00
❑ GA232SD [S]	The Ink Spots' Greatest, Volume 3	1959	40.00

KING
❑ 5001	18 Hits by the Ink Spots	197?	12.00
❑ 535 [M]	Something Old, Something New	1956	400.00
❑ 642 [M]	Songs That Will Live Forever	1959	300.00

—Reissue of 535

LONGINES SYMPHONETTE
| ❑ SYS5830 | 10 of the Best Ink Spots Hits | 197? | 12.00 |

—Label calls this "The Best of the Ink Spots"; also on label is "New Premiun for Mills Bros. V&R Offer

MCA
| ❑ MSM2-35253 | The Beautiful Music Company Presents the Ink Spots | 1991 | 25.00 |
| ❑ 4005 | The Best of the Ink Spots | 197? | 15.00 |

OPEN SKY
| ❑ 3125 | Just Like Old Times | 198? | 12.00 |

PAULA
| ❑ 2212 | The Ink Spots Sing Country | 1972 | 12.00 |

RONDO
| ❑ RS-2010 [S] | The Ink Spots in the Spotlite | 1963 | 18.00 |

— Title on label is "The Ink Spots
| ❑ R-2010 [M] | The Ink Spots in the Spotlite | 1963 | 15.00 |

TOPS
| ❑ L-1561 [M] | The Ink Spots | 1957 | 40.00 |
| ❑ L-1668 [M] | The Ink Spots, Vol. 2 | 1959 | 40.00 |

VERVE
| ❑ MGV-2124 [M] | The Ink Spots' Favorites | 1959 | 30.00 |
| ❑ MGVS-6096 [S] | The Ink Spots' Favorites | 1959 | 40.00 |

VOCALION
❑ VL3725 [M]	Lost in a Dream	1965	15.00
❑ VL73725 [R]	Lost in a Dream	1965	12.00
❑ VL3606 [M]	Sincerely Yours	196?	15.00
❑ VL73606 [R]	Sincerely Yours	196?	12.00

WALDORF MUSIC HALL
| ❑ MH 33-144 [10] | Songs of the South Seas | 195? | 80.00 |
| ❑ MH 33-152 [10] | The Ink Spots Quartet | 195? | 80.00 |

INMAN, AUTRY

EPIC
| ❑ BN26428 | Ballad of Two Brothers | 1968 | 25.00 |

JUBILEE
❑ JGM-2056 [M]	New Year's Eve with Autry Inman	1964	25.00
❑ JGS-2056 [S]	New Year's Eve with Autry Inman	1964	30.00
❑ JGM-2055 [M]	Riscotheque Saturday Night	1964	25.00
❑ JGS-2055 [S]	Riscotheque Saturday Night	1964	30.00

MOUNTAIN DEW
| ❑ 7022 [M] | Autry Inman | 1963 | 25.00 |
| ❑ S-7022 [S] | Autry Inman | 1963 | 30.00 |

SIMS
| ❑ 107 [M] | Autry Inman at the Frontier Club | 1964 | 25.00 |
| ❑ S-107 [S] | Autry Inman at the Frontier Club | 1964 | 30.00 |

INMAN, JERRY

COLUMBIA
| ❑ CL2793 [M] | Lennon-McCartney Country Style R.F.D. | 1967 | 30.00 |
| ❑ CS9593 [S] | Lennon-McCartney Country Style R.F.D. | 1967 | 25.00 |

ELEKTRA
| ❑ 7E-1068 | You Betchum! | 1976 | 15.00 |

INNOCENCE, THE

KAMA SUTRA
| ❑ KLP-8059 [M] | The Innocence | 1967 | 25.00 |
| ❑ KLPS-8059 [S] | The Innocence | 1967 | 30.00 |

INNOCENT, THE

RED LABEL
| ❑ 7300 [B] | Livin' in the Street | 1985 | 80.00 |

INNOCENTS, THE

INDIGO
| ❑ 503 [M] | Inocently Yours | 1961 | 500.00 |

—Plain white cover; promo only
| ❑ 503 [M] | Inocently Yours | 1961 | 80.00 |

INSECT TRUST, THE

ATCO
| ❑ SD 33-313 [B] | Hoboken Saturday Night | 1970 | 60.00 |

CAPITOL
| ❑ SKAO-109 | The Insect Trust | 1968 | 50.00 |

INSIDE OUT

FREDLO
| ❑ 6834 | Bringing It All Back | 1968 | 200.00 |

INTERNATIONAL SUBMARINE BAND, THE

LHI
| ❑ 12001 [B] | Safe at Home | 1968 | 150.00 |

—Counterfeits have white labels, legitimate copies have multi-color labels

RHINO
| ❑ RNLP 069 | Safe at Home | 1985 | 30.00 |

SUNDAZED
| ❑ LP5112 | Safe at Home | 2001 | 15.00 |

—Reissue on 180-gram vinyl

INTERPRETERS, THE

CADET
| ❑ LP-762 [M] | The Knack | 1966 | 18.00 |
| ❑ LPS-762 [S] | The Knack | 1966 | 25.00 |

INTRIGUES, THE

YEW
| ❑ YS-777 | In a Moment | 1970 | 30.00 |

Number	Title	Yr	NM
INTRUDERS, THE (1)			
GAMBLE			
❑ GS-5004 [B]	Cowboys to Girls	1968	50.00
❑ KZ31991	Save the Children	1973	25.00
❑ KZ32131	Super Hits	1973	25.00
❑ G-5001 [M]	The Intruders Are Together	1967	40.00
❑ GS-5001 [S]	The Intruders Are Together	1967	50.00
❑ GS-5005	The Intruders Greatest Hits	1969	40.00
❑ GS-5008	When We Get Married	1970	50.00
PHILADELPHIA INT'L.			
❑ PZ32131	Super Hits	198?	10.00
—Reissue of Gamble 32131			
TSOP			
❑ KZ33149	Energy of Love	1974	18.00
INVADERS, THE			
JUSTICE			
❑ JLP-125	On the Right Track	196?	300.00
INVICTAS, THE			
20TH CENTURY FOX			
❑ TCF-3152 [M]	The Invictas	1964	40.00
INVICTAS			
❑ M80P-5816/7 [M]	The Invictas	196?	250.00
SAHARA			
❑ 101 [M]	The Invictas A-Go-Go	1965	120.00
INVISIBLE MAN'S BAND, THE			
BOARDWALK			
❑ NB1-33238	Really Wanna See Ya	1981	25.00
INXS			
ATCO			
❑ 90115 [EP]	Dekadance	1983	15.00
❑ 90184	INXS	1984	12.00
—U.S. issue of 1980 Australian album			
❑ 90072	Shabooh Shoobah	1983	12.00
❑ 90160	The Swing	1984	12.00
❑ 90185	Underneath the Colours	1984	15.00
—U.S. issue of 1981 Australian album			
ATLANTIC			
❑ R153606	Kick	1987	15.00
—BMG Direct Marketing edition			
❑ 81796	Kick	1987	12.00
❑ R114468	Listen Like Thieves	1985	15.00
—RCA Music Service edition			
❑ 81277	Listen Like Thieves	1985	12.00
❑ A1-82294	Live Baby Live	1991	30.00
—Columbia House version (only U.S. vinyl pressing)			
❑ R164378	X	1990	15.00
—BMG Direct Marketing edition			
❑ 82140	X	1990	12.00
IRIS, DONNIE			
HME			
❑ BFW39949	No Muss... No Fuss	1985	12.00
MCA			
❑ 3272	Back on the Streets	1980	15.00
❑ 5179	Back on the Streets	1981	10.00
—Reissue of 3272			
❑ 5427	Fortune 410	1983	12.00
❑ 5237	King Cool	1981	12.00
❑ 5358	The High and the Mighty	1982	12.00
IRISH ROVERS, THE			
DECCA			
❑ DL75037	All Hung Up	1968	18.00
❑ DL4835 [M]	First	1967	25.00
❑ DL74835 [S]	First	1967	18.00
❑ DL75157	Life of the Rover	1969	18.00
❑ DL75302	On the Shores of Americay	1971	18.00
❑ DL75081	Tales to Warm Your Mind	1969	18.00
❑ DL4951 [M]	The Unicorn	1968	30.00
❑ DL74951 [S]	The Unicorn	1968	18.00
MCA			
❑ 249	First	1973	12.00
—Reissue of Decca 74835			
❑ 4066	Greatest Hits	1976	18.00
❑ 284	Life of the Rover	1973	12.00
—Reissue of Decca 75157			
❑ 175	On the Shores of Americay	1973	12.00
—Reissue of Decca 75302			
❑ 15	The Unicorn	1973	12.00
—Reissue of Decca 74951			
IRON BUTTERFLY			
ATCO			
❑ SD 33-280	Ball	1969	18.00
❑ 33-227 [M]	Heavy	1967	80.00
❑ SD 33-227 [S]	Heavy	1967	30.00
—Brown and purple label			
❑ SD 33-227 [S]	Heavy	1969	18.00
—Yellow label			
❑ 33-250 [M]	In-A-Gadda-Da-Vida	1968	100.00
❑ SD 33-250 [S]	In-A-Gadda-Da-Vida	1968	30.00
—Brown and purple label			
❑ SD 33-250 [S]	In-A-Gadda-Da-Vida	1969	18.00
—Yellow label			
❑ SD 33-250 [S]	In-A-Gadda-Da-Vida	197?	12.00
—Any later Atco label; LP was in print into the late 1980s			
❑ SD 33-318	Iron Butterfly Live	1970	18.00
—Yellow label			
❑ SD 33-318	Iron Butterfly Live	197?	12.00
—Any later Atco label; LP was in print into the late 1980s			
❑ SD 33-339	Metamorphosis	1970	18.00
❑ SD 33-369	The Best of Iron Butterfly/ Evolution	1971	18.00
CLEOPATRA			
❑ CLP1762 [B]	Live at the Galaxy 1967	2014	30.00
MCA			
❑ 465	Scorching Beauty	1975	15.00
❑ 2164	Sun and Steel	1976	15.00
PAIR			
❑ PDL2-1065	Rare Flight	1986	18.00
IRON MAIDEN			
CAPITOL			
❑ 53185	Best of the Beast	1996	80.00
—Box set with booklet; probably a UK pressing stickered with US bar code			
❑ ST-12094	Iron Maiden	198?	15.00
—Reissue of Harvest 12094			
❑ ST-12141	Killers	198?	15.00
—Reissue of Harvest 12141			
❑ SABB-12441	Live After Death	1985	25.00
❑ SQ-15017 [EP]	Maiden Japan	198?	12.00
—Reissue of Harvest 15000			
❑ SEAX-12306 [PD]	Piece of Mind	1983	60.00
❑ ST-12274	Piece of Mind	1983	15.00
❑ SJ-12321	Powerslave	1984	15.00
❑ C1-90258	Seventh Son of a Seventh Son	1988	12.00
❑ SJ-12524	Somewhere in Time	1986	15.00
❑ SEAX-12219 [PD]	The Number of the Beast	1982	60.00
❑ ST-12202	The Number of the Beast	1982	15.00
EPIC			
❑ E46905	No Prayer for the Dying	1990	30.00
—Red vinyl			
HARVEST			
❑ ST-12094 [B]	Iron Maiden	1980	18.00
❑ ST-12141	Killers	1981	18.00
❑ MLP-15000 [EP]	Maiden Japan	1981	12.00
IRVINE, WELDON			
BMG SPECIAL PRODUCTS			
❑ DRL1-1794	Cosmic Vortex	199?	18.00
—Reissue			
❑ DRL1-1795	Sinbad	199?	18.00
—Reissue			
❑ DRL1-1796	Spirit Man	199?	18.00
—Reissue			
NODLEW			
❑ 1001	Liberated Brother	1972	300.00
❑ 1002	Time Capsule	1973	300.00
—Reproductions exist			
RCA VICTOR			
❑ APL1-0703	Cosmic Vortex	1974	120.00
❑ APL1-1363	Sinbad	1976	150.00
❑ APL1-0909	Spirit Man	1975	120.00
STRATA-EAST			
❑ SES-19479	In Harmony	1974	120.00
ISAAK, CHRIS			
REPRISE			
❑ 25837	Heart Shaped World	1989	15.00
WARNER BROS.			
❑ 25336	Chris Isaak	1987	12.00
❑ 25156	Silvertone	1985	12.00
ISLEY BROTHERS, THE			
BUDDAH			
❑ BDS-5652	The Best of the Isley Brothers	1976	18.00
COLLECTABLES			
❑ COL-5103	Shout!	198?	12.00
DEF SOUL			
❑ B0004812-01	Baby Makin' Music	2006	18.00
ISLAND			
❑ 7243 [DJ]	Mission to Please	1996	25.00
—Promo-only vinyl in generic cover			
MOTOWN			
❑ M5-143V1	Doin' Their Thing (Best of the Isley Brothers)	1981	10.00
—Reissue of Tamla 287			
❑ M5-106V1	Motown Superstar Series, Volume 6	1981	10.00
❑ M5-128V1	This Old Heart of Mine	1981	10.00
—Reissue of Tamla 269			
PICKWICK			
❑ SPC-3331	Soul Shout!	197?	12.00
RCA CAMDEN			
❑ ACL1-0861	Rock Around the Clock	1975	15.00
❑ ACL1-0126	Rock On Brother	1973	15.00
RCA VICTOR			
❑ LPM-2156 [M]	Shout!	1959	120.00
—Long Play" label			
❑ LSP-2156 [S]	Shout!	1959	200.00
—Living Stereo" label			
SCEPTER			
❑ SC-552 [M]	Take Some Time Out for the Isley Brothers	1966	30.00
❑ SCS-552 [S]	Take Some Time Out for the Isley Brothers	1966	40.00
SUNSET			
❑ SUS-5257	The Isley Brothers Do Their Thing	1969	18.00
TAMLA			
❑ TS-287	Doin' Their Thing (Best of the Isley Brothers)	1969	25.00
❑ T-275 [M]	Soul on the Rocks	1967	30.00
❑ TS-275 [S]	Soul on the Rocks	1967	30.00
❑ T-269 [M]	This Old Heart of Mine	1966	30.00
❑ TS-269 [S]	This Old Heart of Mine	1966	30.00
T-NECK			
❑ KZ32453	3 + 3	1973	15.00
❑ ZQ32453 [Q]	3 + 3	1974	25.00
❑ PZ32453	3 + 3	197?	10.00
—Reissue with new prefix			
❑ FZ38674	Between the Sheets	1983	12.00
❑ PZ38674	Between the Sheets	1985	10.00
—Budget-line reissue			
❑ TNS-3009	Brother, Brother, Brother	1972	18.00
❑ ASZ137 [DJ]	Everything You Always Wanted to Hear by the Isley Brothers But Were Afraid to Ask For	1976	25.00
—Promo-only compilation			
❑ PZ34452	Forever Gold	1977	12.00
❑ TNS-3006	Get Into Something	1970	18.00
❑ TNS-3008	Givin' It Back	1971	18.00
❑ FZ36305	Go All the Way	1980	12.00
❑ PZ36305	Go All the Way	198?	10.00
—Budget-line reissue			
❑ PZ34432	Go for Your Guns	1977	15.00
—No bar code on cover			
❑ PZQ34432 [Q]	Go for Your Guns	1977	25.00
❑ PZ34432	Go for Your Guns	198?	10.00
—Budget-line reissue with bar code			
❑ FZ37080	Grand Slam	1981	12.00
❑ PZ37080	Grand Slam	198?	10.00
—Budget-line reissue			
❑ FZ39240	Greatest Hits, Vol. 1	1984	12.00
❑ PZ39240	Greatest Hits, Vol. 1	1985	10.00
—Budget-line reissue			
❑ PZ33809	Harvest for the World	1976	15.00
—No bar code on cover			
❑ PZQ33809 [Q]	Harvest for the World	1976	25.00
❑ FZ37533	Inside You	1981	12.00
❑ TNS-3007	In the Beginning (With Jimi Hendrix)	1970	25.00
❑ TNS-3011	Isleys' Greatest Hits	1973	18.00
❑ TNS-3001	It's Our Thing	1969	25.00
❑ PZ33070	Live It Up	1974	15.00
—No bar code on cover			
❑ PZQ33070 [Q]	Live It Up	1974	25.00
❑ JZ34930	Showdown	1978	12.00
❑ PZ34930	Showdown	198?	10.00
—Budget-line reissue			
❑ TNS-3002	The Brothers: Isley	1969	25.00
❑ PZ33536	The Heat Is On	1975	15.00
—No bar code on cover			
❑ PZ33536	The Heat Is On	198?	10.00
—Budget-line reissue with bar code			
❑ TNS-3010	The Isleys Live	1973	25.00
❑ FZ38047	The Real Deal	1982	12.00
❑ KZ235650	Timeless	1978	15.00
❑ PZ236077	Winner Takes All	1979	15.00
UNITED ARTISTS			
❑ UAL-3313 [M]	The Famous Isley Brothers	1963	50.00
❑ UAS-6313 [S]	The Famous Isley Brothers	1963	60.00
❑ UA-LA500-E	The Very Best of the Isley Brothers	1975	12.00
WAND			
❑ WD-653 [M]	Twist & Shout	1962	80.00
❑ WDS-653 [S]	Twist & Shout	1962	100.00
WARNER BROS.			
❑ 25347	Masterpiece	1985	12.00
❑ 25586	Smooth Sailin'	1987	12.00
❑ 25940	Spend the Night	1989	12.00
IVES, BURL			
BELL			
❑ 6055	Time	1971	12.00
COLUMBIA			
❑ CS9728	Burl Ives Christmas Album	1968	15.00
❑ CL980 [M]	Burl Ives Sings Songs for All Ages	1956	30.00

Number	Title	Yr	NM
❏ CL2570 [10]	Children's Favorites	1955	40.00
—House Party Series" issue			
❏ CL6144 [10]	More Folk Songs	1950	50.00
❏ CL1459 [10]	Return of the Wayfaring Stranger	1960	30.00
❏ CS9925 [B]	Softly and Tenderly	1969	15.00
❏ CL6058 [10]	The Return of the Wayfaring Stranger	1949	50.00
❏ CS9675	The Times They Are a-Changin'	1969	15.00
❏ CL6109 [10]	The Wayfaring Stranger	1950	50.00
❏ CL628 [M]	The Wayfaring Stranger	1955	30.00
❏ CS9041 [R]	The Wayfaring Stranger	1964	15.00
DECCA			
❏ DL5080 [10]	A Collection of Ballads and Folk Songs, Volume One	1949	50.00
❏ DL8749 [M]	Australian Folk Songs	1959	30.00
❏ DL5093 [10]	Ballads, Folk and Country Songs	1949	50.00
❏ DL5013 [10]	Ballads and Folk Songs, Volume II	1949	50.00
❏ DL4972 [M]	Big Country Hits	1968	18.00
❏ DL74972 [S]	Big Country Hits	1968	15.00
❏ DL4876 [M]	Broadway	1967	18.00
❏ DL74876 [S]	Broadway	1967	15.00
❏ DL4361 [M]	Burl	1963	18.00
❏ DL74361 [S]	Burl	1963	25.00
❏ DL4850 [M]	Burl Ives' Greatest Hits	1967	18.00
❏ DL74850 [S]	Burl Ives' Greatest Hits	1967	15.00
❏ DL8248 [M]	Burl Ives Sings for Fun	1956	30.00
❏ DL4734 [M]	Burl's Choice	1966	15.00
❏ DL74734 [S]	Burl's Choice	1966	18.00
❏ DL8587 [M]	Captain Burl Ives' Ark	1958	30.00
❏ DL8886 [M]	Cheers	1959	30.00
❏ DL78886 [S]	Cheers	1959	30.00
❏ DL5428 [10]	Christmas Day in the Morning	1952	50.00
❏ DL8391 [M]	Christmas Eve	1957	30.00
❏ DL78391 [R]	Christmas Eve	196?	12.00
❏ DL8080 [M]	Coronation Concert	1953	40.00
❏ DL8245 [M]	Down to the Sea in Ships	1956	30.00
❏ DL5467 [10]	Folk Songs Dramatic and Dangerous	1953	50.00
❏ DL4689 [M]	Have a Holly Jolly Christmas	1965	15.00
❏ DL74689 [S]	Have a Holly Jolly Christmas	1965	18.00
❏ DL8247 [M]	In the Quiet of Night	1956	30.00
❏ DL4279 [M]	It's Just My Funny Way of Laughin'	1962	18.00
❏ DL74279 [S]	It's Just My Funny Way of Laughin'	1962	25.00
❏ DL8125 [M]	Men	1956	30.00
❏ DL4606 [M]	My Gal Sal	1965	15.00
❏ DL74606 [S]	My Gal Sal	1965	18.00
❏ DL8637 [M]	Old Time Varieties	1958	30.00
❏ DL4668 [M]	On the Beach at Waikiki	1965	15.00
❏ DL74668 [S]	On the Beach at Waikiki	1965	10.00
❏ DL4578 [M]	Pearly Shells	1964	18.00
❏ DL74578 [S]	Pearly Shells	1964	25.00
❏ DL4433 [M]	Singin' Easy	1964	18.00
❏ DL74433 [S]	Singin' Easy	1964	25.00
❏ DL4304 [M]	Sing Out, Sweet Land	1962	18.00
❏ DL74304 [S]	Sing Out, Sweet Land	1962	25.00
❏ DL4789 [M]	Something Special	1966	15.00
❏ DL74789 [S]	Something Special	1966	18.00
❏ DL0444 [M]	Songs of Ireland	1958	30.00
❏ DL4179 [M]	Songs of the West	1961	18.00
❏ DL74179 [S]	Songs of the West	1961	25.00
❏ DL4320 [M]	Sunshine in My Soul	1962	18.00
❏ DL74320 [S]	Sunshine in My Soul	1962	25.00
❏ DXSB7167 [S]	The Best of Burl Ives	1961	30.00
❏ DXB167 [M]	The Best of Burl Ives	1961	30.00
❏ DL4390 [M]	The Best of Burl's for Boys and Girls	1963	18.00
❏ DL74390 [S]	The Best of Burl's for Boys and Girls	1963	25.00
❏ DL4152 [M]	The Versatile Burl Ives	1961	18.00
❏ DL74152 [S]	The Versatile Burl Ives	1961	25.00
❏ DL8107 [M]	The Wild Side of Life	1955	30.00
❏ DL4533 [M]	True Love	1964	18.00
❏ DL74533 [S]	True Love	1964	25.00
❏ DL8246 [M]	Women	1956	30.00
❏ DL5490 [10]	Women: Folk Songs About the Fair Sex	1954	50.00
DISNEYLAND			
❏ ST-3927 [M]	Chim Chim Chiree and Other Children's Choices	1964	18.00
❏ STER-3927 [S]	Chim Chim Chiree and Other Children's Choices	1964	25.00
EVEREST ARCHIVE OF FOLK & JAZZ			
❏ 340	Burl Ives Live	1978	12.00
HARMONY			
❏ HS11275	Got the World by the Tail	196?	12.00
❏ HL9507 [M]	The Little White Duck	196?	18.00
❏ HL9551 [M]	The Lollipop Tree	196?	18.00
MCA			
❏ 114	Burl Ives' Greatest Hits	1973	12.00
—Reissue of Decca 74850			
❏ 15002	Have a Holly Jolly Christmas	1973	15.00
—Reissue of Decca 74689; black label with rainbow			
❏ 15002	Have a Holly Jolly Christmas	1980	10.00
—Blue label with rainbow			
❏ 318	Paying My Dues Again	1973	12.00
❏ 15030	Santa Claus Is Coming to Town	198?	12.00
❏ 4034	The Best of Burl Ives	197?	15.00
❏ 4089	The Best of Burl Ives Volume 2	197?	15.00

Number	Title	Yr	NM
NATIONAL GEOGRAPHIC			
❏ 07806	We Americans	1978	15.00
PICKWICK			
❏ SPC-1018	Twelve Days of Christmas	197?	12.00
STINSON			
❏ SLP-1 [10]	The Wayfaring Stranger	1949	60.00
SUNSET			
❏ SUS-5280	Favorites	1970	12.00
UNITED ARTISTS			
❏ UAL3060 [M]	Ballads	1959	18.00
❏ UAS6060 [S]	Ballads	1959	25.00
WORD			
❏ 3259 [M]	Faith and Joy	196?	18.00
❏ 8140 [S]	Faith and Joy	196?	25.00
❏ 8537	How Great Thou Art	1971	15.00
❏ 3391 [M]	I Do Believe	1967	15.00
❏ 8391 [S]	I Do Believe	1967	18.00
❏ 3339 [M]	Shall We Gather at the River	1966	15.00
❏ 8339 [S]	Shall We Gather at the River	1966	18.00
IVORY, JACKIE			
ATCO			
❏ 33-178 [M]	Soul Discovery	1965	25.00
❏ SD 33-178 [S]	Soul Discovery	1965	30.00
IVORY			
PLAYBOY			
❏ 115	Ivory	1973	15.00
TETRAGRAMMATON			
❏ T-104 [B]	Ivory	1968	25.00
IVY LEAGUE, THE			
CAMEO			
❏ C2000 [M]	Tossing and Turning	1965	30.00
❏ CS2000 [R]	Tossing and Turning	1965	30.00
IVY LEAGUE TRIO, THE			
CORAL			
❏ CRL757399 [S]	On and Off Campus	1962	25.00
❏ CRL57399 [M]	On and Off Campus	1962	18.00
❏ CRL757404 [S]	Rare and Well Done	1962	25.00
❏ CRL57404 [M]	Rare and Well Done	1962	18.00
REPRISE			
❏ R9-6087 [R]	Folk Ballads from the World of Edgar Allan Poe	1963	30.00
❏ R-6087 [M]	Folk Ballads from the World of Edgar Allan Poe	1963	25.00

J

Number	Title	Yr	NM
J.F.K. QUINTET, THE			
RIVERSIDE			
❏ RLP-396 [M]	New Frontiers from Washington	1961	30.00
❏ RS-9396 [S]	New Frontiers from Washington	1961	40.00
❏ RLP-424 [M]	Young Ideas	1962	30.00
❏ RS-9424 [S]	Young Ideas	1962	40.00
J.K. AND COMPANY			
BEAT ROCKET			
❏ BR-126	Suddenly One Summer	2000	15.00
—Reissue on 180-gram vinyl			
WHITE WHALE			
❏ WWS-7117 [B]	Suddenly One Summer	1969	100.00
JACINTHA			
GROOVE NOTE			
❏ 2001	Here's to Ben	1999	30.00
—Audiophile vinyl			
JACKS, TERRY			
BELL			
❏ 1307 [B]	Seasons in the Sun	1974	15.00
JACKS, THE			
CROWN			
❏ CLP-5021 [M]	Jumpin' with the Jacks	1960	200.00
❏ CLP-5372 [M]	Jumpin' with the Jacks	1962	100.00
❏ CST-372 [R]	Jumpin' with the Jacks	1962	50.00
RELIC			
❏ 5023	The Jacks' Greatest Hits	198?	12.00
RPM			
❏ LRP-3006 [M]	Jumpin' with the Jacks	1956	2000.00
—VG value 1000; VG+ value 1500			
UNITED			
❏ US-7797	Rock 'n' Roll Hits of the 50's	197?	18.00
JACKSON, ALAN			
ARISTA			
❏ AL8681	Don't Rock the Jukebox	1991	30.00

Number	Title	Yr	NM
—Columbia House vinyl edition			
❏ R143877	Don't Rock the Jukebox	1991	30.00
—BMG Direct Marketing vinyl version			
❏ AL8623	Here in the Real World	1990	25.00
JACKSON, BULL MOOSE			
AUDIO LAB			
❏ AL-1524 [M]	Bull Moose Jackson	1959	600.00
BOGUS			
❏ 6-0214851	Moosemania!	1985	12.00
JACKSON, CALVIN			
COLUMBIA			
❏ CL756 [M]	Calvin Jackson and the All Stars Quartet	1956	50.00
❏ CL824 [M]	Rave Notice	1956	50.00
LIBERTY			
❏ LRP-3071 [M]	Jazz Variations	1957	40.00
X			
❏ LXA-1005 [M]	Calvin Jackson at the Plaza	1954	50.00
JACKSON, CHUBBY, AND BILL HARRIS			
EMARCY			
❏ MG-26012 [M]	Out of the Herd	1965	25.00
❏ SR-66012 [R]	Out of the Herd	1965	15.00
❏ MG-26003 [10]	The Small Herd	1954	200.00
MERCURY			
❏ MG-25076 [10]	Jazz Journey	1950	300.00
JACKSON, CHUBBY			
ARGO			
❏ LP-614 [M]	Chubby's Back	1957	80.00
❏ LPS-614 [S]	Chubby's Back	1959	70.00
❏ LP-625 [M]	I'm Entitled to You	1958	80.00
EVEREST			
❏ LPBR-5009 [M]	Chubby Takes Over	1959	30.00
❏ SDBR-1009 [S]	Chubby Takes Over	1959	40.00
❏ LPBR-5041 [M]	Jazz Then Till Now	1960	30.00
❏ SDBR-1041 [S]	Jazz Then Till Now	1960	40.00
❏ LPBR-5029 [M]	The Big Three	1959	30.00
❏ SDBR-1029 [S]	The Big Three	1959	40.00
LAURIE			
❏ LLP-2011 [M]	Twist Calling	1962	30.00
NEW JAZZ			
❏ NJLP-105 [10]	Chubby Jackson and His All Star Band	1950	800.00
—Original; reissued as Prestige 105			
PRESTIGE			
❏ PRLP-105 [10]	Chubby Jackson and His All Star Band	1951	600.00
❏ PRST-7641	Chubby Jackson Sextet and Big Band	1969	25.00
RAINBOW			
❏ 708 [10]	Chubby Jackson	1951	400.00
STEREO-CRAFT			
❏ RTN-108 [M]	The Big Three	195?	50.00
❏ RTS-108 [S]	The Big Three	195?	50.00
JACKSON, CHUCK, AND MAXINE BROWN			
WAND			
❏ WD-678 [M]	Hold On, We're Coming	1966	30.00
❏ WDS-678 [S]	Hold On, We're Coming	1966	40.00
❏ WD-669 [M]	Say Something	1965	30.00
❏ WDS-669 [S]	Say Something	1965	40.00
JACKSON, CHUCK, AND TAMMI TERRELL			
WAND			
❏ WD-682 [M]	The Early Show	1967	30.00
❏ WDS-682 [S]	The Early Show	1967	30.00
JACKSON, CHUCK			
ABC			
❏ X-798	Through All Times	1973	18.00
ALL PLATINUM			
❏ 3014	Needing You, Wanting You	1976	18.00
COLLECTABLES			
❏ COL-5115	Golden Classics	198?	12.00
EMI AMERICA			
❏ SW-17031	I Wanna Give You Some Love	1980	12.00
GUEST STAR			
❏ GS-1912 [M]	Chuck Jackson	196?	25.00
❏ GSS-1912 [R]	Chuck Jackson	196?	15.00
MOTOWN			
❏ M-667 [M]	Chuck Jackson Arrives!	1967	40.00
❏ MS-667 [S]	Chuck Jackson Arrives!	1967	30.00
❏ MS-687	Goin' Back to Chuck Jackson	1969	30.00
SCEPTER			
❏ 5100	A Tribute to Burt Bacharach	1972	18.00
SPIN-O-RAMA			
❏ 123 [M]	Starring Chuck Jackson	196?	25.00
❏ S-123 [R]	Starring Chuck Jackson	196?	15.00

STRAND

Number	Title	Yr	NM
❑ SL-1125 [M]	The Great Chuck Jackson	196?	30.00
❑ SLS-1125 [S]	The Great Chuck Jackson	196?	30.00

UNITED ARTISTS

Number	Title	Yr	NM
❑ UA-LA499-E	The Very Best of Chuck Jackson	1974	12.00

V.I.P.

Number	Title	Yr	NM
❑ 403	Teardrops Keep Fallin' on My Heart	1970	40.00

WAND

Number	Title	Yr	NM
❑ LP-654 [M]	Any Day Now	1962	40.00
❑ WD-673 [M]	A Tribute to Rhythm and Blues	1966	30.00
❑ WDS-673 [S]	A Tribute to Rhythm and Blues	1966	40.00
❑ WD-676 [M]	A Tribute to Rhythm and Blues, Volume 2	1966	30.00
❑ WDS-676 [S]	A Tribute to Rhythm and Blues, Volume 2	1966	40.00
❑ WD-658 [M]	Chuck Jackson On Tour	1964	40.00
❑ WD-683 [M]	Chuck Jackson's Greatest Hits	1967	25.00
❑ WDS-683 [S]	Chuck Jackson's Greatest Hits	1967	30.00
❑ WD-680 [M]	Dedicated to the King!!	1966	40.00
❑ WDS-680 [S]	Dedicated to the King!!	1966	50.00
❑ WD-655 [M]	Encore	1963	40.00
❑ LP-650 [M]	I Don't Want to Cry	1961	40.00
❑ WDM-667 [M]	Mr. Everything	1965	30.00
❑ WDS-667 [S]	Mr. Everything	1965	40.00

JACKSON, DEON

ATCO

Number	Title	Yr	NM
❑ 33-188 [M]	Love Makes the World Go Round	1966	30.00
❑ SD 33-188 [S]	Love Makes the World Go Round	1966	40.00

COLLECTABLES

Number	Title	Yr	NM
❑ COL-5106	Golden Classics	198?	12.00

JACKSON, FRED

BLUE NOTE

Number	Title	Yr	NM
❑ BLP-4094 [M]	Hootin' 'N Tootin'	1962	250.00
—With 61st St. address on label			
❑ BLP-4094 [M]	Hootin' 'N Tootin'	1963	200.00
—With "New York, USA" address on label			
❑ BST-84094 [S]	Hootin' 'N Tootin'	1962	150.00
—With 61st St. address on label			
❑ BST-84094 [S]	Hootin' 'N Tootin'	1963	100.00
—With "New York, USA" address on label			
❑ BST-84094 [S]	Hootin' 'N Tootin'	1967	25.00
—With "A Division of Liberty Records" on label			

JACKSON, J.J.

CALLA

Number	Title	Yr	NM
❑ C-1101 [M]	But It's Alright/I Dig Girls	1967	25.00
❑ CS-1101 [S]	But It's Alright/I Dig Girls	1967	30.00

CONGRESS

Number	Title	Yr	NM
❑ CS-7000	The Greatest Little Soul Band in the World	1968	30.00

PERCEPTION

Number	Title	Yr	NM
❑ 3	J.J. Jackson's Dilemma	1970	18.00

WARNER BROS.

Number	Title	Yr	NM
❑ WS1797	The Great J.J. Jackson	1969	25.00

JACKSON, JANET

A&M

Number	Title	Yr	NM
❑ SP-3905	Control	1986	10.00
—Second issue; most have a black label			
❑ SP-5106	Control	1986	12.00
—Original issue; silver label with fading A&M logo			
❑ 31454 03991	Design of a Decade 1986/1996	1995	18.00
❑ SP-4962	Dream Street	1984	15.00
❑ SP-6-4907	Janet Jackson	1982	15.00
❑ SP-3920	Janet Jackson's Rhythm Nation 1814	1989	18.00

VIRGIN

Number	Title	Yr	NM
❑ 10144	All for You	2001	18.00
❑ 84404	Damita Jo	2004	18.00

JACKSON, JERMAINE

ARISTA

Number	Title	Yr	NM
❑ AL-8493	Don't Take It Personal	1989	12.00
❑ AL8-8203	Jermaine Jackson	1984	12.00
❑ AL-8421	Jermaine Jackson	1986	10.00
—Budget-line reissue			
❑ AL8-8277	Precious Moments	1986	12.00

MOTOWN

Number	Title	Yr	NM
❑ M-775L	Come Into My Life	1973	12.00
❑ M6-888S1	Feel the Fire	1977	12.00
❑ M7-898R1	Frontiers	1978	12.00
❑ M8-952M1	I Like Your Style	1981	12.00
❑ M-752L	Jermaine	1972	12.00
❑ M8-948M1	Jermaine	1980	12.00
❑ 6017ML	Let Me Tickle Your Fancy	1982	12.00
❑ M7-928R1	Let's Get Serious	1980	12.00
❑ M5-117V1	Motown Superstar Series, Vol. 17	1981	12.00
❑ M6-842S1	My Name Is Jermaine	1976	12.00

JACKSON, JOE

A&M

Number	Title	Yr	NM
❑ SP-3241	Beat Crazy	198?	10.00
—Reissue of SP-4837			
❑ SP-4837	Beat Crazy	1980	12.00
❑ R244331	Big World	1986	18.00
—RCA Music Service edition			
❑ SP-6021	Big World	1986	18.00
❑ R101141	Blaze of Glory	1989	15.00
—BMG Direct Marketing edition			
❑ SP-5249	Blaze of Glory	1989	12.00
❑ SP-5000	Body and Soul	1984	12.00
❑ SP-3286	Body and Soul	1986	10.00
—Reissue of SP-5000			
❑ SP-3221	I'm the Man	198?	10.00
—Reissue of SP-4794			
❑ SP-4794	I'm the Man	1979	12.00
❑ SP-3271	Joe Jackson's Jumpin' Jive	198?	10.00
—Reissue of SP-4871			
❑ SP-4871	Joe Jackson's Jumpin' Jive	1981	12.00
❑ SP-6706	Live: 1980-1986	1988	18.00
❑ R209597	Live 1980-1986	1987	18.00
—BMG Direct Marketing edition			
❑ SP-3187	Look Sharp!	198?	10.00
—Reissue of SP-4743			
❑ SP-4743	Look Sharp!	1979	15.00
❑ SP-3666	Look Sharp!	1979	25.00
—Two 10-inch records in gatefold sleeve with button			
❑ SP-4931	Mike's Murder [Soundtrack]	1983	15.00
❑ SP-4906	Night and Day	1982	12.00
❑ SP-3908	Will Power	1987	15.00

MOBILE FIDELITY

Number	Title	Yr	NM
❑ 1-080	Night and Day	1982	50.00
—Audiophile vinyl			

RYKODISC

Number	Title	Yr	NM
❑ 310921	Rain	2008	18.00

JACKSON, LIL' SON

ARHOOLIE

Number	Title	Yr	NM
❑ 1004 [M]	Lil' Son Jackson	1960	30.00

IMPERIAL

Number	Title	Yr	NM
❑ LP-9142 [M]	Rockin' and Rollin'	1961	400.00

JACKSON, MAHALIA

APOLLO

Number	Title	Yr	NM
❑ 1001/2 [M]	Command Performance	1961	30.00
❑ 499 [M]	Mahalia Jackson	1962	30.00
❑ 482 [M]	No Matter How You Pray	1959	30.00
❑ 201/202 [M]	Spirituals	1954	30.00

COLUMBIA

Number	Title	Yr	NM
❑ CG30744	America's Favorite Hymns	1971	18.00
❑ CS9659	A Mighty Fortress	1968	15.00
❑ CL899 [M]	Bless This House	1956	30.00
❑ CS8761 [R]	Bless This House	1963	15.00
❑ PC8761	Bless This House	198?	10.00
—Budget-line reissue			
❑ CS9727	Christmas with Mahalia	1968	15.00
❑ CL1428 [M]	Come On Children, Let's Sing	1960	25.00
❑ CS8225 [S]	Come On Children, Let's Sing	1960	30.00
❑ CL1643 [M]	Every Time I Feel the Spirit	1961	18.00
❑ CS8443 [S]	Every Time I Feel the Spirit	1961	25.00
❑ CL2546 [M]	Garden of Prayer	1967	18.00
❑ CS9346 [S]	Garden of Prayer	1967	15.00
❑ CL1824 [M]	Great Songs of Love and Faith	1962	18.00
❑ CS8624 [S]	Great Songs of Love and Faith	1962	25.00
❑ KC34073	How I Got Over	1976	12.00
❑ CL1549 [M]	I Believe	1960	18.00
❑ CS8349 [S]	I Believe	1960	25.00
❑ CL2130 [M]	Let's Pray Together	1964	15.00
❑ CS8930 [S]	Let's Pray Together	1964	18.00
❑ CL644 [M]	Mahalia Jackson	1955	40.00
❑ CS8759 [R]	Mahalia Jackson	1963	15.00
❑ CL2690 [M]	Mahalia Jackson In Concert, Easter Sunday 1967	1967	18.00
❑ CS9490 [S]	Mahalia Jackson In Concert, Easter Sunday 1967	1967	15.00
❑ CL2004 [M]	Mahalia Jackson's Greatest Hits	1963	15.00
❑ CS8804 [S]	Mahalia Jackson's Greatest Hits	1963	18.00
❑ PC37710	Mahalia Jackson's Greatest Hits	198?	10.00
❑ CL2452 [M]	Mahalia Sings	1966	15.00
❑ CS9252 [S]	Mahalia Sings	1966	18.00
❑ CL1936 [M]	Make a Joyful Noise Unto the Lord	1962	18.00
❑ CS8736 [S]	Make a Joyful Noise Unto the Lord	1962	25.00
❑ CL2605 [M]	My Faith	1967	18.00
❑ CS9405 [S]	My Faith	1967	15.00
❑ CL1244 [M]	Newport 1958	1959	25.00
❑ CS8071 [S]	Newport 1958	1959	30.00
❑ CL1726 [M]	Recorded in Europe During Her Latest Concert Tour	1962	18.00
❑ CS8526 [S]	Recorded in Europe During Her Latest Concert Tour	1962	25.00
❑ CS9813	Right Out of the Church	1969	15.00
❑ CL1903 [M]	Silent Night	1962	18.00
❑ CS8703 [S]	Silent Night	1962	25.00
❑ 3C38304	Silent Night	1982	10.00
—Reissue			
❑ CL702 [M]	Sweet Little Jesus Boy	1955	40.00
❑ CL1343 [M]	That Great Gettin' Up Morning	1959	25.00
❑ CS8153 [S]	That Great Gettin' Up Morning	1959	30.00
❑ CS9686	The Best-Loved Hymns of Dr. Martin Luther King Jr.	1968	18.00
❑ PC9686	The Best-Loved Hymns of Dr. Martin Luther King Jr.	198?	10.00
—Budget-line reissue			
❑ KG31379	The Great Mahalia Jackson	1972	18.00
❑ CL1473 [M]	The Power and the Glory	1960	25.00
❑ CS8264 [S]	The Power and the Glory	1960	30.00
❑ CS9950	What the World Needs Now	1970	15.00
❑ CL2552 [10]	You'll Never Walk Alone	1955	50.00

COLUMBIA SPECIAL PRODUCTS

Number	Title	Yr	NM
❑ P213200	(HRB Music Proudly Presents) The Best of Mahalia Jackson: Hymns, Spirituals & Songs of Inspiration	1976	18.00

FOLKWAYS

Number	Title	Yr	NM
❑ 31101	I Sing Because I'm Happy, Volume 1	198?	12.00
❑ 31102	I Sing Because I'm Happy, Volume 2	198?	12.00

GRAND AWARD

Number	Title	Yr	NM
❑ GA265SD	I Believe	1966	18.00
—Reissue of 326			
❑ GA 33-326 [M]	Mahalia Jackson	1955	30.00
❑ GA 33-390 [M]	Mahalia Jackson	195?	30.00

HARMONY

Number	Title	Yr	NM
❑ HS11372	Abide with Me	1970	12.00
❑ KH31111	Lord Don't Let Me Fall	1972	12.00
❑ H30019	Sunrise, Sunset	1970	12.00
❑ HS11279	You'll Never Walk Alone	196?	12.00

KENWOOD

Number	Title	Yr	NM
❑ 1001/2	Command Performance	196?	25.00
❑ 501	I Lift My Voice	196?	18.00
❑ 474	In the Upper Room	196?	18.00
❑ 479	Just As I Am	196?	18.00
❑ 486	Mahalia	196?	18.00
❑ 489	Mahalia Jackson With the Greatest Spiritual Singers	196?	18.00
❑ 482	No Matter How You Pray	196?	18.00
❑ 502	Sing Out	196?	18.00
❑ 500	The Best of Mahalia Jackson	196?	18.00

PICKWICK

Number	Title	Yr	NM
❑ SPC-3510	I Believe	197?	12.00

PRIORITY

Number	Title	Yr	NM
❑ PU37710	Mahalia Jackson's Greatest Hits	1981	12.00

JACKSON, MARLON

CAPITOL

Number	Title	Yr	NM
❑ CLT-46942	Baby Tonight	1987	12.00

JACKSON, MARY ANNE

HANOVER

Number	Title	Yr	NM
❑ HM-8009 [M]	The Wild Piano of Mary Anne Jackson	1959	80.00

JACKSON, MICHAEL

EPIC

Number	Title	Yr	NM
❑ OE40600 [B]	Bad	1987	18.00
❑ 9E914043 [PD]	Bad	1987	35.00
❑ E268000 [B]	Blood on the Dance Floor: HIStory in the Mix	1997	60.00
❑ E245400 [B]	Dangerous	1991	30.00
❑ E359000	HIStory: Past, Present and Future -- Book I	1995	30.00
—Box set with 12x12 booklet			
❑ E269400	Invincible	2001	30.00
❑ FE35745 [B]	Off the Wall	1979	25.00
❑ HE47545 [B]	Off the Wall	1982	80.00
—Half-speed mastered edition			
❑ QE38112 [B]	Thriller	1982	30.00
❑ HE48112 [B]	Thriller	1982	100.00
—Half-speed mastered edition			
❑ 8E838867 [PD]	Thriller	1983	100.00

MOTOWN

Number	Title	Yr	NM
❑ M755 [B]	Ben	1972	30.00
—With only Michael Jackson on front cover			
❑ M5-153V1 [B]	Ben	1981	25.00
—Reissue of Motown 755			
❑ M755	Ben	1972	60.00
—With Michael Jackson on top half of cover, rats on the bottom half			
❑ 6101ML [B]	Farewell My Summer Love 1984	1984	30.00
❑ M6-825S [B]	Forever, Michael	1975	30.00
❑ M747	Got to Be There	1972	25.00
❑ M5-130V1	Got to Be There	1981	15.00
—Reissue of Motown 747			
❑ 6099ML	Michael Jackson and The Jackson 5 -- 14 Greatest Hits	1984	15.00
—Picture disc packaged with one glove			

Number	Title	Yr	NM
❏ M5-107V1	Motown Superstar Series, Vol. 7	1981	12.00
❏ M767 [B]	Music and Me	1973	30.00
❏ M8-956M1	One Day in Your Life	1981	15.00
❏ M6-851S	The Best of Michael Jackson	1975	15.00
❏ M5-194V1	The Best of Michael Jackson	1981	12.00
—Reissue of Motown 851			

JACKSON, MICHAEL GREGORY

ARISTA/NOVUS
Number	Title	Yr	NM
❏ AN3015	Heart & Center	1979	18.00

BIJA
| ❏ 1000 | Clarity | 1976 | 30.00 |

ENJA
| ❏ 4026 | Cowboys, Cartoons and Assorted Candy | 1982 | 18.00 |

IAI
| ❏ 373857 | Karmonic Suite | 1978 | 25.00 |

JACKSON, MILLIE, AND ISAAC HAYES

POLYDOR
| ❏ PD-1-6229 | Royal Rappin's | 1979 | 12.00 |

JACKSON, MILLIE

JIVE
Number	Title	Yr	NM
❏ 1016-1-J	An Imitation of Love	1986	10.00
❏ 1186-1-J	Back to the Shit	1989	12.00
❏ 1103-1-J	The Tide Is Turning	1988	10.00
❏ 1447-1-J	Young Man, Older Woman	1991	15.00

SPRING
❏ SP-1-6722	A Moment's Pleasure	1979	12.00
❏ SPR-6703	Caught Up	1974	12.00
❏ SP-6715	Feelin' Bitchy	1977	12.00
❏ SP-1-6727	For Men Only	1980	12.00
❏ SP-1-6719	Get It Out'cha System	1978	12.00
❏ SP-1-6737	Hard Times	1983	12.00
❏ SP-1-6730	I Had to Say It	1981	12.00
❏ SPR-5706	It Hurts So Good	1973	15.00
❏ SP-2-6725	Live & Uncensored	1979	15.00
❏ SP-1-6735	Live and Outrageous (Rated XXX)	1982	12.00
❏ SP-6712	Lovingly Yours	1976	12.00
❏ SPR-6701	Millie	1974	12.00
❏ SPR-6703	Millie Jackson	1972	15.00
❏ SPR-6708	Still Caught Up	1975	12.00

JACKSON, MILT, AND JOHN COLTRANE

ATLANTIC
Number	Title	Yr	NM
❏ 1368 [M]	Bags and Trane	1961	200.00
—Multicolor label, white "fan" logo at right			
❏ 1368 [M]	Bags and Trane	1963	50.00
—Multicolor label, black "fan" logo at right			
❏ SD1368 [S]	Bags and Trane	1961	300.00
—Multicolor label, white "fan" logo at right			
❏ SD1368 [S]	Bags and Trane	1963	80.00
—Multicolor label, black "fan" logo at right			

JACKSON, MILT, AND MONTY ALEXANDER

PABLO
| ❏ 2310804 | Soul Fusion | 1978 | 15.00 |

JACKSON, MILT, AND WES MONTGOMERY

FANTASY
| ❏ OJC-234 | Bags Meets Wes | 198? | 12.00 |

RIVERSIDE
❏ RLP-407 [M]	Bags Meets Wes	1962	25.00
❏ RS-9407 [S]	Bags Meets Wes	1962	30.00
❏ 6058	Bags Meets Wes	197?	15.00

JACKSON, MILT

ABC IMPULSE!
Number	Title	Yr	NM
❏ AS-70 [S]	Jazz n' Samba	1968	18.00
❏ AS-9193	Memphis Jackson	1969	25.00
❏ AS-9230	Milt Jackson Quartet	1973	15.00
❏ AS-14 [S]	Statements	1968	18.00
❏ AS-9189	That's the Way It Is	1969	25.00
❏ AS-9282	The Impulse Years	1974	18.00

ATLANTIC
❏ 1294 [M]	Bags & Flutes	1958	40.00
—Black label			
❏ 1294 [M]	Bags & Flutes	1961	25.00
—Multicolor label, white "fan" logo at right			
❏ 1294 [M]	Bags & Flutes	1963	18.00
—Multicolor label, black "fan" logo at right			
❏ SD1294 [S]	Bags & Flutes	1959	40.00
—Green label			
❏ SD1294 [S]	Bags & Flutes	1961	25.00
—Multicolor label, white "fan" logo at right			
❏ SD1294 [S]	Bags & Flutes	1963	18.00
—Multicolor label, black "fan" logo at right			
❏ 1342 [M]	Ballad Artistry	1960	25.00
—Multicolor label, white "fan" logo at right			
❏ 1342 [M]	Ballad Artistry	1963	18.00
—Multicolor label, black "fan" logo at right			
❏ SD1342 [S]	Ballad Artistry	1960	30.00
—Multicolor label, white "fan" logo at right			
❏ SD1342 [S]	Ballad Artistry	1963	25.00

Number	Title	Yr	NM
—Multicolor label, black "fan" logo at right			
❏ 1242 [M]	Ballads and Blues	1956	40.00
—Black label			
❏ 1242 [M]	Ballads and Blues	1961	25.00
—Multicolor label, white "fan" logo at right			
❏ 1242 [M]	Ballads and Blues	1963	18.00
—Multicolor label, black "fan" logo at right			
❏ 1316 [M]	Bean Bags	1959	40.00
—Black label			
❏ 1316 [M]	Bean Bags	1961	25.00
—Multicolor label, white "fan" logo at right			
❏ 1316 [M]	Bean Bags	1963	18.00
—Multicolor label, black "fan" logo at right			
❏ SD1316 [S]	Bean Bags	1959	40.00
—Green label			
❏ SD1316 [S]	Bean Bags	1961	25.00
—Multicolor label, white "fan" logo at right			
❏ SD1316 [S]	Bean Bags	1963	18.00
—Multicolor label, black "fan" logo at right			
❏ 90465	Bean Bags	1986	12.00
❏ 1269 [M]	Plenty, Plenty Soul	1957	40.00
—Black label			
❏ SD1269 [S]	Plenty, Plenty Soul	1959	40.00
—Green label			
❏ 1269 [M]	Plenty, Plenty Soul	1961	25.00
—Multicolor label, white "fan" logo at right			
❏ 1269 [M]	Plenty, Plenty Soul	1963	18.00
—Multicolor label, black "fan" logo at right			
❏ SD1269 [S]	Plenty, Plenty Soul	1961	25.00
—Multicolor label, white "fan" logo at right			
❏ SD1269 [S]	Plenty, Plenty Soul	1963	18.00
—Multicolor label, black "fan" logo at right			
❏ SD8811	Plenty, Plenty Soul	198?	12.00
❏ SD 2-319	The Art of Milt Jackson	197?	18.00
❏ 1417 [M]	Vibrations	1964	18.00
❏ SD1417 [S]	Vibrations	1964	25.00

BLUE NOTE
❏ BN-LA590-H2	All Star Bags	1976	18.00
❏ BLP-1509 [M]	Milt Jackson	1956	500.00
—Deep groove" version (deep indentation under label on both sides)			
❏ BLP-1509 [M]	Milt Jackson	1956	100.00
—Regular version with Lexington Ave. address on label			
❏ BLP-1509 [M]	Milt Jackson	1963	30.00
—With "New York, USA" address on label			
❏ BST-81509 [R]	Milt Jackson	196?	18.00
—With "A Division of Liberty Records" on label			
❏ B1-81509	Milt Jackson	1987	12.00
—The Finest in Jazz Since 1939" reissue			
❏ BLP-5011 [10]	Wizard of the Vibes	1952	300.00

CTI
❏ 6038	Goodbye	1974	18.00
❏ 6046	Olinga	1974	18.00
❏ 6024	Sunflower	1973	18.00
❏ 8004	Sunflower	197?	12.00
—Reissue of 6024			

DEE GEE
| ❏ 1002 [10] | Milt Jackson | 1952 | 300.00 |

EASTWEST
| ❏ 90991 | Bebop | 1988 | 15.00 |

FANTASY
❏ OJC-366	Big Bags	198?	12.00
❏ OJC-448	Feelings	1990	12.00
❏ OJC-404	For Someone I Love	1989	15.00
❏ OJC-260	Invitation	1987	12.00
❏ OJC-601	It Don't Mean a Thing If You Can't Tap Your Foot to It	1991	18.00
❏ OJC-309	Live" at the Village Gate	1988	12.00
❏ OJC-001	Milt Jackson Quartet	1982	18.00
❏ OJC-375	Montreux '77	198?	12.00

GNP CRESCENDO
| ❏ GNP-9007 | Milt Jackson | 197? | 12.00 |

IMPULSE!
❏ A-70 [M]	Jazz n' Samba	1964	30.00
❏ AS-70 [S]	Jazz n' Samba	1964	30.00
❏ A-14 [M]	Statements	1962	30.00
❏ AS-14 [S]	Statements	1962	30.00

LIMELIGHT
❏ LM-82024 [M]	At the Museum of Modern Art	1965	25.00
❏ LS-86024 [S]	At the Museum of Modern Art	1965	30.00
❏ LM-82045 [M]	Born Free	1966	25.00
❏ LS-86045 [S]	Born Free	1966	30.00
❏ LM-82006 [M]	In a New Setting	1964	25.00
❏ LS-86006 [S]	In a New Setting	1964	30.00

MILESTONE
| ❏ 47006 | Big Band Bags | 1972 | 18.00 |

PABLO
❏ 2310873	Ain't But a Few of Us Left	198?	15.00
❏ 2310932	A London Bridge	1988	15.00
❏ 2310842	Bag's Bag	1979	15.00
❏ 2310867	Big Mouth	198?	15.00
❏ 2310916	Brother Jim	1987	12.00
❏ 2310774	Feelings	1976	15.00
❏ 2310909	It Don't Mean a Thing If You Can't Tap Your Foot to It	1986	18.00
❏ 2310897	Milt Jackson & Co.	198?	15.00

Number	Title	Yr	NM
❏ 2310822	Milt Jackson with Count Basie and the Big Band, Volume 1	1978	15.00
❏ 2310823	Milt Jackson with Count Basie and the Big Band, Volume 2	1978	15.00
❏ 2310832	Soul Believer	1979	15.00
❏ 2405405	The Best of Milt Jackson	198?	12.00
❏ 2310757	The Big 3	1976	15.00
❏ 2310753	The Big 4 at Montreux '75	1976	15.00

PABLO LIVE
❏ 2620103	Kosei Nenkin	197?	18.00
❏ 2308235	Live in London: Memories of Thelonious Monk	198?	15.00
❏ 2308205	Montreux '77	1977	15.00

PABLO TODAY
| ❏ 2312124 | Nightmist | 198? | 15.00 |

PRESTIGE
❏ PRLP-7003 [M]	Milt Jackson	1955	120.00
❏ PRLP-183 [10]	Milt Jackson Quintet	1954	200.00
❏ 24048	Opus de Funk	197?	18.00
❏ PRLP-7224 [M]	Soul Pioneers	1962	40.00
❏ PRST-7655	The Complete Milt Jackson	1969	18.00

QUINTESSENCE
| ❏ 25391 | Milt Jackson (1961-69) | 1980 | 12.00 |

RIVERSIDE
❏ 3021	Bags and Brass	1968	18.00
❏ RLP-429 [M]	Big Bags	1962	25.00
❏ RS-9429 [S]	Big Bags	1962	30.00
❏ RLP-478 [M]	For Someone I Love	1966	25.00
❏ RS-9478 [S]	For Someone I Love	1966	30.00
❏ RLP-446 [M]	Invitation	1963	25.00
❏ RS-9446 [S]	Invitation	1963	30.00
❏ RLP-495 [M]	Live" at the Village Gate	1967	30.00
❏ RS-9495 [S]	Live" at the Village Gate	1967	25.00

SAVOY
❏ MG-12080 [M]	Jackson's Ville	1956	50.00
❏ MG-12070 [M]	Jazz Skyline	1956	50.00
❏ MG-12061 [M]	Meet Milt	1956	50.00
❏ MG-15058 [10]	Milt Jackson	1954	150.00
❏ MG-12046 [M]	Milt Jackson Quartette	1955	50.00
❏ MG-12042 [M]	Roll 'Em Bags	1955	50.00

SAVOY JAZZ
❏ SJL-1130	Bluesology	198?	12.00
❏ SJL-2204	Second Nature	197?	15.00
❏ SJL-1106	The First Q	197?	12.00
❏ SJC-410	The Jazz Skyline	1985	12.00

TRIP
| ❏ 5553 | At the Museum of Modern Art | 197? | 12.00 |

UNITED ARTISTS
| ❏ UAL-4022 [M] | Bags' Opus | 1959 | 40.00 |
| ❏ UAS-5022 [S] | Bags' Opus | 1959 | 30.00 |

VERVE
| ❏ V6 8761 | Milt Jackson and the Hip String Quartet | 1969 | 18.00 |

JACKSON, RANDY

A&M
| ❏ SP-5191 | Randy and the Gypsys | 1989 | 15.00 |
| —As "Randy and the Gypsys" | | | |

JACKSON, SAMMY

ARVEE
| ❏ A-434 [M] | Ladies Man | 1962 | 50.00 |
| ❏ SA-434 [S] | Ladies Man | 1962 | 60.00 |

JACKSON, SHOT

CUMBERLAND
| ❏ MGC-29513 [M] | Bluegrass Dobro | 1965 | 25.00 |
| ❏ SRC-69513 [S] | Bluegrass Dobro | 1965 | 30.00 |

STARDAY
| ❏ SLP-230 [M] | The Singing Strings of Steel Guitar and Dobro | 1962 | 30.00 |

JACKSON, STONEWALL

COLUMBIA
❏ CL2509 [M]	All's Fair in Love 'n' War	1966	18.00
❏ CS9309 [S]	All's Fair in Love 'n' War	1966	25.00
❏ CL2674 [M]	Help Stamp Out Loneliness	1967	30.00
❏ CS9474 [S]	Help Stamp Out Loneliness	1967	25.00
❏ CL2059 [M]	I Love a Song	1963	25.00
❏ CS8859 [S]	I Love a Song	1963	30.00
❏ CS9669	Nothing Takes the Place of Loving You	1968	25.00
❏ CL1770 [M]	Sadness in a Song	1962	25.00
❏ CS8570 [S]	Sadness in a Song	1962	30.00
❏ CL2762 [M]	Stonewall Jackson Country	1967	30.00
❏ CS9562 [S]	Stonewall Jackson Country	1967	25.00
❏ CL2377 [M]	Stonewall Jackson's Greatest Hits	1965	18.00
❏ CS9177 [S]	Stonewall Jackson's Greatest Hits	1965	25.00
❏ CL1391 [M]	The Dynamic Stonewall Jackson	1959	30.00
❏ CS8186 [S]	The Dynamic Stonewall Jackson	1959	30.00
❏ CS9708	The Great Old Songs	1968	25.00
❏ CS9754	The Old Country Church	1969	30.00
❏ C30254	The Real Thing	1971	18.00
❏ CS9880	Tribute to Hank Williams	1969	25.00

Number	Title	Yr	NM
☐ CL2278 [M]	Trouble & Me	1964	18.00
☐ CS9078 [S]	Trouble & Me	1964	25.00
HARMONY			
☐ HS11187	The Exciting Stonewall Jackson	196?	15.00

JACKSON, WALTER

CHI-SOUND
☐ CS-LA656-G	Feeling Good	1976	15.00
☐ CS-LA844-G	Good to See You	1978	15.00
☐ CS-LA733-G	I Want to Come Back As A Song	1977	15.00

COLUMBIA
☐ FC37132	Tell Me Where It Hurts	1981	12.00

EPIC
☐ E34657	Greatest Hits	1977	12.00
☐ PE40434	Greatest Hits	1987	10.00

OKEH
☐ OKM12107 [M]	It's All Over	1965	30.00
☐ OKS14107 [S]	It's All Over	1965	30.00
☐ OKM12120 [M]	Speak Her Name	1967	30.00
☐ OKS14120 [S]	Speak Her Name	1967	30.00
☐ OKS14128	Walter Jackson's Greatest Hits	1969	18.00
☐ OKM12108 [M]	Welcome Home	1966	30.00
☐ OKS14108 [S]	Welcome Home	1966	30.00

JACKSON, WANDA

CAPITOL
☐ ST-554	A Woman Lives for Love	1970	18.00
☐ T2306 [M]	Blues in My Heart	1965	30.00
☐ ST2306 [S]	Blues in My Heart	1965	30.00
☐ ST-11161	Country Keepsakes	1973	18.00
☐ ST2976	Cream of the Crop	1968	18.00
☐ ST-669	I've Gotta Sing!	1971	18.00
☐ ST-11096	I Wouldn't Want You Any Other Way	1972	18.00
☐ T1911 [M]	Love Me Forever	1963	30.00
☐ ST1911 [S]	Love Me Forever	1963	30.00
☐ ST-11023	Praise the Lord	1972	18.00
☐ T2704 [M]	Reckless Love Affair	1967	25.00
☐ ST2704 [S]	Reckless Love Affair	1967	18.00
☐ T1596 [M]	Right or Wrong	1961	40.00
— Black colorband label, Capitol logo at left			
☐ T1596 [M]	Right or Wrong	1962	25.00
— Black colorband label, Capitol logo at top			
☐ ST1596 [S]	Right or Wrong	1961	50.00
— Black colorband label, Capitol logo at left			
☐ ST1596 [S]	Right or Wrong	1962	30.00
— Black colorband label, Capitol logo at top			
☐ T1384 [M]	Rockin' with Wanda	1960	400.00
— Black colorband label, Capitol logo at left			
☐ T1384 [M]	Rockin' with Wanda	1962	250.00
— Gold "Star Line" label			
☐ T1384 [M]	Rockin' with Wanda	1963	150.00
— Black "Star Line" label			
☐ ST2883 [S]	The Best of Wanda Jackson	1968	18.00
☐ T2883 [M]	The Best of Wanda Jackson	1968	40.00
— Red and white "Starline" label			
☐ ST-238 [B]	The Happy Side of Wanda Jackson	1969	18.00
☐ ST-129	The Many Moods of Wanda Jackson	1969	18.00
☐ T1511 [M]	There's a Party Goin' On	1961	250.00
— Black colorband label, Capitol logo at left			
☐ ST1511 [S]	There's a Party Goin' On	1961	400.00
— Black colorband label, Capitol logo at left			
☐ T2030 [M]	Two Sides of Wanda	1964	30.00
☐ ST2030 [S]	Two Sides of Wanda	1964	30.00
☐ T1041 [M]	Wanda Jackson	1958	300.00
— Black colorband label, Capitol logo at left			
☐ T1041 [M]	Wanda Jackson	1962	100.00
— Black colorband label, Capitol logo at top			
☐ ST-434	Wanda Jackson Country!	1970	18.00
☐ ST-345	Wanda Jackson In Person	1970	18.00
☐ ST 8-0345	Wanda Jackson In Person	1970	25.00
— Capitol Record Club edition			
☐ T2606 [M]	Wanda Jackson Salutes the Country Music Hall of Fame	1966	18.00
☐ ST2606 [S]	Wanda Jackson Salutes the Country Music Hall of Fame	1966	25.00
☐ T2438 [M]	Wanda Jackson Sings Country Songs	1965	30.00
☐ ST2438 [S]	Wanda Jackson Sings Country Songs	1965	30.00
☐ T1776 [M]	Wonderful Wanda	1962	30.00
☐ ST1776 [S]	Wonderful Wanda	1962	30.00
☐ T2812 [M]	You'll Always Have My Love	1967	25.00
☐ ST2812 [S]	You'll Always Have My Love	1967	18.00

CLEOPATRA
☐ 6795 [B]	The Queen Of Rockabilly Salutes The King Of Rock N' Roll		25.00

DECCA
☐ DL4224 [M]	Lovin' Country Style	1962	50.00

GUSTO
☐ GT 0057	Greatest Hits	1980	12.00

HILLTOP
☐ 6123	By the Time I Get to Phoenix	1973	12.00
☐ 6074	Leave My Baby Alone	1969	15.00
☐ 6058	Please Help Me I'm Falling	1968	12.00

Number	Title	Yr	NM
☐ 6182	Tears at the Grand Ole Opry	1974	12.00
☐ 6116	We'll Sing in the Sunshine	1972	15.00

MYRRH
☐ MSB-6556	Make Me Like a Child Again	1976	15.00
☐ MSB-6533	Now I Have Everything	1975	15.00
☐ MSB-6513	When It's Time to Fall in Love Again	1974	15.00

PICKWICK
☐ PTP-2053	Wanda Jackson	1974	15.00

SYMPATHY FOR THE RECORD INDUSTRY
☐ SFTRI-724	Heart Trouble	2003	15.00

VARRICK
☐ VR-025	Rock 'n' Roll Away Your Blues	1987	15.00

VOCALION
☐ VL73861 [R]	Nobody's Darlin'	1968	15.00

WORD
☐ WST-8781	Closer to Jesus	1977	15.00
☐ WST-8614	Country Gospel	1973	15.00

JACKSON, WILLIS

ATLANTIC
☐ SD18145	The Way We Were	1975	15.00

CADET
☐ LP-763 [M]	Smoking with Willis	1966	18.00
☐ LPS-763 [S]	Smoking with Willis	1966	25.00

COTILLION
☐ SD9908	Willis Jackson Plays with Feeling	1977	18.00

CTI
☐ 6024	Sunflower	1972	18.00

FANTASY
☐ OJC-220	Cool Gator	198?	12.00
☐ OJC-321	Please, Mr. Jackson	1988	12.00

MOODSVILLE
☐ MVLP-17 [M]	In My Solitude	1961	50.00
— Green label			
☐ MVLP-17 [M]	In My Solitude	1965	30.00
— Blue label, trident logo at right			

MUSE
☐ MR-5162	Bar Wars	1978	15.00
☐ MR-5048	Headed and Gutted	1975	15.00
☐ MR-5100	In the Valley	1976	15.00
☐ MR-5200	Lockin' Horns	1979	15.00
☐ MR-5294	Nothing Butt	198?	12.00
☐ MR-5146	The Gator Horn	1978	15.00
☐ MR-5036	West Africa	1974	15.00
☐ MR-5316	Ya Understand Me?	198?	12.00

PRESTIGE
☐ PRLP-7183 [M]	Blue Gator	1960	50.00
☐ PRST-7850	Blue Gator	197?	18.00
☐ PRLP-7260 [M]	Bossa Nova Plus	1962	30.00
☐ PRST-7260 [S]	Bossa Nova Plus	1962	40.00
☐ PRLP-7329 [M]	Boss Shoutin'	1964	30.00
☐ PRST-7329 [S]	Boss Shoutin'	1964	40.00
☐ PRLP-7211 [M]	Cookin' Sherry	1961	30.00
☐ PRST-7211 [S]	Cookin' Sherry	1961	40.00
☐ PRLP-7172 [M]	Cool Gator	1959	50.00
☐ 2516	Gatorade	198?	15.00
☐ PRST-7648	Gator's Groove	1969	25.00
☐ PRLP-7285 [M]	Grease 'n' Gravy	1963	30.00
☐ PRST-7285 [S]	Grease 'n' Gravy	1963	40.00
☐ PRST-7830	Keep On a-Blowing	1971	25.00
☐ PRLP-7380 [M]	Live! Action	1965	30.00
☐ PRST-7380 [S]	Live! Action	1965	30.00
☐ PRLP-7348 [M]	Live! Jackson's Action	1965	30.00
☐ PRST-7348 [S]	Live! Jackson's Action	1965	30.00
☐ PRLP-7273 [M]	Loose...	1963	30.00
☐ PRST-7273 [S]	Loose...	1963	40.00
☐ PRLP-7317 [M]	More Gravy	1964	30.00
☐ PRST-7317 [S]	More Gravy	1964	40.00
☐ PRLP-7264 [M]	Neapolitan Nights	1963	30.00
☐ PRST-7264 [S]	Neapolitan Nights	1963	40.00
☐ PRLP-7162 [M]	Please, Mr. Jackson	1959	50.00
☐ PRST-7783	Please Mr. Jackson	1970	25.00
☐ PRLP-7196 [M]	Really Groovin'	1961	50.00
☐ PRST-7551	Soul Grabber	1968	25.00
☐ PRLP-7396 [M]	Soul Night -- Live!	1965	30.00
☐ PRST-7396 [S]	Soul Night -- Live!	1965	30.00
☐ PRST-7571	Star Bag	1968	25.00
☐ PRST-7602	Swivel Hips	1969	25.00
☐ PRLP-7412 [M]	Tell It...	1966	25.00
☐ PRST-7412 [S]	Tell It...	1966	30.00
☐ PRST-7702	The Best of Willis Jackson with Brother Jack McDuff	1969	18.00
☐ PRST-7770	The Best -- Soul Stompin'	1971	18.00
☐ PRLP-7296 [M]	The Good Life	1964	30.00
☐ PRST-7296 [S]	The Good Life	1964	40.00
☐ PRLP-7232 [M]	Thunderbird	1962	30.00
☐ PRST-7232 [S]	Thunderbird	1962	40.00
☐ PRLP-7364 [M]	Together Again	1965	30.00
☐ PRST-7364 [S]	Together Again	1965	30.00
☐ PRLP-7428 [M]	Together Again...Again	1966	25.00
☐ PRST-7428 [S]	Together Again...Again	1966	30.00

TRIP
☐ 5028	Funky Reggae	197?	12.00
☐ 5007	Mellow Blues	197?	15.00
☐ 5030	Willis Jackson Plays Around with the Hits	197?	12.00

VERVE
☐ V-8589 [M]	'Gator Tails	1964	18.00
☐ V6-8589 [S]	'Gator Tails	1964	25.00
☐ V6-8782	Willis Jackson	1969	18.00

JACKSON HEIGHTS

MERCURY
☐ SR-61331	King Progress	1970	30.00

VERVE
☐ V6-5089	Jackson Heights	1973	25.00

JACKSONS, THE

EPIC
☐ OE40911	2300 Jackson Street	1989	10.00
☐ JE35552	Destiny	1978	15.00
— Orange label			
☐ JE35552	Destiny	1979	10.00
— Dark blue label			
☐ JE34835	Goin' Places	1977	14.00
— Orange label			
☐ KE237545	Jacksons Live	1981	15.00
☐ PE34229	The Jacksons	1976	14.00
— Orange label			
☐ FE36424	Triumph	1980	10.00
☐ HE46424	Triumph	1982	60.00
— Half-speed mastered edition			
☐ QE38946	Victory	1984	10.00
☐ 8E839576 [PD]	Victory	1984	18.00

MOTOWN
☐ MS709 [B]	ABC	1970	30.00
☐ M5-152V1	ABC	1981	12.00
☐ M7-868	Anthology	1976	25.00
☐ MS713 [B]	Christmas Album	1970	30.00
☐ 5250ML	Christmas Album	1982	10.00
— Reissue of Motown 713			
☐ M6-780	Dancing Machine	1974	18.00
☐ MS700 [B]	Diana Ross Presents the Jackson 5	1969	40.00
☐ M5-129V1	Diana Ross Presents the Jackson Five	1981	12.00
☐ M6-783	Get It Together	1973	18.00
☐ M-742	Goin' Back to Indiana	1971	25.00
☐ M-741	Jackson 5 Greatest Hits	1971	25.00
☐ M5-201V1	Jackson 5 Greatest Hits	1981	12.00
☐ M6-865	Joyful Jukebox Music	1976	18.00
☐ M-750	Lookin' Through the Windows	1972	25.00
☐ M-735	Maybe Tomorrow	1971	25.00
☐ 5228ML	Maybe Tomorrow	1982	12.00
☐ M5-112V1	Motown Superstar Series, Vol. 12	1981	15.00
☐ M6-829	Moving Violation	1975	18.00
☐ M-761	Skywriter	1973	18.00
☐ 374631294-1 [DJ]	Soulsation!	1995	25.00
— Vinyl is promo only; 4-song sampler from box set			
☐ MS718 [B]	Third Album	1970	25.00
☐ M5-157V1	Third Album	1981	12.00

UNIVERSAL MOTOWN
☐ 5316421	ABC	2009	25.00

JACOBI, LOU

CAPITOL
☐ T2596 [M]	Al Tijuana and His Jewish Brass	1966	18.00
☐ ST2596 [S]	Al Tijuana and His Jewish Brass	1966	25.00

JACOBS, DICK

CORAL
☐ CRL57381 [M]	The Electro-Sonic Orchestra Presenting a New Concept in Sound	1958	25.00
☐ CRL757381 [S]	The Electro-Sonic Orchestra Presenting a New Concept in Sound	1958	30.00

JACOBS, FREDDIE

WESTMINSTER
☐ WP-6087 [M]	Swingin' Folk Tunes	195?	30.00

JACOBS, HANK

SUE
☐ LP-1023 [M]	So Far Away	1964	80.00

JACOBY, DON

DECCA
☐ DL4241 [M]	The Swinging Big Sound	1963	18.00
☐ DL74241 [S]	The Swinging Big Sound	1963	25.00

JACQUET, ILLINOIS, AND BEN WEBSTER

CLEF
☐ MGC-680 [M]	The Kid" and "The Brute	1955	200.00

VERVE
☐ MGV-8065 [M]	The Kid" and "The Brute	1957	60.00
— Reissue of Clef 680			
☐ V-8065 [M]	The Kid" and "The Brute	1961	25.00

JACQUET, ILLINOIS, AND LESTER YOUNG

ALADDIN

Number	Title	Yr	NM
❑ LP-701 [10]	Battle of the Saxes	1953	1200.00

JACQUET, ILLINOIS

ALADDIN

Number	Title	Yr	NM
❑ LP-708 [10]	Illinois Jacquet and His Tenor Sax	1954	500.00
❑ LP-803 [M]	Illinois Jacquet and His Tenor Sax	1956	200.00

APOLLO

Number	Title	Yr	NM
❑ LP-104 [10]	Illinois Jacquet Jam Session	1951	600.00

ARGO

Number	Title	Yr	NM
❑ LP-746 [M]	Bosses of the Ballad	1964	40.00
❑ LP-735 [M]	Desert Winds	1964	40.00
❑ LPS-735 [S]	Desert Winds	1964	50.00
❑ LPS-746 [S]	Illinois Jacquet Plays Cole Porter	1964	50.00
❑ LP-722 [M]	The Message	1963	40.00
❑ LPS-722 [S]	The Message	1963	50.00

ATLANTIC

Number	Title	Yr	NM
❑ 81816	Jacquet's Got It!	1988	15.00

BLACK LION

Number	Title	Yr	NM
❑ 146	Genius at Work	197?	25.00

CADET

Number	Title	Yr	NM
❑ LP-746 [M]	Bosses of the Ballad	1966	25.00
— Reissue of Argo 746; fading blue label			
❑ LPS-746 [S]	Bosses of the Ballad	1966	30.00
— Reissue of Argo 746; fading blue label			
❑ LP-735 [M]	Desert Winds	1966	25.00
— Reissue of Argo 735; fading blue label			
❑ LPS-735 [S]	Desert Winds	1966	30.00
— Reissue of Argo 735; fading blue label			
❑ LP-773 [M]	Go Power!	1966	40.00
❑ LPS-773 [S]	Go Power!	1966	50.00
❑ LP-754 [M]	Spectrum	1965	40.00
❑ LPS-754 [S]	Spectrum	1965	50.00
❑ LP-722 [M]	The Message	1966	25.00
— Reissue of Argo 722; fading blue label			
❑ LPS-722 [S]	The Message	1966	30.00
— Reissue of Argo 722; fading blue label			
❑ CA-722 [S]	The Message	197?	25.00
— Yellow and red label			

CHESS

Number	Title	Yr	NM
❑ CH-91554	The Message	1984	12.00
— Reissue			

CLASSIC JAZZ

Number	Title	Yr	NM
❑ 112	Illinois Jacquet with Wild Bill Davis	1978	25.00
❑ 148	Jacquet's Street	1981	25.00

CLEF

Number	Title	Yr	NM
❑ MGC-702 [M]	Groovin' with Jacquet	1956	200.00
❑ MGC-129 [10]	Illinois Jacquet Collates #2	1953	300.00
❑ MGC-112 [10]	Illinois Jacquet Collates	1953	300.00
❑ MGC-676 [M]	Illinois Jacquet Septet	1955	200.00
❑ MGC-167 [10]	Jazz by Jacquet	1954	300.00
❑ MGC-622 [M]	Jazz Moods	1955	200.00
❑ MGC-700 [M]	Jazz Moods by Illinois Jacquet	1956	150.00
❑ MGC-701 [M]	Port of Rico	1956	150.00
❑ MGC-750 [M]	Swing's the Thing	1956	150.00

EPIC

Number	Title	Yr	NM
❑ LA16033 [M]	Illinois Jacquet	1963	40.00
❑ BA17033 [S]	Illinois Jacquet	1963	50.00
❑ BA17033 [S]	Illinois Jacquet	199?	30.00
— Classic Records reissue on audiophile vinyl			

FANTASY

Number	Title	Yr	NM
❑ OJC-417	Bottoms Up!	1990	15.00
❑ OJC-614	The Blues -- That's Me	1991	18.00

GROOVE NOTE

Number	Title	Yr	NM
❑ 2003	Birthday Party	1999	50.00
— Audiophile vinyl; one record has the entire album, the other has two tracks at 45 rpm			

IMPERIAL

Number	Title	Yr	NM
❑ LP-9184 [M]	Flying Home	1962	30.00
❑ LP-12184 [S]	Flying Home	1962	40.00

JAZZ MAN

Number	Title	Yr	NM
❑ 5034	Genius at Work	198?	15.00

JRC

Number	Title	Yr	NM
❑ 11434	Birthday Party	197?	30.00
❑ MGC-112 [10]	Illinois Jacquet Collates	1952	500.00

MOSAIC

Number	Title	Yr	NM
❑ MQ6-165	The Complete Illinois Jacquet Sessions 1945-50	199?	100.00

PRESTIGE

Number	Title	Yr	NM
❑ PRST-7575	Bottoms Up!	1968	40.00
❑ P-24057	How High the Moon	1975	30.00
❑ PRST-7731	The Blues -- That's Me	1969	40.00
❑ PRST-7597	The King!	1968	40.00
❑ PRST-7629	The Soul Explosion	1969	40.00

RCA VICTOR

Number	Title	Yr	NM
❑ LPM-3236 [10]	Black Velvet	1954	500.00

ROULETTE

Number	Title	Yr	NM
❑ R-52035 [M]	Illinois Jacquet Flies Again	1959	70.00
❑ SR-52035 [S]	Illinois Jacquet Flies Again	1959	60.00

SAVOY

Number	Title	Yr	NM
❑ MG-15024 [10]	Tenor Sax	1953	400.00

VERVE

Number	Title	Yr	NM
❑ MGV-8086 [M]	Groovin' with Jacquet	1957	60.00
— Reissue of Clef 702			
❑ V-8086 [M]	Groovin' with Jacquet	1961	30.00
❑ MGV-8061 [M]	Illinois Jacquet and His Orchestra	1957	60.00
— Reissue of Clef 676			
❑ V-8061 [M]	Illinois Jacquet and His Orchestra	1961	30.00
❑ MGV-8084 [M]	Jazz Moods by Illinois Jacquet	1957	60.00
— Reissue of Clef 700			
❑ V-8084 [M]	Jazz Moods by Illinois Jacquet	1961	30.00
❑ MGV-8085 [M]	Port of Rico	1957	60.00
— Reissue of Clef 701			
❑ V-8085 [M]	Port of Rico	1961	30.00
❑ MGV-8023 [M]	Swing's the Thing	1957	60.00
— Reissue of Clef 750			
❑ V-8023 [M]	Swing's the Thing	1961	30.00
❑ VE-2-2544	The Cool Rage	198?	25.00

JACQUET, RUSSELL

KING

Number	Title	Yr	NM
❑ 295-81 [10]	Russell Jacquet and His All Stars	1954	250.00

JADE, FAINE

RSVP

Number	Title	Yr	NM
❑ 8002	Introspection: A Faine Jade Recital	1968	400.00

JADE

GENERAL AMERICAN

Number	Title	Yr	NM
❑ 11311	The Faces of Jade	1968	80.00

JADES, THE

JARRETT

Number	Title	Yr	NM
❑ 21517 [M]	Live at the Disco a-Go-Go	1965	120.00

JAG PANZER

AZRA IRON WORKS

Number	Title	Yr	NM
❑ 1001 [PD]	Ample Destruction	1985	30.00
— Allegedly, 250 were pressed as picture discs			

JAGGER, CHRIS

ASYLUM

Number	Title	Yr	NM
❑ SD5069	Chris Jagger	1973	15.00
❑ 7E-1009	The Adventures of Valentine Vox the Ventriloquist	1974	15.00

JAGGER, MICK

COLUMBIA

Number	Title	Yr	NM
❑ OC40919	Primitive Cool	1987	10.00
❑ FC39940	She's the Boss	1985	12.00

JAGGERZ, THE

GAMBLE

Number	Title	Yr	NM
❑ GS-5006	Introducing the Jaggerz	1969	25.00

KAMA SUTRA

Number	Title	Yr	NM
❑ KSBS-2017	We Went to Different Schools Together	1970	18.00

WOODEN NICKEL

Number	Title	Yr	NM
❑ BWL1-0772	Come Again	1975	15.00

JAIM

ETHEREAL

Number	Title	Yr	NM
❑ 1001	Prophecy Fulfilled	1970	50.00

JALOPY FIVE, THE

MODERN SOUND

Number	Title	Yr	NM
❑ M-561 [M]	I Love That West Coast Sound	1965	50.00
❑ MS-561 [S]	I Love That West Coast Sound	1965	50.00

JAM, THE

POLYDOR

Number	Title	Yr	NM
❑ PD1-6188 [B]	All Mod Cons	1979	30.00
❑ 810751-1 [EP]	Beat Surrender	1982	18.00
❑ PD1-6365 [B]	Dig the New Breed	1982	25.00
❑ PD1-6110 [B]	In the City	1977	30.00
❑ 817124-1	In the City	198?	12.00
— Reissue			
❑ PD1-6249 [B]	Setting Sons	1980	18.00
❑ 815537-1 [B]	Snap!	1983	30.00
❑ PD1-6315 [B]	Sound Affects	1981	18.00
❑ PX1-506 [EP]	The Bitterest Pill	1982	12.00
❑ PD1-6349 [B]	The Gift	1982	18.00
❑ PX1-503 [EP]	The Jam	1982	12.00
❑ PD1-6129 [B]	This Is the Modern World	1978	30.00
❑ 823281-1 [B]	This Is the Modern World	198?	15.00
— Reissue			

JAM FACTORY

EPIC

Number	Title	Yr	NM
❑ BN26521	Sittin' in the Trap	1970	30.00

JAMAL, AHMAD

20TH CENTURY

Number	Title	Yr	NM
❑ T-417	Ahmad Jamal '73	1973	12.00
❑ T-600	Genetic Walk	1980	12.00
❑ T-631	Greatest Hits	1981	12.00
❑ T-622	Intervals	1980	12.00
❑ T-432	Jamaica	1974	12.00
❑ T-459	Jamal Plays Jamal	1975	12.00
❑ T-555	One	1978	12.00
❑ T-515	Steppin' Out with a Dream	1977	12.00

ABC

Number	Title	Yr	NM
❑ S-660	Tranquility	1968	15.00

ABC IMPULSE!

Number	Title	Yr	NM
❑ AS-9176	At the Top -- Poinciana Revisited	1969	18.00
❑ SMAS-92005	At the Top -- Poinciana Revisited	1969	25.00
— Capitol Record Club edition			
❑ AS-9217	Freeflight	1971	15.00
❑ AS-9226	Outertimeinnerspace	1972	15.00
❑ AS-9260	Re-evaluations: The Impulse Years	1975	15.00
❑ AS-9194	The Awakening	1970	18.00
❑ AS-9238	Tranquility	1973	15.00

ARGO

Number	Title	Yr	NM
❑ LP-636 [M]	Ahmad Jamal, Volume IV	1958	30.00
❑ LPS-636 [S]	Ahmad Jamal, Volume IV	1958	40.00
❑ LP-703 [M]	Ahmad Jamal at the Blackhawk	1962	25.00
❑ LPS-703 [S]	Ahmad Jamal at the Blackhawk	1962	30.00
❑ LP-667 [M]	Ahmad Jamal at the Pershing Volume 2	1961	25.00
❑ LPS-667 [S]	Ahmad Jamal at the Pershing Volume 2	1961	30.00
❑ LP-685 [M]	Alhambra	1961	25.00
❑ LPS-685 [S]	Alhambra	1961	30.00
❑ LP-691 [M]	All of You	1962	25.00
❑ LPS-691 [S]	All of You	1962	30.00
❑ LP-628 [M]	But Not for Me/Ahmad Jamal at the Pershing	1958	30.00
❑ LPS-628 [S]	But Not for Me/Ahmad Jamal at the Pershing	1958	40.00
❑ LP-602 [M]	Chamber Music of the New Jazz	1956	50.00
— With "Creative Hi-Fidelity Modern Music" on cover; "ship" label; reissue of Parrot LP			
❑ LP-602 [M]	Chamber Music of the New Jazz	1956	30.00
— Dark green label, gold or silver print			
❑ LP-610 [M]	Count 'Em 88	1957	30.00
❑ LP-758 [M]	Extensions	1965	25.00
❑ LPS-758 [S]	Extensions	1965	30.00
❑ LP-662 [M]	Happy Moods	1960	25.00
❑ LPS-662 [S]	Happy Moods	1960	30.00
❑ LP-646 [M]	Jamal at the Penthouse	1959	30.00
❑ LPS-646 [S]	Jamal at the Penthouse	1959	40.00
❑ LP-673 [M]	Listen to Ahmad Jamal	1961	25.00
❑ LPS-673 [S]	Listen to Ahmad Jamal	1961	30.00
❑ LP-712 [M]	Macanudo	1963	25.00
❑ LPS-712 [S]	Macanudo	1963	30.00
❑ LP-733 [M]	Naked City" Theme	1964	25.00
❑ LPS-733 [S]	Naked City" Theme	1964	30.00
❑ LP-719 [M]	Poin'-ci-an'a	1963	25.00
❑ LPS-719 [S]	Poin'-ci-an'a	1963	30.00
❑ LP-2638 [M]	Portfolio of Ahmad Jamal	1959	40.00
— Textured cover with raised image of Jamal; limited, numbered edition			
❑ LPS-2638 [S]	Portfolio of Ahmad Jamal	1959	50.00
❑ LP-751 [M]	The Roar of the Greasepaint	1965	25.00
❑ LPS-751 [S]	The Roar of the Greasepaint	1965	30.00

ATLANTIC

Number	Title	Yr	NM
❑ 81793	Crystal	1987	12.00
❑ 81258	Digital Works	1985	15.00
❑ 81699	Live at the Montreal Jazz Festival 1985	1986	15.00
❑ 81645	Rossiter Road	1986	12.00

CADET

Number	Title	Yr	NM
❑ LP-636 [M]	Ahmad Jamal, Volume IV	1966	15.00
❑ LPS-636 [S]	Ahmad Jamal, Volume IV	1966	18.00
❑ LP-703 [M]	Ahmad Jamal at the Blackhawk	1966	15.00
❑ LPS-703 [S]	Ahmad Jamal at the Blackhawk	1966	18.00
❑ LP-667 [M]	Ahmad Jamal at the Pershing Volume 2	1966	15.00
❑ LPS-667 [S]	Ahmad Jamal at the Pershing Volume 2	1966	18.00
❑ LP-685 [M]	Alhambra	1966	15.00
❑ LPS-685 [S]	Alhambra	1966	18.00
❑ LP-691 [M]	All of You	1966	15.00
❑ LPS-691 [S]	All of You	1966	18.00
❑ LP-628 [M]	But Not for Me/Ahmad Jamal at the Pershing	1966	15.00
❑ LPS-628 [S]	But Not for Me/Ahmad Jamal at the Pershing	1966	18.00
❑ LP-792 [M]	Cry Young	1967	25.00
❑ LPS-792 [S]	Cry Young	1967	18.00
❑ LP-758 [M]	Extensions	1966	15.00
❑ LPS-758 [S]	Extensions	1965	18.00
❑ CA-758 [S]	Extensions	197?	15.00
— Reissue; yellow and red label with "A Division of All			

Number	Title	Yr	NM
Platinum Record Group" on label			
❑ LP-662 [M]	Happy Moods	1966	15.00
❑ LPS-662 [S]	Happy Moods	1966	18.00
❑ LP-777 [M]	Heat Wave	1966	18.00
❑ LPS-777 [S]	Heat Wave	1966	25.00
—Original with fading blue label			
❑ LPS-777 [S]	Heat Wave	1977	15.00
—Reissue, "a division of All Platinum Record Group" on back cover			
❑ 50035	Inspiration	1974	18.00
❑ LP-646 [M]	Jamal at the Penthouse	1966	15.00
❑ LPS-646 [S]	Jamal at the Penthouse	1966	18.00
❑ LP-673 [M]	Listen to Ahmad Jamal	1966	15.00
❑ LPS-673 [S]	Listen to Ahmad Jamal	1966	18.00
❑ LP-712 [M]	Macanudo	1966	15.00
❑ LPS-712 [S]	Macanudo	1966	18.00
❑ LP-733 [M]	Naked City" Theme	1966	15.00
❑ LPS-733 [S]	Naked City" Theme	1966	18.00
❑ LP-719 [M]	Poin'-ci-an'a	1966	15.00
❑ LPS-719 [S]	Poin'-ci-an'a	1966	18.00
❑ LP-2638 [M]	Portfolio of Ahmad Jamal	1966	18.00
—Cadet issues generally did not have embossed covers			
❑ LPS-2638 [S]	Portfolio of Ahmad Jamal	1966	25.00
—Cadet issues generally did not have embossed covers			
❑ LP-764 [M]	Rhapsody	1966	18.00
❑ LPS-764 [S]	Rhapsody	1966	25.00
❑ LP-786 [M]	Standard Eyes	1967	18.00
❑ LPS-786 [S]	Standard Eyes	1967	25.00
❑ LPS-807	The Bright, the Blue and the Beautiful	1968	18.00
❑ LP-751 [M]	The Roar of the Greasepaint	1966	15.00
❑ LPS-751 [S]	The Roar of the Greasepaint	1966	18.00
CATALYST			
❑ 7606	Live at Oil Can Harry's	1978	15.00
CHESS			
❑ CH-91553	Poinciana	198?	12.00
❑ CH-2-9223	Sun Set	1984	15.00
EPIC			
❑ LN3212 [M]	Ahmad Jamal Trio	1956	50.00
—Yellow label with lines around rim			
❑ BN627 [R]	Ahmad Jamal Trio	196?	25.00
❑ LN3212 [M]	Ahmad Jamal Trio	1963	30.00
—Yellow label, no lines around rim			
❑ LN3631 [M]	The Piano Scene of Ahmad Jamal	1959	30.00
❑ BN634 [S]	The Piano Scene of Ahmad Jamal	1959	25.00
GRP/IMPULSE!			
❑ 226	The Awakening	199?	18.00
—Reissue on audiophile vinyl			
MCA			
❑ 29041	At the Top -- Poinciana Revisited	198?	10.00
—Reissue of Impulse! 9178			
❑ 29043	Freelight	198?	10.00
—Reissue of Impulse! 9217			
❑ 29042	The Awakening	198?	10.00
—Reissue of Impulse! 9194			
MCA/IMPULSE!			
❑ 5644	The Awakening	1986	12.00
—Another reissue of Impulse! 9194			
MOTOWN			
❑ M8-945	Night Song	1981	12.00
PARROT			
❑ 55-245/6 [M]	Ahmad Jamal Plays	1955	1500.00
—VG value 500; VG+ value 1000			

JAMES, BOB, AND EARL KLUGH

Number	Title	Yr	NM
CAPITOL			
❑ SMAS-12244	Two of a Kind	1982	15.00
MOBILE FIDELITY			
❑ 1-124	Two of a Kind	1984	40.00
—Original Master Recording" banner across top of front cover			
TAPPAN ZEE			
❑ HC46241	One on One	198?	30.00
—Half-speed mastered edition			
❑ FC36241	One on One	1979	12.00

JAMES, BOB

Number	Title	Yr	NM
CBS MASTERWORKS			
❑ IM39540	Rameau	1985	15.00
COLUMBIA			
❑ FC38678	The Genie (Themes & Variations from the TV Series "Taxi")	1983	12.00
CTI			
❑ 7074	BJ4	1977	18.00
❑ CTS-6043	One	1974	25.00
❑ CTS-6063	Three	1976	18.00
❑ CTS-6057	Two	1975	30.00
ESP-DISK'			
❑ 1009 [M]	Explosions	1965	40.00
❑ S-1009 [S]	Explosions	1965	50.00
MERCURY			
❑ MG-20768 [M]	Bold Conceptions	1963	40.00
❑ SR-60768 [S]	Bold Conceptions	1963	50.00
TAPPAN ZEE			
❑ FC39580	12	1985	12.00
❑ C2X36786	All Around the Town	1981	15.00
❑ FC36838	BJ4	1981	12.00
—Reissue of CTI 7074			
❑ AS1299 [DJ]	Bob James/Dave Herman Interview	1981	18.00
—Promo-only radio program			
❑ FC38801	Foxie	1983	12.00
❑ JC36422	H	1980	12.00
❑ FC38067	Hands Down	1982	12.00
❑ JC34896	Heads	1977	12.00
❑ JC36056	Lucky Seven	1979	12.00
❑ AS699 [DJ]	Lucky Seven/One on One Sampler	1979	30.00
—Edited selections from both of the above albums; promo only			
❑ FC36835	One	1981	12.00
—Reissue of CTI 6043			
❑ FC37495	Sign of the Times	1981	12.00
❑ HC47495	Sign of the Times	1982	30.00
—Half-speed mastered edition			
❑ FC36837	Three	1981	15.00
—Reissue of CTI 6063			
❑ JC35594	Touchdown	1978	12.00
❑ HC45594	Touchdown	1982	30.00
—Half-speed mastered edition			
❑ FC36836	Two	1981	15.00
—Reissue of CTI 6057			
❑ PC36836	Two	1985	10.00
—Budget-line reissue			
WARNER BROS.			
❑ 26256	Grand Piano Canyon	1990	18.00
❑ 25757	Ivory Coast	1988	12.00
❑ 25495	Obsession	1986	12.00

JAMES, DENNIS

Number	Title	Yr	NM
KAPP			
❑ KL-1009 [M]	Let's All Sing a Song for Christmas	1955	30.00

JAMES, ELMORE

Number	Title	Yr	NM
BELL			
❑ 6037	Elmore James	1969	30.00
CHESS			
❑ LP-1537	Whose Muddy Shoes	1969	30.00
COLLECTABLES			
❑ COL-5112	Golden Classics	198?	15.00
❑ COL-5184	The Complete Fire and Enjoy Sessions, Part 1	198?	12.00
❑ COL-5185	The Complete Fire and Enjoy Sessions, Part 2	198?	12.00
❑ COL-5186	The Complete Fire and Enjoy Sessions, Part 3	198?	12.00
❑ COL-5187	The Complete Fire and Enjoy Sessions, Part 4	198?	12.00
CROWN			
❑ CLP-5168 [M]	Blues After Hours	1961	250.00
—Black label, silver "Crown			
❑ CLP-5168 [M]	Blues After Hours	1962	50.00
—Gray label			
INTERMEDIA			
❑ QS-5034	Red Hot Blues	198?	12.00
KENT			
❑ KLP-9001	Anthology of the Blues Legend	196?	30.00
❑ KLP-5022 [M]	Original Folk Blues	1964	40.00
❑ KST-522 [R]	Original Folk Blues	1964	30.00
❑ KLP-9010	The Resurrection of Elmore James	196?	30.00
SPHERE SOUND			
❑ SR-7008 [M]	I Need You	1966	150.00
❑ SSR-7008 [R]	I Need You	1966	120.00
❑ SR-7002 [M]	The Sky Is Crying	1965	180.00
❑ SSR-7002 [R]	The Sky Is Crying	1965	120.00
UP FRONT			
❑ UP-122	The Great Elmore James	1970	15.00

JAMES, ETTA

Number	Title	Yr	NM
ARGO			
❑ LP-4003 [M]	At Last!	1961	60.00
❑ LPS-4003 [S]	At Last!	1961	80.00
❑ LP-4013 [M]	Etta James	1962	30.00
❑ LPS-4013 [P]	Etta James	1962	40.00
—Two duets with Harvey Fuqua are rechanneled			
❑ LP-4032 [M]	Etta James Rocks the House	1964	100.00
❑ LPS-4032 [S]	Etta James Rocks the House	1964	150.00
❑ LP-4018 [M]	Etta James Sings for Lovers	1962	30.00
❑ LPS-4018 [S]	Etta James Sings for Lovers	1962	40.00
❑ LP-4025 [M]	Etta James Top Ten	1963	30.00
❑ LPS-4025 [S]	Etta James Top Ten	1963	40.00
❑ LP-4040 [M]	The Queen of Soul	1965	30.00
❑ LPS-4040 [S]	The Queen of Soul	1965	40.00
❑ LP-4011 [M]	The Second Time Around	1961	30.00
❑ LPS-4011 [S]	The Second Time Around	1961	40.00
CADET			
❑ LP-4003 [M]	At Last!	1966	15.00
❑ LPS-4003 [S]	At Last!	1966	18.00
❑ LP-4055 [M]	Call My Name	1967	18.00
❑ LPS-4055 [S]	Call My Name	1967	25.00
❑ LP-4013 [M]	Etta James	1966	15.00
❑ LPS-4013 [S]	Etta James	1966	18.00
❑ LP-4018 [M]	Etta James Sings for Lovers	1966	15.00
❑ LPS-4018 [S]	Etta James Sings for Lovers	1966	18.00
❑ LPS-832	Etta James Sings Funk	1969	25.00
❑ LP-4025 [M]	Etta James Top Ten	1966	15.00
❑ LPS-4025 [S]	Etta James Top Ten	1966	18.00
❑ LPS-847	Losers Weepers	1970	18.00
❑ LP-802 [M]	Tell Mama	1968	30.00
❑ LPS-802 [S]	Tell Mama	1968	25.00
❑ LP-4040 [M]	The Queen of Soul	1966	15.00
❑ LPS-4040 [S]	The Queen of Soul	1966	18.00
❑ LP-4011 [M]	The Second Time Around	1966	15.00
❑ LPS-4011 [S]	The Second Time Around	1966	18.00
CHESS			
❑ CH-9266	At Last!	1987	10.00
—Reissue			
❑ CH-60029	Come a Little Closer	1974	18.00
❑ CH-91509	Come a Little Closer	198?	10.00
—Reissue			
❑ ACH-19003	Etta Is Betta Than Evvah!	1976	18.00
❑ CH-50042	Etta James	1973	18.00
❑ CH-9184	Etta James Rocks the House	1986	10.00
—Reissue			
❑ CH-9110	Her Greatest Sides, Vol. 1	1984	12.00
❑ 2CH-60004	Peaches	1971	25.00
❑ CH-9269	Tell Mama	1987	10.00
—Reissue			
❑ CH-9287	The Second Time Around	1989	10.00
—Reissue			
❑ CH2-6028	The Sweetest Peaches	1989	15.00
CROWN			
❑ CLP-5360 [M]	Etta James	1963	30.00
—With Etta smiling on cover			
❑ CLP-5360 [M]	Etta James	1963	30.00
—With Etta somber on cover			
❑ CST-360 [R]	Etta James	1963	25.00
—With Etta smiling on cover			
❑ CST-360 [R]	Etta James	1963	25.00
—With Etta somber on cover			
❑ CLP-5209 [M]	Miss Etta James	1961	100.00
—First edition, with framed picture on cover			
❑ CLP-5209 [M]	Miss Etta James	1962	60.00
—Second edition, all-white cover with "Miss Etta James			
❑ CLP-5234 [M]	The Best of Etta James	1962	60.00
—Black label			
❑ CLP-5234 [M]	The Best of Etta James	1963	30.00
—Gray label			
❑ CLP-5250 [M]	Twist with Etta James	1962	60.00
—Black label			
❑ CLP-5250 [M]	Twist with Etta James	1963	30.00
—Gray label			
INTERMEDIA			
❑ QS-5014	Etta, Red Hot 'N' Live!	198?	12.00
ISLAND			
❑ 91018	Seven Year Itch	1988	12.00
❑ 842926-1	Sticking to My Guns	1990	15.00
KENT			
❑ KLP-5000 [M]	Miss Etta James	1964	30.00
❑ KST-500 [R]	Miss Etta James	1964	80.00
—Red vinyl			
❑ KST-500 [R]	Miss Etta James	1964	30.00
—Black vinyl			
UNITED			
❑ US7712	Etta James Sings	197?	12.00
WARNER BROS.			
❑ BSK3156	Deep in the Night	1978	15.00

JAMES, GREGORY

Number	Title	Yr	NM
INNER CITY			
❑ IC-1050	Alicia	1978	18.00

JAMES, HARRY

Number	Title	Yr	NM
AIRCHECK			
❑ 18	Harry James On the Air	197?	12.00
❑ 33	Harry James On the Air, Vol. 2	1986	12.00
BAINBRIDGE			
❑ BT-6252	Ciribiribin	1982	12.00
CAPITOL			
❑ W654 [M]	Harry James in Hi-Fi	1955	30.00
❑ T1093 [M]	Harry's Choice	1958	30.00
❑ W712 [M]	More Harry James in Hi-Fi	1956	30.00
❑ T1515 [M]	The Hits of Harry James	1961	25.00
—Black colorband label, logo at left			
❑ DT1515 [R]	The Hits of Harry James	1961	15.00
❑ T1515 [M]	The Hits of Harry James	1962	18.00
—Black colorband label, logo at top			
❑ M-1515	The Hits of Harry James	197?	15.00
—Mono reissue			
❑ T1037 [M]	The New James	1958	30.00
❑ T874 [M]	Wild About Harry	1957	30.00

Number	Title	Yr	NM
CIRCLE			
❑ 39	Harry James and His Orchestra 1954	198?	12.00
❑ 5	Harry James and His Orchestra with Dick Haymes	198?	12.00
COLUMBIA			
❑ CL655 [M]	*All Time Favorites	1955	40.00
—Maroon label, gold print			
❑ CL6009 [10]	*All Time Favorites	1949	50.00
❑ CL2630 [M]	*Harry James' Greatest Hits	1967	25.00
❑ CS9430 [R]	*Harry James' Greatest Hits	1967	15.00
—Red "360 Sound" label			
❑ CS9430 [R]	*Harry James' Greatest Hits	1970	12.00
—Orange label			
❑ PC9430	*Harry James' Greatest Hits	198?	10.00
—Budget-line reissue			
❑ CL6088 [10]	Dance Parade	1950	50.00
❑ CL562 [M]	Dancing in Person with Harry James at the Hollywood Palladium	1954	40.00
—Maroon label, gold print			
❑ CL669 [M]	Jazz Session	1955	40.00
❑ CL615 [M]	Juke Box Jamboree	1955	40.00
—Maroon label, gold print			
❑ GL522 [M]	One Night Stand	1953	50.00
—Black label, silver print			
❑ CL522 [M]	One Night Stand	1953	40.00
—Maroon label, gold print			
❑ CL581 [M]	Soft Lights, Sweet Trumpet	1954	40.00
—Maroon label, gold print			
❑ CL6207 [10]	Soft Lights, Sweet Trumpet	1952	50.00
❑ CL2527 [10]	The Man with the Horn	1955	50.00
❑ CL553 [M]	Trumpet After Midnight	1954	40.00
—Maroon label, gold print			
❑ CL6044 [10]	Trumpet Time	1950	50.00
❑ CL6138 [10]	Your Dance Date	1951	50.00
DOT			
❑ DLP-3735 [M]	Harry James and His Western Friends	1966	15.00
❑ DLP-25735 [S]	Harry James and His Western Friends	1966	18.00
❑ DLP-3728 [M]	Live at the Riverboat	1966	15.00
❑ DLP-25728 [S]	Live at the Riverboat	1966	18.00
❑ DLP-3801 [M]	Our Leader	1967	18.00
❑ DLP-25801 [S]	Our Leader	1967	15.00
HARMONY			
❑ KH32018	Best of the Big Bands	1972	12.00
❑ HL7159 [M]	Harry James and His Great Vocalists	196?	18.00
❑ HL7191 [M]	Harry James Plays the Songs That Sold a Million	196?	18.00
❑ HS11245 [R]	Harry James Plays the Songs That Sold a Million	196?	12.00
❑ HL7162 [M]	Harry James Plays Trumpet Rhapsody	196?	18.00
❑ HS11326	Laura	1969	12.00
❑ HL7269 [M]	Strictly Instrumental	196?	18.00
HINDSIGHT			
❑ HSR-102	Harry James and His Orchestra 1943-46	198?	12.00
❑ HSR-123	Harry James and His Orchestra 1943-46	198?	12.00
❑ HSR-141	Harry James and His Orchestra 1943-46, Vol. 4	198?	12.00
❑ HSR-142	Harry James and His Orchestra 1943-53	198?	12.00
❑ HSR-150	Harry James and His Orchestra 1947-49	198?	12.00
❑ HSR-135	Harry James and His Orchestra 1948-49	198?	12.00
❑ HSR-406	Harry James and His Orchestra Play 22 Original Big Band Recordings	198?	15.00
INSIGHT			
❑ 203	Harry James and His Orchestra 1943-53	198?	12.00
JAZZ ARCHIVES			
❑ JA-31	Young Harry James	198?	12.00
LONDON PHASE 4			
❑ SP-44109	Golden Trumpet	1968	18.00
LONGINES SYMPHONETTE			
❑ LS-217	Harry James Dance Band Spectacular	196?	30.00
METRO			
❑ M-536 [M]	Harry Not Jesse	1966	15.00
❑ MS-536 [S]	Harry Not Jesse	1966	15.00
MGM			
❑ E-4214 [M]	25th Anniversary Album	1964	15.00
❑ SE-4214 [S]	25th Anniversary Album	1964	18.00
❑ E-4137 [M]	Double Dixie	1963	18.00
❑ SE-4137 [S]	Double Dixie	1963	25.00
❑ E-3778 [M]	Harry James and His New Swingin' Band	1959	25.00
❑ SE-3778 [S]	Harry James and His New Swingin' Band	1959	30.00
❑ E-3848 [M]	Harry James Today	1960	25.00
❑ SE-3848 [S]	Harry James Today	1960	30.00
❑ E-4274 [M]	In a Relaxed Mood	1965	15.00
❑ SE-4274 [S]	In a Relaxed Mood	1965	18.00
❑ E-4265 [M]	New Versions of Down Beat Favorites	1965	15.00
❑ SE-4265 [S]	New Versions of Down Beat Favorites	1965	18.00
❑ E-4003 [M]	Requests on the Road	1961	25.00
❑ SE-4003 [S]	Requests on the Road	1961	30.00
❑ E-4058 [M]	The Solid Gold Trumpet	1962	18.00
❑ SE-4058 [S]	The Solid Gold Trumpet	1962	25.00
PAIR			
❑ PDL2-1158	Big Band Favorites	1986	15.00
PAUSA			
❑ 9037	More Harry James in Hi-Fi	198?	12.00
PICKWICK			
❑ PC-3006 [M]	Mr. Trumpet	196?	18.00
❑ SPC-3006 [R]	Mr. Trumpet	196?	12.00
❑ SPC-3126	The Shadow of Your Smile	196?	12.00
❑ PC-3044 [M]	You Made Me Love You	196?	18.00
❑ SPC-3044 [R]	You Made Me Love You	196?	12.00
SAVOY JAZZ			
❑ SJL-2262	First Team Player on the Jazz Varsity	198?	15.00
SHEFFIELD LABS			
❑ 6	Comin' From a Good Place	1978	18.00
—Direct-to-disc recording			
❑ 11	Still Harry After All These Years	1979	25.00
—Direct-to-disc recording; comes in box with booklet			
❑ 3	The King James Version	1976	18.00
—Direct-to-disc recording			
SUNBEAM			
❑ 203	Harry James and His Orchestra 1940	197?	12.00
❑ 217	Harry James and His Orchestra 1954	197?	12.00
TIME-LIFE			
❑ STBB-04	Big Bands: Harry James	1983	18.00

JAMES, JIMMY, AND THE VAGABONDS

Number	Title	Yr	NM
ATCO			
❑ 33-222 [M]	The New Religion	1967	40.00
❑ SD 33-222 [S]	The New Religion	1967	25.00
PYE			
❑ 12111	You Don't Stand a Chance If You Can't Dance	1975	12.00

JAMES, JONI

Number	Title	Yr	NM
MGM			
❑ E-3755 [M]	100 Strings and Joni	1959	80.00
—Yellow label			
❑ E-3755 [M]	100 Strings and Joni	1960	40.00
—Black label			
❑ SE-3755 [S]	100 Strings and Joni	1959	120.00
—Yellow label			
❑ SE-3755 [S]	100 Strings and Joni	1960	50.00
—Black label			
❑ E-3840 [M]	100 Strings and Joni In Hollywood	1960	60.00
❑ SE-3840 [S]	100 Strings and Joni In Hollywood	1960	70.00
❑ E-3839 [M]	100 Strings and Joni On Broadway	1960	60.00
❑ SE-3839 [S]	100 Strings and Joni On Broadway	1960	70.00
❑ E-3892 [M]	100 Voices, 100 Strings	1960	50.00
❑ SE-3892 [S]	100 Voices, 100 Strings	1960	60.00
❑ E-4008 [M]	After Hours	1962	50.00
❑ SE-4008 [S]	After Hours	1962	60.00
❑ E-3602 [M]	Among My Souvenirs	1958	80.00
—Yellow label			
❑ E-3602 [M]	Among My Souvenirs	1960	40.00
—Black label			
❑ E-234 [10]	Award Winning Album	1954	200.00
❑ E-3346 [M]	Award Winning Album	1956	80.00
—Yellow label			
❑ E-3346 [M]	Award Winning Album	1960	40.00
—Black label			
❑ E-3706 [M]	Award Winning Album, Volume 2	1958	80.00
—Yellow label			
❑ E-3706 [M]	Award Winning Album, Volume 2	1960	40.00
—Black label			
❑ E-4263 [M]	Beyond the Reef	1964	40.00
❑ SE-4263 [S]	Beyond the Reef	1964	50.00
❑ E-4286 [M]	Bossa Nova Style	1965	40.00
❑ SE-4286 [S]	Bossa Nova Style	1965	50.00
❑ E-4101 [M]	Country Girl Style	1962	50.00
❑ SE-4101 [S]	Country Girl Style	1962	60.00
❑ E-3958 [M]	Folk Songs by Joni James	1961	50.00
❑ SE-3958 [S]	Folk Songs by Joni James	1961	60.00
❑ E-3528 [M]	Give Us This Day	1957	80.00
—Yellow label			
❑ E-3528 [M]	Give Us This Day	1960	40.00
—Black label			
❑ E-4053 [M]	I Feel a Song Comin' On	1962	50.00
❑ SE-4053 [S]	I Feel a Song Comin' On	1962	60.00
❑ E-3837 [M]	I'm in the Mood for Love	1960	60.00
❑ SE-3837 [S]	I'm in the Mood for Love	1960	80.00
❑ E-4054 [M]	I'm Your Girl	1962	50.00
❑ SE-4054 [S]	I'm Your Girl	1962	60.00
❑ E-3328 [M]	In the Still of the Night	1956	80.00
—Yellow label			
❑ E-3328 [M]	In the Still of the Night	1960	40.00
—Black label			
❑ E-3749 [M]	Irish Favorites	1959	80.00
—Yellow label			
❑ E-3749 [M]	Irish Favorites	1960	40.00
—Black label			
❑ SE-3749 [S]	Irish Favorites	1959	120.00
—Yellow label			
❑ SE-3749 [S]	Irish Favorites	1960	50.00
—Black label			
❑ E-4208 [M]	Italianissime!	1963	40.00
❑ SE-4208 [S]	Italianissime!	1963	50.00
❑ E-3718 [M]	Je T'aime (I Love You)	1958	80.00
—Yellow label			
❑ E-3718 [M]	Je T'aime (I Love You)	1960	40.00
—Black label			
❑ SE-3718 [S]	Je T'aime (I Love You)	1958	120.00
—Yellow label			
❑ SE-3718 [S]	Je T'aime (I Love You)	1960	50.00
—Black label			
❑ E-3800 [M]	Joni James at Carnegie Hall	1959	60.00
❑ SE-3800 [S]	Joni James at Carnegie Hall	1959	80.00
❑ E-4255 [M]	Joni James Sings the Gershwins	1964	40.00
❑ SE-4255 [S]	Joni James Sings the Gershwins	1964	50.00
❑ E-3772 [M]	Joni James Swings Sweet	1959	60.00
❑ SE-3772 [S]	Joni James Swings Sweet	1959	80.00
❑ E-222 [10]	Let There Be Love	1953	200.00
❑ E-3348 [M]	Let There Be Love	1956	80.00
—Yellow label			
❑ E-3348 [M]	Let There Be Love	1960	40.00
—Black label			
❑ E-272 [10]	Little Girl Blue	1955	200.00
❑ E-3347 [M]	Little Girl Blue	1956	80.00
—Yellow label			
❑ E-3347 [M]	Little Girl Blue	1960	40.00
—Black label			
❑ E-3468 [M]	Merry Christmas from Joni	1956	120.00
—Yellow label original			
❑ E-3468 [M]	Merry Christmas from Joni	1960	60.00
—Black label reissue			
❑ E-3885 [M]	More Joni Hits	1960	50.00
❑ SE-3885 [S]	More Joni Hits	1960	60.00
❑ E-4200 [M]	My Favorite Things	1963	40.00
❑ SE-4200 [S]	My Favorite Things	1963	50.00
❑ E-4248 [M]	Put On a Happy Face	1964	40.00
❑ SE-4248 [S]	Put On a Happy Face	1964	50.00
❑ E-4158 [M]	Something for the Boys	1963	40.00
❑ SE-4158 [S]	Something for the Boys	1963	50.00
❑ E-3533 [M]	Songs by Jerome Kern and Harry Warren	1957	80.00
—Yellow label			
❑ E-3533 [M]	Songs by Jerome Kern and Harry Warren	1960	40.00
—Black label			
❑ E-3449 [M]	Songs by Victor Young and Frank Loesser	1956	80.00
—Yellow label			
❑ E-3449 [M]	Songs by Victor Young and Frank Loesser	1960	40.00
—Black label			
❑ E-3739 [M]	Songs of Hank Williams	1959	80.00
—Yellow label			
❑ E-3739 [M]	Songs of Hank Williams	1960	40.00
—Black label			
❑ SE-3739 [S]	Songs of Hank Williams	1959	120.00
—Yellow label			
❑ SE-3739 [S]	Songs of Hank Williams	1960	50.00
—Black label			
❑ E-3991 [M]	The Mood Is Blue	1961	50.00
❑ SE-3991 [S]	The Mood Is Blue	1961	60.00
❑ E-3990 [M]	The Mood Is Romance	1961	50.00
❑ SE-3990 [S]	The Mood Is Romance	1961	60.00
❑ E-3987 [M]	The Mood Is Swinging	1961	50.00
❑ SE-3987 [S]	The Mood Is Swinging	1961	60.00
❑ E-4151 [M]	The Very Best of Joni James	1963	40.00
❑ SE-4151 [S]	The Very Best of Joni James	1963	50.00
❑ E-4182 [M]	Three O'Clock in the Morning	1963	40.00
❑ SE-4182 [S]	Three O'Clock in the Morning	1963	50.00
❑ E-3623 [M]	Ti Voglio Bene	1958	80.00
—Yellow label			
❑ E-3623 [M]	Ti Voglio Bene	1960	40.00
—Black label			
❑ E-3240 [M]	When I Fall in Love	1955	80.00
—Yellow label			
❑ E-3240 [M]	When I Fall in Love	1960	40.00
—Black label			

JAMES, LEONARD

Number	Title	Yr	NM
DECCA			
❑ DL8772 [M]	Boppin' and a-Strollin'	1958	50.00

JAMES, RICK

Number	Title	Yr	NM
GORDY			
❑ G7-984 [B]	Bustin' Out of L. Seven	1979	15.00
❑ 6043GL	Cold Blooded	1983	10.00
❑ G7-981 [B]	Come Get It!	1978	15.00
❑ G8-990 [B]	Fire It Up	1979	15.00
❑ G8-995	Garden of Love	1980	12.00
❑ 6135GL	Glow	1985	10.00
❑ 6095GL	Reflections	1984	10.00
❑ G8-1002	Street Songs	1981	10.00
❑ 6005GL	Throwin' Down	1982	10.00

Number	Title	Yr	NM
MOTOWN			
❑ 5263ML	Come Get It!	198?	10.00
❑ 5382ML	Greatest Hits	1986	10.00
REPRISE			
❑ 25659	Wonderful	1988	12.00
UNIVERSAL MOTOWN			
❑ 5316010	Street Songs	2009	25.00

JAMES, SKIP

Number	Title	Yr	NM
VANGUARD			
❑ VSD-79273	Devil Got My Woman	1968	30.00
❑ VRS-9219 [M]	Skip James Today!	1966	30.00
❑ VSD-79219 [S]	Skip James Today!	1966	30.00

JAMES, SONNY

Number	Title	Yr	NM
ABC			
❑ AC-30027	The ABC Collection	1976	15.00
CAPITOL			
❑ ST-629	#1	1970	18.00
❑ T2884 [M]	A World of Our Own	1968	30.00
❑ ST2884 [S]	A World of Our Own	1968	18.00
❑ T2415 [M]	Behind the Tear	1965	25.00
❑ ST2415 [S]	Behind the Tear	1965	30.00
❑ ST-111	Born to Be with You	1968	18.00
❑ SWBB-258	Close-Up	1969	25.00
—Combines ST 2500 and ST 2788 in one package			
❑ ST-734	Empty Arms	1971	18.00
❑ ST2937	Heaven Says Hello	1968	18.00
❑ ST-849	Here Comes Honey Again	1971	18.00
❑ T988 [M]	Honey	1958	50.00
—Turquoise label			
❑ T988 [M]	Honey	1964	25.00
—Black label with colorband, logo on top			
❑ T2317 [M]	I'll Keep Holding On	1965	25.00
❑ ST2317 [S]	I'll Keep Holding On	1965	30.00
❑ T2788 [M]	I'll Never Find Another You	1967	25.00
❑ ST2788 [S]	I'll Never Find Another You	1967	18.00
❑ ST-432	It's Just a Matter of Time	1970	18.00
❑ ST 8-0432	It's Just a Matter of Time	1970	25.00
—Capitol Record Club edition			
❑ T2589 [M]	My Christmas Dream	1966	25.00
❑ ST2589 [S]	My Christmas Dream	1966	30.00
❑ ST 470	My Love/Don't Keep Me Hangin' On	1970	18.00
❑ T2703 [M]	Need You	1967	25.00
❑ ST2703 [S]	Need You	1967	18.00
❑ ST-193	Only the Lonely	1969	18.00
❑ ST 8-0193	Only the Lonely	1969	25.00
—Capitol Record Club edition			
❑ T867 [M]	Sonny	1957	50.00
—Turquoise label			
❑ T867 [M]	Sonny	1964	25.00
—Black label with colorband, logo on top			
❑ SQBO-91357	That Special Country Feeling	196?	30.00
—Capitol Record Club exclusive			
❑ ST-11067	That's Why I Love You Like I Do	1972	18.00
❑ ST-320	The Astrodome Presents In Person Sonny James	1969	18.00
❑ T2615 [M]	The Best of Sonny James	1966	18.00
❑ ST2615 [S]	The Best of Sonny James	1966	25.00
—Black Starline label			
❑ SM-2615	The Best of Sonny James	197?	12.00
❑ SKAO-144	The Best of Sonny James Vol. 2	1969	18.00
❑ ST-11013	The Biggest Hits of Sonny James	1972	18.00
❑ SM-11013	The Biggest Hits of Sonny James	197?	12.00
❑ ST-11144	The Gentleman from the South	1973	15.00
❑ T2017 [M]	The Minute You're Gone	1964	25.00
❑ ST2017 [S]	The Minute You're Gone	1964	30.00
❑ ST-804	The Sensational Sonny James	1971	18.00
❑ T779 [M]	The Southern Gentleman	1957	50.00
—Turquoise label			
❑ T779 [M]	The Southern Gentleman	1964	25.00
—Black label with colorband, logo on top			
❑ T1178 [M]	This Is Sonny James	1959	40.00
—Black label with colorband, logo at left			
❑ T1178 [M]	This Is Sonny James	1964	25.00
—Black label with colorband, logo on top			
❑ T2561 [M]	Till the Last Leaf Shall Fall	1966	25.00
❑ ST2561 [S]	Till the Last Leaf Shall Fall	1966	30.00
❑ ST-11108	Traces	1972	15.00
❑ T2500 [M]	True Love's a Blessing	1966	25.00
❑ ST2500 [S]	True Love's a Blessing	1966	30.00
❑ ST-11196	Young Love	1973	15.00
❑ T2209 [M]	You're the Only World I Know	1965	25.00
❑ ST2209 [S]	You're the Only World I Know	1965	30.00
❑ STBB-535	You're the Only World I Know/I'll Never Find Another You	1970	25.00
—Combines the two listed albums in one package			
COLUMBIA			
❑ PC34035	200 Years of Country Music	1976	15.00
❑ KC33428	A Little Bit South of Saskatoon/Little Band of Gold	1975	15.00
❑ KC33056	A Mi Esposa Con Amor (To My Wife with Love)	1974	15.00
❑ PC33846	Country Male Artist of the Decade	1975	15.00
❑ KC32291	If She Just Helps Me Get Over You	1973	15.00
❑ KC32805	Is It Wrong	1974	15.00
❑ KC35626	Sonny James' Greatest Hits	1978	15.00
❑ PC34706	Sonny James In Prison, In Person	1977	15.00
❑ KC32028	Sonny James Sings the Greatest Country Hits of '72	1973	15.00
❑ KC33477	The Guitars of Sonny James	1975	15.00
❑ KC35379	This Is the Love	1978	15.00
❑ PC34309	When Something Is Wrong with My Baby	1976	15.00
❑ KC31646	When the Snow Is On the Roses	1972	15.00
❑ CG33627	When the Snow Is On the Roses/If She Just Helps Me Get Over You	1975	18.00
❑ PC34472	You're Free to Go	1977	15.00
DOT			
❑ DLP3462 [M]	Young Love	1962	40.00
❑ DLP25462 [S]	Young Love	1962	50.00
DOT/MCA			
❑ 39087	Sonny James	198?	12.00
HILLTOP			
❑ 6067	Invisible Tears	1969	12.00
❑ 6079	Timberline	1969	12.00
PICKWICK			
❑ SPC-3594	Young Love	1977	10.00
RCA CAMDEN			
❑ CAL-2140 [M]	Young Love	1967	18.00
❑ CAS-2140 [S]	Young Love	1967	15.00

JAMES, STAFFORD

Number	Title	Yr	NM
RED RECORD			
❑ VPA-142	Stafford James Ensemble	198?	15.00

JAMES, TOMMY, AND THE SHONDELLS

Number	Title	Yr	NM
RHINO			
❑ R1-70920	Anthology	1989	18.00
ROULETTE			
❑ SR42030	Cellophane Symphony	1969	25.00
❑ SR42023	Crimson and Clover	1969	25.00
❑ SR25357 [S]	Gettin' Together	1968	30.00
❑ R25357 [M]	Gettin' Together	1968	40.00
❑ R25336 [M]	Hanky Panky	1966	30.00
❑ SR25336 [P]	Hanky Panky	1966	30.00
—Hanky Panky" is rechanneled			
❑ R25353 [M]	I Think We're Alone Now	1967	40.00
❑ SR25353 [P]	I Think We're Alone Now	1967	30.00
—Footprints cover; "I Think We're Alone Now" is rechanneled			
❑ SR25353 [P]	I Think We're Alone Now	1967	18.00
—Photo cover			
❑ R25344 [M]	It's Only Love	1967	40.00
❑ SR25344 [S]	It's Only Love	1967	30.00
❑ SR42012 [B]	Mony Mony	1968	25.00
❑ R25355 [M]	Something Special! The Best of Tommy James & The Shondells	1968	80.00
❑ SR42005	Something Special! The Best of Tommy James & The Shondells	1968	18.00
❑ SR25355 [S]	Something Special! The Best of Tommy James & The Shondells	1968	30.00
❑ SR42040	The Best of Tommy James & The Shondells	1969	25.00
—Original versions are in a Unipak (gatefold must be opened to remove record)			
❑ SR42040	The Best of Tommy James & The Shondells	197?	18.00
—Later versions have gatefold covers, but record can be removed without opening it			
❑ SR42044	Travelin'	1970	18.00
SCEPTER CITATION			
❑ CTN-18025	The Best of Tommy James and the Shondells	1973	12.00

JAMES, TOMMY

Number	Title	Yr	NM
FANTASY			
❑ 9509	In Touch	1976	15.00
❑ 9532	Midnight Rider	1977	15.00
MILLENNIUM			
❑ BXL1-7758	Easy to Love	1981	12.00
❑ BXL1-7748	Three Times in Love	1980	12.00
ROULETTE			
❑ SR-3001	Christian of the World	1971	18.00
❑ SR-3007	My Head, My Bed, My Red Guitar	1972	18.00
❑ SR-42061	Tommy James	1970	18.00

JAMES GANG, THE (1)

Number	Title	Yr	NM
ABC			
❑ X-801	16 Greatest Hits	1973	18.00
❑ X-733	James Gang Live in Concert	1971	15.00
❑ S-711 [B]	James Gang Rides Again	1970	30.00
—First pressing with a short version of Ravel's "Bolero" as part of the song "The Bomber"; exists on both promos and early stock copies; no "RE-1" in trail-off wax			
❑ S-711	James Gang Rides Again	1970	15.00
—Standard pressing without "Bolero" as part of "The Bomber"; "RE-1" in trail-off wax			
❑ X-760	Passin' Thru	1972	15.00
❑ X-741	Straight Shooter	1972	15.00
❑ ABCX-774	The Best of the James Gang Featuring Joe Walsh	1973	15.00
—Most copies of this LP contain the edited version of "The Bomber." The full title of the LP is on the spine, and the record's trail-off wax has the number "ABCX-774-A-RE-1".			
❑ ABCX-774	The Best of the James Gang Featuring Joe Walsh	1973	25.00
—A few copies of this LP contain the full version of "The Bomber" with the "Bolero" excerpt. The words "The Best Of" do NOT appear on the spine, and the record's trail-off wax has the number "ABCX-774-A".			
❑ X-721	Thirds	1971	15.00
❑ S-688	Yer' Album	1970	15.00
ATCO			
❑ SD7037	Bang	1973	12.00
❑ SD 36-141	Jesse Come Home	1976	12.00
❑ SD 36-102	Miami	1974	12.00
❑ SD 36-112	Newborn	1975	12.00
BLUESWAY			
❑ BLS-6034 [B]	Yer' Album	1969	30.00
MCA			
❑ 6012	16 Greatest Hits	1980	12.00
—Reissue			
❑ 37111	James Gang Rides Again	1980	10.00
—Reissue			
❑ 37112	The Best of the James Gang Featuring Joe Walsh	1980	10.00
—Reissue			

JAN AND DEAN

Number	Title	Yr	NM
❑ CS9461 [S]	Save for a Rainy Day	1967	4000.00
—LP not known to exist, but an acetate does, and possibly an import on this label and number; VG value 2000; VG+ value 3000			
DEADMAN'S CURVE			
❑ (no #)0	Live at the Keystone Berkeley	1981	50.00
—Plain jacket with front and back cover inserts			
❑ (no #)0	Live at the Keystone Berkeley	1981	30.00
—With front and back covers pasted on			
DORE			
❑ LP-101 [M]	Jan and Dean	1960	400.00
—Original with blue label			
❑ LP-101	Jan and Dean	197?	18.00
—Reissue with black label			
❑ LP-101	Jan and Dean Bonus Photo	1960	120.00
J&D			
❑ 101 [M]	Save for a Rainy Day	1967	300.00
—Private pressing by Dean Torrence of unreleased Columbia album			
LIBERTY			
❑ LRP-3403 [M]	Command Performance/Live in Person	1965	30.00
❑ LST-7403 [S]	Command Performance/Live in Person	1965	40.00
❑ LN-10011	Dead Man's Curve	1980	10.00
—Budget-line reissue			
❑ LRP-3361 [M]	Dead Man's Curve/The New Girl in School	1964	60.00
—Black and white cover with pink tint			
❑ LRP-3361 [M]	Dead Man's Curve/The New Girl in School	1964	40.00
—Full-color cover			
❑ LST-7361 [S]	Dead Man's Curve/The New Girl in School	1964	50.00
—Black and white cover with pink tint			
❑ LST-7361 [S]	Dead Man's Curve/The New Girl in School	1964	40.00
—Full-color cover			
❑ LRP-3339 [M]	Drag City	1963	40.00
❑ LST-7339 [S]	Drag City	1963	50.00
❑ LRP-3441 [M]	Filet of Soul	1966	30.00
❑ LST-7441 [S]	Filet of Soul	1966	40.00
❑ LRP-3431 [M]	Folk 'N' Roll	1965	30.00
❑ LST-7431 [S]	Folk 'N' Roll	1965	40.00
❑ LRP-3444 [M]	Jan and Dean Meet Batman	1966	50.00
❑ LST-7444 [S]	Jan and Dean Meet Batman	1966	70.00
❑ LRP-3248 [M]	Jan and Dean's Golden Hits	1962	30.00
❑ LST-7248 [S]	Jan and Dean's Golden Hits	1962	40.00
❑ LRP-3417 [M]	Jan and Dean's Golden Hits, Volume 2	1965	30.00
❑ LST-7417 [S]	Jan and Dean's Golden Hits, Volume 2	1965	30.00
❑ LRP-3460 [M]	Jan and Dean's Golden Hits, Volume 3	1966	30.00
❑ LST-7460 [S]	Jan and Dean's Golden Hits, Volume 3	1966	30.00
❑ LRP-3294 [M]	Jan and Dean Take Linda Surfin'	1963	50.00
—With correct title on LP spine			
❑ LST-7294 [S]	Jan and Dean Take Linda Surfin'	1963	80.00
—With correct title on LP spine			
❑ LRP-3294 [M]	Jan and Dean Take Linda Surfin'	1963	60.00
—With title on spine "Mr. Bass Man Takes Linda Surfin'			

Number	Title	Yr	NM
❏ LST-7294 [S]	Jan and Dean Take Linda Surfin'	1963	100.00
— With title on spine "Mr. Bass Man Takes Linda Surfin'"			
❏ LRP-3458 [M]	Popsicle	1966	30.00
❏ LST-7458 [S]	Popsicle	1966	40.00
❏ LRP-3368 [M]	Ride the Wild Surf	1964	30.00
❏ LST-7368 [S]	Ride the Wild Surf	1964	40.00
❏ LRP-3314 [M]	Surf City and Other Swingin' Cities	1963	40.00
❏ LST-7314 [S]	Surf City and Other Swingin' Cities	1963	50.00
❏ LN-10115	The Best of Jan and Dean	1981	10.00
❏ LRP-3377 [M]	The Little Old Lady from Pasadena	1964	30.00
❏ LST-7377 [S]	The Little Old Lady from Pasadena	1964	40.00
❏ LN-10151	The Little Old Lady from Pasadena	1982	10.00
— Budget-line reissue			
❏ LRP-3361 [M]	The New Girl in School/ Dead Man's Curve	1964	25.00
— Reissue with reversed title			
❏ LST-7361 [S]	The New Girl in School/ Dead Man's Curve	1964	30.00
— Reissue with reversed title			

PAIR
| ❏ PDL2-1071 | California Gold | 1986 | 15.00 |

RHINO
| ❏ RNDA1498 | One Summer Night -- Live | 1982 | 25.00 |

SUNDAZED
❏ LP5040	Jan and Dean (The Dore Album)	1996	12.00
— Reissue of Dore LP on colored vinyl with extra tracks and poster			
❏ LP5022	Save for a Rainy Day	1996	18.00
— First release to the general public; colored vinyl			

SUNSET
| ❏ SUM-1156 [M] | Jan and Dean | 1967 | 18.00 |
| ❏ SUS-5156 [S] | Jan and Dean | 1967 | 18.00 |

UNITED ARTISTS
❏ UAS-9961	Anthology (Legendary Masters Series, Vol. 3)	1971	30.00
❏ UA-LA341-H2	Gotta Take That One Last Ride	1974	18.00
❏ UA-LA443-E	The Very Best of Jan and Dean	1975	12.00
❏ UA-LA515-E	The Very Best of Jan and Dean, Volume 2	1975	12.00

JAN AND LORRAINE

ABC
| ❏ S-691 | Gypsy People | 1969 | 30.00 |

JANE'S ADDICTION

TRIPLE X
| ❏ 51004 [B] | Jane's Addiction | 1987 | 35.00 |

WARNER BROS.
❏ 25727	Nothing's Shocking	1988	15.00
❏ 25993 [R]	Ritual de lo Habitual	1990	30.00
— First cover, with drawing			
❏ 26223	Ritual de lo Habitual	1990	15.00
Second cover, all white with text of First Amendment			
❏ PRO-A-3369 [DJ]	Words and Music	1990	10.00
— Promo-only interview album			
— "shaded dog" label			

JANIS, JOHNNY

ABC-PARAMOUNT
| ❏ ABC-140 [M] | For the First Time | 1956 | 60.00 |

COLUMBIA
| ❏ CL1674 [M] | The Start of Something Big | 1961 | 30.00 |
| ❏ CS8474 [S] | The Start of Something Big | 1961 | 30.00 |

MONUMENT
| ❏ MLP-8036 [M] | Once in a Blue Moon | 1965 | 18.00 |
| ❏ SLP-18036 [S] | Once in a Blue Moon | 1965 | 25.00 |

JANSSEN, DAVID

EPIC
| ❏ LN24150 [M] | Hidden Island | 1965 | 25.00 |
| ❏ BN26150 [S] | Hidden Island | 1965 | 30.00 |

JAPAN

ARIOLA AMERICA
| ❏ SW-50037 | Adolescent Sex | 1978 | 25.00 |
| ❏ SW-50047 [EP] | Obscure Alternatives | 1979 | 18.00 |

VIRGIN/EPIC
| ❏ ARE37914 | Japan | 1982 | 12.00 |

JARRE, JEAN-MICHEL

DREYFUS/POLYDOR
❏ 833170-1	Concerts Houston/Lyon	1987	12.00
❏ 829456-1	Equinoxe	1987	10.00
❏ 829457-1	Magnetic Fields	1987	10.00
❏ 827885-1	Oxygene	1987	10.00
❏ 829125-1	Rendez-Vous	1986	10.00
❏ 811551-1	The Concerts in China	1983	15.00
❏ 823763-1	Zoolook	1984	10.00

MOBILE FIDELITY
❏ 1-227	Equinoxe	1995	50.00
— Audiophile vinyl			
❏ 1-212	Oxygene	1995	50.00
— Audiophile vinyl			

POLYDOR
❏ PD-1-6175	Equinoxe	1979	12.00
❏ PD-1-6225	Magnetic Fields	1981	12.00
❏ PD-1-6112	Oxygene	1977	12.00

JARREAU, AL

BAINBRIDGE
| ❏ BT-6237 | Al Jarreau 1965 | 1982 | 10.00 |

MOBILE FIDELITY
| ❏ 1-019 | All Fly Home | 1980 | 25.00 |
| — Audiophile vinyl | | | |

REPRISE
❏ MS2248	Glow	1976	12.00
❏ 25778	Heart's Horizon	1988	12.00
❏ MS2224	We Got By	1975	12.00

WARNER BROS.
❏ 25331	Al Jarreau in London	1985	10.00
❏ BSK3229	All Fly Home	1978	12.00
❏ BSK3576	Breakin' Away	1981	10.00
❏ 25106	High Crime	1984	10.00
❏ 23801	Jarreau	1983	10.00
❏ 25477	L Is for Lover	1986	10.00
❏ 2WS3052	Look to the Rainbow/Live in Europe	1977	15.00
❏ BSK3434	This Time	1980	10.00

JARRETT, KEITH, AND JACK DEJOHNETTE

ECM
❏ 1021ST	Ruta & Daitya	1973	18.00
— Original issue; made in Germany?			
❏ ECM-1-1021	Ruta & Daitya	197?	15.00
— Manufactured by Polydor			

JARRETT, KEITH

ABC IMPULSE!
❏ ASH-9305	Backhand	1975	25.00
❏ IA-9334	Bop-Be	1977	15.00
❏ AS-9331	Byablue	1977	15.00
❏ ASD-9301	Death and the Flower	1974	18.00
❏ AS-9240	Fort Yawuh	1973	18.00
❏ ASD-9315	Mysteries	1976	15.00
❏ ASD-9322	Shades	1976	15.00
❏ IA-9348	The Best of Keith Jarrett	1978	12.00
❏ AS-9274	Treasure Island	1974	18.00

ATLANTIC
❏ SD1612	Birth	1972	18.00
❏ SD1673	El Juicio (The Judgment)	1975	15.00
❏ SD1596	Mourning of a Star	1971	25.00
❏ SD8808	Somewhere Before	1981	15.00
— Reissue of Vortex 2012			

COLUMBIA
❏ KG31580	Expectations	1972	25.00
— Original edition			
❏ PG31580	Expectations	198?	15.00
— Reissue with new prefix; some with bar code on cover			

ECM
❏ ECM-1-1070	Arbour Zena	1976	15.00
— Distributed by Polydor			
❏ ECM1-1070	Arbour Zena	197?	12.00
— Distributed by Warner Bros. (reissue)			
❏ 1050ST	Belonging	1974	18.00
— Original, made in Germany?			
❏ 1344/5	Book of Ways	1986	15.00
— Made in Germany			
❏ ECM1-1175	Celestial Hawk	1981	12.00
— Distributed by Warner Bros.			
❏ 1392	Changeless	1990	30.00
— Made in Germany			
❏ 25007	Changes	1984	12.00
— Distributed by Warner Bros.			
❏ 1276	Changes	1984	18.00
— Made in Germany (U.S. version issued on 25007)			
❏ ECM1-1228	Concerts	1982	12.00
— Abridged version of 1227; distributed by Warner Bros.			
❏ ECM3-1227	Concerts	1982	25.00
— Distributed by Warner Bros.; box set			
❏ 1379	Dark Intervals	1988	15.00
— Made in Germany			
❏ ECM-T-1150	Eyes of the Heart	1979	18.00
— Distributed by Warner Bros.			
❏ 1017ST	Facing You	1973	18.00
— Original edition, made in Germany?			
❏ ECM 1-1017	Facing You	197?	15.00
— U.S. pressing, distributed by Polydor			
❏ ECM1-1174	G.I. Gurdjieff Sacred Hymns	1981	12.00
— Distributed by Warner Bros.			
❏ ECM-2-1086	Hymns/Spheres	1977	18.00
— Distributed by Polydor			
❏ 1033/4 ST	In the Light	1976	25.00
— Original edition			
❏ ECM 2-1033	In the Light	197?	18.00

— Reissue with new prefix, distributed by Polydor			
❏ ECM-D-1201	Invocations/The Moth and the Flame	1981	15.00
— Distributed by Warner Bros.			
❏ 1049ST	Luminessence	1974	18.00
— Original, made in Germany			
❏ ECM1-1049	Luminessence	197?	15.00
— Distributed by Warner Bros.			
❏ ECM1-1115	My Song	1978	15.00
— Distributed by Warner Bros.			
❏ ECM2-1171	Nude Ants	1980	18.00
— Distributed by Warner Bros.			
❏ 1382	Personal Mountains	1989	18.00
— Made in Germany			
❏ 1035/6/7 ST	Solo Concerts	1974	30.00
— Original issue, made in Germany?			
❏ ECM-3-1035	Solo Concerts	197?	25.00
— Distributed by Polydor			
❏ 1333/4	Spirits	1986	25.00
— Made in Germany			
❏ ECM-2-1090	Staircase	1977	18.00
— Distributed by Polydor			
❏ 23793	Standards, Volume 1	1983	15.00
— Distributed by Warner Bros.			
❏ 1255	Standards, Volume 1	1983	18.00
— Made in Germany			
❏ 25023	Standards, Volume 2	1985	15.00
— Distributed by Warner Bros.			
❏ 1289	Standards, Volume 2	1985	18.00
— Made in Germany			
❏ 25041	Standards Live	1986	15.00
— Distributed by Warner Bros.			
❏ 1317	Standards Live	1986	18.00
— Made in Germany			
❏ 1360/1	Still Live	1988	30.00
— Made in Germany			
❏ ECM-1-1085	Survivors' Suite	1977	15.00
— Distributed by Polydor			
❏ ECM-2-1064	The Koln Concert	1976	18.00
— Distributed by Polydor			
❏ 1100	The Sun Bear Concerts	1977	150.00
— Made in Germany			

MCA
❏ 29048	Bop-Be	1980	12.00
— Reissue of Impulse 9334			
❏ 29047	Byablue	1980	12.00
— Reissue of Impulse 9331			
❏ 29046	Death and the Flower	1980	12.00
— Reissue of Impulse 9301			
❏ 29044	Fort Yawuh	1980	12.00
— Reissue of Impulse 9240			
❏ 2-4125	Great Moments with Keith Jarrett	1981	25.00
❏ 29045	Treasure Island	1980	12.00
— Reissue of Impulse 9274			
❏ 39106	Treasure Island	198?	30.00
— Another reissue of Impulse 9274			

VORTEX
❏ 2006	Life Between the Exit Signs	1969	30.00
❏ 2008	Restoration Ruin	1969	30.00
❏ 2012	Somewhere Before	1970	30.00

JARRETT, KEITH/MCCOY TYNER

AT EASE
| ❏ MD-11119 | Masters of the Piano | 1978 | 25.00 |
| — Record made for sale at military bases | | | |

JARS OF CLAY

ESSENTIAL/SILVERTONE
| ❏ 83061-0088-1 | Much Afraid | 1997 | 18.00 |

JARVIS, JOHN

CRYSTAL CLEAR
| ❏ 8004 | Evolutions | 1980 | 25.00 |
| — Direct-to-disc recording | | | |

MCA
❏ 5690	So Far So Good	1986	12.00
❏ 5963	Something Constructive	1987	12.00
❏ 6263	Whatever Works	1988	12.00

JASEN, DAVE

BLUE GOOSE
| ❏ 3001 | Fingerbustin' Ragtime | 197? | 15.00 |
| ❏ 3002 | Rompin', Stompin' Ragtime | 197? | 15.00 |

EUPHONIC
| ❏ 1206 | Creative Ragtime | 196? | 15.00 |

FOLKWAYS
| ❏ FC-3561 | Rip-Roarin' Ragtime | 1977 | 12.00 |

JASMINE

WEST 54
| ❏ 8007 | Jasmine | 1980 | 15.00 |

Number	Title	Yr	NM

JASPAR, BOBBY

EMARCY
❏ MG-36105 [M]	Bobby Jaspar and His All Stars	1957	80.00

RIVERSIDE
❏ RLP 12-240 [M]	Bobby Jaspar	1957	80.00
— White label, blue print			
❏ RLP 12-240 [M]	Bobby Jaspar	1959	40.00
— Blue label, microphone label at top			
❏ 6156	Tenor and Flute	198?	15.00

SWING
❏ SW-8413	Bobby Jaspar In Paris	1986	12.00

JASPER WRATH

SUNFLOWER
❏ SNF-5003 [B]	Jasper Wrath	1971	50.00

JAY AND THE AMERICANS

LIBERTY
❏ LM-1010	Jay and the Americans Greatest Hits	1981	10.00
— Another reissue			

RHINO
❏ RNLP70224 [B]	All-Time Greatest Hits	1986	15.00

SUNSET
❏ SUS-5278	Early American Hits	1969	18.00
❏ SUS-5252 [B]	Jay and the Americans!!	1968	15.00

UNART
❏ M-20018 [M]	Jay and the Americans!!	196?	15.00
❏ MS-21018 [S]	Jay and the Americans!!	196?	15.00

UNITED ARTISTS
❏ UAL-3300 [M]	At the Café Wha?	1963	50.00
❏ UAS-6300 [S]	At the Café Wha?	1963	100.00
❏ UAL-3417 [M]	Blockbusters	1965	30.00
❏ UAS-6417 [S]	Blockbusters	1965	30.00
❏ UAS-6762	Capture the Moment	1970	25.00
❏ UAL-3407 [M]	Come a Little Bit Closer	1964	30.00
❏ UAS-6407 [S]	Come a Little Bit Closer	1964	30.00
❏ UAL-3453 [M]	Jay and the Americans Greatest Hits	1965	25.00
❏ UAS-6453 [S]	Jay and the Americans Greatest Hits	1965	30.00
❏ ST-90814 [S]	Jay and the Americans Greatest Hits	1966	30.00
— Capitol Record Club edition			
❏ LM-1010	Jay and the Americans Greatest Hits	1980	12.00
— Reissue			
❏ UAL-3555 [M]	Jay and the Americans Greatest Hits, Volume 2	1966	25.00
❏ UAS-6555 [S]	Jay and the Americans Greatest Hits, Volume 2	1966	25.00
❏ ST-90815 [S]	Jay and the Americans Greatest Hits, Volume 2	1966	30.00
— Capitol Record Club edition			
❏ UAL-3534 [M]	Livin' Above Your Head	1966	25.00
❏ UAS-6534 [S]	Livin' Above Your Head	1966	30.00
❏ UAS-6671	Sands of Time	1969	25.00
❏ UAL-3222 [M]	She Cried	1962	50.00
❏ UAS-6222 [S]	She Cried	1962	100.00
❏ UAL-3474 [M]	Sunday and Me	1966	25.00
❏ UAS-6474 [S]	Sunday and Me	1966	30.00
❏ UA-LA357-E	The Very Best of Jay and the Americans	1975	15.00
❏ UAL-3562 [M]	Try Some of This!	1967	25.00
❏ UAS-6562 [S]	Try Some of This!	1967	40.00
❏ UAS-6719	Wax Museum	1970	25.00
❏ UAS-6751	Wax Museum, Volume 2	1970	25.00

JAY AND THE TECHNIQUES

SMASH
❏ MGS-27095 [M]	Apples, Peaches, Pumpkin Pie	1967	50.00
❏ SRS-67095 [S]	Apples, Peaches, Pumpkin Pie	1967	30.00
— First cover with "live" photo of the band			
❏ SRS-67095 [S]	Apples, Peaches, Pumpkin Pie	1968	25.00
— Second cover with "posed" photo of the band			
❏ SRS-67102 [S]	Love Lost and Found	1968	30.00
❏ MGS-27102 [M]	Love Lost and Found	1968	60.00
— Mono may be white-label promo only			

JAYE, JERRY

HI
❏ SHL-32102	Honky Tonk Women Love Redneck Men	1976	15.00
❏ HL-12038 [M]	My Girl Josephine	1967	25.00
❏ SHL-32038 [S]	My Girl Josephine	1967	25.00

JAYHAWKS, THE (2)

AMERICAN
❏ 43114	Sound of Lies	1997	25.00
❏ 43006	Tomorrow the Green Grass	1995	25.00

BUNKHOUSE
❏ 7001	The Jayhawks	1986	80.00

TWIN/TONE
❏ TTR89151	Blue Earth	1989	18.00

JAYNETTS, THE

TUFF
❏ LP13 [M]	Sally Go 'Round the Roses	1963	300.00

JAZZ ARTISTS GUILD, THE

CANDID
❏ CD-8022 [M]	Newport Rebels	1960	40.00
❏ CS-9022 [S]	Newport Rebels	1960	50.00

JAZZ BROTHERS, THE

RIVERSIDE
❏ RLP-371 [M]	Hey, Baby!	1961	30.00
❏ RS-9371 [S]	Hey, Baby!	1961	30.00
❏ RLP-335 [M]	Jazz Brothers	1960	30.00
❏ RS-9335 [S]	Jazz Brothers	1960	30.00
❏ RLP-405 [M]	Spring Fever	1962	30.00
❏ RS-9405 [S]	Spring Fever	1962	30.00

JAZZ CITY

RAHMP
❏ 2	Jazz City	197?	25.00

JAZZ CITY ALL-STARS, THE

BETHLEHEM
❏ BCP-79 [M]	Jazz City Presents the Jazz City All-Stars	1957	50.00

JAZZ COMPOSERS ORCHESTRA

JCOA
❏ LP-1001/2	Jazz Composers Orchestra	1968	40.00

JAZZ CONTEMPORARIES

STRATA-EAST
❏ SES1972-2	Reasons in Tonality	1972	18.00

JAZZ CORPS, THE

PACIFIC JAZZ
❏ PJ-10116 [M]	The Jazz Corps Under the Direction of Tommy Peltier	1967	30.00
❏ ST-20110 [S]	The Jazz Corps Under the Direction of Tommy Peltier	1967	18.00
❏ LN-10131	The Jazz Corps Under the Direction of Tommy Peltier	198?	12.00
— Budget-line reissue			

JAZZ COURIERS, THE

CARLTON
❏ LP 12-116 [M]	The Couriers of Jazz	1959	50.00
❏ ST 12-116 [S]	The Couriers of Jazz	1959	40.00

JAZZLAND
❏ JLP-34 [M]	Message from Britain	1961	30.00
❏ JLP-934 [S]	Message from Britain	1961	30.00

WHIPPET
❏ WLP-700 [M]	The Jazz Couriers	1956	120.00

JAZZ EXPONENTS, THE

ARGO
❏ LP-622 [M]	The Jazz Exponents	1958	40.00

JAZZ FIVE, THE

RIVERSIDE
❏ RLP-361 [M]	The Hooter	1961	30.00
❏ RS-9361 [S]	The Hooter	1961	30.00

JAZZ INTERACTIONS ORCHESTRA, THE

VERVE
❏ V-8731 [M]	Jazzhattan Suite	1967	25.00
❏ V6-8731 [S]	Jazzhattan Suite	1967	15.00

JAZZ LAB, THE

COLUMBIA
❏ CL998 [M]	Jazz Lab	1957	150.00
❏ CL998 [M]	Jazz Lab	199?	15.00
— 180-gram reissue			
❏ CL1058 [M]	Modern Jazz Perspective/ Jazz Lab, Volume 2	1957	150.00

JAZZLAND
❏ JLP-1 [M]	Jazz Lab	1960	50.00
❏ JLP-901 [S]	Jazz Lab	1960	60.00

JOSIE
❏ JOZ-3500 [M]	Gigi Gryce and Donald Byrd	1962	40.00
— Reissue of Jubilee album			
❏ JS-3500 [R]	Gigi Gryce and Donald Byrd	196?	25.00

JUBILEE
❏ JLP-1059 [M]	Jazz Lab	1958	100.00

RIVERSIDE
❏ RLP 12-229 [M]	Gigi Gryce and the Jazz Lab Quintet	1957	100.00
— White label, blue print			
❏ RLP 12-229 [M]	Gigi Gryce and the Jazz Lab Quintet	1959	50.00
— Blue label, microphone logo at top			
❏ RLP-1110 [S]	Gigi Gryce and the Jazz Lab Quintet	1959	50.00

JAZZ MEMBERS BIG BAND

SEA BREEZE
❏ SB-2028	Live at Fitzgerald	1986	12.00
❏ SB-2014	May Day	1985	12.00

JAZZ O'MANIACS, THE

STOMP OFF
❏ SOS-1046	Have You Ever Felt This Way	198?	12.00
❏ SOS-1071	Sweet Mumtaz	1984	12.00

JAZZ PIANO QUARTET, THE

RCA VICTOR
❏ CPL1-0680	Let It Happen	1974	18.00

JAZZ SYMPHONICS

RENFRO
❏ LP-12369	The Beginning	1968	60.00

JAZZPICKERS, THE

EMARCY
❏ MG-36123 [M]	Command Performance	1958	50.00
❏ MG-36111 [M]	The Jazzpickers	1957	50.00

MERCURY
❏ SR-80013 [S]	For Moderns Only	1959	40.00

JAZZTET, THE

ARGO
❏ LP-672 [M]	Big City Sounds	1961	40.00
❏ LPS-672 [S]	Big City Sounds	1961	50.00
❏ LP-664 [M]	Meet the Jazztet	1960	50.00
❏ LPS-664 [S]	Meet the Jazztet	1960	60.00
❏ LP-684 [M]	The Jazztet and John Lewis	1961	40.00
❏ LPS-684 [S]	The Jazztet and John Lewis	1961	50.00
❏ LP-688 [M]	The Jazztet at Birdhouse	1961	40.00
❏ LPS-688 [S]	The Jazztet at Birdhouse	1961	50.00

CADET
❏ LP-664 [M]	Meet the Jazztet	1966	30.00
❏ LPS-664 [S]	Meet the Jazztet	1966	30.00
— Fading blue label			
❏ CA-664 [S]	Meet the Jazztet	197?	25.00
— Yellow and red label			

CHESS
❏ CH-9159	Meet the Jazztet	198?	15.00
— Reissue			

CONTEMPORARY
❏ C-14020	Back to the City	1987	15.00
❏ C-14034	Real Time	1988	15.00

MERCURY
❏ MG-20737 [M]	Another Git-Together	1962	40.00
❏ SR-60737 [S]	Another Git-Together	1962	50.00
❏ MG-20698 [M]	Here and Now	1962	40.00
❏ SR-60698 [S]	Here and Now	1962	50.00

SOUL NOTE
❏ SN-1066	Moment to Moment	1984	18.00

JAZZY JEFF AND FRESH PRINCE

JIVE
❏ 1188-1-J	And in This Corner...	1989	12.00
❏ 41489-1	Code Red	1993	15.00
— LP in generic black cover with center hole and sticker			
❏ 1091-1-J	He's the D.J., I'm the Rapper	1988	15.00
— Without "Nightmare on My Street" disclaimer on cover			
❏ 1091-1-J RE	He's the D.J., I'm the Rapper	1988	16.00
— With "Nightmare on My Street" disclaimer on cover (much scarcer than original)			
❏ 1392-1-J	Homebase	1991	15.00
❏ JL6-8399	On Fire	1985	15.00
❏ 1026-1-J	Rock the House	1986	12.00
— Reissued in 1989 with same catalog number and one new track			

RAPSTER
❏ RR 008LP	The Magnificent	2002	18.00
— By "DJ Jazzy Jeff"; full-length version with different cover than EP			

WORD UP
❏ WDLP-0001	Rock the House	1985	30.00

JEANNEAU, FRANCOIS

INNER CITY
❏ IC-1022	Techniques Douces	197?	18.00

JEFFERSON, BLIND LEMON

MILESTONE
❏ MLP-2013 [M]	Black Snake Moan	1970	30.00
❏ MLP-2004 [M]	The Immortal Blind Lemon Jefferson	1968	30.00
❏ MLP-2007 [M]	The Immortal Blind Lemon Jefferson, Vol. 2	1969	30.00

RIVERSIDE
❏ RLP 12-136 [M]	Blind Lemon Jefferson, Volume 2	1958	120.00
❏ RLP 12-125 [M]	Blind Lemon Jefferson -- Classic Folk Blues	1957	120.00
❏ 1053 [10]	Penitentiary Blues	1955	250.00

Number	Title	Yr	NM
❏ 1014 [10]	The Folk Blues of Blind Lemon Jefferson	1953	250.00

JEFFERSON, CARTER

TIMELESS

| ❏ 309 | The Rise of Atlantis | 1979 | 15.00 |

JEFFERSON, EDDIE

FANTASY

❏ OJC-396	Body and Soul	1989	15.00
❏ OJC-613	Come Along with Me	1991	15.00
❏ OJC-307	Letter from Home	1988	12.00

INNER CITY

| ❏ IC-1016 | Jazz Singer | 197? | 18.00 |
| ❏ IC-1033 | Main Man | 1978 | 18.00 |

MUSE

❏ MR-5063	Still On the Planet	1976	15.00
❏ MR-5127	The Live-Liest	197?	15.00
❏ MR-5043	Things Are Getting Better	1974	15.00

PRESTIGE

❏ PRST-7619	Body and Soul	1969	25.00
❏ PRST-7698	Come Along with Me	1969	25.00
❏ 24095	There I Go Again	198?	18.00

RIVERSIDE

| ❏ RLP-411 [M] | Letter from Home | 1962 | 30.00 |
| ❏ RS-9411 [S] | Letter from Home | 1962 | 40.00 |

JEFFERSON, RON

CATALYST

| ❏ 7601 | Vous Etes Swing | 1976 | 15.00 |

PACIFIC JAZZ

| ❏ PJ-36 [M] | Love Lifted Me | 1962 | 30.00 |
| ❏ ST-36 [S] | Love Lifted Me | 1962 | 40.00 |

JEFFERSON

JANUS

| ❏ JLS-3006 | Jefferson | 1969 | 18.00 |

JEFFERSON AIRPLANE

DCC COMPACT CLASSICS

| ❏ LPZ-2033 | Surrealistic Pillow | 1997 | 75.00 |
— Audiophile vinyl

EPIC

| ❏ OE45271 | Jefferson Airplane | 1989 | 18.00 |

GRUNT

| ❏ FTR-1001 [B] | Bark | 1971 | 30.00 |
With brown paper bag
| ❏ FTR-1001 | Bark | 1971 | 12.00 |
— Without brown paper bag
❏ AYL1-4386	Bark	1981	10.00
❏ API 1-0437	Early Flight	1974	15.00
❏ CYL2-1255	Flight Log 1966-1976	1977	15.00
❏ FTR-1007	Long John Silver	1972	15.00
❏ BFL1-0147	Thirty Seconds Over Winterland	1973	15.00
❏ AYL1-4391	Thirty Seconds Over Winterland	1981	10.00

MOBILE FIDELITY

| ❏ 1-148 [B] | Crown of Creation | 1984 | 60.00 |
— Audiophile vinyl

PAIR

| ❏ PDL2-1090 | Time Machine | 1986 | 15.00 |

RCA

| ❏ 5724-1-R [B] | 2400 Fulton Street: An Anthology | 1987 | 35.00 |

RCA VICTOR

| ❏ LOP-1511 [M] | After Bathing at Baxter's | 1967 | 150.00 |
| ❏ LSO-1511 [S] | After Bathing at Baxter's | 1967 | 25.00 |
— Black label, dog on top
| ❏ LSO-1511 [S] | After Bathing at Baxter's | 1969 | 15.00 |
— Orange label
| ❏ LSO-1511 [S] | After Bathing at Baxter's | 1975 | 12.00 |
— Tan label
❏ AFL1-4545	After Bathing at Baxter's	1981	10.00
❏ AYL1-4718	After Bathing at Baxter's	1983	10.00
❏ LSP-4133	Bless Its Pointed Little Head	1969	15.00
— Orange label
| ❏ LSP-4133 | Bless Its Pointed Little Head | 1975 | 12.00 |
— Tan label
| ❏ AYL1-3798 | Bless Its Pointed Little Head | 1980 | 10.00 |
| ❏ LSP-4058 | Crown of Creation | 1968 | 30.00 |
— Black label, dog on top
| ❏ LSP-4058 | Crown of Creation | 1969 | 15.00 |
— Orange label
| ❏ LSP-4058 | Crown of Creation | 1975 | 12.00 |
— Tan label
| ❏ AYL1-3797 | Crown of Creation | 1980 | 10.00 |
| ❏ LSP-3584 [S] | Jefferson Airplane Takes Off! | 1966 | 5000.00 |
— Version 1: See Version 1 note under mono version; VG value 2000; VG+ value 3500
| ❏ LPM-3584 [M] | Jefferson Airplane Takes Off! | 1966 | 3000.00 |
— Version 1: With "Runnin' 'Round This World" as last song on side 1. Count the number of bands on Side 1 of the record; don't rely on the cover listing, as some jackets list the title when it's not on the record; VG value 1500; VG+ value 2250
| ❏ LPM-3584 [M] | Jefferson Airplane Takes Off! | 1966 | 1000.00 |
— Version 2: No "Runnin' 'Round This World", but

"questionable" lyrics remain in "Let Me In" ("Don't tell me you want money") and "Run Around" ("That sway as you lay under me"). Until the exact matrix numbers are known, it must be heard to confirm.

Number	Title	Yr	NM
❏ LSP-3584 [S]	Jefferson Airplane Takes Off!	1966	1800.00
— Version 2: See Version 2 note under mono version
| ❏ LPM-3584 [M] | Jefferson Airplane Takes Off! | 1966 | 80.00 |
— Version 3: No "Runnin' 'Round This World", altered lyrics to "Let Me In" ("Don't tell me it's so funny") and "Run Around ("That sway as you stay here by me"). All later versions confirm to Version 3.
| ❏ LSP-3584 [S] | Jefferson Airplane Takes Off! | 1966 | 30.00 |
— Version 3: See Version 3 note under mono version
| ❏ LSP-3584 [S] | Jefferson Airplane Takes Off! | 1969 | 15.00 |
— Orange label
| ❏ LSP-3584 [S] | Jefferson Airplane Takes Off! | 1975 | 12.00 |
— Tan label
❏ AYL1-3739	Jefferson Airplane Takes Off!	1980	10.00
❏ LPM-3766 [M]	Surrealistic Pillow	1967	80.00
❏ LSP-3766 [S]	Surrealistic Pillow	1967	30.00
— Black label, dog on top
| ❏ LSP-3766 [S] | Surrealistic Pillow | 1969 | 15.00 |
— Orange label
| ❏ LSP-3766 [S] | Surrealistic Pillow | 1975 | 12.00 |
— Tan label
❏ AYL1-3738	Surrealistic Pillow	1980	10.00
❏ LSP-4459	The Worst of Jefferson Airplane	1970	15.00
❏ AYL1-3661	The Worst of Jefferson Airplane	1980	10.00
❏ LSP-4238	Volunteers	1969	15.00
— Orange label
| ❏ LSP-4238 | Volunteers | 1975 | 12.00 |
— Tan label
| ❏ APD1-0320 [Q] | Volunteers | 1973 | 100.00 |
— Yellow/orange label
| ❏ APD1-0320 [Q] | Volunteers | 1975 | 60.00 |
— Tan label
| ❏ AYL1-3867 | Volunteers | 1980 | 10.00 |

SUNDAZED

| ❏ LP5187 [M] | After Bathing at Baxter's | 2005 | 18.00 |
— Reissue on 180-gram vinyl
| ❏ LP5186 [M] | Jefferson Airplane Takes Off | 2005 | 18.00 |
— Reissue on 180-gram vinyl

JEFFERSON STARSHIP

DCC COMPACT CLASSICS

| ❏ LPZ-2036 | Red Octopus | 1997 | 40.00 |
— Audiophile vinyl

GRUNT

❏ BFL1-0717	Dragon Fly	1974	12.00
❏ BFD1-0717 [Q]	Dragon Fly	1974	30.00
❏ AYL1-3798	Dragon Fly	1980	10.00
❏ BXL1-2515	Earth	1978	12.00
❏ AYL1-4172	Earth	1981	10.00
❏ BZL1-3452	Freedom at Point Zero	1979	12.00
❏ AYL1-5161	Freedom at Point Zero	1984	10.00
❏ BZL1-3247	Gold	1978	12.00
❏ DJL1-3363 [PD]	Gold	1978	30.00
— Promo-only picture disc
❏ BZL1-3848	Modern Times	1981	12.00
❏ BXL1-4921	Nuclear Furniture	1984	12.00
❏ BFL1-0999	Red Octopus	1975	12.00
❏ BFD1-0999 [Q]	Red Octopus	1975	30.00
❏ AYL1-3660	Red Octopus	1980	10.00
❏ BFL1-1557	Spitfire	1976	12.00
❏ BFD1-1557 [Q]	Spitfire	1976	30.00
❏ AYL1-3953	Spitfire	1981	10.00
❏ BXL1-4372	Winds of Change	1982	12.00

JEFFREY, JOE, GROUP

WAND

| ❏ WDS-686 | My Pledge of Love | 1969 | 30.00 |

JEFFRIES, FRAN

MONUMENT

| ❏ MLP-8069 [M] | This Is Fran Jeffries | 1967 | 25.00 |
| ❏ SLP-18069 [S] | This Is Fran Jeffries | 1967 | 25.00 |

WARWICK

| ❏ W-2020 [M] | Fran Can Really Hang You Up the Most | 1960 | 25.00 |

JEFFRIES, HERB

BETHLEHEM

| ❏ BCP-72 [M] | Say It Isn't So | 1957 | 60.00 |

CORAL

| ❏ CRL56066 [10] | Herb Jeffries Sings Flamingo and Other Songs in a Mellow Mood | 1952 | 120.00 |
| ❏ CRL56044 [10] | Time on My Hands | 1951 | 100.00 |

DOBRE

| ❏ DR-1047 | I Remember the Bing | 1978 | 18.00 |

GOLDEN TONE

| ❏ 14066 [S] | The Devil Is a Woman | 196? | 15.00 |
| ❏ C-4066 [M] | The Devil Is a Woman | 196? | 15.00 |

HARMONY

| ❏ HL7048 [M] | Herb Jeffries | 195? | 18.00 |

MERCURY

Number	Title	Yr	NM
❏ MG-25090 [10]	Herb Jeffries Sings	1950	100.00
❏ MG-25091 [10]	Just Jeffries	1950	100.00
❏ MG-25089 [10]	Magenta Moods	1950	100.00

RCA VICTOR

| ❏ LPM-1608 [M] | Senor Flamingo | 1957 | 40.00 |

RKO UNIQUE

| ❏ ULP-128 [M] | Jamaica | 1956 | 30.00 |

JELLY BEAN BANDITS, THE

MAINSTREAM

| ❏ 56103 [M] | The Jelly Bean Bandits | 1967 | 100.00 |
| ❏ S-6103 [S] | The Jelly Bean Bandits | 1967 | 150.00 |

JELLYBREAD

BLUE HORIZON

| ❏ BH-4801 [B] | First Slice | 1970 | 60.00 |

JENKINS, FLORENCE FOSTER

RCA VICTOR

| ❏ LRT-7001 [10] | A Florence! Foster!! Jenkins!!! Recital!!!! | 195? | 50.00 |
| ❏ LM-2597 [M] | The Glory (????) of the Human Voice | 1961 | 25.00 |

JENKINS, GORDON

BAINBRIDGE

| ❏ BT-1022 [S] | Soul of a People | 1980 | 12.00 |

CAPITOL

| ❏ T1023 [M] | Dream Dust | 1958 | 30.00 |
| ❏ T781 [M] | Night Dreams | 1956 | 30.00 |
— Turquoise label
| ❏ T884 [M] | Stolen Hours | 1956 | 30.00 |
— Turquoise label
| ❏ ST884 [S] | Stolen Hours | 1959 | 30.00 |
| ❏ T766 [M] | The Complete Manhattan Tower | 1956 | 30.00 |
— Turquoise label
❏ DT766 [R]	The Complete Manhattan Tower	196?	15.00
❏ T1048 [M]	Tropicana Holiday	1958	30.00
❏ ST1048 [S]	Tropicana Holiday	1958	30.00

COLUMBIA

❏ CL1764 [M]	Hawaiian Wedding Songs	1962	15.00
❏ CS8564 [S]	Hawaiian Wedding Songs	1962	18.00
❏ CL2009 [M]	In a Tender Mood	1963	15.00
❏ CS8809 [S]	In a Tender Mood	1963	18.00
❏ CL1882 [M]	The Magic World of Gordon Jenkins	1962	15.00
❏ CS8682 [S]	The Magic World of Gordon Jenkins	1962	18.00

DECCA

❏ DL5307 [10]	For You	195?	40.00
❏ DL8116 [M]	Heartbeats	195?	30.00
❏ DL8313 [M]	He Likes to Go Dancing: Music for the Boy Friend	195?	30.00
❏ DL8077 [M]	In the Still of the Night	195?	30.00
❏ DL8011 [M]	Manhattan Tower/California (The Golden State)	1951	30.00
— Black label, gold print
❏ DL78011 [R]	Manhattan Tower/California (The Golden State)	196?	15.00
❏ DL5469 [10]	Me and Juliet/Can-Can	1953	40.00
❏ DL4714 [M]	My Heart Sings	1966	15.00
❏ DL74714 [S]	My Heart Sings	1966	18.00
❏ DL5275 [10]	Playing His Compositions	195?	40.00
❏ DL8109 [M]	P.S. I Love You	195?	30.00

DOT

| ❏ DLP-3752 [M] | Soft Soul | 1966 | 15.00 |
| ❏ DLP-25752 [S] | Soft Soul | 1966 | 18.00 |

GWP

| ❏ 2035 | Way Back Now | 1971 | 12.00 |

KAPP

| ❏ KL1361 [M] | I Live Alone | 196? | 15.00 |
| ❏ KS3361 [S] | I Live Alone | 196? | 18.00 |

MAINSTREAM

| ❏ S-6093 [S] | Soul of a People | 196? | 15.00 |
— Reissue of Time S-2050
| ❏ 56093 [M] | Soul of a People | 196? | 12.00 |
— Reissue of Time 52050

MCA

| ❏ 166 | Manhattan Tower/California (The Golden State) | 1973 | 12.00 |
— Black label with rainbow

MCA CORAL

| ❏ CB-20030 | Romance | 1973 | 12.00 |

PICKWICK

| ❏ PC-3005 [M] | Yours -- The Magic of Gordon Jenkins | 196? | 15.00 |
| ❏ SPC-3005 [S] | Yours -- The Magic of Gordon Jenkins | 196? | 15.00 |

SEARS

| ❏ SPS-403 [S] | The Romantic Moods of Gordon Jenkins | 196? | 18.00 |

SUNSET

| ❏ SUM-1149 [M] | Blue Prelude | 196? | 18.00 |
| ❏ SUS-5149 [S] | Blue Prelude | 196? | 15.00 |

Number	Title	Yr	NM

TIME

Number	Title	Yr	NM
❑ S-2061 [S]	France	196?	18.00
❑ 52061 [M]	France	196?	15.00
❑ 52130 [M]	Paris, I Wish You Love	196?	15.00
❑ S-2130 [S]	Paris, I Wish You Love	196?	18.00
❑ S-2050 [S]	Soul of a People	196?	18.00
❑ 52050 [M]	Soul of a People	196?	15.00

VEE JAY

| ❑ VJLP-1089 [M] | The Great Movie Themes of the 30s, 40s and 50s | 1964 | 15.00 |
| ❑ VJLPS-1089 [S] | The Great Movie Themes of the 30s, 40s and 50s | 1964 | 25.00 |

VOCALION

| ❑ VL3615 [M] | Dreamer's Holiday | 196? | 18.00 |

WARNER BROS.

| ❑ W1464 [M] | Let's Duet | 1963 | 15.00 |
| ❑ WS1464 [S] | Let's Duet | 1963 | 18.00 |

JENKINS, JOHN; CLIFF JORDAN; BOBBY TIMMONS

FANTASY

| ❑ OJC-251 | Jenkins, Jordan & Timmons | 1987 | 15.00 |

NEW JAZZ

❑ NJLP-8232 [M]	Jenkins, Jordan and Timmons	1960	150.00
—Purple label			
❑ NJLP-8232 [M]	Jenkins, Jordan and Timmons	1965	50.00
—Blue label with trident logo			

JENKINS, JOHN

BLUE NOTE

❑ BLP-1573 [M]	John Jenkins with Kenny Burrell	1958	1500.00
—"Deep groove" version; W. 63rd St. address on label			
❑ BLP-1573 [M]	John Jenkins with Kenny Burrell	1958	200.00
—Regular version with W. 63rd St., New York address on label			
❑ BLP-1573 [M]	John Jenkins with Kenny Burrell	1963	40.00
—With "New York, USA" address on label			
❑ BST-1573 [S]	John Jenkins with Kenny Burrell	1959	1500.00
—"Deep groove" version; W. 63rd St. address on label			
❑ BST-1573 [S]	John Jenkins with Kenny Burrell	1959	120.00
—Regular version with W. 63rd St., New York address on label			
❑ BST-1573 [S]	John Jenkins with Kenny Burrell	1963	40.00
—With "New York, USA" address on label			
❑ BST-81573 [S]	John Jenkins with Kenny Burrell	1967	30.00
—With "A Division of Liberty Records" on label			

REGENT

| ❑ MG-6056 [M] | Jazz Eyes | 1957 | 150.00 |

SAVOY

| ❑ MG-12201 [M] | Jazz Eyes | 196? | 40.00 |

JENKINS, MARV

OROVOX

| ❑ 1001 [M] | Marv Jenkins Arrives | 196? | 40.00 |
| ❑ S-1001 [S] | Marv Jenkins Arrives | 196? | 40.00 |

REPRISE

| ❑ R-6077 [M] | Good Little Man at the Rubaiyat Room | 1963 | 25.00 |
| ❑ R9-6077 [S] | Good Little Man at the Rubaiyat Room | 1963 | 30.00 |

JENNEY, JACK

COLUMBIA

| ❑ GL100 [10] | The Golden Era | 1949 | 50.00 |

COLUMBIA MASTERWORKS

| ❑ ML4803 [M] | Jack Jenney | 195? | 80.00 |

JENNINGS, BILL

AUDIO LAB

| ❑ AL-1514 [M] | Guitar/Vibes | 1959 | 100.00 |

KING

❑ 398-527 [M]	Billy in the Lion's Den	1956	600.00
❑ 295-105 [10]	Jazz Interlude	195?	400.00
❑ 398-508 [M]	Mood Indigo	1955	100.00
❑ 295-106 [10]	The Fabulous Guitar of Bill Jennings	195?	250.00

PRESTIGE

❑ PRST-7788	Enough Said	1970	15.00
❑ PRLP-7164 [M]	Enough Said!	1959	150.00
❑ PRLP-7177 [M]	Glide On	1960	50.00
❑ PRST-7836	Glide On	1971	15.00

JENNINGS, WAYLON; WILLIE NELSON; JESSI COLTER; TOMPALL GLASER

RCA VICTOR

❑ APL1-1321	Wanted! The Outlaws	1976	15.00
—Tan label			
❑ APL1-1321	Wanted! The Outlaws	1976	12.00
—Black label, dog near top			

| ❑ AAL1-1321 | Wanted! The Outlaws | 198? | 10.00 |
| *—Reissue* | | | |

JENNINGS, WAYLON

A&M

| ❑ SP-4238 | Don't Think Twice | 1969 | 40.00 |

BAT

| ❑ 1001 [M] | Waylon Jennings at JD's | 1964 | 700.00 |
| *—Approximately 500 copies pressed* | | | |

COLUMBIA

❑ FC40056	Highwayman	1985	12.00
—Waylon Jennings/Willie Nelson/Johnny Cash/Kris Kristofferson			
❑ C45240	Highwayman 2	1990	18.00
—Waylon Jennings/Willie Nelson/Johnny Cash/Kris Kristofferson			
❑ 1P-8030	The Eagle	1990	30.00
—Vinyl released only through Columbia House			

MCA

❑ 42038	A Man Called Hoss	1987	12.00
❑ 42038 [DJ]	A Man Called Hoss	1987	60.00
—Promo-only edition with letter and 48-page book			
❑ 42222	Full Circle	1988	12.00
❑ 5911	Hangin' Tough	1987	12.00
❑ 42287	New Classic Waylon	1989	12.00
❑ 731	Waylon Jennings	198?	15.00
—Reissue of Vocalion LP			
❑ 5688	Will the Wolf Survive	1986	12.00

MCA CORAL

| ❑ VL73873 | Waylon Jennings | 197? | 15.00 |
| *—Reissue of Vocalion 73873; cover still says "Vocalion" but label is "MCA Coral"* | | | |

PAIR

❑ PDL1-1033	A Couple More Years	1986	15.00
❑ PDL1-1110	Honly Tonk Hero	1986	15.00
❑ PDL1-1005	Waylon!	1986	15.00

PICKWICK

❑ CAS-2556	Heartaches by the Number	197?	10.00
—Reissue of RCA Camden CAS-2556			
❑ ACL-0306	Only Daddy That'll Walk the Line	197?	10.00
—Reissue of RCA Camden LP			
❑ ACL-7019 [S]	The Dark Side of Fame	1976	12.00
—Reissue of RCA Camden CAS-2183			

RCA

| ❑ 5620-1-RB | The Best of Waylon | 1987 | 12.00 |
| ❑ 9561-1-R | The Early Years (1965-1969) | 1989 | 12.00 |

RCA CAMDEN

❑ CAS-2556	Heartaches by the Number	1972	15.00
❑ ACL1-0306	Only Daddy That'll Walk the Line	1973	12.00
❑ CAS-2608	Ruby, Don't Take Your Love to Town	1972	15.00
❑ CAS-2183 [S]	The One and Only Waylon Jennings	1967	15.00
❑ CAL-2183 [M]	The One and Only Waylon Jennings	1967	18.00

RCA VICTOR

❑ APL1-1816	Are You Ready for the Country	1976	12.00
❑ AYL1-3663	Are You Ready for the Country	1980	10.00
—Budget-line reissue			
❑ AFL1-1816	Are You Ready for the Country	1977	10.00
—Black label, dog near side; new prefix			
❑ AHL1-4247	Black On Black	1982	12.00
❑ LSP-4567	Cedartown, Georgia	1971	25.00
❑ AHL1-5473	Collector's Series	1985	12.00
❑ LSP-4180	Country-Folk	1969	30.00
❑ APL1-1062	Dreaming My Dreams	1975	12.00
❑ AYL1-4072	Dreaming My Dreams	1981	10.00
—Budget-line reissue			
❑ LPM-3523 [M]	Folk-Country	1966	30.00
❑ LSP-3523 [S]	Folk-Country	1966	40.00
❑ LSP-4647	Good Hearted Woman	1972	25.00
❑ AHL1-3378	Greatest Hits	1979	12.00
❑ LPM-3918 [M]	Hangin' On	1968	100.00
❑ LSP-3918 [S]	Hangin' On	1968	30.00
❑ APL1-0240	Honky Tonk Heroes	1973	18.00
❑ AYL1-3897	Honky Tonk Heroes	1980	10.00
—Budget-line reissue			
❑ AHL1-4673	It's Only Rock & Roll	1983	12.00
❑ AFL1-2979	I've Always Been Crazy	1978	12.00
❑ AYL1-4164	I've Always Been Crazy	1981	10.00
—Budget-line reissue			
❑ LSP-4085	Jewels	1968	30.00
❑ LSP-4137	Just to Satisfy You	1969	30.00
❑ LSP-4751	Ladies Love Outlaws	1972	25.00
❑ LPM-3620 [M]	Leavin' Town	1966	30.00
❑ LSP-3620 [S]	Leavin' Town	1966	40.00
❑ LSP-4854	Lonesome, On'ry and Mean	1973	18.00
—Original issue; orange label			
❑ AFL1-4854	Lonesome, On'ry and Mean	197?	12.00
—Reissue with new prefix			
❑ LPM-3825 [M]	Love of the Common People	1967	30.00
❑ LSP-3825 [S]	Love of the Common People	1967	30.00
❑ AHL1-3602	Music Man	1980	12.00
❑ AYL1-4250	Music Man	1982	10.00

—Budget-line reissue			
❑ LPM-3736 [M]	Nashville Rebel	1967	40.00
❑ LSP-3736 [S]	Nashville Rebel	1967	50.00
❑ AHL1-5017	Never Could Toe the Mark	1984	12.00
❑ AYL1-7046	Never Could Toe the Mark	1985	10.00
—Budget-line reissue			
❑ APL1-2317	Ol' Waylon	1977	12.00
❑ AAL1-2317	Ol' Waylon	198?	10.00
—Reissue			
❑ AYL1-5126	Ol' Waylon	1984	10.00
—Budget-line reissue			
❑ LPM-4023 [M]	Only the Greatest	1968	150.00
❑ LSP-4023 [S]	Only the Greatest	1968	30.00
❑ LSP-4418	Singer of Sad Songs	1970	25.00
❑ AHL1-7184	Sweet Mother Texas	1986	12.00
❑ LSP-4341	The Best of Waylon Jennings	1970	25.00
❑ AYL1-4828	The Best of Waylon Jennings	1983	10.00
—Budget-line reissue			
❑ APL1-0734	The Ramblin' Man	1974	15.00
—Original issue; tan label			
❑ AYL1-4073	The Ramblin' Man	1981	10.00
—Budget-line reissue			
❑ AFL1-0734	The Ramblin' Man	197?	12.00
—Reissue with new prefix			
❑ LSP-4487	The Taker/Tulsa	1971	25.00
❑ APL1-0539	This Time	1974	15.00
❑ AHL1-5428	Turn the Page	1985	12.00
❑ LSP-4260	Waylon	1970	25.00
❑ AHL1-4826	Waylon and Company	1983	12.00
❑ AYL1-5433	Waylon and Company	1985	10.00
—Budget-line reissue			
❑ APL1-1108	Waylon Live	1976	12.00
❑ AYL1-4163	Waylon Live	1981	10.00
—Budget-line reissue			
❑ AHL1-5325	Waylon's Greatest Hits, Vol. 2	1984	12.00
❑ LPM-3660 [M]	Waylon Sings Ol' Harlan	1967	30.00
❑ LSP-3660 [S]	Waylon Sings Ol' Harlan	1967	40.00
❑ AHL1-3493	What Goes Around Comes Around	1979	12.00

SOUNDS

| ❑ 1001 [M] | Waylon Jennings at JD's | 1964 | 500.00 |
| *—Approximately 500 copies pressed; reissue of Bat 1001* | | | |

TIME-LIFE

| ❑ STW-102 | Country Music | 1981 | 12.00 |

JENSEN, DICK

PHILADELPHIA INT'L.

| ❑ KZ31794 [B] | Dick Jensen | 1973 | 35.00 |

JENSEN, KRIS

HICKORY

| ❑ LP110 [M] | Torture | 1963 | 80.00 |

JENSEN, KURT

HOLLYWOOD

| ❑ LPH-137 [M] | An Evening with Jayne | 195? | 60.00 |
| *—Collectible for its "cheesecake" cover of Jayne Mansfield* | | | |

JEREMY AND THE SATYRS

REPRISE

❑ R-6282 [M]	Jeremy and the Satyrs	1968	40.00
—Mono is white label promo only			
❑ RS-6282 [S]	Jeremy and the Satyrs	1968	25.00

JEREMY'S FRIENDS

WARWICK

| ❑ W-2019 [M] | Jeremy's Friends | 1960 | 50.00 |

JERICHO

AMPEX

| ❑ A-10112 | Jericho | 1971 | 30.00 |

JESSE J. AND THE BANDITS

RECAR

| ❑ 2011 [M] | Top Teen Hits | 1965 | 100.00 |

JESUS AND MARY CHAIN, THE

REPRISE

| ❑ 25383 | Psychocandy | 1985 | 15.00 |

WARNER BROS.

❑ 26015	Automatic	1989	14.00
❑ 25729	Barbed Wire Kisses	1988	15.00
❑ 25656	Darklands	1987	15.00

JESUS JONES

SBK

❑ SPRO-05348/9 [DJ]	A Conversation with Jesus	1990	25.00
—Generic cover with sticker			
❑ K1-94480	Liquidizer	1989	18.00

JETHRO TULL

CHRYSALIS

| ❑ V5X41653 | 20 Years of Jethro Tull | 1988 | 80.00 |

Number	Title	Yr	NM
❑ VX241655	20 Years of Jethro Tull	1989	30.00
—Abridged version of Chrysalis 41653			
❑ CHR1301	A	1980	12.00
❑ PV41301	A	1983	10.00
❑ CHR1040 [B]	A Passion Play	1973	20.00
—Green label, "3300 Warner Blvd." address			
❑ CHR1040	A Passion Play	1977	12.00
—Blue label, New York address			
❑ PV41040	A Passion Play	1983	10.00
❑ CHR1044	Aqualung	1973	15.00
—Green label, "3300 Warner Blvd." address			
❑ CHR1044	Aqualung	1977	12.00
—Blue label, New York address			
❑ CH41044 [Q]	Aqualung	1974	60.00
❑ FV41044	Aqualung	1983	10.00
❑ CHR1043	Benefit	1973	15.00
—Green label, "3300 Warner Blvd." address			
❑ CHR1043	Benefit	1977	12.00
—Blue label, New York address			
❑ PV41043	Benefit	1983	10.00
❑ FV41590	Crest of a Knave	1987	12.00
❑ CHR1175	Heavy Horses	1978	12.00
❑ PV41175	Heavy Horses	1983	10.00
❑ CHR21201	Jethro Tull Live -- Bursting Out	1978	15.00
❑ V2X41201	Jethro Tull Live -- Bursting Out	1983	15.00
❑ 2CH1035 [B]	Living in the Past	1972	30.00
—Two-record set with booklet; green labels			
❑ CHR1035 [B]	Living in the Past	1977	25.00
—Blue label, New York address			
❑ KV241035	Living in the Past	1983	15.00
❑ CHR1082	Minstrel in the Gallery	1975	15.00
—Green label, "3300 Warner Blvd." address			
❑ CHR1082	Minstrel in the Gallery	1977	12.00
—Blue label, New York address			
❑ PV41082	Minstrel in the Gallery	1983	10.00
❑ CHR1078	M.U. -- The Best of Jethro Tull	1975	15.00
—Green label, "3300 Warner Blvd." address			
❑ CHR1078	M.U. -- The Best of Jethro Tull	1977	12.00
—Blue label, New York address			
❑ FV41078	M.U. -- The Best of Jethro Tull	1983	10.00
❑ FV41515	Original Masters	1985	12.00
❑ CHR1135	Repeat -- The Best of Jethro Tull, Vol. II	1977	12.00
❑ FV41135	Repeat -- The Best of Jethro Tull, Vol. II	1983	10.00
❑ PV41135	Repeat -- The Best of Jethro Tull, Vol. II	1986	10.00
❑ FI-21700	Rock Island	1989	12.00
❑ CHR1132	Songs from the Wood	1977	12.00
❑ PV41132	Songs from the Wood	1983	10.00
❑ CHR1042	Stand Up	1973	15.00
—Green label, "3300 Warner Blvd." address			
❑ CHR1042	Stand Up	1977	12.00
—Blue label, New York address			
❑ PV41042	Stand Up	1983	10.00
❑ CHR1238	Stormwatch	1979	12.00
❑ PV41238	Stormwatch	1983	10.00
❑ CHR1380	The Broadsword and the Beast	1982	12.00
❑ FV41380	The Broadsword and the Beast	1983	10.00
❑ PV41380	The Broadsword and the Beast	1986	10.00
❑ PRO623 [DJ]	The Jethro Tull Radio Show	1975	60.00
❑ CHR1003	Thick as a Brick	1973	15.00
—Green label, "3300 Warner Blvd." address			
❑ CHR1003	Thick as a Brick	1977	12.00
—Blue label, New York address			
❑ FV41003	Thick as a Brick	1983	10.00
❑ PV41003	Thick as a Brick	1986	10.00
❑ CHR1041	This Was	1973	15.00
—Green label, "3300 Warner Blvd." address			
❑ CHR1041	This Was	1977	12.00
—Blue label, New York address			
❑ PV41041	This Was	1983	10.00
❑ CHR1111	Too Old to Rock 'N' Roll; Too Young to Die!	1976	15.00
—Green label, "3300 Warner Blvd." address			
❑ CHR1111	Too Old to Rock 'N' Roll; Too Young to Die!	1977	12.00
—Blue label, New York address			
❑ PV41111	Too Old to Rock 'N' Roll; Too Young to Die!	1983	10.00
❑ FV41461	Under Wraps	1984	12.00
❑ PV41461	Under Wraps	1986	10.00
❑ CHR1067	War Child	1974	15.00
—Green label, "3300 Warner Blvd." address			
❑ CHR1067	War Child	1974	12.00
—Blue label, New York address			
❑ CH41067 [Q]	War Child	1974	60.00
❑ PV41067	War Child	1983	10.00

DCC COMPACT CLASSICS

Number	Title	Yr	NM
❑ LPZ2033	Aqualung	1997	100.00
—Audiophile vinyl			
❑ LPZ-2059	Original Masters	1998	40.00
—Audiophile vinyl			

MOBILE FIDELITY

Number	Title	Yr	NM
❑ 1-061 [B]	Aqualung	1980	100.00
—Audiophile vinyl			
❑ 1-092 [B]	The Broadsword and the Beast	1982	60.00
—Audiophile vinyl			
❑ 1-187 [B]	Thick as a Brick	1985	80.00
—Audiophile vinyl			

REPRISE

Number	Title	Yr	NM
❑ MS2035	Aqualung	1971	18.00
❑ RS6400	Benefit	1970	25.00
—Two-tone orange label with "r:" and "W7" logos on label			
❑ RS6400	Benefit	1970	18.00
—All-one-color (orange/brown) label with no "W7" on label			
❑ R1536858 [B]	Benefit	2013	30.00
❑ 2MS2106 [B]	Living in the Past	1972	30.00
—Two-record set with booklet; original edition, rather than using cardboard outer sleeve for the records, has record sleeves attached to enclosed booklet, and thus is difficult to find intact			
❑ RS6360	Stand Up	1969	25.00
—Two-tone orange label with "r:" and "W7" logos on label; band "stands up" when gatefold is opened			
❑ RS6360 [B]	Stand Up	1970	18.00
—All-one-color (orange/brown) label with no "W7" on label			
❑ MS2072	Thick as a Brick	1972	18.00
❑ RS6336	This Was	1969	25.00
—Two-tone orange label with "r:" and "W7" logos on label			
❑ RS6336	This Was	1970	18.00
—All-one-color (orange/brown) label with no "W7" on label			

JETT, JOAN, AND THE BLACKHEARTS

BLACKHEART

Number	Title	Yr	NM
❑ 48337 53161 [B]	Glorious Results Of A Misspent Youth	2014	30.00
❑ BFZ40544	Good Music	1986	15.00
❑ JJ707 [B]	Joan Jett	1980	80.00
❑ Z47488	Notorious	1991	30.00
❑ Z45473	The Hit List	1990	18.00
❑ FZ44146	Up Your Alley	1988	12.00

BOARDWALK

Number	Title	Yr	NM
❑ FW37065	Bad Reputation	1981	15.00
—Essentially a reissue of Blackheart JJ 707			
❑ NB1-33251	Bad Reputation	1982	12.00
—Reissue of FW 37065			
❑ NB1-33243 [B]	I Love Rock-n-Roll	1982	18.00
—First pressing contains "Little Drummer Boy," which was replaced on second pressings			
❑ NB1 33243	I Love Rock-n-Roll	1982	15.00
—Second pressing, with "Oh Woe Is Me			

MCA

Number	Title	Yr	NM
❑ 5437	Album	1983	15.00
❑ R163731	Glorious Results of a Misspent Youth	1984	16.00
—RCA Music Service edition			
❑ 5476	Glorious Results of a Misspent Youth	1984	15.00

REPRISE

Number	Title	Yr	NM
❑ 45567	Pure and Simple	1994	25.00

JEWEL

ATLANTIC

Number	Title	Yr	NM
❑ 82700	Pieces of You	1997	30.00
—Contains five songs not on the 1995 CD of the same name			
❑ 82950	Spirit	1998	30.00
❑ 83519-1	This Way	2001	50.00

JIM & JESSE

COLUMBIA LIMITED EDITION

Number	Title	Yr	NM
❑ LE10542	All-Time Great Country Instrumentals	197?	12.00

EPIC

Number	Title	Yr	NM
❑ BN26394	All-Time Great Country Instrumentals	1968	25.00
❑ BN26176 [S]	Berry Pickin' the Country	1965	30.00
❑ LN24176 [M]	Berry Pickin' the Country	1965	25.00
❑ LN24074 [M]	Bluegrass Classics	1963	25.00
❑ BN26074 [S]	Bluegrass Classics	1963	30.00
❑ LN24031 [M]	Bluegrass Special	1963	25.00
❑ BN26031 [S]	Bluegrass Special	1963	30.00
❑ LN24314 [M]	Diesel on My Tail	1967	25.00
❑ BN26314 [S]	Diesel on My Tail	1967	30.00
❑ BN26465	Saluting the Louvin Brothers	1969	25.00
❑ LN24204 [M]	Sing Unto Him	1966	25.00
❑ BN26204 [S]	Sing Unto Him	1966	30.00
❑ LN24107 [M]	The Old Country Church	1964	25.00
❑ BN26107 [S]	The Old Country Church	1964	30.00
❑ LN24144 [M]	Y'All Come	1964	25.00
❑ BN26144 [S]	Y'All Come	1964	30.00

JIMENEZ, JOSE

A&M

Number	Title	Yr	NM
❑ SP-4144 [B]	Mashuganishi Yogi	1968	25.00

CAPITOL

Number	Title	Yr	NM
❑ ST-404 [B]	Hoo Ha! Direct from Noshville	1970	25.00

KAPP

Number	Title	Yr	NM
❑ KL-1402 [M]	Bill Dana in Las Vegas	1964	25.00
❑ KL1238 [M]	Jose Jimenez at the Hungry I	196?	18.00
—Reissue with new title			
❑ KS3238 [S]	Jose Jimenez at the Hungry I	196?	18.00
—Reissue with new title			
❑ KL-1332 [M]	Jose Jimenez in Jollywood	1963	25.00
❑ KS-3332 [S]	Jose Jimenez in Jollywood	1963	30.00
❑ KL-1257 [M]	Jose Jimenez in Orbit -- Bill Dana on Earth	1961	25.00
❑ KS-3257 [S]	Jose Jimenez in Orbit -- Bill Dana on Earth	1961	30.00
❑ KL-1320 [M]	Jose Jimenez -- Our Secret Weapon	1963	25.00
❑ KL1304 [M]	Jose Jimenez Talks to Teenagers of All Ages	1962	25.00
❑ KS3304 [S]	Jose Jimenez Talks to Teenagers of All Ages	1962	30.00
❑ KL1238 [M]	Jose Jimenez -- The Astronaut (The First Man in Space)	1961	25.00
❑ KS3238 [S]	Jose Jimenez -- The Astronaut (The First Man in Space)	1961	30.00
❑ KL1215 [M]	Jose Jimenez the Submarine Officer	1961	30.00
—Original title			
❑ KL1215 [M]	More Jose Jimenez	1961	25.00

ROULETTE

Number	Title	Yr	NM
❑ R25161 [M]	My Name…Jose Jimenez	1961	25.00
—Reissue of Signature LP			

SIGNATURE

Number	Title	Yr	NM
❑ SM1013 [M]	My Name…Jose Jimenez	1960	30.00

JIVE FIVE, THE

AMBIENT SOUND

Number	Title	Yr	NM
❑ FZ37717	Here We Are	1982	18.00

AMBIENT SOUND/ROUNDER

Number	Title	Yr	NM
❑ ASR-801	Way Back	1985	15.00

COLLECTABLES

Number	Title	Yr	NM
❑ COL-5022	Greatest Hits	198?	12.00

RELIC

Number	Title	Yr	NM
❑ 5020	The Jive Five's Greatest Hits (1961-1963)	198?	12.00

UNITED ARTISTS

Number	Title	Yr	NM
❑ UAL-3455 [M]	The Jive Five	1965	50.00
❑ UAS-6455 [S]	The Jive Five	1965	75.00

JO JO GUNNE

ASYLUM

Number	Title	Yr	NM
❑ SD5065	Bite Down Hard	1973	18.00
❑ SD5053	Jo Jo Gunne	1972	18.00
❑ SD5071 [B]	Jumpin' the Gunne	1973	25.00
—Gatefold cover			
❑ SD5071	Jumpin' the Gunne	1974	12.00
—Regular cover			
❑ 7E-1022	So…Where's the Show?	1974	12.00

JOE & EDDIE

GNP CRESCENDO

Number	Title	Yr	NM
❑ GNP-96 [M]	Coast to Coast	1964	25.00
❑ GNPS-96 [S]	Coast to Coast	1964	30.00
❑ GNP-75 [M]	Joe & Eddie	1963	25.00
❑ GNP-99 [M]	Joe & Eddie, Volume 4	1964	25.00
❑ GNPS-99 [S]	Joe & Eddie, Volume 4	1964	30.00
❑ GNP-2007 [M]	Joe & Eddie Live in Hollywood	1965	18.00
❑ GNPS-2007 [S]	Joe & Eddie Live in Hollywood	1965	25.00
❑ GNP-2005 [M]	Tear Down the Walls	1965	18.00
❑ GNPS-2005 [S]	Tear Down the Walls	1965	25.00
❑ GNP-2032 [M]	The Best of Joe & Eddie	1966	18.00
❑ GNPS-2032 [S]	The Best of Joe & Eddie	1966	25.00
❑ GNP-2021 [M]	The Magic of Their Singing	1966	18.00
❑ GNPS-2021 [S]	The Magic of Their Singing	1966	25.00
❑ GNP-86 [M]	There's a Meetin' Here Tonite	1963	25.00
❑ GNP-2014 [M]	Walkin' Down the Line	1965	18.00
❑ GNPS-2014 [S]	Walkin' Down the Line	1965	25.00

JOEL, BILLY

COLUMBIA

Number	Title	Yr	NM
❑ FC35609	52nd Street	1978	12.00
❑ PC35609	52nd Street	1985	10.00
❑ HC45609	52nd Street	1982	30.00
—Half-speed mastered edition			
❑ QC38837	An Innocent Man	1983	12.00
❑ HC48837	An Innocent Man	1983	30.00
—Half-speed mastered edition			
❑ AS1343 [DJ]	Billy Joel Interview	1982	25.00
❑ PC38984	Cold Spring Harbor	1983	10.00
—Remixed, remastered version of Family Productions album			
❑ FC36384	Glass Houses	1980	12.00
❑ PC36384	Glass Houses	1986	10.00
❑ C240121	Greatest Hits, Volumes 1 and 2	1985	15.00
❑ AS402 [DJ]	Inter Chords/Billy Joel Interview	1977	25.00
—Promo-only interview album			
❑ C240996	KOHUEPT	1987	18.00
❑ KC32544	Piano Man	1973	15.00
—Some copies have the first song spelled "Travelin' Prayer," others have it "Travellin' Prayer." No difference in value.			
❑ PC32544	Piano Man	1976	12.00
—No bar code on back cover			

Number	Title	Yr	NM
❑ PC32544	Piano Man	1979	10.00
— With bar code on back cover			
❑ CQ32544 [Q]	Piano Man	1974	25.00
❑ TC37461	Songs in the Attic	1981	12.00
❑ PC37461	Songs in the Attic	1984	10.00
❑ HC47461	Songs in the Attic	1982	70.00
— Half-speed mastered edition			
❑ AS326 [DJ]	Souvenir	1976	25.00
— Promo-only LP with one side live, one side a compilation of studio tracks			
❑ OC44366	Storm Front	1989	15.00
❑ PC33146	Streetlife Serenade	1975	12.00
— No bar code on back cover			
❑ PCQ33146 [Q]	Streetlife Serenade	1975	25.00
❑ PC33146	Streetlife Serenade	1979	10.00
— With bar code on back cover			
❑ OC40402	The Bridge	1986	12.00
❑ QC38200	The Nylon Curtain	1982	12.00
❑ JC34987	The Stranger	1977	12.00
❑ PC34987	The Stranger	1979	10.00
❑ HC34987	The Stranger	1981	30.00
— Original pressing of half-speed mastered edition			
❑ HC44987	The Stranger	1982	30.00
— Half-speed mastered edition (reissue)			
❑ PC33848	Turnstiles	1976	12.00
— No bar code on back cover			
❑ PC33848	Turnstiles	1976	10.00
— With bar code on back cover			
❑ PCQ33848 [Q]	Turnstiles	1976	25.00

FAMILY PRODUCTIONS

Number	Title	Yr	NM
❑ FPS-2700	Cold Spring Harbor	1971	40.00
— Authentic copies have mostly dark blue labels; when reissued on Columbia, the entire LP was remixed and remastered, and "You Can Make Me Free" was shortened by three minutes			

MOBILE FIDELITY

Number	Title	Yr	NM
❑ MFSL2-384 [B]	52nd Street	2013	60.00
❑ MFSL2-388 [B]	An Innocent Man	2013	60.00
❑ MFSL2-385 [B]	Glass Houses	2013	60.00
❑ MFSL2-386 [B]	Songs in the Attic	2014	40.00
❑ MFSL2-387 [B]	The Nylon Curtain	2014	40.00
❑ MFSL2-383 [B]	The Stranger	2013	60.00

JOHN, ELTON

COLUMBIA SPECIAL PRODUCTS

Number	Title	Yr	NM
❑ P16196	The Best of Elton John, Volume One	1981	15.00
❑ P16197	The Best of Elton John, Volume Two	1981	15.00
— Both of the above "Distributed Exclusively by Scott Distributing Corp.			

DCC COMPACT CLASSICS

Number	Title	Yr	NM
❑ LPZ-2013	Elton John's Greatest Hits	1995	100.00
— Audiophile vinyl			
❑ LPZ-2004	Madman Across the Water	1994	120.00
— Audiophile vinyl			

DIRECT DISC

Number	Title	Yr	NM
❑ SD-16614	Goodbye Yellow Brick Road	1980	50.00
— Audiophile vinyl			

GEFFEN

Number	Title	Yr	NM
❑ GHS24031 [DJ]	Breaking Hearts	1984	30.00
— Promo pressing on Quiex II vinyl			
❑ GHS24031 [B]	Breaking Hearts	1984	12.00
❑ GHS24153	Elton John's Greatest Hits, Vol. 3, 1979-1987	1987	12.00
❑ GHS24077	Ice on Fire	1985	12.00
❑ GHS2013	Jump Up!	1982	12.00
❑ GHS24114	Leather Jackets	1986	12.00
❑ PRO-A-2176 [DJ]	Sasson Presents Elton John	1983	30.00
— One-sided promo with four tracks on A-side and an etched facsimile autograph on B-side			
❑ GHS2002	The Fox	1981	12.00
❑ GHS4006	Too Low for Zero	1983	12.00

MCA

Number	Title	Yr	NM
❑ 5121	21 at 33	1980	12.00
— Originals have custom labels			
❑ 772	21 at 33	1981	10.00
❑ 619	11/17/1970	1979	10.00
❑ 2015	11/17/1970	1973	12.00
❑ 3065	A Single Man	1978	12.00
❑ 14951 [PD]	A Single Man	1978	25.00
— Stock picture disc			
❑ L33-1995 [PD]	A Single Man	1978	40.00
— Promo picture disc			
❑ 37068	A Single Man	1979	10.00
❑ 6011	Blue Moves	1979	12.00
❑ 2142	Captain Fantastic and the Brown Dirt Cowboy	1975	15.00
— With custom label, two booklets and poster			
❑ 2142 [DJ]	Captain Fantastic and the Brown Dirt Cowboy	1975	300.00
— Brown vinyl promo, autographed by Elton John and Bernie Taupin			
❑ 37066	Captain Fantastic and the Brown Dirt Cowboy	1979	10.00
❑ 2116	Caribou	1974	12.00
❑ 37065	Caribou	1979	10.00
❑ 2100	Don't Shoot Me, I'm Only the Piano Player	1973	25.00
— With all-black label (no rainbow) and booklet			
❑ 2100	Don't Shoot Me, I'm Only the Piano Player	1973	12.00
— With black rainbow label and booklet			
❑ 37113	Don't Shoot Me, I'm Only the Piano Player	1979	10.00
❑ 2012	Elton John	1973	12.00
❑ 37067	Elton John	1979	10.00
❑ 2128	Elton John's Greatest Hits	1974	12.00
❑ 5224	Elton John's Greatest Hits	1981	10.00
❑ 37215	Elton John's Greatest Hits	1983	10.00
❑ 37216	Elton John's Greatest Hits	1983	10.00
❑ 1689	Elton John's Greatest Hits	198?	10.00
❑ 3027	Elton John's Greatest Hits, Volume 2	1977	12.00
❑ 5225	Elton John's Greatest Hits, Volume 2	1981	10.00
❑ 2130	Empty Sky	1975	12.00
— First American issue of his 1969 debut			
❑ 620	Empty Sky	1979	10.00
❑ 2-10003	Goodbye Yellow Brick Road	1973	18.00
❑ 6894	Goodbye Yellow Brick Road	1980	12.00
❑ R231711	Greatest Hits Volumes One and Two	198?	18.00
— RCA Music Service exclusive; combines both MCA greatest-hits sets			
❑ 2197	Here and There	1976	12.00
❑ 622	Here and There	1979	10.00
❑ 2017	Honky Chateau	1973	12.00
❑ 37064	Honky Chateau	1979	10.00
❑ 8022	Live in Australia with the Melbourne Symphony Orchestra	1987	18.00
❑ 2016	Madman Across the Water	1973	12.00
— With booklet			
❑ 3003	Madman Across the Water	1977	10.00
❑ 37200	Madman Across the Water	1982	10.00
❑ 6240	Reg Strikes Back	1988	12.00
❑ 2163	Rock of the Westies	1975	12.00
❑ 621	Rock of the Westies	1979	10.00
❑ 6321	Sleeping with the Past	1989	12.00
❑ 39115	The Complete Thom Bell Sessions	1989	30.00
❑ 13921 [EP]	The Thom Bell Sessions	1979	10.00
❑ 2014	Tumbleweed Connection	1973	12.00
— With booklet			
❑ 3001	Tumbleweed Connection	1977	10.00
❑ 37199	Tumbleweed Connection	1982	10.00
❑ 5104	Victim of Love	1979	12.00
❑ 771	Victim of Love	1981	10.00
❑ 4L33-1848 [DJ]	Victim of Love	1979	100.00
— Promo-only collection of the entire album as four 12-inch singles			
❑ 37266	Your Songs	1986	12.00

MERCURY

Number	Title	Yr	NM
❑ 5310374	Goodbye Yellow Brick Road	2008	30.00

MOBILE FIDELITY

Number	Title	Yr	NM
❑ 2-160	Goodbye Yellow Brick Road	1984	60.00
— Audiophile vinyl			

NAUTILUS

Number	Title	Yr	NM
❑ NR-42	Elton John's Greatest Hits	198?	100.00
— Audiophile vinyl			

PARAMOUNT

Number	Title	Yr	NM
❑ PAS6004 [B]	Friends (Soundtrack)	1971	30.00
— Whitish gray label original			
❑ PAS6004 [B]	Friends (Soundtrack)	1975	40.00
— Dark blue label with "Paramount" logo at top and ABC Records reference along edge; much rarer than the original			

ROCKET

Number	Title	Yr	NM
❑ 2-11004	Blue Moves	1976	18.00
— Originals have light blue labels with a train at the top of the label			
❑ L33-1173/4 [DJ]	Get Up and Dance	1977	100.00
— Promo-only sampler from "Blue Moves" LP; blue vinyl			
❑ 526915-1	Made in England	1995	25.00
— U.S. version is on 180-gram vinyl, distributed by Classic Records			

UNI

Number	Title	Yr	NM
❑ 93105	11/17/1970	1971	18.00
❑ 73090 [B]	Elton John	1970	25.00
❑ 93090	Elton John	1971	15.00
❑ 93135	Honky Chateau	1972	25.00
— With "(P) 1972 MCA Records, Inc." on label			
❑ 93135	Honky Chateau	1972	18.00
— With "(P) 1972 This Record Co., Ltd." on label			
❑ 93120	Madman Across the Water	1971	18.00
— With booklet			
❑ 73096 [B]	Tumbleweed Connection	1971	25.00
— With booklet			
❑ 93096	Tumbleweed Connection	1971	15.00
— With booklet			

JOHN, LITTLE WILLIE

BLUESWAY

Number	Title	Yr	NM
❑ BLS-6069	Free at Last	1973	30.00

KING

Number	Title	Yr	NM
❑ 802 [M]	Come On and Join Little Willie John	1962	120.00
❑ 395-564 [M]	Fever	1956	1000.00
— Nurse with thermometer" cover			
❑ 564 [M]	Fever	1957	600.00
— White cover with "Fever" in large colorful letters			
❑ KS-1081	Free at Last	1970	40.00
❑ 691 [M]	Little Willie John In Action	1960	250.00
❑ 949 [M]	Little Willie Sings All Originals	1966	100.00
❑ KS-949 [S]	Little Willie Sings All Originals	1966	150.00
❑ 603 [M]	Mister Little Willie John	1958	250.00
❑ 739 [M]	Sure Things	1961	150.00
❑ 596 [M]	Talk to Me	1958	300.00
❑ 895 [M]	These Are My Favorite Songs	1964	100.00
❑ 767 [M]	The Sweet, the Hot, the Teenage Beat	1961	150.00

JOHN, ROBERT

COLUMBIA

Number	Title	Yr	NM
❑ CS9687 [S]	If You Don't Want My Love	1968	25.00
❑ CS9687 [M]	If You Don't Want My Love	1968	50.00
— Mono is white label promo only with stereo number; "Special Mono Radio Station Copy" sticker is on front cover			

EMI AMERICA

Number	Title	Yr	NM
❑ SW-17027	Back on the Street	1980	12.00
❑ SW-17007	Robert John	1979	12.00

HARMONY

Number	Title	Yr	NM
❑ KH31353	On the Way Up	1972	15.00

JOHNNIE AND JACK

DECCA

Number	Title	Yr	NM
❑ DL4308 [M]	Smiles and Tears	1962	25.00
❑ DL74308 [S]	Smiles and Tears	1962	30.00

RCA CAMDEN

Number	Title	Yr	NM
❑ CAL-747 [M]	Johnny & Jack Sing "Poison Love" and Other Country Favorites	1963	30.00
❑ CAS-747 [R]	Johnny & Jack Sing "Poison Love" and Other Country Favorites	1963	15.00
❑ CAL-822 [M]	Sincerely	1964	30.00
❑ CAS-822 [R]	Sincerely	1964	15.00

RCA VICTOR

Number	Title	Yr	NM
❑ VPM-6022	All the Best of Johnnie & Jack	1970	30.00
❑ LPM-2017 [M]	Hits by Johnnie & Jack	1959	30.00
❑ LSP-2017 [R]	Hits by Johnnie & Jack	1959	25.00
❑ LPM-1587 [M]	The Tennessee Mountain Boys	1957	40.00

JOHNNY AND THE BLUE BEATS

WINSOR

Number	Title	Yr	NM
❑ 1001	Smile	196?	40.00

JOHNNY AND THE HURRICANES

ATILA

Number	Title	Yr	NM
❑ 1030 [M]	Live at the Star-Club	1964	300.00

BIG TOP

Number	Title	Yr	NM
❑ 12-1302 [M]	The Big Sound of Johnny and the Hurricanes	1960	250.00
❑ ST 12-1302 [S]	The Big Sound of Johnny and the Hurricanes	1960	300.00

WARWICK

Number	Title	Yr	NM
❑ W-2007 [M]	Johnny and the Hurricanes	1959	150.00
❑ W-2007ST [S]	Johnny and the Hurricanes	1959	300.00
❑ W-2010 [M]	Stormsville	1960	150.00
❑ W-2010ST [S]	Stormsville	1960	250.00

JOHN'S CHILDREN

WHITE WHALE

Number	Title	Yr	NM
❑ WWS7128 [B]	Orgasm	1970	350.00

JOHNSON, ALPHONSO

EPIC

Number	Title	Yr	NM
❑ PE34118	Moonshadows	1975	12.00
❑ JE34869	Spellbound	1977	12.00
❑ JE36521	The Best of Alphonso Johnson	1979	12.00
❑ PE34364	Yesterday's Dreams	1976	12.00

JOHNSON, BETTY

ATLANTIC

Number	Title	Yr	NM
❑ 8017 [M]	Betty Johnson	1958	50.00
❑ 8027 [M]	The Song You Heard When You Fell in Love	1959	50.00
— Black label			
❑ SD8027 [S]	The Song You Heard When You Fell in Love	1959	80.00
— Green label			
❑ 8027 [M]	The Song You Heard When You Fell in Love	1960	25.00
— White "fan" logo on right			
❑ SD8027 [S]	The Song You Heard When You Fell in Love	1960	30.00
— White "fan" logo on right			

JOHNSON, BLIND WILLIE

FOLKWAYS

Number	Title	Yr	NM
❑ FG-3585 [M]	Blind Willie Johnson: His Story	1957	100.00

Number	Title	Yr	NM

RBF

| ❏ 10 [M] | Blind Willie Johnson 1927-1930 | 1965 | 70.00 |

JOHNSON, BOB, AND THE LONESOME TRAVELERS

PARKWAY

| ❏ P-7017 [M] | 12 Shades of Bluegrass | 1962 | 50.00 |

JOHNSON, BUBBER

KING

| ❏ 624 [M] | Bubber Johnson Sings Sweet Love Songs | 1959 | 150.00 |
| ❏ 569 [M] | Come Home | 1957 | 200.00 |

JOHNSON, BUDD

ARGO

❏ LP-721 [M]	French Cookin'	1963	30.00
❏ LPS-721 [S]	French Cookin'	1963	30.00
❏ LP-748 [M]	Off the Wall	1965	30.00
❏ LPS-748 [S]	Off the Wall	1965	30.00
❏ LP-736 [M]	Ya! Ya!	1964	30.00
❏ LPS-736 [S]	Ya! Ya!	1964	30.00

FANTASY

| ❏ OJC-209 | Budd Johnson and the Four Brass Giants | 1985 | 12.00 |
| ❏ OJC-1720 | Let's Swing | 198? | 12.00 |

FELSTED

| ❏ FAJ-7007 [M] | Blues A La Mode | 1959 | 60.00 |
| ❏ SJA-2007 [S] | Blues A La Mode | 1959 | 80.00 |

MASTER JAZZ

| ❏ 8119 | Blues A La Mode | 197? | 15.00 |

RIVERSIDE

| ❏ RLP-343 [M] | Budd Johnson and the Four Brass Giants | 1960 | 40.00 |
| ❏ RS-9343 [S] | Budd Johnson and the Four Brass Giants | 1960 | 50.00 |

SWINGVILLE

❏ SVLP-2015 [M]	Let's Swing	1961	50.00
—Purple label			
❏ SVLP-2015 [M]	Let's Swing	1965	30.00
—Blue label, trident logo at right			

JOHNSON, BUDDY & ELLA

MERCURY

| ❏ MG-20347 [M] | Swing Me | 195? | 80.00 |

ROULETTE

| ❏ R25085 [M] | Go Ahead and Rock and Roll | 1959 | 80.00 |
| ❏ SR25085 [S] | Go Ahead and Rock and Roll | 1959 | 120.00 |

JOHNSON, BUDDY

MCA

| ❏ 1356 | Fine Brown Frame | 198? | 12.00 |

MERCURY

❏ MG-20330 [M]	Buddy Johnson Wails	195?	80.00
❏ SR-60072 [S]	Buddy Johnson Wails	195?	100.00
❏ MG-20209 [M]	Rock 'N' Roll	195?	80.00
❏ MG-20347 [M]	Swing Me	195?	80.00
❏ MG-20322 [M]	Walkin'	196?	80.00

WING

❏ MGW-12234 [M]	Buddy Johnson Wails	196?	30.00
❏ MGW-12005 [M]	Rock 'N' Roll	1956	150.00
❏ MGW-12111 [M]	Rock 'n' Roll Stage Show	1963	40.00

JOHNSON, BUNK, AND LU WATTERS

GOOD TIME JAZZ

| ❏ L-12024 [M] | Bunk and Lu | 195? | 40.00 |

JOHNSON, BUNK

AMERICAN MUSIC

| ❏ 644 [10] | Bunk Johnson Talking | 1952 | 60.00 |
| ❏ 638 [10] | Bunk Plays the Blues -- The Spirituals | 1951 | 60.00 |

COLUMBIA

❏ CL829 [M]	Bunk Johnson	1955	40.00
—Red and black label with six "eye" logos			
❏ GL520 [M]	Bunk Johnson and His Band	1952	60.00
—Black label, silver print			
❏ CL520 [M]	Bunk Johnson and His Band	1953	50.00
—Maroon label, gold print			
❏ CL520 [M]	Bunk Johnson and His Band	1955	40.00
—Red and black label with six "eye" logos			

COLUMBIA MASTERWORKS

| ❏ ML4802 [M] | The Last Testament of a Great New Orleans Jazzman | 1950 | 80.00 |

COMMODORE

| ❏ DL-30007 [M] | The Bunk Johnson Band | 1952 | 50.00 |

FOLKLYRIC

| ❏ 9047 | Bunk Johnson and His New Orleans Jazz Band | 1986 | 12.00 |

GHB

| ❏ 101 | Spicy Advice | 198? | 12.00 |

GOOD TIME JAZZ

| ❏ L-12048 [M] | Bunk Johnson and His Superior Jazz Band | 1962 | 30.00 |
| ❏ L-17 [10] | Bunk Johnson and the Yerba Buena Jazz Band | 1953 | 50.00 |

MAINSTREAM

| ❏ 56039 [M] | Bunk Johnson -- A Legend | 1965 | 25.00 |
| ❏ S-6039 [R] | Bunk Johnson -- A Legend | 1965 | 15.00 |

TRIP

| ❏ J-2 | Bunk Johnson | 1970 | 15.00 |

JOHNSON, CANDY

CANJO

| ❏ LP-1002 [M] | Bikini Beach | 1964 | 40.00 |
| ❏ LP-1001 [M] | The Candy Johnson Show | 1964 | 40.00 |

JOHNSON, CHARLIE

X

| ❏ LVA-3026 [10] | Harlem in the Twenties, Vol. 2 | 1954 | 60.00 |

JOHNSON, DAVID EARLE; JAN HAMMER; JOHN ABERCROMBIE

PLUG

| ❏ 1 | The Midweek Blues | 1986 | 15.00 |

JOHNSON, DAVID EARLE

CMP

| ❏ CMP-14-ST | Hip Address | 1980 | 15.00 |
| ❏ CMP-20-ST | Skin Deep -- Yeah! | 1981 | 15.00 |

VANGUARD

| ❏ VSD-79401 | Time Free | 197? | 12.00 |

JOHNSON, DICK

CONCORD JAZZ

❏ CJ-107	Dick Johnson Plays Alto Sax & Flute & Soprano Sax & Clarinet	1979	15.00
❏ CJ-146	Piano Mover	1980	15.00
❏ CJ-135	Spider's Blues	1980	15.00
❏ CJ-167	Swing Shift	1981	15.00

EMARCY

| ❏ MG-36081 [M] | Music for Swinging Moderns | 1956 | 100.00 |

RIVERSIDE

| ❏ RLP 12-253 [M] | Most Likely... | 1957 | 80.00 |

JOHNSON, J.J., AND KAI WINDING

A&M

❏ SP-3016	Betwixt and Between	1969	25.00
—As "J & K"			
❏ SP-3008	Israel	1968	25.00
—As "K. & J.J."			
❏ SP9-3008	Israel	1983	18.00
—As "K. & J.J."; "Audio Master Plus" reissue			

ABC IMPULSE!

| ❏ AS-1 [S] | The Great Kai & J.J. | 1968 | 15.00 |

BETHLEHEM

❏ BCP-6001 [M]	K + J.J. (East Coast Jazz/7)	1955	50.00
—With the number "BCP 13" on the upper right corner of the front cover and "BCP 6001" stickers on the back cover and "BCP 6001" on the labels			
❏ BCP-13 [M]	K + J.J. (East Coast Jazz/7)	1955	100.00
—With "BCP 13" on the label as well as the cover			
❏ BCP-6001 [M]	The Finest Kai Winding and J.J. Johnson	197?	15.00
—Reissue with new title, distributed by RCA Victor			

COLUMBIA

❏ CL973 [M]	Jay and Kai	1957	50.00
—Red and black label with six "eye" logos			
❏ CL973 [M]	Jay and Kai	1963	25.00
—Red label with "Guaranteed High Fidelity" or "360 Sound Mono" at bottom			
❏ CL892 [M]	J.J. Johnson, Kai Winding + 6	1956	50.00
—Red and black "6-eye" label			
❏ CL892 [M]	J.J. Johnson, Kai Winding + 6	1963	25.00
—Red label with "Guaranteed High Fidelity" or "360 Sound Mono" at bottom			
❏ CL2573 [10]	Kai + J.J.	1955	80.00
❏ CL742 [M]	Trombone for Two	1956	50.00
—Red label with "360 Sound Stereo" in black or white at bottom			
❏ CL742 [M]	Trombone for Two	1963	25.00
—Red label with "Guaranteed High Fidelity" or "360 Sound Mono" at bottom			

COLUMBIA JAZZ ODYSSEY

| ❏ PC37001 [M] | J.J. Johnson, Kai Winding + 6 | 198? | 12.00 |

IMPULSE!

| ❏ A-1 [M] | The Great Kai & J.J. | 1961 | 40.00 |
| ❏ AS-1 [S] | The Great Kai & J.J. | 1961 | 50.00 |

MCA

| ❏ 29061 | The Great Kai & J.J. | 1980 | 12.00 |

PRESTIGE

| ❏ PRLP-195 [10] | Jay and Kai | 1954 | 200.00 |

❏ PRLP-7253 [M]	Looking Back	1963	50.00
❏ PRST-7253 [R]	Looking Back	1963	30.00
❏ PRLP-109 [10]	Modern Jazz Trombones	1951	200.00

SAVOY

❏ MG-15038 [10]	Jay and Kai	1954	120.00
❏ MG-12010 [M]	Jay and Kai	1955	80.00
❏ MG-15048 [10]	Jay and Kai, Volume 2	1955	100.00
❏ MG-15049 [10]	Jay and Kai, Volume 3	1955	100.00
❏ MG-12106 [M]	J.J. Johnson's Jazz Quintets	1957	80.00

X

| ❏ LXA-1040 [M] | An Afternoon at Birdland | 1956 | 80.00 |

JOHNSON, J.J., AND NAT ADDERLEY

PABLO LIVE

| ❏ 2620109 | Yokohama Concert | 1977 | 18.00 |

JOHNSON, J.J.; KAI WINDING; BENNIE GREEN

DEBUT

❏ DEB-126 [M]	Four Trombones	1958	100.00
❏ DLP-5 [10]	Jazz Workshop, Volume 1	1953	200.00
❏ DLP-14 [10]	Jazz Workshop, Volume 2	1955	200.00

FANTASY

❏ 6005 [M]	Four Trombones	1963	50.00
—Red vinyl			
❏ 6005 [M]	Four Trombones	1963	30.00
—Black vinyl			
❏ 86005 [R]	Four Trombones	1963	40.00
—Blue vinyl			
❏ 86005 [R]	Four Trombones	1963	25.00
—Black vinyl			
❏ OJC-091	Trombones by Three	198?	12.00

PRESTIGE

❏ PRLP-7030 [M]	J.J. Johnson, Kai Winding, Bennie Green	1956	150.00
—Yellow label with W. 50th St. address			
❏ PRLP-7023 [M]	Trombone by Three	1956	750.00
—Yellow label with W. 50th St. address. Andy Warhol cover.			
❏ 16-4 [M]	Trombone by Three	1956	500.00
—This album plays at 16 2/3 rpm and is marked as such; white label			

JOHNSON, J.J.

ABC IMPULSE!

❏ AS-68 [S]	Proof Positive	1968	25.00
—Black label with red ring			
❏ AS-68 [S]	Proof Positive	1975	15.00
—Green, blue, purple "target" label			

BLUE NOTE

❏ BLP-5057 [10]	Jay Jay Johnson, Volume 2	1955	700.00
❏ BLP-5070 [10]	Jay Jay Johnson, Volume 3	1955	700.00
❏ BLP-5028 [10]	Jay Jay Johnson All Stars	1953	700.00
❏ BLP-1505 [M]	The Eminent Jay Jay Johnson, Volume 1	1955	300.00
—Deep groove" version; Lexington Ave. address on label			
❏ BLP-1505 [M]	The Eminent Jay Jay Johnson, Volume 1	1958	200.00
—Deep groove" version, W. 63rd St. address on label			
❏ BLP-1505 [M]	The Eminent Jay Jay Johnson, Volume 1	1963	50.00
—New York, USA" address on label			
❏ BST-81505 [R]	The Eminent Jay Jay Johnson, Volume 1	1967	25.00
—A Division of Liberty Records" on label			
❏ BLP-1506 [M]	The Eminent Jay Jay Johnson, Volume 2	1958	200.00
—Deep groove" version, W. 63rd St. address on label			
❏ BLP-1506 [M]	The Eminent Jay Jay Johnson, Volume 2	1955	300.00
—Deep groove" version; Lexington Ave. address on label			
❏ BLP-1506 [M]	The Eminent Jay Jay Johnson, Volume 2	1963	50.00
—New York, USA" address on label			
❏ BST-81506 [R]	The Eminent Jay Jay Johnson, Volume 2	1967	25.00
—A Division of Liberty Records" on label			
❏ B1-81505	The Eminent J.J. Johnson, Volume 1	1989	18.00
—The Finest in Jazz Since 1939" reissue			
❏ B1-81506	The Eminent J.J. Johnson, Volume 2	1989	18.00
—The Finest in Jazz Since 1939" reissue			

COLUMBIA

❏ CL1737 [M]	A Touch of Satin	1962	40.00
—Red and black label with six "eye" logos			
❏ CL1737 [M]	A Touch of Satin	1963	18.00
—Red label with "Guaranteed High Fidelity" or "360 Sound Mono" at bottom			
❏ CS8537 [S]	A Touch of Satin	1962	50.00
—Red and black label with six "eye" logos			
❏ CS8537 [S]	A Touch of Satin	1963	25.00
—Red label with "360 Sound Stereo" in black or white at bottom			
❏ CL1303 [M]	Blue Trombone	1959	40.00
—Red and black label with six "eye" logos			
❏ CL1303 [M]	Blue Trombone	1963	15.00
—Red label with "Guaranteed High Fidelity" or "360 Sound Mono" at bottom			
❏ CS8109 [S]	Blue Trombone	1959	50.00
—Red and black label with six "eye" logos			

Number	Title	Yr	NM
❑ CS8109 [S]	Blue Trombone	1963	18.00
—Red label with "360 Sound Stereo" in black or white at bottom			
❑ CL1084 [M]	Dial J.J. 5	1957	50.00
—Red and black label with six "eye" logos			
❑ CL1084 [M]	Dial J.J. 5	1963	18.00
—Red label with "Guaranteed High Fidelity" or "360 Sound Mono" at bottom			
❑ CL1030 [M]	First Place	1957	50.00
—Red and black label with six "eye" logos			
❑ CL1030 [M]	First Place	1963	18.00
—Red label with "Guaranteed High Fidelity" or "360 Sound Mono" at bottom			
❑ CL935 [M]	J" Is for Jazz	1956	50.00
—Red and black label with six "eye" logos			
❑ CL935 [M]	J" Is for Jazz	1963	18.00
—Red label with "Guaranteed High Fidelity" or "360 Sound Mono" at bottom			
❑ CL1606 [M]	J.J. Inc	1961	30.00
—Red and black label with six "eye" logos			
❑ CL1606 [M]	J.J. Inc	1963	15.00
—Red label with "Guaranteed High Fidelity" or "360 Sound Mono" at bottom			
❑ CS8406 [S]	J.J. Inc	1961	40.00
—Red and black label with six "eye" logos			
❑ CS8406 [S]	J.J. Inc	1963	18.00
—Red label with "360 Sound Stereo" in black or white at bottom			
❑ CL1161 [M]	J.J. In Person	1958	50.00
—Red and black label with six "eye" logos			
❑ CL1161 [M]	J.J. In Person	1963	18.00
—Red label with "Guaranteed High Fidelity" or "360 Sound Mono" at bottom			
❑ CS8009 [S]	J.J. In Person	1959	40.00
—Red and black label with six "eye" logos			
❑ CS8009 [S]	J.J. In Person	1963	15.00
—Red label with "360 Sound Stereo" in black or white at bottom			
❑ CL1383 [M]	Really Livin'	1959	40.00
—Red and black label with six "eye" logos			
❑ CL1383 [M]	Really Livin'	1963	15.00
—Red label with "Guaranteed High Fidelity" or "360 Sound Mono" at bottom			
❑ CS8170 [S]	Really Livin'	1959	50.00
—Red and black label with six "eye" logos			
❑ CS8178 [S]	Really Livin'	1963	18.00
—Red label with "360 Sound Stereo" in black or white at bottom			
❑ CL1547 [M]	Trombones and Voices	1960	30.00
—Red and black label with six "eye" logos			
❑ CL1547 [M]	Trombones and Voices	1963	15.00
—Red label with "Guaranteed High Fidelity" or "360 Sound Mono" at bottom			
❑ CS8347 [S]	Trombones and Voices	1960	40.00
—Red and black label with six "eye" logos			
❑ CS8347 [S]	Trombones and Voices	1963	18.00
—Red label with "360 Sound Stereo" in black or white at bottom			
COLUMBIA JAZZ ODYSSEY			
❑ PC36808	J.J. Inc.	1979	12.00
IMPULSE!			
❑ A-68 [M]	Proof Positive	1965	40.00
❑ AS-68 [S]	Proof Positive	1965	50.00
MCA			
❑ 29072	Proof Positive	1980	12.00
MILESTONE			
❑ M-9093	Pinnacles	1979	15.00
MOSAIC			
❑ MQ11-169	The Complete Columbia J.J. Johnson Small Group Sessions	199?	300.00
PABLO TODAY			
❑ 2312123	Concepts in Blue	1980	15.00
PRESTIGE			
❑ 24067	Early Bones	197?	18.00
RCA VICTOR			
❑ LPM-3544 [M]	Broadway Express	1966	25.00
❑ LSP-3544 [S]	Broadway Express	1966	30.00
❑ LPM-3458 [M]	Goodies	1965	25.00
❑ LSP-3458 [S]	Goodies	1965	30.00
❑ LPM-3350 [M]	J.J.!	1965	25.00
❑ LSP-3350 [S]	J.J.!	1965	30.00
❑ LPM-3833 [M]	The Total J.J. Johnson	1967	30.00
❑ LSP-3833 [S]	The Total J.J. Johnson	1967	25.00
REGENT			
❑ MG-6001 [M]	Jazz South Pacific	1956	50.00
SAVOY			
❑ MG-12205 [M]	Jazz South Pacific	196?	25.00
—Reissue of Regent 6001			
SAVOY JAZZ			
❑ SJL-2232	Mad Bebop	198?	15.00
VERVE			
❑ V-8530 [M]	J.J.'s Broadway	1963	25.00
❑ V6-8530 [S]	J.J.'s Broadway	1963	30.00

JOHNSON, J.J./BENNIE GREEN

Number	Title	Yr	NM
PRESTIGE			
❑ PRLP-123 [10]	Modern Jazz Trombones, Volume 2	1952	200.00

JOHNSON, JACK

Number	Title	Yr	NM
UNIVERSAL REPUBLIC			
❑ 1058001	Sleep Through the Static	2008	30.00

JOHNSON, JAMES P.

Number	Title	Yr	NM
BIOGRAPH			
❑ 1003	Rare Piano Rolls	1972	15.00
❑ 1009	Rare Piano Rolls, Volume 2	1972	15.00
BLUE NOTE			
❑ BLP-7012 [10]	Jazz Band Ball	1951	300.00
❑ BLP-7011 [10]	Stomps, Rags and Blues	1951	300.00
COLUMBIA			
❑ CL1780 [M]	Father of the Stride Piano	1961	30.00
—Red and black label with six "eye" logos			
❑ CL1780 [M]	Father of the Stride Piano	1963	18.00
—All-red label, "Guaranteed High Fidelity" or "360 Sound Mono" at bottom			
DECCA			
❑ DL5228 [10]	James P. Johnson Plays Fats Waller Favorites	1951	100.00
❑ DL5190 [10]	The Daddy of the Piano	1950	100.00
FOLKWAYS			
❑ FJ-2816	Striding in Dixieland	196?	25.00
❑ FJ-2850	The Original James P. Johnson	196?	25.00
❑ FJ-2842 [M]	Yamekraw	1962	25.00
RIVERSIDE			
❑ RLP 12-151 [M]	Backwater Blues	1955	60.00
—White label, blue print			
❑ RLP 12-151 [M]	Backwater Blues	1959	40.00
—Blue label, microphone logo at top			
❑ RLP-1046 [10]	Early Harlem Piano, Vol. 2	1954	120.00
❑ RLP-1056 [10]	Harlem Rent Party	1955	100.00
❑ RLP 12-105 [M]	Rediscovered Early Solos	1955	60.00
—White label, blue print			
❑ RLP 12-105 [M]	Rediscovered Early Solos	1959	40.00
—Blue label, microphone logo at top			
❑ RLP-1011 [10]	Rent Party	1953	120.00
SOUNDS			
❑ 1204	Father of the Stride Piano	196?	18.00
STINSON			
❑ SLP-21 [10]	New York Jazz	1950	120.00
❑ SLP-21 [M]	New York Jazz	195?	50.00
TIME-LIFE			
❑ STL-J-18	Giants of Jazz	1981	25.00

JOHNSON, LONNIE, AND VICTORIA SPIVEY

Number	Title	Yr	NM
BLUESVILLE			
❑ BVLP-1044 [M]	Idle Hours	1962	150.00
—Blue label, silver print			
❑ BVLP-1044 [M]	Idle Hours	1964	50.00
—Blue label with trident logo at right			
❑ BVLP-1054 [M]	Woman Blues	1962	150.00
—Blue label, silver print			
❑ BVLP-1054 [M]	Woman Blues	1964	50.00
—Blue label with trident logo at right			
FANTASY			
❑ OBC-518	Idle Hours	198?	15.00

JOHNSON, LONNIE

Number	Title	Yr	NM
BLUESVILLE			
❑ BVLP-1062 [M]	Another Night to Cry	1963	200.00
—Blue label, silver print			
❑ BVLP-1062 [M]	Another Night to Cry	1964	60.00
—Blue label with trident logo at right			
❑ BVLP-1011 [M]	Blues and Ballads	1960	200.00
—Blue label, silver print			
❑ BVLP-1011 [M]	Blues and Ballads	1964	60.00
—Blue label with trident logo at right			
❑ BVLP-1007 [M]	Blues by Lonnie	1960	200.00
—Blue label, silver print			
❑ BVLP-1007 [M]	Blues by Lonnie	1964	60.00
—Blue label with trident logo at right			
❑ BVLP-1024 [M]	Losing Game	1961	200.00
—Blue label, silver print			
❑ BVLP-1024 [M]	Losing Game	1964	60.00
—Blue label with trident logo at right			
COLUMBIA			
❑ C46221	Steppin' On the Blues	1990	25.00
FANTASY			
❑ OBC-531	Blues and Ballads	1990	15.00
❑ OBC-502	Blues by Lonnie	198?	15.00
KING			
❑ 520 [M]	Lonesome Road	1958	2000.00
—VG value 750; VG+ value 1375			
❑ 958 [M]	Lonnie Johnson 24 Twelve-Bar Blues	1966	60.00
❑ KS-958 [R]	Lonnie Johnson 24 Twelve-Bar Blues	1966	60.00
❑ KS-1083	Tomorrow Night	1970	30.00
PRESTIGE			
❑ PRST-7724	The Blues of Lonnie Johnson	1970	25.00

JOHNSON, MARV

Number	Title	Yr	NM
UNITED ARTISTS			
❑ UAL3187 [M]	I Believe	1962	150.00
❑ UAS6187 [S]	I Believe	1962	200.00
❑ UAL3081 [M]	Marvelous Marv Johnson	1960	150.00
❑ UAS6081 [S]	Marvelous Marv Johnson	1960	200.00
❑ UAL3118 [M]	More Marv Johnson	1961	150.00
❑ UAS6118 [S]	More Marv Johnson	1961	200.00

JOHNSON, MICHAEL

Number	Title	Yr	NM
ATCO			
❑ SD7028	There Is a Breeze	1973	18.00
EMI AMERICA			
❑ SW-17035	Call Me Blue	1980	12.00
❑ SW-17010	Dialogue	1979	12.00
❑ SW-17057	Home Free	1981	12.00
❑ SW-17104	Lifetime Guarantee	1983	12.00
❑ SW-17002	The Michael Johnson Album	1978	12.00
RCA			
❑ 6715-1-R	That's That	1988	10.00
RCA VICTOR			
❑ AEL1-9501	Wings	1986	10.00
SANSKRIT			
❑ (# unknown)	There Is a Breeze	1973	50.00

JOHNSON, OSIE

Number	Title	Yr	NM
BETHLEHEM			
❑ BCP-66 [M]	The Happy Jazz of Osie Johnson	1957	50.00
PERIOD			
❑ SPL-1112 [10]	Johnson's Whacks	1955	80.00
❑ SPL-1108 [10]	Osie's Oasis	1955	80.00
RCA VICTOR			
❑ LPM-1369 [M]	A Bit of the Blues	1957	40.00

JOHNSON, PETE

Number	Title	Yr	NM
BLUE NOTE			
❑ BLP-7019 [10]	Boogie Woogie Blues and Skiffle	1952	300.00
BRUNSWICK			
❑ BL58041 [10]	Boogie Woogie Mood	1953	80.00
MCA			
❑ 1333	Boogie Woogie Mood	198?	12.00
MOSAIC			
❑ MR1-119 [B]	The Pete Johnson/Earl Hines/Teddy Bunn Blue Note Sessions	199?	25.00
RIVERSIDE			
❑ RLP-1056 [10]	Jumpin' with Pete Johnson	1955	80.00
SAVOY			
❑ MG-14018 [M]	Pete's Blues	1958	120.00
SAVOY JAZZ			
❑ SJL-414	Pete's Blues	1985	12.00

JOHNSON, PETE/HADDA BROOKS

Number	Title	Yr	NM
CROWN			
❑ CLP-5058 [M]	Boogie	195?	25.00

JOHNSON, PLAS

Number	Title	Yr	NM
CAPITOL			
❑ T1503 [M]	Mood for the Blues	1961	30.00
❑ ST1503 [S]	Mood for the Blues	1961	30.00
❑ T1281 [M]	This Must Be the Plas!	1960	30.00
❑ ST1281 [S]	This Must Be the Plas!	1960	30.00
CONCORD JAZZ			
❑ CJ-15	Blues	1975	12.00
❑ CJ-24	Positively	1976	12.00
TAMPA			
❑ TP-24 [M]	Bop Me, Daddy	1957	100.00
—Colored vinyl			
❑ TP-24 [M]	Bop Me, Daddy	1958	50.00
—Black vinyl			

JOHNSON, ROBERT

Number	Title	Yr	NM
COLUMBIA			
❑ CL1654 [M]	King of the Delta Blues Singers	1961	500.00
—Red and black label with six "eye" logos			
❑ CL1654 [M]	King of the Delta Blues Singers	1963	50.00
—Guaranteed High Fidelity" label			
❑ CL1654 [M]	King of the Delta Blues Singers	1965	30.00
—360 Sound Mono" label			
❑ CL1654 [M]	King of the Delta Blues Singers	1970	15.00
—Orange label with "Columbia" circling the edge			
❑ CL1654 [M]	King of the Delta Blues Singers	1998	12.00
—Red label, "Columbia" in white at top, "Sony Music" under side numbers			

Number	Title	Yr	NM
❑ CL1654 [M]	King of the Delta Blues Singers	2001	18.00

—Reissue on 180-gram vinyl (sealed copies have a sticker indicating this)

Number	Title	Yr	NM
❑ C30034 [M]	King of the Delta Blues Singers, Volume 2	1970	25.00
❑ PC30034 [M]	King of the Delta Blues Singers, Volume 2	1979	12.00
❑ C346222	Robert Johnson -- The Complete Recordings	1990	50.00

JOHNSON, RUDOLPH

BLACK JAZZ

Number	Title	Yr	NM
❑ 11	Second Coming	1972	30.00
❑ 4	Spring Rain	1971	30.00

OVATION

Number	Title	Yr	NM
❑ OV-1805	Time and Space	1977	18.00

JOHNSON, SYL

TWINIGHT

Number	Title	Yr	NM
❑ LPS-1002	Is It Because I'm Black?	1968	60.00

JOHNSTON, BRUCE

COLUMBIA

Number	Title	Yr	NM
❑ PC34459	Going Public	1976	18.00
❑ CL2057 [M]	Surfin' 'Round the World	1963	200.00
❑ CS8857 [S]	Surfin' 'Round the World	1963	300.00

DEL-FI

Number	Title	Yr	NM
❑ DFLP-1228 [M]	Surfers' Pajama Party	1963	200.00
❑ DFST-1228 [S]	Surfers' Pajama Party	1963	300.00

JOHNSTON, COLONEL JUBILATION B., AND THE MYSTIC KNIGHTS BAND AND STREET SINGERS

COLUMBIA

Number	Title	Yr	NM
❑ CL2532 [M]	Moldy Goldies	1966	30.00
❑ CS9332 [S]	Moldy Goldies	1966	30.00

JOLLY, PETE

A&M

Number	Title	Yr	NM
❑ SP-4184	Give a Damn	1970	15.00
❑ SP-4145	Herb Alpert Presents Pete Jolly	1968	15.00
❑ SP-3033	Seasons	1969	15.00

AVA

Number	Title	Yr	NM
❑ A-51 [M]	Hello Jolly	1964	25.00
❑ AS-51 [S]	Hello Jolly	1964	30.00
❑ A-22 [M]	Little Bird	1963	25.00
❑ AS 22 [S]	Little Bird	1963	30.00
❑ A-39 [M]	Sweet September	1963	25.00
❑ AS-39 [S]	Sweet September	1963	30.00

CHARLIE PARKER

Number	Title	Yr	NM
❑ PLP-825 [M]	Pete Jolly Gasses Everybody	1962	25.00
❑ PLP-825S [S]	Pete Jolly Gasses Everybody	1962	30.00

COLUMBIA

Number	Title	Yr	NM
❑ CL2397 [M]	Too Much, Baby	1965	25.00
❑ CS9197 [S]	Too Much, Baby	1965	30.00

MAINSTREAM

Number	Title	Yr	NM
❑ S-6114	The Best of Pete Jolly	196?	18.00

METROJAZZ

Number	Title	Yr	NM
❑ E-1014 [M]	Impossible	1958	35.00
❑ SE-1014 [S]	Impossible	1958	35.00

MGM

Number	Title	Yr	NM
❑ E-4127 [M]	5 O'Clock Shadows	1963	25.00
❑ SE-4127 [S]	5 O'Clock Shadows	1963	30.00

RCA VICTOR

Number	Title	Yr	NM
❑ LPM-1125 [M]	Duo, Trio, Quartet	1955	50.00
❑ LPM-1105 [M]	Jolly Jumps In	1955	50.00
❑ LPM-1367 [M]	When Lights Are Low	1957	50.00

STEREO FIDELITY

Number	Title	Yr	NM
❑ SFS-11000 [S]	Continental Jazz	1960	30.00

TRIP

Number	Title	Yr	NM
❑ TLP-5817	A Touch of Jazz	197?	12.00

JOLSON, AL

DECCA

Number	Title	Yr	NM
❑ DLP5030 [10]	Al Jolson, Vol. III	1949	30.00
❑ DLP5026 [10]	Al Jolson In Songs He Made Famous	1949	30.00
❑ DL9095 [M]	Al Jolson with Oscar Levant at the Piano	1961	30.00
❑ DL79095 [R]	Al Jolson with Oscar Levant at the Piano	196?	15.00
❑ DL9050 [M]	Among My Souvenirs	1957	30.00

—Black label, silver print

Number	Title	Yr	NM
❑ DL9050 [M]	Among My Souvenirs	196?	18.00

—Black label with color bars

Number	Title	Yr	NM
❑ DL79050 [R]	Among My Souvenirs	196?	15.00
❑ DL9099 [M]	Jolie	196?	30.00

—Black label, silver print

Number	Title	Yr	NM
❑ DLP5006 [10]	Jolson Sings Again	1949	30.00
❑ DL9038 [M]	Memories	1957	30.00

—Black label, silver print

Number	Title	Yr	NM
❑ DL9038 [M]	Memories	1957	18.00

—Black label with color bars

Number	Title	Yr	NM
❑ DL79038 [R]	Memories	196?	15.00
❑ DL9070 [M]	Overseas	1959	30.00

—Black label, silver print

Number	Title	Yr	NM
❑ DL9070 [M]	Overseas	196?	18.00

—Black label with color bars

Number	Title	Yr	NM
❑ DL79070 [R]	Overseas	196?	15.00
❑ DL9036 [M]	Rainbow 'Round My Shoulder	1957	30.00

—Black label, silver print

Number	Title	Yr	NM
❑ DL9036 [M]	Rainbow 'Round My Shoulder	196?	18.00

—Black label with color bars

Number	Title	Yr	NM
❑ DL79036 [R]	Rainbow 'Round My Shoulder	196?	15.00
❑ DL9035 [M]	Rock-a-Bye Your Baby	1957	30.00

—Black label, silver print

Number	Title	Yr	NM
❑ DL9035 [M]	Rock-a-Bye Your Baby	196?	18.00

—Black label with color bars

Number	Title	Yr	NM
❑ DL79035 [R]	Rock-a-Bye Your Baby	196?	15.00
❑ DLP5029 [10]	Souvenir Album, Vol. II	1949	30.00
❑ DLP5031 [10]	Souvenir Album, Vol. IV	1949	30.00
❑ DL5314 [10]	Souvenir Album, Vol. V	1951	30.00
❑ DL5315 [10]	Souvenir Album, Vol. VI	1951	30.00
❑ DL5308 [10]	Stephen Foster Songs	1950	100.00
❑ DXA169 [M]	The Best of Jolson	196?	30.00
❑ DXSA7169 [R]	The Best of Jolson	196?	18.00
❑ DL9063 [M]	The Immortal Al Jolson	1958	30.00

—Maroon label, silver print

Number	Title	Yr	NM
❑ DL9063 [M]	The Immortal Al Jolson	196?	18.00

—Black label with color bars

Number	Title	Yr	NM
❑ DL9074 [M]	The World's Greatest Entertainer	1959	30.00

—Black label, silver print

Number	Title	Yr	NM
❑ DL9074 [M]	The World's Greatest Entertainer	196?	18.00

—Black label with color bars

Number	Title	Yr	NM
❑ DL79074 [R]	The World's Greatest Entertainer	196?	15.00
❑ DL9037 [M]	You Ain't Heard Nothin' Yet!	1957	30.00

—Black label, silver print

Number	Title	Yr	NM
❑ DL9037 [M]	You Ain't Heard Nothin' Yet!	1957	18.00

—Black label with color bars

Number	Title	Yr	NM
❑ DL79037 [R]	You Ain't Heard Nothin' Yet!	196?	15.00
❑ DL9034 [M]	You Made Me Love You	1957	30.00

—Black label, silver print

Number	Title	Yr	NM
❑ DL9034 [M]	You Made Me Love You	196?	18.00

—Black label with color bars

Number	Title	Yr	NM
❑ DL79034 [R]	You Made Me Love You	196?	15.00

MCA

Number	Title	Yr	NM
❑ 2064	Among My Souvenirs	197?	12.00
❑ 2061	Memories	197?	12.00
❑ 27055	Memories	198?	10.00
❑ 2059	Rainbow 'Round My Shoulder	197?	12.00
❑ 27053	Rainbow 'Round My Shoulder	198?	10.00
❑ 2058	Rock-a-Bye Your Baby	197?	12.00
❑ 27052	Rock-a-Bye Your Baby	198?	10.00
❑ 10002	The Best of Jolson	1973	15.00
❑ 2066	The Immortal Al Jolson	197?	12.00
❑ 27057	The Immortal Al Jolson	198?	10.00
❑ 2067	The World's Greatest Entertainer	197?	12.00
❑ 27058	The World's Greatest Entertainer	198?	10.00
❑ 2060	You Ain't Heard Nothin' Yet!	197?	12.00
❑ 27054	You Ain't Heard Nothin' Yet!	198?	10.00
❑ 2057	You Made Me Love You	197?	12.00
❑ 27051	You Made Me Love You	198?	10.00

SUNBEAM

Number	Title	Yr	NM
❑ 505	California, Here I Come	197?	12.00
❑ 503	Steppin' Out	197?	12.00

TOTEM

Number	Title	Yr	NM
❑ 1006 [B]	Al Jolson On the Air, Volume 1	197?	15.00
❑ 1012 [B]	Al Jolson On the Air, Volume 2	197?	15.00
❑ 1019 [B]	Al Jolson On the Air, Volume 3	197?	15.00
❑ 1030 [B]	Al Jolson On the Air, Volume 4	197?	15.00
❑ 1040 [B]	Al Jolson On the Air, Volume 5	197?	15.00

JON AND ROBIN AND THE IN CROWD

ABNAK

Number	Title	Yr	NM
❑ ABST-2070	Elastic Event	1968	25.00
❑ ABM-2068 [M]	Soul of a Boy and Girl	1967	50.00
❑ ABST-2068 [S]	Soul of a Boy and Girl	1967	25.00

JONES, ANN, AND HER AMERICAN SWEETHEARTS

AUDIO LAB

Number	Title	Yr	NM
❑ AL-1521 [M]	Ann Jones and Her American Sweethearts	1959	150.00
❑ AL-1556 [M]	Hit and Run	1960	150.00

JONES, ANTHONY ARMSTRONG

CHART

Number	Title	Yr	NM
❑ 1047	Greatest Hits, Vol. 1	1971	18.00
❑ 1019	Proud Mary	1969	18.00
❑ 1036	Sugar in the Flowers	1970	18.00
❑ 1027	Take a Letter Maria	1970	18.00

JONES, BOBBY

ENJA

Number	Title	Yr	NM
❑ 2046	Hill Country Suite	1975	18.00

JONES, BOOGALOO JOE

PRESTIGE

Number	Title	Yr	NM
❑ 10072	Black Whip	1973	30.00
❑ PRST-7697	Boogaloo Joe	1969	25.00
❑ PRST-7557	Mind Bender	1968	25.00
❑ PRST-7617	My Fire! More of the Psychedelic Soul Jazz Guitar of Joe Jones	1968	25.00

—As "Joe Jones

Number	Title	Yr	NM
❑ 10004	No Way!	1971	30.00
❑ PRST-7766	Right On Brother!	1970	25.00
❑ 10056	Snake Rhythm Rock	1972	30.00
❑ 10035	What It Is	1971	30.00

JONES, BRIAN

ROLLING STONES

Number	Title	Yr	NM
❑ COC49100 [B]	Brian Jones Presents the Pipes of Pan at Joujouka	1971	100.00

JONES, CARMELL

PACIFIC JAZZ

Number	Title	Yr	NM
❑ PJ-53 [M]	Business Meetin'	1962	40.00
❑ ST-53 [S]	Business Meetin'	1962	50.00

—Black vinyl

Number	Title	Yr	NM
❑ ST-53 [S]	Business Meetin'	1962	80.00

—Yellow vinyl

Number	Title	Yr	NM
❑ PJ-29 [M]	The Remarkable Carmell Jones	1961	40.00
❑ ST-29 [S]	The Remarkable Carmell Jones	1961	50.00

PRESTIGE

Number	Title	Yr	NM
❑ PRST-7669	Carmell Jones in Europe	1969	25.00
❑ PRLP-7401 [M]	Jay Hawk Talk	1965	30.00
❑ PRST-7401 [S]	Jay Hawk Talk	1965	40.00

JONES, CONNIE

JAZZOLOGY

Number	Title	Yr	NM
❑ J-49	Connie Jones with the Crescent City Jazz Band	197?	12.00

JONES, CURTIS

BLUESVILLE

Number	Title	Yr	NM
❑ BVLP-1022 [M]	Trouble Blues	1961	80.00

—Blue label, silver print

Number	Title	Yr	NM
❑ BVLP-1022 [M]	Trouble Blues	1964	30.00

—Blue label, trident logo at right

DELMARK

Number	Title	Yr	NM
❑ DL-605 [M]	Lonesome Bedroom Blues	1963	40.00

JONES, DALINE

TBA

Number	Title	Yr	NM
❑ TBA-220	Secret Fantasy	1986	15.00
❑ TBA-231	Share the Love	1987	15.00

JONES, DAVID LYNN

MERCURY

Number	Title	Yr	NM
❑ 832518-1	Hard Times on Easy Street	1987	10.00

JONES, DAVY

BELL

Number	Title	Yr	NM
❑ 6067 [B]	Davy Jones	1971	30.00

COLPIX

Number	Title	Yr	NM
❑ CP493 [M]	David Jones	1965	30.00
❑ CPS493 [S]	David Jones	1965	50.00

—This album charted in 1967 thanks to the singer's membership in The Monkees

JONES, DEAN

VALIANT

Number	Title	Yr	NM
❑ VLM-407 [M]	Introducing Dean Jones	196?	25.00
❑ VLS-407 [S]	Introducing Dean Jones	196?	25.00

JONES, ELVIN, AND THE JIMMY GARRISON SEXTETTE

IMPULSE!

Number	Title	Yr	NM
❑ A-49 [M]	Illumination	1963	30.00
❑ AS-49 [S]	Illumination	1963	30.00

JONES, ELVIN

ABC IMPULSE!

Number	Title	Yr	NM
❑ AS-88 [S]	Dear John C.	1968	18.00
❑ AS-9160	Heavy Sounds	1968	25.00
❑ AS-9283	The Impulse Years	197?	18.00

ATLANTIC

Number	Title	Yr	NM
❑ 1443 [M]	And Then Again	1965	25.00
❑ SD1443 [S]	And Then Again	1965	30.00
❑ 1485 [M]	Midnight Walk	1967	25.00
❑ SD1485 [S]	Midnight Walk	1967	30.00

BLUE NOTE

Number	Title	Yr	NM
❑ BST-84361	Coalition	1970	30.00
❑ BST-84414	Elvin Jones	1972	25.00
❑ BST-84369	Genesis	1971	25.00
❑ BN-LA015-G	Live at the Lighthouse	1973	25.00
❑ BN-LA110-F	Mr. Jones	1973	18.00
❑ BST-84331	Poly-Currents	1969	30.00
❑ BST-84331	Poly-Currents	1986	12.00

—The Finest in Jazz Since 1939" reissue

Number	Title	Yr	NM
❏ BN-LA506-H2	Prime Element	1976	25.00
❏ BST-84282	Puttin' It Together	1968	30.00
❏ BST-84305	The Ultimate Elvin Jones	1969	30.00

ENJA

❏ 2036	Live at the Vanguard	1974	18.00

FANTASY

❏ OJC-259	Elvin!	1987	12.00

IMPULSE!

❏ A-88 [M]	Dear John C.	1965	30.00
❏ AS-88 [S]	Dear John C.	1965	30.00

MCA

❏ 29068	Dear John C.	1980	12.00

PAUSA

❏ 7052	Rememberance	1979	12.00

PM

❏ 004	Live at Town Hall	197?	18.00
❏ 005	On the Mountain	197?	18.00

QUICKSILVER

❏ QS-4001	Brother John	198?	12.00

RIVERSIDE

❏ RLP-409 [M]	Elvin!	1962	30.00
❏ RS-9409 [S]	Elvin!	1962	30.00
❏ 6192	Elvin!	198?	15.00

VANGUARD

❏ VSD-79372	Main Force	1976	18.00
❏ VSD-79362	New Agenda	1975	18.00
❏ VSD-79389	Time Capsule	1977	18.00

JONES, ETTA

FANTASY

Number	Title	Yr	NM
❏ OJC-298	Don't Go to Strangers	198?	12.00
❏ OJC-221	Something Nice	198?	12.00

KING

❏ 707 [M]	Etta Jones Sings	1960	80.00
❏ 544 [M]	The Jones Girl...Etta	1956	150.00

MUSE

❏ MR-5411	Christmas with Etta Jones	1989	15.00
❏ MR-5333	Fine and Mellow	1987	12.00
❏ MR-5175	If You Could See Me Now	1979	15.00
❏ MR-5351	I'll Be Seeing You	1989	15.00
❏ MR-5262	Love Me with All of Your Heart	198?	12.00
❏ MR-5145	Mother's Eyes	1977	15.00
❏ MR-5099	Ms. Jones to You	197?	15.00
❏ MR-5214	Save Your Love for Me	1981	12.00
❏ MR-5379	Sugar	1989	15.00

PRESTIGE

❏ PRLP-7186 [M]	Don't Go to Strangers	1960	40.00
— Yellow label			
❏ PRLP-7186 [M]	Don't Go to Strangers	1964	25.00
— Blue label, trident logo at right			
❏ PRST-7186 [S]	Don't Go to Strangers	1960	50.00
— Silver label			
❏ PRST-7186 [S]	Don't Go to Strangers	1964	30.00
— Blue label, trident logo at right			
❏ PRLP-7443 [M]	Etta Jones' Greatest Hits	1967	30.00
❏ PRST-7443 [M]	Etta Jones' Greatest Hits	1967	25.00
❏ PRLP-7214 [M]	From the Heart	1961	40.00
— Yellow label			
❏ PRLP-7214 [M]	From the Heart	1964	25.00
— Blue label, trident logo at right			
❏ PRST-7214 [S]	From the Heart	1961	50.00
— Silver label			
❏ PRST-7214 [S]	From the Heart	1964	30.00
— Blue label, trident logo at right			
❏ PRLP-7284 [M]	Holler!	1963	40.00
— Yellow label			
❏ PRI-7284 [M]	Holler!	1964	25.00
— Blue label, trident logo at right			
❏ PRST-7284 [S]	Holler!	1963	50.00
— Silver label			
❏ PRST-7284 [S]	Holler!	1964	30.00
— Blue label, trident logo at right			
❏ PRLP-7241 [M]	Lonely and Blue	1962	40.00
— Yellow label			
❏ PRLP-7241 [M]	Lonely and Blue	1964	25.00
— Blue label, trident logo at right			
❏ PRST-7241 [S]	Lonely and Blue	1962	50.00
— Silver label			
❏ PRST-7241 [S]	Lonely and Blue	1964	30.00
— Blue label, trident logo at right			
❏ PRLP-7272 [M]	Love Shout	1963	40.00
— Yellow label			
❏ PRLP-7272 [M]	Love Shout	1964	25.00
— Blue label, trident logo at right			
❏ PRST-7272 [S]	Love Shout	1963	50.00
— Silver label			
❏ PRST-7272 [S]	Love Shout	1964	30.00
— Blue label, trident logo at right			
❏ PRLP-7194 [M]	Something Nice	1961	50.00
— Yellow label			
❏ PRLP-7194 [M]	Something Nice	1964	30.00
— Blue label, trident logo at right			
❏ PRLP-7204 [M]	So Warm -- Etta Jones and Strings	1961	40.00
— Yellow label			

Number	Title	Yr	NM
❏ PRLP-7204 [M]	So Warm -- Etta Jones and Strings	1964	25.00
— Blue label, trident logo at right			
❏ PRST-7204 [S]	So Warm -- Etta Jones and Strings	1961	50.00
— Silver label			
❏ PRST-7204 [S]	So Warm -- Etta Jones and Strings	1964	30.00
— Blue label, trident logo at right			

ROULETTE

❏ R-25329 [M]	Etta Jones Sings	1965	25.00
❏ SR-25329 [S]	Etta Jones Sings	1965	30.00

WESTBOUND

❏ 203	Etta Jones '75	1975	25.00

JONES, GEORGE, AND JOHNNY PAYCHECK

EPIC

❏ JE35783	Double Trouble	1980	12.00

JONES, GEORGE, AND MARGIE SINGLETON

MERCURY

❏ MG-20747 [M]	Duets Country Style	1962	30.00
❏ SR-60747 [S]	Duets Country Style	1962	40.00

JONES, GEORGE, AND MELBA MONTGOMERY

GUEST STAR

❏ GS1465 [M]	George Jones and Melba Montgomery	196?	15.00
—Contains two solo records by each artist (no duets!) and assorted stuff by others			

LIBERTY

❏ LN-10169	Singing What's In Our Hearts	1981	10.00

MUSICOR

❏ MM-2109 [M]	Close Together (As You and Me)	1966	25.00
❏ MS-3109 [S]	Close Together (As You and Me)	1966	30.00
❏ MM-2127 [M]	Let's Get Together/Boy Meets Girl	1967	30.00
❏ MS-3127 [S]	Let's Get Together/Boy Meets Girl	1967	25.00
❏ MM-2127 [M]	Party Pickin'	1967	30.00
—Alternate title			
❏ MS-3127 [S]	Party Pickin'	1967	25.00
—Alternate title			

UNITED ARTISTS

❏ UAL-3352 [M]	Bluegrass Hootenanny	1964	30.00
❏ UAS-6352 [S]	Bluegrass Hootenanny	1964	30.00
❏ UAL-3472 [M]	Blue Moon of Kentucky	1966	25.00
❏ UAS-6472 [S]	Blue Moon of Kentucky	1966	30.00
❏ T-90832 [M]	Blue Moon of Kentucky	1966	30.00
—Capitol Record Club edition			
❏ UAL-3301 [M]	Singing What's In Our Hearts	1963	30.00
❏ UAS-6301 [S]	Singing What's In Our Hearts	1963	30.00

JONES, GEORGE, AND TAMMY WYNETTE

EPIC

❏ FE37348	Encore	1981	12.00
❏ PE37348	Encore	198?	10.00
—Budget-line reissue			
❏ KE33351	George & Tammy & Tina	1975	18.00
❏ KE34291	Golden Ring	1976	15.00
—Orange label			
❏ PE34291	Golden Ring	198?	10.00
—Dark blue label			
❏ KE34716	Greatest Hits	1977	15.00
❏ PE34716	Greatest Hits	198?	10.00
—Budget-line reissue			
❏ KE32113	Let's Build a World Together	1973	18.00
❏ KE31554	Me and the First Lady	1972	18.00
—Yellow label			
❏ KE31554	Me and the First Lady	1973	15.00
—Orange label			
❏ JE36764	Together Again	1980	12.00
❏ PE36764	Together Again	198?	10.00
—Budget-line reissue			
❏ KE30802	We Go Together	1971	18.00
❏ EQ30802 [Q]	We Go Together	1971	30.00
❏ BG33752	We Go Together/Me and the First Lady	1976	18.00
❏ KE31719	We Love to Sing About Jesus	1972	18.00
—Yellow label			
❏ KE31719	We Love to Sing About Jesus	1973	15.00
—Orange label			
❏ KE32757	We're Gonna Hold On	1973	18.00

JONES, GEORGE; MELBA MONTGOMERY; GENE PITNEY

MUSICOR

❏ MM-2079 [M]	Famous Country Duets	1965	25.00
❏ MS-3079 [S]	Famous Country Duets	1965	30.00

JONES, GEORGE; MELBA MONTGOMERY; JUDY LYNN

UNITED ARTISTS

❏ UAL-3367 [M]	A King and Two Queens	1964	25.00
❏ UAS-6367 [S]	A King and Two Queens	1964	30.00

JONES, GEORGE

ACCORD

❏ SN-7201	Tender Years	1982	12.00

ALLEGIANCE

❏ AV-5015	Cold Cold Heart	198?	12.00

BULLDOG

❏ BDL-2009	20 Golden Pieces of George Jones	198?	12.00

EPIC

❏ PE34692	All-Time Greatest Hits Volume 1	1977	15.00
—Orange label			
❏ PE34692	All-Time Greatest Hits Volume 1	198?	10.00
—Dark blue label			
❏ KE34290	Alone Again	1976	15.00
❏ KE238323	Anniversary -- 10 Years of Hits	1982	15.00
❏ KE31718	A Picture of Me (Without You)	1972	18.00
—Yellow label			
❏ KE31718	A Picture of Me (Without You)	1973	15.00
—Orange label			
❏ KE35414	Bartender's Blues	1978	15.00
❏ PE35414	Bartender's Blues	198?	10.00
—Budget-line reissue			
❏ FE39546	By Request	1984	12.00
❏ FE37346	Encore	1981	12.00
❏ FE39899	First Time Live!	1985	12.00
❏ KE31321	George Jones	1972	18.00
—Yellow label			
❏ KE31321	George Jones	1973	15.00
—Orange label			
❏ BG33749	George Jones/A Picture of Me (Without You)	1976	18.00
❏ JE36586	I Am What I Am	1980	15.00
❏ KE32563	In a Gospel Way	1974	18.00
❏ PE34717	I Wanta Sing	1977	15.00
—Orange label			
❏ PE34717	I Wanta Sing	198?	10.00
—Dark blue label			
❏ FE38978	Jones Country	1983	12.00
❏ PE38978	Jones Country	1985	10.00
—Budget-line reissue			
❏ FE39272	Ladies' Choice	1984	12.00
❏ KE33547	Memories of Us	1975	18.00
❏ JE35544	My Very Special Guests	1979	15.00
❏ PE35544	My Very Special Guests	198?	10.00
—Budget-line reissue			
❏ KE32412	Nothing Ever Hurt Me (Half As Bad As Losing You)	1973	18.00
❏ FE44078	One Woman Man	1989	12.00
❏ FE38406	Shine On	1983	12.00
❏ PE38406	Shine On	198?	10.00
—Budget-line reissue			
❏ FE37106	Still the Same Old Me	1981	12.00
❏ PE37106	Still the Same Ole Me	198?	10.00
—Budget-line reissue			
❏ FE40776	Super Hits	1987	12.00
❏ KE34034	The Battle	1976	15.00
❏ KE33352	The Best of George Jones	1975	18.00
❏ PE33352	The Best of George Jones	1981	10.00
—Budget-line reissue			
❏ KE33083	The Grand Tour	1974	18.00
❏ FE40781	Too Wild Too Long	1988	12.00
❏ FE39598	Who's Gonna Fill Their Shoes	1985	12.00
❏ FE40413	Wine Colored Roses	1986	12.00
❏ FE39002	You've Still Got a Place in My Heart	1984	12.00

EVEREST ARCHIVE OF FOLK & JAZZ

❏ 353	George Jones Sings Country Hits	198?	12.00

HILLTOP

❏ 6092	Heartaches by the Number	1969	18.00
❏ 6133	Oh Lonesome Me	1970	18.00
❏ 6048	You're In My Heart	1968	18.00

INTERMEDIA

❏ QS-5061	How I Love These Old Songs	198?	12.00
❏ QS-5044	I Can't Change Overnight	198?	12.00

LIBERTY

❏ LN-10168	I Get Lonely in a Hurry	1981	10.00
❏ LN-10167	Trouble in Mind	1981	10.00

MCA

❏ 10398	And Along Came Jones	1991	25.00
—Vinyl issued only through Columbia House			

MERCURY

❏ MG-20306 [M]	14 Country Favorites	1957	150.00
❏ MG-20906 [M]	Blue and Lonesome	1964	30.00
❏ SR-60906 [S]	Blue and Lonesome	1964	30.00
❏ MG-20624 [M]	Country and Western Hits	1961	40.00
❏ SR-60624 [P]	Country and Western Hits	1961	50.00

Number	Title	Yr	NM
❑ MG-20937 [M]	Country and Western No. 1 Male Singer	1964	30.00
❑ SR-60937 [S]	Country and Western No. 1 Male Singer	1964	30.00
❑ MG-20462 [M]	Country Church Time	1959	200.00
❑ MG-20621 [M]	George Jones' Greatest Hits	1961	40.00
❑ SR-60621 [P]	George Jones' Greatest Hits	1961	50.00
❑ MG-21048 [M]	George Jones' Greatest Hits Volume 2	1965	30.00
❑ SR-61048 [S]	George Jones' Greatest Hits Volume 2	1965	30.00
❑ MG-20596 [M]	George Jones Salutes Hank Williams	1960	80.00
❑ SR-60257 [S]	George Jones Salutes Hank Williams	1960	100.00
❑ 822646-1	George Jones Salutes Hank Williams	1985	12.00
❑ MG-20694 [M]	George Jones Sings From the Heart	1962	40.00
❑ SR-60694 [S]	George Jones Sings From the Heart	1962	50.00
❑ MG-20477 [M]	George Jones Sings White Lightning and Other Favorites	1959	150.00
❑ ML-8014	Greatest Hits	1980	15.00
❑ 826248-1	Greatest Hits	1986	12.00
❑ MG-20990 [M]	Heartaches and Tears	1965	30.00
❑ SR-60990 [S]	Heartaches and Tears	1965	30.00
❑ MG-20282 [M]	Hillbilly Hit Parade, Volume 1	1957	150.00
— Five tracks by George Jones, one by George Jones with Bonny Barnes, and four by other artists			
❑ 826095-1	Rockin' the Country	1985	12.00
❑ MG-21029 [M]	Singing the Blues	1965	30.00
❑ SR-61029 [S]	Singing the Blues	1965	30.00
❑ MG-20836 [M]	The Ballad Side of George Jones	1963	40.00
❑ SR-60836 [S]	The Ballad Side of George Jones	1963	50.00
❑ MG-20793 [M]	The Novelty Side of George Jones	1963	80.00
❑ SR-60793 [S]	The Novelty Side of George Jones	1963	100.00

MUSICOR

Number	Title	Yr	NM
❑ MM-2124 [M]	Cup of Loneliness	1967	30.00
❑ MS-3124 [S]	Cup of Loneliness	1967	25.00
❑ MM-2116 [M]	George Jones' Greatest Hits	1967	30.00
❑ MS-3116 [S]	George Jones' Greatest Hits	1967	30.00
❑ MS-3194	George Jones With Love	1971	25.00
❑ MM-2128 [M]	Hits by George	1967	30.00
❑ MS-3128 [S]	Hits by George	1967	25.00
❑ MS-3158	If My Heart Had Windows	1968	25.00
❑ MS-3177	I'll Share My World with You	1969	25.00
❑ MM-2099 [M]	I'm a People	1966	30.00
❑ MS-3099 [S]	I'm a People	1966	30.00
❑ MM-2088 [M]	Love Bug	1966	30.00
❑ MS-3088 [S]	Love Bug	1966	40.00
❑ MM-2046 [M]	Mr. Country and Western Music	1965	30.00
❑ MS-3046 [S]	Mr. Country and Western Music	1965	40.00
❑ M2O 0160	My Country	1969	30.00
❑ MM-2060 [M]	New Country Hits	1965	30.00
❑ MS-3060 [S]	New Country Hits	1965	40.00
❑ MM-2061 [M]	Old Brush Arbors	1966	30.00
❑ MS-3061 [S]	Old Brush Arbors	1966	40.00
❑ MS-3191	The Best of George Jones	1970	25.00
❑ MS-3203	The Best of Sacred Music	1971	25.00
❑ M2S-3159 [B]	The George Jones Story: The Musical Loves, Life and Sorrows of America's Great Country Star	1968	30.00
❑ MS-3204	The Great Songs of Leon Payne	1971	25.00
❑ MS-3149	The Songs of Dallas Frazier	1968	25.00
❑ MM-2119 [M]	Walk Through This World with Me	1967	30.00
❑ MS-3119 [S]	Walk Through This World with Me	1967	25.00
❑ MM-2106 [M]	We Found Heaven Right Here on Earth	1966	30.00
❑ MS-3106 [S]	We Found Heaven Right Here on Earth	1966	30.00
❑ MS-3181	Where Grass Won't Grow	1969	25.00
❑ MS-3188	Will You Visit Me on Sunday?	1970	25.00

NASHVILLE

Number	Title	Yr	NM
❑ 2076	Seasons of My Heart	1970	18.00

PAIR

Number	Title	Yr	NM
❑ PDL2-1080	Country, By George!	1986	15.00
❑ PDL2-1074	The Best of George Jones	1986	15.00

POWER PAK

Number	Title	Yr	NM
❑ 271	The Crown Prince of Country Music	197?	12.00

QUICKSILVER

Number	Title	Yr	NM
❑ QS-1011	Frozen in Time	198?	12.00
❑ QS-1012	If My Heart Had Windows	198?	12.00

RCA CAMDEN

Number	Title	Yr	NM
❑ CAS-2591	Flowers for Mama	1973	15.00
❑ ACL1-0377	The Race Is On	1973	15.00

RCA VICTOR

Number	Title	Yr	NM
❑ LSP-4716	Best of George Jones Vol. I	1972	18.00
❑ APL1-0316	Best of George Jones Vol. II	1973	18.00
❑ LSP-4727	Country Singer	1972	18.00
❑ LSP-4672	First in the Hearts of Country Music Lovers	1972	18.00
❑ LSP-4785	Four-O Thirty-Three	1972	18.00
❑ LSP-4733	George Jones And Friends	1972	18.00
❑ APL1-0612	His Songs	1974	18.00
❑ APL1-0815	I Can Love You Enough	1974	18.00
❑ LSP-4847	I Can Still See Him	1973	18.00
❑ LSP-4726	I Made Leaving (Easy for You)	1972	18.00
❑ LSP-4725	Poor Man's Riches	1972	18.00
❑ LSP-4787	Take Me	1972	18.00
❑ LSP-4786	Tender Years	1972	18.00
❑ APL1-1113	The Best of the Best	1975	18.00
❑ LSP-4801	Wrapped Around Her Finger	1973	18.00
❑ APL1-0486	You Gotta Be My Baby	1974	18.00

ROUNDER

Number	Title	Yr	NM
❑ SS-15	Burn the Honky Tonk Down	198?	12.00
❑ SS-17	Heartaches & Hangovers	198?	12.00

SEARS

Number	Title	Yr	NM
❑ SPS-125	Maybe, Little Baby	196?	25.00

STARDAY

Number	Title	Yr	NM
❑ 3021	16 Greatest Hits	197?	12.00
❑ SLP335 [M]	George Jones	1965	40.00
❑ SLP150 [M]	George Jones Sings His Greatest Hits	1962	50.00
❑ DT-90080 [R]	George Jones Sings His Greatest Hits	1964	80.00
— Capitol Record Club edition			
❑ SLP344 [M]	Long Live King George	1965	40.00
❑ DT-90611 [R]	The Crown Prince of Country Music	196?	40.00
— Capitol Record Club edition			
❑ SLP125 [M]	The Crown Prince of Country Music	1960	160.00
❑ SLP151 [M]	The Fabulous Country Music Sound of George Jones	1962	50.00
❑ SLP401 [M]	The George Jones Song Book & Picture Album	1967	30.00
— Without book			
❑ SLP401	The George Jones Song Book & Picture Album	1967	50.00
— With book			
❑ SLP366 [M]	The George Jones Story	1966	30.00
❑ SLP366	The George Jones Story Bonus Photo	1966	25.00
❑ SLP440 [M]	The Golden Country Hits of George Jones	1969	30.00
❑ SLP101 [M]	The Grand Ole Opry's New Star	1958	1200.00

TIME-LIFE

Number	Title	Yr	NM
❑ STW-103	Country Music	1981	12.00

UNITED ARTISTS

Number	Title	Yr	NM
❑ UAL-3532 [M]	George Jones' Golden Hits, Volume 1	1966	25.00
❑ UAS-6532 [S]	George Jones' Golden Hits, Volume 1	1966	30.00
❑ UAL-3566 [M]	George Jones' Golden Hits, Volume 2	1967	30.00
❑ UAS-6566 [S]	George Jones' Golden Hits, Volume 2	1967	25.00
❑ UAS-6696	George Jones' Golden Hits, Volume 3	1968	25.00
❑ UAL-3221 [M]	George Jones Sings Bob Wills	1962	40.00
❑ UAS-6221 [S]	George Jones Sings Bob Wills	1962	50.00
❑ UAL-3364 [M]	George Jones Sings Like the Dickens	1964	40.00
❑ UAS-6364 [S]	George Jones Sings Like the Dickens	1964	50.00
❑ UAL-3218 [M]	George Jones Sings the Hits of His Country Cousins	1962	30.00
❑ UAS-6218 [S]	George Jones Sings the Hits of His Country Cousins	1962	40.00
❑ UXS-85	George Jones Superpak	1972	25.00
❑ UAL-3219 [M]	Homecoming in Heaven	1962	30.00
❑ UAS-6219 [S]	Homecoming in Heaven	1962	40.00
❑ UAL-3388 [M]	I Get Lonely in a Hurry	1964	30.00
❑ UAS-6388 [S]	I Get Lonely in a Hurry	1964	40.00
❑ UAL-3270 [M]	I Wish the Night Would Never End	1963	30.00
❑ UAS-6270 [S]	I Wish the Night Would Never End	1963	30.00
❑ UAL-3442 [M]	King of Broken Hearts	1965	30.00
❑ UAS-6442 [S]	King of Broken Hearts	1965	40.00
❑ UAL-3338 [M]	More New Favorites	1964	30.00
❑ UAS-6328 [S]	More New Favorites	1964	30.00
❑ UAL-3220 [M]	My Favorites of Hank Williams	1962	30.00
❑ UAS-6220 [S]	My Favorites of Hank Williams	1962	40.00
❑ UAL-3291 [M]	The Best of George Jones	1963	30.00
❑ UAS-6291 [S]	The Best of George Jones	1963	30.00
❑ UAL-3457 [M]	The Great George Jones	1966	30.00
❑ UAS-6457 [S]	The Great George Jones	1966	40.00
❑ UAL-3193 [M]	The New Favorites of George Jones	1962	30.00
❑ UAS-6193 [S]	The New Favorites of George Jones	1962	40.00
❑ UAL-3422 [M]	The Race Is On	1965	30.00
— With photo of George Jones on front			
❑ UAL-3422 [M]	The Race Is On	1965	25.00
— With cartoon on front			
❑ UAS-6422 [S]	The Race Is On	1965	40.00
— With photo of George Jones on front			
❑ UAS-6422 [S]	The Race Is On	1965	30.00
— With cartoon on front			
❑ T-90829 [M]	The Race Is On	1965	30.00
— Capitol Record Club edition; photo on front			
❑ ST-90829 [S]	The Race Is On	1965	40.00
— Capitol Record Club edition; photo on front			
❑ UAL-3558 [M]	The Young George Jones	1967	30.00
❑ UAS-6558 [S]	The Young George Jones	1967	25.00
❑ UAL-3408 [M]	Trouble in Mind	1965	30.00
❑ UAS-6408 [S]	Trouble in Mind	1965	40.00

WING

Number	Title	Yr	NM
❑ MGW-12266 [M]	The Great George Jones	196?	18.00
❑ SRW-16266 [S]	The Great George Jones	196?	18.00

JONES, GRANDPA

DECCA

Number	Title	Yr	NM
❑ DL4364 [M]	An Evening with Grandpa Jones	1963	30.00
❑ DL74364 [S]	An Evening with Grandpa Jones	1963	30.00

KING

Number	Title	Yr	NM
❑ 822 [M]	16 Sacred Gospel Songs	1963	60.00
❑ 845 [M]	Do You Remember?	1963	60.00
❑ 554 [M]	Grandpa Jones Sings His Biggest Hits	1958	100.00
❑ 809 [M]	Rollin' Along with Grandpa Jones	1963	60.00
❑ 625 [M]	Strictly Country Tunes	1959	100.00
❑ KS-1042	The Living Legend of Country Music	1969	25.00
❑ 888 [M]	The Other Side of Grandpa Jones	1964	60.00

MONUMENT

Number	Title	Yr	NM
❑ SLP-18083	Everybody's Grandpa	1968	25.00
❑ MLP-4006 [M]	Grandpa Jones Makes the Rafters Ring	1962	30.00
❑ SLP-14006 [S]	Grandpa Jones Makes the Rafters Ring	1962	30.00
❑ MLP-8041 [M]	Grandpa Jones Remembers the Brown's Ferry Four	1966	30.00
❑ SLP-18041 [S]	Grandpa Jones Remembers the Brown's Ferry Four	1966	30.00
❑ SLP-18131	Grandpa Jones Sings Hits from Hee Haw	1969	25.00
❑ MLP-8021 [M]	Real Folk Songs	1964	25.00
❑ SLP-18021 [S]	Real Folk Songs	1964	30.00
❑ MLP-8001 [M]	Yodeling Hits	1963	25.00
❑ SLP-18001 [S]	Yodeling Hits	1963	30.00

JONES, HANK, AND RED MITCHELL

TIMELESS

Number	Title	Yr	NM
❑ SJP-283	Duo	1990	18.00

JONES, HANK; RAY BROWN; JIMMIE SMITH

CONCORD JAZZ

Number	Title	Yr	NM
❑ CJ-32	Hank Jones/Ray Brown/ Jimmie Smith	197?	15.00

JONES, HANK

ABC-PARAMOUNT

Number	Title	Yr	NM
❑ ABC-496 [M]	This Is Ragtime Now	1964	25.00
❑ ABCS-496 [S]	This Is Ragtime Now	1964	30.00

ARGO

Number	Title	Yr	NM
❑ LP-728 [M]	Here's Love	1963	25.00
❑ LPS-728 [S]	Here's Love	1963	30.00

CAPITOL

Number	Title	Yr	NM
❑ T1175 [M]	Porgy and Bess	1959	40.00
❑ ST1175 [S]	Porgy and Bess	1959	30.00
❑ T1044 [M]	The Talented Touch of Hank Jones	1958	40.00
❑ ST1044 [S]	The Talented Touch of Hank Jones	1958	30.00

CLEF

Number	Title	Yr	NM
❑ MGC-100 [10]	Hank Jones Piano	1953	120.00
❑ MGC-707 [M]	Urbanity -- Piano Solos by Hank Jones	1956	100.00

CONCORD JAZZ

Number	Title	Yr	NM
❑ CJ-391	Lazy Afternoon	1989	15.00

FANTASY

Number	Title	Yr	NM
❑ OJC-471	Just for Fun	1990	15.00

GALAXY

Number	Title	Yr	NM
❑ 5123	Ain't Misbehavin'	1979	15.00
❑ 5105	Just for	1977	15.00
❑ 5108	Tiptoe Tapdance	1978	15.00

GOLDEN CREST

Number	Title	Yr	NM
❑ GC-3042 [M]	Hank Jones Swings "Gigi	1958	50.00
❑ GC-5002 [S]	Hank Jones Swings "Gigi	1959	40.00
❑ GCS-3042 [S]	Hank Jones Swings "Gigi	196?	25.00

INNER CITY

Number	Title	Yr	NM
❑ IC-6020	Hanky Panky	197?	15.00

MERCURY

Number	Title	Yr	NM
❑ MG-25022 [10]	Hank Jones Piano	1950	200.00
❑ MG-35014 [10]	Hank Jones Piano	1950	200.00
❑ MGC-100 [10]	Hank Jones Piano	195?	150.00

MUSE

Number	Title	Yr	NM
❑ MR-5123	Bop Redux	1977	15.00
❑ MR-5169	Grovin' High	1979	15.00

PAUSA

Number	Title	Yr	NM
❑ 7051	Have You Met This Jones?	1979	12.00

PROGRESSIVE

Number	Title	Yr	NM
❑ 7004	Arigato	1976	15.00

RCA VICTOR

Number	Title	Yr	NM
❑ LPM-2570 [M]	Arrival Time	1962	30.00
❑ LSP-2570 [S]	Arrival Time	1962	30.00

SAVOY

Number	Title	Yr	NM
❑ MG-12037 [M]	Hank Jones Quartet-Quintet	1955	80.00
❑ MG-12087 [M]	Hank Jones Trio	1956	80.00

Number	Title	Yr	NM
❑ MG-12084 [M]	Have You Met Hank Jones	1956	80.00
❑ MG-12053 [M]	The Trio	1956	80.00

SAVOY JAZZ

Number	Title	Yr	NM
❑ SJL-1193	Bluebird	198?	12.00
❑ SJL-1124	Hank Jones	198?	12.00
❑ SJL-1138	Relaxin' at Camarillo	198?	12.00

VERVE

Number	Title	Yr	NM
❑ MGV-8091 [M]	Urbanity -- Piano Solos by Hank Jones	1957	80.00
❑ V-8091 [M]	Urbanity -- Piano Solos by Hank Jones	1961	30.00

JONES, HOWARD

ELEKTRA

Number	Title	Yr	NM
❑ R133246 [EP]	Action Replay	1986	10.00
—RCA Music Service edition			
❑ 60466 [EP]	Action Replay	1986	10.00
❑ 60794	Cross That Line	1989	12.00
❑ 60794 [DJ]	Cross That Line	1989	15.00
—Promo-only white label audiophile vinyl			
❑ R143992	Dream into Action	1985	12.00
—RCA Music Service edition			
❑ 60390	Dream into Action	1985	10.00
❑ 60346	Human's Lib	1984	10.00
❑ R134013	One to One	1986	12.00
—RCA Music Service edition			
❑ 60499	One to One	1986	12.00

JONES, JACK

CAPITOL

Number	Title	Yr	NM
❑ T2100 [M]	In Love	1964	18.00
❑ ST2100 [S]	In Love	1964	25.00
—Reissue of 1274			
❑ T1274 [M]	This Love of Mine	1959	30.00
❑ ST1274 [S]	This Love of Mine	1959	30.00

KAPP

Number	Title	Yr	NM
❑ KL-1365 [M]	Bewitched	1964	15.00
❑ KS-3365 [S]	Bewitched	1964	18.00
❑ KL-1328 [M]	Call Me Irresponsible	1963	15.00
❑ KS-3328 [S]	Call Me Irresponsible	1963	18.00
❑ KS-3566	Curtain Time	1968	15.00
❑ KL-1415 [M]	Dear Heart	1964	15.00
❑ KS-3415 [S]	Dear Heart	1964	18.00
❑ KL-1465 [M]	For the "In" Crowd	1966	15.00
❑ KS-3465 [S]	For the "In" Crowd	1966	18.00
❑ KS-3559	Greatest Hits	1968	15.00
❑ KL-1559 [M]	Greatest Hits	1968	25.00
—May exist only as a white label promo; covers are stereo with a "Mono" sticker			
❑ KS-3602	Greatest Hits Vol. 2	1970	15.00
❑ KL-1265 [M]	I've Got a Lot of Livin' to Do	1962	15.00
❑ KS-3265 [S]	I've Got a Lot of Livin' to Do	1962	18.00
❑ KS-3590	Jack Jones in Hollywood	1969	15.00
❑ KL-1500 [M]	Jack Jones Sings	1966	15.00
❑ KS-3500 [S]	Jack Jones Sings	1966	18.00
❑ KL-1511 [M]	Lady	1967	18.00
❑ KS-3511 [S]	Lady	1967	15.00
❑ KL-1259 [M]	Lollipops and Roses	196?	15.00
—Revised title			
❑ KS-3259 [S]	Lollipops and Roses	196?	18.00
—Revised title			
❑ KL-1433 [M]	My Kind of Town	1965	15.00
❑ KS-3433 [S]	My Kind of Town	1965	18.00
❑ KL-1531 [M]	Our Song	1967	18.00
❑ KS-3531 [S]	Our Song	1967	15.00
❑ KL-1228 [M]	Shall We Dance	1961	15.00
❑ KS-3228 [S]	Shall We Dance	1961	18.00
❑ KL-1337 [M]	She Loves Me	1963	15.00
❑ KS-3337 [S]	She Loves Me	1963	18.00
❑ KXS-5009	The Best of Jack Jones	196?	18.00
❑ KL-1486 [M]	The Impossible Dream	1966	15.00
❑ KS-3486 [S]	The Impossible Dream	1966	18.00
❑ KL1399 [M]	The Jack Jones Christmas Album	1964	15.00
❑ KS3399 [S]	The Jack Jones Christmas Album	1964	18.00
❑ KL-1435 [M]	There's Love & There's Love & There's Love	1965	15.00
❑ KS-3435 [S]	There's Love & There's Love & There's Love	1965	18.00
❑ KL-1259 [M]	This Was My Love	1962	25.00
—Original title			
❑ KS-3259 [S]	This Was My Love	1962	30.00
—Original title			
❑ KS-3551 [S]	What the World Needs Now Is Love!	1968	15.00
❑ KL-1551 [M]	What the World Needs Now Is Love!	1968	25.00
—May only exist as a white label promo; covers are stereo with "Mono" sticker			
❑ KL-1396 [M]	Where Love Has Gone	1964	15.00
❑ KS-3396 [S]	Where Love Has Gone	1964	18.00
❑ KL-1352 [M]	Wives and Lovers	1963	15.00
❑ KS-3352 [S]	Wives and Lovers	1963	18.00

MCA

Number	Title	Yr	NM
❑ 4115	The Best of Jack Jones	197?	15.00
—Reissue of Kapp KXS-5009			
❑ 15014	The Jack Jones Christmas Album	197?	12.00
—Reissue			
❑ 15036	White Christmas	198?	10.00

MGM

Number	Title	Yr	NM
❑ MG-1-5024	Don't Stop Now	1980	12.00
❑ MG-1-5023	Nobody Does It Better	1979	12.00

PICKWICK

Number	Title	Yr	NM
❑ SPC-3041	A Very Precious Love	196?	12.00
❑ PC-3001 [M]	This Love of Mine	196?	15.00
❑ SPC-3001 [S]	This Love of Mine	196?	15.00

RCA CAMDEN

Number	Title	Yr	NM
❑ ACL1-0255	Christmas with Jack Jones	1973	15.00
—Reissue of RCA Victor LSP-4234			

RCA VICTOR

Number	Title	Yr	NM
❑ LSP-4234	A Jack Jones Christmas	1969	18.00
❑ LSP-4613	A Song for You	1971	15.00
❑ LSP-4209	A Time for Us	1969	15.00
❑ LSP-4692	Bread Winners	1972	12.00
❑ APL1-0408	Harbour	1974	12.00
❑ LPM-3969 [M]	If You Ever Leave Me	1968	25.00
❑ LSP-3969 [S]	If You Ever Leave Me	1968	15.00
❑ LSP-4413	In Person at the Sands, Las Vegas	1970	15.00
❑ LSP-4480	Jack Jones Sings Michel Legrand	1970	15.00
❑ ANL1-1081	Jack Jones Sings Michel Legrand	1975	10.00
—Reissue			
❑ LSP-4108	L.A. Break Down	1969	15.00
❑ APL1-2067	The Full Life	1976	12.00
❑ APL1-0139	Together	1973	12.00
❑ APL1-1111	What I Did for Love	1975	12.00
❑ LSP-4048	Where Is Love	1968	15.00
❑ APL1-2361	With One More Look at You	1977	12.00
❑ LPM-3911 [M]	Without Her	1967	25.00
❑ LSP-3911 [S]	Without Her	1967	15.00
❑ APL1-0773	Write Me a Love Song, Charlie	1975	12.00

VOCALION

Number	Title	Yr	NM
❑ VL73913	Jack Jones Showcase	1970	12.00

JONES, JIMMY

JEN JILLUS

Number	Title	Yr	NM
❑ 1001	The Handy Man's Back in Town	1977	15.00

MGM

Number	Title	Yr	NM
❑ E-3847 [M]	Good Timin'	1960	120.00
❑ SE-3847 [S]	Good Timin'	1960	160.00

JONES, JO

EVEREST

Number	Title	Yr	NM
❑ LPBR-5023 [M]	Jo Jones Trio	1959	30.00
❑ SDBR-1023 [S]	Jo Jones Trio	1959	30.00
❑ LPBR-5110 [M]	Percussion and Bass	1960	30.00
❑ SDBR-1110 [S]	Percussion and Bass	1960	30.00
❑ LPBR-5099 [M]	Vamp Till Ready	1960	30.00
❑ SDBR-1099 [S]	Vamp Till Ready	1960	30.00

EVEREST ARCHIVE OF FOLK & JAZZ

Number	Title	Yr	NM
❑ 329	Jo Jones	197?	12.00

JAZZTONE

Number	Title	Yr	NM
❑ J-1242 [M]	Jo Jones Special	1956	50.00

PABLO

Number	Title	Yr	NM
❑ 2310799	Main Man	1976	18.00

VANGUARD

Number	Title	Yr	NM
❑ VRS-8525 [M]	Jo Jones Plus Two	1959	40.00
❑ VSD-2031 [S]	Jo Jones Plus Two	1959	30.00
❑ VRS-8503 [M]	Jo Jones Special	1955	60.00

JONES, JOE

ROULETTE

Number	Title	Yr	NM
❑ R25143 [M]	You Talk Too Much	1961	150.00
❑ SR25143 [R]	You Talk Too Much	1961	100.00

JONES, JOHN PAUL

COLUMBIA

Number	Title	Yr	NM
❑ KC32047	John Paul Jones	1973	25.00

JONES, JONAH, AND EARL "FATHA" HINES

CHIAROSCURO

Number	Title	Yr	NM
❑ 118	Back on the Street	1973	15.00

JONES, JONAH

ANGEL

Number	Title	Yr	NM
❑ ANG.60005 [10]	Jonah Wails -- 1st Blast	1954	75.00
❑ ANG.60006 [10]	Jonah Wails -- 2nd Blast	1954	75.00

BETHLEHEM

Number	Title	Yr	NM
❑ BCP-1014 [10]	Jonah Jones Sextet	1954	80.00

CAPITOL

Number	Title	Yr	NM
❑ T1948 [M]	And Now, In Person -- Jonah Jones	1963	18.00
❑ ST1948 [S]	And Now, In Person -- Jonah Jones	1963	25.00
❑ T1405 [M]	A Touch of Blue	1960	25.00
❑ ST1405 [S]	A Touch of Blue	1960	30.00
❑ T2087 [M]	Blowin' Up a Storm	1964	18.00
❑ ST2087 [S]	Blowin' Up a Storm	1964	25.00
❑ T1641 [M]	Broadway Swings Again	1961	25.00
❑ ST1641 [S]	Broadway Swings Again	1961	30.00
❑ T1557 [M]	Great Instrumental Hits Styled by Jonah Jones	1961	25.00
❑ ST1557 [S]	Great Instrumental Hits Styled by Jonah Jones	1961	30.00
❑ T1375 [M]	Hit Me Again!	1960	25.00
❑ ST1375 [S]	Hit Me Again!	1960	30.00
❑ T1193 [M]	I Dig Chicks	1959	25.00
❑ ST1193 [S]	I Dig Chicks	1959	30.00
❑ T1773 [M]	Jazz Bonus	1962	18.00
❑ ST1773 [S]	Jazz Bonus	1962	25.00
❑ T1660 [M]	Jonah Jones/Glenn Gray	1961	25.00
❑ ST1660 [S]	Jonah Jones/Glenn Gray	1961	30.00
❑ SM-1660	Jonah Jones/Glenn Gray	197?	12.00
❑ T1115 [M]	Jonah Jumps Again	1959	30.00
❑ ST1115 [S]	Jonah Jumps Again	1959	30.00
❑ T1404 [M]	Jumpin' with a Shuffle	1960	25.00
❑ ST1404 [S]	Jumpin' with a Shuffle	1960	30.00
❑ T1039 [M]	Jumpin' with Jonah	1958	30.00
❑ ST1039 [S]	Jumpin' with Jonah	1958	30.00
❑ T839 [M]	Muted Jazz	1957	40.00
❑ T1083 [M]	Swingin' at the Cinema	1958	30.00
❑ ST1083 [S]	Swingin' at the Cinema	1958	30.00
❑ T963 [M]	Swingin' On Broadway	1958	40.00
❑ T1237 [M]	Swingin' 'Round the World	1959	25.00
❑ ST1237 [S]	Swingin' 'Round the World	1959	30.00
❑ T2594 [M]	The Best of Jonah Jones	1966	18.00
❑ ST2594 [S]	The Best of Jonah Jones	1966	15.00
❑ T1532 [M]	The Unsinkable Molly Brown	1961	25.00
❑ ST1532 [S]	The Unsinkable Molly Brown	1961	30.00

CIRCLE

Number	Title	Yr	NM
❑ CLP-83	1944: Butterflies in the Rain	198?	12.00

DECCA

Number	Title	Yr	NM
❑ DL4638 [M]	Hello Broadway	1965	15.00
❑ DL74638 [S]	Hello Broadway	1965	18.00
❑ DL74918	Jazz Tropical!	1968	15.00
❑ DL4688 [M]	On the Sunny Side of the Street	1966	15.00
❑ DL74688 [S]	On the Sunny Side of the Street	1966	18.00
❑ DL4800 [M]	Sweet with a Beat	1967	18.00
❑ DL74800 [S]	Sweet with a Beat	1967	15.00
❑ DL4765 [M]	Tijuana Taxi	1966	15.00
❑ DL74765 [S]	Tijuana Taxi	1966	18.00

GROOVE

Number	Title	Yr	NM
❑ LG-1001 [M]	Jonah Jones at the Embers	1956	50.00

HALL OF FAME

Number	Title	Yr	NM
❑ 613	After Hours Jazz	198?	12.00

JAZZ MAN

Number	Title	Yr	NM
❑ 5009	Confessin'	1981	12.00

MOTOWN

Number	Title	Yr	NM
❑ M-683	Along Came Jonah	1969	40.00
❑ M-690	Little Dis, Little Dat	1970	40.00

PICKWICK

Number	Title	Yr	NM
❑ SPC-3008	Swing Along	196?	15.00

RCA CAMDEN

Number	Title	Yr	NM
❑ CAS-2328	Jonah Jones Quartet	1969	15.00

RCA VICTOR

Number	Title	Yr	NM
❑ LPM-2004 [M]	Jonah Jones at the Embers	1959	40.00
—Reissue of Groove and Vik LP			

SWING

Number	Title	Yr	NM
❑ 8408	Paris 1954	198?	12.00

VIK

Number	Title	Yr	NM
❑ LXA-1135 [M]	Jonah Jones at the Embers	1958	40.00
—Reissue of Groove LP			

JONES, JONAH/CHARLIE SHAVERS

BETHLEHEM

Number	Title	Yr	NM
❑ BCP-6034 [M]	Sounds of the Trumpets	1959	40.00

JONES, NORAH

BLUE NOTE

Number	Title	Yr	NM
❑ BTE32088	Come Away with Me	2004	18.00
—Standard-weight issue with lyrics on back cover; "Manufactured by Caroline Distribution" on back			
❑ BTE84800	Feels Like Home	2004	18.00
—Standard-weight edition; "Manufactured by Caroline Distribution" on back cover			

CLASSICRECORDS.COM

Number	Title	Yr	NM
❑ JP-5004	Come Away with Me	2002	30.00
—Audiophile pressing; heavyweight vinyl with gatefold cover			

JONES, PAUL

CAPITOL

Number	Title	Yr	NM
❑ T2795 [M]	Paul Jones Sings Songs from the Film "Privilege" and Others	1967	60.00
❑ ST2795 [S]	Paul Jones Sings Songs from the Film "Privilege" and Others	1967	30.00

LONDON

Number	Title	Yr	NM
❑ XPS605	Crucifix in a Horseshoe	1971	15.00

JONES, PHILLY JOE, AND ELVIN JONES

ATLANTIC

Number	Title	Yr	NM
❑ 1428 [M]	Together	1964	30.00
❑ SD1428 [S]	Together	1964	30.00

JONES, PHILLY JOE

ATLANTIC

Number	Title	Yr	NM
❑ 1340 [M]	Philly Joe's Beat	1960	30.00
—Multicolor label, white "fan" logo on right			
❑ 1340 [M]	Philly Joe's Beat	1963	18.00
—Multicolor label, black "fan" logo on right			

Number	Title	Yr	NM
❑ SD1340 [S]	Philly Joe's Beat	1960	30.00
—Multicolor label, white "fan" logo on right			
❑ SD1340 [S]	Philly Joe's Beat	1963	18.00
—Multicolor label, black "fan" logo on right			
BLACK LION			
❑ 142	Trailways Express	197?	15.00
FANTASY			
❑ OJC-230	Blues for Dracula	198?	12.00
❑ OJC-484	Showcase	1991	15.00
GALAXY			
❑ 5122	Advance!	1980	15.00
❑ 5153	Drum Song	1985	12.00
❑ 5112	Philly Mignon	1978	15.00
RIVERSIDE			
❑ RLP 12-282 [M]	Blues for Dracula	1958	50.00
❑ 6055	Blues for Dracula	197?	18.00
❑ RLP 12-302 [M]	Drums Around the World	1959	50.00
❑ RLP-1147 [S]	Drums Around the World	1959	40.00
❑ RLP 12-313 [M]	Showcase	1959	50.00
❑ RLP-1159 [S]	Showcase	1959	40.00
❑ 6193	Showcase	198?	15.00
UPTOWN			
❑ 27.15	Look, Stop, Listen	198?	15.00
❑ 27.11	To Tadd with Love	198?	15.00

JONES, QUINCY

Number	Title	Yr	NM
A&M			
❑ SP-3617	Body Heat	1974	12.00
❑ QU-53617 [Q]	Body Heat	1974	12.00
❑ SP-3191	Body Heat	1982	10.00
—Budget-line reissue			
❑ SP-3030	Gula Matari	1970	15.00
❑ SP-3705	I Heard That!!	1976	15.00
❑ SP-6507	I Heard That!!	198?	12.00
—Budget-line reissue			
❑ SP-4526	Mellow Madness	1975	12.00
❑ QU-54526 [Q]	Mellow Madness	1975	12.00
❑ SP-4626	Roots	1977	12.00
❑ SP-3037	Smackwater Jack	1971	15.00
❑ SP-4685	Sounds…And Stuff Like That!	1978	12.00
❑ SP-3249	Sounds…And Stuff Like That!	198?	10.00
—Budget-line reissue			
❑ SP-3200	The Best	1982	10.00
❑ SP-3278	The Best, Vol. 2	1985	10.00
❑ SP-3721	The Dude	1981	12.00
❑ SP-3248	The Dude	198?	10.00
—Budget-line reissue			
❑ SP-3023	Walking in Space	1969	15.00
❑ SP-3041	You've Got It Bad Girl	1973	15.00
❑ QU-53041 [Q]	You've Got It Bad Girl	1974	12.00
ABC			
❑ D-782	Mode	1973	15.00
ABC IMPULSE!			
❑ IA-9342	Quintessential Charts	1978	15.00
❑ AS-11 [S]	The Quintessence	1968	18.00
ABC-PARAMOUNT			
❑ 186 [M]	Go West, Man!	1957	100.00
❑ 149 [M]	This Is How I Feel About Jazz	1956	100.00
CHESS			
❑ CH-91562	The Music of Quincy Jones	198?	12.00
COLGEMS			
❑ COM-107 [M]	In Cold Blood	1967	25.00
❑ COS-107 [S]	In Cold Blood	1967	30.00
EMARCY			
❑ MG-36083 [M]	Jazz Abroad	1956	100.00
❑ 818177-1	The Birth of a Band	1984	15.00
GRP/IMPULSE!			
❑ 222	The Quintessence	199?	18.00
—Reissue on audiophile vinyl			
IMPULSE!			
❑ A-11 [M]	The Quintessence	1962	25.00
❑ AS-11 [S]	The Quintessence	1962	30.00
LIBERTY			
❑ LOM-16004 [M]	Enter Laughing	1967	30.00
❑ LOS-17004 [S]	Enter Laughing	1967	30.00
MCA			
❑ 4145	Quintessential Charts	198?	12.00
—Reissue of ABC Impulse 9342			
❑ 5578	The Slugger's Wife	1985	15.00
MCA/IMPULSE!			
❑ 5728	The Quintessence	1986	10.00
MERCURY			
❑ PPS-2014 [M]	Around the World	1961	30.00
❑ PPS-6014 [S]	Around the World	1961	40.00
❑ MG-20751 [M]	Big Band Bossa Nova	1962	30.00
❑ SR-60751 [S]	Big Band Bossa Nova	1962	40.00
❑ MG-20444 [M]	Birth of a Band	1959	50.00
❑ SR-60129 [S]	Birth of a Band	1959	60.00
❑ MG-20938 [M]	Golden Boy	1964	25.00
❑ SR-60938 [S]	Golden Boy	1964	30.00
❑ MG-20612 [M]	I Dig Dancers	1960	40.00
❑ SR-60612 [S]	I Dig Dancers	1960	50.00
❑ MG-21025 [M]	Mirage	1965	25.00
❑ SR-61025 [S]	Mirage	1965	30.00
❑ SRM-2-623	Ndeda	1972	18.00
❑ MG-20653 [M]	Quincy Jones at Newport '61	1961	30.00
❑ SR-60653 [S]	Quincy Jones at Newport '61	1961	40.00
❑ MG-20863 [M]	Quincy Jones Explores the Music of Henry Mancini	1964	25.00
❑ SR-60863 [S]	Quincy Jones Explores the Music of Henry Mancini	1964	30.00
❑ MG-21050 [M]	Quincy Jones Plays for Pussycats	1965	25.00
❑ SR-61050 [S]	Quincy Jones Plays for Pussycats	1965	30.00
❑ MG-20799 [M]	Quincy Jones Plays Hip Hits	1963	30.00
❑ SR-60799 [S]	Quincy Jones Plays Hip Hits	1963	40.00
❑ MG-21063 [M]	Quincy's Got a Brand New Bag	1965	25.00
❑ SR-61063 [S]	Quincy's Got a Brand New Bag	1965	30.00
❑ MG-21070 [M]	Slender Thread	1966	25.00
❑ SR-61070 [S]	Slender Thread	1966	30.00
❑ MG-20561 [M]	The Great, Wide World of Quincy Jones	1960	50.00
❑ SR-60221 [S]	The Great, Wide World of Quincy Jones	1960	60.00
❑ MG-21011 [M]	The Pawnbroker	1964	25.00
❑ SR-61011 [S]	The Pawnbroker	1964	30.00
MOBILE FIDELITY			
❑ 1-078	You've Got It Bad Girl	1981	30.00
—Audiophile vinyl			
NAUTILUS			
❑ NR-52	The Dude	198?	40.00
—Audiophile vinyl			
PRESTIGE			
❑ PRLP-172 [10]	Quincy Jones with the Swedish-American All Stars	1953	200.00
QWEST			
❑ 26020	Back on the Block	1989	15.00
❑ 25356	The Color Purple	1985	25.00
—Boxed set on purple vinyl			
❑ 25389	The Color Purple	1985	18.00
—Gatefold package on purple vinyl			
TRIP			
❑ 5554	Live at Newport '61	197?	10.00
❑ 5514	The Great Wide World of Quincy Jones	1974	10.00
UNITED ARTISTS			
❑ UAS-5214	They Call Me Mister Tibbs	1970	30.00
WING			
❑ SRW-16398	Around the World	1969	15.00

JONES, RICHARD

Number	Title	Yr	NM
PAX			
❑ 6010 [10]	New Orleans Style	1954	80.00
RIVERSIDE			
❑ RLP-1017 [10]	Richard P. Jones and Clarence Williams	1953	80.00

JONES, RICKIE LEE

Number	Title	Yr	NM
GEFFEN			
❑ GHS24246	Flying Cowboys	1989	12.00
MOBILE FIDELITY			
❑ 1-089	Rickie Lee Jones	1982	200.00
—Audiophile vinyl			
❑ MFSL2-45010 [B]	Rickie Lee Jones	2013	60.00
WARNER BROS.			
❑ 23805 [10]	Girl at Her Volcano	1983	10.00
❑ 23805 [10]	Girl at Her Volcano	1983	18.00
—Promo-only version on Quiex II vinyl			
❑ BSK3432	Pirates	1981	10.00
❑ BSK3296	Rickie Lee Jones	1979	10.00
❑ 25117	The Magazine	1984	10.00

JONES, SAM

Number	Title	Yr	NM
FANTASY			
❑ OJC-6008	Right Down in Front	198?	12.00
INTERPLAY			
❑ 7720	The Bassist	1979	15.00
MUSE			
❑ MR-5149	Something in Common	1977	18.00
RIVERSIDE			
❑ RLP-432 [M]	Down Home	1962	30.00
❑ RS-9432 [S]	Down Home	1962	40.00
❑ 6079	Soul Society	197?	18.00
❑ RLP-358 [M]	The Chant!	1961	30.00
❑ RS-9358 [S]	The Chant!	1961	40.00
❑ RLP 12-324 [M]	The Soul Society	1960	40.00
❑ RLP-1172 [S]	The Soul Society	1960	40.00
SEA BREEZE			
❑ 2004	Something New	1979	15.00
STEEPLECHASE			
❑ SCS-1097	Visitation	198?	15.00
XANADU			
❑ 129	Cello Again	197?	15.00
❑ 150	Changes and Things	1978	15.00

JONES, SPIKE, AND THE CITY SLICKERS

Number	Title	Yr	NM
CORNOGRAPHIC			
❑ 1001	King of Corn	197?	12.00
GOLDBERG & O'REILY			
❑ MF205/4	The Craziest Show on Earth	1977	25.00
—Collection of radio show performances			
HINDSIGHT			
❑ HSR-185	The Uncollected Spike Jones 1946	198?	12.00
LIBERTY			
❑ LRP-3154 [M]	60 Years of Music America Hates Best	1960	50.00
❑ LST-7154 [S]	60 Years of Music America Hates Best	1960	75.00
❑ LRP-3370 [M]	My Man	1964	25.00
❑ LST-7370 [S]	My Man	1964	30.00
❑ LRP-3140 [M]	Omnibust	1959	50.00
❑ LST-7140 [S]	Omnibust	1959	75.00
—Black vinyl			
❑ LST-7140 [S]	Omnibust	1959	150.00
—Red vinyl			
❑ LRP-3349 [M]	Spike Jones' New Band	1964	30.00
❑ LST-7349 [S]	Spike Jones' New Band	1964	40.00
❑ LRP-3401 [M]	Spike Jones Plays Hank Williams Hits	1965	25.00
❑ LST-7401 [S]	Spike Jones Plays Hank Williams Hits	1965	30.00
❑ LRP-3338 [M]	Washington Square	1963	25.00
❑ LST-7338 [S]	Washington Square	1963	30.00
RCA GOLD SEAL			
❑ AGL1-4142	Spike Jones Is Murdering the Classics!	1982	10.00
—Reissue			
RCA RED SEAL			
❑ LSC-3235 [R]	Spike Jones Is Murdering the Classics!	1971	25.00
RCA VICTOR			
❑ LPM-3054 [10]	Bottoms Up	1952	200.00
❑ LPM-3128 [10]	Spike Jones Murders Carmen and Kids the Classics	1953	200.00
❑ LPT-18 [10]	Spike Jones Plays the Charleston	1952	200.00
❑ LPM-2224 [M]	Thank You Music Lovers	1960	50.00
—RCA Victor" in silver above dog, "Long 33 1/3 Play" at bottom of label			
❑ LPM-2224 [M]	Thank You Music Lovers	1965	30.00
—RCA Victor" in white above dog, "Monaural" at bottom of label			
❑ LPM-3849 [M]	The Best of Spike Jones	1967	30.00
❑ LSP-3849 [R]	The Best of Spike Jones	1967	25.00
❑ ANL1-1035	The Best of Spike Jones	1975	12.00
—Reissue			
❑ AYL1-3748	The Best of Spike Jones, Volume 1	1980	10.00
—Best Buy Series" reissue			
❑ AYL1-3870	The Best of Spike Jones, Volume 2	1981	10.00
—Best Buy Series" reissue			
❑ ANL1-2312	The Best of Spike Jones, Volume 2	1977	12.00
—Reissue			
RHINO			
❑ R170261	Dinner Music…For People Who Aren't Very Hungry	1988	15.00
❑ R170196	It's a Spike Jones Christmas	1988	15.00
UNITED ARTISTS			
❑ UA-LA439-E	The Very Best of Spike Jones	1975	15.00
VERVE			
❑ MGV-4005 [M]	Dinner Music…For People Who Aren't Very Hungry	1957	50.00
❑ V-4005 [M]	Dinner Music…For People Who Aren't Very Hungry	1961	30.00
❑ MGV-2021 [M]	Let's Sing a Song for Christmas	1956	50.00
❑ V-2021 [M]	Let's Sing a Song for Christmas	1961	30.00
WARNER BROS.			
❑ W1332 [M]	Spike Jones in Hi-Fi	1959	40.00
❑ WS1332 [S]	Spike Jones in Hi-Fi	1959	50.00
— This is the title on the front of the LP cover, but the spine says "Spike Jones in Stereo			

JONES, STAN

Number	Title	Yr	NM
BUENA VISTA			
❑ BV-3306 [M]	Ghost Riders in the Sky	1961	30.00
—Reissue of Disneyland WDL-3015			
DISNEYLAND			
❑ WDL-3015 [M]	Creakin' Leather	1958	40.00
❑ WDL-1005 [M]	Songs of the National Parks	1958	40.00
—Sold only at national parks			
❑ WDL-3033 [M]	This Was the West -- The Story and the Songs	1958	40.00

JONES, TAMIKO

Number	Title	Yr	NM
A&M			
❑ SP-3011	I'll Be Anything for You	1969	30.00
ARISTA			
❑ AL-4040	Love Trip	1975	30.00
DECEMBER			
❑ DR-8500	Tamiko	1968	30.00

METROMEDIA

Number	Title	Yr	NM
❑ MD1030	Tamiko Jones in Muscle Shoals	1970	30.00

JONES, THAD, AND MEL LEWIS

ARTISTS HOUSE

Number	Title	Yr	NM
❑ 3	Quartet	1980	15.00

BLUE NOTE

Number	Title	Yr	NM
❑ BST-84346	Consummation	1970	30.00
❑ BN-LA392-H	Thad Jones/Mel Lewis	1975	18.00
❑ BST-89905	The Jazz Wave Ltd. On Tour (Volume 1)	1970	30.00

HORIZON

Number	Title	Yr	NM
❑ SP-724	Live in Munich	1978	15.00
❑ SP-707	New Life	1976	15.00
❑ SP-701	Suite for Pops	1975	15.00

MOSAIC

Number	Title	Yr	NM
❑ MQ7-151	The Complete Solid State Recordings of the Thad Jones-Mel Lewis Orchestra	199?	150.00

PAUSA

Number	Title	Yr	NM
❑ 7012	Thad Jones-Mel Lewis Orchestra and Manuel De Sica	198?	12.00

PHILADELPHIA INT'L.

Number	Title	Yr	NM
❑ KZ33152 [B]	Potpourri	1974	35.00

RCA VICTOR

Number	Title	Yr	NM
❑ AFL1-3423	Thad Jones/Mel Lewis and Umo	1980	25.00

SOLID STATE

Number	Title	Yr	NM
❑ SS-18058	Central Park North	1969	18.00
❑ SM-17016 [M]	Live at the Village Vanguard	1967	30.00
❑ SS-18016 [S]	Live at the Village Vanguard	1967	25.00
❑ SS-18048	Monday Night	1969	18.00
❑ SM-17003 [M]	Presenting Thad Jones, Mel Lewis and the Jazz Orchestra	1966	25.00
❑ SS-18003 [S]	Presenting Thad Jones, Mel Lewis and the Jazz Orchestra	1966	25.00
❑ SS-18041	Thad Jones and Mel Lewis Featuring Miss Ruth Brown	1968	18.00

JONES, THAD, AND PEPPER ADAMS

MILESTONE

Number	Title	Yr	NM
❑ MLP-1001 [M]	Mean What You Say	1966	25.00
❑ MSP-9001 [S]	Mean What You Say	1966	30.00

JONES, THAD

BIOGRAPH

Number	Title	Yr	NM
❑ 12059	Greetings and Salutations	197?	15.00

BLUE NOTE

Number	Title	Yr	NM
❑ BLP-1513 [M]	Detroit-New York Junction	1956	500.00
—Deep groove" version; Lexington Ave. address on label			
❑ BLP-1513 [M]	Detroit-New York Junction	1958	400.00
—Deep groove" version, W. 63rd St. address on label			
❑ BLP-1513 [M]	Detroit-New York Junction	1963	50.00
—With "New York, USA" address on label			
❑ BST-81513 [R]	Detroit-New York Junction	1967	25.00
—With "A Division of Liberty Records" on label			
❑ BLP-1527 [M]	The Magnificent Thad Jones	1956	500.00
—Deep groove" version; Lexington Ave. address on label			
❑ BLP-1527 [M]	The Magnificent Thad Jones	1956	150.00
—Deep groove" version, W. 63rd St. address on label			
❑ BLP-1527 [M]	The Magnificent Thad Jones	1963	50.00
—With "New York, USA" address on label			
❑ BST-81527 [R]	The Magnificent Thad Jones	1967	25.00
—With "A Division of Liberty Records" on label			
❑ BLP-1546 [M]	The Magnificent Thad Jones, Volume 3	1957	400.00
—Deep groove" version; W. 63rd St. address on label			
❑ BLP-1546 [M]	The Magnificent Thad Jones, Volume 3	1957	200.00
—Regular version, W. 63rd St., NY address on label			
❑ BLP-1546 [M]	The Magnificent Thad Jones, Volume 3	1963	50.00
—With "New York, USA" address on label			
❑ BST-81546 [R]	The Magnificent Thad Jones, Volume 3	1967	25.00
—With "A Division of Liberty Records" on label			

DEBUT

Number	Title	Yr	NM
❑ DLP-17 [10]	Jazz Collaborations	1954	600.00
❑ DEB-127 [M]	Thad Jones	1958	300.00
❑ DLP-12 [10]	The Fabulous Thad Jones	1954	600.00

FANTASY

Number	Title	Yr	NM
❑ 6004 [M]	The Fabulous Thad Jones	1962	50.00
—Red vinyl			
❑ 6004 [M]	The Fabulous Thad Jones	1962	30.00
—Black vinyl			
❑ 86004 [R]	The Fabulous Thad Jones	1962	30.00
—Blue vinyl			
❑ 86004 [R]	The Fabulous Thad Jones	1962	18.00
—Black vinyl			
❑ OJC-625	The Fabulous Thad Jones	1991	18.00

MOSAIC

Number	Title	Yr	NM
❑ MQ5-172	The Complete Blue Note/UA/Roulette Recordings of Thad Jones	199?	100.00

PERIOD

Number	Title	Yr	NM
❑ SPL-1208 [M]	Mad Thad	1956	250.00

PRESTIGE

Number	Title	Yr	NM
❑ PRLP-7118 [M]	After Hours	1957	300.00
—Yellow label with W. 50th St. address			
❑ P-24017	After Hours	197?	25.00
❑ MPP-2506	Thad Jones and Charles Mingus	1980	18.00

STEEPLECHASE

Number	Title	Yr	NM
❑ SCS-1197	Three and One	198?	15.00

UNITED ARTISTS

Number	Title	Yr	NM
❑ UAL-4025 [M]	Motor City Scene	1959	80.00
❑ UAS-5025 [S]	Motor City Scene	1959	60.00

JONES, TOM

EPIC

Number	Title	Yr	NM
❑ PE34383	Classic Tom Jones	1976	15.00
❑ PE34468	Say You'll Stay Until Tomorrow	1977	15.00
❑ PE34720	Tom Is Love	1977	12.00
❑ JE35023	What a Night	1978	12.00

JIVE

Number	Title	Yr	NM
❑ 1214-1-J	Move Closer	1989	15.00

LONDON

Number	Title	Yr	NM
❑ PS717	The Country Side of Tom Jones	1978	12.00
❑ 820234-1	This Is Tom Jones	1985	10.00
❑ LC-50002	Tom Jones' Greatest Hits	1977	15.00
❑ 820319-1	Tom Jones' Greatest Hits	1985	12.00

MCA

Number	Title	Yr	NM
❑ 37114	Rescue Me	1980	10.00
❑ 3182	Tom Jones	1979	12.00

MERCURY

Number	Title	Yr	NM
❑ SRM-1-4010	Darlin'	1981	12.00
❑ 814448-1	Don't Let Our Dreams Die Young	1983	12.00
❑ 822701-1	Love Is on the Radio	1984	12.00
❑ 826140-1	Tender Loving Care	1985	12.00
❑ 830409-1	Things That Matter Most to Me	1987	12.00
❑ SRM-1-4062	Tom Jones Country	1982	12.00

PARROT

Number	Title	Yr	NM
❑ PA61007 [M]	A-Tom-Ic Jones	1966	18.00
❑ PAS71007 [S]	A-Tom-Ic Jones	1966	18.00
❑ XPAS71055	Close Up	1972	15.00
❑ PA61011 [M]	Funny Familiar Forgotten Feelings	1967	18.00
❑ PAS71011 [S]	Funny Familiar Forgotten Feelings	1967	18.00
❑ PA61009 [M]	Green, Green Grass of Home	1967	18.00
❑ PAS71009 [S]	Green, Green Grass of Home	1967	18.00
❑ PAS71025	Help Yourself	1969	15.00
❑ PA61004 [M]	It's Not Unusual	1965	18.00
❑ PAS71004 [S]	It's Not Unusual	1965	18.00
❑ PAS71039	I (Who Have Nothing)	1970	15.00
❑ 2XPAS71049/50	Live at Caesar's Palace	1971	15.00
❑ PAS71031	Live in Las Vegas	1969	15.00
❑ PAS71068	Memories Don't Leave Like People Do	197?	15.00
❑ PAS71046	She's a Lady	1971	15.00
❑ PAS71066	Somethin' 'Bout You Baby I Like	1974	15.00
❑ XPAS-1 [DJ]	Special Tom Jones Interview	1970	100.00
—Promo-only open-end interview with gatefold cover and script			
❑ XPAS71060	The Body and Soul of Tom Jones	197?	15.00
❑ PAS71019	The Tom Jones Fever Zone	1968	15.00
❑ PAS71028	This Is Tom Jones	1969	15.00
❑ ST-92025	This Is Tom Jones	1969	18.00
—Capitol Record Club edition			
❑ PAS71037	Tom	1970	15.00
❑ SW-93186	Tom	197?	18.00
—Capitol Record Club edition			
❑ XPAS71062	Tom Jones' Greatest Hits	1973	15.00
❑ PAS71014 [S]	Tom Jones Live	1967	18.00
❑ PA61014 [M]	Tom Jones Live	1967	18.00
❑ PA61006 [M]	What's New Pussycat?	1965	18.00
❑ PAS71006 [S]	What's New Pussycat?	1965	18.00

JONES BOYS, THE

MUSICOR

Number	Title	Yr	NM
❑ MM-2017 [M]	Country and Western Songbook	1964	30.00
❑ MS-3017 [S]	Country and Western Songbook	1964	30.00
❑ MS-3182	My Boys, the Jones Boys	1970	25.00

JONES BOYS, THE (2)

PERIOD

Number	Title	Yr	NM
❑ SPL-1210 [M]	The Jones Bash	1954	80.00

JONES BROTHERS, THE

METROJAZZ

Number	Title	Yr	NM
❑ E-1003 [M]	Keepin' Up with the Joneses	1958	80.00
❑ SE-1003 [S]	Keepin' Up with the Joneses	1958	60.00

JOOK, THE

SING SING

Number	Title	Yr	NM
❑ SING053 [B]	The Jook	2013	25.00
—featuring members of John's Children, Sparks, Jet			

JOPLIN, JANIS

COLUMBIA

Number	Title	Yr	NM
❑ AS1377 [DJ]	A Collection	1982	25.00
❑ PC37569	Farewell Song	1982	12.00
❑ KCS9913 [B]	I Got Dem Ol' Kozmik Blues Again Mama!	1969	30.00
—360 Sound Stereo" on label			
❑ KCS9913	I Got Dem Ol' Kozmik Blues Again Mama!	1970	15.00
—Orange label			
❑ PC9913	I Got Dem Ol' Kozmik Blues Again Mama!	198?	10.00
—Budget-line reissue			
❑ PG33345 [B]	Janis	1975	18.00
❑ CG33345	Janis	198?	15.00
❑ KC32168	Janis Joplin's Greatest Hits	1973	18.00
❑ PC32168	Janis Joplin's Greatest Hits	197?	10.00
❑ C2X31160 [B]	Joplin in Concert	1972	30.00
❑ CG31160	Joplin in Concert	198?	15.00
❑ KC30322	Pearl	1971	18.00
❑ PC30322	Pearl	1975	15.00
—Reissue without bar code			
❑ CQ30322 [Q]	Pearl	1974	40.00
❑ PC30322	Pearl	198?	10.00
—Reissue with bar code			

COLUMBIA SPECIAL PRODUCTS

Number	Title	Yr	NM
❑ 2P13792	The Greatest Hits of Janis Joplin	1977	25.00

JORDAN, CLIFFORD

ATLANTIC

Number	Title	Yr	NM
❑ 1444 [M]	These Are My Roots	1965	30.00
❑ SD1444 [S]	These Are My Roots	1965	30.00

BEE HIVE

Number	Title	Yr	NM
❑ BH-7018	Dr. Chicago	1986	12.00

BLUE NOTE

Number	Title	Yr	NM
❑ BLP-1549 [M]	Blowing In from Chicago	1957	200.00
—Deep groove" version (deep indentation under label on both sides)			
❑ BLP-1549 [M]	Blowing In from Chicago	1957	80.00
—Regular version, W. 63rd St., NY address on label			
❑ BLP-1549 [M]	Blowing In from Chicago	1963	30.00
—With "New York, USA" address on label			
❑ BST-81549 [R]	Blowing In from Chicago	1967	15.00
—With "A Division of Liberty Records" on label			
❑ BLP-1582 [M]	Cliff Craft	1958	1000.00
—Deep groove" version (deep indentation under label on both sides)			
❑ BLP-1582 [M]	Cliff Craft	1958	600.00
—Regular version, W. 63rd St., NY address on label			
❑ BLP-1582 [M]	Cliff Craft	1963	30.00
—With "New York, USA" address on label			
❑ BST-1582 [S]	Cliff Craft	1959	350.00
—Deep groove" version (deep indentation under label on both sides)			
❑ BST-1582 [S]	Cliff Craft	1959	60.00
—Regular version, W. 63rd St., NY address on label			
❑ BST-1582 [S]	Cliff Craft	1963	25.00
—With "New York, USA" address on label			
❑ BST-81582 [S]	Cliff Craft	1967	18.00
—With "A Division of Liberty Records" on label			
❑ BST-81582 [S]	Cliff Craft	199?	30.00
—Classic Records reissue on audiophile vinyl			
❑ BLP-1565 [M]	Clifford Jordan	1957	800.00
—Deep groove" version (deep indentation under label on both sides)			
❑ BLP-1565 [M]	Clifford Jordan	1957	80.00
—Regular version, W. 63rd St., NY address on label			
❑ BLP-1565 [M]	Clifford Jordan	1963	30.00
—With "New York, USA" address on label			
❑ BST-1565 [S]	Clifford Jordan	1959	800.00
—Deep groove" version (deep indentation under label on both sides)			
❑ BST-1565 [S]	Clifford Jordan	1959	60.00
—Regular version, W. 63rd St., NY address on label			
❑ BST-1565 [S]	Clifford Jordan	1963	25.00
—With "New York, USA" address on label			
❑ BST-81565 [S]	Clifford Jordan	1967	18.00
—With "A Division of Liberty Records" on label			

FANTASY

Number	Title	Yr	NM
❑ OJC-494	Bearcat	1991	18.00
❑ OJC-147	Starting Time	198?	12.00

INNER CITY

Number	Title	Yr	NM
❑ IC-2033	Firm Roots	197?	18.00
❑ IC-2047	The Highest Mountain	197?	18.00

JAZZLAND

Number	Title	Yr	NM
❑ JLP-40 [M]	A Story Tale	1961	30.00
❑ JLP-940 [S]	A Story Tale	1961	40.00
❑ JLP-69 [M]	Bearcat	1962	30.00
❑ JLP-969 [S]	Bearcat	1962	40.00
❑ JLP-52 [M]	Starting Time	1961	30.00
❑ JLP-952 [S]	Starting Time	1961	40.00

MUSE

Number	Title	Yr	NM
❑ MR-5128	Inward Fire	197?	15.00
❑ MR-5076	Night of the Mark VII	197?	15.00
❑ MR-5105	Remembering Me-Me	197?	15.00
❑ MR-5163	The Adventurer	197?	15.00

Number	Title	Yr	NM
RIVERSIDE			
❏ RLP-340 [M]	Spellbound	1960	40.00
❏ RS-9340 [S]	Spellbound	1960	30.00
SOUL NOTE			
❏ SN-1084	Repetition	1984	15.00
STEEPLECHASE			
❏ SCS-1033	Film Roots	198?	15.00
❏ SCS-1198	Half Note	198?	15.00
❏ SCS-1071	On Stage, Volume 1	197?	15.00
❏ SCS-1092	On Stage, Volume 2	198?	15.00
❏ SCS-1104	On Stage, Volume 3	198?	15.00
❏ SCS-1047	The Highest Mountain	198?	15.00
STRATA-EAST			
❏ SES19737/8	Glass Bead Games	1974	30.00
❏ SES1972-1	In the World	1972	25.00
VORTEX			
❏ 2010	Soul Fountain	1970	25.00
JORDAN, DUKE			
BLUE NOTE			
❏ BLP-4046 [M]	Flight to Jordan	1960	500.00
—With W. 63rd St., NY address on label			
❏ BLP-4046 [M]	Flight to Jordan	1963	30.00
—With "New York, USA" address on label			
❏ BST-84046 [S]	Flight to Jordan	1960	60.00
—With W. 63rd St., NY address on label			
❏ BST-84046 [S]	Flight to Jordan	1963	25.00
—With "New York, USA" address on label			
❏ BST-84046 [S]	Flight to Jordan	1967	18.00
—With "A Division of Liberty Records" on label			
CHARLIE PARKER			
❏ PLP-805 [M]	East and West of Jazz	1962	30.00
❏ PLP-805S [S]	East and West of Jazz	1962	30.00
INNER CITY			
❏ IC-2046	Duke's Delight	197?	18.00
❏ IC-2011	Flight to Denmark	197?	18.00
❏ IC-2024	Two Loves	197?	18.00
NEW JAZZ			
❏ NJ-810 [10]	Jordu	195?	200.00
PRESTIGE			
❏ PRST-7849	Jordu	1970	15.00
SAVOY			
❏ MG-12149 [M]	Duke Jordan	1959	80.00
SAVOY JAZZ			
❏ SJL-1169	Flight to Jordan	1986	12.00
SIGNAL			
❏ S-1202 [M]	Duke Jordan	1955	250.00
STEEPLECHASE			
❏ SCS-1135	Change of Pace	1979	15.00
❏ SCS-1103	Duke's Artistry	1978	15.00
❏ SCS-1046	Duke's Delight	198?	15.00
❏ SCS-1011	Flight to Denmark	198?	15.00
❏ SCS-1088	Flight to Japan	198?	15.00
❏ SCS-1150	Great Session	198?	15.00
❏ SCS-1063/4	Live in Japan	198?	18.00
❏ SCS-1127	Lover Man	198?	15.00
❏ SCS-1143	Midnight Moonlight	198?	15.00
❏ SCS-1053	Misty Thursday	198?	15.00
❏ SCS-1165	Thinking of You	198?	15.00
❏ SCS-1189	Tivol One	198?	15.00
❏ SCS-1193	Tivol Two	198?	15.00
❏ SCS-1175	Truth	198?	15.00
❏ SCS-1024	Two Loves	198?	15.00
❏ SCS-1211	Wait and See	198?	15.00
JORDAN, DUKE/HALL OVERTON			
SAVOY			
❏ MG-12145 [M]	Do It Yourself Jazz	1959	100.00
❏ MG-12146 [M]	Jazz Laboratory Series	1959	100.00
SIGNAL			
❏ S-101/2 [M]	Jazz Laboratory Series	1955	250.00
—Deduct 20 percent if book is missing			
JORDAN, KING			
CORAL			
❏ CRL57372 [M]	Phantom Guitar	1962	25.00
❏ CRL757372 [S]	Phantom Guitar	1962	30.00
JORDAN, LOUIS			
CIRCLE			
❏ 53	Louis Jordan and the Tympany Five: 1944-45	198?	12.00
❏ 97	More Louis Jordan and His Tympany Five	198?	12.00
CLASSIC JAZZ			
❏ 148	I Believe in Music	198?	15.00
DECCA			
❏ DL5035 [M]	Greatest Hits	1968	30.00
❏ DL75035 [M]	Greatest Hits	1968	18.00
❏ DL8551 [M]	Let the Good Times Roll	1958	100.00
—Black label, silver print			
MCA			
❏ 274	Greatest Hits	197?	12.00
❏ 1337	Greatest Hits, Vol. 2	1980	12.00
❏ 4079	The Best of Louis Jordan	197?	15.00

Number	Title	Yr	NM
MERCURY			
❏ MG-20331 [M]	Man, We're Wailin'	1958	120.00
❏ MG-20242 [M]	Somebody Up There Digs Me	1957	120.00
SCORE			
❏ SLP-4007 [M]	Go Blow Your Horn	1957	200.00
TANGERINE			
❏ 1503 [M]	Hallelujah	1964	25.00
❏ S-1503 [S]	Hallelujah	1964	30.00
WING			
❏ MGW-12126 [M]	Somebody Up There Digs Me	1962	30.00
JORDAN, SHEILA			
BLACKHAWK			
❏ BKH-50501	The Crossing	1986	12.00
BLUE NOTE			
❏ BLP-9002 [M]	Portrait of Sheila Jordan	1962	150.00
—With W. 63rd St., NY address on label			
❏ BLP-9002 [M]	Portrait of Sheila Jordan	1963	30.00
—With "New York, USA" address on label			
❏ BST-89002 [R]	Portrait of Sheila Jordan	1967	15.00
—With "A Division of Liberty Records" on label			
MUSE			
❏ MR-5390	Lost and Found	1990	18.00
❏ MR-5366	Old Time Feeling	1989	15.00
PALO ALTO			
❏ PA-8038	Old Time Feeling	1982	15.00
STEEPLECHASE			
❏ SCS-1081	Sheila	1978	15.00
WAVE			
❏ W-1 [M]	Looking Out	1961	60.00
❏ WS-1 [S]	Looking Out	1961	80.00
JORDAN, STANLEY			
BLUE NOTE			
❏ B1-92356	Cornucopia	1990	18.00
❏ BT-85101	Magic Touch	1985	12.00
❏ BT-85130	Standards Volume 1	1986	12.00
❏ SPRO-9434/5 [DJ]	Stanley Jordan	1985	25.00
—Promo-only live recordings			
EMI MANHATTAN			
❏ E1-48682	Flying Home	1988	12.00
TANGENT			
❏ 1001	Touch Sensitive	1982	100.00
JORDAN, TAFT			
MERCURY			
❏ MG-20429 [M]	The Moods of Taft Jordan	1959	40.00
❏ SR-60101 [S]	The Moods of Taft Jordan	1959	40.00
MOODSVILLE			
❏ MVLP-21 [M]	Mood Indigo -- Taft Jordan Plays Duke Ellington	1961	50.00
—Green label			
❏ MVLP-21 [M]	Mood Indigo -- Taft Jordan Plays Duke Ellington	1965	30.00
—Blue label, trident logo at right			
STATUS			
❏ 21 [M]	Mood Indigo -- Taft Jordan Plays Duke Ellington	196?	30.00
—Reissue of Moodsville 21			
JORDAN BROTHERS, THE			
JBP			
❏ ASM-416	Today's Yesterdays Volume 1	1980	30.00
JORDANAIRES, THE			
CAPITOL			
❏ T1167 [M]	Gloryland	1959	60.00
❏ T1011 [M]	Heavenly Spirit	1958	60.00
❏ T1311 [M]	Land of Jordan	1960	60.00
❏ ST1311 [S]	Land of Jordan	1960	60.00
❏ T1742 [M]	Spotlight on the Jordanaires	1962	50.00
❏ ST1742 [S]	Spotlight on the Jordanaires	1962	50.00
❏ T1559 [M]	To God Be the Glory	1961	50.00
❏ ST1559 [S]	To God Be the Glory	1961	50.00
CLASSIC			
❏ CCR1935	Christmas to Elvis from the Jordanaires	1978	15.00
COLUMBIA			
❏ CL2458 [M]	The Big Country Hits	1966	25.00
❏ CS9258 [S]	The Big Country Hits	1966	30.00
❏ CL2214 [M]	This Land	1964	25.00
❏ CS9014 [S]	This Land	1964	30.00
DECCA			
❏ DL8681 [M]	Peace in the Valley	1957	50.00
RCA VICTOR			
❏ LPM-3081 [10]	Beautiful City	1953	100.00
SESAC			
❏ 1401/2 [M]	Of Rivers and Plains	195?	80.00

Number	Title	Yr	NM
JORGENSON, CHRISTINE			
J RECORDS			
❏ J-1 [M]	Christine Jorgenson Reveals	1958	50.00
JOSEFUS			
HOOKAH			
❏ 330	Dead Man	1969	300.00
MAINSTREAM			
❏ S-6127	Josefus	1970	100.00
JOSEPH, MARGIE			
ATLANTIC			
❏ SD19182	Feeling My Way	1978	25.00
❏ SD18126	Margie	1975	25.00
❏ SD7248	Margie Joseph	1973	30.00
❏ SD7277	Sweet Surrender	1974	25.00
COTILLION			
❏ SD9906	Hear the Words, Feel the Feeling	1976	30.00
❏ 90158	Ready for the Night	1984	18.00
H.C.R.C.			
❏ HLP-20009	Knockout	1983	15.00
ICHIBAN			
❏ 1027	Stay	1988	18.00
VOLT			
❏ VOS-6012	Margie Joseph Makes a New Impression	1971	30.00
❏ VOS-6016	Phase II	1971	30.00
JOSEPH			
SCEPTER			
❏ SRS-674 [B]	Stoned Age Man	1970	100.00
JOSHUA FOX			
TETRAGRAMMATON			
❏ T-125	Joshua Fox	1969	30.00
JOSIE AND THE PUSSYCATS			
CAPITOL			
❏ ST-665	Josie and the Pussycats	1970	200.00
JOURNEY			
COLUMBIA			
❏ AS1606 [DJ]	A Candid Conversation with Journey	1983	30.00
—Promo-only interview and songs LP			
❏ KC237016 [B]	Captured	1981	15.00
❏ FC36339	Departure	1980	10.00
❏ HC46339 [B]	Departure	1980	30.00
—Half-speed mastered edition			
❏ HC47998 [B]	Dream After Dream	1982	35.00
—Half-speed mastered edition			
❏ FC37998	Dream After Dream	1982	15.00
❏ PC37998	Dream After Dream	1986	10.00
—Budget-line reissue			
❏ TC37408	Escape	1981	10.00
❏ HC47408 [B]	Escape	1982	30.00
—Half-speed mastered edition			
❏ FC35797	Evolution	1979	10.00
❏ QC38504	Frontiers	1983	10.00
❏ HC48504 [B]	Frontiers	1983	35.00
—Half-speed mastered edition			
❏ OC44493	Greatest Hits	1988	12.00
❏ JC34912	Infinity	1978	12.00
—No bar code on cover			
❏ HC44912 [B]	Infinity	1982	35.00
—Half-speed mastered edition			
❏ C236324 [B]	In the Beginning	1979	15.00
❏ PC33388	Journey	1975	12.00
—No bar code on cover			
❏ AS914 [DJ]	Journey	1981	25.00
—Promo-only four-song sampler			
❏ PC33904	Look Into the Future	1976	12.00
—No bar code on cover			
❏ PC34311	Next	1977	12.00
—No bar code on cover			
❏ OC39936	Raised on Radio	1986	10.00
MOBILE FIDELITY			
❏ 1-144	Escape	1984	200.00
—Audiophile vinyl			
JOURNEYMEN, THE (1)			
CAPITOL			
❏ T1770 [M]	Coming Attraction -- Live!	1962	30.00
❏ ST1770 [S]	Coming Attraction -- Live!	1962	30.00
❏ T1951 [M]	New Directions in Folk Music	1963	30.00
❏ ST1951 [S]	New Directions in Folk Music	1963	30.00
❏ T1629 [M]	The Journeymen	1961	30.00
❏ ST1629 [S]	The Journeymen	1961	30.00
JOY DIVISION			
FACTORY			
❏ FACT US6 [B]	Closer	1980	80.00
—Purple tint vinyl			

Number	Title	Yr	NM
❏ FACT US6 [B]	Closer	1980	60.00
—Red tint vinyl			
❏ FACT US1 [B]	Unknown Pleasures	1979	50.00
QWEST			
❏ 25841 [B]	Closer	1989	18.00
—Reissue of FACT US 6			
❏ 25747	Substance	1988	30.00
❏ 25840	Unknown Pleasures	1989	18.00
—Reissue of FACT US 1			

JOY STRINGS, THE

EPIC

Number	Title	Yr	NM
❏ LN24321 [M]	Well Seasoned	1967	25.00
❏ BN26321 [S]	Well Seasoned	1967	25.00

JOY UNLIMITED

BASF

Number	Title	Yr	NM
❏ 21090	Butterflies	1972	30.00
MERCURY			
❏ SR-61283	Joy Unlimited	1970	30.00

JOYCE, JIMMY

WARNER BROS.

Number	Title	Yr	NM
❏ W1237 [M]	A Christmas to Remember	1958	18.00
❏ WS1237 [S]	A Christmas to Remember	1959	25.00
❏ W1566 [M]	This Is Christmas: A Complete Collection of the Alfred S. Burt Carols	1964	18.00
❏ WS1566 [S]	This Is Christmas: A Complete Collection of the Alfred S. Burt Carols	1964	25.00

JOYOUS NOISE

CAPITOL

Number	Title	Yr	NM
❏ SMAS-844	Joyous Noise	1971	18.00

J'S WITH JAMIE, THE

COLUMBIA

Number	Title	Yr	NM
❏ CL2005 [M]	Hey, Look Us Over!	1963	30.00
❏ CS8805 [S]	Hey, Look Us Over!	1963	40.00
❏ CS8949 [S]	The Remarkable J's with Jamie	1964	40.00
❏ CL2149 [M]	The Remarkable J's with Jamie	1964	30.00

JUDAS PRIEST

COLUMBIA

Number	Title	Yr	NM
❏ JC36443	British Steel	1980	12.00
❏ FC38219	Defenders of the Faith	1984	10.00
❏ 9C939926 [PD]	Great Vinyl and Concert Hits	1984	60.00
❏ JC35706	Hell Bent for Leather	1979	12.00
❏ FC37052	Point of Entry	1981	10.00
❏ C240794	Priest ... Live!	1987	12.00
❏ FC44244	Ram It Down	1988	10.00
❏ AS991543 [DJ]	Screaming for Vengeance	1982	25.00
—Promo-only "world tour" picture disc; plays the correct LP			
❏ AS991543 [DJ]	Screaming for Vengeance	1982	30.00
—Promo-only "world tour" picture disc; plays Neil Diamond's "Heartlight" LP in error			
❏ FC38160	Screaming for Vengeance	1982	10.00
❏ PC34787	Sin After Sin	1977	15.00
—Originals have no bar code on back cover			
❏ JC35296	Stained Class	1978	12.00
❏ OC40158	Turbo	1986	10.00
❏ JC36179	Unleashed in the East (Live in Japan)	1979	10.00
JANUS			
❏ JXS-7019	Sad Wings of Destiny	1976	25.00
❏ JXS-7019 [DJ]	Sad Wings of Destiny	1976	30.00
—Promo version, with "Specially faded for easier programming" sticker on cover			
MOBILE FIDELITY			
❏ MOFI1-036 [B]	Killing Machine	2014	30.00
❏ MOFI1-038 [B]	Screaming for Vengeance	2014	35.00
❏ MOFI1-037 [B]	Stained Class	2014	35.00
OVATION			
❏ OV-1751	Sad Wings of Destiny	1980	18.00
RCA VICTOR			
❏ CYL1-5399	Hero, Hero	1985	25.00
❏ AYL1-5041	Rocka-Rolla	1984	12.00
—Reissue of Visa 7001 with new cover			
❏ AYL1-4747	Sad Wings of Destiny	1983	12.00
—Reissue of Ovation LP			
❏ AYL1-4933	The Best of Judas Priest	1984	10.00
VISA			
❏ IMP-7001	Rocka Rolla	1979	18.00
—First U.S. issue of unreleased Gull LP; front cover has a bottle-cap motif			

JUDD, WYNONNA

MCA

Number	Title	Yr	NM
❏ 1P-8201	Wynonna	1992	30.00
—Only released on vinyl through Columbia House; label misspells her name as "Wyonna"!			

JUDDS, THE

HEARTLAND

Number	Title	Yr	NM
❏ HL-2041	Classic Gold	1992	25.00

RCA

Number	Title	Yr	NM
❏ 6422-1-R	Christmas Time with the Judds	1987	12.00
❏ 8318-1-R	Greatest Hits	1988	12.00
❏ 5916-1-R	Heartland	1987	12.00
❏ 9595-1-R	River of Time	1989	15.00
RCA VICTOR			
❏ AHL1-7042	Rockin' with the Rhythm	1985	12.00
❏ MHL1-8515 [EP]	The Judds	1984	10.00
❏ AHL1-5319	Why Not Me	1984	12.00

JULIAN'S TREATMENT

DECCA

Number	Title	Yr	NM
❏ DL75224 [B]	A Time Before This	1970	30.00

JULY

EPIC

Number	Title	Yr	NM
❏ BN26416	July	1969	200.00

JULY

PARLOPHONE

Number	Title	Yr	NM
❏ 825646335329 [B]	July	2014	50.00

JUNIOR'S EYES

A&M

Number	Title	Yr	NM
❏ SP-4189 [B]	Junior's Eyes	1970	50.00

JUSTIS, BILL

HARMONY

Number	Title	Yr	NM
❏ KH31189	Enchanted Sea	1972	15.00
MONUMENT			
❏ MLP8078 [M]	The Eternal Sea	1967	18.00
❏ SLP18078 [S]	The Eternal Sea	1967	18.00
PHILLIPS INTERNATIONAL			
❏ PLP-1950 [M]	Cloud Nine	1959	400.00
SMASH			
❏ MGS-27021 [M]	Bill Justis Plays 12 Big Instrumental Hits (Alley Cat/Green Onions)	1962	18.00
❏ 3R3-07021 [S]	Dill Justis Plays 12 Big Instrumental Hits (Alley Cat/Green Onions)	1962	25.00
❏ MGS-27030 [M]	Bill Justis Plays 12 More Big Instrumental Hits (Telstar/The Lonely Bull)	1963	18.00
❏ SRS-67030 [S]	Bill Justis Plays 12 More Big Instrumental Hits (Telstar/The Lonely Bull)	1963	25.00
❏ MGS-27043 [M]	Bill Justis Plays 12 Other Instrumental Hits	1964	18.00
❏ SRS-67043 [S]	Bill Justis Plays 12 Other Instrumental Hits	1964	25.00
❏ MGS-27031 [M]	Bill Justis Plays 12 Smash Instrumental Hits	1963	18.00
❏ SRS-67031 [S]	Bill Justis Plays 12 Smash Instrumental Hits	1963	25.00
❏ MGS-27036 [M]	Bill Justis Plays 12 Top Tunes	1963	18.00
❏ SRS-67036 [S]	Bill Justis Plays 12 Top Tunes	1963	25.00
❏ MGS-27047 [M]	Dixieland Folk Style	1964	18.00
❏ SRS-67047 [S]	Dixieland Folk Style	1964	25.00
❏ MGS-27065 [M]	More Instrumental Hits	1965	18.00
❏ SRS-67065 [S]	More Instrumental Hits	1965	25.00
❏ 830898-1	Raunchy	1987	12.00
❏ MGS-27077 [M]	Taste of Honey/The "In" Crowd	1966	18.00
❏ SRS-67077 [S]	Taste of Honey/The "In" Crowd	1966	25.00
SUN			
❏ LP-109	Raunchy	1969	15.00

K

K.C. AND THE SUNSHINE BAND

EPIC

Number	Title	Yr	NM
❏ FE38073	All in a Night's Work	1982	12.00
❏ PE38073 [B]	All in a Night's Work	1984	10.00
—Budget-line reissue			
❏ FE37490	The Painter	1981	12.00
❏ PE37490 [B]	The Painter	1982	10.00
—Budget-line reissue			
MECA			
❏ 8301	KC Ten	1984	12.00
SUNSHINE SOUND			
❏ 614	Space Cadet/Solo Flight	1981	12.00
T.K.			
❏ 500	Do It Good	1974	15.00
❏ 611	Do You Wanna Go Party	1979	12.00
❏ 612	Greatest Hits	1980	12.00
❏ 603	K.C. and the Sunshine Band	1975	12.00
❏ 605	Part 3	1976	12.00
❏ 604 [B]	The Sound of Sunshine	1975	12.00
—By "The Sunshine Band" (all instrumental)			
❏ 607	Who Do Ya (Love)	1978	12.00

K-CI AND JOJO

MCA

Number	Title	Yr	NM
❏ 113069	Emotional	2002	18.00
❏ 11937	It's Real	1999	15.00
❏ 11613	Love Always	1997	15.00

K-DOE, ERNIE

JANUS

Number	Title	Yr	NM
❏ JLS-3030 [B]	Ernie K-Doe	1971	30.00
MINIT			
❏ LP-0002 [M]	Mother-in-Law	1961	250.00
—Orange label			
❏ LP-24002 [R]	Mother-in-Law	196?	150.00
—Black label, not issued until after Imperial bought Minit			

KAJAGOOGOO

EMI AMERICA

Number	Title	Yr	NM
❏ ST-17169	Crazy People's Right to Speak	1985	12.00
—As "Kaja"			
❏ MLP-19012 [EP]	Extra Play	1984	15.00
—Original issue			
❏ ST-17157 [EP]	Extra Play	1984	12.00
—Reissue of 19012			
❏ ST-17094	White Feathers	1983	15.00

KAK

EPIC

Number	Title	Yr	NM
❏ BN26429	Kak	1969	250.00
—Beware -- a reissue that looks almost identical to the original and sells for around $12 appeared in stores in 2000-2001			

KALABASH CORP., THE

UNCLE BILL

Number	Title	Yr	NM
❏ KB-3114	The Kalabash Corp.	1970	80.00

KALEIDOSCOPE, THE

EPIC

Number	Title	Yr	NM
❏ LN24333 [M]	Beacon from Mars	1967	60.00
❏ BN26333 [S]	Beacon from Mars	1967	100.00
❏ BN26508	Bernice	1970	30.00
❏ BN26467	Incredible Kaleidoscope	1969	30.00
❏ LN24304 [M]	Side Trips	1967	30.00
❏ BN26304 [S]	Side Trips	1967	40.00
PACIFIC ARTS			
❏ 102	When Scopes Collide	1978	15.00

KALIN TWINS, THE

DECCA

Number	Title	Yr	NM
❏ DL8812 [M]	The Kalin Twins	1959	100.00
VOCALION			
❏ VL3771 [M]	When	1966	18.00
❏ VL73771 [R]	When	1966	15.00

KALLAO, ALEX

BATON

Number	Title	Yr	NM
❏ BL-1205 [M]	Alex Kallao in Concert, University of Ottawa	1957	60.00
RCA VICTOR			
❏ LJM-1011 [M]	Evening at the Embers	1954	50.00

KALLEN, KITTY

COLUMBIA

Number	Title	Yr	NM
❏ CL1662 [M]	Honky Tonk Angel	1961	25.00
❏ CS8462 [S]	Honky Tonk Angel	1961	30.00
❏ CL1404 [M]	If I Give My Heart to You	1960	25.00
❏ CS8204 [S]	If I Give My Heart to You	1960	30.00
DECCA			
❏ DL8397 [M]	It's a Lonesome Old Town	1958	40.00
MERCURY			
❏ MG25206 [10]	Pretty Kitty Kallen Sings	1955	50.00
MOVIETONE			
❏ S-72026 [S]	Delightfully	1967	18.00
❏ 71026 [M]	Delightfully	1967	18.00
RCA VICTOR			
❏ LPM-2640 [M]	My Coloring Book	1963	25.00
❏ LSP-2640 [S]	My Coloring Book	1963	30.00
VOCALION			
❏ VL3679 [M]	Little Things Mean a Lot	1959	30.00
WING			
❏ MGW-12241 [M]	Kitty Kallen Sings	196?	18.00
❏ SRW-16241 [R]	Kitty Kallen Sings	196?	15.00

KALLMAN, DICK

RCA VICTOR

Number	Title	Yr	NM
❏ LPM-3485 [M]	Dick Kallman Drops In as Hank	1966	25.00
❏ LSP-3485 [S]	Dick Kallman Drops In as Hank	1966	30.00

Number	Title	Yr	NM

KAMINSKY, MAX

CHIAROSCURO

| □ 176 | When Summer Is Gone | 1977 | 15.00 |

COMMODORE

| □ FL-20019 [10] | Max Kaminsky | 1952 | 50.00 |

CONCERT HALL JAZZ

| □ 1009 [10] | Windy City Jazz | 1955 | 50.00 |

JAZZTONE

| □ J-1208 [M] | Chicago Style | 1955 | 40.00 |

MGM

| □ E-261 [10] | When the Saints Go Marching In | 1954 | 50.00 |

RCA VICTOR

| □ LJM-3003 [10] | Jazz on the Campus, Ltd. | 1954 | 50.00 |

UNITED ARTISTS

| □ UAL-3174 [M] | Max Goes East | 1961 | 25.00 |
| □ UAS-6174 [S] | Max Goes East | 1961 | 30.00 |

KAMUCA, RICHIE

CONCORD JAZZ

□ CJ-96	Charlie	1979	30.00
□ CJ-39	Drop Me Off in Harlem	1977	18.00
□ CJ-41	Richie	1977	25.00

FANTASY

| □ OJC-1760 | West Coast Jazz in Hi-Fi | 198? | 15.00 |

HIFI

□ R-604 [M]	Jazz Erotica	1957	200.00
□ J-609 [M]	West Coast Jazz in Hi-Fi	1959	60.00
□ JS-609 [S]	West Coast Jazz in Hi-Fi	1959	50.00

JAZZZ

| □ 104 | Richie Kamuca 1976 | 1976 | 15.00 |

MODE

| □ LP-102 [M] | Richie Kamuka Quartet | 1957 | 200.00 |

KANE, BIG DADDY

COLD CHILLIN'

□ 25941	It's a Big Daddy Thing	1989	30.00
□ 25731	Long Live the Kane	1988	40.00
□	Prince of Darkness	1991	30.00
PRO-A-5205 [DJ]			
— Vinyl is promo only			
□ 26303	Taste of Chocolate	1990	25.00

LABEL

| □ 371801-1 | Veteranz Day | 1998 | 18.00 |

MCA

| □ 11102 [DJ] | Daddy's Home | 1994 | 18.00 |

KANE, KIERAN

ELEKTRA

| □ E1-60004 | Kieran Kane | 1982 | 12.00 |

KANE, MADLEEN

CHALET

| □ CH 0702 | Don't Wanna Lose You | 1981 | 12.00 |
| □ CH 0701 | Sounds of Love | 1980 | 12.00 |

WARNER BROS.

| □ BSK3315 | Cheri | 1979 | 15.00 |
| □ BSK3188 | Rough Diamond | 1978 | 15.00 |

KANE'S COUSINS

SHOVE LOVE

| □ 9827 | Undergum Bubbleground | 1969 | 40.00 |

KANGAROO

MGM

| □ SE-4586 [B] | Kangaroo | 1968 | 35.00 |

KANNIBAL KOMIX

COLOSSUS

| □ 1004 | Kannibal Komix | 1970 | 25.00 |

KANO

EMERGENCY

| □ EMLP7505 | Kano | 1980 | 15.00 |

MIRAGE

| □ WTG19327 | New York Cake | 1981 | 12.00 |

KANSAS

CBS ASSOCIATED

| □ QZ38733 | Drastic Measures | 1983 | 10.00 |
| □ QZ39283 | The Best of Kansas | 1984 | 10.00 |

KIRSHNER

□ FZ36588	Audio-Visions	1980	12.00
□ PZ36588	Audio-Visions	198?	10.00
— Budget-line reissue			
□ KZ32817	Kansas	1974	15.00
□ PZ32817	Kansas	197?	10.00
— Reissue			

□ JZ34224 [B]	Leftoverture	1976	12.00
□ HZ44224	Leftoverture	1982	40.00
— Half-speed mastered edition			
□ PZ34224	Leftoverture	198?	10.00
— Budget-line reissue			
□ PZ33806	Masque	1975	15.00
— Without bar code on cover			
□ PZ33806	Masque	198?	10.00
— With bar code on cover			
□ FZ36008	Monolith	1979	12.00
□ HZ46008	Monolith	1982	50.00
— Half-speed mastered edition			
□ PZ36008	Monolith	198?	10.00
— Budget-line reissue			
□ JZ34929	Point of Know Return	1977	12.00
□ HZ44929	Point of Know Return	1982	40.00
— Half-speed mastered edition			
□ PZ33385 [B]	Song for America	1975	15.00
— Without bar code on cover			
□ PZ33385	Song for America	198?	10.00
— With bar code on cover			
□ PZ235660	Two for the Show	1978	18.00
□ AS555 [DJ]	Two for the Show (Sampler)	1978	25.00
— Promo-only single disc of selections from 35660			
□ FZ38002	Vinyl Confessions	1982	12.00
□ HZ48002	Vinyl Confessions	1982	100.00
— Half-speed mastered edition			
□ PZ38002	Vinyl Confessions	198?	10.00
— Budget-line reissue			

MCA

| □ 6254 | In the Spirit of Things | 1988 | 10.00 |
| □ 5838 | Power | 1986 | 10.00 |

KANTNER, PAUL, AND GRACE SLICK

GRUNT

□ BXL1-0148 [B]	Baron Von Tollbooth and the Chrome Nun	1973	25.00
— Original prefix			
□ AYL1-3799	Baron Von Tollbooth and the Chrome Nun	1980	10.00
— Budget-line reissue			
□ BFL1-0148	Baron Von Tollbooth and the Chrome Nun	1977	12.00
— Reissue with new prefix			
□ FTR-1002	Sunfighter	1971	18.00
— With booklet (deduct 33% if missing)			

KANTNER, PAUL

RCA VICTOR

| □ AFL1-4320 | The Planet Earth Rock and Roll Orchestra | 1983 | 12.00 |

KANTNER, PAUL/JEFFERSON STARSHIP

RCA VICTOR

□ LSP-4448 [B]	Blows Against the Empire	1970	25.00
□ LSP-4448 [DJ]	Blows Against the Empire	1970	100.00
— Clear vinyl promo			
□ AYL1-3868	Blows Against the Empire	1981	10.00
— Budget-line reissue			
□ AFL1-4448	Blows Against the Empire	1977	12.00
— Reissue of LSP-4448			

KAPLAN, ARTIE

HOPI

| □ VHS901 | Confessions of a Male Chauvinist Pig | 1971 | 30.00 |

KAPLAN, GABRIEL

ABC

□ ABCD-905	Holes and Mello-Rolls	1976	15.00
— Reissue with photo of the "Welcome Back, Kotter" cast on cover			
□ ABCD-815	Holes and Mellow Rolls	1974	18.00

— Original release with painting of ice-cream bars on cover			
□ ABC-102 [10]	Holes and Mellow Rolls	1974	18.00
— Promo-only 10-inch sampler			

KARLOFF, BORIS

CAEDMON

□ TC-1221 [M]	Aesop's Fables	1967	25.00
□ TC-1038 [M]	Just So Stories and Other Tales	195?	30.00
□ TC-1100 [M]	Kipling's Jungle Books: How Fear Came	196?	30.00
□ TC-1176 [M]	Kipling's Jungle Books: Toomai of the Elephants	196?	30.00
□ TC-1088 [M]	More of Kipling's Just So Stories	196?	30.00
□ TC-1139 [M]	The Cat That Walked By Herself	196?	30.00
□ TC-1117 [M]	The Little Match Girl and Other Tales	196?	30.00
□ TC-1075 [M]	The Pied Piper; The Hunting of the Snarks	196?	30.00
□ TC-1074 [M]	The Reluctant Dragon	196?	30.00
□ TC-1129 [M]	The Three Bears, Henny Penny and Other Fairy Tales	1962	30.00
□ TC-1109 [M]	The Ugly Duckling and Other Tales	196?	30.00

DECCA

| □ DL4833 [M] | An Evening with Boris Karloff and His Friends | 1967 | 25.00 |
| □ DL74833 [S] | An Evening with Boris Karloff and His Friends | 1967 | 30.00 |

MERCURY

□ MG-20815 [M]	Tales of the Frightened, Volume 1	1963	40.00
□ SR-60815 [S]	Tales of the Frightened, Volume 1	1963	50.00
□ MG-20816 [M]	Tales of the Frightened, Volume 2	1963	40.00
□ SR-60816 [S]	Tales of the Frightened, Volume 2	1963	50.00

KARMA

HORIZON

| □ SP-713 | Celebration | 1976 | 18.00 |
| □ SP-723 | For Everybody | 1977 | 18.00 |

KARMEN, STEVE

JUBILEE

| □ JGM-2048 [M] | This Is a City? | 1963 | 25.00 |

STRUTTIN'

| □ STR-104 | Reconnecting | 1977 | 15.00 |

KARUKAS

OPTIMISM

| □ OP-3101 | The Nightowl | 1988 | 12.00 |

KASAI, KIMIKO

CATALYST

| □ 7900 | One for the Lady | 1977 | 15.00 |

KASANDRA

CAPITOL

| □ ST-157 | A Higher Plateau | 1969 | 18.00 |
| □ ST-2957 | John W. Anderson Presents KaSandra | 1968 | 18.00 |

RESPECT

□ TAS-2603	Beautiful New World	1972	18.00
□ TAS-2602	Color Me Human	1972	18.00
□ TAS-2605	The Mod Messiah	1974	18.00
□ TAS-2604	True Genius	1972	18.00

KASENETZ-KATZ SINGING ORCHESTRAL CIRCUS

BUDDAH

□ BDS-5020 [S]	Kasenetz-Katz Singing Orchestral Circus	1968	18.00
□ BDM-1020 [M]	Kasenetz-Katz Singing Orchestral Circus	1968	100.00
— Mono is promo only; in stereo cover with "Mono" sticker			
□ BDS-5028	Kasenetz-Katz Super Circus	1969	18.00

KASSEL, ART

HINDSIGHT

| □ HSR-162 | Kassels In The Air Orchestra 1944 | 198? | 12.00 |
| □ HSR-170 | Kassels In The Air Orchestra 1945 | 198? | 12.00 |

KAPP

| □ KL-1248 [M] | Dance to the Music of Art Kassel | 1962 | 25.00 |
| □ KS-3248 [S] | Dance to the Music of Art Kassel | 1962 | 30.00 |

KAT MANDU

MARLIN

| □ 2233 | Kat Mandu | 1979 | 25.00 |

KATALINA

THUMP

| □ 9958 | Sonic Groove | 1996 | 18.00 |

Number	Title	Yr	NM

KATINDIG, BOY

PAUSA
❑ 7137	Midnight Lady	198?	12.00

KATMANDU

MAINSTREAM
❑ S-6131	Katmandu	1971	40.00

KATRINA AND THE WAVES

CAPITOL
❑ ST-12400	Katrina and the Waves	1985	12.00
❑ ST-12478	Waves	1986	12.00

SBK
❑ K1-92649	Break of Hearts	1989	15.00

KATZ, BRUCE

AUDIOQUEST
❑ AQ-1012	Crescent Crawl	199?	15.00
❑ AQ-1026	Transformation	1994	15.00

KATZ, DICK; DEREK SMITH; RENE URTREGER

ATLANTIC
❑ 1287 [M]	John Lewis Presents Jazz Piano International	1958	40.00
—Black label			
❑ 1287 [M]	John Lewis Presents Jazz Piano International	1961	30.00
—Multicolor label, white "fan" logo at right			

KATZ, DICK

ATLANTIC
❑ 1314 [M]	Piano and Pin	1959	40.00
—Black label			
❑ 1314 [M]	Piano and Pin	1961	30.00
—Multicolor label, white "fan" logo at right			
❑ SD1314 [S]	Piano and Pin	1959	40.00
—Green label			
❑ SD1314 [S]	Piano and Pin	1961	25.00
—Multicolor label, white "fan" logo at right			

KATZ, FRED

DECCA
❑ DL9213 [M]	4-5-6 Trio	1958	40.00
❑ DL79213 [S]	4-5-6 Trio	1958	30.00
❑ DL9217 [M]	Fred Katz and Jammers	1958	40.00
❑ DL79217 [S]	Fred Katz and Jammers	1958	30.00
❑ DL9202 [M]	Soulo Cello	1958	40.00
❑ DL79202 [S]	Soulo Cello	1958	30.00

WARNER BROS.
❑ W1277 [M]	Folk Songs for Far Out Folks	1959	30.00
❑ WS1277 [S]	Folk Songs for Far Out Folks	1959	30.00

KATZ, MICKEY

CAPITOL
❑ T1603 [M]	At the U.N.	1961	25.00
—Black colorband label, logo at left			
❑ ST1603 [S]	At the U.N.	1961	30.00
—Black colorband label, logo at left			
❑ W1307 [M]	Comin' Round the Katzkills	1959	30.00
—Black colorband label, logo at left			
❑ W1257 [M]	Katz Pajamas	1959	30.00
—Black colorband label, logo at left			
❑ T1021 [M]	Katz Plays Music for Weddings, Bar Mitzvahs and Brisses	1958	30.00
—Turquoise or gray label			
❑ T934 [M]	Katz Puts On the Dog	1958	30.00
—Turquoise or gray label			
❑ H298 [10]	Mickey Katz: The Star of Broadway's Borschtcapades	195?	40.00
❑ T799 [M]	Mish Mosh	1957	30.00
—Turquoise or gray label			
❑ T1744 [M]	Sing Along with Mickele	1962	25.00
❑ ST1744 [S]	Sing Along with Mickele	1962	30.00
❑ T1445 [M]	The Borscht Jester	1960	25.00
—Black colorband label, logo at left			
❑ ST1445 [S]	The Borscht Jester	1960	30.00
—Black colorband label, logo at left			
❑ H457 [10]	The Family Danced	195?	40.00
❑ T1102 [M]	The Most Mishige	1959	30.00
—Black colorband label, logo at left			
❑ T298 [M]	The Very Best of Mickey Katz	195?	30.00
—Turquoise or gray label			

RCA VICTOR
❑ LPM-3193 [10]	Borscht	1954	40.00

KAUFMANN, BOB

LHI
❑ 12002	Trip Through a Blown Mind	1967	60.00

KAUKONEN, PETER

GRUNT
❑ FTR1006 [B]	Black Kangaroo	1972	25.00

KAWAGUCHI, GEORGE, AND ART BLAKEY

STORYVILLE
❑ 4100	Killer Joe	1982	15.00

KAWASAKI, RYO

INNER CITY
❑ IC-6006	Eight Mile Road	197?	18.00
❑ IC-6016	Prism	197?	18.00

RCA VICTOR
❑ APL1-1855	Juice	1977	18.00

KAY-GEES, THE

DE-LITE
❑ 9510	Burn Me Up	1979	12.00
❑ 9505	Kilowatt	1978	12.00

GANG
❑ 102	Find a Friend	1975	12.00
❑ 101	Keep On Bumpin' & Masterplan	1975	12.00

KAYAK

HARVEST
❑ ST-11305	See See the Sun	1973	18.00

JANUS
❑ NXS-7039 [B]	Phantom of the Night	1979	12.00
❑ (no #)0 [PD]	Phantom of the Night	1979	30.00
—Numbered limited edition of 3,000			
❑ NXS-7023	Royal Bed Bouncer	1975	12.00
❑ NXS-7034	Starlight Dancer	1978	12.00

MERCURY
❑ SRM-1-3824	Periscope Life	1980	12.00

KAYE, DANNY

CAPITOL
❑ T937 [M]	Mommy Gimme a Drinka Water	1958	40.00

COLUMBIA
❑ CL6023 [10]	Danny Kaye	1949	50.00
❑ CL6249 [10]	Danny Kaye Entertains	195?	50.00

DECCA
❑ DL8461 [M]	Danny at the Palace	1957	50.00
—Black label, silver print			

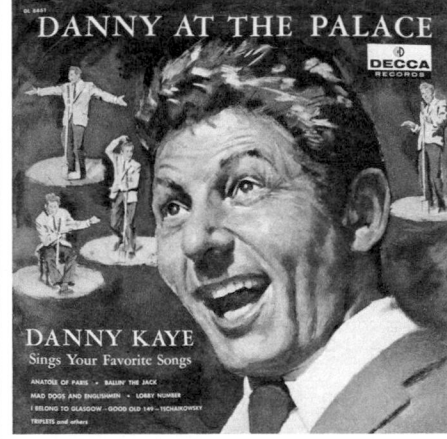

❑ DL8461 [M]	Danny at the Palace	1960	30.00
—Black label with color bars			
❑ DLP5033 [10]	Danny Kaye	1950	50.00
❑ DL8726 [M]	Danny Kaye for Children	1959	30.00
—Black label, silver print			
❑ DL8726 [M]	Danny Kaye for Children	1960	30.00
—Black label with color bars			
❑ DL5094 [10]	Gilbert and Sullivan and Danny Kaye	1950	50.00
❑ DXB175 [M]	The Best of Danny Kaye	1965	30.00
❑ DSXB175 [R]	The Best of Danny Kaye	1965	18.00
❑ DL8212 [M]	The Court Jester	1955	50.00
—Black label, silver print			

KAYE, MARY, TRIO

20TH CENTURY FOX
❑ TFM-3117 [M]	Night Life	1964	15.00
❑ TFS-4117 [S]	Night Life	1964	18.00

COLUMBIA
❑ CL1910 [M]	Our Hawaii	1962	18.00
❑ CS8710 [S]	Our Hawaii	1962	25.00

DECCA
❑ DL8434 [M]	Music on a Silver Platter	1957	30.00
❑ DL8238 [M]	The Mary Kaye Trio	1956	30.00
❑ DL8650 [M]	You Don't Know What Love Is	1958	30.00

MOVIETONE
❑ S72027 [S]	Just Us	1967	15.00
❑ 71027 [M]	Just Us	1967	15.00

VERVE
❑ V-8446 [M]	For the Record	1962	25.00
❑ V6-8446 [S]	For the Record	1962	30.00
❑ MGV-2142 [M]	Up Front!	1960	40.00

WARNER BROS.
❑ W1263 [M]	Jackpot	1959	25.00
❑ WS1263 [S]	Jackpot	1959	30.00
❑ W1342 [M]	The Mary Kaye Trio on the Sunset Strip	1959	25.00
❑ WS1342 [S]	The Mary Kaye Trio on the Sunset Strip	1959	30.00
❑ B1222 [M]	Too Much!	1958	25.00

KAYE, MILTON

GOLDEN CREST
❑ GC-31032	Ragtime at the Rosebud	197?	15.00
❑ CRS-4127	The Classic Rags of Joe Lamb	197?	15.00
—Single-sided LP in gatefold sleeve (B-side is blank)			

KAYE, SAMMY

COLUMBIA
❑ CL2541 [10]	Christmas Serenade	1955	40.00
—House Party Series" issue			
❑ CL1571 [M]	Dancing on a Silken Cloud	1960	18.00
❑ CS8371 [S]	Dancing on a Silken Cloud	1960	25.00
❑ CL668 [M]	Music, Maestro, Please!	195?	30.00
❑ CL885 [M]	My Fair Lady (For Dancing)	1956	25.00
❑ CL1018 [M]	Popular American Waltzes	1957	25.00
❑ CL1236 [M]	Strauss Waltzes for Dancing	1959	18.00
❑ CL6155 [10]	Sunday Serenade	1953	40.00
❑ CL964 [M]	Sunday Serenade	1957	25.00
❑ CL561 [M]	Swing and Sway with Sammy Kaye	195?	30.00
❑ CL891 [M]	What Makes Sammy Swing and Sway	1956	25.00

DECCA
❑ DL4070 [M]	Christmas Day with Sammy Kaye	1960	15.00
❑ DL74070 [S]	Christmas Day with Sammy Kaye	1960	18.00
❑ DL4502 [M]	Come Dance to the Hits	1964	15.00
❑ DL74502 [S]	Come Dance to the Hits	1964	18.00
❑ DL4357 [M]	Come Dance with Me	1963	15.00
❑ DL74357 [S]	Come Dance with Me	1963	18.00
❑ DL4590 [M]	Come Dance with Me (Vol. 2)	1965	15.00
❑ DL74590 [S]	Come Dance with Me (Vol. 2)	1965	18.00
❑ DL4924 [M]	Dance and Be Happy	1967	18.00
❑ DL74924 [S]	Dance and Be Happy	1967	15.00
❑ DL4655 [M]	Dancetime	1965	15.00
❑ DL74655 [S]	Dancetime	1965	18.00
❑ DL4121 [M]	Dance to My Golden Favorites	1961	15.00
❑ DL74121 [S]	Dance to My Golden Favorites	1961	18.00
❑ DL4424 [M]	Dreamy Serenades	1963	15.00
❑ DL74424 [S]	Dreamy Serenades	1963	18.00
❑ DL4306 [M]	For Your Dancing Pleasure	1962	15.00
❑ DL74306 [S]	For Your Dancing Pleasure	1962	18.00
❑ DL4970 [M]	Glory of Love	1967	18.00
❑ DL74970 [S]	Glory of Love	1967	15.00
❑ DL4823 [M]	Let's Face the Music	1967	15.00
❑ DL74823 [S]	Let's Face the Music	1967	18.00
❑ DL4247 [M]	New Twists on Old Favorites	1962	15.00
❑ DL74247 [S]	New Twists on Old Favorites	1962	18.00
❑ DL4215 [M]	Sexy Strings and Subtle Saxes	1962	15.00
❑ DL74215 [S]	Sexy Strings and Subtle Saxes	1962	18.00
❑ DL4754 [M]	Shall We Dance	1966	15.00
❑ DL74754 [S]	Shall We Dance	1966	18.00
❑ DL4071 [M]	Sing and Sway with Sammy Kaye	1960	15.00
❑ DL74071 [S]	Sing and Sway with Sammy Kaye	1960	18.00
❑ DL4154 [M]	Songs I Wish I Had Played…The First Time Around	1961	15.00
❑ DL74154 [S]	Songs I Wish I Had Played…The First Time Around	1961	18.00
❑ DL4862 [M]	Swing & Sway in Hawaii	1967	18.00
❑ DL74862 [S]	Swing & Sway in Hawaii	1967	15.00
❑ DL4687 [M]	Swing and Sway Au-Go-Go	1965	15.00
❑ DL74687 [S]	Swing and Sway Au-Go-Go	1965	18.00
❑ DL75106	The 30's Are Here to Stay	1968	15.00

HARMONY
❑ HS11261	All-Time Waltz Favorites	1968	15.00
❑ HL7357 [M]	Beautiful Waltzes for Dancing	196?	18.00
❑ HS11157 [R]	Beautiful Waltzes for Dancing	196?	15.00
❑ KH32013	Best of the Big Bands	1971	12.00
❑ HL7187 [M]	Dancing with Sammy Kaye in Hi-Fi	196?	18.00
❑ HS11087 [R]	Dancing with Sammy Kaye in Hi-Fi	196?	15.00
❑ HS11377	Harbor Lights	1970	12.00
❑ HL7230 [M]	In a Dancing Mood	196?	18.00
❑ HS11121 [R]	My Fair Lady	1964	15.00
❑ HL7321 [M]	My Fair Lady	1964	18.00

Number	Title	Yr	NM
HINDSIGHT			
HSR-402	22 Original Big Band Recordings	198?	15.00
HSR-158	1940-41	198?	12.00
HSR-163	1942-43	198?	12.00
HSR-207	1944-46	198?	12.00
MCA			
191	Dance to My Golden Favorites	1973	12.00
— Reissue of Decca 74121			
205	Plays Swing & Sway	1973	12.00
— Reissue of Decca 74306			
278	The 30's Are Here to Stay	197?	12.00
— Reissue of Decca material			
4027	The Best of Sammy Kaye	197?	15.00
PROJECT 3			
PR-5065SD	If You've Got the Time	1972	12.00
PR-5065QD [Q]	If You've Got the Time	1972	18.00
RCA CAMDEN			
CAL-261 [M]	Music for Dancing	1956	25.00
CAL-355 [M]	Swing and Sway with Sammy Kaye	1957	25.00
RCA VICTOR			
LPM15 [10]	Sammy Kaye Plays Irving Berlin for Dancing	1950	50.00
LPM-3966 [M]	The Best of Sammy Kaye	1967	25.00
LSP-3966 [R]	The Best of Sammy Kaye	1967	15.00
VPM-6070	This Is Sammy Kaye	1972	15.00
VOCALION			
VL73919	Theme from "Love Story"	1971	12.00

KAZ, FRED

Number	Title	Yr	NM
ATLANTIC			
1335 [M]	Eastern Exposure	1960	30.00
— Multicolor label, white "fan" logo at right			
SD1335 [S]	Eastern Exposure	1960	30.00
— Multicolor label, white "fan" logo at right			

KAZAN, LAINIE

Number	Title	Yr	NM
MGM			
E-4385 [M]	Lainie Kazan	1966	25.00
SE-4385 [S]	Lainie Kazan	1966	30.00
SE-4496	Love Is	1968	25.00
E-4340 [M]	Right Now	1966	25.00
SE-4340 [S]	Right Now	1966	30.00
SE-4631	The Best of Lainie Kazan	1969	25.00
E-4451 [M]	The Love Album	1967	30.00
SE-4451 [S]	The Love Album	1967	25.00

KEANE BROTHERS, THE

Number	Title	Yr	NM
20TH CENTURY			
T-536	The Keane Brothers	1977	18.00
ABC			
AA-1122	Taking Off	1979	18.00

KEARNEY, RAMSEY

Number	Title	Yr	NM
NASHCO			
646	Broken Heart	1986	18.00
616	God Made Them All	1981	18.00
613	I Write the Words	1981	18.00
611	Lots to Look Back On	198?	18.00
654	Red White and Blue USA	1987	18.00
615	Reflections of You	1981	18.00
600	Together in a Song	198?	18.00

KEATING, JOHNNY

Number	Title	Yr	NM
BALLY			
BAL-12001 [M]	English Jazz	1956	50.00
DOT			
DLP-3066 [M]	Swinging Scots	1957	40.00

KEENE, BOB

Number	Title	Yr	NM
ANDEX			
S-4001 [M]	Solo for 7	1958	50.00
DEL-FI			
DFLP-1222 [M]	Twist to Radio KRLA	1962	30.00
DFLP-1202 [M]	Unforgettable Love Songs of the 50's	1959	40.00
GENE NORMAN			
GNP-149 [10]	Bob Keene	1954	50.00

KEITH

Number	Title	Yr	NM
MERCURY			
MG-21102 [M]	98.6/Ain't Gonna Lie	1967	30.00
SR-61102 [S]	98.6/Ain't Gonna Lie	1967	25.00
MG-21129 [M]	Out of Crank	1967	30.00
SR-61129 [S]	Out of Crank	1967	25.00
RCA VICTOR			
LSP-4143	The Adventures of Keith	1969	25.00

KEITH AND DONNA

Number	Title	Yr	NM
ROUND			
RX-104	Keith and Donna	1975	30.00

KELLAWAY, ROGER

Number	Title	Yr	NM
A&M			
SP-3034	Cello Quartet	1970	15.00

Number	Title	Yr	NM
SP-3040	Center of the Circle	1972	18.00
SP-3618	Come to the Meadow	1974	12.00
CHOICE			
CRS-6833	Ain't Misbehavin'	1989	12.00
DISCWASHER			
003	Nostalgia Suite	1979	25.00
DOBRE			
1045	Say That Again	1978	12.00
PACIFIC JAZZ			
PJ-10122 [M]	Spirit Feel	196?	25.00
ST-20122 [S]	Spirit Feel	196?	18.00
LN-10070	Spirit Feel	198?	10.00
— Budget-line reissue			
PRESTIGE			
PRLP-7399 [M]	The Roger Kellaway Trio	1965	30.00
PRST-7399 [S]	The Roger Kellaway Trio	1965	30.00
REGINA			
R-298 [M]	Portraits	1964	25.00
RS-298 [S]	Portraits	1964	30.00
VOSS			
VLP1-42935	Nostalgia Suite	1988	12.00
WORLD PACIFIC			
WP-21861 [M]	Stride	1967	25.00
WPS-21861 [S]	Stride	1967	18.00

KELLER, ALLEN

Number	Title	Yr	NM
CHARLIE PARKER			
PLP-817 [M]	A New Look at the World	1962	30.00
PLP-817S [S]	A New Look at the World	1962	30.00

KELLER, HAL

Number	Title	Yr	NM
SAND			
7 [M]	Hal Keller Debut	1957	50.00
SOUND			
602 [M]	Hal Keller Debut	1959	40.00

KELLER, JERRY

Number	Title	Yr	NM
KAPP			
KL-1178 [M]	Here Comes Jerry Keller	1959	40.00
KS-3178 [S]	Here Comes Jerry Keller	1959	50.00

KELLERMAN, SALLY

Number	Title	Yr	NM
DECCA			
DL75359 [B]	Roll with the Feelin'	1972	25.00

KELLEY, PAT

Number	Title	Yr	NM
NOVA			
8704-1	Views of the Future	1988	12.00

KELLEY, PECK

Number	Title	Yr	NM
COMMODORE			
XF2-17017	Peck Kelley Jam	198?	15.00

KELLIN, MIKE

Number	Title	Yr	NM
VERVE FORECAST			
FT-3028 [M]	Mike Kellin	1967	30.00
FTS-3028 [S]	Mike Kellin	1967	30.00

KELLUM, MURRY

Number	Title	Yr	NM
PLANTATION			
531	Country Comedy	1978	15.00

KELLY, BEVERLY

Number	Title	Yr	NM
AUDIO FIDELITY			
AFLP-1874 [M]	Beverly Kelly Sings	1958	30.00
AFSD-5874 [S]	Beverly Kelly Sings	1958	40.00
RIVERSIDE			
RLP-345 [M]	Bev Kelly In Person	1960	30.00
RS-9345 [S]	Bev Kelly In Person	1960	30.00
6042	Bev Kelly In Person	197?	15.00
RLP-328 [M]	Love Locked Out	1960	30.00
RS-9328 [S]	Love Locked Out	1960	30.00
6052	Love Locked Out	197?	15.00

KELLY, CASEY

Number	Title	Yr	NM
ELEKTRA			
EKS-75040	Casey Kelly	1972	18.00
EKS-75072	For Sale	1974	18.00

KELLY, EMMETT

Number	Title	Yr	NM
ROULETTE			
R-25130 [M]	Sing Along with Emmett Kelly	1962	30.00
SR-25130 [S]	Sing Along with Emmett Kelly	1962	30.00

KELLY, JACK

Number	Title	Yr	NM
JUBILEE			
JLP-21 [10]	Jack Kelly's Badinage	1955	50.00

KELLY, MONTY

Number	Title	Yr	NM
ALSHIRE			
SAS610	Passport to Romance	196?	12.00

Number	Title	Yr	NM
CARLTON			
LP 12-111 [M]	Porgy and Bess	1959	25.00
STLP 12-111 [S]	Porgy and Bess	1959	30.00
LP 12-123 [M]	Summer Set	1960	25.00
STLP 12-123 [S]	Summer Set	1960	30.00
ESSEX			
ESLP-106 [10]	I Love	1954	30.00
ESLP-108 [10]	Monty Kelly Takes Me to Far Away Places	1954	30.00
ESLP-203 [M]	Tropicana	1955	30.00
SOMERSET			
P7300 [M]	Tropicana	196?	12.00
— Reissue of Trans World 203			
TRANS WORLD			
TWLP-203 [M]	Tropicana	1956	25.00
— Reissue of Essex 203			

KELLY, PAUL

Number	Title	Yr	NM
HAPPY TIGER			
1015	Stealing in the Name of the Lord	1970	18.00
WARNER BROS.			
BS2605	Dirt	1972	15.00
BS2689	Don't Burn Me	1973	15.00
BS2812	Hooked, Hogtied & Collared	1974	15.00
BS3026	Stand on the Positive Side	1976	15.00

KELLY, R.

Number	Title	Yr	NM
JIVE			
41625	R.	1998	25.00
41579	R. Kelly	1995	18.00
41748	TP-2.com	2000	18.00

KELLY, WYNTON

Number	Title	Yr	NM
BLUE NOTE			
BLP-5025 [10]	Piano Interpretations by Wynton Kelly	1953	400.00
DELMARK			
DS-441	The Last Trio Session	1989	25.00
EPITAPH			
E-4007	Wynton Kelly 1931-1971	1975	25.00
FANTASY			
OJC-033	Kelly Blue	198?	15.00
OJC-401	Wynton Kelly Piano	1989	18.00
JAZZLAND			
JLP-83 [M]	Whisper Not	1962	40.00
JLP-983 [S]	Whisper Not	1962	50.00
MILESTONE			
MSP-9004	Full View	1968	30.00
M-47026	Keep It Moving	1975	30.00
RIVERSIDE			
RLP 12-298 [M]	Kelly Blue	1959	60.00
RLP-1142 [S]	Kelly Blue	1959	50.00
6114	Kelly Blue	197?	18.00
6043	Whisper Not	197?	18.00
RLP 12-254 [M]	Wynton Kelly Piano	1957	70.00
TRIP			
TLX-5010	Smokin'	197?	18.00
VEE JAY			
VJ-1086 [M]	Best of Wynton Kelly	1964	40.00
VJS-1086 [S]	Best of Wynton Kelly	1964	50.00
VJS-3072-2	Final Notes	1977	30.00
LP-3011 [M]	Kelly at Midnite	1960	80.00
SR-3011 [S]	Kelly at Midnite	1960	100.00
LP-1016 [M]	Kelly Great	1960	80.00
SR-1016 [S]	Kelly Great	1960	100.00
LP-3004 [M]	Kelly Great	1960	60.00
— Reissue of LP-1016			
SR-3004 [S]	Kelly Great	1960	80.00
— Reissue of SR-1016			
VJS-3038	Someday My Prince Will Come	1977	25.00
LP-3022 [M]	Wynton Kelly	1961	50.00
SR-3022 [S]	Wynton Kelly	1961	60.00
VJS-3071	Wynton Kelly In Concert	1977	25.00
VERVE			
V-8576 [M]	Comin' In the Back Door	1964	30.00
V6-8576 [S]	Comin' In the Back Door	1964	40.00
V-8588 [M]	It's All Right	1964	30.00
V6-8588 [S]	It's All Right	1964	30.00
V-8633 [M]	Smokin' at the Half Note	1965	25.00
V6-8633 [S]	Smokin' at the Half Note	1965	30.00
V-8622 [M]	Undiluted	1965	40.00
V6-8622 [S]	Undiluted	1965	50.00
XANADU			
198	Blues On Purpose	198?	12.00

KELLY BROTHERS, THE

Number	Title	Yr	NM
EXCELLO			
LPS-8007	Sweet Soul	1968	50.00
KING			
810 [M]	The Kelly Brothers Sing a Page of Songs from the Good Book	1962	100.00

Number	Title	Yr	NM

KEMP, WAYNE

DECCA
| ☐ DL75290 | Wayne Kemp | 1971 | 18.00 |

MCA
| ☐ 369 | Kentucky Sunshine | 1973 | 15.00 |

KENDALL, CHARLES S.

DOT
| ☐ DLP3083 [M] | Christmas Chimes | 1958 | 18.00 |

KENDALLS, THE

DOT
| ☐ DLP-26001 | Two Divided by Love | 1972 | 18.00 |

EPIC
| ☐ E245249 | 20 Favorites | 1989 | 18.00 |

GUSTO
| ☐ GT 0001 | 1978 Grammy Award Winners -- Best Country Duo | 1978 | 12.00 |

MCA
| ☐ 27021 | Never Ending Song of Love | 198? | 12.00 |

MCA CURB
| ☐ 5724 | Fire at First Sight | 1986 | 10.00 |

MERCURY
☐ SRM-1-6005	Lettin' You In on a Feelin'	1981	12.00
☐ 812779-1	Movin' Train	1983	10.00
☐ SRM-1-4046	Stickin' Together	1982	12.00
☐ 826307-1	Thank God for the Radio... And All the Hits	1986	10.00
☐ 824250-1	Two Heart Harmony	1985	10.00

OVATION
☐ 1746	Heart of the Matter	1979	15.00
☐ 1719	Heaven's Just a Sin Away	1977	15.00
☐ 1739 [B]	Just Like Real People	1979	15.00
☐ 1733 [B]	Old Fashioned Love	1978	15.00
☐ 1756	The Best of the Kendalls	1980	15.00

POWER PAK
| ☐ PO-218 | Leavin' on a Jet Plane | 197? | 12.00 |

STEP ONE
| ☐ 0023 | Break the Routine | 1987 | 12.00 |

STOP
| ☐ 1020 | Meet the Kendalls | 1970 | 25.00 |

KENDRICKS, EDDIE

ARISTA
| ☐ AB4250 | Something More | 1979 | 12.00 |
| ☐ AB4170 | Vintage '78 | 1978 | 12.00 |

ATLANTIC
| ☐ SD19294 | Love Keys | 1981 | 12.00 |

MOTOWN
☐ M5-151V1	Eddie Kendricks	1981	10.00
— Reissue of Tamla 327			
☐ M5-196V1	He's a Friend	1981	10.00
— Reissue of Tamla 343			

TAMLA
☐ T-309	All By Myself	1971	12.00
☐ T330V1	Boogie Down!	1974	12.00
☐ T327L	Eddie Kendricks	1973	12.00
☐ T7-354	Eddie Kendricks at His Best	1977	12.00
☐ T6-335	For You	1974	12.00
☐ T6-346	Goin' Up in Smoke	1976	12.00
☐ T6-343	He's a Friend	1976	12.00
☐ T315L	People...Hold On	1972	12.00
☐ 18-356	Slick	1978	12.00
☐ T6-338	The Hit Man	1975	12.00

KENNEDY, DAVE

COULEE
| ☐ 1001 [M] | Breaking Up Is Hard to Do | 1964 | 50.00 |

KENNEDY, GENE, AND KAREN JEGLUM

DOOR KNOB
| ☐ 1004 | Gene Kennedy and Karen Jeglum | 1981 | 15.00 |

KENNEDY, HARRISON

INVICTUS
| ☐ ST9806 [B] | Hypnotic Music | 1972 | 60.00 |

KENNEDY, JERRY

SMASH
☐ MGS-27004 [M]	Dancing Guitars Rock Elvis' Hits	1962	30.00
☐ SRS-67004 [S]	Dancing Guitars Rock Elvis' Hits	1962	40.00
☐ MGS-27066 [M]	From Nashville to Soulville	1965	25.00
☐ SRS-67066 [S]	From Nashville to Soulville	1965	30.00
☐ MGS-27024 [M]	Jerry Kennedy's Guitars and Strings Play the Golden Standards	1963	25.00
☐ SRS-67024 [S]	Jerry Kennedy's Guitars and Strings Play the Golden Standards	1963	30.00

KENNEDY, JOHN FITZGERALD

20TH CENTURY
| ☐ TCF3127 [M] | The Presidential Years 1960-1963 | 1963 | 25.00 |
| — Narrated by David Teig | | | |

CAEDMON
| ☐ TC-2021 | Self-Portrait | 196? | 25.00 |

CAPITOL
☐ ST2486 [S]	Years of Lightning, Day of Drums	1966	30.00
☐ T2486 [M]	Years of Lightning, Day of Drums	1966	25.00
— Narrated by Gregory Peck; U.S. Information Agency movie soundtrack			

COLPIX
| ☐ CP2500 [M] | Four Days That Shocked the World | 1964 | 50.00 |
| — Narrated by Reid Collins; covers Nov. 22-25, 1963 | | | |

DECCA
| ☐ DL9116 [M] | That Was The Week That Was | 1963 | 25.00 |
| — BBC show's tribute to JFK, broadcast Nov. 23, 1963 | | | |

DIPLOMAT
| ☐ 10000 [M] | John F. Kennedy -- A Memorial Album | 1963 | 18.00 |

DOCUMENTARIES UNLIMITED
| ☐ (no #)0 [M] | JFK The Man, The President | 1963 | 25.00 |
| — Narrated by Barry Gray | | | |

HARMONICA
| ☐ HLP-3005 [M] | Kennedy Speaks | 1963 | 25.00 |

LEGACY
| ☐ L2L1017 [M] | John Fitzgerald Kennedy... As We Remember Him | 1965 | 30.00 |
| — Narrated by Charles Kuralt; with 240-page book | | | |

PICKWICK
| ☐ 169 [M] | The Presidential Years (1960-1963) | 1963 | 18.00 |

PREMIER
| ☐ 2099 [M] | A Memorial Album | 1963 | 25.00 |
| — From WMCA Radio, New York, Nov. 22, 1963 | | | |

RCA VICTOR
| ☐ VDM-101 [M] | The Kennedy Wit | 1964 | 18.00 |
| — Narrated by David Brinkley with introduction by Adlai E. Stevenson | | | |

SOMERSET
| ☐ 16100 [M] | Actual Speeches of Franklin D. Roosevelt and John F. Kennedy | 1963 | 18.00 |
| — One side has FDR speeches, the other, JFK speeches | | | |

KENNEDY, MIKE

ABC
| ☐ ABCX-754 | Louisianna | 1972 | 25.00 |

KENNEDY, RAY (1)

ARC
| ☐ NJC36395 | Ray Kennedy | 1980 | 15.00 |

CREAM
| ☐ CR9001 | Raymond Louis Kennedy | 1972 | 18.00 |

KENNEDY, ROBERT FRANCIS

COLUMBIA
| ☐ C2S792 | A Memorial | 1968 | 25.00 |

KENNER, CHRIS

ATLANTIC
| ☐ 8117 [M] | Land of 1,000 Dances | 1965 | 50.00 |

COLLECTABLES
| ☐ COL-5116 | Golden Classics: I Like It Like That | 198? | 15.00 |

KENNEY, BEVERLY

DECCA
☐ DL8743 [M]	Beverly Kenney Sings for Playboys	1958	400.00
☐ DL8850 [M]	Born to Be Blue	1959	250.00
☐ DL8948 [M]	Like Yesterday	1960	200.00
☐ DL78948 [S]	Like Yesterday	1960	300.00

ROOST
☐ RST-2206 [M]	Beverly Kenney Sings for Johnny Smith	1956	300.00
☐ RST-2218 [M]	Beverly Kenney with Jimmy Jones and the Basie-ites	1957	300.00
☐ RST-2212 [M]	Come Swing with Me	1956	300.00

KENNY, BILL

WARWICK
| ☐ W-2021 [M] | Mr. Ink Spot | 1960 | 30.00 |

KENNY AND THE KASUALS

MARK
☐ 7000 [S]	Garage Kings	1979	30.00
☐ 6000 [M]	Teen Dreams	1978	250.00
— Red vinyl; numbered, signed limited edition			
☐ 5000 [M]	The Impact Sound of Kenny and the Kasuals Live at the Studio Club	1966	1000.00
☐ 5000 [M]	The Impact Sound of Kenny and the Kasuals Live at the Studio Club	1977	30.00
— "Reissue, 1977" appears on cover			

KENNY G

ARISTA
☐ AL8-8427	Duotones	1986	10.00
☐ AL8-8192	G Force	1984	10.00
☐ AL8-8282	Gravity	1985	10.00
☐ AL9608	Kenny G	1982	12.00
☐ ALB6-8299	Kenny G	1985	10.00
— Reissue of 9608			
☐ A2L-8613	Kenny G Live	1989	15.00
☐ AL-8457	Silhouette	1988	10.00

KENSINGTON MARKET

WARNER BROS.
| ☐ WS1780 | Aardvark | 1969 | 25.00 |
| ☐ WS1754 | Avenue Road | 1968 | 25.00 |

KENT, GEORGE

SHANNON
| ☐ 1003 | George Kent | 1974 | 25.00 |

KENT, MARSHALL

HERWIN
| ☐ 301 | Pallet on the Floor | 197? | 18.00 |

KENTON, STAN, AND TEX RITTER

CAPITOL
| ☐ T1757 [M] | Stan Kenton/Tex Ritter | 1962 | 60.00 |
| ☐ ST1757 [S] | Stan Kenton/Tex Ritter | 1962 | 80.00 |

KENTON, STAN

CAPITOL
☐ T1985 [M]	Adventures in Blues	1963	15.00
— Black label with colorband, Capitol logo at top			
☐ ST1985 [S]	Adventures in Blues	1963	18.00
— Black label with colorband, Capitol logo at top			
☐ T1796 [M]	Adventures in Jazz	1962	15.00
— Black label with colorband, Capitol logo at top			
☐ ST1796 [S]	Adventures in Jazz	1962	18.00
— Black label with colorband, Capitol logo at top			
☐ T1844 [M]	Adventures in Time	1963	15.00
— Black label with colorband, Capitol logo at top			
☐ ST1844 [S]	Adventures in Time	1963	18.00
— Black label with colorband, Capitol logo at top			
☐ T1621 [M]	A Merry Christmas	1961	18.00
☐ ST1621 [S]	A Merry Christmas	1961	25.00
☐ H172 [10]	A Presentation of Progressive Jazz	1950	60.00
☐ T172 [M]	A Presentation of Progressive Jazz	195?	40.00
☐ T1931 [M]	Artistry in Bossa Nova	1963	15.00
☐ ST1931 [S]	Artistry in Bossa Nova	1963	18.00
☐ M-11027	Artistry in Jazz	1972	12.00
☐ H167 [10]	Artistry in Rhythm	1950	60.00
☐ T167 [M]	Artistry in Rhythm	195?	40.00
— Turquoise label			
☐ T167 [M]	Artistry in Rhythm	1959	18.00
— Black label with colorband, Capitol logo at left			
☐ T167 [M]	Artistry in Rhythm	1962	15.00
— Black label with colorband, Capitol logo at top			
☐ DT167 [R]	Artistry in Rhythm	1969	12.00
☐ SM-167 [R]	Artistry in Rhythm	1975	10.00
— Reissue with new prefix			
☐ T2132 [M]	Artistry in Voices and Brass	1964	15.00
— Black label with colorband, Capitol logo at top			
☐ ST2132 [S]	Artistry in Voices and Brass	1964	18.00
— Black label with colorband, Capitol logo at top			
☐ T995 [M]	Back to Balboa	1958	40.00
— Turquoise label			
☐ H353 [10]	City of Glass	1952	60.00
☐ T736 [M]	City of Glass/This Modern World	1956	40.00
— Combination of 353 and 460 onto one 12-inch LP, turquoise label			
☐ H358 [10]	Classics	1952	60.00
☐ T358 [M]	Classics	195?	40.00
— Turquoise label			
☐ T666 [M]	Contemporary Concepts	1955	40.00
— Turquoise label			
☐ T731 [M]	Cuban Fire!	1956	40.00
— Turquoise label			
☐ T731 [M]	Cuban Fire!	1959	25.00
— Black label with colorband, Capitol logo at left			
☐ T731 [M]	Cuban Fire!	1962	18.00
— Black label with colorband, Capitol logo at top			
☐ SM-11794 [M]	Cuban Fire!	1978	12.00
— Reissue of Capitol T 731			
☐ T656 [M]	Duet	1955	40.00
— With June Christy; turquoise label			
☐ H155 [10]	Encores	1950	60.00
☐ T155 [M]	Encores	195?	40.00

Number	Title	Yr	NM
— *Turquoise label*			
❑ ST2974	Finian's Rainbow	1968	15.00
❑ P189 [10]	Innovations in Modern Music	1950	60.00
❑ ST2932	Jazz Compositions of Dee Barton	1968	15.00
❑ T1460 [M]	Kenton at the Las Vegas Tropicana	1961	30.00
— *Black label with colorband, Capitol logo at left*			
❑ ST1460 [S]	Kenton at the Las Vegas Tropicana	1961	25.00
— *Black label with colorband, Capitol logo at left*			
❑ W724 [M]	Kenton in Hi-Fi	1956	40.00
— *Gray label*			
❑ W724 [M]	Kenton in Hi-Fi	1959	25.00
— *Black label with colorband, logo at left*			
❑ SW724 [S]	Kenton in Hi-Fi	1959	50.00
— *Black label with colorband, logo at left; one fewer track than mono version*			
❑ SW724 [S]	Kenton in Hi-Fi	1962	30.00
— *Black label with colorband, logo at top; one fewer track than mono version*			
❑ T2655 [M]	Kenton Plays for Today	1966	15.00
— *Black label with colorband, Capitol logo at top*			
❑ ST2655 [S]	Kenton Plays for Today	1966	18.00
— *Black label with colorband, Capitol logo at top*			
❑ TAO2217 [M]	Kenton Plays Wagner	1964	15.00
— *Black label with colorband, Capitol logo at top*			
❑ STAO2217 [S]	Kenton Plays Wagner	1964	18.00
— *Black label with colorband, Capitol logo at top*			
❑ W524 [M]	Kenton Showcase	1954	40.00
❑ H526 [10]	Kenton Showcase -- The Music of Bill Holman	1954	60.00
❑ H525 [10]	Kenton Showcase -- The Music of Bill Russo	1954	60.00
❑ T1609 [M]	Kenton's West Side Story	1961	30.00
— *Black label with colorband, Capitol logo at left*			
❑ ST1609 [S]	Kenton's West Side Story	1961	25.00
— *Black label with colorband, Capitol logo at left*			
❑ T1609 [M]	Kenton's West Side Story	1961	18.00
— *Black label with colorband, Capitol logo at top*			
❑ ST1609 [S]	Kenton's West Side Story	1961	15.00
— *Black label with colorband, Capitol logo at top*			
❑ SM-12037	Kenton's West Side Story	1979	12.00
— *Reissue of Capitol ST 1609*			
❑ T810 [M]	Kenton with Voices	1957	40.00
— *Turquoise label*			
❑ T1130 [M]	Lush Interlude	1959	30.00
— *Black label with colorband, Capitol logo at left*			
❑ ST1130 [S]	Lush Interlude	1959	25.00
— *Black label with colorband, Capitol logo at left*			
❑ H190 [10]	Milestones	1950	60.00
❑ T190 [M]	Milestones	195?	40.00
— *Turquoise label*			
❑ T190 [M]	Milestones	196?	30.00
— *Black colorband label, logo at left*			
❑ ST-305	Music from "Hair	1969	18.00
❑ H303 [10]	New Concepts of Artistry in Rhythm	1953	60.00
❑ T383 [M]	New Concepts of Artistry in Rhythm	195?	40.00
— *Turquoise label*			
❑ H421 [10]	Popular Favorites	1953	60.00
❑ T421 [M]	Popular Favorites	195?	40.00
— *Turquoise label*			
❑ H462 [10]	Portraits on Standards	1953	60.00
❑ T462 [M]	Portraits on Standards	195?	40.00
— *Turquoise label*			
❑ T462 [M]	Portraits on Standards	196?	30.00
— *Black colorband label, logo at left*			
❑ H386 [10]	Prologue: This Is an Orchestra	1953	60.00
❑ T932 [M]	Rendezvous with Kenton	1957	40.00
— *Turquoise label*			
❑ TBO1327 [M]	Road Show	1960	40.00
— *Black label with colorband, Capitol logo at left*			
❑ STBO1327 [S]	Road Show	1960	30.00
— *Black label with colorband, Capitol logo at left*			
❑ TBO1327 [M]	Road Show	1962	25.00
— *Black label with colorband, Capitol logo at top*			
❑ STBO1327 [S]	Road Show	1962	18.00
— *Black label with colorband, Capitol logo at top*			
❑ H426 [10]	Sketches on Standards	1953	60.00
❑ T426 [M]	Sketches on Standards	195?	40.00
— *Turquoise label*			
❑ T1394 [M]	Standards in Silhouette	1960	30.00
— *Black label with colorband, Capitol logo at left*			
❑ ST1394 [S]	Standards in Silhouette	1960	25.00
— *Black label with colorband, Capitol logo at left*			
❑ T1394 [M]	Standards in Silhouette	1962	18.00
— *Black label with colorband, Capitol logo at top*			
❑ ST1394 [S]	Standards in Silhouette	1962	15.00
— *Black label with colorband, Capitol logo at top*			
❑ STCL-575	Stan Kenton	1970	25.00
❑ MAS2424 [M]	Stan Kenton Conducts the Los Angeles Neophonic Orchestra	1966	15.00
— *Black label with colorband, Capitol logo at top*			
❑ SMAS2424 [S]	Stan Kenton Conducts the Los Angeles Neophonic Orchestra	1966	18.00
— *Black label with colorband, Capitol logo at top*			
❑ L248 [10]	Stan Kenton Presents	1951	60.00
❑ T248 [M]	Stan Kenton Presents	195?	40.00
— *Turquoise label*			
❑ T248 [M]	Stan Kenton Presents	196?	30.00
— *Black colorband label, logo at left*			
❑ T248 [M]	Stan Kenton Presents	196?	18.00
— *Black colorband label, logo at top*			
❑ T2327 [M]	Stan Kenton's Greatest Hits	1965	15.00
— *Black label with colorband, Capitol logo at top*			
❑ DT2327 [R]	Stan Kenton's Greatest Hits	1965	12.00
— *Black label with colorband, Capitol logo at top*			
❑ SM-2327	Stan Kenton's Greatest Hits	197?	10.00
— *Reissue with new prefix*			
❑ N-16182	Stan Kenton's Greatest Hits	1984	10.00
— *Budget-line reissue*			
❑ T1068 [M]	The Ballad Style of Stan Kenton	1959	30.00
— *Black label with colorband, Capitol logo at left*			
❑ ST1068 [S]	The Ballad Style of Stan Kenton	1959	25.00
— *Black label with colorband, Capitol logo at left*			
❑ T1068 [M]	The Ballad Style of Stan Kenton	1962	18.00
— *Black label with colorband, Capitol logo at top*			
❑ ST1068 [S]	The Ballad Style of Stan Kenton	1962	15.00
— *Black label with colorband, Capitol logo at top*			
❑ STB-12016	The Comprehensive Kenton	1979	18.00
❑ TDB569 [M]	The Kenton Era	1955	100.00
— *Box set with 44-page book*			
❑ WDX569 [M]	The Kenton Era	196?	70.00
— *Box set with 44-page book; limited edition reissue with black label, Capitol logo at left*			
❑ PRO-206/7 [DJ]	The Kenton Era (Excerpts)	1955	40.00
❑ T1276 [M]	The Kenton Touch	1960	30.00
— *Black label with colorband, Capitol logo at left*			
❑ ST1276 [S]	The Kenton Touch	1960	25.00
— *Black label with colorband, Capitol logo at left*			
❑ T1533 [M]	The Romantic Approach	1961	30.00
— *Black label with colorband, Capitol logo at left*			
❑ ST1533 [S]	The Romantic Approach	1961	25.00
— *Black label with colorband, Capitol logo at left*			
❑ T1533 [M]	The Romantic Approach	1961	18.00
— *Black label with colorband, Capitol logo at top*			
❑ ST1533 [S]	The Romantic Approach	1961	15.00
— *Black label with colorband, Capitol logo at top*			
❑ T1674 [M]	The Sophisticated Approach	1962	15.00
— *Black label with colorband, Capitol logo at top*			
❑ ST1674 [S]	The Sophisticated Approach	1962	18.00
— *Black label with colorband, Capitol logo at top*			
❑ T1166 [M]	The Stage Door Swings	1959	30.00
— *Black label with colorband, Capitol logo at left*			
❑ ST1166 [S]	The Stage Door Swings	1959	25.00
— *Black label with colorband, Capitol logo at left*			
❑ STCL2989	The Stan Kenton Deluxe Set	1968	25.00
❑ ST2810	The World We Know	1968	15.00
❑ H460 [10]	This Modern World	1953	60.00
❑ W1305 [M]	Viva Kenton!	1960	30.00
— *Black label with colorband, Capitol logo at left*			
❑ SW1305 [S]	Viva Kenton!	1960	25.00
— *Black label with colorband, Capitol logo at left*			

CREATIVE WORLD

Number	Title	Yr	NM
❑ ST1070	7.5 on the Richter Scale	1973	12.00
❑ ST1037 [R]	A Concert in Progessive Jazz	197?	10.00
— *Reissue of Capitol T 172*			
❑ ST1012	Adventures in Blues	197?	12.00
— *Reissue of Capitol ST 1985*			
❑ ST1010	Adventures in Jazz	197?	12.00
— *Reissue of Capitol ST 1796*			
❑ ST1025	Adventures in Standards	197?	12.00
❑ ST1011	Adventures in Time	197?	12.00
— *Reissue of Capitol ST 1844*			
❑ ST1045	Artistry in Bossa Nova	197?	12.00
❑ ST1043 [R]	Artistry in Rhythm	197?	10.00
— *Reissue of Capitol DT 167*			
❑ ST1038	Artistry in Voices and Brass	197?	12.00
— *Reissue of Capitol ST 2132*			
❑ ST1031	Back to Balboa	197?	12.00
— *Reissue of Capitol T 995*			
❑ ST1065	Birthday in Britain	1973	12.00
❑ ST1006 [R]	City of Glass/This Modern World	197?	10.00
— *Reissue of Capitol T 736*			
❑ ST1027 [R]	Collector's Choice	197?	10.00
❑ ST1003 [R]	Contemporary Concepts	197?	10.00
— *Reissue of Capitol T 666*			
❑ ST1008 [R]	Cuban Fire!	197?	10.00
— *Reissue of Capitol T 731*			
❑ ST1048 [R]	Duet	197?	10.00
— *Reissue of Capitol T 656*			
❑ ST1034 [R]	Encores	197?	10.00
— *Reissue of Capitol T 155*			
❑ ST1073	Fire, Fury and Fun	1974	12.00
❑ ST1074	Hits in Concert	197?	12.00
❑ ST1009 [R]	Innovations in Modern Music	197?	10.00
— *Reissue of Capitol P 189*			
❑ ST1022	Jazz Compositions of Dee Barton	197?	12.00
— *Reissue of Capitol ST 2932*			
❑ ST1077	Journey Into Capricorn	1977	12.00
❑ ST1076	Kenton '76	1976	12.00
❑ ST1032	Kenton at the Las Vegas Tropicana	197?	12.00
— *Reissue of Capitol ST 1460*			
❑ ST1036 [R]	Kenton By Request, Vol. I	197?	10.00
❑ ST1040 [R]	Kenton By Request, Vol. II	197?	10.00
❑ ST1062 [R]	Kenton By Request, Vol. III	197?	10.00
❑ ST1064 [R]	Kenton By Request, Vol. IV	197?	10.00
❑ ST1066 [R]	Kenton By Request, Vol. V	197?	10.00
❑ ST1069	Kenton By Request, Vol. VI	197?	12.00
❑ ST1004 [R]	Kenton in Stereo	197?	12.00
— *Reissue of Capitol W 724*			
❑ ST1072	Kenton Plays Chicago	1974	12.00
❑ ST1024	Kenton Plays Wagner	197?	12.00
— *Reissue of Capitol STAO 2217*			
❑ ST1001	Kenton's Christmas	1970	15.00
❑ ST1026 [R]	Kenton Showcase	197?	10.00
— *Reissue of Capitol W 524*			
❑ ST1007	Kenton's West Side Story	197?	12.00
— *Reissue of Capitol ST 1609*			
❑ ST1039 [Q]	Live at Brigham Young	1971	18.00
❑ ST1058 [Q]	Live at Butler University	1972	25.00
❑ ST1015	Live at Redlands University	1971	12.00
❑ ST1005	Lush Interlude	197?	12.00
— *Reissue of Capitol ST 1130*			
❑ ST1047 [R]	Milestones	197?	10.00
— *Reissue of Capitol T 190*			
❑ ST1060 [Q]	National Anthems of the World	1972	25.00
❑ ST1002 [R]	New Concepts of Artistry in Rhythm	197?	12.00
— *Reissue of Capitol T 383*			
❑ ST1042 [R]	Portraits on Standards	197?	10.00
— *Reissue of Capitol T 462*			
❑ ST1057	Rendezvous with Kenton	197?	12.00
— *Reissue of Capitol T 932*			
❑ ST1019	Road Show, Volume 1	197?	12.00
— *Partial reissue of Capitol STBO 1327*			
❑ ST1020	Road Show, Volume 2	197?	12.00
— *Partial reissue of Capitol STBO 1327*			
❑ ST1041 [R]	Sketches on Standards	197?	10.00
— *Reissue of Capitol T 426*			
❑ ST1071	Solo	1973	12.00
❑ ST1029 [R]	Some Women I've Known	197?	10.00
❑ ST1049	Standards in Silhouette	197?	12.00
— *Reissue of Capitol ST 1394*			
❑ ST1013	Stan Kenton Conducts the Los Angeles Neophonic Orchestra	197?	12.00
— *Reissue of Capitol SMAS 2424*			
❑ ST1061 [R]	Stan Kenton -- Formative Years	197?	10.00
— *Reissue of Decca DL 8259*			
❑ ST1023 [R]	Stan Kenton Presents	197?	10.00
— *Reissue of Capitol T 248*			
❑ CW-3005	Stan Kenton Presents Gabe Baltazar	1979	12.00
❑ ST1046	Stan Kenton with Jean Turner	197?	12.00
❑ ST1059 [Q]	Stan Kenton with the Four Freshmen at Butler University	1972	25.00
❑ ST1079	Street of Dreams	197?	12.00
❑ ST1068	The Ballad Style of Stan Kenton	197?	10.00
— *Reissue of Capitol ST 1068*			
❑ ST1035 [R]	The Christy Years	197?	10.00
❑ ST1080	The Exciting Stan Kenton	197?	12.00
❑ ST1028 [R]	The Fabulous Alumni of Stan Kenton	197?	10.00
❑ ST1078 [R]	The Jazz Compositions of Stan Kenton	197?	10.00
❑ ST1030 [R]	The Kenton Era	197?	25.00
— *Reissue of Capitol TDB 569*			
❑ ST1033	The Kenton Touch	197?	12.00
— *Reissue of Capitol ST 1276*			
❑ ST1050 [R]	The Lighter Side of Stan Kenton	197?	10.00
❑ ST1017	The Romantic Approach	197?	10.00
— *Reissue of Capitol ST 1533*			
❑ ST1018	The Sophisticated Approach	197?	12.00
— *Reissue of Capitol ST 1674*			
❑ ST1044	The Stage Door Swings	197?	12.00
— *Reissue of Capitol ST 1166*			
❑ ST1067	Too Much	197?	12.00
❑ ST1063	Viva Kenton!	197?	12.00
— *Reissue of Capitol SW 1305*			

DECCA

Number	Title	Yr	NM
❑ DL8259 [M]	Stan Kenton -- Formative Years	195?	30.00
— *All-black label with silver print*			
❑ DL8259 [M]	Stan Kenton -- Formative Years	1960	18.00
— *Black label with color bars*			

HINDSIGHT

Number	Title	Yr	NM
❑ HSR-118	Stan Kenton 1941	1984	10.00
❑ HSR-124	Stan Kenton 1941, Volume 2	1984	10.00
❑ HSR-136	Stan Kenton 1943-44	1984	10.00
❑ HSR-147	Stan Kenton 1944-45	1984	10.00
❑ HSR-157	Stan Kenton 1945-47	1984	10.00
❑ HSR-195	Stan Kenton 1962	1984	10.00

Number	Title	Yr	NM
INSIGHT			
❑ 206	Stan Kenton and His Orchestra, Volume 1	197?	12.00
❑ 217	Stan Kenton and His Orchestra, Volume 2	197?	12.00
LONDON PHASE 4			
❑ ST-44276	Live in Europe	1976	12.00
❑ BP44179/80	Stan Kenton Today	1972	40.00
MOBILE FIDELITY			
❑ 1-091	Kenton Plays Wagner	1982	30.00
—Audiophile vinyl			
MOSAIC			
❑ MR6-136	The Complete Capitol Recordings of the Holman and Russo Charts	199?	120.00
❑ MQ10-163	The Complete Capitol Studio Recordings of Stan Kenton 1943-47	199?	200.00
SUNBEAM			
❑ 213	Artistry in Rhythm, 1944-45	197?	12.00
TIME-LIFE			
❑ STBB-13	Big Bands: Stan Kenton	1984	18.00

KENTON, STAN/JUNE CHRISTY/THE FOUR FRESHMEN

Number	Title	Yr	NM
CAPITOL			
❑ STCL-575	Stan Kenton/June Christy/ The Four Freshmen	1970	30.00
—Reissue of an album by each artist in a 3-LP box -- ST 1796 (Kenton), ST 516 (Christy), ST 1008 (Four Freshmen)			

KENTUCKY COLONELS, THE

Number	Title	Yr	NM
BRIAR			
❑ BT-7202	Livin' in the Past	1975	30.00
❑ 109	The New Sounds of Bluegrass America	1976	40.00
WORLD PACIFIC			
❑ T1821 [M]	Appalachian Swing	1964	50.00
❑ ST1821 [S]	Appalachian Swing	1964	60.00

KENTUCKY HEADHUNTERS, THE

Number	Title	Yr	NM
MERCURY			
❑ 838744-1	Pickin' on Nashville	1989	18.00

KENYATTA, ROBIN

Number	Title	Yr	NM
ATLANTIC			
❑ SD1633	Gypsy Man	1972	25.00
❑ SD1656	Stompin' at the Savoy	1974	18.00
❑ SD1644	Terra Nova	1973	18.00
ECM			
❑ 1008 [B]	The Girl from Martinique	197?	25.00
MUSE			
❑ MR-5095	Beggars	1979	15.00
❑ MR-5062	Nomusa	1975	15.00
VORTEX			
❑ 2005	Until	1969	25.00

KEPPARD, FREDDIE

Number	Title	Yr	NM
HERWIN			
❑ 101	Freddie Keppard 1926	197?	15.00
MILESTONE			
❑ 2014	Freddie Keppard and Tommy Ladnier	197?	15.00

KEROUAC, JACK

Number	Title	Yr	NM
DOT			
❑ DLP-3154 [M]	Poetry for the Beat Generation	1959	10000.00
—Acknowledged to be extremely rare; approximately 130 copies were distributed and only a small handful are known to exist today; the same performance is on Hanover 5000; VG value 5000; VG+ value 7500			
HANOVER			
❑ HML-5006 [M]	Blues and Haikus	1959	250.00
—AL COHN and ZOOT SIMS play saxophones behind Kerouac on this album			

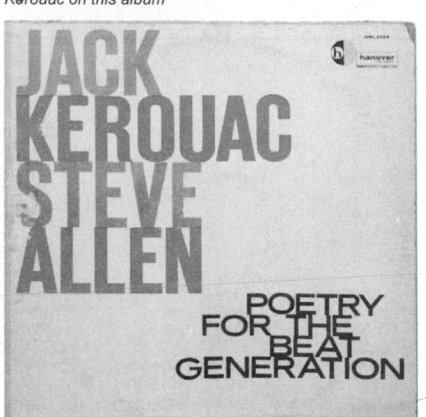

Number	Title	Yr	NM
❑ HML-5000 [M]	Poetry for the Beat Generation	1959	400.00
—Reissue of Dot LP with new cover; STEVE ALLEN plays piano on this record			
RHINO			
❑ R1-70939	The Jack Kerouac Collection	1990	60.00
—Box set compiling the Hanover and Verve LPs plus an LP of unreleased material			
VERVE			
❑ MGV-15005 [M]	Readings on the Beat Generation	1960	250.00

KERR, BROOKS, AND PAUL QUINICHETTE

Number	Title	Yr	NM
FAMOUS DOOR			
❑ 106	Preview	197?	18.00

KERR, BROOKS

Number	Title	Yr	NM
CHIAROSCURO			
❑ 2001	Soda Fountain Rag	197?	15.00

KERSHAW, DOUG

Number	Title	Yr	NM
SCOTTI BROTHERS			
❑ SB7115	Instant Hero	1981	15.00
❑ FZ37428	Instant Hero	1981	12.00
WARNER BROS.			
❑ BS2851	Alive & Pickin'	1975	15.00
❑ WS1820	Cajun Way	1969	25.00
—Green label, "W7" box logo at top			
❑ WS1820	Cajun Way	1970	18.00
—Green label, "WB" shield logo at top			
❑ BS2649	Devil's Elbow	1973	18.00
❑ WS1906	Doug Kershaw	1971	18.00
—Green label			
❑ BS2725	Douglas James Kershaw	1973	18.00
❑ BS3025	Flip, Flop & Fly	1977	15.00
❑ BSK3166	Louisiana Man	1978	15.00
❑ BS2793	Mama Kershaw's Boy	1974	18.00
❑ BS2910	Ragin' Cajun	1976	15.00
❑ WS1861	Spanish Moss	1970	18.00
—Green label			
❑ BS2581	Swamp Grass	1972	18.00
—Green label			

KERSHAW, NIK

Number	Title	Yr	NM
MCA			
❑ 39020	Human Racing	1984	12.00
❑ 5930	Radio Musicola	1986	15.00
—May only exist as a Canadian pressing			
❑ 5548	The Riddle	1985	12.00

KERSHAW, RUSTY AND DOUG

Number	Title	Yr	NM
HICKORY			
❑ LPM-103 [M]	Rusty and Doug Sing Louisiana Man	1960	120.00
HICKORY/MGM			
❑ H3G-4506	Louisiana Man	1974	25.00

KESEY, KEN

Number	Title	Yr	NM
SOUND CITY			
❑ 27690 [M]	The Acid Test	1967	500.00
—THE GRATEFUL DEAD appear on this LP			

KESL, LENNIE

Number	Title	Yr	NM
REVELATION			
❑ 29	Walkin' On Air	1978	15.00

KESSEL, BARNEY, AND HERB ELLIS

Number	Title	Yr	NM
CONCORD JAZZ			
❑ CJ-34	Butterfly	1976	15.00

KESSEL, BARNEY, AND RED MITCHELL

Number	Title	Yr	NM
JAZZ MAN			
❑ 5025	Two Way Conversation	198?	12.00

KESSEL, BARNEY, AND STEPHANE GRAPPELLI

Number	Title	Yr	NM
BLACK LION			
❑ 173	Limehouse Blues	197?	18.00

KESSEL, BARNEY

Number	Title	Yr	NM
BLACK LION			
❑ 310	Blue Soul	197?	18.00
❑ 210	Summertime in Montreux	197?	15.00
❑ 130	Swinging Easy	197?	15.00
CONCORD JAZZ			
❑ CJ-9	Barney Plays Kessel	197?	15.00
❑ CJ-164	Jellybeans	1981	12.00
❑ CJ-33	Soaring	1976	15.00
❑ CJ-221	Solo	1982	12.00
CONTEMPORARY			
❑ C-2508 [10]	Barney Kessel, Volume 1	1953	120.00
❑ C-2514 [10]	Barney Kessel, Volume 2	1954	120.00
❑ M-3563 [M]	Barney Kessel Plays "Carmen"	1959	40.00
❑ S-7563 [S]	Barney Kessel Plays "Carmen"	1959	30.00
❑ C-3511 [M]	Easy Like	1956	80.00
❑ M-3618 [M]	Feeling Free	1965	25.00
❑ S-7618 [S]	Feeling Free	1965	30.00
❑ C-3512 [M]	Kessel Plays Standards	1956	80.00
❑ M-3603 [M]	Let's Cook!	1962	30.00
❑ S-7603 [S]	Let's Cook!	1962	30.00
❑ C-3521 [M]	Music to Listen to Barney Kessel By	1956	60.00
❑ S-7521 [S]	Music to Listen to Barney Kessel By	1959	40.00
❑ C-14044	Red Hot and Blues	198?	12.00
❑ M-3565 [M]	Some Like It Hot	1959	40.00
❑ S-7565 [S]	Some Like It Hot	1959	30.00
❑ C-14033	Spontaneous Combustion	1987	12.00
❑ M-3613 [M]	Swingin' Party	1963	25.00
❑ S-7613 [S]	Swingin' Party	1963	30.00
❑ C-3513 [M]	To Swing or Not to Swing	1956	80.00
❑ M-3585 [M]	Workin' Out!	1960	40.00
❑ S-7585 [S]	Workin' Out!	1960	30.00
EMERALD			
❑ 1401 [M]	On Fire	1965	18.00
❑ 2401 [S]	On Fire	1965	25.00
FANTASY			
❑ OJC-269	Barney Kessel Plays "Carmen"	198?	12.00
❑ OJC-153	Easy Like	198?	12.00
❑ OJC-179	Feeling Free	198?	12.00
❑ OJC-238	Kessel Plays Standards	198?	12.00
❑ OJC-168	Some Like It Hot	198?	12.00
❑ OJC-317	To Swing or Not to Swing	1987	12.00
RCA CAMDEN			
❑ CAS-2404	Guitarra	1970	12.00
REPRISE			
❑ R-6049 [M]	Bossa Nova	1962	18.00
❑ R9-6049 [S]	Bossa Nova	1962	25.00
❑ R-6019 [M]	Breakfast at Tiffany's	1961	18.00
❑ R9-6019 [S]	Breakfast at Tiffany's	1961	25.00
❑ R-6073 [M]	Kessel/Jazz	1963	18.00
❑ R9-6073 [S]	Kessel/Jazz	1963	25.00
STEREO RECORDS			
❑ S-7001 [S]	Music to Listen to Barney Kessel By	1958	50.00

KESSLER, SIEGFRIED, AND DAUNIK LAZRO

Number	Title	Yr	NM
HAT HUT			
❑ 3502	Aeros	1982	15.00

KEYMEN, THE

Number	Title	Yr	NM
ABC-PARAMOUNT			
❑ 258 [M]	Dance with Dick Clark	1958	30.00
❑ S-258 [S]	Dance with Dick Clark	1958	50.00
❑ 288 [M]	Dance with Dick Clark, Volume 2	1959	30.00
❑ S-288 [S]	Dance with Dick Clark, Volume 2	1959	50.00
CORAL			
❑ CRL57112 [M]	Vocal Sounds of the Keymen	1957	30.00
GOLDUST			
❑ LPS-153 [M]	The Keymen Live	196?	50.00

KEYS, CALVIN

Number	Title	Yr	NM
BLACK JAZZ			
❑ 5 [B]	Shawn-neeq	1972	30.00
OVATION			
❑ OV-1804	Criss Cross	1978	15.00

KHAN, CHAKA

Number	Title	Yr	NM
REPRISE			
❑ PRO-A-8478 [DJ]	Epiphany: The Best of Chaka Khan Sampler	1996	18.00
—Promo-only six-song sampler			
WARNER BROS.			
❑ BSK3245 [B]	Chaka	1978	12.00
❑ 23729	Chaka Khan	1982	12.00
❑ 25707	C.K.	1988	12.00
❑ 25425	Destiny	1986	12.00
❑ 25162	I Feel for You	1984	12.00
❑ 25946	Life Is a Dance: The Remix Project	1989	18.00
❑ BSK3385	Naughty	1980	12.00
❑ HS3526	What Cha' Gonna Do for Me	1981	12.00

KHAN, STEVE

Number	Title	Yr	NM
ANTILLES			
❑ AN-1020	Casa Loco	198?	12.00
❑ AN-1018	Eyewitness	198?	12.00
ARISTA/NOVUS			
❑ AN3023	Evidence	1980	15.00
COLUMBIA			
❑ JC36129	Arrows	1979	12.00
❑ JC36406	The Best of Steve Khan	1980	12.00
❑ JC35539	The Blue Man	1978	12.00
❑ JC34857	Tightrope	1977	12.00

KHAN

Number	Title	Yr	NM
PVC			
❑ 7902 [B]	Space Shanty	1978	30.00
—first US release for rare 1972 prog album			

Number	Title	Yr	NM

KHAZAD DOOM

LPL
❑ 892	Level 6 1/2	1970	1000.00

KICKSTANDS, THE

CAPITOL
❑ T2078 [M]	Black Boots and Bikes	1964	120.00
❑ ST2078 [S]	Black Boots and Bikes	1964	150.00
❑ T/ST2078	Black Boots and Bikes Bonus Fold-Out	1964	50.00

KID CREOLE AND THE COCONUTS

ANTILLES
❑ AN7078	Off the Coast of Me	1980	15.00

SIRE
❑ 23977	Doppelganger	1983	12.00
❑ SRK3534	Fresh Fruit in Foreign Places	1981	12.00
❑ 25579	I, Too, Have Seen the Woods	1987	12.00
❑ 25298	In Praise of Older Women and Other Crimes	1985	12.00
❑ SRK3681	Wise Guy	1982	12.00

KID FROST

VIRGIN
❑ 91377	Hispanic Causing Panic	1990	18.00

KID 'N PLAY

SELECT
❑ 21628	2 Hype	1988	15.00
❑ 61206	Face the Nation	1991	15.00
❑ 21638	Kid 'N Play's Funhouse	1990	15.00

KID ROCK

ATLANTIC
❑ 83482	Cocky	2001	25.00
❑ 83119	Devil Without a Cause	1999	25.00
❑ 83685	Kid Rock	2003	18.00
❑ 83314	The History of Rock	2000	25.00

JIVE
❑ 1409-1	Grits Sandwiches for Breakfast	1990	25.00

KID STUFF REPERTORY COMPANY, THE

KID STUFF
❑ KS 090	A Christmas Carol	1978	15.00

KID THOMAS

AMERICAN MUSIC
❑ 642 [10]	Kid Thomas	1952	90.00

ARHOOLIE
❑ 1016	New Orleans Jazz	1967	15.00

GHB
❑ GHB-80	Kid Thomas and His Algiers Stompers	1977	15.00
❑ GHB-291	Kid Thomas in England	198?	12.00
❑ GHB-24 [M]	Kid Thomas + The Hall Brothers Jazz Band	196?	25.00

JAZZOLOGY
❑ JCE-13	Sonnets from Algiers	1967	15.00

NEW ORLEANS
❑ NOR7201	Kid Thomas at Kohlman's Tavern	1972	15.00
—Label calls this "Thomas Valentine at Kohlman's Tavern			

RIVERSIDE
❑ RLP-365 [M]	Kid Thomas and His Algiers Stompers	1961	30.00
❑ RS-9365 [R]	Kid Thomas and His Algiers Stompers	1961	25.00
❑ RLP-386 [M]	Kid Thomas and His Algiers Stompers	1961	30.00
❑ RS-9386 [R]	Kid Thomas and His Algiers Stompers	1961	25.00

KIHN, GREG, BAND

BESERKLEY
❑ JBZ 0052	Again	1978	12.00
—Third issue, distributed by Janus			
❑ PZ34779	Again	1977	18.00
—Second issue, distributed by CBS			
❑ 60117	Again	1982	10.00
—Reissue			
❑ BZ 0052	Again	1977	15.00
—First issue, distributed by Playboy			
❑ BZ10068	Glass House Rock	1980	12.00
❑ JBZ 0046	Greg Kihn Band	1978	12.00
—Third issue, distributed by Janus			
❑ BZ 0046 [B]	Greg Kihn Band	1976	25.00
—First issue, distributed by Playboy			
❑ BZ10069	Greg Rockihnroll Band	1981	10.00
❑ 60224	Kihnspiracy	1983	10.00
❑ 60354	Kihntagious	1984	10.00
❑ 60101	Kihntinued	1982	10.00
❑ JBZ 0056	Next of Kihn	1978	12.00
—Original issue, distributed by Janus			
❑ 60116	Next of Kihn	1982	10.00
—Reissue			

Number	Title	Yr	NM
❑ BZ10063	With the Naked Eye	1979	12.00

EMI AMERICA
❑ SJ-17152	Citizen Kihn	1985	10.00
❑ ST-17180	Love and Rock and Roll	1986	10.00

RHINO
❑ R1-70900	Kihnsolidation: The Best of Greg Kihn	1989	15.00

KILGORE, MERLE

STARDAY
❑ SLP-251 [M]	There's Gold in Them Thar Hills	1963	30.00

WING
❑ MGW-12316 [M]	Tall Texan	196?	18.00
❑ SRW-16316 [S]	Tall Texan	196?	15.00

KILIMANJARO

PHILO
❑ 9001	Kilimanjaro	1979	15.00
❑ 9005	Kilimanjaro 2	1981	15.00

KILLING FLOOR

SIRE
❑ SES-97019 [B]	Killing Floor	1970	75.00

KIM, ANDY

ABC DUNHILL
❑ DSDP-50193	Andy Kim's Greatest Hits	1974	15.00
—Reissue of Steed 37008			

CAPITOL
❑ ST-11318	Andy Kim	1974	15.00
❑ ST-11368	The Pilot	1975	15.00

STEED
❑ ST37008	Andy Kim's Greatest Hits	1970	18.00
❑ ST37004	Baby I Love You	1969	18.00
❑ ST-7001 [M]	How Did We Ever Get This Way?	1968	40.00
—In stereo cover with "Monaural" sticker			
❑ STS-37001 [S]	How Did We Ever Get This Way?	1968	18.00
❑ STS-37002	Rainbow Ride	1969	18.00

UNI
❑ 73137	Andy Kim	1972	15.00

KIMBERLYS, THE

HAPPY TIGER
❑ HT-1014	New Horizon	1970	18.00
❑ HT-1006	The Kimberlys	1970	18.00

KIME, WARREN, AND HIS BRASS IMPACT ORCHESTRA

COMMAND
❑ 33-910 [M]	Brass Impact	1967	12.00
❑ SD 910 [S]	Brass Impact	1967	15.00
❑ 33-919 [M]	Explosive Brass Impact	1967	12.00
❑ SD-919 [S]	Explosive Brass Impact	1967	15.00

KINCAID, BRADLEY

VARSITY
❑ 6988 [10]	American Ballads	1955	60.00
❑ 34 [M]	Bradley Kincaid Sings American Ballads and Folk Songs	1957	40.00

KINCAIDE, DEAN

WEATHERS
❑ 5610 [M]	Arranged for You	1954	50.00

KINES, TOM

ELEKTRA
❑ EKL-137 [M]	Of Maids and Mistresses	1958	30.00

KING, ALBERT

ATLANTIC
❑ SD8213	King of the Blues Guitar	1969	30.00

FANTASY
❑ 9633	I'm in a Phone Booth, Baby	1984	12.00
❑ 9627	San Francisco '83	1983	12.00

KING
❑ 852 [M]	Big Blues	1963	500.00
❑ KS-1060	Travelin' to California	1969	30.00

MODERN BLUES
❑ MBLP-723	Let's Have a Natural Ball	198?	12.00

STAX
❑ MPS-8546	Blues at Sunrise	1988	12.00
❑ MPS-8504	Blues for Elvis	1981	12.00
—Retitled reissue of 2015			
❑ ST-723 [M]	Born Under a Bad Sign	1967	80.00
❑ STS-723 [S]	Born Under a Bad Sign	1967	120.00
❑ STS-3009	I'll Play the Blues for You	1972	25.00
❑ MPS-8513	I'll Play the Blues for You	1981	12.00
—Reissue of 3309			
❑ STS-5505	I Wanna Get Funky	1974	18.00
❑ MPS-8536	I Wanna Get Funky	1987	12.00
—Reissue of 5505			

Number	Title	Yr	NM
❑ STS-2015	King Does the King's Thing	1969	30.00
❑ STS-2003	Live Wire/Blues Power	1968	50.00
❑ STX-4128 [B]	Live Wire/Blues Power	1979	12.00
—Reissue of 2003			
❑ STS-2040	Lovejoy	1971	25.00
❑ MPS-8517	Lovejoy	1981	12.00
—Reissue of 2040			
❑ STS-5520	Montreux Festival	1975	18.00
❑ STX-4132	Montreux Festival	1980	12.00
—Retitled reissue of 5520			
❑ MPS-8534	The Lost Session	1986	12.00
❑ STX-4101	The Pinch	1977	15.00
❑ MPS-8557	Tuesday Night in San Francisco	1990	12.00
❑ MPS-8556	Wednesday Night in San Francisco	1990	12.00
❑ STS-2010	Years Gone By	1969	30.00
❑ MPS-8522	Years Gone By	1982	12.00
—Reissue of 2010			

SUNDAZED
❑ LP5031	Born Under a Bad Sign	1999	18.00
—Reissue on 180-gram vinyl			
❑ 5429 [B]	The Big Blues		30.00

TOMATO
❑ TOM-6002	King Albert	1978	15.00
❑ TOM-7022	New Orleans Heat	1979	15.00

UTOPIA
❑ BUL1-1731	Albert	1976	15.00
❑ CUL2-2205	Albert Live	1977	18.00
❑ BUL1-1387	Truckload of Lovin'	1976	15.00

KING, ALBERT/LITTLE MILTON

STAX
❑ STX-4123	Chronicle	1979	15.00
—One side devoted to each artist			

KING, ALBERT/OTIS RUSH

CHESS
❑ LPS1538	Door to Door	1969	30.00
❑ CH-9322	Door to Door	1990	12.00
—Reissue			

KING, ALBERT/STEVE CROPPER/POP STAPLES

STAX
❑ STS-2020	Jammed Together	1969	30.00
❑ MPS-8544	Jammed Together	1988	12.00
—Reissue			

KING, ANNA

SMASH
❑ MGS-27059 [M]	Back to Soul	1964	100.00
❑ SRS-67059 [S]	Back to Soul	1964	120.00

KING, B.B.

CLEOPATRA
❑ 2849 [B]	King of the Blues		25.00
❑ 8143 [B]	King of the Blues		30.00
—picture disc			

KING, B.B.

ABC
❑ D-878	Back in the Alley	1975	15.00
—Reissue of BluesWay 6050			
❑ D-730	B.B. King in London	1971	15.00
❑ D-704	Blues Is King	1970	15.00
—Reissue of BluesWay 6001			
❑ D-709	Blues on Top of Blues	1970	15.00
—Reissue of BluesWay 6011			
❑ D-868	Completely Well	1975	15.00
—Reissue of BluesWay 6037			
❑ D-825	Friends	1974	15.00
❑ X-759	Guess Who	1972	15.00
❑ D-813	His Best/The Electric B.B. King	1974	15.00
—Reissue of BluesWay 6022			
❑ D-713	Indianola Mississippi Seeds	1970	15.00
❑ AB-977	King Size	1977	15.00
❑ D-743	L.A. Midnight	1972	15.00
❑ D-819	Live and Well	1974	15.00
—Reissue of BluesWay 6031			
❑ D-724	Live at the Regal	1971	15.00
—Reissue of ABC-Paramount 509			
❑ D-723	Live in Cook County Jail	1971	15.00
❑ D-712	Lucille	1970	15.00
—Reissue of BluesWay 6016			
❑ D-898	Lucille Talks Back	1975	15.00
❑ AA-1061	Midnight Believer	1978	15.00
❑ X-767	The Best of B.B. King	1973	15.00
❑ X-794	To Know You Is to Love You	1973	15.00

ABC-PARAMOUNT
❑ 528 [M]	Confessin' the Blues	1965	30.00
❑ S-528 [S]	Confessin' the Blues	1965	40.00
❑ 509 [M]	Live at the Regal	1965	40.00
❑ S-509 [S]	Live at the Regal	1965	50.00
❑ 456 [M]	Mr. Blues	1963	30.00
❑ S-456 [S]	Mr. Blues	1963	40.00

Number	Title	Yr	NM
BLUESWAY			
❑ BLS-6050 [B]	Back in the Alley	1970	25.00
❑ BL-6001 [M]	Blues Is King	1967	40.00
❑ BLS-6001 [S]	Blues Is King	1967	30.00
❑ BLS-6011 [S]	Blues on Top of Blues	1968	30.00
❑ BL-6011 [M]	Blues on Top of Blues	1968	50.00
—Mono is white label promo only			
❑ BLS-6037	Completely Well	1969	25.00
❑ BLS-6022	His Best/The Electric B.B. King	1969	25.00
❑ BLS-6031 [B]	Live and Well	1969	25.00
❑ BLS-6016	Lucille	1968	30.00
COMMAND			
❑ CQD-40022 [Q]	Friends	1974	25.00
CROWN			
❑ CLP-5359 [M]	B.B. King	1963	40.00
—Gray label, black "Crown			
❑ CLP-5359 [M]	B.B. King	196?	15.00
—Black label, multi-color "Crown			
❑ CST-359 [P]	B.B. King	1963	15.00
—Half of the album is in stereo, half is rechanneled			
❑ CLP-5119 [M]	B.B. King Sings Spirituals	1960	60.00
—Gray label, black "Crown			
❑ CLP-5119 [M]	B.B. King Sings Spirituals	196?	15.00
—Black label, multi-color "Crown			
❑ CST-152 [R]	B.B. King Sings Spirituals	1960	15.00
—Black vinyl			
❑ CST-152 [R]	B.B. King Sings Spirituals	1960	100.00
—Red vinyl			
❑ CLP-5115 [M]	B.B. King Wails	1959	80.00
—Black label, silver "Crown			
❑ CLP-5115 [M]	B.B. King Wails	1963	25.00
—Gray label, black "Crown			
❑ CLP-5115 [M]	B.B. King Wails	196?	15.00
—Black label, multi-color "Crown			
❑ CST-147 [R]	B.B. King Wails	1960	15.00
—Black vinyl			
❑ CST-147 [R]	B.B. King Wails	1960	100.00
—Red vinyl			
❑ CLP-5309 [M]	Blues in My Heart	1963	40.00
—Gray label, black "Crown			
❑ CLP-5309 [M]	Blues in My Heart	196?	15.00
—Black label, multi-color "Crown			
❑ CST-309 [R]	Blues in My Heart	1963	15.00
❑ CLP-5286 [M]	Easy Listening Blues	1962	60.00
—Gray label, black "Crown			
❑ CLP-5286 [M]	Easy Listening Blues	196?	15.00
—Black label, multi-color "Crown			
❑ CLP-5167 [M]	King of the Blues	1961	60.00
—Gray label, black "Crown			
❑ CLP-5167 [M]	King of the Blues	196?	15.00
—Black label, multi-color "Crown			
❑ CST-195 [S]	King of the Blues	1961	25.00
—Black vinyl; this album is in true stereo, contrary to prior reports			
❑ CST-195 [S]	King of the Blues	1961	120.00
—Red vinyl; this album is in true stereo, contrary to prior reports			
❑ CLP-5230 [M]	More B.B. King	1962	60.00
—Gray label, black "Crown			
❑ CLP-5230 [M]	More B.B. King	196?	15.00
—Black label, multi-color "Crown			
❑ CLP-5188 [M]	My Kind of Blues	1961	60.00
—Gray label, black "Crown			
❑ CLP-5188 [M]	My Kind of Blues	196?	15.00
—Black label, multi-color "Crown			
❑ CLP-5020 [M]	Singin' the Blues	1957	100.00
—Black label, silver "Crown			
❑ CLP-5020 [M]	Singin' the Blues	1963	25.00
—Gray label, black "Crown			
❑ CLP-5020 [M]	Singin' the Blues	196?	15.00
—Black label, multi-color "Crown			
❑ CLP-5063 [M]	The Blues	1958	80.00
—Black label, silver "Crown			
❑ CLP-5063 [M]	The Blues	1963	25.00
—Gray label, black "Crown			
❑ CLP-5063 [M]	The Blues	196?	15.00
—Black label, multi-color "Crown			
❑ CLP-5143 [M]	The Great B.B. King	1961	60.00
—Gray label, black "Crown			
❑ CLP-5143 [M]	The Great B.B. King	196?	15.00
—Black label, multi-color "Crown			
❑ CLP-5248 [M]	Twist with B.B. King	1962	60.00
—Gray label, black "Crown			
❑ CLP-5248 [M]	Twist with B.B. King	196?	15.00
—Black label, multi-color "Crown			
CRUSADERS			
❑ 16013	Live in London	1982	30.00
—Part of MCA's "Audiophile Series			
CUSTOM			
❑ CM-2046 [M]	Blues for Me	196?	15.00
❑ CM-2049 [M]	I Love You So	196?	15.00
❑ CM-2052 [M]	The Soul of B.B. King	196?	15.00
DIRECT DISK			
❑ SD-16616	Midnight Believer	1980	50.00
—Audiophile vinyl			

Number	Title	Yr	NM
GALAXY			
❑ 202 [M]	16 Greatest Hits	1963	60.00
❑ 8202 [S]	16 Greatest Hits	1963	80.00
GRP			
❑ GR-9637	Live at the Apollo	1991	18.00
KENT			
❑ KST-565	B.B. King Live	1972	18.00
❑ KLP-5015 [M]	B.B. King Live on Stage	1965	25.00
❑ KST-515 [R]	B.B. King Live on Stage	1965	18.00
❑ KST-561	Better Than Ever	1971	18.00
❑ KLP-5029 [M]	Boss of the Blues	1968	25.00
❑ KST-529 [R]	Boss of the Blues	1968	18.00
❑ KST-563	Doing My Thing, Lord	1971	18.00
❑ KST-533 [B]	From the Beginning	1969	25.00
❑ KST-552	Greatest Hits, Volume 1	1971	18.00
❑ KLP-2008	Incredible Soul of B.B. King	1987	15.00
❑ KLP-5013 [M]	Let Me Love You	1965	25.00
❑ KST-513 [R]	Let Me Love You	1965	18.00
❑ KLP-5017 [M]	Pure Soul	1966	25.00
❑ KST-517 [R]	Pure Soul	1966	18.00
❑ KLP-5012 [M]	Rock Me Baby	1964	25.00
❑ KST-512 [R]	Rock Me Baby	1964	18.00
❑ KST-539	The Incredible Soul of B.B. King	1970	18.00
❑ KLP-5021 [M]	The Jungle	1967	25.00
❑ KST-521 [R]	The Jungle	1967	18.00
❑ KST-568	The Original Sweet Sixteen	1972	18.00
❑ KLP-5016 [M]	The Soul of B.B. King	1966	25.00
❑ KST-516 [R]	The Soul of B.B. King	1966	18.00
❑ KST-548	Turn On to B.B. King	1970	18.00
❑ KST-535	Underground Blues	1969	18.00
MCA			
❑ 27010	Back in the Alley	1980	10.00
—Reissue of ABC 878			
❑ 5413	Blues 'N' Jazz	1983	12.00
❑ 27009	Completely Well	1980	10.00
—Reissue of ABC 868			
❑ 27007	His Best/The Electric B.B. King	1980	10.00
—Reissue of ABC 813			
❑ 27008	Live and Well	1980	10.00
—Reissue of ABC 819			
❑ 6455	Live at San Quentin	1990	15.00
❑ 27006	Live at the Regal	1980	10.00
—Reissue of ABC 724			
❑ 27005	Live in Cook County Jail	1980	10.00
—Reissue of ABC 723			
❑ 5307	Love Me Tender	1982	12.00
❑ 27011	Midnight Believer	1980	10.00
—Reissue of ABC 1061			
❑ 2-8016	Now Appearing" at Ole Miss	1980	15.00
❑ 5616	Six Silver Strings	1985	12.00
❑ 3151	Take It Home	1979	12.00
❑ 27028	Take It Home	1981	10.00
—Reissue of MCA 3151			
❑ 27074	The Best of B.B. King	1984	10.00
—Reissue of ABC 767			
❑ 42183	The King of the Blues: 1989	1989	12.00
❑ 5162	There Must Be a Better World Somewhere	1981	12.00
❑ 27034	There Must Be a Better World Somewhere	1983	10.00
—Reissue of MCA 5162			
MCA IMPULSE!			
❑ MCA2-4124	Great Moments with B.B. King	1981	15.00
MOBILE FIDELITY			
❑ 1-235	Lucille	1995	50.00
—Audiophile vinyl			
PICKWICK			
❑ SPC-3593	Live at the Regal	197?	10.00
❑ SPC-3654	Live in Cook County Jail	197?	10.00
STAX			
❑ ORS-4508	16 Original Big Hits	198?	10.00
UNITED			
❑ US-7788	9 x 9	197?	10.00
❑ US-7736	B.B. King Live on Stage	197?	10.00
—Reissue of Kent 515			
❑ US-7708	Blues for Me	197?	10.00
—Reissue of Custom 2046			
❑ US-7750	Boss of the Blues	197?	10.00
—Reissue of Kent 529			
❑ US-7705	Easy Listening Blues	197?	10.00
—Reissue of Crown 5286			
❑ US-7766	Greatest Hits, Volume 1	197?	10.00
—Reissue of Kent 552			
❑ US-7703	Heart Full of Blues	197?	10.00
❑ US-7711	I Love You So	197?	10.00
—Reissue of Custom 2049			
❑ US-7734	Let Me Love You	197?	10.00
—Reissue of Kent 513			
❑ US-7724	My Kind of Blues	197?	10.00
—Reissue of Crown 5188			
❑ US-7733	Rock Me, Baby	197?	10.00
—Reissue of Kent 5012			
❑ US-7726	Singin' the Blues	197?	10.00
—Reissue of Crown 5020			
❑ US-7721	Swing Low	197?	10.00
❑ US-7732	The Blues	197?	10.00
—Reissue of Crown 5063			

Number	Title	Yr	NM
❑ US-7728	The Great B.B. King	197?	10.00
—Reissue of Crown 5143			
❑ US-7756	The Incredible Soul of B.B. King	197?	10.00
—Reissue of Kent 539			
❑ US-7742	The Jungle	197?	10.00
—Reissue of Kent 521			
❑ US-7773	The Original Sweet Sixteen	197?	10.00
—Reissue of Kent 568			
❑ US-7714	The Soul of B.B. King	197?	10.00
—Reissue of Custom 2052			
❑ US-7763	Turn On with B.B. King	197?	10.00
—Reissue of Kent 548			

KING, BEN E.

Number	Title	Yr	NM
ATCO			
❑ 33-165 [M]	Ben E. King's Greatest Hits	1964	30.00
❑ SD 33-165 [S]	Ben E. King's Greatest Hits	1964	40.00
—Purple and brown label			
❑ SD 33-165 [S]	Ben E. King's Greatest Hits	1969	15.00
—Yellow label			
❑ SD 33-165 [S]	Ben E. King's Greatest Hits	197?	10.00
—Any other color label			
❑ 33-137 [M]	Ben E. King Sings for Soulful Lovers	1962	40.00
❑ SD 33-137 [S]	Ben E. King Sings for Soulful Lovers	1962	60.00
❑ 33-142 [M]	Don't Play That Song	1962	40.00
❑ SD 33-142 [S]	Don't Play That Song	1962	60.00
❑ 33-174 [M]	Seven Letters	1965	40.00
❑ SD 33-174 [S]	Seven Letters	1965	50.00
❑ 33-133 [M]	Spanish Harlem	1961	125.00
—Yellow label with harp			
❑ 33-133 [M]	Spanish Harlem	1962	75.00
—Gold and gray label			
❑ SD 33-133 [S]	Spanish Harlem	1961	150.00
—Yellow label with harp			
❑ SD 33-133 [S]	Spanish Harlem	1962	50.00
—Purple and brown label			
ATLANTIC			
❑ SD18169	I Have a Love	1976	15.00
❑ SD19200	Let Me Live in Your Life	1978	15.00
❑ SD19269	Music Trance	1980	12.00
❑ SD18191	Rhapsody	1976	15.00
❑ 81716	Stand By Me: The Best of Ben E. King	1987	10.00
—Includes seven Ben E. King tracks and three by the Drifters			
❑ SD19300	Street Tough	1981	12.00
❑ SD18132 [B]	Supernatural	1975	15.00
CLARION			
❑ 606 [M]	Young Boy Blues	1966	30.00
❑ SD606 [S]	Young Boy Blues	1966	30.00
MANDALA			
❑ MLP-3008 [DJ]	Audio Biography	1972	30.00
—Promo-only interview by Richard Robinson			
❑ MLP3007	The Beginning of It All for Ben E. King	1972	25.00
MAXWELL			
❑ ML-88001	Rough Edges	1969	25.00

KING, CAROLE

Number	Title	Yr	NM
ATLANTIC			
❑ SD19344	One to One	1982	12.00
❑ 80118	Speeding Time	1983	12.00
CAPITOL			
❑ C1-90885	City Streets	1989	15.00
❑ SOO-12073	Pearls -- Songs of Goffin and King	1980	12.00
❑ SMAS-11667 [B]	Simple Things	1977	12.00
❑ SN-16057	Simple Things	1980	10.00
—Budget-line reissue			
❑ SWAK-11963	Touch the Sky	1979	12.00
❑ SN-16059	Touch the Sky	1980	10.00
—Budget-line reissue			
❑ ST-11953	Touch the Sky	1979	12.00
❑ SPRO-9103/4 [EP]	Touch the Sky Sampler	1979	18.00
—Promo-only four-song excerpt from "Touch the Sky			
❑ SW-11785	Welcome Home	1978	12.00
❑ SN-16058	Welcome Home	1980	10.00
—Budget-line reissue			
❑ SW-11785	Welcome Home	1978	12.00
MOBILE FIDELITY			
❑ MFSL1-414 [B]	Tapestry	2013	30.00
ODE			
❑ PE34944	Carole King: Writer	1977	12.00
—Reissue of 77006			
❑ SP-77018 [B]	Fantasy	1973	18.00
❑ PE34962	Fantasy	1977	12.00
—Reissue of 77018			
❑ JE34967	Her Greatest Hits	1978	12.00
❑ SP-77013 [B]	Music	1971	25.00
❑ QU-88013 [Q]	Music	1974	50.00
❑ PE34949	Music	1977	12.00
—Reissue of 77013			
❑ SP-77027	Really Rosie	1975	15.00
❑ PE34955 [B]	Really Rosie	1977	12.00
—Reissue of 77027			

Number	Title	Yr	NM

Number	Title	Yr	NM
❑ SP-77016 [B]	Rhymes and Reasons	1972	18.00
❑ PE34950	Rhymes and Reasons	1977	12.00
— Reissue of 77016			
❑ SP-77009	Tapestry	1971	15.00
❑ PE34946	Tapestry	1977	12.00
— Reissue of 77009			
❑ HE44946	Tapestry	1980	50.00
—Half-speed mastered edition			
❑ FE34946	Tapestry	1979	12.00
— Reissue with new prefix			
❑ SP-77034	Thoroughbred	1976	15.00
❑ PE34963	Thoroughbred	1977	12.00
— Reissue of 77034			
❑ SP-77024	Wrap Around Joy	1974	15.00
❑ PE34953	Wrap Around Joy	1977	12.00
— Reissue of 77024			
❑ SP-77006	Writer: Carole King	1970	15.00

KING, CLAUDE

COLUMBIA

Number	Title	Yr	NM
❑ C30804	Chip 'n' Dale's Place	1971	18.00
❑ CS1024	Friend, Lover, Woman, Wife	1970	18.00
❑ CS9789	I Remember Johnny Horton	1968	18.00
— 360 Sound Stereo" on red label			
❑ CL1810 [M]	Meet Claude King	1962	30.00
— Six "eye" logos on label			
❑ CS8610 [S]	Meet Claude King	1962	40.00
— Six "eye" logos on label			
❑ CL1810 [M]	Meet Claude King	1963	18.00
— Guaranteed High Fidelity" or "Mono" on red label			
❑ CS8610 [S]	Meet Claude King	1963	25.00
— 360 Sound Stereo" on red label			
❑ CL2415 [M]	Tiger Woman	1965	25.00
❑ CS9215 [S]	Tiger Woman	1965	30.00
— 360 Sound Stereo" on red label			

HARMONY

Number	Title	Yr	NM
❑ HS11300	The Best of Claude King	1969	15.00

KING, EVELYN "CHAMPAGNE

EMI

Number	Title	Yr	NM
❑ E1-92049	The Girl Next Door	1989	15.00

EMI MANHATTAN

| ❑ E1-46968 | Flirt | 1988 | 10.00 |

RCA VICTOR

❑ AFL1-7015	A Long Time Coming (A Change Is Gonna Come)	1985	12.00
❑ AFL1-3543	Call On Me	1980	12.00
❑ AFL1-4725	Face to Face	1983	10.00
❑ AFL1-4337	Get Loose	1982	10.00
— As "Evelyn King			
❑ AFL1-3962	I'm in Love	1981	12.00
— As "Evelyn King			
❑ AFL1-3033	Music Box	1979	12.00
❑ APL1-2466	Smooth Talk	1978	12.00
❑ AFL1-5308	So Romantic	1984	10.00

KING, FREDDIE

COTILLION

Number	Title	Yr	NM
❑ 3D9004	Freddie King Is a Blues Master	1969	30.00
❑ SD9016	My Feeling for the Blues	1970	30.00

KING

❑ 964 [M]	24 Vocals and Instrumentals	1966	30.00
❑ 928 [M]	A Bonanza of Instrumentals	1965	50.00
❑ KS-928 [S]	A Bonanza of Instrumentals	1965	60.00
❑ 821 [M]	Bossa Nova and Blues	1962	150.00
❑ 856 [M]	Freddie King Goes Surfin'	1963	80.00
❑ KS-856 [S]	Freddie King Goes Surfin'	1963	120.00
❑ 762 [M]	Freddie King Sings the Blues	1961	250.00
❑ KS-1059	Hide Away	1969	18.00
❑ 773 [M]	Let's Hide Away and Dance Away	1961	250.00

MCA

| ❑ 690 | The Best of Freddie King | 1979 | 10.00 |
| *— Reissue of Shelter 52021* | | | |

MODERN BLUES

| ❑ MBLP-722 | Freddie King Sings | 198? | 12.00 |
| ❑ MB2LP-721 | Just Pickin' | 198? | 18.00 |

RSO

❑ SD4803	Burglar	1974	15.00
❑ RS-1-3025	Freddie King 1934-1976	1977	15.00
❑ SD4811	Larger Than Life	1975	15.00

SHELTER

❑ SW-8905	Getting Ready	1971	18.00
❑ SW-8913	Texas Cannonball	1972	18.00
❑ 2140	The Best of Freddie King	1975	18.00
— Original with MCA distribution			
❑ SRL52021	The Best of Freddie King	1977	15.00
— Second edition with ABC distribution			
❑ SW-8919	Woman Across the River	1973	18.00

STARDAY/GUSTO

| ❑ 5012 | 17 Original Hits | 1977 | 12.00 |
| ❑ 5033 | Hide Away | 1978 | 12.00 |

KING, FREDDIE/LULA REED/BOBBY THOMPSON

KING

| ❑ 777 [M] | Boy-Girl-Boy | 1962 | 250.00 |

KING, JEAN

HANNA-BARBERA

Number	Title	Yr	NM
❑ HLP-8505 [M]	Jean King Sings for the In Crowd	1966	25.00

KING, JONATHAN

PARROT

❑ PA61013 [M]	Jonathan King Or Then Again....	1967	80.00
❑ PAS71013 [P]	Jonathan King Or Then Again....	1967	60.00
— Only "Where the Sun Has Never Shown" is rechanneled.			

U.K.

| ❑ 53101 [B] | Bubble Rock Is Here to Stay | 1972 | 45.00 |
| ❑ 53104 [B] | Pandora's Box | 1973 | 30.00 |

KING, MORGANA

ASCOT

❑ AM13020 [M]	Everybody Loves Saturday Night	1965	30.00
❑ AS16020 [S]	Everybody Loves Saturday Night	1965	30.00
❑ AM13025 [M]	More Morgana	1965	30.00
❑ AS16025 [S]	More Morgana	1965	30.00
❑ AM13019 [M]	The End of a Love Affair	1965	30.00
— Reissue of United Artists 30020			
❑ AS16019 [S]	The End of a Love Affair	1965	30.00
— Reissue of United Artists 40020			
❑ AM13014 [M]	The Winter of My Discontent	1964	30.00
❑ AS16014 [S]	The Winter of My Discontent	1964	30.00

EMARCY

| ❑ MG-36079 [M] | For You, For Me, For Evermore | 1956 | 120.00 |

MAINSTREAM

❑ MRL-355	Cuore di Mama	1974	18.00
❑ 56052 [M]	Miss Morgana King	1965	25.00
❑ S-6052 [S]	Miss Morgana King	1965	30.00
❑ MRL-321	Taste of Honey	1972	18.00
❑ 56015 [M]	With a Taste of Honey	1964	25.00
❑ S-6015 [S]	With a Taste of Honey	1964	30.00

MERCURY

| ❑ MG-20231 [M] | Morgana King Sings the Blues | 1958 | 80.00 |

MUSE

❑ MR-5339	Another Time, Another Space	1988	12.00
❑ MR-5190	Everything Must Change	1978	12.00
❑ MR-5224	Higher Ground	1979	12.00
❑ MR-5257	Looking Through the Eyes of Love	1981	12.00
❑ MR-5301	Portraits	1983	12.00
❑ MR-5326	Simply Eloquent	1986	12.00
❑ MR-5166	Stretchin' Out	1977	12.00

PARAMOUNT

| ❑ PAS-6067 | New Beginnings | 1973 | 15.00 |

RCA CAMDEN

| ❑ CAL-543 [M] | The Greatest Songs Ever Swung | 1959 | 25.00 |
| ❑ CAS-543 [S] | The Greatest Songs Ever Swung | 1959 | 30.00 |

REPRISE

❑ R6257 [M]	Gemini Changes	1967	25.00
❑ RS6257 [S]	Gemini Changes	1967	30.00
❑ R6192 [M]	It's a Quiet Thing	1966	25.00
❑ RS6192 [S]	It's a Quiet Thing	1966	30.00
❑ R6205 [M]	Wild Is Love	1966	25.00
❑ RS6205 [S]	Wild Is Love	1966	30.00

TRIP

| ❑ 5533 | Morgana King Sings | 197? | 12.00 |

UNITED ARTISTS

❑ UAL3028 [M]	Folk Songs A La King	1960	80.00
❑ UAS6028 [S]	Folk Songs A La King	1960	100.00
❑ UAL30020 [M]	Let Me Love You	1960	100.00
❑ UAS30020-S [S]	Let Me Love You	1960	120.00

VERVE

| ❑ V-5061 [M] | I Know How It Feels | 1968 | 30.00 |
| ❑ V6-5061 [S] | I Know How It Feels | 1968 | 30.00 |

WING

| ❑ MGW-12307 [M] | More Morgana King | 1965 | 18.00 |
| ❑ SRW-16307 [S] | More Morgana King | 1965 | 25.00 |

KING, PEE WEE

BRIAR

| ❑ 102 | Golden Olde Tyme Dances | 1975 | 60.00 |

LONGHORN

| ❑ 1236 [M] | The Legendary Pee Wee King | 1967 | 30.00 |

RCA CAMDEN

| ❑ CAL-876 [M] | Country Barn Dance | 1965 | 25.00 |
| ❑ CAS-876 [R] | Country Barn Dance | 1965 | 15.00 |

RCA VICTOR

❑ LPM-3028 [10]	Pee Wee King	195?	80.00
❑ LPM-3280 [10]	Swing West	195?	80.00
❑ LPM-1237 [M]	Swing West	1956	40.00
❑ LPM-3109 [10]	Waltzes	195?	80.00
❑ LPM-3071 [10]	Western Hits	195?	80.00

STARDAY

Number	Title	Yr	NM
❑ SLP-284 [M]	Back Again with the Songs That Made Them Famous	1964	30.00

KING, PEGGY

COLUMBIA

| ❑ CL2549 [10] | Wish Upon a Star | 1955 | 50.00 |

IMPERIAL

| ❑ LP-9078 [M] | Lazy Afternoon | 1959 | 25.00 |
| ❑ LP-12026 [S] | Lazy Afternoon | 1959 | 30.00 |

STASH

| ❑ 246 | Peggy King Sings Jerome Kern: Till the Clouds Roll By | 198? | 10.00 |

KING, REV. MARTIN LUTHER

20TH CENTURY

| ❑ TCF-3110 [M] | Freedom March on Washington | 1963 | 30.00 |
| ❑ S-3201 | The Rev. Dr. Martin Luther King, Jr. | 1968 | 25.00 |

BUDDAH

| ❑ BDS-2002 | Man of Love | 1968 | 25.00 |

CREED

| ❑ 3201 [M] | I Have a Dream | 1968 | 25.00 |

DOOTO

| ❑ DTL-831 [M] | Martin Luther King at Zion Hill | 1962 | 30.00 |
| ❑ DTL-841 [B] | The American Dream | 1968 | 25.00 |

GORDY

❑ G-929	...Free at Last	1968	30.00
— Original with gatefold cover			
❑ G-908 [M]	The Great March on Washington	1963	40.00
— "Gordy" in script at top of label			
❑ G-908 [M]	The Great March on Washington	1968	18.00
— Later pressings			
❑ G-906 [M]	The Great March to Freedom	1963	40.00
— "Gordy" in script at top of label			
❑ G-906 [M]	The Great March to Freedom	1968	18.00
— Later pressings			

MERCURY

| ❑ SR-61170 | In Search of Freedom | 1968 | 25.00 |

MR. MAESTRO

| ❑ 1000 [M] | The March on Washington | 1963 | 30.00 |

SUNSET

| ❑ 21033 | The Struggle for Freedom | 1968 | 18.00 |

UNART

| ❑ S21033 | In the Struggle for Freedom and Human Dignity | 1968 | 25.00 |

KING, SANDRA

AUDIOPHILE

| ❑ AP-197 | Songs by Vernon Duke | 1984 | 15.00 |

KING, TEDDI, AND DAVE McKENNA

INNER CITY

| ❑ IC-1044 | This Is New | 1977 | 25.00 |

KING, TEDDI

AUDIOPHILE

| ❑ AP-117 | Lovers and Losers | 1976 | 18.00 |
| ❑ AP-150 | Someone to Light Up Your Life | 1979 | 15.00 |

CORAL

| ❑ CRL57278 [M] | All the King's Songs | 1959 | 60.00 |
| ❑ CRL757278 [S] | All the King's Songs | 1959 | 80.00 |

RCA VICTOR

❑ LPM-1454 [M]	A Girl and Her Songs	1957	80.00
❑ LPM-1147 [M]	Bidin' My Time	1956	80.00
❑ LPM-1313 [M]	To You from Teddi King	1957	100.00

STORYVILLE

❑ STLP-903 [M]	Now In Vogue	1956	150.00
❑ STLP-302 [10]	'Round Midnight	1954	250.00
❑ STLP-314 [10]	Storyville Presents Teddi King	1954	200.00

KING, WAYNE

DECCA

| ❑ DL4438 [M] | Have Yourself a Merry Little Christmas | 1963 | 18.00 |
| ❑ DL74438 [S] | Have Yourself a Merry Little Christmas | 1963 | 16.00 |

KING BISCUIT BOY

EPIC

| ❑ KE32891 | King Biscuit Boy | 1974 | 15.00 |

PARAMOUNT

❑ PAS-6023 [B]	Gooduns	1972	10.00
❑ PAS-5030	Official Music	1970	18.00
— As "King Biscuit Boy with Crowbar			

KING CRIMSON

ATLANTIC

Number	Title	Yr	NM
❑ 8245 [M]	In the Court of the Crimson King – An Observation by King Crimson	1969	150.00
—Mono is white label promo only; comes in stereo cover with "DJ Copy Monaural" sticker on front			
❑ SD19155	In the Court of the Crimson King – An Observation by King Crimson	1978	15.00
—Reissue of Atlantic 8245			
❑ SD8245 [B]	In the Court of the Crimson King – An Observation by King Crimson	1969	35.00
❑ SD8266 [B]	In the Wake of Poseidon	1970	30.00
❑ SD7212 [B]	Islands	1972	30.00
❑ SD7263 [B]	Larks' Tongues in Aspic	1973	30.00
❑ SD8278 [B]	Lizard	1971	30.00
❑ SD18110 [B]	Red	1974	30.00
❑ SD7298 [B]	Starless and Bible Black	1974	30.00
❑ SD18136 [B]	USA	1975	25.00

EDITIONS EG

Number	Title	Yr	NM
❑ EGKC-1	In the Court of the Crimson King – An Observation by King Crimson	1985	15.00
—Reissue of Atlantic 19155			
❑ EGKC-2	In the Wake of Poseidon	1985	15.00
—Reissue of Atlantic 8266			
❑ EGKC-4	Islands	1985	15.00
—Reissue of Atlantic 7212			
❑ EGKC-6	Lark's Tongue in Aspic	1985	15.00
—Reissue of Atlantic 7263			
❑ EGKC-3	Lizard	1985	15.00
—Reissue of Atlantic 8278			
❑ EGKC-8	Red	1985	15.00
—Reissue of Atlantic 18110			
❑ EGKC-7	Starless and Bible Black	1985	15.00
—Reissue of Atlantic 7298			
❑ EGKC-10 [B]	The Young Person's Guide to King Crimson	1985	40.00
❑ EGKC-9	USA	1985	15.00
—Reissue of Atlantic 18135			

MOBILE FIDELITY

Number	Title	Yr	NM
❑ 1-075	In the Court of the Crimson King – An Observation by King Crimson	1981	120.00
—Audiophile vinyl			

WARNER BROS.

Number	Title	Yr	NM
❑ 23692	Beat	1982	12.00
❑ BSK3629	Discipline	1981	12.00
❑ WBMS-119 [DJ]	The Return of King Crimson	1981	35.00
—Promo-only interview and music show			
❑ 25071	Three of a Perfect Pair	1984	12.00

KING CURTIS

ATCO

Number	Title	Yr	NM
❑ SD 33-385	Everybody's Talkin'	1972	25.00
❑ SD 33-338	Get Ready	1970	25.00
❑ 33-113 [M]	Have Tenor Sax, Will Blow	1959	40.00
❑ SD 33-113 [S]	Have Tenor Sax, Will Blow	1959	60.00
❑ SD 33-293	Instant Groove	1969	25.00
❑ 33-231 [M]	King Size Soul	1967	30.00
❑ SD 33-231 [S]	King Size Soul	1967	25.00
❑ SD 33-359	Live at Fillmore West	1971	25.00
❑ 33-198 [M]	Live at Small's Paradise	1966	25.00
❑ SD 33-198 [S]	Live at Small's Paradise	1966	30.00
❑ 33-247 [M]	Sweet Soul	1968	30.00
❑ SD 33-247 [S]	Sweet Soul	1968	25.00
❑ 33-189 [M]	That Lovin' Feeling	1966	25.00
❑ SD 33-189 [S]	That Lovin' Feeling	1966	30.00
❑ SD 33-266	The Best of King Curtis	1968	25.00
❑ 33-211 [M]	The Great Memphis Hits	1967	25.00
❑ SD 33-211 [S]	The Great Memphis Hits	1967	30.00

ATLANTIC

Number	Title	Yr	NM
❑ SD1637	Blues Montreux	1973	15.00

CAPITOL

Number	Title	Yr	NM
❑ T1756 [M]	Country Soul	1963	30.00
❑ ST1756 [S]	Country Soul	1963	40.00
❑ T2341 [M]	King Curtis Plays the Hits Made Famous by Sam Cooke	1965	30.00
❑ ST2341 [S]	King Curtis Plays the Hits Made Famous by Sam Cooke	1965	30.00
❑ T2095 [M]	Soul Serenade	1964	30.00
❑ ST2095 [S]	Soul Serenade	1964	30.00
❑ SM-11798	Soul Serenade	1978	12.00
—Reissue			
❑ T2858 [M]	The Best of King Curtis	1968	50.00
—Red and white "Starline" label; may be promo only			
❑ SM-11963	The Best of King Curtis	1979	12.00
—Reissue			
❑ ST2858 [S]	The Best of King Curtis	1968	30.00

CLARION

Number	Title	Yr	NM
❑ 615 [M]	The Great "K" Curtis	1966	25.00
❑ SD615 [S]	The Great "K" Curtis	1966	30.00

COLLECTABLES

Number	Title	Yr	NM
❑ COL-5156	Golden Classics: Enjoy… The Best of King Curtis	198?	12.00
❑ COL-5119	Soul Twist	198?	12.00

ENJOY

Number	Title	Yr	NM
❑ ENLP-2001 [M]	Soul Twist	1962	50.00

EVEREST

Number	Title	Yr	NM
❑ LPBR-5121 [M]	Azure	1961	50.00
❑ SDBR-1121 [S]	Azure	1961	75.00

FANTASY

Number	Title	Yr	NM
❑ OJC-198	The New Scene of King Curtis	1985	12.00
—Reissue of New Jazz 8237			
❑ OBC-512	Trouble in Mind	1988	12.00
—Reissue of Tru-Sound 15001			

NEW JAZZ

Number	Title	Yr	NM
❑ NJLP-8237 [M]	The New Scene of King Curtis	1960	60.00
—Purple label			
❑ NJLP-8237 [M]	The New Scene of King Curtis	1965	30.00
—Blue label with trident logo on right			

PRESTIGE

Number	Title	Yr	NM
❑ 24033	Jazz Groove	198?	18.00
❑ PRST-7789	King Soul	1970	18.00
❑ PRLP-7222 [M]	Soul Meeting	1962	50.00
❑ PRST-7222 [S]	Soul Meeting	1962	75.00
❑ PRST-7833	Soul Meeting	1971	18.00
—Reissue of 7222			
❑ PRST-7709	The Best of King Curtis	1969	18.00
❑ PRST-7775	The Best of King Curtis – One More Time	1970	18.00

RCA CAMDEN

Number	Title	Yr	NM
❑ CAS-2242	Sax in Motion	1968	18.00

RCA VICTOR

Number	Title	Yr	NM
❑ LPM-2494 [M]	Arthur Murray's Music for Dancing: The Twist!	1962	30.00
❑ LSP-2494 [S]	Arthur Murray's Music for Dancing: The Twist!	1962	30.00

TRU-SOUND

Number	Title	Yr	NM
❑ TS-15009 [M]	Doin' the Dixie Twist	1962	50.00
❑ TS-15008 [M]	It's Party Time	1962	50.00
❑ TS-15001 [M]	Trouble in Mind	1961	50.00

KING FAMILY, THE

CAPITOL

Number	Title	Yr	NM
❑ T2352 [M]	Love at Home	1965	18.00
❑ DT2352 [R]	Love at Home	1965	15.00

FANNY FARMER/FLEETWOOD

Number	Title	Yr	NM
❑ FCLP3039	Fanny Farmer Presents The King Family Christmas Album	196?	15.00

HARMONY

Number	Title	Yr	NM
❑ HS11293	The Wonderful King Family	196?	12.00

WARNER BROS.

Number	Title	Yr	NM
❑ W1627 [M]	Christmas with the King Family	1965	15.00
❑ WS1627 [S]	Christmas with the King Family	1965	18.00
❑ W1633 [M]	Sunday with the King Family	1966	15.00
❑ WS1633 [S]	Sunday with the King Family	1966	18.00
❑ W1613 [M]	The King Family Album	1965	15.00
❑ WS1613 [S]	The King Family Album	1965	18.00
❑ W1601 [M]	The King Family Show!	1965	15.00
❑ WS1601 [S]	The King Family Show!	1965	18.00

KING HARVEST

A&M

Number	Title	Yr	NM
❑ SP-4540	King Harvest	1975	12.00

PERCEPTION

Number	Title	Yr	NM
❑ 36	Dancing in the Moonlight	1973	15.00

KING PINS, THE (1)

KING

Number	Title	Yr	NM
❑ 865 [M]	It Won't Be This Way Always	1963	300.00

KING PLEASURE

EVEREST ARCHIVE OF FOLK AND JAZZ

Number	Title	Yr	NM
❑ FS-262 [M]	King Pleasure	197?	15.00

FANTASY

Number	Title	Yr	NM
❑ OJC-1771 [S]	Golden Days	1991	18.00

HIFI

Number	Title	Yr	NM
❑ J-425 [M]	Golden Days	1960	40.00
❑ JS-425 [S]	Golden Days	1960	50.00

PRESTIGE

Number	Title	Yr	NM
❑ PRLP-208 [10]	King Pleasure Sings	1955	500.00
❑ PRLP-7586	Original Moody's Mood	1968	30.00
❑ PR-24017	The Source	1972	30.00

SOLID STATE

Number	Title	Yr	NM
❑ SS-18021 [S]	Mr. Jazz	1968	30.00
—Reissue of United Artists 15031			

UNITED ARTISTS

Number	Title	Yr	NM
❑ UAS-5634 [S]	Moody's Mood for Love	1972	25.00
❑ UAJ-14031 [M]	Mr. Jazz	1962	40.00
❑ UAJS-15031 [S]	Mr. Jazz	1962	50.00

KING PLEASURE/ANNIE ROSS

FANTASY

Number	Title	Yr	NM
❑ OJC-217 [M]	King Pleasure Sings/Annie Ross Sings	198?	15.00

PRESTIGE

Number	Title	Yr	NM
❑ PRLP-7128 [M]	King Pleasure Sings/Annie Ross Sings	1957	150.00
—Yellow label, W. 50th Street address on label			
❑ PRLP-7128 [M]	King Pleasure Sings/Annie Ross Sings	1958	80.00
—Yellow label, Bergenfield, N.J. address on label			
❑ PRLP-7128 [M]	King Pleasure Sings/Annie Ross Sings	1965	40.00
—Blue label, trident logo at right			

KING SISTERS, THE

CAPITOL

Number	Title	Yr	NM
❑ T808 [M]	Aloha	1957	30.00
—Turquoise or gray label			
❑ T919 [M]	Imagination	1958	30.00
—Turquoise or gray label			
❑ T1205 [M]	Warm and Wonderful	1959	25.00
—Black colorband label, logo at left			
❑ ST1205 [S]	Warm and Wonderful	1959	30.00
—Black colorband label, logo at left			

KINGBEES, THE

RSO

Number	Title	Yr	NM
❑ RS1-3097	The Big Rock	1981	18.00
❑ RS1-3075	The Kingbees	1980	18.00

KINGDOM

SPECIALTY

Number	Title	Yr	NM
❑ SPS-2135	Kingdom	1970	60.00

KINGFISH

ROUND

Number	Title	Yr	NM
❑ RX-108	Kingfish	1976	16.00

KINGS, THE

ELEKTRA

Number	Title	Yr	NM
❑ 5E-543	Amazon Beach	1981	15.00
❑ 6E-277	The Kings Are Here	1980	30.00

KING'S MEN FIVE, THE

CUCA

Number	Title	Yr	NM
❑ 1130 [M]	The King's Men Five	1965	25.00

KING'S ROAD

PICKWICK

Number	Title	Yr	NM
❑ SPC-3537	A Million or More! '75	1975	12.00
❑ SPC-3547	A Million or More! '75, Vol. 2	1975	12.00
❑ SPC-3513	A Million or More in '74	1975	12.00
❑ SPC-3560	A Million or More in '76	1976	12.00
❑ SPC-3516	Elton John Rock Hits	197?	12.00
❑ SPC-3509	Lucy in the Sky with Diamonds	197?	12.00
❑ SPC-3135	Plays Today's Pops	197?	12.00
❑ SPC-3507	Song Hits of Neil Diamond	1976	12.00
❑ SPC-3904	Super Hits, Vol. 3	197?	12.00
❑ SPC-3905	Super Hits, Vol. 4	197?	12.00
❑ SPC-3906	Super Hits, Vol. 5	197?	12.00
❑ SPC-3907	Super Hits, Vol. 6	197?	12.00
❑ SPC-3908	Super Hits, Vol. 7	197?	12.00
❑ SPC-3909	Super Hits, Vol. 8	197?	12.00
❑ SPC-3910	Super Hits, Vol. 9	197?	12.00
❑ PTP-2062	The Beatles 1962-1970	1973	18.00
❑ SPC-3506	The Hits of Simon and Garfunkel	1976	12.00
❑ SPC-3239	The Long and Winding Road	197?	12.00
❑ SPC-3557	The Neil Sedaka Songbook	197?	12.00
❑ SPC-3551	Today's T.V. Hits	1976	12.00
❑ SPC-3355	Watkins Glen	1973	12.00

KINGSLEY, GERSHON

AUDIO FIDELITY

Number	Title	Yr	NM
❑ AFSD-6222	Music to Moog By	1969	40.00

KINGSMEN, THE (1)

RHINO

Number	Title	Yr	NM
❑ RNLP-126	The Best of the Kingsmen	1985	12.00

SCEPTER

Number	Title	Yr	NM
❑ CTN-18002	The Best of the Kingsmen	1972	12.00

WAND

Number	Title	Yr	NM
❑ WDM-674 [M]	15 Great Hits	1966	25.00
❑ WDS-674 [P]	15 Great Hits	1966	30.00
❑ WDM-662 [M]	The Kingsmen, Volume 3	1965	30.00
❑ WDS-662 [S]	The Kingsmen, Volume 3	1965	30.00
❑ WDM-659 [M]	The Kingsmen, Volume II	1964	30.00
—With "Death of an Angel			
❑ WDM-659 [M]	The Kingsmen, Volume II	1964	40.00
—Without "Death of an Angel" (replaced by untitled instrumental)			
❑ WDS-659 [S]	The Kingsmen, Volume II	1964	40.00
—With "Death of an Angel			
❑ WDS-659 [S]	The Kingsmen, Volume II	1964	50.00
—Without "Death of an Angel" (replaced by untitled instrumental)			
❑ WDM-657 [M]	The Kingsmen In Person	1964	30.00
❑ WDS-657 [P]	The Kingsmen In Person	1964	40.00
❑ WDM-670 [M]	The Kingsmen On Campus	1965	30.00
❑ WDS-670 [S]	The Kingsmen On Campus	1965	30.00

Number	Title	Yr	NM
❑ WDM-681 [M]	The Kingsmen's Greatest Hits	1967	18.00
❑ WDS-681 [S]	The Kingsmen's Greatest Hits	1967	25.00
❑ WDM-675 [M]	Up and Away	1966	25.00
❑ WDS-675 [S]	Up and Away	1966	30.00
❑ ST-91011 [S]	Up and Away	1966	30.00
—Capitol Record Club edition			

KINGSTON TRIO, THE

CAPITOL

Number	Title	Yr	NM
❑ T2081 [M]	Back in Town	1964	18.00
❑ ST2081 [S]	Back in Town	1964	25.00
❑ T1642 [M]	Close-Up	1961	30.00
—Black label with colorband, Capitol logo at left			
❑ T1642 [M]	Close-Up	1962	18.00
—Black label with colorband, Capitol logo at top			
❑ ST1642 [S]	Close-Up	1961	40.00
—Black label with colorband, Capitol logo at left			
❑ ST1642 [S]	Close-Up	1962	25.00
—Black label with colorband, Capitol logo at top			
❑ T1658 [M]	College Concert	1962	25.00
❑ ST1658 [S]	College Concert	1962	30.00
❑ T1612 [M]	Encores	1961	30.00
—Black label with colorband, Capitol logo at left			
❑ T1612 [M]	Encores	1962	18.00
—Black label with colorband, Capitol logo at top			
❑ DT1612 [R]	Encores	1961	25.00
—Black label with colorband, Capitol logo at left			
❑ DT1612 [R]	Encores	1962	12.00
—Black label with colorband, Capitol logo at top			
❑ T1107 [M]	From the Hungry I	1959	40.00
—Black label with colorband, Capitol logo at left			
❑ T1107 [M]	From the Hungry I	1962	25.00
—Black label with colorband, Capitol logo at top			
❑ M-11968	From the Hungry I	1979	12.00
❑ T1564 [M]	Goin' Places	1961	30.00
—Black label with colorband, Capitol logo at left			
❑ T1564 [M]	Goin' Places	1962	18.00
—Black label with colorband, Capitol logo at top			
❑ ST1564 [S]	Goin' Places	1961	40.00
—Black label with colorband, Capitol logo at left			
❑ ST1564 [S]	Goin' Places	1962	25.00
—Black label with colorband, Capitol logo at top			
❑ T1258 [M]	Here We Go Again!	1959	30.00
—Black label with colorband, Capitol logo at left			
❑ T1258 [M]	Here We Go Again!	1962	18.00
—Black label with colorband, Capitol logo at top			
❑ ST1258 [S]	Here We Go Again!	1959	40.00
—Black label with colorband, Capitol logo at left			
❑ ST1258 [S]	Here We Go Again!	1962	25.00
—Black label with colorband, Capitol logo at top			
❑ T1474 [M]	Make Way!	1961	30.00
—Black label with colorband, Capitol logo at left			
❑ T1474 [M]	Make Way!	1962	18.00
—Black label with colorband, Capitol logo at top			
❑ ST1474 [S]	Make Way!	1961	40.00
—Black label with colorband, Capitol logo at left			
❑ ST1474 [S]	Make Way!	1962	25.00
—Black label with colorband, Capitol logo at top			
❑ T1809 [M]	New Frontier	1962	25.00
❑ ST1809 [S]	New Frontier	1962	30.00
❑ SN-16186	Scarlet Ribbons	1981	10.00
❑ KAO2005 [M]	Sing a Song with the Kingston Trio	1963	30.00
❑ SKAO2005 [S]	Sing a Song with the Kingston Trio	1963	30.00
❑ T1352 [M]	Sold Out	1960	30.00
—Black label with colorband, Capitol logo at left			
❑ T1352 [M]	Sold Out	1962	18.00
—Black label with colorband, Capitol logo at top			
❑ ST1352 [S]	Sold Out	1960	40.00
—Black label with colorband, Capitol logo at left			
❑ ST1352 [S]	Sold Out	1962	25.00
—Black label with colorband, Capitol logo at top			
❑ T1747 [M]	Something Special	1962	25.00
❑ ST1747 [S]	Something Special	1962	30.00
❑ ST1183 [S]	Stereo Concert	1959	50.00
—Black label with colorband, Capitol logo at left			
❑ ST1183 [S]	Stereo Concert	1962	30.00
—Black label with colorband, Capitol logo at top			
❑ T1407 [M]	String Along	1960	30.00
—Black label with colorband, Capitol logo at left			
❑ T1407 [M]	String Along	1962	18.00
—Black label with colorband, Capitol logo at top			
❑ ST1407 [S]	String Along	1960	40.00
—Black label with colorband, Capitol logo at left			
❑ ST1407 [S]	String Along	1962	25.00
—Black label with colorband, Capitol logo at top			
❑ T1935 [M]	Sunny Side!	1963	25.00
❑ ST1935 [S]	Sunny Side!	1963	30.00
❑ T1705 [M]	The Best of the Kingston Trio	1962	25.00
❑ ST1705 [P]	The Best of the Kingston Trio	1962	25.00
❑ SM-1705	The Best of the Kingston Trio	197?	12.00
❑ SN-16183	The Best of the Kingston Trio	1981	10.00
—Budget-line reissue			
❑ T2280 [M]	The Best of the Kingston Trio, Volume 2	1965	18.00
❑ ST2280 [S]	The Best of the Kingston Trio, Volume 2	1965	25.00
❑ SM-2280	The Best of the Kingston Trio, Volume 2	197?	12.00
❑ SN-16184	The Best of the Kingston Trio, Volume 2	1981	10.00
—Budget-line reissue			
❑ T2614 [M]	The Best of the Kingston Trio, Volume 3	1966	18.00
❑ ST2614 [S]	The Best of the Kingston Trio, Volume 3	1966	25.00
❑ SM-2614	The Best of the Kingston Trio, Volume 3	197?	12.00
❑ TCL2180 [M]	The Folk Era	1964	40.00
—Box set with booklet			
❑ STCL2180 [S]	The Folk Era	1964	50.00
—Box set with booklet			
❑ T1871 [M]	The Kingston Trio #16	1963	25.00
❑ ST1871 [S]	The Kingston Trio #16	1963	30.00
❑ T996 [M]	The Kingston Trio	1958	50.00
—Turquoise label			
❑ T996 [M]	The Kingston Trio	1958	40.00
—Black label with colorband, Capitol logo at left			
❑ T996 [M]	The Kingston Trio	1962	25.00
—Black label with colorband, Capitol logo at top			
❑ M-11577	The Kingston Trio	1976	12.00
❑ DT996 [R]	The Kingston Trio	196?	15.00
❑ T1199 [M]	The Kingston Trio at Large	1959	30.00
—Black label with colorband, Capitol logo at left, "Long Playing High-Fidelity			
❑ T1199 [M]	The Kingston Trio at Large	1962	18.00
—Black label with colorband, Capitol logo at top			
❑ ST1199 [S]	The Kingston Trio at Large	1959	40.00
—Black label with colorband, Capitol logo at left			
❑ ST1199 [S]	The Kingston Trio at Large	1962	25.00
—Black label with colorband, Capitol logo at top			
❑ T1199 [M]	The Kingston Trio at Large	1960	30.00
—Black label with colorband, Capitol logo at left, white line replaces "Long Playing High-Fidelity			
❑ T1446 [M]	The Last Month of the Year	1960	30.00
❑ ST1446 [S]	The Last Month of the Year	1960	40.00
—Same as above, but in stereo			
❑ T2011 [M]	Time to Think	1964	18.00
❑ ST2011 [S]	Time to Think	1964	25.00
❑ N-16185	Tom Dooley	1981	10.00
❑ STBB-513	Tom Dooley/Scarlet Ribbons	1970	25.00

DECCA

Number	Title	Yr	NM
❑ DL4758 [M]	Children of the Morning	1966	30.00
❑ DL74758 [S]	Children of the Morning	1966	30.00
❑ DL4694 [M]	Somethin' Else	1965	30.00
❑ DL74694 [S]	Somethin' Else	1965	30.00
❑ DL4656 [M]	Stay Awhile	1965	30.00
❑ DL74656 [S]	Stay Awhile	1965	30.00
❑ DL4613 [M]	The Kingston Trio (Nick-Bob-John)	1965	30.00
❑ DL74613 [S]	The Kingston Trio (Nick-Bob-John)	1965	30.00

FOLK ERA

Number	Title	Yr	NM
❑ FE-2036	Hidden Treasures	198?	12.00
❑ FE-2001	Rediscover the Kingston Trio	198?	12.00

NAUTILUS

Number	Title	Yr	NM
❑ NR-2	Aspen Gold	1979	40.00
—Audiophile vinyl			

PAIR

Number	Title	Yr	NM
❑ PDL2-1067	Early American Heroes	1986	15.00

PICKWICK

Number	Title	Yr	NM
❑ SPC-3260	Tom Dooley	196?	15.00

TETRAGRAMMATON

Number	Title	Yr	NM
❑ T-5101	Once Upon a Time	1969	30.00

XERES

Number	Title	Yr	NM
❑ 1-10001	25 Years Non-Stop	1982	15.00

KINKS, THE

4 MEN WITH BEARDS

Number	Title	Yr	NM
❑ 4M801LP [B]	Kinda Kinks		25.00

ARISTA

Number	Title	Yr	NM
❑ SP-85 [EP]	A Fistful of Kinks	1980	30.00
—Promo-only four-song sampler from "One for the Road			
❑ AL118428	Come Dancing with the Kinks	1986	15.00
❑ AL9567	Give the People What They Want	1981	12.00
❑ ALB68328	Give the People What They Want	1985	10.00
—Budget-line reissue			
❑ AB4240	Low Budget	1979	12.00
❑ ALB68300	Low Budget	1985	10.00
—Budget-line reissue			
❑ SP-69 [DJ]	Low Budget Radio Interview	1979	30.00
—Promo-only radio show featuring Ray Davies			
❑ AL4167 [DJ]	Misfits	1978	30.00
—White label promo			
❑ AL4167 [B]	Misfits	1978	12.00
❑ ALB68377	Misfits	1985	10.00
—Budget-line reissue			
❑ AL138041	One for the Road	1983	12.00
—Reissue of 8609			
❑ A2L8401	One for the Road	1980	18.00
—Original edition has this number			
❑ A2L8609	One for the Road	198?	15.00
—Second edition of 8401			
❑ AL4106 [DJ]	Sleepwalker	1977	30.00
—White label promo			
❑ AL4106 [B]	Sleepwalker	1977	12.00
❑ ALB68375	Sleepwalker	1985	10.00
—Budget-line reissue			
❑ AL 8-8018	State of Confusion	1983	12.00
❑ AL8264	Word of Mouth	1984	12.00

COMPLEAT

Number	Title	Yr	NM
❑ CPL2-2003	20th Anniversary Edition	1984	15.00
❑ CPL2-2001	A Compleat Collection	1984	15.00

MCA

Number	Title	Yr	NM
❑ L33-17281 [DJ]	A Look at "Think Visual	1987	30.00
—Promo only in white jacket			
❑ 42107	Live: The Road	1988	12.00
❑ 5822	Think Visual	1987	12.00
❑ 6337	UK Jive	1989	15.00

MOBILE FIDELITY

Number	Title	Yr	NM
❑ 1-070	Misfits	1981	40.00
—Audiophile vinyl			

PICKWICK

Number	Title	Yr	NM
❑ ACL-7072	Preservation Act 1	197?	15.00
—Reissue of RCA Victor LPL1-5002			

PYE

Number	Title	Yr	NM
❑ 505	The Kinks	1975	15.00
❑ 509	The Kinks, Vol. 2	1976	15.00

RCA VICTOR

Number	Title	Yr	NM
❑ APL1-1743	Celluloid Heroes (The Kinks' Greatest)	1976	12.00
❑ AYL1-3869	Celluloid Heroes (The Kinks' Greatest)	1981	10.00
—Budget-line reissue			
❑ VPS-6065	Everybody's in Showbiz	1972	25.00
—Orange label			
❑ VPS-6065	Everybody's in Showbiz	1975	15.00
—Brown label			
❑ LSP-4644	Muswell Hillbillies	1971	30.00
❑ AYL1-4558	Muswell Hillbillies	1982	10.00
—Budget-line reissue			
❑ LPL1-5002	Preservation Act 1	1973	18.00
❑ CPL2-5040	Preservation Act 2	1974	25.00
❑ LPL1-5102	Schoolboys in Disgrace	1975	12.00
❑ AYL1-3749	Schoolboys in Disgrace	1980	10.00
—Budget-line reissue			
❑ APL1-3520	Second Time Around	1980	12.00
❑ AYL1-4719	Second Time Around	1983	10.00
—Budget-line reissue			
❑ LPL1-5081	Soap Opera	1975	18.00
—Orange label			
❑ LPL1-5081	Soap Opera	1975	12.00
—Brown label			
❑ AYL1-3750	Soap Opera	1980	10.00
—Budget-line reissue			

REPRISE

Number	Title	Yr	NM
❑ SMAS-93034	Arthur (Or The Decline and Fall of the British Empire)	1970	40.00
—Capitol Record Club edition			
❑ RS-6366	Arthur (Or The Decline and Fall of the British Empire)	1969	30.00
—Two-tone orange label with "r: and "W7" logos with steamboat			
❑ RS-6366	Arthur (Or The Decline and Fall of the British Empire)	1971	12.00
—Orange label with "r:" and steamboat at top			
❑ R-6228 [M]	Face to Face	1967	50.00
❑ RS-6228 [P]	Face to Face	1967	30.00
—Pink, gold and green label			
❑ RS-6228 [P]	Face to Face	1971	12.00
—Orange label with "r:" and steamboat at top			
❑ PRO328 [P]	God Save the Kinks	1969	600.00
—Mail-order box with decal, postcard, bag of grass, two pins, letter, Kinks consumer guide and "Then Now and In Between" LP. Price is for complete package.			
❑ R-6173 [M]	Kinda Kinks	1965	200.00
—White label promo			
❑ R-6173 [M]	Kinda Kinks	1965	50.00
❑ RS-6173 [R]	Kinda Kinks	1965	30.00
❑ R-6184 [M]	Kinks Kinkdom	1965	200.00
—White label promo			
❑ R-6184 [M]	Kinks Kinkdom	1965	60.00
❑ RS-6184 [R]	Kinks Kinkdom	1965	30.00
❑ R-6158 [M]	Kinks-Size	1965	200.00
—White label promo			
❑ R-6158 [M]	Kinks-Size	1965	50.00
❑ RS-6158 [R]	Kinks-Size	1965	30.00
❑ RS-6423	Lola Versus Powerman and the Moneygoround, Part One	1970	18.00
—Original pressings have blue printing on a white cover			
❑ RS-6423	Lola Versus Powerman and the Moneygoround, Part One	1971	12.00
—Later pressings have black printing on a white cover			
❑ R-6279 [M]	Something Else by the Kinks	1968	300.00
—White label promo; no stock copies were issued in mono			
❑ RS-6279 [S]	Something Else by the Kinks	1968	30.00
—Pink, gold and green label			
❑ RS-6279 [S]	Something Else by the Kinks	1968	25.00

Number	Title	Yr	NM
— Two-tone orange label with "r: and "W7" logos with steamboat			
❑ RS-6279 [S]	Something Else by the Kinks	1971	12.00
— Orange label with "r:" and steamboat at top			
❑ MS-2127	The Great Lost Kinks Album	1973	50.00
❑ R-6197 [M]	The Kink Kontroversy	1966	200.00
— White label promo			
❑ R-6197 [M]	The Kink Kontroversy	1966	60.00
❑ RS-6197 [R]	The Kink Kontroversy	1966	30.00
❑ 2XS-6454	The Kink Kronicles	1972	18.00
❑ RS-6327	The Kinks Are the Village Green Preservation Society	1969	30.00
— Two-tone orange label with "r: and "W7" logos with steamboat			
❑ RS-6327	The Kinks Are the Village Green Preservation Society	1971	12.00
— Orange label with "r:" and steamboat at top			
❑ R-6217 [M]	The Kinks Greatest Hits!	1966	40.00
❑ RS-6217 [R]	The Kinks Greatest Hits!	1966	30.00
— Pink, gold and green label			
❑ RS-6217 [R]	The Kinks Greatest Hits!	1971	12.00
— Orange label with "r:" and steamboat at top			
❑ R-6260 [M]	The Live Kinks	1967	40.00
❑ RS-6260 [S]	The Live Kinks	1967	30.00
— Pink, gold and green label			
❑ RS-6260 [S]	The Live Kinks	1971	12.00
— Orange label with "r:" and steamboat at top			
❑ PRO328 [P]	Then Now and In Between	1969	100.00
— Album that came with above box is sometimes found by itself without all the other goodies.			
❑ R-6143 [M]	You Really Got Me	1965	400.00
— White label promo			
❑ R-6143 [M]	You Really Got Me	1965	60.00
❑ RS-6143 [P]	You Really Got Me	1965	80.00
— Pink, gold and green label			
❑ RS-6143 [P]	You Really Got Me	1971	12.00
— Orange label with "r:" and steamboat at top			

RHINO

Number	Title	Yr	NM
❑ R170316	Kinda Kinks	1988	15.00
❑ R170318	Kinks Kinkdom	1988	15.00
❑ R170317	Kinks-Size	1988	15.00
❑ R170086	The Kinks Greatest Hits! Vol. 1	1989	15.00
❑ R170315	You Really Got Me	1988	15.00

KINSEY, TONY

LONDON

Number	Title	Yr	NM
❑ LL1672 [M]	Kinsey Come On	1957	50.00

KIRBY, JOHN

CIRCLE

Number	Title	Yr	NM
❑ 14	John Kirby and His Orchestra 1941	198?	12.00
❑ 64	John Kirby and His Orchestra 1941-42	198?	12.00

CLASSIC JAZZ

Number	Title	Yr	NM
❑ 22	The Biggest Little Band in the Land	197?	12.00

COLUMBIA

Number	Title	Yr	NM
❑ CG33557	Boss of the Bass	1975	18.00
❑ GL502 [M]	John Kirby and His Orchestra	1951	50.00
— Black label, silver print			
❑ CL502 [M]	John Kirby and His Orchestra	1953	40.00
— Maroon label, gold print			

COLUMBIA MASTERWORKS

Number	Title	Yr	NM
❑ ML4801 [10]	John Kirby and His Orchestra	195?	60.00

EPITAPH

Number	Title	Yr	NM
❑ E-4004	John Kirby 1908-1952	1975	15.00

HARMONY

Number	Title	Yr	NM
❑ HL7124 [M]	Intimate Swing	1958	25.00

TRIP

Number	Title	Yr	NM
❑ 5802	The Biggest Little Band	197?	12.00

KIRK, ANDY

CORAL

Number	Title	Yr	NM
❑ CRL56019 [10]	Andy Kirk Souvenir Album -- Vol. 1	1951	100.00

DECCA

Number	Title	Yr	NM
❑ DL79232	Instrumentally	1968	18.00

MAINSTREAM

Number	Title	Yr	NM
❑ MRL-399	Mar-36	1975	15.00

MCA

Number	Title	Yr	NM
❑ 1308	Instrumentally Speaking	198?	12.00
❑ 4105	The Best of Andy Kirk and the Clouds of Joy	197?	15.00
❑ 1343	The Lady Who Swings the Band	198?	12.00

RCA VICTOR

Number	Title	Yr	NM
❑ LPM-1302 [M]	A Mellow Bit of Rhythm	1956	40.00

KIRK, RAHSAAN ROLAND

ABC

Number	Title	Yr	NM
❑ AA-1106	Cry	1978	15.00

ARGO

Number	Title	Yr	NM
❑ LP-669 [M]	Introducing Roland Kirk	1960	60.00
❑ LPS-669 [S]	Introducing Roland Kirk	1960	80.00

ATLANTIC

Number	Title	Yr	NM
❑ SD1630	A Meeting of the Times	1973	18.00
— With Al Hibbler			
❑ SD1601	Blacknuss	1972	18.00
❑ SD 2-907	Bright Moments	1974	25.00
❑ 3007 [M]	Here Comes the Whistle Man	1967	30.00
❑ SD3007 [S]	Here Comes the Whistle Man	1967	18.00
❑ SD1518	Left and Right	1969	18.00
❑ SD1578	Natural Black Inventions	1971	18.00
❑ SD1686	Other Folks' Music	1976	15.00
❑ SD1640	Prepare Thyself to Deal with a Miracle	1974	18.00
❑ SD1575	Rahsaan Rahsaan	1970	18.00
❑ SD 2-303	The Art of Rahsaan Roland Kirk	1973	25.00
❑ SD1592	The Best of Rahsaan Roland Kirk	1972	18.00
❑ SD1674	The Case of the 3-Sided Dream in Audio Color	1975	18.00
❑ 1502 [M]	The Inflated Tear	1968	30.00
❑ SD1502 [S]	The Inflated Tear	1968	18.00
❑ 90045	The Inflated Tear	1983	12.00
❑ SD 2-1003	Vibration	1978	18.00
❑ SD1534	Volunteered Slavery	1969	18.00

BETHLEHEM

Number	Title	Yr	NM
❑ BCP-6016	Early Roots	197?	25.00
— Reissue of 6064, distributed by RCA Victor			
❑ BCP-6064 [M]	Third Dimension	1962	250.00

EMARCY

Number	Title	Yr	NM
❑ EMS-2-411	Kirk's Works	1975	25.00

FANTASY

Number	Title	Yr	NM
❑ OJC-459	Kirk's Work	1990	18.00

KING

Number	Title	Yr	NM
❑ 539 [M]	Triple Threat	1956	400.00

LIMELIGHT

Number	Title	Yr	NM
❑ LM-82008 [M]	I Talk with the Spirits	1964	60.00
❑ LS-86008 [S]	I Talk with the Spirits	1964	80.00
— Reproductions exist			
❑ LM-82027 [M]	Rip, Rig and Panic	1965	50.00
❑ LS-86027 [S]	Rip, Rig and Panic	1965	60.00
❑ LM-82033 [M]	Slightly Latin	1966	50.00
❑ LS-86033 [S]	Slightly Latin	1966	60.00

MERCURY

Number	Title	Yr	NM
❑ MG-20748 [M]	Domino	1962	30.00
❑ SR-60748 [S]	Domino	1962	40.00
❑ MG-20939 [M]	Gifts and Messages	1964	30.00
❑ SR-60939 [S]	Gifts and Messages	1964	40.00
❑ MG-20894 [M]	Kirk in Copenhagen	1963	30.00
❑ SR-60894 [S]	Kirk in Copenhagen	1963	40.00
❑ MG-20800 [M]	Reeds and Deeds	1963	30.00
❑ SR-60800 [S]	Reeds and Deeds	1963	40.00
❑ MG-20844 [M]	Roland Kirk Meets the Benny Golson Orchestra	1963	30.00
❑ SR-60844 [S]	Roland Kirk Meets the Benny Golson Orchestra	1963	40.00
❑ MG-20679 [M]	We Free Kings	1962	30.00
❑ SR-60679 [S]	We Free Kings	1962	40.00
❑ 826455-1	We Free Kings	1986	15.00

PRESTIGE

Number	Title	Yr	NM
❑ PRLP-7450 [M]	Funk Underneath	1967	50.00
❑ PRST-7450 [R]	Funk Underneath	1967	30.00
❑ PRLP-7210 [M]	Kirk's Work	1961	100.00
❑ 24080	Pre-Rahsaan	1978	18.00

TRIP

Number	Title	Yr	NM
❑ TLP-5503	Domino	197?	25.00
❑ TLP-5512	Kirk in Copenhagen	197?	25.00
❑ TLP-5541	We Free Kings	197?	25.00

VERVE

Number	Title	Yr	NM
❑ V-8709 [M]	Now Please Don't You Cry, Beautiful Edith	1967	100.00
❑ V6-8709 [S]	Now Please Don't You Cry, Beautiful Edith	1967	80.00

WARNER BROS.

Number	Title	Yr	NM
❑ BSK3035	Boogie-Woogie String Along for Real	1977	12.00
❑ BS2982	Kirkatron	1977	12.00
❑ BS2918	The Return of the 5,000 Pound Man	1976	12.00

KIRKLAND, LEROY

IMPERIAL

Number	Title	Yr	NM
❑ LP-9198 [M]	Twistin', Mashin' and All That Jazz	1962	18.00
❑ LP-12198 [S]	Twistin', Mashin' and All That Jazz	1962	25.00

KISS

CASABLANCA

Number	Title	Yr	NM
❑ NBLP7020	Alive!	1975	40.00
— Dark blue labels; with booklet			
❑ NBLP7020	Alive!	1976	25.00
— Tan labels with desert scene, "Casablanca" label			
❑ NBLP7020	Alive!	1977	18.00
— Tan labels with desert scene, "Casablanca Record and FilmWorks" label			
❑ 822780-1	Alive!	1984	12.00
— Reissue			
❑ NBLP7076	Alive II	1977	18.00
— Without inserts			
❑ NBLP7076 [B]	Alive II	1977	500.00
— With 8-page booklet, tattoo insert and "Combat Gear" order form; back cover lists three tracks -- "Take Me," "Hooligan" and "Do You Love Me" -- that were not included on the record; no records with these tracks were made; perhaps as few as 50 copies of this cover were made			
❑ NBLP7076 [B]	Alive II	1977	60.00
— With 8-page booklet, tattoo insert and "Combat Gear" order form; back cover contents are correct			
❑ 822781-1	Alive II	1984	12.00
— Reissue			
❑ NB20128 [DJ]	A Taste of Platinum	1978	50.00
— Promo-only sampler from Double Platinum			
❑ NBLP7270	Creatures of the Night	1982	40.00
— Original version has band with makeup			
❑ 824154-1	Creatures of the Night	1984	10.00
— Reissue; features band without its makeup on cover			
❑ 824154-1 [B]	Creatures of the Night	1994	45.00
— Reissue; glow-in-the-dark vinyl; gatefold edition; makeup cover restored			
❑ NBLP7025	Destroyer	1976	30.00
— Dark blue label			
❑ NBLP7025	Destroyer	1976	18.00
— Tan label with desert scene, "Casablanca" label			
❑ NBLP7025	Destroyer	1977	15.00
— Tan label with desert scene, "Casablanca Record and FilmWorks" label			
❑ 824149-1	Destroyer	1984	10.00
— Reissue			
❑ NBLP7100	Double Platinum	1978	40.00
— With "platinum award" cardboard insert and "Double Platinum Kiss Gear" order form			
❑ NBLP7100	Double Platinum	1978	18.00
— Without inserts			
❑ 824155-1	Double Platinum	1984	12.00
— Reissue			
❑ NBLP7016	Dressed to Kill	1975	30.00
— Dark blue label			
❑ NBLP7016	Dressed to Kill	1976	18.00
— Tan label with desert scene, "Casablanca" label			
❑ NBLP7016 [B]	Dressed to Kill	1977	15.00
— Tan label with desert scene, "Casablanca Record and FilmWorks" label			
❑ 824148-1	Dressed to Kill	1984	10.00
— Reissue			
❑ NBLP7152	Dynasty	1979	18.00
— With poster and merchandise order form			
❑ NBLP7152	Dynasty	1979	12.00
— With neither poster nor order form			
❑ 812770-1	Dynasty	1983	10.00
— Reissue			
❑ NBLP7006	Hotter Than Hell	1974	30.00
— Dark blue label			
❑ NBLP7006	Hotter Than Hell	1976	18.00
— Tan label with desert scene, "Casablanca" label			
❑ NBLP7006	Hotter Than Hell	1977	15.00
— Tan label with desert scene, "Casablanca Record and FilmWorks" label			
❑ 824147-1	Hotter Than Hell	1984	10.00
— Reissue			
❑ NB9001	Kiss	1974	80.00
— First Warner Bros.-distributed version does NOT have "Kissin' Time"			
❑ NBLP7001	Kiss	1974	30.00
— All renumbered versions have "Kissin' Time"; dark blue label			
❑ NBLP7001	Kiss	1976	18.00
— Tan label with desert scene, "Casablanca" label			
❑ NBLP7001	Kiss	1977	15.00
— Tan label with desert scene, "Casablanca Record and FilmWorks" label			
❑ 824146-1	Kiss	1984	10.00
— Reissue			
❑ NB9001	Kiss	1974	50.00
— Second Warner Bros.-distributed version DOES have "Kissin' Time" on Side 2 (RE-1 on label)			
❑ NBLP7225 [B]	Kiss Unmasked	1980	25.00
— With poster and "Kiss Essential Gear" order form			
❑ NBLP7225	Kiss Unmasked	1980	12.00
— With neither poster nor order form			
❑ NBLP7057	Love Gun	1977	40.00
— with "Hot Goods from the Supply Depot" order form, unpunched-out cardboard gun and "Bang!" sticker. All items must be intact to get top dollar for this.			
❑ NBLP7057	Love Gun	1977	15.00
— Without inserts			
❑ 824151-1	Love Gun	1984	10.00
— Reissue			
❑ NBLP7261	Music from The Elder	1981	30.00
— Various editions have paper or plastic innersleeves, lyric sheets, even incorrect track listings on the back cover; no difference in value is noted between variations			
❑ 824153-1	Music from The Elder	1984	10.00
— Reissue			
❑ NB20137 [DJ]	Peter Criss, Ace Frehley, Gene Simmons, Paul Stanley	1978	60.00
— Promo-only sampler from the band's solo albums			
❑ NBLP7037	Rock and Roll Over	1976	25.00
— Tan label with desert scene, "Casablanca" label; comes with sticker and Kiss Army paraphenalia order form			
❑ NBLP7037	Rock and Roll Over	1977	15.00

Number	Title	Yr	NM
— Tan label with desert scene, "Casablanca Record and FilmWorks" label, with inserts			
❑ 824150-1	Rock and Roll Over	1984	10.00
— Reissue			
❑ NBLP737 [DJ]	Rock and Roll Over Special Edition	1977	120.00
— Five-track sampler from the LP			
❑ Kiss '76 [DJ]	Special Kiss Tour Album	1976	100.00
— Special four-track sampler			
❑ NBLP7032 [B]	The Originals	1976	200.00
— Tan label with desert scene, "Casablanca" label; with booklet, six Kiss cards, a Kiss Army sticker			
❑ NBLP7032	The Originals	1976	100.00
— Tan label with desert scene, "Casablanca" label; without extras			
❑ NBLP7032	The Originals	1977	100.00
— Tan label with desert scene, "Casablanca Record and FilmWorks" label; "Second Printing" on cover; with extras listed above			
❑ NBLP7032	The Originals	1977	50.00
— Tan label with desert scene, "Casablanca Record and FilmWorks" label; "Second Printing" on cover; without extras			
❑ 826242-1	Unmasked	1985	10.00
— Reissue			

MERCURY

Number	Title	Yr	NM
❑ 8227801	Alive!	2008	30.00
❑ 522647-1	Alive III	1994	30.00
— Limited edition black vinyl			
❑ 522647-1	Alive III	1994	30.00
— Limited edition white vinyl			
❑ 522647-1	Alive III	1994	30.00
— Limited edition blue vinyl			
❑ 522647-1	Alive III	1994	30.00
— Limited edition red vinyl			
❑ 822495-1	Animalize	1984	15.00
❑ 826099-1	Asylum	1985	12.00
❑ 832632-1	Crazy Nights	1987	12.00
❑ 832903-1 [PD]	Crazy Nights	1987	30.00
❑ 528674-1 [PD]	Creatures of the Night	1995	35.00
— Reissue; picture disc of makeup cover			
❑ 792-1 [DJ]	First Kiss, Last Licks	1990	100.00
— Promo-only sampler			
❑ 838913-1	Hot in the Shade	1989	12.00
❑ 814297-1	Lick It Up	1983	15.00
❑ 528950-1	MTV Unplugged	1996	25.00
— First editions are on black vinyl			
❑ 528950-1 [B]	MTV Unplugged	1996	50.00
— Second editions are on yellow marbled vinyl			
❑ 836427-1	Smashes, Thrashes and Hits	1988	12.00
❑ 836887-1 [PD]	Smashes, Thrashes and Hits	1988	30.00
❑ 532741-1	You Wanted the Best, You Got the Best!!	1996	25.00

KIT KATS, THE

JAMIE

Number	Title	Yr	NM
❑ LPM-3029 [M]	It's Just a Matter of Time	1966	30.00
❑ LPS-3029 [S]	It's Just a Matter of Time	1966	30.00
❑ LPM-3032 [M]	The Kit Kats Do Their Thing -- Live!	1967	30.00
❑ LPS-3032 [S]	The Kit Kats Do Their Thing -- Live!	1967	40.00
❑ JLPS-3034	To Understand Is to Love	1970	30.00
— As "New Hope			

KITAEV, ANDREI, AND BILL DOUGLASS

REFERENCE RECORDINGS

Number	Title	Yr	NM
❑ RR-6	First Takes	198?	25.00

KITCHEN CINQ, THE

LHI

Number	Title	Yr	NM
❑ E-12000 [M]	Everything But the Kitchen Cinq	1967	30.00
❑ E7-12000 [S]	Everything But the Kitchen Cinq	1967	40.00

KITT, EARTHA

CAEDMON

Number	Title	Yr	NM
❑ TC-1267	Folk Tales of the Tribes of Africa	1969	25.00

DECCA

Number	Title	Yr	NM
❑ DL4635 [M]	Eartha Kitt Sings in Spanish	1965	30.00
❑ DL74635 [S]	Eartha Kitt Sings in Spanish	1965	40.00

GNP CRESCENDO

Number	Title	Yr	NM
❑ GNPS-2008 [S]	At the Plaza	1965	25.00
❑ GNP-2008 [M]	At the Plaza	1965	18.00

KAPP

Number	Title	Yr	NM
❑ KL-1192 [M]	Eartha Kitt Revisited	1960	30.00
❑ KS-3192 [S]	Eartha Kitt Revisited	1960	30.00
❑ KL-1162 [M]	The Fabulous Eartha Kitt	1959	30.00
❑ KS-3046 [S]	The Fabulous Eartha Kitt	1959	30.00

MCA

Number	Title	Yr	NM
❑ 1554	The Best of Eartha Kitt	1983	15.00

MGM

Number	Title	Yr	NM
❑ E-4009 [M]	Bad But Beautiful	1962	30.00
❑ SE-4009 [S]	Bad But Beautiful	1962	30.00

RCA VICTOR

Number	Title	Yr	NM
❑ LPM-1109 [M]	Down to Eartha	1955	50.00
❑ LPM-3062 [10]	RCA Victor Presents Eartha Kitt	1953	80.00
❑ LPM-1661 [M]	St. Louis Blues	1958	40.00
❑ LSP-1661 [S]	St. Louis Blues	1958	50.00
❑ LPM-3187 [10]	That Bad Eartha	1953	80.00
❑ LPM-1153 [M]	That Bad Eartha	1955	50.00
❑ LPM-1300 [M]	Thursday's Child	1956	50.00

STANYAN

Number	Title	Yr	NM
❑ SR-10037	Best of All Possible Worlds	1972	18.00
❑ SR-10040	For Always	1975	18.00

SUNNYVIEW

Number	Title	Yr	NM
❑ SUN-4902	I Love Men	1984	12.00

KITTYHAWK

EMI AMERICA

Number	Title	Yr	NM
❑ SW-17029	Kittyhawk	1980	15.00
❑ ST-17053	Race for the Oasis	1981	15.00

ZEBRA

Number	Title	Yr	NM
❑ ZR-5001	Fanfare	198?	15.00

KITZJIMA, OSAMU

ANTILLES

Number	Title	Yr	NM
❑ AN7016 [B]	Benzaiten	1976	35.00

KLAATU

CAPITOL

Number	Title	Yr	NM
❑ ST-12080	Endangered Species	1980	15.00
❑ ST-11633 [B]	Hope	1977	15.00
❑ SN-16061	Hope	1980	10.00
— Budget-line reissue			
❑ ST-11542	Klaatu	1976	18.00
❑ SN-16060	Klaatu	1980	10.00
— Budget-line reissue			
❑ SW-11836	Sir Army Suit	1978	15.00
❑ SN-16062	Sir Army Suit	1980	10.00
— Budget-line reissue			

KLARK KENT

KRYPTONE/I.R.S.

Number	Title	Yr	NM
❑ SP70600 [EP]	Music Madness from the Kinetic Kid	1980	25.00
— Green vinyl 10" in die-cut 12" sleeve			

KLEMMER, JOHN, AND EDDIE HARRIS

CRUSADERS

Number	Title	Yr	NM
❑ 16015	Two Tone	1982	30.00
— Part of MCA's "Audiophile Series			

KLEMMER, JOHN

ABC

Number	Title	Yr	NM
❑ AA-1068	Arabesque	1978	12.00
❑ ABCD-950	Barefoot Ballet	1976	12.00
❑ AA-1116	Brazilia	1979	12.00
❑ AA-1106	Cry	1978	12.00
❑ ABCD-836	Fresh Feathers	1974	18.00
❑ AB-1007	LifeStyle (Living & Loving)	1977	12.00
❑ ABCD-922	Touch	1975	12.00

ABC IMPULSE!

Number	Title	Yr	NM
❑ AS-9214	Constant Throb	1973	18.00
❑ AS-9244	Intensity	1974	25.00
❑ AS-9269	Magic and Movement	1974	25.00
❑ AS-9220	Waterfalls	1973	18.00

ARISTA/NOVUS

Number	Title	Yr	NM
❑ AN2-3500	Nexus	1979	18.00

BLUEBIRD

Number	Title	Yr	NM
❑ 6577-1-RB	Nexus One	1987	12.00

CADET

Number	Title	Yr	NM
❑ LPS808	And We Were Lovers	1968	25.00
❑ LP797 [M]	Involvement	1967	40.00
❑ LPS797 [S]	Involvement	1967	25.00
— Fading blue label			
❑ CA-797 [S]	Involvement	197?	18.00
— Pink and yellow label reissue			

CADET CONCEPT

Number	Title	Yr	NM
❑ LPS326	All the Children Cried	1970	25.00
❑ LPS321	Blowin' Gold	1969	30.00
❑ LPS330	Eruptions	1971	25.00

CHESS

Number	Title	Yr	NM
❑ CH2-92501	Blowin' Gold	1984	15.00
— Reissue of CH-8300			
❑ CH-8300	Blowin' Gold	1982	15.00
— Compilation of tracks from three Cadet Concept LPs			
❑ 2ACMJ-401	Magic Moments	1976	18.00

ELEKTRA

Number	Title	Yr	NM
❑ 5E-527	Hush	1981	12.00
❑ 6E-284	Magnificent Madness	1980	12.00
❑ 5E-566	Solo Saxophone II: Life	1982	12.00

ELEKTRA/MUSICIAN

Number	Title	Yr	NM
❑ 60197	Finesse	1983	12.00

MCA

Number	Title	Yr	NM
❑ 37015	Arabesque	1980	10.00
— Reissue of ABC 1068			
❑ 1585	Arabesque	198?	10.00
— Reissue of MCA 37015			
❑ 37013	Barefoot Ballet	1980	10.00
— Reissue of ABC 950			
❑ AA-1116	Brazilia	1979	10.00
— Reissue of ABC 1116			
❑ 37115	Brazilia	1980	10.00
— Reissue of MCA 1116			
❑ 1639	Brazilia	198?	10.00
— Reissue of MCA 37115			
❑ 37017	Constant Throb	1980	10.00
— Reissue of ABC Impulse 9214			
❑ 37016	Cry	1980	10.00
— Reissue of ABC 1106			
❑ 37012	Fresh Feathers	1980	12.00
— Reissue of ABC 836			
❑ 37019	Intensity	1980	12.00
— Reissue of ABC Impulse 9244			
❑ 37014	LifeStyle (Living & Loving)	1980	10.00
— Reissue of ABC 1007			
❑ 37020	Magic and Movement	1980	12.00
— Reissue of ABC Impulse 9269			
❑ 6246	Music	1989	15.00
❑ 8014	The Best of John Klemmer, Volume One/Mosaic	1979	15.00
❑ 6007	The Best of John Klemmer, Volume One/Mosaic	198?	12.00
— Reissue of MCA 8014			
❑ 6017	The Best of John Klemmer, Volume Two/The Impulse Years	1982	15.00
❑ 37152	Touch	198?	10.00
— Reissue of ABC 922			
❑ 1654	Touch	198?	10.00
— Reissue of MCA 37152			
❑ 37018	Waterfalls	1980	12.00
— Reissue of ABC Impulse 9220			

MOBILE FIDELITY

Number	Title	Yr	NM
❑ 1-006	Touch	1979	30.00
— Original Master Recording" at top of front cover; audiophile vinyl			

NAUTILUS

Number	Title	Yr	NM
❑ NR-22	Finesse	1981	80.00
— SuperDisc" audiophile vinyl			
❑ NR-4	Straight from the Heart	1980	80.00
— Super Disc" audiophile vinyl			

KLF, THE

TVT

Number	Title	Yr	NM
❑ 4040	History of the JAMS a.k.a. The Timelords	1988	25.00
— As "The JAMs			

WAX TRAX!

Number	Title	Yr	NM
❑ 7155 [B]	Chill Out	1990	25.00

KLINK, AL/BOB ALEXANDER

GRAND AWARD

Number	Title	Yr	NM
❑ GA 33-525 [M]	Progressive Jazz	1956	80.00
— With removable outer cover			
❑ GA 33-525 [M]	Progressive Jazz	1956	30.00
— Without removable outer cover			

KLOSS, ERIC, AND BARRY MILES

MUSE

Number	Title	Yr	NM
❑ MR-5112	Together	1976	18.00

KLOSS, ERIC, AND GIL GOLDSTEIN

OMNISOUND

Number	Title	Yr	NM
❑ 1044	Sharing	1981	15.00

KLOSS, ERIC

COBBLESTONE

Number	Title	Yr	NM
❑ 9006	Doors	1972	25.00

MUSE

Number	Title	Yr	NM
❑ MR-5077	Bodies' Warmth	1975	18.00
❑ MR-5196	Celebration	1979	15.00
❑ MR-5291	Doors	198?	15.00
— Reissue of Cobblestone 9006			
❑ MR-5038	Essence	1974	18.00
❑ MR-5147	Now	1978	15.00
❑ MR-5019	One, Two, Free	1973	18.00

PRESTIGE

Number	Title	Yr	NM
❑ PRST-7793	Consciousness!	1970	18.00
❑ PRLP-7520 [M]	First Class Kloss	1967	30.00
❑ PRST-7520 [S]	First Class Kloss	1967	25.00
❑ PRLP-7486 [M]	Grits & Gravy	1967	30.00
❑ PRST-7486 [S]	Grits & Gravy	1967	25.00
❑ PRST-7627	In the Land of the Giants	1969	18.00
❑ PRLP-7442 [M]	Introducing Eric Kloss	1966	25.00
❑ PRST-7442 [S]	Introducing Eric Kloss	1966	30.00
❑ PRST-7535	Life Force	1968	25.00
❑ PRLP-7469 [M]	Love and All That Jazz	1966	25.00
❑ PRST-7469 [S]	Love and All That Jazz	1966	30.00
❑ PRST-7594	Sky Shadows	1969	18.00
❑ PRST-7689	To Hear Is to See!	1970	18.00
❑ PRST-7565	We're Goin' Up	1968	18.00

KLOWNS, THE

Number	Title	Yr	NM
RCA VICTOR			
❑ LSP-4438	The Klowns	1970	12.00

KLUGH, EARL

Number	Title	Yr	NM
BLUE NOTE			
❑ BN-LA596-G	Earl Klugh	1976	12.00
❑ LN-10163	Earl Klugh	198?	10.00
—Budget-line reissue			
❑ BN-LA737-H	Finger Paintings	1977	12.00
❑ LO-737	Finger Paintings	198?	10.00
—Reissue with new prefix			
❑ BN-LA667-G	Living Inside Your Love	1976	12.00
❑ LO-667	Living Inside Your Love	198?	10.00
—Reissue with new prefix			
CAPITOL			
❑ ST-12405	Key Notes (Greatest Hits)	1985	12.00
❑ ST-12253	Low Ride	1983	12.00
❑ ST-12372	Nightsongs	1984	12.00
❑ ST-12323	Wishful Thinking	1984	12.00
LIBERTY			
❑ LT-51113	Crazy for You	1981	12.00
❑ LN-10308	Crazy for You	1986	10.00
—Budget-line reissue			
❑ LN-10257	Finger Paintings	198?	10.00
—Budget-line reissue			
❑ LO-942	Heart String	198?	10.00
—Reissue of United Artists 942			
❑ LN-10231	Heart String	198?	10.00
—Budget-line reissue			
❑ LT-1079	Late Night Guitar	1980	12.00
❑ LN-10233	Living Inside Your Love	198?	10.00
—Budget-line reissue			
❑ LMAS-877	Magic in Your Eyes	198?	10.00
—Reissue of United Artists 877			
MOBILE FIDELITY			
❑ 1-025	Finger Paintings	1979	30.00
—Audiophile vinyl			
❑ UHQR 1-025	Finger Paintings	1982	120.00
—Ultra High Quality" audiophile vinyl in box			
❑ 1-076	Late Night Guitar	1981	50.00
—Audiophile vinyl			
NAUTILUS			
❑ NR-46 [B]	Crazy for You	198?	40.00
—Audiophile vinyl			
UNITED ARTISTS			
❑ LT-1026	Dream Come True	1980	12.00
❑ UA-LA942-H	Heart String	1979	12.00
❑ UA-LA877-H	Magic in Your Eyes	1978	12.00
WARNER BROS.			
❑ 25478	Life Stories	1986	12.00
❑ 25262	Soda Fountain Shuffle	1985	12.00
❑ 26018	Solo Guitar	1989	15.00
❑ 25902	Whispers and Promises	1989	15.00

KNEE, BERNIE

Number	Title	Yr	NM
AUDIOPHILE			
❑ AP-144	Bernie Knee	198?	15.00

KNEPPER, JIMMY

Number	Title	Yr	NM
BETHLEHEM			
❑ BCP-77 [M]	A Swinging Introduction to Jimmy Knepper	1957	60.00
❑ BCP-6031	Idol of the Flies	197?	15.00
—Reissue, distributed by RCA Victor			
INNER CITY			
❑ IC-6047	Knepper in L.A.	197?	15.00
SOUL NOTE			
❑ SN-1092	I Dream Too Much	1984	15.00
STEEPLECHASE			
❑ SCS-1061	Cunningbird	1977	15.00

KNICKERBOCKERS, THE

Number	Title	Yr	NM
CHALLENGE			
❑ CH-621 [M]	Jerk and Twine Time	1965	400.00
❑ CH-622 [M]	Lies	1966	100.00
❑ CHS-622 [S]	Lies	1966	200.00
❑ LP-12664 [M]	Lloyd Thaxton Presents the Knickerbockers	1965	200.00
SUNDAZED			
❑ LP-5154	Rockin' with the Knickerbockers	2003	15.00
❑ LP-5000	The Great Lost Knickerbockers Album	1990	15.00
—Blue vinyl			

KNIGHT, CHRIS, AND MAUREEN MCCORMICK

Number	Title	Yr	NM
PARAMOUNT			
❑ PAS-6062	Chris Knight and Maureen McCormick	1973	120.00

KNIGHT, FREDERICK

Number	Title	Yr	NM
STAX			
❑ STS-3011	I've Been Lonely So Long	1973	25.00

KNIGHT, GLADYS, AND THE PIPS

Number	Title	Yr	NM
ACCORD			
❑ SN-7103	Every Beat of My Heart	1981	12.00
❑ SN-7131	I Feel a Song	1981	12.00
❑ SN-7188	It's Showtime	1982	12.00
❑ SN-7105	Letter Full of Tears	1981	12.00
ALLEGIANCE			
❑ AV-5002	Glad to Be...	198?	12.00
BELL			
❑ 1323	In the Beginning	1975	15.00
❑ 6013	Tastiest Hits	1968	25.00
BUDDAH			
❑ BDS-5639	2nd Anniversary	1975	15.00
❑ BDS-5602	Claudine	1974	30.00
❑ BDS-5612	I Feel a Song	1974	15.00
❑ BDS-5141	Imagination	1973	15.00
❑ BDS-5714	Miss Gladys Knight	1978	15.00
❑ BDS-5676	Pipe Dreams	1976	15.00
❑ BDS-5689	Still Together	1977	15.00
❑ BDS-5653	The Best of Gladys Knight & The Pips	1976	15.00
❑ BDS-5701	The One and Only	1978	15.00
CASABLANCA			
❑ NBLP7081	At Last…The Pips	1977	12.00
—As "The Pips			
❑ NBLP7113	Callin'	1978	12.00
—As "The Pips			
COLLECTABLES			
❑ COL-5154	Golden Classics: Letter Full of Tears	198?	12.00
COLUMBIA			
❑ JC36387	About Love	1980	12.00
❑ PC36387	About Love	198?	10.00
—Budget-line reissue			
❑ JC35704	Gladys Knight	1979	12.00
❑ PC35704	Gladys Knight	198?	10.00
—Budget-line reissue			
❑ FC40376	Greatest Hits	1986	12.00
❑ FC39423	Life	1985	12.00
❑ PC39423	Life	198?	10.00
—Budget-line reissue			
❑ FC38114	That Special Time of Year	1982	12.00
❑ PC38114	That Special Time of Year	1983	10.00
—Same as above with new prefix			
❑ FC40878	The Best of Gladys Knight and the Pips/The Columbia Years	1988	12.00
❑ FC37086	Touch	1981	12.00
❑ PC37086	Touch	198?	10.00
—Budget-line reissue			
❑ FC38205	Visions	1983	12.00
❑ PC38205	Visions	198?	10.00
—Budget-line reissue			
FURY			
❑ 1003 [M]	Letter Full of Tears	1962	500.00
LOST-NITE			
❑ LLP-17 [10]	The Best of Gladys Knight and the Pips	1981	15.00
—Red vinyl			
MAXX			
❑ 3000 [M]	Gladys Knight and the Pips	1964	150.00
MCA			
❑ 42004	All Our Love	1987	12.00
❑ 10329	Good Woman	1991	18.00
MOTOWN			
❑ MOT5303	All the Great Hits of Gladys Knight and the Pips	198?	10.00
❑ M792S2	Anthology	1974	18.00
❑ M5-126V1	Everybody Needs Love	1981	15.00
—Reissue of Soul 706			
❑ M5-113V	Motown Superstar Series, Vol. 13	1981	12.00
❑ M5-193V1	Neither One of Us	1981	15.00
—Reissue of Soul 737			
❑ M5-148V1	Nitty Gritty	1981	15.00
—Reissue of Soul 713			
NATURAL RESOURCES			
❑ NR4004T1	Silk N' Soul	1978	12.00
—Reissue of Soul 711			
PAIR			
❑ PDL2-1198	The Best of Gladys Knight and the Pips	1987	15.00
PICKWICK			
❑ SPC-3349	Every Beat of My Heart	197?	12.00
SOUL			
❑ S744	A Little Knight Music	1975	15.00
❑ SS730	All in a Knight's Work	1970	18.00
❑ S739L	All I Need Is Time	1973	18.00
❑ S706 [M]	Everybody Needs Love	1967	25.00
❑ SS706 [S]	Everybody Needs Love	1967	30.00
❑ S707 [M]	Feelin' Bluesy	1968	40.00
—Mono copies are white label promo only; cover has "Monaural Record DJ Copy" sticker			
❑ SS707 [S]	Feelin' Bluesy	1968	30.00
❑ SS723	Gladys Knight and the Pips Greatest Hits	1970	18.00
❑ SS731	If I Were Your Woman	1971	18.00
❑ S741	Knight Time	1974	15.00
❑ S737L [B]	Neither One of Us	1973	18.00
❑ SS713	Nitty Gritty	1969	30.00
❑ SS711	Silk N' Soul	1968	30.00
❑ S736L	Standing Ovation	1971	18.00
SPHERE SOUND			
❑ SR-7006 [M]	Gladys Knight and the Pips	196?	200.00
❑ SSR-7006 [R]	Gladys Knight and the Pips	196?	120.00
SPRINGBOARD			
❑ SPB-4035	Early Hits	1972	12.00
❑ SPB-4050	How Do You Say Goodbye	1973	12.00
TRIP			
❑ TLP-9509	It Hurt Me So Bad	1973	12.00
UNITED ARTISTS			
❑ UA-LA503-E	The Very Best of Gladys Knight and the Pips	1975	15.00
UPFRONT			
❑ UPF130	Gladys Knight and the Pips	197?	12.00
❑ UPF185	Gladys Knight and the Pips	197?	12.00
VEE JAY			
❑ D1-74796	Every Beat of My Heart: The Greatest Hits of the Early Years	1989	18.00

KNIGHT, JEAN

Number	Title	Yr	NM
COTILLION			
❑ SD5230	Jean Knight and Premium	1981	18.00
MIRAGE			
❑ 90282	My Toot Toot	1985	12.00
STAX			
❑ STS-2045	Mr. Big Stuff	1971	40.00
❑ MPS-8554	Mr. Big Stuff	198?	12.00

KNIGHT, ROBERT

Number	Title	Yr	NM
RISING SONS			
❑ RSM-7000 [M]	Everlasting Love	1967	30.00
❑ RSS-17000 [S]	Everlasting Love	1967	40.00

KNIGHT, SONNY

Number	Title	Yr	NM
AURA			
❑ AR-3001 [M]	If You Want This Love	1964	30.00
❑ AS-3001 [S]	If You Want This Love	1964	35.00

KNIGHT, TED

Number	Title	Yr	NM
RANWOOD			
❑ R-8149 [B]	Hi Guys!	1976	30.00

KNIGHT, TERRY, AND THE PACK

Number	Title	Yr	NM
ABKCO			
❑ AB-4217 [B]	Mark, Don and Terry 1966-67	1972	30.00
CAMEO			
❑ C2007 [M]	Reflections	1967	25.00
—Reissue of Lucky Eleven LE-8001			
❑ CS2007 [S]	Reflections	1967	30.00
—Reissue of Lucky Eleven LES-8001			
LUCKY ELEVEN			
❑ LE-8001 [M]	Reflections	1967	30.00
❑ LES-8001 [S]	Reflections	1967	60.00
❑ LE-8000 [M]	Terry Knight and the Pack	1966	60.00
❑ LES-8000 [R]	Terry Knight and the Pack	1966	30.00

KNIGHTS, THE

Number	Title	Yr	NM
ACE			
❑ 200854	Across the Board	1966	400.00
❑ 4763	Cold Days, Hot Knights	196?	400.00
❑ 201302	The Knights 1967	1967	400.00
CAPITOL			
❑ T2189 [M]	Hot Rod High	1964	400.00
❑ DT2189 [R]	Hot Rod High	1964	400.00
JUSTICE			
❑ JLP-156	On the Move	196?	300.00

KNIGHTS OF DIXIELAND, THE

Number	Title	Yr	NM
JAZZOLOGY			
❑ J-4 [M]	A Night with the Knights of Dixieland	1964	18.00

KNOCKOUTS, THE (1)

Number	Title	Yr	NM
TRIBUTE			
❑ 1202 [M]	Go Ape with the Knockouts	1964	200.00

KNOPF, PAUL

Number	Title	Yr	NM
PLAYBACK			
❑ PLP-502 [M]	And the Walls Came Tumbling Down	1960	40.00
❑ PLP-502ST [S]	And the Walls Came Tumbling Down	1960	50.00
❑ PLP-501 [M]	Enigma of a Day	1959	40.00
❑ PLP-501ST [S]	Enigma of a Day	1959	50.00
❑ PLP-600 [M]	Music from the Morgue	1961	40.00
❑ PLP-600ST [S]	Music from the Morgue	1961	50.00
❑ PLP-503 [M]	Paul Knoft Trio	1960	40.00
❑ PLP-503ST [S]	Paul Knoft Trio	1960	50.00
❑ PLP-500 [M]	The Outcat	1959	40.00
❑ PLP-500ST [S]	The Outcat	1959	50.00

Number	Title	Yr	NM

KNOWBODY ELSE

HIP
| ❏ HIS-7003 | Knowbody Else | 1969 | 40.00 |

KNOX, BUDDY

ACCORD
| ❏ SN-7218 | Party Doll and Other Hits | 1981 | 12.00 |

LIBERTY
| ❏ LRP-3251 [M] | Buddy Knox's Golden Hits | 1962 | 30.00 |
| ❏ LST-7251 [S] | Buddy Knox's Golden Hits | 1962 | 50.00 |

ROULETTE
❏ R25003 [M]	Buddy Knox	1957	200.00
—Black label, all silver print (original)			
❏ R25003 [M]	Buddy Knox	1957	150.00
—Black label, red and silver print			
❏ R25003 [M]	Buddy Knox	1959	100.00
—White label with colored spokes			
❏ R25048 [M]	Buddy Knox and Jimmy Bowen	1959	200.00
—Black label, red and silver print			
❏ R25048 [M]	Buddy Knox and Jimmy Bowen	1959	100.00
—White label with colored spokes			

UNITED ARTISTS
| ❏ UAS6689 | Gypsy Man | 1969 | 30.00 |

KOALA, THE

CAPITOL
| ❏ SKAO-176 | The Koala | 1969 | 60.00 |

KODAKS, THE / THE STARLITES

SPHERE SOUND
| ❏ SSR-7005 [M] | The Kodaks Vs. the Starlites | 1965 | 200.00 |

KOERNER, RAY AND GLOVER

AUDIOPHILE
| ❏ AP-78 [M] | Blues, Rags and Hollers | 1963 | 50.00 |
| —Includes four songs not on the Elektra reissue | | | |

ELEKTRA
❏ EKL-240 [M]	Blues, Rags and Hollers	1963	30.00
—Not issued in stereo on Elektra			
❏ EKL-267 [M]	Lots More Blues, Rags and Hollers	1964	25.00
❏ EKS-7267 [S]	Lots More Blues, Rags and Hollers	1964	30.00
❏ EKL-305 [M]	The Return of Koerner, Ray and Glover	1965	25.00
❏ EKS-7305 [S]	The Return of Koerner, Ray and Glover	1965	30.00

KOERNER, SPIDER JOHN, AND WILLIE MURPHY

ELEKTRA
| ❏ EKS-74041 | Running, Jumping, Standing Still | 1969 | 25.00 |

KOERNER, SPIDER JOHN

ELEKTRA
| ❏ EKL-290 [M] | Spider Blues | 1965 | 25.00 |
| ❏ EKS-7290 [S] | Spider Blues | 1965 | 30.00 |

SWEET JANE
❏ SJL-5872	Music Is Just a Bunch of Notes	1972	100.00
—With Willie and the Bumblebees and BONNIE RAITT			
❏ SJL-1074	Some American Folksongs Like They Used To	1974	30.00

KOFFMAN, MOE

ASCOT
| ❏ AM13001 [M] | Moe Koffman Plays for the Teens | 1962 | 25.00 |
| ❏ AS16001 [S] | Moe Koffman Plays for the Teens | 1962 | 30.00 |

JANUS
| ❏ 7037 | Museum Pieces | 1978 | 12.00 |

JUBILEE
❏ JLP-1037 [M]	Cool and Hot Sax	1957	40.00
❏ JGS-8009	Moe Koffman Goes Electric	1968	30.00
❏ JLP-1074 [M]	The Shepherd Swings Again	1958	40.00
❏ JGS-8016	Turned On	1968	30.00

KAMA SUTRA
| ❏ KSBS-2018 [B] | Moe's Curried Soul | 1970 | 18.00 |

SOUNDWINGS/DUKE STREET
| ❏ SW2108 | Oop-Pop-A-Da | 1988 | 15.00 |
| —With Dizzy Gillespie | | | |

UNITED ARTISTS
| ❏ UAJ-14029 [M] | Tales of Koffman | 1963 | 30.00 |
| ❏ UAJS-15029 [S] | Tales of Koffman | 1963 | 30.00 |

KOHLMAN, FREDDIE

MGM
| ❏ E-297 [10] | New Orleans Now -- New Orleans Then | 1955 | 80.00 |

KOKI, SAM, AND THE PARADISE ISLANDERS

KAPP
| ❏ KL-1321 [M] | Surfin' at Waikiki | 1963 | 18.00 |
| ❏ KS-3321 [S] | Surfin' at Waikiki | 1963 | 25.00 |

KOKOMO (1)

FELSTED
| ❏ FL7513 [M] | Asia Minor | 1961 | 40.00 |
| ❏ FS17513 [S] | Asia Minor | 1961 | 50.00 |

KOKOMO (2)

COLUMBIA
| ❏ PC33442 [B] | Kokomo | 1975 | 18.00 |
| ❏ PC34031 [B] | Rise and Shine! | 1976 | 18.00 |

KOLBY, DIANE

COLUMBIA
| ❏ KC31386 | Diane Kolby | 1972 | 18.00 |

KOLE, JERRY, AND THE STRINGERS

CROWN
| ❏ CLP-5385 [M] | Hot Rod Alley | 1963 | 30.00 |
| ❏ CST-385 [S] | Hot Rod Alley | 1963 | 40.00 |

KOLLER, HANS

DISCOVERY
| ❏ DL-2005 [10] | Hans Koller | 1954 | 80.00 |

VANGUARD
| ❏ VRS-8509 [M] | Hans Across the Sea | 1956 | 50.00 |

KOLOC, BONNIE

OVATION
❏ OVQD 14-21 [Q]	After All This Time	1971	18.00
❏ OVQD 14-29 [Q]	Bonnie Koloc	1973	18.00
❏ OVQD 14-26 [Q]	Hold On to Me	1972	18.00
❏ OVQD 14-38 [Q]	You're Gonna Love Yourself in the Morning	1974	18.00

KOMACK, JAMES

RCA VICTOR
| ❏ LPM-1501 [M] | Inside Me | 1957 | 30.00 |

KON KAN

ATLANTIC
| ❏ 81984 | Move to Move | 1989 | 15.00 |

KONGOS, JOHN

ELEKTRA
| ❏ EKS 75019 [B] | Kongos | 1971 | 18.00 |

JANUS
| ❏ JLS3032 [B] | Confusions About a Goldfish | 1970 | 30.00 |

KONITZ, LEE, AND HAL GALPER

INNER CITY
| ❏ IC-2057 | Windows | 1976 | 18.00 |

STEEPLECHASE
| ❏ SCS-1057 | Windows | 198? | 15.00 |

KONITZ, LEE, AND MARTIAL SOLAL

PAUSA
| ❏ 7138 | Duo: Live at Berlin Jazz Days 1980 | 198? | 12.00 |

KONITZ, LEE, AND RED MITCHELL

INNER CITY
| ❏ IC-2018 | I Concentrate on You | 1975 | 18.00 |

STEEPLECHASE
| ❏ SCS-1018 | I Concentrate on You | 198? | 15.00 |

KONITZ, LEE

ATLANTIC
❏ SD8235	Duets	1969	18.00
❏ 1258 [M]	Inside Hi-Fi	1957	60.00
—Black label			
❏ 1258 [M]	Inside Hi-Fi	1961	30.00
—Multicolor label, white "fan" logo at right			
❏ SD1258 [S]	Inside Hi-Fi	1958	60.00
—Green label			
❏ SD1258 [S]	Inside Hi-Fi	1961	25.00
—Multicolor label, white "fan" logo at right			
❏ 1217 [M]	Lee Konitz with Warne Marsh	1955	80.00
—Black label			
❏ 1217 [M]	Lee Konitz with Warne Marsh	1961	30.00
—Multicolor label, white "fan" logo at right			
❏ 90050	Lee Konitz with Warne Marsh	198?	12.00
❏ 1273 [M]	The Real Lee Konitz	1958	50.00
—Black label			
❏ 1273 [M]	The Real Lee Konitz	1961	30.00
—Multicolor label, white "fan" logo at right			

CHIAROSCURO
| ❏ 186 | The Nonet | 1977 | 15.00 |
| ❏ 166 | The Quartet | 1976 | 15.00 |

CHOICE
| ❏ 1019 | Tenorlee | 1977 | 15.00 |

FANTASY
| ❏ OJC-466 | Duets | 1990 | 15.00 |
| ❏ OJC-186 | Subconscious-Lee | 198? | 12.00 |

GROOVE MERCHANT
| ❏ GM-3306 [B] | Chicago 'n All That Jazz! | 1975 | 25.00 |

IAI
| ❏ 373845 | Pyramid | 1977 | 18.00 |

INNER CITY
| ❏ IC-2035 | Lone-Lee | 1975 | 18.00 |

JAZZTONE
| ❏ J-1275 [M] | Jazz at Storyville | 1957 | 40.00 |
| | Jazz at Storyville | | |

MILESTONE
❏ MSP-9025	Peacemeal	1968	25.00
❏ MSP-9060	Satori	1975	25.00
❏ MSP-9038	Spirits	1969	25.00
❏ MSP-9013	The Lee Konitz Duets	1968	25.00

PAUSA
| ❏ 7019 | Lee Konitz Meets Warne Marsh Again | 198? | 12.00 |

PRESTIGE
❏ 24081	First Sessions 1949-50	198?	18.00
❏ PRLP-7004 [M]	Lee Konitz Groups	1955	150.00
❏ PRLP-116 [10]	Lee Konitz -- The New Sounds	1951	400.00
❏ PRLP-7250 [M]	Subconscious-Lee	1962	50.00

PROGRESSIVE
| ❏ 7003 | Figure and Spirit | 1977 | 18.00 |

ROOST
| ❏ LP-416 [10] | Originalee | 1953 | 200.00 |

ROULETTE
| ❏ SR-5006 | The Nonet | 1976 | 18.00 |

SOUL NOTE
❏ 121119	Ideal Scene	198?	15.00
❏ SN-1069	Live at Laren	198?	15.00
❏ 121169	The New York Album	1990	15.00

STEEPLECHASE
❏ SCS-1072	Jazz & Juan	198?	15.00
❏ SCS-1035	Lone-Lee	198?	15.00
❏ SCS-1119	Yes, Yes Nonet	1979	15.00

STORYVILLE
❏ STLP-313 [10]	Konitz	1954	250.00
❏ STLP-304 [10]	Lee Konitz at Storyville	1954	250.00
❏ STLP-901 [M]	Lee Konitz at Storyville	1956	120.00
❏ STLP-323 [10]	Lee Konitz in Harvard Square	1955	200.00

SUNNYSIDE
| ❏ SSC 1003 | Dovetail | 1985 | 12.00 |

VERVE
❏ MGV-8286 [M]	An Image -- Lee Konitz with Strings	1958	40.00
❏ V-8286 [M]	An Image -- Lee Konitz with Strings	1961	30.00
❏ MGVS-6035 [S]	An Image -- Lee Konitz with Strings	1959	30.00
❏ V6-8286 [S]	An Image -- Lee Konitz with Strings	1961	25.00
❏ MGV-8335 [M]	Lee Konitz Meets Jimmy Giuffre	1959	40.00
❏ V-8335 [M]	Lee Konitz Meets Jimmy Giuffre	1961	25.00
❏ MGVS-6073 [S]	Lee Konitz Meets Jimmy Giuffre	1959	30.00
❏ V6-8335 [S]	Lee Konitz Meets Jimmy Giuffre	1961	18.00
❏ V-8399 [M]	Motion	1961	25.00
❏ V6-8399 [S]	Motion	1961	30.00
❏ UMV-2563	Motion	198?	12.00
❏ MGV-8281 [M]	Tranquility	1958	50.00
❏ V-8281 [M]	Tranquility	1961	30.00
❏ MGV-8209 [M]	Very Cool	1958	50.00
❏ V-8209 [M]	Very Cool	1961	30.00
❏ MGV-8362 [M]	You and Lee	1960	40.00
❏ V-8362 [M]	You and Lee	1961	25.00
❏ MGVS-6131 [S]	You and Lee	1960	30.00
❏ V6-8362 [S]	You and Lee	1961	18.00

KONITZ, LEE/MILES DAVIS/TEDDY CHARLES

NEW JAZZ
❏ NJLP-8295 [M]	Ezz-Thetic	1962	50.00
—Purple label			
❏ NJLP-8295 [M]	Ezz-Thetic	1965	30.00
—Blue label, trident logo at right			

PRESTIGE
| ❏ PRST-7827 | Ezz-Thetic | 1970 | 15.00 |

KOOL AND THE GANG

DE-LITE
❏ 8505	As One	1982	12.00
❏ 822535-1	As One	1984	10.00
—Reissue			
❏ 9518	Celebrate!	1980	12.00
❏ 822538-1	Celebrate!	1984	10.00
—Reissue			
❏ 822943-1	Emergency	1984	10.00
❏ 9509	Everybody's Dancin'	1979	12.00
❏ 2012	Good Times	1973	15.00

Number	Title	Yr	NM
❑ MK-48 [DJ]	History of Kool and the Gang	1979	18.00
❑ 8508	In the Heart	1983	12.00
❑ 814351-1	In the Heart	1984	10.00
—Reissue			
❑ 2015	Kool & The Gang Greatest Hits!	1975	12.00
❑ 9507	Kool & The Gang Spin Their Top Ten Hits	1978	12.00
❑ 822536-1	Kool & The Gang Spin Their Top Ten Hits	1984	10.00
—Reissue			
❑ 2003	Kool and the Gang	1969	30.00
❑ 4001	Kool Jazz	1973	12.00
❑ 9513 [B]	Ladies Night	1979	12.00
❑ 822537-1	Ladies Night	1984	10.00
—Reissue			
❑ 2014	Light of Worlds	1974	12.00
❑ 2010	Live at PJ's	1971	18.00
❑ 2008	Live at the Sex Machine	1971	18.00
❑ 2018	Love and Understanding	1976	12.00
❑ 2011	Music Is the Message	1972	15.00
❑ 2023	Open Sesame	1976	12.00
❑ 8502	Something Special	1981	12.00
❑ 822534-1	Something Special	1984	10.00
—Reissue			
❑ 2016	Spirit of the Boogie	1975	12.00
❑ 2009	The Best of Kool and the Gang	1971	18.00
❑ 9501	The Force	1978	12.00
❑ 2013	Wild and Peaceful	1973	12.00

MERCURY

Number	Title	Yr	NM
❑ 834780-1	Everything's Kool & the Gang: Greatest Hits & More	1988	10.00
❑ 830398-1	Forever	1986	10.00
❑ 838233-1	Sweat	1989	10.00

KOOPER, AL

COLUMBIA

Number	Title	Yr	NM
❑ KC31159	A Possible Projection of the Future/Childhood's End	1972	18.00
❑ FC38137	Championship Wrestling	1982	12.00
❑ G30031	Easy Does It	1970	25.00
❑ CS9718 [B]	I Stand Alone	1969	25.00
—"360 Sound" label			
❑ CS9718	I Stand Alone	1970	12.00
—Orange label			
❑ CS9951	Kooper Session	1970	18.00
—With Shuggie Otis; "360 Sound" label			
❑ CS9951	Kooper Session	1970	12.00
—With Shuggie Otis; orange label			
❑ KC31723	Naked Songs	1973	18.00
❑ KC30506	New York City (You're a Woman)	1971	18.00
❑ PG33169	Unclaimed Freight (Al's Big Deal)	1975	18.00
❑ CS9855 [B]	You Never Know Who Your Friends Are	1969	25.00
—"360 Sound" label			
❑ CS9855	You Never Know Who Your Friends Are	1970	12.00
—Orange label			

UNITED ARTISTS

Number	Title	Yr	NM
❑ UA-LA702-G	Act Like Nothing's Wrong	1976	15.00

KORNER, ALEXIS

COLUMBIA

Number	Title	Yr	NM
❑ PC33427	Get Off of My Cloud	1975	18.00

JUST SUNSHINE

Number	Title	Yr	NM
❑ 13 [B]	All Star Blues Incorporated	1974	18.00

MOBILE FIDELITY

Number	Title	Yr	NM
❑ 1-265	Blues at the Marquee	1996	40.00
—Audiophile vinyl			

WARNER BROS.

Number	Title	Yr	NM
❑ BS2647	Accidentally Borne in New Orleans	1972	18.00
❑ 2XS1966	Bootleg Him	1972	30.00

KOSTELANETZ, ANDRE

COLUMBIA

Number	Title	Yr	NM
❑ CS9740	Andre Kostelanetz' Greatest Hits	1969	12.00
❑ KG31491	Andre Kostelanetz Plays Cole Porter	1972	18.00
❑ KG32825	Andre Kostelanetz Plays Gershwin	1974	15.00
❑ KC32580	Andre Kostelanetz Plays Legrand's Greatest Hits	1974	12.00
❑ CQ32147 [Q]	A Quadraphonic Concert	1972	18.00
❑ CL864 [M]	Beautiful Dreamer	1956	25.00
—Red and black label with six "eye" logos			
❑ CL758 [M]	Bravo!	1956	25.00
—Red and black label with six "eye" logos			
❑ CL863 [M]	Café Continental	1956	25.00
—Red and black label with six "eye" logos			
❑ CL811 [M]	Calendar Girl	1956	25.00
—Red and black label with six "eye" logos			
❑ CL2688 [M]	Concert in the Park	1967	12.00
❑ CS9488 [S]	Concert in the Park	1967	12.00
❑ PC34352	Dance with Me	1977	12.00
❑ C30037	Everything Is Beautiful	1970	12.00
❑ CL2581 [M]	Exotic Nights	1966	12.00
❑ CS9381 [S]	Exotic Nights	1966	12.00
❑ C30672	For All We Know	1971	12.00
❑ CS9691 [S]	For the Young at Heart	1968	12.00
❑ CL2891 [M]	For the Young at Heart	1968	18.00
❑ CL1495 [M]	Gershwin: Rhapsody in Blue; Previn: Concerto in F	1960	15.00
❑ CS8286 [S]	Gershwin: Rhapsody in Blue; Previn: Concerto in F	1960	18.00
❑ CL2133 [M]	Gershwin Wonderland	1964	12.00
❑ CS8933 [S]	Gershwin Wonderland	1964	15.00
❑ CS9973	Greatest Hits of the 60's	1970	12.00
❑ CL1431 [M]	Gypsy Passion	1960	15.00
❑ CS8228 [S]	Gypsy Passion	1960	18.00
❑ CS9724	Hits from Funny Girl, Finian's Rainbow, and Star!	1968	12.00
❑ CS9998	I'll Never Fall in Love Again	1970	12.00
❑ KC34157	I'm Easy and Other Themes	1976	12.00
❑ CL2185 [M]	I Wish You Love	1964	12.00
❑ CS8985 [S]	I Wish You Love	1964	15.00
❑ CL1528 [M]	Joy to the World: Music for Christmas	1959	18.00
❑ CS8328 [S]	Joy to the World: Music for Christmas	1959	25.00
—Red and black label with six "eye" logos			
❑ CL2078 [M]	Kostelanetz in Wonderland	1964	12.00
❑ CS8878 [S]	Kostelanetz in Wonderland	1964	15.00
❑ C31002	Kostelanetz Plays Chicago	1971	12.00
❑ KC32451	Kostelanetz Plays Great Hits of Today	1973	12.00
❑ CL797 [M]	La Boheme for Orchestra	1956	25.00
—Red and black label with six "eye" logos			
❑ KC32187	Last Tango in Paris	1973	12.00
❑ C30501	Love Story	1971	12.00
❑ CL780 [M]	Lure of the Tropics	1956	25.00
—Red and black label with six "eye" logos			
❑ KZ1 [M]	Meet Andre Kostelanetz	1955	25.00
—Red and black label with six "eye" logos			
❑ CL704 [M]	Mood for Love	1956	25.00
—Red and black label with six "eye" logos			
❑ KC33061	Musical Reflections of Broadway and Hollywood	1974	12.00
❑ AK1 [M]	Musical Tour of the World	195?	25.00
❑ KC33954	Music from A Chorus Line and Treemonisha	1975	12.00
❑ PC34660	Music of Charlie Chaplin and Duke Ellington	1977	12.00
❑ CL768 [M]	Music of Irving Berlin	1956	25.00
—Red and black label with six "eye" logos			
❑ C33550	Never Can Say Goodbye	1975	10.00
❑ KC33550	Never Can Say Goodbye	1975	12.00
❑ CL2250 [M]	New Orleans Wonderland	1965	12.00
❑ CS9050 [S]	New Orleans Wonderland	1965	15.00
❑ CL2138 [M]	New York Wonderland	1964	12.00
❑ CS8938 [S]	New York Wonderland	1964	15.00
❑ KC33437	Orient Express	1975	12.00
❑ CL720 [M]	Peter and the Wolf; Carnival of the Animals	1956	25.00
—Red and black label with six "eye" logos			
❑ CQ32856 [Q]	Quadraphonic Pop Concert	1973	18.00
❑ CL1220 [M]	Romantic Music of...	1958	18.00
❑ CS9623 [S]	Scarborough Fair	1968	12.00
❑ CL2823 [M]	Scarborough Fair	1968	18.00
❑ CL806 [M]	Show Boat/South Pacific/ Slaughter on 10th Avenue	1956	25.00
—Red and black label with six "eye" logos			
❑ GP10	Sounds of Love	1969	15.00
❑ CL781 [M]	Stardust	1956	25.00
—Red and black label with six "eye" logos			
❑ CL1718 [M]	Star-Spangled Marches	1962	15.00
❑ CS8518 [S]	Star-Spangled Marches	1962	18.00
❑ CL1354 [M]	Strauss Waltzes	1959	15.00
❑ CS8162 [S]	Strauss Waltzes	1959	18.00
❑ KG33065	Strike Up the Band	1974	15.00
❑ JC35788	Superman	1979	10.00
❑ CL1199 [M]	Theatre Party	1958	18.00
❑ CL2609 [M]	The Kostelanetz Sound of Today	1967	12.00
❑ CS9409 [S]	The Kostelanetz Sound of Today	1967	12.00
❑ CL1335 [M]	The Lure of Paradise	1959	15.00
❑ CS8144 [S]	The Lure of Paradise	1959	18.00
❑ CL765 [M]	The Music of Victor Herbert	1956	25.00
—Red and black label with six "eye" logos			
❑ CL734 [M]	The Music of Victor Youmans	1956	25.00
—Red and black label with six "eye" logos			
❑ C2L11 [M]	The Romantic Music of Tchaikovsky	195?	30.00
—Red and black label with six "eye" logos			
❑ CL2467 [M]	The Shadow of Your Smile and Other Great Movie Themes	1966	12.00
❑ CS9267 [S]	The Shadow of Your Smile and Other Great Movie Themes	1966	12.00
❑ CL843 [M]	The Very Thought of You	1956	25.00
—Red and black label with six "eye" logos			
❑ KG32002	The World's Greatest Love Songs	1973	15.00
❑ CL2359 [M]	Thunder (The Spectacular Sound of John Philip Sousa)	1965	12.00
❑ CS9159 [S]	Thunder (The Spectacular Sound of John Philip Sousa)	1965	15.00
❑ CL2534 [M]	Today's Golden Hits	1966	12.00
❑ CS9334 [S]	Today's Golden Hits	1966	15.00
❑ CL2756 [M]	Today's Greatest Movie Hits	1967	15.00
❑ CS9556 [S]	Today's Greatest Movie Hits	1967	12.00
❑ CS9823	Traces	1969	12.00
❑ JC36382	Various Themes	1980	10.00
❑ CL2068 [M]	Wonderland of Christmas	1963	15.00
❑ CS8868 [S]	Wonderland of Christmas	1963	18.00
❑ CL2039 [M]	Wonderland of Golden Hits	1963	12.00
❑ CS8839 [S]	Wonderland of Golden Hits	1963	15.00
❑ CL1995 [M]	Wonderland of Opera	1963	12.00
❑ CS8795 [S]	Wonderland of Opera	1963	15.00
❑ CL1657 [M]	Wonderland of Sound	1961	15.00
❑ CS8457 [S]	Wonderland of Sound	1961	18.00
❑ CL1827 [M]	Wonderland of Sound (Broadway's Greatest Hits)	1962	15.00
❑ CS8627 [S]	Wonderland of Sound (Broadway's Greatest Hits)	1962	18.00
❑ CL1898 [M]	Wonderland of Sound (Fire and Jealousy)	1962	15.00
❑ CS8698 [S]	Wonderland of Sound (Fire and Jealousy)	1962	18.00
❑ CL1938 [M]	Wonderland of Sound (The World's Greatest Waltzes)	1963	12.00
❑ CS8738 [S]	Wonderland of Sound (The World's Greatest Waltzes)	1963	15.00
❑ JC35328	You Light Up My Life	1978	12.00

COLUMBIA LIMITED EDITION

Number	Title	Yr	NM
❑ LE10083	Joy to the World: Music for Christmas	197?	12.00
—Reissue of CS 8328			
❑ LE10086	Wonderland of Christmas	197?	12.00
—Reissue of CS 8868			

COLUMBIA MASTERWORKS

Number	Title	Yr	NM
❑ ML4455 [M]	An American in Paris	195?	25.00
❑ MS7108 [S]	Andre Kostelanetz Conducts Great Romantic Ballads	196?	12.00
❑ ML4409 [M]	Bizet: L'arlesienne Suites 1 & 2	195?	25.00
❑ ML4082 [M]	Carnival Tropicana	195?	25.00
❑ ML2056 [10]	Chopin-Kostelanetz	195?	30.00
❑ ML4066 [M]	Clair de Lune	195?	25.00
❑ MS7427	Extravaganza	1970	12.00
❑ ML6226 [M]	Favorite Romantic Concertos	1961	15.00
❑ MS6826 [S]	Favorite Romantic Concertos	1961	18.00
❑ ML4065 [M]	Favorites	195?	25.00
❑ M35114	Festive Overtures	1978	10.00
❑ ML4822 [M]	Lure of the Tropics	1956	25.00
❑ ML2022 [10]	Motion Picture Favorites	195?	30.00
❑ M37019	Musical Evenings	1969	12.00
❑ M30075	Music for Strings	1970	12.00
❑ ML4253 [M]	Music of Fritz Kreisler and Sigmund Romberg	195?	25.00
❑ ML2007 [10]	Music of Stephen Foster	195?	30.00
❑ MS6106 [S]	Offenbach: Gaite Parisienne; Bizet: Carmen (Highlights)	195?	25.00
❑ ML6206 [M]	Promenade Favorites	1966	15.00
❑ MS6806 [S]	Promenade Favorites	1966	18.00
❑ ML6111 [M]	Romantic Strings	1960	15.00
❑ MS6711 [S]	Romantic Strings	1960	18.00
❑ ML6224 [M]	Romantic Waltzes of Tchaikovsky	1961	15.00
❑ MS6824 [S]	Romantic Waltzes of Tchaikovsky	1961	18.00
❑ ML6129 [M]	Showstoppers	1960	15.00
❑ MS6729 [S]	Showstoppers	1960	18.00
❑ ML2014 [10]	Songs of Cole Porter	195?	30.00
❑ ML4308 [M]	Swan Lake (Highlights)	195?	25.00
❑ MS7087	Vienna, City of Dreams	1968	15.00
❑ ML2011 [10]	Waltzes of Johann Strauss	195?	30.00
❑ ML6179 [M]	Wishing You a Merry Christmas	1960	15.00
❑ MS6779 [S]	Wishing You a Merry Christmas	1960	18.00

COLUMBIA SPECIAL PRODUCTS

Number	Title	Yr	NM
❑ P13286	Scarborough Fair	197?	10.00
❑ C10975	Wishing You a Merry Christmas	1972	12.00
—Reissue of Columbia Masterworks MS 6779			

HARMONY

Number	Title	Yr	NM
❑ KH31571	Andre Kostelanetz Plays Richard Rogers	1973	12.00
❑ H30014	Be My Love	1970	12.00
❑ HL7371 [M]	Broadway Theatre Party	196?	12.00
❑ HS11171 [S]	Broadway Theatre Party	196?	12.00
❑ HL7395 [M]	Grand Canyon Suite	196?	12.00
❑ HS11195 [S]	Grand Canyon Suite	196?	12.00
❑ KH31414	Greatest Hits of Broadway and Hollywood	1972	12.00
❑ HL7432 [M]	Joy to the World: Music for Christmas	1967	15.00
—Reissue of Columbia 1528			
❑ HS11232 [S]	Joy to the World: Music for Christmas	1967	15.00
—Reissue of Columbia 8328			
❑ KH31500	Love Theme from "The Godfather	1972	12.00
❑ KH32170	Strike Up the Band	1973	12.00
❑ HS11281	The Magic of Music	1968	12.00
❑ HL7368 [M]	You and the Night and the Music	196?	12.00
❑ HS11168 [S]	You and the Night and the Music	196?	12.00

READER'S DIGEST

Number	Title	Yr	NM
❑ RD-120-A	The Best of Andre Kostelanetz	197?	30.00

KOTTKE, LEO

CAPITOL

Number	Title	Yr	NM
❑ ST-11446 [B]	Chewing Pine	1975	15.00
❑ SN-16188	Chewing Pine	1980	10.00
—Budget-line reissue			

Number	Title	Yr	NM
❑ ST-11335 [B]	Dreams and All That Stuff	1974	15.00
❑ SN-16187	Dreams and All That Stuff	1980	10.00
—Budget-line reissue			
❑ ST-11000 [B]	Greenhouse	1972	15.00
❑ SN-16065	Greenhouse	1979	10.00
—Budget-line reissue			
❑ ST-11262 [B]	Ice Water	1974	15.00
❑ SN-16064	Ice Water	1979	10.00
—Budget-line reissue			
❑ ST-11576	Leo Kottke 1971-1976 -- Did You Hear Me?	1976	12.00
❑ SN-16189	Leo Kottke 1971-1976 -- Did You Hear Me?	1980	10.00
—Budget-line reissue			
❑ ST-682	Mudlark	1971	15.00
❑ SN-16063	Mudlark	1979	10.00
—Budget-line reissue			
❑ ST-11164 [B]	My Feet Are Smiling	1973	15.00
❑ SWBC-11867	The Best of Leo Kottke	1979	15.00

CHRYSALIS

Number	Title	Yr	NM
❑ CHR1234	Balance	1979	12.00
❑ PV41234	Balance	1985	10.00
—Budget-line reissue			
❑ CHR1191	Burnt Lips	1978	12.00
❑ PV41191	Burnt Lips	1985	10.00
—Budget-line reissue			
❑ CHR1328	Guitar Music	1981	12.00
❑ PV41328	Guitar Music	1983	10.00
—Budget-line reissue			
❑ CHR1106	Leo Kottke	1977	12.00
❑ PV41106	Leo Kottke	1985	10.00
—Budget-line reissue			
❑ FV41411	Time Step	1983	12.00
❑ PV41411	Time Step	1986	10.00
—Budget-line reissue			

OBLIVION

Number	Title	Yr	NM
❑ S-1	12-String Blues/Live at the Scholar Coffee House	1969	30.00

PRIVATE MUSIC

Number	Title	Yr	NM
❑ 2007-1-P	A Shout Toward Noon	1986	12.00
❑ 2050-1-P	My Father's Face	1989	12.00
❑ 2025-1-P	Regards from Chuck Pink	1988	12.00

SYMPOSIUM

Number	Title	Yr	NM
❑ 2001	Circle Round the Sun	1970	15.00

TAKOMA

Number	Title	Yr	NM
❑ 1024	6 and 12 String Guitar	1969	15.00

KOTTKE, LEO/PETER LANG/JOHN FAHEY

TAKOMA

Number	Title	Yr	NM
❑ 1040	Leo Kottke/Peter Lang/John Fahey	1974	15.00

KRAFTWERK

ASTRALWERKS

Number	Title	Yr	NM
❑ A3W00011	Minimum-Maximum	2005	30.00
—Box set; each LP is in a cardboard inner sleeve and paper sleeve			

CAPITOL

Number	Title	Yr	NM
❑ ST-11457	Radio Activity	1975	25.00
❑ SN-16380	Radio-Activity	1986	12.00
—Reissue			
❑ SW-11728	The Man-Machine	1978	25.00
❑ SN-16302	The Man-Machine	198?	12.00
—Reissue			
❑ SW11603	Trans-Europe Express	1977	25.00
❑ SN-16301	Trans-Europe Express	198?	18.00
—Reissue			

ELEKTRA

Number	Title	Yr	NM
❑ 60797	Autobahn	1988	18.00
—Still another reissue of this album			
❑ 60789	Computer World	1988	18.00
—Reissue			
❑ 60798	Electric Cafe	1988	18.00
—Reissue			
❑ 60869	The Mix	1991	25.00

MERCURY

Number	Title	Yr	NM
❑ SRM-1-3704 [B]	Autobahn	1977	25.00
—Reissue of Vertigo VEL-2003			

MUTE/KLING KLANG

Number	Title	Yr	NM
❑ STUMM306 [B]	The Man Machine	2009	30.00
❑ STUMM305 [B]	Trans Europe Express	2009	30.00

VERTIGO

Number	Title	Yr	NM
❑ VEL-2003 [B]	Autobahn	1974	40.00
❑ VEL-2006 [B]	Ralf & Florian	1976	50.00
—Recorded in 1973			

WARNER BROS.

Number	Title	Yr	NM
❑ 25326	Autobahn	1985	15.00
—Another reissue of Vertigo VEL-2003			
❑ HS3549	Computer World	1981	12.00
❑ 25525	Electric Cafe	1986	15.00

KRAINIA CONSORT

MERCURY LIVING PRESENCE

Number	Title	Yr	NM
❑ SR90397 [S]	Music in Shakespeare's England	196?	60.00
—Maroon label, no "Vendor: Mercury Record Corporation			

Number	Title	Yr	NM
❑ SR90397 [S]	Music in Shakespeare's England	196?	25.00
—Maroon label, with "Vendor: Mercury Record Corporation			
—aroon label, with "Vendor: Mercury Record Corporation			

KRAL, IRENE

AVA

Number	Title	Yr	NM
❑ A-33 [M]	Better Than Anything	1963	40.00
❑ AS-33 [S]	Better Than Anything	1963	50.00

CATALYST

Number	Title	Yr	NM
❑ 7625	Kral Speace	1977	15.00

CHOICE

Number	Title	Yr	NM
❑ CRS1020	Gentle Rain	197?	15.00
❑ CRS1012	Where Is Love?	197?	15.00

DRG

Number	Title	Yr	NM
❑ MRS-505	Irene Kral and the Junior Mance Trio	198?	12.00

MAINSTREAM

Number	Title	Yr	NM
❑ 56058 [M]	Wonderful Life	1965	30.00
❑ S-6058 [S]	Wonderful Life	1965	40.00

UNITED ARTISTS

Number	Title	Yr	NM
❑ UAL-3052 [M]	Steve Irene O!	1959	120.00
❑ UAS-6052 [S]	Steve Irene O!	1959	150.00
❑ UAL-4016 [M]	The Band and I	1959	120.00
❑ UAS-5016 [S]	The Band and I	1959	150.00

KRALL, DIANA

VERVE

Number	Title	Yr	NM
❑ 1243301	Quiet Nights	2009	25.00

KRAMER, BILLY J., AND THE DAKOTAS

CAPITOL

Number	Title	Yr	NM
❑ SM-11897 [P]	The Best of Billy J. Kramer and the Dakotas	1979	12.00

IMPERIAL

Number	Title	Yr	NM
❑ LP9273 [M]	I'll Keep You Satisfied/From a Window	1964	30.00
❑ LP12273 [P]	I'll Keep You Satisfied/From a Window	1964	40.00
❑ LP9267 [M]	Little Children	1964	50.00
—Black label with stars			
❑ LP9267 [M]	Little Children	1964	30.00
—Black and pink label			
❑ LP12267 [P]	Little Children	1964	80.00
—Black label with silver print			
❑ LP12267 [P]	Little Children	1964	40.00
—Black and pink label			
❑ LP9291 [M]	Trains and Boats and Planes	1965	30.00
❑ LP12921 [R]	Trains and Boats and Planes	1965	30.00

KRAUSS, ALISON, AND UNION STATION

MOBILE FIDELITY

Number	Title	Yr	NM
❑ MFSL 2-276	So Long, So Wrong	2004	40.00
—Original Master Recording" at top of cover			

ROUNDER

Number	Title	Yr	NM
❑ 0275	I've Got That Old Feeling	1990	18.00
❑ 0325	Now That I've Found You: A Collection	1995	18.00
❑ 0235	Too Late to Cry	1987	18.00
❑ 0265	Two Highways	1989	18.00

KRAVITZ, LENNY

VIRGIN

Number	Title	Yr	NM
❑ 39169	Are You Gonna Go My Way	1993	30.00
—Clear-vinyl LP plus bonus CD with 8 unreleased tracks			
❑ 91290	Let Love Rule	1989	15.00

KRAZY KATS, THE

DAMON

Number	Title	Yr	NM
❑ 12478 [M]	Movin' Out!! With the Krazy Kats	1964	120.00

KREED

VISION OF SOUND

Number	Title	Yr	NM
❑ 71-56	Kreed	1971	1200.00

KRESS, CARL

CAPITOL

Number	Title	Yr	NM
❑ H368 [10]	Classics in Jazz	1953	50.00

KRESTON, JUDY, AND DAVID LAHM

PLUG

Number	Title	Yr	NM
❑ PLUG-6	Here In Love Lies the Answer	1986	15.00

KRISTOFFERSON, KRIS, AND RITA COOLIDGE

A&M

Number	Title	Yr	NM
❑ SP-4403	Full Moon	1973	15.00
❑ SP-4690	Natural Act	1979	12.00
❑ PR-4690	Natural Act	1979	18.00
—Picture disc			

MONUMENT

Number	Title	Yr	NM
❑ PZ33278	Breakaway	1974	15.00

KRISTOFFERSON, KRIS

COLUMBIA

Number	Title	Yr	NM
❑ PZ31302	Border Lord	1976	10.00
—Reissue			
❑ JZ35310	Easter Island	1978	15.00
❑ FC40056	Highwayman	1985	12.00
—Waylon Jennings/Willie Nelson/Johnny Cash/Kris Kristofferson			
❑ C45240	Highwayman 2	1990	18.00
—Waylon Jennings/Willie Nelson/Johnny Cash/Kris Kristofferson			
❑ PZ31909	Jesus Was a Capricorn	1976	10.00
—Reissue			
❑ PZ30817	Me and Bobby McGee	1976	10.00
—Reissue			
❑ JZ36135	Shake Hands with the Devil	1979	15.00
❑ PZ34687	Songs of Kristofferson	1977	15.00
❑ PZ32914	Spooky Lady's Sideshow	1976	10.00
—Reissue			
❑ PZ30679	The Silver Tongued Devil and I	1976	10.00
—Reissue			
❑ JZ36885	To the Bone	1980	15.00
❑ PZ33379	Who's to Bless…And Who's to Blame	1976	10.00
—Reissue			

MERCURY

Number	Title	Yr	NM
❑ 830406-1	Repossessed	1987	12.00

MONUMENT

Number	Title	Yr	NM
❑ KZ31302	Border Lord	1972	15.00
❑ ZQ31302 [Q]	Border Lord	1972	25.00
❑ KZ31909	Jesus Was a Capricorn	1972	15.00
❑ ZQ31909 [Q]	Jesus Was a Capricorn	1973	25.00
❑ SLP-18139	Kristofferson	1970	30.00
—Original label is light green with a yellow ring			
❑ Z30817	Me and Bobby McGee	1971	15.00
—Reissue of 18139 with new title			
❑ PW38392	Songs of Kristofferson	1982	10.00
—Reissue of 34687			
❑ PZ32914	Spooky Lady's Sideshow	1974	15.00
❑ PZQ32914 [Q]	Spooky Lady's Sideshow	1974	25.00
❑ PZ34254	Surreal Thing	1976	15.00
❑ Z30679	The Silver Tongued Devil and I	1971	15.00
❑ ZQ30679 [Q]	The Silver Tongued Devil and I	1972	25.00
❑ PZ33379	Who's to Bless…And Who's to Blame	1975	15.00

PAIR

Number	Title	Yr	NM
❑ PDL2-1078	My Songs	1986	15.00

KRISTYL

(NO LABEL)

Number	Title	Yr	NM
❑ (no #)0	Kristyl	1975	200.00

KRONOS QUARTET

LANDMARK

Number	Title	Yr	NM
❑ LLP-1505	Monk Suite (Music of Monk & Ellington)	1985	15.00
❑ LLP-1510	Music of Bill Evans	1986	15.00

NONESUCH

Number	Title	Yr	NM
❑ 979111-1F [B]	Kronos Quartet	1986	18.00

REFERENCE RECORDINGS

Number	Title	Yr	NM
❑ RR-9	In Formation	198?	30.00
—Audiophile vinyl			

KRUPA, GENE, AND CHARLIE VENTURA

COMMODORE

Number	Title	Yr	NM
❑ FL-20028 [10]	The Krupa-Ventura Trio	1950	100.00

KRUPA, GENE; LIONEL HAMPTON; TEDDY WILSON

CLEF

Number	Title	Yr	NM
❑ MGC-681 [M]	Selections from "The Benny Goodman Story	1956	80.00

VERVE

Number	Title	Yr	NM
❑ MGV-8066 [M]	Gene Krupa-Lionel Hampton-Teddy Wilson with Red Callender	1957	50.00
—Reissue of Clef 681 with new title			
❑ V-8066 [M]	Gene Krupa-Lionel Hampton-Teddy Wilson with Red Callender	1961	30.00

KRUPA, GENE

AIRCHECK

Number	Title	Yr	NM
❑ 35	Gene Krupa on the Air, 1944-46	198?	12.00

AMERICAN RECORDING SOCIETY

Number	Title	Yr	NM
❑ L-427 [M]	Drummer Man	1957	40.00
❑ L-411 [M]	Gene Krupa Quartet	1956	40.00

CLEF

Number	Title	Yr	NM
❑ MGC-703 [M]	Drum Boogie	1956	60.00
❑ MGC-514 [10]	Gene Krupa Trio	1953	80.00
❑ MGC-684 [M]	Krupa and Rich	1955	60.00
❑ MGC-627 [M]	Sing, Sing, Sing -- The Rocking Mr. Krupa and His Orchestra	1954	60.00

Number	Title	Yr	NM
❑ MGC-728 [M]	The Driving Gene Krupa Plays with His Sextet	1956	60.00
❑ MGC-687 [M]	The Exciting Gene Krupa and His Quartet	1956	60.00
❑ MGC-668 [M]	The Gene Krupa Quartet	1955	60.00
❑ MGC-147 [10]	The Gene Krupa Sextet #1	1954	80.00
❑ MGC-152 [10]	The Gene Krupa Sextet #2	1954	80.00
❑ MGC-631 [M]	The Gene Krupa Sextet #3	1954	60.00
❑ MGC-500 [M]	The Gene Krupa Trio at Jazz at the Philharmonic	1953	60.00
❑ MGC-121 [10]	The Gene Krupa Trio Collates	1953	80.00

—With either Clef or Mercury cover

COLUMBIA

Number	Title	Yr	NM
❑ CL6066 [10]	Dance Parade	1949	100.00
❑ CL2515 [10]	Drummin' Man	1955	50.00
❑ C2L29 [M]	Drummin' Man	1962	50.00

—Red and black labels with six "eye" logos; box set with booklet; deduct 20 percent if book is missing

Number	Title	Yr	NM
❑ C2L29 [M]	Drummin' Man	1963	25.00

—Red labels, "Guaranteed High Fidelity" or "360 Sound Mono" on label

Number	Title	Yr	NM
❑ CL6017 [10]	Gene Krupa	1949	100.00
❑ CL735 [M]	Gene Krupa	1956	30.00

—Red and black label with six "eye" logos

Number	Title	Yr	NM
❑ CL735 [M]	Gene Krupa	1963	18.00

—Red label, "Guaranteed High Fidelity" or "360 Sound Mono" on label

Number	Title	Yr	NM
❑ KG32663	Gene Krupa, His Orchestra and Anita O'Day	1974	18.00
❑ CL641 [M]	Gene Krupa's Sidekicks	1955	40.00

—Maroon label, gold print

Number	Title	Yr	NM
❑ CL641 [M]	Gene Krupa's Sidekicks	1955	30.00

—Red and black label with six "eye" logos

COLUMBIA SPECIAL PRODUCTS

Number	Title	Yr	NM
❑ P14379	Krupa Swings	197?	12.00

ENCORE

Number	Title	Yr	NM
❑ EE22027	That Drummer's Band	196?	18.00

HARMONY

Number	Title	Yr	NM
❑ HL7252 [M]	The Gene Krupa Story in Music	1960	18.00

INTERMEDIA

Number	Title	Yr	NM
❑ QS-5050	Hot Drums	198?	12.00

MERCURY

Number	Title	Yr	NM
❑ MGC-514 [10]	Gene Krupa Trio	1953	120.00
❑ MGC-500 [M]	The Gene Krupa Trio at Jazz at the Philharmonic	1953	80.00
❑ MGC-121 [10]	The Gene Krupa Trio Collates	1953	120.00

—With Mercury cover and Mercury labels

METRO

Number	Title	Yr	NM
❑ M-518 [M]	Gene Krupa	1965	18.00
❑ MS-518 [R]	Gene Krupa	1965	15.00

MGM

Number	Title	Yr	NM
❑ GAS-132	Gene Krupa (Golden Archive Series)	1970	15.00

RCA CAMDEN

Number	Title	Yr	NM
❑ CAL-340 [M]	Mutiny in the Parlor	1958	25.00

SUNBEAM

Number	Title	Yr	NM
❑ 225	The World's Greatest Drummer	197?	12.00

TIME-LIFE

Number	Title	Yr	NM
❑ STBB-12	Big Bands: Gene Krupa	1984	18.00

VERVE

Number	Title	Yr	NM
❑ MGV-8310 [M]	Big Noise from Winnetka -- Gene Krupa at the London House	1959	50.00
❑ MGVS-6042 [S]	Big Noise from Winnetka -- Gene Krupa at the London House	1960	40.00
❑ V-8310 [M]	Big Noise from Winnetka -- Gene Krupa at the London House	1961	30.00
❑ V6-8310 [S]	Big Noise from Winnetka -- Gene Krupa at the London House	1961	25.00
❑ V-8450 [M]	Classics in Percussion	1962	18.00
❑ V6-8450 [S]	Classics in Percussion	1962	25.00
❑ MGV-8087 [M]	Drum Boogie	1957	50.00
❑ V-8087 [M]	Drum Boogie	1961	30.00
❑ 827843-1	Drummer Man	1986	12.00
❑ MGV-2008 [M]	Drummer Man -- Gene Krupa in Highest-Fi	1956	60.00

—Orange label

Number	Title	Yr	NM
❑ MGV-2008 [M]	Drummer Man -- Gene Krupa in Highest-Fi	1957	50.00

—Black label

Number	Title	Yr	NM
❑ V-2008 [M]	Drummer Man -- Gene Krupa in Highest-Fi	1961	30.00
❑ MGV-8292 [M]	Gene Krupa Plays Gerry Mulligan Arrangements	1958	50.00
❑ MGVS-6008 [S]	Gene Krupa Plays Gerry Mulligan Arrangements	1959	40.00
❑ V-8292 [M]	Gene Krupa Plays Gerry Mulligan Arrangements	1961	30.00
❑ V6-8292 [S]	Gene Krupa Plays Gerry Mulligan Arrangements	1961	25.00
❑ MGV-8300 [M]	Hey! Here's Gene Krupa	1959	50.00
❑ V-8300 [M]	Hey! Here's Gene Krupa	1961	30.00
❑ MGV-8069 [M]	Krupa and Rich	1957	50.00
❑ V-8069 [M]	Krupa and Rich	1961	30.00
❑ V-8400 [M]	Krupa and Rich	1961	30.00
❑ V6-8400 [S]	Krupa and Rich	1961	25.00
❑ MGV-8276 [M]	Krupa Rocks	1958	50.00
❑ V-8276 [M]	Krupa Rocks	1961	30.00
❑ V-8571 [M]	Let Me Off Uptown -- The Essential Gene Krupa	1964	18.00
❑ V6-8571 [S]	Let Me Off Uptown -- The Essential Gene Krupa	1964	25.00
❑ V-8414 [M]	Percussion King	1961	18.00
❑ V6-8414 [S]	Percussion King	1961	25.00
❑ MGV-8190 [M]	Sing, Sing, Sing	1957	50.00
❑ V-8190 [M]	Sing, Sing, Sing	1961	30.00
❑ VSP-4 [M]	That Drummer's Band	1966	18.00
❑ VSPS-4 [R]	That Drummer's Band	1966	15.00
❑ MGV-8107 [M]	The Driving Gene Krupa	1957	50.00
❑ V-8107 [M]	The Driving Gene Krupa	1961	30.00
❑ MGV-8369 [M]	The Drum Battle	1960	50.00
❑ UMV-2594	The Exciting Gene Krupa	198?	12.00
❑ MGV-8071 [M]	The Exciting Gene Krupa and His Quartet	1957	50.00
❑ V-8071 [M]	The Exciting Gene Krupa and His Quartet	1961	30.00
❑ MGV-8031 [M]	The Gene Krupa Trio	1957	50.00
❑ V-8031 [M]	The Gene Krupa Trio	1961	30.00
❑ V-8584 [M]	The Great New Gene Krupa Quartet Featuring Charlie Ventura	1964	18.00
❑ V6-8584 [S]	The Great New Gene Krupa Quartet Featuring Charlie Ventura	1964	25.00
❑ MGV-8204 [M]	The Jazz Rhythms of Gene Krupa	1957	50.00
❑ V-8204 [M]	The Jazz Rhythms of Gene Krupa	1961	30.00
❑ V-8484 [M]	The Original Drum Battle	1962	18.00
❑ V6-8484 [R]	The Original Drum Battle	196?	15.00
❑ V-8594 [M]	Verve's Choice -- The Best of Gene Krupa	1964	18.00
❑ V6-8594 [S]	Verve's Choice -- The Best of Gene Krupa	1964	15.00

KUBAN, BOB, AND THE IN-MEN

MUSICLAND U.S.A.

Number	Title	Yr	NM
❑ LP-3500 [M]	Look Out for the Cheater	1966	30.00
❑ SLP-3500 [S]	Look Out for the Cheater	1966	40.00

KUHN, JOACHIM

ATLANTIC

Number	Title	Yr	NM
❑ SD1695	Springfever	1976	15.00
❑ SD19193	Sunshower	1978	12.00

CMP

Number	Title	Yr	NM
❑ CMP-26-ST	Distance	1987	12.00
❑ CMP-22-ST	I'm Not Dreaming	1986	12.00
❑ CMP-29-ST	Wandlungen/ Transformations	1987	12.00

KUHN, ROLF

URANIA

Number	Title	Yr	NM
❑ US-1220 [M]	Sound of Jazz	1962	30.00
❑ US-41220 [S]	Sound of Jazz	1962	30.00

VANGUARD

Number	Title	Yr	NM
❑ VRS-8510 [M]	Streamline	1955	40.00

KUHN, ROLF AND JOACHIM

ABC IMPULSE!

Number	Title	Yr	NM
❑ AS-9150	Impressions of New York	1968	25.00

KUHN, STEVE, AND SHEILA JORDAN

ECM

Number	Title	Yr	NM
❑ 1159	Playground	1979	15.00

KUHN, STEVE, AND TOSHIKO AKIYOSHI

DAUNTLESS

Number	Title	Yr	NM
❑ DM-4308 [M]	The Country & Western Sound for Jazz Pianos	1963	25.00
❑ DS-6308 [S]	The Country & Western Sound for Jazz Pianos	1963	30.00

KUHN, STEVE

ABC IMPULSE!

Number	Title	Yr	NM
❑ AS-9136 [S]	The October Suite	1968	15.00

BUDDAH

Number	Title	Yr	NM
❑ BDS-5098	Steve Kuhn	1972	18.00

CONTACT

Number	Title	Yr	NM
❑ CM-5 [M]	Steve Kuhn Trio Featuring Steve Swallow and Pete LaRoca	1965	25.00
❑ CS-5 [S]	Steve Kuhn Trio Featuring Steve Swallow and Pete LaRoca	1965	30.00

ECM

Number	Title	Yr	NM
❑ ECM-1-1058	Ecstasy	1975	15.00
❑ 1213	Last Year's Waltz	1982	12.00
❑ 1094	Motility	1977	15.00
❑ 1124	Non-Fiction	1978	15.00
❑ 1052	Trance	197?	15.00

IMPULSE!

Number	Title	Yr	NM
❑ A-9136 [M]	The October Suite	1967	40.00
❑ AS-9136 [S]	The October Suite	1967	30.00

MUSE

Number	Title	Yr	NM
❑ MR-5106	Raindrops/Live in New York	1978	15.00

PRESTIGE

Number	Title	Yr	NM
❑ PRST-7694	Steve Kuhn in Europe	1969	18.00

KUSTBANDET

STOMP OFF

Number	Title	Yr	NM
❑ SOS-1178	The New Call of the Freaks	1989	15.00

KUSTOM KINGS, THE

SMASH

Number	Title	Yr	NM
❑ MGS-27051 [M]	Kustom City, U.S.A.	1964	120.00
❑ SRS-67051 [S]	Kustom City, U.S.A.	1964	200.00

KWESKIN, JIM

MOUNTAIN RAILROAD

Number	Title	Yr	NM
❑ MR-52782	Jim Kweskin Lives Again	198?	12.00
❑ MR-52672	Jug Band Blues	198?	12.00
❑ MR-52790	Side by Side	198?	12.00
❑ MR-52793	Swing on a Star	198?	12.00

REPRISE

Number	Title	Yr	NM
❑ RS6464 [B]	America	1971	18.00
❑ R6266 [M]	Garden of Joy	1967	25.00
❑ RS6266 [S]	Garden of Joy	1967	18.00

VANGUARD

Number	Title	Yr	NM
❑ VSD13/14	Greatest Hits	1970	18.00
❑ VRS-9139 [M]	Jim Kweskin and the Jug Band	1963	25.00
❑ VSD-2158 [S]	Jim Kweskin and the Jug Band	1963	30.00
❑ VRS-9163 [M]	Jug Band Music	1965	25.00
❑ VSD-79163 [S]	Jug Band Music	1965	30.00
❑ VRS-9243 [M]	Jump for Joy	1967	25.00
❑ VSD-79243 [S]	Jump for Joy	1967	25.00
❑ VRS-9188 [M]	Relax Your Mind	1966	25.00
❑ VSD-79188 [S]	Relax Your Mind	1966	30.00
❑ VRS-9234 [M]	See Reverse Side for Title	1967	25.00
❑ VSD-79234 [S]	See Reverse Side for Title	1967	30.00
❑ VRS-9270 [M]	The Best of Jim Kweskin and the Jug Band	1968	40.00
❑ VSD-79270 [S]	The Best of Jim Kweskin and the Jug Band	1968	18.00

KYNARD, CHARLES

FANTASY

Number	Title	Yr	NM
❑ OJC-333	Reelin' with the Feelin'	1988	12.00

MAINSTREAM

Number	Title	Yr	NM
❑ MRL-331	Charles Kynard	1972	25.00
❑ MRL-366 [B]	Woga	1973	25.00
❑ MRL-389	Your Mama Don't Dance	1973	25.00

PACIFIC JAZZ

Number	Title	Yr	NM
❑ PJ-72 [M]	Where It's At!	1963	30.00
❑ ST-72 [S]	Where It's At!	1963	40.00

PRESTIGE

Number	Title	Yr	NM
❑ PRST-7796	Afro-disiac	1970	25.00
❑ PRST-7599	Professor Soul	1968	25.00
❑ PRST-7688	Reelin' with the Feelin'	1969	25.00
❑ PRST-7630	The Soul Brotherhood	1969	25.00
❑ 10008	Wa-tu-wa-zui	1971	25.00

WORLD PACIFIC

Number	Title	Yr	NM
❑ WP-1823 [M]	Warm Winds	1964	30.00
❑ ST-1823 [S]	Warm Winds	1964	30.00

KYSER, KAY

CAPITOL

Number	Title	Yr	NM
❑ T1692 [M]	Kay Kyser's Greatest Hits	196?	15.00
❑ ST1692 [S]	Kay Kyser's Greatest Hits	196?	18.00

COLUMBIA

Number	Title	Yr	NM
❑ CL6012 [10]	Campus Favorites	1948	80.00
❑ CG33572	The World of Kay Kyser	1976	18.00

HARMONY

Number	Title	Yr	NM
❑ HL7136 [M]	Campus Rally	196?	18.00
❑ HL7041 [M]	Kay Kyser	196?	18.00

SUNBEAM

Number	Title	Yr	NM
❑ SB-218 [M]	Kay Kyser and His Orchestra 1935-39	198?	15.00

L

L.A. 4

CONCORD JAZZ

Number	Title	Yr	NM
❑ CJ-215	Executive Suite	1982	12.00
❑ CJ-1001	Just Friends	1980	25.00

—Direct-to-disc recording

Number	Title	Yr	NM
❑ CJ-199	Just Friends	1981	12.00

—Regular version

Number	Title	Yr	NM
❑ CJ-100	Live at Montreux, 1979	1980	12.00
❑ CJ-156	Montage	1981	12.00
❑ CJ-8	Scores	197?	18.00
❑ CJ-18	The L.A. 4	197?	15.00
❑ CJ-63	Watch What Happens	1978	15.00
❑ CJ-130	Zaca	1980	12.00

EAST WIND

Number	Title	Yr	NM
❑ 10004	Going Home	197?	30.00

—Audiophile issue

Number	Title	Yr	NM
❑ 10003	Pavanne Pour Une Infante Defunte	197?	30.00

—Audiophile issue

Number	Title	Yr	NM

L.A. GUNS

CLEOPATRA
❏ 8691 [B]	Hollywood Forever		25.00
❏ 8796 [B]	Riot On Sunset - The Best Of		25.00

L.A. JAZZ CHOIR, THE

MOBILE FIDELITY
| ❏ 1-096 | Listen | 1982 | 80.00 |
—Audiophile vinyl

PAUSA
| ❏ 7184 | From All Sides | 1986 | 15.00 |

L.L. COOL J

DEF JAM
❏ C253325	14 Shots to the Dome	1993	18.00
❏ 524125-1	All World	1996	18.00
❏ FC40793	Bigger and Deffer	1987	15.00
❏ 546819-1	G.O.A.T. Featuring James T. Smith the Greatest of All Time	2000	18.00
❏ C46888	Mama Said Knock You Out	1990	18.00
❏ 523845-1	Mr. Smith	1995	15.00
❏ 539186-1	Phenomenon	1997	18.00
❏ FC40239	Radio	1985	15.00
❏ OC45173	Walking with a Panther	1989	18.00

L.T.D.

A&M
❏ SP-4771	Devotion	1979	12.00
❏ SP-3660	Gittin' Down	1975	15.00
❏ SP-4881	Love Magic	1981	12.00
❏ SP-4589	Love to the World	1976	12.00
❏ SP-3146	Love to the World	198?	10.00
—Budget-line reissue
| ❏ SP-3602 | L.T.D. | 1974 | 15.00 |
| ❏ SP-3119 | L.T.D. | 198? | 10.00 |
—Budget-line reissue
❏ SP-4819	Shine On	1980	12.00
❏ SP-4646	Something to Love	1977	12.00
❏ SP-3148	Something to Love	198?	10.00
—Budget-line reissue
| ❏ SP-4705 | Togetherness | 1978 | 12.00 |

L7

EPITAPH
| ❏ 86401 [B] | L7 | 1988 | 60.00 |
—Original press with Donita Sparks' head cut off

SLASH
| ❏ 45624 [B] | Hungry for Stink | 1994 | 18.00 |

SUB POP
| ❏ 79 [EP] | Smell the Magic | 1990 | 50.00 |
—First 1,000 on purple vinyl
| ❏ 79 [EP] | Smell the Magic | 1990 | 18.00 |

LA COSTA

CAPITOL
❏ ST-12090	Changin' All the Time	1980	15.00
❏ ST-11345	Get On My Love Train	1974	15.00
❏ ST-11713	La Costa	1977	15.00
❏ ST-11569	Lovin' Somebody	1975	15.00
❏ ST-11391	With All My Love	1975	15.00

LABELLE, PATTI, AND THE BLUE BELLES

ATLANTIC
❏ 8147 [M]	Dreamer	1967	60.00
❏ SD8147 [S]	Dreamer	1967	50.00
❏ 8119 [M]	Over the Rainbow	1966	40.00
❏ SD8119 [S]	Over the Rainbow	1966	50.00

MISTLETOE
| ❏ MLP-1204 | Merry Christmas from LaBelle | 1976 | 25.00 |

NEWTOWN
| ❏ 632 [M] | Sleigh Bells, Jingle Bells and Blue Bells | 1963 | 300.00 |
| ❏ 631 [M] | Sweethearts of the Apollo | 1963 | 400.00 |

PARKWAY
| ❏ P-7043 [M] | The Bluebelles On Stage | 1965 | 150.00 |
—With bonus single
| ❏ P-7043 [M] | The Bluebelles On Stage | 1965 | 120.00 |
—Without bonus single

TRIP
❏ 9525	Early Hits	197?	12.00
❏ 3508	Patti LaBelle and the Bluebelles	197?	12.00
❏ 8000	Patti LaBelle and the Bluebelles' Greatest Hits	1971	12.00

UNITED ARTISTS
| ❏ UA-LA504-E | The Very Best of Patti LaBelle and the Bluebelles | 1975 | 12.00 |

LABELLE, PATTI

EPIC
| ❏ FE36997 | Best of Patti LaBelle | 1981 | 12.00 |
| ❏ PE36997 | Best of Patti LaBelle | 198? | 10.00 |
—Budget-line reissue
| ❏ JE35772 | It's Alright with Me | 1979 | 15.00 |

| ❏ PE34847 | Patti LaBelle | 1977 | 18.00 |
—Original with no bar code and orange label
| ❏ PE34847 | Patti LaBelle | 1986 | 10.00 |
—Reissue with bar code and dark blue label
| ❏ JE36381 | Released | 1980 | 15.00 |
| ❏ JE35335 | Tasty | 1978 | 18.00 |

MCA
❏ 6292	Be Yourself	1989	12.00
❏ 10439	Burnin'	1991	15.00
❏ 5737	Winner in You	1986	12.00

PHILADELPHIA INT'L.
❏ FZ38539	I'm in Love Again	1983	15.00
❏ FZ40020	Patti	1985	15.00
❏ FZ37380	The Spirit's In It	1981	15.00
❏ PZ37380	The Spirit's In It	198?	10.00
—Budget-line reissue

LABELLE

EPIC
| ❏ PE34189 | Chameleon | 1976 | 12.00 |
—Original with no bar code and orange label
| ❏ PE34189 | Chameleon | 198? | 10.00 |
—Reissue with bar code and dark blue label
| ❏ KE33075 | Nightbirds | 1974 | 15.00 |
| ❏ PE33075 | Nightbirds | 197? | 10.00 |
—Reissue with new prefix
❏ PEQ33075 [Q]	Nightbirds	1975	30.00
❏ PE33579	Phoenix	1975	12.00
❏ PEQ33579 [Q]	Phoenix	1975	30.00

RCA VICTOR
| ❏ AYL1-4176 | Pressure Cookin' | 1982 | 10.00 |
—Best Buy Series" reissue
| ❏ APL1-0205 | Pressure Cookin' | 1973 | 15.00 |

WARNER BROS.
| ❏ WS1943 | LaBelle | 1971 | 18.00 |
| ❏ BS2618 [B] | Moonshadow | 1972 | 18.00 |

LACEWING

MAINSTREAM
| ❏ S-6132 | Lacewing | 1971 | 50.00 |

LACY, STEVE, AND MAL WALDRON

HAT ART
| ❏ 2015 | Herbe de L'Oubli & Snake-Out | 1986 | 18.00 |

HAT HUT
| ❏ 3501 | Snake-Out | 198? | 15.00 |

LACY, STEVE, AND MICHAEL SMITH

IAI
| ❏ 373847 | Sidelines | 197? | 18.00 |

LACY, STEVE

ADELPHI
| ❏ 5004 | Raps | 1977 | 15.00 |

BARNABY
| ❏ BR-5013 | The Straight Horn of Steve Lacy | 1977 | 15.00 |

BLACK SAINT
| ❏ BSR-0008 | Trickles | 198? | 15.00 |
| ❏ BSR-0035 | Troubles | 198? | 15.00 |

CANDID
| ❏ CD-8007 [M] | The Straight Horn of Steve Lacy | 1960 | 40.00 |
| ❏ CS-9007 [S] | The Straight Horn of Steve Lacy | 1960 | 50.00 |

EMANEM
❏ 3310	Saxophone Special	1975	18.00
❏ 3316	School Days	1975	18.00
❏ 301	Steve Lacy Solo	1973	18.00
❏ 304	The Crust	1974	18.00

ESP-DISK'
| ❏ 1060 [M] | The Forest and the Zoo | 1967 | 60.00 |
| ❏ S-1060 [S] | The Forest and the Zoo | 1967 | 50.00 |

FANTASY
❏ OJC-1755	Evidence	198?	15.00
❏ OJC-063	Reflections: Steve Lacy Plays Thelonious Monk	198?	15.00
❏ OJC-130	Steve Lacy Soprano Sax	198?	15.00

HAT ART
❏ 2006	Blinks	1986	18.00
❏ 2022	Futurities	1986	18.00
❏ 2014	N.Y. Capers	1986	18.00
❏ 2029	The Way	1987	18.00

HAT HUT
❏ 1982/3	Ballets	1982	18.00
❏ 14	Capers	1980	18.00
❏ 0F	Clinkers	1977	18.00
❏ 2001	Prospectus	198?	18.00
❏ 1985/86	Songs	1982	18.00
❏ UK/L	Stamps	1978	25.00
❏ 03	The Way	1979	25.00
❏ 20	Tips	1980	15.00

NEW JAZZ
| ❏ NJLP-8271 [M] | Evidence | 1962 | 150.00 |
—Purple label

| ❏ NJLP-8271 [M] | Evidence | 1965 | 50.00 |
—Blue label, trident logo at right
| ❏ NJLP-8206 [M] | Reflections: Steve Lacy Plays Thelonious Monk | 1958 | 200.00 |
—Purple label
| ❏ NJLP-8206 [M] | Reflections: Steve Lacy Plays Thelonious Monk | 1965 | 50.00 |
—Blue label, trident logo at right

NOVUS
❏ 3079-1-N	Anthem	1990	15.00
❏ 3021-1-N	Momentum	1988	12.00
❏ 3049-1-N	The Door	1989	15.00

PRESTIGE
| ❏ 2505 | Evidence | 198? | 15.00 |
| ❏ PRLP-7125 [M] | Steve Lacy Soprano Sax | 1956 | 200.00 |

QED
| ❏ 997 | School Days | 197? | 15.00 |

RED
| ❏ VPA-120 | Axieme Vol. 1 | 198? | 15.00 |
| ❏ VPA-121 | Axieme Vol. 2 | 198? | 15.00 |

SILKHEART
| ❏ SH-103 | One Fell Swoop | 198? | 12.00 |
| ❏ SH-102 | The Gleam | 198? | 12.00 |

SOUL NOE
| ❏ SN-1035 | The Flame | 198? | 15.00 |

SOUL NOTE
❏ 121210	More Monk	199?	18.00
❏ 121100	Only Monk	199?	18.00
❏ 121135	The Condor	1990	18.00
❏ 121185	The Window	199?	18.00

STATUS
| ❏ ST-8308 [M] | Wynton Kelly with Steve Lacy | 1965 | 60.00 |

LADD, CHERYL

CAPITOL
| ❏ SW-11808 | Cheryl Ladd | 1978 | 15.00 |
| ❏ ST-11927 | Dance Forever | 1979 | 15.00 |

LADNIER, TOMMY

RIVERSIDE
❏ RLP-1026 [10]	Early Ladnier	1954	100.00
❏ RLP-1019 [10]	Ida Cox with Tommy Ladnier	1953	100.00
❏ RLP-1044 [10]	Tommy Ladnier Plays the Blues	1954	100.00

X
| ❏ LVA-3027 [M] | Tommy Ladnier | 1954 | 60.00 |

LADY FLASH

RSO
| ❏ RS-1-3002 | Beauties in the Night | 1976 | 15.00 |

LAFARGE, PETER

COLUMBIA
| ❏ CL1795 [M] | Ira Hayes and Other Ballads | 1962 | 25.00 |
| ❏ CS8595 [S] | Ira Hayes and Other Ballads | 1962 | 30.00 |

VERVE FOLKWAYS
| ❏ FV-9004 [M] | Peter LaFarge Sings Women Blues | 1965 | 25.00 |
| ❏ FVS-9004 [S] | Peter LaFarge Sings Women Blues | 1965 | 30.00 |

LAFORGE, JACK

AUDIO FIDELITY
| ❏ AFLP-2161 [M] | Hit the Road Jack | 196? | 18.00 |
| ❏ AFSD-6161 [S] | Hit the Road Jack | 196? | 25.00 |

REGINA
❏ R-309 [M]	Comin' Home Baby	196?	25.00
❏ RS-309 [S]	Comin' Home Baby	196?	30.00
❏ R-319 [M]	Goldfinger	1965	25.00
❏ RS-319 [S]	Goldfinger	1965	30.00
❏ R-716 [M]	Hawaii and I	196?	25.00
❏ RS-716 [S]	Hawaii and I	196?	30.00
❏ R-282 [M]	I Remember You	196?	25.00
❏ RS-282 [S]	I Remember You	196?	30.00
❏ R-314 [M]	Jazz Portrait of Jack LaForge	196?	25.00
❏ RS-314 [S]	Jazz Portrait of Jack LaForge	196?	30.00
❏ R-327 [M]	Our Crazy Affair	196?	25.00
❏ RS-327 [S]	Our Crazy Affair	196?	30.00
❏ R-313 [M]	Promise Her Anything	196?	25.00
❏ RS-313 [S]	Promise Her Anything	196?	30.00
❏ R-288 [M]	Unchain My Heart	196?	25.00
❏ RS-288 [S]	Unchain My Heart	196?	30.00
❏ R-301 [M]	You Fascinate Me So	196?	25.00
❏ RS-301 [S]	You Fascinate Me So	196?	30.00

LAINE, CLEO, AND DUDLEY MOORE

FINESSE
| ❏ FW38091 | Smilin' Through | 1983 | 15.00 |

LAINE, CLEO, AND JAMES GALWAY

RCA RED SEAL
| ❏ ARL1-3628 | Sometimes When We Touch | 198? | 12.00 |

LAINE, CLEO

BUDDAH

Number	Title	Yr	NM
❑ BDS-5607	Day By Day	1972	18.00

CBS

Number	Title	Yr	NM
❑ FM39211	Let the Music Take You	1984	12.00
❑ FM39736	That Old Feeling	1985	12.00

DRG

Number	Title	Yr	NM
❑ MR2S-608	An Evening with Cleo Lane and the John Dankworth Quartet	198?	15.00
❑ DARC2-2101	Cleo at Carnegie: The 10th Anniversary Concert	198?	15.00
❑ MRS-502	Cleo Lane with John Dankworth's Orchestra	198?	12.00
❑ SL-5198	One More Day	198?	12.00

FONTANA

Number	Title	Yr	NM
❑ MGF-27531 [M]	Shakespeare and All That Jazz	1966	18.00
❑ SRF-67531 [S]	Shakespeare and All That Jazz	1966	25.00
❑ MGF-27552 [M]	Woman to Woman	1967	25.00
❑ SRF-67552 [S]	Woman to Woman	1967	18.00

GNP CRESCENDO

Number	Title	Yr	NM
❑ GNPS-9024	Cleo's Choice	197?	12.00

JAZZ MAN

Number	Title	Yr	NM
❑ 5033	Live at Wavendon Festival	198?	12.00

RCA

Number	Title	Yr	NM
❑ 7702-1-R	Cleo Sings Sondheim	1988	12.00

RCA VICTOR

Number	Title	Yr	NM
❑ CPL1-5059	A Beautiful Thing	1974	18.00
❑ AFL1-5059	A Beautiful Thing	1978	12.00
—Reissue with new prefix			
❑ AYL1-3805	A Beautiful Thing	1980	10.00
—Budget-line reissue			
❑ APL1-1937	Best Friends	1976	15.00
❑ AFL1-1937	Best Friends	1978	12.00
—Reissue with new prefix			
❑ LPL1-5113	Born Friday	197?	15.00
❑ AFL1-5113	Born Friday	1978	12.00
—Reissue with new prefix			
❑ AFL1-2926	Gonna Get Through	1978	12.00
❑ LPL1-5000	I Am a Song	1973	18.00
❑ AFL1-5000	I Am a Song	1978	12.00
—Reissue with new prefix			
❑ LPL1-5015	Live at Carnegie Hall	1973	18.00
❑ AFL1-5015	Live at Carnegie Hall	1978	12.00
—Reissue with new prefix			
❑ AYL1-3751	Live at Carnegie Hall	1980	10.00
—Budget-line reissue			
❑ APL1-2407	Return to Carnegie Hall	1977	15.00
❑ AFL1-2407	Return to Carnegie Hall	1978	12.00
—Reissue with new prefix			

STANYAN

Number	Title	Yr	NM
❑ 10067	Day By Day	197?	15.00
❑ 10122	Easy Livin'	197?	15.00

LAINE, DENNY

CAPITOL

Number	Title	Yr	NM
❑ ST-11588 [B]	Holly Days	1977	30.00

REPRISE

Number	Title	Yr	NM
❑ MS2190 [B]	Ah, Laine!	1972	18.00

TAKOMA

Number	Title	Yr	NM
❑ 7034 [B]	Japanese Tears	1983	15.00

LAINE, FRANKIE

ABC

Number	Title	Yr	NM
❑ 604 [M]	I'll Take Care of Your Cares	1967	15.00
❑ S-604 [S]	I'll Take Care of Your Cares	1967	18.00
❑ 608 [M]	I Wanted Someone to Love	1967	15.00
❑ S-608 [S]	I Wanted Someone to Love	1967	18.00
❑ S-657	Take Me Back to Laine Country	1968	18.00
❑ 628 [M]	To Each His Own	1968	25.00
❑ S-628 [S]	To Each His Own	1968	18.00
❑ S-682	You Gave Me a Mountain	1969	18.00

AMOS

Number	Title	Yr	NM
❑ 7013	Brand New Day	1971	15.00
❑ 7009	Frankie Laine's Greatest Hits	1970	15.00

BULLDOG

Number	Title	Yr	NM
❑ BDL-1035	All of Me	198?	12.00

CAPITOL

Number	Title	Yr	NM
❑ T2277 [M]	I Believe	1965	15.00
❑ ST2277 [S]	I Believe	1965	18.00

COLUMBIA

Number	Title	Yr	NM
❑ CL1829 [M]	Call of the Wild	1962	18.00
❑ CS8629 [S]	Call of the Wild	1962	25.00
❑ CL625 [M]	Command Performance	1954	40.00
❑ CL1696 [M]	Deuces Wild	1962	25.00
—Red and black label with six "eye" logos			
❑ CL1696 [M]	Deuces Wild	1962	18.00
—Guaranteed High Fidelity" or "360 Sound Mono" label			
❑ CS8496 [S]	Deuces Wild	1962	30.00
—Red and black label with six "eye" logos			
❑ CS8496 [S]	Deuces Wild	1962	25.00
—360 Sound Stereo" label			
❑ CL1116 [M]	Foreign Affair	1958	30.00
❑ CL1393 [M]	Frankie Laine, Balladeer	1960	25.00
❑ CS8188 [S]	Frankie Laine, Balladeer	1960	30.00
❑ CL1231 [M]	Frankie Laine's Greatest Hits	1958	30.00
—Red and black label with six "eye" logos			
❑ CL1231 [M]	Frankie Laine's Greatest Hits	1962	18.00
—Guaranteed High Fidelity" or "360 Sound Mono" label			
❑ CS8636 [R]	Frankie Laine's Greatest Hits	1963	15.00
❑ PC8636	Frankie Laine's Greatest Hits	198?	10.00
—Reissue with new prefix			
❑ CL1615 [M]	Hell Bent for Leather!	1961	25.00
—Red and black label with six "eye" logos			
❑ CL1615 [M]	Hell Bent for Leather!	1962	18.00
—Guaranteed High Fidelity" or "360 Sound Mono" label			
❑ CS8415 [S]	Hell Bent for Leather!	1961	30.00
—Red and black label with six "eye" logos			
❑ CS8415 [S]	Hell Bent for Leather!	1962	25.00
—360 Sound Stereo" label			
❑ CL808 [M]	Jazz Spectacular	1956	30.00
❑ CL2504 [10]	Lover's Laine	1955	40.00
❑ CL6278 [10]	Mr. Rhythm	1954	50.00
❑ CL6200 [10]	One for My Baby	1952	50.00
❑ CL2548 [10]	One for My Baby	1955	40.00
❑ CL1277 [M]	Reunion in Rhythm	1959	25.00
❑ CS8087 [S]	Reunion in Rhythm	1959	30.00
❑ CL975 [M]	Rockin'	1957	30.00
❑ CL1176 [M]	Torchin'	1959	25.00
❑ CS8024 [S]	Torchin'	1959	30.00
❑ CL1962 [M]	Wanderlust	1963	18.00
❑ CS8762 [S]	Wanderlust	1963	25.00
❑ CL1317 [M]	You Are My Love	1960	25.00
❑ CS8119 [S]	You Are My Love	1960	30.00

GALAXY SERIES

Number	Title	Yr	NM
❑ 4821 [M]	Frankie Laine Sings	195?	15.00

HARMONY

Number	Title	Yr	NM
❑ H30406	High Noon	1971	15.00
❑ HS11345	I'm Gonna Live 'Til I Die	1969	15.00
❑ HL7425 [M]	Memories	196?	15.00
❑ HS11225 [S]	Memories	196?	15.00
❑ HL7329 [M]	Roving Gambler	196?	15.00
❑ HS11129 [S]	Roving Gambler	196?	15.00
❑ HL7382 [M]	That's My Desire	196?	15.00
❑ HS11182 [S]	That's My Desire	196?	15.00

HINDSIGHT

Number	Title	Yr	NM
❑ HSR-216	Frankie Laine with Carl Fischer and His Orchestra, 1947	1985	12.00

MERCURY

Number	Title	Yr	NM
❑ MG-25082 [10]	Christmas Favorites	1951	50.00
❑ MG-20085 [M]	Concert Date	1957	40.00
❑ MG-25007 [10]	Favorites	1949	50.00
❑ MG-25025 [10]	Frankie Laine	1950	50.00
❑ MG-25026 [10]	Frankie Laine	1950	50.00
❑ MG-25027 [10]	Frankie Laine	1950	50.00
❑ MG-20587 [M]	Frankie Laine's Golden Hits	1960	30.00
❑ SR-60587 [R]	Frankie Laine's Golden Hits	196?	15.00
❑ MG-20083 [M]	Frankie Laine Sings For Us	1957	40.00
❑ MG-25124 [10]	Listen to Laine	1952	50.00
❑ MG-25097 [10]	Mr. Rhythm Sings	1951	50.00
❑ MG-20069 [M]	Songs by Frankie Laine	1956	40.00
❑ MG-25024 [10]	Songs from the Heart	1950	50.00
❑ MG-20080 [M]	That's My Desire	1957	40.00
❑ PKW-2-111	The Great Years	1969	18.00
❑ MG-20105 [M]	With All My Heart	1957	40.00

PICKWICK

Number	Title	Yr	NM
❑ SPC-3526	That Lucky Old Sun	197?	12.00
❑ SPC-3601	You Gave Me a Mountain	197?	12.00

TOWER

Number	Title	Yr	NM
❑ T5092 [M]	Memory Laine	1967	15.00
❑ ST5092 [S]	Memory Laine	1967	18.00

WING

Number	Title	Yr	NM
❑ MGW12110 [M]	All-Time Favorites	196?	18.00
❑ SRW16110 [R]	All-Time Favorites	196?	15.00
❑ MGW12158 [M]	Singing the Blues	196?	18.00
❑ SRW16158 [R]	Singing the Blues	196?	15.00
❑ MGW12202 [M]	That's My Desire	196?	18.00
❑ SRW16202 [R]	That's My Desire	196?	15.00

LAIRD, RICK

TIMELESS

Number	Title	Yr	NM
❑ 308	Soft Focus	197?	15.00

LAKE, GREG

CHRYSALIS

Number	Title	Yr	NM
❑ CHR1357	Greg Lake	1981	10.00

LAKE, OLIVER

ARISTA/FREEDOM

Number	Title	Yr	NM
❑ AF1008	Heavy Spirits	1975	18.00
❑ AF1024	Ntu	1976	18.00

ARISTA/NOVUS

Number	Title	Yr	NM
❑ AN3010	Focus	1979	15.00
❑ AN3003	Life Dance Of Is	1978	15.00

BLACK SAINT

Number	Title	Yr	NM
❑ BSR-0054	Clevont Fitzhubert	198?	15.00
❑ BSR-0044	Prophet	198?	15.00

GRAMAVISION

Number	Title	Yr	NM
❑ 8106	Oliver Lake & Jump Up	198?	12.00
❑ 8206	Plug It	198?	12.00

LALA, MIKE

GHB

Number	Title	Yr	NM
❑ GHB-120	Mike Lala and His Dixie Six	198?	12.00

LAMARCH, SUSAN

STOMP OFF

Number	Title	Yr	NM
❑ SOS-1032	Vamp 'Til Ready	198?	12.00

LAMARE, NAPPY, AND KID ORY

MODERN

Number	Title	Yr	NM
❑ 2010 [10]	Modern Records Volume 10	195?	60.00
—No printing on back cover			

LAMAS, FERNANDO

ROULETTE

Number	Title	Yr	NM
❑ R-25041 [M]	With Love, Fernando Lamas	1958	40.00

LAMB, JOSEPH

FOLKWAYS

Number	Title	Yr	NM
❑ FJ-3562 [M]	Classic Ragtime	1960	25.00

LAMB, NATALIE, AND SAMMY PRICE

GHB

Number	Title	Yr	NM
❑ GHB-84	Natalie Lamb and Sammy Price and the Blues	198?	12.00

LAMB

FILLMORE

Number	Title	Yr	NM
❑ F30003	Sign of Change	1970	25.00

WARNER BROS.

Number	Title	Yr	NM
❑ WS1952	Bring Out the Sun	1972	25.00
❑ WS1920	Cross Between	1971	25.00

LAMBERT, DAVE

UNITED ARTISTS

Number	Title	Yr	NM
❑ UAL-3084 [M]	Dave Lambert Sings and Swings Alone	1959	40.00
❑ UAS-6084 [S]	Dave Lambert Sings and Swings Alone	1959	50.00

LAMBERT, DONALD

JAZZOLOGY

Number	Title	Yr	NM
❑ JCE-59	Giant Stride	197?	12.00

LAMBERT, HENDRICKS AND BAVAN

BLUEBIRD

Number	Title	Yr	NM
❑ 6282-1-RB	Swingin' Til the Girls Come Home	1987	12.00

RCA VICTOR

Number	Title	Yr	NM
❑ LPM-2747 [M]	Lambert, Hendricks and Bavan at Newport	1963	30.00
❑ LSP-2747 [S]	Lambert, Hendricks and Bavan at Newport	1963	40.00
❑ LPM-2861 [M]	Lambert, Hendricks and Bavan at the Village Gate	1964	30.00
❑ LSP-2861 [S]	Lambert, Hendricks and Bavan at the Village Gate	1964	40.00
❑ LPM-2635 [M]	Live at Basin Street East	1963	30.00
❑ LSP-2635 [S]	Live at Basin Street East	1963	40.00

LAMBERT, HENDRICKS AND ROSS

ABC IMPULSE!

Number	Title	Yr	NM
❑ AS-83 [S]	Sing a Song of Basie	1968	18.00

ABC-PARAMOUNT

Number	Title	Yr	NM
❑ ABC-223 [M]	Sing a Song of Basie	1958	50.00
❑ ABCS-223 [S]	Sing a Song of Basie	1958	50.00

COLUMBIA

Number	Title	Yr	NM
❑ CL1675 [M]	High Flying	1961	30.00
—Black and red label with six "eye" logos			
❑ CS8475 [S]	High Flying	1961	40.00
—Black and red label with six "eye" logos			
❑ CL1675 [M]	High Flying	1963	18.00
—Red label with "Guaranteed High Fidelity" or "360 Sound Mono" at bottom			
❑ CS8475 [S]	High Flying	1963	25.00
—Red label with "360 Sound Stereo" at bottom			
❑ CL1510 [M]	Lambert, Hendricks and Ross Sing Ellington	1960	30.00
—Black and red label with six "eye" logos			
❑ CS8310 [S]	Lambert, Hendricks and Ross Sing Ellington	1960	40.00
—Black and red label with six "eye" logos			
❑ CL1510 [M]	Lambert, Hendricks and Ross Sing Ellington	1963	18.00
—Red label with "Guaranteed High Fidelity" or "360 Sound Mono" at bottom			
❑ CS8310 [S]	Lambert, Hendricks and Ross Sing Ellington	1963	25.00
—Red label with "360 Sound Stereo" at bottom			
❑ KC32911	The Best of Lambert, Hendricks and Ross	1974	18.00

Number	Title	Yr	NM
❏ C32911	The Best of Lambert, Hendricks and Ross	197?	12.00
— First reissue with new prefix			
❏ PC32911	The Best of Lambert, Hendricks and Ross	198?	10.00
— Second reissue with new prefix and bar code			
❏ CL1403 [M]	The Hottest New Group in Jazz	1959	30.00
— Black and red label with six "eye" logos			
❏ CL1403 [M]	The Hottest New Group in Jazz	1963	18.00
— Red label with "Guaranteed High Fidelity" or "360 Sound Mono" at bottom			
❏ CS8198 [S]	The Hottest New Group in Jazz	1959	40.00
— Black and red label with six "eye" logos			
❏ CS8198 [S]	The Hottest New Group in Jazz	1963	25.00
— Red label with "360 Sound Stereo" at bottom			

COLUMBIA JAZZ ODYSSEY

❏ PC37020	Lambert, Hendricks and Ross with the Ike Isaacs Trio	1983	12.00

IMPULSE!

❏ A-83 [M]	Sing a Song of Basie	1965	30.00
— Reissue of ABC-Paramount ABC-223			
❏ AS-83 [S]	Sing a Song of Basie	1965	30.00
— Reissue of ABC-Paramount ABCS-223			

MCA

❏ 29049	Sing a Song of Basie	1980	10.00

ODYSSEY

❏ 32160292	Way-Out Voices	1968	18.00

ROULETTE

❏ R-52018 [M]	Sing Along with Basie	1959	40.00
❏ SR-52018 [S]	Sing Along with Basie	1959	50.00

WORLD PACIFIC

❏ WP-1264 [M]	The Swingers!	1959	40.00
❏ ST-1025 [S]	The Swingers!	1959	50.00

LAMBSON, ROGER

SEA BREEZE

❏ SB-2035	Dreams of Mexico	198?	12.00

LAMEGO, DANNY, AND HIS JUMPIN' JACKS

FORGET-ME-NOT

❏ 105 [M]	The Big Weekend	1964	100.00

LAMM, ROBERT

COLUMBIA

❏ PC33095	Skinny Boy	1974	15.00

LAMOND, DON

COMMAND

❏ RS 33-842 [M]	Off Beat Percussion	1962	18.00
❏ RS832SD [S]	Off Beat Percussion	1962	25.00

PROGRESSIVE

❏ PRO-7067	Extraordinary	198?	12.00

LAMONT, CHARLES

UNI

❏ 73076	A Legend in His Own Mind	1970	30.00
— As "Lamont"			

LAMOUR, DOROTHY

DECCA

❏ DL5115 [10]	Favorite Hawaiian Songs	1950	80.00

LANCASTER, BYARD

VORTEX

❏ 2003	It's Not Up to Us	1968	30.00

LANCE, HERB

CHESS

❏ LP-1506 [M]	The Comeback	1966	30.00
❏ LPS-1506 [S]	The Comeback	1966	30.00

LANCE, LYNDA K.

ROYAL AMERICAN

❏ RA2801	A Woman's Side of Love	1969	18.00

LANCE, MAJOR

KAT FAMILY

❏ FZ38898	The Major's Back	1983	15.00

OKEH

❏ OKM-12110 [M]	Major's Greatest Hits	1965	40.00
❏ OKS-14110 [S]	Major's Greatest Hits	1965	40.00
❏ OKM-12105 [M]	The Monkey Time	1963	60.00
❏ OKS-14105 [S]	The Monkey Time	1963	50.00
❏ OKM-12106 [M]	Um, Um, Um, Um, Um, Um	1964	60.00
❏ OKS-14106 [S]	Um, Um, Um, Um, Um, Um	1964	50.00

SOUL

❏ S7-751	Now Arriving	1978	15.00

Number	Title	Yr	NM

LANCELOT LINK AND THE EVOLUTION REVOLUTION

ABC

❏ S-715	Lancelot Link and the Evolution Revolution	1970	40.00

LANCERS, THE

CORAL

❏ CRL57100 [M]	Dixieland Ball	1957	30.00

IMPERIAL

❏ LP-9075 [M]	Concert in Contrasts	1959	30.00
❏ LP-12023 [S]	Concert in Contrasts	1959	40.00

TREND

❏ TL-1009 [10]	The Lancers	1954	40.00

LANCHESTER, ELSA

HIFI

❏ 406 [M]	Songs for a Shuttered Parlor	1958	25.00
❏ 405 [M]	Songs for a Smoke-Filled Room	1957	25.00

VERVE

❏ MGV-15015 [M]	Cockney London	1960	30.00
❏ MGV-15024 [M]	Herself	1962	30.00

LAND, HAROLD, AND BLUE MITCHELL

CONCORD JAZZ

❏ CJ-44	Mapenzi	1977	15.00

LAND, HAROLD

BLUE NOTE

❏ LT-1057	Take Aim	1980	12.00

CADET

❏ LPS-813	The Peace-Maker	1968	18.00

CONTEMPORARY

❏ M-3550 [M]	Grooveyard	1959	60.00
— Reissue with new title			
❏ S-7550 [S]	Grooveyard	1959	50.00
❏ C-3550 [M]	Harold in the Land of Hi-Fi	1958	80.00
❏ M-3619 [M]	The Fox	1965	25.00
❏ S-7619 [S]	The Fox	1965	30.00

FANTASY

❏ OJC-493	Eastward Ho! Harold Land in New York	1991	15.00
❏ OJC-162 [B]	In the Land of Jazz	1984	60.00
❏ OJC-343	The Fox	198?	12.00
❏ OJC-146	West Coast Blues!	198?	12.00

HIFI

❏ J-612 [M]	The Fox	1960	100.00
❏ SJ-612 [S]	The Fox	1960	80.00

IMPERIAL

❏ LP-9247 [M]	Jazz Impressions of Folk Music	1963	30.00
❏ LP-12247 [S]	Jazz Impressions of Folk Music	1963	30.00

JAZZLAND

❏ JLP-33 [M]	Eastward Ho! Harold Land in New York	1961	40.00
❏ JLP-933 [S]	Eastward Ho! Harold Land in New York	1961	50.00
❏ JLP-20 [M]	West Coast Blues!	1960	40.00
❏ JLP-920 [S]	West Coast Blues!	1960	50.00

MAINSTREAM

❏ MRL-344	Choma (Burn)	1972	18.00
❏ MRL-367	Damisi	1973	18.00
❏ MRL-314	New Shade of Blue	1971	18.00

MUSE

❏ MR-5272	Xocia's Dance	198?	12.00

LANDE, ART, AND JAN GARBAREK

ECM

❏ 1038	Red Lanta	197?	18.00

LANDE, ART; DAVE SAMUELA; PAUL McCANDLESS

ECM

❏ 1208	Skylight	1982	15.00

LANDE, ART

1750 ARCH

❏ 1769	The Eccentricities of Earl Dant	1978	18.00
❏ 1778	The Story of Ba-Ku	1979	18.00

ECM

❏ 1106	Desert	197?	18.00
❏ 1081	Rubisa Patrol	197?	18.00

LANDSLIDE

CAPITOL

❏ ST-11006	Two-Sided Fantasy	1972	40.00

LANE, ABBE

MERCURY

❏ MG-20643 [M]	Abbe Lane with Xavier Cugat and His Orchestra	1961	30.00

Number	Title	Yr	NM
❏ SR-60643 [S]	Abbe Lane with Xavier Cugat and His Orchestra	1961	30.00
❏ SR-60930 [S]	The Many Sides of Abbe Lane	1964	30.00
❏ MG-20930 [M]	The Many Sides of Abbe Lane	1964	25.00

RCA VICTOR

❏ LPM-1554 [M]	Be Mine Tonight	1957	30.00
❏ LSP-1554 [S]	Be Mine Tonight	1958	40.00
❏ LPM-1688 [M]	The Lady in Red	1958	30.00
❏ LSP-1688 [S]	The Lady in Red	1958	40.00

LANE, CRISTY

ARRIVAL

❏ NU9640	One Day at a Time: 14 Songs of Inspiration and Harmony	1983	12.00

LANE

❏ LPS-101	Cristy Lane Salutes the G.I.'s of Vietnam	197?	30.00

LIBERTY

❏ LT-51117	Amazing Grace	1982	10.00
❏ LT-1023	Ask Me to Dance	1981	10.00
— Reissue of United Artists 1023			
❏ LN-10226	Christmas with Cristy	198?	12.00
❏ LT-51153	Cristy Lane At Her Best	1984	10.00
❏ LT-51148	Footprints in the Sand	1983	10.00
❏ LT-51112	Fragile -- Handle with Care	1981	10.00
❏ LT-51137	Here's to Us	1982	10.00
❏ LT-1083	I Have a Dream	1981	10.00
❏ LI-978	Simple Little Words	1981	10.00
— Reissue of United Artists 978			

LS

❏ 1987	Christmas Gold	1987	12.00
❏ SLL-8358	Christmas Is the Man from Galilee	1983	12.00
❏ 2002	Country Classics Vol. 2	198?	12.00
❏ 2003	Country Classics Vol. 3	198?	12.00
❏ 8027	Cristy Lane Is the Name	1978	15.00
❏ 9227	Cristy Lane Salutes the G.I.'s of Vietnam	198?	12.00
❏ 1001	Easy to Love	198?	12.00
❏ SLL-8385	Greatest Hits	198?	12.00
❏ 8028	Love Lies	1979	15.00
❏ SLL-8386	One Day at a Time	198?	12.00
❏ SLL-8334	The Sweetest Voice This Side of Heaven	198?	12.00

RIVERSONG

❏ 2413	14 Golden Hymns	198?	12.00

SUFFOLK MARKETING

❏ SLL-8289	One Day at a Time	198?	12.00

UNITED ARTISTS

❏ LT-1023	Ask Me to Dance	1980	12.00
❏ UA-LA978-H	Simple Little Words	1979	12.00

LANE, JERRY "MAX

CHART

❏ CHS-1025	Lover's Lane	1970	18.00

LANE, RED

RCA VICTOR

❏ LSP-4576	The World Needs a Melody	1971	18.00

LANE, ROBIN, AND THE CHARTBUSTERS

RERON

❏ 77 [EP]	Heart Connection	1984	15.00
— Robin Lane solo			

WARNER BROS.

❏ MINI3495	Five Live	1980	18.00
❏ BSK3537	Imitation Life	1981	18.00
❏ BSK3424	Robin Lane and the Chartbusters	1980	18.00

LANE, STEVE, AND THE SOUTHERN STOMPERS

STOMP OFF

❏ SOS-1040	Snake Rag	198?	12.00

LANEGAN, MARK

SUB POP

❏ SP419	Scraps at Midnight	1998	25.00
❏ SP61	The Winding Sheet	1990	30.00
— First 1,000 on red vinyl			
❏ SP61	The Winding Sheet	1990	12.00
— Black vinyl. Among the backing musicians are Kurt Cobain and Krist Novoselic of NIRVANA.			
❏ SP132	Whisky for the Holy Ghost	1994	25.00

LANG, EDDIE

YAZOO

❏ 1059	Virtuoso	198?	12.00

LANG, K.D.

BUMSTEAD

❏ BUM-842	A Truly Western Experience	1984	35.00
— Canadian import; first issue			

Number	Title	Yr	NM

Number	Title	Yr	NM
☐ BUM-86 [B]	A Truly Western Experience	1984	30.00

—*Canadian import; reissue of Bumstead 842*

SIRE
☐ 25877	Absolute Torch and Twang	1989	15.00
☐ R160100	Angel with a Lariat	1987	15.00

—*BMG Direct Marketing edition*

☐ 25441	Angel with a Lariat	1987	12.00
☐ R134567	Shadowland	1988	15.00

—*BMG Direct Marketing edition*

☐ 25724	Shadowland	1988	12.00
☐ PRO-A-3120 [DJ]	The Making of Shadowland	1988	25.00

—*Interview album*

WARNER BROS.
☐ 46034	All You Can Eat	1995	25.00

LANG, RONNIE

TOPS
☐ L-1521 [M]	Modern Jazz	1958	30.00

LANGDON, DORY

VERVE
☐ MGV-2101 [M]	Leprechauns Are Upon Me	1957	40.00

LANGDON, JIM

CUCA
☐ 1100 [M]	Jim Langdon Trio	1965	25.00

LANGFORD, BILL

FANTASY
☐ 8396	Gangbusters and Lollipops	197?	12.00

LANGNER SISTERS, THE

STUDIO CITY
☐ 9012	It's the Country Life for Me	1967	30.00
☐ 9011	The Langner Sisters	1966	30.00

LANIN, LESTER

AUDIO FIDELITY
☐ AFSD-6180 [S]	Thoroughly Modern	1968	15.00
☐ AFLP-2180 [M]	Thoroughly Modern	1968	18.00

EPIC
☐ LN3617 [M]	Christmas Dance Party (Volume 9)	1959	18.00
☐ BN547 [S]	Christmas Dance Party (Volume 9)	1959	25.00
☐ LN3531 [M]	Cocktail Dancing	1959	18.00
☐ BN516 [S]	Cocktail Dancing	1959	25.00
☐ LN24317 [M]	Cole Porter's Greatest Hits	1967	15.00
☐ BN26317 [S]	Cole Porter's Greatest Hits	1967	15.00
☐ LN3656 [M]	Dance to the Lester Lanin Beat	1960	18.00
☐ BN556 [S]	Dance to the Lester Lanin Beat	1960	25.00
☐ LN3340 [M]	Dance to the Music of Lester Lanin	1957	18.00
☐ BN633 [R]	Dance to the Music of Lester Lanin	1962	15.00
☐ LN24016 [M]	Dancing Theatre Party	1962	15.00
☐ BN26016 [S]	Dancing Theatre Party	1962	18.00
☐ LN3525 [M]	Have Band, Will Travel	1958	18.00
☐ BN517 [S]	Have Band, Will Travel	1959	25.00
☐ LN3699 [M]	High Society	1961	15.00
☐ BN570 [S]	High Society	1961	18.00
☐ LN3242 [M]	Lester Lanin and His Orchestra	1956	18.00
☐ BN628 [R]	Lester Lanin and His Orchestra	1962	15.00
☐ LN3410 [M]	Lester Lanin at the Tiffany Ball	1957	18.00
☐ BN505 [S]	Lester Lanin at the Tiffany Ball	1959	25.00
☐ LN3474 [M]	Lester Lanin Goes to College	1958	18.00
☐ BN501 [S]	Lester Lanin Goes to College	1959	25.00

Number	Title	Yr	NM
☐ LN24105 [M]	Richard Rogers Hits	1964	15.00
☐ BN26105 [S]	Richard Rogers Hits	1964	18.00
☐ SN6046 [M]	The Dance Album	1964	18.00
☐ BSN146 [S]	The Dance Album	1964	25.00
☐ LN3825 [M]	Twistin' in High Society!	1961	15.00
☐ BN620 [S]	Twistin' in High Society!	1961	18.00

HARMONY
☐ HS11262	Everybody Dance	1968	12.00

HINDSIGHT
☐ HSR-210	Dance Instrumentals: 1960-1962	198?	10.00

METROMEDIA
☐ MD-1006	Narrowing the Generation Gap	1969	15.00

PHILIPS
☐ PHM200145 [M]	Dancing at the Discotheque	1964	12.00
☐ PHS600145 [S]	Dancing at the Discotheque	1964	15.00
☐ PHM200211 [M]	Forty Beatles Hits	1966	15.00
☐ PHS600211 [S]	Forty Beatles Hits	1966	18.00
☐ PHM200181 [M]	Hits for Dancing	1965	12.00
☐ PHS600181 [S]	Hits for Dancing	1965	15.00
☐ PHM200165 [M]	I Had a Ball	1965	12.00
☐ PHS600165 [S]	I Had a Ball	1965	15.00
☐ PHM200192 [M]	Lester Lanin at the Country Club	1966	12.00
☐ PHS600192 [S]	Lester Lanin at the Country Club	1966	15.00
☐ PHM200132 [M]	Lester Lanin Plays for Dancing	1964	12.00
☐ PHS600132 [S]	Lester Lanin Plays for Dancing	1964	15.00

LANZA, MARIO

PAIR
☐ PDL2-1059	The Voice of the Century	1986	15.00

PICKWICK
☐ CAS-777(e) [R]	Christmas Hymns and Carols	1977	10.00

—*Same contents as RCA Camden CAS-777(e)*

RCA CAMDEN
☐ CAL-777 [M]	Christmas Hymns and Carols	196?	18.00
☐ CAS-777(e) [R]	Christmas Hymns and Carols	196?	15.00
☐ CAL-450 [M]	You Do Something to Me	195?	18.00
☐ CAS-450(e) [R]	You Do Something to Me	195?	15.00

RCA RED SEAL
☐ CRL1-1750	A Legendary Performer	1976	12.00
☐ ARL1-0134	Lanza Sings Caruso	1973	12.00
☐ VCS-6192	Mario Lanza's Greatest Hits	1970	30.00
☐ VCS-7073	Opera's Greatest Hits	1971	25.00
☐ ANL1-2874	Pure Gold	1978	12.00
☐ ARL1-4405	The Great Caruso	198?	10.00
☐ CRM5-4158	The Mario Lanza Collection	1981	60.00

RCA VICTOR RED SEAL
☐ LM-1860 [M]	A Kiss" and Other Love Songs	1955	40.00
☐ LSC-1860(e) [R]	A Kiss" and Other Love Songs	196?	15.00
☐ LM-2454 [M]	A Mario Lanza Program	1960	18.00
☐ LSC-2454 [S]	A Mario Lanza Program	1960	25.00
☐ LSC-3289	Be My Love	1972	15.00
☐ LM-2090 [M]	Cavalcade of Show Tunes	1957	30.00
☐ LSC-2090(e) [R]	Cavalcade of Show Tunes	196?	15.00
☐ LM-2422 [M]	Double Feature -- Mario Lanza	1960	25.00
☐ LM-2338 [M]	For the First Time	1959	18.00
☐ LSC-2338 [S]	For the First Time	1959	25.00
☐ LM-2932 [M]	His Favorite Arias	196?	15.00
☐ LSC-2932 [S]	His Favorite Arias	196?	18.00
☐ LM-2790 [M]	If You Are But a Dream	196?	15.00
☐ LSC-2790 [S]	If You Are But a Dream	196?	18.00
☐ LM-2720 [M]	I'll See You in My Dreams	1964	15.00
☐ LSC-2720 [S]	I'll See You in My Dreams	1964	18.00
☐ LM-2607 [M]	I'll Walk with God	1962	25.00
☐ LSC-2607(e) [R]	I'll Walk with God	1962	15.00
☐ LM-2070 [M]	Lanza on Broadway	1956	30.00
☐ LSC-2070(e) [R]	Lanza on Broadway	196?	15.00
☐ LSC-2333 [S]	Lanza Sings Christmas Carols	1959	25.00

—*Original copies have "shaded dog" on labels*

☐ LM-2333 [M]	Lanza Sings Christmas Carols	1959	18.00
☐ LM-1188 [M]	Love Songs and a Neapolitan Serenade	195?	40.00
☐ LSC-1188(e) [R]	Love Songs and a Neapolitan Serenade	196?	15.00
☐ LM-1943 [M]	Magic Mario	1955	40.00
☐ LM-2331 [M]	Mario	1959	25.00
☐ LSC-2331 [S]	Mario!	1959	30.00
☐ LSC-3101	Mario Lanza in Opera	1969	18.00
☐ LSC-3102	Mario Lanza Memories	1969	18.00
☐ LM-2393 [M]	Mario Lanza Sings Caruso Favorites	1960	18.00
☐ LSC-2393 [S]	Mario Lanza Sings Caruso Favorites	1960	25.00
☐ LM-155 [10]	Mario Lanza Sings Christmas Songs	1951	50.00
☐ LM1837 [M]	Mario Lanza Sings the Hit Songs from "The Student Prince" and Other Great Musical Comedies	1955	40.00
☐ LSC1837(e) [R]	Mario Lanza Sings the Hit Songs from "The Student Prince" and Other Great Musical Comedies	196?	15.00

Number	Title	Yr	NM
☐ LSC-3103	Mario Lanza...Speak to Me of Love	1969	18.00
☐ LM-1996 [M]	Serenade	1956	40.00
☐ LM-2211 [M]	Seven Hills of Rome	1958	30.00
☐ LM-2748 [M]	The Best of Mario Lanza	1964	15.00
☐ LSC-2748 [S]	The Best of Mario Lanza	1964	18.00
☐ LM-2998 [M]	The Best of Mario Lanza, Volume 2	1968	25.00
☐ LSC-2998 [S]	The Best of Mario Lanza, Volume 2	1968	18.00
☐ LM-2440 [M]	The Desert Song	1960	18.00
☐ LSC-2440 [S]	The Desert Song	1960	25.00
☐ LM-1127 [M]	The Great Caruso	195?	40.00
☐ LSC-1127(e) [R]	The Great Caruso	196?	15.00
☐ LM-2339 [M]	The Student Prince	1959	18.00
☐ LSC-2339 [S]	The Student Prince	1959	25.00
☐ LSC-3216	The Student Prince	1971	15.00
☐ LM-1927 [M]	The Touch of Your Hand	1955	40.00
☐ LSC-1927(e) [R]	The Touch of Your Hand	196?	15.00
☐ LM-2509 [M]	The Vagabond King	1961	18.00
☐ LSC-2509 [S]	The Vagabond King	1961	25.00
☐ LSC-3049	Younger Than Springtime	1968	15.00

LAPORTA, JOHN

DEBUT
☐ DLP-10 [10]	The John LaPorta Quintet	1954	400.00
☐ DEB-122 [M]	Three Moods	1955	300.00

EVEREST
☐ LPBR-5037 [M]	The Most Minor	1959	50.00
☐ SDBR-1037 [S]	The Most Minor	1959	60.00

FANTASY
☐ 3228 [M]	Conceptions	1956	80.00

—*Red vinyl*

☐ 3228 [M]	Conceptions	1956	40.00

—*Black vinyl*

☐ 3237 [M]	South American Brothers	1956	80.00

—*Red vinyl*

☐ 3237 [M]	South American Brothers	1956	40.00

—*Black vinyl*

☐ 3248 [M]	The Clarinet Artistry of John LaPorta	1957	80.00

—*Red vinyl*

☐ 3248 [M]	The Clarinet Artistry of John LaPorta	1957	40.00

—*Black vinyl*

MUSIC MINUS ONE
☐ 4003 [M]	Eight Men In Search of a Drummer	1961	30.00

LAREDO, JAIME

RCA VICTOR RED SEAL
☐ LSC-2414 [S]	Brahms: Violin Sonata No. 3; Bach: Partita No. 3	1960	80.00

—*Original with "shaded dog" label*

☐ LSC-2472 [S]	Bruch: Violin Concerto No. 1; Mozart: Violin Concerto No. 3	1961	40.00

—*Original with "shaded dog" label*

☐ LSC-2373 [S]	Presenting Jaime Laredo	1960	40.00

—*Original with "shaded dog" label*

LARKIN, BILLY

AURA
☐ AR83003 [M]	Blue Lights	196?	25.00
☐ ARS23003 [S]	Blue Lights	196?	30.00
☐ 23002 [S]	Pigmy	1964	30.00

—*As "The Delegates*

☐ 83002 [M]	Pigmy	1964	25.00

—*As "The Delegates*

BRYAN
☐ 105	Billy Larkin	1975	18.00

SUNBIRD
☐ SN50107	All My Best	1981	12.00

WORLD PACIFIC
☐ WP-1843 [M]	Ain't That a Groove	1966	25.00
☐ WPS-21843 [S]	Ain't That a Groove	1966	30.00
☐ WP-1863 [M]	Don't Stop!	1967	30.00
☐ WPS-21863 [S]	Don't Stop!	1967	25.00
☐ WP-1850 [M]	Hold On	1967	25.00
☐ WPS-21850 [S]	Hold On	1967	30.00
☐ WP-1837 [M]	Hole in the Wall	1966	25.00
☐ WPS-21837 [S]	Hole in the Wall	1966	30.00
☐ WPS-21883	The Best of Billy Larkin & the Delegates	1968	25.00

LARKINS, ELLIS

ANTILLES
☐ DGTL-101	Ellis Larkins	198?	18.00

CLASSIC JAZZ
☐ 145	Smooth One	1977	15.00

DECCA
☐ DL9211 [M]	Blue and Sentimental	1958	30.00
☐ DL79211 [S]	Blue and Sentimental	1958	30.00
☐ DL5391 [10]	Blues in the Night	1952	50.00
☐ DL8303 [M]	Manhattan at Midnight	1956	40.00
☐ DL9205 [M]	The Soft Touch	1958	30.00
☐ DL79205 [S]	The Soft Touch	1958	30.00

Number	Title	Yr	NM
STANYAN			
❏ 10074	Ellis Larkins Plays Bacharach and McKuen	197?	18.00
❏ 10011	Hair	1969	15.00
❏ 10024	Lost in the Wood	197?	15.00
STORYVILLE			
❏ STLP-913 [M]	Do Nothin' Till You Hear from Me	1956	50.00
❏ STLP-316 [10]	Perfume and Rain	1955	80.00
LARKINS, ELLIS/LEE WILEY			
STORYVILLE			
❏ STLP-911 [M]	Duologue	1956	60.00
LARKS, THE (1)			
COLLECTABLES			
❏ COL-5176	Golden Classics: The Jerk	198?	12.00
MONEY			
❏ LP-1107 [M]	Soul Kaleidoscope	1966	40.00
❏ ST-1107 [S]	Soul Kaleidoscope	1966	50.00
❏ LP-1110 [M]	Superslick	1967	40.00
❏ ST-1110 [S]	Superslick	1967	50.00
❏ LP-1102 [M]	The Jerk	1965	40.00
❏ ST-1102 [S]	The Jerk	1965	50.00
LAROCA, PETE			
BLUE NOTE			
❏ B1-32091	Basra	1995	18.00
— The Finest in Jazz Since 1939" reissue			
❏ BLP-4205 [M]	Basra	1965	30.00
❏ BST-84205 [S]	Basra	1965	40.00
— With "New York, USA" address on label			
❏ BST-84205 [S]	Basra	1967	18.00
— With "A Division of Liberty Records" on label			
DOUGLAS			
❏ SD782	Turkish Woman at the Bath	1969	18.00
MUSE			
❏ MR-5011	Bliss	197?	15.00
LAROCCA, NICK			
SOUTHLAND			
❏ 230 [M]	Nick LaRocca and His Dixieland Band	196?	25.00
LAROSA, JULIUS			
AUDIOPHILE			
❏ AP-190	It's a Wrap!	1985	15.00
CADENCE			
❏ CLP1007 [M]	Julius LaRosa (Julie's Best)	1955	40.00
FORUM			
❏ F-16012 [M]	Just Say I Love Her	1960	18.00
❏ FS-16012 [S]	Just Say I Love Her	1960	25.00
KAPP			
❏ KL-1245 [M]	The New Julie LaRosa	1961	18.00
❏ KS-3245 [S]	The New Julie LaRosa	1961	25.00
METROMEDIA			
❏ MD-1036	Words	1971	15.00
MGM			
❏ E-4437 [M]	Hey Look Me Over	1967	15.00
❏ SE-4437 [S]	Hey Look Me Over	1967	18.00
❏ E-4398 [M]	You're Gonna Hear From Me	1966	15.00
❏ SE-4398 [S]	You're Gonna Hear From Me	1966	18.00
RCA VICTOR			
❏ LPM-1299 [M]	Julius LaRosa	1956	40.00
ROULETTE			
❏ R25054 [M]	Love Songs A LaRosa	1959	25.00
❏ SR25054 [S]	Love Songs A LaRosa	1959	30.00
❏ R25083 [M]	On the Sunny Side	1960	25.00
❏ SR25083 [S]	On the Sunny Side	1960	30.00
LARRY AND HANK			
PRESTIGE			
❏ PRLP-7472 [M]	The Blues/A New Generation	1965	25.00
❏ PRST-7472 [S]	The Blues/A New Generation	1965	30.00
LARRY AND LENORE			
REQUEST			
❏ 10037 [M]	Traveling Guitars	1959	100.00
LARSEN, MORTON G.			
STOMP OFF			
❏ SOS-1009	Morton G. Larsen Plays Robert Clemente	198?	12.00
LARSEN, NEIL			
A&M			
❏ SP-3117	High Gear	1980	12.00
❏ SP-3116	Jungle Fever	1980	12.00
— Reissue of Horizon 733			
HORIZON			
❏ SP-738	High Gear	1979	18.00
❏ SP-733	Jungle Fever	1978	18.00
LARSON, NICOLETTE			
MCA			
❏ 5719	Rose of My Heart	1986	10.00
❏ 5556	... Say When	1985	10.00

Number	Title	Yr	NM
WARNER BROS.			
❏ BSK3678	All Dressed Up & No Place to Go	1982	12.00
❏ HS3370	In the Nick of Time	1979	12.00
❏ BSK3243	Nicolette	1978	12.00
❏ BSK3502	Radioland	1980	12.00
LASALLE, DENISE			
ABC			
❏ D-966	Second Breath	1976	15.00
❏ D-1027	The Bitch Is Bad	1977	15.00
❏ AA-1087	Under the Influence	1978	15.00
MALACO			
❏ 7412	A Lady in the Street	198?	12.00
❏ 7447	Hittin' Where It Hurts	198?	12.00
❏ 7441	It's Lying Time Again	198?	12.00
❏ 7464	Love Me Right	198?	12.00
❏ 7422	Love Talkin'	198?	12.00
❏ 7434	Rain and Fire	198?	12.00
❏ 7417	Right Place, Right Time	1984	12.00
❏ 7454	Still Trapped	198?	12.00
MCA			
❏ 3239	I'm So Hot	1980	12.00
❏ 760	I'm So Hot	198?	10.00
— Reissue of 3239			
❏ 3089	Unwrapped	1979	10.00
❏ 759	Unwrapped	198?	10.00
— Reissue of 3089			
WESTBOUND			
❏ 209	Here I Am Again	1975	15.00
❏ 2016	On the Loose	1973	18.00
❏ 2012	Trapped by a Thing Called Love	1972	18.00
LASHA, PRINCE			
CONTEMPORARY			
❏ S-7617	Firebirds	1968	30.00
❏ M-3610 [M]	The Cry	1963	30.00
❏ S-7610 [S]	The Cry	1963	30.00
LASHLEY, BARBARA, AND RAY SKJELBRED			
STOMP OFF			
❏ SOS-1152	Sweet and Lowdown	1988	12.00
LASK, ULRICH			
ECM			
❏ 1217	Lask	198?	15.00
❏ 1268	Sucht und Ordnung	1985	15.00
LAST, JAMES			
POLYDOR			
❏ 24-4505	Classics Up to Date	1970	15.00
❏ 24-4509	El Condor Pasa	1971	15.00
❏ 24-4512	Good Times	1971	15.00
❏ 24-6004	Hair	1969	15.00
❏ PD-5512	Love Must Be the Reason	1972	12.00
❏ PD-5538	M.O.R.	1973	12.00
❏ PD-5505	Music from Across the Way	1972	12.00
❏ PD-5534	Non Stop Dancing	1973	12.00
❏ PD-1-6283	Seduction	1980	12.00
❏ 24-4507	Soft Rock	1970	15.00
❏ PD-5506	The Love Album	197?	12.00
❏ PD-6040	Well Kept Secret	1975	12.00
LAST CALL OF SHILOH, THE			
LAST CALL			
❏ 5136	The Last Call	196?	200.00
LAST EXIT			
CELLULOID			
❏ CELL-8140	Cassette Recordings '87	1988	15.00
ENEMY			
❏ 88561-8176-1	Last Exit	1986	25.00
❏ 88561-8178-1	The Noise of Trouble	1987	18.00
VENTURE			
❏ 91015	Iron Path	1988	15.00
LAST POETS, THE			
BLUE THUMB			
❏ BT-52	At Last	1973	30.00
❏ BT-39	Chastisement	1972	30.00
CASABLANCA			
❏ NBLP7051	Delights of the Garden	1977	30.00
CELLULOID			
❏ 6136	Delights of the Garden	198?	12.00
❏ 6108	Oh My People	198?	12.00
❏ 6101 [B]	The Last Poets	198?	12.00
❏ 6105 [B]	This Is Madness	198?	12.00
COLLECTABLES			
❏ COL-6500	Right On!	198?	12.00
DOUGLAS			
❏ 3 [B]	The Last Poets	1970	60.00
❏ Z30811 [B]	The Last Poets	1971	50.00
❏ Z30583 [B]	This Is Madness	1971	60.00
JUGGERNAUT			
❏ 8802	Right On!	1971	50.00
— As "The Original Last Poets			

Number	Title	Yr	NM
LASWELL, BILL, AND PETER BROTZMANN			
CELLULOID			
❏ CELL-5016	Low Life	198?	15.00
LASWELL, BILL			
ELEKTRA/MUSICIAN			
❏ 60221	Basslines	1984	12.00
VENTURE			
❏ 90888	Hear No Evil	1988	12.00
LATARSKI, DON			
INNER CITY			
❏ IC-1114	Haven	198?	15.00
PAUSA			
❏ 7146	Lifeline	1983	12.00
LATEEF, YUSEF			
ABC IMPULSE!			
❏ AS-84 [S]	1984	1968	25.00
❏ AS-9117 [S]	A Flat, G Flat and C	1968	25.00
❏ ASD-9310	Club Date	1976	40.00
❏ AS-56 [S]	Jazz Around the World	1968	25.00
❏ AS-69 [S]	Live at Pep's	1968	30.00
❏ AS-92 [S]	Psychicemotus	1968	25.00
❏ AS-9259	Re-evaluations: The Impulse Years	1974	30.00
❏ AS-9125 [S]	The Golden Flute	1968	25.00
❏ IA-9353	The Live Session	1978	30.00
ALA			
❏ AJ-502	Archives of Jazz, Vol. 2	198?	12.00
ARGO			
❏ LP-634 [M]	Live at Cranbrook	1959	80.00
ATLANTIC			
❏ SD 2-1000	10 Years Hence	1977	30.00
❏ 81663	Concerto for Yusef Lateef	1988	15.00
❏ SD1635	Hush 'n' Thunder	1973	25.00
❏ 81977	Nocturnes	1989	18.00
❏ SD1650	Part of the Search	1974	18.00
❏ SD1563	Suite 16	1970	30.00
❏ SD1591	The Best of Yusef Lateef	1971	25.00
— 1841 Broadway" address on label			
❏ SD1591	The Best of Yusef Lateef	1976	15.00
— 75 Rockefeller Plaza" address on label			
❏ SD1508	The Blue Lateef	1968	30.00
— Blue and green label			
❏ SD1508	The Blue Lateef	1969	25.00
— Red and green label			
❏ SD1499	The Complete Lateef	1968	40.00
— Blue and green label			
❏ SD1499	The Complete Lateef	1969	25.00
— Red and green label			
❏ SD1548	The Diverse Lateef	1970	30.00
❏ SD1685	The Doctor Is In... And Out	1976	25.00
❏ SD1602	The Gentle Giant	1972	30.00
❏ SD1525	Yusef Lateef's Detroit	1969	100.00
— Reproductions exist			
❏ 81717	Yusef Lateef's Little Symphony	1987	18.00
CADET			
❏ LPS-816	Live at Cranbrook	1969	30.00
❏ LP-634 [M]	Live at Cranbrook	1966	40.00
CHARLIE PARKER			
❏ PLP-814 [M]	Lost in Sound	1962	50.00
❏ PLP-814S [S]	Lost in Sound	1962	60.00
CTI			
❏ 7082	Autophysiopsychic	1977	25.00
❏ 7088	In a Temple Garden	1979	25.00
DELMARK			
❏ DL-407 [M]	Yusef!	1965	40.00
❏ DS-407 [S]	Yusef!	1965	50.00
EVEREST ARCHIVE OF FOLK & JAZZ			
❏ FS-285	Yusef Lateef	197?	12.00
FANTASY			
❏ OJC-482	Cry! Tender	1991	15.00
— Reissue of Prestige 7748			
❏ OJC-612	Eastern Sounds	1991	18.00
— Reissue of Prestige 7139			
❏ OJC-399	Other Sounds	1989	12.00
IMPULSE!			
❏ A-84 [M]	1984	1965	30.00
❏ AS-84 [S]	1984	1965	40.00
❏ A-9117 [M]	A Flat, G Flat and C	1966	50.00
❏ AS-9117 [S]	A Flat, G Flat and C	1966	60.00
❏ A-56 [M]	Jazz Around the World	1963	40.00
❏ AS-56 [S]	Jazz Around the World	1963	50.00
❏ A-69 [M]	Live at Pep's	1964	50.00
❏ AS-69 [S]	Live at Pep's	1964	60.00
❏ MAS-90216 [M]	Live at Pep's	1964	60.00
— Capitol Record Club edition			
❏ A-92 [M]	Psychicemotus	1966	50.00
❏ AS-92 [S]	Psychicemotus	1966	60.00
❏ A-9125 [M]	The Golden Flute	1966	50.00
❏ AS-9125 [S]	The Golden Flute	1966	60.00
LANDMARK			
❏ LLP-502	Yusef Lateef in Nigeria	1985	25.00

Number	Title	Yr	NM

MCA
| ❏ 4146 | Live Session | 198? | 18.00 |

— *Reissue of ABC Impulse! 9353*

MILESTONE
| ❏ M-47009 | The Many Faces of Yusef Lateef | 1973 | 30.00 |

MOODSVILLE
| ❏ MVLP-22 [M] | Eastern Sounds | 1961 | 100.00 |

— *Green label, silver print*

| ❏ MVST-22 [S] | Eastern Sounds | 1961 | 120.00 |

— *Green label, silver print*

NEW JAZZ
| ❏ NJLP-8234 [M] | Cry! Tender | 1960 | 200.00 |

— *Purple label*

| ❏ NJLP-8234 [M] | Cry! Tender | 1965 | 80.00 |

— *Blue label, trident logo at right*

| ❏ NJLP-8272 [M] | Into Something | 1962 | 200.00 |

— *Purple label*

| ❏ NJLP-8272 [M] | Into Something | 1965 | 80.00 |

— *Blue label, trident logo at right*

| ❏ NJLP-8218 [M] | Other Sounds | 1959 | 200.00 |

— *Purple label*

| ❏ NJLP-8218 [M] | Other Sounds | 1965 | 80.00 |

— *Blue label, trident logo at right*

| ❏ NJLP-8261 [M] | The Sounds of Yusef | 1961 | 100.00 |

— *Reissue of Prestige 7122; purple label*

| ❏ NJLP-8261 [M] | The Sounds of Yusef | 1965 | 50.00 |

— *Blue label, trident logo at right*

PRESTIGE
❏ P-24035	Blues for the Orient	1974	18.00
❏ PRST-7748	Cry! Tender	1970	25.00
❏ PRLP-7319 [M]	Eastern Sounds	1964	60.00
❏ PRST-7319 [S]	Eastern Sounds	1964	70.00

— *Reissue of Moodsville 22*

❏ PRST-7653	Expressions	1969	40.00
❏ PRST-7832	Imagination	1971	30.00
❏ PRST-7637	Into Something	1968	18.00
❏ PR-24007	Lateef	1972	30.00
❏ PRLP-7122 [M]	The Sounds of Yusef	1957	200.00

— *Yellow label*

❏ PRLP-7090 [M]	The Sounds of Yusef	1966	20.00
❏ PRST-7398 [S]	The Sounds of Yusef Lateef	1966	40.00
❏ PRLP-7447 [M]	Yusef Lateef Plays for Lovers	1967	30.00
❏ PRST-7447 [S]	Yusef Lateef Plays for Lovers	1967	30.00
❏ P-24105	Yusef's Bag	1981	30.00

RIVERSIDE
❏ RLP-337 [M]	The Centaur and the Phoenix	1960	80.00
❏ RLP-9337 [S]	The Centaur and the Phoenix	1960	60.00
❏ RS-3011	This Is Yusef Lateef	1968	40.00
❏ RLP 12-325 [M]	Three Faces of Yusef Lateef	1960	200.00
❏ RLP-1176 [S]	Three Faces of Yusef Lateef	1960	150.00

SAVOY
❏ MG-12120 [M]	Jazz and the Sounds of Nature	1958	100.00
❏ MG-12109 [M]	Jazz for the Thinker	1957	100.00
❏ MG-12103 [M]	Jazz Mood	1957	100.00
❏ MG-12117 [M]	Prayer to the East	1957	100.00
❏ MG-12139 [M]	The Dreamer	1958	100.00
❏ SR-13007 [S]	The Dreamer	1959	100.00
❏ MG-12140 [M]	The Fabric of Jazz	1958	100.00
❏ SR-13008 [S]	The Fabric of Jazz	1959	100.00

SAVOY JAZZ
❏ SJL-2238	Angel Eyes	1979	30.00
❏ SJL-2226	Gong!	1978	30.00
❏ SJL-2205	Morning: The Savoy Sessions	1976	25.00

TRIP
| ❏ 5018 | Outside Blues | 1973 | 15.00 |

UPFRONT
| ❏ UPF-183 | Dexterity | 197? | 12.00 |

VERVE
| ❏ MGV-8217 [M] | Before Dawn | 1958 | 200.00 |
| ❏ V-8217 [M] | Before Dawn | 1961 | 40.00 |

VJ INTERNATIONAL
| ❏ VJS-3052 [M] | Contemplation | 1974 | 50.00 |

— *Reissue of Vee-Jay 3010, which was originally credited to LOUIS HAYES.*

LATIMORE

GLADES
❏ 7515	Dig a Little Deeper	1978	12.00
❏ 7509	It Ain't Where You Been	1976	12.00
❏ 6502	Latimore	1973	15.00
❏ 7505	Latimore 3	1975	15.00
❏ 6503	More, More, More	1974	15.00

MALACO
❏ 7468	Catchin' Up	1993	15.00
❏ 7436	Every Way But Wrong	198?	12.00
❏ 7423	Good Time Man	198?	12.00
❏ 7414	I'll Do Anything for You	198?	12.00
❏ 7409	Singing in the Key of Love	198?	12.00
❏ 7443	Slow Down	198?	12.00
❏ 7456	The Only Way Is Up	198?	12.00

Number	Title	Yr	NM

LATIN ALL-STARS, THE

CROWN
| ❏ CLP5159 [M] | Jazz Heat-Bongo Beat | 1959 | 30.00 |

LATIN JAZZ QUINTET, THE

NEW JAZZ
| ❏ NJLP-8251 [M] | Caribe | 1960 | 50.00 |

— *Purple label*

| ❏ NJLP-8251 [M] | Caribe | 1965 | 30.00 |

— *Blue label, trident logo at right*

STATUS
| ❏ ST-8321 [M] | Latin Soul | 1965 | 40.00 |

TRIP
| ❏ 8008 | Oh! Pharaoh Speak | 197? | 15.00 |

TRU-SOUND
| ❏ TRU-15003 [M] | Hot Sauce | 1962 | 40.00 |
| ❏ TRU-15012 [M] | The Latin Jazz Quintet | 1962 | 40.00 |

UNITED ARTISTS
| ❏ UAL-4071 [M] | The Latin Jazz Quintet | 1960 | 100.00 |
| ❏ UAS-5071 [S] | The Latin Jazz Quintet | 1960 | 90.00 |

LATIN SOULS, THE

KAPP
❏ KL-1524 [M]	Boo-Ga-Loo and Shing-a-Ling	1967	30.00
❏ KS-3524 [S]	Boo-Ga-Loo and Shing-a-Ling	1967	25.00
❏ KS-3553	Tigar Boo-Ga-Loo	1968	25.00

LATTISAW, STACY, AND JOHNNY GILL

COTILLION
| ❏ 90136 | Perfect Combination | 1984 | 12.00 |

LATTISAW, STACY

COTILLION
❏ 90280	I'm Not the Same Girl	1985	12.00
❏ SD5219	Let Me Be Your Angel	1980	12.00
❏ 90106	Sixteen	1983	12.00
❏ 90002	Sneakin' Out	1982	12.00
❏ SD16049	With You	1981	12.00
❏ SD5214	Young and In Love	1979	15.00

MOTOWN
| ❏ 6247ML | Personal Attention | 1988 | 10.00 |
| ❏ 6212ML | Take Me All the Way | 1986 | 10.00 |

LAUER, CHRISTOF

CMP
| ❏ CMP-39-ST | Christof Lauer | 1990 | 15.00 |

LAUGHTON, CHARLES

CAPITOL
| ❏ TBO1650 [M] | The Story Teller | 1962 | 30.00 |
| ❏ STBO1650 [S] | The Story Teller | 1962 | 30.00 |

DECCA
| ❏ DLP8010 [M] | A Christmas Carol/Mr. Pickwick's Christmas | 1955 | 25.00 |

— *A-side read by Ronald Colman*

| ❏ DL8031 [M] | Readings from the Bible | 195? | 30.00 |

MCA
| ❏ 15010 | A Christmas Carol/Mr. Pickwick's Christmas | 1955 | 25.00 |

— *A-side read by Ronald Colman; reissue of Decca LP*

LAUPER, CYNDI

EPIC
| ❏ OE44318 | A Night to Remember | 1989 | 12.00 |

PORTRAIT

| ❏ BFR38930 [B] | She's So Unusual | 1983 | 15.00 |
| ❏ 9R939610 | She's So Unusual | 1984 | 25.00 |

— *Picture disc in plastic sleeve with sticker*

Number	Title	Yr	NM

| ❏ FR38930 | She's So Unusual | 1984 | 10.00 |

— *Reissue with new prefix*

| ❏ OR40313 | True Colors | 1986 | 12.00 |

LAUREN, ROD

RCA VICTOR
| ❏ LPM-2176 [M] | I'm Rod Lauren | 1961 | 40.00 |
| ❏ LSP-2176 [S] | I'm Rod Lauren | 1961 | 50.00 |

LAURENCE, BABY

CLASSIC JAZZ
| ❏ 30 | Dancemaster | 197? | 12.00 |

LAURIE, ANNIE

AUDIO LAB
| ❏ AL-1510 [M] | It Hurts to Be in Love | 1959 | 300.00 |

LAURIE SISTERS, THE

RCA CAMDEN
| ❏ CAL-545 [M] | Hits of the Great Girl Groups | 1960 | 30.00 |
| ❏ CAS-545 [S] | Hits of the Great Girl Groups | 1960 | 30.00 |

LAVERNE, ANDY

STEEPLECHASE
| ❏ SCS-1086 | Another World | 198? | 15.00 |

LAVETTE, BETTY

ANTI
| ❏ 86873-1 | Scene of the Crime | 2007 | 18.00 |

— *As "Bettye LaVette"; comes with a certificate for a free MP3 download of the album*

DBK WORKS
| ❏ DBK116 | I've Got My Own Hell to Raise | 2005 | 18.00 |

— *As "Bettye LaVette"*

MOTOWN
| ❏ 6000ML | Tell Me a Lie | 1982 | 15.00 |

— *As "Bettye LaVette"*

SUNDAZED
| ❏ LP5208 | Do Your Duty | 2006 | 18.00 |

— *As "Bettye LaVette"; compilation of recordings for Silver Fox and SSS International*

LAVITZ, T.

INTIMA
| ❏ D1-73512 | T. Lavitz and the Bad Habits | 1989 | 15.00 |

LAWRENCE, ARNIE

DOCTOR JAZZ
| ❏ FW38445 | Arnie Lawrence and Treasure Island | 1983 | 12.00 |

EMBRYO
| ❏ SD525 | Inside an Hour Glass | 1970 | 25.00 |

PROJECT 3
| ❏ PR-5028 | Look Toward a Dream | 1968 | 25.00 |
| ❏ PR-5011 | You're Gonna Hear From Me | 1967 | 25.00 |

LAWRENCE, AZAR

PRESTIGE
❏ 10086	Bridge Into a New Age	1973	18.00
❏ 10099	People Moving	1976	18.00
❏ 10097	Summer Solstice	1975	18.00

LAWRENCE, BILL

TOPS
| ❏ L-1576 [M] | Bill Lawrence Sings I'm in the Mood for Love | 1957 | 25.00 |

LAWRENCE, CAROL

CAMEO
| ❏ C-1077 [M] | An Evening with Carol Lawrence | 1964 | 25.00 |
| ❏ SC-1077 [S] | An Evening with Carol Lawrence | 1964 | 30.00 |

CHANCELLOR
| ❏ CHL-5015 [M] | Tonight at 8:30 | 1960 | 25.00 |
| ❏ CHLS-5015 [S] | Tonight at 8:30 | 1960 | 30.00 |

LAWRENCE, EDDIE

CORAL
❏ CRL57155 [M]	Eddie "The Old Philosopher" Lawrence	1957	30.00
❏ CRL57411 [M]	Seven Characters In Search of Eddie Lawrence	1962	30.00
❏ CRL757411 [S]	Seven Characters In Search of Eddie Lawrence	1962	40.00
❏ CRL57203 [M]	The Kingdom of Eddie Lawrence	1958	30.00
❏ CRL57103 [M]	The Old Philosopher	1956	30.00
❏ CRL57371 [M]	The Side Splitting Personality of Eddie Lawrence	1961	30.00

EPIC
| ❏ LN24149 [M] | Is That What's Bothering You Bunkie? | 1965 | 30.00 |

Number	Title	Yr	NM
❑ BN26149 [S]	Is That What's Bothering You Bunkie?	1965	40.00

SIGNATURE

Number	Title	Yr	NM
❑ SM-1003 [M]	The Garden of Eddie Lawrence	1960	40.00

LAWRENCE, ELLIOT

DECCA

Number	Title	Yr	NM
❑ DL5274 [10]	College Prom	1950	50.00
❑ DL5353 [10]	Moonlight on the Campus	1951	50.00

FANTASY

Number	Title	Yr	NM
❑ 3290 [M]	Big Band Sound	1959	40.00
— Red vinyl			
❑ 3290 [M]	Big Band Sound	1959	30.00
— Black vinyl, red label, non-flexible vinyl			
❑ 3290 [M]	Big Band Sound	196?	18.00
— Black vinyl, red label, flexible vinyl			
❑ 8031 [S]	Big Band Sound	196?	30.00
— Blue vinyl			
❑ 8031 [S]	Big Band Sound	196?	25.00
— Black vinyl, blue label, non-flexible vinyl			
❑ 8031 [S]	Big Band Sound	196?	15.00
— Black vinyl, blue label, flexible vinyl			
❑ 3226 [M]	Dream	1956	50.00
— Red vinyl			
❑ 3226 [M]	Dream	1956	30.00
— Black vinyl, red label, non-flexible vinyl			
❑ 3226 [M]	Dream	196?	25.00
— Black vinyl, red label, flexible vinyl			
❑ 3261 [M]	Dream On -- Dance On	1958	40.00
— Red vinyl			
❑ 3261 [M]	Dream On -- Dance On	1958	30.00
— Black vinyl, red label, non-flexible vinyl			
❑ 3261 [M]	Dream On -- Dance On	196?	18.00
— Black vinyl, red label, flexible vinyl			
❑ 8002 [S]	Dream On -- Dance On	196?	30.00
— Blue vinyl			
❑ 8002 [S]	Dream On -- Dance On	196?	25.00
— Black vinyl, blue label, non-flexible vinyl			
❑ 8002 [S]	Dream On -- Dance On	196?	15.00
— Black vinyl, blue label, flexible vinyl			
❑ 3246 [M]	Elliot Lawrence Plays for Swinging Dancers	1957	40.00
— Red vinyl			
❑ 3246 [M]	Elliot Lawrence Plays for Swinging Dancers	1957	30.00
— Black vinyl, red label, non-flexible vinyl			
❑ 3246 [M]	Elliot Lawrence Plays for Swinging Dancers	196?	18.00
— Black vinyl, red label, flexible vinyl			
❑ 8021 [S]	Elliot Lawrence Plays for Swinging Dancers	196?	30.00
— Blue vinyl			
❑ 8021 [S]	Elliot Lawrence Plays for Swinging Dancers	196?	25.00
— Black vinyl, blue label, non-flexible vinyl			
❑ 8021 [S]	Elliot Lawrence Plays for Swinging Dancers	196?	15.00
— Black vinyl, blue label, flexible vinyl			
❑ 3206 [M]	Elliot Lawrence Plays Gerry Mulligan Arrangements	1956	50.00
— Red vinyl			
❑ 3206 [M]	Elliot Lawrence Plays Gerry Mulligan Arrangements	1956	30.00
— Black vinyl, red label, non-flexible vinyl			
❑ 3206 [M]	Elliot Lawrence Plays Gerry Mulligan Arrangements	196?	25.00
— Black vinyl, red label, flexible vinyl			
❑ OJC-117	Elliot Lawrence Plays Gerry Mulligan Arrangements	198?	12.00
❑ 3219 [M]	Elliot Lawrence Plays Tiny Kahn and Johnny Mandel Arrangements	1956	50.00
— Red vinyl			
❑ 3219 [M]	Elliot Lawrence Plays Tiny Kahn and Johnny Mandel Arrangements	1956	30.00
— Black vinyl, red label, non-flexible vinyl			
❑ 3219 [M]	Elliot Lawrence Plays Tiny Kahn and Johnny Mandel Arrangements	196?	25.00
— Black vinyl, red label, flexible vinyl			
❑ 3236 [M]	Swinging at the Steel Pier	1956	50.00
— Red vinyl			
❑ 3236 [M]	Swinging at the Steel Pier	1956	30.00
— Black vinyl, red label, non-flexible vinyl			
❑ 3236 [M]	Swinging at the Steel Pier	196?	25.00
— Black vinyl, red label, flexible vinyl			

HINDSIGHT

Number	Title	Yr	NM
❑ HSR-182	Elliot Lawrence and His Orchestra 1946	1982	12.00

JAZZTONE

Number	Title	Yr	NM
❑ J-1279 [M]	Big Band Modern	1958	60.00

MOBILE FIDELITY

Number	Title	Yr	NM
❑ 2-229	The Music of Elliot Lawrence	1995	40.00
— Original Master Recording" at top of cover			

SESAC

Number	Title	Yr	NM
❑ N-1153 [M]	Jump Steady	1960	30.00
❑ SN-1153 [S]	Jump Steady	1960	40.00

SURREY

Number	Title	Yr	NM
❑ S-1019 [M]	Winds on Velvet	196?	15.00
❑ SS-1019 [S]	Winds on Velvet	196?	18.00

TOP RANK

Number	Title	Yr	NM
❑ RM-304 [M]	Music for Trapping (Tender, That Is)	1959	60.00

VIK

Number	Title	Yr	NM
❑ LX-1124 [M]	Hi-Fi-ing Winds	1958	40.00
❑ LX-1113 [M]	Jazz Goes Broadway	1958	60.00

LAWRENCE, GARY

BLUE GOOSE

Number	Title	Yr	NM
❑ 2020	Gary Lawrence and His Sizzling Syncopators	1979	12.00

LAWRENCE, GERTRUDE

DECCA

Number	Title	Yr	NM
❑ DL8673 [M]	A Remembrance	1958	30.00
— Black label, silver print			
❑ DL5418 [10]	Souvenir Album	1952	50.00

LAWRENCE, MIKE

OPTIMISM

Number	Title	Yr	NM
❑ OP-3104	Nightwind	198?	12.00

LAWRENCE, STEVE, AND EYDIE GORME

ABC

Number	Title	Yr	NM
❑ X-764	20 Golden Performances	1974	15.00

ABC-PARAMOUNT

Number	Title	Yr	NM
❑ 469 [M]	Our Best to You	1964	18.00
❑ S-469 [S]	Our Best to You	1964	25.00
❑ 311 [M]	Steve and Eydie Sing the Golden Hits	1960	25.00
❑ S-311 [S]	Steve and Eydie Sing the Golden Hits	1960	30.00
❑ 300 [M]	We Got Us	1960	25.00
❑ S-300 [S]	We Got Us	1960	30.00

CALENDAR

Number	Title	Yr	NM
❑ KOM-1001 [M]	Golden Rainbow	1968	30.00
❑ KOS-1001 [S]	Golden Rainbow	1968	40.00

COLUMBIA

Number	Title	Yr	NM
❑ CL2730 [M]	Bonfa and Brazil	1968	18.00
❑ CS9530 [S]	Bonfa and Brazil	1968	15.00
❑ CL2021 [M]	Steve and Eydie at the Movies	1964	15.00
❑ CS8821 [S]	Steve and Eydie at the Movies	1964	18.00
❑ CL2636 [M]	Steve and Eydie Together On Broadway	1967	15.00
❑ CS9436 [S]	Steve and Eydie Together On Broadway	1967	18.00
❑ CL2262 [M]	That Holiday Feeling	1964	15.00
❑ CS9062 [S]	That Holiday Feeling	1964	18.00

CORAL

Number	Title	Yr	NM
❑ CRL57226 [M]	Steve and Eydie	1962	25.00

HARMONY

Number	Title	Yr	NM
❑ H30292	Something's Gotta Give	1971	12.00

MATI-MOR

Number	Title	Yr	NM
❑ 8003	It's Us Again	196?	25.00
— Promotional item for Silvirkin shampoo			

MGM

Number	Title	Yr	NM
❑ SE-4881	Feelin'	1973	12.00
❑ SE-4803	The World of Steve Lawrence and Eydie Gorme	1972	12.00

RCA VICTOR

Number	Title	Yr	NM
❑ LSP-4393	A Man and a Woman	1971	15.00
❑ LSP-4107	Real True Lovin'	1969	15.00
❑ VPS-6035	This Is Steve Lawrence and Eydie Gorme	1971	18.00
❑ VPS-6050	This Is Steve Lawrence and Eydie Gorme, Vol. 2	1972	18.00
❑ LSP-4115	What It Was, Was Love	1969	15.00

STAGE 2

Number	Title	Yr	NM
❑ 712	Hallelujah	198?	12.00

UNITED ARTISTS

Number	Title	Yr	NM
❑ WWL-4509 [M]	Cozy	1961	25.00
❑ WWS-8509 [S]	Cozy	1961	30.00
❑ UAL-3191 [M]	The Very Best of Eydie and Steve	1962	25.00
❑ UAS-6191 [S]	The Very Best of Eydie and Steve	1962	30.00
❑ UAL-3268 [M]	Two on the Aisle	1963	25.00
❑ UAS-6268 [S]	Two on the Aisle	1963	30.00

VOCALION

Number	Title	Yr	NM
❑ VL3825 [M]	Presenting Steve and Eydie	1968	15.00
❑ VL73825 [R]	Presenting Steve and Eydie	1968	12.00

LAWRENCE, STEVE

ABC-PARAMOUNT

Number	Title	Yr	NM
❑ 290 [M]	Swing Softly with Me	1959	30.00
❑ S-290 [S]	Swing Softly with Me	1959	30.00
❑ 392 [M]	The Best of Steve Lawrence	1960	25.00
❑ S-392 [S]	The Best of Steve Lawrence	1960	30.00

APPLAUSE

Number	Title	Yr	NM
❑ 1001	Take It On Home	1981	12.00

COLUMBIA

Number	Title	Yr	NM
❑ CL2121 [M]	Academy Award Losers	1964	15.00
❑ CS8921 [S]	Academy Award Losers	1964	18.00
❑ CL2227 [M]	Everybody Knows	1964	15.00
❑ CS9027 [S]	Everybody Knows	1964	18.00
❑ PC9565	Greatest Hits	198?	10.00
— Reissue with new prefix			
❑ CS9565	Greatest Hits	1968	15.00
❑ CL2540 [M]	Of Love and… Sad Young Men	1966	15.00
❑ CS9340 [S]	Of Love and… Sad Young Men	1966	18.00
❑ CL2419 [M]	The Steve Lawrence Show	1965	15.00
❑ CS9219 [S]	The Steve Lawrence Show	1965	18.00
❑ CL1953 [M]	Winners!	1963	15.00
❑ CS8753 [S]	Winners!	1963	18.00

CORAL

Number	Title	Yr	NM
❑ CRL57050 [M]	About That Girl	1956	40.00
❑ CRL57268 [M]	All About Love	1959	30.00
❑ CRL757268 [S]	All About Love	1959	40.00
❑ CRL57204 [M]	Here's Steve Lawrence	1958	40.00
❑ CRL57182 [M]	Songs by Steve Lawrence	1957	40.00
❑ CRL57434 [M]	Songs Everybody Knows	1963	30.00
❑ CRL757434 [S]	Songs Everybody Knows	1963	30.00

HARMONY

Number	Title	Yr	NM
❑ HS11397	Love Me	1970	12.00
❑ HS11257	Moon River	196?	12.00
❑ HS11327	Ramblin' Rose	1969	12.00

KING

Number	Title	Yr	NM
❑ 593 [M]	Steve Lawrence	1959	80.00

MGM

Number	Title	Yr	NM
❑ SE-4824	Portrait	1973	12.00

RCA VICTOR

Number	Title	Yr	NM
❑ LSP-4167	I've Gotta Be Me	1969	15.00
❑ LSP-4347	On a Clear Day	1970	15.00

UNITED ARTISTS

Number	Title	Yr	NM
❑ UAL-3265 [M]	People Will Say We're in Love	1963	25.00
❑ UAS-6265 [S]	People Will Say We're in Love	1963	30.00
❑ UAL-3150 [M]	Portrait of My Love	1961	25.00
❑ UAS-6150 [S]	Portrait of My Love	1961	30.00
❑ UAL-3368 [M]	Steve Lawrence Conquers Broadway	1964	18.00
❑ UAS-6368 [S]	Steve Lawrence Conquers Broadway	1964	25.00
❑ UAL-3114 [M]	Steve Lawrence Goes Latin	1960	25.00
❑ UAS-6114 [S]	Steve Lawrence Goes Latin	1960	30.00
❑ UAL-3098 [M]	The Steve Lawrence Sound	1960	25.00
❑ UAS-6098 [S]	The Steve Lawrence Sound	1960	30.00
❑ UAL-3190 [M]	The Very Best of Steve Lawrence	1962	25.00
❑ UAS-6190 [S]	The Very Best of Steve Lawrence	1962	30.00

VOCALION

Number	Title	Yr	NM
❑ VL3775 [M]	Here's Steve Lawrence	196?	15.00
❑ VL73775 [R]	Here's Steve Lawrence	196?	12.00
❑ VL73886	The More I See You	1970	12.00

LAWRENCE, T.J.

EAGLE

Number	Title	Yr	NM
❑ SM-4194	Illuminations	1985	12.00

LAWRENCE, VICKI

BELL

Number	Title	Yr	NM
❑ 1120	The Night the Lights Went Out in Georgia	1973	15.00

LAWRENCE UNIVERSITY CONCERT CHOIR

(NO LABEL)

Number	Title	Yr	NM
❑ DRS86-630	Christmas at Lawrence	1986	10.00

LAWS, HUBERT

ATLANTIC

Number	Title	Yr	NM
❑ 1452 [M]	Flute By-Laws	1966	25.00
❑ SD1452 [S]	Flute By-Laws	1966	25.00
❑ SD1509	Laws Cause	1970	30.00
❑ 1432 [M]	The Laws of Jazz	1965	25.00
❑ SD1432 [S]	The Laws of Jazz	1965	30.00
— Red and purple label			
❑ SD8813	The Laws of Jazz	1981	10.00
— Reissue of 1432			
❑ SD1432 [S]	The Laws of Jazz	1969	18.00
— Red and green label			
❑ SD1624	Wild Flower	1973	18.00

CBS

Number	Title	Yr	NM
❑ M39858	Blanchard: New Earth Sonata; Telemann: Suite in A; Amazing Grace	1985	12.00

COLUMBIA

Number	Title	Yr	NM
❑ JC36396	Family	1980	18.00
❑ JC35708	Land of Passion	1979	12.00
❑ FC38850	Make It Last	1983	12.00
❑ PC34330	Romeo and Juliet	1976	15.00
❑ JC35022	Say It with Silence	1978	12.00
❑ FC36365	The Best of Hubert Laws	1981	12.00

CTI

Number	Title	Yr	NM
❑ 6006	Afro-Classic	1971	25.00
❑ 8019	Afro-Classic	198?	12.00
— Reissue of 6006			
❑ 6025	Carnegie Hall	1973	18.00
❑ 1002	Crying Song	1970	30.00
— Original issue			

Number	Title	Yr	NM
❑ 6000	Crying Song	1970	18.00
— Reissue of 1002			
❑ CTX-3+ 3	In the Beginning	1974	25.00
❑ 6022	Morning Star	1972	18.00
❑ 6012	Rite of Spring	1972	18.00
❑ 8020	Rite of Spring	198?	12.00
— Reissue of 6012			
❑ 6058	The Chicago Theme	1975	18.00
❑ 8015	The Chicago Theme	198?	12.00
— Reissue of 6058			
❑ 6065	Then There Was Light, Vol. 1	1976	15.00
— Half of "In the Beginning," originally issued as part of CTX 3+3			
❑ 6066	Then There Was Light, Vol. 2	1976	15.00
— Half of "In the Beginning," originally issued as part of CTX 3+3			
❑ 7071	The San Francisco Concert	1977	18.00

LAWS, RONNIE

BLUE NOTE
❑ BN-LA628-G	Fever	1976	15.00
❑ BN-LA730-H	Friends and Strangers	1977	12.00
❑ BN-LA452-G	Pressure Sensitive	1975	18.00

CAPITOL
❑ ST-12375	Classic Masters	1984	12.00
❑ ST-512375	Classic Masters	1984	15.00
— Columbia House edition			
❑ ST-12261	Mr. Nice Guy	1983	12.00

COLUMBIA
❑ FC40902	All Day Rhythm	1987	12.00
❑ BFC40089	Mirror Town	1986	12.00

LIBERTY
❑ LT-1001	Every Generation	1981	10.00
— Reissue of United Artists 1001			
❑ LO-628	Fever	198?	10.00
— Reissue of Blue Note 628			
❑ LN-10255	Fever	198?	10.00
— Budget-line reissue			
❑ LO-881	Flame	198?	10.00
— Reissue of United Artists 881			
❑ LN-10232	Flame	198?	10.00
— Budget-line reissue			
❑ LW-730	Friends and Strangers	198?	10.00
— Reissue of Blue Note 730			
❑ LN-10164	Pressure Sensitive	198?	10.00
— Reissue of Blue Note 452			
❑ LO-51087	Solid Ground	1981	12.00
❑ LN-10307	Solid Ground	1986	10.00
— Budget-line reissue			

UNITED ARTISTS
❑ LT-1001	Every Generation	1980	15.00
❑ UA-LA881-H	Flame	1978	12.00

LAWSON, DEE

ROULETTE
❑ R-52017 [M]	'Round Midnight	1958	30.00
❑ SR-52017 [S]	'Round Midnight	1958	40.00

LAWSON, HUGH

SOUL NOTE
❑ SN-1052	Colour	1983	15.00

STORYVILLE
❑ 4078	Prime Time	198?	12.00

LAWSON, JANET

INNER CITY
❑ IC-1118	Janet Lawson Quintet	1981	15.00

OMNISOUND
❑ 1052	Dreams Can Be	1983	15.00

LAWSON, LINDA

CHANCELLOR
❑ CHL-5010 [M]	Introducing Linda Lawson	1960	30.00

LAWSON, STELLA

STASH
❑ 235	Goin' For It	198?	12.00

LAWSON, YANK, AND BOB HAGGART

ATLANTIC
❑ SD1570	Live at the Roosevelt Grill	1970	18.00
❑ SD1582	What's New?	1971	18.00

DECCA
❑ DL5456 [10]	Blues on the River	1952	60.00
❑ DL8196 [M]	Blues on the River	1955	40.00
❑ DL8801 [M]	Boppin' at the Hop	1959	30.00
❑ DL78801 [S]	Boppin' at the Hop	1959	40.00
❑ DL5427 [10]	College Fight Songs	1952	60.00
❑ DL8453 [M]	Hold That Tiger	1956	30.00
❑ DL5439 [10]	Lawson-Haggart Band	1952	60.00
❑ DL5368 [10]	Lawson-Haggart Band Play Jelly Roll's Jazz	1952	60.00
❑ DL8182 [M]	Lawson-Haggart Band Play Jelly Roll's Jazz	1955	40.00
❑ DL5437 [10]	Lawson-Haggart Band Play King Oliver's Jazz	1952	60.00

Number	Title	Yr	NM
❑ DL8195 [M]	Lawson-Haggart Band Play King Oliver's Jazz	1955	40.00
❑ DL5533 [10]	Louis' Hot Fives and Sevens	1954	60.00
❑ DL8200 [M]	Louis' Hot Fives and Sevens	1955	40.00
❑ DL5529 [10]	South of the Mason-Dixon Line	1954	60.00
❑ DL8197 [M]	South of the Mason-Dixon Line	1955	40.00
❑ DL5502 [10]	Windy City Jazz	1953	60.00
❑ DL8198 [M]	Windy City Jazz	1955	40.00

EVEREST
❑ LPBR-5084 [M]	Dixieland Goes West	1960	25.00
❑ SDBR-1084 [S]	Dixieland Goes West	1960	30.00
❑ LPBR-5040 [M]	Junior Prom	1959	30.00
❑ SDBR-1040 [S]	Junior Prom	1959	25.00

PROJECT 3
❑ PR-5039	Extra	1969	25.00
❑ PR-5033	The World's Greatest Jazz Band	1968	25.00

STINSON
❑ SLP-59 [10]	Lawson-Haggart with Jerry Jerome and His Orchestra	1957	30.00

LAWSON, YANK

ABC-PARAMOUNT
❑ ABC-518 [M]	Big Yank Is Here	1965	18.00
❑ ABCS-518 [S]	Big Yank Is Here	1965	25.00
❑ ABC-567 [M]	Ole Dixie	1965	18.00
❑ ABCS-567 [S]	Ole Dixie	1965	25.00

AUDIOPHILE
❑ AP-221	Yank Lawson Plays Mostly Blues	1986	12.00

BRUNSWICK
❑ BL58035 [10]	Yank Lawson	1953	60.00

DOCTOR JAZZ
❑ FW40064	That's a Plenty	1985	12.00

RIVERSIDE
❑ RLP-2509 [10]	Yank Lawson's Dixieland Jazz	1954	80.00

LAY, RODNEY

CHURCHILL
❑ 9423	Heartbreak	1982	12.00

SUN
❑ 1022	Rockabilly Nuggets	1979	15.00
❑ 1027	Silent Partners	1981	15.00
— All copies on yellow vinyl			

LAY, SAM

BLUE THUMB
❑ BTS14	Sam Lay in Bluesland	1970	30.00

LAYTON, EDDIE

EPIC
❑ LN24118 [M]	Organ Music for Christmas	1964	15.00
❑ BN26118 [S]	Organ Music for Christmas	1964	18.00

LAZAR, SAM

ARGO
❑ LP-4015 [M]	Playback	1962	30.00
❑ LPS-4015 [S]	Playback	1962	40.00
❑ LP-714 [M]	Soul Merchant	1963	30.00
❑ LPS-714 [S]	Soul Merchant	1963	30.00
❑ LP-4002 [M]	Space Flight	1961	30.00
❑ LPS-4002 [S]	Space Flight	1961	40.00

LAZARUS

AMAZON
❑ 1001	Lazarus	1970	25.00

LAZRO, DAUNIK

HAT ART
❑ 2010	Sweet Zee	1986	18.00

HAT HUT
❑ 11	Entrance Gates Tshee Park	198?	18.00

LAZY LESTER

EXCELLO
❑ LP-8006 [M]	True Blues	1967	400.00
❑ LPS-8006 [M]	True Blues	196?	60.00
— Says "Stereo" but plays mono			

LAZY SMOKE

ONYX
❑ 6003	Corridor of Faces	1967	1200.00

LEA, BARBARA, AND BOB DOROUGH

AUDIOPHILE
❑ AP-165	Hoagy's Children	1981	15.00

LEA, BARBARA

AUDIOPHILE
❑ AP-86	A Woman in Love	197?	15.00
❑ AP-175	Do It Again	1984	12.00
❑ AP-125	Remembering Lee Wiley	197?	15.00
❑ AP-119	The Devil Is Afraid of Music	197?	15.00

Number	Title	Yr	NM
FANTASY			
❑ OJC-1713	Barbara Lea	198?	12.00
❑ OJC-1742	Lea in Love	1990	15.00
PRESTIGE			
❑ PRLP-7065 [M]	Barbara Lea	1956	150.00
❑ PRLP-7100 [M]	Lea in Love	1957	150.00
RIVERSIDE			
❑ RLP-2518 [10]	A Woman in Love	1955	200.00

LEA, TERREA

ABC-PARAMOUNT
❑ ABC-141 [M]	Terrea Lea and Her Singing Guitar	1956	30.00

HIFI
❑ R-404 [M]	Folk Songs and Ballads	1957	30.00

LEACH, CURTIS

LONGHORN
❑ 003	Indescribable	1965	50.00

LEADBELLY

ALLEGRO
❑ L-4027 [10]	Sinful Songs	195?	250.00

CAPITOL
❑ H369 [10]	Classics in Jazz	1953	250.00
❑ T1821 [M]	Leadbelly: Huddie Ledbetter's Best	1962	40.00

CLEOPATRA
❑ 2068 [B]	Where Did You Sleep Last Night?		25.00

ELEKTRA
❑ EKL-301/2	The Library of Congress Recordings	1966	30.00

FOLKWAYS
❑ FA-3106 [M]	Leadbelly Sings Folk Songs	196?	30.00
❑ FP-241 [M]	Leadbelly's Last Sessions, Vol. 1	196?	40.00
❑ FP-242 [M]	Leadbelly's Last Sessions, Vol. 2	196?	40.00
❑ FA-2941 [M]	Leadbelly's Last Sessions, Vol. 3	196?	30.00
❑ FA-2942 [M]	Leadbelly's Last Sessions, Vol. 4	196?	30.00
❑ FP-4 [10]	Lead Belly's Legacy, Vol. 1: Take This Hammer	1950	120.00
❑ FA-2004 [10]	Lead Belly's Legacy, Vol. 1: Take This Hammer	195?	50.00
— Reissue of FP-4			
❑ FP-14 [10]	Lead Belly's Legacy, Vol. 2: Rock Island Line	1951	120.00
❑ FA-2014 [10]	Lead Belly's Legacy, Vol. 2: Rock Island Line	195?	50.00
— Reissue of FP-14			
❑ FP-24 [10]	Lead Belly's Legacy, Vol. 3: Early Recordings	1951	120.00
❑ FA-2024 [10]	Lead Belly's Legacy, Vol. 3: Early Recordings	195?	50.00
— Reissue of FP-24			
❑ FP-34 [10]	Lead Belly's Legacy, Vol. 4: Easy Rider	1951	120.00
❑ FA-2034 [10]	Lead Belly's Legacy, Vol. 4: Easy Rider	195?	50.00
— Reissue of FP-34			

RCA VICTOR
❑ LPV-505 [M]	Midnight Special	1964	40.00

ROYALE
❑ 18131 [10]	Blues Songs	1954	120.00
— As "The Lonesome Blues Singer"			

VERVE FOLKWAYS
❑ FT-3019 [M]	From the Last Sessions	1967	30.00
❑ FTS-3019 [R]	From the Last Sessions	1967	18.00
❑ FV-9021 [M]	Keep Your Hands Off Her	1965	30.00
❑ FVS-9021 [R]	Keep Your Hands Off Her	1965	18.00
❑ FV-9001 [M]	Take This Hammer	1965	30.00
❑ FVS-9001 [R]	Take This Hammer	1965	18.00

LEADERS, THE

BLACK SAINT
❑ 120119	Out Here Like This	1989	18.00
❑ 120129	Unforeseen Blessings	1990	18.00

LEAHEY, HARRY

OMNISOUND
❑ 1042	Silver Threads	198?	12.00
❑ 1031	Still Waters	198?	12.00

LEAHY, JOE

TOWER
❑ T5057 [M]	A Taste of Trumpets, A Touch of Voices	1967	25.00
❑ ST5057 [S]	A Taste of Trumpets, A Touch of Voices	1967	30.00
❑ T5014 [M]	Tabasco and Trumpets	1966	25.00
❑ ST5014 [S]	Tabasco and Trumpets	1966	30.00

LEAPER, BOB

LONDON
❑ LL3391 [M]	Big Band Beatle Songs	1964	30.00
❑ SP44056 [S]	Big Band Beatle Songs	1964	40.00

Number	Title	Yr	NM

LEAPY LEE

DECCA
❏ DL75237	Leapy Lee	1970	18.00
❏ DL75076	Little Arrows	1968	25.00

LEARY, DR. TIMOTHY

DOUGLAS
❏ 1 [B]	You Can Be Anyone This Time Around	1969	150.00

ESP-DISK'
❏ 1027 [M]	Turn On, Tune In, Drop Out	1966	200.00

MERCURY
❏ MG-21131 [M]	Turn On, Tune In, Drop Out	1967	100.00
❏ SR-61131 [S]	Turn On, Tune In, Drop Out	1967	50.00

PIXIE
❏ CA-1069 [M]	L.S.D.	1966	80.00

LEARY, JAMES

VITAL MUSIC
❏ VTL-003	James	199?	18.00
❏ VTL-005	James II	199?	18.00

LEATHERCOATED MINDS, THE

VIVA
❏ V-6003 [M]	Trip Down Sunset Strip	1967	60.00
❏ V-36003 [S]	Trip Down Sunset Strip	1967	80.00

LEAVES, THE

CAPITOL
❏ T2638 [M]	All the Good That's Happening	1967	60.00
❏ ST2638 [S]	All the Good That's Happening	1967	30.00

MIRA
❏ LP-3005 [M]	Hey Joe	1966	40.00
❏ LPS-3005 [S]	Hey Joe	1966	50.00

SURREY
❏ LPS-3005	Hey Joe	196?	150.00
— Issued in Mira jackets

LED ZEPPELIN

ATLANTIC
❏ 83061	BBC Sessions	2000	60.00
— Classic Records limited edition; each LP is in its own cardboard sleeve inside a box with a sheet of liner notes
❏ 532632R1 [B]	Celebration Day	2013	80.00
❏ 83268	Early Days: The Best of Led Zeppelin Vol. 1	1999	18.00
❏ 7255 [M]	Houses of the Holy	1973	1000.00
— White label promo only
❏ SD7255 [S]	Houses of the Holy	1973	18.00
— 1841 Broadway" address on label
❏ SD7255 [S]	Houses of the Holy	1974	12.00
— 75 Rockefeller Plaza" address on label
❏ SD19130	Houses of the Holy	1977	10.00
❏ SD7255 [S]	Houses of the Holy	2001	150.00
— Classic Records reissue on audiophile vinyl
❏ 83278	Latter Days: The Best of Led Zeppelin Vol. 2	2000	18.00
❏ SD8216 [S]	Led Zeppelin	1969	250.00
— Possible mispress with purple and brown labels
❏ 8216 [M]	Led Zeppelin	1969	400.00
— White label promo only
❏ SD8216 [DJ]	Led Zeppelin	1969	200.00
— Stereo white label promo
❏ SD8216 [S]	Led Zeppelin	1969	25.00
— 1841 Broadway" address on label
❏ SD8216 [S]	Led Zeppelin	1974	12.00
— 75 Rockefeller Plaza" address on label
❏ SD19126	Led Zeppelin	1977	10.00
❏ SD8216 [S]	Led Zeppelin	2000	125.00
— Classic Records reissue on audiophile vinyl
❏ 82144	Led Zeppelin (Box Set)	1990	100.00
❏ 8236 [M]	Led Zeppelin II	1969	200.00
— White label promo only
❏ SD8236 [DJ]	Led Zeppelin II	1969	300.00
— Stereo white label promo
❏ SD8236 [S]	Led Zeppelin II	1969	25.00
— 1841 Broadway" address on label
❏ SD8236 [S]	Led Zeppelin II	1974	12.00
— 75 Rockefeller Plaza" address on label
❏ SD19127	Led Zeppelin II	1977	10.00
❏ SD8236 [S]	Led Zeppelin II	2000	50.00
— Classic Records reissue on audiophile vinyl
❏ 7201 [M]	Led Zeppelin III	1970	500.00
— White label promo only
❏ SD7201 [DJ]	Led Zeppelin III	1970	200.00
— Stereo white label promo
❏ SD7201 [S]	Led Zeppelin III	1970	25.00
— Die-cut cover with movable wheel; "1841 Broadway" address on label
❏ SD7201 [S]	Led Zeppelin III	1974	12.00
— 75 Rockefeller Plaza" address on label
❏ SD19128	Led Zeppelin III	1977	10.00
❏ SD7201 [S]	Led Zeppelin III	2001	100.00
— Classic Records reissue on audiophile vinyl
❏ 7208 [M]	Led Zeppelin (IV) (Runes)	1971	300.00

— White label promo only
❏ SD7208 [DJ]	Led Zeppelin (IV) (Runes)	1971	150.00
— Stereo white label promo
❏ SD7208 [S]	Led Zeppelin (IV) (Runes)	1971	18.00
— 1841 Broadway" address on label
❏ SD7208 [S]	Led Zeppelin (IV) (Runes)	1974	12.00
— 75 Rockefeller Plaza" address on label
❏ SD19129	Led Zeppelin (IV) (Runes)	1977	10.00
❏ SMAS-94019	Led Zeppelin (IV) (Runes)	1972	40.00
— Capitol Record Club edition
❏ SD7208 [S]	Led Zeppelin (IV) (Runes)	2001	200.00
— Classic Records reissue on audiophile vinyl

ATLANTIC CATALOGUE GROUP

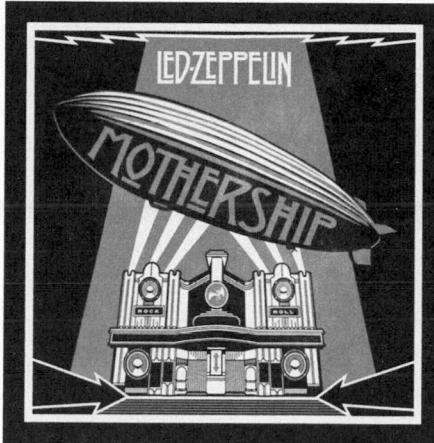

❏ 344700 [B]	Mothership	2008	60.00
❏ 371900 [B]	The Song Remains the Same	2008	200.00

ATLANTIC/RHINO
❏ R1536123 [B]	Led Zeppelin	2014	40.00
❏ R1536180 [B]	Led Zeppelin II	2014	40.00

MOBILE FIDELITY
❏ 1-065	Led Zeppelin II	1981	100.00
— Audiophile vinyl

SWAN SONG
❏ 90051	Coda	1982	14.00
❏ 90051-1 [B]	Coda	2001	75.00
— Classic Records reissue on audiophile vinyl
❏ SS16002 [B]	In Through the Out Door	1979	30.00
— Letter "A" on spine; add 50% if brown paper bag is still with jacket
❏ SS16002 [B]	In Through the Out Door	1979	30.00
— Letter "B" on spine; add 50% if brown paper bag is still with jacket
❏ SS16002 [B]	In Through the Out Door	1979	30.00
— Letter "C" on spine; add 50% if brown paper bag is still with jacket
❏ SS16002 [B]	In Through the Out Door	1979	30.00
— Letter "D" on spine; add 50% if brown paper bag is still with jacket
❏ SS16002 [B]	In Through the Out Door	1979	30.00
— Letter "E" on spine; add 50% if brown paper bag is still with jacket
❏ SS16002 [B]	In Through the Out Door	1979	30.00
— Letter "F" on spine; add 50% if brown paper bag is still with jacket
❏ SS16002 [B]	In Through the Out Door	2003	150.00
— Classic Records reissue on 200-gram vinyl; contains a 12-page insert with all six covers; we don't know if the label actually pressed these with six different covers
❏ SS 2-200	Physical Graffiti	1975	25.00
❏ SS 2-200	Physical Graffiti	2002	200.00
— Classic Records reissue on audiophile vinyl
❏ SS8416	Presence	1976	18.00
❏ SS8416 [B]	Presence	2002	150.00
— Classic Records reissue on audiophile vinyl
❏ SS2-201 [B]	The Song Remains The Same	2005	200.00
— Classic Records reissue on audiophile vinyl
❏ SS 2-201	The Song Remains the Same	1976	25.00
❏ SS 2-201	The Song Remains the Same	2003	40.00
— Classic Records edition on 200-gram vinyl

LEDOUX, CHRIS

AMERICAN COWBOY SONGS
❏ ACS23001	Chris LeDoux and the Saddle Boogie Band	198?	25.00
❏ ACS20001	Melodies and Memories	1984	30.00
❏ ACS17001	Thirty Dollar Cowboy	1983	30.00

LUCKY MAN
❏ NR9175	Chris LeDoux Sings Western Country	1978	30.00
❏ LM10193	Paint Me Back Home in Wyoming	1978	30.00
❏ NR4249	Rodeo Songs Old and New	1973	30.00
❏ ACS5524	Sing Me a Song, Mr. Rodeo Man	197?	30.00
❏ NR7648	Songs of the American West	1976	30.00
❏ LM10194	Western Tunesmith	1980	30.00

LEE, ALVIN

21 RECORDS
❏ 90517	Detroit Diesel	1986	12.00

ATLANTIC
❏ SD19287	Free Fall	1980	12.00
❏ SD19306	RX5	1981	12.00

COLUMBIA
❏ PG33187	In Flight	1974	18.00
❏ KC32729 [B]	On the Road to Freedom	1973	15.00
— With Mylon LeFevre
❏ PC32729	On the Road to Freedom	197?	10.00
— With Mylon LeFevre; reissue with new prefix
❏ PC33796	Pump Iron!	1975	15.00

RSO
❏ RS-1-3049	Ride On	1979	15.00
— With "Ten Years Later
❏ RS-1-3033	Rocket Fuel	1978	15.00
— With "Ten Years Later

LEE, ARTHUR

A&M
❏ SP-4356	Vindicator	1972	30.00

RHINO
❏ RNLP 020	Arthur Lee	1981	12.00

LEE, BRENDA

DECCA
❏ DL4757 [M]	10 Golden Years	1966	30.00
— With gatefold cover
❏ DL4757 [M]	10 Golden Years	196?	18.00
— With regular cover
❏ DL74757 [S]	10 Golden Years	1966	30.00
— With gatefold cover
❏ DL74757 [S]	10 Golden Years	196?	25.00
— With regular cover
❏ ST-90997 [S]	10 Golden Years	1966	30.00
— Capitol Record Club edition
❏ DL4370 [M]	All Alone Am I	1963	30.00
❏ DL74370 [S]	All Alone Am I	1963	30.00
❏ DL4176 [M]	All the Way	1961	30.00
❏ DL74176 [S]	All the Way	1961	30.00
❏ DL4326 [M]	Brenda, That's All	1962	30.00
❏ DL74326 [S]	Brenda, That's All	1962	30.00
❏ DL4039 [M]	Brenda Lee	1960	30.00
❏ DL74039 [S]	Brenda Lee	1960	30.00
❏ DL4755 [M]	Bye Bye Blues	1966	25.00
❏ DL74755 [O]	Bye Bye Blues	1966	30.00
❏ DL4509 [M]	By Request	1964	25.00
❏ DL74509 [S]	By Request	1964	30.00
❏ DL4825 [M]	Coming On Strong	1966	18.00
❏ DL74825 [S]	Coming On Strong	1966	25.00
❏ DL4104 [M]	Emotions	1961	30.00
❏ DL74104 [S]	Emotions	1961	30.00
❏ DL74955 [S]	For the First Time	1968	18.00
— With Pete Fountain
❏ DL8873 [M]	Grandma, What Great Songs You Sang	1960	40.00
❏ DL78873 [S]	Grandma, What Great Songs You Sang	1960	50.00
❏ DL75111	Johnny One Time	1969	18.00
❏ ST-92062	Johnny One Time	1969	25.00
— Capitol Record Club edition
❏ DL4439 [M]	Let Me Sing	1963	30.00
❏ DL74439 [S]	Let Me Sing	1963	30.00
❏ DL75232	Memphis Portrait	1970	18.00
❏ DL4583 [M]	Merry Christmas from Brenda Lee	1964	25.00
❏ DL74583 [S]	Merry Christmas from Brenda Lee	1964	30.00
❏ R103619 [S]	Merry Christmas from Brenda Lee	1971	25.00
— RCA Music Service edition
❏ DL4941 [M]	Reflections in Blue	1967	25.00
❏ DL74941 [S]	Reflections in Blue	1967	18.00
❏ DL4216 [M]	Sincerely	1962	30.00
❏ DL74216 [S]	Sincerely	1962	30.00
❏ DL4661 [M]	The Versatile Brenda Lee	1965	25.00
❏ DL74661 [S]	The Versatile Brenda Lee	1965	30.00
❏ DL4082 [M]	This Is…Brenda	1960	30.00
❏ DL74082 [S]	This Is…Brenda	1960	30.00
❏ DL4684 [M]	Too Many Rivers	1965	25.00
❏ DL74684 [S]	Too Many Rivers	1965	30.00
❏ DL4626 [M]	Top Teen Hits	1965	25.00
❏ DL74626 [S]	Top Teen Hits	1965	30.00

MCA
❏ 305	Brenda	1973	18.00
❏ 433	Brenda Lee Now	1974	15.00
❏ 3211	Even Better	1979	12.00
❏ 758	Even Better	198?	10.00
— Reissue of 3211
❏ 5626	Feels So Right	1985	12.00
❏ 5342	Greatest Country Hits	1982	12.00
❏ 2233	L.A. Sessions	1976	12.00
❏ 232 [S]	Merry Christmas from Brenda Lee	1973	15.00

Number	Title	Yr	NM
❑ 15021 [S]	Merry Christmas from Brenda Lee	197?	12.00
❑ 373	New Sunrise	1973	15.00
❑ 5278	Only When I Laugh	1981	12.00
❑ 824	Only When I Laugh	1982	10.00
— Reissue of 5278			
❑ 15038	Rockin' Around the Christmas Tree	198?	12.00
❑ 477	Sincerely, Brenda Lee	1975	12.00
❑ 5143	Take Me Back	1980	12.00
❑ 2-4012	The Brenda Lee Story -- Her Greatest Hits	1973	25.00

MCA CORAL
❑ CB-20044	Let It Be Me	197?	12.00

VOCALION
❑ VL3795 [M]	Here's Brenda Lee	1967	15.00
❑ VL73795 [S]	Here's Brenda Lee	1967	15.00
❑ VL73890	Let It Be Me	1970	15.00

LEE, BYRON, AND THE DRAGONAIRES

ATCO
❑ 33-182 [M]	Jump Up	1966	25.00
❑ SD 33-182 [S]	Jump Up	1966	30.00

BMN
❑ 004	Dance the Ska	196?	25.00

JAD
❑ JS-1004	Byron Lee and the Dragonaires	1968	25.00

TOWERS HALL
❑ 006	The Sounds of Jamaica	196?	25.00

LEE, DICKEY

MERCURY
❑ SRM-1-5020	Dickey Lee	1979	12.00
❑ SRM-1-5026	Dickey Lee Again	1980	12.00

RCA VICTOR
❑ APL1-1725	Angels, Roses and Rain	1976	15.00
❑ LSP-4715	Ashes of Love	1972	15.00
❑ LSP-4791	Baby, Bye Bye	1972	15.00
❑ LSP-4857	Crying Over You	1973	15.00
❑ LSP-4637	Never Ending Song of Love	1971	15.00
❑ APL1-1240	Rocky	1975	15.00
❑ APL1-0311	Sparklin' Brown Eyes	1974	15.00

SMASH
❑ MGS-27020 [M]	The Tale of Patches	1962	30.00
❑ SRS-67020 [S]	The Tale of Patches	1962	40.00

TCF HALL
❑ TCF-8001 [M]	Dickey Lee Sings "Laurie" and "The Girl from Peyton Place	1965	25.00
❑ TCF-9001 [S]	Dickey Lee Sings "Laurie" and "The Girl from Peyton Place	1965	30.00

LEE, EDDIE

GEORGIAN
❑ GR2001 [M]	Windy City Profile	1958	40.00

LEE, JACKIE (1)

MIRWOOD
❑ MW-7000 [M]	The Duck	1966	25.00
❑ SW-7000 [S]	The Duck	1966	30.00

LEE, JEANNE, AND RAN BLAKE

BLUEBIRD
❑ 6461-1-RB	The Legendary Duets	1987	15.00

RCA VICTOR
❑ LPM-2500 [M]	The Newest Sound Around	1962	30.00
❑ LSP-2500 [S]	The Newest Sound Around	1962	40.00

LEE, JOHN, AND GERRY BROWN

BLUE NOTE
❑ BN-LA541-G	Mango Sunrise	1976	15.00
❑ BN-LA701-G	Still Can't Say Enough	1977	15.00

LEE, JOHNNY

ACCORD
❑ 7219	Country Party	1983	10.00

ASYLUM
❑ 6E-309	Lookin' for Love	1980	12.00

CURB
❑ 10617	New Directions	1989	12.00

FULL MOON
❑ 23899	Hey Bartender	1983	10.00

FULL MOON/ASYLUM
❑ 5E-541	Bet Your Heart on Me	1981	10.00
❑ 60147	Sounds Like Love	1982	10.00

PLANTATION
❑ 45	Party Time	1981	12.00

WARNER BROS.
❑ 23967	Greatest Hits	1983	10.00
❑ 25210	Keep Me Hangin' On	1985	10.00
❑ 6E-309	Lookin' for Love	198?	10.00
— Reissue of Asylum 6E-309			
❑ 25056	'Til the Bars Burn Down	1984	10.00
❑ 25125	Workin' for a Livin'	1984	10.00

LEE, JONI

MCA
❑ 2194	Joni Lee	1976	15.00

LEE, JULIA

CAPITOL
❑ H228 [10]	Party Time	1950	120.00
❑ T228 [M]	Party Time	195?	100.00

PAUSA
❑ 9020	Julia Lee and Her Boyfriends	198?	12.00

LEE, KATIE

HORIZON
❑ WP-1604 [M]	The Best of Katie Lee	1962	25.00
❑ WP-1604Stereo [S]	The Best of Katie Lee	1962	30.00

REPRISE
❑ R-6025 [M]	Songs of Coach and Consultation	1961	30.00

SPECIALTY
❑ SP-5000 [M]	Spicy Songs for Cool Knights	1959	30.00

LEE, LAURA

CHESS
❑ CH-50031	Love More Than Pride	1972	25.00

HOT WAX
❑ HA-714	Laura Lee	1972	18.00
❑ HA-715	The Best of Laura Lee	1973	18.00
❑ HA-708	Women's Love Rights	1971	18.00

INVICTUS
❑ KZ33133	Laura Lee	1974	12.00

LEE, LONDON

PHILIPS
❑ PHS600322	The Rich Kid	1969	18.00

LEE, MICHELE

COLUMBIA
❑ CL2486 [M]	A Taste of the Fantastic	1966	18.00
❑ CS9286 [S]	A Taste of the Fantastic	1966	25.00
❑ CS9682	L. David Sloane and Other Hits of Today	1968	25.00

LEE, PEGGY

A&M
❑ SP-4547	Mirrors	1975	15.00

ATLANTIC
❑ SD18108	Let's Love	1974	15.00

CAPITOL
❑ T1366 [M]	All Aglow Again	1960	25.00
— Black label with colorband, Capitol logo at left			
❑ T1366 [M]	All Aglow Again	1962	15.00
— Black label with colorband, Capitol logo at top			
❑ ST1366 [S]	All Aglow Again	1960	30.00
— Black label with colorband, Capitol logo at left			
❑ ST1366 [S]	All Aglow Again	1962	18.00
— Black label with colorband, Capitol logo at top			
❑ T1213 [M]	Alright, Okay, You Win	1959	30.00
❑ ST1213 [S]	Alright, Okay, You Win	1959	30.00
❑ ST-183	A Natural Woman	1969	18.00
❑ T1520 [M]	Basin Street East	1961	25.00
— Black label with colorband, Capitol logo at left			
❑ T1520 [M]	Basin Street East	1962	15.00
— Black label with colorband, Capitol logo at top			
❑ ST1520 [S]	Basin Street East	1961	30.00
— Black label with colorband, Capitol logo at left			
❑ ST1520 [S]	Basin Street East	1962	18.00
— Black label with colorband, Capitol logo at top			
❑ SM-1520	Basin Street East	1977	12.00
— Reissue with new prefix			
❑ T1219 [M]	Beauty and the Beat	1959	30.00
— With George Shearing; black label with colorband, Capitol logo at left			
❑ ST1219 [S]	Beauty and the Beat	1959	30.00
— With George Shearing; black label with colorband, Capitol logo at left			
❑ T1219 [M]	Beauty and the Beat	1962	18.00
— With George Shearing; black label with colorband, Capitol logo at top			
❑ ST1219 [S]	Beauty and the Beat	1962	25.00
— With George Shearing; black label with colorband, Capitol logo at top			
❑ T1743 [M]	Bewitching-Lee!	1962	30.00
— Black "The Star Line" label			
❑ DT1743 [R]	Bewitching-Lee!	1962	18.00
❑ T2475 [M]	Big $pender	1966	18.00
❑ ST2475 [S]	Big $pender	1966	25.00
❑ T1671 [M]	Blue Cross Country	1962	25.00
❑ ST1671 [S]	Blue Cross Country	1962	30.00
❑ ST-463	Bridge Over Troubled Water	1970	15.00
❑ T1423 [M]	Christmas Carousel	1960	25.00
❑ ST1423 [S]	Christmas Carousel	1960	30.00
❑ T2732 [M]	Extra Special	1967	25.00
❑ ST2732 [S]	Extra Special	1967	18.00
❑ STBB-517	Folks Who Live on the Hill/ Broadway Ala Lee	1970	18.00

Number	Title	Yr	NM
❑ T2469 [M]	Guitars Ala Lee	1966	18.00
❑ ST2469 [S]	Guitars Ala Lee	1966	25.00
❑ T2390 [M]	Happy Holiday	1965	15.00
❑ ST2390 [S]	Happy Holiday	1965	18.00
❑ T1630 [M]	If You Go	1962	25.00
❑ ST1630 [S]	If You Go	1962	30.00
❑ T1131 [M]	I Like Men	1959	30.00
❑ ST1131 [S]	I Like Men	1959	30.00
❑ T1857 [M]	I'm a Woman	1963	25.00
❑ ST1857 [S]	I'm a Woman	1963	30.00
❑ SM-1857	I'm a Woman	1977	12.00
— Reissue with new prefix			
❑ T1969 [M]	In Love Again	1963	25.00
❑ ST1969 [S]	In Love Again	1963	30.00
❑ T2096 [M]	In the Name of Love	1964	18.00
❑ ST2096 [S]	In the Name of Love	1964	25.00
❑ ST-386	Is That All There Is?	1969	15.00
❑ SM-386	Is That All There Is?	197?	12.00
— Reissue with new prefix			
❑ T979 [M]	Jump for Joy	1958	40.00
— Turquoise or gray label			
❑ T979 [M]	Jump for Joy	1959	30.00
— Black label with colorband, Capitol logo at left			
❑ ST979 [S]	Jump for Joy	1959	30.00
❑ T1290 [M]	Latin Ala Lee!	1960	25.00
— Black label with colorband, Capitol logo at left			
❑ T1290 [M]	Latin Ala Lee!	1962	15.00
— Black label with colorband, Capitol logo at top			
❑ ST1290 [S]	Latin Ala Lee!	1960	30.00
— Black label with colorband, Capitol logo at left			
❑ ST1290 [S]	Latin Ala Lee!	1962	18.00
— Black label with colorband, Capitol logo at top			
❑ SM-1290	Latin Ala Lee!	1977	12.00
— Reissue with new prefix			
❑ ST-622	Make It with You	1970	15.00
❑ T1850 [M]	Mink Jazz	1963	25.00
❑ ST1850 [S]	Mink Jazz	1963	30.00
❑ H204 [10]	My Best to You	1952	100.00
❑ T204 [M]	My Best to You	1954	50.00
— Turquoise or gray label			
❑ T204 [M]	My Best to You	1959	30.00
— Black label with colorband, Capitol logo at left			
❑ ST-11077	Norma Deloris Egstrom from Jamestown, North Dakota	1972	15.00
❑ T1475 [M]	Ole Ala Lee!	1961	25.00
❑ ST1475 [S]	Ole Ala Lee!	1961	30.00
❑ T2320 [M]	Pass Me By	1965	18.00
❑ ST2320 [S]	Pass Me By	1965	25.00
❑ STCL-576	Peggy Lee	1970	30.00
❑ DKAO-377	Peggy Lee's Greatest	1969	15.00
❑ SN-16140	Peggy Lee Sings Songs of Cy Coleman	198?	10.00
❑ T1401 [M]	Pretty Eyes	1960	25.00
— Black label with colorband, Capitol logo at left			
❑ T1401 [M]	Pretty Eyes	1962	15.00
— Black label with colorband, Capitol logo at top			
❑ ST1401 [S]	Pretty Eyes	1960	30.00
— Black label with colorband, Capitol logo at left			
❑ ST1401 [S]	Pretty Eyes	1962	18.00
— Black label with colorband, Capitol logo at top			
❑ H151 [10]	Rendezvous with Peggy Lee	1952	100.00
❑ T151 [M]	Rendezvous with Peggy Lee	1954	50.00
— Turquoise or gray label			
❑ T151 [M]	Rendezvous with Peggy Lee	1959	30.00
— Black label with colorband, Capitol logo at left			
❑ ST2781	Somethin' Groovy	1968	18.00
❑ T1772 [M]	Sugar 'n' Spice	1962	25.00
❑ ST1772 [S]	Sugar 'n' Spice	1962	30.00
❑ T2388 [M]	That Was Then, Now Is Now	1965	18.00
❑ ST2388 [S]	That Was Then, Now Is Now	1965	25.00
❑ ST2887	The Hits of Peggy Lee	1968	18.00
❑ T864 [M]	The Man I Love	1957	50.00
— Turquoise label			

❑ T864 [M]	The Man I Love	1959	30.00
— Black label with colorband, Capitol logo at left			
❑ ST864 [S]	The Man I Love	1959	30.00
❑ T1049 [M]	Things Are Swingin'	1958	30.00

Number	Title	Yr	NM
❑ ST1049 [S]	Things Are Swingin'	1959	30.00
❑ ST-105 [B]	Two Shows Nightly	1969	500.00

— *Withdrawn immediately after release; most of the known copies have the word "FREE" stamped diagonally in the upper right corner of the cover*

❑ ST-810	Where Did They Go	1971	15.00

COLUMBIA

❑ CL6033 [10]	Benny Goodman and Peggy Lee	1949	60.00

DECCA

❑ DL5482 [10]	Black Coffee	1953	100.00
❑ DL8358 [M]	Black Coffee	1956	60.00
❑ DL8411 [M]	Dream Street	1957	60.00
❑ DL4458 [M]	Lover	1964	30.00
❑ DL74458 [R]	Lover	1964	18.00
❑ DL8816 [M]	Miss Wonderful	1959	60.00
❑ DL8591 [M]	Sea Shells	1958	60.00
❑ DL5539 [10]	Songs in an Intimate Style	1953	80.00
❑ DXB164 [M]	The Best of Peggy Lee	1964	30.00
❑ DXSB7164 [R]	The Best of Peggy Lee	1964	25.00
❑ DL4461 [M]	The Fabulous Peggy Lee	1964	30.00
❑ DL74461 [R]	The Fabulous Peggy Lee	1964	18.00

DRG

❑ SL-5190	Close Enough for Love	1979	15.00

EVEREST ARCHIVE OF FOLK & JAZZ

❑ 294	Peggy Lee	197?	12.00

GLENDALE

❑ 6023	You Can Depend on Me	1982	12.00

HARMONY

❑ H30024	Miss Peggy Lee	1970	12.00
❑ HL7005 [M]	Peggy Lee Sings with Benny Goodman	195?	30.00

HINDSIGHT

❑ HSR-220	Peggy Lee with the David Barbour and Billy May Bands, 1948	1985	12.00

MCA

❑ 4049	The Best of Peggy Lee	197?	15.00

MERCURY

❑ SRM-1-1172	Live in London	1977	15.00

MUSICMASTERS

❑ 5005	Peggy Sings the Blues	1988	15.00

PAUSA

❑ PR-9043	Sugar 'n' Spice	1985	12.00

PICKWICK

❑ SPC-3192	I've Got the World	1971	12.00
❑ SPC-3090	Once More with Feeling	196?	12.00

S&P

❑ 602	Bewitching-Lee!	2003	30.00

— *Reissue on 180-gram vinyl*

❑ 504	Latin Ala Lee!	2004	30.00

— *Reissue on 180-gram vinyl*

TIME-LIFE

❑ SLCD 07	Legendary Singers: Peggy Lee	1985	10.00

VOCALION

❑ VL73903	Crazy in the Heart	1969	12.00
❑ VL3776 [M]	So Blue	1966	18.00
❑ VL73776 [R]	So Blue	1966	12.00

LEE, PERRY

ROULETTE

❑ R-52080 [M]	A Night at Count Basie's	1962	18.00
❑ SR-52080 [S]	A Night at Count Basie's	1962	25.00

LEE, PINKY

DECCA

❑ DL8421 [M]	The Surprise Party	1957	40.00

LEE, ROBIN

ATLANTIC AMERICA

❑ 90906	This Old Flame	1988	12.00

DOT

❑ DLP-3661 [M]	Robin Lee	1965	30.00

EVERGREEN

❑ 1001	Robin Lee	1986	15.00

LEEDS, ERIC

PAISLEY PARK

❑ 27499	Times Square	1991	18.00

LEES, GENE, AND ROGER KELLAWAY

CHOICE

❑ CRS-6832	Leaves on the Water	1986	12.00

LEES, GENE

STASH

❑ ST-269	Gene Lees Sings the Gene Lees Songbook	1987	12.00

LEESE, TIM

MUSIC IS MEDICINE

❑ 9036	After Hours	198?	15.00

LEFEBVRE, DAVE

JAZZ HOUNDS

❑ 0001	Marble Dust	198?	15.00

LEFEBVRE, GARY

DISCOVERY

❑ DS-849	Gary LeFebvre Quartet	1981	15.00

LEFEVERE, KAMIEL

MERCURY LIVING PRESENCE

❑ SR90189 [S]	The Magic of the Bells	196?	50.00

— *Maroon label, no "Vendor: Mercury Record Corporation*

LEFEVRE, RAYMOND

4 CORNERS OF THE WORLD

❑ FCS-4250	La La La (He Gives Me Love)	1968	15.00
❑ FCL-4239 [M]	Love Me, Please Love Me	1967	15.00
❑ FCS-4239 [S]	Love Me, Please Love Me	1967	15.00
❑ FCS-4257	Merry Christmas	1968	15.00
❑ FCS-4244	Soal Coaxing (Ame Caline)	1968	15.00

ATLANTIC

❑ 8044 [M]	Romantica	1961	25.00
❑ SD8044 [S]	Romantica	1961	30.00

BUDDAH

❑ BDS-5109	Oh Happy Day	1972	12.00
❑ BDS-5095	Raymond Lefevre	1971	12.00

KAPP

❑ KL-1510 [M]	You Don't Have to Stay	1967	18.00
❑ KS-3510 [S]	You Don't Have to Stay	1967	15.00

MONUMENT

❑ MLP-8067 [M]	Paris Cancan	1967	30.00
❑ SLP-18067 [S]	Paris Cancan	1967	15.00

LEFT BANKE, THE

RHINO

❑ RNLP-123	History of the Left Banke	1985	12.00

SMASH

❑ SRS-67113	The Left Banke, Too	1968	50.00
❑ MGS-27088 [M]	Walk Away Renee/Pretty Ballerina	1967	60.00
❑ SRS-67088 [S]	Walk Away Renee/Pretty Ballerina	1967	40.00
❑ SRS-67088 [B]	Walk Away Renee/Pretty Ballerina	198?	12.00

— *Reissue with thinner vinyl*

LEGARDE TWINS, THE

KOALA

❑ K10001	Andaleigha Mia	197?	18.00

LEGEND

BELL

❑ 6027	Legend	1969	50.00

MEGAPHONE

❑ 101	Legend	1970	80.00

LEGENDS, THE

CAPITOL

❑ T1925 [M]	The Legends Let Loose	1963	60.00
❑ ST1925 [S]	The Legends Let Loose	1963	80.00

COLUMBIA

❑ CL1707 [M]	Hit Sounds of Today's Smash Hit Combos	1961	30.00
❑ CS8507 [S]	Hit Sounds of Today's Smash Hit Combos	1961	40.00

ERMINE

❑ LP-101 [M]	The Legends Let Loose	1963	200.00

LEGGE, WADE

BLUE NOTE

❑ BLP-5031 [10]	New Faces New Sounds	1953	600.00

LEGGIO, CARMEN

DREAMSTREET

❑ 103	Aerial View	1979	15.00

FAMOUS DOOR

❑ 125	Tarytown Tenor	1978	15.00

GOLDEN CREST

❑ GCS-1000	Jazz	196?	25.00

PROGRESSIVE

❑ PRO-7010	Smile	1980	12.00

LEGRAND, MICHEL

BELL

❑ 6071	Brian's Song Themes & Variations	1972	12.00
❑ 4200	Twenty Songs of the Century	1974	15.00

COLUMBIA

❑ CL888 [M]	Castles in Spain	1956	30.00
❑ CL647 [M]	Holiday in Rome	1955	30.00
❑ CL555 [M]	I Love Paris	1954	40.00
❑ CL1437 [M]	I Love Paris	1960	30.00

Number	Title	Yr	NM
❑ CS8237 [S]	I Love Paris	1960	25.00
❑ PC9237	I Love Paris	1987	10.00

— *Reissue with new prefix*

❑ CL1139 [M]	Legrand in Rio	1957	30.00
❑ CL1250 [M]	Legrand Jazz	1958	40.00

— *Miles Davis appears on this record*

❑ CS8079 [S]	Legrand Jazz	1959	40.00

— *Miles Davis appears on this record*

❑ CL1115 [M]	Michel Legrand Plays Cole Porter	1957	30.00
❑ CL706 [M]	Vienna Holiday	1955	30.00

GRYPHON

❑ 786	Jazz Grand	1978	12.00

HARMONY

❑ KH31549	Cole Porter, Volume I	1972	12.00
❑ KH31540	Cole Porter, Volume II	1972	12.00
❑ HL7331 [M]	I Love Paris	196?	15.00
❑ HS11131 [S]	I Love Paris	196?	15.00

MERCURY

❑ MG20342 [M]	C'est Magnifique	1958	25.00

MGM

❑ SE-4491	Cinema La Grand	1967	18.00

MOBILE FIDELITY

❑ 1-504	Jazz Grand	198?	50.00

— *Audiophile vinyl*

PABLO TODAY

❑ 2312139	After the Rain	198?	12.00

PHILIPS

❑ PHM200143 [M]	Michel Legrand Sings	1964	30.00
❑ PHS600143 [S]	Michel Legrand Sings	1964	30.00
❑ PHM200074 [M]	The Michel Legrand Big Band Plays Richard Rogers	1963	25.00
❑ PHS600074 [S]	The Michel Legrand Big Band Plays Richard Rogers	1963	30.00

RCA VICTOR

❑ BGL1-1028	Concert	1976	12.00
❑ BXL1-1028	Concert	1978	10.00

— *Reissue with new prefix*

❑ BGL1-0850	Jimmy's	1975	12.00
❑ BXL1-0850	Jimmy's	1978	10.00

— *Reissue with new prefix*

❑ BGL1-1392	Michel Legrand and Friends	1976	12.00
❑ BXL1-1392	Michel Legrand and Friends	1978	10.00

— *Reissue with new prefix*

VERVE

❑ V6-8760	Michel Legrand at Shelly's Mann-Hole	1969	15.00

LEGS DIAMOND

CREAM

❑ CR1010	Fire Power	1979	30.00

MERCURY

❑ SRM-1-1191	A Diamond is a Hard Rock	1977	30.00
❑ SRM-1-1136	Legs Diamond	1977	30.00

LEHRER, TOM

LEHRER

❑ TL-202 [M]	An Evening Wasted with Tom Lehrer	1959	30.00
❑ TL-202S [S]	An Evening Wasted with Tom Lehrer	1959	40.00
❑ TL-102 [M]	More of Tom Lehrer	1958	40.00
❑ TL-102S [S]	More of Tom Lehrer	1959	40.00
❑ TLP-1 [10]	Songs by Tom Lehrer	1953	100.00
❑ TL-101 [M]	Songs by Tom Lehrer	1959	40.00
❑ TL-201 [M]	Tom Lehrer Revisited	1959	30.00

REPRISE

❑ R6199 [M]	An Evening Wasted with Tom Lehrer	1966	25.00

— *Reissue of Lehrer 202*

❑ RS6199 [S]	An Evening Wasted with Tom Lehrer	1966	30.00

— *Reissue of Lehrer 202*

❑ R-6216 [M]	Songs by Tom Lehrer	1966	25.00
❑ RS-6216 [S]	Songs by Tom Lehrer	1966	30.00
❑ R-6179 [M]	That Was the Year That Was	1965	25.00
❑ RS-6179 [S]	That Was the Year That Was	1965	30.00

— *Pink, yellow and green label*

❑ RS-6179 [S]	That Was the Year That Was	1968	18.00

— *Two-tone orange label with "W7" and "r:" logos*

❑ RS-6179 [S]	That Was the Year That Was	1970	12.00

— *Orange/tan label with "r:" logo*

LEIBER, JERRY

KAPP

❑ KL-1127 [M]	Scooby-Doo	1959	50.00

LEIBER AND STOLLER BIG BAND, THE

ATLANTIC

❑ 8047 [M]	Yakety Yak	1960	60.00

— *White "fan" logo on right side of label*

❑ SD8047 [S]	Yakety Yak	1960	60.00

— *White "fan" logo on right side of label*

❑ 8047 [M]	Yakety Yak	1962	40.00

— *Black "fan" logo on right side of label*

❑ SD8047 [S]	Yakety Yak	1962	40.00

— *Black "fan" logo on right side of label*

Number	Title	Yr	NM

LEIBERT, DICK

RCA CAMDEN

| ADL2-0243 | Christmas at Radio City Music Hall | 1973 | 18.00 |

RCA VICTOR

| LPM-2558 [M] | The Sound of Christmas on the Radio City Music Hall Organ | 1962 | 15.00 |
| LSP-2558 [S] | The Sound of Christmas on the Radio City Music Hall Organ | 1962 | 18.00 |

WESTMINSTER

WST15020 [S]	A Merry Wurlitzer Christmas	195?	25.00
WST15034 [S]	Leibert Takes a Holiday	195?	25.00
WST15006 [S]	Leibert Takes Broadway	195?	25.00
WST15009 [S]	Leibert Takes Richmond	195?	25.00
WST15043 [S]	Leibert Takes You Dancing	195?	25.00
WST15050 [S]	Sing a Song with Leibert	195?	25.00

LEIGH, CAROL

GHB

152	Blame It on the Blues	198?	15.00
167	Go Back Where You Stayed Last Night	198?	15.00
GHB-88	Wild Women Don't Have the Blues	197?	15.00
136	You've Got to Give Me Some	1980	15.00

STOMP OFF

| SOS-1064 | If You Don't Know, I Know Who Will | 1983 | 12.00 |
| SOS-1087 | I'm Busy and You Can't Come In | 1985 | 12.00 |

LEIGH, RICHARD

UNITED ARTISTS

| LT-1036 | Richard Leigh | 1980 | 12.00 |

LEIGHTON, BERNIE

CAMEO

| C-1005 [M] | Dizzy Fingers | 1959 | 30.00 |

COLUMBIA

| CL6112 [10] | East Side Rendezvous | 1950 | 80.00 |

MONMOUTH-EVERGREEN

| 7068 | Bernie Leighton Plays Duke Ellington Live at Jimmy Weston's | 197? | 15.00 |

LEIGHTON, BERNIE/JOHNNY GUARNIERI

EMARCY

| MG-26018 [10] | Piano Stylings | 1954 | 80.00 |

LEITCH, PETER

PAUSA

| 7132 | Jump Street | 1981 | 12.00 |

LELLIS, TOM

INNER CITY

| IC-1090 | And In This Corner | 198? | 18.00 |

LEMER, PETER

ESP-DISK'

| 1057 | Local Colour | 1968 | 30.00 |

LEMMON, JACK

CAPITOL

| T1943 [M] | Jack Lemmon Plays Piano Selections from Irma La Douce | 1963 | 30.00 |
| ST1943 [S] | Jack Lemmon Plays Piano Selections from Irma La Douce | 1963 | 35.00 |

EPIC

LN3491 [M]	A Twist of Lemmon	1959	30.00
BN523 [S]	A Twist of Lemmon	1959	30.00
LN3559 [M]	Jack Lemmon Sings and Plays Music from Some Like It Hot	1959	30.00
BN528 [S]	Jack Lemmon Sings and Plays Music from Some Like It Hot	1959	30.00

LEMON PIPERS, THE

BUDDAH

BDS-5009 [S]	Green Tambourine	1968	30.00
BDM-1009 [M]	Green Tambourine	1968	30.00
BDS-5016 [S]	Jungle Marmalade	1968	30.00
BDM-1016 [M]	Jungle Marmalade	1968	40.00

— *Mono is promo only; in stereo cover with "Mono" sticker*

LEMONGELLO, PETER

PRIVATE STOCK

| PS-2018 | Do I Love You | 1976 | 25.00 |

RAPP

| LR8899 | Love '76 | 1976 | 30.00 |

LEMONHEADS, THE

ATLANTIC

| SAM1267 [DJ] | Come On Feel the Lemonheads | 1993 | 30.00 |

— *Promo-only four-song sampler*

| 82537 | Come On Feel the Lemonheads | 1993 | 30.00 |

— *5,000 copies pressed, all on green vinyl; imports sell for less*

| 82137 | Lovey | 1990 | 25.00 |

— *U.S. edition; imports with a similar number go for less*

TAANG!

| 23 | Creator | 1988 | 18.00 |
| 15 | Hate Your Friends | 1987 | 40.00 |

— *The first 3,000 were on black vinyl, yellow lettering on sleeve, yellow label*

| 15 | Hate Your Friends | 1987 | 30.00 |

— *The second 2,000 are on black vinyl, red lettering on sleeve, yellow label*

| 15 | Hate Your Friends | 1987 | 30.00 |

— *Third pressing: Black vinyl, red lettering on sleeve, red label*

| 15 | Hate Your Friends | 1987 | 30.00 |

— *Fourth pressing: Black vinyl, red lettering on sleeve, blue and green label*

| 15 | Hate Your Friends | 1987 | 25.00 |

— *Fifth pressing: Yellow vinyl, yellow lettering on sleeve, yellow label*

| 15 | Hate Your Friends | 1987 | 15.00 |

— *Any edition not listed among the first five pressings above*

| 32 | Lick | 1989 | 18.00 |

TAG/ATLANTIC

| 92726 | Car Button Cloth | 1996 | 25.00 |

TPM/RHINO EXCLUSIVE

| 138 | It's a Shame About Ray | 2008 | 18.00 |

LENNON, JOHN

ADAM VIII

| A-8018 | John Lennon Sings the Great Rock & Roll Hits (Roots) | 1975 | 1000.00 |

— *Counterfeits abound. On authentic copies, cover is posterboard (not slicks); labels are normal size (not overly large); printing on cover is sharp, not blurry; the word "Greatest" does NOT appear on the spine. Authentic copies usually have ad sleeve also.*

APPLE

| SW-3379 [B] | Imagine | 1971 | 30.00 |

— *With either of two postcard inserts, lyric sleeve, poster*

| SW-3379 | Imagine | 1975 | 25.00 |

— *All Rights Reserved" label*

| SW-3372 | John Lennon Plastic Ono Band | 1970 | 25.00 |
| SW-3362 | Live Peace in Toronto 1969 | 1970 | 18.00 |

— *By "The Plastic Ono Band" -- without calendar*

| SW-3362 [B] | Live Peace in Toronto 1969 | 1970 | 30.00 |

— *By "The Plastic Ono Band"; with calendar*

SW-3414	Mind Games	1973	25.00
SK-3419	Rock 'N' Roll	1975	25.00
SW-3421	Shaved Fish	1975	25.00
SVBB-3392 [B]	Some Time in New York City	1972	35.00

— *By John and Yoko; with photo card and petition*

| SVBB-3392 [DJ] | Some Time in New York City | 1972 | 1000.00 |

— *White label promo*

| T-5001 | Two Virgins -- Unfinished Music No. 1 | 1968 | 50.00 |

— *With Yoko Ono; without brown bag*

| T-5001 | Two Virgins -- Unfinished Music No. 1 | 1968 | 150.00 |

— *With Yoko Ono; price with brown bag*

| T-5001 | Two Virgins -- Unfinished Music No. 1 | 1968 | 150.00 |

— *With Yoko Ono; with die-cut bag*

| T-5001 | Two Virgins -- Unfinished Music No. 1 | 1985 | 18.00 |

— *With Yoko Ono; reissue, flat label*

| SW-3416 [B] | Walls and Bridges | 1974 | 30.00 |

— *With fold-open segmented front cover*

| SMAX-3361 | Wedding Album | 1969 | 150.00 |

— *With photo strip, postcard, poster of wedding photos, poster of lithographs, "Bagism" bag, booklet, photo of slice of wedding cake. Missing inserts reduce the value.*

CAPITOL

| C1-91425 | Double Fantasy | 1989 | 25.00 |

— *Very briefly available reissue*

| C1-591425 | Double Fantasy | 1989 | 60.00 |

— *Columbia House edition of reissue*

| SW-3379 | Imagine | 1978 | 12.00 |

— *Purple label, large Capitol logo*

| SW-3379 | Imagine | 1986 | 30.00 |

— *Black label, print in colorband*

| SW-3379 | Imagine | 1987 | 30.00 |

— *Black label, print in colorband; "Digitally Re-Mastered" at top of front cover*

| SW-3379 | Imagine | 1988 | 30.00 |

— *Purple label, small Capitol logo*

| C1-90803 | Imagine: Music from the Motion Picture | 1988 | 25.00 |
| SW-3372 | John Lennon Plastic Ono Band | 1978 | 15.00 |

— *Purple label, large Capitol logo*

| SW-3372 | John Lennon Plastic Ono Band | 1982 | 25.00 |

— *Black label, print in colorband*

| SW-3372 | John Lennon Plastic Ono Band | 1988 | 30.00 |

— *Purple label, small Capitol logo*

| SV-12451 | Live in New York City | 1986 | 15.00 |
| SV-512451 | Live in New York City | 1986 | 18.00 |

— *Columbia House edition*

| R144497 | Live in New York City | 1986 | 18.00 |

— *RCA Music Service edition*

| ST-12239 | Live Peace in Toronto 1969 | 1983 | 50.00 |

— *By "The Plastic Ono Band"; reissue, black Capitol label*

| ST-12239 | Live Peace in Toronto 1969 | 1982 | 12.00 |

— *By "The Plastic Ono Band"; reissue, purple Capitol label*

| SJ-12533 | Menlove Ave. | 1986 | 18.00 |
| R144136 | Menlove Ave. | 1986 | 50.00 |

— *RCA Music Service edition*

| R144136 | Menlove Ave. | 198? | 50.00 |

— *BMG Direct Marketing edition*

| SW-3414 | Mind Games | 1978 | 40.00 |

— *Purple label, large Capitol logo*

| SN-16068 | Mind Games | 1980 | 15.00 |

— *Budget-line reissue*

| SN-16069 | Rock 'N' Roll | 1980 | 15.00 |

— *Budget-line reissue*

| SK-3419 | Rock 'N' Roll | 1978 | 40.00 |

— *Purple label, large Capitol logo*

| SW-3421 | Shaved Fish | 1978 | 15.00 |

— *Purple Capitol label with Apple logo on cover*

| SW-3421 | Shaved Fish | 1978 | 40.00 |

— *Purple Capitol label with Capitol logo on cover*

| SW-3421 | Shaved Fish | 1983 | 25.00 |

— *Black Capitol label with Apple logo on cover*

| SW-3421 | Shaved Fish | 1983 | 40.00 |

— *Black Capitol label with Capitol logo on cover*

| SW-3421 | Shaved Fish | 1989 | 40.00 |

— *Purple Capitol label (small logo) with Capitol logo on cover*

| SVBB-3392 | Some Time in New York City | 197? | 30.00 |

— *By John and Yoko; purple label, large Capitol logo*

| SVBB-3392 | Some Time in New York City | 197? | 100.00 |

— *Both discs in single-pocket gatefold (the other pocket is glued shut)*

| SW-3416 | Walls and Bridges | 1978 | 18.00 |

— *Purple label, large Capitol logo; standard front cover*

| SW-3416 | Walls and Bridges | 1982 | 30.00 |

— *Black label, print in colorband*

| SW-3416 | Walls and Bridges | 1989 | 30.00 |

— *Purple label, small Capitol logo*

GEFFEN

| GHS2001 | Double Fantasy | 1986 | 50.00 |

— *Same as above, but with black Geffen label*

| GHS2001 | Double Fantasy | 1981 | 75.00 |

— *Columbia House edition (all have corrected back cover) with "CH" on label*

| GHS2001 | Double Fantasy | 1980 | 12.00 |

— *Seven tracks by John, seven by Yoko; off-white label; titles on back cover out of order*

| GHS2001 | Double Fantasy | 1981 | 15.00 |

— *Off-white label, titles in order on the back cover*

| GHS2001 | Double Fantasy | 1981 | 15.00 |

— *Columbia House edition (all have corrected back cover) without "CH" on label*

| R104689 | Double Fantasy | 1981 | 40.00 |

— *RCA Music Service edition*

| GHSP2023 [DJ] | The John Lennon Collection | 1982 | 50.00 |

— *Promo only on Quiex II audiophile vinyl*

| GHSP2023 | The John Lennon Collection | 1982 | 25.00 |
| GHSP2023 [DJ] | The John Lennon Collection | 1982 | 50.00 |

— *Promo only on Quiex II audiophile vinyl*

MOBILE FIDELITY

| MFSL 1-277 | Imagine | 2004 | 30.00 |

— *Original Master Recording" at top of front cover*

| 1-153 [B] | Imagine | 1984 | 150.00 |

— *Audiophile vinyl*

| MFSL 1-280 | John Lennon Plastic Ono Band | 2004 | 30.00 |

— *Original Master Recording" at top of front cover*

NAUTILUS

| NR-47 | Double Fantasy | 1982 | 80.00 |

— *Half-speed master*

| NR-47 | Double Fantasy | 1982 | 2000.00 |

— *Half-speed master; alternate experimental cover with yellow and red added to black and white front*

PARLOPHONE

| 21954 | Lennon Legend | 1998 | 25.00 |

— *Made in U.S.A." on back cover*

POLYDOR

| 817238-1 | Heart Play (Unfinished Dialogue) | 1983 | 15.00 |

— *Interviews with John Lennon and Yoko Ono*

| 817160-1 | Milk and Honey | 1983 | 12.00 |

— *Six tracks by John, six by Yoko*

| 817160-1 | Milk and Honey | 1984 | 150.00 |

— *Yellow or green vinyl; unauthorized "inside jobs"*

SILHOUETTE

| SM-10012 | Reflections and Poetry | 1984 | 30.00 |

ZAPPLE

| ST-3357 | Life with the Lions -- Unfinished Music No. 2 | 1969 | 25.00 |

— *With Yoko Ono*

Number	Title	Yr	NM

LENNON, JULIAN

ATLANTIC

| ❏ 81928 | Mr. Jordan | 1989 | 12.00 |
| ❏ PR2693 [DJ] | Mr. Jordan According to Mr. Lennon | 1989 | 18.00 |

— Promo-only interview album

| ❏ 81640 [B] | The Secret Value of Daydreaming | 1986 | 12.00 |
| ❏ 81084 [B] | Valotte | 1984 | 12.00 |

LENNON SISTERS, THE

BRUNSWICK

| ❏ BL54039 [M] | Lawrence Welk Presents the Lennon Sisters | 1958 | 30.00 |
| ❏ BL54031 [M] | Let's Get Acquainted | 1957 | 30.00 |

DOT

❏ DLP-3250 [M]	Best-Loved Catholic Hymns	1959	18.00
❏ DLP-25250 [S]	Best-Loved Catholic Hymns	1959	25.00
❏ DLP-3417 [M]	Can't Help Falling in Love	1962	15.00
❏ DLP-25417 [S]	Can't Help Falling in Love	1962	18.00
❏ DLP3343 [M]	Christmas with the Lennon Sisters	1961	18.00
❏ DLP25343 [S]	Christmas with the Lennon Sisters	1961	25.00
❏ DLP-3557 [M]	Dominique and Other Great Folk Songs	1964	15.00
❏ DLP-25557 [S]	Dominique and Other Great Folk Songs	1964	18.00
❏ DLP-3589 [M]	No. 1 Hits of the 1960s	1964	15.00
❏ DLP-25589 [S]	No. 1 Hits of the 1960s	1964	18.00
❏ DLP-3398 [M]	Sad Movies (Make Me Cry)	1961	18.00
❏ DLP-25398 [S]	Sad Movies (Make Me Cry)	1961	25.00
❏ DLP-3659 [M]	Solos	1965	15.00
❏ DLP-25659 [S]	Solos	1965	18.00
❏ DLP-3797 [M]	Somethin' Stupid	1967	18.00
❏ DLP-25797 [S]	Somethin' Stupid	1967	15.00
❏ DLP-3481 [M]	The Lennon Sisters' Favorites	1963	15.00
❏ DLP-25481 [S]	The Lennon Sisters' Favorites	1963	18.00
❏ DLP-3292 [M]	The Lennon Sisters Sing 12 Great Hits	1960	18.00
❏ DLP-25292 [S]	The Lennon Sisters Sing 12 Great Hits	1960	25.00
❏ DLP-3622 [M]	Twelve Great Hits, Volume 2	1965	15.00
❏ DLP-25622 [S]	Twelve Great Hits, Volume 2	1965	18.00

HAMILTON

| ❏ HLP-119 [M] | Melody of Love | 196? | 15.00 |
| ❏ HLP-12119 [S] | Melody of Love | 196? | 15.00 |

MERCURY

| ❏ SR-61201 | Pop Country | 1969 | 15.00 |
| ❏ SR-61164 | The Lennon Sisters Today!! | 1968 | 15.00 |

PICKWICK

❏ PTP 2014	America's Sweethearts	1973	15.00
❏ SPC-3110	Goodnight Sweetheart	197?	12.00
❏ SPC-3084	Our Favorite Songs	196?	12.00

RANWOOD

❏ 7027	22 Songs of Faith and Inspiration	198?	12.00
❏ 8205	Best of the Lennon Sisters	198?	10.00
❏ 8212	How Great Thou Art	198?	10.00

VOCALION

| ❏ VL73887 | The Lennon Sisters with Lawrence Welk | 1970 | 12.00 |
| ❏ VL73864 | Too Marvelous for Words | 1969 | 12.00 |

LENOIR, J.B.

CHESS

| ❏ CH-9323 | Natural Man | 1990 | 15.00 |
| ❏ LP-410 | Natural Man | 1970 | 40.00 |

POLYDOR

| ❏ 24-4011 | J.B. Lenoir | 1970 | 18.00 |

LENYA, LOTTE

COLUMBIA MASTERWORKS

| ❏ ML5056 [M] | Berlin Theater Songs by Kurt Weill | 1957 | 30.00 |
| ❏ KL5229 [M] | September Song | 1958 | 30.00 |

LEONARD, HARLAN

RCA VICTOR

| ❏ LPV-531 [M] | Harlan Leonard and His Rockets | 1965 | 30.00 |

LEONARD, HARVEY

KEYNOTE

| ❏ 1102 [M] | Jazz Ecstasy | 1955 | 50.00 |

LEONARD, JACK E.

VIK

| ❏ LX-1080 [M] | Rock 'n Roll for People Over Sixteen | 1957 | 50.00 |

LEONHART, JAY

SUNNYSIDE

| ❏ SSC-1032 | The Double Cross | 1989 | 15.00 |
| ❏ SSC-1006 | There's Gonna Be Trouble | 1985 | 12.00 |

LEOPARDS, THE

MOON

| ❏ (# unknown)0 | Kansas City Slickers | 1977 | 30.00 |

LES DJINNS SINGERS

ABC-PARAMOUNT

| ❏ ABC-397 [M] | Joyeaux Noel | 1961 | 18.00 |
| ❏ ABCS-397 [S] | Joyeaux Noel | 1961 | 25.00 |

LES JAZZ MODES

ATLANTIC

| ❏ 1306 [M] | Les Jazz Modes | 1959 | 60.00 |

— Black label

| ❏ 1306 [M] | Les Jazz Modes | 1961 | 30.00 |

— Multicolor label, white "fan" logo at right

| ❏ SD-1306 [S] | Les Jazz Modes | 1959 | 60.00 |

— Green label

| ❏ SD-1306 [S] | Les Jazz Modes | 1961 | 30.00 |

— Multicolor label, white "fan" logo at right

| ❏ 1280 [M] | The Most Happy Fella | 1958 | 80.00 |

— Black label

| ❏ 1280 [M] | The Most Happy Fella | 1961 | 30.00 |

— Multicolor label, white "fan" logo at right

DAWN

❏ DLP-1101 [M]	Jazzville	1956	100.00
❏ DLP-1108 [M]	Les Jazz Modes	1956	100.00
❏ DLP-1117 [M]	Mood in Scarlet	1957	100.00

SEECO

| ❏ CELP-466 [M] | Smart Jazz for the Smart Set | 1960 | 30.00 |

LESBERG, JACK

FAMOUS DOOR

| ❏ 120 | Hollywood | 1977 | 15.00 |

LESLIE, BILL

ARGO

| ❏ LP-710 [M] | Diggin' the Chicks | 1962 | 30.00 |
| ❏ LPS-710 [S] | Diggin' the Chicks | 1962 | 30.00 |

LESMANA, INDRA

ZEBRA

| ❏ ZEB-5709 | For Earth and Heaven | 1986 | 12.00 |
| ❏ ZR-5005 | Indra Lesmana and Nebula | 1984 | 15.00 |

LESTER, KETTY

AVI

| ❏ 6116 | A Collection of Her Best | 1982 | 18.00 |

ERA

| ❏ EL-108 [M] | Love Letters | 1962 | 40.00 |
| ❏ ES-108 [S] | Love Letters | 1962 | 60.00 |

PETE

| ❏ 1109 | Ketty Lester | 1969 | 18.00 |

RCA VICTOR

❏ LPM-2945 [M]	The Soul of Me	1964	30.00
❏ LSP-2945 [S]	The Soul of Me	1964	30.00
❏ LPM-3326 [M]	Where Is Love	1965	30.00
❏ LSP-3326 [S]	Where Is Love	1965	30.00

SHEFFIELD

| ❏ 15 | Ketty Lester In Concert | 1977 | 10.00 |

TOWER

| ❏ T5029 [M] | When a Woman Loves a Man | 1966 | 30.00 |
| ❏ ST5029 [S] | When a Woman Loves a Man | 1966 | 30.00 |

LETMAN, JOHN

BETHLEHEM

| ❏ BCP-6053 [M] | The Many Angles of John Letman | 1961 | 30.00 |
| ❏ SBCP-6053 [S] | The Many Angles of John Letman | 1961 | 40.00 |

LETTERMEN, THE

APPLAUSE

| ❏ 1006 | Love Is... | 198? | 12.00 |

CAPITOL

| ❏ SPRO-4798/9 [DJ] | A Collection of Their Finest Songs | 1969 | 30.00 |

— Promo-only collection of excerpts of 20 songs

❏ T2013 [M]	A Lettermen Kind of Love	1964	15.00
❏ ST2013 [S]	A Lettermen Kind of Love	1964	18.00
❏ SW-11183	Alive" Again ... Naturally	1973	12.00
❏ SW-11249	All-Time Greatest Hits	1973	12.00
❏ SN-16312	All-Time Greatest Hits	198?	10.00

— Budget-line reissue

| ❏ SN-16191 | And I Love Her | 1981 | 10.00 |

— Budget-line reissue

❏ T2496 [M]	A New Song for Young Love	1966	15.00
❏ ST2496 [S]	A New Song for Young Love	1966	18.00
❏ T1669 [M]	A Song for Young Love	1962	18.00
❏ ST1669 [S]	A Song for Young Love	1962	25.00
❏ SWBB-251	Close-Up	1969	18.00

— Reissue of ST 2013 and ST 2083 in one package

❏ T1829 [M]	College Standards	1963	18.00
❏ ST1829 [S]	College Standards	1963	25.00
❏ ST-634	Everything's Good About You	1971	15.00
❏ SW-781	Feelings	1971	15.00
❏ T2587 [M]	For Christmas This Year	1966	15.00
❏ ST2587 [S]	For Christmas This Year	1966	18.00
❏ ST-8-2587 [S]	For Christmas This Year	1966	25.00

— Capitol Record Club edition

| ❏ ST2865 | Goin' Out of My Head | 1968 | 18.00 |
| ❏ SM-11970 | Goin' Out of My Head | 1979 | 10.00 |

— Reissue of 2865

| ❏ ST-269 | Hurt So Bad | 1969 | 15.00 |
| ❏ SM-11678 | Hurt So Bad | 1977 | 10.00 |

— Reissue of 269

| ❏ ST 8-0269 | Hurt So Bad | 1969 | 18.00 |

— Capitol Record Club edition

❏ ST-202	I Have Dreamed	1969	15.00
❏ T1761 [M]	Jim, Tony and Bob	1962	18.00
❏ ST1761 [S]	Jim, Tony and Bob	1962	25.00
❏ SW-11508	Kind of Country	1976	12.00
❏ SN-16190	Let It Be Me	1981	10.00

— Budget-line reissue

❏ STBB-710	Let It Be Me/And I Love Her	1971	18.00
❏ SW-11010	Lettermen 1	1972	12.00
❏ ST-836	Love Book	1971	15.00
❏ SW-11424	Make Time	1975	12.00
❏ T2428 [M]	More Hit Sounds of the Lettermen!	1966	15.00
❏ ST2428 [S]	More Hit Sounds of the Lettermen!	1966	18.00
❏ SW-11319	Now and Forever	1974	12.00
❏ T1711 [M]	Once Upon a Time	1962	18.00
❏ ST1711 [S]	Once Upon a Time	1962	25.00
❏ T2270 [M]	Portrait of My Love	1965	15.00
❏ ST2270 [S]	Portrait of My Love	1965	18.00
❏ ST-147	Put Your Head on My Shoulder	1968	18.00
❏ SM-147	Put Your Head on My Shoulder	1977	10.00

— Reissue with new prefix

| ❏ ST-496 | Reflections | 1970 | 15.00 |
| ❏ ST 8-0496 | Reflections | 1970 | 18.00 |

— Capitol Record Club edition

❏ T2142 [M]	She Cried	1964	15.00
❏ ST2142 [S]	She Cried	1964	18.00
❏ ST2934	Special Request	1968	18.00
❏ SW-11124	Spin Away	1972	12.00
❏ T2711 [M]	Spring!	1967	18.00
❏ ST2711 [S]	Spring!	1967	18.00
❏ SM-2711	Spring!	1977	10.00

— Reissue with new prefix

❏ T2554 [M]	The Best of the Lettermen	1966	15.00
❏ ST2554 [S]	The Best of the Lettermen	1966	18.00
❏ SN-16071	The Best of the Lettermen	1980	10.00

— Budget-line reissue

| ❏ SKAO-138 | The Best of the Lettermen, Vol. 2 | 1969 | 15.00 |
| ❏ SN-16222 | The Best of the Lettermen, Vol. 2 | 198? | 10.00 |

— Budget-line reissue

❏ T2359 [M]	The Hit Sounds of the Lettermen	1965	15.00
❏ ST2359 [S]	The Hit Sounds of the Lettermen	1965	18.00
❏ STCL-577	The Lettermen	1970	30.00
❏ T2758 [M]	The Lettermen!!!... And "Live!	1967	25.00
❏ ST2758 [S]	The Lettermen!!!... And "Live!	1967	18.00
❏ SM-11814	The Lettermen!!! ... And "Live!	1978	10.00

— Reissue of 2758

❏ T1936 [M]	The Lettermen In Concert	1963	18.00
❏ ST1936 [S]	The Lettermen In Concert	1963	25.00
❏ T2083 [M]	The Lettermen Look at Love	1964	15.00
❏ ST2083 [S]	The Lettermen Look at Love	1964	18.00
❏ SW-11364	There Is No Greater Love	1974	12.00
❏ SW-11470	The Time Is Right	1975	12.00
❏ ST-390	Traces/Memories	1970	15.00
❏ T2633 [M]	Warm	1967	18.00
❏ ST2633 [S]	Warm	1967	18.00
❏ T2213 [M]	You'll Never Walk Alone	1965	15.00
❏ ST2213 [S]	You'll Never Walk Alone	1965	18.00

LONGINES SYMPHONETTE

| ❏ 220 | A Time for Us | 1972 | 30.00 |

PICKWICK

| ❏ SPC-3294 | Soft Hits | 1972 | 12.00 |
| ❏ SPC-3565 | With Love | 1978 | 10.00 |

LEVEL 42

A&M

| ❏ SP-4995 | Standing in the Light | 1984 | 15.00 |

POLYDOR

| ❏ 821935-1 | Level 42 | 1986 | 15.00 |

— First U.S. issue of early U.K. LP

| ❏ 841399-1 | Level Best | 1989 | 12.00 |
| ❏ R16226 | Running in the Family | 1987 | 14.00 |

— BMG Direct Marketing edition

| ❏ 831593-1 | Running in the Family | 1987 | 15.00 |
| ❏ 813865-1 | Standing in the Light | 1986 | 10.00 |

— Reissue

❏ 837247-1	Staring at the Sun	1988	12.00
❏ PD1-6359	The Pursuit of Accidents	1982	16.00
❏ 810015-1	The Pursuit of Accidents	1986	10.00

— Reissue

| ❏ 823932-1 | True Colours | 1986 | 15.00 |
| ❏ 827487-1 | World Machine | 1986 | 15.00 |

LEVEY, STAN

BETHLEHEM

| ❏ BCP-71 [M] | Grand Stan | 1957 | 50.00 |

Number	Title	Yr	NM
❑ BCP-1017 [10]	Stan Levey Plays	1954	120.00
❑ BCP-6030 [M]	Stanley the Steamer	197?	18.00
—Reissue of 37, distributed by RCA Victor			
❑ BCP-37 [M]	This Time the Dream's On Me	1956	50.00

MODE

Number	Title	Yr	NM
❑ LP-101 [M]	Stan Levey Quartet	1957	80.00

LEVIATHAN

MACH

Number	Title	Yr	NM
❑ XMA-12501 [B]	Leviathan	1974	40.00

LEVIN, MARC

SAVOY

Number	Title	Yr	NM
❑ MG-12190 [M]	The Dragon Suite	1967	30.00

SWEET DRAGON

Number	Title	Yr	NM
❑ 1	Songs, Dances and Prayers	197?	25.00

LEVIN, PETE

GRAMAVISION

Number	Title	Yr	NM
❑ R1-79456	Party in the Basement	1990	18.00

LEVINE, HENRY

RCA CAMDEN

Number	Title	Yr	NM
❑ CAL-321 [M]	Lower Basin Street	1958	30.00

RCA VICTOR

Number	Title	Yr	NM
❑ LPM-1283 [M]	Dixieland Jazz Band	1956	50.00

LEVINSON, MARK

MARK LEVINSON

Number	Title	Yr	NM
❑ 7	Jazz at Long Wharf	1979	30.00
—Audiophile edition pressed at 45 rpm			

LEVISTER, ALONZO

DEBUT

Number	Title	Yr	NM
❑ DEB-125 [M]	Manhattan Moondrama	1956	150.00

LEVITT, ROD

RCA VICTOR

Number	Title	Yr	NM
❑ LPM-3615 [M]	42nd Street	1966	18.00
❑ LSP-3615 [S]	42nd Street	1966	25.00
❑ LPM-3372 [M]	Insight	1965	18.00
❑ LSP-3372 [S]	Insight	1965	25.00
❑ LPM-3448 [M]	Solid Ground	1965	18.00
❑ LSP-3448 [S]	Solid Ground	1965	25.00

RIVERSIDE

Number	Title	Yr	NM
❑ RLP-471 [M]	The Dynamic Sound Patterns of the Rod Levitt Orchestra	1964	18.00
❑ RS-9471 [S]	The Dynamic Sound Patterns of the Rod Levitt Orchestra	1964	25.00

LEVITTS, THE

ESP-DISK'

Number	Title	Yr	NM
❑ S-1095	We Are the Levitts	1970	30.00

LEVY, LOU

DOBRE

Number	Title	Yr	NM
❑ 1042	A Touch of Class	1978	15.00

INTERPLAY

Number	Title	Yr	NM
❑ 7711	Tempus Fugue It	197?	12.00

JUBILEE

Number	Title	Yr	NM
❑ JLP-1101 [M]	Lou Levy Plays Baby Grand Jazz	1959	40.00
❑ SDJLP-1101 [S]	Lou Levy Plays Baby Grand Jazz	1959	40.00

NOCTURNE

Number	Title	Yr	NM
❑ NLP-10 [10]	Lou Levy Trio	1954	100.00

PHILIPS

Number	Title	Yr	NM
❑ PHM200056 [M]	The Hymn	1962	18.00
❑ PHS600056 [S]	The Hymn	1962	25.00

RCA VICTOR

Number	Title	Yr	NM
❑ LPM-1491 [M]	A Most Musical Fella	1957	50.00
❑ LPM-1319 [M]	Jazz in Four Colors	1956	50.00
❑ LPM-1267 [M]	Solo Scene	1956	50.00

LEVY, LOU/CONTE CANDOLI

ATLANTIC

Number	Title	Yr	NM
❑ 1268 [M]	West Coast Wailers	1957	50.00
—Black label			
❑ 1268 [M]	West Coast Wailers	1961	30.00
—Multicolor label, white "fan" logo at right			

LEVY, O'DONEL

GROOVE MERCHANT

Number	Title	Yr	NM
❑ 501	Black Velvet	1971	30.00
❑ 507	Breeding of Mind	1972	30.00
❑ 518	Dawn of a New Day	1973	30.00
❑ 535	Everything I Do Gonna Be Funky	1975	30.00
❑ 4408	Hands of Fire	197?	30.00
❑ 526	Simba	1974	30.00
❑ 3313	Windows	197?	25.00

LEWD

ICI

Number	Title	Yr	NM
❑ CF200	American Wino	1982	40.00

LEWES, WILSON

DIPLOMAT

Number	Title	Yr	NM
❑ D-2369 [M]	The "In" Crowd	1965	12.00
❑ DS-2369 [S]	The "In" Crowd	1965	15.00
❑ D-2378 [M]	The Shadow of Your Smile	1966	12.00
❑ DS-2378 [S]	The Shadow of Your Smile	1966	15.00

LEWIS, BARBARA

ATLANTIC

Number	Title	Yr	NM
❑ 8110 [M]	Baby, I'm Yours	1965	40.00
❑ SD8110 [S]	Baby, I'm Yours	1965	50.00
❑ 8086 [M]	Hello Stranger	1963	40.00
❑ SD8086 [S]	Hello Stranger	1963	50.00
❑ 8118 [M]	It's Magic	1966	30.00
❑ SD8118 [S]	It's Magic	1966	40.00
❑ 8090 [M]	Snap Your Fingers	1964	40.00
❑ SD8090 [S]	Snap Your Fingers	1964	50.00
❑ SD8286 [S]	The Best of Barbara Lewis	1971	25.00
❑ 8286 [M]	The Best of Barbara Lewis	1971	40.00
—Mono is white label promo only; front cover has "d/j copy monaural" sticker			
❑ SD8173	Workin' on a Groovy Thing	1968	30.00

COLLECTABLES

Number	Title	Yr	NM
❑ COL-5104	Golden Classics	198?	12.00

ENTERPRISE

Number	Title	Yr	NM
❑ ENS-1006	The Many Grooves of Barbara Lewis	1970	30.00

LEWIS, BOBBY (1)

BELTONE

Number	Title	Yr	NM
❑ 4000 [M]	Tossin' and Turnin'	1961	200.00

LEWIS, BOBBY (2)

ACE OF HEARTS

Number	Title	Yr	NM
❑ 1002	Too Many Memories	1974	18.00

RPA

Number	Title	Yr	NM
❑ 1002	Portrait in Love	1976	12.00
❑ 1013	Soul Full of Music	1977	12.00

UNITED ARTISTS

Number	Title	Yr	NM
❑ UAS-6629	An Ordinary Miracle	1968	25.00
❑ UAS-6616	A World of Love from Bobby Lewis	1967	25.00
❑ UAS-6673	From Heaven to Heartache	1968	25.00
❑ UAL-3582 [M]	How Long Has It Been	1967	30.00
❑ UAS-6582 [S]	How Long Has It Been	1967	30.00
❑ UAS-6717	Thanks for You and I	1969	25.00
❑ UAS-6760	The Best of Bobby Lewis, Vol. 1	1970	18.00

LEWIS, DAVE

A&M

Number	Title	Yr	NM
❑ LP-105 [M]	Little Green Thing	1964	25.00
❑ SP-4105 [S]	Little Green Thing	1964	30.00

JERDEN

Number	Title	Yr	NM
❑ JRL-7006 [M]	Dave Lewis Plays Herb Alpert and the Tijuana Brass	1966	25.00
❑ JRLS-7006 [S]	Dave Lewis Plays Herb Alpert and the Tijuana Brass	1966	30.00

LEWIS, FURRY

AMPEX

Number	Title	Yr	NM
❑ A-10140	Live at the Gaslight	1971	30.00

BLUESVILLE

Number	Title	Yr	NM
❑ BVLP-1036 [M]	Back on My Feet Again	1961	100.00
—Blue label, silver print			
❑ BVLP-1036 [M]	Back on My Feet Again	1964	30.00
—Blue label, trident logo at right			
❑ BVLP-1037 [M]	Done Changed My Mind	1961	100.00
—Blue label, silver print			
❑ BVLP-1037 [M]	Done Changed My Mind	1964	30.00
—Blue label, trident logo at right			

LEWIS, GARY, AND THE PLAYBOYS

LIBERTY

Number	Title	Yr	NM
❑ LRP-3419 [M]	A Session with Gary Lewis and the Playboys	1965	25.00
❑ LST-7419 [S]	A Session with Gary Lewis and the Playboys	1965	30.00
❑ LST-7606	Close Cover Before Playing	1969	18.00
❑ LRP-3428 [M]	Everybody Loves a Clown	1965	25.00
❑ LST-7428 [S]	Everybody Loves a Clown	1965	30.00
❑ LST-7568	Gary Lewis Now!	1968	18.00
❑ LRP-3468 [M]	Golden Greats	1966	18.00
❑ LST-7468 [S]	Golden Greats	1966	25.00
—Side 2 plays as listed			
❑ LST-7468 [S]	Golden Greats	1966	30.00
—Side 2, Song 2 claims to be "I Won't Make That Mistake Again" but it plays "You've Got to Hide Your Love Away			
❑ LN-10241	Golden Greats	198?	10.00
—Budget-line reissue			
❑ LRP-3452 [M]	Hits Again!	1966	18.00
❑ LST-7452 [S]	Hits Again!	1966	25.00
❑ LST-7633	I'm On the Right Road Now	1970	18.00
❑ LST-7524 [S]	Listen	1967	18.00
❑ LRP-3524 [M]	Listen!	1967	18.00
❑ LST-7589	More Golden Greats	1968	18.00
❑ LRP-3519 [M]	New Directions	1967	18.00
❑ LST-7519 [S]	New Directions	1967	18.00
❑ LST-7623	Rhythm of the Rain	1969	18.00
❑ LRP-3435 [M]	She's Just My Style	1966	18.00
❑ LST-7435 [S]	She's Just My Style	1966	25.00
❑ LRP-3408 [M]	This Diamond Ring	1965	25.00
❑ LST-7408 [S]	This Diamond Ring	1965	30.00
❑ LM-1003	This Diamond Ring	1981	10.00
—Reissue of United Artists 1008			
❑ LRP-3487 [M]	(You Don't Have to) Paint Me a Picture	1967	18.00
—Side 1 plays as listed			
❑ LRP-3487 [M]	(You Don't Have to) Paint Me a Picture	1967	25.00
—Side 1, Song 4 claims to be "Tina" but plays "Ice Melts in the Sun			
❑ LST-7487 [S]	(You Don't Have to) Paint Me a Picture	1967	25.00
—Side 1 plays as listed			
❑ LST-7487 [S]	(You Don't Have to) Paint Me a Picture	1967	30.00
—Side 1, Song 4 claims to be "Tina" but plays "Ice Melts in the Sun			

RHINO

Number	Title	Yr	NM
❑ RNLP-163	Greatest Hits (1965-1968)	1985	12.00

SUNSET

Number	Title	Yr	NM
❑ SUM-1168 [M]	Gary Lewis and the Playboys	1967	15.00
❑ SUS-5168 [S]	Gary Lewis and the Playboys	1967	15.00
❑ SUS-5262	Rhythm!	1969	15.00

UNITED ARTISTS

Number	Title	Yr	NM
❑ UA-LA430-E	The Very Best of Gary Lewis and the Playboys	1975	12.00
❑ LM-1003	This Diamond Ring	1980	12.00
—Edited reissue of Liberty 7408			

LEWIS, GEORGE (1)

AMERICAN MUSIC

Number	Title	Yr	NM
❑ 645 [10]	George Lewis with Kid Shots Madison	1952	80.00
❑ 639 [10]	The George Lewis Band In the French Quarter	1951	80.00

ATLANTIC

Number	Title	Yr	NM
❑ 1411 [M]	The George Lewis Band	1963	18.00
❑ SD1411 [S]	The George Lewis Band	1963	25.00

BIOGRAPH

Number	Title	Yr	NM
❑ CEN-1	George Lewis and His Mustache Stompers	197?	12.00

BLUE NOTE

Number	Title	Yr	NM
❑ BLP-1205 [M]	George Lewis and His New Orleans Stompers, Volume 1	1955	250.00
—Deep groove" version (deep indentation under label on both sides)			
❑ BLP-1205 [M]	George Lewis and His New Orleans Stompers, Volume 1	1955	100.00
—Regular version, Lexington Ave. address on label			
❑ BLP-1205 [M]	George Lewis and His New Orleans Stompers, Volume 1	1963	30.00
—With "New York, USA" address on label			
❑ BST-81205 [R]	George Lewis and His New Orleans Stompers, Volume 1	1967	15.00
—With "A Division of Liberty Records" on label			
❑ BLP-1206 [M]	George Lewis and His New Orleans Stompers, Volume 2	1955	350.00
—Deep groove" version (deep indentation under label on both sides)			
❑ BLP-1206 [M]	George Lewis and His New Orleans Stompers, Volume 2	1955	100.00
—Regular version, Lexington Ave. address on label			
❑ BLP-1206 [M]	George Lewis and His New Orleans Stompers, Volume 2	1963	30.00
—With "New York, USA" address on label			
❑ BST-81206 [R]	George Lewis and His New Orleans Stompers, Volume 2	1967	15.00
—With "A Division of Liberty Records" on label			
❑ BLP-1208 [M]	George Lewis Concert!	1955	450.00
—Deep groove" version (deep indentation under label on both sides)			
❑ BLP-1208 [M]	George Lewis Concert!	1955	100.00
—Regular version, Lexington Ave. address on label			
❑ BLP-1208 [M]	George Lewis Concert!	1963	30.00
—With "New York, USA" address on label			
❑ BST-81208 [R]	George Lewis Concert!	1967	15.00
—With "A Division of Liberty Records" on label			
❑ BLP-7010 [10]	George Lewis' New Orleans Stompers, Volume 1	1951	250.00
❑ BLP-7013 [10]	George Lewis' New Orleans Stompers, Volume 2	1951	250.00
❑ BLP-7027 [10]	George Lewis' New Orleans Stompers, Volume 3	1954	250.00
❑ BLP-7028 [10]	George Lewis' New Orleans Stompers, Volume 4	1954	250.00

CAVALIER

Number	Title	Yr	NM
❑ CVLP-6004 [M]	George Lewis in Hi-Fi	1956	60.00

CIRCLE

Number	Title	Yr	NM
❑ L-421 [10]	George Lewis and His New Orleans All-Stars	1951	80.00

DELMAR

Number	Title	Yr	NM
❑ DL-201 [M]	Doctor Jazz	195?	50.00
❑ DL-202 [M]	On Parade	195?	50.00

Number	Title	Yr	NM
DELMARK			
❑ DL-203	George Lewis Memorial Album	196?	25.00
❑ DL-202	George Lewis' New Orleans Stompers	196?	30.00
DISC JOCKEY			
❑ DDL-100 [M]	Jazz at Ohio Union	195?	1200.00
— Box set with booklet			
EMPIRICAL			
❑ EM-107 [10]	Spirituals in Ragtime	1956	80.00
EVEREST ARCHIVE OF FOLK & JAZZ			
❑ 240	George Lewis	197?	12.00
FANTASY			
❑ OJC-1739	George Lewis of New Orleans	198?	12.00
❑ OJC-1736	Jazz at Vespers	198?	12.00
FOLKLYRIC			
❑ 9030	George Lewis and His New Orleans Ragtime Jazz Band	198?	12.00
GHB			
❑ GHB-10	City of a Million Dreams	1964	15.00
❑ GHB-29	Easy Riders Jazz Band	1965	15.00
❑ GHB-39	Easy Riders Jazz Band	1968	15.00
❑ GHB-37	For Dancers Only	1968	15.00
❑ GHB-5	George Lewis and His Ragtime Stompers	196?	15.00
❑ GHB-14	George Lewis in Japan, Volume 1	1965	15.00
❑ GHB-15	George Lewis in Japan, Volume 2	1965	15.00
❑ GHB-16	George Lewis in Japan, Volume 3	1965	15.00
❑ GHB-68	The Big Four	1970	15.00
JAZZ CRUSADE			
❑ 2004	Jazzology Poll	1965	15.00
JAZZ MAN			
❑ LP-1 [10]	George Lewis' Ragtime Band	1953	80.00
— Limited First Pressing Dec. 25, 1953" on label at left			
❑ LJ-331 [10]	New Orleans Music	1954	80.00
JAZZOLOGY			
❑ JCE-19	Endless the Trek	1967	15.00
❑ JCE-3 [M]	George Lewis and His Ragtime Stompers	196?	18.00
❑ SJCE-3 [S]	George Lewis and His Ragtime Stompers	196?	15.00
❑ JCE-27	George Lewis at Congo Square	196?	15.00
MOSAIC			
❑ MR5-132	The Complete Blue Note Recordings of George Lewis	199?	100.00
PARADOX			
❑ LP-6001 [10]	George Lewis	1951	80.00
RIVERSIDE			
❑ RLP-2507 [10]	George Lewis	1954	100.00
❑ RLP 12-283 [M]	George Lewis of New Orleans	1958	40.00
❑ RLP-2512 [10]	George Lewis with Guest Artist Red Allen	1955	100.00
❑ RLP 12-230 [M]	Jazz at Vespers	1957	50.00
— White label, blue print			
❑ RLP 12-230 [M]	Jazz at Vespers	1959	30.00
— Blue label, microphone logo at top			
❑ RLP 12-207 [M]	Jazz in the Classic New Orleans Tradition	1956	50.00
— White label, blue print			
❑ RLP 12-207 [M]	Jazz in the Classic New Orleans Tradition	1959	30.00
— Blue label, microphone logo at top			
SOUTHLAND			
❑ SLP-208 [10]	George Lewis	1955	80.00
STORYVILLE			
❑ 4022	George Lewis and His Ragtime Band In Concert	197?	15.00
❑ 4055	George Lewis at Club Hangover, Volume 1	198?	12.00
❑ 4061	George Lewis at Club Hangover, Volume 3	198?	12.00
❑ 4049	Jazz from New Orleans	198?	12.00
VERVE			
❑ MGV-1019 [M]	Blues from the Bayou	1957	50.00
❑ V-1019 [M]	Blues from the Bayou	1961	25.00
❑ MGVS-6113 [S]	Blues from the Bayou	1960	40.00
❑ V6-1019 [S]	Blues from the Bayou	1961	18.00
❑ MGV-1021 [M]	Doctor Jazz	1957	50.00
❑ V-1021 [M]	Doctor Jazz	1961	25.00
❑ MGVS-6122 [S]	Doctor Jazz	1960	40.00
❑ V6-1021 [S]	Doctor Jazz	1961	18.00
❑ MGV-8232 [M]	George Lewis and Turk Murphy at Newport	1958	50.00
❑ V-8232 [M]	George Lewis and Turk Murphy at Newport	1961	25.00
❑ MGV-1027 [M]	George Lewis' Dixieland Band	1957	50.00
❑ V-1027 [M]	George Lewis' Dixieland Band	1961	25.00
❑ MGV-1024 [M]	Hot Time in the Old Town Tonight	1957	50.00
❑ V-1024 [M]	Hot Time in the Old Town Tonight	1961	25.00
❑ V6-1024 [S]	Hot Time in the Old Town Tonight	1961	25.00
❑ MGV-8325 [M]	Oh, Didn't He Ramble	1959	50.00
❑ MGVS-6064 [S]	Oh, Didn't He Ramble	1960	40.00
❑ V-8325 [M]	Oh, Didn't He Ramble	1961	25.00
❑ V6-8325 [S]	Oh, Didn't He Ramble	1961	18.00
❑ MGV-8303 [M]	On Stage: George Lewis Concert, Volume 1	1959	50.00
❑ V-8303 [M]	On Stage: George Lewis Concert, Volume 1	1961	25.00
❑ MGV-8304 [M]	On Stage: George Lewis Concert, Volume 2	1959	50.00
❑ V-8304 [M]	On Stage: George Lewis Concert, Volume 2	1961	25.00
❑ MGV-8277 [M]	The Perennial George Lewis	1958	50.00
❑ V-8277 [M]	The Perennial George Lewis	1961	25.00
❑ UMV-2621	Verve at Newport	198?	15.00

LEWIS, GEORGE (2), AND DOUGLAS EWART

Number	Title	Yr	NM
BLACK SAINT			
❑ BSR-0026	The Imaginary Suite	198?	15.00

LEWIS, GEORGE (2)

Number	Title	Yr	NM
BLACK SAINT			
❑ BSR-0029	Homage to Charles Parker	198?	15.00
❑ BSR 0016	Monads	198?	15.00
LOVELY			
❑ VR-1101	Chicago Slow Dance	198?	18.00

LEWIS, HUEY, AND THE NEWS

Number	Title	Yr	NM
CHRYSALIS			
❑ 8V842795 [EP]	84 Sports Tour	1984	18.00
— Three-song picture disc numbered as if it were a single			
❑ OV41534	Fore!	1986	10.00
❑ CHR1292	Huey Lewis and the News	1980	15.00
❑ FV41292	Huey Lewis and the News	1983	10.00
— Reissue of 1292			
❑ CHR1340 [B]	Picture This	1982	12.00
❑ FV41340	Picture This	1983	10.00
— Reissue of 1340			
❑ OV41622	Small World	1988	10.00
❑ FV41412	Sports	1983	10.00
MOBILE FIDELITY			
❑ 1-181	Sports	1985	30.00
— Original Master Recording" on front cover			

LEWIS, HUGH X.

Number	Title	Yr	NM
KAPP			
❑ KS-3563	Country Fever	1968	30.00
❑ KS-3545	Just a Prayer Away	1968	30.00
❑ KL-1494 [M]	Just Before Dawn	1966	25.00
❑ KS-3494 [S]	Just Before Dawn	1966	30.00
❑ KS-3522 [S]	My Kind of Country	1967	30.00
❑ KL-1522 [M]	My Kind of Country	1967	30.00
❑ KL-1462 [M]	The Hugh X. Lewis Album	1966	25.00
❑ KS-3462 [S]	The Hugh X. Lewis Album	1966	30.00

LEWIS, JERRY

Number	Title	Yr	NM
DECCA			
❑ DL8936 [M]	Big Songs for Little People	1959	50.00
❑ DL78936 [S]	Big Songs for Little People	1959	60.00
❑ DL8410 [M]	Jerry Lewis Just Sings	1956	60.00
❑ DL8595 [M]	More Jerry Lewis	1957	60.00
DOT			
❑ DLP3664 [M]	The Jerry Lewis Singers	1964	18.00
❑ DLP25664 [S]	The Jerry Lewis Singers	1964	25.00

LEWIS, JERRY LEE, AND LINDA GAIL LEWIS

Number	Title	Yr	NM
SMASH			
❑ SRS-67126	Together	1969	25.00

LEWIS, JERRY LEE

Number	Title	Yr	NM
ACCORD			
❑ SN-7133	I Walk the Line	1981	12.00
DESIGN			
❑ DLP-165 [M]	Rockin' with Jerry Lee Lewis	1963	30.00
❑ DST-165 [R]	Rockin' with Jerry Lee Lewis	1963	25.00
ELEKTRA			
❑ 6E-184	Jerry Lee Lewis	1979	15.00
❑ 6E-291	Killer Country	1980	15.00
❑ 60191	The Best of Jerry Lee Lewis Featuring 39 and Holding	1982	12.00
❑ 6E-254	When Two Worlds Collide	1980	15.00
HILLTOP			
❑ 6110	Roll Over Beethoven	1972	12.00
❑ 6120	Rural Route #1	1972	12.00
❑ 6102	Sunday After Church	1971	12.00
MCA			
❑ 5478	I Am What I Am	1984	12.00
❑ 5387	My Fingers Do the Talkin'	1983	12.00
MERCURY			
❑ 690 [DJ]	A Jerry Lee Lewis Radio Special	1973	50.00
❑ SRM-1-1030	Boogie Woogie Country Man	1975	18.00
❑ SRM-1-1109	Country Class	1976	18.00
❑ SRM-1-5004	Country Memories	1977	18.00
❑ 826251-1	Greatest Hits	198?	12.00
❑ SRM-1-710	I-40 Country	1974	18.00
❑ SR-61318	In Loving Memories	1970	30.00
❑ SRM-1-5010	Jerry Lee Lewis Keeps Rockin'	1978	18.00
❑ 836935-1	Killer: The Mercury Years Volume One, 1963-1968	1989	15.00
❑ 836941-1	Killer: The Mercury Years Volume Three, 1973-1977	1989	15.00
❑ 836938-1	Killer: The Mercury Years Volume Two, 1969-1972	1989	15.00
❑ SR-61278	Live at the International, Las Vegas	1970	18.00
❑ SRM-1-1064	Odd Man In	1975	18.00
❑ SRM-1-677	Sometimes a Memory Ain't Enough	1973	18.00
❑ SRM-1-690	Southern Roots -- Back Home to Memphis	1973	18.00
❑ SRM-1-637	The "Killer" Rocks On	1972	18.00
❑ SRM-1-5006 [B]	The Best of Jerry Lee Lewis Volume II	1978	18.00
❑ 822789-1	The Best of Jerry Lee Lewis Volume II	198?	12.00
❑ SR-61323	There Must Be More to Love Than This	1971	18.00
❑ SRM-2-803	The Session	1973	25.00
❑ SR-61343	Touching Home	1971	18.00
— With photo of Jerry Lee in front of a brick wall			
❑ SR 61343	Touching Home	1971	25.00
— With drawing on cover and small photo of Jerry Lee			
❑ SR-61366	Who's Gonna PlayThis Old Piano… (Think About It Darlin')	1972	18.00
❑ 830399-1	Would You Take Another Chance on Me	1987	12.00
— Reissue of 61346			
❑ SR-61346	Would You Take Another Chance on Me?	1971	18.00
PAIR			
❑ PDL2-1132	Solid Gold	1986	15.00
PICKWICK			
❑ SPC-3344	Drinking Wine Spo-Dee-O-Dee	1973	12.00
❑ SPC-3224	High Heel Sneakers	1970	12.00
❑ PTP-2055	Jerry Lee Lewis	1973	15.00
POLYDOR			
❑ 839516-1	Great Balls of Fire!	1989	15.00
❑ 826139-1	I'm on Fire	1985	12.00
POWER PAK			
❑ 247	From the Vaults of Sun	1974	12.00
RHINO			
❑ R1-70656	Jerry Lee Lewis	1989	15.00
— Reissue of Sun 1230			
❑ R1-70657	Jerry Lee's Greatest	1989	15.00
— Reissue of Sun 1265			
❑ RNDA-1499	Milestones	1985	18.00
❑ R1-71499	Milestones	1989	15.00
— Reissue of 1499			
❑ RNDF-255 [PD]	Original Sun Greatest Hits	1983	18.00
❑ R1-70255	Original Sun Greatest Hits	1989	12.00
— Reissue of 255 on black vinyl			
❑ R1-70899	Wild One: Rare Tracks from Jerry Lee Lewis	1989	15.00
SEARS			
❑ SPS-610	Hound Dog	1970	30.00
SMASH			
❑ SRS-67071	All Country	1969	18.00
— Retitled reissue			
❑ SRS-67104	Another Place Another Time	1968	25.00
❑ MGS-27086 [M]	By Request -- More of the Greatest Live Show on Earth	1966	30.00
❑ SRS-67086 [S]	By Request -- More of the Greatest Live Show on Earth	1966	40.00
❑ MGS-27071 [M]	Country Songs for City Folks	1965	30.00
❑ SRS-67071 [S]	Country Songs for City Folks	1965	30.00
❑ SL-7001	Golden Hits	1980	15.00
❑ SRS-67117	Jerry Lee Lewis Sings the Country Music Hall of Fame Hits, Vol. 1	1969	25.00
❑ SRS-67118	Jerry Lee Lewis Sings the Country Music Hall of Fame Hits, Vol. 2	1969	25.00
❑ MGS-27079 [M]	Memphis Beat	1966	30.00
❑ SRS-67079 [S]	Memphis Beat	1966	30.00
❑ SRS-67128	She Even Woke Me Up to Say Goodbye	1970	25.00
❑ SRS-67112 [B]	She Still Comes Around (To Love What's Left of Me)	1969	25.00
❑ MGS-27097 [M]	Soul My Way	1967	30.00
❑ SRS-67097 [S]	Soul My Way	1967	40.00
❑ SRS-67131	The Best of Jerry Lee Lewis	1970	25.00
❑ MGS-27040 [M]	The Golden Hits of Jerry Lee Lewis	1964	30.00
❑ SRS-67040 [S]	The Golden Hits of Jerry Lee Lewis	1964	30.00
❑ SRS-67040 [S]	The Golden Rock Hits of Jerry Lee Lewis	1969	18.00
— Retitled reissue			
❑ MGS-27056 [M]	The Greatest Live Show on Earth	1964	100.00
❑ SRS-67056 [S]	The Greatest Live Show on Earth	1964	150.00
❑ MGS-27063 [M]	The Return of Rock	1965	30.00
❑ SRS-67063 [S]	The Return of Rock	1965	40.00
SUN			
❑ LP-114 [B]	A Taste of Country	1970	18.00
❑ SUN-1011	Duets	1978	18.00
— As "Jerry Lee Lewis and Friends"; gold vinyl			
❑ SLP-1230 [M]	Jerry Lee Lewis	1958	200.00
❑ SLP-1265 [M]	Jerry Lee's Greatest	1961	250.00

Number	Title	Yr	NM
❑ SLP-1265 [M]	Jerry Lee's Greatest	1961	800.00
—*White label promo*			
❑ LP-124	Monsters	1971	18.00
❑ LP-121	Ole Tyme Country Music	1971	18.00
❑ LP-102	Original Golden Hits — Volume 1	1969	18.00
❑ LP-103	Original Golden Hits — Volume 2	1969	18.00
❑ LP-128	Original Golden Hits — Volume 3	1972	18.00
❑ LP-107	Rockin' Rhythm and Blues	1969	18.00
❑ SUN-145	Roots	1982	15.00
❑ SUN-108	The Golden Cream of the Country	1969	18.00
❑ SUN-108 [M]	The Golden Cream of the Country	1969	40.00
—*Mono version is white label promo only; the word "MONO" appears at 9 o'clock on the label*			
❑ 1005	The Original	1978	15.00
❑ 1018	Trio +	1979	15.00
—*With Carl Perkins, Charlie Rich and (uncredited) Orion*			
SUNNYVALE			
❑ 905	The Sun Story, Vol. 5	1977	12.00
WING			
❑ SRW-16340	In Demand	1968	12.00
❑ PKW2-125	The Legend of Jerry Lee Lewis	1969	30.00
❑ MGW-12340 [M]	The Return of Rock	1967	15.00
❑ SRW-16340 [S]	The Return of Rock	1967	15.00
❑ SRW-16406	Unlimited	1968	15.00

LEWIS, JOHN, AND BILL PERKINS

PACIFIC JAZZ

Number	Title	Yr	NM
❑ PJ-1217 [M]	Grand Encounter: 2' East, 3' West	1956	200.00
❑ PJ-44 [M]	Grand Encounter: 2' East, 3' West	1962	60.00
—*Reissue with new number*			
PAUSA			
❑ 9019	Grand Encounter: 2' East, 3' West	198?	15.00
WORLD PACIFIC			
❑ WP-1217 [M]	Grand Encounter: 2' East, 3' West	1959	120.00

LEWIS, JOHN, AND HANK JONES

LITTLE DAVID

Number	Title	Yr	NM
❑ LD1079	An Evening with Two Grand Pianos	1979	15.00

LEWIS, JOHN, AND SACHA DISTEL

ATLANTIC

Number	Title	Yr	NM
❑ 1267 [M]	Afternoon in Paris	1964	18.00
—*Multicolor label, black "fan" logo at right*			
❑ 1267 [M]	Afternoon in Paris	1957	40.00
—*Black label*			
❑ 1267 [M]	Afternoon in Paris	1961	25.00
—*Multicolor label, white "fan" logo at right*			

LEWIS, JOHN

ATLANTIC

Number	Title	Yr	NM
❑ 1402 [M]	Animal Dance	1963	18.00
❑ SD1402 [S]	Animal Dance	1963	25.00
❑ 1425 [M]	Essence	1964	18.00
❑ SD1425 [S]	Essence	1964	25.00
❑ 1392 [M]	European Encounter	1963	18.00
❑ SD1392 [S]	European Encounter	1963	25.00
❑ 90533	European Encounter	1986	12.00
❑ 1313 [M]	Improvised Meditations and Excursions	1959	40.00
—*Black label*			
❑ 1313 [M]	Improvised Meditations and Excursions	1961	25.00
—*Multicolor label, white "fan" logo at right*			
❑ 1313 [M]	Improvised Meditations and Excursions	1964	18.00
—*Multicolor label, black "fan" logo at right*			
❑ SD1313 [S]	Improvised Meditations and Excursions	1959	50.00
—*Green label*			
❑ SD1313 [S]	Improvised Meditations and Excursions	1961	25.00
—*Multicolor label, white "fan" logo at right*			
❑ SD1313 [S]	Improvised Meditations and Excursions	1964	18.00
—*Multicolor label, black "fan" logo at right*			
❑ 1365 [M]	John Lewis Presents Jazz Abstractions	1961	30.00
—*Multicolor label, white "fan" logo at right*			
❑ 1365 [M]	John Lewis Presents Jazz Abstractions	1964	18.00
—*Multicolor label, black "fan" logo at right*			
❑ SD1365 [S]	John Lewis Presents Jazz Abstractions	1961	30.00
—*Multicolor label, white "fan" logo at right*			
❑ SD1365 [S]	John Lewis Presents Jazz Abstractions	1964	25.00
—*Multicolor label, black "fan" logo at right*			
❑ 1370 [M]	Original Sin	1961	30.00
—*Multicolor label, white "fan" logo at right*			
❑ 1370 [M]	Original Sin	1964	18.00
—*Multicolor label, black "fan" logo at right*			

Number	Title	Yr	NM
❑ SD1370 [S]	Original Sin	1961	30.00
—*Multicolor label, white "fan" logo at right*			
❑ SD1370 [S]	Original Sin	1964	25.00
—*Multicolor label, black "fan" logo at right*			
❑ 1334 [M]	The Golden Striker	1960	30.00
—*Multicolor label, white "fan" logo at right*			
❑ 1334 [M]	The Golden Striker	1964	18.00
—*Multicolor label, black "fan" logo at right*			
❑ SD1334 [S]	The Golden Striker	1960	30.00
—*Multicolor label, white "fan" logo at right*			
❑ SD1334 [S]	The Golden Striker	1964	25.00
—*Multicolor label, black "fan" logo at right*			
❑ 1272 [M]	The John Lewis Piano	1958	40.00
—*Black label*			
❑ 1272 [M]	The John Lewis Piano	1961	25.00
—*Multicolor label, white "fan" logo at right*			
❑ 1272 [M]	The John Lewis Piano	1964	18.00
—*Multicolor label, black "fan" logo at right*			
❑ 1375 [M]	The Wonderful World of Jazz	1961	30.00
—*Multicolor label, white "fan" logo at right*			
❑ SD1375 [S]	The Wonderful World of Jazz	1961	30.00
—*Multicolor label, white "fan" logo at right*			
❑ 1375 [M]	The Wonderful World of Jazz	1964	18.00
—*Multicolor label, black "fan" logo at right*			
❑ SD1375 [S]	The Wonderful World of Jazz	1964	25.00
—*Multicolor label, black "fan" logo at right*			
❑ 90979	The Wonderful World of Jazz	1989	15.00
COLUMBIA			
❑ PC33534	P.O.V.	1976	12.00
EMARCY			
❑ 838036-1	Midnight in Paris	1990	15.00
❑ 834478-1	The Garden of Delight: Delaunay's Dilemma	1989	15.00
FINESSE			
❑ FW37681	Album for Nancy Harrow	1982	12.00
❑ FW38187	Kansas City Breaks	1983	12.00
PHILIPS			
❑ 836821-1	Bach: Preludes and Fugues, Vol. 3	1989	15.00
❑ 824381-1	John Lewis Plays Bach's "Well-Tempered Clavier	1985	12.00
❑ 826698-1	The Bridge Game	1986	12.00
❑ 832015-1	The Chess Game	1987	15.00
❑ 832588-1	The Chess Game, Volume 2	1988	15.00
RCA VICTOR			
❑ LPM-1742 [M]	European Windows	1958	50.00

LEWIS, KATHARINE HANDY

FOLKWAYS

Number	Title	Yr	NM
❑ FJ-3540 [M]	W.C. Handy Blues	1958	30.00

LEWIS, LINDA GAIL

SMASH

Number	Title	Yr	NM
❑ SRS-67119	Two Sides of Linda Gail Lewis	1969	30.00

LEWIS, MEADE LUX, AND LOUIS BELLSON

CLEF

Number	Title	Yr	NM
❑ MGC-632 [M]	Boogie Woogie Piano and Drums	1954	80.00

LEWIS, MEADE LUX

ABC-PARAMOUNT

Number	Title	Yr	NM
❑ ABC-164 [M]	Out of the Roaring 20's	1956	50.00
ATLANTIC			
❑ ALS-133 [10]	Boogie-Woogie Interpretations	1952	250.00
BLUE NOTE			
❑ BLP-7018 [10]	Boogie-Woogie Classics	1952	600.00
DISC			
❑ DLP-352 [10]	Meade Lux Lewis at the Philharmonic	195?	400.00
❑ MGD-7 [M]	Yancey's Last Ride	1956	60.00
FANTASY			
❑ OJC-1759	The Blues Piano Artistry of Meade Lux Lewis	198?	15.00
MERCURY			
❑ MG-25158 [10]	Meade Lux Lewis	1951	250.00
MUSE			
❑ MR-5063	Still On the Planet	1976	25.00
PHILIPS			
❑ PHM200044 [M]	Boogie Woogie House Party	196?	25.00
❑ PHS600044 [S]	Boogie Woogie House Party	196?	30.00
RIVERSIDE			
❑ RLP-402 [M]	The Blues Piano Artistry of Meade Lux Lewis	1962	40.00
❑ RS-9402 [S]	The Blues Piano Artistry of Meade Lux Lewis	1962	40.00
STINSON			
❑ 25 [M]	Meade Lux Lewis	196?	30.00
TOPS			
❑ L-1533 [M]	Barrelhouse Piano	195?	40.00

VERVE

Number	Title	Yr	NM
❑ MGV-1006 [M]	Cat House Piano	1957	80.00
❑ V-1006 [M]	Cat House Piano	1961	40.00
❑ MGV-1007 [M]	Meade Lux Lewis	1957	70.00
❑ V-1007 [M]	Meade Lux Lewis	1961	30.00

LEWIS, MEL

ATLANTIC

Number	Title	Yr	NM
❑ 81655	20th Anniversary	1986	12.00
FINESSE			
❑ FW37987	Make Me Smile	1984	12.00
HORIZON			
❑ SP-716	Mel Lewis and Friends	1976	15.00
MODE			
❑ LP-103 [M]	Mel Lewis Sextet	1957	120.00
PAUSA			
❑ 7115	Live in Montreux	1981	12.00
SAN FRANCISCO			
❑ 2 [M]	Got 'Cha	1957	150.00
TELARC			
❑ DG-10044	Naturally	1980	15.00
VEE JAY			
❑ VJS-3062	Gettin' Together	1974	25.00

LEWIS, RAMSEY, AND JEAN DUSHON

ARGO

Number	Title	Yr	NM
❑ 750 [M]	You Better Believe Me	1965	30.00
❑ 750S [S]	You Better Believe Me	1965	30.00

LEWIS, RAMSEY, AND NANCY WILSON

COLUMBIA

Number	Title	Yr	NM
❑ FC39326	The Two of Us	1984	12.00

LEWIS, RAMSEY

ARGO

Number	Title	Yr	NM
❑ LP-645 [M]	An Hour with the Ramsey Lewis Trio	1959	40.00
❑ LPS-645 [S]	An Hour with the Ramsey Lewis Trio	1959	50.00
❑ LP-732 [M]	Bach to the Blues	1964	30.00
❑ LPS-732 [S]	Bach to the Blues	1964	30.00
❑ LP-723 [M]	Barefoot Sunday Blues	1963	30.00
❑ LPS-723 [S]	Barefoot Sunday Blues	1963	30.00
❑ LP-705 [M]	Bossa Nova	1962	30.00
❑ LPS-705 [S]	Bossa Nova	1962	30.00
❑ LP-755 [M]	Choice! The Best of the Ramsey Lewis Trio	1965	30.00
❑ LPS-755 [S]	Choice! The Best of the Ramsey Lewis Trio	1965	40.00
❑ LP-701 [M]	Country Meets the Blues	1962	30.00
❑ LPS-701 [S]	Country Meets the Blues	1962	30.00
❑ LP-627 [M]	Gentleman of Jazz	1958	50.00
❑ LPS-627 [S]	Gentleman of Jazz	1959	60.00
❑ LP-611 [M]	Gentleman of Swing	1958	50.00
❑ LPS-611 [S]	Gentleman of Swing	1959	60.00
❑ LP-680 [M]	More Music from the Soil	1961	40.00
❑ LPS-680 [S]	More Music from the Soil	1961	50.00
❑ LP-745 [M]	More Sounds of Christmas	1964	30.00
❑ LPS-745 [S]	More Sounds of Christmas	1964	30.00
❑ LP-715 [M]	Pot Luck	1963	30.00
❑ LPS-715 [S]	Pot Luck	1963	30.00
❑ LP-687 [M]	Sound of Christmas	1961	40.00
❑ LPS-687 [S]	Sound of Christmas	1961	50.00
❑ LP-665 [M]	Stretching Out	1960	40.00
❑ LPS-665 [S]	Stretching Out	1960	50.00
❑ LP-757 [M]	The In Crowd	1965	30.00
❑ LPS-757 [S]	The In Crowd	1965	30.00
❑ LP-741 [M]	The Ramsey Lewis Trio at the Bohemian Caverns	1964	30.00
❑ LPS-741 [S]	The Ramsey Lewis Trio at the Bohemian Caverns	1964	30.00
❑ LP-671 [M]	The Ramsey Lewis Trio in Chicago	1961	40.00
❑ LPS-671 [S]	The Ramsey Lewis Trio in Chicago	1961	50.00
❑ LP-642 [M]	The Ramsey Lewis Trio with Lee Winchester	1959	40.00
❑ LPS-642 [S]	The Ramsey Lewis Trio with Lee Winchester	1959	50.00
❑ LP-693 [M]	The Sound of Spring	1962	30.00
❑ LPS-693 [S]	The Sound of Spring	1962	30.00
CADET			
❑ LP-645 [M]	An Hour with the Ramsey Lewis Trio	1966	15.00
❑ LPS-645 [S]	An Hour with the Ramsey Lewis Trio	1966	18.00
❑ LPS-827	Another Voyage	1969	18.00
❑ LP-732 [M]	Bach to the Blues	1966	15.00
❑ LPS-732 [S]	Bach to the Blues	1966	18.00
❑ 60001	Back to the Roots	1971	15.00
❑ LP-723 [M]	Barefoot Sunday Blues	1966	15.00
❑ LPS-723 [S]	Barefoot Sunday Blues	1966	18.00
❑ LP-705 [M]	Bossa Nova	1966	15.00
❑ LPS-705 [S]	Bossa Nova	1966	18.00
❑ LP-755 [M]	Choice! The Best of the Ramsey Lewis Trio	1965	18.00
❑ LPS-755 [S]	Choice! The Best of the Ramsey Lewis Trio	1965	25.00
❑ LP-701 [M]	Country Meets the Blues	1966	15.00
❑ LPS-701 [S]	Country Meets the Blues	1966	18.00
❑ LP-794 [M]	Dancing in the Street	1967	25.00
❑ LPS-794 [S]	Dancing in the Street	1967	18.00
❑ LP-627 [M]	Gentleman of Jazz	1966	15.00

Number	Title	Yr	NM
❑ LPS-627 [S]	Gentleman of Jazz	1966	18.00
❑ LP-611 [M]	Gentleman of Swing	1966	15.00
❑ LPS-611 [S]	Gentleman of Swing	1966	18.00
❑ LP-790 [M]	Goin' Latin	1967	25.00
❑ LPS-790 [S]	Goin' Latin	1967	18.00
❑ 50020	Groover	1973	15.00
❑ LP-761 [M]	Hang On Ramsey!	1966	18.00
❑ LPS-761 [S]	Hang On Ramsey!	1966	25.00
❑ 60018	Inside Ramsey Lewis	1972	18.00
❑ LPS-811	Maiden Voyage	1968	18.00
❑ LP-680 [M]	More Music from the Soil	1966	15.00
❑ LPS-680 [S]	More Music from the Soil	1966	18.00
❑ LPS-680 [S]	More Music from the Soil	197?	15.00

—Reissue with "A Division of All Platinum Record Group" on label

Number	Title	Yr	NM
❑ LP-745 [M]	More Sounds of Christmas	1966	18.00
❑ LPS-745 [S]	More Sounds of Christmas	1966	25.00
❑ LPS-821	Mother Nature's Son	1969	18.00
❑ LP-715 [M]	Pot Luck	1966	15.00
❑ LPS-715 [S]	Pot Luck	1966	18.00
❑ LPS-836	Ramsey Lewis, The Piano Player	1970	18.00
❑ 50058	Solid Ivory	1974	18.00
❑ LP-687X [M]	Sound of Christmas	1966	25.00

—Reissue of Argo 687

Number	Title	Yr	NM
❑ LPS-687X [S]	Sound of Christmas	1966	25.00

—Reissue of Argo 687-S

Number	Title	Yr	NM
❑ LP-665 [M]	Stretching Out	1966	15.00
❑ LPS-665 [S]	Stretching Out	1966	18.00
❑ LP-771 [M]	Swingin'	1966	18.00
❑ LPS-771 [S]	Swingin'	1966	25.00
❑ LPS-839	The Best of Ramsey Lewis	1970	18.00
❑ LP-757 [M]	The In Crowd	1965	15.00
❑ LPS-757 [S]	The In Crowd	1965	18.00
❑ LPS-844	Them Changes	1970	18.00
❑ LP-782 [M]	The Movie Album	1967	25.00
❑ LPS-782 [S]	The Movie Album	1967	18.00
❑ LP-741 [M]	The Ramsey Lewis Trio at the Bohemian Caverns	1966	15.00
❑ LPS-741 [S]	The Ramsey Lewis Trio at the Bohemian Caverns	1966	18.00
❑ LP-671 [M]	The Ramsey Lewis Trio in Chicago	1966	15.00
❑ LPS-671 [S]	The Ramsey Lewis Trio in Chicago	1966	18.00
❑ LP-693 [M]	The Sound of Spring	1966	15.00
❑ LPS-693 [S]	The Sound of Spring	1966	18.00
❑ LPS-799	Up Pops Ramsey Lewis	1968	18.00
❑ LP-774 [M]	Wade in the Water	1966	18.00
❑ LPS-774 [S]	Wade in the Water	1966	25.00
❑ LP-750 [M]	You Better Believe It	1966	15.00
❑ LPS-750 [S]	You Better Believe It	1966	18.00

CBS

Number	Title	Yr	NM
❑ FM42661	A Classic Encounter	1988	12.00

CHESS

Number	Title	Yr	NM
❑ 9001	Solid Ivory	197?	15.00

—Reissue of Cadet 50058

Number	Title	Yr	NM
❑ CH9716	Sound of Christmas	1984	12.00

—Reissue of Argo 687-S

COLUMBIA

Number	Title	Yr	NM
❑ FC38294	Chance Encounter	1983	12.00
❑ PC33800	Don't It Feel Good	1975	12.00

—Originals have no bar code

Number	Title	Yr	NM
❑ PC33800	Don't It Feel Good	198?	10.00

—Budget-line reissue with bar code

Number	Title	Yr	NM
❑ FC40108	Fantasy	1985	12.00
❑ KC32030	Funky Serenity	1973	15.00
❑ FC40677	Keys to the City	1987	12.00
❑ JC35483	Legacy	1978	12.00
❑ PC35483	Legacy	198?	10.00

—Budget-line reissue

Number	Title	Yr	NM
❑ FC38787	Les Fleurs	1983	12.00
❑ FC37687	Live at the Savoy	1982	12.00
❑ PC37687	Live at the Savoy	198?	10.00

—Budget-line reissue

Number	Title	Yr	NM
❑ HC47687	Live at the Savoy	1982	80.00

—Half-speed mastered edition

Number	Title	Yr	NM
❑ PC34696	Love Notes	1977	12.00
❑ JC35815	Ramsey	1979	12.00
❑ KC32490	Ramsey Lewis' Newly Recorded All-Time, Non-Stop Golden Hits	1973	15.00
❑ PC32490	Ramsey Lewis' Newly Recorded All-Time, Non-Stop Golden Hits	197?	10.00

—Reissue with new prefix

Number	Title	Yr	NM
❑ FC39158	Reunion	1983	12.00
❑ JC36423	Routes	1980	12.00
❑ PC36423	Routes	198?	10.00

—Budget-line reissue

Number	Title	Yr	NM
❑ PC34173	Salongo	1976	12.00

—Originals have no bar code

Number	Title	Yr	NM
❑ PC34173	Salongo	198?	10.00

—Budget-line reissue with bar code

Number	Title	Yr	NM
❑ KC32897	Solar Wind	1974	15.00
❑ KC33194	Sun Goddess	1974	12.00
❑ PC33194	Sun Goddess	197?	10.00

—Reissue with new prefix

Number	Title	Yr	NM
❑ HC43194	Sun Goddess	1982	50.00

—Half-speed mastered edition

Number	Title	Yr	NM
❑ JC35018	Tequila Mockingbird	1977	12.00
❑ FC36364	The Best of Ramsey Lewis	1980	12.00
❑ FC37153	Three Piece Suite	1981	12.00
❑ KC31096	Upendo Ni Pamoja	1972	15.00
❑ CQ31096 [Q]	Upendo Ni Pamoja	1972	25.00
❑ CG33663	Upendo Ni Pamoja/Funky Serenity	1975	15.00
❑ FC44190	Urban Renewal	1989	18.00

COLUMBIA JAZZ ODYSSEY

Number	Title	Yr	NM
❑ PC37019	Blues for the Night Owl	1981	12.00

EMARCY

Number	Title	Yr	NM
❑ MG-36150 [M]	Down to Earth	1958	40.00
❑ SR-80029 [S]	Down to Earth	1958	50.00

MERCURY

Number	Title	Yr	NM
❑ MG-20536 [M]	Down to Earth	1965	25.00
❑ SR-60536 [S]	Down to Earth	1965	30.00

LEWIS, ROBERT Q.

ATCO

Number	Title	Yr	NM
❑ 33-212 [M]	I'm Just Wild About Vaudeville	1963	30.00
❑ SD 33-212 [S]	I'm Just Wild About Vaudeville	1963	30.00

X

Number	Title	Yr	NM
❑ LXA-1033 [M]	Robert Q. Lewis and His Gang	1956	50.00

LEWIS, SHARI

RCA CAMDEN

Number	Title	Yr	NM
❑ CAL-1052 [M]	Jack and the Beanstalk and Other Stories	1964	30.00
❑ CAS-1052 [S]	Jack and the Beanstalk and Other Stories	1964	30.00

RCA VICTOR

Number	Title	Yr	NM
❑ LBY-1006 [M]	Fun in Shariland	1954	80.00

LEWIS, SMILEY

IMPERIAL

Number	Title	Yr	NM
❑ LP-9141 [M]	I Hear You Knocking	1961	600.00

—Black vinyl

Number	Title	Yr	NM
❑ LP-9141 [M]	I Hear You Knocking	1961	6000.00

—Green vinyl (one copy known)

LEWIS, TED

BIOGRAPH

Number	Title	Yr	NM
❑ C-7	Ted Lewis' Orchestra, Volume 1	198?	12.00
❑ C-8	Ted Lewis' Orchestra, Volume 2	198?	12.00

COLUMBIA

Number	Title	Yr	NM
❑ CL6127 [10]	Classic Jazz	1950	50.00

DECCA

Number	Title	Yr	NM
❑ DL8321 [M]	Is Everybody Happy?	1956	40.00
❑ DL5114 [10]	Ted Lewis and His Orchestra	195?	60.00
❑ DL4905 [M]	Ted Lewis' Greatest Hits	1967	30.00
❑ DL74905 [R]	Ted Lewis' Greatest Hits	1967	18.00
❑ DL8322 [M]	The Medicine Man for the Blues	1956	40.00

EPIC

Number	Title	Yr	NM
❑ LN3170 [M]	Everybody's Happy!	1955	40.00

MCA

Number	Title	Yr	NM
❑ 2-4101	The Best of Ted Lewis	1976	18.00

—Black rainbow labels

OLYMPIC

Number	Title	Yr	NM
❑ OL-7127	Me and My Shadow	1974	12.00

RKO

Number	Title	Yr	NM
❑ ULP-108 [M]	Me and My Shadow	195?	25.00

LEWIS, WILLIE

SWING

Number	Title	Yr	NM
❑ 8400/1	Willie Lewis and His Entertainers	198?	15.00

LEWIS AND CLARKE EXPEDITION, THE

COLGEMS

Number	Title	Yr	NM
❑ COM-105 [M]	The Lewis and Clarke Expedition	1967	30.00
❑ COS-105 [S]	The Lewis and Clarke Expedition	1967	30.00

LEWIS CONNECTION, THE

(NO LABEL)

Number	Title	Yr	NM
❑ (no #)0	The Lewis Connection	1979	400.00

LEWIS FAMILY, THE

STARDAY

Number	Title	Yr	NM
❑ SLP-252 [M]	All Night Singing Convention	1963	30.00
❑ SLP-161 [M]	Anniversary Celebration	1962	30.00
❑ SLP-433	Did You Ever Go Sailing	1969	25.00
❑ SLP-422	Golden Gospel Banjo	1968	25.00
❑ SLP-450	Golden Gospel of the Lewis Family	1970	25.00
❑ SLP-193 [M]	Gospel Special	1962	30.00
❑ SLP-395 [M]	Shall We Gather at the River	1966	30.00
❑ SLP-289 [M]	Singin' in My Soul	1964	30.00
❑ SLP-121 [M]	Singin' Time Down South	1960	30.00
❑ SLP-238 [M]	Sing Me a Gospel Song	1962	30.00
❑ SLP-331 [M]	The First Family of Gospel Music	1965	30.00
❑ SLP-381 [M]	The Lewis Family Album	1965	30.00
❑ SLP-364 [M]	The Lewis Family Sings the Gospel with Carl Story	1965	30.00
❑ SLP-408 [M]	Time Is Moving On	1966	30.00

LIBERACE, GEORGE

COLUMBIA

Number	Title	Yr	NM
❑ CL587 [M]	A Musical Journey with George Liberace	1954	40.00

—Maroon label, gold print

CROWN

Number	Title	Yr	NM
❑ CST-218 [S]	Hawaiian Paradise	196?	30.00

—Black label; red vinyl

Number	Title	Yr	NM
❑ CLP-5218 [M]	Hawaiian Paradise	196?	18.00

—Black label

IMPERIAL

Number	Title	Yr	NM
❑ LP-9039 [M]	George Liberace Goes Teenage	1957	50.00

LIBERACE

ABC

Number	Title	Yr	NM
❑ 4002	16 Great Performances	1974	15.00

AVI

Number	Title	Yr	NM
❑ 1023	Candlelight Classics	1973	15.00
❑ 1029	The World of Liberace	1974	15.00

CBS

Number	Title	Yr	NM
❑ FM42244	Concert Favorites	1986	12.00

COLUMBIA

Number	Title	Yr	NM
❑ CL6239 [10]	An Evening with Liberace	1953	80.00
❑ CL589 [M]	Christmas at Liberace's	1954	50.00

—Maroon label, gold print

Number	Title	Yr	NM
❑ CL6269 [10]	Concertos for You	1953	80.00
❑ CL6283 [10]	Concertos for You, Volume 2	1953	80.00
❑ CL645 [M]	Hollywood Bowl Encore	1955	40.00
❑ CL2592 [10]	Kiddin' on the Keys	1955	60.00
❑ CL896 [M]	Liberace at Home	1956	50.00
❑ CL600 [M]	Liberace at the Hollywood Bowl	1955	40.00
❑ CL6217 [10]	Liberace at the Piano	1952	80.00
❑ CL575 [M]	Liberace at the Piano	1954	40.00

—Maroon label, gold print

Number	Title	Yr	NM
❑ CL6251 [10]	Liberace by Candlelight	1953	80.00
❑ CL661 [M]	Liberace by Candlelight	1955	40.00
❑ CL6327 [10]	Liberace Plays Chopin	1954	80.00
❑ CL6328 [10]	Liberace Plays Chopin, Volume 2	1954	80.00
❑ CS9845	Liberace's Greatest Hits	1969	15.00

—Red "360 Sound" label

Number	Title	Yr	NM
❑ CS9845	Liberace's Greatest Hits	1970	12.00

—Orange label

Number	Title	Yr	NM
❑ CL2516 [10]	Piano Reverie	1955	60.00
❑ CL800 [M]	Sincerely Yours	1956	50.00
❑ CL1118 [M]	South Pacific	1957	30.00

CORAL

Number	Title	Yr	NM
❑ CRL57392 [M]	As Time Goes By	1962	15.00
❑ CRL757392 [S]	As Time Goes By	1962	18.00
❑ CRL57452 [M]	Golden Themes from Hollywood	1964	15.00
❑ CRL757452 [S]	Golden Themes from Hollywood	1964	18.00
❑ CRL57346 [M]	Liberace at the Palladium	1961	15.00
❑ CRL757346 [S]	Liberace at the Palladium	1961	18.00
❑ CRL57344 [M]	My Inspiration	1961	15.00
❑ CRL757344 [S]	My Inspiration	1961	18.00
❑ CRL57377 [M]	My Parade of Golden Favorites	1961	15.00
❑ CRL757377 [S]	My Parade of Golden Favorites	1961	18.00
❑ CRL57292 [M]	Piano Song Book -- Movie Themes	1959	18.00
❑ CRL757292 [S]	Piano Song Book -- Movie Themes	1959	25.00
❑ CRL57395 [M]	Rhapsody by Candlelight	1962	15.00
❑ CRL757395 [S]	Rhapsody by Candlelight	1962	18.00
❑ CXB9 [M]	The Best of Liberace	1965	18.00
❑ 7CXB9 [S]	The Best of Liberace	1965	25.00
❑ CRL57305 [M]	The Magic Pianos of Liberace	1960	15.00
❑ CRL757305 [S]	The Magic Pianos of Liberace	1960	18.00
❑ CRL57305 [M]	The Magic Pianos of Liberace	1960	18.00
❑ CRL757305 [S]	The Magic Pianos of Liberace	1960	25.00

DOT

Number	Title	Yr	NM
❑ DLP-3550 [M]	A Liberace Christmas	1964	15.00
❑ DLP-25550 [S]	A Liberace Christmas	1964	18.00
❑ DLP-3595 [M]	Liberace at the Americana, Volume 1	1965	15.00
❑ DLP-25595 [S]	Liberace at the Americana, Volume 1	1965	18.00
❑ DLP-3596 [M]	Liberace at the Americana, Volume 2	1965	15.00
❑ DLP-25596 [S]	Liberace at the Americana, Volume 2	1965	18.00
❑ DLP-3816 [M]	Liberace Now!	1967	18.00
❑ DLP-25816 [S]	Liberace Now!	1967	18.00
❑ DLP-3547 [M]	Mr. Showmanship	1964	15.00
❑ DLP-25547 [S]	Mr. Showmanship	1964	18.00
❑ DLP-3563 [M]	My Most Requested	1965	15.00
❑ DLP-25563 [S]	My Most Requested	1965	18.00
❑ DLP-3755 [M]	New Sounds	1966	15.00
❑ DLP-25755 [S]	New Sounds	1966	18.00
❑ DLP-9502 [M]	Silver Anniversary	1965	15.00
❑ DLP-29502 [S]	Silver Anniversary	1965	18.00
❑ DLP-25901	Sound of Love	1969	15.00
❑ DLP-25858	The Love Album	1968	15.00

Number	Title	Yr	NM
HARMONY			
❑ HL7361 [M]	Concerto by Candlelight	196?	15.00
❑ HS11161 [R]	Concerto by Candlelight	196?	15.00
❑ HL7237 [M]	Rhapsody in Blue	196?	15.00
❑ HL11175 [R]	Rhapsody in Blue	196?	12.00
❑ HS11325	Tenderly	1969	12.00
❑ HL7154 [M]	The Liberace Show	1959	18.00
❑ HS11054 [R]	The Liberace Show	196?	12.00
❑ HS11391	The Very Thought of You	1970	12.00
MCA			
❑ 740	Here's Liberace	198?	10.00
—Reissue of Vocalion 73821			
❑ 4167	The Artistry of Liberace	198?	15.00
❑ 4060	The Best of Liberace	197?	15.00
MISTLETOE			
❑ MLP-1208	Twas the Night Before Christmas	1974	12.00
PARAMOUNT			
❑ PAS-1032	Liberace In Concert	1974	18.00
❑ PAS-1009	The Best of Liberace	1973	15.00
PICKWICK			
❑ SPC-3208	By the Time I Get to Phoenix	197?	12.00
❑ SPC-3124	Strangers in the Night	196?	12.00
❑ SPC-3159	What Now My Love	1969	12.00
❑ SPC-3085	You Made Me Love You	196?	12.00
VOCALION			
❑ VL3821 [M]	Here's Liberace	196?	15.00
❑ VL73821 [R]	Here's Liberace	196?	15.00
WARNER BROS.			
❑ WS1847	A Brand New Me	1969	15.00
❑ WS1889	Love and Music Festival "Live	1970	15.00

LIBERMAN, JEFFERY

Number	Title	Yr	NM
LIBRAH			
❑ 1545	Jeffery Liberman	1975	80.00
❑ 6969	Solitude Within	1975	120.00
❑ 12157	Synergy	1976	120.00

LIDSTROM, JACK

Number	Title	Yr	NM
WORLD PACIFIC			
❑ PJ-1235 [M]	Look, Dad! They're Comin' Down the Street in Hi-Fi	1957	40.00

LIEBERMAN, LORI

Number	Title	Yr	NM
CAPITOL			
❑ ST-11297	A Piece of Time	1974	15.00
❑ ST-11203	Becoming	1973	15.00
❑ ST-11081	Lori Lieberman	1972	15.00

LIEBMAN, DAVE

Number	Title	Yr	NM
ARTISTS HOUSE			
❑ 8	Pendulum	1978	15.00
CMP			
❑ CMP-40-ST	Chant	1990	18.00
❑ CMP-9-ST	Dedications	198?	15.00
❑ CMP-24-ST	The Loneliness of a Long-Distance Runner	1987	15.00
COLUMBIA			
❑ JC36581	What It Is	1979	12.00
ECM			
❑ 1046	Drum Ode	1975	18.00
❑ 1039	Lookout Farm	197?	18.00
—As "David Liebman			
HEADS UP			
❑ HUP-3005	The Energy of the Chance	1989	18.00
HORIZON			
❑ SP-709	Fantasies	1976	15.00
❑ SP-721	Light'n Up, Please!	1977	15.00
❑ SP-702	Sweet Hands	1976	15.00
PM			
❑ PMR-022	Memories, Dreams and Reflections	1986	15.00
❑ PMR-023	Picture Show	1986	15.00
WEST 54			
❑ 8012	First Visit	1979	15.00

LIFE WITHOUT BUILDINGS

Number	Title	Yr	NM
TUGBOAT			
❑ TUGS016 [B]	Any Other City	2014	30.00

LIFEGUARDS, THE (U)

Number	Title	Yr	NM
WYNCOTE			
❑ W-9043 [M]	C'mon and Swim	1964	15.00
❑ SW-9043 [S]	C'mon and Swim	1964	18.00

LIGGINS, JOE

Number	Title	Yr	NM
MERCURY			
❑ MG-20731 [M]	Honeydripper	1962	80.00
❑ SR-60731 [S]	Honeydripper	1962	100.00

LIGHT, ENOCH

Number	Title	Yr	NM
ABC WESTMINSTER/GRAND AWARD			
❑ 68008	Sing Along with the Original Roaring 20's	1974	12.00
❑ 68009	The Flirty 30's	1974	12.00
❑ 68012	The Torchy Thirties	1974	12.00
COMMAND			
❑ 33-854 [M]	1963 -- The Year's Most Popular Themes	1963	15.00
❑ 854SD [S]	1963 -- The Year's Most Popular Themes	1963	18.00
❑ QD-40002 [Q]	A New Concept	1972	18.00
❑ 33-844 [M]	Big Band Bossa Nova	1962	15.00
❑ 844SD [S]	Big Band Bossa Nova	1962	18.00
❑ 33-818 [M]	Big Bold and Brassy	1961	15.00
❑ 818SD [S]	Big Bold and Brassy	1961	18.00
❑ 33-868 [M]	Command Performances	1964	15.00
❑ 868SD [S]	Command Performances	1964	18.00
❑ 915SD	Command Performances, Volume 2	1969	18.00
❑ 33-867 [M]	Dimension "3	1964	15.00
❑ 867SD [S]	Dimension "3	1964	18.00
❑ 873SD [S]	Discotheque Dance...Dance...Dance	1964	18.00
❑ 33-873 [M]	Discotheque Dance...Dance...Dance	1964	15.00
❑ 882SD [S]	Discotheque Dance...Dance...Dance, Volume 2	1965	18.00
❑ 33-882 [M]	Discotheque Dance...Dance...Dance, Volume 2	1965	15.00
❑ 33-840 [M]	Enoch Light and His Orchestra At Carnegie Hall Play Irving Berlin	1962	15.00
❑ 840SD [S]	Enoch Light and His Orchestra At Carnegie Hall Play Irving Berlin	1962	18.00
❑ 33-822 [M]	Far Away Places	1961	15.00
❑ 822SD [S]	Far Away Places	1961	18.00
❑ 33-850 [M]	Far Away Places, Volume 2	1963	15.00
❑ 850SD [S]	Far Away Places, Volume 2	1963	18.00
❑ 33-879 [M]	Great Cole Porter Songs	1965	15.00
❑ 879SD [S]	Great Cole Porter Songs	1965	18.00
❑ 33-835 [M]	Great Themes from Hit Films	1962	15.00
❑ 835SD [S]	Great Themes from Hit Films	1962	18.00
❑ 33-871 [M]	Great Themes from Hit Films	1964	15.00
❑ 871SD [S]	Great Themes from Hit Films	1964	18.00
❑ 33-851 [M]	Let's Dance the Bossa Nova	1963	15.00
❑ 851SD [S]	Let's Dance the Bossa Nova	1963	18.00
❑ 33-887 [M]	Magnificent Movie Themes	1965	15.00
❑ 887SD [S]	Magnificent Movie Themes	1965	18.00
❑ 33-805 [M]	Paperback Ballet	1960	15.00
❑ 805SD [S]	Paperback Ballet	1960	18.00
❑ 33-800 [M]	Persuasive Percussion	1960	15.00
—By "Terry Snyder and the All-Stars			
❑ 800SD [S]	Persuasive Percussion	1960	18.00
—By "Terry Snyder and the All-Stars			
❑ 33-808 [M]	Persuasive Percussion, Volume 2	1960	15.00
—By "Terry Snyder and the All-Stars			
❑ 808SD [S]	Persuasive Percussion, Volume 2	1960	18.00
—By "Terry Snyder and the All-Stars			
❑ 33-817 [M]	Persuasive Percussion, Volume 3	1961	15.00
—By "The Command All-Stars			
❑ 817SD [S]	Persuasive Percussion, Volume 3	1961	18.00
—By "The Command All-Stars			
❑ 33-830 [M]	Persuasive Percussion, Volume 4	1962	15.00
❑ 830SD [S]	Persuasive Percussion, Volume 4	1962	18.00
❑ 33-895 [M]	Persuasive Percussion 1966	1966	15.00
❑ 895SD [S]	Persuasive Percussion 1966	1966	18.00
❑ 33-814 [M]	Pertinent Percussion Cha-Cha's	1960	15.00
❑ 814SD [S]	Pertinent Percussion Cha-Cha's	1960	18.00
❑ 33-806 [M]	Provocative Percussion	1960	15.00
—By "The Command All-Stars			
❑ 806SD [S]	Provocative Percussion	1960	18.00
—By "The Command All-Stars			
❑ 33-810 [M]	Provocative Percussion, Volume 2	1960	15.00
❑ 810SD [S]	Provocative Percussion, Volume 2	1960	18.00
❑ 33-821 [M]	Provocative Percussion, Volume 3	1961	15.00
❑ 821SD [S]	Provocative Percussion, Volume 3	1961	18.00
❑ 33-834 [M]	Provocative Percussion, Volume 4	1962	15.00
❑ 834SD [S]	Provocative Percussion, Volume 4	1962	18.00
❑ 33-863 [M]	Rome 35/MM	1964	15.00
❑ 863SD [S]	Rome 35/MM	1964	18.00
❑ 826SD [S]	Stereo 35/MM	1961	18.00
❑ 831SD [S]	Stereo 35/MM, Volume Two	1962	18.00
❑ 33-804 [M]	The Sound of Strings	1960	15.00
❑ 804SD [S]	The Sound of Strings	1960	18.00
❑ 33-833 [M]	Vibrations	1962	15.00
❑ 833SD [S]	Vibrations	1962	18.00
GRAND AWARD			
❑ GA 33-399 [M]	All the Things You Are	1959	25.00
❑ GA-236SD [S]	All the Things You Are	1959	30.00
❑ GA-214SD [S]	Around the World in 80 Days	1958	30.00
❑ GA-237SD [S]	Come to Hawaii	1959	30.00
❑ GA 33-405 [M]	Come to Hawaii	1959	25.00
❑ GA-215SD [S]	Gigi	1958	30.00
❑ GA 33-381 [M]	Glenn Miller's Song Hits	1958	25.00
❑ GA-207SD [S]	Glenn Miller's Song Hits	1958	30.00
❑ GA 33-391 [M]	Happy Cha Cha's, Vol. 2	1959	25.00
❑ GA-227SD [S]	Happy Cha Cha's, Vol. 2	1959	30.00
❑ GA 33-388 [M]	I Want to Be Happy Cha Cha's	1959	25.00
❑ GA-222SD [S]	I Want to Be Happy Cha Cha's	1959	30.00
❑ GA-246SD [S]	Just for Kicks	1959	30.00
❑ GA-216SD [S]	My Fair Lady	1958	30.00
❑ GA-224SD [S]	New World Symphony	1958	30.00
❑ GA-217SD [S]	Oklahoma/South Pacific	1958	30.00
❑ GA 33-380 [M]	Paris Spectacular	1958	25.00
❑ GA-228SD [S]	Show Spectacular	1959	30.00
❑ GA 33-419 [M]	Sing Along with the Original Roaring 20's	1959	25.00
❑ GA-251SD [S]	Sing Along with the Original Roaring 20's	1959	30.00
❑ GA 33-410 [M]	Something to Remember You By	1959	25.00
❑ GA-242SD [S]	Something to Remember You By	1959	30.00
❑ GA-202SD [S]	The Flirty Thirties	1958	30.00
❑ GA 33-371 [M]	The Flirty Thirties	1958	25.00
❑ GA-225SD [S]	The Great Themes of America's Great Bands	1958	30.00
❑ GA 33-392 [M]	The Great Themes of America's Great Bands	1958	25.00
❑ GA-201SD [S]	The Roaring Twenties	1958	30.00
❑ GA 33-327 [M]	The Roaring Twenties	1958	25.00
❑ GA-211SD [S]	The Roaring Twenties, Volume 2	1958	30.00
❑ GA 33-353 [M]	The Roaring Twenties, Volume 3	1959	25.00
❑ GA-229SD [S]	The Roaring Twenties, Volume 3	1959	30.00
❑ GA-220SD [S]	The Torchy Thirties	1958	30.00
❑ GA-206SD [S]	Tommy Dorsey's Song Hits	1958	30.00
❑ GA 33-382 [M]	Tommy Dorsey's Song Hits	1958	25.00
❑ GA 33-372 [M]	Waltzes for Dancing	1958	25.00
❑ GA-203SD [S]	Waltzes for Dancing	1958	30.00
❑ GA 33-406 [M]	With My Eyes Wide Open I'm Dreaming	1959	25.00
❑ GA-238SD [S]	With My Eyes Wide Open I'm Dreaming	1959	30.00
PROJECT 3			
❑ PR4C-5068 [Q]	4 Channel Dynamite!	1973	18.00
❑ PR-6034	20 Great Movie Themes	1980	18.00
❑ PR-5084SD	Beatles Classics	1974	15.00
❑ PR4C-5084 [Q]	Beatles Classics	1974	18.00
❑ PR-5046SD	Best of the Movie Themes 1970	1970	15.00
❑ PR4C-5046 [Q]	Best of the Movie Themes 1970	1973	18.00
❑ PR-5056SD	Big Band Hits of the 30's & 40's!	1971	15.00
❑ PR4C-5056 [Q]	Big Band Hits of the 30's & 40's!	1973	18.00
❑ PR-6005/6	Big Band Hits of the 30's, 40's & 50's	1974	18.00
❑ PR4C-6005/6 [Q]	Big Band Hits of the 30's, 40's & 50's	1974	25.00
❑ PR-5049SD	Big Band Hits of the 30's	1971	15.00
❑ PR4C-5049 [Q]	Big Band Hits of the 30's	1973	18.00
❑ PR-5089SD	Big Band Hits of the 30's, Volume 2	1975	15.00
❑ PR4C-5089 [Q]	Big Band Hits of the 30's, Volume 2	1975	18.00
❑ PR-6013/14	Big Band Hits of the 30's and 40's	197?	18.00
❑ PR4C-6013/14 [Q]	Big Band Hits of the 30's and 40's	197?	25.00
❑ PR4C-5076 [Q]	Big Band Hits of the 40's & 50's	1973	18.00
❑ PR-5059SD	Big Hits of the 20's	1971	15.00
❑ PR4C-5059 [Q]	Big Hits of the 20's	1973	18.00
❑ PR-6003/4	Big Hits of the Seventies	1974	18.00
❑ PR4C-6003/4 [Q]	Big Hits of the Seventies	1974	25.00
❑ PR4C-5073 [Q]	Charge!	1973	18.00
❑ PR4C-5092 [Q]	Disco Disque	197?	18.00
❑ PR-5092SD	Disco Disque	197?	15.00
❑ PR-5036SD	Enoch Light and the Brass Menagerie	1969	15.00
❑ PR4C-5036 [Q]	Enoch Light and the Brass Menagerie	1973	18.00
❑ PR-5042SD	Enoch Light and the Brass Menagerie, Volume 2	1969	15.00
❑ PR4C-5042 [Q]	Enoch Light and the Brass Menagerie, Volume 2	1973	18.00
❑ PR-5060SD	Enoch Light and the Brass Menagerie 1973	1972	15.00
❑ PR4C-5060 [Q]	Enoch Light and the Brass Menagerie 1973	1973	18.00
❑ PR-5013SD	Film Fame	1968	15.00
❑ PR-5005SD	Film on Film -- Great Movie Themes	1967	15.00
❑ PR4C-5077 [Q]	Future Sound Shock	1973	18.00
❑ PR-5038SD	Glittering Guitars	1969	15.00
❑ PR-5086SD	Great Hits from the Gatsby Era	1974	15.00
❑ PR4C-5086 [Q]	Great Hits from the Gatsby Era	1974	18.00
❑ PR-5051SD	Hit Movie Themes	1971	15.00
❑ PR4C-5051 [Q]	Hit Movie Themes	1973	18.00
❑ PR-5004SD	It's Happening	1967	15.00
❑ PR-5100	Let It Be	197?	15.00
❑ PR-5063SD	Movie Hits!	1972	15.00
❑ PR4C-5063 [Q]	Movie Hits!	1973	18.00
❑ PR-6011/12	Music Maestro, Please	197?	18.00
❑ PR-5048SD	Permissive Polyphonics	1970	15.00
❑ PR4C-5048 [Q]	Permissive Polyphonics	1973	18.00
❑ PR-5043SD [B]	Spaced Out	1970	15.00
❑ PR4C-5043 [Q]	Spaced Out	1973	18.00

Number	Title	Yr	NM
❏ PR-5000SD	Spanish Strings	1967	15.00
❏ PR4C-5000 [Q]	Spanish Strings	1973	18.00
❏ PR-5027SD	The Best of Hollywood '68-'69	1968	15.00
❏ PR-5109	The Most Beautiful Music in the World	1981	15.00
❏ PR-5021SD	Twelve Smash Hits	1968	15.00
❏ PR-5030SD	Whoever You Are, I Love You	1968	15.00

SEAGULL

❏ LG-8204	Blowin' in the Wind	198?	12.00
❏ LG-8207	Music from the Movies	198?	12.00

LIGHT CRUST DOUGHBOYS, THE

AUDIO LAB

❏ AL-1525 [M]	The Light Crust Doughboys	1959	150.00

LIGHTFOOT, GORDON

LIBERTY

❏ LN-10040	Back Here on Earth	198?	10.00
—Budget-line reissue			
❏ LN-10041	Did She Mention My Name	198?	10.00
—Budget-line reissue			
❏ LN-10044	Lightfoot	198?	10.00
—Budget-line reissue			
❏ LN-10039	Sunday Concert	198?	10.00
—Budget-line reissue			
❏ LN-10038	The Best of Lightfoot	198?	10.00
—Budget-line reissue			
❏ LN-10043	The Way I Feel	198?	10.00
—Budget-line reissue			

MOBILE FIDELITY

❏ 1-018	Sundown	1979	40.00
—Audiophile vinyl			

PAIR

❏ PDL2-1081	Songbook	1986	15.00

REPRISE

❏ MS2206	Cold on the Shoulder	1975	15.00
❏ MS4-2206 [Q]	Cold on the Shoulder	1975	30.00
❏ MS2056	Don Quixote	1972	15.00
❏ 2RS2237	Gord's Gold	1975	18.00
❏ RS6392	If You Could Read My Mind	1971	12.00
—Retitled version			
❏ MS2116	Old Dan's Records	1972	15.00
❏ RS6392	Sit Down Young Stranger	1970	18.00
❏ ST-93228	Sit Down Young Stranger	1970	25.00
—Capitol Record Club edition			
❏ MS2037	Summer Side of Life	1971	15.00
❏ MS2246	Summertime Dream	1976	15.00
❏ MS2177	Sundown	1974	15.00
❏ MS4-2177 [Q]	Sundown	1974	30.00

UNITED ARTISTS

❏ UAS-6672	Back Here on Earth	1969	25.00
❏ UAS-5510	Classic Lightfoot (The Best of Lightfoot Volume 2)	1971	18.00
❏ UAS-6649 [B]	Did She Mention My Name	1968	25.00
❏ UAL-3487 [M]	Lightfoot	1966	25.00
❏ UAS-6487 [S]	Lightfoot	1966	30.00
❏ UAS-6714	Sunday Concert	1969	18.00
❏ UAS-6754	The Best of Gordon Lightfoot	1970	18.00
❏ UA-LA243-G	The Very Best of Gordon Lightfoot	1974	15.00
❏ UAL-3587 [M]	The Way I Feel	1967	25.00
❏ UAS-6587 [S]	The Way I Feel	1967	30.00

WARNER BROS.

❏ HS3426	Dream Street Rose	1980	12.00
❏ 25482	East of Midnight	1986	12.00
❏ BSK3149	Endless Wire	1978	12.00
❏ 25784	Gord's Gold, Volume II	1989	15.00
❏ 23901	Salute	1983	12.00
❏ BSK3633	Shadows	1982	12.00

LIGHTFOOT, PAPA

VAULT

❏ 130	Natchez Trace	1969	18.00
—As "Papa George Lightfoot"			

LIGHTHOUSE

EVOLUTION

❏ 3014	Lighthouse Live!	1972	25.00
❏ 3007 [B]	One Fine Morning	1971	30.00
❏ 3016	Sunny Days	1973	18.00
❏ 3010 [B]	Thoughts of Movin' On	1972	25.00

JANUS

❏ JSX-7025	The Best of Lighthouse	1976	15.00

POLYDOR

❏ PD-5056	Can You Feel It	1973	15.00
❏ PD-1-6028	Good Day	1974	15.00

RCA VICTOR

❏ LSP-4173	Lighthouse	1969	18.00
❏ LSP-4325	Peacing It All Together	1970	18.00
❏ LSP-4241	Suite Feeling	1969	18.00

LIGHTNIN' SLIM

EXCELLO

❏ LPS8018	High and Low Down	1971	18.00
❏ LP8004 [M]	Lightnin' Slim's Bell Ringer	1965	300.00

❏ LPS8004 [M]	Lightnin' Slim's Bell Ringer	196?	50.00
—Thogh labeled "Electronic Stereo," this record is mono			
❏ LPS8023	London Gumbo	1972	18.00
❏ LP8000 [M]	Rooster Blues	1960	800.00
❏ LPS8000 [M]	Rooster Blues	196?	50.00
—Thogh labeled "Electronic Stereo," this record is mono			

INTERMEDIA

❏ QS-5062	That's All Right	198?	12.00

LIGHTNING

P.I.P.

❏ 6807 [B]	Lightning	1971	35.00

LIGHTNING SEEDS, THE

MCA

❏ 6404	Cloudcuckooland	1990	18.00

LIGHTSEY, KIRK

SUNNYSIDE

❏ SSC-1020	Everything Is Changed	198?	15.00
❏ SSC-1002	Lightsey 1	1985	15.00
❏ SSC-1005	Lightsey 2	1985	15.00
❏ SSC-1014	Lightsey Live	1987	15.00

LIL BOW WOW

SO SO DEF

❏ C269981	Beware of Dog	2000	18.00

LIL' KIM

UNDEAS

❏ 92733	Hard Core	1996	25.00
❏ 92840	The Notorious K.I.M.	2000	18.00

LIL' ROMEO

SME/PRIORITY

❏ 50198	Lil' Romeo	2001	18.00

LI'L WALLY

JAY JAY

❏ 5080 [S]	A Polka Christmas	1966	15.00
❏ 1080 [M]	A Polka Christmas	1966	18.00
❏ 8003	Christmas from Poland	19??	15.00
❏ 5026 [S]	Christmas Time	196?	15.00
❏ 1039 [M]	Christmas Time	196?	18.00
❏ 6012 [S]	Dance Around the Christmas Tree	196?	15.00
❏ 1026 [M]	Dance Around the Christmas Tree	196?	18.00
❏ 1023 [M]	Polish Christmas Carols	196?	18.00
❏ 5011 [S]	Polish Christmas Carols	196?	15.00
❏ 1017 [M]	Polish Christmas Carols	195?	18.00

LILLIE, BEATRICE

DECCA

❏ DL 5453 [10]	Souvenir Album	1954	50.00

LIBERTY MUSIC SHOP

❏ 1002 [10]	Thirty Minutes with Bea Lillie	1954	50.00

LONDON

❏ LL1373 [M]	An Evening with Bea Little	1956	30.00
❏ 5471 [M]	Auntie Bea	1959	30.00

LILLY BROTHERS, THE

FOLKLORE

❏ FL-14010 [M]	Bluegrass Breakdown	1963	25.00
❏ FLS-14010 [S]	Bluegrass Breakdown	1963	30.00
❏ FL-14035 [M]	Country Songs	1964	25.00
❏ FLS-14035 [S]	Country Songs	1964	30.00

FOLKWAYS

❏ FA-2433 [M]	Folk Songs from the Southern Mountains	196?	25.00

LIMEHOUSE JAZZ BAND, THE

STOMP OFF

❏ SOS-1014	Rhythm Is Our Business	1981	12.00

LIMELITERS, THE

ELEKTRA

❏ EKM-180 [M]	The Limeliters	1960	25.00
❏ EKS-7180 [S]	The Limeliters	1960	30.00

GNP CRESCENDO

❏ GNPS-2188	Alive! In Concert, Vol. 1	1986	12.00
❏ GNPS-2190	Alive! In Concert, Vol. 2	1987	12.00

LEGACY

❏ 113	Their First Historic Album	1970	15.00

RCA CAMDEN

❏ ACL1-0602	This Train	1974	12.00

RCA VICTOR

❏ LPM-2547 [M]	Folk Matinee	1962	25.00
❏ LSP-2547 [S]	Folk Matinee	1962	30.00
❏ LPM-2671 [M]	Fourteen 14K Folk Songs	1963	25.00
❏ LSP-2671 [S]	Fourteen 14K Folk Songs	1963	30.00
❏ LPM-2906 [M]	Leave It to the Limeliters	1964	18.00
❏ LSP-2906 [S]	Leave It to the Limeliters	1964	25.00
❏ LPM-2907 [M]	London Concert	1964	18.00
❏ LSP-2907 [S]	London Concert	1964	25.00
❏ LPM-2588 [M]	Makin' a Joyful Noise	1963	25.00

❏ LSP-2588 [S]	Makin' a Joyful Noise	1963	30.00
❏ LPM-2844 [M]	More of Everything!	1964	18.00
❏ LSP-2844 [S]	More of Everything!	1964	25.00
❏ LPM-2609 [M]	Our Men in San Francisco	1963	25.00
❏ LSP-2609 [S]	Our Men in San Francisco	1963	30.00
❏ ANL1-2336	Pure Gold	1977	10.00
❏ LPM-2445 [M]	Sing Out!	1962	25.00
❏ LSP-2445 [S]	Sing Out!	1962	30.00
❏ LPM-2889 [M]	The Best of the Limeliters	1964	18.00
❏ LSP-2889 [S]	The Best of the Limeliters	1964	25.00
❏ LPM-3385 [M]	The Limeliters Look at Love… In Depth	1965	18.00
❏ LSP-3385 [S]	The Limeliters Look at Love… In Depth	1965	25.00
❏ LSP-4100	The Original "Those Were the Days	1969	18.00
❏ LPM-2393 [M]	The Slightly Fabulous Limeliters	1961	25.00
❏ LSP-2393 [S]	The Slightly Fabulous Limeliters	1961	30.00
❏ LPM-2512 [M]	Through Children's Eyes	1962	25.00
❏ LSP-2512 [S]	Through Children's Eyes	1962	30.00
❏ LPM-2272 [M]	Tonight: In Person	1961	25.00
❏ LSP-2272 [S]	Tonight: In Person	1961	30.00

WEST KNOLL

❏ WK-1001	Alive! In Concert, Vol. 1	198?	12.00
❏ WK-1002	Alive! In Concert, Vol. 2	198?	12.00

LIMOUSINE

GSF

❏ 1002	Limousine	1972	25.00

LINCOLN, ABBEY

BARMABY

❏ KZ31037	Straight Ahead	1972	30.00

CANDID

❏ CD-8015 [M]	Straight Ahead	1960	80.00
❏ CS-9015 [S]	Straight Ahead	1960	100.00

ENJA

❏ 4060	Talking to the Sun	1983	25.00

FANTASY

❏ OJC-069	Abbey Is Blue	1983	15.00
❏ OJC-205	It's Magic	1985	15.00
❏ OJC-085	That's Him!	198?	15.00

INNER CITY

❏ IC-1117	Golden Lady	198?	30.00
❏ IC-6040	The People in Me	1978	25.00

JAZZ MAN

❏ 5043	Straight Ahead	198?	18.00
—Reissue of Barnaby 31037			

LIBERTY

❏ LRP-3025 [M]	Abbey Lincoln's Affair	1957	70.00

RIVERSIDE

❏ RLP 12-308 [M]	Abbey Is Blue	1959	60.00
❏ RLP-1153 [S]	Abbey Is Blue	1959	80.00
❏ 6088	Abbey Is Blue	197?	25.00
❏ RLP 12-277 [M]	It's Magic	1958	50.00
❏ RLP 12-251 [M]	That's Him!	1957	150.00
❏ RLP-1107 [S]	That's Him!	1958	40.00

LINCOLN, PHILAMORE

EPIC

❏ BN26497	North Wind Blew South	1970	30.00

LINCOLN STREET EXIT

MAINSTREAM

❏ S-6126	Drive It	1970	100.00

LIND, BOB

CAPITOL

❏ ST-780	Since There Were Circles	1971	18.00

VERVE FOLKWAYS

❏ FT-3005 [M]	The Elusive Bob Lind	1966	40.00
❏ FTS-3005 [S]	The Elusive Bob Lind	1966	40.00

WORLD PACIFIC

❏ WP-1841 [M]	Don't Be Concerned	1966	25.00
❏ ST-21841 [S]	Don't Be Concerned	1966	30.00
❏ WP-1851 [M]	Photographs of Feeling	1966	25.00
❏ ST-21851 [S]	Photographs of Feeling	1966	30.00

LINDBERG, JOHN

BLACK SAINT

❏ BSR-0062	Dimension 5	1982	15.00
❏ BSR-0072	Give and Take	1983	15.00
❏ BSR-0082	Trilogy of Works for Eleven Instrumentalists	1985	15.00

SOUND ASPECTS

❏ SAS-001	The East Side Suite	1985	15.00

LINDBERG, NILS

CAPITOL

❏ T10363 [M]	Trisection	196?	25.00
❏ ST10363 [S]	Trisection	196?	30.00

LINDE, DENNIS

INTREPID

❏ 4004 [M]	Linde Manor	1966	25.00
❏ 74004 [S]	Linde Manor	1966	30.00

Number	Title	Yr	NM

LINDEN, KATHY

FELSTED
❏ 7501 [M]	That Certain Boy	1959	60.00

LINDH, JAYSON

JAS
❏ JAS-4000	Second Carneval	1975	25.00

METRONOME
❏ DIX-3001	Cous-Cous	1973	30.00
❏ DIX-3000	Ramadan	1972	30.00
❏ DIX-3002	Sissel	1974	30.00

STORYVILLE
❏ 4132	Atlantis	1983	15.00

— As "Bjorn J-Son Lindh"

VANGUARD
❏ VSD-79434	A Day at the Surface	1979	15.00

— As "Bjorn J-Son Lindh"

LINDISFARNE

ATCO
❏ SD 38-108	Back and Fourth	1978	15.00

ELEKTRA
❏ EKS-75043 [B]	Dingly Dell	1972	20.00
❏ EKS-75021 [B]	Fog on the Tyne	1972	25.00
❏ 7E-1018 [B]	Happy Daze	1975	18.00
❏ EKS-74099 [B]	Nicely Out of Tune	1971	20.00
❏ EKS-75077	Roll On, Ruby	1974	18.00

LINDSAY, MARK

COLUMBIA
❏ CS9986	Arizona	1970	18.00

— Red "360 Sound" label

❏ CS9986	Arizona	1970	15.00

— Orange label

❏ C30111	Silver Bird	1970	15.00
❏ C30735	You've Got a Friend	1971	15.00

LINDSEY, GEORGE

CAPITOL
❏ ST-230	96 Miles to Bakersfield	1969	30.00
❏ ST2965	Goober Sings!	1968	30.00

LINDSEY, LAWANDA

CAPITOL
❏ ST-11306	This Is LaWanda Lindsey	1974	15.00

CHART
❏ CHS-1048	LaWanda Lindsey's Greatest Hits, Volume 1	1971	18.00
❏ CHS-1015	Swingin' and Singin' My Song	1969	18.00
❏ CHS-1035	We'll Sing in the Sunshine	1970	18.00

LINGLE, PAUL

EUPHONIC
❏ 1217	Dance of the Witch Hazels	198?	12.00
❏ 1220	The Legend of Lingle	198?	12.00

LINKLETTER, ART

COLUMBIA
❏ CL703 [M]	Howlers, Boners and Shockers	1956	40.00

LINN, RAY

DISCOVERY
❏ DS-823	Empty Suit Blues	1981	12.00

TREND
❏ 515	Chicago Jazz	1980	25.00

— Direct-to-disc recording

LINN COUNTY

MERCURY
❏ SR-61218	Fever Shot	1969	25.00
❏ SR-61181	Proud Flesh Soothsear	1968	25.00

PHILIPS
❏ PHS600326	Till the Break of Dawn	1970	18.00

LINTON, SHERWIN

BLACK GOLD
❏ 7116	I'm Not Johnny Cash	1972	30.00

BREAKER
❏ BR-4001	Christmas Memories	1987	15.00

RE-CAR
❏ 2108	Sherwin Linton and the Cotton Kings	1968	60.00

LIPPS, INC.

CASABLANCA
❏ NBLP7262	Designer Music	1981	12.00
❏ 811022-1	Four	1983	12.00
❏ NBLP7197	Mouth to Mouth	1980	12.00
❏ NBLP7242	Pucker Up	1980	12.00

LIPSCOMB, MANCE

ARHOOLIE
❏ 1033 [M]	Mance Lipscomb, Vol. 4	1966	40.00
❏ 1049	Mance Lipscomb, Vol. 5	1970	30.00
❏ 1069	Mance Lipscomb, Vol. 6	1975	30.00
❏ 1001 [M]	Texas Sharecropper and Songster	1960	50.00
❏ 1023 [M]	Texas Songster, Vol. 2	1963	40.00
❏ 1026 [M]	Texas Songster, Vol. 3	1965	40.00

REPRISE
❏ R-2012 [M]	Trouble in Mind	1961	100.00
❏ R9-2012 [S]	Trouble in Mind	1961	150.00
❏ RS-6404	Trouble in Mind	1969	30.00

LIPSTIQUE

TOM N JERRY
❏ TJ-4701	At the Discotheque	1978	25.00

LIPTON, PEGGY

ODE
❏ Z1244006 [B]	Peggy Lipton	1968	30.00

LIQUID SMOKE

AVCO EMBASSY
❏ AVE-33005	Liquid Smoke	1970	30.00

LISA LISA AND CULT JAM

COLUMBIA
❏ FC40135	Lisa Lisa and Cult Jam with Full Force	1985	10.00

— Second prefix

❏ BFC40135	Lisa Lisa and Cult Jam with Full Force	1985	15.00

— Original prefix

❏ FC40477	Spanish Fly	1987	10.00
❏ OC44378	Straight to the Sky	1989	12.00

LIST, EUGENE

MERCURY LIVING PRESENCE
❏ SR90290 [S]	Gershwin Favorites	196?	25.00

— Maroon label, no "Vendor: Mercury Record Corporation"

LIST, GARRETT

LOVELY
❏ VR-1201	Fire and Ice	198?	15.00

LISTEN (2)

INNER CITY
❏ IC-1055	Growing	1978	18.00
❏ IC-1025	Listen	1977	18.00

LISTENING

VANGUARD
❏ VSD-6504	Listening	1968	60.00

LISTON, MELBA

METROJAZZ
❏ E-1013 [M]	Melba Liston and Her Bones	1958	80.00
❏ SE-1013 [S]	Melba Liston and Her Bones	1958	60.00

LITE STORM, THE

BEVERLY HILLS
❏ 1135	Lite Storm Warning	1973	60.00

LITTER

EVA
❏ 12013	Rare Tracks	1983	18.00

HEXAGON
❏ 681	$100 Fine	1968	400.00

PROBE
❏ 4504	Emerge	1969	50.00

WARICK
❏ 671	Distortions	1967	500.00

LITTLE, BIG TINY

CORAL
❏ CRL57391 [M]	Christmas with Big Tiny Little	1961	18.00
❏ CRL757391 [S]	Christmas with Big Tiny Little	1961	25.00

LITTLE, BOOKER, AND BOOKER ERVIN

TCB
❏ 1003	Sounds of Inner City	197?	40.00

LITTLE, BOOKER

BAINBRIDGE
❏ BT-1041	Booker Little	1981	12.00

BARNABY
❏ BR-5019	Out Front	1977	18.00

BETHLEHEM
❏ BCP-6061 [M]	Booker Little and Friends	1962	300.00
❏ BCP-6034	Victory and Sorrow	197?	30.00

— Reissue of 6061, distributed by RCA Victor

CANDID
❏ CD-8027 [M]	Out Front	1961	120.00
❏ CS-9027 [S]	Out Front	1961	80.00

TIME
❏ 52011 [M]	Booker Little	1960	150.00
❏ S-2011 [S]	Booker Little	1960	200.00

UNITED ARTISTS
❏ UAL-4034 [M]	The Booker Little Four	1959	120.00
❏ UAS-5034 [S]	The Booker Little Four	1959	100.00

LITTLE, PEGGY

DOT
❏ DLP-25948	A Little Bit of Peggy	1969	18.00
❏ DLP-25982	More Than a Little	1971	18.00

LITTLE ANTHONY AND THE IMPERIALS

ACCORD
❏ SN-7216	Tears on My Pillow	1983	12.00

AVCO
❏ AV-11012	On a New Street	1973	25.00

DCP
❏ DCL-3808 [M]	Goin' Out of My Head	1965	30.00
❏ DCS-6808 [S]	Goin' Out of My Head	1965	30.00
❏ DCL-3801 [M]	I'm On the Outside Looking In	1964	30.00
❏ DCS-6801 [S]	I'm On the Outside Looking In	1964	30.00
❏ DCL-3809 [M]	The Best of Little Anthony and the Imperials	1965	25.00
❏ DCS-6809 [S]	The Best of Little Anthony and the Imperials	1965	30.00

END
❏ LP311 [M]	Shades of the 40's	1960	200.00
❏ LP303 [M]	We Are The Imperials Featuring Little Anthony	1959	250.00

FORUM
❏ F-9107 [M]	Little Anthony and the Imperials' Greatest Hits	196?	18.00
❏ FS-9107 [R]	Little Anthony and the Imperials' Greatest Hits	196?	15.00

LIBERTY
❏ LM-1017	Out of Sight, Out of Mind	1981	10.00

— Reissue of United Artists 1017

❏ LN-10133	The Best of Little Anthony and the Imperials	1981	10.00

— Budget-line reissue

PICKWICK
❏ SPC-3029	The Hits of Little Anthony and the Imperials	196?	15.00

RHINO
❏ R1-70919	The Best of Little Anthony and the Imperials	1989	15.00

ROULETTE
❏ SR-42007	Forever Yours	1968	18.00
❏ R-25294 [M]	Little Anthony and the Imperials' Greatest Hits	1965	30.00
❏ SR-25294 [R]	Little Anthony and the Imperials' Greatest Hits	1965	25.00

SONGBIRD
❏ 3245	Daylight	1980	12.00

SUNSET
❏ SUS-5287	Little Anthony and the Imperials	1970	18.00

UNITED ARTISTS
❏ UA-LA026-G	Legendary Masters Series	1972	30.00
❏ UAS6720	Out of Sight, Out of Mind	1969	25.00
❏ LM-1017	Out of Sight, Out of Mind	1980	12.00

— Reissue of United Artists 6720

❏ UA-LA255-G	The Very Best of Little Anthony and the Imperials	1974	12.00

VEEP
❏ VP13511 [M]	Goin' Out of My Head	1966	18.00
❏ VPS16511 [S]	Goin' Out of My Head	1966	25.00
❏ VP13510 [M]	I'm On the Outside Looking In	1966	18.00
❏ VPS16510 [S]	I'm On the Outside Looking In	1966	25.00
❏ VP13516 [M]	Movie Grabbers	1967	18.00
❏ VPS16516 [S]	Movie Grabbers	1967	25.00
❏ VP13513 [M]	Payin' Our Dues	1966	18.00
❏ VPS16513 [S]	Payin' Our Dues	1966	25.00
❏ VP13514 [M]	Reflections	1967	18.00
❏ VPS16514 [S]	Reflections	1967	25.00
❏ VPS16519	The Best of Little Anthony, Volume 2	1968	18.00
❏ VP13512 [M]	The Best of Little Anthony and the Imperials	1966	18.00
❏ VPS16512 [S]	The Best of Little Anthony and the Imperials	1966	25.00
❏ ST-90840 [S]	The Best of Little Anthony and the Imperials	1966	30.00

— Capitol Record Club edition

LITTLE BILL AND THE BLUENOTES

CAMELOT
❏ 102 [M]	The Fiesta Club Presents Little Bill and the Bluenotes	1960	400.00

Number	Title	Yr	NM

LITTLE BOY BLUES

FONTANA
☐ SRF-67578	In the Woodland of Weir	1968	30.00

LITTLE CAESAR AND THE ROMANS

DEL-FI
☐ DFLP-1218 [M]	Memories of Those Oldies But Goodies	1961	300.00

LITTLE EVA

DIMENSION
☐ DLP-6000 [M]	LLLLLoco-Motion	1962	150.00
—Without "Keep Your Hands Off My Baby"			
☐ DLP-6000 [M]	LLLLLoco-Motion	1962	200.00
—With "Keep Your Hands Off My Baby"			
☐ DLPS-6000 [R]	LLLLLoco-Motion	1962	150.00
—Without "Keep Your Hands Off My Baby"			
☐ DLPS-6000 [R]	LLLLLoco-Motion	1962	200.00
—With "Keep Your Hands Off My Baby"			

LITTLE FEAT

MOBILE FIDELITY
☐ 1-013	Waiting for Columbus	1979	80.00
—Audiophile vinyl			

NAUTILUS
☐ NR-24	Time Loves a Hero	198?	50.00
—Audiophile vinyl			

TPM/RHINO EXCLUSIVE
☐ 299	Little Feat	2008	25.00

WARNER BROS.
☐ BS2686	Dixie Chicken	1973	18.00
—Burbank" palm trees label			
☐ BS2686	Dixie Chicken	1979	10.00
—Tan or white label			
☐ HS3345	Down on the Farm	1979	12.00
☐ BS2748	Feats Don't Fail Me Now	1974	18.00
—Burbank" palm trees label			
☐ BS2748	Feats Don't Fail Me Now	1979	10.00
—Tan or white label			
☐ 2BSK3538	Hoy-Hoy!	1981	15.00
☐ PRO-A-984 [DJ]	Hoy-Hoy!	1981	25.00
—Single-album sampler of 2-LP set			
☐ 25750	Let It Roll	1988	12.00
☐ WS1890	Little Feat	1971	25.00
—Green "WB" label; with photo on back cover			
☐ WS1890	Little Feat	1971	18.00
—Green "WB" label; without photo on back cover			
☐ WS1890	Little Feat	1973	12.00
—Burbank" palm trees label			
☐ WS1890	Little Feat	1979	10.00
—Tan or white label			
☐ 26263	Representing the Mambo	1990	18.00
☐ BS2600	Sailin' Shoes	1972	18.00
—Green "WB" label			
☐ BS2600	Sailin' Shoes	1973	12.00
—Burbank" palm trees label			
☐ BS2600	Sailin' Shoes	1979	10.00
—Tan or white label			
☐ 307	Sailin' Shoes	2008	25.00
☐ BS2884	The Last Record Album	1975	18.00
—Burbank" palm trees label			
☐ BS2884	The Last Record Album	1979	10.00
—Tan or white label			
☐ BS3015	Time Loves a Hero	1977	15.00
—Burbank" palm trees label			
☐ BS3015	Time Loves a Hero	1979	10.00
—Tan or white label			
☐ 2WS3140	Waiting for Columbus	1978	18.00
—Burbank" palm trees label			
☐ 2WS3140	Waiting for Columbus	1979	12.00
—Tan or white label			

ZOO/CLASSIC
☐ 11097	Ain't Had Enough Fun	1995	25.00
—180-gram vinyl			
☐ 11097	Ain't Had Enough Fun	1995	25.00
—150-gram vinyl			

LITTLE GIRLS

FTM ENTERPRISES
☐ 0(no #) [EP]	Little Girls 1985	1985	100.00
—Promo-only three-song EP, with all songs on same side, on clear vinyl in clear plastic sleeve; also contains two black & white photos of the group and three pages of biographical notes and reviews; 100 pressed			

PVC
☐ 5904 [EP]	Thank Heaven!	1983	25.00

LITTLE JOE

BRUNSWICK
☐ BL754135	Little Joe (Sure Can Sing)	1968	25.00

LITTLE MILTON

CHECKER
☐ LP-3011 [B]	Grits Ain't Groceries	1969	30.00
☐ LP-3012	If Walls Could Talk	1970	30.00
☐ LP-3002 [M]	Little Milton Sings Big Blues	1966	50.00
☐ LP-2995 [M]	We're Gonna Make It	1965	100.00
—Black label			
☐ LP-2995 [M]	We're Gonna Make It	1966	70.00
—Blue label with red and black checkers			
☐ LP-2995 [M]	We're Gonna Make It	196?	30.00
—Blue, fading to white, label			

CHESS
☐ CH-9289	If Walls Could Talk	1989	12.00
—Reissue of Checker 3012			
☐ 204	Little Milton	1976	18.00
☐ CH-50013	Little Milton's Greatest Hits	1972	18.00
☐ CH-9265	Little Milton Sings Big Blues	1987	12.00
—Reissue of Checker 3002			
☐ CH-9252	We're Gonna Make It	1986	12.00
—Reissue of Checker 2995			

GLADES
☐ 7508	Friend of Mine	1976	15.00
☐ 7511	Me for You, You for Me	1977	15.00

MALACO
☐ 7435	Annie Mae's Café	198?	15.00
☐ 7448	Back to Back	198?	15.00
☐ 7427	I Will Survive	198?	15.00
☐ 7445	Movin' to the Country	198?	15.00
☐ 7419	Playin' for Keeps	198?	15.00
☐ 7453	Too Much Pain	198?	15.00

MCA
☐ 5414	Age Ain't Nothin' But a Number	1983	12.00

ROUNDER
☐ SS-35	The Sun Masters	198?	15.00

STAX
☐ 5514	Blues 'n' Soul	1974	25.00
☐ MPS-8518	Blues 'n' Soul	1981	12.00
—Reissue of 5514			
☐ MPS-8529	Grits Ain't Groceries	198?	12.00
—Despite the title, this is NOT a reissue of Checker 3011, but a later live recording			
☐ STS-3012	Waiting for Little Milton	1973	25.00
☐ 4117	Waiting for Little Milton	1978	15.00
—Reissue of 3012			
☐ MPS-8514	Walking the Back Streets	1981	12.00
☐ MPS-8550	What It Is	198?	12.00

LITTLE MISS CORNSHUCKS

CHESS
☐ LP-1453 [M]	The Loneliest Gal in Town	1961	200.00

LITTLE RICHARD

20TH FOX
☐ FXG-5010 [M]	Little Richard Sings Gospel	1959	100.00
☐ SGM-5010 [S]	Little Richard Sings Gospel	1959	150.00

ACCORD
☐ SN-7123	Tutti Frutti	1981	12.00

AUDIO ENCORES
☐ 1002	Little Richard	1980	30.00

BUDDAH
☐ BDS-7501	Little Richard	1969	30.00

CLEOPATRA
☐ 3427 [B]	Tutti Frutti - Greatest Hits		25.00

CORAL
☐ CRL57446 [M]	Coming Home	1963	40.00
☐ CRL757446 [S]	Coming Home	1963	50.00

CROWN
☐ CLP-5362 [M]	Little Richard Sings Freedom Songs	1963	25.00

CUSTOM
☐ 2061 [M]	Little Richard Sings Spirituals	196?	15.00

EPIC
☐ EG30428	Cast a Long Shadow	1971	25.00
☐ PE40389	Little Richard's Greatest Hits	1986	12.00
☐ PE40390	The Explosive Little Richard	1986	12.00

EXACT
☐ 206	The Best of Little Richard	1980	12.00

GNP CRESCENDO
☐ GNP-9033	The Big Hits	1974	15.00

GRT
☐ 2103	The Original Little Richard	1977	12.00

GUEST STAR
☐ GS-1429 [M]	Little Richard with Sister Rosetta Tharpe	196?	15.00
☐ GSS-1429 [R]	Little Richard with Sister Rosetta Tharpe	196?	15.00

KAMA SUTRA
☐ KSBS-2023	Little Richard	1970	30.00

MERCURY
☐ MG-20656 [M]	It's Real	1961	50.00
☐ SR-60656 [S]	It's Real	1961	60.00

MODERN
☐ 100 [M]	His Greatest Hits/Recorded Live	1966	25.00
☐ 1000 [S]	His Greatest Hits/Recorded Live	1966	30.00

☐ 103 [M]	The Explosive Little Richard	1966	25.00
☐ 1003 [S]	The Explosive Little Richard	1966	30.00

OKEH
☐ OKM12121 [M]	Little Richard's Greatest Hits	1967	30.00
☐ OKS14121 [S]	Little Richard's Greatest Hits	1967	25.00
☐ OKS14117 [S]	The Explosive Little Richard	1967	25.00
☐ OKM12117 [M]	The Explosive Little Richard	1967	30.00

PICKWICK
☐ SPC-3258	King of the Gospel Singers	197?	12.00

RCA CAMDEN
☐ CAS-2430(e)	Every Hour with Little Richard	1970	15.00
☐ CAL-420 [M]	Little Richard	1956	200.00

REPRISE
☐ RS6462	King of Rock and Roll	1972	25.00
☐ RS6406	The Rill Thing	1971	25.00
☐ MS2107	The Second Coming	1973	25.00

RHINO
☐ R1-70236	Shut Up! A Collection of Rare Tracks, 1951-1964	1988	15.00

SCEPTER CITATION
☐ CTN-18020	The Best of Little Richard	1972	15.00

SPECIALTY
☐ 100 [M]	Here's Little Richard	1957	700.00
☐ SP-2100 [M]	Here's Little Richard	1957	200.00
—Thick vinyl			
☐ SP-2103 [M]	Little Richard	1958	150.00
—Front cover photo occupies the entire cover			
☐ SP-2103 [M]	Little Richard	196?	100.00
—Front cover photo partially obscured by a black triangle at upper right; thick vinyl			
☐ SP-2103 [M]	Little Richard	197?	25.00
—Reissue with thinner vinyl			
☐ SP-2111 [M]	Little Richard -- His Biggest Hits	1963	50.00
—Thick vinyl			
☐ SP-2111 [M]	Little Richard -- His Biggest Hits	197?	25.00
—Reissue with thinner vinyl			
☐ SP-2113	Little Richard's Grooviest 17 Original Hits	1968	30.00
—Thick vinyl			
☐ SP-2104 [M]	The Fabulous Little Richard	1958	150.00
—Thick vinyl			
☐ SP-2104 [M]	The Fabulous Little Richard	197?	25.00
—Reissue with thinner vinyl			
☐ SP-8508	The Specialty Sessions	1989	40.00
☐ SP-2136	Well Alright!	1970	25.00

SPIN-O-RAMA
☐ 119 [M]	Clap Your Hands	196?	15.00

TRIP
☐ 8013	Greatest Hits	1972	15.00

UNITED
☐ US-7775	His Greatest Hits/Recorded Live	197?	12.00
☐ US-7777	The Wild and Frantic Little Richard	197?	12.00

UNITED ARTISTS
☐ UA-LA497-E	The Very Best of Little Richard	1975	12.00

UPFRONT
☐ UPF-197	Little Richard Sings Gospel	197?	12.00
☐ UPF-123	The Best of Little Richard	197?	12.00

VEE JAY
☐ LP-1107 [M]	Little Richard Is Back!	1964	50.00
☐ LPS-1107 [S]	Little Richard Is Back!	1964	70.00
☐ VJLP-1107	Little Richard's Back	198?	12.00
—Reissue with thin vinyl			
☐ LP-1124 [M]	Little Richard's Greatest Hits	1965	30.00
☐ LPS-1124 [S]	Little Richard's Greatest Hits	1965	40.00
☐ VJLP-1124	Little Richard's Greatest Hits	198?	12.00
—Reissue with thin vinyl			
☐ DY-7304	Talkin' 'Bout Soul	198?	15.00

VEE JAY/CHAMELEON
☐ D1-74797	Rip It Up	1989	15.00

WARNER BROS.
☐ 25529	Lifetime Friend	1986	15.00

WING
☐ MGW-12288 [M]	King of the Gospel Singers	1964	18.00
☐ SRW-16288 [S]	King of the Gospel Singers	1964	25.00

LITTLE RIVER BAND

CAPITOL
☐ SN-16072	After Hours	1979	12.00
—First U.S. issue of their second Australian LP			
☐ SWBK-12061	Backstage Pass	1980	12.00
☐ SN-16141	Beginnings	1980	12.00
☐ SN-16142	Beginnings, Vol. 2	1980	12.00
☐ SOO-11954	First Under the Wire	1979	10.00
☐ ST-12247	Greatest Hits	1982	10.00
☐ ST-12480	No Reins	1986	10.00
☐ SJ-12365	Playing to Win	1985	10.00
—As "LRB"			
☐ ST-12273	The Net	1983	10.00
☐ ST-12163	Time Exposure	1981	10.00

HARVEST
☐ SW-11645 [B]	Diamantina Cocktail	1977	12.00

Number	Title	Yr	NM
❑ ST-11512	Little River Band	1976	12.00
❑ SW-11783	Sleeper Catcher	1978	12.00
MCA			
❑ 6269	Get Lucky	1990	15.00
❑ 42193	Monsoon	1989	12.00
MOBILE FIDELITY			
❑ 1-036	First Under the Wire	1980	30.00
—Audiophile vinyl			
LITTLE SISTERS, THE			
MGM			
❑ E-4116 [M]	The Joys of Love	1963	30.00
❑ SE-4116 [S]	The Joys of Love	1963	30.00
LITTLE SONNY			
ENTERPRISE			
❑ ENS-1018	Black and Blue	1971	40.00
❑ ENS-1036	Hard Goin' Up	1973	40.00
❑ ENS-1005	New King of the Blues Harmonica	1970	40.00
LITTLE WALTER			
CHECKER			
❑ LP-1428 [M]	The Best of Little Walter	1957	500.00
—Black or maroon label			
❑ LP-3004 [M]	The Best of Little Walter	1967	50.00
—Reissue of 1428			
CHESS			
❑ 2CH-60014	Boss Blues Harmonica	1972	25.00
❑ CHV-416 [M]	Confessin' the Blues	1974	15.00
❑ LP-1535 [M]	Hate to See You Go	1969	30.00
❑ 2ACMB-202	Little Walter	1976	25.00
—Reissue of 60014			
LIVE			
RADIOACTIVE			
❑ RAR2-11590	Secret Samadhi	1997	18.00
—White vinyl; includes poster			
❑ RAR2-11590	Secret Samadhi	1997	18.00
—Clear vinyl; includes poster			
❑ RAR-10997	Throwing Copper	1994	45.00
—Clear vinyl			
❑ RAR-10997	Throwing Copper	1994	25.00
—Black vinyl			
LIVELY ONES, THE			
DEL-FI			
❑ DFLP-1237 [M]	Surf City	1963	40.00
❑ DFST-1237 [S]	Surf City	1963	50.00
❑ DLF1237	Surf City	1997	15.00
❑ DFLP-1231 [M]	Surf Drums	1963	50.00
❑ DFST-1231 [S]	Surf Drums	1963	70.00
❑ DLF1231	Surf Drums	1997	15.00
❑ DFLP-1240 [M]	Surfin' South of the Border	1964	40.00
❑ DFST-1240 [S]	Surfin' South of the Border	1964	50.00
❑ DFLP-1226 [M]	Surf Rider	1963	100.00
❑ DFST-1226 [S]	Surf Rider	1963	150.00
MGM			
❑ E-4449 [M]	Bugalu Party	1967	25.00
❑ SE-4449 [S]	Bugalu Party	1967	30.00
LIVERPOOL BEATS, THE			
RONDO			
❑ 2026 [M]	The New Merseyside Sound	1964	30.00
LIVERPOOL FIVE, THE			
RCA VICTOR			
❑ LPM-3682 [M]	Out of Sight	1967	30.00
❑ LSP-3682 [S]	Out of Sight	1967	30.00
❑ LPM-3583 [M]	The Liverpool Five Arrive	1966	30.00
❑ LSP-3583 [S]	The Liverpool Five Arrive	1966	30.00
LIVERPOOL SCENE, THE			
EPIC			
❑ LN24336 [M]	The Incredible New Liverpool Scene	1967	35.00
❑ BN26336 [S]	The Incredible New Liverpool Scene	1967	30.00
LIVERPOOLS, THE			
WYNCOTE			
❑ W-9001 [M]	Beatle Mania! In the U.S.A.	1964	30.00
❑ SW-9001 [S]	Beatle Mania! In the U.S.A.	1964	40.00
❑ W-9061 [M]	The Hit Sounds from England	1964	18.00
❑ SW-9061 [S]	The Hit Sounds from England	1964	40.00
LIVIN' BLUES			
DWARF			
❑ 2003	Dutch Treat	1971	30.00
LIVING COLOUR			
EPIC			
❑ E46202	Time's Up	1990	12.00
—Yellow vinyl			

Number	Title	Yr	NM
LIVING JAZZ			
RCA CAMDEN			
❑ CAL-985 [M]	A Lover's Concerto	1966	12.00
❑ CAS-985 [S]	A Lover's Concerto	1966	15.00
❑ CAL-878 [M]	Dear Heart and Other Favorites	1965	12.00
❑ CAS-878 [S]	Dear Heart and Other Favorites	1965	15.00
❑ CAS-2298	Fool on the Hill	1969	12.00
❑ CAS-2436	Hot Butter and Soul	1970	12.00
❑ ACL1-0202	Manha de Carnival	1973	12.00
❑ CAL-2196 [M]	Ode to Young Lovers	1968	15.00
❑ CAS-2196 [S]	Ode to Young Lovers	1968	12.00
❑ CAL-914 [M]	Quiet Nights	1965	12.00
❑ CAS-914 [S]	Quiet Nights	1965	15.00
❑ CAL-848 [M]	The Girl from Ipanema and Other Hits	1964	12.00
❑ CAS-848 [S]	The Girl from Ipanema and Other Hits	1964	15.00
❑ CAL-2135 [M]	The Soul of Brazil	1967	15.00
❑ CAS-2135 [S]	The Soul of Brazil	1967	12.00
RCA VICTOR			
❑ APL1-2386	Hello Young Lovers	1977	12.00
LLOYD, CHARLES			
4 MEN WITH BEARDS			
❑ 4M-119	Love-In	2003	18.00
—180-gram audiophile reissue			
A&M			
❑ SP-3046	Geeta	1973	25.00
❑ SP-3044	Waves	1973	18.00
ATLANTIC			
❑ SD1500	Charles Lloyd in Europe	1969	25.00
❑ SD1571	Charles Lloyd in the Soviet Union	1971	25.00
❑ 1459 [M]	Dream Weaver	1966	18.00
❑ SD1459 [S]	Dream Weaver	1966	25.00
—Blue and green label			
❑ SD1459 [S]	Dream Weaver	1969	15.00
—Red and green label, white stripe through center hole			
❑ SD1586	Flowering of the Original Charles Lloyd Quintet	1972	25.00
❑ 1473 [M]	Forest Flower	1967	30.00
❑ SD1473 [S]	Forest Flower	1967	30.00
❑ SD1493	Journey Within	1968	30.00
❑ 1481 [M]	Love-In	1967	40.00
❑ SD1481 [S]	Love-In	1967	40.00
❑ SD1519	Soundtrack	1970	25.00
❑ SD1556	The Best of Charles Lloyd	1970	18.00
BLUE NOTE			
❑ BT-85104	A Night in Copenhagen	1985	18.00
COLUMBIA			
❑ CL2267 [M]	Discovery!	1965	30.00
❑ CS9067 [S]	Discovery!	1965	30.00
❑ CS9609 [M]	Nirvana	1968	50.00
—White label promo; "Special Mono Radio Station Copy" sticker on stereo cover			
❑ CS9609 [S]	Nirvana	1968	30.00
❑ CL2412 [M]	Of Course, Of Course	1966	30.00
❑ CS9212 [S]	Of Course, Of Course	1966	30.00
❑ PC36981 [S]	Of Course, Of Course	1980	12.00
—Reissue of CS 9212			
DESTINY			
❑ 10003	Autumn in New York Volume 1	1979	18.00
ECM			
❑ 1398	Fish Out of Water	1990	25.00
—Made in Germany			
ELEKTRA/MUSICIAN			
❑ 60220	Montreux '82	1983	15.00
KAPP			
❑ KS-3634	Moon Man	1971	18.00
❑ KS-3647	Warm Waters	1971	30.00
PACIFIC ARTS			
❑ 7-139	Big Sur Tapestry	1979	15.00
❑ 7-123	Weavings	1978	15.00
LLOYD, DAVID			
EPIC			
❑ LN24151 [M]	Confidential (Sounds for a Secret Agent)	1965	25.00
❑ BN26151 [S]	Confidential (Sounds for a Secret Agent)	1965	30.00
LLOYD, HAROLD, JR.			
CORAL			
❑ CRL57471 [M]	The Intimate Style of Harold Lloyd, Jr.	1963	18.00
❑ CRL757471 [S]	The Intimate Style of Harold Lloyd, Jr.	1963	25.00
LOADING ZONE, THE			
RCA VICTOR			
❑ LSP-3959	The Loading Zone	1968	30.00
UMBRELLA			
❑ US-101	One for All	1967	80.00

Number	Title	Yr	NM
LOBO			
BIG TREE			
❑ BT89505	A Cowboy Afraid of Horses	1975	15.00
❑ 2101	Calumet	1973	18.00
❑ 2003	Introducing Lobo	1971	18.00
❑ 2100	Introducing Lobo	1973	15.00
—Reissue of 2003 with new cover			
❑ BT89501	Just a Singer	1974	15.00
❑ 2013	Of a Simple Man	1972	18.00
❑ BT89513	The Best of Lobo	1976	15.00
MCA			
❑ 3194	Lobo	1979	12.00
LOBO (2)			
A&M			
❑ SP-3035	Sergio Mendes Presents Lobo	1970	30.00
LOCASCIO, JOE			
CMG			
❑ CML-8002	Gliders	1988	12.00
❑ CML-8015	Marionette	1989	15.00
LOCKE, JOE			
CADENCE JAZZ			
❑ CJR-1034	Scenario	1988	12.00
LOCKLIN, HANK			
DESIGN			
❑ DLP-603 [M]	Hank Locklin	196?	18.00
HILLTOP			
❑ JM-6003 [M]	Born to Ramble	196?	18.00
❑ JS-6003 [R]	Born to Ramble	196?	15.00
❑ JM-6041 [M]	Hank Locklin Sings Hank Locklin	196?	18.00
❑ JS-6041 [R]	Hank Locklin Sings Hank Locklin	196?	15.00
❑ JM-6083	Queen of Hearts	196?	18.00
KING			
❑ 738 [M]	Encores	1961	60.00
❑ 672 [M]	The Best of Hank Locklin	1961	60.00
METRO			
❑ M541 [M]	Down Texas Way	196?	18.00
❑ MS541 [R]	Down Texas Way	196?	15.00
RCA CAMDEN			
❑ CAL-705 [M]	Hank Locklin	1962	18.00
❑ CAL-912 [M]	My Kind of Country Music	196?	18.00
❑ CAS-912 [R]	My Kind of Country Music	196?	15.00
RCA VICTOR			
❑ LPM-2597 [M]	A Tribute to Roy Acuff, the King of Country Music	1962	30.00
❑ LSP-2597 [S]	A Tribute to Roy Acuff, the King of Country Music	1962	30.00
❑ LPM-3946 [M]	Country Hall of Fame	1968	100.00
❑ LSP-3946 [S]	Country Hall of Fame	1968	25.00
❑ LPM-1673 [M]	Foreign Love	1958	60.00
❑ LPM-3391 [M]	Hank Locklin Sings Eddy Arnold	1965	25.00
❑ LSP-3391 [S]	Hank Locklin Sings Eddy Arnold	1965	30.00
❑ LPM-2997 [M]	Hank Locklin Sings Hank Williams	1964	25.00
❑ LSP-2997 [S]	Hank Locklin Sings Hank Williams	1964	30.00
❑ LPM-2464 [M]	Happy Journey	1962	30.00
❑ LSP-2464 [S]	Happy Journey	1962	30.00
❑ LPM-2801 [M]	Irish Songs, Country Style	1964	25.00
❑ LSP-2801 [S]	Irish Songs, Country Style	1964	30.00
❑ LSP-4191	Lookin' Back	1969	18.00
❑ LSP-4030	My Love Song for You	1968	25.00
❑ LPM-3841 [M]	Nashville Women	1967	30.00
❑ LSP-3841 [S]	Nashville Women	1967	25.00
❑ LPM-3465 [M]	Once Over Lightly	1965	25.00
❑ LSP-3465 [S]	Once Over Lightly	1965	30.00
❑ LPM-2291 [M]	Please Help Me, I'm Falling	1960	30.00
❑ LSP-2291 [S]	Please Help Me, I'm Falling	1960	40.00
❑ LPM-3770 [M]	Send Me the Pillow You Dream On	1967	30.00
❑ LSP-3770 [S]	Send Me the Pillow You Dream On	1967	25.00
❑ LSP-4113	Softly	1969	25.00
❑ LPM-3559 [M]	The Best of Hank Locklin	1966	25.00
❑ LSP-3559 [S]	The Best of Hank Locklin	1966	30.00
❑ LPM-3588 [M]	The Girls Get Prettier	1966	25.00
❑ LSP-3588 [S]	The Girls Get Prettier	1966	30.00
❑ LPM-3656 [M]	The Gloryland Way	1966	25.00
❑ LSP-3656 [S]	The Gloryland Way	1966	30.00
❑ LPM-2680 [M]	The Ways of Life	1963	30.00
❑ LSP-2680 [S]	The Ways of Life	1963	30.00
SEARS			
❑ SPS-104	Send Me the Pillow You Dream On	196?	30.00
STEREO-SPECTRUM			
❑ SDLP-603 [R]	Hank Locklin	196?	15.00
—Stereo" version of Design DLP-603			
WRANGLER			
❑ 1004 [M]	Hank Locklin	1962	30.00
LOCKWOOD, DIDIER			
GRAMAVISION			
❑ 18-8412	Didier Lockwood Group	1984	12.00
❑ 18-8504	Out of the Blue	1985	12.00

Number	Title	Yr	NM
INNER CITY			
❏ IC-1092	Surya	1982	15.00
PAUSA			
❏ 7125	Fasten Seat Belts	1981	12.00
❏ 7094	Live in Montreux	1981	12.00
❏ 7046	New World	1979	12.00
LOCKWOOD, ROBERT, JR.			
TRIX			
❏ 3307	Contrasts	197?	25.00
LOCO, JOE			
FANTASY			
❏ 3277 [M]	Cha-Cha-Cha	1958	30.00
— Red vinyl			
❏ 3277 [M]	Cha-Cha-Cha	1958	25.00
— Black vinyl, red label, non-flexible vinyl			
❏ 3277 [M]	Cha-Cha-Cha	196?	18.00
— Black vinyl, red label, flexible vinyl			
❏ 8022 [S]	Cha-Cha-Cha	1962	30.00
— Blue vinyl			
❏ 8022 [S]	Cha-Cha-Cha	1962	25.00
— Black vinyl, blue label, non-flexible vinyl			
❏ 8022 [S]	Cha-Cha-Cha	196?	18.00
— Black vinyl, blue label, flexible vinyl			
❏ 3280 [M]	Going Loco	1958	30.00
— Red vinyl			
❏ 3280 [M]	Going Loco	1958	25.00
— Black vinyl, red label, non-flexible vinyl			
❏ 3280 [M]	Going Loco	196?	18.00
— Black vinyl, red label, flexible vinyl			
❏ 8042 [S]	Going Loco	1962	30.00
— Blue vinyl			
❏ 8042 [S]	Going Loco	1962	25.00
— Black vinyl, blue label, non-flexible vinyl			
❏ 8042 [S]	Going Loco	196?	18.00
— Black vinyl, blue label, flexible vinyl			
❏ 3215 [M]	Invitation to the Mambo	1956	30.00
— Red vinyl			
❏ 3215 [M]	Invitation to the Mambo	1956	25.00
— Black vinyl, red label, non-flexible vinyl			
❏ 3215 [M]	Invitation to the Mambo	196?	18.00
— Black vinyl, red label, flexible vinyl			
❏ 3294 [M]	Latin Jewels	1959	30.00
— Red vinyl			
❏ 3294 [M]	Latin Jewels	1959	25.00
— Black vinyl, red label, non-flexible vinyl			
❏ 3294 [M]	Latin Jewels	196?	18.00
— Black vinyl, red label, flexible vinyl			
❏ 8041 [S]	Latin Jewels	1962	30.00
— Blue vinyl			
❏ 8041 [S]	Latin Jewels	1962	25.00
— Black vinyl, blue label, non-flexible vinyl			
❏ 8041 [S]	Latin Jewels	196?	18.00
— Black vinyl, blue label, flexible vinyl			
❏ 3285 [M]	Ole, Ole, Ole	1959	30.00
— Red vinyl			
❏ 3285 [M]	Ole, Ole, Ole	1959	25.00
— Black vinyl, red label, non-flexible vinyl			
❏ 3285 [M]	Ole, Ole, Ole	196?	18.00
— Black vinyl, red label, flexible vinyl			
❏ 8028 [S]	Ole, Ole, Ole	1962	30.00
— Blue vinyl			
❏ 8028 [S]	Ole, Ole, Ole	1962	25.00
— Black vinyl, blue label, non-flexible vinyl			
❏ 8028 [S]	Ole, Ole, Ole	196?	18.00
— Black vinyl, blue label, flexible vinyl			
❏ 3321 [M]	Pachanga with Joe Loco	1961	30.00
— Red vinyl			
❏ 3321 [M]	Pachanga with Joe Loco	1961	25.00
— Black vinyl, red label, non-flexible vinyl			
❏ 3321 [M]	Pachanga with Joe Loco	196?	18.00
— Black vinyl, red label, flexible vinyl			
❏ 8064 [S]	Pachanga with Joe Loco	1962	30.00
— Blue vinyl			
❏ 8064 [S]	Pachanga with Joe Loco	1962	25.00
— Black vinyl, blue label, non-flexible vinyl			
❏ 8064 [S]	Pachanga with Joe Loco	196?	18.00
— Black vinyl, blue label, flexible vinyl			
❏ 3303 [M]	The Best of Joe Loco	1960	30.00
— Red vinyl			
❏ 3303 [M]	The Best of Joe Loco	1960	25.00
— Black vinyl, red label, non-flexible vinyl			
❏ 3303 [M]	The Best of Joe Loco	196?	18.00
— Black vinyl, red label, flexible vinyl			
❏ 8048 [S]	The Best of Joe Loco	1962	30.00
— Blue vinyl			
❏ 8048 [S]	The Best of Joe Loco	1962	25.00
— Black vinyl, blue label, non-flexible vinyl			
❏ 8048 [S]	The Best of Joe Loco	196?	18.00
— Black vinyl, blue label, flexible vinyl			
IMPERIAL			
❏ LP-12019 [S]	Happy Go Loco	1959	30.00
❏ LP-9073 [M]	Happy Go Loco	1959	25.00
❏ LP-12014 [S]	Let's Go Loco	1959	30.00
❏ LP-9070 [M]	Let's Go Loco	1959	25.00
❏ LP-9166 [M]	Pachanga Twist	1962	25.00
❏ LP-12079 [S]	Pachanga Twist	1962	30.00

Number	Title	Yr	NM
TICO			
❏ LP-132 [10]	Instrumental Mambos (Vol. 7)	1955	40.00
❏ LP-1008 [M]	Make Mine Mambo	1955	30.00
❏ LP-123 [10]	Mambo Dance Favorites, Vol. 5	195?	40.00
❏ LP-1012 [M]	Mambo Fantasy	1956	30.00
❏ LP-1006 [M]	Mambo Moods	1955	30.00
❏ LP-109 [10]	Mambos, Vol. 1	195?	40.00
❏ LP-111 [10]	Mambos, Vol. 2	195?	40.00
❏ LP-121 [10]	Mambos, Vol. 3	195?	40.00
❏ LP-122 [10]	Mambos, Vol. 4	195?	40.00
❏ LP-129 [10]	Mambos U.S.A.	1954	40.00
❏ LP-1013 [M]	Viva Mambo!	1956	30.00
LODGE, JOHN			
LONDON			
❏ PS683	Natural Avenue	1977	15.00
LODI			
MOWEST			
❏ MW101L [B]	Happiness	1972	30.00
LOEB, LISA, AND NINE STORIES			
GEFFEN			
❏ GEF24734	Tails	1996	15.00
— CD and cassette released in 1995			
LOFGREN, NILS			
A&M			
❏ SP-8362 [DJ]	Authorized Bootleg	1976	45.00
❏ SP-4573	Cry Tough	1976	12.00
❏ SP-3145	Cry Tough	198?	10.00
— Reissue of 4573			
❏ SP-4628	I Came to Dance	1977	12.00
❏ SP-3707	Night After Night	1977	15.00
❏ SP-6509	Night After Night	198?	12.00
— Reissue of 3707			
❏ SP-4756	Nils	1979	12.00
❏ SP-4509	Nils Lofgren	1975	12.00
❏ SP-3201	The Best	1982	12.00
BACKSTREET			
❏ 5251	Night Fades Away	1981	12.00
❏ 5421	Wonderland	1983	12.00
COLUMBIA			
❏ BFC39982	Flip	1985	12.00
LOFTON, CLARENCE			
RIVERSIDE			
❏ RLP-1037 [10]	Honky Tonk and Boogie-Woogie Piano	1954	80.00
LOFTON, TRICKY, AND CARMELL JONES			
PACIFIC JAZZ			
❏ PJ-49 [M]	Brass Bag	1962	40.00
❏ ST-49 [S]	Brass Bag	1962	50.00
LOGGINS, DAVE			
EPIC			
❏ KE32833	Apprentice (In a Musical Workshop)	1974	12.00
❏ PE33946	Country Suite	1975	12.00
❏ JE35792	David Loggins	1979	12.00
❏ PE34713	One Way	1977	12.00
VANGUARD			
❏ VSD-6580	Personal Belongings	1972	18.00
LOGGINS, KENNY			
COLUMBIA			
❏ OC40535	Back to Avalon	1988	12.00
❏ PC34655	Celebrate Me Home	1977	12.00
— Originals have no bar code			
❏ PC34655	Celebrate Me Home	1979	10.00
— Reissues have bar code			
❏ AS946 [DJ]	For Radio Only	1980	18.00
— Promo-only four-song sampler from "Kenny Loggins Alive"			
❏ TC38127	High Adventure	1982	12.00
❏ JC36172	Keep the Fire	1979	12.00
❏ PC36172	Keep the Fire	198?	10.00
— Budget-line reissue			
❏ C2X36738	Kenny Loggins Alive	1980	15.00
❏ AS569 [DJ]	Kenny Loggins Live	1980	18.00
— One-sided promo with three otherwise unavailable live recordings			
❏ HC45387	Nightwatch	198?	70.00
— Half-speed mastered edition			
❏ JC35387	Nightwatch	1978	12.00
— Originals have no bar code			
❏ PC35387	Nightwatch	198?	10.00
— Reissue with new prefix			
❏ FC39174	Vox Humana	1985	12.00
LOGGINS AND MESSINA			
COLUMBIA			
❏ JG34167	Finale	1977	15.00
❏ KC32540	Full Sail	1973	12.00
❏ CQ32540 [Q]	Full Sail	1973	30.00
❏ PC32540	Full Sail	197?	10.00

Number	Title	Yr	NM
— Reissue with new prefix			
❏ C31044	Kenny Loggins with Jim Messina Sittin' In	1972	12.00
❏ PC31044	Kenny Loggins with Jim Messina Sittin' In	197?	10.00
— Reissue with new prefix			
❏ KC31748	Loggins and Messina	1972	12.00
❏ CQ31748 [Q]	Loggins and Messina	1973	30.00
❏ PC31748	Loggins and Messina	197?	10.00
— Reissue with new prefix			
❏ PC33175	Mother Lode	1974	12.00
— Original with no bar code			
❏ PC33175	Mother Lode	198?	10.00
— With bar code			
❏ PC33578	Native Sons	1976	12.00
— Original with no bar code			
❏ PCQ33578 [Q]	Native Sons	1976	30.00
❏ PC33578	Native Sons	198?	10.00
— With bar code			
❏ PG32848	On Stage	1974	15.00
— Original with no bar code			
❏ PG32848	On Stage	198?	12.00
— With bar code			
❏ PC33810	So Fine	1975	12.00
— Original with no bar code			
❏ PC33810	So Fine	198?	10.00
— With bar code			
❏ PC34388	The Best of Friends	1976	12.00
— Original with no bar code			
❏ HC44388	The Best of Friends	1982	50.00
— Half-speed mastered edition			
❏ PC34388	The Best of Friends	198?	10.00
— With bar code			
DIRECT DISC			
❏ SD16606	Full Sail	198?	30.00
— Audiophile vinyl			
EPIC			
❏ PC34388	The Best of Friends	1976	25.00
— Mispressing with wrong label			
LOGSDON, JIMMIE			
KING			
❏ 843 [M]	Howdy Neighbors	1963	60.00
LOLITA			
KAPP			
❏ KL-1219 [M]	Sailor	1961	30.00
❏ KS-3219 [S]	Sailor	1961	30.00
❏ KL-1229 [M]	Songs You Will Never Forget	1961	30.00
❏ KS-3229 [S]	Songs You Will Never Forget	1961	30.00
LOLLIPOP SHOPPE, THE			
UNI			
❏ 73019	The Lollipop Shoppe	1968	80.00
LOLLIPOP SINGERS, THE			
PETER PAN			
❏ 8112	The Candy Man Can	197?	18.00
LOMAX, JACKIE			
APPLE			
❏ ST-3354	Is This What You Want?	1969	25.00
CAPITOL			
❏ ST-11668	Did You Ever	1977	12.00
❏ ST-11558	Livin' for Lovin'	1976	12.00
WARNER BROS.			
❏ PRO520 [DJ]	An Interview with Jackie Lomax	1972	30.00
❏ WS1914	Home Is In My Head	1971	15.00
❏ BS2591	Three	1972	15.00
LOMBARDO, GUY			
CAPITOL			
❏ T916 [M]	A Decade on Broadway 1935-45	1958	25.00
— Turquoise label			
❏ T916 [M]	A Decade on Broadway 1935-45	1958	18.00
— Black colorband label, logo at left			
❏ T916 [M]	A Decade on Broadway 1935-45	1962	15.00
— Black colorband label, logo at top			
❏ DT916 [R]	A Decade on Broadway 1935-45	196?	12.00
— Black colorband label, logo at top			
❏ T788 [M]	A Decade on Broadway 1946-56	1956	25.00
— Turquoise label			
❏ T788 [M]	A Decade on Broadway 1946-56	1958	18.00
— Black colorband label, logo at left			
❏ T738 [M]	A Decade on Broadway 1946-56	1962	15.00
— Black colorband label, logo at left			
❏ DT788 [R]	A Decade on Broadway 1946-56	196?	12.00
— Black colorband label, logo at top			
❏ T2481 [M]	A Wonderful Year	1966	15.00

Number	Title	Yr	NM
❑ ST2481 [S]	A Wonderful Year	1966	18.00
❑ T1019 [M]	Berlin by Lombardo	1958	25.00
— Turquoise or gray label			
❑ ST1019 [S]	Berlin by Lombardo	1959	30.00
— Black colorband label, logo at left			
❑ T1019 [M]	Berlin by Lombardo	1959	18.00
— Black colorband label, logo at left			
❑ T1019 [M]	Berlin by Lombardo	1962	12.00
— Black colorband label, logo at top			
❑ ST1019 [S]	Berlin by Lombardo	1962	15.00
— Black colorband label, logo at top			
❑ T1121 [M]	Dancing Room Only	1959	18.00
— Black colorband label, logo at left			
❑ ST1121 [S]	Dancing Room Only	1959	25.00
— Black colorband label, logo at left			
❑ ST1121 [S]	Dancing Room Only	1962	15.00
— Black colorband label, logo at top			
❑ T1121 [M]	Dancing Room Only	1962	12.00
— Black colorband label, logo at top			
❑ SN-16192	Dancing Room Only	198?	10.00
— Budget-line reissue			
❑ T1593 [M]	Drifting and Dreaming	1961	18.00
— Black colorband label, logo at left			
❑ ST1593 [S]	Drifting and Dreaming	1961	25.00
— Black colorband label, logo at left			
❑ ST1593 [S]	Drifting and Dreaming	1962	15.00
— Black colorband label, logo at top			
❑ T1593 [M]	Drifting and Dreaming	1962	12.00
— Black colorband label, logo at top			
❑ SM-1593	Drifting and Dreaming	1976	10.00
— Reissue with new prefix			
❑ STCL-578	Guy Lombardo	1970	30.00
❑ T2350 [M]	Guy Lombardo and His Royal Canadians Play Songs of Carmen Lombardo	1965	15.00
❑ DT2350 [R]	Guy Lombardo and His Royal Canadians Play Songs of Carmen Lombardo	1965	12.00
❑ ST1393 [S]	Guy Lombardo at Harrah's Club	1960	25.00
❑ T1393 [M]	Guy Lombardo at Harrah's Club	1960	18.00
❑ T2298 [M]	Guy Lombardo Presents Kenny Gardner	1965	15.00
❑ ST2298 [S]	Guy Lombardo Presents Kenny Gardner	1965	18.00
❑ T2559 [M]	Guy Lombardo's Broadway	1966	15.00
❑ ST2559 [S]	Guy Lombardo's Broadway	1966	18.00
❑ ST-340	Is That All There Is?	1969	12.00
❑ SM-340	Is That All There Is?	1976	10.00
— Reissue with new prefix			
❑ T892 [M]	Lively Guy	1957	25.00
— Turquoise label			
❑ T892 [M]	Lively Guy	1958	18.00
— Black colorband label, logo at left			
❑ T892 [M]	Lively Guy	1962	15.00
— Black colorband label, logo at top			
❑ DT892 [R]	Lively Guy	196?	12.00
❑ T2777 [M]	Lombardo Country	1967	18.00
❑ ST2777 [S]	Lombardo Country	1967	15.00
❑ W738 [M]	Lombardo in Hi-Fi	1956	25.00
— Gray label			
❑ W738 [M]	Lombardo in Hi-Fi	1958	18.00
— Black colorband label, logo at left			
❑ W738 [M]	Lombardo in Hi-Fi	1962	15.00
— Black colorband label, logo at top			
❑ ST2825	Medleys on Parade	1968	12.00
❑ KAO1443 [M]	Sing the Songs of Christmas	1960	18.00
— Black colorband label, logo at left			
❑ SKAO1443 [S]	Sing the Songs of Christmas	1960	25.00
— Black colorband label, logo at left			
❑ TAO1443 [M]	Sing the Songs of Christmas	1962	15.00
— Black colorband label, logo at top			
❑ STAO1443 [S]	Sing the Songs of Christmas	1962	18.00
— Black colorband label, logo at top			
❑ T1461 [M]	The Best of Guy Lombardo	1961	25.00
— Black colorband label, logo at left			
❑ DT1461 [R]	The Best of Guy Lombardo	1961	12.00
— Black colorband label, logo at top			
❑ T1461 [M]	The Best of Guy Lombardo	1962	15.00
— Black colorband label, logo at left			
❑ SKAO2940	The Best of Guy Lombardo, Vol. 2	1968	12.00
❑ T2052 [M]	The Lombardo Touch	1964	15.00
❑ ST2052 [S]	The Lombardo Touch	1964	18.00
❑ TDL2181 [M]	The Lombardo Years	1964	30.00
❑ STDL2181 [S]	The Lombardo Years	1964	30.00
❑ ST-128	The New Songs -- The New Sounds	1969	12.00
❑ T1947 [M]	The Sweetest Medleys This Side of Heaven	1963	15.00
❑ DT1947 [R]	The Sweetest Medleys This Side of Heaven	1963	12.00
❑ T2639 [M]	The Sweetest Sounds Today	1967	18.00
❑ ST2639 [S]	The Sweetest Sounds Today	1967	15.00
❑ T1306 [M]	The Sweetest Waltzes This Side of Heaven	1960	18.00
— Black colorband label, logo at left			
❑ ST1306 [S]	The Sweetest Waltzes This Side of Heaven	1960	25.00
— Black colorband label, logo at left			
❑ ST1306 [S]	The Sweetest Waltzes This Side of Heaven	1962	15.00
— Black colorband label, logo at top			
❑ T1306 [M]	The Sweetest Waltzes This Side of Heaven	1962	12.00
— Black colorband label, logo at top			
❑ SN-16193	The Sweetest Waltzes This Side of Heaven	198?	10.00
— Budget-line reissue			
❑ ST2829	They're Playing Our Songs	1968	12.00
❑ T1738 [M]	Waltzing with Guy Lombardo	1962	15.00
❑ ST1738 [S]	Waltzing with Guy Lombardo	1962	18.00
❑ T739 [M]	Your Guy Lombardo Medley	1956	25.00
— Turquoise label			
❑ T739 [M]	Your Guy Lombardo Medley	1958	18.00
— Black colorband label, logo at left			
❑ T739 [M]	Your Guy Lombardo Medley	1962	15.00
— Black colorband label, logo at top			
❑ DT739 [R]	Your Guy Lombardo Medley	196?	12.00
❑ SM-739	Your Guy Lombardo Medley	1976	10.00
— Reissue with new prefix			
❑ T1244 [M]	Your Guy Lombardo Medley, Vol. 2	1960	18.00
— Black colorband label, logo at left			
❑ ST1244 [S]	Your Guy Lombardo Medley, Vol. 2	1960	25.00
— Black colorband label, logo at left			
❑ T1244 [M]	Your Guy Lombardo Medley, Vol. 2	1962	12.00
— Black colorband label, logo at top			
❑ ST1244 [S]	Your Guy Lombardo Medley, Vol. 2	1962	15.00
— Black colorband label, logo at top			
❑ T1598 [M]	Your Guy Lombardo Medley, Vol. 3	1961	18.00
— Black colorband label, logo at left			
❑ ST1598 [S]	Your Guy Lombardo Medley, Vol. 3	1961	25.00
— Black colorband label, logo at left			
❑ ST1598 [S]	Your Guy Lombardo Medley, Vol. 3	1962	15.00
— Black colorband label, logo at top			
❑ T1598 [M]	Your Guy Lombardo Medley, Vol. 3	1962	12.00
— Black colorband label, logo at top			

DECCA

Number	Title	Yr	NM
❑ DL8070 [M]	A Night at the Roosevelt	195?	25.00
— Black label, silver print			
❑ DL8070 [M]	A Night at the Roosevelt	1961	15.00
— Black label with color bars			
❑ DL4280 [M]	By Special Request	1962	15.00
❑ DL74280 [S]	By Special Request	1962	18.00
❑ DL4735 [M]	Dance Medley Time	1966	12.00
❑ DL74735 [S]	Dance Medley Time	1966	15.00
❑ DL4180 [M]	Dance to the Songs Everybody Knows	1961	15.00
❑ DL74180 [S]	Dance to the Songs Everybody Knows	1961	18.00
❑ DL4288 [M]	Dancing Piano	1962	15.00
❑ DL74288 [S]	Dancing Piano	1962	18.00
❑ DL8136 [M]	Enjoy Yourself	1955	25.00
— Black label, silver print			
❑ DL8136 [M]	Enjoy Yourself	1961	15.00
— Black label with color bars			
❑ DL5329 [10]	Enjoy Yourself	195?	30.00
❑ DL8254 [M]	Everybody Dance	1956	25.00
— Black label, silver print			
❑ DL8254 [M]	Everybody Dance	1961	15.00
— Black label with color bars			
❑ DL5442 [10]	Everybody Dance, Vol. 2	1952	30.00
❑ DL5434 [10]	Everybody Dance to the Music of Guy Lombardo	1952	30.00
❑ DL4149 [M]	Far Away Places	1961	15.00
❑ DL74149 [S]	Far Away Places	1961	18.00
❑ DL4430 [M]	Golden Folk Songs	1964	12.00
❑ DL74430 [S]	Golden Folk Songs	1964	15.00
❑ DL4593 [M]	Golden Medleys	1965	12.00
❑ DL74593 [S]	Golden Medleys	1965	15.00
❑ DL4380 [M]	Golden Minstrel Songs for Dancing	1963	15.00
❑ DL74380 [S]	Golden Minstrel Songs for Dancing	1963	18.00
❑ DL4812 [M]	Guy Lombardo's Greatest Hits	1966	12.00
❑ DL74812 [S]	Guy Lombardo's Greatest Hits	1966	15.00
❑ DL5156 [10]	Hawaiian Songs	1950	30.00
❑ DL8843 [M]	Instrumentally Yours	1959	25.00
— Black label, silver print			
❑ DL8843 [M]	Instrumentally Yours	1961	15.00
— Black label with color bars			
❑ DL4516 [M]	Italian Songs Everybody Knows	1964	12.00
❑ DL74516 [S]	Italian Songs Everybody Knows	1964	15.00
❑ DL8354 [M]	Jingle Bells	1956	25.00
— Black label, silver print			
❑ DL78354 [R]	Jingle Bells	196?	12.00
❑ DL8354 [M]	Jingle Bells	1961	15.00
— Black label with color bars			
❑ DL5430 [10]	Jingle Bells	1952	30.00
❑ DL5127 [10]	Latin Rhythms	195?	30.00
❑ DL8249 [M]	Lombardoland	1956	25.00
— Black label, silver print			
❑ DL8249 [M]	Lombardoland	1961	15.00
— Black label with color bars			
❑ DL5041 [10]	Lombardoland	1949	40.00
❑ DL8097 [M]	Lombardoland, U.S.A.	195?	25.00
— Black label, silver print			
❑ DL8097 [M]	Lombardoland, U.S.A.	1961	15.00
— Black label with color bars			
❑ DL5328 [10]	Lombardoland, Vol. 2	195?	30.00
❑ DL4177 [M]	New Year's Eve with Guy Lombardo	1961	15.00
❑ DL74177 [S]	New Year's Eve with Guy Lombardo	1961	18.00
❑ DL8255 [M]	Oh! How We Danced	1956	25.00
— Black label, silver print			
❑ DL8255 [M]	Oh! How We Danced	1961	15.00
— Black label with color bars			
❑ DL4371 [M]	Play a Happy Song	1963	15.00
❑ DL74371 [S]	Play a Happy Song	1963	18.00
❑ DL5024 [10]	Sidewalks of New York	1949	40.00
❑ DL8333 [M]	Silver Jubilee	1956	25.00
— Black label, silver print			
❑ DL8333 [M]	Silver Jubilee	1961	15.00
— Black label with color bars			
❑ DL5235 [10]	Silver Jubilee -- 1925-1950	1950	30.00
❑ DL4567 [M]	Snuggled on Your Shoulder	1965	12.00
❑ DL74567 [S]	Snuggled on Your Shoulder	1965	15.00
❑ DL8135 [M]	Soft and Sweet	1955	25.00
— Black label, silver print			
❑ DL8135 [M]	Soft and Sweet	1961	15.00
— Black label with color bars			
❑ DL5097 [10]	Song Hits from Broadway Shows	1949	40.00
❑ DL5322 [10]	Souvenirs	195?	30.00
❑ DL5277 [10]	Square Dances (Without Calls)	195?	30.00
❑ DL8208 [M]	The Band Played On	1955	25.00
— Black label, silver print			
❑ DL8208 [M]	The Band Played On	1961	15.00
— Black label with color bars			
❑ DXB185 [M]	The Best of Guy Lombardo	1964	25.00
❑ DXSB7185 [R]	The Best of Guy Lombardo	1964	18.00
❑ DL4268 [M]	The Best Songs Are the Old Songs	1962	18.00
❑ DL74268 [R]	The Best Songs Are the Old Songs	196?	15.00
❑ DL8894 [M]	The Sidewalks of New York	1959	25.00
— Black label, silver print			
❑ DL8894 [M]	The Sidewalks of New York	1961	15.00
— Black label with color bars			
❑ DL5330 [10]	The Sweetest Music This Side of Heaven	195?	30.00
❑ DL8962 [M]	The Sweetest Music This Side of Heaven (A Musical Biography 1926-1932)	1960	18.00
— Black label, silver print			
❑ DL8962 [M]	The Sweetest Music This Side of Heaven (A Musical Biography 1926-1932)	1960	12.00
— Black label with color bars			
❑ DL78962 [S]	The Sweetest Music This Side of Heaven (A Musical Biography 1926-1932)	1960	25.00
— Black label, silver print			
❑ DL78962 [S]	The Sweetest Music This Side of Heaven (A Musical Biography 1926-1932)	1960	15.00
— Black label with color bars			
❑ DL4229 [M]	The Sweetest Music This Side of Heaven (A Musical Biography 1932-1939)	1962	15.00
❑ DL74229 [S]	The Sweetest Music This Side of Heaven (A Musical Biography 1932-1939)	1962	18.00
❑ DL4328 [M]	The Sweetest Music This Side of Heaven (A Musical Biography 1944-1948)	1962	15.00
❑ DL74328 [S]	The Sweetest Music This Side of Heaven (A Musical Biography 1944-1948)	1962	18.00
❑ DL4329 [M]	The Sweetest Music This Side of Heaven (A Musical Biography 1949-1954)	1962	15.00
❑ DL74329 [S]	The Sweetest Music This Side of Heaven (A Musical Biography 1949-1954)	1962	18.00
❑ DL4123 [M]	The Sweetest Pianos This Side of Heaven	1961	15.00
❑ DL74123 [S]	The Sweetest Pianos This Side of Heaven	1961	18.00
❑ DLP5002 [10]	The Twin Pianos -- Vol. 1	1949	40.00
— Both record and sleeve have "DLP" prefix			
❑ DL5002 [10]	The Twin Pianos -- Vol. 1	195?	30.00
— Record has "DL" prefix; sleeve may or may not have "DL			
❑ DLP5003 [10]	The Twin Pianos -- Vol. 2	1949	40.00
— Both record and sleeve have "DLP" prefix			
❑ DL5003 [10]	The Twin Pianos -- Vol. 2	195?	30.00
— Record has "DL" prefix; sleeve may or may not have "DL			
❑ DL8251 [M]	Twin Piano Magic	1956	25.00
— Black label, silver print			
❑ DL8251 [M]	Twin Piano Magic	1961	15.00
— Black label with color bars			
❑ DL5447 [10]	Twin Piano Magic	195?	30.00
❑ DL8119 [M]	Twin Pianos	195?	25.00
— Black label, silver print			
❑ DL8119 [M]	Twin Pianos	1961	15.00
— Black label with color bars			
❑ DL5193 [10]	Waltzes	195?	30.00
❑ DL8256 [M]	Waltzland	1956	25.00
— Black label, silver print			
❑ DL8256 [M]	Waltzland	1961	15.00
— Black label with color bars			

Number	Title	Yr	NM
❑ DL5325 [10]	Waltzland	1951	30.00
❑ DL8205 [M]	Waltz Time	1955	25.00
—Black label, silver print			
❑ DL8205 [M]	Waltz Time	1961	15.00
—Black label with color bars			

HINDSIGHT

Number	Title	Yr	NM
❑ HSR-187	Guy Lombardo and His Royal Canadians 1950	198?	12.00

LONDON

Number	Title	Yr	NM
❑ XPS904	Every Night Is New Year's Eve	1973	12.00

MCA

Number	Title	Yr	NM
❑ 15031	Auld Lang Syne	198?	12.00
❑ 242	Dance Medley Time	197?	10.00
—Reissue of Decca 74735			
❑ 197	Dance to the Songs Everybody Knows	1973	10.00
—Reissue of Decca 74180			
❑ 103	Golden Medleys	1973	10.00
—Reissue of Decca 74593			
❑ 245	Guy Lombardo's Greatest Hits	197?	10.00
—Reissue of Decca 74812			
❑ 15035	I Saw Mommy Kissing Santa Claus	198?	12.00
❑ 15012	Jingle Bells	197?	12.00
—Reissue of Decca 78354; black rainbow label			
❑ 15012	Jingle Bells	1977	10.00
—Tan label			
❑ 15012	Jingle Bells	1980	10.00
—Blue rainbow label			
❑ 15000	New Year's Eve with Guy Lombardo	1974	12.00
—Reissue of MCA 195; black rainbow label			
❑ 195	New Year's Eve with Guy Lombardo	1973	15.00
—Reissue of Decca 74177			
❑ 15000	New Year's Eve with Guy Lombardo	1977	10.00
—Tan label			
❑ 15000	New Year's Eve with Guy Lombardo	1980	10.00
—Blue rainbow label			
❑ 4041	The Best of Guy Lombardo	197?	15.00
—Black rainbow labels			
❑ 4041	The Best of Guy Lombardo	1977	12.00
—Tan labels			
❑ 4041	The Best of Guy Lombardo	1980	12.00
—Blue rainbow labels			
❑ 4082	The Best of Guy Lombardo, Vol. 2	197?	15.00
—Black rainbow labels			
❑ 4082	The Best of Guy Lombardo, Vol. 2	1977	12.00
—Tan labels			
❑ 4082	The Best of Guy Lombardo, Vol. 2	1980	12.00
—Blue rainbow labels			
❑ 89	The Best Songs Are the Old Songs	1973	10.00
—Reissue of Decca 74268			
❑ 201	The Sweetest Music This Side of Heaven	1973	10.00
—Reissue of Decca 78962?			

MCA CORAL

Number	Title	Yr	NM
❑ CR20105	Here's Guy Lombardo	197?	12.00

PAIR

Number	Title	Yr	NM
❑ PDL2-1046	Guy Lombardo	1986	15.00

PICKWICK

Number	Title	Yr	NM
❑ SPC-3358	Alley Cat	197?	10.00
❑ SPC1011	Deck the Halls	196?	12.00
—Silver label			
❑ SPC1011	Deck the Halls	197?	10.00
—Reissue on black label			
❑ SPC-3193	Enjoy Yourself	196?	12.00
❑ SPC-3257	Red Roses for a Blue Lady	197?	10.00
❑ SPC-3530	Seems Like Old Times	197?	10.00
❑ SPC-3530	Seems Like Old Times	197?	10.00
❑ SPC-3073	Sweet and Heavenly	196?	12.00
❑ SPC-3312	The Impossible Dream	197?	10.00
❑ PTP-2009	The Sweet Sounds	197?	12.00

RCA CAMDEN

Number	Title	Yr	NM
❑ CAL-445 [M]	An Evening with Guy Lombardo	195?	18.00
❑ CAS-445 [R]	An Evening with Guy Lombardo	196?	12.00
❑ CAL-255 [M]	Guy Lombardo Plays	195?	18.00
❑ CAS-255 [R]	Guy Lombardo Plays	196?	12.00
❑ CAL-578 [M]	He's My Guy	195?	18.00

RCA VICTOR

Number	Title	Yr	NM
❑ CPL1-2047(e)	A Legendary Performer	1977	12.00
❑ VPM-6071	This Is Guy Lombardo	197?	15.00
❑ LPT-3059 [10]	This Is Guy Lombardo and His Orchestra	1954	40.00

SUNBEAM

Number	Title	Yr	NM
❑ 308	On the Air 1935	197?	12.00

VOCALION

Number	Title	Yr	NM
❑ VL3605 [M]	Dance in the Moonlight	1958	18.00
❑ VL73605 [R]	Dance in the Moonlight	196?	12.00
❑ VL73833	Here's Guy Lombardo	1968	12.00

LONDON, JULIE

LIBERTY

Number	Title	Yr	NM
❑ LRP-3043 [M]	About the Blues	1957	40.00
—Green label			
❑ LST-7012 [S]	About the Blues	1958	70.00
—Black label, silver print			
❑ LRP-3043 [M]	About the Blues	1960	25.00
—Black label, colorband and logo at left			
❑ LST-7012 [S]	About the Blues	1960	30.00
—Black label, colorband and logo at left			
❑ LRP-3434 [M]	All Through the Night	1965	30.00
❑ LST-7434 [S]	All Through the Night	1965	30.00
❑ LRP-3164 [M]	Around Midnight	1960	30.00
❑ LST-7164 [S]	Around Midnight	1960	40.00
❑ SCR-1 [S]	By Myself	196?	30.00
—Columbia Record Club exclusive			
❑ MCR-1 [M]	By Myself	196?	30.00
—Columbia Record Club exclusive			
❑ SL-9002 [M]	Calendar Girl	1956	100.00
❑ LST-7546	Easy Does It	1968	25.00
❑ LRP-3416 [M]	Feeling Good	1965	30.00
❑ LST-7416 [S]	Feeling Good	1965	30.00
❑ LRP-3478 [M]	For the Night People	1966	30.00
❑ LST-7478 [S]	For the Night People	1966	30.00
❑ LRP-3096 [M]	Julie	1957	40.00
—Green label			
❑ LST-7004 [S]	Julie	1958	70.00
—Black label, silver print			
❑ LRP-3152 [M]	Julie…At Home	1960	30.00
❑ LST-7152 [S]	Julie…At Home	1960	100.00
—Blue vinyl			
❑ LST-7152 [S]	Julie…At Home	1960	40.00
—Black vinyl			
❑ LRP-3006 [M]	Julie Is Her Name	1956	50.00
—Green label			
❑ LST-7027 [S]	Julie Is Her Name	1958	100.00
—Blue vinyl			
❑ LST-7027 [S]	Julie Is Her Name	1958	100.00
—Red vinyl			
❑ LST-7027 [S]	Julie Is Her Name	1958	40.00
—Black label, silver print			
❑ LRP-3006 [M]	Julie Is Her Name	1960	25.00
—Black label, colorband and logo at left			
❑ LST-7027 [S]	Julie Is Her Name	1960	30.00
—Black label, colorband and logo at left			
❑ LRP-3100 [M]	Julie Is Her Name, Volume 2	1958	40.00
—Green label			
❑ LST-7100 [S]	Julie Is Her Name, Volume 2	1958	40.00
—Black label, silver print			
❑ LRP-3100 [M]	Julie Is Her Name, Volume 2	1960	25.00
—Black label, colorband and logo at left			
❑ LST-7100 [S]	Julie Is Her Name, Volume 2	1960	30.00
—Black label, colorband and logo at left			
❑ LRP-3342 [M]	Julie London	1964	30.00
❑ LST-7342 [S]	Julie London	1964	30.00
❑ LRP-3375 [M]	Julie London In Person at the Americana	1964	30.00
❑ LST-7375 [S]	Julie London In Person at the Americana	1964	30.00
❑ LRP-3291 [M]	Julie's Golden Greats	1963	30.00
—White cover			
❑ LRP-3291 [M]	Julie's Golden Greats	1963	30.00
—Black cover			
❑ LST-7291 [S]	Julie's Golden Greats	1963	30.00
—White cover			
❑ LST-7291 [S]	Julie's Golden Greats	1963	30.00
—Black cover			
❑ LRP-3278 [M]	Latin in a Satin Mood	1963	30.00
❑ LST-7278 [S]	Latin in a Satin Mood	1963	30.00
❑ LRP-3105 [M]	London By Night	1958	30.00
—Green label			
❑ LST-7105 [S]	London By Night	1958	40.00
—Black label, silver print			
❑ LRP-3012 [M]	Lonely Girl	1956	50.00
—Green label			
❑ LST-7029 [S]	Lonely Girl	1958	40.00
—Black label, silver print			
❑ LRP-3012 [M]	Lonely Girl	1960	25.00
—Black label, colorband and logo at left			
❑ LST-7029 [S]	Lonely Girl	1960	30.00
—Black label, colorband and logo at left			
❑ LRP-3231 [M]	Love Letters	1962	30.00
❑ LST-7231 [S]	Love Letters	1962	30.00
❑ LRP-3249 [M]	Love on the Rocks	1963	30.00
❑ LST-7249 [S]	Love on the Rocks	1963	30.00
❑ LRP-3060 [M]	Make Love to Me	1957	40.00
—Green label			
❑ LST-7060 [S]	Make Love to Me	1958	40.00
—Black label, silver print			
❑ LRP-3060 [M]	Make Love to Me	1960	25.00
—Black label, colorband and logo at left			
❑ LST-7060 [S]	Make Love to Me	1960	30.00
—Black label, colorband and logo at left			
❑ LRP-3493 [M]	Nice Girls Don't Stay for Breakfast	1967	30.00
❑ LST-7493 [S]	Nice Girls Don't Stay for Breakfast	1967	30.00
❑ LRP-3392 [M]	Our Fair Lady	1965	30.00
❑ LST-7392 [S]	Our Fair Lady	1965	30.00
❑ LRP-3171 [M]	Send for Me	1961	30.00
❑ LST-7171 [S]	Send for Me	1961	40.00
❑ LRP-3203 [M]	Sophisticated Lady	1962	30.00
❑ LST-7203 [S]	Sophisticated Lady	1962	30.00
❑ LRP-3119 [M]	Swing Me an Old Song	1959	30.00
—Green label			
❑ LST-7119 [S]	Swing Me an Old Song	1959	40.00
—Black label, silver print			
❑ L-5501 [M]	The Best of Julie London	1962	30.00
❑ S-6601 [S]	The Best of Julie London	1962	40.00
❑ LRP-3300 [M]	The End of the World	1963	30.00
❑ LST-7300 [S]	The End of the World	1963	30.00
❑ LRP-3324 [M]	The Wonderful World of Julie London	1963	30.00
❑ LST-7324 [S]	The Wonderful World of Julie London	1963	30.00
❑ LRP-3192 [M]	Whatever Julie Wants	1961	30.00
❑ LST-7192 [S]	Whatever Julie Wants	1961	40.00
❑ LRP-3514 [M]	With Body and Soul	1967	30.00
❑ LST-7514 [S]	With Body and Soul	1967	30.00
❑ LRP-3130 [M]	Your Number Please	1959	30.00
—Green label			
❑ LST-7130 [S]	Your Number Please	1959	40.00
—Black label, silver print			
❑ LRP-3130 [M]	Your Number Please	1960	25.00
—Black label, colorband and logo at left			
❑ LST-7130 [S]	Your Number Please	1960	30.00
—Black label, colorband and logo at left			
❑ LST-7609	Yummy, Yummy, Yummy	1969	25.00

SUNSET

Number	Title	Yr	NM
❑ SUS-5207	Gone with the Wind	196?	15.00
❑ SUM-1104 [M]	Julie London	196?	15.00
❑ SUS-5104 [S]	Julie London	196?	18.00
❑ SUM-1161 [M]	Soft and Sweet	196?	15.00
❑ SUS-5161 [S]	Soft and Sweet	196?	18.00

UNITED ARTISTS

Number	Title	Yr	NM
❑ UA-LA437-E	The Very Best of Julie London	1975	15.00

LONDON, LAURIE

CAPITOL

Number	Title	Yr	NM
❑ T10169 [M]	England's 14 Year Old Singing Sensation -- Laurie London	1958	50.00

LONDON POPS ORCHESTRA (FREDERICK FENNELL, CONDUCTOR)

MERCURY LIVING PRESENCE

Number	Title	Yr	NM
❑ SR90439 [S]	Coates: Three Elizabeths; London Suite; Four Ways Suite	1965	25.00
—Maroon label, with "Vendor: Mercury Record Corporation			

LONDON PROMS SYMPHONY ORCHESTRA (CHARLES MACKERRAS, CONDUCTOR)

RCA VICTOR RED SEAL

Number	Title	Yr	NM
❑ LSC-2336 [S]	Sibelius: Finlandia	1960	40.00
—Original with "shaded dog" label			
❑ LSC-2336 [S]	Sibelius: Finlandia	199?	30.00
—Classic Records reissue			

LONDON PROMS SYMPHONY ORCHESTRA (RAYMOND AGOULT, CONDUCTOR)

RCA VICTOR RED SEAL

Number	Title	Yr	NM
❑ LSC-2326 [S]	Clair de Lune	1960	220.00
—Original with "shaded dog" label			
❑ LSC-2326 [S]	Clair de Lune	199?	30.00
—Classic Records reissue			

LONDON PROMS SYMPHONY ORCHESTRA (ROBERT SHARPLES, CONDUCTOR)

RCA VICTOR RED SEAL

Number	Title	Yr	NM
❑ LSC-2299 [S]	Lehar: Waltzes	1959	30.00
—Original with "shaded dog" label			

LONDON RAGTIME ORCHESTRA, THE

STOMP OFF

Number	Title	Yr	NM
❑ SOS-1081	Bouncing Around	1985	12.00

LONDON SOUND 70 ORCHESTRA AND CHORUS

DECCA

Number	Title	Yr	NM
❑ DEB7-7	The Sounds of Christmas	1970	30.00

LONDON SYMPHONY ORCHESTRA

HALLMARK

Number	Title	Yr	NM
❑ 6250	Hallmark Presents: The Best Loved Christmas Carols	1985	15.00
—Sold only at Hallmark Cards dealers. Also see other "Hallmark Presents:" LPs in the various artists section.			

RCA VICTOR

Number	Title	Yr	NM
❑ XRL1-7067	A Classic Case: The London Symphony Orchestra Plays Music of Jethro Tull	1985	15.00
—Ian Anderson of Jethro Tull appears			

LONDON SYMPHONY ORCHESTRA (ALEXANDER GIBSON, CONDUCTOR)

RCA VICTOR RED SEAL

Number	Title	Yr	NM
❑ LSC-2405 [S]	Sibelius: Symphony No. 5	1960	220.00

Number	Title	Yr	NM

—Original with "shaded dog" label
- ❑ LSC-2405 [S] — Sibelius: Symphony No. 5 — 199? — 30.00
—Classic Records reissue

LONDON SYMPHONY ORCHESTRA (ANTAL DORATI, CONDUCTOR)

MERCURY LIVING PRESENCE
- ❑ SR90311 [S] — Bartok: Bluebeard's Castle — 196? — 25.00
—Maroon label, no "Vendor: Mercury Record Corporation
- ❑ SR90378 [S] — Bartok: Concerto for Orchestra — 196? — 400.00
—Maroon label, no "Vendor: Mercury Record Corporation
- ❑ SR90426 [S] — Bartok: The Wooden Prince — 196? — 40.00
—Maroon label, no "Vendor: Mercury Record Corporation
- ❑ SR90426 [S] — Bartok: The Wooden Prince — 196? — 25.00
—Maroon label, with "Vendor: Mercury Record Corporation
- ❑ SR90317 [S] — Beethoven: Symphony No. 5; Egmont Overture; Consecration of the House Overture — 196? — 80.00
—Maroon label, no "Vendor: Mercury Record Corporation
- ❑ SR90317 [S] — Beethoven: Symphony No. 5; Egmont Overture; Consecration of the House Overture — 196? — 30.00
—Maroon label, with "Vendor: Mercury Record Corporation
- ❑ SR90278 [S] — Berg: Suites from Lulu and Wozzeck — 196? — 60.00
—Maroon label, no "Vendor: Mercury Record Corporation
- ❑ SR90278 [S] — Berg: Suites from Lulu and Wozzeck — 196? — 30.00
—Maroon label, with "Vendor: Mercury Record Corporation
- ❑ SR90122 [S] — Borodin: Polovetsian Dances; Rimsky-Korsakov: Coq d-Or — 1960 — 30.00
—Maroon label, no "Vendor: Mercury Record Corporation
- ❑ SR90437 [S] — Brahms: 16 Hungarian Dances — 1965 — 25.00
—Maroon label, with "Vendor: Mercury Record Corporation
- ❑ SR90154 [S] — Brahms: Haydn Variations; Hungarian Dances — 196? — 30.00
—Maroon label, no "Vendor: Mercury Record Corporation
- ❑ SR90268 [S] — Brahms: Symphony No. 1 — 196? — 50.00
—Maroon label, no "Vendor: Mercury Record Corporation
- ❑ SR90246 [S] — Copland: Appalachian Spring; Billy the Kid — 196? — 80.00
—Maroon label, no "Vendor: Mercury Record Corporation
- ❑ SR90246 [S] — Copland: Appalachian Spring; Billy the Kid — 196? — 80.00
—Maroon label, with "Vendor: Mercury Record Corporation
- ❑ SR90246 [S] — Copland: Appalachian Spring; Billy the Kid — 196? — 25.00
—Third edition: Dark red (not maroon) label
- ❑ SR90236 [S] — Dvorak: Symphony No. 4 (8) in G; Carnaval Overture — 196? — 120.00
—Maroon label, no "Vendor: Mercury Record Corporation
- ❑ SR90158 [S] — Handel-Harty: Water Music Suite; Royal Fireworks Music — 196? — 50.00
—Maroon label, no "Vendor: Mercury Record Corporation
- ❑ SR90155 [S] — Haydn: Symphonies 100 and 101 — 196? — 100.00
—Maroon label, no "Vendor: Mercury Record Corporation
- ❑ SR90415 [S] — Haydn: Symphony No. 100 in G; Beethoven: Symphony No. 6 in F — 196? — 25.00
—Maroon label, no "Vendor: Mercury Record Corporation
- ❑ SR90209 [S] — Khachaturian: Gayne Ballet Suite; Tchaikovsky: Romeo and Juliet — 196? — 30.00
—Maroon label, no "Vendor: Mercury Record Corporation
- ❑ SR90209 [S] — Khachaturian: Gayne Ballet Suite; Tchaikovsky: Romeo and Juliet — 196? — 30.00
—Maroon label, with "Vendor: Mercury Record Corporation
- ❑ SR90235 [S] — Liszt: Hungarian Rhapsodies No. 2 and 3; Enescu: Rumanian Rhapsodies No. 1 and 2 — 196? — 60.00
—Maroon label, with "Vendor: Mercury Record Corporation
- ❑ SR90235 [S] — Liszt: Hungarian Rhapsodies No. 2 and 3; Enescu: Rumanian Rhapsodies No. 1 and 2 — 196? — 60.00
—Maroon label, no "Vendor: Mercury Record Corporation
- ❑ SR90235 [S] — Liszt: Hungarian Rhapsodies No. 2 and 3; Enescu: Rumanian Rhapsodies No. 1 and 2 — 196? — 25.00
—Third edition: Dark red (not maroon) label
- ❑ SR90371 [S] — Liszt: Hungarian Rhapsodies Nos. 1, 4, 5 and 6 — 196? — 400.00
—Maroon label, no "Vendor: Mercury Record Corporation
- ❑ SR90371 [S] — Liszt: Hungarian Rhapsodies Nos. 1, 4, 5 and 6 — 196? — 60.00
—Maroon label, with "Vendor: Mercury Record Corporation
- ❑ SR90371 [S] — Liszt: Hungarian Rhapsodies Nos. 1, 4, 5 and 6 — 196? — 30.00
—Third edition: Dark red (not maroon) label
- ❑ SR90214 [S] — Liszt: Les Preludes; Smetana: The Moldau; Mussorgsky: Night on Bald Mountain; Sibelius: Valse Triste — 196? — 40.00
—Maroon label, no "Vendor: Mercury Record Corporation

Number	Title	Yr	NM

- ❑ SR90123 [S] — Mendelssohn: Symphony No. 3; Fingel's Cave Overture — 1960 — 40.00
—Maroon label, no "Vendor: Mercury Record Corporation
- ❑ SR90280 [S] — Mozart: Symphony No. 40; Haydn: Symphony No. 45 — 196? — 25.00
—Maroon label, no "Vendor: Mercury Record Corporation
- ❑ SR90435 [S] — Paris 1917-1938 — 1965 — 100.00
—Maroon label, with "Vendor: Mercury Record Corporation
- ❑ SR90435 [S] — Paris 1917-1938 — 196? — 25.00
—Maroon label, oval "Mercury" logo
- ❑ SR90006 [S] — Prokofiev: Love for Three Oranges Suite; Scythian Suite — 195? — 300.00
- ❑ SR90006 [S] — Prokofiev: Love for Three Oranges Suite; Scythian Suite — 199? — 30.00
—Classic Records reissue
- ❑ SR90153 [S] — Respighi: The Birds; Brazilian Impressions — 196? — 200.00
—Maroon label, no "Vendor: Mercury Record Corporation
- ❑ SR90153 [S] — Respighi: The Birds; Brazilian Impressions — 196? — 50.00
—Maroon label, with "Vendor: Mercury Record Corporation
- ❑ SR90265 [S] — Rimsky-Korsakov: Capriccio Espagnol; Russian Easter Overture; Borodin: Prince Igor Overture — 196? — 50.00
—Maroon label, no "Vendor: Mercury Record Corporation
- ❑ SR90226 [S] — Stravinsky: The Firebird — 196? — 250.00
—Maroon label, no "Vendor: Mercury Record Corporation
- ❑ SR90226 [S] — Stravinsky: The Firebird — 196? — 30.00
—Maroon label, with "Vendor: Mercury Record Corporation
- ❑ SR90226 [S] — Stravinsky: The Firebird — 196? — 30.00
—Third edition: Dark red (not maroon) label
- ❑ SR90226 [S] — Stravinsky: The Firebird — 199? — 30.00
—Classic Records reissue
- ❑ SR90387 [S] — Stravinsky: Song of the Nightingale; Fireworks; Scherzo; Four Etudes — 196? — 100.00
—Maroon label, no "Vendor: Mercury Record Corporation
- ❑ SR90387 [S] — Stravinsky: Song of the Nightingale; Fireworks; Scherzo; Four Etudes — 196? — 40.00
—Maroon label, with "Vendor: Mercury Record Corporation
- ❑ SR90409 [S] — Tchaikovsky: Rococo Variations; Saint-Saens: Cello Concerto No. 1 — 196? — 100.00
—Maroon label, no "Vendor: Mercury Record Corporation
- ❑ SR90409 [S] — Tchaikovsky: Rococo Variations; Saint-Saens: Cello Concerto No. 1 — 196? — 40.00
—Maroon label, with "Vendor: Mercury Record Corporation
- ❑ SR90255 [S] — Tchaikovsky: Symphony No. 5 — 196? — 150.00
—Maroon label, no "Vendor: Mercury Record Corporation
- ❑ SR90279 [S] — Tchaikovsky: Symphony No. 4 in F — 196? — 300.00
—Maroon label, no "Vendor: Mercury Record Corporation
- ❑ SR90312 [S] — Tchaikovsky: Symphony No. 6 — 196? — 50.00
—Maroon label, no "Vendor: Mercury Record Corporation
- ❑ SR90312 [S] — Tchaikovsky: Symphony No. 6 — 196? — 50.00
—Maroon label, with "Vendor: Mercury Record Corporation
- ❑ SR90156 [S] — Verdi: Overtures — 196? — 25.00
—Maroon label, no "Vendor: Mercury Record Corporation
- ❑ SR90316 [S] — Vienna 1908-1914 — 196? — 200.00
—Maroon label, no "Vendor: Mercury Record Corporation
- ❑ SR90316 [S] — Vienna 1908-1914 — 196? — 120.00
—Maroon label, with "Vendor: Mercury Record Corporation
- ❑ SR90287 [S] — Wagner: Mesitersinger Prelude; Tannhauser Overture; Parsifal; Lohengrin Selections — 196? — 40.00
—Maroon label, no "Vendor: Mercury Record Corporation
- ❑ SR90287 [S] — Wagner: Mesitersinger Prelude; Tannhauser Overture; Parsifal; Lohengrin Selections — 196? — 30.00
—Maroon label, no "Vendor: Mercury Record Corporation
- ❑ SR90234 [S] — Wagner: Tristan und Isolde Prelude and Liebestod; Tannhauser Overture; Lohengrin Prelude — 196? — 30.00
—Maroon label, no "Vendor: Mercury Record Corporation

LONDON SYMPHONY ORCHESTRA (ARTHUR BLISS, CONDUCTOR)

RCA VICTOR RED SEAL
- ❑ LSC-2257 [S] — Elgar: Pomp and Circumstance Marches 1-5 — 1959 — 100.00
—Original with "shaded dog" label

LONDON SYMPHONY ORCHESTRA (HANS SCHMIDT-ISSERSTEDT, CONDUCTOR)

MERCURY LIVING PRESENCE
- ❑ SR90184 [S] — Mozart: Symphonies No. 39 and 41 — 196? — 120.00
—Maroon label, no "Vendor: Mercury Record Corporation
- ❑ SR90184 [S] — Mozart: Symphonies No. 39 and 41 — 196? — 30.00
—Maroon label, with "Vendor: Mercury Record Corporation

Number	Title	Yr	NM

LONDON SYMPHONY ORCHESTRA (JEAN MARTINON, CONDUCTOR)

RCA VICTOR RED SEAL
- ❑ LSC-2298 [S] — Borodin: Symphony No. 2; Rimsky-Korsakov: Capriccio Espagnole — 1960 — 70.00
—Original with "shaded dog" label
- ❑ LSC-2298 [S] — Borodin: Symphony No. 2; Rimsky-Korsakov: Capriccio Espagnole — 199? — 30.00
—Classic Records reissue
- ❑ LSC-2419 [S] — Dvorak: Slavonic Dances — 1960 — 180.00
—Original with "shaded dog" label
- ❑ LSC-2419 [S] — Dvorak: Slavonic Dances — 199? — 30.00
—Classic Records reissue
- ❑ LSC-2322 [S] — Shostakovich: Symphony No. 1 — 1960 — 100.00
—Original with "shaded dog" label
- ❑ LSC-2322 [S] — Shostakovich: Symphony No. 1 — 199? — 30.00
—Classic Records reissue

LONDON SYMPHONY ORCHESTRA (PIERRE MONTEUX, CONDUCTOR)

RCA VICTOR RED SEAL
- ❑ LSC-2489 [S] — Dvorak: Symphony No. 2 — 196? — 30.00
—Original with "shaded dog" label
- ❑ LSC-2489 [S] — Dvorak: Symphony No. 2 — 199? — 30.00
—Classic Records reissue
- ❑ LSC-2418 [S] — Elgar: Enigma Variations — 1960 — 80.00
—Original with "shaded dog" label
- ❑ LSC-2418 [S] — Elgar: Enigma Variations — 199? — 30.00
—Classic Records reissue
- ❑ LSC-2208 [S] — Rimsky-Korsakov: Scheherazade — 1959 — 30.00
—Original with "shaded dog" label
- ❑ LSC-2342 [S] — Sibelius: Symphony No. 2 — 1960 — 25.00
—Original with "shaded dog" label
- ❑ LSC-2342 [S] — Sibelius: Symphony No. 2 — 199? — 30.00
—Classic Records reissue
- ❑ LSC-2177 [S] — Tchaikovsky: Sleeping Beauty (Excerpts) — 1959 — 30.00
—Original with "shaded dog" label

LONDON SYMPHONY ORCHESTRA (WALTER SUSSKIND, HANS SCHMIDT-ISSERSTEDT, CONDUCTORS)

MERCURY LIVING PRESENCE
- ❑ SR90196 [S] — Schubert: Symphonies No. 4 and 6 — 196? — 25.00
—Maroon label, no "Vendor: Mercury Record Corporation

LONDONBEAT

RADIOACTIVE
- ❑ 10192 — In the Blood — 1991 — 15.00

LONE JUSTICE

GEFFEN
- ❑ GHS24060 — Lone Justice — 1985 — 12.00
- ❑ GHS24122 — Shelter — 1986 — 12.00

LONE STAR RAMBLERS, THE

LONGHORN
- ❑ LP-600 [M] — Texas Square Dancing with Red at the 60 Club — 196? — 30.00

LONESOME PINE FIDDLERS, THE

STARDAY
- ❑ SLP-155 [M] — 14 Mountain Songs Featuring 5-String Banjo — 1961 — 40.00
- ❑ SLP-194 [M] — Bluegrass — 1962 — 40.00
- ❑ SLP-222 [M] — More Bluegrass — 1963 — 40.00

LONESOME RHODES

RCA VICTOR
- ❑ LPM-3759 [M] — Lonesome Rhodes — 1967 — 30.00
- ❑ LSP-3759 [S] — Lonesome Rhodes — 1967 — 25.00

LONESOME STRANGERS, THE

HIGHTONE
- ❑ 8016 — The Lonesome Strangers — 1989 — 15.00

LONESOME SUNDOWN

EXCELLO
- ❑ LPS-8012 — Lonesome Lonely Blues — 1970 — 30.00

LONG, BARBARA

SAVOY
- ❑ MG-12161 [M] — Soul — 1961 — 30.00

LONG, DANNY

CAPITOL
- ❑ T1988 [M] — Jazz Furlough — 1963 — 18.00
- ❑ ST1988 [S] — Jazz Furlough — 1963 — 25.00

Number	Title	Yr	NM

LONG, JOHNNY

CIRCLE

| ❑ 56 | Johnny Long and His Orchestra 1941-1942 | 198? | 12.00 |

LONG, SHORTY (1)

SOUL

| ❑ SS-709 [S] | Here Comes the Judge | 1968 | 25.00 |
| ❑ SM-709 [M] | Here Comes the Judge | 1968 | 50.00 |

—Mono is white label promo only; mono sticker on stereo cover

| ❑ SS-719 [B] | The Prime of Shorty Long | 1969 | 18.00 |

LONG, SHORTY (2)

FORD

| ❑ FXM-712 [M] | Country Jamboree | 1963 | 25.00 |

LONGBRANCH PENNYWHISTLE

AMOS

| ❑ AAS-7007 [B] | Longbranch Pennywhistle | 1969 | 60.00 |

LONGET, CLAUDINE

A&M

❑ LP-121 [M]	Claudine	1967	18.00
❑ SP-4121 [S]	Claudine	1967	15.00
❑ SP-4163	Colours	1969	15.00
❑ SP-4142	Love Is Blue	1968	15.00
❑ SP-4232	Run Wild, Run Free	1970	15.00
❑ LP-128 [M]	The Look of Love	1967	18.00
❑ SP-4128 [S]	The Look of Love	1967	15.00

BARNABY

| ❑ KZ31383 | Let's Spend the Night Together | 1972 | 15.00 |
| ❑ Z30377 | We've Only Just Begun | 1971 | 15.00 |

LONGMIRE, WILBERT

COLUMBIA

| ❑ JC35754 | Champagne | 1979 | 12.00 |
| ❑ JC35365 | Sunny Side Up | 1978 | 12.00 |

PACIFIC JAZZ

| ❑ ST-20161 | Revolution | 1969 | 25.00 |

LONGNON, JEAN-LOUP

ATLANTIC

| ❑ 81829 | Jean-Loup Longnon and His New Your Orchestra | 1988 | 12.00 |

LONGO, MIKE

GROOVE MERCHANT

| ❑ 525 | Funkia | 1974 | 25.00 |

MAINSTREAM

| ❑ MRL 004 | Matrix | 1972 | 18.00 |
| ❑ MRL-357 | The Awakening | 1972 | 18.00 |

PABLO

| ❑ 2310769 | Talk with Spirits | 197? | 18.00 |

LONGO, PAT

TOWN HALL

❑ 33	Billy May for President	198?	12.00
❑ 25	Chain Reaction	1980	12.00
❑ 30	Crocodile Tears	1981	12.00

LONZO AND OSCAR

COLUMBIA

| ❑ CS9587 | Mountain Dew | 1968 | 25.00 |

DECCA

| ❑ DL4363 [M] | Country Comedy Time | 1963 | 25.00 |

STARDAY

| ❑ SLP-119 [M] | America's Greatest Country Comedians | 1960 | 40.00 |
| ❑ SLP-244 [M] | Country Music Time | 1963 | 40.00 |

LOOKING GLASS

EPIC

| ❑ KE31320 | Looking Glass | 1972 | 18.00 |
| ❑ KE32167 | Subway Serenade | 1973 | 18.00 |

LOOKOFSKY, HARRY

ATLANTIC

| ❑ 1319 [M] | Stringville | 1959 | 40.00 |

—Black label

| ❑ 1319 [M] | Stringville | 1961 | 25.00 |

—Multicolor label, white "fan" logo at right

| ❑ 1319 [M] | Stringville | 1964 | 18.00 |

—Multicolor label, black "fan" logo at right

| ❑ SD1319 [S] | Stringville | 1959 | 40.00 |

—Green label

| ❑ SD1319 [S] | Stringville | 1961 | 18.00 |

—Multicolor label, white "fan" logo at right

| ❑ SD1319 [S] | Stringville | 1964 | 15.00 |

—Multicolor label, black "fan" logo at right

LOOSE

NOCTURNE

| ❑ 906 | Freaky Billie, The Wheelie King | 1970 | 30.00 |

LOOSE FUR

DRAG CITY

| ❑ DC203 | Loose Fur | 2003 | 30.00 |

LOPEZ, TRINI

CAPITOL

| ❑ SK11009 | Viva | 1972 | 12.00 |

GUEST STAR

| ❑ GS-1499 [M] | Trini Lopez and Scott Gregory | 1964 | 50.00 |

—"Scott Gregory" is said to be a pseudonym for BILL HALEY.

HARMONY

| ❑ H30012 | Bye Bye Love | 1970 | 12.00 |

KING

❑ 962 [M]	24 Songs by the Great Trini Lopez	1966	30.00
❑ 877 [M]	More of Trini Lopez	1964	60.00
❑ 863 [M]	Teenage Love Songs	1963	60.00

REPRISE

❑ R-6226 [M]	Greatest Hits!	1966	15.00
❑ RS-6226 [S]	Greatest Hits!	1966	18.00
❑ RS-6285 [S]	It's a Great Life	1968	15.00
❑ R-6285 [M]	It's a Great Life	1968	30.00

—Mono is white label promo only

❑ R-6134 [M]	Live at Basin St. East	1964	15.00
❑ RS-6134 [S]	Live at Basin St. East	1964	18.00
❑ R-6103 [M]	More Trini Lopez at PJ's	1963	15.00
❑ RS-6103 [S]	More Trini Lopez at PJ's	1963	18.00
❑ R-6112 [M]	On the Move	1964	15.00
❑ RS-6112 [S]	On the Move	1964	18.00
❑ R-6147 [M]	The Folk Album	1965	15.00
❑ RS-6147 [S]	The Folk Album	1965	18.00
❑ R-6125 [M]	The Latin Album	1964	15.00
❑ RS-6125 [S]	The Latin Album	1964	18.00
❑ R-6165 [M]	The Love Album	1965	15.00
❑ RS-6165 [S]	The Love Album	1965	18.00
❑ R-6171 [M]	The Rhythm & Blues Album	1965	15.00
❑ RS-6171 [S]	The Rhythm & Blues Album	1965	18.00
❑ R-6215 [M]	The Second Latin Album	1966	15.00
❑ RS-6215 [S]	The Second Latin Album	1966	18.00
❑ R-6183 [M]	The Sing-Along World of Trini Lopez	1965	15.00
❑ RS-6183 [S]	The Sing-Along World of Trini Lopez	1965	18.00
❑ RS 6361	The Trini Lopez Show	1970	18.00
❑ RS-6337	The Whole Enchilada	1969	15.00
❑ R-6196 [M]	Trini	1966	15.00
❑ RS-6196 [S]	Trini	1966	10.00
❑ R-6093 [M]	Trini Lopez at PJ's	1963	15.00
❑ R9-6093 [S]	Trini Lopez at PJ's	1963	18.00
❑ R-6238 [M]	Trini Lopez in London	1967	18.00
❑ RS-6238 [S]	Trini Lopez in London	1967	15.00
❑ R-6255 [M]	Trini Lopez — Now!	1967	18.00
❑ RS-6255 [S]	Trini Lopez — Now!	1967	15.00
❑ RS-6300	Welcome to Trini Country	1968	15.00

ROULETTE

| ❑ 3020 | Transformed by Time | 1978 | 12.00 |

LORBER, JEFF

ARISTA

| ❑ AL9545 | Galaxian | 1981 | 12.00 |
| ❑ AL8119 | Galaxian | 198? | 10.00 |

—Reissue of 9545

❑ AL8-8025	In the Heat of the Night	1984	12.00
❑ AL9583	It's a Fact	1982	12.00
❑ AL8218	It's a Fact	198?	10.00

—Reissue of 9583

❑ AL8393	Lift Off	1986	12.00
❑ AL8-8269	Step by Step	1985	12.00
❑ AB4234	Water Sign	1979	12.00
❑ AL8360	Water Sign	198?	10.00

—Reissue of 4234

| ❑ AL9516 | Wizard Island | 1980 | 12.00 |
| ❑ AL8340 | Wizard Island | 198? | 10.00 |

—Reissue of 9516

INNER CITY

| ❑ IC-1026 | Jeff Lorber Fusion | 1977 | 18.00 |
| ❑ IC-1056 | Soft Space | 1978 | 18.00 |

WARNER BROS.

| ❑ 25492 | Private Passion | 1986 | 12.00 |

LORD, BOBBY

DECCA

| ❑ DL75246 [B] | Bobby Lord | 1970 | 18.00 |

HARMONY

| ❑ HL7322 [M] | Bobby Lord's Best | 1964 | 30.00 |

HICKORY

| ❑ LP-126 [M] | The Bobby Lord Show | 1965 | 25.00 |

LORD SITAR

CAPITOL

| ❑ ST2916 [B] | Lord Sitar | 1968 | 50.00 |

LORDS OF THE NEW CHURCH

I.R.S.

❑ SP-70039 [B]	Is Nothing Sacred?	1983	18.00
❑ 5726 [B]	Killer Lords	1986	18.00
❑ SP-70029 [B]	The Lords of the New Church	1982	25.00
❑ SP-70049	The Method to Our Madness	1984	15.00

—As "The Lords

LOREN, DONNA

CAPITOL

| ❑ T2323 [M] | Beach Blanket Bingo | 1965 | 40.00 |
| ❑ ST2323 [S] | Beach Blanket Bingo | 1965 | 50.00 |

LORIMER, MICHAEL

DANCING CAT

| ❑ DC-3002 | Remembranza | 198? | 15.00 |

LORING, GLORIA

ATLANTIC

| ❑ 81852 | Full Moon, No Hesitation | 1988 | 10.00 |
| ❑ 81679 | Gloria Loring | 1986 | 10.00 |

MGM

| ❑ SE-4499 | Today | 1968 | 25.00 |

LOS ADMIRADORES

COMMAND

| ❑ 809SD [S] | Bongos Bongos Bongos | 1960 | 18.00 |
| ❑ 812SD [S] | Bongos/Flutes/Guitars | 1960 | 18.00 |

LOS ANGELES PHILHARMONIC (ZUBIN MEHTA, CONDUCTOR)

MOBILE FIDELITY

| ❑ 1-008 | Suites from "Star Wars" and "Close Encounters of the Third Kind" | 1979 | 50.00 |

—Audiophile vinyl

LOS BRAVOS

PARROT

| ❑ PAS71021 | Bring a Little Lovin' | 1968 | 80.00 |

—Among the other tracks, "Black Is Black" in in true stereo.

PRESS

| ❑ PR73003 [M] | Black Is Black | 1966 | 60.00 |
| ❑ PRS83003 [R] | Black Is Black | 1966 | 40.00 |

LOS INDIOS TABAJARAS

RCA CAMDEN

| ❑ CXS-9031 | Los Indios Tabajaras | 1973 | 18.00 |

RCA INTERNATIONAL

| ❑ IL5-7367 | Los Grandes Exitos | 198? | 15.00 |

RCA VICTOR

❑ LPM 2012 [M]	Always in My Heart	1964	18.00
❑ LSP-2912 [S]	Always in My Heart	1964	25.00
❑ AFL1-2912	Always in My Heart	1977	12.00

—Reissue with new prefix

❑ AFL1-3990	Beautiful Sounds	1981	12.00
❑ LPM-3505 [M]	Casually Classical	1966	18.00
❑ LSP-3505 [S]	Casually Classical	1966	25.00
❑ AFL1-3505	Casually Classical	1977	12.00

—Reissue with now prefix

| ❑ CPL1-0668 | Classical Guitars | 1974 | 15.00 |
| ❑ AFL1-0668 | Classical Guitars | 1977 | 12.00 |

—Reissue with new prefix

❑ LSP-4365	Dreams of Love	1970	18.00
❑ LPM-3909 [M]	Fascinating Rhythms of Their Brazil	1968	25.00
❑ LSP-3909 [S]	Fascinating Rhythms of Their Brazil	1968	18.00
❑ APL1-0210	Favorite Movie Themes	1973	15.00
❑ AFL1-0210	Favorite Movie Themes	1977	12.00

—Reissue with new prefix

❑ AFL1-4649	Guitars on the Go	1983	12.00
❑ LSP-4013	In a Sentimental Mood	1968	18.00
❑ ANL1-2321	In a Sentimental Mood	1977	12.00
❑ LPM-3413 [M]	Many-Splendored Guitars	1965	18.00
❑ LSP-3413 [S]	Many-Splendored Guitars	1965	25.00
❑ LPM-2822 [M]	Maria Elena	1963	25.00

—Reissue of LPM-1788

| ❑ LSP-2822 [S] | Maria Elena | 1963 | 30.00 |

—Reissue of LSP-1788

| ❑ FSP-296 | Maria Elena | 1971 | 15.00 |
| ❑ ANL1-1179 | Maria Elena | 1976 | 12.00 |

—Reissue

❑ AFL1-2526	Masterpieces	1978	15.00
❑ APL1-2082	Mellow Nostalgia	1977	15.00
❑ AFL1-4273	Music for Romance	1982	12.00
❑ AFL1-3535	Rainbows	1980	12.00
❑ APL1-1033	Secret Love	1975	15.00
❑ AFL1-1033	Secret Love	1977	12.00

—Reissue with new prefix

❑ FSP-300	Siempre En Mi Corazon	1972	15.00
❑ FSP-310	Softly	1972	15.00
❑ LSP-4129	Song of the Islands	1969	18.00
❑ LPM-1788 [M]	Sweet and Savage	1958	40.00
❑ LSP-1788 [S]	Sweet and Savage	1958	50.00
❑ LSP-4007	The Best of Los Indios Tabajaras	1968	18.00
❑ AFL1-4007	The Best of Los Indios Tabajaras	1977	12.00

—Reissue with new prefix

| ❑ LPM-3723 [M] | Their Very Special Touch | 1967 | 18.00 |
| ❑ LSP-3723 [S] | Their Very Special Touch | 1967 | 25.00 |

Number	Title	Yr	NM
❏ LSP-4496	The Very Thought of You	1971	18.00
❏ LPM-2959 [M]	Twin Guitar Moods	1964	18.00
❏ LSP-2959 [S]	Twin Guitar Moods	1964	25.00
❏ LPM-3611 [M]	Twin Guitars -- In a Mood for Lovers	1966	18.00
❏ LSP-3611 [S]	Twin Guitars -- In a Mood for Lovers	1966	25.00
❏ AFL1-3241	Two Guitars	1979	12.00
❏ LSP-4615	What the World Needs Now	1971	15.00

LOS LOBOS

NEW VISTAS
❏ 1001	Just Another Band from East L.A.	1978	250.00

SLASH
❏ 23963 [EP]	And a Time to Dance	1983	15.00
❏ R144507	By the Light of the Moon	1987	15.00
— RCA Music Service edition			
❏ 25523	By the Light of the Moon	1987	12.00
❏ 25177	How Will the Wolf Survive?	1984	12.00
❏ 25790	La Pistola y El Corazon	1988	18.00
❏ 26131	The Neighborhood	1990	25.00

LOS LOCOS DEL RITMO

DIMSA
❏ 8178	Rock!	196?	100.00

LOS SEVEN DAYS

ECO
❏ 314	Sha-La-La	196?	50.00

LOST & FOUND

INTERNATIONAL ARTISTS
❏ IA-3	Everybody's Here	1968	100.00
— Original pressing, no "Masterfonics" in dead wax			
❏ IA-3	Everybody's Here	1979	18.00
— Reissue with "Masterfonics" in trail-off wax			

LOST NATION, THE

RARE EARTH
❏ RS-518	Paradise Lost	1970	25.00

LOTHAR AND THE HAND PEOPLE

CAPITOL
❏ ST2997 [B]	Presenting Lothar and the Hand People	1968	60.00
❏ SM-2997	Presenting Lothar and the Hand People	1977	10.00
— Reissue with new prefix			
❏ ST-247 [B]	Space Hymn	1969	60.00

LOTTRIDGE, RICHARD, AND JOAN WILDMAN

UNIVERSITY OF WISCONSIN
❏ UW-102	Something New: The Unique Sounds of Jazz Bassoon	1986	18.00

LOUDERMILK, JOHN D.

RCA VICTOR
❏ LPM-3497 [M]	A Bizarre Collection of the Most Unusual Songs	1965	25.00
❏ LSP-3497 [S]	A Bizarre Collection of the Most Unusual Songs	1965	30.00
❏ LSP-4040	Country Love Songs	1968	25.00
❏ LPM-2434 [M]	Language of Love	1961	30.00
❏ LSP-2434 [S]	Language of Love	1961	30.00
❏ LPM-3807 [M]	Suburban Attitudes in Country Music	1967	30.00
❏ LSP-3807 [S]	Suburban Attitudes in Country Music	1967	25.00
❏ LSP-4097	The Open Mind of John D. Loudermilk	1968	25.00
❏ LPM-2539 [M]	Twelve Sides of Loudermilk	1962	25.00
❏ LSP-2539 [S]	Twelve Sides of Loudermilk	1962	30.00

WARNER BROS.
❏ WS1922	Volume 1, Elloree	1971	18.00

LOUDON, DOROTHY

CORAL
❏ CRL57265 [M]	At the Blue Angel	1959	25.00
❏ CRL757265 [S]	At the Blue Angel	1959	30.00

LOUIE AND THE LOVERS

EPIC
❏ E30026 [B]	Rise	1970	30.00

LOUISE, TINA

CONCERT HALL
❏ H-1503 [M]	Her Portrait in Hi-Fi	1958	50.00
❏ H-1521 [M]	It's Time for Tina	1958	200.00

URANIA
❏ USD-2005 [S]	It's Time for Tina	1959	300.00
❏ ULM-2005 [M]	It's Time for Tina	1959	200.00

LOUISIANA HONEY DRIPPERS, THE

PRESTIGE
❏ PR-13035 [M]	Bluegrass	1961	30.00

LOUISIANA RED

ROULETTE
❏ R-25200 [M]	The Lowdown Back Porch Blues	1963	40.00

LOUNGE LIZARDS, THE

EDITIONS EG
❏ EGS-108	The Lounge Lizards	1981	15.00

EUROPA
❏ JP-2012	Live from the Drunken Boat	1983	18.00

ISLAND
❏ 90529	Live in Tokyo -- Big Heart	1986	12.00
❏ 90592	No Pain for Cakes	1987	12.00

LOUVIN, CHARLIE, AND MELBA MONTGOMERY

CAPITOL
❏ ST-808	Baby, You've Got What It Takes	1971	25.00
❏ ST-686	Somethin' to Brag About	1971	25.00

LOUVIN, CHARLIE

CAPITOL
❏ ST-416	Here's a Toast to Mama	1970	25.00
❏ ST-142	Hey Daddy	1969	25.00
❏ ST-8-0142	Hey Daddy	1969	30.00
— Capitol Record Club edition			
❏ T2787 [M]	I Forgot to Cry	1967	30.00
❏ ST2787 [S]	I Forgot to Cry	1967	30.00
❏ T2689 [M]	I'll Remember Always	1967	30.00
❏ ST2689 [S]	I'll Remember Always	1967	30.00
❏ T2208 [M]	Less and Less and I Don't Love You Anymore	1965	25.00
❏ ST2208 [S]	Less and Less and I Don't Love You Anymore	1965	30.00
❏ T2482 [M]	Lonesome Is Me	1966	25.00
❏ ST2482 [S]	Lonesome Is Me	1966	30.00
❏ ST-555	Ten Times Charlie	1970	25.00
❏ ST-248	The Kind of Man I Am	1969	25.00
❏ T2437 [M]	The Many Moods of Charlie Louvin	1966	25.00
❏ ST2437 [S]	The Many Moods of Charlie Louvin	1966	30.00
❏ ST2958	Will You Visit Me on Sundays	1068	25.00

UNITED ARTISTS
❏ UA-LA248-G	It Almost Felt Like Love	1974	18.00

LOUVIN, IRA

CAPITOL
❏ T2413 [M]	The Unforgettable Ira Louvin	1965	30.00
❏ ST2413 [S]	The Unforgettable Ira Louvin	1965	30.00

LOUVIN BROTHERS, THE

CAPITOL
❏ T1449 [M]	A Tribute to the Delmore Brothers	1960	80.00
— Black colorband label, logo at left			
❏ T1449 [M]	A Tribute to the Delmore Brothers	1962	30.00
— Black colorband label, logo at top			
❏ T1616 [M]	Country Christmas	1961	50.00
— Black rainbow label with "Capitol" at left			
❏ ST1616 [S]	Country Christmas	1961	80.00
— Black rainbow label with "Capitol" at left			
❏ T1616 [M]	Country Christmas	1962	25.00
— Black rainbow label with "Capitol" at top			
❏ ST1616 [S]	Country Christmas	1962	30.00
— Black rainbow label with "Capitol" at top			
❏ T1106 [M]	Country Love Ballads	1959	80.00
— Black colorband label, logo at left			
❏ T1106 [M]	Country Love Ballads	1962	30.00
— Black colorband label, logo at top			
❏ T1547 [M]	Encore	1961	80.00
— Black colorband label, logo at left			
❏ T1547 [M]	Encore	1962	30.00
— Black colorband label, logo at top			
❏ T910 [M]	Ira and Charlie	1958	100.00
— Turquoise label			
❏ T910 [M]	Ira and Charlie	1959	40.00
— Black colorband label, logo at left			
❏ T910 [M]	Ira and Charlie	1962	30.00
— Black colorband label, logo at top			
❏ T1834 [M]	Keep Your Eyes on Jesus	1963	40.00
❏ ST1834 [S]	Keep Your Eyes on Jesus	1963	50.00
❏ T1385 [M]	My Baby's Gone	1960	80.00
— Black colorband label, logo at left			
❏ T1385 [M]	My Baby's Gone	1962	30.00
— Black colorband label, logo at top			
❏ T825 [M]	Nearer My God to Thee	1957	100.00
— Turquoise label			
❏ T825 [M]	Nearer My God to Thee	1959	40.00
— Black colorband label, logo at left			
❏ T825 [M]	Nearer My God to Thee	1962	30.00
— Black colorband label, logo at top			
❏ T1277 [M]	Satan Is Real	1960	80.00
— Black colorband label, logo at left			
❏ T1277 [M]	Satan Is Real	1962	30.00
— Black colorband label, logo at top			
❏ T2331 [M]	Thank God for My Christian Home	1965	30.00

Number	Title	Yr	NM
❏ ST2331 [S]	Thank God for My Christian Home	1965	30.00
❏ T1061 [M]	The Family Who Prays	1958	80.00
— Black colorband label, logo at left			
❏ T1061 [M]	The Family Who Prays	1962	30.00
— Black colorband label, logo at top			
❏ DT1061 [R]	The Family Who Prays	196?	25.00
❏ ST2827 [S]	The Great Roy Acuff Songs	1967	30.00
❏ T2827 [M]	The Great Roy Acuff Songs	1967	40.00
❏ T2091 [M]	The Louvin Brothers Sing and Play Their Current Hits	1964	30.00
❏ ST2091 [S]	The Louvin Brothers Sing and Play Their Current Hits	1964	30.00
❏ T769 [M]	Tragic Songs of Life	1956	100.00
— Turquoise label			
❏ T769 [M]	Tragic Songs of Life	1959	40.00
— Black colorband label, logo at left			
❏ T769 [M]	Tragic Songs of Life	1962	30.00
— Black colorband label, logo at top			
❏ DT769 [R]	Tragic Songs of Life	196?	25.00
❏ T1721 [M]	Weapon of Prayer	1962	40.00
❏ ST1721 [S]	Weapon of Prayer	1962	50.00

METRO
❏ M-598 [M]	The Louvin Brothers	1966	30.00
❏ MS-598 [R]	The Louvin Brothers	1966	25.00

MGM
❏ E-3426 [M]	The Louvin Brothers	1957	200.00

SEARS
❏ SP-119 [M]	Ira & Charles Louvin	196?	25.00
❏ SPS-119 [R]	Ira & Charles Louvin	196?	18.00

TOWER
❏ DT5122	Country Heart and Soul	1968	25.00
❏ T5038 [M]	Two Different Worlds	1966	30.00
❏ DT5038 [R]	Two Different Worlds	1966	25.00

LOVANO, JOE

SOUL NOTE
❏ 121132	Tones, Shapes and Colors	1985	15.00
❏ 121182	Village Rhythm	1988	15.00

LOVE, DARLENE

COLUMBIA
❏ FC40605	Paint Another Picture	1988	15.00

LOVE, HOLLY

ACE
❏ LP-1022 [M]	My Love Confessions	1962	30.00

LOVE, PRESTON

KENT
❏ KST-540	Omaha Bar-B-Q	1968	25.00

LOVE

BLUE THUMB
❏ BTS-8822 [B]	False Start	1970	30.00
❏ BTS-9000 [B]	Out Here	1969	40.00

ELEKTRA
❏ EKL-4005 [M]	Da Capo	1967	300.00
❏ EKS-74005 [S]	Da Capo	1967	40.00
— Brown label			
❏ EKS-74005 [S]	Da Capo	1969	18.00
— Red label with large stylized "E			
❏ EKS-74005 [S]	Da Capo	1971	15.00
— Butterfly label			
❏ EKL-4013 [M]	Forever Changes	1967	350.00
❏ EKL-4013 [M]	Forever Changes	1967	350.00
— White label promo			
❏ EKS-74013 [S]	Forever Changes	1967	30.00
— Brown label			
❏ EKS-74013 [S]	Forever Changes	1969	18.00
— Red label with large stylized "E			
❏ EKS-74013 [S]	Forever Changes	1971	15.00
— Butterfly label			
❏ EKS-74013 [S]	Forever Changes	1980	12.00
— Red label, small "E," Warner Communications logo on label			
❏ EKS-74013 [S]	Forever Changes	1984	10.00
— Red and black label			
❏ EKS-74049 [DJ]	Four Sail	1969	80.00
— White label promo			
❏ EKS-74049	Four Sail	1969	30.00
— Red label with large stylized "E			
❏ EKS-74049	Four Sail	1971	15.00
— Butterfly label			
❏ EKL-4001 [M]	Love	1966	300.00
❏ EKL-4001 [M]	Love	1966	350.00
— White label promo			
❏ EKS-74001 [S]	Love	1966	50.00
— Brown label			
❏ EKS-74001 [S]	Love	1969	18.00
— Red label with large stylized "E			
❏ EKS-74001 [S]	Love	1971	15.00
— Butterfly label			
❏ EKS-74058	Revisited	1970	30.00
— Red label with large stylized "E			
❏ EKS-74058	Revisited	1971	15.00
— Butterfly label			
❏ EKS-74058	Revisited	1984	10.00
— Red and black label			

Number	Title	Yr	NM
❑ EKS-74058	Revisited	198?	12.00

—Red label, small "E," Warner Communications logo on label

MCA

Number	Title	Yr	NM
❑ 27025	Studio/Live	1982	12.00

RHINO

Number	Title	Yr	NM
❑ RNLP-800	Best of Love	1980	12.00
❑ RNDF-251 [PD]	Love Live	1981	18.00
❑ RNLP-70175	The Best of Love (1966-1969) (Golden Archive Series)	1987	12.00

RSO

Number	Title	Yr	NM
❑ SO4804	Reel to Real	1974	18.00

SUNDAZED

Number	Title	Yr	NM
❑ LP5101	Da Capo	2001	15.00

—Reissue on 180-gram vinyl

Number	Title	Yr	NM
❑ LP5102	Forever Changes	2001	15.00

—Reissue on 180-gram vinyl

Number	Title	Yr	NM
❑ LP5103	Four Sail	2004	15.00
❑ LP5100	Love	2001	15.00

—Reissue on 180-gram vinyl

Number	Title	Yr	NM
❑ LP5104	Revisited	2001	15.00

—Reissue on 180-gram vinyl

LOVE AND ROCKETS

BEGGARS BANQUET

Number	Title	Yr	NM
❑ 9715-1-R	Love and Rockets	1989	12.00

BIG TIME/RCA

Number	Title	Yr	NM
❑ 6058-1-B8	Earth.Sun.Moon	1987	12.00
❑ 6011-1-B	Express	1986	15.00

RCA

Number	Title	Yr	NM
❑ 8507-1-R	Seventh Dream of Teenage Heaven	1988	12.00

LOVE EXCHANGE, THE

TOWER

Number	Title	Yr	NM
❑ ST5115 [S]	The Love Exchange	1968	30.00
❑ T5115 [M]	The Love Exchange	1968	60.00

LOVE GENERATION, THE

IMPERIAL

Number	Title	Yr	NM
❑ LP-12364	A Generation of Love	1968	25.00
❑ LP-12408	Montage	1968	25.00
❑ LP-9351 [M]	The Love Generation	1967	50.00
❑ LP-12351 [S]	The Love Generation	1967	25.00

LOVE SCULPTURE

EMI AMERICA

Number	Title	Yr	NM
❑ SQ-17208	Blues Helping	1986	15.00

—Reissue of Rare Earth LP

PARROT

Number	Title	Yr	NM
❑ PAS71035 [B]	Forms and Feelings	1970	35.00

RARE EARTH

Number	Title	Yr	NM
❑ RS 506 [B]	Blues Helping	1969	60.00

LOVE UNLIMITED

20TH CENTURY

Number	Title	Yr	NM
❑ T-443	In Heat	1974	12.00
❑ T-414	Under the Influence of…	1973	12.00

MCA

Number	Title	Yr	NM
❑ 181	Love Unlimited	1973	15.00

—Reissue of Uni 73131

UNI

Number	Title	Yr	NM
❑ 73131	Love Unlimited	1972	18.00

UNLIMITED GOLD

Number	Title	Yr	NM
❑ 101	He's All I Got	1977	12.00
❑ JZ36130	Love Is Back	1979	12.00

LOVE UNLIMITED ORCHESTRA

20TH CENTURY

Number	Title	Yr	NM
❑ T-582	Movie Themes	1978	12.00
❑ T-480	Music Maestro Please	1975	12.00
❑ T-554	My Musical Bouquet	1978	12.00
❑ T-517	My Sweet Summer Suite	1976	12.00
❑ T-433	Rhapsody in White	1974	12.00
❑ T-101	Together Brothers	1974	15.00
❑ T-458	White Gold	1974	12.00

UNLIMITED GOLD

Number	Title	Yr	NM
❑ FZ38366	Rise	1983	12.00
❑ FZ37425	Welcome Aboard	1981	12.00

LOVELESS, PATTY

MCA

Number	Title	Yr	NM
❑ 42223	Honky Tonk Angel	1988	12.00
❑ 42092	If My Heart Had Windows	1988	12.00
❑ 5915	Patty Loveless	1987	12.00

LOVELITES, THE

UNI

Number	Title	Yr	NM
❑ 73081 [B]	The Lovelites	1970	30.00

LOVERBOY

COLUMBIA

Number	Title	Yr	NM
❑ OC45411	Big Ones	1989	15.00
❑ FC37638	Get Lucky	1981	10.00
❑ QC38703	Keep It Up	1983	10.00
❑ JC36762	Loverboy	1980	10.00
❑ A2S1256 [DJ]	Loverboy Live from Dayton, Ohio	1981	25.00

—Promo-only release; three sides have music, the fourth side has the band's autographs etched into the record

Number	Title	Yr	NM
❑ FC39953	Lovin' Every Minute of It	1985	10.00
❑ OC40893	Wildside	1987	10.00

LOVETT, LEE

STRAND

Number	Title	Yr	NM
❑ SL-1055 [M]	Jazz Dance Party	1962	25.00
❑ SLS-1055 [S]	Jazz Dance Party	1962	30.00
❑ SL-1059 [M]	Misty	1962	25.00
❑ SLS-1059 [S]	Misty	1962	30.00

WYNNE

Number	Title	Yr	NM
❑ WLP-108 [M]	Jazz Dance Party	195?	30.00

LOVETT, LYLE

MCA/CURB

Number	Title	Yr	NM
❑ R133603	Lyle Lovett	1986	15.00

—RCA Music Service edition

Number	Title	Yr	NM
❑ 5748	Lyle Lovett	1986	12.00
❑ R100932	Lyle Lovett And His Large Band	1989	15.00

—BMG Direct Marketing edition

Number	Title	Yr	NM
❑ 42263	Lyle Lovett And His Large Band	1989	12.00
❑ 17355 [EP]	Not Exactly Mr. Showbiz	1987	18.00

—Promo-only five-song EP with special sleeve

Number	Title	Yr	NM
❑ R153258	Pontiac	1988	15.00

—BMG Direct Marketing edition

Number	Title	Yr	NM
❑ 42028	Pontiac	1988	12.00

LOVICH, LENE

STIFF/EPIC

Number	Title	Yr	NM
❑ JE36308	Flex	1980	15.00
❑ 5E37452 [EP]	New Toy	1981	18.00
❑ ARE38399	No Man's Land	1983	12.00
❑ JE36102 [B]	Stateless	1979	30.00

—Red vinyl

Number	Title	Yr	NM
❑ JE36102 [B]	Stateless	1979	18.00

LOVIN' SPOONFUL, THE

51 WEST

Number	Title	Yr	NM
❑ Q16023	... So Nice	1979	12.00

ACCORD

Number	Title	Yr	NM
❑ SN-7196	Distant Echoes	1981	12.00

BUDDAH

Number	Title	Yr	NM
❑ BDM-5706	The Best of the Lovin' Spoonful	197?	15.00
❑ BLB6-8339	The Best of the Lovin' Spoonful	198?	12.00

—Reissue of 5706

KAMA SUTRA

Number	Title	Yr	NM
❑ KLPS-750-2	24 Karat Hits	1968	25.00
❑ KLP-8051 [M]	Daydream	1966	40.00
❑ KLPS-8051 [S]	Daydream	1966	30.00
❑ T-90675 [M]	Daydream	1966	30.00

—Capitol Record Club edition

Number	Title	Yr	NM
❑ ST-90675 [S]	Daydream	1966	40.00

—Capitol Record Club edition

Number	Title	Yr	NM
❑ KLP-8050 [M]	Do You Believe in Magic	1965	35.00
❑ KLPS-8050 [S]	Do You Believe in Magic	1965	30.00
❑ T-90597 [M]	Do You Believe in Magic	1965	30.00

—Capitol Record Club edition

Number	Title	Yr	NM
❑ ST-90597 [S]	Do You Believe in Magic	1965	40.00

—Capitol Record Club edition

Number	Title	Yr	NM
❑ KLPS-8061 [S]	Everything Playing	1968	25.00
❑ KLP-8061 [M]	Everything Playing	1968	60.00
❑ KLP-8054 [M]	Hums of the Lovin' Spoonful	1966	40.00
❑ KLPS-8054 [S]	Hums of the Lovin' Spoonful	1966	30.00
❑ ST-90988 [S]	Hums of the Lovin' Spoonful	1966	40.00

—Capitol Record Club edition

Number	Title	Yr	NM
❑ KSBS-2029	Once Upon a Time	1971	18.00
❑ KLPS-8073	Revelation: Revolution '69	1969	30.00
❑ KSBS-2608	The Best…Lovin' Spoonful	1976	25.00
❑ KLP-8056 [M]	The Best of the Lovin' Spoonful	1967	18.00

—Came with four bonus photos of the band, which are priced separately

Number	Title	Yr	NM
❑ KLPS-8056 [S]	The Best of the Lovin' Spoonful	1967	18.00

—Came with four bonus photos of the band, which are priced separately

Number	Title	Yr	NM
❑ KAO-91102 [M]	The Best of the Lovin' Spoonful	1967	30.00

—Capitol Record Club edition

Number	Title	Yr	NM
❑ SKAO-91102 [S]	The Best of the Lovin' Spoonful	1967	25.00

—Capitol Record Club edition

Number	Title	Yr	NM
❑ KLP-8064 [M]	The Best of the Lovin' Spoonful, Volume 2	1968	50.00
❑ KLPS-8064 [S]	The Best of the Lovin' Spoonful, Volume 2	1968	25.00
❑ KLP/S-8056	The Best of the Lovin' Spoonful Bonus Photos (4)	1967	12.00
❑ KSBS-2011	The John Sebastian Song Book	1970	18.00
❑ KSBS-2013	The Very Best of the Lovin' Spoonful	1970	18.00
❑ KLP-8053 [M]	What's Up, Tiger Lily?	1966	40.00
❑ KLPS-8053 [S]	What's Up, Tiger Lily?	1966	30.00
❑ KLP-8058 [M]	You're a Big Boy Now	1967	60.00
❑ KLPS-8058 [S]	You're a Big Boy Now	1967	25.00
❑ ST-91198 [S]	You're a Big Boy Now	1967	30.00

—Capitol Record Club edition

KOALA

Number	Title	Yr	NM
❑ KO14221	Day Dream	1979	12.00

PAIR

Number	Title	Yr	NM
❑ PDL2-1200	The Best of the Lovin' Spoonful	1986	15.00

RHINO

Number	Title	Yr	NM
❑ RNLP-114	The Best of the Lovin' Spoonful, Vol. 2	1985	12.00

SUNDAZED

Number	Title	Yr	NM
❑ LP5160	Daydream	2002	18.00

—Reissue on 180-gram vinyl

Number	Title	Yr	NM
❑ LP5159	Do You Believe in Magic	2002	18.00

—Reissue on 180-gram vinyl

Number	Title	Yr	NM
❑ LP5166	Hums of the Lovin' Spoonful	2003	18.00

—Reissue on 180-gram vinyl

LOWE, BERNIE, ORCHESTRA

CAMEO

Number	Title	Yr	NM
❑ C-1057 [M]	Encore	1963	25.00
❑ C-4005 [M]	If the Big Bands Were Here Today	1962	25.00
❑ SC-4005 [S]	If the Big Bands Were Here Today	1962	30.00
❑ C-4007 [M]	If the Big Bands Were Here Today, Vol. 2	1962	25.00
❑ SC-4007 [S]	If the Big Bands Were Here Today, Vol. 2	1962	30.00

LOWE, JIM

DOT

Number	Title	Yr	NM
❑ DLP-3681 [M]	Songs They Sing Behind the Green Door	1965	30.00
❑ DLP-25881 [S]	Songs They Sing Behind the Green Door	1965	30.00
❑ DLP-3051 [M]	The Green Door	1956	150.00
❑ DLP-3114 [M]	Wicked Women	1958	100.00

MERCURY

Number	Title	Yr	NM
❑ MG-20246 [M]	The Door of Fame	1957	150.00

LOWE, MUNDELL

CHARLIE PARKER

Number	Title	Yr	NM
❑ PLP-822 [M]	Blues for a Stripper	1962	40.00
❑ PLP-822S [S]	Blues for a Stripper	1962	50.00

DOBRE

Number	Title	Yr	NM
❑ 1018	Incomparable	1978	18.00

FAMOUS DOOR

Number	Title	Yr	NM
❑ HL-102	California Guitar	1974	30.00

JAZZLAND

Number	Title	Yr	NM
❑ JLP-8 [M]	Low-Down Guitar	1960	60.00

OFFBEAT

Number	Title	Yr	NM
❑ OLP-3010 [M]	Tacet for Neurotics	1960	80.00
❑ OS-93010 [S]	Tacet for Neurotics	1960	100.00

PAUSA

Number	Title	Yr	NM
❑ 7152	Mundell Lowe Presents Transit West	1983	18.00

RCA CAMDEN

Number	Title	Yr	NM
❑ CAL-490 [M]	Porgy and Bess	1959	18.00
❑ CAS-490 [S]	Porgy and Bess	1959	25.00
❑ CAL-522 [M]	TV Action Jazz!	1959	18.00
❑ CAS-522 [S]	TV Action Jazz!	1959	25.00
❑ CAL-627 [M]	TV Action Jazz! -- Volume 2	1960	30.00
❑ CAS-627 [S]	TV Action Jazz! -- Volume 2	1960	30.00

RCA VICTOR

Number	Title	Yr	NM
❑ LJM-3002 [10]	The Mundell Lowe Quintet	1954	120.00

RIVERSIDE

Number	Title	Yr	NM
❑ RLP 12-238 [M]	A Grand Night for Swinging	1957	80.00

—White label, blue print

Number	Title	Yr	NM
❑ RLP 12-238 [M]	A Grand Night for Swinging	1959	50.00

—Blue label, microphone logo at top

Number	Title	Yr	NM
❑ RLP 12-208 [M]	Guitar Moods	1956	60.00

—White label, blue print

Number	Title	Yr	NM
❑ RLP 12-208 [M]	Guitar Moods	1959	50.00

—Blue label, microphone logo at top

Number	Title	Yr	NM
❑ 6089	Mundell Lowe Quintet	197?	18.00
❑ RLP 12-219 [M]	New Music of Alec Wilder	1956	80.00

—White label, blue print

Number	Title	Yr	NM
❑ RLP 12-219 [M]	New Music of Alec Wilder	1959	50.00

—Blue label, microphone logo at top

Number	Title	Yr	NM
❑ RLP 12-204 [M]	The Mundell Lowe Quartet	1956	80.00

—White label, blue print

Number	Title	Yr	NM
❑ RLP 12-204 [M]	The Mundell Lowe Quartet	1959	50.00

—Blue label, microphone logo at top

LOWE, NICK

COLUMBIA

Number	Title	Yr	NM
❑ AS1400 [DJ]	An Interrogation of Nick Lowe	1990	30.00

—Promo-only interview album

Number	Title	Yr	NM
❑ AS1400 [DJ]	An Interrogation of Nick Lowe	1990	30.00

—Promo-only interview album

Number	Title	Yr	NM

LOWE, NICK (continued)

Number	Title	Yr	NM
❏ JC36087	Labour of Lust	1979	12.00
❏ PC36087	Labour of Lust	198?	10.00
— Budget-line reissue			
❏ FC39371	Nick Lowe and His Cowboy Outfit	1984	15.00
❏ PC39371	Nick Lowe and His Cowboy Outfit	1986	10.00
— Budget-line reissue			
❏ FC37932	Nick the Knife	1982	15.00
❏ PC37932	Nick the Knife	198?	10.00
— Budget-line reissue			
❏ FC40381	Pinker and Prouder Than Previous	1988	14.00
❏ JC35529	Pure Pop for Now People	1978	25.00
❏ PC35529	Pure Pop for Now People	198?	10.00
— Budget-line reissue			
❏ FC38589	The Abominable Showman	1983	15.00
❏ PC38589	The Abominable Showman	1986	10.00
— Budget-line reissue			
❏ FC39958	The Rose of England	1985	15.00
REPRISE			
❏ 26132	Party of One	1990	15.00

LOWE, SAMMY

RCA VICTOR
| ❏ LPM-2770 [M] | Hitsville U.S.A. | 1963 | 25.00 |
| ❏ LSP-2770 [S] | Hitsville U.S.A. | 1963 | 30.00 |

LOWRY, RON

REPUBLIC
| ❏ 1303 | Marry Me | 1970 | 18.00 |

LRY

CONGRESS OF THE CROW
| ❏ 8031002 | The LRY Record | 1968 | 200.00 |

LUBOFF, NORMAN, CHOIR

COLUMBIA
❏ CL2545 [10]	Carols for Christmas	1955	30.00
— House Party Series			
❏ CL6272 [10]	Christmas Carols	1953	40.00
❏ CL545 [M]	Easy to Remember	1954	25.00
— Maroon label, gold print			
❏ CL926 [M]	Songs of Christmas	1957	18.00
— Six LPs pictured on back cover: "exciting moments from Columbia's treasury of jazz			
❏ CS8846 [R]	Songs of Christmas	1963	15.00
❏ CL926 [M]	Songs of Christmas	1957	18.00
— Six LPs pictured on back cover: "dazzling performances of music from Hollywood			

RCA VICTOR
| ❏ LPM-2941 [M] | Christmas with the Norman Luboff Choir | 1964 | 15.00 |
| ❏ LSP-2941 [S] | Christmas with the Norman Luboff Choir | 1964 | 18.00 |

LUCAS, BUDDY

UNITED ARTISTS
| ❏ UAL-3482 [M] | Fifty Fabulous Harmonica Favorites | 1966 | 25.00 |
| ❏ UAS-6482 [S] | Fifty Fabulous Harmonica Favorites | 1966 | 30.00 |

LUCAS, DOUG

SHADY BROOK
| ❏ SB 33-004 | Niara | 1975 | 15.00 |

LUCAS, NICK

CAVALIER
| ❏ CAV-5003 [10] | Tip-Toe Thru the Tulips | 195? | 80.00 |
| *— Green vinyl* | | | |
DECCA
| ❏ DL8653 [M] | Painting the Clouds with Sunshine | 1957 | 40.00 |

LUCAS, REGGIE

INNER CITY
| ❏ IC-6010 | Survival Themes | 197? | 18.00 |

LUCEY, CHRIS

SURREY
| ❏ SS-1027 [M] | Songs of Protest and Anti-Protest | 197? | 40.00 |

LUCIE, LAWRENCE

TOY
❏ 1001	Cool and Warm Guitar	197?	18.00
❏ 1006	Mixed Emotions	1980	15.00
❏ 1003	Sophisticated Lady/After Sundown	1978	15.00
❏ 1005	This Is It	1979	15.00

LUCRAFT, HOWARD

DECCA
| ❏ DL8679 [M] | Showcase for Modern Jazz | 1958 | 30.00 |

LUDDEN, ALLEN

RCA VICTOR
| ❏ LPM-2934 [M] | Allen Ludden Sings His Favorite Songs | 1964 | 25.00 |
| ❏ LSP-2934 [S] | Allen Ludden Sings His Favorite Songs | 1964 | 30.00 |

LUDI, WERNER

HAT ART
| ❏ 2018 | Lunatico | 1986 | 18.00 |

LUDWIG, GENE

MUSE
| ❏ MR-5164 | Now's the Time | 1979 | 15.00 |

LUKE

LIL' JOE
| ❏ 260 | Luke's Booty Calls & Chants | 2000 | 18.00 |
LUKE
❏ 7694 [DJ]	Changin' the Game	1997	18.00
— Vinyl is promo only			
❏ 6996	Freak for Life 6996	1994	18.00
— Vinyl may be promo only			
❏ 91830	I Got Shit on My Mind	1992	18.00
❏ 91842	I Got Sumthin' on My Mind	1992	18.00
— Clean version of 91830			
❏ 200	In the Nude	1993	15.00
❏ 201	In the Nude (Edited)	1993	18.00
LUTHER CAMPBELL
❏ 161000-1	Uncle Luke	1996	15.00

LULU

ALFA
| ❏ 10006 | Lulu | 1981 | 15.00 |
ATCO
❏ SD 33-330 [S]	Melody Fair	1970	15.00
❏ 33-330 [M]	Melody Fair	1970	35.00
— White label promo, "DJ Copy Monaural" on cover; no stock copies were issued in mono			
❏ 33-310 [M]	New Routes	1970	30.00
— White label promo; no stock copies were issued in mono			
❏ SD 33-310 [S]	New Routes	1970	15.00
CHELSEA
❏ CHL-518	Heaven and Earth and the Stars	1976	25.00
❏ BCL1-0144	Lulu	1973	15.00
EPIC
❏ BN26536	It's Lulu	1970	15.00
❏ LN24339 [M]	To Sir with Love	1967	30.00
❏ BN26339 [P]	To Sir with Love	1967	30.00
HARMONY
❏ H30249	To Love Somebody	1970	25.00
PARROT
❏ PA61016 [M]	From Lulu with Love	1967	60.00
❏ PAS71016 [S]	From Lulu with Love	1967	80.00
PICKWICK
❏ SPC-3237	Lulu	1973	10.00
ROCKET
❏ BXL1-3073	Don't Take Love for Granted	1978	15.00

LULU BELLE AND SCOTTY

STARDAY
❏ SLP-285 [M]	Down Memory Lane	1964	40.00
❏ SLP-351 [M]	Lulu Belle & Scotty	1965	40.00
❏ SLP-206 [M]	The Sweethearts of Country Music	1963	40.00
SUPER
❏ 6201 [M]	Lule Belle & Scotty	1963	50.00

LUMAN, BOB

EPIC
❏ BN26393	Ain't Got Time to Be Unhappy	1968	25.00
❏ KE34445	Alive and Well!	1976	15.00
❏ KE32759	Bob Luman's Greatest Hits	1974	18.00
❏ E30923	Chain Don't Take to Me	1972	25.00
❏ BN26463 [B]	Come On Home and Sing the Blues	1969	25.00
❏ BN26541	Gettin' Back	1970	25.00
❏ E30617	Is It Any Wonder	1971	25.00
❏ KE31746	Lonely Women Make Good Lovers	1972	25.00
❏ KE32192	Neither One of Us	1973	18.00
❏ KE33942	Satisfied Mind	1975	15.00
❏ KE31375	When You Say Love	1972	25.00
HARMONY
❏ KH32006	Bob Luman	1973	15.00
HICKORY
❏ LPM-124 [M]	Livin' Lovin' Sounds	1965	30.00
❏ LPS-124 [S]	Livin' Lovin' Sounds	1965	30.00
HICKORY/MGM
❏ H3G-4508	Still Loving You	1974	18.00
POLYDOR
❏ PD-1-6135	Bob Luman	1978	15.00

WARNER BROS.

| ❏ W1396 [M] | Let's Think About Livin' | 1960 | 50.00 |
| ❏ WS1396 [S] | Let's Think About Livin' | 1960 | 70.00 |

LUMLEY, RUFUS

RCA VICTOR
| ❏ LPM-3898 [M] | Rufus Lumley | 1967 | 50.00 |
| ❏ LSP-3898 [S] | Rufus Lumley | 1967 | 40.00 |

LUNA

ARHOOLIE
| ❏ ST-8001 | Space Swell | 1968 | 25.00 |

LUNCEFORD, JIMMIE

AIRCHECK
| ❏ 8 | Victory | 197? | 12.00 |
ALLEGRO ELITE
| ❏ 0(# unknown) [10] | Jimmie Lunceford Plays | 195? | 40.00 |
CIRCLE
| ❏ 11 | Jimmie Lunceford and His Orchestra 1940 | 198? | 12.00 |
| ❏ CLP-92 | Jimmie Lunceford and His Orchestra 1944 | 198? | 12.00 |
COLUMBIA
❏ GL104 [10]	Lunceford Special	1950	80.00
❏ CL2715 [M]	Lunceford Special	1967	30.00
❏ CS9515 [R]	Lunceford Special	1967	18.00
— Red "360 Sound" label			
❏ CL634 [M]	Lunceford Special	1955	50.00
— Maroon label, gold print			
❏ CL634 [M]	Lunceford Special	1956	40.00
— Red and black label with six "eye" logos			
COLUMBIA MASTERWORKS
❏ ML4804 [M]	Lunceford Special	195?	60.00
DECCA
❏ DL5393 [10]	For Dancers Only	1952	60.00
❏ DL9238 [M]	Harlem Shout	1968	40.00
❏ DL79238 [R]	Harlem Shout	1968	25.00
❏ DL8050 [M]	Jimmie Lunceford and His Orchestra	1954	40.00
❏ DL9237 [M]	Rhythm Is Our Business	1968	40.00
❏ DL79237 [R]	Rhythm Is Our Business	1968	25.00
MCA
❏ 1314	Blues in the Night	198?	12.00
❏ 1307	For Dancers Only	198?	12.00
❏ 1305	Harlem Shout	198?	12.00
❏ 1320	Jimmie's Legacy	198?	12.00
❏ 1321	Last Sparks	198?	12.00
❏ 1302	Rhythm Is Our Business	198?	12.00
PICKWICK
❏ SPC-3531	Blues in the Night	197?	12.00
SUNBEAM
❏ 221	Jimmie Lunceford and Band 1939-42	197?	12.00
TIME-LIFE
❏ STBB-27	Big Bands: Jimmie Lunceford	1986	18.00
X
❏ LX-3002 [M]	Jimmie Lunceford and His Chickasaw Syncopators	1954	60.00

LUNCH, LYDIA

RUBY
| ❏ JRR806 [B] | 13.13 | 1982 | 50.00 |
ZE/BUDDAH
| ❏ 33006 [B] | Queen of Siam | 1980 | 50.00 |

LUND, GARRETT

(NO LABEL)
| ❏ (no #)0 | Almost Grown | 1975 | 300.00 |

LUNDY, PAT

COLUMBIA
| ❏ CS9588 | Soul Ain't Nothin' But the Blues | 1968 | 25.00 |

LUNN, ROBERT

STARDAY
| ❏ SLP-228 [M] | The Original Talking Blues Man | 1962 | 30.00 |

LUSCIOUS JACKSON

GRAND ROYAL
❏ GR 038	Fever In Fever Out	1996	15.00
❏ GR 001 [EP]	In Search of Manny	1993	10.00
❏ GR 009	Natural Ingredients	1994	12.00

LUTCHER, NELLIE

CAPITOL
| ❏ H232 [10] | Real Gone | 1950 | 60.00 |
| ❏ T232 [M] | Real Gone | 1955 | 40.00 |
EPIC
| ❏ LN1108 [10] | Whee! Nellie | 1955 | 50.00 |

Number	Title	Yr	NM
LIBERTY			
❏ LRP-3014 [M]	Our New Nellie	1956	40.00
LUTHERAN BROTHERHOOD SINGERS, THE			
LUTHERAN BROTHERHOOD			
❏ E-504	Christmas with the Lutheran Brotherhood Singers	197?	12.00
LUV'D ONES, THE			
SUNDAZED			
❏ LP5033	Truth Gotta Stand	199?	15.00
LYLE, BOBBY			
ATLANTIC			
❏ 81938	Ivory Dreams	1989	15.00
CAPITOL			
❏ ST-11627	Genie	1976	12.00
❏ SW-11809	New Warrior	1978	12.00
LYMAN, ABE			
HINDSIGHT			
❏ HSR-184	Abe Lyman and His Orchestra 1941	198?	12.00
LYMAN, ARTHUR			
GNP CRESCENDO			
❏ GNP-607 [M]	Cast Your Fate to the Wind	1965	18.00
❏ GNPS-607 [S]	Cast Your Fate to the Wind	1965	25.00
❏ GNP-605 [M]	Exotic Sounds	1963	18.00
❏ GNPS-605 [S]	Exotic Sounds	1963	25.00
❏ GNP-606 [M]	Paradise	1964	18.00
❏ GNPS-606 [S]	Paradise	1964	25.00
❏ GNPS-2091	Puka Shells	1975	12.00
HIFI			
❏ R-818 [M]	Arthur Lyman On Broadway	1960	25.00
❏ SR-818 [S]	Arthur Lyman On Broadway	1960	30.00
❏ R-815 [M]	Bahia	1959	25.00
❏ SR-815 [S]	Bahia	1959	30.00
❏ R-808 [M]	Bwan-A	1959	25.00
❏ SR-808 [S]	Bwan-A	1959	30.00
❏ R-807 [M]	Hawaiian Sunset	1959	25.00
❏ SR-807 [S]	Hawaiian Sunset	1959	30.00
❏ R-607 [M]	Leis of Jazz	1958	25.00
❏ SR-607 [S]	Leis of Jazz	1958	30.00
❏ R-806 [M]	Taboo	1958	25.00
❏ SR-806 [S]	Taboo	1958	30.00
❏ R-822 [M]	Taboo (Volume 2)	1960	25.00
❏ SR-822 [S]	Taboo (Volume 2)	1960	30.00
❏ R-813 [M]	The Legend of Pele	1959	25.00
❏ SR-813 [S]	The Legend of Pele	1959	30.00
LIFE			
❏ L1034 [M]	Aloha, Amigo	1966	18.00
❏ CL1034 [C]	Aloha, Amigo	1966	25.00
❏ SL1038	Aphrodisia	1968	18.00
❏ L1036 [M]	Arthur Lyman at the Port of L.A.	1967	18.00
❏ SL1036 [S]	Arthur Lyman at the Port of L.A.	1967	25.00
❏ L1014 [M]	Blowin' in the Wind	1963	25.00
❏ SL1014 [S]	Blowin' in the Wind	1963	30.00
❏ L1024 [M]	Call of the Midnight Sun	1964	25.00
❏ SL1024 [S]	Call of the Midnight Sun	1964	30.00
❏ L1010 [M]	Cotton Fields	1963	25.00
❏ SL1010 [S]	Cotton Fields	1963	30.00
❏ L1030 [M]	Greatest Hits	1965	15.00
❏ SL1030 [S]	Greatest Hits	1965	18.00
❏ L1025 [M]	Hawaiian Sunset, Volume 2	1965	18.00
❏ SL1025 [S]	Hawaiian Sunset, Volume 2	1965	25.00
❏ SL1035 [S]	Ilikai	1967	25.00
❏ SL1035 [M]	Ilikai	1967	18.00
❏ L1023 [M]	Isle of Enchantment	1964	25.00
❏ SL1023 [S]	Isle of Enchantment	1964	30.00
❏ L1009 [M]	I Wish You Love	1963	25.00
❏ SL1009 [S]	I Wish You Love	1963	30.00
❏ SL1037	Latitude 20	1968	18.00
❏ L1009 [M]	Love for Sale!	1963	30.00
—Alternate title			
❏ SL1009 [S]	Love for Sale!	1963	30.00
—Alternate title			
❏ L1031 [M]	Lyman '66	1965	18.00
❏ SL1031 [S]	Lyman '66	1965	25.00
❏ L1018 [M]	Mele Kalikimaka (Merry Christmas)	1963	25.00
❏ SL1018 [S]	Mele Kalikimaka (Merry Christmas)	1963	30.00
❏ L1004 [M]	Percussion Spectacular	1961	30.00
❏ SL1004 [S]	Percussion Spectacular	1961	40.00
❏ L1027 [M]	Polynesia	1965	18.00
❏ SL1027 [S]	Polynesia	1965	25.00
❏ L1005 [M]	The Colorful Percussions of Arthur Lyman	1962	25.00
❏ SL1005 [S]	The Colorful Percussions of Arthur Lyman	1962	30.00
❏ L1007 [M]	The Many Moods of Arthur Lyman	1962	25.00
❏ SL1007 [S]	The Many Moods of Arthur Lyman	1962	30.00
❏ L1033 [M]	The Shadow of Your Smile	1966	18.00
❏ SL1033 [S]	The Shadow of Your Smile	1966	25.00
❏ SL1040	Today's Greatest Hits	1970	18.00
❏ SL1039	Winner's Circle	1969	18.00
❏ L1004 [M]	Yellow Bird	1961	25.00
—Reissue with new title reflecting the hit single			
❏ SL1004 [S]	Yellow Bird	1961	30.00

Number	Title	Yr	NM
—Reissue with new title reflecting the hit single			
LYMON, FRANKIE, AND THE TEENAGERS			
ACCORD			
❏ SN-7203	Why Do Fools Fall in Love	1982	12.00
GEE			
❏ GLP-701 [M]	The Teenagers Featuring Frankie Lymon	1956	500.00
—Red label			
❏ GLP-701 [M]	The Teenagers Featuring Frankie Lymon	1961	150.00
—Gray label			
❏ GLP-701 [M]	The Teenagers Featuring Frankie Lymon	197?	15.00
—White label on thinner vinyl			
MURRAY HILL			
❏ 148	Frankie Lymon and the Teenagers	198?	70.00
RHINO			
❏ R1-70918	The Best of Frankie Lymon and the Teenagers	1989	15.00
LYMON, FRANKIE			
GUEST STAR			
❏ GS-1406 [M]	Rock & Roll Party Starring Frankie Lymon	196?	30.00
—Various-artists compilation; retitled, black and white cover			
❏ GS-1406 [M]	Teen Time Tunes Starring Frankie Lymon	1959	40.00
—Various-artists compilation; color cover			
ROULETTE			
❏ R-25013 [M]	Frankie Lymon at the London Palladium	1958	300.00
❏ R-25250 [M]	Frankie Lymon's Greatest	1964	30.00
❏ SR-25250 [R]	Frankie Lymon's Greatest	1964	30.00
❏ R-25036 [M]	Rock 'N' Roll	1958	300.00
LYMON, LEWIS, AND THE TEENCHORDS			
COLLECTABLES			
❏ COL-5049	Lewis Lymon and the Teenchords Meet the Kodaks	198?	12.00
LOST-NITE			
❏ LLP-13 [10]	Lewis Lymon and the Teenchords	1981	12.00
—Red vinyl			
LYNN, BARBARA			
ATLANTIC			
❏ 8171 [M]	Here Is Barbara Lynn	1968	50.00
❏ SD8171 [S]	Here Is Barbara Lynn	1968	40.00
❏ JLP-3023 [M]	You'll Lose a Good Thing	1962	50.00
❏ JLPS-3023 [R]	You'll Lose a Good Thing	1962	50.00
LYNN, DIANA			
CAPITOL			
❏ H180 [10]	Piano Moods	1950	60.00
LYNN, DONNA			
CAPITOL			
❏ T2085 [M]	Java Jones/My Boyfriend Got a Beatle Haircut	1964	25.00
❏ ST2085 [S]	Java Jones/My Boyfriend Got a Beatle Haircut	1964	30.00
LYNN, JUDY			
AMARET			
❏ AST-5014	Naturally	197?	18.00
❏ ST-5011	Parts of Love	1971	18.00
COLUMBIA			
❏ CS9879	Judy Lynn Sings at Caesar's Palace	1968	18.00
MUSICOR			
❏ MM-2126 [M]	Golden Nuggets	1967	18.00
❏ MS-3126 [S]	Golden Nuggets	1967	18.00
❏ MM-2112 [M]	Honey Stuff	1966	18.00
❏ MS-3112 [S]	Honey Stuff	1966	25.00
❏ MS-3096 [S]	The Judy Lynn Show Plays Again	1966	25.00
❏ MM-2096 [M]	The Judy Lynn Show Plays Again	1966	18.00
UNART			
❏ 20009 [M]	Judy Lynn in Las Vegas	1967	18.00
❏ 21009 [S]	Judy Lynn in Las Vegas	1967	15.00
UNITED ARTISTS			
❏ UAL-3342 [M]	America's Number One Most Promising Country and Western Girl Singer	1964	18.00
❏ UAS-6342 [S]	America's Number One Most Promising Country and Western Girl Singer	1964	25.00
❏ UAL-3288 [M]	Here Is Our Gal, Judy Lynn	1963	18.00
❏ UAS-6288 [S]	Here Is Our Gal, Judy Lynn	1963	25.00
❏ UAL-3226 [M]	Judy Lynn Sings at the Golden Nugget	1962	25.00
❏ UAS-6226 [S]	Judy Lynn Sings at the Golden Nugget	1962	30.00
❏ UAL-3461 [M]	The Best of Judy Lynn	1966	18.00
❏ UAS-6461 [S]	The Best of Judy Lynn	1966	25.00

Number	Title	Yr	NM
❏ UAL-3390 [M]	The Judy Lynn Show	1964	18.00
❏ UAS-6390 [S]	The Judy Lynn Show	1964	25.00
❏ UAL-3443 [M]	The Judy Lynn Show Act 2	1965	18.00
❏ UAS-6443 [S]	The Judy Lynn Show Act 2	1965	25.00
LYNN, LORETTA			
DECCA			
❏ DL4541 [M]	Before I'm Over You	1964	30.00
❏ DL74541 [S]	Before I'm Over You	1964	40.00
❏ DL4665 [M]	Blue Kentucky Girl	1965	30.00
❏ DL74665 [S]	Blue Kentucky Girl	1965	40.00
❏ DL75253	Coal Miner's Daughter	1971	25.00
❏ DL4817 [M]	Country Christmas	1966	30.00
❏ DL74817 [S]	Country Christmas	1966	30.00
❏ DL4842 [M]	Don't Come Home a-Drinkin' (With Lovin' on Your Mind)	1967	30.00
❏ DL74842 [S]	Don't Come Home a-Drinkin' (With Lovin' on Your Mind)	1967	30.00
❏ DL75351	Fist City	1968	30.00
❏ DL4997 [M]	Fist City	1968	50.00
—Mono version appears to exist only as a white label promo			
❏ DL75351	God Bless America Again	1972	25.00
❏ DL75381	Here I Am Again	1972	25.00
❏ DL4695 [M]	Hymns	1965	30.00
❏ DL74695 [S]	Hymns	1965	40.00
❏ DL4744 [M]	I Like 'Em Country	1966	30.00
❏ DL74744 [S]	I Like 'Em Country	1966	30.00
❏ DL75282	I Wanna Be Free	1971	25.00
❏ DL75000	Loretta Lynn's Greatest Hits	1968	30.00
❏ ST-91604	Loretta Lynn's Greatest Hits	1968	30.00
—Capitol Record Club edition			
❏ DL4457 [M]	Loretta Lynn Sings	1963	60.00
❏ DL74457 [S]	Loretta Lynn Sings	1963	80.00
❏ DL75198	Loretta Lynn Writes 'Em and Sings 'Em	1970	30.00
❏ DL75334	One's On the Way	1972	25.00
❏ DL4930 [M]	Singin' with Feelin'	1967	30.00
❏ DL74930 [S]	Singin' with Feelin'	1967	30.00
❏ DL4620 [M]	Songs from My Heart	1965	30.00
❏ DL74620 [S]	Songs from My Heart	1965	40.00
❏ DL4928 [M]	Who Says God Is Dead!	1967	40.00
❏ DL74928 [S]	Who Says God Is Dead!	1967	30.00
❏ DL75163	Wings Upon Your Horns	1970	30.00
❏ DL75113	Woman of the World/To Make a Man	1969	30.00
❏ DL4783 [M]	You Ain't Woman Enough	1966	30.00

Number	Title	Yr	NM
❏ DL74783 [S]	You Ain't Woman Enough	1966	30.00
❏ DL75310	You're Lookin' at Country	1971	25.00
❏ DL75084	Your Squaw Is On the Warpath	1969	40.00
—First editions had a track called "Barney"			
❏ DL75084	Your Squaw Is On the Warpath	1969	30.00
—Later editions delete the track "Barney"			
MCA			
❏ 35013	Allis-Chalmers Presents Loretta Lynn	1978	40.00
—Special products compilation			
❏ 735	Alone with You	198?	12.00
❏ 471	Back to the Country	198?	15.00
❏ 15032	Christmas Without Daddy	198?	15.00
❏ 2342	Coal Miner's Daughter	1978	15.00
—Reissue			
❏ 37236	Coal Miner's Daughter	198?	10.00
—Budget-line reissue			
❏ 15022	Country Christmas	1980	12.00
—Blue rainbow label			
❏ 248	Country Christmas	1973	18.00
—First reissue of Decca LP			
❏ 15022	Country Christmas	1974	15.00
—Second reissue of Decca LP; black rainbow label			
❏ 35018	Crisco Presents Loretta Lynn's Country Classics	1979	40.00
—Special products compilation			
❏ 113	Don't Come Home a-Drinkin' (With Lovin' on Your Mind)	1973	18.00
—Reissue of Decca 74842			

Number	Title	Yr	NM
❑ 300	Entertainer of the Year -- Loretta	1973	18.00
❑ 58	Here I Am Again	1973	18.00
— Reissue of Decca 75381			
❑ 2146	Home	1975	15.00
❑ 5	Hymns	1973	18.00
— Reissue of Decca 74695			
❑ 5293	I Lie	1982	12.00
❑ 2265	I Remember Patsy	1977	15.00
❑ 37080	I Remember Patsy Cline	198?	10.00
— Budget-line reissue			
❑ 5613	Just a Woman	1985	12.00
❑ 5148	Lookin' Good	1980	12.00
❑ 3217	Loretta	1980	12.00
❑ 37165	Loretta	198?	10.00
— Budget-line reissue			
❑ L33-1934 [DJ]	Loretta Lynn	1974	40.00
— Promo-only compilation			
❑ 1	Loretta Lynn's Greatest Hits	1973	18.00
— Reissue of Decca 75000			
❑ 2341	Loretta Lynn's Greatest Hits	1978	15.00
— Reissue of MCA 1			
❑ 37235	Loretta Lynn's Greatest Hits	198?	10.00
— Budget-line reissue			
❑ 420	Loretta Lynn's Greatest Hits Vol. II	1974	18.00
❑ 2353	Loretta Lynn's Greatest Hits Vol. II	1978	15.00
— Reissue of MCA 420			
❑ 37205	Loretta Lynn's Greatest Hits Vol. II	198?	10.00
— Budget-line reissue			
❑ 355	Love Is the Foundation	1973	18.00
❑ 5426	Lyin', Cheatin', Woman Chasin', Honky Tonkin', Whiskey Drinkin' You	1983	12.00
❑ 2330	Out of My Head and Back in My Bed	1978	15.00
❑ 2228	Somebody Somewhere	1976	15.00
❑ 630	Somebody Somewhere	198?	10.00
— Budget-line reissue			
❑ 444	They Don't Make 'Em Like My Daddy	1974	18.00
❑ 3073	We've Come a Long Way, Baby	1979	15.00
❑ 721	We've Come a Long Way, Baby	198?	10.00
— Budget-line reissue			
❑ 2179	When the Tingle Becomes a Chill	1976	15.00
❑ 628	When the Tingle Becomes a Chill	198?	10.00
— Budget-line reissue			
❑ 7	Who Says God Is Dead!	1973	18.00
— Reissue of Decca 74928			
❑ 42174	Who Was That Stranger	1988	12.00
❑ 6	You Ain't Woman Enough	1973	18.00
— Reissue of Decca 74783			

VOCALION
| ❑ VL73853 | Here's Loretta Lynn | 1968 | 18.00 |

LYNN, VERA

LONDON
❑ LL3294 [M]	Golden Hits	196?	25.00
❑ LL1510 [M]	If I Am Dreaming	195?	25.00
❑ LPB-58 [10]	Sincerely Yours	195?	60.00
❑ LB-690 [10]	Sincerely Yours Vol. 2	195?	60.00
❑ LL1306 [M]	Vera Lynn Concert	195?	25.00
❑ LL3142 [M]	Vera Lynn Sings Songs of the Twenties	196?	25.00
❑ PS156 [S]	Vera Lynn Sings Songs of the Twenties	196?	30.00
❑ LL3359 [M]	Wonderful Vera	1964	25.00
❑ PS359 [S]	Wonderful Vera	1964	25.00

MGM
❑ E-3889 [M]	As Time Goes By	1961	25.00
❑ SE-3889 [S]	As Time Goes By	1961	30.00
❑ E-3887 [M]	Yours	1961	25.00
❑ SE-3887 [S]	Yours	1961	30.00

STANYAN
❑ 10123	Among My Souvenirs	197?	18.00
❑ 10080	Vera Lynn Remembers the World at War	197?	18.00
❑ 10032	When the Lights Go On Again	197?	18.00

SUFFOLK MARKETING
| ❑ SMI-1-28 | All My Best (Her World Famous Recordings) | 198? | 12.00 |

UNITED ARTISTS
| ❑ UAL-3591 [M] | It Hurts to Say Goodbye | 1967 | 30.00 |
| ❑ UAS-6591 [S] | It Hurts to Say Goodbye | 1967 | 18.00 |

LYNNE, GLORIA

ABC IMPULSE!
| ❑ ASD-9311 | I Don't Know How to Love Him | 1976 | 15.00 |

CANYON
| ❑ 7709 | Happy and In Love | 1970 | 18.00 |

COLLECTABLES
| ❑ COL-5138 | Golden Classics | 198? | 12.00 |

DESIGN
| ❑ D-177 [M] | My Funny Valentine | 196? | 12.00 |

Number	Title	Yr	NM
❑ DS-177 [S]	My Funny Valentine	196?	15.00

EVEREST
❑ EV-5230 [M]	After Hours	1965	25.00
❑ EV-1230 [S]	After Hours	1965	30.00
❑ LPBR-5101 [M]	Day In, Day Out	1961	25.00
❑ SDBR-1101 [S]	Day In, Day Out	1961	30.00
❑ EV-5220 [M]	Gloria, Marty & Strings	1963	25.00
❑ EV-1220 [S]	Gloria, Marty & Strings	1963	30.00
❑ LPBR-5203 [M]	Gloria Blue	1962	25.00
❑ SDBR-1203 [S]	Gloria Blue	1962	30.00
❑ EV-5238 [M]	Gloria Lynne '66	1966	18.00
❑ EV-1238 [S]	Gloria Lynne '66	1966	25.00
❑ LPBR-5132 [M]	Gloria Lynne at Basin Street East	1962	25.00
❑ SDBR-1132 [S]	Gloria Lynne at Basin Street East	1962	30.00
❑ LPBR-5208 [M]	Gloria Lynne at the Las Vegas Thunderbird	1963	25.00
❑ SDBR-1208 [S]	Gloria Lynne at the Las Vegas Thunderbird	1963	30.00
❑ E-5001 [M]	Gloria Lynne Live! Take 1	1959	30.00
❑ ES-1001 [S]	Gloria Lynne Live! Take 1	1959	40.00
❑ EV-5228 [M]	Glorious Gloria Lynne	1964	25.00
❑ EV-1228 [S]	Glorious Gloria Lynne	1964	30.00
❑ EV-5237 [M]	Go! Go! Go!	1965	18.00
❑ EV-1237 [S]	Go! Go! Go!	1965	25.00
❑ LPBR-5128 [M]	He Needs Me	1961	25.00
❑ SDBR-1128 [S]	He Needs Me	1961	30.00
❑ LPBR-5126 [M]	I'm Glad There Is You	1961	25.00
❑ SDBR-1126 [S]	I'm Glad There Is You	1961	30.00
❑ EV-5226 [M]	I Wish You Love	1964	25.00
❑ EV-1226 [S]	I Wish You Love	1964	30.00
❑ ST-90057 [M]	I Wish You Love	196?	30.00
— Capitol Record Club edition			
❑ LPBR-5063 [M]	Lonely and Sentimental	1960	25.00
❑ SDBR-1063 [S]	Lonely and Sentimental	1960	30.00
❑ LPBR-5022 [M]	Miss Gloria Lynne	1959	25.00
❑ SDBR-1022 [S]	Miss Gloria Lynne	1959	30.00
❑ EV-5231 [M]	The Best of Gloria Lynne	1965	18.00
❑ EV-1231 [S]	The Best of Gloria Lynne	1965	25.00
❑ LPBR-5131 [M]	This Little Boy of Mine	1961	25.00
❑ SDBR-1131 [S]	This Little Boy of Mine	1961	30.00
❑ LPBR-5090 [M]	Try a Little Tenderness	1960	25.00
❑ SDBR-1090 [S]	Try a Little Tenderness	1960	30.00

FONTANA
❑ MGF-27561 [M]	Gloria	1966	18.00
❑ SRF-67561 [S]	Gloria	1966	25.00
❑ SRF-67577	Here, There and Everywhere	1968	18.00
❑ MGF-27528 [M]	Intimate Moments	1964	18.00
❑ SRF-67528 [S]	Intimate Moments	1964	25.00
❑ MGF-27546 [M]	Love and a Woman	1965	18.00
❑ SRF-67546 [S]	Love and a Woman	1965	25.00
❑ MGF-27541 [M]	Soul Serenade	1965	18.00
❑ SRF-67541 [S]	Soul Serenade	1965	25.00
❑ MGF-27571 [M]	The Other Side of Gloria Lynne	1967	25.00
❑ SRF-67571 [S]	The Other Side of Gloria Lynne	1967	18.00
❑ MGF-27555 [M]	Where It's At	1966	18.00
❑ SRF-67555 [S]	Where It's At	1966	25.00

HIFI
❑ SR-441	Greatest Hits	1969	18.00
❑ L-440 [M]	The Gloria Lynne Calendar	1966	18.00
❑ SL-440 [S]	The Gloria Lynne Calendar	1966	25.00

INTERMEDIA
| ❑ QS-5069 | Classics | 198? | 12.00 |

MERCURY
| ❑ SRM-1-633 | A Very Gentle Sound | 1972 | 18.00 |

MUSE
| ❑ MR-5381 | A Time for Love | 198? | 12.00 |

SUNSET
❑ SUM-1145 [M]	Gloria Lynne	1966	15.00
❑ SUS-5145 [S]	Gloria Lynne	1966	15.00
❑ SUS-5221	Golden Greats	1968	15.00
❑ SUM-1171 [M]	I Wish You Love	1967	15.00
❑ SUS-5171 [S]	I Wish You Love	1967	15.00

UPFRONT
| ❑ 146 | Gloria Lynne | 197? | 15.00 |

LYNNE, JEFF

REPRISE
| ❑ 26184 [B] | Armchair Theater | 1990 | 25.00 |

LYNOTT, PHIL

WARNER BROS.
| ❑ BSK3405 | Solo in Soho | 1980 | 25.00 |
| ❑ 23745 | The Philip Lynott Album | 1982 | 24.00 |

LYNYRD SKYNYRD

ATLANTIC
| ❑ A1-82258 | Lynyrd Skynyrd 1991 | 1991 | 25.00 |
| — The only U.S. vinyl version was released through Columbia House | | | |

GEFFEN
| ❑ MCA1686 | Second Helping | 2008 | 25.00 |

MCA
❑ 5370	Best of the Rest	1982	12.00
— Original version			
❑ 1448	Best of the Rest	1985	10.00
❑ 2170	Gimme Back My Bullets	1976	15.00

Number	Title	Yr	NM
❑ 37069	Gimme Back My Bullets	1980	10.00
❑ 3022	Gimme Back My Bullets	1977	12.00
— Reissue with new number on black rainbow label			
❑ 11008	Gold & Platinum	1979	15.00
— Originals with embossed gatefold cover			
❑ 6898	Gold & Platinum	1985	12.00
— Most, if not all, of these pressings have no gatefold			
❑ 42084	Legend	1987	12.00
❑ 2137	Nuthin' Fancy	1975	15.00
❑ 3021	Nuthin' Fancy	1976	12.00
— Reissue with new number on black rainbow label			
❑ 37070	Nuthin' Fancy	1980	10.00
❑ L33-1946 [DJ]	One More From the Road	1976	30.00
— Promo only on black vinyl			
❑ L33-1946 [DJ]	One More From the Road	1976	50.00
— Promo on blue, gold, purple or red vinyl (each has the same value)			
❑ 6001	One More From the Road	1976	18.00
— Originals with black rainbow label and gatefold cover			
❑ 10014	One More From the Road	1980	12.00
— Second reissue			
❑ 6897	One More From the Road	1985	12.00
— Most, if not all, of these pressings have no gatefold			
❑ 8011	One More From the Road	1977	15.00
— First reissue with new number			
❑ 363	(pronounced leh-nerd skin-nerd)	1975	15.00
— Reissue on black rainbow label			
❑ 3019	(pronounced leh-nerd skin-nerd)	1976	12.00
— Second reissue with new number on black rainbow label			
❑ 5221	(pronounced leh-nerd skin-nerd)	1980	10.00
❑ 37211	(pronounced leh-nerd skin-nerd)	1985	10.00
❑ 413	Second Helping	1975	15.00
— Reissue on black rainbow label			
❑ 3020	Second Helping	1976	12.00
— Second reissue with new number on black rainbow label			
❑ 5222	Second Helping	1980	10.00
❑ 37212	Second Helping	1985	10.00
❑ L33-1988 [DJ]	Skynyrd's First and...Last	1978	30.00
— Promo sampler			
❑ 3047	Skynyrd's First and...Last	1978	15.00
— Originals with tan labels and gatefold cover			
❑ 37071	Skynyrd's First and...Last	1980	10.00
❑ 42293	Skynyrd's Innyrds	1989	15.00
❑ 8027	Southern by the Grace of God	1988	15.00
❑ 3029	Street Survivors	1977	30.00
— Originals with the band in flames on the front cover and a smaller band photo on the back cover			
❑ 3029	Street Survivors	1977	12.00
— After the band's plane crash, the "flames" photo was replaced with the back cover photo; the back cover is black with only the song titles			
❑ 5223	Street Survivors	1980	10.00
❑ 37213	Street Survivors	1985	10.00

MOBILE FIDELITY
| ❑ MFSL1-400 [B] | (Pronounced 'Lĕh-'nérd 'Skin-'nérd) | 2013 | 30.00 |

SOUNDS OF THE SOUTH
❑ 363	(pronounced leh-nerd skin-nerd)	1973	25.00
❑ 413	Second Helping	1974	25.00
— Both of the above are original pressings with yellow labels			

LYON, JIMMY

FINNADAR
| ❑ 9034 | Johnny Lyon Plays Cole Porter's Steinway and Music | 198? | 18.00 |

LYONS, JIMMY

BLACK SAINT
| ❑ BSR-0087 | Give It Up | 1986 | 15.00 |
| ❑ 120125 | Something in Return | 1990 | 18.00 |

HAT ART
| ❑ 2028 | Jump Up/What to Do About | 1986 | 18.00 |
| — Reissue of Hat Hut 21 | | | |

HAT HUT
❑ 21	Jump Up/What to Do About	198?	25.00
❑ 0Y/Z/Z	Push	1979	30.00
❑ 3503	Riffs	198?	15.00

LYONS, MARIE

DELUXE
| ❑ 12001 | Soul Fever | 1970 | 30.00 |

LYTLE, JOHNNY

FANTASY
| ❑ OJC-110 | The Village Caller | 198? | 12.00 |

JAZZLAND
❑ JLP-22 [M]	Blue Vibes	1960	30.00
❑ JLP-922 [S]	Blue Vibes	1960	30.00
❑ JLP-44 [M]	Happy Ground	1961	30.00
❑ JLP-944 [S]	Happy Ground	1961	30.00
❑ JLP-81 [M]	Moon Child	1962	30.00
❑ JLP-981 [S]	Moon Child	1962	30.00
❑ JLP-67 [M]	Nice and Easy	1962	30.00
❑ JLP-967 [S]	Nice and Easy	1962	30.00

Number	Title	Yr	NM
MILESTONE			
❏ 9043	People and Love	197?	18.00
❏ 9036	Soulful Rebel	197?	18.00
MUSE			
❏ MR-5158	Everything Must Change	1978	15.00
❏ MR-5185	Fast Hands	1981	12.00
❏ MR-5271	Good Vibes	1982	12.00
❏ MR-5387	Happy Ground	1991	18.00
RIVERSIDE			
❏ RM-3003 [M]	A Groove	1967	30.00
❏ RS-3003 [S]	A Groove	1967	25.00
❏ RLP-456 [M]	Got That Feeling	1963	25.00
❏ RS-9456 [S]	Got That Feeling	1963	30.00
❏ RLP-470 [M]	Happy Ground	1964	25.00
❏ RS-9470 [S]	Happy Ground	1964	30.00
❏ RS-3017	Moon Child	1968	18.00
❏ RLP-480 [M]	The Village Caller	1965	25.00
❏ RS-9480 [S]	The Village Caller	1965	30.00
SOLID STATE			
❏ SS-18014	A Man and a Woman	1967	25.00
❏ SS-18044	Be Proud	1969	25.00
❏ SS-18056	Close Enough	1969	25.00

LYTTELTON, HUMPHREY

Number	Title	Yr	NM
ANGEL			
❏ ANG.60008 [10]	Some Like It Hot	1955	60.00
BETHLEHEM			
❏ BCP-6063 [M]	Humph Plays Standards	1961	30.00
LONDON			
❏ LL3132 [M]	Humph Dedicates	195?	30.00
❏ PS178 [S]	Humph Dedicates	1959	30.00
❏ LL3101 [M]	I Play As I Please	195?	30.00
SACKVILLE			
❏ 3033	Humphrey Lyttelton in Canada	198?	15.00
STOMP OFF			
❏ SOS-1160	Delving Back and Forth with Humph	1989	12.00
❏ SOS-1111	Scatterbrains	1986	12.00

LYTTLE, KEVIN

Number	Title	Yr	NM
ATLANTIC			
❏ 83699	Kevin Lyttle	2004	18.00

M

Number	Title	Yr	NM
M			
SIRE			
❏ SRK3672	Famous Last Words	1982	12.00
❏ SRK6084	New York-London-Paris-Munich	1979	15.00
❏ SRK6099	The Official Secrets Act	1981	12.00

MABERN, HAROLD

Number	Title	Yr	NM
FANTASY			
❏ OJC-330	Rakin' and Scrapin'	1988	12.00
PRESTIGE			
❏ PRST-7568 [B]	A Few Miles from Memphis	1968	70.00
❏ PRST-7764 [B]	Greasy Kid Stuff	1970	50.00
❏ PRST-7624 [B]	Rakin' and Scrapin'	1969	50.00
❏ PRST-7687 [B]	Workin' and Wailin'	1969	50.00
SACKVILLE			
❏ 2016	Live at Café Des Copains	198?	15.00

MABLEY, MOMS

Number	Title	Yr	NM
CHESS			
❏ LP-1479 [M]	I Got Somethin' to Tell You!	1963	30.00
❏ LP-1447 [M]	Moms Mabley, Funniest Woman in the World, Onstage	1961	30.00
❏ LP-1463 [M]	Moms Mabley at Geneva Conference	1962	30.00
❏ LP-1452 [M]	Moms Mabley at the "UN"	1961	30.00
❏ LP-1460 [M]	Moms Mabley at the Playboy Club	1961	30.00
❏ LP-1472 [M]	Moms Mabley Breaks It Up	1962	30.00
❏ LPS-1525	Moms Mabley Breaks Up the Network	1968	25.00
❏ LPS-1530	Moms Mabley Sings	1969	25.00
❏ LP-1486 [M]	Moms Wows	1964	30.00

Number	Title	Yr	NM
❏ LP-1487 [M]	The Best of Moms	1964	30.00
❏ LP-1482 [M]	The Funny Sides of Moms Mabley	1963	30.00
❏ LP-1497 [M]	The Man in My Life	1965	25.00
❏ LP-1477 [M]	Young Men, Si -- Old Men, No	1962	30.00
MERCURY			
❏ SR-61235	Abraham, Martin and John	1969	18.00
❏ SR-61205	Her Young Thing	1969	18.00
❏ SR-61263	Live at Sing Sing	1970	18.00
❏ MG-21090 [M]	Moms Mabley at the White House	1966	18.00
❏ SR-61090 [S]	Moms Mabley at the White House	1966	25.00
❏ MG-20907 [M]	Moms the Word	1964	18.00
❏ SR-60907 [S]	Moms the Word	1964	25.00
❏ MG-21012 [M]	Now Hear This	1965	18.00
❏ SR-61012 [S]	Now Hear This	1965	25.00
❏ MG-20889 [M]	Out on a Limb	1964	18.00
❏ SR-60889 [S]	Out on a Limb	1964	25.00
❏ MG-21139 [M]	The Best of Moms Mabley	1967	30.00
❏ SR-61139 [S]	The Best of Moms Mabley	1967	18.00
❏ SR-61229 [B]	The Youngest Teenager	1969	18.00

MABON, WILLIE

Number	Title	Yr	NM
CHESS			
❏ LP 1439 [M]	Willie Mabon	1958	400.00
— Black label			

MACARTHUR, DOUGLAS

Number	Title	Yr	NM
ATCO			
❏ 8095 [M]	The Life of General MacArthur	1964	40.00

MACDONALD, JEANETTE, AND NELSON EDDY

Number	Title	Yr	NM
RCA VICTOR			
❏ LPM-1738 [M]	Favorites in Hi-Fi	1958	40.00
❏ LPV-526 [M]	Rose Marie	1965	30.00
❏ LPT-16 [10]	Rose Marie	1952	60.00

MACDONALD, KEITH

Number	Title	Yr	NM
LANDMARK			
❏ LLP-1503	This Is Keith MacDonald	1985	12.00
❏ LLP-1509	Waiting	1986	12.00

MACDOWELL, AL

Number	Title	Yr	NM
GRAMAVISION			
❏ R1-79450	Time Peace	1990	15.00

MACEO AND ALL THE KING'S MEN

Number	Title	Yr	NM
EXCELLO			
❏ LPS-8022	Funky Music Machine	1972	30.00
HOUSE OF FOX			
❏ LP-1	Doing Their Own Thing	1971	30.00

MACEO AND THE MACKS

Number	Title	Yr	NM
PEOPLE			
❏ PE-6601	Us	1973	30.00

MACERO, TEO

Number	Title	Yr	NM
AMERICAN CLAVE			
❏ 1002	Teo	198?	18.00
COLUMBIA			
❏ CL842 [M]	What's New?	1956	80.00
— Red and black label with six "eye" logos			
DEBUT			
❏ DLP-6 [10]	Explorations by Teo Macero	1954	500.00
DOCTOR JAZZ			
❏ FW40111	Acoustical Suspension	1986	18.00
FANTASY			
❏ OJC-1715	Teo -- Teo Macero with the Prestige Jazz Quartet	198?	15.00

Number	Title	Yr	NM
FINNADAR			
❏ SR9024	Time Plus 7	1979	25.00
PALO ALTO			
❏ PA-8046	Impressions of Charles Mingus	1984	25.00
PRESTIGE			
❏ PRLP-7104 [M]	Teo -- Teo Macero with the Prestige Jazz Quartet	1957	150.00

MACGREGOR, BYRON

Number	Title	Yr	NM
WESTBOUND			
❏ WB-1000	Americans	1974	12.00

MACGREGOR, MARY

Number	Title	Yr	NM
ARIOLA AMERICA			
❏ SW-50025	In Your Eyes	1978	15.00
❏ SMAS-50015	Torn Between Two Lovers	1977	15.00
RSO			
❏ RS-1-3083	Mary MacGregor	1979	15.00

MACHITO

Number	Title	Yr	NM
CLEF			
❏ MGC-505 [10]	Afro-Cuban Jazz	1953	150.00
❏ MGC-689 [M]	Afro-Cuban Jazz	1956	100.00
❏ MGC-511 [10]	Machito Jazz with Flip and Bird	1953	150.00
CORAL			
❏ CRL57258 [M]	Vacation at the Concord	1959	40.00
❏ CRL757258 [S]	Vacation at the Concord	1959	30.00
DECCA			
❏ DL5157 [10]	Machito's Afro-Cuban	1950	200.00
FORUM			
❏ F-9043 [M]	Asia Minor	196?	15.00
— Reissue of Tico 1033			
❏ SF-9043 [S]	Asia Minor	196?	15.00
❏ F-9038 [M]	Mi Amigo, Machito	196?	15.00
— Reissue of Tico 1053			
❏ SF-9038 [S]	Mi Amigo, Machito	196?	15.00
GNP CRESCENDO			
❏ GNPS-58 [R]	Machito at the Crescendo	198?	10.00
❏ GNPS-72 [R]	The World's Greatest Latin Band	198?	10.00
MERCURY			
❏ MGC-505 [10]	Afro-Cuban Jazz	1951	200.00
❏ MG-25009 [10]	Jungle Drums	1950	200.00
❏ MGC-511 [10]	Machito Jazz with Flip and Bird	1952	200.00
❏ MG-25020 [10]	Rhumbas	1950	200.00
RCA VICTOR			
❏ LPM-3944 [M]	Machito Goes Memphis	1968	40.00
❏ LSP-3944 [S]	Machito Goes Memphis	1968	25.00
ROULETTE			
❏ R-52006 [M]	Kenya	1958	40.00
❏ SR-52006 [S]	Kenya	1958	30.00
❏ R-52026 [M]	With Flute to Boot	1959	40.00
❏ SR-52026 [S]	With Flute to Boot	1959	30.00
TICO			
❏ LP-1074 [M]	A Night with Machito	1960	50.00
❏ LPS-1074 [S]	A Night with Machito	1960	60.00
❏ LP-1029 [M]	Asia Minor Cha Cha Cha	1956	80.00
❏ LP-1002 [M]	Cha Cha Cha at the Palladium	1955	80.00
❏ LP-138 [10]	El Niche	1956	150.00
❏ LP-1045 [M]	Inspired by "The Sun Also Rises"	1957	80.00
❏ LP-1062 [M]	Irving Berlin in Latin America	1959	60.00
❏ CLP-1314	Latin Soul Plus Jazz	1973	25.00
❏ CLP-1328	Lo Mejor De Machito Y Sus AfroCubans Con Graciela	1974	25.00
❏ LP-1053 [M]	Mi Amigo, Machito	1959	60.00
❏ LP-1033 [M]	Si Si, No No	1957	80.00
❏ LP-1084 [M]	The New Sound of Machito (El Sonido Nuevo de Machito)	1962	40.00
❏ LPS-1084 [S]	The New Sound of Machito (El Sonido Nuevo de Machito)	1962	50.00
❏ LP-1094 [M]	Tremendo Cumban!	1963	40.00
❏ LPS-1094 [S]	Tremendo Cumban!	1963	50.00
❏ LP-1090 [M]	Variedades	1963	40.00
❏ LPS-1090 [S]	Variedades	1963	50.00
TIMELESS			
❏ LPSJP-183	Machito and His Salsa Big Band	1990	15.00
VERVE			
❏ MGV-8073 [M]	Afro-Cuban Jazz	1957	50.00
❏ V-8073 [M]	Afro-Cuban Jazz	1961	25.00
❏ VSP-19 [M]	Soul Source	1966	25.00
❏ VSPS-19 [R]	Soul Source	1966	15.00

MACK, DAVID

Number	Title	Yr	NM
SEREMUS			
❏ SRE-1009 [M]	New Directions	1965	25.00
❏ SRS-12000 [S]	New Directions	1965	30.00

MACK, LONNIE

Number	Title	Yr	NM
ALLIGATOR			
❏ AL-4786	Live!: Attack of the Killer V	1990	15.00
❏ AL-4750	Second Sight	1987	12.00

Number	Title	Yr	NM
❏ AL-4739	Strike Like Lightning	1985	12.00
❏ AL-3903	The Wham of That Memphis Man	1987	12.00
—Reissue of Fraternity LP			
CAPITOL			
❏ ST-11619	Home at Last	1976	15.00
❏ ST-11703	Lonnie Mack and Pismo	1977	15.00
ELEKTRA			
❏ EKS-74077	For Collectors Only	1970	30.00
❏ EKS-74040	Glad I'm In the Band	1969	30.00
❏ EKS-74102	The Hills of Indiana	1971	30.00
❏ EKS-74050	Whatever's Right	1969	30.00
EPIC			
❏ FE44075	Roadhouses and Dance Halls	1989	15.00
FRATERNITY			
❏ SF-1014 [M]	The Wham of That Memphis Man	1963	120.00
❏ SSF-1014 [S]	The Wham of That Memphis Man	1963	300.00
TRIP			
❏ TLX-9522	The Memphis Sounds of Lonnie Mack	1975	15.00

MACK, WARNER

Number	Title	Yr	NM
DECCA			
❏ DL4883 [M]	Drifting Apart	1967	30.00
❏ DL74883 [S]	Drifting Apart	1967	25.00
❏ DL75165	I'll Still Be Missing You	1969	25.00
❏ DL4912 [M]	Songs We Sand in Church and Home	1967	30.00
❏ DL74912 [S]	Songs We Sand in Church and Home	1967	25.00
❏ DL4692 [M]	The Bridge Washed Out	1965	25.00
❏ DL74692 [S]	The Bridge Washed Out	1965	30.00
❏ DL75092	The Country Beat of Warner Mack	1969	25.00
❏ DL4766 [M]	The Country Touch	1966	25.00
❏ DL74766 [S]	The Country Touch	1966	30.00
❏ DL74995	The Many Country Moods of Warner Mack	1968	25.00
KAPP			
❏ KL-1461 [M]	Everybody's Country Favorites	196?	18.00
❏ KS-3461 [S]	Everybody's Country Favorites	196?	25.00
❏ KL-1255 [M]	Golden Country Hits	1961	25.00
❏ KS-3255 [S]	Golden Country Hits	1961	30.00
❏ KL-1279 [M]	Golden Country Hits, Vol. 2	1962	25.00
❏ KS-3279 [S]	Golden Country Hits, Vol. 2	1962	30.00

MACKAY, BRUCE

Number	Title	Yr	NM
ORO			
❏ 1	Bruce Mackay	196?	25.00

MACKAY, DAVID, AND VICKI HAMILTON

Number	Title	Yr	NM
ABC IMPULSE!			
❏ AS-9184	David MacKay and Vicki Hamilton	1969	25.00
DISCOVERY			
❏ 868	Hands	1982	12.00

MACKENZIE, GISELE

Number	Title	Yr	NM
EVEREST			
❏ LPBR-5069 [M]	In Person at the Empire Room	1959	30.00
❏ SDBR-1069 [S]	In Person at the Empire Room	1959	30.00
GLENDALE			
❏ GL-6017	Gisele MacKenzie Sings	1978	15.00
RCA VICTOR			
❏ LPM-2006 [M]	Christmas with Gisele	1959	30.00
❏ LSP-2006 [S]	Christmas with Gisele	1959	40.00
❏ LPM-1790 [M]	Gisele	1958	30.00
❏ LSP-1790 [S]	Gisele	1958	40.00
SUNSET			
❏ SUM-1155 [M]	In Person at the Empire Room	196?	15.00
❏ SUS-5155 [S]	In Person at the Empire Room	196?	18.00
VIK			
❏ LX-1099 [M]	Christmas with Gisele	1957	40.00
❏ LX-1055 [M]	Gisele MacKenzie	1956	40.00
❏ LX-1075 [M]	Mam'selle MacKenzie	1956	40.00

MACLAINE, SHIRLEY

Number	Title	Yr	NM
COLUMBIA			
❏ PC34223	Live at the Palace	1976	15.00

MACON, UNCLE DAVE

Number	Title	Yr	NM
DECCA			
❏ DL4760 [M]	Uncle Dave Macon	1966	30.00

MACPHERSON, FRASER

Number	Title	Yr	NM
CONCORD JAZZ			
❏ CJ-224	Indian Summer	1983	12.00
❏ CJ-269	Jazz Prose	1985	12.00
❏ CJ-92	Live at the Planetarium	1976	12.00

MACRAE, GORDON

Number	Title	Yr	NM
ALLEGRO ROYALE			
❏ 1606 [M]	Gordon MacRae	1952	25.00
ANGEL			
❏ S37319	The Desert Song	1973	12.00
—Operetta with Dorothy Kirsten; reissue of Capitol SW 1842			
❏ S37320	The New Moon	1973	12.00
—Operetta with Dorothy Kirsten; reissue of Capitol SW 1966			
❏ S37318	The Student Prince	1973	12.00
—Operetta with Dorothy Kirsten; reissue of Capitol SW 1841			
CAPITOL			
❏ L485 [10]	3 Sailors and a Girl	1953	60.00
—With Jane Powell and Gene Nelson			
❏ H422 [10]	By the Light of the Silvery Moon	1953	40.00
—With June Hutton; not the soundtrack from the movie because MacRae and movie co-star Doris Day were on different labels			
❏ T834 [M]	Cowboy's Lament	1957	30.00
—Turquoise or gray label			
❏ T980 [M]	Gordon MacRae in Concert	1957	30.00
—Turquoise or gray label			
❏ ST980 [S]	Gordon MacRae in Concert	1959	40.00
—Black colorband label, logo at left			
❏ H231 [10]	Gordon MacRae Sings	1951	40.00
❏ T1466 [M]	Hallowed Be Thy Name	1960	18.00
—Black colorband label, Capitol logo at left			
❏ ST1466 [S]	Hallowed Be Thy Name	1960	25.00
—Black colorband label, Capitol logo at left			
❏ T2578 [M]	If She Walked Into My Life	1966	15.00
❏ ST2578 [S]	If She Walked Into My Life	1966	18.00
❏ W2022 [M]	Kismet	1964	15.00
—Operetta with Dorothy Kirsten			
❏ SW2022 [S]	Kismet	1964	18.00
—Operetta with Dorothy Kirsten			
❏ T875 [M]	Motion Picture Soundstage	1957	30.00
—Turquoise or gray label			
❏ L468 [10]	Naughty Marietta	1954	40.00
—Operetta with Marguerite Piazza			
❏ T551 [M]	Naughty Marietta and The Red Mill	1955	30.00
—Turquoise label original			
❏ T219 [M]	New Moon and The Vagabond King	195?	30.00
—Operettas with Lucille Norman; turquoise label			
❏ P219 [M]	New Moon and The Vagabond King	1951	30.00
—Operettas with Lucille Norman; original			
❏ ST-125	Only Love	1969	15.00
❏ T681 [M]	Operetta Favorites	1956	30.00
—Turquoise or gray label			
❏ T1353 [M]	Our Love Story	1960	18.00
—With Sheila MacRae; black colorband label, Capitol logo at left			
❏ ST1353 [S]	Our Love Story	1960	25.00
—With Sheila MacRae; black colorband label, Capitol logo at left			
❏ L334 [10]	Roberta	1952	40.00
—Operetta with Lucille Norman and Anne Triola			
❏ T537 [M]	Romantic Ballads	1955	30.00
—Turquoise or gray label			
❏ T1251 [M]	Songs for an Evening at Home	1959	18.00
—Black colorband label, Capitol logo at left			
❏ ST1251 [S]	Songs for an Evening at Home	1959	25.00
—Black colorband label, Capitol logo at left			
❏ T765 [M]	The Best Things in Life Are Free	1956	30.00
—Turquoise or gray label			
❏ L351 [10]	The Desert Song	1953	40.00
—Operetta with Lucille Norman and Bob Sands			
❏ W1842 [M]	The Desert Song	1963	15.00
—Operetta with Dorothy Kirsten			
❏ SW1842 [S]	The Desert Song	1963	18.00
—Operetta with Dorothy Kirsten			
❏ T394 [M]	The Desert Song and Roberta	195?	30.00
—Turquoise label original			
❏ L335 [10]	The Merry Widow	1952	40.00
—With Lucille Norman			
❏ W1966 [M]	The New Moon	1963	15.00
—Operetta with Dorothy Kirsten			
❏ SW1966 [S]	The New Moon	1963	18.00
—Operetta with Dorothy Kirsten			
❏ L530 [10]	The Red Mill	1954	40.00
—Operetta with Lucille Norman			
❏ T1146 [M]	The Seasons of Love	1959	18.00
—Black colorband label, Capitol logo at left			
❏ ST1146 [S]	The Seasons of Love	1959	25.00
—Black colorband label, Capitol logo at left			
❏ L407 [10]	The Student Prince	1953	40.00
—Operetta with Dorothy Warenskjold and Harry Stanton			
❏ W1841 [M]	The Student Prince	1963	15.00
—Opertta with Dorothy Kirsten			
❏ SW1841 [S]	The Student Prince	1963	18.00
—Operetta with Dorothy Kirsten			
❏ T437 [M]	The Student Prince and The Merry Widow	195?	30.00
—Turqiouse label original			
❏ P437 [M]	The Student Prince and The Merry Widow	1953	40.00
—Original			
❏ H218 [10]	The Vagabond King	1951	50.00
—Operetta with Lucille Norman			
❏ T1050 [M]	This Is Gordon MacRae	1958	30.00
—Turquoise label			
COLORTONE			
❏ 4939 [M]	Gordon MacRae Sings	1958	18.00
EVON			
❏ 320 [M]	Gordon MacRae Sings	1958	18.00
—Reissue of Allegro Royale LP			
GALAXY			
❏ 4805 [M]	Gordon MacRae	1958	18.00
—Reissue of Allegro Royale LP			
RONDO-LETTE			
❏ A5 [M]	Gordon MacRae	1958	18.00
—Reissue of Allegro Royale LP			
ROYALE			
❏ 18155 [10]	Gordon MacRae and Orchestra	195?	30.00
❏ 18106 [10]	Gordon MacRae and Walter Gross Orchestra	195?	30.00
SUTTON			
❏ SU292 [M]	Gordon MacRae Sings Broadway's Best!	196?	12.00
❏ SSU292 [R]	Gordon MacRae Sings Broadway's Best!	196?	12.00

MACRAE, SHEILA

Number	Title	Yr	NM
ABC			
❏ ABCS-611	How Sweet She Is	1968	30.00

MAD LADS, THE

Number	Title	Yr	NM
STAX			
❏ MPS-8525	The Best of the Mad Lads	198?	12.00
VOLT			
❏ VOS-6020	A New Beginning	1973	25.00
❏ VOS-6005	The Mad, Mad, Mad, Mad, Mad Lads	1969	30.00
❏ 414 [M]	The Mad Lads In Action	1966	50.00
❏ S-414 [S]	The Mad Lads In Action	1966	60.00

MAD RIVER

Number	Title	Yr	NM
CAPITOL			
❏ ST2985	Mad River	1968	75.00
❏ ST-185	Paradise Bar and Grill	1969	75.00

MADDOX, JOHNNY

Number	Title	Yr	NM
DOT			
❏ DLP-102 [10]	Authentic Ragtime	1952	40.00
❏ DLP-3289 [M]	Crazy Otto Piano	1960	15.00
❏ DLP-25289 [S]	Crazy Otto Piano	1960	18.00
❏ DLP-3131 [M]	Dieieland Blues	1959	18.00
❏ DLP-25131 [S]	Dieieland Blues	1959	25.00
❏ DLP-3005 [M]	Johnny Maddox Plays	1956	30.00
❏ DLP-3314 [M]	Johnny Maddox Plays More Million Sellers	1960	15.00
❏ DLP-25314 [S]	Johnny Maddox Plays More Million Sellers	1960	18.00
❏ DLP-3122 [M]	Johnny Maddox Plays the Million Sellers	1958	18.00
❏ DLP-25122 [S]	Johnny Maddox Plays the Million Sellers	1959	25.00
❏ DLP-3549 [M]	Johnny Maddox Plays the Million Sellers, Volume 3	1963	15.00
❏ DLP-25549 [S]	Johnny Maddox Plays the Million Sellers, Volume 3	1963	18.00
❏ DLP-3044 [M]	King of Ragtime	1957	25.00
❏ DLP-3539 [M]	Memphis	1963	15.00
❏ DLP-25539 [S]	Memphis	1963	18.00
❏ DLP-3645 [M]	More Ragtime Twenties	1965	15.00
❏ DLP-25645 [S]	More Ragtime Twenties	1965	18.00
❏ DLP-3067 [M]	My Old Flames	1957	25.00
❏ DLP-3334 [M]	Near You	1960	15.00
❏ DLP-3198 [M]	Old Fashioned Love	1959	18.00
❏ DLP-25198 [S]	Old Fashioned Love	1959	25.00
❏ DLP-3621 [M]	Raggin' the Hits	1965	15.00
❏ DLP-25621 [M]	Raggin' the Hits	1965	18.00
❏ DLP-3633 [M]	Ragtime by Request	1965	15.00
❏ DLP-25633 [S]	Ragtime by Request	1965	18.00
❏ DLP-3521 [M]	Ragtime Duets	1963	15.00
—With Glenn Rowell			
❏ DLP-25521 [S]	Ragtime Duets	1963	18.00
—With Glenn Rowell			
❏ DLP-3000 [M]	Ragtime Melodies	1955	30.00
❏ DLP-3724 [M]	Ragtime Memories	1966	15.00
❏ DLP-25724 [S]	Ragtime Memories	1966	18.00
❏ DLP-3108 [M]	Ragtime Piano 1917-18	1958	18.00
❏ DLP-3739 [M]	Ragtime Piano Man	1966	15.00
❏ DLP-25739 [S]	Ragtime Piano Man	1966	18.00
❏ DLP-3493 [M]	Ragtime Twenties	1963	15.00
❏ DLP-25493 [S]	Ragtime Twenties	1963	18.00
❏ DLP-3378 [M]	Sabre Dance	1961	15.00
❏ DLP-25378 [S]	Sabre Dance	1961	18.00
❏ DLP-3817 [M]	Second Hand Rose	1967	18.00
❏ DLP-25817 [S]	Second Hand Rose	1967	18.00
❏ DLP-3008 [M]	Tap Dance Rhythms	1956	30.00
❏ DLP-3063 [M]	The Thirties in Ragtime	1957	25.00
❏ DLP-3321 [M]	The World's Greatest Piano Rolls	1960	15.00

Number	Title	Yr	NM
❏ DLP-25321 [S]	The World's Greatest Piano Rolls	1960	18.00
❏ DLP-3476 [M]	World's Greatest Piano Rolls, Volume 2	1962	15.00
❏ DLP-25476 [S]	World's Greatest Piano Rolls, Volume 2	1962	18.00
❏ DLP-3477 [M]	World's Greatest Piano Rolls, Volume 3	1962	15.00
❏ DLP-25477 [S]	World's Greatest Piano Rolls, Volume 3	1962	15.00
❏ DLP-3478 [M]	World's Greatest Piano Rolls, Volume 4	1962	15.00
❏ DLP-25478 [S]	World's Greatest Piano Rolls, Volume 4	1962	18.00
❏ DLP-3720 [M]	World's Greatest Piano Rolls, Volume 5	1966	15.00
❏ DLP-25720 [S]	World's Greatest Piano Rolls, Volume 5	1966	18.00
❏ DLP-3721 [M]	World's Greatest Piano Rolls, Volume 6	1966	15.00
❏ DLP-25721 [S]	World's Greatest Piano Rolls, Volume 6	1966	18.00
❏ DLP-3722 [M]	World's Greatest Piano Rolls, Volume 7	1966	15.00
❏ DLP-25722 [S]	World's Greatest Piano Rolls, Volume 7	1966	18.00

HAMILTON

❏ HLP-115 [M]	12 Ragtime Greats	1964	12.00
❏ HLP-12115 [S]	12 Ragtime Greats	1964	15.00
❏ HLP-150 [M]	Great Marches and Waltzes	1964	12.00
❏ HLP-12150 [S]	Great Marches and Waltzes	1964	15.00

PARAMOUNT

❏ PAS-2-1029	Piano Roll Greats	1974	15.00

PICKWICK

❏ SPC-3097 [S]	Alley Cat and Other Piano Roll Favorites	196?	12.00
❏ PC-3097 [M]	Alley Cat and Other Piano Roll Favorites	196?	15.00

MADDOX, LESTER

LEFEVRE

❏ MLSP-3485	God, Family and Country	197?	40.00

MADDOX, ROSE

CAPITOL

❏ T1540 [M]	A Big Bouquet of Roses	1961	30.00
❏ ST1548 [S]	A Big Bouquet of Roses	1961	40.00
❏ T1993 [M]	Alone with You	1963	30.00
❏ ST1993 [S]	Alone with You	1963	40.00
❏ T1437 [M]	Glorybound Train	1960	30.00
❏ ST1437 [S]	Glorybound Train	1960	40.00
❏ T1799 [M]	Rose Maddox Sings Bluegrass	1962	40.00
❏ ST1799 [S]	Rose Maddox Sings Bluegrass	1962	50.00
❏ T1312 [M]	The One Rose	1960	30.00
❏ ST1312 [S]	The One Rose	1960	40.00

COLUMBIA

❏ CL1159 [M]	Precious Memories	1958	40.00

MADDOX BROTHERS AND ROSE

KING

❏ 669 [M]	A Collection of Standard Sacred Songs	1959	150.00
❏ 752 [M]	I'll Write Your Name in the Sand	1961	120.00
❏ 677 [M]	The Maddox Brothers and Rose	1960	120.00

WRANGLER

❏ W-1003 [M]	The Maddox Brothers and Rose	1962	30.00
❏ WS-1003 [S]	The Maddox Brothers and Rose	1962	40.00

MADIGAN, BETTY

MGM

❏ E-3448 [M]	Am I Blue?	1956	40.00

MADISON, AL

GOLDEN CREST

❏ GC-3048 [M]	Meet Al Madison	196?	30.00

MADISON, JIMMY

ADELPHI

❏ 5007	Bumps	1978	15.00

MADNESS

GEFFEN

❏ GHS4022	Keep Moving	1984	12.00
❏ GHS4003	Madness	1983	12.00
❏ GHS24079	Mad Not Mad	1985	12.00

SIRE

❏ SRK6094	Absolutely	1980	12.00
❏ SRK6085	One Step Beyond	1979	15.00

MADONNA

MAVERICK

❏ PRO-A-7311 [DJ]	Bedtime Stories	1994	100.00
— Promo only on pink vinyl			
❏ PRO-A-5904 [DJ]	Erotica	1992	60.00
— Vinyl is promo only			

Number	Title	Yr	NM
❏ PRO-A-100871 [DJ]	GHV2 Remixed -- The Best of 1991-2001	2001	40.00
— Promo-only remixes of 12 songs from the "GHV2" CD; comes in generic black jacket with hole in center			
❏ PRO-A-100500-A [DJ]	Music	2000	50.00
— Vinyl is promo only; generic white die-cut sleeve			
❏ PRO-A-9378 [DJ]	Ray of Light	1998	60.00
— Vinyl is promo only; generic cover with sticker			

SIRE

❏ 26209	I'm Breathless	1990	12.00
❏ W1-26209	I'm Breathless	1990	18.00
— Columbia House edition			
❏ R100572	I'm Breathless	1990	18.00
— BMG Direct Marketing edition			
❏ 25844 [B]	Like a Prayer	1989	18.00
❏ W1-25844	Like a Prayer	1989	18.00
— Columbia House edition			
❏ R101029	Like a Prayer	1989	18.00
— BMG Direct Marketing edition			
❏ 25157	Like a Virgin	1984	60.00
— White vinyl with silver colored spine			
❏ 25157 [B]	Like a Virgin	1984	60.00
— White vinyl with cream colored spine			
❏ W1-25157	Like a Virgin	1985	18.00
— Columbia House edition			
❏ R161153	Like a Virgin	1985	18.00
— RCA Music Service edition			
❏ 25157	Like a Virgin	1984	12.00
❏ 23867 [B]	Madonna	1983	50.00
— First pressing with 4:48 version of "Burning Up"; this version has only been found on copies with a gold promo stamp on the cover			
❏ 23867 [B]	Madonna	1983	18.00
— Second pressing with 3:49 version of "Burning Up"			
❏ W1-23867	Madonna	1984	18.00
— Columbia House edition			
❏ R164288	Madonna	1984	18.00
— RCA Music Service edition			
❏ 26440	The Immaculate Collection	1990	18.00
❏ W1-26440	The Immaculate Collection	1990	25.00
— Columbia House edition			
❏ R254164	The Immaculate Collection	1990	25.00
— BMG Direct Marketing edition			
❏ 25442	True Blue	1986	15.00
— With poster			
❏ 25442	True Blue	1986	10.00
— Without poster			
❏ W1-25442	True Blue	1986	18.00
— Columbia House edition; issued with poster			
❏ R143811	True Blue	1986	18.00
RCA Music Service edition; issued with poster			
❏ 25535	You Can Dance	1987	15.00
— With gold obi "Madonna and Dancing"			
❏ 25535	You Can Dance	1987	10.00
— Without gold obi			
❏ PRO-A-2892 [B]	You Can Dance	1987	50.00
Promo only; contains single edits of the seven songs on the stock editions			
❏ W1-25535	You Can Dance	1987	18.00
Columbia House edition; not issued with obi			
❏ R134536	You Can Dance	1987	18.00
— RCA Music Service edition; not issued with obi			

WARNER BROS.

❏ 49460-1	Confessions on a Dance Floor	2005	40.00
— All copies on pink vinyl			
❏ 42916-0	Confessions Remixed	2005	40.00
— Six remixes of five different songs from "Confessions on a Dance Floor"			

MAESTRO, JOHNNY

BUDDAH

❏ BDS-5091	The Johnny Maestro Story	1971	40.00
— With inserts; deduct 40% if missing			

MAGAZINE

I.R.S.

❏ SP-70030	After the Fact	1982	12.00
❏ SP-70020	Magic, Murder and the Weather	1981	15.00
❏ SP-70015	Play	1981	15.00

VIRGIN

❏ 90891	Rays & Hail 1978-1981	1987	18.00
❏ VA13144	The Correct Use of Soap	1980	12.00

VIRGIN INTERNATIONAL

❏ VI-2100	Real Life	1978	18.00
❏ VI-2121	Secondhand Daylight	1979	14.00

MAGGARD, CLEDUS

MERCURY

❏ SRM-1-1072	The White Knight	1976	15.00

MAGI, THE

UNCLE DIRTY

❏ 6102-N13	Win or Lose	1975	300.00

Number	Title	Yr	NM
MAGIC			

ARMADILLO

❏ 8031	Enclosed	1970	400.00

RARE EARTH

❏ RS-527	Magic	1971	30.00

MAGIC FERN, THE

PANORAMA

❏ 108	The Magic Fern	1980	150.00

MAGIC LANTERNS

ATLANTIC

❏ SD8217	Shame, Shame	1969	25.00

MAGIC SAM

DELMARK

❏ DL-620	Black Magic	1969	30.00
❏ DL-615	West Side Soul	1968	30.00

MAGIC SAND

UNI

❏ 73094 [B]	Magic Sand	1971	30.00

MAGNIFICENT MEN, THE

CAPITOL

❏ T2775 [M]	The Magnificent Men "Live!	1967	25.00
❏ ST2775 [S]	The Magnificent Men "Live!	1967	18.00
❏ T2678 [M]	The Magnificent Men	1967	25.00
❏ ST2678 [S]	The Magnificent Men	1967	18.00
❏ T2846 [M]	World of Soul	1968	30.00
❏ ST2846 [S]	World of Soul	1968	18.00

MERCURY

❏ SR-61252	Better Than a Ten Cent Movie	1970	18.00

MAHAL, TAJ

COLUMBIA

❏ PC34466	Anthology Volume 1	1977	15.00
❏ GP18	Giant Step/De Ole Folks at Home	1969	25.00
— Red "360 Sound" label			
❏ GP18	Giant Step/De Ole Folks at Home	1971	18.00
— Orange label			
❏ CG18	Giant Step/De Ole Folks at Home	198?	12.00
— Reissue with new prefix			
❏ C30767	Happy to Be Like I Am	1971	15.00
❏ PC30767	Happy to Be Like I Am	198?	10.00
— Budget-line reissue			
❏ KC33051	Mo' Roots	1974	15.00
❏ PC33051	Mo' Roots	198?	10.00
— Budget-line reissue			
❏ PC33801	Music Keeps Me Together	1975	15.00
❏ KC32600	Oooh So Good 'N Blues	1973	15.00
❏ PC32600	Oooh So Good 'N Blues	198?	10.00
— Budget-line reissue			
❏ KC31605	Recycling the Blues & Other Related Stuff	1972	15.00
❏ PC31605	Recycling the Blues & Other Related Stuff	198?	10.00
— Budget-line reissue			
❏ PC34103	Satisfied & Tickled Too	1976	15.00
❏ CL2779 [M]	Taj Mahal	1967	60.00
❏ CS9579 [S]	Taj Mahal	1967	18.00
— Red "360 Sound" label			
❏ CS9579 [S]	Taj Mahal	1971	15.00
— Orange label			
❏ PC9579 [S]	Taj Mahal	198?	10.00
— Reissue with new prefix			
❏ FC36528	The Best of Taj Mahal	1981	12.00
❏ PC36528	The Best of Taj Mahal	198?	10.00
— Budget-line reissue			
❏ 88765494151 [B]	The Hidden Treasures Of Taj Mahal (1969-1973)	2013	25.00
❏ CS9698	The Natch'l Blues	1968	18.00
— Red "360 Sound" label			
❏ CS9698	The Natch'l Blues	1971	15.00
— Orange label			
❏ PC9698	The Natch'l Blues	198?	10.00
— Reissue with new prefix			
❏ 88883700461 [B]	The Natch'l Blues	2013	25.00
❏ G30619	The Real Thing	1971	25.00
❏ CG30619	The Real Thing	198?	12.00
— Reissue with new prefix			

CRYSTAL CLEAR

❏ 5011 [B]	Live and Direct	1980	30.00
— Direct-to-disc recording			

WARNER BROS.

❏ BS3024	Brothers	1977	12.00
❏ BS3094	Evolution (Recent)	1978	12.00
❏ BS2994	Music Fuh Ya' (Musica Para Tu)	1977	12.00

MAHAN, LARRY

WARNER BROS.

❏ BS2959	King of the Rodeo	1976	25.00

Number	Title	Yr	NM

MAHARIS, GEORGE

EPIC

☐ LN24191 [M]	A New Route: George Maharis	1966	15.00
☐ BN26191 [S]	A New Route: George Maharis	1966	18.00
☐ LN24001 [M]	George Maharis Sings!	1962	15.00
☐ BN26001 [S]	George Maharis Sings!	1962	18.00
☐ LN24037 [M]	Just Turn Me Loose!	1963	15.00
☐ BN26037 [S]	Just Turn Me Loose!	1963	18.00
☐ LN24079 [M]	Make Love to Me	1964	15.00
☐ BN26079 [S]	Make Love to Me	1964	18.00
☐ LN24021 [M]	Portrait in Music	1962	15.00
☐ BN26021 [S]	Portrait in Music	1962	18.00
☐ LN24111 [M]	Tonight You Belong to Me	1964	15.00
☐ BN26111 [S]	Tonight You Belong to Me	1964	18.00
☐ LN24064 [M]	Where Can You Go for a Broken Heart?	1963	15.00
☐ BN26064 [S]	Where Can You Go for a Broken Heart?	1963	18.00

MAHOGANY RUSH

20TH CENTURY

☐ T-451	Child of the Novelty	1974	30.00
☐ T-463	Maxoom	1975	30.00
—Reissue of Nine 936			
☐ T-482 [B]	Strange Universe	1975	25.00

COLUMBIA

☐ JC35257	Frank Marino & Mahogany Rush Live	1978	18.00
☐ PC35257	Frank Marino & Mahogany Rush Live	198?	10.00
—Budget-line reissue			
☐ PC34190	Mahogany Rush IV	1976	18.00
—Original with no bar code			
☐ PC34190	Mahogany Rush IV	198?	10.00
—Reissue with bar code			
☐ JC35753	Tales of the Unexpected	1979	18.00
☐ PC35753	Tales of the Unexpected	198?	10.00
—Budget-line reissue			
☐ JC36204	What's Next	1980	18.00
☐ PC36204	What's Next	198?	10.00
—Budget-line reissue			
☐ PC34677	World Anthem	1977	18.00
—Original with no bar code			
☐ PC34677	World Anthem	198?	10.00
—Reissue with bar code			

NINE

☐ 936	Maxoom	1973	50.00

MAHONES, GILDO

PRESTIGE

☐ PRLP-16004 [M]	Shooting High	1964	40.00
☐ PRLP-7339 [M]	The Soulful Piano of Gildo Mahones	1964	30.00
☐ PRST-7339 [S]	The Soulful Piano of Gildo Mahones	1964	40.00

MAIDEN, SIDNEY

BLUESVILLE

☐ BVLP-1035 [M]	Trouble An' Blues	1961	80.00
—Blue label, silver print			
☐ BVLP-1035 [M]	Trouble An' Blues	1964	25.00
—Blue label, trident logo at right			

MAIN ATTRACTION, THE

TOWER

☐ ST-5117 [S]	And Now...The Main Attraction	1968	30.00
☐ T-5117 [M]	And Now...The Main Attraction	1968	50.00

MAIN INGREDIENT, THE

COLLECTABLES

☐ COL-5101	Golden Classics	198?	12.00

POLYDOR

☐ 841249-1	I Just Wanna Love You	1989	15.00

RCA VICTOR

☐ LSP-4834	Afrodisiac	1973	15.00
☐ LSP-4677	Bitter Sweet	1972	15.00
☐ LSP-4483	Black Seeds	1971	15.00
☐ APL1-0335	Euphrates River	1974	15.00
☐ APD1-0335 [Q]	Euphrates River	1974	25.00
☐ APL1-0314	Greatest Hits	1974	15.00
☐ AFL1-3963	I Only Have Eyes for You	1981	12.00
☐ APL1-1558	Music Maximus	1977	15.00
☐ AFL1-3641	Ready for Love	1980	12.00
☐ APL1-0644	Rolling Down a Mountainside	1975	15.00
☐ ANL1-2667	Rolling Down a Mountainside	1978	12.00
—Reissue of APL1-0644			
☐ APL1-1003	Shame On the World	1975	15.00
☐ APL1-1858	Super Hits	1977	15.00
☐ LSP-4412	Tasteful Soul	1971	15.00
☐ LSP-4253	The Main Ingredient L.T.D.	1970	15.00

MAINER, J.E.

ARHOOLIE

☐ F5002	J.E. Mainer's Mountaineers	197?	15.00

BLUE JAY

☐ 101	70th Happy Birthday	1968	25.00
☐ 102	Precious Memories	1968	25.00

KING

☐ 666 [M]	Good Ole Mountain Music	1960	100.00
☐ 666	Good Ole Mountain Music	197?	15.00
—Gusto reissue			
☐ 765 [M]	Variety Album	1961	100.00

OLD HOMESTEAD

☐ 146	J.E. Mainer at Home with Family and Friends, Vol. 1	197?	18.00

OLD TIMEY

☐ 107	J.E. Mainer's Mountaineers, Vol. 2	197?	15.00

RURAL RHYTHM

☐ RRJE-191	More Old Time Mountain Music	198?	15.00
☐ RRJE-198	The Legendary J.E. Mainer, Vol. 3	198?	15.00
☐ RRJE-225	The Legendary J.E. Mainer, Vol. 7	198?	15.00
☐ RRJE-246	The Legendary J.E. Mainer, Vol. 16	198?	15.00
☐ RRJE-250	The Legendary J.E. Mainer, Vol. 20	198?	15.00
☐ RRJE-185	The Legendary J.E. Mainer and His Mountaineers	198?	15.00

MAINER, WADE

KING

☐ 769 [M]	Soulful Sacred Songs	1961	100.00

OLD HOMESTEAD

☐ 4000	From the Maple to the Hill	1976	25.00
☐ 90123	Old Time Songs	1980	18.00
☐ 90016	Sacred Songs Mountain Style	197?	18.00
☐ 90001	Sacred Songs of Mother and Home	1971	18.00

MAIZE, JOE

DECCA

☐ DL8817 [M]	Hawaiian Dreams	1959	25.00
☐ DL78817 [S]	Hawaiian Dreams	1959	30.00
☐ DL4555 [M]	Isle of Dreams	1965	25.00
☐ DL74555 [S]	Isle of Dreams	1965	30.00
☐ DL8590 [M]	Presenting Joe Maize and His Cordsmen	1958	30.00

MAJIC SHIP, THE

BEL AMI

☐ BA-711	The Majic Ship	1968	500.00

MAJORS, THE (1)

IMPERIAL

☐ LP-9222 [M]	Meet the Majors	1963	125.00
☐ LP-12222 [S]	Meet the Majors	1963	200.00

MAKEBA, MIRIAM

KAPP

☐ KL-1274 [M]	The Many Voices of Miriam Makeba	1962	25.00
☐ KS-3274 [S]	The Many Voices of Miriam Makeba	1962	30.00

MERCURY

☐ MG-21095 [M]	All About Miriam	1967	15.00
☐ SR-61095 [S]	All About Miriam	1967	18.00
☐ MG-21082 [M]	The Magnificent Miriam Makeba	1966	15.00
☐ SR-61082 [S]	The Magnificent Miriam Makeba	1966	18.00

MERCURY/URBAN AFRICA

☐ 838208-1	Welela	1989	15.00

PETERS INT'L.

☐ PLD2082	Miriam Makeba in Concert	1977	15.00

RCA VICTOR

☐ LPM-3321 [M]	Makeba Sings	1965	18.00
☐ LSP-3321 [S]	Makeba Sings	1965	25.00
☐ LPM-2267 [M]	Miriam Makeba	1960	25.00
☐ LSP-2267 [S]	Miriam Makeba	1960	30.00
☐ LPM-3982 [M]	The Best of Miriam Makeba	1968	30.00
☐ LSP-3982 [S]	The Best of Miriam Makeba	1968	15.00
☐ LPM-3512 [M]	The Magic of Makeba	1966	18.00
☐ LSP-3512 [S]	The Magic of Makeba	1966	25.00
☐ LPM-2845 [M]	The Voice of Africa	1964	18.00
☐ LSP-2845 [S]	The Voice of Africa	1964	25.00
☐ LPM-2750 [M]	The World of Miriam Makeba	1963	18.00
☐ LSP-2750 [S]	The World of Miriam Makeba	1963	25.00

REPRISE

☐ RS-6381	Keep Me in Mind	1970	15.00
☐ RS-6310	Makeba!	1968	15.00
☐ R-6253 [M]	Miriam Makeba In Concert!	1967	18.00
☐ RS-6253 [S]	Miriam Makeba In Concert!	1967	15.00
☐ R-6274 [M]	Pata Pata	1967	18.00
☐ RS-6274 [S]	Pata Pata	1967	15.00

WARNER BROS.

☐ 25673	Sangoma	1988	12.00

MAKEM, TOMMY

TRADITION

☐ TLP-1044 [M]	Songs of Tommy Makem	1961	30.00
☐ TLPS-1044 [S]	Songs of Tommy Makem	1961	40.00

MAKOWICZ, ADAM, AND GEORGE MRAZ

STASH

☐ ST-216	Classic Jazz Duets	198?	12.00

MAKOWICZ, ADAM

CHOICE

☐ 1028	From My Window	198?	15.00

COLUMBIA

☐ JC35320	Adam	1978	12.00

NOVUS

☐ 3003-1-N	Moonray	1986	12.00
☐ 3022-1-N	Naughty Baby	1988	12.00

SHEFFIELD LABS

☐ 21	The Name Is Makowicz (ma-ko-vitch)	1984	25.00
—Audiophile vinyl			

MALACHI

VERVE

☐ V-5024 [M]	Holy Music	1967	50.00
☐ V6-5024 [S]	Holy Music	1967	40.00

MALCHAK, TIM

ALPINE

☐ 1001	Colorado Moon	1987	15.00

UNIVERSAL

☐ UVL-76002	Different Circles	1989	12.00

MALCOLM X

DOUGLAS

☐ Z30743 [M]	By Any Means Necessary	1971	35.00
☐ SD797 [B]	His Wit and Wisdom	196?	35.00
☐ SD795 [M]	Malcolm X Talks to Young People	1968	35.00

PAUL WINLEY

☐ 135	The Ballot or the Bullet	197?	25.00

RCA

☐ 66132	Words from the Frontlines: Excerpts from the Great Speeches of Malcolm X	1992	25.00

UPFRONT

☐ UPF-152 [B]	Malcolm X Speaks to the People in Harlem	197?	18.00

WARNER BROS.

☐ BS2619 [B]	Malcolm X	1972	30.00
☐	Malcolm X Speaks	1992	25.00
PRO-A-5943 [DJ]			
☐ PRO-A-5957 [DJ]	Music and Dialog from the Historic 1992 Documentary Film Malcolm X	1992	25.00

MALTBY, RICHARD

COLUMBIA

☐ CL1341 [M]	Hello Young Lovers	1959	25.00
☐ CS8151 [S]	Hello Young Lovers	1959	30.00
☐ CL1271 [M]	Swingin' Down the Lane	1959	25.00
☐ CS8083 [S]	Swingin' Down the Lane	1959	30.00

RCA CAMDEN

☐ CAL-526 [M]	A Bow to the Big Name Bands	1959	25.00
☐ CAL-711 [M]	Most Requested	1961	25.00
☐ CAL-600 [M]	Music from Mr. Lucky	1960	25.00

ROULETTE

☐ R-25178 [M]	Brilliant Big Band Ballads and Blues	1962	25.00
☐ SR-25178 [S]	Brilliant Big Band Ballads and Blues	1962	30.00
☐ R-25129 [M]	Richard Maltby Swings for Dancers	1960	25.00
☐ R-25148 [M]	Swing Folksongs	1961	25.00
☐ SR-25148 [S]	Swing Folksongs	1961	30.00

VIK

☐ LX-1051 [M]	Hue-Fi Moods by Maltby	1957	30.00
☐ LX-1071 [M]	Maltby with Strings Attached	1958	30.00
☐ LX-1068 [M]	Manhattan Bandstand	1957	30.00

X

☐ LX-1038 [M]	Make Mine Maltby	1956	30.00

MALVIN, ARTIE

WALDORF MUSIC HALL

☐ 33-149 [10]	Rock and Roll	1955	120.00

MAMA LION

FAMILY PRODUCTIONS

☐ FPS-2713	Give It Everything I've Got	1973	25.00
☐ FPS-2702	Mama Lion	1972	25.00

MAMAS AND THE PAPAS, THE

ABC

☐ AC-30005	The ABC Collection	1976	18.00

ABC DUNHILL

☐ DS-50064	16 of Their Greatest Hits	1969	18.00
☐ DSX-50145	20 Golden Hits	1973	25.00
☐ DS-50073	A Gathering of Flowers	1970	30.00

Number	Title	Yr	NM
❑ DS-50025 [B]	Farewell to the First Golden Era	1968	15.00
❑ DS-50038	Golden Era, Volume 2	1968	25.00
❑ DS-50006	If You Can Believe Your Eyes and Ears	1968	15.00
❑ DSX-50100	Monterey International Pop Festival	1970	18.00
❑ SMAS-93470	Monterey International Pop Festival	1970	30.00
— Capitol Record Club edition; label has the old-style "Dunhill" logo without the "ABC" as part of it			
❑ DSX-50106	People Like Us	1971	15.00
❑ DS-50010	The Mamas and the Papas	1968	15.00
❑ DS-50014	The Mamas and the Papas Deliver	1968	15.00
❑ DS-50031 [B]	The Papas and the Mamas	1968	18.00
— The five LPs above are reissues of records originally without the ABC logo			
DUNHILL			
❑ D-50025 [M]	Farewell to the First Golden Era	1967	25.00
❑ DS-50025 [S]	Farewell to the First Golden Era	1967	35.00
❑ D-50006 [M]	If You Can Believe Your Eyes and Ears	1966	150.00
— With toilet completely visible in lower right			
❑ D-50006 [M]	If You Can Believe Your Eyes and Ears	1966	50.00
— With scroll over toilet			
❑ DS-50006 [S]	If You Can Believe Your Eyes and Ears	1966	100.00
— With toilet completely visible in lower right			
❑ DS-50006 [S]	If You Can Believe Your Eyes and Ears	1966	30.00
— With scroll over toilet proclaiming "Includes California Dreamin'			
❑ DS-50006 [S]	If You Can Believe Your Eyes and Ears	1966	50.00
— Black cover with photo cropped to render toilet invisible			
❑ ST-90797 [S]	If You Can Believe Your Eyes and Ears	1966	50.00
— Capitol Record Club edition; known copies have scroll proclaiming "Includes California Dreamin'.			
❑ DS-50006 [S]	If You Can Believe Your Eyes and Ears	1966	30.00
— With scroll over toilet proclaiming "Includes California Dreamin'... Monday Monday... I Call Your Name			
❑ D-50006 [M]	If You Can Believe Your Eyes and Ears	1966	60.00
— Black cover with photo cropped to render toilet invisible			
❑ T-90797 [M]	If You Can Believe Your Eyes and Ears	1966	50.00
— Capitol Record Club edition; known copies have scroll proclaiming "Includes California Dreamin'.			
❑ D-50010 [M]	The Mamas and the Papas	1966	35.00
❑ DS-50010 [S]	The Mamas and the Papas	1966	30.00
❑ T-90924 [M]	The Mamas and the Papas	1966	35.00
— Capitol Record Club edition			
❑ ST-90924 [S]	The Mamas and the Papas	1966	40.00
— Capitol Record Club edition			
❑ D-50014 [M]	The Mamas and the Papas Deliver	1967	35.00
❑ DS-50014 [S]	The Mamas and the Papas Deliver	1967	30.00
❑ DS-50031	The Papas and the Mamas	1968	30.00
MCA			
❑ 37145	16 of Their Greatest Hits	1980	10.00
❑ 709	Farewell to the First Golden Era	1980	10.00
❑ 6019	The Best of the Mamas and the Papas	1986	15.00
❑ 710	The Papas and the Mamas	1980	10.00
PICKWICK			
❑ SPC-3352	California Dreaming	1972	15.00
SUNDAZED			
❑ LP5446 [B]	Deliver	2013	25.00
❑ LP5445 [B]	The Mamas and the Papas	2013	25.00
MAN			
PHILIPS			
❑ PHS600313	Revelation	1969	25.00
— As "Manpower			
MANCE, JUNIOR			
ATLANTIC			
❑ SD1521	At the Top	1969	18.00
❑ 1479 [M]	Harlem Lullaby	1967	25.00
❑ SD1479 [S]	Harlem Lullaby	1967	18.00
❑ 1496 [M]	I Believe to My Soul	1968	30.00
❑ SD1496 [S]	I Believe to My Soul	1968	18.00
❑ SD1562	With a Lotta Help from My Friends	1970	18.00
BEE HIVE			
❑ BH-7015	Truckin' and Trakin'	198?	15.00
CAPITOL			
❑ T2092 [M]	Get Ready, Set, Jump!	1964	25.00
❑ ST2092 [S]	Get Ready, Set, Jump!	1964	30.00
❑ T2218 [M]	Straight Ahead	1965	18.00
❑ ST2218 [S]	Straight Ahead	1965	25.00
❑ T2393 [M]	That's Where It Is	1965	18.00
❑ ST2393 [S]	That's Where It Is	1965	25.00
FANTASY			
❑ OJC-204	Junior Mance Trio at the Village Vanguard	198?	12.00

Number	Title	Yr	NM
INNER CITY			
❑ IC-6018	Holy Mama	197?	18.00
JAZZLAND			
❑ JLP-53 [M]	Big Chief!	1961	30.00
❑ JLP-953 [S]	Big Chief!	1961	30.00
❑ JLP-77 [M]	Happy Time	1962	30.00
❑ JLP-977 [S]	Happy Time	1962	30.00
❑ JLP-41 [M]	Junior Mance Trio at the Village Vanguard	1961	30.00
❑ JLP-941 [S]	Junior Mance Trio at the Village Vanguard	1961	30.00
❑ JLP-63 [M]	The Jazz Soul of Hollywood	1961	30.00
❑ JLP-963 [S]	The Jazz Soul of Hollywood	1961	30.00
❑ JLP-30 [M]	The Soulful Piano of Junior Mance	1960	30.00
❑ JLP-930 [S]	The Soulful Piano of Junior Mance	1960	30.00
MILESTONE			
❑ M-9041	That Lovin' Feelin'	197?	18.00
POLYDOR			
❑ PD-5051	Touch	1974	18.00
RIVERSIDE			
❑ RLP-447 [M]	Junior's Blues	1963	30.00
❑ RS-9447 [S]	Junior's Blues	1963	30.00
❑ 6059	Soulful Piano	197?	15.00
SACKVILLE			
❑ 3031	For Dancers Only	198?	12.00
VERVE			
❑ MGV-8319 [M]	Junior	1959	40.00
❑ MGVS-6057 [S]	Junior	1960	30.00
❑ V-8319 [M]	Junior	1961	25.00
❑ V6-8319 [S]	Junior	1961	18.00
MANCHESTER, MELISSA			
ARISTA			
❑ AL4067	Better Days & Happy Endings	1976	12.00
❑ AQ4067 [Q]	Better Days & Happy Endings	1976	18.00
❑ AL4011	Bright Eyes	1975	12.00
— Reissue of Bell 1303			
❑ AB4186	Don't Cry Out Loud	1978	12.00
❑ AL8373	Don't Cry Out Loud	198?	10.00
— Budget-line reissue of 4186			
❑ AL8094	Emergency	1983	12.00
❑ AL9533	For the Working Girl	1980	12.00
❑ AL9611	Greatest Hits	1983	12.00
❑ AL8293	Greatest Hits	198?	10.00
— Budget-line reissue of 9611			
❑ AL4095	Help Is On the Way	1976	12.00
❑ AL9574	Hey Ricky	1982	12.00
❑ AL8350	Hey Ricky	198?	10.00
— Budget-line reissue of 9574			
❑ AL4006	Home to Myself	1975	12.00
— Reissue of Bell 1123			
❑ AL4031	Melissa	1975	12.00
❑ AQ4031 [Q]	Melissa	1975	18.00
❑ AL8055	Melissa	1983	10.00
— Budget-line reissue of 4031			
❑ AL9506	Melissa Manchester	1979	12.00
❑ AL4136	Singin'	1977	12.00
BELL			
❑ 1303	Bright Eyes	1974	15.00
❑ 1123	Home to Myself	1973	15.00
MCA			
❑ 5587	Mathematics	1985	12.00
MIKA			
❑ 841273-1	Tribute	1989	15.00
MOBILE FIDELITY			
❑ 1-028 [B]	Melissa	1980	30.00
— Audiophile vinyl			
NAUTILUS			
❑ NR-33	Don't Cry Out Loud	198?	40.00
— Audiophile vinyl			
PAIR			
❑ PDL2-1086	The Many Moods of Melissa Manchester	1986	15.00
MANCHESTERS, THE (1)			
DIPLOMAT			
❑ D-2307 [M]	Beatlerama	1964	18.00
— No artist credited on label or cover			
❑ D-2307 [M]	Beatlerama	1964	18.00
— With artist credited			
❑ DS-2307 [S]	Beatlerama	1964	25.00
— No artist credited on label or cover			
❑ DS-2307 [S]	Beatlerama	1964	25.00
— With artist credited			
GUEST STAR			
❑ G-2307 [M]	Beatlerama	1964	18.00
❑ GS-2307 [S]	Beatlerama	1964	25.00
MANCINI, HENRY			
AVCO EMBASSY			
❑ AVE 0110	Sunflower	1970	18.00
DECCA			
❑ DL79185	Sometimes a Great Notion	1971	18.00

Number	Title	Yr	NM
LIBERTY			
❑ LRP-3121 [M]	The Versatile Henry Mancini	1959	25.00
❑ LST-7121 [S]	The Versatile Henry Mancini	1959	30.00
❑ LT-51135	Trail of the Pink Panther	1982	12.00
MCA			
❑ 6222	The Glass Menagerie	1987	12.00
❑ 2085	The Great Waldo Pepper	1975	15.00
PAIR			
❑ PDL2-1092	The Mancini Collection (Film Music)	1986	15.00
PARAMOUNT			
❑ PAS-6000	The Molly Maguires	1970	25.00
RCA CAMDEN			
❑ CAS-2510	Dream of You	1971	12.00
❑ CXS-9034	Everybody's Favorite	1972	12.00
❑ ACL2-0293	Film Music	1973	15.00
❑ CXS-9005	Mancini Magic	1971	15.00
❑ CAL-2158 [M]	Mancini Plays Mancini and Other Composers	1968	15.00
❑ CAS-2158 [S]	Mancini Plays Mancini and Other Composers	1968	12.00
❑ CAL-928 [M]	The Second Time Around and Others	1966	15.00
❑ CAS-928 [S]	The Second Time Around and Others	1966	15.00
RCA SPECIAL PRODUCTS			
❑ DPL1-0678	Taking It Easy	1984	18.00
— Manufactured for Abbott Laboratories			
RCA VICTOR			
❑ PRM-175 [M]	Academy Award Songs, Volume Two	1965	18.00
— Made for the B.F. Goodrich tire company			
❑ PRS-175 [S]	Academy Award Songs, Volume Two	1965	25.00
— Made for the B.F. Goodrich tire company			
❑ CPL1-1843	A Legendary Performer	1976	12.00
❑ LPM-3612 [M]	A Merry Mancini Christmas	1966	12.00
— Original front cover has a photo of Henry Mancini and family			
❑ LSP-3612 [S]	A Merry Mancini Christmas	1966	15.00
— Same as above, but in stereo			
❑ ANL1-1928 [S]	A Merry Mancini Christmas	1976	10.00
— Reissue with new number and new front cover			
❑ LPM-3623 [M]	Arabesque	1966	15.00
❑ LSP-3623 [S]	Arabesque	1966	18.00
❑ LSP-4140	A Warm Shade of Ivory	1969	18.00
❑ AFL1-4140	A Warm Shade of Ivory	1977	10.00
— Reissue with new prefix			
❑ AYL1-3757	A Warm Shade of Ivory	1980	10.00
— Best Buy Series" reissue			
❑ LSP-4630	Big Screen -- Little Screen	1972	18.00
❑ APL1-0098	Brass, Ivory and Strings	1973	15.00
❑ APD1-0098 [Q]	Brass, Ivory and Strings	1973	25.00
❑ LSP-4629	Brass on Ivory	1972	15.00
❑ AFL1-4629	Brass on Ivory	1977	10.00
— Reissue with new prefix			
❑ AYL1-3756	Brass on Ivory	1980	10.00
— Best Buy Series" reissue			
❑ LPM-2362 [M]	Breakfast at Tiffany's	1961	25.00
❑ LSP-2362 [S]	Breakfast at Tiffany's	1961	30.00
❑ LPM-2755 [M]	Charade	1963	18.00
❑ LSP-2755 [S]	Charade	1963	25.00
❑ LPM-2258 [M]	Combo!	1960	25.00
❑ LSP-2258 [S]	Combo!	1960	30.00
❑ APL1-1379	Concert of Film Music	1975	12.00
❑ APL1-1896	Cop Show Themes	1976	12.00
❑ APL1-0270	Country Gentlemen	1973	15.00
❑ AFL1-0270	Country Gentlemen	1977	12.00
— Reissue with new prefix			
❑ APD1-0270 [Q]	Country Gentlemen	1973	25.00
❑ AYL1-3954	Country Gentlemen	1981	10.00
— Best Buy Series" reissue			
❑ LPM-2990 [M]	Dear Heart and Other Songs About Love	1965	15.00
❑ LSP-2990 [S]	Dear Heart and Other Songs About Love	1965	18.00
❑ LPM-3887 [M]	Encore! More of the Concert Sound of Henry Mancini	1967	25.00
❑ LSP-3887 [S]	Encore! More of the Concert Sound of Henry Mancini	1967	18.00
❑ LPM-2442 [M]	Experiment in Terror	1962	30.00
— Original cover has Lee Remick under attack			
❑ LPM-2442 [M]	Experiment in Terror	1962	25.00
— Reissue cover has two mannequins			
❑ LSP-2442 [S]	Experiment in Terror	1962	40.00
— Original cover has Lee Remick under attack			
❑ LSP-2442 [S]	Experiment in Terror	1962	30.00
— Reissue cover has two mannequins			
❑ LPM-3840 [M]	Gunn	1967	25.00
❑ LSP-3840 [S]	Gunn	1967	30.00
❑ CPL1-0672	Hangin' Out	1974	15.00
❑ AFL1-0672	Hangin' Out	1977	12.00
— Reissue with new prefix			
❑ APD1-0672 [Q]	Hangin' Out	1974	25.00
❑ LPM-2559 [M]	Hatari!	1962	25.00
❑ LSP-2559 [S]	Hatari!	1962	30.00
❑ LPM-3694 [M]	Mancini '67	1967	18.00
❑ LSP-3694 [S]	Mancini '67	1967	18.00
❑ LSP-4542	Mancini Concert	1971	18.00
❑ AFL1-4542	Mancini Concert	1977	12.00
— Reissue with new prefix			
❑ LSP-4307	Mancini Country	1970	18.00
❑ AFL1-4307	Mancini Country	1977	12.00
— Reissue with new prefix			

Number	Title	Yr	NM
❑ AYL1-3668	Mancini Country	1980	10.00
—Best Buy Series" reissue			
❑ LSP-4466	Mancini Plays the Theme from Love Story	1971	18.00
❑ ANL1-2484	Mancini Plays the Theme from Love Story	1977	12.00
—Reissue of LSP-4466			
❑ APL1-0013	Mancini Salutes Sousa	1972	15.00
❑ APD1-0013 [Q]	Mancini Salutes Sousa	1973	25.00
❑ APL1-2290	Mancini's Angels	1977	12.00
❑ LPM-2040 [M]	More Music from Peter Gunn	1959	25.00
❑ LSP-2040 [S]	More Music from Peter Gunn	1959	30.00
❑ LPM-2360 [M]	Mr. Lucky Goes Latin	1961	25.00
❑ LSP-2360 [S]	Mr. Lucky Goes Latin	1961	30.00
❑ LPM-2198 [M]	Music from Mr. Lucky	1960	25.00
❑ LSP-2198 [S]	Music from Mr. Lucky	1960	30.00
❑ LPM-3713 [M]	Music of Hawaii	1966	15.00
❑ LSP-3713 [S]	Music of Hawaii	1966	18.00
❑ AFL1-3713	Music of Hawaii	1977	12.00
—Reissue with new prefix			
❑ AYL1-3877	Music of Hawaii	1981	10.00
—Best Buy Series" reissue			
❑ APL1-0271	Oklahoma Crude	1973	15.00
❑ LPM-2604 [M]	Our Man in Hollywood	1963	18.00
❑ LSP-2604 [S]	Our Man in Hollywood	1963	25.00
❑ LPM-3997 [M]	Party	1968	30.00
❑ LSP-3997 [S]	Party	1968	18.00
❑ ANL1-0980	Pure Gold	1975	12.00
❑ AYL1-3667	Pure Gold	1980	10.00
—Best Buy Series" reissue			
❑ ABL1-0968	Return of the Pink Panther	1975	15.00
❑ ABD1-0968 [Q]	Return of the Pink Panther	1975	25.00
❑ LSP-4239	Six Hours Past Sunset	1969	18.00
❑ APL1-1025	Symphonic Soul	1975	12.00
❑ APD1-1025 [Q]	Symphonic Soul	1975	25.00
❑ AFL1-1025	Symphonic Soul	1977	10.00
—Reissue with new prefix			
❑ LPM-6013 [M]	The Academy Award Songs	1966	18.00
❑ LSP-6013 [S]	The Academy Award Songs	1966	25.00
❑ LPM-2693 [M]	The Best of Mancini	1964	15.00
❑ LSP-2693 [S]	The Best of Mancini	1964	18.00
❑ AFL1-2693	The Best of Mancini	1977	12.00
—Reissue with new prefix			
❑ AYL1-3822	The Best of Mancini	1981	10.00
—Best Buy Series" reissue			
❑ LPM-3557 [M]	The Best of Mancini, Volume 2	1966	15.00
❑ LSP-3557 [S]	The Best of Mancini, Volume 2	1966	18.00
❑ AFL1-3557	The Best of Mancini, Volume 2	1977	12.00
—Reissue with new prefix			
❑ AQL1-3347	The Best of Mancini, Volume 3	1979	12.00
❑ LSP-4049	The Big Latin Band of Henry Mancini	1968	18.00
❑ LPM-2147 [M]	The Blues and the Beat	1960	30.00
❑ LSP-2147 [S]	The Blues and the Beat	1960	30.00
❑ LPM-2897 [M]	The Concert Sound of Henry Mancini	1964	15.00
❑ LSP-2897 [S]	The Concert Sound of Henry Mancini	1964	18.00
❑ LPM-3402 [M]	The Great Race	1965	15.00
❑ LSP-3402 [S]	The Great Race	1965	18.00
❑ LPM-3356 [M]	The Latin Sound of Henry Mancini	1965	15.00
❑ LSP-3356 [S]	The Latin Sound of Henry Mancini	1965	18.00
❑ LSP-4689	The Mancini Generation	1972	15.00
❑ LPM-3943 [M]	The Mancini Sound	1968	25.00
❑ LSP-3943 [S]	The Mancini Sound	1968	18.00
❑ LPM-2101 [M]	The Mancini Touch	1959	25.00
❑ LSP-2101 [S]	The Mancini Touch	1959	30.00
❑ LSP-4350	Theme from "Z" and Other Film Music	1970	18.00
❑ LPM-1956 [M]	The Music from Peter Gunn	1959	40.00
—Original cover is a "block" design with "Peter Gunn" at top			
❑ LPM-1956 [M]	The Music from Peter Gunn	1959	25.00
—First reissue cover is green/blue on front with huge "Peter Gunn" in center; back cover has a figure with a gun and a small photo of Henry Mancini at the lower left positioned so that it appears the gun is aimed at his head; catalog number on back cover is followed by "RE			
❑ LSP-1956 [S]	The Music from Peter Gunn	1959	50.00
—Original cover is a "block" design with "Peter Gunn" at top			
❑ LSP-1956 [S]	The Music from Peter Gunn	1959	30.00
—First reissue cover is green/blue on front with huge "Peter Gunn" in center; back cover has a figure with a gun and a small photo of Henry Mancini at the lower left positioned so that it appears the gun is aimed at his head; catalog number on back cover is followed by "RE			
❑ LPM-1956 [M]	The Music from Peter Gunn	1959	15.00
—Second reissue cover is green/blue on front with huge "Peter Gunn" in center; back cover has a figure with a gun and a large photo of Henry Mancini at the upper left; catalog number on back is followed by "RE 2			
❑ LSP-1956 [S]	The Music from Peter Gunn	1959	18.00
—Second reissue cover is green/blue on front with huge "Peter Gunn" in center; back cover has a figure with a gun and a large photo of Henry Mancini at the upper left; catalog number on back is followed by "RE 2			
❑ LPM-2795 [M]	The Pink Panther	1964	18.00
❑ LSP-2795 [S]	The Pink Panther	1964	25.00
❑ AQL1-3052	The Theme Scene	1978	12.00
❑ VPS-6029	This Is Henry Mancini	1970	25.00
❑ VPS-6053	This Is Henry Mancini, Volume 2	1972	25.00
❑ LPM-3802 [M]	Two for the Road	1967	25.00
❑ LSP-3802 [S]	Two for the Road	1967	18.00
❑ LPM-2692 [M]	Uniquely Mancini	1963	18.00
❑ LSP-2692 [S]	Uniquely Mancini	1963	25.00
❑ ABL1-0231	Visions of Eight	1973	15.00
❑ LPM-3648 [M]	What Did You Do in the War, Daddy?	1966	15.00
❑ LSP-3648 [S]	What Did You Do in the War, Daddy?	1966	18.00

SUNSET

Number	Title	Yr	NM
❑ SUM-1105 [M]	Sounds and Voices	1966	15.00
❑ SUS-5105 [S]	Sounds and Voices	1966	15.00

UNITED ARTISTS

Number	Title	Yr	NM
❑ UAS-5210	The Hawaiians	1970	15.00
❑ SW-93297	The Hawaiians	1970	25.00
—Capitol Record Club edition			
❑ UA-LA694-G	The Pink Panther Strikes Again	1976	18.00

WARNER BROS.

Number	Title	Yr	NM
❑ BSK3399	10	1979	18.00
❑ W1491 [M]	Marches	1963	18.00
❑ WS1491 [S]	Marches	1963	25.00
❑ W1312 [M]	March Step in Hi-Fi	1959	25.00
❑ WS1312 [S]	March Step in Stereo	1959	30.00
❑ W1465 [M]	Sousa's Greatest Marches	1962	18.00
❑ WS1465 [S]	Sousa's Greatest Marches	1962	25.00
❑ BS2700	The Thief Who Came to Dinner	1973	18.00

MANCUSO, GUS

FANTASY

Number	Title	Yr	NM
❑ 3223 [M]	Introducing Gus Mancuso	1956	60.00
—Red vinyl			
❑ 3223 [M]	Introducing Gus Mancuso	1956	40.00
—Black vinyl			
❑ 3282 [M]	Music from New Faces	1958	40.00
—Red vinyl			
❑ 3282 [M]	Music from New Faces	1958	25.00
—Black vinyl			
❑ 8025 [S]	Music from New Faces	1960	30.00
—Blue vinyl			
❑ 8025 [S]	Music from New Faces	1960	18.00
—Black vinyl			

MANDEL, HARVEY

EDITIONS EG

Number	Title	Yr	NM
❑ CAROL-1535-1	Cristo Redentor	198?	12.00
—Reissue of Philips 600-281			

JANUS

Number	Title	Yr	NM
❑ JLS-3017	Baby Batter	1970	25.00
❑ JSX-3067	Feel the Sound of Harvey Mandel	1974	25.00
❑ JLS-3047	Shangrenade	1973	25.00
❑ JXS-7014	The Best of Harvey Mandel	1975	18.00
❑ JLS-3037	The Snake	1972	25.00

OVATION

Number	Title	Yr	NM
❑ OV-1415	Get Off in Chicago	1971	18.00

PHILIPS

Number	Title	Yr	NM
❑ PHS600281	Cristo Redentor	1969	30.00
❑ PHS600325	Games Guitars Play	1970	30.00
❑ PHS600306	Righteous	1969	30.00

MANDEL, MIKE

VANGUARD

Number	Title	Yr	NM
❑ VSD-79409	Sky Music	1978	15.00
❑ VSD-79437	Utopia Parkway	1979	15.00

MANDO AND THE CHILI PEPPERS

GOLDEN CREST

Number	Title	Yr	NM
❑ CR-3023 [M]	On the Road with Rock and Roll	1957	500.00

MANDRAKE MEMORIAL

POPPY

Number	Title	Yr	NM
❑ PYS40002 [B]	Mandrake Memorial	1968	50.00
❑ PYS40003	Medium	1969	40.00
❑ PYS40006	Puzzle	1970	40.00

MANDRELL, BARBARA, AND LEE GREENWOOD

MCA

Number	Title	Yr	NM
❑ 5477	Meant for Each Other	1984	10.00

MANDRELL, BARBARA

ABC

Number	Title	Yr	NM
❑ AB-1088	Moods	1978	15.00
❑ AB-1119	The Best of Barbara Mandrell	1979	15.00

ABC DOT

Number	Title	Yr	NM
❑ DO-2076	Lovers, Friends and Strangers	1977	15.00
❑ DO-2098	Love's Ups and Downs	1977	15.00
❑ DOSD-2067	Midnight Angel	1976	15.00
❑ DOSD-2045	This Is Barbara Mandrell	1976	15.00

CAPITOL

Number	Title	Yr	NM
❑ C1-90416	I'll Be Your Jukebox Tonight	1988	12.00
❑ C1-91977	Morning Sun	1990	15.00

COLUMBIA

Number	Title	Yr	NM
❑ FC37437	Looking Back	1982	12.00
❑ PC37437	Looking Back	198?	10.00
—Budget-line reissue			
❑ PC34876	The Best of Barbara Mandrell	1977	15.00
—No bar code on cover			
❑ PC34876	The Best of Barbara Mandrell	198?	10.00
—Reissue with bar code on cover			
❑ KC32743	The Midnight Oil	1973	18.00
❑ PC32743	The Midnight Oil	198?	10.00
—Budget-line reissue			
❑ KC32959 [B]	This Time I Almost Made It	1974	18.00
❑ C30967	Treat Him Right	1971	25.00

COLUMBIA LIMITED EDITION

Number	Title	Yr	NM
❑ LE10550	Treat Him Right	197?	12.00

EMI AMERICA

Number	Title	Yr	NM
❑ ET-46956	Sure Feels Good	1987	12.00

MCA

Number	Title	Yr	NM
❑ 5243	Barbara Mandrell Live	1981	12.00
❑ 37224	Barbara Mandrell Live	198?	10.00
—Budget-line reissue			
❑ 5519	Christmas at Our House	1984	15.00
❑ 5474	Clean Cut	1984	12.00
❑ 5619	Get to the Heart	1985	12.00
❑ 5566	Greatest Hits	1985	12.00
❑ 5330	He Set My Life to Music	1982	12.00
❑ 5295	...In Black and White	1982	12.00
❑ 3165	Just for the Record	1979	12.00
❑ 37173	Just for the Record	198?	10.00
—Budget-line reissue			
❑ 5136	Love Is Fair	1980	12.00
❑ 673	Lovers, Friends and Strangers	198?	10.00
—Reissue of ABC Dot 2076			
❑ 674	Love's Ups and Downs	198?	10.00
—Reissue of ABC Dot 2098			
❑ 641	Midnight Angel	198?	10.00
—Reissue of ABC Dot 2067			
❑ 3280	Moods	1980	10.00
—Reissue of ABC 1088			
❑ 5377	Spun Gold	1983	12.00
❑ 672	This Is Barbara Mandrell	198?	10.00
—Reissue of ABC Dot 2045			

PAIR

Number	Title	Yr	NM
❑ PDL1-1079	The Best of Barbara Mandrell	1986	15.00

TIME-LIFE

Number	Title	Yr	NM
❑ STW-104	Country Music	1981	12.00

MANDRELL, LOUISE, AND R.C. BANNON

RCA VICTOR

Number	Title	Yr	NM
❑ AHL1-4059	Me and My RC	1982	12.00
❑ AHL1-4377	(You're My) Super Woman/ (You're My) Incredible Man	1982	12.00

MANDRELL, LOUISE

EPIC

Number	Title	Yr	NM
❑ FE37242	Louise Mandrell	1981	12.00
❑ PE37242	Louise Mandrell	198?	10.00
—Budget-line reissue			

RCA

Number	Title	Yr	NM
❑ 5622-1-R	Dreamin'	1987	12.00
❑ 6714-1-R	The Best of Louise Mandrell	1988	10.00

RCA VICTOR

Number	Title	Yr	NM
❑ MHL1-8601 [EP]	Close Up	1983	10.00
❑ AHL1-5015	I'm Not Through Loving You Yet	1984	12.00
❑ AHL1-5454	Maybe My Baby	1985	12.00
❑ AHL1-4820	Too Hot to Sleep	1983	12.00
❑ AYL1-5434	Too Hot to Sleep	1985	10.00
—Best Buy Series" reissue			

MANDRILL

ARISTA

Number	Title	Yr	NM
❑ AL9527	Getting In the Mood	1980	12.00
❑ AL4195	New Worlds	1978	12.00
❑ AL4144	We Are One	1977	12.00

LIBERTY

Number	Title	Yr	NM
❑ LN-10196	Rebirth	1983	10.00

MONTAGE

Number	Title	Yr	NM
❑ ST-72008	Energize	1982	15.00

POLYDOR

Number	Title	Yr	NM
❑ PD-5043 [B]	Composite Truth	1973	18.00
❑ PD-5059 [B]	Just Outside of Town	1973	18.00
❑ 24-4060 [B]	Mandrill	1971	18.00
❑ PD-2-9002	Mandrilland	1976	18.00
❑ PD-5025 [B]	Mandrill Is	1972	18.00
❑ PD-1-6047	The Best of Mandrill	1975	15.00

UNITED ARTISTS

Number	Title	Yr	NM
❑ UA-LA577-G	Beast from the East	1976	15.00
❑ UA-LA408-G	Solid	1975	15.00

MANGIONE, CHUCK

A&M

Number	Title	Yr	NM
❑ SP-4911	70 Miles Young	1982	12.00

Number	Title	Yr	NM
❑ SP-6701	An Evening of Magic -- Chuck Mangione Live at the Hollywood Bowl	1979	15.00
❑ SP-4557	Bellavia	1975	12.00
❑ QU-54557 [Q]	Bellavia	1975	25.00
❑ SP-4518	Chase the Clouds Away	1975	12.00
❑ QU-54518 [Q]	Chase the Clouds Away	1975	25.00
❑ SP-6700	Children of Sanchez	1978	15.00
❑ SP-4658	Feels So Good	1977	12.00
❑ SP-3715	Fun and Games	1980	12.00
❑ SP-4612	Main Squeeze	1976	12.00
❑ SP-6513	Tarantella	1981	15.00
❑ SP-3282	The Best of Chuck Mangione	1985	12.00
COLUMBIA			
❑ FC39479	Disguise	1984	12.00
❑ FC40984	Eyes of the Veiled Temptress	1988	12.00
❑ FC38686	Journey to a Rainbow	1983	12.00
❑ FC38101	Love Notes	1982	12.00
❑ FC40254	Save Tonight for Me	1986	12.00
FANTASY			
❑ OJC-495	Recuerdo	1991	15.00
—Reissue of Jazzland 984			
JAZZLAND			
❑ JLP-84 [M]	Recuerdo	1962	40.00
❑ JLP-984 [S]	Recuerdo	1962	50.00
MERCURY			
❑ SRM-1-650	Alive!	1973	15.00
❑ 824301-1	Alive!	198?	10.00
—Reissue of 650			
❑ SRM-1-1050	Encore/The Chuck Mangione Concerts	1975	12.00
❑ SRM-2-800	Friends & Love -- A Chuck Mangione Concert	1971	18.00
❑ SRM-1-681	Friends & Love/Highlights	1973	15.00
❑ SRM-1-684	Land of Make Believe	1973	15.00
❑ SRM-2-8601	The Best of Chuck Mangione	1978	15.00
❑ SRM-1-631	The Chuck Mangione Quartet	1972	15.00
❑ SRM-2-7501	Together: A New Chuck Mangione Concert	1971	18.00
MILESTONE			
❑ 47042	Jazz Brother	1977	15.00
—Reissue of material issued by "The Jazz Brothers			
MOBILE FIDELITY			
❑ 1-068 [B]	Feels So Good	1981	30.00
—Audiophile vinyl			

MANGIONE, GAP

Number	Title	Yr	NM
A&M			
❑ SP-4762	Dancin' Is Makin' Love	1979	12.00
❑ SP-4621	Gap Mangione!	197?	12.00
❑ SP-3407	She and I	1974	12.00
❑ SP-4694	Suite Lady	1978	12.00
FEELS SO GOOD			
❑ FSG9002	The Boys from Rochester	1987	15.00
GRC			
❑ 9001	Diana in the Autumn Wind	1968	30.00
MERCURY			
❑ SRM-1-647	Sing Along Junk	1972	15.00

MANHATTAN JAZZ ALL-STARS, THE

Number	Title	Yr	NM
COLUMBIA			
❑ CL1426 [M]	Swinging Guys and Dolls	1960	30.00
❑ CS8223 [S]	Swinging Guys and Dolls	1960	30.00

MANHATTAN JAZZ SEPTETTE, THE

Number	Title	Yr	NM
CORAL			
❑ CRL57090 [M]	The Manhattan Jazz Septette	1956	80.00

MANHATTAN RHYTHM KINGS

Number	Title	Yr	NM
INNER CITY			
❑ IC-1124	Manhattan Rhythm Kings	198?	15.00

MANHATTAN TRANSFER

Number	Title	Yr	NM
ATLANTIC			
❑ 80104	Bodies and Souls	1983	12.00
❑ 81233	Bop Doo-Wopp	1984	15.00
❑ 81803	Brasil	1987	12.00
❑ SD18183	Coming Out	1976	12.00
❑ SD19258	Extensions	1979	12.00
❑ 81723	Live	1987	12.00
❑ SD16036	Mecca for Moderns	1981	12.00
❑ SD19163	Pastiche	1978	12.00
❑ SD19319	The Best of the Manhattan Transfer	1981	12.00
❑ SD18133	The Manhattan Transfer	1975	12.00
❑ 81266	Vocalese	1985	12.00
CAPITOL			
❑ ST-778	Jukin'	1971	18.00
—With Gene Pistilli			
❑ ST-11405	Jukin'	1975	12.00
—With Gene Pistilli; reissue of 778			
❑ SN-16223	Jukin'	198?	10.00
—With Gene Pistilli; budget-line reissue			
COLUMBIA			
❑ C47079	The Offbeat of Avenues	1991	18.00
MOBILE FIDELITY			
❑ 1-199	Extensions	1994	30.00
—Audiophile vinyl			
❑ 1-022 [B]	Manhattan Transfer Live	1979	40.00
—Audiophile vinyl			

MANHATTANS, THE (1)

Number	Title	Yr	NM
CARNIVAL			
❑ CMLP-201 [M]	Dedicated to You	1966	250.00
❑ CSLP-201 [S]	Dedicated to You	1966	500.00
❑ CMLP-202 [M]	For You and Yours	1967	150.00
❑ CSLP-202 [S]	For You and Yours	1967	300.00
COLLECTABLES			
❑ COL-5135	Dedicated to You: Golden Carnival Classics, Part One	198?	12.00
❑ COL-5136	For You and Yours: Golden Carnival Classics, Part Two	198?	12.00
COLUMBIA			
❑ JC36411	After Midnight	1980	15.00
❑ PC35693	After Midnight	198?	10.00
—Budget-line reissue			
❑ FC37156	Black Tie	1981	12.00
❑ PC37156	Black Tie	198?	10.00
—Budget-line reissue			
❑ FC38600	Forever By Your Side	1983	12.00
❑ PC34450	It Feels So Good	1977	15.00
—No bar code on back cover			
❑ PCQ34450 [Q]	It Feels So Good	1977	25.00
❑ PC34450	It Feels So Good	198?	10.00
—With bar code on back cover			
❑ JC35693	Love Talk	1979	15.00
❑ JC36861	Manhattans Greatest Hits	1980	15.00
❑ KC33064	That's How Much I Love You	1975	18.00
❑ PC33820	The Manhattans	1976	15.00
—No bar code on back cover			
❑ PC33820	The Manhattans	198?	10.00
—With bar code on back cover			
❑ JC35252	There's No Good in Goodbye	1978	15.00
❑ KC32444	There's No Me Without You	1973	18.00
❑ PC32444	There's No Me Without You	198?	10.00
—Budget-line reissue			
❑ FC39277	Too Hot to Stop It	1985	12.00
DELUXE			
❑ 12004	A Million to One	1972	30.00
❑ 12000	With These Hands	1971	30.00
SOLID SMOKE			
❑ 8007	Follow Your Heart	1981	12.00
VALLEY VUE			
❑ D1-72946	Sweet Talk	1989	15.00

MANILLA ROAD

Number	Title	Yr	NM
ROADSTER			
❑ MR1003	Crystal Logic	1983	50.00
❑ MR1001	Invasion	1980	100.00
❑ MR1002	Metal	1982	100.00

MANILOW, BARRY

Number	Title	Yr	NM
ARISTA			
❑ AL8-8254	2:00 A.M. Paradise Café	1984	10.00
❑ AL9537	Barry	1980	10.00
❑ AL-8570	Barry Manilow	1989	10.00
❑ AL8-8102	Barry Manilow/Greatest Hits, Vol. II	1983	10.00
❑ AL4007	Barry Manilow I	1975	12.00
—Revised version of Bell 1129 with new cover; "Could It Be Magic" especially is noticeably different between the Bell and Arista versions			
❑ AB4007	Barry Manilow I	1977	10.00
—Reissue of AL 4007 with new prefix			
❑ AL4016	Barry Manilow II	1975	12.00
—Reissue of Bell 1314			
❑ AQ4016 [Q]	Barry Manilow II	1975	18.00
❑ AB4016	Barry Manilow II	1977	10.00
—Reissue of AL 4016 with new prefix			
❑ AL8500	Barry Manilow/Live	1977	15.00
❑ AL13-8049	Barry Manilow/Live	1983	12.00
❑ AL-8644	Because It's Christmas	1990	18.00
❑ AB4164	Even Now	1978	10.00
❑ A2L8601	Greatest Hits	1978	15.00
❑ A2L8601 [PD]	Greatest Hits	1979	40.00
—Entire contents on two picture discs (yes, it has the same number as the regular issue)			
❑ AL13-8039	Greatest Hits	1983	12.00
❑ AL-8598	Greatest Hits, Vol. 1	1989	12.00
❑ AL-8599	Greatest Hits, Vol. 2	1989	12.00
❑ AL-8600	Greatest Hits, Vol. 3	1989	12.00
❑ AL-9610	Here Comes the Night	1982	10.00
❑ AL9573	If I Should Love Again	1981	10.00
❑ AL-8638	Live on Broadway	1990	25.00
❑ NU9740	Manilow Magic	1982	15.00
—Manufactured by K-Tel			
❑ AB2500 [EP]	Oh, Julie!	1982	25.00
❑ AL9505	One Voice	1979	10.00
❑ AL-8527	Swing Street	1987	10.00
❑ AL9-8274	The Manilow Collection -- 20 Classic Hits	1985	10.00
❑ AL4090	This One's for You	1976	12.00
❑ AB4090	This One's for You	1977	10.00
—Reissue of AL 4090 with new prefix			
❑ AQ4090 [Q]	This One's for You	1976	25.00
❑ AL4060	Tryin' to Get the Feeling	1975	12.00
❑ AQ4060 [Q]	Tryin' to Get the Feeling	1975	18.00
❑ AB4060	Tryin' to Get the Feeling	1977	10.00
—Reissue of AL 4060 with new prefix			
BELL			
❑ 1129	Barry Manilow	1973	30.00
❑ 1314	Barry Manilow II	1974	18.00
MOBILE FIDELITY			
❑ 1-097 [B]	Barry Manilow I	1981	35.00
—Audiophile vinyl			
RCA VICTOR			
❑ AFL1-7044	Manilow	1985	10.00

MANN, AIMEE

Number	Title	Yr	NM
MOBILE FIDELITY			
❑ MFSL 1-278	Lost in Space	2003	30.00
—Original Master Recording" at top of front cover			

MANN, BARRY

Number	Title	Yr	NM
ABC-PARAMOUNT			
❑ 399 [M]	Who Put the Bomp	1963	120.00
❑ S-399 [S]	Who Put the Bomp	1963	300.00
CASABLANCA			
❑ NBLP7226	Barry Mann	1980	12.00
NEW DESIGN			
❑ Z30876	Lay It All Out	1971	15.00
RCA VICTOR			
❑ DJL1-1162 [DJ]	Flo and Eddie Interview Barry Mann	1975	50.00
❑ APL1-0860	Survivor	1975	15.00

MANN, CARL

Number	Title	Yr	NM
PHILLIPS INT'L.			
❑ PLP-1960 [M]	Like Mann	1960	600.00

MANN, DAVID

Number	Title	Yr	NM
ANTILLES			
❑ 90628	Games	1988	12.00
❑ 91050	Insight	1989	15.00

MANN, ED

Number	Title	Yr	NM
CMP			
❑ CMP-38-ST	Get Up	1988	12.00

MANN, HERBIE, AND BUDDY COLLETTE

Number	Title	Yr	NM
INTERLUDE			
❑ MO-503 [M]	Flute Fraternity	1959	40.00
—Reissue of Mode 114			
❑ ST-1103 [S]	Flute Fraternity	1959	30.00
MODE			
❑ LP-114 [M]	Flute Fraternity	1957	70.00

MANN, HERBIE, AND JOAO GILBERTO

Number	Title	Yr	NM
ATLANTIC			
❑ 8105 [M]	Herbie Mann and Joao Gilberto with Antonio Carlos Jobim	1965	25.00
❑ SD8105 [S]	Herbie Mann and Joao Gilberto with Antonio Carlos Jobim	1965	25.00

MANN, HERBIE, AND MACHITO

Number	Title	Yr	NM
ROULETTE			
❑ R-52122 [M]	Afro-Jazziac	1963	18.00
❑ SR-52122 [S]	Afro-Jazziac	1963	25.00

MANN, HERBIE

Number	Title	Yr	NM
A&M			
❑ LP-2003 [M]	Glory of Love	1967	30.00
❑ SP-3003 [S]	Glory of Love	1967	18.00
❑ SP9-3003	Glory of Love	1983	25.00
—Audio Master Plus" reissue			
ATLANTIC			
❑ 80077	Astral Island	1983	12.00
❑ SD18209	Bird in a Silver Cage	1977	12.00
❑ SD19169	Brazil -- Once Again	1978	12.00
❑ SD1540	Concerto Grosso in D Blues	1969	15.00
❑ SD1670	Discotheque	1975	15.00
❑ 1397 [M]	Do the Bossa Nova with Herbie Mann	1962	18.00
❑ SD1397 [S]	Do the Bossa Nova with Herbie Mann	1962	25.00
❑ SD1658	First Light	1974	15.00
❑ SD19112	Herbie Mann & Fire Island	1977	12.00
❑ 1380 [M]	Herbie Mann at the Village Gate	1962	18.00
❑ SD1380 [S]	Herbie Mann at the Village Gate	1962	25.00
❑ 1413 [M]	Herbie Mann Live at Newport	1963	18.00
❑ SD1413 [S]	Herbie Mann Live at Newport	1963	25.00
❑ 1407 [M]	Herbie Mann Returns to the Village Gate	1963	18.00

Number	Title	Yr	NM
❑ SD1407 [S]	Herbie Mann Returns to the Village Gate	1963	25.00
❑ 1454 [M]	Herbie Mann Today	1966	18.00
❑ SD1454 [S]	Herbie Mann Today	1966	25.00
❑ SD1632	Hold On, I'm Comin'	1973	15.00
❑ QD1632 [Q]	Hold On, I'm Comin'	1973	25.00
❑ 1475 [M]	Impressions of the Middle East	1967	25.00
❑ SD1475 [S]	Impressions of the Middle East	1967	18.00
❑ 1422 [M]	Latin Fever	1964	18.00
❑ SD1422 [S]	Latin Fever	1964	25.00
❑ SD1536	Live at the Whisky A-Go-Go	1969	15.00
❑ SD1648	London Underground	1974	15.00
❑ 8141 [M]	Mann and a Woman	1967	25.00
❑ SD8141 [S]	Mann and a Woman	1967	18.00
❑ SD16046	Mellow	1981	12.00
❑ SD1522	Memphis Underground	1969	15.00
❑ SD1610	Mississippi Gambler	1972	15.00
❑ 1462 [M]	Monday Night at the Village Gate	1966	18.00
❑ SD1462 [S]	Monday Night at the Village Gate	1966	25.00
❑ 1433 [M]	My Kinda Groove	1965	18.00
❑ SD1433 [S]	My Kinda Groove	1965	25.00
❑ 1471 [M]	New Mann at Newport	1967	25.00
❑ SD1471 [S]	New Mann at Newport	1967	18.00
❑ 1426 [M]	Nirvana	1964	18.00
❑ SD1426 [S]	Nirvana	1964	25.00
❑ 90141	Nirvana	1984	12.00
❑ 1464 [M]	Our Mann Flute	1966	18.00
❑ SD1464 [S]	Our Mann Flute	1966	25.00
❑ SD1655	Reggae	1974	15.00
❑ 1384 [M]	Right Now	1962	18.00
❑ SD1384 [S]	Right Now	1962	25.00
❑ 81285	See Through Spirits	1986	12.00
❑ 1445 [M]	Standing Ovation at Newport	1965	18.00
❑ SD1445 [S]	Standing Ovation at Newport	1965	25.00
❑ SD19221	Super Mann	1979	12.00
❑ SD1682	Surprises	1976	15.00
❑ 1483 [M]	The Beat Goes On	1967	25.00
❑ SD1483 [S]	The Beat Goes On	1967	18.00
❑ SD1544	The Best of Herbie Mann	1970	15.00
❑ 1343 [M]	The Common Ground	1960	18.00
❑ SD1343 [S]	The Common Ground	1960	25.00
❑ SD 2-300 [S]	The Evolution of Mann	1972	18.00
❑ 2-300 [M]	The Evolution of Mann	1972	40.00

—Mono is white label promo only with "d/j copy monaural" sticker on front cover

Number	Title	Yr	NM
❑ 1371 [M]	The Family of Mann	1961	18.00
❑ SD1371 [S]	The Family of Mann	1961	25.00
❑ 1490 [M]	The Herbie Mann String Album	1968	30.00
❑ SD1490 [S]	The Herbie Mann String Album	1968	18.00
❑ 1513 [M]	The Inspiration I Feel	1969	30.00

—Mono is promo only

Number	Title	Yr	NM
❑ SD1513 [S]	The Inspiration I Feel	1969	18.00
❑ 1437 [M]	The Roar of the Greasepaint, The Smell of the Crowd	1965	18.00
❑ SD1437 [S]	The Roar of the Greasepaint, The Smell of the Crowd	1965	25.00
❑ SD1642	Turtle Bay	1973	15.00
❑ SD1497	Wailing Dervishes	1968	18.00
❑ SD1676	Waterbed	1975	15.00
❑ SD1507	Windows Open	1969	15.00
❑ SD19252	Yellow Fever	1980	12.00

BETHLEHEM

Number	Title	Yr	NM
❑ BCP-6011	Early Mann	1976	12.00

—Reissue of older material; distributed by Caytronics

Number	Title	Yr	NM
❑ BCP-1018 [10]	East Coast Jazz 4	1954	120.00
❑ BCP-24 [M]	Flamingo, My Goodness -- Four Flutes, Vol. 2	1955	50.00
❑ BCP-58 [M]	Herbie Mann Plays	1956	50.00
❑ BCP-63 [M]	Love and the Weather	1956	150.00
❑ BCP-6067 [M]	The Epitome of Jazz	1963	30.00
❑ BCP-40 [M]	The Herbie Mann-Sam Most Quintet	1956	50.00
❑ BCP-6020 [M]	The Mann with the Most	1960	40.00

COLUMBIA

Number	Title	Yr	NM
❑ CS1068	Big Boss	1970	15.00
❑ CL2388 [M]	Latin Mann	1965	18.00
❑ CS9188 [S]	Latin Mann	1965	25.00

COLUMBIA SPECIAL PRODUCTS

Number	Title	Yr	NM
❑ JCS9188	Latin Mann	197?	15.00

—Part of "Jazz Greats" Collectors' Series

EMBRYO

Number	Title	Yr	NM
❑ 531	Memphis Two-Step	1971	15.00
❑ 526	Muscle Shoals Nitty Gritty	1970	15.00
❑ 532	Push Push	1971	15.00
❑ 520	Stone Flute	1970	15.00

EPIC

Number	Title	Yr	NM
❑ LN3499 [M]	Herbie Mann with the Ilcken Trio	1958	60.00
❑ LN3395 [M]	Salute to the Flute	1957	60.00

FINNADAR

Number	Title	Yr	NM
❑ 9014	Gagaku and Beyond	197?	12.00

HERBIE MANN MUSIC

Number	Title	Yr	NM
❑ HMM-1	Herbie Mann Music	1981	30.00

—Direct-to-disc recording

JAZZLAND

Number	Title	Yr	NM
❑ JLP-5 [M]	Herbie Mann Quintet	1960	30.00

—Reissue of Riverside 245

MILESTONE

Number	Title	Yr	NM
❑ 47010	Let Me Tell You	1973	15.00

NEW JAZZ

Number	Title	Yr	NM
❑ NJLP-8211 [M]	Just Walkin'	1958	50.00

—Purple label

Number	Title	Yr	NM
❑ NJLP-8211 [M]	Just Walkin'	1964	30.00

—Blue label with trident logo

PRESTIGE

Number	Title	Yr	NM
❑ PRLP-7124 [M]	Flute Flight	1957	100.00
❑ PRLP-7101 [M]	Flute Souffle	1957	100.00
❑ PRST-7659	Herbie Mann in Sweden	1969	15.00
❑ PRLP-7136 [M]	Mann in the Morning	1958	80.00
❑ PRLP-7432 [M]	The Best of Herbie Mann	1965	18.00
❑ PRST-7432 [R]	The Best of Herbie Mann	1965	15.00

RIVERSIDE

Number	Title	Yr	NM
❑ RLP 12-245 [M]	Great Ideas of Western Mann	1957	40.00
❑ 6084	Great Ideas of Western Mann	197?	12.00
❑ S-3029	Moody Mann	1969	15.00
❑ RLP 12-234 [M]	Sultry Serenade	1957	60.00

—Blue on white label

Number	Title	Yr	NM
❑ RLP 12-234 [M]	Sultry Serenade	1958	40.00

—Blue label with reel and microphone logo

SAVOY

Number	Title	Yr	NM
❑ MG-12102 [M]	Flute Suite	1957	50.00
❑ MG-12107 [M]	Mann Alone	1957	50.00
❑ MG-12108 [M]	Yardbird Suite	1957	50.00

SAVOY JAZZ

Number	Title	Yr	NM
❑ SJL-1102	Be Bop Synthesis	197?	12.00

SOLID STATE

Number	Title	Yr	NM
❑ SS-18020	Jazz Impressions of Brazil	1968	15.00
❑ SS-18023	St. Thomas	1968	15.00

SURREY

Number	Title	Yr	NM
❑ S-1015 [M]	Big Band	1965	18.00
❑ SS-1015 [S]	Big Band	1965	25.00

TRIP

Number	Title	Yr	NM
❑ 5031	Super Mann	1974	12.00

UNITED ARTISTS

Number	Title	Yr	NM
❑ UAL-4042 [M]	African Suite	1959	30.00
❑ UAS-5042 [S]	African Suite	1959	40.00
❑ UAJ-14009 [M]	Brasil, Bossa Nova and Blue	1962	30.00
❑ UAJS-15009 [S]	Brasil, Bossa Nova and Blue	1962	40.00
❑ UAS-5638	Brazil Blues	1972	15.00
❑ UAJ-14022 [M]	St. Thomas	1962	30.00
❑ UAJS-15022 [S]	St. Thomas	1962	40.00

VERVE

Number	Title	Yr	NM
❑ VSP-19 [M]	Big Band Mann	1966	18.00
❑ VSPS-19 [R]	Big Band Mann	1966	15.00
❑ VSP-8 [M]	Bongo, Conga and Flute	1966	18.00
❑ VSPS-8 [R]	Bongo, Conga and Flute	1966	15.00
❑ V6-8821	Et Tu Flute	1973	18.00
❑ MGV-8336 [M]	Flautista! -- Herbie Mann Plays Afro-Cuban Jazz	1959	40.00
❑ MGVS-6074 [S]	Flautista! -- Herbie Mann Plays Afro-Cuban Jazz	1960	30.00
❑ V-8336 [M]	Flautista! -- Herbie Mann Plays Afro-Cuban Jazz	1961	25.00
❑ V6-8336 [S]	Flautista! -- Herbie Mann Plays Afro-Cuban Jazz	1961	18.00
❑ MGV-8392 [M]	Flute, Brass, Vibes and Percussion	1960	30.00
❑ V-8392 [M]	Flute, Brass, Vibes and Percussion	1961	25.00
❑ MGV-8247 [M]	The Magic Flute of Herbie Mann	1958	40.00
❑ V-8247 [M]	The Magic Flute of Herbie Mann	1961	25.00
❑ V-8527 [M]	The Sound of Mann	1963	25.00
❑ V6-8527 [S]	The Sound of Mann	1963	18.00

MANN, JOHNNY, SINGERS

EPIC

Number	Title	Yr	NM
❑ KE31954	Stand Up and Cheer!	1973	15.00

LIBERTY

Number	Title	Yr	NM
❑ LRP-3134 [M]	Alma Mater	1959	18.00
❑ LST-7134 [S]	Alma Mater	1959	25.00
❑ LRP-3198 [M]	Ballads of the King	1961	18.00
❑ LST-7198 [S]	Ballads of the King	1961	25.00
❑ LRP-3217 [M]	Ballads of the King, Volume 2	1961	18.00
❑ LST-7217 [S]	Ballads of the King, Volume 2	1961	25.00
❑ LRP-3447 [M]	Daydream	1966	15.00
❑ LST-7447 [S]	Daydream	1966	18.00
❑ LST-7629	Golden	1969	15.00
❑ LRP-3253 [M]	Golden Folk Song Hits	1963	15.00
❑ LST-7253 [S]	Golden Folk Song Hits	1963	18.00
❑ LRP-3296 [M]	Golden Folk Song Hits, Volume 2	1963	15.00
❑ LST-7296 [S]	Golden Folk Song Hits, Volume 2	1963	18.00
❑ LRP-3355 [M]	Golden Folk Song Hits, Volume 3	1964	15.00
❑ LST-7355 [S]	Golden Folk Song Hits, Volume 3	1964	18.00
❑ LRP-3411 [M]	If I Loved You	1965	15.00
❑ LST-7411 [S]	If I Loved You	1965	18.00
❑ LRP-3436 [M]	I'll Remember You	1965	15.00
❑ LST-7426 [S]	I'll Remember You	1965	18.00
❑ LRP-3387 [M]	Invisible Tears	1964	15.00
❑ LST-7387 [S]	Invisible Tears	1964	18.00
❑ LRP-3149 [M]	Roar Along with the Singing Twenties	1960	18.00
❑ LST-7149 [S]	Roar Along with the Singing Twenties	1960	25.00
❑ LRP-3156 [M]	Swing Along with the Singing Thirties	1960	18.00
❑ LST-7156 [S]	Swing Along with the Singing Thirties	1960	25.00
❑ LRP-3391 [M]	The Ballad Sound (Beatle Songs)	1964	18.00
❑ LST-7391 [S]	The Ballad Sound (Beatle Songs)	1964	25.00
❑ LMM-13017 [M]	The Great Bands with Great Voices Swing the Great Voices of the Great Bands	1962	18.00
❑ LSS-14017 [S]	The Great Bands with Great Voices Swing the Great Voices of the Great Bands	1962	25.00
❑ LRP-3523 [M]	We Can Fly! Up-Up and Away	1967	15.00
❑ LST-7523 [S]	We Can Fly! Up-Up and Away	1967	18.00
❑ LRP-3522 [M]	We Wish You a Merry Christmas	1967	18.00
❑ LST-7522 [S]	We Wish You a Merry Christmas	1967	18.00

SUNSET

Number	Title	Yr	NM
❑ SUS-5288	At Our Best	1970	15.00
❑ SUS-5231	Country Style	1969	15.00
❑ SUS-5196	Heart Full of Song	1968	15.00
❑ SUM-1115 [M]	The Flowing Voices of the Johnny Mann Singers	196?	12.00
❑ SUS-5115 [S]	The Flowing Voices of the Johnny Mann Singers	196?	15.00

UNITED ARTISTS

Number	Title	Yr	NM
❑ UXS-87	The Johnny Mann Singers Superpak	1972	18.00

MANN, LORENE

RCA VICTOR

Number	Title	Yr	NM
❑ LSP-4243	A Mann Named Lorene	1969	18.00

MANN, MANFRED

ASCOT

Number	Title	Yr	NM
❑ AM-13024 [M]	Mann Made	1966	40.00
❑ AS-16024 [S]	Mann Made	1966	50.00
❑ AM-13021 [M]	My Little Red Book of Winners	1965	40.00
❑ AS-16021 [S]	My Little Red Book of Winners	1965	50.00
❑ AM-13018 [M]	The Five Faces of Manfred Mann	1965	50.00
❑ AS-16018 [P]	The Five Faces of Manfred Mann	1965	50.00
❑ AM-13015 [M]	The Manfred Mann Album	1964	50.00
❑ AS-16015 [P]	The Manfred Mann Album	1964	50.00

CAPITOL

Number	Title	Yr	NM
❑ SM-11688	The Best of Manfred Mann	1977	12.00
❑ SN-16073	The Best of Manfred Mann	1980	10.00

JANUS

Number	Title	Yr	NM
❑ JXS-3064	The Best of Manfred Mann	1974	15.00

MERCURY

Number	Title	Yr	NM
❑ SR-61168	The Mighty Quinn	1968	30.00

POLYDOR

Number	Title	Yr	NM
❑ 24-4013	Chapter Three	1970	18.00

SUNDAZED

Number	Title	Yr	NM
❑ LP5454 [B]	Mann Made	2013	30.00
❑ LP5453 [B]	My Little Red Book Of Winners	2013	30.00
❑ LP5455 [B]	Pretty Flamingo	2013	30.00
❑ LP5452 [B]	The Five Faces Of Manfred Mann	2013	30.00
❑ LP5451 [B]	The Manfred Mann Album	2013	30.00

UNITED ARTISTS

Number	Title	Yr	NM
❑ 94 [DJ]	Manfred Mann Interview	1966	200.00

—Promotional album in plain white jacket

Number	Title	Yr	NM
❑ UAL3551 [M]	Manfred Mann's Greatest Hits	1966	30.00
❑ UAS6551 [P]	Manfred Mann's Greatest Hits	1966	40.00

—Do Wah Diddy Diddy," "Sha La La," "I Got You Babe" and "Satisfaction" are rechanneled.

Number	Title	Yr	NM
❑ UAL3549 [M]	Pretty Flamingo	1966	30.00
❑ UAS6549 [S]	Pretty Flamingo	1966	40.00

MANN, MANFRED'S, EARTH BAND

ARISTA

Number	Title	Yr	NM
❑ AL8194	Somewhere in Afrika	1983	12.00

POLYDOR

Number	Title	Yr	NM
❑ PD-5050	Get Your Rocks Off	1973	18.00
❑ PD-5031	Glorified, Magnified	1972	18.00
❑ PD-5015	Manfred Mann's Earth Band	1971	18.00
❑ PD-1-6019	Solar Fire	1974	18.00

WARNER BROS.

Number	Title	Yr	NM
❑ BSK3302	Angel Station	1979	12.00
❑ BSK3498	Chance	1980	12.00
❑ BS2877	Nightingales and Bombers	1975	15.00
❑ BS2826	The Good Earth	1974	15.00
❑ BS2965	The Roaring Silence	1976	15.00

—Orange cover

Number	Title	Yr	NM
❑ BSK3055	The Roaring Silence	1977	12.00

—Blue cover; re-recording of "Spirit in the Night" is added

Number	Title	Yr	NM
❑ BSK3157	Watch	1978	12.00

Number	Title	Yr	NM

MANN, REV. COLUMBUS

TAMLA
| ❏ T-227 [M] | They Shall Be Mine | 1962 | 4000.00 |

— *VG value 2000; VG+ value 3000*

WINGATE
| ❏ 701 [M] | He Satisfies Me | 196? | 900.00 |

MANN, SHADOW

TOMORROW
| ❏ TPS-69001 | Come Live with Me | 1974 | 60.00 |

MANNA, CHARLIE

DECCA
❏ DL4213 [M]	Manna Live!!	1962	30.00
❏ DL74213 [R]	Manna Live!!	1962	18.00
❏ DL4159 [M]	Manna Overboard!!	1961	30.00
❏ DL74159 [R]	Manna Overboard!!	1961	18.00

VERVE
| ❏ V-15051 [M] | The Rise and Fall of the Great Society | 1966 | 15.00 |
| ❏ V6-15051 [S] | The Rise and Fall of the Great Society | 1966 | 18.00 |

MANNE, SHELLY

ABC IMPULSE!
| ❏ AS-20 [S] | 2 3 4 | 1968 | 25.00 |

— *Black label with red ring*

ATLANTIC
❏ 1469 [M]	Boss Sounds!	1967	18.00
❏ SD1469 [S]	Boss Sounds!	1967	15.00
❏ 8157 [M]	Daktari	1968	30.00
❏ SD8157 [S]	Daktari	1968	15.00
❏ 1487 [M]	Jazz Gunn	1967	25.00
❏ SD1487 [S]	Jazz Gunn	1967	15.00

CAPITOL
❏ T2313 [M]	Manne, That's Gershwin	1965	18.00
❏ ST2313 [S]	Manne, That's Gershwin	1965	25.00
❏ T2173 [M]	My Fair Lady" with Un-Original Cast	1964	18.00
❏ ST2173 [S]	My Fair Lady" with Un-Original Cast	1964	25.00
❏ SM-2173	My Fair Lady" with Un-Original Cast	1976	12.00

— *Reissue with new prefix*

| ❏ T2610 [M] | Shelly Manne Sounds | 1966 | 15.00 |
| ❏ ST2610 [S] | Shelly Manne Sounds | 1966 | 18.00 |

CONCORD JAZZ
| ❏ CJ-21 | Perk Up | 1976 | 15.00 |

CONTEMPORARY
❏ C-3559 [M]	Bells Are Ringing	1958	40.00
❏ S-7559 [S]	Bells Are Ringing	1959	30.00
❏ M-3599 [M]	Checkmate	1961	30.00
❏ S-7599 [S]	Checkmate	1961	30.00
❏ C-3536 [M]	Concerto for Clarinet and Combo	1957	50.00
❏ C-3533 [M]	Li'l Abner	1957	50.00
❏ S-7533 [S]	Li'l Abner	1959	40.00
❏ M-3593/4 [M]	Live! Shelly Manne and His Men at the Manne-Hole	1961	40.00
❏ S-7593/4 [S]	Live! Shelly Manne and His Men at the Manne-Hole	1961	50.00
❏ C-3527 [M]	Modern Jazz Performance of Songs from "My Fair Lady	1957	50.00
❏ S-7527 [S]	Modern Jazz Performance of Songs from "My Fair Lady	1959	40.00
❏ C-3519 [M]	More Swinging Sounds, Vol. 5	1957	70.00
❏ M-3609 [M]	My Son, the Jazz Drummer!	1962	30.00
❏ S-7609 [S]	My Son, the Jazz Drummer!	1962	30.00
❏ M-3624 [M]	Outside	1966	30.00
❏ S-7624 [S]	Outside	1966	30.00
❏ C-3525 [M]	Shelly Manne and His Friends	1957	50.00
❏ C-2503 [10]	Shelly Manne and His Men	1953	150.00
❏ C-2511 [10]	Shelly Manne and His Men, Volume 2	1954	150.00
❏ M-3577 [M]	Shelly Manne and His Men at the Black Hawk, Vol. 1	1960	40.00
❏ S-7577 [S]	Shelly Manne and His Men at the Black Hawk, Vol. 1	1960	30.00
❏ M-3578 [M]	Shelly Manne and His Men at the Black Hawk, Vol. 2	1960	40.00
❏ S-7578 [S]	Shelly Manne and His Men at the Black Hawk, Vol. 2	1960	30.00
❏ M-3579 [M]	Shelly Manne and His Men at the Black Hawk, Vol. 3	1960	40.00
❏ S-7579 [S]	Shelly Manne and His Men at the Black Hawk, Vol. 3	1960	30.00
❏ M-3580 [M]	Shelly Manne and His Men at the Black Hawk, Vol. 4	1960	40.00
❏ S-7580 [S]	Shelly Manne and His Men at the Black Hawk, Vol. 4	1960	30.00
❏ C-14018	Shelly Manne in Zurich	1986	12.00
❏ C-3560 [M]	Shelly Manne Plays "Peter Gunn	1958	50.00
❏ S-7025 [S]	Shelly Manne Plays "Peter Gunn	1959	40.00
❏ M-3566 [M]	Son of Gunn	1959	40.00
❏ S-7566 [S]	Son of Gunn	1959	30.00
❏ M-5006 [M]	Sounds Unheard Of	1962	30.00
❏ S-9006 [S]	Sounds Unheard Of	1962	40.00
❏ C-3516 [M]	Swinging Sounds, Vol. 4	1956	70.00
❏ S-7519 [S]	Swinging Sounds in Stereo	1959	50.00
❏ C-3557 [M]	The Gambit	1958	50.00

Number	Title	Yr	NM
❏ S-7557 [S]	The Gambit	1959	40.00
❏ C-2516 [10]	The Three	1954	150.00
❏ M-3584 [M]	The Three and The Two	1960	30.00
❏ C-2518 [10]	The Two	1954	150.00
❏ C-3507 [M]	The West Coast Sound	1955	60.00

DEE GEE
| ❏ 1003 [10] | Here's That Manne | 1952 | 300.00 |

DISCOVERY
| ❏ 909 | Manne, That's Gershwin! | 1986 | 12.00 |

— *Reissue of Capitol ST 2313*

| ❏ 783 | Rex | 1976 | 15.00 |

DOCTOR JAZZ
| ❏ FW38728 | Shelly Manne and His Friends | 1983 | 12.00 |

FANTASY
❏ OJC-336	Modern Jazz Performance of Songs from "My Fair Lady	198?	12.00
❏ OJC-320	More Swinging Sounds, Vol. 5	198?	12.00
❏ OJC-240	Shelly Manne and His Men at the Black Hawk, Vol. 1	198?	12.00
❏ OJC-267	Swinging Sounds, Vol. 4	1987	12.00
❏ OJC-176	The Three and The Two	198?	12.00
❏ OJC-152	The West Coast Sound	198?	12.00

FLYING DUTCHMAN
| ❏ FD-10150 | Signature: Shelly Manne & Co. | 1973 | 18.00 |

— *Reissue of 1940s recordings in mono*

GALAXY
| ❏ 5101 | Essence | 1978 | 15.00 |
| ❏ 5124 | French Concert | 1979 | 15.00 |

IMPULSE!
| ❏ A-20 [M] | 2 3 4 | 1962 | 40.00 |
| ❏ AS-20 [S] | 2 3 4 | 1962 | 60.00 |

MAINSTREAM
| ❏ MRL-375 | Mannekind | 1972 | 18.00 |

MCA
| ❏ 29073 | 2 3 4 | 1980 | 10.00 |

STEREO RECORDS
❏ S-7019 [S]	Li'l Abner	1958	50.00
❏ S-7002 [S]	Modern Jazz Performance of Songs from "My Fair Lady	1958	50.00
❏ S-7025 [S]	Shelly Manne Plays "Peter Gunn	1958	50.00
❏ S-7007 [S]	Swinging Sounds in Stereo	1958	80.00
❏ S-7030 [S]	The Gambit	1958	50.00

TREND
❏ 526	Double Piano Jazz Quartet	1980	15.00
❏ 527	Double Piano Jazz Quartet, Volume 2	1980	15.00
❏ 525	Interpretations of Bach and Mozart	1980	15.00

MANNE, SHELLY/BILL RUSSO

SAVOY
| ❏ MG-12045 [M] | Deep Purple | 1955 | 50.00 |

MANNHEIM STEAMROLLER

AMERICAN GRAMAPHONE
❏ AG-1988	A Fresh Aire Christmas	1988	18.00
❏ AG355	Fresh Aire	1975	12.00
❏ AG359	Fresh Aire II	1977	12.00
❏ AG365	Fresh Aire III	1979	12.00
❏ AG373	Fresh Aire Interludes	1981	15.00
❏ AG370	Fresh Aire IV	1981	12.00
❏ AG385	Fresh Aire V	1983	12.00
❏ AG386	Fresh Aire VI	1986	15.00
❏ AG-1984	Mannheim Steamroller Christmas	1984	12.00

— *There are at least two label variations (red and brown) and many cover variations ("American Gramaphone Records" along top edge, no bar code on back cover, bar-code sticker on back cover, bar code as part of the art on the back cover, various stickers on front including "Now Available in Sheet Music" and "Grammy Nominee"); as yet, there's no difference in value we can see between the variations*

| ❏ AG2086 | Saving the Wildlife | 1986 | 12.00 |

MANNING, TERRY

ENTERPRISE
| ❏ ENS-1008 | Home Sweet Home | 1969 | 40.00 |

MANONE, WINGY

DECCA
| ❏ DL8473 [M] | Trumpet on the Wing | 1957 | 40.00 |

IMPERIAL
| ❏ LP-9190 [M] | Wingy Manone on the Jazzband Bus | 1962 | 30.00 |
| ❏ LP-12190 [S] | Wingy Manone on the Jazzband Bus | 1962 | 40.00 |

MCA
| ❏ 1364 | Jam and Jive | 1983 | 15.00 |

RCA VICTOR
| ❏ LPV-563 [M] | Wingy Manone, Volume 1 | 1969 | 25.00 |

STORYVILLE
| ❏ 4066 | Wingy Manone with Papa Bue's Viking Jazzband | 198? | 12.00 |

X
| ❏ LVA-3014 [10] | Wingy Manone, Vol. 1 | 1954 | 50.00 |

Number	Title	Yr	NM

MANSFIELD, JAYNE

20TH CENTURY

| ❏ FOX-3049 [M] | Jayne Mansfield Busts Up Las Vegas | 1961 | 200.00 |

MGM
| ❏ E-4202 [M] | Shakespeare, Tchaikovsky and Me | 1964 | 40.00 |
| ❏ SE-4202 [S] | Shakespeare, Tchaikovsky and Me | 1964 | 60.00 |

MANSON, CHARLES

AWARENESS
| ❏ LP-2144 | Lie: The Love and Terror Cult | 197? | 40.00 |
| ❏ 08903-1056 | Lie: The Love and Terror Cult | 1987 | 25.00 |

ESP-DISK'
| ❏ 2003 [B] | Lie: The Love and Terror Cult | 1970 | 300.00 |

MANSON, MARILYN

NOTHING
| ❏ 069490790-1 | Holywood | 2000 | 35.00 |
| ❏ 90273 | Mechanical Animals | 1998 | 35.00 |

— *One record on blue vinyl, the other on red; packaged in two separate cardboard covers in the same shrink wrap*

MANTLE, MICKEY

RCA VICTOR
| ❏ LPM-1704 [M] | My Favorite Hits | 1958 | 400.00 |

MANTLER, MICHAEL

ECM
| ❏ 23786 | Something There | 1984 | 12.00 |

WATT
| ❏ 3 | 13 & 3/4 | 197? | 25.00 |
| ❏ 4 [B] | Hapless Child | 1976 | 50.00 |

— *musical settings to Edward Gorey stories*

❏ 7	Movies	1978	18.00
❏ 2	No Answer	197?	25.00
❏ 5	Silence	197?	25.00

MANTOVANI

BAINBRIDGE
| ❏ BT-6277 | Mantovani's Italia | 1988 | 10.00 |
| ❏ 8001 | The Magic of Mantovani: Live at the Royal Festival Hall | 1982 | 15.00 |

FLEETWOOD
| ❏ FMS1019 | 90 Minutes with Mantovani | 1978 | 15.00 |

— *Side 1: Great Songs of Christmas (reissue of London recordings); Side 2: Great Songs for All Seasons*

HOLIDAY
| ❏ HDY1928 | Holy Night | 1981 | 12.00 |

LONDON
❏ LL3122/3 [M]	All-American Showcase	1959	25.00
❏ PS165/6 [S]	All-American Showcase	1959	30.00
❏ XPS906	All-Time Greatest Hits, Volume 1	1973	12.00
❏ XPS915	American Encores	1976	12.00
❏ LL3260 [M]	American Waltzes	1962	12.00
❏ PS248 [S]	American Waltzes	1962	15.00
❏ LL766 [M]	An Enchanted Evening with Mantovani	1953	25.00
❏ XPS902	An Evening with Mantovani	1973	12.00
❏ XPS610 [S]	Annunzio Paolo Mantovani (25th Anniversary)	1972	15.00
❏ LL1502 [M]	Candlelight	195?	18.00
❏ LL913 [M]	Christmas Carols	1953	18.00

— *Original recordings in mono*

| ❏ PS142 [S] | Christmas Carols | 196? | 18.00 |

— *Reissue with white back cover*

| ❏ LL913 [M] | Christmas Carols | 1959 | 15.00 |

Number	Title	Yr	NM
—Mono versions of stereo re-recordings			
❏ PS142 [S]	Christmas Carols	1959	25.00
—Originals have blue back cover, "Stereophonic" on upper left front cover and dark blue "FFSS" labels			
❏ BP720/1	Christmas Favorites	19??	18.00
❏ LL3338 [M]	Christmas Greetings from Mantovani	1963	15.00
❏ PS338 [S]	Christmas Greetings from Mantovani	1963	18.00
❏ LL3269 [M]	Classical Encores	1963	12.00
❏ PS269 [S]	Classical Encores	1963	15.00
❏ LL3004 [M]	Concert Encores	1958	18.00
❏ PS133 [S]	Concert Encores	1959	25.00
❏ LL3095 [M]	Continental Encores	1959	18.00
❏ PS147 [S]	Continental Encores	1959	25.00
❏ PS921	Favorite Melodies from Opera	1978	12.00
❏ LL1700 [M]	Film Encores	1957	25.00
❏ PS124 [S]	Film Encores	1959	18.00
❏ LL3117 [M]	Film Encores, Vol. 2	1959	15.00
❏ PS164 [S]	Film Encores, Vol. 2	1959	25.00
❏ LL3360 [M]	Folk Songs Around the World	1964	12.00
❏ PS360 [S]	Folk Songs Around the World	1964	15.00
❏ XPS585/6 [S]	From Monty with Love	1971	18.00
❏ LL3032 [M]	Gems Forever	1958	18.00
❏ PS106 [S]	Gems Forever	1959	25.00
❏ LL1262 [M]	Gershwin: Concerto	1955	25.00
❏ LL1262 [M]	Gershwin: Rhapsody in Blue	1955	25.00
❏ PS570	Greensleeves	1970	15.00
❏ LL570 [M]	Greensleeves (A Selection of Favorite Waltzes)	1952	25.00
❏ XPS900	Gypsy Soul	1972	12.00
❏ LL3239 [M]	Italia Mia	1961	15.00
❏ PS232 [S]	Italia Mia	1961	18.00
❏ PM55001 [M]	Kismet	1964	15.00
❏ LL3295 [M]	Latin Rendezvous	1963	12.00
❏ PS295 [S]	Latin Rendezvous	1963	15.00
❏ LL1259 [M]	Lonely Ballerina (Musical Modes)	1956	25.00
❏ LL3516 [M]	Mantovani/Hollywood	1967	15.00
❏ PS516 [S]	Mantovani/Hollywood	1967	15.00
❏ PS578 [S]	Mantovani In Concert	1970	15.00
❏ LL3448 [M]	Mantovani Magic	1966	12.00
❏ PS448 [M]	Mantovani Magic	1966	15.00
❏ LL3328 [M]	Mantovani/Manhattan	1963	12.00
❏ PS328 [S]	Mantovani/Manhattan	1963	15.00
❏ PS542 [S]	Mantovani…Memories	1968	15.00
❏ LL3422 [M]	Mantovani Ole	1965	12.00
❏ PS422 [S]	Mantovani Ole	1965	15.00
❏ LL3231 [M]	Mantovani Plays Music from Exodus and Other Great Themes	1960	15.00
❏ PS224 [S]	Mantovani Plays Music from Exodus and Other Great Themes	1960	18.00
❏ LL768 [M]	Mantovani Plays Tangos	1953	25.00
❏ LL3483 [M]	Mantovani's Golden Hits	1967	15.00
❏ PS483 [S]	Mantovani's Golden Hits	1967	15.00
❏ 820085-1	Mantovani's Golden Hits	198?	10.00
—Reissue of 483			
❏ SS1 [S]	Mantovani Stereo Showcase	1959	25.00
❏ PS532 [S]	Mantovani/Tango	1968	15.00
❏ 820333-1	Mantovani/Tango	198?	10.00
—Reissue of 532			
❏ PS572 [S]	Mantovani Today	1970	15.00
❏ LL3261 [M]	Moon River and Other Great Film Themes	1962	12.00
❏ PS249 [S]	Moon River and Other Great Film Themes	1962	15.00
❏ XPS914	More Golden Hits	197?	12.00
❏ LL3474 [M]	Mr. Music…Mantovani	1966	12.00
❏ PS474 [S]	Mr. Music…Mantovani	1966	15.00
❏ APS907	Musical Moments	1974	12.00
❏ LL1525 [M]	Music from the Ballet	1956	25.00
❏ LL1513 [M]	Music from the Films	1956	25.00
❏ PS112 [S]	Music from the Films	1959	18.00
❏ LL1331 [M]	Operatic Arias	1955	25.00
❏ LL3181 [M]	Operetta Memories	1960	15.00
❏ PS202 [S]	Operetta Memories	1960	18.00
❏ BP910/1	Romantic Hits	197?	15.00
❏ LL979 [M]	Romantic Melodies	1954	25.00
❏ LL1219 [M]	Song Hits from Theatreland	1955	25.00
❏ PS125 [S]	Song Hits from Theatreland	1959	18.00
❏ LL3251 [M]	Songs of Praise	1961	12.00
❏ PS245 [S]	Songs of Praise	1961	15.00
❏ LL3149 [M]	Songs to Remember	1960	15.00
❏ PS193 [S]	Songs to Remember	1960	18.00
❏ LL3270 [M]	Stop the World--I Want to Get Off/Oliver	1962	12.00
❏ PS270 [S]	Stop the World--I Want to Get Off/Oliver	1962	15.00
❏ LL685 [M]	Strauss Waltzes	1953	25.00
❏ PS118 [S]	Strauss Waltzes	1959	25.00
❏ XPS917	Strictly Mantovani	1977	12.00
❏ LL3136 [M]	The American Scene	1960	15.00
❏ PS182 [S]	The American Scene	1960	18.00
❏ XPS913	The Greatest Gift Is Love	197?	12.00
❏ LL3392 [M]	The Incomparable Mantovani	1964	12.00
❏ PS392 [S]	The Incomparable Mantovani	1964	15.00
❏ 820334-1	The Incomparable Mantovani	198?	10.00
—Reissue of 392			
❏ PS548 [S]	The Mantovani Scene	1969	15.00
❏ LL3419 [M]	The Mantovani Sound -- Big Hits from Broadway and Hollywood	1965	12.00
❏ PS419 [S]	The Mantovani Sound -- Big Hits from Broadway and Hollywood	1965	15.00
❏ LL3526 [M]	The Mantovani Touch	1968	18.00
❏ PS526 [S]	The Mantovani Touch	1968	15.00
❏ LL3250 [M]	Themes from Broadway (Carnival)	1961	15.00
❏ PS242 [S]	Themes from Broadway (Carnival)	1961	18.00
❏ LL3123 [M]	The Music of Irving Berlin and Rudolf Friml	1959	18.00
❏ PS166 [S]	The Music of Irving Berlin and Rudolf Friml	1959	25.00
❏ LL1150 [M]	The Music of Rudolf Frimi	1955	25.00
❏ LL3122 [M]	The Music of Victor Herbert and Sigmund Romberg	1959	18.00
❏ PS165 [S]	The Music of Victor Herbert and Sigmund Romberg	1959	25.00
❏ PS565 [S]	The World of Mantovani	1969	15.00
❏ LL1748 [M]	The World's Favorite Love Songs	1957	25.00
❏ LL3280 [M]	The World's Great Love Songs	1963	12.00
❏ PS280 [S]	The World's Great Love Songs	1963	15.00
❏ XPS598 [S]	To Lovers Everywhere U.S.A.	1971	15.00
❏ PS119 [S]	Waltz Encores	1959	25.00
❏ LL1452 [M]	Waltzes of Irving Berlin	1956	25.00
❏ LL1094 [M]	Waltz Time	1954	25.00
LONDON PHASE 4			
❏ SP-44043 [S]	Kismet	1964	18.00
❏ BP44302/3	Million Sellers	1978	15.00

MANZAREK, RAY

A&M

Number	Title	Yr	NM
❏ SP-4945	Carmina Burana	1984	12.00

MERCURY

Number	Title	Yr	NM
❏ SRM-1-703	The Golden Scarab	1974	15.00
❏ SRM-1-1014	The Whole Thing Started with Rock & Roll Now It's Out of Control	1975	15.00

MAPHIS, JOE

COLUMBIA

Number	Title	Yr	NM
❏ CL1005 [M]	Fire on the Strings	1957	100.00

HARMONY

| ❏ HL7180 [M] | Hi-Fi Holiday for Banjo | 1959 | 30.00 |
| ❏ HS11032 [S] | Hi-Fi Holiday for Banjo | 1959 | 30.00 |

KAPP

| ❏ KL-1347 [M] | Hootenanny Star | 1964 | 25.00 |
| ❏ KS-3347 [S] | Hootenanny Star | 1964 | 30.00 |

MACGREGOR

| ❏ MGR-1205 [M] | King of the Strings | 196? | 80.00 |

MOSRITE

| ❏ MA-400 [M] | The New Sound of Joe Maphis | 1967 | 30.00 |
| ❏ MS-400 [S] | The New Sound of Joe Maphis | 1967 | 30.00 |

STARDAY

❏ SLP-373 [M]	Country Guitar Goes to the Jimmy Dean Show	1966	60.00
—Deduct 1/3 if instruction book is missing			
❏ SLP-316 [M]	King of the Strings	1966	50.00

MAPHIS, JOE AND ROSE LEE

CAPITOL

| ❏ T1778 [M] | Rose Lee and Joe Maphis | 1962 | 30.00 |
| ❏ ST1778 [S] | Rose Lee and Joe Maphis | 1962 | 40.00 |

STARDAY

| ❏ SLP-322 [M] | Golden Gospel | 1966 | 30.00 |
| ❏ SLP-286 [M] | Mr. and Mrs. Country Music | 1964 | 30.00 |

MAPHIS, ROSE LEE

COLUMBIA

| ❏ CL1598 [M] | Rose Lee Maphis | 1961 | 35.00 |
| ❏ CS8398 [S] | Rose Lee Maphis | 1961 | 40.00 |

MAR-KEYS

ATLANTIC

❏ 8062 [M]	Do the Pop-Eye with the Mar-Keys	1962	60.00
❏ SD8062 [R]	Do the Pop-Eye with the Mar-Keys	1966	40.00
❏ 8055 [M]	Last Night	1961	125.00
—White "fan" logo on right			
❏ 8055 [M]	Last Night	1962	80.00
—Black "fan" logo on right			
❏ SD8055 [R]	Last Night	1966	60.00

STAX

❏ STS-2025	Damifiknew	1969	25.00
❏ STS-2036	Memphis Experience	1971	25.00
❏ ST-707 [M]	The Great Memphis Sound	1966	60.00
❏ STS-707 [R]	The Great Memphis Sound	1966	40.00

MAR-KEYS/BOOKER T. AND THE MG'S

STAX

| ❏ ST-720 [M] | Back to Back | 1967 | 30.00 |
| ❏ STS-720 [S] | Back to Back | 1967 | 50.00 |

MARABLE, LAWRENCE

JAZZ WEST

Number	Title	Yr	NM
❏ LP-8 [M]	Tenor Man	1956	500.00
—Deep Groove			

MARAIS, JOSEPH, AND MIRANDA

DECCA

❏ DL9047 [M]	Africana Suite and Songs of Spirit and Humor	1956	30.00
❏ DL5268 [10]	Ballads of Many Lands	1950	50.00
❏ DL9030 [M]	Christmas with Joseph and Miranda	1955	30.00
❏ DL9026 [M]	Marais and Miranda In Person, Vol. 1	1955	30.00
❏ DL9027 [M]	Marais and Miranda In Person, Vol. 2	1955	30.00
❏ DL8711 [M]	Sundown Songs	1957	30.00

MARAIS, JOSEPH

DECCA

❏ DL5083 [10]	Songs from the Veld, Vol. 2	1950	50.00
❏ DL5106 [10]	Songs of Many Lands	1950	50.00
❏ DL5014 [10]	South African Veld	1949	50.00

MARATHONS, THE (1)

ARVEE

| ❏ A-428 [M] | Peanut Butter | 1961 | 180.00 |

MARBLE PHROGG, THE

DERRICK

| ❏ 8868 | The Marble Phrogg | 1968 | 1000.00 |

MARCEAU, MARCEL

GONE

| ❏ LP1F | The Best of Marcel Marceau | 196? | 50.00 |

MGM

| ❏ SE-4 | The Best of Marcel Marceau | 196? | 40.00 |
| *—The above records are identical: 38 minutes of silence and 2 minutes of applause!* | | | |

MARCELS, THE

COLPIX

❏ CP-416 [M]	Blue Moon	1961	350.00
—Gold label			
❏ CP-416 [M]	Blue Moon	1963	120.00
—Blue label			

MARCH, HAL

DOT

| ❏ DLP-3092 [M] | The Moods of March | 1958 | 30.00 |
| ❏ DLP-25092 [S] | The Moods of March | 1958 | 40.00 |

HAMILTON

❏ HLP-101 [M]	Hal March Conducts	1960	18.00
❏ HLP-12101 [S]	Hal March Conducts	1960	25.00
—Reissue of Dot LP			

MARCH, LITTLE PEGGY

RCA VICTOR

❏ LPM-2732 [M]	I Will Follow Him	1963	60.00
❏ LSP-2732 [S]	I Will Follow Him	1963	80.00
❏ LPM-3883 [M]	No Foolin'	1968	40.00
❏ LSP-3883 [S]	No Foolin'	1968	30.00

MARCH, LITTLE PEGGY/BENNIE THOMAS

RCA VICTOR

| ❏ LPM-3408 [M] | In Our Fashion | 1965 | 40.00 |
| ❏ LSP-3408 [S] | In Our Fashion | 1965 | 50.00 |

MARCHAN, BOBBY

COLLECTABLES

| ❏ COL-5113 | Golden Classics | 198? | 12.00 |

SPHERE SOUND

| ❏ SSR-7004 [M] | There's Something on Your Mind | 1964 | 300.00 |

MARCUS, LEW

SAVOY

| ❏ MG-15006 [10] | Back Room Piano | 1951 | 50.00 |

MARCUS, STEVE

FLYING DUTCHMAN

| ❏ BDL1-1461 | Sometime Other Than Now | 1976 | 15.00 |

VORTEX

❏ 2009	The Count's Rock Band	1969	25.00
❏ 2013	The Lord's Prayer	1969	25.00
❏ 2001	Tomorrow Never Knows	1968	25.00

MARCUS, WADE

ABC IMPULSE!

| ❏ AS-9318 | Metamorphosis | 197? | 15.00 |

MARDIN, ARIF

ATLANTIC

| ❏ SD1661 | Journey | 1974 | 15.00 |

Number	Title	Yr	NM

MARESCA, ERNIE

SEVILLE
| SV77001 [M] | Shout! Shout! Knock Yourself Out | 1962 | 120.00 |
| SV87001 [S] | Shout! Shout! Knock Yourself Out | 1962 | 200.00 |

MARGITZA, RICK

BLUE NOTE
| B1-92279 | Color | 1989 | 15.00 |

MARGOLIN, STUART

WARNER BROS.
| BSK3439 | And the Angel Sings | 1980 | 25.00 |

MARGULIS, CHARLIE

CARLTON
| LP 12-103 [M] | Marvelous Margulis | 1958 | 30.00 |
| STLP 12-103 [S] | Marvelous Margulis | 1959 | 30.00 |

MARIAH

UNITED ARTISTS
| UA-LA493-G | Mariah | 1975 | 18.00 |

MARIANI

SONOBEAT
| HEC411/2 | Perpetuum Mobile | 197? | 2500.00 |
—Issued in generic white cover; the band and label names are stamped on the jacket, and each of the 50 copies is numbered and autographed by the members of the band; VG value 1000; VG+ value 1750

MARIANO, CHARLIE, AND JERRY DODGION

WORLD PACIFIC
| WP-1245 [M] | Beauties of 1918 | 1958 | 50.00 |

MARIANO, CHARLIE

ATLANTIC
| SD1608 | The Mirror | 197? | 18.00 |

BETHLEHEM
BCP-25 [M]	Alto Sax for Young Moderns	1956	100.00
BCP-49 [M]	Charlie Mariano Plays Chloe	1957	300.00
BCP-1022 [10]	Charlie Mariano Sextet	1955	150.00

CATALYST
| 7915 | Reflections | 197? | 18.00 |

CMP
| CMP-10-ST | Crystal Balls | 198? | 12.00 |
| CMP-2-ST | October | 198? | 12.00 |

ECM
| 1256 | Charlie Mariano with the Karnataka College of Percussion | 1985 | 15.00 |

FANTASY
| OJC-1745 | Charlie Mariano Boston All Stars | 1990 | 15.00 |
| 3-10 [10] | Charlie Mariano Sextet | 1953 | 180.00 |

IMPERIAL
| IMP-3006 [10] | Charlie Mariano Quintet Volume 1 | 1955 | 150.00 |
| IMP-3007 [10] | Charlie Mariano Quintet Volume 2 | 1955 | 150.00 |

INNER CITY
| IC-1024 | October | 1977 | 18.00 |

INTUITION
| C1-90787 | Mariano | 1988 | 12.00 |

PRESTIGE
| PRLP-130 [10] | Charlie Mariano | 1952 | 200.00 |
| PRLP-153 [10] | Charlie Mariano Boston All Stars | 1953 | 200.00 |

REGINA
| R-286 [M] | A Jazz Portrait of Charlie Mariano | 1963 | 30.00 |
| RS-286 [S] | A Jazz Portrait of Charlie Mariano | 1963 | 30.00 |

MARIENTHAL, ERIC

GRP
| GR-9586 | Round Trip | 1989 | 15.00 |
| GR-1052 | Voices of the Heart | 1988 | 12.00 |

MARINERS, THE

CADENCE
| CLP-1008 [M] | The Mariners Sing Spirituals | 1956 | 40.00 |

COLUMBIA
| CL609 [M] | Hymns | 1955 | 40.00 |

MARK-ALMOND

ABC
| D-945 | To the Heart | 1976 | 12.00 |

BLUE THUMB
| BTS27 | Mark-Almond | 1971 | 15.00 |
—Reissue of 8827
BTS-8827	Mark-Almond	1971	18.00
BTS32	Mark-Almond II	1971	15.00
BTS50	The Best of Mark-Almond	1973	15.00

COLUMBIA
KC32486	Mark-Almond 73	1973	15.00
KC31917	Rising	1972	15.00
PC31917	Rising	198?	10.00
—Budget-line reissue
| CG33648 | Rising/Mark-Almond 73 | 1976 | 18.00 |

HORIZON
| SP-730 | Other People's Rooms | 1978 | 12.00 |

MCA
| 711 | Mark-Almond II | 198? | 10.00 |
—Reissue of Blue Thumb 32
| 792 | The Best of Mark-Almond | 198? | 10.00 |
—Reissue of Blue Thumb 50
| 793 | To the Heart | 198? | 10.00 |
—Reissue of ABC 945

PACIFIC ARTS
| 7-142 | The Best of the Mark-Almond Band…Live | 1980 | 12.00 |

MARKAY, GRACE

CAPITOL
| ST2687 [S] | Grace Markay | 1967 | 18.00 |
| T2687 [M] | Grace Markay | 1967 | 25.00 |

UNITED ARTISTS
| UAS-6722 | Please Come Back | 1969 | 25.00 |

MARKETTS, THE

LIBERTY
| LRP-3226 [M] | Surfer's Stomp | 1962 | 40.00 |
—Add 20% if "Surfer's Stomp" instruction sheet is enclosed
| LST-7226 [S] | Surfer's Stomp | 1962 | 50.00 |
—Add 20% if "Surfer's Stomp" instruction sheet is enclosed
| LRP-3226 [M] | The Surfing Scene | 196? | 30.00 |
—Retitled version of above
| LST-7226 [S] | The Surfing Scene | 196? | 40.00 |
—Retitled version of above

MERCURY
| SRM-1-679 | AM, FM, Etc. | 1973 | 18.00 |

WARNER BROS.
W1537 [M]	Out of Limits!	1964	30.00
WS1537 [S]	Out of Limits!	1964	40.00
W1642 [M]	The Batman Theme	1966	40.00
WS1642 [S]	The Batman Theme	1966	50.00
W1509 [M]	The Marketts Take to Wheels	1963	40.00
WS1509 [S]	The Marketts Take to Wheels	1963	50.00

WORLD PACIFIC
| WP-1870 [M] | Sun Power | 1967 | 30.00 |
| WPS-21870 [S] | Sun Power | 1967 | 25.00 |

MARKEWICH, REESE

MODERN AGE
| MA-134 [M] | New Designs in Jazz | 1958 | 50.00 |

MARKHAM, JOHN

FAMOUS DOOR
| 121 | San Francisco Jazz | 1977 | 15.00 |

MARKHAM, PIGMEAT

CHESS
LP-1467 [M]	Anything Goes	1962	30.00
LP-1521 [M]	Backstage	1968	25.00
LPS-1521 [S]	Backstage	1968	25.00
LPS-1534	Bag	1970	18.00
LPS-1525	Here Comes the Judge	1968	25.00
CH-9166	Here Comes the Judge	1985	12.00
—Reissue of 1525
LPS-1529	Hustlers	1969	18.00
LP-1505 [M]	If You Can't Be Good, Be Careful	1966	18.00
LPS-1505 [S]	If You Can't Be Good, Be Careful	1966	25.00
LP-1493 [M]	Mr. Funny Man	1965	30.00
LP-1515 [M]	Mr. Vaudeville	1967	18.00
LPS-1515 [S]	Mr. Vaudeville	1967	25.00
LP-1484 [M]	Open the Door, Richard	1964	30.00
LP-1462 [M]	Pigmeat Markham At the Party	1962	30.00
LP-1517 [M]	Save Your Soul, Baby	1967	25.00
LPS-1517 [S]	Save Your Soul, Baby	1967	25.00
LP-1451 [M]	The Trial	1961	30.00
LP-1475 [M]	The World's Greatest Clown	1963	30.00
LP-1500 [M]	This'll Kill Ya	1965	30.00
LPS-1526	Tune Me In	1968	18.00

JEWEL
| 5007 | Crap-Shootin' Rev | 1972 | 15.00 |
| 5012 | Will the Real Pigmeat Markham Please Sit Down | 1973 | 15.00 |

MARKIE, BIZ

COLD CHILLIN'
45261	All Samples Cleared!	1993	18.00
CDC5003	Biz's Baddest Beats	1995	18.00
CDC9001	Goin' Off	1995	15.00
—Reissue of 25675
| 25675 | Goin' Off | 1988 | 18.00 |
| CDC9000 | I Need a Haircut | 1995 | 15.00 |
—Reissue with banned track, "Alone Again," deleted
| | I Need a Haircut | 1991 | 40.00 |
| PRO-A-5179 [DJ] | | | |
—Promo-only issue on vinyl; includes "Alone Again," which sampled the Gilbert O'Sullivan hit without authorization and resulted in the entire album's withdrawal from sale
| CDC9009 | The Biz Never Sleeps | 1995 | 15.00 |
—Reissue of 26003
| 26003 | The Biz Never Sleeps | 1989 | 18.00 |

LANDSPEED
| LSR8802 | Best of Cold Chillin' | 2000 | 25.00 |

MARKLEY

FORWARD
| 1007 | A Group | 1969 | 30.00 |

MARKOWITZ, MARKIE

FAMOUS DOOR
| 111 | Marky's Vibes | 197? | 18.00 |

MARKS, GUY

ABC
549 [M]	Hollywood Sings	1966	18.00
S-549 [S]	Hollywood Sings	1966	18.00
S-648	Loving You Has Made Me Bananas	1968	25.00

MARKS, J., AND SHIPEN LEBZELTER

COLUMBIA MASTERWORKS
| M30006 | First National Nothing | 1970 | 25.00 |
| MS7193 | Rock and Other Four-Letter Words | 1969 | 30.00 |

MARLEY, BOB, AND THE WAILERS

ACCORD
| SN-7211 | Jamaican Storm | 1982 | 12.00 |

CALLA
| ZX34760 | Early Music | 1977 | 12.00 |
—Reissue of Record 2 of Calla 1240
| CAS-1240 | The Birth of a Legend | 1976 | 18.00 |
| ZX34759 | The Birth of a Legend | 1977 | 12.00 |
—Reissue of Record 1 of Calla 1240

CLEOPATRA
| 3397 [B] | Lee "Scratch" Perry Masters | | 25.00 |
| 8235 [B] | Reggae Classics | | 30.00 |
—picture disc
| 5541 [B] | Soul Rebel | | 25.00 |
| CLP1830 [B] | Soul Revolution Part 2: Dub | 2014 | 25.00 |

COLUMBIA
| PZ34760 | Early Music | 198? | 10.00 |
—Budget-line reissue of Calla 34760
| PZ34759 | The Birth of a Legend | 198? | 10.00 |
—Budget-line reissue of Calla 34759

COTILLION
| SD5228 | Chances Are | 1981 | 12.00 |

ISLAND
| 90029 | Babylon by Bus | 1983 | 15.00 |
| ISLD11 | Babylon by Bus | 1978 | 10.00 |
—Island distribution
| ISLD11 | Babylon by Bus | 1979 | 15.00 |
—Warner Bros. distribution
| 90031 | Burnin' | 1983 | 10.00 |
| SMAS-9338 | Burnin' | 1973 | 25.00 |
—Capitol distribution
| ILPS9256 | Burnin' | 1974 | 18.00 |
—Island distribution
| ILPS9256 | Burnin' | 1978 | 15.00 |
—Warner Bros. distribution
5488941	Burnin'	2008	25.00
90030	Catch a Fire	1983	10.00
SW-9329	Catch a Fire	1973	100.00
—Cigarette lighter" cover with flip-open top; Capitol distribution
| 462011 | Catch a Fire | 2009 | 25.00 |
—Reissue with standard cover; Island distribution
| ILPS9241 | Catch a Fire | 1978 | 15.00 |
—Reissue; Warner Bros. distribution
546404-1 [B]	Chant Down Babylon	1999	25.00
90085	Confrontation	1983	12.00
524419-1	Dreams of Freedom	1997	15.00
90034	Exodus	1983	10.00
ILPS9498	Exodus	1977	15.00
—Island distribution (all have multicolor labels)
| ILPS9498 | Exodus | 1978 | 12.00 |
—Warner Bros. distribution
5318419	Exodus	2009	25.00
90035	Kaya	1983	10.00
ILPS9517	Kaya	1978	15.00
—Island distribution
| ILPS9517 | Kaya | 1979 | 12.00 |
—Warner Bros. distribution
90169	Legend	1984	12.00
5303052	Legend	2009	25.00
90032	Live!	1983	10.00
ILPS9376	Live!	1975	15.00
—Island distribution
| ILPS9376 | Live! | 1978 | 12.00 |

Number	Title	Yr	NM
—Warner Bros. distribution			
❑ 90037	Natty Dread	1983	10.00
—90029-90037 are reissues with Atco distribution			
❑ ILPS9281	Natty Dread	1974	18.00
—Island distribution			
❑ ILPS9281	Natty Dread	1978	15.00
—Warner Bros. distribution			
❑ 90033	Rastaman Vibration	1983	10.00
❑ ILPS9383 [DJ]	Rastaman Vibration	1976	100.00
—Promotional package with burlap box and press kit			
❑ ILPS9383	Rastaman Vibration	1976	15.00
—Island distribution			
❑ ILPS9383	Rastaman Vibration	1978	12.00
—Warner Bros. distribution			
❑ 90520	Rebel Music	1986	12.00
❑ ILPS9542	Survival	1979	15.00
❑ 90036	Uprising	1983	10.00
❑ ILPS9596	Uprising	1980	15.00
MOBILE FIDELITY			
❑ 1-236	Catch a Fire	1995	100.00
—Audiophile vinyl			
❑ 1-221	Exodus	1995	100.00
—Audiophile vinyl			
TUFF GONG			
❑ 846197-1	Babylon by Bus	1990	18.00
❑ 846200-1	Burnin'	1990	15.00
❑ 846201-1	Catch a Fire	1990	15.00
❑ 846207-1	Confrontation	1990	15.00
❑ 846208-1	Exodus	1990	15.00
❑ 846209-1	Kaya	1990	15.00
❑ 846210-1	Legend	1990	15.00
❑ 846203-1	Live!	1990	15.00
❑ 846204-1	Natty Dread	1990	15.00
❑ 524103-1	Natural Mystic	1995	18.00
❑ 846205-1	Rastaman Vibration	1990	15.00
❑ 846206-1	Rebel Music	1990	15.00
❑ 846202-1	Survival	1990	15.00
❑ 848243-1	Talkin' Blues	1991	15.00
❑ 846211-1	Uprising	1990	15.00

MARLO, MICKI

ABC-PARAMOUNT

Number	Title	Yr	NM
❑ 295 [M]	Married I Can Always Get	1959	25.00
❑ S-295 [S]	Married I Can Always Get	1959	30.00

MARLOW, JANET

CMG

Number	Title	Yr	NM
❑ CML-8003	Outside the City	198?	12.00

MARLOWE, MARION, AND FRANK PARKER

COLUMBIA

Number	Title	Yr	NM
❑ CL576 [M]	Arthur Godfrey's TV Sweethearts	1954	30.00
—Maroon label, gold print			

MARLOWE, MEXIE

KING

Number	Title	Yr	NM
❑ 799 [M]	Meet Mexie Marlowe	1962	100.00

MARMALADE, THE

EPIC

Number	Title	Yr	NM
❑ BN26553	The Best of the Marmalade	1970	25.00
LONDON			
❑ PS575 [B]	Reflections of My Life	1970	30.00

MARMAROSA, DODO

ARGO

Number	Title	Yr	NM
❑ LP-4012 [M]	Dodo's Back	1961	250.00
—Deep Groove			
❑ LPS-4012 [S]	Dodo's Back	1961	30.00
PHOENIX			
❑ 20	Piano Man	197?	15.00
SPOTLITE			
❑ 108	Dodo Marmarosa Trio	197?	12.00

MARMAROSA, DODO/ERROLL GARNER

CONCERT HALL JAZZ

Number	Title	Yr	NM
❑ 1001 [10]	Piano Contrasts	1955	50.00
DIAL			
❑ LP-208 [10]	Piano Contrasts	1950	250.00

MAROCCO, FRANK

DISCOVERY

Number	Title	Yr	NM
❑ 797	Jazz Accordion	1979	15.00
❑ 854	Road to Marocco	198?	12.00
❑ 838	The Trio	198?	12.00
TREND			
❑ 516	New Colors	1980	18.00
—Direct-to-disc recording			

MAROHNIC, CHUCK

STEEPLECHASE

Number	Title	Yr	NM
❑ SCS-4002	Copenhagen Suite	198?	15.00
❑ SCS-1155	Permutations	198?	15.00

MAROON 5

OCTONE/J

Number	Title	Yr	NM
❑ 50001	Songs About Jane	2004	18.00

MARR, HANK

KING

Number	Title	Yr	NM
❑ KSD-1061	Greasy Spoon	1969	25.00
❑ 1011 [M]	Hank Marr Plays 24 Originals	1966	25.00
❑ 899 [M]	Live at Club 502	1964	40.00
❑ 933 [M]	On and Off Stage	1965	30.00
❑ 1025 [M]	Sounds from the Marr-Ket Place	1968	25.00
❑ 829 [M]	Teentime Dance Steps	1963	30.00

MARROW, ESTHER

FANTASY

Number	Title	Yr	NM
❑ 9414	Sister Woman	1972	18.00

MARS, CHRIS

SMASH

Number	Title	Yr	NM
❑ 513198-1 [DJ]	Horseshoes and Hand Grenades	1992	25.00
— Vinyl is promo only			

MARS, SYLVIA

LYRIC

Number	Title	Yr	NM
❑ 124	Blues Walk Right In	196?	60.00

MARS VOLTA, THE

UNIVERSAL MOTOWN

Number	Title	Yr	NM
❑ 1061601	The Bedlam in Gotham	2008	30.00

MARSALA, JOE

JAZZOLOGY

Number	Title	Yr	NM
❑ J-106	Joe Marsala and His Jazz Band, 1944	198?	12.00

MARSALA, JOE/BUD FREEMAN

BRUNSWICK

Number	Title	Yr	NM
❑ BL58037 [10]	Battle of Jazz, Vol. 1	1953	50.00

MARSALIS, BRANFORD

CBS MASTERWORKS

Number	Title	Yr	NM
❑ M42122	Romances for Saxophone	1986	15.00
COLUMBIA			
❑ OC44055	Random Abstract	1988	12.00
❑ FC40711	Renaissance	1987	12.00
❑ FC40363	Royal Garden Blues	1986	12.00
❑ FC38951	Scenes in the City	1984	12.00
❑ CX244199	Trio Jeepy	1989	18.00
❑ CAS1628 [DJ]	Trio Jeepy Interchords Special	1989	18.00
JAZZ PLANET			
❑ JP-5004	The Dark Keys	1996	30.00

MARSALIS, ELLIS

SPINDLETOP

Number	Title	Yr	NM
❑ ST-105	Homecoming	1986	12.00

MARSALIS, WYNTON

CBS

Number	Title	Yr	NM
❑ IM42137	Carnaval	1987	12.00
COLUMBIA			
❑ FC40009	Black Codes (From the Underground)	1985	12.00
❑ FC45287	Crescent City Christmas Card	1989	12.00
❑ FC39530	Hot House Flowers	1984	12.00
❑ FC40308	J Mood	1986	12.00
❑ PC240675	Live at Blues Alley	1988	15.00
❑ FC40461	Marsalis Standard Time	1987	12.00
❑ C47346	Standard Time Vol. 2 -- Intimacy Calling	1991	18.00
❑ C46143	Standard Time Vol. 3 -- The Resolution of Romance	1990	15.00
❑ OC45091	The Majesty of the Blues	1989	15.00
❑ FC38641	Think of One	1983	12.00
❑ HC47574	Wynton Marsalis	198?	30.00
—Half-speed mastered edition			
❑ FC37574	Wynton Marsalis	1982	12.00
WHO'S WHO IN JAZZ			
❑ 21024	Wynton Marsalis with Art Blakey and His Jazz Messengers	1981	18.00

MARSH, GEORGE, AND JOHN ABERCROMBIE

1750 ARCH

Number	Title	Yr	NM
❑ 1804	Drum Strum	198?	15.00

MARSH, GEORGE

1750 ARCH

Number	Title	Yr	NM
❑ 1791	Marshland	1982	15.00

MARSH, HUGH

SOUNDWINGS/DUKE STREET

Number	Title	Yr	NM
❑ SW-210	Shaking the Pumpkin	1988	15.00

MARSH, MILTON

STRATA-EAST

Number	Title	Yr	NM
❑ SES-19758	Monism	1975	25.00

MARSH, WARNE, AND SAL MOSCA

INTERPLAY

Number	Title	Yr	NM
❑ 7725	How Deep/How High	1980	15.00

MARSH, WARNE; CLARE FISCHER; GARY FOSTER

REVELATION

Number	Title	Yr	NM
❑ 17	First Symposium on Relaxed Improvisation	197?	18.00

MARSH, WARNE

ATLANTIC

Number	Title	Yr	NM
❑ 1291 [M]	Warne Marsh	1958	150.00
—Black label			
❑ 1291 [M]	Warne Marsh	1961	30.00
—Multicolor label, white "fan" logo at right			
❑ SD1291 [S]	Warne Marsh	1958	200.00
—Green label			
❑ SD1291 [S]	Warne Marsh	1961	25.00
—Multicolor label, white "fan" logo at right			
DISCOVERY			
❑ 863	How Deep/How High	198?	12.00
IMPERIAL			
❑ LP-9027 [M]	Jazz of Two Cities	1957	80.00
❑ LP-12013 [S]	The Winds of Warne Marsh	1959	60.00
—Retitled version in stereo?			
INTERPLAY			
❑ 8604	Posthumous	1986	15.00
❑ 8602	Two Days in the Life of Warne Marsh	1986	15.00
❑ 7709	Warne Out	197?	15.00
MODE			
❑ LP-125 [M]	Music for Prancing	1957	250.00
NESSA			
❑ N-7	All Music	1977	15.00
REVELATION			
❑ R-12	Ne Plus Ultra	1970	25.00
❑ 22	The Art of Improvising	197?	15.00
❑ 27	The Art of Improvising, Vol. 3	197?	15.00
STORYVILLE			
❑ 4001	Jazz Exchange, Vol. 1	197?	15.00
❑ 4026	Jazz Exchange, Vol. 2: Live at the Montmartre Club	198?	15.00
XANADU			
❑ 151	Live in Hollywood	197?	15.00

MARSHALL, CHUCK

DECCA

Number	Title	Yr	NM
❑ DL4267 [M]	Twist to Songs Everybody Knows	1962	18.00
❑ DL74267 [S]	Twist to Songs Everybody Knows	1962	25.00

MARSHALL, EDDIE

TIMELESS

Number	Title	Yr	NM
❑ 315	Dance of the Sun	1977	15.00

MARSHALL, JACK

CAPITOL

Number	Title	Yr	NM
❑ T1108 [M]	18th Century Jazz	1959	25.00
❑ ST1108 [S]	18th Century Jazz	1959	30.00
❑ T1939 [M]	My Son the Surf Nut	1963	30.00
❑ ST1939 [S]	My Son the Surf Nut	1963	40.00
❑ T1601 [M]	Songs Without Words	1961	25.00
❑ ST1601 [S]	Songs Without Words	1961	30.00
❑ T1194 [M]	Soundsville!	1959	25.00
❑ ST1194 [S]	Soundsville!	1959	30.00
❑ T1351 [M]	The Marshall Swings	1960	25.00
❑ ST1351 [S]	The Marshall Swings	1960	30.00
❑ T1727 [M]	The Twangy, Shoutin', Fantastic Big-Band Sounds of Tuff Jack	1962	30.00
❑ ST1727 [S]	The Twangy, Shoutin', Fantastic Big-Band Sounds of Tuff Jack	1962	40.00

MARSHALL, PENNY, AND CINDY WILLIAMS

ATLANTIC

Number	Title	Yr	NM
❑ SD18203	Laverne and Shirley Sing	1979	25.00

MARSHALL, PETER

DOT

Number	Title	Yr	NM
❑ DLP-25930	For the Love of Pete	1969	25.00

MARSHALL TUCKER BAND, THE

CAPRICORN

Number	Title	Yr	NM
❑ CP 0124	A New Life	1974	15.00
❑ CPK 0180	Carolina Dreams	1977	15.00
❑ CPN-0214	Greatest Hits	1978	15.00
❑ CP 0170	Long Hard Ride	1976	15.00
❑ CP 0161 [B]	Searchin' for a Rainbow	1975	15.00
❑ CP 0112	The Marshall Tucker Band	1973	15.00

Number	Title	Yr	NM
❑ CP 0205	Together Forever	1978	15.00
❑ 2CP 0145	Where We All Belong	1974	18.00

MERCURY

Number	Title	Yr	NM
❑ 832794-1	Still Holdin' On	1988	12.00

WARNER BROS.

Number	Title	Yr	NM
❑ BSK3662	A New Life	1982	12.00
—Reissue of Capricorn 0124			
❑ BSK3610	Carolina Dreams	1982	12.00
—Reissue of Capricorn 0180			
❑ HS3525	Dedicated	1981	12.00
❑ BSK3611	Greatest Hits	1982	12.00
—Reissue of Capricorn 0214			
❑ 23803	Just Us	1983	12.00
❑ BSK3663	Long Hard Ride	1982	12.00
—Reissue of Capricorn 0170			
❑ BSK3317	Running Like the Wind	1979	12.00
❑ BSK3609	Searchin' for a Rainbow	1982	12.00
—Reissue of Capricorn 0161			
❑ HS3410	Tenth	1980	12.00
❑ BSK3606	The Marshall Tucker Band	1982	12.00
—Reissue of Capricorn 0112			
❑ BSK3664	Together Forever	1982	12.00
—Reissue of Capricorn 0205			
❑ BSK3684	Tuckerized	1982	12.00
❑ 2WS3608	Where We All Belong	1982	15.00
—Reissue of Capricorn 0145			

MARSHMALLOW WAY

UNITED ARTISTS

Number	Title	Yr	NM
❑ UAS-6708	Marshmallow Way	1969	25.00

MARTELL, LINDA

PLANTATION

Number	Title	Yr	NM
❑ 9	Color Me Country	1970	18.00

MARTHA AND THE MUFFINS

RCA VICTOR

Number	Title	Yr	NM
❑ AFL1-4664	Danseparc	1983	12.00

VIRGIN

Number	Title	Yr	NM
❑ VA13145	Metro Music	1980	12.00

MARTHA AND THE VANDELLAS

GORDY

Number	Title	Yr	NM
❑ GS-958	Black Magic	1972	25.00
❑ G-902 [M]	Come and Get These Memories	1963	400.00
❑ GS-902 [S]	Come and Get These Memories	1963	800.00
❑ G-915 [M]	Dance Party	1965	50.00
❑ GS-915 [S]	Dance Party	1965	60.00
❑ G-917 [M]	Greatest Hits	1966	30.00
❑ GS-917 [S]	Greatest Hits	1966	30.00
❑ G-907 [M]	Heat Wave	1963	150.00
❑ GS-907 [S]	Heat Wave	1963	400.00
Mono cover with "Stereo" sticker			
❑ GS-907 [R]	Heat Wave	1963	150.00
—Stereo" banner pre-printed on cover			
❑ G-925 [M]	Martha and the Vandellas Live!	1967	30.00
❑ GS-925 [S]	Martha and the Vandellas Live!	1967	30.00
❑ GS-952	Natural Resources	1970	25.00
❑ G-926 [M]	Ridin' High	1968	60.00
—Mono is promo only			
❑ GS-926 [S]	Ridin' High	1968	25.00
❑ GS-944	Sugar 'N Spice	1969	25.00
❑ G-920 [M]	Watchout!	1966	30.00
❑ GS-920 [S]	Watchout!	1966	30.00

MOTOWN

Number	Title	Yr	NM
❑ M7-778	Anthology	1974	18.00
❑ M5-204V1	Greatest Hits	1981	12.00
—Reissue of Gordy 917			
❑ M5-145V1	Heat Wave	1981	12.00
—Reissue of Gordy 907			
❑ M5-111V1	Motown Superstar Series, Vol. 11	1981	12.00

MARTIN, ARCH

ZEPHYR

Number	Title	Yr	NM
❑ 12009 [M]	Arch Martin Quintet	1959	30.00

MARTIN, BENNY

STARDAY

Number	Title	Yr	NM
❑ SLP-131 [M]	Country Music's Sensational Entertainer	1961	50.00

MARTIN, BOBBI

BUDDAH

Number	Title	Yr	NM
❑ BDS-5090	Tomorrow	1971	15.00

CORAL

Number	Title	Yr	NM
❑ CRL57472 [M]	Don't Forget I Still Love You	1965	18.00
❑ CRL757472 [S]	Don't Forget I Still Love You	1965	25.00
❑ CRL57478 [M]	I Love You So	1965	18.00
❑ CRL757478 [S]	I Love You So	1965	25.00

SUNSET

Number	Title	Yr	NM
❑ SUS-5319	Thinking of You	197?	12.00

UNITED ARTISTS

Number	Title	Yr	NM
❑ UAS-6700	For the Love of Him	1969	15.00
❑ UAS-6668	Harper Valley P.T.A.	1968	15.00
❑ UAS-6755	With Love	1970	15.00

VOCALION

Number	Title	Yr	NM
❑ VL73906	Have You Ever Been Lonely	196?	12.00

MARTIN, DEAN

CAPITOL

Number	Title	Yr	NM
❑ T1285 [M]	A Winter Romance	1959	25.00
❑ ST1285 [S]	A Winter Romance	1959	30.00
❑ T1702 [M]	Cha Cha De Amor	1962	25.00
❑ ST1702 [S]	Cha Cha De Amor	1962	30.00
❑ W1580 [M]	Dean Martin	1961	25.00
❑ SW1580 [S]	Dean Martin	1961	30.00
❑ H401 [10]	Dean Martin Sings	1953	100.00
❑ T401 [M]	Dean Martin Sings	1953	50.00
❑ T2297 [M]	Dean Martin Sings -- Sinatra Conducts	1965	18.00
❑ ST2297 [S]	Dean Martin Sings -- Sinatra Conducts	1965	25.00
❑ T2333 [M]	Dean Martin -- Southern Style	1965	18.00
❑ DT2333 [R]	Dean Martin -- Southern Style	1965	15.00
❑ T1659 [M]	Dino -- Italian Love Songs	1962	25.00
❑ ST1659 [S]	Dino -- Italian Love Songs	1962	30.00
❑ SM-1659	Dino -- Italian Love Songs	197?	12.00
—Reissue with new prefix			
❑ T2212 [M]	Hey Brother Pour the Wine	1964	25.00
❑ DT2212 [R]	Hey Brother Pour the Wine	1964	15.00
❑ TT2343 [M]	Holiday Cheer	1965	18.00
—Reissue of 1285 with one fewer track			
❑ STT2343 [S]	Holiday Cheer	1965	25.00
—Some copies of this LP have labels that state the title as "Baby, It's Cold Outside."			
❑ T849 [M]	Pretty Baby	1957	30.00
❑ T1150 [M]	Sleep Warm	1959	30.00
❑ ST1150 [S]	Sleep Warm	1959	30.00
❑ T576 [M]	Swingin' Down Yonder	1955	30.00
❑ T2601 [M]	The Best of Dean Martin	1966	18.00
❑ DT2601 [R]	The Best of Dean Martin	1966	15.00
❑ SM-2601	The Best of Dean Martin	197?	12.00
—Reissue with new prefix			
❑ SKAO-140	The Best of Dean Martin, Vol. 2	1968	18.00
❑ TCL2815 [M]	The Dean Martin Deluxe Set	1967	30.00
❑ DTCL2815 [R]	The Dean Martin Deluxe Set	1967	25.00
❑ T1047 [M]	This Is Dean Martin	1958	30.00
❑ DT1047 [R]	This Is Dean Martin	196?	15.00
❑ ST1442 [S]	This Time I'm Swingin'	1961	30.00
❑ T1442 [M]	This Time I'm Swingin'	1961	25.00
❑ STBB-523	You're Nobody 'Til Somebody Loves You/ Return to Me	1970	25.00

LONGINES SYMPHONETTE

Number	Title	Yr	NM
❑ LS-124A	Memories Are Made of This	197?	30.00
—Records are indiividually numbered SYS 5230, 5231, 5232, 5233 and 5234			

PAIR

Number	Title	Yr	NM
❑ PDL2-1029	Dreams and Memories	198?	15.00

PICKWICK

Number	Title	Yr	NM
❑ PTP-2051	Dean Martin	197?	15.00
❑ SPC-3203	Deluxe	197?	12.00
❑ SPC-3089	I Can't Give You Anything But Love	196?	12.00
❑ SPC-3057	You Can't Love 'Em All	196?	12.00
❑ SPC-3136	Young and Foolish	196?	12.00
❑ SPC-3175	You Were Made for Love	197?	12.00

REPRISE

Number	Title	Yr	NM
❑ R-6061 [M]	Country Style	1963	18.00
❑ R9-6061 [S]	Country Style	1963	25.00
❑ R-6085 [M]	Dean "Tex" Martin Rides Again	1963	18.00
❑ R9-6085 [S]	Dean "Tex" Martin Rides Again	1963	25.00
❑ R-6146 [M]	Dean Martin Hits Again	1965	15.00
❑ RS-6146 [S]	Dean Martin Hits Again	1965	18.00
❑ RS-6301	Dean Martin's Greatest Hits! Vol. 1	1968	18.00
❑ RS-6320	Dean Martin's Greatest Hits! Vol. 2	1968	18.00
❑ MS2053	Dino	1972	18.00
❑ SW-94345	Dino	1972	25.00
—Capitol Record Club edition			
❑ R-6054 [M]	Dino Latino	1962	18.00
❑ R9-6054 [S]	Dino Latino	1962	25.00
❑ R-6123 [M]	Dream with Dean	1964	15.00
❑ RS-6123 [S]	Dream with Dean	1964	18.00
❑ R-6130 [M]	Everybody Loves Somebody	1964	15.00
❑ RS-6130 [S]	Everybody Loves Somebody	1964	18.00
❑ RS-6428	For the Good Times	1971	18.00
❑ R-6021 [M]	French Style	1962	18.00
❑ R9-6021 [S]	French Style	1962	25.00
❑ RS-6330 [S]	Gentle on My Mind	1968	18.00
❑ R-6330 [M]	Gentle on My Mind	1968	30.00
❑ R-6242 [M]	Happiness Is Dean Martin	1967	18.00
❑ RS-6242 [S]	Happiness Is Dean Martin	1967	18.00
❑ R-6181 [M]	Houston	1965	15.00
❑ RS-6181 [S]	Houston	1965	18.00
❑ RS-6338	I Take a Lot of Pride in What I Am	1969	18.00
❑ RS-6403	My Woman, My Woman, My Wife	1970	18.00
❑ MS2267	Once in a Lifetime	1978	15.00
❑ R-6170 [M]	(Remember Me) I'm the One Who Loves You	1965	15.00
❑ RS-6170 [S]	(Remember Me) I'm the One Who Loves You	1965	18.00
❑ MS2113	Sittin' on Top of the World	1973	18.00
❑ R-6201 [M]	Somewhere There's a Someone	1966	15.00
❑ RS-6201 [S]	Somewhere There's a Someone	1966	18.00
❑ R6222 [M]	The Dean Martin Christmas Album	1966	18.00
❑ RS6222 [S]	The Dean Martin Christmas Album	1966	25.00
❑ R-6233 [M]	The Dean Martin TV Show	1966	15.00
❑ RS-6233 [S]	The Dean Martin TV Show	1966	18.00
❑ R-6140 [M]	The Door Is Still Open to My Heart	1964	15.00
❑ RS-6140 [S]	The Door Is Still Open to My Heart	1964	18.00
❑ R-6213 [M]	The Hit Sound of Dean Martin	1966	15.00
❑ RS-6213 [S]	The Hit Sound of Dean Martin	1966	18.00
❑ R-6211 [M]	The Silencers	1966	25.00
❑ RS-6211 [S]	The Silencers	1966	30.00
❑ R-6250 [M]	Welcome to My World	1967	18.00
❑ RS-6250 [S]	Welcome to My World	1967	18.00
❑ MS2174	You're the Best Thing That Ever Happened to Me	1973	18.00

TOWER

Number	Title	Yr	NM
❑ T5036 [M]	Happy in Love	1966	18.00
❑ ST5036 [S]	Happy in Love	1966	25.00
❑ T5018 [M]	Relaxin'	1966	25.00
❑ DT5018 [R]	Relaxin'	1966	18.00
❑ T5006 [M]	The Lush Years	1965	25.00
❑ DT5006 [R]	The Lush Years	1965	18.00

WARNER BROS.

Number	Title	Yr	NM
❑ 23870	The Nashville Sessions	1983	15.00

MARTIN, DEWEY, AND MEDICINE BALL

UNI

Number	Title	Yr	NM
❑ 73088	Dewey Martin and Medicine Ball	1970	30.00

MARTIN, FREDDY

CAPITOL

Number	Title	Yr	NM
❑ T2347 [M]	As Time Goes By	1965	12.00
❑ ST2347 [S]	As Time Goes By	1965	15.00
❑ T2098 [M]	Best of the New Favorites	1964	12.00
❑ ST2098 [S]	Best of the New Favorites	1964	15.00
❑ T1269 [M]	C'mon, Let's Dance	1960	15.00
—Black colorband label, logo at left			
❑ T1269 [M]	C'mon, Let's Dance	1962	12.00
—Black colorband label, logo at top			
❑ ST1269 [S]	C'mon, Let's Dance	1960	18.00
—Black colorband label, logo at left			
❑ ST1269 [S]	C'mon, Let's Dance	1962	15.00
—Black colorband label, logo at top			
❑ T2028 [M]	Freddy Martin Plays the Hits	1964	12.00
❑ ST2028 [S]	Freddy Martin Plays the Hits	1964	15.00
❑ T2163 [M]	Freddy Martin Plays the Hits, Vol, 2	1964	12.00
❑ ST2163 [S]	Freddy Martin Plays the Hits, Vol, 2	1964	15.00
❑ T1889 [M]	In a Sentimental Mood	1963	12.00
❑ ST1889 [S]	In a Sentimental Mood	1963	15.00
❑ T1486 [M]	Seems Like Old Times	1961	15.00
—Black colorband label, logo at left			
❑ T1486 [M]	Seems Like Old Times	1962	12.00
—Black colorband label, logo at top			
❑ ST1486 [S]	Seems Like Old Times	1961	18.00
—Black colorband label, logo at left			
❑ ST1486 [S]	Seems Like Old Times	1962	15.00
—Black colorband label, logo at top			
❑ T1582 [M]	The Hits of Freddie Martin	1962	12.00
❑ ST1582 [S]	The Hits of Freddie Martin	1962	15.00
❑ T2018 [M]	Tonight We Love	1964	12.00
❑ ST2018 [S]	Tonight We Love	1964	15.00

DECCA

Number	Title	Yr	NM
❑ DL74908 [R]	Freddy Martin's Greatest Hits	1967	12.00
❑ DL4908 [M]	Freddy Martin's Greatest Hits	1967	18.00
❑ DL4839 [M]	The Most Requested	1967	18.00
❑ DL74839 [R]	The Most Requested	1967	12.00

HINDSIGHT

Number	Title	Yr	NM
❑ HSR-151	Freddy Martin and His Orchestra 1940	198?	12.00
❑ HSR-169	Freddy Martin and His Orchestra 1944-46	198?	12.00
❑ HSR-205	Freddy Martin and His Orchestra 1948, 1952	198?	12.00
❑ HSR-190	Freddy Martin and His Orchestra 1952	198?	12.00

KAPP

Number	Title	Yr	NM
❑ KL-1286 [M]	Dancing Tonight	1963	15.00
❑ KS-3286 [S]	Dancing Tonight	1963	18.00
❑ KL-1261 [M]	Great Waltzes of the World	1962	15.00
❑ KS-3261 [S]	Great Waltzes of the World	1962	18.00
❑ KL-1271 [M]	Great Waltzes of the World, Volume 2	1962	15.00
❑ KS-3271 [S]	Great Waltzes of the World, Volume 2	1962	18.00
❑ KL-1490 [M]	The Most Beautiful Girl in the World	1966	12.00
❑ KS-3490 [S]	The Most Beautiful Girl in the World	1966	15.00

Number	Title	Yr	NM
MCA			
❑ 4021	54 Great Waltzes	197?	15.00
❑ 258	Freddy Martin's Greatest Hits	197?	10.00
❑ 4080	The Best of Freddy Martin	197?	15.00
RCA VICTOR			
❑ LPM-1414 [M]	Freddy Martin at the Cocoanut Grove	1957	25.00
❑ LSP-4044 [R]	The Best of Freddy Martin	1969	12.00
❑ VPM-6072	This Is Freddy Martin	197?	18.00
SUNBEAM			
❑ 313	Music in the Martin Manner 1933-39	197?	12.00

MARTIN, GEORGE

Number	Title	Yr	NM
UNITED ARTISTS			
❑ UAL3383 [M]	A Hard Day's Night	1964	50.00
❑ UAS6383 [S]	A Hard Day's Night	1964	60.00
❑ UAL3420 [M]	George Martin	1965	50.00
❑ UAS6420 [S]	George Martin	1965	50.00
❑ UAL3448 [M]	George Martin Plays "Help	1965	50.00
❑ UAS6448 [S]	George Martin Plays "Help	1965	80.00
❑ UAL3539 [M]	George Martin Salutes the Beatle Girls	1966	50.00
❑ UAS6539 [S]	George Martin Salutes the Beatle Girls	1966	80.00
❑ UAL3647 [M]	London by George	1967	30.00
❑ UAS6647 [S]	London by George	1967	40.00
❑ UAL3377 [M]	Off the Beatle Track	1964	100.00
❑ UAS6377 [S]	Off the Beatle Track	1964	125.00

MARTIN, GRADY

Number	Title	Yr	NM
DECCA			
❑ DL4072 [M]	Big City Lights	1960	25.00
❑ DL74072 [S]	Big City Lights	1960	30.00
❑ DL5566 [10]	Dance-O-Rama	1955	200.00
❑ DL8883 [M]	Hot Time Tonight	1959	25.00
❑ DL78883 [S]	Hot Time Tonight	1959	30.00
❑ DL8292 [M]	Juke Box Jamboree	1956	30.00
❑ DL8181 [M]	Powerhouse Dance Party	1955	30.00
❑ DL4476 [M]	Songs Everybody Knows	1963	18.00
❑ DL74476 [S]	Songs Everybody Knows	1963	25.00
❑ DL4286 [M]	Swingin' Down the River	1962	18.00
❑ DL74286 [S]	Swingin' Down the River	1962	25.00
❑ DL8648 [M]	The Roaring Twenties	1957	30.00

MARTIN, JIMMY

Number	Title	Yr	NM
DECCA			
❑ DL4891 [M]	Big and Country Instrumentals	1967	25.00
❑ DL74891 [S]	Big and Country Instrumentals	1967	25.00
❑ DL4285 [M]	Country Music Time	1962	30.00
❑ DL74285 [S]	Country Music Time	1962	30.00
❑ DL4016 [M]	Good 'n Country	1960	30.00
❑ DL74016 [S]	Good 'n Country	1960	30.00
❑ DL4769 [M]	Mr. Good 'n Country Music	1966	25.00
❑ DL74769 [S]	Mr. Good 'n Country Music	1966	30.00
❑ DL4643 [M]	Sunny Side of the Mountain	1965	25.00
❑ DL74643 [S]	Sunny Side of the Mountain	1965	30.00
❑ DL74996 [S]	Tennessee	1968	25.00
❑ DL4996 [M]	Tennessee	1968	60.00
—Mono is white label promo only			
❑ DL4360 [M]	This World Is Not My Home	1963	30.00
❑ DL74360 [S]	This World Is Not My Home	1963	30.00
❑ DL4536 [M]	Widow Maker	1964	25.00
❑ DL74536 [S]	Widow Maker	1964	30.00

MARTIN, JUAN

Number	Title	Yr	NM
NOVUS			
❑ 3005-1-N	Painter in Sound	1986	12.00
❑ 3036-1-N	Through the Moving Window	1988	12.00

MARTIN, MARILYN

Number	Title	Yr	NM
ATLANTIC			
❑ 81292	Marilyn Martin	1986	10.00
❑ 81814	This Is Serious	1988	10.00

MARTIN, MARY

Number	Title	Yr	NM
COLUMBIA MASTERWORKS			
❑ ML2061 [10]	Mary Martin Sings for You	1949	50.00
DISNEYLAND			
❑ WD-3038 [M]	Hi-Ho!	1958	25.00
❑ STER-3038 [S]	Hi-Ho!	1959	30.00
❑ WDL-4016 [M]	Hi-Ho!	1958	25.00
❑ STER-4016 [S]	Hi-Ho!	1959	30.00
❑ WDL-1038 [M]	Hi-Ho -- Mary Martin Sings and Swings Walt Disney Favorites	1958	25.00
❑ WD-3031 [M]	Mary Martin Sings a Musical Love Story	1958	25.00
❑ STER-3031 [S]	Mary Martin Sings a Musical Love Story	1959	30.00
❑ DQ-1296 [M]	Mary Martin Songs from Rodgers and Hammerstein's The Sound of Music	1966	18.00
❑ STER-1296 [S]	Mary Martin Songs from Rodgers and Hammerstein's The Sound of Music	1966	25.00
❑ ST-3936 [M]	Mary Martin Songs from Rodgers and Hammerstein's The Sound of Music	1966	18.00
❑ STER-3936 [S]	Mary Martin Songs from Rodgers and Hammerstein's The Sound of Music	1966	25.00
❑ ST-2002 [M]	The Little Lame Lamb	1958	50.00
❑ ST-3911 [M]	The Story of Sleeping Beauty	1958	30.00
—Back cover art features Sleeping Beauty and prince			
❑ ST-3911 [M]	The Story of Sleeping Beauty	1969	25.00
—Back cover art features pictures from the booklet			

MARTIN, RAY

Number	Title	Yr	NM
CAPITOL			
❑ T10101 [M]	Global Hop	195?	18.00
❑ T10067 [M]	High Barbaree	195?	18.00
❑ T10066 [M]	International Vibrations	195?	18.00
❑ T10056 [M]	My London	195?	18.00
❑ T10017 [M]	Rainy Night in London	195?	18.00
COLUMBIA			
❑ CL529 [M]	Pop Concert	1953	30.00
ESSEX			
❑ ESLP-105 [10]	I Love	1954	30.00
IMPERIAL			
❑ LP-9085 [M]	Boots and Saddle	1959	15.00
❑ LP-12020 [S]	Boots and Saddle	1959	18.00
❑ LP-9083 [M]	Love of My Life	1959	15.00
❑ LP-12018 [S]	Love of My Life	1959	18.00
❑ LP-9087 [M]	Martin Goes Latin	1959	15.00
❑ LP-12022 [S]	Martin Goes Latin	1959	18.00
JUBILEE			
❑ JLP-1055 [M]	Witchcraft	1958	18.00
LONDON PHASE 4			
❑ SP-44040 [S]	The Sound of Sight: Music for an Experiment in Imagination	1964	25.00
MONUMENT			
❑ LP8068 [M]	Romance in Vienna	1966	12.00
❑ LP18068 [S]	Romance in Vienna	1966	15.00
RCA CAMDEN			
❑ CAL-2102 [M]	Comic Strip Favorites	1967	15.00
❑ CAS-2102 [S]	Comic Strip Favorites	1967	12.00
❑ CAL-913 [M]	Goldfinger and Other Music from James Bond Thrillers	1965	12.00
❑ CAS-913 [S]	Goldfinger and Other Music from James Bond Thrillers	1965	15.00
❑ CAL-976 [M]	Michelle Going for Baroque	1966	12.00
❑ CAS-976 [S]	Michelle Going for Baroque	1966	15.00
❑ CAL-927 [M]	Thunderball and Other Thriller Music	1965	12.00
❑ CAS-927 [S]	Thunderball and Other Thriller Music	1965	15.00
❑ CAL-2181 [M]	Up-Up and Away	1967	15.00
❑ CAS-2181 [S]	Up-Up and Away	1967	12.00
RCA VICTOR			
❑ LSA-2287 [S]	Dynamica	1961	18.00
❑ LPM-2287 [M]	Dynamica	1961	15.00
❑ LSA-2422 [S]	Excitement, Incorporated	1961	18.00
❑ LPM-2422 [M]	Excitement, Incorporated	1961	15.00
❑ LPM-1771 [M]	Pop Goes the Swingin' Marchin' Band	1958	15.00
❑ LSP-1771 [S]	Pop Goes the Swingin' Marchin' Band	1958	25.00
❑ LPM-2130 [M]	The Rockin' Strings of Ray Martin	1959	15.00
❑ LSP-2130 [S]	The Rockin' Strings of Ray Martin	1959	18.00
STRAND			
❑ SL-1037 [M]	Dancing After Dark	1962	15.00

MARTIN, TONY

Number	Title	Yr	NM
20TH CENTURY FOX			
❑ TFM-3138 [M]	Live at Carnegie Hall	1964	15.00
❑ TFS-4138 [S]	Live at Carnegie Hall	1964	18.00
APPLAUSE			
❑ APLP-1003	I'll See You in My Dreams	1982	12.00
❑ R134276	I'll See You in My Dreams	1982	15.00
—RCA Music Service edition			
AUDIO FIDELITY			
❑ AFSD-6200	Tony Martin	1968	18.00
CHART			
❑ CHS-1029	Tony Martin in Nashville	1970	25.00
DECCA			
❑ DL8366 [M]	In the Spotlight	195?	30.00
—Black label, silver print			
❑ DL8286 [M]	Melody Lane	195?	30.00
—Black label, silver print			
❑ DL8287 [M]	Our Love Affair	195?	30.00
—Black label, silver print			
❑ DL5189 [10]	Tony Martin Sings, Vol. 1	1950	40.00
DOT			
❑ DLP-3360 [M]	His Greatest Hits	1961	18.00
❑ DLP-25360 [S]	His Greatest Hits	1961	25.00
KOALA			
❑ KO14140	I'm Always Chasing Rainbows	198?	15.00
MCA			
❑ 1515 [M]	Tony Martin Collectibles	198?	15.00
MCA CORAL			
❑ CB-20019	Melody	1973	15.00
MERCURY			
❑ MG-20079 [M]	Dream Music	195?	30.00
❑ MG-20644 [M]	Golden Hits by Tony Martin	1961	18.00
❑ MG-60644 [S]	Golden Hits by Tony Martin	1961	18.00
❑ MG-20075 [M]	Mr. Song Man	195?	30.00
❑ MG-25004 [10]	Tony Martin	1950	40.00
MOVIETONE			
❑ MTM-1007 [M]	Live at Carnegie Hall	196?	12.00
—Reissue of 20th Century Fox 3138			
❑ MTS-2007 [S]	Live at Carnegie Hall	196?	15.00
—Reissue of 20th Century Fox 4138			
RCA CAMDEN			
❑ CAL-412 [M]	I Get Ideas	195?	18.00
❑ CAL-576 [M]	Tonight	195?	18.00
❑ CAL-484 [M]	Tony Martin Sings of Love	195?	18.00
RCA SPECIAL PRODUCTS			
❑ DML2-0999	The Greatest Singer of Them All!	1991	18.00
RCA VICTOR			
❑ LPM-1357 [M]	A Night at the Copacabana with Tony Martin	1956	30.00
❑ LPM-2107 [M]	Dream a Little Dream	1960	25.00
❑ LSP-2107 [S]	Dream a Little Dream	1960	30.00
❑ LPM-3136 [10]	One for My Baby	195?	40.00
❑ LPM-1263 [M]	Speak to Me of Love	1956	30.00
❑ LPM-1218 [M]	The Night Was Made for Love	1956	30.00
❑ LPM-2146 [M]	Tony Martin at the Desert Inn	1960	25.00
❑ LSP-2146 [S]	Tony Martin at the Desert Inn	1960	30.00
❑ LPM-3126 [10]	World-Wide Favorites	195?	40.00
VOCALION			
❑ VL3610 [M]	Tony Martin	196?	18.00
WING			
❑ MGW-12115 [M]	It's Just Love	196?	15.00
❑ MGW-12203 [M]	Mr. Song Man	196?	15.00

MARTIN, TRADE

Number	Title	Yr	NM
BUDDAH			
❑ BDS-5126	Let Me Touch You	1972	18.00

MARTIN, VINCE, AND FRED NEIL

Number	Title	Yr	NM
ELEKTRA			
❑ EKL-248 [M]	Tear Down the Walls	1964	50.00
❑ EKS-7248 [S]	Tear Down the Walls	1964	60.00

MARTINDALE, WINK

Number	Title	Yr	NM
DOT			
❑ DLP-3403 [M]	Big Bad John	1962	18.00
❑ DLP-25403 [S]	Big Bad John	1962	25.00
❑ DLP-3245 [M]	Deck of Cards	1960	25.00
❑ DLP-25245 [S]	Deck of Cards	1960	30.00
❑ DLP-3692 [M]	Giddyup Go	1966	18.00
❑ DLP-25692 [S]	Giddyup Go	1966	25.00
❑ DLP-3571 [M]	My True Love	1964	18.00
❑ DLP-25571 [S]	My True Love	1964	25.00
❑ DLP-3293 [M]	The Bible Story	1960	18.00
❑ DLP-25293 [S]	The Bible Story	1960	25.00

MARTINELLI, DINO

Number	Title	Yr	NM
HARMONY			
❑ HS11010 [S]	Dino Martinelli Plays Music for Christmas	1959	18.00

MARTINEZ, TONY

Number	Title	Yr	NM
DEL-FI			
❑ DFLP-1205 [M]	The Many Sides of Pepino	1959	30.00
❑ DFLP-1205S [S]	The Many Sides of Pepino	1959	40.00

MARTINO, AL

Number	Title	Yr	NM
20TH CENTURY FOX			
❑ SF-3025 [M]	Al Martino	1959	30.00
❑ SFX-3025 [S]	Al Martino	1959	30.00
❑ TF-4168 [M]	Al Martino Sings	196?	25.00
❑ TFS-4168 [S]	Al Martino Sings	196?	30.00
❑ SF-3032 [M]	Sing Along with Al Martino	1959	30.00
❑ SFX-3032 [S]	Sing Along with Al Martino	1959	30.00
❑ XG-5009 [M]	When Your Lover Has Gone	1963	25.00
❑ SXG-5009 [S]	When Your Lover Has Gone	1963	30.00
CAPITOL			
❑ STCL-572	Al Martino	1971	30.00
❑ T2165 [M]	A Merry Christmas from Al Martino	1964	15.00
❑ ST2165 [S]	A Merry Christmas from Al Martino	1964	18.00
❑ ST-405	Can't Help Falling in Love	1970	15.00
❑ T2733 [M]	Daddy's Little Girl	1967	18.00
❑ ST2733 [S]	Daddy's Little Girl	1967	18.00
❑ STBB-526	Here in My Heart/Yesterday	1970	18.00
❑ T1914 [M]	I Love You Because	1963	15.00
❑ ST1914 [S]	I Love You Because	1963	18.00
❑ T2107 [M]	I Love You More and More Every Day/Tears and Roses	1964	15.00
❑ ST2107 [S]	I Love You More and More Every Day/Tears and Roses	1964	18.00
❑ STBB-713	I Wish You Love/Losing You	1971	18.00
❑ ST-11302	I Won't Last a Day Without You	1974	12.00
❑ ST-379	Jean	1969	15.00
❑ T2040 [M]	Living a Lie	1964	15.00
❑ ST2040 [S]	Living a Lie	1964	18.00
❑ ST2908	Love Is Blue	1968	18.00
❑ ST-11071	Love Theme from "The Godfather	1972	12.00

Number	Title	Yr	NM
❑ SM-11071	Love Theme from "The Godfather	1977	10.00
—Reissue with new prefix			
❑ T2780 [M]	Mary in the Morning	1967	18.00
❑ ST2780 [S]	Mary in the Morning	1967	18.00
❑ T2362 [M]	My Cherie	1965	15.00
❑ ST2362 [S]	My Cherie	1965	18.00
❑ ST-497	My Heart Sings	1970	15.00
❑ T1975 [M]	Painted, Tainted Rose	1963	15.00
❑ ST1975 [S]	Painted, Tainted Rose	1963	18.00
❑ ST-180	Sausalito	1969	15.00
❑ ST-11572	Sing My Love Songs	1976	12.00
❑ T2312 [M]	Somebody Else Is Taking My Place	1965	15.00
❑ ST2312 [S]	Somebody Else Is Taking My Place	1965	18.00
❑ T2435 [M]	Spanish Eyes	1966	15.00
❑ ST2435 [S]	Spanish Eyes	1966	18.00
❑ ST-793	Summer of '42	1971	15.00
❑ SKAO2946	The Best of Al Martino	1968	18.00
❑ SM-2946	The Best of Al Martino	197?	12.00
—Reissue with new prefix			
❑ SN-16074	The Best of Al Martino	1981	10.00
—Budget-line reissue			
❑ T1774 [M]	The Exciting Voice of Al Martino	1962	18.00
❑ ST1774 [S]	The Exciting Voice of Al Martino	1962	25.00
❑ T1907 [M]	The Italian Voice of Al Martino	1963	18.00
❑ ST1907 [S]	The Italian Voice of Al Martino	1963	25.00
❑ ST-11741	The Next Hundred Years	1978	12.00
❑ SQBO-91280	The Romantic World of Al Martino	196?	25.00
—Capitol Record Club exclusive			
❑ T2528 [M]	Think I'll Go Somewhere and Cry Myself to Sleep	1966	15.00
❑ ST2528 [S]	Think I'll Go Somewhere and Cry Myself to Sleep	1966	18.00
❑ ST2843	This Is Al Martino	1968	18.00
❑ T2592 [M]	This Is Love	1966	15.00
❑ ST2592 [S]	This Is Love	1966	18.00
❑ T2654 [M]	This Love for You	1967	18.00
❑ ST2654 [S]	This Love for You	1967	18.00
❑ ST-11366	To the Door of the Sun	1975	12.00
❑ SM-11679	To the Door of the Sun	1977	10.00
—Reissue of 11366			
❑ ST2983	Wake Up to Me Gentle	1968	18.00
❑ T2200 [M]	We Could	1964	15.00
❑ ST2200 [S]	We Could	1964	18.00

MOVIETONE

❑ MTM2015 [M]	All of Me	1967	25.00
❑ MTS72015 [S]	All of Me	1967	18.00
❑ MTM2002 [M]	That Old Feeling	196?	18.00
❑ MTS72002 [S]	That Old Feeling	196?	25.00

PICKWICK

❑ SPC-3049	Don't Go to Strangers	196?	15.00
❑ SPC-3276	Mary in the Morning	197?	12.00

SPRINGBOARD

❑ 4074	Time After Time	1978	10.00

MARTINO, PAT

COBBLESTONE

❑ 9015	The Visit	1972	25.00

FANTASY

❑ OJC-355	Baiyina (The Clear Evidence)	198?	12.00
❑ OJC-397	Desperado	1989	15.00
❑ OJC-248	East!	198?	12.00
❑ OJC-195	El Hombre	198?	12.00
❑ OJC-223	Strings!	198?	12.00

MUSE

❑ MR-5039	Consciousness	1975	15.00
❑ MR-5075	Exit	1976	15.00
❑ MR-5096	Footprints	1977	15.00
❑ MR-5026	Live!	1974	15.00
❑ MR-5328	The Return	198?	12.00
❑ MR-5090	We'll Be Together Again	1977	15.00

PRESTIGE

❑ PRST-7589	Baiyina (The Clear Evidence)	1968	18.00
❑ PRST-7795	Desperado	1970	18.00
❑ PRST-7562	East!	1968	18.00
❑ PRST-7513 [S]	El Hombre	1967	18.00
❑ PRLP-7513 [M]	El Hombre	1967	30.00
❑ PRLP-7547 [M]	Strings!	1967	30.00
❑ PRST-7547 [S]	Strings!	1967	18.00

WARNER BROS.

❑ BS2977	Joyous Lake	1977	12.00
❑ BS2921	Starbright	1976	12.00

MARTYN, JOHN & BEVERLEY

4 MEN WITH BEARDS

❑ 4M803LP [B]	Stormbringer!		25.00

MARVELETTES, THE

MOTOWN

❑ M7-827	Anthology	1975	18.00
❑ M5-180V1	Greatest Hits	1981	12.00
—Reissue of Tamla 253			
❑ 5266ML	Please Mr. Postman	1982	12.00
—Reissue of Tamla 228			

TAMLA

❑ T-253 [M]	Greatest Hits	1966	30.00
—Yellow cover			
❑ T-253 [M]	Greatest Hits	1967	30.00
—Green cover			
❑ TS-253 [S]	Greatest Hits	1966	40.00
—Yellow cover			
❑ TS-253 [S]	Greatest Hits	1967	25.00
—Green cover			
❑ TS-288	In Full Bloom	1969	18.00
❑ T-231 [M]	Playboy	1962	500.00
—Yellow label with overlapping record and globe logo			
❑ T-231 [M]	Playboy	1963	250.00
—Yellow label with side-by-side globes logo			
❑ T-231 [M]	Playboy	1962	600.00
—White label			
❑ T-228 [M]	Please Mr. Postman	1961	600.00
—White label			
❑ T-228 [M]	Please Mr. Postman	1963	300.00
—Yellow label with globes logo			
❑ T-243 [M]	Recorded Live on Stage	1963	80.00
❑ TS-305	Return of the Marvelettes	1970	18.00
❑ T-229 [M]	Smash Hits of 62'	1962	1200.00
—Title as listed on front cover; large black "M" with song titles in circles; VG value 600; VG+ value 900			
❑ T-286 [M]	Sophisticated Soul	1968	40.00
❑ TS-286 [S]	Sophisticated Soul	1968	25.00
❑ T-229 [M]	The Marveletts Sing	1962	500.00
—Title as listed on front cover (misspelled); all-black cover with white circles			
❑ T-229 [M]	The Marveletts Sing	1963	250.00
—Yellow label with side-by-side globes logo			
❑ T-274 [M]	The Marvelettttes	1967	30.00
❑ TS-274 [S]	The Marvelettttes	1967	25.00
❑ T-237 [M]	The Marvelous Marvelettes	1963	150.00

MARVELOWS, THE

ABC

❑ S-643	The Mighty Marvelows	1968	30.00

MARVIN AND JOHNNY

CROWN

❑ CLP-5381 [M]	Marvin and Johnny	1963	50.00
❑ CST-381 [R]	Marvin and Johnny	1963	15.00

MARX, BILL

VEE JAY

❑ LP-3032 [M]	Jazz Kaleidoscope	1962	25.00
❑ SR-3032 [S]	Jazz Kaleidoscope	1962	30.00
❑ LP-3035 [M]	My Son, the Folk Swinger	1963	25.00
❑ SR-3035 [S]	My Son, the Folk Swinger	1963	30.00

MARX, DICK, AND JOHN FRIGO

BRUNSWICK

❑ BL54006 [M]	Two Much Piano	1955	40.00

MARX, DICK

OMEGA

❑ OML-1002 [M]	Marx Makes Broadway	1958	40.00
❑ OSL-2 [S]	Marx Makes Broadway	1959	30.00
—The front cover of the above LP spells his last name "Marks," though it is spelled correctly on the label and back cover			

MARX, GROUCHO

DECCA

❑ DL5405 [10]	Hooray for Captain Spaulding	1954	250.00

MARX, HARPO

MERCURY

❑ MG-20363 [M]	Harpo at Work!	1959	80.00
❑ SR-60016 [S]	Harpo at Work!	1959	100.00
❑ MG-20232 [M]	Harpo in Hi-Fi	1957	100.00

RCA VICTOR

❑ LPM-27 [10]	Harp by Harpo	1952	250.00

WING

❑ MGW-12164 [M]	Harpo	1960	40.00

MARX, RICHARD

CAPITOL

❑ C1-595874	Rush Street	1992	30.00
—Columbia House edition; only U.S. vinyl version			

EMI

❑ E1-90380	Repeat Offender	1989	10.00
❑ E1-590380	Repeat Offender	1989	12.00
—Columbia House edition			

MANHATTAN

❑ ST-53049	Richard Marx	1987	10.00
❑ ST-553049	Richard Marx	1987	12.00
—Columbia House edition			
❑ R134073	Richard Marx	1987	15.00
—BMG Direct Marketing edition			

MARY BUTTERWORTH

CUSTOM FIDELITY

❑ 2092	Mary Butterworth	1969	300.00

MARYLAND JAZZ BAND

GHB

❑ GHB-178	25 Years of Jazz with the Maryland Jazz Band	1987	12.00

MAS, JEAN-PIERRE, AND CESARIUS ALVIM

INNER CITY

❑ IC-1014	Lourmel	197?	18.00

MASEKELA, HUGH

ABC IMPULSE!

❑ IA-9343	African Connection	1978	15.00

BLUE THUMB

❑ BT-6003	Home Is Where the Music Is	1973	12.00
❑ BT-6015	I Am Not Afraid	1974	12.00
❑ BT-62	Introducing Hedzoleh Sounds	1972	12.00

CASABLANCA

❑ NBLP7023	Colonial Man	1976	12.00
❑ NBLP7036	Melody Maker	1977	12.00
❑ NBLP7017	The Boy's Doin' It	1975	12.00
❑ NBLP7079	You Told Your Mama	1978	12.00

CHISA

❑ CS-803	Reconstruction	1970	15.00
❑ CS-808	Union of South Africa	1971	15.00

JIVE

❑ JL-8210	Techno Bush	1984	12.00
❑ JL-8382	Waiting for the Rain	1985	12.00

MERCURY

❑ SR-61109	Grr	1969	15.00
❑ MG-20797 [M]	The Trumpet of Hugh Masekela	1963	18.00
❑ SR-60797 [S]	The Trumpet of Hugh Masekela	1963	25.00

MGM

❑ GAS-116	Hugh Masekela (Golden Archive Series)	1970	15.00
❑ E-4415 [M]	Hugh Masekela's Next Album	1966	15.00
❑ SE-4415 [S]	Hugh Masekela's Next Album	1966	18.00
❑ E-4372 [M]	The Americanization of Ooga Booga	1966	15.00
❑ SE-4372 [S]	The Americanization of Ooga Booga	1966	18.00
❑ E-4468 [M]	The Lasting Impression of Hugh Masekela	1967	18.00
❑ SE-4468 [S]	The Lasting Impression of Hugh Masekela	1967	15.00

NOVUS

❑ 3070-1-R	Uptownship	1990	15.00

UNI

❑ 3015 [M]	Hugh Masekela Is Alive and Well at the Whisky	1967	25.00
❑ 73015 [S]	Hugh Masekela Is Alive and Well at the Whisky	1967	15.00
❑ 3010 [M]	Hugh Masekela's Latest	1967	18.00
❑ 73010 [S]	Hugh Masekela's Latest	1967	15.00
❑ 73041	Masekela	1969	15.00
❑ 73051	Masekela — Vol. 2	1970	15.00
❑ 73028	The Promise of a Future	1968	15.00

VERVE

❑ V6-8651	24 Karat Hits	1968	18.00

WARNER BROS.

❑ 25566	Tomorrow	1987	12.00

MASHMAKHAN

EPIC

❑ E30235	Mashmakhan	1970	16.00
❑ E30813	The Family	1971	16.00

MASKED MARAUDERS, THE

DEITY

❑ RS6378	The Masked Marauders	1969	18.00

MASLAK, KESHAVAN

BLACK SAINT

❑ BSR-0079	Blaster Master	198?	15.00

MASON, BARBARA, AND BUNNY SIGLER

CURTOM

❑ CU5014	Locked in This Position	1977	18.00

MASON, BARBARA

ARCTIC

❑ ALPS-1004	Oh, How It Hurts	1968	80.00
❑ ALP-1000 [M]	Yes, I'm Ready	1965	80.00
❑ ALPS-1000 [P]	Yes, I'm Ready	1965	120.00

BUDDAH

❑ BDS-5117	Give Me Your Love	1972	18.00
❑ BDS-5140	Lady Love	1973	25.00
❑ BDS-5628	Love's the Thing	1975	25.00
❑ BDS-5610	Transition	1974	25.00

NATIONAL GENERAL

❑ 2001	If You Knew Him Like I Do	1970	60.00

PRELUDE

❑ 12159	I Am Your Woman, She Is Your Wife	1978	25.00

Number	Title	Yr	NM

MASON, CHRISTOPHER

OPTIMISM
Number	Title	Yr	NM
❑ OP-3218	Something Beautiful	198?	12.00

MASON, DAVE, AND CASS ELLIOT

BLUE THUMB
❑ BTS-8825	Dave Mason and Cass Elliot	1971	25.00

MASON, DAVE

BLUE THUMB
❑ BTS-19	All Together	1970	200.00
—Erroneous pressing of "Alone Together"			
❑ BTS-19	Alone Together	1970	25.00
—Originals on multicolored vinyl			
❑ BTS-8819	Alone Together	1971	50.00
—Capitol-distributed black vinyl reissue			
❑ BTS-19	Alone Together	1975	15.00
—Multicolor label with "ABC" logo			
❑ ABCD-880	Dave Mason At His Best	1975	12.00
❑ BTS-54	Dave Mason Is Alive!	1973	18.00
❑ BTS-34	Headkeeper	1972	18.00
❑ BT-6013	The Best of Dave Mason	1974	12.00
❑ BT-6032	Very Best of Dave Mason	1978	12.00

CHUMLEY
❑ 00101	Some Assembly Required	1987	12.00

COLUMBIA
❑ PG34174	Certified Live	1976	15.00
❑ PC33096	Dave Mason	1974	12.00
—No bar code on cover			
❑ PCQ33096 [Q]	Dave Mason	1974	25.00
❑ PC33096	Dave Mason	198?	10.00
—Budget-line reissue with bar code			
❑ KC31721	It's Like You Never Left	1973	12.00
❑ CQ31721 [Q]	It's Like You Never Left	1973	25.00
❑ PC31721	It's Like You Never Left	197?	10.00
—Reissue with new prefix			
❑ PC34680	Let It Flow	1977	12.00
—No bar code on cover			
❑ PC34680	Let It Flow	198?	10.00
—Budget-line reissue with bar code			
❑ JC35285	Mariposa de Oro	1978	12.00
❑ JC36144	Old Crest on a New Wave	1980	12.00
❑ PC33698	Split Coconut	1975	12.00
❑ PCQ33698 [Q]	Split Coconut	1975	25.00
❑ FC37089	The Best of Dave Mason	1981	12.00
❑ PC37089	The Best of Dave Mason	1983	10.00
—Budget-line reissue			

MCA
❑ 27035	Alone Together	198?	10.00
—Reissue of Blue Thumb 19			
❑ 11319	Alone Together	1995	25.00
—"Heavy Vinyl" gatefold reissue			
❑ 714	Dave Mason At His Best	198?	10.00
—Reissue of Blue Thumb 880			
❑ 713	Dave Mason Is Alive	198?	10.00
—Reissue of Blue Thumb 54			
❑ 712	Headkeeper	198?	10.00
—Reissue of Blue Thumb 34			
❑ 800	The Best of Dave Mason	1981	10.00
—Reissue of Blue Thumb 6013			
❑ 42086	Two Hearts	1988	12.00
❑ 715	Very Best of Dave Mason	198?	10.00
—Reissue of Blue Thumb 6032			

S&P
❑ 503	It's Like You Never Left	2003	25.00
—Reissue on 180-gram vinyl			

MASON, JACKIE

VERVE
❑ V-15045 [M]	Great Moments in Comedy	1964	25.00
❑ V-15033 [M]	I'm the Greatest Comedian in the World Only Nobody Knows It Yet	1962	25.00
❑ V-15034 [M]	I Want to Leave You with the Words of a Great Comedian	1963	25.00

WARNER BROS.
❑ 25603	The World According to Me!	1987	12.00

MASON, JAMES

CHIAROSCURO
❑ 189	Rhythm of Life	1978	15.00

MASON DIXON

CAPITOL
❑ C1-90120	Exception to the Rule	1989	12.00

MASON PROFFIT

AMPEX
❑ A-10138	Last Night I Had the Strangest Dream	1971	30.00

HAPPY TIGER
❑ HT-1019	Movin' Toward Happiness	1971	25.00
❑ HT-1009	Wanted! Mason Proffit	1970	30.00

WARNER BROS.
❑ BS2704 [B]	Bareback Rider	1973	25.00

Number	Title	Yr	NM
❑ 2WS2746	Come and Gone	1974	25.00
❑ BS2657 [B]	Rockfish Crossing	1972	25.00

MASQUERADERS, THE

ABC/HBS
❑ ABCD-921	Everybody Wanna Live On	1975	18.00
❑ AB-962	Love Anonymous	1976	18.00

BANG
❑ NJZ36321	The Masqueraders	1980	18.00

MASSEY, WAYNE

POLYDOR
❑ PD-1-6309	One Life to Live	1980	15.00

MASTER CYLINDER

INNER CITY
❑ IC-1112	Elsewhere	198?	30.00

MASTER FLEET

SUSSEX
❑ SRA-8028	High on the Sea	1974	40.00

MASTER P

NO LIMIT/PRIORITY
❑ P150969	The Ghettos Tryin to Kill Me!	1997	18.00
—Generic black sleeve with center hole			

MASTERS, JOE

COLUMBIA
❑ CS9398 [S]	The Jazz Mass	1967	25.00
❑ CL2598 [M]	The Jazz Mass	1967	30.00

DISCOVERY
❑ 785	The Jazz Mass	197?	18.00

MASTERS, MARK

SEA BREEZE
❑ SB-2022	Early Start	198?	15.00
❑ SB-2033	Silver Threads Among the Blues	1987	15.00

MASTERSOUNDS, THE

FANTASY
❑ 3316 [M]	A Date with the Mastersounds	1961	40.00
—Red vinyl			
❑ 3316 [M]	A Date with the Mastersounds	1962	30.00
—Black vinyl			
❑ 8062 [S]	A Date with the Mastersounds	1961	30.00
—Blue vinyl			
❑ 8062 [S]	A Date with the Mastersounds	1962	25.00
—Black vinyl			
❑ OJC-282	A Date with the Mastersounds	1987	12.00
❑ OJC-280	Swinging with the Mastersounds	1987	12.00
❑ 3305 [M]	Swingin' with the Mastersounds	1960	40.00
—Red vinyl			
❑ 3305 [M]	Swingin' with the Mastersounds	1962	30.00
—Black vinyl			
❑ 8050 [S]	Swingin' with the Mastersounds	1961	30.00
—Blue vinyl			
❑ 8050 [S]	Swingin' with the Mastersounds	1962	25.00
—Black vinyl			
❑ 3327 [M]	The Mastersounds on Tour	1961	40.00
—Red vinyl			
❑ 3327 [M]	The Mastersounds on Tour	1962	30.00
—Black vinyl			
❑ 8066 [S]	The Mastersounds on Tour	1961	30.00
—Blue vinyl			
❑ 8066 [S]	The Mastersounds on Tour	1962	25.00
—Black vinyl			

PACIFIC JAZZ
❑ PJM-403 [M]	Introducing the Mastersounds	1957	50.00
❑ PJM-405 [M]	The King and I	1958	50.00

WORLD PACIFIC
❑ WP-1260 [M]	Ballads and Blues	1959	40.00
❑ ST-1019 [S]	Ballads and Blues	1959	30.00
❑ WP-1252 [M]	Flower Drum Song	1958	40.00
❑ ST-1012 [S]	Flower Drum Song	1958	30.00
❑ WP-1280 [M]	Happy Holidays from Many Lands	1959	40.00
❑ ST-1030 [S]	Happy Holidays from Many Lands	1959	30.00
❑ WP-1271 [M]	Jazz Showcase	1959	30.00
—Reissue of Pacific Jazz 403			
❑ WP-1243 [M]	Kismet	1958	40.00
❑ ST-1010 [S]	Kismet	1958	30.00
❑ WP-1272 [M]	The King and I	1959	30.00
—Reissue of Pacific Jazz 405			
❑ ST-1017 [S]	The King and I	1959	30.00

Number	Title	Yr	NM
❑ WP-1269 [M]	The Mastersounds in Concert	1959	40.00
❑ ST-1026 [S]	The Mastersounds in Concert	1959	30.00
❑ WP-1284 [M]	The Mastersounds Play Horace Silver	1960	40.00
❑ ST-1284 [S]	The Mastersounds Play Horace Silver	1960	30.00

MATCHBOX 20

LAVA
❑ 92721	Yourself or Someone Like You	1997	15.00

MATHEWS, MAT

AUDIOPHILE
❑ AP-219	Mat Mathews and Friends	1987	12.00

BRUNSWICK
❑ BL54013 [M]	Bag's Groove	1956	80.00

DAWN
❑ DLP-1104 [M]	The Modern Art of Jazz	1956	100.00

MATHEWS, RONNIE

BEE HIVE
❑ 7011	Legacy	197?	15.00
❑ 7008	Roots, Branches and Dances	197?	15.00

PRESTIGE
❑ PRLP-7303 [M]	Doin' the Thang	1964	30.00
❑ PRST-7303 [S]	Doin' the Thang	1964	40.00

TIMELESS
❑ LPSJP-304	Selena's Dance	1990	15.00

MATHIS, COUNTRY JOHNNY

HILLTOP GOSPEL
❑ GS-7004	Country Johnny Mathis	1965	30.00

LITTLE DARLIN'
❑ 8007	He Keeps Me Singin'	1967	25.00

MATHIS, JOHNNY

COLUMBIA
❑ FC38718	A Special Part of Me	1984	12.00
❑ FC40447	Christmas Eve with Johnny Mathis	1986	12.00
❑ 3C38306	Christmas with Johnny Mathis	1982	10.00
—Reissue of Columbia LE 10196 with same contents			
❑ C30210	Close to You	1970	15.00
❑ JC36505	Different Kinda Different	1980	12.00
❑ CL1422 [M]	Faithfully	1959	25.00
—Red and black label with six "eye" logos			
❑ CL1422 [M]	Faithfully	1962	18.00
—Red label with either "Guaranteed High Fidelity" or "360 Sound Mono			
❑ CS8219 [S]	Faithfully	1959	30.00
—Red and black label with six "eye" logos			
❑ CS8219 [S]	Faithfully	1962	25.00
—Red "360 Sound" label			
❑ PC33887	Feelings	1975	12.00
❑ PC39468	For Christmas	1984	10.00
❑ FC37748	Friends in Love	1982	12.00
❑ CS9923	Give Me Your Love for Christmas	1969	15.00
❑ CL1119 [M]	Good Night, Dear Lord	1958	30.00
—Red and black label with six "eye" logos			
❑ CL1119 [M]	Good Night, Dear Lord	1962	18.00
—Red label with either "Guaranteed High Fidelity" or "360 Sound Mono			
❑ CS8012 [S]	Good Night, Dear Lord	1958	40.00
—Red and black label with six "eye" logos			
❑ CS8012 [S]	Good Night, Dear Lord	1962	25.00
—Red "360 Sound" label			
❑ CL1351 [M]	Heavenly	1959	25.00
—Red and black label with six "eye" logos			
❑ CL1351 [M]	Heavenly	1962	18.00
—Red label with either "Guaranteed High Fidelity" or "360 Sound Mono			
❑ CS8152 [S]	Heavenly	1959	30.00
—Red and black label with six "eye" logos			
❑ CS8152 [S]	Heavenly	1962	25.00
—Red "360 Sound" label			
❑ CS8152 [S]	Heavenly	1971	12.00
—Orange label			
❑ CG33621	Heavenly/Faithfully	1975	15.00
❑ PC34872	Hold Me, Thrill Me, Kiss Me	1977	12.00
❑ CL1623 [M]	I'll Buy You a Star	1961	18.00
—Red and black label with six "eye" logos			
❑ CL1623 [M]	I'll Buy You a Star	1962	15.00
—Red label with either "Guaranteed High Fidelity" or "360 Sound Mono			
❑ CS8423 [S]	I'll Buy You a Star	1961	25.00
—Red and black label with six "eye" logos			
❑ CS8423 [S]	I'll Buy You a Star	1962	18.00
—Red "360 Sound" label			
❑ CL2143 [M]	I'll Search My Heart and Other Great Hits	1964	15.00
❑ CS8943 [S]	I'll Search My Heart and Other Great Hits	1964	18.00
—Red "360 Sound" label			
❑ KC32435	I'm Coming Home	1973	12.00
❑ CQ32435 [Q]	I'm Coming Home	1973	25.00

Number	Title	Yr	NM
❑ PC32435	I'm Coming Home	198?	10.00
—Budget-line reissue			
❑ OC44336	In the Still of the Night	1989	15.00
❑ PC34117	I Only Have Eyes for You	1976	12.00
❑ CL2044 [M]	Johnny	1963	15.00
❑ CS8844 [S]	Johnny	1963	18.00
—Red "360 Sound" label			
❑ CL887 [M]	Johnny Mathis	1957	50.00
❑ KG31345	Johnny Mathis' All-Time Greatest Hits	1972	18.00
❑ PC34667	Johnny Mathis' Greatest Hits	1977	12.00
❑ KG30979	Johnny Mathis In Person	1972	18.00
❑ 2CQ30979 [Q]	Johnny Mathis In Person	1972	30.00
❑ FC38699	Johnny Mathis Live	1983	12.00
❑ G30350	Johnny Mathis Sings the Music of Bacharach & Kaempfert	1970	18.00
❑ CL1133 [M]	Johnny's Greatest Hits	1958	30.00
—Red and black label with six "eye" logos			
❑ CL1133 [M]	Johnny's Greatest Hits	1962	18.00
—Red label with either "Guaranteed High Fidelity" or "360 Sound Mono			
❑ CS8634 [R]	Johnny's Greatest Hits	1963	15.00
❑ CL1526 [M]	Johnny's Mood	1960	25.00
—Red and black label with six "eye" logos			
❑ CL1526 [M]	Johnny's Mood	1962	18.00
—Red label with either "Guaranteed High Fidelity" or "360 Sound Mono			
❑ CS8326 [S]	Johnny's Mood	1960	30.00
—Red and black label with six "eye" logos			
❑ CS8326 [S]	Johnny's Mood	1962	25.00
—Red "360 Sound" label			
❑ CL2016 [M]	Johnny's Newest Hits	1963	15.00
❑ CS8816 [S]	Johnny's Newest Hits	1963	18.00
—Red "360 Sound" label			
❑ KC32258	Killing Me Softly with Her Song	1973	12.00
❑ CL1711 [M]	Live It Up!	1962	18.00
—Red and black label with six "eye" logos			
❑ CL1711 [M]	Live It Up!	1962	15.00
—Red label with either "Guaranteed High Fidelity" or "360 Sound Mono			
❑ CS8511 [S]	Live It Up!	1962	25.00
—Red and black label with six "eye" logos; add 1/3 if portrait is there			
❑ CS8511 [S]	Live It Up!	1962	18.00
—Red "360 Sound" label			
❑ CS9637 [S]	Love Is Blue	1968	18.00
❑ CL2837 [M]	Love Is Blue	1968	30.00
❑ C30499	Love Story	1971	15.00
❑ PC30499	Love Story	198?	10.00
—Budget-line reissue			
❑ CS9909	Love Theme from "Romeo and Juliet	1969	18.00
—Red "360 Sound" label			
❑ CS9909	Love Theme from "Romeo and Juliet	1971	12.00
—Orange label			
❑ PC34441	Mathis Is…	1977	12.00
❑ JC36216	Mathis Magic	1979	12.00
❑ KC32114	Me and Mrs. Jones	1973	12.00
❑ CQ32114 [Q]	Me and Mrs. Jones	1973	25.00
❑ CL1195 [M]	Merry Christmas	1958	40.00
—Original cover has Johnny standing, holding skis and poles			
❑ CS8021 [S]	Merry Christmas	1959	30.00
—Original cover has Johnny standing, holding skis and poles; red and black label with six "eye" logos			
❑ CL1195 [M]	Merry Christmas	196?	30.00
—Second cover has Johnny sitting, with skis and poles in snow			
❑ CS8021 [S]	Merry Christmas	196?	25.00
—Second cover has Johnny sitting, with skis and poles in snow			
❑ CL1344 [M]	More Johnny's Greatest Hits	1959	30.00
—Red and black label with six "eye" logos			
❑ CL1344 [M]	More Johnny's Greatest Hits	1962	18.00
—Red label with either "Guaranteed High Fidelity" or "360 Sound Mono			
❑ CS8150 [S]	More Johnny's Greatest Hits	1959	30.00
—Red and black label with six "eye" logos			
❑ CS8150 [S]	More Johnny's Greatest Hits	1962	25.00
—Red "360 Sound" label			
❑ CS8150 [S]	More Johnny's Greatest Hits	1971	12.00
—Orange label			
❑ OC44156	Once in a While	1988	12.00
❑ CL1270 [M]	Open Fire, Two Guitars	1959	30.00
—Red and black label with six "eye" logos			
❑ CL1270 [M]	Open Fire, Two Guitars	1962	18.00
—Red label with either "Guaranteed High Fidelity" or "360 Sound Mono			
❑ CS8056 [S]	Open Fire, Two Guitars	1959	40.00
—Red and black label with six "eye" logos			
❑ CS8056 [S]	Open Fire, Two Guitars	1962	25.00
—Red "360 Sound" label			
❑ CS9871	People	1969	18.00
❑ CL1644 [M]	Portrait of Johnny	1961	18.00
—Red and black label with six "eye" logos; add 1/3 if portrait is there			
❑ CL1644 [M]	Portrait of Johnny	1962	15.00
—Red label with either "Guaranteed High Fidelity" or "360 Sound Mono			
❑ CS8444 [S]	Portrait of Johnny	1961	25.00
—Red and black label with six "eye" logos; add 1/3 if portrait is there			
❑ CS8444 [S]	Portrait of Johnny	1962	18.00
—Red "360 Sound" label			
❑ CS1005	Raindrops Keep Fallin' on My Head	1970	15.00
❑ CL1915 [M]	Rapture	1962	15.00
❑ CS8715 [S]	Rapture	1962	18.00
—Red "360 Sound" label			
❑ FC39601	Right from the Heart	1985	12.00
❑ CL2098 [M]	Romantically	1963	15.00
❑ CS8898 [S]	Romantically	1963	18.00
—Red "360 Sound" label			
❑ C35578	Romantically	1978	10.00
❑ KC31626	Song Sung Blue	1972	15.00
❑ CQ31626 [Q]	Song Sung Blue	1972	25.00
❑ CL1165 [M]	Swing Softly	1958	30.00
—Red and black label with six "eye" logos			
❑ CL1165 [M]	Swing Softly	1962	18.00
—Red label with either "Guaranteed High Fidelity" or "360 Sound Mono			
❑ CS8023 [S]	Swing Softly	1958	40.00
—Red and black label with six "eye" logos			
❑ CL2223 [M]	The Ballads of Broadway	1964	15.00
❑ CS9023 [S]	The Ballads of Broadway	1964	18.00
—Red "360 Sound" label			
❑ CS9024 [S]	The Ballads of Broadway	1964	18.00
—Red "360 Sound" label			
❑ JC35649	The Best Days of My Life	1979	12.00
❑ PC35649	The Best Days of My Life	1985	10.00
—Budget-line reissue			
❑ JC36871	The Best of Johnny Mathis 1975-1980	1980	12.00
❑ C2X37440	The First 25 Years -- The Silver Anniversary Album	1981	15.00
❑ KC31342	The First Time Ever (I Saw Your Face)	1972	15.00
❑ CQ31342 [Q]	The First Time Ever (I Saw Your Face)	1972	25.00
❑ PC31342	The First Time Ever (I Saw Your Face)	198?	10.00
—Budget-line reissue			
❑ C2L34 [M]	The Great Years	1964	18.00
❑ C2S834 [S]	The Great Years	1964	25.00
—Red "360 Sound" label			
❑ KC33251	The Heart of a Woman	1974	12.00
❑ FC40372	The Hollywood Musicals	1986	12.00
—With Henry Mancini			
❑ CS9872	The Impossible Dream	1969	18.00
—Red "360 Sound" label			
❑ CS9872	The Impossible Dream	1971	12.00
—Orange label			
❑ C2L17 [M]	The Rhythms and Ballads of Broadway	1960	30.00
—Red and black label with six "eye" logos			
❑ C2L17 [M]	The Rhythms and Ballads of Broadway	1962	25.00
—Red label with either "Guaranteed High Fidelity" or "360 Sound Mono			
❑ C2S803 [S]	The Rhythms and Ballads of Broadway	1960	30.00
—Red and black label with six "eye" logos			
❑ C2S803 [S]	The Rhythms and Ballads of Broadway	1962	30.00
—Red "360 Sound" label			
❑ CL2224 [M]	The Rhythms of Broadway	1964	15.00
❑ CS9705 [S]	Those Were the Days	1968	18.00
❑ CL2905 [M]	Those Were the Days	1968	40.00
❑ CL2726 [M]	Up, Up and Away	1967	18.00
❑ CS9526 [S]	Up, Up and Away	1967	18.00
❑ CL1078 [M]	Warm	1957	30.00
—Red and black label with six "eye" logos			
❑ CL1078 [M]	Warm	1962	18.00
—Red label with either "Guaranteed High Fidelity" or "360 Sound Mono			
❑ CS8039 [S]	Warm	1958	40.00
—Red and black label with six "eye" logos			
❑ CS8039 [S]	Warm	1962	25.00
—Red "360 Sound" label			
❑ GP2	Warm/Open Fire, Two Guitars	1969	18.00
❑ C32963	What'll I Do	1974	12.00
❑ PC33420	When Will I See You Again	1975	12.00
❑ CL1028 [M]	Wonderful Wonderful	1957	30.00
—Red and black label with six "eye" logos			
❑ CL1028 [M]	Wonderful Wonderful	1962	18.00
—Red label with either "Guaranteed High Fidelity" or "360 Sound Mono			
❑ CS9046 [R]	Wonderful Wonderful	1964	15.00
❑ JC35359	You Light Up My Life	1978	12.00
❑ PC35259	You Light Up My Life	1986	10.00
—Budget-line reissue			
❑ C30740	You've Got a Friend	1971	15.00
❑ CQ30740 [Q]	You've Got a Friend	1972	25.00
❑ PC30740	You've Got a Friend	198?	10.00
—Budget-line reissue			

COLUMBIA LIMITED EDITION

Number	Title	Yr	NM
❑ LE10196	Christmas with Johnny Mathis	1976	12.00
—Reissue of Harmony KH 30684 with same contents			
❑ LE10003	Portrait of Johnny	197?	12.00

COLUMBIA MUSICAL TREASURY

Number	Title	Yr	NM
❑ 6P6030	The Johnny Mathis Treasury	197?	30.00

COLUMBIA SPECIAL PRODUCTS

Number	Title	Yr	NM
❑ P14658	Holidays at the Fireside	197?	25.00
—Bonus album with box set 14628			
❑ P414971	Johnny	197?	30.00
❑ C10896	Merry Christmas	1972	15.00
—Reissue			
❑ P614628	Misty Memories: The Complete Johnny Mathis Treasury	197?	30.00
—Maunfactured for Candelite Music			
❑ P311837	Romantically, Johnny Mathis	197?	30.00
❑ P11477	Romantically, Johnny Mathis	197?	15.00
❑ P14908	The Heart of Johnny Mathis	197?	18.00
—Bonus album with box set 14628			

HARMONY

Number	Title	Yr	NM
❑ KH30684	Christmas with Johnny Mathis	1971	15.00
—Reissue of Mercury SR 60837 with two fewer tracks			
❑ KH30017	Johnny Mathis	1970	12.00
❑ KH31935	Something for Everyone	1973	12.00

MERCURY

Number	Title	Yr	NM
❑ MG-20988 [M]	Johnny Mathis Ole	1965	15.00
❑ SR-60988 [S]	Johnny Mathis Ole	1965	18.00
❑ MG-21107 [M]	Johnny Mathis Sings	1967	18.00
❑ SR-61107 [S]	Johnny Mathis Sings	1967	18.00
❑ MG-20991 [M]	Love Is Everything	1965	15.00
❑ SR-60991 [S]	Love Is Everything	1965	18.00
❑ MG-21093 [M]	So Nice	1966	15.00
❑ SR-61093 [S]	So Nice	1966	18.00
❑ MG20837 [M]	Sounds of Christmas	1963	15.00
❑ SR60837 [S]	Sounds of Christmas	1963	18.00
❑ MG-20890 [M]	Tender Is the Night	1964	15.00
❑ SR-60890 [S]	Tender Is the Night	1964	18.00
❑ MG-21073 [M]	The Shadow of Your Smile	1966	15.00
❑ SR-61073 [S]	The Shadow of Your Smile	1966	18.00
❑ MG-21041 [M]	The Sweetheart Tree	1965	15.00
❑ SR-61041 [S]	The Sweetheart Tree	1965	18.00
❑ MG-20913 [M]	The Wonderful World of Make Believe	1964	15.00
❑ SR-60913 [S]	The Wonderful World of Make Believe	1964	18.00
❑ MG-20942 [M]	This Is Love	1964	15.00
❑ SR-60942 [S]	This Is Love	1964	18.00

MOBILE FIDELITY

Number	Title	Yr	NM
❑ 1-171	Heavenly	1985	30.00
—Audiophile vinyl			

READER'S DIGEST

Number	Title	Yr	NM
❑ RB4-097	His Greatest Hits and Finest Performances	198?	30.00

TIME-LIFE

Number	Title	Yr	NM
❑ SLGD-08	Legendary Singers: Johnny Mathis	1985	18.00

MATHIS, JOHNNY/DENIECE WILLIAMS

COLUMBIA

Number	Title	Yr	NM
❑ JC35435	That's What Friends Are For	1978	12.00
❑ PC35435	That's What Friends Are For	198?	10.00
—Budget-line reissue			

MATLOCK, MATTY

RCA VICTOR

Number	Title	Yr	NM
❑ LPM-1413 [M]	Pete Kelly at Home	1957	40.00

WARNER BROS.

Number	Title	Yr	NM
❑ W1280 [M]	Four Button Dixie	1958	30.00
❑ WS1280 [S]	Four Button Dixie	1958	40.00

X

Number	Title	Yr	NM
❑ LXA-3035 [10]	Sports Parade	1955	50.00

MATRIX

PABLO TODAY

Number	Title	Yr	NM
❑ 2312121	Harvest	1980	15.00

MATTEA, KATHY

MERCURY

Number	Title	Yr	NM
❑ R110791	A Collection of Hits	1990	25.00
—Only released on vinyl by BMG Direct Marketing			
❑ 824308-1	From My Heart	1985	12.00
❑ 818560-1	Kathy Mattea	1984	12.00
❑ 832793-1	Untasted Honey	1987	12.00
❑ 830405-1	Walk the Way the Wind Blows	1986	12.00
❑ 836950-1	Willow in the Wind	1989	15.00

MATTHEWS, DAVE, BAND

RCA

Number	Title	Yr	NM
❑ 67660	Before These Crowded Streets	1998	200.00

MATTHEWS, DAVID

CTI

Number	Title	Yr	NM
❑ 5005	Dune	1977	15.00

GNP CRESCENDO

Number	Title	Yr	NM
❑ GNP-2153	Delta Lady	198?	12.00
❑ GNP-2162	Grand Connection	198?	12.00
❑ GNP-2157	Grand Cross	198?	12.00
❑ GNP-2174	Ice Fuse One	198?	12.00
❑ GNP-2185	Speed Demon	1986	12.00
❑ GNP-2169	Super Funky Sax	198?	12.00

Number	Title	Yr	NM
KUDU			
❏ 30	Shoogie Wanna Boogie	1976	18.00
MUSE			
❏ MR-5073	David Matthews' Big Band at the 5 Spot	1976	12.00
❏ MR-5096	Flight	1977	12.00

MATTHEWS, IAN

Number	Title	Yr	NM
COLUMBIA			
❏ PC34102	Go for Broke	1976	12.00
❏ PC34671	Hit and Run	1977	12.00
ELEKTRA			
❏ EKS-75078	Some Days You Eat the Bear	1974	15.00
❏ EKS-75051	Valley Hi	1973	15.00
MUSHROOM			
❏ MRS-5014	Siamese Friends	1979	12.00
❏ MRS-5012	Stealin' Home	1978	12.00
RSO			
❏ RS-1-3092	A Spot of Interference	1980	12.00
VERTIGO			
❏ VEL-1002 [B]	If You Saw Thro' My Eyes	1971	25.00
❏ VEL-1010 [B]	Tigers Will Survive	1972	25.00
WINDHAM HILL			
❏ WD-1070	Walking a Changing Line: The Songs of Jules Shear	1987	12.00

MATTHEWS, ONZY

Number	Title	Yr	NM
CAPITOL			
❏ T2099 [M]	Blues with a Touch of Elegance	1964	18.00
❏ ST2099 [S]	Blues with a Touch of Elegance	1964	25.00

MATTHEWS, WALT

Number	Title	Yr	NM
FRETLESS			
❏ 158	The Dance in Your Eye	198?	15.00

MATTHEWS' SOUTHERN COMFORT

Number	Title	Yr	NM
DECCA			
❏ DL75264	Later That Same Year	1971	15.00
❏ DL75191 [B]	Matthews' Southern Comfort	1970	18.00
❏ DL75242	Second Spring	1970	15.00
PICKWICK			
❏ SPC-3698	Later That Same Year	197?	10.00

MATTSON, PHIL

Number	Title	Yr	NM
DOCTOR JAZZ			
❏ FW40349	Setting Standards	1986	12.00

MATZ, PETER

Number	Title	Yr	NM
PROJECT 3			
❏ PR5007SD	Peter Matz Brings 'Em Back	1967	18.00

MAUDS, THE

Number	Title	Yr	NM
MERCURY			
❏ MG-21135 [M]	The Mauds Hold On	1967	25.00
❏ SR-61135 [S]	The Mauds Hold On	1967	30.00

MAULAWI

Number	Title	Yr	NM
STRATA-EAST			
❏ SES104-74	Maulawi	1974	30.00

MAUPIN, BENNIE

Number	Title	Yr	NM
ECM			
❏ 1043	The Jewel in the Lotus	197?	18.00
MERCURY			
❏ SRM-1-3717	Moonscapes	1978	12.00
❏ SRM-1-1148	Slow Traffic	1976	12.00

MAVERICKS, THE

Number	Title	Yr	NM
MCA			
❏ 11257	Music for All Occasions	1995	12.00

MAXIMILLIAN

Number	Title	Yr	NM
ABC			
❏ S-696	Maximillian	1969	40.00

MAXTED, BILLY

Number	Title	Yr	NM
BRUNSWICK			
❏ BL58052 [10]	Honky Tonk Piano	1953	60.00
CADENCE			
❏ CLP-1005 [M]	Billy Maxted Plays Hi-Fi Keyboard	1955	40.00
❏ CLP-1013 [M]	Dixieland Manhattan Style	1955	40.00
❏ CLP-3013 [M]	Dixieland Manhattan Style	1958	30.00
❏ CLP-1012 [M]	Jazz at Nick's	1955	40.00
LIBERTY			
❏ LRP-3474 [M]	Maxted Makes It	1966	15.00
❏ LST-7474 [S]	Maxted Makes It	1966	18.00
❏ LRP-3492 [M]	Satin Doll	1967	18.00
❏ LST-7492 [S]	Satin Doll	1967	15.00
SEECO			
❏ CELP-458 [M]	Art of Jazz	1960	25.00
❏ CELP-4580 [S]	Art of Jazz	1960	30.00

Number	Title	Yr	NM
❏ CELP-438 [M]	Bourbon St. Billy and the Blues	1960	25.00
❏ CELP-4380 [S]	Bourbon St. Billy and the Blues	1960	30.00

MAXWELL, DIANE

Number	Title	Yr	NM
CHALLENGE			
❏ CHL-607 [M]	Almost Seventeen	1959	40.00
❏ CHS-2501 [S]	Almost Seventeen	1959	50.00

MAXWELL, JIMMIE

Number	Title	Yr	NM
CIRCLE			
❏ 50	Let's Fall in Love	198?	12.00

MAXWELL, ROBERT

Number	Title	Yr	NM
COMMAND			
❏ SD913 [S]	Anytime	1967	15.00
❏ 33-913 [M]	Anytime	1967	18.00
DECCA			
❏ DL4723 [M]	Let's Get Away from It All	1966	15.00
❏ DL74723 [S]	Let's Get Away from It All	1966	18.00
❏ DL4563 [M]	Peg o' My Heart	1964	15.00
❏ DL74563 [S]	Peg o' My Heart	1964	18.00
❏ DL4421 [M]	Shangri-La	1964	15.00
❏ DL74421 [S]	Shangri-La	1964	18.00
❏ DL4609 [M]	Songs for All Seasons	1965	15.00
❏ DL74609 [S]	Songs for All Seasons	1965	18.00
MGM			
❏ E-4246 [M]	The Very Best of Robert Maxwell	1964	15.00
❏ SE-4246 [S]	The Very Best of Robert Maxwell	1964	18.00

MAY, BILLY

Number	Title	Yr	NM
BAINBRIDGE			
❏ ST1001	I Believe in You	197?	15.00
CAPITOL			
❏ H349 [10]	A Band Is Born!	1952	40.00
❏ T349 [M]	A Band Is Born!	195?	30.00
— Turquoise label original			
❏ H374 [10]	Bacchanalia!	1953	40.00
❏ T374 [M]	Bacchanalia!	195?	30.00
— Turquoise label original			
❏ L329 [10]	Big Band Bash	1952	40.00
❏ T329 [M]	Big Band Bash	195?	30.00
— Turquoise label original			
❏ T1043 [M]	Big Fat Brass	1958	25.00
— Black colorband label, Capitol logo at left			
❏ ST1043 [S]	Big Fat Brass	1958	30.00
— Black colorband label, Capitol logo at left			
❏ T1888 [M]	Bill's Bag	1963	18.00
❏ ST1888 [S]	Bill's Bag	1963	25.00
❏ T771 [M]	Billy May Plays for Fancy Dancin'	1956	30.00
❏ H487 [10]	Billy May's Naughty Operetta!	1953	40.00
❏ T487 [M]	Billy May's Naughty Operetta!	195?	30.00
— Turquoise label original			
❏ T2560 [M]	Billy May Today	1965	15.00
❏ ST2560 [S]	Billy May Today	1965	18.00
❏ ST1329 [S]	Cha Cha!	1959	30.00
— Black colorband label, Capitol logo at left			
❏ T1329 [M]	Cha Cha!	1959	25.00
— Black colorband label, Capitol logo at left			
❏ T1367 [M]	Cha Cha Mambos	1959	25.00
— Black colorband label, logo at left			
❏ TAO924 [M]	Jimmie Lunceford in Hi-Fi: Authentic Re-Creations of the Lunceford Style	1958	30.00
— Turquoise label original			
❏ STAO924 [S]	Jimmie Lunceford in Hi-Fi: Authentic Re-Creations of the Lunceford Style	1958	40.00
— Black colorband label, Capitol logo at left			
❏ H237 [10]	Join the Band	1951	40.00
❏ T1377 [M]	Pow!	1959	25.00
— Gold "The Star Line" label			
❏ T677 [M]	Sorta-Dixie!	195?	30.00
— Turquoise label original			
❏ M11885 [M]	Sorta-Dixie!	197?	12.00
— Reissue of Capitol 677			
❏ T562 [M]	Sorta-May	195?	30.00
— Turquoise label original			
❏ M562 [M]	Sorta-May	197?	12.00
— Reissue with new prefix			
❏ T1417 [M]	The Girls and Boys on Broadway	1960	18.00
— Black colorband label, Capitol logo at left			
❏ ST1417 [S]	The Girls and Boys on Broadway	1960	25.00
— Black colorband label, Capitol logo at left			
❏ T1581 [M]	The Great Jimmie Lunceford: Authentic Re-Creations of the Lunceford Style by Billy May	1961	18.00
— Gold "The Star Line" label			
❏ ST1581 [S]	The Great Jimmie Lunceford: Authentic Re-Creations of the Lunceford Style by Billy May	1961	25.00

Number	Title	Yr	NM
— Gold "The Star Line" label			
❏ T1709 [M]	The Sweetest Swingin' Sounds of No Strings	196?	18.00
❏ ST1709 [S]	The Sweetest Swingin' Sounds of No Strings	196?	25.00
CREATIVE WORLD			
❏ ST-1054	Sorta-Dixie!	197?	15.00
❏ ST-1051 [M]	Sorta-May	197?	15.00
IMPERIAL			
❏ LP-9042 [M]	Fuzzy Pink Nightgown	1957	50.00
— Movie soundtrack			
PAUSA			
❏ PR9035	A Band Is Born!	198?	12.00
— Reissue of Capitol T 349			
PICKWICK			
❏ PC-3010 [M]	Hey It's May	196?	18.00
❏ SPC-3010 [R]	Hey It's May	196?	10.00
STEREO SOUNDS			
❏ SA-12	Music for Uptight Guys	196?	18.00
TIME			
❏ 52064 [M]	Billy May and His Orchestra	1962	18.00
❏ S-2064 [S]	Billy May and His Orchestra	1962	25.00
TIME-LIFE			
❏ STL-340	The Swing Era: 1930-1936	197?	25.00
— Box set with hardcover book; re-creations of original big-band charts, with some contributions by the Glenn Gray Orchestra			
❏ STL-341	The Swing Era: 1936-1937	197?	25.00
— Box set with hardcover book; re-creations of original big-band charts, with some contributions by the Glenn Gray Orchestra			
❏ STL-342	The Swing Era: 1937-1938	197?	25.00
— Box set with hardcover book; re-creations of original big-band charts, with some contributions by the Glenn Gray Orchestra			
❏ STL-343	The Swing Era: 1938-1939	197?	25.00
— Box set with hardcover book; re-creations of original big-band charts, with some contributions by the Glenn Gray Orchestra			
❏ STL-344	The Swing Era: 1939-1940	197?	25.00
— Box set with hardcover book; re-creations of original big-band charts, with some contributions by the Glenn Gray Orchestra			
❏ STL-345	The Swing Era: 1940-1941	197?	25.00
— Box set with hardcover book; re-creations of original big-band charts, with some contributions by the Glenn Gray Orchestra			
❏ STL-346	The Swing Era: 1941-1942	197?	25.00
— Box set with hardcover book; re-creations of original big-band charts, with some contributions by the Glenn Gray Orchestra			
❏ STL-347	The Swing Era: 1942-1944	197?	25.00
— Box set with hardcover book; re-creations of original big-band charts, with some contributions by the Glenn Gray Orchestra			
❏ STL-348	The Swing Era: 1944-1945	197?	25.00
— Box set with hardcover book; re-creations of original big-band charts, with some contributions by the Glenn Gray Orchestra			
❏ STL-352	The Swing Era: Curtain Call	197?	25.00
— Box set with hardcover book; re-creations of original big-band charts, with some contributions by the Glenn Gray Orchestra			
❏ STL-351	The Swing Era: Encore!	197?	25.00
— Box set with hardcover book; re-creations of original big-band charts, with some contributions by the Glenn Gray Orchestra			
❏ STL-350	The Swing Era: Into the '50s	197?	25.00
— Box set with hardcover book; re-creations of original big-band charts, with some contributions by the Glenn Gray Orchestra			
❏ STL-353	The Swing Era: One More Time	197?	25.00
— Box set with hardcover book; re-creations of original big-band charts, with some contributions by the Glenn Gray Orchestra			
❏ STL-349	The Swing Era: The Postwar Years	197?	25.00
— Box set with hardcover book; re-creations of original big-band charts, with some contributions by the Glenn Gray Orchestra			

MAY BLITZ

Number	Title	Yr	NM
PARAMOUNT			
❏ PAS-5020	May Blitz	1970	30.00

MAYALL, JOHN

Number	Title	Yr	NM
ABC			
❏ D-958	A Banquet in Blues	1976	12.00
❏ D-1039	A Hard Core Package	1977	12.00
❏ D-1086	Last of the British Blues	1978	12.00
❏ D-992	Lots of People	1977	12.00
❏ ABCD-926	Notice to Appear	1976	12.00
ACCORD			
❏ SN-7209	Roadshow Blues Band	1982	12.00
BLUE THUMB			
❏ BTS-6019	New Year, New Band, New Company	1975	12.00
DECAL			
❏ LIK-1	Some of My Best Friends Are Blues	1986	12.00

Number	Title	Yr	NM
DJM			
❏ 29	No More Interviews	1979	12.00
❏ 23	The Bottom Line	1979	12.00
GNP CRESCENDO			
❏ 2184	Behind the Iron Curtain	1986	12.00
ISLAND			
❏ 842795-1	A Sense of Place	1990	15.00
❏ 91005	Chicago Line	1988	12.00
LONDON			
❏ LL3502 [M]	A Hard Road	1967	50.00
❏ PS502 [S]	A Hard Road	1967	25.00
❏ PS537	Bare Wires	1968	18.00
❏ LL3492 [M]	Blues Breakers with Eric Clapton	1966	150.00
❏ PS492 [S]	Blues Breakers with Eric Clapton	1966	80.00
❏ LC-50009	Blues Breakers with Eric Clapton	1977	12.00
— Reissue of London PS 492			
❏ 800086-1	Blues Breakers with Eric Clapton	1983	10.00
— Reissue of London 50009			
❏ PS545	Blues from Laurel Canyon	1969	18.00
❏ LL3529 [M]	Crusade	1967	50.00
❏ PS529 [S]	Crusade	1967	30.00
❏ 2PS618 [B]	Down the Line	1973	18.00
❏ PS589	Live in Europe	1971	15.00
❏ PS562	Looking Back	1969	18.00
❏ 820331-1	Looking Back	1985	10.00
— Reissue of London PS 562			
❏ 820320-1	Primal Solos	1985	10.00
❏ PS543	Raw Blues	1968	18.00
❏ 820342-1	Raw Blues	1985	10.00
— Reissue of London PS 543			
❏ PS534	The Blues Alone	1968	18.00
❏ PS570	The Diary of a Band	1970	15.00
❏ 2PS600 [B]	Through the Years	1971	18.00
MCA			
❏ 795	Hard Core	1980	10.00
— Reissue of ABC 1039			
❏ 716	Last of the British Blues	1980	10.00
— Reissue of ABC 1086			
MOBILE FIDELITY			
❏ 1-183 [B]	Blues Breakers Featuring Eric Clapton	1985	80.00
— Audiophile vinyl			
❏ 1-246	The Blues Alone	1996	30.00
— Audiophile vinyl			
POLYDOR			
❏ 837127-1	Archive to the Eighties	1988	10.00
❏ 25-3002 [B]	Back to the Roots	1971	18.00
❏ 24-4010	Empty Rooms	1970	12.00
❏ PD 5027	Jazz-Blues Fusion	1972	12.00
❏ PD-5012	Memories	1971	12.00
❏ PD 5036	Moving On	1972	12.00
❏ PD2-3005 [B]	Ten Years Are Gone	1973	18.00
❏ PD2-3006 [B]	The Best of John Mayall	1973	18.00
❏ PD-6030	The Latest Edition	1974	15.00
❏ 24-4004	The Turning Point	1970	12.00
❏ 823305-1	The Turning Point	1985	10.00
— Reissue of Polydor 24-4004			
❏ 24-4022	U.S.A. Union	1970	12.00
❏ SKAO-93398	U.S.A. Union	1970	18.00
— Capitol Record Club edition			
MAYER, JOHN			
COLUMBIA			
❏ C86185	Heavier Things	2003	15.00
❏ C85293	Room for Squares	2001	15.00
MAYER, NATHANIEL			
FORTUNE			
❏ 8014 [M]	Goin' Back to the Village of Love	1964	300.00
— Light blue label			
❏ 8014 [M]	Goin' Back to the Village of Love	196?	150.00
— Purple label			
❏ 8014 [M]	Goin' Back to the Village of Love	196?	60.00
— Yellow label			
❏ 8014 [M]	Goin' Back to the Village of Love	197?	18.00
— Bluish purple label, with much more flexible vinyl than earlier pressings			
MAYERL, BILLY			
FLAPPER			
❏ 704/5	The Versatility of Billy Mayerl	198?	18.00
MAYFIELD, CURTIS			
BOARDWALK			
❏ NB1-33256	Honesty	1982	12.00
❏ NB1-33239	Love Is the Place	1981	12.00
CRC			
❏ 2001	We Come in Peace with a Message of Love	1985	15.00
CURTOM			
❏ CRS-8015	Back to the World	1973	18.00

Number	Title	Yr	NM
❏ CRS-8005	Curtis	1970	18.00
❏ CRS-8018	Curtis in Chicago	1973	18.00
❏ CRS-8008	Curtis/Live!	1971	25.00
❏ CUK5022	Do It All Night	1978	15.00
❏ CU5007	Give, Get, Take and Have	1976	15.00
❏ CRS-8604	Got to Find a Way	1974	15.00
❏ CUR-2902	Greatest Hits of All Time (Classic Collection)	198?	15.00
❏ CUR-2901	Live in Europe	198?	15.00
❏ CU5013	Never Say You Can't Survive	1977	15.00
❏ CRS-8009	Roots	1971	18.00
❏ CUR-2005	Something to Believe In	198?	10.00
— Reissue of RSO 3077			
❏ CRS-8014	Superfly	1972	25.00
❏ CRS-8601	Sweet Exorcist	1974	15.00
❏ CUR-2008	Take It to the Street	198?	12.00
❏ CU5001	There's No Place Like America Today	1975	15.00
❏ CUR-2003	There's No Place Like America Today	198?	10.00
— Reissue of 5001			
RHINO			
❏ 8122796557 [B]	Curtis	2013	30.00
RSO			
❏ RS-1-3053	Heartbeat	1979	12.00
❏ RS-1-3077	Something to Believe In	1980	12.00
MAYFIELD, PERCY			
BRUNSWICK			
❏ BL754145	Walking on a Tightrope	1968	25.00
INTERMEDIA			
❏ QS-5010	Please Send Me Someone to Love	198?	12.00
RCA VICTOR			
❏ LSP-4558 [B]	Blues And Then Some	1971	18.00
❏ LSP-4269	Percy Mayfield Sings Percy Mayfield	1970	18.00
❏ LSP-4444	Weakness Is a Thing Called Man	1970	18.00
SPECIALTY			
❏ SP-7001	Poet of the Blues	1990	18.00
❏ SPS-2126	The Best of Percy Mayfield	1970	25.00
TANGERINE			
❏ TRC-1510 [M]	Bought Blues	1967	30.00
❏ TRCS-1510 [S]	Bought Blues	1967	50.00
❏ TRC-1505 [M]	My Jug and I	1966	30.00
❏ TRCS-1505 [S]	My Jug and I	1966	50.00
MAYL, GENE			
BLACKBIRD			
❏ 12006	A Trip to Waukesha	1969	18.00
JAZZOLOGY			
❏ J-6 [M]	Gene Mayl's Dixieland Rhythm Kings	1964	18.00
MAYPOLE			
COLOSSUS			
❏ C3-1007	Maypole	1971	60.00
MAYS, BILL			
TREND			
❏ TR-532	Tha's Delights	1984	15.00
MAYS, LYLE			
GEFFEN			
❏ GHS24007	Lyle Mays	1986	12.00
❏ GHS24204	Street Dreams	1988	12.00
MAZE			
MTA			
❏ 5012	Armageddon	1969	100.00
MAZZY STAR			
CAPITOL			
❏ C1-27224	Among My Swan	1996	80.00
ROUGH TRADE			
❏ RUS771	She Hangs Brightly	1990	100.00
MC5			
ALIVE			
❏ 0008 [10]	Ice Pick Slim/Mad Like Eldridge Cleaver	1994	15.00
❏ 0005 [10]	Power Trip	1994	15.00
ATLANTIC			
❏ SD8247	Back in the USA	1970	50.00
❏ SD8285	High Time	1971	50.00
CLEOPATRA			
❏ 8387 [B]	Kick Out The Jams! 1966-1970		30.00
— picture disc			
ELEKTRA			
❏ EKS-74042 [B]	Kick Out the Jams	1969	100.00
— Gatefold cover with John Sinclair liner notes in center spread; brownish label			
❏ EKS-74042	Kick Out the Jams	1969	25.00
— All other editions			

Number	Title	Yr	NM
SUNDAZED			
❏ LP5093	Back in the USA	2002	25.00
— Reissue on 180-gram vinyl			
❏ LP5094	High Time	2002	25.00
— Reissue on 180-gram vinyl			
❏ LP5092	Kick Out the Jams	2001	25.00
— Reissue of original Elektra album, complete with uncensored liner notes			
TOTAL ENERGY			
❏ 2001 [10]	The American Ruse	1994	15.00
MCANALLY, MAC			
ARIOLA AMERICA			
❏ ST-50019	Mac McAnally	1977	15.00
❏ SW-50029	No Problem	1978	15.00
GEFFEN			
❏ 24191	Finish Lines	1988	12.00
❏ GHS2033	Nothing But the Truth	1983	12.00
RCA VICTOR			
❏ AFL1-3519	Cuttin' Corners	1980	15.00
MCAULIFFE, LEON			
ABC-PARAMOUNT			
❏ ABC-394 [M]	Cozy Inn	1961	40.00
❏ ABCS-394 [S]	Cozy Inn	1961	60.00
CAPITOL			
❏ T2148 [M]	Everybody Dance! Everybody Swing!	1964	30.00
❏ ST2148 [S]	Everybody Dance! Everybody Swing!	1964	40.00
❏ T2016 [M]	The Dancin'est Band Around	1964	30.00
❏ ST2016 [S]	The Dancin'est Band Around	1964	40.00
CIMARRON			
❏ CLP-2002 [M]	The Swingin' Western Strings of Leon McAuliff	1960	50.00
DOT			
❏ DLP-3689 [M]	Golden Country Hits	1966	40.00
❏ DLP-25689 [R]	Golden Country Hits	1966	30.00
❏ DLP-3139 [M]	Take Off	1958	60.00
SESAC			
❏ (# unknown) [M]	Just a Minute	1957	100.00
❏ 1601 [M]	Points West	1957	100.00
STARDAY			
❏ SLP-171 [M]	Mr. Western Swing	1962	50.00
❏ SLP-309 [M]	The Swingin' Western Strings of Leon McAuliff	1964	40.00
❏ SLP-280 [M]	The Swingin' West with Leon McAuliff	1964	40.00
MCBEE, CECIL			
ENJA			
❏ 3041	Compassion	198?	15.00
INDIA NAVIGATION			
❏ IN-1043	Alternate Spaces	197?	18.00
❏ IN-1053	Flying Out	198?	18.00
INNER CITY			
❏ IC-3023	Music from the Source	197?	18.00
STRATA-EAST			
❏ SES-7417	Mutima	1975	30.00
MCBRIDE, DALE			
CON BRIO			
❏ 051	The Ordinary Man Album	1977	15.00
MCBROWNE, LENNY			
PACIFIC JAZZ			
❏ PJ-1 [M]	The Four Souls	1960	30.00
❏ ST-1 [S]	The Four Souls	1960	40.00
RIVERSIDE			
❏ RLP-346 [M]	Eastern Lights	1960	30.00
❏ RS-9346 [S]	Eastern Lights	1960	40.00
MCCALL, C.W.			
MGM			
❏ M3G-5008	Black Bear Road	1975	12.00
❏ M3G-4989	Wolf Creek Pass	1975	12.00
POLYDOR			
❏ PD-1-6190	C.W. McCall & Co.	1979	12.00
❏ PD-1-6156	Greatest Hits	1978	12.00
❏ 825793-1	Greatest Hits	198?	10.00
— Reissue of 6156			
❏ PD-1-6125	Roses for Mama	1978	12.00
❏ PD-1-6094	Rubber Duck	1977	12.00
❏ PD-1-6069	Wilderness	1976	12.00
MCCALL, DARRELL			
COLUMBIA			
❏ KC34718	Lily Dale	1977	15.00
WAYSIDE			
❏ 1030	Meet Darrell McCall	1969	25.00
MCCALL, MARY ANN			
CORAL			
❏ CRL57276 [M]	Melancholy Baby	1959	60.00
❏ CRL757276 [S]	Melancholy Baby	1959	80.00

Number	Title	Yr	NM
DISCOVERY			
❑ 3011 [10]	Mary Ann McCall Sings	1950	300.00
JUBILEE			
❑ JLP-1078 [M]	Detour to the Moon	1958	60.00
REGENT			
❑ MG-6040 [M]	Easy Living	1957	80.00
SAVOY JAZZ			
❑ SJL-1178	Easy Living	198?	18.00

MCCALL, TOUSSAINT

Number	Title	Yr	NM
RONN			
❑ 7527 [M]	Nothing Can Take the Place of You	1967	30.00
❑ 7527S [S]	Nothing Can Take the Place of You	1967	40.00

MCCALLUM, DAVID

Number	Title	Yr	NM
CAPITOL			
❑ T2748 [M]	McCallum	1967	18.00
❑ ST2748 [S]	McCallum	1967	18.00
❑ T2498 [M]	Music: A Bit More of Me	1966	15.00
❑ ST2498 [S]	Music: A Bit More of Me	1966	18.00
❑ T2651 [M]	Music: It's Happening Now	1967	18.00
❑ ST2651 [S]	Music: It's Happening Now	1967	18.00
❑ T2432 [M]	Music -- A Part of Me	1966	15.00
❑ ST2432 [S]	Music -- A Part of Me	1966	18.00

MCCANN, HOOPS

Number	Title	Yr	NM
MCA			
❑ 42202	The Hoops McCann Band Plays the Music of Steely Dan	1988	12.00

MCCANN, LES, AND EDDIE HARRIS

Number	Title	Yr	NM
ATLANTIC			
❑ SD1583	Second Movement	1971	18.00
❑ SD1537	Swiss Movement	1969	18.00

MCCANN, LES

Number	Title	Yr	NM
A&M			
❑ SP-4780	Tall, Dark and Handsome	1979	12.00
❑ SP-4718	The Man	1978	12.00
ABC IMPULSE!			
❑ AS-9333	Live at the Roxy	1978	12.00
❑ AS-9329	The Music Lets Me Be	1977	12.00
ATLANTIC			
❑ SD1666	Another Beginning	1974	15.00
❑ SD1547	Comment	1970	18.00
❑ SD1679	Hustle to Survive	1975	15.00
❑ SD1603 [S]	Invitation to Openness	1972	15.00
❑ 1603 [M]	Invitation to Openness	1972	30.00
—Mono is white label promo only with "d/j copy monaural" sticker on front cover			
❑ SD1646	Layers	1973	15.00
❑ SD 2-312	Live at Montreux	1974	18.00
❑ SD1516	Much Les	1969	18.00
❑ SD1690	River High, River Low	1976	15.00
❑ SD1619	Talk to the People	1972	15.00
JAM			
❑ 019	Les McCann's Music Box	1984	12.00
❑ 012	The Longer You Wait	1984	12.00
LIMELIGHT			
❑ LM-82031 [M]	Beaux J. Pooboo	1966	18.00
❑ LS-86031 [S]	Beaux J. Pooboo	1966	25.00
❑ LM-82043 [M]	Bucket O' Grease	1967	25.00
❑ LS-86043 [S]	Bucket O' Grease	1967	18.00
❑ LM-82016 [M]	But Not Really	1965	18.00
❑ LS-86016 [S]	But Not Really	1965	25.00
❑ LM-82041 [M]	Les McCann Plays the Hits	1966	18.00
❑ LS-86041 [S]	Les McCann Plays the Hits	1966	25.00
❑ LM-82036 [M]	Live at Shelly's Manne-Hole	1966	18.00
❑ LS-86036 [S]	Live at Shelly's Manne-Hole	1966	25.00
❑ LM-82046 [M]	Live at the Bohemian Caverns, Washington, D.C.	1967	25.00
❑ LS-86046 [S]	Live at the Bohemian Caverns, Washington, D.C.	1967	18.00
❑ LM-82025 [M]	Poo Boo	1965	18.00
❑ LS-86025 [S]	Poo Boo	1965	25.00
PACIFIC JAZZ			
❑ PJ-10107 [M]	A Bag of Gold	1966	18.00
❑ ST-20107 [S]	A Bag of Gold	1966	25.00
❑ PJ-81 [M]	Jazz Waltz	1964	18.00
❑ ST-81 [S]	Jazz Waltz	1964	25.00
❑ PJ-45 [M]	Les McCann in New York	1962	25.00
❑ ST-45 [S]	Les McCann in New York	1962	30.00
❑ LN-10078	Les McCann in New York	1980	10.00
—Budget-line reissue			
❑ PJ-16 [M]	Les McCann in San Francisco	1961	30.00
❑ ST-16 [S]	Les McCann in San Francisco	1961	30.00
❑ LN-10077	Les McCann in San Francisco	1980	10.00
—Budget-line reissue			
❑ PJ-31 [M]	Les McCann Sings	1961	25.00
❑ ST-31 [S]	Les McCann Sings	1961	30.00
❑ PJ-84 [M]	McCanna	1964	18.00
❑ ST-84 [S]	McCanna	1964	25.00
❑ PJ-91 [M]	McCann/Wilson	1965	18.00
—With Gerald Wilson			
❑ ST-91 [S]	McCann/Wilson	1965	25.00
—With Gerald Wilson			
❑ PJ-56 [M]	On Time	1962	40.00
—Yellow vinyl			
❑ PJ-56 [M]	On Time	1962	25.00
—Black vinyl			
❑ ST-56 [S]	On Time	1962	50.00
—Yellow vinyl			
❑ ST-56 [S]	On Time	1962	30.00
—Black vinyl			
❑ PJ-25 [M]	Pretty Lady	1961	25.00
❑ ST-25 [S]	Pretty Lady	1961	30.00
❑ PJ-63 [M]	Shampoo	1962	18.00
❑ ST-63 [S]	Shampoo	1962	25.00
❑ PJ-78 [M]	Soul Hits	1963	18.00
❑ ST-78 [S]	Soul Hits	1963	25.00
❑ LN-10079	Soul Hits	1980	10.00
—Budget-line reissue			
❑ PJ-10097 [M]	Spanish Onions	1966	18.00
❑ ST-20097 [S]	Spanish Onions	1966	25.00
❑ PJ-69 [M]	The Gospel Truth	1963	18.00
❑ ST-69 [S]	The Gospel Truth	1963	25.00
❑ PJ-7 [M]	The Shout	1960	30.00
❑ ST-7 [S]	The Shout	1960	30.00
❑ LN-10083	The Shout	1980	10.00
—Budget-line reissue			
❑ PJ-2 [M]	The Truth	1960	30.00
❑ ST-2 [S]	The Truth	1960	30.00
STONE			
❑ 1906	Butterfly	1988	12.00
SUNSET			
❑ SUS-5214	Django	1969	12.00
❑ SUS-5296	Unlimited	1970	12.00
WORLD PACIFIC			
❑ ST-20173	Les McCann Sings & Plays in the Big City	1970	18.00
❑ ST-20166	More Or Les McCann	1969	18.00

MCCARTERS, THE

Number	Title	Yr	NM
WARNER BROS.			
❑ 25737	The Gift	1988	12.00

MCCARTHY, JOHN, CHORALE

Number	Title	Yr	NM
RCA MUSIC SERVICE			
❑ R114285	The Greatest Songs of Christmas	1973	15.00

MCCARTNEY, PAUL

Number	Title	Yr	NM
APPLE			
❑ SO-3415	Band on the Run	1973	25.00
—Credited to "Paul McCartney and Wings"; with photo innersleeve and poster			
❑ SPRO-6210 [DJ]	Brung to Ewe By	1971	400.00
—Promo-only radio spots for "Ram"; counterfeits have uneven spacing between tracks			
❑ STAO-3363	McCartney	1970	30.00
—McCartney" and "Paul McCartney" on separate lines on label; New York address on back cover			
❑ STAO-3363	McCartney	1970	30.00
—McCartney" and "Paul McCartney" on separate lines on label; California address on back cover			
❑ STAO-3363	McCartney	1970	80.00
—Apple label with small Capitol logo on B-side			
❑ STAO-3363	McCartney	1970	25.00
—Only "McCartney" on label; back cover does NOT say "An Abkco managed company			
❑ STAO-3363	McCartney	1970	30.00
—Only "McCartney" on label; back cover says "An Abkco managed company			
❑ SMAS-3363	McCartney	197?	25.00
—New prefix on label			
❑ SMAS-3363	McCartney	1975	100.00
—With "All Rights Reserved" on label			
❑ MAS-3375 [M]	Ram	1971	4000.00
—Credited to "Paul and Linda McCartney"; mono record in stereo cover for radio station use only			
❑ SMAS-3375	Ram	1971	18.00
—Credited to "Paul and Linda McCartney"; unsliced apple on one label, sliced apple on other			
❑ SMAS-3375	Ram	1971	30.00
—Credited to "Paul and Linda McCartney"; unsliced apple on both labels			
❑ SMAS-3375	Ram	1971	50.00
—Credited to "Paul and Linda McCartney"; Apple label with small Capitol logo on B-side			
❑ SMAS-3375	Ram	1975	100.00
—Credited to "Paul and Linda McCartney"; with "All Rights Reserved" on label			
❑ SMAL-3409	Red Rose Speedway	1973	25.00
—Credited to "Paul McCartney and Wings"; with bound-in booklet			
❑ SW-3386	Wild Life	1971	18.00
—Credited to "Wings			
CAPITOL			
❑ CLW-48287	All the Best!	1987	25.00
❑ SO-3415	Band on the Run	1975	25.00
—Credited to "Paul McCartney and Wings"; custom label with MPL logo			
❑ SO-3415	Band on the Run	197?	50.00
—Credited to "Paul McCartney and Wings"; black label, "Manufactured by Capitol Records...			
❑ SO-3415	Band on the Run	197?	25.00
—Credited to "Paul McCartney and Wings"; black label, "Maunfactured by MPL Communications Inc." at top			
❑ SEAX-11901 [PD]	Band on the Run	1978	40.00
—Credited to "Paul McCartney and Wings"; picture disc			
❑ 99176	Band on the Run	1999	40.00
—Limited-edition 180-gram reissue with original LP on one record and interviews and "The Making of.." on the second			
❑ C1-56500	Flaming Pie	1997	30.00
❑ C1-91653	Flowers in the Dirt	1989	25.00
❑ SW-11777	London Town	1978	18.00
—Credited to "Wings"; custom label with poster			
❑ SMAS-3363	McCartney	1976	30.00
—Black label, "Manufactured by McCartney Music Inc" at top			
❑ SMAS-3363	McCartney	1976	25.00
—Black label, "Manufactured by MPL Communications Inc" at top			
❑ PJAS-12475	Press to Play	1986	15.00
❑ SMAS-3375	Ram	1976	30.00
—Credited to "Paul and Linda McCartney"; black label, "Manufactured by McCartney Music Inc" at top			
❑ SMAS-3375	Ram	197?	25.00
—Credited to "Paul and Linda McCartney"; black label, "Manufactured by MPL Communications Inc" at top			
❑ SMAS-3375	Ram	197?	40.00
—Credited to "Paul and Linda McCartney"; black label, "Manufactured by Capitol Records..." on label			
❑ SMAL-3409	Red Rose Speedway	1976	30.00
—Credited to "Paul McCartney and Wings"; black label, "Manufactured by McCartney Music Inc" at top			
❑ SMAL-3409	Red Rose Speedway	197?	30.00
—Credited to "Paul McCartney and Wings"; black label, "Manufactured by MPL Communications Inc" at top			
❑ ST-11642	Thrillington	1977	100.00
—Credited to "Percy 'Thrills' Thrillington"; instrumental versions of songs from Ram LP			
❑ C1-94778	Tripping the Live Fantastic	1990	60.00
❑ C1-595379	Tripping the Live Fantastic -- Highlights!	1990	30.00
—Released on vinyl only through Columbia House; with U.S. address on back cover			
❑ C1-595379	Tripping the Live Fantastic -- Highlights!	1990	30.00
—Released on vinyl only through Columbia House; with Canada address on back cover, this was sold in the U.S. by Columbia House			
❑ SMAS-11419	Venus and Mars	1975	18.00
—Credited to "Wings"; with two posters and two stickers			
❑ SW-3386	Wild Life	1976	30.00
—Credited to "Wings"; black label, "Manufactured by McCartney Music Inc" at top			
❑ SW-3386	Wild Life	197?	25.00
—Credited to "Wings"; black label, "Manufactured by MPL Communications Inc" at top			
❑ SW-11525	Wings at the Speed of Sound	1976	12.00
—Credited to "Wings"; custom label			
❑ SW-11525 [DJ]	Wings at the Speed of Sound	1976	300.00
—Credited to "Wings"; white label advance promo			
❑ SOO-11905	Wings Greatest	1978	18.00
—Credited to "Wings"; custom label with poster			
❑ SOO-11905 [DJ]	Wings Greatest	1978	400.00
—Credited to "Wings"; white label advance promo/test pressing			
❑ SWCO-11593	Wings Over America	1976	30.00
—Credited to "Wings"; custom labels with poster			
COLUMBIA			
❑ FC36057	Back to the Egg	1979	12.00
—Credited to "Wings"; custom label			
❑ FC36057 [DJ]	Back to the Egg	1979	40.00
—Credited to "Wings"; "Demonstration -- Not for Sale" on custom label			
❑ PC36057	Back to the Egg	1984	30.00
—Credited to "Wings"; "PC" cover with "FC" label			
❑ PC36057	Back to the Egg	1984	40.00
—Credited to "Wings"; "PC" cover with "PC" label			
❑ JC36482	Band on the Run	1980	18.00
—Credited to "Paul McCartney and Wings"; custom label			
❑ JC36482	Band on the Run	198?	100.00
—Credited to "Paul McCartney and Wings"; white "MPL" logo on lower left front cover			
❑ PC36482	Band on the Run	198?	25.00
—Credited to "Paul McCartney and Wings"; "PC" cover with "JC" label			
❑ PC36482	Band on the Run	198?	30.00
—Credited to "Paul McCartney and Wings"; "PC" cover with "PC" label			
❑ HC46382	Band on the Run	1981	50.00
—Credited to "Paul McCartney and Wings"; half-speed mastered edition			
❑ SC39613	Give My Regards to Broad Street	1984	18.00
❑ JC36478	McCartney	1979	18.00
❑ PC36478	McCartney	1984	18.00
—Budget-line reissue			
❑ FC36511 [DJ]	McCartney II	1980	30.00
—White label promo			
❑ FC36511	McCartney II	1980	12.00
—Add 80% if bonus single of "Coming Up (Live at Glasgow)" (AE7 1204) is with package			

Number	Title	Yr	NM
❑ PC36511	McCartney II	1984	30.00
—"PC" cover with "FC" label			
❑ PC36511	McCartney II	1984	100.00
—"PC" cover with "PC" label			
❑ QC39149	Pipes of Peace	1983	15.00
❑ JC36479	Ram	1980	18.00
—Credited to "Paul and Linda McCartney"			
❑ PC36479	Ram	1984	18.00
—Credited to "Paul and Linda McCartney"; budget-line reissue			
❑ JC36481	Red Rose Speedway	1980	18.00
—Credited to "Paul McCartney and Wings"; flat or glossy cover			
❑ PC36481	Red Rose Speedway	1984	18.00
—Credited to "Paul McCartney and Wings"; not issued with booklet			
❑ A2S821 [DJ]	The McCartney Interview	1980	40.00
—Promo-only set; one LP is the entire interview, the other is banded for airplay; white labels with black print; counterfeits have blank white labels			
❑ PC36987	The McCartney Interview	1980	15.00
—Stock release of interview originally intended for promotional use only			
❑ TC37462	Tug of War	1982	12.00
❑ PC37462	Tug of War	1984	30.00
—Custom label; "PC" cover with "TC" label			
❑ PC37462	Tug of War	1984	100.00
—Regular Columbia label; "PC" cover with "PC" label			
❑ JC36801	Venus and Mars	1980	18.00
—Credited to "Wings"; with one poster and two stickers			
❑ PC36801	Venus and Mars	1982	18.00
—Credited to "Wings"; budget-line reissue, not issued with inserts			
❑ JC36480	Wild Life	1980	18.00
—Credited to "Wings			
❑ PC36480	Wild Life	1982	18.00
—Credited to "Wings"; budget-line reissue			
❑ PC37409	Wings at the Speed of Sound	1982	18.00
—Credited to "Wings"; regular Columbia label, budget-line reissue			
❑ FC37409	Wings at the Speed of Sound	1981	18.00
—Credited to "Wings"; custom label			
❑ C3X37990	Wings Over America	1982	50.00
—Credited to "Wings"; custom labels, no poster			

HEAR MUSIC

❑ HMLP-30383	Memory Almost Full	2007	18.00

MPL/PARLOPHONE

❑ 888072040406 [B]	New	2013	30.00
❑ HRM33452-01 [Mono]	Ram	2012	30.00
—reissue of 1971 promo			
❑ 96413	Unplugged (The Official Bootleg)	1991	75.00
—No U.S. pressings; "American" copies were U.K. imports with liner notes in Spanish!			

NATIONAL FEATURES CORP.

❑ 2955/6	Band on the Run Radio Interview Special	1973	1500.00
—Promo-only interview disc			

MCCLINTON, DELBERT

ABC

❑ ABCD-959	Genuine Cowhide	1976	25.00
❑ AB-991 [B]	Love Rustler	1977	25.00
❑ ABCD-907	Victim of Life's Circumstances	1975	25.00

ACCORD

❑ SN-7145	Wake Up Baby	198?	12.00

ALLIGATOR

❑ AL-3902	Honky Tonkin' (I Done Me Some)	1986	12.00
❑ AL-4773	Live from Austin	1989	15.00

CAPITOL/MSS

❑ ST-12188	Playin' from the Heart	1981	15.00
❑ ST-12115	The Jealous Kind	1980	15.00

CAPRICORN

❑ CPN-0223	Keeper of the Flame	1979	18.00
❑ CPN-0201	Second Wind	1978	25.00

INTERMEDIA

❑ QS-5029	Feelin' Alright!	198?	12.00

MCA

❑ 5197	The Best of Delbert McClinton	1981	12.00

MCCLINTON, O.B.

ENTERPRISE

❑ ENS-1023	Country	1972	30.00
❑ ENS-7506	If You Loved Her That Way	1974	30.00
❑ ENS-1037	Live at Randy's Rodeo	1973	30.00
❑ ENS-1029	Obie from Senatobie	1973	30.00

EPIC

❑ FE40674	The Only One	1987	12.00

HOMETOWN

❑ 104	Album No. 1	198?	15.00

MCCONNELL, ROB

PAUSA

❑ 7148	Again, Vol. 1	1983	12.00
❑ 7140	Big Band Jazz Vol. 1	198?	12.00
❑ 7141	Big Band Jazz Vol. 2	198?	12.00
❑ 7067	Present Perfect	1980	12.00
❑ 7031	The Rob McConnell and Boss Brass Jazz Album	1979	12.00
❑ 7106	Trubute	198?	12.00

MCCOO, MARILYN, AND BILLY DAVIS, JR.

ABC

❑ ABCD-952	I Hope We Get to Love in Time	1976	15.00
❑ AB-1026	The Two of Us	1977	15.00

COLUMBIA

❑ JC35603	Marilyn and Billy	1978	18.00

MCCOO, MARILYN

RCA VICTOR

❑ AFL1-4863	Solid Gold	1983	12.00

MCCORKLE, SUSANNAH

CONCORD JAZZ

❑ CJ-370	No More Blues	1989	15.00

INNER CITY

❑ IC-1141	Music of Harry Warren	198?	15.00
❑ IC-1151	People You Never Get to Love	1984	15.00
❑ IC-1101	Songs of Johnny Mercer	198?	15.00
❑ IC-1131	Songs of Yip Harburg	198?	15.00

PAUSA

❑ 7195	How Do You Keep the Music Playing?	1986	12.00
❑ 7175	Thanks for the Memory	1985	12.00

MCCORMICK, GAYLE

ABC DUNHILL

❑ DS-50109	Gayle McCormick	1971	15.00

DECCA

❑ DL75364	Flesh and Blood	1972	15.00

FANTASY

❑ 9467	One More Hour	1974	15.00

MCCORMICK BROTHERS, THE

HICKORY

❑ LP-108 [M]	Authentic Bluegrass Hits	1962	60.00
❑ LP-102 [M]	Songs for Home Folks	1961	80.00

METROMEDIA

❑ MM-1019	Grass Meets Brass	1969	25.00

MCCOY, CLYDE

CAPITOL

❑ H311 [10]	Sugar Blues	195?	100.00
❑ T311 [M]	Sugar Blues	1955	50.00
—Turquoise or gray label			
❑ T311 [M]	Sugar Blues	1959	40.00
—Black colorband label, logo at left			
❑ T311 [M]	Sugar Blues	1963	30.00
—Black colorband label, logo at top			
❑ DT311 [R]	Sugar Blues	196?	15.00
❑ SM-311 [R]	Sugar Blues	197?	12.00

CIRCLE

❑ CLP-82	Sugar Blues, 1951	198?	12.00

DESIGN

❑ DLP-28 [M]	The Golden Era of the Sugar Blues	196?	15.00

HINDSIGHT

❑ HSR-180	Clyde McCoy and His Orchestra 1936	198?	12.00

MERCURY

❑ MG-20730 [M]	Blue Prelude	1962	18.00
❑ SR-60730 [S]	Blue Prelude	1962	25.00
❑ MG25141 [10]	Date for Dancing	195?	30.00
❑ SR-60677 [S]	Really McCoy	1961	25.00
❑ MG-20677 [M]	Really McCoy	1961	18.00
❑ MG25034 [10]	Sugar Blues	195?	40.00
❑ MG-20110 [M]	The Blues	195?	40.00

TODD

❑ MT-5000 [M]	Clyde McCoy and His Waaa Waaa Dixieland Band	196?	25.00

TOP RANK

❑ RM-350 [M]	Dixieland's Best Friend	1961	30.00
❑ RS-650 [S]	Dixieland's Best Friend	1961	40.00

WING

❑ MGW-12260 [M]	Dancing to the Blues	196?	15.00
❑ SRW-16260 [S]	Dancing to the Blues	196?	15.00

MCCOY, FREDDIE

COBBLESTONE

❑ 9004	Gimme Some	1972	25.00

PRESTIGE

❑ PRST-7542	Beans and Greens	1968	30.00
❑ PRLP-7470 [M]	Funk Drops	1967	30.00
❑ PRST-7470 [S]	Funk Drops	1967	30.00
❑ PRST-7582	Listen Here	1968	30.00
❑ PRLP-7395 [M]	Lonely Avenue	1965	25.00
❑ PRST-7395 [S]	Lonely Avenue	1965	30.00
❑ PRLP-7487 [M]	Peas 'N' Rice	1967	30.00
❑ PRST-7487 [S]	Peas 'N' Rice	1967	30.00
❑ PRST-7561	Soul Yogi	1968	30.00
❑ PRLP-7444 [M]	Spider Man	1966	50.00
❑ PRST-7444 [S]	Spider Man	1966	40.00
❑ PRST-7706	The Best of Freddie McCoy	1969	25.00

MCCOY, VAN

AVCO

❑ AV-69006	Disco Baby	1975	12.00
❑ AV-69002	Love Is the Answer	1974	12.00
❑ AV-69009	The Disco Kid	1975	12.00

BUDDAH

❑ BDS-5648	From Disco to Love	1975	12.00
—Retitled reissue of 5103			
❑ BDS-5103	Soul Improvisations	1971	18.00

COLUMBIA

❑ CL2497 [M]	Night Time Is the Lonely Time	1966	35.00
❑ CS9297 [S]	Night Time Is the Lonely Time	1966	30.00

H&L

❑ HL-69006	Disco Baby	1976	10.00
—Reissue of Avco 69006			
❑ HL-69002	Love Is the Answer	1976	10.00
—Reissue of Avco 69002			
❑ HL-69014	Rhythms of the World	1976	12.00
❑ HL-69009	The Disco Kid	1976	10.00
—Reissue of Avco 69009			
❑ HL-69016	The Hustle and Best of Van McCoy	1976	12.00
❑ HL-69012	The Real McCoy	1976	12.00
❑ HL-69022	Van McCoy and His Magnificent Movie Machine	1977	12.00

MCA

❑ 3054	A Woman Called Moses	1978	12.00
❑ 3071	Lovely Dancer	1979	12.00
❑ 3036	My Favorite Fantasy	1978	12.00

MCCOYS, THE

BANG

❑ BLP-212 [M]	Hang On Sloopy	1965	60.00
❑ BLPS-212 [S]	Hang On Sloopy	1965	40.00
❑ BLP-213 [M]	You Make Me Feel So Good	1966	60.00
❑ BLPS-213 [S]	You Make Me Feel So Good	1966	40.00

MERCURY

❑ SR-61207	Human Ball	1969	30.00
❑ SR-61163	Infinite McCoys	1968	30.00

MCCRACKLIN, JIMMY

CHESS

❑ LP-1464 [M]	Jimmy McCracklin Sings	1961	150.00

CROWN

❑ CLP-5244 [M]	Twist with Jimmy McCracklin	1962	50.00
—Black label, silver "Crown			
❑ CLP-5244 [M]	Twist with Jimmy McCracklin	1962	30.00
—Gray label			
❑ CLP-5244 [M]	Twist with Jimmy McCracklin	196?	18.00
—Black label, multi-color "Crown			

EVEJIM

❑ EJR-4013	Same Lovin'	198?	15.00

IMPERIAL

❑ LP-9285 [M]	Every Night, Every Day	1965	30.00
❑ LP-12285 [S]	Every Night, Every Day	1965	30.00
❑ LP-9219 [M]	I Just Gotta Know	1964	30.00
❑ LP-12219 [S]	I Just Gotta Know	1964	30.00
❑ LP-9306 [M]	My Answer	1966	30.00
❑ LP-12306 [S]	My Answer	1966	30.00
❑ LP-9316 [M]	The New Soul of Jimmy McCracklin	1966	30.00
❑ LP-12316 [S]	The New Soul of Jimmy McCracklin	1966	30.00
❑ LP-9297 [M]	Think	1965	30.00
❑ LP-12297 [S]	Think	1965	30.00

MINIT

❑ LP-24011	Let's Get Together	1968	30.00
❑ LP-24017	Stinger Man	1969	30.00
❑ LP-4009 [M]	The Best of Jimmy McCracklin	1967	30.00
❑ LP-24009 [S]	The Best of Jimmy McCracklin	1967	30.00

STAX

❑ MPS-8506	High on the Blues	1980	12.00
❑ STS-2047	Yesterday Is Gone	1972	25.00

MCCRAE, GEORGE

GOLD MOUNTAIN

❑ GM80008	Own the Night	1984	12.00

T.K.

❑ 606	Diamond Touch	1977	12.00
❑ 602	George McCrae	1975	12.00
❑ 501	Rock Your Baby	1974	12.00

MCCRAE, GEORGE AND GWEN

CAT

❑ 2606	Together	1976	12.00

Number	Title	Yr	NM
MCCRAE, GWEN			
ATLANTIC			
❏ 80014	On My Way	1982	12.00
CAT			
❏ 2603	Gwen McCrae	1974	12.00
❏ 2605	Rockin' Chair	1975	12.00
❏ 2608	Something So Right	1976	12.00
MCCULLOCH, DANNY			
CAPITOL			
❏ ST-174	Wings of a Man	1969	25.00
MCCURDY, ED; JACK ELLIOTT; OSCAR BRAND; DICK WILDER			
ELEKTRA			
❏ EKL-129 [M]	Badmen, Heroes and Pirate Songs	1957	25.00
MCCURDY, ED; JACK ELLIOTT; OSCAR BRAND			
ELEKTRA			
❏ EKL-14 [10]	Badmen and Heroes	1955	50.00
MCCURDY, ED			
DAWN			
❏ DLP-1127 [M]	The Folk Singer	195?	30.00
ELEKTRA			
❏ EKL-205 [M]	A Treasure Chest of American Folk Song	1961	25.00
❏ EKL-108 [M]	Blood Booze 'n' Bones	1956	25.00
❏ EKL-24 [10]	Sin Songs -- Pro and Con	1955	30.00
❏ EKL-124 [M]	Sin Songs -- Pro and Con	1957	25.00
—Reissue of EKL-24 with extra tracks			
❏ EKL-112 [M]	Songs of the Old West	1956	25.00
❏ EKL-170 [M]	Son of Dalliance	1959	25.00
❏ EKL-213 [M]	The Best of Dalliance	1961	25.00
❏ EKL-110 [M]	When Dalliance Was In Flower 1	1956	25.00
❏ EKL-140 [M]	When Dalliance Was In Flower 2	1958	25.00
❏ EKL-160 [M]	When Dalliance Was In Flower 3	1959	25.00
❏ EKS-7160 [S]	When Dalliance Was In Flower 3	1959	30.00
RIVERSIDE			
❏ RLP 12-601 [M]	The Ballad Record	195?	30.00
TRADITION			
❏ TLP-1003 [M]	A Ballad Singer's Choice	195?	30.00
❏ TLP-1027 [M]	Children's Songs	195?	30.00
❏ TLP-2061 [M]	Songs of the West	196?	25.00
MCCURN, GEORGE			
A&M			
❏ LP-102 [M]	Country Boy Goes to Town!!!!!	1963	30.00
MCDANIEL, WILLARD			
CROWN			
❏ CLP-5024 [M]	88 A La Carte	1958	100.00
MCDANIELS, GENE			
ATLANTIC			
❏ SD8281	Headless Heroes	1971	18.00
❏ SD8259	Outlaw	1970	18.00
LIBERTY			
❏ LRP-3191 [M]	100 Lbs. of Clay!	1961	30.00
❏ LST-7191 [S]	100 Lbs. of Clay!	1961	40.00
❏ LRP-3204 [M]	Gene McDaniels Sings Movie Memories	1962	30.00
❏ LST-7204 [S]	Gene McDaniels Sings Movie Memories	1962	40.00
❏ LRP-3258 [M]	Hit After Hit	1962	30.00
❏ LST-7258 [S]	Hit After Hit	1962	40.00
❏ LRP-3146 [M]	In Times Like These	1960	30.00
❏ LST-7146 [S]	In Times Like These	1960	200.00
—Blue vinyl			
❏ LST-7146 [S]	In Times Like These	1960	40.00
—Black vinyl			
❏ LRP-3175 [M]	Sometimes I'm Happy, Sometimes I'm Blue	1960	30.00
❏ LST-7175 [S]	Sometimes I'm Happy, Sometimes I'm Blue	1960	40.00
❏ LRP-3275 [M]	Spanish Lace	1963	30.00
❏ LST-7275 [S]	Spanish Lace	1963	30.00
❏ LRP-3311 [M]	The Wonderful World of Gene McDaniels	1963	30.00
❏ LST-7311 [S]	The Wonderful World of Gene McDaniels	1963	30.00
❏ LRP-3215 [M]	Tower of Strength	1962	30.00
❏ LST-7215 [S]	Tower of Strength	1962	40.00
ODE			
❏ SP-77028	Natural Juices	1975	15.00
SUNSET			
❏ SUM-1122 [M]	Facts of Life	1967	15.00
❏ SUS-5122 [S]	Facts of Life	1967	18.00
UNITED ARTISTS			
❏ UA-LA447-E	The Very Best of Gene McDaniels	1975	12.00

Number	Title	Yr	NM
MCDONALD, KATHI			
CAPITOL			
❏ ST-11224	Insane Asylum	1974	30.00
MCDONALD, MARIE			
RCA VICTOR			
❏ LPM-1585 [M]	The Body Sings!, The	1957	50.00
MCDONALD, MICHAEL			
ARISTA			
❏ ABM-2006	That Was Then -- The Early Recordings of Michael McDonald	1982	50.00
MOBILE FIDELITY			
❏ 1-149	If That's What It Takes	1985	40.00
—Audiophile vinyl			
REPRISE			
❏ 25979	Take It to Heart	1990	18.00
WARNER BROS.			
❏ 23703	If That's What It Takes	1982	12.00
❏ 25291	No Lookin' Back	1985	12.00
MCDONALD, SKEETS			
CAPITOL			
❏ T1040 [M]	Goin' Steady with the Blues	1958	80.00
COLUMBIA			
❏ CL2170 [M]	Call Me Skeets	1964	30.00
❏ CS8970 [S]	Call Me Skeets	1964	30.00
FORTUNE			
❏ 3001	The Tattooed Lady and Other Songs	1969	50.00
SEARS			
❏ SPS-116 [R]	Skeets	196?	30.00
MCDOWELL, MISSISSIPPI FRED			
ARHOOLIE			
❏ F-1021 [M]	Delta Blues	1964	50.00
❏ F-1027 [M]	Delta Blues, Volume 2	1966	50.00
❏ F 1068	Keep Your Lamp Trimmed and Burning	1973	25.00
❏ F-1046	Mississippi Fred McDowell and His Blues Boys	1970	30.00
CAPITOL			
❏ ST-403	I Do Not Play No Rock and Roll	1970	30.00
JUST SUNSHINE			
❏ JSS-4	Mississippi Fred McDowell 1904-1972	1973	18.00
MILESTONE			
❏ MLP-3003 [M]	Long Way from Home	1966	30.00
❏ MLS-93003 [S]	Long Way from Home	1966	40.00
SIRE			
❏ SES-97018	Mississippi Fred McDowell in London	1970	30.00
MCDOWELL, RONNIE			
CURB			
❏ 10602	I'm Still Missing You	1988	10.00
EPIC			
❏ FE38981	Country Boy's Heart	1983	12.00
❏ PE38981	Country Boy's Heart	1985	10.00
—Budget-line reissue with new prefix			
❏ JE36821	Going, Going ... Gone	1980	12.00
❏ PE36821	Going, Going ... Gone	198?	10.00
—Budget-line reissue with new prefix			
❏ FE37399	Good Time Lovin' Man	1981	12.00
❏ PE37399	Good Time Lovin' Man	198?	10.00
—Budget-line reissue with new prefix			
❏ FE38314	Greatest Hits	1983	12.00
❏ FE39954	In a New York Minute	1985	12.00
❏ JE36336	Love So Many Ways	1980	12.00
❏ FE38017	Love to Burn	1982	12.00
❏ PE38017	Love to Burn	198?	10.00
—Budget-line reissue with new prefix			
❏ PE40643	Older Women and Other Greatest Hits	1987	12.00
❏ FE38514	Personally	1983	12.00
❏ PE38514	Personally	1985	10.00
—Budget-line reissue with new prefix			
❏ JE36142	Rockin' You Easy, Lovin' You Slow	1979	12.00
❏ PE36142	Rockin' You Easy, Lovin' You Slow	198?	10.00
—Budget-line reissue with new prefix			
❏ FE39329	Willing	1984	12.00
MCA CURB			
❏ 5725	All Tied Up in Love	1986	10.00
SCORPION			
❏ 8028	I Love You, I Love You, I Love You	1978	18.00
❏ 0010	Live at the Fox	1978	18.00
❏ 8021	The King Is Gone	1977	25.00
MCDUFF, JACK			
ATLANTIC			
❏ 1463 [M]	A Change Is Gonna Come	1966	18.00
❏ SD1463 [S]	A Change Is Gonna Come	1966	25.00

Number	Title	Yr	NM
❏ SD1498	Double Barreled Soul	1968	18.00
❏ 1472 [M]	Tobacco Road	1967	30.00
❏ SD1472 [S]	Tobacco Road	1967	18.00
BLUE NOTE			
❏ BST-84322	Down Home Style	1969	18.00
❏ BST-84334	Moon Rappin'	1970	18.00
❏ BST-84348	To Seek a New Home	1970	18.00
❏ BST-84358	Who Knows	1971	18.00
CADET			
❏ CH-50024	Check This Out	1973	15.00
❏ CH-50051	Fourth Dimension	1974	15.00
❏ LPS-817	Getting Our Thing Together	1969	18.00
❏ LPS-831	Gin and Orange	1970	18.00
❏ CH-60031	Magnetic Feel	1975	15.00
❏ LPS-812	Natural Thing	1968	18.00
❏ CH-60017	The Healin' System	1972	15.00
CHESS			
❏ 19004	Sophisticated Funk	1976	15.00
FANTASY			
❏ OJC-326	Brother Jack Meets the Boss	1988	12.00
—Reissue of Prestige 7228			
❏ OJC-222	The Honeydripper	198?	12.00
—Reissue of Prestige 7199			
❏ OJC-324	Tough 'Duff	1988	12.00
—Reissue of Prestige 7185			
MUSE			
❏ MR-5361	The Re-Entry	1989	15.00
PRESTIGE			
❏ PRST-7771	Best of the Big Soul Band	1970	18.00
❏ PRLP-7174 [M]	Brother Jack	1960	50.00
❏ PRST-7174	Brother Jack	1970	18.00
❏ PRLP-7481 [M]	Brother Jack McDuff's Greatest Hits	1967	30.00
❏ PRST-7481 [S]	Brother Jack McDuff's Greatest Hits	1967	25.00
❏ PRLP-7220 [M]	Goodnight, It's Time to Go	1961	40.00
❏ PRST-7220 [S]	Goodnight, It's Time to Go	1961	40.00
❏ PRLP-7492 [M]	Hallelujah Time!	1967	30.00
❏ PRST-7492 [S]	Hallelujah Time!	1967	25.00
❏ PRLP-7422 [M]	Hot Barbeque	1966	25.00
❏ PRST-7422 [S]	Hot Barbeque	1966	30.00
❏ PRST-7642	I Got a Woman	1969	25.00
❏ PRST-7596	Jack McDuff Plays for Beautiful People	1969	25.00
❏ PRLP-7274 [M]	Live!	1963	40.00
❏ PRST-7274 [S]	Live!	1963	40.00
❏ PRLP-7286 [M]	Live! At the Jazz Workshop	1964	40.00
❏ PRST-7286 [S]	Live! At the Jazz Workshop	1964	40.00
❏ PRST 7703	Live! The Best of Brother Jack McDuff	1969	25.00
❏ PRLP-7228 [M]	Mellow Gravy -- Brother Jack Meets the Boss	1962	40.00
❏ PRST-7228 [S]	Mellow Gravy -- Brother Jack Meets the Boss	1962	40.00
❏ PRST-7851	On With It	1973	15.00
❏ PRLP-7333 [M]	Prelude	1964	30.00
❏ PRST-7333 [S]	Prelude	1964	30.00
❏ 24013	Rock Candy	1972	18.00
❏ PRLP-7259 [M]	Screamin'	1963	40.00
❏ PRST-7259 [S]	Screamin'	1963	40.00
❏ PRLP-7404 [M]	Silk and Soul	1965	30.00
❏ PRST-7404 [S]	Silk and Soul	1965	30.00
❏ PRLP-7265 [M]	Somethin' Slick!	1963	40.00
❏ PRST-7265 [S]	Somethin' Slick!	1963	40.00
❏ PRST-7567	Soul Circle	1968	25.00
❏ PRST-7666	Steppin' Out	1969	25.00
❏ PRLP-7362 [M]	The Concert McDuff Recorded Live!	1965	30.00
❏ PRST-7362 [S]	The Concert McDuff Recorded Live!	1965	30.00
❏ PRLP-7323 [M]	The Dynamic Jack McDuff	1964	40.00
❏ PRST-7323 [S]	The Dynamic Jack McDuff	1964	40.00
❏ PRLP-7199 [M]	The Honeydripper	1961	50.00
❏ PRST-7529	The Midnight Sun	1968	25.00
❏ PRST-7814	Tough Duff	1971	18.00
❏ PRLP-7185 [M]	Tough 'Duff	1960	50.00
❏ PRLP-7476 [M]	Walk On By	1967	30.00
❏ PRST-7476 [S]	Walk On By	1967	25.00
MCENTIRE, REBA			
MCA			
❏ 1P-8162	For My Broken Heart	1991	30.00
—Only released on vinyl through Columbia House			
❏ 5585	Have I Got a Deal for You	1985	10.00
❏ 5475	Just a Little Love	1984	10.00
❏ 42031	Merry Christmas to You	1987	12.00
❏ R164184	Merry Christmas to You	1987	15.00
—BMG Direct Marketing edition			
❏ 5516	My Kind of Country	1984	10.00
❏ 42134	Reba	1988	10.00
❏ R244602	Reba Live	1989	30.00
—BMG Direct Marketing version; no regular retail version			
❏ 2P-7933	Reba Live	1989	30.00
—Columbia House edition; no regular retail version			
❏ 5979	Reba McEntire's Greatest Hits	1987	10.00
❏ 10016	Rumor Has It	1990	25.00
❏ 6294	Sweet Sixteen	1989	12.00
❏ 42030	The Last One to Know	1987	10.00
❏ 5807	What Am I Gonna Do About You	1986	10.00
❏ 5691	Whoever's in New England	1986	10.00
MERCURY			
❏ 812781-1	Behind the Scene	1983	25.00

Number	Title	Yr	NM
❏ SRM-1-5029	Feel the Fire	1980	30.00
❏ 822887-1	Feel the Fire	1986	12.00
— Reissue			
❏ SRM-1-6003	Heart to Heart	1981	30.00
❏ SRM-1-5017	Out of a Dream	1979	40.00
❏ SRM-1-1177	Reba McEntire	1977	100.00
❏ SRM-1-5002	Reba McEntire	1977	40.00
— Reissue of 1177			
❏ 822455-1	Reba Nell McEntire	1986	12.00
❏ 824342-1	The Best of Reba McEntire	1985	12.00
❏ SRM-1-4047	Unlimited	1982	30.00
❏ 822882-1	Unlimited	1986	12.00
— Reissue			

MCEUEN, JOHN

WARNER BROS.
❏ 25266	John McEuen	1985	10.00

MCFADDEN, BOB

BRUNSWICK
❏ BL54056 [M]	Songs Our Mummy Taught Us	1959	200.00
❏ BL754056 [S]	Songs Our Mummy Taught Us	1959	300.00

MCFADDEN AND WHITEHEAD

PHILADELPHIA INT'L.
❏ JZ35800	McFadden and Whitehead	1979	15.00

TSOP
❏ JZ36773	I Heard It in a Love Song	1980	15.00

MCFARLAND, GARY

ABC IMPULSE!
❏ AS-46 [S]	Points of Departure	1968	18.00
❏ AS-9112 [S]	Profiles	1968	18.00
❏ AS-9122 [S]	Simpatico	1968	18.00
❏ AS-9104 [S]	Tijuana Jazz	1968	18.00

BUDDAH
❏ BDS95001	Butterscotch Rum	1967	25.00

COBBLESTONE
❏ CST9019	Requiem for Gary McFarland	1972	25.00

IMPULSE!
❏ A-46 [M]	Point of Departure	1963	30.00
❏ AS-46 [S]	Points of Departure	1963	40.00
❏ A-9112 [M]	Profiles	1966	30.00
❏ AS-9112 [S]	Profiles	1966	40.00
❏ A-9122 [M]	Simpatico	1966	30.00
❏ AS-9122 [S]	Simpatico	1966	40.00
❏ A-9104 [M]	Tijuana Jazz	1966	25.00
❏ AS-9104 [S]	Tijuana Jazz	1966	30.00

SKYE
❏ SK-8	America the Beautiful	1969	25.00
❏ SK-2	Does the Sun Really Shine on the Moon?	1968	25.00
❏ SK-11	Slaves	1970	30.00
❏ SK-14	Today	1970	30.00
❏ V-8443 [M]	How to Succeed in Business Without Really Trying	1962	25.00
❏ V6-8443 [S]	How to Succeed in Business Without Really Trying	1962	30.00
❏ V-8738 [M]	Scorpio and Other Signs	1967	50.00
❏ V6-8738 [S]	Scorpio and Other Signs	1967	40.00
❏ V-8603 [M]	Soft Samba	1964	30.00
❏ V6-8603 [S]	Soft Samba	1964	30.00
❏ V-8682 [M]	Soft Samba Strings	1966	30.00
❏ V6-8682 [S]	Soft Samba Strings	1966	30.00
❏ V6-8786	Sympathetic Vibrations	1969	30.00
❏ V-8632 [M]	The "In" Sound	1965	40.00
❏ V6-8632 [S]	The "In" Sound	1965	50.00
❏ V-8518 [M]	The Gary McFarland Orchestra with Special Guest Soloist Bill Evans	1963	30.00
❏ V6-8518 [S]	The Gary McFarland Orchestra with Special Guest Soloist Bill Evans	1963	30.00

MCFERRIN, BOBBY

BLUE NOTE
❏ BT-85110	Spontaneous Inventions	1986	15.00

ELEKTRA/MUSICIAN
❏ E1-60023	Bobby McFerrin	1982	12.00
❏ 60366	The Voice	1985	12.00

EMI MANHATTAN
❏ E1-48059	Simple Pleasures	1988	10.00
❏ E1-548059	Simple Pleasures	1988	12.00
— Columbia House edition			

MCGARITY, LOU

ARGO
❏ LP-654 [M]	Blue Lou	1960	30.00
❏ LPS-654 [S]	Blue Lou	1960	40.00

JUBILEE
❏ JGM-1108 [M]	Some Like It Hot	1959	50.00

MCGEE, SAM AND KIRK, AND THE CROOK BROTHERS

STARDAY
❏ SLP-182 [M]	Opry Old Timers	1962	40.00

MCGHEE, BROWNIE

BLUESVILLE
❏ BVLP-1042 [M]	Brownie's Blues	1962	80.00
— Blue label, silver print			
❏ BVLP-1042 [M]	Brownie's Blues	1964	30.00
— Blue label, trident logo at right			

FANTASY
❏ OBC-505	Brownie's Blues	198?	15.00

FOLKWAYS
❏ FP-30 [10]	Brownie McGhee Blues	1951	120.00
❏ FA-2030 [10]	Brownie McGhee Blues	1951	100.00
❏ 3557	Brownie McGhee Sings the Blues	197?	15.00
❏ 2421/2	Traditional Blues Vol. 1 and 2	197?	18.00

SAVOY JAZZ
❏ SJL-1204	Jumpin' the Blues	1989	15.00

MCGHEE, HOWARD

ARGO
❏ LP-4020 [M]	House Warmin'	1963	30.00
❏ LPS-4020 [S]	House Warmin'	1963	30.00

BETHLEHEM
❏ BCP-6055 [M]	Dusty Blue	1961	50.00
❏ BCPS-6055 [S]	Dusty Blue	1961	60.00
❏ BCP-61 [M]	Life Is Just a Bowl of Cherries	1957	80.00
❏ BCP-6039	That Bop Thing	197?	15.00
— Reissue of 42, distributed by RCA Victor			
❏ BCP-42 [M]	The Return of Howard McGhee	1956	80.00

BLACK LION
❏ 305	Shades of Blue	197?	15.00

BLUE NOTE
❏ BLP-5024 [10]	Howard McGhee, Volume 2	1953	300.00
❏ BLP-5012 [10]	Howard McGhee's All Stars/ Howard McGhee-Fats Navarro Sextet	1952	300.00

CADET
❏ LP-4020 [M]	House Warmin'	1966	15.00
❏ LPS-4020 [S]	House Warmin'	1966	18.00

CONTEMPORARY
❏ M-3596 [M]	Maggie's Back in Town	1961	40.00
❏ S-7596 [S]	Maggie's Back in Town	1961	50.00

DIAL
❏ LP-217 [10]	Night Music	1951	300.00

HI-LO
❏ HL-6001 [10]	Jazz Goes to the Battlefront, Vol. 1	1952	250.00
❏ HL-6002 [10]	Jazz Goes to the Battlefront, Vol. 2	1952	250.00

SAVOY
❏ MG-12026 [M]	Howard McGhee and Milt Jackson	1955	80.00

SAVOY JAZZ
❏ SJL-2219	Maggie	197?	18.00

STEEPLECHASE
❏ SCS-1024	Just Be There	198?	15.00

STORYVILLE
❏ 4077	Jazzbrothers	198?	15.00
❏ 4080	Young at Heart	198?	15.00

UNITED ARTISTS
❏ UAJ-14028 [M]	Nobody Knows You When You're Down and Out	1963	30.00
❏ UAS-15028 [S]	Nobody Knows You When You're Down and Out	1963	40.00

ZIM
❏ 2004	Cookin' Time	197?	15.00
❏ 2006	Live at Emerson's	197?	15.00

MCGHEE, STICK, AND JOHN LEE HOOKER

AUDIO LAB
❏ AL-1520 [M]	Highway of Blues	1959	350.00

MCGOVERN, MAUREEN

20TH CENTURY
❏ T-474	Academy Award Performances	1975	15.00
❏ T-439	Nice to Be Around	1974	15.00
❏ T-419	The Morning After	1973	15.00

CBS
❏ BFM42314	Another Woman in Love	1987	12.00
❏ BFM44500	State of the Heart	1988	12.00

WARNER BROS.
❏ BSK3329	Maureen McGovern	1979	12.00

MCGOVERN, PATTY, AND THOMAS TALBERT

ATLANTIC
❏ 1245 [M]	Wednesday's Child	1956	50.00
— Black label			
❏ 1245 [M]	Wednesday's Child	1961	30.00
— Multicolor label, white "fan" logo at right			

MCGRATH, BAT, AND DON POTTER

EPIC
❏ BN26499	Introducing	1969	18.00

MCGRAW, TIM

CURB
❏ 77886-2P [DJ]	Everywhere	1997	30.00
— Promo-only picture disc			

MCGREGOR, CHRIS, BROTHERHOOD OF BREATH

VENTURE
❏ 90988	Country Cooking	1988	12.00

MCGRIFF, JIMMY, AND JUNIOR PARKER

CAPITOL
❏ ST-569	Dudes Doin' Business	1971	18.00

UNITED ARTISTS
❏ UAS-6814 [B]	100 Proof Black Magic	1971	25.00
❏ UAS-5597 [B]	Jimmy McGriff and Junior Parker	1972	30.00

MCGRIFF, JIMMY

BLUE NOTE
❏ BST-84374	Black Pearl	1971	18.00
❏ BST-84350	Electric Funk	1970	18.00
❏ BST-84364	Something to Listen To	1971	18.00

CAPITOL
❏ ST-616	Soul Sugar	1970	18.00

COLLECTABLES
❏ COL-5147	Blues for Mr. Jimmy	198?	12.00

GROOVE MERCHANT
❏ 2203	Black and Blues	1971	18.00
❏ 520	Come Together	1973	15.00
❏ 509	Fly Dude	1973	18.00
❏ 4403 [B]	Flyin' Time	197?	25.00
❏ 3300	Giants of the Organ In Concert	1974	18.00
❏ 2205	Good Things Don't Happen Every Day	1971	18.00
❏ 503	Groove Grease	1972	18.00
❏ 529	If You're Ready Come Go with Me	1974	15.00
❏ 506	Let's Stay Together	1972	18.00
❏ 534	Main Squeeze	1975	15.00
❏ 3311	Mean Machine	1976	15.00
❏ 3309	Stump Juice	1976	15.00

JAM
❏ 002	City Lights	1982	15.00
❏ 005	Movin' Upside the Blues	1983	15.00

LRC
❏ 9320	Outside Looking In	1978	18.00
❏ 0316	Tailgunner	1977	18.00

MILESTONE
❏ M-9163	Blue to the 'Bone	1988	12.00
❏ M-9116	Countdown	1984	12.00
❏ M-9120	Skywalk	1985	12.00
❏ M-9135	State of the Art	1986	12.00
❏ M-9140	The Starting Five	1987	12.00

QUINTESSENCE
❏ 25061	Soul	1978	15.00

SOLID STATE
❏ SS-18017	A Bag Full of Blues	1968	25.00
❏ SM-17002 [M]	A Bag Full of Soul	1966	18.00
❏ SS-18002 [S]	A Bag Full of Soul	1966	25.00
❏ SS-18060	A Thing to Come By	1969	25.00
❏ SM-17006 [M]	Cherry	1967	25.00
❏ SS-18006 [S]	Cherry	1967	25.00
❏ SS-18036	Honey	1968	25.00
❏ SS-18030	I've Got a New Woman	1968	25.00
❏ SS-18053	Step I	1969	25.00
❏ SM-17001 [M]	The Big Band of Jimmy McGriff	1966	18.00
❏ SS-18001 [S]	The Big Band of Jimmy McGriff	1966	25.00
❏ SS-18063	The Way You Look Tonight	1970	25.00
❏ SS-18045	The Worm	1968	25.00

SUE
❏ LP-1039 [M]	Blues for Mister Jimmy	1965	30.00
❏ STLP-1039 [S]	Blues for Mister Jimmy	1965	40.00
❏ LP-1018 [M]	Christmas with McGriff	1963	30.00
❏ STLP-1018 [S]	Christmas with McGriff	1963	40.00
❏ LP-1012 [M]	I've Got a Woman	1962	30.00
❏ STLP-1012 [S]	I've Got a Woman	1962	40.00
❏ LP-1017 [M]	Jimmy McGriff at the Apollo	1963	30.00
❏ STLP-1017 [S]	Jimmy McGriff at the Apollo	1963	40.00
❏ LP-1020 [M]	Jimmy McGriff at the Organ	1963	30.00
❏ STLP-1020 [S]	Jimmy McGriff at the Organ	1963	40.00
❏ LP-1013 [M]	One of Mine	1963	30.00
❏ STLP-1013 [S]	One of Mine	1963	40.00
❏ LP-1043 [M]	Toast to Greatest Hits	1966	25.00
❏ STLP-1043 [S]	Toast to Greatest Hits	1966	30.00
❏ LP-1033 [M]	Topkapi	1964	30.00
❏ STLP-1033 [S]	Topkapi	1964	40.00

SUNSET
❏ SUS-5264	The Great Jimmy McGriff	1969	12.00

VEEP
❏ VP-13522 [M]	Greatest Organ Hits	1967	30.00
❏ VPS-13522 [S]	Greatest Organ Hits	1967	25.00
❏ VP-13515 [M]	Live Where the Action Is	1966	25.00
❏ VPS-16515 [S]	Live Where the Action Is	1966	30.00

Number	Title	Yr	NM

MCGUINN, CLARK, & HILLMAN

CAPITOL
☐ ST-12043	City	1980	15.00
☐ SW-11910	McGuinn, Clark & Hillman	1979	15.00

MCGUINN, ROGER

ARISTA
☐ AL8648	Back from Rio	1991	18.00

COLUMBIA
☐ PC34154	Cardiff Rose	1976	15.00
☐ KC32956	Peace On You	1974	15.00
☐ PC33541	Roger McGuinn & Band	1975	15.00
☐ KC31946	Roger McGuinn	1973	15.00
☐ AS353 [DJ]	The Roger McGuinn Airplay Anthology	1977	30.00
—Promo only; also includes Byrds tracks			
☐ PC34656	Thunderbyrd	1977	15.00

MCGUINN AND HILLMAN

CAPITOL
☐ SOO-12108	McGuinn and Hillman	1980	12.00

MCGUIRE, BARRY, AND BARRY KANE

HORIZON
☐ WP-1608 [M]	Barry and Barry: Here and Now!	1962	30.00
☐ SWP-1608 [S]	Barry and Barry: Here and Now!	1962	30.00

MCGUIRE, BARRY

ABC DUNHILL
☐ DS-50033	The World's Last Private Citizen	1968	30.00

DUNHILL
☐ D-50003 [M]	Eve of Destruction	1965	50.00
☐ DS-50003 [S]	Eve of Destruction	1965	60.00
☐ D-50005 [M]	This Precious Time	1966	30.00
☐ DS-50005 [S]	This Precious Time	1966	30.00

HORIZON
☐ WP-1636 [M]	The Barry McGuire Album	1963	30.00
☐ ST-1636 [S]	The Barry McGuire Album	1963	40.00

MIRA
☐ LP-3000 [M]	The Barry McGuire Album	1965	25.00
—Reissue of Horizon LP			
☐ LPS-3000 [S]	The Barry McGuire Album	1965	30.00
—Reissue of Horizon LP			

MYRRH
☐ MSA-6531	Lighten Up	1975	15.00
☐ MSA-6519	Seeds	1974	15.00

ODE
☐ SP-77004	Barry McGuire with the Doctor	1970	18.00

MCGUIRE, PHYLLIS

ABC-PARAMOUNT
☐ 552 [M]	Phyllis McGuire Sings	1966	18.00
☐ S-552 [S]	Phyllis McGuire Sings	1966	25.00

MCGUIRE SISTERS, THE

ABC-PARAMOUNT
☐ 530 [M]	The McGuire Sisters Today	1966	18.00
☐ S-530 [S]	The McGuire Sisters Today	1966	25.00

CORAL
☐ CRL56123 [10]	By Request	1955	50.00
☐ CRL57097 [M]	Children's Holiday	1956	40.00
☐ CRL57026 [M]	Do You Remember When	1956	40.00
☐ CRL57225 [M]	Greetings from the McGuire Sisters	1958	30.00
☐ CRL57033 [M]	He	1956	40.00
☐ CRL57337 [M]	His and Hers	1960	25.00
☐ CRL757337 [S]	His and Hers	1960	30.00
☐ CRL57303 [M]	In Harmony with Him	1959	30.00
☐ CRL757303 [S]	In Harmony with Him	1959	40.00
☐ CRL57385 [M]	Just for Old Times' Sake	1961	25.00
☐ CRL757385 [S]	Just for Old Times' Sake	1961	30.00
☐ CRL57296 [M]	May You Always	1959	25.00
☐ CRL757296 [S]	May You Always	1959	30.00
☐ CRL57180 [M]	Musical Magic	1957	30.00
☐ CRL57349 [M]	Our Golden Favorites	1961	25.00
☐ CRL757349 [S]	Our Golden Favorites	196?	15.00
☐ CRL57443 [M]	Showcase	196?	25.00
☐ CRL757443 [S]	Showcase	196?	15.00
☐ CRL57052 [M]	Sincerely	1956	40.00
☐ CRL57415 [M]	Songs Everybody Knows	1962	18.00
☐ CRL757415 [S]	Songs Everybody Knows	1962	25.00
☐ CRL57398 [M]	Subways Are for Sleeping	1961	18.00
☐ CRL757398 [S]	Subways Are for Sleeping	1961	25.00
☐ CRL57217 [M]	Sugartime	1958	30.00
☐ CRL57028 [M]	'S Wonderful	1956	40.00
☐ CRL57134 [M]	Teenage Party	1957	30.00
☐ CXB6 [M]	The Best of the McGuire Sisters	1965	30.00
☐ 7CXB6 [P]	The Best of the McGuire Sisters	1965	30.00
☐ CRL57145 [M]	While the Lights Are Low	1957	30.00

MCA
☐ 4119	The Best of the McGuire Sisters	1978	15.00
—Reissue of Coral 6			

VOCALION
☐ VL3685 [M]	Children's Holiday	1960	25.00
☐ VL3798 [M]	The McGuire Sisters	1967	18.00
☐ VL73798 [R]	The McGuire Sisters	1967	15.00

MCHARGUE, ROSY

JUMP
☐ JL-8 [10]	Dixie Combo	1955	50.00

MCINTOSH, LADD

SEA BREEZE
☐ 2007	Energy	198?	12.00

MCINTYRE, HAL

COLUMBIA
☐ CL6124 [10]	Dance Date	1950	50.00

FORUM
☐ F-9018 [M]	It Seems Like Only Yesterday	196?	15.00
☐ SF-9018 [S]	It Seems Like Only Yesterday	196?	18.00

HINDSIGHT
☐ HSR-172	Hal McIntyre and His Orchestra 1943-45	198?	12.00

ROULETTE
☐ R-25079 [M]	It Seems Like Only Yesterday	1959	25.00
☐ SR-25079 [S]	It Seems Like Only Yesterday	1959	30.00

MCINTYRE, KALAPARUSHA MAURICE

BLACK SAINT
☐ BSR-0037	Peace and Blessings	198?	15.00

DELMARK
☐ DS-425	Forces and Feelings	197?	25.00
☐ DS-419	Humility	1969	25.00

MCINTYRE, KEN

FANTASY
☐ OJC-252	Looking Ahead	1987	15.00

INNER CITY
☐ IC-2014	Hindsight	1976	40.00
☐ IC-2039	Home	197?	30.00
☐ IC-2065	Introducing the Vibrations	1977	30.00
☐ IC-2049	Open Horizon	1976	25.00

NEW JAZZ
☐ NJLP-8247 [M]	Looking Ahead	1960	150.00
—Purple label			
☐ NJLP-8247 [M]	Looking Ahead	1965	30.00
—Blue label, trident logo at right			
☐ NJLP-8259 [M]	Stone Blues	1961	80.00
—Purple label			
☐ NJLP-8259 [M]	Stone Blues	1965	30.00
—Blue label, trident logo at right			

STEEPLECHASE
☐ SCS-1114	Chasing the Sun	198?	18.00
☐ SCS-1014	Hindsight	198?	25.00
☐ SCS-1039	Home	198?	18.00
☐ SCS-1065	Introducing the Vibrations	198?	18.00
☐ SCS-1049	Open Horizon	198?	18.00

UNITED ARTISTS
☐ UAL-3336 [M]	Way Way Out	1964	80.00
☐ UAS-6336 [S]	Way Way Out	1964	100.00
☐ UAJ-14015 [M]	Year of the Iron Sheep	1962	50.00
☐ UAJS-15015 [S]	Year of the Iron Sheep	1962	60.00

MCKAY, SCOTTY

ACE
☐ LP-1017 [M]	Tonight In Person	1961	80.00

MCKAY, STUART

RCA VICTOR
☐ LJM-1021 [M]	Stuart McKay and His Woods	1955	40.00

MCKENDREE SPRING

DECCA
☐ DL75104	McKendree Spring	1969	18.00
☐ DL75332	McKendree Spring 3	1972	18.00
☐ DL75230	Second Thoughts	1970	18.00
☐ DL75385	Tracks	1972	18.00

MCA
☐ 277	McKendree Spring	1973	12.00
—Reissue of Decca 75104			
☐ 44	McKendree Spring 3	1973	12.00
—Reissue of Decca 75332			
☐ 370	Spring Suite	1973	15.00
☐ 50	Tracks	1973	12.00
—Reissue of Decca 75385			

PYE
☐ 12108	Get Me to the Country	1975	15.00
☐ 12124	Too Young to Feel This Old	1976	15.00

MCKENNA, DAVE, AND HALL OVERTON

BETHLEHEM
☐ BCP-6049 [M]	Dual Piano Jazz	1960	30.00
☐ BCPS-6049 [S]	Dual Piano Jazz	1960	30.00

MCKENNA, DAVE; SCOTT HAMILTON; JAKE HANNA

CONCORD JAZZ
☐ CJ-97	No Bass Hit	1979	15.00

MCKENNA, DAVE

ABC-PARAMOUNT
☐ ABC-104 [M]	Solo Piano	1956	40.00

CHIAROSCURO
☐ 175	Dave "Fingers" McKenna	197?	15.00
☐ 136	Dave McKenna Quartet Featuring Zoot Sims	197?	18.00
☐ 202	McKenna	1978	15.00
☐ 119	Piano Solos	197?	18.00

CONCORD JAZZ
☐ CJ-227	Celebration of Hoagy Carmichael	1984	12.00
☐ CJ-292	Dancing in the Dark	1986	12.00
☐ CJ-174	Dave McKenna Plays Music of Harry Warren	198?	12.00
☐ CJ-99	Giant Strides	1979	15.00
☐ CJ-123	Left Handed Complement	1980	15.00
☐ CJ-313	My Friend the Piano	1987	12.00
☐ CJ-365	No More Ouzo for Puzo	1989	15.00
☐ CJ-261	The Key Man	1985	12.00

EPIC
☐ LN3558 [M]	Dave McKenna	1959	30.00
☐ BN527 [S]	Dave McKenna	1959	30.00

FAMOUS DOOR
☐ 122	No Holds Barred	1978	15.00

HALCYON
☐ 108	Cookin' at Michael's Pub	197?	18.00

SHIAH
☐ MK-1	By Myself	198?	15.00

MCKENZIE, BOB AND DOUG

MERCURY
☐ SRM-1-4034	Great White North	1981	15.00

MCKENZIE, RED, AND EDDIE CONDON

JAZZOLOGY
☐ J-110	Chicagoans (1944)	198?	12.00

MCKENZIE, SCOTT

ODE
☐ SP-77007	Stained Glass Morning	1970	18.00
☐ Z1244002 [S]	The Voice of Scott McKenzie	1967	25.00
☐ Z1244001 [M]	The Voice of Scott McKenzie	1967	60.00

MCKINLEY, RAY, AND EDDIE SAUTER

SAVOY
☐ MG-12024 [M]	Borderline	1955	50.00

MCKINLEY, RAY

ALLEGRO ELITE
☐ 4129 [10]	Ray McKinley and His Famous Orchestra	195?	100.00
☐ 4015 [10]	Ray McKinley Plays Sauter and Others	195?	50.00

SAVOY JAZZ
☐ SJK-2261	The Most Versatile Band in the World	198?	15.00

MCKINLEY, RAY/JOE MARSALA

DECCA
☐ DL5262 [10]	Dixieland Jazz Battle, Vol. 2	1950	50.00

MCKINLEY, TOM, AND ED SCHULLER

GM
☐ 3001	Life Cycle	1982	12.00

MCKINNEY, HAROLD

TRIBE
☐ 2233	Voices and Rhythms	197?	40.00

MCKINNEY'S COTTON PICKERS

RCA VICTOR
☐ LPT-24 [10]	McKinney's Cotton Pickers	1952	60.00

X
☐ LVA-3031 [10]	McKinney's Cotton Pickers	1954	50.00

MCKUEN, ROD; TAK SHINDO; JULIE MEREDITH

IMPERIAL
☐ LP-9092 [M]	The Yellow Unicorn	1960	40.00
☐ LP-12036 [S]	The Yellow Unicorn	1960	50.00

MCKUEN, ROD

BUDDAH
☐ BDS-5138	Cycles	197?	15.00

CAPITOL
☐ ST2838 [S]	Love Movement	1968	18.00
☐ T2838 [M]	Love Movement	1968	30.00
☐ T2079 [M]	Rod McKuen Sings Rod McKuen	1964	18.00
☐ ST2079 [S]	Rod McKuen Sings Rod McKuen	1964	25.00

Number	Title	Yr	NM

DECCA
❏ DL8946 [M]	Alone After Dark	1959	25.00
❏ DL78946 [S]	Alone After Dark	1959	30.00
❏ DL8882 [M]	Anywhere I Wander	1958	25.00
❏ DL78882 [S]	Anywhere I Wander	1958	30.00
❏ DL4969 [M]	Very Warm	1968	25.00
❏ DL74969 [S]	Very Warm	1968	18.00

EPIC
| ❏ BN26370 [S] | In Search of Eros | 1968 | 18.00 |
| ❏ BN26370 [S] | In Search of Eros | 1968 | 30.00 |

— *White label promo only; in stereo cover with "Epic Mono" sticker*

EVEREST
| ❏ 3208 | Desire Has No Special Time | 1968 | 18.00 |
| ❏ 3267 | Life Is | 197? | 18.00 |

HIFI
❏ R419 [M]	Beatsville	1960	25.00
❏ SR419 [S]	Beatsville	1960	30.00
❏ R407 [M]	Time of Desire	1958	25.00
❏ SR407 [S]	Time of Desire	1958	30.00

HORIZON
❏ WP-1612 [M]	New Sounds in Folk Music	1963	25.00
❏ ST-1612 [S]	New Sounds in Folk Music	1963	30.00
❏ WPLP-1632 [M]	There's a Hoot Tonight	1963	25.00
❏ WPLP-1632 [S]	There's a Hoot Tonight	1963	30.00

IN
| ❏ 1003 [M] | Seasons in the Sun | 1964 | 25.00 |
| ❏ S-1003 [S] | Seasons in the Sun | 1964 | 30.00 |

JUBILEE
| ❏ J-5013 [M] | Mr. Oliver Twist | 1962 | 25.00 |
| ❏ SJ-5013 [S] | Mr. Oliver Twist | 1962 | 30.00 |

KAPP
| ❏ KL-1538 [M] | In a Lonely Place | 1967 | 25.00 |
| ❏ KS-3538 [S] | In a Lonely Place | 1967 | 18.00 |

LIBERTY
| ❏ LRP-3011 [M] | Lazy Afternoon | 1956 | 40.00 |

RCA VICTOR
❏ LSP-4010	A Single Man	1968	18.00
❏ LPM-3863 [M]	Listen to the Warm	1967	25.00
❏ LSP-3863 [S]	Listen to the Warm	1967	18.00
❏ LPM-3635 [M]	Other Kinds of Songs	1966	18.00
❏ LSP-3635 [S]	Other Kinds of Songs	1966	25.00
❏ LPM-3424 [M]	Rod McKuen Sings His Own	1965	18.00
❏ LSP-3424 [S]	Rod McKuen Sings His Own	1965	25.00
❏ LSP-4127	The Best of Rod McKuen	1969	18.00
❏ LPM-3508 [M]	The Loner	1966	18.00
❏ LSP-3508 [S]	The Loner	1966	25.00
❏ LPM-3786 [M]	Through European Windows	1967	25.00
❏ LSP-3786 [S]	Through European Windows	1967	18.00

STANYAN
❏ 5010	A Boy Named Charlie Brown	1970	18.00
❏ 5051	Amsterdam Concert	1972	18.00
❏ 5072	A Portrait of Rod McKuen	1972	15.00
❏ 4010	A Single Man	197?	12.00
❏ 5005	Blessings in Shades of Green	1970	15.00
❏ 10009	Concerto No. 1; Four Statements	197?	15.00
❏ 9001	Concerto No. 1 for Four Harpsichords and Orchestra	197?	15.00
❏ 9006	Concerto No. 2 for Guitar and Orchestra; Five Pieces	197?	15.00
❏ 9012	Concerto No. 3 for Piano and Orchestra	1972	15.00
❏ 5040	Evening in Vienna	1972	15.00
❏ 5006	Folk Album	1970	15.00
❏ 5032	Have a Nice Day	1973	15.00
❏ STS-001	In Concert	197?	18.00

— *Originals are numbered, limited editions*
❏ 5048	Listen to the Warm	197?	18.00
❏ 5075	Live at the Sydney Opera House	197?	15.00
❏ 5016	Live in London!	1971	18.00
❏ 5009	Love's Been Good to Me	1970	15.00
❏ 9010	McKuen Conducts McKuen	1972	15.00
❏ 1894	Pastorale	197?	15.00
❏ 5047	Pastures Green	197?	15.00
❏ 9008	Piano Variations	197?	15.00
❏ 5025	Rod	197?	15.00
❏ 5042	Rod McKuen Grand Tour, Vol. 3	1972	15.00
❏ 5031	Rod McKuen's Greatest Hits, Vol. 3	197?	15.00
❏ 2688	Rod McKuen's Greatest Hits, Vol. 4	197?	12.00
❏ 2560	Rod McKuen's Greatest Hits 2	197?	12.00
❏ 5022	Rod McKuen Sings Jacques Brel	197?	15.00
❏ 9015	Seascapes; Plains of My Country	197?	15.00
❏ STS-003	Seasons in the Sun	197?	18.00
❏ 5004	Seasons in the Sun Vol. 2	197?	15.00
❏ 5046	Seasons in the Sun Vols. 1 and 2	197?	18.00
❏ 9005	Symphony No. 1: "All Men Love Something"	197?	15.00
❏ 5020	Try Rod McKuen in Your Own Home	197?	15.00

SUNSET
| ❏ SUS-5273 | In the Beginning | 1970 | 12.00 |

TRADITION
| ❏ 2063 [M] | A San Francisco Hippie Trip | 1967 | 30.00 |

WARNER BROS.
❏ BS2817	Alone	1974	15.00
❏ 2WS2731	Back to Carnegie Hall	1973	18.00
❏ WS1722	Beautiful Strangers	1968	18.00
❏ WS1772	Greatest Hits of Rod McKuen	1969	18.00
❏ ST-92042	Greatest Hits of Rod McKuen	1969	25.00

— *Capitol Record Club edition*
❏ WS1758	Lonesome Cities	1968	18.00
❏ BS2931	McKuen Country	1976	12.00
❏ WS1837	New Ballads	1970	15.00
❏ BS2638	Odyssey	1973	15.00
❏ 2WS1894	Pastorale	1971	18.00
❏ 2WS1794	Rod McKuen at Carnegie Hall	1969	25.00
❏ 2WS1947	Rod McKuen Grand Tour	1971	18.00
❏ BS2688	Rod McKuen's Greatest Hits, Vol. 4	1973	15.00
❏ BS2560	Rod McKuen's Greatest Hits 2	1970	15.00
❏ BS2785	Seasons in the Sun	1974	15.00

MCKUSICK, HAL

BETHLEHEM
| ❏ BCP-16 [M] | East Coast Jazz/8 | 1955 | 200.00 |

CORAL
| ❏ CRL57131 [M] | Hal McKusick Quintet | 1957 | 120.00 |
| ❏ CRL57116 [M] | Jazz at the Academy | 1957 | 80.00 |

DECCA
| ❏ DL9209 [M] | Cross Section -- Saxes | 1958 | 100.00 |
| ❏ DL79209 [S] | Cross Section -- Saxes | 1958 | 100.00 |

MCA
| ❏ 1379 | Hal McKusick Quintet Featuring Art Farmer 1957 | 198? | 15.00 |

PRESTIGE
| ❏ PRLP-7135 [M] | Triple Exposure | 1957 | 400.00 |

RCA VICTOR
| ❏ LPM-1164 [M] | Hal McKusick in the 20th Century Drawing Room | 1956 | 80.00 |
| ❏ LPM-1366 [M] | The Jazz Workshop | 1957 | 120.00 |

MCLACHLAN, SARAH

ARISTA
| ❏ RTH-2013 | Afterglow | 2004 | 30.00 |

— *Audiophile vinyl issue by Classic Records*
| ❏ RTH-2000 | Fumbling Toward Ecstasy and The Freedom Sessions | 1997 | 40.00 |

— *Audiophile vinyl issue of both CDs on 2-LP set by Classic Records, with one bonus track*
| ❏ RTH 2005 | Solace | 2002 | 30.00 |

— *Audiophile vinyl reissue by Classic Records*
| ❏ RTH-18970 | Surfacing | 1999 | 30.00 |

— *Audiophile vinyl issue by Classic Records*
| ❏ AL0601 | Touch | 1989 | 25.00 |
| ❏ RTH-2004 | Touch | 2002 | 30.00 |

— *Audiophile vinyl reissue by Classic Records*

MCLAIN, DENNY

CAPITOL
| ❏ ST2881 | Denny McLain at the Organ | 1968 | 30.00 |
| ❏ ST-204 | Denny McLain In Las Vegas | 1969 | 30.00 |

MCLAIN, TOMMY

CRAZY CAJUN
| ❏ 1050 | Good Mornin' Lousiana | 1978 | 30.00 |

JIN
| ❏ 9009 | Tommy McLain | 1975 | 30.00 |

STARFLITE
| ❏ 36028 | Backwoods Bayou Adventure | 1979 | 18.00 |

MCLAUGHLIN, JOHN

CBS
| ❏ FM45578 | Mediterranean Concerto | 1989 | 18.00 |

CELLULOID
| ❏ CEL-5010 | Devotion | 198? | 12.00 |

— *Reissue of Douglas 31568*

COLUMBIA
| ❏ PC34372 | A Handful of Beauty | 1977 | 15.00 |

— *No bar code on cover*
| ❏ JC35785 | Electric Dreams | 1979 | 12.00 |
| ❏ JC35326 | Electric Guitarist | 1978 | 15.00 |

— *No bar code on cover*
| ❏ FC37152 | Friday Night in San Francisco | 1981 | 12.00 |

— *With Al DiMeola and Paco De Lucia*
| ❏ JC34980 | Natural Elements | 1977 | 15.00 |

— *No bar code on cover*
| ❏ FC38645 | Passion, Grace & Fire | 1983 | 12.00 |

— *With Al DiMeola and Paco De Lucia*
| ❏ PC34162 | Shakti with John McLaughlin | 1976 | 15.00 |

— *No bar code on cover*
| ❏ JC36355 | The Best of John McLaughlin | 1980 | 15.00 |
| ❏ PC36355 | The Best of John McLaughlin | 198? | 10.00 |

— *Reissue with new prefix*

DOUGLAS
| ❏ KZ31568 | Devotion | 1972 | 18.00 |

— *Reissue of 4*
| ❏ 4 | Devotion | 1970 | 25.00 |
| ❏ KZ30766 | My Goals Beyond | 1971 | 18.00 |

— *Original issue*

DOUGLAS CASABLANCA
| ❏ ADLP-6003 | My Goals Beyond | 1976 | 15.00 |

— *Reissue of Douglas 30766; second issue of this album*

ELEKTRA/MUSICIAN
| ❏ E1-60031 | My Goals Beyond | 1982 | 15.00 |

— *Third issue of this album*

POLYDOR
| ❏ PD-5510 | Extrapolation | 1972 | 25.00 |
| ❏ PD-1-6074 | Extrapolation | 1972 | 15.00 |

— *Reissue of 5510*

PYE
| ❏ 12103 | Where Fortune Smiles | 1975 | 25.00 |

— *Recorded in 1970; this was the first U.S. issue of this material*

RELATIVITY
| ❏ 88561-8061-1 | Adventures in Radioland | 1986 | 15.00 |

RYKO ANALOGUE
| ❏ RALP-0051 | My Goals Beyond | 1987 | 25.00 |

— *Clear vinyl; fourth issue of this album*

WARNER BROS.
❏ BSK3619	Belo Horizonte	1981	18.00
❏ 25190	Mahavishnu	1985	12.00
❏ 23723	Music Spoken Here	1982	12.00

MCLAWLER, SARAH

VEE JAY
| ❏ LP-1030 [M] | At the Break of Day | 1961 | 60.00 |

— *With Richard Otto*

MCLEAN, DON

ARISTA
| ❏ AL4149 | Prime Time | 1978 | 12.00 |

CAPITOL
| ❏ C1-48080 | Love Tracks | 1988 | 12.00 |

EMI AMERICA
| ❏ ST-17255 | Don McLean's Greatest Hits, Then and Now | 1987 | 12.00 |

LIBERTY
| ❏ LN-10037 | American Pie | 1980 | 10.00 |

— *Reissue of United Artists 5535*
| ❏ LN-10211 | Homeless Brother | 198? | 10.00 |

— *Reissue of United Artists 315*
| ❏ LN-10167 | Tapestry | 1982 | 10.00 |

— *Reissue of United Artists 5522*

MEDIARTS
| ❏ 41-4 | Tapestry | 1970 | 25.00 |

MILLENNIUM
| ❏ BXL1-7762 | Believers | 1981 | 12.00 |
| ❏ BXL1-7756 | Chain Lightning | 1981 | 12.00 |

UNITED ARTISTS
❏ UAS-5535	American Pie	1971	15.00
❏ UAS-5651	Don McLean	1972	15.00
❏ UA-LA315-G	Homeless Brother	1974	15.00
❏ UA-LA161-F	Playin' Favorites	1973	15.00
❏ UA-LA652-H2	Solo	1976	18.00
❏ UAS-5522	Tapestry	1971	15.00

— *Reissue of Mediarts LP*

MCLEAN, JACKIE, AND MICHAEL CARVIN

INNER CITY
| ❏ IC-2028 | Antiquity | 197? | 18.00 |

STEEPLECHASE
| ❏ SCS-1028 | Antiquity | 198? | 15.00 |

MCLEAN, JACKIE

ADLIB
| ❏ ADL-6601 [M] | The Jackie McLean Quintet | 1955 | 2000.00 |

BLUE NOTE
| ❏ BLP-4218 [M] | Action Action Action | 1965 | 120.00 |

— *With "New York, USA" address on label*
| ❏ BST-84218 [S] | Action Action Action | 1965 | 100.00 |

— *With "New York, USA" address on label*
| ❏ BST-84218 [S] | Action Action Action | 1967 | 30.00 |

— *With "A Division of Liberty Records" on label*
| ❏ BLP-4089 [M] | A Fickle Sonance | 1961 | 400.00 |

— *With W. 63rd St. address on label*
| ❏ BLP-4089 [M] | A Fickle Sonance | 1963 | 150.00 |

— *With "New York, USA" address on label*
| ❏ BST-84089 [S] | A Fickle Sonance | 1961 | 250.00 |

— *With W. 63rd St. address on label*
| ❏ BST-84089 [S] | A Fickle Sonance | 1963 | 100.00 |

— *With "New York, USA" address on label*
| ❏ BST-84089 [S] | A Fickle Sonance | 1967 | 40.00 |

— *With "A Division of Liberty Records" on label*
| ❏ BLP-4067 [M] | Bluesnik | 1961 | 400.00 |

Number	Title	Yr	NM
— With W. 63rd St. address on label			
❑ BLP-4067 [M]	Bluesnik	1963	40.00
— With "New York, USA" address on label			
❑ BST-84067 [S]	Bluesnik	1961	200.00
— With W. 63rd St. address on label			
❑ BST-84067 [S]	Bluesnik	1963	60.00
— With "New York, USA" address on label			
❑ BST-84067 [S]	Bluesnik	1967	30.00
— With "A Division of Liberty Records" on label			
❑ B1-84067 [S]	Bluesnik	1989	15.00
— The Finest in Jazz Since 1939" reissue			
❑ BST-84284	'Bout Soul	1968	80.00
— With "A Division of Liberty Records" on label			
❑ BLP-4038 [M]	Capuchin Swing	1960	600.00
— Deep groove; with "W. 63rd St." address on label			
❑ BLP-4038 [M]	Capuchin Swing	1960	150.00
— W. 63rd St. address on label, either with no "deep groove" or with the groove on only one side			
❑ BLP-4038 [M]	Capuchin Swing	1963	40.00
— With "New York, USA" address on label			
❑ BST-84038 [S]	Capuchin Swing	1960	250.00
— With W. 63rd St. address on label			
❑ BST-84038 [S]	Capuchin Swing	1963	60.00
— With "New York, USA" address on label			
❑ BST-84038 [S]	Capuchin Swing	1967	30.00
— With "A Division of Liberty Records" on label			
❑ LT-994	Consequences	1979	12.00
❑ BST-84345	Demon's Dance	1969	80.00
— With "A Division of Liberty Records" on label			
❑ BST-84345	Demon's Dance	198?	12.00
— The Finest in Jazz Since 1939" reissue			
❑ BLP-4165 [M]	Destination... Out!	1964	120.00
— With "New York, USA" address on label			
❑ BST-84165 [S]	Destination... Out!	197?	18.00
— Dark blue label with white stylized "B			
❑ BST-84165 [S]	Destination... Out!	1964	100.00
— With "New York, USA" address on label			
❑ BST-84165 [S]	Destination... Out!	1967	40.00
— With "A Division of Liberty Records" on label			
❑ BN-LA483-J2	Hipnosis	1975	30.00
❑ BLP-4179 [M]	It's Time!	1964	60.00
— With "New York, USA" address on label			
❑ BST-84179 [S]	It's Time!	1964	100.00
— With "New York, USA" address on label			
❑ BST-84179 [S]	It's Time!	1967	30.00
— With "A Division of Liberty Records" on label			
❑ BLP-4051 [M]	Jackie's Bag	1960	700.00
— Deep groove; with W. 63rd St. address on label			
❑ BLP-4051 [M]	Jackie's Bag	1963	50.00
— With "New York, USA" address on label			
❑ BST-84051 [S]	Jackie's Bag	1960	250.00
— With W. 63rd St. address on label			
❑ BST-84051 [S]	Jackie's Bag	1963	60.00
— With "New York, USA" address on label			
❑ BST-84051 [S]	Jackie's Bag	1967	30.00
— With "A Division of Liberty Records" on label			
❑ BST-84051 [S]	Jackie's Bag	1985	15.00
— The Finest in Jazz Since 1939" reissue			
❑ BN-LA457-H2	Jackknife	1975	30.00
— First issue of unreleased material from 1960s			
❑ BLP-4106 [M]	Let Freedom Ring	1962	300.00
— With "New York, USA" address on label			
❑ BST-84106 [S]	Let Freedom Ring	1962	200.00
— With "New York, USA" address on label			
❑ BST-84106 [S]	Let Freedom Ring	1967	40.00
— With "A Division of Liberty Records" on label			
❑ BST-84106 [S]	Let Freedom Ring	198?	15.00
— The Finest in Jazz Since 1939" reissue			
❑ BLP-4262 [M]	New and Old Gospel	1967	250.00
— With "A Division of Liberty Records" on label			
❑ BST-84262 [S]	New and Old Gospel	1967	120.00
— With "A Division of Liberty Records" on label			
❑ BLP-4013 [M]	New Soil	1959	500.00
— Deep groove" version; W. 63rd St. address on label			
❑ BLP-4013 [M]	New Soil	1959	300.00
— Regular version, W. 63rd St. address on label			
❑ BLP-4013 [M]	New Soil	1963	50.00
— With "New York, USA" address on label			
❑ BST-4013 [S]	New Soil	1959	300.00
— Deep groove" version; W. 63rd St. address on label			
❑ BST-4013 [S]	New Soil	1959	200.00
— Regular version, W. 63rd St. address on label			
❑ BST-4013 [S]	New Soil	1963	40.00
— With "New York, USA" address on label			
❑ BST-84013 [S]	New Soil	1967	30.00
— With "A Division of Liberty Records" on label			
❑ B1-84013 [S]	New Soil	1989	15.00
— The Finest in Jazz Since 1939" reissue			
❑ BLP-4137 [M]	One Step Beyond	1963	120.00
— With "New York, USA" address on label			
❑ BST-84137 [S]	One Step Beyond	1963	100.00
— With "New York, USA" address on label			
❑ BST-84137 [S]	One Step Beyond	1967	40.00
— With "A Division of Liberty Records" on label			
❑ BST-84137 [S]	One Step Beyond	198?	15.00
— The Finest in Jazz Since 1939" reissue			
❑ BST-84137 [S]	One Step Beyond	197?	18.00
— Dark blue label with black stylized "B			

Number	Title	Yr	NM
❑ BLP-4215 [M]	Right Now!	1965	80.00
— With "New York, USA" address on label			
❑ BST-84215 [S]	Right Now!	1965	100.00
— With "New York, USA" address on label			
❑ BST-84215 [S]	Right Now!	1967	30.00
— With "A Division of Liberty Records" on label			
❑ BLP-4024 [M]	Swing, Swang, Swingin'	1959	800.00
— Deep groove" version; W. 63rd St. address on label			
❑ BLP-4024 [M]	Swing, Swang, Swingin'	1959	500.00
— Regular version, W. 63rd St. address on label			
❑ BLP-4024 [M]	Swing, Swang, Swingin'	1963	50.00
— With "New York, USA" address on label			
❑ BST-84024 [S]	Swing, Swang, Swingin'	1959	400.00
— With W. 63rd St. address on label			
❑ BST-84024 [S]	Swing, Swang, Swingin'	1963	80.00
— With "New York, USA" address on label			
❑ BST-84024 [S]	Swing, Swang, Swingin'	1967	30.00
— With "A Division of Liberty Records" on label			
❑ BST-84427	Tippin' the Scales	198?	18.00
❑ LT-1085	Vertigo	1980	12.00
BOPLICITY			
❑ BOP-2	Swing, Swang, Swingin'	198?	12.00
FANTASY			
❑ OJC-056	4, 5 and 6	198?	15.00
❑ OJC-253	A Long Drink of the Blues	1987	15.00
❑ OJC-074	Jackie McLean & Co.	198?	15.00
❑ OJC-1717	Jackie's Pal -- Introducing Bill Hardman	198?	15.00
❑ OJC-426	Lights Out!	1990	18.00
❑ OJC-197	Makin' the Changes	1985	15.00
❑ OJC-098	McLean's Scene	198?	15.00
❑ OJC-354	Strange Blues	198?	15.00
INNER CITY			
❑ IC-2013	Ghetto Lullaby	197?	18.00
❑ IC-2001	Live at Montmartre	197?	18.00
❑ IC-6029	New Wine	1978	18.00
❑ IC-2023	New York Calling	197?	18.00
❑ IC-2009	Ode to Super	197?	18.00
JOSIE			
❑ JJM-3503 [M]	Jackie McLean Sextet	1963	60.00
❑ JJM-3507 [M]	Jackie McLean Sextet	1963	60.00
❑ JLPS-3503 [S]	Jackie McLean Sextet	1963	40.00
❑ JLPS-3507 [S]	Jackie McLean Sextet	1963	40.00
JUBILEE			
❑ JLP-1093 [M]	Jackie McLean Plays Fat Jazz	1959	200.00
❑ JLP-1064 [M]	The Jackie McLean Quintet	1958	150.00
MOSAIC			
❑ MQ6-150	The Complete Blue Note 1964-66 Jackie McLean Sessions	1993	200.00
— Limited edition of 5,000			
NEW JAZZ			
❑ NJLP-8279 [M]	4, 5 and 6	1962	100.00
— Purple label			
❑ NJLP-8279 [M]	4, 5 and 6	1965	40.00
— Blue label, trident logo at right			
❑ NJLP-8253 [M]	A Long Drink of the Blues	1961	150.00
— Purple label			
❑ NJLP-8253 [M]	A Long Drink of the Blues	1965	40.00
— Blue label, trident logo at right			
❑ NJLP-8263 [M]	Lights Out!	1961	100.00
— Purple label			
❑ NJLP-8263 [M]	Lights Out!	1965	40.00
— Blue label, trident logo at right			
❑ NJLP-8231 [M]	Makin' the Changes	1960	150.00
— Purple label			
❑ NJLP-8231 [M]	Makin' the Changes	1965	40.00
— Blue label, trident logo at right			
❑ NJLP-8212 [M]	McLean's Scene	1958	150.00
— Purple label			
❑ NJLP-8212 [M]	McLean's Scene	1965	40.00
— Blue label, trident logo at right			
❑ NJLP-8290 [M]	Steeplechase	1962	100.00
— Purple label			
❑ NJLP-8290 [M]	Steeplechase	1965	40.00
— Blue label, trident logo at right			
PRESTIGE			
❑ PRLP-7048 [M]	4, 5 and 6	1956	300.00
— 446 W. 50th St., N.Y.C." address on yellow label			
❑ PRLP-7114 [M]	Alto Madness	1957	250.00
— Yellow label			
❑ MPP-2512	Alto Madness	198?	15.00
❑ P-24076	Contour	1977	25.00
❑ PRLP-7087 [M]	Jackie McLean & Co.	1957	500.00
— 446 W. 50th St., N.Y.C." address on label			
❑ PRLP-7068 [M]	Jackie's Pal -- Introducing Bill Hardman	1956	300.00
— 446 W. 50th St., N.Y.C." address on yellow label			
❑ PRLP-7035 [M]	Lights Out!	1956	300.00
— 446 W. 50th St., N.Y.C." address on yellow label			
❑ PRST-7757	Lights Out!	1970	30.00
❑ PRLP-7500 [M]	Strange Blues	1967	40.00
❑ PRST-7500 [R]	Strange Blues	1967	30.00
RCA VICTOR			
❑ AFL1-3230 [S]	Monuments	1979	30.00
ROULETTE			
❑ RE-129	Echoes of an Era (Tune-Up)	1976	18.00

Number	Title	Yr	NM
STATUS			
❑ ST-8312 [M]	Alto Madness	1965	60.00
❑ ST-8323 [M]	Jackie McLean & Co.	1965	60.00
STEEPLECHASE			
❑ SCS-1013	A Ghetto Lullaby	198?	15.00
❑ SCC-6005	Dr. Jackie	198?	15.00
❑ SCS-1001	Live at Montmartre	198?	15.00
❑ SCS-1023	New York Calling	198?	15.00
❑ SCS-1009	Ode to Super	198?	15.00
❑ SCS-1006	The Meeting	198?	15.00
❑ SCS-1020	The Source	198?	15.00
TRIP			
❑ TLX-5027	Two Sides of Jackie McLean	197?	25.00

MCLEAN, RENE

Number	Title	Yr	NM
INNER CITY			
❑ IC-2037	Watch Out	197?	18.00
STEEPLECHASE			
❑ SCS-1037	Watch Out!	198?	15.00

MCLOLLIE, OSCAR

Number	Title	Yr	NM
CROWN			
❑ CLP-5016 [M]	Oscar McLollie and His Honey Jumpers	1956	400.00
— Opinions differ as to whether this LP actually exists. Value is probably conservative.			

MCLUHAN, MARSHALL

Number	Title	Yr	NM
COLUMBIA			
❑ CL2701 [M]	The Medium Is the Message	1967	30.00
❑ CS9501 [S]	The Medium Is the Message	1967	30.00

MCLUHAN

Number	Title	Yr	NM
BRUNSWICK			
❑ BL754177	Anomaly	1972	25.00

MCMAHON, ED

Number	Title	Yr	NM
CAMEO			
❑ C-2009 [M]	And Me...I'm Ed McMahon	1967	30.00
❑ SC-2009 [S]	And Me...I'm Ed McMahon	1967	30.00
RCA CAMDEN			
❑ CAL-1083 [M]	What Do You Want to Be When You Grow Up?	1965	25.00
❑ CAS-1083 [S]	What Do You Want to Be When You Grow Up?	1965	30.00

MCNABB, TED

Number	Title	Yr	NM
EPIC			
❑ LN3663 [M]	Ted McNabb and Company	1959	50.00
❑ BN558 [S]	Ted McNabb and Company	1959	40.00

MCNAIR, BARBARA

Number	Title	Yr	NM
AUDIO FIDELITY			
❑ AFSD-6222	More Today Than Yesterday	1969	25.00
❑ ST-92074	More Today Than Yesterday	1969	30.00
— Capitol Record Club edition			
MOTOWN			
❑ 644 [M]	Here I Am	1966	50.00
❑ S-644 [S]	Here I Am	1966	60.00
❑ S-680	The Real Barbara McNair	1969	30.00
SIGNATURE			
❑ SM1042 [M]	Love Talk	1960	40.00
❑ SS1042 [S]	Love Talk	1960	50.00
WARNER BROS.			
❑ W1541 [M]	I Enjoy Being a Girl	1964	30.00
❑ WS1541 [S]	I Enjoy Being a Girl	1964	30.00
❑ W1570 [M]	The Livin' End	1964	30.00
❑ WS1570 [S]	The Livin' End	1964	30.00

MCNEELY, BIG JAY

Number	Title	Yr	NM
COLLECTABLES			
❑ COL-5133	Golden Classics	198?	12.00
FEDERAL			
❑ 295-96 [10]	Big Jay McNeely	1955	3000.00
❑ 395-530 [M]	Big Jay McNeely in 3-D	1956	800.00
KING			
❑ 650 [M]	Big "J" in 3-D	1959	500.00
SAVOY			
❑ MG-15045 [10]	A Rhythm and Blues Concert	1955	2000.00
— VG value 1000; VG+ value 1500			
WARNER BROS.			
❑ W1533 [M]	Big Jay McNeely	1963	80.00
❑ WS1533 [S]	Big Jay McNeely	1963	100.00

MCNEILL, DON

Number	Title	Yr	NM
CORAL			
❑ CRL57288 [M]	Book, Candle, Prayer	1958	30.00
❑ CRL57291 [M]	March Around the Breakfast Table	1958	30.00

MCNEILL, LLOYD

Number	Title	Yr	NM
ASHA			
❑ 3	Washington Suite	1976	18.00

Number	Title	Yr	NM
MCNICHOL, KRISTY AND JIMMY			
RCA VICTOR			
❏ AFL1-2875	Kristy and Jimmy McNichol	1978	25.00
MCPARTLAND, JIMMY/PAUL BARBARIN			
JAZZTONE			
❏ J-1241 [M]	Dixieland Now and Then	195?	30.00
MCPARTLAND, MARIAN, AND GEORGE SHEARING			
SAVOY			
❏ MG-12016 [M]	Great Britain's Marion McPartland and George Shearing	1955	40.00
MCPARTLAND, MARIAN			
ARGO			
❏ LP-640 [M]	Marion McPartland at the London House	1959	40.00
❏ LPS-640 [S]	Marion McPartland at the London House	1959	30.00
BAINBRIDGE			
❏ 1045	Marian McPartland with Ben Tucker	198?	12.00
CAPITOL			
❏ T699 [M]	After Dark	1956	40.00
❏ T574 [M]	Marion McPartland at the Hickory House	1955	40.00
❏ T785 [M]	Marion McPartland Trio	1957	40.00
CONCORD JAZZ			
❏ CJ-86	From This Moment On	1979	12.00
❏ CJ-118	Marian McPartland at the Festival	1981	12.00
❏ CJ-326	Marian McPartland Plays the Music of Billy Strayhorn	1987	12.00
❏ CJ-202	Personal Choice	1982	12.00
❏ CJ-101	Portrait of Marian McPartland	1980	12.00
❏ CJ-272	Willow Creek and Other Ballads	1985	12.00
DOT			
❏ DLP-25907	My Old Flame	1969	18.00
HALCYON			
❏ 103	Ambience	1971	18.00
❏ 105	Delicate Balance	1972	18.00
❏ 100	Interplay	1970	18.00
❏ 117	Live at the Carlyle	1979	15.00
❏ 109	Marian McPartland Plays Alec Wilder	197?	18.00
❏ 115	Now's the Time	1978	15.00
❏ 111	Solo Concert at Haverford	197?	15.00
IMPROV			
❏ 7115	A Fine Romance	1976	15.00
SAVOY			
❏ MG-15019 [10]	Jazz at Storyville, Volume 3	1952	80.00
❏ MG-15032 [10]	Jazz at the Hickory House	1953	80.00
❏ MG-12006 [M]	Lullaby of Birdland	1955	50.00
❏ MG-15027 [10]	Marion McPartland	1953	80.00
❏ MG-12004 [M]	Marion McPartland in Concert	1955	50.00
❏ MG-15021 [10]	Piano Moods	1952	80.00
SAVOY JAZZ			
❏ SJL-2248	Marian McPartland at the Hickory House	198?	18.00
TIME			
❏ 52073 [M]	Bossa Nova Plus Soul	1963	30.00
❏ S-2073 [S]	Bossa Nova Plus Soul	1963	30.00
❏ 52189 [M]	West Side Story	196?	30.00
❏ S-2189 [S]	West Side Story	196?	30.00
MCPHATTER, CLYDE			
ALLEGIANCE			
❏ AV-5029	The Pretty One	198?	12.00
ATLANTIC			
❏ 8031 [M]	Clyde	1959	500.00
—Black label			
❏ 8031 [M]	Clyde	1960	400.00
—White "bullseye" label			
❏ 8031 [M]	Clyde	1960	200.00
—Brown and purple label			
❏ 8024 [M]	Love Ballads	1958	500.00
—Black label			
❏ 8024 [M]	Love Ballads	1960	200.00
—Brown and purple label			
❏ 8024 [M]	Love Ballads	1960	400.00
—White "bullseye" label			
❏ 8077 [M]	The Best of Clyde McPhatter	1963	200.00
DECCA			
❏ DL75231	Welcome Home	1970	30.00
MERCURY			
❏ MG-20783 [M]	Clyde McPhatter's Greatest Hits	1963	30.00
❏ SR-60783 [S]	Clyde McPhatter's Greatest Hits	1963	40.00
❏ MG-20655 [M]	Golden Blues Hits	1961	50.00
❏ SR-60655 [S]	Golden Blues Hits	1961	70.00
❏ MG-20915 [M]	Live at the Apollo	1964	30.00
❏ SR-60915 [S]	Live at the Apollo	1964	40.00
❏ MG-20711 [M]	Lover Please	1962	50.00

Number	Title	Yr	NM
❏ SR-60711 [S]	Lover Please	1962	70.00
❏ MG-20750 [M]	Rhythm and Soul	1962	50.00
❏ SR-60750 [S]	Rhythm and Soul	1962	70.00
❏ MG-20902 [M]	Songs of the Big City	1964	30.00
❏ SR-60902 [S]	Songs of the Big City	1964	40.00
❏ MG-20597 [M]	Ta Ta	1960	50.00
❏ SR-60262 [S]	Ta Ta	1960	70.00
MGM			
❏ E-3866 [M]	Clyde McPhatter's Greatest Hits	1960	70.00
❏ SE-3866 [S]	Clyde McPhatter's Greatest Hits	1960	80.00
❏ E-3775 [M]	Let's Start Over Again	1959	150.00
❏ SE-3775 [S]	Let's Start Over Again	1959	200.00
WING			
❏ MGW-12224 [M]	May I Sing for You?	1962	30.00
❏ SRW-16224 [S]	May I Sing for You?	1962	30.00
MCPHEE, JOE			
CJR			
❏ 2	Nation Time	197?	30.00
❏ 4	Pieces of Light	197?	30.00
❏ 3	Trinity	197?	30.00
HAT ART			
❏ 2033	Po Music: A Future Retrospective	1987	18.00
HAT HUT			
❏ 0A	Black Magic Man	1974	30.00
❏ 0P	Glasses	1978	25.00
❏ 0I/J	Graphics	1977	30.00
❏ 01	Old Eyes	1979	25.00
❏ 0D	Rotation	1977	25.00
❏ 0C	Tenor	1976	25.00
❏ 1987/8	Topology	1981	30.00
❏ 0O	Variations on a Blue Line/Round Midnight	1978	25.00
MCPHERSON, CHARLES			
MAINSTREAM			
❏ MRL-329	Charles McPherson	1972	18.00
❏ MRL-365	Siku Ya Bibi	1973	18.00
❏ MRL-395	Today's Man	1974	18.00
PRESTIGE			
❏ PRLP-7359 [M]	Bebop Revisited	1965	30.00
❏ PRST-7359 [S]	Bebop Revisited	1965	40.00
❏ PRLP-7427 [M]	Con Alma!	1966	30.00
❏ PRST-7427 [S]	Con Alma!	1966	40.00
❏ PRST-7559	From This Moment On	1968	30.00
❏ PRST-7603	Horizons	1969	30.00
❏ PRST-7743	McPherson's Mood	1970	25.00
❏ PRLP-7480 [M]	The Charles McPherson Quintet Live!	1967	40.00
❏ PRST-7480 [S]	The Charles McPherson Quintet Live!	1967	30.00
XANADU			
❏ 115	Beautiful	1976	15.00
❏ 170	Free Bop	1979	15.00
❏ 131	Live in Tokyo	1977	15.00
❏ 149	New Horizons	1978	15.00
MCRAE, CARMEN			
ACCORD			
❏ SN-7152	Love Songs	1981	12.00
ATLANTIC			
❏ 8143 [M]	For Once in My Life	1967	25.00
❏ SD8143 [S]	For Once in My Life	1967	18.00
❏ SD1568	Just a Little Lovin'	1971	15.00
❏ 8165 [M]	Portrait of Carmen	1968	30.00
❏ SD8165 [S]	Portrait of Carmen	1968	18.00
❏ SD 2-904	The Great American Songbook	1971	25.00
❏ SD8200 [S]	The Sound of Silence	1968	18.00
❏ 8200 [M]	The Sound of Silence	1968	30.00
—Mono is white label promo only; "d/j copy monaural" sticker on front cover			
BAINBRIDGE			
❏ 6221	The Sound of Silence	198?	12.00
BETHLEHEM			
❏ BCP-1023 [10]	Carmen McRae	1955	100.00
BLUE NOTE			
❏ BN-LA635-G	Can't Hide Love	1976	15.00
❏ BN-LA462-G	I Am Music	1975	15.00
❏ BN-LA709-H2	The Great Music Hall	1977	18.00
❏ LWB-709	The Great Music Hall	1981	15.00
—Reissue of BN-LA709-H2			
BUDDAH			
❏ B2D-6501	I'm Coming Home Again	1980	18.00
CATALYST			
❏ 7904	As Time Goes By	197?	15.00
COLUMBIA			
❏ CL1730 [M]	Lover Man	1962	25.00
❏ CS8530 [S]	Lover Man	1962	30.00
❏ CL1943 [M]	Something Wonderful	1962	25.00
❏ CS8743 [S]	Something Wonderful	1962	30.00
CONCORD JAZZ			
❏ CJ-342	Fine and Mellow	1988	12.00
❏ CJ-128	Two for the Road	1980	12.00
❏ CJ-235	You're Looking at Me: A Collection of Nat King Cole Songs	1984	12.00

Number	Title	Yr	NM
DECCA			
❏ DL8583 [M]	After Glow	1957	50.00
—Black label, silver print			
❏ DL8583 [M]	After Glow	1960	25.00
—Black label with color bars			
❏ DL8815 [M]	Birds of a Feather	1959	50.00
—Black label, silver print			
❏ DL8815 [M]	Birds of a Feather	1960	25.00
—Black label with color bars			
❏ DL8347 [M]	Blue Moon	1957	100.00
—Black label, silver print			
❏ DL8347 [M]	Blue Moon	1960	25.00
—Black label with color bars			
❏ DL8173 [M]	By Special Request	1955	50.00
—Black label, silver print			
❏ DL8173 [M]	By Special Request	1960	25.00
—Black label with color bars			
❏ DL8738 [M]	Carmen for Cool Ones	1958	50.00
—Black label, silver print			
❏ DL8738 [M]	Carmen for Cool Ones	1960	25.00
—Black label with color bars			
❏ DL8662 [M]	Mad About the Man	1958	50.00
—Black label, silver print			
❏ DL8662 [M]	Mad About the Man	1960	25.00
—Black label with color bars			
❏ DL8267 [M]	Torchy!	1956	50.00
—Black label, silver print			
❏ DL8267 [M]	Torchy!	1960	25.00
—Black label with color bars			
FOCUS			
❏ FL-334 [M]	Bittersweet	1964	18.00
❏ FS-334 [S]	Bittersweet	1964	25.00
GROOVE MERCHANT			
❏ 522	A Whole Lot of Human Feeling	1973	15.00
❏ 531	Ms. Jazz	1974	15.00
❏ 4401	Velvet Soul	197?	18.00
HARMONY			
❏ KH32177	Carmen McRae Sings Billie Holiday	1972	12.00
❏ HL7452 [M]	Yesterdays	1968	25.00
❏ HS11252 [S]	Yesterdays	1968	15.00
JAZZ MAN			
❏ 5004	Carmen McRae and the Kenny Clarke/Francy Boland Big Band	198?	12.00
KAPP			
❏ KL-1117 [M]	Book of Ballads	1958	30.00
❏ KS-3000 [S]	Book of Ballads	1958	30.00
❏ KL-1169 [M]	Something to Swing About	1960	30.00
❏ KS-3053 [S]	Something to Swing About	1960	30.00
❏ KL-1541 [M]	This Is Carmen McRae	1967	25.00
❏ KS-3541 [S]	This Is Carmen McRae	1967	18.00
❏ KL-1125 [M]	When You're Away	1959	30.00
❏ KS-3018 [S]	When You're Away	1959	30.00
MAINSTREAM			
❏ 56084 [M]	Alfie	1966	18.00
❏ S-6084 [S]	Alfie	1966	25.00
❏ 800	Alive!	1974	18.00
❏ 309	Carmen McRae	1971	15.00
❏ 352	Carmen McRae In Person	1972	15.00
❏ 338	Carmen's Gold	1972	15.00
❏ 56044 [M]	Haven't We Met?	1965	18.00
❏ S-6044 [S]	Haven't We Met?	1965	25.00
❏ 56091 [M]	In Person/San Francisco	1967	30.00
❏ S-6091 [S]	In Person/San Francisco	1967	18.00
❏ 387	I Want You	1972	15.00
❏ S-6110	Live & Wailin'	1968	18.00
❏ 403	Live and Doin' It	1974	15.00
❏ 56028 [M]	Second to None	1965	18.00
❏ S-6028 [S]	Second to None	1965	25.00
❏ 56065 [M]	Woman Talk	1966	18.00
❏ S-6065 [S]	Woman Talk	1966	25.00
MCA			
❏ 4111	The Greatest of Carmen McRae	197?	15.00
NOVUS			
❏ 3086-1-N	Carmen Sings Monk	1990	15.00
PAUSA			
❏ 9003	Can't Hide Love	198?	12.00
QUINTESSENCE			
❏ 25021	Ms. Jazz	1978	12.00
—Reissue of Groove Merchant 531			
STANYAN			
❏ 10115	Mad About the Man	197?	15.00
TEMPONIC			
❏ 29562	Carmen	1972	15.00
TIME			
❏ 52104 [M]	Live at Sugar Hill	1960	25.00
❏ S-2104 [S]	Live at Sugar Hill	1960	30.00
VOCALION			
❏ VL3697 [M]	Carmen McRae	1963	18.00
❏ VL73828	My Foolish Heart	1969	15.00
MCRITCHIE, GREG			
CADET			
❏ LP-4058 [M]	Fighting Back	1967	30.00
❏ LPS-4058 [S]	Fighting Back	1967	18.00

Number	Title	Yr	NM
ZEPHYR			
❏ 12005 [M]	Easy Jazz on a Fish Beat Bass	1959	250.00
MCSHANN, JAY			
ATLANTIC			
❏ SD8804	The Big Apple Bash	1979	15.00
❏ 90047	The Big Apple Bash	198?	12.00
—Reissue of 8804			
❏ SD8800	The Last of Jay McShann	197?	15.00
CAPITOL			
❏ T2645 [M]	McShann's Piano	1967	25.00
❏ ST2645 [S]	McShann's Piano	1967	25.00
CLASSIC JAZZ			
❏ 128	Confessin' the Blues	197?	15.00
DECCA			
❏ DL5503 [10]	Kansas City Memories	1954	500.00
—CHARLIE PARKER appears on this LP			
❏ DL9236 [M]	Kansas City Memories	1958	200.00
❏ DL79236 [R]	Kansas City Memories	196?	18.00
MASTER JAZZ			
❏ 8113	Going to Kansas City	197?	18.00
MCA			
❏ 1338	The Early Bird	198?	12.00
SACKVILLE			
❏ 3040	Airmail Special	198?	12.00
❏ 3019	A Tribute to Fats Waller	198?	12.00
❏ 3011	Crazy Legs and Friday Strut	1977	12.00
❏ 3035	Just a Little So and So	198?	12.00
❏ 3021	Kansas City Hustle	198?	12.00
❏ 3006	The Man from Muskogee	198?	12.00
❏ 3025	Tuxedo Junction	1980	12.00
MCTELL, BLIND WILLIE			
BLUESVILLE			
❏ BVLP-1040 [M]	Last Session	1962	120.00
—Blue label, silver print			
❏ BVLP-1040 [M]	Last Session	1964	30.00
—Blue label, trident logo at right			
MELODEON			
❏ 7323 [M]	1940	1956	150.00
MCTELL, RALPH			
CAPITOL			
❏ ST-240	Eight Frames a Second	1969	15.00
REPRISE			
❏ MS2121	Not Till Tomorrow	1973	12.00
MCVIE, CHRISTINE			
SIRE			
❏ SASD-7522	The Legendary Christine Perfect Album	1976	18.00
—Original with ABC distribution			
❏ SR6022	The Legendary Christine Perfect Album	1978	12.00
—Reissue with Warner Bros. distribution			
WARNER BROS.			
❏ 25059	Christine McVie	1984	10.00
❏ 25059 [DJ]	Christine McVie	1984	30.00
—Promo on Quiex II vinyl			
MCWILLIAMS, DAVID			
KAPP			
❏ KS-3547 [B]	Days of Pearly Spencer	1968	30.00
MEADER, VAUGHN			
CADENCE			
❏ CLP3060 [M]	The First Family	1962	12.00
❏ CLP3065 [M]	The First Family, Volume Two	1963	25.00
❏ CLP25065 [S]	The First Family, Volume Two	1963	30.00
KAMA SUTRA			
❏ KSBS-2038	The Second Coming	1971	18.00
LAURIE			
❏ LLP-2035 [M]	Take That!	1966	18.00
VERVE			
❏ V-15042 [M]	Have Some Nuts	1964	18.00
❏ V6-15042 [S]	Have Some Nuts	1964	25.00
❏ V-15050 [M]	If the Shoe Fits	1965	18.00
MEADOW			
PARAMOUNT			
❏ PAS-6066	The Friend Ship	1973	25.00
MEADOWS, DOROTHY, AND JOHN EASTMAN			
INTERNATIONAL AWARD SERIES			
❏ AK-X-8 [M]	Christmas Songs for the Family	196?	15.00
MEAT LOAF			
ATLANTIC			
❏ 81698	Blind Before I Stop	1986	10.00

Number	Title	Yr	NM
CLEVELAND INT'L.			
❏ FE36007	Dead Ringer	1981	10.00
EPIC			
❏ PE34974	Bat Out of Hell	1977	12.00
—Orange label; originals do not have bar code on back cover			
❏ JE34974	Bat Out of Hell	1979	10.00
—Dark blue label			
❏ E9934974 [PD]	Bat Out of Hell	1978	25.00
❏ HE44974	Bat Out of Hell	1981	40.00
—Half-speed mastered edition			
❏ FE38444	Midnight at the Lost and Found	1983	10.00
RCA VICTOR			
❏ AFL1-5451	Bad Attitude	1985	10.00
VIRGIN			
❏ 09463-63147-1	Bat Out of Hell III: The Monster Is Loose	2006	25.00
MEAT PUPPETS			
LONDON			
❏ 1109 [10]	Raw Meat	1994	25.00
—Promo-only five-song 10-inch EP			
❏ 828484-1	Too High to Die	1994	25.00
—Includes bonus 10-inch EP (double value for DJ stamp on cover)			
MERCURY			
❏ 828665-1	No Joke!	1995	18.00
SST			
❏ 150 [B]	Huevos	1987	30.00
❏ 009 [B]	Meat Puppets	1982	30.00
❏ 019 [B]	Meat Puppets II	1984	30.00
❏ 100 [B]	Mirage	1986	25.00
❏ 253	Monsters	1989	18.00
❏ 265	No Strings Attached	1990	25.00
❏ 049 [10]	Out My Way	1986	25.00
—10-inch EP			
❏ 039 [B]	Up on the Sun	1985	30.00
MEATMEN, THE			
HOMESTEAD			
❏ 009	War of the Superbikes	198?	18.00
TOUCH & GO			
❏ TGLP 001	We're the Meatmen...And You Suck	198?	18.00
MECCA, LOU			
BLUE NOTE			
❏ BLP-5067 [10]	Lou Mecca Quartet	1955	300.00
MECKI MARK MEN, THE			
LIMELIGHT			
❏ LS-86068	Running in the Summer Night	1969	30.00
❏ LS-86054	The Mecki Mark Men	1968	30.00
MECO			
ARISTA			
❏ AL8-8098	Ewok Celebration	1983	15.00
❏ AL5-8235	Ewok Celebration	198?	12.00
—Reissue of 8098			
❏ AL9598	Pop Goes the Movies	1982	15.00
❏ AL9605	Swingtime's Greatest Hits	1982	12.00
CASABLANCA			
❏ NBLP7260	Meco's Impressions of An American Werewolf in London	1981	15.00
❏ NBLP7155	Moondancer	1979	15.00
❏ NBLP7196	Music from Star Trek and Music from The Black Hole	1980	15.00
❏ NBLP7136	Superman and Other Galactic Heroes	1979	15.00
MILLENNIUM			
❏ MNLP8004	Encounters of Every Kind	1977	15.00
❏ MNLP8001	Star Wars and Other Galactic Funk	1977	15.00
❏ MNLP8009	The Wizard of Oz	1978	15.00
—Black vinyl			
❏ MNLP8009	The Wizard of Oz	1978	30.00
—Gold vinyl			
RSO			
❏ RO-1-3086 [10]	Meco Plays Music from The Empire Strikes Back	1980	18.00
MEDIUM			
GAMMA			
❏ GS-503	Medium	196?	100.00
MEDLEY, BILL			
A&M			
❏ SP-3505	A Song for You	1971	15.00
❏ SP-3517	Smile	1972	15.00
LIBERTY			
❏ LT-1097	Sweet Thunder	1981	10.00
—Reissue of United Artists 1097			
MGM			
❏ E-4583 [M]	Bill Medley 100%	1968	50.00

Number	Title	Yr	NM
—Mono is yellow label promo only			
❏ SE-4583 [S]	Bill Medley 100%	1968	25.00
❏ SE-4741	Gone	1970	18.00
❏ SE-4702	Nobody Knows	1970	18.00
❏ SE-4603	Soft and Soulful	1969	25.00
❏ SE-4640	Someone Is Standing Outside	1969	25.00
RCA VICTOR			
❏ MHL1-8519 [EP]	I Still Do	1985	10.00
❏ BXL1-4434	Right Here and Now	1982	12.00
❏ CPL1-5352	Still Hung Up on You	1984	12.00
UNITED ARTISTS			
❏ UA-LA929-H	Lay a Little Lovin' on Me	1978	12.00
❏ LT-1097	Sweet Thunder	1980	12.00
MEEUWSEN, TERRY ANN			
SANDY			
❏ SRS-9003	Meet Terry	1976	30.00
MEHEGAN, JOHN, AND EDDIE COSTA			
SAVOY			
❏ MG-12049 [M]	A Pair of Pianos	1956	40.00
MEHEGAN, JOHN			
EPIC			
❏ LA16007 [M]	Act of Jazz	1960	25.00
❏ BA17007 [S]	Act of Jazz	1960	30.00
PERSPECTIVE			
❏ PR-1 [M]	From Barrelhouse to Bop	195?	50.00
SAVOY			
❏ MG-12028 [M]	Reflections	1956	40.00
❏ MG-15054 [10]	The Last Mehegan	1955	60.00
TJ			
❏ LP-1 [M]	Casual Affair	1959	40.00
MEISNER, RANDY			
ASYLUM			
❏ 6E-140	Randy Meisner	1978	12.00
EPIC			
❏ NJE36748 [B]	One More Song	1980	12.00
❏ FE38121	Randy Meisner	1982	12.00
MEL AND TIM			
BAMBOO			
❏ BMS-8001	Good Guys Only Win in the Movies	1970	30.00
STAX			
❏ STS-5501	Mel and Tim	1974	25.00
❏ STS-3007	Starting All Over Again	1972	25.00
MELACHRINO, GEORGE			
RCA VICTOR			
❏ LPM-1045 [M]	Christmas in High Fidelity	1954	30.00
❏ LPM-1329 [M]	I'll Walk Beside You	1956	25.00
❏ LPM-1110 [M]	Immortal Ladies	1955	25.00
❏ LPM-1762 [M]	Lisbon at Twilight	1958	18.00
❏ LSP-1762 [S]	Lisbon at Twilight	1958	25.00
❏ LPM-1184 [M]	Masquerade	1955	25.00
❏ LPM-1307 [M]	Melachrino on Broadway	1956	25.00
❏ LPM-1005 [M]	Music for Courage and Confidence	195?	30.00
❏ LPM-1028 [M]	Music for Daydreaming	195?	30.00
❏ LPM-1000 [M]	Music for Dining	195?	30.00
❏ LPM-1002 [M]	Music for Reading	195?	30.00
❏ LPM-1001 [M]	Music for Relaxation	195?	30.00
❏ LPM-1027 [M]	Music for Two People Alone	195?	30.00
❏ LPM-1006 [M]	Music to Help You Sleep	195?	30.00
❏ LPM-1029 [M]	Music to Work or Study By	195?	30.00
❏ LPM-1008 [M]	Show Tunes	195?	30.00
❏ LPM-1261 [M]	Sounds of Paris	1956	25.00
❏ LPM-1757 [M]	Strauss Waltzes	1958	18.00
❏ LSP-1757 [S]	Strauss Waltzes	1958	25.00
❏ LPM-1330 [M]	Those Beautiful Strings	1956	25.00
MELANIE			
ABC			
❏ ABND-879	From the Beginning/Twelve Great Performances	1975	12.00
ACCORD			
❏ SN-7191	Beautiful People	1982	12.00
❏ SN-7109	What Have They Done to My Song Ma	1981	12.00
AMHERST			
❏ AMH-3302	Am I Real or What	1985	12.00
ATLANTIC			
❏ SD18190	Photograph	1976	12.00
BLANCHE			
❏ BL6177	Arabesque	1982	12.00
BUDDAH			
❏ BDS-5024	Born to Be	1969	18.00
❏ BDS-5060	Candles in the Rain	1970	18.00
❏ BDS-95005	Four Sides of Melanie	1972	18.00
❏ BDS-5095	Garden in the City	1971	15.00
❏ BDS-5066	Leftover Wine	1970	18.00
❏ BDS-5041	Melanie	1969	18.00
❏ BDS-5074	My First Album	1971	15.00
❏ BDS-5132	Please Love Me	1973	15.00
❏ B2D-5664	The Best...Melanie	197?	18.00

Number	Title	Yr	NM
❑ BDS-95000	The Good Book	1971	18.00

MIDSONG

Number	Title	Yr	NM
❑ MCA-3033	Phonogenic: Not Just Another Pretty Face	1978	12.00

NEIGHBORHOOD

Number	Title	Yr	NM
❑ 3000	As I See It Now	1974	15.00
❑ 47001	Gather Me	1971	15.00
❑ 48001	Madrugada	1974	15.00
❑ 49001	Melanie at Carnegie Hall	1973	18.00
❑ 47005	Stoneground Words	1972	15.00
❑ 3001	Sunsets and Other Beginnings	1975	15.00

PICKWICK

Number	Title	Yr	NM
❑ SPC-3317	Try the Real Thing	197?	12.00

TOMATO

Number	Title	Yr	NM
❑ TOM-2-9003	Ballroom Streets	1979	15.00

MELCHER, TERRY

REPRISE

Number	Title	Yr	NM
❑ MS2185	Terry Melcher	1974	18.00

MELDONIAN, DICK

PROGRESSIVE

Number	Title	Yr	NM
❑ 7062	Plays Gene Roland Music	198?	12.00
❑ 7033	Some of These Days	1979	15.00
❑ 7058	The Jersey Swing Concerts	198?	12.00

STATINAS

Number	Title	Yr	NM
❑ SLP-8076	It's a Wonderful World	1985	12.00

MELILLO, MIKE

RED RECORD

Number	Title	Yr	NM
❑ VPA-188	'Live and Well	1986	15.00
❑ VPA-170	Piano Solo	198?	15.00

MELIS, JOSE

DIPLOMAT

Number	Title	Yr	NM
❑ DS-2260 [S]	Jose Melis and the Metropolitan Strings	196?	12.00
❑ D-2260 [M]	Jose Melis and the Metropolitan Strings	196?	12.00

HARMONY

Number	Title	Yr	NM
❑ HL7150 [M]	Exciting TV Star Jose Melis	195?	15.00

MERCURY

Number	Title	Yr	NM
❑ MG20008 [M]	Classics the South American Way	195?	18.00
❑ MG20738 [M]	Everybody's Favorites	1962	15.00
❑ SR60738 [S]	Everybody's Favorites	1962	18.00
❑ MG25035 [10]	Jose Melis	195?	30.00
❑ MG20709 [M]	Jose Melis at the Opera	1962	15.00
❑ SR60709 [S]	Jose Melis at the Opera	1962	18.00
❑ MG20684 [M]	Jose Melis at the Pops Concert	1962	15.00
❑ SR60684 [S]	Jose Melis at the Pops Concert	1962	18.00
❑ SR60648 [S]	Jose Melis in Movieland	1961	18.00
❑ MG20648 [M]	Jose Melis in Movieland	1961	15.00
❑ MG20610 [M]	Jose Melis on Broadway	1961	15.00
❑ SR60610 [S]	Jose Melis on Broadway	1961	18.00
❑ MG25119 [10]	Latin-American Piano	195?	30.00
❑ MG20127 [M]	Latin American Stylings	195?	18.00
❑ MG20275 [M]	Tonight It's Music	195?	18.00

MGM

Number	Title	Yr	NM
❑ E-3527 [M]	Jose Melis of the Jack Paar Show	1957	18.00
❑ E-262 [10]	The Jose Melis Trio	1955	30.00

MUSICOR

Number	Title	Yr	NM
❑ MS-3071 [S]	Piano Classics the South American Way	1967	15.00
❑ MM-2071 [M]	Piano Classics the South American Way	1967	15.00

PALACE

Number	Title	Yr	NM
❑ P-84 [M]	Dance Party with Jose Melis	195?	15.00

SEECO

Number	Title	Yr	NM
❑ CELP423 [M]	Christmas with Melis	1959	18.00
❑ CELP-414 [M]	Jose Melis at Midnight	1959	18.00
❑ CELP-4140 [S]	Jose Melis at Midnight	1959	25.00
❑ CELP-4620 [S]	Jose Melis Plays Jack Paar's Favorites	1960	18.00
❑ CELP-462 [M]	Jose Melis Plays Jack Paar's Favorites	1960	15.00
❑ CELP-445 [M]	Jose Melis Plays the Latin Way	1960	15.00
❑ CELP-4450 [S]	Jose Melis Plays the Latin Way	1960	18.00
❑ CELP-471 [M]	Our Love	1961	15.00
❑ CELP-4710 [S]	Our Love	1961	18.00
❑ CELP-4360 [S]	The Many Moods of Jose Melis	1960	18.00
❑ CELP-436 [M]	The Many Moods of Jose Melis	1960	15.00
❑ CELP-411 [M]	Tonight with Jose Melis	1958	18.00

MELLE, GIL

BLUE NOTE

Number	Title	Yr	NM
❑ BLP-5033 [10]	Gil Melle Quintet, Volume 2	1953	800.00
❑ BLP-5054 [10]	Gil Melle Quintet, Volume 3	1954	800.00
❑ BLP-5063 [10]	Gil Melle Quintet, Volume 4 -- Five Impressions of Color	1954	800.00
❑ BLP-5020 [10]	Gil Melle Quintet/Sextet	1953	800.00
❑ B1-92168	Mindscape	1989	18.00
❑ BLP-1517 [M]	Patterns in Jazz	1956	600.00

—Deep groove" version; Lexington Ave. address on label

GIL MELLE *patterns in jazz with Eddie Bert Joe Cinderella Oscar Pettiford Ed Thigpen blue note 1517*

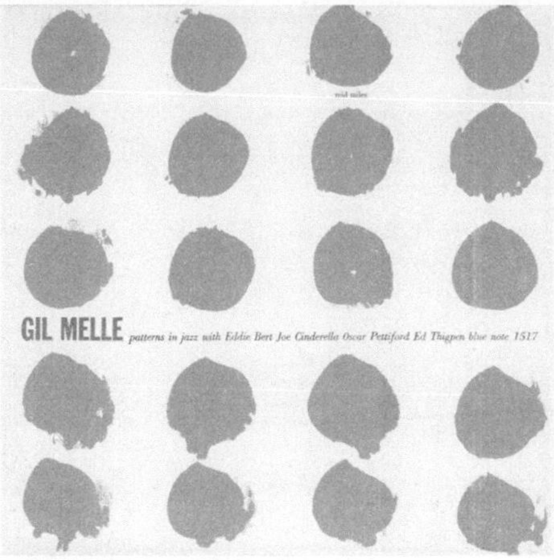

Number	Title	Yr	NM
❑ BLP-1517 [M]	Patterns in Jazz	1956	400.00

—Regular version, Lexington Ave. address on label

FANTASY

Number	Title	Yr	NM
❑ OJC-1753	Gil's Guests	198?	18.00
❑ OJC-1712	Melle Plays Primitive Modern	198?	18.00

PRESTIGE

Number	Title	Yr	NM
❑ PRLP-7063 [M]	Gil's Guests	1956	150.00

— Yellow label with W. 50th St. address

Number	Title	Yr	NM
❑ PRLP-7040 [M]	Melle Plays Primitive Modern	1956	200.00

— Yellow label with W. 50th St. address

Number	Title	Yr	NM
❑ PRLP-7097 [M]	Quadrama	1957	150.00

— Yellow label

VERVE

Number	Title	Yr	NM
❑ V6-8744	Tome VI	1968	40.00

MELLENCAMP, JOHN

COLUMBIA

Number	Title	Yr	NM
❑ C69602	John Mellencamp	1998	18.00

HEAR MUSIC

Number	Title	Yr	NM
❑ HRM30895	Life, Death, Love and Freedom	2008	25.00

MCA

Number	Title	Yr	NM
❑ 2225 [B]	Chestnut Street Incident	1977	30.00

—As "Johnny Cougar"

MERCURY

Number	Title	Yr	NM
❑ 838220-1	Big Daddy	1989	12.00
❑ 832465-1	The Lonesome Jubilee	1987	10.00

MOBILE FIDELITY

Number	Title	Yr	NM
❑ 1-222	The Lonesome Jubilee	1995	40.00

—Audiophile vinyl

RIVA

Number	Title	Yr	NM
❑ RVL7501 [B]	American Fool	1982	12.00

—As "John Cougar"

Number	Title	Yr	NM
❑ RVL7401 [B]	John Cougar	1979	18.00

—As "John Cougar"

Number	Title	Yr	NM
❑ RVL7403	Nothin' Matters and What If It Did	1980	12.00

—As "John Cougar"

Number	Title	Yr	NM
❑ 824865-1	Scarecrow	1985	10.00

—As "John Cougar Mellencamp"

Number	Title	Yr	NM
❑ RVL7504	Uh-Huh	1983	10.00

—As "John Cougar Mellencamp"

MELLO-KINGS, THE

COLLECTABLES

Number	Title	Yr	NM
❑ COL-5020 [B]	Greatest Hits	198?	15.00

HERALD

Number	Title	Yr	NM
❑ H-1013 [M]	Tonight-Tonight	1960	500.00

— Yellow label

Number	Title	Yr	NM
❑ H-1013 [M]	Tonight-Tonight	196?	300.00

— Multi-color label

RELIC

Number	Title	Yr	NM
❑ LP-5035	Greatest Hits	198?	15.00

MELLO-LARKS, THE

RCA CAMDEN

Number	Title	Yr	NM
❑ CAL-530 [M]	Just for a Lark	1959	40.00

MELROSE, FRANK

ABC-PARAMOUNT

Number	Title	Yr	NM
❑ (# unknown)0 [M]	Kansas City Frank Melrose	1956	50.00

MELTON, LEVY, AND THE DEY BROTHERS

COLUMBIA

Number	Title	Yr	NM
❑ KC31279	Levy Melton and the Dey Brothers	1972	25.00

MELTZER, DAVID AND TINA

VANGUARD

Number	Title	Yr	NM
❑ VSD-6619	Poet Song	1969	30.00

MELVIN, HAROLD, AND THE BLUE NOTES

ABC

Number	Title	Yr	NM
❑ AB-1041	Now Is the Time	1978	12.00
❑ AB-969	Reaching for the World	1977	12.00

MCA

Number	Title	Yr	NM
❑ 5261	All Things Happen in Time	1981	12.00

PHILADELPHIA INT'L.

Number	Title	Yr	NM
❑ KZ32407	Black & Blue	1973	15.00
❑ ZQ32407 [Q]	Black & Blue	1973	25.00
❑ PZ34232	Collector's Item -- All Their Greatest Hits!	1976	15.00
❑ KZ31648	Harold Melvin and the Blue Notes	1972	15.00
❑ PZ33148	To Be True	1975	15.00
❑ PZ33808	Wake Up Everybody	1975	15.00
❑ PZQ33808 [Q]	Wake Up Everybody	1975	25.00

PHILLY WORLD

Number	Title	Yr	NM
❑ 90187	Talk It Up (Tell Everybody)	1985	12.00

SOURCE

Number	Title	Yr	NM
❑ 3197	The Blue Album	1980	12.00

MEMBERS ONLY

MUSE

Number	Title	Yr	NM
❑ MR-5332	Members Only	1987	12.00
❑ MR-5348	Members Only...Too: The Way You Make Me Feel	1989	15.00

MEMPHIS MINNIE

MCA

Number	Title	Yr	NM
❑ 1370	Moanin' the Blues	198?	18.00

PORTRAIT

Number	Title	Yr	NM
❑ RJ44072	I Ain't No Bad Gal	1988	18.00

MEMPHIS SLIM

BATTLE

Number	Title	Yr	NM
❑ BM-6118 [M]	Alone with My Friends	1963	50.00
❑ BM-6122 [M]	Baby Please Come Home	1963	50.00

BLUESVILLE

Number	Title	Yr	NM
❑ BVLP-1053 [M]	All Kinds of Blues	1962	100.00

— Blue label, silver print

Number	Title	Yr	NM
❑ BVLP-1053 [M]	All Kinds of Blues	1964	30.00

—Blue label, trident logo at right

Number	Title	Yr	NM
❑ BVLP-1018 [M]	Just Blues	1961	120.00

— Blue label, silver print

Number	Title	Yr	NM
❑ BVLP-1018 [M]	Just Blues	1964	30.00

—Blue label, trident logo at right

Number	Title	Yr	NM
❑ BVLP-1031 [M]	No Strain	1961	120.00

— Blue label, silver print

Number	Title	Yr	NM
❑ BVLP-1031 [M]	No Strain	1964	30.00

—Blue label, trident logo at right

Number	Title	Yr	NM
❑ BVLP-1075 [M]	Steady Rollin' Blues	1963	100.00

—Blue label, silver print

Number	Title	Yr	NM
❑ BVLP-1075 [M]	Steady Rollin' Blues	1964	30.00

—Blue label, trident logo at right

BUDDAH

Number	Title	Yr	NM
❑ BDS-7505	Mother Earth	1969	25.00

CANDID

Number	Title	Yr	NM
❑ CM-8024 [M]	Memphis Slim U.S.A.	1962	60.00
❑ CS-9024 [S]	Memphis Slim U.S.A.	1962	80.00
❑ CM-8023 [M]	Slim's Tribute to Big Bill Broonzy	1961	60.00
❑ CS-9023 [S]	Slim's Tribute to Big Bill Broonzy	1961	80.00

CHESS

Number	Title	Yr	NM
❑ LP-1455 [M]	Memphis Slim	1961	150.00

—Black label

Number	Title	Yr	NM
❑ LP-1510 [M]	The Real Folk Blues	1966	80.00

DISC

Number	Title	Yr	NM
❑ D-105 [M]	If the Rabbit Had a Gun	1964	40.00

FOLKWAYS

Number	Title	Yr	NM
❑ FG-3536 [M]	Chicago Blues	1961	100.00
❑ FG-3535 [M]	Memphis Slim...And the Real Honky Tonk	1960	100.00
❑ FG-3524 [M]	The Real Boogie Woogie	1959	100.00

JUBILEE

Number	Title	Yr	NM
❑ JGM-8003 [M]	Legend of the Blues	1967	30.00
❑ JGS-8003 [S]	Legend of the Blues	1967	30.00

KING

Number	Title	Yr	NM
❑ 885 [M]	Memphis Slim Sings Folk Blues	1964	50.00

SCEPTER

Number	Title	Yr	NM
❑ SM-535 [M]	Self Portrait	1966	25.00
❑ SMS-535 [S]	Self Portrait	1966	30.00

SPIN-O-RAMA

Number	Title	Yr	NM
❑ 149 [M]	Lonesome Blues	196?	25.00

STRAND

Number	Title	Yr	NM
❑ SL-1046 [M]	The World's Foremost Blues Singer	1962	40.00
❑ SLS-1046 [S]	The World's Foremost Blues Singer	1962	50.00

Number	Title	Yr	NM

UNITED ARTISTS

❏ UAL-3137 [M]	Broken Soul Blues	1961	60.00
❏ UAS-6137 [S]	Broken Soul Blues	1961	80.00

VEE JAY

❏ LP-1012 [M]	Memphis Slim at the Gate of the Horn	1959	200.00

—Maroon label

❏ LP-1012 [M]	Memphis Slim at the Gate of the Horn	1961	120.00

—Black rainbow label, oval logo

MEMPHIS WILLIE B

BLUESVILLE

❏ BVLP-1048 [M]	Hard Working Man Blues	1962	100.00

—Blue label, silver print

❏ BVLP-1048 [M]	Hard Working Man Blues	1964	30.00

—Blue label, trident logo at right

❏ BVLP-1034 [M]	Introducing Memphis Willie B	1961	100.00

—Blue label, silver print

❏ BVLP-1034 [M]	Introducing Memphis Willie B	1964	30.00

—Blue label, trident logo at right

MEN, THE

SNAT-5

❏ 2001 [B]	Hermeneutics	1981	30.00

MEN AT WORK

COLUMBIA

❏ ARC37978	Business as Usual	1982	10.00
❏ HC47978	Business as Usual	1983	30.00

—Half-speed mastered edition

❏ HC48660	Cargo	1983	30.00

—Half-speed mastered edition

❏ A2S1650 [DJ]	Cargo (World Premiere Weekend)	1983	25.00

—Promo-only two-record package of interviews and music

❏ FC40078	Two Hearts	1985	10.00

MOBILE FIDELITY

❏ MFSLP1025 [D]	Cargo	2014	30.00

MEN WITHOUT HATS

BACKSTREET

❏ 39002	Rhythm of Youth	1983	15.00
❏ 5436	Rhythm of Youth	1983	12.00

—Reissue

MCA

❏ 5487	Folk of the 80's, Part 3	1984	12.00

MERCURY

❏ 842000-1	In the 21st Century	1989	12.00

STIFF

❏ TEES-12-01 [EP]	Folk of the 80's	1981	30.00

—Reissue of Trend 10-inch EP

TREND

❏ HATS-001 [10]	Folk of the 80's	1981	30.00

—10-inch four-song EP; possibly released only in Canada

MENDES, SERGIO

A&M

❏ SP-5250	Arara	1989	15.00
❏ SP-4984	Confetti	1984	12.00
❏ SP-4197	Crystal Illusions	1969	18.00
❏ LP-122 [M]	Equinox	1967	18.00
❏ SP-4122 [S]	Equinox	1967	18.00
❏ SP-4160	Fool on the Hill	1968	18.00
❏ SP-3108	Fool on the Hill	198?	10.00

—Budget-line reissue

❏ SP-4252	Greatest Hits	1970	18.00
❏ SP-3258	Greatest Hits	198?	10.00

—Budget-line reissue

❏ SP-4137	Look Around	1968	18.00
❏ SP-4315	Pais Tropical	1971	15.00
❏ SP-4353	Primal Roots	1972	15.00
❏ SP-4937	Sergio Mendes	1983	12.00
❏ LP-116 [M]	Sergio Mendes and Brasil '66	1966	15.00
❏ SP-4116 [S]	Sergio Mendes and Brasil '66	1966	18.00
❏ SP-5135	Sergio Mendes and Brasil '86	1986	12.00
❏ SP-4284	Stillness	1970	18.00
❏ SP-3522	The Sergio Mendes Foursider	1973	18.00
❏ SP-6012	The Sergio Mendes Foursider	198?	12.00

—Budget-line reissue

❏ SP-4236	Ye-Me-Le	1969	18.00

ATLANTIC

❏ 1466 [M]	Great Arrival	1966	18.00
❏ SD1466 [S]	Great Arrival	1966	25.00
❏ 8177 [M]	Sergio Mendes' Favorite Things	1968	40.00

—White label promo only

❏ SD8177 [S]	Sergio Mendes' Favorite Things	1968	25.00

❏ 8112 [M]	Sergio Mendes In Person at the El Matador	1967	25.00
❏ SD8112 [S]	Sergio Mendes In Person at the El Matador	1967	18.00
❏ 1480 [M]	The Beat of Brazil	1967	25.00
❏ SD1480 [S]	The Beat of Brazil	1967	18.00
❏ 1434 [M]	The Swinger from Rio	1965	18.00
❏ SD1434 [S]	The Swinger from Rio	1965	25.00

BELL

❏ 1119	Love Music	1973	12.00
❏ 1305	Vintage 74	1974	12.00

CAPITOL

❏ T2294 [M]	In a Brazilan Bag	1965	50.00
❏ ST2294 [S]	In a Brazilan Bag	1965	60.00

ELEKTRA

❏ 7E-1055	Homecooking	1976	12.00
❏ 6E-214	Magic Lady	1980	12.00
❏ 7E-1027	Sergio Mendes	1975	12.00
❏ EQ-1027 [Q]	Sergio Mendes	1975	18.00
❏ 6E-134	Sergio Mendes and Brasil '88	1978	12.00
❏ 7E-1102	Sergio Mendes and the New Brasil '77	1977	12.00

MOBILE FIDELITY

❏ 1-118	Sergio Mendes and Brasil '66	1984	50.00

—Audiophile vinyl

PHILIPS

❏ PHM200263 [M]	Quiet Nights	1968	25.00
❏ PHS600263 [S]	Quiet Nights	1968	18.00

PICKWICK

❏ SPC-3149	So Nice	1972	12.00

TOWER

❏ T5052 [M]	In a Brazilan Bag	1966	40.00

—Reissue of Capitol 2294

❏ ST5052 [S]	In a Brazilan Bag	1966	50.00

—Reissue of Capitol 2294

MENGELBERG, MISHA

SOUL NOTE

❏ SN-1104	Change of Season	1985	15.00

MENTAL AS ANYTHING

A&M

❏ SP-4946	Creatures of Leisure	1983	15.00
❏ SP-4921	If You Leave Me, Can I Come Too?	1982	15.00

COLUMBIA

❏ C45367	Cyclone Raymond	1989	12.00
❏ BFC40299	Fundamental	1985	12.00
❏ FC44144	Mouth to Mouth	1988	12.00

MENUHIN, YEHUDI

MERCURY LIVING PRESENCE

❏ SR90003 [S]	Bartok: Violin Concerto No. 2	1959	70.00

—With Antal Dorati/Minneapolis Symphony Orch.; maroon label, no "Vendor: Mercury Record Corporation

❏ SR90003 [S]	Bartok: Violin Concerto No. 2	196?	30.00

—With Antal Dorati/Minneapolis Symphony Orch.; maroon label, with "Vendor: Mercury Record Corporation

MENZA, DON

CATALYST

❏ 7617	First Flight	1976	18.00

PALO ALTO

❏ PA-8010	Flip Pocket	1981	15.00

PAUSA

❏ 7170	Horn of Plenty	1985	12.00

REAL TIME

❏ RT-301	Burnin'	198?	18.00

VOSS

❏ VLP1-42931	Horn of Plenty	1988	12.00

MENZLES, HAMISH

MUSIC IS MEDICINE

❏ 9028	Jazz Tracks	1979	15.00

MEPHISTOPHELES

REPRISE

❏ RS6355 [B]	In Frustration I Hear Singing	1969	60.00

MERCER, JOHNNY

CAPITOL

❏ T907 [M]	Ac-Cent-Tchu-Ate the Positive	1957	50.00
❏ H214 [10]	Johnny Mercer Sings	1950	80.00
❏ H210 [10]	Music of Jerome Kern	1950	80.00

JUPITER

❏ JLP-1001 [M]	Johnny Mercer Sings Just for Fun	1956	50.00

PAUSA

❏ PR9062	Jonny Mercer Sings Jonny Mercer	1986	12.00

—Name is indeed misspelled on the label as "Jonny

MERCER, MABEL, AND BOBBY SHORT

ATLANTIC

❏ SD 2-604	Mabel Mercer and Bobby Short at Town Hall	1968	25.00

MERCER, MABEL

ATLANTIC

❏ 1213 [M]	Mabel Mercer Sings Cole Porter	1955	40.00

—Black label

❏ 1213 [M]	Mabel Mercer Sings Cole Porter	1961	25.00

—Multicolor label, white "fan" logo at right

❏ 1213 [M]	Mabel Mercer Sings Cole Porter	1963	18.00

—Multicolor label, black "fan" logo at right

❏ 81264	Mabel Mercer Sings Cole Porter	1985	12.00
❏ 1322 [M]	Merely Marvelous Mabel Mercer	1960	40.00

—Black label

❏ SD1322 [S]	Merely Marvelous Mabel Mercer	1960	50.00

—Green label

❏ 1322 [M]	Merely Marvelous Mabel Mercer	1961	25.00

—Multicolor label, white "fan" logo at right

❏ 1322 [M]	Merely Marvelous Mabel Mercer	1963	18.00

—Multicolor label, black "fan" logo at right

❏ SD1322 [S]	Merely Marvelous Mabel Mercer	1961	30.00

—Multicolor labels, white "fan" logo at right

❏ SD1322 [S]	Merely Marvelous Mabel Mercer	1963	25.00

—Multicolor labels, black "fan" logo at right

❏ 1244 [M]	Midnight at Mabel Mercer's	1956	40.00

—Black label

❏ 1244 [M]	Midnight at Mabel Mercer's	1961	25.00

—Multicolor label, white "fan" logo at right

❏ 1244 [M]	Midnight at Mabel Mercer's	1963	18.00

—Multicolor label, black "fan" logo at right

❏ 1301 [M]	Once in a Blue Moon	1959	40.00

—Black label

❏ SD1301 [S]	Once in a Blue Moon	1959	50.00

—Green label

❏ 1301 [M]	Once in a Blue Moon	1961	25.00

—Multicolor label, white "fan" logo at right

❏ 1301 [M]	Once in a Blue Moon	1963	18.00

—Multicolor label, black "fan" logo at right

❏ SD1301 [S]	Once in a Blue Moon	1961	30.00

—Multicolor labels, white "fan" logo at right

❏ SD1301 [S]	Once in a Blue Moon	1963	25.00

—Multicolor labels, black "fan" logo at right

❏ ALS-402 [10]	Songs by Mabel Mercer, Volume 1	1954	80.00
❏ ALS-403 [10]	Songs by Mabel Mercer, Volume 2	1954	80.00
❏ 2-602 [M]	The Art of Mabel Mercer	1959	60.00

—Black labels

❏ 2-602 [M]	The Art of Mabel Mercer	1961	30.00

—Multicolor labels, white "fan" logo at right

❏ 2-602 [M]	The Art of Mabel Mercer	1963	25.00

—Multicolor labels, black "fan" logo at right

❏ SD 2-605	The Second Town Hall Concert	1969	25.00

—Red and green label with "1841 Broadway" address

❏ SD 2-605	The Second Town Hall Concert	1975	15.00

—Red and green label with "75 Rockefeller Plaza" address

AUDIOPHILE

❏ AP-161/2	Echoes of My Life	197?	18.00

DECCA

❏ DL4472 [M]	Mabel Mercer Sings	1964	18.00
❏ DL74472 [S]	Mabel Mercer Sings	1964	25.00

STANYAN

❏ SR10108 [M]	For Always	1974	15.00

MERCHANTS OF DREAM, THE

A&M

❏ SP-4149	Strange Night Voyage	1969	30.00

MERCURY, FREDDIE

COLUMBIA

❏ FC40071 [B]	Mr. Bad Guy	1985	18.00

MERCURY REV

COLUMBIA

❏ C53030	Yerself Is Steam	1992	15.00

MERCY

SUNDI

❏ SRLP-803 [B]	The Mercy & Love (Can Make You Happy)	1969	30.00

—Has the original version of the title song plus filler instrumentals

WARNER BROS.

❏ WS1799	Love (Can Make You Happy)	1969	18.00

—Love (Can Make You Happy)" was re-recorded for this LP

MERCY DEE

ARHOOLIE

Number	Title	Yr	NM
❏ F-1007 [M]	Mercy Dee	1961	60.00

BLUESVILLE

Number	Title	Yr	NM
❏ BVLP-1039 [M]	A Pity and a Shame	1962	80.00

— *Blue label, silver print*

❏ BVLP-1039 [M]	A Pity and a Shame	1964	30.00

— *Blue label, trident logo at right*

MEREDITH, BUDDY

STARDAY

Number	Title	Yr	NM
❏ SLP-225 [M]	Sing Me a Heart Song	1963	30.00

MEREDITH, BURGESS

COLPIX

Number	Title	Yr	NM
❏ CP-452 [M]	Burgess Meredith Sings Songs from "How the West Was Won"	1964	25.00
❏ SCP-452 [S]	Burgess Meredith Sings Songs from "How the West Was Won"	1964	30.00

EPIC

❏ LN3656 [M]	Songs and Stories of the Gold Rush	1961	30.00
❏ BN590 [S]	Songs and Stories of the Gold Rush	1961	30.00

MERIAN, LEON

SEECO

Number	Title	Yr	NM
❏ CELP-459 [M]	Fiorello!	1960	18.00
❏ CELP-4590 [S]	Fiorello!	1960	25.00
❏ CELP-447 [M]	This Time the Swing's On Me	1960	18.00
❏ CELP-4470 [S]	This Time the Swing's On Me	1960	25.00

MERIWETHER, ROY

CAPITOL

Number	Title	Yr	NM
❏ ST-102	Soul Knight	1969	30.00

COLUMBIA

❏ CL2498 [M]	Popcorn and Soul Groovin' at the Movies	1966	18.00
❏ CS9298 [S]	Popcorn and Soul Groovin' at the Movies	1966	25.00
❏ CL2744 [M]	Soul Invader	1968	30.00
❏ CS9544 [S]	Soul Invader	1968	18.00
❏ CL2433 [M]	Soup and Onions (Soul Cookin')	1966	18.00
❏ CS9233 [S]	Soup and Onions (Soul Cookin')	1966	25.00
❏ CL2584 [M]	Stone Truth	1967	25.00
❏ CS9384 [S]	Stone Truth	1967	18.00

MERKIN

WINDI

Number	Title	Yr	NM
❏ 1004/5	Music from Merkin	1972	400.00

MERMAN, ETHEL

DECCA

Number	Title	Yr	NM
❏ DXA153 [M]	A Musical Autobiography	195?	40.00

— *Black label, silver print*

❏ DL8178 [M]	A Musical Autobiography, Volume 1	195?	30.00

— *Black label, silver print*

❏ DL8179 [M]	A Musical Autobiography, Volume 2	195?	30.00

— *Black label, silver print*

❏ DL9028 [M]	Memories	1955	40.00
❏ DL5053 [10]	Songs She Made Famous	1950	60.00

MERRILL, HELEN, AND JOHN LEWIS

MERCURY

Number	Title	Yr	NM
❏ SRM-1-1150	Helen Merrill and John Lewis	197?	15.00

MERRILL, HELEN

ATCO

Number	Title	Yr	NM
❏ 33-112 [M]	American Country Songs	1959	150.00

CATALYST

❏ 7912	Autumn Love	197?	30.00
❏ 7903	Helen Sings, Teddy Swings	197?	30.00

DRG

❏ SL-5204	The Rodgers & Hammerstein Album	1987	15.00

EMARCY

❏ MG-36078 [M]	Dream of You	1956	150.00

— *Blue label with drummer logo*

❏ MG-36078 [M]	Dream of You	1958	100.00

— *Blue label, double oval at top, "Emarcy Jazz" between the two ovals under "Mercury"*

❏ MG-36006 [M]	Helen Merrill	1955	300.00

— *Blue label with drummer logo*

❏ MG-36057 [M]	Helen Merrill with Strings	1955	100.00

— *Blue label with drummer logo*

❏ MG-36107 [M]	Merrill at Midnight	1957	150.00

— *Blue label with drummer logo*

❏ MG-36107 [M]	Merrill at Midnight	1958	30.00

— *Blue label, double oval at top, "Emarcy Jazz" between the two ovals under "Mercury"*

❏ MG-36134 [M]	The Nearness of You	1958	50.00

INNER CITY

❏ IC-1125	Casa Forte	198?	18.00
❏ IC-1080	Chasin' the Bird	198?	18.00
❏ IC-1060	Something Special	1978	18.00

LANDMARK

❏ LLP-1308	A Shade of Difference	1986	15.00

MAINSTREAM

❏ 56014 [M]	The Artistry of Helen Merrill	1965	30.00
❏ S-6014 [S]	The Artistry of Helen Merrill	1965	30.00

MERCURY

❏ 826340-1	The Complete Helen Merrill on Mercury	1985	80.00

METROJAZZ

❏ E-1010 [M]	You've Got a Date with the Blues	1958	40.00
❏ SE-1010 [S]	You've Got a Date with the Blues	1958	50.00

MILESTONE

❏ M-9019	Shade of Difference	1969	25.00
❏ MLP-1003 [M]	The Feeling Is Mutual	1967	40.00
❏ MLS-9003 [S]	The Feeling Is Mutual	1967	30.00

OWL

❏ 044	Music Makers	1986	30.00

TRIP

❏ TLP-5526	Helen Merrill Sings	197?	18.00
❏ TLP-5552	Helen Merrill with Strings	197?	18.00

MERRILL, TONI

RAMA

Number	Title	Yr	NM
❏ RLP-5004 [M]	Songs from the Heart	1957	80.00

MERRY-GO-ROUND, THE

A&M

Number	Title	Yr	NM
❏ LP-132 [M]	The Merry-Go-Round	1967	60.00
❏ SP-4132 [S]	The Merry-Go-Round	1967	30.00

RHINO

❏ RNLP126	The Best of the Merry-Go-Round	1985	12.00

MERRYWEATHER, NEIL

CAPITOL

Number	Title	Yr	NM
❏ SKAO-220	Merryweather	1969	18.00
❏ STBB-278	Word of Mouth	1969	25.00

KENT

❏ KST-546	Neil Merryweather and the Boers	197?	18.00

MERCURY

❏ SRM-1-1024	Kryptonite	1975	15.00
❏ SRM-1-1007 [B]	Space Rangers	1974	15.00

MERRYWEATHER AND CAREY

RCA VICTOR

Number	Title	Yr	NM
❏ LSP-4442	Ivar Avenue Reunion	1970	18.00
❏ LSP-4485	Vacuum Cleaner	1971	18.00

MERSEYBEATS, THE

ARC INTERNATIONAL

Number	Title	Yr	NM
❏ 834 [M]	England's Best Sellers	1964	40.00

MERSEYBOYS, THE

VEE JAY

Number	Title	Yr	NM
❏ VJ-1101 [M]	The 15 Greatest Songs of the Beatles	1964	100.00

— *With typographical error on label "Saluting Their Return to Amercia"; this album is not known to exist in stereo*

❏ VJ-1101 [M]	The 15 Greatest Songs of the Beatles	1964	100.00

— *Without typographical error on label "Saluting Their Return To America"; this album is not known to exist in stereo*

❏ VJ-1101 [DJ]	The 15 Greatest Songs of the Beatles	1964	150.00

— *White label, blue and black print; with typographical error on label: "Saluting Their Return to Amercia"*

❏ VJ-1101 [DJ]	The 15 Greatest Songs of the Beatles	1964	150.00

— *White label, all-blue print; without typographical error on label: "Saluting Their Return To America"*

MERTENS, TEDDY

4 CORNERS OF THE WORLD

Number	Title	Yr	NM
❏ FCL-4229 [M]	Trumpet in the Night	1966	18.00
❏ FCS-4229 [S]	Trumpet in the Night	1966	25.00

MESHEL, BILLY

PROBE

Number	Title	Yr	NM
❏ CPLP-4502	The Love Songs of A. Wilbur Meshel	1969	25.00

MESMERIZING EYE, THE

SMASH

Number	Title	Yr	NM
❏ MGS-27090 [M]	Psychedelia -- A Musical Light Show	1967	100.00
❏ SRS-67090 [S]	Psychedelia -- A Musical Light Show	1967	70.00

MESSENGERS, THE (1)

RARE EARTH

Number	Title	Yr	NM
❏ RS-509	The Messengers	1969	25.00

MESSINA, JIM

AUDIO FIDELITY

Number	Title	Yr	NM
❏ DFM-3037 [M]	The Dragsters	1964	80.00
❏ DFS-7037 [S]	The Dragsters	1964	100.00

COLUMBIA

❏ JC36141	Oasis	1979	12.00

THIMBLE

❏ TLP-3	Jim Messina	197?	18.00

WARNER BROS.

❏ BSK3559	Messina	1981	12.00
❏ BSK3559 [DJ]	Messina	1981	25.00

— *Promo-only version on Quiex II vinyl*

❏ 23825	One More Mile	1983	12.00

MESSNER, JOHNNY

HINDSIGHT

Number	Title	Yr	NM
❏ HSR-186	Johnny Messner and His Hotel McAlpin Orchestra 1939-40	198?	12.00

METALLICA

ELEKTRA

Number	Title	Yr	NM
❏ 60812	...And Justice for All	1988	30.00
❏ 60757 [EP]	Garage Days Re-Revisited	1987	50.00
❏ 62299	Garage Inc.	1998	30.00
❏ 60766	Kill 'Em All	1987	18.00

— *Reissue of Megaforce 069 with two extra tracks*

❏ 61923	Load	1996	25.00
❏ 60439	Master of Puppets	1986	25.00
❏ 61113	Metallica	1991	60.00
❏ 62126	Re-Load	1997	30.00
❏ 60396	Ride the Lightning	1984	25.00
❏ 62504	S&M	1999	25.00
❏ 62853	St. Anger	2003	30.00

MEGAFORCE

❏ MRI 069	Kill 'Em All	1983	40.00
❏ MRI 069 [PD]	Kill 'Em All	1983	50.00

— *Un-numbered version*

❏ MRI 069 [PD]	Kill 'Em All	1983	100.00

— *Numbered limited edition version*

❏ MRI769	Ride the Lightning	1984	40.00

RHINO

❏ R1-76156	Vinyl Box Set	2004	200.00

— *Limited edition of 5,000 numbered copies; includes their first four albums pressed on two records each, the "Garage Days Re-Revisited" EP and the picture disc "Creeping Death"*

WARNER BROS.

❏ 470780	...And Justice for All	2008	50.00
❏ 470716	...And Justice for All	2008	25.00
❏ 508732	Death Magnetic	2008	25.00
❏ 512119	Death Magnetic	2008	100.00

— *Deluxe box*

❏ 343676	Kill 'Em All	2008	30.00
❏ 470908	Master of Puppets	2008	30.00
❏ 511830	Metallica	2008	25.00
❏ 424572	Ride the Lightning	2008	16.00

METERS, THE

JOSIE

Number	Title	Yr	NM
❏ JOS-4011	Look-Ka Py Py	1970	80.00
❏ JOS-4012 [B]	Struttin'	1970	80.00
❏ JOS-4010	The Meters	1969	80.00

REPRISE

❏ MS2076	Cabbage Alley	1972	50.00
❏ MS2228	Fire on the Bayou	1975	40.00
❏ MS2200	Rejuvenation	1974	40.00
❏ MS2252	Trick Bag	1976	40.00

ROUNDER

❏ 2104	Good Old Funky Music	1990	25.00
❏ 2103	Look-Ka Py Py	1990	25.00

— *Reissue of Josie 4011*

SUNDAZED

❏ LP5081	Kickback	2001	15.00

VIRGO

❏ 12002	The Best of the Meters	1972	50.00

WARNER BROS.

❏ BS3042	New Directions	1977	30.00

METHENY, MIKE

HEADFIRST

Number	Title	Yr	NM
❏ 9712	Blue Jay Sessions	198?	25.00

MCA/IMPULSE!

❏ 5755	Day In, Night Out	1986	12.00

METHENY, PAT, AND LYLE MAYS

ECM

Number	Title	Yr	NM
❏ ECM1-1190	As Falls Wichita, So Falls Wichita Falls	1981	12.00

— *Distributed by Warner Bros.*

Number	Title	Yr	NM

METHENY, PAT, AND ORNETTE COLEMAN

GEFFEN

❑ GHS24096	Song X	1986	12.00

METHENY, PAT

ECM

❑ ECM2-1180	80/81	1980	18.00
— Distributed by Warner Bros.			
❑ ECM1-1155	American Garage	1979	12.00
— Distributed by Warner Bros.			
❑ PRO-A-810 [DJ]	An Hour with Pat Metheny	1979	60.00
— Promo-only music and interviews			
❑ ECM-1-1073	Bright Size Life	1976	15.00
— Distributed by Polydor			
❑ ECM-1-1073	Bright Size Life	1979	12.00
— Reissue, distributed by Warner Bros.			
❑ 25008	First Circle	1984	12.00
❑ 1278	First Circle	1984	15.00
— Made in Germany			
❑ PRO 030 [DJ]	Live in Concert	1977	60.00
— Promo-only release			
❑ ECM1-1131	New Chautauqua	1979	12.00
— Distributed by Warner Bros.			
❑ ECM1-1216	Offramp	1982	12.00
— Distributed by Warner Bros.			
❑ ECM1-1114	Pat Metheny Group	1978	12.00
— Distributed by Warner Bros.			
❑ 25006	Rejoicing	1984	12.00
❑ 1271	Rejoicing	1984	15.00
— Made in Germany			
❑ 23791	Travels	1983	18.00
❑ 1252/3	Travels	1983	25.00
— Made in Germany			
❑ ECM-1-1097	Watercolors	1977	15.00
— Distributed by Warner Bros.			
❑ 823270-1	Works	1984	15.00
— Made in West Germany (not issued in U.S.)			

GEFFEN

❑ GHS24245	Letter from Home	1989	18.00
❑ GHS24293	Question and Answer	1990	25.00
❑ GHS24145	Still Life (Talking)	1987	12.00

WARNER BROS.

❑ WBMS-106 [DJ]	Live on Tour	1979	30.00
— Part of "The Warner Bros. Music Show" series; promo only			

METHOD ACTOR

(LABEL UNKNOWN)

❑ 0(# unknown)	Method Actor	1988	500.00

METRONOMES, THE (U)

STRAND

❑ SL-1057 [M]	The Fabulous Metronomes Sing the Standard Hits	1962	30.00
❑ SLS-1057 [S]	The Fabulous Metronomes Sing the Standard Hits	1962	40.00

WYNNE

❑ 106 [M]	And Now... The Metronomes	1960	120.00

METROPOLITAN JAZZ OCTET

ARGO

❑ LP-659 [M]	The Legend of Bix	1960	30.00

METROPOLITAN OPERA MADRIGAL SINGERS, THE

MET

❑ 202	Welcome, Welcome Every Guest	1980	15.00

METROS, THE (1)

RCA VICTOR

❑ LPM-3776 [M]	Sweetest One	1967	80.00
❑ LSP-3776 [S]	Sweetest One	1967	100.00

METROS, THE (3)

MTM

❑ ST-71054	The Metros	1986	15.00

METROTONES, THE

COLUMBIA

❑ CL6341 [10]	Tops in Rock and Roll	1955	250.00

MEXICALI BRASS, THE

CUSTOM

❑ CS10 [S]	Jingle Bells	196?	15.00

MEYERS, AUGIE

ATLANTIC AMERICA

❑ 90856	My Main Squeeze	1988	12.00

PARAMOUNT

❑ PAS-6065	You Ain't Rollin' Your Roll Rite	1973	25.00

POLYDOR

❑ 24-4069	Western Head Music Co.	1971	25.00

TEXAS RE-CORD

❑ 1002	Live at the Longneck	197?	30.00

MEZZROW, MEZZ

BLUE NOTE

❑ BLP-7023 [10]	Mezz Mezzrow and His Band	1952	300.00

LONDON

❑ TKL-93092 [10]	A La Schola Cantorum	195?	60.00

RCA VICTOR

❑ LJM-1006 [M]	Mezzin' Around	1954	50.00

SWING

❑ SW-8409	Paris 1955, Volume 1	1986	12.00

X

❑ LVA-3027 [10]	Mezz Mezzrow	1954	100.00
❑ LVA-3015 [10]	Mezz Mezzrow's Swing Session	1954	100.00

MFG

HAT HUT

❑ 0S/T	MFG in Minnesota	1978	30.00

MFSB

PHILADELPHIA INT'L.

❑ KZ32707	Love Is the Message	1974	12.00
❑ ZQ32707 [Q]	Love Is the Message	1974	25.00
❑ KZ32046	MFSB	1973	12.00
❑ PZ33845	Philadelphia Freedom	1975	12.00
❑ PZQ33845 [Q]	Philadelphia Freedom	1975	25.00
❑ PZ34238	Summertime	1976	12.00
❑ PZ34658	The End of Phase One	1977	12.00
❑ JZ35516	The Gamble-Huff Orchestra	1978	12.00
❑ PZ33158	Universal Love	1975	12.00

TSOP

❑ JZ36405	Mysteries of the World	1980	12.00

MIAMI SOUND MACHINE

AUDIOFON

❑ AUS5426	Live Again -- Renacer	1977	300.00
— First 600 have a cover where the backdrop is clearly visible			
❑ AUS5426	Live Again -- Renacer	1977	200.00
— The rest have a cover with a blue and yellow "tropical" background			
❑ AUS5427	Miami Sound Machine	1978	200.00
— Spanish-language version			

CBS INTERNATIONAL

❑ DSL10335	7Up Presenta Los Hits de Miami Sound Machine	1983	150.00
— Only available in the Miami area from 7Up dealers			
❑ DIL10349	A Toda Maquina	1984	40.00
— Spanish-language version of "Eyes of Innocence," their first all-English LP			
❑ DML10306	Imported	1980	50.00
— Reissue of 10455			
❑ DKL10455	Imported	1979	100.00
— Reissue of MSM album			
❑ DHL10311	Miami Sound Machine	1980	100.00
— Different album than Electric Cat 226 and its later issues			
❑ DIL10320	Otra Vez	1981	50.00
❑ DIL10375	Primitive Love	1985	30.00
— Edition mostly distributed in Puerto Rico, with three Spanish-language tracks replacing three English tracks			
❑ DIL10330	Rio	1982	50.00

ELECTRIC CAT

❑ ECS226 [B]	Miami Sound Machine	1978	250.00
— Mostly English-language version			

EPIC

❑ BFE39622	Eyes of Innocence	1984	18.00
— Original issue			
❑ PE39622	Eyes of Innocence	1986	10.00
— Reissue with new prefix			
❑ BFE40131	Primitive Love	1985	15.00
— The band's breakthrough LP to non-Hispanic audiences, and the last one not to have Gloria Estefan prominently credited; original issue			
❑ FE40131	Primitive Love	1986	10.00
— Reissue with new prefix			

MSM

❑ ERK 0714	Imported	1979	200.00

TOP HITS

❑ TH-AM2185	Live Again -- Renacer	1982	80.00
— Reissue of Audiofon LP of the same name			
❑ TH-AM2228	Lo Mejor De Miami Sound Machine -- A Portrait of the Originals	1983	50.00
— Compilation from first two Spanish-language LPs			
❑ TH-AM2187	Miami Sound Machine	1982	100.00
— Reissue of Electric Cat LP of the same name			

MICHAEL, GEORGE

COLUMBIA

❑ OC40867	Faith	1987	12.00
❑ C46898	Listen Without Prejudice (Volume 1)	1990	15.00

MICHAELS, HILLY

WARNER BROS.

❑ BSK3431 [B]	Calling All Girls	1980	18.00

WARNER BROS.

❑ BSK3566 [B]	Lumia	1981	15.00

MICHAELS, LEE

A&M

❑ SP-4302	5th	1971	18.00
❑ SP-4249	Barrel	1970	18.00
❑ SP-4140	Carnival of Life	1968	40.00
❑ SP-4199	Lee Michaels	1969	18.00
❑ SP-3158	Lee Michaels	198?	10.00
— Budget-line reissue			
❑ SP-3518	Live	1973	18.00
❑ SP-4152	Recital	1968	25.00
❑ SP-4336	Space and First Takes	1972	18.00

COLUMBIA

❑ KC32275	Nice Day for Something	1973	15.00
❑ CQ32275 [Q]	Nice Day for Something	1973	40.00
❑ KC32846	Tailface	1974	15.00

MICKEY AND SYLVIA

RCA CAMDEN

❑ CAL-863 [M]	Love Is Strange	1965	50.00
❑ CAS-863(e) [R]	Love Is Strange	1965	30.00

RCA VICTOR

❑ APM1-0327	Do It Again	1973	15.00

VIK

❑ LX-1102 [M]	New Sounds	1957	400.00

MIDDLE OF THE ROAD

RCA VICTOR

❑ LSP-4674	Acceleration	1972	15.00

MIDDLEBROOKS, HARRY

AVI

❑ AV-6033	Give It Time	107?	15.00

CAPITOL

❑ T2850 [M]	Funny How Time Slips Away	1968	30.00
❑ ST-2850 [S]	Funny How Time Slips Away	1968	15.00

MIDDLETON, EDDIE

EPIC

❑ PE34882	Eddie Middleton	1977	12.00

MIDLER, BETTE

ATLANTIC

❑ 81933	Beaches	1988	12.00
❑ SD7270	Bette Midler	1973	15.00
— 1841 Broadway" address on label; with poster			
❑ SW-95507	Bette Midler	1973	25.00
— Longines Record Club edition			
❑ SD19151	Broken Blossom	1977	12.00
❑ SD16022	Divine Madness	1980	12.00
❑ SD 2-9000	Live! At Last	1977	15.00
❑ PR275 [DJ]	Live! At Last Specially Edited for Air Play	1977	18.00
— Promo-only 14-track sampler			
❑ 81291	Mud Will Be Flung Tonight!	1985	12.00
❑ R163898	Mud Will Be Flung Tonight!	1985	15.00
— RCA Music Service edition			
❑ 80070	No Frills	1983	12.00
❑ 82129	Some People's Lives	1990	15.00
❑ SD18155	Songs for the New Depression	1976	12.00
❑ 7238 [M]	The Divine Miss M	1972	30.00
— Mono is promo only; white label, "dj copy monaural" sticker on stereo cover			
❑ QD7238 [Q]	The Divine Miss M	1973	25.00
❑ SD7238 [S]	The Divine Miss M	1972	12.00
— 1841 Broadway" address on label			
❑ SD16010	The Rose	1979	12.00
❑ SD16004	Thighs and Whispers	1979	12.00

MOBILE FIDELITY

❑ MOFI1-022 [B]	The Rose - The Original Soundtrack Recording	2012	30.00

MIDNIGHT OIL

COLUMBIA

❑ BFC38996	10,9,8,7,6,5,4,3,2,1	1983	15.00
❑ C45398	Blue Sky Mining	1990	15.00
— All copies on blue vinyl			
❑ BFC40967	Diesel and Dust	1987	15.00
❑ FC40967	Diesel and Dust	1988	12.00
— Reissue; "02" added to rear-cover bar code			
❑ BFC39987	Red Sails in the Sunset	1984	15.00

MIDNIGHT STAR

SOLAR

❑ 60454	Headlines	1986	12.00
❑ D1-72564	Midnight Star	1988	12.00
❑ 60241	No Parking on the Dance Floor	1983	12.00
❑ 60384	Planetary Invasion	1984	12.00
❑ S-19	Standing Together	1981	15.00
❑ BXL1-3491	The Beginning	1980	25.00
❑ 60145	Victory	1982	15.00

Number	Title	Yr	NM

MIDNIGHTERS, THE

FEDERAL
| ❑ 295-90 [10] | Their Greatest Hits | 1954 | 8000.00 |

—VG value 4000; VG+ value 6000

| ❑ 541 [M] | Their Greatest Hits | 1955 | 1500.00 |

—Red cover

| ❑ 541 [M] | Their Greatest Hits | 1955 | 1000.00 |

— Yellow cover

| ❑ 581 [M] | The Midnighters, Volume 2 | 1955 | 1200.00 |

KING
| ❑ 541 [M] | Their Greatest Jukebox Hits | 1958 | 400.00 |

— Crownless black label, "King" is two inches wide on label

| ❑ 541 [M] | Their Greatest Jukebox Hits | 196? | 300.00 |

— Crownless black label, "King" is three inches wide on label. Above two have a girl on the cover.

| ❑ 541 [M] | Their Greatest Jukebox Hits | 196? | 200.00 |

— Reissue with Hank Ballard on cover

| ❑ 581 [M] | The Midnighters, Volume 2 | 1958 | 300.00 |

— Crownless black label, "King" is two inches wide on label

| ❑ 581 [M] | The Midnighters, Volume 2 | 196? | 200.00 |

— Crownless black label, "King" is three inches wide on label

MIGHTY BABY

HEAD
| ❑ LPS-025 | Mighty Baby | 1969 | 100.00 |

MIGHTY FAITH INCREASERS, THE

KING
| ❑ 814 [M] | A Festival of Spiritual Songs | 1962 | 150.00 |
| ❑ 806 [M] | The Mighty Faith Increasers with Willa Dorsey | 1962 | 150.00 |

MIGHTY LEMON DROPS, THE

REPRISE
| ❑ 26017 | Laughter | 1989 | 12.00 |

SIRE
❑ 25788	Happy Head	1988	12.00
❑ 25595	Out of Hand	1987	12.00
❑ 25532	The Mighty Lemon Drops	1986	12.00

MIGHTY MIGHTY BOSSTONES

BIG RIG
| ❑ BR101 | Don't Know How to Party | 1993 | 50.00 |

— Includes one 12-inch plaid picture disc and a 10-inch record called "Skacore"

| ❑ BR102 [10] | Question the Answers | 1994 | 50.00 |

— Two 10 inch records; includes one song not on the CD version

BIG RIG/ISLAND
| ❑ 314 542451-1 | Pay Attention | 2000 | 80.00 |

SIDE ONE DUMMY
| ❑ SDLP-1234 | A Jackknife to a Swan | 2002 | 30.00 |

TAANG!
| ❑ 44 | Devils Night Out | 1991 | 30.00 |
| ❑ 49 | More Noise & Other Disturbances | 1991 | 30.00 |

MIKE + THE MECHANICS

ATLANTIC
| ❑ 81923 | Living Years | 1989 | 12.00 |
| ❑ PR820 [DJ] | Mike on Mike | 1985 | 25.00 |

— Promo-only music and interviews

| ❑ PR2543 [DJ] | Mike on Mike II | 1989 | 18.00 |

— Promo-only music and interviews

| ❑ 81287 | Mike + The Mechanics | 1985 | 12.00 |

MIL-COMBO, THE

CAPITOL
| ❑ T579 [M] | The Mil-Combo | 1955 | 50.00 |

— nals on "shaded dog" label

MILBURN, AMOS

ALADDIN
| ❑ LP-704 [10] | Rockin' the Boogie | 1952 | 8000.00 |

— Red vinyl, blue cover

| ❑ LP-704 [10] | Rockin' the Boogie | 1952 | 4000.00 |

— Black vinyl

IMPERIAL
| ❑ LP-9176 [M] | Million Sellers | 1962 | 500.00 |

MOSAIC
| ❑ MQ10-155 | The Complete Aladdin Recordings of Amos Milburn | 199? | 180.00 |

— Limited editon of 3,500

MOTOWN
| ❑ 608 [M] | The Return of Amos Milburn, "The" Blues Boss | 1963 | 900.00 |
| ❑ LP-4012 [M] | Let's Have a Party | 1957 | 800.00 |

MILBURN, AMOS/WYNONIE HARRIS/ETC.

ALADDIN
| ❑ LP-703 [10] | Party After Hours | 1952 | 8000.00 |

— Red vinyl, blue cover

| ❑ LP-703 [10] | Party After Hours | 1952 | 4000.00 |

— Black vinyl

MILES, BARRY

CENTURY
| ❑ 1070 | Fusion Is… | 1979 | 25.00 |

— Audiophile edition

CHARLIE PARKER
| ❑ PLP-804 [M] | Miles of Genius | 1962 | 30.00 |
| ❑ PLP-804S [S] | Miles of Genius | 1962 | 30.00 |

GRYPHON
| ❑ 783 | Fusion Is… | 1978 | 15.00 |

LONDON
| ❑ XPS661 | Magic Theatre | 1975 | 15.00 |
| ❑ XPS651 | Silverlight | 1975 | 15.00 |

MAINSTREAM
| ❑ MRL-382 | Scatbird | 1974 | 18.00 |
| ❑ MRL-353 | White Heat | 1973 | 18.00 |

POPPY
| ❑ PY-40009 | Barry Miles | 1970 | 25.00 |

RCA VICTOR
| ❑ BGL1-2200 | Sky Train | 1977 | 15.00 |

MILES, BUDDY

ATLANTIC
| ❑ SD 2-4000 | Sneak Attack | 1982 | 15.00 |

CASABLANCA
| ❑ NBLP7024 | Bicentennial Gathering of the Tribes | 1976 | 12.00 |
| ❑ NBLP7019 | More Miles Per Gallon | 1975 | 12.00 |

COLUMBIA
❑ KC33089	All the Faces	1974	15.00
❑ KC32694	Booger Bear	1973	15.00
❑ CQ32694 [Q]	Booger Bear	1973	25.00
❑ KC32048	Chapter VII	1973	15.00
❑ CQ32048 [Q]	Chapter VII	1973	25.00

MERCURY
❑ SRM-1-608	A Message to the People	1971	18.00
❑ SRM-2-7500	Buddy Miles Live	1971	18.00
❑ SR-61222	Electric Church	1969	25.00
❑ SR-61196	Expressway to Your Skull	1968	25.00
❑ SR-61280	Them Changes	1970	18.00
❑ SR-61313	We Got to Live Together	1970	18.00

MILES, BUTCH

DREAMSTREET
| ❑ 102 | Lady Be Good | 1980 | 15.00 |

FAMOUS DOOR
❑ 132	Butch Miles Salutes Chick Webb	1979	15.00
❑ 142	Butch Miles Salutes Gene Krupa	1982	12.00
❑ 126	Butch Miles Swings Some Standards	1981	12.00
❑ 124	Encore	1978	15.00
❑ 145	Hail to the Chief	1982	12.00
❑ 117	Miles of Swing	1977	15.00
❑ 150	More Miles… More Standards	1985	12.00

MILES, DICK

CAPITOL
| ❑ ST2925 | The Last Goodbye | 1968 | 18.00 |

MILES, LIZZIE

COOK
❑ 1183 [M]	Hot Songs My Mother Taught Me	195?	60.00
❑ 1182 [M]	Moans and Blues	195?	60.00
❑ 1181 [10]	Queen Mother of the Rue Royale	1955	80.00
❑ 1184 [M]	Torchy Lullabies My Mother Taught Me	195?	60.00

— Black vinyl

| ❑ 1184 [M] | Torchy Lullabies My Mother Taught Me | 195? | 200.00 |

— Rose-colored vinyl

MILES, LUKE "LONG GONE"

WORLD PACIFIC
| ❑ WP-1820 [M] | Country Born | 1964 | 30.00 |
| ❑ ST-1820 [S] | Country Born | 1964 | 30.00 |

MILESTONE JAZZSTARS, THE

MILESTONE
| ❑ 55006 | Milestone Jazzstars In Concert | 1978 | 18.00 |

MILKWOOD (1)

A&M
| ❑ SP-4226 | Under Milkwood | 1969 | 300.00 |

MILKWOOD (2)

PARAMOUNT
| ❑ PAS-6046 [B] | How's the Weather? | 1973 | 45.00 |

MILKWOOD TAPESTRY

METROMEDIA
| ❑ MD-1007 | Milkwood Tapestry | 1969 | 75.00 |

MILL CITY SEVEN, THE

JAZZOLOGY
| ❑ J-19 | The Mill City Seven | 1974 | 12.00 |

MILLARD & DYCE

KAYMAR
| ❑ KS-7-265 | Open | 1973 | 60.00 |

MILLENNIUM

COLUMBIA
| ❑ CS9663 | Begin | 1968 | 30.00 |

MILLER, ASHLEY

COMMAND
| ❑ COM-K-1SD [S] | Christmas Carols with Organ and Chimes | 1963 | 18.00 |

— Sold only at Korvettes department stores

| ❑ COM-K-1 [M] | Christmas Carols with Organ and Chimes | 1963 | 15.00 |

— Sold only at Korvettes department stores

MILLER, CHUCK

MERCURY
| ❑ MG-20195 [M] | After Hours | 1956 | 80.00 |

MILLER, CLARENCE "BIG"

COLUMBIA
❑ CL1808 [M]	Big Miller Sings, Twists, Shouts and Preaches	1962	30.00
❑ CS8608 [S]	Big Miller Sings, Twists, Shouts and Preaches	1962	30.00
❑ CL1611 [M]	Revelation and the Blues	1961	30.00
❑ CS8411 [S]	Revelation and the Blues	1961	30.00

UNITED ARTISTS
| ❑ UAL-3047 [M] | Did You Ever Hear the Blues? | 1959 | 40.00 |
| ❑ UAS-6047 [S] | Did You Ever Hear the Blues? | 1959 | 60.00 |

MILLER, DON

KING
| ❑ 712 [M] | The Don Miller Quartet | 1960 | 60.00 |

MILLER, EDDIE, AND ARMAND HUG

LAND O' JAZZ
| ❑ 5876 | Just Friends | 1979 | 15.00 |

MILLER, EDDIE

CAPITOL
| ❑ T614 [M] | Classics in Jazz | 1955 | 50.00 |

FAMOUS DOOR
| ❑ 131 | It's Miller Time | 1979 | 15.00 |

MILLER, EDDIE/GEORGE VAN EPS

JUMP
| ❑ JL-5 [10] | Eddie Miller/George Van Eps | 1953 | 50.00 |

MILLER, FRANKIE

AUDIO LAB
| ❑ AL-1562 [M] | The Fine Country Singing of Frankie Miller | 1963 | 150.00 |

STARDAY
❑ SLP-339 [M]	Blackland Farmer	1965	60.00
❑ SLP-134 [M]	Country Music's Great New Star	1961	100.00
❑ SLP-199 [M]	The True Country Style of Frankie Miller	1962	100.00

MILLER, GLENN, ORCHESTRA

GRP
| ❑ GRP-A-1002 | In the Digital Mood | 1983 | 12.00 |

MILLER, GLENN, ORCHESTRA (BUDDY DEFRANCO, DIRECTOR)

EPIC
| ❑ LN24206 [M] | Something New | 1966 | 15.00 |
| ❑ BN26206 [S] | Something New | 1966 | 18.00 |

PARAMOUNT
| ❑ PAS-5034 | The Glenn Miller Orchestra | 1970 | 15.00 |

RCA VICTOR
❑ LPM-3819 [M]	In the Mod	1967	18.00
❑ LSP-3819 [S]	In the Mod	1967	15.00
❑ LPM-3971 [M]	The Glenn Miller Orchestra Makes the Goin' Great	1968	40.00
❑ LSP-3971 [S]	The Glenn Miller Orchestra Makes the Goin' Great	1968	15.00
❑ LPM-3880 [M]	The Glenn Miller Orchestra Returns to the Glen Island Casino	1968	25.00
❑ LSP-3880 [S]	The Glenn Miller Orchestra Returns to the Glen Island Casino	1968	15.00

MILLER, GLENN, ORCHESTRA (RAY MCKINLEY, DIRECTOR)

EPIC
| ❑ LN24133 [M] | Glenn Miller Time -- 1965 | 1965 | 18.00 |

Number	Title	Yr	NM
❑ BN26133 [S]	Glenn Miller Time -- 1965	1965	25.00
❑ LN24157 [M]	Great Songs of the 60's	1965	18.00
❑ BN26157 [S]	Great Songs of the 60's	1965	25.00
RCA VICTOR			
❑ LPM-2193 [M]	Dance, Anyone?	1960	30.00
❑ LSP-2193 [S]	Dance, Anyone?	1960	30.00
❑ LPM-2519 [M]	Echoes of Glenn Miller	1962	30.00
❑ LSP-2519 [S]	Echoes of Glenn Miller	1962	30.00
❑ LPM-2436 [M]	Glenn Miller Time	1961	30.00
❑ LSP-2436 [S]	Glenn Miller Time	1961	30.00
❑ LPM-1948 [M]	On Tour with the New Glenn Miller Orchestra	1959	30.00
❑ LSP-1948 [S]	On Tour with the New Glenn Miller Orchestra	1959	40.00
❑ LPM-1678 [M]	Something Old, New, Borrowed and Blue	1958	30.00
❑ LSP-1678 [S]	Something Old, New, Borrowed and Blue	1958	40.00
❑ LPM-2270 [M]	The Authentic Sound of the New Glenn Miller Orchestra -- Today	1961	30.00
❑ LSP-2270 [S]	The Authentic Sound of the New Glenn Miller Orchestra -- Today	1961	30.00
❑ LPM-2080 [M]	The Great Dance Bands of the 30's and 40's	1960	30.00
❑ LSP-2080 [S]	The Great Dance Bands of the 30's and 40's	1960	30.00
❑ ANL1-2975(e) [S]	The Great Dance Bands of the 30's and 40's	1978	10.00
—Reissue of LSP-2080			
❑ LPM-1852 [M]	The Miller Sound	1959	30.00
❑ LSP-1852 [S]	The Miller Sound	1959	40.00
❑ LPM-1522 [M]	The New Glenn Miller Orchestra in Hi-Fi	1957	30.00
❑ LSP-1522 [S]	The New Glenn Miller Orchestra in Hi-Fi	1958	40.00

MILLER, GLENN

Number	Title	Yr	NM
20TH CENTURY			
❑ T2-904	Remember Glenn	197?	18.00
20TH CENTURY FOX			
❑ TFM-3159 [M]	This Is Glenn Miller and His Greatest Orchestra, Volume 1	1964	18.00
❑ TFS-4159 [R]	This Is Glenn Miller and His Greatest Orchestra, Volume 1	1964	12.00
❑ TFM-3160 [M]	This Is Glenn Miller and His Greatest Orchestra, Volume 2	1964	18.00
❑ TFS-4160 [R]	This Is Glenn Miller and His Greatest Orchestra, Volume 2	1964	12.00
20TH FOX			
❑ TCF-100-2 [M]	Glenn Miller and His Orchestra Original Film Sound Tracks	1958	30.00
❑ TCF-100-2S [R]	Glenn Miller and His Orchestra Original Film Sound Tracks	1961	25.00
❑ FOX3020 [M]	Glenn Miller's Original Film Soundtracks, Volume 1	1958	25.00
—Half of 101			
❑ FOX3021 [M]	Glenn Miller's Original Film Soundtracks, Volume 2	1958	25.00
—Half of 101			
BANDSTAND			
❑ BS-7136	A Million Dreams Ago	198?	12.00
BLUEBIRD			
❑ 6360-1-RB	Maj. Glenn Miller and the Army Air Force Band	1987	12.00
❑ AXM2-5512	The Complete Glenn Miller Volume 1, 1938-39	1975	15.00
❑ AXM2-5514	The Complete Glenn Miller Volume 2, 1939	1976	15.00
❑ AXM2-5534	The Complete Glenn Miller Volume 3, 1939-40	1976	15.00
❑ AXM2-5558	The Complete Glenn Miller Volume 4, 1940	1978	15.00
❑ AXM2-5565	The Complete Glenn Miller Volume 5, 1940	1979	15.00
❑ AXM2-5569	The Complete Glenn Miller Volume 6, 1940-41	1980	15.00
❑ AXM2-5570	The Complete Glenn Miller Volume 7, 1941	1980	15.00
❑ AXM2-5571	The Complete Glenn Miller Volume 8, 1941-42	1980	15.00
❑ AXM2-5574	The Complete Glenn Miller Volume 9, 1939-42	1980	15.00
❑ 9785-1-RB	The Popular Recordings 1938-1942	1989	30.00
EPIC			
❑ LA16002 [M]	Glenn Miller	1960	25.00
EVEREST			
❑ 4005/5	His Complete Recordings on Columbia (1928-1938) As Player and Conductor	1982	30.00
—Box set with 8-page booklet			
HARMONY			
❑ HS11393 [R]	Collector's Choice	1970	15.00
INTERMEDIA			
❑ QS-5045	A String of Pearls	198?	10.00
KOALA			
❑ AW14186	Chattanooga Choo Choo	1979	15.00

Number	Title	Yr	NM
MERCURY			
❑ 826635-1	Glenn Miller In Hollywood	1986	15.00
—Reissue of material formerly on 20th Century			
MOVIETONE			
❑ MTM-1003 [M]	Glenn Miller's Shindig	1965	18.00
❑ MTS-72003 [R]	Glenn Miller's Shindig	1965	12.00
❑ MTS-72018 [R]	The Glenn Miller Years	1967	15.00
PAIR			
❑ PDL2-1003	Original Recordings, Volume 1	1986	15.00
❑ PDL2-1036	Original Recordings, Volume 2	1986	15.00
PICKWICK			
❑ DL2-0168	A String of Pearls	197?	12.00
—Reissue of RCA Camden ACL2-0168			
❑ ACL-7009	Parade of Hits	1976	10.00
RCA CAMDEN			
❑ ACL2-0168	A String of Pearls	1973	15.00
❑ CXS-9004	Sunrise Serenade	197?	15.00
❑ CAL-751 [M]	The Great Glenn Miller	1963	18.00
❑ CAS-751(e) [R]	The Great Glenn Miller	1963	15.00
❑ CAL-2128 [M]	The Nearness of You and Others	1967	18.00
❑ CAS-2128 [R]	The Nearness of You and Others	1967	15.00
❑ CAS-2267	The One and Only Glenn Miller	1968	12.00
❑ CAL-829 [M]	The Original Recordings	1964	18.00
❑ CAS-829(e) [R]	The Original Recordings	1964	15.00
❑ ACL-0503	This Time the Dream's On Me	1974	10.00
RCA SPECIAL PRODUCTS			
❑ DMM4-0322	Glenn Miller	1978	25.00
—Box set; mail-order offer			
RCA VICTOR			
❑ CPM2-0693	A Legendary Performer	1974	15.00
❑ CPL1-2080	A Legendary Performer, Volume 2	1976	12.00
❑ CPL1-2495	A Legendary Performer, Volume 3	1977	12.00
❑ LPM-3657 [M]	Blue Moonlight	1966	18.00
❑ LSP 3657 [R]	Blue Moonlight	1966	12.00
❑ LPM-6100 [M]	For the Very First Time…	195?	50.00
—Black "Long Play" labels in leatherette spiral-bound binder			
❑ LPT-31 [10]	Glenn Miller	1951	60.00
❑ VPM-6019	Glenn Miller: A Memorial 1944-1969	1969	18.00
❑ LPT-6700 [M]	Glenn Miller and His Orchestra Limited Edition	1953	150.00
—Silver labels with red print in leatherette spiral-bound binder			
❑ LPT-6700 [M]	Glenn Miller and His Orchestra Limited Edition -- Second Pressing	195?	60.00
—Black "Long Play" labels in leatherette spiral-bound binder			
❑ LPT-6701 [M]	Glenn Miller and His Orchestra Limited Edition Volume Two	1954	120.00
—Black "Long Play" labels in leatherette spiral-bound binder			
❑ LPT-6701 [M]	Glenn Miller and His Orchestra Limited Edition Volume Two -- Second Pressing	195?	60.00
—Black "Long Play" labels in leatherette spiral-bound binder; identified as "Second Pressing" throughout			
❑ LPT-6702 [M]	Glenn Miller Army Air Force Band	1955	120.00
—Black "Long Play" labels in leatherette spiral-bound binder			
❑ LPT-6702 [M]	Glenn Miller Army Air Force Band	195?	60.00
—Same as above, but in box rather than in binder			
❑ LPM-1193 [M]	Glenn Miller Concert	1956	40.00
❑ LPT-16 [10]	Glenn Miller Concert -- Volume 1	1951	60.00
❑ LPT-30 [10]	Glenn Miller Concert -- Volume 2	1951	60.00
❑ LPT-3001 [10]	Glenn Miller Concert -- Volume 3	195?	60.00
❑ LPM-6101 [M]	Glenn Miller On the Air	1963	40.00
❑ LSP-6101 [R]	Glenn Miller On the Air	1963	30.00
❑ LPM-2767 [M]	Glenn Miller On the Air Volume 1	1963	18.00
❑ LSP-2767 [R]	Glenn Miller On the Air Volume 1	1963	12.00
❑ LPM-2768 [M]	Glenn Miller On the Air Volume 2	1963	18.00
❑ LSP-2768 [R]	Glenn Miller On the Air Volume 2	1963	12.00
❑ LPM-2769 [M]	Glenn Miller On the Air Volume 3	1963	18.00
❑ LSP-2769 [R]	Glenn Miller On the Air Volume 3	1963	12.00
❑ PR-114 [M]	Glenn Miller Originals	1962	25.00
—Promotional item for Salada Foods Inc.			
❑ LPT-1016 [M]	Juke Box Saturday Night	1955	40.00
❑ LPM-1494 [M]	Marvelous Miller Moods	1957	40.00
❑ PRM-181 [M]	Moonlight Serenade	1965	18.00
❑ ANL1-0974	Pure Gold	1975	10.00
❑ LPM-1192 [M]	Selections from "The Glenn Miller Story" and Other Hits	1956	40.00
❑ LSP-1192(e) [R]	Selections from "The Glenn Miller Story" and Other Hits	196?	18.00
—Black label, dog on top			
❑ AFL1-1192	Selections from "The Glenn Miller Story" and Other Hits	1977	10.00
❑ LPT-3057 [10]	Selections from the Film "The Glenn Miller Story	1954	60.00
❑ LPT-3067 [10]	Sunrise Serenade	1954	60.00

Number	Title	Yr	NM
❑ LPM-3377 [M]	The Best of Glenn Miller	1965	18.00
❑ LSP-3377(e) [R]	The Best of Glenn Miller	1965	12.00
—Black label			
❑ LSP-3377(e) [R]	The Best of Glenn Miller	1969	10.00
—Orange label			
❑ LPM-3564 [M]	The Best of Glenn Miller Volume 2	1966	18.00
❑ LSP-3564 [R]	The Best of Glenn Miller Volume 2	1966	12.00
❑ LSP-4125 [R]	The Best of Glenn Miller Volume 3	1969	15.00
❑ AFL1-2825	The Best of Glenn Miller Volume 3	1978	10.00
❑ LPM-3873 [M]	The Chesterfield Broadcasts, Volume 1	1967	18.00
❑ LSP-3873 [R]	The Chesterfield Broadcasts, Volume 1	1967	12.00
❑ ANL1-1139	The Chesterfield Broadcasts, Volume 1	1975	10.00
❑ LSP-3981 [R]	The Chesterfield Broadcasts, Volume 2	1968	15.00
❑ LPM-1506 [M]	The Glenn Miller Carnegie Hall Concert	1957	40.00
❑ LOP-1005 [M]	The Marvelous Miller Medleys	1958	40.00
❑ LPM-1973 [M]	The Marvelous Miller Medleys	1959	30.00
❑ LSP-1973 [R]	The Marvelous Miller Medleys	196?	18.00
❑ LPT-1031 [M]	The Nearness of You	1955	40.00
❑ LPM-1189 [M]	The Sound of Glenn Miller	1956	40.00
❑ LPT-3002 [10]	This Is Glenn Miller	195?	60.00
❑ LPM-1190 [M]	This Is Glenn Miller	1956	40.00
❑ VPM-6080	This Is Glenn Miller's Army Air Force Band	1972	18.00
❑ LPT-3036 [10]	This Is Glenn Miller -- Volume 2	195?	60.00
READER'S DIGEST			
❑ RD4-64 [R]	The Unforgettable Glenn Miller	1968	25.00
SANDY HOOK			
❑ SH2055	Uncle Sam Presents the Band of the Army Air Forces Training Command	1981	12.00
SPRINGBOARD			
❑ SPX-6013	Remember Glenn	1973	15.00
SUNBEAM			
❑ SB-232	Glenn Miller and His Chesterfield Orchestra	1984	12.00
TIME-LIFE			
❑ STBB-01	Big Bands: Glenn Miller	1983	18.00
❑ STBB-29	Big Bands: Glenn Miller: Take Two	1986	18.00
❑ STBB-17	Big Bands: Major Glenn Miller	1985	18.00

MILLER, JODY

Number	Title	Yr	NM
CAPITOL			
❑ T2412 [M]	Home of the Brave	1965	18.00
❑ ST2412 [S]	Home of the Brave	1965	25.00
❑ T2446 [M]	Jody Miller Sings the Great Hits of Buck Owens	1966	18.00
❑ ST2446 [S]	Jody Miller Sings the Great Hits of Buck Owens	1966	25.00
❑ T2349 [M]	Queen of the House	1965	18.00
❑ ST2349 [S]	Queen of the House	1965	25.00
❑ ST-11169	The Best of Jody Miller	1973	15.00
❑ ST2996	The Nashville Sound of Jody Miller	1968	18.00
❑ T1913 [M]	Wednesday's Child Is Full of Woe	1963	30.00
❑ ST1913 [S]	Wednesday's Child Is Full of Woe	1963	40.00
EPIC			
❑ KE33349	Country Girl	1975	15.00
❑ KE32386	Good News!	1973	15.00
❑ PE34446	Here's Jody	1977	15.00
❑ E30659	He's So Fine	1971	15.00
❑ KE32569	House of the Rising Sun	1974	15.00
❑ E30282	Look at Mine	1971	15.00
❑ KE31706	There's a Party Goin' On	1972	15.00
❑ KE33934	Will You Love Me Tomorrow?	1976	15.00

MILLER, MARCUS

Number	Title	Yr	NM
WARNER BROS.			
❑ 25074	Marcus Miller	1984	15.00
❑ 23806	Suddenly	1983	18.00

MILLER, MICKEY

Number	Title	Yr	NM
FOLKWAYS			
❑ FA-2393 [M]	American Folk Songs	1959	30.00

MILLER, MITCH

Number	Title	Yr	NM
ATLANTIC			
❑ SD8277	Peace Sing Along with Mitch	1970	15.00
COLUMBIA			
❑ G30250	34 All Time Great Sing Along Selections	1970	15.00
❑ CL1205 [M]	Christmas Sing Along with Mitch	1958	18.00
—Originals have gatefold cover with eight detachable lyric sheets inside			
❑ CS8027 [S]	Christmas Sing Along with Mitch	1959	25.00
—Originals have gatefold cover with eight detachable lyric			

Number	Title	Yr	NM
sheets inside			
❑ PC39298	Christmas Sing Along with Mitch	1984	10.00
❑ CL1773 [M]	Family Sing Along with Mitch	1962	15.00
❑ CS8573 [S]	Family Sing Along with Mitch	1962	18.00
❑ CL1389 [M]	Fireside Sing Along with Mitch	1959	18.00
❑ CS8184 [S]	Fireside Sing Along with Mitch	1959	25.00
❑ CL1316 [M]	Folk Songs Sing Along with Mitch	1959	18.00
❑ CS8118 [S]	Folk Songs Sing Along with Mitch	1959	25.00
❑ CL1568 [M]	Happy Times! Sing Along with Mitch	1961	15.00
❑ CS8368 [S]	Happy Times! Sing Along with Mitch	1961	18.00
❑ CL1701 [M]	Holiday Sing Along with Mitch	1961	15.00
❑ CS8501 [S]	Holiday Sing Along with Mitch	1961	18.00
❑ 3C39297	Holiday Sing Along with Mitch	1984	10.00
❑ CL2063 [M]	Hymn Sing Along with Mitch	1963	15.00
❑ CS8863 [S]	Hymn Sing Along with Mitch	1963	18.00
❑ CL779 [M]	It's So Peaceful in the Country	1956	25.00
— Red and black label with 6 "eye" logos			
❑ CL1475 [M]	March Along with Mitch	1960	15.00
❑ CL1542 [M]	Memories Sing Along with Mitch	1960	15.00
❑ CS8342 [S]	Memories Sing Along with Mitch	1960	18.00
❑ CL6222 [10]	Mitch Miller with Horns and Chorus	195?	30.00
❑ CL1544 [M]	Mitch's Greatest Hits	1961	15.00
❑ CS8638 [R]	Mitch's Greatest Hits	1963	12.00
❑ CL1102 [M]	Mitch's Marches	1957	18.00
❑ CL601 [M]	Mmmmitch!	1954	25.00
— Maroon label, gold print			
❑ CL1243 [M]	More Sing Along with Mitch	1958	18.00
❑ CS8043 [S]	More Sing Along with Mitch	1959	25.00
❑ CL1864 [M]	Night Time Sing Along with Mitch	1963	15.00
❑ CS8664 [S]	Night Time Sing Along with Mitch	1963	18.00
❑ CL1331 [M]	Party Sing Along with Mitch	1959	18.00
❑ CS8138 [S]	Party Sing Along with Mitch	1959	25.00
❑ CL1727 [M]	Rhythm Sing Along with Mitch	1962	15.00
❑ CS8527 [S]	Rhythm Sing Along with Mitch	1962	18.00
❑ CL1414 [M]	Saturday Night Sing Along with Mitch	1960	15.00
❑ CS8211 [S]	Saturday Night Sing Along with Mitch	1960	18.00
❑ CL1457 [M]	Sentimental Sing Along with Mitch	1960	15.00
❑ CS8251 [S]	Sentimental Sing Along with Mitch	1960	18.00
❑ CL1160 [M]	Sing Along with Mitch	1958	18.00
❑ CS8004 [S]	Sing Along with Mitch	1959	25.00
— Red and black label with 6 "eye" logos			
❑ CS8004	Sing Along with Mitch	1963	15.00
— Red label			
❑ CS8004	Sing Along with Mitch	1970	10.00
— Orange label			
❑ CL1283 [M]	Still More! Sing Along with Mitch	1959	18.00
❑ CS8099 [S]	Still More! Sing Along with Mitch	1959	25.00
❑ CL1628 [M]	TV Sing Along with Mitch	1961	15.00
❑ CS8428 [S]	TV Sing Along with Mitch	1961	18.00
❑ CL1671 [M]	Your Request Sing Along with Mitch	1961	15.00
❑ CS8471 [S]	Your Request Sing Along with Mitch	1961	18.00

DECCA

Number	Title	Yr	NM
❑ DL4777 [M]	Dance and Sing Along with Mitch	1966	12.00
❑ DL74777 [S]	Dance and Sing Along with Mitch	1966	15.00

HARMONY

Number	Title	Yr	NM
❑ HS11273	Everybody Sing Along with Mitch	1968	12.00
❑ HS11241	Fireside Sing Along with Mitch	1968	12.00
❑ HL7404 [M]	March Along with Mitch	1967	12.00
❑ HS11204 [S]	March Along with Mitch	1967	15.00
❑ HS11242	Memories Sing Along with Mitch	1968	12.00
❑ HS11354	Night Time Sing Along with Mitch	1970	12.00

MILLER, MRS.

AMARET

Number	Title	Yr	NM
❑ 5000	Mrs. Miller Does Her Thing	1969	25.00

CAPITOL

Number	Title	Yr	NM
❑ T2494 [M]	Mrs. Miller's Greatest Hits	1966	30.00
❑ ST2494 [S]	Mrs. Miller's Greatest Hits	1966	30.00
❑ T2734 [M]	The Country Soul of Mrs. Miller	1967	30.00
❑ ST2734 [S]	The Country Soul of Mrs. Miller	1967	30.00
❑ T2579 [M]	Will Success Spoil Mrs. Miller?	1966	30.00
❑ ST2579 [S]	Will Success Spoil Mrs. Miller?	1966	30.00

MILLER, MULGREW

LANDMARK

Number	Title	Yr	NM
❑ LLP-1525	From Day to Day	1990	15.00
❑ LLP-1507	Keys to the City	198?	12.00
❑ LLP-1519	The Countdown	1989	15.00
❑ LLP-1515	Wingspan	1988	12.00
❑ LLP-1511	Work!	1986	12.00

MILLER, NED

CAPITOL

Number	Title	Yr	NM
❑ ST2914	In the Name of Love	1968	18.00
❑ T2330 [M]	Ned Miller Sings the Songs of Ned Miller	1965	25.00
❑ ST2330 [S]	Ned Miller Sings the Songs of Ned Miller	1965	30.00
❑ T2586 [M]	Teardrop Lane	1967	25.00
❑ ST2586 [S]	Teardrop Lane	1967	25.00
❑ T2414 [M]	The Best of Ned Miller	1966	18.00
❑ ST2414 [S]	The Best of Ned Miller	1966	25.00

FABOR

Number	Title	Yr	NM
❑ FLP-1001 [M]	From a Jack to a King	1963	40.00
— Black vinyl			
❑ FLP-1001 [M]	From a Jack to a King	1963	100.00
— Colored vinyl			

MILLER, PUNCH

HERWIN

Number	Title	Yr	NM
❑ 108	Jazz Rarities 1929-30	197?	12.00

IMPERIAL

Number	Title	Yr	NM
❑ LP-9160 [M]	Hongo Fongo	1962	30.00

JAZZ CRUSADE

Number	Title	Yr	NM
❑ 2016	Oh Lady Be Good	196?	18.00

JAZZOLOGY

Number	Title	Yr	NM
❑ JCE-12	Kid Punch	1967	18.00
❑ J-17	River's in Mourning	197?	12.00

MILLER, ROGER

20TH CENTURY

Number	Title	Yr	NM
❑ T-592	Making a Name for Myself	1979	15.00

COLUMBIA

Number	Title	Yr	NM
❑ KC32449	Dear Folks Sorry I Haven't Written Lately	1973	18.00
❑ KC33472	Supersongs	1975	18.00

HILLTOP

Number	Title	Yr	NM
❑ 6109	King of the Road	197?	12.00
❑ 6131	Little Green Apples	197?	12.00

MCA

Number	Title	Yr	NM
❑ 5722	Roger Miller	1986	12.00

MERCURY

Number	Title	Yr	NM
❑ SR-61297	A Trip in the Country	1970	18.00
❑ 826261-1	Golden Hits	198?	10.00
— Reissue of Smash 67073			
❑ SR-61361	The Best of Roger Miller	1971	18.00

NASHVILLE

Number	Title	Yr	NM
❑ 2046	The Amazing Roger Miller	196?	15.00

PICKWICK

Number	Title	Yr	NM
❑ SPC-3226	Engine #9	197?	12.00
❑ PTP-2057	King High	1973	15.00

RCA CAMDEN

Number	Title	Yr	NM
❑ CAL-851 [M]	Roger Miller	1964	15.00
❑ CAS-851 [S]	Roger Miller	1964	18.00
❑ CAL-903 [M]	The One and Only Roger Miller	1965	15.00
❑ CAS-903 [S]	The One and Only Roger Miller	1965	18.00

SMASH

Number	Title	Yr	NM
❑ SRS-67103	A Tender Look at Love	1968	25.00
❑ MGS-27049 [M]	Dang Me	196?	15.00
— Yet another retitled version of "Roger and Out			
❑ SRS-67049 [S]	Dang Me	196?	18.00
— Yet another retitled version of "Roger and Out			
❑ SRS-67049 [S]	Dang Me/Chug-a-Lug	196?	18.00
— Retitled version of "Roger and Out			
❑ MGS-27049 [M]	Dang Me/Chug-a-Lug	196?	15.00
— Retitled version of "Roger and Out			
❑ MGS-27073 [M]	Golden Hits	1965	18.00
❑ SRS-67073 [S]	Golden Hits	1965	25.00
❑ MGS-27049 [M]	Roger and Out	1964	18.00
❑ SRS-67049 [S]	Roger and Out	1964	25.00
❑ SRS-67123	Roger Miller	1969	25.00
❑ SRS-67129	Roger Miller 1970	1970	25.00
❑ MGS-27068 [M]	The 3rd Time Around	1965	18.00
❑ SRS-67068 [S]	The 3rd Time Around	1965	25.00
❑ MGS-27061 [M]	The Return of Roger Miller	1965	18.00
❑ SRS-67061 [S]	The Return of Roger Miller	1965	25.00
❑ MGS-27092 [M]	Walkin' in the Sunshine	1967	25.00
❑ SRS-67092 [S]	Walkin' in the Sunshine	1967	25.00
❑ MGS-27096 [M]	Waterhole #3	1967	30.00
❑ SRS-67096 [S]	Waterhole #3	1967	25.00
❑ MGS-27075 [M]	Words and Music	1966	18.00
❑ SRS-67075 [S]	Words and Music	1966	25.00

STARDAY

Number	Title	Yr	NM
❑ 3011	Painted Poetry	1978	12.00
❑ SLP-318 [M]	The Country Side of Roger Miller	196?	30.00
— Retitled version of "Wild Child			
❑ SLP-318 [M]	Wild Child Roger Miller	1965	30.00
❑ T-90241 [M]	Wild Child Roger Miller	1965	40.00
— Capitol Record Club edition			
❑ DT-90241 [R]	Wild Child Roger Miller	1965	40.00
— Capitol Record Club edition			

WINDSONG

Number	Title	Yr	NM
❑ BHL1-2337	Off the Wall	1977	15.00

MILLER, STEVE, BAND

CAPITOL

Number	Title	Yr	NM
❑ ST-12216	Abracadabra	1982	12.00
❑ SVBB-11114	Anthology	1972	18.00
❑ R223186	Anthology	197?	18.00
— RCA Music Service edition			
❑ SO-11630	Book of Dreams	1977	12.00
❑ SEAX-11903 [PD]	Book of Dreams	1978	18.00
❑ SN-16323	Book of Dreams	1984	10.00
❑ C1-48303	Born 2 B Blue	1988	12.00
❑ SKAO-184 [B]	Brave New World	1969	30.00
— Black label with colorband			
❑ SKAO-184	Brave New World	1970	18.00
— Green label			
❑ SN-16078	Brave New World	1980	10.00
❑ SKAO-8-0184	Brave New World	1969	30.00
— Capitol Record Club edition; black label with colorband			
❑ SKAO2920	Children of the Future	1968	30.00
— Black label with colorband			
❑ SKAO2920	Children of the Future	1970	18.00
— Green label			
❑ SN-16262	Children of the Future	1982	10.00
❑ STBB-717	Children of the Future/Living in the U.S.A.	1971	18.00
— Repackage of 2920 and 2984 (with new title for the latter)			
❑ ST-12121	Circle of Love	1981	12.00
❑ SN-16357	Circle of Love	1985	10.00
❑ ST-11497	Fly Like an Eagle	1976	12.00
❑ SN-16339	Fly Like an Eagle	1984	10.00
❑ 21185	Fly Like an Eagle	1999	25.00
— Limited-edition reissue on 180-gram vinyl			
❑ SOO-11872 [DJ]	Greatest Hits 1974-1978	1978	30.00
— Promo only on blue vinyl			
❑ SOO-11872	Greatest Hits 1974-1978	1978	12.00
❑ SN-16321	Greatest Hits 1974-1978	1984	10.00
❑ SJ-12339	Italian X-Rays	1985	12.00
❑ PJ-12445	Living in the 20th Century	1987	12.00
❑ SKAO-436	Number 5	1970	18.00
❑ SKAO-80436	Number 5	1970	25.00
— Capitol Record Club edition			
❑ SMAS-11022	Recall the Beginning…A Journey from Eden	1972	18.00
❑ SW-748	Rock Love	1971	18.00
❑ ST2984	Sailor	1968	30.00
— Black label with colorband			
❑ ST2984	Sailor	1970	18.00
— Green label			
❑ SN-16263	Sailor	1982	10.00
❑ ST-12263	Steve Miller Live	1983	12.00
❑ SMAS-11235	The Joker	1973	12.00
❑ ST-331 [B]	Your Saving Grace	1969	30.00
❑ SN-16079	Your Saving Grace	1980	10.00

DCC COMPACT CLASSICS

Number	Title	Yr	NM
❑ LPZ-2028	Greatest Hits 1974-1978	1996	50.00
— Audiophile vinyl			

MOBILE FIDELITY

Number	Title	Yr	NM
❑ 1-021	Fly Like an Eagle	1979	50.00
— Audiophile vinyl			

MILLER, STEVE, BAND/QUICKSILVER MESSENGER SERVICE/THE BAND

CAPITOL

Number	Title	Yr	NM
❑ STCR-288 [B]	Sailor/Quicksilver Messenger Service/Music from Big Pink	1969	50.00
— Special 3-LP box set combining these three LPs, also listed separately in each group's listing, in one package			

MILLER, STEVEN

HIPPOCKET

Number	Title	Yr	NM
❑ HP-102	Singing Whale Songs in a Low Voice	1983	15.00

WINDHAM HILL

Number	Title	Yr	NM
❑ WH-0102	Singing Whale Songs in a Low Voice	1987	12.00
— Reissue of HipPocket 102			

MILLI VANILLI

ARISTA

Number	Title	Yr	NM
❑ AL8592	Girl You Know It's True	1989	12.00
❑ AL8622	The Remix Album	1990	15.00

MILLMAN, JACK

DECCA

Number	Title	Yr	NM
❑ DL8156 [M]	Jazz Studio 4	1955	50.00

ERA

Number	Title	Yr	NM
❑ EL-20005 [M]	Blowing Up a Storm	1956	60.00
— Red vinyl			
❑ EL-20005 [M]	Blowing Up a Storm	1956	40.00
— Black vinyl			

LIBERTY

Number	Title	Yr	NM
❑ LJH-6007 [M]	Shades of Things to Come	1956	50.00

MILLS, ALAN

FOLKWAYS

Number	Title	Yr	NM
❑ FC-7677 [M]	Animals, Vol. 1	1956	30.00
❑ FW-3000 [M]	Canada's Story in Song	1960	40.00
❑ FC-7750 [M]	Christmas Songs from Many Lands	1956	30.00
❑ FP-29 [10]	Folk Songs of French Canada	1952	50.00
❑ FW-6929 [M]	Folk Songs of French Canada	195?	30.00
❑ FP-831 [10]	Folk Songs of Newfoundland	1953	50.00
❑ FW-6831 [M]	Folk Songs of Newfoundland	195?	30.00
❑ FC-7208 [M]	French Folk Songs for Children	1957	30.00
❑ FC-7018 [M]	French Folk Songs for Children in English	1957	30.00
❑ FC-7642 [M]	More Animals, Vol. 2	1956	30.00
❑ FW-3001 [M]	O Canada: A History in Song	1956	30.00
❑ FA-2313 [M]	Songs of the Sea	1957	30.00
❑ FW-8771 [M]	We'll Rant and We'll Roar: Songs of Newfoundland	1958	30.00

SCHOLASTIC

Number	Title	Yr	NM
❑ FC-7750 [M]	Christmas Songs from Many Lands	196?	18.00

—Reissue of Folkways album with same contents

MILLS, FRANK

CAPITOL

Number	Title	Yr	NM
❑ SN-16290	A Special Christmas	198?	10.00
❑ ST-12388	Music Box Dancer	1985	10.00
❑ ST-12421	Traveler	1985	10.00

POLYDOR

Number	Title	Yr	NM
❑ PD-1-6192	Music Box Dancer	1979	12.00
❑ PD-1-6225	Sunday Morning	1980	12.00
❑ PD-1-6305	The Frank Mills Album	1982	12.00

MILLS, HAYLEY

BUENA VISTA

Number	Title	Yr	NM
❑ BV-3311 [M]	Let's Get Together	1962	40.00
❑ STER-3311 [S]	Let's Get Together	1962	40.00

MILLS, MRS.

LIBERTY

Number	Title	Yr	NM
❑ LRP-3359 [M]	My Mother -- The Ragtime Piano Player	1964	15.00
❑ LST-7359 [S]	My Mother -- The Ragtime Piano Player	1964	18.00

MILLS, STEPHANIE

20TH CENTURY

Number	Title	Yr	NM
❑ T-700	Stephanie	1981	12.00
❑ T-603	Sweet Sensation	1980	12.00
❑ T-583	Whatcha Gonna Do ... With My Lovin'?	1979	12.00

ABC

Number	Title	Yr	NM
❑ ABCD-869	Movin' in the Right Direction	1975	18.00

CASABLANCA

Number	Title	Yr	NM
❑ 832519-1	In My Life: Greatest Hits	1987	12.00
❑ 822421-1	I've Got the Cure	1984	12.00
❑ 811364-1	Merciless	1983	12.00
❑ NBLP7265	Tantalizingly Hot	1982	12.00

MCA

Number	Title	Yr	NM
❑ 6312	Home	1989	12.00
❑ 5996	If I Were Your Woman	1987	10.00
❑ 10690	Something Real	1992	18.00
❑ 5669	Stephanie Mills	1985	10.00

MOTOWN

Number	Title	Yr	NM
❑ M6-859S1	For the First Time	1975	15.00
❑ M5-227-V1	For the First Time	1982	10.00

—Reissue of 859

Number	Title	Yr	NM
❑ 6033ML	Love Has Lifted Me	1983	50.00

MILLS BROTHERS, THE

ABC

Number	Title	Yr	NM
❑ 4004	16 Great Performances	1975	12.00
❑ 1027	The Best of the Mills Brothers, Volume 2	1978	15.00

ABC SONGBIRD

Number	Title	Yr	NM
❑ SBDP-255	Inspiration	1974	12.00

DECCA

Number	Title	Yr	NM
❑ DL5050 [10]	Barber Shop Ballads	1950	50.00
❑ DL5051 [10]	Barber Shop Ballads	1950	50.00
❑ DL8890 [M]	Barber Shop Harmony	1959	30.00
❑ DL5516 [10]	Four Boys and a Guitar	1954	50.00
❑ DL8827 [M]	Glow with the Mills Brothers	1958	30.00
❑ DL75174 [R]	Golden Favorites, Volume 2	1970	12.00
❑ DL8892 [M]	Harmonizin' with the Mills Brothers	1959	30.00
❑ DL5506 [10]	Meet the Mills Brothers	1954	50.00
❑ DL8219 [M]	Memory Lane	1956	30.00
❑ DL8491 [M]	One Dozen Roses	1957	30.00
❑ DL4084 [M]	Our Golden Favorites	1960	25.00
❑ DL74084 [R]	Our Golden Favorites	196?	15.00
❑ DL8209 [M]	Singin' and Swingin'	1956	30.00
❑ DL5102 [10]	Souvenir Album	1950	50.00
❑ DL8148 [M]	Souvenir Album	1955	30.00
❑ DXB193 [M]	The Best of the Mills Brothers	1965	25.00
❑ DXSB7193 [R]	The Best of the Mills Brothers	1965	18.00
❑ DL8664 [M]	The Mills Brothers in Hi-Fi	1958	30.00
❑ DL5337 [10]	Wonderful Words	1951	50.00

DOT

Number	Title	Yr	NM
❑ DLP-3465 [M]	Beer Barrel Polka and Other Hits	1962	15.00
❑ DLP-25465 [S]	Beer Barrel Polka and Other Hits	1962	18.00
❑ DLP-25927	Dream	1969	18.00
❑ DLP-25809	Fortuosity	1968	18.00
❑ DLP-3565 [M]	Gems by the Mills Brothers	1964	15.00
❑ DLP-25565 [S]	Gems by the Mills Brothers	1964	18.00
❑ DLP-3208 [M]	Great Barbershop Hits	1959	25.00
❑ DLP-25208 [S]	Great Barbershop Hits	1959	30.00
❑ DLP-3368 [M]	Great Hawaiian Hits	1961	18.00
❑ DLP-25368 [S]	Great Hawaiian Hits	1961	25.00
❑ DLP-3568 [M]	Hymns We Love	1964	15.00
❑ DLP-25568 [S]	Hymns We Love	1964	18.00
❑ DLP-25232 [S]	Merry Christmas	1959	30.00

—Same as above, but in stereo; with cursive "Dot" logo

Number	Title	Yr	NM
❑ DLP-3232 [M]	Merry Christmas	1959	25.00
❑ DLP-25232 [S]	Merry Christmas	1968	15.00

—With "Dot"/"Paramount" logo

Number	Title	Yr	NM
❑ DLP-3103 [M]	Mmmm, The Mills Brothers	1958	25.00
❑ DLP-25103 [S]	Mmmm, The Mills Brothers	1958	30.00
❑ DLP-25872	My Shy Violet	1968	18.00
❑ DLP-3363 [M]	San Antonio Rose	1961	18.00
❑ DLP-25363 [S]	San Antonio Rose	1961	25.00
❑ DLP-3592 [M]	Say Si Si and Other Great Latin Hits	1964	15.00
❑ DLP-25592 [S]	Say Si Si and Other Great Latin Hits	1964	18.00
❑ DLP-3652 [M]	Ten Years of Hits 1954-1964	1965	15.00
❑ DLP-25652 [S]	Ten Years of Hits 1954-1964	1965	18.00
❑ DLP-3744 [M]	That Country Feeling	1966	15.00
❑ DLP-25744 [S]	That Country Feeling	1966	18.00
❑ DLP-3508 [M]	The End of the World	1963	15.00
❑ DLP-25508 [S]	The End of the World	1963	18.00
❑ DLP-3157 [M]	The Mills Brothers' Great Hits	1958	25.00
❑ DLP-25157 [S]	The Mills Brothers' Great Hits	1958	30.00

—Black vinyl

Number	Title	Yr	NM
❑ DLP-25157 [S]	The Mills Brothers' Great Hits	195?	60.00

—Blue vinyl

Number	Title	Yr	NM
❑ DLP-3308 [M]	The Mills Brothers' Great Hits, Volume 2	1960	18.00
❑ DLP-25308 [S]	The Mills Brothers' Great Hits, Volume 2	1960	25.00
❑ DLP-25960	The Mills Brothers In Motion	1970	18.00
❑ DLP-3783 [M]	The Mills Brothers Live	1967	18.00
❑ DLP-25783 [S]	The Mills Brothers Live	1967	18.00
❑ DLP-3237 [M]	The Mills Brothers Sing	1960	25.00
❑ DLP-25237 [S]	The Mills Brothers Sing	1960	30.00
❑ DL-3766 [M]	The Mills Brothers Today	1966	15.00
❑ DLP-25766 [S]	The Mills Brothers Today	1966	18.00
❑ DLP-3699 [M]	These Are the Mills Brothers	1966	15.00
❑ DLP-25699 [S]	These Are the Mills Brothers	1966	18.00
❑ DLP-3338 [M]	Yellow Bird	1960	18.00
❑ DLP-25338 [S]	Yellow Bird	1960	25.00

EVEREST ARCHIVE OF FOLK & JAZZ

Number	Title	Yr	NM
❑ 300	The Mills Brothers	197?	12.00
❑ 328	The Mills Brothers, Volume 2	197?	12.00

GNP CRESCENDO

Number	Title	Yr	NM
❑ GNP-9106	Four Boys and a Guitar	197?	12.00

HAMILTON

Number	Title	Yr	NM
❑ HL-116 [M]	The Mills Brothers Sing for You	1964	15.00
❑ HS-12116 [S]	The Mills Brothers Sing for You	1964	15.00

MARK 56

Number	Title	Yr	NM
❑ 709	Original Radio Broadcasts	197?	12.00

MCA

Number	Title	Yr	NM
❑ 717	16 Great Performances	1980	10.00
❑ 132	Golden Favorites, Volume 2	1973	12.00
❑ 15029	Merry Christmas	198?	12.00
❑ 188	Old Golden Favorites	1973	12.00
❑ 4039	The Best of the Mills Brothers	197?	15.00
❑ 1556	The Mills Brothers	198?	12.00
❑ 27083	The Mills Brothers Great Hits	1980	10.00
❑ 28116	Were You There	198?	10.00

MCA SPECIAL MARKETS

Number	Title	Yr	NM
❑ MSM2-35067	Classic Mills Brothers	198?	12.00

PARAMOUNT

Number	Title	Yr	NM
❑ PAS-6038	A Donut and a Dream	1973	15.00
❑ PAS-5025	No Turnin' Back	1971	15.00
❑ PAS-1010	The Best of the Mills Brothers	1973	15.00
❑ PAS-1027	The Best of the Mills Brothers, Volume 2	1974	18.00
❑ PAS-6024	What a Wonderful World	1972	15.00

PICKWICK

Number	Title	Yr	NM
❑ SPC-3076	14 Karat Gold	196?	12.00
❑ SPC-3107	Anytime	197?	12.00
❑ SPC-3220	Cab Driver	197?	12.00
❑ SPC-3137	Dream a Little Dream	197?	12.00
❑ SPC-1025	Merry Christmas	1979	12.00

—Reissue of Dot album with one fewer track

Number	Title	Yr	NM
❑ 2008	Songs You Remember	197?	12.00
❑ 2030	The Mills Brothers	1973	12.00
❑ SPC-3556	The Mills Brothers	1976	10.00
❑ SPC-3158	Till We Meet Again	197?	12.00

RANWOOD

Number	Title	Yr	NM
❑ 7035	22 Great Hits	1985	12.00
❑ 8152	50th Anniversary	197?	12.00
❑ 8123	Cab Driver	197?	12.00
❑ 8198	Command Performance	198?	10.00
❑ 8139	Country's Greatest Hits	197?	12.00
❑ 8133	The Mills Brothers Story	197?	12.00

SUNNYVALE

Number	Title	Yr	NM
❑ 1023	Timeless	1978	12.00

VOCALION

Number	Title	Yr	NM
❑ VL3607 [M]	In a Mellow Tone	196?	15.00
❑ VL73607 [R]	In a Mellow Tone	196?	12.00
❑ VL73859 [R]	Such Sweet Singing	1969	12.00

MILSAP, RONNIE

PAIR

Number	Title	Yr	NM
❑ PDL2-1105	Back on My Mind Again	1986	15.00
❑ PDL2-1031	Believe It!	1986	15.00

PICKWICK

Number	Title	Yr	NM
❑ JS-6179	Plain and Simple	197?	12.00

RCA

Number	Title	Yr	NM
❑ R183710	Back to the Grindstone	1991	25.00

—Only released on vinyl through BMG Direct Marketing

Number	Title	Yr	NM
❑ 9588-1-R	Stranger Things Have Happened	1989	12.00

RCA VICTOR

Number	Title	Yr	NM
❑ APL1-1666	20-20 Vision	1976	15.00
❑ APL1-0846	A Legend in My Time	1975	18.00
❑ APD1-0846 [Q]	A Legend in My Time	1975	25.00
❑ 5624-1-R	Christmas with Ronnie Milsap	1986	12.00
❑ CPL1-7166	Collector's Series	1986	10.00
❑ AHL1-3772	Greatest Hits	1980	12.00
❑ AHL1-5425	Greatest Hits, Vol. 2	1985	12.00
❑ 6425-1-R	Heart and Soul	1987	12.00
❑ 7618-1-R	Heart and Soul	1988	10.00

—Reissue of 6245

Number	Title	Yr	NM
❑ AHL1-3346	Images	1979	15.00
❑ AYL1-4171	Images	1981	10.00

—Best Buy Series" reissue

Number	Title	Yr	NM
❑ AHL1-4311	Inside Ronnie Milsap	198?	12.00
❑ AYL1-5142	Inside Ronnie Milsap	1984	10.00

—Best Buy Series" reissue

Number	Title	Yr	NM
❑ AFL1-2439	It Was Almost Like a Song	1977	15.00
❑ AYL1-5139	It Was Almost Like a Song	1984	10.00

—Best Buy Series" reissue

Number	Title	Yr	NM
❑ AHL1-4670	Keyed Up	1983	12.00
❑ AYL1-5435	Keyed Up	1985	10.00

—Best Buy Series" reissue

Number	Title	Yr	NM
❑ AHL1-7194	Lost in the Fifties Tonight	1986	12.00
❑ AHL1-3563	Milsap Magic	1980	12.00
❑ APL1-1223	Night Things	1975	18.00
❑ AHL1-5016	One More Try for Love	1984	12.00
❑ AFL1-2780	Only One Love in My Life	1978	15.00
❑ AAL1-3932	Out Where the Bright Lights Are Glowing	1981	12.00
❑ APL1-0500	Pure Love	1974	18.00
❑ APD1-0500 [Q]	Pure Love	1974	25.00
❑ AYL1-3899	Pure Love	1981	10.00

—Best Buy Series" reissue

Number	Title	Yr	NM
❑ APL1-2043	Ronnie Milsap Live	1976	15.00
❑ AYL1-4255	Ronnie Milsap Live	1982	10.00

—Best Buy Series" reissue

Number	Title	Yr	NM
❑ AHL1-4060	There's No Gettin' Over Me	1981	12.00
❑ AYL1-5140	There's No Gettin' Over Me	1984	10.00

—Best Buy Series" reissue

Number	Title	Yr	NM
❑ APL1-0338	Where My Heart Is	1973	25.00
❑ AYL1-3760	Where My Heart Is	1980	10.00

—Best Buy Series" reissue

TIME-LIFE

Number	Title	Yr	NM
❑ STW-110	Country Music	1981	12.00

WARNER BROS.

Number	Title	Yr	NM
❑ BS2870	A Rose By Any Other Name	1975	18.00
❑ WS1934	Ronnie Milsap	1971	25.00

MILTON, ROY

KENT

Number	Title	Yr	NM
❑ KLP-5054 [M]	The Great Roy Milton	1963	50.00
❑ KST-554 [R]	The Great Roy Milton	196?	30.00

MIMMS, GARNET, AND THE ENCHANTERS

ARISTA

Number	Title	Yr	NM
❑ AL4153	Garnet Mimms Has It All	1978	15.00

UNITED ARTISTS

Number	Title	Yr	NM
❑ UAL3396 [M]	As Long As I Have You	1964	50.00
❑ UAS6396 [S]	As Long As I Have You	1964	70.00
❑ UAL3305 [M]	Cry Baby and 11 Other Hits	1963	80.00
❑ UAS6305 [S]	Cry Baby and 11 Other Hits	1963	100.00
❑ UAL3498 [M]	I'll Take Good Care of You	1966	50.00
❑ UAS6498 [S]	I'll Take Good Care of You	1966	70.00

MIND EXPANDERS, THE

DOT

Number	Title	Yr	NM
❑ DLP-3773 [M]	What's Happening	1967	120.00
❑ DLP-25773 [S]	What's Happening	1967	80.00

MIND GARAGE, THE

RCA VICTOR

Number	Title	Yr	NM
❑ LSP-4218	The Mind Garage	1969	30.00

Number	Title	Yr	NM
❑ LSP-4319	The Mind Garage Again!	1970	30.00

MINDBENDERS, THE

FONTANA

Number	Title	Yr	NM
❑ MGF-27554 [M]	A Groovy Kind of Love	1966	40.00
—With "Don't Cry No More			
❑ MGF-27554 [M]	A Groovy Kind of Love	1966	30.00
—With "Ashes to Ashes			
❑ SRF-67554 [R]	A Groovy Kind of Love	1966	30.00
—With "Don't Cry No More			
❑ SRF-67554 [R]	A Groovy Kind of Love	1966	25.00
—With "Ashes to Ashes			

MINEO, SAL

EPIC

Number	Title	Yr	NM
❑ LN3405 [M]	Sal	1958	150.00

MINGUS, CHARLES

ABC IMPULSE!

Number	Title	Yr	NM
❑ AS-35 [S]	Black Saint and Sinner Lady	1968	25.00
—Black label with red ring			
❑ AS-60 [S]	Charlie Mingus Plays Piano	1968	25.00
—Black label with red ring			
❑ AS-54 [S]	Mingus, Mingus, Mingus, Mingus, Mingus	1968	25.00
—Black label with red ring			
❑ AS-9234	Reevaluation -- The Impulse Years	1973	18.00

ATLANTIC

Number	Title	Yr	NM
❑ SD1700	3 or 4 Shades	1977	15.00
❑ 1305 [M]	Blues & Roots	1959	80.00
—White "bullseye" label			
❑ 1305 [M]	Blues & Roots	1961	30.00
—Multicolor label, white "fan" logo at right			
❑ 1305 [M]	Blues & Roots	1964	30.00
—Multicolor label, black "fan" logo at right			
❑ SD1305 [S]	Blues & Roots	1959	80.00
—White "bullseye" label			
❑ SD1305 [S]	Blues & Roots	1961	30.00
—Multicolor label, white "fan" logo at right			
❑ SD1305 [S]	Blues & Roots	1964	25.00
—Multicolor label, black "fan" logo at right			
❑ SD1677	Changes 1	1975	15.00
❑ SD1678	Changes 2	1975	15.00
❑ SD3001	Charles Mingus at Antibes	1979	18.00
❑ SD8801	Cumbia & Jazz Fusion	197?	15.00
❑ SD8803	Me, Myself An Eye	1979	15.00
❑ SD1667	Mingus at Carnegie Hall	1974	15.00
❑ SD1653	Mingus Moves	1974	15.00
❑ 1377 [M]	Oh, Yeah	1961	30.00
—Multicolor label, white "fan" logo at right			
❑ 1377 [M]	Oh, Yeah	1964	25.00
—Multicolor label, black "fan" logo at right			
❑ SD1377 [S]	Oh, Yeah	1961	40.00
—Multicolor label, white "fan" logo at right			
❑ SD1377 [S]	Oh, Yeah	1964	30.00
—Multicolor label, black "fan" logo at right			
❑ SD 3-600	Passions of a Man: The Charles Mingus Anthology	1980	25.00
❑ 1237 [M]	Pithecanthropus Erectus	1956	80.00
—Black label			
❑ 1237 [M]	Pithecanthropus Erectus	1961	30.00
—Multicolor label, white "fan" logo at right			
❑ 1237 [M]	Pithecanthropus Erectus	1964	25.00
—Multicolor label, black "fan" logo at right			
❑ SD8809	Pithecanthropus Erectus	1981	15.00
❑ SD8805	Something Like a Bird	1979	15.00
❑ SD 2-302	The Art of Charles Mingus	1973	18.00
❑ SD1555	The Best of Charles Mingus	1970	18.00
❑ 1260 [M]	The Clown	1957	80.00
—Black label			
❑ 1260 [M]	The Clown	1961	30.00
—Multicolor label, white "fan" logo at right			
❑ 1260 [M]	The Clown	1964	25.00
—Multicolor label, black "fan" logo at right			
❑ 90142	The Clown	198?	12.00
❑ 1417 [M]	Tonight at Noon	1964	30.00
❑ SD1417 [S]	Tonight at Noon	1964	30.00

BARNABY

Number	Title	Yr	NM
❑ BR-5012	Charles Mingus Presents	1978	15.00
❑ Z30561	Charles Mingus Presents the Quartet	1971	18.00
❑ BR-6015	Stormy Weather	1976	15.00
❑ KZ31034	The Candid Recordings	1972	18.00

BETHLEHEM

Number	Title	Yr	NM
❑ BCP-6026 [M]	A Modern Jazz Symposium of Jazz and Poetry	1958	100.00
❑ BCP-6019 [M]	East Coasting	1957	100.00
❑ BCP-6019	East Coasting	197?	18.00
—Reissue, distributed by RCA Victor			
❑ BCP-65 [M]	The Jazz Experiment of Charlie Mingus	1956	100.00

BLUEBIRD

Number	Title	Yr	NM
❑ 5644-1-RB	New Tijuana Moods	1986	18.00

CANDID

Number	Title	Yr	NM
❑ CD-8005 [M]	Charles Mingus Presents Charles Mingus	1960	40.00
❑ CS-9005 [S]	Charles Mingus Presents Charles Mingus	1960	50.00
❑ CD-8021 [M]	Mingus	1960	40.00
❑ CS-9021 [S]	Mingus	1960	50.00

CHARLES MINGUS

Number	Title	Yr	NM
❑ JWS-001/2	Mingus at Monterey	1966	700.00
—Single-pocket jacket with sepia-tone photo on front			
❑ JWS-001/2	Mingus at Monterey	1966	300.00
—Gatefold jacket with color photo on front; "This album can be purchased only by mail" on back cover			
❑ JWS-001/2	Mingus at Monterey	1968	60.00
—Gatefold jacket with color photo on front; distributed by Fantasy			
❑ JWS-005	My Favorite Quintet	1966	300.00
—This album can be purchased only by mail" on back cover			
❑ JWS-013/14	Special Music Written For (But Not Heard At) Monterey	1966	1000.00
—Single-pocket jacket; "This album can be purchased only by mail" on back cover			
❑ JWS-009	Town Hall Concert 1964, Vol. 1	1966	300.00
—This album can be purchased only by mail" on back cover			

COLUMBIA

Number	Title	Yr	NM
❑ G30628	Better Git It in Your Soul	1971	25.00
❑ CG30628	Better Git It in Your Soul	197?	15.00
—Reissue with new prefix			
❑ KG31814	Charles Mingus and Friends	1973	25.00
❑ KC31039	Let My Children Hear Music	1972	18.00
❑ PC31039	Let My Children Hear Music	198?	10.00
—Reissue with new prefix			
❑ CL1370 [M]	Mingus Ah Um	1959	80.00
—Red and black label with six "eye" logos			
❑ CL1370 [M]	Mingus Ah Um	1963	40.00
—Red label with "Guaranteed High Fidelity" at bottom			
❑ CL1370 [M]	Mingus Ah Um	1966	30.00
—Red label with "360 Sound Mono" at bottom			
❑ CS8171 [S]	Mingus Ah Um	1959	120.00
—Red and black label with six "eye" logos			
❑ CS8171 [S]	Mingus Ah Um	1963	50.00
—Red label with "360 Sound Stereo" in black at bottom			
❑ CS8171 [S]	Mingus Ah Um	1966	40.00
—Red label with "360 Sound Stereo" in white at bottom			
❑ CS8171 [S]	Mingus Ah Um	1971	18.00
—Orange label, "Columbia" repeated along edge			
❑ PC8171	Mingus Ah Um	198?	10.00
—Budget-line reissue with new prefix			
❑ CS8171 [S]	Mingus Ah Um	199?	30.00
—Classic Records reissue on audiophile vinyl			
❑ CL1440 [M]	Mingus Dynasty	1960	30.00
—Red and black label with six "eye" logos			
❑ CL1440 [M]	Mingus Dynasty	1963	25.00
—Red label with "Guaranteed High Fidelity" at bottom			
❑ CL1440 [M]	Mingus Dynasty	1966	18.00
—Red label with "360 Sound Mono" at bottom			
❑ CS8236 [S]	Mingus Dynasty	1960	40.00
—Red and black label with six "eye" logos			
❑ CS8236 [S]	Mingus Dynasty	1963	30.00
—Red label with "360 Sound Stereo" in black at bottom			
❑ CS8236 [S]	Mingus Dynasty	1966	25.00
—Red label with "360 Sound Stereo" in white at bottom			
❑ CS8236 [S]	Mingus Dynasty	1971	15.00
—Orange label, "Columbia" repeated along edge			
❑ JG35717	Nostalgia in Times Square	1979	18.00

COLUMBIA JAZZ MASTERPIECES

Number	Title	Yr	NM
❑ CJ40648	Mingus Ah Um	1987	12.00
❑ CJ44050	Shoes of the Fisherman's Wife	1988	12.00

DEBUT

Number	Title	Yr	NM
❑ DEB-123 [M]	Mingus at the Bohemia	1956	200.00
❑ DLP-1 [10]	Strings and Keys	1953	500.00

ENJA

Number	Title	Yr	NM
❑ 3077	Mingus in Europe	198?	15.00

EVEREST ARCHIVE OF FOLK & JAZZ

Number	Title	Yr	NM
❑ 235	Charlie Mingus	1969	15.00

FANTASY

Number	Title	Yr	NM
❑ 6002 [M]	Chazz!	1962	50.00
—Red vinyl			
❑ 6002 [M]	Chazz!	1962	30.00
—Black vinyl			
❑ 86002 [R]	Chazz!	196?	30.00
—Blue vinyl			
❑ 86002 [R]	Chazz!	196?	18.00
—Black vinyl			
❑ JWS-001/2	Mingus at Monterey	1969	25.00
—Reissue of Charles Mingus 001/2			
❑ OJC-045	Mingus at the Bohemia	198?	12.00
❑ JWS-005	My Favorite Quintet	1969	18.00
—Reissue of Charles Mingus 005			
❑ 6017 [M]	Right Now -- Live at the Jazz Workshop	1966	30.00
❑ 86017 [S]	Right Now -- Live at the Jazz Workshop	1966	30.00
❑ OJC-237	Right Now -- Live at the Jazz Workshop	198?	12.00
❑ 6009 [M]	The Charlie Mingus Quartet + Max Roach	1963	30.00
❑ 86009 [R]	The Charlie Mingus Quartet + Max Roach	196?	18.00
❑ OJC-440	The Charlie Mingus Quartet + Max Roach	1990	15.00
❑ OJC-042	Town Hall Concert 1964	198?	12.00
❑ JWS-009	Town Hall Concert 1964, Vol. 1	1969	18.00
—Reissue of Charles Mingus 009			

GATEWAY

Number	Title	Yr	NM
❑ 7026	His Final Work	1979	15.00

GRP/IMPULSE!

Number	Title	Yr	NM
❑ 217	Charlie Mingus Plays Piano	1997	25.00
—Reissue on audioiphile vinyl			

IMPULSE!

Number	Title	Yr	NM
❑ A-35 [M]	Black Saint and Sinner Lady	1963	30.00
❑ AS-35 [S]	Black Saint and Sinner Lady	1963	40.00
❑ A-60 [M]	Charlie Mingus Plays Piano	1964	30.00
❑ AS-60 [S]	Charlie Mingus Plays Piano	1964	40.00
❑ A-54 [M]	Mingus, Mingus, Mingus, Mingus, Mingus	1963	30.00
❑ AS-54 [S]	Mingus, Mingus, Mingus, Mingus, Mingus	1963	40.00

JAZZ MAN

Number	Title	Yr	NM
❑ 5002	Mingus	198?	15.00
❑ 5048	Mingus Presents	198?	15.00

JAZZTONE

Number	Title	Yr	NM
❑ J-1226 [M]	Jazz Experiment	1956	60.00
❑ J-1271 [M]	The Jazz Experiments of Charlie Mingus	1957	50.00

JOSIE

Number	Title	Yr	NM
❑ JOZ-3508 [M]	Mingus Three	1963	30.00
❑ JLPS-3508 [R]	Mingus Three	1963	25.00

JUBILEE

Number	Title	Yr	NM
❑ JLP-1054 [M]	Mingus Trio	1958	80.00

LIMELIGHT

Number	Title	Yr	NM
❑ LM-82015 [M]	Mingus Revisited	1965	30.00
❑ LS-86105 [S]	Mingus Revisited	1965	30.00

MCA IMPULSE!

Number	Title	Yr	NM
❑ MCA-39119	Mingus, Mingus, Mingus, Mingus, Mingus	198?	12.00
❑ MCA-5649	The Black Saint and the Sinner Lady	1986	12.00

MERCURY

Number	Title	Yr	NM
❑ MG-20627 [M]	Pre-Bird	1961	30.00
❑ SR-60627 [S]	Pre-Bird	1961	40.00

MOSAIC

Number	Title	Yr	NM
❑ MQ4-143	The Complete 1959 CBS Charles Mingus Sessions	199?	150.00
❑ MR4-111	The Complete Candid Recordings of Charles Mingus	199?	200.00
—Limited editon of 7,500			

PERIOD

Number	Title	Yr	NM
❑ SPL-1107 [10]	Jazzical Moods, Volume 1	1955	200.00
❑ SLP-1111 [10]	Jazzical Moods, Volume 2	1955	200.00

PRESTIGE

Number	Title	Yr	NM
❑ 24010	Charles Mingus	197?	18.00
❑ 24100	Mingus at Monterey	198?	18.00
❑ 24002	Portrait	1980	18.00
❑ 24028	Reincarnation of a Lovebird	197?	18.00
❑ 34001	The Great Concert	197?	25.00

QUINTESSENCE

Number	Title	Yr	NM
❑ 25171	Soul Fusion	197?	15.00

RCA VICTOR

Number	Title	Yr	NM
❑ LPM-2533 [M]	Tijuana Moods	1962	40.00
❑ LSP-2533 [S]	Tijuana Moods	1962	50.00
❑ APL1-0939	Tijuana Moods	1974	15.00
—Reissue of 2533			
❑ LSP-2533 [S]	Tijuana Moods	199?	30.00
—Classic Records reissue on audiophile vinyl			

SAVOY

Number	Title	Yr	NM
❑ MG-15050 [10]	Charlie Mingus	1955	200.00
❑ MG-12059 [M]	Jazz Composers Workshop	1956	100.00

SAVOY JAZZ

Number	Title	Yr	NM
❑ SJL-1113	Jazz Workshop	197?	12.00

SOLID STATE

Number	Title	Yr	NM
❑ SS-18024	Town Hall Concert	1968	25.00
❑ SS-18019	Wonderland	1968	25.00

TRIP

Number	Title	Yr	NM
❑ 5040	Charles Mingus Trio and Sextet	197?	12.00
❑ 5017	Mingus Moods	197?	12.00
❑ 5513	Mingus Revisited	197?	12.00

UNITED ARTISTS

Number	Title	Yr	NM
❑ UAL-4036 [M]	Jazz Portraits	1959	40.00
❑ UAS-5036 [S]	Jazz Portraits	1959	50.00
❑ UAJ-14024 [M]	Town Hall Concert	1963	40.00
❑ UAJS-15024 [S]	Town Hall Concert	1963	50.00
❑ UAJ-14005 [M]	Wonderland	1962	40.00
❑ UAJS-15005 [S]	Wonderland	1962	50.00
❑ UAS-5637	Wonderland	1972	15.00

WHO'S WHO IN JAZZ

Number	Title	Yr	NM
❑ 21005	Lionel Hampton Presents Charles Mingus	1978	18.00

MINION, FRANK

BETHLEHEM

Number	Title	Yr	NM
❑ BCP-6033 [M]	Forward Sound	1959	40.00
❑ BCP-6052 [M]	The Soft Land of Make Believe	1961	40.00
❑ BCPS-6052 [S]	The Soft Land of Make Believe	1961	50.00

Number	Title	Yr	NM

MINISTRY

ARISTA
❏ AL6608	With Sympathy	1983	14.00
❏ AL68016	With Sympathy	198?	12.00
—Reissue			

SIRE
❏ 25799	The Land of Rape and Honey	1988	15.00
❏ 26004	The Mind Is a Terrible Thing to Taste	1989	15.00
❏ 25309	Twitch	1986	15.00

WARNER BROS.
❏ 45838	Filth Pig	1996	25.00

WAX TRAX!
❏ 035	Twelve Inch Singles 1981-84	1985	18.00

MINK DEVILLE

ATLANTIC
❏ SD19311	Coup De Grace	1981	15.00
❏ 81623	Sportin' Life	1985	10.00
❏ 80115	Where Angels Fear to Tread	1983	12.00

CAPITOL
❏ ST-11955	Le Chat Bleu	1980	15.00
❏ ST-11631	Mink DeVille	1977	15.00
❏ SW-11780	Return to Magenta	1978	15.00
❏ SN-16282	Return to Magenta	1982	10.00
—Budget-line reissue			
❏ SN-16281	Savoir Faire	1982	10.00
—Budget-line reissue of self-titled album			

MINNELLI, LIZA

A&M
❏ SP-4164	Come Saturday Morning	1969	18.00
❏ SP-4345	Live at the Olympia	1971	18.00
❏ SP-4141 [M]	Liza Minnelli	1968	30.00
—Mono copies have stereo numbers, but the labels are mono white label promos			
❏ SP-4141 [S]	Liza Minnelli	1968	18.00
❏ SP-3524	Liza Minnelli Foursider	1973	18.00
❏ SP-6013	Liza Minnelli Foursider	198?	12.00
—Reissue of 3524			
❏ SP-4272	New Feelin'	1970	18.00

CAPITOL
❏ T2271 [M]	It Amazes Me	1965	25.00
❏ ST2271 [S]	It Amazes Me	1965	30.00
❏ SM-2271	It Amazes Me	1976	12.00
—Reissue with new prefix			
❏ T2174 [M]	Liza! Liza!	1964	25.00
❏ ST2174 [S]	Liza! Liza!	1964	30.00
❏ ST-11080	Maybe This Time	1972	15.00
❏ SM-11080	Maybe This Time	197?	12.00
—Reissue with new prefix			
❏ T2448 [M]	There Is a Time	1966	25.00
❏ ST2448 [S]	There Is a Time	1966	30.00
❏ SM-11803	There Is a Time	1978	12.00
—Reissue of ST 2448			

COLUMBIA
❏ PC32854	Live at the Winter Garden	1974	18.00
❏ KC32149	Liza Minnelli The Singer	1973	18.00
❏ PC32149	Liza Minnelli The Singer	198?	10.00
—Budget-line reissue			
❏ CQ32149 [Q]	Liza Minnelli The Singer	1973	25.00
❏ KC31762	Liza with a "Z"	1972	18.00
❏ PC31762	Liza with a "Z"	198?	10.00
—Budget-line reissue			
❏ PC34887	Tropical Nights	1977	15.00

EPIC
❏ OE45098	Results	1989	18.00

TELARC
❏ 15502	Liza Minnelli at Carnegie Hall	1987	18.00

MINNIE PEARL

STARDAY
❏ SLP-380 [M]	America's Beloved Minnie Pearl	1965	40.00
❏ SLP-224 [M]	Howdee!	1963	40.00
❏ SLP-397 [M]	The Country Music Story	1966	30.00

MINOR THREAT

DISCHORD
❏ 10 [B]	Out of Step	1983	50.00
—Second stock pressing, gray back cover with photos			
❏ 10 [DJ]	Out of Step	1983	500.00
—Test pressing of 50; black silkscreen cover with sheep logo; paste-on back cover; blank labels; plain innersleeve with rubber stamp			
❏ 10 [B]	Out of Step	1983	70.00
—First stock pressing, black back cover with lyrics			
❏ 12 [EP]	The First Two 7" On a 12	1984	35.00

MINT CONDITION

PERSPECTIVE
❏ 2896810011	Meant to Be Mint	1991	18.00

MINT TATTOO

DOT
❏ DLP-25918 [B]	Mint Tattoo	1969	40.00

MINUTEMEN

NEW ALLIANCE
❏ 017 [B]	The Politics of Time	1984	40.00

SST
❏ 058 [B]	3-Way Tie (For Last)	1985	30.00
❏ 068 [B]	Ballot Result	1987	30.00
❏ 016 [EP]	Buzz or Howl Under the Influence of Heat	1983	30.00
❏ 028 [B]	Double Nickels on the Dime	1984	30.00
❏ PSST E-28 [DJ]	Excerpts from Double Nickels on the Dime	1984	45.00
—One-sided promo LP with etched B-side and sticker on blank cover			
❏ 034 [EP]	Project Mersh	1985	30.00
❏ 277 [B]	The Politics of Time	198?	25.00
—Reissue of New Alliance 017			
❏ 004 [B]	The Punch Line	1981	40.00
❏ 004 [B]	The Punch Line	1981	50.00
—Original copies have white labels			
❏ 014 [B]	What Makes a Man Start Fires?	1983	30.00
❏ 014 [B]	What Makes a Man Start Fires?	1983	40.00
—Original version has yellow labels and no UPC code			

MIRACLES, THE

COLUMBIA
❏ PC34460	Love Crazy	1977	15.00
❏ PCQ34460 [Q]	Love Crazy	1977	50.00
❏ JC34910	The Miracles	1978	15.00

MOTOWN
❏ M5-136V1	Away We a Go-Go	1981	10.00
—Reissue of Tamla 271			
❏ 5254ML	Christmas with the Miracles	1982	10.00
—Reissue of Tamla 236			
❏ M5-217V1	Doin' Mickey's Monkey	1981	10.00
—Reissue of Tamla 245			
❏ M5-133V1	Do It Baby	1981	10.00
—Reissue of Tamla 334			
❏ M5-210V1	Greatest Hits, Vol. 2	1981	10.00
—Reissue of Tamla 280			
❏ M8-238M2	Greatest Hits from the Beginning	1982	15.00
—Reissue of Tamla 254			
❏ M5-160V1	Hi, We're the Miracles	1981	10.00
—Reissue of Tamla 220			
❏ M5-220V1	Recorded Live on Stage	1981	10.00
—Reissue of Tamla 241			
❏ M793R3	Smokey Robinson and the Miracles Anthology	1974	25.00
❏ 5253ML	The Season for Miracles	1982	10.00
—Reissue of Tamla 307			
❏ M5-156V1	The Tears of a Clown	1981	10.00
—Reissue of Tamla 276			

TAMLA
❏ TS320	1957-1972	1972	25.00
❏ TS306	A Pocket Full of Miracles	1970	18.00
❏ T271 [M]	Away We a Go-Go	1966	30.00
❏ TS271 [S]	Away We a Go-Go	1966	30.00
❏ T236 [M]	Christmas with the Miracles	1963	300.00
—Originals have two globes on the top of the label			
❏ T6-339	City of Angels	1975	15.00
❏ T223 [M]	Cookin' with the Miracles	1962	800.00
—White label			
❏ T245 [M]	Doin' Mickey's Monkey	1963	200.00
❏ TS245 [S]	Doin' Mickey's Monkey	1963	300.00
❏ T6-334	Do It Baby	1974	15.00
❏ T6-336	Don't Cha Love It	1975	15.00
❏ TS318	Flying High Together	1972	18.00
❏ TS297	Four in Blue	1969	25.00
❏ T267 [M]	Going to a Go-Go	1966	30.00
❏ TS267 [S]	Going to a Go-Go	1966	40.00
❏ T7-357	Greatest Hits	1977	15.00
❏ TS280	Greatest Hits, Vol. 2	1968	30.00
❏ T254 [M]	Greatest Hits from the Beginning	1965	60.00
❏ TS254 [P]	Greatest Hits from the Beginning	1965	40.00
❏ T220 [M]	Hi We're the Miracles	1961	600.00
—White label			
❏ T230 [M]	I'll Try Something New	1962	600.00
—White label			
❏ TS289	Live!	1969	25.00
❏ T276 [M]	Make It Happen	1967	30.00
❏ TS276 [M]	Make It Happen	1967	30.00
❏ TS312	One Dozen Roses	1971	18.00
❏ T325F	Renaissance	1973	15.00
❏ T290 [M]	Special Occasion	1968	70.00
❏ TS290 [S]	Special Occasion	1968	25.00
❏ T238 [M]	The Fabulous Miracles	1963	300.00
❏ T241 [M]	The Miracles On Stage	1963	200.00
❏ T6-344	The Power of Music	1976	15.00
❏ TS307	The Season for Miracles	1970	18.00
❏ TS276 [S]	The Tears of a Clown	1970	18.00
—Retitled version of "Make It Happen"			
❏ TS295	Time Out for Smokey Robinson & the Miracles	1969	25.00

❏ TS301	What Love Has…Joined Together	1970	18.00
❏ T238 [M]	You've Really Got a Hold on Me	1963	200.00
—Retitled version of "The Fabulous Miracles			

MIRETTES, THE

REVUE
❏ RS-7205	In the Midnight Hour	1968	18.00

UNI
❏ 73062	Whirlpool	1969	18.00

MIRROR IMAGE

PICKWICK
❏ SPC-1026	Disco Noel	1979	12.00
❏ SPC-1027	Yuletide Disco	1979	12.00

MISFITS, THE

CAROLINE
❏ 7515	Collection II	1995	100.00
—Clear vinyl (500 made); sealed copies have bar code at upper right or not at all			
❏ 7515	Collection II	1995	40.00
—Red vinyl (6,000 made); sealed copies have bar code roughly 1 inch from the bottom of back cover			
❏ 7515	Collection II	1995	30.00
—Green vinyl (3,500 made); sealed copies have bar code roughly 1/4 to 1/2 inch from bottom of back cover			
❏ 7520	Static Age	1997	100.00
—Purple vinyl (500 made)			
❏ 7520	Static Age	1997	40.00
—Red vinyl (2,000 made)			
❏ 7520	Static Age	1997	30.00
—Yellow vinyl (1,000 made)			

GEFFEN
❏ GEF25126 [B]	American Psycho	1997	50.00

PLAN 9
❏ PL9-03 [EP]	Die, Die My Darling	1984	250.00
—500 on purple vinyl			
❏ PL9-03 [EP]	Die, Die My Darling	1984	250.00
—500 on white vinyl (distributed by Caroline)			
❏ PL9-03 [EP]	Die, Die My Darling	1984	15.00
—Common issue on black vinyl (distributed by Caroline)			
❏ PL9-02	Earth A.D.	1983	800.00
—200 on dark purple vinyl			
❏ PL9-02	Earth A.D.	1983	500.00
—500 on yellow vinyl			
❏ PL9-02	Earth A.D.	1983	600.00
—200 on clear vinyl with red and blue swirls			
❏ PL9-02	Earth A.D.	1983	1500.00
—100 on green vinyl			
❏ PL9-02	Earth A.D.	1983	15.00
—At least 10,000 on black vinyl (distributed by Caroline)			
❏ PL9-08 [EP]	Evilive	1987	100.00
—2,000 on green vinyl (distributed by Caroline)			
❏ PL9-08 [EP]	Evilive	1987	25.00
—Black vinyl (distributed by Caroline)			
❏ PL9-06	Legacy of Brutality	1986	500.00
—500 on red vinyl			
❏ PL9-06	Legacy of Brutality	1986	300.00
—500 on white vinyl			
❏ PL9-06	Legacy of Brutality	1986	5000.00
—16 (!!) on pink vinyl; VG value 2000; VG+ value 3500			
❏ PL9-06	Legacy of Brutality	1986	25.00
—Black vinyl (distributed by Caroline)			
❏ PL9-09	Misfits	1988	15.00

ROADRUNNER
❏ RR8658-1	Famous Monsters	1999	25.00
—Picture disc			

RUBY/SLASH
❏ JRR804	Walk Among Us	1982	100.00
—Original red cover; has custom innersleeve and insert			
❏ JRR804	Walk Among Us	1982	50.00
—Purple cover with innersleeve and insert			

SLASH
❏ 25756	Walk Among Us	1988	25.00
—Reissue of JRR 804; some copies came with a Halloween bag, which can double or even triple the value!			

MISSING PERSONS

CAPITOL
❏ ST-12465	Color in Your Life	1986	12.00
❏ MLP-15001 [EP]	Missing Persons	1982	15.00
❏ ST-12315	Rhyme & Reason	1984	12.00
❏ SN-16359	Rhyme & Reason	1985	10.00
—Budget-line reissue			
❏ ST-12228	Spring Session M	1982	15.00
❏ SN-16460	Spring Session M	1987	10.00
—Budget-line reissue			

MISSOURI

PANAMA
❏ 1022	Missouri	1977	30.00

Number	Title	Yr	NM

MISSOURIANS, THE

X

| ❏ LVA-3020 [10] | Harlem in the Twenties, Volume 1 | 1954 | 50.00 |

MITCHELL, BILLY

CATALYST

| ❏ 7611 | Now's the Time | 1976 | 15.00 |

OPTIMISM

| ❏ OP-2501 | Faces | 1987 | 12.00 |
| ❏ OP-2502 | In Focus | 1988 | 12.00 |

PAUSA

| ❏ 7158 | Blue City Jam | 198? | 12.00 |
| ❏ 7192 | Night Theme | 1986 | 12.00 |

SMASH

❏ MGS-27042 [M]	A Little Juicy	1962	30.00
❏ SRS-67042 [S]	A Little Juicy	1962	30.00
❏ MGS-27027 [M]	This Is Billy Mitchell	1962	30.00
❏ SRS-67027 [S]	This Is Billy Mitchell	1962	30.00

TRIP

| ❏ 5534 | Billy Mitchell with Bobby Hutcherson | 197? | 12.00 |

XANADU

| ❏ 158 | Colossus of Detroit | 1978 | 15.00 |
| ❏ 182 | De Lawd's Blues | 198? | 12.00 |

MITCHELL, BLUE

ABC IMPULSE!

| ❏ AS-9328 | African Violet | 1977 | 18.00 |
| ❏ IA-9347 | Summer Soft | 1978 | 18.00 |

BLUE NOTE

❏ BST-84324	Bantu Village	1969	40.00
—With "A Division of Liberty Records" on label			
❏ BLP-4257 [M]	Boss Horn	1967	50.00
—With "A Division of Liberty Records" on label			
❏ BST-84257 [S]	Boss Horn	1967	30.00
—With "A Division of Liberty Records" on label			
❏ BLP-4228 [M]	Bring It Home to Me	1966	50.00
—New York, USA" on label			
❏ BST-84228 [S]	Bring It Home to Me	1966	50.00
—With "New York, USA" address on label			
❏ BST-84228 [S]	Bring It Home to Me	1967	30.00
—With "A Division of Liberty Records" on label			
❏ BST-84300	Collision in Black	1968	30.00
—With "A Division of Liberty Records" on label			
❏ BLP-4214 [M]	Down With It	1965	60.00
—New York, USA" on label			
❏ BST-84214 [S]	Down With It	1965	50.00
—With "New York, USA" address on label			
❏ BST-84214 [S]	Down With It	1967	30.00
—With "A Division of Liberty Records" on label			
❏ BST-84272	Heads Up!	1968	30.00
—With "A Division of Liberty Records" on label			
❏ LT-1082	Step Lightly	1980	25.00
❏ BLP 4178 [M]	The Thing to Do	1964	150.00
—New York, USA" on label			
❏ BST-84178 [S]	The Thing to Do	1964	80.00
—With "New York, USA" address on label			
❏ BST-84178 [S]	The Thing to Do	1967	30.00
—With "A Division of Liberty Records" on label			
❏ BST-84178 [S]	The Thing to Do	1985	15.00
—The Finest in Jazz Since 1939" reissue			

FANTASY

| ❏ OJC-6009 | Blues on My Mind | 198? | 15.00 |
| ❏ OJC-615 | The Big Six | 1991 | 18.00 |

FORTISSIMO

| ❏ XK8006 | Brasses and Strings | 1961 | 80.00 |
| —Red vinyl; record plays from the inside out | | | |

JAM

| ❏ 5002 | Last Dance | 1977 | 25.00 |

MAINSTREAM

❏ MRL-315	Blue Mitchell	1971	50.00
❏ MRL-374	Blue's Blues	1973	40.00
❏ MRL-413	Booty	1974	30.00
❏ MRL-400	Graffiti Blues	1974	40.00
❏ MRL-392	Last Tango = Blues	1973	80.00
—Reproductions exist			
❏ MRL-402	Many Shades of Blue Mitchell	1974	40.00
❏ MRL-343	Vital	1972	50.00

MCA

| ❏ 29050 | African Violet | 1980 | 12.00 |
| ❏ 29051 | Summer Soft | 1980 | 12.00 |

MILESTONE

| ❏ M-47055 | A Blue Time | 1979 | 30.00 |

MOSAIC

| ❏ MQ6-178 | The Complete Blue Note Sessions | 199? | 100.00 |

RCA VICTOR

| ❏ APL1-1493 | Funktion Junction | 1976 | 25.00 |
| ❏ APL1-1109 | Stratosonic Nuances | 1975 | 30.00 |

RIVERSIDE

❏ RLP-414 [M]	A Sure Thing	1962	60.00
❏ RS-9414 [S]	A Sure Thing	1962	80.00
❏ RLP-336 [M]	Blue's Moods	1960	80.00

Number	Title	Yr	NM
❏ RS-9336 [S]	Blue's Moods	1960	80.00
❏ 6045	Blue's Moods	197?	18.00
❏ RLP 12-309 [M]	Blue Soul	1959	100.00
❏ RLP-1155 [S]	Blue Soul	1959	80.00
❏ RLP 12-293 [M]	Out of the Blue	1958	100.00
❏ RLP-1131 [S]	Out of the Blue	1959	80.00
❏ RLP-367 [M]	Smooth as the Wind	1961	60.00
❏ RS-9367 [S]	Smooth as the Wind	1961	80.00
❏ RLP 12-273 [M]	The Big Six	1958	100.00
❏ RLP-439 [M]	The Cup Bearers	1963	60.00
❏ RS-9439 [S]	The Cup Bearers	1963	80.00

MITCHELL, CHAD, TRIO

COLPIX

❏ CP-463 [M]	Everybody's Listening	1964	25.00
❏ SCP-463 [S]	Everybody's Listening	1964	30.00
❏ CP-411 [M]	The Chad Mitchell Trio	1961	25.00
❏ SCP-411 [S]	The Chad Mitchell Trio	1961	30.00

KAPP

❏ KL-1313 [M]	Chad Mitchell Trio In Action	1963	25.00
❏ KS-3313 [S]	Chad Mitchell Trio In Action	1963	30.00
❏ KL-1262 [M]	Mighty Day on Campus	1962	25.00
❏ KS-3262 [S]	Mighty Day on Campus	1962	30.00
❏ KGP-102BI [M]	My Gift to You	196?	50.00
—Three-record boxed set containing KL-1262, KL-1281 and KL-1313 on mid-1960s reissue labels (black with white circle and "Kapp" vertical logo at top)			
❏ KL-1334 [M]	The Best of Chad Mitchell Trio	1963	25.00
❏ KS-3334 [S]	The Best of Chad Mitchell Trio	1963	30.00
❏ KL-1281 [M]	The Chad Mitchell Trio at the Bitter End	1962	25.00
❏ KS-3281 [S]	The Chad Mitchell Trio at the Bitter End	1962	30.00

MERCURY

❏ MG-20891 [M]	Reflecting	1964	18.00
❏ SR-60891 [S]	Reflecting	1964	25.00
❏ MG-20838 [M]	Singin' Our Mind	1963	18.00
❏ SR-60838 [S]	Singin' Our Mind	1963	25.00

MITCHELL, CHAD

BELL

| ❏ 6028 | Chad | 1969 | 18.00 |

WARNER BROS.

❏ W1706 [M]	A Feeling of Love	1967	25.00
❏ WS1706 [S]	A Feeling of Love	1967	10.00
❏ W1667 [M]	Chad Mitchell Himself	1966	18.00
❏ WS1667 [S]	Chad Mitchell Himself	1966	25.00

MITCHELL, FREDDIE

ALLEGRO ROYALE

| ❏ 1600 [M] | That Boogie Beat | 195? | 60.00 |

MITCHELL, GROVER

STASH

| ❏ ST-277 | Truckin' with Grover Mitchell and His Orchestra | 1988 | 12.00 |

MITCHELL, GUY

COLUMBIA

❏ CL1211 [M]	Guy In Love	1958	40.00
❏ CS8011 [S]	Guy in Love	1959	50.00
❏ CL1226 [M]	Guy's Greatest Hits	1959	50.00
—Red and black label with six "eye" logos			
❏ CL1226 [M]	Guy's Greatest Hits	1962	30.00
—Guaranteed High Fidelity" on red label			
❏ CL1226 [M]	Guy's Greatest Hits	1965	25.00
—360 Sound Mono" on red label			
❏ CL6231 [10]	Open Spaces	1953	70.00
❏ CL1552 [M]	Sunshine Guitar	1960	30.00
❏ CS8352 [S]	Sunshine Guitar	1960	40.00

KING

| ❏ 644 [M] | Sincerely Yours | 1959 | 300.00 |

NASHVILLE

| ❏ 2074 | Heartaches | 1970 | 15.00 |

STARDAY

| ❏ 432 | Singin' Up a Storm | 1969 | 25.00 |
| ❏ 412 | Traveling Shoes | 1968 | 25.00 |

MITCHELL, JONI

ASYLUM

❏ 7E-1001	Court and Spark	1974	12.00
❏ EQ-1001 [Q]	Court and Spark	1974	60.00
❏ BB-701	Don Juan's Reckless Daughter	1977	15.00
❏ SD5057	For the Roses	1972	12.00
❏ 7E-1087	Hejira	1976	12.00
❏ AB-202 [B]	Miles of Aisles	1974	12.00
❏ 5E-505	Mingus	1979	12.00
❏ BB-704	Shadows and Light	1980	15.00
❏ 7E-1051	The Hissing of Summer Lawns	1975	12.00
❏ EQ-1051 [Q]	The Hissing of Summer Lawns	1975	60.00
❏ LPZ-2044	Court and Spark	1997	120.00
—Audiophile vinyl			

GEFFEN

| ❏ GHS24172 | Chalk Mark in a Rain Storm | 1988 | 10.00 |
| ❏ GHS24074 | Dog Eat Dog | 1985 | 10.00 |

Number	Title	Yr	NM
❏ GEF24302	Night Ride Home	1991	18.00
❏ GHS2019	Wild Things Run Fast	1982	10.00
❏	Wild Things Run Fast	1982	15.00
PRO-A-1081 [DJ]	Sampler		
—Promo-only 4-song EP			

NAUTILUS

| ❏ NR-11 | Court and Spark | 1980 | 60.00 |
| —Audiophile vinyl | | | |

REPRISE

❏ MS2038	Blue	1970	18.00
❏ RS6341	Clouds	1969	25.00
—With "W7" and "r" logos on two-tone orange label			
❏ RS6341	Clouds	1970	15.00
—With only "r" logo on all-orange (tan) label			
❏ RS6293 [S]	Joni Mitchell	1968	25.00
—With "W7" and "r" logos on two-tone orange label			
❏ RS6293 [S]	Joni Mitchell	1970	15.00
—With only "r" logo on all-orange (tan) label			
❏ R6293 [M]	Joni Mitchell	1968	100.00
—White label promo; evidently, no stock copies were issued in mono			
❏ RS6376	Ladies of the Canyon	1970	25.00
—With "W7" and "r" logos on two-tone orange label			
❏ RS6376	Ladies of the Canyon	1970	15.00
—With only "r:" logo on all-orange (tan) label			

RHINO VINYL

| ❏ 74842 | Blue | 2007 | 30.00 |
| —Reissue on 180-gram vinyl; has replica Reprise label | | | |

MITCHELL, RED, AND HAROLD LAND

ATLANTIC

❏ 1376 [M]	Hear Ye!	1961	30.00
—Multicolor label, white "fan" logo at right			
❏ 1376 [M]	Hear Ye!	1964	25.00
—Multicolor label, black "fan" logo at right			
❏ SD1376 [S]	Hear Ye!	1961	40.00
—Multicolor label, white "fan" logo at right			
❏ SD1376 [S]	Hear Ye!	1964	30.00
—Multicolor label, black "fan" logo at right			

MITCHELL, RED

BETHLEHEM

| ❏ BCP-1033 [10] | Happy Minors | 1955 | 400.00 |
| ❏ BCP-38 [S] | Jam for Your Bread | 1956 | 100.00 |

CONTEMPORARY

| ❏ C-3538 [M] | Presenting Red Mitchell | 1957 | 120.00 |

FANTASY

| ❏ OJC-158 | Presenting Red Mitchell | 198? | 15.00 |

PACIFIC JAZZ

| ❏ PJ-22 [M] | Rejoice | 1961 | 30.00 |
| ❏ ST-22 [S] | Rejoice | 1961 | 40.00 |

PAUSA

| ❏ 7018 | Red Mitchell Meets Manusardi | 198? | 12.00 |

STEEPLECHASE

| ❏ SCS-1161 | Chocolate Cadillac | 198? | 15.00 |

MITCHELL, ROSCOE

BLACK SAINT

| ❏ BSR-0050 | 3 X 4 Eye | 198? | 15.00 |
| ❏ BSR-0070 | Roscoe Mitchell and Sound and Space Ensembles | 198? | 15.00 |

DELMARK

| ❏ D-408 [M] | Roscoe Mitchell Sextet | 1966 | 30.00 |
| ❏ DS-408 [S] | Roscoe Mitchell Sextet | 1966 | 25.00 |

NESSA

❏ N-2	Congliptious	1968	30.00
❏ N-14/15	L-R-G/The Maze/S II Examples	1980	25.00
❏ N-9/10	Nonaah	1977	30.00
❏ N-5	Old/Quartet	197?	18.00
❏ N-20	Snurdy McGurdy and Her Dancin' Shoes	1981	18.00

MITCHELL, WHITEY

ABC-PARAMOUNT

| ❏ ABC-126 [M] | Whitey Mitchell Sextette | 1956 | 50.00 |

MITCHELL, WILLIE

BEARSVILLE

| ❏ BRK3520 | ... Listen ... Dance | 1980 | 12.00 |

HI

❏ HL-32029 [M]	Driving Beat	1966	30.00
❏ SHL-32029 [S]	Driving Beat	1966	30.00
❏ HL-32021 [M]	Hold It	1964	30.00
❏ SHL-32021 [S]	Hold It	1964	30.00
❏ HL-32026 [M]	It's Dance Time	1965	30.00
❏ SHL-32036 [S]	It's Dance Time	1965	30.00
❏ SHL-32048	On Top	1969	30.00
❏ HL-32039 [M]	Ooh Baby, You Turn Me On	1967	30.00
❏ SHL-32039 [S]	Ooh Baby, You Turn Me On	1967	30.00
❏ SHL-32058	Robin's Nest	1970	30.00
❏ SHL-32035	Solid Soul	1968	30.00
❏ SHL-32050	Soul Bag	1969	30.00
❏ HL-32010 [M]	Sunrise Serenade	1963	40.00
❏ SHL-32010 [S]	Sunrise Serenade	1963	30.00
❏ SHL-32068/9	The Best of Willie Mitchell	1971	30.00

Number	Title	Yr	NM
❑ HL-32034 [M]	The Hit Sound of Willie Mitchell	1967	30.00
❑ SHL-32034 [S]	The Hit Sound of Willie Mitchell	1967	30.00
❑ SHL-32056	The Many Moods of Willie Mitchell	1970	30.00
❑ SHL-32042	Willie Mitchell Live	1968	30.00
❑ 8002	Willie Mitchell Live	1977	12.00

MITCHELL-RUFF DUO, THE

ATLANTIC

Number	Title	Yr	NM
❑ 1458 [M]	After This Message	1966	25.00
❑ SD1458 [S]	After This Message	1966	30.00
❑ 1374 [M]	The Catbird Seat	1961	25.00
— Multicolor label, white "fan" logo at right			
❑ 1374 [M]	The Catbird Seat	1964	18.00
— Multicolor label, black "fan" logo at right			
❑ SD1374 [S]	The Catbird Seat	1961	30.00
— Multicolor label, white "fan" logo at right			
❑ SD1374 [S]	The Catbird Seat	1964	25.00
— Multicolor label, black "fan" logo at right			

EPIC

Number	Title	Yr	NM
❑ LN3318 [M]	Campus Concert	1956	40.00
❑ LN3221 [M]	The Mitchell-Ruff Duo	1956	40.00

FORUM

Number	Title	Yr	NM
❑ F-9031 [M]	Jazz Mission to Moscow	196?	15.00
— Reissue of Roulette R-52034			
❑ SF-9031 [S]	Jazz Mission to Moscow	196?	18.00
— Reissue of Roulette SR-52034			

MAINSTREAM

Number	Title	Yr	NM
❑ MRL-335	Strayhorn	1972	18.00

ROULETTE

Number	Title	Yr	NM
❑ R-52002 [M]	Appearing Nightly	1958	40.00
❑ SR-52002 [S]	Appearing Nightly	1959	30.00
❑ R-52025 [M]	Jazz for Juniors	1959	30.00
❑ SR-52025 [S]	Jazz for Juniors	1959	30.00
❑ R-52034 [M]	Jazz Mission to Moscow	1959	30.00
❑ SR-52034 [S]	Jazz Mission to Moscow	1959	30.00
❑ R-52013 [M]	The Mitchell-Ruff Duo Plus Strings and Brass	1958	40.00
❑ SR-52013 [S]	The Mitchell-Ruff Duo Plus Strings and Brass	1959	30.00
❑ R-52037 [M]	The Sound of Music	1960	30.00
❑ SR-52037 [S]	The Sound of Music	1960	30.00

MITCHELL TRIO, THE

MERCURY

Number	Title	Yr	NM
❑ MG-21049 [M]	That's the Way It's Gonna Be	1965	18.00
❑ SR-61049 [S]	That's the Way It's Gonna Be	1965	25.00
❑ MG-20944 [M]	The Slightly Irreverent Mitchell Trio	1964	18.00
❑ SR-60944 [S]	The Slightly Irreverent Mitchell Trio	1964	25.00
❑ MG-20992 [M]	Typical American Boys	1965	18.00
❑ SR-60992 [S]	Typical American Boys	1965	25.00
❑ MG-21067 [M]	Violets of Dawn	1966	18.00
❑ SR-61067 [S]	Violets of Dawn	1966	25.00

REPRISE

Number	Title	Yr	NM
❑ R-6258 [M]	Alive	1967	25.00
❑ RS-6258 [S]	Alive	1967	18.00

MITCHELLS, THE

METROJAZZ

Number	Title	Yr	NM
❑ E-1012 [M]	Get Those Elephants Out'a Here	1958	120.00
❑ SE-1012 [S]	Get Those Elephants Out'a Here	1958	100.00

MITCHUM, ROBERT

CAPITOL

Number	Title	Yr	NM
❑ T853 [M]	Calypso -- Is Like So...	1957	100.00

MONUMENT

Number	Title	Yr	NM
❑ MLP-8066 [M]	That Man, Robert Mitchum, Sings	1967	30.00
❑ SLP-18066 [S]	That Man, Robert Mitchum, Sings	1967	30.00

MIXTURES, THE (1)

LINDA

Number	Title	Yr	NM
❑ 3301 [M]	Stompin' at the Rainbow	1962	100.00

MIZE, BILLY

IMPERIAL

Number	Title	Yr	NM
❑ LP-12441	This Time and Place	1969	25.00

UNITED ARTISTS

Number	Title	Yr	NM
❑ UAS-6781	You're Alright with Me	1971	18.00

ZODIAC

Number	Title	Yr	NM
❑ 5007	Love 'n' Stuff	1976	15.00

MJT + 3

ARGO

Number	Title	Yr	NM
❑ LP-621 [M]	Daddy-O Presents MJT + 3	1957	40.00

TRIP

Number	Title	Yr	NM
❑ 5025	Branching Out	197?	15.00

VEE JAY

Number	Title	Yr	NM
❑ LP-3008 [M]	Make Everybody Happy	1960	30.00
❑ SR-3008 [S]	Make Everybody Happy	1960	30.00
❑ LP-3014 [M]	MJT + 3	1961	30.00
❑ SR-3014 [S]	MJT + 3	1961	30.00
❑ LP-1013 [M]	Walter Perkins' MJT + 3	1959	30.00
❑ SR-1013 [S]	Walter Perkins' MJT + 3	1959	40.00

MOB, THE

COLOSSUS

Number	Title	Yr	NM
❑ CS-1006	The Mob	1971	25.00

MGM

Number	Title	Yr	NM
❑ SE-4839	The Mob	1972	18.00

PRIVATE STOCK

Number	Title	Yr	NM
❑ PS-2005	The Mob	1975	15.00

MOBLEY, HANK

BLUE NOTE

Number	Title	Yr	NM
❑ BLP-4230 [M]	A Caddy for Daddy	1966	150.00
— With "New York, USA" address on label			
❑ BST-84230 [S]	A Caddy for Daddy	1966	100.00
— With "New York, USA" address on label			
❑ BST-84230 [S]	A Caddy for Daddy	1967	40.00
— With "A Division of Liberty Records" on label			
❑ BST-84431	Another Workout	1986	25.00
❑ B1-33582	A Slice Off the Top	1995	18.00
— The Finest in Jazz Since 1939" reissue			
❑ BLP-4209 [M]	Dippin'	1965	150.00
— With "New York, USA" address on label			
❑ BST-84209 [S]	Dippin'	1965	100.00
— With "New York, USA" address on label			
❑ BST-84209 [S]	Dippin'	1967	40.00
— With "A Division of Liberty Records" on label			
❑ BST-84425	Far Away Lands	1985	25.00
❑ BLP-1560 [M]	Hank	1957	1000.00
— Deep groove" version (deep indentation under label on both sides)			
❑ BLP-1560 [M]	Hank	1957	300.00
— Regular version, W. 63rd St. address on label			
❑ BLP-1560 [M]	Hank	1963	40.00
— With "New York, USA" address on label			
❑ BST-81560 [R]	Hank	1967	25.00
— With "A Division of Liberty Records" on label			
❑ BLP-1550 [M]	Hank Mobley	1957	800.00
— Deep groove" version; W. 63rd St. address on label			
❑ BLP-1550 [M]	Hank Mobley	1957	300.00
— Regular version, W. 63rd St. address on label			
❑ BLP-1550 [M]	Hank Mobley	1963	40.00
— With "New York, USA" address on label			
❑ BST-81550 [R]	Hank Mobley	1967	25.00
— With "A Division of Liberty Records" on label			
❑ BLP-1568 [M]	Hank Mobley	1957	4000.00
— Deep groove" version; W. 63rd St. address on label			
❑ BLP-1568 [M]	Hank Mobley	1957	800.00
— Regular version, W. 63rd St. address on label			
❑ BLP-1568 [M]	Hank Mobley	1963	40.00
— With "New York, USA" address on label			
❑ BST-1568 [S]	Hank Mobley	1959	400.00
— Deep groove" version; W. 63rd St. address on label			
❑ BST-1568 [S]	Hank Mobley	1959	200.00
— Regular version, W. 63rd St. address on label			
❑ BST-1568 [S]	Hank Mobley	1963	40.00
— With "New York, USA" address on label			
❑ BST-81568 [S]	Hank Mobley	1967	25.00
— With "A Division of Liberty Records" on label			
❑ BLP-1568 [M]	Hank Mobley	200?	30.00
— 200-gram reissue, distributed by Classic Records			
❑ BLP-1544 [M]	Hank Mobley and His All Stars	1957	800.00
— Deep groove" version; W. 63rd St. address on label			
❑ BLP-1544 [M]	Hank Mobley and His All Stars	1957	300.00
— Regular version, W. 63rd St. address on label			
❑ BLP-1544 [M]	Hank Mobley and His All Stars	1963	40.00
— With "New York, USA" address on label			
❑ BST-81544 [R]	Hank Mobley and His All Stars	1967	25.00
— With "A Division of Liberty Records" on label			
❑ BLP-5066 [10]	Hank Mobley Quartet	1955	1500.00
❑ BLP-1540 [M]	Hank Mobley with Donald Byrd and Lee Morgan	1957	700.00
— Deep groove" version; W. 63rd St. address on label			
❑ BLP-1540 [M]	Hank Mobley with Donald Byrd and Lee Morgan	1957	1000.00
— Deep groove" version, Lexington Ave. address on label			
❑ BLP-1540 [M]	Hank Mobley with Donald Byrd and Lee Morgan	1963	50.00
— With "New York, USA" address on label			
❑ BST-81540 [R]	Hank Mobley with Donald Byrd and Lee Morgan	1967	25.00
— With "A Division of Liberty Records" on label			
❑ BST-84273	High Voltage	1986	15.00
— The Finest in Jazz Since 1939" reissue			
❑ BLP-4273 [M]	Hi Voltage	1968	500.00
— With "A Division of Liberty Records" address on label			
❑ BST-84273 [S]	Hi Voltage	1968	100.00
— With "A Division of Liberty Records" on label			
❑ BLP-4149 [M]	No Room for Squares	1963	200.00
— With "New York, USA" address on label			
❑ BST-84149 [S]	No Room for Squares	1963	100.00
— With "New York, USA" address on label			
❑ BST-84149 [S]	No Room for Squares	1967	40.00
— With "A Division of Liberty Records" on label			
❑ B1-84149	No Room for Squares	1989	18.00
— The Finest in Jazz Since 1939" reissue			
❑ BLP-1574 [M]	Peckin' Time	1958	1200.00
— Deep groove" version; W. 63rd St. address on label			
❑ BLP-1574 [M]	Peckin' Time	1958	300.00
— Regular version, W. 63rd St. address on label			
❑ BLP-1574 [M]	Peckin' Time	1963	40.00
— With "New York, USA" address on label			
❑ BST-81574 [R]	Peckin' Time	1967	25.00
— With "A Division of Liberty Records" on label			
❑ B1-81574	Peckin' Time	1988	15.00
— The Finest in Jazz Since 1939" reissue			
❑ BST-84288	Reach Out!	1968	80.00
— With "A Division of Liberty Records" on label			
❑ BLP-4058 [M]	Roll Call	1961	400.00
— With W. 63rd St. address on label			
❑ BLP-4058 [M]	Roll Call	1963	60.00
— With "New York, USA" address on label			
❑ BST-84058 [S]	Roll Call	1961	200.00
— With W. 63rd St. address on label			
❑ BST-84058 [S]	Roll Call	1963	40.00
— With "New York, USA" address on label			
❑ BST-84058 [S]	Roll Call	1967	30.00
— With "A Division of Liberty Records" on label			
❑ BST-84058	Roll Call	199?	30.00
— 180-gram reissue; distributed by Classic Records			
❑ LT-995	Slice Off the Top	1979	25.00
❑ BLP-4031 [M]	Soul Station	1960	600.00
— Deep groove" version; W. 63rd St. address on label			
❑ BLP-4031 [M]	Soul Station	1960	200.00
— Regular version, W. 63rd St. address on label			
❑ BLP-4031 [M]	Soul Station	1963	40.00
— With "New York, USA" address on label			
❑ BST-84031 [S]	Soul Station	1960	200.00
— With W. 63rd St. address on label			
❑ BST-84031 [S]	Soul Station	1963	40.00
— With "New York, USA" address on label			
❑ BST-84031 [S]	Soul Station	1967	30.00
— With "A Division of Liberty Records" on label			
❑ BST-84031	Soul Station	1987	18.00
— The Finest in Jazz Since 1939" reissue			
❑ BST-84435	Straight No Filter	1986	30.00
❑ BST-84329	The Flip	1969	80.00
— With "A Division of Liberty Records" on label			
❑ BLP-4186 [M]	The Turnaround!	1964	200.00
— With "New York, USA" address on label			
❑ BST-84186 [S]	The Turnaround!	1964	100.00
— With "New York, USA" address on label			
❑ BST-84186 [S]	The Turnaround!	1967	40.00
— With "A Division of Liberty Records" on label			
❑ B1-84186	The Turnaround!	1989	18.00
— The Finest in Jazz Since 1939" reissue			
❑ LT-1045	Thinking of Home	1980	30.00
❑ LT-1081	Third Season	1981	30.00
❑ BLP-4080 [M]	Workout	1961	1000.00
— With W. 63rd St. address on label			
❑ BLP-4080 [M]	Workout	1963	600.00
— With "New York, USA" address on label			
❑ BST-84080 [S]	Workout	1961	200.00
— With W. 63rd St. address on label			
❑ BST-84080 [S]	Workout	1963	150.00
— With "New York, USA" address on label			
❑ BST-84080 [S]	Workout	1967	30.00
— With "A Division of Liberty Records" on label			
❑ B1-84080	Workout	1988	15.00
— The Finest in Jazz Since 1939" reissue			

PRESTIGE

Number	Title	Yr	NM
❑ PRST-7661	Hank Mobley's Message	1969	30.00
❑ P-24063	Messages	1976	30.00
❑ PRLP-7061 [M]	Mobley's Message	1956	500.00
— Yellow label with W. 50th St. address			
❑ PRLP-7082 [M]	Mobley's Second Message	1957	500.00
— Yellow label with W. 50th St. address			
❑ PRST-7667	Mobley's Second Message	1969	30.00

SAVOY

Number	Title	Yr	NM
❑ MG-12092 [M]	Jazz Message #2	1956	400.00

STATUS

Number	Title	Yr	NM
❑ ST-8311 [M]	52nd Street Theme	1965	80.00

MOBY GRAPE

COLUMBIA

Number	Title	Yr	NM
❑ MGS1	Grape Jam	1968	25.00
❑ C31098	Great Grape	1972	18.00
❑ CL2698 [M]	Moby Grape	1967	120.00
— Cover has Don Stephenson "giving the finger" on his washboard			
❑ CS9498 [S]	Moby Grape	1967	100.00
— Cover has Don Stephenson "giving the finger" on his washboard			
❑ CL2698 [M]	Moby Grape	1967	25.00
— Cover has offending finger airbrushed out			
❑ CS9498 [S]	Moby Grape	1967	25.00
— Cover has offending finger airbrushed out			
❑ CS9498	Moby Grape	1971	15.00
— Orange label; with poster			
❑ CS9696	Moby Grape '69	1969	25.00

Number	Title	Yr	NM
❑ 2698/9498	Moby Grape Poster	1967	18.00
—Poster has Don Stephenson "giving the finger" on his washboard			
❑ 2698/9498	Moby Grape Poster	1967	10.00
—Poster has offending finger airbrushed out			
❑ CS9912	Truly Fine Citizen	1969	25.00
❑ CS9613 [M]	Wow	1968	40.00
—Special Mono Radio Station Copy" with white label			
❑ CS9613	Wow	1968	25.00
❑ CXS3	Wow/Grape Jam	1968	30.00
—Joint release of the two albums under one cover			
❑ CXS3	Wow/Grape Jam	1971	18.00
—Orange labels			

ESCAPE

Number	Title	Yr	NM
❑ ESA1	Live Grape	1978	18.00

HARMONY

Number	Title	Yr	NM
❑ KH30392	Omaha	1971	18.00

REPRISE

Number	Title	Yr	NM
❑ RS6460	20 Granite Creek	1971	25.00

SUNDAZED

Number	Title	Yr	NM
❑ LP-5227	Grape Jam	2007	25.00
—Reissue of Columbia MGS 1			
❑ LP-5225 [M]	Moby Grape	2007	30.00
—Reissue of Columbia 2698 with poster			
❑ LP-5228	Moby Grape '69	2007	18.00
—Reissue of Columbia 9696			
❑ LP-5226	Wow	2007	25.00
—Reissue of Columbia 9613			

MOD AND THE ROCKERS

JUSTICE

Number	Title	Yr	NM
❑ JLP-153	Mod and the Rockers Now!	1967	400.00

MODELS, THE

GEFFEN

Number	Title	Yr	NM
❑ GHS24100	Out of Mind Out of Sight	1986	12.00

WINDSONG

Number	Title	Yr	NM
❑ BXL1-3642	Yes with My Body	1980	15.00

MODERN ENGLISH

SIRE

Number	Title	Yr	NM
❑ 23821	After the Snow	1982	12.00
❑ 25066	Ricochet Days	1984	12.00
❑ 26343	Stop Start	1986	12.00

TVT

Number	Title	Yr	NM
❑ 2810	Pillow Lips	1990	12.00

MODERN FOLK QUARTET, THE

WARNER BROS.

Number	Title	Yr	NM
❑ W1546 [M]	Changes	1964	30.00
❑ WS1546 [S]	Changes	1964	30.00
❑ W1511 [M]	The Modern Folk Quartet	1963	30.00
❑ WS1511 [S]	The Modern Folk Quartet	1963	30.00

MODERN JAZZ DISCIPLES, THE

NEW JAZZ

Number	Title	Yr	NM
❑ NJLP-8222 [M]	Modern Jazz Disciples	1959	50.00
—Purple label			
❑ NJLP-8222 [M]	Modern Jazz Disciples	1965	30.00
—Blue label, trident logo at right			
❑ NJLP-8240 [M]	Right Down Front	1960	50.00
—Purple label			
❑ NJLP-8240 [M]	Right Down Front	1965	30.00
—Blue label, trident logo at right			

MODERN JAZZ QUARTET, THE

APPLE

Number	Title	Yr	NM
❑ STAO-3360	Space	1970	30.00
❑ STAO-5-3360	Space	1970	50.00
—Capitol Record Club edition			
❑ ST-3353	Under the Jasmine Tree	1969	30.00
❑ ST-5-3353	Under the Jasmine Tree	1969	50.00
—Capitol Record Club edition			

ATLANTIC

Number	Title	Yr	NM
❑ 1420 [M]	A Quartet Is a Quartet Is a Quartet	1964	18.00
❑ SD1420 [S]	A Quartet Is a Quartet Is a Quartet	1964	25.00
—Multicolor label, black "fan" logo at right			
❑ SD1420 [S]	A Quartet Is a Quartet Is a Quartet	1969	12.00
—Red and green label			
❑ 1468 [M]	Blues at Carnegie Hall	1967	18.00
❑ SD1468 [S]	Blues at Carnegie Hall	1967	18.00
—Blue and green label, black "fan" logo at right			
❑ SD1468 [S]	Blues at Carnegie Hall	1969	15.00
—Red and green label			
❑ SD1652	Blues on Bach	1974	15.00
❑ SQ1652 [Q]	Blues on Bach	1974	25.00
❑ 1429 [M]	Collaboration -- The Modern Jazz Quartet with Laurindo Almeida	1964	15.00
❑ SD1429 [S]	Collaboration -- The Modern Jazz Quartet with Laurindo Almeida	1969	12.00
—Red and green label			
❑ SD1429 [S]	Collaboration -- The Modern Jazz Quartet with Laurindo Almeida	1964	18.00
—Multicolor label, black "fan" logo at right			
❑ 1231 [M]	Fontessa	1956	40.00
—Black label			
❑ 1231 [M]	Fontessa	1960	25.00
—Multicolor label, white "fan" logo at right			
❑ 1231 [M]	Fontessa	1963	18.00
—Multicolor label, black "fan" logo at right			
❑ SD1231 [S]	Fontessa	1958	30.00
—Green label			
❑ SD1231 [S]	Fontessa	1960	18.00
—Multicolor label, white "fan" logo at right			
❑ SD1231 [S]	Fontessa	1963	15.00
—Multicolor label, black "fan" logo at right			
❑ SD1231 [S]	Fontessa	1969	12.00
—Red and green label			
❑ 1449 [M]	Jazz Dialogue	1966	15.00
❑ SD1449 [S]	Jazz Dialogue	1966	18.00
—Multicolor label, black "fan" logo at right			
❑ SD1449 [S]	Jazz Dialogue	1969	12.00
—Red and green label			
❑ SD1623	Legendary Profile	1973	15.00
❑ 1486 [M]	Live at the Lighthouse	1967	25.00
❑ SD1486 [S]	Live at the Lighthouse	1967	15.00
—Multicolor label, black "fan" logo at right			
❑ SD1486 [S]	Live at the Lighthouse	1969	12.00
—Red and green label			
❑ 1381 [M]	Lonely Woman	1962	18.00
❑ SD1381 [S]	Lonely Woman	1962	25.00
—Multicolor label, black "fan" logo at right			
❑ SD1381 [S]	Lonely Woman	1969	12.00
—Red and green label			
❑ SD8806	More from the Last Concert	198?	12.00
❑ 1284 [M]	No Sun in Venice	1958	40.00
—Black label			
❑ 1284 [M]	No Sun in Venice	1960	25.00
—Multicolor label, white "fan" logo at right			
❑ 1284 [M]	No Sun in Venice	1963	18.00
—Multicolor label, black "fan" logo at right			
❑ SD1284 [S]	No Sun in Venice	1958	30.00
—Green label			
❑ SD1284 [S]	No Sun in Venice	1960	18.00
—Multicolor label, white "fan" logo at right			
❑ SD1284 [S]	No Sun in Venice	1963	15.00
—Multicolor label, black "fan" logo at right			
❑ SD1284 [S]	No Sun in Venice	1969	12.00
—Red and green label			
❑ SD1589	Plastic Dreams	1972	15.00
❑ 1325 [M]	Pyramid	1960	40.00
—Black label			
❑ 1325 [M]	Pyramid	1961	25.00
—Multicolor label, white "fan" logo at right			
❑ 1325 [M]	Pyramid	1963	18.00
—Multicolor label, black "fan" logo at right			
❑ SD1325 [S]	Pyramid	1960	30.00
—Green label			
❑ SD1325 [S]	Pyramid	1961	18.00
—Multicolor label, white "fan" logo at right			
❑ SD1325 [S]	Pyramid	1963	15.00
—Multicolor label, black "fan" logo at right			
❑ SD1325 [S]	Pyramid	1969	12.00
—Red and green label			
❑ SD 2-301	The Art of the Modern Jazz Quartet	1973	18.00
❑ SD1546	The Best of the Modern Jazz Quartet	1970	15.00
❑ 1390 [M]	The Comedy	1963	18.00
❑ SD1390 [S]	The Comedy	1963	25.00
—Multicolor label, black "fan" logo at right			
❑ SD1390 [S]	The Comedy	1969	12.00
—Red and green label			
❑ 2-603 [M]	The European Concert	1961	30.00
—Multicolor labels, white "fan" logo at right			
❑ 2-603 [M]	The European Concert	1963	25.00
—Multicolor labels, black "fan" logo at right			
❑ SD 2-603 [S]	The European Concert	1961	40.00
—Multicolor labels, white "fan" logo at right			
❑ SD 2-603 [S]	The European Concert	1963	30.00
—Multicolor labels, black "fan" logo at right			
❑ SD 2-603 [S]	The European Concert	1969	18.00
—Red and green labels			
❑ 1385 [M]	The European Concert, Volume 1	1962	18.00
❑ SD1385 [S]	The European Concert, Volume 1	1962	25.00
—Multicolor label, black "fan" logo at right			
❑ SD1385 [S]	The European Concert, Volume 1	1969	12.00
—Red and green label			
❑ 1386 [M]	The European Concert, Volume 2	1962	18.00
❑ SD1386 [S]	The European Concert, Volume 2	1962	25.00
—Multicolor label, black "fan" logo at right			
❑ SD1386 [S]	The European Concert, Volume 2	1969	12.00
—Red and green label			
❑ SD 2-909	The Last Concert	1975	18.00
❑ SQ 2-909 [Q]	The Last Concert	1975	30.00
❑ 1265 [M]	The Modern Jazz Quartet	1957	40.00
—Black label			
❑ 1265 [M]	The Modern Jazz Quartet	1960	25.00
—Multicolor label, white "fan" logo at right			
❑ 1265 [M]	The Modern Jazz Quartet	1963	18.00
—Multicolor label, black "fan" logo at right			
❑ 1359 [M]	The Modern Jazz Quartet and Orchestra	1961	25.00
—Multicolor label, white "fan" logo at right			
❑ 1359 [M]	The Modern Jazz Quartet and Orchestra	1963	15.00
—Multicolor label, black "fan" logo at right			
❑ SD1359 [S]	The Modern Jazz Quartet and Orchestra	1961	30.00
—Multicolor label, white "fan" logo at right			
❑ SD1359 [S]	The Modern Jazz Quartet and Orchestra	1963	18.00
—Multicolor label, black "fan" logo at right			
❑ SD1359 [S]	The Modern Jazz Quartet and Orchestra	1969	12.00
—Red and green label			
❑ 1247 [M]	The Modern Jazz Quartet at the Music Inn	1956	40.00
—Black label			
❑ 1247 [M]	The Modern Jazz Quartet at the Music Inn	1960	25.00
—Multicolor label, white "fan" logo at right			
❑ 1247 [M]	The Modern Jazz Quartet at the Music Inn	1963	18.00
—Multicolor label, black "fan" logo at right			
❑ 90049	The Modern Jazz Quartet at the Music Inn	1983	12.00
❑ 1299 [M]	The Modern Jazz Quartet at the Music Inn, Volume 2	1958	40.00
—Black label			
❑ 1299 [M]	The Modern Jazz Quartet at the Music Inn, Volume 2	1960	25.00
—Multicolor label, white "fan" logo at right			
❑ 1299 [M]	The Modern Jazz Quartet at the Music Inn, Volume 2	1963	18.00
—Multicolor label, black "fan" logo at right			
❑ SD1299 [S]	The Modern Jazz Quartet at the Music Inn, Volume 2	1958	30.00
—Green label			
❑ SD1299 [S]	The Modern Jazz Quartet at the Music Inn, Volume 2	1960	18.00
—Multicolor label, white "fan" logo at right			
❑ SD1299 [S]	The Modern Jazz Quartet at the Music Inn, Volume 2	1963	15.00
—Multicolor label, black "fan" logo at right			
❑ SD1299 [S]	The Modern Jazz Quartet at the Music Inn, Volume 2	1969	12.00
—Red and green label			
❑ 1440 [M]	The Modern Jazz Quartet Plays Gershwin's "Porgy and Bess	1965	15.00
❑ SD1440 [S]	The Modern Jazz Quartet Plays Gershwin's "Porgy and Bess	1965	18.00
—Multicolor label, black "fan" logo at right			
❑ SD1440 [S]	The Modern Jazz Quartet Plays Gershwin's "Porgy and Bess	1969	12.00
—Red and green label			
❑ 1414 [M]	The Sheriff	1964	18.00
❑ SD1414 [S]	The Sheriff	1964	25.00
—Multicolor label, black "fan" logo at right			
❑ SD1414 [S]	The Sheriff	1969	12.00
—Red and green label			
❑ 1345 [M]	Third Stream Music	1960	25.00
—Multicolor label, white "fan" logo at right			
❑ 1345 [M]	Third Stream Music	1963	15.00
—Multicolor label, black "fan" logo at right			
❑ SD1345 [S]	Third Stream Music	1960	30.00
—Multicolor label, white "fan" logo at right			
❑ SD1345 [S]	Third Stream Music	1963	18.00
—Multicolor label, black "fan" logo at right			
❑ SD1345 [S]	Third Stream Music	1969	12.00
—Red and green label			
❑ 81761	Three Windows	1987	12.00

EASTWEST

Number	Title	Yr	NM
❑ 90826	For Ellington	1988	12.00

FANTASY

Number	Title	Yr	NM
❑ OJC-002	Concorde	1982	12.00
❑ OJC-057	Django	198?	12.00
❑ OJC-125	Modern Jazz Quartet/Milt Jackson Quintet	198?	12.00

LITTLE DAVID

Number	Title	Yr	NM
❑ LD3001	In Memoriam	1975	15.00
❑ 90130	In Memoriam	198?	12.00

MOBILE FIDELITY

Number	Title	Yr	NM
❑ 1-206	Blues at Carnegie Hall	1994	30.00
—Audiophile vinyl			
❑ 1-090	Live at the Lighthouse	1982	50.00
—Audiophile vinyl			
❑ 1-205	The Modern Jazz Quartet	1994	30.00
—Audiophile vinyl			
❑ 1-228	The Modern Jazz Quartet at the Music Inn, Volume 2	1995	60.00
—Audiophile vinyl			

PABLO

Number	Title	Yr	NM
❑ 2405423	The Best of the Modern Jazz Quartet	198?	12.00

Number	Title	Yr	NM
❑ 2310917	Topsy: This One's for Basie	198?	12.00

PABLO LIVE

Number	Title	Yr	NM
❑ 2308243	Reunion at Budokan	198?	12.00
❑ 2308244	Together Again... At Montreux Jazz Festival	198?	12.00

PABLO TODAY

| ❑ 2312142 | Together Again | 1984 | 12.00 |

PRESTIGE

| ❑ PRLP-7005 [M] | Concorde | 1955 | 70.00 |

— Yellow label originals

| ❑ 16-1 [M] | Concorde | 1955 | 500.00 |

— This album plays at 16 2/3 rpm and is marked as such; white label; one side has the Modern Jazz Quartet, the other side has Milt Jackson

| ❑ PRLP-7057 [M] | Django | 1956 | 70.00 |

— Yellow label originals

| ❑ PRST-7749 | First Recordings | 1970 | 15.00 |
| ❑ PRLP-7059 [M] | Modern Jazz Quartet/Milt Jackson Quintet | 1956 | 70.00 |

— Yellow label originals

❑ 24005	The Modern Jazz Quartet	197?	18.00
❑ PRLP-170 [10]	The Modern Jazz Quartet, Volume 2	1953	120.00
❑ PRLP-7421 [M]	The Modern Jazz Quartet Play for Lovers	1966	25.00
❑ PRST-7421 [R]	The Modern Jazz Quartet Play for Lovers	1966	15.00
❑ PRLP-7425 [M]	The Modern Jazz Quartet Plays Jazz Classics	1966	25.00
❑ PRST-7425 [R]	The Modern Jazz Quartet Plays Jazz Classics	1966	15.00
❑ PRLP-160 [10]	The Modern Jazz Quartet with Milt Jackson	1953	120.00

SAVOY

| ❑ MG-12046 [M] | Modern Jazz Quartet | 1955 | 50.00 |

SOLID STATE

| ❑ SS-18035 | The Modern Jazz Quartet on Tour | 1968 | 15.00 |

UNITED ARTISTS

| ❑ UAL-4072 [M] | Patterns | 1960 | 30.00 |
| ❑ UAS-5072 [S] | Patterns | 1960 | 30.00 |

MODERN JAZZ SEXTET, THE

AMERICAN RECORDING SOCIETY

| ❑ G-429 [M] | The Modern Jazz Sextet | 1957 | 40.00 |

NORGRAN

| ❑ MGN-1076 [M] | The Modern Jazz Sextet | 1956 | 100.00 |

VERVE

❑ VE-1-2533	Dizzy Meets Sonny	197?	15.00
❑ MGV-8166 [M]	The Modern Jazz Sextet	1957	60.00
❑ V-8166 [M]	The Modern Jazz Sextet	1961	30.00

MODERN JAZZ SOCIETY, THE

AMERICAN RECORDING SOCIETY

| ❑ G-432 [M] | A Concert of Contemporary Music | 1957 | 40.00 |

NORGRAN

| ❑ MGN-1040 [M] | A Concert of Contemporary Music | 1955 | 100.00 |

VERVE

❑ MGV-8131 [M]	A Concert of Contemporary Music	1957	60.00
❑ V-8131 [M]	A Concert of Contemporary Music	1961	30.00
❑ VSP-18 [M]	Little David's Fugue	1966	25.00

— As "The Modern Jazz Ensemble"

| ❑ VSPS-18 [R] | Little David's Fugue | 1966 | 15.00 |

— As "The Modern Jazz Ensemble"

MODERNAIRES, THE

COLUMBIA

❑ CL2584 [10]	Juke Box Saturday Night	1955	40.00
❑ CL2490 [M]	The Modernaires Salute Herb Alpert and the Tijuana Brass	1966	15.00
❑ CS9290 [S]	The Modernaires Salute Herb Alpert and the Tijuana Brass	1966	18.00
❑ CL6043 [10]	Tributes in Tempo	1950	40.00

HARMONY

| ❑ HL7023 [M] | Juke Box Saturday Night | 195? | 25.00 |

LIBERTY

| ❑ LN-10215 | The Modernaires Sing the Great Glenn Miller Instrumentals | 198? | 12.00 |

MERCURY

| ❑ MG-20546 [M] | Like Swung | 1960 | 18.00 |
| ❑ SR-60220 [S] | Like Swung | 1960 | 25.00 |

UNITED ARTISTS

❑ WWS8510 [S]	The Modernaires Sing the Great Glenn Miller Instrumentals	196?	25.00
❑ WW3510 [S]	The Modernaires Sing the Great Glenn Miller Instrumentals	196?	18.00
❑ WW7524 [M]	We Remember Tommy Dorsey, Too!	196?	18.00
❑ WWS8524 [S]	We Remember Tommy Dorsey, Too!	196?	25.00

WING

| ❑ SRW-16231 [S] | Like Swung | 196? | 18.00 |
| ❑ MGW-12231 [M] | Like Swung | 196? | 15.00 |

MODULATIONS, THE

BUDDAH

| ❑ BDS-5638 [B] | It's Rough Out Here | 1975 | 80.00 |

— Reproductions exist

MOER, PAUL

DEL-FI

| ❑ DFLP-1212 [M] | Contemporary Jazz Classics | 1961 | 25.00 |
| ❑ DFST-1212 [S] | Contemporary Jazz Classics | 1961 | 30.00 |

MOFFATT, HUGH

PHILO

| ❑ PH-1111 | Loving You | 1987 | 12.00 |
| ❑ PH-1127 | Troubadour | 1989 | 15.00 |

MOFFATT, KATY

COLUMBIA

| ❑ PC34172 | Katy Moffatt | 1976 | 18.00 |
| ❑ JC34774 | Kissin' in the California Sun | 1977 | 18.00 |

PHILO

| ❑ PH-1133 | Child Bride | 1990 | 15.00 |
| ❑ PH-1128 | Walkin' on the Moon | 1989 | 15.00 |

MOFFETT, CHARLES

SAVOY

| ❑ MG-12194 | The Gift | 1969 | 25.00 |

MOJO MEN, THE

GRT

| ❑ 10003 | Mojo Magic | 1969 | 30.00 |

MOLE, MIFF

JAZZOLOGY

| ❑ J-105 | Milt Mole and His World Jam Session Band, 1944 | 198? | 12.00 |
| ❑ JCE-5 [M] | The Immortal Miff Mole | 1964 | 18.00 |

MOLE, MIFF/EDMUND HALL

BRUNSWICK

| ❑ BL58042 [10] | Battle of Jazz, Volume 4 | 1953 | 60.00 |

MOLENAT, CLAUDE

VANGUARD

| ❑ VSD-319 | Trumpet/Organ/Rhythm | 197? | 15.00 |

MOLLY HATCHET

CAPITOL

| ❑ C1-92114 | Lightning Strikes Twice | 1989 | 15.00 |

EPIC

| ❑ AS99844 [DJ] | Beatin' the Odds | 1980 | 40.00 |

— Promo-only picture disc

❑ FE36572	Beatin' the Odds	1980	12.00
❑ E240137	Double Trouble Live	1985	18.00
❑ AS99694 [DJ]	Flirtin' with Disaster	1979	40.00

— Promo-only picture disc

| ❑ JE36110 | Flirtin' with Disaster | 1979 | 12.00 |
| ❑ JE35347 | Molly Hatchet | 1978 | 15.00 |

— Orange label

| ❑ JE35347 | Molly Hatchet | 1979 | 12.00 |

— Dark blue label

| ❑ PE35347 | Molly Hatchet | 198? | 10.00 |

— Budget-line reissue with new prefix

| ❑ FE38429 | No Guts... No Glory | 1983 | 12.00 |
| ❑ PE38429 | No Guts... No Glory | 198? | 10.00 |

— Budget-line reissue with new prefix

| ❑ AS991320 [DJ] | Take No Prisoners | 1981 | 30.00 |

— Promo-only picture disc

| ❑ FE37480 | Take No Prisoners | 1981 | 12.00 |
| ❑ PE37480 | Take No Prisoners | 198? | 10.00 |

— Budget-line reissue with new prefix

| ❑ FE39621 | The Deed Is Done | 1984 | 12.00 |

MOLOCH

ENTERPRISE

| ❑ ENS-1002 | Moloch | 1969 | 30.00 |

MOMENTS, THE

CHESS

| ❑ CH2-92517 | Greatest Hits | 198? | 15.00 |

POLYDOR

❑ PD-1-6240	Ray, Goodman & Brown	1979	12.00
❑ PD-1-6299	Ray, Goodman & Brown II	1980	12.00
❑ PD-1-6341	Stay	1981	12.00

STANG

❑ ST-1003	A Moment with the Moments	1970	30.00
❑ 2ST-1033	Greatest Hits	1977	25.00
❑ ST-1015	Live at the Miss Black America Pageant	1972	25.00
❑ ST-1026	Look at Me	1975	18.00
❑ ST-1004	Moments Greatest Hits	1971	25.00
❑ ST-1030	Moments With You	1976	18.00
❑ ST-1022	My Thing	1973	18.00
❑ ST-1000	Not On the Outside, But On the Inside Strong	1969	30.00
❑ ST-1034	Sharp	1978	18.00
❑ ST-1019	The Best of the Moments	1975	18.00
❑ ST-1006	The Moments Live at the New York State Womans Prison	1971	30.00
❑ ST-1002	The Moments On Top	1970	30.00
❑ ST-1009	The Other Side of the Moments	1972	30.00
❑ ST-1023	The Sexy Moments	1974	18.00

MOM'S APPLE PIE

BROWN BAG

| ❑ BB-LA073-F | Mom's Apple Pie #2 | 1973 | 18.00 |
| ❑ 14200 [B] | Mom's Apple Pie | 1972 | 40.00 |

— With vulva showing in the apple pie

| ❑ 14200 [B] | Mom's Apple Pie | 1972 | 30.00 |

— With barbed wire wall covering the former opening. This is much rarer than the first version, though less sought-after

MONCUR, GRACHAN, III

BLUE NOTE

| ❑ BLP-4153 [M] | Evolution | 1963 | 30.00 |
| ❑ BST-84153 [S] | Evolution | 1963 | 30.00 |

— With "New York, USA" address on label

| ❑ BST-84153 [S] | Evolution | 1967 | 18.00 |

— With "A Division of Liberty Records" on label

| ❑ BST-84153 [S] | Evolution | 1986 | 12.00 |

— The Finest in Jazz Since 1939" reissue

| ❑ BLP-4177 [M] | Some Other Stuff | 1964 | 30.00 |
| ❑ BST-84177 [S] | Some Other Stuff | 1964 | 30.00 |

— With "New York, USA" address on label

| ❑ BST-84177 [S] | Some Other Stuff | 1967 | 18.00 |

— With "A Division of Liberty Records" on label

JCOA

| ❑ 1009 | Echoes of Prayer | 197? | 18.00 |

PICCADILLY

| ❑ 3520 | African Concepts | 198? | 12.00 |

MONDAY BLUES

VAULT

| ❑ 133 | The Phil Spector Song Book | 1970 | 25.00 |

MONEY, EDDIE

COLUMBIA

| ❑ FC40096 | Can't Hold Back | 1986 | 12.00 |
| ❑ PC34909 | Eddie Money | 1977 | 15.00 |

— No bar code on back cover

| ❑ JC34909 | Eddie Money | 198? | 10.00 |

— Reissue with bar code on back cover

| ❑ PC34909 | Eddie Money | 1977 | 15.00 |

— No bar code on back cover

| ❑ 1P-7982 | Greatest Hits Sound of Money | 1989 | 18.00 |

— Columbia House edition; only U.S. vinyl version

| ❑ JC35598 | Life for the Taking | 1979 | 12.00 |
| ❑ PC35598 | Life for the Taking | 198? | 10.00 |

— Budget-line reissue with new prefix

❑ FC37960	No Control	1982	12.00
❑ OC44302	Nothing to Lose	1988	12.00
❑ FC36514	Playing for Keeps	1980	12.00
❑ C46756	Right Here	1991	18.00
❑ FC38862	Where's the Party?	1983	12.00

MONEY, ZOOT

EPIC

| ❑ LN24241 [M] | All Happening Zoot Money's Big Roll Band at Klooks Kleek | 1966 | 35.00 |

MONICA, CORBETT

DOT

| ❑ DLP-3303 [M] | For Laughs1 | 1960 | 30.00 |

MONITORS, THE (1)

SOUL

| ❑ SS-714 | Greetings, We're the Monitors | 1969 | 60.00 |

MONK, THELONIOUS, AND JOHN COLTRANE

FANTASY

| ❑ OJC-039 | Thelonious Monk with John Coltrane | 198? | 15.00 |

JAZZLAND

| ❑ JLP-46 [M] | Thelonious Monk with John Coltrane | 1961 | 100.00 |
| ❑ JLP-946 [S] | Thelonious Monk with John Coltrane | 1961 | 80.00 |

MILESTONE

| ❑ M-47011 | Monk/Trane | 1973 | 25.00 |

RIVERSIDE

| ❑ RLP-490 [M] | Thelonious Monk with John Coltrane | 1965 | 50.00 |

— Reissue of Jazzland 46

| ❑ RS-9490 [S] | Thelonious Monk with John Coltrane | 1965 | 40.00 |

— Reissue of Jazzland 946

Number	Title	Yr	NM
MONK, THELONIOUS			
ANALOGUE PRODUCTIONS			
❑ AP-37	The Riverside Tenor Sessions	1999	250.00
BANDSTAND			
❑ BDLP-1516	April in Paris	1992	15.00
❑ BDLP-1505	Blue Monk	1992	15.00
BLACK LION			
❑ 152	Something in Blue	1972	25.00
❑ 197	The Man I Love	1973	25.00
BLUE NOTE			
❑ BLP-5002 [10]	Genius of Modern Music, Vol. 1	1952	800.00
❑ BLP-1510 [M]	Genius of Modern Music, Vol. 1	1956	400.00
—Deep groove" version; Lexington Ave. address on label			
❑ BLP-1510 [M]	Genius of Modern Music, Vol. 1	1958	200.00
—Deep groove" edition, W. 63rd St. address on label			
❑ BLP-1510 [M]	Genius of Modern Music, Vol. 1	1963	40.00
—New York, USA" address on label			
❑ BLP-81510 [R]	Genius of Modern Music, Vol. 1	1968	25.00
—A Division of Liberty Records" on label			
❑ BST-81510	Genius of Modern Music, Vol. 1	1985	15.00
—The Finest in Jazz Since 1939" reissue			
❑ BLP-5009 [10]	Genius of Modern Music, Vol. 2	1952	800.00
❑ BLP-1511 [M]	Genius of Modern Music, Vol. 2	1956	400.00
—Deep groove" version; Lexington Ave. address on label			
❑ BLP-1511 [M]	Genius of Modern Music, Vol. 2	1958	200.00
—Deep groove" edition, W. 63rd St. address on label			
❑ BLP-1511 [M]	Genius of Modern Music, Vol. 2	1963	40.00
—New York, USA" address on label			
❑ BLP-81511 [R]	Genius of Modern Music, Vol. 2	1968	25.00
—A Division of Liberty Records" on label			
❑ BST-81511	Genius of Modern Music, Vol. 2	1985	15.00
—The Finest in Jazz Since 1939" reissue			
❑ BN-LA579-H2	The Complete Genius	1976	25.00
❑ LWB-579	The Complete Genius	1981	18.00
—Reissue of BN-LA579-H2			
COLUMBIA			
❑ JG35720	Always Know	1979	25.00
❑ CL2038 [M]	Criss-Cross	1963	30.00
—Guaranteed High Fidelity" on label			
❑ CS8838 [S]	Criss-Cross	1963	60.00
—360 Sound Stereo" in black on label			
❑ CL2038 [M]	Criss-Cross	1966	25.00
—360 Sound Mono" on label			
❑ CL2038 [M]	Criss-Cross	199?	15.00
—180-gram reissue			
❑ CS8838 [S]	Criss-Cross	1966	30.00
—360 Sound Stereo" in white on label			
❑ CS9775	Greatest Hits	1969	25.00
—Red "360 Sound" label			
❑ CS9775	Greatest Hits	1971	15.00
—Orange label			
❑ PC9775	Greatest Hits	198?	10.00
—Reissue with new prefix			
❑ CL2184 [M]	It's Monk's Time	1964	30.00
—Guaranteed High Fidelity" on label			
❑ CS8984 [S]	It's Monk's Time	1964	70.00
—360 Sound Stereo" in black on label			
❑ CL2184 [M]	It's Monk's Time	1966	25.00
—360 Sound Mono" on label			
❑ CS8984 [S]	It's Monk's Time	1966	30.00
—360 Sound Stereo" in white on label			
❑ CS8984 [S]	It's Monk's Time	199?	15.00
—180-gram reissue			
❑ C238030	Live at the It Club	1983	30.00
—Original edition			
❑ C238030	Live at the It Club	199?	18.00
—180-gram reissue			
❑ C238269	Live at the Jazz Workshop	1983	30.00
❑ CL2416 [M]	Misterioso	1966	30.00
—360 Sound Mono" on label			
❑ CS9216 [S]	Misterioso	1966	30.00
—360 Sound Stereo" on red label			
❑ CL2416 [M]	Misterioso	199?	15.00
—180-gram reissue			
❑ CL2291 [M]	Monk	1965	30.00
—Guaranteed High Fideilty" on label			
❑ CS9091 [S]	Monk	1965	50.00
—360 Sound Stereo" in black on label			
❑ CS9091 [S]	Monk	1966	30.00
—360 Sound Stereo" in white on label			
❑ CS9091 [S]	Monk	199?	15.00
—180-gram reissue			
❑ CL2291 [M]	Monk	1966	25.00
—360 Sound Mono" on label			
❑ CL2164 [M]	Monk Big Band and Quartet In Concert	1964	30.00
—Guaranteed High Fideility" on label			
❑ CS8964 [S]	Monk Big Band and Quartet In Concert	1964	80.00
—360 Sound Stereo" in black on label			
❑ CL2164 [M]	Monk Big Band and Quartet In Concert	1966	25.00
—360 Sound Mono" on label			
❑ CS8964 [S]	Monk Big Band and Quartet In Concert	1966	30.00
—360 Sound Stereo" in white on label			
❑ CS8964 [S]	Monk Big Band and Quartet In Concert	199?	15.00
—180-gram reissue			
❑ CS9806	Monk's Blues	1969	80.00
—Red "360 Sound" label			
❑ CS9806	Monk's Blues	1971	18.00
—Orange label			
❑ PC9806	Monk's Blues	198?	10.00
—Reissue with new prefix; most have bar codes on back cover			
❑ PC9806	Monk's Blues	199?	15.00
—180-gram reissue			
❑ CL1965 [M]	Monk's Dream	1963	30.00
—Guaranteed High Fideilty" on label			
❑ CS8765 [S]	Monk's Dream	1963	70.00
—360 Sound Stereo" in black on label			
❑ CL1965 [M]	Monk's Dream	1966	25.00
—360 Sound Mono" on label			
❑ CS8765 [S]	Monk's Dream	1966	30.00
—360 Sound Stereo" in white on label			
❑ CS8765 [S]	Monk's Dream	199?	15.00
—180-gram reissue			
❑ CL2349 [M]	Solo Monk	1965	30.00
—360 Sound Mono" on label			
❑ CS9149 [S]	Solo Monk	1965	40.00
—Red "360 Sound" label			
❑ CS9149	Solo Monk	1971	15.00
—Orange label			
❑ PC9149	Solo Monk	198?	10.00
—Reissue with new prefix; most have bar codes			
❑ PC9149	Solo Monk	199?	15.00
—180-gram reissue			
❑ CL2651 [M]	Straight No Chaser	1967	50.00
—Red label with "Mono			
❑ CS9451 [S]	Straight No Chaser	1967	40.00
—Red "360 Sound" label			
❑ CS9451	Straight No Chaser	1971	15.00
—Orange label			
❑ PC9451	Straight No Chaser	198?	10.00
—Reissue with new prefix			
❑ PC9451	Straight No Chaser	199?	15.00
—180-gram reissue			
❑ C238510	The Tokyo Concerts	1984	25.00
—Original edition			
❑ C238510	The Tokyo Concerts	199?	18.00
—180-gram reissue			
❑ CS9632 [S]	Underground	1968	30.00
—Red "360 Sound" label			
❑ CS9632	Underground	1971	15.00
—Orange label			
❑ PC9632	Underground	198?	10.00
—Reissue with new prefix			
❑ CS9632 [M]	Underground	1968	50.00
—White label promo only with stereo number; "Special Mono Radio Station Copy" sticker on stereo cover			
❑ PC9632	Underground	199?	15.00
—180-gram reissue			
❑ KG32892	Who's Afraid of the Big Band Monk	1974	30.00
❑ KG32892	Who's Afraid of the Big Band Monk	199?	18.00
—180-gram reissue			
COLUMBIA JAZZ MASTERPIECES			
❑ CJ40786	Monk's Dream	1987	12.00
❑ CJ44297	The Composer	1988	15.00
❑ CJ40785	Underground	1987	12.00
COLUMBIA LIMITED EDITION			
❑ LE10122	Criss-Cross	197?	15.00
COLUMBIA MUSICAL TREASURY			
❑ DS338	Monk's Miracles	1967	30.00
—Columbia Record Club exclusive			
EVEREST ARCHIVE OF FOLK & JAZZ			
❑ FS-336	Piano Solos	1978	15.00
FANTASY			
❑ OJC-362	5 By Monk By 5	1989	15.00
❑ OJC-231	Alone in San Francisco	1987	15.00
❑ OJC-026	Brilliant Corners	198?	15.00
❑ OJC-206	Misterioso	1985	15.00
❑ OJC-016	Monk	198?	15.00
❑ OJC-488	Monk in Italy	1991	15.00
❑ OJC-084	Monk's Music	198?	15.00
❑ OJC-301	Mulligan Meets Monk	1988	15.00
❑ OJC-254	Thelonious Himself	1987	15.00
❑ OJC-103	Thelonious in Action	198?	15.00
❑ OJC-305	Thelonious Monk at the Blackhawk	1988	15.00
❑ OJC-135	Thelonious Monk at Town Hall	1984	15.00
❑ OJC-024	Thelonious Monk Plays Duke Ellington	198?	15.00
❑ OJC-059	Thelonious Monk/Sonny Rollins	198?	15.00
❑ OJC-010	Thelonious Monk Trio	198?	15.00
❑ OJC-064	The Unique Thelonious Monk	198?	15.00
GATEWAY			
❑ GSLP-7023	Monk's Music	197?	18.00
GNP CRESCENDO			
❑ 9008	Thelonious Monk	197?	18.00
JAZZ MAN			
❑ 5017	Something in Blue	1980	15.00
MILESTONE			
❑ M-47060	April in Paris/Live	198?	25.00
❑ M-9124	Blues Five Spot	1984	18.00
❑ M-47023	Brilliance	1975	30.00
❑ M-9115	Evidence	1983	15.00
❑ M-47064	Memorial Album	1982	25.00
❑ M-47004	Pure Monk	1972	25.00
❑ M-47067	'Round Midnight	198?	25.00
❑ M-47043	Thelonious Monk at the Five Spot	1978	25.00
❑ M-47033	Thelonious Monk In Person	1976	30.00
❑ M-47052	The Riverside Trios	1980	25.00
MOSAIC			
❑ MR4-112	The Complete Black Lion and Vogue Recordings	199?	250.00
—Limited edition of 7,500			
❑ MR4-101	The Complete Blue Note Recordings of Thelonious Monk	198?	200.00
—Limited edition of 7,500			
PICCADILLY			
❑ 3521	Monkisms	198?	15.00
PRESTIGE			
❑ PRST-7848	Blue Monk, Volume 2	197?	18.00
❑ PRLP-7053 [M]	Monk	1956	1200.00
—Reissue of 150; yellow label with W. 50th St. address. Andy Warhol cover.			
❑ PRLP-7159 [M]	Monk's Moods	1959	80.00
—Reissue of 7027; yellow label with Bergenfield, N.J. address			
❑ PRST-7751	Reflections, Volume 1	1970	25.00
❑ PRST-7656	The Genius of Thelonious Monk	1969	25.00
❑ PRLP-7363 [M]	The Golden Monk	1965	30.00
—Reissue of 7245			
❑ PRST-7363 [R]	The Golden Monk	1965	25.00
❑ PRLP-7508 [M]	The High Priest	1967	50.00
—Reissue of 7159			
❑ PRST-7508 [R]	The High Priest	1967	25.00
❑ PRLP-7027 [M]	Thelonious Monk	1956	300.00
—Reissue of 142 and 189 on one 12-inch record; yellow label with W. 50th St. address; label calls this "Thelonious Monk Trio			
❑ PR-24006	Thelonious Monk	1971	25.00
❑ PRLP-180 [10]	Thelonious Monk Quintet	1954	800.00
❑ PRLP-166 [10]	Thelonious Monk Quintet with Sonny Rollins and Julius Watkins	1953	800.00
❑ PRLP-7075 [M]	Thelonious Monk/Sonny Rollins	1957	200.00
—Reissue of 166; yellow label with W. 50th St. address			
❑ PRLP-142 [10]	Thelonious Monk Trio	1953	800.00
❑ PRLP-189 [10]	Thelonious Monk Trio	1954	800.00
❑ PRLP-7245 [M]	We See	1962	80.00
—Reissue of 7053			
❑ PRLP-7169 [M]	Work	1959	80.00
—Reissue of 7075			
RIVERSIDE			
❑ RLP 12-305 [M]	5 By Monk By 5	1959	60.00
—Blue label with reel and microphone logo			
❑ RLP1150 [S]	5 By Monk By 5	1959	80.00
—Black label with reel and microphone logo			
❑ 6086	5 By Monk By 5	197?	15.00
❑ 6163	Alone in San Francisco	198?	15.00
❑ RS-3037	Best of Thelonious Monk	1969	18.00
❑ RLP 12-226 [M]	Brilliant Corners	1957	400.00
—White label with blue print			
❑ RLP 12-226 [M]	Brilliant Corners	1958	100.00
—Blue label with reel and microphone logo			
❑ RS-3009 [R]	CT Meets Monk	1968	18.00
❑ 6107	Meet Thelonious Monk and Gerry Mulligan	197?	15.00
❑ RM-3000 [M]	Mighty Monk	1967	40.00
❑ RS-3000 [S]	Mighty Monk	1967	30.00
❑ RLP 12-279 [M]	Misterioso	1958	100.00
—Blue label with reel-and-microphone logo			
❑ RLP1133 [S]	Misterioso	1958	70.00
—Black label with reel and microphone logo			
❑ 6119	Misterioso	197?	15.00
❑ RLP-491 [M]	Monk in France	1965	30.00
❑ RS-9491 [S]	Monk in France	1965	30.00
❑ RS-3015 [R]	Monk Plays Duke	1968	18.00
❑ RLP 12-242 [M]	Monk's Music	1957	400.00
—White label with blue print			
❑ RLP 12-242 [M]	Monk's Music	1958	100.00
—Blue label with reel and microphone logo			
❑ RLP1101 [S]	Monk's Music	1959	60.00
—Black label with reel and microphone logo			
❑ RM-3004 [M]	Monk's Music	1967	30.00
❑ RS-3004 [S]	Monk's Music	1967	25.00
❑ 6207	Monk's Music	1983	15.00
❑ RLP 12-247 [M]	Mulligan Meets Monk	1957	400.00

Number	Title	Yr	NM
—White label with blue print			
❑ RLP 12-247 [M]	Mulligan Meets Monk	1958	100.00
—Blue label with reel and microphone logo			
❑ RLP1106 [S]	Mulligan Meets Monk	1959	60.00
—Black label with reel and microphone logo			
❑ RS-3047	Panorama!	1970	15.00
❑ R-022	The Complete Riverside Recordings	1987	500.00
❑ RLP 12-312 [M]	Thelonious Alone in San Francisco	1959	60.00
—Blue label with reel and microphone logo			
❑ RLP1158 [S]	Thelonious Alone in San Francisco	1959	70.00
—Black label with reel and microphone logo			
❑ RLP 12-235 [M]	Thelonious Himself	1957	400.00
—White label with blue print			
❑ RLP 12-235 [M]	Thelonious Himself	1958	100.00
—Blue label with reel and microphone logo			
❑ 6053 [M]	Thelonious Himself	197?	15.00
❑ 6102	Thelonious in Action	197?	15.00
❑ RLP 12-262 [M]	Thelonious in Action Recorded at the Five Spot Café, New York, With Johnny Griffin	1958	80.00
—Blue label with reel and microphone logo			
❑ RLP1190 [S]	Thelonious in Action Recorded at the Five Spot Café, New York, With Johnny Griffin	1960	70.00
—Black label with reel and microphone logo			
❑ 6198	Thelonious Monk at the Blackhawk	198?	15.00
❑ 6183	Thelonious Monk at Town Hall	198?	15.00
❑ RLP-443 [M]	Thelonious Monk in Italy	1963	30.00
❑ RS-9443 [S]	Thelonious Monk in Italy	1963	40.00
❑ RLP 12-201 [M]	Thelonious Monk Plays Duke Ellington	1955	600.00
—White label with blue print			

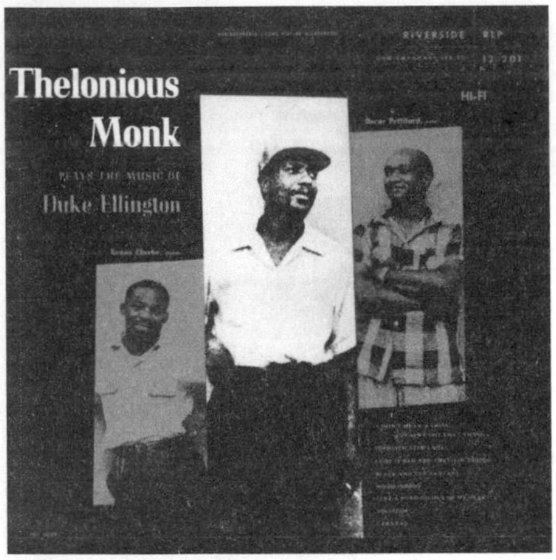

Number	Title	Yr	NM
❑ RLP 12-201 [M]	Thelonious Monk Plays Duke Ellington	1958	100.00
—Blue label with reel and microphone logo			
❑ 6039 [M]	Thelonious Monk Plays Duke Ellington	197?	15.00
❑ RLP 12-323 [M]	Thelonious Monk Quartet Plus Two at the Blackhawk	1960	60.00
—Blue label with reel and microphone logo			
❑ RLP1171 [S]	Thelonious Monk Quartet Plus Two at the Blackhawk	1960	70.00
—Black label with reel and microphone logo			
❑ RLP-421 [M]	Thelonious Monk's Greatest Hits	1962	30.00
❑ RS-9421 [S]	Thelonious Monk's Greatest Hits	1962	30.00
❑ RLP 12-300 [M]	The Thelonious Monk Orchestra at Town Hall	1959	60.00
—Blue label with reel and microphone logo			
❑ RLP1138 [S]	The Thelonious Monk Orchestra at Town Hall	1959	70.00
—Black label with reel and microphone logo			
❑ RS-9483/4 [S]	The Thelonious Monk Story	1965	60.00
❑ RLP-9483/4 [M]	The Thelonious Monk Story	1965	70.00
❑ RLP-483 [M]	The Thelonious Monk Story, Volume 1	1965	30.00
❑ RS-9483 [S]	The Thelonious Monk Story, Volume 1	1965	30.00
❑ RLP-484 [M]	The Thelonious Monk Story, Volume 2	1965	30.00
❑ RS-9484 [S]	The Thelonious Monk Story, Volume 2	1965	30.00
❑ RLP 12-209 [M]	The Unique Thelonious Monk	1956	500.00
—White label with blue print			
❑ RLP 12-209 [M]	The Unique Thelonious Monk	1958	100.00
—Blue label with reel and microphone logo			
❑ 6068 [M]	The Unique Thelonious Monk	197?	15.00
❑ RLP-460/1 [M]	Two Hours with Thelonious Monk	1963	60.00
❑ RS-9460/1 [S]	Two Hours with Thelonious Monk	1963	80.00
❑ RS-3020X [R]	Two Hours with Thelonious Monk	1969	30.00

TRIP

Number	Title	Yr	NM
❑ 5022	Pure Monk	1974	15.00

XANADU

Number	Title	Yr	NM
❑ 202	Live at the Village Gate	1985	18.00

MONKEES, THE

ARISTA

Number	Title	Yr	NM
❑ AL-8525	More of the Monkees	1988	15.00
❑ AL-8524	The Monkees	1988	15.00
❑ AL4089	The Monkees' Greatest Hits	1976	15.00
—Reissue of Bell LP			
❑ AL8-8313	The Monkees' Greatest Hits	198?	10.00
—Reissue of Arista 4089			
❑ AL9-8432	Then & Now...The Best of the Monkees	1986	15.00

BELL

Number	Title	Yr	NM
❑ 6081	Re-Focus	1972	30.00

COLGEMS

Number	Title	Yr	NM
❑ SCOS-1001	A Barrel Full of Monkees	1971	75.00
❑ COS-119	Changes	1970	80.00
❑ COSO-5008	Head	1968	50.00
❑ COS-113	Instant Replay	1969	40.00
❑ COM-102 [M]	More of the Monkees	1966	30.00
❑ COS-102 [S]	More of the Monkees	1966	25.00
❑ COS-104 [S]	Pisces, Aquarius, Capricorn & Jones Ltd.	1967	25.00
❑ COM-104 [M]	Pisces, Aquarius, Capricorn & Jones Ltd.	1967	100.00
❑ COM-109 [M]	The Birds, the Bees & the Monkees	1968	140.00
❑ COS-109 [S]	The Birds, the Bees & the Monkees	1968	25.00
❑ COM-101 [M]	The Monkees	1966	40.00
—First pressing: Side 1, Song 5 listed as "Papa Jean's Blues			
❑ COM-101 [M]	The Monkees	1966	30.00
—Second pressing: Side 1, Song 5 listed as "Papa Gene's Blues" (RE after number on upper right back cover)			
❑ COS-101 [S]	The Monkees	1966	30.00
—First pressing: Side 1, Song 5 listed as "Papa Jean's Blues			
❑ COS-101 [S]	The Monkees	1966	25.00
—Second pressing: Side 1, Song 5 listed as "Papa Gene's Blues" (RE after number on upper right back cover)			
❑ PRS-329	The Monkees' Golden Hits	1971	100.00
—RCA Special Products edition			
❑ COS-115	The Monkees Greatest Hits	1969	40.00
❑ COM-103 [M]	The Monkees' Headquarters	1967	60.00
—First pressing: Back cover, center bottom photo is of two of the LP's producers			
❑ COS-103 [S]	The Monkees' Headquarters	1967	25.00
—First pressing: Back cover, center bottom photo is of two of the LP's producers			
❑ COM-103 [M]	The Monkees' Headquarters	1967	30.00
—Second pressing: Back cover, center bottom photo is of producers plus the Monkees with beards; "RE" on upper right back cover			
❑ COS-103 [S]	The Monkees' Headquarters	1967	30.00
—Second pressing: Back cover, center bottom photo is of producers plus the Monkees with beards; "RE" on upper right back cover			
❑ COS-117	The Monkees Present	1969	50.00

FSH

Number	Title	Yr	NM
❑ 71110	Live, 20th Anniversary Tour	1987	25.00
—Live album sold at tour stops			

LAURIE HOUSE

Number	Title	Yr	NM
❑ LH-8009	The Monkees	1974	25.00
—TV mail-order offer			

PAIR

Number	Title	Yr	NM
❑ ARPDL2-1109	Hit Factory	1986	25.00

RCA SPECIAL PRODUCTS

Number	Title	Yr	NM
❑ DPL2-0188	The Monkees	1976	30.00
—TV mail-order offer			

RHINO

Number	Title	Yr	NM
❑ RNLP-70148	Changes	1986	15.00
❑ RNLP-145	Head	1985	15.00
❑ RNLP-146	Instant Replay	1985	15.00
❑ RNLP-70139	Live 1967	1987	15.00
❑ RNLP-70150	Missing Links	1987	15.00
❑ RNLP-701 [PD]	Monkee Business	1982	18.00
❑ RNLP-113	Monkee Flips	1984	15.00
❑ RNLP-70142	More of the Monkees	1986	15.00
❑ RNLP-70141	Pisces, Aquarius, Capricorn & Jones Ltd.	1986	15.00
❑ RNIN-70706	Pool It!	1987	12.00
❑ RNLP-144	The Birds, the Bees and the Monkees	1985	15.00
❑ RNLP-70140	The Monkees	1986	15.00
❑ RNLP-70143	The Monkees' Headquarters	1986	15.00
❑ RNLP-147	The Monkees Present	1985	15.00

SILHOUETTE

Number	Title	Yr	NM
❑ SM-10012 [PD]	Tails of the Monkees	1983	18.00

SILVER EAGLE

Number	Title	Yr	NM
❑ SE-1048	The Best of the Monkees	1986	18.00
—TV mail-order offer			

SUNDAZED

Number	Title	Yr	NM
❑ LP5046	More of the Monkees	1996	12.00
❑ LP5048	Pisces, Aquarius, Capricorn & Jones Ltd.	1996	12.00
❑ LP5049	The Birds, the Bees, and the Monkees	1996	12.00
—All of the above are on colored vinyl with bonus tracks and posters			
❑ LP5045	The Monkees	1996	12.00
❑ LP5047	The Monkees Headquarters	1996	12.00

MONOCHROME SET

4 MEN WITH BEARDS

Number	Title	Yr	NM
❑ 4M531LP [B]	Love Zombies		25.00
❑ 4M530LP [B]	Strange Boutique		25.00

MONRO, MATT

CAPITOL

Number	Title	Yr	NM
❑ SKAO-152	Best of Matt Monro	1969	12.00
❑ T2608 [M]	Here's to My Lady	1966	15.00
❑ ST2608 [S]	Here's to My Lady	1966	18.00
❑ T2683 [M]	Invitation to Broadway	1967	15.00
❑ ST2683 [S]	Invitation to Broadway	1967	18.00
❑ T2730 [M]	Invitation to the Movies/Born Free	1967	18.00
❑ ST2730 [S]	Invitation to the Movies/Born Free	1967	15.00
❑ T2801 [M]	These Years	1968	18.00
❑ ST2801 [S]	These Years	1968	15.00
❑ T2540 [M]	This Is the Life	1966	15.00
❑ ST2540 [S]	This Is the Life	1966	18.00

LIBERTY

Number	Title	Yr	NM
❑ LRP-3423 [M]	All My Loving	1965	15.00
❑ LST-7423 [S]	All My Loving	1965	18.00
❑ LRP-3256 [M]	From Hollywood With Love	1962	18.00
❑ LST-7256 [S]	From Hollywood With Love	1962	25.00
❑ LRP-3240 [M]	Matt Monro	1962	18.00
❑ LST-7240 [S]	Matt Monro	1962	25.00
❑ LRP-3459 [M]	Matt Monro's Best	1966	15.00
❑ LST-7459 [S]	Matt Monro's Best	1966	18.00
❑ LRP-3402 [M]	Walk Away	1965	15.00
❑ LST-7402 [S]	Walk Away	1965	18.00
❑ LRP-3437 [M]	Yesterday	1966	15.00
❑ LST-7437 [S]	Yesterday	1966	18.00

LONDON

Number	Title	Yr	NM
❑ LL1611 [M]	Blue and Sentimental	1957	30.00

PICKWICK

Number	Title	Yr	NM
❑ SPC-3147	This Is All I Ask	197?	12.00

WARWICK

Number	Title	Yr	NM
❑ W2045 [M]	My Kind of Girl	1961	30.00
❑ WST2045 [S]	My Kind of Girl	1961	50.00

MONROE, BILL

COLUMBIA

Number	Title	Yr	NM
❑ FC38904	Columbia Historic Editions	1983	15.00

DECCA

Number	Title	Yr	NM
❑ DL75135	A Voice from On High	1969	25.00
❑ DL75010	Bill Monroe's Greatest Hits	1968	25.00
❑ DL4601 [M]	Bluegrass Instrumentals	1965	25.00
❑ DL74601 [S]	Bluegrass Instrumentals	1965	30.00
❑ DL4266 [M]	Bluegrass Ramble	1962	30.00
❑ DL74266 [S]	Bluegrass Ramble	1962	40.00
❑ DL4382 [M]	Bluegrass Special	1963	30.00
❑ DL74382 [S]	Bluegrass Special	1963	30.00
❑ DL4896 [M]	Bluegrass Time	1967	30.00
❑ DL74896 [S]	Bluegrass Time	1967	25.00
❑ DL75281	Country Music Hall of Fame	1972	25.00
❑ DL4537 [M]	I'll Meet You in Chuch Sunday Morning	1964	30.00
❑ DL74537 [S]	I'll Meet You in Church Sunday Morning	1964	30.00
❑ DL8769 [M]	I Saw the Light	1959	50.00
❑ DL78769 [S]	I Saw the Light	1959	70.00
❑ DL75213	Kentucky Bluegrass	1970	25.00
❑ DL8731 [M]	Knee Deep in Bluegrass	1958	50.00
❑ DL78731 [S]	Knee Deep in Bluegrass	1958	70.00
❑ DL4080 [M]	Mr. Bluegrass	1960	30.00
❑ DL74080 [S]	Mr. Bluegrass	1960	40.00
❑ DL4327 [M]	My All Time Country Favorites	1962	30.00
❑ DL74327 [S]	My All Time Country Favorites	1962	30.00
❑ DL4780 [M]	The High Lonesome Sound of Bill Monroe	1966	25.00
❑ DL74780 [S]	The High Lonesome Sound of Bill Monroe	1966	30.00

HARMONY

Number	Title	Yr	NM
❑ HL7315 [M]	Bill Monroe's Best	1964	25.00
❑ HL7290 [M]	The Great Bill Monroe and His Bluegrass Boys	1961	30.00
❑ HS11335 [R]	The Great Bill Monroe and His Bluegrass Boys	1969	18.00
❑ HL7338 [M]	The Original Bluegrass Sound	1965	25.00

MCA

Number	Title	Yr	NM
❑ 131	A Voice from On High	1973	15.00
—Reissue of Decca 75135			
❑ 8002	Bean Blossom	1973	25.00
❑ 3209	Bean Blossom '79	1979	18.00
❑ 765	Bean Blossom '79	198?	12.00
—Reissue of 3209			
❑ 5435	Bill Monroe and Friends	1984	15.00
❑ 5625	Bill Monroe and the Stars of the Bluegrass Hall of Fame	1985	15.00
❑ 17	Bill Monroe's Greatest Hits	1973	15.00
—Reissue of Decca 75010			

Number	Title	Yr	NM
❑ 2251	Bill Monroe Sings Bluegrass, Body and Soul	1977	18.00
❑ 708	Bill Monroe Sings Bluegrass, Body and Soul	198?	12.00
—Reissue of 2251			
❑ 104	Bluegrass Instrumentals	1973	15.00
—Reissue of Decca 74601			
❑ 2315	Bluegrass Memories	1978	18.00
❑ 88	Bluegrass Ramble	1973	15.00
—Reissue of Decca 74266			
❑ 97	Bluegrass Special	1973	15.00
—Reissue of Decca 74382			
❑ 116	Bluegrass Time	1973	15.00
—Reissue of Decca 74896			
❑ 140	Country Music Hall of Fame	1973	15.00
—Reissue of Decca 75281			
❑ 226	I'll Meet You in Church Sunday Morning	1973	15.00
—Reissue of Decca 74537			
❑ 527	I Saw the Light	197?	15.00
—Reissue of Decca 78769			
❑ 136	Kentucky Bluegrass	1973	15.00
—Reissue of Decca 75213			
❑ 82	Mr. Bluegrass	1973	15.00
—Reissue of Decca 74080			
❑ 426	Road of Life	1974	18.00
❑ 4090	The Best of Bill Monroe	197?	18.00
❑ 110	The High Lonesome Sound of Bill Monroe	1973	15.00
—Reissue of Decca 74780			
❑ 500	Uncle Pen	197?	15.00
❑ 2173	Weary Traveler	1976	18.00
❑ 707	Weary Traveler	198?	12.00
—Reissue of 2173			
RCA CAMDEN			
❑ CAL-719 [M]	Father of Bluegrass Music	1962	30.00
MONROE, CHARLIE			
STARDAY			
❑ SLP-372 [M]	Charlie Monroe Sings Again	1966	30.00
❑ SLP-361 [M]	Lord, Build Me a Cabin	1965	30.00
MONROE, MARILYN			
20TH CENTURY			
❑ T-901 [B]	Remember Marilyn	1973	30.00
20TH FOX			
❑ FXG-5000 [M]	Marilyn	1962	150.00
❑ SXG-5000 [R]	Marilyn	1962	100.00
❑ F/SXG-5000	Marilyn Bonus Photo	1962	50.00
ASCOT			
❑ AM-13008 [M]	Marilyn Monroe	1963	60.00
❑ AS-16008 [S]	Marilyn Monroe	1963	50.00
CLEOPATRA			
❑ 5250 [D]	Diamonds Are A Girl's Best Friend		18.00
❑ 8202 [B]	Diamonds Are A Girl's Best Friend - 50th Anniversary Edition		30.00
—picture disc			
❑ 8992 [B]	Golden Collection		30.00
❑ 5364 [B]	Greatest Moments		25.00
❑ 3042 [B]	The Essential Masters		25.00
MOVIETONE			
❑ 1016 [M]	The Unforgettable Marilyn Monroe	1967	30.00
❑ 72016 [R]	The Unforgettable Marilyn Monroe	1967	25.00
SANDY HOOK			
❑ SH-2013 [PD]	Rare Recordings 1948-1962	1980	30.00
STET			
❑ DS-15005	Never Before and Never Again	1980	18.00
MONROE, VAUGHN			
DOT			
❑ DLP-3548 [M]	Great Gospels -- Great Hymns	1963	15.00
❑ DLP-25548 [S]	Great Gospels -- Great Hymns	1963	18.00
❑ DLP-3470 [M]	Great Themes of Famous Bands and Famous Singers	1962	15.00
❑ DLP-25470 [S]	Great Themes of Famous Bands and Famous Singers	1962	18.00
❑ DLP-3431 [M]	His Greatest Hits	1962	15.00
❑ DLP-25431 [S]	His Greatest Hits	1962	18.00
❑ DLP-3584 [M]	His Greatest Hits, Volume 2	1964	15.00
❑ DLP-25584 [S]	His Greatest Hits, Volume 2	1964	18.00
❑ DLP-3419 [M]	Surfer's Stomp	1962	30.00
❑ DLP-25419 [S]	Surfer's Stomp	1962	40.00
HAMILTON			
❑ HLP-137 [M]	Racing with the Moon	1965	12.00
❑ HLP-12137 [S]	Racing with the Moon	1965	15.00
RCA CAMDEN			
❑ CAL-329 [M]	Dance with Me	1956	25.00
❑ CAL-354 [M]	Dreamland Special	1956	25.00
RCA VICTOR			
❑ LPM-1493 [M]	House Party	1957	30.00
❑ LPM-3817 [M]	The Best of Vaughn Monroe	1967	25.00
❑ LSP-3817 [R]	The Best of Vaughn Monroe	1967	15.00
❑ ANL1-1140	The Best of Vaughn Monroe	1976	10.00

Number	Title	Yr	NM
❑ LPM-1799 [M]	There I Sing, Swing It Again	1958	25.00
❑ LSP-1799 [S]	There I Sing, Swing It Again	1958	30.00
❑ VPM-6073	This Is Vaughn Monroe	1972	18.00
❑ LPM-3048 [10]	Vaughn Monroe Caravan	1952	40.00
❑ LPM-13 [10]	Vaughn Monroe Plays Victor Herbert for Dancing	1952	40.00
MONROE BROTHERS, THE			
BLUEBIRD			
❑ AXM2-5510	Feast Here Tonight	197?	18.00
MONROES, THE			
ALFA			
❑ AAE-15015 [EP]	The Monroes	1982	25.00
MONTAGE			
LAURIE			
❑ SLP-2049	Montage	1969	25.00
MONTANA, PATSY			
SIMS			
❑ 122 [M]	The New Sound of Patsy Montana	1964	50.00
STARDAY			
❑ SLP-376 [M]	Cowboy's Sweetheart	1966	30.00
MONTANA			
LABOR			
❑ 5	Montana	198?	15.00
MONTANA ORCHESTRA			
MJS			
❑ 3302	Merry Christmas/Happy New Year's	1981	12.00
MONTANA SLIM			
DECCA			
❑ DL8917 [M]	I'm Ragged But I'm Right	1959	60.00
❑ DL4092 [M]	The Dynamite Trail	1960	50.00
❑ DL74092 [S]	The Dynamite Trail	1960	60.00
RCA CAMDEN			
❑ CAL-846 [M]	32 Wonderful Years	1965	25.00
❑ CAS-846 [R]	32 Wonderful Years	1965	15.00
❑ CAL-668 [M]	Reminiscin' with Montana Slim	1962	30.00
❑ CAL-527 [M]	Wilf Carter/Montana Slim	1958	40.00
STARDAY			
❑ SLP-389 [M]	Wilf Carter	1966	30.00
❑ SLP-300 [M]	Wilf Carter As Montana Slim	1964	30.00
MONTE, LOU			
RCA CAMDEN			
❑ CAL-455 [M]	Here's Lou Monte	195?	15.00
RCA VICTOR			
❑ LPM-3705 [M]	Good Time Songs	1967	18.00
❑ LSP-3705 [S]	Good Time Songs	1967	15.00
❑ LPM-1976 [M]	Italian House Party	1959	25.00
❑ LSP-1976 [S]	Italian House Party	1959	30.00
❑ LPM-1651 [M]	Lou Monte Sings for You	1957	30.00
❑ LPM-1877 [M]	Songs for Pizza Lovers	1958	30.00
❑ LPM-3672 [M]	The Best of Lou Monte	1966	18.00
❑ LSP-3672 [S]	The Best of Lou Monte	1966	15.00
REPRISE			
❑ R-6005 [M]	Great Italian-American Hits	1961	25.00
❑ R9-6005 [S]	Great Italian-American Hits	1961	30.00
❑ R-6014 [M]	Live in Person	1961	25.00
❑ R9-6014 [S]	Live in Person	1961	30.00
❑ R-6099 [M]	More Italian Fun Songs	1963	25.00
❑ R9-6099 [S]	More Italian Fun Songs	1963	30.00
❑ R-6058 [M]	Pepino The Italian Mouse & Other Italian Fun Songs	1962	25.00
❑ R9-6058 [S]	Pepino The Italian Mouse & Other Italian Fun Songs	1962	30.00
❑ R-6118 [M]	The Golden Hits of Lou Monte	1964	18.00
❑ RS-6118 [S]	The Golden Hits of Lou Monte	1964	25.00
ROULETTE			
❑ R-25126 [M]	Italiano U.S.A.	1960	25.00
❑ SR-25126 [S]	Italiano U.S.A.	1960	30.00
❑ R-25257 [M]	The Magic World of Italy	1963	18.00
❑ SR-25257 [S]	The Magic World of Italy	1963	25.00
MONTEGO JOE			
ESP-DISK'			
❑ S-1067	Montego Joe's HARYOU Percussion Ensemble	1968	30.00
PRESTIGE			
❑ PRLP-7336 [M]	Arriba Con Montego Joe	1964	30.00
❑ PRST-7336 [S]	Arriba Con Montego Joe	1964	30.00
❑ PRLP-7413 [M]	Wild and Warm	1966	30.00
❑ PRST-7413 [S]	Wild and Warm	1966	30.00
MONTENEGRO, HUGO			
20TH CENTURY FOX			
❑ S-4204	Lady in Cement	1968	25.00

Number	Title	Yr	NM
20TH FOX			
❑ 3018 [M]	The 20th Century Strings, Volume 1	1959	25.00
BAINBRIDGE			
❑ 1002	American Musical Theatre, Volume 1 (1924-1935)	198?	10.00
❑ 1003	American Musical Theatre, Volume 2 (1935-1945)	198?	10.00
❑ 1004	American Musical Theatre, Volume 3 (1946-1952)	198?	10.00
❑ 1005	American Musical Theatre, Volume 4 (1953-1960)	198?	10.00
❑ 1009	Big Band Boogie	198?	10.00
❑ 1021	Camelot	198?	10.00
❑ 1028	Hugo Montenegro Plays the Movies	198?	10.00
GWP			
❑ 2003	The Dawn of Dylan	1971	18.00
MAINSTREAM			
❑ 56101 [M]	Camelot	1967	18.00
❑ S-6101 [S]	Camelot	1967	15.00
RCA CAMDEN			
❑ CAS-2309	Hawaiian Wedding Song	1969	12.00
❑ CAL-729 [M]	In a Sentimental Mood	196?	15.00
❑ CAS-729 [S]	In a Sentimental Mood	196?	15.00
RCA VICTOR			
❑ LSP-4273	Colours of Love	1970	15.00
❑ LPM-3540 [M]	Come Spy with Me	1966	15.00
❑ LSP-3540 [S]	Come Spy with Me	1966	18.00
❑ LSP-4104	Good Vibrations	1969	18.00
❑ LPM-4022 [M]	Hang 'Em High	1968	40.00
❑ LSP-4022 [S]	Hang 'Em High	1968	18.00
❑ APL1-0413	Hugo in Wonderland	1974	15.00
❑ ARD1-0413 [Q]	Hugo in Wonderland	1974	18.00
❑ ARD1-0001 [Q]	Love Theme from "The Godfather	1972	15.00
❑ LSP-4631	Mammy Blue	1971	15.00
❑ LSP-4170	Moog Power	1969	25.00
❑ LPM-3927 [M]	Music from A Fistful of Dollars & For a Few Dollars More & The Good, The Bad and The Ugly	1968	25.00
❑ LSP-3927 [S]	Music from A Fistful of Dollars & For a Few Dollars More & The Good, The Bad and The Ugly	1968	18.00
❑ ANL1-1094	Music from A Fistful of Dollars & For a Few Dollars More & The Good, The Bad and The Ugly	1975	12.00
❑ ARD1-0132 [Q]	Neil's Diamonds	1973	18.00
❑ ARD1-0784 [Q]	Others by Brothers	1974	18.00
❑ LSP-4537	People…One to One	1971	15.00
❑ APL1-1024	Rocket Man	1975	15.00
❑ APD1-1024 [Q]	Rocket Man	1975	25.00
❑ APD1-0025 [Q]	Scenes and Themes	1973	25.00
❑ LSP-4361	The Best of Hugo Montenegro	1970	15.00
❑ AFL1-4361	The Best of Hugo Montenegro	1977	12.00
❑ ANL1-2348	The Neil Diamond Songbook	1977	12.00
❑ LSP-2958 [S]	The Young Beat of Rome	1964	18.00
❑ LPM-2958 [M]	The Young Beat of Rome	1964	15.00
❑ VPS-6036	This Is Hugo Montenegro	1971	18.00
TIME			
❑ 52035 [M]	American Musical Theatre, Volume 1 (1924-1935)	196?	15.00
❑ S-2035 [S]	American Musical Theatre, Volume 1 (1924-1935)	196?	18.00
❑ 52036 [M]	American Musical Theatre, Volume 2 (1935-1945)	196?	15.00
❑ S-2036 [S]	American Musical Theatre, Volume 2 (1935-1945)	196?	18.00
❑ 52037 [M]	American Musical Theatre, Volume 3 (1946-1952)	1961	15.00
❑ S-2037 [S]	American Musical Theatre, Volume 3 (1946-1952)	1961	18.00
❑ 52038 [M]	American Musical Theatre, Volume 4 (1953-1960)	1961	15.00
❑ S-2038 [S]	American Musical Theatre, Volume 4 (1953-1960)	1961	18.00
❑ 52030 [M]	Arriba	196?	18.00
❑ S-2030 [S]	Arriba	196?	25.00
❑ 52020 [M]	Boogie Woogie and Bongos	196?	18.00
❑ S-2020 [S]	Boogie Woogie and Bongos	196?	25.00
❑ 52018 [M]	Cha Chas for Dancing	196?	18.00
❑ S-2018 [S]	Cha Chas for Dancing	196?	25.00
❑ 52044 [M]	Great Songs from Motion Pictures Vol. 1 (1927-1937)	1961	15.00
❑ S-2044 [S]	Great Songs from Motion Pictures Vol. 1 (1927-1937)	1961	18.00
❑ 52045 [M]	Great Songs from Motion Pictures Vol. 2 (1938-1944)	1961	15.00
❑ S-2045 [S]	Great Songs from Motion Pictures Vol. 2 (1938-1944)	1961	18.00
❑ 52046 [M]	Great Songs from Motion Pictures Vol. 3 (1945-1960)	1961	15.00
❑ S-2046 [S]	Great Songs from Motion Pictures Vol. 3 (1945-1960)	1961	18.00
❑ TDM3003 [M]	Italy - Ciao	196?	18.00
❑ TDS3003 [S]	Italy - Ciao	196?	25.00
❑ 52051 [M]	Montenegro in Italy	196?	15.00
❑ S-2051 [S]	Montenegro in Italy	196?	18.00
VIK			
❑ LX-1106 [M]	Ellington Fantasy	1957	30.00
❑ LX-1089 [M]	Loves of My Life	1957	30.00

Number	Title	Yr	NM

MONTEROSE, J.R.

BLUE NOTE
❑ BLP-1536 [M]	J.R. Monterose	1956	1500.00
—*Deep groove" version; Lexington Ave. address on label*			
❑ BLP-1536 [M]	J.R. Monterose	1956	800.00
—*Deep groove" version, W. 63rd St. address on label*			
❑ BLP-1536 [M]	J.R. Monterose	1963	150.00
—*With "New York, USA" address on label*			
❑ BST-81536 [R]	J.R. Monterose	1967	18.00
—*With "A Division of Liberty Records" on label*			
❑ BLP-1536 [M]	J.R. Monterose	2003	30.00
—*200-gram reissue; distributed by Classic Records*			

CADENCE JAZZ
❑ CJ-1013	Bebop Loose and Live	198?	25.00

JARO
❑ JAM-5004 [M]	The Message	1959	800.00
❑ JAS-8004 [S]	The Message	1959	1000.00

PROGRESSIVE
❑ PRO7049	Lush Life	1979	30.00

STUDIO 4
❑ 100 [M]	J.R. Monterose in Action	195?	1500.00

UPTOWN
❑ 27.02	J.R. Monterose in Albany	1980	18.00
❑ 27.06	J.R. Monterose in Duo with Tommy Flanagan….And a Little Pleasure	198?	18.00

XANADU
❑ 126	Straight Ahead	197?	25.00

MONTEZ, CHRIS

A&M
❑ LP-128 [M]	Foolin' Around	1967	18.00
❑ SP-4128 [S]	Foolin' Around	1967	25.00
❑ LP-115 [M]	The More I See You/Call Me	1966	25.00
❑ ST-4115 [S]	The More I See You/Call Me	1966	30.00
❑ LP-120 [M]	Time After Time	1966	18.00
❑ SP-4120 [S]	Time After Time	1966	25.00
❑ LP-157 [M]	Watch What Happens	1967	18.00
❑ SP-4157 [S]	Watch What Happens	1967	25.00

MONOGRAM
❑ M-100 [M]	Let's Dance and Have Some Kinda' Fun!!!	1963	400.00

MONTGOMERY, BUDDY

ABC IMPULSE!
❑ AS-9192	This Rather Than That	1970	25.00

BEAN
❑ 102	Ties	197?	18.00

LANDMARK
❑ LLP-1518	So Why Not?	1989	15.00
❑ LLP-1512	Ties of Love	1987	12.00

MILESTONE
❑ M-9015	Two-Sided Album	1969	25.00

MONTGOMERY, DAVID, AND CECIL LYTLE

KLAVIER
❑ 533	Rags and Blues	197?	15.00

SONIC ARTS
❑ 6	Ragtime Piano for Four Hands	197?	25.00
—*Direct-to-disc recording*			

MONTGOMERY, LITTLE BROTHER

BLUESVILLE
❑ BVLP-1012 [M]	Tasty Blues	1961	80.00
—*Blue label, silver print*			
❑ BVLP-1012 [M]	Tasty Blues	1964	30.00
—*Blue label with trident logo at right*			

RIVERSIDE
❑ RS-9410 [S]	Little Brother Montgomery, Chicago Living Legend	1962	40.00
❑ RLP-410 [M]	Little Brother Montgomery, Chicago Living Legend	1962	30.00

MONTGOMERY, MARIAN

CAPITOL
❑ T1962 [M]	Let There Be Love, Let There Be Swing, Let There Be Marian Montgomery	1963	30.00
❑ ST1962 [S]	Let There Be Love, Let There Be Swing, Let There Be Marian Montgomery	1963	30.00
❑ T2185 [M]	Lovin' Is Livin'	1964	30.00
❑ ST2185 [S]	Lovin' Is Livin'	1964	30.00
❑ T1884 [M]	Marian Montgomery Swings for Winners and Losers	1963	30.00
❑ ST1884 [S]	Marian Montgomery Swings for Winners and Losers	1963	30.00

DECCA
❑ DL4773 [M]	What's New?	1965	25.00
❑ DL74773 [S]	What's New?	1965	30.00

MONTGOMERY, MELBA

CAPITOL
❑ ST-468	Don't Keep Me Lonely Too Long	1970	18.00
❑ ST-328	The Big, Wonderful Country World of Melba Montgomery	1969	18.00
—*This is the title on the cover; the label calls this "The Big, Beautiful Country World of Melba Montgomery*			

ELEKTRA
❑ CM-2	Don't Let the Good Times Fool You	1975	12.00
❑ EKS-75069	Melba Montgomery	1973	15.00
❑ EKS-75079	No Charge	1974	12.00
❑ CM-6	The Greatest Gift of All	1975	12.00

HILLTOP
❑ JS-6031	Miss Country Music	196?	15.00

MUSICOR
❑ MM-2074 [M]	Country Girl	1966	18.00
❑ MS-3074 [S]	Country Girl	1966	25.00
❑ MM-2114 [M]	Don't Keep Me Lonely Too Long	1967	25.00
❑ MS-3114 [S]	Don't Keep Me Lonely Too Long	1967	25.00
❑ MM-2113 [M]	Melba Toast	1967	25.00
❑ MS-3113 [S]	Melba Toast	1967	25.00
❑ MM-2097 [M]	The Hallelujah Road	1966	18.00
❑ MS-3097 [S]	The Hallelujah Road	1966	25.00

STARDAY
❑ SLP-352 [M]	Queen of Country Music	1965	30.00

UNITED ARTISTS
❑ UAL-3341 [M]	America's Number One Country and Western Girl Singer	1964	25.00
❑ UAS-6341 [S]	America's Number One Country and Western Girl Singer	1964	30.00
❑ UAL-3369 [M]	Down Home	1964	25.00
❑ UAS-6369 [S]	Down Home	1964	30.00
❑ UAL-3391 [M]	I Can't Get Used to Being Lonely	1965	25.00
❑ UAS-6391 [S]	I Can't Get Used to Being Lonely	1965	30.00

MONTGOMERY, MONK

CHISA
❑ CS-806	Bass Odyssey	1971	25.00
❑ CS-801	It's Never Too Late	1970	25.00

PHILADELPHIA INT'L.
❑ KZ33153 [B]	Reality	1974	30.00

MONTGOMERY, WES

A&M
❑ LP-2001 [M]	A Day in the Life	1967	25.00
❑ SP-3001 [S]	A Day in the Life	1967	15.00
❑ SP9-3001	A Day in the Life	1983	18.00
—*Audio Master Plus" reissue*			
❑ SP-3006	Down Here on the Ground	1968	18.00
❑ SP9-3006	Down Here on the Ground	1983	18.00
—*Audio Master Plus" reissue*			
❑ SP-4247	Greatest Hits	1970	18.00
❑ SP-3012	Road Song	1968	18.00
❑ SP9-3012	Road Song	1984	18.00
—*Audio Master Plus" reissue*			

ACCORD
❑ SN-7170	The Classic Sound of Wes Montgomery	1981	12.00

BLUE NOTE
❑ BN-LA531-H2	Beginnings	1976	30.00
❑ LWB-531	Beginnings	1981	30.00
—*Reissue of BN-LA531-H2*			

DCC COMPACT CLASSICS
❑ LPZ-2014	Goin' Out of My Head	1996	40.00
—*Audiophile vinyl*			

FANTASY
❑ OJC-034	A Dynamic New Sound	198?	15.00
❑ OJC-261	Boss Guitar	1987	15.00
❑ OJC-106	Full House	198?	15.00
❑ OJC-368	Fusion! Wes Montgomery with Strings	198?	15.00
❑ OJC-489	Guitar on the Go	1991	18.00
❑ OJC-089	Movin' Along	198?	15.00
❑ OJC-144	Portrait of Wes	198?	15.00
❑ OJC-233	So Much Guitar!	198?	15.00
❑ OJC-036	The Incredible Jazz Guitar of Wes Montgomery	198?	15.00

MGM
❑ GAS-120	Wes Montgomery (Golden Archive Series)	1970	18.00

MILESTONE
❑ 9110	Encores	1983	12.00
❑ 47051	Groove Brothers	1979	15.00
❑ 47040	Movin'	197?	15.00
❑ 47030	Pretty Blue	197?	15.00
❑ 47065	The Alternative Wes Montgomery	1982	15.00
❑ 47013	Wes Montgomery and Friends	1973	18.00
❑ 47003	While We're Young	1972	18.00
❑ 47057	Yesterdays	198?	15.00

MOBILE FIDELITY
❑ MFSL-508	Bumpin'	198?	40.00
—*Original Master Recording" at top of cover*			

PACIFIC JAZZ
❑ PJ-10104 [M]	Easy Groove	1966	18.00
❑ ST-20104 [S]	Easy Groove	1966	25.00
❑ PJ-10130 [M]	Kismet	1967	25.00
❑ ST-20130 [S]	Kismet	1967	18.00
❑ PJ-5 [M]	Montgomeryland	1960	30.00
❑ ST-5 [S]	Montgomeryland	1960	40.00
❑ ST-20137	Portrait of Wes Montgomery	1968	18.00

PICCADILLY
❑ 3584	Jazz Guitar	198?	12.00

RIVERSIDE
❑ RLP 12-310 [M]	A Dynamic New Sound	1959	80.00
❑ RLP-459 [M]	Boss Guitar	1963	80.00
❑ RS-9459 [S]	Boss Guitar	1963	30.00
❑ 6111	Boss Guitar	197?	12.00
❑ RLP-434 [M]	Full House	1962	30.00
❑ RS-9434 [S]	Full House	1962	30.00
❑ 6069	Full House	197?	12.00
❑ RLP-472 [M]	Fusion! Wes Montgomery with Strings	1964	25.00
❑ RS-9472 [S]	Fusion! Wes Montgomery with Strings	1964	30.00
❑ 6210	Fusion! Wes Montgomery with Strings	198?	12.00
❑ RLP-494 [M]	Guitar on the Go	1965	18.00
❑ RS-9494 [S]	Guitar on the Go	1965	25.00
❑ 6168	Guitar on the Go	198?	12.00
❑ RM-3002 [M]	In the Wee Small Hours	1967	25.00
—*Reissue of 472*			
❑ RS-3002 [S]	In the Wee Small Hours	1967	18.00
—*Reissue of 9472*			
❑ RS-3036	March 6, 1925-June 15, 1968	1968	18.00
❑ RLP-342 [M]	Movin' Along	1960	30.00
❑ RS-9342 [S]	Movin' Along	1960	30.00
❑ 6199	Movin' Along	198?	12.00
❑ RLP1156 [S]	New Concepts in Jazz Guitar	1959	30.00
❑ RS-3046	Panorama	1969	18.00
❑ RLP-492 [M]	Portrait of Wes	1965	18.00
❑ RS-9492 [S]	Portrait of Wes	1965	25.00
❑ 6202	Portrait of Wes	198?	12.00
❑ RS-3014	'Round Midnight	1968	18.00
—*Reissue of 1156*			
❑ RLP-382 [M]	So Much Guitar!	1961	30.00
❑ RS-9382 [S]	So Much Guitar!	1961	30.00
❑ 6100	So Much Guitar!	197?	12.00
❑ RS-3039	The Best of Wes Montgomery	1968	15.00
❑ 6080	The Dynamic New Jazz Sound of Wes Montgomery	197?	12.00
❑ RLP 12-320 [M]	The Incredible Jazz Guitar of Wes Montgomery	1960	60.00
❑ RLP1169 [S]	The Incredible Jazz Guitar of Wes Montgomery	1960	30.00
❑ 6046	The Incredible Jazz Guitar of Wes Montgomery	197?	12.00
❑ RS-3012	This Is Wes Montgomery	1968	18.00
—*Reissue of 9459*			

VERVE
❑ V-8625 [M]	Bumpin'	1965	18.00
❑ V6-8625 [S]	Bumpin'	1965	25.00
❑ V-8672 [M]	California Dreaming	1967	25.00
❑ V6-8672 [S]	California Dreaming	1967	18.00
❑ V6-8796	Eulogy	1970	18.00
❑ V-8642 [M]	Goin' Out of My Head	1966	18.00
❑ V6-8642 [S]	Goin' Out of My Head	1966	25.00
❑ V6-8804	Just Walkin'	1971	15.00
❑ V-8610 [M]	Movin' Wes	1965	18.00
❑ V6-8610 [S]	Movin' Wes	1965	25.00
❑ V3HB-8839	Return Engagement	1974	18.00
❑ VE-2-2513	Small Group Recording	197?	18.00
❑ V-8653 [M]	Tequila	1966	18.00
❑ V6-8653 [S]	Tequila	1966	25.00
❑ V-8714 [M]	The Best of Wes Montgomery	1967	25.00
❑ V6-8714 [S]	The Best of Wes Montgomery	1967	18.00
❑ V6-8757	The Best of Wes Montgomery, Vol. 2	1968	18.00
❑ V6-8813	The History of Wes Montgomery	1972	18.00
❑ V6-8765	Willow Weep for Me	1969	18.00

MONTGOMERY BROTHERS, THE

FANTASY
❑ OJC-138	Groove Yard	198?	12.00
❑ 3308 [M]	The Montgomery Brothers	1960	50.00
—*Red vinyl*			
❑ 3308 [M]	The Montgomery Brothers	1960	30.00
—*Black vinyl*			
❑ 8052 [S]	The Montgomery Brothers	1960	40.00
—*Blue vinyl*			
❑ 8052 [S]	The Montgomery Brothers	1960	30.00
—*Black vinyl*			
❑ 3323 [M]	The Montgomery Brothers in Canada	1961	50.00
—*Red vinyl*			
❑ 3323 [M]	The Montgomery Brothers in Canada	1961	30.00
—*Black vinyl*			

Number	Title	Yr	NM
❏ 8066 [S]	The Montgomery Brothers in Canada	1961	40.00
—Blue vinyl			
❏ 8066 [S]	The Montgomery Brothers in Canada	1961	30.00
—Black vinyl			
❏ OJC-283	The Montgomery Brothers in Canada	1987	12.00
❏ 3376 [M]	Wes' Best	1967	25.00
❏ 8376 [S]	Wes' Best	1967	18.00
PACIFIC JAZZ			
❏ PJ-17 [M]	Wes, Buddy and Monk Montgomery	1961	30.00
RIVERSIDE			
❏ RLP-362 [M]	Groove Yard	1961	30.00
❏ RS-9362 [S]	Groove Yard	1961	30.00
❏ 6141	Groove Yard	198?	15.00
WORLD PACIFIC			
❏ PJ-1240 [M]	The Montgomery Brothers and Five Others	1957	80.00
❏ WP-1240 [M]	The Montgomery Brothers and Five Others	1958	60.00
—Reissue with new prefix			

MONTROSE, JACK

ATLANTIC

Number	Title	Yr	NM
❏ 1223 [M]	Arranged, Played, Composed by Jack Montrose with Bob Gordon	1956	80.00
—Black label			
❏ 1223 [M]	Arranged, Played, Composed by Jack Montrose with Bob Gordon	1961	30.00
—Multicolor label, white "fan" logo at right			
❏ 1223 [M]	Arranged, Played, Composed by Jack Montrose with Bob Gordon	1964	18.00
—Multicolor label, black "fan" logo at right			
PACIFIC JAZZ			
❏ PJ-1208 [M]	Jack Montrose Sextet	1955	150.00
—Red vinyl			
❏ PJ-1208 [M]	Jack Montrose Sextet	1955	80.00
—Black vinyl			
RCA VICTOR			
❏ LPM-1451 [M]	Blues and Vanilla	1957	50.00
❏ LPM-1572 [M]	The Horns Full	1957	50.00
WORLD PACIFIC			
❏ WP-1208 [M]	Jack Montrose Sextet	1958	50.00

MONTROSE

ENIGMA

Number	Title	Yr	NM
❏ ST-73204	Mean	1987	12.00
❏ D1-73323	Speed of Sound	1988	12.00
WARNER BROS.			
❏ BS2963	Jump On It	1976	12.00
❏ BS2740	Montrose	1974	15.00
❏ BSK3106	Montrose	1978	10.00
—Reissue of 2740			
❏ BS2823	Paper Money	1974	12.00
❏ BS2892	Warner Bros. Presents Montrose!	1975	12.00

MONTY PYTHON

ARISTA

Number	Title	Yr	NM
❏ AL4039 [B]	Matching Tie & Handkerchief	1975	30.00
—Side 2 is "trick tracked," with two different routines depending on where you place the needle at the start			
❏ AL8357	Matching Tie and Handkerchief	198?	10.00
—Reissue; we don't know whether Side 2 maintains the trick groove on this issue			
❏ AL4073	Monty Python Live! At City Center	1976	25.00
❏ AL8353	Monty Python Live! At City Center	198?	10.00
—Reissue			
❏ AB9536	Monty Python's Contractual Obligation Album	1980	25.00
❏ AL8343	Monty Python's Contractual Obligation Album	198?	10.00
—Reissue			
❏ SP-101 [DJ]	Monty Python's Contractual Obligation Sampler	1980	30.00
—One side is censored, the other is uncensored			
❏ AL4050	The Album of the Soundtrack of the Trailer of the Film of "Monty Python and the Holy Grail"	1975	25.00
❏ AL8355	The Album of the Soundtrack of the Trailer of the Film of "Monty Python and the Holy Grail"	198?	10.00
—Reissue			
❏ AB9580	The Monty Python Instant Record Collection	1981	18.00
❏ AL8296	The Monty Python Instant Record Collection	198?	10.00
—Reissue			
BBC			
❏ 22073	Monty Python's Flying Circus	1980	25.00

Number	Title	Yr	NM
—Excerpts from TV shows; pressed by Columbia, possibly for exclusive use by the record club			
BUDDAH			
❏ BDS5656	The Worst of Monty Python	1976	25.00
—Repackage of the two Charisma LPs			
CHARISMA			
❏ CAS1049 [B]	Another Monty Python Record	1972	30.00
❏ CAS1063 [B]	Monty Python's Previous Record	1972	30.00
MCA			
❏ 6121	Monty Python and the Meaning of Life	1983	15.00
PYE			
❏ 12116	Monty Python's Flying Circus	1975	25.00
VIRGIN			
❏ 90865	The Final Rip Off	1988	25.00
WARNER BROS.			
❏ BSK3396	Life of Brian	1979	18.00

MOODY, CLYDE

KING

Number	Title	Yr	NM
❏ 891 [M]	The Best of Clyde Moody	1964	80.00
OLD HOMESTEAD			
❏ 90013	Moody's Blues -- Bluesy Bluegrass	197?	18.00

MOODY, JAMES

ARGO

Number	Title	Yr	NM
❏ LP-695 [M]	Another Bag	1962	30.00
❏ LPS-695 [S]	Another Bag	1962	40.00
❏ LP-740 [M]	Comin' On Strong	1964	30.00
❏ LPS-740 [S]	Comin' On Strong	1964	30.00
❏ LP-603 [M]	Flute 'n the Blues	1956	40.00
—Reissue of Creative 603			
❏ LP-725 [M]	Great Day	1963	30.00
❏ LPS-725 [S]	Great Day	1963	30.00
❏ LP-666 [M]	Hey! It's James Moody	1960	30.00
❏ LPS-666 [S]	Hey! It's James Moody	1960	40.00
❏ LP-648 [M]	James Moody	1959	40.00
❏ LPS-648 [S]	James Moody	1959	30.00
❏ LP-637 [M]	Last Train from Overbrook	1959	40.00
❏ LPS-637 [S]	Last Train from Overbrook	1959	30.00
❏ LP-613 [M]	Moody's Mood for Love	1957	40.00
❏ LP-679 [M]	Moody with Strings	1961	30.00
❏ LPS-679 [S]	Moody with Strings	1961	40.00
BLUE NOTE			
❏ BLP-5006 [10]	James Moody and His Modernists	1952	300.00
❏ BLP-5005 [10]	James Moody with Strings	1952	300.00
CADET			
❏ LP-695 [M]	Another Bag	1966	15.00
❏ LPS-695 [S]	Another Bag	1966	18.00
❏ LP-740 [M]	Comin' On Strong	1966	15.00
❏ LPS-740 [S]	Comin' On Strong	1966	18.00
❏ LP-756 [M]	Cookin' the Blues	1965	25.00
❏ LPS-756 [S]	Cookin' the Blues	1965	30.00
❏ 2CA-60010	Everything About Sax and Flute	1972	25.00
❏ LP-603 [M]	Flute 'n the Blues	1966	18.00
❏ LP-725 [M]	Great Day	1966	15.00
❏ LPS-725 [S]	Great Day	1966	18.00
❏ LP 666 [M]	Hey! It's James Moody	1966	15.00
❏ LPS-666 [S]	Hey! It's James Moody	1966	18.00
❏ LP-648 [M]	James Moody	1966	15.00
❏ LPS-648 [S]	James Moody	1966	18.00
❏ LP-637 [M]	Last Train from Overbrook	1966	15.00
❏ LPS-637 [S]	Last Train from Overbrook	1966	18.00
❏ LP-613 [M]	Moody's Mood for Love	1966	18.00
❏ LP-679 [M]	Moody with Strings	1966	15.00
❏ LPS-679 [S]	Moody with Strings	1966	18.00
CHESS			
❏ CH-91548	Flute 'n' the Blues	198?	12.00
❏ 2ACMJ-403	Moody's Mood	1976	18.00
❏ CH-91522	The Great Day	198?	12.00
CREATIVE			
❏ LP-603 [M]	Flute 'n Blues	1956	150.00
DIAL			
❏ LP-209 [10]	James Moody, His Saxophone and His Band	1950	400.00
EMARCY			
❏ MG-26040 [10]	Moodsville	1954	150.00
❏ MG-26004 [10]	The Moody Story	1954	150.00
❏ MG-36031 [M]	The Moody Story	1955	100.00
FANTASY			
❏ OJC-188	James Moody's Moods	1985	12.00
MILESTONE			
❏ M-9023	Blues and Other Colors	1970	25.00
❏ M-9005	Brass Figures	1968	25.00
MUSE			
❏ MR-5020	Feelin' It Together	1974	15.00
❏ MR-5001	Never Again!	1973	15.00
NOVUS			
❏ 3026-1-N	Moving Forward	1988	12.00
❏ 3004-1-N	Something Special	1986	12.00
❏ 3063-1-N	Sweet and Lovely	1989	15.00

Number	Title	Yr	NM
PAULA			
❏ LPS-4003	Sax and Flute Man	197?	15.00
PAUSA			
❏ 7029	Too Heavy for Words	1979	12.00
PRESTIGE			
❏ PRST-7625	Don't Look Away Now!	1969	18.00
❏ PRLP-7011 [M]	Hi-Fi Party	1955	100.00
❏ PRST-7740	Hi-Fi Party, Volume 2	1970	18.00
❏ 24015	James Moody	197?	18.00
❏ PRLP-198 [10]	James Moody and His Band	1954	150.00
❏ PRLP-110 [10]	James Moody Favorites, No. 1	1951	200.00
❏ PRLP-125 [10]	James Moody Favorites, No. 2	1952	200.00
❏ PRLP-146 [10]	James Moody Favorites, No. 3	1953	200.00
❏ PRLP-7431 [M]	James Moody's Greatest Hits	1967	30.00
❏ PRST-7431 [R]	James Moody's Greatest Hits	1967	18.00
❏ PRLP-7441 [M]	James Moody's Greatest Hits, Volume 2	1967	30.00
❏ PRST-7441 [R]	James Moody's Greatest Hits, Volume 2	1967	18.00
❏ PRLP-7056 [M]	James Moody's Moods	1956	100.00
❏ PRLP-7072 [M]	Moody	1956	100.00
❏ PRLP-157 [10]	Moody in France	1953	150.00
❏ PRLP-192 [10]	Moody's Mood	1954	150.00
❏ PRST-7554	Moody's Moods	1968	18.00
❏ PRLP-7179 [M]	Moody's Workshop	1960	50.00
❏ PRST-7663	Moody's Workshop	1969	18.00
❏ PRLP-7036 [M]	Wail, Moody, Wail	1956	100.00
❏ PRST-7853	Wail Moody Wail, Volume 3	1971	18.00
ROOST			
❏ RST-405 [10]	James Moody in France	1951	250.00
SCEPTER			
❏ SRM-525 [M]	Running the Gamut	1965	25.00
❏ SPS-525 [S]	Running the Gamut	1965	30.00
TRIP			
❏ 5521	The Moody Story (1951-52)	197?	12.00
VANGUARD			
❏ VSD-79404	Beyond	1978	15.00
❏ VSD-79381	Sun Journey	1976	15.00
❏ VSD-79366	Timeless	1975	15.00

MOODY, JAMES/GEORGE WALLINGTON

BLUE NOTE

Number	Title	Yr	NM
❏ B-6503 [M]	The Beginning and End of Bop	1969	30.00

MOODY, PHIL

SOMERSET

Number	Title	Yr	NM
❏ P-10400 [M]	Intimate Jazz	1959	30.00

MOODY BLUES, THE

COMPLEAT

Number	Title	Yr	NM
❏ 672008	Early Blues	1985	18.00
—Reissue of London 1964-66 material			
DERAM			
❏ DE16012 [M]	Days of Future Passed	1968	350.00
❏ DES18012 [S]	Days of Future Passed	1968	25.00
—With large "DERAM" on top half of label			
❏ 820006-1 [S]	Days of Future Passed	1985	10.00
❏ DES18012 [S]	Days of Future Passed	1968	30.00
—With "LONDON" under "DERAM" on top half of label			
❏ DES18017	In Search of the Lost Chord	1968	25.00
—Originals have gatefold covers			
❏ 820168-1	In Search of the Lost Chord	1985	10.00
❏ DES18051 [R]	In the Beginning	1971	25.00
❏ DES18025	On the Threshold of a Dream	1969	25.00
—Originals have gatefold covers and lyric booklet			
❏ 820170-1	On the Threshold of a Dream	1985	10.00
LONDON			
❏ PS690/1	Caught Live + 5	1977	15.00
❏ 820161-1	Caught Live + 5	1985	10.00
❏ LL3428 [M]	Go Now -- The Moody Blues #1	1965	50.00
❏ PS428 [R]	Go Now -- The Moody Blues #1	1965	40.00
❏ PS708 [DJ]	Octave	1978	30.00
—Promo only on blue vinyl			
❏ PS708	Octave	1978	12.00
❏ 820329-1	Octave	1986	10.00
MOBILE FIDELITY			
❏ 1-042	Days of Future Passed	1980	60.00
—Audiophile vinyl			
❏ 1-232	Every Good Boy Deserves Favour	1995	30.00
—Audiophile vinyl			
❏ 1-215	On the Threshold of a Dream	1994	30.00
—Audiophile vinyl			
❏ 1-151	Seventh Sojourn	1984	70.00
—Audiophile vinyl			
❏ 1-253	To Our Children's Children's Children	1996	60.00
—Audiophile vinyl			
NAUTILUS			
❏ NR-21	On the Threshold of a Dream	1981	60.00
—Audiophile vinyl			

Number	Title	Yr	NM
❑ NR-21 [B]	On the Threshold of a Dream	1981	50.00
—Audiophile vinyl; DBX-encoded version			
POLYDOR			
❑ 840 659-1	Greatest Hits (1967-1988)	1989	18.00
❑ 835 756-1	Sur La Mer	1988	15.00
❑ 829 179-1	The Other Side of Life	1986	12.00
THRESHOLD			
❑ THS3	A Question of Balance	1970	18.00
—White label with purple logo; gatefold cover			
❑ THS3	A Question of Balance	197?	12.00
—Blue label; no gatefold			
❑ 820211-1	A Question of Balance	1985	10.00
❑ SMAS-93329	A Question of Balance	1971	25.00
—Capitol Record Club edition			
❑ THS5	Every Good Boy Deserves Favour	1971	18.00
—White label with purple logo; gatefold cover			
❑ THS5	Every Good Boy Deserves Favour	197?	15.00
—Blue label; gatefold cover			
❑ 820160-1	Every Good Boy Deserves Favour	1985	10.00
❑ THS5	Every Good Boy Deserves Favour	197?	12.00
—Blue label; no gatefold			
❑ TR-1-2901	Long Distance Voyager	1981	12.00
❑ 820105-1	Long Distance Voyager	1985	10.00
❑ THS7	Seventh Sojourn	1972	18.00
—White label with purple logo; gatefold cover			
❑ THS7	Seventh Sojourn	197?	15.00
—Blue label; gatefold cover			
❑ 820159-1	Seventh Sojourn	1985	10.00
❑ THS7	Seventh Sojourn	197?	12.00
—Blue label; no gatefold			
❑ THX-100 [DJ]	Special Interview Kit	1971	150.00
—Includes script			
❑ TR-1-2902	The Present	1982	12.00
❑ 810119-1	The Present	1983	10.00
❑ THS12/13	This Is the Moody Blues	1974	18.00
❑ 820007-1	This Is the Moody Blues	1985	10.00
❑ THS1	To Our Children's Children's Children	1969	18.00
—White label with purple logo; gatefold cover			
❑ THS1	To Our Children's Children's Children	197?	12.00
—Blue label; no gatefold			
❑ 820155-1	Voices in the Sky/The Best of the Moody Blues	1985	12.00

MOOG MACHINE, THE

Number	Title	Yr	NM
COLUMBIA			
❑ CS9959	Christmas Becomes Electric	1969	25.00
❑ CS9921	Switched-On Rock	1969	25.00

MOON, KEITH

Number	Title	Yr	NM
TRACK/MCA			
❑ 2136	Two Sides of the Moon	1975	25.00

MOON, THE

Number	Title	Yr	NM
IMPERIAL			
❑ LP-12444	The Moon	1969	40.00
❑ LP-12381	Without Earth	1968	40.00

MOONDOG

Number	Title	Yr	NM
COLUMBIA			
❑ KC30897	Moondog 2	1971	50.00
—With booklet (deduct 20 percent if missing)			
COLUMBIA MASTERWORKS			
❑ MS7335	Moondog	1969	30.00
—Gray label with "360 Sound Stereo" at bottom			
❑ MS7335	Moondog	2001	15.00
—180-gram reissue			
EPIC			
❑ LG1002 [10]	Moondog and His Friends	1954	300.00
FANTASY			
❑ OJC-1741	Moondog	1990	18.00
MOONDOG			
❑ 1	Snaketime Series by Moondog	1956	800.00
—With paper insert; deduct 25 percent if it is missing			
MUSICAL HERITAGE SOCIETY			
❑ MHS3803	Moondog	1978	40.00
PRESTIGE			
❑ PRLP-7042 [M]	Moondog	1956	200.00
—Yellow label with W. 50th St. address			
❑ PRLP-7069 [M]	More Moondog	1957	200.00
—Yellow label with W. 50th St. address			
❑ PRLP-7099 [M]	The Story of Moondog	1957	500.00
—Yellow label with W. 50th St. address. Andy Warhol cover.			

MOONEY, ART

Number	Title	Yr	NM
CORONET			
❑ CXS-138 [S]	Cha Cha Cha with Art Mooney	196?	15.00
❑ CX-138 [M]	Cha Cha Cha with Art Mooney	196?	12.00

Number	Title	Yr	NM
❑ CX-220 [M]	Dance and Dream	196?	15.00
❑ CXS-220 [S]	Dance and Dream	196?	15.00
DECCA			
❑ DL4207 [M]	Songs Everybody Knows	1962	15.00
❑ DL74207 [S]	Songs Everybody Knows	1962	18.00
DIPLOMAT			
❑ DS-2218 [S]	Cha Cha Cha with Art Mooney	196?	15.00
❑ DS-2246 [S]	Sing Along	196?	15.00
HURRAH			
❑ H-1002 [M]	Big Band Dance Time	1962	12.00
❑ HS-1002 [S]	Big Band Dance Time	1962	15.00
KAPP			
❑ KL-1405 [M]	Jump for Joy!	1964	15.00
❑ KS-3405 [S]	Jump for Joy!	1964	18.00
❑ KL-1421 [M]	Sentimental Love Songs of World War II	1965	15.00
❑ KS-3421 [S]	Sentimental Love Songs of World War II	1965	18.00
LION			
❑ L-70062 [M]	Those Happy Banjos	1958	18.00
MGM			
❑ E-3649 [M]	Art Mooney and His Orchestra in Hi-Fi Play for Dancing	1958	25.00
—Reissue of 3628 with new cover and title			
❑ E-3616 [M]	Art Mooney in Hi-Fi Dixieland	1957	25.00
❑ E-3431 [M]	Art Mooney Presents the Happy Minstrels	1956	30.00
❑ E-206 [10]	Banjo Bonanza	1953	30.00
❑ E-3899 [M]	Spectacular Voices with Banjos	1961	15.00
❑ SE-3899 [S]	Spectacular Voices with Banjos	1961	18.00
❑ E-3628 [M]	Sunrise to Sunrise	1958	40.00
—Quickly deleted and reissued as 3649 with a new title			
❑ E-121 [10]	Sunset to Sunrise	1952	30.00
PIROUETTE			
❑ FM-45 [M]	Cha Cha Cha with Art Mooney	196?	12.00
PROMENADE			
❑ 2218 [M]	Cha Cha Cha with Art Mooney	196?	12.00
❑ 2246 [M]	Sing Along	196?	12.00
RCA VICTOR			
❑ LPM-3739 [M]	The Best of Art Mooney	1967	25.00
❑ LSP-3739 [S]	The Best of Art Mooney	1967	15.00
SPIN-O-RAMA			
❑ MK-3079 [M]	Cha Cha Cha with Art Mooney	196?	12.00
❑ S-45 [S]	Cha Cha Cha with Art Mooney	196?	15.00
❑ M-93 [M]	Dancetime	196?	12.00
❑ S-93 [S]	Dancetime	196?	15.00
TIARA			
❑ TM-7545 [M]	Cha Cha Cha with Art Mooney	196?	12.00

MOONEY, JOE

Number	Title	Yr	NM
ATLANTIC			
❑ 1255 [M]	Lush Life	1958	40.00
—Black label			
❑ 1255 [M]	Lush Life	1961	25.00
—Multicolor label, white "fan" logo at right			
COLUMBIA			
❑ CL2186 [M]	The Greatness of Joe Mooney	1964	18.00
❑ CS8986 [S]	The Greatness of Joe Mooney	1964	25.00
❑ CL2345 [M]	The Happiness of Joe Mooney	1965	15.00
❑ CS9145 [S]	The Happiness of Joe Mooney	1965	18.00
DECCA			
❑ DL8468 [M]	On the Rocks	1957	40.00
❑ DL5555 [10]	You Go to My Head	1955	50.00

MOONGLOWS, THE

Number	Title	Yr	NM
CHESS			
❑ LP1430 [M]	Look! It's the Moonglows	1959	500.00
❑ CH-9193	Look! It's the Moonglows	1987	15.00
—Reissue of 1430			
❑ LP1471 [M]	The Best of Bobby Lester & the Moonglows	1962	300.00
—Black label			
❑ LP1471 [M]	The Best of Bobby Lester & the Moonglows	1966	50.00
—Blue, fading to white label			
❑ CH-9111	Their Greatest Sides	1986	15.00
CONSTELLATION			
❑ C-2 [M]	Collectors Showcase -- The Moonglows	1964	100.00
—Light blue lettering			
❑ C-2 [M]	Collectors Showcase -- The Moonglows	1964	50.00
—Dark blue lettering			
LOST-NITE			
❑ LP-23 [10]	The Moonglows	1981	15.00

Number	Title	Yr	NM
RCA VICTOR			
❑ LSP-4722	The Return of the Moonglows	1972	18.00

MOONLIGHTERS, THE

Number	Title	Yr	NM
CENTURY			
❑ 29132	An Evening with the Moonlighters	197?	25.00

MOONRAKERS, THE

Number	Title	Yr	NM
SHAMLEY			
❑ 704	Together	1968	40.00

MOONSHINERS, THE

Number	Title	Yr	NM
VILLAGE GATE			
❑ 2002 [M]	Breakout!	1964	25.00

MOOR, DET

Number	Title	Yr	NM
GALLANT			
❑ GT4001 [M]	Great Jazz from Great TV	1962	40.00

MOORE, ADA

Number	Title	Yr	NM
DEBUT			
❑ DLP-15 [10]	Jazz Workshop	1955	200.00
FANTASY			
❑ OJC-1701	Ada Moore	1985	12.00

MOORE, BOB

Number	Title	Yr	NM
HICKORY			
❑ LP-131 [M]	Viva Bob Moore	1965	18.00
❑ LPS-131 [S]	Viva Bob Moore	1965	25.00
MONUMENT			
❑ MLP-8008 [M]	Mexico	1967	15.00
❑ SLP-18008 [S]	Mexico	1967	18.00
❑ MLP-4005 [M]	Mexico and Other Great Hits!	1961	25.00
❑ SLP-4005 [S]	Mexico and Other Great Hits!	1961	30.00

MOORE, BOBBY, AND THE RHYTHM ACES

Number	Title	Yr	NM
CHECKER			
❑ LP-3000 [M]	Searching for My Love	1966	30.00
❑ LPS-3000 [R]	Searching for My Love	1966	25.00

MOORE, BREW

Number	Title	Yr	NM
FANTASY			
❑ 3264 [M]	Brew Moore	1958	50.00
—Red vinyl			
❑ 3264 [M]	Brew Moore	1958	30.00
—Black vinyl			
❑ OJC-049	Brew Moore	198?	12.00
❑ 6013 [M]	Brew Moore in Europe	1962	100.00
—Red vinyl			
❑ 6013 [M]	Brew Moore in Europe	1962	35.00
—Black vinyl			
❑ 86013 [S]	Brew Moore in Europe	1962	80.00
—Blue vinyl			
❑ 86013 [S]	Brew Moore in Europe	1962	25.00
—Black vinyl			
❑ 3222 [M]	The Brew Moore Quintet	1956	80.00
—Red vinyl			
❑ 3222 [M]	The Brew Moore Quintet	1956	40.00
—Black vinyl			
❑ OJC-100	The Brew Moore Quintet	198?	12.00
SAVOY			
❑ MG-9028 [10]	Tenor Sax	1953	150.00
STEEPLECHASE			
❑ SCS-6016	If I Had You	198?	15.00
❑ SCS-6019	I Should Care	198?	15.00
STORYVILLE			
❑ 4019	No More Brew	198?	12.00

MOORE, CHARLIE, AND BILL NAPIER

Number	Title	Yr	NM
KING			
❑ 1021 [M]	Brand New Country & Western Songs	1967	30.00
❑ KS-1021 [S]	Brand New Country & Western Songs	1967	25.00
❑ 992 [M]	City Folks Back on the Farm	1966	30.00
❑ KS-992 [S]	City Folks Back on the Farm	1966	40.00
❑ 917 [M]	Country Hymnal	1964	40.00
❑ 982 [M]	Country Music Goes to Viet Nam	1966	30.00
❑ KS-982 [S]	Country Music Goes to Viet Nam	1966	40.00
❑ 828 [M]	Folk 'n' Hill	1963	50.00
❑ 1017 [M]	Gospel and Sacred Songs	1967	30.00
❑ KS-1017 [S]	Gospel and Sacred Songs	1967	25.00
❑ 936 [M]	Songs of the Lonesome Truck Drivers	1965	30.00
❑ KS-936 [S]	Songs of the Lonesome Truck Drivers	1965	40.00
❑ 1014 [M]	Spectacular Instrumentals	1967	30.00
❑ KS-1014 [S]	Spectacular Instrumentals	1967	25.00
❑ 880 [M]	The Best of Charlie Moore and Bill Napier	1964	50.00

Number	Title	Yr	NM
MOORE, DANNY			
EVEREST			
❏ LPBR-5211 [M]	Folk Songs from Here and There	1963	25.00
❏ SDBR-1211 [S]	Folk Songs from Here and There	1963	30.00
MOORE, DEBBY			
TOP RANK			
❏ RM-12-301 [M]	My Kind of Blues	1959	40.00
MOORE, DOROTHY			
MALACO			
❏ 6359	Definitely Dorothy	1979	15.00
❏ 6353	Dorothy Moore	1977	18.00
❏ 7455	Feel the Love	1990	15.00
❏ 6351	Misty Blue	1976	15.00
❏ 6356	Once More with Feeling	1978	15.00
❏ 7363	Talk to Me	1980	18.00
REJOICE/A&M			
❏ WR8326	Givin' It Straight to You	1986	18.00
VOLT			
❏ 3401	Time Out for Me	1988	15.00
❏ 3405	Winner	1989	15.00
MOORE, DUDLEY			
ATLANTIC			
❏ 1403 [M]	Beyond the Fringe and All That Jazz	1963	35.00
❏ SD1403 [S]	Beyond the Fringe and All That Jazz	1963	30.00
LONDON			
❏ PS558	Dudley Moore Trio	1969	30.00
MOORE, GATEMOUTH			
AUDIO FIDELITY			
❏ AFLP-1921 [M]	Revival!	196?	60.00
❏ AFSD-5921 [S]	Revival!	196?	80.00
BLUESWAY			
❏ BLS6074	After 21 Years	1973	25.00
KING			
❏ 684 [M]	Gatemouth Moore Sings Blues	1960	5000.00
MOORE, GLEN, AND DAVID FRIESEN			
VANGUARD			
❏ VSD-79383	Glen Moore and David Friesen In Concert	1976	15.00
MOORE, JACKIE			
ATLANTIC			
❏ SD7285	Sweet Charlie Babe	1973	18.00
COLUMBIA			
❏ JC35991	On My Way	1979	12.00
❏ JC36455	With Your Love	1980	12.00
KAYVETTE			
❏ 801	Make Me Feel Like a Woman	1975	18.00
MOORE, JERRY			
ESP-DISK'			
❏ 1061	Life Is a Constant Journey Home	1968	25.00
MOORE, LATTIE			
AUDIO LAB			
❏ AL-1573 [M]	Country Side	1962	150.00
❏ AL-1555 [M]	The Best of Lattie Moore	1960	200.00
DERBYTOWN			
❏ 102 [M]	Lattie Moore	196?	40.00
MOORE, MARILYN			
BETHLEHEM			
❏ BCP-73 [M]	Moody	1957	80.00
MOORE, MELBA			
ACCORD			
❏ SN-7129	Sweet Melba	1981	12.00
BUDDAH			
❏ BDS-5720	Dancin' with Melba	1979	12.00
❏ BDS-5677	Melba	1976	12.00
❏ BDS-5629	Peach Melba	1975	12.00
❏ BDS-5695	Portrait of Melba Moore	1977	12.00
❏ BDS-5657	This Is It	1976	12.00
CAPITOL			
❏ ST-12471	A Lot of Love	1986	12.00
❏ ST-12305	Never Say Never	1983	12.00
❏ ST-12382	Read My Lips	1985	12.00
❏ C1-92355	Soul Exposed	1990	15.00
❏ ST-12243	The Other Side of the Rainbow	1982	12.00
EMI AMERICA			
❏ ST-17060	What a Woman Needs	1981	12.00
EPIC			
❏ JE36128	Burn	1979	12.00

Number	Title	Yr	NM
❏ JE36412	Closer	1980	12.00
❏ JE35507	Melba	1978	12.00
MERCURY			
❏ SR-61287	I Got Love	1970	18.00
❏ SRM-1-622	Live!	1972	15.00
❏ SR-61255	Living to Give	1970	18.00
❏ SR-61321	Look What You're Doing to the Man	1971	18.00
MOORE, OSCAR			
CHARLIE PARKER			
❏ PLP-830 [M]	The Fabulous Oscar Moore Guitar	1962	30.00
❏ PLP-830S [S]	The Fabulous Oscar Moore Guitar	1962	30.00
SKYLARK			
❏ SKLP-19 [M]	Oscar Moore Trio	1954	100.00
TAMPA			
❏ TP-22 [M] —Colored vinyl	Galivantin' Guitar	1957	80.00
❏ TP-22 [M] —Black vinyl	Galivantin' Guitar	1958	50.00
❏ TP-16 [M] —Colored vinyl	Oscar Moore Trio	1957	80.00
❏ TP-16 [M] —Black vinyl	Oscar Moore Trio	1958	50.00
MOORE, PHIL, JR.			
ATLANTIC			
❏ SD1530	Right On	1969	18.00
MOORE, PHIL			
CLEF			
❏ MGC-635 [M]	Music for Moderns	1954	100.00
STRAND			
❏ SL-1004 [M]	Polynesian Paradise	1959	40.00
❏ SLS-1004 [S]	Polynesian Paradise	1959	50.00
MOORE, RALPH			
LANDMARK			
❏ LLP-1526	Furthermore	1990	15.00
❏ LLP-1520	Images	1988	12.00
MOORE, REGGIE			
MAINSTREAM			
❏ MRL-380	Furioso	1972	25.00
❏ MRL-341	Wishbone	1971	25.00
MOORE, SCOTTY			
EPIC			
❏ LN24103 [M]	The Guitar That Changed the World	1964	65.00
❏ BN26103 [S]	The Guitar That Changed the World	1964	75.00
GUINNESS			
❏ GNS-36038 [B]	What's Left	1977	25.00
MOORE, SHELLEY			
ARGO			
❏ LP-4016 [M]	For the First Time	1962	30.00
❏ LPS-4016 [S]	For the First Time	1962	40.00
MOORE, THURSTON			
DGC			
❏ 24810	Psychic Hearts	1995	16.00
MOORE, TIM			
ABC DUNHILL			
❏ DSX-50132	Of Woodstock and Other Places	1973	15.00
A SMALL RECORD COMPANY			
❏ SRS-10001	Tim Moore	1974	30.00
ASYLUM			
❏ 7E-1042	Behind the Eyes	1975	12.00
❏ 6E-179	High Contrast	1979	12.00
❏ 7E-1019	Tim Moore	1974	12.00
❏ 7E-1088	White Shadows	1977	12.00
ELEKTRA			
❏ 60463	Flash Forward	1985	12.00
MOORE, WILD BILL			
JAZZLAND			
❏ JLP-54 [M]	Bottom Groove	1961	30.00
❏ JLP-954 [S]	Bottom Groove	1961	40.00
❏ JLP-38 [M]	Wild Bill's Beat	1961	30.00
❏ JLP-938 [S]	Wild Bill's Beat	1961	40.00
MOORMAN, DENNIS			
INDIA NAVIGATION			
❏ IN-1055	Circles of Destiny	198?	15.00
MORAN, GAYLE			
WARNER BROS.			
❏ BSK3339	I Loved You Then, I Love You Now	1980	12.00

Number	Title	Yr	NM
MORAN, PAT			
AUDIO FIDELITY			
❏ AFLP-1875 [M]	This Is Pat Moran	1958	40.00
❏ AFSD-5875 [S]	This Is Pat Moran	1958	50.00
BETHLEHEM			
❏ BCP-6007 [M]	Pat Moran Quartet	1956	50.00
❏ BCP-6018 [M]	While at Birdland	1957	50.00
MORATH, MAX			
EPIC			
❏ LN24066 [M]	Celebrated Maestro	1963	18.00
❏ BN26066 [S]	Celebrated Maestro	1963	25.00
JAZZOLOGY			
❏ JCE-52 [M]	All Play Together	1969	15.00
RCA VICTOR			
❏ LSO-1159	Max Morath at the Turn of the Century	1969	30.00
SAVOY			
❏ MG-12091 [M]	Introducing Max Morath	196?	25.00
VANGUARD			
❏ VSD-79378	Jonah Man and Others of the Bert Williams Era	1976	12.00
❏ VSD-79391	Living a Ragtime Life: A One-Man Show	1977	15.00
❏ VSD-79418	Max Morath in Jazz Country	1979	12.00
❏ VSD-83/84	Max Morath Plays Ragtime	197?	18.00
❏ VSD-79402	Ragtime Women	1977	12.00
❏ VRS-39/40	The Best of Scott Joplin and Other Rag Classics	1972	18.00
❏ VSD-73106	The Best of Scott Joplin and Other Rag Classics	198?	15.00
❏ VSD-79429	The Great American Piano Bench	1980	12.00
❏ VSD-310	The World of Scott Joplin	197?	15.00
❏ VSD-351	The World of Scott Joplin, Vol. 2	197?	15.00
MOREL, TERRY			
BETHLEHEM			
❏ BCP-47 [M]	Songs of a Woman in Love	1956	150.00
MORELLO, JOE, AND GARY BURTON			
OVATION			
❏ OV-1714	Percussive Jazz	197?	15.00
MORELLO, JOE			
INTRO			
❏ 608 [M]	Joe Morello Sextet	1957	150.00
OVATION			
❏ OV-1197	Joe Morello	197?	18.00
RCA VICTOR			
❏ LPM-2486 [M]	It's About Time	1961	30.00
❏ LSP-2486 [S]	It's About Time	1961	30.00
MORENO, RITA			
STRAND			
❏ L-1039 [M]	Rita Moreno Sings	1962	30.00
❏ 3L-1030 [S]	Rita Moreno Sings	1962	40.00
WYNNE			
❏ WLP-103 [M]	Warm, Wild, Wonderful	1964	25.00
❏ WLP-703 [S]	Warm, Wild, Wonderful	1964	30.00
MOREY STORE BAND, THE			
SOUND MACHINE			
❏ 49007	Cry for the Dreamer	197?	100.00
MORGAN, DICK			
RIVERSIDE			
❏ RLP 12-329 [M]	Dick Morgan at the Showboat	1960	40.00
❏ RLP-1183 [S]	Dick Morgan at the Showboat	1960	40.00
❏ RLP-347 [M]	See What I Mean?	1960	30.00
❏ RS-9347 [S]	See What I Mean?	1960	40.00
❏ RLP-383 [M]	Settin' In	1961	30.00
❏ RS-9383 [S]	Settin' In	1961	40.00
MORGAN, FRANK			
ANTILLES			
❏ 91320	Mood Indigo	1989	15.00
CONTEMPORARY			
❏ C-14026	Bebop Lives!	1987	12.00
❏ C-14045	Double Image	1988	12.00
❏ C-14013	Easy Living	198?	12.00
❏ C-14021	Lament	1986	12.00
❏ C-14039	Major Changes	1988	12.00
❏ C-14052	Reflections	1989	15.00
❏ C-14045	Yardbird Suite	1988	12.00
GENE NORMAN			
❏ GNP-12 [M] —Red vinyl	Frank Morgan	1955	120.00
GNP CRESCENDO			
❏ GNPS-9014	Frank Morgan with Conte Candoli	197?	12.00
SAVOY JAZZ			
❏ SJL-1201	Bird Calls	198?	12.00

WHIPPET

Number	Title	Yr	NM
❑ WLP-704 [M]	Frank Morgan	1956	100.00

MORGAN, GEORGE

4 STAR

Number	Title	Yr	NM
❑ 002	From This Moment On	1975	15.00

COLUMBIA

Number	Title	Yr	NM
❑ CL1631 [M]	Golden Memories	1961	30.00
❑ CS8431 [S]	Golden Memories	1961	30.00
❑ CL1044 [M]	Morgan, By George	1957	50.00
❑ CL2333 [M]	Red Roses for a Blue Lady	1965	25.00
❑ CS9133 [S]	Red Roses for a Blue Lady	1965	30.00
❑ PC33894	Remembering George Morgan	1975	15.00
❑ CL2111 [M]	Tender Lovin' Care	1964	25.00
❑ CS8911 [S]	Tender Lovin' Care	1964	30.00

MCA

Number	Title	Yr	NM
❑ 461	Candy Mountain Melody	1974	15.00
❑ 422	Red Rose from the Blue Side of Town/Somewhere Around Midnight	1974	15.00

STARDAY

Number	Title	Yr	NM
❑ SLP-417	Barbara	1969	25.00
❑ SLP-400	Candy Kisses	1967	30.00
❑ SLP-410	Country Hits by Candelight	1967	30.00
❑ SLP-413	Steal Away	1968	25.00

STOP

Number	Title	Yr	NM
❑ 10009	George Morgan Sings Like a Bird	1969	18.00

MORGAN, JANE

ABC

Number	Title	Yr	NM
❑ S-638	A Jane Morgan Happening	1968	15.00

COLPIX

Number	Title	Yr	NM
❑ CP497 [M]	The Jane Morgan Album	1966	18.00
❑ SCP497 [S]	The Jane Morgan Album	1966	25.00
❑ CP469 [M]	The Last Time I Saw Paris	1964	25.00
❑ SCP469 [S]	The Last Time I Saw Paris	1964	30.00

EPIC

Number	Title	Yr	NM
❑ LN24211 [M]	Fresh Flavor	1966	15.00
❑ BN26211 [S]	Fresh Flavor	1966	18.00
❑ LN24166 [M]	In My Style	1965	15.00
❑ BN26166 [S]	In My Style	1965	18.00
❑ LN24247 [M]	Kiss Tomorrow Goodbye	1967	18.00
❑ BN26247 [S]	Kiss Tomorrow Goodbye	1967	15.00
❑ LN24190 [M]	Today's Hits…Tomorrow's Golden Favorites	1966	15.00
❑ BN26190 [S]	Today's Hits…Tomorrow's Golden Favorites	1966	18.00

HARMONY

Number	Title	Yr	NM
❑ HS11398	Sounds of Silence	1970	12.00

KAPP

Number	Title	Yr	NM
❑ KL-1080 [M]	All the Way	1958	30.00
❑ KL-1191 [M]	Ballads of Lady Jane	1960	18.00
❑ KS-3191 [S]	Ballads of Lady Jane	1960	25.00
❑ KL-1247 [M]	Big Hits from Broadway	1961	18.00
❑ KS-3247 [S]	Big Hits from Broadway	1961	25.00
❑ KS-3001 [S]	Broadway in Stereo	1959	30.00
❑ KL-1066 [M]	Fascination	1957	30.00
❑ KS-3017 [S]	Fascination	1959	30.00
❑ KS-3066 [S]	Fascination	1962	25.00
❑ UXL-5006 [M]	Great Songs from the Great Shows of the Century	195?	40.00
❑ KL-1129 [M]	Jane in Spain	1959	30.00
❑ KS-3014 [S]	Jane in Spain	1959	30.00
❑ KL-1023 [M]	Jane Morgan	1956	30.00
❑ KL-1093 [M]	Jane Morgan	1958	30.00
❑ KL-1268 [M]	Jane Morgan at the Cocoanut Grove	1962	18.00
❑ KS-3268 [S]	Jane Morgan at the Cocoanut Grove	1962	25.00
❑ KL-1329 [M]	Jane Morgan's Greatest Hits	1963	15.00
❑ KS-3329 [S]	Jane Morgan's Greatest Hits	1963	18.00
❑ KL-1170 [M]	Jane Morgan Time	1959	25.00
❑ KS-3054 [S]	Jane Morgan Time	1959	30.00
❑ KL-1250 [M]	Love Makes the World Go 'Round	1961	18.00
❑ KS-3250 [S]	Love Makes the World Go 'Round	1961	25.00
❑ KL-1275 [M]	More Golden Hits	1962	18.00
❑ KS-3275 [S]	More Golden Hits	1962	25.00
❑ KJM-1 [DJ]	Radio Station Sampler	196?	30.00
—Promo only, gatefold cover			
❑ KL-1239 [M]	Second Time Around	1961	18.00
❑ KS-3239 [S]	Second Time Around	1961	25.00
❑ KL-1089 [M]	Something Old, New, Borrowed, Blue	1958	30.00
❑ KL-1089S [S]	Something Old, New, Borrowed, Blue	1958	40.00
❑ KL-1105 [M]	The Day the Rains Came	1958	30.00
❑ KL-1105S [S]	The Day the Rains Came	1958	40.00
❑ KL-1246 [M]	The Great Golden Hits	1961	18.00
❑ KS-3246 [S]	The Great Golden Hits	1961	25.00
❑ KL-1296 [M]	What Now My Love	1962	18.00
❑ KS-3296 [S]	What Now My Love	1962	25.00

MCA

Number	Title	Yr	NM
❑ 537	Jane Morgan's Greatest Hits	197?	12.00

RCA VICTOR

Number	Title	Yr	NM
❑ LSP-4322	Jane Morgan in Nashville	1970	15.00
❑ LSP-4171	Traces of Love	1969	15.00

MORGAN, JAYE P.

ALLEGRO ELITE

Number	Title	Yr	NM
❑ 4111 [M]	Jaye P. Morgan Sings	195?	15.00

BEVERLY HILLS

Number	Title	Yr	NM
❑ 24	What Are You Doing the Rest of Your Life	1970	30.00

MAYFAIR

Number	Title	Yr	NM
❑ 9739 [M]	Life Is Just a Bowl of Cherries	195?	18.00

MGM

Number	Title	Yr	NM
❑ E-3867 [M]	Down South	1960	30.00
❑ SE-3867 [S]	Down South	1960	30.00
❑ E-3774 [M]	Slow and Easy	1959	30.00
❑ SE-3774 [S]	Slow and Easy	1959	30.00
❑ E-3940 [M]	That Country Sound	1961	30.00
❑ SE-3940 [S]	That Country Sound	1961	30.00
❑ E-3830 [M]	Up North	1960	30.00
❑ SE-3830 [S]	Up North	1960	30.00

RCA VICTOR

Number	Title	Yr	NM
❑ LPM-1155 [M]	Jaye P. Morgan	1955	50.00
❑ LPM-1682 [M]	Just You, Just Me	1958	40.00

RONDO-LETTE

Number	Title	Yr	NM
❑ A-13 [M]	Jaye P. Morgan Sings	1958	30.00

ROYALE

Number	Title	Yr	NM
❑ 18147 [10]	Jaye P. Morgan and Orchestra	195?	25.00

TOPS

Number	Title	Yr	NM
❑ L-1739 [M]	Life Is Just a Bowl of Cherries	195?	18.00

MORGAN, LEE

BLUE NOTE

Number	Title	Yr	NM
❑ BLP-1590 [M]	Candy	1958	2000.00
—Deep groove" version; W. 63rd St. address on label			
❑ BLP-1590 [M]	Candy	1958	250.00
—Regular edition, W. 63rd St. address on label			
❑ BST-1590 [S]	Candy	1959	1000.00
—Deep groove" version; W. 63rd St. address on label			
❑ BST-1590 [S]	Candy	1959	200.00
—Regular edition, W. 63rd St. address on label			
❑ BLP-1590 [M]	Candy	1963	50.00
—New York, USA" address on label			
❑ BST-1590 [S]	Candy	1963	40.00
—New York, USA" address on label			
❑ BST-84289	Caramba!	1969	80.00
—A Division of Liberty Records" on label			
❑ BST-84312	Charisma	1969	50.00
—A Division of Liberty Records" on label			
❑ BLP-1575 [M]	City Lights	1958	600.00
—Deep groove" version; W. 63rd St. address on label			
❑ BLP-1575 [M]	City Lights	1958	200.00
—Regular edition, W. 63rd St. address on label			
❑ BST-1575 [S]	City Lights	1959	800.00
—Deep groove" version; W. 63rd St. address on label			
❑ BST-1575 [S]	City Lights	1959	150.00
—Regular edition, W. 63rd St. address on label			
❑ BLP-1575 [M]	City Lights	1963	50.00
—New York, USA" address on label			
❑ BST-1575 [S]	City Lights	1963	30.00
—New York, USA" address on label			
❑ BLP-4222 [M]	Cornbread	1967	80.00
—New York, USA" on label			
❑ BST-84222 [S]	Cornbread	1967	80.00
—New York, USA" address on label			
❑ BST-84222 [S]	Cornbread	1968	30.00
—A Division of Liberty Records" on label			
❑ BLP-4243 [M]	Delightfulee Morgan	1967	120.00
❑ BST-84243 [S]	Delightfulee Morgan	1967	60.00
—New York, USA" address on label			
❑ BST-84243 [S]	Delightfulee Morgan	1968	30.00
—A Division of Liberty Records" on label			
❑ BST-84243	Delightfulee Morgan	198?	15.00
—The Finest in Jazz Since 1939" reissue			
❑ LT-1091	Infinity	1981	40.00
❑ BST-84901	Lee Morgan	1972	30.00
—A Division of Unted Artists" on blue and white labels			
❑ BLP-1541 [M]	Lee Morgan, Volume 2	1957	1000.00
—Deep groove" version; Lexington Ave. address on label			
❑ BLP-1541 [M]	Lee Morgan, Volume 2	1957	700.00
—Deep groove" edition, W. 63rd St. address on label			
❑ BLP-1541 [M]	Lee Morgan, Volume 2	1963	50.00
—New York, USA" address on label			
❑ BLP-1557 [M]	Lee Morgan, Volume 3	1957	900.00
—Deep groove" version; W. 63rd St. address on label			
❑ BLP-1557 [M]	Lee Morgan, Volume 3	1957	300.00
—Regular edition, W. 63rd St. address on label			
❑ BLP-1557 [M]	Lee Morgan, Volume 3	1963	50.00
—New York, USA" address on label			
❑ BST-89906	Lee Morgan at the Lighthouse	1970	50.00
❑ BLP-1538 [M]	Lee Morgan Indeed!	1957	2500.00
—Deep groove" version; Lexington Ave. address on label			
❑ BLP-1538 [M]	Lee Morgan Indeed!	1957	1000.00
—Deep groove" edition, W. 63rd St. address on label			
❑ BLP-1538 [M]	Lee Morgan Indeed!	1963	50.00
—New York, USA" address on label			
❑ BLP-1538 [M]	Lee Morgan Indeed!	200?	30.00
—200-gram edition; distributed by Classic Records			
❑ BLP-4034 [M]	Lee-Way	1960	500.00
—Deep groove" version; W. 63rd St. address on label			
❑ BLP-4034 [M]	Lee-Way	1960	300.00
—Regular edition, W. 63rd St. address on label			
❑ BST-84034 [S]	Lee-Way	1960	150.00
—Regular edition, W. 63rd St. address on label			
❑ BLP-4034 [M]	Lee-Way	1963	50.00
—New York, USA" address on label			
❑ BST-84034 [S]	Lee-Way	1963	40.00
—New York, USA" address on label			
❑ BST-84034 [S]	Lee-Way	1968	30.00
—A Division of Liberty Records" on label			
❑ B1-32089	Lee-Way	1995	25.00
❑ BN-LA224-G	Memorial Album	1974	25.00
❑ BN-LA582-J2	Procrastinator	1977	30.00
❑ BLP-4169 [M]	Search for the New Land	1965	120.00
—New York, USA" on label			
❑ BST-84169 [S]	Search for the New Land	1965	80.00
—New York, USA" address on label			
❑ BST-84169 [S]	Search for the New Land	1968	30.00
—A Division of Liberty Records" on label			
❑ LT-987	Sonic Boom	1979	30.00
❑ LT-1031	Taru	1980	40.00
❑ B1-91138	The Best of Lee Morgan	1988	18.00
❑ BLP-1578 [M]	The Cooker	1958	400.00
—Deep groove" version; W. 63rd St. address on label			
❑ BLP-1578 [M]	The Cooker	1958	200.00
—Regular edition, W. 63rd St. address on label			
❑ BST-1578 [S]	The Cooker	1959	300.00
—Deep groove" version; W. 63rd St. address on label			
❑ BST-1578 [S]	The Cooker	1959	200.00
—Regular edition, W. 63rd St. address on label			
❑ BLP-1578 [M]	The Cooker	1963	50.00
—New York, USA" address on label			
❑ BST-1578 [S]	The Cooker	1963	40.00
—New York, USA" address on label			
❑ BST-81578 [S]	The Cooker	1968	30.00
—A Division of Liberty Records" on label			
❑ BLP-4212 [M]	The Gigolo	1966	100.00
—New York, USA" on label			
❑ BST-84212 [S]	The Gigolo	1966	80.00
—New York, USA" address on label			
❑ BST-84212 [S]	The Gigolo	1968	30.00
—A Division of Liberty Records" on label			
❑ BST-84212	The Gigolo	1986	15.00
—The Finest in Jazz Since 1939" reissue			
❑ B1-33579	The Procrastinator	1995	25.00
❑ BST-84426	The Rajah	1984	50.00
❑ BLP-4199 [M]	The Rumproller	1966	100.00
—New York, USA" on label			
❑ BST-84199 [S]	The Rumproller	1966	80.00
—New York, USA" address on label			
❑ BST-84199 [S]	The Rumproller	1968	30.00
—A Division of Liberty Records" on label			
❑ BLP-4157 [M]	The Sidewinder	1964	100.00
—New York, USA" on label			
❑ BST-84157 [S]	The Sidewinder	1964	80.00
—New York, USA" address on label			
❑ BST-84157 [S]	The Sidewinder	1968	30.00
—A Division of Liberty Records" on label			
❑ LN-10075	The Sidewinder	1981	18.00
—Budget-line reissue			
❑ BST-84157	The Sidewinder	1985	15.00
—The Finest in Jazz Since 1939" reissue			
❑ B1-46137	The Sidewinder	1997	25.00
❑ BST-84335	The Sixth Sense	1969	60.00
—A Division of Liberty Records" on label			
❑ LT-1058	Tom Cat	1980	40.00

FANTASY

Number	Title	Yr	NM
❑ OJC-310	Take Twelve	198?	15.00

GNP CRESCENDO

Number	Title	Yr	NM
❑ GNP-2079	Lee Morgan	1973	25.00

JAZZLAND

Number	Title	Yr	NM
❑ JLP-80 [M]	Take Twelve	1962	50.00
❑ JLP-980 [S]	Take Twelve	1962	60.00

MOSAIC

Number	Title	Yr	NM
❑ MQ6-162	The Complete Blue Note Lee Morgan Fifties Sessions	1995	300.00

PRESTIGE

Number	Title	Yr	NM
❑ MPP-2510	Take Twelve	198?	15.00

SAVOY

Number	Title	Yr	NM
❑ MG-12091 [M]	Introducing Lee Morgan	1956	400.00

SUNSET

Number	Title	Yr	NM
❑ SUS-5269	All the Way	1969	18.00

TRADITION

Number	Title	Yr	NM
❑ 2079	The Genius of Lee Morgan	1969	25.00

TRIP

Number	Title	Yr	NM
❑ 5037	A Date with Lee	1974	18.00
❑ 5041	Live Sessions	1975	30.00
❑ 5029	One of a Kind	1974	18.00
❑ 5020	Speedball	1974	18.00
❑ 5003	Two Sides of Lee Morgan	1974	30.00

VEE JAY

Number	Title	Yr	NM
❑ LP-3015 [M]	Expoobident	1960	80.00
❑ SR-3015 [S]	Expoobident	1960	120.00
❑ LP-3007 [M]	Here's Lee Morgan	1960	150.00
❑ SR-3007 [S]	Here's Lee Morgan	1960	80.00
❑ VJS-3007	Here's Lee Morgan	1986	18.00
—Reissue on reactivated label			
❑ E-4000	Lee Morgan 1938-1972	198?	25.00
❑ VJ-2508 [M]	Lee Morgan Quintet	1965	60.00
❑ VJS-2508 [S]	Lee Morgan Quintet	1965	80.00

MORGAN, LORRIE

RCA

Number	Title	Yr	NM
❑ 9594-1-R	Leave the Light On	1989	15.00
❑ R183848	Something in Red	1991	25.00
—Only available on vinyl through BMG Direct Marketing			

MORGAN, RUSS

CAPITOL

Number	Title	Yr	NM
❑ T1703 [M]	Medleys in the Morgan Manner	1962	15.00
❑ ST1703 [S]	Medleys in the Morgan Manner	1962	18.00
❑ T2158 [M]	Music in the Country Manner	1964	15.00
❑ ST2158 [S]	Music in the Country Manner	1964	18.00

CIRCLE

Number	Title	Yr	NM
❑ CLP-87	Music in the Morgan Manner (1938)	198?	12.00
❑ C-9	Russ Morgan and His Orchestra 1936	198?	12.00

DECCA

Number	Title	Yr	NM
❑ DL8423 [M]	A Lovely Way to Spend an Evening (Songs of Jimmy McHugh)	1957	25.00
—Black label, silver print			
❑ DL8423 [M]	A Lovely Way to Spend an Evening (Songs of Jimmy McHugh)	196?	15.00
—Black label with color bars			
❑ DL8581 [M]	Cheerful Little Earful (Songs of Harry Warren)	195?	25.00
—Black label, silver print			
❑ DL8581 [M]	Cheerful Little Earful (Songs of Harry Warren)	196?	15.00
—Black label with color bars			
❑ DL5278 [10]	College Marching Songs	195?	30.00
❑ DL8332 [M]	Does Your Heart Beat for Me	1956	25.00
—Black label, silver print			
❑ DL8332 [M]	Does Your Heart Beat for Me	196?	15.00
—Black label with color bars			
❑ DL4503 [M]	Does Your Heart Beat for Me	1964	15.00
❑ DL74503 [S]	Does Your Heart Beat for Me	1964	18.00
❑ DL8337 [M]	Everybody Dance	1956	25.00
—Black label, silver print			
❑ DL8337 [M]	Everybody Dance	196?	15.00
—Black label with color bars			
❑ DL5406 [10]	Everybody Dance to the Music of Russ Morgan	195?	30.00
❑ DL8746 [M]	Kitten on the Keys	195?	25.00
—Black label, silver print			
❑ DL8746 [M]	Kitten on the Keys	196?	15.00
—Black label with color bars			
❑ DL5324 [10]	Morgan-Airs	1951	30.00
❑ DL5098 [10]	Music in the Morgan Manner	1950	30.00
❑ DL8828 [M]	Songs Everybody Knows	1958	25.00
—Black label, silver print			
❑ DL8828 [M]	Songs Everybody Knows	196?	15.00
—Black label with color bars			
❑ DL78828 [S]	Songs Everybody Knows	1958	30.00
—Black label, silver print			
❑ DL78828 [S]	Songs Everybody Knows	196?	18.00
—Black label with color bars			
❑ DL8336 [M]	Tap Dancing for Pleasure	1956	25.00
—Black label, silver print			
❑ DL8336 [M]	Tap Dancing for Pleasure	196?	15.00
—Black label with color bars			
❑ DXB196 [M]	The Best of Russ Morgan	1965	25.00
❑ DXSB7196 [R]	The Best of Russ Morgan	1965	18.00
❑ DL8642 [M]	Velvet Violins	1957	25.00
—Black label, silver print			
❑ DL8642 [M]	Velvet Violins	196?	15.00
—Black label with color bars			

EVEREST

Number	Title	Yr	NM
❑ LPBR-5083 [M]	Dance Along	1960	15.00
❑ SDBR-1083 [S]	Dance Along	1960	18.00
❑ LPBR-5055 [M]	Let's All Sing with Russ Morgan and Eddie Wilser	1959	15.00
❑ SDBR-1055 [S]	Let's All Sing with Russ Morgan and Eddie Wilser	1959	18.00
❑ LPBR-5129 [M]	Morgan Time	1961	15.00
❑ SDBR-1129 [S]	Morgan Time	1961	18.00
❑ LPBR-5054 [M]	Music in the Morgan Manner	1959	15.00
❑ SDBR-1054 [S]	Music in the Morgan Manner	1959	18.00
❑ LPBR-5095 [M]	Russ Morgan and His Wolverine Band	1960	15.00
❑ SDBR-1095 [S]	Russ Morgan and His Wolverine Band	1960	18.00
❑ LPBR-5130 [M]	Russ Morgan at Catalina	1961	15.00
❑ SDBR-1130 [S]	Russ Morgan at Catalina	1961	18.00

GNP CRESCENDO

Number	Title	Yr	NM
❑ GNPS-9015	The Best of Russ Morgan	197?	12.00

HINDSIGHT

Number	Title	Yr	NM
❑ HSR-145	Russ Morgan and His Orchestra 1937-38	198?	12.00
❑ HSR-404	Russ Morgan and His Orchestra Play 22 Original Big Band Recordings	198?	15.00

MCA

Number	Title	Yr	NM
❑ 92	Golden Favorites	1973	12.00
❑ 4036	The Best of Russ Morgan	197?	15.00

PICKWICK

Number	Title	Yr	NM
❑ PC-3030 [M]	Dance Along	196?	12.00
❑ SPC-3030 [S]	Dance Along	196?	15.00
❑ PC-3016 [M]	There Goes That Song	196?	12.00
❑ SPC-3016 [S]	There Goes That Song	196?	15.00

RUSS MORGAN PRESENTS

Number	Title	Yr	NM
❑ RMP-1000	Russ Morgan Presents "Music in the Morgan Manner	1967	18.00

SEARS

Number	Title	Yr	NM
❑ SPS-413 [R]	Does Your Heart Beat for Me?	196?	12.00

SUNSET

Number	Title	Yr	NM
❑ SUM-1142 [M]	Does Your Heart Beat for Me	1967	15.00
❑ SUS-5142 [S]	Does Your Heart Beat for Me	1967	12.00

VEE JAY

Number	Title	Yr	NM
❑ VJ-1125 [M]	His Greatest Hits	1964	18.00
❑ VJS-1125 [S]	His Greatest Hits	1964	25.00
❑ VJ-1139 [M]	Red Roses for a Blue Lady	1965	18.00
❑ VJS-1139 [S]	Red Roses for a Blue Lady	1965	25.00
❑ E-4009 [M]	Russ Morgan 1904-1969	1975	18.00

VOCALION

Number	Title	Yr	NM
❑ VL3695 [M]	Hoop-De-Doo Polkas and Waltzes	196?	15.00
❑ VL3601 [M]	Let's Dance	195?	15.00
❑ VL3792 [M]	Music in the Morgan Manner	196?	15.00
❑ VL73792 [R]	Music in the Morgan Manner	196?	12.00

MORGEN

PROBE

Number	Title	Yr	NM
❑ CPLP-4507	Morgen	1969	150.00

MORISSETTE, ALANIS

MAVERICK

Number	Title	Yr	NM
❑ 47094	Supposed Former Infatuation Junkie	1998	18.00

MORLY GREY

STARSHINE

Number	Title	Yr	NM
❑ 69000	The Only Truth	1969	200.00

MORMON TABERNACLE CHOIR

BOOK-OF-THE-MONTH

Number	Title	Yr	NM
❑ 71-6406	Christmas Celebration	1980	30.00
—Contains 20-page lyric booklet			

CBS MASTERWORKS

Number	Title	Yr	NM
❑ XM38299	Christmas Carols Around the World	1982	10.00
❑ IM39034	Faith of Our Fathers	1984	12.00
❑ FM37297	Gloria!	1982	12.00
❑ M37828	Serenade	1985	12.00
❑ IM37206	Silent Night -- The Greatest Hits of Christmas	1981	15.00
❑ M2X39102	The Great Choruses of Bach and Handel	1984	15.00
❑ MG37853	The Greatest Hits of Christmas	198?	18.00
❑ IM36661	The Power and the Glory	1981	12.00
❑ FM37286	The Twenties	1982	12.00
❑ FM37200	When You Wish Upon a Star	1981	12.00

COLUMBIA HOUSE

Number	Title	Yr	NM
❑ 1P6075	Christmas with the Mormon Tabernacle Choir	1973	12.00
❑ 6P6007	The Mormon Tabernacle Choir	1973	30.00
❑ 2P7437	The Mormon Tabernacle Choir Christmas Treasury	1982	18.00
❑ 3P6240	The Mormon Tabernacle Choir's Greatest Hits (Includes Christmas with the Mormon Tabernacle Choir)	1974	25.00
❑ 1P6008	What Child Is This	1973	15.00

COLUMBIA LIMITED EDITION

Number	Title	Yr	NM
❑ LE10091 [B]	Christmas Carols Around the World	1976	12.00
❑ LE10461	Hymns and Songs of Brotherhood	197?	10.00

COLUMBIA MASTERWORKS

Number	Title	Yr	NM
❑ M34134	A Jubilant Song	1976	12.00
❑ ML5497 [M]	A Mighty Fortress	1960	15.00
—Gray and black label with six "eye" logos			
❑ MS6162 [S]	A Mighty Fortress	1960	18.00
—Gray and black label with six "eye" logos			
❑ ML6461 [M]	Anvil Chorus: Favorite Opera Choruses	1967	15.00
❑ MS7061 [S]	Anvil Chorus: Favorite Opera Choruses	1967	15.00
❑ MS7149	Beautiful Dreamer	1968	15.00
—Gray "360 Sound" label			
❑ ML6079 [M]	Beloved Choruses Volume Two	1964	15.00
❑ MS6679 [S]	Beloved Choruses Volume Two	1964	18.00
❑ M35868	Beyond the Blue Horizon	1980	12.00
❑ ML6235 [M]	Bless This House	1966	12.00
❑ MS6835 [S]	Bless This House	1966	15.00
❑ M2L286 [M]	Brahms: A German Requiem Sung in English	1963	18.00
❑ M2S686 [S]	Brahms: A German Requiem Sung in English	1963	25.00
—Gray label, "360 Sound Stereo" in black			
❑ ML5684 [M]	Christmas Carols Around the World	1961	15.00
❑ MS6284 [S]	Christmas Carols Around the World	1961	18.00
—Same as ML 5684, but in stereo			
❑ M32227	Cielito Lindo -- The Mormon Tabernacle Choir En Espanol	1973	15.00
❑ M30647	Climb Every Mountain	1971	12.00
❑ ML5048 [M]	Concert of Sacred Music	1955	25.00
❑ ML6121 [M]	God Bless America	1965	15.00
❑ MS6721 [S]	God Bless America	1965	18.00
❑ M30054	God of Our Fathers	1970	15.00
❑ M35120	Hail to the Victors!	1978	12.00
❑ MS7292	Hallelujah Chorus: The Great Handel Choruses	1969	15.00
—Gray "360 Sound" label			
❑ M2L263 [M]	Handel: Messiah	1959	25.00
—Gray and black labels with six "eye" logos			
❑ M2S607 [S]	Handel: Messiah	1959	30.00
—Gray and black labels with six "eye" logos			
❑ ML5714 [M]	Hymns and Songs of Brotherhood	1962	15.00
❑ MS6314 [S]	Hymns and Songs of Brotherhood	1962	18.00
❑ MS7405	Jesu, Joy of Man's Desiring: The Great Bach Choruses	1970	15.00
—Gray "360 Sound" label			
❑ M30077	Joy to the World	1970	15.00
❑ XM30077	Joy to the World	197?	12.00
—Reissue of M 30077			
❑ M35825	Memories: Songs America Loves Best	1980	12.00
❑ M33440	Music and the Spoken Word	1975	12.00
❑ M35148	Robertson: Oratorio from the Book of Mormon	1978	12.00
❑ MG33710	Rock of Ages	1975	15.00
❑ ML6308 [M]	Sing Unto God	1966	12.00
❑ MS6908 [S]	Sing Unto God	1966	15.00
❑ ML5203 [M]	Songs of Faith and Devotion	1957	25.00
❑ M34538	Songs of Thanks	1977	12.00
❑ ML5659 [M]	Songs of the North & South 1861-1865	1961	15.00
—Gray and black label with six "eye" logos			
❑ MS6259 [S]	Songs of the North & South 1861-1865	1961	18.00
—Gray and black label with six "eye" logos			
❑ M32298	Stars & Stripes Forever	1973	12.00
❑ ML5364 [M]	The Beloved Choruses	1958	18.00
—Gray and black label with six "eye" logos			
❑ MS6058 [S]	The Beloved Choruses	1958	25.00
—Gray and black label with six "eye" logos			
❑ M32935	The Great "Messiah" Choruses	1974	12.00
❑ ML5592 [M]	The Holly and the Ivy	1960	15.00
❑ MS6192 [S]	The Holly and the Ivy	1960	18.00
—Same as ML 5592, but in stereo			
❑ MS6499 [S]	The Joy of Christmas	1963	18.00
—Same as ML 5899, but in stereo			
❑ ML5899 [M]	The Joy of Christmas	1963	15.00
—With the New York Philharmonic conducted by Leonard Bernstein			
❑ ML5302 [M]	The Lord Is My Shepherd	1958	18.00
—Gray and black label with six "eye" logos			
❑ MS6019 [S]	The Lord Is My Shepherd	1958	25.00
—Gray and black label with six "eye" logos			
❑ ML5386 [M]	The Lord's Prayer	1959	18.00
—Gray and black label with six "eye" logos			
❑ MS6068 [S]	The Lord's Prayer	1959	25.00
—Gray and black label with six "eye" logos			
❑ ML5767 [M]	The Lord's Prayer Volume II	1962	15.00
❑ MS6367 [S]	The Lord's Prayer Volume II	1962	18.00
❑ MG31081	The Mormon Tabernacle Choir Album	1972	18.00
❑ ML6019 [M]	The Mormon Tabernacle Choir at the World's Fair	1964	25.00
❑ MS6619 [S]	The Mormon Tabernacle Choir at the World's Fair	1964	30.00
❑ ML2077 [10]	The Mormon Tabernacle Choir of Salt Lake City	1949	40.00
—Their first album			
❑ ML4789 [M]	The Mormon Tabernacle Choir of Salt Lake City	195?	30.00
—Reissue of two 10-inch LPs onto one 12-inch LP			
❑ ML2098 [10]	The Mormon Tabernacle Choir of Salt Lake City Volume II	1950	30.00
❑ ML6351 [M]	The Mormon Tabernacle Choir's Greatest Hits	1966	12.00
❑ MS6951 [S]	The Mormon Tabernacle Choir's Greatest Hits	1966	15.00
—Same as ML 6351, but in stereo			
❑ ML6486 [M]	The Mormon Tabernacle Choir's Greatest Hits, Volume 2	1967	15.00
❑ MS7086 [S]	The Mormon Tabernacle Choir's Greatest Hits, Volume 2	1967	15.00
❑ MS7399	The Mormon Tabernacle Choir's Greatest Hits, Volume 3	1970	15.00
❑ ML5222 [M]	The Mormon Tabernacle Choir Sings Christmas Carols	1957	25.00
❑ ML6177 [M]	The Mormon Tabernacle Choir Sings Christmas Carols	1965	15.00
—A new recording of ML 5222			
❑ MS6777 [S]	The Mormon Tabernacle Choir Sings Christmas Carols	1965	18.00
—Same as ML 6177, but in stereo			

Number	Title	Yr	NM
❑ ML6412 [M]	The Old Beloved Songs	1967	15.00
❑ MS7012 [S]	The Old Beloved Songs	1967	15.00
❑ ML5423 [M]	The Spirit of Christmas	1959	15.00
❑ MS6100 [S]	The Spirit of Christmas	1959	18.00
—Same as ML 5500, but in stereo			
❑ ML5819 [M]	This Is My Country	1962	15.00
❑ MS6419 [S]	This Is My Country	1962	18.00
❑ M2L303 [M]	This Is My Country	1963	18.00
❑ M2S703 [S]	This Is My Country	1963	25.00
—Gray label, "360 Sound Stereo" in black; not to be confused with the single-record LP of the same name			
❑ ML6147 [M]	This Land Is Your Land	1965	15.00
❑ MS6747 [S]	This Land Is Your Land	1965	18.00
❑ M34546	White Christmas	1977	15.00
—In box with insert of Christmas recipes			

COLUMBIA SPECIAL PRODUCTS

Number	Title	Yr	NM
❑ P14245	For All the Saints	1977	15.00
—Mfg by CBS for Covenant Recordings			
❑ P14247	I Know That My Redeemer Lives	1977	15.00
—Mfg by CBS for Covenant Recordings			
❑ P14303	It's Christmas!	1977	15.00
—Mfg by CBS for Covenant Recordings			
❑ P14244	Lift Thine Eyes	1977	15.00
—Mfg by CBS for Covenant Recordings			
❑ P14243	Nearer My God to Thee	1977	15.00
—Mfg by CBS for Covenant Recordings			
❑ P14246	Now the Day Is Over	1977	15.00
—Mfg by CBS for Covenant Recordings			
❑ P15935	Songs of Faith	1983	12.00
❑ CSS1667	The Mormon Tabernacle Choir in South Carolina -- Tricentennial Concert	1970	25.00

FRANKLIN MINT

Number	Title	Yr	NM
❑ (no #)0	The Greatest Songs of Christmas	1980	30.00
—Maroon vinyl; the choir's first digital recording			

HARMONY

Number	Title	Yr	NM
❑ HS11370	Faith of Our Fathers	1970	15.00
❑ HS11272	Onward Christian Soldiers	1968	12.00
❑ KH30673	The Mormon Tabernacle Choir Sings Songs of Christmas	1971	12.00

READER'S DIGEST

Number	Title	Yr	NM
❑ P215176/7	50th Anniversary Album	1980	25.00
❑ RBA-128/A	Climb Ev'ry Mountain: The Mormon Tabernacle Choir Sings Great Songs of Inspiration	1988	30.00
❑ RD4A-221-1	Merry Christmas from the Mormon Tabernacle Choir	1981	12.00
❑ RD4-093	The Mormon Tabernacle Choir Sings	1973	30.00

REALM

Number	Title	Yr	NM
❑ 3V8039	The Mormon Tabernacle Choir's Greatest Hits (Includes Christmas with the Mormon Tabernacle Choir)	197?	18.00
—Reissue of Columbia House 6240			

TIME-LIFE

Number	Title	Yr	NM
❑ SMT104	Christmas Celebration	1987	25.00
—Same contents as Book-of-the-Month LP. Side 1, 2 and 6 are identical; Side 3 is BOTM's Side 5, Side 4 is BOTM's Side 3, and Side 5 is BOTM's Side 4.			

MORNING DEW, THE

ROULETTE

Number	Title	Yr	NM
❑ SR-42049	The Morning Dew	1970	300.00

MORNING GLORY

FONTANA

Number	Title	Yr	NM
❑ SRF-67573 [B]	Two Suns Worth	1968	35.00

MORNINGLORY

TOYA

Number	Title	Yr	NM
❑ STLP-003	Growing	1972	40.00

MORRIS, AUDREY

BETHLEHEM

Number	Title	Yr	NM
❑ BCP-6010 [M]	The Voice of Audrey Morris	1956	120.00

MORRIS, GREG

DOT

Number	Title	Yr	NM
❑ DLP-25881	For You	1968	25.00

MORRIS, MARLOWE

COLUMBIA

Number	Title	Yr	NM
❑ CL1819 [M]	Play the Thing	1962	25.00
❑ CS8619 [S]	Play the Thing	1962	30.00

MORRISON, HAROLD

DECCA

Number	Title	Yr	NM
❑ DL4680 [M]	Hoss, He's the Boss	1965	18.00
❑ DL74680 [S]	Hoss, He's the Boss	1965	25.00

MORRISON, SAM

CHIAROSCURO

Number	Title	Yr	NM
❑ 184	Natural Layers	197?	15.00

INNER CITY

Number	Title	Yr	NM
❑ IC-6017	Dune	197?	18.00

MORRISON, VAN

BANG

Number	Title	Yr	NM
❑ BLP-218 [M]	Blowin' Your Mind	1967	70.00
—With the true "Brown Eyed Girl" lyric, "Makin' love in the green grass behind the stadium with you.			
❑ BLPS-218 [S]	Blowin' Your Mind	1967	40.00
—With the true "Brown Eyed Girl" lyric, "Makin' love in the green grass behind the stadium with you.			
❑ BLBS-218 [S]	Blowin' Your Mind	1968	25.00
—With the censored "Brown Eyed Girl" lyric, "Laughin' and a-runnin', hey hey, behind the stadium with you," part of which was spliced in from another part of the song!			
❑ BLB-218 [M]	Blowin' Your Mind	1968	70.00
—With the censored "Brown Eyed Girl" lyric, "Laughin' and a-runnin', hey hey, behind the stadium with you," part of which was spliced in from another part of the song. This has been confirmed to exist in mono.			
❑ BLPS-400	T.B. Sheets	1973	25.00
❑ BLPS-222	The Best of Van Morrison	1970	18.00

DIRECT DISK

Number	Title	Yr	NM
❑ SD-16604	Moondance	1981	100.00
—Audiophile vinyl			

LOST HIGHWAY

Number	Title	Yr	NM
❑ B0005968-01	Pay the Devil	2006	15.00

MERCURY

Number	Title	Yr	NM
❑ 822895-1	A Sense of Wonder	1985	10.00
❑ 839262-1	Avalon Sunset	1989	12.00
❑ 847100-1	Enlightenment	1990	18.00
❑ 834496-1	Irish Heartbeat	1988	10.00
—With the Chieftains			
❑ 818336-1	Live at the Grand Opera House, Belfast	1985	12.00
❑ 830077-1	No Guru, No Method, No Teacher	1986	10.00
❑ 832585-1	Poetic Champions Compose	1987	10.00
❑ 841970-1	The Best of Van Morrison	1990	18.00

POLYDOR

Number	Title	Yr	NM
❑ 8391661	It's Too Late to Stop Now	2008	30.00
❑ 1775313	Tupelo Honey	2008	25.00

WARNER BROS.

Number	Title	Yr	NM
❑ BS2987	A Period of Transition	1977	15.00
—Burbank" palm-tree labels			
❑ BS2987	A Period of Transition	1979	10.00
—Later white or tan label			
❑ WS1768	Astral Weeks	1968	30.00
—With "W7" logo on green label			
❑ WS1768	Astral Weeks	1970	15.00
—With "WB" logo on green label			
❑ WS1768	Astral Weeks	1973	12.00
—Burbank" palm-tree label			
❑ WS1768	Astral Weeks	1979	10.00
—Later white or tan label			
❑ BSK3652	Beautiful Vision	1981	15.00
❑ BSK3462	Common One	1980	15.00
❑ BS2712	Hard Nose the Highway	1973	15.00
—Burbank" palm-tree label			
❑ BS2712	Hard Nose the Highway	1979	10.00
—Later white or tan label			
❑ WS1884	His Band and the Street Choir	1970	18.00
—With "WB" logo on green label			
❑ WS1884	His Band and the Street Choir	1973	12.00
—Burbank" palm-tree label			
❑ WS1884	His Band and the Street Choir	1979	10.00
—Later white or tan label			
❑ 23802	Inarticulate Speech of the Heart	1983	15.00
❑ HS3390	Into the Music	1979	15.00
❑ 2BS2760	It's Too Late to Stop Now	1974	18.00
—Burbank" palm-tree labels			
❑ 2BS2760	It's Too Late to Stop Now	1979	10.00
—Later white or tan label			
❑ WBMS-102 [DJ]	Live at the Roxy	1978	40.00
❑ WS1835	Moondance	1969	25.00
—With "W7" logo on green label			
❑ WS1835	Moondance	1970	15.00
—With "WB" logo on green label			
❑ WS1835	Moondance	1973	12.00
—Burbank" palm-tree label			
❑ BSK3103	Moondance	1977	12.00
—Reissue with new number; "Burbank" palm-tree label			
❑ BSK3103	Moondance	1979	10.00
—Later white or tan label			
❑ WS2633	Saint Dominic's Preview	1972	18.00
—With "WB" logo on green label			
❑ WS2633	Saint Dominic's Preview	1973	12.00
—Burbank" palm-tree label			
❑ WS2633	Saint Dominic's Preview	1979	10.00
—Later white or tan label			
❑ WS1950	Tupelo Honey	1971	18.00
—With "WB" logo on green label, plus poster			
❑ WS1950	Tupelo Honey	1973	12.00
—Burbank" palm-tree label			
❑ WS1950	Tupelo Honey	1979	10.00
—Later white or tan label			
❑ BS2805	Veedon Fleece	1974	15.00
—Burbank" palm-tree labels			
❑ BS2805	Veedon Fleece	1979	10.00
—Later white or tan label			
❑ BSK3212	Wavelength	1978	15.00

MORRISSEY, PAT

MERCURY

Number	Title	Yr	NM
❑ MG-20197 [M]	I'm Pat Morrissey, I Sing	1957	100.00

MORRISSEY

ATTACK

Number	Title	Yr	NM
❑ 86001	You Are the Quarry	2004	30.00

DECCA

Number	Title	Yr	NM
❑ SKL6003	Greatest Hits	2008	30.00

LOST HIGHWAY

Number	Title	Yr	NM
❑ 1257801	Years of Refusal	2009	25.00

PARLOPHONE

Number	Title	Yr	NM
❑ 825646299485 [B]	Vauxhall and I	2014	35.00
❑ 825646348831 [B]	Your Arsenal	2014	30.00

SIRE

Number	Title	Yr	NM
❑ R153729 [B]	Viva Hate	1988	30.00
—BMG Direct Marketing edition			
❑ 25699 [B]	Viva Hate	1988	18.00

MORROW, BUDDY

EPIC

Number	Title	Yr	NM
❑ LN24095 [M]	Big Band Beatlemania	1964	30.00
❑ BN26095 [S]	Big Band Beatlemania	1964	30.00
❑ LN24171 [M]	Campus After Dark	1965	15.00
❑ BN26171 [S]	Campus After Dark	1965	18.00

HINDSIGHT

Number	Title	Yr	NM
❑ HSR-154	Buddy Morrow 1963-64	198?	12.00

MERCURY

Number	Title	Yr	NM
❑ MG-20764 [M]	A Collection of 33 All-Time Dance Favorites	1963	18.00
❑ SR-60764 [S]	A Collection of 33 All-Time Dance Favorites	1963	25.00
❑ MG-20204 [M]	A Salute to the Fabulous Dorseys	1957	30.00
❑ MG-20221 [M]	Golden Trombone	1956	30.00
❑ MG-20372 [M]	Just We Two	195?	30.00
❑ SR-60018 [S]	Just We Two	1958	40.00
❑ MG-20396 [M]	Night Train	195?	30.00
❑ SR-60009 [S]	Night Train	1958	40.00
❑ MG-20702 [M]	Night Train Goes to Hollywood	1962	30.00
❑ SR-60702 [S]	Night Train Goes to Hollywood	1962	30.00
❑ MG-20062 [M]	Shall We Dance?	195?	30.00
❑ MG-20290 [M]	Tribute to Tommy Dorsey	1957	30.00

RCA VICTOR

Number	Title	Yr	NM
❑ LPM-2018 [M]	Big Band Guitar	1959	30.00
❑ LSP-2018 [S]	Big Band Guitar	1959	40.00
❑ LPM-1925 [M]	Dancing Tonight To Morrow	1958	30.00
❑ LSP-1925 [S]	Dancing Tonight To Morrow	1958	40.00
❑ LPM-2180 [M]	Double Impact	1960	30.00
❑ LSP-2180 [S]	Double Impact	1960	40.00
❑ LPM-2042 [M]	Impact	1959	30.00
❑ LSP-2042 [S]	Impact	1959	40.00
❑ LPM-1427 [M]	Night Train	1956	40.00
❑ LPM-2208 [M]	Poe for Moderns	1960	30.00
❑ LSP-2208 [S]	Poe for Moderns	1960	40.00

WING

Number	Title	Yr	NM
❑ MGW-12102 [M]	Dance Date	196?	15.00
❑ SRW-16102 [R]	Dance Date	196?	15.00
❑ MGW-12105 [M]	Tribute to a Sentimental Gentleman	196?	15.00

MORSE, ELLA MAE

CAPITOL

Number	Title	Yr	NM
❑ H513 [10]	Barrelhouse Boogie and the Blues	1954	400.00
❑ T513 [M]	Barrelhouse Boogie and the Blues	1955	250.00
❑ T1802 [M]	Hits of Ella Mae Morse and Freddie Slack	1962	100.00
❑ ST1802 [S]	Hits of Ella Mae Morse and Freddie Slack	1962	120.00
❑ M-11971 [M]	Hits of Ella Mae Morse and Freddie Slack	197?	18.00
—Reissue			
❑ T898 [M]	Morse Code	1957	150.00
—Turquoise label			

MORSE, ROBERT, AND CHARLES NELSON REILLY

CAPITOL

Number	Title	Yr	NM
❑ T1862 [M]	A Jolly Theatrical Christmas	1963	25.00
❑ ST1862 [S]	A Jolly Theatrical Christmas	1963	30.00

MORTIMER, AZIE

BETHLEHEM

Number	Title	Yr	NM
❑ BLP-10006	The Feeling of Jazz	197?	18.00

MORTIMER

PHILIPS

Number	Title	Yr	NM
❑ PHS600267	Mortimer	1969	30.00

Number	Title	Yr	NM
MORTON, ANN J.			
PRAIRIE DUST			
☐ 1661	My Friends Call Me Annie	197?	18.00
MORTON, BENNY / JIMMY HAMILTON			
MOSAIC			
☐ MR1-115	The Benny Morton and Jimmy Hamilton Blue Note Swingtets	199?	30.00
—Limited edition of 7,500			
MORTON, JELLY ROLL			
BIOGRAPH			
☐ 1004	Rare Piano Rolls 1924-1926	197?	12.00
BLUEBIRD			
☐ 6588-1-RB	Jelly Roll Morton & His Red Hot Peppers	1988	15.00
CIRCLE			
☐ L-14001 [M]	The Saga of Mr. Jelly Lord Volume 1: Jazz Started in New Orelans	1951	120.00
☐ L-14002 [M]	The Saga of Mr. Jelly Lord Volume 2: Way Down Yonder	1951	120.00
☐ L-14003 [M]	The Saga of Mr. Jelly Lord Volume 3: Jazz Is Strictly Music	1951	120.00
☐ L-14004 [M]	The Saga of Mr. Jelly Lord Volume 4: The Spanish Tinge	1951	120.00
☐ L-14005 [M]	The Saga of Mr. Jelly Lord Volume 5: Bad Man Ballads	1951	120.00
☐ L-14006 [M]	The Saga of Mr. Jelly Lord Volume 6: Jazz Piano Soloist #1	1951	120.00
☐ L-14007 [M]	The Saga of Mr. Jelly Lord Volume 7: Everyone Had His Style	1951	120.00
☐ L-14008 [M]	The Saga of Mr. Jelly Lord Volume 8: Jelly and the Blues	1951	120.00
☐ L-14009 [M]	The Saga of Mr. Jelly Lord Volume 9: Alabama Bound	1951	120.00
☐ L-14010 [M]	The Saga of Mr. Jelly Lord Volume 10: Jazz Piano Soloist #2	1951	120.00
☐ L-14011 [M]	The Saga of Mr. Jelly Lord Volume 11: In New Orleans	1951	120.00
☐ L-14012 [M]	The Saga of Mr. Jelly Lord Volume 12. I'm the Winin' Boy	1951	120.00
COMMODORE			
☐ DL-30000 [M]	New Orleans Memories	1950	100.00
☐ XFL-14942	New Orleans Memories	198?	15.00
EVEREST ARCHIVE OF FOLK & JAZZ			
☐ 267	Jelly Roll Morton	197?	12.00
JAZZ PANORAMA			
☐ 1804 [10]	Peppers	1951	100.00
☐ 1810 [10]	Peppers	1951	100.00
MAINSTREAM			
☐ 56020 [M]	Jelly Roll Morton	1965	30.00
☐ S-6020 [R]	Jelly Roll Morton	1965	15.00
MILESTONE			
☐ M-2003 [M]	Immortal Jelly Roll Morton	1970	15.00
☐ 47018	Jelly Roll Morton 1923-24	197?	18.00
RCA VICTOR			
☐ LPT-32 [10]	A Treasury of Immortal Performances	1952	100.00
☐ LPV-524 [M]	Hot Jazz, Pop Jazz, Hokum and Hilarity	1965	25.00
☐ LPV-559 [M]	I Thought I Heard Buddy Bolden Say	1966	25.00
☐ LPV-546 [M]	Mr. Jelly Lord	1966	25.00
☐ LPV-508 [M]	Stomps and Joys	1965	25.00
☐ LPM-1649 [M]	The King of New Orleans Jazz	1957	50.00
RIVERSIDE			
☐ RLP-1038 [10]	Classic Jazz Piano, Volume 1	1954	100.00
☐ RLP-1041 [10]	Classic Jazz Piano, Volume 2	1954	100.00
☐ RLP 12-111 [M]	Classic Piano Solos	1955	50.00
☐ RLP 12-133 [M]	Jelly Roll Morton Plays and Sings	1956	50.00
☐ RLP-1027 [M]	Jelly Roll Morton's Kings of Jazz: His Rarest Recordings	1954	100.00
☐ RLP-9001 [M]	Library of Congress Recordings Volume 1	1955	50.00
☐ RLP-9002 [M]	Library of Congress Recordings Volume 2	1955	50.00
☐ RLP-9003 [M]	Library of Congress Recordings Volume 3	1955	50.00
☐ RLP-9004 [M]	Library of Congress Recordings Volume 4	1955	50.00
☐ RLP-9005 [M]	Library of Congress Recordings Volume 5	1955	50.00
☐ RLP-9006 [M]	Library of Congress Recordings Volume 6	1955	50.00
☐ RLP-9007 [M]	Library of Congress Recordings Volume 7	1955	50.00
☐ RLP-9008 [M]	Library of Congress Recordings Volume 8	1955	50.00
☐ RLP-9009 [M]	Library of Congress Recordings Volume 9	1955	50.00
☐ RLP-9010 [M]	Library of Congress Recordings Volume 10	1955	50.00

Number	Title	Yr	NM
☐ RLP-9011 [M]	Library of Congress Recordings Volume 11	1955	50.00
☐ RLP-9012 [M]	Library of Congress Recordings Volume 12	1955	50.00
☐ RLP 12-132 [M]	Mr. Jelly Lord	1956	50.00
☐ RLP 12-140 [M]	Rags and Blues	1956	50.00
☐ RLP-1018 [10]	Rediscovered Solos	1953	100.00
☐ RLP 12-128 [M]	The Incomparable Jelly Roll Morton	1956	50.00
☐ RLP 12-102 [M]	The New Orleans Rhythm Kings with Jelly Roll Morton	1955	50.00
TIME-LIFE			
☐ STL-J-07	Giants of Jazz	1979	25.00
TRIP			
☐ J-1	Piano Roll Solos	197?	12.00
X			
☐ LX-3008 [10]	Red Hot Peppers, Volume 1	1954	100.00
☐ LVA-3028 [10]	Red Hot Peppers, Volume 2	1954	100.00
MOSBY, JOHNNY AND JONIE			
CAPITOL			
☐ ST-286	Hold Me	1969	18.00
☐ ST-414	I'll Never Be Free	1970	18.00
☐ ST-170	Just Hold My Hand	1969	18.00
☐ ST2903	Make a Left and Then a Right	1968	18.00
☐ ST-556	My Happiness	1970	18.00
☐ ST-737	Oh, Love of Mine	1971	18.00
COLUMBIA			
☐ CL2297 [M]	Mr. & Mrs. Country Music	1965	18.00
☐ CS9097 [S]	Mr. & Mrs. Country Music	1965	25.00
HARMONY			
☐ HS11389	Mr. & Mrs. Country Music	1970	12.00
STARDAY			
☐ SLP-328 [M]	The New Sweethearts of Country Music	1965	30.00
MOSCA, SAL			
CHOICE			
☐ 1022	For You	1979	15.00
INTERPLAY			
☐ 7712	Sal Mosca Music	197?	15.00
MOSCHNER, PINGUIN			
SOUND ASPECTS			
☐ 005	Tuba Love Story	1986	15.00
MOSES, BOB			
GRAMAVISION			
☐ 8307	Visit with the Great Spirit	1983	12.00
☐ 8203	When Elephants Dream of Music	198?	12.00
MOSES, KATHRYN			
PM			
☐ 017	Music in My Heart	1979	15.00
MOSHER, JIMMY			
DISCOVERY			
☐ 860	A Chick from Chelsea	1981	12.00
MOSLEY, BOB			
REPRISE			
☐ MS2068 [B]	Bob Mosley	1972	30.00
MOSS, GENE			
RCA VICTOR			
☐ LPM-2977 [M]	Dracula's Greatest Hits	1964	30.00
☐ LSP-2977 [S]	Dracula's Greatest Hits	1964	40.00
MOSSE, SANDY			
ARGO			
☐ LP-609 [M]	Chicago Scene	1957	40.00
☐ LP-639 [M]	Relaxin' with Sandy Mosse	1959	30.00
☐ LPS-639 [S]	Relaxin' with Sandy Mosse	1959	40.00
MOST, ABE			
LIBERTY			
☐ LJH-6004 [M]	Mister Clarinet	1955	50.00
MOST, SAM			
BETHLEHEM			
☐ BCP-18 [M]	I'm Nuts About the Most: East Coast Jazz, Volume 7	1955	50.00
☐ BCP-6008 [M]	Musically Yours	1956	50.00
☐ BCP-75 [M]	Sam Most Plays Bird, Bud, Monk and Miles	1957	50.00
☐ BCP-78 [M]	The Amazing Sam Most with Strings	1958	50.00
CATALYST			
☐ 7609	But Beautiful	1976	15.00
DEBUT			
☐ DLP-11 [10]	Sam Most Sextet	1954	300.00
VANGUARD			
☐ VRS-8014 [10]	Sam Most Sextet	1954	80.00

Number	Title	Yr	NM
XANADU			
☐ 141	Flute Flight	1977	15.00
☐ 173	Flute Talk	1980	15.00
☐ X-3001	Flute Talk	1980	30.00
—Audiophile edition			
☐ 160	From the Attic of My Mind	198?	12.00
☐ 133	Mostly Flute	1976	15.00
MOTELS, THE			
CAPITOL			
☐ ST-12177	All Four One	1982	12.00
☐ SN-16420	All Four One	198?	10.00
—Budget-line reissue			
☐ ST-12177 [DJ]	All Four One	1982	25.00
—Promo-only high-grade vinyl pressing (different front cover)			
☐ ST-12070	Careful	1980	12.00
☐ SN-16347	Careful	1985	10.00
—Budget-line reissue			
☐ ST-12288	Little Robbers	1983	12.00
☐ SN-16355	Little Robbers	1985	10.00
—Budget-line reissue			
☐ SJ-12378	Shock	1985	12.00
☐ ST-11996	The Motels	1979	12.00
☐ SN-16343	The Motels	1985	10.00
—Budget-line reissue			
MOTEN, BENNIE			
BLUEBIRD			
☐ 9768-1-RB	Bennie Moten's Kansas City Orchestra	1989	15.00
HISTORICAL			
☐ 9	Bennie Moten's Kansas City Orchestra	1966	25.00
RCA VICTOR			
☐ LPV-514 [M]	Bennie Moten's Great Band of 1930-32	1965	25.00
X			
☐ LX-3004 [10]	Kansas City Jazz, Volume 1	1954	60.00
☐ LVA-3025 [10]	Kansas City Jazz, Volume 2	1954	60.00
☐ LVA-3038 [10]	Kansas City Jazz, Volume 3	1954	60.00
MOTHER EARTH			
MERCURY			
☐ SR-61194	Living with the Animals	1968	30.00
☐ SR-61226	Make a Joyful Noise	1969	25.00
☐ SR-61270	Satisfied	1970	25.00
☐ SR-61230	Tracy Nelson Country	1969	25.00
REPRISE			
☐ RS6431	Bring Me Home	1971	18.00
☐ MS2054	Tracy Nelson/Mother Earth	1972	18.00
MOTHER LOVE BONE			
POLYDOR			
☐ 843191-1	Apple	1990	40.00
STARDOG			
☐ 839011-1 [EP]	Shine	1989	40.00
—Four songs on side one, the same four songs on side two			
MOTHERLODE			
BUDDAH			
☐ BDS-5108	Tapped Out	1970	18.00
☐ BDS-5046	When I Die	1969	18.00
MOTHER'S BOYS			
AUDIOPHILE			
☐ AP-100	Stompin' Hot! Singin' Sweet!	1970	15.00
MOTIAN, PAUL			
ECM			
☐ 1028	Conception Vessel	197?	18.00
☐ 1108	Dance	1977	12.00
☐ 1283	It Should Have Happened a Long Time Ago	1985	15.00
☐ 1138	Le Voyage	1979	12.00
☐ 1222	Psalm	198?	12.00
☐ 1048	Tribute	197?	15.00
SOUL NOTE			
☐ SN-1124	Jack of Clubs	1986	15.00
☐ 121224	One Time Out	1990	18.00
☐ SN-1074	The Story of Maryam	1983	15.00
MOTIONS, THE (3)			
PHILIPS			
☐ PHS600317	Electric Baby	1969	25.00
MOTLEY CRUE			
ELEKTRA			
☐ 60829	Dr. Feelgood	1989	15.00
☐ 60725	Girls, Girls, Girls	1987	12.00
☐ 60395 [EP]	Helter Skelter	1984	40.00
—Picture disc with four songs; includes poster and insert (deduct 50 percent if missing)			
☐ 60289	Shout at the Devil	1982	12.00
☐ 60418	Theatre of Pain	1985	12.00
☐ 60174	Too Fast for Love	1982	15.00
—Reissue of Leathur LP with slight revisions			

Number	Title	Yr	NM

LEATHUR
| ❑ LR-1281 | Too Fast for Love | 1981 | 200.00 |

— First pressing with white lettering on cover
| ❑ LR-1281 | Too Fast for Love | 1981 | 150.00 |

— Second pressing with red lettering on cover. Both Leathur pressings contain "Stick to Your Guns," which was not on the Elektra reissue

MOTLEY/HIP-O SELECT
| ❑ B0004791-01 | Too Fast for Love | 2005 | 25.00 |

— Reissue of Leathur LP with bonus 7-inch single, Stick to Your Guns/Toast of the Town

MOTORHEAD

CLEOPATRA
| ❑ 9335 [B] | Roundhouse - February 18, 1978 | | 25.00 |

EMI AMERICA
| ❑ LN-10340 | On Parole | 1986 | 25.00 |

— First U.S. issue of early U.K. LP

ENIGMA
| ❑ D1-75405 | No Sleep at All | 1988 | 15.00 |
| ❑ D1-73536 | The Birthday Party | 1990 | 18.00 |

ISLAND
| ❑ 90233 | No Remorse | 1984 | 25.00 |

— Regular cover
| ❑ 90236 | No Remorse | 1984 | 35.00 |

— Leather cover

MERCURY
❑ SRM-1-4011	Ace of Spades	1980	18.00
❑ 811365-1	Another Perfect Day	1983	18.00
❑ SRM-1-4042	Iron Fist	1982	18.00

PROFILE
| ❑ PRO-3243 | Ace of Spades | 1986 | 12.00 |

— Reissue of Mercury 4011
| ❑ PRO-3242 | Bomber | 1986 | 12.00 |

— First U.S. issue of early U.K. LP
| ❑ PRO-3244 | No Sleep 'Til Hammersmith | 1986 | 12.00 |

— Reissue of Mercury 4023
| ❑ PAL-1223 | Orgasmatron | 1986 | 15.00 |
| ❑ PRO-3241 | Overkill | 1986 | 12.00 |

— First U.S. issue of early U.K. LP
| ❑ PAL-1240 | Rock 'N' Roll | 1987 | 12.00 |

SANCTUARY
| ❑ 5312076 | No Sleep 'Til Hammersmith | 2008 | 25.00 |

WTG
| ❑ N46858 [B] | 1916 | 1991 | 30.00 |

MOTORS, THE

VIRGIN
❑ JZ35348	Approved by the Motors	1978	12.00
❑ VA13139	Tenement Steps	1980	12.00
❑ PZ34924	The Motors	1977	15.00

MOTT THE HOOPLE

ATLANTIC
❑ SD8304 [B]	Brain Capers	1972	30.00
❑ SD8272 [B]	Mad Shadows	1970	30.00
❑ SD8258 [B]	Mott the Hoople	1970	30.00

— With "1841 Broadway" address and no mention of Warner Communications on label
| ❑ SD8258 | Mott the Hoople | 198? | 10.00 |

— With Warner Communications "W" logo on label
| ❑ SD7297 | Rock and Roll Queen | 1974 | 25.00 |
| ❑ SD8284 [B] | Wildlife | 1971 | 30.00 |

COLUMBIA
| ❑ KC31750 | All the Young Dudes | 1972 | 18.00 |
| ❑ PC31750 | All the Young Dudes | 198? | 10.00 |

— Budget-line reissue
| ❑ PC33705 [B] | Drive On | 1975 | 18.00 |

— released under the abbreviated name Mott
| ❑ KC32425 | Mott | 1973 | 18.00 |
| ❑ PC32425 | Mott | 198? | 10.00 |

— Budget-line reissue
| ❑ PC33282 | Mott the Hoople Live | 1974 | 18.00 |

— No bar code on cover
| ❑ PC33282 | Mott the Hoople Live | 198? | 10.00 |

— Reissue with bar code on cover
| ❑ PC34368 | Mott the Hoople's Greatest Hits | 1976 | 15.00 |

— No bar code on cover
| ❑ PC34368 | Mott the Hoople's Greatest Hits | 198? | 10.00 |

— Reissue with bar code on cover
| ❑ PC34236 [B] | Shouting and Pointing | 1976 | 18.00 |

— released under the abbreviated name Mott
| ❑ PC32871 | The Hoople | 1974 | 18.00 |
| ❑ PCQ32871 [Q] | The Hoople | 1974 | 30.00 |

MOULD, BOB

VIRGIN
| ❑ 91395 | Black Sheets of Rain | 1990 | 15.00 |
| ❑ PR3512 [EP] | Rust Bucket Coliseum | 1990 | 18.00 |

— Promo-only five-track release
| ❑ 91240 | Workbook | 1989 | 15.00 |

MOULE, KEN

LONDON
| ❑ LL1673 [M] | Ken Moule Arranges for... | 1957 | 50.00 |

— Label calls this "Cool Moule"

MOUNT ALVERNIA SEMINARY CHOIR

ABC-PARAMOUNT
| ❑ 211 [M] | Christmas in a Monastery: The Sons of St. Francis Sing | 1957 | 25.00 |

MOUNT RUSHMORE

DOT
| ❑ DLP-25898 | High on Mount Rushmore | 1968 | 25.00 |
| ❑ DLP-25934 | Mount Rushmore '69 | 1969 | 25.00 |

MOUNTAIN

COLUMBIA
❑ KC33008	Avalanche	1974	15.00
❑ CQ33008 [Q]	Avalanche	1974	35.00
❑ PC33008	Avalanche	197?	10.00

— Budget-line reissue
❑ KC32079	The Best of Mountain	1973	15.00
❑ CQ32079 [Q]	The Best of Mountain	1973	35.00
❑ PC32079	The Best of Mountain	198?	10.00

— Budget-line reissue
| ❑ CG32818 | Twin Peaks | 1974 | 18.00 |
| ❑ PG32818 | Twin Peaks | 198? | 12.00 |

— Budget-line reissue

SCOTTI BROTHERS
| ❑ FZ40006 | Go for Your Life | 1985 | 12.00 |

WINDFALL
❑ 5501	Flowers of Evil	1971	18.00
❑ 4501	Mountain Climbing!	1970	18.00
❑ 5502	Mountain Live (The Road Goes Ever On)	1972	18.00
❑ 5500	Nantucket Sleighride	1971	18.00

— Deduct 20% if inserts are missing

MOUNTAIN BUS

GOOD
| ❑ 101 | Sundance | 1971 | 200.00 |

MOUNTAIN RAMBLERS, THE

ATLANTIC
| ❑ 1347 [M] | Blue Ridge Mountain Music | 1962 | 30.00 |
| ❑ SD1347 [S] | Blue Ridge Mountain Music | 1962 | 30.00 |

MOURNING REIGN, THE

BEAT ROCKET
| ❑ BR102 | The Mourning Reign | 1999 | 15.00 |

MOUTH AND MACNEIL

PHILIPS
| ❑ PHS700000 | How Do You Do? | 1972 | 15.00 |
| ❑ PHS700003 | Mouth & MacNeil II | 1973 | 15.00 |

MOVE, THE

A&M
| ❑ SP-4259 [B] | Shazam | 1969 | 30.00 |
| ❑ SP-3181 | Shazam | 1982 | 12.00 |

— Budget-line reissue of 4259
| ❑ SP-3625 [B] | The Best of the Move | 1974 | 30.00 |

CAPITOL
| ❑ ST-658 [B] | Looking On | 1971 | 30.00 |
| ❑ ST-811 [B] | Message from the Country | 1971 | 30.00 |

UNITED ARTISTS
| ❑ UAS-5666 | Split Ends | 1972 | 18.00 |

MOVIEES, THE

SUNDAZED
| ❑ LP5073 | Become One of Them | 2000 | 15.00 |

MOVING SIDEWALKS, THE

TANTARA
| ❑ 6919 [B] | Flash | 1968 | 350.00 |

MOYE, DON

AECO
| ❑ 001 | Sun Percussion, Vol. 1 | 1980 | 18.00 |

MOYET, ALISON

COLUMBIA
| ❑ BFC39956 | Alf | 1985 | 12.00 |
| ❑ BFC40653 | Raindancing | 1987 | 12.00 |

MOZIAN, ROGER KING

CLEF
| ❑ MGC-166 [10] | The Colorful Music of Roger King Mozian | 1954 | 100.00 |

MOZZ, THE

MESA
| ❑ R1-79018 | Mystique and Identity | 1989 | 18.00 |

MR. BIG (1)

ARISTA
| ❑ AL4083 [B] | Photographic Smile | 1976 | 18.00 |

MR. BIG (2)

ATLANTIC
| ❑ A1-82209 | Lean Into It | 1991 | 25.00 |

— U.S. version issued on vinyl only through Columbia House
| ❑ 81990 | Mr. Big | 1989 | 12.00 |

MR. BUNGLE

WARNER BROS.
| ❑ 45963 | Disco Volante | 1995 | 25.00 |

— Originals have bonus 7-inch single (listed separately)

MR. GASSER AND THE WEIRDOS

CAPITOL
❑ T2010 [M]	Hot Rod Hootenanny	1963	100.00
❑ ST2010 [S]	Hot Rod Hootenanny	1963	120.00
❑ T2057 [M]	Rods n' Ratfinks	1963	100.00

— Add 25% if ratfink decal is enclosed
| ❑ ST2057 [S] | Rods n' Ratfinks | 1963 | 120.00 |

— Add 25% if ratfink decal is enclosed
| ❑ T2114 [M] | Surfink! | 1964 | 150.00 |

— With bonus single in pocket on cover: "Santa Barbara"/"Midnight Run" by the Super Stocks
| ❑ T2114 [M] | Surfink! | 1964 | 100.00 |

— Without bonus single
| ❑ ST2114 [S] | Surfink! | 1964 | 200.00 |

— With bonus single in pocket on cover: "Santa Barbara"/"Midnight Run" by the Super Stocks
| ❑ ST2114 [S] | Surfink! | 1964 | 150.00 |

— Without bonus single

MR. MISTER

RCA
❑ 6276-1-R	Go On	1987	10.00
❑ AFL1-4864	I Wear the Face	1984	12.00
❑ AFL1-7180	Welcome to the Real World	1985	10.00

— Reissue
| ❑ NFL1-8045 | Welcome to the Real World | 1985 | 15.00 |

— Original issue

MR. SHORT STUFF

SPIVEY
| ❑ 1005 | Mr. Short Stuff | 196? | 25.00 |

MU

CAS
| ❑ 300 | Mu | 1971 | 300.00 |

MUDHONEY

REPRISE
| ❑ 45477 | Five Dollar Bob's Mock Cooter Stew | 1993 | 18.00 |
| ❑ 45840 | My Brother the Cow | 1994 | 18.00 |

SUB POP
| ❑ 105PD [PD] | Every Good Boy Deserves Fudge | 1991 | 30.00 |

— Picture disc -- limited edition of 2,500
| ❑ SP500 [B] | March to Fuzz | 2000 | 35.00 |
| ❑ 44 | Mudhoney | 1989 | 30.00 |

— First 3,000 have gatefold sleeve and poster
| ❑ 44 | Mudhoney | 1989 | 25.00 |

— Without gatefold and poster
❑ 70765 [B]	Mudhoney	2008	18.00
❑ SP-555 [B]	Since We've Become Translucent	2002	25.00
❑ 21 [EP]	Superfuzz Bigmuff	1988	30.00

— With poster
| ❑ 21 [EP] | Superfuzz Bigmuff | 1988 | 25.00 |

— Without poster

SUPER ELECTRO
| ❑ SE10 | Tomorrow Hit Today | 1998 | 15.00 |

MUGWUMPS, THE

WARNER BROS.
| ❑ W1697 [M] | The Mugwumps | 1967 | 60.00 |
| ❑ WS1697 [S] | The Mugwumps | 1967 | 30.00 |

MUHAMMAD, IDRIS

FANTASY
❑ F-9581	Foxhuntin'	1979	18.00
❑ F-9598	Make It Count	1980	18.00
❑ F-9566	You Ain't No Friend of Mine	1978	18.00

KUDU
❑ 38	Boogie to the Top	1978	25.00
❑ 27	House of the Rising Sun	1976	30.00
❑ 17	Power of Soul	1974	30.00
❑ 34	Turn This Mutha Out	1977	25.00

PRESTIGE
| ❑ 10005 | Black Rhythm Revolution | 1971 | 40.00 |
| ❑ 10036 | Peace and Rhythm | 1971 | 30.00 |

THERESA
| ❑ 110 | Kabsha | 198? | 18.00 |

Number	Title	Yr	NM

MULCAY, JIMMY AND MILDRED

JUBILEE
| ❏ JGM-5017 [M] | Magic Millions | 1962 | 30.00 |

MULDAUR, GEOFF & MARIA

CARTHAGE
| ❏ CGLP-4428 | Pottery Pie | 198? | 12.00 |

REPRISE
| ❏ MS2073 | Sweet Potatoes | 1972 | 15.00 |

MULDAUR, GEOFF

FOLKLORE
| ❏ FRLP-14004 [M] | Sleepy Man Blues | 1964 | 30.00 |
| ❏ FRST-14004 [S] | Sleepy Man Blues | 1964 | 40.00 |

PRESTIGE
| ❏ PRST-7727 | Sleepy Man Blues | 1969 | 25.00 |
| —Reissue of Folklore LP | | | |

MULDAUR, MARIA

MYRRH
| ❏ MSB-6685 | There Is a Love | 1984 | 12.00 |

REPRISE
❏ MS2148	Maria Muldaur	1973	15.00
❏ MS2235	Sweet Harmony	1976	15.00
❏ MS2194	Waitress in a Donut Shop	1974	15.00
❏ MS4-2194 [Q]	Waitress in a Donut Shop	1974	25.00

TAKOMA
| ❏ 7084 | Gospel Nights | 1980 | 12.00 |

TUDOR
| ❏ 109902 | Sweet & Sour | 1983 | 12.00 |

WARNER BROS.
| ❏ BSK3305 | Open Your Eyes | 1979 | 12.00 |
| ❏ BSK3162 | Southern Winds | 1978 | 12.00 |

MULL, MARTIN

ABC
| ❏ AB-997 | I'm Everyone I've Ever Loved | 1977 | 12.00 |
| ❏ AA-1064 | Sex and Violins | 1978 | 12.00 |

CAPRICORN
❏ CP 0155	Days of Wine and Neurosis	1975	15.00
❏ CP 0106	Martin Mull	1972	15.00
❏ CP 0117	Martin Mull and His Fabulous Furniture	1973	15.00
❏ CP 0195	No Hits Four Errors	1977	12.00
❏ CP 0126	Normal	1974	15.00

ELEKTRA
| ❏ 6E-200 | Near Perfect | 1979 | 12.00 |

MCA
| ❏ 795 | I'm Everyone I've Ever Loved | 1980 | 10.00 |
| —Reissue of ABC 997 | | | |

MULLER, WERNER

DECCA
❏ DL8388 [M]	O, Tannenbaum (Christmas on the Rhine)	1956	25.00
—Black label, silver print			
❏ DL8388 [M]	O, Tannenbaum (Christmas on the Rhine)	1960	15.00
—Black label with color bars; album credited to "Mixed Chorus and Orchestra" (Muller's name is on the jacket spine only); revised contents thus:			
❏ DL78388 [S]	O, Tannenbaum (Christmas on the Rhine)	1960	18.00

MCA
| ❏ 15023 | O, Tannenbaum (Christmas on the Rhine) | 197? | 10.00 |
| —Reissue still credited to "Mixed Chorus and Orchestra" | | | |

MULLICAN, MOON

AUDIO LAB
| ❏ AL-1568 [M] | Instrumentals | 1962 | 150.00 |

CORAL
| ❏ CRL57235 [M] | Moon Over Mullican | 1958 | 500.00 |

HILLTOP
| ❏ JS-6033 | Good Times Gonna Roll Again | 1966 | 30.00 |

KAPP
| ❏ KS-3600 | Showcase | 1968 | 30.00 |

KING
❏ 628 [M]	Moon Mullican Plays and Sings 16 of His Favorite Tunes	1959	150.00
❏ 937 [M]	Moon Mullican Sings 24 of His Favorite Tunes	1965	50.00
❏ 555 [M]	Moon Mullican Sings His All-Time Greatest Hits	1958	200.00
❏ 681 [M]	The Many Moods of Moon Mullican	1960	150.00

NASHVILLE
| ❏ 2080 | I'll Sail My Ship Alone | 1970 | 25.00 |

SPAR
| ❏ SP-3005 [M] | Mister Honky Tonk Man | 1965 | 100.00 |

STARDAY
❏ SLP-267 [M]	Mister Piano Man	1964	50.00
❏ SLP-135 [M]	Playin' and Singin'	1963	100.00
❏ SLP-398 [M]	The Unforgettable Moon Mullican	1967	40.00

STERLING
| ❏ ST-601 [M] | I'll Sail My Ship Alone | 1958 | 200.00 |

MULLIGAN, GERRY, AND CHET BAKER

CTI
| ❏ 6054 | The Carnegie Hall Concert, Volume 1 | 1976 | 15.00 |
| ❏ 6055 | The Carnegie Hall Concert, Volume 2 | 1976 | 15.00 |

JAZZTONE
| ❏ J-1253 [M] | Mulligan and Baker! | 1957 | 40.00 |

MULLIGAN, GERRY, AND SHORTY ROGERS

CAPITOL
❏ T691 [M]	Modern Sounds	1956	80.00
❏ T2025 [M]	Modern Sounds	1963	25.00
❏ DT2025 [R]	Modern Sounds	1963	15.00

MULLIGAN, GERRY

A&M
| ❏ SP-3036 | The Age of Steam | 1971 | 18.00 |

CAPITOL
| ❏ H439 [10] | Gerry Mulligan and His Ten-Tette | 1953 | 250.00 |

CHIAROSCURO
| ❏ 155 | Idol Gossip | 1977 | 15.00 |

COLUMBIA
❏ CL1932 [M]	Jeru	1963	30.00
—Red label "Guaranteed High Fidelity" at bottom			
❏ CS8732 [S]	Jeru	1963	30.00
—Red label, "360 Sound Stereo" in black at bottom			
❏ CL1932 [M]	Jeru	1965	15.00
—Red label, "360 Sound Mono" at bottom			
❏ CS8732 [S]	Jeru	1965	18.00
—Red label, "360 Sound Stereo" in white at bottom			
❏ CL1932 [M]	Jeru	1963	50.00
—Red and black label with six "eye" logos			
❏ JC34803	The Arranger (1946-57)	1977	15.00
❏ CL1307 [M]	What Is There to Say?	1959	40.00
—Red and black label with six "eye" logos			
❏ CS8116 [S]	What Is There to Say?	1959	40.00
—Red and black label with six "eye" logos			
❏ CL1307 [M]	What Is There to Say?	1963	15.00
—Red label, "Guaranteed High Fidelity" or "360 Sound Mono" at bottom			
❏ CS8116 [S]	What Is There to Say?	1963	18.00
—Red label, "360 Sound Stereo" at bottom			

CONCORD JAZZ
| ❏ CJ-300 | Soft Lights and Sweet Music | 1986 | 12.00 |

CROWN
| ❏ CLP-5363 [M] | The Great Gerry Mulligan | 196? | 18.00 |
| ❏ CST-363 [R] | The Great Gerry Mulligan | 196? | 15.00 |

DRG
| ❏ MRS-506 | Gerry Mulligan and Dave Grusin | 198? | 12.00 |
| ❏ SL-5194 | Walk on the Water | 1980 | 12.00 |

EMARCY
| ❏ MG-36101 [M] | Mainstream of Jazz | 1956 | 150.00 |
| ❏ MG-36056 [M] | Presenting the Gerry Mulligan Sextet | 1955 | 150.00 |

FANTASY
❏ 3-6 [10]	Gerry Mulligan Quartet	1953	200.00
—Green vinyl			
❏ 3-6 [10]	Gerry Mulligan Quartet	1953	200.00
—Red vinyl			
❏ 3-6 [10]	Gerry Mulligan Quartet	1953	150.00
—Black vinyl			
❏ OJC-003	Mulligan Plays Mulligan	1982	12.00

GENE NORMAN
| ❏ GNP-3 [10] | Gerry Mulligan Quartet | 1952 | 250.00 |

GRP
| ❏ GR-1003 | Little Big Horn | 198? | 12.00 |

LIMELIGHT
❏ LM-82004 [M]	Butterfly with Hiccups	1964	30.00
❏ LS-86004 [S]	Butterfly with Hiccups	1964	30.00
❏ LM-82030 [M]	Feelin' Good	1965	30.00
❏ LS-86030 [S]	Feelin' Good	1965	30.00
❏ LM-82021 [M]	If You Can't Beat 'Em, Join 'Em	1965	30.00
❏ LS-86021 [S]	If You Can't Beat 'Em, Join 'Em	1965	30.00
❏ LM-82040 [M]	Something Borrowed, Something Blue	1966	25.00
❏ LS-86040 [S]	Something Borrowed, Something Blue	1966	30.00

MERCURY
| ❏ MG-20453 [M] | A Profile of Gerry Mulligan | 1959 | 60.00 |

MOBILE FIDELITY
❏ 1-179	At the Village Vanguard	1985	50.00
—Audiophile vinyl			
❏ 1-241	Blues in Time	1996	45.00
—Audiophile vinyl			

| ❏ 1-234 | Gerry Mulligan Meets Ben Webster | 1995 | 50.00 |
| —Audiophile vinyl | | | |

MOSAIC
| ❏ MR5-102 | The Complete Pacific Jazz and Capitol Recordings of the Original Gerry Mulligan Quartet and Tentette | 198? | 100.00 |

ODYSSEY
| ❏ 32160290 | Jeru | 1968 | 15.00 |
| ❏ 32160258 | What Is There to Say? | 1968 | 15.00 |

PACIFIC JAZZ
❏ PJ-50 [M]	California Concerts	1962	30.00
❏ PJ-1228 [M]	Gerry Mulligan at Storyville	1957	150.00
❏ PJLP-1 [10]	Gerry Mulligan Quartet	1953	300.00
❏ PJLP-5 [10]	Gerry Mulligan Quartet	1953	300.00
❏ PJ-1201 [M]	Gerry Mulligan Sextet	1955	150.00
❏ PJ-38 [M]	Konitz Meets Mulligan	1962	30.00
❏ PJLP-10 [10]	Lee Konitz and the Gerry Mulligan Quartet	1954	250.00
❏ PJLP-2 [10]	Lee Konitz Plays with the Gerry Mulligan Quartet	1953	300.00
❏ PJM-406 [M]	Lee Konitz with the Gerry Mulligan Quartet	1956	150.00
❏ PJ-1210 [M]	Paris Concert	1956	150.00
❏ PJ-10102 [M]	Paris Concert	1966	25.00
❏ ST-20102 [S]	Paris Concert	1966	25.00
❏ PJ-47 [M]	Reunion with Chet Baker	1962	30.00
❏ ST-47 [S]	Reunion with Chet Baker	1962	30.00
❏ T90061 [M]	Reunion with Chet Baker	196?	30.00
—Capitol Record Club edition			
❏ PJ-8 [M]	The Genius of Gerry Mulligan	1960	40.00
❏ ST-20140 [R]	The Genius of Gerry Mulligan	1968	18.00
❏ PJ-1207 [M]	The Original Mulligan Quartet	1955	150.00
❏ PJ-75 [M]	Timeless	1963	30.00

PAR
| ❏ PAD-703 | Symphonic Dreams | 1987 | 12.00 |

PAUSA
| ❏ 9010 | The Genius of Gerry Mulligan | 198? | 12.00 |

PHILIPS
❏ PHM200108 [M]	Night Lights	1963	25.00
❏ PHS600108 [S]	Night Lights	1963	30.00
❏ PHM200077 [M]	Spring Is Sprung	1963	25.00
❏ PHS600077 [S]	Spring Is Sprung	1963	30.00

PRESTIGE
❏ PRLP-120 [10]	Gerry Mulligan Blows	1952	300.00
❏ PRLP-7251 [M]	Historically Speaking	1963	40.00
—Yellow label			
❏ 24016	Mulligan/Baker	1972	18.00
❏ PRLP-7006 [M]	Mulligan Plays Mulligan	1956	100.00
—Yellow label			
❏ PRLP 141 [10]	Mulligan Too Blows	1953	300.00

SUNSET
| ❏ SUM-1117 [M] | Concert Days | 1966 | 18.00 |
| ❏ SUS-5117 [S] | Concert Days | 1966 | 15.00 |

TRIP
| ❏ 5581 | Gerry Mulligan Sextet | 197? | 12.00 |
| ❏ 5531 | Profile (1955-56) | 197? | 12.00 |

UNITED ARTISTS
| ❏ UAL-4085 [M] | Nightwatch | 1960 | 40.00 |
| ❏ UAS-5085 [S] | Nightwatch | 1960 | 50.00 |

VERVE
❏ V-8478 [M]	Blues in Time	1962	25.00
❏ V6-8478 [S]	Blues in Time	1962	30.00
❏ V-8515 [M]	Gerry Mulligan '63 -- The Concert Jazz Band	1963	25.00
❏ V6-8515 [S]	Gerry Mulligan '63 -- The Concert Jazz Band	1963	30.00
❏ MGV-8388 [M]	Gerry Mulligan and the Concert Jazz Band	1960	40.00
❏ V6-8388 [S]	Gerry Mulligan and the Concert Jazz Band	1961	30.00
❏ V-8388 [M]	Gerry Mulligan and the Concert Jazz Band	1961	25.00
❏ MGV-8396 [M]	Gerry Mulligan and the Concert Jazz Band at the Village Vanguard	1960	40.00
❏ V6-8396 [S]	Gerry Mulligan and the Concert Jazz Band at the Village Vanguard	1961	30.00
❏ V-8396 [M]	Gerry Mulligan and the Concert Jazz Band at the Village Vanguard	1961	25.00
❏ UMV-2057	Gerry Mulligan and the Concert Jazz Band at the Village Vanguard	198?	15.00
❏ V-8415 [M]	Gerry Mulligan and the Concert Jazz Band Presents a Concert in Jazz	1961	30.00
❏ V6-8415 [S]	Gerry Mulligan and the Concert Jazz Band Presents a Concert in Jazz	1961	30.00
❏ MGV-8343 [M]	Gerry Mulligan Meets Ben Webster	1959	40.00
❏ MGVS-6104 [S]	Gerry Mulligan Meets Ben Webster	1960	40.00
❏ V-8343 [M]	Gerry Mulligan Meets Ben Webster	1961	25.00
❏ V-8534 [M]	Gerry Mulligan Meets Ben Webster	1963	18.00
❏ V6-8534 [S]	Gerry Mulligan Meets Ben Webster	1963	25.00

Number	Title	Yr	NM
❑ UMJ-3093	Gerry Mulligan Meets Ben Webster	198?	15.00
❑ MGV-8367 [M]	Gerry Mulligan Meets Johnny Hodges	1960	40.00
❑ V6-8367 [S]	Gerry Mulligan Meets Johnny Hodges	1961	30.00
❑ V-8367 [M]	Gerry Mulligan Meets Johnny Hodges	1961	25.00
❑ V-8536 [M]	Gerry Mulligan Meets Johnny Hodges	1963	18.00
❑ V6-8536 [S]	Gerry Mulligan Meets Johnny Hodges	1963	25.00
❑ V-8535 [M]	Gerry Mulligan Meets Stan Getz	1963	18.00
❑ V6-8535 [S]	Gerry Mulligan Meets Stan Getz	1963	25.00
❑ UMV-2652	Gerry Mulligan Presents a Concert in Jazz	198?	15.00
❑ VSP-6 [M]	Gerry's Time	1966	18.00
❑ VSPS-6 [R]	Gerry's Time	1966	15.00
❑ MGV-8249 [M]	Getz Meets Mulligan in Hi-Fi	1958	40.00
❑ MGVS-6003 [S]	Getz Meets Mulligan in Hi-Fi	1960	40.00
❑ V-8249 [M]	Getz Meets Mulligan in Hi-Fi	1961	25.00
❑ V6-8249 [S]	Getz Meets Mulligan in Hi-Fi	1961	30.00
❑ VE-2-2537	Mulligan & Getz & Desmond	1980	18.00
❑ V-8567 [M]	The Essential Gerry Mulligan	1964	15.00
❑ V6-8567 [S]	The Essential Gerry Mulligan	1964	18.00
❑ V-8438 [M]	The Gerry Mulligan Concert Jazz Band On Tour with Guest Soloist Zoot Sims	1962	30.00
❑ V6-8438 [S]	The Gerry Mulligan Concert Jazz Band On Tour with Guest Soloist Zoot Sims	1962	30.00
❑ MGV-8246 [M]	The Gerry Mulligan-Paul Desmond Quartet	1958	50.00
❑ V-8246 [M]	The Gerry Mulligan-Paul Desmond Quartet	1961	25.00
❑ V-8466 [M]	The Gerry Mulligan Quartet	1962	30.00
❑ V6-8466 [S]	The Gerry Mulligan Quartet	1962	30.00

WHO'S WHO IN JAZZ

❑ 21007	Lionel Hampton Presents Gerry Mulligan	1978	15.00

WING

❑ MGW-12335 [M]	Night Lights	1964	15.00
❑ SRW-16335 [S]	Night Lights	1964	18.00

WORLD PACIFIC

❑ WP-1201 [M]	California Concerts	1958	80.00
❑ WP-1228 [M]	Gerry Mulligan at Storyville	1958	80.00
❑ ST-1006 [S]	Gerry Mulligan at Storyville	1958	100.00
❑ WP-1273 [M]	Lee Konitz Plays with the Gerry Mulligan Quartet	1959	80.00
—Reissue of 406			
❑ PJM-406 [M]	Lee Konitz with the Gerry Mulligan Quartet	1958	80.00
❑ WP-1210 [M]	Paris Concert	1958	80.00
❑ PJ-1241 [M]	Reunion with Chet Baker	1957	120.00
❑ WP-1241 [M]	Reunion with Chet Baker	1958	80.00
❑ ST-1007 [S]	Reunion with Chet Baker	1958	100.00
❑ PJ-1237 [M]	The Gerry Mulligan Songbook, Volume 1	1957	120.00
❑ WP-1237 [M]	The Gerry Mulligan Songbook, Volume 1	1958	80.00
❑ ST-1001 [S]	The Gerry Mulligan Songbook, Volume 1	1958	100.00
❑ WP-1207 [M]	The Original Mulligan Quartet	1958	80.00

MULLIGAN, GERRY/BUDDY DEFRANCO

GENE NORMAN

❑ GNP-26 [M]	The Gerry Mulligan Quartet with Chet Baker/Buddy DeFranco Quartet	1957	80.00
—Combined reissue of two 10-inch LPs			
❑ GNP-56 [M]	The Gerry Mulligan Quartet with Chet Baker/Buddy DeFranco Quartet	196?	40.00
—Reissue of 26			

GNP CRESCENDO

❑ GNPS-56 [R]	The Gerry Mulligan Quartet with Chet Baker/Buddy DeFranco Quartet	196?	12.00

MULLIGAN, GERRY/KAI WINDING/RED RODNEY

STATUS

❑ ST-8306 [M]	Broadway	1965	40.00

MULLIGAN, GERRY/PAUL DESMOND

FANTASY

❑ 3220 [M]	Gerry Mulligan Quartet/Paul Desmond Quintet	1956	80.00
—Red vinyl; combined reissue of two 10-inch LPs			
❑ 3220 [M]	Gerry Mulligan Quartet/Paul Desmond Quintet	1956	40.00
—Black vinyl			

MULLINS, DEE

PLANTATION

❑ PLP-4	The Continuing Story	1969	18.00

MULLINS, ROB

FLYING PIANO

❑ FPR102	Red Shoes	1982	18.00

NOVA

❑ 8810	5th Gear	1988	12.00

MULLOY, BOB

CLASSIC CHRISTMAS

❑ CCR-1932	The Musical Magic of Christmas Organ and Chimes	1977	12.00

MULTIPLICATION ROCK (SOUNDTRACK)

CAPITOL

❑ SJA-11174	Multiplication Rock	1973	40.00

MUMY, BILL

BB

❑ 103	Bill Mumy	1980	30.00

MUNGO JERRY

JANUS

❑ JLS-3027	Memoirs of a Stockbroker	1972	18.00
❑ JLS3027 [B]	Memoirs of a Stockbroker	1971	18.00
❑ JXS-7000	Mungo Jerry	1970	18.00

MUNOZ

INDIA NAVIGATION

❑ IN-1034	Rendezvous with Now	1978	18.00

MUNSON, ESTELLA

MEL-SO'NANCE

❑ SLP-33-100	Christmas Is In the Air	1968	15.00

MUNSTERS, THE

DECCA

❑ DL4588 [M]	The Munsters	1964	100.00
❑ DL74588 [S]	The Munsters	1964	150.00

MURE, BILLY

EVEREST

❑ LPBR-5067 [M]	A String of Trumpets	1960	25.00
❑ SDBR-1067 [S]	A String of Trumpets	1960	30.00
❑ LPBR-5072 [M]	Songs of Hank Williams	1960	25.00
❑ SDBR-1072 [S]	Songs of Hank Williams	1960	30.00
❑ LPBR-5120 [M]	Strictly Cha-Cha-Cha	1961	25.00
❑ SDBR-1120 [S]	Strictly Cha-Cha-Cha	1961	30.00

KAPP

❑ KL-1253 [M]	Tough Strings	1961	25.00
❑ KS-3253 [S]	Tough Strings	1961	30.00

MGM

❑ E-4406 [M]	Happy Guitars	1966	25.00
❑ SE-4406 [S]	Happy Guitars	1966	30.00
❑ E-4189 [M]	Maria Elena and Other Great Songs	1964	25.00
❑ SE-4189 [S]	Maria Elena and Other Great Songs	1964	30.00
❑ E-3780 [M]	Supersonic Guitars	1959	30.00
❑ SE-3780 [S]	Supersonic Guitars	1959	50.00
❑ E-3807 [M]	Supersonic Guitars, Vol. 2	1959	30.00
❑ SE-3807 [S]	Supersonic Guitars, Vol. 2	1959	50.00
❑ E-4131 [M]	Teen Bossa Nova	1963	25.00
❑ SE-4131 [S]	Teen Bossa Nova	1963	30.00

PREMIER

❑ PM-9014 [M]	Blue Hawaii	196?	12.00
—Side 1 by Billy Mure; Side 2 by Harry Kaapuni and His Royal Hawaiians			

RCA VICTOR

❑ LPM-1694 [M]	Fireworks	1958	30.00
❑ LSP-1694 [S]	Fireworks	1958	40.00
❑ LPM-1536 [M]	Supersonic Guitars in Hi-Fi	1957	40.00
❑ LPM-1869 [M]	Supersonic in Flight	1959	30.00
❑ LSP-1869 [S]	Supersonic in Flight	1959	50.00

SPIN-O-RAMA

❑ S147 [M]	Blue Hawaii	196?	12.00
—Side 1 by Billy Mure; Side 2 by Harry Kaapuni and His Royal Hawaiians			
❑ S157 [M]	Hawaiian Moods	196?	12.00
—One side by Billy Mure; one side by Luke Leilani			

STRAND

❑ SL-1010 [M]	Hawaiian Percussion	1961	30.00
❑ SLS-1010 [S]	Hawaiian Percussion	1961	40.00
❑ SL-1070 [M]	Pink Hawaii	1962	25.00
❑ SLS-1070 [S]	Pink Hawaii	1962	30.00
❑ SL-1021 [M]	'Round the World in Percussion	1961	30.00
❑ SLS-1021 [S]	'Round the World in Percussion	1961	40.00

SUNSET

❑ SUS-5173	Songs of Hank Williams	196?	15.00
—Reissue of Everest SDBR-1072 with fewer tracks			

UNITED ARTISTS

❑ UAL-3031 [M]	Bandstand Record Hop	1959	40.00
❑ UAS-6031 [S]	Bandstand Record Hop	1959	60.00

MURMAIDS, THE

CHATTAHOOCHEE

❑ CHLP-628 [M]	The Mermaids Resurface!	1981	30.00

MURPHEY, MICHAEL

A&M

❑ SP-4388	Cosmic Cowboy Souvenir	1973	15.00
❑ SP-3137	Cosmic Cowboy Souvenir	198?	10.00
—Budget-line reissue			
❑ SP-4358	Geronimo's Cadillac	1972	15.00
❑ SP-3134	Geronimo's Cadillac	198?	10.00
—Budget-line reissue			

EMI AMERICA

❑ ST-17143	The Best of Michael Martin Murphey	1984	12.00
❑ LN-10310	The Heart Never Lies	1986	10.00
—Budget-line reissue			

EPIC

❑ KE33290	Blue Sky -- Night Thunder	1975	12.00
❑ PE33290	Blue Sky -- Night Thunder	197?	10.00
—Reissue with new prefix & dark blue label			
❑ PE34220	Flowing Free Forever	1976	12.00
❑ JE35013	Lonewolf	1978	12.00
❑ KE32835	Michael Murphey	1974	15.00
❑ JE35742	Peaks, Valleys, Honky-Tonks & Alleys	1979	12.00
❑ PE33851	Swans Against the Sun	1975	12.00
❑ PEQ33851 [Q]	Swans Against the Sun	1975	16.00

LIBERTY

❑ LT-51120	Michael Martin Murphey	1982	12.00
❑ LT-51150	The Heart Never Lies	1983	12.00

WARNER BROS.

❑ 25500	Americana	1987	12.00
❑ 25894	Land of Enchantment	1989	15.00
❑ 25644	River of Time	1988	12.00
❑ 25369	Tonight We Ride	1986	12.00

MURPHY, EDDIE

COLUMBIA

❑ FC39005	Comedian	1983	12.00
❑ AS991763 [DJ]	Comedian	1983	25.00
—Promo-only picture disc			
❑ 9C939151	Comedian	1983	18.00
—Stock version of picture disc			
❑ FC39952	How Could It Be	1985	12.00
❑ OC40970	So Happy	1989	15.00

THE ENTERTAINMENT COMPANY

❑ FC38180	Eddie Murphy	1982	12.00
❑ AS1607 [EP]	Special Censored Versions	1982	15.00
—Promo-only collection of "safe for airplay" routines from FC 38180			

MURPHY, ELLIOTT

POLYDOR

❑ PD-5061	Aquashow	1973	25.00
—First edition with "Like a Great Gatsby" listed as a song title			

RCA VICTOR

❑ APL1-0916	Lost Generation	1975	25.00
—Orange or tan labels			
❑ APL1-1318	Night Lights	1976	25.00
—Orange or tan labels			

MURPHY, LYLE

CONTEMPORARY

❑ C-3506 [M]	Gone with the Woodwinds	1955	60.00

GENE NORMAN

❑ GNP-9 [10]	Four Saxophones in Twelve Tones	1954	120.00
❑ GNP-152 [M]	Four Saxophones in Twelve Tones	195?	50.00
❑ GNP-33 [M]	New Orbits in Sound	1957	50.00

INNER CITY

❑ IC-1133	Ultimate Odyssey	198?	18.00

MURPHY, MARK

AUDIOPHILE

❑ AP-132	Mark Murphy Sings Dorothy Fields and Cy Coleman	197?	12.00

CAPITOL

❑ T1299 [M]	Hip Parade	1960	30.00
❑ ST1299 [S]	Hip Parade	1960	30.00
❑ T1458 [M]	Playing the Field	1960	30.00
❑ ST1458 [S]	Playing the Field	1960	30.00
❑ T1177 [M]	This Could Be the Start of Something	1959	30.00
❑ ST1177 [S]	This Could Be the Start of Something	1959	30.00

DECCA

❑ DL8632 [M]	Let Yourself Go	1958	40.00
❑ DL8390 [M]	Meet Mark Murphy	1957	50.00

FANTASY

❑ OJC-141	Rah	198?	12.00
❑ OJC-367	That's How I Love the Blues	198?	12.00

FONTANA

❑ MGF-27537 [M]	A Swingin' Singin' Affair	1965	25.00
❑ SRF-67537 [S]	A Swingin' Singin' Affair	1965	30.00

MILESTONE

❑ M-9145	Night Mood	1987	12.00
❑ M-9154	September Ballads	1988	12.00

Number	Title	Yr	NM
MUSE			
❏ MR-5355	Beauty and the Beast	198?	12.00
❏ MR-5253	Bop for Kerouac	1981	15.00
❏ MR-5297	Brazil Song (Cancoes do Brasil)	1983	12.00
❏ MR-5009	Bridging a Gap	197?	15.00
❏ MR-5359	Kerouac, Then and Now	198?	15.00
❏ MR-5345	Living Room	1986	12.00
❏ MR-5041	Mark II	197?	15.00
❏ MR-5078	Mark Murphy Sings	1975	15.00
❏ MR-5308	Mark Murphy Sings Nat's Choice	1985	12.00
❏ MR-5320	Mark Murphy Sings Nat's Choice, Vol. 2	1986	12.00
❏ MR-5213	Satisfaction Guaranteed	1980	12.00
❏ MR-5102	Stolen Moments	1978	15.00
❏ MR-5286	The Artistry of Mark Murphy	1982	12.00
PAUSA			
❏ 7023	Midnight Mood	1979	12.00
❏ 9042	This Could Be the Start of Something	1985	12.00
RIVERSIDE			
❏ RLP-395 [M]	Rah	1961	30.00
❏ RS-9395 [S]	Rah	1961	30.00
❏ 6064	Rah	197?	15.00
❏ 6091	That's How I Love the Blues	197?	15.00
❏ RLP-441 [M]	That's How I Love the Blues!	1962	30.00
❏ RS-9441 [S]	That's How I Love the Blues!	1962	30.00

MURPHY, ROSE

AUDIOPHILE			
❏ AP-70	Rose Murphy	198?	15.00
MCA			
❏ 1558	Rose Murphy Sings Again	1983	18.00
ROYALE			
❏ VLP-6079 [10]	Chi-Chi Girl	195?	80.00
❏ 1835 [10]	Rose Murphy and Quartette	195?	80.00
UNITED ARTISTS			
❏ UAJ-14025 [M]	Jazz, Joy and Happiness	1962	50.00
❏ UAJS-15025 [S]	Jazz, Joy and Happiness	1962	60.00
VERVE			
❏ MGV-2070 [M]	Not Cha-Cha But Chi-Chi	1957	50.00
❏ V-2070 [M]	Not Cha-Cha But Chi-Chi	1961	30.00

MURPHY, TURK

ATLANTIC			
❏ SD1613	The Many Faces of Ragtime	1972	15.00
COLUMBIA			
❏ CL6257 [10]	Barrelhouse Jazz	1953	50.00
❏ CL595 [M]	Barrelhouse Jazz	1954	40.00
—Maroon label, gold print			
❏ CL595 [M]	Barrelhouse Jazz	1955	30.00
—Red and black label with six "eye" logos			
❏ CL650 [M]	Dancing Jazz	1955	40.00
—Maroon label, gold print			
❏ CL650 [M]	Dancing Jazz	1955	30.00
—Red and black label with six "eye" logos			
❏ CL559 [M]	The Music of Jelly Roll Morton	1954	40.00
—Maroon label, gold print			
❏ CL559 [M]	The Music of Jelly Roll Morton	1955	30.00
—Red and black label with six "eye" logos			
❏ CL546 [M]	When the Saints Go Marching In	1953	40.00
—Maroon label, gold print			
❏ CL546 [M]	When the Saints Go Marching In	1955	30.00
—Red and black label with six "eye" logos			
FORUM			
❏ F-9017 [M]	Turk Murphy and His Jazz Band at the Roundtable	196?	15.00
—Reissue of Roulette R-25076			
❏ SF-9017 [S]	Turk Murphy and His Jazz Band at the Roundtable	196?	18.00
—Reissue of Roulette SR-25076			
GHB			
❏ 91	Turk Murphy, Volume 1	198?	12.00
❏ 92	Turk Murphy, Volume 2	198?	12.00
❏ 93	Turk Murphy, Volume 3	198?	12.00
GOOD TIME JAZZ			
❏ L-12026 [M]	San Francisco Jazz, Volume 1	1955	40.00
❏ L-12027 [M]	San Francisco Jazz, Volume 2	1955	40.00
❏ L-7 [10]	Turk Murphy with Claire Austin	1952	50.00
MERRY MAKERS			
❏ S-105	Turk Murphy San Francisco Jazz Band	197?	18.00
❏ S-106	Turk Murphy's Jazz Band	197?	18.00
MOTHERLODE			
❏ 0103	Turk Murphy's Jazz Band, Vol. 1	1973	15.00
❏ 0104	Turk Murphy's Jazz Band, Vol. 2	1973	15.00
MPS			
❏ MC-22097	Live!	197?	18.00

Number	Title	Yr	NM
RCA VICTOR			
❏ LPM-2501 [M]	Let the Good Times Roll	1962	25.00
❏ LSP-2501 [S]	Let the Good Times Roll	1962	30.00
ROULETTE			
❏ R-25088 [M]	Music for Wise Guys	1960	25.00
❏ SR-25088 [S]	Music for Wise Guys	1960	30.00
❏ R-25076 [M]	Turk Murphy and His Jazz Band at the Roundtable	1959	25.00
❏ SR-25076 [S]	Turk Murphy and His Jazz Band at the Roundtable	1959	30.00
SONIC ARTS			
❏ 14	Natural High	1979	18.00
STOMP OFF			
❏ SOS-1161	Southern Stomps	1989	12.00
❏ SOS-1155	Turk at Carnegie	1988	12.00
VERVE			
❏ MGV-1013 [M]	Music for Losers	1957	40.00
❏ V-1013 [M]	Music for Losers	1961	25.00
❏ MGV-1015 [M]	Turk Murphy on Easy Street	1957	40.00
❏ V-1015 [M]	Turk Murphy on Easy Street	1961	25.00

MURPHY, WALTER

MCA			
❏ 6114	Themes from E.T. and More	1982	12.00
PRIVATE STOCK			
❏ PS2015	A Fifth of Beethoven	1976	12.00
❏ PS7010	Phantom of the Opera	1978	12.00
❏ PS2028	Rhapsody in Blue	1977	12.00

MURRAY, ANNE, AND GLEN CAMPBELL

CAPITOL			
❏ SW-869	Anne Murray/Glen Campbell	1971	15.00
❏ SN-16144	Anne Murray/Glen Campbell	1980	10.00
—Budget-line reissue			

MURRAY, ANNE

CAPITOL			
❏ ST-12039	A Country Collection	1980	12.00
❏ SN-16338	A Country Collection	198?	10.00
—Budget-line reissue			
❏ ST-12301	A Little Good News	1983	12.00
❏ ST-667	Anne Murray	1971	15.00
❏ SOO-12110	Anne Murray's Greatest Hits	1980	12.00
❏ ST-11024	Annie	1972	12.00
❏ C1-48764	As I Am	1988	12.00
❏ C1-90886	Christmas	1987	10.00
❏ SN-16232	Christmas Wishes	1981	12.00
—Original issue was on the budget-line series			
❏ ST-11324	Country	1974	12.00
❏ SN-16213	Country	1981	10.00
—Budget-line reissue			
❏ ST-11172	Danny's Song	1973	12.00
❏ SN-16211	Danny's Song	1981	10.00
—Budget-line reissue			
❏ ST-12072	Greatest Hits Volume II	1989	15.00
❏ PJ-12562	Harmony	1987	12.00
❏ SJ-12303	Heart Over Mind	1984	12.00
❏ ST-11354	Highly Prized Possession	1974	12.00
❏ SN-16081	Highly Prized Possession	1980	10.00
—Budget-line reissue			
❏ SOO-12012	I'll Always Love You	1979	12.00
❏ ST-11559	Keeping in Touch	1976	12.00
❏ SN-16082	Keeping in Touch	1980	10.00
—Budget-line reissue			
❏ ST-11743	Let's Keep It That Way	1978	12.00
❏ SN-16341	Let's Keep It That Way	198?	10.00
—Budget-line reissue			
❏ ST-11266	Love Song	1974	12.00
❏ SN-16212	Love Song	1981	10.00
—Budget-line reissue			
❏ SW-11849	New Kind of Feeling	1979	12.00
❏ SN-16283	New Kind of Feeling	1982	10.00
—Budget-line reissue			
❏ ST-579	Snowbird	1970	15.00
❏ SOO-12064	Somebody's Waiting	1980	12.00
❏ SJ-12466	Something to Talk About	1986	12.00
❏ ST-821	Talk It Over in the Morning	1971	15.00
❏ SN-16080	Talk It Over in the Morning	1980	10.00
—Budget-line reissue			
❏ ST-12225	The Hottest Night of the Year	1982	12.00
❏ SN-16233	There's a Hippo in My Tub	1981	12.00
—Original issue was on the budget-line series			
❏ ST-11433	Together	1975	12.00
❏ SN-16282	Together	1982	10.00
—Budget-line reissue			
❏ SOO-12144	Where Do You Go When You Dream	1981	12.00
CAPITOL NASHVILLE			
❏ R173232	You Will	1990	25.00
—Only released on vinyl through BMG Direct Marketing			
PICKWICK			
❏ SPC-3350	What About Me	197?	10.00

MURRAY, DAVID

ADELPHI			
❏ 5002	Low Class Conspiracy	1976	18.00
BLACK SAINT			
❏ BSR-0089	Children	1986	15.00

Number	Title	Yr	NM
❏ BSR-0055	Home	198?	15.00
❏ BSR-0018	Interboogieology	198?	18.00
❏ 120105	I Want to Talk About You	1990	18.00
❏ BSR-0085	Live at Sweet Basil, Vol. 1	1985	15.00
❏ 120095	Live at Sweet Basil, Vol. 2	1986	15.00
❏ BSR-0045	Ming	198?	15.00
❏ BSR-0075	Morning Song	1984	15.00
❏ BSR-0065	Murray's Steps	1983	15.00
❏ BSR-0039	Sweet Lovely	198?	15.00
❏ 120110	The Hill	1990	18.00
HAT ART			
❏ 2016	3D Family	1986	18.00
HAT HUT			
❏ 0U/V	The Third Family	1979	25.00
INDIA NAVIGATION			
❏ IN-1026	Flowers for Albert	197?	18.00
❏ IN-1044	Live, Volume 2	1979	18.00
❏ IN-1032	Live at the Ocean Club	1978	18.00
PORTRAIT			
❏ OR44432	Ming's Samba	1989	15.00
RED RECORD			
❏ VPA-129	Last of the Hipman	198?	15.00

MURRAY, SUNNY

ESP-DISK'			
❏ 1032 [M]	Sunny Murray	1966	25.00
❏ S-1032 [S]	Sunny Murray	1966	30.00
JIHAD			
❏ 663 [M]	Sunny's Time Now	1967	200.00

MUSCLE SHOALS HORNS, THE

BANG			
❏ BLP-403 [B]	Born to Get Down	1975	25.00

MUSIC ASYLUM, THE

UNITED ARTISTS			
❏ UAS-6778	Commit Thyself	1970	25.00

MUSIC CITY SINGERS, THE

HALO			
❏ 1003	Christmas Favorites	196?	18.00
—Includes Bobby Russell, Bill Pursell, Boots Randolph, Willie Ackerman, The Jordanaires and the Anita Kerr Singers, among others			

MUSIC CITY SOUNDS, THE

MGM			
❏ SE-4672	The Music City Sounds Featuring Lloyd Green and Pete Wade	1970	18.00

MUSIC COMPANY, THE

CRESTVIEW			
❏ CRS-3057	Hard and Heavy	1968	30.00
MIRWOOD			
❏ M-7002 [M]	Rubber Soul Jazz	1966	25.00
❏ MS-7002 [S]	Rubber Soul Jazz	1966	30.00

MUSIC EMPORIUM, THE

SENTINEL			
❏ 69001	The Music Emporium	1969	2000.00
SUNDAZED			
❏ LP5078	The Music Emporium	2001	18.00
—First legitimate reissue of the original			

MUSIC EXPLOSION, THE

LAURIE			
❏ LLP-2040 [M]	Little Bit O'Soul	1967	25.00
❏ SLLP-2040 [S]	Little Bit O'Soul	1967	30.00

MUSIC IMPROVISATION COMPANY, THE

ECM			
❏ 1005	The Music Improvisation Company	197?	18.00

MUSIC MACHINE, THE

ORIGINAL SOUND			
❏ 5015 [M]	(Turn On) The Music Machine	1966	40.00
❏ 8875 [S]	(Turn On) The Music Machine	1966	50.00
SUNDAZED			
❏ LP5038	Ignition	2000	15.00
WARNER BROS.			
❏ W1732 [M]	Bonniwell's Music Machine	1967	60.00
❏ WS1732 [S]	Bonniwell's Music Machine	1967	40.00

MUSICAL YOUTH

MCA			
❏ 5454 [B]	Different Style	1983	15.00
❏ 5389 [B]	The Youth of Today	1983	15.00

MUSSELWHITE, CHARLIE

VANGUARD			
❏ VSD-79287	Charlie Musselwhite	1968	25.00

Number	Title	Yr	NM
❏ VRS-9232 [M]	Stand Back! Here Comes Charlie Musselwhite's South Side Band	1966	25.00
❏ VSD-79232 [S]	Stand Back! Here Comes Charlie Musselwhite's South Side Band	1966	30.00
❏ VSD-6258	Tennessee Woman	1969	25.00

MUSSO, VIDO

CROWN
❏ CLP-5029 [M]	Teenage Dance Party	1957	50.00
❏ CLP-5007 [M]	The Swingin'st	1957	50.00
—Reissue of Modern LP			

MODERN
| ❏ MLP-1207 [M] | The Swingin'st | 1956 | 100.00 |

MUSSULLI, BOOTS

CAPITOL
| ❏ H6506 [10] | Boots Mussulli | 1955 | 120.00 |
| ❏ T6506 [M] | Boots Mussulli | 1955 | 50.00 |

MUSTANGS, THE

PROVIDENCE
| ❏ PLP-001 [M] | Dartell Stomp | 1964 | 50.00 |

MUTZIE

SUSSEX
| ❏ SUX-7001 | Light of Your Shadow | 1970 | 30.00 |

MY BLOODY VALENTINE

CREATION/RELATIVITY
| ❏ 1006 [B] | Isn't Anything | 1989 | 35.00 |

MYA

INTERSCOPE
| ❏ 490640-1 | Fear of Flying | 2000 | 18.00 |
| ❏ 90166 | Mya | 1998 | 15.00 |

MYERS, DAVE

CAROLE
| ❏ 8002 [M] | Greatest Racing Themes | 1967 | 50.00 |

DEL-FI
❏ DFLP-1239 [M]	Hangin' Twenty	1963	80.00
❏ DFST-1239 [S]	Hangin' Twenty	1963	180.00
❏ DLF-1239	Hangin' Twenty	1998	15.00

MYERSON, BESS

MGM
| ❏ E-3785 [M] | Fashions in Music | 1959 | 30.00 |
| ❏ SE-3785 [S] | Fashions in Music | 1959 | 40.00 |

MYLES, ALANNAH

ATLANTIC
| ❏ 81956 | Alannah Myles | 1989 | 15.00 |

MYRICK, BERL

STRATA-EAST
| ❏ SES-102-74 | Live 'n Well | 1974 | 30.00 |

MYRICK, GARY, AND THE FIGURES

EPIC
❏ NJE36524	Gary Myrick and the Figures	1980	15.00
❏ JE36524	Gary Myrick and the Figures	1981	12.00
—Reissue with amended prefix			
❏ B5E38637 [EP]	Language	1983	12.00
❏ AS1389 [DJ]	Live Sampler	1982	16.00
—Four live tracks, including one unreleased song			
❏ ARE37429	Living in a Movie	1981	12.00
❏ AS912 [DJ]	Talks in Stereo	1981	40.00
—Side one has studio tracks, side two has live versions of songs on side one			

GEFFEN
| ❏ GHS24076 | Stand for Love | 1985 | 12.00 |

MYSTERIOUS FLYING ORCHESTRA, THE

RCA VICTOR
| ❏ APL1-2137 | The Mysterious Flying Orchestra | 1977 | 25.00 |

MYSTIC ASTROLOGICAL CRYSTAL BAND, THE

CAROLE
❏ S-8003	Clip Out, Put On Book	1968	30.00
❏ 8001 [M]	Mystic Astrological Crystal Band	1967	30.00
❏ S-8001 [S]	Mystic Astrological Crystal Band	1967	30.00

MYSTIC SIVA

VO
| ❏ 19713 | Mystic Siva | 1971 | 1000.00 |

MYSTICS, THE

AMBIENT SOUND
| ❏ FZ37716 | Crazy for You | 1982 | 12.00 |

COLLECTABLES
| ❏ COL-5043 | 16 Golden Classics | 198? | 12.00 |

N

N.E.R.D.

VIRGIN
| ❏ 91457 [B] | Fly or Die | 2004 | 18.00 |
| ❏ 12622 [B] | In Search of... | 2002 | 30.00 |

N.W.A.

PRIORITY
| ❏ SPRO30080 [DJ] | Greatest Hits/In-Store Play | 1996 | 25.00 |
| —Promo-only "clean" versions for retailer use | | | |

RUTHLESS
❏ 7224 [EP]	100 Miles and Runnin'	1990	18.00
❏ 57126	Efil4zaggin (Niggaz4life)	1991	25.00
❏ 50561	Greatest Hits	1996	18.00
❏ 57119	N.W.A. and the Posse	1990	18.00
—Reissue of MRC 1057			
❏ MRC1057	N.W.A. and the Posse	1987	30.00

"STRAIGHT OUTTA COMPTON"

| ❏ 57102 [B] | Straight Outta Compton | 1989 | 25.00 |

NABORS, JIM

CAPITOL SPECIAL MARKETS
| ❏ SL-8136 | 20 All-Time Favorites | 1977 | 12.00 |

COLUMBIA
❏ KC33401	A Very Special Love Song	1974	15.00
❏ PC33401	A Very Special Love Song	1979	10.00
—Budget-line reissue			
❏ C30129	Everything Is Beautiful	1970	15.00
❏ C30449	For the Good Times/The Jim Nabors Hour	1971	15.00
❏ CS9817	Galveston	1969	15.00
❏ KG31591	Great Love Songs	1972	18.00
❏ PG31591	Great Love Songs	198?	12.00
—Budget-line reissue			
❏ C30810	Help Me Make It Through the Night	1971	15.00
❏ CQ30810 [Q]	Help Me Make It Through the Night	1971	25.00
❏ C30671	How Great Thou Art	1971	15.00
❏ 3C30671	How Great Thou Art	198?	10.00
—Budget-line reissue			
❏ KC32950	It's My Life	1973	15.00
❏ CL2665 [M]	Jim Nabors By Request	1967	15.00
❏ CS9465 [S]	Jim Nabors By Request	1967	18.00
❏ CL2731 [M]	Jim Nabors' Christmas Album	1967	15.00
❏ CS9531 [S]	Jim Nabors' Christmas Album	1967	15.00
—Originals with "360 Sound" label			
❏ CS9531	Jim Nabors' Christmas Album	1970	12.00
—Later editions with orange label			
❏ CL2558 [M]	Jim Nabors Sings Love Me with All Your Heart	1966	15.00
❏ CS9358 [S]	Jim Nabors Sings Love Me with All Your Heart	1966	18.00
❏ CS9620	Kiss Me Goodbye	1968	15.00
❏ C31630	Merry Christmas	1972	12.00
❏ KC32909	Peace in the Valley	1973	15.00
❏ PC32909	Peace in the Valley	1979	10.00
—Budget-line reissue			
❏ CL2368 [M]	Shazam! (Gomer Pyle, U.S.M.C.)	1965	25.00
❏ CS9168 [S]	Shazam! (Gomer Pyle, U.S.M.C.)	1965	30.00
❏ CS1020	The Jim Nabors Hour	1970	15.00
❏ PC9716	The Lord's Prayer	1979	10.00
—Budget-line reissue			

Number	Title	Yr	NM
❏ CS9716	The Lord's Prayer and Other Sacred Songs	1968	15.00
❏ CG33618	The Lord's Prayer/How Great Thou Art	1975	18.00
❏ CL2703 [M]	The Things I Love	1967	15.00
❏ CS9503 [S]	The Things I Love	1967	18.00
❏ KC32377	The Twelfth of Never	1972	15.00
❏ KC31336	The Way of Love	1972	15.00
❏ KG31973	The World of Jim Nabors	1972	18.00
❏ PG31973	The World of Jim Nabors	1979	12.00
—Budget-line reissue			

COLUMBIA SPECIAL PRODUCTS
| ❏ P13507 | Somewhere My Love | 1977 | 12.00 |

HARMONY
| ❏ KH30398 | More | 1971 | 12.00 |

PAIR
| ❏ PDL2-1097 | On the Country Side | 1986 | 15.00 |
| ❏ PDL2-1077 | The Very Special Warmth of Jim Nabors | 1986 | 15.00 |

RANWOOD
❏ R-7017	22 Great Hymn and Country Favorites	1984	15.00
❏ R-8178	I See God	1977	12.00
❏ R-8157	Old Time Religion	1976	12.00
❏ R-8176	Sincerely	1977	12.00
❏ R-8164	Town & Country	1976	12.00

REALM
| ❏ 1V-8170 | Christmas with Jim Nabors | 1982 | 10.00 |

NAGLE, RON

WARNER BROS.
| ❏ WS1902 [B] | Bad Rice | 1970 | 25.00 |

NAKED EYES

EMI AMERICA
| ❏ ST-17116 | Fuel for the Fire | 1984 | 12.00 |
| ❏ ST-17089 | Naked Eyes | 1983 | 15.00 |

NAKED RAYGUN

CAROLINE
❏ 1348	Jettison	1988	25.00
❏ 1642	Raygun...Naked Raygun	1990	25.00
❏ 1371	Understand?	1989	25.00

HAUNTED TOWN
| ❏ HTR11 | Free Shit | 2001 | 12.00 |

HOMESTEAD
❏ HMS 045	All Rise	1985	30.00
❏ HMS 008	Throb Throb	1984	30.00
—First edition has lyric sheet			
❏ HMS 008	Throb Throb	1984	25.00
—Second edition has lyric innersleeve			

RUTHLESS
| ❏ 03 [EP] | Basement Screams | 1983 | 80.00 |

NAMYSLOVSKI, ZBIGNIEW

INNER CITY
| ❏ IC-1130 | Air Condition | 198? | 15.00 |
| ❏ IC-1048 | Namyslovski | 197? | 18.00 |

NANCE, RAY

SOLID STATE
| ❏ SS-18062 [B] | Body and Soul | 1969 | 25.00 |

NANTON, MORRIS

PRESTIGE
❏ PRLP-7345 [M]	Preface	1964	25.00
❏ PRST-7345 [S]	Preface	1964	30.00
❏ PRLP-7409 [M]	Something We've Got	1965	25.00
❏ PRST-7409 [S]	Something We've Got	1965	30.00
❏ PRLP-7467 [M]	Soul Fingers	1966	25.00
❏ PRST-7467 [S]	Soul Fingers	1966	30.00

WARNER BROS.
❏ W-1256 [M]	Flower Drum Song	1958	30.00
❏ WS-1256 [S]	Flower Drum Song	1958	30.00
❏ W-1279 [M]	The Original Jazz Performance of "Roberta	1959	30.00
❏ WS-1279 [S]	The Original Jazz Performance of "Roberta	1959	30.00

NAPOLEON, PHIL

CAPITOL
❏ ST1428 [S]	In the Land of Dixie	1961	30.00
❏ T1428 [M]	In the Land of Dixie	1961	25.00
❏ T1344 [M]	Phil Napoleon and the Memphis Five	1960	30.00
❏ ST1344 [S]	Phil Napoleon and the Memphis Five	1960	25.00
❏ ST1535 [S]	Tenderloin Dixieland	1961	30.00
❏ T1535 [M]	Tenderloin Dixieland	1961	25.00

COLUMBIA
| ❏ CL2505 [10] | Two-Beat | 1955 | 80.00 |

EMARCY
❏ MG-26008 [10]	Dixieland Classics Vol. 1	1954	100.00
❏ MG-36033 [M]	Dixieland Classics Vol. 1	1955	80.00
❏ MG-26009 [10]	Dixieland Classics Vol. 2	1954	100.00

Number	Title	Yr	NM

JOLLY ROGER
| ❏ 5006 [10] | Dixieland By Phil Napoleon | 1954 | 50.00 |

MERCURY
| ❏ MG-25078 [10] | Dixieland Classics Vol. 1 | 1953 | 100.00 |
| ❏ MG-25079 [10] | Dixieland Classics Vol. 2 | 1953 | 100.00 |

NAPOLEON XIV

RHINO
| ❏ RNLP816 | They're Coming to Take Me Away, Ha-Haaa! | 1985 | 15.00 |

WARNER BROS.
| ❏ W1661 [M] | They're Coming to Take Me Away, Ha-Haaa! | 1966 | 80.00 |
| ❏ WS1661 [S] | They're Coming to Take Me Away, Ha-Haaa! | 1966 | 100.00 |

NARELL, ANDY

HIPPOCKET
❏ HP-103	Light in Your Eyes	1983	15.00
—Original issue			
❏ HP-105	Slow Motion	1985	15.00
—Original issue			
❏ HP-101	Stickman	1981	15.00
—Original issue			

INNER CITY
| ❏ IC-1053 | Hidden Treasure | 1979 | 18.00 |

WINDHAM HILL
❏ WH-0103	Light in Your Eyes	1987	12.00
—Reissue of HipPocket 103			
❏ WH-0120	Little Secrets	1989	15.00
❏ WH-0105	Slow Motion	1987	12.00
—Reissue of HipPocket 105			
❏ WH-0101	Stickman	1987	12.00
—Reissue of HipPocket 101			
❏ WH-0107	The Hammer	1987	12.00

NARZ, JACK

DOT
| ❏ DLP-3244 [M] | Sing the Folk Hits with Jack Narz | 1960 | 30.00 |
| ❏ DLP-25244 [S] | Sing the Folk Hits with Jack Narz | 1960 | 30.00 |

NAS

COLUMBIA
❏ C286930	God's Son	2002	18.00
❏ C2S41881 [DJ]	I Am	1999	25.00
—Promo-only version in generic black sleeve			
❏ C268773	I Am	1999	18.00
❏ C57694	Illmatic	1994	30.00
❏ C292072	Illmatic	2004	18.00
—10th anniversary reissue with bonus material			
❏ C67015	It Was Written	1996	15.00
❏ C285530	Nastradamus	1999	10.00
❏ C285736	Stillmatic	2001	18.00
❏ C492065	Street's Disciple	2004	30.00
❏ C285275	The Lost Tapes	2002	18.00

NASCIMENTO, MILTON

A&M
❏ SP-3019	Courage	1969	25.00
❏ SP9-3019	Courage	198?	18.00
—Audiophile reissue (clearly marked as such)			
❏ SP-4719	Journey to Dawn	1979	18.00
❏ SP-4611	Milton	1976	12.00
❏ LP-0(# unknown) [M]	Milton Nascimento	1967	30.00
❏ SP-0(# unknown) [S]	Milton Nascimento	1967	25.00

COLUMBIA
| ❏ FC45239 | Miltons | 1989 | 15.00 |
| ❏ FC44277 | Yauarate | 1987 | 12.00 |

INTUITION
| ❏ B1-90790 | Milagre Dos Peixes | 1988 | 15.00 |
| —Originally issued in Brazil in 1973 | | | |

POLYDOR
| ❏ 827638-1 | Encontros E Despedidas | 1986 | 15.00 |

VERVE
| ❏ 831349-1 | A Barca Dos Amantes | 1986 | 15.00 |

NASH, GRAHAM, AND DAVID CROSBY

ABC
❏ AA-1042	Crosby/Nash -- Live	1977	12.00
❏ AA-1102	The Best of Crosby/Nash	1978	12.00
❏ ABCD-956 [B]	Whistling Down the Wire	1976	12.00
❏ ABCD-902 [B]	Wind on the Water	1975	12.00

ATLANTIC
| ❏ SD7220 | Graham Nash/David Crosby | 1972 | 15.00 |

MCA
❏ 37008	The Best of Crosby/Nash	198?	10.00
—Reissue of ABC 1102			
❏ 37007	Wind on the Water	198?	10.00
—Reissue of ABC 902			

NASH, GRAHAM

ATLANTIC
❏ 81633	Innocent Eyes	1986	10.00
❏ SD7204	Songs for Beginners	1971	15.00
❏ SD7288	Wild Tales	1974	12.00

CAPITOL
| ❏ SWAK-12014 | Earth & Sky | 1980 | 12.00 |

NASH, JOHNNY

ABC-PARAMOUNT
❏ 299 [M]	I Got Rhythm	1959	30.00
❏ S-299 [S]	I Got Rhythm	1959	40.00
❏ 244 [M]	Johnny Nash	1958	30.00
❏ S-244 [S]	Johnny Nash	1959	40.00
❏ 344 [M]	Let's Get Lost	1960	30.00
❏ S-344 [S]	Let's Get Lost	1960	40.00
❏ 276 [M]	Quiet Hour	1959	30.00
❏ S-276 [S]	Quiet Hour	1959	40.00
❏ 383 [M]	Studio Time	1961	30.00
❏ S-383 [S]	Studio Time	1961	40.00

ARGO
| ❏ LP-4038 [M] | Composer's Choice | 1964 | 25.00 |
| ❏ LPS-4038 [S] | Composer's Choice | 1964 | 30.00 |

EPIC
❏ PE32828	Celebrate Life	1974	18.00
❏ KE31607	I Can See Clearly Now	1972	18.00
—Yellow label			
❏ KE31607	I Can See Clearly Now	1973	15.00
—Orange label			
❏ KE32158	My Merry-Go-Round	1973	18.00

JAD
❏ JS-1006 [B]	Folk Soul	1970	30.00
❏ JS-1207	Hold Me Tight	1968	30.00
❏ JS-1001 [B]	Prince of Peace	1969	30.00

NASH, PAUL

REVELATION
| ❏ 32 | A Jazz Composer's Ensemble | 1980 | 18.00 |

SOUL NOTE
| ❏ SN-1107 | Second Impression | 1986 | 15.00 |

NASH, TED & DICK

LIBERTY
| ❏ LJH-6011 [M] | The Brothers Nash | 1956 | 50.00 |

NASH, TED

COLUMBIA
| ❏ CL989 [M] | Star Eyes | 1957 | 40.00 |

CONCORD JAZZ
| ❏ CJ-106 | Conception | 1980 | 12.00 |

STARLITE
| ❏ LP-6001 [10] | Ted Nash | 1954 | 50.00 |

NASHVILLE ALL STARS, THE

RCA VICTOR
| ❏ LPM-2302 [M] | After the Riot at Newport | 1960 | 40.00 |
| ❏ LSP-2302 [S] | After the Riot at Newport | 1960 | 50.00 |

RCA VICTOR RECORD CLUB
❏ CPM-0114 [M]	All-Time Country and Western Hits	1966	15.00
❏ CSP-0114 [S]	All-Time Country and Western Hits	1966	18.00
❏ CPM-0126 [M]	That Happy Nashville Sound	1967	18.00
❏ CSP-0126 [S]	That Happy Nashville Sound	1967	15.00

NASHVILLE GUITARS, THE

MONUMENT
❏ MLP-8058 [M]	The Nashville Guitars	1966	18.00
❏ SLP-18058 [S]	The Nashville Guitars	1966	25.00
❏ MLP-18093	The Nashville Guitars at Home	1968	18.00

NASHVILLE JAZZ MACHINE, THE

AM-PM
| ❏ 14 | Where's Eli? | 1986 | 12.00 |

NASHVILLE PUSSY

AMPHETAMINE REPTILE
| ❏ AMREP-69 | Let Them Eat Pussy | 1999 | 30.00 |

RESERVATION
| ❏ REZP-1 [PD] | Say Something Nasty | 2003 | 18.00 |
| —Picture disc; 1,000 pressed | | | |

TVT
| ❏ 3340-1 | High as Hell | 2000 | 30.00 |

NASHVILLE TEENS, THE

LONDON
| ❏ LL3407 [M] | Tobacco Road | 1964 | 120.00 |
| ❏ PS407 [R] | Tobacco Road | 1964 | 80.00 |

NASTOS, NICK

STRAND
| ❏ SL-1097 [M] | Guitars on Fire | 1962 | 25.00 |
| ❏ SLS-1097 [S] | Guitars on Fire | 1962 | 30.00 |

NATAL, NANETTE

BENYO
| ❏ BY-3335 | Hi-Fi Baby | 198? | 15.00 |
| ❏ BY-3334 | Wild in Reverie | 198? | 15.00 |

NATIONAL LAMPOON

BANANA
❏ BTS6006 [B]	Lemmings	1973	25.00
❏ BTS6008	Missing White House Tapes	1974	18.00
❏ BTS38 [B]	Radio Dinner	1972	25.00

EPIC
❏ PE33410	Gold Turkey	1974	15.00
—Orange label			
❏ PE33410 [B]	Gold Turkey	1979	10.00
—Dark blue label			
❏ PE33956	Goodbye Pop	1975	15.00
—Orange label			
❏ PE33956	Goodbye Pop	1979	10.00
—Dark blue label			

LABEL 21
❏ IMP-2001	That's Not Funny, That's Sick!	1978	12.00
❏ PIC-2001 [PD]	That's Not Funny, That's Sick!	1978	25.00
❏ IMP-2002	The White Album	1979	12.00

MCA
| ❏ 27023 | Lemmings | 198? | 10.00 |
| ❏ 27024 | Radio Dinner | 198? | 10.00 |

PASSPORT
| ❏ PB6018 | Sex, Drugs, Rock and Roll and the End of the World | 1982 | 12.00 |

VISA
❏ 7008 [B]	Greatest Hits of the National Lampoon	1978	15.00
❏ 2001	That's Not Funny, That's Sick!	198?	10.00
❏ 2002	The White Album	198?	10.00

NATIONAL SYMPHONY ORCHESTRA (HOWARD MITCHELL, CONDUCTOR)

RCA VICTOR RED SEAL
| ❏ LSC-2261 [S] | Shostakovich: Symphony No. 5 | 1959 | 50.00 |
| —Original with "shaded dog" label | | | |

NATIONAL YOUTH JAZZ ORCHESTRA

RCA VICTOR
| ❏ LPL1-5116 | 11 Plus | 197? | 18.00 |

NATURAL ESSENCE

FANTASY
| ❏ F-9440 | In Search of Happiness | 1974 | 15.00 |

NATURAL FOUR, THE

CURTOM
| ❏ CU5004 | Heaven Right Here on Earth | 1975 | 25.00 |
| ❏ CRT-8600 | The Natural Four | 1974 | 25.00 |

NATURAL LIFE

ASI
❏ 5006	All Music	1977	15.00
❏ 5001	Natural Life	1977	15.00
❏ 5005	Unnamed Land	1977	15.00

CELEBRATION
| ❏ 5001 | Natural Life | 197? | 18.00 |
| ❏ 5005 | Unnamed Land | 1975 | 18.00 |

NATURAL PROGRESSIONS

PALO ALTO/TBA
| ❏ TBA-248 | Rumor Has It | 1989 | 15.00 |

NAUGHTON, BOBBY

OTIC
❏ 1009	Nauxtagram	1979	15.00
❏ 1005	The Haunt	1976	18.00
❏ 1003	Understanding	197?	18.00

NAUGHTY BY NATURE

ARISTA
| ❏ 19047 | Nineteen Naughty Nine -- Nature's Fury | 1999 | 25.00 |

TOMMY BOY
❏ TBLP-1069	19 Naughty III	1993	25.00
❏ TBLP-1310	Nature's Finest: Naughty by Nature's Greatest Hits	1999	18.00
❏ TBLP-1051	Naughty By Nature	1991	18.00
❏ TBLP-1111	Poverty's Paradise	1995	15.00

NAVARRO, FATS

BLUE NOTE
❏ BLP-5004 [10]	Fats Navarro Memorial Album	1952	1000.00
❏ BN-LA507-H2	Prime Source	1976	18.00
❏ BLP-1531 [M]	The Fabulous Fats Navarro, Vol. 1	1956	500.00
—"Deep groove" version; Lexington Ave. address on label			

Number	Title	Yr	NM
❑ BLP-1531 [M]	The Fabulous Fats Navarro, Vol. 1	1956	200.00
—Deep groove" version, W. 63rd St. address on label			
❑ BLP-1531 [M]	The Fabulous Fats Navarro, Vol. 1	1963	40.00
—With "New York, USA" address on label			
❑ BST-81531 [R]	The Fabulous Fats Navarro, Vol. 1	196?	15.00
—With "A Divison of Liberty Records" on label			
❑ BST-81531	The Fabulous Fats Navarro, Vol. 1	1985	15.00
—The Finest in Jazz Since 1939" reissue			
❑ BLP-1532 [M]	The Fabulous Fats Navarro, Vol. 2	1956	500.00
—Deep groove" version; Lexington Ave. address on label			
❑ BLP-1532 [M]	The Fabulous Fats Navarro, Vol. 2	1956	200.00
—Deep groove" version, W. 63rd St. address on label			
❑ BLP-1532 [M]	The Fabulous Fats Navarro, Vol. 2	1963	40.00
—With "New York, USA" address on label			
❑ BST-81532 [R]	The Fabulous Fats Navarro, Vol. 2	196?	15.00
—With "A Divison of Liberty Records" on label			
❑ BST-81532	The Fabulous Fats Navarro, Vol. 2	1985	15.00
—The Finest in Jazz Since 1939" reissue			

RIVERSIDE

Number	Title	Yr	NM
❑ RS-3019	Good Bait	1968	25.00

SAVOY

Number	Title	Yr	NM
❑ MG-12011 [M]	Fats Navarro Memorial	1955	150.00
❑ MG-9005 [10]	New Sounds in Modern Music	1952	400.00
❑ MG-9019 [10]	New Trends Of Jazz	1952	400.00
❑ MG-12133 [M]	Nostalgia	1958	100.00

SAVOY JAZZ

Number	Title	Yr	NM
❑ SJL-2216	Fat Girl	197?	15.00
❑ SJC-416	Memorial Album	1985	12.00

NAVARRO, FATS/KAI WINDING/BREW MOORE

SAVOY

Number	Title	Yr	NM
❑ MG-12119 [M]	In the Beginning…Bebop	1957	60.00

NAVARRO, JOEY

ANTILLES

Number	Title	Yr	NM
❑ 90985	On the Rocks	1988	12.00

NAVARRO, TOMMY, AND THE SUNDIALERS

URANIA

Number	Title	Yr	NM
❑ UR-900 [M]	Twist Around the Town	1961	150.00
❑ US-5900 [S]	Twist Around the Town	1961	200.00

NAZARETH

A&M

Number	Title	Yr	NM
❑ SP-4901	2XS	1982	12.00
❑ SP-4562	Close Enough for Rock 'N' Roll	1976	12.00
❑ SP-3109	Close Enough for Rock 'N' Roll	1981	10.00
—Budget-line reissue			
❑ SP-3168	Exercises	1982	10.00
—Reissue of Warner Bros. 2639			
❑ SP-4666	Expect No Mercy	1977	12.00
❑ SP-4511	Hair of the Dog	1975	12.00

Number	Title	Yr	NM
❑ SP-3225 [B]	Hair of the Dog	1984	10.00
—Budget-line reissue			
❑ SP-4643	Hot Tracks	1977	12.00
❑ SP-3226	Hot Tracks	1984	10.00
—Budget-line reissue			
❑ SP-3609	Loud 'N' Proud	1974	12.00
❑ SP-4799	Malice in Wonderland	1980	12.00
❑ SP-3169	Nazareth	1982	10.00
—Reissue of Warner Bros. 2615			
❑ SP-4741	No Mean City	1979	12.00
❑ SP-4610	Play 'N' the Game	1976	12.00

Number	Title	Yr	NM
❑ SP-3641	Rampant	1974	12.00
❑ SP-4396	Razamanaz	1973	18.00
—First edition with brown label			
❑ SP-4396	Razamanaz	1974	12.00
❑ SP-6703	'Snaz	1981	15.00
❑ SP-4844	The Fool Circle	1981	12.00

MCA

Number	Title	Yr	NM
❑ 5458	Sound Elixir	1983	12.00

WARNER BROS.

Number	Title	Yr	NM
❑ BS2639 [B]	Exercises	1972	30.00
❑ BS2615 [B]	Nazareth	1972	30.00

NAZZ (1)

RHINO

Number	Title	Yr	NM
❑ RNLP109	Nazz	1984	18.00
❑ RNLP111	Nazz III	1984	18.00
❑ RNLP110	Nazz Nazz	1984	18.00
❑ RNLP116	The Best of Nazz	1984	18.00
❑ R170116	The Best of Nazz	1987	15.00

SGC

Number	Title	Yr	NM
❑ SD5001	Nazz	1968	40.00
❑ SD5004	Nazz III	1970	40.00
❑ 5002 [M]	Nazz Nazz	1969	80.00
—Promo-only mono pressing on red vinyl			
❑ SD5002 [S]	Nazz Nazz	1969	40.00
—Red vinyl			
❑ SD5002 [S]	Nazz Nazz	1969	80.00
—Black vinyl			

NBC SYMPHONY ORCHESTRA (LEOPOLD STOKOWSKI, COND.)

RCA VICTOR RED SEAL

Number	Title	Yr	NM
❑ LSC-2555 [S]	The Sound of Stokowski and Wagner	1961	60.00
—Originals with "shaded dog" label			
❑ LSC-2555 [S]	The Sound of Stokowski and Wagner	1964	30.00
—Second editions with "white dog" label			

NDEGEOCELLO, ME'SHELL

MAVERICK

Number	Title	Yr	NM
❑ PRO-A-6622 [DJ]	Plantation Lullabies	1993	25.00
—Promo-only U.S. vinyl release			

NECKBONES, THE

FAT POSSUM

Number	Title	Yr	NM
❑ 80304-1 [B]	Souls On Fire	1997	18.00

NECROS

RESTLESS

Number	Title	Yr	NM
❑ 72203	Tangled Up	1986	15.00

TOUCH & GO

Number	Title	Yr	NM
❑ 2	Conquest for Death	1983	70.00

NEELY, DON

MERRY MAKERS

Number	Title	Yr	NM
❑ 108	Don Neely's Royal Society Jazz Orchestra	197?	12.00

STOMP OFF

Number	Title	Yr	NM
❑ SOS-1208	Ain't That a Grand and Glorious Feeling?	1991	15.00

NEELY, JIMMY

TRU-SOUND

Number	Title	Yr	NM
❑ TRU-15002 [M]	Misirlou	1962	40.00

NEELY, SAM

A&M

Number	Title	Yr	NM
❑ SP-3626	Sam Neely	1974	15.00

CAPITOL

Number	Title	Yr	NM
❑ ST-873	Long Road to Texas	1972	18.00
❑ ST-11097	Loving You Just Crossed My Mind	1972	15.00
—Reissued version of ST-873			
❑ SMAS-11143	Sam Neely -- 2	1973	15.00

NEFF, HILDEGARDE

LONDON

Number	Title	Yr	NM
❑ PS596	From Here On It Gets Rough	1971	25.00

NEGATIVLAND

SEELAND

Number	Title	Yr	NM
❑ 003	A Big 10-8 Place	1985	15.00
❑ 001 [B]	Negativland	1981	35.00
—Every copy has a different cover			
❑ 002	Points	1982	15.00
—Black vinyl			
❑ 002	Points	1982	18.00
—Blue vinyl			

SST

Number	Title	Yr	NM
❑ 133	Escape from Noise	1987	25.00
—With booklet			
❑ 292 [EP]	Guns	1992	10.00

Number	Title	Yr	NM
❑ 252	Helter Stupid	1989	15.00
❑ 272 [EP]	U2	1990	300.00
—Withdrawn thanks to pressure from the record company of U2 (the band)			

NEIDLINGER, BUELL

ANTILLES

Number	Title	Yr	NM
❑ AN-1014	Swingrass '83	1983	12.00

NEIGHBORHOOD, THE

BIG TREE

Number	Title	Yr	NM
❑ 2001	Debut	1970	18.00

NEIGHB'RHOOD CHILDREN

ACTA

Number	Title	Yr	NM
❑ 8005 [M]	The Neighb'rhood Children	1968	80.00
❑ 38005 [S]	The Neighb'rhood Children	1968	100.00

SUNDAZED

Number	Title	Yr	NM
❑ LP5023	Long Years in Space	199?	18.00

NEIL, FRED

CAPITOL

Number	Title	Yr	NM
❑ ST-294	Everybody's Talkin'	1969	30.00
❑ T2665 [M]	Fred Neil	1966	30.00
❑ ST2665 [S]	Fred Neil	1966	40.00
—With color photo on back			
❑ ST2665 [S]	Fred Neil	1967	30.00
—With black & white photo on back			
❑ T2862 [M]	Fred Neil Sessions	1968	40.00
❑ ST2862 [S]	Fred Neil Sessions	1968	30.00

ELEKTRA

Number	Title	Yr	NM
❑ EKL-293 [M]	Bleecker and MacDougal	1965	30.00
❑ EKS-7293 [S]	Bleecker and MacDougal	1965	40.00
❑ EKS-74073	Little Bit of Rain	1970	25.00
—Reissue of 7293			

SUNDAZED

Number	Title	Yr	NM
❑ LP5107	Bleecker and MacDougal	2002	15.00

NEKTAR

CLEOPATRA

Number	Title	Yr	NM
❑ 9223 [B]	A Spoonful Of Time		35.00
❑ CLP0514 [B]	A Tab In The Ocean	2013	35.00
❑ 9958 [B]	Journey To The Centre Of The Eye		25.00
❑ CLP9958 [B]	Journey To The Centre Of The Eye	2013	35.00
❑ 741157064414 [B]	Magic is a Child	2014	30.00
❑ 9296 [B]	Recycled - Deluxe Edition		30.00
❑ CLP0297 [B]	Remember the Future	2013	35.00
❑ CLP0676 [B]	...Sounds Like This	2013	35.00
❑ CLP0495 [B]	Time Machine	2013	35.00

PASSPORT

Number	Title	Yr	NM
❑ PPSD-98017 [B]	A Tab in the Ocean	1976	25.00
❑ PPSD-98005 [B]	Down to Earth	1975	25.00
❑ PPSD-98011 [B]	Recycled	1976	25.00
❑ PPS-98002 [B]	Remember the Future	1974	25.00

POLYDOR

Number	Title	Yr	NM
❑ PD-1-6115	Magic Is a Child	1977	12.00

VISA

Number	Title	Yr	NM
❑ IMP9001	Thru the Ears	1979	15.00

NELSON, OLIVER, AND LOU DONALDSON

CHESS

Number	Title	Yr	NM
❑ 2ACMJ-404	Back Talk	1976	18.00
❑ CH2-92515	Back Talk	198?	15.00

NELSON, OLIVER; KING CURTIS; JIMMY FORREST

PRESTIGE

Number	Title	Yr	NM
❑ PRLP-7223 [M]	Soul Battle	1962	60.00
—Yellow label			
❑ PRST-7223 [S]	Soul Battle	1962	70.00

NELSON, OLIVER

ABC IMPULSE!

Number	Title	Yr	NM
❑ AS-9132 [S]	Happenings	1968	25.00
—With Hank Jones; black label with red ring			
❑ AS-9153 [S]	Live From Los Angeles	1968	25.00
—Black label with red ring			
❑ AS-9113 [S]	Michelle	1968	25.00
—Black label with red ring			
❑ AS-75 [S]	More Blues and the Abstract Truth	1968	25.00
—Black label with red ring			
❑ AS-75 [S]	More Blues and the Abstract Truth	1975	15.00
—Green, blue, purple "target" label			
❑ AS-9168 [S]	Soulful Brass	1968	30.00
—Black label with red ring			
❑ AS-9129 [S]	Sound Pieces	1968	25.00
—Black label with red ring			
❑ AS-5 [S]	The Blues and the Abstract Truth	1968	25.00
—Black label with red ring			
❑ AS-9144 [S]	The Kennedy Dream	1968	25.00

Number	Title	Yr	NM
—Black label with red ring			
❑ AS-9147 [S]	The Spirit of '67	1968	25.00
—With Pee Wee Russell; black label with red ring			
❑ IA-9335-2	Three Dimensions	1978	25.00
ARGO			
❑ LP-737 [M]	Fantabulous	1964	50.00
❑ LPS-737 [S]	Fantabulous	1964	50.00
BLUEBIRD			
❑ 6993-1-RB	Black, Brown and Beautiful	1989	18.00
—Reissue of Flying Dutchman 10116			
CADET			
❑ LPS-737 [S]	Fantabulous	1966	18.00
—Fading blue label			
❑ LP-737 [M]	Fantabulous	1966	30.00
—Fading blue label			
FANTASY			
❑ OJC-227	Meet Oliver Nelson	198?	15.00
❑ OJC-089	Screamin' the Blues	198?	15.00
❑ OJC-325	Soul Battle	1988	15.00
❑ OJC-099	Straight Ahead	198?	15.00
FLYING DUTCHMAN			
❑ FD-10134	Berlin Dialogue	1972	30.00
❑ FD-10116	Black, Brown and Beautiful	1971	40.00
—Reissue of 116			
❑ FD-116	Black, Brown and Beautiful	1970	60.00
❑ CYL2-1449	Dream Deferred	1976	30.00
❑ BDL1-0592	Oliver Nelson in London	1974	30.00
❑ BDL1-0825	Skull Session	1975	80.00
—Reproductions exist			
❑ FD-10149	Swiss Suite	1973	30.00
GRP IMPULSE!			
❑ IMP-212	More Blues and the Abstract Truth	1997	25.00
—Reissue on audiophile vinyl			
❑ IMP-154	The Blues and the Abstract Truth	1995	18.00
—Reissue on audiophile vinyl			
IMPULSE!			
❑ A-9132 [M]	Happenings	1967	40.00
—With Hank Jones			
❑ AS-9132 [S]	Happenings	1967	30.00
—With Hank Jones			
❑ A-9153 [M]	Live From Los Angeles	1967	80.00
❑ AS-9153 [S]	Live From Los Angeles	1967	30.00
❑ A-9113 [M]	Michelle	1966	30.00
❑ AS-9113 [S]	Michelle	1966	40.00
❑ A-75 [M]	More Blues and the Abstract Truth	1964	100.00
❑ AS-75 [S]	More Blues and the Abstract Truth	1964	100.00
❑ A-9129 [M]	Sound Pieces	1966	40.00
❑ AS-9129 [S]	Sound Pieces	1966	40.00
❑ A-5 [M]	The Blues and the Abstract Truth	1961	100.00
—Original cover has an abstract painting and lists Bill Evans' name first			
❑ AS-5 [S]	The Blues and the Abstract Truth	1961	120.00
—Original cover has an abstract painting and lists Bill Evans' name first			
❑ A-5 [M]	The Blues and the Abstract Truth	196?	40.00
—Later cover has Oliver Nelson clearly indicated as leader and features a photo of him at the right			
❑ AS-5 [S]	The Blues and the Abstract Truth	196?	50.00
—Later cover has Oliver Nelson clearly indicated as leader and features a photo of him at the right			
❑ A-9144 [M]	The Kennedy Dream	1967	40.00
❑ AS-9144 [S]	The Kennedy Dream	1967	30.00
❑ A-9147 [M]	The Spirit of '67	1967	50.00
—With Pee Wee Russell			
❑ AS-9147 [S]	The Spirit of '67	1967	30.00
—With Pee Wee Russell			
INNER CITY			
❑ IC-6008	Stolen Moments	1977	18.00
MCA			
❑ 29052	More Blues and the Abstract Truth	1980	12.00
❑ 5888	More Blues and the Abstract Truth	1987	12.00
—Another reissue			
❑ 29063	The Blues and the Abstract Truth	1980	12.00
❑ 4148	Three Dimensions	1980	15.00
MCA IMPULSE!			
❑ MCA-5888	More Blues and the Abstract Truth	1987	12.00
❑ MCA-5659	The Blues and the Abstract Truth	1985	15.00
MOODSVILLE			
❑ MVLP-13 [M]	Nocturne	1960	100.00
—Green label			
❑ MVLP-13 [M]	Nocturne	1965	50.00
—Blue label, trident logo at right			
NEW JAZZ			
❑ NJLP-8224 [M]	Meet Oliver Nelson	1959	120.00
—Purple label			

Number	Title	Yr	NM
❑ NJLP-8224 [M]	Meet Oliver Nelson	1965	50.00
—Blue label, trident logo at right			
❑ NJLP-8243 [M]	Screamin' the Blues	1960	120.00
—Purple label			
❑ NJLP-8243 [M]	Screamin' the Blues	1965	50.00
—Blue label, trident logo at right			
❑ NJLP-8255 [M]	Straight Ahead	1961	120.00
—Purple label			
❑ NJLP-8255 [M]	Straight Ahead	1965	50.00
—Blue label, trident logo at right			
❑ NJLP-8233 [M]	Takin' Care of Business	1960	120.00
—Purple label			
❑ NJLP-8233 [M]	Takin' Care of Business	1965	50.00
—Blue label, trident logo at right			
PRESTIGE			
❑ PRLP-7225 [M]	Afro/American Sketches	1962	50.00
❑ PRST-7225 [S]	Afro/American Sketches	1962	60.00
❑ P-24060	Images	1976	25.00
❑ PRLP-7236 [M]	Main Stem	1962	60.00
❑ PRST-7236 [S]	Main Stem	1962	80.00
STATUS			
❑ ST-8324 [M]	Screamin' the Blues	1965	50.00
UNITED ARTISTS			
❑ UAJ-14019 [M]	Impressions of Phaedra	1962	50.00
❑ UAJS-15019 [S]	Impressions of Phaedra	1962	80.00
VERVE			
❑ V-8508 [M]	Full Nelson	1963	40.00
❑ V6-8508 [S]	Full Nelson	1963	50.00
❑ V6-8743 [S]	Leonard Feather Presents the Sound of Feeling and the Sound of Oliver Nelson	1968	100.00

NELSON, OZZIE

Number	Title	Yr	NM
AIRCHECK			
❑ 19	Ozzie Nelson and His Orchestra On the Air	198?	12.00
HINDSIGHT			
❑ HSR-189	Ozzie Nelson and His Orchestra 1937	198?	12.00
❑ HSR-208	Ozzie Nelson and His Orchestra 1938	198?	12.00
❑ HSR-107	Ozzie Nelson and His Orchestra 1940-42	198?	12.00

NELSON, RICK "COUGAR

Number	Title	Yr	NM
JAZZOLOGY			
❑ J-123	Steppin' Out	198?	12.00

NELSON, RICKY

Number	Title	Yr	NM
CAPITOL			
❑ SOO-12109	Playing to Win	1981	12.00
DECCA			
❑ DL4944 [M]	Another Side of Rick	1967	30.00
❑ DL74944 [S]	Another Side of Rick	1967	30.00
❑ DL4660 [M]	Best Always	1965	30.00
❑ DL74660 [S]	Best Always	1965	40.00
❑ DL4779 [M]	Bright Lights and Country Music	1966	30.00
❑ DL74779 [S]	Bright Lights and Country Music	1966	30.00
❑ DL4827 [M]	Country Fever	1967	30.00
❑ DL74827 [S]	Country Fever	1967	30.00
❑ DL4419 [M]	For Your Sweet Love	1963	30.00
❑ DL74419 [S]	For Your Sweet Love	1963	40.00
❑ DL75391	Garden Party	1972	30.00
❑ DL4678 [M]	Love and Kisses	1965	30.00
❑ DL74678 [S]	Love and Kisses	1965	40.00
❑ DL5014 [M]	Perspective	1968	70.00
—Mono copies are promo only			
❑ DL75014 [S]	Perspective	1968	30.00
❑ DL75162	Rick Nelson In Concert	1970	30.00
❑ DL4479 [M]	Rick Nelson Sings "For You	1963	35.00

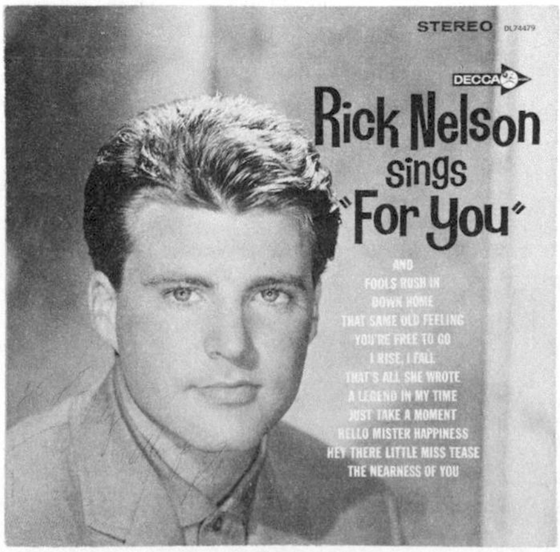

Number	Title	Yr	NM
❑ DL74479 [S]	Rick Nelson Sings "For You	1963	45.00
❑ DL75236	Rick Sings Nelson	1970	30.00
—Deduct 20 percent if poster is missing			

Number	Title	Yr	NM
❑ DL75297	Rudy the Fifth	1971	30.00
❑ DL4608 [M]	Spotlight on Rick	1964	30.00
❑ DL74608 [S]	Spotlight on Rick	1964	40.00
❑ DL4559 [M]	The Very Thought of You	1964	30.00
❑ DL74559 [S]	The Very Thought of You	1964	40.00
EMI AMERICA			
❑ SQ-17192	The Very Best of Rick Nelson	1986	12.00
—Reissue of United Artists UA-LA330			
EPIC			
❑ JE34420	Intakes	1977	15.00
❑ FE40388	The Memphis Sessions	1986	12.00
EPIC/NU-DISK			
❑ 3E36868 [10]	Four You	1981	15.00
IMPERIAL			
❑ LP9167 [M]	Album Seven by Rick	1962	40.00
—Black label with stars			
❑ LP9167 [M]	Album Seven by Rick	1964	30.00
—Black label with pink and white at left			
❑ LP9167 [M]	Album Seven by Rick	1966	25.00
—Black label with green and white at left			
❑ LP12082 [S]	Album Seven by Rick	1962	100.00
—Black label with silver print			
❑ LP12082 [S]	Album Seven by Rick	1964	40.00
—Black label with pink and white at left			
❑ LP12082 [S]	Album Seven by Rick	1966	30.00
—Black label with green and white at left			
❑ LP9244 [M]	A Long Vacation	1963	40.00
—Black label with stars			
❑ LP9244 [M]	A Long Vacation	1964	30.00
—Black label with pink and white at left			
❑ LP9244 [M]	A Long Vacation	1966	25.00
—Black label with green and white at left			
❑ LP12244 [R]	A Long Vacation	1964	25.00
—Black label with pink and white at left			
❑ LP12244 [R]	A Long Vacation	1966	18.00
—Black label with green and white at left			
❑ LP12218 [R]	Best Sellers	1964	25.00
—Black label with pink and white at left			
❑ LP12218 [R]	Best Sellers	1966	18.00
—Black label with green and white at left			
❑ LP9218 [M]	Best Sellers by Rick Nelson	1963	40.00
—Black label with stars			
❑ LP9218 [M]	Best Sellers by Rick Nelson	1964	30.00
—Black label with pink and white at left			
❑ LP9218 [M]	Best Sellers by Rick Nelson	1966	25.00
—Black label with green and white at left			
❑ LP9223 [M]	It's Up to You	1963	40.00
—Black label with stars			
❑ LP9223 [M]	It's Up to You	1964	30.00
—Black label with pink and white at left			
❑ LP9223 [M]	It's Up to You	1966	25.00
—Black label with green and white at left			
❑ LP9232 [M]	Million Sellers	1963	40.00
—Black label with stars			
❑ LP9232 [M]	Million Sellers	1964	30.00
—Black label with pink and white at left			
❑ LP9232 [M]	Million Sellers	1966	25.00
—Black label with green and white at left			
❑ LP12232 [R]	Million Sellers	1964	25.00
—Black label with pink and white at left			
❑ LP12232 [R]	Million Sellers	1966	18.00
—Black label with green and white at left			
❑ LP9122 [M]	More Songs by Ricky	1960	75.00
—Black label with stars			
❑ LP9122 [M]	More Songs by Ricky	1964	30.00
—Black label with pink and white at left			
❑ LP9122 [M]	More Songs by Ricky	1966	25.00
—Black label with green and white at left			
❑ LP12059 [DJ]	More Songs by Ricky	1960	1000.00
—Promo copy on blue vinyl. Add 20 percent for enclosed poster.			
❑ LP12059 [S]	More Songs by Ricky	1960	100.00
—Black label with silver print			
❑ LP12059 [S]	More Songs by Ricky	1964	40.00
—Black label with pink and white at left			
❑ LP12059 [S]	More Songs by Ricky	1966	30.00
—Black label with green and white at left			
❑ LP9152 [M]	Rick Is 21	1961	40.00
—Black label with stars			
❑ LP9152 [M]	Rick Is 21	1964	30.00
—Black label with pink and white at left			
❑ LP9152 [M]	Rick Is 21	1966	25.00
—Black label with green and white at left			
❑ LP12071 [S]	Rick Is 21	1961	100.00
—Black label with silver print			
❑ LP12071 [S]	Rick Is 21	1964	40.00
—Black label with pink and white at left			
❑ LP12071 [S]	Rick Is 21	1966	30.00
—Black label with green and white at left			
❑ LP9251 [M]	Rick Nelson Sings for You	1964	40.00
—Black label with stars			
❑ LP9251 [M]	Rick Nelson Sings for You	1964	30.00
—Black label with pink and white at left			
❑ LP9251 [M]	Rick Nelson Sings for You	1966	25.00
—Black label with green and white at left			
❑ LP12251 [R]	Rick Nelson Sings for You	1964	30.00
—Black label with silver print			

Number	Title	Yr	NM
❑ LP12251 [R]	Rick Nelson Sings for You	1964	25.00
—Black label with pink and white at left			
❑ LP12251 [R]	Rick Nelson Sings for You	1966	18.00
—Black label with green and white at left			
❑ LP9048 [M]	Ricky	1957	100.00
—Black label with stars			
❑ LP9048 [M]	Ricky	1964	30.00
—Black label with pink and white at left			
❑ LP9048 [M]	Ricky	1966	25.00
—Black label with green and white at left			
❑ LP12392 [R]	Ricky	1968	18.00
—Rechanneled reissue of 9048			
❑ LP9050 [M]	Ricky Nelson	1958	100.00
—Black label with stars			
❑ LP9050 [M]	Ricky Nelson	1964	30.00
—Black label with pink and white at left			
❑ LP9050 [M]	Ricky Nelson	1966	25.00
—Black label with green and white at left			
❑ LP12393 [R]	Ricky Nelson	1968	18.00
—Rechanneled reissue of 9050			
❑ LP9061 [M]	Ricky Sings Again	1959	100.00
—Black label with stars			
❑ LP9061 [M]	Ricky Sings Again	1964	30.00
—Black label with pink and white at left			
❑ LP9061 [M]	Ricky Sings Again	1966	25.00
—Black label with green and white at left			
❑ LP12090 [S]	Ricky Sings Again	1962	150.00
—Black label with silver print			
❑ LP12090 [S]	Ricky Sings Again	1964	40.00
—Black label with pink and white at left			
❑ LP12090 [S]	Ricky Sings Again	1966	30.00
—Black label with green and white at left			
❑ LP9082 [M]	Songs by Ricky	1959	75.00
—Black label with stars			
❑ LP9082 [M]	Songs by Ricky	1964	30.00
—Black label with pink and white at left			
❑ LP9082 [M]	Songs by Ricky	1966	25.00
—Black label with green and white at left			
❑ LP12030 [S]	Songs by Ricky	1959	200.00
—Black label with silver print			
❑ LP12030 [S]	Songs by Ricky	1964	40.00
—Black label with pink and white at left			
❑ LP12030 [S]	Songs by Ricky	1966	30.00
—Black label with green and white at left			

LIBERTY

Number	Title	Yr	NM
❑ LN-10304	I Need You	1986	10.00
—Reissue of Sunset 5205			
❑ LXB-9960	Legendary Masters	198?	15.00
—Reissue of United Artists 9960			
❑ LM-1004	Ricky	1981	10.00
—Reissue of United Artists 1004			
❑ LM-51004	Ricky	1983	10.00
—Reissue of Liberty 1004			
❑ LN-10305	Ricky Nelson	1986	10.00
—Another reissue			
❑ LN-10134	Ricky Sings Again	1982	12.00
—Reissue of Imperial 12090			
❑ LN-10205	Souvenirs	1983	10.00
❑ LN-10253	Teen Age Idol	1984	10.00

MCA

Number	Title	Yr	NM
❑ 6163	All My Best	1986	12.00
❑ 62	Garden Party	1973	15.00
—Reissue of Decca 75391			
❑ 2-4004	Rick Nelson Country	1973	18.00
❑ 3	Rick Nelson In Concert	1973	15.00
—Reissue of Decca 75162			
❑ 25983	Rick Nelson In Concert The Troubadour, 1969	1987	12.00
—Reissue of MCA 3 with revised title			
❑ 20	Rick Sings Nelson	1973	15.00
—Reissue of Decca 75236			
❑ 37	Rudy the Fifth	1973	15.00
—Reissue of Decca 75297			
❑ 1517	The Decca Years	1982	10.00
❑ 383	Windfall	1974	18.00

RHINO

Number	Title	Yr	NM
❑ RNLP215	Greatest Hits	1985	15.00
❑ R1-70215	Greatest Hits	1987	12.00
❑ RNDF259 [PD]	Greatest Hits	1985	18.00
❑ R1-71114	Live 1983-1985	1989	15.00

SUNSET

Number	Title	Yr	NM
❑ SUS-5205	I Need You	1968	18.00
❑ SUM-1118 [M]	Ricky Nelson	1966	18.00
❑ SUS-5118 [P]	Ricky Nelson	1966	25.00

TIME-LIFE

Number	Title	Yr	NM
❑ SRNR31	Rick Nelson: 1957-1972	1989	18.00

UNITED ARTISTS

Number	Title	Yr	NM
❑ UAS-9960	Legendary Masters	1971	30.00
❑ LM-1004	Ricky	1980	12.00
—Reissue of Imperial 9048			
❑ UA-LA330-E	The Very Best of Rick Nelson	1974	15.00

VERVE

Number	Title	Yr	NM
❑ V2083 [M]	Teen Time	1957	500.00
—Has three Ricky Nelson songs plus tracks by four others; usually treated as Rick's LP because of his prominence on the cover			

NELSON, SANDY

IMPERIAL

Number	Title	Yr	NM
❑ LP9329 [M]	Beat That #!!@* Drum	1966	15.00
❑ LP12329 [S]	Beat That #!!@* Drum	1966	18.00
❑ LP9237 [M]	Beat That Drum	1963	18.00
❑ LP12237 [S]	Beat That Drum	1963	25.00
❑ LP9258 [M]	Be True to Your School	1964	18.00
❑ LP12258 [S]	Be True to Your School	1964	25.00
❑ LP12367	Boogaloo Beat	1968	15.00
❑ LP9298 [M]	Boss Beat	1965	18.00
❑ LP12298 [S]	Boss Beat	1965	25.00
❑ LP9340 [M]	Cheetah Beat	1967	15.00
❑ LP12340 [S]	Cheetah Beat	1967	18.00
❑ LP9204 [M]	Compelling Percussion	1962	25.00
❑ LP12204 [S]	Compelling Percussion	1962	30.00
❑ LP9203 [M]	Country Style	1962	25.00
❑ LP12203 [S]	Country Style	1962	30.00
❑ LP9283 [M]	Drum Discotheque	1965	18.00
❑ LP12283 [S]	Drum Discotheque	1965	25.00
❑ LP9189 [M]	Drummin' Up a Storm	1962	25.00
❑ LP12189 [S]	Drummin' Up a Storm	1962	30.00
❑ LP9287 [M]	Drums A Go-Go	1965	18.00
❑ LP12287 [S]	Drums A Go-Go	1965	25.00
❑ LP9168 [M]	Drums Are My Beat!	1962	25.00
—Black label with stars			
❑ LP12083 [S]	Drums Are My Beat!	1962	30.00
❑ LP9168 [M]	Drums Are My Beat!	1964	18.00
—Pink, white and black label			
❑ LP9202 [M]	Golden Hits	1962	25.00
❑ LP12202 [P]	Golden Hits	1962	30.00
❑ LP12451	Groovy	1970	15.00
❑ LP9136 [M]	He's a Drummer Boy	1961	30.00
❑ LP12089 [R]	He's a Drummer Boy	1962	30.00
❑ LP9305 [M]	In" Beat	1966	18.00
❑ LP12305 [S]	In" Beat	1966	25.00
❑ LP9159 [M]	Let There Be Drums	1962	30.00
❑ LP12080 [R]	Let There Be Drums	1962	30.00
❑ LP9272 [M]	Live! In Las Vegas	1964	25.00
❑ LP12272 [R]	Live! In Las Vegas	1964	18.00
❑ LP12439	Manhattan Spiritual	1969	15.00
❑ LP9203 [M]	On the Wild Side	1966	18.00
—Same LP as above, but new title on cover			
❑ LP12203 [S]	On the Wild Side	1966	25.00
—Same LP as above, but new title on cover			
❑ LP12424	Rebirth of the Beat	1969	15.00
❑ LP12400	Rock and Roll Revival	1968	15.00
❑ LP9249 [M]	Sandy Nelson Plays	1963	18.00
❑ LP12249 [S]	Sandy Nelson Plays	1963	25.00
❑ LP9105 [M]	Sandy Nelson Plays Teen Beat	1960	30.00
❑ LP12044 [S]	Sandy Nelson Plays Teen Beat	1960	40.00
❑ LP9362 [M]	Soul Drums	1967	18.00
❑ LP12362 [S]	Soul Drums	1967	15.00
❑ LP9314 [M]	Super Drums	1966	18.00
❑ LP12314 [S]	Super Drums	1966	25.00
❑ LP9215 [M]	Teenage House Party	1963	25.00
❑ LP12215 [S]	Teenage House Party	1963	30.00
❑ LP9278 [M]	Teen Beat '65	1965	18.00
❑ LP12278 [S]	Teen Beat '65	1965	25.00
❑ LP9345 [M]	The Beat Goes On	1967	15.00
❑ LP12345 [S]	The Beat Goes On	1967	18.00
❑ LP9224 [M]	The Best of the Beats	1963	18.00
❑ LP12224 [S]	The Best of the Beats	1963	25.00
—Black label			
❑ LP12224 [S]	The Best of the Beats	1963	18.00
—Black, pink and white label			

LIBERTY

Number	Title	Yr	NM
❑ LN-10209	Collectors' Gems, Vol. 2	1983	10.00
❑ LN-10172	The Very Best of Sandy Nelson	1982	10.00

PICKWICK

Number	Title	Yr	NM
❑ SPC-3605	And Then There Were Drums	1978	12.00

SUNSET

Number	Title	Yr	NM
❑ SUS-5224	And There Were Drums (Drums and More Drums)	1968	12.00
❑ SUS-5261	Heavy Drums	1969	12.00
❑ SUS-5291	Sandy Nelson Plays Fats Domino Hits	1970	12.00
❑ SUM-1166 [M]	Teen Drums	1967	12.00
❑ SUS-5166 [S]	Teen Drums	1967	15.00
❑ SUM-1114 [M]	Walking Beat	1966	12.00
❑ SUS-5114 [S]	Walking Beat	1966	15.00

UNITED ARTISTS

Number	Title	Yr	NM
❑ UA-LA440-E	The Very Best of Sandy Nelson	1975	15.00

NELSON, TRACY

ADELPHI

Number	Title	Yr	NM
❑ 4119	Doin' It My Way	1981	12.00

ATLANTIC

Number	Title	Yr	NM
❑ SD7310 [B]	Tracy Nelson	1974	15.00

COLUMBIA

Number	Title	Yr	NM
❑ KC31759	Poor Man's Paradise	1973	15.00

FLYING FISH

Number	Title	Yr	NM
❑ FF-209	Come See About Me	1980	12.00
❑ FF-052	Homemade Songs	1978	12.00

MCA

Number	Title	Yr	NM
❑ 494	Sweet Soul Music	1975	15.00
❑ 2203	Time Is On My Side	1976	15.00

PRESTIGE

Number	Title	Yr	NM
❑ PRLP7393 [M]	Deep Are the Roots	1965	30.00
❑ PRST7393 [S]	Deep Are the Roots	1965	30.00
❑ PRST7726	Deep Are the Roots	1969	18.00

NELSON, WILLIE, AND DAVID ALLAN COE

PLANTATION

Number	Title	Yr	NM
❑ PLP41	Willie and David	1980	12.00
—One side is solo songs by Willie Nelson, the other side solo songs by David Allan Coe			

NELSON, WILLIE, AND FARON YOUNG

COLUMBIA

Number	Title	Yr	NM
❑ FC39484	Funny How Time Slips Away	1984	12.00
❑ PC39484	Funny How Time Slips Away	1985	10.00
—Budget-line reissue			

NELSON, WILLIE, AND HANK SNOW

COLUMBIA

Number	Title	Yr	NM
❑ FC39977	Brand on My Heart	1984	12.00
❑ PC39977	Brand on My Heart	1985	10.00
—Budget-line reissue			

NELSON, WILLIE, AND KRIS KRISTOFFERSON

COLUMBIA

Number	Title	Yr	NM
❑ FC39531	Music from Songwriter	1984	12.00

NELSON, WILLIE, AND LEON RUSSELL

COLUMBIA

Number	Title	Yr	NM
❑ KC236064	One for the Road	1979	18.00

NELSON, WILLIE, AND RAY PRICE

COLUMBIA

Number	Title	Yr	NM
❑ JC36476	San Antonio Rose	1980	12.00
❑ PC36476	San Antonio Rose	198?	10.00
—Budget-line reissue			

NELSON, WILLIE, AND ROGER MILLER

COLUMBIA

Number	Title	Yr	NM
❑ FC38013	Old Friends	1982	12.00
❑ PC38013	Old Friends	198?	10.00
—Budget-line reissue			

NELSON, WILLIE, AND WEBB PIERCE

COLUMBIA

Number	Title	Yr	NM
❑ FC38095	In the Jailhouse Now	1982	12.00
❑ PC38095	In the Jailhouse Now	198?	10.00
—Budget-line reissue			

NELSON, WILLIE

ALLEGIANCE

Number	Title	Yr	NM
❑ AV-5010	Wild & Willie	1983	12.00
❑ AV-5005	Willie or Won't He	1983	12.00

ATLANTIC

Number	Title	Yr	NM
❑ SD7291	Phases and Stages	1974	25.00
❑ SD7262	Shotgun Willie	1973	25.00

COLUMBIA

Number	Title	Yr	NM
❑ FC45046	A Horse Called Music	1989	12.00
❑ FC37951	Always on My Mind	1982	12.00
❑ HC47951	Always on My Mind	1982	50.00
—Half-speed mastered edition			
❑ 9C939943 [PD]	Always on My Mind	1985	25.00
❑ PC37951	Always on My Mind	1984	10.00
—Budget-line reissue			
❑ FC39363	Angel Eyes	1984	12.00
❑ PC39363	Angel Eyes	1985	10.00
—Budget-line reissue			
❑ FC39145	City of New Orleans	1984	12.00
❑ PC39145	City of New Orleans	1985	10.00
—Budget-line reissue			
❑ FC39990	Half Nelson	1985	12.00
—Duets with 10 different artists			
❑ PC39990	Half Nelson	1986	10.00
—Budget-line reissue			
❑ FC40056	Highwayman	1985	12.00
—Waylon Jennings/Willie Nelson/Johnny Cash/Kris Kristofferson			
❑ C45240	Highwayman 2	1990	18.00
—Waylon Jennings/Willie Nelson/Johnny Cash/Kris Kristofferson			
❑ S236752	Honeysuckle Rose	1980	15.00
—Over half of the LP is by Willie			
❑ FC40487	Island in the Sea	1987	12.00
❑ FC40008	Me and Paul	1985	12.00
❑ PC40008	Me and Paul	1986	10.00
—Budget-line reissue			
❑ FC39894	Partners	1986	12.00
❑ PC39894	Partners	1987	10.00
—Budget-line reissue			
❑ JC36189	Pretty Paper	1979	12.00
❑ KC33482	Red Headed Stranger	1975	18.00
—No bar code on back cover			
❑ HC43482	Red Headed Stranger	1982	40.00
—Half-speed mastered edition			

Number	Title	Yr	NM

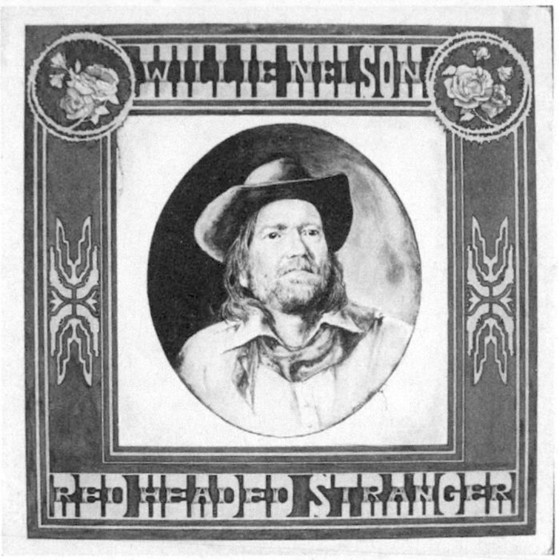

Number	Title	Yr	NM
❑ PC33482 [B]	Red Headed Stranger	1979	10.00
—With bar code on back cover; budget-line reissue			
❑ FC36883	Somewhere Over the Rainbow	1981	12.00
❑ JC35305 [B]	Stardust	1978	12.00
❑ HC45305	Stardust	1981	70.00
—Half-speed mastered edition			
❑ JC35305	Stardust	2000	30.00
—Classic Records reissue on audiophile vinyl			
❑ JS36327	The Electric Horseman	1979	12.00
—Side 2 by Dave Grusin			
❑ FC40327	The Promiseland	1986	12.00
❑ PC34092	The Sound in Your Mind	1976	15.00
—No bar code on back cover			
❑ PC34092	The Sound in Your Mind	1979	10.00
—With bar code on back cover; budget-line reissue			
❑ KC34112	The Troublemaker	1976	15.00
—No bar code on back cover			
❑ PC34112	The Troublemaker	1979	10.00
—With bar code on back cover; budget-line reissue			
❑ JC34695	To Lefty From Willie	1977	15.00
❑ PC34695	To Lefty From Willie	1979	10.00
—Budget-line reissue			
❑ QC38248	Tougher Than Leather	1983	12.00
❑ HC48248	Tougher Than Leather	1983	50.00
—Half-speed mastered edition			
❑ PC38248	Tougher Than Leather	1984	10.00
—Budget-line reissue			
❑ FC44431	What a Wonderful World	1988	12.00
❑ KC235642	Willie and Family Live	1978	18.00
❑ CX38250	Willie Nelson	1980	120.00
❑ KC237542	Willie Nelson's Greatest Hits (& Some That Will Be)	1981	15.00
❑ JC36188	Willie Nelson Sings Kristofferson	1979	12.00
❑ PC36188	Willie Nelson Sings Kristofferson	1980	10.00
—Budget-line reissue			
❑ FC39110	Without a Song	1983	12.00
❑ PC39110	Without a Song	1984	10.00
—Budget-line reissue			
DELTA			
❑ DLP-1157	Diamonds in the Rough	1982	12.00
HEARTLAND			
❑ HL1038/9	The Best of Willie Nelson	1987	18.00
LIBERTY			
❑ LRP-3239 [M]	...And Then I Wrote	1962	40.00
❑ LST-7239 [S]	...And Then I Wrote	1962	50.00
❑ LN-10013	Country Willie	1980	10.00
—Budget-line reissue			
❑ LRP-3308 [M]	Here's Willie Nelson	1963	40.00
❑ LST-7308 [S]	Here's Willie Nelson	1963	50.00
❑ LN-10118	The Best of Willie Nelson	1982	10.00
—Budget-line reissue			
LOST HIGHWAY			
❑ B0004706-01	Countryman	2005	15.00
❑ B0006939-01	Songbird	2006	18.00
❑ B0006079-01	You Don't Know Me: The Songs of Cindy Walker	2006	15.00
PAIR			
❑ PDL2-1007	Country Winners	1986	15.00
❑ PDL2-1114	Good Hearted Woman	1986	15.00
❑ PDL2-1032	Once More with Feeling	1986	15.00
PICKWICK			
❑ ACL1-7018	Columbus Stockade Blues	1976	10.00
❑ ACL1-0326	Country Winners	1976	10.00
❑ SPC-3584	Hello Walls	1978	12.00
❑ ACL1-0705	Spotlight on Willie Nelson	1976	10.00
PLANTATION			
❑ PLP-24 [B]	The Longhorn Jamboree Presents: Willie Nelson & His Friends	1976	12.00
—Also includes tracks by David Allan Coe, Jerry Lee Lewis and Carl Perkins			

Number	Title	Yr	NM
RCA CAMDEN			
❑ CAS-2444	Columbus Stockade Blues	1970	18.00
❑ ACL1-7018	Columbus Stockade Blues	1975	12.00
❑ ACL1-0326	Country Winners	1973	15.00
❑ ACL1-0705	Spotlight on Willie Nelson	1974	15.00
RCA VICTOR			
❑ APL1-2210	Before His Time	1977	12.00
❑ AYL1-3671	Before His Time	1980	10.00
—Best Buy Series" reissue			
❑ LSP-4294	Both Sides Now	1970	25.00
❑ AHL1-5470	Collector's Series	1985	12.00
❑ LPM-3528 [M]	Country Favorites, Willie Nelson Style	1966	25.00
❑ LSP-3528 [S]	Country Favorites, Willie Nelson Style	1966	30.00
❑ LPM-3659 [M]	Country Music Concert	1966	25.00
❑ LSP-3659 [S]	Country Music Concert	1966	30.00
❑ LPM-3418 [M]	Country Willie -- His Own Songs	1965	25.00
❑ LSP-3418 [S]	Country Willie -- His Own Songs	1965	30.00
❑ AHL1-3549	Danny Davis & Willie Nelson with the Nashville Brass	1980	12.00
❑ CPL1-5174	Don't You Ever Get Tired of Hurting Me	1984	12.00
❑ LSP-4057	Good Times	1968	25.00
❑ LSP-4404	Laying My Burdens Down	1970	25.00
❑ LPM-3748 [M]	Make Way for Willie Nelson	1967	25.00
❑ LSP-3748 [S]	Make Way for Willie Nelson	1967	30.00
❑ LSP-4111	My Own Peculiar Way	1969	25.00
❑ AHL1-4819	My Own Way	1983	12.00
❑ AYL1-5438	My Own Way	1985	10.00
—Best Buy Series" reissue			
❑ AHL1-3243	Sweet Memories	1979	12.00
❑ AYL1-4300	Sweet Memories	1982	10.00
—Best Buy Series" reissue			
❑ LPM-3937 [M]	Texas in My Soul	1968	100.00
❑ LSP-3937 [S]	Texas in My Soul	1968	25.00
❑ AHL1-4420	The Best of Willie Nelson	1982	12.00
❑ AYL1-5143	The Best of Willie Nelson	1984	10.00
—Best Buy Series" reissue			
❑ AHL1-4045	The Minstrel Man	1981	12.00
❑ LPM-3858 [M]	The Party's Over and Other Great Willie Nelson Songs	1967	30.00
❑ LSP-3858 [S]	The Party's Over and Other Great Willie Nelson Songs	1967	25.00
❑ LSP-4653	The Picture	1972	25.00
❑ LSP-4760	The Willie Way	1972	25.00
❑ APL1-1234	What Can You Do to Me Now	1975	15.00
❑ AYL1-3958	What Can You Do to Me Now	1981	10.00
—Best Buy Series" reissue			
❑ CPL1-7158	Willie	1986	12.00
❑ LSP-4489	Willie Nelson & Family	1971	25.00
❑ APL1-1487	Willie Nelson Live	1976	15.00
❑ AYL1-4165	Willie Nelson Live	1981	10.00
—Best Buy Series" reissue			
❑ LSP-4568	Yesterday's Wine	1971	25.00
❑ AYL1-3800	Yesterday's Wine	1980	10.00
—Best Buy Series" reissue			
❑ ANL1-1102	Yesterday's Wine	1975	12.00
SONGBIRD			
❑ 3258	Family Bible	1980	12.00
SUNSET			
❑ SUM-1138 [M]	Hello Walls	1966	18.00
❑ SUS-5138 [S]	Hello Walls	1966	25.00
TAKOMA			
❑ TAK-7104	The Legend Begins	1983	12.00
TIME-LIFE			
❑ P16946	Country and Western Classics	1983	25.00
UNITED ARTISTS			
❑ UA-LA410-G	Country Willie	1975	18.00
❑ UA-LA574-H2	Texas Country	1975	25.00
❑ UA-LA086-E	The Best of Willie Nelson	1973	18.00
—Reissue of Liberty tracks			
❑ UA-LA930-G	There'll Be No Teardrops Tonight	1978	18.00

NELSON

Number	Title	Yr	NM
DGC			
❑ DGC-24290	After the Rain	1990	18.00

NENA

Number	Title	Yr	NM
EPIC			
❑ BFE39294	99 Luftballons	1984	15.00
❑ PE39294	99 Luftballons	198?	10.00
—Budget-line reissue with new prefix			
❑ FE40144	It's All in the Game	1985	12.00

NEON PHILHARMONIC, THE

Number	Title	Yr	NM
WARNER BROS.			
❑ WS1769	The Moth Confesses	1968	30.00
❑ WS1804 [B]	The Neon Philharmonic	1969	18.00

NEP-TUNES, THE

Number	Title	Yr	NM
FAMILY			
❑ FLP-152 [M]	Surfer's Holiday	1963	200.00
❑ SFLP-152 [S]	Surfer's Holiday	1963	300.00

NEPTUNE, JOHN KAIZAN

Number	Title	Yr	NM
FORTUNA			
❑ 17030	Dance for the One in Six	198?	12.00
INNER CITY			
❑ IC-6077	Bamboo	198?	15.00
❑ IC-6078	Shogun	198?	15.00
MILESTONE			
❑ M-9113	West of Somewhere	1981	15.00

NERO, PAUL

Number	Title	Yr	NM
SUNSET			
❑ LP-303 [M]	Play the Music of Paul Nero and His Hi-Fiddles	1956	60.00

NERO, PETER

Number	Title	Yr	NM
ARISTA			
❑ AL4034	Disco, Dance and Love Themes	1976	12.00
BAINBRIDGE			
❑ BT-6268	The Sounds of Love	1987	12.00
COLUMBIA			
❑ PC33136	Greatest Hits	1974	12.00
❑ CS1009	I'll Never Fall in Love Again	1970	12.00
❑ CS9800	I've Gotta Be Me	1969	15.00
❑ C30586	Love Story	1971	12.00
❑ KC32689	Say, Has Anybody Seen My Sweet Gypsy Rose	1973	12.00
❑ KC31105	Summer of '42	1971	12.00
❑ CQ31105 [Q]	Summer of '42	1971	18.00
❑ KC31335	The First Time Ever (I Saw Your Face)	1972	12.00
❑ C231982	The World of Peter Nero	1972	15.00
CONCORD JAZZ			
❑ CJ-48	Now	1978	12.00
CRYSTAL CLEAR			
❑ 6001	The Wiz	198?	25.00
—Direct-to-disc recording			
MODE			
❑ LP-117 [M]	Bernie Nerow Trio	1957	120.00
—As "Bernie Nerow			
PREMIER			
❑ PM 2011 [M]	Just for You	1963	25.00
❑ PS-2011 [R]	Just for You	1963	15.00
RCA CAMDEN			
❑ CAL-2228 [M]	If Ever I Would Leave You	1968	18.00
❑ CAS-2228 [S]	If Ever I Would Leave You	1968	15.00
❑ CAL-2139 [M]	Peter Nero Plays Born Free and Others	1967	18.00
❑ CAS-2139 [S]	Peter Nero Plays Born Free and Others	1967	15.00
RCA VICTOR			
❑ LPM-3313 [M]	Career Girls	1965	18.00
❑ LSP-3313 [S]	Career Girls	1965	25.00
❑ LPM-2536 [M]	For the Nero-Minded	1962	18.00
❑ LSP-2536 [S]	For the Nero-Minded	1962	25.00
❑ LPM-2638 [M]	Hail the Conquering Nero	1963	18.00
❑ LSP-2638 [S]	Hail the Conquering Nero	1963	25.00
❑ LSP-4072	Impressions (Great Songs of Burt Bacharach and Hal David)	1968	15.00
❑ LSP-4205	Love Trip	1969	15.00
❑ ADL1-0284	Music Festival of Hits	1973	15.00
❑ LPM-3871 [M]	Nero-ing In on the Hits	1968	18.00
❑ LSP-3871 [S]	Nero-ing In on the Hits	1968	15.00
❑ LPM-2383 [M]	New Piano in Town	1961	18.00
❑ LSP-2383 [S]	New Piano in Town	1961	25.00
❑ LPM-2710 [M]	Peter Nero in Person	1963	18.00
❑ LSP-2710 [S]	Peter Nero in Person	1963	25.00
❑ LPM-3610 [M]	Peter Nero On Tour	1966	15.00
❑ LSP-3610 [S]	Peter Nero On Tour	1966	18.00
❑ LSP-3936 [S]	Peter Nero Plays Love Is Blue and Ten Other Great Songs	1968	15.00
❑ LPM-3936 [M]	Peter Nero Plays Love Is Blue and Ten Other Great Songs	1968	18.00
❑ LPM-3550 [M]	Peter Nero -- Up Close	1966	15.00
❑ LSP-3550 [S]	Peter Nero -- Up Close	1966	18.00
❑ LPM-2334 [M]	Piano Forte	1961	18.00
❑ LSP-2334 [S]	Piano Forte	1961	25.00
❑ LPM-3720 [M]	Plays a Salute to Herb Alpert and the Tijuana Brass	1967	18.00
❑ LSP-3720 [S]	Plays a Salute to Herb Alpert and the Tijuana Brass	1967	15.00
❑ LPM-2853 [M]	Reflections	1964	18.00
❑ LSP-2853 [S]	Reflections	1964	25.00
❑ LPM-2935 [M]	Songs You Won't Forget	1964	18.00
❑ LSP-2935 [S]	Songs You Won't Forget	1964	25.00
❑ LPM-2827 [M]	Sunday in New York	1964	18.00
❑ LSP-2827 [S]	Sunday in New York	1964	25.00
❑ PRM-241 [M]	Tender Is the Night	1967	18.00
❑ PRS-241 [S]	Tender Is the Night	1967	25.00
—Special-products release			
❑ LPM-2978 [M]	The Best of Peter Nero	1965	18.00
❑ LSP-2978 [S]	The Best of Peter Nero	1965	25.00
❑ LPM-2618 [M]	The Colorful Peter Nero	1963	18.00
❑ LSP-2618 [S]	The Colorful Peter Nero	1963	25.00
❑ LPM-3496 [M]	The Screen Scene	1966	15.00
❑ LSP-3496 [S]	The Screen Scene	1966	18.00
❑ LPM-3814 [M]	Xochimilico	1967	18.00
❑ LSP-3814 [S]	Xochimilico	1967	15.00

Number	Title	Yr	NM
❏ LPM-2484 [M]	Young and Warm and Wonderful	1962	18.00
❏ LSP-2484 [S]	Young and Warm and Wonderful	1962	25.00

NERVOUS EATERS

ACE OF HEARTS
❏ 1007	Hot Steel and Acid	1986	12.00

ELEKTRA
❏ 6E-282	Nervous Eaters	1980	18.00

NESBITT, JIM

CHART
❏ CHS-1031 [B]	Runnin' Bare	1970	25.00
❏ CHM-1005 [M]	Truck Drivin' Cat with Nine Wives	1968	30.00
❏ CHS-1005 [S]	Truck Drivin' Cat with Nine Wives	1968	25.00

NESMITH, MICHAEL

PACIFIC ARTS
❏ 7-116	And the Hits Just Keep On Comin'	1978	18.00
—Reissue of RCA 4695			
❏ 7-106	Compilation	1976	25.00
❏ 7-107	From a Radio Engine to the Photon Wing	1977	15.00
❏ ILPA-9486	From a Radio Engine to the Photon Wing	1977	18.00
—Original issue			
❏ 7-130 [B]	Infinite Rider on the Big Dogma	1979	18.00
❏ 7-118	Live at the Palais	1978	18.00
❏ 7-117	Pretty Much Your Standard Ranch Stash	1978	18.00
—Reissue of RCA APL1-0164			
❏ (no #) [DJ]	The Michael Nesmith Radio Special	1979	40.00
❏ 11-101A	The Prison	197?	50.00
—Boxed set with booklet			
❏ 7-101	The Prison	197?	25.00
—Standard cover			

RCA VICTOR
❏ LSP-4695	And the Hits Just Keep On Comin'	1972	30.00
❏ LSP-4415	Loose Salute	1970	30.00
❏ LSP-4371	Magnetic South	1970	30.00
❏ LSP-4497	Nevada Fighter	1971	30.00
❏ APL1-0164	Pretty Much Your Standard Ranch Stash	1973	30.00
❏ LSP-4563	Tantamount to Treason	1971	30.00

RHINO
❏ R1-70168	The Newer Stuff	1989	15.00

NESTICO, SAMMY

MARK
❏ 32244	Swingaphonic	1969	25.00

SEA BREEZE
❏ SBD-103	Night Flight	1986	12.00

NETHERWORLD

R.E.M.
❏ 4441 [B]	Netherworld	196?	75.00

NEUMANN, ROGER

SEA BREEZE
❏ SBD-102	Introducing Roger Neumann's Rather Large Band	1983	12.00

NEUSTADT, LISA, AND THE ANGEL BAND WITH JEAN REDPATH

PHILO
❏ 1068	Shout for Joy: An Unusual Collection of Traditional Carols	1980	15.00

NEVIL, ROBBIE

EMI MANHATTAN
❏ E1-48359	A Place Like This	1988	12.00

MANHATTAN
❏ ST-53006	Robbie Nevil	1986	12.00

NEVILLE, AARON

MINIT
❏ LP40007 [M]	Like It 'Tis	1967	60.00
❏ LP24007 [R]	Like It 'Tis	1967	30.00

PAR-LO
❏ 1 [M]	Tell It Like It Is	1967	150.00
❏ 1 [S]	Tell It Like It Is	1967	200.00

NEVILLE BROTHERS, THE

CAPITOL
❏ ST-11865	The Neville Brothers	1978	30.00

NEW APOCALYPSE, THE

M.T.A.
❏ S-5017	Stainless Soul	1970	25.00

NEW BIRTH, THE

ARIOLA AMERICA
❏ SW-50062	Platinum City	1979	12.00

BUDDAH
❏ BDS-5636	Blind Baby	1975	12.00

COLLECTABLES
❏ COL-5100	Golden Classics	1988	12.00

RCA VICTOR
❏ LSP-4526	Ain't No Big Thing, But It's Growing	1971	18.00
❏ LSP-4797	Birth Day	1973	15.00
❏ ANL1-2145	Birth Day	1977	12.00
—Reissue of 4797			
❏ APL1-0494	Comin' From All Ends	1974	12.00
❏ LSP-4697	Coming Together	1972	18.00
❏ AFL1-4411	I'm Back	1982	12.00
❏ APL1-0285 [B]	It's Been a Long Time	1974	12.00
❏ APD1-0285 [Q]	It's Been a Long Time	1974	25.00
❏ APL1-1021	The Best of the New Birth	1975	12.00
❏ LSP-4450	The New Birth	1970	18.00

WARNER BROS.
❏ BSK3071	Behold the Mighty Army	1977	12.00
❏ BS2953	Love Potion	1976	12.00

NEW CHRISTY MINSTRELS, THE

COLUMBIA
❏ CL2369 [M]	Chim Chim Cher-ee	1965	25.00
❏ CS9169 [S]	Chim Chim Cher-ee	1965	30.00
❏ CS9709	Chitty Chitty Bang Bang	1969	25.00
❏ CS9356 [S]	Christmas with the Christies	1966	30.00
❏ CL2556 [M]	Christmas with the Christies	1966	25.00
❏ CL2303 [M]	Cowboys and Indians	1965	25.00
❏ CS9103 [S]	Cowboys and Indians	1965	30.00
❏ CL2479 [M]	Greatest Hits	1966	25.00
❏ CS9279 [S]	Greatest Hits	1966	30.00
❏ CL2531 [M]	In Italy...In Italian	1966	25.00
❏ CS9331 [S]	In Italy...In Italian	1966	30.00
❏ CL2187 [M]	Land of Giants	1964	25.00
❏ CS8987 [S]	Land of Giants	1964	30.00
❏ CL2096 [M]	Merry Christmas	1963	25.00
❏ CS8896 [S]	Merry Christmas	1963	30.00
❏ CL2542 [M]	New Kick	1967	25.00
❏ CS9342 [S]	New Kick	1967	30.00
❏ CS9616 [M]	On Tour Through Motortown	1968	50.00
—White label promo only; "Special Mono Radio Station Copy" sticker on front			
❏ CS9616 [S]	On Tour Through Motortown	1968	25.00
❏ CL2055 [M]	Ramblin' Feturing Green, Green	1963	25.00
❏ CS8855 [S]	Ramblin' Feturing Green, Green	1963	30.00
❏ CL2017 [M]	Tall Tales! Legends & Nonsense	1963	25.00
❏ CS8817 [S]	Tall Tales! Legends & Nonsense	1963	30.00
❏ CL1872 [M]	The New Christy Minstrels	1962	25.00
❏ CS8672 [S]	The New Christy Minstrels	1962	30.00
❏ CL1941 [M]	The New Christy Minstrels In Person	1963	25.00
❏ CS8741 [S]	The New Christy Minstrels In Person	1963	30.00
❏ CL2280 [M]	The Quiet Sides of the New Christy Minstrels	1965	25.00
❏ CS9080 [S]	The Quiet Sides of the New Christy Minstrels	1965	30.00
❏ CL2384 [M]	The Wandering Minstrels	1965	25.00
❏ CS9184 [S]	The Wandering Minstrels	1965	30.00
❏ CL2159 [M]	Today	1964	25.00
❏ CS8959 [S]	Today	1964	30.00

GREGAR
❏ 102 [B]	You Need Someone to Love	1970	18.00

NEW COLONY SIX, THE

MERCURY
❏ SR-61228 [B]	Attacking a Straw Man	1969	30.00
❏ SR-61165 [B]	Revelations	1968	30.00

SENTAR
❏ LP-101 [M]	Breakthrough	1966	500.00
❏ ST-3001 [M]	Colonization	1967	50.00
❏ SST-3001 [S]	Colonization	1967	60.00

SUNDAZED
❏ LP5007	At the River's Edge	1995	12.00

NEW DAWN, THE

HOOT
❏ GR 704569	There's a New Dawn	1970	1000.00

NEW DIMENSIONS, THE

SUNDAZED
❏ LP-5025	The Best of the New Dimensions	199?	12.00

SUTTON
❏ SU-331 [M]	Deuces and Eights	1963	80.00
❏ SSU-331 [S]	Deuces and Eights	1963	100.00
❏ SU-336 [M]	Soul Surf	1964	40.00
❏ SSU-336 [S]	Soul Surf	1964	50.00
❏ SU-332 [M]	Surf 'N' Bongos	1963	40.00
❏ SSU-332 [S]	Surf 'N' Bongos	1963	50.00

NEW EDITION

MCA
❏ 5679	All for Love	1985	10.00
❏ 39040 [EP]	Christmas All Over the World	1985	10.00
❏ 42207	Heart Break	1988	10.00
❏ 11480	Home Again	1996	18.00
❏ 5515	New Edition	1984	10.00
❏ 5912	Under the Blue Moon	1986	10.00

STREETWISE
❏ 3301	Candy Girl	1983	15.00

NEW KIDS ON THE BLOCK

COLUMBIA
❏ BFC40985	Hangin' Tough	1988	15.00
—Original with three-letter prefix on spine and short bar code on back cover; all versions have only a "C" prefix on the label			
❏ FC40985	Hangin' Tough	1988	10.00
—Reissue with only "FC" on spine and longer bar code on back cover; all versions have only a "C" prefix on the label			
❏ OC40985	Hangin' Tough	1988	15.00
—Yet another version with a different prefix on spine and a long bar code on back cover; all versions have only a "C" prefix on the label			
❏ FC45280	Merry Merry Christmas	1989	15.00
❏ BFC40475	New Kids on the Block	1987	15.00
—Original with short bar code on back cover			
❏ FC40475	New Kids on the Block	1988	10.00
—Reissue with longer bar code on back cover; both versions have only the "C" prefix on the label			
❏ C45129	Step by Step	1990	15.00

NEW LEGION ROCK SPECTACULAR, THE

SPECTACULAR
❏ 7777	Wild Ones!	1975	60.00

NEW LONDON CHORALE, THE

MYRRH
❏ 6658	The Young Messiah	1981	15.00

NEW MCKINNEY'S COTTON PICKERS, THE

BOUNTIFUL
❏ 38000	The New McKinney's Cotton Pickers	1972	18.00
❏ 38001	You're Driving Me Crazy	1974	18.00

NEW MIX, THE

UNITED ARTISTS
❏ UAS-6678	The New Mix	1968	25.00

NEW ORDER

FACTORY
❏ FACTUS8 [EP]	1981-1982	1983	25.00
❏ FACTUS50	Movement	1981	25.00
—Originals have no bar code			
❏ FACTUS50	Movement	1981	50.00
—Purple vinyl (looks more black, but will appear purple when held to a light)			
❏ FACTUS50	Movement	198?	15.00
—With bar code on cover			
❏ FACTUS12 [B]	Power, Corruption and Lies	1983	25.00

QWEST
❏ 25511 [B]	Brotherhood	1986	15.00
❏	In Order	1993	50.00
PRO-A-5970 [DJ]			
—Promo only six-song, 44-minute compilation; orange vinyl			
❏ 25289	Low Life	1985	12.00
❏ 25308	Power, Corruption and Lies	1985	12.00
—Reissue of Factory FACTUS 12			
❏ 25621 [B]	Substance	1987	30.00
❏ R100938	Technique	1989	15.00
—BMG Direct Marketing edition			
❏ 25845	Technique	1989	15.00

NEW ORLEANS ALL STARS, THE

DIXIELAND JUBILEE
❏ DJ-502	In Concert	196?	18.00

NEW ORLEANS CREOLE ORCHESTRA

SOUTHLAND
❏ 234 [M]	New Orleans Creole Jazz Band	1962	18.00

NEW ORLEANS HERITAGE HALL JAZZ BAND

DIXIELAND JUBILEE
❏ DJ-512	New Orleans Heritage Hall Jazz Band	197?	15.00

NEW ORLEANS NIGHTHAWKS, THE

GHB
❏ 98	The New Orleans Nighthawks	1979	12.00

NEW ORLEANS RAGTIME ORCHESTRA

ARHOOLIE
❏ 1058	New Orleans Ragtime Orchestra	197?	15.00

Number	Title	Yr	NM
DELMARK			
❑ DS-214	Grace and Beauty	197?	15.00
VANGUARD			
❑ VSD-69/70	New Orleans Ragtime Orchestra	197?	18.00

NEW ORLEANS RASCALS, THE

Number	Title	Yr	NM
STOMP OFF			
❑ SOS-1074	Love Song of the Nile	1984	12.00
❑ SOS-1113	The New Orleans Rascals at Preservation Hall	1986	12.00

NEW ORLEANS RHYTHM KINGS

Number	Title	Yr	NM
BRUNSWICK			
❑ BL58011 [10]	Dixieland Jazz	1950	120.00
KINGS OF JAZZ			
❑ NLJ-18009/10	New Orleans Rhythm Kings Heritage	198?	18.00
MILESTONE			
❑ 47020	New Orleans Rhythm Kings	197?	18.00

NEW ORLEANS SHUFFLERS, THE

Number	Title	Yr	NM
KINGSWAY			
❑ KL-700 [M]	The New Orleans Shufflers	1955	40.00

NEW RENAISSANCE SOCIETY, THE

Number	Title	Yr	NM
HANNA-BARBERA			
❑ HLP-9504 [M]	Baroque n' Stones	1966	25.00
❑ HST-9504 [S]	Baroque n' Stones	1966	30.00

NEW RIDERS OF THE PURPLE SAGE

Number	Title	Yr	NM
A&M			
❑ SP-4818	Feelin' All Right	1981	12.00
COLUMBIA			
❑ PC33145	Brujo	1974	18.00
— *Originals have no bar code*			
❑ KC31930	Gypsy Cowboy	1972	18.00
❑ PC31930	Gypsy Cowboy	1979	10.00
— *Budget-line reissue*			
❑ PC32870	Home, Home on the Road	1974	18.00
— *Originals have no bar code*			
❑ KC30888	New Riders of the Purple Sage	1971	18.00
❑ PC30888 [B]	New Riders of the Purple Sage	1979	10.00
— *Budget-line reissue*			
❑ PC33688	Oh, What a Mighty Time	1975	18.00
— *Originals have no bar code*			
❑ KC31284	Powerglide	1972	18.00
❑ PC31284	Powerglide	1979	10.00
— *Budget-line reissue*			
❑ KC32450 [B]	The Adventures of Panama Red	1973	18.00
❑ CQ32450 [Q]	The Adventures of Panama Red	1974	25.00
❑ PC32450	The Adventures of Panama Red	1979	10.00
— *Budget-line reissue*			
❑ PC34367	The Best of New Riders of the Purple Sage	1976	15.00
— *Originals have no bar code*			
❑ PC34367	The Best of New Riders of the Purple Sage	1979	10.00
— *Budget-line reissue with bar code*			
MCA			
❑ 2307	Marin County Line	1977	15.00
❑ 632	Marin County Line	1980	10.00
— *Reissue of 2307*			
❑ 2196	New Riders	1976	15.00
❑ 2248	Who Are These Guys	1977	15.00
RELIX			
❑ RRLP-2024	Before Time Began	1986	10.00
❑ RRLP-2025	Vintage NRPS	1987	10.00

NEW SEEKERS, THE

Number	Title	Yr	NM
ELEKTRA			
❑ EKS-74088	Beautiful People	1971	15.00
❑ EKS-75034	Circles	1972	15.00
❑ EKS-74108 [B]	New Colours	1971	15.00
❑ EKS-75051	The Best of the New Seekers	1973	15.00
❑ EQ-5051 [Q]	The Best of the New Seekers	1973	25.00
❑ EKS-74115	We'd Like to Teach the World to Sing	1971	15.00
MGM VERVE			
❑ V5090	Come Softly to Me	1972	12.00
❑ V5098	Pinball Wizards	1973	12.00
❑ V5095	The History of the New Seekers	1973	12.00

NEW SOCIETY, THE

Number	Title	Yr	NM
RCA VICTOR			
❑ LPM-3676 [M]	The Barock Sound of the New Society	1966	30.00
❑ LSP-3676 [S]	The Barock Sound of the New Society	1966	30.00

NEW STRANGERS, THE

Number	Title	Yr	NM
FOLKLORE			
❑ FRLP-14027 [M]	Meet the New Strangers	1964	25.00
❑ FRST-14027 [S]	Meet the New Strangers	1964	30.00

NEW SUNSHINE JAZZ BAND

Number	Title	Yr	NM
BIOGRAPH			
❑ 12058	Too Much Mustard	197?	15.00
FLYING DUTCHMAN			
❑ BDL1-0549	Old Rags	1974	15.00

NEW SYMPHONY ORCHESTRA OF LONDON (ALEXANDER GIBSON, CONDUCTOR)

Number	Title	Yr	NM
RCA VICTOR RED SEAL			
❑ LSC-2225 [S]	Witches' Brew	1959	400.00
— *Original with "shaded dog" label*			
❑ LSC-2225 [S]	Witches' Brew	199?	30.00
— *Classic Records reissue*			

NEW SYMPHONY ORCHESTRA OF LONDON (RAYMOND AGOULT, CONDUCTOR)

Number	Title	Yr	NM
RCA VICTOR RED SEAL			
❑ LSC-2134 [S]	Overture! Overture!	1959	50.00
— *Original with "shaded dog" label; issued with two different covers*			
❑ LSC-2134 [S]	Overture! Overture!	199?	30.00
— *Classic Records reissue*			

NEW SYMPHONY ORCHESTRA OF LONDON (RONALD BINGE, CONDUCTOR)

Number	Title	Yr	NM
RCA VICTOR RED SEAL			
❑ LSC-2399 [S]	Mendelssohniana	1960	300.00
— *Originals with "shaded dog" label*			

NEW TROUBADOURS, THE

Number	Title	Yr	NM
LORIAN			
❑ 39340	Festival of Light: A Collection of Original Christmas Songs	1980	15.00

NEW TWEEDY BROTHERS, THE

Number	Title	Yr	NM
RIDON			
❑ 234	The New Tweedy Brothers	1968	2000.00
— *With oversized hexagonal cover designed to look like a sugar cube*			
❑ 234	The New Tweedy Brothers	1968	400.00
— *With plain white cover*			

NEW VAUDEVILLE BAND, THE

Number	Title	Yr	NM
FONTANA			
❑ MGF-27600 [M]	The New Vaudeville Band on Tour	1967	15.00
❑ SRF-67688 [P]	The New Vaudeville Band on Tour	1967	15.00
❑ MGF-27560 [M]	Winchester Cathedral	1966	18.00
— *With "Whatever Happened to Phyllis Puke" and "Diana Goodbye"*			
❑ MGF-27560 [M]	Winchester Cathedral	1966	18.00
— *With "Oh, Donna Clara"; record has mono number and actually plays in mono; the number "27560" is in the trail-off*			
❑ SRF-67560 [P]	Winchester Cathedral	1966	18.00
— *With "Whatever Happened to Phyllis Puke" and "Diana Goodbye"*			
❑ SRF-67560 [P]	Winchester Cathedral	1966	15.00
— *With "Oh, Donna Clara"*			
❑ MGF-27560 [P]	Winchester Cathedral	1966	15.00
— *With "Oh, Donna Clara"; record has mono number, but plays stereo; the number "2/67560" is in trail-off area*			

NEW WAVE, THE

Number	Title	Yr	NM
CANTERBURY			
❑ CLPS-1501	The New Wave	1967	30.00

NEW YANKEE RHYTHM KINGS, THE

Number	Title	Yr	NM
STOMP OFF			
❑ SOS-1015	Jazz Band	198?	12.00
❑ SOS-1050	Live at the Strata-Capitol	1982	12.00
❑ SOS-1067	Together at Last	1984	12.00

NEW YORK ART QUARTET, THE

Number	Title	Yr	NM
ESP-DISK'			
❑ 1004 [M]	The New York Art Quartet	1965	25.00
❑ S-1004 [S]	The New York Art Quartet	1965	30.00

NEW YORK BASS VIOLIN CHOIR

Number	Title	Yr	NM
STRATA-EAST			
❑ SES-8003	New York Bass Violin Choir	1980	18.00

NEW YORK CITY

Number	Title	Yr	NM
CHELSEA			
❑ BCL1-0198	I'm Doin' Fine Now	1973	18.00
❑ CHL500	Soulful Road	1974	18.00
❑ CHL514	The Best of New York City	1977	15.00

NEW YORK CITY GAY MEN'S CHORUS

Number	Title	Yr	NM
PRO ARTE			
❑ 159	A Festival of Song	198?	15.00

NEW YORK DOLLS

Number	Title	Yr	NM
CLEOPATRA			
❑ 8124 [B]	Trashed In Paris '73		30.00
— *picture disc*			
MERCURY			
❑ SRM-1-1001	In Too Much Too Soon	1974	40.00
❑ SRM-1-675	New York Dolls	1973	40.00
❑ 1786413	New York Dolls	2008	25.00
❑ 826094-1 [B]	Night of the Living Dolls	1985	15.00

NEW YORK JAZZ GUITAR ENSEMBLE, THE

Number	Title	Yr	NM
CHOICE			
❑ CRS-6831	4 On 6 x 5	1986	15.00

NEW YORK JAZZ QUARTET, THE (1)

Number	Title	Yr	NM
CORAL			
❑ CRL57136 [M]	Music For Suburban Living	1958	200.00
❑ CRL757136 [S]	Music For Suburban Living	1958	150.00
ELEKTRA			
❑ EKL-118 [M]	Gone Native	1957	50.00
❑ EKL-115 [M]	The New York Jazz Quartet	1957	50.00
SAVOY			
❑ MG-12172 [M]	Adam's Theme	1960	30.00
❑ MG-12175 [M]	Gone Native	1961	30.00

NEW YORK JAZZ QUARTET, THE (2)

Number	Title	Yr	NM
ENJA			
❑ 3083	Oasis	1981	15.00
INNER CITY			
❑ IC-3024	Blues for Sarka	1978	18.00
❑ IC-3011	Surge	197?	18.00
SALVATION			
❑ 703	Concert in Japan	197?	15.00

NEW YORK JAZZ SEXTET, THE

Number	Title	Yr	NM
SCEPTER			
❑ S-526 [M]	New York Jazz Sextet	1964	25.00
❑ SS-526 [S]	New York Jazz Sextet	1964	30.00

NEW YORK MARY

Number	Title	Yr	NM
ARISTA/FREEDOM			
❑ AF1019	New York Mary	1975	18.00
❑ AF1035	Piece of the Apple	1976	18.00

NEW YORK ORIGINATORS, THE

Number	Title	Yr	NM
PARAMOUNT			
❑ RS-201 [10]	The New York Style	1952	60.00

NEW YORK PHILHARMONIC ORCHESTRA (BRUNO WALTER, CONDUCTOR)

Number	Title	Yr	NM
COLUMBIA MASTERWORKS			
❑ ML4001 [M]	Mendelssohn: Violin Concerto	1948	40.00
— *Violinist: Nathan Milstein; the very first modern microgroove LP!*			
❑ ML4001 [M]	Mendelssohn: Violin Concerto	1999	30.00
— *Violinist: Nathan Milstein; Classic Records commemorative reissue*			

NEW YORK PRO MUSICA ANTIQUA

Number	Title	Yr	NM
COUNTERPOINT/ESOTERIC			
❑ CPT521 [M]	English Medieval Christmas Carols	196?	25.00
❑ CPTS5521 [S]	English Medieval Christmas Carols	196?	18.00

NEW YORK ROCK ENSEMBLE, THE

Number	Title	Yr	NM
ATCO			
❑ SD 33-294	Faithful Friends	1969	18.00
❑ SD 33-312	Reflections	1970	18.00
❑ SD 33-240	The New York Rock 'n' Roll Ensemble	1968	18.00
COLUMBIA			
❑ KC31317	Freedomburger	1972	18.00
❑ C30033	Roll Over	1970	18.00

NEW YORK SAXOPHONE QUARTET, THE

Number	Title	Yr	NM
20TH CENTURY FOX			
❑ TFM-3150 [M]	The New York Saxophone Quartet	1964	25.00
❑ TFS-3150 [S]	The New York Saxophone Quartet	1964	30.00
MARK			
❑ 32322	The New York Saxophone Quartet	1969	25.00
STASH			
❑ ST-220	An American Experience	198?	12.00
❑ ST-210	New York Saxophone Quartet	198?	12.00

NEW YORK VOICES

GRP

Number	Title	Yr	NM
❑ GR-9589	New York Voices	1989	15.00

NEWBEATS, THE

HICKORY

Number	Title	Yr	NM
❑ LPM122 [M]	Big Beat Sounds by the Newbeats	1965	50.00
❑ LPS122 [S]	Big Beat Sounds by the Newbeats	1965	100.00
❑ LPM120 [M]	Bread and Butter	1964	50.00
❑ LPS120 [S]	Bread and Butter	1964	150.00
❑ T90701 [M]	Bread and Butter	1965	150.00
—Capitol Record Club edition			
❑ DT90701 [R]	Bread and Butter	1965	150.00
—Capitol Record Club edition			
❑ ST90701 [S]	Bread and Butter	1965	200.00
—Capitol Record Club edition			
❑ LPM128 [M]	Run Baby Run	1965	50.00
❑ LPS128 [S]	Run Baby Run	1965	100.00

NEWBORN, PHINEAS

ATLANTIC

Number	Title	Yr	NM
❑ 1235 [M]	Here Is Phineas	1956	50.00
—Black label			
❑ SD1235 [S]	Here Is Phineas	1958	50.00
—Green label			
❑ 1235 [M]	Here Is Phineas	1961	25.00
—Multicolor label, white "fan" logo at right			
❑ SD1235 [S]	Here Is Phineas	1961	18.00
—Multicolor label, white "fan" logo at right			
❑ 1235 [M]	Here Is Phineas	1964	18.00
—Multicolor label, black "fan" logo at right			
❑ SD1235 [S]	Here Is Phineas	1964	15.00
—Multicolor label, black "fan" logo at right			
❑ SD1672	Solo Piano	1975	15.00
❑ 90534	The Piano Artistry of Phineas Newborn	1986	12.00

CONTEMPORARY

Number	Title	Yr	NM
❑ C-7648	Back Home	198?	15.00
❑ M-3611 [M]	Great Jazz Piano	1962	25.00
❑ S-7611 [S]	Great Jazz Piano	1962	30.00
❑ S-7622 [S]	Please Send Me Someone to Love	1969	25.00
❑ M-3615 [M]	The Newborn Touch	1964	25.00
❑ S-7615 [S]	The Newborn Touch	1964	30.00
❑ M-3600 [M]	The World of Piano!	1961	25.00
❑ S-7600 [S]	The World of Piano!	1961	30.00

FANTASY

Number	Title	Yr	NM
❑ OJC-175	A World of Piano	198?	12.00
❑ OJC-388	Great Jazz Piano	1989	15.00
❑ OJC-270	The Newborn Touch	1988	12.00
❑ OJC-175	The World of Piano!	198?	12.00

PABLO

Number	Title	Yr	NM
❑ 2310801	Look Out, Phineas Is Back	197?	15.00

RCA VICTOR

Number	Title	Yr	NM
❑ LPM-1873 [M]	Fabulous Phineas	1958	50.00
❑ LSP-1873 [S]	Fabulous Phineas	1958	40.00
❑ LPM-1589 [M]	Phineas Newborn Plays Jamaica	1957	50.00
❑ LPM-1421 [M]	Phineas' Rainbow	1957	50.00
❑ LPM-1474 [M]	While the Lady Sleeps	1957	50.00

ROULETTE

Number	Title	Yr	NM
❑ R-52043 [M]	I Love a Piano	1960	30.00
❑ SR-52043 [S]	I Love a Piano	1960	30.00
❑ R-52031 [M]	Piano Portraits	1959	30.00
❑ SR-52031 [S]	Piano Portraits	1959	30.00

NEWBURY, MICKEY

ABC HICKORY

Number	Title	Yr	NM
❑ HA-44011	Eye on the Sparrow	1978	12.00
❑ HA-44002	Rusty Tracks	1977	12.00
❑ HB-44017	The Sailor	1979	12.00

ELEKTRA

Number	Title	Yr	NM
❑ EKS-74107 [B]	'Frisco Mabel Joy	1971	12.00
❑ EQ-4107 [Q]	'Frisco Mabel Joy	1974	25.00
❑ EKS-75055	Heaven Help the Child	1973	12.00
❑ 7E-1007	I Came to Hear the Music	1974	12.00
❑ 7E-1030	Lovers	1975	12.00
❑ EK-PROMO20 [DJ]	Recorded Live at Montezuma Hall, San Diego State University, March 6, 1973	1973	40.00

MCA

Number	Title	Yr	NM
❑ 803	Eye on the Sparrow	198?	10.00
—Reissue			
❑ 802	Rusty Tracks	198?	10.00
—Reissue			
❑ 945	Sweet Memories	1985	12.00
❑ 804	The Sailor	198?	10.00
—Reissue			

MERCURY

Number	Title	Yr	NM
❑ SR61236	Looks Like Rain	1969	18.00

RCA VICTOR

Number	Title	Yr	NM
❑ LSP-4043	Harlequin Melodies	1968	18.00

NEWHART, BOB

HARMONY

Number	Title	Yr	NM
❑ HS11344	The Very Funny Bob Newhart	196?	15.00

MURRAY HILL

Number	Title	Yr	NM
❑ OP2529	The Best of the Button-Down Mind	197?	25.00

WARNER BROS.

Number	Title	Yr	NM
❑ W1417 [M]	Behind the Button-Down Mind of Bob Newhart	1961	30.00
❑ WS1417 [S]	Behind the Button-Down Mind of Bob Newhart	1961	25.00
❑ W1517 [M]	Bob Newhart Faces Bob Newhart (Faces Bob Newhart)	1964	30.00
❑ W1672 [M]	The Best of Bob Newhart	1966	30.00
❑ WS1672 [S]	The Best of Bob Newhart	1966	30.00
—Gold label			
❑ WS1672 [S]	The Best of Bob Newhart	1968	25.00
—Green "W7" label			
❑ WS1672 [S]	The Best of Bob Newhart	1970	18.00
—Green "WB" label			
❑ WS1672 [S]	The Best of Bob Newhart	1973	15.00
—Burbank" palm-trees label			
❑ WS1672 [S]	The Best of Bob Newhart	1979	10.00
—White or tan label			
❑ 2N1399 [M]	The Bob Newhart Deluxe Edition	1961	50.00
❑ 2NS1399 [S]	The Bob Newhart Deluxe Edition	1961	40.00
❑ W1379 [M]	The Button-Down Mind of Bob Newhart	1960	30.00
❑ WS1379 [S]	The Button-Down Mind of Bob Newhart	1960	30.00
❑ W1467 [M]	The Button-Down Mind on TV	1962	30.00
❑ WS1467 [S]	The Button-Down Mind on TV	1962	25.00
❑ W1393 [M]	The Button-Down Mind Strikes Back!	1960	30.00
❑ WS1393 [S]	The Button-Down Mind Strikes Back!	1960	30.00
❑ W1588 [M]	The Windmills Are Weakening	1965	30.00
❑ W1717 [M]	This Is It	1967	30.00

NEWLEY, ANTHONY

LONDON

Number	Title	Yr	NM
❑ LL3461 [M]	Genius	1966	15.00
❑ PS461 [S]	Genius	1966	18.00
❑ LL3156 [M]	Love Is a Now and Then Thing	1960	25.00
❑ LL3262 [M]	This Is Tony Newley	1962	18.00
❑ LL3252 [M]	Tony	1962	18.00
❑ PS244 [S]	Tony	1962	30.00

RCA VICTOR

Number	Title	Yr	NM
❑ LPM-3839 [M]	Doctor Dolittle	1967	15.00
❑ LSP-3839 [S]	Doctor Dolittle	1967	18.00
❑ LPM-2925 [M]	In My Solitude	1964	18.00
❑ LSP-2925 [S]	In My Solitude	1964	25.00
❑ LPM-3614 [M]	Newly Recorded	1966	15.00
❑ LSP-3614 [S]	Newly Recorded	1966	18.00
❑ LSP-4163	The Best of Anthony Newley	1969	15.00
❑ LPM-3347 [M]	Who Can I Turn To	1965	15.00
❑ LSP-3347 [S]	Who Can I Turn To	1965	18.00

NEWMAN, BOB

AUDIO LAB

Number	Title	Yr	NM
❑ AL-1536 [M]	The Kentucky Colonel	1959	200.00

NEWMAN, DAVID "FATHEAD

ATLANTIC

Number	Title	Yr	NM
❑ SD1505	Bigger and Better	1968	25.00
❑ 1399 [M]	Fathead Comes On	1962	30.00
❑ SD1399 [S]	Fathead Comes On	1962	40.00
❑ 81965	Fire! Live at the Village Vanguard	1989	15.00
❑ 81725	Heads Up	1987	12.00
❑ SD1489	House of David	1968	25.00
❑ SD1600	Lonely Avenue	1972	18.00
❑ SD1524	Many Facets	1969	18.00
❑ SD1662	Newmanism	1974	15.00
❑ 1304 [M]	Ray Charles Presents David "Fathead" Newman	1959	40.00
—Black label			
❑ 1304 [M]	Ray Charles Presents David "Fathead" Newman	1961	18.00
—Multicolor label with white "fan" logo			
❑ 1304 [M]	Ray Charles Presents David "Fathead" Newman	1964	15.00
—Multicolor label with black "fan" logo			
❑ SD1304 [S]	Ray Charles Presents David "Fathead" Newman	1959	50.00
—Green label			
❑ SD1304 [S]	Ray Charles Presents David "Fathead" Newman	1961	25.00
—Multicolor label with white "fan" logo			
❑ SD1304 [S]	Ray Charles Presents David "Fathead" Newman	1964	18.00
—Multicolor label with black "fan" logo			
❑ 1366 [M]	Straight Ahead	1961	30.00
—Multicolor label with white "fan" logo			
❑ 1366 [M]	Straight Ahead	1964	15.00
—Multicolor label with black "fan" logo			
❑ SD1366 [S]	Straight Ahead	1961	40.00
—Multicolor label with white "fan" logo			
❑ SD1366 [S]	Straight Ahead	1964	18.00
—Multicolor label with black "fan" logo			
❑ SD1590	The Best of David "Fathead" Newman	1972	18.00
❑ SD1638	The Weapon	1973	18.00

COTILLION

Number	Title	Yr	NM
❑ SD18002	Captain Buckles	1970	25.00

MUSE

Number	Title	Yr	NM
❑ MR-5234	Resurgence	1981	12.00
❑ MR-5283	Still Hard Times	1982	12.00

PRESTIGE

Number	Title	Yr	NM
❑ 10104	Concrete Jungle	1978	18.00
❑ 10106	Keep the Dream Alive	1978	18.00
❑ 10108	Scratch My Back	1979	18.00

WARNER BROS.

Number	Title	Yr	NM
❑ BS2984	Front Money	1977	12.00
❑ BS2917	Mr. Fathead	1976	12.00

NEWMAN, JIMMY

DECCA

Number	Title	Yr	NM
❑ DL4748 [M]	Artificial Rose	1966	25.00
❑ DL74748 [S]	Artificial Rose	1966	30.00
❑ DL75065	Born to Love You	1968	25.00
❑ DL4398 [M]	Folk Songs of the Bayou Country	1963	40.00
❑ DL74398 [S]	Folk Songs of the Bayou Country	1963	50.00
❑ DL4221 [M]	Jimmy Newman	1962	30.00
❑ DL74221 [S]	Jimmy Newman	1962	30.00
❑ DL4781 [M]	Jimmy Newman Sings Country Songs	1966	25.00
❑ DL74781 [S]	Jimmy Newman Sings Country Songs	1966	30.00
❑ DL4960 [M]	The Jimmy Newman Way	1967	30.00
❑ DL74960 [S]	The Jimmy Newman Way	1967	25.00
❑ DL4885 [M]	The World of Country Music	1967	30.00
❑ DL74885 [S]	The World of Country Music	1967	25.00

DOT

Number	Title	Yr	NM
❑ DLP-3690 [M]	A Fallen Star	1965	30.00
❑ DLP-3736 [M]	Country Crossroads	1966	30.00
❑ DLP-25736 [R]	Country Crossroads	1966	25.00

MGM

Number	Title	Yr	NM
❑ E-4045 [M]	Songs by Jimmy Newman	1962	30.00
❑ SE-4045 [S]	Songs by Jimmy Newman	1962	30.00
❑ E-3777 [M]	This Is Jimmy Newman	1959	30.00
❑ SE-3777 [S]	This Is Jimmy Newman	1959	30.00

NEWMAN, JOE, AND JOE WILDER

CONCORD JAZZ

Number	Title	Yr	NM
❑ CJ-262	Joe Newman and Joe Wilder	1985	15.00

NEWMAN, JOE

AMERICAN RECORDING SOCIETY

Number	Title	Yr	NM
❑ G-447 [M]	Basically Swing	1958	40.00
❑ G-451 [M]	New Sounds In Swing	1958	40.00

CORAL

Number	Title	Yr	NM
❑ CRL57208 [M]	Soft Swingin' Jazz	1958	50.00
❑ CRL57121 [M]	The Happy Cats	1957	50.00

FANTASY

Number	Title	Yr	NM
❑ OJC-185	Good 'N Groovy	1985	12.00
❑ OJC-419	Jive At Five	1990	15.00

JAZZTONE

Number	Title	Yr	NM
❑ J-1217 [M]	New Sounds In Swing	1956	40.00
❑ J-1265 [M]	Swing Lightly	1957	40.00
❑ J-1220 [M]	The Count's Men	1956	40.00

MERCURY

Number	Title	Yr	NM
❑ MG-20696 [M]	Joe Newman At Count Basie's	1962	30.00
❑ SR-60696 [S]	Joe Newman At Count Basie's	1962	30.00

PRESTIGE

Number	Title	Yr	NM
❑ 2509	Jive At Five	198?	15.00

RAMA

Number	Title	Yr	NM
❑ LP-1003 [M]	Locking Horns	1957	120.00

RCA VICTOR

Number	Title	Yr	NM
❑ LPM-1118 [M]	All I Want To Do Is Swing	1955	100.00
❑ LPM-1198 [M]	I'm Still Swinging	1956	500.00
—Andy Warhol cover.			
❑ LPM-1324 [M]	Salute To Satch	1956	80.00

ROULETTE

Number	Title	Yr	NM
❑ R-52014 [M]	Joe Newman With Woodwinds	1958	40.00
❑ SR-52014 [S]	Joe Newman With Woodwinds	1958	30.00
❑ R-52009 [M]	Locking Horns	1958	40.00
❑ SR-52009 [S]	Locking Horns	1958	30.00

STASH

Number	Title	Yr	NM
❑ ST-219	In a Mellow Mood	198?	12.00

STORYVILLE

Number	Title	Yr	NM
❑ STLP-905 [M]	I Feel Like a Newman	1956	100.00
❑ STLP-318 [10]	Joe Newman and the Boys In the Band	1955	150.00

SWINGVILLE

Number	Title	Yr	NM
❑ SVLP-2019 [M]	Good 'N Groovy	1961	50.00
—Purple label			

Number	Title	Yr	NM
❑ SVLP-2019 [M]	Good 'N Groovy	1965	30.00
—Blue label, trident logo at right			
❑ SVLP-2011 [M]	Jive At Five	1961	50.00
—Purple label			
❑ SVLP-2011 [M]	Jive At Five	1965	30.00
—Blue label, trident logo at right			
❑ SVLP-2027 [M]	Joe's Hap'nin's	1961	60.00
—Purple label			
❑ SVST-2027 [S]	Joe's Hap'nin's	1961	60.00
—Red label			
❑ SVLP-2027 [M]	Joe's Hap'nin's	1965	30.00
—Blue label, trident logo at right			
❑ SVST-2027 [S]	Joe's Hap'nin's	1965	30.00
—Blue label, trident logo at right			

TRIP

Number	Title	Yr	NM
❑ 5548	Live at Basie's	197?	12.00

VANGUARD

| ❑ VRS-8007 [10] | Joe Newman and His Band | 1954 | 200.00 |

VIK

| ❑ LX-1060 [M] | The Midgets | 1957 | 80.00 |

WORLD PACIFIC

| ❑ WP-1288 [M] | Countin' | 1960 | 40.00 |
| ❑ ST-1288 [S] | Countin' | 1960 | 40.00 |

NEWMAN, PHYLLIS

SIRE

| ❑ SES-97002 | Those Were the Days | 1969 | 25.00 |

NEWMAN, RANDY

REPRISE

Number	Title	Yr	NM
❑ RS6373	12 Songs	1970	18.00
—With "W7" and "r:" logos on two-tone orange label			
❑ RS6373	12 Songs	1970	12.00
—With only "r:" logo on all-orange (tan) label			
❑ MS2193	Good Old Boys	1974	12.00
❑ MS42193 [Q]	Good Old Boys	1974	18.00
❑ 25773	Land of Dreams	1988	12.00
❑ RS6286	Randy Newman	1968	25.00
—Cover with Randy standing in the clouds			
❑ RS6286	Randy Newman	1968	18.00
—Cover with close-up of Randy's face; "W7" and "r:" logos on two-tone orange label			
❑ RS6286	Randy Newman	1970	15.00
—With only "r:" logo on all-orange (tan) label			
❑ RS6459	Randy Newman/Live	1971	12.00
❑ MS2064	Sail Away	1972	18.00
—With no song titles listed on back			
❑ MS2064	Sail Away	1972	12.00
—With song titles listed on back			

RHINO

| ❑ R16286 [B] | Randy Newman | 2014 | 25.00 |

WARNER BROS.

❑ HS3346 [B]	Born Again	1979	12.00
❑ BSK3079	Little Criminals	1977	12.00
❑ 23755	Trouble in Paradise	1983	12.00

NEWPORT ALL STARS, THE

BASF

| ❑ 20717 | A Tribute to Duke | 1972 | 18.00 |

BLACK LION

| ❑ 303 | Newport All Stars | 197? | 15.00 |

CONCORD JAZZ

| ❑ CJ-343 | European Tour | 1988 | 12.00 |
| *—As "The Newport Jazz Festival All-Stars* | | | |

NEWTON, CAM

INNER CITY

| ❑ IC-1059 | The Motive Behind the Smile | 1979 | 18.00 |
| ❑ IC-1079 | Welcome Aliens | 1980 | 18.00 |

NEWTON, JAMES

BLUE NOTE

| ❑ BT-85109 | The African Flower | 1986 | 15.00 |

CELESTIAL HARMONIES

❑ CEL-012	Echo Canyon	1984	15.00
❑ 13012	Echo Canyon	198?	12.00
—Reissue with new number			
❑ 14030	James Newton in Venice	1988	15.00

ECM

| ❑ 1214 | Axum | 1981 | 12.00 |

GRAMAVISION

| ❑ 8205 | James Newton | 1982 | 12.00 |
| ❑ GR-8304 | Luella | 1983 | 12.00 |

INDIA NAVIGATION

❑ IN-1046	Mystery School	1980	15.00
❑ IN-1037	Paseo Del Mar	197?	18.00
❑ IN-1051	Portraits	198?	15.00

NEWTON, JUICE

CAPITOL

❑ ST-11682	Come to Me	1977	18.00
❑ SN-16242	Come to Me	1982	10.00
—Budget-line reissue			

Number	Title	Yr	NM
❑ ST-12294	Dirty Looks	1983	12.00
❑ SN-16356	Dirty Looks	1985	10.00
—Budget-line reissue			
❑ SJ-12353	Greatest Hits	1984	12.00
❑ SN-16471	Greatest Hits	1987	10.00
—Budget-line reissue			
❑ ST-12136	Juice	1981	12.00
❑ SN-16313	Juice	1984	10.00
—Budget-line reissue			
❑ ST-12210	Quiet Lies	1982	12.00
❑ SN-16314	Quiet Lies	1984	10.00
—Budget-line reissue			
❑ ST-12000	Take Heart	1980	18.00
❑ SN-16244	Take Heart	1982	10.00
—Budget-line reissue			
❑ ST-11811	Well-Kept Secret	1978	18.00
❑ SN-16243	Well-Kept Secret	1982	10.00
—Budget-line reissue			

RCA

❑ 8376-1-R	Ain't Gonna Cry	1989	12.00
❑ 6371-1-R	Emotion	1987	12.00
❑ 5646-1-R	Old Flame	1986	12.00
—Reissue of 5493 with slightly different lineup			

RCA VICTOR

❑ APL1-1722	After Dust Settled	1977	18.00
❑ AYL1-4038	After Dust Settled	1982	10.00
—Best Buy Series" reissue			
❑ AFL1-4995	Can't Wait All Night	1984	12.00
❑ APL1-1004	Juice Newton and Silver Spur	1975	25.00
❑ AYL1-4037	Juice Newton and Silver Spur	1982	10.00
—Best Buy Series" reissue			
❑ AFL1-5493	Old Flame	1985	15.00

NEWTON, LAUREN

HAT HUT

| ❑ 3511 | Timbre | 1982 | 18.00 |

NEWTON, WAYNE

20TH CENTURY

| ❑ T-576 | Change of Heart | 1979 | 12.00 |

ARIES II

| ❑ WY201 | Wayne Newton Christmas | 1979 | 12.00 |

CAPITOL

Number	Title	Yr	NM
❑ T1973 [M]	Danke Schoen	1963	18.00
❑ ST1973 [S]	Danke Schoen	1963	25.00
❑ SM-11972	Danke Schoen	1979	12.00
—Reissue			
❑ T2832 [M]	God Is Alive	1968	25.00
❑ ST2832 [S]	God Is Alive	1968	18.00
❑ ST-617	How I Got This Way	1971	18.00
❑ T2635 [M]	It's Only the Good Times	1967	18.00
❑ ST2635 [S]	It's Only the Good Times	1967	25.00
❑ STBB-487	Merry Christmas to You	1970	18.00
❑ T2335 [M]	Red Roses for a Blue Lady	1965	18.00
❑ ST2335 [S]	Red Roses for a Blue Lady	1965	25.00
❑ SM 2335	Red Roses for a Blue Lady	197?	12.00
—Reissue			
❑ T2714 [M]	Song of the Year...Wayne Newton Style	1967	25.00
❑ ST2714 [S]	Song of the Year...Wayne Newton Style	1967	18.00
❑ T2588 [M]	Songs for a Merry Christmas	1966	15.00
❑ ST2588 [S]	Songs for a Merry Christmas	1966	18.00
❑ T2389 [M]	Summer Wind	1965	18.00
❑ ST2389 [S]	Summer Wind	1965	25.00
❑ T2797 [M]	The Best of Wayne Newton	1967	25.00
❑ ST2797 [S]	The Best of Wayne Newton	1967	18.00
❑ SN-16083	The Best of Wayne Newton	1980	10.00
—Budget-line reissue			
❑ SKAO-137	The Best of Wayne Newton, Volume 2	1968	18.00
❑ T2563 [M]	The Old Rugged Cross	1966	18.00
❑ ST2563 [S]	The Old Rugged Cross	1966	25.00
❑ SM-2563	The Old Rugged Cross	197?	12.00
—Reissue			
❑ T2029 [M]	Wayne Newton In Person	1964	18.00
❑ ST2029 [S]	Wayne Newton In Person	1964	25.00
❑ T2445 [M]	Wayne Newton -- Now!	1966	18.00
❑ ST2445 [S]	Wayne Newton -- Now!	1966	25.00
❑ T2130 [M]	Wayne Newton Sings Hit Songs	1964	18.00
❑ ST2130 [S]	Wayne Newton Sings Hit Songs	1964	25.00
❑ T2847 [M]	Wayne Newton -- The Greatest	1968	25.00
❑ ST2847 [S]	Wayne Newton -- The Greatest	1968	18.00

CAPITOL PICKWICK SERIES

❑ PC-3459 [M]	Everybody Loves Somebody	196?	12.00
❑ SPC-3459 [S]	Everybody Loves Somebody	196?	12.00
❑ PC-3461 [M]	Michelle	196?	12.00
❑ SPC-3461 [S]	Michelle	196?	12.00
❑ PC-3455 [M]	Somewhere My Love	196?	12.00
❑ SPC-3455 [S]	Somewhere My Love	196?	12.00
❑ PC-3464 [M]	Wow! Wayne Newton Live	196?	12.00
❑ SPC-3464 [S]	Wow! Wayne Newton Live	196?	12.00

CHELSEA

| ❑ CHE1003 | Can't You Hear the Song? | 1972 | 15.00 |
| ❑ CHE1001 | Daddy Don't You Walk So Fast | 1972 | 15.00 |

Number	Title	Yr	NM
❑ CHL-513	Daddy Don't You Walk So Fast	1976	12.00
—Reissue of 1001			
❑ CHL-507	Midnight Idol	1975	12.00
❑ BCL1-0367	Pour Me a Little More Wine	1973	15.00
❑ CHL-504	The Best of Wayne Newton Live	1974	12.00
❑ CHL-512	Tomorrow	1976	12.00
❑ CHE1006	While We're Still Young	1973	15.00

CURB

| ❑ 10607 | Coming Home | 1989 | 15.00 |

MGM

❑ SE-4593	Christmas Isn't Christmas Without You	1968	15.00
❑ SE-4594	Dreams of the Everyday Housewife/Town and Country	1969	15.00
❑ E-4549 [M]	One More Time	1968	25.00
❑ SE-4549 [S]	One More Time	1968	15.00
❑ E-4523 [M]	Walking on New Grass	1968	25.00
❑ SE-4523 [S]	Walking on New Grass	1968	15.00

WORD

| ❑ WST-8586 | Only Believe | 1972 | 15.00 |

NEWTON, WOOD

ELEKTRA

| ❑ 6E-176 | Wood Newton | 1979 | 12.00 |

NEWTON-JOHN, OLIVIA

GEFFEN

| ❑ GHS24257 | Warm and Tender | 1989 | 15.00 |

MCA

Number	Title	Yr	NM
❑ 2148	Clearly Love	1975	12.00
❑ 3015	Clearly Love	1977	10.00
—Reissue			
❑ 37061	Clearly Love	1980	10.00
—Reissue			
❑ 2186	Come On Over	1976	12.00
❑ 3016	Come On Over	1977	10.00
—Reissue			
❑ 37062	Come On Over	1980	10.00
—Reissue			
❑ 2223	Don't Stop Believin'	1976	12.00
❑ 3017	Don't Stop Believin'	1977	10.00
—Reissue			
❑ 37063	Don't Stop Believin'	1980	10.00
—Reissue			
❑ 2133	Have You Never Been Mellow	1975	12.00
❑ 3014	Have You Never Been Mellow	1977	10.00
—Reissue			
❑ 411	If You Love Me Let Me Know	1974	18.00
—Originals have incorrect song title: "I Love You, I Honestly Love You			
❑ 411	If You Love Me Let Me Know	1974	12.00
—With corrected song title: "I Honestly Love You			
❑ 3013	If You Love Me Let Me Know	1977	10.00
—Reissue			
❑ 389	Let Me Be There	1973	18.00
❑ 3012	Let Me Be There	1977	10.00
—Reissue			
❑ 2280	Making a Good Thing Better	1977	12.00
❑ 3018	Making a Good Thing Better	1977	10.00
—Reissue			
❑ 3028	Olivia Newton-John's Greatest Hits	1977	12.00
❑ 5347	Olivia's Greatest Hits, Vol. 2	1982	10.00
❑ 5229	Physical	1981	10.00
❑ 16011	Physical	1982	30.00
—Audiophile edition			
❑ 6151	Soul Kiss	1985	10.00
❑ 6245	The Rumour	1988	10.00
❑ 3067	Totally Hot	1978	12.00
❑ 37123	Totally Hot	1981	10.00
—Reissue			

MOBILE FIDELITY

| ❑ 1-040 [B] | Totally Hot | 1980 | 25.00 |
| *—Audiophile vinyl* | | | |

UNI

| ❑ 73117 | If Not for You | 1971 | 80.00 |

NEXT MORNING, THE

CALLA

| ❑ SC-2002 | The Next Morning | 1972 | 100.00 |

NICE, THE

COLUMBIA SPECIAL PRODUCTS

❑ P11634	Ars Longa Vita Brevis	1973	15.00
❑ P11635	The Nice	1973	15.00
❑ P11633	Thoughts of Emerlist Davjack	1973	15.00

IMMEDIATE

❑ Z12-52020 [B]	Ars Longa Vita Brevis	1969	30.00
❑ Z12-52022 [B]	The Nice	1969	30.00
❑ Z1252004 [B]	Thoughts of Emerlist Davjack	1968	30.00

MERCURY

| ❑ SR61324 | Elegy | 1971 | 15.00 |

Number	Title	Yr	NM
❑ SR61295	Five Bridges	1970	15.00
❑ SRM-2-6500	Keith Emerson with The Nice	1972	18.00

SIRE

❑ SASH-3710	The Vintage Years	1975	18.00

NICHOLAS, ALBERT

DELMARK

❑ DS-209	Albert Nicholas with Art Hodes' All-Star Stompers	1964	25.00

GHB

❑ 64	The Albert Nicholas/John Defferary Jazztet	197?	15.00

NICHOLAS, ALBERT/SIDNEY BECHET

RIVERSIDE

❑ RLP-12-216 [M]	Creole Reeds	1956	80.00
— White label, blue print			
❑ RLP-12-216 [M]	Creole Reeds	1959	40.00
— Blue label, microphone logo at top			

NICHOLAS, GEORGE "BIG NICK

INDIA NAVIGATION

❑ IN-1061	Big and Warm	1985	15.00
❑ IN-1066	Big Nick	1986	15.00

NICHOLAS, JOSEPH "WOODEN JOE

AMERICA MUSIC

❑ 640 [10]	A Nite at Artesian Hall With Wooden Joe	1951	60.00

NICHOLAS, PAUL

RSO

❑ RS-1-3028	Paul Nicholas	1977	15.00

NICHOLAS BROTHERS, THE

MERCURY

❑ MG-20355 [M]	We Do Sing, Too	1958	30.00

NICHOLS, HERBIE

BETHLEHEM

❑ BCP-81 [M]	Love Gloom Cash and Love	1957	250.00
❑ BCP-6028	The Bethlehem Years	197?	18.00
— Distributed by RCA Victor			

BLUE NOTE

❑ BLP-1519 [M]	Herbie Nichols Trio	1956	600.00
— Deep groove" version, Lexington Ave. address on label			
❑ BLP-1519 [M]	Herbie Nichols Trio	1956	500.00
— Deep groove" edition, W. 63rd St. address on label			
❑ BLP-1519 [M]	Herbie Nichols Trio	1963	60.00
— With "New York, USA" address on label			
❑ BST-81519 [R]	Herbie Nichols Trio	1967	25.00
— With "A Division of Liberty Records" on label			
❑ BLP-1519 [M]	Herbie Nichols Trio	1971	40.00
— A Division of United Artists" on label			
❑ BLP-5068 [10]	The Prophetic Herbie Nichols, Volume 1	1955	1200.00
❑ BLP-5069 [10]	The Prophetic Herbie Nichols, Volume 2	1955	1200.00
❑ BN-LA485-H2	Third World	1975	40.00

MOSAIC

❑ MR5-118	The Complete Blue Note Recordings of Herbie Nichols	1987	200.00
— Limited edition of 7,500			

NICHOLS, KEITH

STOMP OFF

❑ SOS-1159	Chitterlin' Strut	1988	12.00
❑ SOS-1135	Doctors Jazz	1987	12.00

NICHOLS, MIKE, AND ELAINE MAY

MERCURY

❑ OCM2200 [M]	An Evening with Mike Nichols and Elaine May	1961	30.00
❑ OCS6200 [S]	An Evening with Mike Nichols and Elaine May	1961	40.00
❑ MG20376 [M]	Improvisations to Music	1959	30.00
❑ SR60040 [S]	Improvisations to Music	1959	40.00
❑ MG20680 [M]	Nichols and May Examine Doctors	1962	30.00
❑ SR60680 [S]	Nichols and May Examine Doctors	1962	30.00
❑ SRM-2-628	Retrospect	1972	25.00
❑ SR60997 [S]	The Best of Nichols and May	1965	30.00
❑ MG20997 [M]	The Best of Nichols and May	1965	25.00

NICHOLS, NICHELLE

EPIC

❑ BN26351 [S]	Down to Earth	1968	40.00
❑ LN24351 [M]	Down to Earth	1968	80.00
— White label promo only; in stereo cover with "Mono" sticker			

NICHOLS, RED, AND THE FIVE PENNIES

AUDIOPHILE

❑ AP-1 [M]	Red Nichols and Band	195?	50.00

❑ AP-7 [M]	Syncopated Chamber Music, Volume 1	195?	50.00
❑ AP-8 [M]	Syncopated Chamber Music, Volume 2	195?	50.00

BRUNSWICK

❑ BL58008 [10]	Classics, Volume 1	1950	80.00
❑ BL58009 [10]	Classics, Volume 2	1950	80.00
❑ BL54008 [M]	For Collectors Only	1954	50.00
❑ BL54047 [M]	The Red Nichols Story	1959	50.00
❑ BL58027 [10]	Volume 3	1951	80.00

CAPITOL

❑ T2065 [M]	Blues and Old-Time Rags	1963	18.00
❑ ST2065 [S]	Blues and Old-Time Rags	1963	25.00
❑ T1297 [M]	Dixieland Dinner Dance	1960	18.00
❑ ST1297 [S]	Dixieland Dinner Dance	1960	25.00
❑ T775 [M]	Hot Pennies	1956	50.00
❑ H215 [10]	Jazz Time	1950	80.00
❑ T1051 [M]	Parade of the Pennies	1958	25.00
❑ ST1051 [S]	Parade of the Pennies	1958	30.00
❑ T1803 [M]	The All-Time Hits of Red Nichols	1962	18.00
❑ ST1803 [S]	The All-Time Hits of Red Nichols	1962	25.00

CIRCLE

❑ CLP-110	Red Nichols and His Orchestra 1936	1987	12.00

CONCERT DISC

❑ CS-53	Red Nichols and His Five Pennies	1961	18.00

HALL OF FAME

❑ 619	Red Nichols and His Five Pennies	197?	12.00

JAZZOLOGY

❑ J-90	Red Nichols and His Five Pennies	198?	12.00

MARK 56

❑ 612	Red Nichols and His Five Pennies	197?	15.00

MCA

❑ 1518	The Rarest Brunswick Masters	198?	12.00

MOBILE FIDELITY

❑ 1-093 [B]	Red Nichols and the Five Pennies at Marineland	1982	25.00
— Audiophile vinyl			

PAUSA

❑ 9022	All Time Hits	198?	12.00

PICCADILLY

❑ 3570	Big Band Series/Original Recordings	198?	12.00

STARDUST

❑ SD-122 [M]	Red Nichols and His "Five Pennies	196?	15.00
❑ SDS-122 [S]	Red Nichols and His "Five Pennies	196?	15.00

SUNBEAM

❑ 12	Popular Concert 1928-32	197?	15.00
❑ 137	Red Nichols and His Five Pennies 1929-31	1973	12.00

NICHOLS-JACOBY DREAMLAND SYNCOPATORS

STOMP OFF

❑ SOS-1150	Territory Jazz	1988	12.00

NICKEL BAG, THE

KAMA SUTRA

❑ KLPS-8066 [S]	Doing Their Love Thing	1968	30.00
❑ KLP-8066 [M]	Doing Their Love Thing	1968	60.00
— Both stock and promo copies exist			

NICKS, STEVIE

ATLANTIC

❑ 1P-8160	TimeSpace -- The Best of Stevie Nicks	1991	25.00
— Columbia House edition; only US vinyl version			

MOBILE FIDELITY

❑ 1-121	Bella Donna	1984	50.00
— Audiophile vinyl			

MODERN

❑ MR 38-139	Bella Donna	1981	12.00
❑ PR-2881 [DJ]	Reflections from the Other Side of the Mirror	1989	25.00
— Promo-only interview album with script			
❑ 90479	Rock a Little	1985	12.00
❑ 91245	The Other Side of the Mirror	1989	12.00
❑ 90084	The Wild Heart	1983	12.00

NICO

4 MEN WITH BEARDS

❑ 4M138LP [B]	Chelsea Girl		25.00
❑ 4M113LP [B]	Desertshore		25.00
❑ 4M113 [B]	Desertshore	2013	25.00

CLEOPATRA

❑ 8916 [B]	All Tomorrow's Parties		30.00
— picture disc			
❑ 9925 [B]	Reims Cathedral - December 13, 1974	2012	25.00

ELEKTRA

❑ EKS-74029 [B]	The Marble Index	1968	50.00
❑ EKS74029 [B]	The Marble Index	1968	50.00

ISLAND

❑ ILPS-9311 [B]	The End	1975	35.00
❑ ILPS9311 [B]	The End	1974	35.00

PVC

❑ 8938 [B]	Camera Obscura	1985	30.00

REPRISE

❑ RS6424 [B]	Desertshore	1970	35.00
❑ RS6424 [B]	Desert Shore	1970	35.00

VERVE

❑ V-5032 [M]	Chelsea Girl	1967	100.00
❑ V6-5032 [S]	Chelsea Girl	1967	40.00
❑ V5032 [Mono]	Chelsea Girl	1967	100.00
❑ V65032 [S]	Chelsea Girl	1967	40.00

NIEBLA, EDUARDO, AND ANTONIO FORCIONE

VENTURE

❑ 90655	Celebration	1988	12.00

NIEHAUS, LENNIE

CAMBRIA

❑ C-1016	Shades of Dring	1981	25.00

CONTEMPORARY

❑ C-2513 [10]	Lennie Niehaus, Vol. 1: The Quintet	1954	250.00
❑ C-2517 [10]	Lennie Niehaus, Vol. 2: The Octet	1954	250.00
❑ C-3503 [M]	Lennie Niehaus, Vol. 3: The Octet No. 2	1955	150.00
❑ C-3510 [M]	Lennie Niehaus, Vol. 4: The Quintets & Strings	1956	120.00
❑ C-3524 [M]	Lennie Niehaus, Vol. 5: The Sextet	1956	100.00
❑ C-3518 [M]	The Lennie Niehaus Quintet	1956	120.00
❑ C-3540 [M]	Zounds! Lennie Niehaus, Vol. 2: The Octet	1957	100.00

EMARCY

❑ MG-36118 [M]	I Swing for You	1957	100.00

FANTASY

❑ OJC-319	The Lennie Niehaus Quintet	198?	15.00

MERCURY

❑ MG-20555 [M]	I Swing for You	1960	60.00
❑ SR-60123 [S]	I Swing for You	1960	50.00

NIELSEN, GERTRUDE

DECCA

❑ DL5138 [10]	Gertrude Nielsen	1951	50.00

NIEMACK, JUDY, AND SIMON WETTENHALL

INNER CITY

❑ IC-1115	Night Sprite	198?	15.00

SEA BREEZE

❑ 2001	By Heart	1980	15.00

NIEWOOD, GERRY

A&M

❑ SP-3409	Slow, Hot Wind	1977	12.00

HORIZON

❑ SP-719	Gerry Niewood and Timepiece	1976	15.00

NIGHT

PLANET

❑ P-10	Long Distance	1980	15.00
❑ P-2	Night	1979	15.00

NIGHT OWLS, THE

VALMOR

❑ 79 [M]	Twisting the Oldies	1962	100.00

NIGHT RANGER

BOARDWALK

❑ NB1-33259	Dawn Patrol	1982	15.00

MCA

❑ 5460	Dawn Patrol	1984	10.00
— Reissue of Boardwalk LP			
❑ 5456	Midnight Madness	1984	10.00

MCA CAMEL

❑ 5593 [B]	7 Wishes	1985	10.00
❑ 5839	Big Life	1987	10.00

NIGHT SHADOWS, THE

HOTTRAX

❑ 1450	Invasion of the Acid Eaters	1982	30.00
❑ 1430	Live at the Spot	1981	30.00
❑ 1414 [B]	The Square Root of Two	1979	50.00
— Reissue of Spectrum LP			

SPECTRUM

❑ 2001	The Square Root of Two	1968	1000.00
— With neither bonus 45 nor psychedelic poster			
❑ 2001	The Square Root of Two	1968	1100.00
— With bonus 45, but no poster			

Number	Title	Yr	NM
❑ 2001	The Square Root of Two	1968	1200.00
— With poster, but no 45			
❑ 2001	The Square Root of Two	1968	1500.00
— With both 45 and poster			

NIGHTCAPS, THE

VANDAN
| ❑ VRLP-8124 | Wine, Wine, Wine | 196? | 150.00 |

NIGHTCRAWLERS, THE

KAPP
| ❑ KL-1520 [M] | The Little Black Egg | 1967 | 60.00 |
| ❑ KS-3520 [S] | The Little Black Egg | 1967 | 40.00 |

NIGHTHAWKS, THE

ALADDIN
| ❑ LP-101 | Rock and Roll | 197? | 200.00 |

NIGHTINGALE, MAXINE

HIGHRISE
| ❑ HR101 | It's a Beautiful Thing | 198? | 15.00 |
RCA VICTOR
| ❑ AFL1-3528 | Bittersweet | 1980 | 12.00 |
UNITED ARTISTS
| ❑ UA-LA731-G | Night Life | 1977 | 15.00 |
| ❑ UA-LA626-G | Right Back Where We Started From | 1976 | 15.00 |
WINDSONG
| ❑ BXL1-3404 | Lead Me On | 1979 | 12.00 |

NIGHTWIND

PAUSA
| ❑ 7127 | Casual Romance | 198? | 12.00 |

NILES, JOHN JACOB

BOONE-TOLLIVER
| ❑ BTR-22 [10] | American Folk Songs to Dulcimer Accompaniment | 195? | 50.00 |
| ❑ BTR-23 [10] | Ballads | 195? | 50.00 |
RCA CAMDEN
❑ CAL-330 [M]	50th Anniversary Album	195?	30.00
❑ CAL-219 [M]	American Folk and Gambling Songs	195?	30.00
❑ CAL-245 [M]	American Folk Songs	195?	30.00
TRADITION
❑ TLP-1036 [M]	An Evening with John Jacob Niles	195?	30.00
❑ TLP-1023 [M]	I Wonder As I Wander	1957	30.00

NILSSON

MUSICOR
| ❑ MUS-2505 [S] | Early Tymes | 1977 | 18.00 |
PICKWICK
| ❑ SPC-3321 [B] | Rock 'N' Roll | 1977 | 12.00 |
RAPPLE
| ❑ ABL1-0220 | Son of Dracula | 1974 | 15.00 |
RCA VICTOR
❑ LPM-3956 [M]	Aerial Ballet	1968	50.00
❑ LSP-3956 [S]	Aerial Ballet	1968	25.00
— Stereo" on black label			
❑ LSP-3956 [S]	Aerial Ballet	1969	18.00
— Orange label, non-flexible vinyl			
❑ LSP-4543	Aerial Pandemonium Ballet	1971	15.00
— Collection of tracks from 3874 and 3956, remixed with, in some cases, new vocals			
❑ APL1-0097	A Little Touch of Schmilsson in the Night	1973	15.00
❑ AYL1-3761	A Little Touch of Schmilsson in the Night	1980	10.00
— Best Buy Series" reissue			
❑ APL1-0817	Duit On Mon Dei	1975	15.00
❑ APD1-0817 [Q]	Duit On Mon Dei	1975	25.00
❑ AFL1-2798	Greatest Hits	1978	15.00
❑ LSP-4197	Harry	1969	18.00
— Orange label, non-flexible vinyl			
❑ AFL1-2276	Knnillssonn	1977	15.00
❑ LSP-4515 [B]	Nilsson Schmilsson	1971	15.00
❑ APD1-0319 [Q]	Nilsson Schmilsson	1974	25.00
❑ ANL1-3464	Nilsson Schmilsson	1979	10.00
❑ APL1-0203	Nilsson Sings Newman	1974	12.00
— Reissue of LSP-4289			
❑ LSP-4289	Nilsson Sings Newman	1970	15.00
— Orange label, non-flexible vinyl			
❑ LPM-3874 [M]	Pandemonium Shadow Show	1967	40.00
❑ LSP-3874 [S]	Pandemonium Shadow Show	1967	25.00
— Stereo" on black label			
❑ LSP-3874 [S]	Pandemonium Shadow Show	1969	18.00
— Orange label			
❑ CPL1-0570	Pussy Cats	1974	25.00
❑ APD1-0570 [Q]	Pussy Cats	1974	30.00
❑ APL1-1031	Sandman	1976	15.00
❑ APD1-1031 [Q]	Sandman	1976	25.00
❑ SPS-33-567 [DJ]	Scatalogue	197?	100.00

Number	Title	Yr	NM
❑ LSP-4717	Son of Schmilsson	1972	15.00
— With custom black "Victor" label			
❑ AYL1-3812	Son of Schmilsson	1980	10.00
— Best Buy Series" reissue			
❑ APL1-1119	That's the Way It Is	1976	15.00
❑ LSPX-1003	The Point!	1971	15.00
❑ AYL1-3811	The Point!	1980	10.00
— Best Buy Series" reissue			
❑ LSP-4417	The Point!	1971	12.00
— Reissue of LSPX-1003			
❑ (no #)0 [M]	The True One	1967	200.00
— Boxed set with mono copy of RCA Victor 3874, two photos, button, poster, sticker, bios			
SUNDAZED
❑ LP5468 [B]	Aerial Ballet	2014	30.00
❑ LP5467 [B]	Pandemonium Shadow Show	2014	30.00
TOWER
❑ T5095 [M]	Spotlight on Nilsson	1967	25.00
❑ ST5095 [S]	Spotlight on Nilsson	1967	25.00
❑ DT5165 [R]	Spotlight on Nilsson	1969	18.00

NIMMONS, PHIL

VERVE
❑ MGV-8376 [M]	Nimmons 'n' Nine	1960	30.00
❑ V-8376 [M]	Nimmons 'n' Nine	1961	25.00
❑ MGV-8025 [M]	The Canadian Scene Via Phil Nimmons	1957	30.00
❑ V-8025 [M]	The Canadian Scene Via Phil Nimmons	1961	25.00

NIMOY, LEONARD

CAEDMON
❑ TC-1526	Green Hills of Earth	1977	30.00
❑ TC-1479	The Illustrated Man	1976	30.00
❑ TC-1466	The Martian Chronicles	1976	30.00
❑ TC-1520	War of the Worlds	1977	30.00
DOT
❑ DLP3794 [M]	Mr. Spock's Music from Outer Space	1967	50.00

❑ DLP25794 [S]	Mr. Spock's Music from Outer Space	1967	80.00
❑ DLP25966	The New World of Leonard Nimoy	1969	60.00
❑ DLP25910	The Touch of Leonard Nimoy	1969	60.00
❑ DLP3883 [M]	The Way I Feel	1968	80.00
— Stereo cover with "Monaural" sticker; label is black stock copy			
❑ DLP25883 [S]	The Way I Feel	1968	60.00
❑ DLP3835 [M]	Two Sides of Leonard Nimoy	1968	50.00
❑ DLP25835 [S]	Two Sides of Leonard Nimoy	1968	80.00
JRT
❑ (# unknown)0	The Mysterious Golem	1982	40.00
PARAMOUNT
❑ PAS-1030	Outer Space/Inner Mind	1970	50.00
PICKWICK
❑ SPC-3199	Space Odyssey	197?	50.00
SEARS
❑ SPS-491	Leonard Nimoy	196?	80.00

NINE INCH NAILS

NOTHING
| ❑ 1169701 [S] | The Downward Spiral | 2008 | 30.00 |
NOTHING/INTERSCOPE
❑ 490473	The Fragile	1999	100.00
— Also called "Halo Fourteen"			
❑ 490744	Things Falling Apart	2000	25.00
— Also called "Halo Sixteen"			
❑ B0004553-01	With Teeth	2005	30.00
NOTHING/TVT
❑ 2610	Pretty Hate Machine	1990	25.00
— Also called "Halo Two"			

Number	Title	Yr	NM
NOTHING/TVT/INTERSCOPE
❑ DMD1903 [EP]	Broken	1992	40.00
— Also called "Halo Five"; promo-only vinyl release; six songs on one side of a 12-inch record and two bonus tracks, "Physical (You're So)" and "Suck," on a bonus 7-inch record			
❑ 96093 [EP]	Fixed	1992	40.00
— Also called "Halo Six			
❑ PR5509 [DJ]	The Downward Spiral	1994	60.00
— Also called "Halo Eight"; vinyl is promo only			
RYKODISC
❑ RLP10386-1	Pretty Hate Machine	2006	25.00
— Reissue of TVT album of the same title			

999

POLYDOR
❑ PD1-6256	Biggest Prize in Sport	1980	14.00
❑ PD1-6307	Biggest Tour in Sport	1980	14.00
❑ PD1-6322	Concrete	1981	15.00
PVC
❑ 7999 [B]	High Energy Plan	1979	15.00

1910 FRUITGUM COMPANY

BUDDAH
❑ BDS-5022	1,2,3 Red Light	1968	30.00
❑ BDS-5032	Goody, Goody Gumdrops	1969	30.00
❑ BDS-5043	Hard Ride	1969	30.00
❑ BDS-5036	Indian Giver	1969	30.00
❑ BDS-5057 [B]	Juiciest Fruitgum	1970	30.00
❑ BDM-5010 [M]	Simon Says	1968	50.00
— Appears to be promo only; "Mono" sticker on stereo cover			
❑ BDS-5010 [S]	Simon Says	1968	30.00

NINETEENTH WHOLE, THE

EASTBOUND
| ❑ EB-9003 | Smilin' | 1970 | 200.00 |

94 EAST

HOT PINK
| ❑ HLP3223 | Minneapolis Genius -- 94 East | 1977 | 40.00 |
| — Deduct 25% for cut-outs | | | |

98 DEGREES

MOTOWN
| ❑ 3145307961 | 98 Degrees | 1997 | 18.00 |

NIRVANA

DGC
❑ 25105	From the Muddy Banks of the Wishkah	1996	25.00
❑ 24504	Incesticide	1992	30.00
— All copies on blue swirl vinyl			
❑ 24607 [B]	In Utero	1993	30.00
— All copies on clear vinyl			
❑ 24727	MTV Unplugged in New York	1994	25.00
— White vinyl version			
❑ 24727 [B]	MTV Unplugged in New York	1994	40.00
— Black vinyl, issued simultaneously with white vinyl version; color of vinyl cannot be determined without opening the shrink wrap			

| ❑ 24425 [B] | Nevermind | 1991 | 30.00 |
| — All copies on black vinyl | | | |
MOBILE FIDELITY
| ❑ 1-258 | Nevermind | 1996 | 200.00 |
| — Audiophile vinyl | | | |
SUB POP
❑ SP34	Bleach	1989	200.00
— First 1,000 were pressed on white vinyl			
❑ SP34	Bleach	1989	200.00

Number	Title	Yr	NM

—Second 1,000 were pressed on black vinyl and include a poster

Number	Title	Yr	NM
❏ SP34 [B]	Bleach	1989	60.00
—Red vinyl			
❏ SP34 [B]	Bleach	1989	70.00
—Pink vinyl			
❏ SP34	Bleach	1989	150.00
—Red and white swirl vinyl			
❏ SP34 [B]	Bleach	1989	70.00
—Purple vinyl			
❏ 70034 [B]	Bleach	2000	30.00
—Reissue			

NIRVANA (1)

BELL
❏ 6024 [B]	All of Us	1969	60.00
❏ 6015 [B]	The Story of Simon Simopath	1968	60.00

NIRVANA (2)

METROMEDIA
❏ MD-1018	Nirvana	1970	30.00

NISTICO, SAL

BEE HIVE
❏ BH-7006	Neo/Nistico	1980	15.00

JAZZLAND
❏ JLP-66 [M]	Heavyweights	1962	30.00
❏ JLP-966 [S]	Heavyweights	1962	40.00

RIVERSIDE
❏ RLP-457 [M]	Comin' On Up	1963	30.00
❏ RS-9457 [S]	Comin' On Up	1963	40.00

NITE-LITERS, THE

RCA VICTOR
❏ LSP-4580	Instrumental Directions	1972	18.00
❏ LSP-4493	Morning, Noon & The Nite-Liters	1971	18.00

NITTY GRITTY DIRT BAND

LIBERTY
❏ LST-7611	Alive	1969	30.00
❏ LMAS-5553	All the Good Times	1981	10.00
❏ LO-974	An American Dream	1981	10.00
❏ LKCL-670	Dirt, Silver and Gold	1981	15.00
❏ LT-51146	Let's Go	1982	12.00
❏ LT-1042	Make a Little Magic	1981	10.00
❏ LST-7540	Rare Junk	1968	30.00
❏ LRP-3516 [M]	Ricochet	1967	30.00
❏ LST-7516 [S]	Ricochet	1967	30.00
❏ LWB-184	Stars and Stripes Forever	1981	12.00
❏ LRP-3501 [M]	The Nitty Gritty Dirt Band	1967	30.00
❏ LST-7501 [S]	The Nitty Gritty Dirt Band	1967	30.00
❏ LST-7642 [DJ]	Uncle Charlie and His Dog Teddy	1970	120.00

—Leatherette promo pack with LP, two other discs, photos, booklet

❏ LST-7642 [B]	Uncle Charlie and His Dog Teddy	1970	30.00

—Standard issue of LP

❏ LTAO-7642	Uncle Charlie and His Dog Teddy	1981	10.00
❏ LWCL-51158	Will the Circle Be Unbroken	1986	18.00

MCA
❏ 6407	The Rest of the Dream	1990	15.00

UNITED ARTISTS
❏ UAS-5553	All the Good Times	1972	18.00
❏ UA-LA974-H	An American Dream	1979	12.00
❏ UA-LA670-L3	Dirt, Silver and Gold	1976	25.00
❏ UA-LA469-G	Dream	1975	15.00
❏ LW-1106	Jealousy	1981	12.00
❏ LT-1042	Make a Little Magic	1980	12.00
❏ UA-LA184-J2	Stars and Stripes Forever	1974	18.00
❏ UA-LA830-H	The Chicken Chronicles	1978	12.00
❏ UA-LA854-H	The Dirt Band	1978	12.00
❏ UAS-9801	Will the Circle Be Unbroken	1972	30.00

UNIVERSAL
❏ UVL2-12500	Will the Circle Be Unbroken, Volume Two	1989	25.00

WARNER BROS.
❏ 25573	Hold On	1987	10.00
❏ 25830	More Great Dirt: The Best of the Nitty Gritty Dirt Band, Vol. 2	1989	12.00
❏ 25304	Partners, Brothers and Friends	1985	10.00
❏ 25113	Plain Dirt Fashion	1984	10.00
❏ 25382	Twenty Years of Dirt: The Best of the Nitty Gritty Dirt Band	1986	10.00
❏ 25722	Workin' Band	1988	10.00

NITZINGER

20TH CENTURY
❏ T-518 [B]	Live Better Electrically	1976	15.00

CAPITOL
❏ SMAS-11091	Nitzinger	1972	25.00
❏ SMAS-11122	One Foot in History	1973	25.00

NITZSCHE, JACK

REPRISE
❏ R6200 [M]	Chopin '66	1966	30.00
❏ RS6200 [S]	Chopin '66	1966	30.00
❏ R6115 [M]	Dance to the Hits of the Beatles	1964	50.00
❏ RS6115 [S]	Dance to the Hits of the Beatles	1964	60.00
❏ MS2092	St. Giles Cripplegate	1972	25.00
❏ R6101 [M]	The Lonely Surfer	1963	75.00
❏ R9-6101 [S]	The Lonely Surfer	1963	150.00
—Pink, gold and green label			
❏ RS6101 [S]	The Lonely Surfer	197?	25.00
—With only "r:" logo on all-orange (tan) label			

NIX, DON

CREAM
❏ 1001	Gone Too Long	1979	12.00

ELEKTRA
❏ EKS-74101	Living by the Days	1971	15.00

ENTERPRISE
❏ ENS-1032	Hobos, Heroes and Street Corner Clowns	1974	15.00

NIXON, MOJO, AND SKID ROPER

ENIGMA
❏ ST-73272	Bo-Day-Shus!!!	1987	15.00

RESTLESS
❏ 72127	Frenzy	1986	15.00
❏ 72185 [EP]	Get Out of My Way	1986	12.00
—Clear vinyl			
❏ 72056	Mojo Nixon and Skid Roper	1985	15.00

NIXON, NICK

MERCURY
❏ SRM-1-1175	Nick Nixon	1977	12.00

NKRUMAH, KWAME

COLUMBIA
❏ CS9863	Ninth Son	1969	30.00

NO DOUBT

TRAUMA/INTERSCOPE
❏ 069-490441-1	Return of Saturn	2000	18.00
❏ 069-493195-1	Rock Steady	2001	40.00

❏ 92580-1 [B]	Tragic Kingdom	1995	100.00

NOACK, EDDIE

WIDE WORLD
❏ 2001	Remembering Jimmie Rodgers	1970	30.00

NOBLE, NICK

COLUMBIA
❏ CS9810	I'm Gonna Make You Love Me	1969	18.00

LIBERTY
❏ LRP-3302 [M]	Relax	1963	25.00
❏ LST-7302 [M]	Relax	1963	30.00

MERCURY
❏ MG-20182 [M]	You Don't Know What Love Is	1956	30.00

WING
❏ MGW-12184 [M]	Music for Lovers	196?	18.00

NOBLES, CLIFF

MOON SHOT
❏ 601	Pony the Horse	1969	40.00

PHIL-L.A. OF SOUL
❏ 4001	The Horse	1968	60.00

NOCK, MIKE

ECM
❏ 1220	Ondas	1981	12.00

IAI
❏ 373851	Almanac	197?	18.00

TIMELESS
❏ 313	In Out and Around	1978	15.00

TOMATO
❏ TOM-8009	Climbing	1979	18.00

NOCTURNES, THE

MGM
❏ E-154 [10]	Melodies from Far Away Places	195?	60.00

NOEL (1)

4TH & B'WAY
❏ 4009	Noel	1988	12.00

NO/GAP JAZZ BAND, THE

NO/GAP
❏ 7444001	Live	197?	18.00
❏ 7444002	No/Gap Jazz Band	197?	18.00

NOGUEZ, JACKY

JAMIE
❏ JLP-3007 [M]	Chow Chow Bambina	1959	25.00
❏ JLPS-3007 [S]	Chow Chow Bambina	1959	30.00
❏ JLP-3013 [M]	Dance Along with Jacky Noguez	1960	25.00
❏ JLPS-3013 [S]	Dance Along with Jacky Noguez	1960	30.00
❏ JLP-3012 [M]	Jacky Noguez	1960	25.00
❏ JLPS-3012 [S]	Jacky Noguez	1960	30.00

NOLAND, TERRY

BRUNSWICK
❏ BL54041 [M]	Terry Noland	1958	600.00
—Buddy Holly plays guitar			

NOONE, JIMMIE

BRUNSWICK
❏ BL58006 [10]	The Apex Club Orchestra	1950	50.00

MCA
❏ 1313	Jimmie Noone and Earl Hines at the Apex Club	198?	12.00

NOONE, JIMMY, JR.

STOMP OFF
❏ SOS-1121	Jimmy Remembers Jimmie	1986	12.00

NOONE, PETER

JOHNSTON
❏ ARZ37369	One of the Glory Boys	1982	12.00

NORDINE, KEN

BLUE THUMB
❏ BTS-33	How Are Things in Your Town?	1971	60.00
❏ BTS-35	Ken Nordine	1972	50.00

DECCA
❏ DL8550 [M]	Concert in the Sky	1957	60.00

DOT
❏ DLP-3115 [M]	Love Words	1958	100.00
❏ DLP-25115 [S]	Love Words	1959	120.00
❏ DLP-3142 [M]	My Baby	1959	50.00
❏ DLP-25142 [S]	My Baby	1959	80.00
❏ DLP-3196 [M]	Next!	1959	50.00
❏ DLP-25196 [S]	Next!	1959	80.00
❏ DLP-3096 [M]	Son of Word Jazz	1958	100.00
❏ DLP-25096 [S]	Son of Word Jazz	1959	120.00
❏ DLP-25880	The Best of Word Jazz	1968	40.00
❏ DLP-3075 [M]	Word Jazz	1958	100.00
❏ DLP-25075 [S]	Word Jazz	1959	120.00
❏ DLP-3301 [M]	Word Jazz, Vol. 2	1960	60.00
❏ DLP-25301 [S]	Word Jazz, Vol. 2	1960	100.00

FM
❏ 304 [M]	Passion In the Desert	1963	30.00
❏ S-304 [S]	Passion In the Desert	1963	40.00

HAMILTON
❏ HL-102 [M]	The Voice of Love	1964	30.00
❏ HL-12102 [S]	The Voice of Love	1964	40.00

PHILIPS
❏ PHM200224 [M]	Colors	1966	80.00
❏ PHS600224 [S]	Colors	1966	100.00
❏ PHM200258 [M]	Ken Nordine Does Robert Shure's "Twink	1967	30.00
❏ PHS600258 [S]	Ken Nordine Does Robert Shure's "Twink	1967	40.00

SNAIL
❏ SR-1003	Grandson of Word Jazz	1987	30.00
❏ SR-1001	Stare with Your Ears	1979	30.00

VERSION
❏ VLP101 [10]	Passion In the Desert	1957	200.00

Number	Title	Yr	NM

NORMA JEAN

HARMONY

❏ HL7363 [M]	Country's Favorite	1966	25.00
❏ HS11163 [R]	Country's Favorite	1966	18.00

RCA CAMDEN

❏ CAL-2218 [M]	Heaven Help the Working Girl	1968	40.00
❏ CAS-2218 [S]	Heaven Help the Working Girl	1968	18.00
❏ CAS-2511	It Wasn't God Who Made Honky Tonk Angels	1972	18.00

RCA VICTOR

❏ LSP-4341	Another Man Loved Me Last Night	1970	25.00
❏ LSP-3977	Body and Mind	1968	30.00
❏ LSP-4146	Country Giants	1969	30.00
❏ LPM-3910 [M]	Heaven's Just a Prayer Away	1967	50.00
❏ LSP-3910 [S]	Heaven's Just a Prayer Away	1967	30.00
❏ LSP-4745	I Guess That Comes From Being Poor	1972	25.00
❏ LSP-4446	It's Time for Norma Jean	1970	30.00
❏ LPM-3836 [M]	Jackson Ain't a Very Big Town	1967	30.00
❏ LSP-3836 [S]	Jackson Ain't a Very Big Town	1967	30.00
❏ LPM-2961 [M]	Let's Go All the Way	1964	30.00
❏ LSP-2961 [S]	Let's Go All the Way	1964	30.00
❏ LSP-4060	Love's a Woman's Job	1968	30.00
❏ LSP-4510	Norma Jean	1971	25.00
❏ LSP-4587	Norma Jean Sings	1971	25.00
❏ LPM-3664 [M]	Norma Jean Sings a Tribute to Kitty Wells	1966	30.00
❏ LSP-3664 [S]	Norma Jean Sings a Tribute to Kitty Wells	1966	30.00
❏ LPM-3700 [M]	Norma Jean Sings Porter Wagoner	1967	30.00
❏ LSP-3700 [S]	Norma Jean Sings Porter Wagoner	1967	30.00
❏ LPM-3541 [M]	Please Don't Hurt Me	1966	30.00
❏ LSP-3541 [S]	Please Don't Hurt Me	1966	30.00
❏ LPM-3449 [M]	Pretty Miss Norma Jean	1965	30.00
❏ LSP-3449 [S]	Pretty Miss Norma Jean	1965	30.00
❏ LSP-4691	Thank You for Loving Me	1972	25.00
❏ LSP-4227	The Best of Norma Jean	1969	30.00
❏ APL1-0170	The Only Way to Hold Your Man	1973	18.00

NORMAN, GENE, GROUP

GNP CRESCENDO

❏ GNP-2015 [M]	Dylan Jazz	1965	25.00
❏ GNPS-2015 [S]	Dylan Jazz	1965	30.00

NORMAN, JESSYE

PHILIPS

❏ 420180-1	Christmastide	1987	12.00
—Pressed in Europe for export			

NORMAN, LARRY

AB

❏ 777	Streams of White Light Into Darkened Corners	1977	30.00

CAPITOL

❏ ST-446	Upon This Rock	1970	30.00

IMPACT

❏ 3121 [B]	Upon This Rock	197?	25.00

MGM

❏ SE-4942	So Long Ago the Garden	1974	40.00

ONE WAY

❏ 4847	Bootleg	1972	40.00
—Gatefold cover			
❏ 900	Bootleg	1972	30.00
—Regular cover			
❏ 7397	Street Level	1971	30.00

PHYDEAUX

❏ BONE-777-6	Almost So Long Ago the Garden	1981	18.00
❏ ARF-777-6	Almost So Long Ago the Garden	1984	15.00

SOLID ROCK

❏ 2001 [B]	In Another Land	1976	18.00
❏ 2007	Something New Under the Son	1981	18.00

STREET LEVEL

❏ ROCK-888-5	Only Visiting This Planet	1978	18.00
—Gatefold cover			
❏ ROCK-888-5	Only Visiting This Planet	1978	15.00
—Regular cover			

VERVE

❏ V6-5092	Only Visiting This Planet	1973	30.00
—Tri-fold cover			
❏ V6-5092	Only Visiting This Planet	1973	40.00
—Gatefold cover			

NORRIS, WALTER, AND ALADAR PAGE

INNER CITY

❏ IC-3028	Synchronicity	1979	18.00

NORRIS, WALTER, AND GEORGE MRAZ

ENJA

❏ 2044	Drifting	197?	18.00

NORRIS, WALTER

ENJA

❏ 2044	Drifting	198?	15.00

PROGRESSIVE

❏ PRO-7039	Stepping on Cracks	198?	15.00

NORTH, FREDDIE

MANKIND

❏ 205 [B]	Cuss the Wind	1973	40.00
❏ 204	Friend	1971	30.00

NORTH, JAY

KEM

❏ 27	Look Who's Singing!	1960	100.00

NORTHCOTT, TOM

UNI

❏ 73108	Upside Downside	1971	25.00

NORTHERN FRONT

KADER

❏ (# unknown)0	Furniture Store	1975	100.00

NORVO, RED, AND ROSS TOMPKINS

CONCORD JAZZ

❏ CJ-90	Red Norvo and Ross Tompkins	1979	12.00

NORVO, RED

ALLEGRO

❏ 1739 [M]	Red Norvo Jazz Trio	195?	40.00

BLUEBIRD

❏ 6278-1-RB	Just a Mood	1987	12.00

CAPITOL

❏ T616 [M]	Classics in Jazz	1955	80.00

CHARLIE PARKER

❏ PLP-833 [M]	Pretty Is the Only Way To Fly	1962	30.00
❏ PLP-833S [S]	Pretty Is the Only Way To Fly	1962	30.00

CIRCLE

❏ 3	Red Norvo and His Orchestra 1938	198?	12.00

COMMODORE

❏ FL-20023 [10]	Town Hall Concert, Volume 1	1952	150.00
❏ FL-20027 [10]	Town Hall Concert, Volume 2	1952	150.00

CONTEMPORARY

❏ C-3534 [M]	Music To Listen To Red Norvo By	1957	50.00
❏ S-7009 [S]	Music To Listen To Red Norvo By	1959	40.00

CONTINENTAL

❏ C-16005 [M]	Mainstream Jazz	1962	18.00
❏ CS-16005 [S]	Mainstream Jazz	1962	25.00

DECCA

❏ DL5501 [10]	Dancing on the Ceiling	1953	120.00

DIAL

❏ LP-903 [M]	Fabulous Jazz Session	1951	600.00

DISCOVERY

❏ DL-3012 [10]	Red Norvo Trio	1950	150.00
❏ DL-3018 [10]	Red Norvo Trio	1952	150.00
❏ DL-4005 [M]	Red Norvo Trio, Volume 1	1951	120.00

DOT

❏ DLP-3126 [M]	Windjammer City Style	1958	30.00
❏ DLP-25126 [S]	Windjammer City Style	1958	40.00

EMARCY

❏ MG-26002 [10]	Improvisation	1954	150.00

ENCORE

❏ EE-22009	Original 1933-38 Recordings	1968	18.00

EPIC

❏ LN3128 [M]	Red Norvo and His All Stars	1955	50.00

FAMOUS DOOR

❏ 116	Red Norvo in New York	197?	15.00
❏ 108	Second Time Around	197?	15.00
❏ 105	Vibes A La Red	197?	15.00

FANTASY

❏ OJC-155	Music To Listen To Red Norvo By	198?	12.00
❏ 3-12 [10]	Red Norvo Trio	1953	150.00
—Colored vinyl			
❏ 3-12 [10]	Red Norvo Trio	1953	100.00
—Black vinyl			
❏ 3-19 [M]	Red Norvo Trio	1955	80.00
—Red vinyl			
❏ 3-19 [M]	Red Norvo Trio	195?	40.00
—Black vinyl			
❏ OJC-641	Red Norvo Trio	1991	15.00
❏ 3218 [M]	Red Norvo With Strings	1956	80.00
—Red vinyl			
❏ 3218 [M]	Red Norvo With Strings	195?	40.00

—Black vinyl			
❏ 3244 [M]	The Red Norvo Trios	1957	80.00
—Red vinyl			
❏ 3244 [M]	The Red Norvo Trios	195?	40.00
—Black vinyl			

LIBERTY

❏ LRP-3035 [M]	Ad Lib	1957	40.00
❏ LJH-6012 [M]	Vibe-rations In Hi-Fi	1956	50.00

MERCURY

❏ 830966-1	Improvisations	1987	12.00

PAUSA

❏ 9015	All Star Sessions	198?	12.00

PRESTIGE

❏ 24108	The Trios	198?	18.00

RAVE

❏ 101 [M]	Red Norvo Quintet	1956	80.00

RCA VICTOR

❏ LPM-1420 [M]	Hi Five	1957	40.00
❏ LSP-1711 [S]	Red Norvo In Stereo	1958	50.00
❏ LPM-1729 [M]	Red Plays the Blues	1958	40.00
❏ LSP-1729 [S]	Red Plays the Blues	1958	50.00
❏ LPM-1449 [M]	Some of My Favorites	1957	40.00

REFERENCE RECORDINGS

❏ RR-8	The Forward Look	1983	25.00
❏ RR-8-UHGR	The Forward Look	1983	40.00

RONDO-LETTE

❏ A-28 [M]	Red Norvo Trio	1958	30.00

SAVOY

❏ MG-12093 [M]	Midnight On Cloud 69	1956	80.00
❏ MG-12088 [M]	Move!	1956	80.00

SAVOY JAZZ

❏ SJL-2212	Red Norvo Trio	197?	15.00

SPOTLITE

❏ 107	Fabulous Jam	197?	12.00

STASH

❏ ST-230	Just Friends	1984	12.00

STEREO RECORDS

❏ S-7009 [S]	Music To Listen To Red Norvo By	1958	50.00

TAMPA

❏ TP-35 [M]	Norvo Naturally	1957	100.00
—Colored vinyl			
❏ TP-35 [M]	Norvo Naturally	1958	50.00
—Black vinyl			

TIME-LIFE

❏ STL-J-14	Giants of Jazz	1980	25.00

X

❏ LXA-3034 [M]	Red's Blue Room	1955	150.00

XANADU

❏ 199	Time in His Hands	198?	12.00

NORVO, RED/CAL TJADER

JAZZTONE

❏ J-1277 [M]	Dolightfully Light	195?	40.00

NORVO, RED/GEORGIE AULD

GOLDEN ERA

❏ 15016 [M]	The Great Dance Bands, Vol. 2	195?	40.00

NORWOOD, DOROTHY

I AM

❏ 4002-1-M	A Wonderful Day	1990	18.00

JEWEL

❏ 0134	He's a Friend	1978	18.00

SAVOY

❏ SL-14598	Answer Me Dear Jesus	198?	18.00
❏ MG14190 [M]	Bereaved Child	196?	30.00
❏ MG14244	Brother Came Too Late	196?	30.00
❏ MG14309	Come By Here	1973	30.00
❏ MG14140 [M]	Denied Mother	196?	30.00
❏ MG14266	Despondent Wife	196?	30.00
❏ SL-14515	Faithful Daughter	198?	18.00
❏ SL-14557	God Can	198?	18.00
❏ MG14127 [M]	He Will Never Let Go My Hand	196?	30.00
❏ MG14259	Jesus Picked Up the Pieces	196?	30.00
❏ MG14083 [M]	Johnny and Jesus	196?	30.00
❏ MG14217	Just in Time	196?	30.00
❏ MG14295	Just the Two of Us	1972	30.00
—With Lois Snead			
❏ SL-14630	Look What They've Done to My Child	198?	18.00
❏ MG14157 [M]	Soldier from Vietnam	196?	30.00
❏ SL-14651	Somebody Here	198?	18.00
—With the Allen Darling Ensemble			
❏ MG14107 [M]	The Bell Didn't Toll	196?	30.00
❏ MG14169 [M]	The Dorothy Norwood Singers	196?	30.00
❏ SL-7042	The Mountain Climbers	1979	25.00
❏ MG14093 [M]	The Old Lady's House	196?	30.00
❏ MG14175 [M]	The Singing Slave	196?	30.00
❏ MG14212	The Stories Behind the Songs	196?	30.00
❏ MG14282	Three Little Pigs	197?	30.00

Number	Title	Yr	NM

— With Lois Snead

SL-14716 Up Where We Belong — 1983 — 18.00
WORD
WR-8420 Mother's Son — 1988 — 12.00

NOSY PARKER

(NO LABEL)
(no #)0 Nosy Parker — 1975 — 250.00

NOTES FROM THE UNDERGROUND

VANGUARD
VSD-6502 Notes from the Underground — 1970 — 80.00

NOTHING, CHARLIE

TAKOMA
C-1015 The Psychedelic Saxophone of Charlie Nothing — 1967 — 50.00

NOTO, SAM

XANADU
127 Act One — 1976 — 15.00
103 Entrance! — 1975 — 15.00
144 Notes to You — 1977 — 15.00
168 Noto-Riety — 198? — 12.00

NOTRE DAME GLEE CLUB

ND
JPJ5655 A-Caroling — 1977 — 15.00

NOVA LOCAL, THE

DECCA
DL74977 Nova 1 — 1968 — 70.00

NOVAC, JERRY

EMBRYO
527 The 5th Word — 1970 — 30.00

NOVELLS, THE

MOTHER'S
MLPS-73 A Happening — 1968 — 50.00

NOW CREATIVE ARTS JAZZ ENSEMBLE, THE

ARHOOLIE
8002 Now — 1969 — 25.00

NOZERO, LARRY

STRATA
109-75 Time — 1975 — 25.00

NRBQ

ANNUIT COEPTIS
1001/2 Scraps/Workshop — 1976 — 25.00
— Reissue of Kama Sutra LPs

BEARSVILLE
23817 Grooves in Orbit — 1983 — 12.00
COLUMBIA
CS9858 NRBQ — 1969 — 30.00
— 360 Sound Stereo" label
CS9858 NRBQ — 1970 — 15.00
— Orange label
PC9858 NRBQ — 198? — 10.00
— Budget-line reissue

KAMA SUTRA
KSBS-2045 [B] Scraps — 1972 — 30.00
KSBS-2065 [B] Workshop — 1973 — 40.00
MERCURY
SRM-1-3712 NRBQ at Yankee Stadium — 1978 — 18.00
824462-1 NRBQ at Yankee Stadium — 1984 — 12.00
— Reissue

RED ROOSTER
101 All Hopped Up — 1977 — 18.00
ROUNDER
3029 All Hopped Up — 1979 — 15.00
EP-2501 [EP] Christmas Wish — 1985 — 15.00
3108 God Bless Us All — 1988 — 12.00
3030 Kick Me Hard — 1979 — 15.00
3109 Live! Diggin' Uncle Q — 1988 — 12.00
3098 Lou and the Q — 1986 — 12.00
— With pro wrestler Captain Lou Albano
3090 RC Cola & a Moon Pie — 1987 — 12.00
3055 Scraps — 1982 — 12.00
3066 Tapdancin' Bats — 1983 — 12.00
3048 Tiddlywinks — 1980 — 15.00
SUNDAZED
LP-5162 Atsa My Band — 2003 — 18.00
LP-5184 Scraps — 2007 — 18.00
— Reissue of Kama Sutra 2045
LP-5185 Workshop — 2007 — 18.00
— Reissue of Kama Sutra 2065

VIRGIN
91291 Wild Weekend — 1989 — 12.00

NU SHOOZ

ATLANTIC
81647 Poolside — 1986 — 12.00
81804 Told U So — 1988 — 12.00

NUBIN, KATI BELL

MGV-3004 [M] Soul, Soul Searchin' — 1960 — 80.00
V-3004 [M] Soul, Soul Searchin' — 1961 — 40.00
V6-3004 [S] Soul, Soul Searchin' — 1961 — 50.00

NUCLEUS

MAINSTREAM
S-6120 Nucleus — 1969 — 50.00

NUDIE

NUDIE
3203 Nudie and His Mandolin — 196? — 40.00

NUGENT, TED

ATLANTIC
81812 If You Can't Lick 'Em... Lick 'Em — 1988 — 12.00
81632 Little Miss Dangerous — 1986 — 12.00
SD19365 Nugent — 1982 — 12.00
80125 Penetrator — 1984 — 12.00
EPIC
JE34700 Cat Scratch Fever — 1977 — 15.00
— Orange label
PE34700 [B] Cat Scratch Fever — 198? — 10.00
— Reissue with dark blue label and bar code
KE235069 Double Live Gonzo! — 1978 — 18.00
— Orange labels
PE34121 [B] Free-for-All — 1976 — 15.00
— Orange label
PEQ34121 [Q] Free-for-All — 1976 — 25.00
PE34121 Free-for-All — 1979 — 10.00
— Reissue with dark blue label and bar code
FE37667 Great Gonzos! The Best of Ted Nugent — 1981 — 12.00
PE37667 Great Gonzos! The Best of Ted Nugent — 198? — 10.00
— Budget-line reissue
FE37084 Intensities in 10 Cities — 1981 — 12.00
PE37084 Intensities in 10 Cities — 198? — 10.00
— Budget-line reissue
FE36404 Scream Dream — 1980 — 12.00
FE36000 State of Shock — 1979 — 12.00
AS99-607 [PD] State of Shock — 1979 — 30.00
— Promo-only picture disc
PE36000 [B] State of Shock — 198? — 10.00
— Budget-line reissue
PE33692 Ted Nugent — 1975 — 15.00
— Orange label
PE33692 Ted Nugent — 1979 — 10.00
— Reissue with dark blue label and bar code
FE35551 Weekend Warriors — 1978 — 15.00
— Orange label
PE35551 [B] Weekend Warriors — 198? — 10.00
— Reissue with dark blue label and bar code

NUMAN, GARY

ATCO
SD 38-143 Dance — 1981 — 12.00
90014 [B] I, Assassin — 1982 — 15.00
SD 38-117 Replicas — 1979 — 12.00
— With Tubeway Army
SD 32-103 Telekon — 1980 — 12.00
SD 38-120 [B] The Pleasure Principle — 1979 — 15.00
SD 32-106 Tubeway Army: The First Album — 1980 — 12.00
— First American issue of U.K. debut
I.R.S.
82003 New Anger — 1988 — 12.00
NUMA
1005 Strange Charm — 1985 — 12.00

NUNEZ, FLIP

CATALYST
7603 My Own Time and Space — 1976 — 15.00

NUNS, THE

BOMP!
4010 [B] The Nuns — 1980 — 30.00
POSH BOY
105 [B] The Nuns — 1980 — 30.00
— Same album as the Bomp! release

NUROCK, KIRK

LABOR
13 Natural Sound — 1981 — 15.00

NUTMEGS, THE

COLLECTABLES
COL-5018 Greatest Hits — 198? — 12.00

QUICKSILVER
QS-1001 Shoo-Wop-a-Doo-Wop — 198? — 12.00
RELIC
LP-5011 Greatest Hits (1955-1959) — 198? — 12.00
LP-5002 The Nutmegs Featuring Leroy Griffin — 198? — 12.00

NUTTER, MAYF

CAPITOL
ST-11194 The First Batch — 1973 — 15.00
GNP CRESCENDO
GNPS-2104 Goin' Skinny Dippin' — 1976 — 15.00

NUTTY SQUIRRELS, THE

COLUMBIA
CL1589 [M] Bird Watching — 1961 — 30.00
CS8389 [S] Bird Watching — 1961 — 40.00
HANOVER
HML-8014 [M] The Nutty Squirrels — 1960 — 50.00
MGM
E-4272 [M] A Hard Day's Night — 1964 — 30.00
SE-4272 [S] A Hard Day's Night — 1964 — 30.00

NYE, LOUIS

RIVERSIDE
RLP-842 [M] Heigh-Ho, Madison Avenue — 1960 — 30.00

NYRO, LAURA

COLUMBIA
KC30259 Christmas and the Beads of Sweat — 1970 — 18.00
— 360 Sound Stereo" label
KC30259 Christmas and the Beads of Sweat — 1970 — 12.00
— Orange label
PC30259 Christmas and the Beads of Sweat — 198? — 10.00
— Budget-line reissue
CL2826 [M] Eli and the Thirteenth Confession — 1968 — 40.00
CS9626 [S] Eli and the Thirteenth Confession — 1968 — 18.00
— 360 Sound Stereo" label
CS9626 Eli and the Thirteenth Confession — 1970 — 12.00
— Orange label
PC9626 [B] Eli and the Thirteenth Confession — 198? — 10.00
— Budget-line reissue
KC30987 Gonna Take a Miracle — 1971 — 18.00
PC30987 [B] Gonna Take a Miracle — 197? — 10.00
— Budget-line reissue
FC39215 Mother's Spiritual — 1984 — 12.00
JC35449 Nested — 1978 — 15.00
PC35449 Nested — 198? — 10.00
— Budget-line reissue
CS9737 [B] New York Tendaberry — 1969 — 18.00
— 360 Sound Stereo" label
CS9737 New York Tendaberry — 1970 — 12.00
— Orange label
PC9737 [B] New York Tendaberry — 198? — 10.00
— Budget-line reissue
PC234331 [DJ] Season of Lights...Laura Nyro in Concert — 1977 — 50.00
— Promo only in plain cardboard jacket; this LP was edited to one LP for release
JC34786 Season of Lights...Laura Nyro in Concert — 1977 — 15.00
— Edited version of above
PC33912 Smile — 1976 — 15.00
— No bar code on cover
KC31410 The First Songs — 1973 — 18.00
— Reissue of Verve Forecast 3020
PC31410 The First Songs — 197? — 10.00
— Budget-line reissue

VERVE FOLKWAYS
FT-3020 [M] Laura Nyro -- More Than a New Discovery — 1967 — 30.00
FTS-3020 [S] Laura Nyro -- More Than a New Discovery — 1967 — 30.00
ST93036 Laura Nyro -- More Than a New Discovery — 1968 — 30.00
— Capitol Record Club edition
FTS-3020 [S] Laura Nyro (The First Songs) — 1967 — 25.00
— The First Songs" is found on the label and back cover, but not on the front cover or the spine; this has the same material as the Verve Folkways LP but in a different order

Number	Title	Yr	NM

O

O.C.

PAYDAY
❏ 524399-1	Jewelz	1997	15.00

WILD PITCH
❏ E1-30928	Word...Life	1994	25.00

OAK RIDGE BOYS, THE

ABC
❏ AA-1135	Have Arrived	1979	15.00
❏ AA-1065	Room Service	1978	12.00

ABC/DOT
❏ DA-2093	Y'all Come Back Saloon	1977	12.00

ACCORD
❏ SN-7138	Spiritual Jubilee	198?	12.00
❏ SN-7159	Spiritual Jubilee -- Volume 2	198?	12.00
❏ SN-7199	Spiritual Jubilee -- Volume 3	198?	12.00

CADENCE
❏ CLP-3019 [M]	The Oak Ridge Quartet	1958	60.00

CANAAN
❏ 9625	Together	1966	25.00
—With the Harvesters			

COLUMBIA
❏ FC37737	All Our Favorite Songs	1981	12.00
❏ KC33935	Old Fashioned, Down Home, Hand Clappin', Foot Stompin', Southern Style, Gospel Quartet Music	1976	15.00
❏ PC37711	Old Fashoned Gospel Quartet Music	1984	10.00
❏ KC33057	Sky High	1975	15.00
❏ PC33057	Sky High	197?	10.00
—Reissue			
❏ PC38467	Smoky Mountain Gospel	1984	10.00
❏ PC35202	The Best of the Oak Ridge Boys	1978	12.00
❏ KC32742	The Oak Ridge Boys	1974	15.00
❏ PC32742	The Oak Ridge Boys	197?	10.00
—Reissue			

HEARTWARMING
❏ HWS3091	International	1971	18.00
❏ HWS3036	Thanks	1971	18.00
❏ HWS3159	The Light	1972	18.00

INTERMEDIA
❏ QS-5012	Glory Train	198?	12.00

LIBERTY
❏ LN-10046	The Oak Ridge Boys at Their Best	1981	10.00

MCA
❏ 42311	American Dreams	1989	12.00
❏ 5390	American Made	1983	12.00
❏ 1447	American Made	1985	10.00
—Budget-line reissue			
❏ 5294	Bobbie Sue	1982	12.00
❏ 5365	Christmas	1982	12.00
❏ 5799	Christmas Again	1986	12.00
❏ 5455	Deliver	1983	12.00
❏ 1446	Deliver	1985	10.00
—Budget-line reissue			
❏ 5209 [B]	Fancy Free	1981	12.00
❏ 5150	Greatest Hits	1980	12.00
❏ 5496	Greatest Hits 2	1984	12.00
❏ AA-1135	Have Arrived	1979	12.00
❏ 37221	Have Arrived	1984	10.00
—Budget-line reissue			
❏ 42036	Heartbeat	1987	12.00
❏ 42205	Monongahela	1988	12.00
❏ 37153	Room Service	198?	10.00
—Budget-line reissue			
❏ 5714	Seasons	1986	12.00
❏ L33-2-1276 [DJ]	Step On Out" World Premiere	1985	30.00
—Promo-only interview and music LP with no script or cover			
❏ 5555	Step On Out	1985	12.00
❏ 3220	Together	1980	12.00
❏ 37223	Together	1984	10.00
—Budget-line reissue			
❏ 5945	Where the Fast Lane Ends	1987	12.00
❏ 37222	Y'all Come Back Saloon	1984	10.00
—Budget-line reissue			

NASHVILLE
❏ 2086	Higher Power	1970	18.00

POWER PAK
❏ 716	The Oak Ridge Boys	197?	12.00

PRIORITY
❏ PU37711	Old Fashoned Gospel Quartot Music	1981	12.00
❏ PU38467	Smoky Mountain Gospel	1983	12.00

RCA
❏ R164223	Unstoppable	1991	18.00
—Only released on vinyl through BMG Direct Marketing			

SKYLITE
❏ RLP-6030 [M]	I Wouldn't Take Nothing for My Journey Now	1965	25.00
❏ SRLP-6030 [S]	I Wouldn't Take Nothing for My Journey Now	1965	30.00
❏ RLP-6045 [M]	River of Love	1967	25.00
❏ SRLP-6045 [S]	River of Love	1967	30.00
❏ RLP-6020 [M]	The Oak Ridge Boys Sing for You	1964	25.00
❏ SRLP-6020 [S]	The Oak Ridge Boys Sing for You	1964	30.00
❏ RLP-6040 [M]	The Solid Gospel Sound of the Oak Ridge Boys	1966	25.00
❏ SRLP-6040 [S]	The Solid Gospel Sound of the Oak Ridge Boys	1966	30.00

STARDAY
❏ SLP-356 [M]	The Sensational Oak Ridge Boys	1965	30.00

UNITED ARTISTS
❏ UAL3554 [M]	The Oak Ridge Boys at Their Best	1966	25.00
❏ UAS6554 [S]	The Oak Ridge Boys at Their Best	1966	30.00
❏ LN-10046	The Oak Ridge Boys at Their Best	1979	12.00

WARNER BROS.
❏ W1521 [M]	Folk-Minded Spirituals for Spiritual-Minded Folks	1963	25.00
❏ WS1521 [S]	Folk-Minded Spirituals for Spiritual-Minded Folks	1963	30.00
❏ W1497 [M]	With Sounds of Nashville	1963	25.00
❏ WS1497 [S]	With Sounds of Nashville	1963	30.00

OAKEY, PHILIP AND GIORGIO MORODER

A&M
❏ SP-5080	Philip Oakey and Giorgio Moroder	1985	10.00

OAKLEY, LEON

GHB
❏ GHB-153	Leon Oakley and the Flying Duces	198?	12.00

STOMP OFF
❏ SOS-1013	New Orleans Joys	198?	12.00

OAKTOWN'S 3.5.7.

BUST IT
❏ C1-92996	Fully Loaded	1991	18.00

CAPITOL
❏ C1-90926	Wild and Loose	1989	12.00

OASIS

EPIC
❏ E94493	Don't Believe the Truth	2005	25.00

HELTER SKELTER
❏ 88697-00754-1	Stop the Clocks	2006	50.00
—Pressed in Europe but imported by Sony BMG for U.S. distribution			

O'BANION, JOHN

ELEKTRA
❏ 6E-342	John O'Danion	1981	12.00

OBEIDO, RAY

WINDHAM HILL
❏ WH-0115	Perfect Crime	1989	15.00

OBOLER, ARCH

CAPITOL
❏ T1763 [M]	Drop Dead! An Exercise in Horror	1962	30.00
❏ ST1763 [S]	Drop Dead! An Exercise in Horror	1962	30.00

O'BRIAN, HUGH

ABC-PARAMOUNT
❏ ABC-203 [M]	TV's Wyatt Earp Sings	1957	60.00

O'BRIEN, HOD

UPTOWN
❏ 27.08	Bits and Pieces	198?	12.00

O'BRYAN

CAPITOL
❏ ST-12332	Be My Lover	1984	12.00
❏ ST-12192	Doin' Alright	1982	12.00
❏ ST-12520	Surrender	1986	12.00
❏ ST-12256	You and I	1983	12.00

O'BRYANT, JIMMY

BIOGRAPH
❏ 12002 [M]	Jimmy O'Bryant's Washboard Wonders 1924-26	1968	15.00

O'BRYANT, JOAN

FOLKWAYS
❏ FA-2338 [M]	American Ballads and Folksongs	1958	30.00
❏ FA-2134 [M]	Folksongs and Ballads of Kansas	1957	30.00

OCASEK, RIC

GEFFEN
❏ GHS2022	Beatitude	1983	10.00
❏ R144634	This Side of Paradise	1986	12.00
—RCA Music Service edition			
❏ 24098	This Side of Paradise	1986	10.00

OCEAN, BILLY

EPIC
❏ FE38129	Inner Feelings	1982	18.00
❏ PE38129	Inner Feelings	1985	10.00
—Budget-line reissue with new prefix			
❏ FE37406	Nights (Feel Like Gettin' Down)	1981	18.00
❏ PE37406	Nights (Feel Like Gettin' Down)	1985	10.00
—Budget-line reissue with new prefix			

JIVE
❏ 1271-1-J	Greatest Hits	1989	12.00

JIVE/ARISTA
❏ JL8-8409	Love Zone	1986	10.00
❏ JL8-8213	Suddenly	1986	10.00
—Original cover: Photo of Billy Ocean on blue background			
❏ JL8-8213	Suddenly	1984	10.00
—Second cover: Drawing of Billy Ocean on white background			
❏ JL8-8495	Tear Down These Walls	1988	10.00

OCEAN

KAMA SUTRA
❏ KSBS-2064	Give Tomorrow's Children One More Chance	1972	15.00
❏ KSBS-2033	Put Your Hand in the Hand	1971	15.00

OCEAN BLUE, THE

SIRE
❏ 25906	The Ocean Blue	1989	15.00

OCHS, PHIL

A&M
❏ SP-6511	Chords of Fame	1976	18.00
—Reissue of 4599			
❏ SP-4599	Chords of Fame	1974	30.00
—Original edition			
❏ SP-4253	Phil Ochs Greatest Hits	1970	25.00
❏ SP-3125 [B]	Phil Ochs Greatest Hits	198?	10.00
—Budget-line reissue			
❏ LP-133 [M]	Pleasures of the Harbor	1967	30.00
❏ SP-4133 [S]	Pleasures of the Harbor	1967	25.00
❏ SP-4181	Rehearsals for Retirement	1969	25.00
❏ SP-4148 [S]	Tape from California	1968	25.00
❏ LP-148 [M]	Tape from California	1968	50.00
—Mono is white label promo only; "Monaural" sticker at upper right corner of stereo cover			

CARTHAGE
❏ CGLP-4427	All the News That's Fit to Sing	198?	12.00
❏ CGLP-4422	I Ain't Marching Anymore	198?	12.00

ELEKTRA
❏ EKL-269 [M]	All the News That's Fit to Sing	1964	30.00
—Gold label with "guitar player" logo			
❏ EKL-269 [M]	All the News That's Fit to Sing	1966	25.00
—Gold label with stylized "E" logo			
❏ EKS-7269 [S]	All the News That's Fit to Sing	1964	40.00
—Gold label with "guitar player" logo			
❏ EKS-7269 [S]	All the News That's Fit to Sing	1966	30.00
—Gold label with stylized "E" logo			
❏ EKL-287 [M]	I Ain't Marching Anymore	1965	30.00
—Gold label with "guitar player" logo			
❏ EKL-287 [M]	I Ain't Marching Anymore	1966	25.00
—Gold label with stylized "E" logo			
❏ EKS-7287 [S]	I Ain't Marching Anymore	1965	40.00
—Gold label with "guitar player" logo			
❏ EKS-7287 [S]	I Ain't Marching Anymore	1966	30.00
—Gold label with stylized "E" logo			
❏ EKS-7287 [S]	I Ain't Marching Anymore	1975	15.00
—Butterfly label with small Warner Communications logo			
❏ EKL-310 [M]	Phil Ochs in Concert	1966	25.00
❏ EKS-7310 [S]	Phil Ochs in Concert	1966	30.00

FOLKWAYS
❏ FD-5362	Broadside Tapes 1 (#14)	1979	15.00
❏ FB-5321	Phil Ochs Interviews	197?	15.00
❏ FB-5320	Phil Ochs Sings Songs for Broadside (#10)	1976	15.00

PICKWICK
❏ SPC-3707	Rehearsals for Retirement	197?	12.00

RHINO
❏ RNLP-70080	A Toast to Those Who Are Gone	1986	12.00

SMITHSONIAN/FOLKWAYS
❏ SF-40008	Broadside Tapes 1 (#14)	1989	15.00

Number	Title	Yr	NM

O'CONNELL, BILL

INNER CITY

| ❏ IC-1035 | Searching | 197? | 18.00 |

O'CONNELL, HELEN

MARK 56

| ❏ 711 | Christmas with Helen O'Connell | 19?? | 15.00 |

VIK

| ❏ LX-1093 [M] | Green Eyes | 1957 | 40.00 |

O'CONNOR, CARROLL

A&M

| ❏ SP-4340 | Remembering You | 1972 | 30.00 |

AUDIO FIDELITY

| ❏ AFSD-6727 | Carroll O'Connor Sings for Old P.F.A.R.T.S. | 1976 | 30.00 |

O'CONNOR, SINEAD

CHRYSALIS

❏ R133512	I Do Not Want What I Haven't Got	1990	18.00
—BMG Direct Marketing edition			
❏ F1-21759	I Do Not Want What I Haven't Got	1990	15.00
❏ R163660	The Lion and the Cobra	1988	12.00
—BMG Direct Marketing edition			
❏ BFV41612	The Lion and the Cobra	1987	10.00
❏ F1-21612	The Lion and the Cobra	1989	15.00
—Reissue			

OCTOBER COUNTRY

EPIC

| ❏ BN26381 [B] | October Country | 1968 | 25.00 |

ODA

LOUD

| ❏ A 0011 | Oda | 1973 | 200.00 |

O'DAY, ALAN

PACIFIC

| ❏ PC4300 | Appetizers | 1977 | 12.00 |
| ❏ PC4301 | Oh Johnny! | 1979 | 12.00 |

VIVA

| ❏ VV2679 | Caress Me Pretty Music | 1973 | 18.00 |

O'DAY, ANITA

ADVANCE

| ❏ LSP-8 [10] | Anita O'Day Specials | 1951 | 250.00 |

AMERICAN RECORDING SOCIETY

| ❏ G-426 [M] | For Oscar | 1957 | 40.00 |

BASF

| ❏ MB20750 | Recorded Live at the Berlin Jazz Festival | 1973 | 25.00 |

BOB THIELE MUSIC

| ❏ BBM1-0595 [M] | Hi Ho Trailus Boot Whip | 1974 | 18.00 |

CLEF

| ❏ MGC-130 [10] | Anita O'Day Collates | 1953 | 150.00 |

CORAL

| ❏ CRL-56073 [10] | Singin' and Swingin' | 1953 | 150.00 |

DOCTOR JAZZ

| ❏ FW39418 | Hi Ho Trailus Boot Whip | 198? | 12.00 |

EMILY

❏ 13081	Angel Eyes	1981	15.00
❏ 83084	A Song for You	1984	15.00
❏ 92685	Big Band Concert 1985	1985	15.00
❏ 11579	Live at Mingos	1979	18.00
❏ 102479	Live at the City	1979	18.00
❏ 42181	Live at the City: The Second Set	1981	15.00
❏ 9579	Live at Tokyo	1979	18.00
❏ 11279	My Ship	1979	18.00
❏ 32383	The Night Has a Thousand Eyes	1983	15.00

GLENDALE

| ❏ 6001 | Anita O'Day | 197? | 15.00 |
| ❏ 6000 | Once Upon a Summertime | 197? | 15.00 |

GNP CRESCENDO

| ❏ GNPS-2126 | Mello' Day | 197? | 12.00 |

NORGRAN

❏ MGN-1057 [M]	An Evening With Anita	1956	100.00
❏ MGN-1049 [M]	Anita O'Day	1955	120.00
❏ MGN-30 [10]	Songs By Anita O'Day	1954	150.00

PAUSA

| ❏ 7092 | Anita O'Day in Berlin | 198? | 12.00 |

VERVE

❏ V-8442 [M]	All the Sad Young Men	1962	30.00
❏ V6-8442 [S]	All the Sad Young Men	1962	40.00
❏ MGV-2050 [M]	An Evening With Anita O'Day	1957	60.00
❏ V-2050 [M]	An Evening With Anita O'Day	1961	25.00
❏ MGV-2000 [M]	Anita	1956	80.00
❏ V-2000 [M]	Anita	1961	25.00
❏ 829261-1	Anita	1986	12.00

❏ MGV-2141 [M]	Anita O'Day and Billy May Swing Rodgers and Hart	1960	60.00
❏ V-2141 [M]	Anita O'Day and Billy May Swing Rodgers and Hart	1961	25.00
❏ V6-2141 [S]	Anita O'Day and Billy May Swing Rodgers and Hart	1961	30.00
❏ V-8514 [M]	Anita O'Day and the Three Sounds	1963	30.00
❏ V6-8514 [S]	Anita O'Day and the Three Sounds	1963	30.00
❏ MGV-2113 [M]	Anita O'Day At Mr. Kelly's	1958	50.00
❏ MGVS-6043 [S]	Anita O'Day At Mr. Kelly's	1960	60.00
❏ V-2113 [M]	Anita O'Day At Mr. Kelly's	1961	25.00
❏ V6-2113 [S]	Anita O'Day At Mr. Kelly's	1961	30.00
❏ UMV-2550	Anita O'Day At Mr. Kelly's	198?	15.00
❏ MGV-8283 [M]	Anita O'Day Sings the Winners	1958	50.00
❏ MGVS-6002 [S]	Anita O'Day Sings the Winners	1960	60.00
❏ V 8283 [M]	Anita O'Day Sings the Winners	1961	25.00
❏ V6-8283 [S]	Anita O'Day Sings the Winners	1961	30.00
❏ V-8485 [M]	Anita O'Day Sings the Winners	1962	25.00
❏ V6-8485 [S]	Anita O'Day Sings the Winners	1962	30.00
❏ UMV-2536	Anita O'Day Sings the Winners	198?	15.00
❏ MGV-2118 [M]	Anita O'Day Swings Cole Porter	1959	50.00
❏ MGVS-6059 [S]	Anita O'Day Swings Cole Porter	1960	60.00
❏ V-2118 [M]	Anita O'Day Swings Cole Porter	1961	25.00
❏ V6-2118 [S]	Anita O'Day Swings Cole Porter	1961	30.00
❏ MGV-8259 [M]	Anita Sings the Most	1958	50.00
❏ V-8259 [M]	Anita Sings the Most	1961	25.00
❏ MGV-8312 [M]	Cool Heat -- Anita O'Day Sings Jimmy Giuffre Arrangements	1959	50.00
❏ MGVS-6046 [S]	Cool Heat -- Anita O'Day Sings Jimmy Giuffre Arrangements	1960	60.00
❏ V-8312 [M]	Cool Heat -- Anita O'Day Sings Jimmy Giuffre Arrangements	1961	25.00
❏ V6-8312 [S]	Cool Heat -- Anita O'Day Sings Jimmy Giuffre Arrangements	1961	30.00
❏ UMV-2679	Cool Heat -- Anita O'Day Sings Jimmy Giuffre Arrangements	198?	15.00
❏ V-8572 [M]	Incomparable! Anita O'Day	1964	30.00
❏ V6-8572 [S]	Incomparable! Anita O'Day	1964	30.00
❏ MGV-2043 [M]	Pick Yourself Up With Anita O'Day	1957	80.00
❏ V-2043 [M]	Pick Yourself Up With Anita O'Day	1961	25.00
❏ VE-2-2534	The Big Band Sessions	1979	18.00
❏ MGV-2049 [M]	The Lady Is a Tramp	1957	60.00
❏ V-2049 [M]	The Lady Is a Tramp	1961	25.00
❏ V-8483 [M]	This Is Anita	1962	30.00
❏ V6-8483 [R]	This Is Anita	1962	18.00
❏ V-8472 [M]	Time For Two	1962	30.00
❏ V6-8472 [S]	Time For Two	1962	40.00
❏ UMJ-3287	Time For Two	198?	15.00
❏ MGV-2157 [M]	Trav'lin' Light	1960	50.00
❏ V-2157 [M]	Trav'lin' Light	1961	25.00
❏ V6-2157 [S]	Trav'lin' Light	1961	30.00
❏ MGV-2145 [M]	Waiter, Make Mine Blues	1960	60.00
❏ V-2145 [M]	Waiter, Make Mine Blues	1961	25.00
❏ V6-2145 [S]	Waiter, Make Mine Blues	1961	30.00

O'DAY, MOLLY

AUDIO LAB

| ❏ AL-1544 [M] | Music for the Country Folks | 1960 | 30.00 |

HARMONY

| ❏ HL7299 [M] | The Unforgettable Molly O'Day | 1963 | 25.00 |

STARDAY

| ❏ SLP-367 [B] | The Living Legend of Country Music | 1966 | 30.00 |

O'DAY, TOMMY

NU TRAYL

| ❏ NLP-6005 | Tommy O'Day | 1977 | 18.00 |
| ❏ NLP-6006 | Tommy O'Day Sings Today's Woman | 1978 | 18.00 |

ODD SQUAD

RAP-A-LOT

| ❏ SPRO50781 [EP] | Hot Club Wax | 1994 | 15.00 |
| —Promo-only six-song sampler | | | |

O'DELL, DOYE

ERA

❏ EL-20004 [M]	Doye	1956	50.00
—Red vinyl			
❏ EL-20004 [M]	Doye	1956	30.00
—Black vinyl			

SAGE

| ❏ C-36 [M] | Crossroads | 195? | 30.00 |

O'DELL, KENNY

CAPRICORN

| ❏ CP 0140 | Kenny O'Dell | 1974 | 15.00 |
| ❏ CPN 0211 | Let's Shake Hands and Come Out Lovin' | 1978 | 15.00 |

VEGAS

| ❏ 401 | Beautiful People | 1968 | 30.00 |

ODETTA

ALCAZAR

| ❏ ALC-104 | Christmas Spirituals | 198? | 12.00 |

EVEREST ARCHIVE OF FOLK & JAZZ

| ❏ 273 | Odetta | 1973 | 15.00 |

FANTASY

❏ 3-15 [10]	Odetta and Larry	1955	50.00
❏ F-3252 [M]	Odetta and Larry	1957	50.00
Dark red vinyl			
❏ F-3252 [M]	Odetta and Larry	1958	30.00
❏ F-8345	Odetta and Larry	1963	15.00
—Reissue of 3252			
❏ OBC-509	Odetta and the Blues	198?	12.00
—Reissue of Riverside LP			

RCA VICTOR

❏ LPM-2792 [M]	It's a Mighty World	1964	18.00
❏ LSP-2792 [S]	It's a Mighty World	1964	25.00
❏ LPM-3457 [M]	Odetta in Japan	1965	18.00
❏ LSP-3457 [S]	Odetta in Japan	1965	25.00
❏ LPM-3324 [M]	Odetta Sings Dylan	1965	18.00
❏ LSP-3324 [S]	Odetta Sings Dylan	1965	25.00
❏ LPM-2643 [M]	Odetta Sings Folk Songs	1963	25.00
❏ LSP-2643 [S]	Odetta Sings Folk Songs	1963	30.00
❏ LPM-2923 [M]	Odetta Sings of Many Things	1964	18.00
❏ LSP-2923 [S]	Odetta Sings of Many Things	1964	25.00
❏ LPM-2573 [M]	Sometimes I Feel Like Crying	1962	25.00
❏ LSP-2573 [S]	Sometimes I Feel Like Crying	1962	30.00

RIVERSIDE

| ❏ RLP-417 [M] | Odetta and the Blues | 1962 | 30.00 |
| ❏ RS-9417 [S] | Odetta and the Blues | 1962 | 30.00 |

ROSE QUARTZ

| ❏ RQ-101 | Movin' It On | 1987 | 12.00 |

TRADITION

❏ TRP-1025 [M]	Odetta at the Gate of Horn	1958	30.00
❏ TRP-1010 [M]	Odetta Sings Ballads and Blues	1957	30.00
❏ TRP-1052 [M]	The Best of Odetta	1967	25.00
❏ TRS-2052 [R]	The Best of Odetta	1967	18.00

VANGUARD

❏ VRS-9066 [M]	Ballads for Americans	1960	25.00
❏ VSD-2057 [S]	Ballads for Americans	1960	30.00
❏ VRS-9079 [M]	Christmas Spirituals	1961	25.00
❏ VSD-2079 [S]	Christmas Spirituals	1961	30.00
❏ VSD-43/44	Essential Odetta	1973	18.00
❏ VRS-9059 [M]	My Eyes Have Seen	1960	25.00
❏ VSD-2046 [S]	My Eyes Have Seen	1960	30.00
❏ VRS-9076 [M]	Odetta at Carnegie Hall	1961	25.00
❏ VSD-2072 [S]	Odetta at Carnegie Hall	1961	30.00
❏ VRS-3003 [M]	Odetta at Carnegie Hall	1967	18.00
❏ VSD-73003 [S]	Odetta at Carnegie Hall	1967	25.00
❏ VRS-9103 [M]	Odetta at Town Hall	1962	25.00
❏ VSD-2109 [S]	Odetta at Town Hall	1962	30.00
❏ VRS-9137 [M]	One Grain of Sand	1963	25.00
❏ VSD-2153 [S]	One Grain of Sand	1963	30.00

ODRICH, RON

CLASSIC JAZZ

| ❏ 35 | Blackstick | 1978 | 15.00 |

ODYSSEY

RCA VICTOR

❏ AFL1-3526	Hang Together	1980	12.00
❏ AFL1-4240	Happy Together	1982	12.00
❏ AFL1-3031	Hollywood Party Tonight	1978	12.00

Number	Title	Yr	NM
❏ AFL1-3910	I Got the Melody	1981	12.00
❏ APL1-2204	Odyssey	1977	12.00

O'FARRILL, CHICO

ABC IMPULSE!
❏ AS-9135 [S]	Nine Flags	1968	18.00

CLEF
❏ MGC-131 [10]	Afro-Cuban	1953	200.00
❏ MGC-132 [10]	Chico O'Farrill Jazz	1953	200.00
❏ MGC-699 [M]	Chico O'Farrill Jazz	1956	80.00

IMPULSE!
❏ AS-9135 [S]	Nine Flags	1967	25.00
❏ A-9135 [M]	Nine Flags	1967	30.00

NORGRAN
❏ MGN-31 [10]	Chico O'Farrill	1954	80.00
❏ MGN-28 [10]	Latino Dance Sessions	1954	80.00
❏ MGN-27 [10]	Mambo Dance Sessions	1954	80.00
❏ MGN-9 [10]	The Second Afro-Cuban Jazz Suite	1954	150.00

VERVE
❏ MGV-8083 [M]	Jazz North of the Border and South of the Border	1957	50.00
❏ V-8083 [M]	Jazz North of the Border and South of the Border	1961	30.00
❏ MGV-2003 [M]	Mambo/Latino Dances	1956	50.00
❏ V-2003 [M]	Mambo/Latino Dances	1961	30.00
❏ MGV-2024 [M]	Music From South America	1956	50.00
❏ V-2024 [M]	Music From South America	1961	30.00

OFF BROADWAY USA

ATLANTIC
❏ SD19263	On	1980	25.00
❏ SD19287	Quick Turns	1981	18.00

OFFSPRING, THE

COLUMBIA
❏ C69661 [B]	Americana	1998	30.00
❏ C61419	Conspiracy of One	2000	18.00
❏ C67810	Ixnay on the Hombre	1997	18.00
❏ C89026	Splinter	2003	18.00

EPITAPH
❏ 86424 [B]	Ignition	1992	30.00
❏ 86432	Smash	1994	18.00

NEMESIS
❏ 6	The Offspring	1989	100.00

— Original issue, 5,000 copies pressed

NITRO
❏ 06460	The Offspring	1995	15.00

— Reissue of Nemesis LP

OGERMAN, CLAUS, AND MICHAEL BRECKER

ECM
❏ 23698	Cityscape	1982	12.00

OGERMAN, CLAUS

JAZZ MAN
❏ 5015	Aranjuez	198?	15.00

RCA VICTOR
❏ LPM-3640 [M]	Saxes Mexicano	1966	25.00
❏ LSP-3640 [S]	Saxes Mexicano	1966	30.00
❏ LPM-3366 [M]	Soul Searchin'	1965	25.00
❏ LSP-3366 [S]	Soul Searchin'	1965	30.00
❏ LPM-3455 [M]	Watusi Trumpets	1965	25.00
❏ LSP-3455 [S]	Watusi Trumpets	1965	30.00

UNITED ARTISTS
❏ UAL-3206 [M]	Sing Along in German	1962	25.00
❏ UAS-6206 [S]	Sing Along in German	1962	30.00

WARNER BROS.
❏ BS3006	Gate of Dreams	1977	12.00

O'GWYNN, JAMES

MERCURY
❏ MG-20727 [M]	The Best of James O'Gwynn	1962	30.00
❏ SR-60727 [S]	The Best of James O'Gwynn	1962	40.00

PLANTATION
❏ 21	Greatest Hits	197?	15.00

WING
❏ MGW-12290 [M]	Heartaches and Memories	1964	25.00
❏ SRW-16290 [S]	Heartaches and Memories	1964	30.00

O'HARA, MAUREEN

COLUMBIA
❏ CL1750 [M]	Maureen O'Hara Sings Her Favorite Irish Songs	1962	40.00
❏ CS8550 [S]	Maureen O'Hara Sings Her Favorite Irish Songs	1962	50.00

RCA VICTOR
❏ LPM-1953 [M]	Love Letters	1959	50.00
❏ LSP-1953 [S]	Love Letters	1959	60.00

OHIO EXPRESS, THE

BUDDAH
❏ BDS5026	Chewy, Chewy	1969	25.00
❏ BDS5037 [B]	Mercy	1969	25.00
❏ BDM1018 [M]	The Ohio Express	1968	40.00

— Stereo cover with "mono" sticker attached; white label promo
❏ BDS5018 [S]	The Ohio Express	1968	25.00
❏ BDS5058	The Very Best of the Ohio Express	1970	25.00

CAMEO
❏ C20000 [M]	Beg, Borrow and Steal	1967	30.00
❏ CS20000 [S]	Beg, Borrow and Steal	1967	40.00

OHIO PLAYERS, THE

ACCORD
❏ SN-7102	Young and Ready	1981	10.00

ARISTA
❏ AB4226	Everybody Up	1979	10.00

BOARDWALK
❏ FW37090	Tenderness	1981	10.00

CAPITOL
❏ ST-192	Observations in Time	1969	50.00
❏ ST-11291	The Ohio Players	1974	15.00

— Reissue of 192

MERCURY
❏ SRM-1-3701	Angel	1977	12.00
❏ SRM-1-1088	Contradiction	1976	12.00
❏ SRM-1-1013	Fire	1974	12.00
❏ SRM-1-1038	Honey	1975	12.00
❏ SRM-1-3730	Jass-Ay-Lay-Dee	1978	12.00
❏ SRM-1-3707	Mr. Mean	1977	12.00
❏ SRM-1-1122	Ohio Players Gold	1976	12.00
❏ 824461-1	Ohio Players Gold	198?	10.00

— Reissue of 1122
❏ SRM-1-705	Skin Tight	1974	15.00

— Red label
❏ SRM-1-705 [B]	Skin Tight	1974	12.00

— Chicago skyline label

TRACK
❏ TRK58810	Back	1988	12.00

TRIP
❏ 8029	First Impression	1972	15.00

UNITED ARTISTS
❏ UA-LA502-E	The Very Best of The Ohio Players	1975	15.00

WESTBOUND
❏ 1003	Climax	1974	18.00
❏ 2021	Ecstasy	1973	25.00
❏ 222	Ecstasy	1976	15.00

— Reissue of 2021
❏ 1005	Ohio Players Greatest Hits	1975	18.00
❏ 2015	Pain	1972	25.00
❏ 219	Pain	1976	15.00

— Reissue of 2015
❏ 2017	Pleasure	1973	25.00
❏ 220	Pleasure	1976	15.00

— Reissue of 2017
❏ 211	Rattlesnake	1975	15.00
❏ 304	The Best of the Early Years	1977	18.00

OHLSON, CURTIS

INTIMA
❏ D1-73358	Better Than Ever	1989	15.00
❏ SJE-73274	So Fast	1987	12.00

OHNO, SHUNZO

INNER CITY
❏ IC-1108	Quarter Moon	198?	15.00

OINGO BOINGO

A&M
❏ SP-4959	Good for Your Soul	1983	12.00
❏ SP-3252	Good for Your Soul	1984	10.00

— Reissue of 4959
❏ SP-4903	Nothing to Fear	1982	12.00
❏ SP-3251	Nothing to Fear	1984	10.00

— Reissue of 4930
❏ SP-4863	Only a Lad	1981	12.00
❏ SP-3250 [B]	Only a Lad	1984	10.00

— Reissue of 4863
❏ SP-5217	Skeletons in the Closet	1988	12.00

I.R.S.
❏ SP-70400 [10]	Oingo Boingo	1980	15.00

— Four-song 10-inch EP
❏ SP-70400	Oingo Boingo	1980	15.00

— Limited edition 12" version

MCA
❏ 5811	BOI-NGO	1987	12.00
❏ 8030	Boingo Alive	1988	15.00
❏ 6365	Dark at the End of the Tunnel	1990	12.00
❏ L33-18137 [DJ]	Dark at the End of the Tunnel	1990	40.00

— Promo-only picture disc
❏ 5665	Dead Man's Party	1985	12.00

O'JAYS, THE

BELL
❏ 6014	Back on Top	1968	25.00
❏ 6082	The O'Jays	1973	15.00

EMI
❏ E1-93390	Emotionally Yours	1991	18.00
❏ E1-96420	Home for Christmas	1991	18.00
❏ E1-90921	Serious	1989	12.00

IMPERIAL
❏ LP9290 [M]	Comin' Through	1965	40.00
❏ LP12290 [S]	Comin' Through	1965	50.00

KORY
❏ 1006	The O'Jays	1977	12.00

LIBERTY
❏ LN-10119	Greatest Hits	1980	10.00

— Budget-line reissue of Imperial material

MINIT
❏ LP-40008 [M]	Soul Sounds	1967	40.00
❏ LP-24008 [S]	Soul Sounds	1967	50.00

NEPTUNE
❏ 202	The O'Jays in Philadelphia	1969	30.00

PHILADELPHIA INT'L.
❏ KZ31712 [B]	Back Stabbers	1972	15.00
❏ ASZ140 [DJ]	Everything You Always Wanted to Hear by the O'Jays But Were Afraid to Ask For	1975	18.00
❏ PZ33807	Family Reunion	1975	15.00

— No bar code on back cover
❏ PZQ33807 [Q]	Family Reunion	1975	18.00
❏ PZ33807	Family Reunion	198?	12.00

— Budget-line reissue with bar code
❏ FZ39251	Greatest Hits	1984	12.00
❏ FZ36027	Identify Yourself	1979	12.00
❏ 53036	Let Me Touch You	1987	12.00
❏ 53015	Love Fever	1985	12.00
❏ PZ34245	Message in the Music	1976	12.00
❏ FZ37999	My Favorite Person	1982	12.00
❏ KZ32408	Ship Ahoy	1973	12.00
❏ PZQ32408 [Q]	Ship Ahoy	1974	18.00
❏ PZ32408	Ship Ahoy	198?	10.00

— Budget-line reissue
❏ JZ35355	So Full of Love	1978	12.00
❏ PZ35355	So Full of Love	198?	10.00

— Budget-line reissue
❏ PZ33150	Survival	1975	12.00
❏ PZG35024	The O'Jays: Collector's Items	1978	15.00
❏ Z235024	The O'Jays. Collector's Items	198?	12.00

— Reissue
❏ KZ32120	The O'Jays in Philadelphia	1973	15.00

— Reissue of Neptune LP
❏ KZ32953	The O'Jays Live in London	1974	12.00
❏ PZQ32953 [Q]	The O'Jays Live in London	1974	18.00
❏ PZ34684	Travelin' at the Speed of Thought	1977	12.00
❏ FZ38518	When Will I See You Again	1983	12.00
❏ PZ38518	When Will I See You Again	1985	10.00

— Budget-line reissue

SUNSET
❏ SUS-5222	Full of Soul	1968	18.00

— Reissue of Imperial LP

TSOP
❏ FZ36416	The Year 2000	1980	12.00

UNITED ARTISTS
❏ UAS-5655	The O'Jays Greatest Hits	1972	15.00

VOLCANO
❏ 31149	Love You to Tears	1997	18.00

O'KANES, THE

COLUMBIA
❏ BFC40459	The O'Kanes	1986	10.00
❏ FC44066	Tired of the Runnin'	1988	10.00

O'KAYSIONS, THE

ABC
❏ S-664	Girl Watcher	1968	40.00

O'KEEFE, DANNY

ATLANTIC
❏ SD7264	Breezy Stories	1973	15.00
❏ SD18125	So Long, Harry Truman	1975	15.00

COTILLION
❏ SD9036	Danny O'Keefe	1971	18.00

FIRST AMERICAN
❏ 7700	The Seattle Tapes	1977	15.00
❏ 7721	The Seattle Tapes, Volume 2	1979	15.00

PANORAMA
❏ 105	Introducing Danny O'Keefe	1966	40.00

SIGNPOST
❏ SD8404	O'Keefe	1972	15.00

WARNER BROS.
❏ BS3050	American Roulette	1977	12.00
❏ BSK3314	Global Blues	1978	12.00
❏ PRO760 [DJ]	The O'Keefe File	1977	18.00

OL' DIRTY BASTARD

ELEKTRA
❏ ED6187 [DJ]	N***a Please	1999	25.00

Number	Title	Yr	NM
—Promo-only version			
❑ 62414	Nigga Please	1999	18.00
❑ 61659	Return to the 36 Chambers: The Dirty Version	1995	18.00
❑ ED5796 [DJ]	Return to the 36 Chambers: The Dirty Version	1995	18.00
—Promo-only version			

OL' SKOOL

UNIVERSAL
| ❑ 53104 | Ol' Skool | 1998 | 15.00 |

OLA AND THE JANGLERS

GNP CRESCENDO
| ❑ GNPS-2050 | Let's Dance/What a Way to Die | 1969 | 25.00 |

OLAY, RUTH

ABC
| ❑ ABC-573 [M] | Soul In the Night | 1966 | 25.00 |
| ❑ ABCS-573 [S] | Soul In the Night | 1966 | 30.00 |
EMARCY
| ❑ MG-36125 [M] | Olay! The New Sound Of Ruth Olay | 1958 | 50.00 |
EVEREST
| ❑ LPBR-5218 [M] | Olay! OK | 1963 | 30.00 |
| ❑ SDBR-1218 [S] | Olay! OK | 1963 | 30.00 |
LAUREL
| ❑ 501 | Ruth Olay Sings Jazz Today | 198? | 15.00 |
MERCURY
| ❑ MG-20390 [M] | Easy Living | 1959 | 40.00 |
| ❑ SR-60069 [S] | Easy Living | 1959 | 50.00 |
UNITED ARTISTS
| ❑ UAL-3115 [M] | Ruth Olay In Person | 1960 | 30.00 |
| ❑ UAS-4115 [S] | Ruth Olay In Person | 1960 | 40.00 |

OLD & IN THE WAY

ROUND
| ❑ RX-103 | Old & in the Way | 1975 | 30.00 |
SUGAR HILL
| ❑ SH-3746 | Old & In the Way | 1987 | 12.00 |
| —Reissue of Round LP | | | |

OLD AND NEW DREAMS

BLACK SAINT
| ❑ 120113 | A Tribute to Blackwell | 1990 | 18.00 |
| ❑ BSR-0013 | Old and New Dreams | 198? | 18.00 |
ECM
❑ ECM1-1154	Old and New Dreams	1979	18.00
—Distributed by Warner Bros.			
❑ ECM1-1205	Playing	1981	18.00
—Distributed by Warner Bros.			

OLDFIELD, MIKE

VIRGIN
❑ VR13143 [B]	Airborn	1980	30.00
—U.S.-only compilation, which may make it much more valuable overseas			
❑ 91270	Earth Moving	1990	15.00
❑ VR 13-109	Hergest Ridge	1974	15.00
—First issue of this album			
❑ VR 13-109 [DJ]	Hergest Ridge	1974	25.00
—Promo only; banded for airplay			
❑ 90590	Hergest Ridge	1987	10.00
—Reissue of Virgin International 2013			
❑ 90645	Islands	1988	12.00
❑ PZ33913	Ommadawn	1975	15.00
—Original U.S. issue of this album			
❑ PZ33913 [DJ]	Ommadawn	1975	25.00
—Promo only; banded for airplay			
❑ PZQ33913 [Q]	Ommadawn	1975	60.00
❑ 90591	The Killing Fields	1987	12.00
❑ 90894	The Orchestral Tubular Bells	1989	12.00
—Reissue of 13-115			
❑ VR 13-115	The Orchestral Tubular Bells	1975	15.00
❑ VR 13-105	Tubular Bells	1973	18.00
—First stereo issue of this album			
❑ QD 13-105 [Q]	Tubular Bells	1974	75.00
❑ VR13135	Tubular Bells	1979	12.00
—Third stereo issue of this album			
❑ PZ34116	Tubular Bells	1976	15.00
—Second stereo issue of this album (note the "PZ" prefix)			
❑ 90589	Tubular Bells	1987	10.00
—Fifth stereo issue of this album			
VIRGIN/EPIC
❑ ARE37983	Five Miles Out	1982	12.00
❑ FE37358	QE2	1981	12.00
❑ PE34116	Tubular Bells	1982	10.00
—Fourth stereo issue of this album (note the "PE" prefix)			
❑ HE44116	Tubular Bells	1982	30.00
—Half-speed mastered edition			
VIRGIN INTERNATIONAL
❑ VI-2013	Hergest Ridge	1979	12.00
—Reissue of 13-109; not to be confused with UK pressings that have only a "V" prefix			

Number	Title	Yr	NM
❑ VI-2043	Ommadawn	1979	12.00
—Reissue of 33913; not to be confused with UK pressings that have only a "V" prefix			

OLDHAM, ANDREW

LONDON
| ❑ LL3457 [M] | The Rolling Stones Songbook | 1965 | 100.00 |
| ❑ PS457 [S] | The Rolling Stones Songbook | 1965 | 150.00 |
PARROT
| ❑ PA61003 [M] | East Meets West | 1965 | 200.00 |
| ❑ PAS71003 [S] | East Meets West | 1965 | 250.00 |

OLDHAM, DOUG

IMPACT
| ❑ R3193 | Christmas with Doug Oldham | 1972 | 15.00 |

OLENN, JOHNNY

LIBERTY
| ❑ LRP-3029 [M] | Just Rollin' with Johnny Olenn | 1956 | 300.00 |

O'LENO, LARRY

PAINTED SMILES
| ❑ 1348 | Larry O'Leno Sings Billy Strayhorn | 198? | 15.00 |

OLIPHANT, GRASELLA

ATLANTIC
| ❑ 1438 [M] | The Grass Roots | 1965 | 18.00 |
| ❑ SD-1438 [S] | The Grass Roots | 1965 | 25.00 |

OLIVA, TONY

KUBANY
| ❑ SD-600 | My Favorite Music | 1966 | 30.00 |

OLIVER, DAVID

MERCURY
❑ SRM-1-1183	David Oliver	1978	12.00
❑ SRM-1-3831	Here's to You	1980	12.00
❑ SRM-1-3747	Mind Magic	1979	12.00
❑ SRM-1-3784	Rain Fire	1979	12.00

OLIVER, JIMMY

SUE
| ❑ LP-1041 [M] | Hits A-Go-Go | 1966 | 25.00 |
| ❑ STLP-1041 [S] | Hits A-Go-Go | 1966 | 30.00 |

OLIVER, KING

BRUNSWICK
| ❑ BL58020 [10] | King Oliver | 1950 | 120.00 |
DECCA
| ❑ DL79246 | Papa Joe | 1969 | 18.00 |
EPIC
❑ LA16003 [M]	King Oliver and His Orchestra	1960	30.00
❑ BA17003 [R]	King Oliver and His Orchestra	1960	25.00
❑ LN3208 [M]	King Oliver Featuring Louis Armstrong	1956	50.00
HERWIN
❑ 106	Zulus Ball/Working Man Blues	197?	15.00
LONDON
❑ AL3510 [10]	King Oliver Plays the Blues	195?	80.00
MCA
❑ 1309	Papa Joe	198?	12.00
MILESTONE
❑ M-2006	The Immortal King Oliver	197?	18.00
RCA VICTOR
❑ LPV-529 [M]	King Oliver In New York	1965	30.00
RIVERSIDE
❑ RLP-1007 [10]	King Oliver Plays the Blues	1953	80.00
X
❑ LVA-3018 [10]	King Oliver's Uptown Jazz	1954	100.00

OLIVER, SY

MOBILE FIDELITY
| ❑ 1-242 | Oliver's Twist/Easy Walkin' | 1996 | 30.00 |
| —Audiophile vinyl | | | |

OLIVER

CREWE
| ❑ CR-1333 | Good Morning Starshine | 1969 | 18.00 |
| ❑ CR-1344 | Oliver Again | 1970 | 18.00 |
UNITED ARTISTS
| ❑ UAS-5511 | Prisms | 1971 | 18.00 |

OLIVER AND THE TWISTERS

COLPIX
| ❑ CP-423 [M] | Look Who's Twistin' Everybody | 1961 | 40.00 |

Number	Title	Yr	NM
OLIVOR, JANE			
COLUMBIA			
❑ PC34917	Chasing Rainbows	1977	12.00
—Original issue with no bar code			
❑ PC34274	First Night	1977	12.00
—Original issue with no bar code			
❑ FC37938	In Concert	1982	10.00
❑ JC35437	Stay the Night	1978	10.00
❑ JC36335	The Best Side of Goodbye	1980	10.00

OLLIE AND THE NIGHTINGALES

STAX
| ❑ STS-2021 | Ollie and the Nightingales | 1969 | 50.00 |

OLSEN, DOROTHY

RCA VICTOR
| ❑ LPM-1606 [M] | I Know Where I'm Going | 1957 | 30.00 |

OLSEN, GEORGE

RCA VICTOR
| ❑ LPV-549 [M] | George Olsen and His Music | 1968 | 25.00 |

OLSHER, LESLEY

VITAL
| ❑ VTL-011 | Lesley | 1993 | 25.00 |

OLSSON, NIGEL

BANG
| ❑ JZ36491 | Changing Tides | 1980 | 12.00 |
| ❑ JZ35792 | Nigel | 1979 | 12.00 |
ROCKET
❑ L33-1962 [DJ]	Drummers Can Sing Too!	1975	25.00
—Promo-only interview album			
❑ PIG-2158	Nigel Olsson	1975	15.00
UNI
❑ 73113	Nigel Olsson's Drum Orchestra	1971	18.00

OLYMPIA BRASS BAND OF NEW ORLEANS

AUDIOPHILE
| ❑ AP-108 | Olympia Brass Band of New Orleans | 197? | 15.00 |
BASF
| ❑ 20678 | New Orleans Street Parade | 197? | 15.00 |
BIOGRAPH
| ❑ VPS-4 | Here Come Da Great Olympia Jazz Band | 197? | 15.00 |

OLYMPIC RUNNERS

LONDON
❑ PS668	Don't Let Up	1975	18.00
❑ PS678	Hot to Trot	1977	18.00
❑ PS658	Out in Front	1975	18.00
❑ PS653	Put the Music Where Your Mouth Is	1974	18.00
POLYDOR
❑ PD-1-6196	Dancealot	1979	15.00

OLYMPICS, THE

ARVEE
❑ A-424 [M]	Dance by the Light of the Moon	1961	120.00
❑ A-423 [M]	Doin' the Hully Gully	1960	160.00
❑ A-429 [M]	Party Time	1961	120.00
EVEREST
❑ 4109	The Olympics	1981	12.00
MIRWOOD
❑ MW-7003 [M]	Something Old, Something New	1966	40.00
❑ MS-7003 [S]	Something Old, Something New	1966	50.00
POST
❑ 8000	The Olympics Sing	196?	30.00
RHINO
❑ RNDF-207	The Official Record Album of the Olympics	1983	15.00
TRI-DISC
❑ 1001 [M]	Do the Bounce	1963	80.00

O'MALLEY, LENORE

POLYDOR
| ❑ PD-1-6253 | First Be a Woman | 1980 | 18.00 |
| ❑ PD-1-6321 | Lenore | 1981 | 18.00 |

OMAR AND THE HOWLERS

AMAZING
| ❑ AM1003 | Big Leg Beat | 1980 | 30.00 |
AUSTIN
| ❑ 8401 | I Told You So | 1984 | 15.00 |
COLUMBIA
| ❑ BFC40815 | Hard Times in the Land of Plenty | 1987 | 12.00 |
| ❑ FC44102 | Wall of Pride | 1988 | 12.00 |

Number	Title	Yr	NM
OMNIBUS			
UNITED ARTISTS			
❏ UAS-6743	Omnibus	1970	40.00
ONE			
VILLAGE			
❏ (# unknown)0	Creation Earth	1977	50.00
— Includes posters			
ONE 2 MANY			
A&M			
❏ SP-5237	Mirror	1988	10.00
ONE CAUSE ONE EFFECT			
CAPITOL			
❏ C1-94847	Drop the Axxe	1991	18.00
101 STRINGS			
ALSHIRE			
❏ S-7100	The Glory of Christmas	1966	15.00
❏ XM-4	The Glory of Christmas	197?	10.00
— Reissue of 7100			
100 PROOF AGED IN SOUL			
HOT WAX			
❏ 712	100 Proof Aged in Soul	1971	18.00
❏ 704	Somebody's Been Sleeping in My Bed	1970	18.00
100 VOICES OF CHRISTMAS, THE			
DESIGN			
❏ SDLP-X-15 [S]	Silent Night	196?	18.00
— Same as above, but in stereo			
❏ DLP-X-15 [M]	Silent Night	196?	15.00
101 NORTH			
CAPITOL			
❏ C1-90911	101 North	1988	12.00
— Reissue of Valley Vue 72945			
❏ C1-92510	Forever Yours	1991	18.00
VALLEY VUE			
❏ D1-72945	101 North	1988	18.00
ONE TO ONE			
WARNER BROS.			
❏ 25090	Forward Your Emotions	1986	15.00
112			
BAD BOY			
❏ 73039 [B]	Part III	2000	15.00
❏ 73021 [B]	Room 112	1998	18.00
ONE WAY			
CAPITOL			
❏ C1-48990	New Beginning	1988	15.00
— As "Al Hudson and One Way"			
MCA			
❏ 5247	Fancy Dancer	1981	12.00
❏ 5470	Lady	1984	12.00
❏ 5163	Love Is ... One Way	1981	12.00
❏ 5127	One Way Featuring Al Hudson	1980	12.00
— Not the same album as 3178			
❏ 3178	One Way Featuring Al Hudson	1979	12.00
❏ 5823	One Way IX	1986	12.00
❏ 5428	Shine on Me	1983	12.00
❏ 5279	Who's Foolin' Who	1982	12.00
❏ 5369	Wild Night	1982	12.00
❏ 5552	Wrap Your Body	1985	12.00
O'NEAL, ALEXANDER			
TABU			
❏ FZ39331	Alexander O'Neal	1985	10.00
❏ OZ44492	All Mixed Up	1989	12.00
❏ Z45349	All True Man	1991	18.00
❏ FZ40320	Hearsay	1987	10.00
❏ OZ45016	My Gift to You	1988	12.00
O'NEAL, JOHNNY			
CONCORD JAZZ			
❏ CJ-228	Coming Out	198?	12.00
O'NEAL, SHAQUILLE			
JIVE			
❏ 41520	Shaq Diesel	1993	18.00
— Issued in generic cover			
❏ 41550	Shaq-Fu: Da Return	1994	15.00
T.W.ISM.			
❏ INT2-90087	You Can't Stop the Reign	1996	18.00
❏ 6064 [EP]	You Can't Stop the Reign	1996	10.00
— Promo only four-track sampler			

Number	Title	Yr	NM
ONENESS OF JUJU			
BLACK FIRE			
❏ (# unknown)0 [B]	African Rhythms	1975	60.00
❏ (# unknown)0	Space Jungle Luv	1976	60.00
STRATA-EAST			
❏ SES-19735	A Message from Mozambique	1973	100.00
— As "Juju			
❏ SES-7420	Chapter 2: Nia	1974	100.00
— As "Juju			
ONO, YOKO			
APPLE			
❏ SVBB-3399 [B]	Approximately Infinite Universe	1973	50.00
❏ SW-3412 [B]	Feeling the Space	1973	35.00
❏ SVBB-3380 [B]	Fly	1971	50.00
❏ SW-3373 [B]	Yoko Ono Plastic Ono Band	1970	30.00
CAPITOL			
❏ SPRO-11219 [DJ]	Rising Mixes	1996	30.00
— Promo-only vinyl EP of six remixes from the CD "Rising			
GEFFEN			
❏ GHS2004	Season of Glass	1981	15.00
POLYDOR			
❏ PD-1-6364	It's Alright (I See Rainbows)	1982	12.00
❏ 823289-1	It's Alright (I See Rainbows)	1984	10.00
— Reissue			
❏ 827530-1 [B]	Starpeace	1985	15.00
ONYX			
DEF JAM			
❏ 536988-1	Shut 'Em Down	1998	18.00
❏ 230 [DJ]	Shut 'Em Down	1998	25.00
— Promo-only version in generic cover			
JMJ/RAL			
❏ 529265-1	All We Got Iz Us	1995	15.00
OPA			
MILESTONE			
❏ M-9069	Goldenwings	1976	15.00
❏ M-9078	Magic Time	1977	15.00
OPAFIRE			
NOVUS			
❏ 3084-1-N	Opafire Featuring Norman Engelnitner	1990	15.00
OPEN SKY			
PM			
❏ PMR-001	Open Sky	1974	18.00
❏ PMR-003	Spirit in the Sky	1975	18.00
OPHELIA RAGTIME ORCHESTRA			
STOMP OFF			
❏ SOS-1108	Echoes from the Snowball Club	1986	12.00
OPUS			
POLYDOR			
❏ 827953-1	Up and Down	1985	12.00
OPUS SEVEN			
SOURCE			
❏ 27000	Thoughts	1979	18.00
ORANG UTAN			
BELL			
❏ 6054	Orang Utan	1971	40.00
ORANGE COLORED SKY			
UNI			
❏ 73031	Orange Colored Sky	1968	50.00
ORANGE THEN BLUE			
GM RECORDINGS			
❏ GM-3006	Music for Jazz Orchestra	1987	12.00
ORANGE WEDGE			
(NO LABEL)			
❏ (no #)0	No One Left But Me	1975	300.00
❏ (no #)0	Wedge	1975	300.00
ORBACH, JERRY			
MGM			
❏ E-4056 [M]	Jerry Orbach Off Broadway	1963	25.00
❏ SE-4056 [S]	Jerry Orbach Off Broadway	1963	30.00
ORBISON, ROY			
ACCORD			
❏ SN-7150	Ooby Dooby	1981	10.00

Number	Title	Yr	NM
ASYLUM			
❏ 6E-198	Laminar Flow	1979	15.00
BUCKBOARD			
❏ BBS-1015	Roy Orbison's Golden Hits	197?	12.00
CANDELITE			
❏ P212946	The Living Legend of Roy Orbison	1976	18.00
DCC COMPACT CLASSICS			
❏ LPZ-2042	The All-Time Greatest Hits of Roy Orbison	1997	120.00
— Audiophile vinyl			
DESIGN			
❏ DLP-164 [M]	Orbiting with Roy Orbison	196?	18.00
❏ DLPS-164 [R]	Orbiting with Roy Orbison	196?	12.00
HALLMARK			
❏ SHM-824	The Exciting Roy Orbison	197?	10.00
HITS UNLIMITED			
❏ 233-0	My Spell on You	1982	10.00
MERCURY			
❏ SRM-1-1045	I'm Still in Love with You	1975	15.00
MGM			
❏ E-4514 [M]	Cry Softly, Lonely One	1967	30.00
❏ SE-4514 [S]	Cry Softly, Lonely One	1967	35.00
❏ SE-4683	Hank Williams the Roy Orbison Way	1970	30.00
❏ SE-4867	Memphis	1972	18.00
❏ SE-4934	Milestones	1973	18.00
❏ SE-4835	Roy Orbison Sings	1972	18.00
❏ E-4424 [M]	Roy Orbison Sings Don Gibson	1967	30.00
❏ SE-4424 [S]	Roy Orbison Sings Don Gibson	1967	35.00
❏ T-91173 [M]	Roy Orbison Sings Don Gibson	1967	35.00
— Capitol Record Club edition			
❏ ST-91173 [S]	Roy Orbison Sings Don Gibson	1967	35.00
— Capitol Record Club edition			
❏ E-4379 [M]	The Classic Roy Orbison	1966	30.00
❏ SE-4379 [S]	The Classic Roy Orbison	1966	35.00
❏ T-90928 [M]	The Classic Roy Orbison	1966	35.00
— Capitol Record Club edition			
❏ ST-90928 [S]	The Classic Roy Orbison	1966	35.00
— Capitol Record Club edition			
❏ SE-4659	The Great Songs of Roy Orbison	1970	30.00
❏ SE-4636	The Many Moods of Roy Orbison	1969	30.00
❏ E-4322 [M]	The Orbison Way	1965	30.00
❏ SE-4322 [S]	The Orbison Way	1965	35.00
❏ T-90631 [M]	The Orbison Way	1965	35.00
— Capitol Record Club edition			
❏ ST-90631 [S]	The Orbison Way	1965	35.00
— Capitol Record Club edition			
❏ E-4308 [M]	There Is Only One Roy Orbison	1965	30.00
❏ SE-4308 [S]	There Is Only One Roy Orbison	1965	35.00
❏ T-90454 [M]	There Is Only One Roy Orbison	1965	40.00
— Capitol Record Club edition			
❏ ST-90454 [S]	There Is Only One Roy Orbison	1965	40.00
— Capitol Record Club edition			
MONUMENT			
❏ M-4007 [M]	Crying	1962	120.00
❏ SM-14007 [S]	Crying	1962	600.00
❏ MLP-8023 [M]	Early Orbison	1964	30.00
❏ SLP-18023 [S]	Early Orbison	1964	50.00
❏ MLP-8003 [M]	In Dreams	1963	50.00
— White and rainbow label			
❏ MLP-8003 [M]	In Dreams	1964	30.00
— Green and gold label			
❏ SLP-18003 [S]	In Dreams	1963	100.00
— White and rainbow label			
❏ SLP-18003 [S]	In Dreams	1964	50.00
— Green and gold label			
❏ MC-6620	In Dreams	1977	15.00

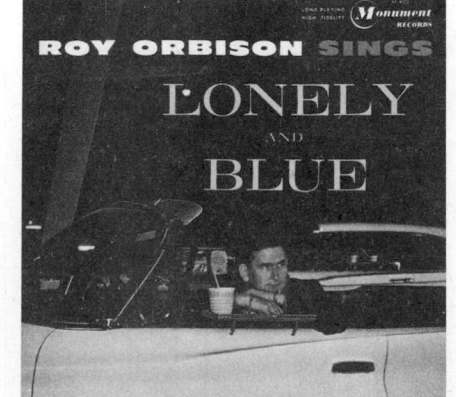

Number	Title	Yr	NM
❏ M-4002 [M]	Lonely and Blue	1961	150.00
❏ SM-14002 [S]	Lonely and Blue	1961	600.00
❏ MLP-8024 [M]	More of Roy Orbison's Greatest Hits	1964	30.00
❏ SLP-18024 [S]	More of Roy Orbison's Greatest Hits	1964	40.00
❏ MC-6621	More of Roy Orbison's Greatest Hits	1977	15.00
❏ MLP-8035 [M]	Orbisongs	1965	30.00
❏ SLP-18035 [S]	Orbisongs	1965	35.00
❏ MG-7600	Regeneration	1976	18.00
❏ M-4009 [M]	Roy Orbison's Greatest Hits	1962	50.00
❏ MLP-8000 [M]	Roy Orbison's Greatest Hits	1963	30.00
❏ SM-14009 [S]	Roy Orbison's Greatest Hits	1962	80.00
❏ SLP-18000 [S]	Roy Orbison's Greatest Hits	1963	40.00
❏ MC-6619	Roy Orbison's Greatest Hits	1977	15.00
❏ KZG31484	The All-Time Greatest Hits of Roy Orbison	1972	30.00
❏ MP-8600	The All-Time Greatest Hits of Roy Orbison	1977	16.00
❏ KWG38384	The All-Time Greatest Hits of Roy Orbison	1982	12.00
❏ MLP-8045 [M]	The Very Best of Roy Orbison	1966	30.00
❏ SLP-18045 [P]	The Very Best of Roy Orbison	1966	35.00
—"It's Over" is rechanneled			
❏ MC-6622	The Very Best of Roy Orbison	1977	15.00
RHINO			
❏ R171493	For the Lonely: A Roy Orbison Anthology	1988	15.00
❏ R170711	The Classic Roy Orbison	1989	15.00
❏ R170916	The Sun Years	1989	18.00
S&P			
❏ 507	The All-Time Greatest Hits of Roy Orbison	2004	40.00
—Reissue on 180-gram vinyl			
SUN			
❏ LP-1260 [M]	Roy Orbison at the Rock House	1961	600.00
❏ 113	The Original Sound	1969	15.00
TIME-LIFE			
❏ SRNR34	Roy Orbison 1960-1965	1990	25.00
—Box set in "The Rock 'n' Roll Era" series			
TRIP			
❏ TLX-8505	The Best of Roy Orbison	197?	10.00
VIRGIN			
❏ 91295	A Black and White Night	1990	18.00
❏ 90604	In Dreams: The Greatest Hits	1987	15.00
—Re-recordings of his original hits			
❏ 91058	Mystery Girl	1989	12.00

ORCHESTRA OF THE EIGHTH DAY

Number	Title	Yr	NM
FLYING FISH			
❏ FF-292	Music for the End	1982	18.00

ORCHESTRA U.S.A.

Number	Title	Yr	NM
COLPIX			
❏ CP-448 [M]	Orchestra U.S.A. Debut	1964	40.00
❏ SCP-448 [S]	Orchestra U.S.A. Debut	1964	50.00
COLUMBIA			
❏ CL2247 [M]	Jazz Journey	1963	30.00
❏ CS9047 [S]	Jazz Journey	1963	30.00
RCA VICTOR			
❏ LPM-3498 [M]	The Sextet Of Orchestra U.S.A.	1965	25.00
❏ LSP-3498 [S]	The Sextet Of Orchestra U.S.A.	1965	30.00

ORCHESTRAL MANOEUVRES IN THE DARK

Number	Title	Yr	NM
A&M			
❏ SP-5077	Crush	1985	10.00
❏ SP6-5027	Junk Culture	1984	10.00
❏ R184156	The Best of O.M.D.	1988	15.00
—BMG Direct Marketing edition			
❏ SP-5186	The Best of O.M.D.	1988	12.00
❏ R114546	The Pacific Age	1986	15.00
—RCA Music Service edition			
❏ SP-5144	The Pacific Age	1986	12.00
VIRGIN			
❏ 91006	Dazzle Ships	1988	12.00
—Reissue			
❏ 90611	Orchestral Manoeuvres in the Dark	1987	12.00
—Reissue			
❏ 90612	Organisation	1987	12.00
—First U.S. issue of early LP			
VIRGIN/EPIC			
❏ ARE37721	Architecture and Morality	1981	18.00
❏ FE37411	Orchestral Manoeuvres in the Dark	1981	18.00
VIRGIN/EPIC			
❏ BFE38543	Dazzle Ships	1983	15.00

ORCHIDS, THE (U)

Number	Title	Yr	NM
ROULETTE			
❏ R-25169 [M]	Twistin' at the Roundtable	1962	40.00
❏ SR-25169 [S]	Twistin' at the Roundtable	1962	35.00

OREGON

Number	Title	Yr	NM
ECM			
❏ 25025	Crossing	1985	12.00
❏ 23796	Oregon	1983	12.00
ELEKTRA			
❏ AB-304	In Performance	1979	18.00
❏ 6E-154	Out of the Woods	1978	12.00
❏ 6E-224	Roots in the Sky	1979	12.00
MOBILE FIDELITY			
❏ 1-514	Distant Hills	198?	70.00
—Audiophile vinyl			
PORTRAIT			
❏ OR44465	45th Parallel	1989	15.00
TERRA			
❏ T-1	Music of Another Present Era	1985	12.00
VANGUARD			
❏ VSD-79341	Distant Hills	1973	15.00
❏ VSQ-40031 [Q]	Distant Hills	1974	30.00
❏ VSD-79370	Friends	1976	15.00
❏ VSD-79358	In Concert	1975	15.00
❏ VSD-79419	Moon and Mind	1979	15.00
❏ VSD-79326	Music of Another Present Era	197?	15.00
❏ VSD-79432	Our First Record	1980	15.00
❏ VSD-109/10	The Essential Oregon	198?	18.00
❏ VSD-79397	Violin	1978	15.00
❏ VSD-79350	Winter Light	1974	15.00

OREGON AND ELVIN JONES

Number	Title	Yr	NM
VANGUARD			
❏ VSD-79377	Together	1977	15.00

ORGAN GRINDERS, THE

Number	Title	Yr	NM
MERCURY			
❏ SR-61282	Out of the Egg	1970	30.00

ORGANIZED KONFUSION

Number	Title	Yr	NM
HOLLYWOOD			
❏ HB-61406	Stress: The Extinction Agenda	1994	30.00
—Vinyl may be promo only			
PRIORITY			
❏ 50560	The Equinox	1997	15.00

ORIENT EXPRESS, THE

Number	Title	Yr	NM
MAINSTREAN			
❏ S-6117	The Orient Express	1969	80.00

ORIGINAL CAMELLIA JAZZ BAND

Number	Title	Yr	NM
NEW ORLEANS			
❏ 7207	Original Camellia Jazz Band	198?	12.00

ORIGINAL CASTE, THE

Number	Title	Yr	NM
T-A			
❏ 5003	One Tin Soldier	1970	18.00

ORIGINAL DIXIELAND JAZZ BAND, THE

Number	Title	Yr	NM
GHB			
❏ GHB-100	Original Dixieland Jazz Band 1943	198?	12.00
RCA VICTOR			
❏ LPV-547 [M]	The Original Dixieland Jazz Band	1968	25.00
X			
❏ LX-3007 [M]	The Original Dixieland Jazz Band	1954	50.00

ORIGINAL MEMPHIS FIVE, THE

Number	Title	Yr	NM
FOLKWAYS			
❏ RBF-26	The Original Memphis Five	197?	18.00

ORIGINAL SALTY DOGS, THE

Number	Title	Yr	NM
BLACKBIRD			
❏ 12003	Traditional Classics	1967	18.00
GHB			
❏ 58	Free Wheeling	1968	18.00
❏ 44	The Original Salty Dogs	1967	18.00
❏ 62	The Right Track	197?	15.00
STOMP OFF			
❏ SOS-1115	Honky Tonk Town	1987	12.00

ORIGINAL TWISTERS, THE

Number	Title	Yr	NM
WING			
❏ MGW-12217 [M]	Come On and Twist	1962	25.00
❏ SRW-16217 [S]	Come On and Twist	1962	30.00

ORIGINAL WASHBOARD BAND, THE

Number	Title	Yr	NM
RCA VICTOR			
❏ LSP-1958 [S]	Scrubbin' and Pickin'	1959	30.00
❏ LPM-1958 [M]	Scrubbin' and Pickin'	1959	25.00

ORIGINALS, THE (1)

Number	Title	Yr	NM
FANTASY			
❏ F-9546	Another Time, Another Place	1978	12.00
❏ F-9577	Come Away with Me	1979	12.00
MOTOWN			
❏ M7-826	California Sunset	1975	18.00
❏ M5-110V	Motown Superstar Series, Vol. 10	1982	12.00
PHASE II			
❏ JW37075	Yesterday and Today	1981	15.00
SOUL			
❏ SS-716	Baby I'm for Real	1969	40.00
❏ S7-746	Communique	1976	18.00
❏ SS-734	Definitions	1971	25.00
❏ S7-749	Down to Love Town	1977	18.00
❏ SS-729	Naturally Together	1971	30.00
❏ SS-724	Portrait of the Originals	1970	30.00
❏ SS-740	The Game Called…	1973	18.00

ORIGINOO GUNN CLAPPAZ

Number	Title	Yr	NM
PRIORITY			
❏ 50577	Da Storm	1996	18.00

ORIOLES, THE

Number	Title	Yr	NM
BIG A			
❏ LP-2001	The Orioles' Greatest All-Time Hits	1969	30.00
CHARLIE PARKER			
❏ PLP-816 [M]	Modern Sounds of the Orioles	1962	80.00
❏ PLP-816S [S]	Modern Sounds of the Orioles	1962	100.00
COLLECTABLES			
❏ COL-5014	Sonny Til and the Orioles' Greatest Hits	198?	15.00
MURRAY HILL			
❏ M61234	For Collectors Only	1983	40.00

ORION, P.J., AND THE MAGNATES

Number	Title	Yr	NM
MAGNATE			
❏ 122459	P.J. Orion and the Magnates	196?	150.00

ORION

Number	Title	Yr	NM
SUN			
❏ 1028 [B]	Fresh	1983	12.00
❏ 1025	Glory	1982	12.00
❏ 1019	Orion Country	1980	12.00
❏ 1012	Orion Reborn	1978	30.00
—White cover, also known as the "coffin cover"			
❏ 1012	Orion Reborn	1978	12.00
—Blue cover			
❏ 1021	Rockabilly	1981	12.00
❏ 1017	Sunrise	1979	12.00

ORION THE HUNTER

Number	Title	Yr	NM
PORTRAIT			
❏ BFR39239	Orion the Hunter	1984	18.00

ORLANDO, JAY

Number	Title	Yr	NM
DOBRE			
❏ 1040	Jay Orlando Loves Earl Bostic	197?	15.00

ORLANDO, TONY

Number	Title	Yr	NM
CASABLANCA			
❏ NBLP7153	I Got Rhythm	1979	12.00
❏ NBLP7209	Living for the Music	1980	12.00
EPIC			
❏ BG33785	Before Dawn	1975	18.00
❏ BN611 [S]	Bless You and 11 Other Great Hits	1961	40.00
❏ LN3808 [M]	Bless You and 11 Other Great Hits	1961	30.00

ORLEANS

Number	Title	Yr	NM
ABC			
❏ AA-1058-2	Before the Dance	1977	15.00
❏ ABCX-795	Orleans	1973	18.00
❏ AC-30011	The ABC Collection	1976	12.00
ASYLUM			
❏ 7E-1029	Let There Be Music	1975	12.00
❏ 7E-1070	Waking and Dreaming	1976	12.00
INFINITY			
❏ INF-9006	Forever	1979	12.00
MCA			
❏ 5767	Grown Up Children	1986	10.00
❏ 5110	Orleans	1980	12.00
RADIO			
❏ 90012	One of a Kind	1982	12.00

ORLONS, THE

Number	Title	Yr	NM
CAMEO			
❏ C1033 [M]	All the Hits by the Orlons	1962	60.00
❏ C1073 [M]	Down Memory Lane with the Orlons	1964	50.00
❏ C1054 [M]	Not Me	1963	50.00

Number	Title	Yr	NM
❑ C1041 [M]	South Street	1963	60.00
❑ C1061 [M]	The Orlons' Biggest Hits	1964	50.00
❑ C1020 [M]	The Wah-Watusi	1962	60.00

ORLONS, THE / THE DOVELLS

CAMEO
❑ C1067 [M]	Golden Hits of the Orlons and the Dovells	1964	50.00

ORNBERG, THOMAS

STOMP OFF
❑ SOS-1043	Come Back, Sweet Papa	198?	12.00

ORPHAN EGG

CAROLE
❑ CARS-8004	Orphan Egg	1968	40.00

ORPHANN

O.M.I.
❑ 70021	Up for Adoption	1977	100.00

ORPHEON CELESTA

STOMP OFF
❑ SOS-1083	Gare de Lyon	1985	12.00
❑ SOS-1095	Shim-Me-Sha-Wabble	1985	12.00

ORPHEUS

MGM
❑ SE-4569 [S]	Ascending	1968	25.00
❑ E-4569 [M]	Ascending	1968	60.00

— Known copies are yellow label promos with "DJ Monaural" sticker on stereo cover

❑ SE-4599	Joyful	1969	25.00
❑ E-4524 [M]	Orpheus	1968	60.00
❑ SE-4524 [S]	Orpheus	1968	18.00

ORR, BENJAMIN

ELEKTRA
❑ R152406	The Lace	1986	15.00

— RCA Music Service edition
❑ 60460	The Lace	1986	12.00

ORRALL, ROBERT ELLIS

RCA VICTOR
❑ AFL1-4853	Contain Yourself	1984	10.00
❑ AFL1-4081	Fixation	1981	10.00
❑ MFL1-8502 [EP]	Special Pain	1983	10.00

ORSTED PEDERSEN, NIELS-HENNING, AND KENNETH KNUDSEN

STEEPLECHASE
❑ SCS-1068	Pictures	198?	15.00

ORSTED PEDERSEN, NIELS-HENNING, AND SAM JONES

INNER CITY
❑ IC-2055	Double Bass	197?	18.00

STEEPLECHASE
❑ SCS-1055	Double Bass	198?	15.00

ORSTED PEDERSEN, NIELS-HENNING

INNER CITY
❑ IC-2041	Jaywalkin'	197?	18.00

STEEPLECHASE
❑ SCS-1125	Dancing on the Tables	1979	15.00
❑ SCS-1041	Jaywalkin'	198?	15.00
❑ SCS-1083	Trio 1	198?	15.00
❑ SCS-1093	Trio 2	198?	15.00

ORTEGA, ANTHONY

BETHLEHEM
❑ BCP-79 [M]	Jazz For Young Moderns	1957	50.00

DISCOVERY
❑ 788	Rain Dance	1978	15.00

HERALD
❑ HLP-0101 [M]	A Man and His Horn	1956	60.00

REVELATION
❑ REV-M3 [M]	New Dance	1968	40.00
❑ REV-3 [S]	New Dance	1968	25.00

VANTAGE
❑ VLP-2 [10]	Anthony Ortega	1954	120.00

ORTEGA, FRANKIE

DOBRE
❑ 1043	Smokin'	197?	15.00

IMPERIAL
❑ LP-9025 [M]	Piano Stylings	1956	30.00
❑ LP-12011 [S]	Piano Stylings	1959	25.00

JUBILEE
❑ JLP-1106 [M]	77 Sunset Strip	1959	30.00
❑ JGS-1106 [S]	77 Sunset Strip	1959	40.00
❑ JGM-1112 [M]	Frankie Ortega at the Embers	1960	25.00
❑ JGS-1112 [S]	Frankie Ortega at the Embers	1960	30.00

❑ JLP-1080 [M]	Swingin' Abroad	1958	25.00
❑ SDJLP-1080 [S]	Swingin' Abroad	1958	30.00
❑ JLP-1051 [M]	Twinkling Pinkies	1958	30.00

ORTEGA/DOMANICO/WEST/GOODWIN

REVELATION
❑ REV-7 [S]	Permutations	1969	30.00

ORY, KID

COLUMBIA
❑ CL6145 [10]	Kid Ory & His Creole Dixieland Band	1950	100.00
❑ CL835 [M]	Kid Ory	1955	50.00

DIXIELAND JUBILEE
❑ DJ-519	Kid Ory at the Dixieland Jubilee	198?	12.00

FOLKLYRIC
❑ 9008	Kid Ory's Creole Jazz Band	197?	12.00

GOOD TIME JAZZ
❑ L-12022 [M]	Kid Ory's Creole Jazz Band, 1944-45	1955	40.00
❑ L-21 [10]	Kid Ory's Creole Jazz Band, 1953	1954	50.00
❑ L-12004 [M]	Kid Ory's Creole Jazz Band, 1954	1954	40.00
❑ L-12008 [M]	Kid Ory's Creole Jazz Band, 1955	1955	40.00
❑ L-12016 [M]	Kid Ory's Creole Jazz Band, 1956	1955	40.00
❑ L-12041/2 [M]	Kid Ory's Favorites!	1961	50.00
❑ S-10041/2 [S]	Kid Ory's Favorites!	1961	60.00
❑ M-12045 [M]	This Kid's the Greatest!	1962	30.00

STORYVILLE
❑ 4064	Kid Ory Plays the Blues	198?	12.00

VAULT
❑ 9006	Kid Ory Live!	196?	18.00

VERVE
❑ MGV-1022 [M]	Dance with Kid Ory or Just Listen	1957	50.00
❑ MGVS-6125 [S]	Dance with Kid Ory or Just Listen	1960	40.00
❑ V-1022 [M]	Dance with Kid Ory or Just Listen	1961	25.00
❑ V6-1022 [S]	Dance with Kid Ory or Just Listen	1961	18.00
❑ MGV-1026 [M]	Dixieland Marching Songs	1957	50.00
❑ V-1026 [M]	Dixieland Marching Songs	1961	25.00
❑ V6-1026 [S]	Dixieland Marching Songs	1961	18.00
❑ MGV 8254 [M]	Kid Ory In Europe	1958	50.00
❑ V-8254 [M]	Kid Ory In Europe	1961	25.00
❑ MGV-1017 [M]	Kid Ory Plays W.C. Handy	1957	50.00
❑ MGVS-6061 [S]	Kid Ory Plays W.C. Handy	1960	40.00
❑ V-1017 [M]	Kid Ory Plays W.C. Handy	1961	25.00
❑ V6-1017 [S]	Kid Ory Plays W.C. Handy	1961	18.00
❑ MGV-1014 [M]	Song of the Wanderer	1957	50.00
❑ MGVS-6011 [S]	Song of the Wanderer	1960	40.00
❑ V-1014 [M]	Song of the Wanderer	1961	25.00
❑ V6-1014 [S]	Song of the Wanderer	1961	18.00
❑ V-8456 [M]	Storyville Nights	1962	30.00
❑ V6-8456 [S]	Storyville Nights	1962	25.00
❑ MGV-1016 [M]	The Kid From New Orleans	1957	50.00
❑ V-1016 [M]	The Kid From New Orleans	1961	25.00
❑ MGV-1023 [M]	The Original Jazz	1957	50.00
❑ V-1023 [M]	The Original Jazz	1961	25.00
❑ V6-1023 [S]	The Original Jazz	1961	18.00

ORY, KID/JOHNNY WITTWER

JAZZ MAN
❑ LP-2 [10]	Kid Ory's Creole Band/ Johnny Wittwer Trio	1954	50.00

OSBORNE, JEFFREY

A&M
❑ SP-5017	Don't Stop	1984	10.00
❑ SP-5103	Emotional	1986	10.00
❑ SP-4896	Jeffrey Osborne	1982	10.00
❑ SP-5205	One Love -- One Dream	1988	10.00
❑ SP-4940	Stay with Me Tonight	1983	10.00

ARISTA
❑ AL8620	Only Human	1990	18.00

OSBORNE, JIMMIE

AUDIO LAB
❑ AL-1527 [M]	Singing Songs He Wrote	1959	100.00

KING
❑ 782 [M]	Golden Harvest	1963	50.00
❑ 941 [M]	Jimmie Osborne's Golden Harvest	1965	40.00
❑ 730 [M]	The Legendary Jimmy Osborne	1961	50.00
❑ 892 [M]	The Very Best of Jimmie Osborne	1964	40.00

OSBORNE, MARY

STASH
❑ ST-215	Now and Then	198?	12.00

WARWICK
❑ W-2004 [M]	A Girl and Her Guitar	1960	100.00
❑ W-2004ST [S]	A Girl and Her Guitar	1960	120.00

OSBORNE, WILL

AIRCHECK
❑ 37	Will Osborne and His Orchestra On the Air	198?	12.00

HINDSIGHT
❑ HSR-197	Will Osborne and His Orchestra 1936	198?	12.00

OSBORNE AND GILES

RED LABEL
❑ ST-73103	Stranger in the Night	1985	10.00

OSBORNE BROTHERS, THE

CMH
❑ 6206 [B]	#1	197?	12.00
❑ 9011	Bluegrass Collection	1978	18.00
❑ 6231	Bluegrass Concerto	197?	15.00
❑ 6256	Bobby and His Mandolin	1981	15.00
❑ 9008	From Rocky Top to Muddy Bottom	1977	18.00
❑ 4501	Greatest Bluegrass Hits, Vol. 1	198?	15.00
❑ 6244	Kentucky Calling Me	1980	15.00
❑ 9016	The Essential Bluegrass Album	1979	18.00

— With MacWiseman

DECCA
❑ DL75356	Bobby & Sonny	1972	18.00
❑ DL75321	Country Roads	1971	18.00
❑ DL75079	Favorite Hymns by the Osborne Brothers	1969	25.00
❑ DL4903 [M]	Modern Sounds of Bluegrass Music	1967	18.00
❑ DL74903 [S]	Modern Sounds of Bluegrass Music	1967	25.00
❑ DL75204	Ru-Beeeee	1970	25.00
❑ DL75271	The Osborne Brothers	1971	18.00
❑ DL4767 [M]	Up This Hill and Down	1966	18.00
❑ DL74767 [S]	Up This Hill and Down	1966	25.00
❑ DL75128	Up to Date and Down to Earth	1969	25.00
❑ DL4602 [M]	Voices in the Bluegrass	1965	18.00
❑ DL74602 [S]	Voices in the Bluegrass	1965	25.00
❑ DL4993 [M]	Yesterday, Today and The Osborne Brothers	1968	30.00
❑ DL74993 [S]	Yesterday, Today and The Osborne Brothers	1968	25.00

MCA
❑ 125	Favorite Hymns by the Osborne Brothers	1973	15.00

— Reissue of Decca 75079
❑ 135	Ru-Beeeee	1973	15.00

— Reissue of Decca 75204
❑ 4086	The Best of the Osborne Brothers	1974	18.00
❑ 105	Voices in the Bluegrass	1973	15.00

— Reissue of Decca 74602
❑ 119	Yesterday, Today and The Osborne Brothers	1973	15.00

— Reissue of Decca 74993

MGM
❑ E-4090 [M]	Bluegrass Instrumentals	1962	30.00
❑ SE-4090 [S]	Bluegrass Instrumentals	1962	30.00
❑ E-4018 [M]	Bluegrass Music	1962	30.00
❑ SE-4018 [S]	Bluegrass Music	1962	30.00
❑ E-3734 [M]	Country Pickin' and Hillside Singin'	1959	50.00
❑ E-4149 [M]	Cuttin' Grass	1963	30.00
❑ SE-4149 [S]	Cuttin' Grass	1963	30.00
❑ GAS140	The Osborne Brothers (Golden Archives Series)	1970	25.00

RCA VICTOR
❑ AHL1-4324	Bluegrass Spectacular	1982	12.00
❑ AYL1-5436	Bluegrass Spectacular	1985	10.00

— Best Buy Series" reissue

ROUNDER
❑ SS-04	The Osborne Brothers	198?	15.00
❑ SS-03	The Osborne Brothers with Red Allen	1981	15.00

SUGAR HILL
❑ SH-3754	Once More, Vol. 1	1986	12.00
❑ SH-3758	Once More, Vol. 2	1987	12.00
❑ SH-3764	Singing, Shouting Praises	1988	12.00
❑ SH-3740	Some Things I Want to Sing About	1984	12.00

OSBOURNE, OZZY

CBS ASSOCIATED
❑ FZ38987	Bark at the Moon	1983	12.00
❑ PZ38987	Bark at the Moon	1985	10.00

— Budget-line reissue with new prefix
❑ AS1828 [DJ]	Interview with Ozzy	1984	30.00
❑ Z46795	No More Tears	1991	25.00
❑ FZ44245	No Rest for the Wicked	1988	12.00
❑ ZX240714	Ozzy Osbourne/Randy Rhoads Tribute	1987	15.00
❑ 9Z940543 [EP]	The Ultimate Live Ozzy	1986	40.00

— Picture disc with live material
❑ FZ40026	The Ultimate Sin	1986	12.00

JET
❑ JZ36812	Blizzard of Ozz	1981	12.00

Number	Title	Yr	NM
❑ AS991372 [PD]	Diary of a Madman	1981	40.00
—Promo-only picture disc			
❑ FZ37492	Diary of a Madman	1981	12.00
❑ 8Z837640 [EP]	Mr. Crowley	1982	30.00
—Three-song picture disc with live material			
❑ ZX238350	Speak of the Devil	1982	18.00

O'SHEA, MILO

COLUMBIA

❑ CS9647	An Evening in Dublin	1969	25.00

OSIBISA

ANTILLES

❑ 7058	Ojah Awake	1978	12.00
❑ 7051	Welcome Home	1978	12.00

BUDDAH

❑ BDS-5136	Super Fly T.N.T.	1973	30.00

DECCA

❑ DL75368	Heads	1972	18.00
❑ DL75285	Osibisa	1971	18.00
❑ DL75327	Woyaya	1972	18.00

ISLAND

❑ ILPS9411	Ojah Awake	1977	12.00
❑ ILPS9355	Welcome Home	1976	12.00

MCA

❑ 32	Osibisa	1973	12.00
—Reissue of Decca 75285			
❑ 43	Woyaya	1973	12.00
—Reissue of Decca 75327			

WARNER BROS.

❑ BS2732	Happy Children	1973	12.00
❑ BS2802	Osibirock	1974	12.00

OSIRIS

MARLIN

❑ 2234	O-Zone	1979	25.00

WARNER BROS.

❑ BSK3311	Since Before Our Time	1978	25.00

OSKAR, LEE

ELEKTRA

❑ 6E-150	Before the Rain	1978	12.00
❑ 5E-526	My Road, Our Road	1981	12.00

UNITED ARTISTS

❑ UA-LA594-G	Lee Oskar	1976	12.00

OSLIN, K.T.

RCA

❑ 5924-1-R	80's Ladies	1987	12.00
❑ 8369-1-R	This Woman	1988	12.00

OSMOND, DONNY

CAPITOL

❑ C1-92354	Donny Osmond	1989	15.00
❑ C1-94051	Eyes Don't Lie	1990	18.00

MGM

❑ SE-4886	Alone Together	1973	30.00
—With tear-off 10x10 photo intact; deduct 60 percent if missing			
❑ M3G-4930	A Time for Us	1973	12.00
❑ M3G-4978	Donny	1974	12.00
❑ SE-4872	My Best to You	1972	12.00
❑ SE-4820	Portrait of Donny	1972	12.00
❑ SE-4782	The Donny Osmond Album	1971	15.00
❑ SE-4854	Too Young	1972	12.00
❑ SE-4797	To You with Love, Donny	1971	12.00

POLYDOR

❑ PD-1-6067	Disco Train	1976	10.00
❑ PD-1-6109	Donald Clark Osmond	1977	10.00

OSMOND, DONNY AND MARIE

MGM

❑ M3G-4968	I'm Leaving It All Up to You	1974	12.00
❑ M3G-4996	Make the World Go Away	1975	12.00

POLYDOR

❑ PD-1-6068	Donny & Marie -- Featuring Songs from Their Television Show	1976	10.00
❑ PD-1-6083	Donny & Marie -- New Season	1976	10.00
❑ PD-1-6169	Goin' Coconuts	1978	10.00
❑ PD-1-6127	Winning Combination	1978	10.00

OSMOND, JIMMY

MGM

❑ SE-4855	Killer Joe	1972	12.00
❑ M3G-4916	Little Arrows	1975	15.00

OSMOND, MARIE

CAPITOL

❑ C1-48968	All in Love	1988	10.00
❑ ST-12516	I Only Wanted You	1986	10.00
❑ C1-91781	Steppin' Stone	1989	12.00
❑ ST-12414	There's No Stopping Your Heart	1985	10.00

Number	Title	Yr	NM
MGM			
❑ M3G-4944	In My Little Corner of the World	1974	15.00
❑ SE-4910	Paper Roses	1973	15.00
❑ M3G-4979	Who's Sorry Now	1975	15.00
POLYDOR			
❑ PD-1-6099	This Is the Way That I Feel	1977	10.00

OSMONDS, THE

ELEKTRA

❑ 60180	The Osmond Brothers	1982	12.00

MERCURY

❑ SRM-1-3766	Steppin' Out	1979	12.00

METRO

❑ M543 [M]	We Sing You a Merry Christmas	1965	18.00
—Reissue of 4187 with one track missing and remaining contents rearranged			
❑ MS543 [S]	We Sing You a Merry Christmas	1965	25.00

MGM

❑ MG-2-5012	Around the World -- Live in Concert	1975	15.00
❑ SE-4851	Crazy Horses	1972	15.00
❑ SE-4770	Homemade	1971	30.00
—With tear-off poster intact; deduct 60 percent if poster is not attached			
❑ M3G-4939	Love Me for a Reason	1974	12.00
❑ SE-4724	Osmonds	1971	15.00
❑ SE-4796	Phase-III	1972	15.00
❑ E-4146 [M]	Songs We Sang on the Andy Williams Show	1963	30.00
❑ SE-4146 [S]	Songs We Sang on the Andy Williams Show	1963	30.00
—As "The Osmond Brothers"			
❑ E-4291 [M]	The New Sound of the Osmond Brothers	1965	25.00
❑ SE-4291 [S]	The New Sound of the Osmond Brothers	1965	30.00
❑ T90403 [M]	The New Sound of the Osmond Brothers	1965	40.00
—Capitol Record Club edition			
❑ ST90403 [S]	The New Sound of the Osmond Brothers	1965	40.00
—Capitol Record Club edition			
❑ E-4235 [M]	The Osmond Brothers Sing the All-Time Hymn Favorites	1964	25.00
❑ SE-4235 [S]	The Osmond Brothers Sing the All-Time Hymn Favorites	1964	30.00
❑ SE-4826	The Osmonds "Live"	1972	18.00
❑ SE-4902	The Plan	1973	12.00
❑ M3G-4993	The Proud One	1975	12.00
❑ PM-7 [M]	The Travels of Jaimie McPheeters	1963	50.00
—Side 1: Dialogue from TV show; Side 2: Osmond Brothers tracks. AC Spark Plugs promo.			
❑ E-4187 [M]	We Sing You a Merry Christmas	1963	30.00
—As "The Osmond Brothers"			
❑ SE-4187 [S]	We Sing You a Merry Christmas	1963	30.00
❑ PM-9 [M]	We Sing You a Merry Christmas	1963	40.00
—Special-products issue for AC Spark Plug dealers			

POLYDOR

❑ PD-1-6077	Brainstorm	1976	12.00
❑ PD-2-8001	The Osmond Christmas Album	1976	18.00
—Includes group, solo and duet recordings			
❑ PD-2-9005	The Osmonds Greatest Hits	1977	15.00

WARNER BROS.

❑ 25070	One Way Rider	1984	10.00

OSTERWALD, HAZY

BALLY

❑ BAL-12004 [M]	Swiss Jazz	1956	40.00

O'SULLIVAN, GILBERT

EPIC

❑ JE37013	Off Centre	1981	12.00

MAM

❑ 5	Back to Front	1972	18.00
❑ 4	Gilbert O'Sullivan -- Himself	1972	18.00
❑ 7	I'm a Writer, Not a Fighter	1973	18.00
❑ 10	Stranger in My Own Backyard	1974	18.00

OSWALD, LEE HARVEY

EYEWITNESS

❑ 1002	Lee Harvey Oswald Speaks	1967	80.00

INCA

❑ 1001	Oswald: Self Portrait in Red	1965	100.00

KEY

❑ 880	The President's Assassin Speaks	1964	100.00

OTB

BLUE NOTE

❑ BT-85128	Inside Track	1986	15.00
❑ B1-85141	Live at Mt. Fuji	1987	15.00
❑ BT-85118	Out of the Blue	1985	15.00
❑ B1-93006	Spiral Staircase	1989	18.00

Number	Title	Yr	NM
OTHER HALF, THE (1)			
ACTA			
❑ 38004	The Other Half	1968	100.00

OTHER HALF, THE (2)

7/2

❑ (no #)0	The Other Half	1966	1500.00
—Album has been counterfeited, but those records are translucent when held to a light, originals are not			

OTIS, JOHNNY

ALLIGATOR

❑ AL-4726	The New Johnny Otis Show	1982	12.00

CAPITOL

❑ C1-92858	The Capitol Years	1989	18.00
❑ T940 [M]	The Johnny Otis Show	1958	250.00

DIG

❑ 104 [M]	Rock and Roll Hit Parade, Volume 1	1957	900.00
—Gold cover with thick cardboard and thick vinyl records. Counterfeits have noticeably thinner vinyl.			
❑ 104 [M]	Rock and Roll Hit Parade, Volume 1	1958	600.00
—Yellow cover with thick cardboard and thick vinyl records. Counterfeits have noticeably thinner vinyl.			

EPIC

❑ BN26524 [B]	Cuttin' Up	1970	30.00
❑ EG30473	The Johnny Otis Show Live at Monterey	1971	30.00

KENT

❑ KST-534	Cold Shot	1968	30.00

SAVOY

❑ SJL-2230	The Original Johnny Otis Show	1978	18.00
❑ SJL-2252	The Original Johnny Otis Show, Vol. 2	1980	18.00

OTIS, SHUGGIE

EPIC

❑ KE30752	Freedom Flight	1971	18.00
❑ BN26511	Here Comes Shuggie Otis	1970	18.00
❑ PE33059	Inspiration Information	1975	18.00

OTIS AND CARLA

STAX

❑ ST-716 [M]	King and Queen	1967	35.00
❑ STS-716 [S]	King and Queen	1967	50.00

SUNDAZED

❑ LP5069 [S]	King and Queen	2001	15.00
—Reissue on 180-gram vinyl			

OTTE, HANS

KUCKUCK

❑ KU-069/70	Das Buch der Klange	1984	18.00

OTTO'S CHEMICAL LOUNGE

HOMESTEAD

❑ HMS 023	Spillover	1985	15.00

OTWAY, JOHN

STIFF

❑ NEW3 [B]	I Did It Otway	1981	15.00

STIFF/EPIC

❑ USE5 [B]	Deep Thought	1980	18.00

OUSLEY, HAROLD

BETHLEHEM

❑ BCP-6059 [M]	Tenor Sax	1961	30.00
❑ SBCP-6059 [S]	Tenor Sax	1961	40.00

COBBLESTONE

❑ 9017	The Kid!	1971	30.00

MUSE

❑ MR-5141	Sweet Double Hipness	1979	15.00
❑ MR-5107	The People's Groove	197?	18.00

OUTCASTS, THE (2)

CICADELIC

❑ CIC-988	Live! Standing Room Only	1985	18.00
❑ CIC-987	Meet the Outcasts	1985	18.00

OUTFIELD, THE

COLUMBIA

❑ OC40619	Bangin'	1987	10.00
❑ BFC40027	Play Deep	1985	10.00
❑ OC44449	Voices of Babylon	1989	12.00

MCA

❑ 10111	Diamond Days	1990	15.00

OUTKAST

LAFACE

❑ 26053	Aquemini	1998	18.00
❑ 6153 [DJ]	Aquemini	1998	25.00
—Promo-only censored version			

Number	Title	Yr	NM
❑ 26029	Atliens	1996	18.00
❑ 26072	Stankonia	2000	18.00

OUTLAW BLUES BAND, THE

BLUESWAY

Number	Title	Yr	NM
❑ BLS-6020	Breakin' In	1969	30.00
❑ BLS-6021	The Outlaw Blues Band	1968	30.00

OUTLAWS

ARISTA

Number	Title	Yr	NM
❑ A2L8300	Bring It Back Alive	1978	15.00
❑ A2L8608	Bring It Back Alive	198?	12.00
—Reissue			
❑ A2L8114	Bring It Back Alive	198?	12.00
—Second reissue			
❑ AL9542	Ghost Riders	1980	12.00
❑ AL9614	Greatest Hits of the Outlaws/ High Tides Forever	1982	12.00
❑ AL8319	Greatest Hits of the Outlaws/ High Tides Forever	198?	10.00
—Reissue			
❑ AL4135	Hurry Sundown	1977	12.00
❑ AL8369	Hurry Sundown	198?	10.00
—Reissue			
❑ AL9507	In the Eye of the Storm	1979	12.00
❑ AL4070 [B]	Lady in Waiting	1976	12.00
❑ AQ4070 [Q]	Lady in Waiting	1976	18.00
❑ AL9584	Los Hombres Malo	1982	12.00
❑ AL4042	Outlaws	1975	12.00
❑ AL8301	Outlaws	198?	10.00
—Reissue			
❑ AB4205	Playin' to Win	1978	12.00
❑ SP-132 [EP]	Radio Remixes	1982	15.00
—Promo-only four-song sampler			

DIRECT DISC

Number	Title	Yr	NM
❑ SD16617	Outlaws	198?	50.00
—Audiophile vinyl			

PAIR

Number	Title	Yr	NM
❑ PDL2-1050	The Outlaws	1986	15.00

PASHA

Number	Title	Yr	NM
❑ BFZ40512	Soldiers of Fortune	1986	10.00

OUTSIDERS, THE

CAPITOL

Number	Title	Yr	NM
❑ T2745 [M]	Happening "Live!	1967	30.00
❑ ST2745 [S]	Happening "Live!	1967	30.00
❑ T2636 [M]	In	1967	30.00
❑ ST2636 [S]	In	1967	30.00
❑ T2568 [M]	The Outsiders Album #2	1966	30.00
❑ ST2558 [S]	The Outsiders Album #2	1966	30.00
❑ T2501 [M]	Time Won't Let Me	1966	30.00
❑ ST2501 [S]	Time Won't Let Me	1966	30.00

RHINO

Number	Title	Yr	NM
❑ RNLP-70132	The Best of the Outsiders (1965-1968)	1986	12.00

OVATIONS, THE (1)

MGM

Number	Title	Yr	NM
❑ SE-4945	Having a Party	1973	18.00

SOUNDS OF MEMPHIS

Number	Title	Yr	NM
❑ 7001	Hooked on a Feeling	1972	25.00

OVERKILL

MEGAFORCE

Number	Title	Yr	NM
❑ MRI1469	Feel the Fire	1985	15.00

MEGAFORCE/ATLANTIC

Number	Title	Yr	NM
❑ 81792 [EP]	Fuck You!	1987	12.00
❑ 81735	Taking Over	1987	12.00
❑ 82045	The Years of Decay	1989	15.00
❑ 81865	Under the Influence	1988	12.00

OVERSTREET, PAUL

RCA

Number	Title	Yr	NM
❑ R150526	Heroes	1991	18.00
—Only available on vinyl through BMG Direct Marketing			
❑ 9717-1-R	Sowin' Love	1989	15.00

RCA VICTOR

Number	Title	Yr	NM
❑ NFL1-8007	Paul Overstreet	1983	15.00

OVERSTREET, TOMMY

ABC

Number	Title	Yr	NM
❑ AB-1066	Better Me	1978	15.00

ABC DOT

Number	Title	Yr	NM
❑ DOSD-2027	Greatest Hits Vol. One	1975	18.00
❑ DO-2086	Hangin' 'Round	1977	15.00
❑ DOSD-2016 [B]	I'm a Believer	1975	18.00
❑ DOSD-2038	The Tommy Overstreet Show Live from the Silver Slipper	1975	18.00
❑ DOSD-2056	Turn On to Tommy Overstreet	1976	18.00
❑ DO-2071	Vintage '77	1977	15.00

DOT

Number	Title	Yr	NM
❑ DLP-25992	Gwen (Congratulations)	1971	25.00
❑ DLP-26003	Heaven Is My Woman's Love	1972	25.00
❑ DOS-26010	My Friends Call Me T.O.	1973	25.00
❑ DLP-25994	This Is Tommy Overstreet	1972	25.00
❑ DOS-26021	Woman, Your Name Is My Song	1974	25.00

ELEKTRA

Number	Title	Yr	NM
❑ 6E-178	I'll Never Let You Down	1979	12.00
❑ 6E-292	The Best of Tommy Overstreet	1980	12.00
❑ 6E-226	The Real Tommy Overstreet	1979	12.00

MCA

Number	Title	Yr	NM
❑ 797	Better Me	198?	10.00
—Reissue			
❑ 646	Hangin' 'Round	198?	10.00
—Reissue			
❑ 645	Vintage '77	198?	10.00
—Reissue			

OWEN, JIM

EPIC

Number	Title	Yr	NM
❑ PEG34852	A Song for Us All: A Salute to Hank Williams	1977	25.00

OWEN, REG

DECCA

Number	Title	Yr	NM
❑ DL8859 [M]	Under Paris Skies	1959	25.00
❑ DL78859 [S]	Under Paris Skies	1959	30.00

PALETTE

Number	Title	Yr	NM
❑ PZ-1018 [M]	Fiorello!	1960	25.00
❑ SPZ-31018 [S]	Fiorello!	1960	30.00
❑ PZ-1004 [M]	Get Happy	1960	25.00
❑ SPZ-31004 [S]	Get Happy	1960	30.00
❑ 1001 [M]	Manhattan Spiritual	1959	30.00
❑ S-1001 [S]	Manhattan Spiritual	1959	40.00

RCA VICTOR

Number	Title	Yr	NM
❑ LPM-1582 [M]	Coffee Break	1958	25.00
❑ LSP-1582 [S]	Coffee Break	1958	30.00
❑ LPM-1914 [M]	Cuddle Up a Little Closer	1959	25.00
❑ LSP-1914 [S]	Cuddle Up a Little Closer	1959	30.00
❑ LPM-1907 [M]	Deep in a Dream	1959	30.00
❑ LPM-1580 [M]	Dreaming	1958	30.00
❑ LPM-1908 [M]	Girls Were Made to Take Care of Boys	1959	25.00
❑ LSP-1908 [S]	Girls Were Made to Take Care of Boys	1959	30.00
❑ LPM-1597 [M]	Holiday Abroad in Dublin	1958	25.00
❑ LSP-1597 [S]	Holiday Abroad in Dublin	1958	30.00
❑ LPM-1599 [M]	Holiday Abroad in London	1958	25.00
❑ LSP-1599 [S]	Holiday Abroad in London	1958	30.00
❑ LPM-1906 [M]	I'll Sing You 1,000 Love Songs	1959	25.00
❑ LSP-1906 [S]	I'll Sing You 1,000 Love Songs	1959	30.00
❑ LPM-1542 [M]	The Best of Irving Berlin	1957	30.00
❑ LPM-1675 [M]	The British Isles	1958	25.00
❑ LSP-1675 [S]	The British Isles	1958	30.00
❑ LPM-1915 [M]	You Don't Know Paree	1959	30.00

OWEN-B

MUS-I-COL

Number	Title	Yr	NM
❑ 101209	Owen-B	1970	60.00

OWENS, BONNIE

CAPITOL

Number	Title	Yr	NM
❑ T2600 [M]	All of Me Belongs to You	1967	30.00
❑ ST2600 [S]	All of Me Belongs to You	1967	30.00
❑ T2403 [M]	Don't Take Advantage of Me	1965	25.00
❑ ST2403 [S]	Don't Take Advantage of Me	1965	30.00
❑ ST-341	Hi-Fi to Cry By	1969	30.00
❑ ST-195	Lead Me On	1969	30.00
❑ ST-557	Mother's Favorite Hymns	1970	30.00
❑ ST2861	Somewhere Between	1968	30.00

OWENS, BUCK, AND SUSAN RAYE

CAPITOL

Number	Title	Yr	NM
❑ ST-558	Great White Horse	1970	18.00
❑ ST-837	Merry Christmas from Buck Owens and Susan Raye	1971	18.00
❑ ST-11084	The Best of Buck Owens and Susan Raye	1972	18.00
❑ ST-11204	The Good Old Days (Are Here Again)	1973	18.00
❑ ST-448	We're Gonna Get Together	1970	25.00

OWENS, BUCK

CAPITOL

Number	Title	Yr	NM
❑ C1-92893	Act Naturally	1989	18.00
❑ SMAS-11180	Ain't It Amazing, Gracie	1973	18.00
❑ STBB-486	A Merry "Hee Haw" Christmas	1970	30.00
❑ ST2902	A Night on the Town	1968	30.00
❑ ST-194	Anywhere U.S.A.	1969	25.00
❑ ST-11222	Arms Full of Empty	1972	18.00
❑ T2353 [M]	Before You Go/No One But You	1965	30.00
❑ ST2353 [S]	Before You Go/No One But You	1965	30.00
❑ ST-685	Bridge Over Troubled Water	1971	18.00
❑ T1489 [M]	Buck Owens	1961	40.00
—Black colorband label, Capitol logo at left			
❑ STCL-574	Buck Owens	1970	40.00
❑ T1489 [M]	Buck Owens	1962	30.00
—Black colorband label, Capitol logo at top			
❑ ST2994	Buck Owens, The Guitar Player	1968	30.00
❑ T2715 [M]	Buck Owens and His Buckaroos in Japan	1967	25.00
❑ ST2715 [S]	Buck Owens and His Buckaroos in Japan	1967	30.00
❑ ST-232	Buck Owens in London	1969	25.00
❑ ST 8-0232	Buck Owens in London	1969	30.00
—Capitol Record Club edition			
❑ T1482 [M]	Buck Owens Sings Harlan Howard	1961	40.00
❑ ST1482 [S]	Buck Owens Sings Harlan Howard	1961	50.00
❑ T1989 [M]	Buck Owens Sings Tommy Collins	1963	40.00
❑ ST1989 [S]	Buck Owens Sings Tommy Collins	1963	50.00
❑ T2556 [M]	Carnegie Hall Concert	1966	25.00
❑ ST2556 [S]	Carnegie Hall Concert	1966	30.00
❑ ST2977	Christmas Shopping	1968	30.00
❑ T2396 [M]	Christmas with Buck Owens and His Buckaroos	1965	25.00
❑ ST2396 [S]	Christmas with Buck Owens and His Buckaroos	1965	30.00
❑ SWBB-257	Close-Up	1969	25.00
—Reissue of "Together Again" and "No One But You			
❑ T2497 [M]	Dust on Mother's Bible	1966	25.00
❑ ST2497 [S]	Dust on Mother's Bible	1966	30.00
❑ C1-91132	Hot Dog!	1988	15.00
❑ T2186 [M]	I Don't Care	1964	30.00
❑ ST2186 [S]	I Don't Care	1964	30.00
❑ ST-11136	In the Palm of Your Hand	1973	18.00
❑ ST2841 [S]	It Takes People Like You to Make People Like Me	1968	30.00
❑ T2841 [M]	It Takes People Like You to Make People Like Me	1968	40.00
❑ T2283 [M]	I've Got a Tiger by the Tail	1965	30.00
❑ ST2283 [S]	I've Got a Tiger by the Tail	1965	30.00
❑ ST-131	I've Got You on My Mind Again	1969	25.00
❑ ST-628	I Wouldn't Live in New York City	1970	25.00
❑ ST-11105	Live at the White House	1972	18.00
❑ SPRO2980/1 [DJ]	Minute Masters	1966	50.00
—Promo-only excerpts of 24 songs			
❑ ST-11332	Monster's Holiday	1974	18.00
❑ T1879 [M]	On the Bandstand	1963	40.00
❑ ST1879 [S]	On the Bandstand	1963	50.00
❑ T2650 [M]	Open Up Your Heart	1967	25.00
❑ ST2650 [S]	Open Up Your Heart	1967	30.00
❑ T2443 [M]	Roll Out the Red Carpet for Buck Owens & The Buckaroos	1966	25.00
❑ ST2443 [S]	Roll Out the Red Carpet for Buck Owens & The Buckaroos	1966	30.00
❑ ST2962	Sweet Rosie Jones	1968	30.00
❑ ST-212	Tall Dark Stranger	1969	25.00
❑ T2105 [M]	The Best of Buck Owens	1964	30.00
❑ ST2105 [S]	The Best of Buck Owens	1964	30.00
❑ ST2897	The Best of Buck Owens, Vol. 2	1968	30.00
❑ ST-830	The Best of Buck Owens, Vol. 4	1971	18.00
❑ SKAO-145	The Best of Buck Owens, Volume 3	1969	25.00
❑ ST-11471	The Best of Buck Owens, Volume 6	1976	18.00
❑ ST-11273	The Best of Buck Owens Volume 5	1973	18.00
❑ T2367 [M]	The Instrumental Hits of Buck Owens & the Buckaroos	1965	30.00
❑ ST2367 [S]	The Instrumental Hits of Buck Owens & the Buckaroos	1965	30.00
❑ ST-476	The Kansas City Song	1970	25.00
❑ T2135 [M]	Together Again/My Heart Skips a Beat	1964	30.00
❑ ST2135 [S]	Together Again/My Heart Skips a Beat	1964	30.00
❑ DT1489 [R]	Under Your Spell Again	1968	30.00
—Duophonic" reissue of mono original with new title			
❑ ST-11390	Weekend Daddy	1974	18.00
❑ T1777 [M]	You're for Me	1962	40.00
❑ ST1777 [S]	You're for Me	1962	50.00
❑ ST-439	Your Mother's Prayer	1970	25.00
❑ T2760 [M]	Your Tender Loving Care	1967	30.00
❑ ST2760 [S]	Your Tender Loving Care	1967	30.00

COUNTRY MUSIC FOUNDATION

Number	Title	Yr	NM
❑ CMF-012	Live at Carnegie Hall	198?	15.00

LABREA

Number	Title	Yr	NM
❑ 1017 [M]	Buck Owens	1961	100.00
❑ 8017 [S]	Buck Owens	1961	150.00

STARDAY

Number	Title	Yr	NM
❑ SLP-324 [B]	Coutnry Hit Maker #1	1964	30.00
❑ SLP-172	The Fabulous Country Music Sound of Buck Owens	1962	50.00

TIME-LIFE

Number	Title	Yr	NM
❑ STW-114	Country Music	1981	12.00

WARNER BROS.

Number	Title	Yr	NM
❑ BS2952	Buck 'Em	1976	15.00
❑ BS3087	Our Old Mansion	1977	15.00

OWENS, CHARLES

DISCOVERY

Number	Title	Yr	NM
❑ 811	Music of Harry Warren, Volume 1	1980	15.00

Number	Title	Yr	NM
❏ 787	Two Quartets	1978	15.00

VAULT

Number	Title	Yr	NM
❏ LP-0(# unknown)	I Stand Alone	196?	50.00

OWENS, JIMMY

ATLANTIC

❏ SD1491	Jimmy Owens-Kenny Barron Quintet	1968	25.00
—Multicolor label, black "fan" logo at right			
❏ SD1491	Jimmy Owens-Kenny Barron Quintet	1969	18.00
—Red and green label			

HORIZON

❏ SP-729	Headin' Home	1978	15.00
❏ SP-712	Jimmy Owens	197?	15.00

OXFORD, VERNON

RCA VICTOR

❏ LPM-3704 [M]	Woman, Let Me Sing You a Song	1967	40.00
❏ LSP-3704 [S]	Woman, Let Me Sing You a Song	1967	30.00

ROUNDER

❏ 0123	His and Hers	198?	18.00
❏ 0091	If I Had My Wife to Love Over	198?	18.00
❏ 0156	Keepin' It Country	1982	18.00

OZ KNOZZ

OZONE

❏ O2-1000	Ruff Mix	1975	500.00

OZARK MOUNTAIN DAREDEVILS

A&M

❏ SP-4662	Don't Look Down	1977	15.00
❏ SP-3654	It'll Shine When It Shines	1974	15.00
❏ SP-3192	It'll Shine When It Shines	198?	10.00
—Budget-line reissue			
❏ SP-6006	It's Alive	1978	18.00
❏ SP-4601	Men from Earth	1976	15.00
❏ SP-3202	The Best of Ozark Mountain Daredevils	1982	12.00
❏ SP-4549	The Car Over the Lake Album	1975	15.00
❏ SP-4411	The Ozark Mountain Daredevils	1973	15.00
❏ SP-3110	The Ozark Mountain Daredevils	198?	10.00
—Budget-line reissue			

COLUMBIA

❏ JC36375	Ozark Mountain Daredevils	1980	12.00

SOUNDS GREAT

❏ SG-5004	The Lost Cabin Sessions	1985	12.00

OZONE, MAKOTO

COLUMBIA

❏ FC40240	After	1986	12.00
❏ BFC39624	Makoto Ozone	1985	12.00
❏ FC40676	Now You Know	1987	12.00

OZONE

MOTOWN

❏ 6037ML	Glasses	1983	25.00
❏ 6011ML	Li'l Suzy	1982	25.00
❏ M8-962M1	Send It	1981	25.00

P

P. FUNK ALL STARS

CBS ASSOCIATED

❏ FZ39168	Urban Dancefloor Guerrilas	1983	18.00

P.F.M.

ASYLUM

❏ 7E-1071 [B]	Chocolate Kings	1976	15.00
❏ 7E-1101 [B]	Jet Lag	1977	15.00

MANTICORE

❏ MA6-502 [B]	P.F.M. 'Cook'	1974	25.00
❏ MC66668 [B]	Photos of Ghosts	1973	25.00
❏ MC66673 [B]	The World Became the World	1974	20.00

P.H. PHACTOR

PICCADILLY

❏ PIC-3343	Merryjuana	1980	100.00
—Cover spells the group's name "Factor" but the label has it "Phactor"			

P.M. DAWN

GEE STREET

❏ 6768 [DJ]	The Bliss Album	1993	25.00
—Promo-only vinyl edition			

P.M. DAWN

GEE STREET

Number	Title	Yr	NM
❏ 524147-1	Jesus Wept	1995	25.00
❏ PRLP-6768-1 [DJ]	The Bliss Album...?	1993	25.00
—Promo-only vinyl edition			

PABLO CRUISE

A&M

❏ SP-4625	A Place in the Sun	1977	12.00
❏ SP-3236	A Place in the Sun	198?	10.00
—Budget-line reissue of 4625			
❏ SP-4575	Lifeline	1976	12.00
❏ SP-4909	Out of Our Hands	1983	12.00
❏ SP-4528	Pablo Cruise	1975	12.00
❏ SP-3111	Pablo Cruise	198?	10.00
—Budget-line reissue of 4528			
❏ SP-3712	Part of the Game	1979	12.00
❏ SP-3726	Reflector	1981	12.00
❏ SP-4697	Worlds Away	1978	12.00
❏ SP-3198	Worlds Away	198?	10.00
—Budget-line reissue of 4697			

MOBILE FIDELITY

❏ 1-029 [B]	A Place in the Sun	1979	25.00
—Audiophile vinyl			

NAUTILUS

❏ NR-6	Lifeline	1980	25.00
—Audiophile vinyl			
❏ NR-28	Worlds Away	1981	25.00
—Audiophile vinyl			

PAC-MAN

KID STUFF

❏ KSS-5029	Christmas Album	1982	18.00
—Written and produced by Patrick McBride and Dana Walden			

PACE, JOHNNY

RIVERSIDE

❏ RLP 12-292 [M]	Chet Baker Introduces Johnny Pace	1958	50.00
❏ RLP-1130 [S]	Chet Baker Introduces Johnny Pace	1959	50.00

PACERS, THE

RAZORBACK

❏ 121 [M]	You Asked For It	1965	100.00

PACHECO, MIKE

INTERLUDE

❏ MO-513 [M]	Hot Skins	1959	40.00
❏ ST-1013 [S]	Hot Skins	1959	30.00

TAMPA

❏ TP-30 [M]	Bongo Date	1957	100.00
—Colored vinyl			
❏ TP-30 [M]	Bongo Date	1958	50.00
—Black vinyl			
❏ TP-21 [M]	Bongo Session	1957	100.00
—Colored vinyl			
❏ TP-21 [M]	Bongo Session	1958	50.00
—Black vinyl			
❏ TP-10 [M]	Bongo Skins	1957	100.00
—Colored vinyl			
❏ TP-10 [M]	Bongo Skins	1958	50.00
—Black vinyl			

PACIFIC COAST RAGTIMERS, THE

CIRCLE

❏ CLP-1376	The Pacific Coast Ragtimers	199?	15.00

PACIFIC DRIFT

DERAM

❏ DES18040	Feelin' Free	1970	25.00

PACIFIC GAS & ELECTRIC

ABC DUNHILL

❏ DSX-50157	Pacific Gas and Electric Starring Charlie Allen	1974	15.00

BRIGHT ORANGE

❏ 701	Get It On	1968	40.00

COLUMBIA

❏ CS1017	Are You Ready	1970	18.00
—360 Sound" label			
❏ CS1017	Are You Ready	1970	15.00
—Orange label			
❏ CS9900	Pacific Gas and Electric	1969	18.00
—360 Sound" label			
❏ CS9900	Pacific Gas and Electric	1970	15.00
—Orange label			
❏ C30362	PG&E	1971	15.00
❏ C32019	The Best of Pacific Gas & Electric	1972	15.00

POWER

❏ 701	Get It On	1969	30.00

PACIFIC OCEAN

V.M.C.

Number	Title	Yr	NM
❏ 135	Pacific Ocean	1969	25.00

PACK, MARSHALL

STARDAY

❏ SLP-120 [M]	Marshall Pack	1960	40.00

PACKERS, THE

PURE SOUL MUSIC

❏ 1001 [S]	Hole in the Wall	1966	25.00

PAGE, GENE

ARISTA

❏ AL4174	Close Encounters	1978	12.00
❏ AL4262	Love Starts After Dark	1980	12.00

ATLANTIC

❏ SD18111	Hot City	1974	15.00
❏ SD18161	Lovelock!	1975	15.00

PAGE, HOT LIPS

CONTINENTAL

❏ 16007 [M]	Hot and Cozy	1962	60.00

ONYX

❏ 207	After Hours	197?	15.00

XANADU

❏ 107	Trumpet at Minton's	197?	15.00

PAGE, JIMMY, AND ROBERT PLANT

ATLANTIC

❏ 82706 [B]	No Quarter	1994	30.00
❏ 83092	Walking Into Clarksdale	1998	25.00
—With all four sides of music correct			
❏ 83092	Walking Into Clarksdale	1998	25.00
—Pressing error with Side 2's music repeated on Side 3			

PAGE, JIMMY

CLEOPATRA

❏ 2914 [B]	Burn Up		25.00
❏ 8207 [B]	Burn Up		30.00
—picture disc			
❏ 1236 [B]	No Introduction Necessary - Deluxe Edition		25.00

GEFFEN

❏ GHS24188	Outrider	1988	12.00

SPRINGBOARD

❏ SPB-4038	Special Early Works	1972	30.00

PAGE, LARRY, ORCHESTRA

RHINO

❏ RNDF-257 [PD]	Kinky Music	1984	15.00
❏ RNLP-058	Kinky Music	1984	12.00

PAGE, MILTON

DIPLOMAT

❏ X-1016	Pipe Organ	196?	12.00
—Reissue of Promenade album with same contents in same order			

PROMENADE

❏ CH-1006	Pipe Organ	196?	18.00

PAGE, PATTI

ACCORD

❏ SN-7206	Special Thoughts	1982	12.00

COLUMBIA

❏ CL2505 [M]	America's Favorite Hymns	1966	15.00
❏ CS9305 [S]	America's Favorite Hymns	1966	18.00
❏ CL2414 [M]	Christmas with Patti Page	1965	15.00
❏ CS9214 [S]	Christmas with Patti Page	1965	18.00
❏ CS9666	Gentle on My Mind	1968	18.00
❏ CS9999	Honey Come Back	1970	15.00
❏ CL2353 [M]	Hush, Hush, Sweet Charlotte	1965	18.00
❏ CS9153 [S]	Hush, Hush, Sweet Charlotte	1965	25.00
❏ CL2132 [M]	Love After Midnight	1964	18.00
❏ CS8932 [S]	Love After Midnight	1964	25.00
❏ CL2526 [M]	Patti Page's Greatest Hits	1966	15.00
❏ CS9326 [S]	Patti Page's Greatest Hits	1966	18.00
—360 Sound" label			
❏ CS9326	Patti Page's Greatest Hits	1970	12.00
—Orange label			
❏ PC9326	Patti Page's Greatest Hits	198?	10.00
—Budget-line reissue			
❏ CL2049 [M]	Say Wonderful Things	1963	18.00
❏ CS8849 [S]	Say Wonderful Things	1963	25.00
❏ CL2761 [M]	Today My Way	1967	25.00
❏ CS9561 [S]	Today My Way	1967	18.00

EMARCY

❏ MG-36074 [M]	In the Land of Hi-Fi	1956	50.00
❏ SR-80000 [S]	In the Land of Hi-Fi	1959	50.00
❏ MG-36116 [M]	The East Side	1957	50.00
❏ MG-36136 [M]	The West Side	1957	50.00

Number	Title	Yr	NM
HARMONY			
❑ KH30407	Green, Green Grass of Home	1971	12.00
❑ HS11381	Stand By Your Man	1970	12.00
MERCURY			
❑ MG-25209 [10]	And I Thought About You	1954	40.00
❑ MG-20909 [M]	Blue Dream Street	1964	25.00
❑ SR-60909 [S]	Blue Dream Street	1964	30.00
❑ MG-25109 [10]	Christmas	1951	40.00
❑ MG20093 [M]	Christmas with Patti Page	1956	30.00
❑ 822740-1	Christmas with Patti Page	1987	12.00
— Reissue			
❑ MG-20615 [M]	Country & Western Golden Hits	1961	25.00
❑ SR-60615 [S]	Country & Western Golden Hits	1961	30.00
❑ MG-25101 [10]	Folksong Favorites	1951	40.00
❑ MG-20712 [M]	Golden Hits of the Boys	1962	25.00
❑ SR-60712 [S]	Golden Hits of the Boys	1962	30.00
❑ MG-20689 [M]	Go On Home	1962	25.00
❑ SR-60689 [S]	Go On Home	1962	30.00
❑ SR-61344	I'd Rather Be Sorry	1971	15.00
❑ MG-20406 [M]	I'll Remember April	1959	30.00
❑ SR-60081 [S]	I'll Remember April	1959	40.00
❑ MG-20405 [M]	Indiscretion	1959	30.00
❑ SR-60059 [S]	Indiscretion	1959	40.00
❑ MG-20388 [M]	I've Heard That Song Before	1957	30.00
❑ SR-60011 [S]	I've Heard That Song Before	1959	40.00
❑ MG-20573 [M]	Just a Closer Walk with Thee	1960	30.00
❑ SR-60233 [S]	Just a Closer Walk with Thee	1960	40.00
❑ MG-25196 [10]	Just Patti	1954	40.00
❑ MG-20387 [M]	Let's Get Away from It All	1957	30.00
❑ SR-60010 [S]	Let's Get Away from It All	1959	40.00
❑ MG-20226 [M]	Manhattan Tower	1956	30.00
❑ MG-20099 [M]	Music for Two in Love	1955	30.00
❑ MG-20095 [M]	Page I	1955	30.00
❑ MG-20096 [M]	Page II	1955	30.00
❑ MG-20097 [M]	Page III	1955	30.00
❑ MG-20101 [M]	Page IV	1955	30.00
❑ MG-20398 [M]	Patti Page On Camera	1958	30.00
❑ SR-60025 [S]	Patti Page On Camera	1959	40.00
❑ MG-20758 [M]	Patti Page On Stage	1963	25.00
❑ SR-60758 [S]	Patti Page On Stage	1963	30.00
❑ MG-20495 [M]	Patti Page's Golden Hits	1960	30.00
❑ SR-60495 [S]	Patti Page's Golden Hits	196?	30.00
❑ MG-20794 [M]	Patti Page's Golden Hits, Volume 2	1963	25.00
❑ SR-60794 [S]	Patti Page's Golden Hits, Volume 2	1963	30.00
❑ MG-20599 [M]	Patti Page Sings and Stars In "Elmer Gantry	1960	30.00
❑ SR-60260 [S]	Patti Page Sings and Stars In "Elmer Gantry	1960	30.00
❑ MG-25185 [10]	Patti Sings for Romance	1954	40.00
❑ MG-25197 [10]	Patti's Songs	1954	40.00
❑ MG-20076 [M]	Romance on the Range	1955	30.00
❑ MG-25210 [10]	So Many Memories	1954	40.00
❑ MG-25059 [10]	Songs	1950	40.00
❑ MG-25187 [10]	Song Souvenirs	1954	40.00
❑ MG-25154 [10]	Tennessee Waltz	1952	40.00
❑ SR-60114 [S]	The East Side	1959	50.00
❑ PKW-118	The Most	1969	18.00
❑ MG-20952 [M]	The Nearness of You	1965	18.00
❑ SR-60952 [S]	The Nearness of You	1965	25.00
❑ MG-20819 [M]	The Singing Rage	1963	25.00
❑ SR-60819 [S]	The Singing Rage	1963	30.00
❑ MG-20100 [M]	The Voice of Patti Page	1955	30.00
❑ MG-20318 [M]	The Waltz Queen	1957	40.00
— With one image of Patti Page on cover; "Custom High Fidelity" and Mercury logo at upper right of front cover			
❑ SR-60049 [S]	The Waltz Queen	1959	40.00
❑ MG-20318 [M]	The Waltz Queen	1959	30.00
— With two images of Patti Page on cover; Mercury logo at upper left of front cover, "High Custom Fidelity" in white strip along bottom front cover			
❑ SR-60113 [S]	The West Side	1959	50.00
❑ MG-20102 [M]	This Is My Song	1955	30.00
❑ MG-20417 [M]	Three Little Words	1960	30.00
❑ SR-60037 [S]	Three Little Words	1960	40.00
❑ MG-20098 [M]	You Go to My Head	1955	30.00
PLANTATION			
❑ 548	Aces	1981	12.00
WING			
❑ MGW12174 [M]	Christmas with Patti Page	196?	25.00
— Same contents and order as Mercury 20093			
❑ MGW12250 [M]	Let's Get Away from It All	196?	15.00
❑ SRW16250 [S]	Let's Get Away from It All	196?	18.00
❑ MGW12121 [M]	The Waltz Queen	196?	15.00
❑ SRW16121 [S]	The Waltz Queen	196?	18.00

PAGE, SID, AND DAVID SHELANDER

Number	Title	Yr	NM
BAINBRIDGE			
❑ 6257	Odyssey	198?	12.00

PAGE, TOMMY

Number	Title	Yr	NM
SIRE			
❑ 26148	Paintings in My Mind	1990	15.00
❑ 25740	Tommy Page	1988	12.00

PAICH, MARTY

Number	Title	Yr	NM
BETHLEHEM			
❑ BCP-44 [M]	Jazz City Workshop	1956	80.00
CADENCE			
❑ CLP-3010 [M]	Marty Paich Big Band	1958	50.00
DISCOVERY			
❑ 829	I Get A Boot Out of You	198?	12.00
❑ 844	New York Scene	198?	12.00
❑ DS-857	What's New	198?	12.00
GENE NORMAN			
❑ GNP-10 [10]	Marty Paich Octet	1955	120.00
— Red vinyl			
❑ GNP-21 [M]	Marty Paich Octet	1956	80.00
INTERLUDE			
❑ MO-514 [M]	Like Wow -- Jazz 1960	1960	30.00
❑ ST-1014 [S]	Like Wow -- Jazz 1960	1960	30.00
❑ MO-509 [M]	Revel Without a Pause	1959	30.00
❑ ST-1009 [S]	Revel Without a Pause	1959	30.00
MODE			
❑ LP-110 [M]	Jazz Band Ball	1957	80.00
❑ LP-105 [M]	Marty Paich Trio	1957	80.00
RCA VICTOR			
❑ LPM-2164 [M]	Piano Quartet	1960	25.00
❑ LSP-2164 [S]	Piano Quartet	1960	30.00
❑ LPM-2259 [M]	Piano Quartet	1960	25.00
❑ LSP-2259 [S]	Piano Quartet	1960	30.00
REPRISE			
❑ RS-6206 [S]	The Rock-Jazz Incident	1966	18.00
❑ R-6206 [M]	The Rock-Jazz Incident	1966	15.00
TAMPA			
❑ TP-23 [M]	Hot Piano	1957	150.00
— Probably the original title			
❑ TP-23 [M]	Jazz for Relaxation	1957	200.00
— Colored vinyl			
❑ TP-23 [M]	Jazz for Relaxation	1958	100.00
— Black vinyl			
❑ TP-28 [M]	Marty Paich Quintet Featuring Art Pepper	1957	800.00
— Red vinyl			
❑ TP-28 [M]	Marty Paich Quintet Featuring Art Pepper	1958	400.00
— Black vinyl			
WARNER BROS.			
❑ W1349 [M]	I Get A Boot Out of You	1959	150.00
❑ WS1349 [S]	I Get A Boot Out of You	1959	180.00
❑ W1296 [M]	The Broadway Bit	1959	1200.00
❑ WS1296 [S]	The Broadway Bit	1959	600.00

PAIGE, JANIS

Number	Title	Yr	NM
BALLY			
❑ BAL-12008 [M]	Let's Fall in Love	1957	40.00

PAIR, THE

Number	Title	Yr	NM
LIBERTY			
❑ LRP-3461 [M]	In"-Citement	1966	18.00
❑ LST-7461 [S]	In"-Citement	1966	25.00
❑ LRP-3504 [M]	It's a Wonderful World	1967	18.00
❑ LST-7504 [S]	It's a Wonderful World	1967	25.00
❑ LRP-3440 [M]	The Pair Extraordinaire	1966	18.00
❑ LST-7440 [S]	The Pair Extraordinaire	1966	25.00
❑ LRP-3410 [M]	The Pair Live! At the Ice House	1965	25.00
❑ LST-7410 [S]	The Pair Live! At the Ice House	1965	30.00

PAISLEYS, THE

Number	Title	Yr	NM
AUDIO CITY			
❑ 70	Cosmic Mind at Play	1970	200.00

PALANCE, JACK

Number	Title	Yr	NM
WARNER BROS.			
❑ WS1865	Palance	1970	30.00

PALEY, TOM

Number	Title	Yr	NM
ELEKTRA			
❑ EKL-12 [M]	Folk Songs from the Southern Appalachians	195?	40.00

PALM BEACH BAND BOYS, THE

Number	Title	Yr	NM
RCA VICTOR			
❑ LPM-3808 [M]	The Palm Beach Band Boys Strike Again	1967	18.00
❑ LSP-3808 [S]	The Palm Beach Band Boys Strike Again	1967	12.00
❑ LPM-3734 [M]	Winchester Cathedral	1966	15.00
❑ LSP-3734 [S]	Winchester Cathedral	1966	12.00

PALMER, BRUCE

Number	Title	Yr	NM
VERVE FORECAST			
❑ FTS-3086 [B]	The Cycle Is Complete	1970	30.00

PALMER, EARL

Number	Title	Yr	NM
LIBERTY			
❑ LRP-3201 [M]	Drumsville	1961	30.00
❑ LST-7201 [S]	Drumsville	1961	40.00
❑ LRP-3227 [M]	Percolator Twist	1962	30.00
❑ LST-7227 [S]	Percolator Twist	1962	40.00

PALMER, JEFF

Number	Title	Yr	NM
AUDIOQUEST			
❑ AQ-LP-1014	Ease On	1993	18.00
STATIRAS			
❑ SLP-8081	Laser Wizzard	1987	15.00

PALMER, ROBERT

Number	Title	Yr	NM
EMI MANHATTAN			
❑ E1-48057	Heavy Nova	1988	12.00
ISLAND			
❑ 842301-1	Addictions Volume I	1990	12.00
❑ 91318	Addictions Volume I	1989	15.00
— Original pressing available only for a short time			
❑ ILPS9595	Clues	1980	12.00
❑ 90493	Clues	1986	10.00
❑ ILPS9476	Double Fun	1978	15.00
— Original copies of the above four albums were NOT distributed by Warner Bros.			
❑ 90494	Double Fun	1986	10.00
❑ ILPS9665	Maybe It's Live	1982	12.00
❑ ILPS9372	Pressure Drop	1976	15.00
❑ 90087	Pressure Drop	1984	10.00
❑ 90065	Pride	1983	12.00
❑ 90471	Riptide	1985	12.00
❑ PRO-819 [DJ]	Secrets	1979	25.00
— Promo-only picture disc			
❑ PRO-819 [DJ]	Secrets	1979	35.00
— Promo-only picture disc			
❑ ILPS9544	Secrets	1979	12.00
❑ 90089	Secrets	1984	10.00
❑ ILPS9294 [B]	Sneakin' Sally Through the Alley	1975	18.00
❑ 90086	Sneakin' Sally Through the Alley	1984	10.00
❑ ILPS9420	Some People Can Do What They Like	1977	15.00
WARNER BROS.			
❑ WBMS-111 [DJ]	Live in Boston	1979	30.00
— Part of "The Warner Bros. Music Show			
❑ WBMS-111 [DJ]	Live in Boston	1979	25.00
— Part of "The Warner Bros. Music Show			

PALMER, ROY

Number	Title	Yr	NM
RIVERSIDE			
❑ RLP-1020 [10]	Roy Palmer's State Street Ramblers	1953	80.00

PALMER, SINGLETON

Number	Title	Yr	NM
DIXIELAND JUBILEE			
❑ DJ-513	At the Opera House	197?	12.00
❑ DJ-511	Dixie by Gaslight	197?	12.00
NORMAN			
❑ NS-206 [S]	At the Opera House	1963	18.00
❑ NL-100 [M]	At the Opera House	1963	15.00
❑ NS-201 [S]	Dixie by Gaslight	1962	18.00
❑ NL-101 [M]	Dixie by Gaslight	1962	15.00
❑ NL-110 [M]	The Best Dixieland Band	1965	15.00
❑ NS-210 [S]	The Best Dixieland Band	1965	18.00

PALMIER, REMO

Number	Title	Yr	NM
CONCORD JAZZ			
❑ CJ-76	Remo Palmier	1979	12.00

PALMIERI, EDDIE

Number	Title	Yr	NM
EPIC			
❑ JE35523	Lucumi Macumba Voodoo	1978	12.00
INTUITION			
❑ C1-91353	Suono	1989	15.00

PAMEIJER, PAM

Number	Title	Yr	NM
STOMP OFF			
❑ SOS-1134	Jelly Roll Morton: 100 Years	1987	12.00
❑ SOS-1194	Little Bits	1989	12.00
❑ SOS-1172	London Blues	1988	12.00

PANDIT, KORLA

Number	Title	Yr	NM
FANTASY			
❑ 3350 [M]	Christmas with Korla Pandit	1962	40.00
— Red vinyl			
❑ 3350 [M]	Christmas with Korla Pandit	1962	30.00
— Black vinyl			
❑ 8350 [S]	Christmas with Korla Pandit	1962	50.00
— Blue vinyl			
❑ 8350 [S]	Christmas with Korla Pandit	1962	30.00
— Black vinyl			
❑ 3329 [M]	Hypnotique	1961	40.00
— Red vinyl			
❑ 3329 [M]	Hypnotique	1961	30.00
— Black vinyl			
❑ 8075 [S]	Hypnotique	1961	50.00
— Blue vinyl			
❑ 8075 [S]	Hypnotique	1961	30.00
— Black vinyl			
❑ 3286 [M]	Korla Pandit at the Pipe Organ	1959	40.00
— Red vinyl			
❑ 3286 [M]	Korla Pandit at the Pipe Organ	1959	30.00
— Black vinyl			
❑ 8018 [S]	Korla Pandit at the Pipe Organ	1960	50.00
— Blue vinyl			

Number	Title	Yr	NM
❏ 8018 [S]	Korla Pandit at the Pipe Organ	1960	30.00
—Black vinyl			
❏ 3304 [M]	Korla Pandit in Concert	1960	40.00
—Red vinyl			
❏ 3304 [M]	Korla Pandit in Concert	1960	30.00
—Black vinyl			
❏ 8049 [S]	Korla Pandit in Concert	1960	50.00
—Blue vinyl			
❏ 8049 [S]	Korla Pandit in Concert	1960	30.00
—Black vinyl			
❏ 3347 [M]	Korla Pandit in Paris	1962	30.00
❏ 8347 [M]	Korla Pandit in Paris	1962	30.00
❏ 3284 [M]	Latin Holiday	1959	40.00
—Red vinyl			
❏ 3284 [M]	Latin Holiday	1959	30.00
—Black vinyl			
❏ 8027 [S]	Latin Holiday	1960	50.00
—Blue vinyl			
❏ 8027 [S]	Latin Holiday	1960	30.00
—Black vinyl			
❏ 3327 [M]	Love Letters	1961	40.00
—Red vinyl			
❏ 3327 [M]	Love Letters	1961	30.00
—Black vinyl			
❏ 8070 [S]	Love Letters	1961	50.00
—Blue vinyl			
❏ 8070 [S]	Love Letters	1961	30.00
—Black vinyl			
❏ 3342 [M]	Music for Meditation	1962	40.00
—Red vinyl			
❏ 3342 [M]	Music for Meditation	1962	30.00
—Black vinyl			
❏ 8342 [S]	Music for Meditation	1962	50.00
—Blue vinyl			
❏ 8342 [S]	Music for Meditation	1962	30.00
—Black vinyl			
❏ 3334 [M]	Music of Hollywood	1962	40.00
—Red vinyl			
❏ 3334 [M]	Music of Hollywood	1962	30.00
—Black vinyl			
❏ 8086 [S]	Music of Hollywood	1962	50.00
—Blue vinyl			
❏ 8086 [S]	Music of Hollywood	1962	30.00
—Black vinyl			
❏ 3320 [M]	Music of Mystery and Romance	1961	40.00
—Red vinyl			
❏ 3320 [M]	Music of Mystery and Romance	1961	30.00
—Black vinyl			
❏ 8061 [S]	Music of Mystery and Romance	1961	50.00
—Blue vinyl			
❏ 8061 [S]	Music of Mystery and Romance	1961	30.00
—Black vinyl			
❏ 3272 [M]	Music of the Exotic East	1958	40.00
—Red vinyl			
❏ 3272 [M]	Music of the Exotic East	1958	30.00
—Black vinyl			
❏ 8013 [S]	Music of the Exotic East	1960	50.00
—Blue vinyl			
❏ 8013 [S]	Music of the Exotic East	1960	30.00
—Black vinyl			
❏ 3293 [M]	Speak to Me of Love	1959	40.00
—Red vinyl			
❏ 3293 [M]	Speak to Me of Love	1959	30.00
—Black vinyl			
❏ 8039 [S]	Speak to Me of Love	1960	50.00
—Blue vinyl			
❏ 8039 [S]	Speak to Me of Love	1960	30.00
—Black vinyl			
❏ 3288 [M]	Tropical Magic	1959	40.00
—Red vinyl			
❏ 3288 [M]	Tropical Magic	1959	30.00
—Black vinyl			
❏ 8034 [S]	Tropical Magic	1960	50.00
—Blue vinyl			
❏ 8034 [S]	Tropical Magic	1960	30.00
—Black vinyl			

NATIONAL CUSTOM

Number	Title	Yr	NM
❏ NCR 12-574	Fantastique!	196?	30.00

SYMPATHY FOR THE RECORD INDUSTRY

Number	Title	Yr	NM
❏ SFTRI387	Exotica 2000	1996	15.00

VITA

Number	Title	Yr	NM
❏ VLP-14 [10]	Rememb'ring with Korla Pandit	195?	80.00

PANICS, THE

CHANCELLOR

Number	Title	Yr	NM
❏ CHL-5026 [M]	Panicsville	1962	30.00
❏ CHLS-5026 [S]	Panicsville	1962	40.00

PHILIPS

Number	Title	Yr	NM
❏ PHM200159 [M]	Discotheque Dance Party	1964	18.00
❏ PHS600159 [S]	Discotheque Dance Party	1964	25.00

PANTERA

EASTWEST

Number	Title	Yr	NM
❏ 92302	Far Beyond Driven	1994	200.00
❏ 62068	Official Live: 101 Proof	1997	100.00
❏ 61908	The Great Southern Trendkill	1996	30.00

ELEKTRA

Number	Title	Yr	NM
❏ 62451	Reinventing the Steel	2000	35.00

METAL MAGIC

Number	Title	Yr	NM
❏ MMR1985	I Am the Night	1985	100.00
❏ MMR1283	Metal Magic	1983	150.00
❏ MMR1988	Power Metal	1988	120.00
❏ MMR1984	Projects in the Jungle	1984	100.00

PAPA DOO RUN RUN

TELARC

Number	Title	Yr	NM
❏ 70501	California Project	1985	12.00

PAPER GARDEN, THE

MUSICOR

Number	Title	Yr	NM
❏ MS-0(# unknown)	The Paper Garden	1968	40.00

PAPER LACE

MERCURY

Number	Title	Yr	NM
❏ SRM-1-1008	Paper Lace	1974	15.00

PAPPALARDI, FELIX

A&M

Number	Title	Yr	NM
❏ SP-4586	Creation	1976	12.00
❏ SP-4729	Don't Worry Me	1979	12.00

PARADISE ISLANDERS, THE

DECCA

Number	Title	Yr	NM
❏ DL4122 [M]	Christmas in Hawaii	1961	15.00
❏ DL74122 [S]	Christmas in Hawaii	1961	18.00

PARAGONS, THE & THE HARPTONES

MUSICTONE

Number	Title	Yr	NM
❏ M-8001 [M]	The Paragons vs. the Harptones	1964	50.00

PARAGONS, THE & THE JESTERS

JOSIE

Number	Title	Yr	NM
❏ 4008 [M]	The Paragons Meet the Jesters	1962	200.00

JUBILEE

Number	Title	Yr	NM
❏ JLP-1098 [M]	The Paragons Meet the Jesters	1959	300.00
—Blue label, black vinyl			
❏ JLP-1098 [M]	The Paragons Meet the Jesters	1959	1500.00
—Multi-color splash vinyl; VG value 750; VG+ value 1125			
❏ JLP-1098 [M]	The Paragons Meet the Jesters	196?	150.00
—Flat black label			
❏ JLP-1098 [M]	The Paragons Meet the Jesters	196?	60.00
—Black label with multi-color logo			

WINLEY

Number	Title	Yr	NM
❏ LP-6003 [M]	War! The Jesters vs. the Paragons	195?	500.00

PARAGONS, THE

COLLECTABLES

Number	Title	Yr	NM
❏ COL-5035	The Best of the Paragons	198?	12.00

LOST-NITE

Number	Title	Yr	NM
❏ LLP-4 [10]	The Best of the Paragons	1981	12.00
—Red vinyl; in die-cut cover with sticker			

PARANOISE

ANTILLES

Number	Title	Yr	NM
❏ 90986	Constant Fear	1988	18.00

PARENTI, TONY

JAZZOLOGY

Number	Title	Yr	NM
❏ J-11 [M]	Downtown Boys	1965	18.00
❏ J-41	Jazz Goes Underground	197?	12.00
❏ J-26	Jean Kittrell with Tony Parenti and His Blues Blowers	196?	18.00
❏ J-31 [M]	Night at Jimmy Ryan's	196?	18.00
❏ J-15	Ragtime	196?	18.00
❏ J-21 [M]	Ragtime Jubilee	1967	18.00
❏ J-71	The Final Bar	197?	12.00
❏ J-1 [M]	Tony Parenti	1962	18.00
❏ JCE-1 [10]	Tony Parenti and His New Orleanians	1962	25.00

RIVERSIDE

Number	Title	Yr	NM
❏ RLP 12-205 [M]	Ragtime	1956	60.00
—White label, blue print			
❏ RLP 12-205 [M]	Ragtime	195?	30.00
—Blue label, microphone logo at top			

PARENTI, TONY/THE DIXIELAND RHYTHM KINGS

JAZZTONE

Number	Title	Yr	NM
❏ J-1273 [M]	Two Beat Bash	195?	40.00

PARHAM, TINY

FOLKLYRIC

Number	Title	Yr	NM
❏ 9028	Hot Chicago Jazz	198?	12.00

X

Number	Title	Yr	NM
❏ LVA-3039 [10]	Tiny Parham's South Side Jazz	1955	60.00

PARIS, BOBBY

TETRAGRAMMATON

Number	Title	Yr	NM
❏ T-105 [S]	Let Me Show You the Way	1968	40.00
❏ M-2105 [M]	Let Me Show You the Way	1968	100.00

PARIS, FREDDIE

RCA VICTOR

Number	Title	Yr	NM
❏ LSP-4064	Lovin' Mood	1968	25.00

PARIS, JACK

2-J

Number	Title	Yr	NM
❏ 101	My Music, My Friends	197?	18.00
❏ 102	Strawberries and Butterflies	197?	18.00

50 STATES

Number	Title	Yr	NM
❏ 1005	Nashville Heart and Soul	197?	18.00
❏ 1002	Southern Session	197?	18.00

PARIS, JACKIE, AND ANNE MARIE MOSS

DIFFERENT DRUMMER

Number	Title	Yr	NM
❏ 1004	Maisonette	197?	18.00

PARIS, JACKIE

ABC IMPULSE!

Number	Title	Yr	NM
❏ AS-17 [S]	The Song Is Paris	1968	25.00

AUDIOPHILE

Number	Title	Yr	NM
❏ 158	Jackie Paris	198?	12.00

BRUNSWICK

Number	Title	Yr	NM
❏ BL-54019 [M]	Skylark	1957	100.00

CORAL

Number	Title	Yr	NM
❏ CRL-56118 [10]	That Paris Mood	195?	80.00

EASTWEST

Number	Title	Yr	NM
❏ 4002 [M]	The Jackie Paris Sound	1958	80.00

EMARCY

Number	Title	Yr	NM
❏ MG-36095 [M]	Songs by Jackie Paris	1956	100.00

IMPULSE!

Number	Title	Yr	NM
❏ A-17 [M]	The Song Is Paris	1962	30.00
❏ AS-17 [S]	The Song Is Paris	1962	40.00

TIME

Number	Title	Yr	NM
❏ T-70009 [M]	Jackie Paris Sings the Lyrics of Ira Gershwin	1959	40.00
❏ ST-70009 [S]	Jackie Paris Sings the Lyrics of Ira Gershwin	1959	50.00

WING

Number	Title	Yr	NM
❏ MGW-60004 [M]	Songs by Jackie Paris	1956	80.00

PARIS, PRISCILLA

HAPPY TIGER

Number	Title	Yr	NM
❏ HT-1002	Priscilla Loves Billy	1968	40.00

YORK

Number	Title	Yr	NM
❏ 4005 [M]	Priscilla Sings Herself	1967	30.00
❏ 4005-S [S]	Priscilla Sings Herself	1967	40.00

PARIS

CAPITOL

Number	Title	Yr	NM
❏ ST-11560	Big Towne, 2061	1976	15.00
❏ ST-11464	Paris	1975	15.00

PARIS CONSERVATOIRE ORCHESTRE (ALBERT WOLFF, CONDUCTOR)

RCA VICTOR RED SEAL

Number	Title	Yr	NM
❏ LSC-2301 [S]	Adam: Giselle	1959	50.00
—Original with "shaded dog" label			

PARIS CONSERVATOIRE ORCHESTRE (ANATOLE FISTOULARI, CONDUCTOR)

RCA VICTOR RED SEAL

Number	Title	Yr	NM
❏ LSC-2400 [S]	Ballet Music from the Opera	1960	400.00
—Original with "shaded dog" label			
❏ LSC-2400 [S]	Ballet Music from the Opera	199?	30.00
—Classic Records reissue			

PARIS CONSERVATOIRE ORCHESTRE (HUGH RIGNOLD, CONDUCTOR)

RCA VICTOR RED SEAL

Number	Title	Yr	NM
❏ LSC-2485 [S]	Delibes: Sylvia and Coppelia Ballet Suites	1961	80.00
—Original with "shaded dog" label			

PARIS CONSERVATOIRE ORCHESTRE (JEAN-PAUL MOREL, CONDUCTOR)

RCA VICTOR RED SEAL

Number	Title	Yr	NM
❏ LSC-6094 [S]	Albaniz: Iberia; Ravel: Rapsodie Espagnole	196?	400.00
—Original with "shaded dog" label			

PARIS CONSERVATOIRE ORCHESTRE (JEAN MARTINON, CONDUCTOR)

RCA VICTOR RED SEAL

Number	Title	Yr	NM
❑ LSC-2272 [S]	Prokofiev: Symphony No. 5	1959	80.00
—Original with "shaded dog" label			
❑ LSC-2288 [S]	Prokofiev: Symphony No. 7	1959	80.00
—Original with "shaded dog" label			
❑ LSC-2288 [S]	Prokofiev: Symphony No. 7	199?	30.00
—Classic Records reissue			

PARIS CONSERVATOIRE ORCHESTRE (PIERRE MONTEUX, CONDUCTOR)

RCA VICTOR RED SEAL

Number	Title	Yr	NM
❑ LSC-2085 [S]	Stravinsky: The Rite of Spring	1958	50.00
—Original with "shaded dog" label			
❑ LSC-2085 [S]	Stravinsky: The Rite of Spring	1964	40.00
—Second issue with "white dog" label			

PARIS PILOT

HIP

Number	Title	Yr	NM
❑ 7004	Paris Pilot	1970	30.00

PARIS SISTERS, THE

REPRISE

Number	Title	Yr	NM
❑ R-6259 [M]	Everything Under the Sun	1967	40.00
❑ RS-6359 [S]	Everything Under the Sun	1967	60.00

SIDEWALK

Number	Title	Yr	NM
❑ T5906 [M]	Golden Hits of the Paris Sisters	1967	50.00
❑ DT5906 [R]	Golden Hits of the Paris Sisters	1967	30.00

UNIFILMS

Number	Title	Yr	NM
❑ 505 [M]	The Paris Sisters Sing Songs from Glass House	1966	40.00
❑ S-505 [S]	The Paris Sisters Sing Songs from Glass House	1966	50.00

PARISH HALL

FANTASY

Number	Title	Yr	NM
❑ 8398	Parish Hall	1969	25.00

PARKER, BILLIE JEAN

RCA VICTOR

Number	Title	Yr	NM
❑ LPM-3967 [M]	The Truth About Bonnie and Clyde	1968	40.00
❑ LSP-3967 [S]	The Truth About Bonnie and Clyde	1968	18.00

PARKER, BILLY (2)

STRATA-EAST

Number	Title	Yr	NM
❑ SES-19754	Freedom of Speech	1975	30.00

PARKER, CHARLIE; DIZZY GILLESPIE; RED NORVO

DIAL

Number	Title	Yr	NM
❑ LP-903 [M]	Fabulous Jam Session	1951	600.00

PARKER, CHARLIE

ALAMAC

Number	Title	Yr	NM
❑ QSR2430	Charlie Parker's All Stars 1950	198?	15.00

AMERICAN RECORDING SOCIETY

Number	Title	Yr	NM
❑ G-441 [M]	Now's the Time	1957	50.00

BARONET

Number	Title	Yr	NM
❑ B-105 [M]	A Handful of Modern Jazz	1962	25.00
❑ BS-105 [R]	A Handful of Modern Jazz	1962	15.00
❑ B-107 [M]	The Early Bird	1962	25.00
❑ BS-107 [R]	The Early Bird	1962	15.00

BIRDLAND

Number	Title	Yr	NM
❑ 425 [10]	A Night at Carnegie Hall	1956	300.00

BLUE NOTE

Number	Title	Yr	NM
❑ BT-85108	Charlie Parker at Storyville	198?	15.00

BLUE RIBBON

Number	Title	Yr	NM
❑ 8011 [M]	The Early Bird	1962	25.00
❑ S-8011 [R]	The Early Bird	1962	15.00

CHARLIE PARKER

Number	Title	Yr	NM
❑ PLP-401 [M]	Bird Is Free	1961	40.00
❑ PLP-407 [M]	Bird Symbols	1961	40.00
❑ PLP-406 [M]	Charlie Parker	1961	40.00
❑ CP-513 [M]	Charlie Parker Plus Strings	196?	40.00
❑ PLP-701	Historical Masterpieces	196?	60.00
❑ CP-2-502 [M]	Live at Rockland Palace, September 26, 1952	1961	50.00
❑ PLP-408 [M]	Once There Was Bird	1961	40.00
❑ PLP-404 [M]	The Happy Bird	1961	40.00

CLEF

Number	Title	Yr	NM
❑ MGC-512 [10]	Bird and Diz	1954	400.00
—Reissue of Mercury 512			
❑ MGC-157 [10]	Charlie Parker	1954	400.00
❑ MGC-609 [M]	Charlie Parker Big Band	1954	400.00
❑ MGC-501 [10]	Charlie Parker with Strings	1954	400.00
—Reissue of Mercury 501			
❑ MGC-675 [M]	Charlie Parker with Strings	1955	400.00
❑ MGC-509 [10]	Charlie Parker with Strings, No. 2	1954	400.00
—Reissue of Mercury 509			
❑ MGC-725 [M]	Night and Day	1956	120.00
❑ MGC-513 [10]	South of the Border	1954	400.00
—Reissue of Mercury 513			
❑ MGC-646 [M]	The Magnificent Charlie Parker	1955	400.00

COLUMBIA

Number	Title	Yr	NM
❑ JC34832	Bird with Strings Live	1977	15.00
❑ JG34808	One Night in Birdland	1977	18.00
❑ C234808	One Night in Birdland	198?	15.00
—Reissue with new prefix			
❑ JC34831	Summit Meeting	1977	15.00

CONCERT HALL JAZZ

Number	Title	Yr	NM
❑ 1017 [10]	The Art of Charlie Parker, Vol. 2	1955	60.00
❑ 1004 [10]	The Fabulous Bird	1955	60.00

CONTINENTAL

Number	Title	Yr	NM
❑ 16004 [M]	Bird Lives	1962	40.00

DEBUT

Number	Title	Yr	NM
❑ DEB-611 [M]	Bird on 52nd Street	196?	50.00

DIAL

Number	Title	Yr	NM
❑ LP-904 [M]	Alternate Masters	1951	600.00
❑ LP-905 [M]	Alternate Masters	1951	600.00
❑ LP-203 [10]	Charlie Parker	1949	800.00
❑ LP-201 [10]	Charlie Parker Quintet	1949	800.00
❑ LP-202 [10]	Charlie Parker Quintet	1949	800.00
❑ LP-207 [10]	Charlie Parker Sextet	1949	800.00
❑ LP-901 [M]	The Bird Blows the Blues	1949	4000.00
—Limited edition of 300 copies on opaque red vinyl; designed as a mail-order offer; issued with a generic gray cover; also has a pale yellow Dial label similiar to the label's 78 rpm design			
❑ LP-901 [M]	The Bird Blows the Blues	1950	600.00
—Commercial version of mail-order album			

ELEKTRA/MUSICIAN

Number	Title	Yr	NM
❑ 60019	One Night in Washington	1982	12.00

ESP-DISK'

Number	Title	Yr	NM
❑ ESP-BIRD-2	Broadcast Performances 1948-1949, Vol. 2	1973	25.00

EVEREST ARCHIVE OF FOLK & JAZZ

Number	Title	Yr	NM
❑ 214	Charlie Parker	1969	15.00
❑ 254	Charlie Parker, Vol. 3	197?	12.00
❑ 295	Charlie Parker, Vol. 4	197?	12.00
❑ 315	Charlie Parker, Vol. 5	197?	12.00
❑ 232	Charlie Parker, Volume 2	1970	12.00

FANTASY

Number	Title	Yr	NM
❑ 6012 [M]	Bird at St. Nick's	1964	30.00
❑ OJC-041	Bird at St. Nick's	1983	12.00
❑ 86012 [R]	Bird at St. Nick's	1964	18.00
❑ 6011 [M]	Bird on 52nd St.	1964	30.00
❑ 86011 [R]	Bird on 52nd St.	1964	18.00
❑ OJC-114	Bird on 52nd St.	198?	12.00
❑ OJC-044	Jazz at Massey Hall	198?	12.00

HALL OF FAME

Number	Title	Yr	NM
❑ 617	Giants of Jazz	197?	12.00
❑ 620	Takin' Off	197?	12.00

JAZZTONE

Number	Title	Yr	NM
❑ J-1204 [M]	Giants of Modern Jazz	1955	50.00
❑ J-0(# unk) [M]	The Art of Charlie Parker, Vol. 2	1955	50.00
❑ J-1214 [M]	The Fabulous Bird	1955	50.00
❑ J-1240 [M]	The Saxes of Stan Getz and Charlie Parker	1957	50.00

JAZZ WORKSHOP

Number	Title	Yr	NM
❑ JWS-500 [M]	Bird at St. Nick's	1958	120.00
❑ JWS-501 [M]	Bird on 52nd Street	1958	120.00

LES JAZZ COOL

Number	Title	Yr	NM
❑ 101 [M]	Les Jazz Cool, Volume 1	1960	50.00
❑ 102 [M]	Les Jazz Cool, Volume 2	1960	50.00
❑ 103 [M]	Les Jazz Cool, Volume 3	1960	50.00

MERCURY

Number	Title	Yr	NM
❑ MGC-512 [10]	Bird and Diz	1952	500.00
❑ MG-35010 [10]	Charlie Parker with Strings	1950	600.00
❑ MGC-101 [10]	Charlie Parker with Strings	1950	500.00
—Reissue of 35010			
❑ MGC-501 [10]	Charlie Parker with Strings	1951	500.00
—Reissue of 101 with new number			
❑ MGC-109 [10]	Charlie Parker with Strings, Volume 2	1950	500.00
❑ MGC-509 [10]	Charlie Parker with Strings, Volume 2	1952	500.00
—Reissue of 109 with new number			
❑ MGC-513 [10]	South of the Border	1952	500.00

MGM

Number	Title	Yr	NM
❑ M3G-4949	Archetypes	1974	15.00

MOSAIC

Number	Title	Yr	NM
❑ MR10-129	The Complete Dean Benedetti Recordings of Charlie Parker	199?	100.00

ONYX

Number	Title	Yr	NM
❑ 221	First Recordings with Jay McShann	197?	15.00

PHOENIX

Number	Title	Yr	NM
❑ 10	New Bird	197?	12.00
❑ 12	New Bird, Vol. 2	197?	12.00
❑ 17	Yardbird in Lotusland	197?	12.00

PICKWICK

Number	Title	Yr	NM
❑ SPC-3054 [R]	Yardbird	196?	12.00
❑ PC-3054 [M]	Yardbird	196?	15.00

PRESTIGE

Number	Title	Yr	NM
❑ 24009	Charlie Parker	197?	18.00
❑ 24024	Parker/Powell/Mingus/Roach	197?	18.00

ROOST

Number	Title	Yr	NM
❑ LP-2210 [M]	All Star Sextet	1958	120.00
❑ LP-2257 [M]	The World of Charlie Parker	1963	40.00

SAVOY

Number	Title	Yr	NM
❑ MG-12152 [M]	An Evening at Home with the Bird	196?	40.00
❑ MG-12138 [M]	Bird's Night -- The Music of Charlie Parker	1958	50.00
❑ MG-9000 [10]	Charlie Parker	1950	500.00
❑ MG-9001 [10]	Charlie Parker, Volume 2	1951	500.00
❑ MG-9010 [10]	Charlie Parker, Volume 3	1952	500.00
❑ MG-9011 [10]	Charlie Parker, Volume 4	1952	500.00
❑ MG-12000 [M]	Charlie Parker Memorial	1955	100.00
❑ MG-12009 [M]	Charlie Parker Memorial, Volume 2	1955	100.00
❑ MG-12186 [M]	Newly Discovered Sides by the Immortal Charlie Parker	1966	30.00
❑ MG-12179 [M]	The "Bird" Returns	196?	30.00
❑ MG-12079 [M]	The Charlie Parker Story	1956	100.00
❑ MG-12014 [M]	The Genius of Charlie Parker	1955	100.00
❑ MG-12001 [M]	The Immortal Charlie Parker	1955	100.00

SAVOY JAZZ

Number	Title	Yr	NM
❑ SJL-2201	Bird: The Savoy Recordings	1976	18.00
❑ SJL-1108	Bird at the Roost	197?	15.00
❑ SJL-1173	Bird at the Roost, Vol. 3	1987	12.00
❑ SJL-2259	Bird at the Roost: The Complete Royal Roost Performances, Vol. 1	198?	18.00
❑ SJL-2260	Bird at the Roost: The Complete Royal Roost Performances, Vol. 2	1986	18.00
❑ SJL-1107	Encores	197?	15.00
❑ SJL-1129	Encores, Vol. 2	198?	12.00
❑ SJL-1132	One Night in Chicago	198?	12.00
❑ SJL-1208	Original Bird: The Best on Savoy	198?	12.00
❑ SJL-5500	The Complete Savoy Studio Sessions	197?	30.00

SPOTLITE

Number	Title	Yr	NM
❑ 101	Charlie Parker on Dial, Vol. 1	197?	12.00
❑ 102	Charlie Parker on Dial, Vol. 2	197?	12.00
❑ 103	Charlie Parker on Dial, Vol. 3	197?	12.00
❑ 104	Charlie Parker on Dial, Vol. 4	197?	12.00
❑ 105	Charlie Parker on Dial, Vol. 5	197?	12.00
❑ 106	Charlie Parker on Dial, Vol. 6	197?	12.00

STASH

Number	Title	Yr	NM
❑ ST-260	Birth of the Bebop	1986	12.00
❑ ST-280	The Bird You Never Heard	1988	12.00

TRIP

Number	Title	Yr	NM
❑ 5020	Birdology	197?	18.00
❑ 5035	The Master	197?	15.00

UPFRONT

Number	Title	Yr	NM
❑ UPF-172	Live Sessions	197?	12.00

VERVE

Number	Title	Yr	NM
❑ MGV-8004 [M]	April in Paris (The Genius of Charlie Parker #2)	1957	80.00
❑ V-8004 [M]	April in Paris (The Genius of Charlie Parker #2)	1961	30.00
❑ V6-8004 [R]	April in Paris (The Genius of Charlie Parker #2)	196?	15.00
❑ 50-5263 [M]	April in Paris (The Genius of Charlie Parker #2)	197?	18.00
—Book-of-the-Month Club edition of 8004			
❑ 837176-1	Bird: The Original Recordings of Charlie Parker	1987	12.00
❑ MGV-8006 [M]	Bird and Diz (The Genius of Charlie Parker #4)	1957	80.00
❑ V-8006 [M]	Bird and Diz (The Genius of Charlie Parker #4)	1961	30.00
❑ V6-8006 [R]	Bird and Diz (The Genius of Charlie Parker #4)	196?	15.00
❑ 817442-1	Bird on Verve, Vol. 1: Charlie Parker with Strings	1985	12.00
❑ 817443-1	Bird on Verve, Vol. 2: Bird and Diz	1985	12.00
❑ 817444-1	Bird on Verve, Vol. 3: More Charlie Parker with Strings	1985	12.00
❑ 817445-1	Bird on Verve, Vol. 4: Afro-Cuban Jazz	1985	12.00
❑ 817446-1	Bird on Verve, Vol. 5: Charlie Parker	1985	12.00
❑ 817447-1	Bird on Verve, Vol. 6: South of the Border	1985	12.00
❑ 817448-1	Bird on Verve, Vol. 7: Big Band	1985	12.00
❑ 817449-1	Bird on Verve, Vol. 8: Charlie Parker in Hi-Fi	1985	12.00
❑ V6-8787 [R]	Bird Set	1969	18.00
❑ VSP-23 [M]	Bird Wings	1966	25.00
❑ VSPS-23 [R]	Bird Wings	1966	15.00
❑ MGV-8007 [M]	Charlie Parker Plays Cole Porter (The Genius of Charlie Parker #5)	1957	80.00
❑ V-8007 [M]	Charlie Parker Plays Cole Porter (The Genius of Charlie Parker #5)	1961	30.00
❑ V6-8007 [R]	Charlie Parker Plays Cole Porter (The Genius of Charlie Parker #5)	196?	15.00

Number	Title	Yr	NM
❏ VE-2-2508	Charlie Parker Sides	197?	18.00
❏ 833564-1	Charlie Parker Sides	198?	12.00
❏ UMV-2562	Charlie Parker with Strings	198?	12.00
❏ MGV-8008 [M]	Fiesta (The Genius of Charlie Parker #6)	1957	80.00
❏ V-8008 [M]	Fiesta (The Genius of Charlie Parker #6)	1961	30.00
❏ V6-8008 [R]	Fiesta (The Genius of Charlie Parker #6)	196?	15.00
❏ UMV-2617	Jazz Perennial	198?	12.00
❏ MGV-8009 [M]	Jazz Perennial (The Genius of Charlie Parker #7)	1957	80.00
❏ V-8009 [M]	Jazz Perennial (The Genius of Charlie Parker #7)	1961	30.00
❏ V6-8009 [R]	Jazz Perennial (The Genius of Charlie Parker #7)	196?	15.00
❏ MGV-8003 [M]	Night and Day (The Genius of Charlie Parker #1)	1957	80.00
❏ V-8003 [M]	Night and Day (The Genius of Charlie Parker #1)	1961	30.00
❏ V6-8003 [R]	Night and Day (The Genius of Charlie Parker #1)	196?	15.00
❏ UMV-2029	Now's the Time	198?	12.00
❏ V6-8005 [R]	Now's the Time (The Genius of Charlie Parker #3)	196?	15.00
❏ V-8005 [M]	Now's the Time (The Genius of Charlie Parker #3)	1961	30.00
❏ MGV-8005 [M]	Now's the Time (The Genius of Charlie Parker #3)	1957	80.00
❏ V3HB-8840	Return Engagement	197?	18.00
❏ UMV-2030	Swedish Schnapps	198?	12.00
❏ MGV-8010 [M]	Swedish Schnapps (The Genius of Charlie Parker #8)	1957	80.00
❏ V-8010 [M]	Swedish Schnapps (The Genius of Charlie Parker #8)	1961	30.00
❏ V6-8010 [R]	Swedish Schnapps (The Genius of Charlie Parker #8)	196?	15.00
❏ MGV-8100-3 [M]	The Charlie Parker Story	1957	150.00
—Combines 8000, 8001 and 8002 in a box set			
❏ V-8100-3 [M]	The Charlie Parker Story	1961	60.00
—Combines 8000, 8001 and 8002 in a box set			
❏ MGV-8000 [M]	The Charlie Parker Story, Volume 1	1957	80.00
❏ V-8000 [M]	The Charlie Parker Story, Volume 1	1961	30.00
❏ V6-8000 [R]	The Charlie Parker Story, Volume 1	196?	15.00
❏ MGV-8001 [M]	The Charlie Parker Story, Volume 2	1957	80.00
❏ V-8001 [M]	The Charlie Parker Story, Volume 2	1961	30.00
❏ V6-8001 [R]	The Charlie Parker Story, Volume 2	196?	15.00
❏ MGV-8002 [M]	The Charlie Parker Story, Volume 3	1957	80.00
❏ V-8002 [M]	The Charlie Parker Story, Volume 3	1961	30.00
❏ V6-8002 [R]	The Charlie Parker Story, Volume 3	196?	15.00
❏ 823250-1	The Cole Porter Songbook	1986	12.00
❏ V-8409 [M]	The Essential Charlie Parker	1961	30.00
❏ V6-8409 [R]	The Essential Charlie Parker	196?	15.00
❏ VE-2-2501	The Verve Years 1948-50	197?	18.00
❏ VE-2-2512	The Verve Years 1950-51	197?	18.00
❏ VE-2-2523	The Verve Years 1952-54	197?	18.00

VOGUE
❏ LAE-12002 [M]	Memorial Album	1955	150.00

WARNER BROS.
❏ 6BS3159	The Complete Dial Recordings	1977	80.00
—Limited edition of 4,000 box sets			
❏ 2WB3198	The Very Best of Bird	1977	25.00

ZIM
❏ 1006	Apartment Jam	197?	15.00
❏ 1003	At the Pershing Ballroom, Chicago, 1950	197?	15.00
❏ 1001	Lullaby in Rhythm	197?	15.00

PARKER, CHARLIE/COLEMAN HAWKINS/GEORGIE AULD

JAM
❏ 5006	Unearthed Masters, Vol. 1	198?	12.00

PARKER, CHARLIE/DIZZY GILLESPIE

EMUS
❏ ES-12027 [R]	Charlie Parker / Dizzy Gillespie	197?	15.00

PARKER, CHARLIE/DIZZY GILLESPIE/BUD POWELL/MAX ROACH

SAVOY
❏ MG-9034 [10]	Bird, Diz, Bud, Max	1953	600.00

PARKER, CHARLIE/STAN GETZ/WARDELL GRAY

DESIGN
❏ DLP-183 [M]	Charlie Parker/Stan Getz/Wardell Gray	196?	18.00

PARKER, FESS

COLUMBIA
❏ CL666 [M]	Walt Disney's Davy Crockett, King of the Wild Frontier	1955	100.00

DISNEYLAND
❏ DQ-1336	Cowboy and Indian Songs	1969	30.00
❏ DQ-1269 [M]	Pecos Bill and Other Stories in Song	1965	30.00

Number	Title	Yr	NM
❏ WDA-3602 [M]	Three Adventures of Davy Crockett	1958	50.00
—Reissue of Columbia 666			
❏ DQ-1315 [M]	Three Adventures of Davy Crockett	1968	30.00
—Another reissue, this time of 1926			
❏ ST-1926 [M]	Three Adventures of Davy Crockett	1963	30.00
—Reissue of 3602			
❏ WDL-3041 [M]	Westward Ho the Wagons	1959	30.00
—Reissue of 4008			
❏ WDL-4006 [M]	Westward Ho the Wagons	1956	80.00
❏ WDL-3006 [M]	Yarns and Songs	1957	40.00
❏ WDL-1007 [M]	Yarns and Songs of the West	1959	30.00
—Reissue of 3006			

RCA VICTOR
❏ LPM-2973 [M]	Fess Parker Sings About Daniel Boone, Davy Crockett and Abe Lincoln	1964	30.00
❏ LSP-2973 [S]	Fess Parker Sings About Daniel Boone, Davy Crockett and Abe Lincoln	1964	30.00

PARKER, GRAHAM

ARISTA
❏ AL9589	Another Grey Area	1982	12.00
❏ AL6-8374	Another Grey Area	1985	10.00
—Budget-line reissue			
❏ SP-63 [DJ]	Live Sparks	1979	35.00
❏ SP-63 [DJ]	Live Sparks	1979	35.00
❏ AL6-8391	Look Back in Anger	1985	12.00
❏ AL4223	Squeezing Out Sparks	1979	15.00
❏ AL6-8363	Squeezing Out Sparks	1985	10.00
—Budget-line reissue			
❏ AL8-8023	The Real Macaw	1983	12.00
❏ AL6-8352	The Real Macaw	1985	10.00
—Budget-line reissue			
❏ AL9517	The Up Escalator	1980	12.00
❏ AL6-8356	The Up Escalator	1985	10.00
—Budget-line reissue			

ELEKTRA
❏ 60388	Steady Nerves	1985	12.00

MERCURY
❏ SRM-1-1117	Heat Treatment	1976	18.00
❏ SRM-1-1095	Howlin' Wind	1976	18.00
❏ 826097-1 [B]	Pourin' It All Out: The Mercury Years	1985	18.00
❏ SRM-1-3706	Stick to Me	1977	18.00
❏ 824808-1	Stick to Me	1985	15.00
—Reissue with new number			
❏ SRM-2-100 [B]	The Parkerilla	1978	25.00
—Originals have gatefold sleeves			

RCA
❏ 9876-1-R	Human Soul	1989	12.00
❏ 8316-1-R	The Mona Lisa's Sister	1988	12.00

ROCK THE HOUSE
❏ RTH-2817-1	12 Haunted Episodes	1995	18.00

PARKER, JACY

VERVE
❏ V-8424 [M]	Spotlight On Jacy Parker	1962	40.00
❏ V6-8424 [S]	Spotlight On Jacy Parker	1962	50.00

PARKER, JOHN

GOLDEN CREST
❏ GC-3051	Dixieland	196?	18.00

PARKER, JUNIOR, AND BOBBY BLAND

ABC DUKE
❏ DLP-72	Blues Consolidated	1974	18.00

DUKE
❏ DLP-72 [M]	Blues Consolidated	1961	150.00

PARKER, JUNIOR

ABC
❏ AC-30010	The ABC Collection	1976	18.00

ABC DUKE
❏ DLP-76	Driving Wheel	1974	18.00
❏ DLP-83	The Best of Junior Parker	1974	18.00

BLUE ROCK
❏ SRB-64004	Honey-Drippin' Blues	1969	18.00

BLUESWAY
❏ BLS-6066	Sometime Tomorrow	1973	18.00

CAPITOL
❏ ST-564	Outside Man	1970	18.00

DUKE
❏ DLP-76 [M]	Driving Wheel	1962	150.00
—With Cadillac on front cover			
❏ DLP-76 [M]	Driving Wheel	196?	100.00
—With Wagon Wheel on front cover			
❏ DLP-83 [M]	The Best of Junior Parker	1967	50.00
❏ DLPS-83 [P]	The Best of Junior Parker	1967	40.00

GROOVE MERCHANT
❏ 513	Love Ain't Nothin'	1974	18.00

MCA
Number	Title	Yr	NM
❏ 27046	The Best of Junior Parker	1980	12.00

MERCURY
❏ MG-21101 [M]	Like It Is	1967	30.00
❏ SR-61101 [S]	Like It Is	1967	30.00

MINIT
❏ 24024	Blues Man	1969	30.00

UNITED ARTISTS
❏ UAS-6823	I Tell Stories Sad and True	1971	18.00

PARKER, KNOCKY, AND SMOKEY MONTGOMERY

CIRCLE
❏ CLP-10001	Texas Swing, Vol. 1: The Barrelhouse	1987	12.00
❏ CLP-10002	Texas Swing, Vol. 2: The Boogie-Woogie	1987	12.00
❏ CLP-10003	Texas Swing, Vol. 3: … And the Blues	1987	12.00
❏ CLP-10004	Texas Swing, Vol. 4: Smokey and the Bearkats	1987	12.00

PARKER, KNOCKY

AUDIOPHILE
❏ AP-28 [M]	Boogie Woogie Maxine	1956	40.00
❏ AP-102/5	The Complete Piano Works of Jelly Roll Morton	196?	50.00
—In box with booklet; it's unknown whether the volumes also were issued individually			

EUPHONIC
❏ 1216	Classic Rags and Nostalgia	198?	12.00
❏ 1215	Eight on Eighty-Eight	198?	12.00

GHB
❏ GHB-19	Knocky Parker	1967	18.00
❏ 150	Knocky Parker and the Cake-Walkin' Jazz Band	1981	12.00

JAZZOLOGY
❏ J-81	Cakewalk to Ragtime	197?	12.00

PROGRESSIVE
❏ PLP-1 [10]	New Orleans Stomps	1954	50.00

PARKER, LEO

BLUE NOTE
❏ BLP-4087 [M]	Let Me Tell You 'Bout It	1961	60.00
—With 61st St. address on label			
❏ BST-84087 [S]	Let Me Tell You 'Bout It	1961	80.00
—With 61st St. address on label			
❏ BLP-4087 [M]	Let Me Tell You 'Bout It	1963	25.00
—With "New York, USA" address on label			
❏ BST-84087 [S]	Let Me Tell You 'Bout It	1963	30.00
—With "New York, USA" address on label			
❏ BST-84087 [S]	Let Me Tell You 'Bout It	1967	18.00
—With "A Division of Liberty Records" on label			
❏ LT-1076	Rollin' with Leo	1980	12.00
❏ BST-84095	Rollin' with Leo	1986	15.00
—Originally scheduled for 1961 release, this was the first issue on its originally assigned number			

CHESS
❏ LPV-413	The Late, Great King of Baritone Sax	1971	18.00

COLLECTABLES
❏ COL-5329	Back to the Baritones	198?	12.00

SAVOY
❏ MG-9009 [10]	Leo Parker	1952	250.00
❏ MG-9018 [10]	New Trends in Modern Music	1952	250.00

PARKER, MAYNARD

PRESTIGE
❏ 10054	Midnight Rider	1973	25.00

PARKER, RAY, JR.

ARISTA
❏ AL9543	A Woman Needs Love	1981	12.00
—As "Ray Parker Jr. and Raydio			
❏ AL8-8266	Chartbusters	1984	12.00
❏ AL9612	Greatest Hits	1982	12.00
❏ AB4163	Raydio	1978	18.00
—As "Raydio			
❏ AB4212	Rock On	1979	18.00
—As "Raydio			
❏ AL8-8280	Sex and the Single Man	1985	12.00
❏ AL9590	The Other Woman	1982	12.00
❏ AL9515	Two Places at the Same Time	1980	12.00
—As "Ray Parker Jr. and Raydio			
❏ AL8-8087	Woman Out of Control	1983	12.00

GEFFEN
❏ GHS24124	After Dark	1987	12.00

MCA
❏ 10327	I Love You Like You Are	1991	15.00

PARKER, ROBERT

NOLA
❏ LP-1001 [M]	Barefootin'	1966	40.00

PARKER FAMILY, THE

Number	Title	Yr	NM
AUDIO LAB			
❑ AL-1548 [M]	Songs for Salvation	196?	150.00
❑ AL-1574 [M]	Songs for Salvation, Vol. 2	196?	150.00
KING			
❑ 932 [M]	Just a Real Nice Family	1965	40.00

PARKINS, LEROY

Number	Title	Yr	NM
BETHLEHEM			
❑ BCP-6047 [M]	LeRoy Parkins and His Yazoo River Band	1960	30.00
❑ SBCP-6047 [S]	LeRoy Parkins and His Yazoo River Band	1960	40.00

PARKS, ANDY

Number	Title	Yr	NM
CAPITOL			
❑ T2799 [M]	Sex, School…And Like Other Pressures	1967	25.00
❑ ST2799 [S]	Sex, School…And Like Other Pressures	1967	25.00

PARKS, MICHAEL

Number	Title	Yr	NM
FIRST AMERICAN			
❑ 7781	You Don't Know Me	1983	12.00
MGM			
❑ SE-4717	Blue	1970	18.00
❑ SE-4646	Closing the Gap	1969	18.00
❑ SE-4662	Long Lonesome Highway	1970	18.00
❑ SE-4784	The Best of Michael Parks	1971	18.00
VERVE			
❑ V6-5079	Lost and Found	1971	18.00

PARKS, VAN DYKE

Number	Title	Yr	NM
SUNDAZED			
❑ LP-5141	Discover America	2002	18.00
— Reissue on 180-gram vinyl			
❑ LP-5140	Song Cycle	2002	18.00
— Reissue on 180-gram vinyl			
WARNER BROS.			
❑ BS2878	Clang of the Yankee Reaper	1975	15.00
❑ BS2589	Discover America	1972	15.00
❑ 23829	Jump!	1984	15.00
❑ WS1727	Song Cycle	1968	30.00
— Gold label			
❑ WS1727 [B]	Song Cycle	1968	30.00
— Green label with "W7" box logo			
❑ WS1727	Song Cycle	1970	15.00
— Green label with "WB" shield logo			
❑ 25968	Tokyo Rose	1989	15.00

PARLAN, HORACE

Number	Title	Yr	NM
BLUE NOTE			
❑ BST-84134	Happy Frame of Mind	1986	15.00
— The Finest in Jazz Since 1939" issue			
❑ BLP-4062 [M]	Headin' South	1961	300.00
— With W. 63rd St. address on label			
❑ BST 84062 [S]	Headin' South	1961	250.00
— With W. 63rd St. address on label			
❑ BLP-4062 [M]	Headin' South	1963	25.00
— With "New York, USA" address on label			
❑ BST-84062 [S]	Headin' South	1963	30.00
— With "New York, USA" address on label			
❑ BST-84062 [S]	Headin' South	1967	18.00
— With "A Division of Liberty Records" on label			
❑ BLP-4028 [M]	Movin' and Groovin'	1960	300.00
— Deep groove" version (deep indentation under label on both sides)			
❑ BLP-4028 [M]	Movin' and Groovin'	1960	150.00
— Regular version, W. 63rd St. address on label			
❑ BST-84028 [S]	Movin' and Groovin'	1960	250.00
— With W. 63rd St. address on label			
❑ BLP-4028 [M]	Movin' and Groovin'	1963	25.00
— With "New York, USA" address on label			
❑ BST-84028 [S]	Movin' and Groovin'	1963	30.00
— With "New York, USA" address on label			
❑ BST-84028 [S]	Movin' and Groovin'	1967	18.00
— With "A Division of Liberty Records" on label			
❑ BLP-4074 [M]	On the Spur of the Moment	1961	150.00
— With W. 63rd St. address on label			
❑ BST-84074 [S]	On the Spur of the Moment	1961	70.00
— With 61st St. address on label			
❑ BLP-4074 [M]	On the Spur of the Moment	1961	60.00
— With 61st St. address on label			
❑ BST-84074 [S]	On the Spur of the Moment	1961	200.00
— With W. 63rd St. address on label			
❑ BLP-4074 [M]	On the Spur of the Moment	1963	25.00
— With "New York, USA" address on label			
❑ BST-84074 [S]	On the Spur of the Moment	1963	30.00
— With "New York, USA" address on label			
❑ BST-84074 [S]	On the Spur of the Moment	1967	18.00
— With "A Division of Liberty Records" on label			
❑ BST-4074	On the Spur of the Moment	199?	30.00
— Classic Records reissue on audiophile vinyl			
❑ BLP-4043 [M]	Speakin' My Piece	1960	100.00
— Deep groove" version (deep indentation under label on both sides)			
❑ BLP-4043 [M]	Speakin' My Piece	1960	80.00
— Regular version, W. 63rd St. address on label			
❑ BST-84043 [S]	Speakin' My Piece	1963	30.00
— With "New York, USA" address on label			
❑ BLP-4043 [M]	Speakin' My Piece	1963	25.00
— With "New York, USA" address on label			
❑ BST-84043 [S]	Speakin' My Piece	1960	80.00
— With W. 63rd St. address on label			
❑ BST-84043 [S]	Speakin' My Piece	1967	18.00
— With "A Division of Liberty Records" on label			
❑ BLP-4082 [M]	Up and Down	1961	60.00
— With 61st St. address on label			
❑ BST-84082 [S]	Up and Down	1961	70.00
— With 61st St. address on label			
❑ BLP-4082 [M]	Up and Down	1963	25.00
— With "New York, USA" address on label			
❑ BST-84082 [S]	Up and Down	1963	30.00
— With "New York, USA" address on label			
❑ BST-84082 [S]	Up and Down	1967	18.00
— With "A Division of Liberty Records" on label			
❑ BLP-4037 [M]	Us Three	1960	1000.00
— Deep groove" version (deep indentation under label on both sides)			
❑ BLP-4037 [M]	Us Three	1960	80.00
— Regular version, W. 63rd St. address on label			
❑ BST-84037 [S]	Us Three	1960	80.00
— With W. 63rd St. address on label			
❑ BLP-4037 [M]	Us Three	1963	25.00
— With "New York, USA" address on label			
❑ BST-84037 [S]	Us Three	1967	18.00
— With "A Division of Liberty Records" on label			
❑ BST-84037 [S]	Us Three	1963	30.00
— With "New York, USA" address on label			
INNER CITY			
❑ IC-2012	Arrival	197?	18.00
❑ IC-2056	No Blues	197?	18.00
MOSAIC			
❑ MQ8-197	The Complete Horace Parlan Blue Note Sessions	2000	150.00
STEEPLECHASE			
❑ SCS-1012	Arrival	198?	15.00
❑ SCS-1124	Blue Parlan	198?	15.00
❑ SCS-1076	Frank-ly Speaking	198?	15.00
❑ SCS-1194	Glad I Met You	198?	15.00
❑ SCS-1178	Like Someone in Love	1983	15.00
❑ SCS-1141	Musically Yours	198?	15.00
❑ SCS-1056	No Blues	198?	15.00
❑ SCS-1167	The Maestro	198?	15.00

PARLET

Number	Title	Yr	NM
CASABLANCA			
❑ NBLP7146	Invasion of the Booty Snatchers	1979	25.00
❑ NBLP7094	Pleasure Principle	1978	25.00

PARLIAMENT

Number	Title	Yr	NM
CASABLANCA			
❑ NBLP7014	Chocolate City	1975	75.00
❑ NBLP7084	Funkentelechy vs. the Placebo Syndrome	1977	65.00
❑ 824501-1	Funkentelechy vs. the Placebo Syndrome	1985	25.00
❑ NBLP7195 [B]	Gloryhallastoopid (Or Pin the Tale on the Funky)	1979	65.00
❑ 822637-1	Greatest Hits	1984	25.00
❑ NBLP7022	Mothership Connection	1976	65.00
❑ 824502-1	Mothership Connection	1985	25.00
❑ NBLP7125	Motor-Booty Affair	1978	65.00
❑ NBPIX7125 [PD]	Motor-Booty Affair	1978	75.00
❑ NBLP7053	Parliament Live/P. Funk Earth Tour	1977	75.00
❑ NBLP7034	The Clones of Dr. Funkenstein	1976	65.00
❑ NBLP7249	Trombipulation	1980	65.00
❑ NBLP9003	Up for the Down Stroke	1974	60.00
— Original pressing, distributed by Warner Bros.			
❑ NBLP7002	Up for the Down Stroke	1974	75.00
INVICTUS			
❑ ST-7302	Osmium	1970	150.00

PARSONS, ALAN, PROJECT

Number	Title	Yr	NM
20TH CENTURY			
❑ T-508 [B]	Tales of Mystery and Imagination - Edgar Allan Poe	1976	18.00
ARISTA			
❑ AL8204	Ammonia Avenue	1984	12.00
❑ AL8289	Ammonia Avenue	1985	10.00
— Reissue			
❑ SP-68 [DJ]	Audio Guide to the Alan Parsons Project	1979	50.00
— Contains first four APP LPs plus a two-record set of other Parsons work			
❑ SP-68 [DJ]	Audio Guide to the Alan Parsons Project	1979	50.00
— Contains first four APP LPs plus a two-record set of other Parsons work			
❑ SP-140 [DJ]	Complete Audio Guide to the Alan Parsons Project	1982	80.00
— Contains first six APP LPs plus a two-record set of other Parsons work			
❑ SP-140 [DJ]	Complete Audio Guide to the Alan Parsons Project	1982	80.00
— Contains first six APP LPs plus a two-record set of other Parsons work			
❑ AB9504	Eve	1979	12.00
❑ AL8318	Eve	1985	10.00
— Reissue			
❑ AL9599	Eye in the Sky	1982	12.00
❑ AL8290	Eye in the Sky	1985	10.00
— Reissue			
❑ AL8448	Gaudi	1987	10.00
❑ AL7002	I Robot	1977	12.00
❑ AL8040	I Robot	1983	10.00
— Reissue			
❑ AB4180	Pyramid	1978	12.00
❑ AL8320	Pyramid	1985	10.00
— Reissue			
❑ AL8384	Stereotomy	1986	18.00
— First editions came in an oversize vinyl jacket			
❑ AL8384	Stereotomy	1986	10.00
— With regular LP jacket			
❑ AL8193	The Best of the Alan Parsons Project	1983	10.00
❑ AL8486	The Best of the Alan Parsons Project, Vol. 2	1987	10.00
❑ AL8487	The Instrumental Works of the Alan Parsons Project	1988	12.00
❑ AL9518	The Turn of a Friendly Card	1980	12.00
❑ AL8315	The Turn of a Friendly Card	1985	10.00
— Reissue			
❑ ALPD8263 [DJ]	Vulture Culture	1985	30.00
— Promo-only picture disc			
❑ ALPD8263 [DJ]	Vulture Culture	1985	30.00
— Promo-only picture disc			
❑ AL8263	Vulture Culture	1985	10.00
CASABLANCA			
❑ 822784-1	Tales of Mystery and Imagination - Edgar Allan Poe	1984	12.00
— Reissue of 20th Century LP			
MOBILE FIDELITY			
❑ 1-084	I Robot	1982	60.00
— Audiophile vinyl			
❑ MFQR 1-084	I Robot	1982	100.00
— Audiophile vinyl; Ultra High Quality pressing in box			
❑ 1-204	Tales of Mystery and Imagination - Edgar Allan Poe	1994	60.00
— Audiophile vinyl			

PARSONS, GRAM

Number	Title	Yr	NM
REPRISE			
❑ MS2123 [B]	G.P.	1973	25.00
❑ MS2171 [B]	Grievous Angel	1974	25.00
RHINO			
❑ R1 541107 [B]	Alternate Takes From GP And Grievous Angel	2014	40.00
❑ R-12123 [B]	GP	2014	30.00
❑ R-12171 [B]	Grievous Angel	2014	30.00
SIERRA			
❑ 8702	Early Years, Volume 1 (1963-65)	1979	12.00
❑ SP-1963	Early Years, Volume 1 (1963-65)	198?	10.00
— Reissue of 8702			
❑ GP-1973	Gram Parsons and the Fallen Angels Live '73	1982	12.00
SUNDAZED			
❑ LP5076	Another Side of This Life	2000	15.00

PARTON, DOLLY

Number	Title	Yr	NM
COLUMBIA			
❑ C46882	Eagle When She Flies	1991	25.00
— Available on vinyl only through Columbia House			
❑ FC40968	Rainbow	1987	12.00
❑ FC44384	White Limozeen	1989	15.00
MONUMENT			
❑ SLP-18136	As Long As I Love	1970	25.00
❑ MLP-8085 [M]	Hello, I'm Dolly	1967	30.00
❑ SLP-18085 [S]	Hello, I'm Dolly	1967	40.00
❑ KZG33876	Hello, I'm Dolly	1975	25.00
❑ 7623	In the Beginning	197?	15.00
❑ KZG31913	The World of Dolly	1972	25.00
PAIR			
❑ PDL2-1009	Just the Way I Am	1986	15.00
❑ PDL2-1116	Portrait	1986	15.00
RCA			
❑ 5706-1-R	The Best of Dolly Parton, Vol. 3	1987	12.00
❑ 6497-1-R	The Best There Is	1987	12.00
RCA CAMDEN			
❑ CAS-2583	Just the Way I Am	1972	12.00
❑ ACL1-0307	Mine	1973	12.00
RCA VICTOR			
❑ AYL1-4830	9 to 5 and Odd Jobs	1984	10.00
— Best Buy Series" reissue			
❑ AHL1-3852	9 to 5 and Odd Jobs	1980	15.00
❑ APL1-1665	All I Can Do	1976	15.00
❑ LSP-4387	A Real Live Dolly	1970	30.00
— Four songs feature Porter Wagoner			

Number	Title	Yr	NM
❑ APD1-0286 [Q]	Bubbling Over	1974	25.00
❑ APL1-0286	Bubbling Over	1973	15.00
❑ AHL1-4691	Burlap & Satin	1983	12.00
❑ AYL1-5437	Burlap & Satin	1985	10.00
—Best Buy Series" reissue			
❑ LSP-4603	Coat of Many Colors	1971	25.00
❑ AHL1-5471	Collector's Series	1985	12.00
❑ APL1-1221	Dolly	1975	15.00
❑ AHL1-3546	Dolly Dolly Dolly	1980	15.00
❑ LSP-4762	Dolly Parton Sings	1972	18.00
❑ LSP-4398	Golden Streets of Glory	1971	25.00
❑ AHL1-3361	Great Balls of Fire	1979	15.00
❑ AHL1-4422	Greatest Hits	1982	15.00
❑ AFL1-2797	Heartbreaker	1978	15.00
❑ AYL1-3665	Heartbreaker	1980	10.00
—Best Buy Series" reissue			
❑ AHL1-4289	Heartbreak Express	1982	15.00
❑ AYL1-4829	Here You Come Again	1984	10.00
—Best Buy Series" reissue			
❑ AFL1-2544	Here You Come Again	1977	15.00
❑ LSP-4099	In the Good Old Days	1969	25.00
❑ AYL1-3898	Jolene	1981	10.00
—Best Buy Series" reissue			
❑ APL1-0473	Jolene	1974	15.00
❑ LSP-4507	Joshua	1971	25.00
❑ LPM-3949 [M]	Just Because I'm a Woman	1968	100.00
❑ LSP-3949 [S]	Just Because I'm a Woman	1968	30.00
—Stereo" on black label			
❑ LSP-3949 [S]	Just Because I'm a Woman	1968	25.00
—Orange label			
❑ APL1-0712	Love Is Like a Butterfly	1974	15.00
❑ LSP-4188	My Blue Ridge Mountain Boy	1969	25.00
❑ LSP-4752	My Favorite Song Writer: Porter Wagoner	1972	25.00
❑ APL1-0033	My Tennessee Mountain Home	1973	15.00
❑ AYL1-3764	My Tennessee Mountain Home	1980	10.00
—Best Buy Series" reissue			
❑ AYL1-3980	New Harvest	1981	10.00
—Best Buy Series" reissue			
❑ APL1-2188	New Harvest...First Gathering	1977	15.00
❑ DJL1-2314 [DJ]	Personal Music Dialogue with Dolly Parton	1976	30.00
❑ AHL1-5414	Real Love	1985	12.00
❑ APL1-0950	The Bargain Store	1975	15.00
❑ LSP-4449	The Best of Dolly Parton	1970	25.00
❑ AYL1-5146	The Best of Dolly Parton	1984	10.00
—Best Buy Series" reissue			
❑ APL1-1117	The Best of Dolly Parton	1975	15.00
❑ LSP-4288	The Fairest of Them All	1970	25.00
❑ AHL1-4940	The Great Pretender	1984	12.00
❑ AHL1-9508	Think About Love	1986	12.00
❑ LSP-4686	Touch Your Woman	1972	25.00
TIME-LIFE			
❑ STW-107	Country Music	1981	12.00

PARTON, DOLLY/FAYE TUCKER

Number	Title	Yr	NM
SOMERSET			
❑ SF-29400	Dolly Parton Sings Country Oldies	1968	18.00
❑ S-9700 [M]	Hits Made Famous by Country Queens	1963	30.00
❑ SF-19700 [S]	Hits Made Famous by Country Queens	1963	30.00
—Dolly Parton sings songs made famous by Kitty Wells			
TIME			
❑ 2108	Country & Western Soul	1963	40.00

PARTON, DOLLY/GEORGE JONES

Number	Title	Yr	NM
STARDAY			
❑ LP429 [P]	Dolly Parton and George Jones	1968	40.00
—One side of Dolly in stereo, one side of "Possum" in rechanneled stereo			

PARTON, DOLLY/LINDA RONSTADT/EMMYLOU HARRIS

Number	Title	Yr	NM
WARNER BROS.			
❑ 25491	Trio	1987	12.00

PARTON, STELLA

Number	Title	Yr	NM
ELEKTRA			
❑ 7E-1111	Country Sweet	1977	15.00
❑ 6E-191	Love Ya	1979	15.00
❑ 6E-126	Stella Parton	1978	15.00
❑ 6E-229	The Best of Stella Parton	1979	15.00
SOUL, COUNTRY & BLUES			
❑ 6006	I Want to Hold You in My Dreams Tonight	1975	25.00
TOWN HOUSE			
❑ ST-7005	So Far So Good	1982	15.00

PARTRIDGE FAMILY, THE

Number	Title	Yr	NM
BELL			
❑ 6066	A Partridge Family Christmas Card	1971	30.00
—With attached Christmas card			
❑ 6066	A Partridge Family Christmas Card	1971	18.00
—Without Christmas card			
❑ 6066	A Partridge Family Christmas Card	1971	40.00
—With Christmas card printed on the cover (later pressing)			
❑ 1137	Bulletin Board	1973	50.00
❑ 1122	Crossword Puzzle	1973	30.00
❑ 6050	The Partridge Family Album	1970	25.00
❑ 6050	The Partridge Family Album Bonus Photo	1970	12.00
❑ 1107 [B]	The Partridge Family At Home with Their Greatest Hits	1972	25.00
❑ 1111	The Partridge Family Notebook	1972	30.00
❑ 6072	The Partridge Family Shopping Bag	1972	25.00
❑ 6072	The Partridge Family Shopping Bag Bonus Shopping Bag	1972	12.00
❑ 6064	The Partridge Family Sound Magazine	1971	25.00
❑ 1319	The World of the Partridge Family	1974	40.00
❑ 6059	Up to Date	1971	25.00
❑ 6059	Up to Date Book Cover	1971	12.00
LAURIE HOUSE			
❑ H-8014	The Partridge Family	197?	50.00

PASSPORT

Number	Title	Yr	NM
ATCO			
❑ SD 36-107	Cross-Collateral	1975	15.00
❑ SD 36-149	Iguacu	1977	12.00
❑ SD 36-132	Infinity Machine	1976	15.00
❑ SD7042	Looking Thru	1974	15.00
ATLANTIC			
❑ SD19304	Blue Tattoo	1981	12.00
❑ SD18162	Doldinger Jubilee '75	1976	15.00
❑ 80034	Earthborn	1982	12.00
❑ SD19233	Garden of Eden	1979	12.00
❑ 81727	Heavy Nights	1986	12.00
❑ 80144	Man in the Mirror	1983	12.00
❑ SD19265	Oceanliner	1980	12.00
❑ 81251	Running in Real Time	1985	12.00
❑ SD19177	Sky Blue	1978	12.00
❑ 81937	Talk Back	1989	12.00
REPRISE			
❑ MS2143	Doldinger	1973	18.00

PASTEL SIX, THE

Number	Title	Yr	NM
ZEN			
❑ 1001 [M]	The Cinnamon Cinder	1963	100.00

PASTICHE

Number	Title	Yr	NM
NOVA			
❑ 8707	That's R & B-Bop	198?	15.00

PATCHEN, KENNETH, WITH THE CHAMBER JAZZ SEXTET

Number	Title	Yr	NM
CADENCE			
❑ CLP-3004 [M]	Kenneth Patchen Reads His Poetry	1957	300.00

PATCHETT, TOM, AND JAY TARSES

Number	Title	Yr	NM
DECCA			
❑ DL75300	Instant Replay (Two Sides of Football)	1971	18.00

PATE, JOHNNY

Number	Title	Yr	NM
GIG			
❑ GLP-100 [M]	Subtle Sounds	1956	100.00
KING			
❑ 611 [M]	A Date with Johnny Pate	1959	80.00
❑ 561 [M]	Jazz Goes Ivy League	1958	80.00
❑ 584 [M]	Swingin' Flute	1958	80.00
STEPHENY			
❑ 4002 [M]	Johnny Pate at the Blue Note	1957	100.00
TALISMAN			
❑ TLP-1 [10]	Johnny Pate Trio	1956	120.00

PATITUCCI, JOHN

Number	Title	Yr	NM
GRP			
❑ GR-1049	John Patitucci	1988	12.00
❑ GR-9583	On the Corner	1989	15.00

PATRON SAINTS, THE

Number	Title	Yr	NM
(NO LABEL)			
❑ JT-1001	Fohhob Bohob	1969	3000.00
—100 copies were pressed; VG value 1000; VG+ value 2000			
PATRON SAINT			
❑ JT-1001	Fohhob Bohob	1997	30.00
—Authorized reissue with bonus 7-inch single; numbered edition of 500			

PATTERSON, DON

Number	Title	Yr	NM
CADET			
❑ LPS-787 [S]	Goin' Down Home	1967	25.00
❑ LP-787 [M]	Goin' Down Home	1967	30.00
MUSE			
❑ MR-5121	Movin' Up	1977	15.00
❑ MR-5005	The Return of Don Patterson	1974	18.00
❑ MR-5032	These Are Soulful Days	1975	18.00
❑ MR-5148	Why Not	1979	15.00
PRESTIGE			
❑ PRST-7772	Best of Jazz Giants	1971	18.00
❑ PRST-7563	Boppin' and Burnin'	1968	25.00
❑ PRST-7738	Brothers-4	1970	18.00
❑ PRST-7816	Donnybrook	1971	18.00
❑ PRST-7533 [S]	Four Dimensions	1967	25.00
❑ PRLP-7533 [M]	Four Dimensions	1967	30.00
❑ PRST-7613	Funk You	1969	25.00
❑ PRST-7349 [S]	Hip Cake Walk	1965	30.00
❑ PRLP-7349 [M]	Hip Cake Walk	1965	30.00
❑ PRST-7415 [S]	Holiday Soul	1965	30.00
❑ PRLP-7415 [M]	Holiday Soul	1966	30.00
❑ PRST-7510 [S]	Mellow Soul	1967	25.00
❑ PRLP-7510 [M]	Mellow Soul	1967	30.00
❑ PRST-7640	Oh, Happy Days!	1969	25.00
❑ PRST-7577	Opus De Don	1968	25.00
❑ PRST-7381 [S]	Patterson's People	1965	30.00
❑ PRLP-7381 [M]	Patterson's People	1965	30.00
❑ PRST-7430 [S]	Satisfaction	1966	30.00
❑ PRLP-7430 [M]	Satisfaction	1966	30.00
❑ PRST-7484 [S]	Soul Happening!	1967	25.00
❑ PRLP-7484 [M]	Soul Happening!	1967	30.00
❑ PRST-7704	The Best of Don Patterson	1969	18.00
❑ PRST-7466 [S]	The Boss Men	1967	30.00
❑ PRLP-7466 [M]	The Boss Men	1967	30.00
❑ PRST-7331 [S]	The Exciting New Organ of Don Patterson	1964	30.00
❑ PRLP-7331 [M]	The Exiting New Organ of Don Patterson	1964	30.00
❑ PRST-7852	Tune Up	1971	18.00

PATTERSON, KELLEE

Number	Title	Yr	NM
BLACK JAZZ			
❑ QD-12	Maiden Voyage	1974	25.00

PATTERSON SINGERS, THE

Number	Title	Yr	NM
ATCO			
❑ SD 33-380	The Patterson Singers	1972	25.00
KING			
❑ 763 [M]	Gospel Songs by the Patterson Singers	1962	50.00
❑ KS-1129	Jesus Knows	1971	25.00
MINIT			
❑ LP-40021	The Soul of Gospel	1969	25.00
VEE JAY			
❑ LP-5017 [M]	My Prayer	1962	30.00
❑ LP-5046 [M]	Songs of Faith	1963	25.00
❑ SR-5046 [S]	Songs of Faith	1963	30.00
❑ LP-5032 [M]	The Lord's Prayer	1963	30.00
❑ LP-5060 [M]	The Soul of the Patterson Singers	1964	25.00

PATTI, SANDI

Number	Title	Yr	NM
IMPACT			
❑ RO3874	The Gift Goes On	1983	15.00

PATTO

Number	Title	Yr	NM
ISLAND			
❑ SW-9322	Roll 'Em, Smoke 'Em, Put Another Line Out	1972	30.00
VERTIGO			
❑ VEL-1008 [B]	Hold Your Fire	1972	35.00
❑ VEL-1001	Patto	1971	35.00

PATTON, "BIG" JOHN

Number	Title	Yr	NM
BLUE NOTE			
❑ BST-84340 [S]	Accent on the Blues	1970	30.00
—With "A Division of Liberty Records" on label			
❑ BLP-4130 [M]	Along Came John	1963	30.00
❑ BST-84130 [S]	Along Came John	1963	40.00
—With "New York, USA" address on label			
❑ BST-84130 [S]	Along Came John	1967	18.00
—With "A Division of Liberty Records" on label			
❑ BST-84143 [S]	Blue John	1986	15.00
—The Finest in Jazz Since 1939" issue; originally scheduled for 1963 release, but canceled			
❑ BLP-4229 [M]	Got a Good Thing Goin'	1966	30.00
❑ BST-84229 [S]	Got a Good Thing Goin'	1966	30.00
—With "New York, USA" address on label			
❑ BST-84229 [S]	Got a Good Thing Goin'	1967	18.00
—With "A Division of Liberty Records" on label			
❑ BLP-4239 [M]	Let 'Em Roll	1966	30.00
❑ BST-84239 [S]	Let 'Em Roll	1966	30.00
—With "New York, USA" address on label			
❑ BST-84239 [S]	Let 'Em Roll	1967	18.00
—With "A Division of Liberty Records" on label			
❑ BLP-4192 [M]	Oh Baby!	1964	30.00
❑ BST-84192 [S]	Oh Baby!	1964	30.00
—With "New York, USA" address on label			
❑ BST-84192 [S]	Oh Baby!	1967	18.00
—With "A Division of Liberty Records" on label			
❑ BST-84281 [S]	That Certain Feeling	1968	30.00
—With "A Division of Liberty Records" on label			
❑ BLP-4174 [M]	The Way I Feel	1964	30.00
❑ BST-84174 [S]	The Way I Feel	1964	30.00
—With "New York, USA" address on label			

Number	Title	Yr	NM
☐ BST-84174 [S]	The Way I Feel	1967	18.00
— With "A Division of Liberty Records" on label			
☐ BST-84306 [S]	Understanding	1969	30.00
— With "A Division of Liberty Records" on label			

PATTON, CHARLEY

ORIGIN JAZZ LIBRARY
Number	Title	Yr	NM
☐ OJL-1 [M]	The Immortal Charley Patton No. 1	1962	30.00
☐ OJL-7 [M]	The Immortal Charley Patton No. 2	1962	30.00

YAZOO
Number	Title	Yr	NM
☐ 2010	Founder of the Delta Blues	197?	30.00
☐ 2001	King of the Delta Blues	197?	30.00

PATTON, JIMMY

MOON
Number	Title	Yr	NM
☐ 101 [M]	Make Room for the Blues	1966	40.00

SIMS
Number	Title	Yr	NM
☐ 127 [M]	Blue Darlin'	1965	40.00

SOURDOUGH
Number	Title	Yr	NM
☐ 127 [M]	Blue Darlin'	1965	50.00

STEREOPHONIC
Number	Title	Yr	NM
☐ LP-1002 [S]	Take 30 Minutes with Jimmy Patton	196?	120.00

PAUL, BILLY

GAMBLE
Number	Title	Yr	NM
☐ SG-5002	Feeling Good at the Cadillac Club	1968	30.00

ICHIBAN
Number	Title	Yr	NM
☐ ICH-1025	Wide Open	198?	12.00

NEPTUNE
Number	Title	Yr	NM
☐ 201	Ebony Woman	1970	25.00

PHILADELPHIA INT'L.
Number	Title	Yr	NM
☐ KZ31793	360 Degrees of Billy Paul	1972	15.00
☐ ZQ31793 [Q]	360 Degrees of Billy Paul	1972	25.00
☐ KZ32118	Ebony Woman	1973	15.00
— Reissue of Neptune LP			
☐ KZ32119	Feeling Good at the Cadillac Club	1973	15.00
— Reissue of Gamble LP			
☐ JZ35756	First Class	1979	12.00
☐ Z30580	Going East	1971	15.00
☐ PZ33157	Got My Head On Straight	1975	12.00
☐ PZ34389	Let 'Em In	1976	12.00
☐ KZ32952	Live in Europe	1974	12.00
☐ ZQ32952 [Q]	Live in Europe	1974	25.00
☐ PZ34923	Only the Strong Survive	1977	12.00
☐ Z236314	The Best of Billy Paul	1980	18.00
☐ KZ32409	War of the Gods	1973	12.00
☐ ZQ32409 [Q]	War of the Gods	1973	30.00
☐ PZ33843	When Love Is New	1975	12.00

TOTAL EXPERIENCE
Number	Title	Yr	NM
☐ TEL8-5711	Lately	1985	12.00

PAUL, JOYCE

UNITED ARTISTS
Number	Title	Yr	NM
☐ UAS-6684	Heartaches, Laughter and Tears	1968	18.00

PAUL, LES, AND MARY FORD

CAPITOL
Number	Title	Yr	NM
☐ H356 [10]	Bye Bye Blues	1952	80.00
☐ T356 [M]	Bye Bye Blues	1955	50.00
☐ H577 [10]	Les and Mary	1955	80.00
☐ W577 [M]	Les and Mary	1955	50.00
☐ H416 [10]	The Hit Makers	1953	80.00
☐ T416 [M]	The Hit Makers	1955	50.00
☐ T1476 [M]	The Hits of Les and Mary	1960	30.00
☐ DT1476 [R]	The Hits of Les and Mary	1960	25.00
☐ H226 [10]	The New Sound, Volume 1	1950	80.00
☐ T226 [M]	The New Sound, Volume 1	1955	50.00
☐ H286 [10]	The New Sound, Volume 2	1951	80.00
☐ T286 [M]	The New Sound, Volume 2	1955	50.00
☐ SM-286	The New Sound, Volume 2	197?	12.00
☐ ST-11308	The World Is Still Waiting for the Sunrise	1974	15.00
☐ SM-11308	The World Is Still Waiting for the Sunrise	197?	12.00
— Reissue with new prefix			
☐ T802 [M]	Time to Dream	1956	50.00

CAPITOL SPECIAL MARKETS
Number	Title	Yr	NM
☐ SLCR-8130	The All-Time Greatest Hits of Les Paul and Mary Ford	1980	25.00
— Produced for Murray Hill Records (979462)			

COLUMBIA
Number	Title	Yr	NM
☐ CL1821 [M]	Bouquet of Roses	1962	25.00
☐ CS8621 [S]	Bouquet of Roses	1962	30.00
☐ CL1276 [M]	Lovers' Luau	1959	25.00
☐ CS8086 [S]	Lovers' Luau	1959	30.00
☐ CL1928 [M]	Swingin' South	1963	18.00
☐ CS8728 [S]	Swingin' South	1963	25.00
☐ CL1688 [M]	Warm and Wonderful	1962	25.00
☐ CS8488 [S]	Warm and Wonderful	1962	30.00

HARMONY
Number	Title	Yr	NM
☐ HL7333 [M]	The Fabulous Les Paul and Mary Ford	1965	15.00
☐ HS11133 [S]	The Fabulous Les Paul and Mary Ford	1965	15.00

PICKWICK
Number	Title	Yr	NM
☐ SPC-3122	Brazil	197?	12.00

PAUL, LES

CAPITOL
Number	Title	Yr	NM
☐ N-16286	Early Les Paul	1982	10.00

DECCA
Number	Title	Yr	NM
☐ DL-5376 [10]	Galloping Guitars	1952	100.00
☐ DL-5018 [10]	Hawaiian Paradise	1949	100.00
☐ DL8589 [M]	More of Les	1957	40.00

GLENDALE
Number	Title	Yr	NM
☐ 6014 [B]	The Les Paul Trio	198?	15.00

LONDON
Number	Title	Yr	NM
☐ 50016	Multi-Trackin'	1979	15.00

LONDON PHASE 4
Number	Title	Yr	NM
☐ SP-44101	Les Paul Now!	1968	18.00

VOCALION
Number	Title	Yr	NM
☐ VL3849 [M]	The Guitar Artistry of Les Paul	196?	18.00
☐ VL73849 [R]	The Guitar Artistry of Les Paul	196?	15.00

PAUL, LOUIS

ENTERPRISE
Number	Title	Yr	NM
☐ ENS-1034	Reflections of the Way It Really Is	1971	18.00

PAUL AND PAULA

PHILIPS
Number	Title	Yr	NM
☐ PHM200101 [M]	Holiday for Teens	1963	35.00
☐ PHS600101 [S]	Holiday for Teens	1963	40.00
☐ PHM200078 [M]	Paul and Paula Sing for Young Lovers	1963	30.00
☐ PHS600078 [S]	Paul and Paula Sing for Young Lovers	1963	40.00
☐ PHM200089 [M]	We Go Together	1963	30.00
☐ PHS600089 [S]	We Go Together	1963	40.00

PAUL MESSIS

STATE RECORDS
Number	Title	Yr	NM
☐ THSLP005 [S]	Case Closed	2013	25.00
— Limited edition; 500 copies pressed on 180-gram vinyl. With a front-laminated flip-back sleeve. Released in the U.K. on April 23, 2013. Pricing based on range seen on amazon.com as of 26 June 2013.			

PAULIN, DOC

FOLKWAYS
Number	Title	Yr	NM
☐ FA2856	Doc Paulin's Marching Band	198?	12.00

PAULO, MICHAEL

MOA
Number	Title	Yr	NM
☐ 42295	One Passion	1989	15.00

PAULSON, PAT

RUBICON/MERCURY
Number	Title	Yr	NM
☐ SR61251	Live at the Ice House	1970	18.00
☐ SR61179	Pat Paulson for President	1968	25.00

PAUPERS, THE

VERVE FORECAST
Number	Title	Yr	NM
☐ FTS-3051	Ellis Island	1968	18.00
☐ FT-3026 [M]	Magic People	1967	25.00
☐ FTS-3026 [S]	Magic People	1967	25.00

PAVAGEAU, ALCIDE "SLOW DRAG

GHB
Number	Title	Yr	NM
☐ GHB-54	Half Fast Jazz Band	196?	18.00

PAVAROTTI, LUCIANO

LONDON
Number	Title	Yr	NM
☐ OS26473	O Holy Night	1976	18.00
— Original U.S.-distributed version has "London" without "ffrr" on upper right front cover and a white back cover			
☐ OS26473	O Holy Night	198?	15.00
— Later pressings have "London/ffrr" on upper right front cover and have a yellow back cover			

PAVLOV'S DOG

ABC
Number	Title	Yr	NM
☐ D-866	Pampered Menial	1975	30.00

COLUMBIA
Number	Title	Yr	NM
☐ PC33964	At the Sound of the Bell	1976	15.00
☐ PC33552	Pampered Menial	1976	15.00
— Reissue of ABC album			

PAVONE, RITA

RCA VICTOR
Number	Title	Yr	NM
☐ LPM-2900 [M]	Rita Pavone	1964	18.00
☐ LSP-2900 [S]	Rita Pavone	1964	25.00
☐ LPM-2996 [M]	Small Wonder	1965	18.00
☐ LSP-2996 [S]	Small Wonder	1965	25.00

PAXTON, GARY

NEW PAX
Number	Title	Yr	NM
☐ NP-33033	More from the Astonishing, Outrageous, Amazing, Incredible, Unbelievable World of Gary S. Paxton	1977	15.00
☐ NP-33080	(Some of) The Best of Gary S. Paxton (So Far)	1980	15.00
☐ NP-33005	The Astonishing, Outrageous, Amazing, Incredible, Unbelievably Different World of Gary S. Paxton	1976	15.00
☐ NP-33048	The Gospel According to Gary S.	1979	15.00

PAX
Number	Title	Yr	NM
☐ R-2411	Gary Sanford Paxton	1979	15.00
☐ R-2406	Terminally Weird but Godly Right/Anchored in the Rock of Ages	1978	15.00

PAXTON, TOM

ELEKTRA
Number	Title	Yr	NM
☐ EKL-298 [M]	Ain't That News	1965	25.00
☐ EKS-7298 [S]	Ain't That News	1965	30.00
☐ EKS-74019	Morning Again	1968	25.00
☐ EKL-317 [M]	Outward Bound	1966	25.00
☐ EKS-7317 [S]	Outward Bound	1966	30.00
☐ EKL-277 [M]	Ramblin' Boy	1964	25.00
☐ EKS-7277 [S]	Ramblin' Boy	1964	30.00
☐ 7E-2003	The Compleat Tom Paxton	1971	25.00
☐ EKS-74043	The Things I Notice Now	1969	18.00
☐ EKS-74066	Tom Paxton 6	1970	18.00

FLYING FISH
Number	Title	Yr	NM
☐ FF-414	And Loving You	1987	12.00
☐ FF-280	Even a Gray Day	1983	12.00
☐ FF-356	One Million Lawyers...And Other Disasters	1986	12.00
☐ FF-486	Politics	199?	15.00
☐ FF-408	The Marvellous Toy and Other Gallimaufry	1987	12.00
☐ FF-519	The Very Best of Tom Paxton	199?	15.00

GASLIGHT
Number	Title	Yr	NM
☐ GV-116 [M]	I'm the Man Who Built the Bridges	1962	80.00

HOGEYE
Number	Title	Yr	NM
☐ 004	Bulletin...We Interrupt This Record	198?	12.00

MOUNTAIN RAILROAD
Number	Title	Yr	NM
☐ 52796	The Paxton Report	198?	15.00
☐ 52792	Up and Up	1980	15.00

PRIVATE STOCK
Number	Title	Yr	NM
☐ PS-2002	Something in My Life	1976	15.00

REPRISE
Number	Title	Yr	NM
☐ RS6443	How Come the Sun	1971	18.00
☐ MS2144	New Songs for Old Friends	1973	18.00
☐ MS2096	Peace Will Come	1972	10.00

VANGUARD
Number	Title	Yr	NM
☐ VSD-79411	Heroes	1978	15.00
☐ VSD-79395	New Songs from the Briarpatch	1977	15.00

PAYCHECK, JOHNNY

ACCORD
Number	Title	Yr	NM
☐ SN-7173	Extra Special	1981	12.00

ALLEGIANCE
Number	Title	Yr	NM
☐ AV-435	I Don't Need to Know That Right Now	198?	10.00

CERTRON
Number	Title	Yr	NM
☐ 7002	Johnny Paycheck Again	1970	18.00

EPIC
Number	Title	Yr	NM
☐ KE33943	11 Months and 29 Days	1975	12.00
☐ KE35444	Armed and Crazy	1978	12.00
☐ FE37345	Encore	1981	12.00
☐ PE37345	Encore	198?	10.00
— Budget-line reissue			
☐ JE36200	Everybody's Got a Family — Meet Mine	1979	12.00
☐ KE33091	Greatest Hits	1974	12.00
☐ PE33091	Greatest Hits	198?	10.00
— Budget-line reissue			
☐ KE35623	Greatest Hits, Volume 2	1978	12.00
☐ PE35623	Greatest Hits, Volume 2	198?	10.00
— Budget-line reissue			
☐ PE39943	John Austin Paycheck	1984	10.00
☐ FE38322	Johnny Paycheck's Biggest Hits	1983	12.00
☐ FE37933	Lovers and Losers	1982	12.00
☐ KE33354	Loving You Beats All I've Ever Seen	1975	12.00
☐ FE36761	Mr. Hag Told My Story	1981	12.00
☐ PE36761	Mr. Hag Told My Story	1981	10.00
— Budget-line reissue			
☐ JE36496	New York Town	1980	12.00
☐ E31141	She's All I Got	1971	15.00
☐ PE34693	Slide Off of Your Satin Sheets	1976	12.00
☐ KE31702	Somebody Loves Me	1972	15.00
☐ KE31449	Someone to Give My Love To	1972	15.00
☐ KE32387	Something About You I Love	1973	15.00

Number	Title	Yr	NM
❏ KE32570	Song and Dance Man	1973	15.00
❏ KE35045	Take This Job and Shove It	1977	12.00
❏ PE35045	Take This Job and Shove It	198?	10.00
—Budget-line reissue			

INTERMEDIA
❏ QS-5018	Back On the Job	198?	10.00

LITTLE DARLIN'
❏ SLD-8010	Country Soul	1968	30.00
❏ LD-4004 [M]	Gospeltime in My Fashion	1967	25.00
❏ SLD-8004 [S]	Gospeltime in My Fashion	1967	30.00
❏ LD-4001 [M]	Johnny Paycheck at Carnegie Hall	1966	25.00
❏ SLD-8001 [S]	Johnny Paycheck at Carnegie Hall	1966	30.00
❏ SLD-8012	Johnny Paycheck's Greatest Hits	1968	30.00
❏ LD-4006 [M]	Johnny Paycheck Sings Jukebox Charlie	1967	30.00
❏ SLD-8006 [S]	Johnny Paycheck Sings Jukebox Charlie	1967	30.00
❏ LD-4003 [M]	The Lovin' Machine	1966	25.00
❏ SLD-8003 [S]	The Lovin' Machine	1966	30.00
❏ SLD-8023	Wherever You Are	1969	30.00

MERCURY
❏ 830404-1	Modern Times	1987	12.00

POWER PAK
❏ PO-284	Johnny Paycheck At His Best	197?	10.00

PAYNE, BENNIE

KAPP
❏ KL-1004 [M]	Bennie Payne Plays and Sings	1955	80.00

PAYNE, CECIL, AND DUKE JORDAN

MUSE
❏ MR-5015	Brooklyn Brothers	1974	18.00

PAYNE, CECIL

CHARLIE PARKER
❏ PLP-801 [M]	Cecil Payne Performing Charlie Parker's Music	1962	40.00
❏ PLP-801S [S]	Cecil Payne Performing Charlie Parker's Music	1962	50.00
❏ PLP-506 [M]	Shaw Nuff	1962	30.00
❏ PLP-506S [S]	Shaw Nuff	1962	30.00

MUSE
❏ MR-5061	Bird Gets the Worm	1976	15.00

SAVOY
❏ MG-12147 [M]	Patterns of Jazz	1959	80.00

SAVOY JAZZ
❏ SJL-1167	Patterns	1986	12.00

SIGNAL
❏ S-1203 [M]	Cecil Payne Quintet and Quartet	1955	200.00

STRATA-EAST
❏ SES-19734	The Zodiac	1973	30.00

PAYNE, DENNIS, AND THE RENEGADES

RED MAN
❏ 1492	We're Indian	1969	150.00

PAYNE, FREDA

ABC
❏ D-901	Out of Payne Comes Love	1976	15.00

ABC DUNHILL
❏ DSX-50176	Payne and Pleasure	1974	18.00

ABC IMPULSE!
❏ AS-53 [S]	After the Lights Go Down Low…And Much More	1968	18.00

CAPITOL
❏ ST-12003	Hot	1979	15.00
❏ ST-11700	Stares and Whispers	1977	15.00
❏ ST-11864	Supernatural	1978	15.00

IMPULSE!
❏ A-53 [M]	After the Lights Go Down Low…And Much More	1964	30.00
❏ AS-53 [S]	After the Lights Go Down Low…And Much More	1964	40.00

INVICTUS
❏ ST-7301 [B]	Band of Gold	1970	25.00
❏ SMAS-7307	Contact	1971	18.00
❏ Z32493	Reaching Out	1973	18.00
❏ ST-9804	The Best of Freda Payne	1972	18.00

MGM
❏ GAS-128	Freda Payne (Golden Archive Series)	1970	18.00
❏ E-4370 [M]	How Do You Say I Don't Love You Anymore	1966	30.00
❏ SE-4370 [S]	How Do You Say I Don't Love You Anymore	1966	30.00

PAYNE, JIMMY

EPIC
❏ BN26372	Woman, Woman! What Does It Take?	1968	25.00

PAYNE, JOHN, AND LOUIS LEVIN

ARISTA/FREEDOM
❏ AF1025	Bedtime	1976	15.00
❏ AF1036	The Razor's Edge	1976	15.00

MERCURY
❏ SRM-1-1166	John Payne/Louis Levin Band	1977	12.00

PAYNE, LEON

STARDAY
❏ SLP-236 [M]	Americana	1963	50.00
❏ SLP-231 [M]	Leon Payne: A Living Legend of Country Music	1963	80.00

PEACE, JOE

RITE
❏ 29917	Finding Peace	1972	200.00

PEACHES AND HERB

COLUMBIA
❏ FC38746	Remember	1983	12.00

DATE
❏ TEM3005 [M]	For Your Love	1967	30.00
❏ TES4005 [S]	For Your Love	1967	25.00
❏ TEM3007 [M]	Golden Duets	1968	30.00
❏ TES4007 [S]	Golden Duets	1968	25.00
❏ TEM3004 [M]	Let's Fall in Love	1967	25.00
❏ TES4004 [S]	Let's Fall in Love	1967	30.00
❏ TES4012	Peaches and Herb's Greatest Hits	1968	25.00

EPIC
❏ E36089	Love Is Strange	1979	12.00
—Reissue of Date material			
❏ JE36099	Peaches and Herb's Greatest Hits	1979	12.00
—Reissue of Date 4012			

MCA
❏ 2261	Peaches and Herb	1977	15.00

POLYDOR
❏ PD-1-6172	2 Hot!	1978	12.00
❏ PD-1-6332	Sayin' Something!	1981	12.00
❏ PD-1-6239	Twice the Fire	1979	12.00
❏ PD-1-6298	Worth the Wait	1980	12.00

PEAGLER, CURTIS

PABLO
❏ 2310930	I'll Be Around	1988	12.00

PEANUT BUTTER CONSPIRACY, THE

CHALLENGE
❏ 2000	For Children of All Ages	1969	30.00

COLUMBIA
❏ CL2790 [M]	The Great Conspiracy	1968	40.00
❏ CS9590 [S]	The Great Conspiracy	1968	30.00
❏ CL2654 [M]	The Peanut Butter Conspiracy Is Spreading	1967	70.00
❏ CS9454 [S]	The Peanut Butter Conspiracy Is Spreading	1967	30.00

PEARL HARBOUR AND THE EXPLOSIONS

WARNER BROS.
❏ BSK3515	Don't Follow Me, I'm Lost Too	1981	12.00
—Pearl Harbor solo, with members of The Clash			
❏ BSK3404	Pearl Harbor and the Explosions	1980	15.00

PEARL JAM

EPIC
❏ E263365	Binaural	2000	50.00
❏ E269752	Live on Two Legs	1998	50.00
❏ E385738	Lost Dogs	2004	30.00
—CD version was issued in 2003			
❏ E67500	No Code	1996	30.00
—Includes one of four sets of six 12x12 trading cards			
❏ E493535	Rearviewmirror: Greatest Hits	2004	50.00
❏ E286825	Riot Act	2002	50.00
❏ E66900	Vitalogy	1994	25.00
❏ E53136	Vs.	1993	25.00
❏ E68164	Yield	1998	50.00

EPIC ASSOCIATED
❏ Z47857	Ten	1991	12.00
—Album not released on U.S. vinyl until 1994			

J
❏ 82876-71467-1	Pearl Jam	2006	25.00
—With 36-page lyric booklet; number is nowhere on the packaging or labels, but is only in the trail-off wax of the records			

PEARLS BEFORE SWINE

4 MEN WITH BEARDS
❏ 4M234 [B]	The Use of Ashes	2013	25.00

ADELPHI
❏ 4111	The Best of Pearls Before Swine	198?	18.00

ESP-DISK
❏ 1075	Balaklava	1968	40.00
❏ 1054 [M]	One Nation Under Ground	1967	80.00
❏ 1054 [S]	One Nation Under Ground	1967	50.00
—Sepia-tone cover with white border			
❏ 1054 [S]	One Nation Under Ground	1967	50.00
—Sepia-tone cover with no border			
❏ 1054 [S]	One Nation Under Ground	1967	50.00
—Black and white cover			
❏ 1054 [S]	One Nation Under Ground	1968	30.00
—Full-color cover			
❏ 1054	One Nation Under Ground Bonus Poster	1967	30.00

REPRISE
❏ RS6467	Beautiful Lies You Could Live In	1971	40.00
❏ RS6442	City of Gold	1971	40.00
❏ RS6364	These Things Too	1969	30.00
❏ RS6405	The Use of Ashes	1970	30.00

PEARSON, ALBIE

VIBRANT
❏ 1501	Albie Pearson	1973	30.00

PEARSON, DUKE

ATLANTIC
❏ 3002 [M]	Honeybuns	196?	18.00
❏ SD3002 [S]	Honeybuns	196?	18.00
❏ SD3005	Prairie Dog	196?	18.00

BLUE NOTE
❏ BST-84344	How Insensitive	1970	25.00
❏ B1-35220	I Don't Care Who Knows It	1996	15.00
❏ BST-84276	Introducing Duke Pearson's Big Band	1968	30.00
❏ BN-LA317-G	It Could Only Happen with You	1974	18.00
❏ BST-84323	Merry Ole Soul	1970	25.00
❏ BST-84308	Now Hear This	1969	30.00
❏ BLP-4022 [M]	Profile -- Duke Pearson	1959	120.00
—Deep groove" version (deep indentation under label on both sides)			
❏ BLP-4022 [M]	Profile -- Duke Pearson	1959	80.00
—Regular version with W. 63rd St. address on label			
❏ BLP-4022 [M]	Profile -- Duke Pearson	1963	30.00
—With New York, USA address on label			
❏ BST-84022 [S]	Profile -- Duke Pearson	1959	60.00
—With W. 63rd St. address on label			
❏ BST-84022 [S]	Profile -- Duke Pearson	1963	25.00
—With New York, USA address on label			
❏ BST-84022 [S]	Profile -- Duke Pearson	1967	15.00
—With "A Division of Liberty Records" on label			
❏ BLP-4252 [M]	Sweet Honey Bee	1966	30.00
❏ BST-84252 [S]	Sweet Honey Bee	1966	30.00
—With New York, USA address on label			
❏ BST-84252 [S]	Sweet Honey Bee	1967	15.00
—With "A Division of Liberty Records" on label			
❏ B1-89792	Sweet Honey Bee	1993	15.00
—Reissue of 84252			
❏ BLP-4035 [M]	Tender Feelin's	1960	120.00
—Deep groove" version (deep indentation under label on both sides)			
❏ BLP-4035 [M]	Tender Feelin's	1960	80.00
—Regular version with W. 63rd St. address on label			
❏ BLP-4035 [M]	Tender Feelin's	1963	30.00
—With New York, USA address on label			
❏ BST-84035 [S]	Tender Feelin's	1960	60.00
—With W. 63rd St. address on label			
❏ BST-84035 [S]	Tender Feelin's	1963	25.00
—With New York, USA address on label			
❏ BST-84035 [S]	Tender Feelin's	1967	15.00
—With "A Division of Liberty Records" on label			
❏ BST-84293	The Phantom	1969	30.00
❏ BST-84267	The Right Touch	1968	30.00
❏ B1-28269	The Right Touch	1994	15.00
—Reissue of 84267			
❏ BLP-4191 [M]	Wahoo!	1965	30.00
❏ BST-84191 [S]	Wahoo!	1965	30.00
—With New York, USA address on label			
❏ BST-84191 [S]	Wahoo!	1967	15.00
—With "A Division of Liberty Records" on label			
❏ B1-84191	Wahoo!	1986	15.00
—The Finest in Jazz Since 1939" reissue			

JAZZTIME
❏ 33-02 [M]	Hush!	1962	40.00

PRESTIGE
❏ PRST-7729	Dedication	1970	18.00

PEBBLES

MCA
❏ 10025	Always	1990	18.00
❏ 42094	Pebbles	1987	12.00

PEBBLES AND BAMM BAMM

HANNA-BARBERA
❏ HLP-2040 [M]	On the Good Ship Lollipop	1966	100.00
❏ HLP-2033 [M]	Pebbles and Bamm-Bamm Sing Songs of Christmas	1965	120.00

Number	Title	Yr	NM

PECORA, SANTO

CLEF

❏ MGC-123 [10]	Santo Pecora Collates	1953	100.00

— With either Mercury or Clef cover; all labels are Clef

SOUTHLAND

| ❏ SLP-213 [M] | Santo Pecora | 1955 | 50.00 |

VIK

| ❏ XLA-1081 [M] | Dixieland Mardi Gras | 1957 | 50.00 |

PEDERSEN, HERB

EPIC

| ❏ PE34933 | Sandman | 1977 | 18.00 |
| ❏ PE34225 | South by Southwest | 1976 | 18.00 |

SUGAR HILL

| ❏ SH-3738 | Lonesome Feeling | 1984 | 15.00 |

PEDICIN, MIKE

APOLLO

| ❏ LP-484 [M] | Musical Medicine | 1957 | 150.00 |

PEEBLES, ANN

HI

❏ XSHL-32079	I Can't Stand the Rain	1974	25.00
❏ HLP-6002	If This Is Heaven	1977	15.00
❏ SHL-32059	Part Time Love	1971	25.00
❏ HLP-8005	Part Time Love	197?	15.00

— Reissue of 32059

| ❏ SHL-32065 | Straight from the Heart | 1972 | 25.00 |
| ❏ HLP-8009 | Straight from the Heart | 197? | 15.00 |

— Reissue of 32065

| ❏ SHL-32091 | Tellin' It | 1975 | 25.00 |
| ❏ HLP-6007 | The Handwriting Is On the Wall | 1978 | 15.00 |

PEEL, DAVE

CHART

| ❏ CHS-1039 | Move Two Mountains | 1971 | 18.00 |

PEEL, DAVID

APPLE

| ❏ SW-3391 [B] | The Pope Smokes Dope | 1972 | 50.00 |

ELEKTRA

| ❏ EKS-74032 [B] | Have a Marijuana | 1968 | 40.00 |
| ❏ EKS-74069 [B] | The American Revolution | 1970 | 40.00 |

PEELS, THE

KARATE

| ❏ 5402 [M] | Juanita Banana | 1966 | 80.00 |

PEGGY SUE

DECCA

| ❏ DL75215 | All American Husband | 1970 | 30.00 |
| ❏ DL75153 | Dynamite! | 1969 | 30.00 |

PEGGY SUE AND SONNY WRIGHT (2)

COUNTRY INT'L.

| ❏ 732 | One Side of Peggy Sue and Sonny Wright | 198? | 25.00 |

PEIFFER, BERNARD

DECCA

❏ DL9203 [M]	Piano Ala Mood	1958	50.00
❏ DL79203 [S]	Piano Ala Mood	1958	40.00
❏ DL8626 [M]	The Astounding Bernard Peiffer	1958	50.00
❏ DL9218 [M]	The Pied Peiffer of the Piano	1959	50.00
❏ DL79218 [S]	The Pied Peiffer of the Piano	1959	40.00

EMARCY

| ❏ MG-36080 [M] | Bernie's Tunes | 1956 | 50.00 |
| ❏ MG-26036 [10] | Le Most | 1954 | 80.00 |

LAURIE

❏ LLP-1008 [M]	Cole Porter's "Can Can"	1960	30.00
❏ SLP-1008 [S]	Cole Porter's "Can Can"	1960	30.00
❏ LLP-1006 [M]	Modern Jazz for People Who Like Original Music	1960	30.00
❏ SLP-1006 [S]	Modern Jazz for People Who Like Original Music	1960	30.00

NORGRAN

| ❏ MGN-11 [10] | Bernard Peiffer Et Son Trio | 1954 | 80.00 |

PELL, DAVE, AND JOE WILLIAMS

GNP CRESCENDO

| ❏ GNPS-2124 | Prez & Joe: In Celebration of Lester Young | 1979 | 12.00 |

PELL, DAVE

ATLANTIC

| ❏ 1216 [M] | Jazz and Romantic Places | 1955 | 100.00 |

— Black label

| ❏ 1216 [M] | Jazz and Romantic Places | 1961 | 30.00 |

— Multicolor label, white "fan" logo at right

| ❏ 1249 [M] | Love Story | 1956 | 80.00 |

— Black label

| ❏ 1249 [M] | Love Story | 1961 | 30.00 |

— Multicolor label, white "fan" logo at right

CAPITOL

| ❏ T925 [M] | I Had the Craziest Dream | 1958 | 30.00 |

— Turquoise label

❏ T1687 [M]	I Remember John Kirby	1962	25.00
❏ ST1687 [S]	I Remember John Kirby	1962	30.00
❏ T1512 [M]	Old South Wails	1961	25.00
❏ ST1512 [S]	Old South Wails	1961	30.00
❏ T1309 [M]	The Big Small Bands	1960	25.00
❏ ST1309 [S]	The Big Small Bands	1960	30.00

CORAL

| ❏ CRL57248 [M] | Swingin' School Songs | 1958 | 30.00 |
| ❏ CRL757248 [S] | Swingin' School Songs | 1958 | 30.00 |

GNP CRESCENDO

| ❏ GNPS-2122 | Prez Conference | 1978 | 12.00 |

HEADFIRST

| ❏ 715 | Live at Alfonse's | 198? | 15.00 |

KAPP

❏ KL-1034 [M]	Dave Pell Plays Burke and Van Heusen	1956	40.00
❏ KL-1036 [M]	Dave Pell Plays Irving Berlin	1957	40.00
❏ KL-1025 [M]	Dave Pell Plays Rodgers and Hart	1956	30.00

LIBERTY

❏ LRP-3321 [M]	Jazz Voices in Video	1963	18.00
❏ LST-7321 [S]	Jazz Voices in Video	1963	25.00
❏ LST-7631 [S]	Man-Ha-Man-Ha	1969	18.00
❏ LST-7298 [S]	Today;s Hits in Jazz	1961	25.00
❏ LRP-3298 [M]	Today's Hits in Jazz	1961	18.00

PRI

❏ 3003 [M]	Dave Pell Plays Artie Shaw's Big Band Sounds	196?	25.00
❏ 3004 [M]	Dave Pell Plays Benny Goodman's Big Band Sounds	196?	25.00
❏ 3007 [M]	Dave Pell Plays Duke Ellington's Big Band Sounds	196?	25.00
❏ 3002 [M]	Dave Pell Plays Harry James' Big Band Sounds	196?	25.00
❏ 3005 [M]	Dave Pell Plays Lawrence Welk's Big Band Sounds	196?	25.00
❏ 3009 [M]	Dave Pell Plays Mantovani's Big Band Sounds	196?	25.00
❏ 3006 [M]	Dave Pell Plays Perez Prado's Big Band Sounds	196?	25.00
❏ 3011 [M]	Dave Pell Plays the Big Band Sounds	196?	25.00
❏ 3010 [M]	Dave Pell Plays the Dorsey Brothers' Big Band Sounds	196?	25.00

RCA VICTOR

❏ LPM-1662 [M]	Campus Hop	1957	50.00
❏ LPM-1320 [M]	Jazz Goes Dancing	1956	50.00
❏ LPM-1524 [M]	Pell of a Time	1957	50.00
❏ LPM-1394 [M]	Swingin' in the Ol' Corral	1957	50.00

TREND

| ❏ TL-1003 [10] | Dave Pell Plays Irving Berlin | 1953 | 120.00 |
| ❏ TL-1501 [M] | Dave Pell Plays Rodgers and Hart | 1954 | 100.00 |

PENDERGRASS, TEDDY

ASYLUM

| ❏ 60317 | Love Language | 1984 | 10.00 |
| ❏ 60447 | Workin' It Back | 1985 | 10.00 |

ELEKTRA

| ❏ 60775 | Joy | 1988 | 10.00 |

PHILADELPHIA INT'L.

❏ FZ39252	Greatest Hits	1984	12.00
❏ FZ38646	Heaven Only Knows	1983	12.00
❏ PZ38646	Heaven Only Knows	1985	10.00

— Budget-line reissue with new prefix

| ❏ HZ47491 | It's Time for Love | 198? | 40.00 |

— Half-speed mastered edition

| ❏ FZ37491 | It's Time for Love | 1981 | 12.00 |
| ❏ PZ37491 | It's Time for Love | 198? | 10.00 |

— Budget-line reissue with new prefix

| ❏ PZ35095 | Life Is a Song Worth Singing | 1978 | 12.00 |

— No bar code on back cover

| ❏ PZ35095 | Life Is a Song Worth Singing | 198? | 10.00 |

— With bar code on back cover

| ❏ FZ36003 | Teddy | 1979 | 12.00 |
| ❏ PZ36003 | Teddy | 198? | 10.00 |

— Budget-line reissue with new prefix

| ❏ KZ236294 | Teddy Live! Coast to Coast | 1979 | 15.00 |
| ❏ PZ34390 | Teddy Pendergrass | 1977 | 12.00 |

— No bar code on back cover

| ❏ PZ34390 | Teddy Pendergrass | 198? | 10.00 |

— With bar code on back cover

| ❏ FZ38118 | This One's for You | 1982 | 12.00 |
| ❏ PZ38118 | This One's for You | 198? | 10.00 |

— Budget-line reissue with new prefix

| ❏ FZ36745 | TP | 1980 | 12.00 |
| ❏ PZ36745 | TP | 198? | 10.00 |

— Budget-line reissue with new prefix

PENGUINS, THE

COLLECTABLES

| ❏ COL-5045 | Golden Classics | 198? | 12.00 |

DOOTO

| ❏ DTL-204 [M] | The Best Vocal Groups... Rhythm and Blues | 1959 | 200.00 |

— Reissue of Dootone 204; blue and yellow label

| ❏ DTL-204 [M] | The Best Vocal Groups... Rhythm and Blues | 196? | 100.00 |

— Black label with gold/orange/blue ring. This is NOT a counterfeit.

| ❏ DTL-242 [M] | The Cool, Cool Penguins | 1959 | 700.00 |

— Red and yellow label

| ❏ DTL-242 [M] | The Cool, Cool Penguins | 1959 | 700.00 |

— Blue and yellow label

| ❏ DTL-242 [M] | The Cool, Cool Penguins | 196? | 200.00 |

— Black label with gold/orange/blue ring. This is NOT a counterfeit.

DOOTONE

| ❏ DTL-204 [M] | The Best Vocal Groups... Rhythm and Blues | 1957 | 1500.00 |

— Also includes tracks by the Medallions, Don Julian and the Meadowlarks, and the Dootones. Flat maroon label.

| ❏ DTL-204 [M] | The Best Vocal Groups... Rhythm and Blues | 195? | 500.00 |

— As above; glossy maroon label

PENNY, HANK

AUDIO LAB

| ❏ AL-1508 [M] | Hank Penny Sings | 1959 | 200.00 |

PENNY AND JEAN

RCA VICTOR

| ❏ LPM-2244 [M] | Two for the Road | 1961 | 25.00 |
| ❏ LSP-2244 [S] | Two for the Road | 1961 | 30.00 |

PENSYL, KIM

OPTIMISM

| ❏ OP-3210 | Pensyl Sketches #1 | 1988 | 12.00 |

PENTAGON

EAST WIND

| ❏ 10002 | Pentagon | 1979 | 25.00 |

PENTANGLE, THE

GREEN LINNET

| ❏ SIF-3048 | So Early in the Spring | 1990 | 15.00 |

REPRISE

| ❏ RS6372 [B] | Basket of Light | 1969 | 30.00 |

— With "W7" and "r:" logos on two-tone orange label

| ❏ RS6372 [B] | Basket of Light | 1970 | 25.00 |

— With only "r:" logo on all-orange (tan) label

❏ RS6430	Cruel Sister	1971	18.00
❏ RS6463	Reflection	1971	18.00
❏ MS2100	Solomon's Seal	1972	18.00
❏ 2RS6334	Sweet Child	1969	30.00

— With "W7" and "r:" logos on two-tone orange label

| ❏ 2RS6334 | Sweet Child | 1970 | 25.00 |

— With only "r:" logo on all-orange (tan) label

| ❏ RS6315 | The Pentangle | 1968 | 25.00 |

— With "W7" and "r:" logos on two-tone orange label

| ❏ RS6315 [B] | The Pentangle | 1970 | 18.00 |

— With "r:" logo on all-orange (tan) label

SHANACHIE

| ❏ 79066 | A Maid That's Deep In Love | 198? | 12.00 |

VARRICK

| ❏ VR-026 | In the Round | 1986 | 12.00 |
| ❏ VR-017 | Open the Door | 1985 | 12.00 |

PEOPLE

CAPITOL

| ❏ ST-151 | Both Sides of People | 1969 | 25.00 |
| ❏ ST2924 | I Love You | 1968 | 25.00 |

PARAMOUNT

| ❏ PAS-5013 | There Are People | 1970 | 25.00 |

PEPPER, ART

ANALOGUE PRODUCTIONS

| ❏ AP 017 | Art Pepper + Eleven: Modern Jazz Classics | 199? | 30.00 |

— Reissue on audiophile vinyl

| ❏ AP 010 | Art Pepper Meets the Rhythm Section | 199? | 30.00 |

— Reissue on audiophile vinyl

| ❏ AP 012 | Smack Up! | 199? | 30.00 |

— Reissue on audiophile vinyl

❏ APR3013	So in Love	199?	18.00
❏ APR3014	The Intimate Art Pepper	199?	18.00
❏ APR3012	The New York Album	199?	18.00

ARTISTS HOUSE

| ❏ AH9412 | So in Love | 1979 | 18.00 |

BLUE NOTE

| ❏ BN-LA591-H2 | Early Art | 1976 | 30.00 |
| ❏ LT-1064 | Omega Alpha | 1980 | 25.00 |

CONTEMPORARY

❏ C-7650	Art Pepper at the Village Vanguard, Vol. 4: More for Les	1986	18.00
❏ M-3568 [M]	Art Pepper + Eleven: Modern Jazz Classics	1959	100.00
❏ S-7568 [S]	Art Pepper + Eleven: Modern Jazz Classics	1959	80.00
❏ C-3532 [M]	Art Pepper Meets the Rhythm Section	1957	100.00

Number	Title	Yr	NM
❏ S-7532 [S]	Art Pepper Meets the Rhythm Section	1959	50.00
❏ S-7643	Friday Night at the Village Vanguard	1980	18.00
❏ M-3573 [M]	Gettin' Together!	1960	60.00
❏ S-7573 [S]	Gettin' Together!	1960	70.00
❏ M-3607 [M]	Intensity	1963	30.00
❏ S-7607 [S]	Intensity	1963	40.00
❏ S-7633	Living Legend	1975	25.00
❏ S-7639	No Limit	1978	25.00
❏ C-7644	Saturday Night at the Village Vanguard	198?	18.00
❏ M-3602 [M]	Smack Up!	1961	60.00
❏ S-7602 [S]	Smack Up!	1961	80.00
❏ S-7638	The Trip	1977	25.00
❏ S-7630	The Way It Was!	1972	30.00
—Originals have orange labels			
❏ S-7642	Thursday Night at the Village Vanguard	1979	25.00

DISCOVERY
❏ DS-837	Among Friends	1981	25.00
❏ 3019 [10]	Art Pepper Quartet	1952	600.00
❏ 3023 [10]	Art Pepper Quintet	1954	600.00

FANTASY
❏ OJC-338	Art Pepper Meets the Rhythm Section	198?	15.00
❏ OJC-474	Art Pepper Today	1990	18.00
❏ OJC-695	Friday Night at the Village Vanguard	199?	15.00
❏ OJC-169	Gettin' Together	198?	15.00
❏ OJC-387	Intensity	1989	15.00
❏ OJC-408	Living Legend	1990	18.00
❏ OJC-341	Modern Jazz Classics	198?	15.00
❏ OJC-411	No Limit	1990	18.00
❏ OJC-696	Saturday Night at the Village Vanguard	199?	15.00
❏ OJC-176	Smack Up!	198?	15.00
❏ OJC-475	Straight Life	1990	18.00
❏ OJC-410	The Trip	1990	18.00
❏ OJC-389	The Way It Was	1989	15.00

GALAXY
❏ GXY-5145	Art Lives	1983	18.00
❏ GXY-5151	Art Pepper Quartet: The Maiden Voyage Sessions, Part 3	198?	25.00
❏ GXY-5119	Art Pepper Today	1979	18.00
❏ GXY-5148	Art Works	1984	18.00
❏ GXY-5143	Goin' Home	1982	18.00
❏ GXY-5128	Landscape	1980	25.00
❏ GXY-5141	One September Afternoon	1981	25.00
❏ GXY-5142	Roadgame	1982	15.00
❏ GXY-5127	Straight Life	1979	15.00
❏ GXY-5147	Tete-a-Tete	198?	18.00
❏ GXY-5154	The New York Album	1985	25.00
❏ GXY-5140	Winter Moon	1980	18.00

INTERLUDE
❏ MO-512 [M]	Art Pepper Quartet	1959	50.00
❏ ST-1012 [S]	Art Pepper Quartet	1959	40.00

INTERPLAY
❏ 7718	Among Friends	1979	25.00

INTRO
❏ 606 [M]	Modern Art	1957	2500.00

JAZZ WEST
❏ JLP-10 [M]	The Return of Art Pepper	1956	600.00

MOSAIC
❏ MR3-105	The Complete Pacific Jazz Small Group Recordings of Art Pepper	198?	80.00

ONYX
❏ 219	Omega Man / Omega Man	197?	12.00

PACIFIC JAZZ
❏ PJ-60 [M]	The Artistry of Pepper	1962	40.00

SAVOY
❏ MG-12089 [M]	Surf Ride	1956	100.00

SAVOY JAZZ
❏ SJL-2217	Discoveries	197?	18.00

SCORE
❏ SLP-4030 [M]	Modern Art	1958	100.00
❏ SLP-4031 [M]	The Art Pepper-Red Norvo Sextet	1958	100.00
❏ SLP-4032 [M]	The Return of Art Pepper	1958	100.00

STEREO RECORDS
❏ S-7018 [S]	Art Pepper Meets the Rhythm Section	1958	80.00

TAMPA
❏ TP-20 [M]	Art Pepper Quartet	1957	500.00
—Red vinyl			
❏ TP-20 [M]	Art Pepper Quartet	1958	250.00
—Black vinyl			
❏ TS-1001 [S]	Art Pepper Quartet	1959	1000.00

XANADU
❏ 108	The Early Show	197?	12.00
❏ 117	The Late Show	198?	12.00

PEPPER, ART/SHELLY MANNE

CHARLIE PARKER
❏ PLP-836 [M]	Pepper/Manne	1963	30.00
❏ PLP-836S [S]	Pepper/Manne	1963	30.00

PEPPER, ART/SONNY REDD

REGENT
❏ MG-6069 [M]	Two Altos	1959	50.00

SAVOY
❏ MG-12215 [M]	Art Pepper-Sonny Redd	1969	25.00

PEPPER, JIM

EMBRYO
❏ SD-731	Pepper's Powwow	196?	40.00

PEPPERMINT, DANNY

CARLTON
❏ LP-20001 [M]	Twist with Danny Peppermint	1962	40.00
❏ STLP-20001 [S]	Twist with Danny Peppermint	1962	50.00

PEPPERMINT RAINBOW, THE

DECCA
❏ DL75129	Will You Be Staying After Sunday	1969	25.00

PEPPERMINT TROLLEY COMPANY, THE

ACTA
❏ A-8007 [M]	The Peppermint Trolley Company	1968	100.00
—In stereo cover with "Monaural" sticker			
❏ A-38007 [S]	The Peppermint Trolley Company	1968	35.00

PEPPERS, THE

EVENT
❏ EV6901	Pepper Box	1974	18.00

PERAZA, ARMANDO

SKYE
❏ S-5D	Wild Thing	1970	18.00

PERE UBU

BLANK
❏ 001 [B]	The Modern Dance	1978	60.00

CHRYSALIS
❏ CHR1207	Dub Housing	1979	30.00

ENIGMA
❏ D1-73343	The Tenement Year	1988	18.00

FONTANA
❏ 838237-1	Cloudland	1989	15.00

ROUGH TRADE
❏ ROUGH US10	390 Degrees of Simulated Stereo	1981	25.00
❏ ROUGH US21	Song of the Bailing Man	1982	25.00
❏ ROUGH US4	The Art of Walking	1980	40.00
—First 1,800 were incorrectly mastered			
❏ ROUGH US4	The Art of Walking	1980	25.00
—Revised version: Vocal added on "Arabia"; "Miles" is shortened			
❏ ROUGH US7	The Modern Dance	1981	25.00
—Reissue of Blank 001			

PERHACS, LINDA

KAPP
❏ KS-3636	Parallelograms	1970	200.00

PERIGEO

RCA VICTOR
❏ TPL1-1228	Fata Morgana	197?	18.00
❏ TPL1-1080	Genealogia	197?	18.00
❏ TPL1-1175	The Valley of the Temples	197?	18.00
❏ APL1-1175	The Valley of the Temples	197?	15.00
—Reissue with new prefix			

PERKINS, BILL, AND RICHIE KAMUCA

LIBERTY
❏ LRP-3051 [M]	Tenors Head On	1957	80.00

PERKINS, BILL, AND THE SAN FRANCISCANS

FAMOUS DOOR
❏ 128	The Other Bill	197?	12.00

PERKINS, BILL; ART PEPPER; RICHIE KAMUCA

PACIFIC JAZZ
❏ PJM-401 [M]	Just Friends	1956	200.00

WORLD PACIFIC
❏ PJM-401 [M]	Just Friends	1958	120.00

PERKINS, BILL

CONTEMPORARY
❏ C-14011	Journey to the East	1985	15.00

INTERPLAY
❏ 7721	Confluence	1979	30.00
❏ 8606	Remembrance of Dino's	1990	15.00

LIBERTY
❏ LRP-3293 [M]	Bossa Nova with Strings Attached	1963	40.00
❏ LST-7293 [S]	Bossa Nova with Strings Attached	1963	50.00

PACIFIC JAZZ
❏ PJ-1221 [M]	The Bill Perkins Octet On Stage	1956	120.00

RIVERSIDE
❏ RS-3052	Quietly There	1969	30.00

SEA BREEZE
❏ SB-2006	Many Ways to Go	1980	12.00

WORLD PACIFIC
❏ WP-1221 [M]	The Bill Perkins Octet On Stage	1958	80.00

PERKINS, CARL

ACCORD
❏ SN-7169	Presenting Carl Perkins	1982	12.00

ALBUM GLOBE
❏ 8118	Country Soul	1980	12.00
❏ 9037	Goin' Back to Memphis	1980	12.00

ALLEGIANCE
❏ AV-5001	The Heart and Soul of Carl Perkins	198?	12.00

BULLDOG
❏ BDL-2034	Twenty Golden Pieces	198?	12.00

COLUMBIA
❏ CS9981	Boppin' the Blues	1970	30.00
—Red "360 Sound Stereo" label			
❏ PC9981	Boppin' the Blues	198?	10.00
—Budget-line reissue			
❏ CS9981	Boppin' the Blues	1970	15.00
—Orange label			
❏ CS9833	Carl Perkins' Greatest Hits	1969	30.00
—Red "360 Sound Stereo" label			
❏ CS9931	Carl Perkins On Top	1969	30.00
—Red "360 Sound Stereo" label			
❏ FC37961	The Survivors	1982	12.00
—With Johnny Cash and Jerry Lee Lewis			
❏ PC37961	The Survivors	198?	10.00
—Budget-line reissue			
❏ CL1234 [M]	Whole Lotta Shakin'	1958	400.00
❏ CL1234 [DJ]	Whole Lotta Shakin'	1958	800.00
—White label promo			

COLUMBIA LIMITED EDITION
❏ LE10117	Carl Perkins' Greatest Hits	1974	15.00
—Limited Edition" brown label			

DESIGN
❏ DLP-611 [M]	Tennessee	1963	30.00
❏ SDLP-611 [R]	Tennessee	1963	25.00

DOLLIE
❏ 4001	Country Boy's Dream	1967	30.00
❏ ST-91428	Country Boy's Dream	1967	40.00
—Capitol Record Club edition			

HARMONY
❏ KH31179	Brown Eyed Handsome Man	1971	15.00
❏ HS11385	Carl Perkins	1970	18.00
❏ KH31792	Greatest Hits	1972	15.00

HILLTOP
❏ 6103	Matchbox	197?	15.00

JET
❏ JZ35604	Ol' Blue Suede's Back	1978	12.00
❏ JT-LA856-H	Ol' Blue Suede's Back	1978	18.00

KOALA
❏ AW14164	Country Soul	198?	12.00

MCA DOT
❏ 39035	Carl Perkins	1985	12.00

MERCURY
❏ SRM-1-691	My Kind of Country	1973	15.00

RHINO
❏ RNLP-70221	Original Sun Greatest Hits (1955-1957)	1986	15.00

ROUNDER
❏ SS-27	Honky Tonk Gal: Rare and Unissued Sun Masters	1989	15.00

SMASH
❏ 830002-1	Class of '55	1986	15.00
—With Jerry Lee Lewis, Roy Orbison and Johnny Cash			

SUEDE
❏ 002	Live at Austin City Limits	1981	12.00

SUN
❏ LP-112	Blue Suede Shoes	1969	15.00
❏ LP-111	Original Golden Hits	1969	15.00
❏ SLP-1225 [M]	Teen Beat -- The Best of Carl Perkins	1961	500.00
—Reissue with new title			
❏ SLP-1225 [M]	The Dance Album of Carl Perkins	1957	1200.00

SUNNYVALE
❏ 9330803	The Sun Story, Vol. 3	1977	15.00

TRIP
❏ TLP-8503	The Best of Carl Perkins	1974	15.00

Number	Title	Yr	NM

UNIVERSAL
| UVL-76001 | Born to Rock | 1989 | 18.00 |

PERKINS, CARL (2)

DOOTO
| DL-211 [M] | Introducing Carl Perkins | 196? | 18.00 |

DOOTONE
DL-211 [M]	Introducing Carl Perkins	1956	120.00
—Black vinyl			
DL-211 [M]	Introducing Carl Perkins	1956	200.00
—Red vinyl			

PERKINS, TONY

EPIC
| LN3394 [M] | Tony Perkins | 1957 | 50.00 |

RCA VICTOR
LPM-1679 [M]	From My Heart	1958	40.00
LSP-1679 [S]	From My Heart	1958	60.00
LPM-1853 [M]	On a Rainy Afternoon	1958	40.00
LSP-1853 [S]	On a Rainy Afternoon	1958	60.00

PERREY, JEAN-JACQUES

PICKWICK
PC-3160 [M]	The Happy Moog	196?	25.00
SPC-3160 [S]	The Happy Moog	196?	30.00
—Silver label			

VANGUARD
| VSD-6549 | Moog Indigo | 1969 | 40.00 |
| VSD-79286 | The Amazing New Electronic Pop Sound of Jean-Jackques Perrey | 1968 | 40.00 |

PERREY-KINGSLEY

VANGUARD
VSD-6525	Kaleidoscopic Vibrations	1969	30.00
VSD-71/72	The Essential Perrey & Kingsley	197?	30.00
VRS-9222 [M]	The In Sound from Way Out!	1966	30.00
VSD-79222 [S]	The In Sound from Way Out!	1966	40.00

PERRINE, PEP

HIDEOUT
| 1003 [M] | Pep Perrine Live and In Person | 196? | 120.00 |

PERRY, STEVE

COLUMBIA
| FC39334 | Street Talk | 1984 | 12.00 |

PERSIP, CHARLIE

BETHLEHEM
BCP-6046 [M]	Charlie Persip and the Jazz Statesmen	1960	40.00
ODOP-0040 [O]	Charlie Persip and the Jazz Statesmen	1960	40.00
BCP 6046	Right Down Front	197?	16.00
—Reissue, distributed by RCA Victor			

SOUL NOTE
| SN-1079 | In Case You Missed It | 1985 | 15.00 |
| 121179 | No Dummies Allowed | 1990 | 18.00 |

STASH
| ST-209 | The Charlie Persip & Gerry LaFum Superband | 198? | 12.00 |

PERSON, HOUSTON

20TH CENTURY
| W-205 | Houston Person | 196? | 30.00 |

FANTASY
| OJC-332 | Goodness! | 1988 | 12.00 |

MERCURY
| SRM-1-1151 | Harmony | 1977 | 15.00 |
| SRM-1-1104 | Pure Pleasure | 1976 | 15.00 |

MUSE
MR-5289	Always on My Mind	1986	12.00
MR-5344	Basics	1989	15.00
MR-5260	Heavy Juice	1982	12.00
MR-5376	Something in Common	1989	15.00
MR-5110	Stolen Sweets	1977	15.00
MR-5199	Suspicions	1980	15.00
MR-5136	The Big Horn	197?	15.00
MR-5178	The Nearness of You	197?	15.00
MR-5331	The Talk of the Town	1987	12.00
MR-5231	Very Personal	1981	12.00
MR-5433	Why Not!	1991	18.00
MR-5161	Wild Flower	1977	15.00

PRESTIGE
PRST-7566 [B]	Blue Odyssey	1968	25.00
10044	Broken Windows, Empty Hallways	1972	25.00
PRST-7517	Chocomotive	1968	25.00
PRST-7678	Goodness!	1969	25.00
10017	Houston Express	1971	25.00
10003	Person to Person	1971	30.00
PRST-7621	Soul Dance!	1969	25.00
10055	Sweet Buns and Barbeque	1973	25.00
PRST-7779	The Best of Houston Person	1970	18.00
PRST-7767	The Truth!	1970	25.00

PRST-7548	Trust in Me	1968	25.00
PRLP-7491 [M]	Underground Soul	1967	30.00
PRST-7491 [S]	Underground Soul	1967	25.00

SAVOY
| 14471 | Gospel Soul | 197? | 15.00 |

WESTBOUND
| 213 | Get Outa My Way | 1975 | 18.00 |
| 205 | Houston Person '75 | 1975 | 18.00 |

PERSSON, AAKE

EMARCY
| MG-26039 [10] | Swedish Modern | 1954 | 200.00 |

PERSSON, AAKE/ARNE DOMNERUS

PRESTIGE
| PRLP-173 [10] | Aake Persson Swedish All Stars | 1953 | 250.00 |

PERSUADERS, THE

ATCO
| SD7046 | Best Thing That Ever Happened to Me | 1974 | 25.00 |
| SD7021 | The Persuaders | 1973 | 25.00 |

CALLA
| PZ34802 | It's All About Love | 1977 | 18.00 |

COLLECTABLES
| COL-5139 | Thin Line Between Love and Hate (Golden Classics) | 198? | 12.00 |

WIN OR LOSE
| SD 33-387 | Thin Line Between Love and Hate | 1972 | 30.00 |

PERSUADERS, THE (2)

SATURN
| SAT-5000 [M] | Surfer's Nightmare | 1963 | 300.00 |
| SATS-5000 [S] | Surfer's Nightmare | 1963 | 400.00 |

PERSUASIONS, THE

A&M
| SP-3656 | I Just Want to Sing with My Friends | 1974 | 15.00 |
| SP-3635 | More Than Before | 1974 | 15.00 |

CAPITOL
ST-11101	Spread the Word	1972	30.00
ST-872	Street Corner Symphony	1972	30.00
ST-791	We Came to Play	1971	30.00
SM-791	We Came to Play	197?	12.00
—Reissue with new prefix			

CATAMOUNT
| 905 | Stardust | 197? | 40.00 |

ELEKTRA
| 7E-1099 | Chirpin' | 1977 | 15.00 |

FLYING FISH
| FF-093 | Comin' At Ya | 1979 | 15.00 |

MCA
| 326 | We Still Ain't Got No Band | 1973 | 18.00 |

REPRISE
| RS6394 | Acapella | 1970 | 30.00 |

ROUNDER
| 3053 | Good News | 1981 | 12.00 |
| 3083 | No Frills | 1984 | 12.00 |

PET SHOP BOYS

EMI
E1-34023	Alternative	1995	60.00
—Box set pressed in UK for import into the US (regular UK pressings have gatefold sleeves)			
E1-28105	Disco 2	1994	15.00

EMI AMERICA
SQ-17246	Disco	1986	12.00
R164390	Please	1986	15.00
—BMG Direct Marketing edition			
PW-17193	Please	1986	12.00

EMI MANHATTAN
R153678	Actually	1987	15.00
—BMG Direct Marketing edition			
ELJ-46972	Actually	1987	12.00
E1-90263	Actually	1988	25.00
—Limited set with bonus 12" record of "Always on My Mind" (SPRO-04055/6) included			
R100681	Introspective	1988	15.00
—BMG Direct Marketing edition			
E1-90868	Introspective	1988	12.00
4233 [DJ]	Special Limited Edition: Introspective Club Mixes	1988	40.00
—Promo-only set of three 12" records of remixes			
E1-90868 [DJ]	Special Limited Edition Club Mixes	1988	100.00
—Promo-only set of three 12-inch singles of remixes, which can also be found separately (SPRO-04231/2; SPRO-04233/41; SPRO-04242/3); this is for the complete package with outer sticker			

PETER, PAUL AND MARY

GOLD CASTLE
| D1-71316 | A Holiday Celebration | 1988 | 12.00 |

R164086	A Holiday Celebration	1988	15.00
—Same as above, except BMG Direct Marketing edition			
171001	No Easy Walk to Freedom	1987	15.00
D1-71301	No Easy Walk to Freedom	1988	12.00
—Reissue of 171001			

PETER, PAUL AND MARY
| 830331 | Such Is Love | 1983 | 25.00 |

WARNER BROS.
W1700 [M]	Album 1700	1967	30.00
WS1700 [S]	Album 1700	1967	30.00
—Gold label			
WS1700 [S]	Album 1700	1968	15.00
—Green "W7" label			
WS1700 [S]	Album 1700	1970	12.00
—Any later Warner Bros. label			
W1589 [M]	A Song Will Rise	1965	25.00
WS1589 [S]	A Song Will Rise	1965	30.00
—Gold label			
WS1589 [S]	A Song Will Rise	1968	12.00
—Any later Warner Bros. label			
W1507 [M]	In the Wind	1963	25.00
WS1507 [S]	In the Wind	1963	30.00
—Gold label			
WS1507 [S]	In the Wind	1968	12.00
—Any later Warner Bros. label			
WS1751	Late Again	1968	18.00
—Green "W7" label			
WS1751	Late Again	1970	12.00
—Any later Warner Bros. label			
W1473 [M]	(Moving)	1963	25.00
WS1473 [S]	(Moving)	1963	30.00
—Gold label			
WS1473 [S]	(Moving)	1968	12.00
—Any later Warner Bros. label (green "W7", green "WB", palm trees, white label)			
W1449 [M]	Peter, Paul and Mary	1962	25.00
WS1449 [S]	Peter, Paul and Mary	1962	30.00
—Gold label			
WS1449 [S]	Peter, Paul and Mary	1968	15.00
—Green "W7" label			
WS1449 [S]	Peter, Paul and Mary	1970	12.00
—Any later Warner Bros. label (green "WB", palm trees, white label)			
W1648 [M]	Peter, Paul and Mary Album	1966	25.00
WS1648 [S]	Peter, Paul and Mary Album	1966	30.00
—Gold label			
WS1648 [S]	Peter, Paul and Mary Album	1968	12.00
—Any later Warner Bros. label			
2W1555 [M]	Peter, Paul and Mary In Concert	1964	30.00
2WS1555 [S]	Peter, Paul and Mary In Concert	1964	30.00
—Gold labels			
2WS1555 [S]	Peter, Paul and Mary In Concert	1968	15.00
—Any later Warner Bros. label			
WS1785	Peter, Paul and Mommy	1969	18.00
—Green "W7" label			
WS1785	Peter, Paul and Mommy	1970	12.00
—Any later Warner Bros. label			
BSK3231	Reunion	1978	12.00
W1615 [M]	See What Tomorrow Brings	1965	25.00
WS1615 [S]	See What Tomorrow Brings	1965	30.00
—Gold label			
WS1615 [S]	See What Tomorrow Brings	1968	12.00
—Any later Warner Bros. label			
BS2552	(Ten) Years Together -- The Best of Peter, Paul and Mary	1970	18.00
—Green "WB" label			
BS2552	(Ten) Years Together -- The Best of Peter, Paul and Mary	1973	15.00
—Burbank" palm-trees label			
BSK3105	(Ten) Years Together -- The Best of Peter, Paul and Mary	1977	12.00
—Burbank" palm-trees label			
BSK3105	(Ten) Years Together -- The Best of Peter, Paul and Mary	1979	10.00
—White or tan label			

PETER AND GORDON

CAPITOL
T2115 [M]	A World Without Love	1964	30.00
ST2115 [S]	A World Without Love	1964	30.00
ST2882 [S]	Hot, Cold and Custard	1968	30.00
T2220 [M]	I Don't Want to See You Again	1964	25.00
ST2220 [S]	I Don't Want to See You Again	1964	30.00
T2324 [M]	I Go to Pieces	1965	25.00
ST2324 [S]	I Go to Pieces	1965	30.00
T2747 [M]	In London for Tea	1967	18.00
ST2747 [S]	In London for Tea	1967	25.00
T2729 [M]	Knight in Rusty Armour	1967	18.00
ST2729 [S]	Knight in Rusty Armour	1967	25.00
T2664 [M]	Lady Godiva	1967	18.00
ST2664 [S]	Lady Godiva	1967	25.00
T2430 [M]	Peter and Gordon Sing the Hits of Nashville	1966	25.00
ST2430 [S]	Peter and Gordon Sing the Hits of Nashville	1966	30.00
T2549 [M]	The Best of Peter and Gordon	1966	18.00

Number	Title	Yr	NM
— Black label with colorband			
❑ ST2549 [P]	The Best of Peter and Gordon	1966	25.00
— Black label with colorband; "Woman" is rechanneled			
❑ T2549 [M]	The Best of Peter and Gordon	1967	15.00
— Starline" label			
❑ ST2549 [P]	The Best of Peter and Gordon	1967	18.00
— Starline" label			
❑ SN-16084 [S]	The Best of Peter and Gordon	1979	10.00
❑ T2368 [M]	True Love Ways	1965	25.00
❑ ST2368 [S]	True Love Ways	1965	30.00
❑ T2477 [M]	Woman	1966	25.00
❑ ST2477 [P]	Woman	1966	30.00
— Woman" is rechanneled			

PETERS, BROCK

UNITED ARTISTS

Number	Title	Yr	NM
❑ UAL-3127 [M]	Brock Peters	1963	25.00
❑ UAS-6127 [S]	Brock Peters	1963	30.00
❑ UAL-3062 [M]	Brock Peters at the Village Gate	1961	30.00
❑ UAS-6062 [S]	Brock Peters at the Village Gate	1961	30.00
❑ UAL-3041 [M]	Sing'a Man	1960	30.00
❑ UAS-6041 [S]	Sing'a Man	1960	40.00

PETERS, RAY

JCW

Number	Title	Yr	NM
❑ 1333	From the Heart	1968	30.00

PETERS, ROBERTA

RCA VICTOR RED SEAL

Number	Title	Yr	NM
❑ LSC-2379 [S]	Roberta Peters in Recital	1960	25.00
— Original with "shaded dog" label			

PETERSEN, EDWARD

DELMARK

Number	Title	Yr	NM
❑ DS-445	Upward Spiral	1990	15.00

PETERSEN, PAUL

COLPIX

Number	Title	Yr	NM
❑ CP-429 [M]	Lollipops and Roses	1962	50.00
❑ SCP-429 [S]	Lollipops and Roses	1962	60.00
❑ CP-442 [M]	My Dad	1963	50.00
❑ SCP-442 [S]	My Dad	1963	60.00

PETERSON, COLLEEN

CAPITOL

Number	Title	Yr	NM
❑ ST-11567	Beginning to Feel Like Home	1976	15.00
❑ ST-11714	Colleen	1978	15.00
❑ ST-11835	Takin' My Boots Off	1978	15.00

PETERSON, HANNIBAL MARVIN

ENJA

Number	Title	Yr	NM
❑ 3085	Angels of Atlanta	1981	15.00

INNER CITY

Number	Title	Yr	NM
❑ IC-3020	Antibes	197?	18.00

PETERSON, JEANNE ARLAND

CELEBRATION

Number	Title	Yr	NM
❑ 5004	Jeanne Arland Peterson	197?	18.00

PETERSON, OSCAR, AND HERB ELLIS

BASF

Number	Title	Yr	NM
❑ 20723	Hello Herbie	1969	18.00

PAUSA

Number	Title	Yr	NM
❑ PR7085	Hello Herbie	1981	12.00
— Reissue			

PETERSON, OSCAR, AND MILT JACKSON

PABLO

Number	Title	Yr	NM
❑ 2310881	Two of the Few	1983	15.00

PETERSON, OSCAR, AND STEPHANE GRAPPELLI

JAZZ MAN

Number	Title	Yr	NM
❑ 5054	Time After Time	1983	15.00

PABLO

Number	Title	Yr	NM
❑ 2310907	Violins No End	198?	15.00
— With Stuff Smith			

PRESTIGE

Number	Title	Yr	NM
❑ 24041	Oscar Peterson Featuring Stephane Grappelli	1974	18.00

PETERSON, OSCAR

AMERICAN RECORDING SOCIETY

Number	Title	Yr	NM
❑ G-415 [M]	An Oscar for Peterson	1957	40.00
❑ G-438 [M]	Oscar Peterson Trio at Newport	1957	40.00

BASF

Number	Title	Yr	NM
❑ 20869	Another Day	1975	18.00
❑ MC20668	A Rare Mood	1976	18.00
❑ 25101	Exclusively for My Friends	1972	18.00
❑ MC21281	Great Connection	1974	18.00
❑ 25156	In a Mellow Mood	1973	18.00
❑ 20905	In Tune	1973	15.00
❑ 20713	Motions and Emotions	1972	15.00
❑ 20908	Reunion Blues	1973	18.00
❑ MC20879	Tracks	1974	18.00
❑ 20734	Tristeza on Piano	1972	15.00
❑ 20868	Walking the Line	1973	15.00

BOOK-OF-THE-MONTH

Number	Title	Yr	NM
❑ 61-7546	Easy Does It	1984	30.00

CLEF

Number	Title	Yr	NM
❑ MGC-698 [M]	An Evening with the Oscar Peterson Duo/Quartet	1956	50.00
❑ MGC-697 [M]	Keyboard Music by Oscar Peterson	1956	50.00
❑ MGC-695 [M]	Nostalgic Memories by Oscar Peterson	1956	50.00
❑ MGC-107 [10]	Oscar Peterson at Carnegie Hall	1951	100.00
❑ MGC-110 [10]	Oscar Peterson Collates	1952	100.00
❑ MGC-127 [10]	Oscar Peterson Collates No. 2	1953	80.00
❑ MGC-106 [10]	Oscar Peterson Piano Solos	1951	100.00
— Reissue of Mercury 25024			
❑ MGC-603 [M]	Oscar Peterson Plays Cole Porter	1953	60.00
❑ MGC-708 [M]	Oscar Peterson Plays Count Basie	1956	50.00
❑ MGC-606 [M]	Oscar Peterson Plays Duke Ellington	1953	60.00
❑ MGC-605 [M]	Oscar Peterson Plays George Gershwin	1953	60.00
❑ MGC-649 [M]	Oscar Peterson Plays Harold Arlen	1955	50.00
❑ MGC-648 [M]	Oscar Peterson Plays Harry Warren	1955	50.00
❑ MGC-604 [M]	Oscar Peterson Plays Irving Berlin	1953	60.00
❑ MGC-623 [M]	Oscar Peterson Plays Jerome Kern	1954	50.00
❑ MGC-650 [M]	Oscar Peterson Plays Jimmy McHugh	1955	50.00
❑ MGC-119 [10]	Oscar Peterson Plays Pretty	1952	100.00
❑ MGC-155 [10]	Oscar Peterson Plays Pretty No. 2	1954	80.00
❑ MGC-624 [M]	Oscar Peterson Plays Richard Rodgers	1954	50.00
❑ MGC-625 [M]	Oscar Peterson Plays Vincent Youmans	1954	50.00
❑ MGC-145 [10]	Oscar Peterson Sings	1954	80.00
❑ MGC-694 [M]	Recital by Oscar Peterson	1956	50.00
❑ MGC-696 [M]	Tenderly -- Music by Oscar Peterson	1956	50.00
❑ MGC-116 [10]	The Oscar Peterson Quartet	1952	100.00
❑ MGC-688 [M]	The Oscar Peterson Quartet	1956	50.00
— Reissue of 116			
❑ MGC-168 [10]	The Oscar Peterson Quartet No. 2	1954	80.00

DCC COMPACT CLASSICS

Number	Title	Yr	NM
❑ LPZ-2021	West Side Story	1996	100.00
— Audiophile vinyl			

EMARCY

Number	Title	Yr	NM
❑ 405	Oscar Peterson Trio Transition	1976	18.00

FANTASY

Number	Title	Yr	NM
❑ OJC-383	Oscar Peterson and the Bassists -- Montreux '77	1989	12.00
❑ OJC-378	Oscar Peterson Jam -- Montreux '77	1989	12.00
❑ OJC-498	Skol	1991	12.00
❑ OJC-627	The Good Life	1991	12.00
❑ OJC-603	Trumpet Summit Meets the Oscar Peterson Big Four	1991	12.00

LIMELIGHT

Number	Title	Yr	NM
❑ LM-82039 [M]	Blues Etude	1966	18.00
❑ LS-86039 [S]	Blues Etude	1966	18.00
❑ LM-82010 [M]	Canadiana Suite	1965	18.00
❑ LS-86010 [S]	Canadiana Suite	1965	25.00
❑ LM-82023 [M]	Eloquence	1965	18.00
❑ LS-86023 [S]	Eloquence	1965	25.00
❑ LM-82044 [M]	Soul Espanol	1967	25.00
❑ LS-86044 [S]	Soul Espanol	1967	18.00
❑ LM-82029 [M]	With Respect to Nat	1966	18.00
❑ LS-86029 [S]	With Respect to Nat	1966	25.00

MERCURY

Number	Title	Yr	NM
❑ MGC-107 [10]	Oscar Peterson at Carnegie Hall	1951	120.00
❑ MGC-110 [10]	Oscar Peterson Collates	1952	120.00
❑ MG-25024 [10]	Oscar Peterson Piano Solos	1950	150.00
❑ MGC-106 [10]	Oscar Peterson Piano Solos	1951	120.00
❑ MGC-603 [M]	Oscar Peterson Plays Cole Porter	1953	100.00
❑ MGC-606 [M]	Oscar Peterson Plays Duke Ellington	1953	100.00
❑ MGC-605 [M]	Oscar Peterson Plays George Gershwin	1953	100.00
❑ MGC-604 [M]	Oscar Peterson Plays Irving Berlin	1953	100.00
❑ MGC-119 [10]	Oscar Peterson Plays Pretty	1952	120.00
❑ MG-20975 [M]	Oscar Peterson Trio + One	1964	30.00
❑ SR-60975 [S]	Oscar Peterson Trio + One	1964	30.00
❑ MGC-116 [10]	The Oscar Peterson Quartet	1952	120.00

MGM

Number	Title	Yr	NM
❑ GAS-133	Oscar Peterson (Golden Archive Series)	1970	15.00

MOBILE FIDELITY

Number	Title	Yr	NM
❑ 1-243	Very Tall	1995	50.00
— Audiophile vinyl			

PABLO

Number	Title	Yr	NM
❑ 2625705	A Salle Pleyel	1975	18.00
❑ 2640101	Freedom Songbook	1983	18.00
❑ 2310796	Giants	1977	15.00
❑ 2625702	History of An Artist	1975	18.00
❑ 2310895	History of An Artist, Volume 2	1983	15.00
❑ 2310918	If You Could See Me Now	1987	12.00
❑ 2310817	Jousts	1979	15.00
❑ 2310940	Live	1990	12.00
❑ 2310747	Montreux '75	1976	15.00
❑ 2310742	Oscar Peterson and Clark Terry	1976	15.00
❑ 2310740	Oscar Peterson and Dizzy Gillespie	1976	15.00
❑ 2310741	Oscar Peterson and Harry Edison	1976	15.00
❑ 2310743	Oscar Peterson and Jon Faddis	1976	15.00
❑ 2310739	Oscar Peterson and Roy Eldridge	1976	15.00
❑ 2310927	Oscar Peterson + Harry Edison + Eddie "Cleanhead" Vinson	1988	12.00
❑ 2625711	Oscar Peterson in Russia	1976	15.00
❑ 2310779	Porgy and Bess	1976	15.00
❑ 2310701	The Trio	1975	15.00

PABLO LIVE

Number	Title	Yr	NM
❑ 2308224	Digital at Montreux	1980	15.00
❑ 2620115	Live at the Northsea Jazz Festival, 1980	1981	18.00
❑ 2308231	Nigerian Marketplace	1982	15.00
❑ 2308213	Oscar Peterson and the Bassists -- Montreux '77	1978	15.00
❑ 2308208	Oscar Peterson Jam -- Montreux '77	1977	15.00
❑ 2308232	Skol	1982	15.00
❑ 2308241	The Good Life	1983	15.00
❑ 2620111	The London Concert	1979	18.00
❑ 2620112	The Paris Concert	1979	18.00

PABLO TODAY

Number	Title	Yr	NM
❑ 2312129	A Royal Wedding Suite	198?	15.00
❑ 2312108	Night Child	1979	15.00
❑ 2313103	Silent Partner	1980	15.00
❑ 2312135	The Personal Touch	1982	15.00

PAUSA

Number	Title	Yr	NM
❑ PR7059	Action	1980	12.00
❑ PR7135	Another Day	1983	12.00
— Reissue of BASF 20869			
❑ PR7064	Girl Talk	1980	12.00
❑ PR7113	Great Connection	1983	12.00
— Reissue of BASF 21281			
❑ PR7073	In Tune	1980	12.00
— Reissue of BASF 20905			
❑ PR7044	Mellow Mood	1979	12.00
❑ PR7102	Motions and Emotions	1982	12.00
— Reissue of BASF 20713			
❑ PR7069	My Favorite Instrument	1980	12.00
❑ PR7099	Reunion Blues	1981	12.00
— Reissue of BASF 20908			
❑ PR7080	The Way I Really Play	1981	12.00
❑ PR7124	Tristeza on Piano	1983	12.00
— Reissue of BASF 20734			

PRESTIGE

Number	Title	Yr	NM
❑ PRST-7690	Easy Walker	1969	18.00
❑ PRST-7649	Oscar Peterson Plays for Lovers	1969	18.00
❑ PRST-7595	Soul-O!	1968	18.00
❑ PRST-7620	The Great Oscar Peterson on Prestige!	1969	18.00

RCA VICTOR

Number	Title	Yr	NM
❑ LPT-3006 [10]	This Is Oscar Peterson	1952	120.00

TRIP

Number	Title	Yr	NM
❑ 5560	Eloquence	197?	12.00

VERVE

Number	Title	Yr	NM
❑ V-8516 [M]	Affinity	1963	30.00
❑ V6-8516 [S]	Affinity	1963	30.00
❑ MGV-2048 [M]	An Evening with Oscar Peterson	1957	40.00
— Reissue of Clef 698			
❑ V-2048 [M]	An Evening with Oscar Peterson	1961	25.00
❑ MGV-8287 [M]	A Night on the Town	1958	40.00
❑ V-8287 [M]	A Night on the Town	1961	25.00
❑ V-8476 [M]	Bursting Out with the All Star Big Band!	1962	30.00
❑ V6-8476 [S]	Bursting Out with the All Star Big Band!	1962	30.00
❑ MGV-2002 [M]	In a Romantic Mood -- Oscar Peterson with Strings	1956	40.00
❑ V-2002 [M]	In a Romantic Mood -- Oscar Peterson with Strings	1961	25.00
❑ MGV-2047 [M]	Keyboard Music by Oscar Peterson	1957	40.00
— Reissue of Clef 697			
❑ V-2047 [M]	Keyboard Music by Oscar Peterson	1961	25.00
❑ 821289-1	Motions and Emotions	1984	12.00
— Reissue			
❑ V-8538 [M]	Night Train	1963	30.00
❑ V6-8538 [S]	Night Train	1963	30.00

Number	Title	Yr	NM
❑ BOMC 70-5601 [S]	Night Train	197?	30.00
—Book-of-the-Month Club edition			
❑ V-8740 [M]	Night Train, Volume 2	1967	25.00
❑ V6-8740 [S]	Night Train, Volume 2	1967	18.00
❑ MGV-2045 [M]	Nostalgic Memories by Oscar Peterson	1957	40.00
—Reissue of Clef 695			
❑ V-2045 [M]	Nostalgic Memories by Oscar Peterson	1961	25.00
❑ UMV-2626	Oscar Peterson at the Concertgebouw	198?	12.00
❑ UMV-2502	Oscar Peterson at the Stratford Shakespearean Festival	198?	12.00
❑ MGV-2119 [M]	Oscar Peterson Plays "My Fair Lady	1958	40.00
❑ MGVS-6060 [S]	Oscar Peterson Plays "My Fair Lady	1960	30.00
❑ V-2119 [M]	Oscar Peterson Plays "My Fair Lady	1961	25.00
❑ V6-2119 [S]	Oscar Peterson Plays "My Fair Lady	1961	18.00
—Reissue of 6060			
❑ V-8581 [M]	Oscar Peterson Plays "My Fair Lady	1964	18.00
❑ V6-8581 [S]	Oscar Peterson Plays "My Fair Lady	1964	25.00
❑ MGV-8092 [M]	Oscar Peterson Plays Count Basie	1957	40.00
—Reissue of Clef 708			
❑ V-8092 [M]	Oscar Peterson Plays Count Basie	1961	25.00
❑ MGV-2052 [M]	Oscar Peterson Plays the Cole Porter Songbook	1957	40.00
—Reissue of Clef 603			
❑ MGVS-6083 [S]	Oscar Peterson Plays the Cole Porter Songbook	1960	30.00
❑ V6-2052 [S]	Oscar Peterson Plays the Cole Porter Songbook	1961	18.00
—Reissue of 6083			
❑ V-2052 [M]	Oscar Peterson Plays the Cole Porter Songbook	1961	25.00
❑ 821987-1	Oscar Peterson Plays the Cole Porter Songbook	1986	12.00
—Reissue of 2053			
❑ MGV-2055 [M]	Oscar Peterson Plays the Duke Ellington Songbook	1957	40.00
—Reissue of Clef 606			
❑ MGVS-6086 [S]	Oscar Peterson Plays the Duke Ellington Songbook	1960	30.00
❑ V-2055 [M]	Oscar Peterson Plays the Duke Ellington Songbook	1961	25.00
❑ V6-2055 [S]	Oscar Peterson Plays the Duke Ellington Songbook	1961	18.00
—Reissue of 6086			
❑ MGV-2054 [M]	Oscar Peterson Plays the George Gershwin Songbook	1957	40.00
—Reissue of Clef 605			
❑ MGVS-6085 [S]	Oscar Peterson Plays the George Gershwin Songbook	1960	30.00
❑ V-2054 [M]	Oscar Peterson Plays the George Gershwin Songbook	1961	25.00
❑ V6-2054 [S]	Oscar Peterson Plays the George Gershwin Songbook	1961	18.00
—Reissue of 6085			
❑ 823249-1	Oscar Peterson Plays the George Gershwin Songbook	1985	12.00
—Reissue of 2054			
❑ MGV-2060 [M]	Oscar Peterson Plays the Harold Arlen Songbook	1957	40.00
—Reissue of Clef 649			
❑ MGVS-6091 [S]	Oscar Peterson Plays the Harold Arlen Songbook	1960	30.00
❑ V-2060 [M]	Oscar Peterson Plays the Harold Arlen Songbook	1961	25.00
❑ V6-2060 [S]	Oscar Peterson Plays the Harold Arlen Songbook	1961	18.00
—Reissue of 6091			
❑ MGV-2059 [M]	Oscar Peterson Plays the Harry Warren Songbook	1957	40.00
—Reissue of Clef 648			
❑ MGVS-6090 [S]	Oscar Peterson Plays the Harry Warren Songbook	1960	30.00
❑ V-2059 [M]	Oscar Peterson Plays the Harry Warren Songbook	1961	25.00
❑ V6-2059 [S]	Oscar Peterson Plays the Harry Warren Songbook	1961	18.00
—Reissue of 6090			
❑ MGV-2053 [M]	Oscar Peterson Plays the Irving Berlin Songbook	1957	40.00
—Reissue of Clef 604			
❑ MGVS-6084 [S]	Oscar Peterson Plays the Irving Berlin Songbook	1960	30.00
❑ V-2053 [M]	Oscar Peterson Plays the Irving Berlin Songbook	1961	25.00
❑ V6-2053 [S]	Oscar Peterson Plays the Irving Berlin Songbook	1961	18.00
—Reissue of 6084			
❑ MGV-2056 [M]	Oscar Peterson Plays the Jerome Kern Songbook	1957	40.00
—Reissue of Clef 623			
❑ MGVS-6087 [S]	Oscar Peterson Plays the Jerome Kern Songbook	1960	30.00
❑ V-2056 [M]	Oscar Peterson Plays the Jerome Kern Songbook	1961	25.00
❑ V6-2056 [S]	Oscar Peterson Plays the Jerome Kern Songbook	1961	18.00
—Reissue of 6087			
❑ 825865-1	Oscar Peterson Plays the Jerome Kern Songbook	1985	12.00

Number	Title	Yr	NM
—Reissue of 2056			
❑ MGV-2061 [M]	Oscar Peterson Plays the Jimmy McHugh Songbook	1957	40.00
—Reissue of Clef 650			
❑ MGVS-6092 [S]	Oscar Peterson Plays the Jimmy McHugh Songbook	1960	30.00
❑ V-2061 [M]	Oscar Peterson Plays the Jimmy McHugh Songbook	1961	25.00
❑ V6-2061 [S]	Oscar Peterson Plays the Jimmy McHugh Songbook	1961	18.00
—Reissue of 6092			
❑ MGV-2057 [M]	Oscar Peterson Plays the Richard Rodgers Songbook	1957	40.00
—Reissue of Clef 624			
❑ MGVS-6088 [S]	Oscar Peterson Plays the Richard Rodgers Songbook	1960	30.00
❑ V-2057 [M]	Oscar Peterson Plays the Richard Rodgers Songbook	1961	25.00
❑ V6-2057 [S]	Oscar Peterson Plays the Richard Rodgers Songbook	1961	18.00
—Reissue of 6088			
❑ V6-8775	Oscars -- Oscar Peterson Plays the Academy Awards	1969	18.00
❑ MGV-2004 [M]	Pastel Moods by Oscar Peterson	1956	40.00
❑ V-2004 [M]	Pastel Moods by Oscar Peterson	1961	25.00
❑ MGV-8340 [M]	Porgy and Bess	1959	40.00
❑ V-8340 [M]	Porgy and Bess	1961	25.00
❑ V6-8340 [S]	Porgy and Bess	1961	18.00
❑ V-8660 [M]	Put On a Happy Face	1966	18.00
❑ V6-8660 [S]	Put On a Happy Face	1966	25.00
❑ MGV-2044 [M]	Recital by Oscar Peterson	1957	40.00
—Reissue of Clef 694			
❑ V-2044 [M]	Recital by Oscar Peterson	1961	25.00
❑ V3HB-8842	Return Engagement	1975	18.00
❑ 833552	Return Engagement	198?	15.00
—Reissue of 8842 (though the labels may still use the old number)			
❑ MGV-2012 [M]	Romance -- The Vocal Styling of Oscar Peterson	1956	40.00
—Reissue of Clef 145			
❑ V-2012 [M]	Romance -- The Vocal Styling of Oscar Peterson	1961	25.00
❑ MGV-2079 [M]	Soft Sands	1957	40.00
❑ V-2079 [M]	Soft Sands	1961	25.00
❑ V-8681 [M]	Something Warm	1966	18.00
❑ V6-8681 [S]	Something Warm	1966	25.00
❑ MGV-8334 [M]	Songs for a Swingin' Affair -- A Jazz Portrait of Sinatra	1959	50.00
❑ MGVS-6071 [S]	Songs for a Swingin' Affair -- A Jazz Portrait of Sinatra	1960	40.00
❑ V-8334 [M]	Songs for a Swingin' Affair -- A Jazz Portrait of Sinatra	1961	25.00
❑ V6-8334 [S]	Songs for a Swingin' Affair -- A Jazz Portrait of Sinatra	1961	18.00
—Reissue of 6071			
❑ 825769-1	Songs for a Swingin' Affair -- A Jazz Portrait of Sinatra	1985	12.00
—Reissue of 8334			
❑ VSP-11 [M]	Stage Right	1966	15.00
❑ VSPS-11 [S]	Stage Right	1966	18.00
❑ MGV-8364 [M]	Swinging Brass with the Oscar Peterson Trio	1959	40.00
❑ MGVS-6119 [S]	Swinging Brass with the Oscar Peterson Trio	1960	30.00
❑ V-8364 [M]	Swinging Brass with the Oscar Peterson Trio	1961	25.00
❑ V6-8364 [S]	Swinging Brass with the Oscar Peterson Trio	1961	18.00
—Reissue of 6119			
❑ MGV-2046 [M]	Tenderly -- Music by Oscar Peterson	1957	40.00
—Reissue of Clef 696			
❑ V-2046 [M]	Tenderly -- Music by Oscar Peterson	1961	25.00
❑ MGV-8351 [M]	The Jazz Soul of Oscar Peterson	1959	40.00
❑ V-8351 [M]	The Jazz Soul of Oscar Peterson	1961	25.00
❑ V-8482 [M]	The Modern Jazz Quartet and the Oscar Petereson Trio at the Opera House	1962	25.00
—Reissue of 8269			
❑ V6-8482 [S]	The Modern Jazz Quartet and the Oscar Petereson Trio at the Opera House	1962	25.00
—Reissue of 8269			
❑ MGV-8366 [M]	The Music from "Fiorello!	1960	40.00
❑ V-8366 [M]	The Music from "Fiorello!	1961	25.00
❑ V3G-8828	The Newport Years	1974	15.00
❑ V6-8810	The Oscar Peterson Collection	1972	18.00
❑ 30-5606 [M]	The Oscar Peterson Quartet #1	197?	15.00
—Book-of-the-Month Club edition			
❑ MGV-8072 [M]	The Oscar Peterson Quartet No. 1	1957	40.00
❑ V-8072 [M]	The Oscar Peterson Quartet No. 1	1961	25.00
❑ MGV-8368 [M]	The Oscar Peterson Trio at J.A.T.P.	1960	40.00
❑ V-8368 [M]	The Oscar Peterson Trio at J.A.T.P.	1961	25.00
❑ MGV-8268 [M]	The Oscar Peterson Trio at the Concertgebouw	1958	40.00
❑ V-8268 [M]	The Oscar Peterson Trio at the Concertgebouw	1961	25.00
❑ MGV-8024 [M]	The Oscar Peterson Trio at the Stratford Shakespearean Festival	1957	40.00

Number	Title	Yr	NM
❑ V-8024 [M]	The Oscar Peterson Trio at the Stratford Shakespearean Festival	1961	25.00
❑ V-8591 [M]	The Oscar Peterson Trio Plays	1964	18.00
❑ V6-8591 [S]	The Oscar Peterson Trio Plays	1964	25.00
❑ 825099-1	The Oscar Peterson Trio Set	1985	12.00
❑ V-8562 [M]	The Oscar Peterson Trio with Nelson Riddle	1963	30.00
❑ V6-8562 [S]	The Oscar Peterson Trio with Nelson Riddle	1963	30.00
❑ MGV-8239 [M]	The Oscar Peterson Trio with Sonny Stitt, Roy Eldredge and Jo Jones at Newport	1958	40.00
❑ V-8239 [M]	The Oscar Peterson Trio with Sonny Stitt, Roy Eldredge and Jo Jones at Newport	1961	25.00
❑ MGV-8269 [M]	The Oscar Peterson Trio with the Modern Jazz Quartet at the Opera House	1958	40.00
❑ MGVS-6069 [S]	The Oscar Peterson Trio with the Modern Jazz Quartet at the Opera House	1960	30.00
❑ V-8269 [M]	The Oscar Peterson Trio with the Modern Jazz Quartet at the Opera House	1961	25.00
❑ V6-8269 [S]	The Oscar Peterson Trio with the Modern Jazz Quartet at the Opera House	1961	18.00
—Reissue of 6069			
❑ V-8480 [M]	The Sound of the Trio	1962	30.00
❑ V6-8480 [S]	The Sound of the Trio	1962	30.00
❑ V-8420 [M]	The Trio -- Live from Chicago	1961	30.00
❑ V6-8420 [S]	The Trio -- Live from Chicago	1961	30.00
❑ V-8700 [M]	Thoroughly Modern '20s	1967	18.00
❑ V6-8700 [S]	Thoroughly Modern '20s	1967	18.00
❑ 821849-1	Tracks	1985	12.00
❑ 821663-1	Travelin' On	1985	12.00
❑ V-8429 [M]	Very Tall	1962	30.00
❑ V6-8429 [S]	Very Tall	1962	30.00
❑ V-8606 [M]	We Get Requests	1965	18.00
❑ V6-8606 [S]	We Get Requests	1965	25.00
❑ 810047-1	We Get Requests	1986	12.00
❑ V-8454 [M]	West Side Story	1962	30.00
❑ V6-8454 [S]	West Side Story	1962	30.00

WING

❑ SRW16351	Canadiana Suite	1969	15.00

PETERSON, OSCAR/GERRY MULLIGAN

VERVE

❑ V-8559 [M]	The Oscar Peterson Trio and the Gerry Mulligan Four at Newport	1963	30.00
❑ V6-8559 [S]	The Oscar Peterson Trio and the Gerry Mulligan Four at Newport	1963	30.00

PETERSON, PAT

ENJA

❑ 4020	Introducing Pat Peterson	1982	15.00

PETERSON, RALPH

BLUE NOTE

❑ B1-92750	Tri-Angular	1989	15.00
❑ B1-91730	V	1989	15.00

PETERSON, RAY

DECCA

❑ DL75307	Ray Peterson Country	1971	25.00

MGM

❑ E-4277 [M]	The Other Side of Ray Peterson	1965	30.00
❑ SE-4277 [S]	The Other Side of Ray Peterson	1965	30.00
❑ E-4250 [M]	The Very Best of Ray Peterson	1964	30.00
❑ SE-4250 [S]	The Very Best of Ray Peterson	1964	30.00

RCA CAMDEN

❑ CAL-2119 [M]	Goodnight My Love	1966	15.00
❑ CAS-2119 [S]	Goodnight My Love	1966	15.00

RCA VICTOR

❑ LPM-2297 [M]	Tell Laura I Love Her	1960	100.00
❑ LSP-2297 [S]	Tell Laura I Love Her	1960	150.00

UNI

❑ 73078	Missing You/Featuring His Greatest Hits!	1969	25.00

PETERSTEIN, SHORTY

WORLD PACIFIC

❑ WP-1274 [M]	The Wide Weird World of Shorty Petterstein	1959	40.00

PETRUCCIANI, MICHEL

BLUE NOTE

❑ B1-48679	Michel Plays Petrucciani	1988	12.00
❑ B1-92563	Music	1989	15.00
❑ BT-85124	Pianism	1987	12.00
❑ BT-85133	Power of Three	1987	12.00

Number	Title	Yr	NM

GEORGE WEIN COLLECTION
| ❏ GW-3001 | 100 Hearts | 1984 | 15.00 |
| ❏ GW-3006 | Live at the Village Vanguard | 1985 | 15.00 |

PETTIFORD, OSCAR

ABC-PARAMOUNT
❏ ABC-227 [M]	O.P.'s Jazz Men: Oscar Pettiford Orchestra in Hi-Fi, Vol. 2	1958	120.00
❏ ABCS-227 [S]	O.P.'s Jazz Men: Oscar Pettiford Orchestra in Hi-Fi, Vol. 2	1958	100.00
❏ ABC-135 [M]	Oscar Pettiford Orchestra in Hi-Fi	1956	100.00

BETHLEHEM
❏ BCP-1019 [10]	Basically Duke	1955	250.00
❏ BCP-1003 [10]	Oscar Pettiford	1954	250.00
❏ BCP-33 [M]	Oscar Pettiford Sextet	1955	150.00
❏ BCP-6007	The Finest of Oscar Pettiford	197?	18.00
— Reissue, distributed by RCA Victor			

DEBUT
| ❏ DLP-8 [10] | Oscar Pettiford Sextet | 1954 | 500.00 |

FANTASY
❏ 6010 [M]	My Little Cello	1964	40.00
❏ 86010 [R]	My Little Cello	1964	25.00
❏ 6015 [M]	The Essen Jazz Festival	1964	40.00
❏ 86015 [R]	The Essen Jazz Festival	1964	25.00
❏ OJC-112	The New Sextet	198?	15.00

JAZZLAND
| ❏ JLP-64 [M] | Last Recordings by the Late, Great Bassist | 1962 | 60.00 |
| ❏ JLP-964 [R] | Last Recordings by the Late, Great Bassist | 1962 | 40.00 |

JAZZ MAN
| ❏ 5036 | Blue Brothers | 1981 | 15.00 |

PRESTIGE
| ❏ PRST-7813 | Memorial Album | 1971 | 25.00 |

SAVOY JAZZ
| ❏ SJL-1172 | Discoveries | 1986 | 15.00 |

PETTIFORD, OSCAR/RED MITCHELL

BETHLEHEM
| ❏ DCP-2 [M] | Jazz Mainstream | 1957 | 200.00 |

PETTIFORD, OSCAR/VINNIE BURKE

BETHLEHEM
| ❏ BCP-6 [M] | Bass by Pettiford/Burke | 1957 | 200.00 |

PETTY, NORMAN, TRIO

COLUMBIA
| ❏ CL1092 [M] | Moondreams | 1958 | 150.00 |

TOP RANK
| ❏ R-639 [M] | Petty for Your Thoughts | 1960 | 30.00 |
| ❏ RS-639 [S] | Petty for Your Thoughts | 1960 | 40.00 |

VIK
| ❏ LX-1073 [M] | Corsage | 1957 | 70.00 |

PETTY, TOM, AND THE HEARTBREAKERS

AMERICAN
| ❏ 44285-1 | Highway Companion | 2007 | 30.00 |
| — 180-gram issue; CD released in 2006 | | | |

BACKSTREET
❏ BSR-5105	Damn the Torpedoes	1979	12.00
❏ BSR-5160	Hard Promises	1981	12.00
❏ BSR-5360	Long After Dark	1982	12.00

MCA
❏ 1486	Damn the Torpedoes	1987	10.00
❏ 6253	Full Moon Fever	1989	12.00
❏ 37239	Hard Promises	1984	10.00
❏ 10317 [B]	Into the Great Wide Open	1991	25.00
❏ 5836	Let Me Up (I've Had Enough)	1987	12.00
❏ 2-8021	Pack Up the Plantation -- Live!	1985	15.00
❏ 5486	Southern Accents	1985	12.00
❏ 37143	Tom Petty and the Heartbreakers	1982	10.00
❏ 37116	You're Gonna Get It!	1982	10.00

REPRISE
| ❏ 544259-1 [B] | Hypnotic Eye | 2014 | 25.00 |

SHELTER
❏ TP-12677 [DJ]	Official Live 'Leg	1977	60.00
— Promo-only live album with letter to radio (has been counterfeited)			
❏ TP-12677 [DJ]	Official Live 'Leg	1977	60.00
— Promo-only live album with letter to radio (has been counterfeited)			
❏ SRL-52006 [B]	Tom Petty and the Heartbreakers	1976	25.00
— Original copies were distributed by ABC			
❏ SRL-52006	Tom Petty and the Heartbreakers	1979	15.00
— Later copies were distributed by MCA			
❏ DA-52029 [DJ]	You're Gonna Get It!	1978	30.00
— Promo only on red vinyl			
❏ DA-52029 [DJ]	You're Gonna Get It!	1978	30.00
— Promo only on red vinyl			

Number	Title	Yr	NM
❏ DA-52029	You're Gonna Get It!	1978	18.00
— Original copies were distributed by ABC			
❏ DA-52029	You're Gonna Get It!	1979	15.00
— Later copies were distributed by MCA			

WARNER BROS.
❏ 47294	Echo	1999	25.00
❏ 46285	Songs and Music from the Motion Picture "She's the One"	1996	12.00
❏ 47955	The Last DJ	2002	25.00
❏ 45759	Wildflowers	1994	30.00

PFEIFER, DIANE

CAPITOL
| ❏ ST-12046 | Diane Pfeifer | 1980 | 12.00 |

PHAFNER

DRAGON
| ❏ LP-101 | Overdrive | 1971 | 3000.00 |
| — VG value 1000; VG+ value 2000 | | | |

PHAIR, LIZ

MATADOR
❏ OLE 051-1	Exile in Guyville	1992	25.00
❏ OLE107-1	Whip-Smart	1994	15.00
❏ OLE191-1	Whitechocolatespaceegg	1998	18.00

PHANTOM'S DIVINE COMEDY

CAPITOL
| ❏ ST-11313 | The Phantom's Divine Comedy, Part One | 1974 | 75.00 |

PHILARMONICS, THE

CAPRICORN
| ❏ CPN 0179 | The Masters in Philadelphia | 1977 | 30.00 |

PHILBIN, REGIS

MERCURY
| ❏ SR-61169 | It's Time for Regis! | 1968 | 30.00 |

PHILLIPS, BARRE

ECM
❏ 1149	Barre Phillips II	198?	15.00
❏ 1257	Call Me When You Get There	198?	15.00
❏ 1076	Mountainscapes	1976	15.00
❏ 1011	Music for Two Basses	197?	18.00

OPUS ONE
| ❏ 2 | Journal Violone | 197? | 18.00 |

PHILLIPS, BILL

DECCA
❏ DL4897 [M]	Bill Phillips' Style	1967	30.00
❏ DL74897 [S]	Bill Phillips' Style	1967	30.00
❏ DL75022	Country Action	1968	25.00
❏ DL75182	Little Boy Sad	1970	25.00
❏ DL4792 [M]	Put It Off Until Tomorrow	1966	30.00
❏ DL74792 [S]	Put It Off Until Tomorrow	1966	40.00

HARMONY
| ❏ HL7309 [M] | Bill Phillips' Best | 1964 | 25.00 |

PHILLIPS, ESTHER

ATLANTIC
❏ 8102 [M]	And I Love Him	1965	50.00
— Cover has a pink Cupid on it			
❏ 8102 [M]	And I Love Him	1966	30.00
— Cover has a black photo on it			
❏ SD8102 [S]	And I Love Him	1965	80.00
— Cover has a pink Cupid on it			
❏ SD8102 [S]	And I Love Him	1966	40.00
— Cover has a black photo on it			
❏ SD1565	Burnin'	1970	30.00
❏ SD1680	Confessin' the Blues	1975	18.00
❏ 90670	Confessin' the Blues	1987	12.00
— Reissue of 1680			
❏ 8122 [M]	Esther	1966	30.00
❏ SD8122 [S]	Esther	1966	40.00
❏ 8130 [M]	The Country Side of Esther Phillips	1966	30.00
— Reissue of Lenox 227			
❏ SD8130 [S]	The Country Side of Esther Phillips	1966	40.00
— Reissue of Lenox S-227			

CBS ASSOCIATED
❏ PZ40935	From a Whisper to a Scream	1988	10.00
— Reissue of Kudu 05			
❏ PZ40710	What a Diff'rence a Day Makes	1987	10.00
— Reissue of Kudu 23			

KING
| ❏ 622 [M] | Memory Lane | 1959 | 4000.00 |

KUDU
❏ 09	Alone Again, Naturally	1972	15.00
❏ 14	Black-Eyed Blues	1973	15.00
❏ 31	Capricorn Princess	1976	15.00
❏ 28	For All We Know	1976	15.00

Number	Title	Yr	NM
❏ 05	From a Whisper to a Scream	1972	15.00
❏ 18	Performance	1974	15.00
❏ 23	What a Diff'rence a Day Makes	1975	15.00

LENOX
| ❏ 227 [M] | Release Me | 1962 | 100.00 |
| ❏ S-227 [S] | Release Me | 1962 | 200.00 |

MERCURY
❏ SRM-1-4005	A Good Black Is Hard to Crack	1981	12.00
❏ SRM-1-3733	All About Esther Phillips	1978	12.00
❏ SRM-1-3769	Here's Esther -- Are You Ready?	1979	12.00
❏ SRM-1-1187	You've Come a Long Way, Baby	1977	12.00

MUSE
| ❏ MR-5302 | A Way to Say Goodbye | 1986 | 15.00 |

SAVOY JAZZ
| ❏ SJL-2258 | The Complete Savoy Recordings | 1984 | 12.00 |

PHILLIPS, FLIP, AND WOODY HERMAN

CENTURY
| ❏ 1090 | Together | 1978 | 18.00 |

PHILLIPS, FLIP

BRUNSWICK
| ❏ BL58032 [10] | Tenor Sax Stylings | 1953 | 150.00 |

CHOICE
| ❏ 1013 | Phillips' Head | 197? | 15.00 |

CLEF
❏ MGC-693 [M]	Flip	1956	120.00
❏ MGC-105 [10]	Flip Phillips	1953	200.00
❏ MGC-109 [10]	Flip Phillips Collates	1953	200.00
❏ MGC-133 [10]	Flip Phillips Collates No. 2	1953	250.00
❏ MGC-691 [M]	Flip Wails	1956	150.00
❏ MGC-158 [10]	Jumping Moods with Flip Phillips	1954	200.00
❏ MGC-740 [M]	Rock with Flip	1956	150.00
❏ MGC-692 [M]	Swinging with Flip Phillips and His Orchestra	1956	120.00
❏ MGC-634 [M]	The Flip Phillips-Buddy Rich Trio	1954	120.00
❏ MGC-037 [M]	The Flip Phillips Quintet	1954	120.00

CONCORD JAZZ
| ❏ CJ-358 | A Real Swinger | 1988 | 12.00 |
| ❏ CJ-334 | A Sound Investment | 1988 | 12.00 |

DOCTOR JAZZ
| ❏ FW39419 | A Melody from the Sky | 198? | 12.00 |

MERCURY
❏ MGC-105 [10]	Flip Phillips	1951	250.00
❏ MGC-109 [10]	Flip Phillips Collates	1952	200.00
❏ MG-25023 [10]	Flip Phillips Quartet	1950	300.00

ONYX
| ❏ 214 | Flip Phillips in Florida | 197? | 15.00 |

PROGRESSIVE
| ❏ PRO-7063 | Flipenstein | 198? | 12.00 |

SUE
| ❏ STLP-1035 [S] | Flip Phillips Revisited | 1965 | 40.00 |
| ❏ LP-1035 [M] | Flip Phillips Revisited | 1965 | 30.00 |

VERVE
❏ MGV-8077 [M]	Flip	1957	80.00
❏ V-8077 [M]	Flip	1961	30.00
❏ MGV-8075 [M]	Flip Wails	1957	80.00
❏ V-8075 [M]	Flip Wails	1961	30.00
❏ MGV-8116 [M]	Rock with Flip	1957	80.00
❏ V-8116 [M]	Rock with Flip	1961	30.00
❏ MGV-8076 [M]	Swingin' with Flip	1957	80.00
❏ V-8076 [M]	Swingin' with Flip	1961	30.00

PHILLIPS, GENE

CROWN
| ❏ CLP-5375 [M] | Gene Phillips and the Rockers | 1963 | 40.00 |

PHILLIPS, JOHN

ABC DUNHILL
| ❏ DS-50077 | John Phillips (John the Wolfking of L.A.) | 1970 | 18.00 |

PHILLIPS, MICHELLE

A&M
| ❏ SP-4651 | Victim of Romance | 1977 | 18.00 |

PHILLIPS, SHAWN

A&M
❏ SP-4402	Bright White	1973	15.00
❏ SP-4324	Collaboration	1972	18.00
❏ SP-4241	Contribution	1970	18.00
❏ SP-4539	Do You Wonder	1975	15.00
❏ SP-4363	Faces	1972	15.00
❏ SP-3135	Faces	198?	10.00
— Budget-line reissue			
❏ SP-3662	Furthermore	1974	15.00
❏ SP-4582	Rumpelstiltskin's Resolve	1976	15.00
❏ SP-4282	Second Contribution	1971	18.00
❏ SP-3128	Second Contribution	198?	10.00
— Budget-line reissue			
❏ SP-4650	Spaced	1977	15.00

Number	Title	Yr	NM
CHAMELEON			
❏ D1-74764	Beyond Here Be Dragons	1988	12.00
RCA VICTOR			
❏ AFL1-3028	Transcendence	1978	12.00
❏ AYL1-3873	Transcendence	1981	10.00
—Best Buy Series" reissue			
PHILLIPS, SONNY			
MUSE			
❏ MR-5157	I Concentrate on You	1979	15.00
❏ MR-5118	My Black Flower	1977	15.00
PRESTIGE			
❏ PRST-7799	Black Magic	1970	25.00
❏ 10007	Black On Black	1971	25.00
❏ PRST-7737	Sure 'Nuff	1970	25.00
PHILLIPS, STU			
CAPITOL			
❏ T2356 [M]	Feels Like Lovin'	1965	30.00
❏ ST2356 [S]	Feels Like Lovin'	1965	30.00
RCA VICTOR			
❏ LPM-3717 [M]	Grassroots Country	1967	30.00
❏ LSP-3717 [S]	Grassroots Country	1967	30.00
❏ LPM-4012 [M]	Our Last Rendezvous	1968	50.00
❏ LSP-4012 [S]	Our Last Rendezvous	1968	30.00
❏ LPM-3619 [M]	Singin' Stu Phillips	1966	25.00
❏ LSP-3619 [S]	Singin' Stu Phillips	1966	30.00
PHILLIPS, WARREN, AND THE ROCKETS			
PARROT			
❏ PAS71044	Rocked Out	1970	30.00
PHILLIPS, WOOLF			
CORAL			
❏ CRL56036 [10]	Woolf Phillips Plays Duke Ellington Songs	1951	50.00
PHILOSOPHERS, THE			
PHILO			
❏ 1001	After Sundown	1969	150.00
PHIPPS FAMILY, THE			
STARDAY			
❏ SLP-248 [M]	Echoes of the Carter Family	1963	30.00
❏ SLP-195 [M]	Old Time Pickin' and Singin'	1962	30.00
❏ SLP-139 [M]	The Phipps Family Sings the Most Requested Sacred Songs of the Carter Family	1961	40.00
PHLUPH			
VERVE			
❏ V6-5054 [B]	Phluph	1968	35.00
PIAF, EDITH			
CAPITOL			
❏ T10210 [M]	Piaf	1959	30.00
❏ T10348 [M]	Piaf and Sarapo at the Bobido	1963	18.00
❏ ST10348 [S]	Piaf and Sarapo at the Bobido	1963	25.00
❏ T10368 [M]	Piaf at the Olympia	1964	18.00
❏ ST10368 [S]	Piaf at the Olympia	1964	25.00
❏ T10283 [M]	Piaf of Paris	1961	18.00
❏ ST10283 [S]	Piaf of Paris	1961	25.00
❏ T10295 [M]	Potpourri Par Piaf	1962	18.00
❏ ST10295 [S]	Potpourri Par Piaf	1962	25.00
❏ DTCL2953	The Edith Piaf Deluxe Set	1968	30.00
COLUMBIA			
❏ CL6223 [10]	Encore Parisiennes	1952	50.00
❏ CL898 [M]	La Vie En Rose	1956	40.00
DECCA			
❏ DL6004 [10]	Chansons de Cafes du Paris	1951	60.00
PHILIPS			
❏ PCC208 [M]	Adieu, Edith Piaf, Little Sparrow	1964	25.00
POLYDOR VOX			
❏ PL3050 [10]	Edith Piaf Sings	195?	80.00
PIANO RED			
ARHOOLIE			
❏ 1064	William Perryman (Alone with Piano)	197?	15.00
EUPHONIC			
❏ 1212	Percussive Piano	198?	12.00
❏ LG-1002 [M]	Piano Red in Concert	1956	600.00
KING			
❏ KS-1117	Happiness Is Piano Red	1970	25.00
RCA CAMDEN			
❏ ACL1-0547	Rockin' with Red	1974	15.00
SOUTHLAND			
❏ 8	Willie Perryman-Piano Red-Dr. Feelgood	1983	18.00
PIANO ROLLS AND VOICES, THE			
RCA VICTOR			
❏ LSP-4000	All Time Christmas Hits	1968	18.00

Number	Title	Yr	NM
PIATIGORSKI, GREGOR			
RCA VICTOR RED SEAL			
❏ LSC-2490 [S]	Dvorak: Cello Concerto	1961	40.00
—With Charles Munch/Boston Symphony Orch.; original with "shaded dog" label			
❏ LSC-2490 [S]	Dvorak: Cello Concerto	199?	30.00
—With Charles Munch/Boston Symphony Orch.; Classic Records reissue			
PICHON, WALTER "FATS			
DECCA			
❏ DL8390 [M]	Appearing Nightly	1956	40.00
PICKARD, SORRELLS			
DECCA			
❏ DL75338	Sorrells Pickard	1972	18.00
PICKETT, BOBBY "BORIS			
GARPAX			
❏ GPX57001 [M]	The Original Monster Mash	1962	150.00
❏ SGP67001 [S]	The Original Monster Mash	1962	250.00
PARROT			
❏ XPAS71063 [R]	The Original Monster Mash	1973	30.00
—Reissue of Garpax LP with four tracks deleted and one added			
PICKETT, WILSON			
ATLANTIC			
❏ SD8300	Don't Knock My Love	1971	18.00
❏ SD8215 [B]	Hey Jude	1969	30.00
❏ SD8175 [B]	I'm in Love	1968	30.00
❏ 8114 [M]	In the Midnight Hour	1965	50.00
❏ SD8114 [R]	In the Midnight Hour	1965	40.00
❏ SD8250	Right On	1970	25.00
❏ 8151 [M]	The Best of Wilson Pickett	1967	40.00
❏ SD8151 [R]	The Best of Wilson Pickett	1967	30.00
❏ 81283	The Best of Wilson Pickett	1985	12.00
❏ 8290 [M]	The Best of Wilson Pickett, Vol. II	1971	35.00
—Mono copies are promo only			
❏ SD8290 [S]	The Best of Wilson Pickett, Vol. II	1971	18.00
❏ 8129 [M]	The Exciting Wilson Pickett	1966	50.00
❏ SD8129 [R]	The Exciting Wilson Pickett	1966	40.00
❏ SD8183 [B]	The Midnight Mover	1968	30.00
❏ 8145 [M]	The Sound of Wilson Pickett	1967	50.00

Number	Title	Yr	NM
❏ SD8145 [P]	The Sound of Wilson Pickett	1967	50.00
❏ 8136 [M]	The Wicked Pickett	1967	50.00
❏ SD8136 [R]	The Wicked Pickett	1967	40.00
❏ SD8270	Wilson Pickett in Philadelphia	1970	25.00
❏ SD 2-501	Wilson Pickett's Greatest Hits	1973	25.00
BIG TREE			
❏ SD76011	Funky Situation	1978	15.00
DOUBLE-L			
❏ DL-2300 [M]	It's Too Late	1963	50.00
❏ SDL-8300 [S]	It's Too Late	1963	70.00
EMI AMERICA			
❏ SW-17019	I Want You	1979	15.00
❏ SW-17043	Right Track	1981	15.00
MOTOWN			
❏ 6244ML	American Soul Man	1987	12.00
RCA VICTOR			
❏ ANL1-2149	Join Me and Let's Be Free	1977	12.00
—Reissue			
❏ APL1-0856	Join Me and Let's Be Free	1975	18.00
❏ APL1-0312	Miz Lena's Boy	1973	18.00
❏ LSP-4858	Mr. Magic Man	1973	18.00
❏ APL1-0495	Pickett in the Pocket	1974	18.00
TRIP			
❏ 8010	Wickedness	1972	12.00

Number	Title	Yr	NM
UPFRONT			
❏ UPF-127 [S]	It's Too Late	197?	12.00
WAND			
❏ WD-672 [M]	Great Wilson Pickett Hits	1966	30.00
❏ WDS-672 [R]	Great Wilson Pickett Hits	1966	25.00
WICKED			
❏ 9001	Chocolate Mountain	1976	30.00
PIECES OF A DREAM			
ELEKTRA			
❏ 60270	Imagine This	1984	12.00
❏ 6E-350	Pieces of a Dream	1981	12.00
❏ 60142	We Are One	1982	12.00
MANHATTAN			
❏ ST-53023	Joyride	1986	12.00
PIERCE, BILLIE AND DEDE			
ARHOOLIE			
❏ 2016	New Orleans Music	197?	12.00
BIOGRAPH			
❏ CEN-15	Billie and Dede Pierce at Luthjen's	197?	12.00
JAZZOLOGY			
❏ JCE-25	New Orleans Legends Live, Vol. 15	196?	18.00
RIVERSIDE			
❏ RLP-394 [M]	Blues and Tonks From the Delta	1961	30.00
❏ RS-9394 [R]	Blues and Tonks From the Delta	1961	18.00
❏ RLP-370 [M]	Blues in the Classic Tradition	1961	30.00
❏ RS-9370 [R]	Blues in the Classic Tradition	1961	18.00
PIERCE, BILLY			
SUNNYSIDE			
❏ SSC-1026	Give and Take	1988	12.00
❏ SSC-1013	William the Conqueror	1986	12.00
PIERCE, BOBBY			
COBBLESTONE			
❏ 9016	Introducing Bobby Pierce	197?	18.00
MUSE			
❏ MR-5030	New York	1974	15.00
❏ MR-5304	Piercing	198?	12.00
PIERCE, DEDE			
BIOGRAPH			
❏ CEN-5	Dede Pierce and the New Orleans Stompers	197?	12.00
PIERCE, NAT; DICK COLLINS; CHARLIE MARIANO			
FANTASY			
❏ OJC-118	Nat Pierce-Dick Collins Nonet/Charlie Mariano Sextet	198?	12.00
❏ 3224 [M]	Nat Pierce-Dick Collins Nonet/Charlie Mariano Sextet	1956	120.00
—Red vinyl			
❏ 3224 [M]	Nat Pierce-Dick Collins Nonet/Charlie Mariano Sextet	195?	60.00
—Black vinyl			
PIERCE, NAT; MILT HINTON; BARRY GALBRAITH; OSIE JOHNSON			
MUSIC MINUS ONE			
❏ Vol.1 [M]	Nat Pierce and Milt Hinton and Barry Galbraith and Osie Johnson	1956	30.00
—With sheet music attached			
PIERCE, NAT			
CORAL			
❏ CRL57128 [M]	Chamber Music for Moderns	1957	40.00
❏ CRL57091 [M]	Kansas City Memories	1957	50.00
FANTASY			
❏ 3-14 [10]	Nat Pierce and the Herdsmen Featuring Dick Collins	1954	80.00
—Red vinyl			
❏ 3-14 [10]	Nat Pierce and the Herdsmen Featuring Dick Collins	1954	80.00
—Blue vinyl			
KEYNOTE			
❏ LP-1101 [M]	Nat Pierce Octet and Tentette	1955	80.00
RCA VICTOR			
❏ LPM-2543 [M]	Big Band at the Savoy Ballroom	1962	30.00
❏ LSP-2543 [S]	Big Band at the Savoy Ballroom	1962	30.00
VANGUARD			
❏ VRS-8017 [10]	Nat Pierce Bandstand	1955	80.00

Number	Title	Yr	NM

ZIM
| ❏ 2003 | Ballad of Jazz Street | 198? | 12.00 |
| ❏ 1005 | Nat Pierce and His Orchestra | 197? | 15.00 |

PIERCE, WEBB; MARVIN RAINWATER; STUART HAMBLEN

AUDIO LAB
| ❏ AL-1563 [M] | Sing for You | 1960 | 200.00 |

PIERCE, WEBB

DECCA
❏ DL8889 [M]	Bound for the Kingdom	1959	40.00
—Black label, silver print			
❏ DL8889 [M]	Bound for the Kingdom	196?	30.00
—Black label with color bar			
❏ DL78889 [S]	Bound for the Kingdom	1959	50.00
—Black label, silver print			
❏ DL78889 [S]	Bound for the Kingdom	196?	30.00
—Black label with color bar			
❏ DL4384 [M]	Bow Thy Head	1963	30.00
❏ DL74384 [S]	Bow Thy Head	1963	30.00
❏ DL4659 [M]	Country Music Time	1965	30.00
❏ DL74659 [S]	Country Music Time	1965	30.00
❏ DL4294 [M]	Cross Country	1962	30.00
❏ DL74294 [S]	Cross Country	1962	40.00
❏ DL4144 [M]	Fallen Angel	1961	30.00
❏ DL74144 [S]	Fallen Angel	1961	40.00
❏ DL4964 [M]	Fool, Fool, Fool	1968	50.00
❏ DL74964 [S]	Fool, Fool, Fool	1968	30.00
❏ DL4110 [M]	Golden Favorites	1961	30.00
❏ DL74110 [S]	Golden Favorites	1961	40.00
❏ DL4218 [M]	Hideaway Heart	1962	30.00
❏ DL74218 [S]	Hideaway Heart	1962	40.00
❏ DL75393	I'm Gonna Be a Swinger	1972	25.00
❏ DL4358 [M]	I've Got a New Heartache	1963	30.00
❏ DL74358 [S]	I've Got a New Heartache	1963	30.00
❏ DL8728 [M]	Just Imagination	1957	50.00
—Black label, silver print			
❏ DL8728 [M]	Just Imagination	196?	30.00
—Black label with color bar			
❏ DL75168	Love Ain't Never Gonna Be No Better	1970	30.00
❏ DL4604 [M]	Memory #1	1965	30.00
❏ DL74604 [S]	Memory #1	1965	30.00
❏ DL75210	Merry-Go-Round World	1970	25.00
❏ DL4486 [M]	Sands of Gold	1964	30.00
❏ DL74486 [S]	Sands of Gold	1964	30.00
❏ DL75071	Saturday Night	1969	30.00
❏ DL4739 [M]	Sweet Memories	1966	30.00
❏ DL74739 [S]	Sweet Memories	1966	30.00
❏ DL5536 [10]	That Wondering Boy	1954	120.00
❏ DL8295 [M]	That Wondering Boy	1956	60.00
—Black label, silver print			
❏ DL8295 [M]	That Wondering Boy	196?	30.00
—Black label with color bar			
❏ DL75280	The Webb Pierce Road Show	1971	25.00
❏ DXB181 [M]	The Webb Pierce Story	1964	30.00
—Deduct 25% if booklet is missing			
❏ DXSB7181 [S]	The Webb Pierce Story	1964	40.00
—Deduct 25% if booklet is missing			
❏ DL4079 [M]	Walking the Streets	1960	30.00
❏ DL74079 [S]	Walking the Streets	1960	40.00
❏ DL8899 [M]	Webb!	1959	40.00
—Black label, silver print			
❏ DL78899 [S]	Webb!	1959	50.00
—Black label, silver print			
❏ DL8899 [M]	Webb!	196?	30.00
—Black label with color bar			
❏ DL78899 [M]	Webb!	196?	30.00
—Black label with color bar			
❏ DL8129 [M]	Webb Pierce	1955	60.00
—Black label, silver print			
❏ DL8129 [M]	Webb Pierce	196?	30.00
—Black label with color bar			
❏ DL74999	Webb Pierce's Greatest Hits	1968	30.00
❏ DL75132	Webb Pierce Sings This Thing	1969	30.00
❏ DL4782 [M]	Webb's Choice	1966	30.00
❏ DL74782 [S]	Webb's Choice	1966	30.00
❏ DL4015 [M]	Webb with a Beat	1960	30.00
❏ DL74015 [S]	Webb with a Beat	1960	40.00
❏ DL4844 [M]	Where'd Ya Stay Last Night	1967	30.00
❏ DL74844 [S]	Where'd Ya Stay Last Night	1967	30.00

KING
| ❏ 648 [M] | The One and Only Webb Pierce | 1959 | 70.00 |

MCA
❏ 130	Greatest Hits	1973	15.00
❏ 513	I'm Gonna Be a Swinger	197?	15.00
—Reissue of Decca 75393			
❏ 4087	The Best of Webb Pierce	1974	18.00

VOCALION
| ❏ VL73911 | Country Favorites | 1970 | 18.00 |
| ❏ VL73830 | Country Songs | 1968 | 15.00 |

PIKE, DAVE

ATLANTIC
| ❏ 1457 [M] | Jazz for the Jet Set | 1966 | 30.00 |
| ❏ SD1457 [S] | Jazz for the Jet Set | 1966 | 25.00 |

BASF
❏ 20739	Infra-Red	1972	18.00
❏ 25112	Riff for Rent	1973	25.00
❏ 21541	Salamao	1974	18.00

COLUMBIA JAZZ ODYSSEY
| ❏ PC37011 | Pike's Peak | 1981 | 12.00 |
| —Reissue of Epic 17025 | | | |

DECCA
| ❏ DL4568 [M] | Manhattan Latin | 1965 | 18.00 |
| ❏ DL74568 [S] | Manhattan Latin | 1965 | 25.00 |

EPIC
| ❏ LA-16025 [M] | Pike's Peak | 1962 | 30.00 |
| ❏ BA-17025 [S] | Pike's Peak | 1962 | 30.00 |

MOODSVILLE
❏ MVLP-36 [M]	Dave Pike Plays the Jazz Version of "Oliver	1963	50.00
—Green label			
❏ MVLP-36 [M]	Dave Pike Plays the Jazz Version of "Oliver	1965	30.00
—Blue label, trident logo at right			

MUSE
❏ MR-5203	Let the Minstrels Play On	1980	12.00
❏ MR-5261	Moon Bird	198?	12.00
❏ MR-5092	Times Out of Mind	197?	15.00

NEW JAZZ
❏ NJLP-8281 [M]	Bossa Nova Carnival	1962	50.00
—Purple label			
❏ NJLP-8281 [M]	Bossa Nova Carnival	1965	30.00
—Blue label, trident logo at right			
❏ NJLP-8284 [M]	Limbo Carnival	1962	50.00
—Purple label			
❏ NJLP-8284 [M]	Limbo Carnival	1965	30.00
—Blue label, trident logo at right			

RIVERSIDE
| ❏ RLP-360 [M] | It's Time for David Pike | 1961 | 30.00 |
| ❏ RS-9360 [S] | It's Time for David Pike | 1961 | 30.00 |

TIMELESS
| ❏ LPSJP-302 | Bluebird | 1990 | 15.00 |

VORTEX
| ❏ 2007 | The Doors of Perception | 1970 | 25.00 |

PIKE, PETE

AUDIO LAB
| ❏ AL-1559 [M] | Pete Pike | 1960 | 100.00 |

PILHOFER, HERB

ARGO
| ❏ LP-657 [M] | Jazz | 1960 | 30.00 |
| ❏ LPS-657 [S] | Jazz | 1960 | 30.00 |

SOUND 80
| ❏ DLR103 | Spaces | 198? | 15.00 |

ZEPHYR
| ❏ ZP-12103-G [M] | Dick and Don Maw Present the Herb Pilhofer Octet -- Jazz from the North Coast, Volume 2 | 1959 | 60.00 |

PILLOW, RAY

ABC
| ❏ ABCS-665 | Ray Pillow Sings | 1968 | 18.00 |

ABC DOT
| ❏ DOSD-2013 | Countryfied | 1975 | 15.00 |

CAPITOL
❏ T2738 [M]	Even When It's Bad, It's Good!	1967	25.00
❏ ST2738 [S]	Even When It's Bad, It's Good!	1967	18.00
❏ T2417 [M]	Presenting Ray Pillow	1965	18.00
❏ ST2417 [S]	Presenting Ray Pillow	1965	25.00

HILLTOP
| ❏ JS-6164 | Wonderful Day | 197? | 15.00 |

MEGA
| ❏ 1017 | Slippin' Around with Ray Pillow | 1972 | 18.00 |

PLANTATION
| ❏ PLP-6 | People Music | 1970 | 18.00 |

PILOT (1)

EMI
| ❏ ST-11488 | January | 1976 | 12.00 |
| ❏ ST-11368 | Pilot | 1975 | 12.00 |

PILOT (2)

RCA VICTOR
| ❏ LSP-4730 | Pilot | 1972 | 15.00 |
| ❏ LSP-4825 | Point of View | 1973 | 25.00 |

PILTZECKER, TED

SEA BREEZE
| ❏ SB-2027 | Destinations | 1986 | 12.00 |

PINDER, MICHAEL

THRESHOLD
| ❏ THS18 | The Promise | 1976 | 15.00 |

PINE, COURTNEY

ANTILLES
❏ 510769-1	Closer to Home	1992	25.00
❏ 90697	Destiny's Song + The Image of Pursuance	1987	15.00
❏ 8700	Journey to the Urge Within	1986	18.00
❏ 91334	The Vision's Tale	1989	15.00

PINERA, MIKE

CAPRICORN
| ❏ CPN 0202 [B] | Isla | 1978 | 18.00 |

SPECTOR
| ❏ 00001 [B] | Forever, Mike Pinera | 1979 | 18.00 |

PINETOPPERS, THE

CORAL
| ❏ CRL56200 [10] | Square Dances | 195? | 40.00 |
| ❏ CRL57048 [M] | The Pinetoppers | 195? | 30.00 |

DECCA
| ❏ DL8348 [M] | Saturday Night Barn Dance | 1956 | 30.00 |

PINK FLOYD

CAPITOL
❏ SN-16337	Atom Heart Mother	1985	12.00
—Budget-line reissue			
❏ SN-16230 [B]	More	1982	15.00
—Budget-line reissue			
❏ SN-16330	Obscured by Clouds	1985	12.00
—Budget-line reissue			
❏ SPRO-8116/7 [DJ]	Pink Floyd Tour '75	1975	120.00
❏ SN-16234 [B]	Relics	1982	18.00
—Budget-line reissue			
❏ SEAX-11902 [PD]	The Dark Side of the Moon	1978	70.00
❏ ST-12276 [B]	Works	1983	15.00

COLUMBIA
❏ TC37680	A Collection of Great Dance Songs	1981	12.00
❏ HC47680	A Collection of Great Dance Songs	1982	50.00
—Half-speed mastered edition			
❏ PC37680	A Collection of Great Dance Songs	198?	10.00
—Budget-line reissue			
❏ OC40599	A Momentary Lapse of Reason	1987	12.00
❏ AP-1 [DJ]	Animals	1977	150.00
—White cover, with the song "Pigs" edited for airplay			
❏ JC34474 [DJ]	Animals	1977	100.00
—Demonstration Not for Sale" on label; also has insert			
❏ JC34474 [B]	Animals	1977	15.00
❏ PC244484 [B]	Delicate Sound of Thunder	1988	30.00
❏ AS736 [DJ]	Off the Wall	1979	150.00
—Sampler from 2-LP set			
❏ C64200	The Division Bell	1994	100.00
—U.S. pressings on blue vinyl			
❏ QC38243	The Final Cut	1983	12.00
❏ AS1636 [DJ]	The Final Cut	1983	30.00
—White label, record banded for airplay			
❏ PC236183	The Wall	1979	18.00
❏ HC246183	The Wall	1983	250.00
—Half-speed mastered edition			
❏ PC33453	Wish You Were Here	1975	15.00
—Standard copy (no blue wraparound) without bar code			
❏ PC33453 [DJ]	Wish You Were Here	1975	300.00
—Blue cover with photo and title on jacket; unbanded record			
❏ PC33453 [B]	Wish You Were Here	1975	35.00
—Original copies had a blue wraparound with title/artist sticker. Most buyers threw this out upon opening the LP!			
❏ PCQ33453 [Q]	Wish You Were Here	1975	250.00
❏ HC33453 [B]	Wish You Were Here	1981	80.00
—Half-speed mastered edition (original)			
❏ HC43453 [B]	Wish You Were Here	1982	50.00
—Half-speed mastered edition (reissue)			
❏ PC33453 [DJ]	Wish You Were Here	1975	250.00
—White cover, "Special DJ Copy"; banded for airplay			

EMI
| ❏ 32700 | Pulse | 1995 | 100.00 |
| —Pressed in U.K. for U.S. release; box set with 12x12 hardback book; identical to British pressings except for American bar code (67065) on shrink wrap | | | |

HARVEST
❏ SABB-11257 [B]	A Nice Pair	1973	35.00
—original sleeve shows uncensored breasts and WR Phang dental surgery			
❏ SABB-11257 [B]	A Nice Pair	1973	25.00
—sleeve censors breasts and replaces Phang dental surgery with a gargling monk			
❏ SKAO-382 [B]	Atom Heart Mother	1970	30.00
—Without title on front cover			
❏ SKAO-382 [B]	Atom Heart Mother	197?	18.00
—With title on front cover			
❏ SMAS-832 [B]	Meddle	1971	18.00
❏ ST-11198	More	1973	15.00
—Reissue of Tower 5169			
❏ ST-11078	Obscured by Clouds	1972	18.00
❏ SW-759 [B]	Relics	1971	30.00

Number	Title	Yr	NM
❑ SMAS-11163 [B]	The Dark Side of the Moon	1973	35.00
— With poster and two stickers			
❑ SMAS-11163	The Dark Side of the Moon	1973	15.00
— With no inserts			
❑ SKBB-388 [B]	Ummagumma	1969	60.00
— With the soundtrack LP from "Gigi" leaning against wall on front cover			
❑ SKBB-388	Ummagumma	1970	25.00
— With white LP cover leaning against wall on front cover			

MOBILE FIDELITY

❑ 1-202 [B]	Atom Heart Mother	1994	75.00
— Audiophile vinyl			
❑ 1-190 [B]	Meddle	1987	175.00
— Audiophile vinyl			
❑ 1-017 [B]	The Dark Side of the Moon	1980	150.00
— Audiophile vinyl			
❑ MFQR-017	The Dark Side of the Moon	1982	300.00
— Audiophile vinyl; "Ultra High Quality Recording" in box			

TOWER

❑ ST5131	A Saucerful of Secrets	1968	80.00
— Orange label			
❑ ST5131	A Saucerful of Secrets	1968	40.00
— Multi-color striped label			
❑ ST5169	More	1968	50.00
❑ T5093 [M]	Pink Floyd (The Piper at the Gates of Dawn)	1967	450.00
❑ ST5093 [S]	Pink Floyd (The Piper at the Gates of Dawn)	1967	80.00
— Orange label			
❑ ST5093 [S]	Pink Floyd (The Piper at the Gates of Dawn)	1968	40.00
— Multi-color striped label			

PINKARD AND BOWDEN

WARNER BROS.

❑ 25299	PG-13	1985	10.00
❑ 25057	Writers in Disguise	1984	10.00

PIPER, WARDELL

MIDSONG INT'L.

❑ MSI-009	Wardell Piper	1979	15.00

PIPKINS, THE

CAPITOL

❑ ST-483	Gimme Dat Ding	1970	30.00

PIRANHAS, THE

CUSTOM FIDELITY

❑ 1452	Somethin' Fishy	1969	150.00

PIRCHNER, WERNER; HARRY PEPL; JACK DEJOHNETTE

ECM

❑ 1237	Trio Recordings	1985	15.00

PIROUETTE ORCHESTRA AND CHORUS, THE

PIROUETTE

❑ XFM-58	Christmas Sing Along	195?	18.00

PISANO, JOHNNY, AND BILLY BEAN

DECCA

❑ DL9206 [M]	Makin' It	1958	30.00
❑ DL79206 [S]	Makin' It	1958	30.00
❑ DL9219 [M]	Take Your Pick	1958	30.00
❑ DL79219 [S]	Take Your Pick	1958	30.00

PITNEY, GENE, AND GEORGE JONES

MUSICOR

❑ MM-2044 [M]	For the First Time! Two Great Singers Together: George Jones and Gene Pitney	1965	30.00
❑ MS-3044 [S]	For the First Time! Two Great Singers Together: George Jones and Gene Pitney	1965	30.00
❑ MM-2065 [M]	It's Country Time Again	1965	30.00
❑ MS-3065 [S]	It's Country Time Again	1965	30.00

PITNEY, GENE, AND MELBA MONTGOMERY

MUSICOR

❑ MM-2077 [M]	Being Together	1966	30.00
❑ MS-3077 [S]	Being Together	1966	30.00

PITNEY, GENE

MUSIC DISC

❑ MDS1006	America's Greatest Country Songs	1969	15.00
❑ MDS1014	Baby, I Need Your Lovin'	1969	15.00
❑ MDS1003	The Man Who Shot Liberty Valance	1969	15.00
❑ MDS1005	Town Without Pity	1969	15.00
❑ MDS1008	Twenty Four Hours from Tulsa	1969	15.00

MUSICOR

❑ MM-2095 [M]	Backstage I'm Lonely	1966	25.00
❑ MS-3095 [S]	Backstage I'm Lonely	1966	30.00

Number	Title	Yr	NM
❑ MM-2085 [M]	Big Sixteen, Vol. 3	1966	25.00
❑ MS-3085 [S]	Big Sixteen, Vol. 3	1966	30.00
❑ MM-2006 [M]	Blue Gene	1963	30.00
❑ MS-3006 [S]	Blue Gene	1963	40.00
❑ MM-2015 [M]	Gene Italiano	1964	30.00
❑ MS-3015 [S]	Gene Italiano	1964	30.00
❑ MM-2072 [M]	Gene Pitney En Espanol	1965	30.00
❑ MS-3072 [S]	Gene Pitney En Espanol	1965	30.00
❑ MM-2007 [M]	Gene Pitney Meets the Fair Young Ladies of Folkland	1964	30.00
❑ MS-3007 [S]	Gene Pitney Meets the Fair Young Ladies of Folkland	1964	40.00
❑ MM-2008 [M]	Gene Pitney's Big Sixteen	1964	30.00
❑ MS-3008 [P]	Gene Pitney's Big Sixteen	1964	40.00
❑ MS-3161	Gene Pitney Sings Burt Bacharach	1968	25.00
❑ MM-2004 [M]	Gene Pitney Sings Just for You	1963	30.00
❑ MS-3004 [S]	Gene Pitney Sings Just for You	1963	40.00
❑ MS-3183	Gene Pitney Sings the Platters' Golden Platters	1970	18.00
❑ MM-2043 [M]	Gene Pitney's More Big Sixteen	1965	30.00
❑ MS-3043 [P]	Gene Pitney's More Big Sixteen	1965	30.00
❑ MS-3193	Gene Pitney Super Star	1971	18.00
❑ MM-2134 [M]	Golden Greats	1967	30.00
❑ MS-3134 [S]	Golden Greats	1967	25.00
❑ MS-3233	Golden Hour	1972	18.00
❑ MM-2102 [M]	Greatest Hits of All Times	1966	25.00
❑ MS-3102 [P]	Greatest Hits of All Times	1966	30.00
❑ MM-2056 [M]	I Must Be Seeing Things	1965	30.00
❑ MS-3056 [S]	I Must Be Seeing Things	1965	30.00
❑ MM-2019 [M]	It Hurts to Be in Love	1964	30.00
❑ MS-3019 [P]	It Hurts to Be in Love	1964	30.00
❑ MM-2117 [M]	Just One Smile	1967	25.00
❑ MS-3117 [S]	Just One Smile	1967	30.00
❑ MM-2069 [M]	Looking Through the Eyes of Love	1965	30.00
❑ MS-3069 [S]	Looking Through the Eyes of Love	1965	30.00
❑ MM-2100 [M]	Messumo Mi Puo Giudicare	1966	25.00
❑ MS-3100 [S]	Messumo Mi Puo Giudicare	1966	30.00
❑ MM-2003 [M]	Only Love Can Break a Heart	1962	40.00
— Brown label			
❑ MM-2003 [M]	Only Love Can Break a Heart	1963	30.00
— Black label			
❑ MS-3003 [S]	Only Love Can Break a Heart	1962	50.00
— Brown label			
❑ MS-3003 [S]	Only Love Can Break a Heart	1963	30.00
— Black label			
❑ MS-3164	She's a Heartbreaker	1968	25.00
❑ MS-3206	Ten Years After	1971	18.00
❑ MUX-4600	The Best of Gene Pitney (Double Gold Series)	1977	18.00
❑ MM-2104 [M]	The Country Side of Gene Pitney	1967	25.00
❑ MS-3104 [S]	The Country Side of Gene Pitney	1967	30.00
❑ MM-2101 [M]	The Gene Pitney Show	1966	25.00
❑ MS-3101 [S]	The Gene Pitney Show	1966	30.00
❑ M2S-3148 [S]	The Gene Pitney Story	1968	30.00
— Add 40% if bonus photo is enclosed			
❑ M2-3148 [M]	The Gene Pitney Story	1968	40.00
— Mono is promo only			
❑ MS-3174	The Greatest Hits of Gene Pitney	1969	25.00
❑ MM-2001 [M]	The Many Sides of Gene Pitney	1962	50.00
— Brown label			
❑ MM-2001 [M]	The Many Sides of Gene Pitney	1963	30.00
— Black label			
❑ MS-3001 [R]	The Many Sides of Gene Pitney	1962	30.00
— Brown label			
❑ MS-3001 [R]	The Many Sides of Gene Pitney	1963	25.00
— Black label			
❑ MM-2005 [M]	World-Wide Winners	1963	30.00
❑ MS-3005 [P]	World-Wide Winners	1963	40.00
❑ MM-2108 [M]	Young and Warm and Wonderful	1967	25.00
❑ MS-3108 [S]	Young and Warm and Wonderful	1967	30.00

RHINO

❑ RNDA-1102	Anthology (1961-1968)	1984	15.00

SPRINGBOARD

❑ SPB-4057	Gene Pitney	1975	12.00

PIXIES

4AD

❑ 70010 [B]	Bossanova	2008	18.00
❑ 71014	Trompe La Monde	2008	18.00

ELEKTRA

❑ 60963	Bossanova	1990	18.00
❑ 60856	Doolittle	1989	25.00
❑ 60856 [DJ]	Doolittle	1989	15.00
— Promo-only on audiophile vinyl			
❑ PR-8127 [DJ]	Live	1989	60.00
— Promo-only seven-song live collection of mostly songs from their pre-Elektra days			

Number	Title	Yr	NM
ROUGH TRADE			
❑ ROUGH US38	Surfer Rosa	1988	25.00

PIXIES THREE, THE

MERCURY

❑ MG-20912 [M]	Party with the Pixies Three	1964	150.00
❑ SR-60912 [S]	Party with the Pixies Three	1964	200.00

PIZZARELLI, BUCKY, AND BUD FREEMAN

FLYING DUTCHMAN

❑ BDL1-1378	Buck & Bud	1976	15.00

PIZZARELLI, BUCKY, AND VINNIE BURKE

SAVOY

❑ MG-12158 [M]	Music Minus Many Men	1960	30.00

PIZZARELLI, BUCKY

FLYING DUTCHMAN

❑ BDL1-1120	Nightwings	1975	15.00

MONMOUTH-EVERGREEN

❑ 7066	Bucky Pizzarelli Plays Beiderbecke, Challis, Kress	197?	18.00
❑ 7093	Bucky Pizzarelli with the Care Pierre Trio	197?	15.00
❑ 7082	Bucky's Bunch	197?	15.00
❑ 7047	Green Guitar Blues	197?	18.00

STASH

❑ ST-213	Love Songs	198?	12.00
❑ ST-263	Solo Flight	1987	12.00

PIZZARELLI, BUCKY AND JOHN JR.

STASH

❑ ST-207	2 x 7 = Pizzarelli	1980	15.00
❑ ST-239	Swinging Sevens	198?	12.00

PIZZARELLI, JOHN JR.

STASH

❑ ST-256	Hit That Jive, Jack!	1985	12.00
❑ ST-226	I'm Hip	1983	12.00
❑ ST-267	Sing! Sing! Sing!	1987	12.00

PIZZI, RAY

DISCOVERY

❑ 853	Espressivo	1982	12.00
❑ 801	The Love Letter	1980	12.00

PABLO

❑ 2310795	Conception	197?	15.00

PLACE, MARY KAY

COLUMBIA

❑ PC34908	Aimin' to Please	1977	12.00
❑ KC34353	Tonite! At the Capri Lounge Loretta Haggers	1976	12.00

PLAIN JANE

HOBBIT

❑ 5000	Plain Jane	1969	30.00

PLANET, JANET

SEA BREEZE

❑ SB-2026	Sweet Thunder	1986	15.00

PLANET P

GEFFEN

❑ GHS4000	Planet P	1983	15.00

MCA

❑ 8019	Pink World	1984	25.00
— As "Planet P Project"			
❑ L33-1227 [EP]	Pink World	1984	15.00
— Promo-only pink vinyl EP			

PLANET PATROL

TOMMY BOY

❑ TBLP-1002	Planet Patrol	1983	40.00
— Originals on purple vinyl			
❑ TBLP-1002	Planet Patrol	1983	18.00
— Black vinyl			

PLANT, ROBERT

ES PARANZA

❑ 90485 [EP]	Little by Little Collector's Edition	1985	10.00
❑ 91336	Manic Nirvana	1990	18.00
❑ PR2244 [DJ]	Non-Stop Go	1988	30.00
— Promo-only interview album			
❑ 90863	Now and Zen	1988	10.00
❑ 90265	Shaken 'n' Stirred	1985	10.00
❑ 90101	The Principle of Moments	1983	10.00

SWAN SONG

❑ SS8512	Pictures at Eleven	1982	12.00

PLANT & SEE

WHITE WHALE

❑ WWS-7120	Plant & See	1969	30.00

Number	Title	Yr	NM

PLASMATICS

CAPITOL
❑ ST-12237	Coup d'Etat	1982	18.00

PVC
❑ 8929	Beyond the Valley of 1984	1983	18.00
—Reissue of Stiff USE-11			
❑ 6908	Metal Priestess	1983	18.00
—Reissue of Stiff WOW-666			

STIFF
❑ USE-11	Beyond the Valley of 1984	1981	30.00
❑ WOW-666 [EP]	Metal Priestess	1981	30.00
❑ USE-9	New Hope for the Wretched	1980	30.00

VICE SQUAD
| ❑ VS105/106 [EP] | Meet the Plasmatics | 1979 | 80.00 |

PLASTER CASTERS, THE

BLUESTIME
| ❑ BTS-9001 [B] | The Plaster Casters Blues Band | 1969 | 60.00 |

PLASTIC BERTRAND

SIRE
| ❑ SRK6061 | Plastic Bertrand | 1978 | 25.00 |

PLASTIC COW, THE

DOT
| ❑ DLP25961 [B] | The Plastic Cow Goes Moooooog | 1969 | 30.00 |

PLATINUM BLONDE

EPIC
| ❑ BFE40147 | Alien Shores | 1985 | 12.00 |
| ❑ BFE40949 | Contact | 1987 | 12.00 |

PLATTERS, THE

CANDELITE MUSIC
| ❑ CMI1000 | The 50 Golden Hits of the Platters | 197? | 40.00 |

COLUMBIA SPECIAL PRODUCTS
| ❑ P11834 [S] | Christmas with the Platters | 1973 | 18.00 |
| —Reissue of Mercury SR-60841 with fewer tracks | | | |

FEDERAL
| ❑ 549 [M] | The Platters | 1957 | 1600.00 |
| —Records on Federal 651 are bootlegs from the 1970s | | | |

KING
❑ 5002	19 Hits of the Platters	197?	15.00
❑ 651 [M]	The Platters	1959	800.00
—Records on Federal 651 are bootlegs from the 1970s			
❑ KLP-651 [M]	The Platters	1987	12.00
—Reissue with "Highland Records" on label			

MERCURY
❑ MG-20933 [M]	10th Anniversary Album	1964	25.00
❑ SR-60933 [S]	10th Anniversary Album	1964	30.00
❑ MG-20841 [M]	Christmas with the Platters	1963	30.00
❑ SR-60841 [S]	Christmas with the Platters	1963	40.00
—Same as above, but in stereo			
❑ MG-20613 [M]	Encore of Broadway Golden Hits	1961	25.00
❑ SR-60613 [S]	Encore of Broadway Golden Hits	1961	30.00
❑ MG-20472 [M]	Encore of Golden Hits	1960	30.00
❑ SR-60243 [P]	Encore of Golden Hits	1960	40.00
—Original: Black label, silver print; 12 songs on LP			
❑ 828254-1	Encore of Golden Hits	198?	10.00
—Reissue			
❑ SR-60243 [P]	Encore of Golden Hits	1965	30.00
—Second edition: Red label, "MERCURY" in white across top; may or may not have "Gold Record Award" insignia on back cover; 12 songs on LP			
❑ SR-60243 [P]	Encore of Golden Hits	1975	15.00
—Chicago skyline label; album has 10 songs			
❑ MG-20893 [M]	Encore of Golden Hits of the Groups	1964	25.00
❑ SR-60893 [S]	Encore of Golden Hits of the Groups	1964	30.00
❑ MG-20589 [M]	Life Is Just a Bowl of Cherries	1960	30.00
❑ SR-60245 [S]	Life Is Just a Bowl of Cherries	1960	30.00
❑ MG-20759 [M]	Moonlight Memories	1963	25.00
❑ SR-60759 [S]	Moonlight Memories	1963	30.00
❑ MG-20591 [M]	More Encore of Golden Hits	1960	30.00
❑ SR-60252 [S]	More Encore of Golden Hits	1960	30.00
❑ 828246-1	More Encore of Golden Hits	198?	10.00
—Reissue			
❑ SRM-1-4050	Platterama	1982	12.00
❑ MG-20481 [M]	Reflections	1960	30.00
❑ SR-60160 [S]	Reflections	1960	30.00
❑ MG-20410 [M]	Remember When?	1959	30.00
❑ SR-60087 [S]	Remember When?	1959	50.00
❑ MG-20669 [M]	Song for the Lonely	1962	25.00
❑ SR-60669 [S]	Song for the Lonely	1962	30.00
❑ MG-20298 [M]	The Flying Platters	1957	100.00
❑ MG-20366 [M]	The Flying Platters Around the World	1958	30.00
❑ SR-60043 [S]	The Flying Platters Around the World	1959	50.00
❑ MG-20983 [M]	The New Soul of the Platters	1965	18.00

❑ SR-60983 [S]	The New Soul of the Platters	1965	25.00
❑ MG-20146 [M]	The Platters	1956	100.00
❑ MG-20216 [M]	The Platters, Volume Two	1956	100.00
❑ MG-20782 [M]	The Platters Present All-Time Movie Hits	1963	25.00
❑ SR-60782 [S]	The Platters Present All-Time Movie Hits	1963	30.00
❑ MG-20808 [M]	The Platters Sing Latino	1963	25.00
❑ SR-60808 [S]	The Platters Sing Latino	1963	30.00

MUSIC DISC
| ❑ MDS-1002 | Only You | 1969 | 15.00 |

MUSICOR
❑ MM-2125 [M]	Going Back to Detroit	1967	18.00
❑ MS-3125 [S]	Going Back to Detroit	1967	18.00
❑ MS-3231	Golden Hour	1973	15.00
❑ MS-3171	I Get the Sweetest Feeling	1968	18.00
❑ MM-2091 [M]	I Love You 1,000 Times	1966	18.00
❑ MS-3091 [S]	I Love You 1,000 Times	1966	25.00
❑ MM-2141 [M]	New Golden Hits of the Platters	1967	25.00
❑ MS-3141 [S]	New Golden Hits of the Platters	1967	18.00
❑ MS-3185	Singing the Great Hits Our Way	1969	18.00
❑ MS-3156	Sweet, Sweet Lovin'	1968	18.00
❑ MS-3254	The Golden Hits of the Platters	1973	15.00
❑ MM-2111 [M]	The Platters Have the Magic Touch	1966	18.00
❑ MS-3111 [S]	The Platters Have the Magic Touch	1966	25.00

PICKWICK
| ❑ PTP-2083 | Only You | 1973 | 15.00 |
| ❑ SPC-3236 | Super Hits | 197? | 12.00 |

RHINO
| ❑ RNFP-71495 | Anthology (1955-1967) | 1986 | 15.00 |

SPRINGBOARD
| ❑ SPB-4059 | The Platters | 197? | 12.00 |

WING
❑ MGW-12346 [M]	10th Anniversary Album	196?	15.00
❑ SRW-16346 [S]	10th Anniversary Album	196?	15.00
❑ MGW-12112 [M]	Encores!	1959	30.00
—With liner notes on back cover			
❑ MGW-12112 [M]	Encores!	196?	18.00
—With photos of other Wing LPs on back cover			
❑ SRW-16112 [R]	Encores!	196?	15.00
❑ MGW-12226 [M]	Flying Platters	1963	15.00
❑ SRW-16226 [S]	Flying Platters	1963	15.00
❑ MGW-12272 [M]	Reflections	1964	15.00
❑ SRW-16272 [S]	Reflections	1964	15.00

PLAXICO, LONNIE

MUSE
| ❑ MR-5389 | Plaxico | 1989 | 15.00 |

PLAYER

CASABLANCA
| ❑ NBLP7217 | Room with a View | 1980 | 12.00 |

RCA VICTOR
| ❑ AFL1-4186 | Spies of Life | 1982 | 12.00 |

RSO
| ❑ RS-1-3036 | Danger Zone | 1978 | 12.00 |
| ❑ RS-1-3026 | Player | 1977 | 12.00 |

PLAYERS, THE

MINIT
| ❑ LP-40006 [M] | He'll Be Back | 1966 | 30.00 |
| ❑ LP-24006 [S] | He'll Be Back | 1966 | 30.00 |

PLAYMATES, THE

FORUM
❑ F-9012 [M]	At Play with the Playmates	196?	15.00
❑ SF-9012 [S]	At Play with the Playmates	196?	18.00
❑ F-9021 [M]	Broadway Show Stoppers	196?	15.00
❑ SF-9021 [S]	Broadway Show Stoppers	196?	18.00
❑ F-16001 [M]	The Playmates Visit West of the Indies	1960	18.00
❑ SF-16001 [S]	The Playmates Visit West of the Indies	1960	25.00

ROULETTE
❑ R-25043 [M]	At Play with the Playmates	1958	30.00
❑ SR-25043 [S]	At Play with the Playmates	1958	30.00
❑ R-25084 [M]	Broadway Show Stoppers	1961	25.00
❑ SR-25084 [S]	Broadway Show Stoppers	1961	30.00
❑ R-25001 [M]	Calypso	1957	30.00
❑ R-25068 [M]	Cuttin' Capers	1960	25.00
❑ SR-25068 [S]	Cuttin' Capers	1960	30.00
❑ R-25059 [M]	Rock and Roll Record Hop	1959	25.00
❑ SR-25059 [S]	Rock and Roll Record Hop	1959	30.00

PLEASURE FAIR, THE

UNI
| ❑ 3008 [M] | The Pleasure Fair | 1967 | 25.00 |
| ❑ 73008 [S] | The Pleasure Fair | 1967 | 25.00 |

PLIMSOULS, THE

BEAT
| ❑ BE-1001 [EP] | Zero Hour | 1980 | 30.00 |

GEFFEN
| ❑ GHS4002 | Everywhere at Once | 1983 | 15.00 |

PLANET

| ❑ 13 [B] | The Plimsouls | 1981 | 30.00 |

PLONSKY, JOHN

GOLDEN CREST
| ❑ GC-3014 [M] | Cool Man, Cool | 1958 | 30.00 |

PLUGZ

FATIMA
| ❑ 80 | Better Luck | 1981 | 30.00 |

PLUG/REAL LIFE
| ❑ 001 | Electrify Me | 1979 | 60.00 |

PLUM NELLY

CAPITOL
| ❑ ST-692 [B] | Deceptive Lines | 1971 | 30.00 |

PLUMMER, BILL

ABC IMPULSE!
| ❑ A-9164 [M] | Bill Plummer and the Cosmic Brotherhood | 1968 | 40.00 |
| ❑ AS-9164 [S] | Bill Plummer and the Cosmic Brotherhood | 1968 | 25.00 |

PO' BOYS, THE

DECCA
❑ DL4725 [M]	Bill Anderson Presents the Po' Boys	1966	25.00
❑ DL74725 [S]	Bill Anderson Presents the Po' Boys	1966	30.00
❑ DL4884 [M]	The Po' Boys Pick Again	1967	30.00
❑ DL74884 [S]	The Po' Boys Pick Again	1967	25.00

MCA
| ❑ 337 | The Rich Sounds of Bill Anderson's Po' Boys | 1973 | 18.00 |

POCO

ABC
❑ D-890	Head Over Heels	1975	12.00
❑ D-989	Indian Summer	1977	12.00
❑ AA-1099	Legend	1978	15.00
❑ D-946	Rose of Cimarron	1976	12.00

ATLANTIC
| ❑ 80008 | Ghost Town | 1982 | 12.00 |
| ❑ 80148 | Inamorata | 1984 | 12.00 |

EPIC
❑ KE31601	A Good Feelin' to Know	1972	18.00
—Yellow label			
❑ KE31601	A Good Feelin' to Know	1973	12.00
—Orange label			
❑ PE31601	A Good Feelin' to Know	198?	10.00
—Budget-line reissue			
❑ PE33192	Cantamos	1974	15.00
—Orange label			
❑ PCQ33192 [Q]	Cantamos	1974	25.00
❑ KE32354	Crazy Eyes	1973	15.00
—Orange label			
❑ EQ32354 [Q]	Crazy Eyes	1973	25.00
❑ PE32354	Crazy Eyes	1979	10.00
—Blue label			
❑ KE30209	Deliverin'	1971	18.00
—Yellow label			
❑ KE30209	Deliverin'	1973	12.00
—Orange label			
❑ EQ30209 [Q]	Deliverin'	1972	25.00
❑ KE30753	From the Inside	1971	18.00
—Yellow label			
❑ KE30753	From the Inside	1973	12.00
—Orange label			
❑ E30753	From the Inside	1973	12.00
—Reissue with new prefix			
❑ PE33336	Live	1976	15.00
—Orange label			
❑ BN26160	Pickin' Up the Pieces	1969	18.00
—Yellow label			
❑ BN26460	Pickin' Up the Pieces	1973	12.00
—Orange label			
❑ BN26522	Poco	1970	18.00
—Yellow label			
❑ BN26522 [B]	Poco	1973	12.00
—Orange label			
❑ KE32895	Seven	1974	15.00
—Orange label			
❑ EQ32895 [Q]	Seven	1974	25.00
❑ JE36210	The Songs of Paul Cotton	1980	12.00
❑ JE36211	The Songs of Richie Furay	1980	12.00
❑ PEG33537	The Very Best of Poco	1975	18.00
—Orange labels			

MCA
❑ 5363	Backtracks	1983	12.00
❑ 5227	Blue and Gray	1981	12.00
❑ 5288	Cowboys & Englishmen	1982	12.00
❑ 37009	Head Over Heels	1980	10.00
—Budget-line reissue			
❑ 37011	Indian Summer	1980	10.00
—Budget-line reissue			
❑ AA-1099	Legend	1979	12.00
—Reissue of ABC 1099			

Number	Title	Yr	NM
❏ 37117	Legend	1981	10.00
—Budget-line reissue			
❏ 37010	Rose of Cimarron	1980	10.00
—Budget-line reissue			
❏ 5132	Under the Gun	1980	12.00
❏ 37160	Under the Gun	198?	10.00
—Budget-line reissue			

MOBILE FIDELITY

Number	Title	Yr	NM
❏ 1-020	Legend	1979	40.00
—Audiophile vinyl			

RCA

Number	Title	Yr	NM
❏ 9694-1-R	Legacy	1989	12.00

PODEWELL, POLLY

AUDIOPHILE

Number	Title	Yr	NM
❏ AP-136	All of Me	1980	12.00

POGUES, THE

ENIGMA

Number	Title	Yr	NM
❏ ST-73225	Red Roses for Me	1986	30.00

ISLAND

| ❏ 90872 | If I Should Fall from Grace With God | 1988 | 15.00 |

RHINO

| ❏ R1542004 [B] | Live in London (with Joe Strummer) | 2014 | 50.00 |
| —credited to the Pogues with Joe Strummer | | | |

STIFF/MCA

| ❏ 36015 [EP] | Poguetry in Motion | 1986 | 25.00 |
| ❏ 5744 | Rum, Sodomy and the Lash | 1985 | 25.00 |

POI DOG PONDERING

COLUMBIA

❏ CAS1856 [DJ]	Interchords	1989	25.00
—Promo-only interview and music			
❏ CAS2219 [EP]	Untitled (Fruitless)	1990	18.00
—Promo-only six-song sampler			
❏ C45403	Wishing Like a Mountain and Thinking Like the Sea	1990	15.00

TEXAS HOTEL

| ❏ 16 [EP] | Circle Around the Sun | 198? | 10.00 |
| ❏ 11 [EP] | Poi Dog Pondering | 1988 | 10.00 |

POINDEXTER, BUSTER

RCA

| ❏ 9665-1-R | Buster Goes Berserk | 1989 | 15.00 |
| ❏ 6633-1-R | Buster Poindexter | 1987 | 15.00 |

POINDEXTER, PONY

EPIC

| ❏ LA-16035 [M] | Pony's Express | 1962 | 60.00 |
| ❏ BA-17035 [S] | Pony's Express | 1962 | 80.00 |

INNER CITY

❏ IC-1062	Poindexter	198?	15.00
❏ NJLP-8285 [M]	Pony Poindexter Plays the Big Ones	1962	80.00
—Purple label			
❏ NJLP-8285 [M]	Pony Poindexter Plays the Big Ones	1965	30.00
—Blue label, trident logo at right			

PRESTIGE

| ❏ PRLP-16001 [M] | Gumbo | 1964 | 40.00 |

POINTER SISTERS, THE

ABC BLUE THUMB

❏ BT-6023	Having a Party	1977	15.00
❏ BT-6021	Steppin	1975	15.00
❏ BTSY-6026	The Best of the Pointer Sisters	1976	18.00

BLUE THUMB

❏ BTS-8002	Live at the Opera House	1974	18.00
❏ BTS-6009	That's a Plenty	1974	15.00
❏ BTS-48	The Pointer Sisters	1973	15.00

MCA

| ❏ 3275 | Retrospect | 1981 | 12.00 |
| —Reissue of Blue Thumb material | | | |

MOTOWN

| ❏ 6287ML | Right Rhythm | 1990 | 15.00 |

PLANET

❏ P-18	Black and White	1981	12.00
❏ BXL1-4705	Break Out	1983	12.00
—Original does not have "I'm So Excited"			
❏ BEL1-4705A	Break Out	1984	10.00
—Reissue has "I'm So Excited" plus a remix of "Jump (For My Love)"			
❏ P-1	Energy	1978	12.00
❏ 60203	Pointer Sisters' Greatest Hits	1982	12.00
❏ P-9003	Priority	1979	12.00
❏ BXL1-4355	So Excited!	1982	12.00
❏ P-9	Special Things	1980	12.00

RCA

| ❏ 5609-1-R | Hot Together | 1986 | 12.00 |
| ❏ 6562-1-R | Serious Slammin' | 1988 | 12.00 |

RCA VICTOR

Number	Title	Yr	NM
❏ AYL1-5092	Black and White	1985	10.00
—Budget-line reissue			
❏ AJL1-5487	Contact	1985	12.00
❏ AYL1-5091	Energy	1985	10.00
—Budget-line reissue			
❏ AYL1-5089	Priority	1985	10.00
—Budget-line reissue			
❏ AYL1-5088	Special Things	1985	10.00
—Budget-line reissue			

POISON

CAPITOL

| ❏ C1-598046 | Swallow This Live | 1991 | 40.00 |
| —Vinyl version available only from Columbia House | | | |

CAPITOL/ENIGMA

❏ C1-91813	Flesh & Blood	1990	15.00
—With blood dripping from letters "Flesh & Blood"			
❏ C1-91813	Flesh & Blood	1990	15.00
—With blood airbrushed out of front cover photo			
❏ C1-591813	Flesh & Blood	1990	15.00
—Columbia House club edition			
❏ ST-12523	Look What the Cat Dragged In	1986	10.00
❏ ST-512523	Look What the Cat Dragged In	1986	12.00
—Columbia House club edition			
❏ R144402	Look What the Cat Dragged In	1986	12.00
—BMG Direct Marketing club edition			
❏ C1-48493	Open Up and Say...Ahh!	1988	15.00
—With uncropped front cover photo (woman's tongue is fully visible)			
❏ C1-48493	Open Up and Say...Ahh!	1988	10.00
—With cropped front cover photo (woman's tongue is cut off; large black bars at top and bottom of cover)			
❏ SPRO79319/22	Open Up and Say...Ahh! World Premiere Weekend	1988	30.00
—Special radio-only version to promote the LP's release			

POITIER, SIDNEY

WARNER BROS.

| ❏ W1561 [M] | Poitier Meets Plato | 1965 | 30.00 |
| ❏ WS1561 [S] | Poitier Meets Plato | 1965 | 30.00 |

POLAD, MIKE

JAZZOLOGY

| ❏ J-77 | The Cascades | 197? | 12.00 |

POLCER, ED

JAZZOLOGY

| ❏ J-150 | In the Condon Tradition | 1987 | 12.00 |

POLICE, THE

A&M

❏ R173924	Every Breath You Take -- The Singles	1986	15.00
—BMG Direct Marketing edition			
❏ SP-3902	Every Breath You Take -- The Singles	1986	12.00
❏ R123571	Ghost in the Machine	1981	15.00
—RCA Music Service edition			
❏ SP-3730	Ghost in the Machine	1981	12.00
❏ SP-3730 [DJ]	Ghost in the Machine	1981	1000.00
—Special prototype picture disc that lights up when placed on a turntable			
❏ R124159	Outlandos d'Amour	1979	15.00
—RCA Music Service edition			
❏ SP-4753	Outlandos d'Amour	1979	15.00
❏ SP-3311	Outlandos d'Amour	198?	10.00
—Reissue			
❏ R153349	Reggatta de Blanc	1979	15.00
—RCA Music Service edition			
❏ SP-3713 [10]	Reggatta de Blanc	1979	40.00
—Two 10" records with poster			
❏ SP-4792	Reggatta de Blanc	1979	15.00
❏ SP-3312	Reggatta de Blanc	198?	10.00
—Reissue			
❏ SP-6018 [10]	Reggatta de Blanc	1980	30.00
—Reissue of SP-3713			
❏ R134070	Synchronicity	1983	15.00
—RCA Music Service edition			
❏ SP-3735	Synchronicity	1983	40.00
—With gold, silver and bronze color bands on cover; used on audiophile pressings			
❏ SP-3735	Synchronicity	1983	12.00
—With blue, yellow and red color bands; 93 versions of this cover exist, none more valuable than any other			
❏ 3937351	Synchronicity	2008	25.00
—Black & white cover			
❏ R130108	Zenyatta Mondatta	1980	15.00
—RCA Music Service edition			
❏ SP-3720	Zenyatta Mondatta	1980	12.00
❏ 1775311	Zenyatta Mondatta	2008	25.00

NAUTILUS

❏ NR-40 [B]	Ghost in the Machine	1982	40.00
—Audiophile vinyl			
❏ NR-19 [B]	Zenyatta Mondatta	1981	50.00

Number	Title	Yr	NM
—Audiophile vinyl			

POLK, LUCY ANN

INTERLUDE

| ❏ MO-504 [M] | Easy Livin' | 1959 | 100.00 |
| ❏ ST-1004 [S] | Easy Livin' | 1959 | 80.00 |

MODE

| ❏ LP-115 [M] | Lucky Lucy Ann | 1957 | 150.00 |

TREND

| ❏ TL-1008 [10] | Lucy Ann Polk with Dave Pell | 1954 | 150.00 |

POLL WINNERS, THE

CONTEMPORARY

❏ M-3581 [M]	Exploring the Scene	1960	40.00
❏ S-7581 [S]	Exploring the Scene	1960	30.00
❏ M-3576 [M]	Poll Winners Three	1960	40.00
❏ S-7576 [S]	Poll Winners Three	1960	30.00
❏ C-3535 [M]	The Poll Winners	1957	50.00
❏ S-7535 [S]	The Poll Winners	1958	40.00
❏ C-3556 [M]	The Poll Winners Ride Again	1958	50.00
❏ S-7556 [S]	The Poll Winners Ride Again	1959	40.00

STEREO RECORDS

| ❏ S-7010 [S] | The Poll Winners | 1958 | 50.00 |
| ❏ S-7029 [S] | The Poll Winners Ride Again | 1958 | 50.00 |

POLLACK, BEN

BRUNSWICK

| ❏ BL58025 [10] | Ben Pollack | 1951 | 60.00 |

SAVOY

| ❏ MG-12207 [M] | Dixieland Strut | 196? | 25.00 |
| ❏ MG-12090 [M] | Pick a Rib Boys | 1956 | 50.00 |

X

| ❏ LX-3003 [10] | Ben Pollack and His Orchestra Featuring Benny Goodman | 1954 | 60.00 |

POLLARD, TERRY

BETHLEHEM

| ❏ BCP-1015 [10] | Terry Pollard | 1954 | 100.00 |

POLLARD, TERRY/BOBBY SCOTT

BETHLEHEM

| ❏ BCP-1 [M] | Young Moderns | 1957 | 50.00 |

POLLUTION

CAPITOL

| ❏ ST-205 | Heir: Pollution | 1969 | 25.00 |

PROPHECY

| ❏ SD6051 | Pollution | 1971 | 25.00 |
| ❏ SD6067 | Pollution II | 1972 | 25.00 |

POLNAREFF, MICHEL

4 CORNERS OF THE WORLD

| ❏ FCL-4240 [M] | French Rock-Blues | 1967 | 18.00 |
| ❏ FCS-4240 [S] | French Rock-Blues | 1967 | 25.00 |

ATLANTIC

| ❏ SD18153 | Michel Polnareff | 1976 | 12.00 |

POLYPHONIC SPREE

CHERRY RED

| ❏ BRED588 [S] | Yes, It's True | 2013 | 19.98 |
| —Released Aug. 6, 2013. | | | |

POMEROY, HERB

ROULETTE

| ❏ R-52001 [M] | Life Is A Many Splendored Gig | 1958 | 120.00 |
| ❏ SR-52001 [S] | Life Is A Many Splendored Gig | 1958 | 100.00 |

SHIAH

| ❏ HP-1 | Pramlatta's Hips | 1980 | 25.00 |

TRANSITION

| ❏ TRLP-1 [M] | Jazz in a Stable | 1956 | 400.00 |
| —Deduct 25 percent if booklet is missing | | | |

UNITED ARTISTS

| ❏ UAL-4015 [M] | Band in Boston | 1959 | 150.00 |
| ❏ UAS-5015 [S] | Band in Boston | 1959 | 120.00 |

PONCE, PONCIE

WARNER BROS.

| ❏ W1453 [M] | Poncie Ponce Sings | 1962 | 25.00 |
| ❏ WS1453 [S] | Poncie Ponce Sings | 1962 | 30.00 |

PONDER, JIMMY

ABC IMPULSE!

| ❏ IA-9313 | Illusions | 197? | 15.00 |
| ❏ IA-9327 | White Room | 197? | 15.00 |

CADET

| ❏ CA-50048 | While My Guitar Gently Weeps | 1974 | 15.00 |

MILESTONE

| ❏ M-9121 | Down Here on the Ground | 1984 | 12.00 |
| ❏ M-9132 | So Many Stars | 1985 | 12.00 |

Number	Title	Yr	NM

MUSE

❏ MR-5347	Jump	1988	12.00
❏ MR-5324	Mean Streets, No Bridges	1987	12.00

PONTY, JEAN-LUC

ATLANTIC

❏ SD19253	A Taste for Passion	1979	12.00
❏ SD18163	Aurora	1976	12.00
❏ SD19158	Aurora	1978	10.00
—Reissue of 18163			
❏ SD16020	Civilized Evil	1980	12.00
❏ SD19189	Cosmic Messenger	1978	12.00
❏ SD19110	Enigmatic Ocean	1977	12.00
❏ 81276	Fables	1985	10.00
❏ SD18195	Imaginary Voyage	1976	12.00
❏ SD19136	Imaginary Voyage	1978	10.00
—Reissue of 18195			
❏ A1-80098	Individual Choice	1983	10.00
❏ SD19229	Jean-Luc Ponty: Live	1979	12.00
❏ SD19333	Mystical Adventures	1982	12.00
❏ 80185	Open Mind	1984	10.00
❏ SD18138	Upon the Wings of Music	1975	12.00

BASF

❏ 21288	Open Strings	1973	25.00
❏ 20645	Sunday Walk	1972	25.00

BLUE NOTE

❏ BN-LA632-H2	Cantaloupe Island	1976	25.00
❏ LWB-632	Cantaloupe Island	1981	15.00
—Reissue of BN-LA632-H2			
❏ LT-1102	Live at Donte's	1981	12.00

COLUMBIA

❏ FC45252	Storytelling	1989	18.00
❏ FC40983	The Gift of Time	1987	10.00

DIRECT DISC

❏ SD-16603	Cosmic Messenger	1980	30.00
—Audiophile vinyl			

INNER CITY

❏ IC-1005	Jean-Luc Ponty and Stephane Grappelli	197?	12.00
❏ IC-1003	Live at Montreux: Sonata Erotica	1976	18.00

PAUSA

❏ PR-7014	Jean-Luc Ponty Meets Giorgio Gaslini	1979	12.00
❏ PR-7065	Open Strings	1980	12.00
—Reissue of BASF 21288			
❏ PR-7033	Sunday Walk	1980	12.00
—Reissue of BASF 20645			
❏ PA9001	The Jean-Luc Ponty Experience	1982	25.00

PRESTIGE

❏ PRST-7676	Critic's Choice	1969	25.00

WORLD PACIFIC

❏ ST-20156	Electric Connection	1969	30.00
❏ ST-20134	More Than Meets the Ear	1969	25.00

WORLD PACIFIC JAZZ

❏ ST-20172	King Kong -- Jean-Luc Ponty Plays the Music of Frank Zappa	1970	40.00
❏ ST-20168	The Jean-Luc Ponty Experience	1969	30.00

POOBAH

A.E.I.

❏ A-LP-1	U.S. Rock	1976	250.00

PEPPERMINT

❏ PP-1180	Steamroller	1979	150.00

RITE

❏ (no #)0	Let Me In	1972	600.00

POOLE, BILLIE

RIVERSIDE

❏ RLP-458 [M]	Confessin' the Blues	1963	30.00
❏ RS-9458 [S]	Confessin' the Blues	1963	40.00
❏ RLP-425 [M]	Sermonette	1962	30.00
❏ RS-9425 [S]	Sermonette	1962	40.00

POOLE, BRIAN, AND THE TREMELOES

AUDIO FIDELITY

❏ AFLP2151 [M]	Brian Poole Is Here	1966	40.00
❏ AFSD2151 [R]	Brian Poole Is Here	1966	30.00
❏ AFLP2177 [M]	The Tremeloes Are Here	1967	60.00
—Reissue of above album with new title			
❏ AFSD2177 [R]	The Tremeloes Are Here	1967	30.00
—Reissue of above album with new title			

POP WILL EAT ITSELF

NOTHING

❏ 95887	Amalgamation	1994	12.00

RCA

❏ 9742-1-R	This Is the Day...This Is the Hour...This Is This!	1989	18.00

ROUGH TRADE

❏ ROUGH033	Box Frenzy!	1988	18.00
❏ ROUGH022	Now for a Feast	198?	18.00

POPCORN BLIZZARD, THE (1)

DE-LITE

❏ DE-2004 [B]	Explode!	1969	50.00

POPE JOHN PAUL II

INFINITY

❏ INF9899	Pope John Paul II Sings at the Festival of Sacrosong	1979	15.00

VOX CHRISTIANA

❏ VC3004/5	Christmas Midnight Mass	1979	18.00
—Recording of the December 24, 1978 Mass at St. Peter's Basilica at the Vatican			

POPE JOHN XXIII

MERCURY

❏ 200 [M]	Pope John XXIII	1963	18.00
—Tribute album released after his death			

POPKIN, LENNY

CHOICE

❏ 1027	Falling Free	198?	12.00

POPPIES, THE

EPIC

❏ LN24200 [M]	Lullaby of Love	1966	40.00
❏ BN26200 [S]	Lullaby of Love	1966	50.00

POPPY FAMILY, THE

LONDON

❏ PS599	Seeds	1971	18.00
❏ PS574	Which Way You Goin' Billy?	1970	18.00

PORCELAIN BEARMEAT

DILL PICKLE

❏ 3468	Free Love, Free Sex, Free Music	1971	25.00

PORNO FOR PYROS

WARNER BROS.

❏ 45228	Porno for Pyros	1993	18.00

PORT OF HARLEM JAZZMEN, THE

MOSAIC

❏ MR1-108	The Complete Recordings of the Port of Harlem Jazzmen	198?	25.00

PORTAL, MICHEL

HARMONIA MUNDI

❏ HM-5186	Turbulence	1987	15.00

PORTER, DAVID

ENTERPRISE

❏ ENS-1012	David Porter...Into a Real Thing	1971	25.00
❏ ENS-1009	Gritty, Groovy, & Gettin' It	1970	25.00
❏ ENS-1026	Sweat and Love	1973	25.00
❏ ENS-1019	Victim of the Joke?	1972	25.00

PORTER, JERRY

MIRROR

❏ SWB-123 [M]	Don't Bother Me!	1966	100.00

PORTER, NOLAN

ABC

❏ ABCX-766	Nolan	1973	120.00

LIZARD

❏ A-20102	No Apologies	1971	30.00
—As "Nolan"			

PORTER, PEPPER

FIRST AMERICAN

❏ FA-7756	Invasion	1980	30.00

PORTER TWIN DISC MUSIC BOX, THE

PORTER

❏ 103	Music Box Nutcracker Suite and More Christmas Favorites	1984	15.00

PORTISHEAD

LONDON/GO BEAT

❏ 539189-1	(Music by) Portishead	1997	15.00

PORTSMOUTH SINFONIA

ANTILLES

❏ AN-7002 [B]	Hallelujah - At The Royal Albert Hall	1974	40.00

POSEY, SANDY

COLUMBIA

❏ KC31594	Why Don't We Go Somewhere and Love	1972	15.00

MGM

❏ E-4418 [M]	Born a Woman	1966	18.00
❏ SE-4418 [S]	Born a Woman	1966	25.00
❏ E-4480 [M]	I Take It Back	1967	25.00
❏ SE-4480 [S]	I Take It Back	1967	25.00
❏ E-4525 [M]	Looking at You	1968	30.00
❏ SE-4525 [S]	Looking at You	1968	18.00
❏ GAS-125	Sandy Posey (Golden Archive Series)	1970	18.00
❏ E-4455 [M]	Single Girl	1967	25.00
❏ SE-4455 [S]	Single Girl	1967	25.00
❏ ST-91110	Single Girl	1967	30.00
—Capitol Record Club issue			
❏ E-4509 [M]	The Best of Sandy Posey	1967	30.00
❏ SE-4509 [S]	The Best of Sandy Posey	1967	25.00

POSEY, SANDY/ SKEETER DAVIS

GUSTO

❏ 0005	The Best of Sandy Posey/ Skeeter Davis	198?	10.00

POSSUM

CAPITOL

❏ ST-648 [B]	Possum	1970	18.00

POSSUM HUNTERS, THE

TAKOMA

❏ C-1010 [B]	Death on Lee Highway	1970	30.00

POST, MIKE

ELEKTRA

❏ 60028 [EP]	Television Theme Songs	1982	10.00

MGM

❏ M3G-5005	Railhead Overture	1975	12.00

POLYDOR

❏ 833985-1	Theme from L.A. Law and Otherwise	1987	10.00

RCA VICTOR

❏ AFL1-5415	Mike Post	1985	12.00

POTLIQUOR

CAPITOL

❏ ST-11998	Potliquor	1979	15.00

JANUS

❏ JLS-3033	Levee Blues	1972	25.00
❏ JLS-3036	Louisiana Rock and Roll	1973	25.00
❏ JLS-3002	Potliquor	1970	25.00

POTTER, CURTIS

DOT

❏ DLP-25988	Here Comes Curtis Potter	1971	25.00

STEP ONE

❏ 0020	All I Need Is Time	1987	25.00
❏ 0004	Down in Texas Today	1984	25.00

POTTER, TOMMY

EASTWEST

❏ 4001 [M]	Tommy Potter's Hard Funk	1958	50.00

POTTS, BILL

COLPIX

❏ CP-451 [M]	Bye Bye Birdie	1963	30.00
❏ SCP-451 [S]	Bye Bye Birdie	1963	40.00

UNITED ARTISTS

❏ UAL-4032 [M]	The Jazz Soul of Porgy and Bess	1959	30.00
❏ UAS-5032 [S]	The Jazz Soul of Porgy and Bess	1959	40.00

POWELL, ADAM CLAYTON

JUBILEE

❏ JGM2062 [M]	Keep the Faith, Baby!	1967	18.00

POWELL, ANDREW, AND THE PHILHARMONIA ORCHESTRA

MOBILE FIDELITY

❏ 1-175	The Best of the Alan Parsons Project	1986	30.00
—Audiophile vinyl			

POWELL, BADEN

BASF

❏ 25155	Canto on Guitar	197?	25.00
❏ 29194	Estudios	197?	18.00
❏ 29057	Images on Guitar	197?	18.00
❏ 29623	Tristeza on Guitar	197?	18.00

COLUMBIA

❏ KC32441	Solitude on Guitar	1974	15.00

PAUSA

❏ 7078	Tristeza on Guitar	198?	12.00

POWELL, BUD

BLACK LION

❏ 153	Invisible Cage	1974	25.00

Number	Title	Yr	NM
BLUE NOTE			
❑ BST-84430	Alternate Takes	1985	25.00
❑ BLP-1571 [M]	Bud!	1957	400.00
—*Deep groove" version; W. 63rd St. address on label*			
❑ BLP-1571 [M]	Bud!	1957	200.00
—*Regular version, W. 63rd St. address on label*			
❑ BST-1571 [S]	Bud!	1959	600.00
—*Deep groove" version; W. 63rd St. address on label*			
❑ BST-1571 [S]	Bud!	1959	150.00
—*Regular version, W. 63rd St. address on label*			
❑ BLP-1571 [M]	Bud!	1963	40.00
—*With "New York, USA" address on label*			
❑ BST-1571 [S]	Bud!	1963	40.00
—*With "New York, USA" address on label*			
❑ BST-81571 [S]	Bud!	1967	30.00
—*With "A Division of Liberty Records" on label*			
❑ BST-81571 [S]	Bud!	1986	15.00
—*The Finest in Jazz Since 1939" reissue*			
❑ BLP-5003 [10]	The Amazing Bud Powell	1951	1000.00
❑ BLP-1503 [M]	The Amazing Bud Powell, Vol. 1	1955	400.00
—*Deep groove" version; Lexington Ave. address on label*			
❑ BLP-1503 [M]	The Amazing Bud Powell, Vol. 1	1958	250.00
—*Deep groove" version, W. 63rd St. address on label*			
❑ BLP-1503 [M]	The Amazing Bud Powell, Vol. 1	1963	40.00
—*With "New York, USA" address on label*			
❑ BST-81503 [R]	The Amazing Bud Powell, Vol. 1	1967	25.00
—*With "A Division of Liberty Records" on label*			
❑ B1-81503 [M]	The Amazing Bud Powell, Vol. 1	1989	18.00
—*The Finest in Jazz Since 1939" reissue*			
❑ BLP-5041 [10]	The Amazing Bud Powell, Vol. 2	1954	1000.00
❑ BLP-1504 [M]	The Amazing Bud Powell, Vol. 2	1955	500.00
—*Deep groove" version; Lexington Ave. address on label*			
❑ BLP-1504 [M]	The Amazing Bud Powell, Vol. 2	1963	40.00
—*With "New York, USA" address on label*			
❑ BLP-1504 [M]	The Amazing Bud Powell, Vol. 2	1958	250.00
—*Deep groove" version, W. 63rd St. address on label*			
❑ BST-81504 [R]	The Amazing Bud Powell, Vol. 2	1967	25.00
—*With "A Division of Liberty Records" on label*			
❑ B1-81504 [M]	The Amazing Bud Powell, Vol. 2	1989	18.00
—*The Finest in Jazz Since 1939" reissue*			
❑ B1-93204	The Best of Bud Powell	1989	18.00
❑ BLP-4009 [M]	The Scene Changes	1959	400.00
—*Deep groove" version; W. 63rd St. address on label*			
❑ BLP-4009 [M]	The Scene Changes	1959	200.00
—*Regular version, W. 63rd St. address on label*			
❑ BST-4009 [S]	The Scene Changes	1959	250.00
—*Deep groove" version; W. 63rd St. address on label*			
❑ BST-4009 [S]	The Scene Changes	1959	150.00
—*Regular version, W. 63rd St. address on label*			
❑ BLP-4009 [M]	The Scene Changes	1963	40.00
—*With "New York, USA" address on label*			
❑ BST-4009 [S]	The Scene Changes	1963	40.00
—*With "New York, USA" address on label*			
❑ BST-84009 [S]	The Scene Changes	1967	25.00
—*With "A Division of Liberty Records" on label*			
❑ BLP-1598 [M]	The Time Waits	1959	400.00
—*Deep groove" version, W. 63rd St. address on label*			
❑ BLP-1598 [M]	The Time Waits	1959	250.00
—*Regular version, W. 63rd St. address on label*			
❑ BST-1598 [S]	The Time Waits	1959	250.00
—*Deep groove" version, W. 63rd St. address on label*			
❑ BST-1598 [S]	The Time Waits	1959	150.00
—*Regular version, W. 63rd St. address on label*			
❑ BLP-1598 [M]	The Time Waits	1963	40.00
—*With "New York, USA" address on label*			
❑ BST-1598 [S]	The Time Waits	1963	40.00
—*With "New York, USA" address on label*			
❑ BST-81598 [S]	The Time Waits	1967	25.00
—*With "A Division of Liberty Records" on label*			
❑ MGC-502 [10]	Bud Powell Piano Solos	1954	400.00
❑ MGC-507 [10]	Bud Powell Piano Solos, No. 2	1954	400.00
❑ MGC-610 [M]	Bud Powell's Moods	1954	300.00
❑ MGC-739 [M]	The Genius of Bud Powell	1956	250.00
COLUMBIA			
❑ CL2292 [M]	A Portrait of Thelonious	1965	40.00
❑ CS9092 [S]	A Portrait of Thelonious	1965	50.00
—*Red label with "360 Sound Stereo*			
COLUMBIA JAZZ ODYSSEY			
❑ PC36805	A Portrait of Thelonious	1980	12.00
COMMODORE			
❑ XFL-14943	The World Is Waiting	198?	18.00
DEBUT			
❑ DLP-3 [10]	Jazz at Massey Hall, Volume 2	1953	800.00
DELMARK			
❑ DL-406 [M]	Bouncing with Bud	1966	40.00
❑ DS-9406 [S]	Bouncing with Bud	1966	50.00
❑ DS-406	Bouncing with Bud	1987	15.00

Number	Title	Yr	NM
DISCOVERY			
❑ 830	Bud Powell in Paris	198?	15.00
ELEKTRA/MUSICIAN			
❑ E1-60030	Inner Fires	1982	15.00
ESP-DISK'			
❑ BUD-1	Broadcast Performances 1953	197?	25.00
❑ 1066 [S]	Bud Powell at the Blue Note Café, Paris	1968	30.00
FANTASY			
❑ 6006 [M]	Bud Powell Trio	1962	80.00
—*Red vinyl*			
❑ 6006 [M]	Bud Powell Trio	1962	40.00
—*Black vinyl*			
❑ 86006 [R]	Bud Powell Trio	1962	40.00
—*Blue vinyl*			
❑ 86006 [R]	Bud Powell Trio	1962	25.00
—*Black vinyl*			
❑ OJC-111	Jazz at Massey Hall, Volume 2	198?	15.00
MAINSTREAM			
❑ MRL-385	Ups 'n' Downs	1973	30.00
MERCURY			
❑ MG-35012 [10]	Bud Powell Piano	1950	600.00
❑ MGC-102 [10]	Bud Powell Piano	1950	500.00
❑ MGC-502 [10]	Bud Powell Piano Solos	1951	500.00
❑ MGC-507 [10]	Bud Powell Piano Solos, No. 2	1951	500.00
❑ MGC-610 [M]	Bud Powell's Moods	1953	400.00
MOSAIC			
❑ MR5-116	The Complete Bud Powell Blue Note Recordings (1949-1958)	199?	250.00
MYTHIC SOUND			
❑ MS-6002	Burning in the USA, 1953-55	199?	15.00
❑ MS-6003	Cookin' at Saint-Germain, 1957-59	199?	15.00
❑ MS-6001	Early Years of a Genius, 1944-48	199?	15.00
❑ MS-6005	Groovin' at the Blue Note, 1959-61	199?	15.00
❑ MS-6008	Holiday in Edenville, 1964	199?	15.00
❑ MS-6004	Relaxin' at Home, 1961-64	199?	15.00
❑ MS-6009	Return to Birdland, 1964	199?	15.00
❑ MS-6007	Tribute to Thelonious, 1964	199?	15.00
❑ MS-6006	Writin' for Duke, 1963	199?	15.00
NORGRAN			
❑ MGN-1098 [M]	Bud Powell '57	1957	200.00
❑ MGN-1064 [M]	Bud Powell's Moods	1956	200.00
❑ MGN-23 [10]	Bud Powell Trio	1954	500.00
❑ MGN-1063 [M]	Jazz Giant	1956	200.00
❑ MGN-1017 [M]	Jazz Original	1955	200.00
❑ MGN-1077 [M]	Piano Interpretations by Bud Powell	1956	200.00
QUINTESSENCE			
❑ 25381	Bud Powell	1980	15.00
RCA VICTOR			
❑ LPM-1423 [M]	Strictly Powell	1957	150.00
—*Reproductions exist*			
❑ LPM-1507 [M]	Swingin' with Bud	1957	120.00
—*Reproductions exist*			
REPRISE			
❑ R-6098 [M]	Bud Powell in Paris	1964	40.00
❑ R9-6098 [S]	Bud Powell in Paris	1964	60.00
ROOST			
❑ LP-401 [10]	Bud Powell Trio	1950	600.00
❑ LP-412 [10]	Bud Powell Trio	1953	500.00
❑ LP-2224 [M]	Bud Powell Trio	1957	150.00
ROULETTE			
❑ R-52115 [M]	The Return of Bud Powell -- His First New Recordings Since 1958	1965	30.00
❑ SR-52115 [S]	The Return of Bud Powell -- His First New Recordings Since 1958	1965	40.00
STEEPLECHASE			
❑ SCC-6001	Bud Powell at the Golden Circle, Vol. 1	198?	18.00
❑ SCC-6002	Bud Powell at the Golden Circle, Vol. 2	198?	18.00
❑ SCC-6009	Bud Powell at the Golden Circle, Vol. 3	198?	18.00
❑ SCC-6014	Bud Powell at the Golden Circle, Vol. 4	198?	18.00
❑ SCC-6017	Bud Powell at the Golden Circle, Vol. 5	198?	18.00
VERVE			
❑ MGV-8218 [M]	Blues in the Closet	1958	50.00
❑ V-8218 [M]	Blues in the Closet	1961	30.00
❑ MGV-8185 [M]	Bud Powell '57	1957	50.00
❑ V-8185 [M]	Bud Powell '57	1961	30.00
❑ UMV-2571	Bud Powell '57	198?	12.00
❑ MGV-8154 [M]	Bud Powell's Moods	1957	60.00
❑ V-8154 [M]	Bud Powell's Moods	1961	30.00
❑ MGV-8153 [M]	Jazz Giant	1957	60.00
❑ V-8153 [M]	Jazz Giant	1961	30.00
❑ MGV-8167 [M]	Piano Interpretations by Bud Powell	1957	60.00
❑ V-8167 [M]	Piano Interpretations by Bud Powell	1961	30.00
❑ UMV-2573	Piano Interpretations by Bud Powell	198?	12.00

Number	Title	Yr	NM
❑ MGV-8115 [M]	The Genius of Bud Powell	1957	50.00
❑ V-8115 [M]	The Genius of Bud Powell	1961	30.00
❑ VE-2-2506	The Genius of Bud Powell, Vol. 1	197?	18.00
❑ VE-2-2526	The Genius of Bud Powell, Vol. 2	197?	18.00
❑ VSP-34 [M]	The Jazz Legacy of Bud Powell	1966	25.00
❑ VSPS-34 [R]	The Jazz Legacy of Bud Powell	1966	15.00
❑ MGV-8301 [M]	The Lonely One…	1959	50.00
❑ V-8301 [M]	The Lonely One…	1961	30.00
❑ VSP-37 [M]	This Was Bud Powell	1966	25.00
❑ VSPS-37 [R]	This Was Bud Powell	1966	15.00
XANADU			
❑ 102	Bud in Paris	1975	18.00
POWELL, DICK			
DECCA			
❑ DL8837 [M]	Song Book	1959	40.00
RPC			
❑ 105 [M]	The Wonderful Teens	1962	30.00
POWELL, JANE			
COLUMBIA MASTERWORKS			
❑ ML2045 [10]	A Date with Jane Powell	1949	80.00
❑ ML2034 [10]	Romance	1949	80.00
LION			
❑ L-70111 [M]	Jane Powell Sings	1960	25.00
MGM			
❑ E-3451 [M]	Something Wonderful	1957	40.00
VERVE			
❑ MGV-2023 [M]	Can't We Be Friends?	1957	40.00
POWELL, LOVEY			
TRANSITION			
❑ TRLP-1 [M]	Lovelady	1956	100.00
—*Deduct 25 percent if booklet is missing*			
POWELL, MEL			
CAPITOL			
❑ T615 [M]	Classics in Jazz	1955	40.00
COMMODORE			
❑ XFL-14943	The World Is Waiting	1979	12.00
PAUSA			
❑ 9023	The Unavailable Mel Powell	198?	12.00
VANGUARD			
❑ VRS-8015 [10]	Bandstand	1954	80.00
❑ VRS-8501 [M]	Borderline	1954	50.00
❑ VRS-8519 [M]	Easy Swing	1955	50.00
❑ VRS-8004 [10]	Mel Powell Septet	1953	80.00
❑ VRS-8506 [M]	Out on a Limb	1955	50.00
❑ VRS-8502 [M]	Thigamagig	1954	50.00
POWELL, ROGER			
ATLANTIC			
❑ SD7251	Cosmic Furnace	1973	18.00
POWELL, SELDON			
ROOST			
❑ LP-2205 [M]	Seldon Powell Plays	1956	200.00
❑ LP-2220 [M]	Seldon Powell Sextet	1956	250.00
POWELL, SPECS			
ROULETTE			
❑ R-52004 [M]	Movin' In	1958	30.00
❑ SR-52004 [S]	Movin' In	1958	30.00
STRAND			
❑ SL-1027 [M]	Specs Powell Presents Big Band Jazz	1961	25.00
❑ SLS-1027 [S]	Specs Powell Presents Big Band Jazz	1961	30.00
POWER STATION, THE			
CAPITOL			
❑ R123577	The Power Station	1985	15.00
—*RCA Music Service edition*			
❑ SJ-12380	The Power Station	1985	12.00
POWERS, JOEY			
AMY			
❑ 8001 [M]	Midnight Mary	1964	30.00
POWERS OF BLUE, THE			
MTA			
❑ 1002 [M]	Flipout	1967	30.00
❑ 5002 [S]	Flipout	1967	30.00
POZAR, ROBERT			
SAVOY			
❑ MG-12189 [M]	Good Golly, Miss Nancy	1967	25.00
POZO-SECO SINGERS, THE			
CERTRON			
❑ CS-7007	Spend Some Time with Me	1970	18.00

COLUMBIA

Number	Title	Yr	NM
❑ CL2600 [M]	I Can Make It with You	1967	25.00
❑ CS9400 [S]	I Can Make It with You	1967	18.00
❑ CS9656	Shades of Time	1968	18.00
❑ CL2515 [M]	Time/I'll Be Gone	1966	18.00
❑ CS9315 [S]	Time/I'll Be Gone	1966	25.00

POWER PAK

Number	Title	Yr	NM
❑ 285	The Pozo-Seco Singers with Don Williams	198?	12.00

PRADO, PEREZ

RCA CAMDEN

Number	Title	Yr	NM
❑ CAL-547 [M]	Latino!	1960	25.00
❑ CAL-409 [M]	Mambo Happy!	1957	25.00

RCA VICTOR

Number	Title	Yr	NM
❑ LPM-2133 [M]	A Touch of Tabasco	1960	25.00
❑ LSP-2133 [S]	A Touch of Tabasco	1960	30.00
❑ LPM-2104 [M]	Big Hits by Prado	1959	30.00
❑ LSP-2104 [S]	Big Hits by Prado	1959	40.00
❑ LPM-3330 [M]	Dance Latino	1965	18.00
❑ LSP-3330 [S]	Dance Latino	1965	25.00
❑ LPM-1883 [M]	Dilo (Ugh!)	1958	30.00
❑ LSP-1883 [S]	Dilo (Ugh!)	1959	40.00
❑ LPM-2571 [M]	Exotic Suite	1962	25.00
❑ LSP-2571 [S]	Exotic Suite	1962	30.00
❑ LPM-1257 [M]	Havana 3 A.M.	1956	40.00
❑ LPM-1459 [M]	Latin Satin	1957	40.00
❑ LPM-3108 [10]	Mambo by the King	1953	60.00
❑ LPM-1196 [M]	Mambo by the King	1956	40.00
❑ LPM-1075 [M]	Mambo Mania	1955	40.00
❑ LPM-2610 [M]	Our Man in Latin America	1963	25.00
❑ LSP-2610 [S]	Our Man in Latin America	1963	30.00
❑ LPM-21 [10]	Perez Prado Plays Mucho Mambo for Dancing	1951	60.00
❑ LPM-2028 [M]	Pops and Prado	1959	30.00
❑ LSP-2028 [S]	Pops and Prado	1959	40.00
❑ LPM-1556 [M]	Prez	1958	30.00
❑ LSP-1556 [S]	Prez	1959	40.00
❑ ANL1-1941	Pure Gold	1975	12.00
❑ LPM-2308 [M]	Rockambo	1961	25.00
❑ LSP-2308 [S]	Rockambo	1961	30.00
❑ LPM-3732 [M]	The Best of Perez Prado	1967	25.00
❑ LSP-3732 [S]	The Best of Perez Prado	1967	18.00
❑ LPM-2379 [M]	The New Dance La Chunga	1961	25.00
❑ LSP-2379 [S]	The New Dance La Chunga	1961	30.00
❑ LPM-2524 [M]	The Twist Goes Latin	1962	25.00
❑ LSP-2524 [S]	The Twist Goes Latin	1962	30.00
❑ VPS-6066	This Is Perez Prado	1972	18.00
❑ LPM-1101 [M]	Voodoo Suite (and Six All-Time Greats)	1955	40.00

UNITED ARTISTS

Number	Title	Yr	NM
❑ LS-61032	Estas Si Viven (The Living End)	196?	18.00

PREACHER ROLLO

KING

Number	Title	Yr	NM
❑ 295-101 [10]	Dixieland	195?	120.00

MGM

Number	Title	Yr	NM
❑ E-3259 [M]	Dixieland Favorites	1955	50.00
❑ E-95 [10]	Preacher Rollo and the Five Saints	1951	80.00
❑ E-217 [10]	Preacher Rollo at the Jazz Band Ball	1953	80.00
❑ E-3403 [M]	Swanee River Jazz	1956	50.00

PREFAB SPROUT

EPIC

Number	Title	Yr	NM
❑ BFE44208	From Langley Park to Memphis	1988	12.00
❑ E46132	Jordan: The Comeback	1990	15.00
❑ BFE40100	Two Wheels Good	1985	12.00

PORTRAIT

Number	Title	Yr	NM
❑ BFR39872	Swoon	1984	12.00

PREMIERS, THE (1)

WARNER BROS.

Number	Title	Yr	NM
❑ W1565 [M]	Farmer John	1964	40.00
❑ WS1565 [S]	Farmer John	1964	50.00

PRESERVATION HALL JAZZ BAND

CBS MASTERWORKS

Number	Title	Yr	NM
❑ FM44856	New Orleans, Vol. 4	1989	15.00
❑ FM37780	New Orleans, Volume 2	1982	12.00
❑ FM38650	New Orleans, Volume 3	1983	12.00
❑ FM44996	The Best of Preservation Hall Jazz Band	1989	15.00

COLUMBIA MASTERWORKS

Number	Title	Yr	NM
❑ M34549	Preservation Hall Jazz Band	1977	15.00

PRESIDENT, THE

ELEKTRA/MUSICIAN

Number	Title	Yr	NM
❑ 60799	Bring Yr Camera	1989	15.00

PRESIDENTS, THE (1)

SUSSEX

Number	Title	Yr	NM
❑ SXBX-7005	5-10-15-20 (25-30 Years of Love)	1970	30.00

PRESLEY, ELVIS

BMG/SUN

Number	Title	Yr	NM
❑ 82876-61205-1	Elvis at Sun	2004	18.00

BOXCAR

Number	Title	Yr	NM
❑ (no #) [B]	Having Fun with Elvis on Stage	1974	200.00

—All-talking record sold at Elvis concerts in 1974

COLLECTABLES

Number	Title	Yr	NM
❑ COL-0165 [B]	Elvis Top Album Collection, Volume 1	2003	150.00

—Contains reproductions, on red vinyl, of five RCA albums (LPM-1254, LPM-1382, LSP-2370, LSP-2426 and APL2-2587) using facsimiles of original labels, covers, inner sleeves and inserts; with poster and all in wooden box

Number	Title	Yr	NM
❑ COL-0166	Elvis Top Album Collection, Volume 2	2003	100.00

—Contains reproductions, on red vinyl, of five RCA albums (LPM-1515, LOC-1035, LSP-2256, LSP-2999 and CPL2-2642) using facsimiles of original labels, covers, inner sleeves and inserts; with poster and all in wooden box

DCC COMPACT CLASSICS

Number	Title	Yr	NM
❑ LPZ-2037 [S]	Elvis Is Back!	1997	120.00

—Audiophile vinyl

FOTOPLAY

Number	Title	Yr	NM
❑ FSP-1001 [PD]	To Elvis: Love Still Burning	1978	30.00

—Tribute-song picture disc of Elvis; in plastic bag with 11x11 insert

Number	Title	Yr	NM
❑ FSP-1001 [PD]	To Elvis: Love Still Burning	1978	30.00

—In white cardboard cover with black printing

Number	Title	Yr	NM
❑ FSP-1001 [PD]	To Elvis: Love Still Burning	1978	18.00

—In black cardboard cover with white printing

GOLDEN EDITIONS

Number	Title	Yr	NM
❑ GEL-101	The First Year (Elvis, Scotty and Bill)	1979	25.00
❑ KING-1	The First Year (Elvis, Scotty and Bill)	1979	18.00

GREAT NORTHWEST

Number	Title	Yr	NM
❑ GNW-4005	The Elvis Tapes	1977	15.00
❑ GV-2004	The King Speaks (February 1961, Memphis, Tennessee)	1977	12.00

—Label says this is on "Green Valley" while sleeve says "Great Northwest

Number	Title	Yr	NM
❑ GNW-4006 [B]	The King Speaks (February 1961, Memphis, Tennessee)	1977	15.00

—Both label and sleeve say this is on "Great Northwest

GREEN VALLEY

Number	Title	Yr	NM
❑ GV-2001	Elvis Exclusive Live Press Conference (Memphis, Tennessee, February 1961)	1977	40.00

—Issued with two slightly different covers

Number	Title	Yr	NM
❑ GV-2001/3	Elvis (Speaks to You)	1978	30.00

—Elvis interviews plus tracks by the Jordanaires

GUSTO

Number	Title	Yr	NM
❑ SD-995	Interviews with Elvis (Canada 1957)	1978	40.00

—Reissue of Great Northwest album

HALW

Number	Title	Yr	NM
❑ HALW-0001	The First Years	1978	30.00

—With stamped, limited edition number

Number	Title	Yr	NM
❑ HALW-0001	The First Years	1978	25.00

—Without limited edition number

K-TEL

Number	Title	Yr	NM
❑ NU9900	Love Songs	1981	25.00

LOUISIANA HAYRIDE

Number	Title	Yr	NM
❑ LH-3061	Beginning Years	1984	25.00

—With booklet and facsimile contract

MARVENCO

Number	Title	Yr	NM
❑ 101	Beginning (1954-1955)	1988	18.00

—Pink vinyl with booklet and facsimile contract

MOBILE FIDELITY

Number	Title	Yr	NM
❑ 1-059	From Elvis in Memphis	1982	50.00

—Audiophile vinyl

MUSIC WORKS

Number	Title	Yr	NM
❑ PB-3601	The First Live Recordings	1984	18.00
❑ PB-3602	The Hillbilly Cat	1984	18.00

OAK

Number	Title	Yr	NM
❑ 1003	Vintage 1955 Elvis	1990	60.00

PAIR

Number	Title	Yr	NM
❑ PDL2-1010	Double Dynamite	1982	25.00
❑ PDL2-1185	Elvis Aron Presley Forever	1988	25.00
❑ PDL2-1037	Remembering	1983	30.00

PICKWICK

Number	Title	Yr	NM
❑ CAS-2440	Almost in Love	1975	12.00
❑ CAS-2595	Burning Love And Hits from His Movies, Vol. 2	1975	15.00

—First cover contains a notice about the upcoming "Aloha from Hawaii" show

Number	Title	Yr	NM
❑ CAS-2595	Burning Love And Hits from His Movies, Vol. 2	1976	10.00

—Reissue deletes the "Aloha from Hawaii" notice

Number	Title	Yr	NM
❑ CAL-2518	C'mon Everybody	1975	12.00
❑ DL2-5001	Double Dynamite	1975	30.00
❑ CAS-2428 [M]	Elvis' Christmas Album	1975	15.00

—Same contents as RCA Camden LP; no Christmas trim on border; despite the "CAS" catalog number, this album is mono

Number	Title	Yr	NM
❑ CAS-2428 [M]	Elvis' Christmas Album	1976	12.00

—Same as above, but with Christmas trim on cover border; despite the "CAS" catalog number, this album is mono

Number	Title	Yr	NM
❑ CAS-2304	Elvis Sings Flaming Star	1976	12.00
❑ CAS-2567	Elvis Sings Hits from His Movies, Volume 1	1975	12.00
❑ ACL-7007	Frankie and Johnny	1976	12.00
❑ CAS-2533	I Got Lucky	1975	12.00
❑ CAS-2408	Let's Be Friends	1975	12.00
❑ ACL-7064	Mahalo from Elvis	1978	25.00
❑ CAS-2611	Separate Ways	1975	12.00
❑ (no #)0	The Pickwick Pack (unofficial title)	1978	60.00

—Seven Pickwick albums in special package and cardboard wrapper; one of the LPs is Elvis' Christmas Album

Number	Title	Yr	NM
❑ (no #)0	The Pickwick Pack (unofficial title)	1979	60.00

—Seven Pickwick albums in special package and cardboard wrapper; one of the LPs is Frankie and Johnny

PREMORE

Number	Title	Yr	NM
❑ PL-589	Early Elvis (1954-1956 Live at the Louisiana Hayride)	1989	30.00

RCA

Number	Title	Yr	NM
❑ 82876-51108-1	2nd to None	2003	25.00
❑ 3114-1-R	Collectors Gold	1991	200.00
❑ 9586-1-R	Elvis Gospel 1957-1971 (Known Only to Him)	1989	40.00
❑ 8468-1-R	Elvis in Nashville (1956-1971)	1988	40.00
❑ 6313-1-R	Elvis Talks!	1987	30.00
❑ 9589-1-R	Essential Elvis, Vol. 2 (Stereo '57)	1989	30.00
❑ 6738-1-R	Essential Elvis: The First Movies	1988	30.00
❑ 5600-1-R	Return of the Rocker	1986	25.00
❑ 6985-1-R	The Alternate Aloha	1988	25.00
❑ 6414-1-R	The Complete Sun Sessions	1987	30.00
❑ 2227-1-R	The Great Performances	1990	40.00
❑ 6221-1-R	The Memphis Record	1987	30.00
❑ 2023-1-R	The Million Dollar Quartet	1990	15.00

—With Jerry Lee Lewis, Carl Perkins, and perhaps Johnny Cash

Number	Title	Yr	NM
❑ 6382-1-R	The Number One Hits	1987	30.00
❑ 6383-1-R	The Top Ten Hits	1987	30.00

RCA CAMDEN

Number	Title	Yr	NM
❑ CAS-2440 [B]	Almost in Love	1970	50.00

—Last song on Side 2 is "Stay Away, Joe

Number	Title	Yr	NM
❑ CAS-2440	Almost in Love	1973	30.00

—Last song on Side 2 is "Stay Away

Number	Title	Yr	NM
❑ CAS-2595	Burning Love And Hits from His Movies, Vol. 2	1972	30.00

—With star on front cover advertising a bonus photo, the presence of which doubles the value of this LP

Number	Title	Yr	NM
❑ CAS-2595 [B]	Burning Love And Hits from His Movies, Vol. 2	1972	15.00

—No star on cover, no bonus photo

Number	Title	Yr	NM
❑ CAL-2518	C'mon Everybody	1971	25.00
❑ CAL-2428 [M]	Elvis' Christmas Album	1970	30.00

—Blue label, non-flexible vinyl

Number	Title	Yr	NM
❑ CAL-2428 [M]	Elvis' Christmas Album	1971	15.00

—Blue label, flexible vinyl

Number	Title	Yr	NM
❑ CAS-2304	Elvis Sings Flaming Star	1969	30.00
❑ CAS-2567	Elvis Sings Hits from His Movies, Volume 1	1972	25.00
❑ CAL-2533	I Got Lucky	1971	30.00
❑ CAS-2408	Let's Be Friends	1970	30.00
❑ CAS-2611	Separate Ways	1973	30.00

RCA SPECIAL PRODUCTS

Number	Title	Yr	NM
❑ SVL3-0710	50 Years -- 50 Hits	1985	30.00
❑ DPL2-0056(e)	Elvis	1973	50.00

—Mustard labels

Number	Title	Yr	NM
❑ DPL2-0056(e)	Elvis	1973	30.00

—Blue labels

Number	Title	Yr	NM
❑ CAL-2428 [M]	Elvis' Christmas Album	1986	30.00

—Reissue for The Special Music Company

Number	Title	Yr	NM
❑ DPL2-0056(e)	Elvis Commemorative Album	1978	80.00

—Reissue of "Elvis" (same number) with new title and gold vinyl

Number	Title	Yr	NM
❑ DPL1-0647	Elvis Country	1984	30.00
❑ DPL2-0168	Elvis in Hollywood	1976	60.00

—Blue labels; with 20-page booklet

Number	Title	Yr	NM
❑ DVM1-0704	Elvis (One Night with You)	1984	60.00

—With poster (deduct 25% if missing)

Number	Title	Yr	NM
❑ SVL2-0824	Good Rockin' Tonight	1988	25.00
❑ DVL2-0728	His Songs of Faith and Inspiration	1986	50.00
❑ DML1-0264	His Songs of Inspiration	1977	18.00
❑ DPL5-0347	Memories of Elvis (A Lasting Tribute to the King of Rock 'N' Roll)	1978	80.00
❑ DML1-0437	Rock 'N Roll Forever	1981	18.00
❑ DML3-0632	The Elvis Presley Collection	1984	80.00

—Available through Candelite Music via mail order

Number	Title	Yr	NM
❑ DML5-0263	The Elvis Story	1977	60.00

—Available through Candelite Music via mail order

Number	Title	Yr	NM
❑ DML1-0413	The Greatest Moments in Music	1980	18.00
❑ DML1-0348	The Greatest Show on Earth	1978	18.00
❑ DVL1-0461	The Legendary Magic of Elvis Presley	1980	18.00
❑ DML6-0412 [B]	The Legendary Recordings of Elvis Presley	1979	120.00

RCA VICTOR

Number	Title	Yr	NM
❑ KKL1-7065	A Canadian Tribute	1978	25.00

—Gold vinyl, embossed cover

Number	Title	Yr	NM
❑ LPM-2011 [M]	A Date with Elvis	1965	50.00

—Monaural" on label

Number	Title	Yr	NM
❑ LSP-2011(e) [R]	A Date with Elvis	1965	50.00
—Black label, "Stereo Electronically Reprocessed" on label			
❑ LPM-2011 [M]	A Date with Elvis	1959	600.00
—Long Play" on label; gatefold cover, no sticker on cover			
❑ LPM-2011 [M]	A Date with Elvis	1959	800.00
—Long Play" on label; gatefold cover, with sticker on cover			
❑ LPM-2011 [M]	A Date with Elvis	1963	200.00
—Mono" on label; no gatefold cover			
❑ LSP-2011(e) [R]	A Date with Elvis	1968	30.00
—Orange label, non-flexible vinyl			
❑ LSP-2011(e) [R]	A Date with Elvis	1971	25.00
—Orange label, flexible vinyl			
❑ LSP-2011(e) [R]	A Date with Elvis	1975	25.00
—Tan label			
❑ LSP-2011(e) [R]	A Date with Elvis	1977	15.00
—Black label, dog near top			
❑ AFL1-2011(e) [R]	A Date with Elvis	1977	15.00
—Black label, dog near top; includes copies with sticker wrapped around spine with new number			
❑ CPM6-5172	A Golden Celebration	1984	100.00
❑ CPL1-0341	A Legendary Performer, Volume 1	1974	30.00
—Includes booklet (deduct 40% if missing); with die-cut hole in front cover			
❑ CPL1-0341	A Legendary Performer, Volume 1	1986	18.00
—No die-cut hole in cover and no booklet			
❑ CPL1-1349	A Legendary Performer, Volume 2	1976	30.00
—Includes booklet (deduct 40% if missing); with die-cut hole in front cover			
❑ CPL1-1349	A Legendary Performer, Volume 2	1976	60.00
—Without false starts and outtakes of "Such a Night" and "Cane and a High Starched Collar," which are supposed to be there. End of matrix number may be "31.			
❑ CPL1-1349	A Legendary Performer, Volume 2	1986	18.00
—No die-cut hole in cover and no booklet			
❑ CPL1-3078 [PD]	A Legendary Performer, Volume 3	1978	30.00
—Picture disc applied to blue vinyl LP; with booklet (deduct 40% if missing)			
❑ CPL1-3082 [B]	A Legendary Performer, Volume 3	1978	30.00
—Includes booklet (deduct 40% if missing); with die-cut hole in front cover			
❑ CPL1-3082	A Legendary Performer, Volume 3	1986	10.00
—No die-cut hole in cover and no booklet			
❑ CPL1-4848	A Legendary Performer, Volume 4	1983	30.00
—Includes booklet (deduct 40% if missing); with die-cut hole in front cover			
❑ CPL1-4848	A Legendary Performer, Volume 4	1986	25.00
—No die-cut hole in cover			
❑ CPL2-2642 [S]	Aloha from Hawaii Via Satellite	2003	25.00
—Red vinyl, "DRL 13359" in trail-off wax, "DRL-23359" on back cover, "BMG Special Products" logo on back cover, from box "Elvis Top Album Collection Volume 2			
❑ VPSX-6089 [Q]	Aloha from Hawaii Via Satellite	1973	120.00
—Dark orange labels, "QuadraDisc" on top, "RCA" on bottom			
❑ VPSX-6089 [Q]	Aloha from Hawaii Via Satellite	1973	5000.00
—Stokely Van Camp employee version with Saturn-shaped sticker on front cover with "Chicken of the Sea" and mermaid (beware: this has been counterfeited); VG value 2500; VG+ value 3750			
❑ VPSX-6089 [Q]	Aloha from Hawaii Via Satellite	1973	40.00
—Lighter orange labels, "RCA" on side			
❑ CPL2-2642 [Q]	Aloha from Hawaii Via Satellite	1984	15.00
—New prefix; single-pocket instead of gatefold jacket			
❑ R213736 [S]	Aloha from Hawaii Via Satellite	1973	70.00
—RCA Record Club edition in stereo instead of quadraphonic; orange labels			
❑ R213736 [S]	Aloha from Hawaii Via Satellite	1975	60.00
—RCA Record Club edition in stereo instead of quadraphonic; tan labels			
❑ R213736 [S]	Aloha from Hawaii Via Satellite	1977	30.00
—RCA Record Club edition in stereo instead of quadraphonic; black labels, dog near top			
❑ AFL1-5430	Always on My Mind	1985	25.00
—All copies on purple vinyl			
❑ AFL1-5353	A Valentine Gift for You	1985	25.00
—Red vinyl			
❑ AFL1-5353	A Valentine Gift for You	1985	12.00
—Black vinyl			
❑ LSP-4429	Back in Memphis	1970	40.00
—Orange label, non-flexible vinyl			
❑ LSP-4429	Back in Memphis	1971	30.00
—Orange label, flexible vinyl			
❑ LSP-4429	Back in Memphis	1975	30.00
—Tan label			
❑ LSP-4429	Back in Memphis	1977	18.00
—Black label, dog near top			
❑ AFL1-4429	Back in Memphis	1977	15.00

Number	Title	Yr	NM
—Black label, dog near top; with sticker wrapped around spine with new number			
❑ LSP-2426 [S]	Blue Hawaii	2003	25.00
—Red vinyl; "DRL 13358" in trail-off wax; "BMG Special Products" logo on back cover; from box "Elvis Top Album Collection Volume 1"			
❑ LSP-2426 [S]	Blue Hawaii	197?	1200.00
—One-of-a-kind blue vinyl pressing with black label, dog near top			
❑ LPM-2426 [M]	Blue Hawaii	1961	150.00
—Long Play" on label; with sticker on cover advertising the presence of "Can't Help Falling in Love" and "Rock-a-Hula Baby			
❑ LPM-2426 [M]	Blue Hawaii	1963	50.00
—Mono" on label			
❑ LPM-2426 [M]	Blue Hawaii	1964	40.00
—Monaural" on label			
❑ LPM-2426 [M]	Blue Hawaii	1962	60.00
—Long Play" on label; no sticker on front cover			
❑ LSP-2426 [S]	Blue Hawaii	1961	200.00
—Living Stereo" on label and upper right front cover; with sticker on cover advertising the presence of "Can't Help Falling in Love" and "Rock-a-Hula Baby			
❑ LSP-2426 [S]	Blue Hawaii	1962	80.00
—Living Stereo" on label and upper right front cover; no sticker on front cover			
❑ LSP-2426 [S]	Blue Hawaii	1964	50.00
—Stereo" on label; "Victor Stereo" on upper right front cover			
❑ LSP-2426 [S]	Blue Hawaii	1968	40.00
—Orange label, non-flexible vinyl			
❑ LSP-2426 [S]	Blue Hawaii	1971	25.00
—Orange label, flexible vinyl			
❑ LSP-2426 [S]	Blue Hawaii	1975	25.00
—Tan label			
❑ LSP-2426 [S]	Blue Hawaii	1977	15.00
—Black label, dog near top			
❑ AFL1-2426 [S]	Blue Hawaii	1977	15.00
—Black label, dog near top; with sticker wrapped around spine with new number			
❑ AYL1-3683 [S]	Blue Hawaii	1980	12.00
—Best Buy Series" reissue			

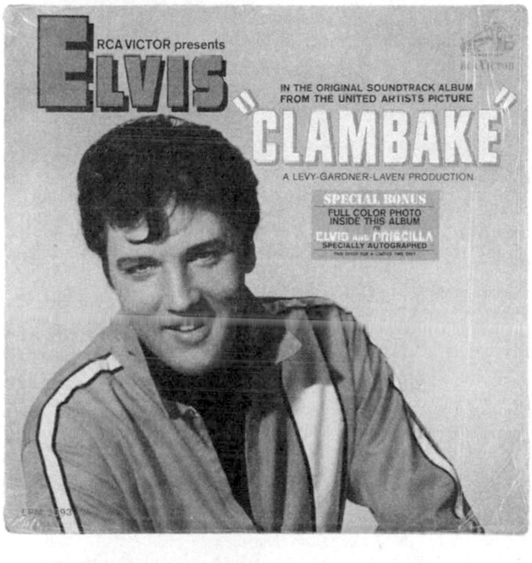
RCA VICTOR presents
ELVIS
IN THE ORIGINAL SOUNDTRACK ALBUM FROM THE UNITED ARTISTS PICTURE
"CLAMBAKE"
A LEVY-GARDNER-LAVEN PRODUCTION
SPECIAL BONUS
FULL COLOR PHOTO INSIDE THIS ALBUM
ELVIS AND PRISCILLA
SPECIALLY AUTOGRAPHED

Number	Title	Yr	NM
❑ LPM-3893 [M]	Clambake	1967	300.00
❑ LSP-3893 [S]	Clambake	1967	60.00
❑ APL1-2565	Clambake	1977	15.00
❑ LPM/LSP-3893	Clambake Bonus Photo	1967	50.00
❑ R233299(e)	Country Classics	1980	40.00
—RCA Music Service exclusive			
❑ R244069	Country Memories	1978	40.00
—RCA Music Service exclusive			
❑ LPM-3787 [M]	Double Trouble	1967	60.00
—With bonus photo announcement on cover			
❑ LPM-3787 [M]	Double Trouble	1967	80.00
—With no bonus photo announcement on cover			
❑ LSP-3787 [S]	Double Trouble	1967	60.00
—With bonus photo announcement on cover			
❑ LSP-3787 [S]	Double Trouble	1967	70.00
—With no bonus photo announcement on cover; black label "Stereo			
❑ LSP-3787 [S]	Double Trouble	1968	40.00
—Orange label, non-flexible vinyl			
❑ LSP-3787 [S]	Double Trouble	1975	25.00
—Tan label			
❑ LSP-3787 [S]	Double Trouble	1977	18.00
—Black label, dog near top			
❑ APL1-2564 [S]	Double Trouble	1977	15.00
—Black label, dog near top; includes copies with sticker wrapped around spine with new number			
❑ LPM/LSP-3787	Double Trouble Bonus Photo	1967	50.00
❑ LPM-1382 [M]	Elvis	2003	25.00
—Red vinyl; "DRC 13271" in trail-off wax; "BMG Special Products" logo on back cover; from box "Elvis Top Album Collection Volume 1			
❑ LPM-1382 [M]	Elvis	1956	400.00
—Back cover has ads for other albums. At least 11 different variations of this are known, all of equal value.			
❑ LPM-1382 [M]	Elvis	1956	400.00
—Back cover has no ads for other albums. "Long Play" on label.			
❑ LPM-1382 [M]	Elvis	1956	1000.00
—With alternate take of "Old Shep" on side 2. Matrix number on the "Old Shep" side ends in "15S," "17S" or "19S," but should be played for positive ID. On alternate take, Elvis sings "he grew old AND his eyes were growing dim" (no AND on standard press)			
❑ LPM-1382 [M]	Elvis	1956	400.00
—With tracks listed on labels as "Band 1" through "Band 6			
❑ LPM-1382 [M]	Elvis	1963	80.00
—Mono" on label			
❑ LPM-1382 [M]	Elvis	1965	60.00
—Monaural" on label			
❑ LSP-1382(e) [R]	Elvis	1962	300.00
—Stereo Electronically Reprocessed" and silver "RCA Victor" on label			
❑ LSP-1382(e) [R]	Elvis	1964	50.00
—Stereo Electronically Reprocessed" and white "RCA Victor" on label			
❑ LSP-1382(e) [R]	Elvis	1968	40.00
—Orange label, non-flexible vinyl			
❑ LSP-1382(e) [R]	Elvis	1971	25.00
—Orange label, flexible vinyl			
❑ LSP-1382(e) [R]	Elvis	1975	18.00
—Tan label			
❑ LSP-1382(e) [R]	Elvis	1976	15.00
—Black label, dog near top			
❑ AFL1-1382(e) [R]	Elvis	1977	15.00
—Black label, dog near top; includes copies with sticker wrapped around spine with new number			
❑ AFM1-5199 [M]	Elvis	1984	25.00
—50th Anniversary reissue in mono with banner			
❑ APL1-0283	Elvis	1973	50.00
❑ CPL8-3699 [B]	Elvis Aron Presley	1980	200.00
—Box set; regular issue with booklet			
❑ CPL8-3699 [B]	Elvis Aron Presley	1980	300.00
—Box set; "Reviewer Series" edition (will be identified as such on the cover)			
❑ DJL1-3729 [DJ]	Elvis Aron Presley (Excerpts)	1980	150.00
—Promo-only excerpts of songs from box set			
❑ DJL1-3781 [DJ]	Elvis Aron Presley (Selections)	1980	150.00
—Promo-only complete versions of songs from box set			
❑ LSP-4776	Elvis As Recorded at Madison Square Garden	1972	30.00
—Orange label			
❑ SPS-33-571 [DJ]	Elvis As Recorded at Madison Square Garden	1972	350.00
—Radio Station Banded Special Version"; came in plain white cover with stickers			
❑ LSP-4776	Elvis As Recorded at Madison Square Garden	1975	25.00
—Tan label			
❑ LSP-4776	Elvis As Recorded at Madison Square Garden	1976	18.00
—Black label, dog near top			
❑ AFL1-4776	Elvis As Recorded at Madison Square Garden	1977	15.00
—Black label, dog near top; includes copies with sticker wrapped around spine with new number			
❑ AQL1-4776	Elvis As Recorded at Madison Square Garden	1980	10.00
—Another reissue with new prefix			
❑ LOC-1035 [M]	Elvis' Christmas Album	2003	25.00
—Red vinyl; not to be mistaken for the unique 1957 version, as this has "DRL 13265" number in trail-off wax and BMG Special Products logo and "This Is a replica of the original packaging" on back cover; from box "Elvis Top Album Collection Volume 2"			
❑ LOC-1035 [M]	Elvis' Christmas Album	1957	600.00
—Gatefold cover; title printed in gold on LP spine; includes bound-in booklet but not sticker			
❑ LOC-1035 [M]	Elvis' Christmas Album	1957	800.00
—Gatefold cover; title printed in silver on LP spine; includes bound-in booklet but not sticker			
❑ LOC-1035 [M]	Elvis' Christmas Album	1957	20000.00
—Red vinyl; unique; VG value 7500; VG+ value 11250			
❑ AFM1-5486 [M]	Elvis' Christmas Album	1985	25.00
—Same as LOC-1035; green vinyl with booklet			
❑ AFM1-5486 [M]	Elvis' Christmas Album	1985	18.00
—Same as LOC-1035; black vinyl with booklet			
❑ LPM-1951 [M]	Elvis' Christmas Album	1958	300.00
—Same contents as LOC-1035, but with non-gatefold blue cover; "Long Play" at bottom of label			
❑ LPM-1951 [M]	Elvis' Christmas Album	1963	150.00
—Mono" at bottom of label: "RE" on lower left front cover (photos on back were altered)			
❑ LPM-1951 [M]	Elvis' Christmas Album	1964	40.00
—Monaural" at bottom of label; "RE" on lower left front cover			
❑ LSP-1951(e) [R]	Elvis' Christmas Album	1968	60.00
—Orange label, non-flexible vinyl			
❑ LSP-1951(e) [R]	Elvis' Christmas Album	1964	50.00
—Black label, dog on top; "Stereo Electronically Reprocessed" at bottom of label			
❑ LOC-1035 [M]	Elvis' Christmas Album Sticker	1957	200.00
—Gold sticker with "To________" and "From________" blanks			
❑ LSP-4460	Elvis Country ("I'm 10,000 Years Old")	1971	40.00
—Orange label, non-flexible vinyl			

Number	Title	Yr	NM
❏ LSP-4460	Elvis Country ("I'm 10,000 Years Old")	1971	30.00

—Orange label, flexible vinyl

| ❏ LSP-4460 | Elvis Country ("I'm 10,000 Years Old") | 1975 | 30.00 |

—Tan label

| ❏ LSP-4460 | Elvis Country ("I'm 10,000 Years Old") | 1976 | 18.00 |

—Black label, dog near top

| ❏ AFL1-4460 | Elvis Country ("I'm 10,000 Years Old") | 1977 | 15.00 |

—Black label, dog near top; includes copies with sticker wrapped around spine with new number

| ❏ AYL1-3956 | Elvis Country ("I'm 10,000 Years Old") | 1981 | 10.00 |

—Best Buy Series" reissue

| ❏ LSP-4460 | Elvis Country ("I'm 10,000 Years Old") Bonus Photo | 1971 | 18.00 |

—Available in either orange-label pressing

| ❏ LPM-3450 [M] | Elvis for Everyone | 1965 | 60.00 |
| ❏ LSP-3450 [P] | Elvis for Everyone | 1965 | 60.00 |

—Black label, "Stereo" on label

| ❏ LSP-3450 [P] | Elvis for Everyone | 1968 | 40.00 |

—Orange label, non-flexible vinyl

| ❏ LSP-3450 [P] | Elvis for Everyone | 1971 | 25.00 |

—Orange label, flexible vinyl

| ❏ LSP-3450 [P] | Elvis for Everyone | 1975 | 25.00 |

—Tan label

| ❏ LSP-3450 [P] | Elvis for Everyone | 1976 | 15.00 |

—Black label, dog near top

| ❏ AFL1-3450 [P] | Elvis for Everyone | 1977 | 15.00 |

—Black label, dog near top; includes copies with sticker wrapped around spine with new number

| ❏ AYL1-4232 [P] | Elvis for Everyone | 1982 | 10.00 |

—Best Buy Series" reissue

| ❏ LPM-1707 [M] | Elvis' Golden Records | 1964 | 40.00 |

—Monaural" on label; "RE2" on back cover

| ❏ LPM-1707 [M] | Elvis' Golden Records | 1958 | 300.00 |

—Title on cover in light blue letters; no song titles listed on front cover

| ❏ LPM-1707 [M] | Elvis' Golden Records | 1958 | 200.00 |

—Title on cover in light blue letters; no song titles listed on front cover; "RE" on back cover

| ❏ LPM-1707 [M] | Elvis' Golden Records | 1963 | 60.00 |

—Mono" on label; title on cover in white letters; song titles added to front cover

| ❏ LSP-1707(e) [R] | Elvis' Golden Records | 1962 | 200.00 |

—Stereo Electronically Reprocessed" and silver "RCA Victor" on label

| ❏ LSP-1707(e) [R] | Elvis' Golden Records | 1964 | 50.00 |

—Stereo Electronically Reprocessed" and white "RCA Victor" on label

| ❏ LSP-1707(e) [R] | Elvis' Golden Records | 1968 | 30.00 |

—Orange label, non-flexible vinyl

| ❏ LSP-1707(e) [R] | Elvis' Golden Records | 1971 | 25.00 |

—Orange label, flexible vinyl

| ❏ LSP-1707(e) [R] | Elvis' Golden Records | 1975 | 25.00 |

—Tan label

| ❏ LSP-1707(e) [R] | Elvis' Golden Records | 1976 | 15.00 |

—Black label, dog near top

| ❏ AFL1-1707(e) [R] | Elvis' Golden Records | 1977 | 15.00 |

—Black label, dog near top; includes copies with sticker wrapped around spine with new number

| ❏ AQL1-1707(e) [R] | Elvis' Golden Records | 1979 | 12.00 |

—Another reissue with new prefix

| ❏ AFM1-5196 [M] | Elvis' Golden Records | 1984 | 25.00 |

—50th Anniversary reissue in mono with banner

| ❏ LPM-2765 [M] | Elvis' Golden Records, Volume 3 | 1963 | 150.00 |

—Mono" on label

| ❏ LPM-2765 [M] | Elvis' Golden Records, Volume 3 | 1964 | 60.00 |

—Monaural" on label

| ❏ LSP-2765 [S] | Elvis' Golden Records, Volume 3 | 1963 | 150.00 |

—Stereo" and silver "RCA Victor" on black label

| ❏ LSP-2765 [S] | Elvis' Golden Records, Volume 3 | 1964 | 50.00 |

—Stereo" and white "RCA Victor" on black label

| ❏ LSP-2765 [S] | Elvis' Golden Records, Volume 3 | 1968 | 40.00 |

—Orange label, non-flexible vinyl

| ❏ LSP-2765 [S] | Elvis' Golden Records, Volume 3 | 1975 | 25.00 |

—Tan label

| ❏ LSP-2765 [S] | Elvis' Golden Records, Volume 3 | 1976 | 15.00 |

—Black label, dog near top

| ❏ AFL1-2765 [S] | Elvis' Golden Records, Volume 3 | 1977 | 15.00 |

—Black label, dog near top; includes copies with sticker wrapped around spine with new number

| ❏ LPM-3921 [M] | Elvis' Gold Records, Volume 4 | 1968 | 2000.00 |

—Monaural" on label

| ❏ LSP-3921 [P] | Elvis' Gold Records, Volume 4 | 1968 | 50.00 |

—Stereo" and white "RCA Victor" on black label

| ❏ LSP-3921 [P] | Elvis' Gold Records, Volume 4 | 1968 | 40.00 |

—Orange label, non-flexible vinyl

| ❏ LSP-3921 [P] | Elvis' Gold Records, Volume 4 | 1975 | 30.00 |

—Tan label

| ❏ LSP-3921 [P] | Elvis' Gold Records, Volume 4 | 1976 | 15.00 |

—Black label, dog near top

| ❏ AFL1-3921 [P] | Elvis' Gold Records, Volume 4 | 1976 | 18.00 |

—Tan label with new prefix

| ❏ AFL1-3921 [P] | Elvis' Gold Records, Volume 4 | 1977 | 15.00 |

—Black label, dog near top; includes copies with sticker wrapped around spine with new number

| ❏ AFL1-4941 | Elvis' Gold Records, Volume 5 | 1984 | 12.00 |
| ❏ LPM-2075 [M] | Elvis' Gold Records Volume 2 -- 50,000,000 Elvis Fans Can't Be Wrong | 1960 | 250.00 |

—Long Play" on label; "Magic Millions" on upper right front cover with RCA Victor logo

| ❏ LPM-2075 [M] | Elvis' Gold Records Volume 2 -- 50,000,000 Elvis Fans Can't Be Wrong | 1963 | 80.00 |

—Mono" on label; "RE" on lower right front cover

| ❏ LPM-2075 [M] | Elvis' Gold Records Volume 2 -- 50,000,000 Elvis Fans Can't Be Wrong | 1964 | 50.00 |

—Monaural" on label; label has words "50,000,000 Elvis Presley Fans Can't Be Wrong"

| ❏ LSP-2075(e) [R] | Elvis' Gold Records Volume 2 – 50,000,000 Elvis Fans Can't Be Wrong | 1964 | 50.00 |

—Stereo Electronically Reprocessed" and white "RCA Victor" on label

| ❏ LPM-2075 [M] | Elvis' Gold Records Volume 2 -- 50,000,000 Elvis Fans Can't Be Wrong | 1964 | 50.00 |

—Monaural" on label; label only has "Elvis' Gold Records - Vol. 2"

| ❏ LSP-2075(e) [R] | Elvis' Gold Records Volume 2 – 50,000,000 Elvis Fans Can't Be Wrong | 1962 | 200.00 |

—Stereo Electronically Reprocessed" on label; label has words "50,000,000 Elvis Presley Fans Can't Be Wrong"

| ❏ LSP-2075(e) [R] | Elvis' Gold Records Volume 2 – 50,000,000 Elvis Fans Can't Be Wrong | 1975 | 30.00 |

—Tan label

| ❏ LSP-2075(e) [R] | Elvis' Gold Records Volume 2 – 50,000,000 Elvis Fans Can't Be Wrong | 1968 | 30.00 |

—Orange label, non-flexible vinyl

| ❏ LSP-2075(e) [R] | Elvis' Gold Records Volume 2 – 50,000,000 Elvis Fans Can't Be Wrong | 1971 | 30.00 |

—Orange label, flexible vinyl

| ❏ LSP-2075(e) [R] | Elvis' Gold Records Volume 2 – 50,000,000 Elvis Fans Can't Be Wrong | 1976 | 15.00 |

—Black label, dog near top

| ❏ AFL1-2075(e) [R] | Elvis' Gold Records Volume 2 – 50,000,000 Elvis Fans Can't Be Wrong | 1977 | 15.00 |

—Black label, dog near top; includes copies with sticker wrapped around spine with new number

| ❏ AFM1-5197 [M] | Elvis' Gold Records Volume 2 – 50,000,000 Elvis Fans Can't Be Wrong | 1984 | 25.00 |

—50th Anniversary reissue in mono with banner

| ❏ APL2-2587 | Elvis in Concert | 2003 | 25.00 |

—Red vinyl; "DRL 13360" in trail-off wax; "This is a replica of the original packaging" on back cover and all inserts; "DRL-23360" on back cover; from box "Elvis Top Album Collection Volume 1"

❏ APL2-2587	Elvis in Concert	1977	30.00
❏ CPL2-2587	Elvis in Concert	1982	40.00
❏ LSP-4428 [B]	Elvis in Person at the International Hotel, Las Vegas, Nevada	1970	60.00

—Orange label, non-flexible vinyl

| ❏ LSP-4428 | Elvis in Person at the International Hotel, Las Vegas, Nevada | 1971 | 40.00 |

—Orange label, flexible vinyl

| ❏ LSP-4428 | Elvis in Person at the International Hotel, Las Vegas, Nevada | 1975 | 30.00 |

—Tan label

| ❏ LSP-4428 | Elvis in Person at the International Hotel, Las Vegas, Nevada | 1976 | 18.00 |

—Black label, dog near top

| ❏ AFL1-4428 | Elvis in Person at the International Hotel, Las Vegas, Nevada | 1977 | 15.00 |

—Black label, dog near top; includes copies with sticker wrapped around spine with new number

| ❏ AYL1-3892 | Elvis in Person at the International Hotel, Las Vegas, Nevada | 1981 | 10.00 |

—Best Buy Series" reissue

| ❏ LPM-2231 [M] | Elvis Is Back! | 1960 | 150.00 |

—With sticker attached to front cover. Side 2, Song 4 is listed as "The Girl Next Door.

| ❏ LPM-2231 [M] | Elvis Is Back! | 1960 | 150.00 |

—With sticker attached to front cover. Side 2, Song 4 is listed as "The Girl Next Door Went a-Walking.

| ❏ LPM-2231 [M] | Elvis Is Back! | 1960 | 200.00 |

—With no sticker attached to front cover. Side 2, Song 4 is listed as "The Girl Next Door.

| ❏ LPM-2231 [M] | Elvis Is Back! | 1960 | 200.00 |

—With no sticker attached to front cover. Side 2, Song 4 is listed as "The Girl Next Door Went a-Walking.

| ❏ LPM-2231 [M] | Elvis Is Back! | 1963 | 60.00 |

—Mono" on label; song titles printed on front cover

| ❏ LPM-2231 [M] | Elvis Is Back! | 1964 | 60.00 |

—Monaural" on label

| ❏ LSP-2231 [S] | Elvis Is Back! | 1960 | 300.00 |

—Living Stereo" on label; with sticker attached to front cover. Side 2, Song 4 is listed as "The Girl Next Door.

| ❏ LSP-2231 [S] | Elvis Is Back! | 1960 | 300.00 |

—Living Stereo" on label; with sticker attached to front cover. Side 2, Song 4 is listed as "The Girl Next Door Went a-Walking.

| ❏ LSP-2231 [S] | Elvis Is Back! | 1960 | 300.00 |

—Living Stereo" on label; with no sticker attached to front cover. Side 2, Song 4 is listed as "The Girl Next Door.

| ❏ LSP-2231 [S] | Elvis Is Back! | 1960 | 300.00 |

—Living Stereo" on label; with no sticker attached to front cover. Side 2, Song 4 is listed as "The Girl Next Door Went a-Walking.

| ❏ LSP-2231 [S] | Elvis Is Back! | 1964 | 60.00 |

—Stereo" on label; song titles printed on front cover

| ❏ LSP-2231 [S] | Elvis Is Back! | 1968 | 40.00 |

—Orange label, non-flexible vinyl

| ❏ LSP-2231 [S] | Elvis Is Back! | 1975 | 25.00 |

—Tan label

| ❏ LSP-2231 [S] | Elvis Is Back! | 1976 | 18.00 |

—Black label, dog on top

| ❏ AFL1-2231 [S] | Elvis Is Back! | 1977 | 15.00 |

—Black label, dog near top; includes copies with sticker wrapped around spine with new number

| ❏ LPM-4088 | Elvis (NBC-TV Special) | 1968 | 40.00 |

—Orange label, non-flexible vinyl

| ❏ LPM-4088 | Elvis (NBC-TV Special) | 1971 | 30.00 |

—Orange label, flexible vinyl

| ❏ LPM-4088 | Elvis (NBC-TV Special) | 1975 | 25.00 |

—Tan label

| ❏ LPM-4088 | Elvis (NBC-TV Special) | 1976 | 18.00 |

—Black label, dog near top

| ❏ AFM1-4088 | Elvis (NBC TV Special) | 1977 | 15.00 |

—Black label, dog near top; includes copies with sticker wrapped around spine with new number

| ❏ AYM1-3894 | Elvis (NBC-TV Special) | 1981 | 10.00 |

—Best Buy Series" reissue

| ❏ LSP-4671 | Elvis Now | 1972 | 30.00 |

—Orange label

| ❏ LSP-4671 | Elvis Now | 1975 | 30.00 |

—Tan label

| ❏ LSP-4671 | Elvis Now | 1976 | 18.00 |

—Black label, dog near top

| ❏ AFL1-4671 | Elvis Now | 1977 | 15.00 |

—Black label, dog near top; includes copies with sticker wrapped around spine with new number

| ❏ LPM-1254 [M] | Elvis Presley | 2003 | 25.00 |

—Red vinyl; "DRL 13272" in trail-off wax; "BMG Special Products" logo on back cover; from box "Elvis Top Album Collection Volume 1"

| ❏ LSP-1254(e) [R] | Elvis Presley | 1968 | 30.00 |

—Orange label, non-flexible vinyl

| ❏ LPM-1254 [M] | Elvis Presley | 1956 | 800.00 |

—Version 1: "Long Play" on label; "Elvis" in pale pink, "Presley" in pale green on cover; pale green logo box in upper right front cover

| ❏ LPM-1254 [M] | Elvis Presley | 1956 | 600.00 |

—Version 2: "Long Play" on label; "Elvis" in pale pink, "Presley" in neon green on cover; neon green logo box in upper right front cover

| ❏ LPM-1254 [M] | Elvis Presley | 1956 | 300.00 |

—Version 3: "Long Play" on label; "Elvis" in pale pink, "Presley" in neon green on cover; black logo box in upper right front cover

| ❏ LPM-1254 [M] | Elvis Presley | 1958 | 300.00 |

—Version 4: "Long Play" on label; "Elvis" in neon pink, almost

Number	Title	Yr	NM
	red, "Presley" in neon green on cover; black logo box in upper right front cover		
❑ LPM-1254 [M]	Elvis Presley	1963	150.00
	—Mono" on label; cover photo is slightly left of center, otherwise same as Version 4 above		
❑ LPM-1254 [M]	Elvis Presley	1964	60.00
	—Monaural" on label		
❑ LSP-1254(e) [R]	Elvis Presley	1965	40.00
	—Stereo Electronically Reprocessed" and white "RCA Victor" on label		
❑ LSP-1254(e) [R]	Elvis Presley	1962	200.00
	—Stereo Electronically Reprocessed" and silver "RCA Victor" on label		
❑ LSP-1254(e) [R]	Elvis Presley	1975	18.00
	—Tan label		
❑ LSP-1254(e) [R]	Elvis Presley	1976	15.00
	—Black label, dog near top		
❑ AFL1-1254(e) [R]	Elvis Presley	1977	15.00
	—Black label, dog near top; includes copies with sticker wrapped around spine with new number		
❑ AFM1-5198 [M]	Elvis Presley	1984	25.00
	—50th Anniversary reissue in mono with banner		
❑ DJM1-0835 [DJ]	Elvis Presley Interview Record: An Audio Self-Portrait	1984	80.00
	—Promotional item for "50th Anniversary" series; later issued as RCA 6313-1-R		
❑ CPL1-0606	Elvis Recorded Live on Stage in Memphis	1974	30.00
	—Orange label		
❑ DJL1-0606 [DJ]	Elvis Recorded Live on Stage in Memphis	1974	350.00
	—Special banded version for radio airplay		
❑ APD1-0606 [Q]	Elvis Recorded Live on Stage in Memphis	1974	250.00
	—RCA QuadraDisc" labels		
❑ CPL1-0606	Elvis Recorded Live on Stage in Memphis	1975	30.00
	—Tan label		
❑ AFL1-0606	Elvis Recorded Live on Stage in Memphis	1977	15.00
	—Black label, dog near top; includes copies with sticker wrapped around spine with new number		
❑ CPL1-2901	Elvis Sings for Children and Grownups Too!	1978	25.00
	—With two slits for removable greeting card on back cover (card should be with package)		
❑ CPL1-2901	Elvis Sings for Children and Grownups Too!	1978	12.00
	—With greeting card graphic printed on back cover, and no slits on back cover		
❑ LSP-4579 [B]	Elvis Sings the Wonderful World of Christmas	1971	40.00
	—Orange label. Bonus postcard is priced separately		
❑ ANL1-1936	Elvis Sings the Wonderful World of Christmas	1975	18.00
	—New number, same contents as LSP-4579. Orange label		
❑ ANL1-1936	Elvis Sings the Wonderful World of Christmas	1976	15.00
	—Tan label		
❑ ANL1-1936	Elvis Sings the Wonderful World of Christmas	1977	12.00
	—Black label, dog near top		
❑ LSP-4579 [B]	Elvis Sings the Wonderful World of Christmas Postcard	1971	30.00
❑ APL1-1039	Elvis Today	1975	60.00
	—Orange label		
❑ APD1-1039 [Q]	Elvis Today	1975	300.00
	—RCA QuadraDisc" labels		
❑ APL1-1039	Elvis Today	1975	30.00
	—Tan label		
❑ APD1-1039 [Q]	Elvis Today	1977	200.00
	—Black label, dog near top; quadraphonic reissue		
❑ AFL1-1039	Elvis Today	1977	15.00
	—Black label, dog near top; includes copies with sticker wrapped around spine with new number		
❑ LPM-1990 [M]	For LP Fans Only	1959	250.00
	—Long Play" on label		
❑ LPM-1990 [M]	For LP Fans Only	1963	80.00
	—Mono" on label		
❑ LPM-1990 [M]	For LP Fans Only	1964	50.00
	—Monaural" on label		
❑ LSP-1990(e) [R]	For LP Fans Only	1965	300.00
	—Stereo Electronically Reprocessed" on label; error cover with same photo on both front and back		
❑ LSP-1990(e) [R]	For LP Fans Only	1965	50.00
	—Stereo Electronically Reprocessed" on label; normal cover with different front and back cover photos		
❑ LSP-1990(e) [R]	For LP Fans Only	1968	30.00
	—Orange label, non-flexible vinyl		
❑ LSP-1990(e) [R]	For LP Fans Only	1975	25.00
	—Tan label		
❑ LSP-1990(e) [R]	For LP Fans Only	1976	15.00
	—Black label, dog near top		
❑ AFL1-1990(e) [R]	For LP Fans Only	1977	15.00
	—Black label, dog near top; includes copies with sticker wrapped around spine with new number		
❑ LPM-3553 [M]	Frankie and Johnny	1966	60.00
❑ LSP-3553 [S]	Frankie and Johnny	1966	60.00
	—Stereo" on black label		
❑ LPM/LSP-3553	Frankie and Johnny Bonus Print	1966	60.00

Number	Title	Yr	NM
❑ LSP-4155	From Elvis in Memphis	1975	30.00
	—Tan label		
❑ LSP-4155	From Elvis in Memphis	1976	18.00
	—Black label, dog near top		
❑ LSP-4155	From Elvis in Memphis	1969	40.00
	—Orange label, non-flexible vinyl		
❑ LSP-4155	From Elvis in Memphis	1971	30.00
	—Orange label, flexible vinyl		
❑ AFL1-4155	From Elvis in Memphis	1977	15.00
	—Black label, dog near top; includes copies with sticker wrapped around spine with new number		
❑ LSP-4155	From Elvis in Memphis Bonus Photo	1969	40.00
❑ APL1-1506	From Elvis Presley Boulevard, Memphis, Tennessee	1976	30.00
	—Tan label		
❑ AFL1-1506	From Elvis Presley Boulevard, Memphis, Tennessee	1977	15.00
	—Black label, dog near top; with sticker wrapped around spine with new number (old number still on label)		
❑ AFL1-1506	From Elvis Presley Boulevard, Memphis, Tennessee	1977	12.00
	—Black label, dog near top; new number is on cover and label		
❑ R234340	From Elvis with Love	1978	40.00
	—RCA Music Service exclusive		
❑ LSP-6020 [B]	From Memphis to Vegas/ From Vegas to Memphis	1969	150.00
	—Orange labels, non-flexible vinyl; with composers of "Words" correctly listed as Barry, Robin and Maurice Gibb		
❑ LSP-6020	From Memphis to Vegas/ From Vegas to Memphis	1969	150.00
	—Orange labels, non-flexible vinyl; with composers of "Words" incorrectly listed as Tommy Boyce and Bobby Hart		
❑ LSP-6020	From Memphis to Vegas/ From Vegas to Memphis	1971	40.00
	—Orange labels, flexible vinyl		
❑ LSP-6020	From Memphis to Vegas/ From Vegas to Memphis Bonus Photos	1969	50.00
	—Four different photos came with LP, but no more than two per set. Value is for any two different of the four photos.		
❑ LSP-6020	From Memphis to Vegas/ From Vegas to Memphis Bonus Photos	1975	30.00
	—Tan labels		
❑ LSP-6020	From Memphis to Vegas/ From Vegas to Memphis Bonus Photos	1976	25.00
	—Black label, dog near top		
❑ LPM-2756 [M]	Fun in Acapulco	1963	80.00
	—Mono" on label		
❑ LPM-2756 [M]	Fun in Acapulco	1964	60.00
	—Monaural" on label		
❑ LSP-2756 [S]	Fun in Acapulco	1963	100.00
	—Stereo" and silver "RCA Victor" on black label		
❑ LSP-2756 [S]	Fun in Acapulco	1964	60.00
	—Stereo" and white "RCA Victor" on black label		
❑ LSP-2756 [S]	Fun in Acapulco	1968	40.00
	—Orange label, non-flexible vinyl		
❑ LSP-2756 [S]	Fun in Acapulco	1975	30.00
	—Tan label		
❑ LSP-2756 [S]	Fun in Acapulco	1976	15.00
	—Black label, dog near top		
❑ AFL1-2756 [S]	Fun in Acapulco	1977	15.00
	—Black label, dog near top; includes copies with sticker wrapped around spine with new number		
❑ LSP-2256 [S]	G.I. Blues	2003	25.00
	—Red vinyl; "DRL 13273" in trail-off wax; "BMG Special Products" logo on back cover; from box "Elvis Top Album Collection Volume 2"		
❑ LPM-2256 [M]	G.I. Blues	1960	500.00
	—Long Play" on label; with sticker on front cover advertising the presence of "Wooden Heart		
❑ LPM-2256 [M]	G.I. Blues	1960	120.00
	—Long Play" on label; with no sticker on front cover		
❑ LPM-2256 [M]	G.I. Blues	1963	100.00
	—Mono" on label		
❑ LPM-2256 [M]	G.I. Blues	1964	50.00
	—Monaural" on label		
❑ LSP-2256 [S]	G.I. Blues	1960	600.00
	—Living Stereo" on label; with sticker on front cover advertising the presence of "Wooden Heart		
❑ LSP-2256 [S]	G.I. Blues	1960	100.00
	—Living Stereo" on label; with no sticker on front cover		
❑ LSP-2256 [S]	G.I. Blues	1964	50.00
	—Stereo" on black label		
❑ LSP-2256 [S]	G.I. Blues	1968	40.00
	—Orange label, non-flexible vinyl		
❑ LSP-2256 [S]	G.I. Blues	1971	25.00
	—Orange label, flexible vinyl		
❑ LSP-2256 [S]	G.I. Blues	1975	30.00
	—Tan label		
❑ LSP-2256 [S]	G.I. Blues	1976	15.00
	—Black label, dog near top		
❑ AYL1-3735 [S]	G.I. Blues	1980	10.00
	—Best Buy Series" reissue		
❑ AFL1-2256 [S]	G.I. Blues	1977	15.00
	—Black label, dog near top; includes copies with sticker wrapped around spine with new number		
❑ LSP-3338 [S]	Girl Happy	1971	25.00

Number	Title	Yr	NM
	—Orange label, flexible vinyl		
❑ LPM-3338 [M]	Girl Happy	1965	60.00
❑ LSP-3338 [S]	Girl Happy	1965	60.00
	—Stereo" on black label		
❑ LSP-3338 [S]	Girl Happy	1968	40.00
	—Orange label, non-flexible vinyl		
❑ LSP-3338 [S]	Girl Happy	1975	30.00
	—Tan label		
❑ LSP-3338 [S]	Girl Happy	1976	15.00
	—Black label, dog near top		
❑ AFL1-3338 [S]	Girl Happy	1977	15.00
	—Black label, dog near top; includes copies with sticker wrapped around spine with new number		
❑ LPM-2621 [M]	Girls! Girls! Girls!	1962	80.00
	—Long Play" on label		
❑ LPM-2621 [M]	Girls! Girls! Girls!	1963	60.00
	—Mono" on label		
❑ LPM-2621 [M]	Girls! Girls! Girls!	1964	40.00
	—Monaural" on label		
❑ LSP-2621 [S]	Girls! Girls! Girls!	1962	200.00
	—Living Stereo" on label		
❑ LSP-2621 [S]	Girls! Girls! Girls!	1964	60.00
	—Stereo" on black label		
❑ LSP-2621 [S]	Girls! Girls! Girls!	1968	40.00
	—Orange label, non-flexible vinyl		
❑ LSP-2621 [S]	Girls! Girls! Girls!	1971	25.00
	—Orange label, flexible vinyl		
❑ LSP-2621 [S]	Girls! Girls! Girls!	1975	30.00
	—Tan label		
❑ LSP-2621 [S]	Girls! Girls! Girls!	1976	15.00
	—Black label, dog near top		
❑ AFL1-2621 [S]	Girls! Girls! Girls!	1977	15.00
	—Black label, dog near top; includes copies with sticker wrapped around spine with new number		
❑ LPM/LSP-2621 [B]	Girls! Girls! Girls! Bonus 1963 Calendar	1962	200.00
	—With listing of other Elvis records on back		
❑ CPL1-0475	Good Times	1974	50.00
	—Orange label		
❑ CPL1-0475	Good Times	1976	15.00
	—Black label, dog near top		
❑ AFL1-0475	Good Times	1977	15.00
	—Black label, dog near top; includes copies with sticker wrapped around spine with new number		
❑ AHL1-2347	Greatest Hits, Volume One	1981	30.00
	—With embossed cover		
❑ AHL1-2347	Greatest Hits, Volume One	1983	18.00
	—Without embossed cover		
❑ AAL1-3917	Guitar Man	1981	30.00
❑ LPM-3468 [M]	Harum Scarum	1965	60.00
❑ LSP-3468 [S]	Harum Scarum	1965	60.00
	—Stereo" on black label		
❑ APL1-2558 [S]	Harum Scarum	1977	15.00
	—Black label, dog near top		
❑ AYL1-3734 [S]	Harum Scarum	1980	10.00
	—Best Buy Series" reissue		
❑ LPM/LSP-3468	Harum Scarum Bonus Photo	1965	60.00
❑ CPM1-0818	Having Fun with Elvis on Stage	1974	30.00
	—Commercial issue of Boxcar LP; orange label		
❑ CPM1-0818	Having Fun with Elvis on Stage	1975	25.00
	—Tan label		
❑ AFM1-0818	Having Fun with Elvis on Stage	1977	30.00
	—Black label, dog near top		
❑ LSP-4690	He Touched Me	1972	40.00
	—Orange label		
❑ LSP-4690	He Touched Me	1975	25.00
	—Tan label		
❑ LSP-4690	He Touched Me	1976	18.00
	—Black label, dog near top		
❑ AFL1-4690	He Touched Me	1977	15.00
	—Black label, dog near top; includes copies with sticker wrapped around spine with new number		
❑ AFL1-2772	He Walks Beside Me	1978	30.00
	—Includes 20-page photo booklet		
❑ LPM-2328 [M]	His Hand in Mine	1960	150.00
	—Long Play" on label		
❑ LPM-2328 [M]	His Hand in Mine	1963	60.00
	—Mono" on label		
❑ LPM-2328 [M]	His Hand in Mine	1964	50.00
	—Monaural" on label		
❑ LSP-2328 [S]	His Hand in Mine	1960	200.00
	—Living Stereo" on label		
❑ LSP-2328 [S]	His Hand in Mine	1964	700.00
	—Stereo" and silver "RCA Victor" on black label		
❑ LSP-2328 [S]	His Hand in Mine	1964	150.00
	—Stereo" and white "RCA Victor" on black label		
❑ LSP-2328 [S]	His Hand in Mine	1968	50.00
	—Orange label, non-flexible vinyl		
❑ LSP-2328 [S]	His Hand in Mine	1975	25.00
	—Tan label		
❑ ANL1-1319 [S]	His Hand in Mine	1976	18.00
	—Reissue with more tightly cropped photo of Elvis on front cover		
❑ AYL1-3935 [S]	His Hand in Mine	1981	10.00
	—Best Buy Series" reissue; includes copies with sticker wrapped around spine with new number		
❑ LPM-3758 [M]	How Great Thou Art	1967	60.00

Number	Title	Yr	NM
—Mono Dynagroove" on label			
❑ LSP-3758 [S]	How Great Thou Art	1967	60.00
—Stereo Dynagroove" on black label			
❑ LSP-3758 [S]	How Great Thou Art	1968	40.00
—Orange label, non-flexible vinyl			
❑ LSP-3758 [S]	How Great Thou Art	1971	30.00
—Orange label, flexible vinyl			
❑ LSP-3758 [S]	How Great Thou Art	1975	25.00
—Tan label			
❑ LSP-3758 [S]	How Great Thou Art	1976	15.00
—Black label, dog near top			
❑ AFL1-3758 [S]	How Great Thou Art	1977	15.00
—Black label, dog near top; includes copies with sticker wrapped around spine with new number			
❑ AQL1-3758 [S]	How Great Thou Art	1979	12.00
—Reissue with new prefix			
❑ (no #)0 [B]	International Hotel, Las Vegas Nevada, Presents Elvis, 1969	1969	3000.00
—Gift box to guests at Elvis' July 31-Aug, 1, 1969 shows. Includes LPM-4088 and LSP-4155; press release; 1969 catalog; three photos; and thank-you note from Elvis and the Colonel. Most of the value is for the box; VG value 1250; VG+ value 1875			
❑ (no #)0 [B]	International Hotel, Las Vegas Nevada, Presents Elvis, 1970	1970	3000.00
—Gift box to guests at Elvis' Jan. 28, 1970 show. Includes LSP-6020 and 47-9791; press release; 1970 catalog; photo; booklet; and dinner menu. Most of the value is for the box; VG value 1250; VG+ value 1875			
❑ LPM-2697 [M]	It Happened at the World's Fair	1963	150.00
❑ LSP-2697 [S]	It Happened at the World's Fair	1963	200.00
—Living Stereo" and silver "RCA Victor" on black label			
❑ LSP-2697 [S]	It Happened at the World's Fair	1964	80.00
—Stereo" and white "RCA Victor" on black label			
❑ APL1-2568 [S]	It Happened at the World's Fair	1977	15.00
❑ LPM/LSP-2697	It Happened at the World's Fair Photo	1963	250.00
❑ AHL1-4678	I Was the One	1983	12.00
❑ LPM-1884 [M]	King Creole	1958	200.00
—Long Play" on label; contrary to some other sources, this was NOT issued with a bonus photo			
❑ LPM-1884 [M]	King Creole	1963	80.00
—Mono" on label			
❑ LPM-1884 [M]	King Creole	1964	60.00
—Monaural" on label			
❑ LSP-1884(e) [R]	King Creole	1962	150.00
—Stereo Electronically Reprocessed" and silver "RCA Victor" on label			
❑ LSP-1884(e) [R]	King Creole	1964	60.00
—Stereo Electronically Reprocessed" and white "RCA Victor" on label			
❑ LSP-1884(e) [R]	King Creole	1968	40.00
—Orange label, non-flexible vinyl			
❑ LSP-1884(e) [R]	King Creole	1971	25.00
—Orange label, flexible vinyl			
❑ LSP-1884(e) [R]	King Creole	1975	25.00
—Tan label			
❑ LSP-1884(e) [R]	King Creole	1976	15.00
—Black label, dog near top			
❑ AFL1-1884(e) [R]	King Creole	1977	15.00
—Black label, dog near top; includes copies with sticker wrapped around spine with new number			
❑ AYL1-3733 [R]	King Creole	1980	10.00
—Best Buy Series" reissue; includes copies with sticker wrapped around spine with new number			
❑ LSP-2894 [S]	Kissin' Cousins	1968	40.00
—Orange label, non-flexible vinyl			
❑ LPM-2894 [M]	Kissin' Cousins	1964	80.00
—Mono" on label; front cover has a small black and white photo of six cast members in lower right			
❑ LPM-2894 [M]	Kissin' Cousins	1964	200.00
—Mono" on label; front cover does NOT have black and white photo in lower right			
❑ LPM-2894 [M]	Kissin' Cousins	1964	100.00
—Monaural" on label; front cover has a small black and white photo of six cast members in lower right			
❑ LPM-2894 [M]	Kissin' Cousins	1964	200.00
—Monaural" on label; front cover does NOT have black and white photo in lower right			
❑ LSP-2894 [S]	Kissin' Cousins	1964	120.00
—Stereo" and silver "RCA Victor" on black label; front cover has a small black and white photo of six cast members in lower right			
❑ LSP-2894 [S]	Kissin' Cousins	1964	200.00
—Stereo" and silver "RCA Victor" on black label; front cover does NOT have black and white photo in lower right			
❑ LSP-2894 [S]	Kissin' Cousins	1964	60.00
—Stereo" and white "RCA Victor" on black label; all front covers have the cast photo in lower right			
❑ LSP-2894 [S]	Kissin' Cousins	1971	25.00
—Orange label, flexible vinyl			
❑ LSP-2894 [S]	Kissin' Cousins	1975	30.00
—Tan label			
❑ LSP-2894 [S]	Kissin' Cousins	1976	15.00
—Black label, dog near top			
❑ AFL1-2894 [S]	Kissin' Cousins	1977	15.00
—Black label, dog near top; includes copies with sticker			

Number	Title	Yr	NM
wrapped around spine with new number			
❑ AYL1-4115 [S]	Kissin' Cousins	1981	10.00
—Best Buy Series" reissue; includes copies with sticker wrapped around spine with new number			
❑ LSP-4530	Love Letters from Elvis	1971	40.00
—Orange label; "Love Letters from" on one line of cover, "Elvis" on a second line			
❑ LSP-4530	Love Letters from Elvis	1971	30.00
—Orange label; "Love Letters" on one line of cover; "from" on a second line, "Elvis" on a third line			
❑ LSP-4530	Love Letters from Elvis	1975	30.00
—Tan label; "Love Letters from" on one line of cover, "Elvis" on a second line			
❑ LSP-4530	Love Letters from Elvis	1975	30.00
—Tan label; "Love Letters" on one line of cover; "from" on a second line, "Elvis" on a third line			
❑ LSP-4530	Love Letters from Elvis	1976	25.00
—Black label, dog near top			
❑ AFL1-4530	Love Letters from Elvis	1977	15.00
—Black label, dog near top; includes copies with sticker wrapped around spine with new number			
❑ LPM-1515 [M]	Loving You	2003	25.00
—Red vinyl; "DRL 13268" in trail-off wax; "BMG Special Products" logo on back cover; from box "Elvis Top Album Collection Volume 2"			
❑ LSP-1515(e) [R]	Loving You	1975	25.00
—Tan label			
❑ LSP-1515(e) [R]	Loving You	1976	15.00
—Black label, dog near top			
❑ LPM-1515 [M]	Loving You	1957	400.00
—Long Play" on label			
❑ LPM-1515 [M]	Loving You	1963	200.00
—Mono" on label			
❑ LPM-1515 [M]	Loving You	1964	50.00
—Monaural" on label			
❑ LSP-1515(e) [R]	Loving You	1962	150.00
—Stereo Electronically Reprocessed" and silver "RCA Victor" on label			
❑ LSP-1515(e) [R]	Loving You	1964	50.00
—Stereo Electronically Reprocessed" and white "RCA Victor" on label			
❑ LSP-1515(e) [R]	Loving You	1968	40.00
—Orange label, non-flexible vinyl			
❑ LSP-1515(e) [R]	Loving You	1971	25.00
—Orange label, flexible vinyl			
❑ AFL1-1515(e) [R]	Loving You	1977	15.00
—Black label, dog near top; includes copies with sticker wrapped around spine with new number			
❑ CPL1-4395	Memories of Christmas	1982	18.00
—With greeting card (deduct 1/3 if missing)			
❑ AFK1-2428 [B]	Moody Blue	1977	5000.00
—Alternate cover slick (never put on an actual cover), with the words "Moody Blue" inside the large word "Elvis." See any late-1970s Elvis inner sleeve for a black and white photo of the scrapped cover; VG value 1500; VG+ value 2250			
❑ AFL1-2428 [DJ]	Moody Blue	1977	2500.00
—Experimental colored vinyl pressings (with no cover), any color or combination except blue or black			
❑ AFL1-2428	Moody Blue	1977	12.00
—Blue vinyl			
❑ AFL1-2428 [B]	Moody Blue	1977	300.00
—Black vinyl			
❑ AQL1-2428	Moody Blue	1979	30.00
—Reissue with new prefix			
❑ LSP-4362	On Stage February, 1970	1970	40.00
—Orange label, non-flexible vinyl			
❑ LSP-4362	On Stage February, 1970	1971	30.00
—Orange label, flexible vinyl			
❑ LSP-4362	On Stage February, 1970	1975	30.00
—Tan label			
❑ LSP-4362	On Stage February, 1970	1976	30.00
—Black label, dog near top			
❑ AFL1-4362	On Stage February, 1970	1977	15.00
—Black label, dog near top; includes copies with sticker wrapped around spine with new number			
❑ AQL1-4362	On Stage February, 1970	1983	10.00
—Reissue with some cover changes			
❑ AQL1-3279 [B]	Our Memories of Elvis	1979	30.00
❑ AQL1-3448	Our Memories of Elvis, Volume 2	1979	25.00
❑ LPM-3643 [M]	Paradise, Hawaiian Style	1966	60.00
❑ LSP-3643 [S]	Paradise, Hawaiian Style	1966	60.00
—Stereo" on black label			
❑ LSP-3643 [S]	Paradise, Hawaiian Style	1968	40.00
—Orange label, non-flexible vinyl			
❑ LSP-3643 [S]	Paradise, Hawaiian Style	1971	25.00
—Orange label, flexible vinyl			
❑ LSP-3643 [S]	Paradise, Hawaiian Style	1975	18.00
—Tan label			
❑ LSP-3643 [S]	Paradise, Hawaiian Style	1976	15.00
—Black label, dog near top			
❑ AFL1-3643 [S]	Paradise, Hawaiian Style	1977	15.00
—Black label, dog near top; includes copies with sticker wrapped around spine with new number			
❑ LPM-2523 [M]	Pot Luck with Elvis	1962	150.00
—Long Play" on label			
❑ LPM-2523 [M]	Pot Luck with Elvis	1964	150.00
—Monaural" on label			
❑ LSP-2523 [S]	Pot Luck with Elvis	1962	150.00
—Living Stereo" on label			

Number	Title	Yr	NM
❑ LSP-2523 [S]	Pot Luck with Elvis	1964	60.00
—Stereo" on black label			
❑ LSP-2523 [S]	Pot Luck with Elvis	1968	40.00
—Orange label, non-flexible vinyl			
❑ LSP-2523 [S]	Pot Luck with Elvis	1975	25.00
—Tan label			
❑ LSP-2523 [S]	Pot Luck with Elvis	1976	15.00
—Black label, dog near top			
❑ AFL1-2523 [S]	Pot Luck with Elvis	1977	15.00
—Black label, dog near top; includes copies with sticker wrapped around spine with new number			
❑ APL1-0873	Promised Land	1975	60.00
—Orange label			
❑ APD1-0873 [Q]	Promised Land	1975	250.00
—RCA QuadraDisc" label			
❑ APL1-0873	Promised Land	1975	25.00
—Tan label			
❑ AFL1-0873	Promised Land	1977	18.00
—Black label, dog near top			
❑ APD1-0873 [Q]	Promised Land	1977	200.00
—Black label, dog near top; quadraphonic reissue			
❑ DJL1-3455 [DJ]	Pure Elvis	1979	800.00
—Promo-only item for Our Memories of Elvis, Volume 2; contains original version of five songs on one side, "unsweetened" versions of same songs on the other			
❑ ANL1-0971(e)	Pure Gold	1975	18.00
—Orange label			
❑ ANL1-0971(e)	Pure Gold	1976	15.00
—Yellow label			
❑ AYL1-3732	Pure Gold	1980	10.00
—Best Buy Series" reissue			
❑ APL1-0388	Raised on Rock/For Ol' Times Sake	1973	30.00
—Orange label			
❑ APL1-0388	Raised on Rock/For Ol' Times Sake	1975	30.00
—Tan label			
❑ APL1-0388	Raised on Rock/For Ol' Times Sake	1977	15.00
—Black label, dog near top			
❑ AFL1-5418	Reconsider Baby	1985	25.00
—All copies on blue vinyl			
❑ AFM1-5182	Rocker	1984	25.00
❑ LSP-2999 [S]	Roustabout	2003	25.00
—Red vinyl, "DRL 13269" in trail-off wax; "BMG Special Products" logo on back cover; from box "Elvis Top Album Collection Volume 2"			

Number	Title	Yr	NM
❑ LPM-2999 [M]	Roustabout	1964	150.00
—Mono" on label			
❑ LPM-2999 [M]	Roustabout	1965	60.00
—Monaural" on label			
❑ LSP-2999 [S]	Roustabout	1964	700.00
—Stereo" and silver "RCA Victor" on black label			
❑ LSP-2999 [S]	Roustabout	1964	60.00
—Stereo" and white "RCA Victor" on black label			
❑ LSP-2999 [S]	Roustabout	1968	40.00
—Orange label, non-flexible vinyl			
❑ LSP-2999 [S]	Roustabout	1971	25.00
—Orange label, flexible vinyl			
❑ LSP-2999 [S]	Roustabout	1975	25.00
—Tan label			
❑ LSP-2999 [S]	Roustabout	1976	15.00
—Black label, dog near top			
❑ AFL1-2999 [S]	Roustabout	1977	15.00
—Black label, dog near top; includes copies with sticker wrapped around spine with new number			
❑ PRS-279 [B]	Singer Presents Elvis Singing Flaming Star and Others	1968	150.00
—Sold only at Singer sewing machine dealers; reissued on RCA Camden 2304			
❑ LSP-2370 [S]	Something for Everybody	2003	25.00
—Red vinyl; "DRL 13270" in trail-off wax; "BMG Special Products" logo on back cover; from box "Elvis Top Album Collection Volume 1"			

Number	Title	Yr	NM
❑ LPM-2370 [M]	Something for Everybody	1961	150.00
—"Long Play" on label; back cover advertises RCA Compact 33 singles and doubles			
❑ LPM-2370 [M]	Something for Everybody	1963	80.00
—"Mono" on label; back cover advertises "Viva Las Vegas" EP			
❑ LPM-2370 [M]	Something for Everybody	1964	50.00
—"Monaural" on label; back cover advertises "Viva Las Vegas" EP			
❑ LSP-2370 [S]	Something for Everybody	1961	250.00
—"Living Stereo" on label; back cover advertises RCA Compact 33 singles and doubles			
❑ LSP-2370 [S]	Something for Everybody	1963	150.00
—"Stereo" and silver "RCA Victor" on black label; back cover advertises Elvis' Christmas Album and His Hand in Mine LPs and "Viva Las Vegas" EP			
❑ LSP-2370 [S]	Something for Everybody	1964	50.00
—"Stereo" and white "RCA Victor" on black label; back cover advertises "Viva Las Vegas" EP			
❑ LSP-2370 [S]	Something for Everybody	1968	40.00
—Orange label, non-flexible vinyl; final back cover change advertises Elvis (NBC-TV Special), Elvis' Christmas Album and His Hand in Mine LPs			
❑ LSP-2370 [S]	Something for Everybody	1971	25.00
—Orange label, flexible vinyl			
❑ LSP-2370 [S]	Something for Everybody	1975	25.00
—Tan label			
❑ LSP-2370 [S]	Something for Everybody	1976	15.00
—Black label, dog near top			
❑ AFL1-2370 [S]	Something for Everybody	1977	15.00
—Black label, dog near top; includes copies with sticker wrapped around spine with new number			
❑ AYL1-4116 [S]	Something for Everybody	1981	10.00
—"Best Buy Series" reissue; includes copies with sticker wrapped around spine with new number			
❑ UNRM-5697/8 [DJ]	Special Christmas Programming	1967	1200.00
—White label promo. Add 25% for script.			
❑ SP-33-461 [DJ]	Special Palm Sunday Programming	1967	1000.00
—White label promo. Add 25% for cue sheet.			
❑ LSP-3989 [S]	Speedway	1971	25.00
—Orange label, flexible vinyl			
❑ LSP-3989 [S]	Speedway	1975	25.00
—Tan label			
❑ LPM-3989 [M]	Speedway	1968	3000.00
❑ LSP-3989 [S]	Speedway	1968	60.00
—"Stereo" on black label			
❑ LSP-3989 [S]	Speedway	1968	40.00
—Orange label, non-flexible vinyl			
❑ LSP-3989 [S]	Speedway	1976	15.00
—Black label, dog near top			
❑ AFL1-3989 [3]	Speedway	1977	15.00
—Black label, dog near top; includes copies with sticker wrapped around spine with new number			
❑ LPM/LSP-3989	Speedway Bonus Photo	1968	50.00
❑ LPM-3702 [M]	Spinout	1966	60.00
❑ LSP-3702 [S]	Spinout	1966	60.00
—"Stereo" on black label			
❑ APL1-2560 [S]	Spinout	1977	15.00
—Black label, dog near top			
❑ AYL1-3684 [S]	Spinout	1980	10.00
—"Best Buy Series" reissue			
❑ LPM/LSP-3702	Spinout Bonus Photo	1966	60.00
❑ LSP-4445	That's the Way It Is	1970	80.00
—Orange label, non-flexible vinyl			
❑ LSP-4445	That's the Way It Is	1971	30.00
—Orange label, flexible vinyl			
❑ LSP-4445	That's the Way It Is	1975	25.00
—Tan label			
❑ LSP-4445	That's the Way It Is	1976	18.00
—Black label, dog near top			
❑ AFL1-4445	That's the Way It Is	1977	15.00
—Black label, dog near top; includes copies with sticker wrapped around spine with new number			
❑ AYL1-4114	That's the Way It Is	1981	10.00
—"Best Buy Series" reissue; includes copies with sticker wrapped around spine with new number			
❑ AHL1-4530	The Elvis Medley	1982	15.00
❑ R244047	The Legendary Concert Performances	1978	40.00
—RCA Music Service exclusive			
❑ APM1-1675	The Sun Sessions	1976	25.00
—Tan label			
❑ APM1-1675	The Sun Sessions	1976	15.00
—Black label, dog near top			
❑ AFM1-1675	The Sun Sessions	1977	18.00
—Black label, dog near top; includes copies with sticker wrapped around spine with new number			
❑ AYM1-3893	The Sun Sessions	1981	10.00
—"Best Buy Series" reissue; includes copies with sticker wrapped around spine with new number			
❑ CPL2-4031	This Is Elvis	1980	18.00
❑ APL1-2274	Welcome to My World	1977	25.00
—Black label, dog near top			
❑ AFL1-2274	Welcome to My World	1977	15.00
—Black label, dog near top; includes copies with sticker wrapped around spine with new number			
❑ AQL1-2274	Welcome to My World	1979	12.00
—Black label, dog near top; includes copies with sticker wrapped around spine with new number			
❑ LPM-6401	Worldwide 50 Gold Award Hits, Vol. 1	1970	80.00

Number	Title	Yr	NM
—Orange labels, non-flexible vinyl; with blurb for photo book on cover			
❑ LPM-6401	Worldwide 50 Gold Award Hits, Vol. 1	1970	80.00
—Orange labels, flexible vinyl; with blurb for photo book on cover			

READER'S DIGEST

❑ RDA-242/D	Elvis Sings Country Favorites	1984	60.00
❑ RD4A-181/D	Elvis Sings Inspirational Favorites	1983	25.00
❑ RBA-072/D	Great Hits of 1956-57	1987	25.00
❑ RD-10/A [B]	His Greatest Hits	1979	400.00
—White box			
❑ 010/A	His Greatest Hits	1990	40.00
—White box			
❑ 010/A	His Greatest Hits	1983	60.00
—Yellow box			
❑ RB4-191/A	The Legend Lives On	1986	60.00

SHOW-LAND

❑ LP-2001	The First of Elvis	1979	100.00

SILHOUETTE

❑ 10001/2	Personally Elvis	1979	30.00
—Interview records; no music			

SUN

❑ 1001 [B]	The Sun Years -- Interviews and Memories	1977	30.00
—With "Memphis, Tennessee" on label			
❑ 1001 [B]	The Sun Years -- Interviews and Memories	1977	15.00
—With "Nashville, U.S.A." on label; white cover with brown print			
❑ 1001 [B]	The Sun Years -- Interviews and Memories	1977	25.00
—With "Nashville, U.S.A." on label; dark yellow cover with brown print			

TIME-LIFE

❑ STW-106	Country Music	1981	25.00
❑ STL-106	Elvis Presley: 1954-1961	1986	30.00
❑ STL-126	Elvis the King: 1954-1965	1989	80.00

PRESNELL, HARVE

MGM

❑ E-4266 [M]	New Echoes of the Old West	1965	25.00
❑ SE-4266 [S]	New Echoes of the Old West	1965	30.00
❑ E-4194 [M]	The World's Greatest Love Songs	1964	25.00
❑ SE-4194 [S]	The World's Greatest Love Songs	1964	30.00

PRESTI, IDA, AND ALEXANDRE LAGOYA

MERCURY LIVING PRESENCE

❑ SR90457 [S]	Baroque Music for Two Guitars	196?	40.00
—Maroon label, with "Vendor: Mercury Record Corporation"			
❑ SR90380 [S]	Four Concertos for Two Guitars by Vivaldi	196?	30.00
—Maroon label, no "Vendor: Mercury Record Corporation"			
❑ SR90427 [S]	Spanish Music for Two Guitars	196?	30.00
—Maroon label, no "Vendor: Mercury Record Corporation"			

PRESTIGE BLUES SWINGERS, THE

PRESTIGE

❑ PRST-7787	Outskirts of Town	1970	18.00
❑ PRLP-7145 [M]	Outskirts of Town	1958	80.00

SWINGVILLE

❑ SVLP-2013 [M]	Stasch	1960	30.00
—Blue label, trident logo at right			
❑ SVLP-2013 [M]	Stasch	1965	50.00
—Purple label			

PRESTIGE JAZZ QUARTET, THE

PRESTIGE

❑ PRLP-7108 [M]	The Prestige Jazz Quartet	1957	50.00

PRESTON, BILLY

A&M

❑ SP-4587	Billy Preston	1976	15.00
❑ SP-3526	Everybody Likes Some Kind of Music	1973	15.00
❑ SP-4657	It's a Whole New Thing	1977	15.00
❑ SP-4532	It's My Pleasure	1975	15.00
❑ SP-3507	I Wrote a Simple Song	1971	15.00
❑ SP-3637	Live European Tour	1974	15.00
❑ SP-3516	Music Is My Life	1972	15.00
❑ SP-3205	The Best of Billy Preston	1982	12.00
❑ SP-3645	The Kids & Me	1974	15.00

APPLE

❑ ST-3370	Encouraging Words	1970	25.00
❑ ST-3359	That's the Way God Planned It	1969	50.00
—Cover has close-up of Billy Preston			
❑ ST-3359	That's the Way God Planned It	1972	25.00
—Cover has multiple images of Billy Preston			

BUDDAH

❑ BDS-7502	Billy Preston	1969	18.00

Number	Title	Yr	NM
❑ T2532 [M]	Wildest Organ in Town!	1966	50.00
❑ ST2532 [S]	Wildest Organ in Town!	1966	40.00

DERBY

❑ LPM-701 [M]	16 Year Old Soul	1963	250.00

EXODUS

❑ 304 [M]	Early Hits of 1965	1965	30.00

GNP CRESCENDO

❑ GNPS-2071	Soul'd Out	1973	18.00

MCA

❑ 28037	Gospel Soul	198?	10.00
—Reissue of Peacock LP			

MOTOWN

❑ M7-958	Billy Preston & Syreeta	1981	12.00
❑ M7-925	Late at Night	1980	12.00
❑ 6020ML	Pressin' On	1982	12.00
❑ M8-941	The Way I Am	1981	12.00

MYRRH

❑ MSB-6605	Behold	1978	15.00
❑ MSB-6607	Universal Love	1979	15.00

PEACOCK

❑ 179	Gospel Soul	197?	15.00

PICKWICK

❑ SPC-3315	Organ Transplant	197?	12.00

VEE JAY

❑ LP-1142 [M]	Greatest Hits	1966	40.00
❑ LPS-1142 [S]	Greatest Hits	1966	60.00
❑ LP-1123 [M]	The Most Exciting Organ Ever	1965	40.00
❑ LPS-1123 [S]	The Most Exciting Organ Ever	1965	60.00

PRESTON, JOHNNY

MERCURY

❑ MG-20609 [M]	Come Rock with Me	1960	100.00
❑ SR-60609 [S]	Come Rock with Me	1960	150.00
❑ MG-20592 [M]	Running Bear	1960	100.00
❑ SR-60250 [S]	Running Bear	1960	150.00
—Black label			
❑ SR-60250 [S]	Running Bear	1981	15.00
—Reissue on Chicago skyline label			

WING

❑ MGW-12246 [M]	Running Bear	1963	25.00
❑ SRW-16246 [S]	Running Bear	1963	30.00

PRETENDERS

NAUTILUS

❑ NR-38	Pretenders	1982	50.00
—Audiophile vinyl			

SIRE

❑ MINI3563 [EP]	Extended Play	1981	12.00
❑ R144453	Get Close	1986	15.00
—RCA Music Service edition			
❑ 25488	Get Close	1986	12.00
❑ 23980	Learning to Crawl	1983	12.00
❑ 23980 [DJ]	Learning to Crawl	1983	30.00
—Promo-only Quiex II pressing; otherwise, same as above			
❑ 26219	Packed!	1990	15.00
❑ SRK6083	Pretenders	1980	12.00
❑ SRK3572	Pretenders II	1981	12.00
❑ R133248	The Singles	1987	15.00
—BMG Direct Marketing edition; otherwise, same as 25664			
❑ 25664	The Singles	1987	12.00

WARNER BROS.

❑ WBMS-142 [DJ]	Get Close Interview	1987	25.00
—Part of "The Warner Bros. Music Show" series			
❑ WBMS-114 [DJ]	Pretenders Live	1980	30.00
—Part of "The Warner Bros. Music Show" series; comes in red die-cut cover			
❑ WBMS-121 [DJ]	Pretenders Live (Star Fleet)	1982	25.00
—Part of "The Warner Bros. Music Show" series; comes in black cover with white sticker			

PRETTY POISON

SVENGALI

❑ SRPP-1 [EP]	Laced	1984	25.00

VIRGIN

❑ R144099	Catch Me I'm Falling	1988	15.00
—BMG Direct Marketing edition			
❑ 90885	Catch Me I'm Falling	1987	12.00

PRETTY THINGS, THE

BIG BEAT

❑ WIK-24 [B]	Live at Heartbreak Hotel	1985	15.00

FONTANA

❑ MGF-27544 [M]	The Pretty Things	1965	80.00
❑ SRF-67544 [P]	The Pretty Things	1965	80.00

NORTON

❑ TED-1001 [10]	Defecting Grey	2000	30.00
❑ 283	Get the Picture?	2000	15.00
❑ 284	Midnight to Six	2000	15.00
❑ 282	The Pretty Things	2000	15.00

RARE EARTH

❑ RS515	Parachute	1970	25.00
❑ R549R2	Real Pretty	1976	18.00

Number	Title	Yr	NM

— The two prior Rare Earth albums in one package
❑ RS506 [B] — S.F. Sorrow — 1969 — 60.00
— Original covers are rounded at top
❑ RS506 — S.F. Sorrow — 1969 — 30.00
— Later copies are standard in shape

SIRE
❑ SASH-3713 [B] — The Vintage Years — 1976 — 30.00
SWAN SONG
❑ SS8414 [B] — Savage Eye — 1976 — 18.00
❑ SS8411 [B] — Silk Torpedo — 1975 — 18.00
WARNER BROS.
❑ BSK3466 [B] — Cross Talk — 1980 — 18.00
❑ BS2680 [B] — Freeway Madness — 1973 — 15.00

PREVIN, ANDRE, AND RUSS FREEMAN

CONTEMPORARY
❑ C-3537 [M] — Double Play! — 1957 — 50.00
❑ S-7011 [S] — Double Play! — 1959 — 40.00
STEREO RECORDS
❑ S-7011 [S] — Double Play! — 1958 — 50.00

PREVIN, ANDRE; HERB ELLIS; SHELLY MANNE; RAY BROWN

COLUMBIA
❑ CL2018 [M] — Four to Go — 1963 — 25.00
❑ CS8818 [S] — Four to Go — 1963 — 30.00

PREVIN, ANDRE

ANGEL
❑ DS-37780 — A Different Kind of Blues — 1981 — 12.00
❑ S-1-37799 — It's a Breeze — 1981 — 12.00
COLUMBIA
❑ CL2034 [M] — Andre Previn in Hollywood — 1963 — 18.00
— Red label with "Guaranteed High Fidelity" at bottom
❑ CS8834 [S] — Andre Previn in Hollywood — 1963 — 25.00
— Red label with "360 Sound Stereo" in black at bottom
❑ CL2034 [M] — Andre Previn in Hollywood — 1966 — 15.00
— Red label with "360 Sound Mono" at bottom
❑ CS8834 [S] — Andre Previn in Hollywood — 1966 — 18.00
— Red label with "360 Sound Stereo" in white at bottom
❑ CL1649 [M] — A Touch of Elegance — 1961 — 25.00
— Red and black label with six "eye" logos
❑ CS8449 [S] — A Touch of Elegance — 1961 — 30.00
— Red and black label with six "eye" logos
❑ CL1569 [M] — Camelot — 1961 — 25.00
— Red and black label with six "eye" logos
❑ CS8369 [S] — Camelot — 1961 — 30.00
— Red and black label with six "eye" logos
❑ CL1569 [M] — Camelot — 1963 — 15.00
— Red label with "Guaranteed High Fidelity" or "360 Sound Mono" at bottom
❑ CS8369 [S] — Camelot — 1963 — 18.00
— Red label with "360 Sound Stereo" at bottom
❑ CL1786 [M] — Faraway Part of Town — 1962 — 25.00
— Red and black label with six "eye" logos
❑ CS8586 [S] — Faraway Part of Town — 1962 — 30.00
— Red and black label with six "eye" logos
❑ CL1786 [M] — Faraway Part of Town — 1963 — 15.00
— Red label with "Guaranteed High Fidelity" or "360 Sound Mono" at bottom
❑ CS8586 [S] — Faraway Part of Town — 1963 — 18.00
— Red label with "360 Sound Stereo" at bottom
❑ CL1530 [M] — Give My Regards to Broadway — 1960 — 25.00
— Red and black label with six "eye" logos
❑ CS8330 [S] — Give My Regards to Broadway — 1960 — 30.00
— Red and black label with six "eye" logos
❑ CL1530 [M] — Give My Regards to Broadway — 1963 — 15.00
— Red label with "Guaranteed High Fidelity" or "360 Sound Mono" at bottom
❑ CS8330 [S] — Give My Regards to Broadway — 1960 — 18.00
— Red label with "360 Sound Stereo" at bottom
❑ CL1437 [M] — Like Love — 1960 — 18.00
— Red and black label with six "eye" logos
❑ CS8233 [S] — Like Love — 1960 — 25.00
— Red and black label with six "eye" logos
❑ CL1437 [M] — Like Love — 1963 — 15.00
— Red label with "Guaranteed High Fidelity" or "360 Sound Mono" at bottom
❑ CS8233 [S] — Like Love — 1963 — 18.00
— Red label with "360 Sound Stereo" at bottom
❑ CL1741 [M] — Mack the Knife and Other Kurt Weill Music — 1962 — 25.00
— Red and black label with six "eye" logos
❑ CS8541 [S] — Mack the Knife and Other Kurt Weill Music — 1962 — 30.00
— Red and black label with six "eye" logos
❑ CL1741 [M] — Mack the Knife and Other Kurt Weill Music — 1963 — 15.00
— Red label with "Guaranteed High Fidelity" or "360 Sound Mono" at bottom
❑ CS8541 [S] — Mack the Knife and Other Kurt Weill Music — 1962 — 18.00
— Red label with "360 Sound Stereo" at bottom
❑ CL2195 [M] — My Fair Lady — 1964 — 18.00
— Red label with "Guaranteed High Fidelity" at bottom

Number	Title	Yr	NM

❑ CS8995 [S] — My Fair Lady — 1964 — 25.00
— Red label with "360 Sound Stereo" in black at bottom
❑ CL2195 [M] — My Fair Lady — 1966 — 15.00
— Red label with "360 Sound Mono" at bottom
❑ CS8995 [S] — My Fair Lady — 1966 — 18.00
— Red label with "360 Sound Stereo" in white at bottom
❑ CL2294 [M] — Popular Previn — 1965 — 18.00
— Red label with "Guaranteed High Fidelity" at bottom
❑ CS9094 [S] — Popular Previn — 1965 — 25.00
— Red label with "360 Sound Stereo" in black at bottom
❑ CS9094 [S] — Popular Previn — 1966 — 18.00
— Red label with "360 Sound Stereo" in white at bottom
❑ CL2294 [M] — Popular Previn — 1966 — 15.00
— Red label with "360 Sound Mono" at bottom
❑ CL1495 [M] — Rhapsody in Blue — 1960 — 18.00
— Red and black label with six "eye" logos
❑ CS8286 [S] — Rhapsody in Blue — 1960 — 25.00
— Red and black label with six "eye" logos
❑ CS8286 [S] — Rhapsody in Blue — 1963 — 18.00
— Red label with "360 Sound Stereo" at bottom
❑ CL1495 [M] — Rhapsody in Blue — 1963 — 15.00
— Red label with "Guaranteed High Fidelity" or "360 Sound Mono" at bottom
❑ CS8733 [S] — Sittin' on a Rainbow: The Music of Harold Arlen — 1963 — 25.00
— Red label, "360 Sound Stereo" in black at bottom
❑ CL1933 [M] — Sittin' on a Rainbow: The Music of Harold Arlen — 1963 — 18.00
— Guaranteed High Fidelity" on label
❑ CL1888 [M] — The Light Fantastic — 1962 — 25.00
— Red and black label with six "eye" logos
❑ CS8688 [S] — The Light Fantastic — 1962 — 30.00
— Red and black label with six "eye" logos
❑ CL1888 [M] — The Light Fantastic — 1963 — 15.00
— Red label with "Guaranteed High Fidelity" or "360 Sound Mono" at bottom
❑ CS8688 [S] — The Light Fantastic — 1963 — 18.00
— Red label with "360 Sound Stereo" at bottom
❑ CL2114 [M] — The Soft and Swinging Music of Jimmy McHugh — 1964 — 18.00
— Red label with "Guaranteed High Fidelity" at bottom
❑ CS8914 [S] — The Soft and Swinging Music of Jimmy McHugh — 1964 — 25.00
— Red label with "360 Sound Stereo" in black at bottom
❑ CS8914 [S] — The Soft and Swinging Music of Jimmy McHugh — 1966 — 18.00
— Red label with "360 Sound Stereo" in white at bottom
❑ CL2114 [M] — The Soft and Swinging Music of Jimmy McHugh — 1966 — 15.00
— Red label with "360 Sound Mono" at bottom
❑ CL1595 [M] — Thinking of You — 1961 — 25.00
— Red and black label with six "eye" logos
❑ CS8395 [S] — Thinking of You — 1961 — 30.00
— Red and black label with six "eye" logos
❑ CL1595 [M] — Thinking of You — 1963 — 15.00
— Red label with "Guaranteed High Fidelity" or "360 Sound Mono" at bottom
❑ CS8395 [S] — Thinking of You — 1963 — 18.00
— Red label with "360 Sound Stereo" at bottom

CONTEMPORARY
❑ M-3586 [M] — Andre Previn Plays Harold Arlen — 1960 — 40.00
❑ S-7586 [S] — Andre Previn Plays Harold Arlen — 1960 — 30.00
❑ M-3567 [M] — Andre Previn Plays Jerome Kern — 1959 — 50.00
❑ S-7567 [S] — Andre Previn Plays Jerome Kern — 1959 — 40.00
❑ M-3558 [M] — Andre Previn Plays Vernon Duke — 1959 — 50.00
❑ S-7558 [S] — Andre Previn Plays Vernon Duke — 1959 — 40.00
❑ C-3548 [M] — Gigi — 1958 — 50.00
❑ S-7548 [S] — Gigi — 1959 — 40.00
❑ M-3570 [M] — Jazz Trio, King Size — 1959 — 50.00
❑ S-7570 [S] — Jazz Trio, King Size — 1959 — 40.00
❑ M-3575 [M] — Like Previn — 1960 — 40.00
❑ S-7575 [S] — Like Previn — 1960 — 30.00
❑ C-3543 [M] — Pal Joey — 1957 — 50.00
❑ S-7543 [S] — Pal Joey — 1959 — 40.00
❑ M-3572 [M] — West Side Story — 1960 — 40.00
❑ S-7572 [S] — West Side Story — 1960 — 30.00
CORONET
❑ 170 — Featuring Andre Previn — 196? — 15.00
❑ 181 — The Magic Sounds of Andre Previn — 196? — 15.00
DECCA
❑ DL4115 [M] — Andre Previn Plays Pretty — 1961 — 15.00
❑ DL74115 [S] — Andre Previn Plays Pretty — 1961 — 18.00
❑ DL4350 [M] — But Beautiful — 1963 — 15.00
❑ DL74350 [S] — But Beautiful — 1963 — 18.00
❑ DL8341 [M] — Hollywood at Midnight — 1957 — 40.00
❑ DL8131 [M] — Let's Get Away from It All — 1955 — 40.00
EVEREST ARCHIVE OF FOLK & JAZZ
❑ 247 — Early Years — 1970 — 12.00
FANTASY
❑ OJC-157 — Double Play! — 198? — 12.00
— Reissue of Contemporary 7011
❑ OJC-170 — Like Previn — 198? — 12.00
— Reissue of Contemporary 7575
❑ OJC-637 — Pal Joey — 1991 — 15.00
❑ OJC-422 — West Side Story — 1990 — 12.00

Number	Title	Yr	NM

GUEST STAR
❑ 1436 — Piano Greats — 196? — 15.00
HARMONY
❑ HL7429 [M] — Camelot — 1967 — 15.00
❑ HS11229 [S] — Camelot — 1967 — 15.00
❑ HL7348 [M] — Misty — 1965 — 15.00
❑ HS11148 [S] — Misty — 1965 — 15.00
❑ HL7407 [M] — Starlight Piano — 196? — 15.00
❑ HS11207 [S] — Starlight Piano — 196? — 15.00
JAZZ ODYSSEY
❑ 32160260 — Mack the Knife and Other Kurt Weill Music — 196? — 15.00
— Reissue of Columbia 8541
MGM
❑ E-4186 [M] — Andre Previn -- Composer, Conductor, Arranger, Pianist — 1964 — 18.00
❑ SE-4186 [S] — Andre Previn -- Composer, Conductor, Arranger, Pianist — 1964 — 25.00
❑ E-3811 [M] — Like Blue — 1960 — 25.00
❑ SE-3811 [S] — Like Blue — 1960 — 30.00
❑ E-3716 [M] — Secret Songs for Young Lovers — 1959 — 25.00
❑ SE-3716 [S] — Secret Songs for Young Lovers — 1959 — 30.00
MOBILE FIDELITY
❑ 1-095 — West Side Story — 1982 — 30.00
— Audiophile vinyl
MONARCH
❑ 203 [10] — All Star Jazz — 1952 — 80.00
❑ 204 [10] — Andre Previn Plays Duke — 1952 — 80.00
PRI
❑ 3026 [S] — The World's Most Honored Pianist — 1962 — 30.00
— Issued on yellow vinyl
RCA CAMDEN
❑ CAL-792 [M] — Love Walked In — 1964 — 15.00
❑ CAS-792 [R] — Love Walked In — 1964 — 12.00
RCA VICTOR
❑ LPM-3806 [M] — All Alone — 1967 — 18.00
❑ LSP-3806 [S] — All Alone — 1967 — 15.00
❑ LPM-36 [10] — Andre Previn By Request — 1951 — 80.00
❑ LPT-3002 [10] — Andre Previn Plays Harry Warren — 1952 — 80.00
❑ LPM-3491 [M] — Andre Previn Plays Music of the Young Hollywood Composers — 1966 — 15.00
❑ LSP-3491 [S] — Andre Previn Plays Music of the Young Hollywood Composers — 1966 — 18.00
❑ LPM-3551 [M] — Andre Previn with Voices — 1966 — 15.00
❑ LSP-3551 [S] — Andre Previn with Voices — 1966 — 18.00
❑ LPM-1011 [M] — Gershwin — 1955 — 40.00
❑ ANL1-2805 — Pure Gold — 1978 — 12.00
❑ LPM-1356 [M] — Three Little Words — 1957 — 40.00
SPRINGBOARD
❑ SPB-4053 — After Dark — 197? — 12.00
STEREO RECORDS
❑ S-7020 [S] — Gigi — 1958 — 50.00
❑ S-7004 [S] — Pal Joey — 1958 — 50.00
STRAND
❑ SL1074 [M] — Andre Previn Plays — 1962 — 15.00
❑ SLS1074 [S] — Andre Previn Plays — 1962 — 18.00
VERVE
❑ V-8565 [M] — The Essential Andre Previn — 1963 — 15.00
❑ V6-8565 [S] — The Essential Andre Previn — 1963 — 18.00

PREVITE, ROBERT

SOUND ASPECTS
❑ SAS 008 — Bump the Renaissance — 1986 — 15.00

PRICE, ALAN

ACCORD
❑ SJA-7904 — It's Priceless — 1982 — 12.00
JET
❑ JT-LA809-H — Alan Price — 1977 — 12.00
— The "H" suffix is on the label, but the front and back cover, inner sleeve and spine have a "G" prefix; it's not known if any labels have a "G" prefix
❑ JZ35710 — Lucky Day — 1979 — 12.00
❑ NJZ36510 — Rising Sun — 1980 — 12.00
PARROT
❑ PAS71018 [P] — The Price Is Right — 1968 — 30.00
TOWNHOUSE
❑ SN-7126 — House of the Rising Sun — 1981 — 12.00
WARNER BROS.
❑ BS2783 [B] — Between Today and Yesterday — 1974 — 18.00
❑ BS2710 [B] — O Lucky Man — 1973 — 18.00

PRICE, KENNY

BOONE
❑ 1211 — One Hit Follows Another — 1967 — 30.00
❑ 1214 — Southern Bound — 1968 — 30.00
DIMENSION
❑ DLP-5000 — The Best of Both — 1980 — 15.00
RCA VICTOR
❑ APL1-0208 — 30 California Women — 1973 — 18.00

Number	Title	Yr	NM
❑ LSP-4605	Charlotte Fever	1971	25.00
❑ LSP-4224	Happy Tracks	1969	25.00
❑ LSP-4373	Northeast Arkansas Mississippi County Bootlegger	1970	25.00
❑ LSP-4839	Sea of Heartbreak	1973	25.00
❑ LSP-4681	Supersideman	1972	25.00
❑ LSP-4292	The Heavyweight	1970	25.00
❑ LSP-4469	The Red Foley Songbook	1971	25.00
❑ LSP-4527	The Sheriff of Boone County	1971	25.00
❑ LSP-4225	Walking on New Grass	1969	25.00
❑ LSP-4763	You Almost Slipped My Mind	1972	25.00

PRICE, LEONTYNE

LONDON

Number	Title	Yr	NM
❑ OS25280 [S]	A Christmas Offering	1961	30.00
❑ 5644 [M]	A Christmas Offering	1961	25.00
❑ 410198-1	Noel! Noel!	1983	12.00

LONDON JUBILEE

Number	Title	Yr	NM
❑ 411614-1	A Christmas Offering	1984	12.00
—Reissue of London 25280			

RCA VICTOR RED SEAL

Number	Title	Yr	NM
❑ LSC-2279 [S]	A Program of Song	1959	25.00
—Original with "shaded dog" label			
❑ LSC-2600 [S]	Swing Low, Sweet Chariot	1962	30.00
—Original with "shaded dog" label			

PRICE, LLOYD

ABC

Number	Title	Yr	NM
❑ X-763	16 Greatest Hits	1972	18.00
❑ DW-94842	16 Greatest Hits	1972	25.00
—Capitol Record Club edition			
❑ S-297	Mr. Personality	1967	18.00
—Reissue on revised label			
❑ S-324 [R]	Mr. Personality's Big 15	1968	18.00
—Reissue on revised label			
❑ AC-30006	The ABC Collection	1976	18.00

ABC-PARAMOUNT

Number	Title	Yr	NM
❑ ABC-382 [M]	Cookin' with Lloyd Price	1961	40.00
❑ ABCS-382 [S]	Cookin' with Lloyd Price	1961	50.00
❑ ABC-366 [M]	Lloyd Price Sings the Million Sellers	1961	40.00
❑ ABCS-366 [S]	Lloyd Price Sings the Million Sellers	1961	50.00
❑ ABC-297 [M]	Mr. Personality	1959	40.00
❑ ABCS-297 [S]	Mr. Personality	1959	80.00
❑ ABC-324 [M]	Mr. Personality's 15 Hits	1960	40.00
—Label calls this "Mr. Personality's Big Hits			
❑ ABC-315 [M]	Mr. Personality Sings the Blues	1960	40.00
❑ ABCS-315 [S]	Mr. Personality Sings the Blues	1960	80.00
❑ ABC-277 [M]	The Exciting Lloyd Price	1959	40.00
❑ ABCS-277 [S]	The Exciting Lloyd Price	1959	100.00
❑ ABC-346 [M]	The Fantastic Lloyd Price	1960	40.00
❑ ABCS-346 [R]	The Fantastic Lloyd Price	196?	30.00

DOUBLE-L

Number	Title	Yr	NM
❑ DL-2303 [M]	Misty	1963	30.00
❑ SDL 8303 [S]	Misty	1963	40.00
❑ DL-2301 [M]	The Lloyd Price Orchestra	1963	30.00
❑ SDL-8301 [S]	The Lloyd Price Orchestra	1963	40.00

GRAND PRIX

Number	Title	Yr	NM
❑ 422 [M]	Mr. Rhythm and Blues	196?	15.00
❑ S-422 [R]	Mr. Rhythm and Blues	196?	12.00

GUEST STAR

Number	Title	Yr	NM
❑ G-1910 [M]	Come to Me	196?	15.00
❑ GS-1910 [R]	Come to Me	196?	12.00

JAD

Number	Title	Yr	NM
❑ 1002	Lloyd Price Now	1969	30.00

LPG

Number	Title	Yr	NM
❑ 001	Music…Music	1976	12.00

MCA

Number	Title	Yr	NM
❑ 1503	Greatest Hits	1982	10.00

MONUMENT

Number	Title	Yr	NM
❑ MLP-8032 [M]	Lloyd Swings for Sammy	1965	30.00
❑ SLP-18032 [S]	Lloyd Swings for Sammy	1965	40.00

PICKWICK

Number	Title	Yr	NM
❑ SPC-3518	Big Hits	197?	10.00

SCEPTER CITATION

Number	Title	Yr	NM
❑ CTN-18006	The Best of Lloyd Price	1972	12.00

SPECIALTY

Number	Title	Yr	NM
❑ SP-2105 [M]	Lloyd Price	1959	180.00
❑ SP-2105	Lloyd Price	198?	15.00
—1980s reissue			

TRIP

Number	Title	Yr	NM
❑ TOP 16-5	16 Greatest Hits	1976	12.00

TURNTABLE

Number	Title	Yr	NM
❑ TTS-5001	Lloyd Price Now	197?	18.00

UPFRONT

Number	Title	Yr	NM
❑ UPF-126	Misty	197?	15.00

PRICE, RAY

ABC DOT

Number	Title	Yr	NM
❑ DOSD-2062	Hank 'n Me	1976	15.00
❑ DO-2053	Rainbows and Tears	1976	15.00
❑ DO-2073	Reunited	1977	15.00
❑ DO-2037	Say I Do	1975	15.00

COLUMBIA

Number	Title	Yr	NM
❑ CL2528 [M]	Another Bridge to Burn	1966	18.00
❑ CS9328 [S]	Another Bridge to Burn	1966	25.00
❑ JC37061	A Tribute to Willie and Kris	1982	12.00
❑ CL2289 [M]	Burning Memories	1965	18.00
❑ CS9089 [S]	Burning Memories	1965	25.00
❑ CL2677 [M]	Danny Boy	1967	25.00
❑ CS9477 [S]	Danny Boy	1967	18.00
❑ CL1494 [M]	Faith	1960	30.00
❑ CS8285 [S]	Faith	1960	40.00
❑ C30106	For the Good Times	1970	15.00
❑ CQ30106 [Q]	For the Good Times	1972	25.00
❑ CG33633	For the Good Times/I Won't Mention It Again	1975	18.00
—Reissue of two LPs in one package			
❑ PC34710	Help Me	1977	15.00
❑ PC33560	If You Change Your Mind	1975	15.00
❑ C30510	I Won't Mention It Again	1971	15.00
❑ CL2189 [M]	Love Life	1964	18.00
❑ CS8989 [S]	Love Life	1964	25.00
❑ CL1971 [M]	Night Life	1963	18.00
❑ CS8771 [S]	Night Life	1963	25.00
❑ KG31364	Ray Price's All-Time Greatest Hits	1972	18.00
❑ CS9861	Ray Price's Christmas Album	1969	18.00
❑ CL1566 [M]	Ray Price's Greatest Hits	1961	30.00
❑ CS8866 [R]	Ray Price's Greatest Hits	1964	15.00
❑ PC8866	Ray Price's Greatest Hits	198?	10.00
—Reissue with new prefix			
❑ CL2670 [M]	Ray Price's Greatest Hits, Volume 2	1967	25.00
❑ CS9470 [S]	Ray Price's Greatest Hits, Volume 2	1967	18.00
❑ CL1015 [M]	Ray Price Sings Heart Songs	1957	50.00
❑ CL1756 [M]	San Antonio Rose	1962	25.00
❑ CS8556 [S]	San Antonio Rose	1962	30.00
❑ KC32033	She's Got to Be a Saint	1973	15.00
❑ PC32033	She's Got to Be a Saint	197?	10.00
—Reissue with new prefix			
❑ CS9733	She Wears My Ring	1968	18.00
❑ CS9822	Sweetheart of the Year	1969	18.00
❑ CL2806 [M]	Take Me As I Am	1968	30.00
❑ CS9606 [S]	Take Me As I Am	1968	18.00
❑ CL1148 [M]	Talk to Your Heart	1958	40.00
❑ PC34160	The Best of Ray Price	1976	15.00
❑ KC31546	The Lonesomest Lonesome	1972	15.00
❑ CL2382 [M]	The Other Woman	1965	18.00
❑ CS9182 [S]	The Other Woman	1965	25.00
❑ GP28	The World of Ray Price	1970	18.00
❑ CL2606 [M]	Touch My Heart	1967	25.00
❑ CS9406 [S]	Touch My Heart	1967	18.00
❑ CG30878	Welcome to My World	1971	18.00
❑ CL2330 [M]	Western Strings	1965	25.00
❑ CS9139 [S]	Western Strings	1965	30.00
❑ KC32777	You're the Best Thing That Ever Happened to Me	1973	15.00
❑ PC32777	You're the Best Thing That Ever Happened to Me	197?	10.00
—Reissue with new prefix			
❑ CS9918	You Wouldn't Know Love	1970	18.00

COLUMBIA LIMITED EDITION

Number	Title	Yr	NM
❑ LE10142	Love Life	197?	12.00
—Reissue of Columbia CS 8989			

HARMONY

Number	Title	Yr	NM
❑ HL7440 [M]	Born to Lose	1967	15.00
❑ HS11240 [S]	Born to Lose	1967	15.00
❑ HL7372 [M]	Collectors' Choice	196?	15.00
❑ HS11172 [R]	Collectors' Choice	196?	15.00
❑ HS11373	I Fall to Pieces	1969	12.00
❑ KH30272	Make the World Go Away	1970	12.00

MONUMENT

Number	Title	Yr	NM
❑ 7633	Always Me	1979	12.00

MYRRH

Number	Title	Yr	NM
❑ 6532	This Time, Lord	1975	15.00

PAIR

Number	Title	Yr	NM
❑ PDL2-1044	Happens to Be the Best	1986	15.00
❑ PDL2-1096	Priceless	1986	15.00
❑ PDL2-1044	Ray Price Happens to Be the Best!	1986	15.00

ROUNDER

Number	Title	Yr	NM
❑ SS-22	The Honky Tonk Years	1986	12.00

WORD

Number	Title	Yr	NM
❑ 8780	How Great Thou Art	1978	15.00
❑ 8723	Precious Memories	197?	15.00

PRICE, RUTH

AVA

Number	Title	Yr	NM
❑ A-54 [M]	Live and Beautiful	1963	40.00
❑ AS-54 [S]	Live and Beautiful	1963	50.00

CONTEMPORARY

Number	Title	Yr	NM
❑ M-3590 [M]	Ruth Price with Shelly Manne at the Manne-Hole	1961	50.00
❑ S-7590 [S]	Ruth Price with Shelly Manne at the Manne-Hole	1961	60.00

KAPP

Number	Title	Yr	NM
❑ KL-1006 [M]	My Name Is Ruth Price. I Sing.	1955	100.00
❑ KL-1054 [M]	The Party's Over	1957	100.00

ROOST

Number	Title	Yr	NM
❑ LP-2217 [M]	Ruth Price Sings!	1956	100.00

PRICE, SAMMY

CIRCLE

Number	Title	Yr	NM
❑ 73	Sammy Price and His Musicians, 1944	1985	12.00

CLASSIC JAZZ

Number	Title	Yr	NM
❑ 106	Fire	198?	12.00

CONCERT HALL JAZZ

Number	Title	Yr	NM
❑ 1008 [10]	Barrelhouse and Blues	1955	50.00

JAZZTONE

Number	Title	Yr	NM
❑ J-1207 [M]	Barrelhouse and Blues	1956	40.00
❑ J-1236 [M]	Les Jeunesses Musicales	1956	40.00
❑ J-1260 [M]	The Price Is Right	1957	40.00

SAVOY

Number	Title	Yr	NM
❑ MG-14004	Rock	196?	18.00

WORLD WIDE

Number	Title	Yr	NM
❑ 20016	Blues and Boogie	196?	18.00

PRICE, VINCENT

CAEDMON

Number	Title	Yr	NM
❑ TC1429	A Graveyard of Ghost Tales	1974	18.00
❑ TC-1059 [M]	Vincent Price Reads Poems of Shelley	196?	30.00

CAPITOL

Number	Title	Yr	NM
❑ SWBB-342	Witchcraft/Magic	1969	30.00

CAPITOL CUSTOM

Number	Title	Yr	NM
❑ SGP-6258/9 [S]	The World of the 21st Century	1965	40.00
—Blue vinyl			
❑ SGP-6256/7 [S]	The World Tomorrow	1965	40.00
—Blue vinyl			

COLUMBIA MASTERWORKS

Number	Title	Yr	NM
❑ ML5668 [M]	America the Beautiful	1961	30.00

DOT

Number	Title	Yr	NM
❑ DLP-3195 [M]	Gallery	1962	30.00
❑ DLP-25195 [S]	Gallery	1962	30.00

NELSON INDUSTRIES

Number	Title	Yr	NM
❑ (# unknown)0	International Cooking Course	1977	40.00

PRICE, VITO

ARGO

Number	Title	Yr	NM
❑ LP-631 [M]	Swingin' the Loop	1958	250.00
❑ LPS-631 [S]	Swingin' the Loop	1958	250.00

PRIDE, CHARLEY

16TH AVENUE

Number	Title	Yr	NM
❑ ST-70550	After All This Time	1987	15.00
❑ D1-70551	I'm Gonna Love Her on the Radio	1988	15.00
❑ D1-70554	Moody Woman	1989	15.00

PAIR

Number	Title	Yr	NM
❑ PDL2-1023	Country in My Soul	1986	15.00

RCA CAMDEN

Number	Title	Yr	NM
❑ CAS-2584	The Incomparable Charley Pride	1972	18.00

RCA VICTOR

Number	Title	Yr	NM
❑ APL1-0397	Amazing Love	1974	18.00
❑ APD1-0397 [Q]	Amazing Love	1974	30.00
❑ AYL1-4074	Amazing Love	1981	10.00
—Best Buy Series" reissue			
❑ LSP-4742	A Sunshiny Day with Charley Pride	1972	25.00
❑ AHL1-5851	Back to the Country	1986	12.00
❑ AHL1-2963	Burgers and Fries	1978	15.00
❑ AYL1-4252	Burgers and Fries	1982	10.00
—Best Buy Series" reissue			
❑ APL1-1038	Charley	1975	18.00
❑ APD1-1038 [Q]	Charley	1975	30.00
❑ LSP-4094	Charley Pride -- In Person	1969	25.00
❑ ANL1-0996	Charley Pride -- In Person	1975	12.00
—Reissue of LSP-4094			
❑ AHL1-4524	Charley Pride Live	1983	12.00
❑ APL1-0315	Charley Pride Presents the Pridesmen	1973	18.00
❑ LSP-4367	Charley Pride's 10th Album	1970	25.00
❑ AHL1-4287	Charley Pride Sings Everybody's Choice	1982	12.00
❑ LSP-4617	Charley Pride Sings Heart Songs	1971	25.00
❑ LSP-4406	Christmas in My Home Town	1970	25.00
❑ ANL1-1934	Christmas in My Home Town	1976	10.00
—Reissue of LSP-4406			
❑ CPL1-7049	Collector's Series	1985	12.00
❑ LPM-3645 [M]	Country Charley Pride	1966	30.00
❑ LSP-3645 [S]	Country Charley Pride	1966	30.00
❑ AHL1-4662	Country Classics	1983	12.00
❑ APL1-0534	Country Feelin'	1974	18.00
❑ LSP-4513	Did You Think to Pray	1971	25.00
❑ LSP-4468	From Me to You	1971	25.00
❑ AHL1-4151	Greatest Hits	1981	12.00
❑ AYL1-5147	Greatest Hits	1984	10.00
—Best Buy Series" reissue			
❑ AHL1-5426	Greatest Hits, Volume 2	1985	12.00
❑ LSP-4560	I'm Just Me	1971	25.00
❑ ANL1-1214	I'm Just Me	1975	12.00
—Reissue of LSP-4560			
❑ AYL1-3874	I'm Just Me	1981	10.00
—Best Buy Series" reissue			

Number	Title	Yr	NM
❏ LSP-4290	Just Plain Charley	1970	25.00
❏ LPM-3952 [M]	Make Mine Country	1968	60.00
❏ LSP-3952 [S]	Make Mine Country	1968	25.00
❏ AHL1-4822	Night Games	1983	12.00
❏ APL1-0757	Pride of America	1974	18.00
❏ APD1-0757 [Q]	Pride of America	1974	30.00
❏ AHL1-3905	Roll On Mississippi	1981	12.00
❏ APL1-2261	She's Just an Old Love Turned Memory	1977	15.00
❏ AYL1-4166	She's Just an Old Love Turned Memory	1981	10.00
—Best Buy Series" reissue			
❏ AHL1-2478	Someone Loves You Honey	1978	15.00
❏ AYL1-3676	Someone Loves You Honey	1980	10.00
—Best Buy Series" reissue			
❏ LSP-4837	Songs of Love by Charley Pride	1973	18.00
❏ LSP-4041	Songs of Pride -- Charley, That Is	1968	25.00
❏ APL1-1359	Sunday Morning with Charley Pride	1976	18.00
❏ APD1-1359 [Q]	Sunday Morning with Charley Pride	1976	30.00
❏ AYL1-3740	Sunday Morning with Charley Pride	1980	10.00
—Best Buy Series" reissue			
❏ APL1-0217	Sweet Country	1973	18.00
❏ APD1-0217 [Q]	Sweet Country	1973	30.00
❏ LSP-4223	The Best of Charley Pride	1969	25.00
❏ AHL1-4223	The Best of Charley Pride	198?	12.00
—Reissue of LSP-4223			
❏ AYL1-5148	The Best of Charley Pride	1984	10.00
—Best Buy Series" reissue			
❏ APL1-2023	The Best of Charley Pride, Vol. III	1976	15.00
❏ LSP-4682	The Best of Charley Pride, Volume 2	1972	25.00
❏ AHL1-4682	The Best of Charley Pride, Volume 2	198?	12.00
—Reissue of LSP-4682			
❏ AHL1-7174	The Best There Is	1986	12.00
❏ LPM-3895 [M]	The Country Way	1967	30.00
❏ LSP-3895 [S]	The Country Way	1967	25.00
❏ APL1-1241	The Happiness of Having You	1975	18.00
❏ APD1-1241 [Q]	The Happiness of Having You	1975	30.00
❏ AYL1-3943	The Happiness of Having You	1981	10.00
—Best Buy Series" reissue			
❏ AHL1-5031	The Power of Love	1984	12.00
❏ LPM-3775 [M]	The Pride of Country Music	1967	30.00
❏ LSP-3775 [S]	The Pride of Country Music	1967	25.00
❏ AHL1-3548	There's a Little Bit of Hank in Me	1980	15.00
❏ AYL1-4831	There's a Little Bit of Hank in Me	1983	10.00
—Best Buy Series" reissue			
❏ LSP-4153	The Sensational Charley Pride	1969	25.00
❏ AHL1-3441	You're My Jamaica	1979	15.00

READER'S DIGEST
| ❏ RDA-217 | Charley Pride's Country | 1979 | 40.00 |

TEE VEE/RCA SPECIAL PRODUCTS
| ❏ DVL2-0208 | Favorites | 1976 | 18.00 |
| —Label calls this "Charley's Favorites" | | | |

TIME-LIFE
| ❏ STW-101 | Country Music | 1981 | 12.00 |

PRIDE

WARNER BROS.
| ❏ WS1848 | Pride | 1970 | 30.00 |

PRIEST, MAXI

VIRGIN
| ❏ 90957 | Maxi Priest | 1988 | 15.00 |

PRIESTER, JULIAN

ECM
❏ 1044	Love, Love	197?	30.00
—Only issued in Germany?			
❏ 1098	Polarization	1977	30.00
—Only issued in Germany?			

JAZZLAND
| ❏ JLP-25 [M] | Spiritsville | 1960 | 50.00 |
| ❏ JLP-925 [S] | Spiritsville | 1960 | 70.00 |

RIVERSIDE
❏ 6081	Keep Swingin'	197?	18.00
❏ RLP 12-316 [M]	Keep Swingin'	1960	80.00
❏ RLP1163 [S]	Keep Swingin'	1960	100.00

PRIMA, LOUIS

BRUNSWICK
| ❏ BL754183 | The Prima Generation '72 | 1972 | 80.00 |

CAPITOL
❏ T1797 [M]	Lake Tahoe Prima Style	1962	30.00
❏ ST1797 [S]	Lake Tahoe Prima Style	1962	30.00
❏ T1010 [M]	Las Vegas Prima Style	1958	50.00
❏ T1132 [M]	Strictly Prima	1959	30.00
❏ T836 [M]	The Call of the Wildest	1957	50.00
❏ T755 [M]	The Wildest	1956	50.00
❏ T1723 [M]	The Wildest Comes Home	1962	30.00

Number	Title	Yr	NM
❏ ST1723 [S]	The Wildest Comes Home	1962	30.00
❏ T908 [M]	The Wildest Show at Tahoe	1957	50.00

COLUMBIA
| ❏ CL1206 [M] | Breakin' It Up! | 1959 | 40.00 |

DOT
❏ DLP-3385 [M]	Blue Moon	1961	30.00
❏ DLP-25385 [S]	Blue Moon	1961	30.00
❏ DLP-3410 [M]	Doin' the Twist	1961	30.00
❏ DLP-25410 [S]	Doin' the Twist	1961	30.00
❏ DLP-3262 [M]	His Greatest Hits	1960	30.00
❏ DLP-25262 [S]	His Greatest Hits	1960	30.00
❏ DLP-3264 [M]	Pretty Music Prima Style	1960	30.00
❏ DLP-25264 [S]	Pretty Music Prima Style	1960	30.00
❏ DLP-3392 [M]	Return of the Wildest!	1961	30.00
❏ DLP-25392 [S]	Return of the Wildest!	1961	30.00
❏ DLP-3272 [M]	The Wildest Clan	1960	30.00
❏ DLP-25272 [S]	The Wildest Clan	1960	30.00
❏ DLP-3352 [M]	Wonderland by Night	1960	30.00
❏ DLP-25352 [S]	Wonderland by Night	1960	30.00

GOLDEN TONE
| ❏ 326 [M] | Italian Favorites | 196? | 12.00 |
| —Label calls this "Italian Songs"; one side is by Louis Prima, the other side by Phil Brito | | | |

HANNA-BARBERA
| ❏ HLP-8502 [M] | The Golden Hits of Louis Prima | 1966 | 30.00 |

MERCURY
| ❏ MG-25142 [10] | Louis Prima Plays | 1953 | 80.00 |

PRIMA
❏ ST 0074	Angelina	1973	30.00
❏ PS3003 [S]	King of Clubs	1964	100.00
❏ PM3003 [M]	King of Clubs	1964	70.00
❏ PM3001 [M]	Prima Show in the Casbar	1963	40.00
❏ PS3001 [S]	Prima Show in the Casbar	1963	60.00
❏ ST 0072	The Prima Generation	1972	50.00

RONDO-LETTE
| ❏ A-25 [M] | Louis Prima Entertains | 1959 | 30.00 |
| ❏ A-9 [M] | Louis Prima in All His Moods | 1959 | 30.00 |

SAVOY JAZZ
| ❏ SJL-2264 | Play Pretty for the People | 198? | 15.00 |

TOPS
| ❏ 9759 [M] | Italian Favorites | 195? | 18.00 |

PRIMUS

CAROLINE
❏ CAROL1619	Frizzle Fry	1990	80.00
—Red vinyl			
❏ CAROL1620	Suck on This	1990	60.00
—Clear vinyl			

INTERSCOPE
❏ 069-490414-01	Antipop	1999	30.00
❏ INT2-90126	Brown Album	1997	50.00
❏ 92553	Tales from the Punchbowl	1995	80.00

MOBILE FIDELITY
| ❏ LMF45-001 [EP] | Animals Should Not Try to Act Like Humans | 2004 | 30.00 |
| —Original Master Recording" at top of cover; plays at 45 rpm | | | |

PRAWN SONG/INTERSCOPE
| ❏ 7-72738-1 [B] | Pork Soda | 1993 | 70.00 |

PRINCE, BOB

RCA VICTOR
| ❏ LPM-2435 [M] | Opus Jazz | 1961 | 25.00 |
| ❏ LSP-2435 [S] | Opus Jazz | 1961 | 30.00 |

WARNER BROS.
❏ W1276 [M]	Charleston 1970	1959	25.00
❏ WS1276 [S]	Charleston 1970	1959	30.00
❏ W1240 [M]	N.Y. Export: Op. Jazz from Ballets U.S.A.; Ballet Music from Leonard Bernstein's West Side Story	1958	25.00
❏ WS1240 [S]	N.Y. Export: Op. Jazz from Ballets U.S.A.; Ballet Music from Leonard Bernstein's West Side Story	1958	30.00

PRINCE

ARISTA
| ❏ 14624 | Rave Un2 the Joy Fantastic | 1999 | 15.00 |

NPG/BELLMARK
| ❏ 71003 [EP] | The Beautiful Experience | 1994 | 25.00 |

NPG/REDLINE
| ❏ 70004 | The Rainbow Children | 2001 | 150.00 |

PAISLEY PARK
❏ R124370	Around the World in a Day	1985	15.00
—RCA Music Service edition			
❏ 25286	Around the World in a Day	1985	12.00
—Original copies have a fold-over flap (deduct 25% or more if missing)			
❏ R234107	Graffiti Bridge	1990	25.00
—Also includes The Time, Tevin Campbell; BMG Direct Marketing edition			
❏ 27493	Graffiti Bridge	1990	18.00
—Also includes The Time, Tevin Campbell			
❏ R154087	Lovesexy	1988	14.00
—BMG Direct Marketing edition			

Number	Title	Yr	NM
❏ 25720	Lovesexy	1988	15.00
❏ 25720-DJ [DJ]	Lovesexy	1988	25.00
—Gold stamped and stickered cover (no UPC) with promo labels; tracks are banded			
❏ R140234	Parade	1986	15.00
—RCA Music Service edition			
❏ 25395	Parade	1986	10.00
❏ 25577	Sign "O" The Times	1987	18.00
❏ W1-25577	Sign "O" The Times	1987	25.00
—Columbia House edition			
❏ R261991	Sign "O" The Times	1987	25.00
—BMG Direct Marketing edition			
❏ 25677	The Black Album	1987	1500.00
—Withdrawn prior to release, though a few copies escaped. Numerous counterfeits exist on other labels and colored vinyl.			
❏ 25677-DJ	The Black Album	1987	3000.00
—Entire album on two 12-inch records that play at 45 RPM			

WARNER BROS.
❏ R252483	1999	1982	25.00
—RCA Music Service edition			
❏ 23720	1999	1982	18.00
❏ R160344	Batman (Soundtrack)	1989	15.00
—BMG Direct Marketing edition			
❏ 25936	Batman (Soundtrack)	1989	12.00
❏	Come	1994	30.00
PRO-A-7270 [DJ]			
—Promo-only vinyl			
❏ BSK3601	Controversy	1981	15.00
❏ BSK3478	Dirty Mind	1980	15.00
❏ BSK3150	For You	1978	25.00
—First edition on Burbank "palm trees" label			
❏ BSK3150	For You	1978	15.00
—White WB label			
❏ BSK3366	Prince	1979	15.00
❏ R160175	Purple Rain	1984	15.00
—RCA Music Service edition; includes poster			
❏ 25110	Purple Rain	1984	50.00
—Purple vinyl; comes with poster			
❏ 25110	Purple Rain	1984	12.00
—With poster			
❏	The Black Album	1994	30.00
PRO-A-7330 [DJ]			
—Promo-only vinyl			
❏ 45793 [DJ]	The Black Album	1994	200.00
—White vinyl; 300 copies, numbered in gold on the label (from 051 to 350)			
❏ 45793 [DJ]	The Black Album	1994	100.00
—Peach vinyl; 1,000 copies			
❏ 45793 [DJ]	The Black Album	1994	500.00
—Gray marbled vinyl; 50 copies			
❏	The Gold Experience	1995	80.00
PRO-A-7835 [DJ]			
—Promo-only gold vinyl with numbered gold foil jacket			

PRINCE BUSTER

RCA VICTOR
| ❏ LPM-3792 [M] | Ten Commandments | 1967 | 60.00 |
| ❏ LSP-3792 [S] | Ten Commandments | 1967 | 35.00 |

PRINCE IGOR AND THE CZAR

DIFFERENT DRUMMER
| ❏ 1002 | From Russia | 197? | 18.00 |

PRINCETON TRIANGLE JAZZ BAND

BIOGRAPH
| ❏ 12014 | College Jazz in the '20s | 1969 | 18.00 |

PRINE, JOHN

ASYLUM
❏ 6E-139	Bruised Orange	1978	15.00
❏ 6E-222	Pink Cadillac	1979	15.00
❏ 6E-286	Storm Windows	1980	15.00

ATLANTIC
❏ SD18127	Common Sense	1975	15.00
❏ SD7240	Diamonds in the Rough	1972	15.00
❏ SD8296	John Prine	1971	15.00
❏ SD19156	John Prine	1978	12.00
—Reissue of 8296			
❏ SD18202	Prime Prine -- The Best of John Prine	1976	15.00
❏ SD7274	Sweet Revenge	1973	15.00

OH BOY
❏ 002	Aimless Love	198?	12.00
❏ OBR-034	Fair & Square	2007	30.00
—Contains four bonus tracks not on the CD version			
❏ 003	German Afternoons	198?	12.00
❏ 005	John Prine Live	1986	18.00

PRINZ, ROSEMARY

PHAROS
| ❏ MN-10001 [M] | TV's Penny Sings | 1966 | 25.00 |
| ❏ SN-30001 [S] | TV's Penny Sings | 1966 | 30.00 |

PRITCHARD, DAVID

INNER CITY
| ❏ IC-1070 | City Dreams | 1979 | 15.00 |
| ❏ IC-1047 | Light-Year | 1978 | 15.00 |

Number	Title	Yr	NM
PRITCHETT, GEORGE			
KINNICKINNICK			
❑ 101	By Request	197?	25.00
PROBY, P.J.			
LIBERTY			
❑ LRP-3497 [M]	Enigma	1967	35.00
❑ LST-7497 [S]	Enigma	1967	30.00
❑ LRP-3515 [M]	Phenomenon	1967	40.00
❑ LST-7515 [S]	Phenomenon	1967	30.00
❑ LRP-3421 [M]	P.J. Proby	1965	25.00
❑ LST-7421 [S]	P.J. Proby	1965	30.00
❑ LRP-3406 [M]	Somewhere/Go Go P.J. Proby	1965	25.00
❑ LST-7406 [S]	Somewhere/Go Go P.J. Proby	1965	30.00
❑ LST-7561 [B]	What's Wrong with My World?	1968	30.00
PROCESSION			
SMASH			
❑ SRS-67122	Procession	1969	25.00
PROCLAIMERS, THE			
CHRYSALIS			
❑ R152320	Sunshine on Leith	1989	14.00
— BMG Music Service edition			
❑ F1-21668	Sunshine on Leith	1989	15.00
❑ FV41602	This Is the Story	1988	15.00
PROCOL HARUM			
A&M			
❑ SP-4179	A Salty Dog	1969	18.00
❑ SP-3123	A Salty Dog	1979	10.00
— Reissue of 4179			
❑ SP-4373	A Whiter Shade of Pale	1972	15.00
— Reissue of Deram 18008 with one more track			
❑ SP-4294	Broken Barricades	1971	15.00
❑ SP-4261	Home	1970	15.00
❑ SP-4335	Procol Harum Live in Concert with the Edmonton Symphony Orchestra	1972	15.00
❑ SP-8503 [DJ]	Procol Harum Lives	197?	300.00
— Promo-only box set with press kit, photos, keychain and interview LP			
❑ SP-8503 [DJ]	Procol Harum Lives	197?	30.00
— Interview LP alone			
❑ SP-4151	Shine On Brightly	1968	30.00
❑ SP-4401	The Best of Procol Harum	1973	15.00
❑ SP-3259	The Best of Procol Harum	198?	10.00
— Reissue of 4401			
CHRYSALIS			
❑ CHR1058	Exotic Birds and Fruit	1974	15.00
— Green label with "3300 Warner Blvd." address			
❑ PV41058	Exotic Birds and Fruit	1985	10.00
❑ CHR1058	Exotic Birds and Fruit	1977	12.00
— Blue label with New York address			
❑ CHR1037	Grand Hotel	1973	15.00
— Green label with "3300 Warner Blvd." address			
❑ PV41037	Grand Hotel	1985	10.00
❑ CHR1037	Grand Hotel	1977	12.00
— Blue label with New York address			
❑ CHR1080	Procol's Ninth	1975	15.00
— Green label with "3300 Warner Blvd." address			
❑ PV41080	Procol's Ninth	1985	10.00
❑ CHR1080	Procol's Ninth	1977	12.00
— Blue label with New York address			
❑ CHR1130	Something Magic	1977	12.00
DERAM			
❑ DE16008 [M]	Procol Harum	1967	120.00
❑ DES18008 [R]	Procol Harum	1967	40.00
❑ DE/ S16008/18008	Procol Harum Poster	1967	30.00
PROCOPE, RUSSELL			
DOT			
❑ DLP3010 [M]	The Persuasive Sax of Russell Procope	1956	40.00
PRODIGY			
MAVERICK			
❑ PRO-A-8929 [DJ]	The Fat of the Land	1997	30.00
— Promo-only U.S. vinyl in generic white sleeve			
PRODUCERS, THE			
MARATHON			
❑ MR111	Run For Your Life	198?	25.00
PORTRAIT			
❑ NJR37097	The Producers	1981	15.00
❑ ARR38060	You Make the Heat	1982	15.00
PROFESSOR LONGHAIR			
ATLANTIC			
❑ SD7225	New Orleans Piano	1972	30.00

Number	Title	Yr	NM
PROVINE, DOROTHY			
WARNER BROS.			
❑ W1394 [M]	The Roaring 20's	1961	25.00
❑ WS1394 [S]	The Roaring 20's	1961	30.00
❑ W1419 [M]	The Vamp of the Roaring 20's	1961	25.00
❑ WS1419 [S]	The Vamp of the Roaring 20's	1961	30.00
PRYOR, RICHARD			
AUDIOFIDELITY			
❑ 349 [PD]	Richard Pryor Live	198?	18.00
DOVE			
❑ RS6325	Richard Pryor	1968	25.00
LAFF			
❑ A196	Are You Serious???	1977	15.00
❑ A200	Black Ben	1978	12.00
❑ 226	Blackjack	198?	10.00
— Reissue of 146			
❑ A146	Craps: After Hours	1971	15.00
❑ A184	Down 'N' Dirty	197?	15.00
❑ A212	Holy Smoke	1980	12.00
❑ A209	Insane	1980	12.00
❑ A206	Outrageous	1979	12.00
❑ A170	Pryor Goes Foxx Hunting	197?	15.00
❑ A216	Rev. Du Rite	1981	12.00
❑ 279	Richard Pryor Live	198?	10.00
❑ A188	Richard Pryor Meets Richard and Willie and the S.L.A.	1976	15.00
❑ 227	Show Biz	198?	10.00
— Reissue of 200			
❑ (# unknown)0	Supernigger	198?	10.00
❑ A221	The Very Best of Richard Pryor	1982	12.00
❑ A198	Who Me? I'm Not Him	1977	15.00
❑ A202	Wizard of Comedy	1978	12.00
PARTEE			
❑ PBS-2404	That Nigger's Crazy	1974	18.00
REPRISE			
❑ MS2227	Is It Something I Said?	1975	15.00
❑ MSK2285	Is It Something I Said?	1977	12.00
— Reissue of 2227			
❑ RS6325	Richard Pryor	197?	15.00
— Reissue of Dove LP			
❑ MS2241	That Nigger's Crazy	197?	15.00
— Reissue of Partee LP			
❑ MSK2287	That Nigger's Crazy	1977	12.00
— Reissue of Reprise 2241			
TIGER LILY			
❑ TL14023	L.A. Jail	1977	15.00
WARNER BROS.			
❑ RS2960	Bicentennial Nigger	1976	15.00
❑ BSK3114	Bicentennial Nigger	1977	12.00
— Reissue of 2960			
❑ 23981	Richard Pryor: Here and Now	1983	12.00
❑ BSK3660	Richard Pryor Live on the Sunset Strip	1982	12.00
❑ BSK3057	Richard Pryor's Greatest Hits	1977	12.00
❑ 2BSK3364	Wanted	1978	15.00
PRYSOCK, ARTHUR			
DECCA			
❑ DL4628 [M]	Showcase	1965	18.00
❑ DL74628 [S]	Showcase	1965	25.00
❑ DL4581 [M]	Strictly Sentimental	1965	18.00
❑ DL74581 [S]	Strictly Sentimental	1965	25.00
KING			
❑ KS-1088	Fly My Love	1970	15.00
❑ KS-1064	The Country Side of Arthur Prysock	1969	15.00
❑ KS-1067	The Lord Is My Shepherd	1970	15.00
❑ KS-1134	Unforgettable	1971	15.00
❑ KS-1066	Where the Soul Trees Go	1970	15.00
MCA			
❑ 3061	Here's To Good Friends	1978	12.00
MGM			
❑ SE-4694	Arthur Prysock	1970	15.00
❑ GAS-134	Arthur Prysock (Golden Archive Series)	1970	15.00
MILESTONE			
❑ M-9139	A Rockin' Good Way	1986	12.00
❑ M-9146	This Guy's in Love with You	1987	12.00
❑ M-9157	Today's Love Songs, Tomorrow's Blues	1988	12.00
OLD TOWN			
❑ LP-2009 [M]	A Double Header with Arthur Prysock	1965	40.00
❑ 12-004	All My Life	1976	15.00
❑ LP-2006 [M]	A Portrait of Arthur Prysock	1963	40.00
❑ T-90604 [M]	A Portrait of Arthur Prysock	1965	40.00
— Capitol Record Club edition			
❑ ST-90604 [S]	A Portrait of Arthur Prysock	1965	40.00
— Capitol Record Club edition			
❑ 12-001	Arthur Prysock '74	1973	15.00
❑ OT12005	Arthur Prysock Does It Again	1977	15.00
❑ LP-2004 [M]	Arthur Prysock Sings Only for You	1962	50.00

Number	Title	Yr	NM
❑ LP-2005 [M]	Coast to Coast	1963	40.00
❑ LP-2007 [M]	Everlasting Songs for Everlasting Lovers	1964	40.00
❑ LP-2010 [M]	In a Mood	1965	40.00
❑ LP-2008 [M]	Intimately Yours	1964	40.00
❑ LP-102 [M]	I Worry About You	1962	50.00
❑ 12-002	Love Makes It Right	1974	15.00
POLYDOR			
❑ PD-2-8901	Silk and Satin	1977	18.00
VERVE			
❑ V6-650	24 Karat Hits	1969	18.00
❑ V-5012 [M]	A Portrait of Arthur Prysock	1967	18.00
❑ V6-5012 [S]	A Portrait of Arthur Prysock	1967	18.00
❑ V-5009 [M]	Art and Soul	1966	15.00
❑ V6-5009 [S]	Art and Soul	1966	18.00
❑ V-5059	I Must Be Doing Something Right	1968	15.00
❑ V-5029 [M]	Love Me	1968	18.00
❑ V6-5029 [S]	Love Me	1968	15.00
❑ V-5014 [M]	Mister Prysock	1967	18.00
❑ V6-5014 [S]	Mister Prysock	1967	18.00
❑ V-5011 [M]	The Best of Arthur Prysock	1967	15.00
❑ V6-5011 [S]	The Best of Arthur Prysock	1967	18.00
❑ V-5038 [M]	The Best of Arthur Prysock, Number 2	1968	25.00
— All mono copies appear to be yellow label promos			
❑ V6-5038 [S]	The Best of Arthur Prysock, Number 2	1968	15.00
❑ V-5070	This Is My Beloved	1969	15.00
❑ V-5048 [M]	To Love or Not to Love	1968	30.00
— May be promo only			
❑ V6-5048 [S]	To Love or Not to Love	1968	15.00
PRYSOCK, ARTHUR/COUNT BASIE			
VERVE			
❑ V-8646 [M]	Arthur Prysock/Count Basie	1966	18.00
❑ V6-8646 [S]	Arthur Prysock/Count Basie	1966	25.00
❑ 827011-1	Arthur Prysock/Count Basie	1985	10.00
— Reissue			
PRYSOCK, RED			
MERCURY			
❑ MG-20211 [M]	Fruit Boots	1957	120.00
❑ MG-20088 [M]	Rock 'n Roll	1955	200.00
❑ MG-20512 [M]	Swing Softly Red	1958	50.00
❑ SR-60188 [S]	Swing Softly Red	1959	80.00
❑ MG-20307 [M]	The Beat	1957	80.00
WING			
❑ MGW-12007 [M]	Fruit Boots	1959	40.00
— Originals have liner notes on back cover			
❑ MGW-12007 [M]	Fruit Boots	196?	25.00
— Reissues have other LPs listed on back cover			
❑ SRW-16007 [R]	Fruit Boots	196?	15.00
PSYCHEDELIC FURS			
COLUMBIA			
❑ FC44377	All of This and Nothing	1988	12.00
❑ FC45412	Book of Days	1989	12.00
❑ ARC38261 [B]	Forever Now	1982	12.00
❑ PC38261	Forever Now	198?	10.00
— Budget-line reissue			
❑ AS1296 [DJ]	Interchorde	1981	30.00
❑ AS1296 [DJ]	Interchords	1981	30.00
❑ CAS1310 [DJ]	Interchords with Richard Butler	1988	25.00
❑ CAS 01310 [DJ]	Interchords with Richard Butler	1988	18.00
❑ FC40466	Midnight to Midnight	1987	12.00
❑ BFC39278	Mirror Moves	1984	12.00
❑ PC39278	Mirror Moves	198?	10.00
— Budget-line reissue			
❑ NFC36791	Psychedelic Furs	1980	15.00
❑ CAS2719 [DJ]	Richard Butler Interview	1987	18.00
❑ CAS2719 [DJ]	Richard Butler Interview	1987	18.00
❑ NFC37339	Talk Talk Talk	1981	12.00
❑ PC37339	Talk Talk Talk	1983	10.00
— Budget-line reissue			
❑ PC36791	The Psychedelic Furs	198?	10.00
— Budget-line reissue			
PSYCHOTIC PINEAPPLE, THE			
RICHMOND			
❑ 6026 [B]	Where's the Party	1980	30.00
PUBLIC ENEMY			
ATOMIC POP			
❑ 0001	There's a Poison Goin' On	1999	30.00
— Red vinyl			
DEF JAM			
❑ C247374	Apocalypse 91... The Enemy Strikes Black	1991	18.00
❑ C45413	Fear of a Black Planet	1990	15.00
❑ C253014	Greatest Misses	1993	18.00
❑ 558130-1	He Got Game	1998	18.00
❑ BFW44303	It Takes a Nation of Millions to Hold Us Back	1988	15.00
❑ 523362-1	Muse Sick-N-Hour Mess Age	1994	12.00
❑ BFC40658	Yo! Bum Rush the Show	1987	15.00

PUBLIC IMAGE LTD.

4 MEN WITH BEARDS

Number	Title	Yr	NM
❑ 4M517LP [B]	Second Edition		30.00
❑ 4M518LP [B]	The Flowers of Romance		25.00

ELEKTRA

Number	Title	Yr	NM
❑ 60491	Live in Tokyo	1985	12.00
❑ 60438	Public Image Ltd. Album	1986	12.00
❑ 60365	This Is What You Want... This Is What You'll Get	1984	12.00

ISLAND

Number	Title	Yr	NM
❑ 2WX3288	Second Edition	1980	25.00

LIGHT IN THE ATTIC

Number	Title	Yr	NM
❑ LITA100 [B]	First Edition	2013	30.00

VIRGIN

Number	Title	Yr	NM
❑ 91062	9	1989	12.00
❑ 90642	Happy	1987	12.00

WARNER BROS.

Number	Title	Yr	NM
❑ BSK3536	Flowers of Romance	1981	15.00
❑ 2WX3288 [B]	Second Edition	198?	30.00

—Reissue

PUCHO AND THE LATIN SOUL BROTHERS

PRESTIGE

Number	Title	Yr	NM
❑ PRST-7555	Big Stick	1968	30.00
❑ PRST-7616	Dateline	1969	30.00
❑ PRST-7572	Heat!	1968	30.00
❑ PRLP-7471 [M]	Pucho and the Latin Soul Brothers	1967	40.00
❑ PRST-7471 [S]	Pucho and the Latin Soul Brothers	1967	30.00
❑ PRLP-7502 [M]	Saffron and Soul	1967	40.00
❑ PRST-7502 [S]	Saffron and Soul	1967	30.00
❑ PRLP-7528 [M]	Shuckin' and Jivin'	1967	50.00
❑ PRST-7528 [S]	Shuckin' and Jivin'	1967	30.00
❑ PRST-7679	The Best of Pucho and the Latin Soul Brothers	1969	30.00

PUCKETT, GARY, AND THE UNION GAP

COLUMBIA

Number	Title	Yr	NM
❑ CS1042	Gary Puckett and the Union Gap's Greatest Hits	1970	25.00
❑ CS9715 [S]	Incredible	1968	25.00
❑ CL2915 [M]	Incredible	1968	60.00

—Red label stock copy with "Mono" on label; this has been confirmed to exist

Number	Title	Yr	NM
❑ C30862	The Gary Puckett Album	1971	18.00
❑ CS9935	The New Gary Puckett and the Union Gap Album	1969	25.00
❑ CS9612 [S]	Woman, Woman	1968	25.00

—As "The Union Gap Featuring Gary Puckett

Number	Title	Yr	NM
❑ CL2812 [M]	Woman, Woman	1968	40.00

—As "The Union Gap Featuring Gary Puckett

Number	Title	Yr	NM
❑ CS9664 [S]	Young Girl	1968	25.00
❑ CL2864 [M]	Young Girl	1968	50.00

—Red label stock copy with "Mono" on label; this has been confirmed to exist

Number	Title	Yr	NM
❑ CS9664 [M]	Young Girl	1968	60.00

—White label promo with stereo number and "Mono" on label; "Special Mono Radio Station Copy" sticker and timing strip on front cover

HARMONY

Number	Title	Yr	NM
❑ KH31184	Lady Willpower	1972	12.00

PUENTE, TITO

CONCORD PICANTE

Number	Title	Yr	NM
❑ CJP-250	El Rey	1984	12.00
❑ CJP-283	Mambo Diablo	1985	12.00
❑ CP-207	On Broadway	1983	12.00
❑ CJP-354	Salsa Meets Jazz	1988	12.00
❑ CJP-301	Sensacion	1987	12.00
❑ CJP-329	Un Poco Loco	1987	12.00

DECCA

Number	Title	Yr	NM
❑ DL74910 [S]	Brasilia Nueve	1967	25.00
❑ DL4910 [M]	Brasilia Nueve	1967	30.00

GNP CRESCENDO

Number	Title	Yr	NM
❑ GNPS-2048 [S]	Puente Now!	197?	12.00

—Reissue of 70

Number	Title	Yr	NM
❑ GNP-70 [M]	The Exciting Tito Puente Band in Hollywood	196?	30.00

RCA VICTOR

Number	Title	Yr	NM
❑ LPM-2187 [M]	Cha Cha at Grossinger's	1959	30.00
❑ LSP-2187 [S]	Cha Cha at Grossinger's	1959	40.00
❑ LPM-1251 [M]	Cuban Carnival	1955	50.00
❑ LPM-1692 [M]	Dance Mania	1958	30.00
❑ LSP-1692 [S]	Dance Mania	1958	40.00
❑ LPM-1874 [M]	Dancing Under Latin Skies	1958	30.00
❑ LSP-1874 [S]	Dancing Under Latin Skies	1958	40.00
❑ LPM-1392 [M]	Let's Cha-Cha with Puente	1957	40.00
❑ LPM-1354 [M]	Mambo on Broadway	1957	40.00
❑ LPM-2113 [M]	Mucho Cha Cha Cha	1959	30.00
❑ LSP-2113 [S]	Mucho Cha Cha Cha	1959	40.00
❑ LPM-1479 [M]	Mucho Puente	1957	40.00
❑ LPM-1447 [M]	Night Beat	1957	40.00
❑ LPM-1312 [M]	Puente Goes Jazz	1956	60.00
❑ LPM-2299 [M]	Revolving Bandstand	1960	30.00
❑ LSP-2299 [S]	Revolving Bandstand	1960	40.00
❑ LPM-2257 [M]	Tambo	1960	30.00
❑ LSP-2257 [S]	Tambo	1960	40.00
❑ LPM-2974 [M]	The Best of Tito Puente	1964	30.00
❑ LSP-2974(e) [P]	The Best of Tito Puente	1964	18.00
❑ LSP-1617 [S]	Top Percussion	1958	40.00
❑ LPM-1617 [M]	Top Percussion	1958	30.00

ROULETTE

Number	Title	Yr	NM
❑ R-25193 [M]	Bossa Nova	1962	25.00
❑ SR-25193 [S]	Bossa Nova	1962	30.00
❑ R-25276 [M]	My Fair Lady" Goes Latin	1964	25.00
❑ SR-25276 [S]	My Fair Lady" Goes Latin	1964	30.00

TICO

Number	Title	Yr	NM
❑ LP-1151 [M]	20th Anniversary	1967	30.00
❑ SLP-1151 [S]	20th Anniversary	1967	25.00
❑ LP-1032 [M]	Basic Cha Cha Cha	1957	50.00
❑ LP-1127 [M]	Carnival in Harlem	196?	25.00
❑ SLP-1127 [S]	Carnival in Harlem	196?	30.00
❑ JMTS-1440	Ce' Magnifique	198?	18.00
❑ LP-128 [10]	Cha Cha Cha, Volume 1	195?	80.00
❑ LP-130 [10]	Cha Cha Cha, Volume 2	195?	80.00
❑ LP-134 [10]	Cha Cha Cha, Volume 3	195?	80.00
❑ LP-1025 [M]	Cha Cha Cha at the El Morocco	1956	60.00
❑ LP-1136 [M]	Cuba Y Puerto Ricon Son	196?	25.00
❑ SLP-1136 [S]	Cuba Y Puerto Ricon Son	196?	30.00
❑ JMTS-1439	Dance Mania 80's	198?	18.00
❑ LP-1010 [M]	Dance the Cha Cha Cha	195?	60.00
❑ LP-1116 [M]	De Mi Para Ti	196?	30.00
❑ SLP-1116 [S]	De Mi Para Ti	196?	30.00
❑ LP-1109 [M]	El Mundo Latino de Tito Puente	196?	30.00
❑ SLP-1109 [S]	El Mundo Latino de Tito Puente	196?	30.00
❑ SLP-1172	El Rey (The King)	1968	25.00
❑ LP-1086 [M]	El Rey Tito: Bravo Puente	1962	30.00
❑ SLP-1086 [S]	El Rey Tito: Bravo Puente	1962	40.00

—This album contains the original version of "Oye Como Va," later a hit for Santana

Number	Title	Yr	NM
❑ SLP-1154 [S]	El Rey Y Yo (The King and I)	1967	25.00
❑ LP-1154 [M]	El Rey Y Yo (The King and I)	1967	30.00
❑ LP-1106 [M]	Excitente Ritmo	196?	30.00
❑ SLP-1106 [S]	Excitente Ritmo	196?	30.00
❑ JMTS-1425	Homenaje a Beny More	1978	18.00
❑ LP-1131 [M]	Homenaje a Rafael Hernandez	196?	25.00
❑ SLP-1131 [S]	Homenaje a Rafael Hernandez	196?	30.00
❑ LP-133 [10]	Instrumental Mambos	195?	80.00
❑ JMTS-1430	La Pareja	1978	18.00
❑ LP-1003 [M]	Mambo and Me	1955	60.00
❑ LP-1001 [M]	Mamborama	1955	60.00
❑ LP-101 [10]	Mambos, Volume 1	1951	100.00
❑ LP-103 [10]	Mambos, Volume 2	1952	80.00
❑ LP-107 [10]	Mambos, Volume 3	195?	80.00
❑ LP-114 [10]	Mambos, Volume 4	195?	80.00
❑ LP-116 [10]	Mambos, Volume 5	195?	80.00
❑ LP-131 [10]	Mambos, Volume 8	195?	80.00
❑ LP-1006 [M]	Mambos for Lovers	1955	60.00
❑ LP-1115 [M]	Mucho Puente	196?	30.00
❑ SLP-1115 [S]	Mucho Puente	196?	30.00
❑ SLP-1083 [S]	Pachanga Con Puente	1961	40.00
❑ LP-1083 [M]	Pachanga Con Puente	1961	30.00
❑ SLP-1214	P'alante!	1970	25.00
❑ CLP-1301	Para Los Rumberos	1972	18.00
❑ LP-1058 [M]	Puente in Love	1959	40.00
❑ LP-1011 [M]	Puente in Percussion	1956	60.00
❑ SLP-1203	The Best of Tito Puente	1969	25.00
❑ LP-120 [10]	The King of the Mambo and His Orchestra	195?	80.00
❑ JMTS-1413	The Legend	1976	18.00
❑ CLP-1308	Tito Puente and His Concert Orchestra	1972	18.00
❑ LP-124 [10]	Tito Puente at the Vibes and His Rhythm Quartet	195?	80.00
❑ LP-1093 [M]	Tito Puente Bailables	1963	30.00
❑ SLP-1093 [S]	Tito Puente Bailables	1963	30.00
❑ SLP-1191	Tito Puente En El Puente (On the Bridge)	1969	25.00
❑ LP-1088 [M]	Tito Puente in Puerto Rico	1963	30.00
❑ SLP-1088 [S]	Tito Puente in Puerto Rico	1963	30.00
❑ SLP-1121 [S]	Tito Puente Swings/The Exciting Lupe Sings	196?	30.00
❑ LP-1121 [M]	Tito Puente Swings/The Exciting Lupe Sings	196?	25.00
❑ LP-1049 [M]	Tito Puente Swings/ Vicentico Valdes Sings	1958	50.00
❑ SLP-1125 [S]	Tu Y Yo (You 'n' Me)	196?	30.00
❑ LP-1125 [M]	Tu Y Yo (You 'n' Me)	196?	25.00
❑ CLP-1322	Unlimited Tito	1974	18.00
❑ LP-1085 [M]	Vaya Puente	1962	30.00
❑ SLP-1085 [S]	Vaya Puente	1962	40.00

PUFF DADDY

BAD BOY

Number	Title	Yr	NM
❑ 73012	No Way Out	1997	15.00

PUGSLEY MUNION

J&S

Number	Title	Yr	NM
❑ SLP-001	Just Like You	1969	100.00

PULLEN, DON, AND MILFORD GRAVES

PULLEN-GRAVES MUSIC

Number	Title	Yr	NM
❑ (# unknown)0	Graves-Pullen Duo	1967	50.00

S.R.P.

Number	Title	Yr	NM
❑ LP-290	Nommo	1968	40.00

PULLEN, WHITEY

CROWN

Number	Title	Yr	NM
❑ CLP-5332 [M]	Whitey Pullen	1963	40.00
❑ CST-332 [R]	Whitey Pullen	1963	15.00

PULLINS, LEROY

KAPP

Number	Title	Yr	NM
❑ KS-3557	Funny Bones and Hearts	1968	30.00
❑ KL-1488 [M]	I'm a Nut	1966	30.00
❑ KS-3488 [S]	I'm a Nut	1966	30.00

PULSE

POISON RING

Number	Title	Yr	NM
❑ 2237	Pulse	1969	30.00

PUMA, JOE

BETHLEHEM

Number	Title	Yr	NM
❑ BCP-1012 [10]	East Coast Jazz 3	1954	200.00

COLUMBIA

Number	Title	Yr	NM
❑ CL1618 [M]	Like Tweet	1961	30.00
❑ CS8418 [S]	Like Tweet	1961	40.00

DAWN

Number	Title	Yr	NM
❑ DLP-1118 [M]	Wild Kitten	1957	100.00

JUBILEE

Number	Title	Yr	NM
❑ JLP-1070 [M]	Joe Puma Jazz	1958	80.00

PURDIE, BERNARD

DATE

Number	Title	Yr	NM
❑ TEM3006 [M]	Soul Drums	1967	25.00
❑ TES4006 [S]	Soul Drums	1967	25.00

PRESTIGE

Number	Title	Yr	NM
❑ 10013	Purdie Good	1971	18.00
❑ 10038	Shaft	1972	25.00

PURE ENERGY

PRISM

Number	Title	Yr	NM
❑ PLP-1007	Pure Energy	1980	25.00

PURE PRAIRIE LEAGUE

CASABLANCA

Number	Title	Yr	NM
❑ NBLP-7212	Firin' Up	1980	12.00
❑ NBLP-7255	Something in the Night	1981	12.00

PAIR

Number	Title	Yr	NM
❑ PDL2-1034	Home on the Range	1986	15.00

RCA VICTOR

Number	Title	Yr	NM
❑ LSP-4769 [B]	Bustin' Out	1972	18.00
❑ AFL1-4769 [B]	Bustin' Out	1977	12.00

—Reissue of LSP-4769

Number	Title	Yr	NM
❑ AYL1-4656	Bustin' Out	1984	10.00

—Best Buy Series" reissue

Number	Title	Yr	NM
❑ AFL1-3335	Can't Hold Back	1979	15.00
❑ APL1-1924	Dance	1976	15.00
❑ AYL1-3723	Dance	1981	10.00

—Best Buy Series" reissue

Number	Title	Yr	NM
❑ APL1-1247	If the Shoe Fits	1976	15.00
❑ APD1-1247 [Q]	If the Shoe Fits	1976	25.00
❑ AYL1-3717	If the Shoe Fits	1981	10.00

—Best Buy Series" reissue

Number	Title	Yr	NM
❑ AFL1-2590	Just Fly	1978	15.00
❑ AYL1-3718	Just Fly	1981	10.00

—Best Buy Series" reissue

Number	Title	Yr	NM
❑ CPL2-2404	Live!! Takin' the Stage	1977	18.00
❑ LSP-4650	Pure Prairie League	1972	15.00
❑ AFL1-4650	Pure Prairie League	1977	12.00

—Reissue of LSP-4650

Number	Title	Yr	NM
❑ AYL1-3719	Pure Prairie League	1981	10.00

—Best Buy Series" reissue

Number	Title	Yr	NM
❑ APL1-0933	Two Lane Highway	1975	15.00
❑ APD1-0933 [Q]	Two Lane Highway	1975	25.00
❑ AYL1-3669	Two Lane Highway	1980	10.00

—Best Buy Series" reissue

PURIFY, JAMES AND BOBBY

BELL

Number	Title	Yr	NM
❑ 6003 [M]	James and Bobby Purify	1966	30.00
❑ S-6003 [S]	James and Bobby Purify	1966	30.00
❑ 6010 [M]	The Pure Sound of the Purifys	1967	30.00
❑ S-6010 [S]	The Pure Sound of the Purifys	1967	30.00

MERCURY

Number	Title	Yr	NM
❑ SRM-1-1134	The Purify Brothers	1977	15.00

PURIM, FLORA, AND AIRTO

CROSSOVER

Number	Title	Yr	NM
❑ CR-5001	The Magicians	1988	12.00
❑ CR-5003	The Sun Is Out	1989	18.00

GEORGE WEIN COLLECTION

Number	Title	Yr	NM
❑ GW-3007	Humble People	1986	12.00

PURIM, FLORA

FANTASY

Number	Title	Yr	NM
❑ OJC-315	Butterfly Dreams	1988	10.00

—Reissue of Milestone 9052

Number	Title	Yr	NM
❑ OJC-619	Stories to Tell	1991	15.00

—Reissue of Milestone 9058

MILESTONE

Number	Title	Yr	NM
❑ M-9070	500 Miles High	1976	15.00
❑ M-9052	Butterfly Dreams	1973	18.00

Number	Title	Yr	NM
❏ M-9077	Encounter	1977	18.00
❏ M-9095	Love Reborn	1980	15.00
❏ M-9075	Nothing Will Be As It Was... Tomorrow	1977	25.00
❏ M-9065	Open Your Eyes You Can Fly	1976	18.00
❏ M-9058	Stories to Tell	1974	18.00
❏ FPM-4005 [Q]	Stories to Tell	1975	30.00
❏ M-9081	That's What She Said	1978	15.00

VIRGIN

❏ 90995	The Midnight Sun	1988	15.00

WARNER BROS.

❏ BSK3344	Carry On	1979	18.00
❏ BSK3168	Everyday, Everynight	1978	15.00
❏ BS2985	Nothing Will Be As It Was... Tomorrow	1977	15.00

PURPLE GANG, THE

SIRE

❏ SES97006 [B]	The Purple Gang Strikes	1969	60.00

PURPLE IMAGE

MAP CITY

❏ 3015	Purple Image	1971	50.00

PURSELL, BILL

COLUMBIA

❏ CL2077 [M]	Chasing a Dream	1964	18.00
❏ CS8877 [S]	Chasing a Dream	1964	25.00
❏ CL1992 [M]	Our Winter Love	1963	18.00
❏ CS8792 [S]	Our Winter Love	1963	25.00
❏ CL2421 [M]	Remembered Love	1965	18.00
❏ CS9221 [S]	Remembered Love	1965	25.00

PUSSY GALORE

BUY OUR RECORDS

❏ 10 [EP]	Pussy Gold 5000	1986	50.00

CAROLINE

❏ CAROL1369	Dial "M" for Motherfucker	1989	30.00
❏ CAROL1337	Right Now!	1987	30.00

SHOVE

❏ 2	Groovy Hate Fuck	1986	50.00

PUTMAN, CURLY

ABC

❏ ABC-618 [M]	Lonesome	1967	30.00
❏ ABCS-618 [S]	Lonesome	1967	18.00
❏ ABCS-686	World of Country Music	1969	18.00

PUZZLE

ABC

❏ ABCS-671	Puzzle	1969	25.00

PYLE, ARTIMUS

MCA

❏ 5010 [D]	A P R	1982	30.00
❏ 39003	Nightcaller	1983	30.00

PYLE, JACK

CAMEO

❏ C-1017 [M]	Listen Son...And Other Readings by Jack Pyle	1963	25.00

PYRAMIDS, THE (1)

BEST

❏ LPM-1001 [M]	The Original Penetration! And Other Favorites	1964	250.00
— Original issue with "Walkin' the Dog"			
❏ BR16501 [M]	The Original Penetration! And Other Favorites	1964	200.00
— Reissue with "Road Runnah"			
❏ BS36501 [R]	The Original Penetration! And Other Favorites	1964	120.00

SUNDAZED

❏ LP-5012	Penetration! The Best of the Pyramids	1995	12.00

Q

Q-FEEL

JIVE/ARISTA

❏ VA66005	Q-Feel	1983	15.00

Q-TIP

ARISTA

❏ 14619	Amplified	1999	18.00

Q

EPIC

❏ PE34691	Dancin' Man	1977	15.00

QKUMBA ZOO

ARISTA

❏ ADP3251 [EP]	Qkumka Zoo	1996	12.00
— Five-song promo-only sampler			

Number	Title	Yr	NM

QUAD CITY DJ'S

BIG BEAT

❏ 82905	Get On Up and Dance	1996	12.00

QUADRANT

PABLO

❏ 2310837	Quardrant	1978	15.00

PABLO TODAY

❏ 2312117	Quardrant Toasts Duke Ellington/All Too Soon	1980	15.00

QUARTERFLASH

GEFFEN

❏ GHS24078 [B]	Back Into Blue	1985	12.00
❏ GHS2003 [B]	Quarterflash	1981	12.00
❏ GHS4011 [B]	Take Another Picture	1983	12.00

QUARTETTE TRES BIEN

ATLANTIC

❏ 1461 [M]	Bully!	1966	15.00
❏ SD1461 [S]	Bully!	1966	18.00

DECCA

❏ DL4547 [M]	Boss Tres Bien	1964	15.00
❏ DL74547 [S]	Boss Tres Bien	1964	18.00
❏ DL4958 [M]	Four of a Kind	1967	18.00
❏ DL74958 [S]	Four of a Kind	1967	15.00
❏ DL4893 [M]	Here It Is	1967	18.00
❏ DL74893 [S]	Here It Is	1967	15.00
❏ DL4791 [M]	In" Motion	1966	15.00
❏ DL74791 [S]	In" Motion	1966	18.00
❏ DL4548 [M]	Kilimanjaro	1964	15.00
❏ DL74548 [S]	Kilimanjaro	1964	18.00
❏ DL75044	Our Thing	1969	15.00
❏ DL4715 [M]	Sky High	1966	15.00
❏ DL74715 [S]	Sky High	1966	18.00
❏ DL4617 [M]	Spring Into Spring	1965	15.00
❏ DL74617 [S]	Spring Into Spring	1965	18.00
❏ DL4675 [M]	Stepping Out	1965	15.00
❏ DL74675 [S]	Stepping Out	1965	18.00
❏ DL4822 [M]	Where It's At	1966	15.00
❏ DL74822 [S]	Where It's At	1966	18.00

GNP

❏ GNP-107 [M]	Kilimanjaro	1963	25.00
❏ GNPS-107 [S]	Kilimanjaro	1963	30.00
❏ GNP-102 [M]	Quartette Tres Bien	1962	25.00
❏ GNPS-102 [S]	Quartette Tres Bien	1962	30.00

QUARTZ

MARLIN

❏ 2216	Quartz	1978	15.00

POLYDOR

❏ PD-1-6203	Camel in the City	1979	18.00

QUATEMAN, DILL

COLUMBIA

❏ KC31761	Bill Quateman	1973	15.00

RCA VICTOR

❏ AFL1-2879	Just Like You	1979	12.00
❏ APL1-2027	Night After Night	1977	12.00
❏ APL1-2434	Shot in the Dark	1977	12.00

QUATERMASS

HARVEST

❏ SKAO-314 [B]	Quatermass	1970	50.00

QUATRO, MICHAEL

EVOLUTION

❏ 3021	Look Deeply Into the Mirror	1973	30.00
— As "Mike Quatro Jam Band"			
❏ 3011	Paintings	1972	30.00
— As "Mike Quatro Jam Band"			

KOALA

❏ KOA14631	Into the Mirror	1979	18.00
— New version of similar 1973 album on Evolution			

PRODIGAL

❏ P6-10010S1 [B]	Dancers, Romancers, Dreamers and Schemers	1976	18.00
❏ P6-10016S1	Gettin' Ready	1977	18.00

SPECTOR

❏ SW-70003	Bottom Line	1981	18.00

UNITED ARTISTS

❏ UA-LA420-G	In Collaboration with the Gods	1975	25.00

QUATRO, SUZI

ARISTA

❏ AL4035 [B]	Your Mama Won't Like Me	1975	15.00

BELL

❏ 1313 [B]	Quatro	1974	18.00
❏ 1302	Suzi Quatro	1974	18.00

DREAMLAND

❏ DL-1-5006	Rock Hard	1980	12.00

RSO

❏ RS-1-3044	If You Knew Suzi...	1979	12.00

Number	Title	Yr	NM
❏ RS-1-3064	Suzi...And Other Four Letter Words	1980	12.00

QUATTLEBAUM, DOUG

BLUESVILLE

❏ BVLP-1065 [M]	Softee Man Blues	1963	60.00
— Blue label, silver print			
❏ BVLP-1065 [M]	Softee Man Blues	1964	25.00
— Blue label, trident logo at right			

QUEBEC, IKE

BLUE NOTE

❏ BLP-4098 [M]	Blue and Sentimental	1962	85.00
— With "New York, USA" address on label			
❏ BST-84098 [S]	Blue and Sentimental	1962	25.00
— With "New York, USA" address on label			
❏ BLP-4098 [M]	Blue and Sentimental	1962	80.00
— With 61st St. address on label			
❏ BST-84098 [S]	Blue and Sentimental	1962	60.00
— With 61st St. address on label			
❏ BST-84098 [S]	Blue and Sentimental	1967	15.00
— With "A Division of Liberty Records" on label			
❏ BST-84098 [S]	Blue and Sentimental	1986	12.00
— The Finest in Jazz Since 1939" reissue			
❏ BLP-4114 [M]	Bossa Nova Soul Samba	1962	30.00
❏ BST-84114 [S]	Bossa Nova Soul Samba	1962	40.00
— With "New York, USA" address on label			
❏ BST-84114 [S]	Bossa Nova Soul Samba	1967	18.00
— With "A Division of Liberty Records" on label			
❏ BST-84103 [S]	Easy Living	1987	15.00
— The Finest in Jazz Since 1939" issue; originally scheduled for 1962 release			
❏ BLP-4093 [M]	Heavy Soul	1962	30.00
— With "New York, USA" address on label			
❏ BST-84093 [S]	Heavy Soul	1961	25.00
— With "New York, USA" address on label			
❏ BLP-4093 [M]	Heavy Soul	1961	80.00
— With 61st St. address on label			
❏ BST-84093 [S]	Heavy Soul	1961	60.00
— With 61st St. address on label			
❏ BST-84093 [S]	Heavy Soul	1967	15.00
— With "A Division of Liberty Records" on label			
❏ B1-32090	Heavy Soul	1995	18.00
— The Finest in Jazz Since 1939" reissue			
❏ BLP-4105 [M]	It Might As Well Be Spring	1962	30.00
❏ BST-84105 [S]	It Might As Well Be Spring	1962	40.00
— With "New York, USA" address on label			
❏ BST-84105 [S]	It Might As Well Be Spring	1967	18.00
— With "A Division of Liberty Records" on label			
❏ BST-84114	Soul Samba	199?	30.00
— Classic Records reissue on audiophile vinyl			
❏ LT-1052	With a Song in My Heart	1980	12.00

MOSAIC

❏ MR3-121	The Complete Blue Note 45 Sessions of Ike Quebec	199?	60.00
❏ MR4-107	The Complete Blue Note Forties Recordings of Ike Quebec and John Hardee	199?	70.00

QUEEN & PAUL RODGERS

HOLLYWOOD

❏ D261601 [B]	The Cosmos Rocks	2008	30.00

QUEEN

CAPITOL

❏ SMAS-12476	A Kind of Magic	1986	12.00
❏ C1-92357	The Miracle	1989	18.00
❏ ST-12322	The Works	1984	12.00

DCC COMPACT CLASSICS

❏ LPZ-2072 [B]	A Night at the Opera	2000	150.00
— Audiophile vinyl			

ELEKTRA

❏ 6E-101 [B]	A Day at the Races	1977	12.00
— Butterfly, red, or red/black labels			
❏ 7E-1053	A Night at the Opera	1975	12.00
— Butterfly, red, or red/black labels			
❏ 60128	Hot Space	1982	12.00
❏ 6E-166 [B]	Jazz	1978	18.00
— With poster of the nude bicycle race			
❏ 6E-166	Jazz	1978	10.00
— Without poster of the nude bicycle race. Some copies had a sticker on the shrink wrap with an address at which the poster was available free.			
❏ BB-702	Live Killers	1979	15.00
❏ 6E-112 [DJ]	News of the World	1977	150.00
— White label promo with oversize cover and press kit			
❏ 6E-112	News of the World	1977	12.00
❏ EKS-75064 [DJ]	Queen	1973	50.00
— White label promo			
❏ EKS-75064	Queen	1973	30.00
— With "Queen" gold-embossed on the cover			
❏ EKS-75064	Queen	1973	12.00
— With "Queen" printed on the cover; butterfly, red, or red/black labels			
❏ EQ-5064 [Q]	Queen	1973	40.00
❏ EKS-75082 [DJ]	Queen II	1974	50.00
— White label promo			

Number	Title	Yr	NM
❏ EKS-75082	Queen II	1974	12.00
—Butterfly, red, or red/black labels			
❏ 5E-564	Queen's Greatest Hits	1981	15.00
❏ 7E-1026 [DJ]	Sheer Heart Attack	1974	50.00
—White label promo			
❏ 7E-1026	Sheer Heart Attack	1974	12.00
—Butterfly, red, or red/black labels			
❏ 5E-513	The Game	1980	18.00
—With shiny, mirrorlike cover; all copies have custom white labels			
❏ 5E-513	The Game	1980	12.00
—With dull gray cover; all copies have custom white labels			
HOLLYWOOD			
❏ D262101	A Day at the Races	2008	25.00
❏ D436601	A Kind of Magic	2009	25.00
❏ D262001	A Night at the Opera	2008	25.00
❏ D436501	Flash Gordon	2009	25.00
❏ D436701	Innuendo	2009	25.00
❏ D002083101 [B]	Live at the Rainbow '74	2014	250.00
❏ 62017	Made in Heaven	1996	25.00
—White vinyl; imported from Europe; the only distinguishing mark to make this a U.S. version is the Hollywood bar code, which was stuck to the shrink wrap			
❏ D436401	News of the World	2009	25.00
❏ D436301	Queen	2009	25.00
❏ ED-62005 [PD]	Queen at the BBC	1995	100.00
—Promo-only picture disc (no U.S. stock vinyl)			
❏ D261801	Queen II	2008	25.00
❏ D261901 [B]	Sheer Heart Attack	2008	25.00
MOBILE FIDELITY			
❏ 1-256 [B]	A Day at the Races	1996	120.00
—Audiophile vinyl			
❏ 1-067 [B]	A Night at the Opera	1980	100.00
—Audiophile vinyl			
❏ 1-211	The Game	1995	90.00
—Audiophile vinyl			

QUEEN CITY RAGTIME ENSEMBLE

STOMP OFF

❏ SOS-1138	Everybody's Rag	1987	12.00

QUEEN LATIFAH

MOTOWN

❏ 530895-1	Order in the Court	1998	18.00
❏ 37463	Order in the Court	1998	18.00
08951 [DJ]			
—Promo-only eight-song sampler from LP			

TOMMY BOY

❏ TB1022	All Hail the Queen	1989	18.00
❏ TB1035	Nature of a Sista'	1991	18.00

QUEEN PEN

INTERSCOPE

❏ INT2-90151	My Melody	1997	18.00
MOTOWN			
❏ 013785-1	Conversations with Queen	2001	15.00

QUEEN'S NECTORINE MACHINE, THE

ABC

❏ S-666	The Mystical Powers of Roving Tarot Gamble	1969	40.00

QUEENS OF THE STONE AGE

IPECAC

❏ IPC-41 [B]	Songs for the Deaf	2002	25.00
MAN'S RUIN			
❏ MR151	Queens of the Stone Age	1998	120.00
—2,500 copies on black vinyl; beware of counterfeits; counterfeits lack "MR 151" in the trail-off wax			
❏ MR151	Queens of the Stone Age	1998	250.00
—Approximately 200 copies on green vinyl			
❏ MR151	Queens of the Stone Age	1998	250.00
—Approximately 200 copies on blue vinyl			
❏ MR151	Queens of the Stone Age	1998	250.00
—Approximately 300 copies on orange-yellow vinyl			

QUEENSRYCHE

206 RECORDS

❏ R-101 [EP]	Queensryche	1983	75.00
EMI			
❏ E1-92806 [B]	Empire	1990	18.00
❏ E1-30711 [B]	Promised Land	1994	30.00
EMI AMERICA			
❏ MLP-19006 [EP]	Queensryche	1983	15.00
❏ SPRO-	Queensryche	1983	40.00
MLP-19006 [DJ]			
—White label version in film can			
❏ ST-17197	Rage for Order	1986	12.00
—Black circle on front cover			
❏ ST-17197	Rage for Order	1986	18.00
—Blue circle on front cover			
❏ ST-17134 [DJ]	The Warning	1984	40.00
—Promo-only "High Quality Vinyl" pressing			
❏ ST-17134	The Warning	1984	12.00

EMI MANHATTAN

❏ E1-48640	Operation: Mindcrime	1988	15.00
❏ SPRO-	Operation: Mindcrime	1988	80.00
04136/7 [PD]			
—Promo-only picture disc			
❏ SPRO-	Speak the Word	1988	25.00
04194 [DJ]			
—Promo-only interview album			

RHINO

❏ R1-73306	Operation: Mindcrime II	2006	25.00

QUEERS, THE

CLEARVIEW

❏ 0(no # ?) [B]	Suck This	1995	30.00
—Picture disc			
HOPELESS			
❏ HR643	Beyond the Valley of the Assfuckers	2000	12.00
❏ HR636 [B]	Punk Rock Confidential	1998	25.00
LOOKOUT!			
❏ LK 081	Beat Off	199?	12.00
❏ LK140	Don't Back Down	1996	12.00
❏ LK 090	Grow Up	1995	12.00
—Reissue of rare Shakin' Street original			
❏ LK 066	Love Songs for the Retarded	199?	12.00
❏ LK114 [B]	Move Back Home	1995	18.00
SELFLESS			
❏ SFLS-28	Rocket to Russia	1994	25.00
—Tour edition; 300 on pink vinyl			
SHAKIN' STREET			
❏ 010	Grow Up	1990	200.00
—Only 100-150 copies exist of a planned pressing of 500 (others were destroyed at the plant)			

? (QUESTION MARK) AND THE MYSTERIANS

CAMEO

❏ C-2004 [M]	96 Tears	1966	100.00
❏ CS-2004 [P]	96 Tears	1966	80.00
—96 Tears," "I Need Somebody," "Up Side" and "8-Teen" are rechanneled			
❏ C-2006 [M]	Action	1967	150.00
❏ CS-2006 [P]	Action	1967	100.00
—Don't Hold It Against Me," "Like a Rose" and "Girl (You Captivate Me)" are rechanneled			
COLLECTABLES			
❏ COL2004 [B]	Featuring 96 Tears	1997	15.00
—Re-recorded tracks; orange vinyl			
NORTON			
❏ 262 [B]	Do You Feel It Baby?	1998	18.00
—Live album recorded in 1997			

QUICKSILVER MESSENGER SERVICE

CAPITOL

❏ SVBB-11165	Anthology	1973	25.00
❏ SMAS-11002	Comin' Thru	1972	18.00
❏ ST-120	Happy Trails	1969	30.00
—Black label with colorband			
❏ ST-120 [B]	Happy Trails	1973	15.00
—Orange label			
❏ SN-16090	Happy Trails	1980	10.00
—Budget-line reissue			
❏ SMAS-498	Just for Love	1970	30.00
—Lime green label			
❏ SMAS-498	Just for Love	1973	15.00
—Orange label			
❏ SN-16093	Just for Love	1980	10.00
—Budget-line reissue			
❏ ST-12496	Peace By Piece	1986	12.00
❏ SW-819	Quicksilver	1971	30.00
—Red label with stylized "C" at top			
❏ SW-819	Quicksilver	1973	15.00
—Orange label			
❏ SN-16091	Quicksilver	1980	10.00
—Budget-line reissue			
❏ ST2904	Quicksilver Messenger Service	1968	40.00
—Black label with colorband; glossy black cover with red and silver foil-like printing			
❏ ST-2904	Quicksilver Messenger Service	1969	25.00
—Lime green or red label			
❏ ST-2904 [B]	Quicksilver Messenger Service	1973	15.00
—Orange label			
❏ SN-16089	Quicksilver Messenger Service	1980	10.00
—Budget-line reissue			
❏ SKAO-391	Shady Grove	1969	30.00
—Lime green label			
❏ SKAO-391	Shady Grove	1973	15.00
—Orange label			
❏ SN-16094	Shady Grove	1980	10.00
—Budget-line reissue			
❏ SM-391	Shady Grove	1976	12.00
—Reissue on yellow label and new prefix			

❏ ST-11462	Solid Silver	1975	18.00
❏ SM-11820	Solid Silver	1978	12.00
—Reissue of 11462			
❏ SMAS-630	What About Me	1970	30.00
—Lime green label			
❏ SMAS-630	What About Me	1973	15.00
—Orange label			
❏ SN-16092	What About Me	1980	10.00
—Budget-line reissue			
CLEOPATRA			
❏ CLP1559 [B]	Fillmore Auditorium, Nov. 5th, 1966	2014	40.00
❏ CLP0432 [B]	Live At The Fillmore June 7,1968	2013	35.00
❏ CLP0795 [B]	Live At The Winterland Ballroom, December 1, 1973	2013	35.00

QUIET RIOT

PASHA

❏ QZ39516 [B]	Condition Critical	1984	10.00
❏ 8Z839203	Metal Health	1983	25.00
—Picture disc in plastic sleeve with sticker			
❏ BFZ38443	Metal Health	1983	10.00
—Original edition with full prefix			
❏ FZ38443 [B]	Metal Health	1983	10.00
—Later edition with shorter prefix			
❏ OZ40321	QR III	1986	10.00
❏ OZ40981	Quiet Riot	1988	10.00

QUIET SUN

ANTILLES

❏ AN-7008 [B]	Mainstream	1975	30.00

QUIGLEY, JACK

SAND

❏ C-30 [M]	Class In Session	196?	30.00
—Red vinyl; may or may not exist on black vinyl			
❏ CS-30 [S]	Class In Session	196?	25.00
❏ C-38 [M]	D'Jever	196?	25.00
❏ CS-38 [S]	D'Jever	196?	30.00
❏ C-28 [M]	Jack Quigley in Hollywood	196?	30.00
—Red vinyl; may or may not exist on black vinyl			
❏ CS-28 [S]	Jack Quigley in Hollywood	196?	25.00
❏ C-32 [M]	Listen! Quigley	196?	30.00
—Red vinyl; may or may not exist on black vinyl			
❏ CS-32 [S]	Listen! Quigley	196?	25.00

QUILL, GENE

ROOST

❏ LP-2229 [M]	Three Bones and a Quill	1958	50.00

QUILL

COTILLION

❏ SD9017 [B]	Quill	1970	30.00

QUINICHETTE, PAUL, AND FRANK FOSTER

DECCA

❏ DL8058 [M]	Jazz Studio 1	1954	100.00

QUINICHETTE, PAUL

BIOGRAPH

❏ BLP-12066	The Kid from Denver	199?	15.00
DAWN			
❏ DLP-1109 [M]	The Kid from Denver	1956	100.00
EMARCY			
❏ MG-36003 [M]	Moods	1955	120.00
❏ MG-26035 [10]	Sequel	1954	250.00
❏ MG-26022 [10]	The Vice 'Pres'	1954	250.00
❏ MG-36027 [M]	The Vice 'Pres'	1955	120.00
FANTASY			
❏ OJC-076	On the Sunny Side	198?	15.00
PRESTIGE			
❏ PRLP-7147 [M]	Basie Reunion	1958	100.00
❏ P-24109	Basie Reunions	198?	18.00
❏ PRLP-7127 [M]	For Basie	1957	120.00
—Yellow label with W. 50th St. address			
❏ PRLP-7103 [M]	On the Sunny Side	1957	150.00
—Yellow label with W. 50th St. address			
STATUS			
❏ ST-2036 [M]	For Basie	1966	25.00
—Reissue of Swingville 2036			
SWINGVILLE			
❏ SVLP-2037 [M]	Basie Reunion	1962	50.00
—Purple label			
❏ SVLP-2037 [M]	Basie Reunion	1965	30.00
—Blue label, trident logo at right			
❏ SVLP-2036 [M]	For Basie	1965	30.00
—Blue label, trident logo at right			
❏ SVLP-2036 [M]	For Basie	1962	50.00
—Purple label			
TRIP			
❏ TLP-5542	The Vice 'Pres'	197?	30.00
UNITED ARTISTS			
❏ UAL-4024 [M]	Like Basie	1959	50.00

Number	Title	Yr	NM
❏ UAS-5024 [S]	Like Basie	1959	40.00
❏ UAL-4054 [M]	Like Who?	1959	40.00
❏ UAS-5054 [S]	Like Who?	1959	30.00
❏ UAL-4077 [M]	Paul Quinichette	1960	40.00
❏ UAS-5077 [S]	Paul Quinichette	1960	50.00

QUINICHETTE, PAUL/GENE ROLAND

DAWN
| ❏ DLP-1112 [M] | Jazzville | 1957 | 100.00 |

QUINN, ANTHONY

CAPITOL
| ❏ ST-116 [B] | In My Own Way... I Love You | 1969 | 30.00 |

R

R.E.M.

A&M
| ❏ B1301501 | Murmur | 2009 | 25.00 |
| ❏ B1302901 | Reckoning | 2009 | 25.00 |

I.R.S.
❏ SP-70502 [EP]	Chronic Town	1982	15.00
—Original pressings have a custom gargoyle label			
❏ SP-70054	Dead Letter Office	1987	15.00
❏ R163503	Document	1987	15.00
—BMG Direct Marketing edition			
❏ 42059 [B]	Document	1987	12.00
❏ R100701	Eponymous	1988	15.00
—BMG Direct Marketing edition			
❏ 6262	Eponymous	1988	12.00
❏ 5592	Fables of the Reconstruction	1985	15.00
❏ R173669	Lifes Rich Pageant	1986	14.00
—RCA Music Service edition			
❏ 5783	Lifes Rich Pageant	1986	15.00
❏ SP-70014	Murmur	1983	15.00
—Reissue?			
❏ SP-70604	Murmur	1983	18.00
—Original number?			
❏ SP-70044	Reckoning	1984	15.00

MOBILE FIDELITY
❏ 1-231	Murmur	1995	50.00
—Audiophile vinyl			
❏ 1-261	Reckoning	1996	80.00
—Audiophile vinyl			

RHINO
| ❏ R1541570 [B] | Unplugged 1991 & 2001 - The Complete Sessions | 2014 | 40.00 |

WARNER BROS.
❏ 418620	Accelerate	2008	30.00
❏ R1-78422	Around the Sun	2004	25.00
❏ 45055 [B]	Automatic for the People	1992	18.00
❏ R100715	Green	1988	15.00
—BMG Direct Marketing edition			
❏ 25795	Green	1988	15.00
❏ W1-25795	Green	1988	18.00
—Columbia House edition			
❏ 45740 [B]	Monster	1994	25.00
❏ 46320 [B]	New Adventures in Hi-Fi	1996	30.00
❏ R124762 [B]	Out of Time	1991	30.00
—BMG Direct Marketing edition; one of the last BMG vinyl releases			
❏ 26496 [B]	Out of Time	1991	25.00
❏ 303740	R.E.M. Live	2008	40.00
❏ 47946	Reveal	2001	25.00
❏ PRO-A-3377 [DJ]	Should We Talk About the Weather?	1988	40.00
—Promo-only interviews and music			
❏ 47112	Up	1998	18.00

R.P.S.

MARS
| ❏ (# unknown)0 | R.P.S. | 197? | 80.00 |

RABBITT, EDDIE

ELEKTRA
❏ CM-3	Eddie Rabbitt	1975	18.00
❏ 6E-276	Horizon	1980	12.00
❏ 6E-181	Loveline	1979	12.00
❏ 7E-1105	Rabbitt	1977	18.00
—Butterfly label			
❏ 7E-1105	Rabbitt	198?	10.00
—Red label			
❏ 60160	Radio Romance	1982	12.00
❏ 7E-1065	Rocky Mountain Music	1976	18.00
—Butterfly label			
❏ 7E-1065	Rocky Mountain Music	198?	10.00
—Red label			
❏ 5E-532	Step by Step	1981	12.00
❏ 6E-235	The Best of Eddie Rabbitt	1979	12.00
❏ 6E-127	Variations	1978	15.00

RCA
| ❏ 6373-1-R | I Wanna Dance with You | 1988 | 10.00 |

RCA VICTOR
| ❏ AHL1-7041 | Rabbitt Trax | 1986 | 10.00 |

WARNER BROS.
❏ 25278	#1's	1985	12.00
❏ 23925	Greatest Hits, Volume II	1983	12.00
❏ 6E-276	Horizon	1983	10.00
—Reissue of Elektra LP			
❏ 6E-181	Loveline	1983	10.00
—Reissue of Elektra LP			
❏ 60160	Radio Romance	1983	10.00
—Reissue of Elektra LP			
❏ 7E-1065	Rocky Mountain Music	1983	10.00
—Reissue of Elektra LP			
❏ 5E-532	Step by Step	1983	10.00
—Reissue of Elektra LP			
❏ 6E-235	The Best of Eddie Rabbitt	1983	10.00
—Reissue of Elektra LP			
❏ 25251	The Best Year of My Life	1984	12.00
❏ 6E-127	Variations	1983	10.00
—Reissue of Elektra LP			

RABBITT, JIMMY

CAPITOL
| ❏ ST-11491 | Jimmy Rabbitt and Renegade | 1976 | 15.00 |

RABBLE, THE

ROULETTE
| ❏ SR-42010 | The Rabble | 1968 | 150.00 |

RACHABANE, BARNEY

JIVE
| ❏ 1253-1-J | Barney's Way | 1989 | 15.00 |

RACKET SQUAD, THE

JUBILEE
| ❏ JGS-8026 | Corners of Your Mind | 1969 | 40.00 |
| ❏ JGS-8015 | The Racket Squad | 1968 | 40.00 |

RACONTEURS, THE

ELEKTRA
❏ 60815 [DJ]	Blind Man's Zoo	1989	18.00
—Promo-only audiophile pressing (promo labels)			
❏ 60738 [DJ]	In My Tribe	1987	15.00
—Promo-only audiophile pressing			
❏ 5270 [DJ]	Interview	1987	30.00
—Lenny Kaye interviews Natalie Merchant; promo only			

RADER, DON

DISCOVERY
| ❏ 796 | Wallflower | 1979 | 15.00 |

PBR
| ❏ 10 | Now | 197? | 15.00 |

RADICE, MARK

PARAMOUNT
| ❏ PAS-6033 | Mark Radice | 1972 | 40.00 |

ROADSHOW
| ❏ RS-LA788-G | Intense | 1977 | 18.00 |

UNITED ARTISTS
| ❏ UA-LA629-G | Ain't Nothin' But a Party | 1976 | 18.00 |

RAE, CHARLOTTE

VANGUARD
| ❏ VRS-9004 [M] | Songs I Taught My Mother | 1956 | 40.00 |

RAE, JOHN

SAVOY
| ❏ MG-12156 [M] | Opus De Jazz, Volume 2 | 1960 | 40.00 |

RAEBURN, BOYD

AIRCHECK
| ❏ 20 | Rhythms by Boyd Raeburn | 197? | 12.00 |

CIRCLE
| ❏ 22 | Boyd Raeburn and His Orchestra 1944-45 | 198? | 12.00 |
| ❏ CLP-113 | More Boyd Raeburn and His Orchestra 1944-45 | 1987 | 12.00 |

COLUMBIA
❏ CL889 [M]	Dance Spectacular	1956	40.00
❏ CL957 [M]	Fraternity Rush	1957	40.00
❏ CL1073 [M]	Teen Rock	1958	50.00

MUSICRAFT
| ❏ 505 | Experiments in Big Band Jazz 1945 | 198? | 12.00 |

SAVOY
❏ MG-12040 [M]	Boyd Meets Stravinsky	1955	80.00
❏ MG-15010 [10]	Innovations by Boyd Raeburn, Volume 1	1951	150.00
❏ MG-15011 [10]	Innovations by Boyd Raeburn, Volume 2	1951	150.00
❏ MG-15012 [10]	Innovations by Boyd Raeburn, Volume 3	1951	150.00
❏ MG-12025 [M]	Man With the Horns	1955	80.00

SAVOY JAZZ
| ❏ SJL-2250 | Jewels Plus | 1980 | 30.00 |
| ❏ SJC-406 | Man With the Horns | 1985 | 18.00 |

RAELETTS, THE

TANGERINE
| ❏ TRCS-1515 | Yesterday, Today, Tomorrow | 1972 | 18.00 |

RAFF, RENEE

AUDIO FIDELITY
| ❏ AFLP-2142 [M] | Among the Stars | 1965 | 18.00 |
| ❏ AFSD-6142 [S] | Among the Stars | 1965 | 25.00 |

RAFFERTY, GERRY

ABC/BLUE THUMB
| ❏ 6031 | Can I Have My Money Back? | 1978 | 15.00 |

BLUE THUMB
| ❏ BTS-58 | Can I Have My Money Back? | 1973 | 25.00 |

LIBERTY
❏ LO-840	City to City	1981	10.00
—Reissue of United Artists 840			
❏ LOO-958	Night and Day	1981	10.00
—Reissue of United Artists 958			
❏ LT-51132	Sleepwalking	1982	12.00
❏ LOO-1039	Snakes and Ladders	1981	10.00
—Reissue of United Artists 1039			

MOBILE FIDELITY
| ❏ 1-058 [B] | City to City | 1980 | 50.00 |
| —Audiophile vinyl | | | |

PARLOPHONE
| ❏ 825646321933 [B] | City to City | 2014 | 30.00 |

POLYDOR
| ❏ 835449-1 | North and South | 1988 | 12.00 |

UNITED ARTISTS
❏ UA-LA840-H	City to City	1978	12.00
❏ UA-LA958-I	Night Owl	1979	12.00
❏ LOO-1039	Snakes and Ladders	1980	12.00

VISA
| ❏ 7006 [B] | Gerry Rafferty | 1978 | 15.00 |
| —Reissue of Blue Thumb material | | | |

RAFFI

MCA
| ❏ 10043 | Raffi's Christmas Album | 1990 | 18.00 |
| —Reissue of Shoreline LP | | | |

SHORELINE
❏ SL-0226	Raffi's Christmas Album	1983	12.00
❏ R154088	Raffi's Christmas Album	198?	18.00
—Same as above, but BMG Direct Marketing edition			

RAGE AGAINST THE MACHINE

EPIC
❏ E57523	Evil Empire	1996	25.00
❏ E52959	Rage Against The Machine	1996	25.00
—CD and cassette released in 1992			
❏ E69630	The Battle of Los Angeles	1999	25.00

RAGTIME BANJO COMMISSION, THE

GHB
| ❏ GHB-154 | The Ragtime Banjo Commission | 1981 | 12.00 |

RAHIM, EMANUEL K., AND THE KAHLIQA

COBBLESTONE
| ❏ 9014 | Total Submission | 1972 | 30.00 |

RAIDERS, THE (3)

LIBERTY
| ❏ LRP-3225 [M] | Twistin' the Country Classics | 1962 | 30.00 |
| ❏ LST-7225 [S] | Twistin' the Country Classics | 1962 | 30.00 |

RAIN

PROJECT 3
| ❏ PR5072SD | New Rock Group | 1972 | 30.00 |

WHAZOO
| ❏ USR-3049 | Live Christmas Night | 1969 | 150.00 |
| —Issued with no cover | | | |

RAINBOW

MERCURY
❏ 815305-1	Bent Out of Shape	1983	12.00
❏ 827987-1	Finyl Vinyl	1986	14.00
❏ SRM-1-4041	Straight Between the Eyes	1982	12.00

OYSTER
❏ OY-2-1801	On Stage	1977	18.00
❏ OY-1-1601	Rainbow Rising	1976	15.00
❏ OY-6049	Ritchie Blackmore's Rainbow	1975	18.00

POLYDOR
❏ PD-1-6316	Difficult to Cure	1981	12.00
❏ 825383-1	Difficult to Cure	1985	10.00
—Reissue			
❏ PD-1-6221	Down to Earth	1979	12.00

Number	Title	Yr	NM
❑ 823705-1	Down to Earth	1985	10.00
—Reissue			
❑ PX-1-502 [EP]	Jealous Lover	1981	10.00
❑ PD-1-6143	Long Live Rock 'n' Roll	1978	12.00
❑ 825090-1	Long Live Rock 'n' Roll	1985	10.00
—Reissue			
❑ 823656-1	On Stage	1985	15.00
—Reissue			
❑ 823655-1	Rainbow Rising	1985	10.00
—Reissue			

RAINBOW (2)

GNP CRESCENDO
❑ GNPS-2049	After the Storm	1969	30.00

RAINBOW (3)

INNER CITY
❑ IC-6001	Crystal Green	197?	18.00

RAINBOW PRESS, THE

MR. G
❑ 9004	Sunday Funnies	1969	30.00
❑ 9003	There's a War On	1968	30.00

RAINBOW PROMISE, THE

NEW WINE
❑ LPS-251-01	The Rainbow Promise	1970	300.00

RAINCOATS, THE

ROUGH TRADE
❑ ROUGH US13 [B]	Odyshape	1981	40.00

SOUNDS LIKE
❑ 12 [EP]	The Raincoats	1994	25.00

RAINDROPS, THE (1)

JUBILEE
❑ JGM-5023 [M]	The Raindrops	1963	150.00
❑ JGS-5023 [S]	The Raindrops	1963	300.00

RAINEY, CHUCK

COBBLESTONE
❑ 9008	Chuck Rainey Coalition	1972	25.00

RAINEY, MA

BIOGRAPH
❑ LP-12001	Blues the World Forgot	1968	18.00
❑ LP-12011	Oh My Babe Blues	197?	15.00
❑ LP-12032	Queen of the Blues	197?	15.00

MILESTONE
❑ 2008	Blame It on the Blues	196?	18.00
❑ 2017	Down in the Basement	197?	15.00
❑ 2001	Immortal Ma Rainey	1967	18.00
❑ 47021	Ma Rainey	197?	18.00

RIVERSIDE
❑ RLP 12-137 [M]	Broken Hearted Blues	1956	100.00
❑ RLP 12-108 [M]	Ma Rainey	1955	200.00
❑ RLP-1003 [10]	Ma Rainey, Vol. 1	1953	250.00
❑ RLP-1016 [10]	Ma Rainey, Vol. 2	1953	250.00
❑ RLP-1045 [10]	Ma Rainey, Vol. 3	1954	250.00

RAINFORD, TINA

EPIC
❑ KE35034	Silver Angel	1977	15.00

RAINWATER, MARVIN

CROWN
❑ CLP-5307 [M]	Marvin Rainwater	196?	15.00
❑ CST-307 [R]	Marvin Rainwater	196?	15.00

GUEST STAR
❑ GS-1435 [M]	Country and Western Star	196?	15.00

MGM
❑ E-4046 [M]	Gonna Find Me a Bluebird	1962	80.00
❑ SE-4046 [R]	Gonna Find Me a Bluebird	1962	50.00
❑ E-3721 [M]	Marvin Rainwater Sings with a Beat	1958	120.00
❑ E-3534 [M]	Songs by Marvin Rainwater	1957	150.00

SPIN-O-RAMA
❑ SPM-109 [M]	Golden Country Hits	196?	15.00

RAINY DAZE, THE

UNI
❑ 3002 [M]	That Acapulco Gold	1967	25.00
❑ 73002 [S]	That Acapulco Gold	1967	30.00

RAITT, BONNIE

CAPITOL
❑ C1-96111	Luck of the Draw	1991	18.00
❑ C1-91268	Nick of Time	1989	15.00

DCC COMPACT CLASSICS
❑ LPZ-2031	Luck of the Draw	1997	80.00
—Audiophile vinyl			
❑ LPZ-2025	Nick of Time	1996	80.00
—Audiophile vinyl			

WARNER BROS.
Number	Title	Yr	NM
❑ WS1953	Bonnie Raitt	1971	18.00
—Green "WB" label			
❑ WS1953	Bonnie Raitt	1973	15.00
—Burbank" palm trees label			
❑ WS1953	Bonnie Raitt	1979	10.00
—White or tan label			
❑ BS2643	Give It Up	1972	18.00
—Green "WB" label			
❑ BS2643	Give It Up	1973	15.00
—Burbank" palm trees label			
❑ BS2643	Give It Up	1979	10.00
—White or tan label			
❑ BSK3630	Green Light	1982	15.00
❑ BS2864	Home Plate	1975	15.00
—Burbank" palm trees label			
❑ BS2864	Home Plate	1979	10.00
—White or tan label			
❑ 25486	Nine Lives	1986	12.00
❑ BS2818	Streetlights	1974	15.00
—Burbank" palm trees label			
❑ BS2818	Streetlights	1979	10.00
—White or tan label			
❑ BS2990	Sweet Forgiveness	1977	15.00
—Burbank" palm trees label			
❑ BS2990	Sweet Forgiveness	1979	10.00
—White or tan label			
❑ BS2729	Takin' My Time	1973	15.00
—Burbank" palm trees label			
❑ BS2729	Takin' My Time	1979	10.00
—White or tan label			
❑ HS3369	The Glow	1979	15.00

RAITT, JOHN

CAPITOL
❑ T583 [M]	Highlights of Broadway	1955	30.00
❑ T714 [M]	Mediterranean Magic	1956	30.00
❑ T1058 [M]	Under Open Skies	1958	30.00
❑ ST1058 [S]	Under Open Skies	1958	40.00

RAKES, PAL

ATLANTIC AMERICA
❑ 90964	Midnight Rain	1988	12.00

RAKIM

UNIVERSAL
❑ U2-53113	The 18th Letter	1997	18.00
—Generic black cover with large sticker			

RALKE, DON

CROWN
❑ CLP-5019 [M]	Bongo Madness	1957	30.00

WARNER BROS.
❑ W1321 [M]	Bourbon Street Beat	1959	30.00
❑ WS1321 [S]	Bourbon Street Beat	1959	30.00
❑ W1360 [M]	But You've Never Heard Gershwin with Bongos	1960	25.00
❑ WS1360 [S]	But You've Never Heard Gershwin with Bongos	1960	30.00
❑ W1398 [M]	The Savage and Sensuous Bongos	1960	30.00
❑ WS1398 [S]	The Savage and Sensuous Bongos	1960	30.00

RALSTON, BOB

RCA CAMDEN
❑ CAL-994 [M]	Christmas Hymns and Carols	196?	15.00
❑ CAS-994 [S]	Christmas Hymns and Carols	196?	18.00

RAM, BUCK

MERCURY
❑ MG-20392 [M]	The Magic Touch	1960	30.00
❑ SR-60067 [S]	The Magic Touch	1960	40.00

RAM

POLYDOR
❑ 24-5013	Where (In Conclusion)	1972	30.00

RAM JAM

EPIC
❑ JE35287	Portrait of the Artist as a Young Ram	1978	14.00
❑ PE34885	Ram Jam	1977	15.00

RAMATAM

ATLANTIC
❑ SD7261	In April Came the Dawning of the Red Suns	1973	18.00
❑ SD7236	Ramatam	1972	18.00

RAMBEAU, EDDIE

DYNO VOICE
❑ 9001 [M]	Concrete and Clay	1965	25.00
❑ DS-9001 [S]	Concrete and Clay	1965	30.00

RAMIREZ, RAM

MASTER JAZZ
Number	Title	Yr	NM
❑ 8122	Rampant Ram	1973	15.00

RAMONE, DEE DEE

SIRE
❑ 25884	Standing in the Spotlight	1988	18.00

RAMONES, THE

RADIOACTIVE
❑ 11273 [B]	Adios Amigos!	1995	30.00
❑ 10615	Mondo Bizarro	1992	18.00

SIRE
❑ 25433	Animal Boy	1986	18.00
❑ 25905	Brain Drain	1989	18.00
❑ SRK6077	End of the Century	1980	18.00
❑ 25641	Halfway to Sanity	1987	18.00
❑ SRK3571	Pleasant Dreams	1981	18.00
❑ PRO-A-996 [DJ]	Pleasant Dreams Radio Sampler	1980	30.00
❑ SASD-7520	Ramones	1976	30.00
—First issue, distributed by ABC			
❑ SR6020 [B]	Ramones	1978	30.00
—Reissue, distributed by Warner Bros.; originals have no bar code			
❑ SA-7528 [B]	Ramones Leave Home	1977	80.00
—First issue, distributed by ABC, with "Carbona Not Glue			
❑ SA-7528	Ramones Leave Home	1977	30.00
—Second issue, distributed by ABC, with "Sheena Is a Punk Rocker" replacing "Carbona Not Glue			
❑ SR6031	Ramones Leave Home	1978	25.00
—Third issue, distributed by Warner Bros., tracks as on second issue; originals have no bar code			
❑ 25709	RamonesMania	1988	25.00
❑ SRK6063	Road to Ruin	1979	18.00
❑ PRO-A-756 [DJ]	Road to Ruin Radio Sampler	1978	35.00
❑ SRK6042	Rocket to Russia	1978	18.00
❑ PRO-A-605 [DJ]	Rock 'n' Roll High School Radio Sampler	1979	30.00
❑ 23800	Subterranean Jungle	1983	18.00
❑ 25187	Too Tough to Die	1984	18.00

RAMPART STREET PARADERS, THE

COLUMBIA
❑ CL785 [M]	Dixieland My Dixieland	1956	30.00
❑ CL648 [M]	Rampart and Vine	1955	40.00
—Maroon label, gold print			
❑ CL648 [M]	Rampart and Vine	1956	30.00
—Red and black label with six "eye" logos			
❑ CL1061 [M]	Texas! U.S.A.	1957	30.00

HARMONY
❑ HL7214 [M]	Real Dixieland	196?	18.00

RAMSAY, OBRAY

PRESTIGE
❑ PRLP-13020 [M]	Folk Songs from the Three Laurels	1961	30.00
❑ PRLP-13009 [M]	Obray Ramsay Sings Jimmie Rodgers Favorites	1960	30.00

RIVERSIDE
❑ RLP-12-649 [M]	Banjo Songs of the Blue Ridge and Great Smokies	196?	30.00

RAND, CHARLES

PREMIER
❑ XMS-10 [S]	Christmas Organ in the Ken Griffin Style	196?	18.00
—Same as above, but in stereo			
❑ XM-10 [M]	Christmas Organ in the Ken Griffin Style	196?	15.00

RANDALL, TONY, AND JACK KLUGMAN

LONDON
❑ XPS903	The Odd Couple Sings	1973	50.00

RANDALL, TONY

IMPERIAL
❑ LP-9090 [M]	Tony Randall	1958	30.00

MERCURY
❑ MG-21108 [M]	Vo, Vo, De Oh, Doe	1967	25.00
❑ SR-61108 [S]	Vo, Vo, De Oh, Doe	1967	30.00
❑ MG-21128 [M]	Warm and Wavery	1967	25.00
❑ SR-61128 [S]	Warm and Wavery	1967	30.00

RANDAZZO, TEDDY

ABC-PARAMOUNT
❑ 352 [M]	Journey to Love	1961	30.00
❑ S-352 [S]	Journey to Love	1961	40.00
❑ 421 [M]	Teddy Randazzo Twists	1962	30.00
❑ S-421 [S]	Teddy Randazzo Twists	1962	40.00

COLPIX
❑ CP-445 [M]	Big Wide World	1963	30.00
❑ SCP-445 [S]	Big Wide World	1963	40.00

VIK
❑ LX-1121 [M]	I'm Confessin'	1958	200.00

Number	Title	Yr	NM

RANDI, DON

CAPITOL
| ☐ ST-287 | Love Theme from Romeo and Juliet | 1969 | 25.00 |

PALOMAR
| ☐ 24002 [M] | Don Randi! | 1965 | 18.00 |
| ☐ 34002 [S] | Don Randi! | 1965 | 25.00 |

POPPY
| ☐ PY-5701 | Don Randi Trio at the Baked Potato | 1972 | 18.00 |

REPRISE
| ☐ R-6229 [M] | Revolver Jazz | 1966 | 25.00 |
| ☐ RS-6229 [S] | Revolver Jazz | 1966 | 30.00 |

VERVE
☐ V-8524 [M]	Last Night With the Don Randi Trio	1963	15.00
☐ V6-8524 [S]	Last Night With the Don Randi Trio	1963	18.00
☐ V-8469 [M]	Where Do We Go From Here?	1962	15.00
☐ V6-8469 [S]	Where Do We Go From Here?	1962	18.00

WORLD PACIFIC
| ☐ WP-1297 [M] | Feelin' Like Blues | 1960 | 30.00 |
| ☐ ST-1297 [S] | Feelin' Like Blues | 1960 | 30.00 |

RANDOLPH, BOOTS

MONUMENT
☐ MLP-8029 [M]	12 Monstrous Sax Hits	1965	18.00
☐ SLP-18029 [S]	12 Monstrous Sax Hits	1965	25.00
☐ SLP18127	Boots and Stockings	1969	18.00
☐ 6610	Boots and Stockings	197?	12.00
—Reissue of 18127			
☐ MLP-8037 [M]	Boots Randolph Plays More Yakety Sax	1965	18.00
☐ SLP-18037 [S]	Boots Randolph Plays More Yakety Sax	1965	25.00
☐ 6602	Boots Randolph Plays More Yakety Sax	197?	12.00
—Reissue of 18037			
☐ KZ31908	Boots Randolph Plays the Great Hits of Today	1972	15.00
☐ 6615	Boots Randolph Plays the Great Hits of Today	197?	12.00
—Reissue of 31908			
☐ MLP-8002 [M]	Boots Randolph's Yakoty Sax	1963	25.00
☐ SLP-18002 [S]	Boots Randolph's Yakety Sax	1963	30.00
☐ 6600	Boots Randolph's Yakety Sax	197?	12.00
—Reissue of 18002			
☐ KZ33298	Boots Randolph's Yakety Sax	1974	15.00
☐ MLP-8082 [M]	Boots Randolph with the Knightsbridge Strings & Voices	1967	25.00
☐ SLP-18082 [S]	Boots Randolph with the Knightsbridge Strings & Voices	1967	18.00
☐ 6606	Boots Randolph with the Knightsbridge Strings & Voices	197?	12.00
—Reissue of 18082			
☐ CLP-10147	Boots with Brass	1970	18.00
☐ 6613	Boots with Brass	197?	12.00
—Reissue of 18147			
☐ MLP-8066 [M]	Boots with Strings	1966	18.00
☐ SLP-18066 [S]	Boots with Strings	1966	25.00
☐ 6604	Boots with Strings	197?	12.00
—Reissue of 18066			
☐ BZ33852	Boots with Strings	1975	18.00
☐ 6618	Cool Boots	197?	12.00
—Reissue of 33803			
☐ KZ33803	Cool Boots	1975	15.00
☐ 6617	Country Boots	197?	12.00
—Reissue of 32912			
☐ KZ32912	Country Boots	1974	15.00
☐ JW38396	Dedication	1983	12.00
☐ 7602	Greatest Hits	1977	12.00
☐ PW38388	Greatest Hits	1983	12.00
☐ MLP-8015 [M]	Hip Boots	1964	18.00
☐ SLP-18015 [S]	Hip Boots	1964	25.00
☐ 6601	Hip Boots	197?	12.00
—Reissue of 18015			
☐ SLP-18144	Hit Boots 1970	1970	18.00
☐ 6612	Hit Boots 1970	197?	12.00
—Reissue of 18144			
☐ Z30678	Homer Louis Randolph, III	1971	15.00
☐ 6614	Homer Louis Randolph, III	197?	12.00
—Reissue of 30678			
☐ DS632	King of Yakety	197?	18.00
—Manufactured by CBS Direct Marketing Services			
☐ 8604	Party Boots	197?	15.00
—Reissue of 34082			
☐ Z234082	Party Boots	1976	18.00
☐ 7627	Put a Little Sax	1978	12.00
☐ 7611	Sax Appeal	1977	12.00
☐ MC6605	Sax-Sational	1976	12.00
—Reissue of 18079			
☐ MLP-8079 [M]	Sax-Sational	1967	25.00
☐ SLP-18079 [S]	Sax-Sational	1967	18.00
☐ KZ32292	Sentimental Journey	1973	15.00
☐ 6616	Sentimental Journey	197?	12.00

—Reissue of 32292			
☐ SLP-18092	Sunday Sax	1968	25.00
☐ 6607	Sunday Sax	197?	12.00
—Reissue of 18092			
☐ MLP-8042 [M]	The Fantastic Boots Randolph	1966	18.00
☐ SLP-18042 [S]	The Fantastic Boots Randolph	1966	25.00
☐ 6603	The Fantastic Boots Randolph	197?	12.00
—Reissue of 18042			
☐ SLP-18099	The Sound of Boots	1968	25.00
☐ 6608	The Sound of Boots	197?	12.00
—Reissue of 18099			
☐ ZG30963	The World of Boots	1971	18.00
☐ SLP-18111	…With Love/The Seductive Sax of Boots Randolph	1969	18.00
☐ 6609	…With Love/The Seductive Sax of Boots Randolph	197?	12.00
—Reissue of 18111			
☐ SLP-18128	Yakety Revisited	1969	18.00
☐ 6611	Yakety Revisited	197?	12.00
—Reissue of 18128			

RCA CAMDEN
☐ CAL-865 [M]	Sweet Talk	1965	18.00
☐ CAS-865 [R]	Sweet Talk	1965	15.00
☐ ACL-9003	Yakety Sax	1972	15.00
☐ CAL-825 [M]	Yakin' Sax Man	1964	18.00
☐ CAS-825 [S]	Yakin' Sax Man	1964	18.00

RCA VICTOR
| ☐ LPM-2165 [M] | Yakety Sax | 1960 | 40.00 |
| ☐ LSP-2165 [S] | Yakety Sax | 1960 | 50.00 |

RANDY AND THE RAINBOWS

AMBIENT SOUND
| ☐ FZ37715 | C'mon, Let's Go | 1982 | 15.00 |
| ☐ ASR-601 | Remember | 1985 | 15.00 |

RANELIN, PHIL

TRIBE
| ☐ PRSD-2226 | Message from the Tribe | 197? | 100.00 |
| ☐ TRCD4006 | The Time Is Now! | 1974 | 80.00 |

RANEY, DOUG

STEEPLECHASE
☐ SCS-1191	Black and White	198?	15.00
☐ SCS-1105	Cuttin' Loose	198?	15.00
☐ SCS-1212	Guitar, Guitar, Guitar	198?	15.00
☐ SCS-1166	I'll Close My Eyes	1982	15.00
☐ SCS-1082	Introducing Doug Raney	1978	15.00
☐ SCS-1200	Lazy Bird	198?	15.00
☐ SCS-1144	Listen	1981	15.00

RANEY, JIMMY

ABC-PARAMOUNT
| ☐ ABC-129 [M] | Jimmy Raney Featuring Bob Brookmeyer | 1956 | 300.00 |
| ☐ ABC-167 [M] | Jimmy Raney in Three Attitudes | 1957 | 150.00 |

BIOGRAPH
| ☐ LP-12060 | Too Marvelous for Words | 198? | 15.00 |

DAWN
| ☐ DLP-1120 [M] | Jimmy Raney Visits Paris | 1958 | 100.00 |

FANTASY
| ☐ OJC-1706 | Jimmy Raney/A | 1985 | 15.00 |

MUSE
| ☐ MR-5004 | Strings and Swings | 1973 | 40.00 |

NEW JAZZ
| ☐ NJLP-1103 [10] | Jimmy Raney Ensemble Introducing Phil Woods | 1953 | 500.00 |
| ☐ NJLP-1101 [10] | Jimmy Raney Quartet Featuring Hall Overton | 1953 | 500.00 |

PAUSA
| ☐ 7021 | Momentum | 197? | 15.00 |

PRESTIGE
☐ PRLP-7089 [M]	Jimmy Raney/A	1957	300.00
—Yellow label with W. 50th St. address			
☐ PRLP-203 [10]	Jimmy Raney in Sweden	1955	400.00
☐ PRLP-179 [10]	Jimmy Raney in Sweden	1954	400.00
☐ PRLP-156 [10]	Jimmy Raney Plays	1953	400.00
☐ PRLP-201 [10]	Jimmy Raney Quartet	1955	400.00
☐ PRLP-199 [10]	Jimmy Raney Quintet	1954	400.00

XANADU
☐ 116	Influence	197?	30.00
☐ 132	Live in Tokyo	197?	30.00
☐ 140	Solo	1977	30.00

RANEY, JIMMY AND DOUG

STEEPLECHASE
☐ SCS-1134	Duets	1980	18.00
☐ SCS-1184	Nardis	198?	18.00
☐ SCS-1118	Stolen Moments	198?	18.00

RANEY, JIMMY/GEORGE WALLINGTON

EMARCY
| ☐ MG-36121 [M] | Swingin' in Sweden | 1958 | 100.00 |

RANEY, SUE, AND BOB FLORENCE

DISCOVERY
| ☐ DS-931 | Flight of Fancy: A Journey of Alan and Marilyn Bergman | 1987 | 12.00 |
| ☐ DS-939 | Quietly There | 1988 | 12.00 |

RANEY, SUE

CAPITOL
☐ T2032 [M]	All By Myself	1964	18.00
☐ ST2032 [S]	All By Myself	1964	25.00
☐ T1335 [M]	Songs for a Raney Day	1960	25.00
☐ ST1335 [S]	Songs for a Raney Day	1960	30.00

DISCOVERY
| ☐ DS-913 | Ridin' High | 1984 | 12.00 |
| ☐ DS-875 | Sue Raney Sings the Music of Johnny Mandel | 1982 | 12.00 |

IMPERIAL
☐ LP-9323 [M]	Alive and In Love	1966	18.00
☐ LP-12323 [S]	Alive and In Love	1966	25.00
☐ LP-9355 [M]	New and Now	1967	30.00
☐ LP-12355 [S]	New and Now	1967	18.00
☐ LP-9376 [M]	With a Little Help from My Friends	1968	30.00
☐ LP-12376 [S]	With a Little Help from My Friends	1968	18.00

RANEY, WAYNE

KING
| ☐ 588 [M] | Songs from the Hills | 1958 | 100.00 |

NASHVILLE
| ☐ NLP-2002 | Radio Gospel and Sacred Favorites | 196? | 18.00 |

STARDAY
| ☐ SLP-279 [M] | Don't Try to Be What You Ain't | 1964 | 40.00 |
| ☐ SLP-124 [M] | Wayne Raney and the Raney Family | 1960 | 40.00 |

RANGELL, NELSON

GRP
| ☐ GR-9593 | Playing for Keeps | 1989 | 15.00 |

RANGER, ANDY

DOT
| ☐ DLP-3028 [M] | The Song That Never Ends | 1956 | 60.00 |

RANK AND FILE

RHINO
| ☐ RNLP70830 | Rank and File | 1987 | 12.00 |

SLASH
☐ 25007	Long Gone Dead	1984	15.00
☐ 23833	Sundown	1983	12.00
☐ SR114	Sundown	1982	15.00

RANKIN, KENNY

ATLANTIC
| ☐ SD19271 | After the Roses | 1980 | 12.00 |

LITTLE DAVID
☐ LD1000	Incido	1975	12.00
☐ LD1003	Like a Seed	1972	12.00
☐ SD3000	Silver Morning	1974	12.00
☐ 90131	Silver Morning	1984	10.00
—Reissue of 3000			
☐ LD1013	The Kenny Rankin Album	1977	12.00

MERCURY
☐ SR-61240	Family	1969	15.00
☐ MG-21141 [M]	Mind Dusters	1967	18.00
☐ SR-61141 [S]	Mind Dusters	1967	15.00

RAPEMAN

TOUCH & GO
| ☐ 19 [B] | Budd | 1988 | 30.00 |
| ☐ 36 [B] | Two Nuns and a Pack Mule | 1989 | 30.00 |

RARE BIRD

ABC
| ☐ X-715 | As Your Mind Flies | 1972 | 18.00 |

POLYDOR
☐ PD6506	Born Again	1974	18.00
☐ PD5530	Epic Forest	1973	18.00
☐ PD6502	Somebody's Watching	1974	18.00

PROBE
| ☐ 4514 | Rare Bird | 1970 | 30.00 |

RARE EARTH

MOTOWN
☐ M5-202V1	Ecology	1981	10.00
☐ 5229ML	Get Ready	1982	10.00
☐ M5-116V1	Motown Superstar Series, Vol. 16	1981	12.00

PRODIGAL
☐ P7-10025	Band Together	1978	12.00
☐ P7-10027	Grand Slam	1979	12.00
☐ P6-10019	Rare Earth	1977	12.00

RARE EARTH
| ☐ R6-548 | Back to Earth | 1975 | 15.00 |

Number	Title	Yr	NM
❏ RS514	Ecology	1970	18.00
❏ RS510	Generation	1970	500.00
—At least one copy of this album has been confirmed to exist			
❏ RS507	Get Ready	1969	30.00
—Original cover has a rounded top			
❏ RS507	Get Ready	1970	15.00
—Regular square cover			
❏ R6-546	Ma	1973	15.00
❏ R7-550	Midnight Lady	1976	15.00
❏ RS520	One World	1971	18.00
❏ R534	Rare Earth in Concert	1971	18.00
❏ R543	Willie Remembers	1972	15.00
VERVE			
❏ V6-5066	Dreams/Answers	1968	50.00

RASCALS, THE

ATLANTIC

Number	Title	Yr	NM
❏ 8134 [M]	Collections	1967	30.00
❏ SD8134 [S]	Collections	1967	30.00
—Green and blue label			
❏ SD8134 [S]	Collections	1969	15.00
—Red and green label			
❏ SD 2-901 [B]	Freedom Suite	1969	40.00
❏ ST-137 [DJ]	Freedom Suite Sampler	1969	50.00
❏ 8148 [M]	Groovin'	1967	30.00
❏ SD8148 [S]	Groovin'	1967	30.00
—Green and blue label			
❏ SD8148 [S]	Groovin'	1969	15.00
—Red and green label			
❏ 8169 [M]	Once Upon a Dream	1968	50.00
❏ SD8169 [S]	Once Upon a Dream	1968	30.00
—Green and blue label			
❏ SD8169 [S]	Once Upon a Dream	1969	15.00
—Red and green label			
❏ 8276 [M]	Search and Nearness	1970	50.00
—Mono is promo only; cover has "dj copy monaural" sticker on front			
❏ SD8276 [S]	Search and Nearness	1970	18.00
❏ 8246 [M]	See	1969	50.00
—Mono is promo only; cover has "dj copy monaural" sticker on front			
❏ SD8246 [S]	See	1969	18.00
❏ 8123 [M]	The Young Rascals	1966	60.00
❏ 3D8123 [S]	The Young Rascals	1966	40.00
—Green and blue label			
❏ SD8123 [S]	The Young Rascals	1966	50.00
—Purple and green label			
❏ SD8123 [S]	The Young Rascals	1969	15.00
—Red and green label			
❏ 8190 [M]	Time Peace/The Rascals' Greatest Hits	1968	50.00
—Mono is promo only			
❏ SD8190 [S]	Time Peace/The Rascals' Greatest Hits	1968	30.00
—Green and blue label			
❏ SD8190 [S]	Time Peace/The Rascals' Greatest Hits	1968	18.00
—Purple and gold label			
❏ SD8190 [S]	Time Peace/The Rascals' Greatest Hits	1969	15.00
—Red and green label			

COLUMBIA

Number	Title	Yr	NM
❏ G30462	Peaceful World	1971	18.00
❏ KC31103	The Island of Real	1972	15.00
PAIR			
❏ PDL2-1106	Rock and Roll Treasures	1986	18.00
RHINO			
❏ RNLP70238	Collections	1988	12.00
❏ R1-70241	Freedom Suite	1988	12.00
❏ RNLP70239	Groovin'	1988	12.00
❏ R1-70240	Once Upon a Dream	1988	12.00
❏ R1-70242	Searching for Ecstasy: The Rest of the Rascals 1969-1972	1988	12.00
❏ RNLP70237	The Young Rascals	1988	12.00
SUNDAZED			
❏ LP5117	Collections	2002	15.00
❏ LP5118	Groovin'	2002	15.00
❏ LP5119	Once Upon a Dream	2002	15.00
❏ LP5116	The Young Rascals	2002	15.00
WARNER SPECIAL PRODUCTS			
❏ SP-2502	24 Greatest Hits	1971	25.00
WES FARRELL			
❏ PFT-1002 [DJ]	Songs from the Rascals	197?	30.00
—Promo-only publisher's demo			

RASPBERRIES

CAPITOL

Number	Title	Yr	NM
❏ ST-11123	Fresh	1972	25.00
❏ SK-11036 [B]	Raspberries	1972	60.00
—Originals have red labels and a "scratch 'n' sniff" cover, the smell of which fades over time			
❏ ST-11036	Raspberries	1973	25.00
—Orange label, "Capitol" at bottom			
❏ ST-11524	Raspberries' Best Featuring Eric Carmen	1976	18.00
❏ SN-16095	Raspberries' Best Featuring Eric Carmen	1979	12.00
❏ SMAS-11220	Side 3	1973	25.00
—With cover cut in the shape of a basket of raspberries			

Number	Title	Yr	NM
❏ ST-11329	Starting Over	1974	25.00
MOBILE FIDELITY			
❏ MOFI1-032 [B]	Raspberries' Best - Featuring Eric Carmen	2013	35.00

RATCHELL

DECCA

Number	Title	Yr	NM
❏ DL75330	Ratchell	1972	18.00
❏ DL75365	Ratchell 2	1972	18.00

RATHBONE, BASIL

CAEDMON

Number	Title	Yr	NM
❏ TC1028 [M]	Basil Rathbone Reads Edgar Allan Poe	195?	30.00
❏ TC1115 [M]	Basil Rathbone Reads Edgar Allan Poe, Vol. 2	195?	30.00
❏ TC1195 [M]	Basil Rathbone Reads Edgar Allan Poe, Vol. 3	196?	30.00
❏ TC1120 [M]	Stories of Hawthorne	195?	30.00
❏ TC1197 [M]	Stories of Hawthorne, Vol. 2	196?	30.00
❏ TC1172 [M]	Stories of Sherlock Holmes, Vol. 1	1963	30.00
❏ TC1208 [M]	Stories of Sherlock Holmes, Vol. 2	1966	30.00
❏ TC1220 [M]	Stories of Sherlock Holmes, Vol. 3	1967	30.00
❏ TC1240 [M]	Stories of Sherlock Holmes, Vol. 4	1967	30.00
❏ TC1044 [M]	The Happy Prince and Other Oscar Wilde Fairy Tales	195?	30.00

COLUMBIA MASTERWORKS

Number	Title	Yr	NM
❏ ML4081 [10]	A Christmas Carol	1950	50.00
❏ ML4038 [10]	Peter and the Wolf; Treasure Island	1949	50.00

CO-STAR

Number	Title	Yr	NM
❏ C-107 [M]	The Brothers Karamazov	196?	25.00
❏ CS-107 [S]	The Brothers Karamazov	196?	30.00

DECCA

Number	Title	Yr	NM
❏ DL9109 [M]	Selections from The Jungle Book	1962	30.00

RATIONALS, THE

CREWE

Number	Title	Yr	NM
❏ CR-1334	The Rationals	1969	40.00

RATTLES, THE

MERCURY

Number	Title	Yr	NM
❏ MG21127 [M]	The Rattles' Greatest Hits	1967	80.00
❏ SR61127 [R]	The Rattles' Greatest Hits	1967	50.00

RATTLESNAKE ANNIE

COLUMBIA

Number	Title	Yr	NM
❏ B6C40678	Rattlesnake Annie	1987	12.00

RAVEN, EDDY

ABC DOT

Number	Title	Yr	NM
❏ DOSD-2031	This Is Eddy Raven	1975	18.00
DIMENSION			
❏ DLP-5001	Eyes	1980	18.00
ELEKTRA			
❏ 5E-545	Desperate Dreams	1981	15.00
LA LOUISIANNE			
❏ 127	That Cajun Country Sound	197?	25.00
MCA			
❏ 910	Thank God for Kids	198?	10.00
RCA			
❏ 5728-1-R	Right Hand Man	1987	10.00
❏ 6815-1-R	The Best of Eddy Raven	1988	10.00
RCA VICTOR			
❏ AHL1-5040	I Could Use Another You	1984	10.00
❏ AHL1-5456	Love and Other Hard Times	1985	10.00
UNIVERSAL			
❏ UVL-76003	Temporary Sanity	1989	12.00
WARNER BROS.			
❏ 5E-545	Desperate Dreams	1983	10.00
—Reissue of Elektra 5E-545			

RAVEN

COLUMBIA

Number	Title	Yr	NM
❏ CS9903	Raven	1969	25.00
DISCOVERY			
❏ 36133	Live at the Inferno	1967	80.00

RAVENS, THE

HARLEM HIT PARADE

Number	Title	Yr	NM
❏ 1007	The Ravens	1975	12.00
REGENT			
❏ MG-6062 [M]	Write Me a Letter	1957	300.00
—Green label			
❏ MG-6062 [M]	Write Me a Letter	195?	150.00
—Red label			
SAVOY JAZZ			
❏ SJL-2227	The Greatest Group of Them All	1978	15.00

RAVENSCROFT, THURL

DOT

Number	Title	Yr	NM
❏ DLP-3430 [M]	Great Hits	1962	30.00
❏ DLP-25430 [S]	Great Hits	1962	40.00

RAW

CORAL

Number	Title	Yr	NM
❏ CRL757515 [B]	Raw Holly	1971	40.00

RAW SPITT

UNITED ARTISTS

Number	Title	Yr	NM
❏ UAS-6795	Maybe You Ain't Black	1971	30.00

RAWLINS, STEVE

SEA BREEZE

Number	Title	Yr	NM
❏ SB-3003	Step Right Up	1985	12.00

RAWLS, LOU

ALLEGIANCE

Number	Title	Yr	NM
❏ AV-5016	Trying As Hard As I Can	198?	12.00
BELL			
❏ 1318	She's Gone	1974	15.00
BLUE NOTE			
❏ B1-91937	At Last	1989	15.00
❏ B1-93841	It's Supposed to Be Fun	1990	18.00
❏ B1-91441	Stormy Monday	1990	15.00
—Reissue of Capitol 1714			
CAPITOL			
❏ T1824 [M]	Black and Blue	1963	25.00
❏ ST1824 [S]	Black and Blue	1963	30.00
❏ ST-479	Bring It on Home	1970	18.00
❏ SWBB-261	Close-Up	1969	25.00
—Reissue of 1824 and 2042 in one package			
❏ STBB-720	Down Here on the Ground/I'd Rather Drink Muddy Water	1971	25.00
❏ T2864 [M]	Feelin' Good	1968	30.00
❏ ST2864 [S]	Feelin' Good	1968	18.00
❏ T2401 [M]	Lou Rawls and Strings	1965	25.00
❏ ST2401 [S]	Lou Rawls and Strings	1965	30.00
❏ T2632 [M]	Lou Rawls Carryin' On!	1966	18.00
❏ ST2632 [S]	Lou Rawls Carryin' On!	1966	25.00
❏ T2459 [M]	Lou Rawls Live!	1966	18.00
❏ ST2459 [S]	Lou Rawls Live!	1966	25.00
❏ SM-2459	Lou Rawls Live!	197?	12.00
—Reissue with new prefix			
❏ SN-16097	Lou Rawls Live!	1980	10.00
—Budget-line reissue			
❏ T2566 [M]	Lou Rawls Soulin'	1966	18.00
❏ ST2566 [S]	Lou Rawls Soulin'	1966	25.00
❏ SM-2566	Lou Rawls Soulin'	197?	12.00
—Reissue with new prefix			
❏ ST2790 [S]	Merry Christmas, Ho, Ho, Ho	1967	15.00
❏ T2790 [M]	Merry Christmas, Ho, Ho, Ho	1967	18.00
❏ T2273 [M]	Nobody But Lou	1965	25.00
❏ ST2273 [S]	Nobody But Lou	1965	30.00
❏ T1714 [M]	Stormy Monday	1962	25.00
❏ ST1714 [S]	Stormy Monday	1962	30.00
❏ SM-1714	Stormy Monday	197?	12.00
—Reissue with new prefix			
❏ T2756 [M]	That's Lou	1967	25.00
❏ ST2756 [S]	That's Lou	1967	18.00
❏ SKBB-11585	The Best from Lou Rawls	1976	15.00
❏ SKAO2948	The Best of Lou Rawls	1968	18.00
❏ SM-2948	The Best of Lou Rawls	197?	12.00
—Reissue with new prefix			
❏ SN-16096	The Best of Lou Rawls	1980	10.00
—Budget-line reissue			
❏ ST-122	The Way It Was	1969	18.00
❏ ST-215	The Way It Was -- The Way It Is	1969	18.00
❏ ST 8-0215	The Way It Was -- The Way It Is	1969	25.00
—Capitol Record Club edition			
❏ T2042 [M]	Tobacco Road	1964	25.00
❏ ST2042 [S]	Tobacco Road	1964	30.00
❏ T2713 [M]	Too Much!	1967	25.00
❏ ST2713 [S]	Too Much!	1967	18.00
❏ ST2927	You're Good for Me	1968	18.00
❏ ST-325	Your Good Thing	1969	18.00
❏ ST-427	You've Made Me So Very Happy	1970	18.00
EPIC			
❏ FE39403	Close Company	1984	12.00
❏ FE40210	Love All Your Blues Away	1986	12.00
❏ FE37448	Now Is the Time	1982	12.00
❏ FE38553	When the Night Comes	1983	12.00
MGM			
❏ SE-4861	A Man of Value	1973	15.00
❏ SE-4965	Live at the Century Plaza	1974	15.00
❏ SE-4771	Natural Man	1971	15.00
❏ SE-4809	Silk & Soul	1972	15.00
PHILADELPHIA INT'L.			
❏ PZ33957	All Things in Time	1976	12.00
—No bar code on cover			
❏ PZ33957	All Things in Time	198?	10.00
—With bar code on cover			
❏ FZ39285	Classics	1984	12.00

Number	Title	Yr	NM
❑ JZ36006	Let Me Be Good to You	1979	12.00
❑ PZ36006	Let Me Be Good to You	198?	10.00
— Budget-line reissue			
❑ PZ235517	Lou Rawls Live	1978	15.00
❑ JZ36774	Shades of Blue	1980	12.00
❑ JZ36304	Sit Down and Talk to Me	1979	12.00
❑ PZ36304	Sit Down and Talk to Me	198?	10.00
— Budget-line reissue			
❑ PZ34488	Unmistakably Lou	1977	12.00
❑ PZ34488	Unmistakably Lou	1986	10.00
— Budget-line reissue			
❑ JZ35036	When You Hear Lou, You've Heard It All	1977	12.00

PICKWICK

❑ SPC-3156	Come On In, Mr. Blues	1971	12.00
❑ SPC-3228	Gee Baby	1972	12.00

POLYDOR

❑ PD-1-6086	Naturally	1976	12.00

RAY, DAVE

ELEKTRA

❑ EKL-319 [M]	Fine Soft Land	1966	25.00
❑ EKS-7319 [S]	Fine Soft Land	1966	30.00
❑ EKL-284 [M]	Snaker's Here	1965	25.00
❑ EKS-7284 [S]	Snaker's Here	1965	30.00

RAY, DIANE

MERCURY

❑ MG-20903 [M]	The Exciting Years	1964	80.00
❑ SR-60903 [S]	The Exciting Years	1964	100.00

RAY, JAMES

CAPRICE

❑ LP-1002 [M]	James Ray	1962	80.00
❑ SLP-1002 [S]	James Ray	1962	120.00

RAY, JOHNNIE

COLUMBIA

❑ CL1093 [M]	At the Desert Inn in Las Vegas	1957	50.00
❑ CL2510 [10]	I Cry for You	1955	70.00
— House Party Series" issue			
❑ CL6199 [10]	Johnnie Ray	1951	80.00
❑ CL1227 [M]	Johnnie Ray's Greatest Hits	1958	40.00
— Red and black label with 6 "eye" logos			
❑ CL1227 [M]	Johnnie Ray's Greatest Hits	1962	30.00
— Guaranteed High Fidelity" on label			
❑ CL1227 [M]	Johnnie Ray's Greatest Hits	1965	18.00
— 360 Sound" label			
❑ CL1385 [M]	On the Trail	1959	40.00
❑ CS8180 [S]	On the Trail	1959	50.00
❑ CL961 [M]	The Big Beat	1957	50.00
❑ CL1225 [M]	'Til Morning	1958	40.00
— Red and black label with six "eye" logos			
❑ CL1225 [M]	'Til Morning	1963	25.00
— Red label with either "Guaranteed High Fidelity" or "360 Sound Mono" at bottom			

COLUMBIA SPECIAL PRODUCTS

❑ P13086	Greatest Hits	197?	12.00

EPIC

❑ LN1120 [10]	Johnnie Ray	1955	80.00

HARMONY

❑ H30609	The Best of Johnnie Ray	1971	15.00

LIBERTY

❑ LRP-3221 [M]	Johnnie Ray	1962	25.00
❑ LST-7221 [S]	Johnnie Ray	1962	30.00

SUNSET

❑ SUM-1125 [M]	Mr. Cry	196?	15.00
❑ SUS-5125 [S]	Mr. Cry	196?	15.00

RAY, WADE

ABC-PARAMOUNT

❑ ABC-539 [M]	A Ray of Country Sun	1966	18.00
❑ ABCS-539 [S]	A Ray of Country Sun	1966	25.00

RCA CAMDEN

❑ CAS-2107	Walk Softly	1969	18.00

RAYBURN, MARGIE

LIBERTY

❑ LRP-3126 [M]	Margie	1959	30.00
❑ LST-7126 [S]	Margie	1959	40.00

RAYE, JERRY

DEVILLE

❑ LP-101 [M]	The Many Sides of Jerry Raye and Fenwyck	1967	600.00

RAYE, MARTHA

EPIC

❑ LG3061 [M]	Here's Martha Raye	1954	40.00

RAYE, SUSAN

CAPITOL

❑ ST-11179	Cheating Game	1973	15.00
❑ ST-11255	Hymns by Susan Raye	1974	15.00
❑ ST-875	(I've Got a) Happy Heart	1972	18.00

Number	Title	Yr	NM
❑ ST-11135	Love Sure Feels Good in My Heart	1973	15.00
❑ ST-11055	My Heart Has a Mind of Its Own	1972	15.00
❑ ST-543	One Night Stand	1970	18.00
❑ ST-807	Pitty, Pitty, Patter	1971	18.00
❑ ST-11223	Plastic Trains, Paper Planes	1973	15.00
❑ ST-11333	Singing	1974	15.00
❑ ST-11282	The Best of Susan Raye	1974	15.00
❑ ST-11393	Whatch Gonna Do with a Dog Like That	1975	15.00
❑ ST-11106	Wheel of Fortune	1972	15.00
❑ ST-736	Willy Jones	1971	18.00

UNITED ARTISTS

❑ UA-LA764-G	Susan Raye	1977	15.00

RAYMOND, LEW

TOPS

❑ L-1583 [M]	For Men Only	1958	40.00
— Jayne Mansfield is the cover model			
❑ L-1647 [M]	Million Sellers	1960	30.00
— Mary Tyler Moore is the cover model			

RE-FLEX

CAPITOL

❑ ST-12314 [DJ]	The Politics of Dancing	1983	18.00
— High-grade vinyl edition (sticker on cover)			
❑ ST-12314	The Politics of Dancing	1983	12.00

REA, CHRIS

COLUMBIA

❑ FC37664	Chris Rea	1981	12.00
❑ JC36435	Tennis	1980	12.00

GEFFEN

❑ GHS24232	New Light Through Old Windows	1989	15.00

MOTOWN

❑ 6245ML	Dancing with Strangers	1987	12.00

UNITED ARTISTS

❑ UA-LA959-H	Deltics	1979	12.00
❑ UA-LA879-H	Whatever Happened to Benny Santini?	1978	15.00

READY FOR THE WORLD

MCA

❑ 5829	Long Time Coming	1986	10.00
❑ 5594	Ready for the World	1985	10.00
❑ 42198	Ruff 'N' Ready	1988	10.00
❑ 10224	Straight Down to Business	1991	18.00

REAGAN, RONALD

DECCA

❑ DL4943 [M]	Freedom's Finest Hour	1967	30.00
❑ DL74943 [S]	Freedom's Finest Hour	1967	30.00

KEY

❑ 690 [M]	Rendezvous with Destiny	1964	30.00

X

❑ LVA-3051 [M]	Tales from the Great Book	1956	40.00

REAL LIFE

CURB

❑ CRB-10624	Let's Fall in Love	1989	12.00
❑ D1-77271	Lifetime	1990	15.00
❑ CRB-10614	Send Me an Angel '89	1989	12.00

MCA CURB

❑ 5834	Down Comes the Hammer	1986	12.00
❑ 5639	Flame	1985	12.00
❑ 5459	Heartland	1983	12.00
❑ 1443	Heartland	1985	10.00
— Budget-line reissue			

REALLY RED

C.I.A.

❑ 006	Teaching You the Fear	1981	80.00

REAVES, GILES, AND JOHN GOIN

MCA

❑ 6283	Letting Go	1989	15.00

REBECCA AND THE SUNNY BROOK FARMERS

MUSICOR

❑ MS-3176 [B]	Rebecca and the Sunny Brook Farmers	1969	50.00

REBILLOT, PAT

ATLANTIC

❑ SD1663	Free Fall	1974	15.00

REBIRTH

AVANT GARDE

❑ AVS-135	Rebirth	1971	50.00

REBIRTH BRASS BAND

ARHOOLIE

❑ 1092	Here to Stay	1986	12.00
— As "Rebirth Jazz Band of New Orleans"			

Number	Title	Yr	NM
ROUNDER			
❑ 2093	Feel Like Funkin' It Up	1989	15.00

REBROFF, IVAN

CBS MASTERWORKS

❑ IM38658	Christmas with Ivan Rebroff	1983	12.00

REBS, THE

FREDLO

❑ 6830	1968 A.D. Break Through	1968	400.00

RECOIL

PAUSA

❑ 7117	Pardon My Fantasy	198?	12.00
❑ 7168	The Fantasy Continues	1985	12.00

RECORD, EUGENE

WARNER BROS.

❑ BS3018	Eugene Record	1977	18.00
❑ BSK3097	Trying to Get to You	1978	18.00
❑ BSK3284	Welcome to My Fantasy	1979	18.00

RECORDS, THE

VIRGIN

❑ VA13140	Crashes	1980	15.00
❑ VA13130 [B]	The Records	1979	25.00
— With bonus 4-song EP "Abracadabra" (deduct 33% if missing)			

VIRGIN INTERNATIONAL

❑ VI2206	Music on Both Sides	1982	12.00

RED, SONNY

BLUE NOTE

❑ BLP-4032 [M]	Out of the Blue	1960	100.00
— Deep groove" version (deep indentation under label on both sides)			
❑ BLP-4032 [M]	Out of the Blue	1960	80.00
— Regular version, W. 63rd St. address on label			
❑ ST-84032 [S]	Out of the Blue	1960	60.00
— With W. 63rd St. address on label			
❑ BLP-4032 [M]	Out of the Blue	1963	30.00
— With "New York, USA" address on label			
❑ ST-84032 [S]	Out of the Blue	1963	25.00
— With "New York, USA" address on label			
❑ ST-84032 [S]	Out of the Blue	1967	18.00
— With "A Division of Liberty Records" on label			

FANTASY

❑ OJC-148	Images	198?	12.00

JAZZLAND

❑ JLP-32 [M]	Breezin'	1960	30.00
❑ JLP-932 [M]	Breezin'	1960	40.00
❑ JLP-74 [M]	Images	1962	30.00
❑ JLP-974 [S]	Images	1962	40.00
❑ JLP-59 [M]	The Mode	1961	30.00
❑ JLP-959 [S]	The Mode	1961	40.00

MAINSTREAM

❑ MRL-324	Sonny Red	1971	18.00

RED, WHITE AND BLUE (GRASS)

GRC

❑ 5002	Red, White and Blue (Grass)	1973	18.00
❑ 10003	Red, White and Blue (Grass) Pickin' Up!	1974	18.00

MERCURY

❑ SRM-1-1165	Red, White and Blue (Grass) and Company	1977	15.00

RED CRAYOLA, THE

INTERNATIONAL ARTISTS

❑ 7	God Bless the Red Crayola	1968	60.00
❑ 7	God Bless the Red Crayola	1979	18.00
— Reissue with "Masterfonics" in trail-off wax			
❑ 2 [M]	Parable of the Arable Land	1968	120.00
❑ 2 [S]	Parable of the Arable Land	1968	80.00
❑ 2	Parable of the Arable Land	1979	18.00
— Reissue with "Masterfonics" in trail-off wax			

RED HOT CHILI PEPPERS

EMI

❑ E1-92152	Mother's Milk	1989	25.00
❑ E1-29665 [B]	Out in L.A.	1994	25.00

EMI AMERICA

❑ ST-17168	Freaky Styley	1985	18.00
❑ ST-17128	Red Hot Chili Peppers	1984	18.00
❑ E1-48036	The Uplift Mofo Party Plan	1987	18.00

EMI MANHATTAN

❑ E1-90869 [EP]	The Abbey Road E.P.	1988	10.00

WARNER BROS.

❑	Blood Sugar Sex Magik	1991	50.00
PRO-A-5170 [DJ]			
Radio ready" version of LP, this is the only U.S. vinyl release of this album			
❑ 48140	By the Way	2002	30.00
❑ 47386	Californication	1999	60.00
❑ 43391-1	Stadium Arcadium	2006	40.00

Number	Title	Yr	NM

—150-gram version; records are contained in two gatefold sleeves inside a slipcase

| ❏ 49996-1 | Stadium Arcadium | 2006 | 80.00 |

—180-gram version; box set contains records in individual sleeves plus two 12x12 booklets

RED ONION JAZZ BAND, THE

BIOGRAPH

| ❏ LP-12012 | There'll Be a Hot Time in the Old Town Tonight | 1969 | 18.00 |

RIVERSIDE

| ❏ RLP 12-260 [M] | Dance Off Both Your Shoes In Hi-Fi | 1958 | 40.00 |

RED RIVER DAVE

CONTINENTAL

| ❏ 1507 [M] | Red River Dave Sings | 1962 | 30.00 |

VARSITY

| ❏ 6962 [10] | Red River Dave | 1951 | 70.00 |

REDBONE, LEON

AUGUST

| ❏ AS8890 | Christmas Island | 1988 | 18.00 |

WARNER BROS.

❏ BS3165	Champagne Charlie	1978	30.00
❏ BS2971	Double Time	1977	25.00
❏ BS2888	On the Track	1975	25.00

REDBONE

EPIC

❏ KE31598	Already Here	1972	18.00
❏ KE33053	Bearded Dreams Through Turquoise Eyes	1974	18.00
❏ EQ33053 [Q]	Bearded Dreams Through Turquoise Eyes	1974	25.00
❏ KEG33456	Come & Get Your Redbone	1975	25.00
❏ KE30815	Message from a Drum	1972	18.00
❏ EQ30815 [Q]	Message from a Drum	1973	25.00
❏ E30109 [B]	Potlatch	1970	18.00
❏ EGP501 [B]	Redbone	1970	30.00
❏ KE32462	Wovoka	1974	18.00

RCA VICTOR

| ❏ AFL1-2352 | Cyclps | 1977 | 15.00 |

REDD, FREDDIE, AND HAMPTON HAWES

FANTASY

| ❏ OJC-1705 | Piano: East/West | 1985 | 12.00 |

PRESTIGE

| ❏ PRLP-7067 [M] | Piano: East/West | 1956 | 80.00 |

STATUS

| ❏ ST-8307 [M] | Movin' | 1965 | 40.00 |

REDD, FREDDIE

BLUE NOTE

| ❏ BLP-4027 [M] | Music From "The Connection | 1960 | 120.00 |

—Deep groove" version (deep indentation under label on both sides)

| ❏ BLP-4027 [M] | Music From "The Connection | 1963 | 30.00 |

—With "New York, USA" address on label

| ❏ BST-84027 [S] | Music From "The Connection | 1967 | 18.00 |

—With "A Division of Liberty Records" on label

| ❏ BLP-4027 [M] | Music From "The Connection | 1960 | 100.00 |

—Regular version, W. 63rd St. address on label

| ❏ BST-84027 [S] | Music From "The Connection | 1960 | 100.00 |

—With W. 63rd St. address on label

| ❏ BST-84027 [S] | Music From "The Connection | 1963 | 25.00 |

—With "New York, USA" address on label

| ❏ BLP-4045 [M] | Shades of Redd | 1960 | 120.00 |

—Deep groove" version (deep indentation under label on both sides)

| ❏ BLP-4045 [M] | Shades of Redd | 1963 | 30.00 |

—With "New York, USA" address on label

| ❏ BLP-4045 [M] | Shades of Redd | 1960 | 100.00 |

—Regular version, W. 63rd St. address on label

FANTASY

| ❏ OJC-1748 | San Francisco Suite For Jazz Trio | 1990 | 15.00 |

INTERPLAY

| ❏ 7715 | Straight Ahead | 1979 | 15.00 |

MOSAIC

| ❏ MR3-124 | The Complete Blue Note Recordings of Freddie Redd | 199? | 30.00 |

PRESTIGE

| ❏ PRLP-197 [10] | Introducing the Freddie Redd Trio | 1954 | 150.00 |

RIVERSIDE

| ❏ RLP 12-250 [M] | San Francisco Suite For Jazz Trio | 1957 | 60.00 |
| ❏ 6184 | San Francisco Suite For Jazz Trio | 198? | 15.00 |

REDD, VI

ATCO

| ❏ 33-157 [M] | Lady Soul | 1963 | 30.00 |
| ❏ SD 33-157 [S] | Lady Soul | 1963 | 40.00 |

UNITED ARTISTS

| ❏ UAJ-14016 [M] | Bird Call | 1962 | 40.00 |
| ❏ UAJS-15016 [S] | Bird Call | 1962 | 50.00 |

REDD KROSS

ATLANTIC

| ❏ 82148 | Third Eye | 1990 | 12.00 |

BIG TIME

| ❏ 6034-1 | Neurotica | 1987 | 15.00 |

FRONTIER

| ❏ 4609-1-L [B] | Born Innocent | 1991 | 25.00 |

—Reissue

| ❏ FLP1018 | Born Innocent | 1986 | 15.00 |

—Reissue

GASATANKA

| ❏ E1170 [B] | Teen Babies from Monsanto | 1984 | 25.00 |

POSH BOY

| ❏ 1010 [EP] | Annette's Got the Hits | 1987 | 25.00 |

—Reissue

| ❏ 1010 [EP] | Red Cross | 1980 | 25.00 |

SMOKE

| ❏ SMK7-103 | Born Innocent | 1982 | 18.00 |

SYMPATHY FOR THE RECORD INDUSTRY

| ❏ 260 [10] | 2,500 Redd Kross Fans Can't Be Wrong | 1993 | 25.00 |

REDDING, GENE

HAVEN

| ❏ ST-9200 | Blood Brother | 1974 | 25.00 |

REDDING, OTIS

4 MEN WITH BEARDS

| ❏ 4M105 | The Great Otis Redding Sings Soul Ballads | 2002 | 18.00 |

—Reissue on 180-gram vinyl

ATCO

| ❏ SD 33-287 | Complete & Unbelievable... The Otis Redding Dictionary of Soul | 1969 | 18.00 |

—Reissue of Volt 415

| ❏ SD 33-261 | History of Otis Redding | 1968 | 18.00 |

—Reissue of Volt 418

| ❏ SD 33-289 | Love Man | 1969 | 18.00 |
| ❏ SD 33-284 | Otis Blue/Otis Redding Sings Soul | 1969 | 18.00 |

—Reissue of Volt 412

| ❏ SD 33-265 | Otis Redding In Person at the Whiskey A-Go-Go | 1968 | 18.00 |
| ❏ SD 33-286 | Otis Redding Live in Europe | 1969 | 18.00 |

—Reissue of Volt 416

❏ R180253 [B]	Pain In My Heart	2014	60.00
❏ 33-161 [M]	Pain in My Heart	1964	250.00
❏ SD 33-161 [R]	Pain in My Heart	1968	250.00
❏ SD 33-333	Tell the Truth	1970	18.00
❏ SD 2-801	The Best of Otis Redding	1972	25.00
❏ SD 33-288 [B]	The Dock of the Bay	1969	25.00

—Reissue of Volt 419

| ❏ SD 33-252 [S] | The Immortal Otis Redding | 1968 | 18.00 |
| ❏ 33-252 [M] | The Immortal Otis Redding | 1968 | 50.00 |

—Mono is white label promo only

| ❏ SD 33-285 | The Soul Album | 1969 | 18.00 |

—Reissue of Volt 413

ATLANTIC

❏ SD19346	Recorded Live	198?	12.00
❏ 81282	The Best of Otis Redding	1985	12.00
❏ 81762	The Otis Redding Story	1987	30.00

PAIR

| ❏ PDL2-1062 | The Legend of Otis Redding | 1984 | 18.00 |

SUNDAZED

| ❏ LP5063 [M] | Complete & Unbelievable ... The Otis Redding Dictionary of Soul | 2001 | 15.00 |

—Reissue on 180-gram vinyl

| ❏ LP5064 [M] | Otis Blue/Otis Redding Sings Soul | 2001 | 15.00 |

—Reissue on 180-gram vinyl

| ❏ LP5133 [S] | Otis Redding In Person at the Whiskey A-Go-Go | 2003 | 15.00 |

—Reissue on 180-gram vinyl

| ❏ LP5134 [S] | Otis Redding Live in Europe | 2003 | 15.00 |

—Reissue on 180-gram vinyl

| ❏ LP5172 [S] | The Dock of the Bay | 2003 | 15.00 |

—Reissue on 180-gram vinyl

| ❏ LP5132 [M] | The Soul Album | 2003 | 15.00 |

—Reissue on 180-gram vinyl

VOLT

❏ 415 [M]	Complete & Unbelievable... The Otis Redding Dictionary of Soul	1966	80.00
❏ S-415 [S]	Complete & Unbelievable... The Otis Redding Dictionary of Soul	1966	60.00
❏ 418 [M]	History of Otis Redding	1967	40.00
❏ S-418 [S]	History of Otis Redding	1967	30.00
❏ 412 [M]	Otis Blue/Otis Redding Sings Soul	1965	80.00
❏ S-412 [S]	Otis Blue/Otis Redding Sings Soul	1965	60.00
❏ 416 [M]	Otis Redding Live in Europe	1967	30.00
❏ S-416 [S]	Otis Redding Live in Europe	1967	40.00
❏ S-419	The Dock of the Bay	1968	30.00
❏ 411 [M]	The Great Otis Redding Sings Soul Ballads	1965	120.00
❏ S-411 [R]	The Great Otis Redding Sings Soul Ballads	1968	120.00
❏ 413 [M]	The Soul Album	1966	80.00
❏ S-413 [S]	The Soul Album	1966	60.00

REDDINGS, THE

BELIEVE IN A DREAM

❏ JZ36875	Awakening	1980	12.00
❏ FZ38690	Back to Basics	1983	12.00
❏ FZ37175	Class	1981	12.00
❏ FZ37974	Steamin' Hot	1982	12.00

POLYDOR

| ❏ 823324-1 | If Looks Could Kill | 1985 | 10.00 |
| ❏ 835292-1 | The Reddings | 1988 | 12.00 |

REDDY, HELEN

CAPITOL

❏ SO-11640	Ear Candy	1977	12.00
❏ ST-11348	Free and Easy	1974	12.00
❏ SN-16249	Free and Easy	198?	10.00

—Budget-line reissue

| ❏ ST-857 | Helen Reddy | 1971 | 18.00 |
| ❏ SN-16098 | Helen Reddy | 1980 | 10.00 |

—Budget-line reissue

| ❏ ST-11467 | Helen Reddy's Greatest Hits | 1975 | 12.00 |

—Orange label

| ❏ SW-11467 | Helen Reddy's Greatest Hits | 1978 | 10.00 |

—Purple label

| ❏ ST-11068 | I Am Woman | 1972 | 12.00 |
| ❏ SN-16099 | I Am Woman | 1980 | 10.00 |

—Budget-line reissue

| ❏ ST-762 | I Don't Know How to Love Him | 1971 | 18.00 |
| ❏ SN-16100 | I Don't Know How to Love Him | 1980 | 10.00 |

—Budget-line reissue

| ❏ SKBO-11873 | Live | 1979 | 15.00 |
| ❏ SN-16250 | Live | 198? | 10.00 |

—Budget-line reissue

| ❏ SMAS-11213 | Long Hard Climb | 1973 | 12.00 |
| ❏ SN-16101 | Long Hard Climb | 1980 | 10.00 |

—Budget-line reissue

| ❏ SO-11284 | Love Song for Jeffrey | 1974 | 12.00 |
| ❏ SN-16195 | Love Song for Jeffrey | 198? | 10.00 |

—Budget-line reissue

❏ ST-11547	Music, Music	1976	12.00
❏ ST-11418	No Way to Treat a Lady	1975	12.00
❏ SN-16196	No Way to Treat a Lady	1980	10.00

—Budget-line reissue

| ❏ SO-11949 | Reddy | 1979 | 12.00 |
| ❏ SN-16200 | Reddy | 1980 | 10.00 |

—Budget-line reissue

| ❏ SOO-12068 | Take What You Find | 1980 | 12.00 |
| ❏ SN-16248 | Take What You Find | 198? | 10.00 |

—Budget-line reissue

| ❏ SW-11759 | We'll Sing in the Sunshine | 1978 | 12.00 |
| ❏ SN-16199 | We'll Sing in the Sunshine | 1980 | 10.00 |

—Budget-line reissue

MCA

| ❏ 5376 | Imagination | 198? | 10.00 |

PAIR

| ❏ PDL2-1066 | Lust for Life | 1986 | 15.00 |

REDEYE

PENTAGRAM

| ❏ PR-10006 [B] | One Man's Poison | 1971 | 25.00 |
| ❏ PE-10003 [B] | Redeye | 1970 | 25.00 |

REDMAN, DEWEY, AND ED BLACKWELL

BLACK SAINT

| ❏ BSR-0093 | Red and Black in Willisau | 1985 | 15.00 |

REDMAN, DEWEY

ABC IMPULSE!

| ❏ AS-9300 | Coincide | 1974 | 18.00 |
| ❏ AS-9250 | The Ear of the Behearer | 1973 | 18.00 |

ARISTA/FREEDOM

| ❏ AF1011 | Look for the Black Star | 1976 | 15.00 |

BLACK SAINT

| ❏ 120123 | Living on the Edge | 1990 | 18.00 |

ECM

| ❏ 1225 | The Struggle Continues | 1981 | 12.00 |

GALAXY

| ❏ 5118 | Musics | 1980 | 15.00 |
| ❏ 5130 | Soundsigns | 198? | 15.00 |

REDMAN, DON

GOLDEN CREST

| ❏ GC-3017 [M] | Park Avenue Patter | 1958 | 40.00 |

Number	Title	Yr	NM
RCA VICTOR			
❑ LPV-520 [M]	Master of the Big Band	1965	25.00
ROULETTE			
❑ R-25070 [M]	Dixieland in High Society	1960	25.00
❑ SR-25070 [S]	Dixieland in High Society	1960	30.00
STEEPLECHASE			
❑ SCC-6020	For Europeans Only	198?	15.00

REDMAN, GEORGE

Number	Title	Yr	NM
SKYLARK			
❑ SKLP-20 [10]	The George Redman Group	1954	150.00

REDMOND, EDGAR

Number	Title	Yr	NM
DISQUE-PHENOMENON			
❑ 2696 [10]	Edgar Redmond & the Modern String Ensemble	1965	30.00

REDPATH, JEAN

Number	Title	Yr	NM
ELEKTRA			
❑ EKL-274 [M]	Laddie Lie Near Me	1964	16.00
❑ EKS-7274 [S]	Laddie Lie Near Me	1964	25.00
❑ EKL-214 [M]	Scottish Ballad Book	1962	25.00
❑ EKL-224 [M]	Songs of Love, Lilt and Laughter	1963	25.00
PRESTIGE			
❑ PR-13041 [M]	Skipping Barefoot Through the Heather	1962	30.00

REECE, DIZZY, AND TUBBY HAYES

Number	Title	Yr	NM
SAVOY			
❑ MG-12111 [M]	Changing the Jazz at Buckingham Palace	1957	100.00

REECE, DIZZY

Number	Title	Yr	NM
BEE HIVE			
❑ BH-7001	Manhattan Project	1978	30.00
BLUE NOTE			
❑ BLP-4006 [M]	Blues in Trinity	1958	400.00
—Deep groove" version; W. 63rd St. address on label			
❑ BLP-4006 [M]	Blues in Trinity	1958	150.00
—Regular version, W. 63rd St. address on label			
❑ BST-4006 [S]	Blues in Trinity	1959	600.00
—Deep groove" version; W. 63rd St. address on label			
❑ BST-4006 [S]	Blues in Trinity	1959	120.00
Regular version, W. 63rd St. address on label			
❑ BLP-4006 [M]	Blues in Trinity	1963	40.00
—With "New York, USA" address on label			
❑ BST-4006 [S]	Blues in Trinity	1963	30.00
—With "New York, USA" address on label			
❑ BST-84006 [S]	Blues in Trinity	1967	30.00
—With "A Division of Liberty Records" on label			
❑ B1-32093	Blues in Trinity	1995	18.00
❑ BLP-4033 [M]	Soundin' Off	1960	400.00
—Deep groove" version; W. 63rd St. address on label			
❑ BLP-4033 [M]	Soundin' Off	1960	200.00
—Regular version, W. 63rd St. address on label			
❑ BST-84033 [S]	Soundin' Off	1960	150.00
—With W. 63rd St. address on label			
❑ BLP-4033 [M]	Soundin' Off	1963	50.00
—With "New York, USA" address on label			
❑ BST-84033 [S]	Soundin' Off	1963	40.00
—With "New York, USA" address on label			
❑ BST-84033 [S]	Soundin' Off	1967	30.00
—With "A Division of Liberty Records" on label			
❑ BLP-4023 [M]	Star Bright	1959	250.00
—Deep groove" version; W. 63rd St. address on label			
❑ BLP-4023 [M]	Star Bright	1959	150.00
—Regular version, W. 63rd St. address on label			
❑ BST-84023 [S]	Star Bright	1959	120.00
—With W. 63rd St. address on label			
❑ BLP-4023 [M]	Star Bright	1963	40.00
—With "New York, USA" address on label			
❑ BST-84023 [S]	Star Bright	1963	40.00
—With "New York, USA" address on label			
❑ BST-84023 [S]	Star Bright	1967	30.00
—With "A Division of Liberty Records" on label			
❑ BLP-4023 [M]	Star Bright	200?	30.00
—200-gram reissue; distributed by Classic Records			
DISCOVERY			
❑ DS-839	Moose the Mooche	1982	25.00
IMPERIAL			
❑ LP-9043 [M]	London Jazz	1957	80.00
NEW JAZZ			
❑ NJLP-8274 [M]	Asia Minor	1962	60.00
—Purple label			
❑ NJLP-8274 [M]	Asia Minor	1965	30.00
—Blue label, trident logo at right			

REED, JERRY

Number	Title	Yr	NM
CAPITOL			
❑ ST-12492	Lookin' at You	1986	10.00
HARMONY			
❑ H30547	I'm Movin' On	1971	12.00
RCA CAMDEN			
❑ CAS-2585	Oh What a Woman!	1972	12.00
❑ ACL1-0331	Tupelo Mississippi Flash	1973	12.00
RCA VICTOR			
❑ APL1-0544	A Good Woman's Love	1974	15.00
❑ LSP-4069	Alabama Wild Man	1968	25.00
❑ LSP-4147	Better Things in Life	1969	25.00
❑ APL1-1861	Both Barrels	1976	15.00
❑ AHL1-5472	Collector's Series	1985	12.00
❑ LSP-4293	Cookin'	1970	25.00
❑ AHL1-4021	Dixie Dreams	1981	15.00
❑ AHL1-2516	East Bound and Down	1977	15.00
❑ AYL1-3677	East Bound and Down	1980	10.00
—Best Buy Series" reissue			
❑ LSP-4391 [B]	Georgia Sunshine	1970	30.00
❑ AHL1-5176	Greatest Hits	1984	12.00
❑ AHL1-3359	Half Singin' & Half Pickin'	1979	15.00
❑ LSP-4838	Hot A' Mighty!	1973	18.00
❑ LSP-4750	Jerry Reed	1972	18.00
❑ LSP-4204	Jerry Reed Explores Guitar Country	1969	25.00
❑ AHL1-3453	Jerry Reed Live!	1979	15.00
❑ AYL1-4167	Jerry Reed Live!	1982	10.00
—Best Buy Series" reissue			
❑ AHL1-2346	Jerry Reed Rides Again	1977	15.00
❑ AHL1-3604	Jerry Reed Sings Jim Croce	1980	15.00
❑ LSP-4596	Ko-Ko Joe	1971	18.00
❑ APL1-0238	Lord, Mr. Ford	1973	15.00
❑ APD1-0238 [Q]	Lord, Mr. Ford	1973	30.00
❑ LSP-4707	Me and Chet	1972	18.00
—With Chet Atkins			
❑ ANL1-2167	Me and Chet	1976	12.00
—Reissue of 4707			
❑ APL1-0787	Mind Your Love	1974	15.00
❑ LPM-3978 [M]	Nashville Underground	1968	50.00
❑ LSP-3978 [S]	Nashville Underground	1968	25.00
❑ AHL1-4692	Ready	1983	12.00
❑ APL1-1226	Red Hot Picker	1975	15.00
❑ LSP-4660	Smell the Flowers	1972	18.00
❑ AHL1-2764	Sweet Love Feelings	1978	15.00
❑ AHL1-3771	Texas Bound and Flyin'	1980	15.00
❑ AYL1-4394	Texas Bound and Flyin'	1982	10.00
—Best Buy Series" reissue			
❑ LSP-4729	The Best of Jerry Reed	1972	18.00
❑ AHL1-4529	The Bird	1982	12.00
❑ AYL1-5151	The Bird	1984	10.00
—Best Buy Series" reissue			
❑ AHL1-4315	The Man with the Golden Thumb	1982	12.00
❑ LPM-3756 [M]	The Unbelievable Guitar and Voice of Jerry Reed	1967	30.00
❑ LSP-3756 [S]	The Unbelievable Guitar and Voice of Jerry Reed	1967	25.00
❑ APL1-0356	The Uptown Poker Club	1973	15.00
❑ LSP-4506	When You're Hot, You're Hot	1971	18.00
❑ ANL1-1345	When You're Hot, You're Hot	1975	12.00
—Reissue of 4506			

REED, JIMMY

Number	Title	Yr	NM
ANTILLES			
❑ 7007	Cold Chills	197?	10.00
BLUESVILLE			
❑ BLS-6054	I Ain't From Chicago	1973	18.00
❑ BLS-6073	Jimmy Reed at Carnegie Hall	1973	25.00
❑ BLS-6067	The Ultimate Jimmy Reed	1973	18.00
BLUESWAY			
❑ BLS-6015	Big Boss Man	1968	25.00
❑ BLS-6024	Down in Virginia	1969	25.00
❑ BL 6009 [M]	Soulin'	1967	25.00
❑ BLS-6009 [S]	Soulin'	1967	25.00
❑ BL-6004 [M]	The New Jimmy Reed Album	1967	25.00
❑ BLS-6004 [S]	The New Jimmy Reed Album	1967	25.00
BUDDAH			
❑ BDS-4003	The Very Best of Jimmy Reed	1969	18.00
—Reissue of Vee Jay 1039			
CHAMELEON			
❑ D1-74762	Bright Lights, Big City	1988	12.00
EVEREST ARCHIVE OF FOLK & JAZZ			
❑ 234	Jimmy Reed	197?	15.00
GNP CRESCENDO			
❑ GNPS-10006	The Best of Jimmy Reed	1974	18.00
SUNSET			
❑ SUS-5218	Somethin' Else	1968	15.00
TRADITION			
❑ 2069	Wailin' the Blues	1969	15.00
TRIP			
❑ 8012	History of Jimmy Reed	1971	18.00
VEE JAY			
❑ VJS-7303	Blues Is My Business	198?	12.00
❑ LP-1022 [M]	Found Love	1959	200.00
—Maroon label			
❑ LP-1022 [M]	Found Love	1961	80.00
—Black label with colorband			
❑ LP-1004 [M]	I'm Jimmy Reed	1958	220.00
—Maroon label			
❑ LP-1004 [M]	I'm Jimmy Reed	1961	80.00
—Black label with colorband			
❑ VJLP-1004	I'm Jimmy Reed	198?	12.00
—Reissue with glossy labels			
❑ 2LP-1035 [M]	Jimmy Reed at Carnegie Hall	1961	50.00
❑ 2SR-1035 [S]	Jimmy Reed at Carnegie Hall	1961	70.00
❑ VJLP2-1035	Jimmy Reed at Carnegie Hall	198?	15.00
—Reissue with glossy labels			
❑ LP-1095 [M]	Jimmy Reed at Soul City	1964	40.00
❑ VJLP-1095	Jimmy Reed at Soul City	198?	12.00
—Reissue with glossy labels			
❑ LP-1050 [M]	Just Jimmy Reed	1962	40.00
❑ SR-1050 [S]	Just Jimmy Reed	1962	60.00
❑ LP-1080 [M]	More of the Best of Jimmy Reed	1964	40.00
❑ SR-1080 [S]	More of the Best of Jimmy Reed	1964	150.00
❑ LP-1025 [M]	Now Appearing	1960	80.00
❑ VJLP-1025	Now Appearing	198?	12.00
—Reissue with glossy labels			
❑ LP-1008 [M]	Rockin' with Reed	1959	200.00
—Maroon label			
❑ LP-1008 [M]	Rockin' with Reed	1961	80.00
—Black label with colorband			
❑ VJLP-1008	Rockin' with Reed	198?	12.00
—Reissue with glossy labels			
❑ LP-1067 [M]	T'Ain't No Big Thing…But He Is Jimmy Reed	1963	40.00
❑ SR-1067 [S]	T'Ain't No Big Thing…But He Is Jimmy Reed	1963	60.00
❑ LP-1073 [M]	The 12 String Guitar Blues	1963	40.00
❑ SR-1073 [S]	The 12 String Guitar Blues	1963	150.00
❑ LP-1039 [M]	The Best of Jimmy Reed	1962	40.00
❑ SR-1039 [S]	The Best of Jimmy Reed	1962	60.00
❑ VJLP-1039	The Best of Jimmy Reed	198?	12.00
—Reissue with glossy labels			
❑ LP-1072 [M]	The Best of the Blues	1963	40.00
❑ LP-8501 [M]	The Legend, The Man	1965	40.00
❑ VJS-8501 [S]	The Legend, The Man	1965	150.00
❑ VJLP-8501	The Legend, The Man	198?	12.00
—Reissue with glossy labels			

REED, LOU, AND JOHN CALE

Number	Title	Yr	NM
SIRE			
❑ 26140 [B]	Songs for Drella	1990	18.00

REED, LOU

Number	Title	Yr	NM
ARISTA			
❑ ALB6-8390	City Lights -- Classic Performances by Lou Reed	1985	12.00
❑ AL9522	Growing Up in Public	1980	15.00
❑ AL8502 [B]	Live! Take No Prisoners	1978	30.00
❑ R252506	Rock and Roll Diary 1967-1980	1980	25.00
—RCA Music Service edition			
❑ A2L8603	Rock and Roll Diary 1967-1980	1980	25.00
❑ AL118434	Rock and Roll Diary 1967-1980	198?	16.00
—Reissue			
❑ AL4100	Rock and Roll Heart	1976	18.00
—Originals on light blue labels			
❑ AL4169	Street Hassle	1978	18.00
❑ AL4220	The Bells	1979	15.00
DIRECT DISK			
❑ (no #)0 [DJ]	The Blue Mask	1982	150.00
—Only exists on test pressings; no stock copies made			
RCA			
❑ 88691958021 [B]	Rock N Roll Animal	2012	30.00
RCA VICTOR			
❑ APL1-0207 [B]	Berlin	1973	35.00
❑ AYL1-4388	Berlin	1983	10.00
—Best Buy Series reissue			
❑ APL1-0915 [B]	Coney Island Baby	1976	25.00
❑ ANL1-2480	Coney Island Baby	1977	10.00
—Reissue			
❑ AYL1-3807	Coney Island Baby	1980	10.00
—Best Buy Series reissue			
❑ AFL1-4568	Legendary Hearts	1983	12.00
❑ LSP-4701 [B]	Lou Reed	1972	30.00
❑ APL1-0959	Lou Reed Live	1975	18.00
❑ AFL1-0959	Lou Reed Live	1977	10.00
—Reissue			
❑ AYL1-3752	Lou Reed Live	1980	10.00
—Best Buy Series reissue			
❑ CPL2-1101 [B]	Metal Machine Music	1975	80.00
—Orange or brown label			
❑ CPD2-1101 [Q]	Metal Machine Music	1975	150.00
❑ AFL1-7190	Mistrial	1986	15.00
❑ AFL1-4998	New Sensations	1984	10.00
❑ APL1-0472	Rock & Roll Animal	1974	15.00
❑ AFL1-0472	Rock & Roll Animal	1977	10.00
—Reissue			
❑ AYL1-3664	Rock & Roll Animal	1980	10.00
—Best Buy Series reissue			
❑ CPL1-0611	Sally Can't Dance	1974	25.00
❑ AFL1-0611	Sally Can't Dance	1977	10.00
—Reissue			
❑ AYL1-4555	Sally Can't Dance	1983	10.00
—Best Buy Series reissue			

Number	Title	Yr	NM
❑ DJL1-4266 [DJ]	Special Radio Series, Vol. XVII	1980	30.00
—Promo-only with insert			
❑ AFL1-4221	The Blue Mask	1982	12.00
❑ AYL1-4780	The Blue Mask	1984	10.00
—Best Buy Series reissue			
❑ DJL1-4267	The Blue Mask Interview Album	1982	30.00
❑ DJL1-4345 [DJ]	The Blue Mask Sampler	1982	15.00
—Three-song EP released to radio			
❑ LSP-4807	Transformer	1972	25.00
❑ AFL1-4807	Transformer	1977	10.00
—Reissue			
❑ AYL1-3806	Transformer	1980	10.00
—Best Buy Series reissue			
❑ APL1-2001	Walk on the Wild Side	1977	15.00
❑ AFL1-2001	Walk on the Wild Side	1978	10.00
—Reissue			
❑ AYL1-3753	Walk on the Wild Side	1980	10.00
—Best Buy Series reissue			
SIRE			
❑ R101058	New York	1989	15.00
—BMG Music Service edition			
❑ 25829	New York	1989	12.00

REED, LUCY

Number	Title	Yr	NM
FANTASY			
❑ 3212 [M]	The Singing Reed	1956	150.00
—Red vinyl			
❑ 3212 [M]	The Singing Reed	195?	80.00
—Black vinyl			
❑ 3243 [M]	This Is Lucy Reed	1957	150.00
—Red vinyl			
❑ 3243 [M]	This Is Lucy Reed	195?	80.00
—Black vinyl			

REED, LULA

Number	Title	Yr	NM
KING			
❑ 604 [M]	Blue and Moody	1958	2000.00

REED, VIVIAN

Number	Title	Yr	NM
EPIC			
❑ BN26412	Vivian Reed	1968	40.00
H&L			
❑ 69017	Brown Sugar	1976	25.00
UNITED ARTISTS			
❑ UA-LA911-H	Another Side	1978	18.00
❑ UA-LA970-H	Ready and Waiting	1979	18.00

REED, WAYMON

Number	Title	Yr	NM
ARTISTS HOUSE			
❑ 10	46th and 8th	1980	15.00

REESE, DELLA

Number	Title	Yr	NM
ABC			
❑ 612 [M]	Della on Strings of Blue	1967	25.00
❑ S-612 [S]	Della on Strings of Blue	1967	18.00
❑ 569 [M]	Della Reese Live	1966	18.00
❑ S-569 [S]	Della Reese Live	1966	25.00
❑ S-636	I Gotta Be Me…This Trip Out	1968	18.00
❑ 589 [M]	One More Time	1967	25.00
❑ S-589 [S]	One More Time	1967	18.00
❑ AC-30002	The ABC Collection	1976	18.00
ABC-PARAMOUNT			
❑ ABC-524 [M]	C'mon and Hear Della Reese	1965	18.00
❑ ABCS-524 [S]	C'mon and Hear Della Reese	1965	25.00
❑ ABC-540 [M]	I Like It Like Dat!	1966	18.00
❑ ABCS-540 [S]	I Like It Like Dat!	1966	25.00
AVCO EMBASSY			
❑ 33004	Black Is Beautiful	1969	18.00
❑ 33017	Right Now	1970	18.00
JAZZ A LA CARTE			
❑ 3	One of a Kind	1978	18.00
JUBILEE			
❑ JLP-1071 [M]	A Date with Della Reese at Mr. Kelly's in Chicago	1959	30.00
—Originals have blue labels			
❑ SDJLP-1071 [S]	A Date with Della Reese at Mr. Kelly's in Chicago	1959	30.00
—Originals have blue labels			
❑ JGM-1071 [M]	A Date with Della Reese at Mr. Kelly's in Chicago	196?	25.00
—Black label with all-silver print			
❑ JGM-1071 [M]	A Date with Della Reese at Mr. Kelly's in Chicago	1963	18.00
—Black label, multi-colored spokes around "jubilee			
❑ SDJLP-1071 [S]	A Date with Della Reese at Mr. Kelly's in Chicago	1959	30.00
—Black label with all-silver print			
❑ SDJLP-1071 [S]	A Date with Della Reese at Mr. Kelly's in Chicago	1962	25.00
—Black label, multi-colored spokes around "jubilee," yellow spoke goes almost to center hole			
❑ JGS-1071 [S]	A Date with Della Reese at Mr. Kelly's in Chicago	1965	18.00
—Black label, multi-colored spokes around "jubilee," yellow spoke goes nowhere near center hole; new prefix			
❑ JLP-1083 [M]	Amen	1959	30.00
❑ SDJLP-1083 [S]	Amen	1959	30.00
❑ JLP-1116 [M]	And That Reminds Me	1960	30.00
❑ JLP-1026 [M]	Melancholy Baby	1957	30.00
❑ JGM-5002 [M]	The Best of Della Reese	196?	18.00
❑ JGS-5002 [S]	The Best of Della Reese	196?	25.00
❑ JLP-1095 [M]	The Story of the Blues	1960	30.00
—Original labels are black with all-silver print			
❑ SDJLP-1095 [S]	The Story of the Blues	1960	30.00
—Original labels are black with all-silver print			
❑ JLP-1095 [M]	The Story of the Blues	1960	25.00
—Black label, multi-colored spokes around "jubilee," yellow spoke goes almost to center hole			
❑ JGM-1095 [M]	The Story of the Blues	1962	18.00
—Black label, multi-colored spokes around "jubilee," yellow spoke goes almost to center hole; new prefix			
❑ JGS-1095 [S]	The Story of the Blues	1964	18.00
—Black label, multi-colored spokes around "jubilee," yellow spoke goes nowhere near center hole			
❑ SDJLP-1095 [S]	The Story of the Blues	1962	30.00
—Black label, multi-colored spokes around "jubilee," yellow spoke goes almost to center hole			
❑ JLP-1109 [M]	What Do You Know About Love	1960	30.00
PICKWICK			
❑ SPC-3058	And That Reminds Me	196?	15.00
RCA VICTOR			
❑ LPM-2157 [M]	Della	1960	25.00
❑ LSP-2157 [S]	Della	1960	30.00
❑ LPM-2204 [M]	Della by Starlight	1960	25.00
❑ LSP-2204 [S]	Della by Starlight	1960	30.00
❑ LPM-2280 [M]	Della Della Cha-Cha-Cha	1961	25.00
❑ LSP-2280 [S]	Della Della Cha-Cha-Cha	1961	30.00
❑ LPM-2568 [M]	Della on Stage	1962	25.00
❑ LSP-2568 [S]	Della on Stage	1962	30.00
❑ LPM-2872 [M]	Della Reese at Basin Street East	1964	25.00
❑ LSP-2872 [S]	Della Reese at Basin Street East	1964	30.00
❑ LPM-2814 [M]	Moody	1963	25.00
❑ LSP-2814 [S]	Moody	1963	30.00
❑ LPM-2391 [M]	Special Delivery	1961	25.00
❑ LSP-2391 [S]	Special Delivery	1961	30.00
❑ LSP-4651	The Best of Della Reese	1972	15.00
❑ LPM-2419 [M]	The Classic Della	1962	25.00
❑ LSP-2419 [S]	The Classic Della	1962	30.00
❑ LPM-2711 [M]	Waltz with Me, Della	1963	25.00
❑ LSP-2711 [S]	Waltz with Me, Della	1963	30.00

REEVES, DEL, AND BILLIE JO SPEARS

Number	Title	Yr	NM
UNITED ARTISTS			
❑ UA-LA649-G	By Request: Del and Billie Jo	1976	18.00

REEVES, DEL, AND BOBBY GOLDSBORO

Number	Title	Yr	NM
UNITED ARTISTS			
❑ UAL3615 [M]	Our Way of Life	1967	50.00
❑ UAS6615 [S]	Our Way of Life	1967	25.00

REEVES, DEL

Number	Title	Yr	NM
KOALA			
❑ KO14188	Del Reeves	1980	15.00
PLAYBACK			
❑ 12002	Here's Del Reeves	1988	18.00
STARDAY			
❑ 998	Greatest Hits	197?	12.00
SUNSET			
❑ SUS-5279	Country Concert Live!	1969	15.00
❑ SUS-5321	Out in the Country	1970	15.00
❑ SUS-5230	Wonderful World of Country Music	1968	15.00
UNITED ARTISTS			
❑ UA-LA687-G	10th Anniversary	1977	15.00
❑ UAS-6830	Before Goodbye	1972	25.00
❑ UAS-6733	Big Daddy Del	1970	25.00
❑ UAL-3441 [M]	Del Reeves Sings Girl on the Billboard	1965	30.00
❑ UAS-6441 [S]	Del Reeves Sings Girl on the Billboard	1965	30.00
❑ UAL-3468 [M]	Del Reeves Sings Jim Reeves	1966	25.00
❑ UAS-6468 [S]	Del Reeves Sings Jim Reeves	1966	30.00
❑ UA-LA364-G	Del Reeves with Strings and Things	1975	18.00
❑ UAL-3458 [M]	Doodle-Oo-Doo-Doo	1965	25.00
❑ UAS-6458 [S]	Doodle-Oo-Doo-Doo	1965	30.00
❑ UAS-6705	Down at Good Time Charlie's	1969	25.00
❑ UAS-6789	Friends and Neighbors	1971	25.00
❑ UAL-3530 [M]	Gettin' Any Feed for Your Chickens?	1966	25.00
❑ UAS-6530 [S]	Gettin' Any Feed for Your Chickens?	1966	30.00
❑ UA-LA204-G	Live at the Palomino Club	1974	18.00
❑ UAS-6674	Looking at the World Through a Windshield	1968	25.00
❑ UAS-6643	Running Wild	1968	25.00
❑ UAL-3528 [M]	Santa's Boy	1966	25.00
❑ UAS-6528 [S]	Santa's Boy	1966	30.00
❑ UAL-3595 [M]	Six of One, Half a Dozen of the Other	1967	30.00
❑ UAS-6595 [S]	Six of One, Half a Dozen of the Other	1967	25.00
❑ UAL-3488 [M]	Special Delivery	1966	25.00
❑ UAS-6488 [S]	Special Delivery	1966	30.00
❑ UAL-3571 [M]	Struttin' My Stuff	1967	30.00
❑ UAS-6571 [S]	Struttin' My Stuff	1967	25.00
❑ UAS-6635	The Best of Del Reeves	1968	25.00
❑ UAS-6758	The Best of Del Reeves, Vol. 2	1970	25.00
❑ UAS-6820	The Del Reeves Album	1971	25.00
❑ UAS-6612 [S]	The Little Church in the Dell	1967	30.00
❑ UAL-3612 [M]	The Little Church in the Dell	1967	30.00
❑ UA-LA235	The Very Best of Del Reeves	1974	18.00
❑ UA-LA044-F	Trucker's Paradise	1973	18.00

REEVES, DIANNE

Number	Title	Yr	NM
BLUE NOTE			
❑ BT-46906	Dianne Reeves	1987	12.00
EMI			
❑ E1-92401	Never Too Far	1990	15.00
PALO ALTO			
❑ PA-8026	Welcome to My Love	1983	18.00
PALO ALTO/TBA			
❑ TB-203	For Every Heart	1984	15.00

REEVES, JIM, AND PATSY CLINE

Number	Title	Yr	NM
MCA			
❑ 5319	Remembering Jim Reeves and Patsy Cline	1982	18.00
RCA VICTOR			
❑ AHL1-4127	Greatest Hits	1981	18.00
❑ AYL1-5152	Greatest Hits	1984	12.00
—Best Buy Series" reissue			

REEVES, JIM

Number	Title	Yr	NM
ABBOTT			
❑ LP-5001 [M]	Jim Reeves Sings	1956	2000.00
—VG value 1000; VG+ value 1500			
COUNTRY MUSIC FOUNDATION			
❑ CMF-008	Live at the Opry	198?	12.00
PAIR			
❑ PDL2-1002	The Country Side of Jim Reeves	1986	15.00
RCA CAMDEN			
❑ CAL-583 [M]	According to My Heart	1960	25.00
❑ CAS-583 [R]	According to My Heart	1960	25.00
❑ CAL-784 [M]	Good 'N' Country	1963	25.00
❑ CAS-784 [S]	Good 'N' Country	1963	25.00
❑ CAL-842 [M]	Have I Told You Lately That I Love You?	1964	25.00
❑ CAS-842 [S]	Have I Told You Lately That I Love You?	1964	25.00
❑ CAX-9001	Jim Reeves	1972	25.00
❑ ACL1-0123	Kimberley Jim	1973	18.00
❑ CAL-686 [M]	The Country Side of Jim Reeves	1962	25.00
❑ CAS-686 [S]	The Country Side of Jim Reeves	1962	25.00
❑ CAS-2532	Young and Country	1971	18.00
RCA VICTOR			
❑ CPL1-1891	A Legendary Performer	1976	25.00
❑ APL1-0039	Am I That Easy to Forget	1973	25.00
❑ AHL1-4865	A Special Collection	1983	15.00
❑ LPM-3987 [M]	A Touch of Sadness	1968	60.00
❑ LSP-3987 [S]	A Touch of Sadness	1968	25.00
❑ LPM-2487 [M]	A Touch of Velvet	1962	30.00
❑ LSP-2487 [S]	A Touch of Velvet	1962	30.00
❑ LPM-1410 [M]	Bimbo	1957	200.00
—Reissue of Abbott LP			
❑ LPM-3793 [M]	Blue Side of Lonesome	1967	30.00
❑ LSP-3793 [S]	Blue Side of Lonesome	1967	25.00
❑ AHL1-5424	Collector's Series	1985	15.00
❑ LPM-3542 [M]	Distant Drums	1966	25.00
❑ LSP-3542 [P]	Distant Drums	1966	30.00
—Overnight" and "The Gods Were Angry with Me" are rechanneled			
❑ AHL1-3454	Don't Let Me Cross Over	1979	18.00
❑ AYL1-4833	Don't Let Me Cross Over	1983	12.00
—Best Buy Series" reissue			
❑ LPM-2223 [M]	Featuring He'll Have to Go and Other Favorites	1960	30.00
—Black and white cover (original)			
❑ LSP-2223 [S]	Featuring He'll Have to Go and Other Favorites	1960	40.00
—Black and white cover (original)			
❑ LPM-2223 [M]	Featuring He'll Have to Go and Other Favorites	1962	25.00
—Color cover (reissue)			
❑ LSP-2223 [S]	Featuring He'll Have to Go and Other Favorites	1962	30.00
—Color cover (reissue)			
❑ LPM-2605 [M]	Gentleman Jim	1963	30.00
❑ LSP-2605 [S]	Gentleman Jim	1963	30.00
❑ LPM-1685 [M]	Girls I Have Known	1958	60.00
❑ LPM-1950 [M]	God Be With You	1958	40.00
❑ LSP-1950 [S]	God Be With You	1958	50.00
❑ APL1-0330	Great Moments with Jim Reeves	1973	25.00
❑ APL1-0537	I'd Fight the World	1974	25.00
❑ APL1-1224	I Love You Because	1976	25.00
❑ AYL1-4835	I Love You Because	1983	12.00
—Best Buy Series" reissue			
❑ APL1-2309	It's Nothin' to Me	1977	18.00

Number	Title	Yr	NM
❑ LPM-1576 [M]	Jim Reeves	1957	80.00
❑ AHL1-2720	Jim Reeves	1978	18.00
❑ LSP-4112	Jim Reeves and Some Friends	1969	25.00
❑ LSP-4062	Jim Reeves On Stage	1968	25.00
❑ LSP-4475	Jim Reeves Writes You a Record	1971	25.00
❑ CPL2-5044	Just for You	1984	18.00
❑ LPM-2780 [M]	Kimberley Jim	1964	30.00
❑ LSP-2780 [S]	Kimberley Jim	1964	30.00
❑ LSP-4749	Missing You	1972	25.00
❑ LPM-2854 [M]	Moonlight and Roses	1964	30.00
❑ LSP-2854 [S]	Moonlight and Roses	1964	30.00
❑ LPM-3903 [M]	My Cathedral	1967	30.00
❑ LSP-3903 [S]	My Cathedral	1967	30.00
❑ LSP-4646	My Friend	1972	25.00
❑ ANL1-3014	Pure Gold, Volume 1	1978	15.00
❑ AYL1-3936	Pure Gold, Volume 1	1980	12.00
— Best Buy Series" reissue			
❑ LPM-1256 [M]	Singing Down the Lane	1956	200.00
❑ LSP-4528	Something Special	1971	25.00
❑ APL1-1037	Songs of Love	1975	25.00
❑ AYL1-4836	Songs of Love	1983	12.00
— Best Buy Series" reissue			
❑ LPM-2001 [M]	Songs to Warm the Heart	1959	40.00
❑ LSP-2001 [S]	Songs to Warm the Heart	1959	50.00
❑ LPM-2339 [M]	Talkin' to Your Heart	1961	30.00
❑ LSP-2339 [S]	Talkin' to Your Heart	1961	30.00
❑ LPM-2284 [M]	Tall Tales and Short Tempers	1961	30.00
❑ LSP-2284 [S]	Tall Tales and Short Tempers	1961	30.00
❑ LPM-2890 [M]	The Best of Jim Reeves	1964	25.00
❑ LSP-2890 [S]	The Best of Jim Reeves	1964	30.00
❑ AYL1-3678	The Best of Jim Reeves	1980	15.00
— Best Buy Series" reissue			
❑ LPM-3482 [M]	The Best of Jim Reeves, Vol. II	1966	25.00
❑ LSP-3482(e) [P]	The Best of Jim Reeves, Vol. II	1966	30.00
— This album is at least partially, and possibly entirely, in rechanneled stereo			
❑ AYL1-4168	The Best of Jim Reeves, Vol. II	1981	12.00
— Best Buy Series" reissue			
❑ AHL1-3271	The Best of Jim Reeves, Volume IV	1979	18.00
❑ AYL1-4075	The Best of Jim Reeves, Volume IV	1981	12.00
— Best Buy Series" reissue			
❑ APL1-0793	The Best of Jim Reeves Sacred Songs	1974	25.00
❑ AYL1-3765	The Best of Jim Reeves Sacred Songs	1980	12.00
— Best Buy Series" reissue			
❑ AYL1-4838	The Best of Jim Reeves, Vol. III	1983	12.00
— Best Buy Series" reissue			
❑ LSP-4187	The Best of Jim Reeves Volume III	1969	25.00
❑ LPM-2704 [M]	The International Jim Reeves	1963	30.00
❑ LSP-2704 [S]	The International Jim Reeves	1963	30.00
❑ LPM-2216 [M]	The Intimate Jim Reeves	1960	30.00
❑ LSP-2216 [S]	The Intimate Jim Reeves	1960	40.00
❑ AHL1-4531	The Jim Reeves Medley	1983	12.00
❑ LPM-2968 [M]	The Jim Reeves Way	1965	25.00
❑ LSP-2968 [S]	The Jim Reeves Way	1965	30.00
❑ AHL1-3827	There's Always Me	1980	15.00
❑ AYL1-4839	There's Always Me	1983	12.00
— Best Buy Series" reissue			
❑ LPM-2758 [M]	Twelve Songs of Christmas	1963	30.00
❑ LSP-2758 [S]	Twelve Songs of Christmas	1963	30.00
❑ ANL1-1927	Twelve Songs of Christmas	1976	10.00
— Reissue of LSP-2758			
❑ LPM-3427 [M]	Up Through the Years	1965	25.00
❑ LSP-3427 [S]	Up Through the Years	1965	30.00
❑ LPM-2552 [M]	We Thank Thee	1962	30.00
❑ LSP-2552 [S]	We Thank Thee	1962	30.00
❑ AYL1-4840	We Thank Thee	1983	12.00
— Best Buy Series" reissue			
❑ LPM-3709 [M]	Yours Sincerely, Jim Reeves	1966	25.00
❑ LSP-3709(e) [P]	Yours Sincerely, Jim Reeves	1966	30.00
— This album is at least partially, and possibly entirely, in rechanneled stereo			

TIME-LIFE

Number	Title	Yr	NM
❑ STW-113	Country Music	1981	12.00

REEVES, MARTHA

ARISTA

Number	Title	Yr	NM
❑ AL4105	The Rest of My Life	1976	15.00

FANTASY

Number	Title	Yr	NM
❑ F-9591	Gotta Keep Moving	1980	15.00
❑ F-9549	We'll Meet Again	1978	15.00

MCA

Number	Title	Yr	NM
❑ 414	Martha Reeves	1974	15.00

REFLECTIONS, THE (1)

GOLDEN WORLD

Number	Title	Yr	NM
❑ 300 [M]	(Just Like) Romeo and Juliet	1964	150.00

REGENT CONCERT ORCHESTRA, THE

REGENT

Number	Title	Yr	NM
❑ 6091 [M]	Amor	1958	50.00
— Cover model is Jayne Mansfield			

REGENTS, THE (1)

GEE

Number	Title	Yr	NM
❑ GLP-706 [M]	Barbara Ann	1961	150.00
❑ SGLP-706 [S]	Barbara Ann	1961	250.00
❑ SGLP-706	Barbara Ann	197?	30.00
— Reissue by Publishers Central Bureau (clearly marked as such on cover)			

REGENTS, THE (U)

CAPITOL

Number	Title	Yr	NM
❑ KAO2153 [M]	Live at the AM-PM Discotheque	1964	50.00
❑ SKAO2153 [S]	Live at the AM-PM Discotheque	1964	60.00

REHAK, FRANK/ALEX SMITH

DAWN

Number	Title	Yr	NM
❑ DLP-1107 [M]	Jazzville, Vol. 2	1956	100.00

REICHMAN, JOE

CIRCLE

Number	Title	Yr	NM
❑ CLP-84	The Pagliacci of the Piano	1986	12.00

HINDSIGHT

Number	Title	Yr	NM
❑ HSR-166	Joe Reichman and His Orchestra 1944-49	198?	12.00

RCA CAMDEN

Number	Title	Yr	NM
❑ CAL-230 [M]	Show Tunes of Broadway	1954	18.00
❑ CAL-133 [M]	Tea for Two	195?	18.00

REID, CLARENCE

ATCO

Number	Title	Yr	NM
❑ SD 33-307	Dancin' with Nobody But You Babe	1969	30.00

REID, IRENE

MGM

Number	Title	Yr	NM
❑ E-4159 [M]	It's Only the Beginning for Irene Reid	1963	25.00
❑ SE-4159 [S]	It's Only the Beginning for Irene Reid	1963	30.00

POLYDOR

Number	Title	Yr	NM
❑ 24-4040	The World Needs What I Need	1971	18.00

VERVE

Number	Title	Yr	NM
❑ V-8621 [M]	Room for One More	1965	18.00
❑ V6-8621 [S]	Room for One More	1965	25.00

REID, RUFUS

SUNNYSIDE

Number	Title	Yr	NM
❑ SSC-1010	Seven Minds	1985	12.00

THERESA

Number	Title	Yr	NM
❑ 111	Perpetual Stroll	1980	15.00

REID, TERRY

4 MEN WITH BEARDS

Number	Title	Yr	NM
❑ 4M106LP [B]	River		25.00

ABC

Number	Title	Yr	NM
❑ X-935	Seed of Memory	1976	15.00

ATLANTIC

Number	Title	Yr	NM
❑ SD7259	River	1973	15.00

CAPITOL

Number	Title	Yr	NM
❑ SW-11857	Rogue Waves	1978	15.00

EPIC

Number	Title	Yr	NM
❑ BN26427	Bang, Bang You're Terry Reid	1968	18.00
❑ BN26477	Terry Reid	1969	18.00

REILLY, JACK

CAROUSEL

Number	Title	Yr	NM
❑ 1001	Blue-Sean-Green	197?	18.00
❑ 1002	Tributes	197?	18.00

REVELATION

Number	Title	Yr	NM
❑ 36	Brinksman	198?	12.00
❑ 35	Together (Again)… For the First Time	198?	12.00

REINER, CARL, AND MEL BROOKS

CAPITOL

Number	Title	Yr	NM
❑ W1618 [M]	2000 and One Years	1961	18.00
❑ SW1618 [S]	2000 and One Years	1961	25.00
❑ W1529 [M]	2000 Years	1961	18.00
❑ SW1529 [S]	2000 Years	1961	25.00
❑ W1815 [M]	At the Cannes Film Festival	1962	18.00
❑ SW1815 [S]	At the Cannes Film Festival	1962	25.00
❑ ST2981	The Best of the 2000 Year Old Man	1968	18.00

WARNER BROS.

Number	Title	Yr	NM
❑ BS2741	2000 and Thirteen	1973	18.00
❑ 3XX2744	The Incomplete Works of Reiner and Brooks	1973	30.00

WORLD PACIFIC

Number	Title	Yr	NM
❑ WP-1401 [M]	2000 Years	1960	30.00

REINHARDT, DJANGO

ANGEL

Number	Title	Yr	NM
❑ ANG-36985	Django Reinhardt and the Quintet of the Hot Club of France	197?	12.00
❑ ANG.60011 [10]	Django's Guitar	1955	150.00
❑ ANG.60003 [10]	Le Jazz Hot	1954	150.00

BLUEBIRD

Number	Title	Yr	NM
❑ 9988-1-RB	Djangology 49	1990	15.00

CAPITOL

Number	Title	Yr	NM
❑ TBO10226 [M]	The Best of Django Reinhardt	1960	50.00
— Black colorband labels, Capitol logo at left			

CLEF

Number	Title	Yr	NM
❑ MGC-516 [10]	The Great Artistry of Django Reinhardt	1954	150.00

COLUMBIA

Number	Title	Yr	NM
❑ C31479	Swing It Lightly	1972	15.00
❑ PC31479	Swing It Lightly	198?	10.00
— Budget-line reissue			

EMARCY

Number	Title	Yr	NM
❑ 66004	Jazz Hot	1967	15.00

EPITAPH

Number	Title	Yr	NM
❑ E-4002	Django Reinhardt 1910-1953	1975	18.00

EVEREST ARCHIVE OF FOLK & JAZZ

Number	Title	Yr	NM
❑ FS-212 [R]	Django Reinhardt	1968	12.00
❑ FS-255	Django Reinhardt, Vol. 3	197?	12.00
❑ FS-306	Django Reinhardt, Vol. 4	197?	12.00
❑ FS-230 [R]	Django Reinhardt, Volume II	1969	12.00

GNP CRESCENDO

Number	Title	Yr	NM
❑ GNP-9031	Django Reinhardt 1934	197?	12.00
❑ GNP-9023	Django Reinhardt 1935	197?	12.00
❑ GNP-9019	Django Reinhardt 1935-39	197?	12.00
❑ GNP-9001	Django Reinhardt and the Quintet of the Hot Club of France	196?	12.00
❑ GNP-9039	Legendary Django Reinhardt	198?	12.00
❑ GNP-9002	Parisian Swing	197?	12.00
❑ GNP-9038	The Immortal Django Reinhardt	198?	12.00

INNER CITY

Number	Title	Yr	NM
❑ IC-1106	Compositions	198?	15.00
❑ IC-1104	Django Reinhardt and the Quintet of the Hot Club of France	198?	15.00
❑ IC-1105	Solos/Duos/Trios, Vol. 2	198?	15.00
❑ IC-7004	The Versatile Giant	198?	15.00

JAY

Number	Title	Yr	NM
❑ 3008 [10]	Django Reinhardt	1954	180.00

MERCURY

Number	Title	Yr	NM
❑ MGC-516 [10]	The Great Artistry of Django Reinhardt	1953	200.00

PERIOD

Number	Title	Yr	NM
❑ SPL-1100 [10]	Django Reinhardt Memorial, Volume 1	1954	120.00
❑ SPL-1101 [10]	Django Reinhardt Memorial, Volume 2	1954	120.00
❑ SPL-1102 [10]	Django Reinhardt Memorial, Volume 3	1954	120.00
❑ SPL-1201 [M]	Django Reinhardt Memorial Album, Volume 1	1956	50.00
❑ SPL-1201 [M]	Django Reinhardt Memorial Album, Volume 2	1956	50.00
❑ SPL-1203 [M]	Django Reinhardt Memorial Album, Volume 3	1956	50.00
❑ SPL-1204 [M]	The Best of Django Reinhardt	1956	50.00
❑ SPL-2204 [R]	The Best of Django Reinhardt	196?	30.00

PRESTIGE

Number	Title	Yr	NM
❑ PRST-7633 [R]	Django Reinhardt and American Jazz Giants	1969	18.00

RCA VICTOR

Number	Title	Yr	NM
❑ LPM-2319 [M]	Djangology	1961	40.00
❑ LSP-2319 [R]	Djangology	196?	30.00
❑ LPM-1100 [M]	Django Reinhardt	1955	100.00

REPRISE

Number	Title	Yr	NM
❑ R-6075 [M]	The Immortal Django Reinhardt	1963	30.00
❑ R9-6075 [R]	The Immortal Django Reinhardt	1963	18.00

SUTTON

Number	Title	Yr	NM
❑ SU-274 [M]	Django Reinhardt and His Guitar	1966	25.00
❑ SSU-274 [R]	Django Reinhardt and His Guitar	1966	15.00

SWING

Number	Title	Yr	NM
❑ SW-8420/7	Djangologie USA Volumes 1-7	1988	60.00

REMAINS, THE

EPIC

Number	Title	Yr	NM
❑ LN24214 [M]	The Remains	1966	200.00
❑ BN26214 [S]	The Remains	1966	300.00

SPOONFED

Number	Title	Yr	NM
❑ SFD-3205	The Remains	1978	18.00
— Red vinyl			

SUNDAZED

Number	Title	Yr	NM
❑ LP5015	A Session with the Remains	199?	12.00
❑ LP5055	The Remains	1999	15.00
❑ SEP 10-162 [10]	The Remains	2000	10.00

Number	Title	Yr	NM

REMINGTON, DAVE

JUBILEE
❏ JLP-1017 [M]	Chicago Jazz Reborn	1956	40.00

TEMPUS
❏ TL-101 [M]	Danceable Dixieland Jazz	1958	40.00

VEE JAY
❏ LP-3030 [M]	Dixie Chicago Style	1962	25.00
❏ SR-3030 [S]	Dixie Chicago Style	1962	30.00
❏ LP-3009 [M]	Dixie on the Rocks	1960	30.00
❏ SR-3009 [S]	Dixie on the Rocks	1960	30.00

REMINGTON, HERB

D
❏ 1376	Herby Remington Plays the Steel	197?	15.00

HILLTOP
❏ JM-6020 [M]	Herby Remington Rides Again	196?	18.00
❏ JS-6020 [S]	Herby Remington Rides Again	196?	15.00

STONEWAY
❏ 138	Pure Remington Steel	197?	15.00

UNITED ARTISTS
❏ UAL-3167 [M]	Steel Guitar Holiday	1961	30.00
❏ UAS-6167 [S]	Steel Guitar Holiday	1961	30.00

REMINGTON, RITA

HILLTOP
❏ JS-6050	The Loretta Lynn Songbook	197?	15.00

PLANTATION
❏ 511	Country Girl Gold	197?	15.00

RENA, KID

CIRCLE
❏ L-409 [10]	Kid Rena Delta Jazz Band	1951	80.00

RENAUD, HENRI

CONTEMPORARY
❏ C-2502 [10]	The Henri Renaud All-Stars	1953	120.00

PERIOD
❏ SPL-1211 [M]	The Birdlanders	1954	80.00
❏ SPL-1212 [M]	The Birdlanders	1954	80.00

RENAY, DIANE

20TH CENTURY FOX
❏ TF-3133 [M]	Navy Blue	1964	80.00
❏ TFS-4133 [S]	Navy Blue	1964	150.00

RENDELL, DON

JAZZLAND
❏ JLP-51 [M]	Roarin'	1961	30.00
❏ JLP-951 [S]	Roarin'	1961	40.00

RENE, GOOGIE

CLASS
❏ LP-5001 [M]	Beautiful Weekend	1957	30.00
❏ LP-200 [M]	Flapjacks	1963	25.00
❏ LP-5003 [M]	Googie Rene Presents Romesville	1959	30.00

RENDEZVOUS
❏ M-1311 [M]	Beautiful Weekend	196?	18.00
❏ M-1313 [M]	Romseville	196?	18.00

RENE, HENRI

IMPERIAL
❏ LP-9096 [M]	Swingin' 59	1960	25.00
❏ LP-12040 [S]	Swingin' 59	1960	30.00
❏ LP-9074 [M]	White Heat	1959	25.00
❏ LP-12021 [S]	White Heat	1959	30.00

RCA CAMDEN
❏ CAL-312 [M]	In Love Again	195?	18.00
❏ CAL-353 [M]	Melodic Magic	195?	18.00
❏ CAL-130 [M]	Portfolio for Easy Listening	195?	18.00

RCA VICTOR
❏ LPM-1947 [M]	Compulsion to Swing	1958	25.00
❏ LSP-1947 [S]	Compulsion to Swing	1958	30.00
❏ LSA-2396 [S]	Dynamic Dimensions	1961	30.00
❏ LPM-3076 [10]	Listen to Rene	1953	40.00
❏ LPM-1046 [M]	Music for Bachelors	1955	120.00
— Cover model is Jayne Mansfield			
❏ LPM-1583 [M]	Music for the Weaker Sex	1957	30.00
❏ LPM-1033 [M]	Passion in Paint	1955	80.00
❏ LPM-2002 [M]	Riot in Rhythm	1959	25.00
❏ LSP-2002 [S]	Riot in Rhythm	1959	30.00
❏ LPM-3049 [10]	Serenade to Love	1953	40.00

RENE AND RENE

WHITE WHALE
❏ WWS-7119	Lo Mucho Que Te Quiero	1968	18.00

RENO, DON, AND BILL HARRELL

JALYN
❏ JLP-108 [M]	Bluegrass Favorites	1964	30.00
❏ JLP-119 [M]	The Most Requested Songs	1966	30.00

KING
❏ KSD-1033	All the Way to Reno	1968	25.00
❏ KSD-1029	A Variety of New Sacred Gospel Songs	1968	25.00
❏ KSD-1068	I'm Using My Bible for a Roadmap	1969	25.00

RENO, JACK

ATCO
❏ SD 33-251	Meet Jack Reno	1968	30.00

DERBYTOWN
❏ 101	Yellow Pages	197?	25.00

DOT
❏ DLP25946	I'm a Good Man in a Bad Frame of Mind	1969	30.00
❏ DLP25921	I Want One	1968	30.00

TARGET
❏ 1313	Hitchin' a Ride	1972	25.00

RENO, RONNIE

MCA
❏ 472	For the First Time	1974	15.00

RENO AND SMILEY

DOT
❏ DLP-3490 [M]	Bluegrass Hits	1963	30.00
❏ DLP-25490 [S]	Bluegrass Hits	1963	30.00

KING
❏ 914 [M]	A Bluegrass Tribute to Cowboy Copas	1964	80.00
❏ 816 [M]	Another Day with Reno and Smiley	1962	80.00
❏ 646 [M]	A Variety of Country Songs	1959	100.00
❏ 787 [M]	Banjo Special	1962	80.00
❏ 776 [M]	Country Singing and Instrumentals	1962	80.00
❏ 701 [M]	Country Songs	1959	100.00
❏ 579 [M]	Folk Ballads and Instrumentals	1958	100.00
❏ 756 [M]	Folk Songs of the Civil War	1961	100.00
❏ 621 [M]	Good Old Country Ballads	1959	100.00
❏ 693 [M]	Hymns Sacred and Gospel	1959	100.00
❏ KSD-1044	I Know You're Married	1969	30.00
❏ 911 [M]	On the Road with Reno and Smiley	1964	80.00
❏ 552 [M]	Reno and Smiley Instrumentals	1958	100.00
❏ 550 [M]	Sacred Songs	1958	120.00
❏ 617 [M]	Someone Will Love Me in Heaven	1959	100.00
❏ 853 [M]	The 15 Greatest Hymns of All Time	1963	80.00
❏ KSD-1091	The Best of Reno and Smiley	1970	30.00
❏ 874 [M]	The True Meaning of Christmas	1963	100.00
❏ 874 [M]	The True Meaning of Christmas	1963	80.00
❏ 861 [M]	The World's Best Five String Banjo	1963	80.00
❏ 718 [M]	Wanted	1961	100.00

REO SPEEDWAGON

EPIC
❏ KE236444	A Decade of Rock and Roll 1970 to 1980	1980	15.00
❏ FE38100	Good Trouble	1982	12.00
❏ PE38100	Good Trouble	198?	10.00
— Budget-line reissue			
❏ HE48100	Good Trouble	1982	30.00
— Half-speed mastered edition			
❏ FE36844	Hi Infidelity	1980	10.00
❏ HE46844	Hi Infidelity	1982	30.00
— Half-speed mastered edition			
❏ FE40444	Life As We Know It	1987	10.00
❏ PE32948	Lost in a Dream	1974	15.00
— Orange label			
❏ PE32948	Lost in a Dream	1979	10.00
— Dark blue label			
❏ PEQ32948 [Q]	Lost in a Dream	1974	25.00
❏ FE35988	Nine Lives	1979	12.00
❏ PE35988	Nine Lives	198?	10.00
— Budget-line reissue			
❏ PE34143	R.E.O.	1976	15.00
— Orange label			
❏ PE34143	R.E.O.	1979	10.00
— Dark blue label			
❏ E31089	REO Speedwagon	1972	18.00
— Yellow label original			
❏ KE31089	REO Speedwagon	1973	15.00
— Orange label			
❏ PE31089	REO Speedwagon	1979	10.00
— Dark blue label			
❏ PEG34494	REO Speedwagon Live/You Get What You Play For	1977	18.00
— Orange labels			
❏ PEG34494	REO Speedwagon Live/You Get What You Play For	1979	15.00
— Dark blue labels			
❏ KE31745	R.E.O./T.W.O.	1972	18.00
— Yellow label original			
❏ KE31745	R.E.O./T.W.O.	1973	15.00
— Orange label			
❏ PE31745	R.E.O./T.W.O.	1979	10.00
— Dark blue label			
❏ KE32378	Ridin' the Storm Out	1973	15.00
— Orange label			
❏ PE32378	Ridin' the Storm Out	1979	10.00
— Dark blue label			
❏ E45246	The Earth, a Small Man, His Dog and a Chicken	1990	15.00
❏ OE44202	The Hits	1988	12.00
❏ PE33338	This Time We Mean It	1975	15.00
— Orange label			
❏ PE33338	This Time We Mean It	1979	10.00
— Dark blue label			
❏ PEQ33338 [Q]	This Time We Mean It	1975	25.00
❏ QE39593	Wheels Are Turnin'	1984	10.00
❏ JE35082	You Can Tune a Piano, But You Can't Tuna Fish	1978	15.00
— Orange label; no bar code on back cover			
❏ JE35082	You Can Tune a Piano, But You Can't Tuna Fish	1978	12.00
— Orange label; with bar code on back cover			
❏ JE35082	You Can Tune a Piano, But You Can't Tuna Fish	1979	10.00
— Dark blue label			
❏ PE35082	You Can Tune a Piano, But You Can't Tuna Fish	198?	10.00
❏ HE45082	You Can Tune a Piano, But You Can't Tuna Fish	198?	40.00
— Half-speed mastered edition			

REPARATA AND THE DELRONS

AVCO EMBASSY
❏ AVE-33008	Rock and Roll Revolution	1970	30.00

WORLD ARTISTS
❏ WAM-2006 [M]	Whenever a Teenager Cries	1965	50.00
❏ WAS-3006 [S]	Whenever a Teenager Cries	1965	60.00

REPLACEMENTS, THE

RHINO
❏ 25557	Pleased to Meet Me	2008	25.00
❏ 25330	Tim	2008	25.00

SIRE
❏	Don't Sell Or Buy...It's Crap	1991	30.00
PRO-A-4632 [DJ]			
— Promo-only 5-track sampler			
❏ R101024	Don't Tell a Soul	1989	18.00
— BMG Music Service edition			
❏ 25831	Don't Tell a Soul	1989	15.00
❏	Live Inconcerated	1989	50.00
PRO-A-3633 [DJ]			
— Five live tracks and one studio track, each of which is repeated on the other side			
❏ 25557	Pleased to Meet Me	1987	15.00
❏ 25330	Tim	1985	15.00

TWIN/TONE
❏ TTR8332 [B]	Hootenanny	1983	30.00
❏ TTR8441 [B]	Let It Be	1984	30.00
❏ TTR8123 [B]	Sorry, Ma, Forgot to Take Out the Trash	1981	30.00
❏ TTR8228 [EP]	The Replacements Stink	1982	30.00

WARNER BROS.
❏ WBMS-148 [DJ]	An Interview with Paul Westerberg	1987	50.00
— Part of "The Warner Bros. Music Show" promotional series			

RESIDENTS, THE

CRYPTIC
❏ S-18335SP-2	For Elsie	1987	100.00
— Green vinyl one-sided LP			

ENIGMA
❏ 73547	The King & Eye	1989	18.00

EPISODE
❏ ED21	The Census Taker (Soundtrack)	1985	80.00
— Red vinyl			
❏ ED21	The Census Taker (Soundtrack)	1985	25.00

RALPH
❏ RR 0278 [B]	Duck Stab	1978	50.00
— First version: Green titles box on back			
❏ RR 0278 [B]	Duck Stab	1978	40.00
— Second version: Yellow titles box on back			
❏ RR87521 [B]	Duck Stab	1988	18.00
— New number, red vinyl			
❏ RR87521	Duck Stab	1988	12.00
— New number, black vinyl			
❏ ESK7906 [B]	Eskimo	1979	60.00
— First version: White vinyl, gatefold cover			
❏ ESK7906 [B]	Eskimo	1979	50.00
— Second version: Black vinyl, gatefold			
❏ ESK7906 [B]	Eskimo	1979	40.00
— Third version: Black vinyl, standard cover			
❏ RZ7906 [PD]	Eskimo	1979	30.00
— Picture disc			
❏ RR1276	Fingerprince	1977	80.00
— First version: Dark brown cover, "First Pressing" written on back cover			
❏ RR1276	Fingerprince	1977	25.00

Number	Title	Yr	NM

— Second version: Lighter brown cover

| RR1276 | Fingerprince | 1977 | 12.00 |

— Third version: Color cover

| RR82761 | Fingerprince | 1988 | 15.00 |

— New number, purple vinyl

| RR82761 | Fingerprince | 1988 | 12.00 |

— New number, black vinyl

| OP-011 [PD] | Freak Show | 1991 | 70.00 |

— Picture disc

| OP-011 [DJ] | Freak Show | 1991 | 150.00 |

— Promo-only black vinyl pressing; 400 made

| RZ8402 | George & James | 1984 | 30.00 |

— First edition: Rejected mix with "Re-1" in trail-off

| RZ8402 | George & James | 1984 | 12.00 |

— Second edition: Approved mix with "Re-5" in trail-off

| RZ8402 | George & James | 1984 | 50.00 |

— Re-5" in trail-off, clear vinyl

| RZ8252 | Intermission | 1982 | 14.00 |

— Red vinyl

| RZ8252 | Intermission | 1982 | 15.00 |
| RZ8152 | Mark of the Mole | 1981 | 50.00 |

— Signed brown vinyl edition with lyrics

| RZ8152 | Mark of the Mole | 1981 | 12.00 |
| RR 0274 | Meet the Residents | 1974 | 200.00 |

— First version: "Meet the Beatles" LP parody cover and "First Edition" on back cover

| RR 0677 [B] | Meet the Residents | 1977 | 150.00 |

— Second version: "She Loves You" picture sleeve parody cover, split "a" Ralph logo

| RR 0677 [B] | Meet the Residents | 1977 | 100.00 |

— Third version: same cover as second version, black "a" Ralph logo

| RR 0677 [B] | Meet the Residents | 1977 | 80.00 |

— Fourth version: same cover as second version, modified and orange back cover

| RR88521 | Meet the Residents | 1988 | 18.00 |

— Original "Meet the Beatles" parody cover restored, white vinyl

| RR88521 | Meet the Residents | 1988 | 15.00 |

— Original "Meet the Beatles" parody cover restored, black vinyl

| RZ7707 [PD] | Meet the Residents | 1986 | 30.00 |

— Picture disc, with original cover on one side, replacement cover on other

| RR1174 | Not Available | 1978 | 30.00 |

— Purple label, mis-mastered, "Re-1" in trail-off vinyl

| RR1174 | Not Available | 1978 | 18.00 |

— Orange label, remastered, "Re-3" in trail-off vinyl

| RR1174 | Not Available | 1978 | 15.00 |

— Green label, address is "444 Grove

| RR1174 | Not Available | 1978 | 12.00 |

— Green label, address is "109 Minna

| DJ7901 [DJ] | Please Do Not Steal It! | 1979 | 40.00 |

— Promo-only sampler

| RZ8302 | Residue | 1983 | 15.00 |
| R78652 | Stars & Hank Forever | 1986 | 40.00 |

— Blue vinyl

| RZ8652 | Stars & Hank Forever | 1986 | 12.00 |
| RZ8552 | The Big Bubble | 1985 | 80.00 |

— Pink vinyl

| RZ8552 | The Big Bubble | 1985 | 15.00 |
| RZ8602 | The Eyeball Show (The 13th Anniversary Show) Live in Japan | 1986 | 80.00 |

— White vinyl

RZ8602	The Eyeball Show (The 13th Anniversary Show) Live in Japan	1986	12.00
Mole Show 001	The Mole Show (The Roxy)	1983	30.00
C-002A	The Mole Show (The Roxy)	1983	40.00

— Picture disc

| RZ8052 | The Residents Commercial Album | 1980 | 25.00 |

— First version: Purple Ralph logo, songs listed in wrong order

| RZ8052 | The Residents Commercial Album | 1980 | 18.00 |

— Second version: Corrected song order, green logo

| RZ8052 | The Residents Commercial Album | 1980 | 15.00 |

— Third version: Green vinyl

| RR1075 | The Third Reich 'N' Roll | 1976 | 200.00 |

— First version of 1,000: Liner notes inside, orange carrot

| RR1075 [B] | The Third Reich 'N' Roll | 1976 | 150.00 |

— Second version: Gray carrot, split "a" Ralph logo

| RR1075 | The Third Reich 'N' Roll | 1976 | 15.00 |

— Third version: Orange carrot, black "a" Ralph logo

| RR1075 | The Third Reich 'N' Roll | 1976 | 12.00 |

— Fourth version: Gray carrot, black "a" Ralph logo

| RR1075 | The Third Reich 'N' Roll | 1976 | 1500.00 |

— Numbered box set on marbled vinyl, silkscreened cover and lithographs inside

| RR1075 [B] | The Third Reich 'N' Roll | 1976 | 100.00 |

— Censored cover with swastikas obscured, pressed in U.S. for export to Germany

| RZ8202 | The Tunes of Two Cities | 1982 | 15.00 |

— First edition: "444 Grove Street" address

| RZ8202 | The Tunes of Two Cities | 1982 | 12.00 |

— Second edition: "109 Minna Street" address

| RR8315 | Title in Limbo | 1983 | 15.00 |

— With Renaldo and The Loaf

| RZ8452 | Whatever Happened to Vileness Fats? | 1984 | 80.00 |

— Red vinyl

| RZ8452 | Whatever Happened to Vileness Fats? | 1984 | 15.00 |

RYKO ANALOGUE

| RALP-0044-2 [B] | God in Three Persons | 1988 | 40.00 |

— Clear vinyl

| RALP-0045-2 | God in Three Persons Instrumental | 1988 | 18.00 |

— Clear vinyl

UWEB

| 0011 | Stranger Than Supper | 1990 | 30.00 |

— Fan club issue

RESNICK, ART

CAPRI

| 74015 | A Gift | 198? | 12.00 |

SYMPOSIUM

| 2005 | Jungleopolis | 197? | 18.00 |

RESTIVO, JOHNNY

RCA VICTOR

| LPM-2149 [M] | Oh, Johnny! | 1959 | 60.00 |
| LSP-2149 [S] | Oh, Johnny! | 1959 | 100.00 |

RESTLESS HEART

RCA

8317-1-R	Big Dreams in a Small Town	1988	10.00
9961-1-R	Fast Movin' Train	1990	15.00
5648-1-R	Wheels	1986	10.00

RCA VICTOR

| CPL1-5369 | Restless Heart | 1985 | 10.00 |

RESTUM, WILLIE

GONE

| LP-5011 [M] | Willie Restum at the Dream Lounge | 1960 | 250.00 |

ROULETTE

| R-25152 [M] | Dream Bar | 1961 | 60.00 |

REVELERS, THE

RONDO-LETTE

| A-50 [M] | Jazz at the Downstairs Club | 1962 | 25.00 |
| SA-50 [S] | Jazz at the Downstairs Club | 1962 | 30.00 |

REVELLS, THE

REPRISE

| R-6160 [M] | The Go Sound of the Slots | 1965 | 150.00 |
| RS-6160 [S] | The Go Sound of the Slots | 1965 | 200.00 |

REVELS, THE (2)

IMPACT

| LPM-1 [M] | Revels on a Rampage | 1964 | 500.00 |

SUNDAZED

| LP5010 | Intoxica! The Best of the Revels | 1994 | 12.00 |

REVENGERS, THE

METRO

| M-565 [M] | Batman and Other Supermen | 1966 | 30.00 |
| MS-565 [S] | Batman and Other Supermen | 1966 | 40.00 |

REVERBERI

PAUSA

| 7003 | Reverberi and ... | 198? | 12.00 |
| 7016 | Timer | 198? | 12.00 |

UNITED ARTISTS

| UA-LA813-H | Stairway to Heaven | 1977 | 15.00 |

REVERE, PAUL, AND THE RAIDERS

COLUMBIA

CL2755 [M]	A Christmas Present... And Past	1967	60.00
CS9555 [S]	A Christmas Present... And Past	1967	30.00
CS9905	Alias Pink Puzz	1969	25.00
KG31464	All-Time Greatest Hits	1972	25.00
CS9964	Collage	1970	25.00
KC31106	Country Wine	1972	18.00
CL2805 [M]	Goin' to Memphis	1968	80.00
CS9605 [S]	Goin' to Memphis	1968	25.00
KCL2662 [M]	Greatest Hits	1967	30.00

— Add 20% if booklet is included; at least some copies actually are stereo with the "XSS" prefix on the label's master numbers rather than "XLP," though we don't know if all of them are

| KCS9462 [P] | Greatest Hits | 1967 | 30.00 |

— Add 20% if booklet is included

PC35593	Greatest Hits	1978	12.00
C30386	Greatest Hits, Volume 2	1971	25.00
CS9753	Hard 'N' Heavy (With Marshmallow)	1969	25.00

— Black and white cover

| CS9753 | Hard 'N' Heavy (With Marshmallow) | 1969 | 30.00 |

— Color cover

| CL2307 [M] | Here They Come! | 1965 | 30.00 |

— Guaranteed High Fidelity" on label

| CL2307 [M] | Here They Come! | 1965 | 25.00 |

— 360 Sound Mono" on label

| CS9107 [S] | Here They Come! | 1965 | 40.00 |

— 360 Sound Stereo" in black on label

| CS9107 [S] | Here They Come! | 1965 | 30.00 |

— 360 Sound Stereo" in white on label

C30768	Indian Reservation	1971	18.00
CL2451 [M]	Just Like Us!	1966	30.00
CS9251 [S]	Just Like Us!	1966	30.00
CL2508 [M]	Midnight Ride	1966	30.00
CS9308 [S]	Midnight Ride	1966	30.00
CL2721 [M]	Revolution!	1967	30.00
CS9521 [S]	Revolution!	1967	30.00
CS9665	Something Happening	1968	25.00
CL2595 [M]	The Spirit of '67	1966	30.00
CS9395 [S]	The Spirit of '67	1966	30.00
GP12	Two All Time Great Selling LPs	1969	30.00

— Combines 9395 and 9521 in one package; red labels

| GP12 | Two All Time Great Selling LPs | 1971 | 25.00 |

— Combines 9395 and 9521 in one package; orange labels

COLUMBIA LIMITED EDITION

| LE10170 [S] | Midnight Ride | 197? | 18.00 |

— Reissue of 9308

COLUMBIA SPECIAL PRODUCTS

| P13512 | Goin' to Memphis | 197? | 18.00 |

ERA

| NU5880 | The Great Raider Reunion | 1983 | 15.00 |

— Re-recordings

GARDENA

| LP-G-1000 | Like, Long Hair | 1961 | 600.00 |

HARMONY

KH30975	Good Thing	1971	15.00
KH31183	Movin' On	1972	15.00
H30089	Paul Revere and the Raiders Featuring Mark Lindsay	1970	15.00

JERDEN

JRL-7004 [M]	Paul Revere and the Raiders In the Beginning	1966	80.00
JRS-7004 [R]	Paul Revere and the Raiders In the Beginning	1966	30.00
T-90709 [M]	Paul Revere and the Raiders In the Beginning	1966	70.00

— Capitol Record Club edition

| DT-90709 [R] | Paul Revere and the Raiders In the Beginning | 1966 | 50.00 |

— Capitol Record Club edition

PICKWICK

| SPC-3176 [R] | Paul Revere and the Raiders | 1969 | 12.00 |

SANDE

| S-1001 [M] | Paul Revere and the Raiders | 1963 | 1200.00 |

— Original version with "Sande" and no mention of "Etiquette" in trail-off area

| S-1001 [M] | Paul Revere and the Raiders | 1979 | 30.00 |

— Legitimate reissue with "Sande" and "Etiquette" in trail-off area

SEARS

| SPS-493 | Paul Revere and the Raiders | 1969 | 30.00 |

REVEREND HORTON HEAT

SUB POP

250	Liquor in the Front	1994	15.00
96 [10]	Smoke 'Em If You Got 'Em	1991	15.00
202	The Full Custom Gospel Sounds of Reverend Horton Heat	1993	15.00

REVOLTING COCKS

WAX TRAX!

7063 [B]	Beers Steers and Queers	1990	18.00
017 [B]	Big Sexy Land	1986	18.00
037 [B]	You Goddamned Son of a Bitch	1988	18.00

REVOLUTIONARY ENSEMBLE, THE

ESP-DISK'

| S-3007 | The Revolutionary Ensemble at Peace Church | 196? | 18.00 |

HORIZON

| SP-708 | People's Republic | 1975 | 15.00 |

INDIA NAVIGATION

| IN-1023 | Manhattan Cycles | 197? | 18.00 |

INNER CITY

| IC-3016 | The Revolutionary Ensemble | 197? | 15.00 |

REX

COLUMBIA

| PC34399 | Rex | 1976 | 18.00 |
| PC34865 | Where Do We Go from Here | 1977 | 18.00 |

Number	Title	Yr	NM

REXROTH, KENNETH, AND LAWRENCE FERLINGHETTI

FANTASY

❑ 7002 [M]	Poetry Readings from the Cellar	1957	200.00
—Red vinyl			
❑ 7002 [M]	Poetry Readings from the Cellar	1957	100.00
—Black vinyl			

REXROTH, KENNETH

FANTASY

❑ 7008 [M]	Poetry and Jazz at the Blackhawk	1958	200.00
—Red vinyl			
❑ 7008 [M]	Poetry and Jazz at the Blackhawk	1958	100.00
—Black vinyl			

REY, ALVINO

CAPITOL

❑ T808 [M]	Aloha	1957	30.00
❑ T1262 [M]	Ping Pong!	1959	25.00
❑ ST1262 [S]	Ping Pong!	1959	30.00
❑ T1085 [M]	Swinging Fling	1958	30.00
❑ ST1085 [S]	Swinging Fling	1958	30.00
❑ T1395 [M]	That Lonely Feeling	1960	25.00
❑ ST1395 [S]	That Lonely Feeling	1960	30.00

HINDSIGHT

❑ HSR-196	Alvino Rey and His Orchestra 1940-41	198?	12.00
❑ HSR-121	Alvino Rey and His Orchestra 1946	198?	12.00
❑ HSR-167	Alvino Rey and His Orchestra 1946, Vol. 2	198?	12.00

REYNOLDS, ART, SINGERS

CAPITOL

❑ ST-191	It's a Wonderful World	1969	25.00
❑ T2811 [M]	Long Dusty Road	1967	30.00
❑ ST2811 [S]	Long Dusty Road	1967	25.00
❑ ST2900	Soul-Gospel Sounds	1968	25.00
❑ T2534 [M]	Tellin' It Like It Is	1966	25.00
❑ ST2534 [S]	Tellin' It Like It Is	1966	30.00

REYNOLDS, BURT

MERCURY

❑ MK-4 [DJ]	A Burt Reynolds Radio Special	1973	30.00
❑ SRM-1-693	Ask Me What I Am	1973	18.00

REYNOLDS, DEBBIE

DOT

❑ DLP-3295 [M]	Am I That Easy to Forget?	1960	30.00
❑ DLP-25295 [S]	Am I That Easy to Forget?	1960	40.00
—Black vinyl			
❑ DLP-25295 [S]	Am I That Easy to Forget?	1960	80.00
—Blue vinyl			
❑ DLP-3191 [M]	Debbie	1959	30.00
❑ DLP-25191 [S]	Debbie	1959	40.00
❑ DLP-3298 [M]	Fine and Dandy	1960	25.00
❑ DLP-25298 [S]	Fine and Dandy	1960	30.00
❑ DLP-3492 [M]	Tammy	1963	25.00
❑ DLP-25492 [S]	Tammy	1963	30.00

K-TEL

❑ NU9190	Do It Debbie's Way	1983	12.00
—Exercise record			

METRO

❑ M-535 [M]	Raise a Ruckus	196?	25.00
❑ MS-535 [S]	Raise a Ruckus	196?	25.00

MGM

❑ E-3806 [M]	From Debbie with Love	1959	40.00

REYNOLDS, LAWRENCE

WARNER BROS.

❑ WS1825	Jesus Is a Soul Man	1969	25.00

REYNOLDS, TEDDY, AND THE TWISTERS

CROWN

❑ CLP-5247 [M]	The Twist	1962	30.00
❑ CST-247 [S]	The Twist	1962	40.00

REYNOLDS, TOMMY

AUDIO LAB

❑ AL-1509 [M]	Dixieland All-Stars	1958	100.00

KING

❑ 395-510 [M]	Jazz for Happy Feet	1956	80.00

ROYALE

❑ 18117 [10]	Tommy Reynolds Orchestra with Bon Bon	195?	80.00

REYS, RITA

COLUMBIA

❑ CL903 [M]	The Cool Voice of Rita Reys with Art Blakey and the Jazz Messengers	1956	150.00

EPIC

❑ LN3522 [M]	Her Name Is Rita Reys	1957	80.00

INNER CITY

❑ IC-1157	Songs of Antonio Carlos Jobim	198?	18.00

REZILLOS, THE

SIRE

❑ SR6057 [B]	Can't Stand the Rezillos	1978	18.00

RHINOCEROS

ELEKTRA

❑ EKS-74075	Better Times Are Coming	1970	25.00
❑ EKS-74030 [B]	Rhinoceros	1968	30.00
❑ EKS-74056	Satin Chickens	1969	25.00

RHODES, EMITT

A&M

❑ SP-4254	The American Dream	1971	18.00
—Reissue contains "Saturday Night" and a framed photo of Rhodes on cover			
❑ SP-4254	The American Dream	1970	30.00
—Original album contains "You're a Very Lovely Woman" and has Rhodes in front of a paint-covered backdrop on cover			

ABC DUNHILL

❑ DS-50089	Emitt Rhodes	1970	15.00
❑ DS-50122	Farewell to Paradise	1972	15.00
❑ DS-50111	Mirror	1971	15.00

RHODES, GEORGE

GROOVE

❑ LG-1005 [M]	Real George!	1956	60.00

RHODES, TODD

KING

❑ 658 [M]	Dance Music	1960	800.00
❑ 295-88 [10]	Todd Rhodes Playing His Greatest Hits	1954	1500.00

RHYNE, MEL

JAZZLAND

❑ JLP-16 [M]	Organizing	1960	30.00
❑ JLP-916 [S]	Organizing	1960	40.00

RHYTHM AND BLU

GRAMAVISION

❑ 18-8608	Rhythm and Blu	1986	15.00

RHYTHM COMBINATION, THE

BASF

❑ 25124	Power Play	197?	18.00
❑ 21751	Waitaminute	197?	18.00

RHYTHM DEVILS, THE

PASSPORT

❑ PB-9844	The Rhythm Devils Play River Music	1980	25.00

RHYTHM MASTERS, THE (1)

ACE

❑ LP-1010 [M]	Hymns and Spirituals	1961	100.00

RHYTHM ROCKERS (1)

CHALLENGE

❑ CHL-617 [M]	Soul Surfin'	1963	90.00

RHYTHMIC UNION, THE

INNER CITY

❑ IC-1100	Gentle Awakening	198?	15.00

RHYZE

20TH CENTURY

❑ T-639	Rhyze to the Top	1981	30.00

RICE, BOBBY G.

AUDIOGRAPH

❑ 6000	Bobby G. Rice	1982	12.00
❑ 7772	Bobby's Back	1982	12.00

DOOR KNOB

❑ 1008	New Beginning	198?	15.00

GRT

❑ 8011	Instant Rice -- The Best of Bobby G.	1976	15.00
❑ 8001	She Sure Laid the Lonelies on Me	1974	15.00
❑ 8016	With Love from Bobby G. Rice	1977	15.00
❑ 8003	Write Me a Letter	1975	15.00

METROMEDIA COUNTRY

❑ BML1-0186	You Lay So Easy on My Mind	1973	25.00

ROYAL AMERICAN

❑ 1003	Hit After Hit	1972	25.00

SUNBIRD

❑ SN-50106	Greatest Hits	1980	15.00

RICE, DARYLE

AUDIOPHILE

❑ AP-141	I Walk with Music	1980	12.00

RICH, BUDDY, AND MAX ROACH

MERCURY

❑ MG-20448 [M]	Rich Versus Roach	1959	60.00
❑ SR-60133 [S]	Rich Versus Roach	1959	70.00

RICH, BUDDY, AND SWEETS EDISON

NORGRAN

❑ MGN-1038 [M]	Buddy Rich and Sweets Edison	1955	100.00

VERVE

❑ MGV-8129 [M]	Buddy and Sweets	1957	50.00
—Reissue of Norgran 1038			
❑ V-8129 [M]	Buddy and Sweets	1961	25.00

RICH, BUDDY

ARGO

❑ LP-676 [M]	Playtime	1961	30.00
❑ LPS-676 [S]	Playtime	1961	40.00

EMARCY

❑ EMS-2-402	Both Sides	1976	18.00
❑ 66006	Driver	1967	25.00

EVEREST ARCHIVE OF FOLK & JAZZ

❑ 260	Buddy Rich	197?	18.00

GREAT AMERICAN

❑ 1030	Class of '78	1978	25.00
—Direct-to-disc version of Gryphon 781			

GROOVE MERCHANT

❑ 3307	The Big Band Machine	1976	15.00
❑ 3303	The Last Blues Album, Vol. 1	1975	15.00
❑ 528	The Roar of '74	1974	15.00
❑ 4407	Tuff Dude!	197?	18.00
❑ 3301	Very Live at Buddy's Place	1974	15.00

GRYPHON

❑ 781	Class of '78	1978	15.00

LIBERTY

❑ 11006	Keep the Customer Satisfied	1970	18.00

MCA

❑ 5186	The Buddy Rich Band	1981	12.00

MERCURY

❑ MG-20451 [M]	Richcraft	1959	60.00
❑ SR-60136 [S]	Richcraft	1959	70.00
❑ MG-20461 [M]	The Voice Is Rich	1959	50.00
❑ SR-60144 [S]	The Voice Is Rich	1959	60.00

NORGRAN

❑ MGN-26 [10]	Buddy Rich Swingin'	1954	120.00
❑ MGN-1031 [M]	Sing and Swing with Buddy Rich	1955	80.00
❑ MGN-1052 [M]	The Swingin' Buddy Rich	1955	60.00
—Reissue of 26			
❑ MGN-1078 [M]	The Wailing Buddy Rich	1956	60.00
❑ MGN-1088 [M]	This One's for Basie	1956	60.00

PACIFIC JAZZ

❑ ST-20126	A New One	1968	25.00
❑ PJ-10117 [M]	Big Swing Face	1967	30.00
❑ ST-20117 [S]	Big Swing Face	1967	25.00
❑ LN-10090	Big Swing Face	1981	10.00
—Budget-line reissue			
❑ PJ-10113 [M]	Swingin' New Big Band	1966	30.00
❑ ST-20113 [S]	Swingin' New Big Band	1966	25.00
❑ LN-10089	Swingin' New Big Band	1981	10.00
—Budget-line reissue			

PAUSA

❑ 9004	Buddy & Soul	1983	12.00

QUINTESSENCE

❑ 25051	Mr. Drums	1978	15.00

RCA VICTOR

❑ LSP-4593	A Different Drummer	1971	15.00
❑ ANL1-1090	A Different Drummer	1975	12.00
—Reissue of 4593			
❑ CPL2-2273	Buddy Rich Plays & Plays & Plays	1977	18.00
❑ LSP-4666	Rich in London	1972	15.00
❑ AFL1-4666	Rich in London	1977	12.00
—Reissue with new prefix			
❑ APL1-1503	Speak No Evil	1976	15.00
❑ LSP-4802	Stick It	1972	15.00
❑ AFL1-4802	Stick It	1977	12.00
—Reissue with new prefix			

UNITED ARTISTS

❑ UXS-86	Buddy Rich Superpak	1972	18.00

VERVE

❑ V-8712 [M]	Big Band Shout	1967	25.00
❑ V6-8712 [S]	Big Band Shout	1967	18.00
❑ V-8425 [M]	Blues Caravan	1962	30.00
❑ V6-8425 [S]	Blues Caravan	1962	30.00
❑ VSP-40 [M]	Buddy Rich at J.A.T.P.	1966	18.00
❑ VSPS-40 [R]	Buddy Rich at J.A.T.P.	1966	15.00
❑ MGV-8285 [M]	Buddy Rich in Miami	1958	60.00
❑ V-8285 [M]	Buddy Rich in Miami	1961	25.00
❑ MGV-2075 [M]	Buddy Rich Just Sings	1957	60.00
❑ V-2075 [M]	Buddy Rich Just Sings	1961	25.00

Number	Title	Yr	NM
❑ MGV-2009 [M]	Buddy Rich Sings Johnny Mercer	1956	60.00
❑ V-2009 [M]	Buddy Rich Sings Johnny Mercer	1961	25.00
❑ V-8471 [M]	Burnin' Beat	1962	30.00
❑ V6-8471 [S]	Burnin' Beat	1962	30.00
❑ V-8484 [M]	Drum Battle: Gene Krupa vs. Buddy Rich	1962	30.00
❑ V6-8484 [S]	Drum Battle: Gene Krupa vs. Buddy Rich	1962	30.00
❑ V6-8824	Monster	1973	18.00
❑ V6-8778	Super Rich	1969	18.00
❑ MGV-8142 [M]	The Swingin' Buddy Rich	1957	50.00
— Reissue of Norgran 1052			
❑ V-8142 [M]	The Swingin' Buddy Rich	1961	25.00
❑ MGV-8168 [M]	The Wailing Buddy Rich	1957	50.00
— Reissue of Norgran 1078			
❑ V-8168 [M]	The Wailing Buddy Rich	1961	25.00
❑ MGV-8176 [M]	This One's for Basie	1957	50.00
— Reissue of Norgran 1086			
❑ V-8176 [M]	This One's for Basie	1961	25.00
WHO'S WHO IN JAZZ			
❑ 21006	Lionel Hampton Presents Buddy Rich	1978	15.00
WORLD PACIFIC			
❑ WPS-20158	Buddy & Soul	1969	18.00
❑ WPS-20133	Mercy, Mercy	1968	18.00
❑ WPS-20169	The Best of Buddy Rich	1970	18.00
❑ WPS-20113	The Buddy Rich Big Band	1968	18.00

RICH, CHARLIE

Number	Title	Yr	NM
BUCKBOARD			
❑ 1019	The Entertainer	197?	12.00
COLUMBIA SPECIAL PRODUCTS			
❑ P213663	Super Hits	197?	18.00
ELEKTRA			
❑ 6E-301	Once a Drifter	1981	12.00
EPIC			
❑ KE32247	Behind Closed Doors	1973	15.00
❑ PE32247	Behind Closed Doors	197?	10.00
— Reissue			
❑ CQ32247 [Q]	Behind Closed Doors	1973	25.00
❑ E30214	Boss Man	1970	25.00
❑ AS50 [DJ]	Charlie Rich	1973	30.00
— Promo-only compilation			
❑ JE35394	Classic Rich, Vol. 1	1978	12.00
❑ JE35624	Classic Rich, Vol. 2	1978	12.00
❑ AS139 [DJ]	Everything You Always Wanted to Hear by Charlie Rich But Were Afraid to Ask For	1976	30.00
— Promo-only sampler			
❑ PE33455	Every Time You Touch Me (I Get High)	1975	15.00
❑ PEQ33455 [Q]	Every Time You Touch Me (I Get High)	1975	25.00
❑ PE34240	Greatest Hits	1976	12.00
— Without bar code on cover			
❑ PE34240	Greatest Hits	1979	10.00
— With bar code on cover			
❑ PE34891	Rollin' with the Flow	1977	12.00
❑ BN26376	Set Me Free	1968	25.00
❑ PE33545	Silver Linings	1976	12.00
❑ PE34444	Take Me	1977	12.00
❑ PE34444	Take Me	1977	12.00
❑ KE31933	The Best of Charlie Rich	1972	18.00
— Yellow label; add 80 percent if bonus record AE7 1065 and its special sleeve are still there			
❑ KE31933	The Best of Charlie Rich	1973	15.00
— Orange label			
❑ CQ31933 [Q]	The Best of Charlie Rich	1972	25.00
❑ BN26516	The Fabulous Charlie Rich	1970	25.00
❑ PE33250	The Silver Fox	1974	15.00
❑ PEQ33250 [Q]	The Silver Fox	1974	25.00
❑ PE32531	Very Special Love Songs	1974	15.00
❑ PEQ32531 [Q]	Very Special Love Songs	1974	25.00
GROOVE			
❑ GM-1000 [M]	Charlie Rich	1964	150.00
❑ GS-1000 [S]	Charlie Rich	1964	300.00
HARMONY			
❑ KH32166	I Do My Swingin' at Home	1973	15.00
HI			
❑ HL12037 [M]	Charlie Rich Sings Country and Western	1967	30.00
❑ SHL32037 [S]	Charlie Rich Sings Country and Western	1967	25.00
❑ SHL32084	Charlie Rich Sings the Songs of Hank Williams & Others	1974	15.00
— Reissue of 32037			
❑ 8006	I'm So Lonesome I Could Cry	198?	10.00
— Reissue of Hi 32084			
HILLTOP			
❑ 6160	Entertainer of the Year	197?	12.00
❑ 6139	Lonely Weekends	197?	12.00
❑ 6149	Songs for Beautiful Girls	1974	12.00
MERCURY			
❑ SRM-2-7505	Fully Realized	1974	18.00
PHILLIPS INTERNATIONAL			
❑ PLP-1970 [M]	Lonely Weekends	1960	600.00

Number	Title	Yr	NM
PICKWICK			
❑ ACL-7001	Too Many Teardrops	1975	12.00
POWER PAK			
❑ PO-245	Arkansas Traveler	197?	12.00
❑ PO-241	There Won't Be Anymore	197?	12.00
❑ PO-252	The Silver Fox	197?	12.00
QUICKSILVER			
❑ QS-1005	Midnight Blue	198?	15.00
RCA CAMDEN			
❑ CAS-2417	The Versatile and Talented Charlie Rich	1970	12.00
RCA VICTOR			
❑ LPM-3537 [M]	Big Boss Man	1966	40.00
❑ LSP-3557 [S]	Big Boss Man	1966	50.00
❑ APL1-2260	Big Boss Man/My Mountain Dew	1977	15.00
❑ AHL1-5496	Collector's Series	1985	10.00
❑ APL1-0857	Greatest Hits	1975	15.00
❑ APL1-1242	Now Everybody Knows	1975	15.00
❑ APL1-0686	She Called Me Baby	1974	15.00
❑ ANL1-2424	She Called Me Baby	1977	12.00
— Reissue of APL1-0686			
❑ LPM-3352 [M]	That's Rich	1965	40.00
❑ LSP-3352 [S]	That's Rich	1965	50.00
❑ APL1-0433	There Won't Be Anymore	1974	15.00
❑ APL1-0258	Tomorrow Night	1973	15.00
❑ ANL1-1542	Tomorrow Night	1976	12.00
— Reissue			
SMASH			
❑ MGS-27078 [M]	The Best Years	1966	30.00
❑ SRS-67070 [S]	The Best Years	1966	40.00
❑ MGS-27070 [M]	The Many New Sides of Charlie Rich	1965	30.00
❑ SRS-67070 [S]	The Many New Sides of Charlie Rich	1965	40.00
SUN			
❑ 1003 [B]	20 Golden Hits	1979	18.00
— Gold vinyl			
❑ LP123 [B]	A Time for Tears	1971	18.00
❑ LP134 [B]	Golden Treasures	1974	18.00
❑ LP110 [B]	Lonely Weekend	1970	18.00
❑ LP135 [B]	Sun's Best of Charlie Rich	1974	18.00
❑ LP132 [B]	The Early Years	1974	18.00
❑ LP133 [B]	The Memphis Sound of Charlie Rich	1974	18.00
❑ 1007	The Original Charlie Rich	1979	12.00
SUNNYVALE			
❑ 9330	The Sun Story Vol. 2	1977	12.00
TIME-LIFE			
❑ STW-115	Country Music	1981	12.00
TRIP			
❑ TLP-8502	The Best of Charlie Rich	1974	15.00
UNITED ARTISTS			
❑ UA-LA876-H	I Still Believe in Love	1978	15.00
❑ UA-LA925-H	The Fool Strikes Again	1978	12.00
WING			
❑ SRW-16375	A Lonely Weekend	1969	15.00

RICH, DAVE

Number	Title	Yr	NM
STOP			
❑ 10007	Soul Brother	196?	30.00

RICH, DON

Number	Title	Yr	NM
CAPITOL			
❑ ST-643	That Fiddlin' Man	1970	30.00

RICHARD, CLIFF

Number	Title	Yr	NM
ABC-PARAMOUNT			
❑ 321 [M]	Cliff Sings	1960	100.00
❑ S-321 [S]	Cliff Sings	1960	120.00
❑ 391 [M]	Listen to Cliff	1961	100.00
❑ S-391 [S]	Listen to Cliff	1961	120.00
EMI AMERICA			
❑ SN-16253	Every Face Tells a Story	1981	10.00
❑ ST-17105	Give a Little Bit More	1983	12.00
❑ SN-16220	Green Light	1981	10.00
❑ SN-16221	I'm Nearly Famous	1981	10.00
❑ SW-17039	I'm No Hero	1980	12.00
❑ ST-17081	Now You See Me, Now You Don't	1982	12.00
❑ SW-17018	We Don't Talk Anymore	1979	12.00
❑ SW-17059	Wired for Sound	1981	12.00
EPIC			
❑ LN24115 [M]	Cliff Richard in Spain	1965	50.00
❑ BN26115 [S]	Cliff Richard in Spain	1965	60.00
❑ LN24089 [M]	It's All in the Game	1964	50.00
❑ BN26089 [S]	It's All in the Game	1964	60.00
❑ LN24063 [M]	Summer Holiday	1963	50.00
❑ BN26063 [S]	Summer Holiday	1963	60.00
❑ LN24145 [Mono]	Swingers' Paradise	1963	40.00
❑ BN24145 [S]	Swingers' Paradise		60.00
ROCKET			
❑ PIG-2268	Every Face Tells a Story	1977	15.00
❑ BXL1-2958	Green Light	1978	15.00
❑ PIG-2210 [B]	I'm Nearly Famous	1976	18.00
WORD			
❑ WR-8306	Walking in the Light	1985	15.00

Number	Title	Yr	NM
RICHARD AND JIM			
CAPITOL			
❑ T2058 [M]	Folk Songs and Country Sounds	1964	25.00
❑ ST2058 [S]	Folk Songs and Country Sounds	1964	30.00
❑ T2287 [M]	Two Boys from Alabama	1965	25.00
❑ ST2287 [S]	Two Boys from Alabama	1965	30.00

RICHARDS, ANN

Number	Title	Yr	NM
ATCO			
❑ 33-136 [M]	Ann, Man!	1961	40.00
❑ SD 33-136 [S]	Ann, Man!	1961	60.00
CAPITOL			
❑ T1087 [M]	I'm Shooting High	1959	50.00
❑ ST1087 [S]	I'm Shooting High	1959	60.00
❑ T1406 [M]	The Many Moods of Ann Richards	1960	60.00
❑ ST1406 [S]	The Many Moods of Ann Richards	1960	80.00
❑ T1495 [M]	Two Much!	1961	60.00
❑ ST1495 [S]	Two Much!	1961	80.00
VEE JAY			
❑ LP-1070 [M]	Live...At the Losers	1963	40.00
❑ SR-1070 [S]	Live...At the Losers	1963	50.00

RICHARDS, EMIL

Number	Title	Yr	NM
ABC IMPULSE!			
❑ AS-9188 [S]	Journey to Bliss	1969	25.00
❑ AS-9182 [S]	Spirit of '76	1968	25.00
UNI			
❑ 3008 [M]	New Sound	1967	30.00
❑ 73008 [S]	New Sound	1967	25.00
❑ 3003 [M]	New Time Element	1967	30.00
❑ 73003 [S]	New Time Element	1967	25.00

RICHARDS, JOHNNY

Number	Title	Yr	NM
BETHLEHEM			
❑ BCP-6011 [M]	Something Else by Johnny Richards	1956	80.00
❑ BCP-6032	Something Else by Johnny Richards	197?	25.00
— Reissue, distributed by RCA Victor			
CAPITOL			
❑ T981 [M]	Experiments In Sound	1958	40.00
— Turquoise label			
❑ T885 [M]	Wide Range	1957	60.00
— Turquoise label			
CORAL			
❑ CRL57304 [M]	Walk Softly/Run Wild	1959	60.00
❑ CRL757304 [S]	Walk Softly/Run Wild	1959	80.00
CREATIVE WORLD			
❑ ST-1052	Wide Range	198?	18.00
DISCOVERY			
❑ DS-915	Je Vous Adore	1986	30.00
ROULETTE			
❑ SR-25351 [S]	Aqui Se Habla Espanol	1967	30.00
❑ R-25351 [M]	Aqui Se Habla Espanol	1967	30.00
❑ R-52114 [M]	My Fair Lady, My Way	1964	30.00
❑ SR-52114 [S]	My Fair Lady, My Way	1964	40.00
❑ R-52008 [M]	The Rites of Diablo	1958	80.00
❑ SR-52008 [S]	The Rites of Diablo	1958	60.00

RICHARDS, KEITH

Number	Title	Yr	NM
VIRGIN			
❑ 90973	Talk Is Cheap	1988	15.00

RICHARDS, RED

Number	Title	Yr	NM
SACKVILLE			
❑ 2017	I'm Shooting High	198?	15.00
WEST 54			
❑ 8005	Mellow Tone	1980	15.00
❑ 8000	Soft Buns	1979	15.00

RICHARDS, SUE

Number	Title	Yr	NM
ABC DOT			
❑ DOSD-2012	A Girl Named Sue	1974	15.00
❑ DOSD-2052	Sweet Sensuous Feelings	1976	15.00

RICHARDS, TREVOR

Number	Title	Yr	NM
STOMP OFF			
❑ SOS-1222	The Trevor Richards New Orleans Trio	1991	15.00

RICHARDS, TRUDY

Number	Title	Yr	NM
CAPITOL			
❑ T838 [M]	Crazy in Love	1957	30.00

RICHARDSON, JEROME

Number	Title	Yr	NM
NEW JAZZ			
❑ NJLP-8205 [M]	Jerome Richardson Sextet	1958	80.00
— Purple label			
❑ NJLP-8205 [M]	Jerome Richardson Sextet	1965	30.00
— Blue label, trident logo at right			
❑ NJLP-8226 [M]	Roamin' with Richardson	1959	80.00
— Purple label			

Number	Title	Yr	NM
❏ NJLP-8226 [M]	Roamin' with Richardson	1965	30.00

—*Blue label, trident logo at right*

UNITED ARTISTS

❏ UAJ-14006 [M]	Going to the Movies	1962	30.00
❏ UAJS-15006 [S]	Going to the Movies	1962	40.00

VERVE

❏ V-8729 [M]	Groove Merchant	1967	25.00
❏ V6-8729 [S]	Groove Merchant	1967	18.00

RICHARDSON, JIMMY

STARDAY

❏ SLP-126 [M]	Sweet with a Beat	1960	30.00

RICHARDSON, RALPH; PAUL SCHOFIELD; AND CAST

CAEDMON

❏ TC91135 [S]	A Christmas Carol	1960	18.00

— *Green, blue and white label; front cover says "Sir Ralph Richardson"; number on jacket is "TC 1135S"*

❏ TC1135 [S]	A Christmas Carol	197?	15.00

—*Blue and white label; front cover says "Ralph Richardson"; 1960 copyright date added to label and jacket*

RICHARDSON, WALLY

PRESTIGE

❏ PRST-7569	Soul Guru	1969	25.00

RICHARDSON, WARREN S., JR.

COTILLION

❏ SD9013	Warren S. Richardson, Jr.	1970	30.00

RICHIE, LIONEL

MOTOWN

❏ MOT-6338	Back to Front	1992	30.00

— *U.S. vinyl available only through Columbia House*

❏ 6059ML	Can't Slow Down	1983	10.00
❏ R110767	Can't Slow Down	1983	12.00

—*RCA Music Service edition*

❏ 6158ML	Dancing on the Ceiling	1986	10.00
❏ 6007ML	Lionel Richie	1982	10.00
❏ 5386ML	The Composer	1986	10.00

— *Includes songs he wrote and performed with the Commodores, plus "Endless Love" with Diana Ross*

RICHMAN, JONATHAN, AND THE MODERN LOVERS

BESERKLEY

❏ JBZ 0060	Back in Your Life	1979	12.00

—*Distributed by Playboy/CBS*

❏ 10060	Back in Your Life	1980	15.00

—*Reissue -- change in distributing label to Elektra*

❏ BZ-0048	Jonathan Richman and the Modern Lovers	1976	30.00

—*Distributed by GRT*

❏ JBZ 0048	Jonathan Richman and the Modern Lovers	1976	30.00

—*Distributed by Playboy/CBS*

❏ JBZ 0055	Modern Lovers "Live	1978	14.00

—*Distributed by Playboy/CBS*

❏ PZ34800	Rock 'N' Roll with the Modern Lovers	1977	14.00

—*Distributed by Playboy/CBS*

❏ BZ-0053	Rock 'N' Roll with the Modern Lovers	1977	25.00

—*Distributed by Janus/GRT*

❏ JBZ 0050	The Modern Lovers	1978	30.00

—*Distributed by Playboy/CBS*

❏ BZ-0050	The Modern Lovers	1976	30.00

—*Distributed by GRT*

BOMP!

❏ 4021	The Original Modern Lovers	1981	25.00

—*Same album as Mohawk releasse*

HOME OF THE HITS

❏ HH-1910	The Modern Lovers	1975	50.00

MOHAWK

❏ SCALP 0002	The Original Modern Lovers	1981	30.00

RHINO

❏ RNLP70095	Back in Your Life	1986	15.00

—*Reissue*

❏ RNLP70092	Jonathan Richman and the Modern Lovers	1986	15.00

—*Reissue*

❏ RNLP70094	Modern Lovers "Live	1986	15.00

—*Reissue*

❏ RNLP70093	Rock 'N' Roll with the Modern Lovers	1986	15.00

—*Reissue*

❏ RNLP70091	The Modern Lovers	1986	15.00

—*Reissue*

ROUNDER

❏ 9024	Jonathan Goes Country	1990	15.00
❏ 9021	Jonathan Richman	1989	15.00
❏ 9014	Modern Lovers '88	1988	15.00

SIRE

❏ 23939	Jonathan Sings!	1983	15.00

VAPOR

❏ 48216	Her Mystery Not of High Heels and Eye Shadow	2001	18.00
❏ 47086	I'm So Confused	1998	18.00

RICHMOND, DANNIE

ABC IMPULSE!

❏ AS-98 [S]	Dannie Richmond	1968	18.00

GATEMOUTH

❏ 1004	Dannie Richmond Quintet	1980	15.00

IMPULSE!

❏ AS-98 [S]	Dannie Richmond	1966	30.00
❏ A-98 [M]	Dannie Richmond	1966	25.00

RED RECORD

❏ VPA-161	Dionysius	198?	15.00

SOUL NOTE

❏ SN-1005	Ode to Mingus	198?	15.00

RICHMOND, MIKE, AND ANDY LAVERNE

STEEPLECHASE

❏ SCS-1101	For Us	198?	15.00

RICHMOND, MIKE

INNER CITY

❏ IC-1065	Dream Waves	1978	15.00

RICKLES, DON

WARNER BROS.

❏ WS1779	Don Rickles Speaks!	1969	18.00
❏ WS1745	Hello Dummy!	1968	18.00

RICKS, JIMMY

JUBILEE

❏ JGS-8021	Tell Her You Love Her	1969	50.00

MAINSTREAM

❏ 56050 [M]	Vibrations	1965	50.00
❏ S-6050 [S]	Vibrations	1965	60.00

SIGNATURE

❏ SM-1032 [M]	Jimmy Ricks	1961	300.00
❏ SM-1032 [M]	Jimmy Ricks	1961	200.00

— *White label promo*

RIDDLE, NELSON

ALSHIRE

❏ 5203	Bridge Over Troubled Water	197?	12.00

AVON

❏ 10170	Avon Wishes You a Happy Holiday and a Joyous New Year	1970	18.00

— *Given to Avon salespeople*

CAPITOL

❏ T1365 [M]	Can-Can	1961	25.00
❏ ST1365 [S]	Can-Can	1961	30.00
❏ T893 [M]	C'mon, Get Happy	1957	30.00
❏ T813 [M]	Hey, Let Yourself Go	1957	30.00
❏ T1817 [M]	Love Is a Game of Poker	1962	25.00
❏ ST1817 [S]	Love Is a Game of Poker	1962	30.00
❏ T1571 [M]	Love Tide	1961	25.00
❏ ST1571 [S]	Love Tide	1961	30.00
❏ T1670 [M]	Magic Moments from "The Gay Life	1962	25.00
❏ ST1670 [S]	Magic Moments from "The Gay Life	1962	30.00
❏ T1869 [M]	More Hit TV Themes	1963	25.00
❏ ST1869 [S]	More Hit TV Themes	1963	30.00
❏ T1771 [M]	Route 66 Theme and Other Great TV Themes	1962	30.00
❏ ST1771 [S]	Route 66 Theme and Other Great TV Themes	1962	30.00
❏ T915 [M]	Sea of Dreams	1958	30.00
❏ TAO1259 [M]	Sing a Song with Riddle	1960	25.00
❏ STAO1259 [S]	Sing a Song with Riddle	1960	30.00
❏ T1990 [M]	The Best of Nelson Riddle	1963	18.00
❏ DT1990 [P]	The Best of Nelson Riddle	1963	18.00
❏ SM-11764	The Best of Nelson Riddle	1976	12.00
❏ T1148 [M]	The Joy of Living	1959	25.00
❏ ST1148 [S]	The Joy of Living	1959	30.00
❏ T753 [M]	The Tender Touch	1956	30.00

DAYBREAK

❏ DS2015	Viva Legrand!	197?	25.00

HARMONY

❏ HS11320	Nelson Riddle and His Orchestra Play the Wonderful Nat King Cole Songs	1969	15.00

LIBERTY

❏ LRP-3508 [M]	The Bright and the Beautiful	1967	18.00
❏ LST-7508 [S]	The Bright and the Beautiful	1967	18.00
❏ LST-3532 [M]	The Riddle of Today	1967	25.00
❏ LST-7532 [S]	The Riddle of Today	1967	18.00

PICKWICK

❏ PC3007 [M]	Witchcraft	1965	20.00
❏ SPC3007 [R]	Witchcraft	1965	15.00

REPRISE

❏ R-6071 [M]	Come Blow Your Horn	1963	18.00
❏ R9-6071 [S]	Come Blow Your Horn	1963	25.00
❏ R-6138 [M]	Great Music, Great Films, Great Sounds	1964	18.00
❏ RS-6138 [S]	Great Music, Great Films, Great Sounds	1964	25.00
❏ R-6162 [M]	Nat	1965	18.00
❏ RS-6162 [S]	Nat	1965	25.00
❏ R-6120 [M]	White on White," "Shangri-La," "Charade" and Other Hits of 1964	1964	18.00
❏ RS-6120 [S]	White on White," "Shangri-La," "Charade" and Other Hits of 1964	1964	25.00

SEARS

❏ SP-406 [M]	Witchcraft	196?	18.00
❏ SPS-406 [R]	Witchcraft	196?	15.00

SOLID STATE

❏ SS-18013	Music for Wives and Lovers	1967	25.00
❏ ST-91083	Music for Wives and Lovers	1967	30.00

— *Capitol Record Club edition*

SUNSET

❏ SUS-5233	The Riddle Touch	1968	15.00

UNITED ARTISTS

❏ UAS6670	The Contemporary Sound of Nelson Riddle	1968	25.00
❏ ST-91566	The Contemporary Sound of Nelson Riddle	1968	30.00

— *Capitol Record Club edition*

RIDERS IN THE SKY

MCA

❏ 42180	Riders Radio Theater	1988	10.00
❏ 42040	The Cowboy Way	1987	10.00
❏ 42305	The Riders Go Commercial	1989	12.00

ROUNDER

❏ 0147	Cowboy Jubilee	1981	12.00
❏ 0186	Live	1984	12.00
❏ 0220	New Trails	1986	12.00
❏ 0170	Prairie Serenade	1982	12.00
❏ 8011	Saddle Pals	1985	12.00
❏ 0102	Three on the Trail	1980	12.00
❏ 1038	Weeds and Water	1983	12.00

RIDLEY, LARRY

STRATA-EAST

❏ SES-19759	Sum of the Parts	1975	30.00

RIEDEL, GEORGE

PHILIPS

❏ PHM200140 [M]	Jazz Ballet	1964	18.00
❏ PHS600140 [S]	Jazz Ballet	1964	25.00

RIEMANN, KURT

INNOVATIVE COMMUNICATION

❏ KS 80.047	Electronic Nightworks	1987	15.00

RIFKIN, JOSHUA

NONESUCH

❏ H-71248	Piano Rags by Scott Joplin	1970	15.00
❏ H-71264	Piano Rags by Scott Joplin, Vol. 2	1971	15.00

RIG

CAPITOL

❏ ST-473 [B]	Rig	1970	30.00

RIGHTEOUS BROTHERS, THE

HAVEN

❏ ST-9201	Give It to the People	1974	18.00
❏ ST-9203	Sons of Mrs. Righteous	1975	18.00

MGM

❏ SE-4885	The History of the Righteous Brothers	1973	18.00
❏ GAS-102	The Righteous Brothers (Golden Archive Series)	1970	18.00

MOONGLOW

❏ MLP-1001 [M]	Right Now!	1963	40.00
❏ MSP-1001 [S]	Right Now!	1963	60.00
❏ MLP-1002 [M]	Some Blue-Eyed Soul	1964	40.00
❏ MSP-1002 [S]	Some Blue-Eyed Soul	1964	60.00
❏ MLP-1004 [M]	The Best of the Righteous Brothers	1966	30.00
❏ MSP-1004 [S]	The Best of the Righteous Brothers	1966	30.00
❏ MLP-1003 [M]	This Is New!	1965	40.00
❏ MSP-1003 [S]	This Is New!	1965	60.00

PHILLES

❏ PHLP-4009 [M]	Back to Back	1965	30.00
❏ PHLPS-4009 [S]	Back to Back	1965	40.00
❏ T-90677 [M]	Back to Back	1965	30.00

—*Capitol Record Club edition*

❏ ST-90677 [S]	Back to Back	1965	40.00

—*Capitol Record Club edition*

❏ PHLP-4008 [M]	Just Once in My Life	1965	30.00
❏ PHLPS-4008 [S]	Just Once in My Life	1965	40.00
❏ PHLP-4007 [M]	You've Lost That Lovin' Feelin'	1964	40.00
❏ PHLPS-4007 [S]	You've Lost That Lovin' Feelin'	1964	50.00
❏ T-90692 [M]	You've Lost That Lovin' Feelin'	1965	50.00

—*Capitol Record Club edition*

Number	Title	Yr	NM
❏ ST-90692 [S]	You've Lost That Lovin' Feelin'	1965	50.00

— Capitol Record Club edition

RHINO

Number	Title	Yr	NM
❏ R1-71488	Anthology	1989	18.00

VERVE

Number	Title	Yr	NM
❏ V-5004 [M]	Go Ahead and Cry	1966	25.00
❏ V6-5004 [S]	Go Ahead and Cry	1966	30.00
❏ ST-90921 [S]	Go Ahead and Cry	1966	30.00

— Capitol Record Club edition

❏ V-5020 [M]	Greatest Hits	1967	30.00
❏ V6-5020 [S]	Greatest Hits	1967	25.00
❏ 823662-1	Greatest Hits	198?	12.00
❏ V6-5071	Greatest Hits, Vol. 2	1969	25.00
❏ V6-5058	One for the Road	1968	30.00

— With The Blossoms credited on the back cover

| ❏ V6-5058 | One for the Road | 1968 | 25.00 |

— Without The Blossoms credited on the back cover

❏ V6-5076	Re-Birth	1970	25.00
❏ V-5010 [M]	Sayin' Somethin'	1967	25.00
❏ V6-5010 [S]	Sayin' Somethin'	1967	30.00
❏ T-91057 [M]	Sayin' Somethin'	1967	30.00

— Capitol Record Club edition

| ❏ ST-91057 [S] | Sayin' Somethin' | 1967 | 30.00 |

— Capitol Record Club edition

❏ V-5001 [M]	Soul and Inspiration	1966	25.00
❏ V6-5001 [S]	Soul and Inspiration	1966	30.00
❏ ST-90669 [S]	Soul and Inspiration	1966	30.00

— Capitol Record Club edition

❏ V-5031 [M]	Souled Out	1967	40.00
❏ V6-5031 [S]	Souled Out	1967	25.00
❏ V6-5051	Standards	1968	25.00

RILEY, BILLY LEE

GNP CRESCENDO

Number	Title	Yr	NM
❏ GNP-2020 [M]	Billy Lee Riley	1966	18.00
❏ GNPS-2020 [S]	Billy Lee Riley	1966	25.00

MERCURY

❏ MG-20974 [M]	Beatlemania Harmonica	1965	25.00
❏ SR-60974 [S]	Beatlemania Harmonica	1965	30.00
❏ MG-20965 [M]	Big Harmonica Special	1964	25.00
❏ SR-60965 [S]	Big Harmonica Special	1964	30.00
❏ MG-20958 [M]	The Whiskey A-Go-Go Presents Billy Lee Riley	1964	25.00
❏ SR-60958 [S]	The Whiskey A-Go-Go Presents Billy Lee Riley	1964	30.00

RILEY, DOUG

PM

Number	Title	Yr	NM
❏ 007	Dreams	1977	15.00

RILEY, JEANNIE C.

ALLEGIANCE

Number	Title	Yr	NM
❏ AV-5026	Tears, Joys and Memories	198?	12.00

CAPITOL

| ❏ ST-177 | The Songs of Jeannie C. Riley | 1969 | 18.00 |

LITTLE DARLIN'

| ❏ SLD8011 | Soul Soul | 1968 | 25.00 |

MGM

❏ SE-4849	Down to Earth	1973	15.00
❏ SE-4805	Give Myself a Party	1972	15.00
❏ SE-4909	Just Jeannie C. Riley	1973	15.00
❏ SE-4891	When Love Has Gone Away	1973	15.00

PICKWICK

| ❏ 6098 | The Girl Most Likely | 197? | 12.00 |
| ❏ 6119 | The World of Country | 197? | 12.00 |

PLANTATION

❏ PLP8	Country Girl	1970	18.00
❏ 508	Country Queens	197?	15.00
❏ PLP1 [S]	Harper Valley P.T.A.	1968	25.00
❏ PLM1 [M]	Harper Valley P.T.A.	1968	60.00
❏ PLP16	Jeannie	1971	18.00
❏ PLP13	Jeannie C. Riley's Greatest Hits	1971	18.00
❏ PLP11	The Generation Gap	1970	18.00
❏ PLP3	Things Go Better with Love	1969	18.00
❏ PLP2	Yearbooks and Yesterdays	1969	18.00

POWER PAK

| ❏ 250 | Country Gold | 197? | 12.00 |

RIMINGTON, SAMMY

GHB

Number	Title	Yr	NM
❏ GHB-181	Sammy Rimington and the Mouldy Five, Vol. 1	1985	12.00
❏ GHB-182	Sammy Rimington and the Mouldy Five, Vol. 2	1985	12.00
❏ GHB-94	Sammy Rimington Plays George Lewis Classics	198?	12.00

JAZZ CRUSADE

| ❏ 1005 | Sammy Rimington Plays George Lewis Classics | 196? | 18.00 |

PROGRESSIVE

| ❏ PRO-7077 | The Exciting Sax of Sammy Rimington | 1987 | 12.00 |

RINCON SURFSIDE BAND, THE

DUNHILL

Number	Title	Yr	NM
❏ D50001 [M]	Surfing Songbook	1965	200.00

Number	Title	Yr	NM
❏ DS50001 [S]	Surfing Songbook	1965	300.00

RIOPELLE, JERRY

CAPITOL

Number	Title	Yr	NM
❏ ST-732	Jerry Riopelle	1971	18.00
❏ ST-863	Second Album	1971	18.00

RIOS, MIGUEL

A&M

Number	Title	Yr	NM
❏ SPX-4267	A Song of Joy	1970	18.00

RIOS, WALDO DE LOS

UNITED ARTISTS

Number	Title	Yr	NM
❏ UAS-5554	Mozartmania	1972	15.00
❏ UAS-6802	Sinfonias	1971	15.00

VAULT

| ❏ VS-126 [B] | International Hits | 1969 | 30.00 |

WARNER BROS.

| ❏ BS2801 | Operas | 1974 | 15.00 |

RIOT

ARIOLA

Number	Title	Yr	NM
❏ ARL5007	Rock City	1977	18.00

CAPITOL

| ❏ ST12081 | Narita | 1979 | 15.00 |
| ❏ SN16271 | Narita | 1982 | 12.00 |

CBS

| ❏ Z45132 | The Privilege of Power | 1990 | 14.00 |
| ❏ BFZ44232 | Thundersteel | 1988 | 15.00 |

ELEKTRA

❏ 55546	Fire Down Under	1981	15.00
❏ 60134	Restless Breed	1982	12.00
❏ 67969	Riot Live	1982	25.00

FIRE-SIGN

| ❏ 87001 | Rock City | 1977 | 30.00 |

GRAND SLAMM

| ❏ SLAM6 | Born In America | 1989 | 14.00 |

QUALITY

| ❏ QUS1008 | Born In America | 1983 | 15.00 |

RIP CHORDS, THE

COLUMBIA

Number	Title	Yr	NM
❏ CL2151 [M]	Hey Little Cobra and Other Hot Rod Hits	1964	40.00

— Guaranteed High Fidelity" on label

| ❏ CS8951 [S] | Hey Little Cobra and Other Hot Rod Hits | 1964 | 50.00 |
| ❏ CL2151 [M] | Hey Little Cobra and Other Hot Rod Hits | 1966 | 30.00 |

— 360 Sound Mono" on label

| ❏ CL2216 [M] | Three Window Coupe | 1964 | 60.00 |
| ❏ CS9016 [S] | Three Window Coupe | 1964 | 70.00 |

RIPERTON, MINNIE

ACCORD

Number	Title	Yr	NM
❏ SN 7205	Wistful Memories	1981	12.00

CAPITOL

| ❏ SN-12005 | Adventures in Paradise | 1979 | 12.00 |

— Reissue of Epic 33454

| ❏ SN-16146 | Adventures in Paradise | 1980 | 10.00 |

— Budget-line reissue

❏ SOO-12097	Love Lives Forever	1980	12.00
❏ SO-11936	Minnie	1979	12.00
❏ SN-12004	Perfect Angel	1979	12.00

— Reissue of Epic 32561

| ❏ SN-16145 | Perfect Angel | 1980 | 10.00 |

— Budget-line reissue

| ❏ SN-12006 | Stay in Love | 1979 | 12.00 |

— Reissue of Epic 34191

| ❏ SN-16147 | Stay in Love | 1980 | 10.00 |

— Budget-line reissue

| ❏ ST-12189 | The Best of Minnie Riperton | 1981 | 12.00 |

EPIC

❏ PE33454	Adventures in Paradise	1975	15.00
❏ PEQ33454 [Q]	Adventures in Paradise	1975	30.00
❏ KE32561	Perfect Angel	1974	15.00
❏ EQ32561 [Q]	Perfect Angel	1974	30.00
❏ PE34191	Stay in Love	1977	15.00

GRT

| ❏ 30001 | Come To My Garden | 1970 | 18.00 |

JANUS

| ❏ 7011 | Come To My Garden | 1974 | 15.00 |

— Reissue of GRT LP

RIPPINGTONS, THE

GRP

Number	Title	Yr	NM
❏ GR-9588	Tourist in Paradise	1989	15.00
❏ GR-9618	Welcome to the St. James Club	1990	18.00

PASSPORT JAZZ

| ❏ PJ88042 | Kilimanjaro | 1988 | 15.00 |
| ❏ PJ88019 | Moonlighting | 1987 | 15.00 |

RIPPY, RODNEY ALLEN

BELL

Number	Title	Yr	NM
❏ 1311	Take Life a Little Easier	1974	25.00

RISERS, THE

IMPERIAL

Number	Title	Yr	NM
❏ LP-9269 [M]	She's a Bad Motorcycle	1964	100.00
❏ LP-12269 [S]	She's a Bad Motorcycle	1964	150.00

RISING SONS, THE

SUNDAZED

Number	Title	Yr	NM
❏ LP5054	The Rising Sons	200?	15.00

RISING STORM, THE

ARF! ARF!

Number	Title	Yr	NM
❏ 007	Alive in Anover Again	1983	120.00

REMNANT

| ❏ BBA-3571 | Calm Before the Rising Storm | 1968 | 1200.00 |

— VG value 600; VG+ value 900

STANTON PARK

| ❏ 001 | Calm Before the Rising Storm | 1991 | 25.00 |

— Reissue of Remnant album

RITCHIE FAMILY, THE

20TH CENTURY

Number	Title	Yr	NM
❏ T-498	Brazil	1975	12.00

CASABLANCA

| ❏ NBLP-7166 | Bad Reputation | 1979 | 12.00 |
| ❏ NBLP-7223 | Give Me a Break | 1980 | 12.00 |

MARLIN

❏ 2206	African Queens	1977	12.00
❏ 2215	American Generation	1978	12.00
❏ 2201	Arabian Nights	1976	12.00
❏ 2203	Life Is Music	1977	12.00

RCA VICTOR

| ❏ AFL1-4601 | All Night, All Night | 1983 | 12.00 |
| ❏ AFL1-4324 | I'll Do My Best | 1982 | 12.00 |

RITENOUR, LEE

ELEKTRA

Number	Title	Yr	NM
❏ 60358	Banded Together	1984	12.00
❏ 6E-192	Feel the Night	1979	12.00
❏ 6E-331	Rit	1981	12.00
❏ 60186	Rit/2	1982	12.00
❏ 6E-136	The Captain's Journey	1978	12.00

ELEKTRA/MUSICIAN

| ❏ 60310 | On the Line | 1983 | 12.00 |
| ❏ 60024 | Rio | 1982 | 12.00 |

EPIC

| ❏ PE34426 | Captain Fingers | 1977 | 12.00 |

— Orange label

| ❏ PE34426 | Captain Fingers | 1979 | 10.00 |

— Dark blue label

| ❏ PE33947 | First Course | 1976 | 12.00 |

— Orange label

| ❏ PE33947 | First Course | 1979 | 10.00 |

— Dark blue label

| ❏ JE36527 | The Best of Lee Ritenour | 1980 | 12.00 |
| ❏ PE36527 | The Best of Lee Ritenour | 198? | 10.00 |

— Budget-line reissue

GRP

❏ GR-9594	Color Rit	1989	15.00
❏ GR-1021	Earth Run	1986	12.00
❏ GR-9570	Festival	1988	12.00
❏ GR-1042	Portrait	1987	12.00
❏ GR-1017	Rio	1986	10.00
❏ GR-9615	Stolen Moments	1990	18.00

MOBILE FIDELITY

| ❏ 1-147 | Captain Fingers | 1985 | 30.00 |

— Audiophile vinyl

NAUTILUS

| ❏ NR-41 | Rit | 198? | 40.00 |

— Audiophile vinyl

RITTER, TEX

BUCKBOARD

Number	Title	Yr	NM
❏ BBS1030	Tex Ritter	198?	12.00

CAPITOL

| ❏ SKC-11241 | An American Legend | 1973 | 30.00 |
| ❏ T1292 [M] | Blood on the Saddle | 1960 | 30.00 |

— Black colorband label, logo at left

| ❏ T1292 [M] | Blood on the Saddle | 1962 | 25.00 |

— Black colorband label, logo at top

| ❏ ST1292 [S] | Blood on the Saddle | 1960 | 40.00 |

— Black colorband label, logo at left

| ❏ ST1292 [S] | Blood on the Saddle | 1962 | 30.00 |

— Black colorband label, logo at top

❏ T1910 [M]	Border Affair	1963	25.00
❏ ST1910 [S]	Border Affair	1963	30.00
❏ T2890 [M]	Bum Tiddil Dee Bum Bum!	1968	50.00
❏ ST2890 [S]	Bum Tiddil Dee Bum Bum!	1968	30.00
❏ ST-213	Chuck Wagon Days	1969	25.00

Number	Title	Yr	NM
❑ ST-11503	Comin' After Jinny	1976	18.00
❑ H4004 [10]	Cowboy Favorites	195?	180.00
❑ ST-11351	Fall Away	1974	18.00
❑ ST-467	Green Green Valley	1970	25.00
❑ T1623 [M]	Hillbilly Heaven	1961	30.00
— Black colorband label, logo at left			
❑ T1623 [M]	Hillbilly Heaven	1962	25.00
— Black colorband label, logo at top			
❑ ST1623 [S]	Hillbilly Heaven	1961	40.00
— Black colorband label, logo at left			
❑ ST1623 [S]	Hillbilly Heaven	1962	30.00
— Black colorband label, logo at top			
❑ SM-1623	Hillbilly Heaven	1976	12.00
— Reissue with new prefix			
❑ T2786 [M]	Just Beyond the Moon	1967	30.00
❑ ST2786 [S]	Just Beyond the Moon	1967	30.00
❑ T1100 [M]	Psalms	1959	50.00
— Black colorband label, logo at left			
❑ T1100 [M]	Psalms	1962	30.00
— Black colorband label, logo at top			
❑ T971 [M]	Songs from the Western Screen	1958	80.00
— Turquoise or gray label			
❑ T971 [M]	Songs from the Western Screen	1959	40.00
— Black colorband label, logo at left			
❑ T971 [M]	Songs from the Western Screen	1962	30.00
— Black colorband label, logo at top			
❑ ST-11037	Supercountrylegendary	1972	18.00
❑ T2743 [M]	Sweet Land of Liberty	1967	30.00
❑ ST2743 [S]	Sweet Land of Liberty	1967	30.00
❑ ST2974	Tex Ritter's Wild West	1968	30.00
❑ T2595 [M]	The Best of Tex Ritter	1966	30.00
❑ DT2595 [R]	The Best of Tex Ritter	1966	18.00
❑ T2402 [M]	The Friendly Voice of Tex Ritter	1965	25.00
❑ ST2402 [S]	The Friendly Voice of Tex Ritter	1965	30.00
❑ W1562 [M]	The Lincoln Hymns	1961	30.00
❑ SW1562 [S]	The Lincoln Hymns	1961	40.00

HILLTOP

Number	Title	Yr	NM
❑ JS-6138	High Noon	196?	15.00
❑ JS-6075	Love You As Big As Texas	196?	15.00
❑ PTP-2020	My Kinda Songs	197?	18.00
❑ JS-6155	Tex	197?	15.00
❑ JS-6043	Tex Ritter Sings His Hits	196?	15.00

LABREA

Number	Title	Yr	NM
❑ L-8036 [M]	Jamboree, Nashville Style	196?	25.00
❑ LS-8036 [S]	Jamboree, Nashville Style	196?	30.00

PREMIER

Number	Title	Yr	NM
❑ 9023	Tex Ritter and the Rio Grande River Boys	196?	15.00

RITZ, LYLE

VERVE

Number	Title	Yr	NM
❑ MGV-8333 [M]	50th State Jazz	1959	50.00
❑ MGVS-6070 [S]	50th State Jazz	1960	40.00
❑ V-8333 [M]	50th State Jazz	1961	30.00
❑ V6-8333 [S]	50th State Jazz	1961	25.00
❑ MGV-2087 [M]	How About Uke?	1957	40.00

RITZ, THE

PAUSA

Number	Title	Yr	NM
❑ 7190	Born to Bop	1986	12.00

RIVERA, HECTOR

WING

Number	Title	Yr	NM
❑ MGW-12197 [M]	Let's Cha Cha Cha	1960	25.00

RIVERA, LUIS, AND DOC BAGBY

KING

Number	Title	Yr	NM
❑ 631 [M]	Battle of the Organs	1959	100.00

RIVERA, LUIS

IMPERIAL

Number	Title	Yr	NM
❑ LP-9139 [M]	Filet of Soul	1961	30.00

RIVERS, JERRY

STARDAY

Number	Title	Yr	NM
❑ SLP-281 [M]	Fantastic Fiddlin' and Tall Tales	1964	30.00

RIVERS, JOHNNY

ATLANTIC

Number	Title	Yr	NM
❑ SD7301	The Road	1974	15.00

BIG TREE

Number	Title	Yr	NM
❑ BT76004	Outside Help	1977	15.00

CAPITOL

Number	Title	Yr	NM
❑ T2161 [M]	The Sensational Johnny Rivers	1964	25.00
❑ ST2161 [S]	The Sensational Johnny Rivers	1964	30.00

COLUMBIA

Number	Title	Yr	NM
❑ FE38429	Not a Through Street	1983	12.00
❑ PE38429	Not a Through Street	1985	10.00
— Budget-line reissue			

EPIC

Number	Title	Yr	NM
❑ PE33681	New Lovers and Old Friends	1975	15.00

IMPERIAL

Number	Title	Yr	NM
❑ LP-9307 [M]	...And I Know You Wanna Dance	1966	25.00
— Black label with pink and white at left			
❑ LP-12307 [S]	...And I Know You Wanna Dance	1966	30.00
— Black label with pink and white at left			
❑ LP-9307 [M]	...And I Know You Wanna Dance	1966	15.00
— Black label with green and white at left			
❑ LP-12307 [S]	...And I Know You Wanna Dance	1966	18.00
— Black label with green and white at left			
❑ LP-12427	A Touch of Gold	1969	25.00
❑ LP-9334 [M]	Changes	1966	18.00
❑ LP-12334 [S]	Changes	1966	25.00
❑ LP-9274 [M]	Here We A-Go-Go Again!	1964	25.00
— Black label with pink and white at left			
❑ LP-12274 [S]	Here We A-Go-Go Again!	1964	30.00
— Black label with pink and white at left			
❑ LP-9274 [M]	Here We A-Go-Go Again!	1966	15.00
— Black label with green and white at left			
❑ LP-12274 [S]	Here We A-Go-Go Again!	1966	18.00
— Black label with green and white at left			
❑ LP-9264 [M]	Johnny Rivers at the Whiskey A-Go-Go	1964	25.00
— Black label with pink and white at left			
❑ LP-12264 [S]	Johnny Rivers at the Whiskey A-Go-Go	1964	30.00
— Black label with pink and white at left			
❑ LP-9264 [M]	Johnny Rivers at the Whiskey A-Go-Go	1966	15.00
— Black label with green and white at left			
❑ LP-12264 [S]	Johnny Rivers at the Whiskey A-Go-Go	1966	18.00
— Black label with green and white at left			
❑ LP-9324 [M]	Johnny Rivers' Golden Hits	1966	18.00
❑ LP-12324 [S]	Johnny Rivers' Golden Hits	1966	25.00
❑ LP-9280 [M]	Johnny Rivers In Action!	1965	25.00
— Black label with pink and white at left			
❑ LP-12280 [S]	Johnny Rivers In Action!	1965	30.00
— Black label with pink and white at left			
❑ LP-9280 [M]	Johnny Rivers In Action!	1966	15.00
— Black label with green and white at left			
❑ LP-12280 [S]	Johnny Rivers In Action!	1966	18.00
— Black label with green and white at left			
❑ LP-9293 [M]	Johnny Rivers Rocks the Folk	1965	25.00
— Black label with pink and white at left			
❑ LP-12293 [S]	Johnny Rivers Rocks the Folk	1965	30.00
— Black label with pink and white at left			
❑ LP-9293 [M]	Johnny Rivers Rocks the Folk	1966	15.00
— Black label with green and white at left			
❑ LP-12293 [S]	Johnny Rivers Rocks the Folk	1966	18.00
— Black label with green and white at left			
❑ LP-9284 [M]	Meanwhile Back at the Whiskey a-Go-Go	1965	25.00
— Black label with pink and white at left			
❑ LP-12284 [S]	Meanwhile Back at the Whiskey a-Go-Go	1965	30.00
— Black label with pink and white at left			
❑ LP-9284 [M]	Meanwhile Back at the Whiskey a-Go-Go	1966	15.00
— Black label with green and white at left			
❑ LP-12284 [S]	Meanwhile Back at the Whiskey a-Go-Go	1966	18.00
— Black label with green and white at left			
❑ LP-12372 [S]	Realization	1968	25.00
❑ LP-9372 [M]	Realization	1968	40.00
❑ LP-9341 [M]	Rewind	1967	25.00
❑ LP-12341 [S]	Rewind	1967	25.00
❑ LP-16001	Slim Slo Slider	1970	25.00

LIBERTY

Number	Title	Yr	NM
❑ LW-12427	A Touch of Gold	198?	10.00
— Budget-line reissue			
❑ LN-10154	Blue Suede Shoes	1981	10.00
— Budget-line reissue			
❑ LN-10121	Changes	1981	10.00
— Budget-line reissue			
❑ LO-12324	Johnny Rivers' Golden Hits	198?	10.00
— Budget-line reissue			
❑ LN-10120	The Best of Johnny Rivers	1981	10.00

MCA

Number	Title	Yr	NM
❑ 917	Greatest Hits	1985	12.00

PICKWICK

Number	Title	Yr	NM
❑ SPC-3191	If You Want It, I Got It	196?	15.00
❑ PC-3022 [M]	Johnny Rivers	196?	18.00
❑ SPC-3022 [R]	Johnny Rivers	196?	15.00
— First pressing covers have no "electronically enhanced for STEREO" at upper right			
❑ SPC-3022 [R]	Johnny Rivers	196?	12.00
— Later covers have "electronically enhanced for STEREO" at upper right			

RSO

Number	Title	Yr	NM
❑ RS-1-3082	Borrowed Time	1980	12.00

SEARS

Number	Title	Yr	NM
❑ SPS-487	Groovin'	1968	30.00
❑ SPS-417	Mr. Teenage	196?	30.00

SOUL CITY

Number	Title	Yr	NM
❑ SC1007-1	Greatest Hits	1998	25.00
— 500 copies, each autographed by Johnny Rivers			

SUNSET

Number	Title	Yr	NM
❑ SUS-5251	The Early Years	1969	12.00
❑ SUS-5157 [S]	Whiskey A-Go-Go Revisited	1967	12.00
❑ SUM-1157 [M]	Whiskey A-Go-Go Revisited	1967	15.00

UNART

Number	Title	Yr	NM
❑ M-20007 [M]	The Great Johnny Rivers	1967	15.00
❑ S-21007 [S]	The Great Johnny Rivers	1967	15.00

UNITED ARTISTS

Number	Title	Yr	NM
❑ UA-LA075-F	Blue Suede Shoes	1973	15.00
❑ UAL-3386 [M]	Go, Johnny, Go	1964	25.00
❑ UAS-6386 [S]	Go, Johnny, Go	1964	30.00
❑ T-90813 [M]	Go, Johnny, Go	1965	30.00
— Capitol Record Club edition			
❑ ST-90813 [S]	Go, Johnny, Go	1965	30.00
— Capitol Record Club edition			
❑ UAS-5532	Home Grown	1971	18.00
❑ USX-93	Johnny Rivers Superpak	1971	25.00
❑ UAS-5650	L.A. Reggae	1972	18.00
❑ UA-LA253-G	The Very Best of Johnny Rivers	1974	15.00
❑ UA-LA387-E	The Very Best of Johnny Rivers	1975	15.00
❑ UA-LA486-G	Wild Night	1976	15.00

WARNER BROS.

Number	Title	Yr	NM
❑ R133498 [S]	Johnny Rivers' Golden Hits	197?	30.00
— RCA Music Service edition of Imperial LP-12324 on "Burbank" palm trees label; why this was pressed on Warner Bros. is anyone's guess, but it doesn't appear to be an error			

RIVERS, MAVIS

CAPITOL

Number	Title	Yr	NM
❑ T1210 [M]	Take a Number	1959	30.00
❑ ST1210 [S]	Take a Number	1959	40.00

DELOS

Number	Title	Yr	NM
❑ DMS-4002	It's a Good Day	1983	15.00

REPRISE

Number	Title	Yr	NM
❑ R-2002 [M]	Mavis	1961	30.00
❑ R9-2002 [S]	Mavis	1961	40.00
❑ R-6074 [M]	Mavis Rivers Meets Shorty Rogers	1963	30.00
❑ RS-6074 [S]	Mavis Rivers Meets Shorty Rogers	1963	30.00

VEE JAY

Number	Title	Yr	NM
❑ VJ-1132 [M]	We Remember Mildred Bailey	1964	30.00
❑ VJS-1132 [S]	We Remember Mildred Bailey	1964	40.00

RIVERS, SAM

ABC IMPULSE!

Number	Title	Yr	NM
❑ AS-9286	Crystals	1974	18.00
❑ AS-9302	Hues	1974	18.00
❑ IA-9352	Sam Rivers Live	1978	18.00
❑ AS-9316	Sizzle	1975	18.00
❑ AS-9251	Streams	1973	18.00

BLACK SAINT

Number	Title	Yr	NM
❑ BSR-0064	Colours	1982	15.00

BLUE NOTE

Number	Title	Yr	NM
❑ BLP-4249 [M]	A New Conception	1966	30.00
❑ BST-84249 [S]	A New Conception	1966	30.00
— With "New York, USA" address on label			
❑ BST-84249 [S]	A New Conception	1967	25.00
— With "A Division of Liberty Records" on label			
❑ BLP-4206 [M]	Contours	1965	30.00
❑ BST-84206 [S]	Contours	1965	30.00
— With "New York, USA" address on label			
❑ BST-84206 [S]	Contours	1967	25.00
— With "A Division of Liberty Records" on label			
❑ BST-84261 [S]	Dimensions and Extensions	1986	15.00
— The Finest in Jazz Since 1939" label; originally scheduled for 1966 release			
❑ BLP-4184 [M]	Fuchsia Swing Song	1964	30.00
❑ BST-84184 [S]	Fuchsia Swing Song	1964	30.00
— With "New York, USA" address on label			
❑ BST-84184 [S]	Fuchsia Swing Song	1967	25.00
— With "A Division of Liberty Records" on label			
❑ BN-LA453-H2	Involution	1975	18.00

ECM

Number	Title	Yr	NM
❑ 1162	Contrasts	1980	15.00

MCA

Number	Title	Yr	NM
❑ 4149	Live Trio Session	198?	15.00

PAUSA

Number	Title	Yr	NM
❑ 7015	The Quest	198?	12.00

RED RECORD

Number	Title	Yr	NM
❑ VPA-106	The Quest	198?	15.00

TOMATO

Number	Title	Yr	NM
❑ TOM-8002	Waves	1979	15.00

RIVERSIDE JAZZ STARS, THE

RIVERSIDE

Number	Title	Yr	NM
❑ RLP-397 [M]	A Jazz Version of "Kean	1961	30.00
❑ RS-9397 [S]	A Jazz Version of "Kean	1961	40.00

Number	Title	Yr	NM

RIVIERAS, THE (1)

POST

| ❏ 2000 | The Rivieras Sing | 196? | 40.00 |

RIVIERAS, THE (2)

RIVIERA

| ❏ 701 [M] | Campus Party | 1964 | 250.00 |

U.S.A.

| ❏ 102 [M] | Let's Have a Party | 1964 | 150.00 |

RIVINGTONS, THE

LIBERTY

| ❏ LRP-3282 [M] | Doin' the Bird | 1963 | 100.00 |
| ❏ LST-7282 [S] | Doin' the Bird | 1963 | 200.00 |

RIZZI, TONY

MILAGRO

| ❏ 1000 | Tony Rizzi Plays Charlie Christian | 197? | 15.00 |

STARLITE

| ❏ 6002 [10] | Tony Rizzi Guitar | 1954 | 50.00 |

ROACH, FREDDIE

BLUE NOTE

❏ BLP-4190 [M]	All That's Good	1965	30.00
❏ BST-84190 [S]	All That's Good	1965	30.00
— With "New York, USA" address on label			
❏ BST-84190 [S]	All That's Good	1967	18.00
— With "A Division of Liberty Records" on label			
❏ BLP-4168 [M]	Brown Sugar	1964	30.00
❏ BST-84168 [S]	Brown Sugar	1964	30.00
— With "New York, USA" address on label			
❏ BST-84168 [S]	Brown Sugar	1967	18.00
— With "A Division of Liberty Records" on label			
❏ BLP-4113 [M]	Down to Earth	1962	30.00
❏ BST-84113 [S]	Down to Earth	1962	30.00
— With "New York, USA" address on label			
❏ BST-84113 [S]	Down to Earth	1967	18.00
— With "A Division of Liberty Records" on label			
❏ BLP-4158 [M]	Good Move	1964	30.00
❏ BST-84158 [S]	Good Move	1964	30.00
— With "New York, USA" address on label			
❏ BST-84158 [S]	Good Move	1967	18.00
— With "A Division of Liberty Records" on label			
❏ BLP-4128 [M]	Mo' Greens, Please	1963	30.00
❏ BST-84128 [S]	Mo' Greens, Please	1963	30.00
— With "New York, USA" address on label			
❏ BST-84128 [S]	Mo' Greens, Please	1967	18.00
— With "A Division of Liberty Records" on label			

PRESTIGE

❏ PRLP-7507 [M]	Mocha Motion	1967	30.00
❏ PRST-7507 [S]	Mocha Motion	1967	25.00
❏ PRLP-7521 [M]	My People -- Soul People	1967	30.00
❏ PRST-7521 [S]	My People -- Soul People	1967	25.00
❏ PRLP-7490 [M]	The Soul Book	1967	30.00
❏ PRST-7490 [S]	The Soul Book	1967	25.00

ROACH, MAX, AND ANTHONY BRAXTON

BLACK SAINT

| ❏ DSR-0024 [B] | Birth and Rebirth | 198? | 18.00 |

HAT HUT

| ❏ 06 | One in Two -- Two in One | 1980 | 25.00 |

ROACH, MAX, AND ARCHIE SHEPP

HAT HUT

| ❏ 13 | The Long March | 1980 | 25.00 |

ROACH, MAX, AND CECIL TAYLOR

SOUL NOTE

| ❏ SN-1100/1 | Historic Concerts | 1985 | 18.00 |

ROACH, MAX, AND CONNIE CROTHERS

NEW ARTISTS

| ❏ NA-1001 | Swish | 198? | 15.00 |

ROACH, MAX, AND STAN LEVEY

LIBERTY

| ❏ LRP-3064 [M] | Drummin' the Blues | 1957 | 80.00 |

ROACH, MAX; SONNY CLARK; GEORGE DUVIVIER

TIME

| ❏ 52101 [M] | Max Roach, Sonny Clark, George Duvivier | 1962 | 30.00 |
| ❏ S-2101 [S] | Max Roach, Sonny Clark, George Duvivier | 1962 | 40.00 |

ROACH, MAX

ABC IMPULSE!

| ❏ AS-16 [S] | It's Time | 1968 | 40.00 |
| ❏ AS-8 [S] | Percussion Bitter Sweet | 1968 | 25.00 |

ARGO

| ❏ LP-623 [M] | Max | 1958 | 50.00 |
| ❏ LPS-623 [S] | Max | 1958 | 50.00 |

Number	Title	Yr	NM

ATLANTIC

❏ 1467 [M]	Drums Unlimited	1966	25.00
❏ SD1467 [S]	Drums Unlimited	1966	30.00
❏ SD1587	Lift Every Voice and Sing	1972	15.00
❏ 1435 [M]	Max Roach Trio Featuring the Legendary Hasaan	1965	25.00
❏ SD1435 [S]	Max Roach Trio Featuring the Legendary Hasaan	1965	30.00
❏ SD1510 [S]	Members Don't Get Weary	1968	25.00

BAINBRIDGE

| ❏ 1042 | Max Roach | 198? | 12.00 |
| ❏ 1044 | Max Roach/George Duvivier/Sonny Clark | 198? | 12.00 |

CANDID

| ❏ CD-8002 [M] | We Insist -- Freedom Now Suite | 1960 | 60.00 |
| ❏ CS-9002 [S] | We Insist -- Freedom Now Suite | 1960 | 60.00 |

DEBUT

| ❏ DLP-13 [10] | Max Roach Quartet Featuring Hank Mobley | 1954 | 400.00 |

EMARCY

❏ MG-36108 [M]	Jazz in 3/4 Time	1957	80.00
❏ SR-80002 [S]	Jazz in 3/4 Time	1959	60.00
❏ 826456-1	Jazz in 3/4 Time	1986	12.00
❏ MG-36132 [M]	Max Roach + 4 on the Chicago Scene	1958	60.00
❏ MG-36098 [M]	Max Roach + 4	1957	100.00
❏ SR-80001 [S]	Max Roach + 4	1959	80.00
❏ MG-36140 [M]	Max Roach Plus Four At Newport	1958	60.00
❏ SR-80010 [S]	Max Roach Plus Four At Newport	1959	50.00
❏ MG-36144 [M]	Max Roach with the Boston Percussion Ensemble	1958	60.00
❏ SR-80015 [S]	Max Roach with the Boston Percussion Ensemble	1959	50.00
❏ 814190-1	Standard Time	198?	15.00
❏ MG-36127 [M]	The Max Roach 4 Plays Charlie Parker	1958	80.00
❏ SR-80019 [S]	The Max Roach 4 Plays Charlie Parker	1959	60.00

FANTASY

❏ OJC-304	Deeds, Not Words	1988	12.00
❏ OJC-202	Max Roach Quartet Featuring Hank Mobley	1985	12.00
❏ 6007 [M]	Speak Brother, Speak	1963	30.00
❏ 86007 [S]	Speak Brother, Speak	1963	30.00

HAT ART

| ❏ 4026 | The Long March | 1986 | 30.00 |

IMPULSE!

❏ A-16 [M]	It's Time	1962	25.00
❏ AS-16 [S]	It's Time	1962	30.00
❏ A-8 [M]	Percussion Bitter Sweet	1961	30.00
❏ AS-8 [S]	Percussion Bitter Sweet	1961	40.00

JAZZLAND

| ❏ JLP-79 [M] | Conversation | 1962 | 30.00 |
| ❏ JLP-979 [S] | Conversation | 1962 | 30.00 |

MCA

| ❏ 29052 | It's Time | 1980 | 12.00 |

MERCURY

❏ MG-20539 [M]	Moon Faced and Starry-Eyed	1960	40.00
❏ SR-60215 [S]	Moon Faced and Starry-Eyed	1960	50.00
❏ MG-20760 [M]	Parisian Sketches	1962	30.00
❏ SR-60760 [S]	Parisian Sketches	1962	40.00
❏ MG-20491 [M]	Quiet As It's Kept	1959	40.00
❏ SR-60170 [S]	Quiet As It's Kept	1959	50.00
❏ MG-20911 [M]	The Many Sides of Max	1964	30.00
❏ SR-60911 [S]	The Many Sides of Max	1964	30.00

MILESTONE

| ❏ 47061 | Conversations | 198? | 18.00 |

RIVERSIDE

❏ RLP 12-280 [M]	Deeds, Not Words	1958	50.00
❏ RLP-1122 [S]	Deeds, Not Words	1959	40.00
❏ RS-3018 [S]	Deeds, Not Words	1968	18.00

SOUL NOTE

❏ SN-1109	Easy Winners	1985	15.00
❏ SN-1053	In the Light	1982	15.00
❏ SN-1003	Pictures in a Frame	198?	15.00
❏ SN-1103	Scott Free	1985	15.00
❏ SN-1093	Survivors	1985	15.00

TIME

❏ T-70003 [M]	Award Winning Drummer	1959	80.00
❏ ST-70003 [S]	Award Winning Drummer	1959	60.00
❏ 52087 [M]	Max Roach	1962	40.00
❏ S-2087 [S]	Max Roach	1962	40.00

TRIP

| ❏ TLP-5559 | Jazz in 3/4 Time | 197? | 15.00 |
| ❏ TLP-5522 | Max Roach + 4 | 197? | 15.00 |

ROACH, MAX/ART BLAKEY

BLUE NOTE

| ❏ BLP-5010 [10] | Max Roach Quintet / Art Blakey and His Band | 1952 | 1000.00 |

ROAD, THE

KAMA SUTRA

❏ KSBS-2032 [B]	Cognition	1970	30.00
❏ KLPS-8075	The Road	1969	25.00
❏ KSBS-2012	The Road	1970	18.00
— Reissue of 8075			

Number	Title	Yr	NM

ROAD RUNNERS, THE

BEAT ROCKET

| ❏ BR104 | The Road Runners | 1999 | 15.00 |

LONDON

| ❏ LL3381 [M] | The New Mustang (And Other Hot Rod Hits) | 1964 | 200.00 |
| ❏ PS381 [S] | The New Mustang (And Other Hot Rod Hits) | 1964 | 300.00 |

ROANE, STEPHEN

LABOR

| ❏ 2 | Siblings | 1980 | 15.00 |

ROARING SEVEN JAZZBAND, THE

STOMP OFF

| ❏ SOS-1019 | Hot Dance | 198? | 12.00 |

ROBBINS, ADELAIDE/MARIAN MCPARTLAND/ BARBARA CARROLL

SAVOY

| ❏ MG-12097 [M] | Lookin' for a Boy | 1957 | 50.00 |

ROBBINS, DENNIS

MCA

| ❏ 5720 | The First of Me | 1986 | 10.00 |

ROBBINS, HARGUS "PIG

CHART

| ❏ CHS-1011 | One More Time | 196? | 18.00 |

ELEKTRA

❏ 7E-1110	Country Instrumentalist of the Year	1977	15.00
❏ 6E-129	Pig in a Poke	1978	15.00
❏ 6E-185	Unbreakable Hearts	1979	15.00

TIME

| ❏ 52107 [M] | A Bit of Country Piano | 1963 | 25.00 |
| ❏ S-2107 [S] | A Bit of Country Piano | 1963 | 30.00 |

ROBBINS, MARTY

ARTCO

| ❏ 110 | The Best of Marty Robbins | 1973 | 40.00 |

CBS SPECIAL PRODUCTS

| ❏ P17730 | The Great Love Songs | 1984 | 12.00 |

COLUMBIA

❏ PC34448	Adios Amigo	1977	15.00
— No bar code on cover			
❏ PC34448	Adios Amigo	198?	10.00
— With bar code on cover			
❏ C238870	A Lifetime of Song 1951-1982	1983	18.00
❏ JC36085	All Around Cowboy	1979	15.00
❏ PC36085	All Around Cowboy	198?	10.00
— Budget-line reissue			
❏ CS31361	All Time Greatest Hits	1972	25.00
❏ FC38309	Biggest Hits	1982	15.00
❏ KC31341	Bound for Old Mexico (Great Hits from South of the Border)	1973	18.00
❏ CL2817 [M]	By the Time I Get to Phoenix	1968	60.00
❏ CS9617 [S]	By the Time I Get to Phoenix	1968	25.00
❏ CS9617 [S]	By the Time I Get to Phoenix	1968	50.00
— Special Mono Radio Station Copy" with stereo number and "Mono" on white label			
❏ CL2735 [M]	Christmas with Marty Robbins	1967	50.00
❏ CS9535 [S]	Christmas with Marty Robbins	1967	30.00
❏ 3C9535	Christmas with Marty Robbins	198?	12.00
— Budget-line reissue			
❏ FC37995	Come Back to Me	1982	15.00
❏ PC37995	Come Back to Me	198?	10.00
— Budget-line reissue			
❏ CL1918 [M]	Devil Woman	1962	30.00
— Red label with "Guaranteed High Fidelity			
❏ CL1918 [M]	Devil Woman	1965	18.00
— Red label with "360 Sound Mono			
❏ CS8718 [S]	Devil Woman	1962	30.00
— Red label with "360 Sound Stereo" in black			
❏ CS8718 [S]	Devil Woman	1965	25.00
— Red label with "360 Sound Stereo" in white			
❏ CS8718 [S]	Devil Woman	1970	12.00
— Orange label			
❏ KC35040	Don't Let Me Touch You	1977	15.00
❏ PC30316	El Paso	198?	10.00
— Reissue of Harmony 30316			
❏ PC34303	El Paso City	198?	10.00
— With bar code on cover			
❏ PC34303	El Paso City	1976	15.00
— No bar code on cover			
❏ FC37353	Encore	1981	15.00
❏ PC37353	Encore	198?	10.00
— Budget-line reissue			
❏ JC36860	Everything I've Always Wanted	1981	15.00
❏ KC35629	Greatest Hits Vol. IV	1978	15.00
❏ CL1349 [M]	Gunfighter Ballads and Trail Songs	1959	30.00
— Red and black label with six "eye" logos			

Number	Title	Yr	NM
❑ CL1349 [M]	Gunfighter Ballads and Trail Songs	1963	18.00
—Red label with "Guaranteed High Fidelity" or "360 Sound Mono			
❑ CS8158 [S]	Gunfighter Ballads and Trail Songs	1959	40.00
—Red and black label with six "eye" logos			
❑ CS8158 [S]	Gunfighter Ballads and Trail Songs	1963	25.00
—Red label with "360 Sound Stereo			
❑ CS8158 [S]	Gunfighter Ballads and Trail Songs	1971	12.00
—Orange label			
❑ PC8158	Gunfighter Ballads and Trail Songs	198?	10.00
—Reissue with new prefix			
❑ CG33630	Gunfighter Ballads and Trail Songs/My Woman, My Woman, My Wife	1976	18.00
❑ KC32586	Have I Told You Lately That I Love You	1974	18.00
❑ CL2040 [M]	Hawaii's Calling Me	1963	30.00
—Red label with "Guaranteed High Fidelity			
❑ CL2040 [M]	Hawaii's Calling Me	1965	18.00
—Red label with "360 Sound Mono			
❑ CS8840 [S]	Hawaii's Calling Me	1963	30.00
—Red label with "360 Sound Stereo" in black			
❑ CS8840 [S]	Hawaii's Calling Me	1965	25.00
—Red label with "360 Sound Stereo" in white			
❑ CL2176 [M]	Island Woman	1964	30.00
—Red label with "Guaranteed High Fidelity			
❑ CS8976 [S]	Island Woman	1964	40.00
—Red label with "360 Sound Stereo" in black			
❑ CL2176 [M]	Island Woman	1965	25.00
—Red label with "360 Sound Mono			
❑ CS8976 [S]	Island Woman	1965	30.00
—Red label with "360 Sound Stereo" in white			
❑ CS9811	It's a Sin	1969	25.00
—Red "360 Sound" label			
❑ CS9811	It's a Sin	1970	12.00
—Orange label			
❑ KC31628	I've Got a Woman's Love	1972	18.00
❑ CS9725	I Walk Alone	1968	25.00
—Red "360 Sound" label			
❑ CS9725	I Walk Alone	1970	12.00
—Orange label			
❑ CL1666 [M]	Just a Little Sentimental	1961	30.00
—Red and black label with six "eye" logos			
❑ CL1666 [M]	Just a Little Sentimental	1963	18.00
—Red label with "Guaranteed High Fidelity" or "360 Sound Mono			
❑ CS8466 [S]	Just a Little Sentimental	1961	30.00
—Red and black label with six "eye" logos			
❑ CS8466 [S]	Just a Little Sentimental	1963	25.00
—Red label with "360 Sound Stereo			
❑ KC239575	Long, Long Ago	1984	18.00
❑ CL1801 [M]	Marty After Midnight	1962	50.00
—Red and black label with six "eye" logos			
❑ CL1801 [M]	Marty After Midnight	1962	25.00
—Red label with "Guaranteed High Fidelity			
❑ CL1801 [M]	Marty After Midnight	1965	18.00
—Red label with "360 Sound Mono			
❑ CS8601 [S]	Marty After Midnight	1962	80.00
—Red and black label with six "eye" logos			
❑ CS8601 [S]	Marty After Midnight	1962	30.00
—Red label with "360 Sound Stereo" in black			
❑ CS8601 [S]	Marty After Midnight	1965	25.00
—Red label with "360 Sound Stereo" in white			
❑ CL1189 [M]	Marty Robbins	1958	80.00
—Red and black label with six "eye" logos			
❑ CL1189 [M]	Marty Robbins	1963	25.00
—Red label with "Guaranteed High Fidelity" or "360 Sound Mono			
❑ KG31361	Marty Robbins' All-Time Greatest Hits	1972	25.00
❑ C30571	Marty Robbins' Greatest Hits Vol. III	1971	18.00
❑ PC30571	Marty Robbins' Greatest Hits Vol. III	198?	10.00
—Budget-line reissue			
❑ GP15	Marty's Country	1969	30.00
❑ CL1325 [M]	Marty's Greatest Hits	1959	80.00
—Red and black label with six "eye" logos			
❑ CL1325 [M]	Marty's Greatest Hits	1963	25.00
—Red label with "Guaranteed High Fidelity" or "360 Sound Mono			
❑ CS8639 [P]	Marty's Greatest Hits	1962	30.00
—Red label with "360 Sound Stereo" in black			
❑ CS8639 [P]	Marty's Greatest Hits	1965	25.00
—Red label with "360 Sound Stereo" in white			
❑ CS8639 [P]	Marty's Greatest Hits	1970	12.00
—Orange label			
❑ PC8639	Marty's Greatest Hits	198?	10.00
—Reissue with new prefix			
❑ CL1635 [M]	More Greatest Hits	1961	30.00
—Red and black label with six "eye" logos			
❑ CL1635 [M]	More Greatest Hits	1963	18.00
—Red label with "Guaranteed High Fidelity" or "360 Sound Mono			
❑ CS8435 [S]	More Greatest Hits	1961	30.00
—Red and black label with six "eye" logos			
❑ CS8435 [S]	More Greatest Hits	1963	25.00
—Red label with "360 Sound Stereo			
❑ CS8435 [S]	More Greatest Hits	1971	12.00
—Orange label			
❑ PC8435	More Greatest Hits	198?	10.00
—Reissue with new prefix			
❑ CL1481 [M]	More Gunfighter Ballads and Trail Songs	1960	40.00
—Red and black label with six "eye" logos			
❑ CL1481 [M]	More Gunfighter Ballads and Trail Songs	1963	18.00
—Red label with "Guaranteed High Fidelity" or "360 Sound Mono			
❑ CS8272 [S]	More Gunfighter Ballads and Trail Songs	1960	40.00
—Red and black label with six "eye" logos			
❑ CS8272 [S]	More Gunfighter Ballads and Trail Songs	1963	25.00
—Red label with "360 Sound Stereo			
❑ CS8272 [S]	More Gunfighter Ballads and Trail Songs	1971	12.00
—Orange label			
❑ PC8272	More Gunfighter Ballads and Trail Songs More	198?	10.00
—Reissue with new prefix			
❑ CL2645 [M]	My Kind of Country	1967	30.00
❑ CS9445 [S]	My Kind of Country	1967	25.00
❑ CS9978	My Woman, My Woman, My Wife	1970	25.00
—Red "360 Sound" label			
❑ CS9978	My Woman, My Woman, My Wife	1970	18.00
—Orange label			
❑ KC33476	No Sign of Loneliness Here	1976	15.00
❑ CL1855 [M]	Portrait of Marty	1962	40.00
❑ CS8655 [S]	Portrait of Marty	1962	50.00
❑ CL1855/CS 8655	Portrait of Marty Bonus Photo	1962	30.00
❑ CL2072 [M]	Return of the Gunfighter	1963	25.00
—Red label with "Guaranteed High Fidelity			
❑ CL2072 [M]	Return of the Gunfighter	1965	18.00
—Red label with "360 Sound Mono			
❑ CS8872 [S]	Return of the Gunfighter	1963	30.00
—Red label with "360 Sound Stereo" in black			
❑ CS8872 [S]	Return of the Gunfighter	1965	25.00
—Red label with "360 Sound Stereo" in white			
❑ CS8872 [S]	Return of the Gunfighter	1970	12.00
—Orange label			
❑ CL2220 [M]	R.F.D.	1964	25.00
—Red label with "Guaranteed High Fidelity			
❑ CL2220 [M]	R.F.D.	1965	18.00
—Red label with "360 Sound Mono			
❑ CS9020 [S]	R.F.D.	1964	30.00
—Red label with "360 Sound Stereo" in black			
❑ CS9020 [S]	R.F.D.	1965	25.00
—Red label with "360 Sound Stereo" in white			
❑ CL2601 [10]	Rock 'N Roll 'N Robbins	1956	1000.00
❑ FC38603	Some Memories Just Won't Die	1983	15.00
❑ CL1087 [M]	Song of the Islands	1957	120.00
—Red and black label with six "eye" logos			
❑ CL1087 [M]	Song of the Islands	1963	25.00
—Red label with "Guaranteed High Fidelity" or "360 Sound Mono			
❑ CS9425 [R]	Song of the Islands	1967	18.00
❑ CL2527 [M]	The Drifter	1966	18.00
❑ CS9327 [S]	The Drifter	1966	25.00
—Red "360 Sound" label			
❑ CS9327 [S]	The Drifter	1970	12.00
—Orange label			
❑ FC37541	The Legend	1982	15.00
❑ PC37541	The Legend	1985	10.00
—Budget-line reissue			
❑ JC35446	The Performer	1979	15.00
❑ CL976 [M]	The Song of Robbins	1957	100.00
—Red and black label with six "eye" logos			
❑ CL976 [M]	The Song of Robbins	1963	25.00
—Red label with "Guaranteed High Fidelity" or "360 Sound Mono			
❑ CS9421 [R]	The Song of Robbins	1967	18.00
—Red "360 Sound" label			
❑ CS9421 [R]	The Song of Robbins	1970	12.00
—Orange label			
❑ G30881	The World of Marty Robbins	1971	25.00
❑ C30816	Today	1971	18.00
❑ CL2725 [M]	Tonight Carmen	1967	30.00
❑ CS9525 [S]	Tonight Carmen	1967	25.00
—Red "360 Sound" label			
❑ CS9525 [S]	Tonight Carmen	1970	12.00
—Orange label			
❑ CL2304 [M]	Turn the Lights Down Low	1965	30.00
—Red label with "Guaranteed High Fidelity			
❑ CL2304 [M]	Turn the Lights Down Low	1965	18.00
—Red label with "360 Sound Mono			
❑ CS9104 [S]	Turn the Lights Down Low	1965	30.00
—Red label with "360 Sound Stereo" in black			
❑ CS9104 [S]	Turn the Lights Down Low	1965	25.00
—Red label with "360 Sound Stereo" in white			
❑ CL2448 [M]	What God Has Done	1966	18.00
❑ CS9248 [S]	What God Has Done	1966	25.00
—Red "360 Sound" label			
❑ CS9248 [S]	What God Has Done	1970	12.00
—Orange label			
❑ JC36507	With Love	1980	15.00
COLUMBIA LIMITED EDITION			
❑ LE10045	By the Time I Get to Phoenix	197?	12.00
❑ LE10579	Devil Woman	197?	12.00
❑ LE10575	From the Heart	197?	12.00
❑ LE10030	It's a Sin	197?	12.00
❑ LE10033	My Kind of Country	197?	12.00
❑ LE10022	Portrait of Marty	197?	12.00
❑ LE10144	R.F.D.	197?	12.00
❑ LE10576	Streets of Laredo	197?	12.00
❑ LE10578	The Song of Robbins	197?	12.00
❑ LE10577	The Story of My Life	197?	12.00
❑ LE10046	Today	197?	12.00
❑ LE10189	Tonight Carmen	197?	12.00
❑ LE10145	Turn the Lights Down Low	197?	12.00
COLUMBIA MUSICAL TREASURY			
❑ P5S5812	Marty	1972	40.00
COLUMBIA RECORD CLUB			
❑ DS445	Bend in the River	1968	40.00
COLUMBIA SPECIAL PRODUCTS			
❑ P17138	Banquet of Songs	1983	12.00
❑ C11311	By the Time I Get to Phoenix	1972	18.00
❑ C11513	By the Time I Get to Phoenix	1973	18.00
❑ C10980 [S]	Christmas with Marty	1972	18.00
—Stereo reissue; "Distributed by Apex Rendezvous, Inc." on back cover			
❑ P13358	Christmas with Marty Robbins	1976	15.00
❑ 3P16578	Classics	1983	25.00
❑ P16914	Country Classics	1983	12.00
❑ P17209	Country Cowboy	1983	12.00
❑ P17136	Forever Yours	1983	12.00
❑ P14035	Legendary Music Man	1977	15.00
❑ P15812	Marty Robbins' Best	1982	12.00
❑ P12416	Marty Robbins' Own Favorites	1974	18.00
❑ C11122	Marty's Greatest Hits	1972	15.00
❑ P16561	Reflections	1982	12.00
❑ P17120	Sincerely	1983	12.00
❑ P17367	Song of the Islands	1983	12.00
❑ P17137	That Country Feeling	1983	12.00
❑ P14613	The Best of Marty Robbins	1978	12.00
❑ P17159	The Great Marty Robbins	1983	12.00
❑ P17206	The Legendary Marty Robbins	1983	12.00
❑ P15594	The Number One Cowboy	1981	12.00
DECCA			
❑ DL75389	This Much a Man	1972	18.00
HARMONY			
❑ KH30316	El Paso	1971	15.00
❑ KH31257	Marty Robbins Favorites	1972	15.00
❑ HS11338	Singing the Blues	1969	18.00
❑ H31258	Songs of the Islands	1972	25.00
❑ KH32286	Streets of Laredo	1973	15.00
❑ HS11409	The Story of My Life	1970	18.00
MCA			
❑ 27060	20th Century Drifter	1983	18.00
—Reissue of older material			
❑ 421	Good'n Country	1974	18.00
❑ 342	Marty Robbins	1973	18.00
❑ 61	This Much a Man	1973	15.00
—Reissue of Decca LP			
READER'S DIGEST			
❑ RDA-054/A	His Greatest Hits and Finest Performances	1983	30.00
TIME-LIFE			
❑ STW-109	Country Music	1981	15.00

ROBBINS, RONNY

Number	Title	Yr	NM
COLUMBIA			
❑ CS9944	Columbia Records Presents Marty Robbins Jr.	1970	30.00
—As "Marty Robbins, Jr.			

ROBBS, THE

Number	Title	Yr	NM
MERCURY			
❑ SR-61130 [S]	The Robbs	1967	30.00
❑ MG-21130 [M]	The Robbs	1967	40.00

ROBERTS, GEORGE

Number	Title	Yr	NM
COLUMBIA			
❑ CL1384 [M]	Meet Mr. Roberts -- George Roberts and His Big Bass Trombone	195?	80.00

ROBERTS, HOWARD

Number	Title	Yr	NM
ABC IMPULSE!			
❑ AS-9207	Antelope Freeway	1972	18.00
❑ AS-9299	Equinox Express Elevator	1974	18.00
CAPITOL			
❑ T2609 [M]	All-Time Great Instrumental Hits	1966	18.00
❑ ST2609 [S]	All-Time Great Instrumental Hits	1966	25.00
❑ T1887 [M]	Color Him Funky	1963	18.00
❑ ST1887 [S]	Color Him Funky	1963	30.00
❑ T2400 [M]	Goodies	1965	18.00
❑ ST2400 [S]	Goodies	1965	25.00
❑ T2824 [M]	Guilty	1967	25.00

Number	Title	Yr	NM
❑ ST2824 [S]	Guilty	1967	18.00
❑ SM-1961 [S]	H.R. Is A Dirty Guitar Player	1976	12.00
— Reissue with new prefix			
❑ T1961 [M]	H.R. Is A Dirty Guitar Player	1963	18.00
❑ ST1961 [S]	H.R. Is A Dirty Guitar Player	1963	25.00
❑ T2716 [M]	Jaunty -- Jolly	1967	30.00
❑ ST2716 [S]	Jaunty -- Jolly	1967	18.00
❑ ST2901 [S]	Out Of Sight -- But In Mind	1968	18.00
❑ T2214 [M]	Something's Cookin'	1965	18.00
❑ ST2214 [S]	Something's Cookin'	1965	25.00
❑ ST-11247	Sounds	1974	15.00
❑ ST-336	Spinning Wheel	1970	18.00
❑ T2478 [M]	Whatever's Fair	1966	18.00
❑ ST2478 [S]	Whatever's Fair	1966	25.00

CONCORD JAZZ

❑ CJ-53	The Real Howard Roberts	1978	12.00

DISCOVERY

❑ 812	Turning to Spring	1980	15.00

VERVE

❑ MGV-8305 [M]	Good Pickin's	1959	50.00
❑ V-8305 [M]	Good Pickin's	1961	30.00
❑ MGV-8192 [M]	Mr. Roberts Plays Guitar	1957	50.00
❑ V-8192 [M]	Mr. Roberts Plays Guitar	1961	30.00
❑ UMV-2673	Mr. Roberts Plays Guitar	198?	15.00
❑ VSP-29 [M]	The Movin' Man	1966	25.00
❑ VSPS-29 [R]	The Movin' Man	1966	15.00
❑ V-8662 [M]	Velvet Groove	1966	25.00
❑ V6-8662 [S]	Velvet Groove	1966	18.00

ROBERTS, KENNY

STARDAY

❑ SLP-434	Country Music Singing Sensation	1969	25.00
❑ SLP-336 [M]	Indian Love Call	1965	40.00
❑ SLP-406 [M]	The Incredible Kenny Roberts	1967	30.00

VOCALION

❑ VL73770	Kenny Roberts Sings Country Songs	196?	15.00

ROBERTS, LUCKEY, AND WILLIE "THE LION" SMITH

GOOD TIME JAZZ

❑ L-12035 [M]	Harlem Piano Solos	1958	40.00
❑ S-10035 [S]	Harlem Piano Solos	1958	30.00

ROBERTS, LUCKEY

PERIOD

❑ RL-1929 [M]	Happy Go Luckey	1956	40.00

ROBERTS, MARCUS

NOVUS

❑ 3078-1-N	Deep in the Shed	1990	18.00
❑ 3051-1-N	The Truth Is Spoken Here	1989	15.00

ROBERTS, PAT

DOT

❑ DLP-26011	This Is Pat Roberts	1970	10.00

ROBERTS, PERNELL

RCA VICTOR

❑ LPM-2662 [M]	Come All Ye Fair and Tender Ladies	1963	30.00
❑ LSP-2662 [S]	Come All Ye Fair and Tender Ladies	1963	40.00

ROBERTS, ROCKY, AND THE AIREDALES

BRUNSWICK

❑ BL754133 [S]	Rocky Roberts and the Airedales	1968	25.00
❑ BL54133 [M]	Rocky Roberts and the Airedales	1968	80.00
— Mono is yellow label promo only			

ROBERTS, WILLIAM NEIL

KLAVIER

❑ 510	Great Scott!	197?	15.00
❑ 516	Scott Joplin Ragtime, Vol. 2	1974	15.00

ROBERTSON, DALE

RCA VICTOR

❑ LPM-2158 [M]	Dale Robertson Presents His Album of Western Classics	1959	80.00
❑ LSP-2158 [S]	Dale Robertson Presents His Album of Western Classics	1959	100.00

ROBERTSON, DON

RCA VICTOR

❑ LPM-3348 [M]	Heart on My Sleeve	1965	25.00
❑ LSP-3348 [S]	Heart on My Sleeve	1965	30.00

ROBERTSON, HERB

JMT

❑ 834420-1	Shades of Bud Powell	1988	12.00

ROBERTSON, PAUL

PALO ALTO

❑ PA-8013	Old Friends, New Friends	1982	12.00
❑ PA-8002	The Song Is You	1981	12.00

ROBERTSON, PERRY

CHIAROSCURO

❑ 190	The Traveler	1977	18.00

ROBERTSON, ROBBIE

GEFFEN

❑ GEF-24160	Robbie Robertson	1987	12.00
❑ GEF24303	Storyville	1991	30.00

ROBERTSON, TEXAS JIM

DESIGN

❑ DLP-115 [M]	Golden Hits of Country and Western Music	196?	15.00
❑ DLP-132 [M]	Sacred Country & Western Songs	196?	15.00

GRAND PRIX

❑ 185 [M]	Texas Jim Robertson Sings the Great Hits of Country & Western	196?	18.00

MASTERSEAL

❑ (# unknown)0 [10]	Eight Top Western Hits	195?	60.00

STRAND

❑ 1016 [M]	Texas Jim Robertson	1961	40.00

ROBESON, PAUL

COLUMBIA MASTERWORKS

❑ ML4105 [10]	Spirituals	1949	80.00
❑ ML2038 [10]	Swing Low Sweet Chariot	1949	80.00

VANGUARD

❑ VSD-79193 [S]	Ballad for Americans: Carnegie Hall Concert, Vol. 2	1965	25.00
❑ VRS-9193 [M]	Ballad for Americans: Carnegie Hall Concert, Vol. 2	1965	25.00
❑ VSD-57/58	Essential Paul Robeson	197?	25.00
❑ VRS-9051 [M]	Paul Robeson at Carnegie Hall	1960	25.00
❑ VRS-9037 [M]	Spirituals and Folksongs	1959	40.00

ROBINS, THE (1)

GNP CRESCENDO

❑ GNPS-9034 [B]	The Best of the Robins	1975	25.00

WHIPPET

❑ WLP-703 [M]	Rock 'n' Roll with the Robins	1958	800.00

ROBINSON, FLOYD

RCA VICTOR

❑ LPM-2162 [M]	Floyd Robinson	1960	80.00
❑ LSP-2162 [S]	Floyd Robinson	1960	120.00

ROBINSON, FREDDY

ENTERPRISE

❑ ENS-1025	Freddy Robinson at the Drive In	1972	15.00

PACIFIC JAZZ

❑ ST-20176	Hot Fun in the Summertime	1971	18.00
❑ ST-20162	The Coming Atlantis	1970	18.00

ROBINSON, JIM, AND BILLIE AND DEDE PIERCE

ATLANTIC

❑ 1409 [M]	Jim Robinson and Billie & DeDe Pierce	1963	25.00
❑ SD1409 [S]	Jim Robinson and Billie & DeDe Pierce	1963	30.00

ROBINSON, JIM

BIOGRAPH

❑ CEN-8	Jim Robinson and His New Orleans Band	197?	12.00
❑ CEN-16	Jim Robinson and His New Orleans Joymakers	197?	12.00

CENTER

❑ PLP-1 [M]	Jim Robinson and His New Orleans Band	196?	18.00

GHB

❑ GHB-196	1944 Revisited	1986	12.00
❑ GHB-185	Big Jim's Little Six	1986	12.00
❑ GHB-28	Jim Robinson at the Jacinto Ballroom	197?	15.00

JAZZ CRUSADE

❑ 2015	1944 Revisited	196?	18.00
❑ 2005	Jim Robinson	1965	18.00
❑ 2010	Jim Robinson's Little Six	196?	18.00

PEARL

❑ PS-5	Economy Hall Breakdown	197?	15.00

RIVERSIDE

❑ RLP-393 [M]	Jim Robinson Plays Spirituals and Blues	1961	30.00
❑ RS-9393 [R]	Jim Robinson Plays Spirituals and Blues	1961	18.00

❑ RLP-369 [M]	Jim Robinson's New Orleans Band	1961	30.00
❑ RS-9369 [R]	Jim Robinson's New Orleans Band	1961	18.00

ROBINSON, JOHNNY

EPIC

❑ BN26528	Memphis High	1970	25.00

ROBINSON, SMOKEY

MOTOWN

❑ M5-197V1	A Quiet Storm	1981	10.00
— Reissue of Tamla 337			
❑ 5349ML	Being with You	1983	10.00
— Reissue of Tamla 375			
❑ M5-154V1	Deep in My Soul	1981	10.00
— Reissue of Tamla 350			
❑ MOT-6268	Love, Smokey	1990	15.00
❑ M5-118V1	Motown Superstar Series, Vol. 18	1981	12.00
❑ MOT-6226	One Heartbeat	1987	12.00
❑ M5-168V1	Pure Smokey	1981	10.00
— Reissue of Tamla 331			
❑ M5-134V1	Smokey	1981	10.00
— Reissue of Tamla 328			
❑ 5267ML	Where There;s Smoke	1982	10.00
— Reissue of Tamla 366			

TAMLA

❑ T6-337	A Quiet Storm	1975	15.00
❑ T8-375	Being with You	1981	12.00
❑ 6064TL	Blame It on Love & All the Great Hits	1983	12.00
❑ T6-350	Deep in My Soul	1977	15.00
❑ 6098TL	Essar	1984	12.00
❑ T7-359	Love Breeze	1978	15.00
❑ T6-331	Pure Smokey	1974	15.00
❑ 6156TL	Smoke Signals	1986	12.00
❑ T328	Smokey	1973	15.00
❑ T6-341	Smokey's Family Robinson	1976	15.00
❑ T9-363	Smokin'	1979	18.00
❑ 6030TL	Touch the Sky	1983	12.00
❑ T8-367	Warm Thoughts	1980	12.00
❑ T7-366	Where There's Smoke	1979	12.00
❑ 6001TL	Yes It's You Lady	1982	12.00

UNIVERSAL MOTOWN

❑ 5316009	A Quiet Storm	2009	25.00

ROBINSON, SPIKE, AND AL COHN

CAPRI

❑ 71787	Henry B. Meets Alvin G.	1987	12.00

ROBINSON, SPIKE

CAPRI

❑ 72185	It's a Wonderful World	1985	12.00
❑ 8984	London Reprise	1984	12.00
❑ 71785	Spring Can Really Hang You Up the Most	1985	12.00

DISCOVERY

❑ 970	This Is Always: The Music of Harry Warren, Vol. 2	198?	12.00

ROBINSON, SUGAR CHILE

CAPITOL

❑ T589 [M]	Boogie Woogie	1955	120.00

ROBINSON, SUGAR RAY

CONTINENTAL

❑ CLP-16009	I'm Still Swinging	195?	25.00

ROBINSON, TOM, BAND

GEFFEN

❑ GHS24053	Hope and Glory	1984	12.00

HARVEST

❑ STBB-11778 [B]	Power in the Darkness	1978	25.00
❑ ST-11930	TRB 2	1979	15.00

I.R.S.

❑ SP-70013	Tom Robinson's Sector 27	1980	15.00

ROBINSON, VICKI SUE

RCA VICTOR

❑ AFL1-2294	Half and Half	1978	15.00
❑ APL1-1256	Never Gonna Let You Go	1976	15.00
❑ AYL1-3949	Turn the Beat Around	1981	10.00
❑ APL1-1829	Vicki Sue Robinson	1977	15.00

ROBINSON, WANDA

PERCEPTION

❑ 18 [B]	Black Ivory	1971	18.00

ROBINSON/LANGWORTHY/AXT JAZZ TRIO, THE

ASHLAND

❑ 4963	The Robinson/Langworthy/ Axt Jazz Trio	198?	15.00

ROBISON, CARSON

COLUMBIA

❑ CL2551 [10]	Square Dance	1955	80.00
❑ CL6029 [10]	Square Dance	1949	80.00

Number	Title	Yr	NM

MGM

❑ E-13 [M]	Call Your Own Square Dances	195?	60.00
❑ E-3594 [M]	Life Gets Tee-Jus, Don't It	1958	50.00
❑ E-3258 [M]	Square Dances	1955	30.00
❑ E-557 [10]	Square Dances with Calls	1952	60.00

RCA VICTOR

❑ LPM-3030 [10]	Square Dances	1952	60.00
❑ LPM-1238 [M]	Square Dances	1956	30.00

ROCHE, BETTY

BETHLEHEM

❑ BCP-64 [M]	Take the "A" Train	1956	120.00
❑ BCP-6026	Take the "A" Train	197?	25.00

— *Reissue, distributed by RCA Victor*

FANTASY

❑ OJC-1718	Singin' and Swingin'	198?	15.00

PRESTIGE

❑ PRLP-7198 [M]	Lightly and Politely	1961	150.00
❑ PRLP-7187 [M]	Singin' and Swingin'	1961	120.00

ROCHES, THE

MCA

❑ 10020	We Three Kings	1990	25.00

RHINO

❑ RNEP-70616 [EP]	No Trespassing	1987	18.00

WARNER BROS.

❑ 25321 [B]	Another World	1985	15.00
❑ 23735 [B]	Keep On Doing	1982	18.00
❑ BSK3475 [B]	Nurds	1980	18.00
❑ BSK3298 [B]	The Roches	1979	18.00

ROCK-A-TEENS, THE

ROULETTE

❑ R-25109 [M]	Woo-Hoo	1960	150.00
❑ SR-25109 [S]	Woo-Hoo	1960	250.00

ROCK ISLAND

PROJECT 3

❑ PR-4005SD	Rock Island	1970	30.00

ROCKATS

ISLAND

❑ ILPS9626	Live at the Ritz	1981	30.00

ROCKETS, THE (4)

WHITE WHALE

❑ WWS-7116	The Rockets	1968	30.00

ROCKETS

ELEKTRA

❑ 6E-351	Back Talk	1981	12.00
❑ 60143	Rocket Roll	1982	12.00

RSO

❑ RS1-3071	No Ballads	1980	15.00
❑ RS1-3047	The Rockets	1979	15.00

TORTOISE INT'L.

❑ BYL1-2572 [B]	Love Transfusion	1977	18.00

ROCKIN' FOO

HOBBIT

❑ HB-5001 [B]	Rockin' Foo	1969	30.00

ROCKIN' REBELS, THE

SWAN

❑ SLP-509 [M]	Wild Weekend	1963	200.00

ROCKIN' SIDNEY

EPIC

❑ B5E40153 [EP]	My Toot Toot	1985	10.00

ZBC

❑ LP-100	A Holiday Celebration with Rockin' Sidney	1983	18.00

ROCKPILE

COLUMBIA

❑ JC36886	Seconds of Pleasure	1980	18.00

— *Includes bonus EP, "Nick Lowe and Dave Edmunds Sing the Everly Brothers.*

ROCKWELL, ROBERT

ASI

❑ 5002	Androids	1977	15.00

CELEBRATION

❑ 5002	Androids	197?	18.00

ROCKWELL

MOTOWN

❑ 6122ML	Captured	1985	12.00
❑ 6052ML	Somebody's Watching Me	1984	12.00
❑ 6178ML	The Genie	1986	12.00

Number	Title	Yr	NM

ROCKY FELLERS, THE

SCEPTER

❑ SP-512 [M]	Killer Joe	1964	30.00
❑ SPS-512 [S]	Killer Joe	1964	40.00

RODGER, MART

GHB

❑ GHB-224	Jazz Tale of Two Cities	198?	12.00

RODGERS, GENE

EMARCY

❑ MG-36145 [M]	Jazz Comes to the Astor	1958	40.00

RODGERS, IKE

RIVERSIDE

❑ RLP-1013 [10]	The Trombone of Ike Rodgers	1953	80.00

RODGERS, JIMMIE (1)

RCA VICTOR

❑ CPL1-2504	A Legendary Performer	1977	12.00
❑ LPM-2531 [M]	Country Music Hall of Fame	1962	80.00
❑ LPM-2213 [M]	Jimmie the Kid	1961	80.00
❑ LPM-2112 [M]	My Rough and Rowdy Ways	1960	80.00
❑ ANL1-1209	My Rough and Rowdy Ways	1976	12.00
❑ LPM-2865 [M]	My Time Ain't Long	1964	50.00
❑ LPM-1232 [M]	Never No Mo' Blues -- A Memorial Album	1955	150.00
❑ LPM-3315 [M]	The Best of the Legendary Jimmie Rodgers	1965	40.00
❑ LSP-3315 [R]	The Best of the Legendary Jimmie Rodgers	1965	25.00
❑ AHL1-3315	The Best of the Legendary Jimmie Rodgers	197?	10.00

— *Reissue with new prefix*

❑ DPL2-0075	The Legendary Jimmie Rodgers, Vol. 1	1974	40.00

— *Special-products issue for Country Music Magazine*

❑ LPM-2634 [M]	The Short But Brilliant Life of Jimmie Rodgers	1963	80.00
❑ VPS-6091(e)	This Is Jimmie Rodgers	1971	25.00
❑ LPM-1640 [M]	Train Whistle Blues	1957	150.00
❑ LPM-3073 [10]	Travelin' Blues	1952	500.00
❑ LPT-3037 [10]	Yodelingly Yours Jimmie Rodgers, Volume 1	1953	500.00
❑ LPT-3038 [10]	Yodelingly Yours Jimmie Rodgers, Volume 2	1953	500.00
❑ LPT-3039 [10]	Yodelingly Yours Jimmie Rodgers, Volume 3	1953	500.00

ROUNDER

❑ 1056	First Sessions 1927-1928	1990	15.00
❑ 1057	The Early Years 1928-1929	1990	15.00

RODGERS, JIMMIE (2)

A&M

❑ SP-130 [M]	Child of Clay	1967	30.00
❑ SP-4130 [S]	Child of Clay	1967	18.00
❑ SP-4242	Troubled Times	1970	18.00
❑ SP-4187	Windmills of Your Mind	1969	18.00

ACCORD

❑ SN-7198	Honeycomb & Other Hits	198?	12.00

DOT

❑ DLP-3579 [M]	12 Great Hits	1964	18.00
❑ DLP-25579 [S]	12 Great Hits	1964	25.00
❑ DLP3657 [M]	Christmas with Jimmie	1965	15.00
❑ DLP25657 [S]	Christmas with Jimmie	1965	25.00
❑ DLP-3710 [M]	Country Music 1966	1966	18.00
❑ DLP-25710 [S]	Country Music 1966	1966	25.00
❑ DLP-3614 [M]	Deep Purple	1965	18.00
❑ DLP-25614 [S]	Deep Purple	1965	25.00
❑ DLP-3815 [M]	Golden Hits/15 Hits of Jimmie Rodgers	1967	25.00
❑ DLP-25815 [S]	Golden Hits/15 Hits of Jimmie Rodgers	1967	18.00
❑ DLP-3525 [M]	Honeycomb & Kisses Sweeter Than Wine	1963	18.00
❑ DLP-25525 [S]	Honeycomb & Kisses Sweeter Than Wine	1963	25.00
❑ DLP-3717 [M]	It's Over	1966	18.00
❑ DLP-25717 [S]	It's Over	1966	25.00
❑ DLP-3496 [M]	Jimmie Rodgers Folk Concert	1963	18.00
❑ DLP-25496 [S]	Jimmie Rodgers Folk Concert	1963	25.00
❑ DLP-3780 [M]	Love Me, Please Love Me	1967	18.00
❑ DLP-25780 [S]	Love Me, Please Love Me	1967	25.00
❑ DLP-3502 [M]	My Favorite Hymns	1963	18.00
❑ DLP-25502 [S]	My Favorite Hymns	1963	25.00
❑ DLP-25453 [S]	No One Will Ever Know	1962	25.00
❑ DLP-3453 [M]	No One Will Ever Know	1962	18.00
❑ DLP-3687 [M]	The Nashville Sound	1966	18.00
❑ DLP-25687 [S]	The Nashville Sound	1966	25.00
❑ DLP-3556 [M]	The World I Used to Know	1964	18.00

— *Retitled version of above*

❑ DLP-25556 [S]	The World I Used to Know	1964	25.00

— *Retitled version of above*

❑ DLP-3556 [M]	Town and Country	1964	25.00
❑ DLP-25556 [S]	Town and Country	1964	30.00

FORUM

❑ F-9025 [M]	At Home with Jimmie Rodgers: An Evening of Folk Songs	196?	15.00

Number	Title	Yr	NM

❑ SF-9025 [S]	At Home with Jimmie Rodgers: An Evening of Folk Songs	196?	15.00
❑ SF-9059 [S]	Jimmie Rodgers Sings Folk Songs	196?	15.00
❑ F-9059 [M]	Jimmie Rodgers Sings Folk Songs	196?	15.00
❑ F-9049 [M]	Just for You	196?	15.00
❑ SF-9049 [S]	Just for You	196?	15.00

HAMILTON

❑ HL-114 [M]	6 Favorite Hymns and 6 Favorite Folk Ballads	1964	15.00
❑ HS-12114 [S]	6 Favorite Hymns and 6 Favorite Folk Ballads	1964	15.00
❑ HL-148 [M]	12 Immortal Songs	196?	15.00
❑ HS-12148 [S]	12 Immortal Songs	196?	15.00

PARAMOUNT

❑ PAS-2-1042	Honeycomb	1974	18.00

PICKWICK

❑ SPC-3106	Am I That Easy to Forget	196?	15.00
❑ SPC-3599	Big Hits	197?	12.00
❑ PC-3040 [M]	Jimmie Rodgers	196?	15.00
❑ SPC-3040 [S]	Jimmie Rodgers	196?	15.00

ROULETTE

❑ R-25179 [M]	15 Million Sellers	1962	30.00
❑ SR-25179 [P]	15 Million Sellers	1962	30.00

— *White label with colored spokes*

❑ SR-25179 [P]	15 Million Sellers	1962	25.00

— *Orange and yellow label*

❑ R-25128 [M]	At Home with Jimmie Rodgers: An Evening of Folk Songs	1960	30.00
❑ SR-25128 [S]	At Home with Jimmie Rodgers: An Evening of Folk Songs	1960	40.00
❑ R-25199 [M]	Folk Songs	1963	25.00
❑ SR-25199 [S]	Folk Songs	1963	30.00
❑ R-25057 [M]	His Golden Year	1959	30.00
❑ R25095 [M]	It's Christmas Once Again	1959	30.00
❑ SR25095 [S]	It's Christmas Once Again	1959	50.00
❑ R-25020 [M]	Jimmie Rodgers	1959	30.00

— *White label with colored spokes*

❑ R-25020 [M]	Jimmie Rodgers	1957	50.00

— *Black label*

❑ R-25042 [M]	Jimmie Rodgers Sings Folk Songs	1958	50.00

— *Black label*

❑ R-25042 [M]	Jimmie Rodgers Sings Folk Songs	1959	30.00

— *White label with colored spokes*

❑ R-25033 [M]	Number One Ballads	1958	50.00

— *Black label*

❑ R-25033 [M]	Number One Ballads	1959	30.00

— *White label with colored spokes*

❑ R-25160 [M]	The Best of Jimmie Rodgers' Folk Tunes	1961	30.00
❑ SR-25160 [S]	The Best of Jimmie Rodgers' Folk Tunes	1961	40.00

— *Black vinyl*

❑ SR-25160 [S]	The Best of Jimmie Rodgers' Folk Tunes	1961	250.00

— *Red vinyl*

❑ R-25150 [M]	The Folk Song World of Jimmie Rodgers	1961	30.00
❑ SR-25150 [S]	The Folk Song World of Jimmie Rodgers	1961	40.00
❑ R-25071 [M]	TV Favorites	1959	30.00
❑ SR-25071 [S]	TV Favorites	1959	50.00
❑ R-25081 [M]	Twilight on the Trail	1959	30.00
❑ SR-25081 [S]	Twilight on the Trail	1959	50.00
❑ R-25103 [M]	When the Spirit Moves You	1960	30.00
❑ SR-25103 [S]	When the Spirit Moves You	1960	40.00
❑ SR-42006	Yours Truly	1968	18.00

RODGERS, PAUL

ATLANTIC

❑ 80121	Cut Loose	1983	10.00

RODITI, CLAUDIO

MILESTONE

❑ M-9158	Gemini Man	198?	12.00
❑ M-9175	Slow Fire	198?	12.00

RODMAN, JUDY

MTM

❑ ST-71060	A Place Called Love	1987	12.00
❑ D1-71069	Goin' to Work	1988	12.00
❑ ST-71050	Judy	1986	12.00

RODNEY, RED, AND IRA SULLIVAN

ELEKTRA/MUSICIAN

❑ 60261	Sprint	198?	12.00
❑ 60020	The Spirit Within	1982	12.00

RODNEY, RED

ARGO

❑ LP-643 [M]	Red Rodney Returns	1959	50.00
❑ LSP-643 [S]	Red Rodney Returns	1959	40.00

FANTASY

❑ 3208 [M]	Modern Music from Chicago	1956	120.00

— *Red vinyl*

❑ 3208 [M]	Modern Music from Chicago	195?	80.00

— *Black vinyl*

Number	Title	Yr	NM
❏ OJC-048	Modern Music from Chicago	198?	12.00

MUSE
Number	Title	Yr	NM
❏ MR-5307	Alive in New York	1986	12.00
❏ MR-5034	Bird Lives!	1975	15.00
❏ MR-5371	Bird Lives!	1989	12.00
❏ MR-5135	Home Free	197?	15.00
❏ MR-5209	Live at the Village Vanguard	1980	15.00
❏ MR-5274	Night and Day	1981	12.00
❏ MR-5088	Red Tornado	1975	15.00
❏ MR-5111	Red White and Blues	1977	15.00
❏ MR-5046	Superbop	197?	15.00
❏ MR-5290	The 3 R's	198?	12.00

ONYX
Number	Title	Yr	NM
❏ 204	Red Arrow	197?	15.00

PRESTIGE
Number	Title	Yr	NM
❏ PRLP-122 [10]	Red Rodney	1952	200.00

SAVOY
Number	Title	Yr	NM
❏ MG-12148 [M]	Fiery Red Rodney	1959	100.00

SIGNAL
Number	Title	Yr	NM
❏ S-1206 [M]	Red Rodney 1957	1957	600.00
❏ S-1206 [S]	Red Rodney 1957	199?	30.00
— Classic Records reissue on audiophile vinyl (in stereo)

RODRIGUEZ, WILLIE

RIVERSIDE
Number	Title	Yr	NM
❏ RLP-469 [M]	Flatjacks	1963	30.00
❏ RS-9469 [S]	Flatjacks	1963	30.00

RODRIQUEZ, BOBBY

SEA BREEZE
Number	Title	Yr	NM
❏ SB-2030	Tell An Amigo	1986	12.00

ROE, TOMMY

ABC
Number	Title	Yr	NM
❏ S-700	12 in a Roe/A Collection of Tommy Roe's Greatest Hits	1969	25.00
❏ X-762	16 Greatest Hits	1972	18.00
❏ S-732	Beginnings	1971	18.00
❏ S-683	Dizzy	1969	25.00
❏ 594 [M]	It's Now Winters Day	1967	25.00
❏ S-594 [S]	It's Now Winters Day	1967	30.00
❏ 610 [M]	Phantasy	1967	40.00
❏ S-610 [S]	Phantasy	1967	40.00
❏ S-467 [R]	Something for Everybody	1968	50.00
— Issued in rechanneled stereo four years after its original release
| ❏ T-90883 [M] | Sweet Pea | 1966 | 40.00 |
— Capitol Record Club issue
| ❏ ST-90883 [S] | Sweet Pea | 1966 | 40.00 |
— Capitol Record Club issue
| ❏ S-714 | We Can Make Music | 1970 | 18.00 |

ABC-PARAMOUNT
Number	Title	Yr	NM
❏ 432 [M]	Sheila	1962	40.00
❏ S-432 [S]	Sheila	1962	50.00
❏ 467 [M]	Something for Everybody	1964	30.00
❏ 575 [M]	Sweet Pea	1966	30.00
❏ S-575 [S]	Sweet Pea	1966	40.00

ACCORD
Number	Title	Yr	NM
❏ SN-7155	Sheila	1981	12.00

MCA
Number	Title	Yr	NM
❏ 1510	Collectibles – Greatest Hits	1982	10.00

MONUMENT
Number	Title	Yr	NM
❏ PZ34182	Energy	1976	15.00
❏ 7604	Energy	1977	12.00
— Reissue of 34182
| ❏ 7614 | Full Bloom | 1977 | 12.00 |

PICKWICK
Number	Title	Yr	NM
❏ SPC-3361	Dizzy	197?	12.00

ROESSLER, GEORGE

EAGLE
Number	Title	Yr	NM
❏ SM-4195	Still Life and Old Dreams	1985	12.00

ROGERS, BOB

INDIGO
Number	Title	Yr	NM
❏ 1501 [M]	All That and This, Too	1961	40.00

ROGERS, DANN

IA
Number	Title	Yr	NM
❏ 5000	Hearts Under Fire	1979	15.00

MCA
Number	Title	Yr	NM
❏ 42025	Still Runnin'	1987	10.00

ROGERS, DAVID

ATLANTIC
Number	Title	Yr	NM
❏ SD7283	Farewell to the Ryman	1973	25.00
❏ SD7306	Hey There Girl	1974	18.00
❏ SD7266	Just Thank Me	1973	18.00

COLUMBIA
Number	Title	Yr	NM
❏ CS1023	A World Called You	1970	18.00
❏ KC31506	Need You	1972	18.00
❏ C30972	She Don't Make Me Cry	1971	18.00

REPUBLIC
Number	Title	Yr	NM
❏ 5907	I'm Gonna Love You Right Out of This World	1976	15.00
❏ 5003	Lovingly	197?	15.00

UNITED ARTISTS
Number	Title	Yr	NM
❏ UA-LA422-G	A Whole Lotta Livin' in a House	1975	15.00

ROGERS, ERIC, CHORALE AND ORCHESTRA

LONDON PHASE 4
Number	Title	Yr	NM
❏ SP44027	The Glory of Christmas	196?	15.00

ROGERS, JULIE

MERCURY
Number	Title	Yr	NM
❏ MG-20981 [M]	Julie Rogers	1965	18.00
❏ SR-60981 [S]	Julie Rogers	1965	25.00

ROGERS, KENNY, AND DOLLY PARTON

RCA VICTOR
Number	Title	Yr	NM
❏ ASL1-5307	Once Upon a Christmas	1984	12.00

ROGERS, KENNY, AND DOTTIE WEST

UNITED ARTISTS
Number	Title	Yr	NM
❏ UA-LA946-H	Classics	1979	12.00
❏ UA-LA864-G	Every Time Two Fools Collide	1978	12.00

ROGERS, KENNY

LIBERTY
Number	Title	Yr	NM
❏ LOO-51115	Christmas	1981	12.00
❏ LN-10240	Christmas	198?	10.00
— Reissue of LOO 51115
| ❏ LO-754 | Daytime Friends | 1981 | 10.00 |
— Reissue of United Artists 754
| ❏ LO-51154 | Duets | 1984 | 10.00 |
| ❏ LOO-1035 | Gideon | 1981 | 10.00 |
— Reissue of United Artists 1035
| ❏ LOO-979 | Kenny | 1981 | 10.00 |
— Reissue of United Artists 979
| ❏ LO-689 | Kenny Rogers | 1981 | 10.00 |
— Reissue of United Artists 689
❏ LOO-1072	Kenny Rogers' Greatest Hits	1980	10.00
❏ LO-51157	Love Is What We Make It	1985	10.00
❏ LO-607	Love Lifted Me	1981	10.00
— Reissue of United Artists 607
| ❏ LO-903 | Love Or Something Like It | 1981 | 10.00 |
— Reissue of United Artists 903
❏ LO-51124	Love Will Turn You Around	1982	10.00
❏ LOO-1108	Share Your Love	1981	10.00
❏ LO-835	Ten Years of Gold	1981	10.00
— Reissue of United Artists 835
| ❏ LO-934 | The Gambler | 1981 | 10.00 |
— Reissue of United Artists 934
| ❏ LV-51152 | Twenty Greatest Hits | 1983 | 10.00 |
| ❏ LO-51143 | We've Got Tonight | 1983 | 10.00 |

MOBILE FIDELITY
Number	Title	Yr	NM
❏ 1-049	Kenny Rogers' Greatest Hits	1981	25.00
— Audiophile vinyl
| ❏ 1-044 | The Gambler | 1981 | 25.00 |
— Audiophile vinyl

RCA
Number	Title	Yr	NM
❏ 8371-1-R	Greatest Hits	1988	10.00
❏ 6484-1-R	I Prefer the Moonlight	1987	10.00
❏ 5833-1-R	They Don't Make Them Like They Used To	1986	10.00

RCA VICTOR
Number	Title	Yr	NM
❏ AFL1-4697	Eyes That See in the Dark	1983	10.00
❏ AFL1-4697	Eyes That See in the Dark	1983	200.00
— Picture disc on one side, regular RCA label on other; possibly an in-house demo at the RCA Indianapolis pressing plant
| ❏ AJL1-7023 | The Heart of the Matter | 1985 | 10.00 |
| ❏ AJL1-5335 | What About Me | 1984 | 10.00 |

REPRISE
Number	Title	Yr	NM
❏ 25973	Christmas in America	1989	15.00
❏ R144593	Love Is Strange	1990	25.00
— Only available on vinyl from BMG Direct Marketing
| ❏ 25792 | Something Inside So Strong | 1989 | 12.00 |

UNITED ARTISTS
Number	Title	Yr	NM
❏ UA-LA754-G	Daytime Friends	1977	12.00
❏ LOO-1035	Gideon	1980	12.00
❏ LWAK-979	Kenny	1979	12.00
❏ UA-LA689-G	Kenny Rogers	1976	12.00
❏ UA-LA607-G	Love Lifted Me	1976	18.00
❏ UA-LA903-H	Love Or Something Like It	1978	12.00
❏ UA-LA835-H	Ten Years of Gold	1978	12.00
❏ UA-LA934-H [B]	The Gambler	1978	12.00

ROGERS, RONNIE

MTM
Number	Title	Yr	NM
❏ ST-71065	Tough Times Don't Last	1988	12.00

ROGERS, ROY, AND DALE EVANS

CAPITOL
Number	Title	Yr	NM
❏ T2818 [M]	Christmas Is Always	1967	30.00
❏ ST2818 [S]	Christmas Is Always	1967	30.00
❏ T1745 [M]	The Bible Tells Me So	1962	40.00
❏ ST1745 [S]	The Bible Tells Me So	1962	50.00

GOLDEN
Number	Title	Yr	NM
❏ A198-7 [M]	16 Great Songs of the Old West	1958	80.00
— Originals have black labels and "198" prefix

Number	Title	Yr	NM
❏ LP7 [M]	A Child's Introduction to the West (16 Great Songs of the Old West)	196?	40.00
— Yellow label, "LP" prefix
| ❏ A298-81 [M] | Peter Cottontail | 1962 | 60.00 |
— Originals have black labels and "298" prefix
| ❏ A198-6 [M] | Roy Rogers' and Dale Evans' Song Wagon | 1958 | 80.00 |
— Originals have black labels and "198" prefix

RCA VICTOR
Number	Title	Yr	NM
❏ LPM-1439 [M]	Sweet Hour of Prayer	1957	80.00

ROGERS, ROY

20TH CENTURY
Number	Title	Yr	NM
❏ T-487	Happy Trails to You	1975	18.00

CAPITOL
Number	Title	Yr	NM
❏ ST-785	A Man from Duck Run	1971	25.00
❏ ST-594	The Country Side of Roy Rogers	1970	25.00

RCA
Number	Title	Yr	NM
❏ 3024-1-RRE [PD]	Roy Rogers Tribute	1991	40.00
— Picture disc; only vinyl edition of this release

RCA CAMDEN
Number	Title	Yr	NM
❏ CAL-1074 [M]	Lore of the West	1966	30.00
❏ CAS-1074(e) [R]	Lore of the West	1966	18.00
❏ CAL-1054 [M]	Pecos Bill	1964	30.00
❏ CAS-1054(e) [R]	Pecos Bill	1964	18.00
❏ CAS-1097 [R]	Peter Cottontail and His Friends	1968	18.00
❏ CAL-1097 [M]	Peter Cottontail and His Friends	1968	30.00

RCA VICTOR
Number	Title	Yr	NM
❏ LPM-3168 [M]	Hymns of Faith	1954	200.00
❏ LBY-1022 [M]	Jesus Loves Me	1959	50.00
— On the "Children's Bluebird Series
| ❏ LPM-3041 [M] | Roy Rogers Souvenir Album | 1952 | 300.00 |

ROGERS, SHORTY, AND ANDRE PREVIN

RCA VICTOR
Number	Title	Yr	NM
❏ LPM-1018 [M]	Collaboration	1954	60.00

ROGERS, SHORTY, AND BUDD SHANK

CONCORD JAZZ
Number	Title	Yr	NM
❏ CJ-223	Yesterday, Today and Forever	1983	12.00

ROGERS, SHORTY

ATLANTIC
Number	Title	Yr	NM
❏ 1232 [M]	Martians, Come Back	1956	50.00
— Black label
| ❏ SD1232 [S] | Martians, Come Back | 1958 | 50.00 |
— Green label
| ❏ 1232 [M] | Martians, Come Back | 1961 | 30.00 |
— Multicolor label, white "fan" logo at right
| ❏ SD1232 [S] | Martians, Come Back | 1961 | 25.00 |
— Multicolor label, white "fan" logo at right
| ❏ 1232 [M] | Martians, Come Back | 1963 | 25.00 |
— Multicolor label, black "fan" logo at right
| ❏ SD1232 [S] | Martians, Come Back | 1963 | 18.00 |
— Multicolor label, black "fan" logo at right
| ❏ 90042 | The Swinging Mr. Rogers | 1983 | 12.00 |
| ❏ 1212 [M] | The Swinging Mr. Rogers | 1955 | 50.00 |
— Black label
| ❏ 1212 [M] | The Swinging Mr. Rogers | 1961 | 30.00 |
— Multicolor label, white "fan" logo at right
| ❏ 1212 [M] | The Swinging Mr. Rogers | 1963 | 25.00 |
— Multicolor label, black "fan" logo at right
| ❏ 1270 [M] | Way Up There | 1957 | 50.00 |
— Black label
| ❏ 1270 [M] | Way Up There | 1961 | 30.00 |
— Multicolor label, white "fan" logo at right
| ❏ 1270 [M] | Way Up There | 1963 | 25.00 |
— Multicolor label, black "fan" logo at right

BLUEBIRD
Number	Title	Yr	NM
❏ 5917-1-RB	Short Stops	1987	18.00

CAPITOL
Number	Title	Yr	NM
❏ T1960 [M]	Gospel Mission	1963	30.00
❏ ST1960 [S]	Gospel Mission	1963	25.00
❏ H294 [10]	Modern Sounds	1952	200.00

DISCOVERY
Number	Title	Yr	NM
❏ 843	Jazz Waltz	1982	12.00

MGM
Number	Title	Yr	NM
❏ E-3798 [M]	Shorty Rogers Meets Tarzan	1960	30.00
❏ SE-3798 [S]	Shorty Rogers Meets Tarzan	1960	40.00

MOSAIC
Number	Title	Yr	NM
❏ MR6-125	The Complete Atlantic and EMI Jazz Recordings of Shorty Rogers	199?	150.00
— Limited edition of 7,500

PAUSA
Number	Title	Yr	NM
❏ 9016	14 Historic Arrangements and Performances	198?	12.00

RCA VICTOR
Number	Title	Yr	NM
❏ LPM-1763 [M]	Afro-Cuban Influence	1958	40.00
❏ LSP-1763 [S]	Afro-Cuban Influence	1958	50.00

Number	Title	Yr	NM
❑ LPM-1975 [M]	Chances Are It Swings	1959	40.00
❑ LSP-1975 [S]	Chances Are It Swings	1959	50.00
❑ LPM-1334 [M]	Collaboration	1956	60.00
❑ LPM-3138 [10]	Cool and Crazy	1953	200.00
❑ LPM-1696 [M]	Gigi Goes Jazz	1958	50.00
❑ LSP-1696 [S]	Gigi Goes Jazz	1958	60.00
❑ LPM-1564 [M]	Portrait of Shorty	1957	60.00
❑ LPM-1195 [M]	Shorty Rogers and His Giants	1956	70.00
❑ LJM-1004 [M]	Shorty Rogers Courts the Count	1954	80.00
❑ LPM-3137 [10]	Shorty Rogers' Giants	1953	200.00
❑ LPM-1428 [M]	Shorty Rogers Plays Richard Rogers	1957	60.00
❑ LPM-1350 [M]	The Big Shorty Rogers Express	1957	60.00
❑ LPM-2110 [M]	The Swingin' Nutcracker	1960	40.00
❑ LSP-2110 [S]	The Swingin' Nutcracker	1960	50.00
❑ LPM-1997 [M]	The Wizard of Oz	1959	40.00
❑ LSP-1997 [S]	The Wizard of Oz	1959	50.00
❑ LPM-1326 [M]	Wherever the Five Winds Blow	1956	70.00

REPRISE

❑ R-6050 [M] Bossa Nova 1962 25.00
❑ R9-6050 [S] Bossa Nova 1962 30.00
❑ R-6060 [M] Jazz Waltz 1962 25.00
❑ R9-6060 [S] Jazz Waltz 1962 30.00

WARNER BROS.

❑ W1443 [M] 4th Dimension Jazz 1961 30.00
❑ WS1443 [S] 4th Dimension Jazz 1961 30.00

XANADU

❑ 148 Popi 198? 12.00

ROGERS, TIMMIE

PHILIPS

❑ PHM200088 [M] If I Were President 1963 30.00
❑ PHS600088 [S] If I Were President 1963 40.00

ROHRS, DONNIE

AD-KORP

❑ 0112 Daddy and Daughter Time 197? 15.00

ROKES, THE

RCA VICTOR INTERNATIONAL

❑ FPM-185 [M] Che Mondo Strano 1967 80.00

ROLAND, GENE

BRUNSWICK

❑ BL54114 [M] Swingin' Friends 1963 40.00
❑ BL754114 [S] Swingin' Friends 1963 50.00

DAWN

❑ DLP-1122 [M] Jazzville, Volume 4 1958 80.00

ROLAND, JOE

BETHLEHEM

❑ BCP-17 [M] Joe Roland Quintet 1955 50.00

SAVOY

❑ MG-15034 [10] Joe Roland Quartet 1954 120.00
❑ MG-15047 [10] Joe Roland Quartet 1954 120.00
❑ MG-12039 [M] Joltin' Joe Roland 1955 50.00

ROLLING STONES, THE

ABKCO

❑ 18771-9477-1 Aftermath UK 2003 25.00
—180-gram vinyl reissue pressed in U.S. by RTI, though cover says "Made in E.U."; with loose outer bag; cover has number "882 323-1

❑ 18771-9539-1 Beggars Banquet 2003 25.00
—180-gram vinyl reissue pressed in U.S. by RTI, though cover says "Made in E.U."; with loose outer bag; cover has number "882 330-1

❑ 18771-9500-1 Between the Buttons UK 2003 25.00
—180-gram vinyl reissue pressed in U.S. by RTI, though cover says "Made in E.U."; with loose outer bag; cover has number "882 326-1

❑ 18771-9001-1 Big Hits (High Tide and Green Grass) 2003 25.00
—180-gram vinyl reissue pressed in U.S. by RTI, though cover says "Made in E.U."; with loose outer bag; number on cover is "002 322-1

❑ 18771-9375-1 England's Newest Hit Makers -- The Rolling Stones 2003 25.00
—180-gram vinyl reissue pressed in U.S. by RTI, though cover says "Made in E.U."; with loose outer bag; cover has number "882 316-1

❑ 18771-9005-1 Get Yer Ya-Ya's Out! 2003 25.00
—180-gram vinyl reissue pressed in U.S. by RTI, though cover says "Made in E.U."; with loose outer bag; cover has number "882 333-1

❑ 18771-9667-1 Hot Rocks 1964-1971 2003 40.00
—180-gram vinyl reissue pressed in U.S. by RTI, though cover says "Made in E.U."; with loose outer bag; cover has number "882 334-1

❑ 18771-9004-1 Let It Bleed 2003 25.00
—180-gram vinyl reissue pressed in U.S. by RTI, though cover says "Made in E.U."; with loose outer bag; cover has number "882 332-1

❑ ANA1 [P] Metamorphosis 1975 15.00
❑ 18771-9006-1 Metamorphosis 2003 25.00
—180-gram vinyl reissue pressed in U.S. by RTI, though cover says "Made in E.U."; with loose outer bag; cover has number "882 344-1

❑ AB-4224 [B] Necrophilia 1973 10000.00
—Canceled; covers exist. Value is for complete tri-fold cover.

❑ 18771-9430-1 Out of Our Heads UK 2003 25.00
—180-gram vinyl reissue pressed in U.S. by RTI, though cover says "Made in E.U."; with loose outer bag; cover has number "882 319-1

❑ 1218-1 Singles Collection: The London Years 1989 50.00
❑ MPD-1 [DJ] Songs of the Rolling Stones 1975 700.00
—Band in field" cover

❑ MPD-1 [DJ] Songs of the Rolling Stones 1975 3000.00
—Rock and Roll Circus" cover; VG value 1000; VG+ value 2000

❑ 18771-9002-1 Their Satanic Majesties Request 2003 25.00
—180-gram vinyl reissue pressed in U.S. by RTI, though cover says "Made in E.U."; with loose outer bag; cover has number "882 329-1

❑ DVL2-0268 [P] The Rolling Stones' Greatest Hits 1977 25.00
—RCA Special Products mail-order offer

EAGLE

❑ ERDVLP070 [B] Some Girls (Live In Texas '78) 2012 40.00
—gatefold sleeve includes DVD

LONDON

❑ LL3402 [M] 12 x 5 1964 200.00
—Maroon label with "London/ffrr" in a box at top

❑ LL3402 [M] 12 x 5 1964 60.00
—Maroon label with "London" unboxed at top

❑ LL3402 [M] 12 x 5 1964 10000.00
—Maroon label with "London" unboxed at top; possibly unique blue vinyl pressing; VG value 5000; VG+ value 7500

❑ LL3402 [M] 12 x 5 1965 40.00
—Red or maroon label with "London" boxed at top

❑ PS402 [R] 12 x 5 1964 30.00
—Dark blue label with "London" unboxed at top

❑ PS402 [R] 12 x 5 1965 12.00
—Dark blue label with "London" boxed at top

❑ LL3476 [M] Aftermath 1966 60.00
❑ PS476 [S] Aftermath 1966 12.00
❑ PS509 Back Behind and In Front 1967 5000.00
—Prototype cover slick for an unreleased LP; the same number was used for "Flowers

❑ PS539 [S] Beggars Banquet 1968 30.00
—With all songs credited to "Jagger-Richard

❑ PS539 [S] Beggars Banquet 1968 12.00
—With "Rev. Wilkins: credited as composer of "Prodigal Son

❑ PS539 Beggars Banquet 1968 10000.00
—Original "toilet graffiti" cover slick (not on a cover)

❑ LL3499 [M] Between the Buttons 1967 80.00
❑ PS499 [S] Between the Buttons 1967 12.00
❑ NP1 [M] Big Hits (High Tide and Green Grass) 1966 8000.00
—With two lines of type on the front cover, all in small letters

❑ NP1 [M] Big Hits (High Tide and Green Grass) 1966 50.00
—With five lines of type on the front cover, all in capital letters

❑ NPS1 [R] Big Hits (High Tide and Green Grass) 1966 12.00
❑ LL3451 [M] December's Children (and Everybody's) 1965 40.00
—Maroon label with "London" unboxed at top

❑ LL3451 [M] December's Children (and Everybody's) 1966 30.00
—Maroon label with "London" boxed at top

❑ PS451 [P] December's Children (and Everybody's) 1965 30.00
—Dark blue label with "London" unboxed at top

❑ PS451 [P] December's Children (and Everybody's) 1966 12.00
—Dark blue label with "London" boxed at top. "Look What You've Done" is in true stereo; all other tracks are rechanneled.

❑ LL3375 [DJ] England's Newest Hit Makers -- The Rolling Stones 1964 3000.00
—White label promo

❑ LL3375 [M] England's Newest Hit Makers -- The Rolling Stones 1964 300.00
—Maroon label with "Full Frequency Range Recording" inside horizontal lines that go through the center hole; lower left-hand corner of cover advertises a bonus photo

❑ PS375 [R] England's Newest Hit Makers -- The Rolling Stones 1964 300.00
—Dark blue label; lower left-hand corner of cover advertises a bonus photo

❑ LL3375 [M] England's Newest Hit Makers -- The Rolling Stones 1965 60.00
—Maroon label with "London" unboxed at top

❑ LL3375 [M] England's Newest Hit Makers -- The Rolling Stones 1966 40.00
—Red or maroon label with "London" boxed at top

❑ PS375 [R] England's Newest Hit Makers -- The Rolling Stones 1965 30.00
—Dark blue label with "London" unboxed at top

❑ PS375 [R] England's Newest Hit Makers -- The Rolling Stones 1966 12.00
—Dark blue label with "London" boxed at top

❑ LL3375 England's Newest Hit Makers -- The Rolling Stones Bonus Photo 1964 200.00
❑ LL3509 [M] Flowers 1967 100.00
❑ PS509 [P] Flowers 1967 12.00
—Have You Seen Your Mother, Baby, Standing in the Shadow?" and "Mother's Little Helper" are rechanneled; all others are true stereo

❑ PS509 [M] Flowers 197? 10.00
—Some later "stereo" copies of this LP are actually entirely in mono

❑ NPS5 [S] Get Yer Ya-Ya's Out! 1970 12.00
❑ LL3493 [M] Got Live If You Want It! 1966 60.00
❑ PS493 [P] Got Live If You Want It! 1966 12.00
—Fortune Teller" is rechanneled (it's actually an early studio recording with overdubbed crowd noise)

❑ 2PS606/7 [P] Hot Rocks 1964-1971 1971 1000.00
—With alternate versions of "Brown Sugar" and "Wild Horses" unavailable elsewhere. The date "11-5-71" or "11-18-71" is in the Side 4 trail-off area.

❑ 2PS606/7 [P] Hot Rocks 1964-1971 1971 25.00
—With regular versions of all tracks. All of Side 1 and "Mothers Little Helper" and "19th Nervous Breakdown" on Side 2 are rechanneled. All of Side 3 and 4 are stereo.

❑ NPS4 [S] Let It Bleed 1969 18.00
—With poster

❑ NPS4 [S] Let It Bleed 1969 12.00
—Without poster

❑ NPS-4 Let It Bleed 1970 10000.00
—One-of-a-kind red/yellow/blue/green vinyl (all on the same record!); VG value 5000; VG+ value 7500

❑ 2PS626/7 [P] More Hot Rocks (Big Hits and Fazed Cookies) 1972 25.00
—All of Sides 1 and 4 are rechanneled; Side 2 and 3, except "Have You Seen Your Mother, Baby, Standing in the Shadow?" are in true stereo

❑ LL3429 [M] Out of Our Heads 1965 200.00
—Maroon label with "London/ffrr" in a box at top

❑ LL3429 [M] Out of Our Heads 1965 40.00
—Maroon label with "London" unboxed at top

❑ LL3429 [M] Out of Our Heads 1966 30.00
—Red or maroon label with "London" boxed at top

❑ PS429 [R] Out of Our Heads 1965 100.00
—Dark blue label with "London/ffrr" in a box at top and "Made in England by the Decca Record Co. Ltd." at top edge

❑ PS429 [R] Out of Our Heads 1965 30.00
—Dark blue label with "London" unboxed at top

❑ PS429 [R] Out of Our Heads 1965 12.00
—Dark blue label with "London" boxed at top

❑ NP2 [M] Their Satanic Majesties Request 1967 300.00
❑ NPS2 [S] Their Satanic Majesties Request 1967 50.00
—With 3-D cover

❑ NPS2 [S] Their Satanic Majesties Request 197? 10.00
—Without 3-D cover

❑ LL3420 [M] The Rolling Stones, Now! 1965 200.00
—Maroon label with "London/ffrr" in a box at top. Add 20% for complete liner notes (or sticker) on back cover (both columns of type about equal in length).

❑ LL3420 [M] The Rolling Stones, Now! 1965 60.00
—Maroon label with "London" unboxed at top and no lines on label. Add 20% for complete liner notes (or sticker) on back cover (both columns of type about equal in length).

❑ LL3420 [M] The Rolling Stones, Now! 1966 40.00
—Red or maroon label with "London" boxed at top and censored liner notes (second column an inch shorter than the first column)

❑ PS420 [R] The Rolling Stones, Now! 1965 30.00
—Dark blue label with "London" unboxed at top. Add 20% for complete liner notes (or sticker) on back cover (both columns of type about equal in length).

❑ PS420 [R] The Rolling Stones, Now! 1966 25.00
—Dark blue label with "London" boxed at top. Add 20% for censored liner notes (or sticker) on back cover (second column an inch shorter than the first column; "offensive" notes were quietly restored in the 1970s).

❑ LL3420 [M] The Rolling Stones, Now! 1965 400.00
—Maroon label with "London" unboxed, but with "ffrr" ear above "London" and "Full Frequency Range Recording" inside horizontal lines that go through the center hole

❑ LL3420 [M] The Rolling Stones, Now! 1965 400.00
—Maroon label with "London" unboxed, with horizontal lines that go through the center hole, but with NO "ffrr" ear at the top and NO "Full Frequency Range Recording" between the horizonal lines

❑ RSD-1 [DJ] The Rolling Stones -- The Promotional Album 1969 3000.00
—Not to be confused with imports of this rare promo; VG value 1000; VG+ value 2000

❑ NPS3 [P] Through the Past, Darkly (Big Hits Vol. 2) 1969 12.00
—With hexagonal cover

❑ NPS3 [P] Through the Past, Darkly (Big Hits Vol. 2) 197? 25.00
—Reissue with regular square cover

❑ NPS3 [PD] Through the Past, Darkly (Big Hits Vol. 2) 1969 6000.00
—Prototype picture discs that used the cover art from "Big Hits (High Tide and Green Grass)" either on one or both sides; VG value 3000; VG+ value 4500

Number	Title	Yr	NM

LONDON/ABKCO

Number	Title	Yr	NM
❏ 74021 [M]	12 x 5	1986	10.00

— *Digitally Remastered from Original Master Recording" on cover; red label*

| ❏ 74761 [S] | Aftermath | 1986 | 10.00 |

— *Digitally Remastered from Original Master Recording" on cover; red label*

| ❏ 75391 [S] | Beggars Banquet | 1986 | 15.00 |

— *Digitally Remastered from Original Master Recording" on cover; red label; original banned "toilet cover" released for the first time on this reissue*

| ❏ 74991 [S] | Between the Buttons | 1986 | 10.00 |

— *Digitally Remastered from Original Master Recording" on cover; red label*

| ❏ 80011 [M] | Big Hits (High Tide and Green Grass) | 1986 | 10.00 |

— *Digitally Remastered from Original Master Recording" on cover; red label*

| ❏ 74511 [M] | December's Children (and Everybody's) | 1986 | 10.00 |

— *Digitally Remastered from Original Master Recording" on cover; red label*

| ❏ 73751 [M] | England's Newest Hit Makers -- The Rolling Stones | 1986 | 10.00 |

— *Digitally Remastered from Original Master Recording" on cover; red label*

| ❏ 75091 [S] | Flowers | 1986 | 10.00 |

— *Digitally Remastered from Original Master Recording" on cover; red label*

| ❏ 80051 | Get Yer Ya-Ya's Out! | 1986 | 10.00 |

— *Digitally Remastered from Original Master Recording" on cover; red label*

| ❏ 74931 [S] | Got Live If You Want It! | 1986 | 10.00 |

— *Digitally Remastered from Original Master Recording" on cover; red label*

| ❏ 62671 [P] | Hot Rocks 1964-1971 | 1986 | 18.00 |

— *Digitally Remastered from Original Master Recording" on cover; red label; same stereo content as original*

| ❏ 80041 | Let It Bleed | 1986 | 10.00 |

— *Digitally Remastered from Original Master Recording" on cover; red label*

| ❏ 62671 [P] | More Hot Rocks (Big Hits and Fazed Cookies) | 1986 | 18.00 |

— *Digitally Remastered from Original Master Recording" on cover; red label*

| ❏ 74291 [P] | Out of Our Heads | 1986 | 10.00 |

— *Digitally Remastered from Original Master Recording" on cover; red label*

| ❏ 80021 [S] | Their Satanic Majesties Request | 1986 | 10.00 |

— *Digitally Remastered from Original Master Recording" on cover; red label*

| ❏ 74201 [P] | The Rolling Stones, Now! | 1986 | 10.00 |

— *Digitally Remastered from Original Master Recording" on cover; red label; four tracks are in true stereo*

| ❏ 80031 [S] | Through the Past, Darkly (Big Hits Vol. 2) | 1986 | 10.00 |

— *Digitally Remastered from Original Master Recording" on cover; red label*

MOBILE FIDELITY

Number	Title	Yr	NM
❏ 1-087	Some Girls	1982	75.00

— *Audiophile vinyl*

| ❏ 1-060 [B] | Sticky Fingers | 1980 | 75.00 |

— *Audiophile vinyl*

| ❏ RC 1 | The Rolling Stones | 1984 | 500.00 |

— *London LPs pressed on audiophile vinyl in box*

RADIO PULSEBEAT NEWS

Number	Title	Yr	NM
❏ 4 [B]	It's Here Luv!!	1965	200.00

— *Ed Rudy interview album; this has been counterfeited, but originals can be identified thus: Charlie Watts' jacket should be completely black with no white marks; the label is very clear; the vinyl is all black*

ROLLING STONES

Number	Title	Yr	NM
❏ COC79104	Black and Blue	1976	12.00
❏ FC40495	Black and Blue	1986	10.00

— *Reissue on CBS*

| ❏ OC40250 | Dirty Work | 1986 | 10.00 |

— *Originals came with red shrink wrap; add 50% if it is still with the package*

| ❏ COC16015 [B] | Emotional Rescue | 1980 | 25.00 |

— *Originally released with a large poster wrapped around the outside of the record jacket*

| ❏ COC16015 | Emotional Rescue | 1980 | 12.00 |

— *Without poster*

| ❏ FC40500 | Emotional Rescue | 1986 | 10.00 |

— *Reissue on CBS*

| ❏ COC 2-2900 | Exile on Main St. | 1973 | 15.00 |

— *Reissue covers have two pockets, one for each record*

| ❏ CG240489 | Exile on Main St. | 1986 | 12.00 |

— *Reissue on CBS*

| ❏ COC 2-2900 [B] | Exile on Main St. | 1972 | 30.00 |

— *Original covers have Unipak design -- cover has to be opened to remove the records. Add 33% for sheet of postcards*

| ❏ C47456 [B] | Flashpoint | 1991 | 30.00 |
| ❏ COC59101 | Goats Head Soup | 1973 | 18.00 |

— *With bonus photo*

| ❏ COC59101 | Goats Head Soup | 1973 | 12.00 |

— *Without bonus photo*

| ❏ COC39106 | Goats Head Soup | 1977 | 10.00 |

— *Reissue on Atlantic*

| ❏ FC40492 | Goats Head Soup | 1986 | 10.00 |

— *Reissue on CBS*

| ❏ PR164 [DJ] | Interview with Mick Jagger by Tom Donahue | 1971 | 200.00 |

— *Yellow label*

| ❏ COC79101 | It's Only Rock 'n' Roll | 1974 | 12.00 |
| ❏ FC40493 | It's Only Rock 'n' Roll | 1986 | 10.00 |

— *Reissue on CBS*

| ❏ COC39100 | Jamming with Edward | 1972 | 18.00 |

— *Not an official Stones album, this includes Jagger, Watts and Wyman with Ry Cooder and Nicky Hopkins*

| ❏ COC39100 [DJ] | Jamming with Edward | 1972 | 175.00 |

— *White label stereo promo*

| ❏ COC39100 [M] | Jamming with Edward | 1972 | 250.00 |

— *White label mono promo*

| ❏ COC 2-9001 | Love You Live | 1977 | 15.00 |
| ❏ CG240496 | Love You Live | 1986 | 12.00 |

— *Reissue on CBS*

| ❏ COC79102 | Made in the Shade | 1975 | 12.00 |
| ❏ COC39107 | Made in the Shade | 1977 | 10.00 |

— *Reissue on Atlantic*

| ❏ FC40494 | Made in the Shade | 1986 | 10.00 |

— *Reissue on CBS*

| ❏ 90176 | Rewind (1971-1984) | 1984 | 30.00 |
| ❏ FC40505 | Rewind (1971-1984) | 1986 | 10.00 |

— *Reissue on CBS*

| ❏ COC39108 | Some Girls | 1978 | 18.00 |

— *With all women's faces visible. Nine different color schemes exist for the front cover.*

| ❏ COC39108 | Some Girls | 1978 | 12.00 |

— *With "cover under reconstruction." Nine different color schemes exist for the front cover.*

| ❏ FC40499 | Some Girls | 1986 | 10.00 |

— *Reissue on CBS*

| ❏ OC45333 | Steel Wheels | 1989 | 12.00 |
| ❏ COC59100 [M] | Sticky Fingers | 1971 | 500.00 |

— *White label mono promo*

| ❏ COC59100 [DJ] | Sticky Fingers | 1971 | 300.00 |

— *White label stereo promo*

| ❏ COC59100 | Sticky Fingers | 1971 | 15.00 |

— *With working zipper*

| ❏ FC40488 | Sticky Fingers | 1986 | 10.00 |

— *Reissue on CBS with photo of zipper only*

| ❏ COC39105 | Sticky Fingers | 1977 | 12.00 |

— *Reissue on Atlantic with working zipper*

| ❏ COC39105 | Sticky Fingers | 1977 | 10.00 |

— *Reissue on Atlantic with photo of zipper only*

❏ COC39113	Still Life (American Concert 1981)	1982	12.00
❏ COC39114 [PD]	Still Life (American Concert 1981)	1982	40.00
❏ FC40503	Still Life (American Concert 1981)	1986	10.00

— *Reissue on CBS*

| ❏ COC16028 | Sucking in the Seventies | 1981 | 12.00 |
| ❏ FC40501 | Sucking in the Seventies | 1986 | 10.00 |

— *Reissue on CBS*

| ❏ COC16052 | Tattoo You | 1981 | 12.00 |
| ❏ FC40502 | Tattoo You | 1986 | 10.00 |

— *Reissue on CBS*

| ❏ 00120 | Undercover | 1983 | 15.00 |

— *With stickers intact*

| ❏ 90120 | Undercover | 1983 | 10.00 |

— *With stickers peeled off*

| ❏ FC40504 | Undercover | 1986 | 10.00 |

— *Reissue on CBS has no stickers on cover*

VIRGIN

Number	Title	Yr	NM
❏ V3012	A Bigger Bang	2005	18.00

— *Alternate number is "00946 3300671 3"; pressed in the EU for U.S. distribution*

| ❏ 8447121 | Bridges to Babylon | 1997 | 80.00 |

— *U.S. versions pressed in U.K., but have "Virgin Records America Inc." on back cover*

| ❏ 47864 | Exile on Main St. | 1999 | 50.00 |

— *Limited-edition reissue with 180-gram vinyl and all original inserts*

| ❏ 8467401 [B] | No Security | 1998 | 30.00 |

— *U.S. versions pressed in U.K., but have "Virgin Records America Inc." on back cover*

| ❏ 47867 | Some Girls | 1999 | 30.00 |

— *Limited-edition reissue with 180-gram vinyl and original inserts (except it has the "cover under reconstruction" inner sleeve)*

| ❏ 47863 | Sticky Fingers | 1999 | 30.00 |

— *Limited-edition reissue with 180-gram vinyl and original working zipper cover*

| ❏ V2801(8 41040 1) | Stripped | 1995 | 25.00 |

— *U.S. versions pressed in U.K., but have UPC code paste-over with "Marketed and Distributed by Caroline Records*

| ❏ V2750(8 39782 1) | Voodoo Lounge | 1994 | 30.00 |

— *U.S. versions pressed in U.K., but have UPC code paste-over and blue sticker "Marketed by Caroline*

ROLLINI, ADRIAN

MERCURY

Number	Title	Yr	NM
❏ MG-20011 [M]	Chopsticks	1953	50.00

SUNBEAM

| ❏ 134 | Adrian Rollini and His Orchestra 1933-34 | 197? | 12.00 |

ROLLINS, SONNY; CLIFFORD BROWN; MAX ROACH

PRESTIGE

Number	Title	Yr	NM
❏ PRST-7821	Three Giants	1971	15.00
❏ PRLP-7291 [M]	Three Giants	1964	40.00
❏ PRST-7291 [R]	Three Giants	1964	30.00

ROLLINS, SONNY

ABC IMPULSE!

Number	Title	Yr	NM
❏ AS-9121 [S]	East Broadway Run Down	1968	18.00

— *Black label with red ring*

| ❏ AS-9236 | Reevaluation: The Impulse Years | 1973 | 25.00 |
| ❏ AS-91 [S] | Sonny Rollins On Impulse! | 1968 | 30.00 |

— *Black label with red ring*

| ❏ IA-9349 | There Will Never Be Another You | 1978 | 18.00 |

ANALOGUE PRODUCTIONS

| ❏ AP 008 | Way Out West | 199? | 30.00 |

— *180-gram audiophile vinyl*

BLUEBIRD

| ❏ 5634-1-RB | The Quartets Featuring Jim Hall | 1986 | 25.00 |

BLUE NOTE

| ❏ BLP-1581 [M] | A Night at the Village Vanguard | 1958 | 800.00 |

— *Deep groove" version; W. 63rd St. address on label*

| ❏ BLP-1581 [M] | A Night at the Village Vanguard | 1958 | 250.00 |

— *Regular version, W. 63rd St. address on label*

| ❏ BLP-1581 [M] | A Night at the Village Vanguard | 1963 | 50.00 |

— *With "New York, USA" address on label*

| ❏ BST-81581 [R] | A Night at the Village Vanguard | 1967 | 18.00 |

— *With "A Division of Liberty Records" on label*

| ❏ BST-81581 [M] | A Night at the Village Vanguard, Vol. 1 | 1987 | 15.00 |

— *The Finest in Jazz Since 1939" reissue*

| ❏ BN-LA475-H2 | More from the Vanguard | 1975 | 18.00 |
| ❏ BLP-4001 [M] | Newk's Time | 1958 | 300.00 |

— *Deep groove" version; W. 63rd St. address on label*

| ❏ BLP-4001 [M] | Newk's Time | 1958 | 150.00 |

— *Regular version, W. 63rd St. address on label*

| ❏ BST-4001 [S] | Newk's Time | 1959 | 250.00 |

— *Deep groove" version; W. 63rd St. address on label*

| ❏ BST-4001 [S] | Newk's Time | 1959 | 120.00 |

— *Regular version, W. 63rd St. address on label*

| ❏ BLP-4001 [M] | Newk's Time | 1963 | 60.00 |

— *With "New York, USA" address on label*

| ❏ BST 4001 [S] | Newk's Time | 1963 | 40.00 |

— *With "New York, USA" address on label*

| ❏ BST-84001 [S] | Newk's Time | 1967 | 25.00 |

— *With "A Division of Liberty Records" on label*

| ❏ BST-84001 [S] | Newk's Time | 198? | 15.00 |

— *The Finest in Jazz Since 1939" reissue*

| ❏ BLP-1542 [M] | Sonny Rollins | 1957 | 1000.00 |

— *Deep groove" version; Lexington Ave. address on label*

| ❏ BLP-1542 [M] | Sonny Rollins | 1958 | 500.00 |

— *Deep groove" version; W. 63rd St. address on label*

| ❏ BLP-1542 [M] | Sonny Rollins | 1963 | 80.00 |

— *With "New York, USA" address on label*

| ❏ BST-81542 [R] | Sonny Rollins | 1967 | 18.00 |

— *With "A Division of Liberty Records" on label*

| ❏ BN-LA401-H2 | Sonny Rollins | 1975 | 30.00 |
| ❏ BST-81542 [M] | Sonny Rollins | 1985 | 15.00 |

— *The Finest in Jazz Since 1939" reissue*

| ❏ BLP-1558 [M] | Sonny Rollins, Volume 2 | 1957 | 1000.00 |

— *Deep groove" version; W. 63rd St. address on label*

| ❏ BLP-1558 [M] | Sonny Rollins, Volume 2 | 1957 | 400.00 |

— *Regular version, W. 63rd St. address on label*

| ❏ BLP-1558 [M] | Sonny Rollins, Volume 2 | 1963 | 80.00 |

— *With "New York, USA" address on label*

| ❏ BST-81558 [R] | Sonny Rollins, Volume 2 | 1967 | 18.00 |

— *With "A Division of Liberty Records" on label*

| ❏ BST-81558 [M] | Sonny Rollins, Volume 2 | 1985 | 15.00 |

— *The Finest in Jazz Since 1939" reissue*

| ❏ B1-93203 | The Best of Sonny Rollins | 1989 | 18.00 |

CONTEMPORARY

❏ C-7651	Alternate Takes	1986	18.00
❏ M-3564 [M]	Sonny Rollins and the Contemporary Leaders	1959	250.00
❏ S-7564 [S]	Sonny Rollins and the Contemporary Leaders	1959	200.00
❏ C-3530 [M]	Way Out West	1957	250.00
❏ S-7530 [S]	Way Out West	1959	150.00

DCC COMPACT CLASSICS

| ❏ LPZ-2008 | Saxophone Colossus | 1995 | 100.00 |

— *180-gram audiophile vinyl*

| ❏ LPZ-2022 | Tenor Madness | 1996 | 150.00 |

— *180-gram audiophile vinyl*

EVEREST ARCHIVE OF FOLK & JAZZ

| ❏ FS-220 [R] | Sonny Rollins with Guest Artist Thad Jones | 1968 | 15.00 |

FANTASY

❏ OJC-067	Freedom Suite	198?	15.00
❏ OJC-314	Horn Culture	198?	15.00
❏ OJC-058	Moving Out	198?	15.00

Number	Title	Yr	NM
❑ OJC-620	Nucleus	1991	18.00
❑ OJC-291	Saxophone Colossus	198?	15.00
❑ OJC-348	Sonny Boy	198?	15.00
❑ OJC-340	Sonny Rollins and the Contemporary Leaders	198?	18.00
❑ OJC-214	Sonny Rollins Plays for Bird	198?	15.00
❑ OJC-243	Sonny Rollins Plus 4	1987	15.00
❑ OJC-011	Sonny Rollins with the Modern Jazz Quartet	1982	15.00
❑ OJC-124	Tenor Madness	198?	15.00
❑ OJC-468	The Cutting Edge: Montreux 1974	198?	15.00
❑ OJC-312	The Next Album	1988	15.00
❑ OJC=029	The Sound of Sonny	198?	15.00
❑ OJC-337	Way Out West	198?	15.00
❑ OJC-007	Work Time	1982	15.00

GATEWAY

Number	Title	Yr	NM
❑ GS-7204	The Sound of Sonny	1977	12.00

GRP IMPULSE!

Number	Title	Yr	NM
❑ IMP-161 [M]	East Broadway Run Down	199?	25.00
—180-gram audiophile reissue			
❑ IMP-223	Sonny Rollins On Impulse!	1997	25.00
—180-gram reissue			

IMPULSE!

Number	Title	Yr	NM
❑ A-9121 [M]	East Broadway Run Down	1967	80.00
❑ AS-9121 [S]	East Broadway Run Down	1967	50.00
❑ A-91 [M]	Sonny Rollins On Impulse!	1966	60.00
❑ AS-91 [S]	Sonny Rollins On Impulse!	1966	80.00

JAZZLAND

Number	Title	Yr	NM
❑ JLP-86 [M]	Shadow Waltz	1962	80.00
❑ JLP-986 [S]	Shadow Waltz	1962	70.00
❑ JLP-72 [M]	Sonny's Time	1962	80.00
❑ JLP-972 [S]	Sonny's Time	1962	70.00

MCA

Number	Title	Yr	NM
❑ 4127	Great Moments with Sonny Rollins	198?	15.00
❑ 29054	Sonny Rollins On Impulse!	1980	12.00
❑ 29055	There Will Never Be Another You	1980	12.00

MCA IMPULSE!

Number	Title	Yr	NM
❑ MCA-5655	Sonny Rollins On Impulse!	1986	12.00

METROJAZZ

Number	Title	Yr	NM
❑ E-1002 [M]	Sonny Rollins and the Big Brass	1958	120.00
❑ SE-1002 [S]	Sonny Rollins and the Big Brass	1958	80.00
❑ E-1011 [M]	Sonny Rollins at Music Inn	1958	120.00
❑ SE-1011 [S]	Sonny Rollins at Music Inn	1958	100.00

MILESTONE

Number	Title	Yr	NM
❑ M-9155	Dancing in the Dark	1988	15.00
❑ M-9090	Don't Ask	1979	15.00
❑ M-55005	Don't Stop the Carnival	1978	25.00
❑ M-9080	Easy Living	1977	15.00
❑ M-9179	Falling in Love with Jazz	1990	18.00
❑ M-47007	Freedom Suite Plus	1973	25.00
❑ M-9150	G-Man	1987	15.00
❑ M-9051	Horn Culture	1974	15.00
❑ M-9098	Love at First Sight	1980	15.00
❑ M-9104	No Problem	1981	12.00
❑ M-9064	Nucleus	1975	15.00
❑ M-9108	Reel Life	1982	12.00
❑ M-9122	Sunny Days, Starry Nights	1984	12.00
❑ M-9059	The Cutting Edge: Montreux 1974	1975	15.00
❑ M-9042	The Next Album	197?	15.00
❑ M-9074	The Way I Feel	1976	15.00

PRESTIGE

Number	Title	Yr	NM
❑ PRLP-7058 [M]	Moving Out	1956	300.00
—Yellow label with W. 50th St. address			
❑ PRLP-7058 [M]	Moving Out	1958	80.00
—Yellow label with Bergenfield, N.J. address			
❑ PRLP-7095 [M]	Rollins Plays for Bird	1957	500.00
—Yellow label with W. 50th St. address			
❑ PRLP-7079 [M]	Saxophone Colossus	1957	400.00
—Yellow label with W. 50th St. address			
❑ PRLP-7326 [M]	Saxophone Colossus	1964	60.00
❑ PRST-7326 [R]	Saxophone Colossus	1964	30.00
❑ P-24050	Saxophone Colossus and More	1974	25.00
❑ PRLP-7269 [M]	Sonny and the Stars	1963	80.00
❑ PRST-7269 [R]	Sonny and the Stars	1963	40.00
❑ PRLP-7207 [M]	Sonny Boy	1961	100.00
❑ PR-24004	Sonny Rollins	1972	30.00
❑ PRLP-190 [10]	Sonny Rollins	1954	600.00
❑ PRST-7553 [R]	Sonny Rollins Plays for Bird	1968	30.00
❑ PRLP-7433 [M]	Sonny Rollins Plays Jazz Classics	1967	100.00
❑ PRST-7433 [R]	Sonny Rollins Plays Jazz Classics	1967	30.00
❑ PRLP-7038 [M]	Sonny Rollins Plus 4	1956	300.00
—Yellow label with W. 50th St. address			
❑ PRLP-137 [10]	Sonny Rollins Quartet	1952	800.00
❑ PRLP-186 [10]	Sonny Rollins Quartet	1954	700.00
❑ PRLP-7029 [M]	Sonny Rollins with the Modern Jazz Quartet	1956	400.00
—Orange cover; original edition has the wrong catalog number at upper left (PR 7020), but the record has the correct number			
❑ PRLP-7029 [M]	Sonny Rollins with the Modern Jazz Quartet	1956	300.00
—Orange cover; second edition has the correct catalog number, "Prestige LP 7029," in upper left inside an orange box			
❑ PRLP-7029 [M]	Sonny Rollins with the Modern Jazz Quartet	1956	250.00
—Brown and yellow cover; catalog number at upper left is "Prestige Hi-Fi LP 7029"; record has yellow label with W. 50th St. address			
❑ P-24082	Taking Care of Business	1978	25.00
❑ PRLP-7047 [M]	Tenor Madness	1956	300.00
—Yellow label with W. 50th St. address			
❑ PRST-7657 [R]	Tenor Madness	1969	30.00
❑ PRLP-7047 [M]	Tenor Madness	1958	200.00
—Yellow label with Bergenfield, N.J. address			
❑ PRST-7856	The First Recordings	1972	15.00
❑ PRLP-7126 [M]	Tour de Force	1957	200.00
—Yellow label with W. 50th St. address			
❑ P-24096	Vintage Sessions	1981	25.00
❑ PRST-7750	Worktime	1970	15.00
❑ PRLP-7020 [M]	Work Time	1956	500.00
—Yellow label with W. 50th St. address			
❑ PRLP-7246 [M]	Work Time	1962	80.00
❑ PRST-7246 [R]	Work Time	1962	40.00

QUINTESSENCE

Number	Title	Yr	NM
❑ QJ-25181	Green Dolphin Street	1978	15.00

RCA VICTOR

Number	Title	Yr	NM
❑ LPM-2927 [M]	Now's the Time	1964	30.00
❑ LSP-2927 [S]	Now's the Time!	1964	30.00
❑ LSP-2927 [S]	Now's the Time!	199?	30.00
—Classic Records reissue on audiophile vinyl			
❑ LPM-2612 [M]	Our Man In Jazz	1962	30.00
❑ LSP-2612 [S]	Our Man In Jazz	1962	60.00
❑ LSP-2612 [S]	Our Man In Jazz	199?	30.00
—Classic Records reissue on audiophile vinyl			
❑ ANL1-2809	Pure Gold	1978	12.00
❑ LPM-2712 [M]	Sonny Meets Hawk!	1963	30.00
❑ LSP-2712 [S]	Sonny Meets Hawk!	1963	60.00
❑ LSP-2712 [S]	Sonny Meets Hawk!	199?	30.00
—Classic Records reissue on audiophile vinyl			
❑ LPM-2527 [M]	The Bridge	1962	40.00
—Black label, dog on top, "Long 33 1/3 Play" at bottom			
❑ LSP-2527 [S]	The Bridge	1962	70.00
—Black label, dog on top, "Living Stereo" at bottom			
❑ APL1-0859	The Bridge	1975	25.00
—Reissue of LSP-2527; orange or tan label			
❑ AFL1-0859	The Bridge	1977	15.00
—Reissue with new prefix; black label, dog at 1 o'clock			
❑ LSP-2527 [S]	The Bridge	199?	30.00
—Classic Records reissue on audiophile vinyl			
❑ LSP-2527-45	The Bridge	1999	60.00
—Classic Records reissue; 4 single-sided LPs that play at 45 rpm			
❑ LPM-3355 [M]	The Standard Sonny Rollins	1965	30.00
❑ LSP-3355 [S]	The Standard Sonny Rollins	1965	30.00
❑ LPM-2572 [M]	What's New?	1962	30.00
❑ LSP-2572 [S]	What's New?	1962	60.00

RIVERSIDE

Number	Title	Yr	NM
❑ RLP-258 [M]	Freedom Suite	1958	200.00
❑ RS-3010 [S]	Freedom Suite	1968	30.00
❑ SMJ-6044	Freedom Suite	1974	25.00
❑ RLP 12-241 [M]	The Sound of Sonny	1957	400.00
—White label, blue print			
❑ RLP 12-241 [M]	The Sound of Sonny	1959	200.00
—Blue label, microphone logo at top			
❑ RLP-1124 [S]	The Sound of Sonny	1959	200.00

STEREO RECORDS

Number	Title	Yr	NM
❑ S-7017 [S]	Way Out West	1958	200.00

VERVE

Number	Title	Yr	NM
❑ V-8430 [M]	Sonny Rollins/Brass, Sonny Rollins/Trio	1962	40.00
❑ V6-8430 [S]	Sonny Rollins/Brass, Sonny Rollins/Trio	1962	30.00
❑ UMV-2555	Sonny Rollins/Brass, Sonny Rollins/Trio	198?	12.00
❑ VSP-32 [M]	Tenor Titan	1966	18.00
❑ VSPS-32 [S]	Tenor Titan	1966	15.00

ROLLINS, SONNY/JIMMY CLEVELAND

PERIOD

Number	Title	Yr	NM
❑ SPL-1204 [M]	Sonny Rollins Plays/Jimmy Cleveland Plays	1956	100.00

ROLLINS BAND, THE

1/4 STICK

Number	Title	Yr	NM
❑ 0002	Turned On	1990	18.00

IMAGO

Number	Title	Yr	NM
❑ 21034	Weight	1994	18.00

ROMAN NEW ORLEANS JAZZ BAND, THE

RCA VICTOR

Number	Title	Yr	NM
❑ LPT-3033 [10]	Around the World in Jazz -- Italy	1953	40.00

ROMANTICS, THE

NEMPEROR

Number	Title	Yr	NM
❑ BFZ38880	In Heat	1983	12.00
❑ JZ36881	National Breakout	1980	12.00
❑ FZ40106	Rhythm Romance	1985	12.00
❑ ARZ37435	Strictly Personal	1981	12.00
❑ JZ36273 [B]	The Romantics	1980	12.00

ROMEO VOID

415 RECORDS

Number	Title	Yr	NM
❑ A-0004	It's a Condition	1981	18.00
❑ A-0007 [EP]	Never Say Never	1981	30.00

COLUMBIA

Number	Title	Yr	NM
❑ ARC38182	Benefactor	1982	12.00
❑ PC38182	Benefactor	198?	10.00
—Reissue			
❑ BFC39155	Instincts	1984	12.00
❑ PC39155	Instincts	1985	10.00
—Reissue			
❑ PC38178 [EP]	Never Say Never	1982	15.00
—Reissue			

ROMEOS, THE (1)

MARK II

Number	Title	Yr	NM
❑ 1001	Precious Memories	1967	30.00

ROMERO, CESAR

TOPS

Number	Title	Yr	NM
❑ L-1631 [M]	Songs by a Latin Lover	1958	30.00

ROMERO, PEPE

MERCURY LIVING PRESENCE

Number	Title	Yr	NM
❑ SR90297 [S]	Flamenco	196?	40.00
—Maroon label, no "Vendor: Mercury Record Corporation			

ROMNEY, HUGH

WORLD PACIFIC

Number	Title	Yr	NM
❑ WP-1805 [M]	Third Stream Humor	1962	30.00
❑ ST-1805 [S]	Third Stream Humor	1962	40.00

RONDO, DON

JUBILEE

Number	Title	Yr	NM
❑ JLP-1081 [M]	Have You Met Don Rondo	195?	25.00
❑ JLP-1052 [M]	Rondo	195?	25.00

VOCALION

Number	Title	Yr	NM
❑ VL73897	Two Different Worlds	1970	15.00

RONETTES, THE

COLPIX

Number	Title	Yr	NM
❑ CP-486 [M]	The Ronettes Featuring Veronica	1965	200.00
—Gold label			
❑ CP-486 [M]	The Ronettes Featuring Veronica	1965	100.00
—Blue label			
❑ SCP-486 [S]	The Ronettes Featuring Veronica	1965	300.00
—Gold label			
❑ SCP-486 [S]	The Ronettes Featuring Veronica	1965	150.00
—Blue label			

PHILLES

Number	Title	Yr	NM
❑ PHLP-4006 [M]	Presenting the Fabulous Ronettes Featuring Veronica	1964	800.00
—Blue and black label			
❑ PHLP-4006 [M]	Presenting the Fabulous Ronettes Featuring Veronica	1964	400.00
—Yellow and red label			
❑ PHLP-ST-4006 [S]	Presenting the Fabulous Ronettes Featuring Veronica	1965	600.00
❑ T-90721 [M]	Presenting the Fabulous Ronettes Featuring Veronica	1965	250.00
—Capitol Record Club edition			
❑ ST-90721 [S]	Presenting the Fabulous Ronettes Featuring Veronica	1965	400.00
—Capitol Record Club edition			

RONEY, WALLACE

MUSE

Number	Title	Yr	NM
❑ MR-5346	Intuition	1989	15.00
❑ MR-5372	The Standard Bearer	1990	15.00
❑ MR-5335	Verses	1987	12.00

RONNIE AND THE DEADBEATS

CHECK

Number	Title	Yr	NM
❑ 103 [M]	Groovin' with Ronnie and the Deadbeats	197?	25.00

RONNIE AND THE POMONA CASUALS

DONNA

Number	Title	Yr	NM
❑ 2113 [M]	Everybody Jerk	1965	30.00

RONNY AND THE DAYTONAS

BEAT ROCKET

Number	Title	Yr	NM
❑ BR119	G.T.O.	199?	15.00
—Reissue of Mala 4001 with four bonus tracks			
❑ BR120	Sandy	199?	15.00
—Reissue of Mala 4002 with three bonus tracks			

MALA

Number	Title	Yr	NM
❑ 4001 [M]	G.T.O.	1964	120.00
❑ 4002 [M]	Sandy	1966	80.00
❑ 4002S [S]	Sandy	1966	100.00

SUNDAZED

Number	Title	Yr	NM
❑ LP5050	G.T.O. -- Best of the Mala Recordings	1997	12.00

Number	Title	Yr	NM

RONSON, MICK

RCA VICTOR
❏ APL1-0681 [B]	Play Don't Worry	1975	18.00
❏ APL1-0353 [B]	Slaughter on 10th Avenue	1974	18.00

RONSTADT, LINDA

ASYLUM
❏ 60765	Canciones De Mi Padre	1988	15.00
❏ SD5064	Don't Cry Now	1973	12.00
❏ 60474	For Sentimental Reasons	1987	12.00
❏ 60185	Get Closer	1982	12.00
❏ 7E-1092	Greatest Hits	1976	15.00
❏ 6E-106	Greatest Hits	1977	12.00
❏ 5E-516	Greatest Hits, Volume 2	1980	12.00
❏ 7E-1072	Hasten Down the Wind	1976	12.00
— Clouds" label			
❏ 7E-1072	Hasten Down the Wind	1976	18.00
— Solid blue label with white stylized "a" at top			
❏ 6E-155	Living in the U.S.A.	1978	12.00
❏ DP-401 [PD]	Living in the U.S.A.	1978	30.00
❏ 60387	Lush Life	1984	12.00
❏ 5E-510	Mad Love	1980	12.00
❏ 7E-1045	Prisoner in Disguise	1975	12.00
❏ 60489	'Round Midnight: The Nelson Riddle Sessions	1987	30.00
❏ 6E-104	Simple Dreams	1977	12.00
❏ 60260	What's New	1983	12.00

CAPITOL
❏ SKBB-11629	A Retrospective	1977	18.00
— Also includes Stone Poneys tracks			
❏ SN-16133	Beginnings	1980	10.00
❏ ST-11269	Different Drum	1974	15.00
— Also includes Stone Poneys tracks			
❏ SN-16299	Different Drum	198?	10.00
— Budget-line reissue			
❏ ST-208	Hand Sown…Home Grown	1969	25.00
— Black label with colorband			
❏ ST-208	Hand Sown…Home Grown	1970	18.00
— Green label			
❏ ST-208	Hand Sown…Home Grown	1971	15.00
— Red label			
❏ SN-16130	Hand Sown…Home Grown	1980	10.00
❏ ST-11358	Heart Like a Wheel	1974	15.00
❏ SW-11358	Heart Like a Wheel	1975	12.00
❏ SMAS-635	Linda Ronstadt	1972	15.00
❏ SN-16132	Linda Ronstadt	1980	10.00
❏ ST-407	Silk Purse	1970	18.00
— Green label			
❏ ST-407	Silk Purse	1971	15.00
— Red label			
❏ SN-16131	Silk Purse	1980	10.00
❏ ST-8-0407	Silk Purse	1970	25.00
— Capitol Record Club edition			

DCC COMPACT CLASSICS
❏ LPZ-2048	Greatest Hits	1997	80.00
— Audiophile vinyl			
❏ LPZ-2065	Greatest Hits, Volume Two	1998	40.00
— Audiophile vinyl			

ELEKTRA
❏ 60872	Cry Like a Rainstorm, Howl Like the Wind	1989	15.00

MOBILE FIDELITY
❏ 1-158	What's New	1984	50.00
— Audiophile vinyl			

NAUTILUS
❏ NR-26	Simple Dreams	1982	50.00
— Audiophile vinyl			

PAIR
❏ PDL2-1070	Prime of Life	1986	15.00
❏ PDL2-1125	Rockfile	1986	15.00

TPM/RHINO EXCLUSIVE
❏ 306	Prisoner in Disguise	2008	25.00

ROOFTOP SINGERS, THE

VANGUARD
❏ VRS-9134 [M]	Good Time	1964	18.00
❏ VSD-79134 [S]	Good Time	1964	25.00
❏ VRS-9190 [M]	Rainy River	1965	18.00
❏ VSD-79190 [S]	Rainy River	1965	25.00
❏ VRS-9123 [M]	Walk Right In	1963	18.00
❏ VSD-2136 [S]	Walk Right In	1963	25.00

ROOMFUL OF BLUES

ANTILLES
❏ 7071	Let's Have a Party!	1980	25.00

BLUE FLAME
❏ 1001	Hot Little Mama	197?	30.00

ISLAND
❏ ILPS9474	Roomful of Blues	1977	30.00

ROONEY, MICKEY

RCA VICTOR
❏ LPM-1520 [M]	Mickey Rooney Sings George M. Cohan	1957	80.00

ROS, EDMUNDO

LONDON
❏ PS114 [S]	Rhythms of the South	195?	18.00

ROSE, BIFF

BUDDAH
❏ BDS-5076	Children of Light	1971	15.00
— Reissue of Tetragrammaton 116			
❏ BDS-5078	Half Live at the Bitter End	1971	15.00
❏ BDS-5069	Ride On!	1970	15.00
❏ BDS-5075	The Thorn in Mrs. Rose's Side	1971	15.00
— Reissue of Tetragrammaton 103			

TETRAGRAMMATON
❏ T-116	Children of Light	1969	18.00
❏ T-103	The Thorn in Mrs. Rose's Side	1968	18.00

UNITED ARTISTS
❏ UAS-5594	Uncle Jesus Auntie Christ	1972	15.00

ROSE, DAVID

CAPITOL
❏ ST2853	Christmas Album	1968	18.00
❏ T2717 [M]	Holiday for Strings	1967	18.00
❏ ST2717 [S]	Holiday for Strings	1967	15.00
❏ ST-124	Something Fresh	1969	18.00
❏ T2627 [M]	The Bible	1966	15.00
❏ ST2627 [S]	The Bible	1966	18.00
❏ ST-290	The Little Drummer Boy	1969	15.00
— Reissue of 2853			

DINO
❏ DP-3001	Miracle	1972	15.00

KAPP
❏ KL-1100 [M]	Great Waltzes of the Fabulous Century	1958	25.00
❏ K-1100-S [S]	Great Waltzes of the Fabulous Century	1958	30.00
❏ KXL-5004 [M]	Songs of the Fabulous Thirties	1958	30.00
❏ KX-5004-S [S]	Songs of the Fabulous Thirties	1958	30.00
❏ KL-1205 [M]	Songs of the Fabulous Thirties, Vol. 1	1960	18.00
❏ KS-3205 [S]	Songs of the Fabulous Thirties, Vol. 1	1960	25.00
❏ KL-1206 [M]	Songs of the Fabulous Thirties, Vol. 2	1960	18.00
❏ KS-3206 [S]	Songs of the Fabulous Thirties, Vol. 2	1960	25.00
❏ KS-3010 [S]	Waltzes in Stereo	1959	30.00

LION
❏ L-70109 [M]	Magic Melodies	1959	25.00

METRO
❏ M585 [M]	Among the Stars	1966	15.00
❏ MS585 [S]	Among the Stars	1966	15.00
❏ M502 [M]	Deep Purple	1965	15.00
❏ MS502 [R]	Deep Purple	1965	15.00

MGM
❏ E-4004 [M]	21 Channel Sound	1962	18.00
❏ SE-4004 [S]	21 Channel Sound	1962	25.00
❏ E-3469 [M]	A Merry Christmas to You	1956	30.00
Yellow label			
❏ E-3469 [M]	A Merry Christmas to You	1960	18.00
— Black label			
❏ E-532 [10]	A Sentimental Journey with David Rose	1950	60.00
❏ E-3592 [M]	Autumn Leaves	1957	30.00
— Yellow label			
❏ SE-3592 [S]	Autumn Leaves	1959	30.00
— Yellow label			
❏ E-3067 [M]	Beautiful Music to Love By	1953	30.00
— Yellow label			
❏ E-3894 [M]	Box-Office Blockbusters	1961	18.00
❏ SE-3894 [S]	Box-Office Blockbusters	1961	25.00
❏ E-3952 [M]	Butterfield-8	1961	18.00
❏ SE-3952 [S]	Butterfield-8	1961	25.00
❏ E-3953 [M]	Cimarron	1961	18.00
❏ SE-3953 [S]	Cimarron	1961	25.00
❏ E-3852 [M]	Concert with a Beat!	1960	18.00
❏ SE-3852 [S]	Concert with a Beat!	1960	25.00
❏ E-3960 [M]	David Rose and His Concert Orchestra Play His Dramatic Music from the NBC-TV Series "Bonanza	1961	30.00
❏ SE-3960 [S]	David Rose and His Concert Orchestra Play His Dramatic Music from the NBC-TV Series "Bonanza	1961	40.00
❏ GAS-129	David Rose and His Orchestra (Golden Archive Series)	1970	12.00
❏ E-85 [10]	David Rose and His Orchestra Play Music of George Gershwin	1951	40.00
❏ E-3748 [M]	David Rose Plays David Rose	1959	30.00
— Yellow label			
❏ SE-3748 [S]	David Rose Plays David Rose	1959	25.00
— Yellow label			
❏ E-3640 [M]	David Rose Plays Music from "Gigi	1958	30.00
— Yellow label			
❏ SE-3640 [S]	David Rose Plays Music from "Gigi	1958	30.00
— Yellow label			
❏ E-3746 [M]	David Rose Plays the Music from "Whoop Up!	1959	25.00
— Yellow label			
❏ SE-3746 [S]	David Rose Plays the Music from "Whoop Up!	1959	30.00
— Yellow label			
❏ E-3950 [M]	Exodus	1961	18.00
❏ SE-3950 [S]	Exodus	1961	25.00
❏ E-3108 [M]	Fiddlin' for Fun	1954	30.00
— Yellow label			
❏ E-3481 [M]	Hi Fiddles	1957	30.00
— Yellow label			
❏ E-3215 [M]	Holiday for Strings	1955	30.00
— Yellow label			
❏ E-506 [10]	Holiday for Strings	1950	60.00
❏ E-3101 [M]	Let's Fall in Love	1954	30.00
— Yellow label			
❏ E-3289 [M]	Lover's Serenade	1955	30.00
— Yellow label			
❏ E-4144 [M]	Love Theme from "Cleopatra" and Music from Other Great Motion Pictures	1963	18.00
❏ SE-4144 [S]	Love Theme from "Cleopatra" and Music from Other Great Motion Pictures	1963	25.00
❏ E-3123 [M]	Love Walked In -- The Music of George Gershwin	1954	30.00
— Yellow label			
❏ E-4099 [M]	More, More, More, Music of the Stripper	1963	18.00
❏ SE-4099 [S]	More, More, More, Music of the Stripper	1963	25.00
❏ E-3612 [M]	Music from Jamaica	1957	30.00
— Yellow label			
❏ E-3397 [M]	Music from Motion Pictures	1956	30.00
— Yellow label			
❏ E-3134 [M]	Nostalgia	1954	30.00
— Yellow label			
❏ E-4285 [M]	Quick, Before It Melts and Other Selections	1965	18.00
❏ SE-4285 [S]	Quick, Before It Melts and Other Selections	1965	25.00
❏ E-3603 [M]	Reflections in the Water	1957	30.00
— Yellow label			
❏ E-3716 [M]	Secret Songs for Young Lovers	1959	25.00
— With Andre Previn; yellow label			
❏ SE-3716 [S]	Secret Songs for Young Lovers	1959	30.00
— With Andre Previn; yellow label			
❏ E-3255 [M]	Sentimental Journey	1955	30.00
— Yellow label			
❏ E-515 [10]	Serenades	1950	60.00
❏ E-3895 [M]	Spectacular Strings	1961	18.00
❏ SE-3895 [S]	Spectacular Strings	1961	25.00
❏ E-4271 [M]	The Americanization of Emily and Other Great Movie Themes	1964	18.00
❏ SE-4271 [S]	The Americanization of Emily and Other Great Movie Themes	1964	25.00
❏ E-196 [10]	The Magic Music Box	1953	40.00
❏ E-3666 [M]	The Song Is You -- Melodies of Jerome Kern	1957	30.00
— Yellow label			
❏ T-90534 [M]	The Stripper and Other Fun Songs for the Family	1965	25.00
— Capitol Record Club edition			
❏ ST-90534 [S]	The Stripper and Other Fun Songs for the Family	1965	25.00
— Capitol Record Club edition			
❏ E-4062 [M]	The Stripper and Other Fun Songs for the Family	1962	18.00
— Black label			
❏ SE-4062 [S]	The Stripper and Other Fun Songs for the Family	1962	25.00
— Black label			
❏ SE-4062 [S]	The Stripper and Other Fun Songs for the Family	1968	15.00
— Blue and gold label			
❏ E-4307 [M]	The Velvet Beat	1965	15.00
❏ SE-4307 [S]	The Velvet Beat	1965	18.00
❏ ST-90754 [S]	The Velvet Beat	1965	25.00
— Capitol Record Club edition			
❏ E-4155 [M]	The Very Best of David Rose	1963	15.00
❏ SE-4155 [S]	The Very Best of David Rose	1963	18.00
❏ E-4077 [M]	The Wonderful World of the Brothers Grimm	1962	18.00
❏ SE-4077 [S]	The Wonderful World of the Brothers Grimm	1962	25.00

ROSE, DAVID (2)

INNER CITY
❏ IC-1058	The Distance Between Dreams	197?	15.00

ROSE, TIM

CAPITOL
❏ ST-673	Love, A Kind of Hate Story	1970	15.00

Number	Title	Yr	NM

COLUMBIA
- CS9772 [B] — Thru Rose Colored Glasses — 1969 — 18.00
- CS9577 [B] — Tim Rose — 1968 — 18.00

PLAYBOY
- P-101 — Tim Rose — 1972 — 15.00

ROSE, WALLY

BLACKBIRD
- 12007 — Wally Rose on Piano — 196? — 15.00
- 12010 — Whippin' the Keys — 197? — 15.00

COLUMBIA
- CL782 [M] — Cake Walk to Lindy Hop — 1956 — 40.00
- CL2535 [10] — Honky-Tonkin' — 1955 — 30.00
— "House Party Series" reissue
- CL6260 [10] — Wally Rose — 1953 — 50.00

GOOD TIME JAZZ
- S-10034 [S] — Ragtime Classics — 1960 — 25.00
- L-12034 [M] — Ragtime Classics — 1960 — 18.00

STOMP OFF
- SOS-1057 — Wally Rose Revisited — 1982 — 12.00

ROSE

MILLENNIUM
- BXL1-7749 — Worlds Apart — 1979 — 18.00

ROSE GARDEN, THE

ATCO
- 33-225 [M] — The Rose Garden — 1968 — 60.00
- SD 33-225 [S] — The Rose Garden — 1968 — 30.00

ROSE MARIE

KAPP
- KFL-4500 [M] — Songs for Single Girls — 1964 — 30.00

ROSE ROYCE

ATLANTIC
- 81944 — Perfect Lover — 1989 — 15.00

EPIC
- FE37939 — Stronger Than Ever — 1982 — 18.00

MONTAGE
- MA110 — Music Magic — 1984 — 10.00

OMNI
- 90557 — Fresh Cut — 1987 — 15.00
- 90641 — The Best of Rose Royce — 1988 — 25.00

WHITFIELD
- WHK3512 — Golden Touch — 1980 — 18.00
- WHK3457 — Greatest Hits — 1980 — 15.00
- WHK3620 — Jump Street — 1981 — 18.00
- WH3074 — Rose Royce II/In Full Bloom — 1977 — 15.00
- WHK3227 — Rose Royce III/Strikes Again! — 1978 — 15.00
- WHS3387 — Rose Royce IV/Rainbow Connection — 1979 — 15.00

ROSELLI, JIMMY

UNITED ARTISTS
- UAS-6665 — 3 A.M. — 1968 — 15.00
- UAS-6635 — Core Napulitano — 1968 — 18.00
- UAS-6698 — Core Spezzato — 1969 — 18.00
- UAS-6775 — I'te Voglio Bene Assale — 1970 — 15.00
- UAS-6747 — It's Been Swell — 1970 — 15.00
- UXS-83 — Jimmy Roselli Superpak — 1972 — 18.00
- UAS-6724 — Let Me Sing — 1969 — 15.00
- UAL-3429 [M] — Life & Love Italian Style — 1965 — 15.00
- UAS-6429 [S] — Life & Love Italian Style — 1965 — 18.00
- UAL-3430 [M] — Mala Femmina — 1965 — 15.00
- UAS-6430 [S] — Mala Femmina — 1965 — 18.00
- UAL-3467 [M] — New York: My Port of Call — 1966 — 15.00
- UAS-6467 [S] — New York: My Port of Call — 1966 — 18.00
- UAL-3451 [M] — Saloon Songs — 1966 — 15.00
- UAS-6451 [S] — Saloon Songs — 1966 — 18.00
- UAL-3585 [M] — Saloon Songs, Vol. 2 — 1967 — 15.00
- UAS-6585 [S] — Saloon Songs, Vol. 2 — 1967 — 18.00
- UAS-5641 — Simmo 'e Napule — 1972 — 15.00
- UAL-3564 [M] — Sold Out — 1967 — 15.00
- UAS-6564 [S] — Sold Out — 1967 — 18.00
- UAS-6645 — The Best of Jimmy Roselli — 1968 — 18.00
- UAL3539 [M] — The Christmas Album — 1966 — 15.00
- UAS6539 [S] — The Christmas Album — 1966 — 18.00
- UAL-3438 [M] — The Great Ones! — 1965 — 15.00
- UAS-6438 [S] — The Great Ones! — 1965 — 18.00
- UAL-3544 [M] — The Italian Album — 1966 — 15.00
- UAS-6544 [S] — The Italian Album — 1966 — 18.00
- UAL-3611 [M] — There Must Be a Way — 1967 — 18.00
- UAS-6611 [S] — There Must Be a Way — 1967 — 18.00

ROSEWOMAN, MICHELE

ENJA
- R1-79607 — Contrast High — 1990 — 18.00

SOUL NOTE
- SN-1072 — The Source — 1984 — 15.00

ROSIE AND THE ORIGINALS

BRUNSWICK
- BL54102 [M] — Lonely Blue Nights with Rosie — 1961 — 150.00
- BL754102 [S] — Lonely Blue Nights with Rosie — 1961 — 200.00

ROSIE O'GRADY'S GOOD TIME BAND

DIRECT DISK
- DD-103 — Dixieland — 1979 — 25.00
— Audiophile recording

ROSNES, RENEE

BLUE NOTE
- B1-93561 — Renee Rosnes — 1990 — 18.00

ROSOLINO, FRANK

BETHLEHEM
- BCP-26 [M] — I Play Trombone — 1955 — 120.00

CAPITOL
- T6509 [M] — Frankly Speaking — 1955 — 100.00
- H6507 [10] — Frank Rosolino — 1954 — 150.00
- T6507 [M] — Frank Rosolino — 1955 — 100.00

INTERLUDE
- MO-500 [M] — The Legend of Frank Rosolino — 1959 — 80.00
- ST-1000 [S] — The Legend of Frank Rosolino — 1959 — 60.00

MODE
- LP-107 [M] — Frank Rosolino Quintet — 1957 — 150.00

REPRISE
- R-6016 [M] — Turn Me Loose — 1961 — 60.00
- R9-6016 [S] — Turn Me Loose — 1961 — 80.00

SACKVILLE
- 2014 — Thinking About You — 198? — 25.00

SPECIALTY
- SPS-2161 — Free for All — 1974 — 40.00

ROSS, ANNIE; DOROTHY DUNN; SHELBY DAVIS

SAVOY
- MG-12060 [M] — Singin' 'N Swingin' — 1956 — 60.00

ROSS, ANNIE

DECCA
- DL4922 [M] — Fill My Heart with Song — 1967 — 40.00
- DL74922 [S] — Fill My Heart with Song — 1967 — 30.00

KIMBERLY
- 2018 [M] — Annie Ross Sings A Song With Mulligan! — 1963 — 40.00
- 11018 [S] — Annie Ross Sings A Song With Mulligan! — 1963 — 40.00

WORLD PACIFIC
- WP-1285 [M] — A Gasser! — 1960 — 80.00
- ST-1285 [S] — A Gasser! — 1960 — 60.00
- WP-1253 [M] — Annie Ross Sings A Song With Mulligan! — 1959 — 70.00
- ST-1020 [S] — Annie Ross Sings A Song With Mulligan! — 1959 — 60.00
- WP-1808 [M] — Gypsy — 1959 — 80.00
- ST-1028 [S] — Gypsy — 1959 — 60.00

ROSS, ARNOLD

DISCOVERY
- DL-2006 [M] — Arnold Ross — 1954 — 50.00

MERCURY
- MGC-134 [10] — Arnold Ross — 1952 — 150.00

ROSS, CHARLIE

ACCORD
- SN-7007 — High Cost of Loving — 1982 — 12.00

ROSS, DIANA, AND MARVIN GAYE

MOTOWN
- M7-803 [B] — Diana & Marvin — 1973 — 25.00
- M5-124V1 — Diana & Marvin — 1981 — 10.00
— Reissue

ROSS, DIANA

MOTOWN
- M13-960C2 — All the Great Hits — 1981 — 15.00
- M7-877R2 — An Evening with Diana Ross — 1977 — 18.00
- M7-890R1 — Baby It's Me — 1977 — 15.00
- M8-936 — Diana — 1980 — 12.00
- MS-719 — Diana! — 1971 — 18.00
- M5-155V1 — Diana! — 1981 — 10.00
— Reissue of 719
- MS-711 — Diana Ross — 1970 — 18.00
- M6-861S1 — Diana Ross — 1976 — 15.00
- M5-135V1 — Diana Ross — 1981 — 10.00
— Reissue of 711
- 5294ML — Diana Ross — 1983 — 10.00
— Reissue of 861
- 6049ML2 — Diana Ross Anthology — 1983 — 18.00
- M6-869S1 — Diana Ross' Greatest Hits — 1976 — 15.00
- M6-801S1 — Diana Ross Live at Caesars Palace — 1974 — 15.00
- M5-169V1 — Diana Ross Live at Caesars Palace — 1981 — 10.00
— Reissue of 801
- M5-214V1 — Duets with Diana — 1981 — 12.00
- MS-724 — Everything Is Everything — 1970 — 18.00
- M-758D — Lady Sings the Blues — 1972 — 18.00
— With booklet; all but four tracks are by Diana Ross
- M7-812V1 — Last Time I Saw Him — 1974 — 15.00
- M7-907R1 — Ross — 1978 — 15.00
- MS-723 — Surrender — 1971 — 18.00
- M8-923M1 — The Boss — 1979 — 12.00
- M5-198V1 — The Boss — 1981 — 10.00
— Reissue of 923
- 37463-6377-1 — The Remixes — 1994 — 15.00
- M8-951M1 — To Love Again — 1981 — 12.00
- M-772L — Touch Me in the Morning — 1973 — 18.00
- M5-163V1 — Touch Me in the Morning — 1981 — 10.00
— Reissue of 772
- MOT-6274 — Workin' Overtime — 1989 — 12.00

NAUTILUS
- NR-37 [B] — Diana — 1981 — 40.00
— Audiophile vinyl

RCA VICTOR
- AFL1-5422 — Eaten Alive — 1985 — 10.00
- 6388-1-R — Red Hot Rhythm and Blues — 1987 — 10.00
- AFL1-4677 — Ross — 1983 — 10.00
- AFL1-4384 — Silk Electric — 1982 — 12.00
- AFL1-5009 — Swept Away — 1984 — 10.00
- AFL1-4153 — Why Do Fools Fall in Love — 1981 — 12.00

ROSS, JACK

DOT
- DLP-3429 [M] — Cinderella — 1962 — 25.00
- DLP-25429 [S] — Cinderella — 1962 — 30.00

ROSS, JACKIE

CHESS
- LP-1489 [M] — In Full Bloom — 1966 — 30.00
- LPS-1489 [S] — In Full Bloom — 1966 — 40.00

ROSS, JERIS

ABC DOT
- DOSD-2046 — Jeris Ross — 1976 — 15.00

ROSS, JOE E.

ROULETTE
- R-25281 [M] — Love Songs from a Cop — 1965 — 30.00
- SR-25281 [S] — Love Songs from a Cop — 1965 — 30.00

ROSS, RONNIE

ATLANTIC
- 1333 [M] — The Jazz Makers — 1960 — 30.00
- SD1333 [S] — The Jazz Makers — 1960 — 40.00

ROSS, SPENCER

COLUMBIA
- CL1525 [M] — Spencer Ross and His Orchestra — 1960 — 25.00
- CS0(# unknown) [S] — Spencer Ross and His Orchestra — 1960 — 30.00

ROSS, STAN

DEL-FI
- DFLP-1233 [M] — My Son the Copy Cat — 1963 — 30.00
- DFST-1233 [S] — My Son the Copy Cat — 1963 — 40.00

ROSS-LEVINE BAND, THE

HEADFIRST
- 9701 — That Summer Something — 198? — 15.00

ROTARY CONNECTION

CADET
- CS-50006 [B] — Hey Love — 1971 — 30.00

CADET CONCEPT
- LPS-317 — Aladdin — 1968 — 30.00
- LSP-328 [B] — Dinner Music — 1970 — 30.00
- LPS318 [B] — Peace — 1969 — 30.00
- LP-312 [M] — Rotary Connection — 1968 — 80.00
— Mono appears to be promo only
- LPS-312 [S] — Rotary Connection — 1968 — 30.00
- LPS-322 [B] — Songs — 1969 — 30.00

ROTH, DAVID LEE

WARNER BROS.
- 26471 — A Little Ain't Enough — 1991 — 18.00
- 25470 — Eat 'Em and Smile — 1986 — 10.00
- 25671 — Skyscraper — 1988 — 10.00

ROTH, LILLIAN

EPIC
- LN3206 [M] — I'll Cry Tomorrow — 1957 — 30.00

TOPS
- L-1567 [M] — Lillian Roth Sings — 1958 — 30.00

ROUND, JONATHAN

WESTBOUND
- 2009 — Jonathan Round — 1971 — 30.00
— Round cover
- 2009 [B] — Jonathan Round — 1972 — 25.00
— Square cover

ROUND ROBIN

CHALLENGE
- LP-620 [M] — The Land of 1,000 Dances — 1965 — 30.00

Number	Title	Yr	NM
DOMAIN			
❏ 101 [M]	Greatest Dance Hits Slauson Style	1964	40.00
ROUSE, CHARLIE, AND PAUL QUINICHETTE			
BETHLEHEM			
❏ BCP-6021 [M]	The Chase Is On	1958	50.00
ROUSE, CHARLIE			
BLUE NOTE			
❏ BLP-4119 [M]	Bossa Nova Bacchanal	1962	30.00
❏ BST-84119 [S]	Bossa Nova Bacchanal	1962	40.00
— With "New York, USA" address on label			
❏ BST-84119 [S]	Bossa Nova Bacchanal	196?	25.00
— With "A Division of Liberty Records" on label			
DOUGLAS			
❏ 7044	Cinnamon Flower	197?	18.00
EPIC			
❏ LA16018 [M]	We Paid Our Dues	1961	40.00
❏ BA17018 [S]	We Paid Our Dues	1961	50.00
❏ LA16012 [M]	Yeah!	1960	500.00
❏ BA17012 [M]	Yeah!	1960	50.00
❏ BA17012 [S]	Yeah!	199?	30.00
— Classic Records reissue on audiophile vinyl			
FANTASY			
❏ OJC-491	Takin' Care of Business	1991	15.00
JAZZLAND			
❏ JLP-19 [M]	Takin' Care of Business	1960	40.00
❏ JLP-919 [S]	Takin' Care of Business	1960	50.00
LANDMARK			
❏ LLP-1521	Epistrophy	1989	15.00
STORYVILLE			
❏ 4079	Moment's Notice	198?	12.00
STRATA-EAST			
❏ SES-19746	Two Is One	1974	30.00
ROUTERS, THE			
WARNER BROS.			
❏ W1524 [M]	1963's Great Instrumental Hits	1964	30.00
❏ WS1524 [S]	1963's Great Instrumental Hits	1964	40.00
❏ W1559 [M]	Charge!	1964	30.00
❏ WS1559 [S]	Charge!	1964	30.00
❏ W1595 [M]	Go Go Go with the Chuck Berry Songbook	1965	25.00
❏ WS1595 [S]	Go Go Go with the Chuck Berry Songbook	1965	30.00
❏ W1490 [M]	Let's Go! with the Routers	1963	40.00
❏ WS1490 [S]	Let's Go! with the Routers	1963	50.00
ROVERS, THE			
CLEVELAND INT'L.			
❏ FE37706	Pain In My Past	1982	12.00
❏ JE37107	Wasn't That a Party	1981	12.00
ROWLAND, DAVE			
ELEKTRA			
❏ 5E-525	Pleasure	1981	10.00
— As "Dave Rowland and Sugar"			
❏ 60011	Sugar Free	1982	10.00
ROWLES, JIMMY, AND GEORGE MRAZ			
PROGRESSIVE			
❏ PRO-7009	Music's the Only Thing on My Mind	1981	18.00
ROWLES, JIMMY			
ANDEX			
❏ A-3007 [M]	Weather in a Jazz Vane	1958	50.00
❏ AS-3007 [S]	Weather in a Jazz Vane	1958	40.00
CAPITOL			
❏ T1831 [M]	Kinda Groovy!	1963	30.00
❏ ST1831 [S]	Kinda Groovy!	1963	40.00
CHOICE			
❏ CRS1014	Grandpaws	1976	25.00
❏ CRS1023	Paws That Refresh	1979	18.00
COLUMBIA			
❏ FC37639	Jimmy Rowles Plays Duke Ellington and Billy Strayhorn	1981	18.00
❏ JC34873	Peacocks	1979	18.00
CONTEMPORARY			
❏ C-14032	I'm Glad There Is You	1988	15.00
❏ C-14016	Jimmy Rowles/Red Mitchell Trio	1986	15.00
HALCYON			
❏ HAL110	Special Magic	197?	12.00
INTERLUDE			
❏ MO-515 [M]	Upper Classmen	1959	60.00
❏ ST-1015 [S]	Upper Classmen	1959	40.00
JAZZZ			
❏ 103	Jazz Is a Fleeting Moment	1976	30.00
LIBERTY			
❏ LRP-3003 [M]	Rare -- But Well Done	1955	150.00

Number	Title	Yr	NM
SIGNATURE			
❏ SM-6011 [M]	Fiorello Uptown, Mary Sunshine Downtown	1960	120.00
❏ SS-6011 [S]	Fiorello Uptown, Mary Sunshine Downtown	1960	150.00
STASH			
❏ ST-227	Peacocks	198?	12.00
TAMPA			
❏ TP-8 [M]	Let's Get Acquainted with Jazz… For People Who Hate Jazz	1957	250.00
— Colored vinyl			
❏ TP-8 [M]	Let's Get Acquainted with Jazz… For People Who Hate Jazz	1958	150.00
❏ TPS-8 [S]	Let's Get Acquainted with Jazz… For People Who Hate Jazz	1958	80.00
XANADU			
❏ 157	Make Such Beautiful Music Together	1980	18.00
ROXETTE			
CAPITOL			
❏ MLP-15018 [EP]	Heartland	1984	40.00
EMI			
❏ E1-91098	Look Sharp!	1989	18.00
ROXY MUSIC			
ATCO			
❏ SD 36-106 [B]	Country Life	1975	30.00
— Original cover shows two semi-naked women on a grassy background			
❏ SD 36-106A	Country Life	1975	12.00
— Revised cover deletes women, leaves only the grassy background			
❏ SD 32-102	Flesh + Blood	1980	12.00
❏ SD 36-134	For Your Pleasure	1975	15.00
— Reissue of Warner Bros. BS 2696; originals have yellow labels			
❏ SD 38-103	Greatest Hits	1977	12.00
❏ SD 38-114	Manifesto	1979	12.00
❏ SD 38-114 [PD]	Manifesto	1979	30.00
— Picture disc			
❏ SD 36-127	Siren	1975	12.00
— Originals have yellow labels			
❏ SD7045	Stranded	1974	15.00
❏ 90122	The Atlantic Years (1973-80)	1983	12.00
❏ SD 36-133 [B]	The First Roxy Music Album	1975	15.00
— Reissue of Reprise MS 2114; originals have yellow labels			
❏ SD 36-139	Viva! Roxy Music (Live)	1976	12.00
— Originals have yellow labels			
REPRISE			
❏ MS2114 [B]	Roxy Music	1972	35.00
❏ 25857	Street Life: 20 Greatest Hits	1989	18.00
— By "Bryan Ferry & Roxy Music"			
WARNER BROS.			
❏ 23686	Avalon	1982	12.00
❏ BS2696	For Your Pleasure	1973	30.00
❏ 23808 [EP]	Musique -- The High Road	1983	10.00
ROYAL, BILLY JOE			
ATLANTIC AMERICA			
❏ 90508	Looking Ahead	1986	12.00
❏ 91064	Tell It Like It Is	1989	12.00
❏ 90658	The Royal Treatment	1987	12.00
COLUMBIA			
❏ CL2781 [M]	Billy Joe Royal	1967	30.00
❏ CS9581 [S]	Billy Joe Royal	1967	30.00
❏ CS9974	Cherry Hill Park	1969	30.00
❏ CL2403 [M]	Down in the Boondocks	1965	25.00
❏ CS9203 [S]	Down in the Boondocks	1965	30.00
KAT FAMILY			
❏ JW37342	Billy Joe Royal	1982	12.00
MERCURY			
❏ SRM-1-3837	Billy Joe Royal	1980	12.00
ROYAL, ERNIE			
URANIA			
❏ UJLP-1203 [M]	Accent on Trumpet	1955	50.00
ROYAL, MARSHALL			
CONCORD JAZZ			
❏ CJ-88	First Chair	1979	12.00
❏ CJ-125	Royal Blue	1980	12.00
EVEREST			
❏ LPBR-5087 [M]	Gordon Jenkins Presents Marshall Royal	1960	30.00
❏ SDBR-1087 [S]	Gordon Jenkins Presents Marshall Royal	1960	30.00
ROYAL GUARDSMEN, THE			
HOLIDAY			
❏ HDY1913	Merry Snoopy's Christmas	1980	12.00
— Reissue of Laurie 2042			
LAURIE			
❏ LLP2042 [M]	Snoopy and His Friends	1967	50.00

Number	Title	Yr	NM
— With "Merry Snoopy's Christmas" poster still attached to back cover			
❏ LLP2042 [M]	Snoopy and His Friends	1967	40.00
— With "Merry Snoopy's Christmas" poster missing			
❏ SLP2042 [S]	Snoopy and His Friends	1967	30.00
— With "Merry Snoopy's Christmas" poster still attached to back cover			
❏ SLP2042 [S]	Snoopy and His Friends	1967	25.00
— With "Merry Snoopy's Christmas" poster missing			
❏ SLP-2046	Snoopy for President	1968	30.00
❏ LLP-2038 [M]	Snoopy vs. the Red Baron	1967	40.00
❏ SLP-2038 [S]	Snoopy vs. the Red Baron	1967	30.00
❏ LLP-2039 [M]	The Return of the Red Baron	1967	50.00
❏ SLP-2039 [S]	The Return of the Red Baron	1967	30.00
ROYAL OPERA HOUSE ORCHESTRA (ALEXANDER GIBSON, CONDUCTOR)			
RCA VICTOR RED SEAL			
❏ LSC-2449 [S]	Gounod: Ballet Music of Faust; Bizet: Carmen	1960	1000.00
— Original with "shaded dog" label			
❏ LSC-2449 [S]	Gounod: Ballet Music of Faust; Bizet: Carmen	199?	30.00
— Classic Records reissue			
ROYAL PHILHARMONIC ORCHESTRA (RENE LEIBOWITZ, CONDUCTOR)			
RCA VICTOR RED SEAL			
❏ VCS-2659 [S]	The Power of the Orchestra	1962	300.00
— Original with "shaded dog" label			
ROYAL PLAYBOYS, THE			
WALDORF			
❏ 33-136 [10]	Rock and Roll/New Orleans Blues	195?	500.00
ROYAL TEENS, THE			
COLLECTABLES			
❏ COL-5094	Short Shorts: Golden Classics	198?	12.00
MUSICOR			
❏ MS-3186	Newies But Oldies	1970	25.00
TRU-GEMS			
❏ 1001	Short Shorts & Others	1975	25.00
ROYALETTES, THE			
MGM			
❏ E-4332 [M]	It's Gonna Take a Miracle	1965	25.00
❏ SE-4332 [S]	It's Gonna Take a Miracle	1965	30.00
❏ E-4366 [M]	The Elegant Sound of the Royalettes	1966	25.00
❏ SE-4366 [S]	The Elegant Sound of the Royalettes	1966	30.00
ROYALS, THE (1)			
FEDERAL			
❏ 567	The Best of the Royals	197?	18.00
— This is a bootleg album			
RUBBER BAND, THE (2)			
GRT			
❏ 10015	Beatles Songbook	1969	30.00
❏ 10000	Cream Songbook	1969	30.00
❏ 10007	Hendrix Songbook	1969	30.00
RUBBER CITY REBELS			
CAPITOL			
❏ ST-12100 [B]	Rubber City Rebels	1980	50.00
RUBBER MEMORY			
R.P.C.			
❏ 69401	Welcome	196?	1000.00
RUBEN AND THE JETS			
MERCURY			
❏ SRM-1-694 [B]	Con Safos	1974	30.00
❏ SRM-1-659 [B]	For Real	1973	35.00
RUBENSTEIN, ARTUR			
RCA VICTOR RED SEAL			
❏ LSC-2120 [S]	Beethoven: Piano Concerto No. 1	1959	30.00
— With Josef Krips/NBC "Symphony of the Air" Orchestra; original with "shaded dog" label			
❏ LSC-2121 [S]	Beethoven: Piano Concerto No. 2	1959	25.00
— With Josef Krips/NBC "Symphony of the Air" Orchestra; original with "shaded dog" label			
❏ LSC-2122 [S]	Beethoven: Piano Concerto No. 3	1959	25.00
— With Josef Krips/NBC "Symphony of the Air" Orchestra; original with "shaded dog" label			
❏ LSC-2123 [S]	Beethoven: Piano Concerto No. 4	1959	25.00
— With Josef Krips/NBC "Symphony of the Air" Orchestra; original with "shaded dog" label			

Number	Title	Yr	NM
❑ LSC-2124 [S]	Beethoven: Piano Concerto No. 5	1959	25.00
—With Josef Krips/NBC "Symphony of the Air" Orchestra; original with "shaded dog" label			
❑ LSC-1831 [S]	Brahms: Piano Concerto No. 1	199?	30.00
—With the Chicago Symphony (Fritz Reiner cond.); Classic Records issue; this album is not known to have been issued in stereo before this			
❑ LSC-2296 [S]	Brahms: Piano Concerto No. 2	1959	25.00
—With Josef Krips/RCA Victor Symphony Orchestra; original with "shaded dog" label			
❑ LSC-2459 [S]	Brahms: Piano Sonata in F; Intermezzo; Romance	1961	40.00
—Original with "shaded dog" label			
❑ LSC-2370 [S]	Chopin: Ballades 1-4	1960	25.00
—Original with "shaded dog" label			
❑ LDS-2554 [S]	Chopin: Piano Sonatas No. 2 and 3	1961	30.00
—Original with "shaded dog" label			
❑ LSC-2368 [S]	Chopin: Scherzos 1-4	1960	25.00
—Original with "shaded dog" label			
❑ LSC-2566 [S]	Grieg: Piano Concerto	1962	25.00
—Original with "shaded dog" label			
❑ LSC-2429 [S]	Grieg: Piano Concerto in A; Lizst: Piano Concerto No. 1	1960	30.00
—Original with "shaded dog" label			
❑ LSC-2636 [S]	Mozart: Piano Concerto No. 17; Schubert: Impromptus	1962	40.00
—Original with "shaded dog" label			
❑ LSC-2068 [S]	Rachmaninoff: Piano Concerto No. 2; Lizst: Piano Conceto No. 1	1958	30.00
—Original with "shaded dog" label			
❑ LSC-2430 [S]	Rachmaninoff: Rhapsody on a Theme of Paganini	1960	25.00
—With Fritz Reiner/Chicago Symphony Orchestra; original with "shaded dog" label			
❑ LSC-2430 [S]	Rachmaninoff: Rhapsody on a Theme of Paganini	199?	30.00
—With Fritz Reiner/Chicago Symphony Orchestra; Classic Records reissue			
❑ LSC-2605 [S]	Rubenstein at Carnegie Hall	1962	25.00
—Original with "shaded dog" label			
❑ LSC-2234 [S]	Saint-Saens: Piano Concerto No. 2	1959	25.00
—With the Symphony of the Air Orchestra (Alfred Wallenstein, conductor); original with "shaded dog" label			
❑ LSC-2234 [S]	Saint-Saens: Piano Concerto No. 2	199?	30.00
—With the Symphony of the Air Orchestra (Alfred Wallenstein, conductor); Classic Records reissue			
❑ LSC-2256 [S]	Schubert: Piano Concerto in A	1959	25.00
—With Josef Krips/RCA Victor Symphony Orchestra; original with "shaded dog" label			
❑ LSC-2265 [S]	The Rubenstein Story	1959	30.00
—With Alfred Wallerstein/NBC Symphony Orchestra; original with "shaded dog" label and gatefold cover			

RUBETTES

STATE
❑ MCA-2193 [B]	Rubettes	1976	18.00

RUBIN, STAN

CORAL
❑ CRL57185 [M]	Dixieland Goes Broadway	1959	30.00
❑ CRL757185 [S]	Dixieland Goes Broadway	1959	30.00

JUBLIEE
❑ JLP-1003 [M]	College Jazz Comes to Carnegie Hall	1955	40.00
❑ JLP-1024 [M]	Stan Rubin in Morocco	1956	40.00
❑ JLP-1001 [M]	The College All Stars at Carnegie Hall	1955	40.00
❑ JLP-4 [10]	The Tigertown Five, Vol. 1	1954	50.00
❑ JLP-5 [10]	The Tigertown Five, Vol. 2	1954	50.00
❑ JLP-6 [10]	The Tigertown Five, Vol. 3	1954	50.00
❑ JLP-1016 [M]	Tigertown Five	1956	40.00

PRINCETON
❑ LP-102 [10]	The Stan Rubin Tigertown Five	1954	60.00

RCA VICTOR
❑ LPM-1200 [M]	Dixieland Bash	1956	40.00
❑ LPM-3277 [10]	Stan Rubin's Dixieland Comes to Carnegie Hall	1955	50.00

RUDD, ROSWELL, AND STEVE LACY

SOUL NOTE
❑ SN-1054	Regeneration	1982	15.00

RUDD, ROSWELL

ABC IMPULSE!
❑ AS-9126 [S]	Everywhere	1968	18.00

ARISTA/FREEDOM
❑ AF1006	Flexible Flyer	1975	15.00
❑ AF1029	Inside Job	1976	15.00

IMPULSE!
❑ A-9126 [M]	Everywhere	1967	30.00
❑ AS-9126 [S]	Everywhere	1967	30.00

JCOA
❑ 1007	The Numatik String Band	197?	18.00

RUEDEBUSCH, DICK

ASCOT
❑ AM-13017 [M]	Dick Ruedebusch	1964	15.00
❑ AS-16017 [S]	Dick Ruedebusch	1964	18.00

JUBILEE
❑ JGS-5015 [S]	Dick Ruedebusch Remembers the Greats	1962	25.00
❑ JGM-5015 [M]	Dick Ruedebusch Remembers the Greats	1962	18.00
❑ JGS-5008 [S]	Meet Mr. Trumpet	1962	25.00
❑ JGM-5008 [M]	Meet Mr. Trumpet	1962	18.00
❑ JGS-5021 [S]	Mr. Trumpet, Volume 2	1963	25.00
❑ JGM-5021 [M]	Mr. Trumpet, Volume 2	1963	18.00

RUFF, WILLIE

COLUMBIA
❑ CS9603	The Smooth Side of Willie Ruff	1968	25.00
—Red "360 Sound" label			

RUFFIN, DAVID

MOTOWN
❑ M7-895	At His Best	1978	15.00
❑ M5-211V1	At His Best	1981	10.00
—Reissue			
❑ M-762	David Ruffin	1973	15.00
❑ M6-866	Everything's Coming Up Love	1976	15.00
❑ MS-696	Feelin' Good	1969	18.00
❑ M6-885	In My Stride	1977	15.00
❑ M6-818	Me 'N' Rock 'N' Roll Are Here to Stay	1974	15.00
❑ MS-685	My Whole World Ended	1969	25.00
❑ M5-146V1	My Whole World Ended	1981	10.00
—Reissue			
❑ M6-849	Who I Am	1975	15.00

WARNER BROS.
❑ BSK3416	Gentleman Ruffin	1980	12.00
❑ BSK3306	So Soon We Change	1979	12.00

RUFFIN, JIMMY

RSO
❑ RS-1-3078	Sunrise	1980	12.00

SOUL
❑ S-708	Ruff'n Ready	1969	30.00
❑ SS-727	The Groove Governor	1970	25.00
❑ 704 [M]	Top Ten	1967	50.00
—One-color cover			
❑ 704 [M]	Top Ten	1967	30.00
—Full-color cover			
❑ S-704 [S]	Top Ten	1967	30.00

RUFFIN, JIMMY AND DAVID

MOTOWN
❑ M5-108V1	Motown Superstar Series, Vol. 8	1981	12.00

SOUL
❑ SS-728	I Am My Brother's Keeper	1970	25.00

RUFUS

ABC
❑ D-975	Ask Rufus	1977	12.00
❑ AA-1098	Numbers	1979	12.00
❑ AA-1098 [PD]	Numbers	1979	25.00
—Promo-only picture disc			
❑ X-809	Rags to Rufus	1974	12.00
❑ X-783	Rufus	1973	12.00
❑ D-909	Rufus Featuring Chaka Khan	1975	12.00
❑ D-837	Rufusized	1974	12.00
❑ AA-1049	Street Player	1978	12.00
❑ AA-1049 [PD]	Street Player	1978	30.00
—Promo-only picture disc			

COMMAND
❑ CQD-40024 [Q]	Rags to Rufus	1974	25.00
❑ CQD-40023 [Q]	Rufusized	1974	25.00
❑ 5270	Camouflage	1982	12.00
❑ 5103	Masterjam	1979	12.00
❑ 5159	Party 'Til You're Broke	1981	12.00
❑ 5339	The Very Best of Rufus	1983	12.00

WARNER BROS.
❑ 23679	Live: Stompin' at the Savoy	1983	15.00
❑ 23753	Seal in Red	1984	12.00

RUFUS AND CARLA

STAX
❑ STX-4124	Chronicle	1979	18.00

RUGBYS, THE

AMAZON
❑ 1000	Hot Cargo	1970	25.00

RUMBLERS, THE

DOT
❑ DLP-3509 [M]	Boss!	1963	50.00
❑ DLP-25509 [S]	Boss!	1963	60.00

DOWNEY
❑ DLP-1001 [M]	Boss!	1963	180.00
❑ DLPS-1001 [S]	Boss!	1963	250.00

RUMMEL, JACK

STOMP OFF
❑ SOS-1118	Back to Ragtime	1986	12.00

RUMOUR, THE

ARISTA
❑ AL4235	Frogs, Sprouts, Clogs & Krauts	1979	15.00

HANNIBAL
❑ 1305	Purity of Essence	1981	18.00

MERCURY
❑ SRM-1-1174	Max	1977	18.00

RUMPLESTILTSKIN

BELL
❑ 6047	Rumpelstiltskin	1970	30.00

RUMSEY, HOWARD

CONTEMPORARY
❑ C-2506 [10]	Howard Rumsey's Lighthouse All-Stars	1953	120.00
❑ C-3508 [M]	Howard Rumsey's Lighthouse All-Stars, Vol. 3	1955	80.00
❑ C-3520 [M]	Howard Rumsey's Lighthouse All-Stars, Vol. 4: Oboe/Flute	1956	80.00
❑ C-3504 [M]	Howard Rumsey's Lighthouse All-Stars, Vol. 6	1955	80.00
❑ C-2513 [10]	Howard Rumsey's Lighthouse All-Stars, Volume 1: The Quintet	1954	120.00
❑ C-2515 [10]	Howard Rumsey's Lighthouse All-Stars, Volume 2: The Octet	1954	120.00
❑ C-2510 [10]	Howard Rumsey's Lighthouse All-Stars, Volume 4	1954	120.00
❑ C-3517 [M]	In the Solo Spotlight	1956	80.00
❑ C-14051	Jazz Invention	1989	15.00
❑ C-3509 [M]	Lighthouse at Laguna	1955	80.00
❑ C-3528 [M]	Music for Lighthousekeeping	1957	80.00
❑ S-7008 [S]	Music for Lighthousekeeping	1959	50.00
❑ C-2501 [10]	Sunday Jazz a la Lighthouse	1953	120.00
❑ C-3501 [M]	Sunday Jazz a la Lighthouse	1955	80.00

FANTASY
❑ OJC-266	Howard Rumsey's Lighthouse All-Stars, Vol. 3	198?	12.00
❑ OJC-154	Howard Rumsey's Lighthouse All-Stars, Vol. 4: Oboe/Flute	198?	12.00
❑ OJC-386	Howard Rumsey's Lighthouse All-Stars, Vol. 6	1989	12.00
❑ OJC-451	In the Solo Spotlight	1990	15.00
❑ OJC-406	Lighthouse at Laguna	1989	12.00
❑ OJC-151	Sunday Jazz a la Lighthouse	198?	12.00

LIBERTY
❑ LRP-3045 [M]	Double or Nothin'	1957	50.00
❑ LST-7014 [S]	Double or Nothin'	1959	40.00

LIGHTHOUSE
❑ LP-300 [M]	Jazz Rolls-Royce	1958	40.00
❑ LP-301 [M]	Sunday Jazz a la Lighthouse	1958	40.00
—Red vinyl			

OMEGA
❑ OML-5 [M]	Jazz Rolls-Royce	1960	30.00
❑ OSL-5 [S]	Jazz Rolls-Royce	1960	30.00

PHILIPS
❑ PHM200012 [M]	Jazz Structures	1961	25.00
❑ PHS600012 [S]	Jazz Structures	1961	30.00

STEREO RECORDS
❑ S-7008 [S]	Music for Lighthousekeeping	1958	70.00

RUN-D.M.C.

ARISTA
❑ 16400	Crown Royal	2001	18.00

PROFILE
❑ PRO-1401 [B]	Back from Hell	1990	18.00
❑ PRO-1205	King of Rock	1985	15.00
❑ PRO-1217	Raising Hell	1986	15.00
❑ PRO-1202	Run-D.M.C.	1984	15.00
❑ PRO-1419	Together Forever: Greatest Hits 1983-1991	1991	18.00
❑ PRO-1265	Tougher Than Leather	1988	15.00

RUNAWAYS, THE

MARILYN
❑ USM1004 [B]	Born to Be Bad	1991	30.00

MERCURY
❑ SRM-1-3740 [B]	Live in Japan	1978	60.00
❑ SRM-1-1126	Queens of Noise	1977	30.00
❑ SRM-1-1090	The Runaways	1976	30.00
❑ SRM-1-3705	Waiting for the Night	1977	30.00

RHINO
❑ RNDF-250 [PD]	Little Lost Girls	1982	30.00
❑ RNLP-70861	Little Lost Girls	1987	15.00
—Reissue of Rhino 250 on regular vinyl			
❑ RNEP-602 [EP]	Mama Weer All Crazee Now	1983	18.00

RUNDGREN, TODD

AMPEX

Number	Title	Yr	NM
❑ A-10105	Runt	1970	150.00
—LP jacket and label list 10 tracks, but the album has 12			
❑ A-10105 [B]	Runt	1970	120.00
—LP jacket and label list 10 tracks, but the album has 11			
❑ A-10105 [B]	Runt	1970	60.00
—LP jacket and label list 10 tracks and album actually has 10			

BEARSVILLE

Number	Title	Yr	NM
❑ BR2133	A Wizard/A True Star	1973	15.00
❑ 2BRX6986	Back to the Bars	1978	15.00
❑ BR6963	Faithful	1976	12.00
❑ BHS3522	Healing	1981	12.00
—Add $5 if bonus 7-inch 33 1/3 single (Time Heals/Tiny Demons) is included			
❑ BRK6981	Hermit of Mink Hollow	1978	12.00
❑ PRO597 [DJ]	Ikon/Todd Rundgren Interview	1974	100.00
❑ BR6957	Initiation	1975	12.00
❑ A-10105	Runt	1971	30.00
—Reissue with new label			
❑ BR2046	Runt	1972	18.00
—Another reissue, after switch from Ampex to Warner Bros. distribution			
❑ 2BX2066	Something/Anything?	1972	30.00
—Regular copy with black vinyl			
❑ 2BX2066	Something/Anything?	1972	200.00
—White label with one record on red vinyl and the other on blue vinyl			
❑ A-10116 [B]	The Ballad of Todd Rundgren	1971	100.00
❑ BR2047	The Ballad of Todd Rundgren	1972	18.00
—Reissue of 10116			
❑ 23732	The Ever Popular Tortured Artist Effect	1983	12.00
❑ PRO524 [DJ]	The Todd Rundgren Radio Show	1972	150.00
❑ 2BR6952	Todd	1974	18.00
❑ PRO-A-788 [DJ]	Todd Rundgren Radio Sampler	1978	50.00
—Highlights of "Back to the Bars" plus interview of Todd by Patti Smith			

MOBILE FIDELITY

Number	Title	Yr	NM
❑ 2-225	Something/Anything?	1995	40.00
—Audiophile vinyl			

RHINO

Number	Title	Yr	NM
❑ R1-71491	Anthology (1968-1985)	1989	25.00
❑ RNLP70864	A Wizard/A True Star	1987	12.00
❑ RNDA71109	Back to the Bars	1987	15.00
❑ RNLP70868	Faithful	1987	12.00
❑ RNLP70874	Healing	1987	12.00
❑ RNLP70871	Hermit of Mink Hollow	1988	12.00
❑ RNLP70866	Initiation	1987	12.00
❑ RNLP70862	Runt	1987	12.00
❑ RNDA71107	Something/Anything?	1987	15.00
❑ RNLP70863	The Ballad of Todd Rundgren	1987	12.00
❑ RNLP70876	The Ever Popular Tortured Artist Effect	1988	12.00
❑ RNDA71108	Todd	1987	15.00

WARNER BROS.

Number	Title	Yr	NM
❑ 25128	A Cappella	1985	12.00
❑ 25881	Nearly Human	1989	18.00

RUSH, MERRILEE

BELL

Number	Title	Yr	NM
❑ 6020 [S]	Angel of the Morning	1968	25.00
❑ 6020 [M]	Angel of the Morning	1968	40.00
—Mono is white label promo only with "Monaural" on label; sticker with "This is a monaural record for radio station play only" on cover			

LIBERTY

Number	Title	Yr	NM
❑ LN-10166	Merilee Rush	1981	10.00
—Budget-line reissue			

UNITED ARTISTS

Number	Title	Yr	NM
❑ UA-LA735-G	Merilee Rush	1977	12.00

RUSH, OTIS

BLUE HORIZON

Number	Title	Yr	NM
❑ BH-4602	Blues Masters, Volume 2	1968	30.00
❑ BH-4805	Chicago Blues	1970	30.00

COTILLION

Number	Title	Yr	NM
❑ SD9006	Mourning in the Morning	1969	30.00

RUSH, TOM

COLUMBIA

Number	Title	Yr	NM
❑ KC33054	Ladies Love Outlaws	1974	15.00
❑ KC31306	Merrimack County	1972	15.00
❑ PC33907	The Best of Tom Rush	1976	15.00
❑ CS9972	Tom Rush	1970	18.00
—Red "360 Sound" label			
❑ CS9972	Tom Rush	1970	15.00
—Orange label			
❑ C30402	Wrong End of the Rainbow	1970	15.00

ELEKTRA

Number	Title	Yr	NM
❑ EKS-74062	Classic Rush	1971	18.00
❑ EKL-308 [M]	Take a Little Walk with Me	1966	18.00
❑ EKS-7308 [S]	Take a Little Walk with Me	1966	18.00
❑ EKS-74018 [B]	The Circle Game	1968	18.00
❑ EKL-288 [M]	Tom Rush	1965	18.00
❑ EKS-7288 [S]	Tom Rush	1965	18.00

FANTASY

Number	Title	Yr	NM
❑ 24709	Tom Rush	1973	18.00
—Reissue of Prestige/Folklore recordings			

FOLKLORE

Number	Title	Yr	NM
❑ FRLP-14003 [M]	Got a Mind to Ramble	1964	25.00
❑ FRST-14003 [S]	Got a Mind to Ramble	1964	30.00

LY CORNU

Number	Title	Yr	NM
❑ SA-70-2	Tom Rush at the Unicorn	1962	100.00

PRESTIGE

Number	Title	Yr	NM
❑ PR-7374 [M]	Blues -- Songs -- Ballads	1965	25.00
❑ PRST-7374 [S]	Blues -- Songs -- Ballads	1965	30.00
❑ PRST-7536	Got a Mind to Ramble	1968	18.00
—Reissue of Folklore LP			

RUSH

ATLANTIC

Number	Title	Yr	NM
❑ 83728	Feedback	2004	16.00
❑ 82040	Presto	1989	18.00
❑ 83531	Vapor Trails	2002	30.00

MERCURY

Number	Title	Yr	NM
❑ SRM-1-1079	2112	1976	12.00
—Chicago skyline" label			
❑ 822545-1	2112	1985	10.00
—Reissue with new number			
❑ SRM-1-1079	2112	1983	10.00
—Black label			
❑ SRM-1-1184	A Farewell to Kings	1977	12.00
—Chicago skyline" label			
❑ 822546-1	A Farewell to Kings	1985	10.00
—Reissue with new number			
❑ SRM-1-1184	A Farewell to Kings	1983	10.00
—Black label			
❑ SRM-2-7508	All the World's a Stage	1976	15.00
—Chicago skyline" labels			
❑ 822552-1	All the World's a Stage	1985	12.00
—Reissue with new number			
❑ SRM-2-7508	All the World's a Stage	1983	12.00
—Black labels			
❑ SRM-3-9200	Archives	1978	25.00
—Chicago skyline" labels			
❑ 822553-1	Archives	1985	18.00
—Reissue with new number			
❑ SRM-3-9200	Archives	1983	25.00
—Black labels			
❑ 836346-1	A Show of Hands	1988	15.00
❑ SRM-1-1046	Caress of Steel	1975	12.00
—Chicago skyline" label			
❑ 822543-1	Caress of Steel	1985	10.00
—Reissue with new number			
❑ SRM-1-1046	Caress of Steel	1983	10.00
—Black label			
❑ MK-32 [DJ]	Everything Your Listener Ever Wanted to Hear by Rush ... But You Were Afraid to Play	1977	150.00
❑ SRM-2-7001	Exit... Stage Left	1981	15.00
❑ 822551-1	Exit...Stage Left	1985	12.00
—Reissue with new number			
❑ SRM-1-1023	Fly by Night	1975	12.00
—Chicago skyline" label			
❑ 822542-1	Fly by Night	1985	10.00
—Reissue with new number			
❑ SRM-1-1023	Fly by Night	1983	10.00
—Black label			
❑ 818476-1	Grace Under Pressure	1984	12.00
❑ SRM-1-3743	Hemispheres	1978	12.00
—Chicago skyline" label; with poster			
❑ SRP-1-1300 [PD]	Hemispheres	1979	40.00
❑ 822547-1	Hemispheres	1985	10.00
—Reissue with new number			
❑ SRM-1-3743	Hemispheres	1983	10.00
—Black label			
❑ 832464-1	Hold Your Fire	1987	12.00
❑ SRM-1-4013	Moving Pictures	1981	12.00
—Custom label			
❑ 822549-1	Moving Pictures	1985	10.00
—Reissue with new number			
❑ SRM-1-4001	Permanent Waves	1980	12.00
—Custom label			
❑ 822548-1	Permanent Waves	1985	10.00
—Reissue with new number			
❑ 826098-1	Power Windows	1985	12.00
❑ SRM-1-1011	Rush	1974	12.00
—Based on the LP's release date, original copies theoretically have red labels, rather than the common "Chicago skyline" labels; those would be worth at least twice this price			
❑ 822541-1	Rush	1985	10.00
—Reissue with new number			
❑ SRM-1-1011	Rush	1983	10.00
—Black label			
❑ MK-185 [DJ]	Rush 'N' Roulette	1981	120.00
—Promo-only six-track EP that has six grooves cut in it; the song it plays is based on where you place the stylus			
❑ SRM-1-4063	Signals	1982	12.00
❑ 822550-1	Signals	1985	10.00
—Reissue with new number			

RUSHEN, PATRICE

ARISTA

Number	Title	Yr	NM
❑ AL-8401	Watch Out!	1987	12.00

ELEKTRA

Number	Title	Yr	NM
❑ 60465	Anthology of Patrice Rushen	1986	12.00
❑ 6E-160	Patrice	1978	12.00
❑ 60360	Patrice Rushen Now	1984	12.00
❑ 6E-243	Pizzazz	1979	12.00
❑ 6E-302	Posh	1980	12.00
❑ 60015	Straight from the Heart	1982	12.00

PRESTIGE

Number	Title	Yr	NM
❑ 10098	Before the Dawn	1976	25.00
❑ 10110	Let There Be Funk	1980	18.00
❑ 10089	Prelusion	1974	25.00
❑ 10101	Shout It Out	1977	18.00

RUSHING, JIMMY; ADA MOORE; BUCK CLAYTON

COLUMBIA

Number	Title	Yr	NM
❑ CL778 [M]	Cat Meets Chick	1956	60.00

RUSHING, JIMMY

AUDIO LAB

Number	Title	Yr	NM
❑ AL-1512 [M]	Two Shades of Blue	1959	120.00

BLUESWAY

Number	Title	Yr	NM
❑ BL-6005 [M]	Everyday I Have the Blues	1967	25.00
❑ BLS 6005 [S]	Everyday I Have the Blues	1967	25.00
❑ BLS-6017	Livin' the Blues	1968	25.00
❑ BLS-6057	Sent for You Yesterday	1973	18.00

COLPIX

Number	Title	Yr	NM
❑ CP-446 [M]	Five Feet of Soul	1963	40.00
❑ SCP-446 [S]	Five Feet of Soul	1963	60.00
—The existence of this record has been confirmed			

COLUMBIA

Number	Title	Yr	NM
❑ CL1605 [M]	Jimmy Rushing and the Smith Girls	1961	30.00
❑ CS8405 [S]	Jimmy Rushing and the Smith Girls	1961	40.00
❑ CL1152 [M]	Little Jimmy Rushing and the Big Brass	1958	40.00
❑ CS8060 [S]	Little Jimmy Rushing and the Big Brass	1958	50.00
❑ C236419	Mister Five by Five	1979	15.00
❑ CL1401 [M]	Rushing Lullabies	1959	40.00
❑ CS8196 [S]	Rushing Lullabies	1959	50.00
❑ CL963 [M]	The Jazz Odyssey of James Rushing, Esq.	1957	40.00

JAZZTONE

Number	Title	Yr	NM
❑ J-1244 [M]	Listen to the Blues	195?	40.00

MASTER JAZZ

Number	Title	Yr	NM
❑ 8104	Gee, Baby	197?	18.00
❑ 8120	Who Was It Sang That Song?	1971	18.00

RCA VICTOR

Number	Title	Yr	NM
❑ LSP-4566	You and Me The Used to Be	1972	18.00

VANGUARD

Number	Title	Yr	NM
❑ VRS-65/66	Essential Jimmy Rushing	197?	18.00
❑ VRS-8518 [M]	Going to Chicago	1957	50.00
❑ VRS-8513 [M]	If This Ain't the Blues	1957	50.00
❑ VSD-2008 [S]	If This Ain't the Blues	1958	60.00
❑ VRS-8011 [10]	Jimmy Rushing Sings the Blues	1955	100.00
❑ VRS-8505 [M]	Listen to the Blues	1955	50.00
❑ VSD-73007	Listen to the Blues	1967	18.00

RUSKIN-SPEAR, ROGER

UNITED ARTISTS

Number	Title	Yr	NM
❑ UA-LA097-F	Electric Shocks	1973	30.00

RUSSELL, ANNA

COLUMBIA MASTERWORKS

Number	Title	Yr	NM
❑ ML4928 [M]	Anna Russell's Guide to Concert Audiences	1955	30.00
❑ ML4594 [M]	Anna Russell Sings?	1953	30.00
❑ ML4733 [M]	Anna Russell Sings! Again?	1954	30.00
❑ ML5295 [M]	A Practical Banana Promotion	1959	50.00
❑ ML5036 [M]	A Square Talk on Popular Music	1956	30.00
❑ ML5195 [M]	In Darkest Africa	1957	30.00
❑ MG31199	The Anna Russell Album?	1972	25.00

RUSSELL, BOBBY

ELF

Number	Title	Yr	NM
❑ 9501	Unlimited	1970	18.00
❑ 9500 [S]	Words, Music, Laughter & Tears	1969	25.00
❑ 9500 [M]	Words, Music, Laughter & Tears	1969	50.00
—Mono copies are white label promo only and say "Monaural" on the label			

UNITED ARTISTS

Number	Title	Yr	NM
❑ UAS-5548	Saturday Morning Confusion	1971	15.00

Number	Title	Yr	NM

RUSSELL, GEORGE

BASF
| ❏ 25125 | Live at Beethoven Hall | 1973 | 18.00 |

BLUE NOTE
| ❏ BT-85132 | So What | 1987 | 18.00 |
| ❏ BT-85103 | The African Game | 198? | 15.00 |

CONCEPT
| ❏ 002 | Listen to the Silence | 197? | 15.00 |

DECCA
❏ DL9220 [M]	George Russell at the Five Spot	1958	50.00
❏ DL79220 [S]	George Russell at the Five Spot	1958	40.00
❏ DL4183 [M]	George Russell in Kansas City	1961	30.00
❏ DL74183 [S]	George Russell in Kansas City	1961	40.00
❏ DL9219 [M]	Jazz in the Space Age	1958	50.00
❏ DL79219 [S]	Jazz in the Space Age	1958	40.00
❏ DL9216 [M]	New York, N.Y.	1958	50.00
❏ DL79216 [S]	New York, N.Y.	1958	40.00

FANTASY
❏ OJC-070	Ezz-thetics	198?	12.00
❏ OJC-232	Stratusphunk	198?	12.00
❏ OJC-616	The Outer View	1991	15.00
❏ OJC-365	The Stratus Seekers	198?	12.00

FLYING DUTCHMAN
❏ FD-10124	Electronic Sonata for Souls Loved by Nature	1971	18.00
❏ FD-124	Electronic Sonata for Souls Loved by Nature	1970	25.00
❏ FD-10122	Othello Ballet Suite/ Electronic Organ Sonata No. 1	1971	18.00
❏ FD-122	Othello Ballet Suite/ Electronic Organ Sonata No. 1	1970	25.00

MCA
| ❏ 4017 | New York, N.Y./Jazz in the Space Age | 1974 | 18.00 |

MGM
| ❏ E-3321 [M] | George Russell Octets | 1955 | 80.00 |

MILESTONE
| ❏ 47027 | Outer Thoughts | 197? | 18.00 |

PETE
| ❏ 1107 | Easy Listening | 1969 | 18.00 |

RCA VICTOR
❏ LPM-1372 [M]	Jazz Workshop	1957	80.00
❏ LPM-2534 [M]	Jazz Workshop	1962	30.00
❏ LSP-2534 [R]	Jazz Workshop	1962	18.00

RIVERSIDE
❏ RLP-375 [M]	Ezz-thetics	1961	30.00
❏ RS-9375 [S]	Ezz-thetics	1961	30.00
❏ 6112	Ezz-thetics	197?	15.00
❏ RS-3043	George Russell Sextet	1970	18.00
❏ RLP-341 [M]	Stratusphunk	1960	30.00
❏ RS-9341 [S]	Stratusphunk	1960	30.00
❏ RLP-440 [M]	The Outer View	1963	30.00
❏ RS-9440 [S]	The Outer View	1963	30.00
❏ RS-3016	The Outer View	1968	25.00
❏ RLP-412 [M]	The Stratus Seekers	1962	30.00
❏ RS-9412 [S]	The Stratus Seekers	1962	30.00

SOUL NOTE
❏ SN-1034	Electronic Sonata for Souls Loved by Nature 1969	198?	15.00
❏ SN-1009	Electronic Sonata for Souls Loved by Nature 1980	1980	15.00
❏ SN-1024	Listen to the Silence (A Mass for Our Time)	198?	15.00
❏ SN-1049	Live in an American Time Spiral	1983	15.00
❏ SN-1039	New York Big Band	198?	15.00
❏ SN-1014	Othello Ballet Suite	198?	15.00
❏ SN-1044/5	The Essence of George Russell	198?	18.00
❏ SN-1029	Trip to Pillar-Guri	198?	15.00
❏ SN-1019	Vertical Form VI	198?	15.00

STRATA-EAST
| ❏ SES-19761 | Electronic Sonata for Souls Loved by Nature | 1976 | 25.00 |

RUSSELL, JANE

MGM
| ❏ E-3715 [M] | Jane Russell | 1959 | 50.00 |
| ❏ SE-3715 [S] | Jane Russell | 1959 | 100.00 |

RUSSELL, JIMMY

CUCA
| ❏ 4100 [M] | Jimmy Russell Trio | 1965 | 30.00 |

DORIAN
| ❏ 1020 | The Swingin'est | 1968 | 18.00 |

RUSSELL, JOHNNY

MERCURY
| ❏ SRM-1-5019 | Perspectives | 1979 | 15.00 |

RCA VICTOR
❏ LSP-4851	Catfish John/Chained	1973	18.00
❏ APL1-1211	Here Comes Johnny Russell	1975	18.00
❏ LSP-4588	Mr. and Mrs. Untrue	1971	18.00

❏ APL1-0345	Rednecks, White Socks and Blue Ribbon Beer	1973	18.00
❏ ANL1-2165	Rednecks, White Socks and Blue Ribbon Beer	1977	12.00
—Reissue			
❏ APL1-0542	She's in Love with a Rodeo Man	1974	18.00

RUSSELL, KURT

CAPITOL
| ❏ SKAO-492 | Kurt Russell | 1970 | 30.00 |

RUSSELL, LEON

MCA
❏ 37114	Best of Leon	1980	10.00
—Reissue of Shelter 52004			
❏ 685	Carney	1979	10.00
—Reissue of Shelter 52011			
❏ 682	Leon Russell	1979	10.00
—Reissue of Shelter 52007			
❏ 683	Leon Russell and the Shelter People	1979	10.00
—Reissue of Shelter 52008			
❏ 686	Will O' the Wisp	1979	10.00
—Reissue of Shelter 52020			

PARADISE
❏ BSK3172	Americana	1978	15.00
❏ 0002	Hank Wilson Vol. II	1984	15.00
❏ BSK3341	Life and Love	1979	15.00
❏ BSK3066	Make Love to the Music	1977	15.00
—As "Leon and Mary Russell"			
❏ BSK3532	The Live Album	1981	12.00
❏ PR2943	Wedding Album	1976	15.00
—As "Leon and Mary Russell"			

SHELTER
❏ 52004	Best of Leon	1976	12.00
❏ SW-8911	Carney	1972	18.00
❏ SR2121	Carney	1974	15.00
—Reissue of 8911			
❏ 52011	Carney	1977	12.00
—Reissue of 2121			
❏ SW-8923	Hank Wilson's Back, Vol. 1	1973	18.00
—As "Hank Wilson"			
❏ 52014	Hank Wilson's Back, Vol. 1	1977	12.00
—Reissue of 8923			
❏ STCO-8917	Leon Live	1973	25.00
❏ SHE-1001	Leon Russell	1968	25.00
❏ SW-8901	Leon Russell	1970	18.00
—Early reissue of 1001			
❏ SR2118	Leon Russell	1974	15.00
—Reissue of 8901			
❏ 52007	Leon Russell	1977	12.00
—Reissue of 2118			
❏ SW-8903	Leon Russell and the Shelter People	1971	18.00
❏ SR2119	Leon Russell and the Shelter People	1974	15.00
—Reissue of 8903			
❏ 52008	Leon Russell and the Shelter People	1977	12.00
—Reissue of 2119			
❏ SR2108	Stop All That Jazz	1974	18.00
❏ 52016	Stop All That Jazz	1977	12.00
—Reissue of 2108			
❏ SR2138	Will O' the Wisp	1975	18.00
❏ 52020	Will O' the Wisp	1977	12.00
—Reissue of 2138			

RUSSELL, PEE WEE, AND RUBY BRAFF

SAVOY
| ❏ MG-12034 [M] | Jazz At Storyville, Volume 1 | 1955 | 50.00 |
| ❏ MG-12041 [M] | Jazz at Storyville, Volume 2 | 1955 | 50.00 |

RUSSELL, PEE WEE

ABC IMPULSE!
❏ AS-96 [S]	Ask Me Now	1968	18.00
❏ AS-9137 [S]	College Concert of Pee Wee Russell with Henry "Red" Allen	1968	18.00
❏ IA-9359	Salute to Newport	1979	18.00

ATLANTIC
| ❏ ALS-126 [10] | Pee Wee Russell All Stars | 1952 | 80.00 |

BARNABY
| ❏ BR-5018 | Jazz Reunion | 197? | 15.00 |

BELL
| ❏ LP-42 [M] | Pee Wee Russell Plays Pee Wee | 1961 | 30.00 |
| ❏ LPS-42 [S] | Pee Wee Russell Plays Pee Wee | 1961 | 30.00 |

COLUMBIA
| ❏ CL1985 [M] | New Groove | 1963 | 18.00 |
| ❏ CS8785 [S] | New Groove | 1963 | 25.00 |

COMMODORE
| ❏ XFL-16440 | Three Deuces and Hot Four: The Pied Piper of Jazz | 198? | 12.00 |

COUNTERPOINT
| ❏ 0(# unknown) [M] | Portrait of Pee Wee | 1957 | 60.00 |

DCC COMPACT CLASSICS
| ❏ LPZ-2024 | Portrait of Pee Wee | 1996 | 30.00 |
| —Audiophile vinyl | | | |

DISC
| ❏ DLP-0(# unknown) [10] | Jazz Ensemble | 195? | 120.00 |

DOT
| ❏ DLP-3253 [M] | Pee Wee Russell Plays | 1960 | 30.00 |
| ❏ DLP-25253 [S] | Pee Wee Russell Plays | 1960 | 25.00 |

ESOTERIC
| ❏ 565 [M] | Pee Wee Russell All Stars | 1959 | 40.00 |
| ❏ 5565 [S] | Pee Wee Russell All Stars | 1959 | 30.00 |

EVEREST ARCHIVE OF FOLK & JAZZ
| ❏ 233 [R] | Pee Wee Russell | 1969 | 12.00 |

FANTASY
| ❏ OJC-1708 | Rhythmakers and Teagarden | 1985 | 12.00 |

IMPULSE!
❏ A-96 [M]	Ask Me Now	1966	30.00
❏ AS-96 [S]	Ask Me Now	1966	30.00
❏ A-9137 [M]	College Concert of Pee Wee Russell with Henry "Red" Allen	1967	30.00
❏ AS-9137 [S]	College Concert of Pee Wee Russell with Henry "Red" Allen	1967	25.00

MAINSTREAM
| ❏ 56026 [M] | A Legend | 1965 | 18.00 |
| ❏ S-6026 [S] | A Legend | 1965 | 25.00 |

MCA
| ❏ 4150 | Salute to Newport | 198? | 15.00 |

PRESTIGE
| ❏ 24051 | Jam Session in Swingville | 198? | 18.00 |
| ❏ PRST-7672 [R] | The Pee Wee Russell Memorial Album | 1969 | 18.00 |

RIVERSIDE
| ❏ RLP 12-141 [M] | Rhythmakers and Teagarden | 1955 | 60.00 |

SAVOY JAZZ
| ❏ SJL-2228 | The Individualism of Pee Wee Russell | 197? | 18.00 |

STEREO-CRAFT
| ❏ RTN-106 [M] | Pee Wee Plays Pee Wee | 196? | 25.00 |
| ❏ RTS-105 [S] | Pee Wee Plays Pee Wee | 196? | 30.00 |

STORYVILLE
| ❏ STLP-308 [10] | Pee Wee Russell | 1954 | 80.00 |
| ❏ STLP-909 [M] | We're In the Money | 1956 | 50.00 |

SWINGVILLE
❏ SVLP-2008 [M]	Swingin' with Pee Wee	1960	50.00
—Purple label			
❏ SVLP-2008 [M]	Swingin' with Pee Wee	1965	30.00
—Blue label, trident logo at right			

TIME-LIFE
| ❏ STL-J-17 | Giants of Jazz | 1981 | 25.00 |

XANADU
| ❏ 192 | Over the Rainbow | 198? | 12.00 |

RUSSELL, PEE WEE/BILLY BANKS

JAZZ PANORAMA
| ❏ 1808 [10] | Pee Wee Russell / Billy Banks | 1951 | 80.00 |

RUSSIN, BABE

DOT
| ❏ DLP-3060 [M] | To Soothe the Savage | 1956 | 50.00 |

RUTLES, THE

WARNER BROS.
❏ HS3151 [B]	The Rutles	1978	30.00
—With bound-in booklet			
❏ PRO-A-723 [DJ]	The Rutles	1978	30.00
—Yellow vinyl with five songs and "banana" label			

RYAN, BUCK, AND SMITTY IRWIN

MONUMENT
| ❏ MLP-8031 [M] | Ballads and Bluegrass | 1965 | 25.00 |
| ❏ SLP-18031 [S] | Ballads and Bluegrass | 1965 | 30.00 |

RYAN, CHARLIE

HILLTOP
| ❏ JM-6006 [M] | Hot Rod Lincoln Drags Again | 1964 | 50.00 |
| ❏ JS-6006 [R] | Hot Rod Lincoln Drags Again | 1964 | 30.00 |

KING
| ❏ 751 [M] | Hot Rod Lincoln | 1961 | 400.00 |

RYDELL, BOBBY

CAMEO
❏ C-2001 [M]	16 Golden Hits	1965	25.00
❏ SC-2001 [R]	16 Golden Hits	1965	25.00
❏ C-1019 [M]	All the Hits	1962	30.00
—Black vinyl			
❏ C-1019 [M]	All the Hits	1962	150.00

Number	Title	Yr	NM
—Red vinyl			
❏ C-1040 [M]	All the Hits, Volume 2	1963	30.00
❏ SC-1040 [P]	All the Hits, Volume 2	1963	40.00
❏ C-1010 [M]	Bobby Rydell Salutes "The Great Ones	1961	30.00
❏ SC-1010 [S]	Bobby Rydell Salutes "The Great Ones	1961	40.00
❏ C-1028 [M]	Bobby Rydell's Biggest Hits, Volume 2	1962	30.00
❏ C-1009 [M]	Bobby's Biggest Hits	1961	80.00
—Original with die-cut cover and textured inner sleeve			
❏ C-1009 [M]	Bobby's Biggest Hits	1961	30.00
—Standard cover			
❏ C-1007 [M]	Bobby Sings	1960	50.00
❏ C-1043 [M]	Bye Bye Birdie	1963	30.00
❏ C-1080 [M]	Forget Him	1964	25.00
❏ SC-1080 [R]	Forget Him	1964	25.00
❏ C-1011 [M]	Rydell at the Copa	1961	30.00
❏ SC-1011 [S]	Rydell at the Copa	1961	40.00
❏ C-1070 [M]	The Top Hits of 1963	1963	25.00
—Came with bonus single, also numbered 1070			
❏ SC-1070 [S]	The Top Hits of 1963	1963	30.00
—Came with bonus single, also numbered 1070			
❏ C-1006 [M]	We Got Love	1959	60.00
❏ C-1055 [M]	Wild (Wood) Days	1963	25.00
❏ SC-1055 [S]	Wild (Wood) Days	1963	30.00
CAPITOL			
❏ T2281 [M]	Somebody Loves You	1965	18.00
❏ ST2281 [S]	Somebody Loves You	1965	25.00
P.I.P.			
❏ 6818	Born with a Smile	1976	12.00
SPIN-O-RAMA			
❏ 143 [M]	Starring Bobby Rydell	196?	15.00
❏ S-143 [S]	Starring Bobby Rydell	196?	15.00
STRAND			
❏ SL-1120 [M]	Bobby Rydell Sings	196?	30.00
❏ SLS-1120 [R]	Bobby Rydell Sings	196?	25.00
VENISE			
❏ 10035 [M]	Twistin'	1962	30.00
—Also includes tracks by Barry Norman and Stephen Garrick			

RYDELL, BOBBY/CHUBBY CHECKER

CAMEO

Number	Title	Yr	NM
❏ C1013 [M]	Bobby Rydell/Chubby Checker	1961	30.00
❏ C-1063 [M]	Chubby Checker and Bobby Rydell	1963	25.00

RYDER, MITCH, AND THE DETROIT WHEELS

CREWE

Number	Title	Yr	NM
❏ CR-1335	All Mitch Ryder Hits!	1969	18.00
—Reissue of New Voice 2004			
NEW VOICE			
❏ 2004 [M]	All Mitch Ryder Hits!	1967	30.00
❏ NVS-2004 [S]	All Mitch Ryder Hits!	1967	25.00
❏ 2002 [M]	Breakout…!!!	1966	30.00
—Without "Devil with a Blue Dress On/Good Golly Miss Molly			
❏ 2002 [M]	Breakout…!!!	1966	25.00
—With "Devil with a Blue Dress On/Good Golly Miss Molly			
❏ S-2002 [S]	Breakout…!!!	1966	30.00
—Without "Devil with a Blue Dress On/Good Golly Miss Molly			
❏ S-2002 [S]	Breakout…!!!	1966	30.00
—With "Devil with a Blue Dress On/Good Golly Miss Molly			
❏ S-2005	Mitch Ryder Sings the Hits	1968	25.00
❏ 2003 [M]	Sock It To Me!	1967	60.00
❏ S-2003 [S]	Sock It To Me!	1967	30.00
❏ 2000 [M]	Take a Ride	1966	30.00
❏ S-2000 [S]	Take a Ride	1966	30.00
RHINO			
❏ R1-70941	Rev Up: The Best of Mitch Ryder and the Detroit Wheels	1989	15.00
SUNDAZED			
❏ LP5083	Breakout … !!!	2001	15.00
—Reissue on 180-gram vinyl			
VIRGO			
❏ 12001	The Best of Mitch Ryder and the Detroit Wheels	1972	15.00

RYDER, MITCH

DYNO VOICE

Number	Title	Yr	NM
❏ 1901 [M]	What Now My Love	1967	60.00
❏ 31901 [S]	What Now My Love	1967	25.00
RIVA			
❏ RV7503	Never Kick a Sleeping Dog	1983	12.00
SEEDS & STEMS			
❏ 7801	How I Spent My Summer Vacation	1978	15.00
❏ 7804	Naked But Not Dead	1980	15.00

RYG, JORGEN

EMARCY

Number	Title	Yr	NM
❏ MG-36099 [M]	Jorgen Ryg Jazz Quartet	1956	50.00

S

SAAD, SUE, AND THE NEXT

PLANET

Number	Title	Yr	NM
❏ 4	Sue Saad and the Next	1979	15.00

SABIEN, RANDY

FLYING FISH

Number	Title	Yr	NM
❏ FF-297	In a Fog	198?	12.00

SABRES, THE

RCA VICTOR

Number	Title	Yr	NM
❏ LPM-1376 [M]	Ridin' High with the Sabres	1956	60.00

SABU, PAUL

MCA

Number	Title	Yr	NM
❏ 3236	Sabu	1980	15.00
—As "Sabu			
OCEAN/ARIOLA AMERICA			
❏ SW-49902	Sabu	1979	30.00
—As "Sabu			

SABU

ALEGRE

Number	Title	Yr	NM
❏ 802 [M]	Jazz Espagnole	195?	300.00
BLUE NOTE			
❏ BLP-1561 [M]	Palo Congo	1957	800.00
—Deep groove" version (deep indentation under label on both sides)			
❏ BLP-1561 [M]	Palo Congo	1957	100.00
—Regular version, W. 63rd St. address on label			
❏ BLP-1561 [M]	Palo Congo	1963	30.00
—With "New York, USA" address on label			
❏ BST-81561 [R]	Palo Congo	1967	18.00
—With "A Division of Liberty Records" on label			

SACBE

DISCOVERY

Number	Title	Yr	NM
❏ 864	Street Corner	198?	12.00
TREND			
❏ TR-521	Aztlan	1979	15.00
❏ TR-544	The Sleeping Lady	1986	12.00

SACHS, AARON

BETHLEHEM

Number	Title	Yr	NM
❏ BCP-1008 [10]	Aaron Sachs Quintet	1954	120.00
DAWN			
❏ DLP-1114 [M]	Jazzville, Volume 3	1957	80.00
RAMA			
❏ LP 1001 [M]	Clarinet and Co.	1957	80.00

SACHS, AARON/HANK D'AMICO

BETHLEHEM

Number	Title	Yr	NM
❏ BCP-7 [M]	We Brought Our "Axes"	1955	80.00

SACRED MUSHROOM, THE

PARALLAX

Number	Title	Yr	NM
❏ P-4001	The Sacred Mushroom	1969	150.00

SADE

EPIC

Number	Title	Yr	NM
❏ OE44210	Stronger Than Pride	1988	12.00
❏ E266686	The Best of Sade	1994	18.00
PORTRAIT			
❏ BFR39581	Diamond Life	1984	15.00
❏ BFR40263	Promise	1985	12.00

SADI, FATS

BLUE NOTE

Number	Title	Yr	NM
❏ BLP-5061 [10]	The Swinging Fats Sadi Combo	1955	300.00

SADLER, SSGT. BARRY

RCA VICTOR

Number	Title	Yr	NM
❏ LPM-3605 [M]	A" Team, The	1966	35.00
❏ LSP-3605 [S]	A" Team, The	1966	25.00
❏ LPM-3691 [M]	Back Home	1967	35.00
❏ LSP-3691 [S]	Back Home	1967	18.00
❏ LPM-3547 [M]	Ballads of the Green Berets	1966	35.00
❏ LSP-3547 [S]	Ballads of the Green Berets	1966	25.00

SAGA

ATLANTIC

Number	Title	Yr	NM
❏ 81794	Wildest Dreams	1987	12.00
POLYDOR			
❏ PD-1-6209	Saga	1979	18.00
PORTRAIT			
❏ BFR40145	Behaviour	1985	10.00
❏ FR38999	Heads or Tales	1983	10.00
❏ ARR38246	Worlds Apart	1982	12.00

Number	Title	Yr	NM
❏ FR38246	Worlds Apart	1982	10.00
—Reissue with new prefix			

SAGITTARIUS

COLUMBIA

Number	Title	Yr	NM
❏ CS9644 [B]	Present Tense	1968	35.00
TOGETHER			
❏ STT-1002 [B]	The Blue Marble	1969	60.00
—With two bonus photos; deduct 25 percent if missing			

SAHL, MORT

FANTASY

Number	Title	Yr	NM
❏ 7005 [M]	Mort Sahl at Sunset	196?	40.00
—Red vinyl			
❏ 7005 [M]	Mort Sahl at Sunset	196?	30.00
—Black vinyl			
GNP CRESCENDO			
❏ GNPS-2070	Sing a Song of Watergate	1973	18.00
MERCURY			
❏ MG-21112 [M]	Anyway…Onward	1967	25.00
❏ SR-61112 [S]	Anyway…Onward	1967	25.00
REPRISE			
❏ R-5003 [M]	Mort Sahl On Relationships	1961	40.00
❏ R9-5003 [S]	Mort Sahl On Relationships	1961	50.00
—Joan Collins appears on the cover			
❏ R-5002 [M]	The New Frontier	1961	25.00
❏ R9-5002 [S]	The New Frontier	1961	30.00
VERVE			
❏ MGV-15004 [M]	1960: Look Forward in Anger	1959	25.00
❏ MGV-15006 [M]	A Way of Life	1960	25.00
❏ V-15049 [M]	Great Moments of Comedy	1965	18.00
❏ MGV-15012 [M]	Mort Sahl at the Hungry I	1960	25.00
❏ MGVS-15012 [S]	Mort Sahl at the Hungry I	1960	30.00
❏ MGV-15002 [M]	The Future Lies Ahead	1959	25.00
❏ V-15021 [M]	The Next President	1961	25.00
❏ V6-15021 [S]	The Next President	1961	30.00

SAHM, DOUG

ABC DOT

Number	Title	Yr	NM
❏ DO-2057	Texas Rock for Country Rollers	1976	18.00
ANTONE'S			
❏ ANT-0008	Juke Box Music	1989	15.00
ATLANTIC			
❏ SD7254	Doug Sahm and Band	1973	18.00
MERCURY			
❏ SRM-1-655 [B]	Rough Edges	1972	35.00
TAKOMA			
❏ TAK-7075	Hell of a Spell	1980	15.00
TEARDROP			
❏ TD-5000	The West Side Sound Rolls Again	1982	15.00
WARNER BROS.			
❏ BS2810	Groovers Paradise	1974	25.00

SAILCAT

ELEKTRA

Number	Title	Yr	NM
❏ EKS-75029	Sailcat	1972	18.00

SAIN, OLIVER

ABAT

Number	Title	Yr	NM
❏ 406	Bus Stop	1974	25.00
❏ 404	Main Man	1973	25.00

SAINT ETIENNE

PLAIN

Number	Title	Yr	NM
❏ PLAIN178 [B]	Foxbase Alpha	2013	30.00
❏ PLAIN179 [B]	So Tough	2013	30.00
❏ PLAIN180 [B]	Tiger Bay	2014	35.00

SAINT STEVEN

PROBE

Number	Title	Yr	NM
❏ CPLP-4506	Over the Hills	1969	75.00

SAINTE-MARIE, BUFFY

ABC

Number	Title	Yr	NM
❏ D-929	Sweet America	1976	15.00
MCA			
❏ 405	Buffy	1974	15.00
❏ 451	Changing Woman	1975	15.00
VANGUARD			
❏ VRS9250 [M]	Fire & Fleet & Candlelight	1967	25.00
❏ VSD79250 [S]	Fire & Fleet & Candlelight	1967	25.00
❏ VSD79300 [B]	Illuminations	1969	25.00
❏ VSD79280 [B]	I'm Gonna Be a Country Girl Again	1968	25.00
❏ VRS9142 [M]	It's My Way	1964	25.00
❏ VSD79142 [S]	It's My Way	1964	25.00
❏ VRS9211 [M]	Little Wheel Spin and Spin	1966	25.00
❏ VSD79211 [S]	Little Wheel Spin and Spin	1966	25.00
❏ VRS9171 [M]	Many a Mile	1965	25.00
❏ VSD79171 [S]	Many a Mile	1965	25.00
❏ VSD79312 [B]	Moon Shot	1972	25.00

Number	Title	Yr	NM
❏ VSQ40003 [Q]	Moon Shot	1972	30.00
❏ VSD79340	Native Child: Odyssey	1974	15.00
❏ VSD79330	Quiet Places	1973	15.00
❏ VSQ40020 [Q]	Quiet Places	1973	30.00
❏ VSD79311 [B]	She Used to Wanna Be a Ballerina	1971	25.00
❏ VSD3/4	The Best of Buffy Sainte-Marie	1970	25.00
❏ VMS73113	The Best of Buffy Sainte-Marie	1985	12.00
❏ VSD33/34	The Best of Buffy Sainte-Marie, Vol. 2	1974	18.00

SAINTS, THE

4 MEN WITH BEARDS
❏ 4M529LP [B]	Eternally Yours		25.00
❏ 4M502LP [B]	(I'm) Stranded		25.00

SIRE
❏ SRK6055 [B]	Eternally Yours	1978	30.00
❏ SR6039	(I'm) Stranded	1977	30.00

TVT
❏ 2111	All Fools Day	1987	12.00
❏ 2121	Prodigal Son	1988	12.00

SAKAMOTO, KYU

CAPITOL
❏ T10349 [M]	Sukiyaki and Other Japanese Hits	1963	30.00
❏ DT10349 [R]	Sukiyaki and Other Japanese Hits	1963	18.00

SALEM MASS

SALEM MASS
❏ SM-101	Witch Burning	1972	250.00

SALES, SOUPY

ABC-PARAMOUNT
❏ 517 [M]	Soupy Sales Sez Do the Mouse and Other Teen Hits	1965	30.00
❏ S-517 [S]	Soupy Sales Sez Do the Mouse and Other Teen Hits	1965	30.00
❏ 503 [M]	Spy with a Pie	1965	30.00
❏ S-503 [S]	Spy with a Pie	1965	30.00

MCA
❏ 5274	Still Soupy After All These Years	1981	15.00

MOTOWN
❏ MS686	A Bag of Soup	1969	30.00

REPRISE
❏ R6010 [M]	The Soupy Sales Show	1961	30.00
❏ R96010 [S]	The Soupy Sales Show	1961	40.00
❏ R6052 [M]	Up in the Air	1962	30.00
❏ R96052 [S]	Up in the Air	1962	40.00

SALIM, A.K.

PRESTIGE
❏ PRLP-7379 [M]	Afro-Soul Drum Orgy	1966	30.00
❏ PRST-7379 [S]	Afro-Soul Drum Orgy	1966	30.00

SAVOY
❏ MG-12132 [M]	Blues Suite	1958	50.00
❏ SST-13001 [S]	Blues Suite	1959	40.00
❏ MG-12118 [M]	Pretty for the People	1957	80.00
❏ MG-12102 [M]	The Flute Suite	1957	80.00

SALIS, ANTONELLO

HAT HUT
❏ 10	Orange Juice/Nice Food	1980	18.00

SALLYANGIE

WARNER BROS.
❏ WS1783 [B]	Children of the Sun	1969	35.00

SALSOUL ORCHESTRA, THE

SALSOUL
❏ SZS5507	Christmas Jollies	1976	15.00
❏ CA-1001	Christmas Jollies	198?	10.00
—Reissue			
❏ SA8547	Christmas Jollies II	1981	15.00
❏ CA-1004	Christmas Jollies II	198?	10.00
—Reissue			
❏ SA-8508	Greatest Disco Hits/Music for Non-Stop Dancing	1978	12.00
❏ SA-8552	Heat It Up	1982	12.00
❏ SA-8528	How High	1980	12.00
❏ SZS5515	Magic Journey	1977	12.00
❏ SZS5502	Nice 'n' Naasty	1976	12.00
❏ SA-8516	Street Sense	1979	12.00
❏ SZS5501	The Salsoul Orchestra	1975	12.00
❏ SA-8500	Up the Yellow Brick Road	1978	12.00

SALT-N-PEPA

LONDON
❏ 828392-1	Very Necessary	1993	15.00

LONDON/RED ANT
❏ 828959-1	Brand New	1997	15.00

NEXT PLATEAU
❏ PL1011	A Salt with a Deadly Pepa	1988	15.00
❏ PL1019	Blacks' Magic	1989	15.00

SALT CITY FIVE, THE

JUBILEE
❏ JLP-13 [10]	Salt City Five	1955	50.00
❏ JLP-1012 [10]	Salt City Five	1956	40.00
❏ JLP-24 [10]	Salt City Five, Volume 2	1955	50.00

SALT WATER TAFFY

BUDDAH
❏ BDS-5021	Finders Keepers	1968	25.00

SALUZZI, DINO

ECM
❏ 1251	Kultrum	198?	15.00
❏ 25042	Once Upon a Time… Far Away in the South	1986	12.00

SALVADOR, DOM

MUSE
❏ MR-5085	My Family	1976	15.00

SALVADOR, SAL

BEE HIVE
❏ BH-7009	Juicy Lucy	1979	15.00
❏ BH-7002	Starfingers	1978	15.00

BETHLEHEM
❏ BCP-59 [M]	Frivolous Sal	1956	50.00
❏ BCP-39 [M]	Shades of Sal Salvador	1956	50.00
❏ BCP-74 [M]	Tribute to the Greats	1957	50.00

BLUE NOTE
❏ BLP-5035 [10]	Sal Salvador Quintet	1954	300.00

CAPITOL
❏ H6505 [10]	Sal Salvador	1954	120.00
❏ T6505 [M]	Sal Salvador	1955	80.00

DAUNTLESS
❏ DM-4307 [M]	You Ain't Heard Nothin' Yet	1963	30.00
❏ DS-6307 [S]	You Ain't Heard Nothin' Yet	1963	40.00

DECCA
❏ DL4026 [M]	Beat for This Generation	1959	40.00
❏ DL74026 [S]	Beat for This Generation	1959	50.00
❏ DL9210 [M]	Colors in Sound	1958	50.00
❏ DL79210 [S]	Colors in Sound	1958	40.00

GOLDEN CREST
❏ GC-1001 [M]	Sal Salvador Quartet	1961	30.00
❏ GCS-1001 [S]	Sal Salvador Quartet	1961	30.00

GP
❏ 5010	Live at the University of Bridgeport	197?	15.00

ROULETTE
❏ R-25262 [M]	Music To Stop Smoking By	1964	25.00
❏ RS-25262 [S]	Music To Stop Smoking By	1964	30.00

STASH
❏ ST-224	In Our Own Sweet Way	198?	12.00
❏ ST-251	Sal Salvador Plays Gerry Mulligan	1985	12.00
❏ ST-234	Sal Salvador Plays the World's Greatest Standards	198?	12.00

SALVATION

ABC
❏ S-653	Gypsy Carnival Caravan	1968	25.00
❏ S-623 [B]	Salvation	1968	30.00

SAM AND DAVE

ATLANTIC
❏ SD8205	I Thank You	1968	30.00
❏ 81718	Soul Men	1987	12.00
—Reissue of Stax 725			
❏ SD8218	The Best of Sam and Dave	1969	25.00
❏ 81279	The Best of Sam and Dave	1985	12.00

GUSTO
❏ 0045	Sweet and Funky Gold	197?	12.00

ROULETTE
❏ R-25323 [M]	Sam and Dave	1966	50.00
❏ SR-25323 [S]	Sam and Dave	1966	40.00

STAX
❏ ST-712 [M]	Double Dynamite	1966	60.00
❏ STS-712 [S]	Double Dynamite	1966	40.00
❏ ST-708 [M]	Hold On, I'm Comin'	1966	60.00
❏ STS-708 [S]	Hold On, I'm Comin'	1966	50.00
❏ ST-725 [M]	Soul Men	1967	60.00
❏ STS-725 [S]	Soul Men	1967	40.00

UNITED ARTISTS
❏ UA-LA524-G	Back At 'Cha!	1975	15.00

SAM THE SHAM AND THE PHARAOHS

ATLANTIC
❏ SD8271	Hard and Heavy	1971	18.00
—As "Sam Samudio"			

MGM
❏ E-4407 [M]	Lil' Red Riding Hood	1966	30.00
❏ SE-4407 [S]	Lil' Red Riding Hood	1966	30.00
❏ E-4477 [M]	Nefertiti	1967	30.00
❏ SE-4477 [S]	Nefertiti	1967	30.00
❏ E-4347 [M]	On Tour	1966	30.00
❏ SE-4347 [S]	On Tour	1966	30.00
❏ SE-4526	Ten of Pentacles	1968	25.00
❏ E-4422 [M]	The Best of Sam the Sham and the Pharoahs	1967	25.00
❏ SE-4422 [S]	The Best of Sam the Sham and the Pharoahs	1967	30.00
❏ E-4317 [M]	Their Second Album	1965	30.00
❏ SE-4317 [S]	Their Second Album	1965	30.00
❏ SE-4477	The Sam The Sham Revue	1968	25.00
—Retitled reissue			
❏ T90422 [M]	Wooly Bully	1965	60.00
—Capitol Record Club edition			
❏ ST90422 [S]	Wooly Bully	1965	50.00
—Capitol Record Club edition			
❏ E-4297 [M]	Wooly Bully	1965	30.00
❏ SE-4297 [S]	Wooly Bully	1965	40.00

POLYDOR
❏ 827917-1	The Best of Sam the Sham and the Pharoahs	1985	12.00

RHINO
❏ RNLP-122	Pharoahization: The Best of Sam the Sham and the Pharoahs (1965-1967)	1986	12.00

SAMHAIN

PLAN 9
❏ PL9-04	Initium	1984	100.00
—500 on red vinyl			
❏ PL9-04	Initium	1984	300.00
—No more than 100 on marbled black and white vinyl			
❏ PL9-04	Initium	1984	50.00
—Black vinyl; "8-84" scrawled in trail-off wax			
❏ PL9-04	Initium	1984	300.00
—100 on white vinyl			
❏ PL9-04	Initium	1984	400.00
—Pink vinyl "error" pressing			
❏ PL9-07	November Coming Fire	1986	150.00
—200 on orange vinyl			
❏ PL9-07	November Coming Fire	1986	30.00
—Regular issue on black vinyl			
❏ PL9-05 [EP]	Unholy Passion	1985	80.00
—Black vinyl, tan cover (original)			
❏ PL9-05 [EP]	Unholy Passion	1985	100.00
—Red vinyl, maroon cover			
❏ PL9-05 [EP]	Unholy Passion	1985	100.00
White vinyl, tan cover			
❏ PL9-05 [EP]	Unholy Passion	1985	15.00
—Black vinyl, maroon cover			

SAMI JO

MGM
❏ M3G-4998	Sami Jo	1975	15.00

MGM SOUTH
❏ S3G703	It Could Have Been Me	1974	15.00

SAMMES, MIKE, SINGERS

COMPOSE
❏ S98032	White Christmas	1970	18.00

SAMPLE, JOE, AND DAVID T. WALKER

CRUSADERS
❏ 16004	Swing Street Café	198?	25.00
—Audiophile vinyl			

MCA
❏ 5785	Swing Street Café	198?	12.00

SAMPLE, JOE; RAY BROWN; SHELLY MANNE

EAST WIND
❏ 10001	The Three	1976	25.00

INNER CITY
❏ IC-6007	The Three	197?	18.00

SAMPLE, JOE

ABC
❏ AA-1126	Carmel	1979	15.00
❏ AA-1050	Rainbow Seeker	1978	12.00

CRUSADERS
❏ 16001	Carmel	198?	25.00
—Audiophile vinyl			

MCA
❏ 37210	Carmel	198?	10.00
—Budget-line reissue			
❏ AA-1126	Carmel	1979	12.00
—Reissue of ABC 1126			
❏ 5481	Oasis	1985	12.00
❏ AA-1050	Rainbow Seeker	1979	10.00
—Reissue of ABC 1050			
❏ 5978	Roles	1987	12.00
❏ 5397	The Hunter	1983	12.00
❏ 5172	Voices in the Rain	1981	12.00
❏ 27077	Voices in the Rain	198?	10.00
—Budget-line reissue			

MOBILE FIDELITY
❏ 1-016	Rainbow Seeker	1979	25.00
—Audiophile vinyl			

Number	Title	Yr	NM
STORYVILLE			
❏ 4000	Fancy Dance	1980	15.00
WARNER BROS.			
❏ 26318	Ashes to Ashes	1990	18.00
❏ 25781	Spellbound	1989	15.00
SAMPLES, JUNIOR			
CHART			
❏ CHS-1045	Best of Junior Samples	1970	18.00
❏ CHS-1007	Bull Session at Bulls Gap	1968	18.00
❏ CHS-1021	That's a Hee Haw	1969	18.00
❏ CHM-1002 [M]	The World of Junior Samples	1967	25.00
❏ CHS-1002 [S]	The World of Junior Samples	1967	25.00
HILLTOP			
❏ JS-6113	Moonshining	197?	12.00
SAMPSON, EDGAR			
CORAL			
❏ CRL57049 [M]	Swing Softly Sweet Sampson	1957	40.00
MCA			
❏ 1354	Sampson Swings Again	198?	12.00
SAMS, GEORGE			
HAT HUT			
❏ 3506	Nomadic Winds	198?	15.00
SAMUELS, DAVID			
MCA			
❏ 6328	Ten Degrees North	1988	12.00
SAN REMO GOLDEN STRINGS			
GORDY			
❏ G-923 [M]	Hungry for Love	1967	30.00
❏ GS-923 [S]	Hungry for Love	1967	30.00
❏ GS-928 [S]	Swing	1968	25.00
❏ GLP-928 [M]	Swing	1968	60.00
— Mono is white label promo only; stereo cover has "Monaural Record DJ Copy" sticker on front			
RIC-TIC			
❏ 901 [M]	Hungry for Love	1966	50.00
❏ S-901 [S]	Hungry for Love	1966	60.00
SAN SEBASTIAN STRINGS, THE			
STANYAN			
❏ 10043	La Mer	1972	12.00
WARNER BROS.			
❏ BS2768	Bouquet -- The Best of the San Sebastian Strings	1974	12.00
❏ WS1705	For Lovers	1969	15.00
❏ WS1764	Home to the Sea	1968	15.00
❏ ST-91618	Home to the Sea	1968	18.00
— Capitol Record Club edition			
❏ 4WS2754	Seasons	1973	25.00
❏ BS2707	Summer	1973	12.00
❏ BS4 2707 [Q]	Summer	1973	18.00
❏ 3WS1827	The Complete Sea	1969	25.00
❏ W1705 [M]	The Earth	1967	18.00
❏ WS1705 [S]	The Earth	1967	15.00
❏ W1670 [M]	The Sea	1967	18.00
❏ WS1670 [S]	The Sea	1967	15.00
❏ 3WS1730	The Sea, The Earth, The Sky	1968	25.00
❏ WS1720	The Sky	1968	15.00
❏ WS1839	The Soft Sea	1970	15.00
❏ BS2622	Winter	1972	12.00
❏ BS2837	With Love	1975	12.00
SANBORN, DAVID			
REPRISE			
❏ 25715	Close-Up	1988	12.00
WARNER BROS.			
❏ 25479	A Change of Heart	1987	12.00
❏ 23650	As We Speak	1982	12.00
❏ 23906	Backstreet	1983	12.00
❏ BSK3189	Heart to Heart	1978	12.00
❏ BSK3379	Hideaway	1980	12.00
❏ BS3051	Promise Me the Moon	1977	12.00
❏ BS2957	Sanborn	1976	12.00
❏ 25150	Straight from the Heart	1985	12.00
❏ BS2873	Taking Off	1975	12.00
❏ BSK3546	Voyeur	1981	12.00
SANCHEZ, PONCHO			
CONCORD PICANTE			
❏ CJP-239	Bien Sabroso	198?	12.00
❏ CJP-286	El Conguero	1985	12.00
❏ CJP-340	Fuente	1988	12.00
❏ CJP-369	La Familia	1989	12.00
❏ CJP-310	Papa Gato	1987	12.00
❏ CJP-201	Sonando	198?	12.00
DISCOVERY			
❏ 799	Poncho	1979	15.00
❏ 813	Straight Ahead	1980	15.00
SANCIOUS, DAVID			
ELEKTRA/MUSICIAN			
❏ 60130	The Bridge	1982	12.00

Number	Title	Yr	NM
SANCTON, TOMMY			
GHB			
❏ GHB-52	Tommy Sancton's Galvanized Washboard Band	1969	15.00
SANCTUARY			
COLUMBIA			
❏ 45085	Into The Mirror Black	1990	16.00
❏ BFE40920	Refuge Denied	1987	12.00
SANDALS, THE			
WORLD PACIFIC			
❏ WP-1818 [M]	Scrambler	1964	80.00
— As "The Sandells			
❏ ST-1818 [S]	Scrambler	1964	100.00
— As "The Sandells"; black vinyl			
❏ ST-1818 [S]	Scrambler	1964	250.00
— As "The Sandells"; red vinyl			
❏ WP-1832 [M]	The Endless Summer	1966	30.00
❏ ST-1832 [S]	The Endless Summer	1966	30.00
❏ ST-21884	The Last of the Ski Bums	1969	30.00
— With skiers' silhouettes on cover			
❏ ST-21884	The Last of the Ski Bums	1969	30.00
— With Volkswagon bus on cover			
SANDBERG, CARL			
COLUMBIA MASTERWORKS			
❏ ML5539 [M]	Flat Rock Ballads	1959	25.00
DECCA			
❏ DL9105 [M]	Cowboy Songs and Negro Spirituals	1964	25.00
❏ DL5135 [10]	The People, Yes	1950	50.00
LYRICHORD			
❏ LL-4 [10]	American Songbag	1951	50.00
❏ LL-66 [M]	The Great Carl Sandburg	1957	30.00
SANDBERG, PAUL			
MANNA			
❏ MS-2068	The Wonder and Warmth of Christmas	1980	12.00
SANDERS, ANNETTE			
SOVEREIGN			
❏ SOV-502	The Time Is Right	198?	15.00
SANDERS, ED			
REPRISE			
❏ MS2105 [B]	Beer Cans on the Moon	1972	30.00
❏ RS-6374 [B]	Sanders' Truckstop	1969	50.00
SANDERS, FELICIA			
COLUMBIA			
❏ CL634 [M]	Felicia Sanders at the Blue Angel	1955	30.00
❏ OL710 [M]	Girl Meets Boy	1955	30.00
DECCA			
❏ DL8762 [M]	That Certain Feeling	1958	30.00
❏ DL78762 [S]	That Certain Feeling	1959	40.00
SANDERS, GEORGE			
ABC-PARAMOUNT			
❏ ABC-231 [M]	The George Sanders Touch	1958	30.00
SANDERS, PHAROAH			
ABC IMPULSE!			
❏ AS-9219	Black Unity	1972	18.00
❏ AQ-9219 [Q]	Black Unity	1974	25.00
❏ AS-9261	Elevation	1974	15.00
❏ AQ-9261 [Q]	Elevation	1974	25.00
❏ AS-9190	Jewels of Thought	1970	25.00
❏ AS-9181	Karma	1969	25.00
❏ AS-9227	Live at the East	1973	18.00
❏ AQ-9227 [Q]	Live at the East	1974	25.00
❏ ASD-9280	Love in Us All	1975	15.00
❏ AQ-9280 [Q]	Love in Us All	1975	25.00
❏ AS-9199	Summun Bukmun Umyum	1970	25.00
❏ A-9138 [M]	Tauhid	1967	30.00
❏ AS-9138 [S]	Tauhid	1967	25.00
❏ AS-9229	The Best of Pharoah Sanders	1973	25.00
❏ AS-9206	Thembi	1971	18.00
❏ AS-9254	Village of the Pharoahs	1974	15.00
❏ AQ-9254 [Q]	Village of the Pharoahs	1974	25.00
❏ AS-9233	Wisdom Through Music	1973	18.00
ARISTA			
❏ AL4161	Love Will Find a Way	1978	15.00
ESP-DISK'			
❏ 1003 [M]	Pharoah's First	1965	30.00
❏ S-1003 [S]	Pharoah's First	1965	30.00
GRP/IMPULSE!			
❏ IMP-219	Black Unity	199?	18.00
— Reissue on audiophile vinyl			
INDIA NAVIGATION			
❏ IN-1027	Pharoah	1977	15.00

Number	Title	Yr	NM
MCA			
❏ 29058	Jewels of Thought	1981	10.00
— Reissue of Impulse 9190			
❏ 29057	Karma	1981	10.00
— Reissue of Impulse 9181			
❏ 29056	Tauhid	1981	10.00
— Reissue of Impulse 9138			
❏ 4151	The Best of Pharoah Sanders	1981	15.00
— Reissue of Impulse 9229			
❏ 29059	Thembi	1981	10.00
— Reissue of Impulse 9206			
SIGNATURE			
❏ FA40952	Oh Lord, Let Me Do No Wrong	1989	15.00
STRATA-EAST			
❏ 19733	Izipho Sam (My Gifts)	1973	18.00
THERESA			
❏ 118	Heart Is a Melody	1986	12.00
❏ 108/9	Journey to the One	1980	18.00
❏ 116	Pharoah Sanders Live	1985	12.00
❏ 112/13	Rejoice	1981	18.00
❏ 121	Shukuru	1986	12.00
TIMELESS			
❏ SJP-253	Africa	1990	15.00
UPFRONT			
❏ 150	Spotlight	1973	15.00
SANDERS, RAY			
IMPERIAL			
❏ LP-12447	Feelin' Good Is Easy	1969	18.00
REPUBLIC			
❏ 5004	I Don't Want to Be Alone Tonight	1977	15.00
UNITED ARTISTS			
❏ UAS-6822	Ray Sanders	1972	15.00
SANDERS, THE			
AIRBORNE			
❏ 61003	Into Every Life	1988	15.00
SANDKE, JORDAN			
STASH			
❏ ST-259	Rhythm Is Our Business	1986	12.00
SANDKE, RANDY			
STASH			
❏ ST-264	New York Stories	1987	12.00
SANDLER AND YOUNG			
CAPITOL			
❏ S1-449	Honey Come Back	1970	15.00
❏ T2802 [M]	More and More	1967	18.00
❏ ST2802 [S]	More and More	1967	15.00
❏ T2000 [M]	On the Move	1967	15.00
❏ ST2686 [S]	On the Move	1967	18.00
❏ ST-241	Pretty Things Come in Twos	1969	15.00
❏ T2598 [M]	Side by Side	1966	15.00
— also known as "Tony Sandler and Ralph Young			
❏ ST2598 [S]	Side by Side	1966	18.00
❏ ST2967	The Christmas World of Sandler and Young	1968	15.00
❏ ST-159	Together	1968	15.00
HOLIDAY			
❏ HDY1942	Happy Holidays!	1981	10.00
— Reissue of True Value 2 (almost identical front cover, different back cover)			
RALTON			
❏ SY200	Re-Discover Christmas	19??	18.00
— Has same contents as "Happy Holidays, Volume 11"; is this the original?			
TRUE VALUE			
❏ 1	Happy Holidays, Album Eleven	1975	12.00
— Sold only at True Value Hardware stores			
❏ 2	Happy Holidays! Album Twelve	1976	12.00
— Sold only at True Value Hardware stores			
SANDOLE, DENNIS			
FANTASY			
❏ 3251 [M]	Compositions and Arrangements for Guitar	1958	30.00
SANDOLE BROTHERS, THE			
FANTASY			
❏ 3209 [M]	Modern Music from Philadelphia	1956	50.00
— Red vinyl			
❏ 3209 [M]	Modern Music from Philadelphia	1957	30.00
— Black vinyl			
SANDOVAL, ARTURO			
GRP			
❏ GR-9634	Flight to Freedom	1991	18.00

SANDPIPERS, THE

A&M

Number	Title	Yr	NM
❑ SP-4328	A Gift of Song	1972	15.00
❑ SP-4262	Come Saturday Morning	1970	15.00
❑ SP-3525	Foursider	1973	15.00
❑ SP-6014	Foursider	198?	12.00
—Reissue of 3525			
❑ SP-4246	Greatest Hits	1970	15.00
❑ LP-117 [M]	Guantanamera	1966	15.00
❑ SP-4117 [S]	Guantanamera	1966	18.00
❑ SP-4135	Misty Roses	1967	15.00
❑ SP-4147	Softly	1968	15.00
❑ LP-125 [M]	The Sandpipers	1967	18.00
❑ SP-4125 [S]	The Sandpipers	1967	15.00
❑ SP-4159	The Spanish Album	1969	15.00
❑ SP-4180	The Wonder of You	1969	15.00

SANDS, EVIE

A&M

Number	Title	Yr	NM
❑ SP-4239 [B]	Any Way That You Want Me	1969	35.00

HAVEN

Number	Title	Yr	NM
❑ ST-9202	Estate of Mind	1975	25.00

RCA VICTOR

Number	Title	Yr	NM
❑ AFL1-2943	Suspended Animation	1979	18.00

SANDS, TOMMY

CAPITOL

Number	Title	Yr	NM
❑ T1426 [M]	Dream with Me	1961	30.00
❑ ST1426 [S]	Dream with Me	1961	40.00
❑ T1364 [M]	Sands at the Sands	1960	30.00
❑ ST1364 [S]	Sands at the Sands	1960	40.00
❑ T1081 [M]	Sands Storm	1959	50.00
❑ T929 [M]	Sing Boy Sing	1958	60.00
❑ T848 [M]	Steady Date with Tommy Sands	1957	60.00
❑ T1123 [M]	This Thing Called Love	1959	30.00
❑ ST1123 [S]	This Thing Called Love	1959	40.00
❑ T1239 [M]	When I'm Thinking of You	1960	30.00
❑ ST1239 [S]	When I'm Thinking of You	1960	40.00

GREEN LINNET

Number	Title	Yr	NM
❑ SIF-3044	Singing of the Times	1989	15.00

SANG, SAMANTHA

LIBERTY

Number	Title	Yr	NM
❑ LN-10017	From Dance to Love	1980	10.00
—Budget-line reissue			

PRIVATE STOCK

Number	Title	Yr	NM
❑ PS-7009	Emotion	1978	12.00

UNITED ARTISTS

Number	Title	Yr	NM
❑ UA-LA965-H	From Dance to Love	1979	12.00

SANGUMA

ODE NEW ZEALAND

Number	Title	Yr	NM
❑ SODE-194	Sanguma	1986	15.00

SANTA CLAUS

CAPITOL

Number	Title	Yr	NM
❑ T2836	Santa's Own Christmas	1967	18.00

SANTA ESMERALDA

CASABLANCA

Number	Title	Yr	NM
❑ NBLP7175	Another Cha-Cha	1979	15.00
❑ NBLP7109	Beauty	1978	15.00
❑ NBLP7216	Don't Be Shy Tonight	1980	15.00
❑ NBLP7080	Don't Let Me Be Misunderstood	1977	15.00
❑ NBLP7088	House of the Rising Sun	1978	15.00

SANTA FE

RTV

Number	Title	Yr	NM
❑ 301	Good Earth	197?	30.00

SANTAMARIA, MONGO

ATLANTIC

Number	Title	Yr	NM
❑ SD8252	Feelin' Alright	1970	15.00
❑ SD1567	Mongo '70	1970	15.00
❑ SD1593	Mongo at Montreux	1972	15.00
❑ SD1581	Mongo's Way	1971	15.00
❑ SD1621 [S]	Up from the Roots	1972	15.00
❑ 1621 [M]	Up from the Roots	1972	30.00
—Mono is white label promo only; "d/j copy monaural" sticker on stereo cover			

BATTLE

Number	Title	Yr	NM
❑ B-6129 [M]	Mongo at the Village Gate	1964	25.00
❑ BS-96129 [S]	Mongo at the Village Gate	1964	30.00
❑ B-6120 [M]	Watermelon Man!	1963	25.00
❑ BS-96120 [S]	Watermelon Man!	1963	30.00

COLUMBIA

Number	Title	Yr	NM
❑ CS9988	All Strung Out	1970	18.00
❑ CL2411 [M]	El Bravo	1966	15.00
❑ CS9211 [S]	El Bravo	1966	18.00
❑ CL2298 [M]	El Pussy Cat	1965	25.00
—With "Guaranteed High Fidelity" in black at bottom of red label			
❑ CS9098 [S]	El Pussy Cat	1965	30.00
—With "360 Sound Stereo" in black at bottom of red label			
❑ CL2298 [M]	El Pussy Cat	1965	15.00
—With "360 Sound Mono" in white at bottom of red label			
❑ CS9098 [S]	El Pussy Cat	1965	18.00
—With "360 Sound Stereo" in white at bottom of red label			
❑ CL2473 [M]	Hey! Let's Party	1966	15.00
❑ CS9273 [S]	Hey! Let's Party	1966	18.00
❑ CL2375 [M]	La Bamba	1965	18.00
❑ CS9175 [S]	La Bamba	1965	25.00
❑ CL2612 [M]	Mongomania	1967	18.00
❑ CS9412 [S]	Mongomania	1967	15.00
❑ CL2770 [M]	Mongo Santamaria Explodes at the Village Gate	1967	18.00
❑ CS9570 [S]	Mongo Santamaria Explodes at the Village Gate	1967	15.00
❑ CS1060	Mongo's Greatest Hits	1970	15.00
❑ PC1060	Mongo's Greatest Hits	198?	10.00
—Reissue with new prefix			
❑ CL2375 [M]	Mr. Watermelon Man	196?	15.00
—Retitled reissue			
❑ CS9175 [S]	Mr. Watermelon Man	196?	18.00
—Retitled reissue			
❑ CS9653	Soul Bag	1968	18.00
❑ CS9780	Stone Soul	1969	18.00
❑ CS9937	Workin' on a Groovy Thing	1969	18.00

CONCORD JAZZ

Number	Title	Yr	NM
❑ CJ-387	Ole Ola	1989	15.00

CONCORD PICANTE

Number	Title	Yr	NM
❑ CJP-362	Soca Me Nice	1988	12.00
❑ CJP-327	Soy Yo	1987	12.00

FANTASY

Number	Title	Yr	NM
❑ 3324 [M]	Arriba!	1961	40.00
—Red vinyl			
❑ 3324 [M]	Arriba!	1961	30.00
—Black vinyl			
❑ 8067 [S]	Arriba!	1962	30.00
—Blue vinyl			
❑ 8067 [S]	Arriba!	1962	25.00
—Black vinyl			
❑ 3328 [M]	Mas Sabroso	1962	40.00
—Red vinyl			
❑ 3328 [M]	Mas Sabroso	1962	30.00
—Black vinyl			
❑ 8071 [S]	Mas Sabroso	1962	30.00
—Blue vinyl			
❑ 8071 [S]	Mas Sabroso	1962	25.00
—Black vinyl			
❑ 8351 [S]	Mighty Mongo	1963	25.00
❑ 3351 [M]	Mighty Mongo	1963	18.00
❑ 3291 [M]	Mongo	1959	40.00
—Red vinyl			
❑ 3291 [M]	Mongo	1959	30.00
—Black vinyl			
❑ 8032 [S]	Mongo	1962	30.00
—Blue vinyl			
❑ 8032 [S]	Mongo	1962	25.00
—Black vinyl			
❑ OJC-490	Mongo at the Village Gate	1991	15.00
—Reissue of Riverside 93529			
❑ 3311 [M]	Mongo in Havana	1960	40.00
—Red vinyl			
❑ 3311 [M]	Mongo in Havana	1960	30.00
—Black vinyl			
❑ 8055 [S]	Mongo in Havana	1962	30.00
—Blue vinyl			
❑ 8055 [S]	Mongo in Havana	1962	25.00
—Black vinyl			
❑ 8373	Mongo Santamaria's Greatest Hits	1967	15.00
❑ MPF-4529	Mongo Santamaria's Greatest Hits	198?	10.00
—Budget-line reissue			
❑ 9431	Mongo Y La Lupe	1974	15.00
❑ 3302 [M]	Our Man in Havana	1960	40.00
—Red vinyl			
❑ 3302 [M]	Our Man in Havana	1960	30.00
—Black vinyl			
❑ 8045 [S]	Our Man in Havana	1962	30.00
—Blue vinyl			
❑ 8045 [S]	Our Man in Havana	1962	25.00
—Black vinyl			
❑ 3314 [M]	Sabroso	1960	40.00
—Red vinyl			
❑ 3314 [M]	Sabroso	1960	30.00
—Black vinyl			
❑ 8058 [S]	Sabroso	1962	30.00
—Blue vinyl			
❑ 8058 [S]	Sabroso	1962	25.00
—Black vinyl			
❑ OJC-281	Sabroso	1987	12.00
—Reissue of 8058			
❑ OJC-626	Summertime	1991	15.00
—Reissue of Pablo 2308 229			
❑ 3335 [M]	Viva Mongo!	1962	40.00
—Red vinyl			
❑ 3335 [M]	Viva Mongo!	1962	30.00
—Black vinyl			
❑ 8087 [S]	Viva Mongo!	1962	30.00
—Blue vinyl			
❑ 8087 [S]	Viva Mongo!	1962	25.00
—Black vinyl			
❑ 3267 [M]	Yambu	1959	40.00
—Red vinyl			
❑ 3267 [M]	Yambu	1959	30.00
—Black vinyl			
❑ 8012 [S]	Yambu	1962	30.00
—Blue vinyl			
❑ 8012 [S]	Yambu	1962	25.00
—Black vinyl			
❑ OJC-276	Yambu	1987	12.00
—Reissue of 8012			

HARMONY

Number	Title	Yr	NM
❑ H30291	The Dock of the Bay	1971	12.00

MILESTONE

Number	Title	Yr	NM
❑ 47038	Skins	1976	18.00
❑ 47012	Watermelon Man	1974	18.00

PABLO

Number	Title	Yr	NM
❑ 2308229	Summertime	1980	15.00

PRESTIGE

Number	Title	Yr	NM
❑ 24018	Afro Roots	1973	18.00

RIVERSIDE

Number	Title	Yr	NM
❑ R-3008 [M]	Explosion	1967	30.00
❑ RS-3008 [S]	Explosion	1968	18.00
❑ RM-3008 [M]	Explosion	1968	30.00
❑ RLP-423 [M]	Go, Mongo!	1962	30.00
❑ RS-9423 [S]	Go, Mongo!	1962	30.00
❑ RM-3529 [M]	Mongo at the Village Gate	1963	25.00
❑ RS-93529 [S]	Mongo at the Village Gate	1963	30.00
❑ RM-3523 [M]	Mongo Introduces La Lupe	1963	25.00
❑ RS-93523 [S]	Mongo Introduces La Lupe	1963	30.00
❑ RM-3530 [M]	Mongo Santamaria Explodes!	1964	25.00
❑ RS-93530 [S]	Mongo Santamaria Explodes!	1964	30.00
❑ RS-3045	Mongo Soul	1969	18.00

TICO

Number	Title	Yr	NM
❑ LP-137 [10]	Chango	1955	80.00
❑ LP-1037 [M]	Chango: Mongo Santamaria's Drums and Chants	1957	60.00
❑ LP-1149 [M]	Mongo Santamaria's Drums and Chants	1967	25.00

SANTANA, CARLOS, AND BUDDY MILES

COLUMBIA

Number	Title	Yr	NM
❑ KC31308	Carlos Santana and Buddy Miles! Live!	1972	15.00
❑ PC31308	Carlos Santana and Buddy Miles! Live!	197?	10.00
—Reissue with new prefix			

SANTANA, CARLOS, AND MAHAVISHNU JOHN MCLAUGHLIN

COLUMBIA

Number	Title	Yr	NM
❑ KC32034	Love Devotion Surrender	1973	12.00
❑ PC32034	Love Devotion Surrender	197?	10.00
—Reissue with new prefix			

SANTANA, CARLOS

COLUMBIA

Number	Title	Yr	NM
❑ FC40875	Blues for Salvador	1987	12.00
❑ FC38642	Havana Moon	1983	12.00
❑ JC35686	Oneness/Silver Dreams-Golden Reality	1979	12.00
❑ AS573 [DJ]	The Solo Guitar of Devadip Carlos Santana	1979	18.00
❑ C236590	The Swing of Delight	1980	15.00

SANTANA

ARISTA

Number	Title	Yr	NM
❑ 19080	Supernatural	2000	40.00
—Classic Records audiophile vinyl issue in gatefold cover with booklet			

CICADELIC

Number	Title	Yr	NM
❑ 1004	Santana '68	1988	15.00

CLEOPATRA

Number	Title	Yr	NM
❑ CLP1816 [B]	1968 San Francisco	2014	30.00
❑ 8203 [B]	The Early San Francisco Years		30.00
—picture disc			

COLUMBIA

Number	Title	Yr	NM
❑ KC30130	Abraxas	1970	18.00
—Original copies have a poster			
❑ KC30130	Abraxas	197?	12.00
—With no poster			
❑ PC30130	Abraxas	1985	10.00
❑ CQ30130 [Q]	Abraxas	1972	30.00
❑ HC40130 [B]	Abraxas	1981	100.00
—Half-speed mastered edition			
❑ JC30130	Abraxas	1977	10.00
❑ PC33576	Amigos	1976	15.00
—No bar code on cover			
❑ PCQ33576 [Q]	Amigos	1976	25.00
❑ PC33576	Amigos	1979	10.00
—With bar code on cover			
❑ FC39527	Beyond Appearances	1985	12.00
❑ PC39527	Beyond Appearances	198?	10.00
—Budget-line reissue			
❑ PC33135	Borboletta	1974	15.00
—No bar code on cover			

Number	Title	Yr	NM
❏ PC33135	Borboletta	1979	10.00
— With bar code on cover			
❏ PCQ33135 [Q]	Borboletta	1974	25.00
❏ KC31610	Caravanserai	1972	15.00
❏ PC31610	Caravanserai	197?	10.00
❏ PCQ31610 [Q]	Caravanserai	1974	30.00
❏ JC34423	Festival	1977	15.00
❏ JCQ34423 [Q]	Festival	1977	25.00
❏ PC34423	Festival	198?	10.00
❏ FC40272	Freedom	1987	12.00
❏ FC35600	Inner Secrets	1978	15.00
❏ PC35600	Inner Secrets	198?	10.00
— Budget-line reissue			
❏ FC36154	Marathon	1979	15.00
❏ PC36154	Marathon	198?	10.00
— Budget-line reissue			
❏ C234914	Moonflower	1977	18.00
❏ CS9781	Santana	1969	18.00
— 360 Sound" on label			
❏ CS9781	Santana	1970	12.00
— Orange label			
❏ PC9781	Santana	198?	10.00
❏ KC30595	Santana	1971	15.00
— Not the same album as CS 9781; this is often called "Santana III"			
❏ CQ30595 [Q]	Santana	1972	30.00
❏ PC30595	Santana	197?	10.00
❏ PCQ32964 [Q]	Santana	1974	30.00
— Quadraphonic issue of their debut album (9781)			
❏ PC33050	Santana's Greatest Hits	1974	15.00
— No bar code on cover			
❏ JC33050	Santana's Greatest Hits	1977	10.00
❏ PCQ33050 [Q]	Santana's Greatest Hits	1974	30.00
❏ FC38122	Shango	1982	15.00
❏ PC38122	Shango	198?	10.00
— Budget-line reissue			
❏ C236590	Swing of Delight	1980	18.00
❏ C3X44344	Viva Santana	1988	25.00
❏ PC32455	Welcome	1973	15.00
— No bar code on cover			
❏ PC32455	Welcome	1979	10.00
— With bar code on cover			
❏ PCQ32455 [Q]	Welcome	1974	30.00
❏ FC37158	Zebop!	1981	15.00
❏ HC47158	Zebop!	1981	40.00
— Half-speed mastered edition			
❏ PC37158	Zebop!	198?	10.00
— Budget-line reissue			

MOBILE FIDELITY

❏ MOFI1-039 [B]	Santana III	2014	40.00

SANTA'S HELPERS

DESIGN

❏ SDLPX-30 [S]	All I Want for Christmas Are My Two Front Teeth	190?	15.00

SANTIAGO, MIKE

CHIAROSCURO

❏ 193	White Trees	1978	15.00

SANTO AND JOHNNY

CANADIAN AMERICAN

❏ CALP-1008 [M]	Around the World with Santo and Johnny	1962	30.00
❏ SCALP-1008 [S]	Around the World with Santo and Johnny	1962	40.00
❏ CALP-1006 [M]	Come On In	1962	30.00
❏ SCALP-1006 [S]	Come On In	1962	40.00
❏ CALP-1002 [M]	Encore	1960	40.00
❏ SCALP-1002 [S]	Encore	1960	50.00
❏ CALP-1004 [M]	Hawaii	1961	40.00
❏ SCALP-1004 [S]	Hawaii	1961	50.00
❏ CALP-1014 [M]	In the Still of the Night	1963	30.00
❏ SCALP-1014 [S]	In the Still of the Night	1963	40.00
❏ CALP-1018 [M]	Mucho	1965	30.00
❏ SCALP-1018 [S]	Mucho	1965	40.00
❏ CALP-1011 [M]	Off Shore	1963	30.00
❏ SCALP-1011 [S]	Off Shore	1963	40.00
❏ CALP-1001 [M]	Santo & Johnny	1959	60.00
❏ SCALP-1001 [S]	Santo & Johnny	1959	80.00
❏ CALP-1017 [M]	The Beatles' Greatest Hits	1965	40.00
❏ SCALP-1017 [S]	The Beatles' Greatest Hits	1965	50.00
❏ CALP-1016 [M]	Wish You Love	1964	30.00
❏ SCALP-1016 [S]	Wish You Love	1964	40.00

IMPERIAL

❏ LP-9363 [M]	Brilliant Guitar Sounds	1967	18.00
❏ LP-12363 [S]	Brilliant Guitar Sounds	1967	25.00
❏ LP-12366	Golden Guitars	1968	18.00
❏ LP-12418	On the Road Again	1968	18.00

SANTOS, LARRY

CASABLANCA

❏ NBLP7061	Don't Let the Music Stop	1977	15.00
❏ NBLP7030	You Are Everything I Need	1976	15.00

EVOLUTION

❏ 2002	Just a Man	1969	25.00
❏ 2015	Morning Sun	1971	18.00

SANTOS, MOACIR

BLUE NOTE

❏ BN-LA483-G	Carnival of the Spirits	1975	18.00

Number	Title	Yr	NM
❏ BN-LA007-F	Maestro	1972	25.00
❏ BN-LA260-G	Saudade	1974	18.00

DISCOVERY

❏ 795	Opus 3, No. 1	1979	15.00

SANTOS BROTHERS, THE

METROJAZZ

❏ E-1015 [M]	Jazz For Two Trumpets	1958	50.00
❏ SE-1015 [S]	Jazz For Two Trumpets	1958	40.00

SAPODILLA PUNCH

PHILIPS

❏ PHS600312	Sapodilla Punch	1969	25.00

SAPPHIRE THINKERS, THE

HOBBIT

❏ HB-5003	From Within	1969	30.00

SAPPHIRES, THE (1)

COLLECTABLES

❏ COL-5007	Who Do You Love	198?	12.00

SWAN

❏ LP-513 [M]	Who Do You Love	1964	300.00

SARACHO

ABC IMPULSE!

❏ AS-9247	En Medio	1974	18.00

SARBIB, SAHEB

CADENCE JAZZ

❏ CJR-1010	Aisha	198?	12.00
❏ CJR-1001	Live at the Public Theatre	198?	12.00
❏ CJR-1008	U.F.O. -- Live on Tour	198?	12.00

SOUL NOTE

❏ SN-1098	It Couldn't Happen Without You	198?	15.00
❏ SN-1048	Sessions	198?	15.00

SARSTEDT, PETER

UNITED ARTISTS

❏ UAS-5558	Every Word You Say Is Written Down	1971	12.00

WORLD PACIFIC

❏ WPS-21899	As Though It Were a Movie	1969	18.00
❏ WPS-21895 [B]	Where Do You Go To, My Lovely	1969	25.00

SASH, LEON

DELMARK

❏ DS-9416	I Remember Newport	1968	18.00

STORYVILLE

❏ STLP-917 [M]	Leon Sash Quartet	1956	50.00

SASKIA AND SERGE

ABC HICKORY

❏ HB-44008	Saskia and Serge	1978	12.00

SATAN AND THE DISCIPLES

GOLDBAND

❏ 7750 [B]	Underground	1969	80.00

SATANS, THE

(NO LABEL)

❏ (no #)0 [M]	Raisin' Hell	1962	300.00

SATAN'S FOUR

B.T. PUPPY

❏ BTS-1010	Mixed Soul	1970	150.00
— With the Cinnamon Angels			

SATCHMO LEGACY BAND, THE

SOUL NOTE

❏ 121116	Salute to Pops, Vol. 1	1990	18.00

SATIN STRINGS

SUTTON

❏ SU101X [M]	Satin Strings Play for Christmas	196?	15.00
❏ SSU101X [S]	Satin Strings Play for Christmas	196?	18.00

SATOH, MASAHIKO

ENJA

❏ 2008	Trinity	197?	18.00

PORTRAIT

❏ OR44194	Amorphism	1989	15.00

SATTERFIELD, ESTHER

A&M

❏ SP-3408	Once I Loved	1974	12.00
❏ SP-3411	The Need to Be	1975	12.00

SAUNDERS, HERM

VOGUE

❏ 101 [10]	Music at the Bantam Cock	1953	200.00

Number	Title	Yr	NM
WARNER BROS.			
❏ W1269 [M]	That Celestial Feeling	1959	25.00
❏ W1234 [M]	The Tinkling Piano in the Next Apartment	1958	25.00

SAUNDERS, MERL

CRYSTAL CLEAR

❏ 5006	Do I Move You	1980	25.00
— Direct-to-disc recording			

FANTASY

❏ 9421	Fire Up	1973	25.00
— With Jerry Garcia and Tom Fogerty			
❏ 8421	Heavy Turbulence	1972	18.00
❏ MPF-4533	Keystone Encores, Vol. 1	1988	15.00
❏ MPF-4534	Keystone Encores, Vol. 2	1988	15.00
❏ 9503	Leave Your Hat On	1976	15.00
❏ 79002	Live at the Keystone	198?	25.00
❏ MPF-4535	Live at the Keystone, Vol. 1	1988	15.00
❏ MPF-4536	Live at the Keystone, Vol. 2	1988	15.00
❏ 9460	Saunders	1974	18.00

GALAXY

❏ 8209	Soul Grooving	197?	18.00

SAUNDERS, TEDDY

DISCOVERY

❏ 809	Sue Blue	1980	15.00

SAUNDERS, TOM

BOUNTIFUL

❏ 38002	Tom Saunders' Surf Side Six	197?	18.00

SAUSSY, TUPPER

MONUMENT

❏ MLP-8034 [M]	A Swinger's Guide to "Mary Poppins	1965	25.00
❏ SLP-18034 [S]	A Swinger's Guide to "Mary Poppins	1965	30.00
❏ MLP-8004 [M]	Discover Tupper Saussy	1964	25.00
❏ SLP-18004 [S]	Discover Tupper Saussy	1964	30.00
❏ MLP-8027 [M]	Said I to Shostakovich	1965	25.00
❏ SLP-18027 [S]	Said I to Shostakovich	1965	30.00

SAUTER-FINEGAN; CHICAGO SYMPHONY ORCHESTRA (FRITZ REINER, CONDUCTOR)

RCA VICTOR RED SEAL

❏ LM-1888 [M]	Concerto for Jazz Band and Orchestra	1954	30.00

SAUTER-FINEGAN

GOLDEN ERA

❏ 15071	Sauter-Finegan Orchestra Revisited	198?	12.00

RCA VICTOR

❏ LPM-1240 [M]	Adventure In Time	1956	60.00
❏ LPM-1051 [M]	Concert Jazz	1955	60.00
❏ LJM-1003 [M]	Inside Sauter-Finegan	1954	80.00
❏ LPM-2473 [M]	Inside Sauter-Finegan Revisited	1961	30.00
❏ LSP-2473 [S]	Inside Sauter-Finegan Revisited	1961	40.00
❏ LPM-1034 [M]	Memories of Goodman and Miller	1958	50.00
❏ LPM-3115 [10]	New Directions in Music	1953	120.00
❏ LPM-1227 [M]	New Directions in Music	1956	60.00
❏ LPM-1104 [M]	Sons of Sauter-Finegan	1955	60.00
❏ LPM-1497 [M]	Straight Down the Middle	1957	50.00
❏ LPM-1009 [M]	The Sound of Sauter-Finegan	1954	80.00
❏ LPM-1341 [M]	Under Analysis	1957	50.00

UNITED ARTISTS

❏ WWR3511 [M]	The Return of the Doodletown Fifers	1959	40.00
❏ WWS7511 [S]	The Return of the Doodletown Fifers	1959	50.00

SAVAGE GRACE

REPRISE

❏ RS6399	Savage Grace	1970	30.00
❏ RS6484 [B]	Savage Grace 2	1971	30.00

SAVAGE RESURRECTION

MERCURY

❏ MG-21156 [M]	Savage Resurrection	1968	200.00
❏ SR-61156 [S]	Savage Resurrection	1968	100.00

SAVAGE ROSE

POLYDOR

❏ 24-6001	In the Plain	1969	25.00
— Gatefold cover			

SAVALAS, TELLY

AUDIO FIDELITY

❏ AFSD-6271	Telly Savalas	1975	18.00

MCA

❏ 436	Telly	1974	18.00
❏ 2160	Who Loves Ya Baby	1976	18.00

Number	Title	Yr	NM

SAVATAGE

ATLANTIC
❏ 81634	Fight for the Rock	1986	12.00
❏ 82008	Gutter Ballet	1990	18.00
❏ 81775	Hall of the Mountain King	1987	12.00
❏ 81247	Power of the Night	1985	15.00

COMBAT
| ❏ 8018 | Sirens | 1986 | 15.00 |

— *Reissue of Par LP with new cover*

| ❏ MX6016 [EP] | The Dungeons Are Calling | 1985 | 18.00 |

PAR
| ❏ PAR-1050 | Sirens | 1983 | 400.00 |

— *Blue vinyl*

| ❏ PAR-1050 | Sirens | 1983 | 200.00 |

— *Black vinyl*

SAVITT, BUDDY

PARKWAY
| ❏ P-7012 [M] | The Most Heard Sax in the World | 1962 | 30.00 |
| ❏ SP-7012 [S] | The Most Heard Sax in the World | 1962 | 100.00 |

SAVITT, JAN

HINDSIGHT
| ❏ HSR-213 | Jan Savitt and His Top Hatters 1939 | 198? | 12.00 |

SAVOY BROWN

GNP CRESCENDO
| ❏ GNPS-2196 | Kings of Boogie | 1989 | 12.00 |
| ❏ GNPS-2193 | Make Me Sweat | 1988 | 12.00 |

LONDON
❏ APS638	Boogie Brothers	1974	12.00
❏ PS718	Savage Return	1978	12.00
❏ PS670	Skin 'n' Bone	1976	12.00
❏ LC-50000	The Best of Savoy Brown	1977	12.00
❏ PS659	Wire Fire	1975	12.00

PARROT
❏ PAS71029	A Step Further	1969	18.00
❏ PAS71027	Blue Matter	1969	30.00
❏ PAS71024	Getting to the Point	1968	30.00
❏ XPAS71052	Hellbound Train	1972	18.00
❏ XPAS71059	Jack the Toad	1973	18.00
❏ XPAS71057	Lion's Share	1972	18.00
❏ PAS71042	Looking In	1970	18.00
❏ PAS71036	Raw Sienna	1970	18.00
❏ PAS71047	Street Corner Talking	1971	18.00

TOWN HOUSE
| ❏ SKBK-7003 | Greatest Hits Live in Concert | 1982 | 18.00 |
| ❏ ST-7002 | Rock 'n' Roll Warriors | 1981 | 15.00 |

SAWBUCK

FILLMORE
| ❏ Z31248 | Sawbuck | 1972 | 25.00 |

SAWYER, RAY

CAPITOL
| ❏ ST-11591 | Ray Sawyer | 1976 | 12.00 |

SAWYER BROWN

CAPITOL
❏ ST-12517	Out Goin' Cattin'	1986	10.00
❏ ST-12391	Sawyer Brown	1985	10.00
❏ ST-12438	Shakin'	1985	10.00
❏ CLT-46923	Somewhere in the Night	1987	10.00
❏ C1-92358	The Boys Are Back	1989	12.00
❏ C1-90417	Wide Open	1988	10.00

SAXON, SKY

GNP CRESCENDO
| ❏ GNP-2040 [M] | A Full Spoon of Seedy Blues | 1967 | 45.00 |
| ❏ GNPS-2040 [S] | A Full Spoon of Seedy Blues | 1967 | 40.00 |

SAXONS, THE

MIRASONIC
| ❏ A-1017 [M] | The Saxons | 1966 | 40.00 |
| ❏ AS-1017 [S] | The Saxons | 1966 | 80.00 |

SAYE, JOE

EMARCY
❏ MG-36147 [M]	A Double Shot of Saye	1958	40.00
❏ SR-80022 [S]	A Double Shot of Saye	1958	30.00
❏ MG-36112 [M]	A Wee Bit of Jazz	1957	40.00
❏ MG-36072 [M]	Scotch on the Rocks	1956	40.00

MERCURY
| ❏ SR-60052 [S] | A Wee Bit of Jazz | 1959 | 30.00 |

SAYER, LEO

CHRYSALIS
| ❏ PV41087 | Another Year | 1985 | 10.00 |

— *Reissue of Warner Bros. 2885*

| ❏ PV41125 | Endless Flight | 1985 | 10.00 |

— *Reissue of Warner Bros. 3101*

| ❏ PV41240 | Here | 1985 | 10.00 |

— *Reissue of Warner Bros. 3374*

| ❏ PV41198 | Leo Sayer | 1985 | 10.00 |

— *Reissue of Warner Bros. 3200*

| ❏ PV41154 | Thunder in My Heart | 1985 | 10.00 |

— *Reissue of Warner Bros. 3089*

WARNER BROS.
❏ BS2885	Another Year	1975	12.00
❏ BS2962	Endless Flight	1976	12.00
❏ BSK3101	Endless Flight	1977	10.00

— *Reissue of 2962*

❏ 25073	Have You Ever Been in Love	1984	12.00
❏ BSK3374	Here	1979	12.00
❏ BS2836	Just a Boy	1974	12.00
❏ BSK3200	Leo Sayer	1978	12.00
❏ BSK3483	Living in a Fantasy	1980	12.00
❏ BS2738	Silverbird	1973	15.00
❏ BSK3089	Thunder in My Heart	1977	12.00
❏ 23560	World Radio	1982	12.00

SAYLES SILVER LEAF RAGTIME

GHB
| ❏ GHB-8 | Sayles Sugar Leaf Ragtime | 196? | 18.00 |

SCAFFOLD, THE

BELL
| ❏ 6018 [S] | Thank U Very Much | 1968 | 60.00 |
| ❏ 6018 [M] | Thank U Very Much | 1968 | 80.00 |

— *Mono copies are promo only*

SCAGGS, BOZ

ATLANTIC
| ❏ SD8239 | Boz Scaggs | 1969 | 15.00 |
| ❏ SD19166 | Boz Scaggs | 1977 | 10.00 |

COLUMBIA
❏ KC30976	Boz Scaggs & Band	1971	12.00
❏ PC30976	Boz Scaggs & Band	197?	10.00
❏ JC37429	Down Two Then Left	1977	12.00
❏ PC37249	Down Two Then Left	198?	10.00

— *Budget-line reissue*

| ❏ FC36841 | Hits! | 1980 | 12.00 |
| ❏ PC36841 | Hits! | 198? | 10.00 |

— *Budget-line reissue*

| ❏ A2S71 [DJ] | KSAN Live Concert | 1974 | 50.00 |

— *Promo-only set released in plain cardboard jacket*

| ❏ FC36106 | Middle Man | 1980 | 12.00 |
| ❏ PC36106 | Middle Man | 198? | 10.00 |

— *Budget-line reissue*

❏ KC30454	Moments	1971	12.00
❏ PC30454	Moments	197?	10.00
❏ KC31384	My Time	1972	12.00
❏ PC31384	My Time	197?	10.00
❏ FC40463	Other Roads	1988	12.00
❏ JC33920	Silk Degrees	1977	12.00

— *Early reissue with new prefix*

| ❏ PC33920 | Silk Degrees | 1985 | 10.00 |

— *Budget-line reissue; bar code on back cover*

| ❏ HC43920 | Silk Degrees | 1981 | 30.00 |

— *Half-speed mastered edition*

| ❏ PC33920 | Silk Degrees | 1976 | 15.00 |

— *Original edition with "PC" prefix and no bar code on back cover*

| ❏ KC32760 | Slow Dancer | 1974 | 15.00 |

— *Original cover has Boz Scaggs on a beach in only a bathing suit*

| ❏ KC32760 | Slow Dancer | 1974 | 12.00 |

— *Second cover has a male dancer who is not Boz Scaggs*

| ❏ PC32760 | Slow Dancer | 197? | 10.00 |
| ❏ AS203 [DJ] | The Boz Scaggs Sampler | 1976 | 25.00 |

SCALETTA, DON

CAPITOL
❏ T2328 [M]	All in Good Time	1965	18.00
❏ ST2328 [S]	All in Good Time	1965	25.00
❏ T2204 [M]	Any Time, Any Groove	1965	18.00
❏ ST2204 [S]	Any Time, Any Groove	1965	25.00

VERVE
| ❏ V-5027 [M] | Sunday Afternoon at the Trident | 1967 | 25.00 |
| ❏ V6-5027 [S] | Sunday Afternoon at the Trident | 1967 | 18.00 |

SCAMPS, THE

PROJECT
| ❏ 8002 [M] | Teen Dance and Sing Along Party | 1962 | 40.00 |

SCANDAL

COLUMBIA
| ❏ 5C38194 [EP] | Scandal | 1983 | 12.00 |
| ❏ 8C839905 [EP] | Scandal featuring Patty Smyth | 1985 | 25.00 |

— *Picture disc EP with four of the group's biggest hits*

| ❏ FC39173 | Warrior | 1984 | 12.00 |

SCANIAZZ

STOMP OFF
❏ SOS-1056	It's Right Here for You	198?	12.00
❏ SOS-1004	Messin' Around	198?	12.00
❏ SOS-1038	Sunset Café Stomp	198?	12.00

SCARBURY, JOEY

ELEKTRA
| ❏ 5E-537 | America's Greatest Hero | 1981 | 12.00 |

SCARS ON BROADWAY

INTERSCOPE
| ❏ 1159201 | Scars on Broadway | 2008 | 25.00 |

SCHAEFER, HAL

DISCOVERY
| ❏ DS781 | Extraordinary Jazz Pianist | 1979 | 15.00 |

RCA VICTOR
| ❏ LPM-1106 [M] | Just Too Much | 1955 | 120.00 |
| ❏ LPM-1199 [M] | The RCA Victor Jazz Workshop | 1956 | 120.00 |

RENAISSANCE
| ❏ 1000 | Extraordinary Jazz Pianist | 197? | 18.00 |

UNITED ARTISTS
| ❏ UAL-3021 [M] | Ten Shades of Blue | 1959 | 60.00 |
| ❏ UAS-6021 [S] | Ten Shades of Blue | 1959 | 50.00 |

SCHAERLI, PETER

HAT ART
| ❏ 2037 | Schnipp Schnapp | 1987 | 18.00 |

SCHAFER, KERMIT

JUBILEE
❏ BL-1 [M]	Blooperama	196?	25.00
❏ JGM-2001 [M]	Comedy of Errors	196?	25.00
❏ JGM-2008 [M]	Foot 'n Mouth Club	196?	25.00
❏ JGM-2007 [M]	Funny Boners	196?	25.00
❏ JGM-2005 [M]	Off the Record	196?	25.00
❏ LP-2 [10]	Pardon My Blooper!	1954	40.00
❏ PMB-1 [M]	Pardon My Blooper! Volume 1	1958	25.00
❏ LP-3 [10]	Pardon My Blooper! Volume 2	1954	40.00
❏ PMB-2 [M]	Pardon My Blooper! Volume 2	1958	25.00
❏ LP-19 [10]	Pardon My Blooper! Volume 3	1955	40.00
❏ PMB-3 [M]	Pardon My Blooper! Volume 3	1958	25.00
❏ PMB-4 [M]	Pardon My Blooper! Volume 4	1958	25.00
❏ PMB-5 [M]	Pardon My Blooper! Volume 5	1959	25.00
❏ PMB-6 [M]	Pardon My Blooper! Volume 6	1959	25.00
❏ PMB-7 [M]	Pardon My Blooper! Volume 7	1959	25.00
❏ PMB-8 [M]	Pardon My Blooper! Volume 8	1959	25.00
❏ QPMB-10 [M]	Pardon My Quiz Blooper!	196?	25.00
❏ SPMB-9 [M]	Pardon My Sports Blooper!	196?	25.00
❏ WPMB-11 [M]	Pardon My Washington Blooper!	196?	25.00
❏ JGM-2003 [M]	Prize Bloopers	196?	25.00
❏ JGM-2002 [M]	Slipped Disks	196?	25.00
❏ JLP-1000 [M]	Special Edition: Pardon My Blooper	195?	30.00
❏ JGM-2006 [M]	Station Breaks	196?	25.00
❏ JGM-2004 [M]	Super Bloopers	196?	25.00
❏ KS-1 [M]	The Best of Bloopers	1959	30.00

SCHECKTER, JANE

DRG
| ❏ MRS-711 | I've Got My Standards | 1989 | 15.00 |

SCHEER MUSIC

PALO ALTO
| ❏ TB-204 | High Rise | 198? | 15.00 |
| ❏ PA-8025 | Rappin' It Up | 198? | 15.00 |

SCHIFRIN, LALO

AMERICAN INT'L.
| ❏ AILP3003 | The Amityville Horror | 1979 | 12.00 |

AUDIO FIDELITY
❏ AFLP-1981 [M]	Bossa Nova -- New Brazilian Jazz	1962	25.00
❏ AFSD-5981 [S]	Bossa Nova -- New Brazilian Jazz	1962	30.00
❏ AFLP-2117 [M]	Eso Es Latino Jazz	1963	25.00
❏ AFSD-6117 [S]	Eso Es Latino Jazz	1963	30.00
❏ AFSD-6195	The Other Side of Lalo Schifrin	1968	18.00

COLGEMS
| ❏ COMO-5003 [M] | Murderer's Row | 1967 | 50.00 |
| ❏ COSO-5003 [S] | Murderer's Row | 1967 | 100.00 |

CTI
| ❏ 5000 | Black Widow | 1976 | 15.00 |
| ❏ 5003 | Towering Toccata | 1977 | 15.00 |

DOT
❏ DLP-3833 [M]	Cool Hand Luke	1968	50.00
❏ DLP-25833 [S]	Cool Hand Luke	1968	50.00
❏ DLP-3831 [M]	Music from Mission: Impossible	1967	30.00
❏ DLP-25831 [S]	Music from Mission: Impossible	1967	40.00
❏ DLP-25852	There's a Whole Lot of Schifrin Goin' On	1968	25.00

Number	Title	Yr	NM

DRG
- SBL-12591 — The Fourth Protocol — 1987 — 18.00

ENTR'ACTE
- ERS-6510 — The Eagle Has Landed/The Four Musketeers — 1980 — 15.00
- ERS-6508 — Voyage of the Damned — 1977 — 30.00

MCA
- 25137 — Liquidator — 1966 — 10.00
- 2374 — Nunzio — 1978 — 15.00
- 2284 — Rollercoaster — 1977 — 18.00
- 25012 — The Cincinnati Kid — 1986 — 10.00
- 5185 — The Competition — 1980 — 12.00

MGM
- E-4156 [M] — Between Broadway and Hollywood — 1963 — 18.00
- SE-4156 [S] — Between Broadway and Hollywood — 1963 — 25.00
- E-4413ST [M] — Liquidator — 1966 — 25.00
- SE-4413ST [S] — Liquidator — 1966 — 30.00
- SE-4742 — Medical Center and Other Great Themes — 1971 — 25.00
- E-4110 [M] — Piano, Strings and Bossa Nova — 1963 — 18.00
- SE-4110 [S] — Piano, Strings and Bossa Nova — 1963 — 25.00
- E-4313 [M] — The Cincinnati Kid — 1965 — 25.00
- SE-4313 [S] — The Cincinnati Kid — 1965 — 30.00

NAUTILUS
- NR-51 — Ins and Outs — 198? — 40.00
- *Audiophile vinyl*

PALO ALTO
- 8055 — Ins and Outs — 1983 — 15.00

PARAMOUNT
- PAS-5004 — Mannix — 1969 — 30.00
- PAS-5002 — More Music from Mission: Impossible — 1969 — 40.00

ROULETTE
- R52088 [M] — Lalo Brilliance — 1962 — 25.00
- SR52088 [S] — Lalo Brilliance — 1962 — 30.00
- SR-42013 — Lalole" -- The Latin Sound — 1968 — 18.00

TABU
- JZ35436 — Gypsies — 1978 — 15.00
- JZ36091 — No One Home — 1979 — 15.00

TETRAGRAMMATON
- T-5006 — Che! — 1969 — 30.00

TICO
- LP-1070 [M] — Piano Espanol — 1960 — 30.00
- LPS-1070 [S] — Piano Espanol — 1960 — 30.00

VARESE SARABANDE
- STV-81198 — The Osterman Weekend — 1983 — 12.00

VERVE
- V6-8785 — Insensatez — 1968 — 18.00
- V-8601 [M] — New Fantasy — 1964 — 18.00
- V6-8601 [S] — New Fantasy — 1964 — 25.00
- V6-8624 [M] — Once a Thief and Other Themes — 1965 — 18.00
- V6-8624 [O] — Once a Thief and Other Themes — 1965 — 25.00
- V6-8801 — Rock Requiem — 1971 — 15.00
- V-8543 [M] — Samba Paros Dos — 1963 — 18.00
- *With Bob Brookmeyer*
- V6-8543 [O] — Samba Paros Dos — 1963 — 25.00
- *With Bob Brookmeyer*
- V-8654 [M] — The Dissection and Reconstruction of Music from the Past — 1966 — 18.00
- V6-8654 [S] — The Dissection and Reconstruction of Music from the Past — 1966 — 25.00

WARNER BROS.
- BSK3328 — Boulevard Nights — 1979 — 12.00
- WS1777 — Bullitt — 1968 — 60.00
- BS2727 — Enter the Dragon — 1973 — 60.00

SCHILLER, LAWRENCE

CAPITOL
- KAO2652 [M] — Homosexuality in the American Male — 1967 — 40.00
- TAO2574 [M] — LSD — 1966 — 100.00
- KAO2630 [M] — Why Did Lenny Bruce Die? — 1967 — 40.00

SCHILLING, PETER

ELEKTRA
- 60265 — Error in the System — 1983 — 12.00
- 60863 — The Different Story — 1989 — 12.00
- 60404 — Things to Come — 1985 — 12.00

SCHLAMME, MARTHA

VANGUARD
- VRS497 [M] — Chansons de Noel — 1956 — 30.00
- VRS-9019 [M] — Folk Songs of Many Lands — 195? — 30.00
- VRS-9011 [M] — Raisins and Almonds and Other Jewish Folk Songs — 195? — 30.00

SCHMIT, TIMOTHY B.

ASYLUM
- 60359 — Playin' It Cool — 1984 — 12.00

MCA
- 6420 — Tell Me the Truth — 1990 — 18.00
- 42049 — Timothy B. — 1987 — 12.00

SCHNEIDER, ERIC, AND EARL HINES

GATEMOUTH
- 1003 — Eric and Earl — 1980 — 15.00

SCHNEIDER, ERIC

GATEMOUTH
- 1005 — Eric's Alley — 1981 — 15.00

SCHNEIDER, FRED

WARNER BROS.
- 25158 — Fred Schneider and the Shake Society — 1984 — 15.00

SCHNEIDER, JOHN

MCA
- 5668 — A Memory Like You — 1986 — 10.00
- 42033 — Greatest Hits — 1987 — 10.00
- 5789 — Take the Long Way Home — 1986 — 10.00
- 5495 — Too Good to Stop Now — 1984 — 10.00
- 5583 — Tryin' to Outrun the Wind — 1985 — 10.00
- 5973 — You Ain't Seen the Last of Me — 1987 — 10.00

SCOTTI BROTHERS
- FZ38712 — If You Believe — 1983 — 12.00
- FZ37400 — Now or Never — 1981 — 12.00
- FZ37956 — Quiet Man — 1982 — 12.00
- FZ37617 — White Christmas — 1981 — 12.00
- 3Z37617 — White Christmas — 198? — 10.00
- *Budget-line reissue with new prefix*

SCHNEIDER, KENT

DELMARK
- DS-418 — Celebration for Modern Man — 197? — 15.00

SCHNITTER, DAVID

MUSE
- MR-5222 — Glowing — 1980 — 15.00
- MR-5153 — Goliath — 1977 — 15.00
- MR-5108 — Invitation — 197? — 15.00
- MR-5197 — Thundering — 1979 — 15.00

SCHOEN, VIC

DECCA
- DL8132 [M] — Letter to Laura — 195? — 30.00
- DL8081 [M] — Music for a Rainy Night — 195? — 30.00

KAPP
- KL-1097 [M] — Great Songs from All Over the World — 1959 — 25.00
- K-1097-S [S] — Great Songs from All Over the World — 1959 — 30.00

MAINSTREAM
- 56036 [M] — Corcovado Trumpets — 196? — 25.00
- S-6036 [S] — Corcovado Trumpets — 196? — 25.00
- MMS705 — Girls with Brass — 197? — 15.00

RCA VICTOR
- LPM-2344 [M] — Brass Laced with Strings — 196? — 18.00
- LSA-2344 [S] — Brass Laced with Strings — 196? — 30.00

SCHOOF, MANFRED

ECM
- 19004 — Scales — 1980 — 15.00

SCHORY, DICK

CONCERT DISC
- SC-21 [M] — Re-Percussion — 1957 — 60.00

RCA VICTOR
- LPM-2806 [M] — Dick Schory on Tour — 1964 — 25.00
- LSP-2806 [S] — Dick Schory on Tour — 1964 — 30.00
- LSA-2485 [S] — Holiday for Percussion — 1962 — 40.00
- LPM-2485 [M] — Holiday for Percussion — 1962 — 30.00
- LPM-1866 [M] — Music for Bang, Barroom and Harp — 1958 — 60.00
- LSP-1866 [S] — Music for Bang, Barroom and Harp — 1958 — 200.00
- LPM-2125 [M] — Music to Break Any Mood — 1960 — 30.00
- LSP-2125 [S] — Music to Break Any Mood — 1960 — 100.00
- LPM-2738 [M] — Politely Percussive — 1963 — 30.00
- LSP-2738 [S] — Politely Percussive — 1963 — 40.00
- LSA-2306 [S] — Runnin' Wild — 1960 — 40.00
- LSA-2382 [S] — Stereo Action Goes Broadway — 1961 — 40.00
- LSP-2613 [S] — Supercussion — 1963 — 40.00
- LPM-2926 [M] — The Happy Hits — 1964 — 25.00
- LSP-2926 [S] — The Happy Hits — 1964 — 30.00
- LPM-2289 [M] — Wild Percussion and Horns A-Plenty — 1960 — 30.00
- LSP-2289 [S] — Wild Percussion and Horns A-Plenty — 1960 — 60.00

SCHULLER, GUNTHER

ANGEL
- S-36060 — Joplin — 197? — 15.00

ATLANTIC
- SD1368 [S] — Jazz Abstractions — 1963 — 18.00
- *Multicolor label, black "fan" logo at right*
- 1368 [M] — Jazz Abstractions — 1961 — 25.00
- *Multicolor label, white "fan" logo at right*
- SD1368 [S] — Jazz Abstractions — 1961 — 30.00

- *Multicolor label, white "fan" logo at right*
- 1368 [M] — Jazz Abstractions — 1963 — 15.00
- *Multicolor label, black "fan" logo at right*

GM RECORDINGS
- GM-3010 — Jumpin' in the Future — 1989 — 15.00

GOLDEN CREST
- 31043 — Happy Feet: A Tribute to Paul Whiteman — 197? — 15.00
- 31042 — The Road from Rags to Jazz — 197? — 18.00

SCHUMANN, WALTER

CAPITOL
- L9016 [10] — Christmas in the Air! — 1952? — 35.00
- *Reissue with red label and new prefix*
- H9016 [10] — Christmas in the Air! — 1951 — 40.00
- *Original issue with purple label*
- H285 [10] — Songs of the Ivy League — 195? — 40.00
- *Purple label original*
- L285 [10] — Songs of the Ivy League — 195? — 30.00
- *Reissue with red label; has the same cover as the original, except the "H" has been blacked out and an "L" stamped next to it*
- H297 [10] — The Voices of Walter Schumann — 195? — 40.00
- T297 [M] — The Voices of Walter Schumann — 1955 — 30.00

PICKWICK
- PCX-1003 [M] — The Christmas Voices of Walter Schumann — 196? — 18.00
- *Reissue of Capitol material; record is not banded*
- SPCX-1003 [R] — The Christmas Voices of Walter Schumann — 196? — 12.00
- *Same as above, except in rechanneled stereo*

RCA VICTOR
- LPM-1025 [M] — Exploring the Unknown — 1955 — 50.00
- LPM-1465 [M] — Scrapbook: The Voices of Walter Schumann — 1957 — 25.00
- LPM-1141 [M] — The Voices of Christmas — 1955 — 25.00
- *Original cover has all-yellow lettering on front cover and eight LP/EP covers on back*
- LPM-1141 [M] — The Voices of Christmas — 1956 — 25.00
- *Second cover has red and yellow lettering on front cover and no LP/EP covers on back*
- LPM-1558 [M] — Walter Schumann Presents the Voices — 1958 — 18.00
- LSP-1558 [S] — Walter Schumann Presents the Voices — 1958 — 25.00
- LPM-1477 [M] — When We Were Young — 1957 — 25.00

SCHUUR, DIANE

GRP
- GR-1010 — Deedles — 1984 — 12.00
- GR-1039 — Diane Schuur and the Count Basie Orchestra — 1987 — 12.00
- GR-9628 — Pure Schuur — 1991 — 18.00
- GR-1022 — Schuur Thing — 1985 — 12.00
- GR-9567 — Talkin' 'Bout You — 1988 — 12.00
- GR-9591 — The Diane Schuur Collection — 1989 — 15.00
- GR-1030 — Timeless — 1986 — 12.00

MUSIC IS MEDICINE
- 9057 — Pilot of My Destiny — 1982 — 25.00

SCHUYLER, KNOBLOCH & BICKHARDT

MTM
- ST-71064 — No Easy Horses — 1987 — 12.00

SCHUYLER, KNOBLOCH & OVERSTREET

MTM
- ST-71058 — S-K-O — 1986 — 12.00

SCHUYLER, THOM

CAPITOL
- SQ-12298 — Brave Heart — 1983 — 12.00

SCHWARTZ, CHARLES

INNER CITY
- IC-1015 — Professor Jive — 197? — 18.00
- IC-1164 — Solo Brothers — 198? — 15.00

PABLO TODAY
- 2312115 — Mother--! Mother--! — 1980 — 18.00

SCHWARTZ, JONATHAN

MUSE
- MR-5325 — Anyone Would Love You — 1986 — 12.00

SCHWARTZ, THORNEL

ARGO
- LP-704 [M] — Soul Cookin' — 1962 — 30.00
- LPS-704 [S] — Soul Cookin' — 1962 — 30.00

SCHWEIZER, IRENE, AND RUDIGER CARL

HAT HUT
- 0X — The Very Centre of Middle Europe — 1979 — 18.00

SCIANNI, JOSEPH

SAVOY
- MG-12185 [M] — New Concepts — 1965 — 30.00

Number	Title	Yr	NM

SCOBEY, BOB

AMERICAN RECORDING SOCIETY
❏ G-408 [M]	Bob Scobey's Frisco Band	1956	40.00

DOWN HOME
❏ MGD-1 [M]	Bob Scobey's Frisco Band with Clancy Hayes	1954	50.00

GOOD TIME JAZZ
❏ L-22 [10]	Bob Scobey's Frisco Band	1954	50.00
❏ L-12032 [M]	Bob Scobey's Frisco Band, Volume 1	1957	40.00
❏ L-12033 [M]	Bob Scobey's Frisco Band, Volume 2	1957	40.00
❏ L-14 [10]	Bob Scobey's Frisco Band Vol. 2	1954	50.00
❏ L-12006 [M]	Bob Scobey's Frisco Band with Clancy Hayes	1955	40.00
❏ L-12023 [M]	Direct from San Francisco	1955	40.00
❏ L-12009 [M]	Scobey and Clancy	1955	40.00

JANSCO
❏ 6250	The Great Bob Scobey, Volume 1	1967	18.00
❏ 6252	The Great Bob Scobey, Volume 2	1967	18.00
❏ 5231	The Great Bob Scobey, Volume 3	1967	18.00

RCA VICTOR
❏ LPM-1344 [M]	Beauty and the Beat	1957	40.00
❏ LPM-1567 [M]	Between 18th and 19th on Any Street	1957	40.00
❏ LPM-1700 [M]	College Classics	1958	40.00
❏ LPM-2086 [M]	Rompin' and Stompin'	1959	30.00
❏ LSP-2086 [S]	Rompin' and Stompin'	1959	40.00
❏ LPM-1889 [M]	Something's Always Happening on the River	1958	40.00
❏ LSP-1889 [S]	Something's Always Happening on the River	1958	60.00
❏ LPM-1448 [M]	Swingin' on the Golden Gate	1957	40.00

VERVE
❏ MGV-1001 [M]	Bob Scobey's Band	1956	40.00
❏ V-1001 [M]	Bob Scobey's Band	1961	25.00
❏ MGV-1009 [M]	Music from Bourbon Street	1956	40.00
❏ V-1009 [M]	Music from Bourbon Street	1961	25.00
❏ MGV-1011 [M]	The San Francisco Jazz of Bob Scobey	1957	40.00
❏ V-1011 [M]	The San Francisco Jazz of Bob Scobey	1961	25.00

SCOFIELD, JOHN

ARISTA/NOVUS
❏ AN3018	Who's Who?	1980	15.00

BLUE NOTE
❏ B1-92894	Time on My Hands	1990	18.00

ENJA
❏ 4038	Out Like a Light	1982	15.00
❏ 4004	Shinola	1981	15.00

GRAMAVISION
❏ 18-8702-1	Blue Matter	1987	12.00
❏ GR-8405	Electric Outlet	1984	12.00
❏ R1-79400	Flat Out	1989	15.00
❏ 18-8508-1	Still Warm	1985	12.00

INNER CITY
❏ IC-3022	John Scofield Live	197?	18.00
❏ IC-3030	Rough House	1979	15.00

SCOOBY DOO

ZEPHYR
❏ ZMP-12002 [M]	Jerry Leiber Presents Scooby Doo	1959	50.00

SCOOBY DOO AND FRIENDS

PETER PAN
❏ 8214	Exciting Christmas Stories	1978	18.00

—*With voices from the TV series: Don Messick, Casey Kasem, Frank Welker, Heather North, Pat Stevens.*

SCORPION

TOWER
❏ ST5171	Scorpion	1969	50.00

SCORPIONS

BILLINGSGATE
❏ 1004 [B]	Lonesome Crow	1974	40.00

MERCURY
❏ SRM-1-3825	Animal Magnetism	1980	12.00
❏ 822556-1	Animal Magnetism	198?	10.00
—*Reissue of 3825*			
❏ 842002-1	Best of Rockers 'N' Ballads	1989	12.00
❏ SRM-1-4039	Blackout	1982	12.00
❏ 818885-1	Blackout	198?	10.00
—*Reissue of 4039*			
❏ 846908-1	Crazy World	1990	18.00
❏ 814981-1	Love at First Sting	1984	12.00
—*With man and woman on cover*			
❏ 822038-1	Love at First Sting	1984	15.00
—*Reissue with band on cover*			
❏ SRM-1-3795	Lovedrive	1979	12.00
❏ 822555-1	Lovedrive	198?	10.00
—*Reissue of 3795*			
❏ 832963-1	Savage Amusement	1988	12.00
❏ 824344-1	World Wide Live	1985	15.00

RCA VICTOR
❏ AFL1-3516	Best of Scorpions	1979	12.00
❏ AFL1-5085	Best of Scorpions, Vol. 2	1984	12.00
❏ PPL1-4025	Fly to the Rainbow	1975	15.00
❏ AFL1-4025	Fly to the Rainbow	1977	12.00
—*Reissue with new prefix*			
❏ AYL1-5057	Fly to the Rainbow	1984	10.00
—*Best Buy Series" reissue*			
❏ PPL1-4128	In Trance	1976	15.00
❏ AFL1-4128	In Trance	1977	12.00
—*Reissue with new prefix*			
❏ AYL1-4657	In Trance	1983	10.00
—*Best Buy Series" reissue*			
❏ AFL1-2628	Taken by Force	1978	15.00
❏ CPL2-3039	Toyko Tapes	1978	18.00
❏ PPL1-4225	Virgin Killer	1977	15.00
❏ AYL1-3659	Virgin Killer	1980	10.00
—*Best Buy Series" reissue*			

SCOT, PATRICIA

ABC-PARAMOUNT
❏ 301 [M]	Once Around the Clock	1959	25.00
❏ S-301 [S]	Once Around the Clock	1959	30.00

SCOTT, BOBBY

ABC-PARAMOUNT
❏ ABC-148 [M]	Bobby Scott and Two Horns	1957	50.00
❏ ABC-102 [M]	Scott Free	1956	50.00

ATLANTIC
❏ 1355 [M]	A Taste of Honey	1960	25.00
—*Multicolor label, white "fan" logo at right*			
❏ SD1355 [S]	A Taste of Honey	1960	30.00
—*Multicolor label, white "fan" logo at right*			
❏ 1341 [M]	The Compleat Musician	1960	25.00
—*Multicolor label, white "fan" logo at right*			
❏ SD1341 [S]	The Compleat Musician	1960	30.00
—*Multicolor label, white "fan" logo at right*			

BETHLEHEM
❏ BCP-1004 [10]	Great Scott	1954	120.00
❏ BCP-8 [M]	The Compositions of Bobby Scott	1957	50.00
❏ BCP-1009 [10]	The Compositions of Bobby Scott, Volume 1	1954	100.00
❏ BCP-1029 [10]	The Compositions of Bobby Scott, Volume 2	1955	100.00

MERCURY
❏ MG-20854 [M]	108 Pounds of Heartache	1963	25.00
❏ SR-60854 [S]	108 Pounds of Heartache	1963	30.00
❏ MG-20995 [M]	I Had a Ball	1964	25.00
❏ SR-60995 [S]	I Had a Ball	1964	30.00
❏ MG-20701 [M]	Joyful Noises	1962	25.00
❏ SR-60701 [S]	Joyful Noises	1962	30.00
❏ MG-20767 [M]	When the Feeling Hits You	1963	25.00
❏ SR-60767 [S]	When the Feeling Hits You	1963	30.00

VERVE
❏ MGV-8326 [M]	Bobby Scott Plays the Music of Leonard Bernstein	1959	50.00
❏ MGVS-6065 [S]	Bobby Scott Plays the Music of Leonard Bernstein	1960	40.00
❏ V-8326 [M]	Bobby Scott Plays the Music of Leonard Bernstein	1961	30.00
❏ V6-8326 [S]	Bobby Scott Plays the Music of Leonard Bernstein	1961	25.00
❏ MGV-2106 [M]	Bobby Scott Sings the Best of Lerner and Loewe	1958	50.00
❏ MGVS-6030 [S]	Bobby Scott Sings the Best of Lerner and Loewe	1960	40.00
❏ V-2106 [M]	Bobby Scott Sings the Best of Lerner and Loewe	1961	30.00
❏ V6-2106 [S]	Bobby Scott Sings the Best of Lerner and Loewe	1961	25.00
❏ MGV-8297 [M]	Serenate -- Bobby Scott, Pianist	1959	50.00
❏ MGVS-6031 [S]	Serenate -- Bobby Scott, Pianist	1960	40.00
❏ V-8297 [M]	Serenate -- Bobby Scott, Pianist	1961	30.00
❏ V6-8297 [S]	Serenate -- Bobby Scott, Pianist	1961	25.00

SCOTT, CALVIN

STAX
❏ STS-2046	I'm Not Blind... I Just Can't See	1972	80.00

SCOTT, CHRISTOPHER

DECCA
❏ DL75243	More Switched-On Bacharach	1970	18.00
❏ DL75141	Switched-On Bacharach	1969	18.00

MCA
❏ 282	Switched-On Bacharach	1973	15.00
—*Reissue of Decca 75141*			

SCOTT, CLIFFORD, AND LES McCANN

PACIFIC JAZZ
❏ PJ-66 [M]	Out Front	1963	40.00
—*Colored vinyl*			
❏ PJ-66 [M]	Out Front	1963	25.00
—*Black vinyl*			
❏ ST-66 [S]	Out Front	1963	50.00
—*Colored vinyl*			
❏ ST-66 [S]	Out Front	1963	30.00
—*Black vinyl*			

SCOTT, CLIFFORD

WORLD PACIFIC
❏ WP-1825 [M]	Lavender Sax	1964	30.00
❏ ST-1825 [S]	Lavender Sax	1964	40.00
❏ WP-1811 [M]	The Big Ones	1964	25.00
—*Black vinyl*			
❏ ST-1811 [S]	The Big Ones	1964	30.00
—*Black vinyl*			
❏ WP-1811 [M]	The Big Ones	1964	60.00
—*Green vinyl*			
❏ ST-1811 [S]	The Big Ones	1964	80.00
—*Green vinyl*			

SCOTT, FREDDIE

COLPIX
❏ CP-461 [M]	Freddie Scott Sings and Sings and Sings	1964	60.00
—*Gold label*			
❏ CP-461 [M]	Freddie Scott Sings and Sings and Sings	1965	40.00
—*Blue label*			
❏ SCP-461 [S]	Freddie Scott Sings and Sings and Sings	1964	120.00
—*Gold label*			
❏ SCP-461 [R]	Freddie Scott Sings and Sings and Sings	1965	30.00
—*Blue label*			

COLUMBIA
❏ CL2258 [M]	Everything I Have Is Yours	1964	25.00
❏ CS9058 [S]	Everything I Have Is Yours	1964	30.00
❏ CL2660 [M]	Lonely Man	1967	25.00
❏ CS9460 [S]	Lonely Man	1967	30.00

PROBE
❏ CPLP-4517	I Shall Be Released	1970	30.00

SHOUT
❏ SLP-501 [M]	Are You Lonely for Me	1967	25.00
❏ SLPS-501 [S]	Are You Lonely for Me	1967	30.00

SCOTT, HAZEL

CAPITOL
❏ H364 [10]	Late Show	1953	80.00

COLUMBIA
❏ CL6090 [10]	Great Scott	1950	80.00

CORAL
❏ CRL56057 [10]	Hazel Scott	1952	80.00

DEBUT
❏ DLP-16 [10]	Relaxed Piano Moods	1955	200.00

DECCA
❏ DL8474 [M]	'Round Midnight	1957	40.00
❏ DL5130 [10]	Swinging the Classics	1950	80.00

FANTASY
❏ OJC-1702	Relaxed Piano Moods	1985	12.00

TIOCH
❏ TD-1013	Afterhours	198?	12.00

SCOTT, JACK

CAPITOL
❏ T2035 [M]	Burning Bridges	1964	80.00
❏ ST2035 [S]	Burning Bridges	1964	150.00
❏ ST-8-2035	Burning Bridges	196?	200.00
—*Capitol Record Club edition*			

CARLTON
❏ LP-12-107 [M]	Jack Scott	1959	150.00
❏ STLP-12-107 [S]	Jack Scott	1959	400.00
—*With "Stereo" in felt letters vertically along the left of cover*			
❏ STLP-12-107 [S]	Jack Scott	1959	300.00
—*With "Stereo" in felt letters horizontally along the top of cover*			
❏ STLP-12-107 [S]	Jack Scott	1959	200.00
—*With "Stereo" printed across the top*			
❏ LP-12-122 [M]	What Am I Living For	1959	120.00
❏ STLP-12-122 [S]	What Am I Living For	1959	320.00

JADE
❏ J33-113	Jack Is Back	198?	18.00
❏ J33-114	The Way I Rock	198?	18.00

PONIE
❏ 563	Jack Scott	1974	18.00
❏ 7055	Jack Scott	1977	18.00

TOP RANK
❏ RM-319 [M]	I Remember Hank Williams	1960	200.00
❏ SM-619 [S]	I Remember Hank Williams	1960	300.00
❏ RM-348 [M]	The Spirit Moves Me	1961	200.00
❏ SM-648 [S]	The Spirit Moves Me	1961	300.00
❏ RM-326 [M]	What in the World's Come Over You	1960	200.00
❏ SM-626 [S]	What in the World's Come Over You	1960	300.00

Number	Title	Yr	NM
SCOTT, JIMMY			
SAVOY			
❏ MG-12181 [M]	If You Only Knew	1963	40.00
❏ MG-12150 [M]	The Fabulous Little Jimmy Scott	1959	40.00
❏ MG-12301 [M]	The Fabulous Songs of Jimmy Scott	1969	18.00
❏ MG-12302 [M]	The Fabulous Voice of Jimmy Scott	1969	18.00
❏ MG-12027 [M]	Very Truly Yours	1955	60.00
❏ MG-12300 [M]	Very Truly Yours	1969	18.00
TANGERINE			
❏ TRC-1501 [M]	Falling in Love Is Wonderful	1963	200.00
❏ TRCS-1501 [S]	Falling in Love Is Wonderful	1963	250.00
SCOTT, LINDA			
CANADIAN AMERICAN			
❏ CALP-1007 [M]	Great Scott!! Her Greatest Hits	1962	100.00
❏ SCALP-1007 [S]	Great Scott!! Her Greatest Hits	1962	150.00
❏ CALP-1005 [M]	Starlight, Starbright	1961	100.00
❏ SCALP-1005 [S]	Starlight, Starbright	1961	150.00
CONGRESS			
❏ CGL-3001 [M]	Linda	1962	40.00
❏ CGS-3001 [S]	Linda	1962	50.00
KAPP			
❏ KL-1424 [M]	Hey, Look at Me Now	1965	40.00
❏ KS-3424 [S]	Hey, Look at Me Now	1965	50.00
SCOTT, LIZABETH			
VIK			
❏ LX-1130 [M]	Lizabeth	1958	100.00
SCOTT, PEGGY, AND JO JO BENSON			
SSS INTERNATIONAL			
❏ 2	Lover's Heaven	1969	30.00
❏ 1	Soulshake	1968	30.00
SCOTT, ROBERT WILLIAM			
WARNER BROS.			
❏ WS1886	Robert William Scott	1970	18.00
SCOTT, SHIRLEY, AND CLARK TERRY			
ABC IMPULSE!			
❏ AS-9133 [S]	Soul Duo	1968	18.00
IMPULSE!			
❏ A-9133 [M]	Soul Duo	1967	30.00
❏ AS-9133 [S]	Soul Duo	1967	25.00
SCOTT, SHIRLEY			
ABC IMPULSE!			
❏ AS-73 [S]	Everybody Loves a Lover	1968	18.00
❏ AS-51 [S]	For Members Only	1968	18.00
❏ AS-67 [S]	Girl Talk	1967	18.00
❏ AS-67 [S]	Great Scott!	1968	18.00
❏ AS-93 [S]	Latin Shadows	1968	18.00
❏ AS-9109 [S]	On a Clear Day	1968	18.00
❏ AS-81 [S]	Queen of the Organ	1968	18.00
❏ AS-9119 [S]	Shirley Scott Plays the Big Bands	1968	18.00
❏ IA-9341	The Great Live Sessions	1978	18.00
ATLANTIC			
❏ SD1561	Something	1970	18.00
❏ SD1532	Soul Saxes	1969	18.00
❏ SD1515	Soul Song	1968	18.00
CADET			
❏ CA-50025	Lean On Me	1972	15.00
❏ CA-50009	Mystical Lady	1972	15.00
❏ CA-50036	Superstition	1973	15.00
FANTASY			
❏ OJC-328	Blue Flames	1988	12.00
IMPULSE!			
❏ A-73 [M]	Everybody Loves a Lover	1964	25.00
❏ AS-73 [S]	Everybody Loves a Lover	1964	30.00
❏ A-51 [M]	For Members Only	1963	25.00
❏ AS-51 [S]	For Members Only	1963	30.00
❏ A-9141 [M]	Girl Talk	1967	30.00
❏ AS-9141 [S]	Girl Talk	1967	25.00
❏ A-67 [M]	Great Scott!	1964	25.00
❏ AS-67 [S]	Great Scott!	1964	30.00
❏ A-93 [M]	Latin Shadows	1965	25.00
❏ AS-93 [S]	Latin Shadows	1965	30.00
❏ A-9109 [M]	On a Clear Day	1967	25.00
❏ AS-9109 [S]	On a Clear Day	1967	30.00
❏ A-81 [M]	Queen of the Organ	1965	25.00
❏ AS-81 [S]	Queen of the Organ	1965	30.00
❏ A-9119 [M]	Shirley Scott Plays the Big Bands	1966	25.00
❏ AS-9119 [S]	Shirley Scott Plays the Big Bands	1966	30.00
MCA			
❏ 4152	The Great Live Sessions	1980	15.00
MOODSVILLE			
❏ MVLP-19 [M]	Like Cozy	1961	50.00
— Green label			
❏ MVST-19 [S]	Like Cozy	1961	50.00
— Green label			
❏ MVLP-19 [M]	Like Cozy	1965	30.00

Number	Title	Yr	NM
— Blue label, trident logo at right			
❏ MVST-19 [S]	Like Cozy	1965	30.00
— Blue label, trident logo at right			
❏ MVLP-5 [M]	Shirley Scott Trio	1960	50.00
— Green label			
❏ MVLP-5 [M]	Shirley Scott Trio	1965	30.00
— Blue label, trident logo at right			
MUSE			
❏ MR-5388	Oasis	1990	15.00
PRESTIGE			
❏ PRLP-7338 [M]	Blue Flames	1965	30.00
❏ PRST-7338 [S]	Blue Flames	1965	30.00
❏ PRLP-7376 [M]	Blue Seven	1965	30.00
❏ PRST-7376 [S]	Blue Seven	1965	30.00
❏ PRLP-7305 [M]	Drag 'Em Out	1964	40.00
❏ PRST-7305 [S]	Drag 'Em Out	1964	50.00
❏ PRLP-7143 [M]	Great Scott!	1958	50.00
❏ PRLP-7262 [M]	Happy Talk	1963	40.00
❏ PRST-7262 [S]	Happy Talk	1963	50.00
❏ PRLP-7205 [M]	Hip Soul	1961	40.00
— Yellow label, Bergenfield, NJ address			
❏ PRLP-7205 [M]	Hip Soul	1965	25.00
— Blue label, trident logo at right			
❏ PRLP-7226 [M]	Hip Twist	1962	40.00
— Yellow label, Bergenfield, NJ address			
❏ PRST-7226 [S]	Hip Twist	1962	50.00
— Silver label, Bergenfield, NJ address			
❏ PRLP-7226 [M]	Hip Twist	1965	25.00
— Blue label, trident logo at right			
❏ PRST-7226 [S]	Hip Twist	1965	30.00
— Blue label, trident logo at right			
❏ PRLP-7182 [M]	Mucho, Mucho	1960	50.00
❏ PRLP-7440 [M]	Now's the Time	1967	30.00
❏ PRST-7440 [S]	Now's the Time	1967	30.00
❏ PRLP-7283 [M]	Satin Doll	1963	40.00
❏ PRST-7283 [S]	Satin Doll	1963	50.00
❏ PRLP-7155 [M]	Scottie	1959	50.00
❏ PRLP-7163 [M]	Scottie Plays Duke	1959	50.00
❏ PRLP-7240 [M]	Shirley Scott Plays Horace Silver	1962	40.00
❏ PRST-7240 [S]	Shirley Scott Plays Horace Silver	1962	50.00
❏ PRLP-7195 [M]	Shirley's Sounds	1961	40.00
❏ PRST-7195 [S]	Shirley's Sounds	1961	50.00
❏ PRLP-7173 [M]	Soul Searching	1960	50.00
❏ PRLP-7312 [M]	Soul Shoutin'	1964	40.00
— Yellow label, Bergenfield, NJ address			
❏ PRST-7312 [S]	Soul Shoutin'	1964	50.00
— Silver label, Bergenfield, NJ address			
❏ PRLP-7312 [M]	Soul Shoutin'	1965	25.00
— Blue label, trident logo at right			
❏ PRST-7312 [S]	Soul Shoutin'	1965	30.00
— Blue label, trident logo at right			
❏ PRLP-7392 [M]	Soul Sisters	1965	30.00
❏ PRST-7392 [S]	Soul Sisters	1965	30.00
❏ PRST-7456 [S]	Stompin'	1968	30.00
❏ PRLP-7360 [M]	Sweet Soul	1965	30.00
❏ PRST-7360 [S]	Sweet Soul	1965	30.00
❏ PRST-7773	The Best for Beautiful People	1970	25.00
❏ PRST-7707 [S]	The Best of Shirley Scott and Stanley Turrentine	1969	25.00
❏ PRLP-7267 [M]	The Soul Is Willing	1963	40.00
— Yellow label, Bergenfield, NJ address			
❏ PRST-7267 [S]	The Soul Is Willing	1963	50.00
— Silver label, Bergenfield, NJ address			
❏ PRLP-7267 [M]	The Soul Is Willing	1965	25.00
— Blue label, trident logo at right			
❏ PRST-7267 [S]	The Soul Is Willing	1965	30.00
— Blue label, trident logo at right			
❏ PRST-7845	The Soul Is Willing	1971	18.00
❏ PRLP-7328 [M]	Travelin' Light	1964	30.00
❏ PRST-7328 [S]	Travelin' Light	1964	30.00
❏ PRLP-7424 [M]	Workin'	1966	30.00
❏ PRST-7424 [S]	Workin'	1966	30.00
STRATA-EAST			
❏ SES-7430	One for Me	197?	25.00
SCOTT, TOM			
A&M			
❏ SP-4330	Great Scott!	1972	18.00
ABC IMPULSE!			
❏ A-9163 [M]	Honeysuckle Breeze	1967	50.00
❏ AS-9163 [S]	Honeysuckle Breeze	1967	40.00
❏ AS-9171	Rural Still Life	1968	30.00
ATLANTIC			
❏ 80106	Target	1983	12.00
COLUMBIA			
❏ FC37419	Apple Juice	1981	12.00
❏ JC35557	Intimate Strangers	1978	12.00
❏ PC35557	Intimate Strangers	198?	10.00
— Budget-line reissue			
❏ JC36137	Street Beat	1979	12.00
❏ JC36352	The Best of Tom Scott	1980	12.00
ELEKTRA/MUSICIAN			
❏ 60162	Desire	1982	12.00
FLYING DUTCHMAN			
❏ 106	Hair	1969	25.00
❏ 114	Paint Your Wagon	1970	25.00
❏ BDL1-0833	Tom Scott in L.A.	1975	15.00

Number	Title	Yr	NM
❏ AYL1-3875	Tom Scott in L.A.	1980	10.00
— Best Buy Series" reissue			
❏ BXL1-0833	Tom Scott in L.A.	197?	12.00
— Second edition; new prefix, "RE" on cover			
GRP			
❏ GR-9571	Flashpoint	1988	12.00
❏ GR-1044	Streamlines	1987	12.00
MCA			
❏ 29060	Rural Still Life	198?	10.00
— Reissue of Impulse 9171			
ODE			
❏ PE34966	Blow It Out	1977	12.00
❏ SP-77033	New York Connection	1976	12.00
❏ PE34959	New York Connection	1977	10.00
— Reissue of 77033			
❏ SP-77029	Tom Cat	1975	12.00
❏ PE34956	Tom Cat	1977	10.00
— Reissue of 77029			
❏ SP-77021	Tom Scott and the L.A. Express	1974	12.00
❏ PE34952	Tom Scott and the L.A. Express	1977	10.00
— Reissue of 77021			
SOUNDWINGS			
❏ SW-202	Tom Scott	1986	12.00
SCOTT, TONY, AND JIMMY KNEPPER			
CARLTON			
❏ LP-12-113 [M]	Free Blown Jazz	1959	50.00
❏ ST-12-113 [S]	Free Blown Jazz	1959	50.00
SCOTT, TONY, AND MAT MATTHEWS			
BRUNSWICK			
❏ BL58057 [10]	Jazz for GI's	1954	120.00
SCOTT, TONY, AND TERRY GIBBS			
BRUNSWICK			
❏ BL58058 [10]	Hi-Fi Jazz	1955	120.00
SCOTT, TONY			
ABC-PARAMOUNT			
❏ ABC-235 [M]	South Pacific	1958	30.00
❏ ABCS-235 [S]	South Pacific	1958	30.00
BRUNSWICK			
❏ BL58040 [10]	Music After Midnight	1953	120.00
❏ BL54021 [M]	Tony Scott In Hi-Fi	1957	80.00
❏ BL58056 [10]	Tony Scott Quartet	1954	120.00
❏ BL54056 [M]	Tony Scott Quartet	1957	120.00
CORAL			
❏ CRL57230 [M]	52nd Street Scene	1958	50.00
❏ CRL757239 [S]	52nd Street Scene	1958	40.00
MUSE			
❏ MR-5230	Golden Moments	198?	12.00
❏ MR-5200	I'll Remember	198?	12.00
PERFECT			
❏ PL-12010 [M]	My Kind of Jazz	1960	40.00
❏ PL-14010 [S]	My Kind of Jazz	1960	50.00
RCA VICTOR			
❏ LPM-1353 [M]	A Touch of Tony Scott	1956	80.00
❏ LPM-1268 [M]	Both Sides of Tony Scott	1956	80.00
❏ LJM-1022 [M]	Scott's Fling	1955	80.00
❏ LPM-1452 [M]	The Complete Tony Scott	1957	80.00
SEECO			
❏ SLP-428 [M]	Hi-Fi Land of Jazz	1959	30.00
❏ SLP-4280 [S]	Hi-Fi Land of Jazz	1959	40.00
❏ SLP-425 [M]	The Modern Art of Jazz	1959	30.00
❏ SLP-4250 [S]	The Modern Art of Jazz	1959	40.00
SIGNATURE			
❏ SM-6001 [M]	Gypsy	1959	50.00
❏ SS-6001 [S]	Gypsy	1959	40.00
SOUL NOTE			
❏ SN-1083	African Bird: Come Back! Mother Africa	1984	15.00
SUNNYSIDE			
❏ SSC-1015	Sung Heroes	1987	12.00
VERVE			
❏ V6-8788 [S]	Homage to Lord Krishna	1969	18.00
❏ V-8742 [S]	Music for Yoga Meditation and Other Joys	1967	25.00
❏ V6-8742 [S]	Music for Yoga Meditation and Other Joys	1967	18.00
❏ V-8634 [M]	Music for Zen Meditation	1965	18.00
❏ V6-8634 [S]	Music for Zen Meditation	1965	25.00
SCOTT, WALTER			
MUSICLAND U.S.A.			
❏ LP-3502 [M]	Great Scott	1967	25.00
❏ SLP-3502 [S]	Great Scott	1967	30.00
WHITE WHALE			
❏ WWS-7131	Walter Scott	1970	25.00
SCOTT-HERON, GIL			
ARISTA			
❏ AL9514	1980	1980	12.00
❏ AL4147	Bridges	1977	12.00

Number	Title	Yr	NM
❑ AL4044	From South Africa to South Carolina	1975	12.00
❑ A2L5001	It's Your World	1976	15.00
❑ AL9606	Moving Target	1982	12.00
❑ AL9540	Real Eyes	1980	12.00
❑ AL9566	Reflections	1981	12.00
❑ AB4189	Secrets	1978	12.00
❑ ALB6-8306	The Best of Gil Scott-Heron	1985	10.00
—Reissue of 8248			
❑ AL8248	The Best of Gil Scott-Heron	1984	12.00
❑ AL4030	The First Minute of a New Day	1975	12.00
❑ AL8301	The Mind of Gil Scott-Heron	1980	18.00

BLUEBIRD

Number	Title	Yr	NM
❑ 6994-1-RB	The Revolution Will Not Be Televised	1988	15.00

FLYING DUTCHMAN

Number	Title	Yr	NM
❑ FD-10153	Free Will	1972	25.00
❑ FD-10143	Pieces of a Man	1971	25.00
❑ BXL1-2834	Pieces of a Man	1978	15.00
—Reissue of 10143			
❑ AYL1-3819	Pieces of a Man	1980	10.00
—Best Buy Series" reissue			
❑ BLD1-0613 [B]	The Revolution Will Not Be Televised	1974	30.00
❑ BXL1-0613	The Revolution Will Not Be Televised	1978	15.00
—Reissue with new prefix			
❑ AYL1-3818	The Revolution Will Not Be Televised	1980	10.00
—Best Buy Series" reissue			

STRATA-EAST

Number	Title	Yr	NM
❑ SES-19742	Winter in America	1974	30.00

SCOTTO, RENATA

RCA RED SEAL

Number	Title	Yr	NM
❑ ARL1-4136	Christmas with Renata Scotto at St. Patrick's Cathedral	1981	12.00

SCOTTSVILLE SQUIRREL BARKERS, THE

CROWN

Number	Title	Yr	NM
❑ CLP-5346 [M]	Bluegrass Favorites	1963	50.00
❑ CST-346 [S]	Bluegrass Favorites	1963	60.00

SCRAMBLERS, THE

CROWN

Number	Title	Yr	NM
❑ CLP-5384 [M]	Cycle Psychos	1964	25.00
❑ CST-384 [S]	Cycle Psychos	1964	30.00

DIPLOMAT

Number	Title	Yr	NM
❑ D-2316 [M]	Motorcycle Scramble	1964	25.00
❑ DS-2316 [S]	Motorcycle Scramble	1964	30.00

WYNCOTE

Number	Title	Yr	NM
❑ W-9048 [M]	Little Honda	1964	25.00
❑ SW-9048 [S]	Little Honda	1964	30.00

SCREAMING BLUE MESSIAHS

ELEKTRA

Number	Title	Yr	NM
❑ 60755 [DJ]	Bikini Red	1987	15.00
—Promo-only pressing on audiophile vinyl			
❑ 60755	Bikini Red	1987	12.00
❑ 60755 [DJ]	Bikini Red	1987	15.00
—Promo-only pressing on audiophile vinyl			
❑ 60488	Gun-Shy	1985	18.00
❑ 60859 [DJ]	Totally Religious	1989	15.00
—Promo-only pressing on audiophile vinyl			
❑ 60859	Totally Religious	1989	12.00
❑ 60859 [DJ]	Totally Religious	1989	15.00
—Promo-only pressing on audiophile vinyl			

SCREAMING GYPSY BANDITS

BAR-B-Q

Number	Title	Yr	NM
❑ 22185	In the Eye	1973	80.00
❑ 004	The Dancer Inside You	1974	80.00

SCREAMING TREES

EPIC

Number	Title	Yr	NM
❑ E48996 [B]	Sweet Oblivion	1992	18.00
❑ E46800 [B]	Uncle Anesthesia	1991	18.00

SST

Number	Title	Yr	NM
❑ 260 [B]	Anthology	1991	30.00
❑ 248 [B]	Buzz Factory	1989	25.00
❑ 132 [B]	Even If and Especially When	1987	25.00
❑ 188 [B]	Invisible Lantern	1988	25.00
❑ 105 [EP]	Other Worlds	1986	25.00
—Reissue of Velvetone cassette-only release			

VELVETONE

Number	Title	Yr	NM
❑ 86002	Clairvoyance	1986	40.00

SCRITTI POLITTI

WARNER BROS.

Number	Title	Yr	NM
❑ R144294	Cupid & Psyche '85	1985	12.00
—RCA Music Service edition			
❑ 25302	Cupid & Psyche '85	1985	10.00
❑ R100460	Provision	1988	15.00
—BMG Direct Marketing edition			
❑ 25686	Provision	1988	12.00

SCROOGE BROTHERS, THE

RHINO

Number	Title	Yr	NM
❑ RNEP70514 [EP]	Commercial Christmasland	1987	10.00
—Reissue of Enigma EP			

SCRUGGS, EARL

COLUMBIA

Number	Title	Yr	NM
❑ FC39586	American Made, World Played	1984	12.00
❑ PC33416	Anniversary Special, Volume One	1975	12.00
❑ JC35319	Bold & New	1978	12.00
❑ JC36509	Country Comfort	1980	12.00
❑ C32268	Dueling Banjos	1973	15.00
❑ PC32268	Dueling Banjos	198?	10.00
—Budget-line reissue with bar code			
❑ PC34346	Family Portrait	1976	12.00
❑ KC31354	I Saw the Light	1972	18.00
❑ C31758	Live at Kansas State	1972	15.00
❑ PC31758	Live at Kansas State	198?	10.00
—Budget-line reissue with bar code			
❑ PC34464	Live from Austin City Limits	1977	12.00
—No bar code on back cover			
❑ PC34464	Live from Austin City Limits	198?	10.00
—Budget-line reissue with bar code			
❑ CS1007	Nashville's Rock	1970	18.00
❑ KC32943	Rockin' 'Cross the Country	1974	15.00
❑ PC34878	Strike Anywhere	1977	12.00
❑ FC39370	Super Jammin'	1984	12.00
❑ KC32426	The Earl Scruggs Revue	1973	15.00
❑ PC34090	The Earl Scruggs Revue, Volume II	1976	12.00
❑ JC36084	Today and Forever	1979	12.00
❑ PC36084	Today and Forever	198?	10.00
—Budget-line reissue with bar code			
❑ FC38295	Top of the World	1983	12.00
❑ PC38295	Top of the World	1985	10.00
—Budget-line reissue with new prefix			

SEA, JOHNNY

HILLTOP

Number	Title	Yr	NM
❑ JM-6018	Everybody's Favorite	196?	15.00

PHILIPS

Number	Title	Yr	NM
❑ PHM200194 [M]	Live at the Bitter End	1965	25.00
❑ PHS600194 [S]	Live at the Bitter End	1965	30.00
❑ PHM200139 [M]	World of a Country Boy	1964	25.00
❑ PHS600139 [S]	World of a Country Boy	1964	30.00

WARNER BROS.

Number	Title	Yr	NM
❑ W1659 [M]	Day for Decision	1966	18.00
❑ WS1659 [S]	Day for Decision	1966	25.00

SEA HAGS

CHRYSALIS

Number	Title	Yr	NM
❑ FV41665	Sea Hags	1989	12.00

SEA LEVEL

ARISTA

Number	Title	Yr	NM
❑ AL9531	Ball Room	1980	12.00

CAPRICORN

Number	Title	Yr	NM
❑ CPN 0198	Cats on the Coast	1978	12.00
❑ CPN 0227	Long Walk on a Short Pier	1979	12.00
❑ CPN 0212	On the Edge	1978	12.00
❑ CP 0178	Sea Level	1977	12.00

SEALS, DAN

CAPITOL

Number	Title	Yr	NM
❑ 1P7999	On Arrival	1990	25.00
—Only available on vinyl from Columbia House			
❑ C1-46976	Rage On	1988	10.00
❑ CLT-48308	The Best	1988	10.00

EMI AMERICA

Number	Title	Yr	NM
❑ PW-17231	On the Front Line	1986	10.00
❑ ST-17131	San Antone	1984	10.00
❑ ST-17166	Won't Be Blue Anymore	1985	10.00

LIBERTY

Number	Title	Yr	NM
❑ LT-51149	Rebel Heart	1983	12.00

SEALS, TROY

ATLANTIC

Number	Title	Yr	NM
❑ SD7281	Now Prresenting Troy Seals	1973	15.00

COLUMBIA

Number	Title	Yr	NM
❑ KC34271	Troy Seals	1976	15.00

SEALS AND CROFTS

K-TEL

Number	Title	Yr	NM
❑ NU9610	Collection: 16 of Their Greatest Hits	1979	15.00

NAUTILUS

Number	Title	Yr	NM
❑ NR-10 [B]	Summer Breeze	1980	35.00
—Audiophile vinyl			

T-A

Number	Title	Yr	NM
❑ 5004	Down Home	1970	30.00
❑ 5001	Seals and Crofts	1969	30.00

WARNER BROS.

Number	Title	Yr	NM
❑ BS2699	Diamond Girl	1973	15.00
—Burbank" palm-tree label			
❑ BS2699	Diamond Girl	1979	10.00
—White or tan label			
❑ BS42699 [Q]	Diamond Girl	1974	30.00
❑ BS2907	Get Closer	1976	12.00
❑ BS2886	Greatest Hits	1975	12.00
❑ BSK3109	Greatest Hits	1977	10.00
—Reissue; any label variation			
❑ BS2848	I'll Play for You	1975	12.00
❑ BS42848 [Q]	I'll Play for You	1975	25.00
❑ 2WS2809 [B]	Seals & Crofts I and II	1974	25.00
—Reissue of the two T-A LPs in one package			
❑ BS2976	Sudan Village	1976	12.00
❑ BS2629	Summer Breeze	1972	15.00
—Green "WB" label			
❑ BS2629	Summer Breeze	1973	12.00
—Burbank" palm-tree label			
❑ BS2629	Summer Breeze	1979	10.00
—White or tan label			
❑ BS42629 [Q]	Summer Breeze	1974	30.00
❑ BSK3165	Takin' It Easy	1978	12.00
❑ BSK3365	The Longest Road	1980	12.00
❑ BS2761	Unborn Child	1974	15.00
❑ BS42761 [Q]	Unborn Child	1974	30.00
❑ BS2568	Year of Sunday	1971	15.00
—Green "WB" label			
❑ BS2568	Year of Sunday	1973	12.00
—Burbank" palm-tree label			

SEALY, JOE

SACKVILLE

Number	Title	Yr	NM
❑ 4007	Clear Vision	198?	12.00

SEARCH PARTY, THE

CENTURY CUSTOM

Number	Title	Yr	NM
❑ 32013	Montgomery Chapel	1969	2000.00

SEARCHERS, THE

KAPP

Number	Title	Yr	NM
❑ KL-1363 [M]	Meet the Searchers	1964	40.00
—With black and blue label			
❑ KS-3363 [S]	Meet the Searchers	1964	50.00
—With black and blue label			
❑ KL-1363 [M]	Meet the Searchers	1964	30.00
—With black label			
❑ KS-3363 [S]	Meet the Searchers	1964	30.00
—With black label			
❑ KL-1477 [M]	Take Me for What I'm Worth	1966	30.00
❑ KS-3477 [S]	Take Me for What I'm Worth	1966	30.00
❑ KL-1412 [M]	The New Searchers LP	1965	30.00
❑ KS-3412 [S]	The New Searchers LP	1965	30.00
❑ KL-1449 [M]	The Searchers No. 4	1965	30.00
❑ KS-3419 [S]	The Searchers No. 4	1965	30.00
❑ KL-1409 [M]	This Is Us	1964	30.00
—Version 1: No sticker on front cover			
❑ KS-3409 [S]	This Is Us	1964	30.00
—Version 1: No sticker on front cover			
❑ KL-1409 [M]	This Is Us	1964	30.00
—Version 2: With sticker on front cover referring to "Love Potion No. 9			
❑ KS-3409 [S]	This Is Us	1964	30.00
—Version 2: With sticker on front cover referring to "Love Potion No. 9			

MERCURY

Number	Title	Yr	NM
❑ MG-20914 [M]	Hear! Hear!	1964	50.00
—White label promo			
❑ MG-20914 [M]	Hear! Hear!	1964	50.00
—Version 1: With only the title on the front cover			
❑ SR-60914 [S]	Hear! Hear!	1964	40.00
—Version 1: With only the title on the front cover			
❑ MG-20914 [M]	Hear! Hear!	1964	40.00
—Version 2: With sticker "Live from the Star Club" on cover			
❑ SR-60914 [S]	Hear! Hear!	1964	30.00
—Version 2: With sticker "Live from the Star Club" on cover			
❑ MG-20914 [M]	Hear! Hear!	1964	30.00
—Version 3: With "Live from the Star Club" imprinted on cover			
❑ SR-60914 [S]	Hear! Hear!	1964	30.00
—Version 3: With "Live from the Star Club" imprinted on cover			
❑ MG-20994 [M]	The Searchers Meet the Rattles	1965	100.00
❑ SR-60994 [S]	The Searchers Meet the Rattles	1965	60.00

PYE

Number	Title	Yr	NM
❑ 501	The Searchers	197?	18.00
—Reissue of Kapp hits			
❑ 508	The Searchers, Vol. 2	1976	18.00

RHINO

Number	Title	Yr	NM
❑ RNLP162	Greatest Hits	1985	12.00
❑ R1-70162	Greatest Hits	1988	10.00
—Reissue of RNLP 162			

SIRE

Number	Title	Yr	NM
❑ SRK3523	Love's Melodies	1981	12.00
❑ SRK6082	The Searchers	1980	12.00

SEARS, AL

AUDIO LAB

Number	Title	Yr	NM
❑ AL-1540 [M]	Dance Music with a Swing Beat	1959	120.00

Number	Title	Yr	NM
SWINGVILLE			
❏ SVLP-2018 [M]	Swing's the Thing	1961	50.00
— Purple label			
❏ SVLP-2018 [M]	Swing's the Thing	1965	30.00
— Blue label, trident logo at right			
SEARS GOLDEN STRINGS, THE			
SEARS			
❏ SPX-503 [M]	White Christmas	196?	15.00
❏ SPSX-503 [S]	White Christmas	196?	18.00
SEATRAIN			
A&M			
❏ SP-4171	Sea Train	1969	18.00
CAPITOL			
❏ SMAS-829	Marblehead Messenger	1971	18.00
❏ SN-16103	Marblehead Messenger	1980	10.00
— Budget-line reissue			
❏ SMAS-650	Seatrain	1970	18.00
❏ SN-16102	Seatrain	1980	10.00
— Budget-line reissue			
WARNER BROS.			
❏ BS2692	Watch	1973	15.00
SEBASTIAN, JOHN			
MGM			
❏ SE-4654	John B. Sebastian	1969	18.00
❏ SE-4720	John Sebastian Live	1970	18.00
REPRISE			
❏ MS2036 [B]	Cheapo-Cheapo Productions Presents Real Live John Sebastian	1971	15.00
❏ RS6379	John B. Sebastian	1969	25.00
— Same album as MGM 4654, but a different mix			
❏ MS2187	Tarzana Kid	1974	15.00
❏ MS2041	The Four of Us	1971	15.00
❏ MS2249	Welcome Back	1976	15.00
RHINO			
❏ R1-70170	The Best of John Sebastian (1969-1976)	1989	15.00
SEBESKY, DON			
CTI			
❏ CTX-6031/2	Giant Box	1974	18.00
❏ 6061	The Rape of El Morro	197?	15.00
DOCTOR JAZZ			
❏ FW40155	Moving Lines	1986	12.00
GNP CRESCENDO			
❏ GNPS-2164	Full Circle	198?	12.00
GRYPHON			
❏ 791	Three Works for Jazz Soloists and Symphony Orchestra	1980	18.00
MOBILE FIDELITY			
❏ 1-503	Three Works for Jazz Soloists and Symphony Orchestra	198?	60.00
— Audiophile vinyl			
VERVE			
❏ V6-8756	Don Sebesky and the Jazz-Rock Syndrome	1968	25.00
SECOND TIME, THE			
TOWER			
❏ ST5146 [B]	Listen to the Music	1968	30.00
SECRET OYSTER			
PETERS INT'L.			
❏ 9003	Furtive Pearl	1973	30.00
❏ 9009	Sea Son	1974	30.00
SEDAKA, NEIL, AND THE TOKENS WITH THE COINS			
CROWN			
❏ CLP-5366 [M]	Neil Sedaka and the Tokens and the Coins	1963	40.00
❏ CST-366 [R]	Neil Sedaka and the Tokens and the Coins	1963	40.00
SEDAKA, NEIL			
51 WEST			
❏ Q16003	I'm a Song	1979	15.00
ACCORD			
❏ SN-7152	Singer, Songwriter, Melody Maker	1981	12.00
ELEKTRA			
❏ 6E-161	All You Need Is Music	1978	12.00
❏ 6E-102	A Song	1977	12.00
❏ 6E-259	In the Pocket	1980	12.00
❏ 6E-348	Neil Sedaka Now	1981	12.00
INTERMEDIA			
❏ QS5015	Superbird	1982	12.00
KIRSHNER			
❏ KES-111	Emergence	1971	18.00
❏ KES-117	Solitaire	1972	18.00

Number	Title	Yr	NM
MCA			
❏ 5466	Come See About Me	1984	12.00
❏ 2357	Sedaka's Back	1978	12.00
— Reissue of Rocket 463			
ORBIT			
❏ RB-17196	Bravo!	1983	12.00
PICKWICK			
❏ ACL-7006	Breaking Up Is Hard to Do	197?	10.00
POLYDOR			
❏ 831235-1	My Friend	1986	12.00
RCA CAMDEN			
❏ ACL-7006	Breaking Up Is Hard to Do	197?	12.00
RCA SPECIAL PRODUCTS			
❏ DPL2-0149	Original Hits	1975	25.00
RCA VICTOR			
❏ LPM-2317 [M]	Circulate	1960	80.00
❏ LSP-2317 [S]	Circulate	1960	100.00
❏ APL1-1789	Emergence	1976	15.00
— Reissue of Kirshner 111			
❏ R133511	Let's Go Steady Again	1976	18.00
— RCA Record Club edition			
❏ LPM-2421 [M]	Little Devil" and His Other Hits	1961	80.00
❏ LSP-2421 [S]	Little Devil" and His Other Hits	1961	100.00
❏ VPL1-1540	Live in Australia	1976	15.00
❏ LPM-2035 [M]	Neil Sedaka	1959	100.00
❏ LSP-2035 [S]	Neil Sedaka	1959	130.00
❏ LPM-2627 [M]	Neil Sedaka Sings His Greatest Hits	1962	60.00
❏ LSP-2627 [S]	Neil Sedaka Sings His Greatest Hits	1962	80.00
— Black label, dog on top, "Living Stereo" at bottom			
❏ APL1-0928	Neil Sedaka Sings His Greatest Hits	1975	15.00
— Reissue of LSP-2627			
❏ AFL1-0928	Neil Sedaka Sings His Greatest Hits	1977	12.00
— Reissue with new prefix			
❏ ANL1-3465	Neil Sedaka Sings His Greatest Hits	1979	10.00
— Reissue of AFL1-0928			
❏ LSP-2627 [S]	Neil Sedaka Sings His Greatest Hits	1969	25.00
— Reissue; orange label			
❏ ANL1-0879	Oh! Carol	1975	12.00
❏ ANL1-1314	Pure Gold	1976	12.00
❏ AFL1-2254	Sedaka -- The '50s and '60s	1977	12.00
❏ APL1-1790	Solitaire	1976	15.00
— Reissue of Kirshner 117			
❏ AFL1-2524	The Many Sides of Neil Sedaka	1978	12.00
ROCKET			
❏ PIG-2297	Neil Sedaka's Greatest Hits	1977	15.00
❏ MCA-463	Sedaka's Back	1974	15.00
❏ PIG-2195	Steppin' Out	1976	15.00
❏ PIG-2157	The Hungry Years	1975	15.00
ROLLER SKATE			
❏ TLA-50172	Is Anybody Gonna Miss You	1982	18.00
SEDUCTION			
VENDETTA			
❏ SP-5280	Nothing Matters Without Love	1989	15.00
SEEDS, THE			
GNP CRESCENDO			
❏ GNP-2040 [M]	A Full Spoon of Seedy Blues	1968	120.00
❏ GNPS-2040 [S]	A Full Spoon of Seedy Blues	1968	30.00
❏ GNP-2033 [M]	A Web of Sound	1967	100.00
❏ GNPS-2033 [S]	A Web of Sound	1967	40.00
❏ ST-91224	A Web of Sound	1968	30.00
— Capitol Record Club edition			
❏ GNPS-2107	Fallin' Off the Edge	1977	12.00
❏ GNP-2038 [M]	Future	1967	100.00
— Deduct 25% if two inserts are missing			
❏ GNPS-2038 [S]	Future	1967	30.00
— Deduct 25% if two inserts are missing			
❏ GNPS-2043	Raw and Alive	1968	30.00
❏ GNP-2023 [M]	The Seeds	1966	70.00
❏ GNPS-2023 [S]	The Seeds	1966	40.00
SEEGER, BERT			
ANTILLES			
❏ AN-7088	Because They Can	198?	12.00
❏ AN-7086	Time to Burn	198?	12.00
SEEGER, PEGGY, BARBARA AND PENNY			
FOLKWAYS			
❏ FC-7553 [10]	American Folk Songs for Christmas	195?	50.00
SCHOLASTIC			
❏ SC7553 [M]	American Folk Songs for Christmas	1966	25.00
— Reissue of Folkways material			
SEEGER, PEGGY			
FOLKLORE			
❏ FRLP-14016 [M]	The Best of Peggy Seeger	196?	30.00

Number	Title	Yr	NM
FOLK-LYRIC			
❏ FL114 [M]	American Folksongs for Banjo	196?	30.00
❏ FL120 [M]	Popular Ballads	196?	30.00
FOLKWAYS			
❏ FC-7551 [10]	Animal Folksongs for Children	1957	100.00
❏ FP-49 [10]	Folk Songs of Courting and Complaint	1955	100.00
❏ FP-2049 [10]	Folk Songs of Courting and Complaint	195?	80.00
❏ FW-8563 [M]	From Where I Stand	1982	12.00
PRESTIGE			
❏ PRLP-13058 [M]	A Song for You and Me	1962	30.00
❏ PRLP-13005 [M]	The Best of Peggy Seeger	1961	30.00
RIVERSIDE			
❏ RLP-12-655 [M]	Folksongs and Ballads	1958	40.00
TOPIC			
❏ 10T-9 [10]	Peggy Seeger	1956	100.00
SEEGER, PETE, PENNY AND MICHAEL			
PRESTIGE			
❏ PRLP-7375 [M]	Pete, Penny and Michael Seeger	1965	25.00
❏ PRST-7375 [S]	Pete, Penny and Michael Seeger	1965	30.00
SEEGER, PETE			
ARAVEL			
❏ AB1006 [M]	Live Hootenanny	1963	18.00
BROADSIDE			
❏ 502	Pete Seeger Sings and Answers Questions	1970	18.00
BULLDOG			
❏ BDL-2011	20 Golden Pieces of Pete Seeger	198?	12.00
CAPITOL			
❏ W2172 [M]	Folk Songs	1964	25.00
❏ DW2172 [R]	Folk Songs	1964	15.00
❏ T2718 [M]	Freight Train	1967	25.00
❏ DT2718 [R]	Freight Train	1967	15.00
COLUMBIA			
❏ CL1947 [M]	Children's Concert at Town Hall	1963	30.00
❏ CS8747 [S]	Children's Concert at Town Hall	1963	30.00
❏ CL2503 [M]	Dangerous Songs?	1966	18.00
❏ CS9303 [S]	Dangerous Songs?	1966	25.00
❏ CL2432 [M]	God Bless the Grass	1966	18.00
❏ CS9232 [S]	God Bless the Grass	1966	25.00
❏ CL2257 [M]	I Can See a New Day	1965	18.00
❏ CS9057 [S]	I Can See a New Day	1965	25.00
❏ CS9717	Pete Seeger Now	1968	18.00
❏ CL2616 [M]	Pete Seeger's Greatest Hits	1967	25.00
❏ CS9416 [S]	Pete Seeger's Greatest Hits	1967	18.00
❏ PC9416	Pete Seeger's Greatest Hits	198?	10.00
— Reissue with new prefix			
❏ CL1668 [M]	Pete Seeger Story Songs	1961	30.00
❏ CS8468 [S]	Pete Seeger Story Songs	1961	30.00
❏ C30739	Rainbow Race	1971	15.00
❏ CL2334 [M]	Strangers and Cousins	1964	30.00
❏ CS9134 [S]	Strangers and Cousins	1964	25.00
❏ CL1916 [M]	The Bitter and the Sweet	1962	30.00
❏ CS8716 [S]	The Bitter and the Sweet	1962	30.00
❏ KG31949	The World of Pete Seeger	1972	18.00
❏ CL2705 [M]	Waist Deep in the Big Muddy	1967	25.00
❏ CS9505 [S]	Waist Deep in the Big Muddy	1967	18.00
❏ CL2101 [M]	We Shall Overcome	1963	18.00
❏ CS8901 [S]	We Shall Overcome	1963	25.00
❏ CS9873	Young vs. Old	1969	18.00
DISC			
❏ D-101 [M]	Sing with Seeger	1964	25.00
EVEREST ARCHIVE OF FOLK & JAZZ			
❏ 201	Pete Seeger	1966	15.00
FOLKWAYS			
❏ FI-8371 [M]	12-String Guitar As Played by Leadbelly	1962	25.00
❏ FA-2319 [M]	American Ballads	1957	30.00
❏ FTS-31017 [R]	American Favorite Ballads	1968	15.00
❏ FA-2320 [M]	American Favorite Ballads, Vol. 1	1957	30.00
❏ FA-2321 [M]	American Favorite Ballads, Vol. 2	1958	30.00
❏ FA-2322 [M]	American Favorite Ballads, Vol. 3	1958	30.00
❏ FA-2323 [M]	American Favorite Ballads, Vol. 4	1961	25.00
❏ FA-2445 [M]	American Favorite Ballads, Vol. 5: Tunes and Songs As Sung by Pete Seeger	1962	25.00
❏ FP-701 [10]	American Folk Songs for Children	195?	100.00
❏ FC-7601 [10]	American Folk Songs for Children	1953	80.00
❏ FC-7674 [M]	American Game and Activity Songs for Children	1962	25.00
❏ FH-5251 [M]	American Industrial Ballads	1956	30.00
❏ FP-43 [10]	A Pete Seeger Sampler	195?	100.00
❏ FA-2043 [10]	A Pete Seeger Sampler	1954	80.00
❏ FH-5485 [M]	Ballads of Sacco and Vanzetti	1963	25.00

Number	Title	Yr	NM
❑ FTS-31040 [R]	Banks of Marble and Other Songs	1974	15.00
❑ FW-6912 [10]	Bantu Choral Folk Songs	1955	80.00
❑ FC-7611 [M]	Birds, Beasts, Bugs and Bigger Fishes	1954	50.00
❑ FP-710 [10]	Birds, Beasts, Bugs and Little Fishes	1954	100.00
❑ FC-7610 [10]	Birds, Beasts, Bugs and Little Fishes	1954	80.00
❑ FH-5302 [M]	Broadside Ballads, Vol. 2	1963	25.00
❑ FA-2456 [M]	Broadsides	1964	25.00
❑ FH-5210 [M]	Champlain Valley Songs	1960	30.00
❑ FP-3 [10]	Darling Corey	1950	100.00
❑ FA-2003 [10]	Darling Corey	1950	80.00
❑ FH-5257	Fifty Sail On Newburgh Bay	1976	15.00
❑ FI-8354 [M]	Folksinger's Guitar Guide Vol. 1: An Instruction Record	1955	30.00
❑ FP-911 [10]	Folk Songs of Four Continents	195?	100.00
❑ FW-6911 [10]	Folk Songs of Four Continents	1955	80.00
❑ 5003	Frontier Ballads	1954	100.00
❑ FA-2175 [10]	Frontier Ballads, Volume 1	1954	80.00
❑ FA-2176 [10]	Frontier Ballads, Volume 2	1954	80.00
❑ FA-2501 [M]	Gazette, Vol. 1	1958	30.00
❑ FA-2502 [M]	Gazette, Vol. 2	1962	25.00
❑ FW-6843 [10]	German Folk Songs	1954	80.00
❑ 37232	God Bless the Grass	1982	15.00
❑ FP-45 [10]	Goofing Off Suite	195?	100.00
❑ FA-2045 [10]	Goofing Off Suite	1954	80.00
❑ FA-2450 [M]	Highlights of Pete Seeger at the Village Gate with Memphis Slim and Willie Dixon	1960	30.00
❑ FN-2511 [M]	Hootenanny Tonight!	195?	30.00
❑ FI-8303 [M]	How to Play the Five String Banjo	195?	30.00
❑ FS-3851 [M]	Indian Summer	1960	30.00
—With Michael Seeger			
❑ FP-10 [10]	Lonesome Valley	195?	100.00
❑ FA-2010 [10]	Lonesome Valley	195?	80.00
❑ FA-2453 [M]	Love Songs for Friends and Foes	1956	30.00
❑ FA-2439 [M]	Nonesuch	196?	25.00
❑ FA-2412 [M]	Pete Seeger and Sonny Terry	1958	30.00
❑ FA-2451 [M]	Pete Seeger at the Village Gate -- Vol. 2	1960	30.00
❑ FH-5702	Pete Seeger Sings and Answers Questions	1968	30.00
❑ FTS-31022 [R]	Pete Seeger Sings Leadbelly	1968	15.00
❑ FTS-31002 [R]	Pete Seeger Sings Woody Guthrie	1968	15.00
❑ FA-2454 [M]	Rainbow Quest	1960	30.00
❑ FXM-36055	Sing Along	1980	18.00
❑ FN-2513 [M]	Sing Out! Hootenanny	1963	25.00
❑ FA-2455 [M]	Sing Out with Pete!	1961	25.00
❑ FC-7526 [M]	Song and Play Time	195?	50.00
❑ FH-5233 [M]	Songs of Struggle and Protest 1930-50	1959	30.00
❑ FH-5436 [M]	Songs of the Spanish Civil War, Vol. 1	1961	25.00
❑ FC-7020 [10]	Songs to Grow On -- Vol. 2	1951	80.00
❑ FC-7027 [10]	Songs to Grow On -- Vol. 3	1951	80.00
❑ FQ-8354 [M]	The Folksinger's Guitar Gude	1955	30.00
❑ FT-35001	The Nativity: By Sholem Asch	1963	18.00
❑ FA-2311 [M]	Traditional Christmas Carols	1956	30.00
❑ FTS-32311 [R]	Traditional Christmas Carols	1967	18.00
❑ FTS-31018 [R]	Wimoweh and Other Songs of Freedom and Protest	1968	15.00
❑ FA-2452 [M]	With Voices Together We Sing	1956	30.00
❑ FH-5595 [M]	WNEW's Story of Selma	1965	25.00
❑ 7527	Zhitkov's How I Hunted the Little Fellows	1980	15.00

HARMONY

Number	Title	Yr	NM
❑ HS11337	John Henry and Other Folk Favorites	1969	15.00

ODYSSEY

Number	Title	Yr	NM
❑ 32160266	3 Saints, 4 Sinners and 6 Other People	1968	18.00

OLYMPIC

Number	Title	Yr	NM
❑ 7102	America's Balladeer	1973	15.00

PAIR

Number	Title	Yr	NM
❑ PDL2-1076	Clearwater Classics	1986	15.00

PHILIPS

Number	Title	Yr	NM
❑ PHM 2-300 [M]	The Story of the Nativity	1963	25.00
❑ PHS 2-300 [S]	The Story of the Nativity	1963	30.00
❑ PHM 2-300 [M]	The Story of the Nativity	1963	25.00
❑ PHS 2-300 [S]	The Story of the Nativity	1963	30.00

SMITHSONIAN FOLKWAYS

Number	Title	Yr	NM
❑ SF-40024	Traditional Christmas Carols	1989	15.00

STINSON

Number	Title	Yr	NM
❑ SLP-57 [10]	A Pete Seeger Concert	1953	100.00
❑ SLP-52 [10]	Lincoln Brigade	1953	100.00
❑ SLP-90 [M]	Pete	1963	30.00

TRADITION

Number	Title	Yr	NM
❑ 2107	Folk Music of the World	1973	15.00

VANGUARD

Number	Title	Yr	NM
❑ VSD-97/98	The Essential Pete Seeger	1978	18.00
❑ VSD-73111	The Essential Pete Seeger, Vol. 1	198?	10.00
❑ VSD-73112	The Essential Pete Seeger, Vol. 2	198?	10.00

VERVE FOLKWAYS

Number	Title	Yr	NM
❑ FV-9013 [M]	Folk Music Live at the Village Gate	1965	25.00
❑ FVS-9013 [S]	Folk Music Live at the Village Gate	1965	30.00
❑ FV-9020 [M]	Little Boxes and Other Broadsides	1965	25.00
❑ FVS-9020 [S]	Little Boxes and Other Broadsides	1965	30.00
❑ FV-9008 [M]	Pete Seeger and Big Bill Broonzy in Concert	1965	25.00
❑ FVS-9008 [S]	Pete Seeger and Big Bill Broonzy in Concert	1965	30.00
❑ FV-9009 [M]	Pete Seeger On Campus	1965	25.00
❑ FVS-9009 [S]	Pete Seeger On Campus	1965	30.00

WARNER BROS.

Number	Title	Yr	NM
❑ BSK3329	Circles and Seasons	1979	15.00

SEEKERS, THE

CAPITOL

Number	Title	Yr	NM
❑ T2369 [M]	A World of Our Own	1965	15.00
❑ DT2369 [R]	A World of Our Own	1965	15.00
❑ T2431 [M]	Georgy Girl	1966	25.00
❑ ST2431 [S]	Georgy Girl	1966	18.00
❑ SM-2746 [P]	The Best of the Seekers	197?	12.00
❑ SN-16104 [P]	The Best of the Seekers	1980	10.00
❑ T2746 [M]	The Best of the Seekers	1967	15.00
❑ ST2746 [P]	The Best of the Seekers	1967	15.00

—Red and white "target" Starline label; though the cover has an "ST" prefix, the record and trail-off wax have a "DT" prefix; "Morningtown Ride," Turn, Turn, Turn," and "We're Moving On" are in stereo

Number	Title	Yr	NM
❑ ST2746 [P]	The Best of the Seekers	196?	12.00
—Red and white "star" Starline label			
❑ T2319 [M]	The New Seekers	1965	15.00
❑ ST2319 [S]	The New Seekers	1965	18.00
❑ ST-135 [S]	The Seekers Live	1969	15.00
❑ SKAO2821 [S]	The Seekers Seen in Green	1968	18.00
❑ KAO2821 [M]	The Seekers Seen in Green	1968	60.00

MARVEL

Number	Title	Yr	NM
❑ 2060 [M]	The Seekers	1965	15.00
❑ 3060 [R]	The Seekers	1965	12.00

SEELY, JEANNIE

DECCA

Number	Title	Yr	NM
❑ DL75093	Jeannie Seely	1969	18.00
❑ DL75228	Please Be My New Love	1970	18.00

HARMONY

Number	Title	Yr	NM
❑ KH31029	Make the World Go Away	1972	15.00

MCA

Number	Title	Yr	NM
❑ 385	Can I Sleep in Your Arms/ Lucky Ladies	1973	15.00

MONUMENT

Number	Title	Yr	NM
❑ KZ31911	Greatest Hits	1973	18.00
❑ 6640	Greatest Hits	1977	15.00
—Reissue of 31911			
❑ SLP-18091	I'll Love You More	1968	25.00
❑ SLP-18104	Little Things	1968	25.00
❑ MLP-8073 [M]	Thanks, Hank!	1967	30.00
❑ SLP-18073 [S]	Thanks, Hank!	1967	25.00
❑ MLP-8057 [M]	The Seely Style	1966	18.00
—Title on label is "The Jeannie Seely Style			
❑ SLP-18057 [S]	The Seely Style	1966	25.00
—Title on label is "The Jeannie Seely Style			

SEGAL, GEORGE

PHILIPS

Number	Title	Yr	NM
❑ PHM200242 [M]	The Yama-Yama Man	1967	25.00
❑ PHS600242 [S]	The Yama-Yama Man	1967	25.00

SIGNATURE

Number	Title	Yr	NM
❑ BSL1-0654	A Touch of Ragtime	1976	18.00

SEGALL, RICKY

BELL

Number	Title	Yr	NM
❑ 1138	Ricky Segall and the Segalls	1973	25.00

SEGER, BOB

CAPITOL

Number	Title	Yr	NM
❑ SOO-12041	Against the Wind	1980	12.00
❑ ST-11378	Beautiful Loser	1975	12.00
—Originals have orange labels			
❑ ST-11378	Beautiful Loser	1978	10.00
—Purple label with large Capitol logo			
❑ SN-16315	Beautiful Loser	1984	10.00
❑ ST-731	Brand New Morning	1971	100.00
❑ SPRO-8433 [DJ]	Consensus Cuts Edited for Airplay from "Live Bullet	1976	30.00
❑ SPRO-8433 [DJ]	Consensus Cuts Edited for Airplay from "Live Bullet	1976	30.00
❑ C1-30334	Greatest Hits	1994	18.00
❑ PT-12398	Like a Rock	1986	12.00
❑ SKBB-11523	Live Bullet	1976	18.00
—Originals have orange labels			
❑ SKBB-11523	Live Bullet	1978	15.00
—Purple label with large Capitol logo			
❑ SKBB-11523	Live Bullet	1983	15.00
—Black label, print in colorband			
❑ STBK-11523	Live Bullet	1988	15.00
—Purple label with smaller Capitol logo			
❑ SKAO-499	Mongrel	1970	30.00
❑ SM-499	Mongrel	1977	10.00
❑ SN-16106	Mongrel	1980	10.00
❑ ST-11557	Night Moves	1976	12.00
❑ (no #)0 [PD]	Night Moves	1977	40.00
—Promo-only picture disc			
❑ STBK-12182	Nine Tonight	1981	18.00
❑ ST-236	Noah	1969	80.00
❑ ST-172 [B]	Ramblin' Gamblin' Man	1969	50.00
—Black label with colorband			
❑ SM-172	Ramblin' Gamblin' Man	1977	10.00
❑ SN-16105	Ramblin' Gamblin' Man	1980	10.00
❑ R124284	Ramblin' Gamblin' Man	197?	25.00

—Orange label, "Capitol"at bottom; RCA Music Service edition with B-side label error listing the title as "Ramblin' Bamblin' Man

Number	Title	Yr	NM
❑ ST-11748	Seven	1978	12.00
❑ SN-16108	Seven	1980	10.00
❑ ST-11746	Smokin' O.P.'s	1978	12.00
❑ SN-16107	Smokin' O.P.'s	1980	10.00
❑ SW-11698	Stranger in Town	1978	12.00
❑ SEAX-11904 [PD]	Stranger in Town	1978	30.00
❑ ST-12254	The Distance	1983	12.00
❑ C1-91134	The Fire Inside	1991	15.00

MOBILE FIDELITY

Number	Title	Yr	NM
❑ 1-127	Against the Wind	1983	40.00
—Audiophile vinyl			
❑ 1-034 [B]	Night Moves	1980	65.00
—Audiophile vinyl			

PALLADIUM

Number	Title	Yr	NM
❑ P-1006	Smokin' O.P.'s	1972	30.00

REPRISE

Number	Title	Yr	NM
❑ MS2126	Back in '72	1973	60.00
❑ MS2184	Seven	1974	25.00
❑ MS2109	Smokin' O.P.'s	1972	18.00

SEGO BROTHERS AND NAOMI, THE

GOSPEL TIME

Number	Title	Yr	NM
❑ 5007	From the Soul	196?	30.00
❑ 5018	Gospel Concert Special	196?	25.00

HARVEST

Number	Title	Yr	NM
❑ 1001	Keeping It Gospel	196?	30.00

HEART WARMING

Number	Title	Yr	NM
❑ 3154	Featuring Naomi	1972	30.00
❑ 3056	Happy Day	196?	30.00
❑ 3433	It Will Be Different the Next Time	1976	30.00
❑ 3144	Meetin' Time	1972	30.00
❑ 3186	Sorry I Never Knew You	1972	30.00
❑ 3206	The Dearest Friend I Ever Had	1973	30.00
❑ 1955	This World Has Turned Me Down	196?	30.00
❑ 3279	What a Happy Time	1974	30.00
❑ 1952	With the Help of God	196?	30.00

RUNA

Number	Title	Yr	NM
❑ 1942	Completely Gospel	196?	30.00
❑ 1941	Gospel Singing	196?	30.00

SCRIPTURE

Number	Title	Yr	NM
❑ 122	Far Above the Starry Skies	196?	30.00
❑ 121	The Best of the Sego Brothers and Naomi	196?	30.00

SILVER STAFF

Number	Title	Yr	NM
❑ 15003	I Pray My Way Out of Trouble	196?	30.00

SIMS

Number	Title	Yr	NM
❑ 134	With the Help of God	196?	40.00

SING

Number	Title	Yr	NM
❑ 9092S [S]	One Day Late	196?	40.00
❑ 9092M [M]	One Day Late	196?	30.00
❑ 9091M [M]	Sego Brothers and Naomi	196?	30.00
❑ 9091S [S]	Sego Brothers and Naomi	196?	40.00

SONGS OF FAITH

Number	Title	Yr	NM
❑ 150	Daddy Sang Bass	1969	30.00
❑ 117	From the Soul	196?	30.00
❑ 158	Golden Hits of the Sego Brothers and Naomi	1970	30.00
❑ 141	Gospel Music On Stage with the Sego Brothers and Naomi	196?	30.00
❑ 133	He'll Walk By Your Side	196?	30.00
❑ 126	Hem of His Garment	196?	30.00
❑ 143	I'm Longing for Home	196?	30.00
❑ 103	Satisfied with Me	196?	30.00
❑ 147	Somebody Touched Me	196?	30.00
❑ 121	The Award Winning Sego Brothers and Naomi	196?	30.00
❑ 168	The Sego Brothers and Naomi at Grandfather Mountain	197?	30.00
❑ 156	The Sego Brothers and Naomi Featuring W.R. Sego	1969	30.00
❑ 110	The Sego Brothers and Naomi Sing the Gospel	1963	30.00
❑ 145	The Sego Brothers and Naomi Sing Weapon of Prayer	196?	25.00
❑ 137	Will the Circle Be Unbroken	196?	30.00

SUPREME

Number	Title	Yr	NM
❑ 33003	I Pray My Way Out of Trouble	196?	30.00

VISTA

Number	Title	Yr	NM
❑ 1224	Old Time Singing	196?	30.00

Number	Title	Yr	NM

SEIFERT, ZBIGNIEW

CAPITOL
| ❏ ST-11618 | Zbigniew Seifert | 197? | 15.00 |

PAUSA
| ❏ 7077 | Man of the Light | 1979 | 12.00 |

SELAH JUBILEE QUARTET, THE

REMINGTON
| ❏ 1023 [10] | Spirituals | 1951 | 200.00 |

SELECTER, THE

CHRYSALIS
❏ CHR1306	Celebrate the Bullet	1981	12.00
❏ PV41306	Celebrate the Bullet	198?	10.00
— Reissue			
❏ CHR1274	Too Much Pressure	1980	12.00
❏ PV41274	Too Much Pressure	1983	10.00
— Reissue			

SELENA

CAPITOL/EMI LATIN
❏ H1-42299 [B]	16 Super Exitos Originales	1990	80.00
❏ H1-42144 [B]	Selena Y Los Dinos	1989	80.00
❏ H1-42359 [B]	Ven Conmingo	1990	80.00
CBS DISCOS
| ❏ RRL80323 [B] | Personal Best | 1990 | 80.00 |
GP
❏ LP-1002	Alpha	1986	500.00
❏ LP-1009	And the Winner Is…	1987	200.00
❏ LP-1005	Menequito De Trapo	1986	300.00
RP
| ❏ LP-8803 | Dulce Amor | 1988 | 150.00 |
| ❏ LP-8801 | Preciosa | 1988 | 150.00 |

SELLARS, MARILYN

KOALA
| ❏ 14154 | Raised on Country Sunshine | 198? | 12.00 |
MEGA
| ❏ MLPS-609 | Gather Me | 1974 | 15.00 |
| ❏ MLPS-602 | One Day at a Time | 1974 | 15.00 |
ZODIAC
| ❏ ZLP-5005 | Marilyn | 1977 | 15.00 |
| ❏ ZLP-5001 | One Day at a Time | 1976 | 15.00 |

SELLERS, BROTHER JOHN

VANGUARD
| ❏ VRS-9036 [M] | Blues and Folk Songs | 1957 | 80.00 |
| ❏ VRS-8005 [10] | Brother John Sellers: Folk Songs and Blues | 1954 | 100.00 |

SELLERS, PETER, AND SOPHIA LOREN

ANGEL
| ❏ 35910 [M] | Peter Sellers and Sophia Loren | 1961 | 40.00 |
| ❏ S35910 [S] | Peter Sellers and Sophia Loren | 1961 | 50.00 |

SELLERS, PETER

ACAPELLA
| ❏ 1 [B] | Fool Brittania | 1963 | 35.00 |
| — With Joan Collins and Anthony Newley | | | |
ANGEL
| ❏ 35884 [M] | The Best of Sellers | 1960 | 30.00 |
| ❏ S35884 [S] | The Best of Sellers | 1960 | 40.00 |
EMI AMERICA
| ❏ SN-16396 | Songs for Swingin' Sellers | 1986 | 25.00 |
| — First American issue of 1959 U.K. LP | | | |

SEMBELLO, MICHAEL

A&M
| ❏ SP-5044 | Without Walls | 1986 | 25.00 |
WARNER BROS.
| ❏ 23920 | Bossa Nova Hotel | 1983 | 12.00 |

SENATOR BOBBY

PARKWAY
| ❏ P7057 [M] | Boston Soul with the Hardly-Worthit Players | 1967 | 25.00 |
| ❏ SP7057 [S] | Boston Soul with the Hardly-Worthit Players | 1967 | 25.00 |

SENENSKY, BERNIE

PM
| ❏ 021 | Free Spirit | 1986 | 12.00 |
| ❏ 006 | New Life | 197? | 15.00 |

SENOFSKY, BERL

RCA VICTOR RED SEAL
| ❏ LSC-2488 [S] | Debussy: Violin Sonata; Faure: Violin Sonata No. 1 in A | 1961 | 40.00 |
| — With Gary Graffman, piano; original with "shaded dog" label | | | |

Number	Title	Yr	NM

SENSATIONS, THE

ARGO
| ❏ LP-4022 [M] | Let Me In/Music, Music, Music | 1963 | 500.00 |

SENTINALS, THE

DEL-FI
❏ DFLP-1232 [M]	Big Surf!	1963	100.00
❏ DFST-1232 [S]	Big Surf!	1963	150.00
❏ DLF1232	Big Surf!	1997	15.00
❏ DFLP-1241 [M]	Surfer Girl	1963	70.00
❏ DFST-1241 [S]	Surfer Girl	1963	100.00
❏ DLF1241	Surfer Girl	1997	15.00
SUTTON
| ❏ SU-338 [M] | Vegas Go-Go | 1964 | 40.00 |
| ❏ SSU-338 [S] | Vegas Go-Go | 1964 | 50.00 |

SERENDIPITY SINGERS, THE

PHILIPS
❏ PHM200190 [M]	Love, Lies and Flying Festoons	1965	18.00
❏ PHS600190 [S]	Love, Lies and Flying Festoons	1965	25.00
❏ PHM200151 [M]	Take Your Shoes Off with the Serendipity Singers	1964	18.00
❏ PHS600151 [S]	Take Your Shoes Off with the Serendipity Singers	1964	25.00
❏ PHM200134 [M]	The Many Sides of the Serendipity Singers	1964	18.00
❏ PHS600134 [S]	The Many Sides of the Serendipity Singers	1964	25.00
❏ PHM200115 [M]	The Serendipity Singers	1964	18.00
❏ PHS600115 [S]	The Serendipity Singers	1964	25.00
❏ PHM200180 [M]	We Belong Together	1965	18.00
❏ PHS600180 [S]	We Belong Together	1965	25.00

SERPENT POWER

VANGUARD
| ❏ VRS-9252 [M] | Serpent Power | 1967 | 200.00 |
| ❏ VSD-79252 [S] | Serpent Power | 1967 | 80.00 |

SERRANO, PAUL

RIVERSIDE
| ❏ RLP-359 [M] | Blues Holiday | 1961 | 30.00 |
| ❏ RS-9359 [S] | Blues Holiday | 1961 | 30.00 |

SERRY, JOHN

CHRYSALIS
| ❏ CHS1279 | Jazziz | 1979 | 12.00 |

SERTL, DOUG

DISCOVERY
| ❏ 920 | Groovin' | 1986 | 12.00 |

SESSIONS, RONNIE

MCA
| ❏ 2285 | Ronnie Sessions | 1977 | 12.00 |

SETE, BOLA

ANALOGUE PRODUCTIONS
| ❏ APR3003 | Tour de Force | 199? | 18.00 |
COLUMBIA
| ❏ KC32375 | Goin' to Rio | 1973 | 15.00 |
DANCING CAT
| ❏ DC-3005 | Jungle Suite | 1985 | 15.00 |
FANTASY
❏ OJC-290	Autentico!	1987	12.00
❏ 3375 [M]	Autentico!	1966	18.00
❏ 8375 [S]	Autentico!	1966	25.00
❏ OJC-286	Bossa Nova	1987	12.00
❏ 3349 [M]	Bossa Nova	1963	18.00
❏ 8349 [S]	Bossa Nova	1963	25.00
❏ 8417	Shebaba	1971	15.00
❏ OJC-288	The Incomparable Bola Sete	1987	12.00
❏ 3364 [M]	The Incomparable Bola Sete	1965	18.00
❏ 8364 [S]	The Incomparable Bola Sete	1965	25.00
❏ 3369 [M]	The Solo Guitar of Bola Sete	1966	18.00
❏ 8369 [S]	The Solo Guitar of Bola Sete	1966	25.00
❏ 7358 [S]	Tour de Force	1965	25.00
❏ 3358 [M]	Tour de Force	1965	18.00
LOST LAKE ARTS
| ❏ LL-82 | Ocean | 1981 | 12.00 |
| — Reissue of Takoma LP | | | |
PARAMOUNT
| ❏ PAS-5011 | Workin' on a Groovy Thing | 1970 | 18.00 |
TAKOMA
| ❏ C-1049 | Ocean | 1975 | 15.00 |
VERVE
| ❏ V-8689 [M] | Bola Sete At the Monterey Jazz Festival | 1967 | 25.00 |
| ❏ V6-8689 [S] | Bola Sete At the Monterey Jazz Festival | 1967 | 18.00 |

SETTLE, MIKE

REPRISE
| ❏ R-6149 [M] | The Mike Settle Shindig | 1965 | 25.00 |
| ❏ RS-6149 [S] | The Mike Settle Shindig | 1965 | 30.00 |

Number	Title	Yr	NM

SETZER, BRIAN

EMI AMERICA
❏ ST-17178	The Knife Feels Like Justice	1986	12.00
❏ ST-517178	The Knife Feels Like Justice	1986	15.00
— Columbia House edition			
EMI MANHATTAN
| ❏ E1-46963 | Live Nude Guitars | 1988 | 15.00 |
INTERSCOPE
| ❏ 90183 | The Dirty Boogie | 1998 | 18.00 |
| — As "The Brian Setzer Orchestra" | | | |
SURFDOG
| ❏ 67124 | Ignition! | 2001 | 18.00 |
| — As "Brian Setzer '68 Comeback Special"; red vinyl | | | |

SEVEN BLENDS, THE

ROULETTE
| ❏ R-25172 [M] | Twistin' at the Miami Beach Peppermint Lounge | 1962 | 25.00 |
| ❏ SR-25172 [S] | Twistin' at the Miami Beach Peppermint Lounge | 1962 | 30.00 |

SEVENTH AVENUE

I.T.I.
| ❏ JL-022 | Heads Up | 1986 | 15.00 |

SEVENTH AVENUE STOMPERS

SAVOY JAZZ
| ❏ SJL-1139 | Fidgety Feet | 198? | 12.00 |

SEVENTH SONS, THE

ESP-DISK'
| ❏ 1078 | The Seventh Sons | 1967 | 30.00 |

SEVENTH WAVE, THE

JANUS
| ❏ 7021 | Psi-Fi | 1975 | 25.00 |
| ❏ 7008 | Things to Come | 1974 | 25.00 |

SEVERINSON, DOC

ABC
| ❏ S-737 [B] | 16 Great Performances | 1971 | 15.00 |
| ❏ X-771 | Trumpets, Crumpets | 1973 | 12.00 |
AMHERST
❏ AMH-3319	Facets	1988	12.00
❏ AMH-3311	The Tonight Show Band with Doc Severinson	1986	12.00
❏ AMH-3312	The Tonight Show Band with Doc Severinson, Vol. II	1987	12.00
COMMAND
❏ RS 33-904 [M]	Command Performances	1966	15.00
❏ RS904SD [S]	Command Performances	1966	15.00
❏ RS937SD	Doc Severinson with Strings	1969	15.00
❏ RS 33-893 [M]	Fever!	1966	15.00
❏ RS893SD [S]	Fever!	1966	18.00
❏ QD-40003 [Q]	Fever!	1972	18.00
❏ RS 33-883 [M]	High, Wide and Wonderful	1965	18.00
❏ RS883SD [S]	High, Wide and Wonderful	1965	25.00
❏ RS 33-901 [M]	Live!	1966	15.00
❏ RS901SD [S]	Live!	1966	18.00
❏ RS 33-909 [M]	Swinging and Singing	1967	18.00
❏ RS909SD [S]	Swinging and Singing	1967	15.00
❏ RS 33-819 [M]	Tempestuous Trumpet	1961	25.00
❏ RS819SD [S]	Tempestuous Trumpet	1961	25.00
❏ RS952SD	The Best of Doc Severinson	1970	15.00
❏ RS 33-837 [M]	The Big Band's Back in Town	1962	18.00
❏ RS837SD [S]	The Big Band's Back in Town	1962	25.00
❏ RS950SD	The Closet	1970	15.00
❏ RS927SD	The Great Arrival	1968	15.00
❏ RS 33-917 [M]	The New Sound	1967	18.00
❏ RS917SD [S]	The New Sound	1967	15.00
❏ RS 33-859 [M]	Torch Songs for Trumpet	1963	18.00
❏ RS859SD [S]	Torch Songs for Trumpet	1963	25.00
EPIC
| ❏ PE34925 | A Brand New Thing | 1977 | 12.00 |
| ❏ PE34078 | Night Journey | 1976 | 12.00 |
EVEREST ARCHIVE OF FOLK & JAZZ
| ❏ 334 | Doc Severinson and Friends | 1978 | 12.00 |
FIRSTLINE
| ❏ FDLP5001 | London Sessions | 1980 | 15.00 |
JUNO
| ❏ 1001 | I Feel Good | 1970 | 15.00 |
MCA
| ❏ 4168 | The Best of Doc Severinson | 198? | 12.00 |
PICKWICK
| ❏ SPC3627 | Tempestuous Trumpet | 1978 | 10.00 |
| ❏ SPC-3608 | Torch Songs for Trumpet | 1978 | 10.00 |
RCA VICTOR
❏ LSP-4522	Brass Roots	1971	15.00
❏ LSP-4669	Doc	1972	15.00
❏ AFL1-4669	Doc	1977	12.00
— Reissue with new prefix			
❏ APL1-0273	Rhapsody for Now!	1973	15.00

Number	Title	Yr	NM

SEVERSON, PAUL

ACADEMY
❏ MWJ-1 [M]	Midwest Jazz	1956	50.00

SEVILLA, JORGE

VERVE
❏ MGV-8342 [M]	The Incredible Guitar of Jorge Sevilla	1959	50.00
❏ MGVS-6103 [S]	The Incredible Guitar of Jorge Sevilla	1960	40.00
❏ V-8342 [M]	The Incredible Guitar of Jorge Sevilla	1961	30.00
❏ V6-8342 [S]	The Incredible Guitar of Jorge Sevilla	1961	25.00

SEVILLE, DAVID

LIBERTY
❏ LRP-3073 [M]	The Music of David Seville	1957	100.00
❏ LRP-3092 [M]	The Witch Doctor	1958	120.00

SEWARD, ALEC

BLUESVILLE
❏ BVLP-1076 [M]	Creepin' Blues	1963	80.00
—Blue label, silver print			
❏ BVLP-1076 [M]	Creepin' Blues	1964	30.00
—Blue label, trident logo at right			

SEX CLARK FIVE

BLOOD MONEY
❏ ERATO59	Battle of Sex Clark Five	1989	25.00

RECORDS TO RUSSIA
❏ LP408	Strum & Drum!	1986	120.00
—Test pressing with 24 tracks			
❏ LP408	Strum & Drum!	1987	25.00
—First pressing: 20 tracks, photos are halftones			
❏ LP408	Strum & Drum!	1987	18.00
—Second pressing: 20 tracks, no halftones, different back photo			

SKYCLAD
❏ (NOT) BM131 [B]	Antedium	1992	25.00

SEX PISTOLS

RESTLESS
❏ 72255 [B]	Better Live Than Dead	1988	25.00
❏ 72511 [B]	Live at Chelmsford Top Security Prison	1990	25.00
❏ 72257	The Ex-Pistols: The Swindle Continues	1988	15.00
❏ 72256 [EP]	The Mini-Album	1988	15.00

RHINO/WARNER BROS.
❏ 3147 [B]	Never Mind the Bollocks Here's the Sex Pistols	2008	25.00

SKYCLAD
❏ SEX6 [B]	We've Cum For Your Children	1988	25.00

WARNER BROS.
❏ BSK3147 [B]	Never Mind the Bollocks Here's the Sex Pistols	1978	50.00
—With sticker "Contains Sub-Mission"			
❏ BSK3147 [B]	Never Mind the Bollocks Here's the Sex Pistols	1978	30.00
—Any other version with custom label			
❏ BSK3147 [B]	Never Mind the Bollocks Here's the Sex Pistols	1978	25.00
—With white WB label			

SEYMOUR, PHIL

BOARDWALK
❏ FW36996	Phil Seymour	1980	15.00
❏ NB1-33252	Phil Seymour 2	1982	18.00

SHA NA NA

ACCORD
❏ SN-7115	Remember Then	1981	12.00
❏ SN-7146	Sh-Boom	1981	12.00

BUDDAH
❏ BDM-5692	Rock & Roll Is Here to Stay!	1978	12.00
❏ BDM-5703	The Best of Sha Na Na	1978	12.00

EMUS
❏ ES-12037	On Stage	1978	12.00

KAMA SUTRA
❏ KSBS-2075	From the Streets of New York	1973	18.00
❏ KSBS-2600	Hot Sox	1974	18.00
❏ KSBS-2010	Rock & Roll Is Here to Stay!	1969	18.00
❏ KSBS-2077	Rock & Roll Is Here to Stay!	1974	18.00
❏ KSBS-2034	Sha Na Na	1971	18.00
❏ KSBS-2605	Sha Na Now	1975	18.00
❏ KSBS-2609	The Best…Sha Na Na	1976	18.00
❏ KSBS-2073	The Golden Age of Rock 'n' Roll	1973	25.00
❏ KSBS-2050	The Night Is Still Young	1972	18.00

NASHVILLE
❏ NR-12348-122	Rockin' in the 80's	1980	15.00

REALM
❏ 2V8058	All-Time Greatest Rock 'n' Roll Hits	1977	18.00
❏ 1V8059	Rock 'n' Roll Dance Party	1977	15.00

SHACKLEFORDS, THE

CAPITOL
❏ T2450 [M]	The Shacklefords	1966	25.00
❏ ST2450 [S]	The Shacklefords	1966	30.00

MERCURY
❏ MG-20806 [M]	Until You've Heard the Shacklefords	1963	25.00
❏ SR-60806 [S]	Until You've Heard the Shacklefords	1963	30.00

SHADES OF BLUE

IMPACT
❏ IM-101 [M]	Happiness Is the Shades of Blue	1966	80.00
❏ IM-1001 [S]	Happiness Is the Shades of Blue	1966	60.00

SHADES OF JOY

FONTANA
❏ SRF-67592	Shades of Joy	1969	25.00

SHADOW PROJECT

LIVELY ART
❏ ARTY37 [B]	Shadow Project	1991	40.00

SHADOWS, THE (1)

ATLANTIC
❏ 8084 [M]	Out of the Shadows	1962	200.00
—Canada-only release?			
❏ 8089 [M]	Surfing with the Shadows	1963	150.00
❏ SD8089 [S]	Surfing with the Shadows	1963	300.00
❏ 8097 [M]	The Shadows Know	1964	100.00
❏ SD8097 [S]	The Shadows Know	1964	200.00

SHADOWS OF KNIGHT, THE

DUNWICH
❏ 667 [M]	Back Door Men	1966	60.00
❏ S-667 [S]	Back Door Men	1966	80.00
❏ 666 [M]	Gloria	1966	80.00
❏ S-666 [S]	Gloria	1966	100.00

SUNDAZED
❏ LP5035	Back Door Men	1999	15.00
—Reissue on 180-gram vinyl			
❏ LP5034	Gloria	1999	15.00
—Reissue on 180-gram vinyl			
❏ LP5006	Raw and Live at the Cellar 1966	1992	12.00

SUPER K
❏ SKS-6002	The Shadows of Knight	1969	50.00

SHADRACK

IGL
❏ 132	Chameleon	1971	300.00

SHAFRAN, DANIEL

RCA VICTOR RED SEAL
❏ LSC-2553 [S]	Shostakovich: Cello Sonata; Schubert: Arpeggione Sonata	1961	120.00
—Original with "shaded dog" label			

SHAGGS, THE (2)

MCM
❏ 1295 [B]	Wink	1967	300.00
—No number on label -- this number is found in the trail-off wax on each side			

SHAGGS, THE (3)

ROUNDER
❏ 3032	Philosophy of the World	1980	30.00
❏ 3056	Shaggs' Own Thing	1982	30.00

THIRD WORLD
❏ 3001	Philosophy of the World	1969	2000.00

SHAGGY

MCA
❏ 112096	Hotshot	2000	18.00
❏ 112827	Hotshot Ultramix	2002	18.00

VIRGIN
❏ 44487	Midnite Lover	1997	15.00

SHAKATAK

POLYDOR
❏ 823017-1	Drivin' Hard	1987	12.00
❏ 839578-1	Manic and Cool	1989	15.00

SHAKERS, THE

AUDIO FIDELITY
❏ AFLP-2155 [M]	The Shakers Break It All	1966	40.00
❏ AFSD-6155 [S]	The Shakers Break It All	1966	50.00

SHAKEY JAKE

BLUESVILLE
❏ BVLP-1008 [M]	Good Times	1960	120.00
—Blue label, silver print			
❏ BVLP-1008 [M]	Good Times	1964	30.00
—Blue label, trident logo at right			
❏ BVLP-1027 [M]	Mouth Harp Blues	1961	120.00
—Blue label, silver print			
❏ BVLP-1027 [M]	Mouth Harp Blues	1964	30.00
—Blue label, trident logo at right			

WORLD PACIFIC
❏ WPS-21886	Blues Makers	196?	30.00

SHAKEY VICK

JANUS
❏ JLS-3000 [B]	Little Woman, You're So Sweet	1970	30.00

SHALAMAR

SOLAR
❏ BXL1-3479	Big Fun	1979	15.00
❏ ST-72556	Circumstantial Evidence	1987	12.00
❏ BXL1-2895	Disco Gardens	1978	18.00
❏ S-28	Friends	1982	12.00
❏ BXL1-3984	Go For It	1981	15.00
❏ BXL1-4262	Greatest Hits	1982	15.00
❏ 60385	Heart Break	1984	12.00
❏ 60239	The Look	1983	12.00
❏ BZL1-3577	Three for Love	1980	12.00
❏ Z75315	Wake Up	1990	15.00

SOUL TRAIN
❏ BVL1-2289	Uptown Festival	1977	18.00

SHAM 69

SIRE
❏ SRK-6060	Tell Us the Truth	1978	18.00

SHANGRI-LAS, THE

COLLECTABLES
❏ COL-5011	Remember…Their Greatest Hits	198?	12.00

MERCURY
❏ MG-21099 [M]	The Shangri-Las' Golden Hits	1966	60.00
❏ SR-61099 [S]	The Shangri-Las' Golden Hits	1966	80.00

POLYDOR
❏ 824807-1	Golden Hits of the Shangri-Las	1985	12.00

POST
❏ 4000	The Shangri-Las Sing	196?	25.00

RED BIRD
❏ 20104 [M]	I Can Never Go Home Anymore	1966	150.00
—Retitled version with title song added and "Sophisticated Boom Boom" dropped			
❏ 20101 [M]	Leader of the Pack	1965	200.00
❏ 20104 [M]	Shangri-Las '65	1965	200.00

SHANK, BUD

BAINBRIDGE
❏ CRS-6830	Live at the Haig	1985	12.00

CONCORD CONCERTO
❏ CC-2002	Explorations 1980: Suite for Flute and Piano	1981	12.00

CONCORD JAZZ
❏ CJ-126	Crystal Comments	1980	12.00
❏ CJ-58	Heritage	1979	15.00
❏ CJ-20	Sunshine Express	1976	15.00

CONTEMPORARY
❏ C-14027	Bud Shank at Jazz Alley	1987	12.00
❏ C-14012	California Concert	1985	12.00
❏ C-14031	Serious Swingers	1988	12.00
—With the Bill Perkins Quartet			
❏ C-14019	That Old Feeling	1986	12.00
❏ C-14048	Tomorrow's Rainbow	1989	12.00

CROWN
❏ CLP-5311 [M]	Bud Shank	1963	18.00
❏ CST-311 [R]	Bud Shank	1963	15.00

KIMBERLY
❏ 2025 [M]	The Talents of Bud Shank	1963	25.00
❏ 11025 [S]	The Talents of Bud Shank	1963	30.00

MUSE
❏ 5309	This Bud's for You	198?	12.00

NOCTURNE
❏ NLP-2 [10]	Compositions of Shorty Rogers	1953	200.00

PACIFIC JAZZ
❏ PJ-58 [M]	Bossa Nova Jazz Samba	1962	30.00
❏ ST-58 [S]	Bossa Nova Jazz Samba	1962	30.00
❏ PJ-64 [M]	Brassamba Bossa Nova	1963	25.00
❏ ST-64 [S]	Brassamba Bossa Nova	1963	30.00
❏ PJLP-20 [10]	Bud Shank and Bob Brookmeyer	1954	120.00
❏ PJ-89 [M]	Bud Shank and His Brazilian Friends	1965	25.00

Number	Title	Yr	NM
ST-89 [S]	Bud Shank and His Brazilian Friends	1965	30.00
PJ-10110 [M]	Bud Shank and the Sax Section	1966	18.00
ST-20110 [S]	Bud Shank and the Sax Section	1966	25.00
LN-10091	Bud Shank and the Sax Section	198?	12.00
PJ-4 [M]	Bud Shank Plays Tenor	1960	30.00
ST-4 [S]	Bud Shank Plays Tenor	1960	30.00
PJ-1205 [M]	Bud Shank/Shorty Rogers	1955	80.00
PJLP-14 [10]	Bud Shank with Three Trombones	1954	120.00
PJ-1226 [M]	Flute 'n Oboe	1957	60.00
PJ-1219 [M]	Jazz at Cal-Tech	1956	60.00
PJ-21 [M]	New Groove	1961	30.00
ST-21 [S]	New Groove	1961	30.00
PJ-1213 [M]	Strings and Trombones	1956	80.00
PJ-1215 [M]	The Bud Shank Quartet	1956	80.00
PJ-1230 [M]	The Bud Shank Quartet	1957	60.00
PJM-411 [M]	The Swing's to TV	1957	60.00
ST-20157	Windmills of Your Mind	1969	18.00

SUNSET

Number	Title	Yr	NM
SUM-1132 [M]	I Hear Music	1967	15.00
SUS-5132 [S]	I Hear Music	1967	15.00

WORLD PACIFIC

Number	Title	Yr	NM
ST-21868	A Spoonful of Jazz	1968	18.00
WP-1855 [M]	Brazil! Brazil! Brazil!	1967	25.00
ST-21855 [S]	Brazil! Brazil! Brazil!	1967	18.00
WP-1864 [M]	Bud Shank Plays Music from Today's Movies	1967	25.00
ST-21864 [S]	Bud Shank Plays Music from Today's Movies	1967	18.00
WP-1205 [M]	Bud Shank/Shorty Rogers	1958	40.00
WP-1845 [M]	California Dreaming	1966	18.00
ST-21845 [S]	California Dreaming	1966	25.00
WP-1827 [M]	Flute, Oboe and Strings	1965	18.00
ST-21827 [S]	Flute, Oboe and Strings	1965	25.00
WP-1286 [M]	Flute 'n Alto	1960	30.00
ST-1286 [S]	Flute 'n Alto	1960	40.00
WP-1226 [M]	Flute 'n Oboe	1958	40.00
WP-1819 [M]	Folk 'n Flute	1965	18.00
ST-21819 [S]	Folk 'n Flute	1965	25.00
WP-1853 [M]	Girl in Love	1967	25.00
ST-21853 [S]	Girl in Love	1967	18.00
WP-1259 [M]	Holiday in Brazil	1959	40.00
ST-1018 [S]	Holiday in Brazil	1959	30.00
WP-1251 [M]	I'll Take Romance	1958	40.00
WP-1416 [M]	Improvisations	1961	30.00
WP-1219 [M]	Jazz at Cal-Tech	1958	40.00
WP-1299 [M]	Koto 'n Flute	1960	30.00
ST-1299 [S]	Koto 'n Flute	1960	40.00
WP-1424 [M]	Koto 'n Flute	1962	30.00
WP-1281 [M]	Latin Contrasts	1959	40.00
ST-1281 [S]	Latin Contrasts	1959	30.00
ST-20170	Let It Be	1970	18.00
ST-21873	Magical Mystery Tour	1968	18.00
WP-1840 [M]	Michelle	1966	18.00
ST-21840 [S]	Michelle	1966	25.00
WP-1215 [M]	The Bud Shank Quartet	1958	40.00
WP-1230 [M]	The Bud Shank Quartet	1958	40.00
WPM-411 [M]	The Swing's to TV	1958	40.00
ST-1002 [S]	The Swing's to TV	1959	30.00
PJM-411 [M]	The Swing's to TV	1958	50.00

SHANK, BUD/CHET BAKER

KIMBERLY

Number	Title	Yr	NM
2016 [M]	Swinging Soundtrack	1963	25.00
11016 [S]	Swinging Soundtrack	1963	30.00

SHANKAR, ANANDA

REPRISE

Number	Title	Yr	NM
RS-6398	Ananda Shankar	1970	25.00

SHANKAR, L.

ZAPPA

Number	Title	Yr	NM
SRZ-1-1602	Touch Me There	1979	25.00

SHANKAR, RAVI

ANGEL

Number	Title	Yr	NM
S36806	Concerto for Sitar and Orchestra	1972	15.00
35468 [M]	Music of India	196?	30.00
DS-37935	Raga-Mala (Sitar Concert No. 2)	1983	12.00
DS-37920	Raga Mishra Piloo	1982	12.00
36418 [M]	West Meets East	1967	30.00
— With Yahudi Menuhin			
S36418 [S]	West Meets East	1967	25.00
— With Yahudi Menuhin			
S36026 [S]	West Meets East, Vol. 2	1968	18.00

APPLE

Number	Title	Yr	NM
SWAO-3384	Raga	1971	30.00
SVBB-3396	Ravi Shankar In Concert	1973	40.00

BLUESVILLE

Number	Title	Yr	NM
BVLP-1078 [M]	The Master Musician of India	1964	30.00

CAPITOL

Number	Title	Yr	NM
T10497 [M]	Exotic Sitar and Sarod	196?	25.00
ST10497 [S]	Exotic Sitar and Sarod	196?	30.00
SP-10561	Raga Parameshwari	1972	15.00
ST10504	Ravi	196?	18.00
T2720 [M]	Three Ragas	1967	25.00
DT2720 [R]	Three Ragas	1967	18.00
T10482 [M]	Two Raga Moods	196?	25.00
ST10482 [S]	Two Raga Moods	196?	30.00

COLUMBIA

Number	Title	Yr	NM
OS3230	Chappaqua	1968	18.00
CL2496 [M]	Sounds of India	1966	18.00
CS9296 [S]	Sounds of India	1966	25.00
CL2760 [M]	The Genius of Ravi Shankar	1967	25.00
CS9560 [S]	The Genius of Ravi Shankar	1967	18.00
WL119 [M]	The Sounds of India	196?	30.00

DARK HORSE

Number	Title	Yr	NM
SP22007	Music Festival from India	1975	15.00
SP22002	Shankar Family and Friends	1974	15.00

DEUTCHE GRAMMOPHON

Number	Title	Yr	NM
2531356	Homage to Mahatma Gandhi; Homage to Baba Allauddin	198?	12.00
2531381	Pad Hasapa, for Koto; etc.	198?	12.00
2531280	Raga Jogeshwari	198?	12.00
2531216	Ragas Hameer & Gara	198?	12.00

FANTASY

Number	Title	Yr	NM
24714	Ragas	1973	18.00

ORIENTAL

Number	Title	Yr	NM
BGRP-108	Raga Sanjh Kalyan	198?	12.00

PRIVATE MUSIC

Number	Title	Yr	NM
2044-1-P	Inside the Kremlin	1989	12.00
2016-1-P	The Shankar Project: Tana Mana	1988	12.00

SPARK

Number	Title	Yr	NM
06	Transmigration Macabre	1973	15.00

WORLD PACIFIC

Number	Title	Yr	NM
ST-21454	Charly	1969	18.00
WPS-26201	His Festival from India	1968	25.00
WP-1422 [M]	India's Master Musician	1965	18.00
ST-21422 [S]	India's Master Musician	1965	25.00
ST-21464	Morning Raga/Evening Raga	1970	18.00
WP-1432 [M]	Portrait of Genius	1966	18.00
ST-21432 [S]	Portrait of Genius	1966	25.00
WP-1431 [M]	Ragas and Talas	1966	18.00
ST-21431 [S]	Ragas and Talas	1966	25.00
WP-1442 [M]	Ravi Shankar at the Monterey International Pop Festival	1967	25.00
ST-21442 [S]	Ravi Shankar at the Monterey International Pop Festival	1967	25.00
ST-21467	Ravi Shankar at Woodstock	1970	18.00
WP-1421 [M]	Ravi Shankar In Concert	1965	18.00
ST-21421 [S]	Ravi Shankar In Concert	1965	25.00
WP-1430 [M]	Ravi Shankar In London	1966	18.00
ST-21430 [S]	Ravi Shankar In London	1966	25.00
WP-1441 [M]	Ravi Shankar in New York	1967	18.00
ST-21441 [S]	Ravi Shankar in New York	1967	25.00
ST-21449	Ravi Shankar in San Francisco	1968	25.00
WP-1434 [M]	Sound of the Sitar	1967	18.00
ST-21434 [S]	Sound of the Sitar	1967	25.00
WP-1438 [M]	Three Ragas	1967	18.00
ST-21438 [S]	Three Ragas	1967	25.00

SHANKAR

ECM

Number	Title	Yr	NM
25016	Song for Everyone	1985	12.00
25039	The Epidemics	1986	12.00
25004	Vision	1985	12.00
1195	Who's to Know	198?	15.00

SHANNON, DEL

AMY

Number	Title	Yr	NM
8006 [M]	1,661 Seconds with Del Shannon	1965	50.00
S-8006 [S]	1,661 Seconds with Del Shannon	1965	80.00
8004 [M]	Del Shannon Sings Hank Williams	1965	50.00
S-8004 [S]	Del Shannon Sings Hank Williams	1965	80.00
8003 [M]	Handy Man	1964	50.00
S-8003 [S]	Handy Man	1964	80.00

BIG TOP

Number	Title	Yr	NM
12-1308 [M]	Little Town Flirt	1963	150.00
12-1308 [B]	Little Town Flirt	1963	1000.00
— One side is mono, one side is stereo; should be played to identify			
12-1308 [S]	Little Town Flirt	1963	1500.00
— Stereo copies are not identified as such on either cover or label; some, but not all, copies have an "S" in the dead wax. Playing is the best way to identify.			
12-1303 [M]	Runaway	1961	300.00
12-1303 [S]	Runaway	1961	1600.00

DOT

Number	Title	Yr	NM
DLP3824 [M]	The Best of Del Shannon	1967	50.00
DLP25824 [R]	The Best of Del Shannon	1967	40.00

ELEKTRA

Number	Title	Yr	NM
5E-568	Drop Down and Get Me	1981	12.00

LIBERTY

Number	Title	Yr	NM
LRP-3539 [M]	The Further Adventures of Charles Westover	1967	50.00
LST-7539 [S]	The Further Adventures of Charles Westover	1967	80.00
LRP-3453 [M]	This Is My Bag	1966	30.00
LST-7453 [S]	This Is My Bag	1966	40.00
LRP-3479 [M]	Total Commitment	1966	30.00
LST-7479 [S]	Total Commitment	1966	40.00

PICKWICK

Number	Title	Yr	NM
SPC-3595 [R]	The Best of Del Shannon	197?	12.00

POST

Number	Title	Yr	NM
9000 [R]	Del Shannon Sings	196?	40.00

RHINO

Number	Title	Yr	NM
RNLP-71056 [M]	Runaway Hits	1986	12.00

SIRE

Number	Title	Yr	NM
SASH-3708 [P]	The Vintage Years	1975	30.00

TWIRL

Number	Title	Yr	NM
5001 [M]	Del Shannon's Greatest Hits	196?	200.00
— LP was never issued; price is for front cover slick, which is known to exist			

UNITED ARTISTS

Number	Title	Yr	NM
UA-LA151-E	Del Shannon Live in England	1973	30.00

SHANNON, HUGH

ATLANTIC

Number	Title	Yr	NM
ALS-406 [10]	Hugh Shannon Sings	195?	100.00

SHANTY BOYS, THE

ELEKTRA

Number	Title	Yr	NM
EKL-142 [M]	Off-Beat Folk Songs	1958	30.00

SHAPIRO, HELEN

EPIC

Number	Title	Yr	NM
LN24075 [M]	A Teenager in Love	1962	40.00
BN26075 [S]	A Teenager in Love	1962	40.00

SHARKEY, FEARGAL

A&M

Number	Title	Yr	NM
SP6-5108	Feargal Sharkey	1985	12.00

VIRGIN

Number	Title	Yr	NM
90895	Wish	1988	12.00

SHARKS

MCA

Number	Title	Yr	NM
351	First Water	1973	18.00
415	Jab It in Your Eye	1974	18.00

SHARON, RALPH

ARGO

Number	Title	Yr	NM
LP-635 [M]	2:38 A.M.	1958	40.00

BETHLEHEM

Number	Title	Yr	NM
BCP-13 [M]	Mr. & Mrs. Jazz	1955	40.00
BCP-41 [M]	Ralph Sharon Trio	1956	40.00

COLUMBIA

Number	Title	Yr	NM
CL2321 [M]	Do I Hear a Waltz?	1965	30.00
CS9121 [S]	Do I Hear a Waltz?	1965	30.00

GORDY

Number	Title	Yr	NM
G-903 [M]	Modern Innovations on Country & Western Themes	1963	200.00

LONDON

Number	Title	Yr	NM
LB-842 [10]	Autumn Leaves	1954	50.00
LL1488 [M]	Easy Jazz	1956	40.00
LB-733 [10]	Spring Fever	1953	50.00
LL1339 [M]	Spring Fever/Autumn Leaves	1955	40.00

RAMA

Number	Title	Yr	NM
RLP-1001 [M]	Jazz Around the World	1957	50.00

SHARP, DEE DEE, AND CHUBBY CHECKER

CAMEO

Number	Title	Yr	NM
C-1029 [M]	Down to Earth	1962	40.00
SC-1029 [S]	Down to Earth	1962	50.00

SHARP, DEE DEE

CAMEO

Number	Title	Yr	NM
C-2002 [M]	18 Golden Hits	1964	40.00
SC-2002 [S]	18 Golden Hits	1964	50.00
C-1027 [M]	All the Hits	1962	40.00
SC-1027 [S]	All the Hits	1962	50.00
C-1032 [M]	All the Hits, Vol. 2	1963	40.00
SC-1032 [S]	All the Hits, Vol. 2	1963	50.00
C-1062 [M]	Biggest Hits	1963	40.00
C-1050 [M]	Do the Bird	1963	40.00
SC-1050 [S]	Do the Bird	1963	50.00
C-1074 [M]	Down Memory Lane	1963	40.00
C-1018 [M]	It's Mashed Potato Time	1962	60.00
C-1022 [M]	Songs of Faith	1962	40.00
SC-1022 [S]	Songs of Faith	1962	50.00

PHILADELPHIA INT'L.

Number	Title	Yr	NM
JZ36370	Dee Dee	1980	12.00
PZ33839	Happy 'Bout the Whole Thing	1976	12.00
PZ34437	What Color Is Love	1977	12.00

SHARP, RANDY

NAUTILUS

Number	Title	Yr	NM
NR-1	First in Line	1980	40.00
— Standard cover			
NR-1	First in Line	1980	50.00
— Styrofoam cover			

Number	Title	Yr	NM
SHARPE, RAY			
AWARD			
❑ LMP-711 [M]	Welcome Back, Linda Lu	1964	120.00
SHARPE, SUNDAY			
UNITED ARTISTS			
❑ UA-LA362-G	I'm Having Your Baby	1975	15.00
SHARROCK, SONNY			
4 MEN WITH BEARDS			
❑ 4M103LP [B]	Black Woman		25.00
VORTEX			
❑ 2014	Black Woman	1970	25.00
SHATNER, WILLIAM			
CLEOPATRA			
❑ 7062 [B]	Seeking Major Tom		60.00
DECCA			
❑ DL5043 [M]	The Transformed Man	1969	150.00
— Mono is white label promo only; in stereo cover with "Monaural" sticker			
❑ DL75043 [S]	The Transformed Man	1969	80.00
K-TEL			
❑ NC494 [B]	Captain of the Starship	1978	60.00
— Reissue of Lemli album			
LEMLI			
❑ 9400 [B]	William Shatner -- Live!	1977	50.00
SHAVER, BILLY JOE			
CAPRICORN			
❑ CPN 0192	Gypsy Boy	1977	15.00
❑ CPN 0171	Wings	1976	15.00
COLUMBIA			
❑ FC37959	Billy Joe Shaver	1982	12.00
❑ FC37078	I'm Just an Old Chunk of Coal	1981	12.00
MONUMENT			
❑ KZ32293	Old Five and Dimers Like Me	1973	18.00
❑ 7621	Old Five and Dimers Like Me	1978	12.00
— Reissue of 32293			
ZOO			
❑ 1104	Unshaven: Live at Smith's Olde Bar	1995	18.00
SHAVERS, CHARLIE			
AAMCO			
❑ 310 [M]	The Most Intimate Charlie Shavers	1959	40.00
BETHLEHEM			
❑ BCP-27 [M]	Gershwin, Shavers and Strings	1955	80.00
❑ BCP-1007 [10]	Horn o' Plenty	1954	100.00
❑ BCP-67 [M]	The Complete Charlie Shavers with Maxine Sullivan	1957	80.00
❑ BCP-6005 [M]	The Finest of Charlie Shavers: The Most Intimate	1976	15.00
— Reissue, distributed by Caytronics			
❑ BCP-1021 [10]	The Most Intimate Charlie Shavers	1955	100.00
❑ BCP-5002 [M]	The Most Intimate Charlie Shavers	1958	80.00
CAPITOL			
❑ T1883 [M]	Excitement Unlimited	1963	25.00
❑ ST1883 [S]	Excitement Unlimited	1963	30.00
EVEREST			
❑ LPBR-5070 [M]	Girl of My Dreams	1960	25.00
❑ SDBR-1070 [S]	Girl of My Dreams	1960	30.00
❑ LPBR-5108 [M]	Here Comes Charlie	1960	25.00
❑ SDBR-1108 [S]	Here Comes Charlie	1960	30.00
❑ LPBR-5127 [M]	Like Charlie	1961	25.00
❑ SDBR-1127 [S]	Like Charlie	1961	30.00
JAZZTONE			
❑ J-1229	Flow Gently, Sweet Rhythm	1956	40.00
MGM			
❑ E-3809 [M]	Charlie Digs Dixie	1960	30.00
❑ SE-3809 [S]	Charlie Digs Dixie	1960	30.00
❑ E-3765 [M]	Charlie Digs Paree	1959	30.00
❑ SE-3765 [S]	Charlie Digs Paree	1959	30.00
PERIOD			
❑ SPL-1113 [10]	Flow Gently, Sweet Rhythm	1955	120.00
PHOENIX			
❑ 21	Trumpet Man	197?	12.00
SHAW, ARTIE			
AIRCHECK			
❑ 11	Artie Shaw and His Orchestra 1939-40	197?	12.00
ALLEGRO			
❑ 1405 [M]	An Hour with Artie Shaw	1955	40.00
❑ 1466 [M]	Artie Shaw Hour	1955	40.00
ALLEGRO EILTE			
❑ 4023 [10]	Artie Shaw Plays	195?	40.00

Number	Title	Yr	NM
❑ 4107 [10]	Artie Shaw Plays Cole Porter	195?	40.00
BLUEBIRD			
❑ AXM2-5580	The Complete Artie Shaw, Volume 7: Retrospective	198?	18.00
❑ AXM2-5517	The Complete Artie Shaw, Volume 1 (1938-39)	197?	18.00
❑ AXM2-5533	The Complete Artie Shaw, Volume 2 (1939)	197?	18.00
❑ AXM2-5556	The Complete Artie Shaw, Volume 3 (1939-40)	1979	18.00
❑ AXM2-5572	The Complete Artie Shaw, Volume 4 (1940-41)	1980	18.00
❑ AXM2-5576	The Complete Artie Shaw, Volume 5 (1941-42)	198?	18.00
❑ AXM2-5579	The Complete Artie Shaw, Volume 6 (1942-45)	198?	18.00
❑ 7637-1-RB	The Complete Gramercy Five Sessions	1989	15.00
CAPITOL			
❑ ST2992	Artie Shaw Re-Creates His Great '38 Band	1968	18.00
CLEF			
❑ MGC-159 [10]	Artie Shaw and His Gramercy Five, Volume 1	1954	60.00
❑ MGC-160 [10]	Artie Shaw and His Gramercy Five, Volume 2	1954	60.00
❑ MGC-630 [M]	Artie Shaw and His Gramercy Five, Volume 3	1954	60.00
❑ MGC-645 [M]	Artie Shaw and His Gramercy Five, Volume 4	1955	60.00
COLUMBIA MASTERWORKS			
❑ ML4260 [M]	Modern Music for Clarinet	1950	50.00
DECCA			
❑ DL5286 [10]	Artie Shaw Dance Program	195?	50.00
❑ DL8309 [M]	Did Someone Say Party?	1956	40.00
— Black label, silver print			
❑ DL5524 [10]	Speak to Me of Love	195?	50.00
ENCORE			
❑ EE22023	Free for All	196?	18.00
EPIC			
❑ LG1102 [10]	Artie Shaw	1955	50.00
❑ LN3150 [M]	Artie Shaw and His Orchestra	1955	40.00
❑ LG1006 [10]	Artie Shaw with Strings	1954	50.00
❑ LN3112 [M]	Artie Shaw with Strings	1955	40.00
❑ LG1017 [10]	Non-Stop Flight	1954	50.00
EVEREST ARCHIVE OF FOLK & JAZZ			
❑ 248	Artie Shaw	1970	12.00
HINDSIGHT			
❑ HSR-139	Artie Shaw and His Orchestra, 1938	198?	12.00
❑ HSR-140	Artie Shaw and His Orchestra, 1938, Volume 2	198?	12.00
❑ HSR-176	Artie Shaw and His Orchestra, 1938-39	198?	12.00
❑ HSR-148	Artie Shaw and His Orchestra, 1939	198?	12.00
❑ HSR-149	Artie Shaw and His Orchestra, 1939, Volume 2	198?	12.00
❑ HSR-401	Artie Shaw and His Orchestra Play 22 Original Big Band Recordings	198?	15.00
INSIGHT			
❑ 204	Artie Shaw and His Orchestra (1938-39)	198?	12.00
LION			
❑ L-70058 [M]	Artie Shaw Plays Irving Berlin and Cole Porter	1958	30.00
MCA			
❑ 4081	The Best of Artie Shaw	197?	15.00
MGM			
❑ E-517 [10]	Artie Shaw Plays Cole Porter	1950	50.00
MUSICRAFT			
❑ 503	Artie Shaw and His Orchestra, Volume 1	198?	12.00
❑ 507	Artie Shaw and His Orchestra, Volume 2	198?	12.00
PAIR			
❑ PDL2-1012	Original Recordings	1986	15.00
RCA CAMDEN			
❑ ACL1-0509	Greatest Hits	1974	12.00
❑ CAL-584 [M]	One Night Stand	1959	25.00
❑ CAL-908 [M]	September Song and Other Favorites	196?	25.00
❑ CAL-465 [M]	The Great Artie Shaw	195?	25.00
RCA VICTOR			
❑ LPM-1648 [M]	A Man and His Dream	1957	40.00
❑ LPM-1570 [M]	Any Old Time	1957	250.00
— although signed AW, this Andy Warhol cover was not fully acknowledged until 2007			
❑ LPM-1241 [M]	Artie Shaw and His Gramercy Five	1956	40.00
❑ LPT-28 [10]	Artie Shaw Favorites	195?	50.00
❑ LPM-1217 [M]	Back Bay Shuffle	1956	40.00
❑ ANL1-2151	Backbay Shuffle	1977	12.00
❑ LPM-1201 [M]	Both Feet in the Groove	1956	400.00
— Andy Warhol cover.			
❑ LPM-30 [10]	Four Star Favorites	1955	50.00
❑ LPT-6000 [M]	In the Blue Room/In the Café Rouge	195?	50.00
— Originals are in a box; silver labels, red print			

Number	Title	Yr	NM
❑ LPM-1244 [M]	Moonglow	1956	40.00
❑ LPT-1020 [M]	My Concerto	195?	40.00
❑ ANL1-1089	The Best of Artie Shaw	1975	12.00
❑ LPM-3675 [M]	The Best of Artie Shaw	1967	25.00
❑ LSP-3675 [R]	The Best of Artie Shaw	1967	15.00
❑ LPT-3013 [10]	This Is Artie Shaw	1952	50.00
❑ VPM-6039	This Is Artie Shaw	197?	18.00
❑ VPM-6062	This Is Artie Shaw, Volume 2	1972	18.00
❑ VPM-6062	This Is Artie Shaw, Volume 2	1976	15.00
— Black labels, dog near top			
ROYALE			
❑ 18135 [10]	The Best in Dance Music	195?	30.00
SUNBEAM			
❑ 207	New Music 1936-37	197?	12.00
TIME-LIFE			
❑ STBB-06	Big Bands: Artie Shaw	1983	18.00
❑ STBB-26	Big Bands: Encore: Artie Shaw	1986	18.00
VERVE			
❑ MGV-2014 [M]	I Can't Get Started	1956	40.00
❑ V-2014 [M]	I Can't Get Started	1961	25.00
❑ MGV-2015 [M]	Sequence in Music	1956	40.00
❑ V-2015 [M]	Sequence in Music	1961	25.00
SHAW, BOBO			
BLACK SAINT			
❑ BSR-0021	Junk Trap	198?	15.00
MUSE			
❑ MR-5268	Bugle Boy Bop	198?	15.00
❑ MR-5232	P'NKJ'ZZ	198?	18.00
SHAW, GENE			
ARGO			
❑ LP-707 [M]	Breakthrough	1962	30.00
❑ LPS-707 [S]	Breakthrough	1962	30.00
❑ LP-743 [M]	Carnival Sketches	1964	30.00
❑ LPS-743 [S]	Carnival Sketches	1964	30.00
❑ LP-726 [M]	Debut In Blues	1963	30.00
❑ LPS-726 [S]	Debut In Blues	1963	30.00
CHESS			
❑ CH-91564	Debut In Blues	198?	12.00
SHAW, GEORGE			
PALO ALTO/TBA			
❑ TBA-218	Encounters	1986	12.00
❑ TBA-223	Let Yourself Go	1987	12.00
SHAW, LEE			
CADENCE JAZZ			
❑ CJR-1021	OK!	198?	12.00
SHAW, MARLENA			
BLUE NOTE			
❑ BN-LA143-F	From the Depths of My Soul	1974	18.00
❑ BN-LA606-G	Just a Matter	1976	18.00
❑ BST-84422	Marlena	1972	18.00
❑ BN-LA397-G	Who Is This Bitch, Anyway?	1975	18.00
CADET			
❑ LPS-803	Different Bags	1968	25.00
❑ LPS-833	Spice of Life	1969	25.00
COLUMBIA			
❑ JC34458	Acting Up	1978	15.00
❑ PC34458	Sweet Beginnings	1977	15.00
❑ JC35632	Take a Bite	1979	15.00
❑ JC36367	The Best of Marlena Shaw	1980	12.00
VERVE			
❑ 831438-1	It Is Love	1987	12.00
❑ 837312-1	Love Is In Flight	1988	12.00
SHAW, ROBERT, CHORALE			
RCA CAMDEN			
❑ CAL-448 [M]	Joy to the World	1958	15.00
— Reissue of RCA Red Seal LM-1112			
RCA VICTOR RED SEAL			
❑ LSC-2598 [S]	23 Glee Club Favorites	1962	40.00
— Original with "shaded dog" label			
❑ LSC-2402 [S]	A Chorus of Love	1960	25.00
— Original with "shaded dog" label or second edition with "white dog" label			
❑ LSC-2199 [S]	A Mighty Fortress	1959	25.00
— Original with "shaded dog" label			
❑ LSC-2273 [S]	Bach, J.S.: Cantata 4	1959	25.00
— Original with "shaded dog" label			
❑ LM-1112 [M]	Christmas Hymns and Carols	1952	30.00
— Original has 2" brown border around all four sides of front cover			
❑ LM-2139 [M]	Christmas Hymns and Carols, Volume 1	1957	25.00
— Original cover has "LM-2139" with "RCA Victor" in box on upper right			
❑ LM-2139 [M]	Christmas Hymns and Carols, Volume 1	1958	16.00
— Second cover has "LM-2139" in lower left corner; small "RE" is on front cover			
❑ LSC-2139 [S]	Christmas Hymns and Carols, Volume 1	1958	25.00
— Original with "shaded dog" label			

Number	Title	Yr	NM
❏ LM-1112 [M]	Christmas Hymns and Carols, Volume I	1954	25.00

— *Mostly pink front cover with "Enhanced Sound" at top and under dog on label*

Number	Title	Yr	NM
❏ LM-1711 [M]	Christmas Hymns and Carols Vol. 2	195?	25.00

— *Pink "ornaments" cover; maroon label, large dog on top*

| ❏ LM-1711 [M] | Christmas Hymns and Carols Volume II | 1954 | 30.00 |

— *Original carolers cover; red label with outline of dog*

| ❏ LSC-2247 [S] | Deep River and Other Spirituals | 1959 | 25.00 |

— *Original with "shaded dog" label*

| ❏ LSC-2580 [S] | I'm Goin' to Sing | 1962 | 40.00 |

— *Original with "shaded dog" label*

| ❏ LSC-2231 [S] | On Stage | 1959 | 25.00 |

— *Original with "shaded dog" label*

| ❏ LSC-2416 [S] | Operatic Choruses | 1960 | 25.00 |

— *Original with "shaded dog" label*

| ❏ LSC-2551 [S] | Sea Shanties | 1961 | 30.00 |

— *Original with "shaded dog" label*

❏ LM-2684 [M]	The Many Moods of Christmas	1963	15.00
❏ LSC-2684 [S]	The Many Moods of Christmas	1963	18.00
❏ LSC-2295 [S]	The Stephen Foster Song Book	1959	25.00

— *Original with "shaded dog" label*

| ❏ LSC-2403 [S] | What Wondrous Love | 1960 | 25.00 |

— *Original with "shaded dog" label*

SHAW, RON

PACIFIC CHALLENGER
| ❏ 152 | Goin' Home | 1978 | 15.00 |

SHAW, SANDIE

REPRISE
❏ R-6191 [M]	Me	1966	80.00
❏ RS-6191 [S]	Me	1966	50.00
❏ R-6166 [M]	Sandie Shaw	1965	60.00
❏ RS-6166 [R]	Sandie Shaw	1965	60.00

SHAW, SERENA

RAMA
| ❏ RLP-5001 [M] | Cry My Love | 1956 | 400.00 |

SHAW, TOMMY

A&M
| ❏ SP-5020 | Girls with Guns | 1984 | 12.00 |
| ❏ SP-5097 | What If | 1985 | 12.00 |

ATLANTIC
| ❏ 81798 | Ambition | 1987 | 12.00 |

SHAW, WOODY

COLUMBIA
❏ FC36303	For Sure	1980	15.00
❏ JC35309	Rosewood	1977	15.00
❏ JC35560	Stepping	1978	15.00
❏ FC36519	The Best of Woody Shaw	1980	12.00
❏ JC35977	Woody III	1979	15.00

CONTEMPORARY
| ❏ C-7627/8 | Blackstone Legacy | 1971 | 25.00 |
| ❏ C-7632 | Song of Songs | 197? | 18.00 |

ELEKTRA/MUSICIAN
| ❏ 60131 | Master of the Art | 1983 | 12.00 |
| ❏ 60299 | Night Music | 1984 | 12.00 |

ENJA
| ❏ 4018 | Lotus Flower | 1982 | 15.00 |

FANTASY
| ❏ OJC-180 | Song of Songs | 198? | 12.00 |

MOSAIC
| ❏ MR4-142 | The Complete CBS Studio Recordings of Woody Shaw | 199? | 80.00 |

MUSE
❏ MR-5139	Concert Ensemble '76	1977	15.00
❏ MR-5338	Imagination	1988	12.00
❏ MR-5298	In the Beginning	198?	12.00
❏ MR-5074	Love Dance	1976	15.00
❏ MR-5058	Moontrane	1975	15.00
❏ MR-5103	Red's Fantasy	197?	15.00
❏ MR-5318	Setting Standards	198?	12.00
❏ MR-5329	Solid	1987	12.00
❏ MR-5160	The Iron Men	198?	15.00

RED RECORD
| ❏ VPA-168 | The Time Is Right | 198? | 15.00 |

SHAWN, DICK

20TH CENTURY FOX
| ❏ TFM-3124 [M] | Dick Shawn Sings with His Little People | 1964 | 25.00 |
| ❏ TFS-4124 [S] | Dick Shawn Sings with His Little People | 1964 | 30.00 |

SHAY, DOROTHY

CAPITOL
| ❏ H517 [10] | Broadway Ditties | 195? | 50.00 |
| ❏ H444 [10] | Park Avenue Hillbilly | 195? | 50.00 |

COLUMBIA
| ❏ CL6089 [10] | Coming 'Round the Mountain | 1950 | 50.00 |
| ❏ CL6003 [10] | Dorothy Shay Sings | 1948 | 50.00 |

— *With envelope-like cover*

HARMONY
| ❏ HL7017 [M] | Coming 'Round the Mountain | 195? | 30.00 |

SHAY, SHERYL

LAUREL
| ❏ LR-506 | Sophisticated Lady | 1985 | 15.00 |

SHEA, GEORGE BEVERLY

RCA CAMDEN
| ❏ CAL-850 [M] | Christmas with George Beverly Shea | 196? | 15.00 |
| ❏ CAS-850 [S] | Christmas with George Beverly Shea | 196? | 15.00 |

RCA VICTOR
❏ LPM-1406 [M]	A Billy Graham Crusade in Song	1956	25.00
❏ LPM-1967 [M]	Blessed Assurance	1959	18.00
❏ LSP-1967 [S]	Blessed Assurance	1959	25.00
❏ LPM-2064 [M]	Christmas Hymns	1959	18.00
❏ LSP-2064 [S]	Christmas Hymns	1959	25.00
❏ LPM-1349 [M]	Evening Prayer	1956	25.00
❏ LPM-1062 [M]	Evening Vespers	1955	25.00
❏ LPM-1564 [M]	George Beverly Shea	1957	25.00
❏ LPM-1187 [M]	Inspirational Songs	1955	25.00
❏ LPM-1235 [M]	Sacred Songs	1956	25.00
❏ LPM-3904 [M]	The Best of George Beverly Shea, Vol. II	1968	30.00
❏ LSP-3904 [S]	The Best of George Beverly Shea, Vol. II	1968	15.00
❏ LPM-1949 [M]	The Love of God	1958	18.00
❏ LSP-1949 [S]	The Love of God	1958	25.00
❏ LPM-1642 [M]	Through the Years	1957	25.00

SHEA, TOM

STOMP OFF
| ❏ SOS-1022 | Little Wabash Special | 198? | 12.00 |

SHEARING, GEORGE, AND MEL TORME

CONCORD JAZZ
❏ CJ-294	An Elegant Evening	1985	12.00
❏ CJ-248	An Evening at Charlie's	1984	12.00
❏ CJ-190	An Evening with George Shearing and Mel Torme	1982	12.00
❏ CJ-341	A Vintage Year	1988	12.00
❏ CJ-219	Top Drawer	1983	12.00

SHEARING, GEORGE, AND THE MONTGOMERY BROTHERS

FANTASY
| ❏ OJC-040 | George Shearing and the Montgomery Brothers | 198? | 12.00 |

JAZZLAND
| ❏ JLP-55 [M] | Love Walked In | 1961 | 30.00 |

— *Cover has Shearing and the brothers*

| ❏ JLP-55 [M] | Love Walked In | 1962 | 30.00 |

— *Cover has a woman*

| ❏ JLP-955 [S] | Love Walked In | 1961 | 40.00 |

— *Cover has Shearing and the brothers*

| ❏ JLP-955 [S] | Love Walked In | 1962 | 30.00 |

— *Cover has a woman*

RIVERSIDE
| ❏ 6087 | George Shearing and the Montgomery Brothers | 197? | 12.00 |

— *Reissue of Jazzland LP*

SHEARING, GEORGE

BASF
❏ MC-25612	Continental Experience	1975	15.00
❏ 25340	Light, Airy and Swinging	1973	15.00
❏ 25351	The Way We Are	1974	15.00

CAPITOL
| ❏ T858 [M] | Black Satin | 1957 | 30.00 |

— *Turquoise label*

| ❏ T858 [M] | Black Satin | 1959 | 25.00 |

— *Black label with colorband, logo on left*

| ❏ T858 [M] | Black Satin | 1962 | 18.00 |

— *Black label with colorband, logo on top*

| ❏ ST858 [S] | Black Satin | 1959 | 25.00 |

— *Black label with colorband, logo on left*

| ❏ ST858 [S] | Black Satin | 1962 | 18.00 |

— *Black label with colorband, logo on top*

| ❏ SM-11800 | Black Satin | 1978 | 12.00 |
| ❏ T1124 [M] | Blue Chiffon | 1959 | 25.00 |

— *Black label with colorband, logo on left*

| ❏ T1124 [M] | Blue Chiffon | 1962 | 18.00 |

— *Black label with colorband, logo on top*

| ❏ ST1124 [S] | Blue Chiffon | 1959 | 30.00 |

— *Black label with colorband, logo on left*

| ❏ ST1124 [S] | Blue Chiffon | 1962 | 25.00 |

— *Black label with colorband, logo on top*

❏ T1873 [M]	Bossa Nova	1963	18.00
❏ ST1873 [S]	Bossa Nova	1963	25.00
❏ T1038 [M]	Burnished Brass	1958	25.00

— *Black label with colorband, logo on left*

| ❏ T1038 [M] | Burnished Brass | 1962 | 18.00 |

— *Black label with colorband, logo on top*

| ❏ ST1038 [S] | Burnished Brass | 1959 | 30.00 |

— *Black label with colorband, logo on left*

| ❏ ST1038 [S] | Burnished Brass | 1962 | 25.00 |

— *Black label with colorband, logo on top*

❏ T1755 [M]	Concerto for My Love	1962	18.00
❏ ST1755 [S]	Concerto for My Love	1962	25.00
❏ T2143 [M]	Deep Velvet	1964	15.00
❏ ST2143 [S]	Deep Velvet	1964	18.00
❏ ST-181	Fool on the Hill	1969	15.00
❏ T1187 [M]	George Shearing On Stage	1959	25.00

— *Black label with colorband, logo on left*

| ❏ T1187 [M] | George Shearing On Stage | 1962 | 18.00 |

— *Black label with colorband, logo on top*

| ❏ ST1187 [S] | George Shearing On Stage | 1959 | 30.00 |

— *Black label with colorband, logo on left*

| ❏ ST1187 [S] | George Shearing On Stage | 1962 | 25.00 |

— *Black label with colorband, logo on top*

❏ T2699 [M]	George Shearing Today	1967	18.00
❏ ST2699 [S]	George Shearing Today	1967	15.00
❏ T2372 [M]	Here and Now	1965	15.00
❏ ST2372 [S]	Here and Now	1965	18.00
❏ T1992 [M]	Jazz Concert	1963	18.00
❏ ST1992 [S]	Jazz Concert	1963	25.00
❏ T1827 [M]	Jazz Moments	1963	18.00
❏ ST1827 [S]	Jazz Moments	1963	25.00
❏ T1275 [M]	Latin Affair	1960	25.00

— *Black label with colorband, logo on left*

| ❏ T1275 [M] | Latin Affair | 1962 | 18.00 |

— *Black label with colorband, logo on top*

| ❏ ST1275 [S] | Latin Affair | 1960 | 30.00 |

— *Black label with colorband, logo on left*

| ❏ ST1275 [S] | Latin Affair | 1962 | 25.00 |

— *Black label with colorband, logo on top*

| ❏ T737 [M] | Latin Escapade | 1957 | 30.00 |

— *Turquoise label*

| ❏ T737 [M] | Latin Escapade | 1959 | 25.00 |

— *Black label with colorband, logo on left*

| ❏ T737 [M] | Latin Escapade | 1962 | 18.00 |

— *Black label with colorband, logo on top*

❏ DT737 [R]	Latin Escapade	196?	15.00
❏ SM-11454	Latin Escapade	197?	12.00
❏ T1082 [M]	Latin Lace	1958	25.00

— *Black label with colorband, logo on left*

| ❏ T1082 [M] | Latin Lace | 1962 | 18.00 |

— *Black label with colorband, logo on top*

| ❏ ST1082 [S] | Latin Lace | 1958 | 30.00 |

— *Black label with colorband, logo on left*

| ❏ ST1082 [S] | Latin Lace | 1962 | 25.00 |

— *Black label with colorband, logo on top*

❏ T2326 [M]	Latin Rendezvous	1965	15.00
❏ ST2326 [S]	Latin Rendezvous	1965	18.00
❏ T1567 [M]	Mood Latino	1961	25.00

— *Black label with colorband, logo on left*

| ❏ T1567 [M] | Mood Latino | 1962 | 18.00 |

— *Black label with colorband, logo on top*

| ❏ ST1567 [S] | Mood Latino | 1961 | 30.00 |

— *Black label with colorband, logo on left*

| ❏ ST1567 [S] | Mood Latino | 1962 | 25.00 |

— *Black label with colorband, logo on top*

| ❏ T943 [M] | Night Mist | 1957 | 30.00 |

— *Turquoise label*

❏ T2048 [M]	Old Gold and Ivory	1964	15.00
❏ ST2048 [S]	Old Gold and Ivory	1964	18.00
❏ T1416 [M]	On the Sunny Side of the Strip	1960	25.00

— *Black label with colorband, logo on left*

| ❏ T1416 [M] | On the Sunny Side of the Strip | 1962 | 18.00 |

— *Black label with colorband, logo on top*

| ❏ ST1416 [S] | On the Sunny Side of the Strip | 1960 | 30.00 |

— *Black label with colorband, logo on left*

| ❏ ST1416 [S] | On the Sunny Side of the Strip | 1962 | 25.00 |

— *Black label with colorband, logo on top*

❏ T2272 [M]	Out of the Woods	1965	15.00
❏ ST2272 [S]	Out of the Woods	1965	18.00
❏ T2447 [M]	Rare Form	1965	15.00
❏ ST2447 [S]	Rare Form	1965	18.00
❏ T1715 [M]	San Francisco Scene	1962	18.00
❏ ST1715 [S]	San Francisco Scene	1962	25.00
❏ T1628 [M]	Satin Affair	1961	25.00

— *Black label with colorband, logo on left*

| ❏ T1628 [M] | Satin Affair | 1962 | 18.00 |

— *Black label with colorband, logo on top*

| ❏ ST1628 [S] | Satin Affair | 1961 | 30.00 |

— *Black label with colorband, logo on left*

| ❏ ST1628 [S] | Satin Affair | 1962 | 25.00 |

— *Black label with colorband, logo on top*

| ❏ T909 [M] | Shearing Piano | 1957 | 30.00 |

— *Turquoise label*

| ❏ T909 [M] | Shearing Piano | 1959 | 25.00 |

— *Black label with colorband, logo on top*

❏ T2567 [M]	That Fresh Feeling	1966	15.00
❏ ST2567 [S]	That Fresh Feeling	1966	18.00
❏ T2104 [M]	The Best of George Shearing	1964	15.00
❏ ST2104 [S]	The Best of George Shearing	1964	18.00

Number	Title	Yr	NM
SM-2104	The Best of George Shearing	1977	12.00
—Reissue with new prefix			
SKAO-139	The Best of George Shearing, Vol. 2	1969	15.00
T648 [M]	The Shearing Spell	1956	30.00
—Turquoise label			
T648 [M]	The Shearing Spell	1959	25.00
—Black label with colorband, logo on left			
T1472 [M]	The Shearing Touch	1961	25.00
—Black label with colorband, logo on left			
T1472 [M]	The Shearing Touch	1962	18.00
—Black label with colorband, logo on top			
ST1472 [S]	The Shearing Touch	1961	30.00
—Black label with colorband, logo on left			
ST1472 [S]	The Shearing Touch	1962	25.00
—Black label with colorband, logo on top			
SM-1472	The Shearing Touch	1977	12.00
—Reissue with new prefix			
T1874 [M]	Touch Me Softly	1963	18.00
ST1874 [S]	Touch Me Softly	1963	25.00
T720 [M]	Velvet Carpet	1956	30.00
—Turquoise label			
T720 [M]	Velvet Carpet	1959	25.00
—Black label with colorband, logo on left			
T720 [M]	Velvet Carpet	1962	18.00
—Black label with colorband, logo on top			
DT720 [R]	Velvet Carpet	196?	15.00
T1334 [M]	White Satin	1960	25.00
—Black label with colorband, logo on left			
T1334 [M]	White Satin	1962	18.00
—Black label with colorband, logo on top			
ST1334 [S]	White Satin	1960	30.00
—Black label with colorband, logo on left			
ST1334 [S]	White Satin	1962	25.00
—Black label with colorband, logo on top			

CONCORD CONCERTO

Number	Title	Yr	NM
CC-2010	George Shearing and Barry Tuckwell Play the Music of Cole Porter	1986	12.00

CONCORD JAZZ

Number	Title	Yr	NM
CJ-171	Alone Together	1981	12.00
CJ-357	A Perfect Match	1988	12.00
—With Ernestine Anderson			
CJ-110	Blues Alley Jazz	1980	12.00
CJ-335	Breakin' Out	1988	12.00
CJ-346	Dexterity	1988	12.00
CJ-177	First Edition	1982	12.00
CJ-388	George Shearing in Dixieland	1989	15.00
CJ-281	Grand Piano	1985	12.00
CJ-246	Live at the Café Carlyle	1984	12.00
CJ-318	More Grand Piano	1987	12.00
CJ-132	On a Clear Day	1981	12.00
—With Brian Torff			
CJ-400	Piano	1989	15.00
CJ-371	The Spirit of 176	1989	15.00
—With Hank Jones			

DISCOVERY

Number	Title	Yr	NM
DL-3002 [10]	George Shearing Quintet	1950	60.00

EVEREST ARCHIVE OF FOLK & JAZZ

Number	Title	Yr	NM
236	The Early Years, Vol. 2	1969	12.00
223	Young George Shearing	1968	12.00

LONDON

Number	Title	Yr	NM
LL1343 [M]	By Request	1956	30.00
LL295 [10]	Souvenirs	1951	60.00

MGM

Number	Title	Yr	NM
E-252 [10]	An Evening with George Shearing	1954	50.00
E-3122 [M]	An Evening with The George Shearing Quintet	1955	30.00
E-90 [10]	A Touch of Genius	1951	50.00
E-155 [10]	I Hear Music	1952	50.00
E-3266 [M]	I Hear Music	1955	30.00
E-4041 [M]	Satin Latin	1962	18.00
SE-4041 [R]	Satin Latin	1962	15.00
E-3175 [M]	Shearing Caravan	1955	30.00
E-3293 [M]	Shearing in Hi-Fi	1955	30.00
E-4043 [M]	Smooth and Swinging	1962	18.00
SE-4043 [R]	Smooth and Swinging	1962	15.00
E-4042 [M]	Soft and Silky	1962	18.00
SE-4042 [R]	Soft and Silky	1962	15.00
E-4169 [M]	The Very Best of George Shearing	1963	18.00
SE-4169 [R]	The Very Best of George Shearing	1963	15.00
E-3265 [M]	Touch of Genius	1955	30.00
E-226 [10]	When Lights Are Low	1953	50.00
E-3264 [M]	When Lights Are Low	1955	30.00
GAS-143	You're Hearing George Shearing	1970	15.00
E-3216 [M]	You're Hearing George Shearing	1955	30.00
E-3796 [M]	You're Hearing the Best of George Shearing	1960	18.00
E-518 [10]	You're Hearing the George Shearing Quartet	1950	60.00

MOSAIC

Number	Title	Yr	NM
MQ7-157	The Complete Capitol Live Recordings of George Shearing	199?	120.00

PAUSA

Number	Title	Yr	NM
7072	500 Miles High	1979	12.00
7088	Getting in the Swing of Things	1981	12.00
9036	Jazz Moments	1985	12.00
9065	Latin Affair	1986	12.00
7035	Light, Airy and Swinging	1977	12.00
7116	On Target	198?	12.00
PR7049	The Reunion	1977	12.00
—With Stephane Grappelli			
9030	The Shearing Touch	198?	12.00

PICKWICK

Number	Title	Yr	NM
SPC-3039	Lullaby of Birdland	197?	12.00
SPC-3100	You Stepped Out of a Dream	197?	12.00

SAVOY

Number	Title	Yr	NM
MG-15003 [10]	Piano Solo	1951	60.00

SAVOY JAZZ

Number	Title	Yr	NM
SJL-1117	So Rare	198?	12.00

SHEBA

Number	Title	Yr	NM
105	As Requested	197?	15.00
107	GAS	197?	15.00
104	George Shearing Quartet	197?	15.00
103	George Shearing Trio	197?	15.00
106	Music to Hear	197?	15.00
101	Out of This World	197?	15.00

VERVE

Number	Title	Yr	NM
VSP-9 [M]	Classic Shearing	1966	18.00
VSPS-9 [R]	Classic Shearing	1966	15.00
827977-1	Lullaby of Birdland	1986	15.00
821664-1	My Ship	198?	12.00

SHEEN, MICKEY

HERALD

Number	Title	Yr	NM
HLP-0105 [M]	Have Swing, Will Travel	1956	60.00

SHELDON, JACK

CAPITOL

Number	Title	Yr	NM
T1851 [M]	Out!	1963	18.00
ST1851 [S]	Out!	1963	25.00
T2029 [M]	Play Buddy, Play!	1966	18.00
ST2029 [S]	Play Buddy, Play!	1966	25.00

CONCORD JAZZ

Number	Title	Yr	NM
CJ-339	Hollywood Heroes	1988	12.00
CJ-229	Stand By for Jack Sheldon	1983	12.00

GENE NORMAN

Number	Title	Yr	NM
GNP-60 [M]	Jack's Groove	1961	40.00

GNP CRESCENDO

Number	Title	Yr	NM
GNPS-60	Jack's Groove	196?	15.00
GNPS-9036	Jack Sheldon and His All-Star Band	197?	12.00
GNPS-2029 [S]	Play, Buddy, Play!	1966	15.00
GNP-2029 [M]	Play, Buddy, Play!	1966	18.00

JAZZ WEST

Number	Title	Yr	NM
JWLP-1 [10]	Get Out of Town	1955	400.00
JWLP-2 [10]	Jack Sheldon Quintet	1955	400.00
JWLP-6 [M]	The Quartet and the Quintet	1956	30.00

REAL TIME

Number	Title	Yr	NM
303	Playin' It Straight	1981	18.00

REPRISE

Number	Title	Yr	NM
R-2004 [M]	A Jazz Profile of Ray Charles	1961	30.00
R9-2004 [S]	A Jazz Profile of Ray Charles	1961	30.00

SHELDON, NINA

PLUG

Number	Title	Yr	NM
PLUG-2	Secret Places	1986	15.00

SHELLS, THE

CANDELITE

Number	Title	Yr	NM
1000	Accapella	197?	18.00

COLLECTABLES

Number	Title	Yr	NM
COL-5077 [B]	Golden Classics	198?	15.00

SHELTON, RICKY VAN

COLUMBIA

Number	Title	Yr	NM
C46855	Backroads	1990	25.00
—Vinyl available only through Columbia House			
FC44221	Loving Proof	1988	10.00
FC45269	Ricky Van Shelton Sings Christmas	1989	15.00
C45250	RVS III	1990	18.00
B6C40602	Wild-Eyed Dream	1987	10.00

SHELTON, ROSCOE

EXCELLO

Number	Title	Yr	NM
LP-8002 [M]	Roscoe Shelton Sings	1961	600.00

SOUND STAGE 7

Number	Title	Yr	NM
SSS-5002 [M]	Soul in His Music, Music in His Soul	1966	40.00
SSS-15002 [S]	Soul in His Music, Music in His Soul	1966	50.00

SHENANDOAH

COLUMBIA

Number	Title	Yr	NM
C48885	Greatest Hits	1992	25.00
—Vinyl available only through Columbia House			
BFC40788	Shenandoah	1987	12.00
FC44468	The Road Not Taken	1989	15.00

SHEP AND THE LIMELITES

HULL

Number	Title	Yr	NM
1001 [M]	Our Anniversary	1962	1200.00

ROULETTE

Number	Title	Yr	NM
R-25350 [M]	Our Anniversary	1967	80.00
SR-25350 [R]	Our Anniversary	1967	50.00

SHEPARD, JEAN, AND RAY PILLOW

CAPITOL

Number	Title	Yr	NM
T2537 [M]	I'll Take the Dog	1966	18.00
ST2537 [S]	I'll Take the Dog	1966	25.00

SHEPARD, JEAN

CAPITOL

Number	Title	Yr	NM
ST2966	A Real Good Woman	1968	18.00
ST-559	A Woman's Hand	1970	18.00
ST-441	Best By Request	1970	18.00
SM-11409	For the Good Times	1975	12.00
T1525 [M]	Got You on My Mind	1961	30.00
ST1525 [S]	Got You on My Mind	1961	30.00
T2690 [M]	Heart, We Did All That We Could	1967	18.00
ST2690 [S]	Heart, We Did All That We Could	1967	18.00
T1663 [M]	Heartaches and Tears	1962	30.00
ST1663 [S]	Heartaches and Tears	1962	30.00
T2871 [M]	Heart to Heart	1968	40.00
ST2871 [S]	Heart to Heart	1968	18.00
ST-738	Here and Now	1971	18.00
ST-171	I'll Fly Away	1969	18.00
T2416 [M]	It's a Man Every Time	1965	15.00
ST2416 [S]	It's a Man Every Time	1965	18.00
ST-815	Just As Soon As I Get Over Loving You	1971	18.00
ST-11049	Just Like Walkin' in the Sunshine	1972	15.00
T2187 [M]	Lighthearted and Blue	1964	18.00
ST2187 [S]	Lighthearted and Blue	1964	25.00
T1126 [M]	Lonesome Love	1959	40.00
T2547 [M]	Many Happy Hangovers	1966	15.00
ST2547 [S]	Many Happy Hangovers	1966	18.00
ST-321	Seven Lonely Days	1969	18.00
T728 [M]	Songs of a Love Affair	1956	60.00
T1922 [M]	The Best of Jean Shepherd	1963	30.00
DT1922 [R]	The Best of Jean Shepherd	1963	18.00
T1253 [M]	This Is Jean Shepard	1959	40.00
T2765 [M]	Your Forevers Don't Last Very Long	1967	25.00
ST2765 [S]	Your Forevers Don't Last Very Long	1967	18.00

HILLTOP

Number	Title	Yr	NM
JS-6068	Under Your Spell Again	197?	12.00

UNITED ARTISTS

Number	Title	Yr	NM
UA-LA307-R	I'll Do Anything It Takes	1974	15.00
UA-LA525-G	I'm a Believer	1975	15.00
UA-LA685-G	Jean Shepard's Greatest Hits	1976	12.00
UA-LA609	Mercy, Ain't Love Good	1976	15.00
UA-LA363-G	Poor Sweet Baby and Ten More Bill Anderson Songs	1975	15.00
UA-LA144-F	Slippin' Away	1973	15.00

SHEPARD, TOMMY

CORAL

Number	Title	Yr	NM
CRL57110 [M]	Shepard's Flock	1957	80.00

SHEPHERD, CYBILL

PARAMOUNT

Number	Title	Yr	NM
PAS-1018	Cybill Does It...to Cole Porter	1974	25.00
—With poster			

SHEPHERD, JEAN

ELEKTRA

Number	Title	Yr	NM
EKL-172 [M]	Jean Shepherd and Other Foibles	1959	50.00

SHEPP, ARCHIE, AND BILL DIXON

SAVOY

Number	Title	Yr	NM
MG-12184 [M]	Archie Shepp and the New Contemporary 5/The Bill Dixon 7-Tette	1964	50.00
—White bordered cover			
MG-12184 [M]	Archie Shepp and the New Contemporary 5/The Bill Dixon 7-Tette	1965	30.00
—Purple bordered cover			
MG-12178 [M]	The Archie Shepp-Bill Dixon Quartet	1962	30.00

SHEPP, ARCHIE, AND DOLLAR BRAND

DENON

Number	Title	Yr	NM
7532	Duet	197?	18.00

SHEPP, ARCHIE, AND HORACE PARLAN

STEEPLECHASE

Number	Title	Yr	NM
SCS-1079	Goin' Home	197?	15.00
SCS-1139	Trouble in Mind	1980	15.00

SHEPP, ARCHIE

ABC IMPULSE!

Number	Title	Yr	NM
❑ AS-9222	Africa Blues	197?	18.00
❑ AS-9231	Cry of My People	1973	18.00
❑ AS-86 [S]	Fire Music	1968	18.00
❑ AS-9188	For Losers	1970	25.00
❑ AS-71 [S]	Four for Trane	1968	18.00
❑ AS-9262	Kwanza	1974	18.00
❑ AS-9118 [S]	Live In San Francisco	1968	18.00
❑ AS-9134 [S]	Mama Too Tight	1968	18.00
❑ AS-97 [S]	On This Night	1968	18.00
❑ AS-9154 [S]	The Magic of Ju Ju	1968	25.00
❑ AS-9170 [S]	The Way Ahead	1969	25.00
❑ AS-9212	Things Have Got to Change	197?	18.00
❑ AS-9162 [S]	Three for a Quarter, One for a Dime	1968	25.00

ARISTA/FREEDOM

Number	Title	Yr	NM
❑ AF1027	Montreux 1	197?	15.00
❑ AF1034	Montreux 2	197?	15.00
❑ AF1016	There's a Trumpet in My Soul	1975	15.00

BASF

Number	Title	Yr	NM
❑ 20651	Donaueschingen Festival	197?	18.00

BLACK SAINT

Number	Title	Yr	NM
❑ BSR-0002	A Sea of Faces	198?	15.00

DELMARK

Number	Title	Yr	NM
❑ DL-409 [M]	Archie Shepp in Europe	1968	30.00
❑ DS-9409 [S]	Archie Shepp in Europe	1968	25.00

DENON

Number	Title	Yr	NM
❑ 7543	Lady Bird	197?	18.00
❑ 7538	Live in Tokyo	197?	18.00

GRP/IMPULSE!

Number	Title	Yr	NM
❑ IMP-218	Four for Trane	199?	18.00
—Reissue on audiophile vinyl			

IMPULSE!

Number	Title	Yr	NM
❑ A-86 [M]	Fire Music	1965	30.00
❑ AS-86 [S]	Fire Music	1965	30.00
❑ A-71 [M]	Four for Trane	1964	30.00
❑ AS-71 [S]	Four for Trane	1964	30.00
❑ A-9118 [M]	Live In San Francisco	1967	30.00
❑ AS-9118 [S]	Live In San Francisco	1967	30.00
❑ A-9134 [M]	Mama Too Tight	1967	30.00
❑ AS-9134 [S]	Mama Too Tight	1967	30.00
❑ A-97 [M]	On This Night	1966	30.00
❑ AS-97 [S]	On This Night	1966	30.00

INNER CITY

Number	Title	Yr	NM
❑ IC-1001	Doodlin'	197?	18.00
❑ IC-3002	Steam	1976	15.00

PRESTIGE

Number	Title	Yr	NM
❑ 10034	Black Gypsy	197?	18.00
❑ 10066	Coral Rock	197?	18.00

SACKVILLE

Number	Title	Yr	NM
❑ 3026	I Know About the Life	198?	12.00

SOUL NOTE

Number	Title	Yr	NM
❑ SN-1102	Down Home in New York	1985	15.00

STEEPLECHASE

Number	Title	Yr	NM
❑ SCS-1140	Looking at Bird	198?	15.00
❑ SCS-1169	Mama Rose	1982	15.00
❑ SCS-6013	The House I Live In	198?	15.00

TIMELESS

Number	Title	Yr	NM
❑ SJP-287	Lover Man	1990	15.00

VARRICK

Number	Title	Yr	NM
❑ VR-005	The Good Life	198?	12.00

SHEPPARD, ANDY

ANTILLES

Number	Title	Yr	NM
❑ 90692	Andy Sheppard	1988	12.00

SHEPPARD, T.G.

COLUMBIA

Number	Title	Yr	NM
❑ FC40796	1ne 4 the $	1987	10.00
❑ FC44307	Biggest Hits (1985-1987)	1988	10.00
❑ FC44421	Crossroads	1989	12.00
❑ FC40310	It Still Rains in Memphis	1986	10.00
❑ FC40007	Livin' on the Edge	1985	10.00

HITSVILLE

Number	Title	Yr	NM
❑ H6-404S1	Solitary Man	1976	15.00

MELODYLAND

Number	Title	Yr	NM
❑ ME6-403S1	Motels and Memories	1976	15.00
❑ ME6-401S1	T.G. Sheppard	1975	15.00

WARNER BROS.

Number	Title	Yr	NM
❑ BSK3353	3/4 Lonely	1979	10.00
❑ BSK3259	Daylight	1978	10.00
❑ BSK3600	Finally!	1982	10.00
❑ 25329	Greatest Hits, Volume 2	1985	10.00
❑ BSK3528	I Love 'Em All	1981	10.00
❑ 25149	One Owner Heart	1984	10.00
❑ 23726	Perfect Stranger	1982	10.00
❑ 23911	Slow Burn	1983	10.00
❑ BSK3423	Smooth Sailin'	1980	10.00
❑ BSK3133	T.G.	1978	12.00
—Burbank" palm trees label			
❑ BSK3133	T.G.	1979	10.00
—White label			
❑ 25282	T.G.	1985	10.00
❑ 23841	T.G. Sheppard's Greatest Hits	1983	10.00

SHEPPARDS, THE

COLLECTABLES

Number	Title	Yr	NM
❑ COL-5078	Golden Classics	198?	12.00

CONSTELLATION

Number	Title	Yr	NM
❑ C-4 [M]	Collectors Showcase: The Sheppards	1964	80.00
❑ CS-4 [R]	Collectors Showcase: The Sheppards	1964	40.00

SOLID SMOKE

Number	Title	Yr	NM
❑ SS-8028	18 Dusty Diamonds	1984	12.00
❑ SS-8004	The Sheppards	1980	12.00

SHERIFF

CAPITOL

Number	Title	Yr	NM
❑ ST-12227	Sheriff	1983	12.00
❑ C1-91216	Sheriff	1988	12.00
—Reissue of 12227			

SHERLEY, GLEN

MEGA

Number	Title	Yr	NM
❑ 1006	Glen Sherley	1971	15.00

SHERMAN, ALLAN

JUBLIEE

Number	Title	Yr	NM
❑ JGM5019 [M]	More Folk Songs by Allan Sherman	1963	25.00
—Two early Allan Sherman sides plus comedy bits by others			

RCA RED SEAL

Number	Title	Yr	NM
❑ LM-2773 [M]	Peter and the Commissar	1964	25.00
❑ LSC-2773 [S]	Peter and the Commissar	1964	30.00
—With Arthur Fiedler and the Boston Pops Orchestra			

RHINO

Number	Title	Yr	NM
❑ RNLP70818	A Gift of Laughter	1986	12.00
❑ RNLP-005	The Best of Allan Sherman	198?	12.00

WARNER BROS.

Number	Title	Yr	NM
❑ W1539 [M]	Allan in Wonderland	1964	15.00
❑ WS1539 [S]	Allan in Wonderland	1964	18.00
—Gold label			
❑ W1649 [M]	Allan Sherman -- Live	1966	15.00
❑ WS1649 [S]	Allan Sherman -- Live	1966	18.00
—Gold label			
❑ W1569 [M]	For Swingin' Livers Only!	1964	15.00
❑ WS1569 [S]	For Swingin' Livers Only!	1964	18.00
❑ W1604 [M]	My Name Is Allan	1965	15.00
❑ WS1604 [S]	My Name Is Allan	1965	18.00
—Gold label			
❑ W1487 [M]	My Son, the Celebrity	1963	18.00
❑ WS1487 [S]	My Son, the Celebrity	1963	25.00
—Gold label			
❑ W1475 [M]	My Son, the Folk Singer	1962	18.00
❑ WS1475 [S]	My Son, the Folk Singer	1962	25.00
—Gold label			
❑ W1501 [M]	My Son, the Nut	1963	18.00
❑ WS1501 [S]	My Son, the Nut	1963	25.00
—Gold label			
❑ W1684 [M]	Togetherness	1967	18.00
❑ WS1684 [S]	Togetherness	1967	25.00
—Gold label			

SHERMAN, BOBBY

METROMEDIA

Number	Title	Yr	NM
❑ MD1014	Bobby Sherman	1969	18.00
❑ MD1038	Bobby Sherman Christmas Album	1970	18.00
❑ KMD1048	Bobby Sherman's Greatest Hits	1972	15.00
❑ MD1045	Getting Together	1971	18.00
❑ MD1028	Here Comes Bobby	1970	18.00
❑ MD1060	Just for You	1973	18.00
❑ MD1040	Portrait of Bobby	1971	18.00
❑ MD1032	With Love, Bobby	1970	18.00

SHERMAN, MARK

COLUMBIA

Number	Title	Yr	NM
❑ BFC40360	A New Balance	1986	12.00

SHERRILL, JOYA

20TH CENTURY FOX

Number	Title	Yr	NM
❑ TFL-3170 [M]	Joya Sherrill Sings Duke Ellington	196?	30.00
❑ TFS-4170 [S]	Joya Sherrill Sings Duke Ellington	196?	30.00

COLUMBIA

Number	Title	Yr	NM
❑ CL1378 [M]	Sugar and Spice	1959	30.00
❑ CS8178 [S]	Sugar and Spice	1960	30.00

DESIGN

Number	Title	Yr	NM
❑ DLP-22 [M]	Joya Sherrill Jumps with Sammy Davis, Jr.	196?	15.00

SHERRYS, THE

GUYDEN

Number	Title	Yr	NM
❑ GLP503 [M]	At the Hop with the Sherrys	1963	250.00

SHERWOOD, BOBBY

CAPITOL

Number	Title	Yr	NM
❑ H463 [10]	Bobby Sherwood	1954	50.00
❑ H320 [10]	Classics in Jazz	1952	60.00
❑ T320 [M]	Classics in Jazz	1955	40.00

IAJRC

Number	Title	Yr	NM
❑ LP35	Out of Sherwood's Forest	198?	12.00

JUBILEE

Number	Title	Yr	NM
❑ JLP-1040 [M]	I'm an Old Cowhand	1957	30.00
❑ JLP-1061 [M]	Pal Joey	1958	30.00
❑ SDJLP-1061 [S]	Pal Joey	1959	30.00

SHEW, BOBBY, AND BILL MAYS

JAZZ HOUNDS

Number	Title	Yr	NM
❑ 0003	Telepathy	198?	12.00

SHEW, BOBBY, AND CHUCK FINDLEY

DELOS

Number	Title	Yr	NM
❑ DMS-4003	Trumpets No End	1984	12.00

SHEW, BOBBY

INNER CITY

Number	Title	Yr	NM
❑ IC-1077	Outstanding in His Field	197?	15.00

JAZZ HOUNDS

Number	Title	Yr	NM
❑ 0002	Play Song	1980	12.00

PAUSA

Number	Title	Yr	NM
❑ 7171	Breakfast Wine	1985	12.00
❑ 7198	Shewhorn	1986	12.00

SHIELDS, BILL

OPTIMISM

Number	Title	Yr	NM
❑ OP-9001	Shieldstone	198?	12.00

SHIELDS, ROGER

TURNABOUT

Number	Title	Yr	NM
❑ 34579	The Age of Ragtime	197?	12.00

SHIGETA, JAMES

CHOREO

Number	Title	Yr	NM
❑ A-7 [M]	We Speak the Same Language	1962	30.00
❑ AS-7 [S]	We Speak the Same Language	1962	30.00

SHIHAB, SAHIB

ARGO

Number	Title	Yr	NM
❑ LP-742 [M]	Summer Dawn	1964	30.00
❑ LPS-742 [S]	Summer Dawn	1964	30.00

CHESS

Number	Title	Yr	NM
❑ CH-91563	Summer Dawn	198?	12.00

SAVOY

Number	Title	Yr	NM
❑ MG-12124 [M]	Jazz Sahib	1957	50.00

SAVOY JAZZ

Number	Title	Yr	NM
❑ SJL-2245	All-Star Sextets	197?	15.00
❑ SJC-409	Jazz Sahib	1985	12.00

SHIHAB, SAHIB/HERBIE MANN

SAVOY

Number	Title	Yr	NM
❑ MG-12112 [M]	The Jazz We Heard Last Summer	1957	50.00

SHILOH

AMOS

Number	Title	Yr	NM
❑ AAS-7015	Shiloh	1971	80.00

SHINER, MERVIN

LITTLE DARLIN'

Number	Title	Yr	NM
❑ 8018	In the Ghetto	1970	18.00

SHIP, THE

ELEKTRA

Number	Title	Yr	NM
❑ EKS-75036 [B]	The Ship	1972	35.00

SHIRELLES, THE

RCA VICTOR

Number	Title	Yr	NM
❑ LSP-4581	Happy and In Love	1971	18.00
❑ LSP-4698	The Shirelles	1972	18.00

RHINO

Number	Title	Yr	NM
❑ RNDA-1101	Anthology (1959-1967)	1984	15.00

SCEPTER

Number	Title	Yr	NM
❑ SPM-505 [M]	A Twist Party	1962	80.00
❑ SPS-505 [S]	A Twist Party	1965	100.00
❑ SPM-504 [M]	Baby It's You	1962	100.00
❑ SPS-504 [S]	Baby It's You	1965	100.00
❑ SPS-569	Eternally Soul	1968	30.00
❑ SPM-511 [M]	Foolish Little Girl	1963	50.00
❑ SPS-511 [S]	Foolish Little Girl	1965	80.00
❑ SPM-514 [M]	It's a Mad, Mad, Mad, Mad World	1963	40.00
❑ SPS-514 [S]	It's a Mad, Mad, Mad, Mad World	1963	50.00
❑ SPS-2-599	Remember When	1972	25.00
❑ SPM-562 [M]	Spontaneous Combustion	1967	40.00
❑ SPS-562 [S]	Spontaneous Combustion	1967	50.00
❑ SPM-507 [M]	The Shirelles' Greatest Hits	1962	40.00
❑ SPS-507 [S]	The Shirelles' Greatest Hits	1965	50.00
❑ SPM-560 [M]	The Shirelles' Greatest Hits, Volume 2	1967	25.00

Number	Title	Yr	NM
❑ SPS-560 [S]	The Shirelles' Greatest Hits, Volume 2	1967	30.00
❑ SPM-516 [M]	The Shirelles Sing the Golden Oldies	1964	40.00
❑ SPS-516 [S]	The Shirelles Sing the Golden Oldies	1964	50.00
❑ S-502 [M]	The Shirelles Sing to Trumpets and Strings	1961	200.00
— Scepter" in scroll at top of label			
❑ SPM-502 [M]	The Shirelles Sing to Trumpets and Strings	1962	60.00
— Scepter Records" at left of label			
❑ SPS-502 [S]	The Shirelles Sing to Trumpets and Strings	1965	100.00
❑ S-501 [M]	Tonight's the Night	1961	200.00
— Scepter" in scroll at top of label			
❑ SPM-501 [M]	Tonight's the Night	1962	60.00
— Scepter Records" at left of label			
❑ SPS-501 [S]	Tonight's the Night	1965	100.00
SPRINGBOARD			
❑ 4006	The Shirelles Sing Their Very Best	1973	10.00
UNITED ARTISTS			
❑ UA-LA340-E	The Very Best of the Shirelles	1974	12.00

SHIRLEY, DON

Number	Title	Yr	NM
AUDIO FIDELITY			
❑ AFLP-1897 [M]	Don Shirley	1959	25.00
❑ AFSD-5897 [S]	Don Shirley	1959	30.00
CADENCE			
❑ CLP-1015 [M]	Don Shirley Duo	1956	40.00
❑ CLP-3035 [M]	Don Shirley Plays Birdland Lullabies	1960	30.00
❑ CLP-3032 [M]	Don Shirley Plays Gershwin	1960	30.00
❑ CLP-3034 [M]	Don Shirley Plays Love Songs	1960	30.00
❑ CLP-3036 [M]	Don Shirley Plays Showtunes	1960	30.00
❑ CLP-3033 [M]	Don Shirley Plays Standards	1960	30.00
❑ CLP-3007 [M]	Don Shirley Solos	1958	30.00
❑ CLP-3008 [M]	Don Shirley with Two Basses	1958	30.00
❑ CLP-3057 [M]	Drown in My Own Tears	1962	25.00
❑ CLP-25057 [S]	Drown in My Own Tears	1962	30.00
❑ CLP-1009 [M]	Orpheus in the Underworld	1956	40.00
❑ CLP-3037 [M]	Orpheus in the Underworld	1960	30.00
— Reissue of 1009			
❑ CLP-3048 [M]	Pianist Extraordinary	1962	25.00
❑ CLP-25048 [S]	Pianist Extraordinary	1962	30.00
❑ CLP-3049 [M]	Piano Arrangements of Spirituals	1962	25.00
❑ CLP-25049 [S]	Piano Arrangements of Spirituals	1962	30.00
❑ CLP-1004 [M]	Piano Perspectives	1955	40.00
❑ CLP-1001 [M]	Tonal Expressions	1955	40.00
❑ CLP-3046 [M]	Trio	1961	25.00
❑ CLP-25046 [S]	Trio	1961	30.00
COLUMBIA			
❑ CL2396 [M]	Water Boy	1965	18.00
❑ CS9196 [S]	Water Boy	1965	25.00

SHIRLEY (AND COMPANY)

Number	Title	Yr	NM
VIBRATION			
❑ 128	Shame Shame Shame	1975	12.00

SHIRLEY AND LEE

Number	Title	Yr	NM
ALADDIN			
❑ 807 [M]	Let the Good Times Roll	1956	1500.00
IMPERIAL			
❑ LP-9179 [M]	Let the Good Times Roll	1962	300.00
— Reissue of Aladdin LP			
SCORE			
❑ SLP-4023 [M]	Let the Good Times Roll	1957	800.00
— Reissue of Aladdin LP			
WARWICK			
❑ W-2028 [M]	Let the Good Times Roll	1961	150.00
❑ W-2028ST [S]	Let the Good Times Roll	1961	300.00

SHIRTS, THE

Number	Title	Yr	NM
CAPITOL			
❑ SW-12085	Inner Sleeve	1980	15.00
❑ ST-11944	Street Light Shine	1979	14.00
❑ SW-11791	The Shirts	1978	14.00

SHIVA'S HEADBAND

Number	Title	Yr	NM
APE			
❑ 1001	Psychedelic Yesterday	1981	25.00
ARMADILLO			
❑ (no #)0	Coming to a Head	1969	250.00
CAPITOL			
❑ ST-538	Take Me to the Mountains	1970	60.00

SHOCKED, MICHELLE

Number	Title	Yr	NM
MERCURY			
❑ 838878-1	Captain Swing	1989	12.00
❑ PRO797 [DJ]	Live	1990	25.00
— Five-song mini-LP for radio stations with custom jacket			
❑ PRO797 [DJ]	Live	1990	25.00
— Five-song mini-LP for radio stations with custom jacket			
❑ 834924-1	Short Sharp Shocked	1988	12.00
❑ 834581-1	The Texas Campfire Tapes	1988	15.00

SHOCKING BLUE, THE

Number	Title	Yr	NM
COLOSSUS			
❑ CS-1000	The Shocking Blue	1970	30.00

SHOEMAKE, CHARLIE, AND BILL HOLMAN

Number	Title	Yr	NM
PAUSA			
❑ 7180	Collaboration	1985	12.00

SHOEMAKE, CHARLIE, AND HAROLD LAND

Number	Title	Yr	NM
CMG			
❑ CML-8016	Stand-Up Guys	1989	15.00

SHOEMAKE, CHARLIE

Number	Title	Yr	NM
DISCOVERY			
❑ 856	Away from the Crowd	198?	12.00
❑ 894	Charlie Shoemake Plays the Music of David Raksin	1986	12.00
❑ 924	I Think We're Almost There	1987	12.00
MUSE			
❑ MR-5221	Blue Shoe	1979	15.00
❑ MR-5193	Sunstroke	1978	15.00

SHOES

Number	Title	Yr	NM
BLACK VINYL			
❑ 51477	Black Vinyl Shoes	1977	80.00
ELEKTRA			
❑ 60146	Boomerang	1982	12.00
❑ 6E-244	Present Tense	1979	12.00
❑ AS11570 [DJ]	Shoes on Ice -- Live	1982	40.00
— Promo-only 7-song live record; issued in generic jacket			
❑ AS11570 [DJ]	Shoes on Ice -- Live	1982	50.00
— Promo-only 7-song live record; issued in generic jacket			
❑ 6E-303	Tongue Twister	1980	12.00
(NO LABEL)			
❑ (no #)0	One in Versailles	1976	120.00
PVC			
❑ 7904	Black Vinyl Shoes	1979	25.00

SHONDELL, TROY

Number	Title	Yr	NM
EVEREST			
❑ 5206 [M]	The Many Sides of Troy Shondell	1963	50.00
❑ 1206 [S]	The Many Sides of Troy Shondell	1963	80.00
SUNSET			
❑ SUM-1174 [M]	This Time	1967	18.00
❑ SUS-5174 [S]	This Time	1967	18.00

SHOOTERS, THE

Number	Title	Yr	NM
EPIC			
❑ FE44326	Solid as a Rock	1989	12.00
❑ FE40885	The Shooters	1987	10.00

SHOOTING STAR

Number	Title	Yr	NM
EPIC			
❑ FE38020	3 Wishes	1982	12.00
❑ BFE38683	Burning	1983	12.00
❑ NFE37407	Hang On for Your Life	1981	12.00
❑ PE37720	Shooting Star	1982	10.00
— Reissue of Virgin VA 13133			
GEFFEN			
❑ GHS24056	Silent Scream	1985	12.00
VIRGIN			
❑ VA13133	Shooting Star	1979	12.00

SHOPPE, THE

Number	Title	Yr	NM
MTM			
❑ ST-71051	The Shoppe	1986	12.00

SHORE, DINAH

Number	Title	Yr	NM
BAINBRIDGE			
❑ 6232	Once Upon a Summertime	198?	12.00
CAPITOL			
❑ T1247 [M]	Dinah, Yes Indeed	1959	25.00
❑ ST1247 [S]	Dinah, Yes Indeed	1959	30.00
❑ T1655 [M]	Dinah Down Home	1962	25.00
❑ ST1655 [S]	Dinah Down Home	1962	30.00
❑ T1422 [M]	Dinah Sings/Previn Plays	1960	25.00
❑ ST1422 [S]	Dinah Sings/Previn Plays	1960	30.00
❑ T1354 [M]	Dinah Sings Some Blues with Red	1960	30.00
❑ ST1354 [S]	Dinah Sings Some Blues with Red	1960	30.00
❑ T1296 [M]	Somebody Loves Me	1959	25.00
❑ ST1296 [S]	Somebody Loves Me	1959	30.00
❑ T1704 [M]	The Fabulous Hits of Dinah Shore	1962	25.00
— Black label with colorband, logo at left			
❑ T1704 [M]	The Fabulous Hits of Dinah Shore	1962	15.00
— Black label with colorband, logo at top			
❑ ST1704 [S]	The Fabulous Hits of Dinah Shore	1962	30.00
— Black label with colorband, logo at left			
❑ ST1704 [S]	The Fabulous Hits of Dinah Shore	1962	18.00
— Black label with colorband, logo at top			
COLUMBIA			
❑ CL6004 [10]	Dinah Shore Sings	1949	50.00
❑ CL6069 [10]	Reminiscing	1949	50.00
❑ C34395	The Best of Dinah Shore	1977	12.00
HARMONY			
❑ HL7188 [M]	Buttons and Bows	195?	18.00
❑ HL7010 [M]	Dinah Shore Sings Cole Porter and Richard Rodgers	195?	25.00
❑ HL7239 [M]	Lavender Blue	1959	18.00
PICKWICK			
❑ SPC-3524	It's So Nice to Have a Man Around the House	197?	10.00
PROJECT 3			
❑ PR-5018SD	Songs for Sometime Losers	1968	18.00
RCA CAMDEN			
❑ CAL-477 [M]	I'm Your Girl	1959	18.00
❑ CAL-572 [M]	Vivacious Dinah Shore	1960	18.00
RCA VICTOR			
❑ LPM-1214 [M]	Bouquet of Blues	1956	30.00
❑ LPM-3103 [10]	Dinah Shore Sings the Blues	1953	40.00
❑ LPM-1154 [M]	Holding Hands at Midnight	1955	30.00
❑ LPM-1719 [M]	Moments Like These	1958	30.00
❑ ANL1-1158	The Best of Dinah Shore	1976	12.00
❑ LPM-3214 [10]	The Dinah Shore TV Show	1954	40.00
REPRISE			
❑ R-6150 [M]	The Lower East Side Revisited	1965	15.00
❑ RS-6150 [S]	The Lower East Side Revisited	1965	18.00
SEAGULL			
❑ LG-8203	Oh Lonesome Me	198?	12.00
STANYAN			
❑ 10071	Dinah Sings the Blues	197?	12.00
❑ 10139	For Always	1977	12.00
❑ 10125	Once Upon a Summertime	197?	12.00

SHORT, BOBBY

Number	Title	Yr	NM
ATLANTIC			
❑ 81715	50 from Bobby Short	1987	30.00
❑ 1230 [M]	Bobby Short	1956	30.00
— Black label			
❑ 1230 [M]	Bobby Short	1961	25.00
— White "fan" logo at right of label			
❑ 1230 [M]	Bobby Short	1963	18.00
— Black "fan" logo at right of label			
❑ SD 2-610	Bobby Short Celebrates Rodgers and Hart	197?	18.00
❑ SD 2-608	Bobby Short Is K-RA-Z-Y for Gershwin	1973	18.00
❑ SD 2-606	Bobby Short Loves Cole Porter	1972	25.00
❑ 81778	Guess Who's in Town: The Lyrics of Andy Razaf	1988	12.00
❑ SD1535	Jump for Joy	1969	15.00
❑ SD 2-609	Live at the Café Carlyle	1974	18.00
❑ SD 2-607	Mad About Noel Coward	1972	25.00
❑ SD1574	Nobody Else But Me	1971	15.00
❑ 1321 [M]	On the East Side	1960	30.00
— Black label			
❑ 1321 [M]	On the East Side	1961	25.00
— White "fan" logo at right of label			
❑ 1321 [M]	On the East Side	1963	18.00
— Black "fan" logo at right of label			
❑ SD1321 [S]	On the East Side	1960	40.00
— Green label			
❑ SD1321 [S]	On the East Side	1961	30.00
— White "fan" logo at right of label			
❑ SD1321 [S]	On the East Side	1963	25.00
— Black "fan" logo at right of label			
❑ SD1689	Personal	1977	15.00
❑ 1285 [M]	Sing Me a Swing Song	1958	30.00
— Black label			
❑ 1285 [M]	Sing Me a Swing Song	1961	25.00
— White "fan" logo at right of label			
❑ 1285 [M]	Sing Me a Swing Song	1963	18.00
— Black "fan" logo at right of label			
❑ 1214 [M]	Songs by Bobby Short	1955	30.00
— Black label			
❑ 1214 [M]	Songs by Bobby Short	1961	25.00
— White "fan" logo at right of label			
❑ 1214 [M]	Songs by Bobby Short	1963	18.00
— Black "fan" logo at right of label			
❑ 1262 [M]	Speaking of Love	1958	30.00
— Black label			
❑ 1262 [M]	Speaking of Love	1961	25.00
— White "fan" logo at right of label			
❑ SD1262 [S]	Speaking of Love	1959	40.00
— Green label			
❑ SD1262 [S]	Speaking of Love	1961	30.00
— White "fan" logo at right of label			
❑ 1302 [M]	The Mad Twenties	1959	30.00
— Black label			
❑ 1302 [M]	The Mad Twenties	1961	25.00
— White "fan" logo at right of label			
❑ 1302 [M]	The Mad Twenties	1963	18.00
— Black "fan" logo at right of label			

Number	Title	Yr	NM
❑ SD1302 [S]	The Mad Twenties	1959	40.00
— Green label			
❑ SD1302 [S]	The Mad Twenties	1961	30.00
— White "fan" logo at right of label			
❑ SD1302 [S]	The Mad Twenties	1963	25.00
— Black "fan" logo at right of label			
❑ SD1664	The Mad Twenties	1974	15.00
❑ SD1620	The Very Best of Bobby Short	1973	15.00

ELEKTRA

❑ E1-60002	Moments Like This	1982	12.00

SHORT CROSS

GRIZZLY

❑ S-16013 [B]	Arising	1970	300.00

SHORTER, ALAN

VERVE

❑ V6-8769	Orgasm	1969	25.00

SHORTER, WAYNE

BLUE NOTE

❑ BST-84232	Adam's Apple	1967	25.00
❑ BST-84232	Adam's Apple	1985	12.00
— The Finest in Jazz Since 1939" reissue			
❑ LT-1056	Etcetera	1980	15.00
❑ B1-33581	Etcetera	1995	18.00
❑ BLP-4182 [M]	Juju	1965	30.00
❑ BST-84182 [S]	Juju	1965	30.00
— With New York, USA address on label			
❑ BST-84182 [S]	Juju	1967	18.00
— With "A Division of Liberty Records" on label			
❑ BST-84182	Juju	198?	12.00
— The Finest in Jazz Since 1939" reissue			
❑ BN-LA014-G	Moto Grosso Feio	1973	18.00
❑ BLP-4173 [M]	Night Dreamer	1964	30.00
❑ BST-84173 [S]	Night Dreamer	1964	30.00
— With New York, USA address on label			
❑ BST-84173 [S]	Night Dreamer	1967	18.00
— With "A Division of Liberty Records" on label			
❑ BST-84297	Schizophrenia	1969	25.00
❑ B1-32096	Schizophrenia	1995	18.00
❑ BLP-4194 [M]	Speak No Evil	1966	30.00
❑ RST-84194 [S]	Speak No Evil	1966	30.00
— With New York, USA address on label			
❑ BST-84194 [S]	Speak No Evil	1967	18.00
— With "A Division of Liberty Records" on label			
❑ B1-46509	Speak No Evil	1997	18.00
— Reissue on 180-gram vinyl			
❑ BST-84332	Super Nova	1970	25.00
❑ BLP-4219 [M]	The All Seeing Eye	1966	30.00
❑ BST-84219 [S]	The All Seeing Eye	1966	30.00
— With New York, USA address on label			
❑ BST-84219 [S]	The All Seeing Eye	1967	18.00
— With "A Division of Liberty Records" on label			
❑ B1-29100	The All Seeing Eye	1994	18.00
❑ B1-91141	The Best of Wayne Shorter	1988	12.00
❑ BST-84363	The Odyssey of Iska	1971	18.00
❑ LT-988	The Soothsayer	1979	18.00

COLUMBIA

❑ FC40055	Atlantis	1985	12.00
❑ FC44110	Joy Ryder	1988	12.00
❑ PC33418	Native Dancer	1975	15.00
— Originals have no bar code			
❑ PC33418	Native Dancer	198?	10.00
— Reissue with bar code			
❑ FC40373	Phantom Navigator	1987	12.00

GNP CRESCENDO

❑ GNPS-2075	Wayne Shorter	1973	18.00

TRIP

❑ 5009	Shorter Moments	1974	15.00

VEE JAY

❑ LP-3006 [M]	Introducing Wayne Shorter	1960	40.00
❑ SR-3006 [S]	Introducing Wayne Shorter	1960	50.00
❑ VJS-3006	Introducing Wayne Shorter	1986	15.00
— 1980s reissue on thinner vinyl			
❑ LP-3057 [M]	Second Genesis	1963	30.00
❑ SR-3057 [S]	Second Genesis	1963	40.00
❑ VJS-3057	Second Genesis	198?	15.00
— 1980s reissue on thinner vinyl			
❑ LP-3029 [M]	Wayning Moments	1962	30.00
❑ SR-3029 [S]	Wayning Moments	1962	40.00
❑ VJS-3029	Wayning Moments	198?	15.00
— 1980s reissue on thinner vinyl			

SHOTGUN LTD.

PROPHESY

❑ 6050	Shotgun Ltd.	1971	25.00

SHOWMEN, THE

COLLECTABLES

❑ COL-5162	Golden Classics	198?	12.00

SHQ

ESP-DISK'

❑ 1080 [S]	The Uhu Sleeps Only During the Day	1969	30.00

SHRINER, HERB

COLUMBIA

❑ CL774 [M]	Herb Shriner On Stage	1957	30.00

DOT

❑ DLP-3149 [M]	Polka Dot Party	1959	30.00
❑ DLP-25149 [S]	Polka Dot Party	1959	40.00

SHU, EDDIE

BETHLEHEM

❑ BCP-1013 [10]	I Only Have Eyes For Shu	1954	100.00

SHU, EDDIE/BOB HARDAWAY

BETHLEHEM

❑ BCP-3 [M]	Jazz Practitioners	1957	180.00

SHU, EDDIE/JOE ROLAND/"WILD" BILL DAVIS

MERCER

❑ LP-1002 [10]	New Stars, New Sounds, Volume 1	1951	150.00

SHULMAN, JOEL

JAMAL

❑ 5162	Peninah	197?	25.00

SHUMATE, TED, AND IRA SULLIVAN

PAUSA

❑ 7188	Gulfstream	1986	12.00

SHYLO

COLUMBIA

❑ PC34161	Flower of the South	1976	15.00

SICKNICKS, THE

AMY

❑ 2 [M]	Sick #2	1961	50.00

SIDE OF THE ROAD GANG, THE

CAPITOL

❑ ST-11526	The Side of the Road Gang	1976	15.00

SIDEKICKS, THE

RCA VICTOR

❑ LPM-3712 [M]	Fifi the Flea	1966	40.00
❑ LSP-3712 [S]	Fifi the Flea	1966	30.00

SIDEWINDERS, THE

RCA VICTOR

❑ LSP-4694	The Sidewinders	1972	25.00

SIDMAN, DAVID

CADENCE JAZZ

❑ CJR-1033	Shades of Meaning	1988	12.00

SIDRAN, BEN

ANTILLES

❑ AN-1012	Bop City	1984	15.00
❑ AN-1004	Old Songs for the New Depression	1981	18.00

ARISTA

❑ AB4178	A Little Kiss in the Night	1978	18.00
❑ AL4081	Free in America	1976	15.00
❑ AB4218	Live at Montreux	1979	15.00
❑ AL4131	The Doctor Is In	1977	15.00

BLUEBIRD

❑ 6575-1-RB	That's Life I Guess	1990	18.00

BLUE THUMB

❑ BTS-6012	Don't Let Go	1974	25.00
❑ BTS-40	I Lead a Life	1972	40.00
❑ BTS-55	Puttin' In Time on Planet Earth	1973	25.00

CAPITOL

❑ ST-825	Feel Your Groove	1971	50.00

HORIZON

❑ SP-741	The Cat and the Hat	1980	15.00

MAGENTA

❑ MA-0204	On the Cool Side	1985	12.00
❑ MA-0206	On the Live Side	1986	12.00

WINDHAM HILL

❑ WH-0108	Too Hot to Touch	1988	15.00

SIEGEL, DAN

CBS ASSOCIATED

❑ OZ44490	Late One Night	1989	15.00
❑ BZ44026	Northern Nights	1987	12.00

INNER CITY

❑ IC-1046	Nite Ride	197?	15.00
❑ IC-1134	Oasis	198?	15.00
❑ IC-1111	The Hot Shot	198?	15.00

PAUSA

❑ 7164	Another Time	1984	12.00
❑ 7179	On the Edge	1985	12.00
❑ 7142	Reflections	198?	12.00

SIEGEL-SCHWALL BAND, THE

VANGUARD

❑ VRS-9249 [M]	Say Siegel-Schwall	1967	30.00
❑ VSD-79249 [S]	Say Siegel-Schwall	1967	25.00
❑ VSD-79289	Shake!	1968	25.00
❑ VSD-6562	Siegel-Schwall '70	1970	25.00
❑ VRS-9235 [M]	The Siegel-Schwall Band	1966	25.00
❑ VSD-79235 [S]	The Siegel-Schwall Band	1966	30.00

WOODEN NICKEL

❑ BWL1-0121	953 West	1973	25.00
❑ BWL1-0288	Last Summer -- Live	1974	25.00
❑ BWL1-0554	R.I.P.	1974	25.00
❑ WNS-1010	Sleepy Hollow	1972	30.00
❑ WNS-1002	The Siegel-Schwall Band	1971	30.00

SIGLER, BUNNY

GOLD MIND

❑ 9503	I've Always Wanted to Sing... Not Just Write Songs	1979	15.00
❑ 7502	Let Me Party with You	1978	15.00

PARKWAY

❑ P-50000 [M]	Let the Good Times Roll	1967	40.00
❑ PS-50000 [S]	Let the Good Times Roll	1967	40.00

PHILADELPHIA INT'L.

❑ KZ33249 [B]	Keep Smilin'	1974	18.00
❑ PZ34267 [B]	My Music	1976	30.00
❑ KZ32589	That's How Long I'll Be Loving You	1974	18.00

SALSOUL

❑ SA-8531	Let It Snow	1980	15.00

SIGNATURES, THE

WARNER BROS.

❑ W1353 [M]	Prepare to Flip!	1959	30.00
❑ WS1353 [S]	Prepare to Flip!	1959	40.00
❑ W1250 [M]	The Signatures Sing In	1958	30.00
❑ WS1250 [S]	The Signatures Sing In	1958	40.00

WHIPPET

❑ WLP-702 [M]	The Signatures -- Their Voices and Instruments	1957	60.00

SIGNORELLI, FRANK

DAVIS

❑ JD-103 [M]	Piano Moods	1951	50.00

SIGUE SIGUE SPUTNIK

EMI

❑ E1-48700 [B]	Dress for Excess	1989	15.00

MANHATTAN

❑ ST-53033 [B]	Flaunt It	1986	15.00

SILHOUETTES, THE

GOODWAY

❑ GLP-100 [B]	The Silhouettes 1958-1968/ Get a Job	1968	500.00

SILK

ABC

❑ S-694	Smooth As Raw Silk	1969	30.00

SILKIE, THE

FONTANA

❑ MGF27548 [M]	You've Got to Hide Your Love Away	1965	80.00
— With full-color cover			
❑ MGF27548 [M]	You've Got to Hide Your Love Away	1965	60.00
— With purplish, black and white cover			
❑ SRF67548 [R]	You've Got to Hide Your Love Away	1965	50.00
— With full-color cover			
❑ SRF67548 [R]	You've Got to Hide Your Love Away	1965	40.00
— With purplish, black and white cover			

SILL, JUDEE

4 MEN WITH BEARDS

❑ 4M121LP [B]	Heart Food		25.00
❑ 4M120LP [B]	Judee Sill		25.00

SILLY SURFERS, THE

MERCURY

❑ MG-20977 [M]	The Sounds of the Silly Surfers	1965	80.00
❑ SR-60977 [S]	The Sounds of the Silly Surfers	1965	100.00

SILLY SURFERS, THE / THE WEIRD-OHS

HAIRY

❑ 101 [M]	The Sounds of the Silly Surfers/The Sounds of the Weird-Ohs	1964	150.00

SILVA, ALAN

CHIAROSCURO

❑ 2015	The Shout: Portrait for a Small Woman	197?	15.00

Number	Title	Yr	NM

ESP-DISK'

❑ 1091 [S] Alan Silva 1969 25.00

SILVA, MARCOS

CROSSOVER

❑ CR-5004 Here We Go 1987 12.00
❑ CR-5006 White and Black 1989 15.00

SILVEIRA, RICARDO

VERVE FORECAST

❑ 835054-1 Long Distance 1988 12.00
❑ 837696-1 Sky Light 1989 15.00

SILVER, HORACE

BLUE NOTE

❑ BLP-4017 [M] Blowin' the Blues Away 1959 300.00
—Deep groove" version; W. 63rd St. address on label
❑ BLP-4017 [M] Blowin' the Blues Away 1959 120.00
—Regular edition, W. 63rd St. address on label
❑ BLP-4017 [M] Blowin' the Blues Away 1963 40.00
—New York, USA" address on label
❑ BST-84017 [S] Blowin' the Blues Away 1959 120.00
—W. 63rd St. address on label
❑ BST-84017 [S] Blowin' the Blues Away 1963 40.00
—New York, USA" address on label
❑ BST-84017 [S] Blowin' the Blues Away 1967 30.00
—A Division of Liberty Records" on label
❑ BST-84017 Blowin' the Blues Away 1985 15.00
—The Finest in Jazz Since 1939" reissue
❑ BLP-4076 [M] Doin' the Thing at the Village Gate 1961 150.00
—W. 63rd St. address on label
❑ BLP-4076 [M] Doin' the Thing at the Village Gate 1963 80.00
—New York, USA" address on label
❑ BST-84076 [S] Doin' the Thing at the Village Gate 1961 120.00
—W. 63rd St. address on label
❑ BST-84076 [S] Doin' the Thing at the Village Gate 1963 80.00
—New York, USA" address on label
❑ BST-84076 [S] Doin' the Thing at the Village Gate 1967 30.00
—A Division of Liberty Records" on label
❑ B1-84076 Doin' the Thing at the Village Gate 1989 15.00
—The Finest in Jazz Since 1939" reissue
❑ BLP-4008 [M] Finger Poppin' 1959 400.00
—Deep groove" version; W. 63rd St. address on label
❑ BLP-4008 [M] Finger Poppin' 1959 120.00
—Regular edition, W. 63rd St. address on label
❑ BLP-4008 [M] Finger Poppin' 1963 40.00
—New York, USA" address on label
❑ BST-4008 [S] Finger Poppin' 1959 500.00
—Deep groove" version; W. 63rd St. address on label
❑ BST-4008 [S] Finger Poppin' 1959 100.00
—Regular edition, W. 63rd St. address on label
❑ BST-4008 [S] Finger Poppin' 1963 40.00
—New York, USA" address on label
❑ BST-84008 [S] Finger Poppin' 1967 25.00
—With "A Division of Liberty Records" on label
❑ B1-84008 Finger Poppin' 198? 15.00
—The Finest in Jazz Since 1939" reissue
❑ BLP-1589 [M] Further Explorations 1958 300.00
—Deep groove" version; W. 63rd St. address on label
❑ BLP-1589 [M] Further Explorations 1958 120.00
—Regular edition, W. 63rd St. address on label
❑ BLP-1589 [M] Further Explorations 1963 40.00
—New York, USA" address on label
❑ BST-1589 [S] Further Explorations 1959 150.00
—Deep groove" version; W. 63rd St. address on label
❑ BST-1589 [S] Further Explorations 1959 100.00
—Regular edition, W. 63rd St. address on label
❑ BST-1589 [S] Further Explorations 1963 40.00
—New York, USA" address on label
❑ BST-81589 [S] Further Explorations 1967 25.00
—With "A Division of Liberty Records" on label
❑ BLP-4042 [M] Horace-Scope 1960 400.00
—Deep groove" version; W. 63rd St. address on label
❑ BLP-4042 [M] Horace-Scope 1960 120.00
—Regular edition, W. 63rd St. address on label
❑ BLP-4042 [M] Horace-Scope 1963 40.00
—New York, USA" address on label
❑ BST-84042 [S] Horace-Scope 1960 120.00
—W. 63rd St. address on label
❑ BST-84042 [S] Horace-Scope 1963 40.00
—New York, USA" address on label
❑ BST-84042 [S] Horace-Scope 1967 30.00
—A Division of Liberty Records" on label
❑ BN-LA402-H2 Horace Silver 1975 30.00
❑ BLP-1518 [M] Horace Silver and the Jazz Messengers 1956 700.00
—Deep groove" version; Lexington Ave. address on label
❑ BLP-1518 [M] Horace Silver and the Jazz Messengers 1956 300.00
—Deep groove" edition, W. 63rd St. address on label
❑ BLP-1518 [M] Horace Silver and the Jazz Messengers 1963 50.00
—New York, USA" address on label
❑ BST-81518 [R] Horace Silver and the Jazz Messengers 1967 30.00
—A Division of Liberty Records" on label
❑ BST-81518 Horace Silver and the Jazz Messengers 1985 18.00
—The Finest in Jazz Since 1939" reissue
❑ BLP-5058 [10] Horace Silver Quintet 1955 700.00
❑ BLP-5062 [10] Horace Silver Quintet 1955 700.00
❑ BLP-5034 [10] Horace Silver Trio, Vol. 2 1954 800.00
❑ BLP-5018 [10] New Faces 1953 800.00
❑ BST-84420 Phase Three "All 1972 50.00
—A Division of United Artists Records" on blue and white label
❑ BST-84277 Serenade to a Soul Sister 1968 80.00
—A Division of Liberty Records" on label
❑ LWB-1033 Silver and Strings Play Music of the Spheres 1980 30.00
❑ BN-LA406-G Silver 'n' Brass 1975 25.00
❑ BN-LA853-H Silver 'n' Percussion 1978 18.00
❑ BN-LA708-G Silver 'n' Voices 1977 25.00
❑ BN-LA581-G Silver 'n' Wood 1976 30.00
❑ BLP-4131 [M] Silver's Serenade 1963 100.00
—New York, USA" on label
❑ BST-84131 [S] Silver's Serenade 1963 80.00
—New York, USA" address on label
❑ BST-84131 [S] Silver's Serenade 1967 30.00
—A Division of Liberty Records" on label
❑ BLP-1539 [M] Six Pieces of Silver 1957 600.00
—Deep groove" version; Lexington Ave. address on label
❑ BLP-1539 [M] Six Pieces of Silver 1957 200.00
—Deep groove" edition, W. 63rd St. address on label
❑ BLP-1539 [M] Six Pieces of Silver 1963 50.00
—New York, USA" address on label
❑ BST-81539 [R] Six Pieces of Silver 1967 25.00
—With "A Division of Liberty Records" on label
❑ B1-81539 Six Pieces of Silver 1988 15.00
—The Finest in Jazz Since 1939" reissue
❑ B1-46548 Song for My Father 1997 18.00
—Reissue on 180-gram vinyl
❑ BLP-4185 [M] Song for My Father (Cantiga Para Meu Pai) 1965 100.00
—New York, USA" on label
❑ BST-84185 [S] Song for My Father (Cantiga Para Meu Pai) 1965 70.00
—New York, USA" address on label
❑ BST-84185 [S] Song for My Father (Cantiga Para Meu Pai) 1967 30.00
—A Division of Liberty Records" on label
❑ BST-84185 Song for My Father (Cantiga Para Meu Pai) 1985 15.00
—The Finest in Jazz Since 1939" reissue
❑ BLP-1520 [M] Spotlight on Drums 1956 600.00
—Deep groove" version; Lexington Ave. address on label
❑ BLP-1520 [M] Spotlight on Drums 1956 300.00
—Deep groove" edition, W. 63rd St. address on label
❑ BLP-1520 [M] Spotlight on Drums 1963 50.00
—New York, USA" address on label
❑ BST-81520 [R] Spotlight on Drums 1967 25.00
—With "A Division of Liberty Records" on label
❑ BN-LA945-H Sterling Silver 1979 18.00
❑ BST-84352 That Healin' Feelin' (Phase 1) 1970 80.00
—A Division of Liberty Records" on label
❑ BST-84325 The Best of Horace Silver 1970 30.00
—A Division of Liberty Records" on label
❑ B1-91143 The Best of Horace Silver 1988 15.00
❑ B1-93206 The Best of Horace Silver, Vol. 2 1989 15.00
❑ BLP-4220 [M] The Cape Verdean Blues 1965 100.00
❑ BST-84220 [S] The Cape Verdean Blues 1965 70.00
—New York, USA" address on label
❑ BST-84220 [S] The Cape Verdean Blues 1967 30.00
—A Division of Liberty Records" on label
❑ B1-81520 The Horace Silver Trio 1989 15.00
—The Finest in Jazz Since 1939" reissue
❑ BLP-4250 [M] The Jody Grind 1966 80.00
—A Division of Liberty Records" on label
❑ BST-84250 [S] The Jody Grind 1966 60.00
—New York, USA" address on label
❑ BST-84250 [S] The Jody Grind 1967 30.00
—A Division of Liberty Records" on label
❑ BN-LA054-F The Pursuit of the 27th Man 1973 18.00
—Dark blue label with black stylized "b" at upper right
❑ BLP-1562 [M] The Stylings of Silver 1957 250.00
—Deep groove" version; W. 63rd St. address on label
❑ BLP-1562 [M] The Stylings of Silver 1957 120.00
—Regular edition, W. 63rd St. address on label
❑ BLP-1562 [M] The Stylings of Silver 1963 40.00
—New York, USA" address on label
❑ BST-1562 [S] The Stylings of Silver 1959 200.00
—Deep groove" version; W. 63rd St. address on label
❑ BST-1562 [S] The Stylings of Silver 1959 100.00
—Regular edition, W. 63rd St. address on label
❑ BST-1562 [S] The Stylings of Silver 1963 40.00
—New York, USA" address on label
❑ BST-81562 [S] The Stylings of Silver 1967 25.00
—With "A Division of Liberty Records" on label
❑ BLP-4110 [M] The Tokyo Blues 1962 100.00
—New York, USA" on label
❑ BST-84110 [S] The Tokyo Blues 1962 80.00
—New York, USA" address on label
❑ BST-84110 [S] The Tokyo Blues 1967 30.00
—A Division of Liberty Records" on label
❑ BST-84368 Total Response (Phase 2) 1971 100.00
❑ BST-84309 You Gotta Take a Little Love 1969 50.00
—A Division of Liberty Records" on label

EPIC

❑ LN3326 [M] Silver's Blue 1956 120.00
❑ LA16006 [M] Silver's Blue 1959 60.00
—Reissue with new cover
❑ BA17006 [R] Silver's Blue 196? 30.00

SILVER

ARISTA

❑ AL4076 Silver 1976 15.00

SILVER APPLES

KAPP

❑ KS-3584 [B] Contact 1969 40.00
❑ KS-3562 [B] Silver Apples 1968 40.00
—Add 1/3 if poster is enclosed

SILVER CONVENTION

MIDLAND INT'L.

❑ BKL1-1824 Madhouse 1976 12.00
❑ BKL1-1129 Save Me 1975 12.00
❑ BKL1-1369 Silver Convention 1976 12.00

MIDSONG INT'L.

❑ BKL1-2296 Golden Girls 1977 12.00
❑ BXL1-2296 Golden Girls 1978 10.00
—Reissue with new prefix
❑ BXL1-1824 Madhouse 1978 10.00
—Reissue with new prefix
❑ BXL1-1129 Save Me 1978 10.00
—Reissue with new prefix
❑ BXL1-1369 Silver Convention 1978 10.00
—Reissue with new prefix

SILVERHEAD

MCA

❑ MCA306 [B] Silverhead 1972 25.00
❑ MCA391 [B] Sixteen and Savaged 1973 25.00

SILVERS, PHIL

COLUMBIA

❑ CL1011 [M] Phil Silvers and the Swinging Brass 1957 50.00

HARMONY

❑ HL7170 [M] Bugle Calls for Big Band 196? 30.00

SILVERSTEIN, SHEL

ATLANTIC

❑ 8072 [M] Inside Folk Songs 1962 30.00
❑ SD8072 [S] Inside Folk Songs 1962 40.00

CADET

❑ LP4054 [M] Drain My Brain 1966 30.00
❑ LPS4054 [S] Drain My Brain 1966 30.00
❑ LP4052 [M] I'm So Good I Don't Have to Brag! 1965 30.00
❑ LPS4052 [S] I'm So Good I Don't Have to Brag! 1965 30.00

COLUMBIA

❑ FC40219 A Light in the Attic 1985 12.00
❑ KC31119 Freakin' at the Freakers' Ball 1972 18.00
❑ PC31119 Freakin' at the Freakers' Ball 1979 10.00
—Budget-line reissue
❑ FC39412 Where the Sidewalk Ends 1984 12.00
❑ 9C939611 [PD] Where the Sidewalk Ends 1984 30.00
—Picture disc

CRESTVIEW

❑ CRV804 [M] Stag Party 1963 30.00
❑ CRS7804 [S] Stag Party 1963 30.00

ELEKTRA

❑ EKL-176 [M] Hairy Jazz 1961 100.00
❑ EKS-7176 [S] Hairy Jazz 1961 150.00

FLYING FISH

❑ FF-211 Conch Train Robbery 1980 15.00

JANUS

❑ 2JLS3052 Crouching on the Outside 1973 18.00

PARACHUTE

❑ 20512 [DJ] Selected Cuts from Songs and Stories 1978 25.00
—Promo-only EP
❑ RRLP-9007 Songs and Stories 1978 15.00

RCA VICTOR

❑ LSP-4192 A Boy Named Sue (And His Other Country Songs) 1969 25.00

SIMEON, OMER

CONCERT HALL JAZZ

❑ 1014 [10] Clarinet A La Creole 195? 50.00

DISC

❑ DLP-748 [10] Omer Simeon Trio With James P. Johnson 195? 200.00

SIMEONE, HARRY, CHORALE

20TH CENTURY FOX

❑ TFM-3100 [M] The Little Drummer Boy 1963 15.00

Number	Title	Yr	NM

—Reissue of FOX-3002 with same contents
- TFS-3100 [S] — The Little Drummer Boy — 1963 — 18.00
—Same as above, but in stereo ("The Little Drummer Boy" is mono)
- T-580 — The Little Drummer Boy — 1978 — 12.00
—Another reissue of S 3100
- 3100 [M] — The Little Drummer Boy — 1966 — 12.00
—Reissue of TFM-3100 (distributed by ABC)
- S-3100 [S] — The Little Drummer Boy — 1966 — 15.00
—Reissue of TFS-3100 (distributed by ABC)

20TH FOX
- FOX-3002 [M] — Sing We Now of Christmas — 1959 — 30.00
—With no mention of "The Little Drummer Boy" at bottom of front cover
- FOX-3002 [M] — Sing We Now of Christmas — 1959 — 25.00
—With "The Little Drummer Boy" mentioned at bottom of front cover
- SFX-3002 [S] — Sing We Now of Christmas — 1959 — 25.00
—Sky blue label

DIPLOMAT
- XS1018 — The Little Drummer Boy — 196? — 15.00
—Abridged reissue of 20th Fox material

KAPP
- KL1450 [M] — The Little Drummer Boy — 1965 — 15.00
—With re-recording of the title song
- KS3450 [S] — The Little Drummer Boy — 1965 — 18.00

MERCURY
- MG20820 [M] — The Wonderful Songs of Christmas — 1963 — 18.00
- SR60820 [S] — The Wonderful Songs of Christmas — 1963 — 25.00

MISTLETOE
- MLP-1201 [S] — The Little Drummer Boy — 1973 — 10.00
—Reissue of TFS 3100 with same contents

SIMMONS, "JUMPIN'" GENE

HI
- HL2018 [M] — Jumpin' Gene Simmons — 1964 — 50.00
- SHL32018 [S] — Jumpin' Gene Simmons — 1964 — 70.00

SIMMONS, GENE

CASABLANCA
- NBLP7120 — Gene Simmons — 1978 — 25.00
- NBPIX7120 [PD] — Gene Simmons — 1978 — 70.00

SIMMONS, JEFF

REPRISE
- RS-6391 — Lucille Has Messed Up My Mind — 1969 — 30.00

STRAIGHT
- STS-1057 — Lucille Has Messed Up My Mind — 1969 — 80.00

SIMMONS, NORMAN

ARGO
- LP-607 [M] — Norman Simmons Trio — 1956 — 40.00

CREATIVE
- LP-607 [M] — Interpolations — 1956 — 80.00

MILLJAC
- MLP-1002 — I'm the Blues — 1981 — 18.00
- MLP-1001 — Midnight Creeper — 1979 — 18.00

SIMMONS, PATRICK

ELEKTRA
- 60225 — Arcade — 1983 — 12.00

SIMMONS, SONNY

ARHOOLIE
- 8003 [S] — Manhattan Egos — 1969 — 18.00

CONTEMPORARY
- S-7625/6 — Burning Spirits — 1970 — 25.00
- M-3623 [M] — Rumasuma — 1966 — 25.00
- S-7623 [S] — Rumasuma — 1966 — 30.00

ESP-DISK'
- 1043 [M] — Music from the Spheres — 1967 — 30.00
- S-1043 [S] — Music from the Spheres — 1967 — 25.00
- 1030 [M] — Sonny Simmons — 1966 — 25.00
- S-1030 [S] — Sonny Simmons — 1966 — 30.00

SIMON, ALAN

CADENCE JAZZ
- CJR-1027 — Rainsplash — 198? — 12.00

SIMON, CARLY

ARISTA
- AL-8443 — Coming Around Again — 1987 — 10.00
- AL-8526 — Greatest Hits Live — 1988 — 10.00
- AL-8650 — Have You Seen Me Lately? — 1990 — 15.00
- AL-8582 — My Romance — 1990 — 15.00

DIRECT DISK
- SD-16608 — Boys In the Trees — 1980 — 50.00
—Audiophile vinyl

ELEKTRA
- 7E-1064 — Another Passenger — 1976 — 12.00

Number	Title	Yr	NM

- EKS-75016 — Anticipation — 1971 — 15.00
- 6E-128 — Boys in the Trees — 1978 — 12.00
- EKS-74082 — Carly Simon — 1971 — 15.00
- EQ-4082 [Q] — Carly Simon — 1974 — 25.00
- 7E-1002 — Hotcakes — 1974 — 12.00
- EQ-1002 [Q] — Hotcakes — 1974 — 25.00
- EKS-75049 — No Secrets — 1972 — 15.00
—With lyrics on innersleeve
- EKS-75049 — No Secrets — 1973 — 12.00
—Without lyrics on innersleeve
- EQ-5049 [Q] — No Secrets — 1974 — 25.00
- 7E-1033 — Playing Possum — 1975 — 12.00
- EQ-1033 [Q] — Playing Possum — 1975 — 25.00
- 5E-506 — Spy — 1979 — 12.00
- 7E-1048 — The Best of Carly Simon — 1975 — 12.00
- EQ-1048 [Q] — The Best of Carly Simon — 1975 — 25.00
- 6E-109 — The Best of Carly Simon — 1977 — 10.00
—Reissue of 7E-1048

EPIC
- FE39970 — Spoiled Girl — 1985 — 12.00

WARNER BROS.
- BSK3443 — Come Upstairs — 1980 — 12.00
- 23886 — Hello Big Man — 1983 — 12.00
- BSK3592 — Torch — 1981 — 12.00

SIMON, FRANK

AUDIO LAB
- AL-1552 [M] — Four Star Hits — 1960 — 150.00

SIMON, FRED

WNDHAM HILL
- WH-1071 — Usually/Always — 1988 — 12.00

SIMON, JOE

BUDDAH
- BDS-7512 — Joe Simon — 1969 — 30.00

COMPLEAT
- 671015-1 — Mr. Right — 1985 — 15.00

POSSE
- 10003 — By Popular Demand — 1982 — 15.00
- 10002 — Glad You Came My Way — 1981 — 15.00

SOUND STAGE 7
- KZ31916 — Greatest Hits — 1972 — 15.00
- SSS-15008 — Joe Simon...Better Than Ever — 1969 — 30.00
- SSS-15004 — No Sad Songs — 1968 — 40.00
- SSM-5003 [M] — Pure Soul — 1967 — 30.00
- SSS-15003 [S] — Pure Soul — 1967 — 40.00
- SSS-15005 — Simon Sings — 1968 — 40.00
- SSS-15009 — The Best of Joe Simon — 1972 — 18.00
- SSS-15006 — The Chokin' Kind — 1969 — 30.00
- ZG33879 — The Chokin' Kind/Joe Simon...Better Than Ever — 1975 — 18.00
- 5000 — The World of Joe Simon — 197? — 15.00
—Reissue of 32536
- ZG32536 — The World of Joe Simon — 1974 — 18.00

SPRING
- SPR-6716 — Bad Case of Love — 1977 — 18.00
- SPR-5702 — Drowning in the Sea of Love — 1972 — 30.00
- SPR-6713 — Easy to Love — 1976 — 18.00
- SPR-6706 — Get Down — 1975 — 18.00
- SPR-6720 — Love Vibrations — 1979 — 18.00
- SPR-6702 — Mood, Heart and Soul — 1974 — 18.00
- SPR-5705 — Simon Country — 1973 — 18.00
- SPR-5704 — The Power of Joe Simon — 1973 — 30.00
- SPR-4701 — The Sounds of Simon — 1971 — 30.00
- SPR-6710 — Today — 1975 — 18.00

SIMON, PAUL

COLUMBIA
- C5X37581 [B] — Collected Works — 1981 — 80.00
—Contains his first four post-S&G solo albums plus the elusive "Paul Simon Songbook," otherwise unavailable in U.S.
- JC35032 — Greatest Hits, Etc. — 1977 — 12.00
- HC45032 [B] — Greatest Hits, Etc. — 1981 — 60.00
—Half-speed mastered edition
- KC30750 — Paul Simon — 1972 — 12.00
- CQ30750 [Q] — Paul Simon — 1974 — 40.00
- PC32855 — Paul Simon in Concert -- Live Rhymin' — 1974 — 12.00
- PC33540 — Still Crazy After All These Years — 1975 — 12.00
—Original release has no bar code on cover
- PCQ33540 [Q] — Still Crazy After All These Years — 1975 — 25.00
- HC43540 [B] — Still Crazy After All These Years — 1981 — 60.00
—Half-speed mastered edition
- PC33540 — Still Crazy After All These Years — 1980 — 10.00
—With bar code on cover
- KC32280 — There Goes Rhymin' Simon — 1973 — 12.00
- CQ32280 [Q] — There Goes Rhymin' Simon — 1974 — 40.00
- PC32280 — There Goes Rhymin' Simon — 1980 — 10.00

DCC COMPACT CLASSICS
- LPZ-2060 — Paul Simon — 1998 — 30.00
—Audiophile vinyl
- LPZ-2062 — There Goes Rhymin' Simon — 1998 — 30.00
—Audiophile vinyl

WARNER BROS.
- 25447 — Graceland — 1986 — 12.00

Number	Title	Yr	NM

- 23942 [DJ] — Hearts and Bones — 1983 — 25.00
—Promo only on Quiex II vinyl
- 23942 [DJ] — Hearts and Bones — 1983 — 25.00
—Promo only on Quiex II vinyl
- 23942 — Hearts and Bones — 1983 — 12.00
- 25789 — Negotiations and Love Songs — 1988 — 18.00
- HS3472 — One-Trick Pony — 1980 — 12.00
- 25588 — Paul Simon — 1988 — 15.00
- 25590 — Paul Simon in Concert -- Live Rhymin' — 1988 — 15.00
- 46814 — Songs from The Capeman — 1997 — 80.00
- 25591 — Still Crazy After All These Years — 1988 — 15.00
- 49982-1 — Surprise — 2006 — 18.00
- WBMS-140 [DJ] — The Paul Simon Interview Show — 1986 — 50.00
—Promo-only "Graceland"-era program in the "Warner Bros. Music Show" series
- 25589 — There Goes Rhymin' Simon — 1988 — 15.00
- 26098 — The Rhythm of the Saints — 1990 — 18.00

SIMON, RALPH

GRAMAVISION
- 8002 — Time Being — 1981 — 12.00

SIMON AND BARD

FLYING FISH
- FF-243 — Musaic — 1980 — 12.00
- FF-262 — Tear It Up — 1982 — 12.00
- FF-321 — The Enormous Radio — 198? — 12.00

SIMON AND GARFUNKEL

CBS
- KCS9914 — Bridge Over Troubled Water — 1970 — 18.00
—360 Sound Stereo" on label; pressed in U.S. for export

COLUMBIA
- KCS9529 [M] — Bookends — 1968 — 30.00
—White label "Special Mono Radio Station Copy"
- KCS9529 [S] — Bookends — 1968 — 15.00
—360 Sound Stereo" on label; add 25% for poster
- KCS9529 [S] — Bookends — 1970 — 12.00
—Orange label
- PC9529 [S] — Bookends — 197? — 10.00
—Budget-line reissue
- KCL2729 [M] — Bookends — 1968 — 100.00
—Red label, "Mono" at bottom
- KCS9914 — Bridge Over Troubled Water — 1970 — 15.00
—360 Sound Stereo" on label
- KCS9914 — Bridge Over Troubled Water — 1970 — 12.00
—Orange label
- PC9914 — Bridge Over Troubled Water — 198? — 10.00
—Budget-line reissue
- HC49914 — Bridge Over Troubled Water — 1982 — 30.00
—Half-speed mastered edition
- CQ30995 [Q] — Bridge Over Troubled Water — 1971 — 30.00
- JC9914 — Bridge Over Troubled Water — 197? — 10.00
—Reissue with new prefix
- KCS9914 — Bridge Over Troubled Water — 2000 — 30.00
—Classic Records reissue on audiophile vinyl
- PCQ30995 [Q] — Bridge Over Troubled Water — 1974 — 30.00
—Reissue with new prefix; possibly the only difference between this and the original is a sticker on the cover with the new number
- C5X37587 — Collected Works — 1981 — 40.00
- CL2563 [M] — Parsley, Sage, Rosemary and Thyme — 1966 — 25.00
- CS9363 [S] — Parsley, Sage, Rosemary and Thyme — 1966 — 18.00
—360 Sound Stereo" on label
- CS9363 [S] — Parsley, Sage, Rosemary and Thyme — 1970 — 12.00
—Orange label
- PC9363 [S] — Parsley, Sage, Rosemary and Thyme — 197? — 10.00
—Budget-line reissue
- KC31350 — Simon and Garfunkel's Greatest Hits — 1972 — 15.00
—Original covers are slightly oversized
- JC31350 — Simon and Garfunkel's Greatest Hits — 197? — 10.00
—Reissue with new prefix
- HC41350 — Simon and Garfunkel's Greatest Hits — 1982 — 30.00
—Half-speed mastered edition
- CS9269 [S] — Sounds of Silence — 1970 — 12.00
—Orange label
- CL2469 [M] — Sounds of Silence — 1966 — 30.00
—With "Simon and Garfunkel" and "Sounds of Silence" in all capital letters on front cover with no list of songs
- CL2469 [M] — Sounds of Silence — 1966 — 25.00
—With "Simon and Garfunkel" and "Sounds of Silence" in large upper and lowercase letters on front cover with all song titles listed; "Tiger Beat" magazine is pictured twice on back cover
- CS9269 [S] — Sounds of Silence — 1966 — 30.00
—With "Simon and Garfunkel" and "Sounds of Silence" in all capital letters on front cover with no list of songs
- CS9269 [S] — Sounds of Silence — 1966 — 25.00
—With "Simon and Garfunkel" and "Sounds of Silence" in large upper and lowercase letters on front cover with all song titles listed; "Tiger Beat" magazine is pictured twice on back cover

Number	Title	Yr	NM
❑ PC9269 [S]	Sounds of Silence	198?	10.00
—Budget-line reissue			
❑ JC9269	Sounds of Silence	197?	10.00
—Reissue with new prefix			
❑ CL2469 [M]	Sounds of Silence	1966	25.00
—With "Simon and Garfunkel" and "Sounds of Silence" in large upper and lowercase letters on front cover with all song titles listed; "Tiger Beat" magazines on back cover are airbrushed out			
❑ CS9269 [S]	Sounds of Silence	1966	15.00
—With "Simon and Garfunkel" and "Sounds of Silence" in large upper and lowercase letters on front cover with all song titles listed; "Tiger Beat" magazines on back cover are airbrushed out			
❑ CL2249 [M]	Wednesday Morning, 3 A.M.	1964	30.00
—Guaranteed High Fidelity" on label			
❑ CL2249 [M]	Wednesday Morning, 3 A.M.	1965	25.00
—Mono" on label			
❑ CS9049 [S]	Wednesday Morning, 3 A.M.	1964	30.00
—360 Sound Stereo" in black on label			
❑ CS9049 [S]	Wednesday Morning, 3 A.M.	1965	18.00
—360 Sound Stereo" in white on label			
❑ CS9049 [S]	Wednesday Morning, 3 A.M.	1970	12.00
—Orange label			
❑ PC9049 [S]	Wednesday Morning, 3 A.M.	197?	10.00
—Budget-line reissue			

MOBILE FIDELITY

Number	Title	Yr	NM
❑ 1-173	Bridge Over Troubled Water	198?	40.00
—Audiophile vinyl			

PICKWICK

Number	Title	Yr	NM
❑ PC-3059 [M]	The Hit Sounds of Simon and Garfunkel	1966	60.00
❑ SPC-3059 [R]	The Hit Sounds of Simon and Garfunkel	1966	30.00

SEARS

Number	Title	Yr	NM
❑ SPS-435	Simon and Garfunkel	196?	30.00

TEE VEE

Number	Title	Yr	NM
❑ TV-2002 [B]	The Complete Collection	1980	80.00
—Alternate number is Columbia Special Products P5-15333; also contains solo material by both Paul Simon and Art Garfunkel, plus a rare true stereo mix of "You Don't Know Where Your Interest Lies			

WARNER BROS.

Number	Title	Yr	NM
❑ 2BSK3654	The Concert in Central Park	1982	15.00

SIMON SISTERS, THE

COLUMBIA

Number	Title	Yr	NM
❑ CC24506	The Lobster Quadrille	1969	25.00
—Special edition with booklet			
❑ CR21525 [B]	The Lobster Quadrille	1969	25.00
❑ CR21539	The Simon Sisters Sing for Children	1972	18.00

KAPP

Number	Title	Yr	NM
❑ KL-1397 [M]	Cuddlebug	1964	40.00
❑ KS-3397 [S]	Cuddlebug	1964	50.00
❑ KL-1359 [M]	Winkin', Blinkin' and Nod	1964	30.00
❑ KS-3359 [S]	Winkin', Blinkin' and Nod	1964	40.00

SIMONE, NINA

ACCORD

Number	Title	Yr	NM
❑ SN-7108	In Concert	1981	12.00

BETHLEHEM

Number	Title	Yr	NM
❑ BCP-6028 [M]	Jazz As Played in an Exclusive Side Street Club	1959	80.00
❑ SBCP-6028 [S]	Jazz As Played in an Exclusive Side Street Club	1959	100.00
❑ BCP-6041 [M]	Nina Simone and Her Friends	1960	40.00
❑ SBCP-6041 [S]	Nina Simone and Her Friends	1960	50.00
—With Carmen McRae and Chris Connor			
❑ BCP-6003	Nina Simone's Finest	197?	15.00
❑ BCP-6028 [M]	The Original Nina Simone	1961	30.00
—Retitled reissue			
❑ SBCP-6028 [S]	The Original Nina Simone	1961	40.00
—Retitled reissue			

CANYON

Number	Title	Yr	NM
❑ 7705	Gifted and Black	1971	18.00

COLPIX

Number	Title	Yr	NM
❑ CP-465 [M]	Folksy Nina	1964	30.00
❑ SCP-465 [S]	Folksy Nina	1964	30.00
❑ CP-419 [M]	Forbidden Fruit	1961	30.00
❑ SCP-419 [S]	Forbidden Fruit	1961	30.00
❑ CP-412 [M]	Nina at Newport	1960	30.00
❑ SCP-412 [S]	Nina at Newport	1960	30.00
❑ CP-409 [M]	Nina at Town Hall	1960	30.00
❑ SCP-409 [S]	Nina at Town Hall	1960	30.00
❑ CP-443 [M]	Nina's Choice	1963	30.00
❑ SCP-443 [S]	Nina's Choice	1963	30.00
❑ CP-455 [M]	Nina Simone at Carnegie Hall	1963	30.00
❑ SCP-455 [S]	Nina Simone at Carnegie Hall	1963	30.00
❑ CP-421 [M]	Nina Simone at the Village Gate	1961	30.00
❑ SCP-421 [S]	Nina Simone at the Village Gate	1961	30.00
❑ CP-425 [M]	Nina Sings Ellington	1962	30.00
❑ SCP-425 [S]	Nina Sings Ellington	1962	30.00
❑ CP-496 [M]	Nina with Strings	1966	30.00
❑ SCP-496 [S]	Nina with Strings	1966	30.00
❑ CP-407 [M]	The Amazing Nina Simone	1959	30.00
❑ SCP-407 [S]	The Amazing Nina Simone	1959	30.00

CTI

Number	Title	Yr	NM
❑ 7084	Baltimore	1978	15.00

PHILIPS

Number	Title	Yr	NM
❑ PHM200148 [M]	Broadway...Blues...Ballads	1964	18.00
❑ PHS600148 [S]	Broadway...Blues...Ballads	1964	25.00
❑ PHM200172 [M]	I Put a Spell on You	1965	18.00
❑ PHS600172 [S]	I Put a Spell on You	1965	25.00
❑ PHM200202 [M]	Let It All Out	1966	18.00
❑ PHS600202 [S]	Let It All Out	1966	25.00
❑ PHM200135 [M]	Nina Simone In Concert	1964	18.00
❑ PHS600135 [S]	Nina Simone In Concert	1964	25.00
❑ PHM200187 [M]	Pastel Blues	1965	18.00
❑ PHS600187 [S]	Pastel Blues	1965	25.00
❑ PHS600298	The Best of Nina Simone	1969	25.00
❑ 822846-1	The Best of Nina Simone	198?	12.00
❑ PHM200219 [M]	The High Priestess of Soul	1967	18.00
❑ PHS600219 [S]	The High Priestess of Soul	1967	25.00
❑ PHM200207 [M]	Wild Is the Wind	1966	18.00
❑ PHS600207 [S]	Wild Is the Wind	1966	25.00

PM

Number	Title	Yr	NM
❑ 018	A Very Rare Evening	1979	15.00

QUINTESSENCE

Number	Title	Yr	NM
❑ 25421	Silk and Soul	1979	12.00

RCA VICTOR

Number	Title	Yr	NM
❑ LSP-4248	Black Gold	1970	18.00
❑ LSP-4757	Emergency Ward!	1972	18.00
❑ LSP-4536	Here Comes the Sun	1971	18.00
❑ AFL1-4536	Here Comes the Sun	1977	12.00
—Reissue with new prefix			
❑ APL1-0241	It Is Finished -- Nina 1974	1974	15.00
❑ AFL1-0241	It Is Finished -- Nina 1974	1977	12.00
—Reissue with new prefix			
❑ LSP-4102	Nina Simone and Piano	1968	18.00
❑ LPM-3789 [M]	Nina Simone Sings the Blues	1967	30.00
❑ LSP-3789 [S]	Nina Simone Sings the Blues	1967	18.00
❑ LSP-4065	'Nuff Said	1968	18.00
❑ APL1-1788	Poets	1976	15.00
❑ AFL1-1788	Poets	1977	12.00
—Reissue with new prefix			
❑ LPM-3837 [M]	Silk and Soul	1967	30.00
❑ LSP-3837 [S]	Silk and Soul	1967	18.00
❑ LSP-4374	The Best of Nina Simone	1970	18.00
❑ AFL1-4374	The Best of Nina Simone	1977	12.00
—Reissue with new prefix			
❑ LSP-4152	To Love Somebody	1969	18.00

SALSOUL

Number	Title	Yr	NM
❑ SA-8546	Little Girl Blue	1982	12.00

TRIP

Number	Title	Yr	NM
❑ 8021	Black Is the Color	1973	15.00
❑ 8020	Live in Europe	1973	15.00
❑ 9521	Portrait	197?	12.00

VERVE

Number	Title	Yr	NM
❑ 831437-1	Let It Be Me	1987	12.00

SIMONE

COLUMBIA

Number	Title	Yr	NM
❑ FC44275	Vicio	1988	15.00

SIMPKINS, ANDY, AND DAVE MACKAY

STUDIO 7

Number	Title	Yr	NM
❑ 403	Happying	197?	15.00

SIMPLE MINDS

A&M

Number	Title	Yr	NM
❑ R209526	Live in the City of Light	1987	25.00
—BMG Direct Marketing edition			
❑ SP-6850	Live in the City of Light	1987	18.00
❑ SP-6-4928	New Gold Dream (81-82-83-84)	1982	15.00
—Originals have gold and purple marbled vinyl			
❑ R142320	Once Upon a Time	1985	15.00
—RCA Music Service edition; has front and back covers reversed			
❑ SP-5092	Once Upon a Time	1985	10.00
❑ SP-6-4981	Sparkle in the Rain	1984	12.00
❑ R101142	Street Fighting Years	1989	15.00
—BMG Direct Marketing edition			
❑ SP-3927	Street Fighting Years	1989	12.00

PVC

Number	Title	Yr	NM
❑ 7910	Life in a Day	1979	25.00

STIFF

Number	Title	Yr	NM
❑ TEES-102	Themes for Great Cities	1982	18.00

VIRGIN

Number	Title	Yr	NM
❑ 90858	Life in a Day	1988	12.00
—Reissue of PVC 7910			
❑ 90859	Real to Real Cacophony	1988	12.00
—First U.S. edition of early LP			
❑ 90610	Sister Feelings Call	1987	12.00
—First U.S. issue of LP originally released in 1981			

SIMPLY RED

ELEKTRA

Number	Title	Yr	NM
❑ R101012	A New Flame	1989	15.00
—BMG Direct Marketing edition			
❑ 60828	A New Flame	1989	12.00
❑ R152858	Men and Women	1987	12.00
—RCA Music Service edition			
❑ 60727	Men and Women	1987	10.00
❑ R153936	Picture Book	1985	12.00
—RCA Music Service edition			
❑ 60452	Picture Book	1985	10.00
❑ ED5236 [DJ]	Simply Red Billboard Interview	1989	40.00
—Nelson George interviews Mick Hucknall and Lamont Dozier; promo-only			
❑ ED5236 [DJ]	Simply Red Interview	1989	30.00
—Nelson George interviews Mick Hucknall and Lamont Dozier; promo-only			

SIMPSON, CAROLE

CAPITOL

Number	Title	Yr	NM
❑ T878 [M]	All About Carole	1957	80.00

TOPS

Number	Title	Yr	NM
❑ L-1732 [M]	Singin' and Swingin'	1960	30.00

SIMPSON, CASS

ABC-PARAMOUNT

Number	Title	Yr	NM
❑ ABC-103 [M]	Cass Simpson	1956	40.00

SIMPSON, RED

CAPITOL

Number	Title	Yr	NM
❑ T2829 [M]	A Bakersfield Dozen	1967	30.00
❑ ST2829 [S]	A Bakersfield Dozen	1967	25.00
❑ ST-11231	A Trucker's Christmas	1973	18.00
❑ ST-881	I'm a Truck	1972	18.00
❑ T2468 [M]	Roll, Truck, Roll	1966	18.00
❑ ST2468 [S]	Roll, Truck, Roll	1966	25.00
❑ T2569 [M]	The Man Behind the Badge	1966	18.00
❑ ST2569 [S]	The Man Behind the Badge	1966	25.00
❑ ST-11093	The Very Real Red Simpson	1973	18.00
❑ T2691 [M]	Truck Drivin' Fool	1967	25.00
❑ ST2691 [S]	Truck Drivin' Fool	1967	25.00

PORTLAND

Number	Title	Yr	NM
❑ 1005 [M]	Hello, I'm a Truck	1965	80.00

SEA SHELL

Number	Title	Yr	NM
❑ 16253	Ramblin' Road	198?	15.00

SIMPSON, VALERIE

TAMLA

Number	Title	Yr	NM
❑ T6-351	Keep It Comin'	1977	15.00
❑ T317	Valerie Simpson	1972	18.00
❑ T311	Valerie Simpson Exposed	1971	18.00

SIMPSONS, THE

GEFFEN

Number	Title	Yr	NM
❑ GHS24308	The Simpsons Sing the Blues	1990	30.00

SIMS, FRANKIE LEE

SPECIALTY

Number	Title	Yr	NM
❑ SPS-2124	Lucy Mae Blues	1970	40.00

SIMS, ZOOT, AND BUDDY RICH

QUINTESSENCE

Number	Title	Yr	NM
❑ 25041	Air Mail Special	197?	15.00

SIMS, ZOOT, AND HARRY "SWEETS" EDISON

FANTASY

Number	Title	Yr	NM
❑ OJC-499	Just Friends	1991	15.00

PABLO

Number	Title	Yr	NM
❑ 2310841	Just Friends	198?	12.00

SIMS, ZOOT, AND JIMMY ROWLES

PABLO

Number	Title	Yr	NM
❑ 2310803	Lucky	1977	15.00

SIMS, ZOOT; JIMMY RANEY; JIM HALL

MAINSTREAM

Number	Title	Yr	NM
❑ MRL-358	Otra Vez	1972	15.00
❑ 56013 [M]	Two Jims and Zoot	1965	25.00
❑ S-6013 [S]	Two Jims and Zoot	1965	30.00

SIMS, ZOOT; TONY SCOTT; AL COHN

JAZZLAND

Number	Title	Yr	NM
❑ JLP-11 [M]	East Coast Sounds	1960	40.00
❑ JLP-911 [S]	East Coast Sounds	1960	40.00

SIMS, ZOOT

ABC IMPULSE!

Number	Title	Yr	NM
❑ AS-9131 [S]	The Waiting Game	1968	30.00
—Black label with red ring			

ABC-PARAMOUNT

Number	Title	Yr	NM
❑ ABC-155 [M]	Zoot Sims Plays Alto, Tenor and Baritone	1957	80.00
❑ ABC-198 [M]	Zoot Sims Plays Four Altos	1957	80.00

ARGO

Number	Title	Yr	NM
❑ LP-608 [M]	Zoot	1956	120.00
—Color cover			

Number	Title	Yr	NM
❏ LP-608 [M]	Zoot	1957	80.00
—Black and white cover			
BETHLEHEM			
❏ BCP-6027	Down Home	197?	25.00
—Reissue, distributed by RCA Victor			
❏ BCP-6051 [M]	Down Home	1960	200.00
❏ SBCP-6051 [S]	Down Home	1960	150.00
BIOGRAPH			
❏ 12062	One to Blow On	198?	12.00
CADET			
❏ LP-608 [M]	Zoot	1966	25.00
—Fading blue label			
CHOICE			
❏ 1006	Party	197?	18.00
CLASSIC JAZZ			
❏ 21	Zoot Sims and Bucky Pizzarelli	197?	15.00
COLPIX			
❏ CP-435 [M]	New Beat Bossa Nova	1962	40.00
❏ SCP-435 [S]	New Beat Bossa Nova	1962	50.00
❏ CP-437 [M]	New Beat Bossa Nova, Volume 2	1962	40.00
❏ SCP-437 [S]	New Beat Bossa Nova, Volume 2	1962	50.00
DAWN			
❏ DLP-1102 [M]	The Modern Art of Jazz	1956	120.00
❏ DLP-1115 [M]	Zoot Sims Goes to Jazzville	1957	120.00
DISCOVERY			
❏ DL-3015 [10]	The Zoot Sims Quartet In Paris	1951	250.00
FAMOUS DOOR			
❏ HL-2000	At Ease	197?	18.00
FANTASY			
❏ OJC-444	The Gershwin Brothers	1990	18.00
❏ OJC-228	Zoot!	198?	15.00
❏ OJC-242	Zoot Sims Quartets	1987	15.00
GROOVE MERCHANT			
❏ 533	Nirvana	197?	18.00
IMPULSE!			
❏ A-9131 [M]	The Waiting Game	1967	50.00
❏ AS-9131 [S]	The Waiting Game	1967	30.00
JAZZLAND			
❏ JLP-2 [M]	Zoot Sims Quintet	1960	40.00
❏ JLP-92 [S]	Zoot Sims Quintet	1960	30.00
MCA			
❏ 29069	Zoot Sims Plays Four Altos	1980	12.00
NEW JAZZ			
❏ NJLP-8280 [M]	Good Old Zoot	1962	50.00
❏ NJLP-1102 [10]	Zoot Sims in Hollywood	1954	300.00
PABLO			
❏ 2310783	Hawthorne Nights	197?	15.00
❏ 2310868	I Wish I Were Twins	198?	12.00
❏ 2310903	Quietly There	198?	12.00
❏ 2310770	Soprano Sax	197?	15.00
❏ 2310898	Suddenly It's Spring	198?	12.00
❏ 2310861	Swinger	198?	12.00
❏ 2405406	The Best of Zoot Sims	198?	12.00
❏ 2310744	The Gershwin Brothers	197?	15.00
❏ 2310872	The Innocent Years	198?	12.00
❏ 2310831	Warm Tenor	1979	15.00
PABLO TODAY			
❏ 2312120	Zoot Sims Plays Duke Ellington/Passion Flower	1980	15.00
PACIFIC JAZZ			
❏ PJ-20 [M]	Choice	1961	40.00
PRESTIGE			
❏ PRST-7817	First Recordings!	1970	18.00
❏ PRLP-117 [10]	Swingin' with Zoot Sims	1951	300.00
❏ PRLP-118 [10]	Tenor Sax Favorites	1951	300.00
❏ PRLP-16009 [M]	Trotting	1963	60.00
❏ P-24061	Zootcase	197?	25.00
❏ PRLP-138 [10]	Zoot Sims All Stars	1953	300.00
❏ PRLP-7026 [M]	Zoot Sims Quartets	1956	200.00
—Yellow label with W. 50th St. address			
❏ PRLP-202 [10]	Zoot Sims Quintet	1955	250.00
RIVERSIDE			
❏ 6103	Zoot	197?	15.00
❏ RLP 12-228 [M]	Zoot!	1957	100.00
SEECO			
❏ CELP-452 [M]	The Modern Art of Jazz	1960	40.00
❏ CELP-4520 [S]	The Modern Art of Jazz	1960	40.00
STATUS			
❏ ST-8280 [M]	Good Old Zoot	1965	40.00
❏ ST-8309 [M]	Koo Koo	1965	40.00
SWING			
❏ SW-8417	Zoot Sims in Paris	1987	12.00
TRIP			
❏ 5548	You 'n Me	197?	12.00
UNITED ARTISTS			
❏ UAL-4040 [M]	A Night at the Half Note	1959	40.00
❏ UAS-5040 [S]	A Night at the Half Note	1959	50.00
❏ UAJ-14013 [M]	Zoot Sims in Paris	1962	40.00
❏ UAJS-15013 [S]	Zoot Sims in Paris	1962	50.00

Number	Title	Yr	NM
ZIM			
❏ 1008	Nash-ville	198?	12.00

SIN SAY SHUNS, THE

Number	Title	Yr	NM
VENETT			
❏ V-940 [M]	I'll Be There	1966	40.00
❏ VS-940 [S]	I'll Be There	1966	50.00

SINATRA, FRANK

Number	Title	Yr	NM
BOOK-OF-THE-MONTH			
❏ (# unknown)	Tommy Dorsey/Frank Sinatra: The Complete Sessions	1983	100.00
CAPITOL			
❏ W894 [M]	A Jolly Christmas from Frank Sinatra	1957	40.00
—Original mono with gray label			
❏ W894 [M]	A Jolly Christmas from Frank Sinatra	1958	30.00
—Black colorband label, logo at left			
❏ W1538 [M]	All the Way	1961	25.00
❏ SW1538 [S]	All the Way	1961	30.00
❏ SN-16205	All the Way	198?	10.00
—Budget-line reissue			
❏ W803 [M]	A Swingin' Affair!	1957	30.00
—Gray label			
❏ W803 [M]	A Swingin' Affair!	1957	25.00
—Black label with colorband			
❏ DW803 [R]	A Swingin' Affair!	196?	15.00
❏ SM-11502	A Swingin' Affair!	1976	12.00
❏ W789 [M]	Close to You	1957	30.00
—Gray label			
❏ W789 [M]	Close to You	1959	25.00
—Black label with colorband			
❏ DW789 [R]	Close to You	196?	15.00
❏ DWBB-254 [R]	Close-Up	1969	25.00
—Reissue in one package of "This Is Sinatra" and "This Is Sinatra, Volume Two			
❏ W1069 [M]	Come Dance with Me!	1959	25.00
❏ SW1069 [S]	Come Dance with Me!	1959	30.00
❏ SN-16203	Come Dance with Me!	198?	10.00
—Budget-line reissue			
❏ W920 [M]	Come Fly with Me	1958	40.00
—Gray label			
❏ W920 [M]	Come Fly with Me	1959	25.00
—Black label with colorband			
❏ SW920 [S]	Come Fly with Me	1959	30.00
❏ SM-920	Come Fly with Me	197?	10.00
❏ SM-11801	Come Swing with Me	1978	12.00
❏ W1594 [M]	Come Swing with Me!	1961	25.00
❏ SW1594 [S]	Come Swing with Me!	1961	30.00
❏ C1-89611	Duets	1993	25.00
❏ T2602 [M]	Forever Frank	1966	25.00
❏ DT2602 [R]	Forever Frank	1966	15.00
❏ T735 [M]	Frank Sinatra Conducts Tone Poems of Color	1956	60.00
—Turquoise label			
❏ T735 [M]	Frank Sinatra Conducts Tone Poems of Color	1959	40.00
—Black label with colorband			
❏ PRO-2974/5 [DJ]	Frank Sinatra Minute Masters	1965	40.00
—Edited version of 20 songs			
❏ DKAO-374 [R]	Frank Sinatra's Greatest Hits	1969	15.00
❏ W1053 [M]	Frank Sinatra Sings for Only the Lonely	1958	40.00
—Gray label			
❏ W1053 [M]	Frank Sinatra Sings for Only the Lonely	1959	25.00
—Black label with colorband			
❏ SW1053 [S]	Frank Sinatra Sings for Only the Lonely	1959	30.00
—Originals do not include "It's a Lonesome Old Town" and "Spring Is Here			
❏ SW1053 [S]	Frank Sinatra Sings for Only the Lonely	196?	30.00
—Later releases restore "It's a Lonesome Old Town" and "Spring Is Here			
❏ SN-16202	Frank Sinatra Sings for Only the Lonely	198?	10.00
—Budget-line reissue			
❏ W581 [M]	In the Wee Small Hours	1955	40.00
—Gray label original			
❏ W581 [M]	In the Wee Small Hours	1959	30.00
—Black label with colorband			
❏ DW581 [R]	In the Wee Small Hours	196?	15.00
❏ SM-581	In the Wee Small Hours	197?	10.00
❏ H1-581 [10]	In the Wee Small Hours, Part 1	1955	100.00
❏ H2-581 [10]	In the Wee Small Hours, Part 2	1955	100.00
❏ W1164 [M]	Look to Your Heart	1959	30.00
❏ DW1164 [R]	Look to Your Heart	196?	15.00
❏ N-16148	Look to Your Heart	198?	10.00
—Budget-line reissue			
❏ N-16112	My One and Only Love	198?	10.00
—Budget-line reissue			
❏ STBB-724	My One and Only Love/ Sentimental Journey	1971	18.00
❏ W1417 [M]	Nice 'N' Easy	1960	25.00

Number	Title	Yr	NM
❏ SW1417 [S]	Nice 'N' Easy	1960	30.00
❏ SN-16204	Nice 'N' Easy	198?	10.00
—Budget-line reissue			
❏ W1221 [M]	No One Cares	1959	25.00
❏ SW1221 [S]	No One Cares	1959	30.00
❏ SM-1221	No One Cares	197?	10.00
❏ ST-11309	One More for the Road	1973	12.00
❏ W1676 [M]	Point of No Return	1962	25.00
❏ SW1676 [S]	Point of No Return	1962	30.00
❏ SM-1676	Point of No Return	197?	10.00
❏ SABB-11367 [P]	Round #1	1974	18.00
❏ PRO-2163/4/5/6 [DJ]	Selections from Sinatra, The Great Years	1962	40.00
❏ W90986 [M]	Sentimental Journey	1966	30.00
—Capitol Record Club issue			
❏ DW90986 [R]	Sentimental Journey	1966	18.00
—Capitol Record Club issue			
❏ SN-16113	Sentimental Journey	198?	10.00
—Budget-line reissue			
❏ WCO1762 [M]	Sinatra, The Great Years	1962	30.00
❏ SWCO1762 [S]	Sinatra, The Great Years	1962	40.00
❏ W1729 [M]	Sinatra Sings…Of Love and Things	1962	25.00
❏ SW1729 [P]	Sinatra Sings…Of Love and Things	1962	25.00
❏ SN-16149	Sinatra Sings…Of Love and Things	198?	10.00
—Budget-line reissue			
❏ W1825 [M]	Sinatra Sings Rodgers and Hart	1963	25.00
❏ DW1825 [R]	Sinatra Sings Rodgers and Hart	1963	15.00
❏ STBB-95191	Sinatra Sings the Great Ones	1973	25.00
—Longines Symphonette (formerly Capitol) Record Club issue			
❏ W2301 [M]	Sinatra Sings the Select Cole Porter	1965	25.00
❏ DW2301 [R]	Sinatra Sings the Select Cole Porter	1965	15.00
❏ T2123 [M]	Sinatra Sings the Select Harold Arlen	1964	100.00
—Only released in Canada, Australia and the UK			
❏ W1994 [M]	Sinatra Sings the Select Johnny Mercer	1963	25.00
❏ DW1994 [R]	Sinatra Sings the Select Johnny Mercer	1963	15.00
❏ W1491 [M]	Sinatra's Swingin' Session!!!	1961	25.00
❏ SW1491 [S]	Sinatra's Swingin' Session!!!	1961	30.00
❏ SM-1491	Sinatra's Swingin' Session!!!	197?	10.00
❏ W653 [M]	Songs for Swingin' Lovers!	1956	50.00
—Gray label; cover has Sinatra facing away from the embracing couple			
❏ W653 [M]	Songs for Swingin' Lovers!	1956	40.00
—Gray label; cover has Sinatra facing toward the embracing couple			
❏ W653 [M]	Songs for Swingin' Lovers!	1959	30.00
—Black label with colorband			
❏ DW653 [R]	Songs for Swingin' Lovers!	196?	15.00
❏ SM-653	Songs for Swingin' Lovers!	197?	10.00
❏ DQBO91261 [R]	Songs for the Young at Heart	196?	30.00
—Capitol Record Club issue			
❏ H488 [10]	Songs for Young Lovers	1954	60.00
❏ W1432 [M]	Songs for Young Lovers	1960	25.00
❏ DW1432 [R]	Songs for Young Lovers	1960	15.00
❏ H528 [10]	Swing Easy	1954	60.00
❏ W1429 [M]	Swing Easy	1960	25.00
❏ DW1429 [R]	Swing Easy	1960	15.00
❏ W587 [M]	Swing Easy/Songs for Young Lovers	1955	40.00
—Gray label original; 12-inch version of two 10-inch LPs			
❏ W587 [M]	Swing Easy/Songs for Young Lovers	1959	30.00
—Black label with colorband			
❏ T1919 [M]	Tell Her You Love Her	1963	25.00
❏ DT1919 [R]	Tell Her You Love Her	1963	15.00
❏ DKAO2900 [R]	The Best of Frank Sinatra	1968	18.00
❏ SN-16109	The Best of Frank Sinatra	198?	10.00
—Budget-line reissue			
❏ C1-94777	The Capitol Years	1990	100.00
—With book and wraparound banner. Only 5,000 were pressed			

Number	Title	Yr	NM
❑ TFL2814 [M]	The Frank Sinatra Deluxe Set	1968	100.00
❑ STFL2814 [P]	The Frank Sinatra Deluxe Set	1968	60.00
❑ T2036 [M]	The Greatest Hits of Frank Sinatra	1964	25.00
❑ DT2036 [R]	The Greatest Hits of Frank Sinatra	1964	15.00
❑ T2700 [M]	The Movie Songs	1967	25.00
❑ DT2700 [R]	The Movie Songs	1967	15.00
❑ SN-16111	The Night We Called It a Day	198?	10.00
—Budget-line reissue			
❑ T894 [M]	The Sinatra Christmas Album	196?	25.00
—Reissue of A Jolly Christmas with Frank Sinatra with same contents; some copies have this cover and "A Jolly Christmas" labels			
❑ SM-894 [R]	The Sinatra Christmas Album	197?	10.00
—Reissue in rechanneled stereo; any color label			
❑ DT894 [R]	The Sinatra Christmas Album	196?	12.00
—Rechanneled reissue of A Jolly Christmas with Frank Sinatra with same contents; some copies have this cover and "A Jolly Christmas" labels			
❑ DNFR7630 [P]	The Sinatra Touch	19??	60.00
❑ T768 [M]	This Is Sinatra!	1956	30.00
—Turquoise label			
❑ T768 [M]	This Is Sinatra!	196?	25.00
—Black "Starline" label			
❑ T768 [M]	This Is Sinatra!	196?	18.00
—Gold "Starline" label			
❑ DT768 [R]	This Is Sinatra!	196?	15.00
❑ M-11883	This Is Sinatra!	1979	12.00
❑ W982 [M]	This Is Sinatra, Volume Two	1958	40.00
—Gray label			
❑ W982 [M]	This Is Sinatra, Volume Two	1959	25.00
—Black label with colorband, logo at left			
❑ DW982 [R]	This Is Sinatra, Volume Two	196?	15.00
❑ DN-16268	This Is Sinatra, Volume Two	198?	10.00
—Budget-line reissue			
❑ DN-16110	What Is This Thing Called Love	198?	10.00
—Budget-line reissue			
❑ STBB-529	What Is This Thing Called Love?/The Night We Called It a Day	1970	18.00
❑ SN-16267	Where Are You	198?	10.00
—Budget-line reissue			
❑ W855 [M]	Where Are You?	1957	30.00
—Gray label			
❑ W855 [M]	Where Are You?	1959	25.00
—Black label with colorband			
❑ SW855 [S]	Where Are You?	1959	40.00
—Originals do not include "I Cover the Waterfront			
❑ SW855 [S]	Where Are You?	196?	30.00
—Later releases restore "I Cover the Waterfront			

CAPITOL PICKWICK SERIES

Number	Title	Yr	NM
❑ PC-3457 [M]	Just One of Those Things	196?	15.00
❑ SPC-3457 [R]	Just One of Those Things	196?	12.00
❑ PC-3463 [M]	My Cole Porter	196?	15.00
❑ SPC-3463 [R]	My Cole Porter	196?	12.00
❑ PC-3456 [M]	Nevertheless	196?	15.00
❑ SPC-3456 [R]	Nevertheless	196?	12.00
❑ PC-3450 [M]	The Nearness of You	196?	15.00
❑ SPC-3450 [R]	The Nearness of You	196?	12.00
❑ PC-3458 [M]	This Love of Mine	196?	15.00
❑ SPC-3458 [R]	This Love of Mine	196?	12.00
❑ PC-3452 [M]	Try a Little Tenderness	196?	15.00
❑ SPC-3452 [R]	Try a Little Tenderness	196?	12.00

COLUMBIA

Number	Title	Yr	NM
❑ CL953 [M]	Adventures of the Heart	1957	30.00
❑ PC40707	Christmas Dreaming	1987	30.00
—Reissue of CL 1032 with an extra track			
❑ CL1032 [M]	Christmas Dreaming	1957	80.00
❑ CL6019 [10]	Christmas Songs by Sinatra	1948	100.00
—With "gingerbread man" cover			
❑ CL6019 [10]	Christmas Songs by Sinatra	1949	80.00
—With green vinylite cover			
❑ CL2542 [10]	Christmas with Sinatra	1955	60.00
—House Party Series" release			
❑ CL1359 [M]	Come Back to Sorrento	1959	30.00
❑ CL6096 [10]	Dedicated to You	1952	100.00
—Three of the tracks on this LP are alternate takes unavailable on vinyl anywhere else			
❑ CL606 [M]	Frankie	1955	30.00
—Cover has drawing of Frank Sinatra wearing a hat			
❑ CL606 [M]	Frankie	1955	30.00
—Cover has Frank with Debbie Reynolds			
❑ CL6059 [10]	Frankly Sentimental	1951	60.00
❑ CL884 [M]	Frank Sinatra Conducts Music of Alec Wilder	1956	40.00
—Reissue of Columbia Masterworks ML 4271			
❑ CL2913 [M]	Frank Sinatra in Hollywood	1968	80.00
❑ CS9713 [R]	Frank Sinatra in Hollywood	1968	15.00
❑ CL2521 [10]	Get Happy	1955	60.00
—House Party Series" release			
❑ CL2474 [M]	Greatest Hits, The Early Years, Vol. 1	1966	18.00
❑ CS9274 [R]	Greatest Hits, The Early Years, Vol. 1	1966	12.00
❑ PC9274	Greatest Hits, The Early Years, Vol. 1	197?	10.00
❑ CL2572 [M]	Greatest Hits, The Early Years, Vol. 2	1966	18.00
❑ CS9372 [R]	Greatest Hits, The Early Years, Vol. 2	1966	12.00
❑ PC9372	Greatest Hits, The Early Years, Vol. 2	197?	10.00
❑ C2X40897	Hello Young Lovers	1988	30.00
❑ KG31358	In the Beginning	1971	40.00
—Original edition; titles of songs at left on front cover			
❑ PG31358	In the Beginning	197?	15.00
—Revised version; titles of songs at right on front cover			
❑ CL6290 [10]	I've Got a Crush on You	1954	60.00
❑ CL2539 [10]	I've Got a Crush on You	1955	60.00
—House Party Series" release; different contents from CL 6290			
❑ CL1241 [M]	Love Is a Kick	1958	30.00
❑ CL1136 [M]	Put Your Dreams Away	1958	30.00
❑ CL1448 [M]	Reflections	1959	60.00
❑ PC44238 [M]	Sinatra Rarities	1989	40.00
❑ CL6143 [10]	Sing and Dance with Frank Sinatra	1953	60.00
❑ CL6087 [10]	Songs by Sinatra, Volume 1	1952	60.00
❑ CL902 [M]	That Old Feeling	1956	30.00
❑ CL1297 [M]	The Broadway Kick	1958	30.00
❑ S3L42 [M]	The Essential Frank Sinatra	1966	100.00
❑ S3S42 [R]	The Essential Frank Sinatra	1966	50.00
❑ CL2739 [M]	The Essential Frank Sinatra, Volume 1	1967	30.00
❑ CS9539 [R]	The Essential Frank Sinatra, Volume 1	1967	15.00
❑ CL2740 [M]	The Essential Frank Sinatra, Volume 2	1967	30.00
❑ CS9540 [R]	The Essential Frank Sinatra, Volume 2	1967	15.00
❑ CL2741 [M]	The Essential Frank Sinatra, Volume 3	1967	30.00
❑ CS9541 [R]	The Essential Frank Sinatra, Volume 3	1967	15.00
❑ C2L6 [M]	The Frank Sinatra Story	1958	30.00
❑ CL743 [M]	The Voice	1956	30.00
❑ CL743 [M]	The Voice	1999	30.00
—Classic Records reissue on audiophile vinyl			
❑ C6X40343	The Voice: The Columbia Years 1943-1952	1986	80.00
❑ CAS2475 [DJ]	The Voice: The Columbia Years Sampler	1986	40.00
❑ CAS2475 [DJ]	The Voice: The Columbia Years Sampler	1986	40.00
❑ CL6001 [10]	The Voice of Frank Sinatra	1949	70.00
—Original in pink paper cover			
❑ CL6001 [10]	The Voice of Frank Sinatra	1950	60.00
—Blue cardboard cover			

COLUMBIA MASTERWORKS

Number	Title	Yr	NM
❑ ML4271 [M]	Frank Sinatra Conducts Music of Alec Wilder	1955	100.00

HARMONY

Number	Title	Yr	NM
❑ HS11390 [R]	Frank Sinatra	1969	18.00
❑ KH30318 [R]	Greatest Hits, Early Years	1971	18.00
❑ HL7400 [M]	Have Yourself a Merry Little Christmas	1967	30.00
❑ HS11200 [R]	Have Yourself a Merry Little Christmas	1967	25.00
—At least two different cover designs exist			
❑ HL7405 [M]	Romantic Scenes from the Early Years	1967	30.00
❑ HS11205 [R]	Romantic Scenes from the Early Years	1967	15.00
❑ HS11277 [R]	Someone to Watch Over Me	1968	18.00

LONGINES SYMPHONETTE

Number	Title	Yr	NM
❑ LS-308A	Sinatra: The Works	1972	75.00
❑ LS-309A	Sinatra: The Works	1973	40.00
—Abridged version of LS-308A			
❑ SYS-5637	Sinatra Like Never Before	1972	30.00
—Bonus LP with purchase of LS-308A			

MOBILE FIDELITY

Number	Title	Yr	NM
❑ 1-135 [M]	A Jolly Christmas from Frank Sinatra	1984	40.00
—Audiophile vinyl using the original title			
❑ 1-086	Nice 'N' Easy	1981	40.00
—Audiophile vinyl			
❑ SC-1	Sinatra	1983	600.00
—Audiophile vinyl; only two of the 16 records in this box were released individually			

PAIR

Number	Title	Yr	NM
❑ PDL2-1027	All-Time Classics	1986	15.00
❑ PDL2-1122	Classic Performances	1986	15.00
❑ PDL2-1028	Timeless	1986	15.00

QWEST

Number	Title	Yr	NM
❑ 25145	L.A. Is My Lady	1984	15.00

RCA VICTOR

Number	Title	Yr	NM
❑ LPT-3063 [10]	Fabulous Frankie	1953	60.00
❑ LPM-1569 [M]	Frankie and Tommy	1957	60.00
—First issue of this LP			
❑ AFL1-4741 [R]	Radio Years (Sinatra/Dorsey/Stordahl)	1983	18.00
❑ CPL2-4334	The Sinatra/Dorsey Sessions, Vol. 1	1982	30.00
❑ CPL2-4335	The Sinatra/Dorsey Sessions, Vol. 2	1982	30.00
❑ CPL2-4336	The Sinatra/Dorsey Sessions, Vol. 3	1982	30.00
❑ LPV-583 [M]	This Love of Mine	1971	40.00
❑ LPM-1569 [M]	Tommy Plays, Frankie Sings	1957	40.00
—Second issue with new title			
❑ LPM-1632 [M]	We Three	1958	60.00
—First issue			
❑ LPM-1632 [M]	We Three	1958	40.00
—Second issue, "RE" on cover			
❑ APL1-0497 [R]	What'll I Do	1974	15.00
❑ ANL1-1050 [R]	What'll I Do	1976	12.00

REPRISE

Number	Title	Yr	NM
❑ F1007 [M]	All Alone	1962	18.00
❑ R91007 [S]	All Alone	1962	25.00
❑ FS1030	A Man Alone & Other Songs of Rod McKuen	1969	18.00
❑ FS1030	A Man Alone & Other Songs of Rod McKuen	1969	400.00
—Signed copies with gatefold cover and hardbound book; 400 made			
❑ SMAS-92081	A Man Alone & Other Songs of Rod McKuen	1969	25.00
—Capitol Record Club edition			
❑ 2F1016 [M]	A Man and His Music	1965	25.00
❑ 2FS1016 [S]	A Man and His Music	1965	30.00
❑ 5004 [DJ]	A Man and His Music, Part II	1966	200.00
—Promotional album for use by Budweiser			
❑ 5004 [DJ]	A Man and His Music, Part II	1966	300.00
—Promotional album for use by Budweiser			
❑ 2F/2FS1016	A Man and His Music Special Box	1965	200.00
—Blue slipcase with embossed silver front, raised letters, plus 4-page booklet and a signed card (deduct 50% if card missing). Add this to LP value.			
❑ FS1027	Cycles	1969	18.00
❑ F1011 [M]	Days of Wine and Roses, Moon River, and Other Academy Award Winners	1964	18.00
❑ FS1011 [S]	Days of Wine and Roses, Moon River, and Other Academy Award Winners	1964	25.00
❑ FS1024	Francis A. and Edward K.	1968	25.00
❑ F1021 [M]	Francis Albert Sinatra & Antonio Carlos Jobim	1967	15.00
❑ FS1021 [S]	Francis Albert Sinatra & Antonio Carlos Jobim	1967	18.00
❑ FS1025	Frank Sinatra's Greatest Hits	1968	18.00
❑ FS1034	Frank Sinatra's Greatest Hits, Vol. 2	1972	18.00
❑ F1022 [M]	Frank Sinatra (The World We Knew)	1967	18.00
❑ FS1022 [S]	Frank Sinatra (The World We Knew)	1967	18.00
❑ F1006 [M]	Great Songs from Great Britain	1962	80.00
—Only released in the UK			
❑ R91006 [S]	Great Songs from Great Britain	1962	100.00
—Only released in the UK			
❑ F1003 [M]	I Remember Tommy	1961	25.00
❑ R91003 [S]	I Remember Tommy	1961	30.00
❑ 5409 [DJ]	I Sing the Songs	1976	50.00
❑ 5409 [DJ]	I Sing the Songs	1976	50.00
❑ F1012 [M]	It Might As Well Be Swing	1964	18.00
❑ FS1012 [S]	It Might As Well Be Swing	1964	25.00
❑ F1018 [M]	Moonlight Sinatra	1966	18.00
❑ FS1018 [S]	Moonlight Sinatra	1966	25.00
❑ F1015 [M]	My Kind of Broadway	1965	18.00
❑ FS1015 [S]	My Kind of Broadway	1965	25.00
❑ FS1029	My Way	1969	18.00
❑ FS41029 [Q]	My Way	1974	30.00
❑ FS2155	Ol' Blue Eyes Is Back	1973	15.00
❑ FS42155 [Q]	Ol' Blue Eyes Is Back	1974	30.00
❑ F1001 [M]	Ring-a-Ding-Ding!	1961	25.00
❑ R91001 [S]	Ring-a-Ding-Ding!	1961	30.00
❑ F1014 [M]	September of My Years	1965	18.00
❑ FS1014 [S]	September of My Years	1965	25.00
❑ FS2305	She Shot Me Down	1981	15.00
❑ F1004 [M]	Sinatra & Strings	1962	18.00
❑ R91004 [S]	Sinatra & Strings	1962	25.00
❑ R6167 [M]	Sinatra '65	1965	18.00
❑ RS6167 [S]	Sinatra '65	1965	25.00
❑ FS1033	Sinatra and Company	1971	18.00
❑ F1005 [M]	Sinatra and Swingin' Brass	1962	18.00
❑ R91005 [S]	Sinatra and Swingin' Brass	1962	25.00
❑ 2F1019 [M]	Sinatra at the Sands	1966	25.00
❑ 2FS1019 [S]	Sinatra at the Sands	1966	30.00
❑ F1008 [M]	Sinatra-Basie	1963	18.00
❑ R91008 [S]	Sinatra-Basie	1963	25.00
❑ F6045 [M]	Sinatra Conducts Music from Pictures and Plays	1962	30.00
❑ R96045 [S]	Sinatra Conducts Music from Pictures and Plays	1962	40.00
❑ FS1028	SinatraJobim	1969	4000.00
—Unreleased; test pressings exist (value is for one of these). 8-track tapes also exist and are 10% of this value; VG value 1000; VG+ value 1000			
❑ R-1010 [M]	Sinatra's Sinatra	1963	18.00
—Gatefold jacket; some copies have a large photo of Sinatra holding a pack of Lucky Strikes at the right side of the inside gatefold; we don't yet know the relative rarity of these variations, or which came first, or whether they also exist on stereo copies			
❑ R-1010 [M]	Sinatra's Sinatra	1963	18.00
—Gatefold jacket; some copies have eight photos of previous Frank Sinatra Reprise LPs at the right side of the inside gatefold; we don't yet know the relative rarity of these variations, or which came first, or whether they also exist on stereo copies			
❑ R91010 [S]	Sinatra's Sinatra	1963	25.00
❑ F1002 [M]	Sinatra Swings	1961	25.00
—Retitled version of "Swing Along with Me"; Capitol threatened legal action because of its "Come Swing With Me!" collection			

Number	Title	Yr	NM
❏ R91002 [S]	Sinatra Swings	1961	30.00

—Retitled version of "Swing Along with Me"; Capitol threatened legal action because of its "Come Swing With Me!" collection

❏ FS2207	Sinatra -- The Main Event Live	1974	15.00
❏ F1013 [M]	Softly, As I Leave You	1964	18.00
❏ FS1013 [S]	Softly, As I Leave You	1964	25.00
❏ FS2195	Some Nice Things I've Missed	1974	15.00
❏ FS42194 [Q]	Some Nice Things I've Missed	1974	30.00
❏ 5230 [DJ]	Songbook, Vol. 1	1971	50.00
❏ 5230 [DJ]	Songbook, Vol. 1	1971	50.00
❏ 5267 [DJ]	Songbook, Vol. 2	1972	100.00
❏ 5267 [DJ]	Songbook, Vol. 2	1972	100.00
❏ F1017 [M]	Strangers in the Night	1966	15.00
❏ FS1017 [S]	Strangers in the Night	1966	18.00
❏ F1002 [M]	Swing Along with Me	1961	40.00

— Original title

❏ R91002 [S]	Swing Along with Me	1961	50.00

— Original title

❏ F1020 [M]	That's Life	1966	15.00
❏ FS1020 [S]	That's Life	1966	18.00
❏ F1009 [M]	The Concert Sinatra	1963	18.00
❏ R91009 [S]	The Concert Sinatra	1963	30.00

— Original pressings declare this was recorded in "35mm Stereo

❏ R91009 [S]	The Concert Sinatra	196?	25.00

— Without cover reference to "35mm Stereo

❏ FS1023	The Sinatra Christmas Album	1967	100.00

— Album never released; value is for cover slick

❏ 3FS2300	Trilogy: Past, Present, Future	1980	25.00
❏ FS1031	Watertown	1970	30.00

— With gatefold and poster

TIME-LIFE

❏ SLGD-02	Legendary Singers: Frank Sinatra	1985	30.00

SINATRA, NANCY

RCA VICTOR

❏ LSP-4645	Nancy and Lee Again	1972	30.00

— With Lee Hazlewood

❏ VPS-6078	This Is Nancy Sinatra	1972	50.00
❏ LSP-4774	Woman	1973	30.00

REPRISE

❏ R-6202 [M]	Boots	1966	30.00
❏ RS-6202 [S]	Boots	1966	35.00
❏ ST-91341 [S]	Boots	1967	50.00

— Capitol Record Club edition

❏ R-6251 [M]	Country, My Way	1967	50.00
❏ RS-6251 [S]	Country, My Way	1967	35.00
❏ R-6207 [M]	How Does That Grab You?	1966	30.00
❏ RS-6207 [S]	How Does That Grab You?	1966	35.00
❏ R-6277 [M]	Movin' with Nancy	1967	50.00
❏ RS-6277 [S]	Movin' with Nancy	1967	35.00
❏ ST-91349 [S]	Movin' with Nancy	1967	40.00

— Capitol Record Club edition

❏ RS-6333 [B]	Nancy	1969	40.00
❏ RS-6273 [B]	Nancy and Lee	1968	35.00

— With Lee Hazlewood

❏ R-6221 [M]	Nancy in London	1966	40.00
❏ RS-6221 [S]	Nancy in London	1966	35.00
❏ RS-6409 [B]	Nancy's Greatest Hits	1970	30.00
❏ R-6239 [M]	Sugar	1967	50.00
❏ RS-6239 [S]	Sugar	1967	35.00

RHINO

❏ RNLP-70227 [B]	Boots: Nancy Sinatra's All-Time Hits (1966-1970)	1987	15.00
❏ R1-70166 [B]	Fairy Tales and Fantasies: The Best of Nancy and Lee	1989	15.00

— With Lee Hazlewood

SINCEROS, THE

COLUMBIA

❏ NFC37349	Pet Rock	1980	12.00
❏ JC36134	The Sound of Sunbathing	1979	15.00

SINFIELD, PETE

MANTICORE

❏ MC66667 [B]	Still	1973	30.00

SING A SONG WITH THE BEATLES

TOWER

❏ KAO5000 [M]	Sing a Song with the Beatles	1965	250.00

— No artist listed on label

❏ DKAO5000 [R]	Sing a Song with the Beatles	1965	300.00

SINGER, HAL, AND CHARLIE SHAVERS

PRESTIGE

❏ PRLP-7153 [M]	Blue Stompin'	1959	80.00

SWINGVILLE

❏ SVLP-2023 [M]	Blue Stompin'	1961	50.00

— Purple label

❏ SVLP-2023 [M]	Blue Stompin'	1965	30.00

— Blue label, trident logo at right

SINGER ORCHESTRA, THE

SINGER

❏ HE-M-1 [M]	Favorite Christmas Songs from Singer	1964	18.00

— Cover photo of the cast of "The Donna Reed Show"

❏ HE-S-1 [S]	Favorite Christmas Songs from Singer	1964	25.00

— Cover photo of the cast of "The Donna Reed Show"

SINGERS UNLIMITED, THE

BASF

❏ 21852	The Four of Us	197?	15.00
❏ 20903	Try to Remember	197?	15.00

PAUSA

❏ 7100	A Cappella I	198?	12.00
❏ 7101	A Cappella II	198?	12.00
❏ 7076	A Cappella III	1979	12.00
❏ 7062	A Special Blend	197?	12.00
❏ 7136	Composer's Corner: The Singers Unlimited Sing Music of Lennon, McCartney and Ellington	198?	15.00
❏ 7109	Easy to Love	198?	12.00
❏ 7118	Eventide	198?	12.00
❏ 7068	Feeling Free	197?	12.00
❏ 7121	Four of Us	198?	12.00
❏ 7039	Friends	197?	12.00
❏ 7048	Just in Time	197?	12.00
❏ 7056	The Singers Unlimited with Rob McConnell and the Boss Brass	197?	12.00

VERVE

❏ 815671-1	A Cappella	1985	12.00
❏ 821859-1	Christmas	198?	15.00
❏ 817486-1	The Singers Unlimited with Rob McConnell and the Boss Brass	198?	12.00

SINGING NUN, THE

PHILIPS

❏ PCC209 [M]	Her Joy, Her Songs	1964	18.00
❏ PCC609 [S]	Her Joy, Her Songs	1964	18.00
❏ PCC203 [M]	Soeur Sourire: The Singing Nun	1963	25.00
❏ PCC603 [S]	Soeur Sourire: The Singing Nun	1963	18.00

SINGING NUNS, THE

SN

❏ 001 [S]	O Bambino	197?	15.00

— No relation to the "Dominique" lady.

SINGLE BULLET THEORY

NEMPEROR

❏ ARZ38368	Single Bullet Theory	1983	12.00

SINGLETON, CHARLIE

RCA CAMDEN

❏ CAL-713 [M]	Big Twist Hits	1962	25.00
❏ CAS-713 [S]	Big Twist Hits	1962	30.00

SINGLETON, MARGIE

ASHLEY

❏ 3003	Margie Singleton Sings Country Music with Soul	1968	18.00

PICKWICK

❏ SPC-3133	Harper Valley P.T.A.	197?	12.00

UNITED ARTISTS

❏ UAL-3459 [M]	Crying Time	1965	18.00
❏ UAS-6459 [S]	Crying Time	1965	25.00

SINGLETON, ZUTTY/ART TATUM

BRUNSWICK

❏ BL58038 [10]	Battle of Jazz, Vol. 2	1953	50.00

SIOUXSIE AND THE BANSHEES

GEFFEN

❏ GHS24049	A Kiss in the Dream House	1984	12.00
❏ GHS24030	Hyaena	1984	12.00
❏ GHS24047	Join Hands	1984	12.00
❏ GHS24050	Juju	1984	12.00

— Reissue of PVC 8903

❏ GHS24048	Kaleidoscope	1984	12.00

— Reissue of PVC 7921

❏ GHS24052	Nocturne	1984	12.00
❏ GHS24051	Once Upon a Time: The Singles	1984	12.00

— Reissue of PVC 8906

❏ GHS24205	Peepshow	1988	12.00
❏ GEF24387 [B]	Superstition	1991	25.00
❏ GEF24630	The Rapture	1995	18.00
❏ GHS24046	The Scream	1984	12.00

— Reissue of Polydor PD1-6207

❏ GHS24134	Through the Looking Glass	1987	12.00
❏ GHS24092	Tinderbox	1986	12.00

POLYDOR

❏ PD1-6207	The Scream	1978	30.00

PVC

❏ 8903	Ju Ju	1981	30.00

— Original copies include bonus single "Israel"/"Red Over White

❏ 7921	Kaleidoscope	1980	30.00
❏ 8906	Once Upon a Time: The Singles	1981	25.00

— With poster and inner sleeve

WARNER BROS.

❏ WBMS-138 [DJ]	The Tinderbox Interview	1986	30.00

— Part of "The Warner Bros. Music Show

SIR DOUGLAS QUINTET

ABC DOT

❏ DO-2057	Texas Rock for Country Rollers	1976	18.00

— As "Sir Doug and the Texas Tornadoes

ATLANTIC

❏ SD7287	Texas Tornado	1974	18.00

— As "Sir Douglas Band

BEAT ROCKET

❏ BR123	The Best of the Sir Douglas Quintet	2000	15.00

— Reissue of Tribe LP on 180-gram vinyl

❏ BR124	The Sir Douglas Quintet Is Back!	2000	15.00

— New compilation of Tribe material on 180-gram vinyl

PHILIPS

❏ PHS600344	1 + 1 + 1 = 4	1970	30.00
❏ PHS600353	The Return of Doug Saldana	1971	30.00

R&M

❏ UDL-2343	The Tracker	1981	25.00

SMASH

❏ SRS-67115	Mendocino	1969	30.00
❏ SRS-67108	Sir Douglas Quintet + 2 = Honkey Blues	1968	30.00
❏ SRS-67130	Together After Five	1970	30.00

TAKOMA

❏ TAK-7088	Border Wave	1981	15.00
❏ TAK-7095	Sir Douglas Quintet Live	1985	15.00
❏ TAK-7086	The Best of the Sir Douglas Quintet	1980	15.00

TRIBE

❏ TR37001 [M]	The Best of the Sir Douglas Quintet	1966	70.00
❏ TRS47001 [R]	The Best of the Sir Douglas Quintet	1966	50.00

VARRICK

❏ 004	Quintessence	1983	15.00

SIR LANCELOT

MERCURY

❏ MG-25159 [10]	Calypso	1952	50.00

SIR LORD BALTIMORE

MERCURY

❏ SR-61328	Kingdom Come	1970	30.00
❏ SRM-1-613	Sir Lord Baltimore	1971	30.00

SIRAVO, GEORGE

AD-LIB

❏ 226 [M]	Out on a Limb	196?	18.00
❏ S-226 [S]	Out on a Limb	196?	25.00

COLUMBIA

❏ CL6146 [10]	Your Dance Date with George Siravo	1951	40.00

DECCA

❏ DL8464 [M]	Portraits in Hi-Fi	1957	30.00

EPIC

❏ LN3803 [M]	Everything Goes	1961	18.00
❏ BN607 [S]	Everything Goes	1961	25.00

KAPP

❏ KL-1016 [M]	Polite Jazz	1956	30.00

MERCURY

❏ MG-20327 [M]	Darling, Please Forgive Me	1958	30.00

RCA CAMDEN

❏ CAL-505 [M]	Siravo Swing Session	1959	18.00
❏ CAS-505 [S]	Siravo Swing Session	1959	25.00

RCA VICTOR

❏ LPM-1970 [M]	Swingin' in Hi-Fi in Studio A	1959	30.00
❏ LSP-1970 [S]	Swingin' in Hi-Fi in Studio A	1959	30.00

TIME

❏ 52115 [M]	And Then I Wrote Richard Rodgers	196?	18.00
❏ S-2115 [S]	And Then I Wrote Richard Rodgers	196?	25.00
❏ S-2019 [S]	Seductive Strings	196?	25.00
❏ 52019 [M]	Seductive Strings	196?	18.00

VIK

❏ LX-1091 [M]	Old But New	1957	30.00
❏ LX-1125 [M]	Swing Hi, Swing Fi	1958	30.00

SIREN

ELEKTRA

❏ EKS-74087	Strange Locomotion	1971	25.00

Number	Title	Yr	NM

SISTER DOUBLE HAPPINESS

REPRISE

❏ PRO05010 [DJ]	Heart and Mind	1991	50.00

—Available as stock copy on cassette and CD only

❏ PRO-A-5010 [DJ]	Heart and Mind	1991	50.00

—Vinyl is promo only

SST

❏ 162	Sister Double Happiness	1988	12.00

SISTER SLEDGE

ATCO

❏ SD 36-105	Circle of Love	1975	25.00

ATLANTIC

❏ 81255	When the Boys Meet the Girls	1985	12.00

COTILLION

❏ SD16027	All American Girls	1981	12.00
❏ 90069	Bet Cha Say That to All the Girls	1983	12.00
❏ SD16012	Love Somebody Today	1980	12.00
❏ SD5231	The Sisters	1982	12.00
❏ SD9919	Together	1976	25.00
❏ SD5209	We Are Family	1979	12.00

SISTERS OF MERCY

ELEKTRA

❏ 60405 [B]	First and Last and Always	1985	25.00
❏ 60762 [B]	Floodland	1987	25.00

MOBILE FIDELITY

❏ MOFI1-021 [B]	Floodland	2013	35.00

SIVUCA

VANGUARD

❏ VSD-79352	Live at the Village Gate	197?	15.00
❏ VSD-79337	Sivuca	197?	18.00

SIX, THE

BETHLEHEM

❏ BCP-28 [M]	The Six	1955	80.00
❏ BCP-57 [M]	The View From Jazzbo's Head	1956	100.00

SIX AND SEVEN-EIGHTHS STRING BAND, THE

FOLKWAYS

❏ FP-2671 [M]	The Six and Seven-Eighths String Band	195?	40.00
❏ FP-671 [M]	The Six and Seven-Eighths String Band	1951	50.00

SIZEMORE, ARTHUR

DECCA

❏ DL4785 [M]	Mountain Ballads and Old Hymns	1966	30.00
❏ DL74785 [S]	Mountain Ballads and Old Hymns	1966	40.00

SKAGGS, RICKY, AND KEITH WHITLEY

REBEL

❏ 1504	Second Generation Bluegrass	1972	25.00
❏ 1550	That's It	1975	25.00

SKAGGS, RICKY

ATLANTIC

❏ 82834	Solid Ground	1995	18.00

EPIC

❏ FE40623	Comin' Home to Stay	1988	10.00
❏ FE39410	Country Boy	1984	12.00
❏ FE39409	Favorite Country Songs	1985	12.00
❏ FE37996	Highways and Heartaches	1982	12.00
❏ FE45027	Kentucky Thunder	1989	12.00
❏ FE40103	Live in London	1985	12.00
❏ FE40309	Love's Gonna Get Ya!	1986	10.00
❏ EAS2022 [DJ]	The Ricky Skaggs Story	1990	30.00

—Promo-only interview record

❏ FE37193	Waitin' for the Sun to Shine	1981	12.00

ROUNDER

❏ 0151	Family and Friends	1982	15.00

SUGAR HILL

❏ SH-3711	Skaggs and Rice	1980	15.00
❏ SH-3706	Sweet Temptation	1979	15.00

SUGAR HILL/EPIC

❏ FE38954	Don't Cheat in Our Hometown	1983	12.00

SKELTON, RED

LIBERTY

❏ LRP-3477 [M]	Music from the Heart	1966	25.00
❏ LST-7477 [S]	Music from the Heart	1966	30.00
❏ LRP-3425 [M]	Red Skelton Conducts	1966	25.00
❏ LST-7425 [S]	Red Skelton Conducts	1966	30.00

SKID ROW (1)

EPIC

❏ E30913	34 Hours	1971	30.00
❏ E30404	Skid Row	1971	30.00

Number	Title	Yr	NM

SKID ROW (2)

ATLANTIC

❏ 81936 [B]	Skid Row	1989	15.00
❏ 1P-8136	Slave to the Grind	1991	30.00

—U.S. vinyl version available only from Columbia House; all copies are the censored version with "Beggars Day"

SKIN ALLEY

STAX

❏ STS-3013	Two Quid Deal	1973	25.00

—With poster

SKINNER, CORNELIA AND OTIS

RCA CAMDEN

❏ CAL-190 [M]	Cornelia Skinner with Otis Skinner	1955	30.00

SKINNER, JIMMIE

DECCA

❏ DL4132 [M]	Country Singer	1961	40.00

MERCURY

❏ MG-20700 [M]	Jimmie Skinner Sings Jimmie Rodgers	1962	30.00
❏ SR-60700 [S]	Jimmie Skinner Sings Jimmie Rodgers	1962	30.00
❏ MG-20352 [M]	Songs That Make the Jukebox Play	1957	80.00

STARDAY

❏ SLP-240 [M]	Jimmie Skinner	1963	40.00

VETCO

❏ 3001 [B]	Jimmie Skinner Sings Bluegrass	1976	25.00

WING

❏ MGW-12277 [M]	Country Blues	1964	30.00
❏ SRW-16277 [R]	Country Blues	1964	18.00

SKIP AND THE CREATIONS

JUSTICE

❏ (# unknown)0	Mobam	196?	400.00

SKJELBRED, RAY

EUPHONIC

❏ 1223	Chicago High Life	198?	12.00

STOMP OFF

❏ SOS-1097	Gin Mill Blues	1985	12.00
❏ SOS-1124	Stompin' 'Em Down	1987	12.00

SKUNKS, THE

TEEN TOWN

❏ TTLP-101	Getting Started	1968	50.00

SKY

RCA VICTOR

❏ LSP-4514	Sailor's Delight	1971	18.00
❏ LSP-4457	Sky	1970	18.00

SKYLARK

CAPITOL

❏ ST-11048	Skylark	1972	18.00
❏ ST-11256	Skylark 2	1973	15.00

SKYLINERS, THE

CALICO

❏ LP-3000 [M]	The Skyliners	1959	600.00

—Yellow and blue label

❏ LP-3000 [M]	The Skyliners	196?	200.00

—Blue label

KAMA SUTRA

❏ KSBS-2026	Once Upon a Time	1971	30.00

ORIGINAL SOUND

❏ OS-5010 [M]	Since I Don't Have You	1963	50.00
❏ OSS-8873 [S]	Since I Don't Have You	1963	70.00
❏ OSS-8873 [S]	Since I Don't Have You	197?	18.00

—Reissue on thinner vinyl

SKYWALK

ZEBRA

❏ ZEB-42204	Paradiso	1988	12.00
❏ ZEB-5680	Silent Witness	1986	12.00

—Reissue of 5004

❏ ZR5004	Silent Witness	1984	15.00
❏ ZEB-5715	The Bohemians	1986	12.00

SLACK, FREDDIE

EMARCY

❏ MG-36094 [M]	Boogie-Woogie on the 88	1956	40.00

PAUSA

❏ 9027	Behind the Eight-Beat	198?	12.00

SLADE

CBS ASSOCIATED

❏ FZ39336	Keep Your Hands Off My Power Supply	1984	12.00

Number	Title	Yr	NM

❏ PZ39336	Keep Your Hands Off My Power Supply	1985	10.00

—Budget-line reissue

❏ FZ39976	Rogues Gallery	1985	15.00
❏ BFZ40908	You Boyz Make Big Noize	1986	15.00

COTILLION

❏ SD9035 [B]	Play It Loud	1970	100.00

FONTANA

❏ SRF-67598 [B]	Ballzy	1969	200.00
❏ SRF-67598 [DJ]	Ballzy	1969	150.00

—White label promo

POLYDOR

❏ PD-5508	Slade Alive!	1972	18.00
❏ PD-5524	Slayed?	1973	18.00

REPRISE

❏ MS2173	Sladest	1973	18.00

WARNER BROS.

❏ BS2936	Nobody's Fools	1976	25.00
❏ BS2865	Slade in Flame	1975	18.00
❏ BS2770	Stomp Your Hands, Clap Your Feet	1974	18.00

SLAGLE, STEVE

ATLANTIC

❏ 81657	Rio Highlife	1986	12.00

SLATER, DAVID

CAPITOL

❏ C1-91181	Be with Me	1989	12.00
❏ C1-48307	Exchange of Hearts	1988	10.00

SLATKIN, FELIX

LIBERTY

❏ LRP-3150 [M]	Fantastic Percussion	1960	18.00
❏ LST-7150 [S]	Fantastic Percussion	1960	25.00
❏ LMM-13021 [M]	Fantastic Strings Play Fantastic Themes	1962	18.00
❏ LSS-14021 [S]	Fantastic Strings Play Fantastic Themes	1962	25.00
❏ LMM-13024 [M]	Hoedown	1963	18.00
❏ LSS-14024 [S]	Hoedown	1963	25.00
❏ LMM-13019 [M]	Inspired Themes from the Inspired Films	1962	18.00
❏ LSS-14019 [S]	Inspired Themes from the Inspired Films	1962	25.00
❏ LMM-13011 [M]	Many Splendored Themes	1962	18.00
❏ LSS-14011 [S]	Many Splendored Themes	1962	25.00
❏ LRP-3287 [M]	Our Winter Love	1963	15.00
❏ LST-7287 [S]	Our Winter Love	1963	18.00
❏ LMM-13001 [M]	Paradise Found	1960	18.00
❏ LSS-14001 [S]	Paradise Found	1960	25.00
❏ LMM-13008 [M]	Street Scene	1961	18.00
❏ LSS-14008 [S]	Street Scene	1961	25.00
❏ LMM-13027 [M]	The Ballad of New Orleans	1963	18.00
❏ LSS-14027 [S]	The Ballad of New Orleans	1963	25.00

SUNSET

❏ SUM-1106 [M]	Love Strings	196?	15.00
❏ SUS-5106 [S]	Love Strings	196?	15.00
❏ SUM-1141 [M]	Seasons Greetings	196?	15.00
❏ SUS-5141 [S]	Seasons Greetings	196?	15.00
❏ SUM-1170 [M]	Tender Strings	196?	15.00
❏ SUS-5170 [S]	Tender Strings	196?	15.00

UNITED ARTISTS

❏ UAS-6818	Classic Country	1971	12.00

SLAUGHTER

CHRYSALIS

❏ R120666 [EP]	Stick It Live	1990	25.00

—Vinyl version available only through BMG Direct Marketing

❏ F1-21702 [DJ]	Stick It To Ya	1990	30.00

—Black generic sleeve with hole; numbered edition of 500 with sticker that says "Limited Edition Special Vinyl Pressing Metal Radio Only"

❏ F1-21911	The Wild Life	1992	25.00

—Vinyl version available only through Columbia House

SLAWSON, BRIAN

CBS/FM

❏ 5M42069 [EP]	A Yule Log	1985	10.00

SLAYER

AMERICAN

❏ C269192	Diabolus in Musica	1998	30.00

COMBAT

❏ MX8020	Hell Awaits	1985	25.00

DEF AMERICAN

❏ DFS24307	Seasons in the Abyss	1990	25.00

DEF JAM

❏ GHS24131	Reign in Blood	1986	25.00
❏ GHS24203	South of Heaven	1988	14.00

METAL BLADE

❏ 72297	Hell Awaits	1988	16.00

—Reissue of Combat LP

❏ MBR1037 [PD]	Live Undead	1984	30.00

—Limited edition picture disc

❏ 72217	Live Undead	1987	25.00
❏ 71034	Show No Mercy	198?	15.00

Number	Title	Yr	NM
— Early reissue of 1034			
❏ E1034	Show No Mercy	1983	25.00
❏ 72214 [PD]	Show No Mercy	1987	30.00
— Picture disc in plastic sleeve			

SLEAZE

SING SING
| ❏ SING0-49 [B] | Sleaze | 2012 | 30.00 |

SLEDD, PATSY

MEGA
| ❏ 1020 | Yours Sincerely | 1973 | 15.00 |

SLEDGE, PERCY

ATLANTIC
❏ SD8180	Take Time to Know Her	1968	50.00
❏ SD8210	The Best of Percy Sledge	1969	30.00
❏ 8146 [M]	The Percy Sledge Way	1967	50.00
❏ SD8146 [S]	The Percy Sledge Way	1967	50.00
❏ 80212	The Ultimate Collection: When a Man Loves a Woman	1983	15.00
❏ 8132 [M]	Warm and Tender Soul	1966	50.00
❏ SD8132 [R]	Warm and Tender Soul	1966	30.00
❏ 8125 [M]	When a Man Loves a Woman	1966	50.00
❏ SD8125 [R]	When a Man Loves a Woman	1966	30.00

CAPRICORN
| ❏ CP 0147 | I'll Be Your Everything | 1974 | 18.00 |

MONUMENT
| ❏ FW38532 | Percy! | 1983 | 15.00 |

SLEEP

TUPELO
| ❏ TUPLP34 | Volume One | 1992 | 24.00 |

SLEEPERS

ADOLESCENT
| ❏ ARTT 007 | Painless Nights | 1981 | 15.00 |

SLEET, DON

JAZZLAND
| ❏ JLP-45 [M] | All Members | 1961 | 30.00 |
| ❏ JLP-945 [S] | All Members | 1961 | 30.00 |

SLICK, GRACE

GRUNT
❏ BFL1-0347 [B]	Manhole	1974	18.00
❏ AYL1-3736	Manhole	1981	10.00
— Best Buy Series" reissue			

RCA VICTOR
❏ AFL1-3544	Dreams	1980	12.00
❏ DJL1-3923 [DJ]	RCA Special Radio Series	1981	25.00
❏ AQL1-3851	Welcome to the Wrecking Ball	1981	12.00
❏ DJL1-3922 [DJ]	Welcome to the Wrecking Ball Interview	1981	25.00

SLICKAPHONICS

ENJA
| ❏ 4024 | Wow Bag | 1982 | 15.00 |

SLICKEE BOYS

DACOIT
| ❏ 1001 | Separated Vegetables | 1977 | 80.00 |
| *— Limited edition of 100 copies* | | | |

GIANT
| ❏ GR16037-1 | Live at Last | 1989 | 12.00 |

LIMP
| ❏ 1003 | Separated Vegetables | 1980 | 30.00 |
| *— Limited edition of 300 copies; reissue with new cover* | | | |

TWIN/TONE
| ❏ TTR8337 | Cybernetic Dreams of Pi | 1983 | 18.00 |
| ❏ TTR8544 | Uh Oh, No Breaks | 1985 | 15.00 |

SLIDER-GLENN

I.T.I.
| ❏ JL-031 | A Whispered Warning | 1986 | 12.00 |

REEL DREAMS
| ❏ 1007 | A Whispered Warning | 1983 | 18.00 |

SLIM JIM

SOMA
| ❏ MG1225 [M] | Slim Jim Sings | 1958 | 40.00 |

SLINGER, CEES

TIMELESS
| ❏ LPSJP-225 | Sling Shot | 1990 | 15.00 |

SLITS, THE

4 MEN WITH BEARDS
| ❏ 4M506LP [B] | Cut | | 25.00 |

ANTILLES
| ❏ AN-7077 | Cut | 1979 | 40.00 |

SLOAN, P.F.

ATCO
| ❏ SD 33-268 | Measure of Pleasure | 1968 | 30.00 |

DUNHILL
❏ D-50004 [M]	Songs of Our Times	1965	30.00
❏ DS-50004 [S]	Songs of Our Times	1965	30.00
❏ D-50007 [M]	Twelve More Times	1966	30.00
❏ DS-50007 [S]	Twelve More Times	1966	30.00

MUMS
| ❏ KZ31260 | Raised on Records | 1972 | 25.00 |

RHINO
| ❏ RNLP-70133 | Precious Times: The Best of P.F. Sloan | 1986 | 12.00 |

SLOANE, CAROL

AUDIOPHILE
| ❏ AP-195 | Sophisticated Lady | 1985 | 12.00 |

CHOICE
| ❏ 1025 | Cottontail | 1979 | 18.00 |

COLUMBIA
❏ CL1923 [M]	Carol Sloane Live at 30th Street	1963	60.00
❏ CS8723 [S]	Carol Sloane Live at 30th Street	1963	80.00
❏ CL1766 [M]	Out of the Blue	1962	60.00
❏ CS8566 [S]	Out of the Blue	1962	80.00

CONTEMPORARY
| ❏ C-14049 | Love You Madly | 1989 | 18.00 |
| ❏ C-14060 | The Real Thing | 1990 | 18.00 |

PROGRESSIVE
| ❏ PRO-7047 | Carol Sings | 1978 | 15.00 |

SLY AND THE FAMILY STONE

EPIC
❏ E237071	Anthology	1981	18.00
❏ LN24324 [M]	A Whole New Thing	1967	80.00
❏ BN26324 [S]	A Whole New Thing	1967	25.00

❏ E30335 [B]	A Whole New Thing	1971	15.00
— Reissue of 26324			
❏ BN26371 [S]	Dance to the Music	1968	18.00
❏ E30334	Dance to the Music	1971	15.00
— Reissue of 26371			
❏ LN24371 [M]	Dance to the Music	1968	80.00
❏ AS264 [DJ]	Everything You Always Wanted to Hear by Sly and the Family Stone But Were Afraid to Ask For	1976	30.00
— Promo-only compilation			
❏ AS264 [DJ]	Everything You Always Wanted to Hear by Sly and the Family Stone But Were Afraid to Ask For	1976	30.00
— Promo-only compilation			
❏ KE32134	Fresh	1973	12.00
— Orange label			
❏ PE34348	Heard Ya Missed Me, Well I'm Back	1976	12.00
— Orange label			
❏ PE33835	High on You	1975	12.00
— Orange label			
❏ PEQ33835 [Q]	High on You	1975	30.00
❏ BN26397	Life	1968	18.00
❏ E30333	Life	1971	15.00
— Reissue of 26397			
❏ KE30325	Sly and the Family Stone's Greatest Hits	1970	15.00
— Yellow label, gatefold cover			
❏ EQ30325 [Q]	Sly and the Family Stone's Greatest Hits	1971	100.00
— Has alternate mixes of "Hot Fun in the Summertime," "Thank You" and "Everybody Is a Star," which are not rechanneled stereo as they are on other LPs			

Number	Title	Yr	NM
❏ PE30325	Sly and the Family Stone's Greatest Hits	1979	10.00
— Budget-line reissue			
❏ PE32930	Small Talk	1974	12.00
— Orange label			
❏ PEQ32930 [Q]	Small Talk	1974	30.00
❏ BN26456	Stand!	1969	18.00
❏ PE26456	Stand!	1986	10.00
— Budget-line reissue			
❏ JE35974	Ten Years Too Soon	1979	12.00
❏ KE30986	There's a Riot Goin' On	1971	15.00
— Yellow label, gatefold cover			

WARNER BROS.
| ❏ 23700 | Ain't But the Right Way | 1983 | 12.00 |
| ❏ BSK3303 | Back on the Right Track | 1979 | 12.00 |

SLY FOX

CAPITOL
❏ ST-12367	Let's Go All the Way	1985	10.00
❏ ST-512367	Let's Go All the Way	1985	12.00
— Columbia House edition			

SMACK, THE

AUDIO HOUSE
| ❏ (# unknown)0 | The Smack | 1968 | 2000.00 |

SMALL, DANNY

UNITED ARTISTS
| ❏ UAJ-14004 [M] | Woman She Was Born for Sorrow | 1962 | 25.00 |
| ❏ UAJS-15004 [S] | Woman She Was Born for Sorrow | 1962 | 30.00 |

SMALL, MILLIE

SMASH
| ❏ MGS-27055 [M] | My Boy Lollipop | 1964 | 60.00 |
| ❏ SRS-67055 [R] | My Boy Lollipop | 1964 | 50.00 |

SMALL FACES

4 MEN WITH BEARDS
| ❏ 4M182LP [B] | From The Beginning | | 25.00 |
| ❏ 4M181LP [R] | Small Faces | | 25.00 |

ACCORD
| ❏ AN-7157 | By Appointment | 1982 | 12.00 |

ATLANTIC
| ❏ SD19171 | 78 in the Shade | 1978 | 12.00 |
| ❏ SD19113 | Playmates | 1977 | 12.00 |

COMPLEAT
❏ 67-2004	Big Music	1985	15.00
❏ 67-5003	Ogden's Nut Gone Flake	1985	12.00
— Reissue			

IMMEDIATE
❏ Z1252008 [S]	Ogden's Nut Gone Flake	1968	60.00
— Originals have a round cover			
❏ 4225	Ogden's Nut Gone Flake	1973	18.00
— Reissue has a standard square cover			
❏ Z1252002 [S]	There Are But Four Small Faces	1967	50.00
— Color cover (counterfeits have either black and white or black and green covers)			

MGM
| ❏ M3F-4955 | Archetypes | 1974 | 15.00 |

PRIDE
| ❏ PRD 0001 [R] | Early Faces | 1972 | 18.00 |
| ❏ PRD 0014 [P] | The History of the Small Faces | 1973 | 15.00 |

SIRE
| ❏ SASH-3709 | The Vintage Years | 1976 | 18.00 |

VARESE SARABANDE
| ❏ 302 067 183 1 [B] | There Are But Four Small Faces | 2013 | 25.00 |

SMALLEY, JUNE

CIRCLE
| ❏ C-6 | June Smalley Swings America | 1979 | 12.00 |

SMALLS, CLIFF

MASTER JAZZ
| ❏ 8131 | Swing and Things | 197? | 15.00 |

SMART SET, THE

WARNER BROS.
| ❏ W-1203 [M] | A New Experience in Vocal Styles | 1958 | 30.00 |
| ❏ WS-1203 [S] | A New Experience in Vocal Styles | 1958 | 40.00 |

SMASHING PUMPKINS

CAROLINE
❏ 45079 [B]	Adore	1998	40.00
— Different cover than CD version, and the entire LP was remixed into mono			
❏ 1705	Gish	1991	60.00
— Originals do not have the word "Remastered" under the			

Number	Title	Yr	NM

bar code

| ❏ 1705 | Gish | 199? | 25.00 |

— With "Remastered" under the bar code

| ❏ 48936 | Machina/The Machines of God | 2000 | 30.00 |

— With bound-in booklet

| ❏ 1767 | Pisces Iscariot | 1994 | 300.00 |

— First 2,000 copies, hand-numbered on back cover, came with a bonus 7-inch single

| ❏ 1767 [B] | Pisces Iscariot | 1994 | 150.00 |

— Regular pressing on colored vinyl, not numbered, no bonus 7-inch single

| ❏ 1740 [B] | Siamese Dream | 1993 | 100.00 |

— Originals have dark red vinyl

| ❏ 1740 | Siamese Dream | 199? | 50.00 |

— Pink marbled vinyl

CONSTANTINOPLE

| ❏ CR 01-04 | Machina II/The Friends and Enemies of Modern Music | 2000 | 3000.00 |

— Exactly 25 copies were pressed as two 12-inch and three 10-inch records, with the presumption that at least some of them would be bootlegged onto CDs and into downloadable files via the Internet. (This has indeed happened, so many fans have heard the music.) It's not known whether any of the 25 copies have left the hands of their original recipients, so the price above is highly speculative and probably conservative; VG value 1000; VG+ value 2000

SMECK, ROY

ABC-PARAMOUNT

❏ ABC-329 [M]	Adventures in Paradise	1960	30.00
❏ ABCS-329 [S]	Adventures in Paradise	1960	40.00
❏ ABC-358 [M]	Adventures in Paradise, Volume 2	1961	30.00
❏ ABCS-358 [S]	Adventures in Paradise, Volume 2	1961	30.00
❏ ABC-414 [M]	Adventures in Paradise, Volume 3	1962	30.00
❏ ABCS-414 [S]	Adventures in Paradise, Volume 3	1962	30.00
❏ ABC-462 [M]	Adventures in Paradise, Volume 4	1963	30.00
❏ ABCS-462 [S]	Adventures in Paradise, Volume 4	1963	30.00
❏ ABC-234 [M]	Hi-Fi Paradise	1958	40.00
❏ ABC-484 [M]	I Love to Hear a Banjo	1964	30.00
❏ ABCS-484 [S]	I Love to Hear a Banjo	1964	30.00
❏ ABC-174 [M]	Melodies with Memories	1957	40.00
❏ ABC-379 [M]	Roy Smeck, His Singing Guitar and Paradise Serenaders	1961	30.00
❏ ABCS-379 [S]	Roy Smeck, His Singing Guitar and Paradise Serenaders	1961	30.00
❏ ABC-119 [M]	South Seas Serenade	1956	40.00
❏ ABC-412 [M]	Stringing Along	1962	30.00
❏ ABCS-412 [S]	Stringing Along	1962	30.00
❏ ABC-309 [M]	The Happy Banjo	1959	30.00
❏ ABCS-309 [S]	The Happy Banjo	1959	40.00
❏ ABC-330 [M]	The Haunting Hawaiian Guitar	1960	30.00
❏ ABCS-330 [S]	The Haunting Hawaiian Guitar	1960	30.00
❏ ABC-279 [M]	The Magic Ukulele	1959	30.00
❏ ABCS-279 [S]	The Magic Ukulele	1959	40.00
❏ ABC-452 [M]	The Many Guitar Moods of Roy Smeck	1963	30.00
❏ ABCS-452 [S]	The Many Guitar Moods of Roy Smeck	1963	30.00

CORAL

| ❏ CRL56013 [10] | Drifting and Dreaming | 195? | 120.00 |

DECCA

| ❏ DL8674 [M] | Memories of You | 1958 | 40.00 |

— Black label, silver print

| ❏ DL5458 [10] | Memory Lane | 1953 | 100.00 |
| ❏ DL5473 [10] | Songs of the Range | 1953 | 100.00 |

X

| ❏ LPA-3016 [10] | Christmas in Hawaii | 195? | 120.00 |
| ❏ LPX-3012 [10] | South of the Border | 1954 | 120.00 |

SMIAROWSKI, MIKE

SMEAR

| ❏ SMR-891 | Island Fantasy | 1990 | 18.00 |

SMILE (1)

PICKWICK

| ❏ SPC-3288 | Smile | 1973 | 30.00 |

SMITH, "FIDDLIN' " ARTHUR

STARDAY

| ❏ SLP-202 [M] | Rare Old Time Fiddle Tunes | 1962 | 30.00 |

SMITH, AL

BLUESVILLE

| ❏ BVLP-1069 [M] | Blues Shout | 196? | 25.00 |
| ❏ BVLP-1001 [M] | Hear My Blues | 1960 | 80.00 |

— Blue label, silver print

| ❏ BVLP-1001 [M] | Hear My Blues | 1964 | 30.00 |

— Blue label, trident logo at right

| ❏ BVLP-1014 [M] | Midnight Special | 1961 | 80.00 |

— Blue label, silver print

| ❏ BVLP-1014 [M] | Midnight Special | 1964 | 30.00 |

— Blue label, trident logo at right

SMITH, ARTHUR "GUITAR BOOGIE

ABC-PARAMOUNT

| ❏ ABC-441 [M] | Arthur "Guitar" Smith and Voices | 1963 | 25.00 |
| ❏ ABCS-441 [S] | Arthur "Guitar" Smith and Voices | 1963 | 30.00 |

DOT

❏ DLP-3769 [M]	A Tribute to Jim Reeves	1966	18.00
❏ DLP-25769 [S]	A Tribute to Jim Reeves	1966	25.00
❏ DLP-3636 [M]	Great Country and Western Hits	1965	18.00
❏ DLP-25636 [S]	Great Country and Western Hits	1965	25.00
❏ DLP-3600 [M]	Original Guitar Boogie	1964	25.00
❏ DLP-25600 [S]	Original Guitar Boogie	1964	30.00
❏ DLP-3642 [M]	Singing on the Mountain with the Crossroads Quartet	1965	25.00
❏ DLP-25642 [S]	Singing on the Mountain with the Crossroads Quartet	1965	30.00

MGM

❏ E-533 [10]	Fingers on Fire	1955	100.00
❏ E-3525 [M]	Fingers on Fire	1957	80.00
❏ E-236 [10]	Foolish Questions	1954	120.00
❏ E-3301 [M]	Specials	1955	80.00

MONUMENT

| ❏ Z32259 | Battling Banjos | 1973 | 15.00 |

STARDAY

❏ SLP-216 [M]	Arthur "Guitar Boogie" Smith Goes to Town	1963	30.00
❏ SLP-186 [M]	Arthur Smith and the Crossroads Quartet	1962	40.00
❏ SLP-266 [M]	Down Home	1964	30.00
❏ SLP-241 [M]	In Person	1963	30.00
❏ SLP-173 [M]	Mister Guitar	1962	30.00

SMITH, BARTON

FOLKWAYS

| ❏ FSP-33856 | Realizations | 198? | 15.00 |

SMITH, BESSIE

COLUMBIA

❏ CG30126	Any Woman's Blues	1971	18.00
❏ CG30818	Empress	1972	18.00
❏ CG30450	Empty Bed Blues	1971	18.00
❏ CG31093	Nobody's Blues But Mine	1972	18.00
❏ GL503 [M]	The Bessie Smith Story, Volume 1	1951	50.00

— Maroon label, gold print

| ❏ CL855 [M] | The Bessie Smith Story, Volume 1 | 1956 | 30.00 |

— Red and black label with six "eye" logos

| ❏ CL855 [M] | The Bessie Smith Story, Volume 1 | 1963 | 18.00 |

— Red label with "Guaranteed High Fidelity" or "360 Sound Mono

| ❏ GL504 [M] | The Bessie Smith Story, Volume 2 | 1951 | 50.00 |

— Maroon label, gold print

| ❏ CL856 [M] | The Bessie Smith Story, Volume 2 | 1956 | 30.00 |

— Red and black label with six "eye" logos

| ❏ CL856 [M] | The Bessie Smith Story, Volume 2 | 1963 | 18.00 |

— Red label with "Guaranteed High Fidelity" or "360 Sound Mono

| ❏ GL505 [M] | The Bessie Smith Story, Volume 3 | 1951 | 50.00 |

— Maroon label, gold print

| ❏ CL857 [M] | The Bessie Smith Story, Volume 3 | 1956 | 30.00 |

— Red and black label with six "eye" logos

| ❏ CL857 [M] | The Bessie Smith Story, Volume 3 | 1963 | 18.00 |

— Red label with "Guaranteed High Fidelity" or "360 Sound Mono

| ❏ GL506 [M] | The Bessie Smith Story, Volume 4 | 1951 | 50.00 |

— Maroon label, gold print

| ❏ CL858 [M] | The Bessie Smith Story, Volume 4 | 1956 | 30.00 |

— Red and black label with six "eye" logos

| ❏ CL858 [M] | The Bessie Smith Story, Volume 4 | 1963 | 18.00 |

— Red label with "Guaranteed High Fidelity" or "360 Sound Mono

| ❏ C247091 | The Complete Recordings Volume 1: Empress of the Blues | 1991 | 25.00 |

— Box set; none of the subsequent volumes came out on vinyl

| ❏ GP33 | The World's Greatest Blues Singer | 1970 | 25.00 |

COLUMBIA MASTERWORKS

❏ ML4801 [M]	The Bessie Smith Story, Volume 1	1954	30.00
❏ ML4802 [M]	The Bessie Smith Story, Volume 2	1954	30.00
❏ ML4809 [M]	The Bessie Smith Story, Volume 3	1954	30.00
❏ ML4810 [M]	The Bessie Smith Story, Volume 4	1954	30.00

TIME-LIFE

| ❏ STL-J-28 | Giants of Jazz | 1982 | 25.00 |

SMITH, BILL

CONTEMPORARY

| ❏ M-3591 [M] | Folk Jazz | 1961 | 25.00 |
| ❏ S-7591 [S] | Folk Jazz | 1961 | 30.00 |

ONARI

| ❏ 004 | Pick a Number | 198? | 15.00 |

SMITH, BOB

KENT

| ❏ KST-551 | The Visit | 1970 | 100.00 |

— Deduct 25 percent if poster is missing

SMITH, BOBBY

CMH

| ❏ 6225 | Smokin' Bluegrass | 198? | 12.00 |

SMITH, BUSTER

ATLANTIC

| ❏ 1323 [M] | The Legendary Buster Smith | 1960 | 50.00 |

— Black label

| ❏ 1323 [M] | The Legendary Buster Smith | 1961 | 25.00 |

— Multi-color label, white "fan" logo

| ❏ SD1323 [S] | The Legendary Buster Smith | 1960 | 50.00 |

— Green label

| ❏ SD1323 [S] | The Legendary Buster Smith | 1961 | 25.00 |

— Multi-color label, white "fan" logo

SMITH, CAL

DECCA

| ❏ DL75369 | I've Found Someone of My Own | 1972 | 18.00 |

KAPP

❏ KL-1504 [M]	All the World Is Lonely Now	1966	30.00
❏ KS-3504 [S]	All the World Is Lonely Now	1966	25.00
❏ KS-3608	Cal Smith Sings It Takes Me All Night Long	1969	25.00
❏ KS-3585	Drinking Champagne	1968	25.00
❏ KL-1537 [M]	Goin' to Cal's Place	1967	30.00
❏ KS-3537 [S]	Goin' to Cal's Place	1967	25.00
❏ KS-3642	The Best of Cal Smith	1969	18.00
❏ KL-1544 [M]	Travelin' Man	1968	40.00

— White label promo only; in stereo cover with "Mono" sticker

| ❏ KS-3544 [S] | Travelin' Man | 1968 | 25.00 |

MCA

| ❏ 344 | Cal Smith | 1973 | 12.00 |

— Reissue of Decca LP

❏ 424	Country Bumpkin	1974	12.00
❏ 2266	I Just Came Home to Count the Memories	1977	12.00
❏ 467	It's Time to Pay the Fiddler	1975	12.00
❏ 2172	Jason's Farm	1976	12.00
❏ 485	My Kind of Country	1975	12.00
❏ 70	The Best of Cal Smith	1973	12.00

— Reissue of Kapp 3642

SMITH, CARL; LEFTY FRIZZELL; MARTY ROBBINS

COLUMBIA

| ❏ CL2544 [10] | Carl, Lefty and Marty | 1955 | 500.00 |

SMITH, CARL

ABC HICKORY

| ❏ HB-44015 | The Silver-Tongued Cowboy | 1978 | 15.00 |
| ❏ HB-44005 | This Lady Loves Me | 1977 | 15.00 |

COLUMBIA

❏ C30548	Bluegrass	1971	25.00
❏ CL2579 [10]	Carl Smith	1955	100.00
❏ FC38906	Carl Smith	198?	12.00
❏ CL1937 [M]	Carl Smith's Greatest Hits	1962	30.00
❏ CS8737 [S]	Carl Smith's Greatest Hits	1962	30.00
❏ CS9807	Carl Smith's Greatest Hits, Vol. 2	1969	25.00
❏ CS9870	Carl Smith Sings a Tribute to Roy Acuff	1969	25.00
❏ C30215	Carl Smith with the Tunesmiths	1970	25.00
❏ CS9688 [S]	Country on My Mind	1968	25.00
❏ CL2888 [M]	Country on My Mind	1968	50.00
❏ CL2822 [M]	Deep Water	1968	30.00
❏ CS9622 [S]	Deep Water	1968	25.00
❏ C31277	Don't Say You're Mine	1972	25.00
❏ CL1740 [M]	Easy to Please	1961	30.00
❏ CS8540 [S]	Easy to Please	1961	25.00
❏ CS9786	Faded Love and Winter Roses	1969	25.00
❏ KC31606	If This Is Goodbye	1972	25.00
❏ CS9898	I Love You Because	1970	25.00
❏ CL2293 [M]	I Want to Live and Love	1965	25.00
❏ CS9093 [S]	I Want to Live and Love	1965	30.00
❏ CL2358 [M]	Kisses Don't Lie	1965	25.00
❏ CS9158 [S]	Kisses Don't Lie	1965	30.00
❏ CL1172 [M]	Let's Live a Little	1958	60.00
❏ CL2501 [M]	Man with a Plan	1966	25.00
❏ CS9301 [S]	Man with a Plan	1966	30.00
❏ CL9023 [10]	Sentimental Songs	195?	100.00
❏ CL1022 [M]	Smith's the Name	1957	60.00
❏ CL9026 [10]	Softly and Tenderly	195?	80.00
❏ CL959 [M]	Sunday Down South	1957	60.00
❏ GP31	The Carl Smith Anniversary Album/20 Years of Hits	1970	30.00

Number	Title	Yr	NM
❑ CL1532 [M]	The Carl Smith Touch	1960	30.00
❑ CS8352 [S]	The Carl Smith Touch	1960	30.00
❑ CL2610 [M]	The Country Gentleman	1967	25.00
❑ CS9410 [S]	The Country Gentleman	1967	30.00
❑ CL2687 [M]	The Country Gentleman Sings His Favorites	1967	30.00
❑ CS9487 [S]	The Country Gentleman Sings His Favorites	1967	25.00
❑ CL2173 [M]	There Stands the Glass	1964	25.00
❑ CS8973 [S]	There Stands the Glass	1964	30.00
❑ CL2091 [M]	The Tall, Tall Gentleman	1963	25.00
❑ CS8891 [S]	The Tall, Tall Gentleman	1963	30.00

HICKORY/MGM

Number	Title	Yr	NM
❑ H3G4522	The Girl I Love	1975	15.00
❑ H3G4518	The Way I Lose My Mind	1975	15.00

ROUNDER

Number	Title	Yr	NM
❑ SS-25	Old Lonesome Times	1988	12.00

SMITH, CARRIE

AUDIOPHILE

Number	Title	Yr	NM
❑ AP-164	Fine and Mellow	198?	12.00

CLASSIC JAZZ

Number	Title	Yr	NM
❑ 139	Do Your Duty	197?	18.00

WEST 54

Number	Title	Yr	NM
❑ 8002	Carrie Smith	197?	18.00

SMITH, CONNIE, AND NAT STUCKEY

RCA VICTOR

Number	Title	Yr	NM
❑ LSP-4300	Sunday Morning	1970	18.00
❑ LSP-4190	Young Love	1969	25.00

SMITH, CONNIE

COLUMBIA

Number	Title	Yr	NM
❑ KC32185	A Lady Named Smith	1973	15.00
❑ KC33414	Connie Smith Sings Hank Williams Gospel	1975	15.00
❑ KC32492	God Is Abundant	1973	15.00
❑ KC34270	I Don't Want to Talk It Over Anymore	1976	15.00
❑ KC33375	I Got a Lot of Hurtin' Done Today/I've Got My Baby on My Mind	1975	15.00
❑ KC33055	I Never Knew (What That Song Meant Before)	1974	15.00
❑ KC32581	That's the Way Love Goes	1974	15.00
❑ KC34877	The Best of Connie Smith	1977	15.00
❑ KC33918	The Song We Fell in Love To	1976	15.00

MONUMENT

Number	Title	Yr	NM
❑ 7624	New Horizons	1978	15.00
❑ 7609	Pure Connie Smith	1977	15.00

RCA CAMDEN

Number	Title	Yr	NM
❑ CAS-2550	City Lights -- Country Favorites	1972	12.00
❑ CAL-2120 [M]	Connie in the Country	1967	18.00
❑ CAS-2120 [S]	Connie in the Country	1967	15.00
❑ ACL1-0250	Even the Bad Times Are Good	1973	12.00
—With Nat Stuckey			
❑ CAS-2495	My Heart Has a Mind of Its Own	1971	12.00

RCA VICTOR

Number	Title	Yr	NM
❑ LSP-4094	Ain't We Having a Good Time	1972	18.00
❑ LSP-4229	Back in Baby's Arms	1969	25.00
❑ LPM-3628 [M]	Born to Sing	1966	25.00
❑ LSP-3628 [S]	Born to Sing	1966	30.00
❑ LSP-4598	Come Along and Walk with Me	1971	25.00
❑ LSP-4132	Connie's Country	1969	25.00
❑ LPM-3341 [M]	Connie Smith	1965	25.00
❑ LSP-3341 [S]	Connie Smith	1965	30.00
❑ APL1-0275	Connie Smith's Greatest Hits, Volume 1	1973	15.00
❑ LPM-3768 [M]	Connie Smith Sings Bill Anderson	1967	30.00
❑ LSP-3768 [S]	Connie Smith Sings Bill Anderson	1967	25.00
❑ LPM-3589 [M]	Connie Smith Sings Great Sacred Songs	1966	25.00
❑ LSP-3589 [S]	Connie Smith Sings Great Sacred Songs	1966	30.00
❑ LPM-3444 [M]	Cute 'n' Country	1965	25.00
❑ LSP-3444 [S]	Cute 'n' Country	1965	30.00
❑ LPM-3725 [M]	Downtown Country	1967	30.00
❑ LSP-3725 [S]	Downtown Country	1967	25.00
❑ APL1-0188	Dream Painter	1973	15.00
❑ LSP-4748	If It Ain't Love" And Other Great Dallas Frazier Songs	1972	18.00
❑ LSP-4002 [S]	I Love Charley Brown	1968	25.00
❑ LPM-4002 [M]	I Love Charley Brown	1968	80.00
❑ LSP-4394	I Never Once Stopped Loving You	1970	25.00
❑ LSP-4537	Just One Time	1971	18.00
❑ LSP-4840	Love Is the Look You're Looking For	1973	18.00
❑ LPM-3520 [M]	Miss Smith Goes to Nashville	1966	25.00
❑ LSP-3520 [S]	Miss Smith Goes to Nashville	1966	30.00
❑ APL1-0607	Now	1974	15.00
❑ LPM-3889 [M]	Soul of Country Music	1968	50.00
❑ LSP-3889 [S]	Soul of Country Music	1968	25.00
❑ LSP-4077	Sunshine and Rain	1968	25.00
❑ LPM-3848 [M]	The Best of Connie Smith	1967	30.00
❑ LSP-3848 [S]	The Best of Connie Smith	1967	25.00
—Black label, dog on top, "Stereo Dynagroove" at bottom			
❑ LSP-3848 [S]	The Best of Connie Smith	1969	15.00
—Orange label			
❑ LSP-4324	The Best of Connie Smith Volume II	1970	25.00
❑ LSP-4474	Where's My Castle	1971	18.00

SMITH, DAN

BIOGRAPH

Number	Title	Yr	NM
❑ LP-12036	God Is Not Dead	197?	12.00

SMITH, DARDEN

COLUMBIA

Number	Title	Yr	NM
❑ CAS3034 [DJ]	Interchords	1988	18.00
—Promo-only interview record			

EPIC

Number	Title	Yr	NM
❑ E40938	Darden Smith	1988	12.00
❑ EAS1282 [EP]	Live Tracks: Darden Smith	1988	18.00
—Promo-only three-song live EP			

REDI MIX

Number	Title	Yr	NM
❑ RM 001	Native Soil	1986	25.00

SMITH, DEREK

PROGRESSIVE

Number	Title	Yr	NM
❑ PRO-7055	Derek Smith Plays Jerome Kern	198?	12.00
❑ PRO-7002	Love for Sale	197?	15.00
❑ PRO-7035	The Man I Love	197?	15.00

SMITH, DWAYNE, AND ART JOHNSON

CAFÉ

Number	Title	Yr	NM
❑ L-729	Heartbound	1985	12.00

SMITH, EFFIE

JUBILEE

Number	Title	Yr	NM
❑ JGM-2057 [M]	Dial That Telephone	1966	30.00

SMITH, ELLIOTT

BONG LOAD

Number	Title	Yr	NM
❑ BL-48	Figure 8	2000	30.00
❑ BL 35	XO	1998	25.00

KILL ROCK STARS

Number	Title	Yr	NM
❑ KRS-269	Either/Or	1997	15.00
❑ KRS-246	Elliott Smith	1995	15.00

SMITH, ETHEL

DECCA

Number	Title	Yr	NM
❑ DL8187 [M]	Christmas Music	1955	25.00
—Black label, silver print			

SMITH, GREG AND BEV

INTIMA

Number	Title	Yr	NM
❑ SJE-73291	Mr. and Mrs. Smith: No Baggage	1987	15.00

SMITH, GREGG, SINGERS

TURNABOUT

Number	Title	Yr	NM
❑ QTV34710 [Q]	The World Rejoices	1977	18.00

SMITH, HAL

JAZZOLOGY

Number	Title	Yr	NM
❑ J-136	Hal Smith and His Rhythmakers with Butch Thompson	1985	12.00

STOMP OFF

Number	Title	Yr	NM
❑ SOS-1078	Do What Ory Say!	1985	12.00

SMITH, HUEY "PIANO

ACE

Number	Title	Yr	NM
❑ LP-1015 [M]	For Dancing	1961	250.00
❑ 2038	Good Old Rock & Roll	198?	18.00
❑ LP-1004 [M]	Having a Good Time	1959	400.00
❑ LP-2021	Rock 'N' Roll Revival	197?	30.00
❑ LP-1027 [M]	'Twas the Night Before Christmas	1962	250.00
❑ LP-1027 [M]	'Twas the Night Before Christmas	198?	18.00
—Reissue with "Dr. John Band" credited on front cover and label			

GRAND PRIX

Number	Title	Yr	NM
❑ K-418 [M]	Huey "Piano" Smith	196?	25.00
❑ KS-418 [R]	Huey "Piano" Smith	196?	15.00

RHINO

Number	Title	Yr	NM
❑ RNLP-70222	Serious Clownin': The History of Huey "Piano" Smith and the Clowns	1986	15.00

SMITH, HURRICANE

CAPITOL

Number	Title	Yr	NM
❑ ST-11139 [B]	Hurricane Smith	1972	15.00

SMITH, JABBO

MCA

Number	Title	Yr	NM
❑ 1347	Ace of Rhythm	198?	12.00

MELODEON

Number	Title	Yr	NM
❑ 7326	Trumpet Ace of the 20s, Vol. 1	197?	15.00
❑ 7327	Trumpet Ace of the 20s, Vol. 2	197?	15.00

SMITH, JACK

BEL CANTO

Number	Title	Yr	NM
❑ BCM-37 [M]	You Asked for It: Jack Smith Sings	1959	30.00
❑ SR-1015 [S]	You Asked for It: Jack Smith Sings	1959	30.00

SMITH, JENNIE

CANADIAN AMERICAN

Number	Title	Yr	NM
❑ CALP-1010 [M]	Nightly Yours on the Steve Allen Show	1963	30.00

COLUMBIA

Number	Title	Yr	NM
❑ CL1242 [M]	Love Among the Young	1959	30.00
❑ CS8028 [S]	Love Among the Young	1959	40.00

DOT

Number	Title	Yr	NM
❑ DLP-3586 [M]	Jennie	1964	18.00
❑ DLP-25586 [S]	Jennie	1964	25.00

RCA VICTOR

Number	Title	Yr	NM
❑ LPM-1523 [M]	Jennie	1957	40.00

SMITH, JERRY

ABC

Number	Title	Yr	NM
❑ ABCS-692	Truck Stop	1969	18.00

DECCA

Number	Title	Yr	NM
❑ DL75241	Drivin' Home, Steppin' Out	1970	18.00
❑ DL75311	The Touch of Love	1972	18.00

RANWOOD

Number	Title	Yr	NM
❑ R-8126	Ragtime	197?	12.00
❑ R-8111	The New Sound of Jerry Smith and His Pianos	197?	12.00

SMITH, JIMMY, AND WES MONTGOMERY

VERVE

Number	Title	Yr	NM
❑ V-8678 [M]	Jimmy and Wes, The Dynamic Duo	1967	25.00
❑ V6-8678 [S]	Jimmy and Wes, The Dynamic Duo	1967	18.00
❑ UMV-2069	Jimmy and Wes, The Dynamic Duo	198?	12.00
—Reissue of 8678			
❑ V6-8766	The Further Adventures of Jimmy Smith and Wes Montgomery	1969	18.00

SMITH, JIMMY

BLUE NOTE

Number	Title	Yr	NM
❑ BLP-1547 [M]	A Date with Jimmy Smith, Vol. 1	1957	200.00
—Deep groove" version (deep indentation under label on both sides)			
❑ BLP-1547 [M]	A Date with Jimmy Smith, Vol. 1	1957	80.00
—Regular edition, W. 63rd St. address on label			
❑ BLP-1547 [M]	A Date with Jimmy Smith, Vol. 1	1963	30.00
—With New York, USA address on label			
❑ BST-81547 [R]	A Date with Jimmy Smith, Vol. 1	1967	15.00
❑ BLP-1548 [M]	A Date with Jimmy Smith, Vol. 2	1957	200.00
—Deep groove" version (deep indentation under label on both sides)			
❑ BLP-1548 [M]	A Date with Jimmy Smith, Vol. 2	1957	80.00
—Regular edition, W. 63rd St. address on label			
❑ BLP-1548 [M]	A Date with Jimmy Smith, Vol. 2	1963	30.00
—With New York, USA address on label			
❑ BST-81548 [R]	A Date with Jimmy Smith, Vol. 2	1967	15.00
❑ BLP-4117 [M]	Back at the Chicken Shack	1963	30.00
❑ BST-84117 [S]	Back at the Chicken Shack	1963	30.00
—With New York, USA address on label			
❑ BST-84117 [S]	Back at the Chicken Shack	1967	18.00
—With "A Division of Liberty Records" on label			
❑ BST-84117	Back at the Chicken Shack	1985	12.00
—The Finest in Jazz Since 1939" reissue			
❑ BLP-4235 [M]	Bucket!	1966	30.00
❑ BST-84235 [S]	Bucket!	1966	30.00
—With New York, USA address on label			
❑ BST-84235 [S]	Bucket!	1967	18.00
—With "A Division of Liberty Records" on label			
❑ LT-992	Confirmation	1979	12.00
❑ LT-1054	Cool Blues	1980	12.00
❑ BLP-4030 [M]	Crazy Baby	1960	200.00
—Deep groove" version (deep indentation under label on both sides)			
❑ BLP-4030 [M]	Crazy Baby	1960	80.00
—Regular edition, W. 63rd St. address on label			
❑ BLP-4030 [M]	Crazy Baby	1963	30.00
—With New York, USA address on label			
❑ BST-84030 [S]	Crazy Baby	1960	50.00
—With W. 63rd St. address on label			
❑ BST-84030 [S]	Crazy Baby	1963	25.00
—With New York, USA address on label			

Number	Title	Yr	NM
❑ BST-84030 [S]	Crazy Baby	1967	18.00
—With "A Division of Liberty Records" on label			
❑ B1-84030	Crazy Baby	1988	12.00
—The Finest in Jazz Since 1939" reissue			
❑ B1-85125	Go For Whatcha Know	198?	12.00
❑ BLP-1585 [M]	Groovin' at Small's Paradise, Vol. 1	1958	250.00
—Deep groove" version (deep indentation under label on both sides)			
❑ BLP-1585 [M]	Groovin' at Small's Paradise, Vol. 1	1958	80.00
—Regular edition, W. 63rd St. address on label			
❑ BLP-1585 [M]	Groovin' at Small's Paradise, Vol. 1	1963	30.00
—With New York, USA address on label			
❑ BST-1585 [S]	Groovin' at Small's Paradise, Vol. 1	1959	300.00
—Deep groove" version (deep indentation under label on both sides)			
❑ BST-1585 [S]	Groovin' at Small's Paradise, Vol. 1	1959	50.00
—Regular edition, W. 63rd St. address on label			
❑ BST-1585 [S]	Groovin' at Small's Paradise, Vol. 1	1963	25.00
—With New York, USA address on label			
❑ BST-81585 [S]	Groovin' at Small's Paradise, Vol. 1	1967	18.00
❑ BST-81586 [S]	Groovin' at Small's Paradise, Vol. 1	1967	18.00
❑ BLP-1586 [M]	Groovin' at Small's Paradise, Vol. 2	1958	300.00
—Deep groove" version (deep indentation under label on both sides)			
❑ BLP-1586 [M]	Groovin' at Small's Paradise, Vol. 2	1958	80.00
—Regular edition, W. 63rd St. address on label			
❑ BLP-1586 [M]	Groovin' at Small's Paradise, Vol. 2	1963	30.00
—With New York, USA address on label			
❑ BST-1586 [S]	Groovin' at Small's Paradise, Vol. 2	1959	400.00
—Deep groove" version (deep indentation under label on both sides)			
❑ BST-1586 [S]	Groovin' at Small's Paradise, Vol. 2	1959	50.00
—Regular edition, W. 63rd St. address on label			
❑ BST-1586 [S]	Groovin' at Small's Paradise, Vol. 2	1963	25.00
—With New York, USA address on label			
❑ BLP-4050 [M]	Home Cookin'	1961	50.00
—With W. 63rd St. address on label			
❑ BLP-4050 [M]	Home Cookin'	1963	25.00
—With New York, USA address on label			
❑ BST-84050 [S]	Home Cookin'	1961	50.00
—With W. 63rd St. address on label			
❑ BST-84050 [S]	Home Cookin'	1963	25.00
—With New York, USA address on label			
❑ BST-84050 [S]	Home Cookin'	1967	18.00
—With "A Division of Liberty Records" on label			
❑ BLP-4002 [M]	House Party	1959	500.00
—Deep groove" version (deep indentation under label on both sides)			
❑ BLP-4002 [M]	House Party	1959	80.00
—Regular edition, W. 63rd St. address on label			
❑ BLP-4002 [M]	House Party	1963	30.00
—With New York, USA address on label			
❑ BST-4002 [S]	House Party	1959	150.00
—Deep groove" version (deep indentation under label on both sides)			
❑ BST-4002 [S]	House Party	1959	50.00
—Regular edition, W. 63rd St. address on label			
❑ BST-4002 [S]	House Party	1963	25.00
—With New York, USA address on label			
❑ BST-84002 [S]	House Party	1967	18.00
❑ BST-84002	House Party	1985	12.00
—The Finest in Jazz Since 1939" reissue			
❑ BLP-4255 [M]	I'm Movin' On	1967	30.00
❑ BST-84255 [S]	I'm Movin' On	1967	25.00
❑ BN-LA400-H2	Jimmy Smith	1975	18.00
❑ BLP-1512 [M]	Jimmy Smith at the Organ, Vol. 1	1956	350.00
—Deep groove" version (deep indentation under label on both sides)			
❑ BLP-1512 [M]	Jimmy Smith at the Organ, Vol. 1	1956	100.00
—Regular edition, Lexington Ave. address on label			
❑ BLP-1512 [M]	Jimmy Smith at the Organ, Vol. 1	1963	30.00
—With New York, USA address on label			
❑ BLP-1551 [M]	Jimmy Smith at the Organ, Vol. 1	1957	200.00
—Deep groove" version (deep indentation under label on both sides)			
❑ BLP-1551 [M]	Jimmy Smith at the Organ, Vol. 1	1957	80.00
—Regular edition, W. 63rd St. address on label			
❑ BLP-1551 [M]	Jimmy Smith at the Organ, Vol. 1	1963	30.00
—With New York, USA address on label			
❑ BST-81512 [R]	Jimmy Smith at the Organ, Vol. 1	1967	15.00
❑ BST-81551 [R]	Jimmy Smith at the Organ, Vol. 1	1967	15.00
❑ BLP-1514 [M]	Jimmy Smith at the Organ, Vol. 2	1956	350.00
—Deep groove" version (deep indentation under label on both sides)			
❑ BLP-1514 [M]	Jimmy Smith at the Organ, Vol. 2	1956	100.00
—Regular edition, Lexington Ave. address on label			
❑ BLP-1514 [M]	Jimmy Smith at the Organ, Vol. 2	1963	30.00
—With New York, USA address on label			
❑ BLP-1552 [M]	Jimmy Smith at the Organ, Vol. 2	1957	200.00
—Deep groove" version (deep indentation under label on both sides)			
❑ BLP-1552 [M]	Jimmy Smith at the Organ, Vol. 2	1957	80.00
—Regular edition, W. 63rd St. address on label			
❑ BLP-1552 [M]	Jimmy Smith at the Organ, Vol. 2	1963	30.00
—With New York, USA address on label			
❑ BST-81514 [R]	Jimmy Smith at the Organ, Vol. 2	1967	15.00
❑ BST-81552 [R]	Jimmy Smith at the Organ, Vol. 2	1967	15.00
❑ BLP-4100 [M]	Jimmy Smith Plays Fats Waller	1962	50.00
—With 61st St. address on label			
❑ BLP-4100 [M]	Jimmy Smith Plays Fats Waller	1963	25.00
—With New York, USA address on label			
❑ BST-84100 [S]	Jimmy Smith Plays Fats Waller	1962	50.00
—With 61st St. address on label			
❑ BST-84100 [S]	Jimmy Smith Plays Fats Waller	1963	25.00
—With New York, USA address on label			
❑ BST-84100 [S]	Jimmy Smith Plays Fats Waller	1967	18.00
—With "A Division of Liberty Records" on label			
❑ BLP-1563 [M]	Jimmy Smith Plays Pretty Just for You	1957	80.00
—Regular edition, W. 63rd St. address on label			
❑ BLP-1563 [M]	Jimmy Smith Plays Pretty Just for You	1957	200.00
—Deep groove" version (deep indentation under label on both sides)			
❑ BLP-1563 [M]	Jimmy Smith Plays Pretty Just for You	1963	30.00
—With New York, USA address on label			
❑ BST-1563 [S]	Jimmy Smith Plays Pretty Just for You	1959	150.00
—Deep groove" version (deep indentation under label on both sides)			
❑ BST-1563 [S]	Jimmy Smith Plays Pretty Just for You	1959	50.00
—Regular edition, W. 63rd St. address on label			
❑ BST-1563 [S]	Jimmy Smith Plays Pretty Just for You	1963	25.00
—With New York, USA address on label			
❑ BST-81563 [S]	Jimmy Smith Plays Pretty Just for You	1967	18.00
❑ BST-89901	Jimmy Smith's Greatest Hits!	1969	30.00
❑ LWB-89901	Jimmy Smith's Greatest Hits!	198?	18.00
❑ BLP-4078 [M]	Midnight Special	1961	50.00
—With 61st St. address on label			
❑ BLP-4078 [M]	Midnight Special	1963	25.00
—With New York, USA address on label			
❑ BST-84078 [S]	Midnight Special	1961	50.00
—With 61st St. address on label			
❑ BST-84078 [S]	Midnight Special	1963	25.00
—With New York, USA address on label			
❑ BST-84078 [S]	Midnight Special	1967	18.00
—With "A Division of Liberty Records" on label			
❑ B1-84078	Midnight Special	1989	12.00
—The Finest in Jazz Since 1939" reissue			
❑ LT-1092	On the Sunny Side	1981	12.00
❑ BST-84269	Open House	1968	25.00
❑ BST-84296	Plain Talk	1969	25.00
❑ BLP-4164 [M]	Prayer Meetin'	1964	30.00
❑ BST-84164 [S]	Prayer Meetin'	1964	30.00
—With New York, USA address on label			
❑ BST-84164 [S]	Prayer Meetin'	1967	18.00
—With "A Division of Liberty Records" on label			
❑ B1-84164	Prayer Meetin'	1988	12.00
—The Finest in Jazz Since 1939" reissue			
❑ BLP-4141 [M]	Rockin' the Boat	1963	30.00
❑ BST-84141 [S]	Rockin' the Boat	1963	30.00
—With New York, USA address on label			
❑ BST-84141 [S]	Rockin' the Boat	1967	18.00
—With "A Division of Liberty Records" on label			
❑ BLP-4200 [M]	Softly as a Summer Breeze	1965	30.00
❑ BST-84200 [S]	Softly as a Summer Breeze	1965	30.00
—With New York, USA address on label			
❑ BST-84200 [S]	Softly as a Summer Breeze	1967	18.00
—With "A Division of Liberty Records" on label			
❑ B1-91140	The Best of Jimmy Smith	1988	12.00
❑ BLP-1528 [M]	The Incredible Jimmy Smith at Club Baby Grand, Wilmington, Delaware, Vol. 1	1956	150.00
—Deep groove" version (deep indentation under label on both sides)			
❑ BLP-1528 [M]	The Incredible Jimmy Smith at Club Baby Grand, Wilmington, Delaware, Vol. 1	1956	100.00
—Regular edition, Lexington Ave. address on label			
❑ BLP-1528 [M]	The Incredible Jimmy Smith at Club Baby Grand, Wilmington, Delaware, Vol. 1	1963	30.00
—With New York, USA address on label			
❑ BST-81528 [R]	The Incredible Jimmy Smith at Club Baby Grand, Wilmington, Delaware, Vol. 1	1967	15.00
❑ BLP-1529 [M]	The Incredible Jimmy Smith at Club Baby Grand, Wilmington, Delaware, Vol. 2	1956	150.00
—Deep groove" version (deep indentation under label on both sides)			
❑ BLP-1529 [M]	The Incredible Jimmy Smith at Club Baby Grand, Wilmington, Delaware, Vol. 2	1956	100.00
—Regular edition, Lexington Ave. address on label			
❑ BLP-1529 [M]	The Incredible Jimmy Smith at Club Baby Grand, Wilmington, Delaware, Vol. 2	1963	30.00
—With New York, USA address on label			
❑ BST-81529 [R]	The Incredible Jimmy Smith at Club Baby Grand, Wilmington, Delaware, Vol. 2	1967	15.00
❑ BLP-1525 [M]	The Incredible Jimmy Smith at the Organ, Vol. 3	1956	150.00
—Deep groove" version (deep indentation under label on both sides)			
❑ BLP-1525 [M]	The Incredible Jimmy Smith at the Organ, Vol. 3	1956	100.00
—Regular edition, Lexington Ave. address on label			
❑ BLP-1525 [M]	The Incredible Jimmy Smith at the Organ, Vol. 3	1963	30.00
—With New York, USA address on label			
❑ BST-81525 [R]	The Incredible Jimmy Smith at the Organ, Vol. 3	1967	15.00
❑ BLP-4011 [M]	The Sermon	1959	120.00
—Deep groove" version (deep indentation under label on both sides)			
❑ BLP-4011 [M]	The Sermon	1959	80.00
—Regular edition, W. 63rd St. address on label			
❑ BLP-4011 [M]	The Sermon	1963	30.00
—With New York, USA address on label			
❑ BST-4011 [S]	The Sermon	1959	80.00
—Deep groove" version (deep indentation under label on both sides)			
❑ BST-4011 [S]	The Sermon	1959	50.00
—Regular edition, W. 63rd St. address on label			
❑ BST-4011 [S]	The Sermon	1963	25.00
—With New York, USA address on label			
❑ BST-84011 [S]	The Sermon	1967	18.00
❑ BLP-1556 [M]	The Sounds of Jimmy Smith	1957	120.00
—Deep groove" version (deep indentation under label on both sides)			
❑ BLP-1556 [M]	The Sounds of Jimmy Smith	1957	80.00
—Regular edition, W. 63rd St. address on label			
❑ BLP-1556 [M]	The Sounds of Jimmy Smith	1963	30.00
—With New York, USA address on label			
❑ BST-81556 [R]	The Sounds of Jimmy Smith	1967	15.00
ELEKTRA/MUSICIAN			
❑ 60301	Keep On Comin'	1984	12.00
❑ 60175	Off the Top	1983	12.00
GUEST STAR			
❑ G1914 [M]	Jimmy Smith	196?	15.00
❑ 1344 [M]	Jimmy Smith	196?	15.00
INNER CITY			
❑ 1121	The Cat Strikes Again	1981	12.00
MERCURY			
❑ SRM-1-1189	It's Necessary	1977	12.00
❑ SRM-1-1127	Sit On It!	1976	12.00
❑ SRM-1-3716	Unfinished Business	1978	12.00
METRO			
❑ M-521 [M]	Jimmy Smith at the Village Gate	1965	15.00
❑ MS-521 [S]	Jimmy Smith at the Village Gate	1965	15.00
❑ M-568 [M]	Live In Concert/The Incredible Jimmy Smith	196?	15.00
❑ M-568 [S]	Live In Concert/The Incredible Jimmy Smith	196?	15.00
MGM			
❑ SE-4751	I'm Gon' Git Myself Together	1971	15.00
❑ GAS-107	Jimmy Smith (Golden Archive Series)	1970	18.00
❑ SE-4709	The Other Side	1970	15.00
MILESTONE			
❑ M-9176	Prime Time	198?	12.00
MOSAIC			
❑ MQ5-154	The Complete February 1957 Jimmy Smith Blue Note Sessions	199?	80.00
PICKWICK			
❑ SPC-3023	Stranger in Paradise	196?	12.00
PRIDE			
❑ 6011	Black Smith	1974	15.00
SUNSET			
❑ SUM-1175 [M]	Jimmy Smith Plays the Standards	1967	18.00
❑ SUS-5175 [S]	Jimmy Smith Plays the Standards	1967	15.00
❑ SUS-5316	Just Friends	1971	15.00
VERVE			
❑ V6-652-2	24 Karat Hits	196?	18.00
❑ V-8552 [M]	Any Number Can Win	1963	30.00
❑ V6-8552 [S]	Any Number Can Win	1963	30.00
❑ V-8474 [M]	Bashin'	1962	30.00
❑ V6-8474 [S]	Bashin'	1962	40.00

Number	Title	Yr	NM
❑ 823308-1	Bashin'	1986	12.00
—Reissue of 8474			
❑ V6-8809	Bluesmith	1973	15.00
❑ V-8604 [M]	Christmas '64	1964	25.00
❑ V6-8604 [S]	Christmas '64	1964	30.00
❑ V-8666 [M]	Christmas Cookin'	1966	25.00
❑ V6-8666 [S]	Christmas Cookin'	1966	30.00
❑ V-8641 [M]	Got My Mojo Workin'	1966	18.00
❑ V6-8641 [S]	Got My Mojo Workin'	1966	25.00
❑ MAS-90751 [M]	Got My Mojo Workin'	1966	25.00
—Capitol Record Club edition			
❑ SMAS-90751 [S]	Got My Mojo Workin'	1966	30.00
❑ V6-8794	Groove Drops	1970	18.00
❑ V6-8814	History of Jimmy Smith	1973	18.00
❑ V-8544 [M]	Hobo Flats	1963	30.00
❑ V6-8544 [S]	Hobo Flats	1963	30.00
❑ V-8667 [M]	Hoochie Coochie Man	1966	18.00
❑ V6-8667 [S]	Hoochie Coochie Man	1966	25.00
❑ V6-8750	Livin' It Up!	1968	18.00
❑ V-8628 [M]	Organ Grinder Swing	1965	18.00
❑ V6-8628 [S]	Organ Grinder Swing	1965	25.00
❑ UMV-2073	Organ Grinder Swing	198?	12.00
—Reissue of 8628			
❑ V-8652 [M]	Peter and the Wolf	1966	25.00
❑ V6-8652 [S]	Peter and the Wolf	1966	30.00
❑ V6-8800	Plain Brown Wrapper	1971	15.00
❑ V6-8832	Portuguese Soul	1974	15.00
❑ V-8705 [M]	Respect	1967	25.00
❑ V6-8705 [S]	Respect	1967	18.00
❑ V6-8806	Root Down	1972	15.00
❑ V6-8745 [S]	Stay Loose	1968	18.00
❑ V-8721 [M]	The Best of Jimmy Smith	1967	25.00
❑ V6-8721 [S]	The Best of Jimmy Smith	1967	18.00
❑ V6-8770	The Boss	1969	18.00
❑ V-8587 [M]	The Cat	1964	30.00
❑ V6-8587 [S]	The Cat	1964	30.00
❑ V-8618 [M]	The Monster	1965	18.00
❑ V6-8618 [S]	The Monster	1965	25.00
❑ SMAS-90643 [S]	The Monster	1965	30.00
—Capitol Record Club edition			
❑ V-8583 [M]	Who's Afraid of Virginia Woolf?	1964	25.00
❑ V6-8583 [S]	Who's Afraid of Virginia Woolf?	1964	30.00

SMITH, JOHNNY

LEGENDE

Number	Title	Yr	NM
❑ 1401 [10]	Annotations of the Muses	1955	100.00

ROOST

Number	Title	Yr	NM
❑ R-410 [10]	A Three-Dimension Sound Recording of Jazz at NBC with the Johnny Smith Quintet	1953	150.00
❑ LP-2239 [M]	Dear Little Sweetheart	1960	30.00
❑ SLP-2239 [S]	Dear Little Sweetheart	1960	40.00
❑ LP-2238 [M]	Designed for You	1960	30.00
❑ SLP-2238 [S]	Designed for You	1960	40.00
❑ LP-2233 [M]	Easy Listening	1959	40.00
❑ SLP-2233 [S]	Easy Listening	1959	30.00
❑ LP-2237 [M]	Favorites	1959	40.00
❑ SLP-2237 [S]	Favorites	1959	30.00
❑ LP-2231 [M]	Flower Drum Song	1958	40.00
❑ SLP-2231 [S]	Flower Drum Song	1958	30.00
❑ LP-2242 [M]	Guitar and Strings	1960	30.00
❑ SLP-2242 [S]	Guitar and Strings	1960	40.00
❑ LP-2254 [M]	Guitar World	1963	30.00
❑ SLP-2254 [S]	Guitar World	1963	30.00
❑ R-421 [10]	In a Mellow Mood	1954	100.00
❑ R-424 [10]	In a Sentimental Mood	1954	100.00
❑ LP-2223 [M]	Johnny Smith Foursome, Volume 1	1956	50.00
❑ LP-2228 [M]	Johnny Smith Foursome, Volume 2	1957	50.00
❑ LP-2201 [M]	Johnny Smith Plays Jimmy Van Heusen	1955	80.00
❑ LP-2250 [M]	Johnny Smith Plays Jimmy Van Heusen	1963	30.00
❑ SLP-2250 [S]	Johnny Smith Plays Jimmy Van Heusen	1963	30.00
❑ LP-2243 [M]	Johnny Smith Plus the Trio	1960	30.00
❑ SLP-2243 [S]	Johnny Smith Plus the Trio	1960	40.00
❑ LP-2203 [M]	Johnny Smith Quartet	1955	80.00
❑ R-413 [10]	Johnny Smith Quintet	1953	120.00
❑ LP-2248 [M]	Man with the Blue Guitar	1962	30.00
❑ SLP-2248 [S]	Man with the Blue Guitar	1962	40.00
❑ LP-2215 [M]	Moods	1956	60.00
❑ LP-2211 [M]	Moonlight in Vermont	1956	80.00
❑ LP-2216 [M]	New Quartet	1956	60.00
❑ LP-2259 [M]	Reminiscing	1965	30.00
❑ SLP-2259 [S]	Reminiscing	1965	30.00
❑ LP-2246 [M]	The Sound of the Johnny Smith Guitar	1961	30.00
❑ SLP-2246 [S]	The Sound of the Johnny Smith Guitar	1961	40.00

VERVE

Number	Title	Yr	NM
❑ V-8692 [M]	Johnny Smith	1967	30.00
❑ V6-8692 [S]	Johnny Smith	1967	25.00
❑ V-8737 [M]	Johnny Smith's Kaleidoscope	1968	30.00
❑ V6-8737 [S]	Johnny Smith's Kaleidoscope	1968	25.00
❑ V6-8767 [S]	Phase II	1969	25.00

SMITH, KATE

RCA VICTOR

Number	Title	Yr	NM
❑ LPM-3607 [M]	The Kate Smith Christmas Album	1966	15.00
❑ LSP-3607 [S]	The Kate Smith Christmas Album	1966	18.00
—Same as above, but in stereo			

TOPS

Number	Title	Yr	NM
❑ L1677 [M]	Christmas with Kate	195?	18.00

SMITH, KEELY

CAPITOL

Number	Title	Yr	NM
❑ W914 [M]	I Wish You Love	1957	50.00
—Turquoise label			
❑ W914 [M]	I Wish You Love	1959	30.00
—Black label with colorband, Capitol logo at left			
❑ W914 [M]	I Wish You Love	1962	18.00
—Black label with colorband, Capitol logo at top			
❑ SW914 [S]	I Wish You Love	1959	30.00
—Black label with colorband, Capitol logo at left			
❑ SW914 [S]	I Wish You Love	1962	18.00
—Black label with colorband, Capitol logo at top			
❑ T1073 [M]	Politely!	1958	40.00
—Black label with colorband, Capitol logo at left			
❑ T1073 [M]	Politely!	1962	18.00
—Black label with colorband, Capitol logo at top			
❑ ST1073 [S]	Politely!	1959	50.00
—Black label with colorband, Capitol logo at left			
❑ ST1073 [S]	Politely!	1962	25.00
—Black label with colorband, Capitol logo at top			
❑ T1145 [M]	Swingin' Pretty	1959	40.00
—Black label with colorband, Capitol logo at left			
❑ T1145 [M]	Swingin' Pretty	1962	18.00
—Black label with colorband, Capitol logo at top			
❑ ST1145 [S]	Swingin' Pretty	1959	50.00
—Black label with colorband, Capitol logo at left			
❑ ST1145 [S]	Swingin' Pretty	1962	25.00
—Black label with colorband, Capitol logo at top			

DOT

Number	Title	Yr	NM
❑ DLP-3345 [M]	A Keely Christmas	1961	30.00
❑ DLP-25345 [S]	A Keely Christmas	1961	30.00
❑ DLP-3415 [M]	Because You're Mine	1962	30.00
❑ DLP-25415 [S]	Because You're Mine	1962	30.00
❑ DLP-3241 [M]	Be My Love	1959	30.00
❑ DLP-25241 [S]	Be My Love	1959	30.00
❑ DLP-3460 [M]	Cherokeely Swings	1962	30.00
❑ DLP-25460 [S]	Cherokeely Swings	1962	30.00
❑ DLP-3287 [M]	Dearly Beloved	1961	30.00
❑ DLP-25287 [S]	Dearly Beloved	1961	30.00
❑ DLP-3265 [M]	Swing, You Lovers	1960	30.00
❑ DLP-25265 [S]	Swing, You Lovers	1960	30.00
❑ DLP-3423 [M]	Twist with Keely Smith	1962	30.00
❑ DLP-25423 [S]	Twist with Keely Smith	1962	30.00
❑ DLP-3461 [M]	What Kind of Fool Am I	1962	30.00
❑ DLP-25461 [S]	What Kind of Fool Am I	1962	30.00

HARMONY

Number	Title	Yr	NM
❑ HS11333	That Old Black Magic	1968	15.00

REPRISE

Number	Title	Yr	NM
❑ R-6142 [M]	Keely Smith Sings the John Lennon/Paul McCartney Songbook	1964	30.00
❑ RS-6142 [S]	Keely Smith Sings the John Lennon/Paul McCartney Songbook	1964	30.00
❑ R-6086 [M]	Little Girl Blue, Little Girl New	1963	25.00
❑ R9-6086 [S]	Little Girl Blue, Little Girl New	1963	30.00
❑ R-6175 [M]	That Old Black Magic	1965	25.00
❑ RS-6175 [S]	That Old Black Magic	1965	30.00
❑ R-6132 [M]	The Intimate Keely Smith	1964	25.00
❑ RS-6132 [S]	The Intimate Keely Smith	1964	30.00

SMITH, KEITH

GHB

Number	Title	Yr	NM
❑ GHB-27	Keith Smith's Climax Jazz Band	196?	15.00

SMITH, LAVERGNE

COOK

Number	Title	Yr	NM
❑ LP-1081 [10]	Angel in the Absinthe House	1955	150.00

SAVOY

Number	Title	Yr	NM
❑ MG-12031 [M]	New Orleans Nightingale	1955	50.00

VIK

Number	Title	Yr	NM
❑ LX-1056 [M]	La Vergne Smith	1956	50.00

SMITH, LEO

BLACK SAINT

Number	Title	Yr	NM
❑ BSR-0053	Go in Numbers	198?	15.00

ECM

Number	Title	Yr	NM
❑ 1143	Divine Love	1979	15.00

KABELL

Number	Title	Yr	NM
❑ CM-1	Creative Music-1	197?	18.00

NESSA

Number	Title	Yr	NM
❑ N-19	Spirit Catcher	1980	18.00

SACKVILLE

Number	Title	Yr	NM
❑ 3030	Rastafari	198?	12.00

SMITH, LONNIE

BLUE NOTE

Number	Title	Yr	NM
❑ BST-84351	Drives	1971	18.00
❑ B1-28266	Drives	1994	18.00
❑ B1-31880	Live at Club Mozambique	1995	18.00
❑ BST-84326	Move Your Hand	1970	18.00
❑ B1-31249	Move Your Hand	1996	18.00
❑ BST-84290	Think!	1968	25.00
❑ BST-84313	Turning Point	1969	25.00

CHIAROSCURO

Number	Title	Yr	NM
❑ 2019	When the Night Is Right	1979	15.00

COLUMBIA

Number	Title	Yr	NM
❑ CL2696 [M]	Finger-Lickin' Good Soul Organ	1967	30.00
❑ CS9496 [S]	Finger-Lickin' Good Soul Organ	1967	25.00

GROOVE MERCHANT

Number	Title	Yr	NM
❑ 3308	Afro-Desia	1975	15.00
❑ 3312	Keep On Lovin'	1976	15.00

KUDU

Number	Title	Yr	NM
❑ 02	Mama Wailer	1972	15.00

SMITH, LONNIE LISTON

BLUEBIRD

Number	Title	Yr	NM
❑ 6996-1-RB	Golden Dreams	1988	12.00

COLUMBIA

Number	Title	Yr	NM
❑ JC35654	Exotic Mysteries	1979	12.00
❑ JC36373	Love Is the Answer	1980	12.00
❑ JC35332	Loveland	1978	12.00
❑ JC36141	Song for the Children	1979	12.00
❑ JC36366	The Best of Lonnie Liston Smith	1980	12.00

DOCTOR JAZZ

Number	Title	Yr	NM
❑ FW38447	Dreams of Tomorrow	1983	12.00
❑ FW40063	Rejuvenation	1985	12.00
❑ FW39420	Silhouettes	1984	12.00

FLYING DUTCHMAN

Number	Title	Yr	NM
❑ 10163	Astral Travelling	1973	15.00
❑ BDL1-0591	Cosmic Funk	1974	15.00
❑ BXL1-0591	Cosmic Funk	1978	10.00
—Reissue with new prefix			
❑ BDL1-0934	Expressions	1975	15.00
❑ BXL1-0934	Expressions	1978	10.00
—Reissue with new prefix			
❑ BDL1-1460	Reflections of a Golden Dream	1976	15.00
❑ BXL1-1460	Reflections of a Golden Dream	1978	10.00
—Reissue with new prefix			
❑ BDL1-1196	Visions of a New World	1975	15.00
❑ BXL1-1196	Visions of a New World	1978	10.00
—Reissue with new prefix			

RCA VICTOR

Number	Title	Yr	NM
❑ APL1-2433	Live!	1977	12.00
❑ AFL1-2433	Live!	1978	10.00
—Reissue with new prefix			
❑ APL1-1822	Renaissance	1976	12.00
❑ AFL1-1822	Renaissance	1978	10.00
—Reissue with new prefix			
❑ AFL1-2897	The Best of Lonnie Liston Smith	1978	12.00

STARTRAK

Number	Title	Yr	NM
❑ STA-4021	Love Goddess	198?	12.00

SMITH, LOUIS

BLUE NOTE

Number	Title	Yr	NM
❑ BLP-1584 [M]	Here Comes Louis Smith	1958	1000.00
—"Deep groove" version (deep indentation under label on both sides)			
❑ BLP-1584 [M]	Here Comes Louis Smith	1958	800.00
—Regular version, W. 63rd St. address on label			
❑ BST-1584 [S]	Here Comes Louis Smith	1959	800.00
—"Deep groove" version (deep indentation under label on both sides)			
❑ BST-1584 [S]	Here Comes Louis Smith	1959	800.00
—Regular version, W. 63rd St. address on label			
❑ BST-81584 [S]	Here Comes Louis Smith	1967	18.00
—With "A Division of Liberty Records" on label			
❑ BLP-1594 [M]	Smithville	1958	100.00
—"Deep groove" version (deep indentation under label on both sides)			
❑ BLP-1594 [M]	Smithville	1958	80.00
—Regular version, W. 63rd St. address on label			
❑ BST-1594 [S]	Smithville	1959	80.00
—"Deep groove" version (deep indentation under label on both sides)			
❑ BST-1594 [S]	Smithville	1959	60.00
—Regular version, W. 63rd St. address on label			
❑ BST-81594 [S]	Smithville	1967	18.00
—With "A Division of Liberty Records" on label			

STEEPLECHASE

Number	Title	Yr	NM
❑ SCS-1096	Just Friends	198?	15.00
❑ SCS-1121	Prancin'	1979	15.00

SMITH, MARGO

20TH CENTURY

Number	Title	Yr	NM
❑ T-490	Margo Smith	1975	15.00

Number	Title	Yr	NM

WARNER BROS.

Number	Title	Yr	NM
❏ BSK3286	A Woman	1979	12.00
❏ BSK3464	Diamonds and Chills	1980	12.00
❏ BSK3173	Don't Break the Heart That Loves You	1978	12.00
❏ BS3049	Happiness	1977	12.00
❏ BSK3388	Just Margo	1979	12.00
❏ BS2955	Song Bird	1976	12.00

SMITH, MARVIN "SMITTY"

CONCORD JAZZ

❏ CJ-325	Keeper of the Drums	1987	12.00
❏ CJ-379	The Road Less Traveled	1989	15.00

SMITH, MICHAEL

STORYVILLE

❏ 4014	Reflection on Progress	1980	15.00

SMITH, MIKE

DELMARK

❏ DS-444	Unit 7: A Tribute to Cannonball Adderley	1990	15.00

SMITH, O.C.

CARIBOU

❏ PZ34471	Together	1977	30.00

COLUMBIA

❏ CS9756	For Once in My Life	1969	15.00
❏ C30664	Help Me Make It Through the Night	1971	25.00
❏ CS9680 [M]	Hickory Holler Revisited	1968	60.00

—White label promo "Special Mono Radio Station Copy" with stereo number

❏ CS9680 [S]	Hickory Holler Revisited	1968	25.00
❏ KC33247	La La Peace Song	1974	25.00
❏ CS9908	O.C. Smith at Home	1969	15.00
❏ C30227	O.C. Smith's Greatest Hits	1970	15.00
❏ CL2714 [M]	The Dynamic O.C. Smith	1967	60.00
❏ CS9514 [S]	The Dynamic O.C. Smith	1967	40.00

FAMILY

❏ 1000	Dreams Come True	1980	18.00

HARMONY

❏ KH30317	O.C. Smith	1971	12.00

MOTOWN

❏ 6019ML	Love Changes	1982	30.00

RENDEZVOUS

❏ 50006	What'cha Gonna Do	1986	18.00

SHADY BROOK

❏ SB-012	Love Is Forever	1978	15.00

SOUTH BAY

❏ SB1001	Love Changes	1982	30.00

SMITH, OSBORNE

ARGO

| ❏ LP-4000 [M] | Eyes of Love | 1960 | 30.00 |
| ❏ LPS-4000 [S] | Eyes of Love | 1960 | 40.00 |

SMITH, PATTI, GROUP

ARISTA

❏ R100469	Dreams of Life	1988	15.00

—BMG Music Service edition

❏ AL8453	Dreams of Life	1988	12.00
❏ AB4171	Easter	1978	15.00
❏ ALB6-8349	Easter	198?	10.00

—Reissue

| ❏ AL4066 [B] | Horses | 1975 | 18.00 |

—With the word "Horses" in white letters on the front cover

| ❏ ALB6-8362 | Horses | 198? | 10.00 |

—Reissue

| ❏ AL4066 [B] | Horses | 1975 | 25.00 |

—With the word "Horses" in black letters on the front cover

| ❏ AL4097 | Radio Ethiopia | 1977 | 15.00 |
| ❏ ALB6-8379 | Radio Ethiopia | 198? | 10.00 |

—Reissue

| ❏ AB4221 | Wave | 1979 | 12.00 |
| ❏ AL8546 | Wave | 1990 | 10.00 |

—Reissue

COLUMBIA

❏ C290330	Trampin'	2004	18.00

SMITH, PAUL; RAY BROWN; LOUIS BELLSON

DISCWASHER

❏ 001	Intensive Care	1979	25.00

SMITH, PAUL

CAPITOL

❏ T665 [M]	Cascades	1955	40.00
❏ T757 [M]	Cool and Sparkling	1956	40.00
❏ T1017 [M]	Delicate Jazz	1958	30.00
❏ ST1017 [S]	Delicate Jazz	1958	30.00
❏ H493 [10]	Liquid Sounds	1954	80.00
❏ T829 [M]	Softly, Baby	1957	40.00

DISCOVERY

| ❏ DL-3009 [10] | Paul Smith | 1950 | 100.00 |
| ❏ DL-3017 [10] | Paul Smith Trio | 1952 | 80.00 |

MGM

| ❏ E-4057 [M] | Memories of Paris | 1962 | 25.00 |
| ❏ SE-4057 [S] | Memories of Paris | 1962 | 30.00 |

OUTSTANDING

❏ 009	Heavy Jazz	197?	15.00
❏ 011	Heavy Jazz, Vol. 2	1978	15.00
❏ 024	Jazz Spotlight on Ellington and Rodgers	1980	18.00
❏ 023	Jazz Spotlight on Porter and Gershwin	1980	18.00
❏ 004	The Art Tatum Touch	197?	15.00
❏ 007	The Art Tatum Touch, Vol. 2	197?	15.00
❏ 005	The Ballad Touch	197?	15.00
❏ 002	The Master Touch	197?	15.00
❏ 012	This One Cooks!	197?	15.00

PAUSA

❏ 7172	Paul Smith Plays Steve Allen	1985	12.00

SAVOY

❏ MG-12094 [M]	By the Fireside	1956	50.00

SKYLARK

❏ SKLP-13 [10]	Paul Smith Quartet	1954	120.00

TAMPA

| ❏ TP-9 [M] | Fine, Sweet and Tasty | 1957 | 100.00 |

—Colored vinyl

| ❏ TP-9 [M] | Fine, Sweet and Tasty | 1958 | 50.00 |

—Black vinyl

VERVE

❏ MGV-4051 [M]	Carnival! In Percussion	1961	30.00
❏ V-4051 [M]	Carnival! In Percussion	1961	25.00
❏ V6-4051 [S]	Carnival! In Percussion	1961	30.00
❏ MGV-2148 [M]	Latin Keyboards and Percussion	1960	40.00
❏ V-2148 [M]	Latin Keyboards and Percussion	1961	25.00
❏ V6-2148 [S]	Latin Keyboards and Percussion	1961	18.00
❏ MGV-2130 [M]	The Big Men	1960	40.00
❏ MGVS-6135 [S]	The Big Men	1960	30.00
❏ V-2130 [M]	The Big Men	1961	25.00
❏ V6-2130 [S]	The Big Men	1961	18.00
❏ MGV-2128 [M]	The Sound of Music	1960	40.00
❏ MGVS-6128 [S]	The Sound of Music	1960	30.00
❏ V-2128 [M]	The Sound of Music	1961	25.00
❏ V6-2128 [S]	The Sound of Music	1961	18.00

VOSS

❏ VLP1-42937	The Good Life	1988	12.00

SMITH, PINE TOP

BRUNSWICK

❏ BL58003 [10]	Pine Top Smith	1950	120.00

SMITH, PLATO

LAND O' JAZZ

❏ 1972	Dixieland Dance Date	1972	12.00

SMITH, RAY

COLUMBIA

| ❏ CL1937 [M] | Ray Smith's Greatest Hits | 1963 | 30.00 |
| ❏ CS8737 [S] | Ray Smith's Greatest Hits | 1963 | 30.00 |

JUDD

❏ JLPA-701 [M]	Travelin' with Ray	1960	700.00

STOMP OFF

❏ SOS-1012	Jungle Blues	198?	15.00

T

❏ 56062 [M]	The Best of Ray Smith	196?	100.00

WIX

❏ 1000	I'm Gonna Rock Some More	197?	18.00

SMITH, RICHARD

CMG

❏ CML-8011	Puma Creek	1988	12.00

SMITH, ROBERT CURTIS

BLUESVILLE

| ❏ BVLP-1064 [M] | Clarksdale Blues | 1963 | 80.00 |

—Blue label, silver print

| ❏ BVLP-1064 [M] | Clarksdale Blues | 1964 | 30.00 |

—Blue label, trident logo at right

SMITH, ROGER

WARNER BROS.

| ❏ W1305 [M] | Beach Romance | 1960 | 40.00 |
| ❏ WS1305 [S] | Beach Romance | 1960 | 50.00 |

SMITH, RUSSELL

CAPITOL

❏ ST-12197	Russell Smith	1982	10.00

EPIC

❏ FE40918	This Little Town	1988	10.00

SMITH, SAMMI

ELEKTRA

| ❏ 7E-1058 | As Long As There's a Sunday | 1976 | 12.00 |
| ❏ 7E-1108 | Mixed Emotions | 1977 | 12.00 |

HARMONY

❏ H30616	The World of Sammi Smith	1971	12.00

MEGA

❏ 31-1000	Help Me Make It Through the Night	1971	15.00
❏ 31-1007	Lonesome	1971	15.00
❏ MLPS-601	Rainbow in Daddy's Eyes	1974	15.00
❏ MLPS-604	Sammi's Greatest Hits	1974	15.00
❏ 31-1011	Something Old, Something New, Something Blue	1972	15.00
❏ 31-1019	The Best of Sammi Smith	1973	15.00
❏ 31-1021	The Toast of '45	1973	15.00
❏ MLPS-612	Today I Started Loving You Again	1975	15.00

PICKWICK

❏ 6167	Help Me Make It Through the Night	197?	12.00

ZODIAC

❏ 5004	Her Way	1976	12.00

SMITH, SOMETHIN', AND THE REDHEADS

EPIC

| ❏ LN3373 [M] | Put the Blame on Mame | 196? | 30.00 |
| ❏ LN3138 [M] | Somethin' Smith and the Redheads | 1959 | 35.00 |

MGM

| ❏ E-3941 [M] | Ain't We Got Fun Kinda Songs | 1961 | 30.00 |
| ❏ SE-3941 [S] | Ain't We Got Fun Kinda Songs | 1961 | 35.00 |

SMITH, STEVE

COLUMBIA

| ❏ FC44334 | Fiafiaga | 1988 | 12.00 |
| ❏ FC38955 | Vital Information | 1983 | 12.00 |

SMITH, STUFF

20TH FOX

| ❏ FTM-3008 [M] | Sweet Singin' Stuff | 1959 | 30.00 |
| ❏ FTS-3008 [S] | Sweet Singin' Stuff | 1959 | 30.00 |

BASF

❏ 20650	Black Violin	197?	18.00

EVEREST ARCHIVE OF FOLK & JAZZ

❏ 238	Stuff Smith/Guest Artist: Stphane Grappelly	1970	12.00

PRESTIGE

❏ PRST-7691 [R]	The Stuff Smith Memorial Album	1969	18.00

STORYVILLE

❏ 4087	Swingin' Stuff	198?	12.00

VERVE

❏ MGV-8339 [M]	Cat on a Hot Fiddle	1959	50.00
❏ MGVS-6097 [S]	Cat on a Hot Fiddle	1960	40.00
❏ V-8339 [M]	Cat on a Hot Fiddle	1961	25.00
❏ V6-8339 [S]	Cat on a Hot Fiddle	1961	18.00
❏ MGV-8282 [M]	Have Violin, Will Swing	1958	50.00
❏ V-8282 [M]	Have Violin, Will Swing	1961	25.00
❏ MGV-8206 [M]	Soft Winds	1958	50.00
❏ V-8206 [M]	Soft Winds	1961	25.00

SMITH, TAB

CHECKER

| ❏ LP-2971 [M] | Tab Smith | 1960 | 600.00 |

—White label promo with multi-color vinyl

| ❏ LP-2971 [M] | Tab Smith | 1960 | 100.00 |

—Regular issue

UNITED

| ❏ LP-001 [10] | Music Styled by Tab Smith | 1955 | 200.00 |
| ❏ LP-003 [10] | Red, Hot and Cool Blues | 1955 | 200.00 |

SMITH, TOMMY

BLUE NOTE

❏ B1-91930	Step by Step	1989	15.00

STOMP OFF

❏ SOS-1162	South Side Strut: A Tribute to Don Ewell	1989	12.00

SMITH, VERDELLE

CAPITOL

| ❏ T2476 [M] | In My Room | 1966 | 200.00 |
| ❏ ST2476 [S] | In My Room | 1966 | 250.00 |

SMITH, WARREN

LIBERTY

| ❏ LRP-3199 [M] | The First Country Collection of Warren Smith | 1961 | 50.00 |
| ❏ LST-7199 [S] | The First Country Collection of Warren Smith | 1961 | 70.00 |

SMITH, WHISTLING JACK

DERAM

| ❏ DE16006 [M] | I Was Kaiser Bill's Batman | 1967 | 30.00 |
| ❏ DES18006 [S] | I Was Kaiser Bill's Batman | 1967 | 25.00 |

SMITH, WILL

COLUMBIA

❏ C268683	Big Willie Style	1997	18.00

Number	Title	Yr	NM
❏ C286189	Born to Reign	2002	18.00
❏ C269985	Willennium	1999	18.00

SMITH, WILLIE "THE LION", AND DON EWELL

SACKVILLE

Number	Title	Yr	NM
❏ 2004	Grand Piano	198?	12.00

SMITH, WILLIE "THE LION

BLACK LION

Number	Title	Yr	NM
❏ 156	Pork and Beans	197?	18.00

BLUE CIRCLE

| ❏ 1500-33 [10] | Willie "The Lion" Smith | 1952 | 80.00 |

CHIAROSCURO

| ❏ 104 | Live at Blues Alley | 197? | 18.00 |

COMMODORE

| ❏ DL-30004 [M] | The Lion of the Piano | 1951 | 100.00 |
| ❏ XFL-15775 | Willie "The Lion" Smith | 198? | 12.00 |

DIAL

| ❏ LP-305 [10] | Harlem Memories | 1953 | 250.00 |

DOT

| ❏ DLP-3094 [M] | The Lion Roars | 1958 | 50.00 |

GNP CRESCENDO

| ❏ GNP-9011 | Willie "The Lion" Smith | 197? | 12.00 |

GRAND AWARD

| ❏ GA-33-368 [M] | The Legend of Willie Smith | 1956 | 50.00 |

MAINSTREAM

| ❏ 56027 [M] | A Legend | 1965 | 30.00 |
| ❏ S-6027 [R] | A Legend | 1965 | 18.00 |

RCA VICTOR

| ❏ LSP-6016 | Memoirs | 1968 | 25.00 |

URANIA

| ❏ UJLP-1207 [M] | Accent On Piano | 1955 | 60.00 |

SMITH, WILLIE

EMARCY

| ❏ MG-26000 [10] | Relaxin' After Hours | 1954 | 100.00 |

GNP CRESCENDO

| ❏ GNPS-2055 | The Best – Alto Saxophone Supreme | 196? | 12.00 |

MERCURY

| ❏ MG-25075 [10] | Alto Sax Artistry | 1950 | 120.00 |

SMITH-GLAMANN QUINTET

BETHLEHEM

| ❏ BCP-22 [M] | Smith-Glamann Quintet | 1955 | 50.00 |

SMITH

ABC DUNHILL

| ❏ DS-50056 | A Group Called Smith | 1969 | 18.00 |
| ❏ DS-50081 | Minus-Plus | 1970 | 18.00 |

SMITHEREENS, THE

CAPITOL

| ❏ C1-91194 | 11 | 1989 | 15.00 |

CAPITOL/ENIGMA

❏ R130120	Green Thoughts	1988	15.00
—BMG Direct Marketing edition			
❏ C1-48375	Green Thoughts	1988	12.00

ENIGMA

❏ 73220 [EP]	Beauty and Sadness	1988	10.00
—Remixed version of Little Ricky 103 with one track deleted			
❏ R164050	Especially for You	1987	15.00
—BMG Direct Marketing edition			
❏ SEAX-73258 [PD]	Especially for You	1986	25.00
—Picture disc in plastic sleeve, sticker on sleeve			
❏ ST-73208	Especially for You	1986	12.00
❏ (no0 [DJ]	Live at the Roxy -- Special Forces Radio Concert	1986	40.00
❏ (no #)0 [DJ]	Live at the Roxy -- Special Forces Radio Concert	1986	40.00

LITTLE RICKY

| ❏ 103 [EP] | Beauty and Sadness | 1983 | 40.00 |

SMITHS, THE

SIRE

❏ 25669	Louder Than Bombs	1987	18.00
❏ 25269	Meat Is Murder	1985	18.00
❏ 25786	Rank	1988	15.00
❏ 25649	Strangeways, Here We Come	1987	14.00
❏ 25426	The Queen Is Dead	1986	18.00
❏ 25065	The Smiths	1984	18.00

WARNER BROS.

❏ WBMS-130 [DJ]	Music and Interviews	1985	60.00
—Part of "The Warner Bros. Music Show" series; one side is The Smiths; the other side is The Blasters			
❏ WBMS-130 [DJ]	The Warner Bros. Music Show	1985	14.00
—One side: The Smiths; the other side: The Blasters			

SMITHSONIAN JAZZ REPERTORY ENSEMBLE, THE

SMITHSONIAN

Number	Title	Yr	NM
❏ N-021	The Music of Fats Waller and James P. Johnson	1988	18.00

SMOKE, THE (1)

SIDEWALK

| ❏ ST5912 | The Smoke | 1968 | 40.00 |

SMOKE, THE (2)

UNI

| ❏ 73052 | The Smoke | 1969 | 30.00 |
| ❏ 73065 | The Smoke at George's Coffee Shop | 1970 | 30.00 |

SMOKE RISE, THE

PARAMOUNT

| ❏ PAS-9000 [B] | The Survival of St. Joan | 1971 | 30.00 |
| —With booklet | | | |

SMOKER, PAUL

SOUND ASPECTS

| ❏ SAS-006 | Mississippi River Rat | 1985 | 15.00 |

SMOKESTACK LIGHTNIN'

BELL

| ❏ 6026 | Off the Wall | 1969 | 25.00 |

SMOKIE

MCA

| ❏ 2152 | Smokey | 1975 | 15.00 |
| —As "Smokey" | | | |

RSO

| ❏ RS-1-3029 | Bright Lights and Back Alleys | 1978 | 12.00 |
| ❏ RS-1-3005 | Midnight Café | 1976 | 12.00 |

SMOKY BABE

BLUESVILLE

❏ BVLP-1063 [M]	Hottest Brand Going	1963	80.00
—Blue label, silver print			
❏ BVLP-1063 [M]	Hottest Brand Going	1964	30.00
—Blue label, trident logo at right			

FOLK-LYRIC

| ❏ FL-108 [M] | Smokey Babe | 196? | 100.00 |

SMOTHERS, SMOKEY

KING

| ❏ 770 [M] | The Backporch Blues | 1962 | 1000.00 |

SMOTHERS BROTHERS, THE

MERCURY

❏ MG 20905 [M]	Aesop's Fables the Smothers Brothers Way	1965	18.00
❏ SR 60005 [O]	Aesop's Fables the Smothers Brothers Way	1965	25.00
❏ MGDJ-20 [DJ]	Best of the Smothers Brothers	1964	40.00
❏ MCDJ-20 [DJ]	Best of the Smothers Brothers	1964	40.00
❏ MG-20862 [M]	Curb Your Tongue, Knave!	1963	18.00
❏ SR-60862 [S]	Curb Your Tongue, Knave!	1963	25.00
❏ MG-21089 [M]	Golden Hits of the Smothers Brothers, Vol. 2	1966	18.00
❏ SR-61089 [S]	Golden Hits of the Smothers Brothers, Vol. 2	1966	25.00
❏ MG-20904 [M]	It Must Have Been Something I Said!	1964	18.00
❏ SR-60904 [S]	It Must Have Been Something I Said!	1964	25.00
❏ MGDJ-25 [DJ]	It's Brothers Smothers Month	1964	40.00
❏ MGDJ-25 [DJ]	It's Brothers Smothers Month	1964	40.00
❏ MG-21051 [M]	Mom Always Liked You Best!	1965	18.00
❏ SR-61051 [S]	Mom Always Liked You Best!	1965	25.00
❏ SR-61193	Smothers Comedy Brothers Hour	1968	25.00
❏ MG-21064 [M]	The Smothers Brothers Play It Straight	1966	18.00
❏ SR-61064 [S]	The Smothers Brothers Play It Straight	1966	25.00
❏ MG-20611 [M]	The Songs and Comedy of the Smothers Brothers!	1962	18.00
❏ SR-60611 [S]	The Songs and Comedy of the Smothers Brothers!	1962	25.00
❏ MG-20675 [M]	The Two Sides of the Smothers Brothers	1962	18.00
❏ SR-60675 [S]	The Two Sides of the Smothers Brothers	1962	25.00
❏ MG-20777 [M]	(Think Ethnic!)	1963	18.00
❏ SR-60777 [S]	(Think Ethnic!)	1963	25.00
❏ MG-20948 [M]	Tour De Farce American History and Other Unrelated Subjects	1964	18.00
❏ SR-60948 [S]	Tour De Farce American History and Other Unrelated Subjects	1964	25.00

RHINO

| ❏ R1-70188 | Sibling Revelry: The Best of the Smothers Brothers | 1988 | 12.00 |

SNAKEFINGER

RALPH

Number	Title	Yr	NM
❏ SN8353	Against the Grain	1983	15.00
❏ SNK7909	Chewing Hides the Sound	1979	15.00
❏ SN8053	Greener Postures	1980	15.00
❏ SN8203	Manual of Errors	1982	15.00

SNAP

ARISTA

| ❏ AL8536 | World Power | 1990 | 15.00 |

SNEAKY PETE

SHILO

| ❏ 4086 | Sneaky Pete | 1979 | 30.00 |

SNELL, TONY

ESP-DISK'

| ❏ 3004 | Medieval and Latter Day Lays | 197? | 25.00 |

SNIFF 'N' THE TEARS

ATLANTIC

❏ SD19242	Fickle Heart	1979	14.00
—With full version of "Driver's Seat"			
❏ SD19242	Fickle Heart	1979	12.00
—Some pressings erroneously contain an edit of "Driver's Seat" with the entire first verse missing			
❏ SD19272	The Game's Up	1980	12.00

MCA

❏ 5242	Love Action	1981	12.00
❏ 821	Love Action	1983	10.00
—Budget-line reissue			

SNOOP DOGG

DEATH ROW/INTERSCOPE

❏ 92279	Doggystyle	1993	50.00
—As "Snoop Doggy Dogg"			
❏ INT2-90038	Tha Doggfather	1996	50.00
—As "Snoop Doggy Dogg"			

GEFFEN

| ❏ B0003763-01 | R&G (Rhythm & Gangsta): The Masterpiece | 2004 | 18.00 |

NO LIMIT

| ❏ 50006 | Da Game Is to Be Sold, Not to Be Told | 1998 | 30.00 |
| ❏ 50062 | No Limit Top Dogg | 1999 | 30.00 |

PRIORITY

| ❏ 39157 | Paid Tha Cost to Be Tha Bo$$ | 2002 | 30.00 |
| ❏ P123225 | Tha Last Meal | 2000 | 30.00 |

SNOW, HANK, AND ANITA CARTER

RCA VICTOR

| ❏ LPM-2580 [M] | Together Again | 1962 | 30.00 |
| ❏ LSP-2580 [S] | Together Again | 1962 | 40.00 |

SNOW, HANK, AND CHET ATKINS

RCA VICTOR

❏ LSP-4254	By Special Request - C.B. Atkins and C.E. Snow	1970	25.00
❏ LPM-2952 [M]	Reminiscing	1964	30.00
❏ LSP-2952 [S]	Reminiscing	1964	30.00

SNOW, HANK, AND KELLY FOXTON

RCA VICTOR

| ❏ AHL1-3496 | Lovingly Yours | 1980 | 12.00 |
| ❏ AYL1-3987 | Win Some, Lose Some, Lonesome | 1981 | 12.00 |

SNOW, HANK; PORTER WAGONER; HANK LOCKLIN

RCA VICTOR

| ❏ LPM-2723 [M] | Three Country Gentlemen | 1963 | 30.00 |
| ❏ LSP-2723 [S] | Three Country Gentlemen | 1963 | 40.00 |

SNOW, HANK

PAIR

| ❏ PDL2-1004 | I'm Movin' On | 1986 | 15.00 |

RCA CAMDEN

❏ ACL1-0540	I'm Movin' On	1974	12.00
❏ CAS-2348	I Went to Your Wedding	1969	15.00
❏ CAS-2513	Lonesome Whistle	1972	15.00
❏ CAS-2443	Memories Are Made of This	1970	15.00
❏ CAL-2160 [M]	My Early Favorites	1967	18.00
❏ CAS-2160 [S]	My Early Favorites	1967	15.00
❏ CAS-2257 [B]	My Nova Scotia Home	1968	15.00
❏ CAL-836 [M]	Old and Great Songs	1964	18.00
❏ CAS-836 [S]	Old and Great Songs	1964	15.00
❏ ACL1-0124	Snowbird	1973	12.00
❏ CAS-2235	Somewhere Along Life's Highway	1968	15.00
❏ CAL-910 [M]	The Highest Bidder	1965	15.00
❏ CAS-910 [S]	The Highest Bidder	1965	18.00
❏ CAL-782 [M]	The Last Ride	1963	30.00
❏ CAS-782 [R]	The Last Ride	1963	18.00
❏ CAS-2560	The Legend of Old Doc Brown	1972	15.00

Number	Title	Yr	NM
❑ CAL-722 [M]	The One and Only Hank Snow	1962	30.00
❑ CAS-722 [R]	The One and Only Hank Snow	1962	18.00
❑ CAL-514 [M]	The Singing Ranger	1959	25.00
❑ CAS-514 [R]	The Singing Ranger	196?	15.00
❑ CAL-680 [M]	The Southern Cannonball	1961	30.00
❑ CAS-680 [R]	The Southern Cannonball	196?	18.00
❑ CXS-9009	The Wreck of the 97	197?	18.00
❑ CAL-964 [M]	Travelin' Blues	1966	15.00
❑ CAS-964 [S]	Travelin' Blues	1966	18.00
❑ ACL2-0337	When My Blue Moon Turns to Gold Again	197?	18.00

RCA VICTOR

Number	Title	Yr	NM
❑ APL1-2400	#104 -- Still Movin' On	1977	15.00
❑ LSP-4601	Award Winners	1971	25.00
❑ LPM-2458 [M]	Big Country Hits	1961	30.00
❑ LSP-2458 [S]	Big Country Hits	1961	40.00
❑ LPM-3826 [M]	Christmas with Hank Snow	1967	30.00
❑ LSP-3826 [S]	Christmas with Hank Snow	1967	30.00
❑ AHL1-5497	Collector's Series	1986	12.00
❑ LPM-1419 [M]	Country and Western Jamboree	1957	80.00
❑ LPM-3026 [10]	Country Classics	1952	200.00
❑ LPM-1233 [M]	Country Classics	1956	80.00
❑ LSP-4379	Cure for the Blues	1970	25.00
❑ LPM-3378 [M]	Gloryland March	1965	30.00
❑ LSP-3378 [S]	Gloryland March	1965	30.00
❑ LPM-3595 [M]	Gospel Train	1966	30.00
❑ LSP-3595 [S]	Gospel Train	1966	40.00
❑ APL1-0162	Grand Ole Opry Favorites	1973	18.00
❑ ANL1-1207	Grand Ole Opry Favorites	1975	12.00
— Reissue of APL1-0162			
❑ LPM-3548 [M]	Guitar Stylings of Hank Snow	1966	40.00
❑ LSP-3548 [S]	Guitar Stylings of Hank Snow	1966	35.00
❑ LPM-3131 [10]	Hank Snow Salutes Jimmie Rodgers	1953	180.00
❑ LPM-3267 [10]	Hank Snow's Country Guitar	1954	180.00
❑ LPM-1435 [M]	Hank Snow's Country Guitar	1957	80.00
❑ LPM-3070 [10]	Hank Snow Sings	1952	180.00
❑ LSP-4306	Hank Snow Sings in Memory of Jimmie Rodgers	1970	25.00
❑ LPM-2043 [M]	Hank Snow Sings Jimmie Rodgers Songs	1959	50.00
❑ LSP-2043 [S]	Hank Snow Sings Jimmie Rodgers Songs	1959	100.00
❑ LPM-1638 [M]	Hank Snow Sings Sacred Songs	1958	60.00
❑ LPM-2285 [M]	Hank Snow Souvenirs	1961	30.00
❑ LSP-2285 [S]	Hank Snow Souvenirs	1961	40.00
❑ LPM-3471 [M]	Heartbreak Trail - A Tribute to the Sons of the Pioneers	1966	30.00
❑ LSP-3471 [S]	Heartbreak Trail - A Tribute to the Sons of the Pioneers	1966	30.00
❑ APL1-0441	Hello Love	1974	18.00
❑ LPM-3965 [M]	Hits, Hits and More Hits	1968	150.00
❑ LSP-3965 [S]	Hits, Hits and More Hits	1968	30.00
❑ AHL1-3511	Instrumentally Yours	1980	15.00
❑ LPM-2675 [M]	I've Been Everywhere	1963	30.00
❑ LSP-2675 [S]	I've Been Everywhere	1963	40.00
❑ LPM-1113 [M]	Just Keep a-Movin'	1955	100.00
❑ APL1-1361	Live from Evangel Temple	1976	15.00
— With Jimmy Snow			
❑ LPM-2812 [M]	More Hank Snow Souvenirs	1964	30.00
❑ LSP-2812 [S]	More Hank Snow Souvenirs	1964	30.00
❑ AHL1-3208	Mysterious Lady	1979	15.00
❑ LPM-1156 [M]	Old Doc Brown and Other Narrations	1955	100.00
❑ LPM-2705 [M]	Railroad Man	1963	30.00
❑ LSP-2705 [S]	Railroad Man	1963	40.00
❑ LSP-4122	Snow in All Seasons	1969	30.00
❑ LPM-3737 [M]	Snow in Hawaii	1967	30.00
❑ LSP-3737 [S]	Snow in Hawaii	1967	30.00
❑ LPM-2901 [M]	Songs of Tragedy	1964	30.00
❑ LSP-2901 [S]	Songs of Tragedy	1964	30.00
❑ LPM-3857 [M]	Spanish Fire Ball and Other Great Hank Snow Stylings	1967	30.00
❑ LSP-3857 [S]	Spanish Fire Ball and Other Great Hank Snow Stylings	1967	30.00
❑ LSP-4032	Tales of the Yukon	1968	30.00
❑ APL1-0608	That's You and Me	1974	18.00
❑ LPM-3478 [M]	The Best of Hank Snow	1966	25.00
❑ LSP-3478 [S]	The Best of Hank Snow	1966	30.00
❑ ANL1-3470	The Best of Hank Snow	1980	10.00
❑ LSP-4798	The Best of Hank Snow, Vol. 2	1972	18.00
❑ LSP-4708	The Jimmie Rodgers Story	1972	18.00
❑ ANL1-2194	The Jimmie Rodgers Story	1977	12.00
— Reissue of 4708			
❑ DPL2-0134	The Living Legend	197?	100.00
— RCA Special Products release			
❑ LPM-6014 [M]	This Is My Story	1966	40.00
❑ LSP-6014 [S]	This Is My Story	1966	50.00
❑ LSP-4501	Tracks and Trains	1971	25.00
❑ APL1-0908	You're Easy to Love	1975	18.00
❑ LPM-3317 [M]	Your Favorite Country Hits	1965	30.00
❑ LSP-3317 [S]	Your Favorite Country Hits	1965	30.00

READER'S DIGEST

Number	Title	Yr	NM
❑ RDA-216	I'm Movin' On	197?	120.00

SCHOOL OF MUSIC

Number	Title	Yr	NM
❑ 1149 [M]	The Guitar	1958	300.00
— Deduct 20 percent if instruction book is missing			

SNOW, PHOEBE

COLUMBIA

Number	Title	Yr	NM
❑ JC35456	Against the Grain	1978	12.00
❑ PC34387	It Looks Like Snow	1976	12.00
— Original with no bar code			
❑ PC34387	It Looks Like Snow	198?	10.00
— Budget-line reissue with bar code			
❑ JC34875	Never Letting Go	1977	12.00
❑ PC33952	Second Childhood	1976	12.00
— Original with no bar code			
❑ PCQ33952 [Q]	Second Childhood	1976	18.00
❑ PC33952	Second Childhood	198?	10.00
— Budget-line reissue with bar code			
❑ JC37091	The Best of Phoebe Snow	1981	12.00
❑ PC37091	The Best of Phoebe Snow	1981	10.00
— Budget-line reissue			

DCC COMPACT CLASSICS

Number	Title	Yr	NM
❑ LPZ-2027	Phoebe Snow	1996	30.00
— Audiophile vinyl			

ELEKTRA

Number	Title	Yr	NM
❑ 60852	Something Real	1989	12.00

MCA

Number	Title	Yr	NM
❑ 37119	Phoebe Snow	198?	10.00
— Budget-line reissue of Shelter LP			

MIRAGE

Number	Title	Yr	NM
❑ SD19297	Rock Away	1981	12.00

SHELTER

Number	Title	Yr	NM
❑ 2109	Phoebe Snow	1974	12.00
❑ 52017	Phoebe Snow	1977	10.00
— Reissue with ABC distribution			

SNOW, VALAIDA

SWING

Number	Title	Yr	NM
❑ SW-8455/6	Swing Is the Thing	198?	15.00

SNOW

EPIC

Number	Title	Yr	NM
❑ BN26435 [B]	Snow	1969	30.00

SNOWDEN, ELMER

FANTASY

Number	Title	Yr	NM
❑ OJC-1756	Harlem Banjo	198?	12.00

IAJRC

Number	Title	Yr	NM
❑ LP12	Elmer Snowden 1924-63	198?	12.00

RIVERSIDE

Number	Title	Yr	NM
❑ RLP-348 [M]	Harlem Banjo	1960	25.00
❑ RS-9348 [S]	Harlem Banjo	1960	30.00

SNUFF

ELEKTRA

Number	Title	Yr	NM
❑ 60149	Snuff	1982	12.00

SOBULE, JILL

MCA

Number	Title	Yr	NM
❑ 6375	Things Here Are Different	1990	16.00

SOCIAL DISTORTION

13TH FLOOR

Number	Title	Yr	NM
❑ SD1301 [B]	Mommy's Little Monster	1983	60.00
— Standard cover with lyric sheet			
❑ SD1301 [B]	Mommy's Little Monster	1983	80.00
— Gatefold cover			

EPIC

Number	Title	Yr	NM
❑ E46055	Social Distortion	1990	25.00
❑ E47948 [B]	Somewhere Between Heaven and Hell	1992	30.00

EPIC/550 MUSIC

Number	Title	Yr	NM
❑ E64380	White Light, White Heat, White Trash	1996	15.00

RESTLESS

Number	Title	Yr	NM
❑ 72251 [B]	Prison Bound	1988	30.00

TIME BOMB

Number	Title	Yr	NM
❑ 43516 [B]	Live at the Roxy	1998	2000.00
❑ 43502 [B]	Mainliner (Wreckage from the Past)	1995	25.00
❑ 43500 [B]	Mommy's Little Monster	1995	30.00
❑ 43501	Prison Bound	1995	18.00

TRIPLE X

Number	Title	Yr	NM
❑ 51019	Mommy's Little Monster	1989	25.00
— Clear vinyl			

SOCIAL UNREST

LIBERTINE

Number	Title	Yr	NM
❑ LSU1 [EP]	Rat in a Maze	1982	30.00
❑ LSU2461 [B]	SU-2000	1985	30.00

SOCIETY OF SEVEN

SILVER SWORD

Number	Title	Yr	NM
❑ 7012	How Has Your Love Life Been?	1970	25.00

SOCOLOW, FRANK

BETHLEHEM

Number	Title	Yr	NM
❑ BCP-70 [M]	Sounds By Socolow	1957	80.00

SOFT CELL

SIRE

Number	Title	Yr	NM
❑ 23694 [EP]	Non-Stop Ecstatic Dancing	1982	15.00
❑ BSK3647	Non-Stop Erotic Cabaret	1981	15.00
❑ 23989 [EP]	Soul Inside	1983	15.00
❑ 23769 [B]	The Art of Falling Apart	1983	25.00
— With limited 12-inch EP			
❑ 25096 [B]	This Last Night	1984	15.00

SOFT MACHINE, THE

ACCORD

Number	Title	Yr	NM
❑ SN-7178	Memories	1981	12.00

COLUMBIA

Number	Title	Yr	NM
❑ KC31604 [B]	5	1972	18.00
❑ C30754 [B]	Fourth	1971	18.00
❑ KC32716	Seven	1974	15.00
❑ KG32260	Six	1973	18.00
❑ G30339 [B]	Third	1970	25.00

COMMAND

Number	Title	Yr	NM
❑ 964SD	Soft Machine	1973	18.00
— Reissue of Probe LPs in one package			

PROBE

Number	Title	Yr	NM
❑ CPLP-4500 [B]	The Soft Machine	1968	60.00
— Cover with moving parts			
❑ CPLP-4500	The Soft Machine	1969	25.00
— Regular cover			
❑ CPLP-4505 [B]	The Soft Machine, Vol. 2	1969	40.00

SOFTWARE

HEADFIRST

Number	Title	Yr	NM
❑ 9707	Marbles	198?	15.00

INNOVATIVE COMMUNICATION

Number	Title	Yr	NM
❑ KS 80.050	Chip-Meditation	1987	18.00
❑ D1-74766	Digital Dance	1988	15.00
❑ KS 80.055	Electronic Universe	1987	25.00
❑ IC 80.064	Syn-Code/Live in Concert	1988	18.00

SOHO

ATCO

Number	Title	Yr	NM
❑ 91585	Goddess	1990	15.00

SOLAL, MARTIAL

CAPITOL

Number	Title	Yr	NM
❑ T10261 [M]	Martial Solal	1960	30.00
❑ ST10261 [S]	Martial Solal	1960	30.00
❑ T10354 [M]	Vive La France! Viva La Jazz! Vive Solal!	1961	25.00
❑ ST10354 [S]	Vive La France! Viva La Jazz! Vive Solal!	1961	30.00

CONTEMPORARY

Number	Title	Yr	NM
❑ C-2512 [10]	French Modern Sounds	1954	80.00

LIBERTY

Number	Title	Yr	NM
❑ LRP-3335 [M]	Martial Solal in Concert	1963	18.00
❑ LST-7335 [S]	Martial Solal in Concert	1963	25.00

MILESTONE

Number	Title	Yr	NM
❑ MSP-9014	On Home Ground	1969	18.00
❑ MLP-1001 [M]	Solal!	1967	30.00
❑ MSP-9001 [S]	Solal!	1967	18.00

PAUSA

Number	Title	Yr	NM
❑ 7061	Four Keys	197?	12.00
❑ 7103	Movability	198?	12.00

RCA VICTOR

Number	Title	Yr	NM
❑ LPM-2777 [M]	Martial Solal at Newport '63	1963	18.00
❑ LSP-2777 [S]	Martial Solal at Newport '63	1963	25.00

SOUL NOTE

Number	Title	Yr	NM
❑ SN-1060	Bluesine	1983	15.00

SOLAR PLEXUS

INNER CITY

Number	Title	Yr	NM
❑ IC-1087	Earth Songs	1980	15.00
❑ IC-1067	Solar Plexus	1979	15.00

SOLOFF, LEW

PROJAZZ

Number	Title	Yr	NM
❑ PAD-601	Hanalei Bay	1986	12.00

SOLUTION, THE

FIRST AMERICAN

Number	Title	Yr	NM
❑ 7776	It's Only Just Begun	198?	12.00

SOMERSET STRINGS, THE

EPIC

Number	Title	Yr	NM
❑ LN3159 [M]	Music for Christmas at Home	1955	25.00

SOMMER, ELKE

MGM

Number	Title	Yr	NM
❑ E-4321 [M]	Love in Any Language	1965	30.00
❑ SE-4321 [S]	Love in Any Language	1965	30.00

SOMMERS, JOANIE

COLUMBIA

Number	Title	Yr	NM
❑ CL2495 [M]	Come Alive	1966	25.00
❑ CS9295 [S]	Come Alive	1966	30.00

Number	Title	Yr	NM

DISCOVERY

| ❏ DS-883 | Dream | 1983 | 15.00 |
— With Bob Florence

WARNER BROS.

| ❏ B1348 [M] | Behind Closed Doors at a Recording Session | 1960 | 150.00 |
— Record comes in a box with a booklet included

❏ W1436 [M]	For Those Who Think Young	1962	30.00
❏ WS1436 [S]	For Those Who Think Young	1962	40.00
❏ W1412 [M]	Joanie Sommers	1961	30.00
❏ WS1412 [S]	Joanie Sommers	1961	40.00
❏ W1470 [M]	Johnny Get Angry	1962	40.00
❏ WS1470 [S]	Johnny Get Angry	1962	50.00
❏ W1474 [M]	Let's Talk About Love	1962	30.00
❏ WS1474 [S]	Let's Talk About Love	1962	40.00
❏ W1346 [M]	Positively the Most	1960	30.00
❏ WS1346 [S]	Positively the Most	1960	40.00
❏ W1575 [M]	Softly, The Brazilian Sound	1964	30.00
❏ WS1575 [S]	Softly, The Brazilian Sound	1964	30.00
❏ W1504 [M]	Sommers' Seasons	1963	30.00
❏ WS1504 [S]	Sommers' Seasons	1963	30.00

SOMOA

PROJAZZ

| ❏ PAD-645 | No Band Is an Island | 1987 | 12.00 |

SON VOLT

WARNER BROS.

| ❏ 46518 | Straightaways | 1997 | 15.00 |
| ❏ 47059 | Wide Swing Tremolo | 1998 | 15.00 |

SONDHEIM, ALAN

ESP-DISK'

| ❏ 1048 [S] | Ritual-All-7-70 | 1969 | 25.00 |
| ❏ 1082 [S] | T'Other Little Tune | 1969 | 25.00 |

SONIC YOUTH

DGC

❏ 24485 [B]	Dirty	1992	35.00
❏ 24632	Experimental Jet Set, Trash and No Star	1994	40.00
❏ 24297	Goo	1990	30.00
❏ 24825	Washing Machine	1995	40.00

ENIGMA

| ❏ 75403 | Daydream Nation | 1988 | 30.00 |

GEFFEN

| ❏ 490650-1 | NYC Ghosts and Flowers | 2000 | 18.00 |

GOOFIN'

❏ GOO 05	Dirty (Deluxe Edition)	2003	30.00
❏ GOO 07	Goo (Deluxe Edition)	2005	30.00
❏ GOO 04	Murray Street	2002	15.00
❏ GOO11	Rather Ripped	2006	15.00
❏ GOO 06	Sonic Nurse	2004	18.00
❏ GOO 08	Sonic Youth	2006	25.00
— Reissue of 1982 debut album with a second record of bonus tracks

HOMESTEAD

| ❏ HMS 016 [B] | Bad Moon Rising | 1985 | 40.00 |
| ❏ HMS 021 [EP] | Death Valley '69 | 1985 | 40.00 |
— With Lydia Lunch

KONKURRENT

| ❏ FISH-9 | In the Fishtank | 2002 | 18.00 |
— With I.C.P. and The Ex; U.S. editions are distributed by Touch and Go Records

MOBILE FIDELITY

| ❏ 1-257 | Goo | 1996 | 100.00 |
— Audiophile vinyl

MY SO-CALLED RECORDS

| ❏ 3 | A Thousand Leaves | 1998 | 18.00 |

NEUTRAL

❏ 9 [B]	Confusion Is Sex	1983	80.00
❏ N-1 [EP]	Sonic Youth	1982	100.00
❏ 001 [EP]	Sonic Youth	1982	100.00

RHINO

| ❏ R171591 [B] | Made in U.S.A. (Soundtrack) | 1995 | 30.00 |
— Clear vinyl record and sleeve; music recorded in 1986

SST

| ❏ 096 [B] | Confusion Is Sex | 1987 | 50.00 |
— Reissue of Neutral 9

❏ 059 [B]	Evol	1986	60.00
❏ 155 [EP]	Master Dik	1988	40.00
❏ 134 [B]	Sister	1987	30.00
❏ 097 [EP]	Sonic Youth	1987	30.00
❏ 080 [EP]	Starpower	1986	50.00

SYR

| ❏ 1 [B] | Anagrama | 1997 | 12.00 |
— Red vinyl

| ❏ 4 | Goodbye 20th Century | 1999 | 18.00 |
| ❏ 3 | Invito Al Cielo | 1998 | 12.00 |
— With Jim O'Rourke; clear vinyl

| ❏ 5 | Kim Gordon - DJ Olive - Ikue Mori | 2000 | 15.00 |
| ❏ 2 [B] | Slaapkamers Met Slagroom | 1997 | 30.00 |
— Teal vinyl

SONICS, THE (2); THE WAILERS; THE GALAXIES

ETIQUETTE

| ❏ ETALB-025 [M] | Merry Christmas | 1965 | 500.00 |
| ❏ ETALB-025 | Merry Christmas | 1984 | 12.00 |
— Flimsier vinyl, with date on back cover

SONICS, THE (2)

BEAT ROCKET

| ❏ BR114 | Introducing the Sonics | 199? | 15.00 |

BOMP!

| ❏ 4011 | Sinderella | 1980 | 18.00 |

BUCKSHOT

| ❏ 001 | Explosives | 1973 | 200.00 |

ETIQUETTE

| ❏ ETALB-024 [M] | Here Are the Sonics!!! | 1965 | 350.00 |
— Red label

| ❏ ETALB-024 [M] | Here Are the Sonics!!! | 1965 | 300.00 |
— Purple label

| ❏ ETLPS-024 [S] | Here Are the Sonics!!! | 1965 | 400.00 |
— Red label

| ❏ ETLPS-024 [S] | Here Are the Sonics!!! | 1965 | 300.00 |
— Purple label

| ❏ ETLPS-024 | Here Are the Sonics!!! | 1984 | 16.00 |
— Purple label, flimsier vinyl, with date on back cover

❏ ETALB-027 [M]	The Sonics Boom	1966	500.00
❏ ETLPS-027 [R]	The Sonics Boom	1966	200.00
❏ ETLPS-027	The Sonics Boom	1984	12.00
— Flimsier vinyl, with date on back cover

FIRST AMERICAN

❏ FA-7779	Fire and Ice	1983	25.00
❏ FA-7715	Original Northwest Punk	1978	25.00
❏ FA-7719	Unreleased	1980	25.00

JERDEN

| ❏ JRL-7007 [M] | Introducing the Sonics | 1967 | 200.00 |
| ❏ JRS-7007 [R] | Introducing the Sonics | 1967 | 150.00 |

SONN, LARRY

CORAL

| ❏ CRL57057 [M] | The Sound of Sonn | 1956 | 40.00 |

DOT

| ❏ DLP-9005 [M] | Jazz Band Having a Ball | 1958 | 30.00 |
| ❏ DLP-29005 [S] | Jazz Band Having a Ball | 1958 | 30.00 |

SONNIER, JO-EL

RCA

❏ 6374-1-R	Come On Joe	1988	10.00
❏ 9718-1-R	Have a Little Faith	1990	15.00
❏ 8396-RDJ [DJ]	Jo-El	1989	18.00
— Promo-only sampler

ROUNDER

| ❏ 3049 | Cajun Life | 1088 | 12.00 |

SONNY

ATCO

| ❏ 33-229 [M] | Inner Views | 1967 | 25.00 |
| ❏ SD 33-229 [S] | Inner Views | 1967 | 25.00 |

SONNY AND CHER

ATCO

❏ 33-214 [M]	Good Times	1967	18.00
❏ SD 33-214 [S]	Good Times	1967	25.00
❏ 33-203 [M]	In Case You're in Love	1967	18.00
❏ SD 33-203 [S]	In Case You're in Love	1967	25.00
❏ 33-177 [M]	Look At Us	1965	40.00
— Without white box that says "Includes Their Big Hit 'I Got You Babe'" (original)

| ❏ SD 33-177 [S] | Look At Us | 1965 | 30.00 |
— Without white box that says "Includes Their Big Hit 'I Got You Babe'" (original)

| ❏ 33-177 [M] | Look At Us | 1965 | 18.00 |
— With white box that says "Includes Their Big Hit 'I Got You Babe'" (second edition)

| ❏ SD 33-177 [S] | Look At Us | 1965 | 18.00 |
— With white box that says "Includes Their Big Hit 'I Got You Babe'" (second edition)

| ❏ A2M5177 [M] | Sonny & Cher's Greatest Hits | 1967 | 35.00 |
— Columbia Record Club exclusive

| ❏ A2S5178 [S] | Sonny & Cher's Greatest Hits | 1967 | 30.00 |
— Columbia Record Club exclusive

❏ SD11000	The Beat Goes On	1975	18.00
❏ 33-219 [M]	The Best of Sonny and Cher	1967	25.00
❏ SD 33-219 [S]	The Best of Sonny and Cher	1967	25.00
— "What Now My Love," "A Beautiful Story," "But You're Mine" and "Laugh at Me" are rechanneled

| ❏ SD 2-804 | The Two of Us | 1972 | 25.00 |
— Combines "Look at Us" and "In Case You're in Love"

| ❏ 33-183 [M] | The Wondrous World of Sonny and Cher | 1966 | 18.00 |
| ❏ SD 33-183 [S] | The Wondrous World of Sonny and Cher | 1966 | 25.00 |

KAPP

| ❏ KS-3660 | All I Ever Need Is You | 1972 | 18.00 |
— Orange and red swirl label

| ❏ ST-94312 | All I Ever Need Is You | 1972 | 25.00 |
— Capitol Record Club edition

| ❏ KS-3660 | All I Ever Need Is You | 1972 | 25.00 |
— Black label with red "Kapp" cap at top

| ❏ KS-3660 | All I Ever Need Is You | 1972 | 30.00 |
— Red label with red "Kapp" cap at top

| ❏ KRS-5560 | All I Ever Need Is You | 1972 | 15.00 |
— Reissue; orange and red swirl label; some of these have a sticker on the front cover with the new number with no difference in value

| ❏ KS-3654 | Sonny & Cher Live | 1971 | 18.00 |

MCA

| ❏ 2021 | All I Ever Need Is You | 1973 | 15.00 |
— Reissue of Kapp 3660

❏ 2117	Greatest Hits	1974	15.00
❏ 2101	Mama Was a Rock & Roll Singer Papa Used to Write All Her Songs	1973	15.00
❏ 2009	Sonny & Cher Live	1973	15.00
— Reissue of Kapp 3654

| ❏ 2-8004 | Sonny & Cher Live in Las Vegas, Vol. 2 | 1973 | 18.00 |

PAIR

| ❏ PDL2-1140 | Sonny & Cher At Their Best | 1986 | 15.00 |

REPRISE

| ❏ R6177 [M] | Baby Don't Go | 1965 | 30.00 |
| ❏ RS6177 [P] | Baby Don't Go | 1965 | 30.00 |
— By "Sonny & Cher & Friends" (also includes The Lettermen, Bill Medley and The Blendells)

TVP

| ❏ TVP-1021 | The Hits of Sonny & Cher | 1977 | 15.00 |

SONNY AND THE DEMONS

UNITED ARTISTS

| ❏ UAL-3316 [M] | Drag Kings | 1964 | 60.00 |
| ❏ UAS-6316 [S] | Drag Kings | 1964 | 70.00 |

SONS OF BIX, THE

JAZZOLOGY

| ❏ J-99 | Copenhagen | 1983 | 12.00 |
| ❏ J-59 | Ostrich Walk | 1979 | 12.00 |

SONS OF CHAMPLIN, THE

ARIOLA AMERICA

❏ ST-50007	A Circle Filled with Love	1976	12.00
❏ SW-50017	Loving Is Why	1977	12.00
❏ SW-50002	The Sons of Champlin	1975	12.00

CAPITOL

| ❏ ST-675 | Follow Your Heart | 1971 | 25.00 |
| ❏ SWBB-200 [B] | Loosen Up Naturally | 1969 | 60.00 |
— With the F-word clearly visible as part of the cover artwork

| ❏ SWBB-200 | Loosen Up Naturally | 1969 | 30.00 |
— With the F-word scratched off the cover artwork

| ❏ SWBB-200 [B] | Loosen Up Naturally | 1969 | 35.00 |
— With the F-word airbrushed off the cover artwork

| ❏ STAO-022 | The Sons | 1969 | 30.00 |

COLUMBIA

| ❏ KC32341 | Welcome to the Dance | 1973 | 18.00 |

GOLDMINE

| ❏ GM04930 | The Sons of Champlin | 1975 | 25.00 |

SONS OF CHAMPLIN

| ❏ (no #) | Minus Seeds and Stems | 1969 | 500.00 |

SONS OF HEROES

MCA

| ❏ 39010 | Sons of Heroes | 1983 | 25.00 |

SONS OF THE PIONEERS

COLUMBIA

| ❏ FC37439 | The Sons of the Pioneers: Columbia Historical Edition | 1981 | 12.00 |

MCA

| ❏ 730 | Tumbleweed Trails | 198? | 12.00 |

RCA CAMDEN

❏ CAL-587 [M]	Room Full of Roses	1960	25.00
❏ CAL-413 [M]	Wagons West	1958	25.00
❏ CAS-413 [R]	Wagons West	1963	15.00

RCA VICTOR

❏ ANL1-2332	A Country-Western Songbook	1977	18.00
❏ LPM-3714 [M]	Campfire Favorites	1967	30.00
❏ LSP-3714 [S]	Campfire Favorites	1967	25.00
❏ LPM-2118 [M]	Cool Water	1960	30.00
❏ LSP-2118 [S]	Cool Water	1960	30.00
❏ AYL1-3679	Cool Water	1980	12.00
❏ LPM-2855 [M]	Country Fare	1964	25.00
❏ LSP-2855 [S]	Country Fare	1964	30.00
❏ LPM-3032 [10]	Cowboy Classics	1952	100.00
❏ LPM-3095 [10]	Cowboy Hymns and Spirituals	1952	100.00
❏ LPM-2957 [M]	Down Memory Trail	1964	25.00
❏ LSP-2957 [S]	Down Memory Trail	1964	30.00
❏ LPM-1130 [M]	Favorite Cowboy Songs	1955	60.00
❏ LPM-1431 [M]	How Great Thou Art	1957	60.00
❏ LPM-2652 [M]	Hymns of the Cowboy	1963	25.00
❏ LSP-2652 [S]	Hymns of the Cowboy	1963	30.00
❏ LPM-3351 [M]	Legends of the West	1965	18.00
❏ LSP-3351 [S]	Legends of the West	1965	25.00
❏ AYM1-4092	Let's Go West Again	1981	12.00

Number	Title	Yr	NM
❏ LPM-2356 [M]	Lure of the West	1961	30.00
❏ LSP-2356 [S]	Lure of the West	1961	30.00
❏ LPM-1483 [M]	One Man's Songs	1957	60.00
❏ LPM-2603 [M]	Our Men Out West	1963	25.00
❏ LSP-2603 [S]	Our Men Out West	1963	30.00
❏ LPM-3964 [M]	South of the Border	1968	80.00
❏ LSP-3964 [S]	South of the Border	1968	25.00
❏ LPM-3476 [M]	The Best of Sons of the Pioneers	1966	18.00
❏ LSP-3476 [S]	The Best of Sons of the Pioneers	1966	25.00
❏ ANL1-3468	The Best of the Sons of the Pioneers	1980	12.00
❏ LPM-3554 [M]	The Songs of Bob Nolan	1966	18.00
❏ LSP-3554 [S]	The Songs of Bob Nolan	1966	25.00
❏ LPM-2737 [M]	Trail Dust	1963	25.00
❏ LSP-2737 [S]	Trail Dust	1963	30.00
❏ LPM-2456 [M]	Tumbleweed Trails	1962	30.00
❏ LSP-2456 [S]	Tumbleweed Trails	1962	30.00
❏ LPM-3162 [10]	Western Classics	1953	100.00
❏ PRM-104 [M]	Westward Ho!	1961	30.00
—Special-products issue			

READER'S DIGEST

Number	Title	Yr	NM
❏ RBA-135-A	Down Memory Trail with the Sons of the Pioneers	1981	60.00

SILVER SPUR

Number	Title	Yr	NM
❏ S581	Celebration: Commemorating 50 Years of the Sons of the Pioneers	1982	18.00

SONS OF THE PURPLE SAGE

TOPS

Number	Title	Yr	NM
❏ L-1588 [M]	Western Favorites	1959	25.00

WALDORF

Number	Title	Yr	NM
❏ 143 [10]	Songs of the Golden West	1955	50.00

SOPHOMORES, THE (1)

SEECO

Number	Title	Yr	NM
❏ CELP-451 [M]	The Sophomores	1958	200.00

SOPRANO SUMMIT

CHIAROSCURO

Number	Title	Yr	NM
❏ 149	Chalumeau Blue	197?	15.00
❏ 178	Crazy Rhythm	1977	15.00

CONCORD JAZZ

Number	Title	Yr	NM
❏ CJ-52	Live at Concord '77	1977	15.00
❏ CJ-29	Soprano Summit in Concert	1976	15.00

JAZZOLOGY

Number	Title	Yr	NM
❏ J-56	Live at Big Horn Jazzfest	197?	12.00

SOPWITH "CAMEL," THE

KAMA SUTRA

Number	Title	Yr	NM
❏ KSBS-2063	Hello Hello	1973	25.00
❏ KLP-8060 [M]	The Sopwith Camel	1967	30.00
❏ KLPS-8060 [S]	The Sopwith Camel	1967	30.00

REPRISE

Number	Title	Yr	NM
❏ MS2108	The Miraculous Hump Returns	1973	30.00

SOSKIN, MARK

PRESTIGE

Number	Title	Yr	NM
❏ 10109	Rhythm Vision	1979	18.00

SOSSON, MARSHALL

TOWN HALL

Number	Title	Yr	NM
❏ M-26	Virtuoso Jazz Violin Classics	197?	15.00

SOTHERN, ANN

CRAFTSMAN

Number	Title	Yr	NM
❏ C-8061 [M]	It's Ann Sothern Time	1961	25.00

TOPS

Number	Title	Yr	NM
❏ L-1611 [M]	Sothern Exposure	1959	30.00

SOUCHON, DR. EDMOND

GHB

Number	Title	Yr	NM
❏ GHB-6	Dr. Edmond Souchon	1963	18.00
❏ GHB-131	Dr. Edmond Souchon and the Milneburg Boys	1969	15.00

GOLDEN CREST

Number	Title	Yr	NM
❏ GC-3021	Dixieland of New Orleans	196?	18.00
❏ GC-3065	Minstrel Days	196?	18.00

SOUTHLAND

Number	Title	Yr	NM
❏ 231	Dr. Edmond Souchon and the Milneburg Boys	1962	18.00

SOUL, DAVID

PRIVATE STOCK

Number	Title	Yr	NM
❏ PS-2019	David Soul	1977	12.00
❏ PS-7001	Playing to an Audience of One	1977	12.00

SOUL, JIMMY

SPQR

Number	Title	Yr	NM
❏ E16001	If You Wanna Be Happy	1963	150.00

SOUL ASYLUM

A&M

Number	Title	Yr	NM
❏ 7503153181 [B]	...And the Horse They Rode In On	1990	25.00

Number	Title	Yr	NM
—Blue vinyl			
❏ SP-5197	Hang Time	1988	18.00

COLUMBIA

Number	Title	Yr	NM
❏ C67618	Candy From a Stranger	1998	15.00
❏ C48898 [B]	Grave Dancers Union	1993	25.00
❏ C57616	Let Your Dim Light Shine	1995	15.00

TWIN/TONE

Number	Title	Yr	NM
❏ TTR88144 [EP]	Clam Dip & Other Delights	1988	25.00
❏ TTR8666 [B]	Made to Be Broken	1986	25.00
❏ TTR8439	Say What You Will, Clarence...Karl Sold the Truck	1984	25.00
❏ TTR8691 [B]	While You Were Out	1986	25.00

SOUL CHILDREN, THE

EPIC

Number	Title	Yr	NM
❏ PE33902	Finders Keepers	1976	18.00
❏ PE34455	Where Is Your Woman Tonight	1977	18.00

STAX

Number	Title	Yr	NM
❏ STX-4120	Chronicle	1979	15.00
❏ STS-5507	Friction	1974	30.00
❏ STS-3003	Genesis	1972	30.00
❏ STX-4105	Open Door Policy	1978	18.00
❏ STS-2018	Soul Children	1969	30.00
❏ STS-2043	The Best of Two Worlds	1971	30.00

SOUL FINDERS, THE

RCA CAMDEN

Number	Title	Yr	NM
❏ CAL-2239 [M]	An Explosive Album of Soul	1968	40.00
❏ CAS-2239 [S]	An Explosive Album of Soul	1968	40.00
❏ CAL-2170 [M]	Sweet Soul Music	1967	40.00
❏ CAS-2170 [S]	Sweet Soul Music	1967	40.00

SOUL FLUTES

A&M

Number	Title	Yr	NM
❏ SP-3009	Trust in Me	1968	25.00

SOUL GENERATION, THE

EBONY SOUNDS

Number	Title	Yr	NM
❏ 2000 [B]	Beyond Body and Soul	1972	30.00

SOUL SET, THE

JOHNSON

Number	Title	Yr	NM
❏ 1001	The Soul Set	196?	30.00

SOUL SISTERS, THE

SUE

Number	Title	Yr	NM
❏ LP-1022 [M]	I Can't Stand It	1964	200.00
❏ STLP-1022 [S]	I Can't Stand It	1964	400.00

SOUL SOCIETY, THE

DOT

Number	Title	Yr	NM
❏ DLP-25842	Satisfaction	1969	30.00

SOUL STIRRERS, THE

SPECIALTY

Number	Title	Yr	NM
❏ SP-2106 [M]	The Soul Stirrers Featuring Sam Cooke	1959	50.00

SOUL SURVIVORS

ATCO

Number	Title	Yr	NM
❏ SD 33-277	Take Another Look	1969	30.00

CRIMSON

Number	Title	Yr	NM
❏ CR-502 [M]	When the Whistle Blows Anything Goes	1967	50.00
❏ CR-502S [S]	When the Whistle Blows Anything Goes	1967	30.00

TSOP

Number	Title	Yr	NM
❏ KZ33186	The Soul Survivors	1975	15.00

SOULFUL STRINGS, THE

CADET

Number	Title	Yr	NM
❏ LPS-805	Another Exposure	1968	15.00
❏ 50022	Best of the Soulful Strings	1973	15.00
❏ LPS-846	Gamble-Huff	1971	12.00
❏ LPS-796	Groovin' with the Soulful Strings	1967	15.00
❏ LPS-820	In Concert/Back by Demand	1969	15.00
❏ LP-776 [M]	Paint It Black	1967	18.00
❏ LPS-776 [S]	Paint It Black	1967	15.00
❏ LPS-834	String Fever	1969	15.00
❏ LPS-814	The Magic of Christmas	1968	15.00

SOUND FOUNDATION

SMOBRO

Number	Title	Yr	NM
❏ 9001	Sound Foundation	1971	30.00

SOUND OF FEELING

LIMELIGHT

Number	Title	Yr	NM
❏ LS-86063	Spleen	1969	25.00

SOUND SYMPOSIUM, THE

DOT

Number	Title	Yr	NM
❏ DLP-25952	Bob Dylan Interpreted	1969	25.00
❏ DLP-3871 [M]	Paul Simon Interpreted	1968	30.00
—Stereo cover with white "Monaural" sticker; label is regular			

Number	Title	Yr	NM
stock copy			
❏ DLP-25871 [S]	Paul Simon Interpreted	1968	25.00

SOUNDGARDEN

A&M

Number	Title	Yr	NM
❏ 7502153741 [B]	Badmotorfinger	1991	60.00
—Limited edition on yellow vinyl			
❏ 31454 0526-1	Down on the Upside	1996	25.00
❏ SP-17951 [DJ]	Louder Than Live	1990	50.00
—Promo-only live album on blue vinyl			
❏ SP-17951 [DJ]	Louder Than Live	1990	80.00
—Promo-only live album on blue vinyl			
❏ SP-5252	Louder Than Love	1989	25.00
—Black vinyl			
❏ SP-5252	Louder Than Love	1989	60.00
—Green vinyl			
❏ SP-5252	Louder Than Love	1989	40.00
—Red vinyl			
❏ 31454 01981	Superunknown	1994	30.00
—Gold vinyl			
❏ 31454 01981	Superunknown	1994	30.00
—Blue vinyl			
❏ 31454 01981	Superunknown	1994	30.00
—Clear vinyl			

SST

Number	Title	Yr	NM
❏ 911 [10]	Flower	1988	30.00
❏ 231 [EP]	Flower	1988	35.00
❏ 201 [B]	Ultramega OK	1988	40.00

SUB POP

Number	Title	Yr	NM
❏ 17 [EP]	Fopp	1988	60.00
❏ 12 [EP]	Screaming Life	1987	250.00
—First 500 copies on orange vinyl			
❏ 12 [EP]	Screaming Life	1987	50.00
—Black vinyl			
❏ 12 [EP]	Screaming Life	1987	35.00
—Reissues on any color vinyl except black or orange			

SOUNDS OF OUR TIMES, THE

CAPITOL

Number	Title	Yr	NM
❏ ST-182	Galveston	1969	15.00
❏ ST-117	Hey Jude	1969	15.00
❏ ST-8-0117	Hey Jude	1969	18.00
—Capitol Record Club edition			
❏ T2817 [M]	Music of the Flower Children	1968	25.00
❏ ST2817 [S]	Music of the Flower Children	1968	15.00
❏ T2892 [M]	The Sounds of Our Time Play "Love Is Blue"	1968	30.00
❏ ST2892 [S]	The Sounds of Our Time Play "Love Is Blue"	1968	15.00

SOUNDS OF SUNSHINE

P.I.P.

Number	Title	Yr	NM
❏ 6823	Nadia's Theme	1976	12.00

RANWOOD

Number	Title	Yr	NM
❏ 8089	Love Means You Never Have to Say You're Sorry	1971	12.00
❏ 8095	Today Is the First Day (Of the Rest of Your Life)	1972	12.00

SOUNDS ORCHESTRAL

JANUS

Number	Title	Yr	NM
❏ JLS-3014 [B]	One More Time	197?	25.00

PARKWAY

Number	Title	Yr	NM
❏ P7046 [M]	Cast Your Fate to the Wind	1965	25.00
❏ SP7046 [S]	Cast Your Fate to the Wind	1965	25.00
❏ P7050 [M]	Impressions of James Bond	1966	35.00
❏ SP7050 [S]	Impressions of James Bond	1966	30.00
❏ P7047 [M]	The Soul of Sounds Orchestral	1965	25.00
❏ SP7047 [S]	The Soul of Sounds Orchestral	1965	25.00

SOUNDSTAGE ALL-STARS, THE

DOT

Number	Title	Yr	NM
❏ DLP-3204 [M]	More "Peter Gunn"	1959	30.00
❏ DLP-25204 [S]	More "Peter Gunn"	1959	30.00

SOUP

ARF ARM

Number	Title	Yr	NM
❏ 1	Soup	1970	120.00

BIG TREE

Number	Title	Yr	NM
❏ BTS2007	The Album Soup	1971	35.00

SOUP DRAGONS

BIG LIFE/MERCURY

Number	Title	Yr	NM
❏ 842985-1	Lovegod	1990	15.00

MERCURY

Number	Title	Yr	NM
❏ 522732-1	Hydrophonic	1994	15.00
—Clear vinyl			

SIRE

Number	Title	Yr	NM
❏ 25666	Hang Ten!	1987	10.00
❏ 25702	This Is Our Art	1988	10.00

SOUTH, EDDIE

CHESS

Number	Title	Yr	NM
❏ ACMJ-415	South Side Jazz	197?	15.00

Number	Title	Yr	NM
MERCURY			
❏ MG-20401 [M]	The Distinguished Violin of Eddie South	1959	30.00
❏ SR-60070 [S]	The Distinguished Violin of Eddie South	1959	30.00
SWING			
❏ SW-8405	Eddie South	1985	12.00
TRIP			
❏ 5803	Dark Angel of the Fiddle	197?	12.00

SOUTH, JOE

Number	Title	Yr	NM
ACCORD			
❏ SN-7119	Party People	1981	12.00
CAPITOL			
❏ ST-11074	A Look Inside	1972	15.00
❏ ST-392	Don't It Make You Want to Go Home	1969	18.00
❏ ST-235	Games People Play	1969	18.00
❏ ST-108	Introspect	1968	25.00
❏ ST-845	Joe South	1972	15.00
❏ ST-450	Joe South's Greatest Hits	1970	18.00
❏ SM-450	Joe South's Greatest Hits	1977	10.00
—Reissue with new prefix			
❏ ST-637	So the Seeds Are Growing	1971	15.00
ISLAND			
❏ ILPS-9328	Midnight Rainbows	1975	12.00
MINE			
❏ MSG-1100	The Joe South Story	1971	18.00
❏ MSG-1100	Walkin' Shoes	1971	15.00
—Reissue with new title			
NASHVILLE			
❏ 2092	You're the Reason	1970	15.00
PICKWICK			
❏ SPC-3314	Games People Play	197?	12.00

SOUTH 40

Number	Title	Yr	NM
METROBEAT			
❏ MBS-1000	Live at the Someplace Else	1968	30.00

SOUTH CENTRAL AVENUE MUNICIPAL BLUES BAND

Number	Title	Yr	NM
BLUESWAY			
❏ BL-6018	The Soul of Bonnie and Clyde	1968	30.00

SOUTH FRISCO JAZZ BAND, THE

Number	Title	Yr	NM
SFJB			
❏ 2-1978	Diggin' Clams	1978	18.00
STOMP OFF			
❏ SOS-1180	Broken Promises	1988	12.00
❏ SOS-1103	Jones Law Blues	1985	12.00
❏ SOS-1027	Live at Earthquake McGoon's	198?	12.00
❏ SOS-1143	Sage Hen Strut	1987	12.00
❏ SOS-1035	These Cats Are Diggin' Us	198?	12.00
VAULT			
❏ S-9008	Hot Tamale Man	196?	18.00

SOUTHER, HILLMAN, FURAY BAND, THE

Number	Title	Yr	NM
ASYLUM			
❏ 7E-1006	The Souther, Hillman, Furay Band	1974	12.00
❏ 7E-1036	Trouble in Paradise	1975	12.00
❏ EQ-1036 [Q]	Trouble in Paradise	1975	25.00

SOUTHER, J.D.

Number	Title	Yr	NM
ASYLUM			
❏ 7E-1059	Black Rose	1976	12.00
❏ SD5055 [B]	John David Souther	1972	18.00
COLUMBIA			
❏ JC36093	You're Only Lonely	1979	12.00
❏ PC36093	You're Only Lonely	198?	10.00
—Budget-line reissue			
WARNER BROS.			
❏ 25081	Home By Dawn	1985	12.00

SOUTHERN, HAL

Number	Title	Yr	NM
SAGE & SAND			
❏ 46	You Got a Man on Your Hands	1967	30.00

SOUTHERN, JERI

Number	Title	Yr	NM
CAPITOL			
❏ T1278 [M]	Jeri Southern at the Crescendo	1960	30.00
—Black colorband label, Capitol logo at left			
❏ ST1278 [S]	Jeri Southern at the Crescendo	1960	40.00
—Black colorband label, Capitol logo at left			
❏ T1278 [M]	Jeri Southern at the Crescendo	1963	18.00
—Black colorband label, Capitol logo at top			
❏ ST1278 [S]	Jeri Southern at the Crescendo	1963	25.00
—Black colorband label, Capitol logo at top			

Number	Title	Yr	NM
❏ T1173 [M]	Jeri Southern Meets Cole Porter	1959	30.00
—Black colorband label, Capitol logo at left			
❏ ST1173 [S]	Jeri Southern Meets Cole Porter	1959	40.00
—Black colorband label, Capitol logo at left			
❏ T1173 [M]	Jeri Southern Meets Cole Porter	1963	18.00
—Black colorband label, Capitol logo at top			
❏ ST1173 [S]	Jeri Southern Meets Cole Porter	1963	25.00
—Black colorband label, Capitol logo at top			
DECCA			
❏ DL5531 [10]	Intimate Songs	1954	80.00
❏ DL8472 [M]	Jeri Southern Gently Jumps	1957	50.00
❏ DL8745 [M]	Prelude to a Kiss	1958	50.00
❏ DL8761 [M]	Southern Hospitality	1958	50.00
❏ DL8055 [M]	Southern Style	1955	50.00
❏ DL8394 [M]	When Your Heart's on Fire	1956	50.00
❏ DL8214 [M]	You Better Go Now	1956	50.00
FORUM			
❏ F-9030 [M]	Jeri Southern Meets Johnny Smith	196?	15.00
❏ SF-9030 [S]	Jeri Southern Meets Johnny Smith	196?	18.00
PAUSA			
❏ PR9054	Jeri Southern Meets Cole Porter	1986	12.00
—Reissue of Capitol ST 1173			
ROULETTE			
❏ R-25039 [M]	Coffee, Cigarettes and Memories	1958	40.00
❏ R-52016 [M]	Jeri Southern Meets Johnny Smith	1958	40.00
❏ RS-52016 [S]	Jeri Southern Meets Johnny Smith	1958	50.00
❏ R-52010 [M]	Southern Breeze	1958	40.00
❏ RS-52010 [S]	Southern Breeze	1958	50.00
STANYAN			
❏ SR10106	You Better Go Now	1974	18.00
—Reissue of Decca DL 8214			

SOUTHERN CALIFORNIA MORMON CHOIR, THE

Number	Title	Yr	NM
CAPITOL			
❏ T2590 [M]	The Southern California Mormon Choir Sings the Songs of Christmas	1966	15.00
❏ ST2590 [S]	The Southern California Mormon Choir Sings the Songs of Christmas	1966	18.00

SOUTHERN CULTURE ON THE SKIDS

Number	Title	Yr	NM
LLOYD STREET			
❏ SO17737	Southern Culture on the Skids	1985	80.00
SAFEHOUSE			
❏ SH-2114-1 [PD]	Ditch Diggin'	1994	30.00
Picture disc			
TEL STAR			
❏ 20	Dirt Track Date	1995	40.00
❏ TR-40 [B]	Liquored Up and Lacquered Down	2000	18.00
❏ TR30	Plastic Seat Sweat	1997	15.00
YEP ROC			
❏ LP-YEP-2120	Double Wide and Live	2006	25.00
❏ 2063	Mojo Box	2004	18.00

SOUTHERN PACIFIC

Number	Title	Yr	NM
WARNER BROS.			
❏ 25409	Killbilly Hill	1986	10.00
❏ 25206	Southern Pacific	1985	10.00
❏ 25609	Zuma	1988	10.00

SOUTHERN STOMPERS, THE

Number	Title	Yr	NM
STOMP OFF			
❏ SOS-1215	Echoes of King Oliver's Jazz Band	1991	12.00

SOUTHSIDE JOHNNY AND THE ASBURY JUKES

Number	Title	Yr	NM
ATLANTIC			
❏ 81654	At Least We Got Shoes	1986	10.00
CYPRESS			
❏ YL-0115	Slow Dance	1988	12.00
EPIC			
❏ JE36246	Havin' a Party with Southside Johnny	1979	12.00
❏ PE36246	Havin' a Party with Southside Johnny	198?	10.00
—Budget-line reissue with new prefix			
❏ JE35488	Hearts of Stone	1978	12.00
—Orange label, no bar code			
❏ PE35488	Hearts of Stone	198?	10.00
—Dark blue label, bar code on back cover			
❏ PE34180	I Don't Want to Go Home	1976	12.00
—Orange label, no bar code			
❏ PE34180	I Don't Want to Go Home	1979	10.00
—Dark blue label, most have bar codes on back cover			
❏ AS275 [DJ]	Jukes Live at the Bottom Line	1976	30.00

Number	Title	Yr	NM
❏ PE34668	This Time It's for Real	1977	12.00
—Orange label, no bar code			
❏ PE34668	This Time It's for Real	198?	10.00
—Dark blue label, bar code on back cover			
MERCURY			
❏ SRM-2-8602	Live -- Reach Out and Touch the Sky	1981	15.00
❏ 826285-1	Live -- Reach Out and Touch the Sky	198?	12.00
—Reissue of 8602			
❏ SRM-1-3836	Love Is a Sacrifice	1980	12.00
❏ SRM-1-3793	The Jukes	1979	12.00
MIRAGE			
❏ 90186	In the Heat	1984	12.00
❏ 90113	Trash It Up!	1983	12.00

SOUTHWEST F.O.B.

Number	Title	Yr	NM
HIP			
❏ 7001 [B]	Smell of Incense	1969	40.00

SOVINE, RED

Number	Title	Yr	NM
CHART			
❏ 2056	It'll Come Back	1974	18.00
❏ 1052	The Greatest Grand Ol' Opry	1972	18.00
DECCA			
❏ DL4736 [M]	Country Music Time	1966	30.00
❏ DL74736 [R]	Country Music Time	1966	25.00
❏ DL4445 [M]	Red Sovine	1963	30.00
❏ DL74445 [R]	Red Sovine	1963	25.00
GUSTO			
❏ 3010	16 All-Time Favorites	1978	15.00
MGM			
❏ E-3465 [M]	Red Sovine	1957	60.00
NASHVILLE			
❏ 2044	A Dear John Letter	196?	15.00
❏ 2056	Anytime	196?	15.00
❏ 2083	Don't Take Your Love to Town	1969	15.00
❏ 2033	Giddy-Up Go	196?	15.00
POWER PAK			
❏ 270	Phantom 309	197?	12.00
STARDAY			
❏ SLP-436	Classic Narrations	1968	25.00
❏ SLP-441	Closing Time 'Til Dawn	1969	25.00
❏ SLP-363 [M]	Giddy-Up Go	1966	25.00
❏ T-90712 [M]	Giddy-Up Go	1966	30.00
—Capitol Record Club edition			
❏ ST-90712 [S]	Giddy-Up Go	1966	30.00
—Capitol Record Club edition			
❏ SLP 197 [M]	Golden Country Ballads of the 1960s	1962	40.00
❏ SLP-405 [M]	I Didn't Jump the Fence	1967	25.00
❏ SLP-459	I Know You're Married But I Love You Still	1970	25.00
❏ SLP-341 [M]	Little Rosa	1965	30.00
❏ SLP-414 [M]	Phantom 309	1967	25.00
❏ 991	Red Sovine's 16 Greatest Hits	1977	18.00
❏ SLP-427	Sunday with Sovine	1968	25.00
❏ 968	Teddy Bear	1976	18.00
❏ SLP-420	Tell Maude I Slipped	1968	25.00
❏ SLP-357	That's Truckdrivin'	196?	25.00
❏ 952	The Best of Red Sovine	197?	18.00
❏ SLP-396 [M]	The Nashville Sound of Red Sovine	1967	25.00
❏ SLP-132 [M]	The One and Only Red Sovine	1961	40.00
❏ SLP-383 [M]	Town and Country Action	1966	25.00
❏ SLP-445	Who Am I	1969	25.00
❏ 970	Woodrow Wilson Sovine	1977	18.00
VOCALION			
❏ VL3829 [M]	The Country Way	196?	18.00
❏ VL73829 [R]	The Country Way	196?	15.00

SPACE

Number	Title	Yr	NM
1750 ARCH			
❏ 1806	An Interesting Breakfast Conversation	198?	15.00
HAND			
❏ 5167	Space	1969	30.00

SPACEK, SISSY

Number	Title	Yr	NM
ATLANTIC AMERICA			
❏ 90100	Hangin' Up My Heart	1983	12.00

SPACEMEN, THE

Number	Title	Yr	NM
ROULETTE			
❏ R-25322 [M]	Music for Batman and Robin	1966	40.00
❏ SR-25322 [S]	Music for Batman and Robin	1966	50.00
❏ R-25275 [M]	Rockin' in the 25th Century	1964	30.00
❏ SR-25275 [S]	Rockin' in the 25th Century	1964	40.00

SPANDAU BALLET

Number	Title	Yr	NM
CHRYSALIS			
❏ CHR1353	Diamond	1982	12.00
❏ FV41353	Diamond	1983	10.00
—Reissue of CHR 1353			
❏ PV41353	Diamond	1986	10.00

Number	Title	Yr	NM
—Reissue of FV 41353 with new prefix			
❑ CHR1331	Journeys to Glory	1981	15.00
❑ FV41331	Journeys to Glory	1983	10.00
—Reissue			
❑ FV41473	Parade	1984	12.00
❑ FV41498	The Singles Collection	1985	12.00
❑ FV41403	TRUE	1983	10.00
—Reissue with new prefix			
❑ B6V41403	TRUE	1983	15.00
—Original prefix			
EPIC			
❑ FE40642	Through the Barricades	1987	15.00
MOBILE FIDELITY			
❑ 1-152	TRUE	1984	25.00
—Audiophile vinyl			

SPANIELS, THE

Number	Title	Yr	NM
LOST-NITE			
❑ LLP-19 [10]	The Spaniels	1981	15.00
—Red vinyl			
VEE JAY			
❑ LP-1002 [M]	Goodnite, It's Time to Go	1958	600.00
—Maroon label; group pictured on cover			
❑ LP-1002 [M]	Goodnite, It's Time to Go	1961	200.00
—Black label; dogs on cover			
❑ VJLP-1002 [M]	Goodnite, It's Time to Go	198?	15.00
—Legitimate reissue on flimsier vinyl than originals			
❑ LP-1024 [M]	The Spaniels	1960	300.00

SPANIER, MUGGSY

Number	Title	Yr	NM
AVA			
❑ A-12 [M]	Columbia, the Gem of the Ocean	1963	15.00
❑ AS-12 [S]	Columbia, the Gem of the Ocean	1963	18.00
COMMODORE			
❑ FL-30016 [M]	Chicago Jazz	1957	50.00
❑ XFL-15777	Muggsy Spanier at Nick's New York, April 1944	198?	12.00
❑ FL-20009 [10]	Spanier's Ragtimers	1950	100.00
DECCA			
❑ DL5552 [10]	Hot Horn	1955	60.00
EMARCY			
❑ MG-26011 [10]	Muggsy Spanier and His Dixieland Band	1954	100.00
EVEREST ARCHIVE OF FOLK & JAZZ			
❑ 226	Muggsy Spanier	1968	12.00
❑ 326	Muggsy Spanier, Vol. 2	197?	12.00
GLENDALE			
❑ GLS6024	One of a Kind	198?	12.00
JAZZ ARCHIVES			
❑ JA-44	Jazz from California	198?	12.00
❑ JA-30	Little David Play Your Harp	198?	12.00
JAZZOLOGY			
❑ J-33	Muggsy Spanier	197?	12.00
❑ J-115	Relaxin' at Touro -- 1952	198?	12.00
LONDON			
❑ AL-3503 [S]	Muggsy, Tesch and the Chicagoans	195?	30.00
❑ LL3528 [M]	Muggsy Spanier and the Bucktown Five	1959	40.00
MERCURY			
❑ MG-25095 [10]	Muggsy Spanier and His Dixieland Band	1953	120.00
❑ MG-20171 [M]	Muggsy Spanier and His Dixieland Band	1956	50.00
RCA VICTOR			
❑ LPM-3043 [10]	Ragtime Favorites	195?	120.00
❑ LPM-1295 [M]	The Great 16	1956	50.00
RIVERSIDE			
❑ RLP 12-107 [M]	Classic Early Recordings	1955	60.00
❑ RLP-1004 [10]	Muggsy Spanier and Frank Teschemacher	1953	120.00
❑ RLP-1035 [10]	Muggsy Spanier and His Bucktown Five	1954	120.00
RKO			
❑ ULP130 [M]	Chicago Jazz	195?	25.00
STINSON			
❑ SLP30 [M]	Muggsy Spanier's Ragtimers, Vol. 1	1962	50.00
—Red vinyl			
❑ SLP30 [M]	Muggsy Spanier's Ragtimers, Vol. 1	1962	30.00
—Black vinyl			
❑ SLP31 [M]	Muggsy Spanier's Ragtimers, Vol. 2	1962	50.00
—Red vinyl			
❑ SLP31 [M]	Muggsy Spanier's Ragtimers, Vol. 2	1962	30.00
—Black vinyl			
STORYVILLE			
❑ 4053	Hot Horn	198?	12.00
❑ 4020	Muggsy Spanier	198?	12.00
❑ 4056	Muggsy Spanier at Club Hangover	198?	12.00
TRIP			
❑ 5532	Dixieland Session	197?	12.00
WEATHERS INDUSTRIES			
❑ W-5401 [M]	Dynamic Dixie	1954	60.00
ZEE GEE			
❑ 101 [10]	Muggsy Spanier's Ragtimers, Vol. 1	195?	120.00
❑ 102 [10]	Muggsy Spanier's Ragtimers, Vol. 2	195?	120.00

SPANKY AND OUR GANG

Number	Title	Yr	NM
EPIC			
❑ PE33580	Change	1975	15.00
MERCURY			
❑ SR-61183	Anything You Choose/ Without Rhyme or Reason	1969	25.00
❑ SR-61161	Like to Get to Know You	1968	25.00
❑ SR-61326	Live	1971	18.00
❑ MG-21124 [M]	Spanky and Our Gang	1967	30.00
❑ SR-61124 [S]	Spanky and Our Gang	1967	25.00
❑ SR-61227	Spanky's Greatest Hit(s)	1969	25.00
RHINO			
❑ RNLP-70131	The Best of Spanky and Our Gang (1967-1969)	1986	15.00

SPANN, LES

Number	Title	Yr	NM
JAZZLAND			
❑ JLP-35 [M]	Gemini	1961	30.00
❑ JLP-935 [S]	Gemini	1961	30.00

SPANN, LUCILLE

Number	Title	Yr	NM
BLUESWAY			
❑ BLS-6070	Cry Before I Go	1974	30.00

SPANN, OTIS

Number	Title	Yr	NM
BARNABY			
❑ Z30246	Otis Spann Is the Blues	1970	25.00
❑ KZ31290	Walking the Blues	1972	25.00
BLUE HORIZON			
❑ BH4802	The Biggest Thing Since Colossus	1970	30.00
BLUES TIME			
❑ 9006	Sweet Giant of the Blues	1970	25.00
BLUESWAY			
❑ BLS-6063	Heart Loaded with Trouble	1973	25.00
❑ BL-6003 [M]	The Blues Is Where It's At	1967	30.00
❑ BLS-6003 [S]	The Blues Is Where It's At	1967	30.00
❑ BLS-6013	The Bottom of the Blues	1968	30.00
CANDID			
❑ CM-8001 [M]	Otis Spann Is the Blues	1966	150.00
❑ CS-9001 [S]	Otis Spann Is the Blues	1966	200.00
LONDON			
❑ PS551	Cracked Spanner Head	1969	30.00
❑ PS543	Raw Blues	1968	30.00
PRESTIGE			
❑ PRST-7719	The Blues Will Never Die	1969	25.00
TESTAMENT			
❑ T-2211	Otis Spann's Chicago Blues	1966	40.00
VANGUARD			
❑ VSD-6514	Cryin' Time	1970	25.00

SPARKS, MELVIN

Number	Title	Yr	NM
MUSE			
❑ MR-5248	Sparkling	1981	18.00
PRESTIGE			
❑ 10039	Akilah!	1973	25.00
❑ 10016	Spark Plug	1972	25.00
❑ 10001	Sparks!	1971	25.00
WESTBOUND			
❑ 204	Melvin Sparks '75	1975	25.00

SPARKS, RANDY

Number	Title	Yr	NM
VERVE			
❑ MGV-2103 [M]	Randy Sparks	1959	30.00
❑ MGV-2143 [M]	Randy Sparks Three	1960	30.00
❑ MGV-2126 [M]	Walkin' the Low Road	1960	30.00

SPARKS

Number	Title	Yr	NM
ANTILLES			
❑ ANT-7044	Kimono My House	198?	12.00
—Reissue of Island 9272			
ATLANTIC			
❑ SD19347	Angst in My Pants	1982	12.00
❑ 80160	Pulling Rabbits Out of a Hat	1984	12.00
❑ 80055	Sparks in Outer Space	1983	12.00
BEARSVILLE			
❑ BR2110 [B]	A Woofer in Tweeter's Clothing	1973	30.00
❑ BV2048 [B]	Halfnelson	1971	50.00
—Original issue of "Sparks" as "Halfnelson			
❑ BV2048 [B]	Sparks	1972	25.00
—Reissue under the group's new name			
COLUMBIA			
❑ PC34359 [B]	Big Beat	1976	15.00
—Originals have no bar code			
❑ PC34901	Introducing Sparks	1977	12.00
—Originals have no bar code			
ELEKTRA			
❑ 6E-186	No. 1 in Heaven	1979	12.00
IN THE RED			
❑ ITR131	Hello Young Lovers	2006	15.00
ISLAND			
❑ ILPS-9345 [B]	Indiscreet	1975	18.00
—Originals have black label and no Warner Bros. distribution			
❑ ILPS-9272 [B]	Kimono My House	1974	18.00
—Originals have multicolor island-scene label			
❑ 5318093	Kimono My House	2009	25.00
❑ ILPS-9312	Propaganda	1975	15.00
—Originals have multicolor island-scene label			
MCA CURB			
❑ 5780	Music That You Can Dance To	1986	12.00
RCA VICTOR			
❑ AFL1-4091	Whomp That Sucker	1981	12.00
RHINO			
❑ R1-70841	Interior Design	1988	12.00

SPARROW, THE

Number	Title	Yr	NM
COLUMBIA			
❑ CS9758	John Kay and Sparrow	1969	40.00
—Red "360 Sound" label			

SPARROWS, THE

Number	Title	Yr	NM
ELKAY			
❑ 3009 [M]	That Mersey Sound	1964	40.00

SPATS, THE

Number	Title	Yr	NM
ABC-PARAMOUNT			
❑ 502 [M]	Cookin' with the Spats	1965	25.00
❑ S-502 [S]	Cookin' with the Spats	1965	30.00

SPAULDING, JAMES

Number	Title	Yr	NM
MUSE			
❑ MR-5369	Brilliant Corners	1989	12.00
❑ MR-5413	Gotstabe a Better Way!	1990	15.00
STORYVILLE			
❑ 4034	Jame Spaulding Plays the Legacy of Duke	1980	15.00

SPEARS, BILLIE JO

Number	Title	Yr	NM
CAPITOL			
❑ ST-560	Country Girl	1970	18.00
❑ ST-688	Just Singin'	1971	18.00
❑ ST-397	Miss Sincerity	1969	18.00
❑ ST-224	Mr. Walker, It's All Over!	1969	18.00
❑ SM-11887	The Best of Billie Jo Spears	1979	12.00
❑ ST-114	The Voice of Billie Jo Spears	1969	25.00
❑ ST-454	With Love	1970	18.00
LIBERTY			
❑ LN-10018	Blanket on the Ground	1980	10.00
❑ LN-10021	If You Want Me	1980	10.00
❑ LN-10020	I Will Survive	1980	10.00
❑ LN-10019	Love Ain't Gonna Wait for Us	1980	10.00
❑ LT-1074	Only the Hits	1981	10.00
UNITED ARTISTS			
❑ UA-LA508-G	Billie Jo	1975	12.00
❑ UA-LA390-G	Blanket on the Ground	1975	12.00
❑ UA-LA748-G	If You Want Me	1977	12.00
❑ UA-LA684-G	I'm Not Easy	1976	12.00
❑ UA-LA859-G	Lonely Hearts Club	1977	12.00
❑ UA-LA921-H	Love Ain't Gonna Wait for Us	1978	12.00
❑ LT-1018	Standing Tall	1980	12.00
❑ LT-983	The Singles Album	1979	12.00
❑ UA-LA608-G	What I've Got in Mind	1976	12.00

SPECIAL EFX

Number	Title	Yr	NM
GRP			
❑ GR-9581	Confidential	1989	15.00
❑ GR-1048	Double Feature	1988	12.00
❑ GR-1014	Modern Manners	1986	12.00
❑ GR-1033	Mystique	1987	12.00
❑ GR-1025	Slice of Life	1987	12.00
❑ GR-1007	Special EFX	1986	12.00

SPECIALS, THE

Number	Title	Yr	NM
CHRYSALIS			
❑ CHR1303	More Specials	1980	15.00
❑ PV41303	More Specials	1983	10.00
—Reissue			
❑ CHR1265	The Specials	1979	18.00
❑ PV41265	The Specials	1986	12.00
—Reissue			

SPECTOR, RONNIE

Number	Title	Yr	NM
COLUMBIA			
❑ C40620	Unfinished Business	1987	12.00
POLISH			
❑ PRG-808	Siren	1980	15.00

SPELLBINDERS, THE

Number	Title	Yr	NM
COLUMBIA			
❑ CL2514 [M]	The Magic of the Spellbinders	1966	25.00

Number	Title	Yr	NM
❏ CS9314 [S]	The Magic of the Spellbinders	1966	30.00

SPENCE, ALEXANDER "SKIP

COLUMBIA
| ❏ CS9831 | Oar | 1969 | 60.00 |
SUNDAZED
| ❏ LP5030 | Oar | 2000 | 25.00 |
—Reissue on 180-gram vinyl

SPENCER, JEREMY

ATLANTIC
| ❏ SD19236 | Flee | 1979 | 12.00 |
COLUMBIA
| ❏ KC31990 | Jeremy Spencer and the Children of God | 1972 | 18.00 |

SPENCER, JON, BLUES EXPLOSION

CAROLINE
| ❏ 1719 [B] | Jon Spencer Blues Explosion | 1992 | 18.00 |
CRYPT
| ❏ 29 [B] | Crypt Style | 1991 | 30.00 |
MATADOR
| ❏ OLE322-1 | Acme | 1998 | 12.00 |
| ❏ (# unknown)0 [DJ] | Controversial Negro | 1997 | 30.00 |
—Promo-only vinyl issue of a Japanese live CD
❏ OLE52-1 [B]	Extra Width	1993	18.00
❏ OLE193-1	Now I Got Worry	1996	12.00
❏ OLE105-1 [B]	Orange	1994	18.00
❏ OLE376-1	Xtra-Acme USA	1999	18.00

SPENCER, LEON, JR.

PRESTIGE
❏ 10042	Bad Walking Woman	1973	25.00
❏ 10033	Louisiana Slim	1972	25.00
❏ 10011	Sneak Preview!	1971	25.00
❏ 10063	Where I'm Coming From	197?	18.00

SPENCER, TRACIE

CAPITOL
| ❏ C1-92153 | Make the Difference | 1990 | 15.00 |
| ❏ C1-48186 | Tracie Spencer | 1988 | 10.00 |

SPHEERIS, JIMMY

COLUMBIA
| ❏ C30988 | The Isle of View | 1972 | 18.00 |
| ❏ KC32157 | The Original Tap Dancing Kid | 1973 | 18.00 |
EPIC
| ❏ PE34276 | Ports of the Heart | 1976 | 15.00 |
| ❏ PE33565 | The Dragon Is Dancing | 1975 | 15.00 |

SPHERE (1)

STRATA
| ❏ 103-74 | Inside Ourselves | 1974 | 18.00 |

SPHERE (2)

ELEKTRA/MUSICIAN
| ❏ 60313 | Flight Path | 1984 | 12.00 |
| ❏ 60166 | Four in One | 1982 | 12.00 |
RED RECORD
| ❏ VPA-191 | Sphere On Tour | 1986 | 15.00 |
VERVE
| ❏ 837032-1 | Bird Songs | 198? | 12.00 |
| ❏ 831674-1 | Four for All | 1987 | 12.00 |

SPHEROE

INNER CITY
| ❏ IC-1034 | Spheroe | 197? | 18.00 |

SPIDER-MAN

LIFESONG
| ❏ LS6001 [B] | Rock Reflections of a Superhero | 1976 | 40.00 |

SPIDERS, THE (1)

IMPERIAL
| ❏ LP-9142 [M] | I Didn't Wanna Do It | 1961 | 600.00 |

SPIEGEL, VICTOR

EAGLE
| ❏ SM-4197 | Wind on the Water | 1985 | 15.00 |

SPIN DOCTORS

EPIC
| ❏ E52907 | Turn It Upside Down | 1994 | 12.00 |

SPINAL TAP

MCA
| ❏ 10514 [PD] | Break Like the Wind | 1992 | 18.00 |
—Picture disc (only U.S. vinyl version of this LP)

SPINNERS, THE

TIME
| ❏ 52092 [M] | Party -- My Pad After Surfin' | 1963 | 30.00 |
| ❏ S-2092 [S] | Party -- My Pad After Surfin' | 1963 | 30.00 |

SPINNERS

ATLANTIC
❏ SD19318	Can't Shake This Feelin'	1981	12.00
❏ SD19256	Dancin' and Lovin'	1980	12.00
❏ SD19219	From Here to Eternally	1979	15.00
❏ 80020	Grand Slam	1982	12.00
❏ SD18181	Happiness is Being with the Spinners	1976	15.00
❏ SD16032	Labor of Love	1981	12.00
❏ SD19270	Love Trippin'	1980	12.00
❏ SD7296	Mighty Love	1974	15.00
❏ SD18118	New and Improved	1974	15.00
❏ QD18118 [Q]	New and Improved	1974	25.00
❏ SD18141	Pick of the Litter	1975	15.00
❏ QD18141 [Q]	Pick of the Litter	1975	25.00
❏ SD7256	Spinners	1973	15.00
❏ QD7256 [Q]	Spinners	1974	25.00
❏ SD19146	Spinners/8	1977	15.00
❏ SD 2-910	Spinners Live!	1975	18.00
❏ SD19179	The Best of the Spinners	1978	15.00
❏ SD19100	Yesterday, Today & Tomorrow	1977	15.00
MIRAGE
| ❏ 90456 | Lovin' Feelings | 1985 | 12.00 |
MOTOWN
❏ M5-109V1	Motown Superstar Series, Vol. 9	1982	10.00
❏ M769	The Best of the Spinners	1973	18.00
❏ M5-199V1	The Best of the Spinners	1981	15.00
—Reissue of Motown 769
❏ M639 [M]	The Original Spinners	1967	30.00
❏ MS639 [P]	The Original Spinners	1967	30.00
❏ M5-132V1	The Original Spinners	1981	15.00
—Reissue of Motown 639
V.I.P.
| ❏ 405 | 2nd Time Around | 1970 | 40.00 |
VOLT
| ❏ V-3403 | Down to Business | 1989 | 15.00 |

SPINORAMA ORCHESTRA AND CHORUS, THE

SPIN-O-RAMA
| ❏ XMK-4012 [M] | Christmas Sing Along | 195? | 18.00 |

SPINOZZA, DAVID

A&M
| ❏ SP-4677 | Spinozza | 1978 | 12.00 |

SPIRAL STARECASE

COLUMBIA
| ❏ CS9852 | More Today Than Yesterday | 1969 | 30.00 |
—.360 Sound" label

SPIRIT

EPIC
| ❏ KE31175 | Feedback | 1972 | 25.00 |
— Yellow label
| ❏ KE31175 | Feedback | 1973 | 12.00 |
— Orange label
| ❏ KEG31457 | Spirit | 1972 | 18.00 |
—Reissue of Ode 44004 and 44016 in one package; yellow labels
| ❏ PEG31457 | Spirit | 197? | 15.00 |
—Reissue with new prefix and orange labels
| ❏ KE32271 | The Best of Spirit | 1973 | 15.00 |
| ❏ PE32271 | The Best of Spirit | 1979 | 10.00 |
—Dark blue label; bar code on cover
| ❏ KE31461 | The Family That Plays Together | 1972 | 15.00 |
—Reissue of Ode 44014 with slightly different cover; yellow label
| ❏ KE31461 | The Family That Plays Together | 1973 | 12.00 |
— Orange label
| ❏ BG33761 [B] | The Family That Plays Together/Feedback | 1976 | 18.00 |
| ❏ E30267 [B] | Twelve Dreams of Dr. Sardonicus | 1970 | 30.00 |
— Yellow label
| ❏ KE30267 | Twelve Dreams of Dr. Sardonicus | 1973 | 12.00 |
— Orange label
| ❏ PE30267 | Twelve Dreams of Dr. Sardonicus | 197? | 10.00 |
— Orange or dark blue label, with or without bar code
I.R.S.
| ❏ 82007 | Rapture in the Chambers | 1989 | 15.00 |
MERCURY
❏ SRM-1-1094	Farther Along	1976	15.00
❏ SRM-1-1122	Future Games	1977	15.00
❏ SRM-1-1053	Son of Spirit	1975	15.00
❏ SRM-2-804 [B]	Spirit of '76	1975	25.00
❏ 818514-1	Spirit of '84	1984	12.00
ODE
❏ Z1244016	Clear Spirit	1969	30.00
❏ Z1244004 [S]	Spirit	1968	30.00
❏ Z1244003 [M]	Spirit	1968	100.00
❏ Z1244014	The Family That Plays Together	1968	30.00
POTATO
| ❏ 2001 | Live | 1978 | 12.00 |
RHINO
| ❏ RNSP-303 | Potatoland | 1981 | 12.00 |
SUNDAZED
❏ LP5082	Clear	2001	16.00
❏ LP5068	Eventide	2000	16.00
❏ LP5067	Now or Anywhere	2000	16.00
❏ LP5085	The Family That Plays Together	2001	16.00

SPIRIT OF NEW ORLEANS JAZZ BAND, THE

GHB
| ❏ GHB-247 | The Spirit of New Orleans Jazz Band | 198? | 12.00 |

SPIRITS AND WORM

A&M
| ❏ SP-4229 | Spirits and Worm | 1969 | 800.00 |

SPIRITUAL CONCEPT

PHILADELPHIA INT'L.
| ❏ KZ32404 [B] | Spiritual Concept | 1973 | 35.00 |

SPITFIRE BAND, THE

COLUMBIA
| ❏ FC39891 | Flight III | 1985 | 12.00 |

SPIVAK, CHARLIE

CIRCLE
❏ 17	Charlie Spivak and His Orchestra: Now!	1981	12.00
❏ 16	Charlie Spivak and His Orchestra 1942	198?	12.00
❏ CLP-80	Charlie Spivak and His Orchestra 1946	1985	12.00
HINDSIGHT
| ❏ HSR-188 | Charlie Spivak and His Orchestra 1941 | 198? | 12.00 |
| ❏ HSR-105 | Charlie Spivak and His Orchestra 1943-46 | 198? | 12.00 |
INSIGHT
| ❏ 215 | Charlie Spivak and His Orchestra 1943-46 | 198? | 12.00 |

SPIVAK, DUBBY

AUDIOPHILE
| ❏ AP-189 | Dubby Swings Lightly | 1986 | 12.00 |

SPIVEY, VICTORIA

SPIVEY
❏ LP-1001 [M]	Basket of Blues	1962	30.00
❏ LP-1009 [M]	Encore for the Chicago Blues	1964	30.00
❏ LP-2001 [M]	Recorded Legacy of the Blues	196?	30.00
❏ LP-1015 [M]	Spivey's Blues Cavalcade	196?	30.00
❏ LP-1012 [M]	Spivey's Blues Parade	196?	30.00
❏ LP-1017 [M]	Spivey's Blues Showcase	196?	30.00
❏ LP-1008 [M]	The Bluesmen of the Muddy Waters Band	1964	30.00
❏ LP-1010 [M]	The Bluesmen of the Muddy Waters Band, Volume Two	1964	30.00
❏ LP-1006 [M]	The Queen and Her Knights	1964	30.00
❏ LP-1004 [M]	Three Kings and a Queen	1964	50.00
—Bob Dylan plays on this LP; no blurb on cover
| ❏ LP-1004 [M] | Three Kings and a Queen | 196? | 30.00 |
—Historic Tracks, Bob Dylan Appears with Big Joe Williams" blurb on cover
| ❏ LP-1014 [M] | Three Kings and a Queen, Volume Two | 196? | 30.00 |
| ❏ LP-1002 [M] | Victoria and Her Blues | 1963 | 30.00 |

SPLINTER

DARK HORSE
❏ SP-22006	Harder to Live	1975	25.00
❏ SP-22001	The Place I Love	1974	25.00
❏ DH3073	Two Man Band	1977	30.00

SPLIT ENZ

A&M
| ❏ SP-4963 | Conflicting Emotions | 1984 | 12.00 |
| ❏ SP-3153 | Frenzy | 1981 | 15.00 |
—First U.S. issue of 1979 recordings
❏ SP-3289	History Never Repeats: The Best of Split Enz	1987	15.00
❏ SP-4894	Time & Tide	1982	15.00
❏ SP-3256	Time & Tide	1984	10.00
—Reissue
| ❏ SP-4822 | True Colours | 1980 | 12.00 |
—All copies are laser etched on one side; mostly purple cover with yellow triangles
| ❏ SP-3235 | True Colours | 1984 | 25.00 |
—Reissue; record is NOT laser etched

Number	Title	Yr	NM
❑ SP-4822	True Colours	1980	12.00

—All copies are laser etched on one side; mostly red cover with green triangles

❑ SP-4822	True Colours	1980	12.00

—All copies are laser etched on one side; mostly yellow cover with blue triangles

❑ SP-4822	True Colours	1980	12.00

—All copies are laser etched on one side; mostly blue cover with orange triangles

❑ SP-4848	Waiata	1981	12.00
❑ SP-3255	Waiata	1984	10.00

—Reissue

CHRYSALIS

❑ CHR1145	Disrythmia	1977	15.00
❑ PV41145	Disrythmia	198?	10.00

—Budget-line reissue of CHR 1145

❑ CHR1131	Mental Notes	1976	15.00
❑ PV41131	Mental Notes	198?	10.00

—Budget-line reissue of CHR 1131

SPOELSTRA, MARK

ELEKTRA

❑ EKL-283 [M]	Five and Twenty Questions	1965	25.00
❑ EKS-7283 [S]	Five and Twenty Questions	1965	30.00
❑ EKL-307 [M]	State of Mind	1966	25.00
❑ EKS-7307 [S]	State of Mind	1966	30.00

VERVE FOLKWAYS

❑ FV-9018 [M]	The Times I've Had	196?	25.00
❑ FVS-9018 [S]	The Times I've Had	196?	30.00

SPOKESMEN, THE

DECCA

❑ DL4712 [M]	The Dawn of Correction	1965	30.00
❑ DL74712 [S]	The Dawn of Correction	1965	30.00

SPONTANEOUS COMBUSTION

CAPITOL

❑ ST-11021	Spontaneous Combustion	1972	30.00

FLYING DUTCHMAN

❑ 102	Spontaneous Combustion	1969	30.00

HARVEST

❑ SW 11095	Triad	1972	30.00

SPONTANEOUS MUSIC ENSEMBLE, THE

EMANEM

❑ 303	Face to Face	1974	25.00

SPOOKY TOOTH

A&M

❑ SP-4225	Ceremony	1970	25.00
❑ SP-4194	Spooky Two	1969	25.00
❑ SP-3124	Spooky Two	198?	10.00

—Budget-line reissue

❑ SP-4266	The Last Puff	1970	25.00
❑ SP-4300	Tobacco Road	1971	18.00

—Reissue of Bell LP

❑ SP-4385	You Broke My Heart So I Busted Your Jaw	1973	18.00

ACCORD

❑ SN-7168	Hell or High Water	1982	12.00

BELL

❑ 6019 [M]	Spooky Tooth	1968	120.00

—Mono is white label promo only; record in stereo cover

❑ 6019 [S]	Spooky Tooth	1968	30.00

ISLAND

❑ SW-9292	The Mirror	1974	15.00
❑ ILPS-9337	Witness	1974	12.00
❑ SW-9255	Witness	1973	15.00

SPOTTS, ROGER HAMILTON

SEA BREEZE

❑ SB-5004	Roger Hamilton Spotts and His Big Band	1986	12.00

SPRAGUE, PETER

CONCORD JAZZ

❑ CJ-237	Musica Del Mar	1984	12.00
❑ CJ-277	Na Pali Coast	1985	12.00

XANADU

❑ 184	Bird Raga	198?	12.00
❑ 176	Dance of the Universe	1980	15.00
❑ 193	Message Sent on the Wind	1982	12.00
❑ 183	The Path	1981	12.00

SPRING

UNITED ARTISTS

❑ UAS-5571 [DJ]	Spring	1972	100.00

—Special promo package in 12x12 folder; includes LP, press kit and a packet of seeds

❑ UAS-5571	Spring	1972	30.00
❑ UAS-5571 [DJ]	Spring	1972	100.00

—Special promo package in 12x12 folder; includes LP, press kit and a packet of seeds

Number	Title	Yr	NM

SPRING STREET STOMPERS, THE

JUBILEE

❑ JLP-1004 [M]	I Go, Hook, Line and Sinker	1955	40.00
❑ JLP-1002 [M]	The Spring Street Stompers at Carnegie Hall	1955	40.00

SPRINGFIELD, BOBBY LEE

EPIC

❑ B6E40816	All Fired Up!	1987	10.00

SPRINGFIELD, DUSTY

4 MEN WITH BEARDS

❑ 4M112	Dusty in Memphis	2002	18.00

—Reissue on 180-gram vinyl

ABC DUNHILL

❑ DSX-50128	Cameo	1973	18.00

ATLANTIC

❑ SD8249	A Brand New Me	1970	18.00
❑ 8249 [DJ]	A Brand New Me	1970	40.00

—Mono white label promo

❑ SD8214 [B]	Dusty in Memphis	1969	35.00

—Originals have purple and brown labels

❑ SD8214	Dusty in Memphis	1969	18.00

—Second pressings have green and red labels

CASABLANCA

❑ NBLP-7271	White Heat	1982	15.00

LIBERTY

❑ LN-10024	It Begins Again	1980	10.00

—Budget-line reissue of United Artists LP of same name

❑ LN-10026	Living Without Your Love	1980	10.00

—Budget-line reissue of United Artists LP of same name

PHILIPS

❑ PHM-200156 [M]	Dusty	1964	35.00
❑ PHS-600156 [P]	Dusty	1964	40.00
❑ PHM-200220 [M]	Dusty Springfield's Golden Hits	1966	30.00

—With "Goin' Back

❑ PHM-200220 [M]	Dusty Springfield's Golden Hits	1967	35.00

—Without "Goin' Back

❑ PHS-600220 [P]	Dusty Springfield's Golden Hits	1966	35.00

—With "Goin' Back

❑ PHS-600220 [P]	Dusty Springfield's Golden Hits	1967	30.00

—Without "Goin' Back

❑ PHM-200303 [M]	Everything's Coming Up Dusty	1967	35.00
❑ PHS-600303 [S]	Everything's Coming Up Dusty	1967	30.00
❑ PHM-200174 [M]	Oooooo Weeeee!	1965	40.00
❑ PHS-600174 [S]	Oooooo Weeeee!	1965	50.00
❑ PHM-200133 [M]	Stay Awhile	1964	35.00
❑ PHS-600133 [P]	Stay Awhile	1964	40.00
❑ PHM-200256 [M]	The Look of Love	1967	35.00
❑ PHS-600256 [S]	The Look of Love	1967	30.00
❑ PHM-200210 [M]	You Don't Have to Say You Love Me	1966	35.00
❑ PHS-600210 [S]	You Don't Have to Say You Love Me	1966	40.00

POLYDOR

❑ 824467-1	Dusty Springfield's Golden Hits	1985	12.00

UNITED ARTISTS

❑ UA-LA791	It Begins Again	1978	18.00
❑ UA-LA936	Living Without Your Love	1979	18.00

WING

❑ SRW-16380	Just Dusty	196?	15.00
❑ PKW-2-120	Something Special	196?	25.00

SPRINGFIELD, RICK

CAPITOL

❑ SMAS-11047	Beginnings	1972	25.00
❑ SN-16251	Beginnings	1981	10.00

—Budget-line reissue

❑ SMAS-11206	Comic Book Heroes	1973	40.00

—Withdrawn and reissued on Columbia

CHELSEA

❑ 515	Wait for Night	1976	18.00

COLUMBIA

❑ KC32704	Comic Book Heroes	1973	18.00
❑ PC32704	Comic Book Heroes	1981	10.00

—Budget-line reissue

MERCURY

❑ 824107-1	Beautiful Feelings	1984	12.00

RCA

❑ 9817-1-R	Rick Springfield's Greatest Hits	1989	15.00
❑ 6620-1-R	Rock of Life	1988	10.00

RCA VICTOR

❑ ABL1-4935	Hard to Hold	1984	12.00

Number	Title	Yr	NM
❑ AFL1-4660	Living in Oz	1983	12.00
❑ AFL1-4125	Success Hasn't Spoiled Me Yet	1982	12.00
❑ AYL1-4767	Success Hasn't Spoiled Me Yet	1983	10.00

—Best Buy Series" reissue

❑ AJL1-5370	Tao	1985	12.00
❑ AFL1-4235	Wait for Night	1982	12.00

—Reissue of Chelsea LP

❑ ARL1-3697	Working Class Dog	1981	12.00
❑ AYL1-4766	Working Class Dog	1983	10.00

—Best Buy Series" reissue

SPRINGFIELD RIFLE, THE

BURDETTE

❑ ST-5159	The Springfield Rifle	1969	30.00

SPRINGFIELDS, THE

PHILIPS

❑ PHM200076 [M]	Folksongs from the Hills	1963	30.00
❑ PHS600076 [S]	Folksongs from the Hills	1963	40.00
❑ PHM200052 [M]	Silver Threads and Golden Needles	1962	30.00
❑ PHS600052 [S]	Silver Threads and Golden Needles	1962	40.00

SPRINGSTEEN, BRUCE

COLUMBIA

❑ C269746 [B]	18 Tracks	1999	30.00
❑ AS978 [DJ]	As Requested Around the World	1981	50.00
❑ AS978 [DJ]	As Requested Around the World	1981	50.00
❑ QC38653	Born in the U.S.A.	1984	12.00
❑ PC33795 [DJ]	Born to Run	1975	1200.00

—Test pressing with "Bruce Springsteen -- Born to Run" in script print. Also includes mailing envelope, letter from CBS and orange patch

❑ PC33795 [DJ]	Born to Run	1975	100.00

—White label promo

❑ PC33795 [DJ]	Born to Run	1975	1200.00

—Test pressing with "Bruce Springsteen -- Born to Run" in script print. Also includes mailing envelope, letter from CBS and orange patch; VG value 400; VG+ value 800

❑ PC33795 [DJ]	Born to Run	1975	100.00

—White label promo

❑ PC33795	Born to Run	1975	30.00

—Jon Landau's name is misspelled "John" on the back cover

❑ PC33795	Born to Run	1975	18.00

—Sticker with the correct spelling of Jon Landau is on the back cover

❑ PC33795	Born to Run	1975	12.00

—Jon Landau's name is correct on the back cover

❑ JC33795	Born to Run	1977	10.00
❑ HC33795 [B]	Born to Run	1981	80.00

—Half-speed mastered edition (original)

❑ HC43795 [B]	Born to Run	1982	60.00

—Half-speed mastered edition (reissue)

❑ PC33795	Born to Run	1999	40.00

—Classic Records reissue, identified as such on back cover; "error" first pressing with no gatefold

❑ PC33795	Born to Run	1999	30.00

—Classic Records reissue, identified as such on back cover; corrected pressing with gatefold

❑ AS1957 [DJ]	Bruce Springsteen	1985	40.00

—Five-song mini-LP with five B-sides of singles from Born in the U.S.A.

❑ AS1957 [DJ]	Bruce Springsteen	1987	30.00

—Five-song mini-LP with five B-sides of singles from Born in the U.S.A.; second pressings say so on the label

❑ AS1957 [DJ]	Bruce Springsteen	1985	40.00

—Five-song mini-LP with five B-sides of singles from Born in the U.S.A.

❑ AS1957 [DJ]	Bruce Springsteen	1987	30.00

—Five-song mini-LP with five B-sides of singles from Born in the U.S.A.; second pressings say so on the label

❑ AS2543 [DJ]	Bruce Springsteen and the E Street Band: Live 1975-1985	1986	30.00

—Sampler from 5-LP live set

❑ C5X40558	Bruce Springsteen and the E Street Band: Live 1975-1985	1986	40.00
❑ CAS2543 [DJ]	Bruce Springsteen and the E Street Band: Live 1975-1985	1986	60.00

—Sampler from 5-LP live set

❑ 3C44445 [EP]	Chimes of Freedom	1988	12.00
❑ JC35318 [DJ]	Darkness on the Edge of Town	1978	100.00

—White label promo

❑ JC35318 [B]	Darkness on the Edge of Town	1978	18.00

—Original pressings have thick paper innersleeves and small titles on back cover

❑ JC35318	Darkness on the Edge of Town	198?	10.00

—Later pressings have thin paper innersleeves and larger titles on back cover

❑ (# unknown)0 [PD]	Darkness on the Edge of Town	1978	200.00

—Promo-only picture disc

❑ JC35318 [DJ]	Darkness on the Edge of Town	1978	100.00

—White label promo

Number	Title	Yr	NM
❏ HC45318 [B]	Darkness on the Edge of Town	1981	60.00
—Half-speed mastered edition			
❏ C293900	Devils and Dust	2005	25.00
❏ C267060 [B]	Greatest Hits	1995	25.00
❏ KC31903 [DJ]	Greetings from Asbury Park, N.J.	1973	200.00
—Promotional copy with timing strip and "Bruce Springsteen Fact Sheet" attached to back cover. Authentic fact sheets are on glossy stock			
❏ KC31903 [DJ]	Greetings from Asbury Park, N.J.	1973	200.00
—Promotional copy with timing strip and "Bruce Springsteen Fact Sheet" attached to back cover. Authentic fact sheets are on glossy stock			
❏ KC31903	Greetings from Asbury Park, N.J.	1973	25.00
❏ PC31903	Greetings from Asbury Park, N.J.	1975	12.00
—Without bar code on cover			
❏ PC31903	Greetings from Asbury Park, N.J.	1979	10.00
—With bar code on cover			
❏ JC31903	Greetings from Asbury Park, N.J.	1977	10.00
—Reissue of the first PC-prefix version			
❏ C53000 [B]	Human Touch	1992	18.00
❏ C385490	Live in New York City	2001	25.00
—As of press date, all known copies contain "Born to Run," but the song is not listed on either the record jacket or label			
❏ C53001 [B]	Lucky Town	1992	18.00
❏ 88697-17060-1	Magic	2007	18.00
❏ TC38358	Nebraska	1982	12.00
❏ C67484	The Ghost of Tom Joad	1995	25.00
❏ C286600	The Rising	2002	25.00
❏ PC236854 [DJ]	The River	1980	80.00
—White label promo, with photocopied letter from CBS			
❏ PC236854 [DJ]	The River	1980	50.00
—White label promo, without letter			
❏ PC236854 [DJ]	The River	1980	80.00
—White label promo, with photocopied letter from CBS			
❏ PC236854 [DJ]	The River	1980	50.00
—White label promo, without letter			
❏ PC236854 [B]	The River	1980	25.00
❏ KC32432	The Wild, the Innocent & the E Street Shuffle	1973	25.00
❏ PC32432	The Wild, the Innocent & the E Street Shuffle	1975	12.00
—Without bar code on cover			
❏ PC32432	The Wild, the Innocent & the E Street Shuffle	1979	10.00
—With bar code on cover			
❏ JC32432	The Wild, the Innocent & the E Street Shuffle	1977	10.00
—Reissue of the first PC-prefix version			
❏ OC40999	Tunnel of Love	1987	12.00

SPUR

CINEMA

❏ CSLP-1500	Spur of the Moment	196?	80.00

SPYRO GYRA

AMHERST

❏ AMH-1014	Spyro Gyra	1978	18.00

GRP

❏ GR-9608	Fast Forward	1990	18.00

INFINITY

❏ INF-9004	Morning Dance	1979	15.00

MCA

❏ 6893	Access All Areas	1984	15.00
❏ 5606	Alternating Currents	1985	12.00
❏ 5753	Breakout	1986	12.00
❏ 37176	Carnaval	198?	10.00
—Budget-line reissue			
❏ 5149	Carnaval	1981	12.00
❏ 16010	Catching the Sun	1982	40.00
—Audiophile vinyl			
❏ 5108	Catching the Sun	1980	12.00
❏ 1445	City Kids	1986	10.00
—Budget-line reissue			
❏ 5431	City Kids	1983	12.00
❏ 5238	Freetime	1981	12.00
❏ 5368	Incognito	1982	12.00
❏ 37148	Morning Dance	198?	10.00
—Reissue of Infinity LP			
❏ 6309	Point of View	1989	15.00
❏ 6235	Rites of Summer	1988	12.00
❏ 37149	Spyro Gyra	198?	10.00
—Reissue of Amherst LP			
❏ 42046	Stories Without Words	1987	12.00

NAUTILUS

❏ NR-9	Morning Dance	1979	40.00
—Audiophile vinyl			

SQUEEZE

A&M

❏ SP-4802	Argybargy	1980	15.00
❏ SP-3232	Argybargy	198?	10.00
—Reissue			
❏ SP-5161	Babylon and On	1987	12.00
❏ SP-4759	Cool for Cats	1979	15.00

Number	Title	Yr	NM
❏ SP-3231	Cool for Cats	198?	10.00
—Reissue			
❏ SP-5085	Cosi Fan Tutti Frutti	1985	12.00
❏ SP-4854	East Side Story	1981	12.00
❏ SP-3253	East Side Story	198?	10.00
—Reissue			
❏ R124200	Frank	1989	15.00
—BMG Music Service edition			
❏ SP-5278	Frank	1989	12.00
❏ SP-4922	Singles 45's and Under	1983	12.00
❏ SP-3413 [EP]	Six Squeeze Songs Crammed Into One 10-Inch Record	1979	18.00
—10-inch EP in 12-inch "squeezed" jacket			
❏ SP-4899	Sweets from a Stranger	1982	12.00
—With flap removed or never there			
❏ SP-4899	Sweets from a Stranger	1982	15.00
—Original pressings have a 2-inch flap on the right side of the front cover with critics' raves			
❏ SP-3254	Sweets from a Stranger	198?	10.00
—Reissue; none of these have 2-inch flap			
❏ SP-4687 [B]	U.K. Squeeze	1978	30.00
—First pressing on red vinyl			
❏ SP-4687	U.K. Squeeze	1978	15.00
—Later pressings on black vinyl			
❏ SP-3185	U.K. Squeeze	198?	10.00
—Reissue			

SQUIRREL NUT ZIPPERS

MAMMOTH

❏ MR 0137	Hot	1996	10.00
❏ MR 0169	Perennial Favorites	1998	10.00
❏ MR 0105	The Inevitable	1995	10.00

SRC

CAPITOL

❏ ST-134 [B]	Milestones	1969	50.00
❏ ST2991 [B]	SRC	1968	80.00
❏ SKAO-273 [B]	Travellers Tale	1970	50.00

ST. ANTHONY'S FIRE

ZONK

❏ (# unknown)0	St. Anthony's Fire	1968	400.00

ST. CLAIRE, BETTY

JUBILEE

❏ JLP-23 [10]	Cool and Clearer	1955	100.00
❏ JLP-15 [10]	Hal McKusick Plays — Betty St. Clair Sings	1955	150.00
❏ JLP-1011 [M]	What Is There to Say?	1956	50.00

SEECO

❏ SLP-456 [M]	Betty St. Claire at Basin Street	1960	40.00
❏ SLP-4560 [S]	Betty St. Claire at Basin Street	1960	40.00

ST. CLOUD, ENDLE

INTERNATIONAL ARTISTS

❏ IA-12	Thank You All Very Much	1970	60.00

ST. CYR, JOHNNY

SOUTHLAND

❏ 212	Johnny St. Cyr and His Hot Five	196?	25.00

ST. GERMAIN

BLUE NOTE

❏ 25114	Tourist	2000	30.00

ST. LOUIS JIMMY

BLUESVILLE

❏ BVLP-1028 [M]	Goin' Down Blues	1961	150.00
—Blue label, silver print			
❏ BVLP-1028 [M]	Goin' Down Blues	1964	60.00
—Blue label, trident logo at right			

ST. LOUIS RAGTIMERS, THE

AUDIOPHILE

❏ AP-122	Songs of the Showboat Era	197?	12.00
❏ AP-116	The St. Louis Ragtimers	1977	12.00

ST. OLAF CHOIRS, THE

ST. OLAF

❏ E-661/2	Born a Child & Yet a King: Christmas at St. Olaf College/Volume II	19??	18.00

ST. PARADISE

WARNER BROS.

❏ BSK3281	St. Paradise	1979	15.00

ST. PATRICK'S CATHEDRAL CHOIR

ROULETTE

❏ R25142 [M]	Sings Christmas Songs (Volume 2)	1960	18.00

Number	Title	Yr	NM
ST. PETERS, CRISPIAN			
JAMIE			
❏ JLPM-3027 [M]	The Pied Piper	1966	30.00
❏ JLPS-3027 [R]	The Pied Piper	1966	25.00
ST. PETER'S CHOIR			
CORAL			
❏ CRL56015 [10]	Hark! The Herald Angels Sing	1950	40.00
ST. SHAW, MIKE			
REPRISE			
❏ R-6128 [M]	The Mike St. Shaw Trio	1964	25.00
❏ RS-6128 [S]	The Mike St. Shaw Trio	1964	30.00
ST JOHN, BRIDGET			
4 MEN WITH BEARDS			
❏ 4M188LP [B]	Ask Me No Questions		25.00
❏ 4M189LP [B]	Songs For The Gentle Man		25.00
❏ 4M190LP [B]	Thank You For...		25.00
STACEY Q			
ATLANTIC			
❏ 81676	Better Than Heaven	1986	12.00
❏ 81802	Hard Machine	1988	12.00
❏ 81962	Nights Like This	1989	12.00
STACKRIDGE			
DECCA			
❏ DL75317	Stackridge	1971	30.00
MCA			
❏ 308 [B]	Friendliness	1973	15.00
SIRE			
❏ SASD-7509 [B]	Extravaganza	1975	15.00
❏ SASD-7503 [B]	Pinafore Days	1974	15.00
STACY, JESS			
AIRCHECK			
❏ 26	Jess Stacy On the Air	198?	12.00
ATLANTIC			
❏ 1225 [M]	A Tribute to Benny Goodman	1956	50.00
—Black label			
❏ 90664	A Tribute to Benny Goodman	1988	12.00
BRUNSWICK			
❏ BL58029 [10]	Piano Solos	1951	80.00
❏ BL54017 [M]	Piano Solos	1956	50.00
CHIAROSCURO			
❏ 177	Stacy's Still Swinging	1978	15.00
❏ 133	Stacy Still Swings	197?	15.00
COLUMBIA			
❏ CL6147 [10]	Piano Moods	1950	100.00
COMMODORE			
❏ XFL-15358	Jess Stacy and Friends	198?	12.00
HANOVER			
❏ HL-8010 [M]	The Return of Jess Stacy	1964	18.00
❏ HS 8010 [S]	The Return of Jess Stacy	1964	25.00
JAZZOLOGY			
❏ JCE-90	Blue Notion	198?	12.00
STADLER, HEINER			
LABOR			
❏ 7001	Brains on Fire	197?	18.00
❏ 7002	Brains on Fire, Vol. 2	1974	18.00
❏ 7003	Ecstasy	197?	18.00
❏ 7006	Jazz Alchemy	197?	18.00
STAETER, TED			
ATLANTIC			
❏ 1218 [M]	Ted Staeter's New York	1955	30.00
—Multicolor label, white "fan" logo at right			
❏ 1218 [M]	Ted Staeter's New York	1961	50.00
—Black label			
STAFFORD, JIM			
MGM			
❏ M3G-4947	Jim Stafford	1974	12.00
❏ M3G-4984	Not Just Another Pretty Foot	1975	12.00
POLYDOR			
❏ PD-1-6072	Jim Stafford	1976	10.00
—Reissue of MGM 4947			
STAFFORD, JO, AND GORDON MACRAE			
CAPITOL			
❏ T423 [M]	Memory Songs	1955	50.00
❏ H247 [10]	Sunday Evening Songs	1952	60.00
❏ T1916 [M]	There's Peace in the Valley	1963	25.00
❏ ST1916 [S]	There's Peace in the Valley	1963	30.00
❏ SM-11890 [B]	There's Peace in the Valley	1978	12.00
—Reissue			
❏ T1696 [M]	Whispering Hope	1962	25.00
❏ ST1696 [S]	Whispering Hope	1962	30.00

STAFFORD, JO

Number	Title	Yr	NM
BAINBRIDGE			
❑ 6234	Look at Me Now	1982	12.00
CAPITOL			
❑ H75 [10]	American Folk Songs	1950	60.00
❑ T1653 [M]	American Folk Songs	1962	25.00
❑ ST1653 [S]	American Folk Songs	1962	30.00
❑ H197 [10]	Autumn in New York	195?	60.00
❑ T197 [M]	Autumn in New York	1955	50.00
— Turquoise or gray label			
❑ T197 [M]	Autumn in New York	1959	30.00
— Black colorband label, Capitol logo at left			
❑ T423 [M]	Memory Songs	1955	50.00
— Turquoise or gray label			
❑ T423 [M]	Memory Songs	1959	30.00
— Black colorband label, Capitol logo at left			
❑ H247 [10]	Songs for Sunday Evening	195?	60.00
❑ H9014 [10]	Songs of Faith	1950	60.00
❑ H435 [10]	Starring Jo Stafford	1953	60.00
❑ T435 [M]	Starring Jo Stafford	1955	50.00
— Turquoise or gray label			
❑ T435 [M]	Starring Jo Stafford	1959	30.00
— Black colorband label, Capitol logo at left			
❑ T2069 [M]	Sweet Hour of Prayer	1964	25.00
❑ ST2069 [S]	Sweet Hour of Prayer	1964	30.00
❑ T1921 [M]	The Hits of Jo Stafford	1963	25.00
❑ ST1921 [S]	The Hits of Jo Stafford	1963	30.00
❑ SM-11889	The Hits of Jo Stafford	1979	12.00
❑ T2166 [M]	The Joyful Season	1964	25.00
❑ ST2166 [S]	The Joyful Season	1964	30.00
❑ SM-1696	Whispering Hope	1977	12.00
— Reissue with new prefix			
COLUMBIA			
❑ CL2591 [10]	A Gal Named Jo	1955	40.00
❑ CL6210 [10]	As You Desire Me	1952	50.00
❑ CL1339 [M]	Ballad of the Blues	1959	30.00
❑ CS8139 [S]	Ballad of the Blues	1959	40.00
❑ CL6286 [10]	Garden of Prayer	1954	50.00
❑ CL691 [M]	Happy Holiday	1955	60.00
❑ CL1262 [M]	I'll Be Seeing You	1959	30.00
❑ CS8080 [S]	I'll Be Seeing You	1959	40.00
❑ CL1561 [M]	Jo + Jazz	1960	40.00
❑ CS8361 [S]	Jo + Jazz	1960	60.00
❑ CL1228 [M]	Jo Stafford's Greatest Hits	1958	40.00
— Red and black label with six "eye" logos			
❑ CL1228 [M]	Jo Stafford's Greatest Hits	1963	25.00
— Red label with "Guaranteed High Fidelity" in black			
❑ CL1228 [M]	Jo Stafford's Greatest Hits	1965	18.00
— Red label with "360 Sound Mono" in white			
❑ CL6238 [10]	Jo Stafford Sings Broadway's Best	1953	50.00
❑ CL584 [M]	Jo Stafford Sings Broadway's Best	1954	40.00
— Maroon label, gold print			
❑ CL584 [M]	Jo Stafford Sings Broadway's Best	1955	30.00
— Red and black label with six "eye" logos			
❑ CL1043 [M]	Jo Stafford Sings Songs of Scotland	1957	40.00
❑ CL6274 [10]	My Heart's in the Highland	1954	50.00
❑ CL578 [M]	New Orleans	1954	40.00
— Maroon label, gold print			
❑ CL6268 [10]	New Orleans	1954	50.00
❑ CL578 [M]	New Orleans	1955	30.00
— Red and black label with six "eye" logos			
❑ CL968 [M]	Once Over Lightly	1957	40.00
❑ CL910 [M]	Ski Trails	1956	40.00
❑ CL2501 [10]	Soft and Sentimental	1955	40.00
❑ CL1124 [M]	Swingin' Down Broadway	1958	40.00
CORINTHIAN			
❑ COR-118	Broadway Revisited	198?	12.00
❑ COR-119	By Request	198?	12.00
❑ COR-105	G.I. Jo	1977	12.00
❑ COR-106	Greatest Hits	1977	12.00
❑ COR-115	International Hits	197?	12.00
❑ COR-114	Jo + Blues	197?	12.00
❑ COR-112	Jo + Broadway	197?	12.00
❑ COR-108	Jo + Jazz	197?	12.00
❑ COR-110	Jo Stafford Sings American Folk Songs	197?	12.00
❑ COR-123	Music of My Life	1986	12.00
❑ COR-113	Ski Trails	197?	12.00
❑ COR-111	Songs of Faith, Hope and Love	197?	12.00
DECCA			
❑ DL74973	Jo Stafford's Greatest Hits	1968	18.00
DOT			
❑ DLP-3673 [M]	Do I Hear a Waltz?	1966	18.00
❑ DLP-25673 [S]	Do I Hear a Waltz?	1966	25.00
❑ DLP-3745 [M]	This Is Jo Stafford	1967	18.00
❑ DLP-25745 [S]	This Is Jo Stafford	1967	25.00
REPRISE			
❑ R-6090 [M]	Getting Sentimental Over Tommy Dorsey	1963	25.00
❑ R9-6090 [S]	Getting Sentimental Over Tommy Dorsey	1963	30.00
STANYAN			
❑ 10073	Look at Me Now	197?	15.00
TIME-LIFE			
❑ SLGD-14	Legendary Singers: Jo Stafford	1986	18.00

Number	Title	Yr	NM
VOCALION			
❑ VL73856 [R]	Happy Holidays	1968	15.00
❑ VL73892	In the Mood for Love	1970	15.00
❑ VL73866 [R]	Sweet Singer of Songs	1969	15.00

STAFFORD, MARILYN, AND THE ERNIE CARSON BAND

Number	Title	Yr	NM
CIRCLE			
❑ C-66	Jazz Goes Country	198?	12.00

STAFFORD, TERRY

Number	Title	Yr	NM
ATLANTIC			
❑ SD7282	Say, Has Anybody Seen My Sweet Gypsy Rose	1974	15.00
CRUSADER			
❑ CLP-1001 [M]	Suspicion!	1964	40.00
❑ CLP-1001S [S]	Suspicion!	1964	60.00

STAINED GLASS

Number	Title	Yr	NM
CAPITOL			
❑ ST-242	Aurora	1969	30.00
❑ ST-154	Crazy Horse Roads	1969	30.00

STALEY, KAREN

Number	Title	Yr	NM
MCA			
❑ 42112	Wildest Dreams	1988	12.00

STALLINGS, MARY, AND CAL TJADER

Number	Title	Yr	NM
FANTASY			
❑ 3325 [M]	Cal Tjader Plays, Mary Stallings Sings	1962	50.00
— Red vinyl			
❑ 3325 [M]	Cal Tjader Plays, Mary Stallings Sings	1962	30.00
— Black vinyl			
❑ 8068 [S]	Cal Tjader Plays, Mary Stallings Sings	1962	40.00
— Blue vinyl			
❑ 8068 [S]	Cal Tjader Plays, Mary Stallings Sings	1962	25.00
— Black vinyl			

STAMEY, CHRIS

Number	Title	Yr	NM
COYOTE			
❑ TTC8564	Christmas Time	1985	12.00

STAMM, MARVIN

Number	Title	Yr	NM
PALO ALTO			
❑ PA-8022	Stampede	198?	12.00
VERVE			
❑ V6-8759	Machinations	1968	25.00

STAMPEDERS

Number	Title	Yr	NM
BELL			
❑ 6068	Sweet City Woman	1971	18.00
CAPITOL			
❑ ST-11288	From the Fire	1973	15.00
❑ ST-11328	New Day	1974	15.00
QUALITY			
❑ 1001	Hit the Road	1976	15.00

STAMPLEY, JOE

Number	Title	Yr	NM
ABC			
❑ AC-30031	The ABC Collection	1976	15.00
ABC DOT			
❑ DOSD-2059	All These Things	1976	15.00
❑ DOSD-2023	Joe Stampley's Greatest Hits Volume 1	1975	15.00
❑ DOSD-2006	Take Me Home to Somewhere	1974	15.00
ACCORD			
❑ SN-7156	Early Years	1982	12.00
DOT			
❑ DLP-26002	If You Touch Me (You've Got to Love Me)	1972	18.00
❑ DLP-26020	I'm Still Loving You	1974	18.00
❑ DLP-26007	Soul Song	1973	18.00
EPIC			
❑ JE36484	After Hours	1980	12.00
❑ FE38364	Backslidin'	1982	12.00
❑ FE38319	Biggest Hits	1982	12.00
❑ PE33546	Billy, Get Me a Woman	1975	15.00
❑ FE37343	Encore	1981	12.00
❑ KE35622	Greatest Hits	1978	12.00
❑ PE35622	Greatest Hits	198?	10.00
— Budget-line reissue with new prefix			
❑ KE36016	I Don't Lie	1979	12.00
❑ FE37927	I'm Goin' Hurtin'	1982	12.00
❑ FE37055	I'm Gonna Love You Back to Loving Me Again	1981	12.00
❑ KE33356	Joe Stampley	1975	15.00
❑ FE38964	Memory Lane	1983	12.00
❑ KE35543	Red Wine and Blue Memories	1978	15.00
❑ PE34732	Saturday Nite Dance	1977	15.00
❑ FE39960	Still Be Lovin' You	1985	10.00
❑ PE34356	Ten Songs About Her	1976	15.00
❑ KE34036	The Sheik of Chicago	1976	15.00

Number	Title	Yr	NM
MCA			
❑ 27022	The Very Best of Joe Stampley	198?	10.00

STANDBACK

Number	Title	Yr	NM
SEA BREEZE			
❑ SB-3004	Norwegian Wood	198?	12.00

STANDELLS, THE

Number	Title	Yr	NM
LIBERTY			
❑ LRP-3384 [M]	The Standells In Person at P.J.'s	1964	80.00
❑ LST-7384 [S]	The Standells In Person at P.J.'s	1964	100.00
RHINO			
❑ RNLP-115	Rarities	1983	12.00
❑ RNLP-107	The Best of the Standells	1983	12.00
❑ RNLP-70176	The Best of the Standells (Golden Archive Series)	1987	12.00
SUNSET			
❑ SUM-1136 [M]	Live and Out of Sight	1966	30.00
❑ SUS-5136 [S]	Live and Out of Sight	1966	30.00
TOWER			
❑ T5027 [M]	Dirty Water	1966	60.00
❑ ST5027 [R]	Dirty Water	1966	50.00
❑ T5049 [M]	The Hot Ones	1966	80.00
❑ ST5049 [S]	The Hot Ones	1966	60.00
❑ T5098 [M]	Try It	1967	80.00
❑ ST5098 [S]	Try It	1967	60.00
❑ T5044 [M]	Why Pick on Me	1966	50.00
❑ ST5044 [S]	Why Pick on Me	1966	60.00

STANKO, TOMASZ

Number	Title	Yr	NM
ECM			
❑ 1071	Balladyna	1976	15.00

STANLEY, MICHAEL, BAND

Number	Title	Yr	NM
ARISTA			
❑ AL4182	Cabin Fever	1978	12.00
❑ AL4236	Greatest Hints	1979	12.00
EMI AMERICA			
❑ SW-17040	Heartland	1980	12.00
❑ SN-16352	Heartland	1985	10.00
— Budget-line reissue			
❑ ST-17071	MSB	1082	12.00
❑ SN-16392	MSB	1986	10.00
— Budget-line reissue			
❑ SW-17056	North Coast	1981	12.00
❑ ST-17100	You Can't Fight Fashion	1983	12.00
❑ SN-16353	You Can't Fight Fashion	1985	10.00
— Budget-line reissue			
EPIC			
❑ PE33917	Ladies' Choice	1976	15.00
— Original with orange label and no bar code			
❑ PE33917	Ladies' Choice	198?	10.00
— Reissue with dark blue label and bar code			
❑ PEG34661	Stagepass	1977	18.00
❑ PE33492	You Break It...You Bought It!	1975	15.00
— Original with orange label and no bar code			
❑ PE33492	You Break It...You Bought It!	198?	10.00
— Reissue with dark blue label and bar code			
MCA			
❑ 372	Friends and Legends	1973	15.00
TUMBLEWEED			
❑ TWS106	Michael Stanley	1972	25.00
— Blue textured cover			

STANLEY, PAUL

Number	Title	Yr	NM
CASABLANCA			
❑ NBLP-7123	Paul Stanley	1978	30.00
❑ NBPIX-7123 [PD]	Paul Stanley	1978	60.00

STANLEY, RALPH

Number	Title	Yr	NM
JALYN			
❑ JLP-118 [M]	Old Time Music	1966	30.00
❑ JLP-129 [M]	Ralph Stanley and the Clinch Mountain Boys	196?	30.00
❑ JLP-120 [M]	The Bluegrass Sound of Ralph Stanley	1966	30.00
KING			
❑ KSD-1028	Brand New Country Songs by Ralph Stanley	1968	25.00
❑ KSD-1046	How Far to Little Rock?	1969	25.00
❑ KSD-1032	Over the Sunset Hill	1968	25.00
❑ KSD-1069	The Hills of Home	1969	25.00

STANLEY BROTHERS, THE

Number	Title	Yr	NM
CABIN CREEK			
❑ LP-203 [M]	Bluegrass Gospel Favorites	1966	60.00
HARMONY			
❑ HL7291 [M]	The Stanley Brothers	1961	30.00
KING			
❑ 963 [M]	A Collection of Gospel and Sacred Songs	1966	30.00
❑ 791 [M]	Award Winners	1962	80.00
❑ KS-791 [S]	Award Winners	1962	100.00

Number	Title	Yr	NM
❑ 864 [M]	Country Folk Music Spotlight	1964	50.00
❑ 690 [M]	Everybody's Country Favorites	1961	80.00
❑ KS-690 [S]	Everybody's Country Favorites	1961	100.00
❑ 872 [M]	Five String Banjo Hootenanny	1964	50.00
❑ 698 [M]	For the Good People	1961	80.00
❑ 805 [M]	Good Old Camp Meeting Songs	1963	80.00
❑ KS-805 [S]	Good Old Camp Meeting Songs	1963	100.00
❑ 645 [M]	Hymns and Sacred Songs	1960	80.00
❑ 918 [M]	Hymns of the Cross	1964	50.00
❑ 834 [M]	Just Because	1964	50.00
❑ 750 [M]	Old Time Camp Meeting	1962	80.00
❑ 953 [M]	The Best of the Stanley Brothers	1966	30.00
❑ 924 [M]	The Remarkable Stanley Brothers Play and Sing Bluegrass Songs for You	1965	50.00
❑ 615 [M]	The Stanley Brothers	1959	100.00
❑ 772 [M]	The Stanley Brothers and the Clinch Mountain Boys Sing the Songs They Like Best	1962	80.00
❑ 1013 [M]	The Stanley Brothers Sing the Best-Loved Sacred Songs of the Carter Family	1967	30.00
❑ KS-1013 [S]	The Stanley Brothers Sing the Best-Loved Sacred Songs of the Carter Family	1967	30.00
❑ 719 [M]	The Stanleys In Person	1961	80.00
❑ KS-719 [S]	The Stanleys In Person	1961	100.00

MERCURY

Number	Title	Yr	NM
❑ MG-20349 [M]	Country Pickin' and Singin'	1958	80.00
❑ MG-20884 [M]	Hard Times	1963	30.00
❑ SR-60884 [S]	Hard Times	1963	30.00

STARDAY

Number	Title	Yr	NM
❑ SLP-384 [M]	Jacob's Vision	1966	30.00
❑ SLP-106 [M]	Mountain Song Favorites	1959	50.00
❑ SLP-122 [M]	Sacred Songs from the Hills	1960	50.00
❑ SLP-201 [M]	The Mountain Music Sound of the Stanley Brothers	1962	40.00

VINTAGE

Number	Title	Yr	NM
❑ ZK-002 [M]	The Stanley Brothers Live at Antioch College	1961	70.00

STANSFIELD, LISA

ARISTA

Number	Title	Yr	NM
❑ R134198	Affection	1990	15.00
—BMG Music Service edition			
❑ AL-8554	Affection	1990	12.00
❑ 19012	The #1 Remixes	1998	18.00

STAPLE SINGERS, THE

20TH CENTURY

Number	Title	Yr	NM
❑ T-636	Hold On to Your Dream	1981	12.00

ARCHIVE OF GOSPEL MUSIC

Number	Title	Yr	NM
❑ 62	The Staple Singers	1968	15.00
❑ 72	The Staple Singers, Vol. 2	1969	15.00

BUDDAH

Number	Title	Yr	NM
❑ BDS-2009	The Best of the Staple Singers	1969	25.00
❑ BDS-7508	Will the Circle Be Unbroken	1969	25.00

CURTOM

Number	Title	Yr	NM
❑ CU5005	Let's Do It Again	1975	15.00

EPIC

Number	Title	Yr	NM
❑ LN24132 [M]	Amen	1965	25.00
❑ BN26132 [S]	Amen	1965	30.00
❑ LN24332 [M]	For What It's Worth	1967	30.00
❑ BN26332 [S]	For What It's Worth	1967	25.00
❑ LN24163 [M]	Freedom Highway	1965	25.00
❑ BN26163 [S]	Freedom Highway	1965	30.00
❑ LN24237 [M]	Pray On	1967	30.00
❑ BN26237 [S]	Pray On	1967	25.00
❑ EG30635	The Staple Singers Make You Happy	1971	25.00
❑ BN26373	What the World Needs Now Is Love	1968	25.00
❑ LN24196 [M]	Why	1966	25.00
❑ BN26196 [S]	Why	1966	30.00

FANTASY

Number	Title	Yr	NM
❑ 9442	The 25th Day of December	1973	18.00
❑ 9423	Use What You Got	1973	18.00

HARMONY

Number	Title	Yr	NM
❑ KH31775	Tell It Like It Is	1972	15.00

MILESTONE

Number	Title	Yr	NM
❑ 47028	A Great Day	197?	18.00

PICKWICK

Number	Title	Yr	NM
❑ 7001	The Staple Singers	197?	12.00

PRIVATE I

Number	Title	Yr	NM
❑ BFZ40109	The Staple Singers	1985	12.00
❑ FZ39460	The Turning Point	1984	12.00

STAX

Number	Title	Yr	NM
❑ STS-3002	Be Altitude: Respect Yourself	1972	18.00
❑ STX-4116	Be Altitude: Respect Yourself	198?	12.00
—Reissue of 3002			
❑ STS-3015	Be What You Are	1973	18.00
❑ MPS-8553	Be What You Are	1990	15.00
—Reissue of 3015			
❑ STX-4119	Chronicle	198?	12.00
❑ STS-5515	City in the Sky	1974	18.00
❑ STS-2004	Soul Folk in Action	1968	30.00
❑ STS-5523	The Best of the Staple Singers	1975	18.00
❑ STS-2034	The Staple Swingers	1971	25.00
❑ MPS-8511	This Time Around	198?	12.00
❑ STS-2016	We'll Get Over	1969	25.00
❑ MPS-8532	We'll Get Over	198?	12.00
—Reissue of 2016			

TRIP

Number	Title	Yr	NM
❑ 7014	Swing Low	197?	12.00
❑ 7019	The Best of the Staple Singers	197?	12.00
❑ 8014	The Other Side of the Staple Singers	1972	12.00
❑ 7000	Uncloudy Day	197?	12.00

VEE JAY

Number	Title	Yr	NM
❑ LP-5019 [M]	Best of the Staple Singers	1962	30.00
❑ LP-5014 [M]	Swing Low	1961	30.00
❑ LP-5030 [M]	Swing Low Sweet Chariot	1963	30.00
❑ LP-5000 [M]	Uncloudy Day	1959	30.00
❑ LP-5008 [M]	Will the Circle Be Unbroken	1960	30.00

VEE JAY/CHAMELEON

Number	Title	Yr	NM
❑ D1-74782	The Best of the Staple Singers	1988	18.00

WARNER BROS.

Number	Title	Yr	NM
❑ BS3084	Family Tree	1977	15.00
—As "The Staples			
❑ BS2945	Pass It On	1976	15.00
—As "The Staples			
❑ BSK3192	Unlock Your Mind	1978	15.00
—As "The Staples			

STAPLES, MAVIS

CURTOM

Number	Title	Yr	NM
❑ CU5019	A Piece of the Action	1977	15.00

PAISLEY PARK

Number	Title	Yr	NM
❑ 25798	Time Waits for No One	1989	15.00

STAX

Number	Title	Yr	NM
❑ STX-4118	Mavis Staples	198?	12.00
—Reissue of Volt 6007			
❑ MPS-8539	Only for the Lonely	1987	12.00
—Reissue of Volt 6010			

VOLT

Number	Title	Yr	NM
❑ VOS-6007	Mavis Staples	1969	25.00
❑ VOS-6010	Only for the Lonely	1970	25.00

WARNER BROS.

Number	Title	Yr	NM
❑ BSK3319	Oh What a Feeling	1979	15.00

STAPLETON, CYRIL

RICHMOND

Number	Title	Yr	NM
❑ S30057 [S]	Children's Christmas Album	196?	18.00

STARCASTLE

EPIC

Number	Title	Yr	NM
❑ 34935 [PD]	Citadel	1978	50.00
—Picture disc, possibly promo only			
❑ PE34935	Citadel	1977	15.00
—Orange label			
❑ PE34075	Fountains of Light	1977	15.00
—Orange label			
❑ AS296 [DJ]	Fountains of Light Banded for Airplay	1977	40.00
—White label, promo-only version with separations between tracks			
❑ JE35441	Real to Reel	1978	15.00
—Orange label			
❑ PE33914 [B]	Starcastle	1976	15.00
—Orange label			

STARCHER, BUDDY

DECCA

Number	Title	Yr	NM
❑ DL4796 [M]	History Repeats Itself	1966	25.00
❑ DL74796 [S]	History Repeats Itself	1966	30.00

STARDAY

Number	Title	Yr	NM
❑ SLP-211 [M]	Buddy Starcher and His Mountain Guitar	1962	30.00
❑ SLP-382 [M]	History Repeats Itself	1966	30.00

STARFIRES, THE (4)

OHIO RECORDING SERVICE

Number	Title	Yr	NM
❑ 34 [M]	The Starfires Play	1964	50.00

STARFIRES, THE (5)

LABREA

Number	Title	Yr	NM
❑ LS-8018 [M]	Teenbeat A-Go-Go	1965	50.00

STARK NAKED

RCA VICTOR

Number	Title	Yr	NM
❑ LSP-4592	Stark Naked	1971	30.00

STARKER, JANOS

MERCURY LIVING PRESENCE

Number	Title	Yr	NM
❑ SR90480 [S]	Bach, J.S.: Three Sonatas	196?	200.00
—Maroon label, with "Vendor: Mercury Record Corporation			
❑ SR90370 [S]	Bach: Suites 2 and 5 for Solo Violin	196?	80.00
—Maroon label, no "Vendor: Mercury Record Corporation			
❑ SR90370 [S]	Bach: Suites 2 and 5 for Solo Violin	196?	40.00
—Third edition: Dark red (not maroon) label			
❑ SR90370 [S]	Bach: Suites 2 and 5 for Solo Violin	196?	60.00
—Maroon label, with "Vendor: Mercury Record Corporation			
❑ SR90405 [S]	Bartok: First Rhapsody; Mendelssohn: Various Concertantes; Martinu: Rossini Variations; et al.	196?	120.00
—Maroon label, no "Vendor: Mercury Record Corporation			
❑ SR90405 [S]	Bartok: First Rhapsody; Mendelssohn: Various Concertantes; Martinu: Rossini Variations; et al.	196?	60.00
—Maroon label, with "Vendor: Mercury Record Corporation			
❑ SR90405 [S]	Bartok: First Rhapsody; Mendelssohn: Various Concertantes; Martinu: Rossini Variations; et al.	196?	40.00
—Third edition: Dark red (not maroon) label			
❑ SR90392 [S]	Brahms: Cello Sonatas No. 1 and 2	196?	150.00
—Maroon label, no "Vendor: Mercury Record Corporation			
❑ SR90392 [S]	Brahms: Cello Sonatas No. 1 and 2	196?	50.00
—Maroon label, with "Vendor: Mercury Record Corporation			
❑ SR90303 [S]	Dvorak: Cello Concerto; Bruch: Kol Nidre	196?	120.00
—With Antal Dorati/London Symphony Orchestra; maroon label, no "Vendor: Mercury Record Corporation			
❑ SR90303 [S]	Dvorak: Cello Concerto; Bruch: Kol Nidre	196?	70.00
—With Antal Dorati/London Symphony Orchestra; maroon label, with "Vendor: Mercury Record Corporation			
❑ SR90303 [S]	Dvorak: Cello Concerto; Bruch: Kol Nidre	196?	40.00
—With Antal Dorati/London Symphony Orchestra; third edition (dark red, not maroon, label)			
❑ SR90320 [S]	Mendelssohn: Cello Sonata; Chopin: Cello Sonata in G	196?	100.00
—Maroon label, no "Vendor: Mercury Record Corporation			
❑ SR90320 [S]	Mendelssohn: Cello Sonata; Chopin: Cello Sonata in G	196?	60.00
—Maroon label, with "Vendor: Mercury Record Corporation			
❑ SR90347 [S]	Schumann: Cello Concerto; Lalo: Cello Concerto	196?	120.00
—With Stanislaw Skrowaczewski/London Symphony Orchestra; maroon label, no "Vendor: Mercury Record Corporation			
❑ SR90347 [S]	Schumann: Cello Concerto; Lalo: Cello Concerto	196?	40.00
—With Stanislaw Skrowaczewski/London Symphony Orchestra; maroon label, with "Vendor: Mercury Record Corporation			

STARLAND VOCAL BAND

WINDSONG

Number	Title	Yr	NM
❑ BXL1-3536	4 x 4	1980	15.00
❑ BXL1-2598	Late Nite Radio	1978	15.00
❑ BHL1-2239	Rear View Mirror	1977	15.00
❑ BHL1-1351	Starland Vocal Band	1976	15.00

STARR, EDWIN

20TH CENTURY

Number	Title	Yr	NM
❑ T-559	Clean	1978	12.00
❑ T-538	Edwin Starr	1977	12.00
❑ T-591	Happy Radio	1979	12.00
❑ T-615	Stronger Than You	1980	12.00
❑ T-634	The Best of Edwin Starr	1981	12.00

GORDY

Number	Title	Yr	NM
❑ GS-940	25 Miles	1969	30.00
❑ GS-956	Involved	1971	25.00
❑ GS-945	Just We Two	1969	25.00
—With Blinky			
❑ GS-931	Soul Master	1968	30.00
❑ GS-948	War & Peace	1970	25.00

GRANITE

Number	Title	Yr	NM
❑ 1005	Free to Be Myself	1975	15.00

MOTOWN

Number	Title	Yr	NM
❑ M5-103V1	Superstar Series, Vol. 3	1981	12.00
❑ M5-170V1	War & Peace	1981	12.00

PICKWICK

Number	Title	Yr	NM
❑ SPC-3387	25 Miles	197?	12.00

STARR, KAY

ABC

Number	Title	Yr	NM
❑ S-631	When the Lights Go On Again	1968	15.00

CAPITOL

Number	Title	Yr	NM
❑ T1468 [M]	All Starr Hits	1961	30.00
❑ ST1468 [S]	All Starr Hits	1961	30.00
❑ T1681 [M]	I Cry by Night	1962	25.00
❑ ST1681 [S]	I Cry by Night	1962	30.00
❑ T580 [M]	In a Blue Mood	1955	50.00
❑ T1795 [M]	Just Plain Country	1962	25.00
❑ ST1795 [S]	Just Plain Country	1962	30.00
❑ ST-8-1795 [S]	Just Plain Country	196?	30.00
—Capitol Record Club edition			
❑ T1438 [M]	Kay Starr, Jazz Singer	1960	30.00

Number	Title	Yr	NM
❑ GT1438 [S]	Kay Starr, Jazz Singer	1960	40.00
❑ ST-11323	Kay Starrs Again	1974	12.00
❑ SM-11323	Kay Starrs Again	1977	10.00
— Reissue with new prefix			
❑ T1303 [M]	Losers Weepers	1960	30.00
❑ ST1303 [S]	Losers Weepers	1960	30.00
❑ T1254 [M]	Movin'	1959	30.00
❑ ST1254 [S]	Movin'	1959	30.00
❑ SM-11880	Movin'	1979	12.00
❑ T1374 [M]	Movin' on Broadway	1960	30.00
❑ ST1374 [S]	Movin' on Broadway	1960	30.00
❑ T1358 [M]	One More Time	1960	30.00
❑ ST1358 [S]	One More Time	1960	30.00
❑ H211 [10]	Songs by Starr	1950	70.00
❑ T211 [M]	Songs by Starr	1955	50.00
❑ T2550 [M]	Tears and Heartaches/Old Records	1966	15.00
❑ ST2550 [S]	Tears and Heartaches/Old Records	1966	18.00
❑ T2106 [M]	The Fabulous Favorites	1964	15.00
❑ ST2106 [S]	The Fabulous Favorites	1964	18.00
❑ H415 [10]	The Hits of Kay Starr	1953	70.00
❑ T415 [M]	The Hits of Kay Starr	1955	50.00
— Turquoise or gray label			
❑ T415 [M]	The Hits of Kay Starr	1958	30.00
— Black label with colorband, Capitol logo at left			
❑ T415 [M]	The Hits of Kay Starr	1962	25.00
— Black label with colorband, Capitol logo at top			
❑ DT415 [R]	The Hits of Kay Starr	196?	15.00
❑ H363 [10]	The Kay Starr Style	1953	70.00
❑ T363 [M]	The Kay Starr Style	1955	50.00
CORONET			
❑ CX-106 [M]	Kay Starr Sings	196?	15.00
❑ CXS-106 [S]	Kay Starr Sings	196?	15.00
GNP CRESCENDO			
❑ GNPS-2090	Back to the Roots	1975	12.00
❑ GNPS-2083	Country	1974	12.00
HINDSIGHT			
❑ HSR-214	Kay Starr 1947	1985	12.00
LIBERTY			
❑ LRP-9001 [M]	Swingin' with the Starr	1956	50.00
❑ LRP-3280 [M]	Swingin' with the Starr	1963	30.00
— Reissue of 9001			
PARAMOUNT			
❑ PAS-5001	How About This	1969	15.00
RCA CAMDEN			
❑ CAL-567 [M]	Kay Starr	196?	15.00
RCA VICTOR			
❑ LPM-1549 [M]	Blue Starr	1957	30.00
❑ LPM-2055 [M]	I Hear the Word	1959	30.00
❑ LSP-2055 [S]	I Hear the Word	1959	30.00
❑ ANL1-1311	Pure Gold	1976	10.00
❑ LPM-1720 [M]	Rockin' with Kay	1958	50.00
❑ LPM-1149 [M]	The One and Only Kay Starr	1955	30.00
RONDO-LETTE			
❑ A-3 [M]	Them There Eyes	1958	30.00
SUNSET			
❑ SUM-1126 [M]	Portrait of a Starr	196?	18.00
❑ SUS-5126 [R]	Portrait of a Starr	196?	12.00

STARR, KAY/ERROLL GARNER

CROWN

Number	Title	Yr	NM
❑ CLP-5003 [M]	Singin' Kay Starr, Swingin' Erroll Garner	1957	30.00

MODERN

Number	Title	Yr	NM
❑ MLP-1203 [M]	Singin' Kay Starr, Swingin' Erroll Garner	1956	80.00

STARR, KENNY

MCA

Number	Title	Yr	NM
❑ 2177	The Blind Man in the Bleachers	1975	12.00

STARR, LUCILLE

A&M

Number	Title	Yr	NM
❑ LP-107 [M]	French Song	1966	30.00

EPIC

Number	Title	Yr	NM
❑ BN26436	Lonely Street	1969	30.00

STARR, RINGO

APPLE

Number	Title	Yr	NM
❑ SMAS-3368 [B]	Beaucoups of Blues	1970	30.00
❑ SW-3422	Blast from Your Past	1975	18.00
❑ SW-3417	Goodnight Vienna	1974	15.00
❑ SWAL-3413	Ringo	1973	25.00
— Standard issue with booklet; Side 1, Song 2 identified on cover as "Hold On			
❑ SWAL-3413	Ringo	1974	30.00
— Later issue with booklet; Side 1, Song 2 identified on cover as "Have You Seen My Baby			
❑ SWAL-3413	Ringo	1973	400.00
— With a 5:26 version of "Six O'Clock." On later copies, the song is shortened to 4:05 though the label still says 5:26. All known copies have a promo punch-hole in top corner of jacket; on Side 2 record, "Six O'Clock" will be the widest track.			
❑ SW-3365 [B]	Sentimental Journey	1970	30.00
ATLANTIC			
❑ SD18193	Ringo's Rotogravure	1976	18.00
— Deduct 2/3 for cut-outs			

Number	Title	Yr	NM
❑ SD18193 [DJ]	Ringo's Rotogravure	1976	30.00
— With "DJ Only" scrawled into trail-off area			
❑ SD19108	Ringo the 4th	1977	18.00
— Deduct 1/2 for cut-outs			
❑ SD19108 [DJ]	Ringo the 4th	1977	30.00
— With "DJ Only" scrawled into trail-off area			
BOARDWALK			
❑ NB1-33246	Stop and Smell the Roses	1981	12.00
— Deduct 1/2 for cut-outs			
CAPITOL			
❑ SN-16235	Beaucoups of Blues	198?	25.00
— Green label budget-line reissue			
❑ SN-16236	Blast from Your Past	198?	18.00
— Green label budget-line reissue			
❑ SN-16219	Goodnight Vienna	198?	30.00
— Green label budget-line reissue			
❑ SN-16114	Ringo	198?	18.00
— Green label budget-line reissue with all errors corrected			
❑ SW-3365	Sentimental Journey	197?	40.00
— Purple label, large Capitol logo			
❑ SN-16218	Sentimental Journey	198?	30.00
— Green label budget-line reissue			
PORTRAIT			
❑ JR35378	Bad Boy	1978	18.00
— Deduct 1/3 for cut-outs			
❑ JR35378 [DJ]	Bad Boy	1978	100.00
— White label promo with "Advance Promotion" on label; in plain white cover			
❑ JR35378 [DJ]	Bad Boy	1978	30.00
— Regular white-label promo in standard jacket			
RHINO			
❑ R170199	Starr Struck: Ringo's Best 1976-1983	1989	30.00
RYKODISC			
❑ RALP 0190	Ringo Starr and His All-Starr Band	1990	30.00
— With limited, numbered obi (deduct $5 if missing)			

STARR, SALLY

ARCADE

Number	Title	Yr	NM
❑ 1001 [M]	Our Gal Sal	1960	80.00

CLYMAX

Number	Title	Yr	NM
❑ 1001 [M]	Our Gal Sal	1959	200.00

STARS ON

21 RECORDS

Number	Title	Yr	NM
❑ 90291	Soul Revue	1985	18.00

RADIO

Number	Title	Yr	NM
❑ RR16044	Stars On Long Play	1981	12.00
❑ RR19314	Stars On Long Play II	1981	12.00
❑ RR19349	Stars On Long Play III	1982	12.00

STARSHIP

GRUNT

Number	Title	Yr	NM
❑ BXL1-5488	Knee Deep in the Hoopla	1985	10.00
❑ 6413-1-G	No Protection	1987	10.00

RCA

Number	Title	Yr	NM
❑ 9693-1-R	Love Among the Cannibals	1989	12.00

STARSHIP ORCHESTRA

COLUMBIA

Number	Title	Yr	NM
❑ NJC36456	Celestial Sky	1980	12.00

STARZ

CAPITOL

Number	Title	Yr	NM
❑ ST-11730	Attention Shoppers!	1978	12.00
❑ ST-11861	Coliseum Rock	1978	12.00
❑ SPRO-8657/8 [DJ]	Live at Municipal Auditorium, Louisville, March 30, 1978	1978	30.00
— Promo-only "Superstars Radio Network Presents" album			
❑ ST-11539	Starz	1976	12.00
❑ SW-11617	Violation	1977	25.00
— Gold vinyl			
❑ SW-11617	Violation	1977	12.00
— Black vinyl			
METAL BLADE			
❑ 73430	Live in Action	1989	15.00
VIOLATION			
❑ 0001	Live in America	1983	18.00

STATE STREET ACES, THE

STOMP OFF

Number	Title	Yr	NM
❑ SOS-1106	Old Folks Shuffle	198?	12.00
❑ SOS-1041	Pass Out Lightly	198?	12.00
❑ SOS-1011	Stuff	198?	12.00

STATE STREET RAMBLERS, THE

HERWIN

Number	Title	Yr	NM
❑ 104	The State Street Ramblers, Vol. 1	197?	15.00
❑ 105	The State Street Ramblers, Vol. 2	197?	15.00

STATLER BROTHERS, THE

COLUMBIA

Number	Title	Yr	NM
❑ CL2449 [M]	Flowers on the Wall	1966	30.00
❑ CS9249 [S]	Flowers on the Wall	1966	30.00
❑ PC9249	Flowers on the Wall	198?	10.00
— Reissue with new prefix			
❑ C31560	How Great Thou Art	197?	12.00
— Reissue of Harmony 31560			
❑ CS9878 [B]	Oh Happy Day	1969	30.00
❑ PC9878	Oh Happy Day	198?	10.00
— Reissue with new prefix			
❑ CL2719 [M]	The Big Hits	1967	30.00
❑ CS9519 [S]	The Big Hits	1967	30.00
❑ PC9519	The Big Hits	198?	10.00
— Reissue with new prefix			
❑ KG31557	The World of the Statler Brothers	1972	25.00
❑ CG31557	The World of the Statler Brothers	198?	15.00
— Reissue with new prefix			
HARMONY			
❑ H30610	Big Country Hits	1971	15.00
❑ KH32256	Do You Love Me Tonight	1973	15.00
❑ KH31560	How Great Thou Art	1972	15.00
MERCURY			
❑ SRM-1-5027	10th Anniversary	1980	15.00
❑ 812282-1	10th Anniversary	1983	10.00
❑ 818652-1	Atlanta Blue	1984	12.00
❑ SR-61317	Bed of Rose's	1970	18.00
❑ 826247-1	Bed of Rose's	1986	10.00
❑ SRM-1-676	Carry Me Back	1973	18.00
❑ 812284-1	Carry Me Back	1983	10.00
❑ SRM-1-5012 [B]	Christmas Card	1978	12.00
❑ 822743-1	Christmas Card	1985	10.00
❑ 824785-1	Christmas Present	1985	10.00
❑ SR-61367	Country Music "Then and Now	1972	18.00
❑ 826260-1	Country Music "Then and Now	1986	10.00
❑ SRM-1-5007	Entertainers...On and Off the Record	1978	15.00
❑ 812283-1	Entertainers...On and Off the Record	1983	10.00
❑ 826782-1	Four for the Show	1986	12.00
❑ SRM-1-1077	Harold, Lew, Phil & Don	1976	18.00
❑ 826269-1	Harold, Lew, Phil & Don	1986	10.00
❑ 3RM-1-1052	Holy Bible: New Testament	1975	18.00
❑ 826268-1	Holy Bible: New Testament	1986	10.00
❑ SRM-1-1051	Holy Bible: Old Testament	1975	18.00
❑ 826267-1	Holy Bible: Old Testament	1986	10.00
❑ SRM-2-101	Holy Bible/The Old and New Testaments	1978	25.00
— Reissue of 1051 and 1052 in one package			
❑ 826264-1	Holy Bible/The Old and New Testaments	1986	12.00
❑ SR-61358	Innerview	1972	18.00
❑ 826259-1	Innerview	1986	10.00
❑ 832404-1	Maple Street Memories	1987	12.00
❑ 824420-1	Pardners in Rhyme	1985	12.00
❑ SR-61349	Pictures of Moments to Remember	1971	18.00
❑ 826710-1	Radio Gospel Favorites	1986	12.00
❑ SRM-1-5001	Short Stories	1977	15.00
❑ 826280-1	Short Stories	1986	10.00
❑ SRM-1-1019	Sons of the Motherland	1975	18.00
❑ 838231-1	Statler Brothers Live -- Sold Out	1989	18.00
❑ SRM-1-707	Thank You World	1974	18.00
❑ SRM-1-1037	The Best of the Statler Brothers	1975	15.00
❑ 822524-1	The Best of the Statler Brothers	1984	10.00
❑ SRM-1-5024	The Best of the Statler Brothers Rides Again, Volume II	1980	15.00
❑ 822525-1	The Best of the Statler Brothers Rides Again, Volume II	1984	10.00
❑ SRM-1-1125	The Country America Loves	1977	18.00
❑ 826275-1	The Country America Loves	1986	10.00
❑ SRM-1-4048	The Legend Goes On	1982	15.00
❑ 826278-1	The Legend Goes On	1986	10.00
❑ SRM-1-5016	The Originals	1979	15.00
❑ 826281-1	The Originals	1986	10.00
❑ SR-61374	The Statler Brothers Sing Country Symphonies in E Major	1973	18.00
❑ 834626-1	The Statlers Greatest Hits	1988	12.00
❑ 812184-1	Today	1983	12.00
❑ SRM-1-6002	Years Ago	1981	15.00
PRIORITY			
❑ PU37709	Country Gospel	1982	12.00
REALM			
❑ 2V8077	The Very Best of the Statler Brothers	1977	18.00
TIME-LIFE			
❑ STW-105	Country Music	1981	12.00

STATON, CANDI

FAME

Number	Title	Yr	NM
❑ 1800	Candi Staton	1972	25.00
❑ ST-4201	I'm a Prisoner	1970	25.00
❑ ST-4202	Stand By Your Man	1971	25.00

WARNER BROS.

Number	Title	Yr	NM
❑ BS2830	Candi	1974	15.00
❑ BSK3428	Candi Staton	1980	15.00
❑ BSK3333	Chance	1979	15.00
❑ BSK3207	House of Love	1978	15.00
❑ BS3040	Music Speaks Louder Than Words	1977	15.00
❑ BS2948	Young Hearts Run Free	1976	15.00

STATON, DAKOTA

CAPITOL

Number	Title	Yr	NM
❑ T1387 [M]	Ballads and the Blues	1960	30.00
—Black label with colorband, Capitol logo at left			
❑ ST1387 [S]	Ballads and the Blues	1960	40.00
—Black label with colorband, Capitol logo at left			
❑ T1387 [M]	Ballads and the Blues	1962	18.00
—Black label with colorband, Capitol logo at top			
❑ ST1387 [S]	Ballads and the Blues	1962	25.00
—Black label with colorband, Capitol logo at top			
❑ T1170 [M]	Crazy He Calls Me	1959	30.00
—Black label with colorband, Capitol logo at left			
❑ T1170 [M]	Crazy He Calls Me	1962	18.00
—Black label with colorband, Capitol logo at top			
❑ ST1170 [S]	Crazy He Calls Me	1959	40.00
—Black label with colorband, Capitol logo at left			
❑ ST1170 [S]	Crazy He Calls Me	1962	25.00
—Black label with colorband, Capitol logo at top			
❑ T1490 [M]	Dakota	1961	30.00
—Black label with colorband, Capitol logo at left			
❑ T1490 [M]	Dakota	1962	18.00
—Black label with colorband, Capitol logo at top			
❑ ST1490 [S]	Dakota	1961	40.00
—Black label with colorband, Capitol logo at left			
❑ ST1490 [S]	Dakota	1962	25.00
—Black label with colorband, Capitol logo at top			
❑ T1649 [M]	Dakota at Storyville	1962	25.00
❑ ST1649 [S]	Dakota at Storyville	1962	30.00
❑ T1054 [M]	Dynamic!	1958	30.00
—Black label with colorband, Capitol logo at left			
❑ T1054 [M]	Dynamic!	1962	18.00
—Black label with colorband, Capitol logo at top			
❑ ST1054 [S]	Dynamic!	1959	40.00
—Black label with colorband, Capitol logo at left			
❑ ST1054 [S]	Dynamic!	1962	25.00
—Black label with colorband, Capitol logo at top			
❑ T1003 [M]	In the Night	1958	50.00
—Turquoise or gray label			
❑ T1003 [M]	In the Night	1959	30.00
—Black label with colorband, Capitol logo at left			
❑ M-1003	In the Night	1976	12.00
—Reissue with new prefix			
❑ T1325 [M]	More Than the Most	1960	30.00
—Black label with colorband, Capitol logo at left			
❑ T1325 [M]	More Than the Most	1962	18.00
—Black label with colorband, Capitol logo at top			
❑ ST1325 [S]	More Than the Most	1960	40.00
—Black label with colorband, Capitol logo at left			
❑ ST1325 [S]	More Than the Most	1962	25.00
—Black label with colorband, Capitol logo at top			
❑ T1597 [M]	'Round Midnight	1961	30.00
—Black label with colorband, Capitol logo at left			
❑ T1597 [M]	'Round Midnight	1962	18.00
—Black label with colorband, Capitol logo at top			
❑ ST1597 [S]	'Round Midnight	1961	40.00
—Black label with colorband, Capitol logo at left			
❑ ST1597 [S]	'Round Midnight	1962	25.00
—Black label with colorband, Capitol logo at top			
❑ T1427 [M]	Softly	1961	30.00
—Black label with colorband, Capitol logo at left			
❑ T1427 [M]	Softly	1962	18.00
—Black label with colorband, Capitol logo at top			
❑ ST1427 [S]	Softly	1961	40.00
—Black label with colorband, Capitol logo at left			
❑ ST1427 [S]	Softly	1962	25.00
—Black label with colorband, Capitol logo at top			
❑ T876 [M]	The Late, Late Show	1957	50.00
—Turquoise or gray label			
❑ T876 [M]	The Late, Late Show	1959	30.00
—Black label with colorband, Capitol logo at left			
❑ T876 [M]	The Late, Late Show	1962	18.00
—Black label with colorband, Capitol logo at top			
❑ DT876 [R]	The Late, Late Show	196?	15.00
❑ SM-876	The Late, Late Show	1977	12.00
—Reissue with new prefix			
❑ T1241 [M]	Time to Swing	1959	30.00
—Black label with colorband, Capitol logo at left			
❑ T1241 [M]	Time to Swing	1962	18.00
—Black label with colorband, Capitol logo at top			
❑ ST1241 [S]	Time to Swing	1959	40.00
—Black label with colorband, Capitol logo at left			
❑ ST1241 [S]	Time to Swing	1962	25.00
—Black label with colorband, Capitol logo at top			

GROOVE MERCHANT

Number	Title	Yr	NM
❑ 4410	Confessin'	197?	18.00
❑ 521	I Want a Country Man	1973	15.00
❑ 510	Madame Foo-Foo	1972	15.00
❑ 532	Ms. Soul	1974	15.00

LONDON

Number	Title	Yr	NM
❑ LL3495 [M]	Dakota '67	1967	25.00
❑ PS495 [S]	Dakota '67	1967	18.00

MUSE

Number	Title	Yr	NM
❑ MR-5401	Dakota Staton	1991	18.00

UNITED ARTISTS

Number	Title	Yr	NM
❑ UAL-3355 [M]	Dakota Staton with Strings	1964	25.00
❑ UAS-6355 [S]	Dakota Staton with Strings	1964	30.00
❑ UAL-3292 [M]	From Dakota with Love	1963	25.00
❑ UAS-6292 [S]	From Dakota with Love	1963	30.00
❑ UAL-3312 [M]	Live and Swinging	1963	25.00
❑ UAS-6316 [S]	Live and Swinging	1963	30.00

VERVE

Number	Title	Yr	NM
❑ V6-8799	I've Been There	1971	18.00

STATUS CYMBAL, THE

RCA VICTOR

Number	Title	Yr	NM
❑ LPM-3993 [M]	In the Morning	1968	50.00
❑ LSP-3993 [S]	In the Morning	1968	25.00

STATUS QUO

A&M

Number	Title	Yr	NM
❑ SP-3615 [B]	Hello!	1974	18.00
❑ SP-4381 [B]	Piledriver	1973	18.00
❑ SP-3649 [B]	Quo	1974	18.00

CADET CONCEPT

Number	Title	Yr	NM
❑ LPS-315 [B]	Messages from the Status Quo	1968	80.00

CAPITOL

Number	Title	Yr	NM
❑ ST-11381	On the Level	1975	12.00
❑ ST-11749	Rockin' All Over the World	1978	12.00
❑ ST-11509	Status Quo	1976	12.00
❑ SKBB-11623	Status Quo Live	1977	15.00

JANUS

Number	Title	Yr	NM
❑ JLS-3018 [B]	Ma Kelly's Greasy Spoon	1970	30.00

MERCURY

Number	Title	Yr	NM
❑ 836651-1	Status Quo	1989	15.00

PYE

Number	Title	Yr	NM
❑ 3301 [B]	Dog of Two Head	1971	30.00

RIVA

Number	Title	Yr	NM
❑ 7402	Now Here This	1980	15.00

STEAGALL, RED

ABC

Number	Title	Yr	NM
❑ AB-1051	Hang On Feelin'	1978	15.00

ABC DOT

Number	Title	Yr	NM
❑ DO-2078	For All Our Cowboy Friends	1977	15.00
❑ DOSD-2055	Lone Star Beer and Bob Wills Music	1976	18.00
❑ DOSD-2068	Texas Red	1976	15.00

CAPITOL

Number	Title	Yr	NM
❑ ST-11321	Finer Things in Life	1974	15.00
❑ ST-11228	If You've Got the Time, I've Got the Song	1973	15.00
❑ ST-11060	Party Dolls and Wine	1972	25.00
❑ ST-11162	Somewhere My Love	1973	15.00

MCA

Number	Title	Yr	NM
❑ 680	For All Our Cowboy Friends	198?	10.00
—Reissue of ABC Dot 2078			
❑ 681	Hang On Feelin'	198?	10.00
—Reissue of ABC 1051			
❑ 985	Lone Star Beer and Bob Wills Music	1986	12.00
—Reissue of ABC Dot 2055			

STEALERS WHEEL

A&M

Number	Title	Yr	NM
❑ SP-4419	Ferguslie Park	1974	15.00
❑ SP-4517	Right or Wrong	1974	15.00
❑ SP-4377 [B]	Stealers Wheel	1973	18.00
❑ SP-4708	Stuck in the Middle with You -- The Best of Stealers Wheel	1978	12.00

STEAM

MERCURY

Number	Title	Yr	NM
❑ SR61254 [B]	Steam	1969	30.00

STEAMHAMMER

EPIC

Number	Title	Yr	NM
❑ BN26490	Reflection	1969	30.00
❑ BN26552	Steamhammer	1970	30.00

STEARNS, JUNE

COLUMBIA

Number	Title	Yr	NM
❑ CS9783	River of Regret	1969	25.00

STEEL

EPIC

Number	Title	Yr	NM
❑ E30875	Steel	1971	25.00

STEELE, JAN & CAGE, JOHN

ANTILLES

Number	Title	Yr	NM
❑ AN-7031 [B]	Voices and Instruments	1976	50.00

STEELE, JOAN, AND JOHN MAGALDI

AUDIOPHILE

Number	Title	Yr	NM
❑ AP-156	Lonesome No More	198?	12.00

STEELE, JOAN

AUDIOPHILE

Number	Title	Yr	NM
❑ AP-94	'Round Midnight	1975	15.00

STEELE, TOMMY

LIBERTY

Number	Title	Yr	NM
❑ LRP-3426 [M]	Everything's Coming Up Broadway	1965	25.00
❑ LST-7426 [S]	Everything's Coming Up Broadway	1965	30.00
❑ LRP-3566 [M]	Sixpenny Millionaire	1968	30.00
—Stereo cover with "Audition Mono LP Not for Sale" sticker attached; label is stock			
❑ LST-7566 [S]	Sixpenny Millionaire	1968	18.00

LONDON

Number	Title	Yr	NM
❑ LL1770 [M]	Rock Around the World	195?	50.00

STEELEYE SPAN

BIG TREE

Number	Title	Yr	NM
❑ BTS2004 [B]	Please to See the King	1971	35.00

CHRYSALIS

Number	Title	Yr	NM
❑ CHR1091	All Around My Hat	1975	18.00
—Green label, "3300 Warner Blvd." address			
❑ CHR1091	All Around My Hat	1977	15.00
—Blue label, New York address			
❑ CHR1008	Below the Salt	1972	18.00
—Green label, "3300 Warner Blvd." address			
❑ CHR1008	Below the Salt	1977	15.00
—Blue label, New York address			
❑ CHR1071	Commoners Crown	1975	18.00
—Green label, "3300 Warner Blvd." address			
❑ CHR1071	Commoners Crown	1977	15.00
—Blue label, New York address			
❑ CHR1120	Hark the Village Wait	1976	18.00
—First US issue of debut LP; green label, "3300 Warner Blvd." address			
❑ CHR1120	Hark the Village Wait	1977	15.00
—Blue label, New York address			
❑ CHR1199	Live at Last	1978	15.00
❑ CHR1053	Now We Are Six	1974	18.00
—Green label, "3300 Warner Blvd." address			
❑ CHR1053	Now We Are Six	1977	15.00
—Blue label, New York address			
❑ CHR1046	Parcel of Rogues	1973	18.00
—Green label, "3300 Warner Blvd." address			
❑ CHR1046	Parcel of Rogues	1977	15.00
—Blue label, New York address			
❑ CHR1119	Please to See the King	1976	18.00
—Reissue of Big Tree LP; green label, "3300 Warner Blvd." address			
❑ CHR1119	Please to See the King	1977	15.00
—Blue label, New York address			
❑ CHR1123	Rocket Cottage	1976	18.00
—Green label, "3300 Warner Blvd." address			
❑ CHR1123	Rocket Cottage	1977	15.00
—Blue label, New York address			
❑ CHR1151	Storm Force Ten	1978	15.00
❑ CHR1121	Ten Man Mop	1976	18.00
—First US issue of third UK LP; green label, "3300 Warner Blvd." address			
❑ CHR1121	Ten Man Mop	1977	15.00
—Blue label, New York address			
❑ CHR21136	The Steeleye Span Story: Original Masters	1977	18.00
❑ V2X41136	The Steeleye Span Story: Original Masters	1984	15.00
—Reissue of 1136			

MOBILE FIDELITY

Number	Title	Yr	NM
❑ 1-027 [B]	All Around My Hat	1980	50.00
—Audiophile vinyl			

PAIR

Number	Title	Yr	NM
❑ CRPDL-2-1021	Dogs and Ferrets	1983	18.00

SHANACHIE

Number	Title	Yr	NM
❑ 79059	All Around My Hat	1989	15.00
❑ 79063	Back in Line	1989	15.00
❑ 79039	Below the Salt	1989	15.00
❑ 79052	Hark the Village Wait	1989	15.00
❑ 79060	Now We Are Six	1989	15.00
❑ 79045	Parcel of Rogues	1989	15.00
❑ 79071/2 [B]	Portfolio	1990	30.00
❑ 64020	Tempted and Tried	1989	15.00
❑ 79049	Ten Man Mop	1989	15.00

TAKOMA

Number	Title	Yr	NM
❑ TAK-7097	Sails of Silver	1981	12.00

STEELY DAN

ABC

Number	Title	Yr	NM
❑ AA-1006	Aja	1977	15.00
❑ 758	Can't Buy a Thrill	1972	15.00
—Black label			
❑ 758	Can't Buy a Thrill	1974	12.00
—Multicolor label			
❑ 779	Countdown to Ecstasy	1973	15.00

Number	Title	Yr	NM

—Black label
| ❏ 779 | Countdown to Ecstasy | 1974 | 12.00 |

—Multicolor label
| ❏ AK-1107 | Greatest Hits | 1978 | 18.00 |
| ❏ 2022-1107 | Greatest Hits | 1978 | 25.00 |

—Canadian import on gold vinyl, widely available in U.S.
| ❏ 846 | Katy Lied | 1975 | 15.00 |
| ❏ 806 [B] | Pretzel Logic | 1974 | 15.00 |

—Black label
| ❏ 806 | Pretzel Logic | 1974 | 12.00 |

—Multicolor label
| ❏ 931 | The Royal Scam | 1976 | 15.00 |

ABC DUNHILL
| ❏ SMAS-94976 | Can't Buy a Thrill | 1973 | 30.00 |

—Capitol Record Club edition pressed on the wrong label

COMMAND
| ❏ QD-40009 [Q] | Can't Buy a Thrill | 1974 | 40.00 |

—Second issue with no border around the cover
| ❏ QD-40009 [Q] | Can't Buy a Thrill | 1974 | 45.00 |

—First issue with wide border around outside of cover
| ❏ QD-40010 [Q] | Countdown to Ecstasy | 1974 | 40.00 |
| ❏ QD-40015 [Q] | Pretzel Logic | 1974 | 40.00 |

GEFFEN
| ❏ MCA1693 | Gaucho | 2008 | 25.00 |

MCA
❏ AA-1006	Aja	1980	12.00
❏ 37040	Can't Buy a Thrill	1980	10.00
❏ 37041	Countdown to Ecstasy	1980	10.00
❏ 6102	Gaucho	1980	12.00
❏ 16009	Gaucho	1981	50.00

—Audiophile pressing
| ❏ 5324 | Gold | 1982 | 12.00 |
| ❏ 16016 | Gold | 1982 | 50.00 |

—Audiophile pressing
❏ 37243	Gold	1984	10.00
❏ 2-6008	Greatest Hits	1980	15.00
❏ 37043	Katy Lied	1980	10.00
❏ 37042	Pretzel Logic	1980	10.00
❏ 37044	The Royal Scam	1980	10.00

MOBILE FIDELITY
| ❏ 1-033 [B] | Aja | 1980 | 80.00 |

—Audiophile vinyl
| ❏ 1-007 [B] | Katy Lied | 1979 | 100.00 |

—Audiophile vinyl

STEGALL, KEITH

EPIC
| ❏ B6E39892 | Keith Stegall | 1985 | 10.00 |

STEIG, JEREMY, AND EDDIE GOMEZ

CMP
❏ CMP-3-ST	Lend Me Your Ears	198?	12.00
❏ CMP-6-ST	Music for Flute and Double Bass	198?	12.00
❏ CMP-12-ST	Rain Forest	198?	12.00

ENJA
| ❏ 2098 | Outlaws | 198? | 15.00 |

INNER CITY
| ❏ IC-3015 | Outlaws | 197? | 15.00 |

STEIG, JEREMY

BLUE NOTE
| ❏ BST-84354 | Wayfaring Stranger | 1970 | 25.00 |

CAPITOL
| ❏ SM-662 | Energy | 1976 | 12.00 |

—Reissue with new prefix
| ❏ ST-662 | Energy | 1971 | 18.00 |

COLUMBIA
❏ CL2136 [M]	Flute Fever	1964	15.00
❏ CS8936 [S]	Flute Fever	1964	18.00
❏ KC32579	Monium	1974	15.00
❏ KC33297	Temple of Birth	1975	15.00

CTI
| ❏ 7075 | Firefly | 1977 | 15.00 |

GROOVE MERCHANT
| ❏ 2204 | Fusion | 197? | 18.00 |

SOLID STATE
| ❏ SS-18068 | Legwork | 1970 | 18.00 |
| ❏ SS-18059 | This Is Jeremy Steig | 1969 | 18.00 |

STEIN, ANDY

STOMP OFF
| ❏ SOS-1146 | Goin' Places | 1987 | 12.00 |

STEIN, HAL, AND WARREN FITZGERALD

PROGRESSIVE
| ❏ PLP-1002 [M] | Hal Stein-Warren Fitzgerald Quintet | 1955 | 500.00 |

STEIN, LOU

AUDIOPHILE
| ❏ AP-198 | Solo Piano | 1984 | 12.00 |

BRUNSWICK
| ❏ BL58053 [10] | Lou Stein | 1953 | 50.00 |

CHIAROSCURO
| ❏ CR-2027 | Temple of the Gods | 1979 | 18.00 |
| ❏ 140 | Tribute to Tatum | 197? | 15.00 |

CORAL
| ❏ CRL57201 [M] | Sing Around the Piano | 1958 | 25.00 |
| ❏ CRL57003 [M] | Sweet and Lovely | 195? | 30.00 |

DREAMSTREET
| ❏ DR-106 | Lou Stein Trio Live at the Dome | 1986 | 12.00 |

EPIC
❏ LN3186 [M]	From Broadway to Paris	1955	40.00
❏ LG3101 [M]	House Top	1955	40.00
❏ LN3148 [M]	Three, Four and Five	1955	40.00

JUBILEE
| ❏ JLP-1019 [M] | Eight for Kicks, Four for Laughs | 1956 | 40.00 |
| ❏ JLP-8 [10] | Six for Kicks | 1954 | 50.00 |

MASTERSEAL
| ❏ MS33-1812 [M] | Mood Music for Beer and Pretzels | 1957 | 18.00 |

MERCURY
❏ SR-60054 [S]	Honky Tonk Piano	1959	25.00
❏ MG-20364 [M]	Honky Tonk Piano	195?	18.00
❏ MG-20159 [M]	Honky Tonk Piano	195?	25.00
❏ MG-20469 [M]	Honky Tonk Piano and a Hot Banjo	1960	15.00
❏ SR-60151 [S]	Honky Tonk Piano and a Hot Banjo	1960	18.00
❏ MG-20271 [M]	Saloon Favorites	195?	18.00

MUSICOR
| ❏ MM-2057 [M] | Hey Louie! Play Melancholy Baby! | 1967 | 18.00 |
| ❏ MS-3057 [S] | Hey Louie! Play Melancholy Baby! | 1967 | 15.00 |

WING
| ❏ SRW-16219 [S] | The Lou Stein-Way of Piano Pleasure | 196? | 18.00 |
| ❏ MGW-12219 [M] | The Lou Stein-Way of Piano Pleasure | 196? | 15.00 |

WORLD JAZZ
| ❏ WJLPS-17 | Lou Stein and Friends | 1980 | 15.00 |

STEINBERG, DAVID

COLUMBIA
| ❏ KC32563 | Booga Booga | 1974 | 12.00 |
| ❏ PC33390 | Goodbye to the Seventies | 1975 | 12.00 |

ELEKTRA
| ❏ EKS-74063 | Disguised as a Normal Person | 1970 | 15.00 |

UNI
| ❏ 73013 | The Incredible Shrinking God | 1968 | 18.00 |

STEINMAN, JIM

CLEVELAND INT'L.
| ❏ FE36531 | Bad for Good | 1981 | 18.00 |

—With bonus 7-inch 33 1/3 small hole single AE7 1232, "The Storm"/"Rock and Roll Dreams Come Through," and its picture sleeve (deduct 50 percent if missing)

STEPHENS, LEIGH

PHILIPS
| ❏ PHS600294 | Red Weather | 1969 | 80.00 |

STEPPENWOLF

ABC
| ❏ AC-30008 | The ABC Collection | 1976 | 18.00 |

ABC DUNHILL
❏ DSX-50135	16 Greatest Hits	1973	25.00
❏ DSX-50053	At Your Birthday Party	1969	25.00
❏ DS-50060	Early Steppenwolf	1969	25.00

—Actually a 1967 concert by Sparrow (pre-Steppenwolf)
❏ DSX-50110	For Ladies Only	1971	25.00
❏ DS-50066	Monster	1969	25.00
❏ DSX-50124	Rest in Peace	1972	25.00
❏ DS-50029 [S]	Steppenwolf	1968	25.00
❏ DSX-50090	Steppenwolf 7	1970	25.00
❏ DSX-50099	Steppenwolf Gold/Their Great Hits	1971	25.00
❏ DSD-50075	Steppenwolf 'Live'	1970	30.00
❏ DS-50037	The Second	1968	30.00

—With chrome border on cover
| ❏ DS-50037 | The Second | 1968 | 30.00 |

—With white border on cover

DUNHILL
| ❏ SKAO-93083 | Monster | 1969 | 30.00 |

—Capitol Record Club edition on old-style Dunhill label
❏ D-50029 [M]	Steppenwolf	1968	150.00
❏ DS-50029 [S]	Steppenwolf	1968	40.00
❏ ST-91487	Steppenwolf	1968	30.00

—Capitol Record Club edition

EPIC
❏ PE33583	Hour of the Wolf	1975	15.00
❏ JE34382	Reborn to Be Wild	1977	15.00
❏ PE34120	Skullduggery	1976	15.00

MCA
| ❏ 37049 | 16 Greatest Hits | 1979 | 10.00 |

| ❏ 1599 | 16 Greatest Hits | 198? | 10.00 |

—Reissue of 37049
❏ 37045	Steppenwolf	1979	10.00
❏ 37047	Steppenwolf 7	1979	10.00
❏ DSX-50099	Steppenwolf Gold/Their Great Hits	1980	15.00

—Columbia House edition on blue rainbow label, but retaining the original ABC Dunhill catalog number
| ❏ 2-6013 | Steppenwolf 'Live' | 198? | 12.00 |
| ❏ 37046 | The Second | 1979 | 10.00 |

MUMS
| ❏ PZ33093 | Slow Flux | 1974 | 18.00 |

NAUTILUS
| ❏ NR-53 | Wolftracks | 198? | 50.00 |

—As "John Kay and Steppenwolf"; audiophile vinyl

PICKWICK
| ❏ SPC-3603 | Best of Steppenwolf | 1978 | 12.00 |

STEPS AHEAD

ELEKTRA/MUSICIAN
❏ 60441	Magnetic	1986	12.00
❏ 60351	Modern Times	1985	12.00
❏ 60168	Steps	1983	12.00

STERLING, ARNOLD

JAM
| ❏ 010 | Here's Brother Sterling | 198? | 15.00 |

STERN, LENI

ENJA
| ❏ R1-79602 | Secrets | 1989 | 15.00 |

STERN, MIKE

ATLANTIC
❏ 82027	Jigsaw	1990	15.00
❏ 81840	Time in Place	1988	12.00
❏ 81656	Upside Downside	1986	12.00

STEVENS, APRIL

AUDIO LAB
| ❏ AL-1534 [M] | Torrid Tunes | 1959 | 200.00 |

IMPERIAL
| ❏ LP-9118 [M] | Teach Me Tiger | 1960 | 60.00 |
| ❏ LP-12055 [S] | Teach Me Tiger | 1960 | 100.00 |

STEVENS, CAT

A&M
❏ SP-4735	Back to Earth	1978	15.00
❏ SP-3623	Buddha and the Chocolate Box	1974	15.00
❏ QU-53623 [Q]	Buddha and the Chocolate Box	1974	25.00
❏ SP-4365	Catch Bull at Four	1972	15.00
❏ SP-3736	Footsteps in the Dark -- Greatest Hits, Volume Two	1984	12.00
❏ SP-3285	Footsteps in the Dark -- Greatest Hits, Volume Two	1986	10.00

—Reissue of 3736
❏ SP-4391	Foreigner	1973	15.00
❏ QU-54391 [Q]	Foreigner	1974	25.00
❏ SP-4519	Greatest Hits	1975	15.00
❏ QU-54519 [Q]	Greatest Hits	1975	25.00
❏ SP-4702	Izitso	1977	15.00
❏ SP-4260	Mona Bone Jakon	1970	15.00

—Brown label
| ❏ SP-4260 | Mona Bone Jakon | 1974 | 12.00 |

—Mostly silver label with gradually fading "A&M"
| ❏ SP-3160 | Mona Bone Jakon | 198? | 10.00 |

—Reissue of 4260
| ❏ SP-4555 | Numbers | 1975 | 15.00 |
| ❏ SP-4280 | Tea for the Tillerman | 1971 | 15.00 |

—Brown label
| ❏ SP-4280 | Tea for the Tillerman | 1974 | 12.00 |

—Mostly silver label with gradually fading "A&M"
| ❏ SP-4313 | Teaser and the Firecat | 1971 | 15.00 |

—Brown label
| ❏ SP-4313 | Teaser and the Firecat | 1974 | 12.00 |

—Mostly silver label with gradually fading "A&M"

DERAM
❏ DE16005 [M]	Matthew and Son	1967	60.00
❏ DES18005 [P]	Matthew and Son	1967	25.00
❏ DES18005/10 [P]	Matthew and Son/New Masters	1971	18.00
❏ DES18010 [S]	New Masters	1968	30.00
❏ DES18061 [P]	Very Young and Early Songs	1972	15.00

LONDON
| ❏ LC-50010 | Cat's Cradle | 1977 | 15.00 |
| ❏ 820321-1 | Cat's Cradle | 1985 | 10.00 |

MOBILE FIDELITY
| ❏ 1-254 | Izitso | 1996 | 30.00 |

—Audiophile vinyl
| ❏ 1-035 [B] | Tea for the Tillerman | 1979 | 60.00 |

—Audiophile vinyl
| ❏ MFQR-035 [B] | Tea for the Tillerman | 1984 | 150.00 |

—Ultra High Quality Recording in a box
| ❏ 1-244 [B] | Teaser and the Firecat | 1996 | 60.00 |

—Audiophile vinyl

Number	Title	Yr	NM

STEVENS, CLIVE

CAPITOL
ST-11263	Atmospheres	1973	18.00
SM-11675	Atmospheres	1976	12.00
ST-11320	Voyage to Uranus	1974	18.00
SM-11676	Voyage to Uranus	1976	12.00

STEVENS, CONNIE

HARMONY
| HS11312 | The Hank Williams Songbook | 1969 | 18.00 |

WARNER BROS.
W1208 [M]	Conchetta	1958	50.00
WS1208 [S]	Conchetta	1958	60.00
W1432 [M]	Connie	1962	30.00
WS1432 [S]	Connie	1962	40.00
W1382 [M]	Connie Stevens from "Hawaiian Eye	1960	30.00
WS1382 [S]	Connie Stevens from "Hawaiian Eye	1960	40.00
W1431 [M]	From Me to You	1962	30.00
WS1431 [S]	From Me to You	1962	40.00
W1460 [M]	The Hank Williams Songbook	1962	30.00
WS1460 [S]	The Hank Williams Songbook	1962	40.00

STEVENS, DODIE

DOT
DLP-3212 [M]	Dodie Stevens	1960	30.00
DLP-25212 [S]	Dodie Stevens	1960	40.00
DLP-3323 [M]	Over the Rainbow	1960	30.00
DLP-25323 [S]	Over the Rainbow	1960	40.00
DLP-3271 [M]	Pink Shoelaces	1961	30.00
DLP-25371 [S]	Pink Shoelaces	1961	40.00

STEVENS, EVEN

DAKAR
| DK-76905 | Even Stevens | 1973 | 30.00 |

ELEKTRA
| 7E-1113 | Thorn on a Rose | 1977 | 15.00 |

STEVENS, LEITH

CORAL
| CRL57283 [M] | Jazz Themes for Cops and Robbers | 1958 | 50.00 |

DECCA
| DL5515 [10] | Jazz Themes in "The Wild One | 1954 | 80.00 |

STEVENS, MIKE

NOVUS
| 3042-1-N | Light Up the Night | 1988 | 12.00 |
| 3080-1-N | Set the Spirit Free | 1990 | 15.00 |

STEVENS, RAY

BARNABY
6003	Boogity Boogity	1974	15.00
Z1235005	Everything Is Beautiful	1970	18.00
KZ32139	Losin' Streak	1972	15.00
6012	Misty	1975	15.00
BR15007	Nashville	1973	15.00
5005	Nashville	1974	12.00
— Reissue of 15007			
Z30770	Ray Stevens' Greatest Hits	1971	15.00
5004	Ray Stevens' Greatest Hits	1974	12.00
— Reissue of 30770			
ZQ30770 [Q]	Ray Stevens' Greatest Hits	1971	25.00
Z30092	Ray Stevens...Unreal!!!	1970	15.00
6018	The Very Best of Ray Stevens	1975	15.00
Z30809	Turn Your Radio On	1972	15.00
ZQ30809 [Q]	Turn Your Radio On	1972	25.00

MCA
42303	Beside Myself	1989	12.00
42020	Crackin' Up!	1987	12.00
5918	Greatest Hits	1987	12.00
42062	Greatest Hits, Volume 2	1987	12.00
5517	He Thinks He's Ray Stevens	1984	12.00
5635	I Have Returned	1985	12.00
42172	I Never Made a Record I Didn't Like	1988	12.00
5795	Surely You Joust	1986	12.00

MERCURY
MG-20732 [M]	1,837 Seconds of Humor	1962	40.00
SR-60732 [S]	1,837 Seconds of Humor	1962	50.00
812780-1	Me	1984	12.00
SR-61272	The Best of Ray Stevens	1968	18.00
MG-20828 [M]	This Is Ray Stevens	1963	30.00
SR-60828 [S]	This Is Ray Stevens	1963	30.00

MONUMENT
SLP-18102	Even Stevens	1968	18.00
SLP-18115	Gitarzan	1969	18.00
SLP-18134	Have a Little Talk with Myself	1970	18.00

PICKWICK
| SPC-3266 | Rock and Roll Show | 1971 | 12.00 |

PRIORITY
| PU38075 | Turn Your Radio On | 1982 | 12.00 |
| — Reissue of Barnaby 30809 | | | |

RCA VICTOR
CPL1-7161	Collector's Series	1986	12.00
AHL1-4288	Don't Laugh Now	1982	12.00
AHL1-4727	Greatest Hits	1983	12.00
AYL1-5153	Greatest Hits	1985	10.00
— Best Buy Series" reissue			
AHL1-3841	One More Last Chance	1981	12.00
AHL1-3574	Shriner's Convention	1980	12.00
AYL1-4253	Shriner's Convention	1982	10.00
— Best Buy Series" reissue			

WARNER BROS.
BS3195	Be Your Own Best Friend	1978	12.00
BS2997	Feel the Music	1977	12.00
BS2914	Just for the Record	1976	12.00
BSK3332	The Feeling's Not Right Again	1979	12.00
BS3098	There Is Something...	1977	12.00

STEVENS, SHAKIN'

EPIC
FE37415	Get Shakin'	1981	14.00
BFE38449	Give Me Your Heart Tonight	1983	12.00
3E36924 [10]	Shakin' Stevens	1981	10.00
BFE39286	The Bop Won't Stop	1983	12.00
ARE38022	You Drive Me Crazy	1982	12.00

STEVENS, TERRI

EVEREST
| LPBR-5088 [M] | It's Been a Long, Long Time | 1960 | 25.00 |
| SDBR-1088 [S] | It's Been a Long, Long Time | 1960 | 30.00 |

STEVENSON, B.W.

MCA
| 3215 | Lifeline | 1980 | 12.00 |

RCA VICTOR
LSP-4685	B.W. Stevenson	1972	18.00
APL1-0410	Calabasas	1974	15.00
APD1-0410 [Q]	Calabasas	1974	25.00
LSP-4794	Lead Free	1972	18.00
APL1-0088	My Maria	1973	15.00
APL1-2394	The Best of B.W. Stevenson	1977	12.00

WARNER BROS.
| BS3012 | Lost | 1977 | 12.00 |
| BS2901 | We Be Sailin' | 1976 | 12.00 |

STEVIE B

LMR
LP-5531	In My Eyes	1989	18.00
2307-1-R	Love & Emotion	1990	18.00
LP-5500	Party Your Body	1988	15.00

STEWARD, ALEC

BLUESVILLE
BVLP-1076 [M]	Creepin' Blues	1963	80.00
— Blue label, silver print			
BVLP-1076 [M]	Creepin' Blues	1964	30.00
— Blue label, trident logo at right			

STEWARD, HERB

AVA
| A-9 [M] | So Pretty | 1962 | 30.00 |
| AS-9 [S] | So Pretty | 1962 | 30.00 |

FAMOUS DOOR
| 139 | Three Horns of Herb Steward | 1981 | 15.00 |

STEWART, AL

ARISTA
AL9520 [B]	24 Carrots	1980	18.00
A2L8607 [B]	Live/Indian Summer	1981	25.00
AL9525	Modern Times	1980	12.00
— Reissue of Janus 7012			
AL9524	Past, Present and Future	1980	12.00
— Reissue of Janus 3063			
AL6-8359	Past, Present and Future	198?	10.00
— Reissue of Arista 9524			
AL4190 [B]	Time Passages	1978	18.00
AL6-8342	Time Passages	198?	10.00
— Reissue of 4190			
AL9503	Year of the Cat	1979	12.00
— Reissue of Janus 7022			
AL6-8326	Year of the Cat	198?	10.00
— Reissue of Arista 9503			

ENIGMA
| D1-73316 [B] | Last Days of the Century | 1988 | 25.00 |

EPIC
| BN26564 [B] | Love Chronicles | 1970 | 40.00 |

JANUS
7012 [B]	Modern Times	1975	35.00
3063 [B]	Past, Present and Future	1974	30.00
7026 [DJ]	The Early Years	1977	30.00
— Promo-only condensation of 2-LP set with rubber-stamp cover			
7026 [B]	The Early Years	1977	25.00
7026 [DJ]	The Early Years	1977	35.00
— Promo-only condensation of 2-LP set with rubber-stamp cover			
7022	Year of the Cat	1976	15.00

MOBILE FIDELITY
1-082	Time Passages	1981	30.00
— Audiophile vinyl			
1-009 [B]	Year of the Cat	1979	80.00
— Audiophile vinyl			

NAUTILUS
| NR-34 | 24 Carrots | 198? | 30.00 |
| — Audiophile vinyl | | | |

PASSPORT
| PB-6042 [B] | Russians and Americans | 1986 | 18.00 |

STEWART, AMII

ARIOLA AMERICA
| SW50054 | Knock on Wood | 1979 | 15.00 |
| SW50072 | Paradise Bird | 1979 | 12.00 |

STEWART, ANDY

CAPITOL
| T10320 [M] | Andy Stewart's Scotland | 196? | 18.00 |
| ST10320 [S] | Andy Stewart's Scotland | 196? | 25.00 |

EPIC
LF18027 [M]	A Scottish Soldier	196?	15.00
BF19027 [S]	A Scottish Soldier	196?	18.00
LF18048 [M]	I'm Off to Bonnie Scotland	196?	15.00
BF19048 [S]	I'm Off to Bonnie Scotland	196?	18.00
LF18031 [M]	Tunes of Glory	196?	15.00
BF19031 [S]	Tunes of Glory	196?	18.00

WARWICK
| W3043 [M] | A Scottish Soldier | 1961 | 25.00 |
| WST3043 [S] | A Scottish Soldier | 1961 | 30.00 |

STEWART, BILLY

CHESS
LPS-1547	Billy Stewart Remembered	1970	30.00
LP-1513 [M]	Billy Stewart Teaches Old Standards New Tricks	1967	30.00
LPS-1513 [S]	Billy Stewart Teaches Old Standards New Tricks	1967	40.00
CH-50059	Cross My Heart	1974	18.00
LP-1496 [M]	I Do Love You	1965	80.00
— Red cover, black "wheel			
LP-1496 [M]	I Do Love You	196?	30.00
— Green "woman" cover			
LPS-1496 [S]	I Do Love You	1965	100.00
— Red cover, black "wheel			
LPS-1496 [S]	I Do Love You	196?	40.00
— Green "woman" cover			
CH-9104	The Greatest Sides	198?	12.00
LP-1499 [M]	Unbelievable	1966	30.00
LPS-1499 [S]	Unbelievable	1966	40.00

STEWART, BOB

DAWN
| DLP-1103 [M] | Let's Talk About Love | 1956 | 50.00 |

JMT
| 834414-1 | First Line | 1988 | 12.00 |

STASH
| ST-266 | In a Sentimental Mood | 1987 | 12.00 |

STEWART, DAVE

ARISTA
| AL9-8626 | Dave Stewart and the Spiritual Cowboys | 1990 | 12.00 |

STEWART, GARY, AND DEAN DILLON

RCA VICTOR
| AHL1-4310 | Brotherly Love | 1982 | 12.00 |
| MHL1-8602 [EP] | Those Were the Days | 1983 | 10.00 |

STEWART, GARY

HIGHTONE
| HT-8014 | Brand New | 1988 | 15.00 |

MCA
| 488 | You're Not the Woman You Used to Be | 1975 | 15.00 |

RCA VICTOR
AHL1-3627	Cactus and a Rose	1980	12.00
AHL1-5498	Collector's Series	1985	10.00
AHL1-3288	Gary	1979	12.00
AYL1-4254	Greatest Hits	1982	10.00
AHL1-2779	Little Junior	1978	12.00
APL1-0900	Out of Hand	1975	12.00
AYL1-3944	Out of Hand	1981	10.00
— Best Buy Series" reissue			
APL1-1225	Steppin' Out	1976	12.00
AYL1-3769	Steppin' Out	1981	10.00
— Best Buy Series" reissue			
APL1-2199	Your Place or Mine	1977	12.00

STEWART, HELYNE

CONTEMPORARY
| M-3601 [M] | Love Moods | 1962 | 30.00 |
| S-7601 [S] | Love Moods | 1962 | 40.00 |

Number	Title	Yr	NM

STEWART, JIMMY

BLACKHAWK
| ❏ BKH-50301 | The Touch | 1986 | 12.00 |

CADENCE JAZZ
| ❏ CJR-1018 | An Engineer of Sounds | 198? | 12.00 |

CATALYST
| ❏ 7621 | Fire Flower | 1977 | 15.00 |

STEWART, JOHN

AFFORDABLE DREAMS
| ❏ AD-01 | Trancas | 1984 | 12.00 |

ALLEGIANCE
| ❏ AV-431 | Blondes | 1982 | 12.00 |

CAPITOL
❏ ST-203	California Bloodlines	1969	18.00
❏ SN-16150	California Bloodlines	198?	10.00
—Budget-line reissue			
❏ ST2975	Signals Through the Glass	1968	25.00
❏ SM-2975	Signals Through the Glass	1977	12.00
—Reissue with new prefix			
❏ ST-540	Willard	1970	18.00
❏ SN-16151	Willard	198?	10.00
—Budget-line reissue			

CYPRESS
| ❏ 661117-1 | Punch the Big Guy | 1987 | 12.00 |

HOMECOMING
❏ HC-0200	Centennial	1984	12.00
❏ HC-0300	The Last Campaign	1985	12.00
❏ HC-0500	The Trio Years	1986	12.00

RCA VICTOR
❏ LSP-4827	Cannons in the Rain	1973	15.00
❏ AYL1-3731	Cannons in the Rain	1981	10.00
—Best Buy Series" reissue			
❏ AFL1-3513	John Stewart in Concert	1980	12.00
❏ CPL2-0265	The Phoenix Concerts -- Live	1974	18.00
❏ APL1-0816	Wingless Angels	1975	15.00

RSO
❏ RS-1-3051	Bombs Away Dream Babies	1979	12.00
❏ RS-1-3074	Dream Babies Go Hollywood	1980	12.00
❏ RS-1-3027	Fire in the Wind	1977	12.00

WARNER BROS.
| ❏ BS2611 | Sunstorm | 1972 | 15.00 |
| ❏ WS1948 | The Lonesome Picker Rides Again | 1971 | 15.00 |

STEWART, REDD

AUDIO LAB
| ❏ AL-1528 [M] | Redd Stewart Sings Favorite Old Time Tunes | 1959 | 200.00 |

HICKORY/MGM
| ❏ H3G-4512 | I Remember | 1974 | 18.00 |

STEWART, REX, AND DICKIE WELLS

RCA VICTOR
| ❏ LPM-2024 [M] | Chatter Jazz | 1959 | 30.00 |
| ❏ LSP-2024 [S] | Chatter Jazz | 1959 | 30.00 |

STEWART, REX

AMERICAN RECORDING SOCIETY
| ❏ G-448 [M] | The Big Challenge | 1958 | 40.00 |

ATLANTIC
| ❏ 1209 [M] | Big Jazz | 1956 | 50.00 |

CONCERT HALL JAZZ
| ❏ 1202 [M] | Dixieland On Location | 1954 | 80.00 |

DIAL
| ❏ LP-215 [10] | Ellingtonia | 1951 | 250.00 |

FELSTED
| ❏ 7001 [M] | Rendezvous with Rex | 1958 | 40.00 |
| ❏ 2001 [S] | Rendezvous with Rex | 1958 | 30.00 |

GRAND AWARD
| ❏ GA 33-414 [M] | Just for Kicks | 195? | 40.00 |

HALL OF FAME
| ❏ 624 | Reunion | 197? | 12.00 |

JAZZOLOGY
| ❏ J-36 | The Irrepressible Rex Stewart | 197? | 15.00 |

JAZZTONE
❏ J-1202 [M]	Dixieland Free-for-All	1956	40.00
❏ J-1268 [M]	The Big Challenge	1957	40.00
❏ J-1285 [M]	The Big Reunion	1957	40.00

MASTER JAZZ
| ❏ 8123 | Rendezvous with Rex | 197? | 15.00 |

PRESTIGE
❏ PRST-7728	Memorial Album	1970	18.00
❏ PRST-7812	Trumpet Jive!	1971	18.00
—With Wingy Manone			

SWING
| ❏ SW-8414 | Porgy and Bess Revisited | 1986 | 12.00 |

SWINGVILLE
| ❏ SVLP-2006 [M] | The Happy Jazz of Rex Stewart | 1960 | 50.00 |
| —Purple label | | | |

| ❏ SVLP-2006 [M] | The Happy Jazz of Rex Stewart | 1965 | 30.00 |
| —Blue label, trident logo at right | | | |

UNITED ARTISTS
| ❏ UAL-4009 [M] | Henderson Homecoming | 1959 | 40.00 |
| ❏ UAS-5009 [S] | Henderson Homecoming | 1959 | 30.00 |

URANIA
| ❏ UJLP-2012 [M] | Cool Fever | 1955 | 60.00 |

WARNER BROS.
| ❏ W1260 [M] | Porgy and Bess Revisited | 1958 | 40.00 |
| ❏ WS1260 [S] | Porgy and Bess Revisited | 1958 | 30.00 |

X
| ❏ LX-3001 [10] | Rex Stewart and His Orchestra | 1954 | 100.00 |

STEWART, REX/ILLINOIS JACQUET

GRAND AWARD
| ❏ GA 33-315 [M] | Rex Stewart Plays Duke/ Uptown Jazz | 1955 | 40.00 |

STEWART, REX/PEANUTS HUCKO

JAZZTONE
| ❏ J-1250 [M] | Dedicated Jazz | 1957 | 40.00 |

STEWART, ROD

ACCORD
| ❏ SN-7142 | Rod the Mod | 1981 | 15.00 |

DCC COMPACT CLASSICS
| ❏ LPZ-2010 | Never a Dull Moment | 1995 | 30.00 |
| —Audiophile vinyl | | | |

J
| ❏ 55710 | As Time Goes By... The Great American Songbook Vol. 2 | 2003 | 18.00 |
| ❏ 62182 | Stardust... The Great American Songbook Volume III | 2004 | 18.00 |

MERCURY
❏ SRM-1-609	Every Picture Tells a Story	1971	18.00
—Original cover has an attached, perforated poster			
❏ SRM-1-609	Every Picture Tells a Story	1971	12.00
—With poster missing; red label			
❏ 822385-1	Every Picture Tells a Story	1984	10.00
❏ SR-61264	Gasoline Alley	1970	25.00
—Cover is textured, most noticeably on the pebbles			
❏ SR-61264	Gasoline Alley	1971	18.00
—Cover is not textured; red label			
❏ 824881-1	Gasoline Alley	1985	10.00
❏ SRM-1-646	Never a Dull Moment	1972	15.00
—Red label			
❏ SRM-1-697	Rod Stewart/Faces Live: Coast to Coast Overtures and Beginners	1973	18.00
—By "Rod Stewart/Faces			
❏ SRM-1-680	Sing It Again Rod	1973	15.00
—Red label			
❏ 824882-1	Sing It Again Rod	1985	10.00
❏ SRM-1-1017	Smiler	1974	15.00
—Chicago skyline label			
❏ SRM-2-7507	The Best of Rod Stewart	1976	18.00
❏ 826287-1	The Best of Rod Stewart	1985	15.00
❏ SRM-2-7509	The Best of Rod Stewart, Volume 2	1977	18.00
❏ 822791-1	The Best of Rod Stewart, Volume 2	1985	15.00
❏ SR-61237	The Rod Stewart Album	1969	30.00
—Cover is yellow with no black border			
❏ SR-61237	The Rod Stewart Album	1971	18.00
—Cover is yellow with black border; red label			

MOBILE FIDELITY
| ❏ 1-054 | Blondes Have More Fun | 1980 | 30.00 |
| —Audiophile vinyl | | | |

PRIVATE STOCK
| ❏ PS-2021 | A Shot of Rhythm and Blues | 1976 | 18.00 |

SPRINGBOARD
| ❏ SPB-4063 | Rod Stewart and Steampacket | 197? | 15.00 |
| ❏ SPB-4030 | Rod Stewart and The Faces | 197? | 15.00 |

TRIP
| ❏ TOP-16-31 | Looking Back/16 Early Hits | 1974 | 15.00 |

UNITED DISTRIBUTORS
| ❏ UDL-2391 | The Day Will Come | 1981 | 25.00 |

WARNER BROS.
❏ 23743 [DJ]	Absolutely Live	1982	35.00
—Promo only on Quiex II vinyl			
❏ 23743	Absolutely Live	1982	15.00
❏ 23743 [DJ]	Absolutely Live	1982	30.00
—Promo only on Quiex II vinyl			
❏ BS2938	A Night on the Town	1976	12.00
❏ BSK3116	A Night on the Town	1977	10.00
—Reissue of 2938			
❏ BS2875	Atlantic Crossing	1975	12.00
❏ BSK3108	Atlantic Crossing	1977	10.00
—Reissue of 2875			
❏ BSK3261	Blondes Have More Fun	1978	12.00
❏ BSP3276 [PD]	Blondes Have More Fun	1978	25.00
❏ 23877	Body Wishes	1983	10.00
❏ 23877 [DJ]	Body Wishes	1983	30.00
—Promo only on Quiex II vinyl			
❏ 25095	Camouflage	1984	10.00
—Issued with 16 different back covers, all of equal value, that, when assembled, form a giant poster			
❏ 26158	Downtown Train: Selections from the Storyteller Anthology	1990	15.00
❏ HS3485	Foolish Behaviour	1980	12.00
❏ BSK3092	Foot Loose and Fancy Free	1977	12.00
❏ 25884	Out of Order	1988	10.00
❏ 25446	Rod Stewart	1986	10.00
❏ HS3373	Rod Stewart Greatest Hits	1979	12.00
❏ BSK3602	Tonight I'm Yours	1981	12.00

STEWART, SANDY

AUDIOPHILE
| ❏ AP-205 | Sandy Stewart Sings Songs of Jerome Kern | 1985 | 12.00 |
| —Accompanied by Dick Hyman on piano | | | |

COLPIX
| ❏ CP-441 [M] | My Coloring Book | 1963 | 30.00 |
| ❏ SCP-441 [S] | My Coloring Book | 1963 | 30.00 |

STEWART, SLAM, AND BUCKY PIZZARELLI

STASH
| ❏ ST-201 | Dialogue | 1978 | 15.00 |

STEWART, SLAM

JAZZ MAN
| ❏ 5010 | Slam Stewart with Milt Buckner and Jo Jones | 198? | 12.00 |

SAVOY
| ❏ MG-12067 [M] | Bowin' Singin' Slam | 1956 | 40.00 |

STEWART, SLY

SCULPTURE
| ❏ SCP-2001 | San Francisco Recordings 1964-1967 | 197? | 25.00 |
| —As "Sly Stone | | | |

STEWART, TOM

ABC-PARAMOUNT
| ❏ ABC-117 [M] | Tom Stewart Sextette/ Quintet | 1956 | 50.00 |

STEWART, WYNN, AND JAN HOWARD

CHALLENGE
| ❏ CHL-611 [M] | Sweethearts of Country Music | 1961 | 50.00 |

STARDAY
| ❏ SLP-421 | Wynn Stewart and Jan Howard Sing Their Hits | 1968 | 30.00 |

STEWART, WYNN, AND WEBB PIERCE

DESIGN
| ❏ DLP-604 [M] | Country and Western Stars | 196? | 15.00 |

STEREO-SPECTRUM
| ❏ SLP-604 [R] | Country and Western Stars | 196? | 15.00 |

STEWART, WYNN

CAPITOL
❏ ST-113	In Love	1969	25.00
❏ T2737 [M]	It's Such a Pretty World Today	1967	25.00
❏ ST2737 [S]	It's Such a Pretty World Today	1967	30.00
❏ ST-214	Let the Whole World Sing It with Me	1969	25.00
❏ T2849 [M]	Love's Gonna Happen to Me	1968	30.00
❏ ST2849 [S]	Love's Gonna Happen to Me	1968	25.00
❏ ST2921	Something Pretty	1968	25.00
❏ T2332 [M]	The Songs of Wynn Stewart	1965	25.00
❏ ST2332 [S]	The Songs of Wynn Stewart	1965	30.00
❏ ST-324	Yours Forever	1969	25.00

HILLTOP
| ❏ JM-6050 [M] | Above and Beyond the Call of Love | 1967 | 18.00 |
| ❏ JS-6050 [S] | Above and Beyond the Call of Love | 1967 | 15.00 |

PLAYBOY
| ❏ PB416 | After the Storm | 1976 | 12.00 |

WRANGLER
| ❏ W-1006 [M] | Wynn Stewart | 1962 | 30.00 |
| ❏ W-31006 [S] | Wynn Stewart | 1962 | 40.00 |

STEWART FAMILY, THE

KING
| ❏ 687 [M] | Country Sacred Songs | 1960 | 30.00 |
| ❏ 695 [M] | Golden Country Favorites | 1960 | 30.00 |

STIDHAM, ARBEE

BLUESVILLE
❏ BVLP-1021 [M]	Tired of Wandering	1961	100.00
—Blue label, silver print			
❏ BVLP-1021 [M]	Tired of Wandering	1964	30.00
—Blue label, trident logo at right			

Number	Title	Yr	NM

FOLKWAYS

Number	Title	Yr	NM
❑ F-31033	There's Always Tomorrow	1973	25.00

STIFF LITTLE FINGERS

4 MEN WITH BEARDS

Number	Title	Yr	NM
❑ 4M526LP [B]	Inflammable Material		25.00

CAROLINE

Number	Title	Yr	NM
❑ 1377	See You Up There	1990	15.00

CHRYSALIS

Number	Title	Yr	NM
❑ CHR1339	Go For It	1981	25.00
❑ CHR1300	Hanx	1980	25.00
❑ CHR1270	Nobody's Heroes	1980	25.00

ROUGH TRADE

Number	Title	Yr	NM
❑ ROUGH US5	Inflammable Material	1980	30.00
—Released in U.K. in 1979			

STILES, DANNY, AND BILL WATROUS

FAMOUS DOOR

Number	Title	Yr	NM
❑ HL-103	In Tandem	1974	25.00
❑ 126	In Tandem -- Into the 80s	1980	18.00
❑ HL-112	One More Time	1977	25.00

STILLROVEN, THE

SUNDAZED

Number	Title	Yr	NM
❑ LP-5020	Cast Thy Burden Upon the Stillroven	199?	12.00

STILLS, STEPHEN

ATLANTIC

Number	Title	Yr	NM
❑ SD7250	Down the Road	1973	15.00
❑ SD 2-903	Manassas	1972	18.00
❑ 80177	Right By You	1984	10.00
❑ SD7202	Stephen Stills	1970	15.00
❑ SD7206	Stephen Stills 2	1971	15.00
❑ SD18156	Stephen Stills Live	1975	15.00
❑ SD18201	Still Stills -- The Best of Stephen Stills	1976	12.00

COLUMBIA

Number	Title	Yr	NM
❑ PC34348	Illegal Stills	1976	12.00
❑ PC33575	Stills	1975	12.00
—No bar code on cover			
❑ PCQ33575 [Q]	Stills	1975	25.00
❑ PC33575	Stills	198?	10.00
—Bar code on cover			
❑ JC35380	Thoroughfare Gap	1978	12.00

STILLS-YOUNG BAND, THE

REPRISE

Number	Title	Yr	NM
❑ MS2253	Long May You Run	1976	12.00

STING

A&M

Number	Title	Yr	NM
❑ SP-3295 [EP]	...Nada Como El Sol	1988	25.00
—Spanish versions of songs from "...Nothing Like the Sun			
❑ R273965	...Nothing Like the Sun	1987	14.00
—BMG Direct Marketing edition			
❑ SP-6402	...Nothing Like the Sun	1987	15.00
❑ R150200	The Dream of the Blue Turtles	1985	15.00
—RCA Music Service edition			
❑ SP 3750	The Dream of the Blue Turtles	1985	12.00
❑ 750216405-1	The Soul Cages	1991	15.00

MOBILE FIDELITY

Number	Title	Yr	NM
❑ 1-185	The Dream of the Blue Turtles	1985	25.00
—Audiophile vinyl			

STINGERS, THE

CROWN

Number	Title	Yr	NM
❑ CLP-5476 [M]	Guitars A Go Go	196?	30.00
❑ CST-476 [S]	Guitars A Go Go	196?	40.00

STINSON BROTHERS, THE

CANADIAN AMERICAN

Number	Title	Yr	NM
❑ CALP-1012 [M]	The Stinson Brothers in Las Vegas	196?	25.00
❑ SCALP-1012 [S]	The Stinson Brothers in Las Vegas	196?	30.00

STITES, GARY

CARLTON

Number	Title	Yr	NM
❑ LP-120 [M]	Lonely for You	1960	80.00
❑ STLP-120 [S]	Lonely for You	1960	120.00

STITT, SONNY

ABC IMPULSE!

Number	Title	Yr	NM
❑ AS-52 [S]	Salt and Pepper	1968	25.00
—With Paul Gonsalves; black label with red ring			
❑ AS-43 [S]	Sonny Stitt Now!	1968	25.00
—Black label with red ring			
❑ AS-43 [S]	Sonny Stitt Now!	1975	15.00
—Green, purple, blue "target" label			

ARGO

Number	Title	Yr	NM
❑ LP-661 [M]	Burnin'	1960	40.00
❑ LPS-661 [S]	Burnin'	1960	50.00
❑ LP-730 [M]	Move On Over	1964	40.00
❑ LPS-730 [S]	Move On Over	1964	50.00
❑ LP-744 [M]	My Main Man	1965	40.00
❑ LPS-744 [S]	My Main Man	1965	50.00
❑ LP-709 [M]	Rearin' Back	1962	40.00
❑ LPS-709 [S]	Rearin' Back	1962	50.00
❑ LP-629 [M]	Sonny Stitt	1958	50.00
❑ LP-683 [M]	Sonny Stitt at the D.J. Lounge	1961	40.00
❑ LPS-683 [S]	Sonny Stitt at the D.J. Lounge	1961	50.00

ATLANTIC

Number	Title	Yr	NM
❑ SD3008	Deuces Wild	1970	25.00
❑ 1395 [M]	Sonny Stitt and the Top Brass	1962	30.00
❑ SD1395 [S]	Sonny Stitt and the Top Brass	1962	30.00
❑ 90139	Sonny Stitt and the Top Brass	198?	15.00
❑ 1418 [M]	Stitt Plays Bird	1964	30.00
❑ SD1418 [S]	Stitt Plays Bird	1964	40.00

BLACKHAWK

Number	Title	Yr	NM
❑ 528	Good Life	1982	15.00

BLACK LION

Number	Title	Yr	NM
❑ 307	Night Work	197?	15.00

CADET

Number	Title	Yr	NM
❑ LP-661 [M]	Burnin'	1966	25.00
—Fading blue label			
❑ LPS-661 [S]	Burnin'	1966	30.00
—Fading blue label			
❑ CA-661	Burnin'	197?	15.00
—Yellow and pink label			
❑ 2CA-50039	I Cover the Waterfront	1974	30.00
❑ LP-760 [M]	Inter-Action	1966	30.00
—Fading blue label			
❑ LPS-760 [S]	Inter-Action	1966	40.00
—Fading blue label			
❑ LP-730 [M]	Move On Over	1966	25.00
—Fading blue label			
❑ LPS-730 [S]	Move On Over	1966	30.00
—Fading blue label			
❑ CA-730 [S]	Move On Over	197?	15.00
—Yellow and pink label			
❑ CA-50026	Mr. Bojangles	1973	40.00
❑ LP-744 [M]	My Main Man	1966	25.00
—Fading blue label			
❑ LPS-744 [S]	My Main Man	1966	30.00
—Fading blue label			
❑ CA-60040	Never Can Say Goodbye	1975	25.00
❑ LP-709 [M]	Rearin' Back	1966	25.00
—Fading blue label			
❑ LPS-709 [S]	Rearin' Back	1966	30.00
—Fading blue label			
❑ CA-709	Rearin' Back	197?	15.00
—Yellow and pink label			
❑ CA-50060	Satan	1974	25.00
❑ LP-629 [M]	Sonny Stitt	1966	25.00
—Fading blue label			
❑ CA-629 [R]	Sonny Stitt	197?	12.00
—Yellow and pink label			
❑ LP-683 [M]	Sonny Stitt at the D.J. Lounge	1966	25.00
—Fading blue label			
❑ LPS-683 [S]	Sonny Stitt at the D.J. Lounge	1966	30.00
—Fading blue label			
❑ CA-683	Sonny Stitt at the D.J. Lounge	197?	15.00
—Yellow and pink label			
❑ LP-770 [M]	Soul In the Night	1966	30.00
—Fading blue label			
❑ LPS-770 [S]	Soul In the Night	1966	40.00
—Fading blue label			

CATALYST

Number	Title	Yr	NM
❑ 7608	Forecast	1976	25.00
—With Red Holloway			
❑ 7616	I Remember Bird	1977	25.00
❑ 7620	Tribute to Duke Ellington	1977	18.00

CHESS

Number	Title	Yr	NM
❑ 2ACMJ-405	Interaction	197?	25.00
—With Zoot Sims			
❑ CH-9317	Sonny Stitt	1990	15.00
❑ CH-91523	Sonny Stitt at the D.J. Lounge	198?	15.00

COBBLESTONE

Number	Title	Yr	NM
❑ CST-9021	Constellation	1973	25.00
❑ CST-9013	Tune-Up	1972	30.00

COLPIX

Number	Title	Yr	NM
❑ CP-499 [M]	Broadway Soul	1964	30.00
❑ SCP-499 [S]	Broadway Soul	1964	40.00

DELMARK

Number	Title	Yr	NM
❑ DS-426	Made for Each Other	1972	25.00

FANTASY

Number	Title	Yr	NM
❑ OJC-060	Kaleidoscope	198?	15.00
❑ OJC-009	Sonny Stitt/Bud Powell/J.J. Johnson	198?	15.00

FLYING DUTCHMAN

Number	Title	Yr	NM
❑ BDL1-1197	Dumpy Mama	1975	30.00
❑ BDL1-1538	Stomp Off Let's Go	1976	25.00

GALAXY

Number	Title	Yr	NM
❑ 8204	In the Beginning	197?	25.00

GRP/IMPULSE!

Number	Title	Yr	NM
❑ IMP-210	Salt and Pepper	1997	18.00
—Reissue on audiophile vinyl			

IMPULSE!

Number	Title	Yr	NM
❑ A-52 [M]	Salt and Pepper	1964	40.00
❑ AS-52 [S]	Salt and Pepper	1964	50.00
—With Paul Gonsalves			
❑ A-43 [M]	Sonny Stitt Now!	1963	50.00
❑ AS-43 [S]	Sonny Stitt Now!	1963	60.00

JAZZLAND

Number	Title	Yr	NM
❑ JLP-71 [M]	Low Flame	1962	40.00
❑ JLP-971 [S]	Low Flame	1962	50.00

JAZZ MAN

Number	Title	Yr	NM
❑ 5040	Night Work	198?	15.00
—Reissue of Black Lion LP			

JAZZTONE

Number	Title	Yr	NM
❑ J-1231 [M]	Early Modern	1956	80.00
❑ J-1263 [M]	Early Modern	1957	60.00

MUSE

Number	Title	Yr	NM
❑ MR-5006	12!	1973	18.00
❑ MR-5129	Blues for Duke	1978	15.00
❑ MR-5323	Constellation	1986	18.00
—Reissue of Cobblestone 9021			
❑ MR-5228	In Style	1982	15.00
❑ MR-5067	Mellow	1975	25.00
❑ MR-5091	My Buddy: Sonny Stitt Plays for Gene Ammons	1976	18.00
❑ MR-5204	Sonny's Back	1981	18.00
❑ MR-5023	The Champ	1974	18.00
❑ MR-5269	The Last Stitt Sessions, Vol. 1	1983	18.00
❑ MR-5280	The Last Stitt Sessions, Vol. 2	1984	18.00
❑ MR-5334	Tune-Up	1987	18.00
—Reissue of Cobblestone 9013			

NEW JAZZ

Number	Title	Yr	NM
❑ NJLP-103 [10]	Sonny Stitt and Bud Powell	1950	500.00

PACIFIC JAZZ

Number	Title	Yr	NM
❑ PJ-71 [M]	My Mother's Eyes	1963	80.00
❑ ST-71 [S]	My Mother's Eyes	1963	80.00

PAULA

Number	Title	Yr	NM
❑ 4004	Soul Girl	1974	15.00

PHOENIX

Number	Title	Yr	NM
❑ 19	Battles	197?	12.00
❑ 15	Superstitt	197?	12.00

PRESTIGE

Number	Title	Yr	NM
❑ PRLP-7248 [M]	All God's Chillun Got Rhythm	1962	80.00
—Yellow label with Bergenfield, N.J. address			
❑ PRLP-7248 [M]	All God's Chillun Got Rhythm	1964	40.00
—Blue label with trident logo			
❑ PRST-7248 [R]	All God's Chillun Got Rhythm	1962	30.00
❑ PRST-7769	Best for Lovers	1970	30.00
❑ P-10032	Black Vibrations	1972	30.00
❑ PRST-7839	Bud's Blues	1974	25.00
❑ PRLP-126 [10]	Favorites, Volume 1	1952	400.00
❑ PRLP-148 [10]	Favorites, Volume 2	1953	400.00
❑ P-24044	Genesis	1974	25.00
❑ 10048	Goin' Down Slow	1973	30.00
❑ PRLP-7077 [M]	Kaleidoscope	1957	120.00
—Yellow label with W. 50th St address			
❑ PRLP-111 [10]	Mr. Saxophone	1951	400.00
❑ PRLP-7436 [M]	Night Crawler	1966	40.00
—Blue label, trident logo at right			
❑ PRST-7436 [S]	Night Crawler	1966	50.00
—Blue label, trident logo at right			
❑ PRST-7759	Night Letter	1970	25.00
❑ PRLP-7452 [M]	'Nuther Fu'ther	1966	40.00
—Blue label, trident logo at right			
❑ PRST-7452 [S]	'Nuther Fu'ther	1966	50.00
—Blue label, trident logo at right			
❑ PRST-7452 [S]	'Nuther Fu'ther	197?	30.00
—Green label			
❑ PRLP-7459 [M]	Pow!	1967	50.00
—Blue label, trident logo at right			
❑ PRST-7459 [S]	Pow!	1967	40.00
—Blue label, trident logo at right			
❑ PRLP-7302 [M]	Primitive Soul!	1964	80.00
—Yellow label with Bergenfield, N.J. address			
❑ PRLP-7302 [M]	Primitive Soul!	1965	40.00
—Blue label with trident logo			
❑ PRST-7302 [S]	Primitive Soul!	1964	70.00
—Silver label			
❑ PRST-7302 [S]	Primitive Soul!	1965	40.00
—Blue label with trident logo			
❑ PRLP-7332 [M]	Shangri-La	1964	40.00
—Blue label, trident logo at right			
❑ PRST-7332 [S]	Shangri-La	1964	50.00
—Blue label, trident logo at right			
❑ P-10074	So Doggone Good	1974	18.00
❑ PRLP-103 [10]	Sonny Stitt Plays	1951	400.00
❑ PRLP-7024 [M]	Sonny Stitt with Bud Powell and J.J. Johnson	1956	150.00
❑ PRST-7635	Soul Electricity	1969	30.00

Number	Title	Yr	NM
❑ PRLP-7372 [M]	Soul People	1965	40.00
—Blue label, trident logo at right			
❑ PRST-7372 [S]	Soul People	1965	50.00
—Blue label, trident logo at right			
❑ PRST-7372 [S]	Soul People	197?	30.00
—Green label			
❑ PRLP-7297 [M]	Soul Shack	1964	80.00
—Yellow label with Bergenfield, N.J. address			
❑ PRLP-7297 [M]	Soul Shack	1965	40.00
—Blue label with trident logo			
❑ PRST-7297 [S]	Soul Shack	1964	70.00
—Silver label with Bergenfield, N.J. address			
❑ PRST-7297 [S]	Soul Shack	1965	40.00
—Blue label with trident logo			
❑ PRLP-7244 [M]	Stitt Meets Brother Jack	1962	80.00
—Yellow label with Bergenfield, N.J. address			
❑ PRLP-7244 [M]	Stitt Meets Brother Jack	1964	40.00
—Blue label with trident logo			
❑ PRST-7244 [S]	Stitt Meets Brother Jack	1962	70.00
❑ PRLP-7133 [M]	Stitt's Bits	1958	120.00
❑ PRST-7585	Stitt's Bits, Volume 1	1968	30.00
❑ PRST-7612	Stitt's Bits, Volume 2	1969	30.00
❑ PRST-7701	The Best of Sonny Stitt with Brother Jack McDuff	1969	30.00
❑ P-10012	Turn It On	1971	30.00

PROGRESSIVE

Number	Title	Yr	NM
❑ PRO-7034	Sonny Stitt Meets Sadik Hakim	1978	30.00

ROOST

Number	Title	Yr	NM
❑ LP-2219 [M]	37 Minutes and 48 Seconds with Sonny Stitt	1957	80.00
❑ LP-2235 [M]	A Little Bit of Stitt	1959	70.00
❑ SLP-2235 [S]	A Little Bit of Stitt	1959	60.00
❑ LP-1203 [M]	Battle of Birdland	1955	120.00
❑ LP-2247 [M]	Feelin's	1962	60.00
❑ SLP-2247 [S]	Feelin's	1962	60.00
❑ LP-418 [10]	Jazz at the Hi-Hat	1954	400.00
❑ LP-2245 [M]	Sonny Side Up	1960	80.00
❑ SLP-2245 [S]	Sonny Side Up	1960	80.00
❑ LP-1208 [M]	Sonny Stitt	1956	120.00
❑ LP-2208 [M]	Sonny Stitt	1957	120.00
❑ LP-2253 [M]	Sonny Stitt Goes Latin	1963	50.00
❑ SLP-2253 [S]	Sonny Stitt Goes Latin	1963	50.00
❑ LP-2252 [M]	Sonny Stitt in Orbit	1963	50.00
❑ SLP-2252 [S]	Sonny Stitt in Orbit	1963	50.00
❑ LP-415 [10]	Sonny Stitt Plays Arrangements from the Pen of Johnny Richards	1952	400.00
❑ LP-2204 [M]	Sonny Stitt Plays Arrangements of Quincy Jones	1957	150.00
❑ LP-2226 [M]	Sonny Stitt with the New Yorkers	1958	80.00
❑ LP-2244 [M]	Stittsville	1960	70.00
❑ SLP-2244 [S]	Stittsville	1960	80.00
❑ LP-2230 [M]	The Saxophone of Sonny Stitt	1959	70.00
❑ SLP-2230 [S]	The Saxophone of Sonny Stitt	1959	60.00
❑ LP-2240 [M]	The Sonny Side of Stitt	1960	70.00
❑ SLP-2240 [S]	The Sonny Side of Stitt	1960	60.00

ROULETTE

Number	Title	Yr	NM
❑ R-25348 [M]	I Keep Comin' Back	1967	40.00
❑ SR-25348 [S]	I Keep Comin' Back	1967	30.00
❑ SR-42035	Make Someone Happy	1969	25.00
❑ SR-25354 [S]	Parallel-O-Stitt	1968	30.00
❑ R-25354 [M]	Parallel-O-Stitt	1968	50.00
❑ SR-42048	Stardust	1970	25.00
❑ SR-5002	Stardust	197?	18.00
—Reissue of 42048			
❑ R-25339 [M]	The Matadors Meet the Bull	1965	40.00
❑ SR-25339 [S]	The Matadors Meet the Bull	1965	50.00
❑ R-25343 [M]	What's New?	1966	30.00
❑ SR-25343 [S]	What's New?	1966	40.00

SAVOY

Number	Title	Yr	NM
❑ MG-9006 [10]	All Star Series: Sonny Stitt	1953	300.00
❑ MG-9012 [10]	New Sounds in Modern Music	1953	300.00
❑ MG-9014 [10]	New Trends Of Jazz	1953	300.00

SAVOY JAZZ

Number	Title	Yr	NM
❑ SJL-1165	Symphony Hall Swing	1986	18.00

SOLID STATE

Number	Title	Yr	NM
❑ SS-18057	Come Hither	1969	25.00
❑ SS-18047	Little Green Apples	1968	25.00

TRIP

Number	Title	Yr	NM
❑ TLX-5008	Two Sides of Sonny Stitt	1974	18.00

UPFRONT

Number	Title	Yr	NM
❑ UPF-196	Sonny's Blues	197?	15.00

VERVE

Number	Title	Yr	NM
❑ MGV-8219 [M]	New York Jazz	1957	50.00
❑ V-8219 [M]	New York Jazz	1961	30.00
❑ UMV-2558	New York Jazz	198?	15.00
❑ MGV-8250 [M]	Only the Blues	1958	50.00
❑ V-8250 [M]	Only the Blues	1961	30.00
❑ UMV-2634	Only the Blues	198?	15.00
❑ MGV-8324 [M]	Personal Appearance	1959	50.00
❑ V-8324 [M]	Personal Appearance	1961	30.00
❑ V6-8837	Previously Unreleased Recordings	1974	15.00
❑ MGV-8377 [M]	Saxophone Supremacy	1960	50.00
❑ V-8377 [M]	Saxophone Supremacy	1961	30.00
❑ V-8380 [M]	Sommy Stitt Swings the Most	1961	30.00
❑ MGV-8262 [M]	Sonny Side Up	1958	60.00
❑ V-8262 [M]	Sonny Side Up	1961	30.00
❑ MGV-8374 [M]	Sonny Stitt Blows the Blues	1960	50.00
❑ MGVS-6149 [S]	Sonny Stitt Blows the Blues	1960	40.00
❑ V-8374 [M]	Sonny Stitt Blows the Blues	1961	30.00
❑ V6-8374 [S]	Sonny Stitt Blows the Blues	1961	25.00
❑ MGVS-6149	Sonny Stitt Blows the Blues	1996	40.00
—Audiophile reissue by Classic Records			
❑ MGVS-6149-45	Sonny Stitt Blows the Blues	1999	40.00
—Audiophile reissue by Classic Records; plays at 45 rpm			
❑ MGV-8309 [M]	Sonny Stitt Plays Jimmy Giuffre Arrangements	1959	50.00
❑ MGVS-6041 [S]	Sonny Stitt Plays Jimmy Giuffre Arrangements	1960	40.00
❑ V-8309 [M]	Sonny Stitt Plays Jimmy Giuffre Arrangements	1961	30.00
❑ V6-8309 [S]	Sonny Stitt Plays Jimmy Giuffre Arrangements	1961	25.00
❑ MGV-8344 [M]	Sonny Stitt Sits In with the Oscar Peterson Trio	1959	50.00
❑ MGVS-6108 [S]	Sonny Stitt Sits In with the Oscar Peterson Trio	1960	40.00
❑ V-8344 [M]	Sonny Stitt Sits In with the Oscar Peterson Trio	1961	30.00
❑ V6-8344 [S]	Sonny Stitt Sits In with the Oscar Peterson Trio	1961	25.00
❑ MGV-8380 [M]	Sonny Stitt Swings the Most	1960	50.00
❑ MGV-8306 [M]	The Hard Swing	1959	50.00
❑ MGVS-6038 [S]	The Hard Swing	1960	40.00
❑ V-8306 [M]	The Hard Swing	1961	30.00
❑ V6-8306 [S]	The Hard Swing	1961	25.00
❑ V-8451 [M]	The Sensual Sound of Sonny Stitt	1962	25.00
❑ V6-8451 [S]	The Sensual Sound of Sonny Stitt	1962	30.00

WHO'S WHO IN JAZZ

Number	Title	Yr	NM
❑ 21022	Sonny, Sweets and Jaws	1981	18.00
❑ 21025	The Bubba's Sessions	1982	18.00

STOECKLEIN, VAL

DOT

Number	Title	Yr	NM
❑ DLP-3904 [M]	Grey Life	1968	100.00
—Label is black, as if stock copy, but record is found inside stereo (25904) cover with "Monaural Promotion Not for Sale" sticker on front			
❑ DLP-25904 [S]	Grey Life	1968	40.00

STOKES, CARL B.

FLYING DUTCHMAN

Number	Title	Yr	NM
❑ FD-130	The Mayor and the People	1970	50.00

STOKOWSKI, LEOPOLD

RCA VICTOR RED SEAL

Number	Title	Yr	NM
❑ LSC-2593 [S]	Inspiration	1962	25.00
—Original with "shaded dog" label			

THE BACH GUILD

Number	Title	Yr	NM
❑ BGS-70696	In Dulci Jubilo: A Baroque Concert	1967	15.00

STOLOFF, MORRIS

DECCA

Number	Title	Yr	NM
❑ DL8574 [M]	This Is Kim	1957	60.00
—Black label, silver print; Kim Novak is the cover model			

STOLTZMAN, RICHARD

RCA

Number	Title	Yr	NM
❑ 5944-1-RC	New York Counterpoint	1987	12.00

RCA VICTOR

Number	Title	Yr	NM
❑ AML1-7124	Begin Sweet World	1986	12.00

STONE, ANGIE

J

Number	Title	Yr	NM
❑ 80813-20013-1	Mahogany Soul	2001	30.00
❑ 82876-56215-1	Stone Love	2004	18.00

STONE, CLIFFIE

CAPITOL

Number	Title	Yr	NM
❑ T1230 [M]	Cool Cowboy	1959	30.00
❑ ST1230 [S]	Cool Cowboy	1959	40.00
❑ T1685 [M]	It's Fun to Square Dance	1962	25.00
❑ ST1685 [S]	It's Fun to Square Dance	1962	30.00
❑ KAO1555 [M]	Original Cowboy Sing-A-Long	1961	30.00
❑ SKAO1555 [S]	Original Cowboy Sing-A-Long	1961	40.00
❑ T1286 [M]	Square Dance Promenade	1960	30.00
❑ ST1286 [S]	Square Dance Promenade	1960	40.00
❑ H4009 [10]	Square Dances	195?	60.00
❑ T1080 [M]	The Party's on Me	1958	40.00

TOWER

Number	Title	Yr	NM
❑ T5073 [M]	Together Again	1967	30.00
❑ ST5073 [S]	Together Again	1967	30.00

STONE, KIRBY, FOUR

CADENCE

Number	Title	Yr	NM
❑ CLP1023 [M]	Man I Flipped	1958	30.00

COLUMBIA

Number	Title	Yr	NM
❑ CL1211 [M]	Baubles, Bangles and Beads	1959	25.00
❑ CS8014 [S]	Baubles, Bangles and Beads	1959	30.00
❑ CL1714 [M]	Guys and Dolls	1961	25.00
❑ CS8514 [S]	Guys and Dolls	1961	30.00
❑ CL1290 [M]	The "Go" Sound of the Kirby Stone Four	1959	25.00
❑ CS8130 [S]	The "Go" Sound of the Kirby Stone Four	1959	30.00
❑ CL1646 [M]	The Kirby Stone Four at the Playboy Club	1960	25.00
❑ CS8446 [S]	The Kirby Stone Four at the Playboy Club	1960	30.00
❑ CL1356 [M]	The Kirby Stone Touch	1959	25.00
❑ CS8164 [S]	The Kirby Stone Touch	1959	30.00

TOPS

Number	Title	Yr	NM
❑ L-1582 [M]	The Kirby Stone Four	1957	30.00

STONE, ROLAND

ACE

Number	Title	Yr	NM
❑ LP-1018 [M]	Just a Moment	1961	150.00

STONE, SLY

CLEOPATRA

Number	Title	Yr	NM
❑ 6612 [B]	I'm Back! Family & Friends		25.00

STONE CIRCUS, THE

MAINSTREAM

Number	Title	Yr	NM
❑ S-6119	The Stone Circus	1969	80.00

STONE COUNTRY

RCA VICTOR

Number	Title	Yr	NM
❑ LSP-3958	Stone Country	1968	25.00

STONE HARBOUR

STONE HARBOUR

Number	Title	Yr	NM
❑ 398	Stone Harbour Emerges	197?	500.00

STONE PONEYS

CAPITOL

Number	Title	Yr	NM
❑ T2763 [M]	Evergreen, Vol. 2	1967	100.00
❑ ST2763 [S]	Evergreen, Vol. 2	1967	30.00
❑ ST2863	Linda Ronstadt/Stone Poneys and Friends Vol. III	1968	50.00
❑ T2666 [M]	The Stone Poneys	1967	80.00
❑ ST2666 [S]	The Stone Poneys	1967	30.00
❑ ST-11383	The Stone Poneys Featuring Linda Ronstadt	1974	12.00

PICKWICK

Number	Title	Yr	NM
❑ SPC-3298	Stoney End	1976	15.00

STONE ROSES, THE

SILVERTONE

Number	Title	Yr	NM
❑ 1184-1-J	The Stone Roses	1989	15.00

STONE TEMPLE PILOTS

ATLANTIC

Number	Title	Yr	NM
❑ 82607 [B]	Purple	1994	25.00
❑ 82871	Tiny Music -- Music from the Vatican Gift Shop	1996	25.00

STONE THE CROWS

POLYDOR

Number	Title	Yr	NM
❑ PD-5037	Continuous Performance	1972	25.00
❑ 24-4019	Stone the Crows	1970	25.00
❑ PD-5020	Teenage Licks	1972	25.00

STONEGROUND

WARNER BROS.

Number	Title	Yr	NM
❑ 2WS1956	Family Album	1971	25.00
❑ WS1895	Stoneground	1971	18.00
❑ BS2645	Stoneground 3	1972	14.00

STONEHILL, RANDY

ONE WAY

Number	Title	Yr	NM
❑ JC-31252	Born Twice	1972	60.00

STONEMANS, THE

MGM

Number	Title	Yr	NM
❑ E-4511 [M]	All in the Family	1968	30.00
❑ SE-4511 [S]	All in the Family	1968	25.00
❑ SE-4613	A Stoneman Christmas	1968	25.00
❑ E-4453 [M]	Stoneman's Country	1967	25.00
❑ SE-4453 [S]	Stoneman's Country	1967	30.00
❑ SE-4578	The Great Stonemans	1968	25.00
❑ GAS-124	The Stonemans (Golden Archive Series)	1970	18.00
❑ E-4363 [M]	Those Singin' Swingin' Stompin' Sensational Stonemans	1966	25.00
❑ SE-4363 [S]	Those Singin' Swingin' Stompin' Sensational Stonemans	1966	30.00

RCA VICTOR

Number	Title	Yr	NM
❑ LSP-4431	California Blues	1970	18.00
❑ LSP-4264	Dawn of the Stonemans' Age	1970	18.00
❑ LSP-4343	In All Honesty	1970	18.00

STARDAY

Number	Title	Yr	NM
❑ SLP-393 [M]	White Lightning	1965	40.00

WORLD PACIFIC

Number	Title	Yr	NM
❑ WP-1828 [M]	Big Ball in Monterey	1964	30.00
❑ ST-1828 [S]	Big Ball in Monterey	1964	40.00

Number	Title	Yr	NM

STONEY AND MEATLOAF

PRODIGAL
| ❑ 10 | Stoney and Meatloaf | 1978 | 15.00 |

RARE EARTH
| ❑ R528 [B] | Stoney and Meatloaf | 1971 | 40.00 |

STOOKEY, PAUL

WARNER BROS.
| ❑ BS2674 | One Night Stand | 1973 | 12.00 |
— *As "Noel Paul Stookey"*
| ❑ WS1912 | Paul and… | 1971 | 12.00 |

STOPAK, BERNIE

STASH
| ❑ ST-274 | Remember Me | 1988 | 12.00 |

STORDAHL, AXEL

DECCA
| ❑ DL8933 [M] | Christmas in Scandinavia | 1960 | 18.00 |
| ❑ DL78933 [S] | Christmas in Scandinavia | 1960 | 25.00 |

STORIES

KAMA SUTRA
| ❑ KSBS-2068 | About Us | 1973 | 30.00 |
— *Gatefold; does NOT contain "Brother Louie*
| ❑ KSBS-2068 | About Us | 1973 | 18.00 |
— *Gatefold cover; "Brother Louie" added as the last song on side 2*
| ❑ KSBS-2068 | About Us | 1973 | 18.00 |
— *Regular cover; "Brother Louie" added as the last song on side 2*
| ❑ KSBS-2051 | Stories | 1972 | 15.00 |
| ❑ KSBS-2078 | Traveling Underground | 1974 | 15.00 |

STORM, BILLY

BUENA VISTA
| ❑ BV-3315 [M] | Billy Storm | 1963 | 100.00 |
| ❑ STER-3315 [S] | Billy Storm | 1963 | 120.00 |

FAMOUS
| ❑ F-504 | This Is the Night | 1969 | 100.00 |

STORM, GALE

DOT
❑ DLP-3011 [M]	Gale Storm	1956	50.00
❑ DLP-3098 [M]	Gale Storm Hits	1958	40.00
❑ DLP-3209 [M]	Gale Storm Sings	1959	30.00
❑ DLP-25209 [S]	Gale Storm Sings	1959	40.00
❑ DLP-3017 [M]	Sentimental Me	1956	50.00
❑ DLP-3197 [M]	Softly and Tenderly	1959	30.00
❑ DLP-25197 [S]	Softly and Tenderly	1959	40.00

HAMILTON
| ❑ HLP-171 [M] | I Don't Want to Walk | 1966 | 15.00 |
| ❑ HLP-12171 [S] | I Don't Want to Walk | 1966 | 18.00 |

MCA
| ❑ 1504 | Gale Storm | 198? | 12.00 |

STORY, CARL

MERCURY
❑ MG-20323 [M]	Gospel Quartet Favorites	1958	40.00
❑ MG-20584 [M]	More Gospel Quartet Favorites	1961	30.00
❑ 3R-60584 [S]	More Gospel Quartet Favorites	1961	40.00

STARDAY
❑ SLP-278 [M]	All Day Sacred Singing	1964	40.00
❑ SLP-137 [M]	All Day Singing with Dinner on the Ground	1961	40.00
❑ SLP-107 [M]	America's Favorite Country Gospel Artist	1959	50.00
❑ SLP-152 [M]	Get Religion	1962	40.00
❑ SLP-127 [M]	Gospel Revival	1961	40.00
❑ SLP-219 [M]	Mighty Close to Heaven	1963	40.00
❑ SLP-411 [M]	My Lord Keeps a Record	1968	30.00
❑ SLP-315 [M]	Sacred Songs of Life and the Hereafter	1965	40.00
❑ SLP-348 [M]	There's Nothing on Earth (That Heaven Can't Cure)	1965	40.00

STORYVILLE STOMPERS, THE

TROPICANA
| ❑ 1204 [M] | New Orleans Jazz | 195? | 40.00 |

STOVER, SMOKEY

ARGO
| ❑ LP-652 [DJ] | Smokey Stover's Original Firemen | 1960 | 60.00 |
— *White label, multi-color vinyl*
| ❑ LP-652 [M] | Smokey Stover's Original Firemen | 1960 | 30.00 |
| ❑ LPS-652 [S] | Smokey Stover's Original Firemen | 1960 | 30.00 |

JAZZOLOGY
| ❑ J-53 | Smokey Stover and the Original Firemen | 197? | 12.00 |

STOWAWAYS, THE

JUSTICE
| ❑ JLP-148 | The Stowaways | 1968 | 500.00 |

STOWELL, JOHN

INNER CITY
| ❑ IC-1030 | Golden Delicious | 197? | 15.00 |

STRADIVARI STRINGS, THE

SPIN-O-RAMA
| ❑ 590 [M] | String Along with Me | 196? | 30.00 |
| ❑ S-590 [S] | String Along with Me | 196? | 40.00 |
— *Cover model on the above LP is Jayne Mansfield*

STRAIT, GEORGE

HEARTLAND
| ❑ HL1172/3 | The Very Best of George Strait | 1991 | 18.00 |

MCA
❑ 5750	#7	1986	12.00
❑ 42266	Beyond the Blue Neon	1989	10.00
❑ R153641	Chill of an Early Fall	1991	25.00
— *Only released on vinyl through BMG Direct Marketing*
❑ 5518	Does Fort Worth Ever Cross Your Mind	1984	12.00
❑ 5567	Greatest Hits	1985	12.00
❑ 42035	Greatest Hits, Volume Two	1987	10.00
❑ 10532	Holding My Own	1992	25.00
— *Only available on vinyl through Columbia House*
❑ 42114	If You Ain't Lovin' You Ain't Livin'	1988	10.00
❑ 6415	Livin' It Up	1990	15.00
❑ 5800	Merry Christmas Strait to You	1986	12.00
❑ R134172	Merry Christmas Strait to You	1986	15.00
— *BMG Direct Marketing version*
❑ 5913	Ocean Front Property	1987	12.00
❑ 5450	Right or Wrong	1983	12.00
❑ 5605	Something Special	1985	12.00
❑ 5248	Strait Country	1981	12.00
❑ 27092	Strait Country	1984	10.00
— *Reissue of 5248*
| ❑ 5320 | Strait from the Heart | 1982 | 12.00 |
| ❑ 10450 | Ten Strait Hits | 1992 | 25.00 |
— *Only available on vinyl through Columbia House*

STRAND, LES

FANTASY
| ❑ 3242 [M] | Jazz Classics on the Baldwin Organ | 1956 | 50.00 |
— *Red vinyl*
| ❑ 3242 [M] | Jazz Classics on the Baldwin Organ | 195? | 25.00 |
— *Black vinyl*
| ❑ 3231 [M] | Les Strand on the Baldwin Organ | 1956 | 50.00 |
— *Red vinyl*
| ❑ 3231 [M] | Les Strand on the Baldwin Organ | 195? | 25.00 |
— *Black vinyl*

STRANGE, BILLY

CHESS
| ❑ CH2-6027 | One More Time | 1988 | 15.00 |

COLISEUM
| ❑ CM-1001 [M] | Limbo Rock | 1962 | 40.00 |

GNP CRESCENDO
❑ GNPS-2039	A James Bond Double Feature	1967	15.00
❑ GNP-2024 [M]	Billy Strange Plays Roger Miller Hits	1966	15.00
❑ GNPS-2024 [S]	Billy Strange Plays Roger Miller Hits	1966	18.00
❑ GNP-2012 [M]	Billy Strange Plays the Hits	1965	15.00
❑ GNPS-2012 [S]	Billy Strange Plays the Hits	1965	18.00
❑ GNP-2030 [M]	Billy Strange with the Challengers	1966	18.00
❑ GNPS-2030 [S]	Billy Strange with the Challengers	1966	25.00
❑ GNPS-2094	Dyn-o-mite Guitar	197?	12.00
❑ GNP-2009 [M]	English Hits of '65	1965	15.00
❑ GNPS-2009 [S]	English Hits of '65	1965	18.00
❑ GNP-98 [M]	Five String Banjo	1964	15.00
❑ GNPS-98 [S]	Five String Banjo	1964	18.00
❑ GNP-2016 [M]	Folk Rock Hits	1965	15.00
❑ GNPS-2016 [S]	Folk Rock Hits	1965	18.00
❑ GNP-2006 [M]	Goldfinger	1965	15.00
❑ GNPS-2006 [S]	Goldfinger	1965	18.00
❑ GNPS-2046	Great Western Themes	1969	15.00
❑ GNP-2022 [M]	In the Mexican Bag	1966	15.00
❑ GNPS-2022 [S]	In the Mexican Bag	1966	18.00
❑ GNP-97 [M]	Mr. Guitar	1963	15.00
❑ GNPS-97 [S]	Mr. Guitar	1963	18.00
❑ GNPS-2041	Railroad Man	1968	15.00
❑ GNP-2019 [M]	Secret Agent File	1966	15.00
❑ GNPS-2019 [S]	Secret Agent File	1966	18.00
❑ GNP-2037 [M]	The Best of Billy Strange	1967	15.00
❑ GNPS-2037 [S]	The Best of Billy Strange	1967	15.00
❑ GNP-2004 [M]	The James Bond Theme	1964	15.00
❑ GNPS-2004 [S]	The James Bond Theme	1964	18.00
❑ GNP-94 [M]	Twelve String Guitar	1963	15.00
❑ GNPS-94 [S]	Twelve String Guitar	1963	18.00

SUNSET
| ❑ SUS-5209 | Mr. Guitar | 1968 | 12.00 |

SURREY
| ❑ SS-1002 | The Best of Billy Strange | 1965 | 18.00 |

TRADITION
| ❑ 2080 | Strange Country | 1969 | 12.00 |

STRANGE, RICHARD

PVC
| ❑ 7917 [B] | The Live Rise of Richard Strange | 1980 | 30.00 |

STRANGE

OUTER GALAXIE
| ❑ 1001 | Raw Power | 1976 | 100.00 |
| ❑ 1000 | Translucent World | 1973 | 100.00 |

STRANGEBREW

ABC
| ❑ ABCS-672 [B] | Very Strangebrew | 1969 | 30.00 |

STRANGELOVES, THE

BANG
| ❑ BLP-211 [M] | I Want Candy | 1965 | 80.00 |
| ❑ BLPS-211 [S] | I Want Candy | 1965 | 100.00 |

STRANGERS, THE

CAPITOL
❑ ST-590	Getting to Know Merle Haggard's Strangers	1970	25.00
❑ ST-796	Honky Tonkin'	1971	25.00
❑ ST-169	Instrumental Sounds of Merle Haggard's Strangers	1969	25.00
❑ ST-445	Introducing My Friends the Strangers	1970	25.00
❑ ST-11141	Totally Instrumental with One Exception…	1973	18.00

STRANGLERS, THE

A&M
| ❑ SP-4706 [B] | Black and White | 1978 | 30.00 |
— *Grey marbled wax; first 75,000 released with white-vinyl EP (FREE-9)*
| ❑ SP-4706 | Black and White | 1978 | 15.00 |
— *Black vinyl without bonus single*
| ❑ SP-4659 [B] | No More Heroes | 1977 | 25.00 |
| ❑ SP-4648 [B] | Rattus Norvegicus | 1977 | 25.00 |
— *With bonus single "Peasant in the Big Shitty"/"Choosie Suzie" (FREE-3)*

EMI AMERICA
| ❑ SQ-17207 | La Folie | 1986 | 18.00 |
— *U.S. issue of 1981 U.K. release*
| ❑ ST-17189 | The Men in Black | 1986 | 18.00 |
— *Reissue*

EPIC
❑ FE44209	All Live and All of the Night	1988	12.00
❑ BFE39080	Aural Sculpture	1985	12.00
❑ BFE40607	Dreamtime	1986	12.00
❑ BFE38642	Feline	1983	15.00
❑ E46120	Stranglers 10	1990	12.00
❑ E47081	The Stranglers Greatest Hits 1977 1990	1990	15.00

I.R.S.
| ❑ SP70011 [B] | Stranglers IV | 1980 | 25.00 |
— *combines tracks from the 1979 "The Raven" LP (unreleased in US) and singles*

STIFF AMERICA
| ❑ USE-10 | The Men in Black | 1981 | 18.00 |

STRATAVARIOUS

ROULETTE
| ❑ RS3019 | Stratavarious | 1976 | 30.00 |

STRATTON, DON

ABC-PARAMOUNT
| ❑ ABC-118 [M] | Modern Jazz with Dixieland Roots | 1956 | 40.00 |

STRAWBERRY ALARM CLOCK

SUNDAZED
❑ LP5441 [B]	Best Of The Strawberry Alarm Clock	2013	25.00
❑ LP5440 [B]	The World In A Sea Shell	2013	25.00
❑ LP5439 [B]	Wake Up...It's Tomorrow	2013	25.00

UNI
❑ 73054	Good Morning Starshine	1969	40.00
❑ 3014 [M]	Incense and Peppermints	1967	80.00
❑ 73014 [S]	Incense and Peppermints	1967	40.00
❑ 73074	The Best of the Strawberry Alarm Clock	1970	40.00
❑ 73035	The World in a Sea Shell	1968	40.00
❑ 73025	Wake Up It's Tomorrow	1968	40.00

VOCALION
| ❑ VL73915 | Changes | 1971 | 50.00 |

STRAWBS, THE

A&M
| ❑ SP-6005 | Best of the Strawbs | 1978 | 15.00 |
| ❑ SP-4383 | Bursting at the Seams | 1973 | 18.00 |

Number	Title	Yr	NM
❑ SP-4304	From the Witchwood	1971	18.00
❑ SP-4506	Ghosts	1975	18.00
❑ SP-4344	Grave New World	1972	18.00
❑ SP-3607	Hero and Heroine	1974	18.00
❑ SP-4288	Just a Collection of Antiques and Curios	1971	18.00
❑ SP-4544	Nomadness	1975	18.00

ARISTA

Number	Title	Yr	NM
❑ AB4172	Deadlines	1978	12.00

OYSTER

Number	Title	Yr	NM
❑ OY-1604	Burning for You	1977	15.00
❑ OY-1603	Deep Cuts	1976	15.00

STRAY CATS

CLEOPATRA

Number	Title	Yr	NM
❑ CLP1747 [B]	Live at the Roxy 1981	2014	25.00

EMI

Number	Title	Yr	NM
❑ R101178	Blast Off	1989	18.00
—BMG Music Service edition			

EMI AMERICA

Number	Title	Yr	NM
❑ ST-17070	Built for Speed	1982	12.00
❑ ST-517070	Built for Speed	1982	12.00
—Columbia House edition			
❑ SO-17102 [B]	Rant 'n' Rave with the Stray Cats	1983	12.00
❑ SN-16354	Rant 'n' Rave with the Stray Cats	1985	10.00
—Budget-line reissue			
❑ ST-17226	Rock Therapy	1986	18.00

STRAYHORN, BILLY

FELSTED

Number	Title	Yr	NM
❑ 7008 [M]	Billy Strayhorn Septet	1958	80.00
❑ 2008 [S]	Billy Strayhorn Septet	1958	60.00

MASTER JAZZ

Number	Title	Yr	NM
❑ 8116	Cue for Sax	197?	18.00

MERCER

Number	Title	Yr	NM
❑ LP-1005 [10]	Billy Strayhorn and All-Stars	1951	200.00
❑ LP-1001 [10]	Billy Strayhorn Trio	1951	200.00

ROULETTE

Number	Title	Yr	NM
❑ R-52119 [M]	Live!	1965	25.00
❑ SR-52119 [S]	Live!	1965	30.00

SOLID STATE

Number	Title	Yr	NM
❑ SS-18031	The Peaceful Side of Billy Strayhorn	1968	18.00

UNITED ARTISTS

Number	Title	Yr	NM
❑ UAJ-14010 [M]	The Peaceful Side of Billy Strayhorn	1962	40.00
❑ UAJS-15010 [S]	The Peaceful Side of Billy Strayhorn	1962	50.00

STREET, MEL

GRT

Number	Title	Yr	NM
❑ 8010	Mel Street's Greatest Hits	1976	15.00
❑ 8004	Smokey Mountain Memories	1975	15.00
❑ 8002	Two Way Street	1974	15.00

METROMEDIA COUNTRY

Number	Title	Yr	NM
❑ 5001	Borrowed Angel	1972	18.00
❑ BML1-0281	The Town Where You Live/ Walk Softly on the Bridges	1973	15.00

POLYDOR

Number	Title	Yr	NM
❑ PD-1-6144	Country Soul	1978	12.00
❑ PD-1-6114	Mel Street	1977	12.00

SUNBIRD

Number	Title	Yr	NM
❑ 1000	Many Moods of Mel	1980	15.00
❑ ST-50102	Some Special Moments	1980	15.00
❑ ST-50101	The Very Best of Mel Street	1980	12.00

STREET NOISE

EVOLUTION

Number	Title	Yr	NM
❑ 2010	Street Noise	1970	25.00

STREET PEOPLE

MUSICOR

Number	Title	Yr	NM
❑ MS-3189	Jennifer Tomkins	1970	25.00

STREET PLAYERS

ARIOLA AMERICA

Number	Title	Yr	NM
❑ SW-50071	Dancin' Fever	1979	25.00

STREETDANCER

DHARMA

Number	Title	Yr	NM
❑ 807	Rising	197?	18.00

FUTURE

Number	Title	Yr	NM
❑ 2001	Streetdancer	197?	18.00

STREISAND, BARBRA

COLUMBIA

Number	Title	Yr	NM
❑ CL2757 [M]	A Christmas Album	1967	30.00
❑ CS9557 [S]	A Christmas Album	1967	25.00
—Red "360 Sound Stereo" label			
❑ CS9557 [S]	A Christmas Album	1970	10.00
—Orange label			
❑ OC45369	A Collection: Greatest Hits.. And More	1989	18.00
❑ CS9710	A Happening in Central Park	1968	18.00
—Red "360 Sound Stereo" label			
❑ CS9710	A Happening in Central Park	1970	12.00
—Orange label			
❑ PC9710	A Happening in Central Park	197?	10.00
—Reissue with new prefix			
❑ JS34403	A Star Is Born	1976	15.00
—With Kris Kristofferson			
❑ KC30792	Barbra Joan Streisand	1971	18.00
❑ CQ30792 [Q]	Barbra Joan Streisand	1972	30.00
❑ PC30792	Barbra Joan Streisand	197?	10.00
—Reissue with new prefix			
❑ KC32655	Barbra Streisand...And Other Musical Instruments	1973	15.00
❑ PC32655	Barbra Streisand...And Other Musical Instruments	197?	10.00
—Reissue with new prefix			
❑ PC32801	Barbra Streisand Featuring The Way We Were and All In Love Is Fair	1974	25.00
—Original version with this title on spine and label, and no title on front cover			
❑ KCS9968	Barbra Streisand's Greatest Hits	1970	18.00
—Red "360 Sound Stereo" label			
❑ KCS9968	Barbra Streisand's Greatest Hits	1970	12.00
—Orange label			
❑ PC9968	Barbra Streisand's Greatest Hits	197?	10.00
—Reissue with new prefix			
❑ FC35679	Barbra Streisand's Greatest Hits, Volume 2	1978	15.00
❑ HC45679	Barbra Streisand's Greatest Hits, Volume 2	1980	30.00
—Half-speed mastered edition			
❑ PC33095	Butterfly	1974	15.00
—Original with no bar code			
❑ PC33095	Butterfly	198?	10.00
—Reissue with bar code			
❑ PCQ33095 [Q]	Butterfly	1974	25.00
❑ CL2478 [M-DJ]	Color Me Barbra	1966	200.00
—Promo only on red vinyl (white label)			
❑ CS9278 [S-DJ]	Color Me Barbra	1966	200.00
—Promo only on red vinyl (white label)			
❑ CL2478 [M]	Color Me Barbra	1966	18.00
❑ CL2478 [M]	Color Me Barbra	1966	200.00
—Promo only on red vinyl (white label)			
❑ CS9278 [S]	Color Me Barbra	1966	25.00
—Red "360 Sound Stereo" label			
❑ CS9278 [S]	Color Me Barbra	1966	200.00
—Promo only on red vinyl (white label)			
❑ CS9278 [S]	Color Me Barbra	1970	12.00
—Orange label			
❑ PC9278	Color Me Barbra	197?	10.00
—Reissue with new prefix			
❑ QC39480	Emotion	1984	12.00
❑ FC36750	Guilty	1980	12.00
❑ HC46750	Guilty	1982	30.00
—Half-speed mastered edition			
❑ CL2547 [M]	Je M'Appelle Barbra	1966	18.00
❑ CS9347 [S]	Je M'Appelle Barbra	1966	25.00
—Red "360 Sound Stereo" label			
❑ CS9347 [S]	Je M'Appelle Barbra	1970	12.00
—Orange label			
❑ PC9347	Je M'Appelle Barbra	197?	10.00
—Reissue with new prefix			
❑ PC33815	Lazy Afternoon	1975	15.00
—Original with no bar code			
❑ PCQ33815 [Q]	Lazy Afternoon	1975	30.00
❑ PC33815	Lazy Afternoon	198?	10.00
—Reissue with bar code			
❑ KC31760	Live Concert at the Forum	1972	18.00
❑ CQ31760 [Q]	Live Concert at the Forum	1972	30.00
❑ PC31760	Live Concert at the Forum	197?	10.00
—Reissue with new prefix			
❑ TC37678	Memories	1981	12.00
❑ HC47678	Memories	1982	30.00
—Half-speed mastered edition			
❑ CL2336 [M]	My Name Is Barbra	1965	25.00
—Guaranteed High Fidelity" on label			
❑ CL2336 [M]	My Name Is Barbra	1966	15.00
—360 Sound Mono" on label			
❑ CS9136 [S]	My Name Is Barbra	1965	30.00
—360 Sound Stereo" in black on label			
❑ CS9136 [S]	My Name Is Barbra	1966	18.00
—360 Sound Stereo" in white on label			
❑ CS9136 [S]	My Name Is Barbra	1970	12.00
—Orange label			
❑ PC9136	My Name Is Barbra	197?	10.00
—Reissue with new prefix			
❑ CL2409 [M]	My Name Is Barbra, Two	1965	18.00
❑ CS9209 [S]	My Name Is Barbra, Two	1965	25.00
—Red "360 Sound Stereo" label			
❑ CS9209 [S]	My Name Is Barbra, Two	1970	12.00
—Orange label			
❑ PC9209	My Name Is Barbra, Two	197?	10.00
—Reissue with new prefix			
❑ OC40788	One Voice	1987	12.00
❑ CL2215 [M]	People	1964	25.00
—Guaranteed High Fidelity" on label			
❑ CL2215 [M]	People	1966	15.00
—360 Sound Mono" on label			
❑ CS9015 [S]	People	1964	30.00
—360 Sound Stereo" in black on label			
❑ CS9015 [S]	People	1966	18.00
—360 Sound Stereo" in white on label			
❑ CS9015 [S]	People	1970	12.00
—Orange label			
❑ PC9015	People	197?	10.00
—Reissue with new prefix			
❑ CL2682 [M]	Simply Streisand	1967	30.00
❑ CS9482 [S]	Simply Streisand	1967	25.00
—Red "360 Sound Stereo" label			
❑ CS9482 [S]	Simply Streisand	1970	12.00
—Orange label			
❑ PC9482	Simply Streisand	197?	10.00
—Reissue with new prefix			
❑ JC35375	Songbird	1978	15.00
❑ PC35275	Songbird	198?	10.00
—Budget-line reissue			
❑ KC30378	Stoney End	1971	18.00
❑ CQ30378 [Q]	Stoney End	1972	30.00
❑ PC30378	Stoney End	197?	10.00
—Reissue with new prefix			
❑ JC34830	Streisand Superman	1977	15.00
❑ PC34830	Streisand Superman	198?	10.00
—Budget-line reissue			
❑ CL2007 [M]	The Barbra Streisand Album	1963	25.00
—Guaranteed High Fidelity" on label			
❑ CL2007 [M]	The Barbra Streisand Album	1966	15.00
—360 Sound Mono" on label			
❑ CS8807 [S]	The Barbra Streisand Album	1963	30.00
—360 Sound Stereo" in black on label			
❑ CS8807 [S]	The Barbra Streisand Album	1966	18.00
—360 Sound Stereo" in white on label			
❑ CS8807 [S]	The Barbra Streisand Album	1970	12.00
—Orange label			
❑ PC8807	The Barbra Streisand Album	197?	10.00
—Reissue with new prefix			
❑ OC40092	The Broadway Album	1985	12.00
❑ AS1779 [DJ]	The Legend of Barbra Streisand	1983	30.00
—Promo-only interview LP for "Yentl			
❑ A2S1779 [DJ]	The Legend of Barbra Streisand	1983	100.00
—Promo-only interview LP for "Yentl			
❑ CL2054 [M-DJ]	The Second Barbra Streisand Album	1963	200.00
—Promo only on blue vinyl (white label)			
❑ CS8854 [S-DJ]	The Second Barbra Streisand Album	1963	200.00
—Promo only on blue vinyl (white label)			
❑ CL2054 [M]	The Second Barbra Streisand Album	1963	200.00
—Promo only on blue vinyl (white label)			
❑ CL2054 [M]	The Second Barbra Streisand Album	1963	25.00
—Guaranteed High Fidelity" on label			
❑ CL2054 [M]	The Second Barbra Streisand Album	1966	15.00
—360 Sound Mono" on label			
❑ CS8854 [S]	The Second Barbra Streisand Album	1963	200.00
—Promo only on blue vinyl (white label)			
❑ CS8854 [S]	The Second Barbra Streisand Album	1963	30.00
—360 Sound Stereo" in black on label			
❑ CS8854 [S]	The Second Barbra Streisand Album	1966	18.00
—360 Sound Stereo" in white on label			
❑ CS8854 [S]	The Second Barbra Streisand Album	1970	12.00
—Orange label			
❑ PC8854	The Second Barbra Streisand Album	197?	10.00
—Reissue with new prefix			
❑ CL2154 [M]	The Third Album	1964	25.00
—Guaranteed High Fidelity" on label			
❑ CL2154 [M]	The Third Album	1966	15.00
—360 Sound Mono" on label			
❑ CS8954 [S]	The Third Album	1964	30.00
—360 Sound Stereo" in black on label			
❑ CS8954 [S]	The Third Album	1966	18.00
—360 Sound Stereo" in white on label			
❑ CS8954 [S]	The Third Album	1970	12.00
—Orange label			
❑ PC8954	The Third Album	197?	10.00
—Reissue with new prefix			
❑ PC32801	The Way We Were	1974	15.00
—Revised version; has this title on spine, label and front cover			
❑ PCQ32801 [Q]	The Way We Were	1974	30.00
❑ HC42801	The Way We Were	1982	30.00
—Half-speed mastered edition			
❑ JC32801	The Way We Were	197?	10.00
—Reissue with new prefix			
❑ OC40880	Till I Loved You	1988	12.00
❑ FC36258	Wet	1979	12.00
❑ CS9816	What About Today?	1969	18.00
—Red "360 Sound Stereo" label			
❑ CS9816	What About Today?	1970	12.00
—Orange label			
❑ PC9816	What About Today?	197?	10.00
—Reissue with new prefix			
❑ JS39152	Yentl	1983	12.00

Number	Title	Yr	NM
COLUMBIA MASTERWORKS			
❑ M33452	Classical Barbra	1976	15.00
STRENGTH, "TEXAS" BILL			
RE-CAR			
❑ 2022	Greatest Hits	1967	30.00
STRIDER			
WARNER BROS.			
❑ BS2722 [B]	Exposed	1973	30.00
STRING-A-LONGS, THE			
ATCO			
❑ SD 33-241 [S]	Wide World Hits	1969	30.00
❑ 33-241 [M]	Wide World Hits	1969	50.00
—Mono is white label promo only			
DOT			
❑ DLP-3723 [M]	Great Instrumental Hits	1966	25.00
❑ DLP-25723 [S]	Great Instrumental Hits	1966	30.00
❑ DLP-3463 [M]	Matilda	1962	30.00
❑ DLP-25463 [S]	Matilda	1962	30.00
WARWICK			
❑ W-2036 [M]	Pick-A-Hit Featuring "Wheels	1961	50.00
❑ W-2036ST [S]	Pick-A-Hit Featuring "Wheels	1961	80.00
STRING CHEESE			
WOODEN NICKEL			
❑ WNS-1001 [B]	String Cheese	1971	30.00
STRINGBEAN			
STARDAY			
❑ SLP-215 [M]	A Salute to Uncle Dave Macon	1963	50.00
❑ SLP-142 [M]	Old Time Pickin' and Singin' with Stringbean	1961	60.00
❑ SLP-179 [M]	Stringbean	1962	50.00
❑ SLP-260 [M]	Way Back in the Hills of Old Kentucky	1964	50.00
STROLLERS, THE			
SCORE			
❑ SLP-4026 [M]	Swinging Flute in Hi-Fi	1958	50.00
STRONG, BARRETT			
CAPITOL			
❑ ST-11376 [B]	Stronghold	1975	18.00
STRONG, NOLAN, AND THE DIABLOS			
FORTUNE			
❑ LP-8010 [M]	Fortune of Hits	1961	220.00
—Purple label, thick vinyl			
❑ LP-8010 [M]	Fortune of Hits	196?	50.00
—Yellow label			
❑ LP-8010 [M]	Fortune of Hits	197?	18.00
—Purple label, thinner, more flexible vinyl			
❑ LP-8012 [M]	Fortune of Hits, Vol. 2	1962	220.00
—Purple label, thick vinyl			
❑ LP-8012 [M]	Fortune of Hits, Vol. 2	196?	50.00
—Yellow label			
❑ LP-8012 [M]	Fortune of Hits, Vol. 2	197?	18.00
—Purple label, thinner, more flexible vinyl			
❑ LP-8015 [M]	Mind Over Matter	1963	250.00
—Purple label, thick vinyl			
❑ LP-8015 [M]	Mind Over Matter	196?	60.00
—Yellow label			
❑ LP-8015 [M]	Mind Over Matter	197?	25.00
—Purple label, thinner, more flexible vinyl			
STROZIER, FRANK			
INNER CITY			
❑ IC-2066	Remember Me	197?	18.00
JAZZLAND			
❑ JLP-56 [M]	Long Night	1961	30.00
❑ JLP-956 [S]	Long Night	1961	30.00
❑ JLP-70 [M]	March of the Siamese Children	1962	30.00
❑ JLP-970 [S]	March of the Siamese Children	1962	30.00
STEEPLECHASE			
❑ SCS-1066	Remember Me	198?	15.00
VEE JAY			
❑ LP-3005 [M]	Fantastic Frank Strozier	1960	30.00
❑ SR-3005 [S]	Fantastic Frank Strozier	1960	40.00
STRUMMER, JOE			
EPIC			
❑ E45372	Earthquake Weather	1989	15.00
STRUNK, JUD			
COLUMBIA			
❑ CS9990	Downeast Viewpoint	1970	18.00
HARMONY			
❑ KH32344	Mr. Bojangles and Other Favorites	1973	12.00

Number	Title	Yr	NM
MCA			
❑ 2309	A Semi-Reformed Tequila Crazed Gypsy	1977	12.00
MGM			
❑ SE-4898	Daisy a Day	1973	15.00
❑ SE-4790	Jones General Store	1972	15.00
STRUNZ & FARAH			
MILESTONE			
❑ M-9123	Frontera	1984	12.00
❑ M-9136	Guitarras	1985	12.00
STRYPER			
ENIGMA			
❑ D1-73317	In God We Trust	1988	12.00
❑ 72077	Soldiers Under Command	1985	25.00
—White vinyl			
❑ 72077	Soldiers Under Command	1985	15.00
—Black vinyl			
❑ ST-73217	Soldiers Under Command	1985	12.00
—Reissue with new number			
❑ ST-73207	The Yellow and Black Attack	1985	25.00
—Reissue with eight tracks; blue vinyl, round sleeve			
❑ E-1064	The Yellow and Black Attack	1984	40.00
—Original with six tracks; yellow vinyl			
❑ 71064	The Yellow and Black Attack	1984	25.00
—Original with six tracks; black vinyl			
❑ ST-73207	The Yellow and Black Attack	1985	12.00
—Reissue with eight tracks; black vinyl, square sleeve			
❑ PJAS-73237	To Hell with the Devil	1986	25.00
—Cover has band as winged angels in battle			
❑ SEAX-73277	To Hell with the Devil	1986	30.00
—Picture disc in plastic sleeve			
❑ PJAS-73237	To Hell with the Devil	1986	12.00
—Cover is black			
STUART, MARTY			
COLUMBIA			
❑ B6C40302	Marty Stuart	1986	30.00
MCA			
❑ 42312	Hillbilly Rock	1989	18.00
❑ R170076	Tempted	1990	30.00
—Vinyl version available only through BMG Direct Marketing			
RIDGE RUNNER			
❑ RRR 0013	Marty	1978	30.00
SUGAR HILL			
❑ 3726	Busy Bee Café	1981	30.00
STUART, MARY			
BELL			
❑ 1133	Mary Stuart	1973	25.00
COLUMBIA			
❑ CL6333 [10]	Joanne Sings	1954	40.00
STUART, RORY			
CADENCE JAZZ			
❑ CJR-1016	Nightwork	1983	12.00
SUNNYSIDE			
❑ SSC-1021	Hurricane	1988	12.00
STUARTI, ENZO			
MISTLETOE			
❑ MLP-1237	Comin' Home for Christmas	1978	12.00
STUBBLEFIELD, JOHN			
SOUL NOTE			
❑ SN-1095	Confessin'	1985	15.00
STORYVILLE			
❑ 4011	Prelude	197?	15.00
STUCKEY, NAT			
MCA			
❑ 2184	Independence	1976	15.00
PAULA			
❑ LP-2196 [M]	All My Tomorrows	1967	25.00
❑ LPS-2196 [S]	All My Tomorrows	1967	30.00
❑ LPS-2203	Country Favorites	1968	30.00
❑ LP-2192 [M]	Nat Stuckey Sings	1966	25.00
❑ LPS-2192 [S]	Nat Stuckey Sings	1966	30.00
RCA CAMDEN			
❑ ACL1-0780	In the Ghetto	1974	12.00
RCA VICTOR			
❑ LSP-4389	Country Fever	1970	18.00
❑ LSP-4635	Forgive Me for Calling You Darling	1972	18.00
❑ LSP-4743 [B]	Is It Any Wonder That I Love You	1972	18.00
❑ LSP-4123	Keep 'Em Country	1969	25.00
❑ LSP-4090	Nat Stuckey Sings	1968	25.00
❑ LSP-4226	New Country Roads	1969	25.00
❑ LSP-4330	Old Man Willie	1970	18.00
❑ LSP-4559	Only a Woman Like You	1971	18.00
❑ LSP-4477	She Wakes Me with a Kiss Every Morning	1971	18.00

Number	Title	Yr	NM
❑ APD1-0080 [Q]	Take Time to Love Her/I Used It All on You	1973	30.00
—QuadraDisc"; may not exist in regular stereo			
❑ APL1-0541	The Best of Nat Stuckey	1974	18.00
STUDDARD, RUBEN			
J			
❑ 54639	Soulful	2003	18.00
STUERMER, DARYL			
GRP			
❑ GR-9573	Steppin' Out	1988	12.00
STUFFY AND HIS FROZEN PARACHUTE BAND			
PARAMOUNT			
❑ PAS-6070 [B]	Stuffy and His Frozen Parachute Band	1974	30.00
—Reissue of Water Street 1002			
WATER STREET			
❑ WST1002 [B]	Stuffy and His Frozen Parachute Band	1974	60.00
STURR, JIMMY			
STARR			
❑ R-BS-116	Polka Christmas in My Home Town	1979	18.00
STUTTGART BAROQUE ENSEMBLE (MARCEL COURAND, CONDUCTOR)			
MERCURY LIVING PRESENCE			
❑ SR90402 [S]	Couperin: Les Nations (selections); Rameau: Concerts en Sextuor Nos. 1, 4, 5 and 6	196?	50.00
—Maroon label, no "Vendor: Mercury Record Corporation			
STYLE COUNCIL, THE			
GEFFEN			
❑ GHS24103	Home and Abroad	1986	12.00
❑ GHS24061	Internationalists	1985	12.00
❑ GHS4029	My Ever Changing Moods	1984	12.00
POLYDOR			
❑ 835785-1	Confessions of a Pop Group	1988	15.00
❑ 815277-1 [EP]	Introducing the Style Council	1983	10.00
❑ 831443-1	The Cost of Loving	1987	15.00
STYLISTICS, THE			
AMHERST			
❑ AMH-744	All-Time Classics	1986	12.00
❑ AMH-746	Greatest Love Hits	1986	12.00
❑ AMH-743	The Best of the Stylistics	1986	12.00
❑ AMH-745	The Best of the Stylistics, Vol. 2	1986	12.00
AVCO			
❑ AV-69004	Heavy	1974	18.00
❑ AV-69001	Let's Put It All Together	1974	18.00
❑ 11010	Rockin' Roll Baby	1973	25.00
❑ 11006	Round 2: The Stylistics	1972	25.00
❑ 69008	Thank You Baby	1975	18.00
❑ AV-69005	The Best of the Stylistics	1975	18.00
❑ AV-33023	The Stylistics	1971	25.00
❑ 69010	You Are Beautiful	1975	18.00
H&L			
❑ 69013	Fabulous	1976	15.00
❑ 69032	Wonder Woman	1978	15.00
MERCURY			
❑ SRM-1-3727	In Fashion	1978	15.00
❑ SRM-1-3753	Love Spell	1979	15.00
PHILADELPHIA INT'L.			
❑ FZ37955	1982	1982	12.00
TSOP			
❑ FZ37458	Closer Than Close	1981	12.00
❑ JZ36470	Hurry Up This Way Again	1980	12.00
STYX			
A&M			
❑ SP-6514	Caught in the Act	1984	15.00
❑ SP-3711	Cornerstone	1979	30.00
—Silver vinyl pressing, reportedly for fan club members			
❑ SP-3711	Cornerstone	1979	12.00
❑ SP-3239	Cornerstone	1984	10.00
❑ SP-4604	Crystal Ball	1976	12.00
❑ SP-3218	Crystal Ball	1984	10.00
❑ 7502153271	Edge of the Century	1990	25.00
❑ SP-4559	Equinox	1975	12.00
❑ SP-3217	Equinox	1984	10.00
❑ SP-3734	Kilroy Was Here	1983	12.00
❑ SP-3719	Paradise Theater	1981	12.00
❑ SP-3240	Paradise Theater	1984	10.00
—3200 series LPs are reissues			
❑ SP-4724	Pieces of Eight	1978	12.00
❑ SP-3224	Pieces of Eight	1984	10.00
❑ PR-4724 [PD]	Pieces of Eight	1978	30.00
❑ SP-17222 [DJ]	Radio Sampler and Interview Album	1983	30.00
—Promo only; with "Kilroy Was Here" album graphic on cover			
❑ SP-17053 [DJ]	Styx Radio Special	1978	40.00
—Promo-only box set			

Number	Title	Yr	NM
❑ SP-17053 [DJ]	Styx Radio Special	1978	40.00
—Promo-only box set			
❑ SP-4637	The Grand Illusion	1977	12.00
❑ SP-3223	The Grand Illusion	1984	10.00
❑ SP-8431 [DJ]	The Styx Radio Special	1977	30.00
—Promo only; green cover			

MOBILE FIDELITY
❑ 1-026	The Grand Illusion	1979	30.00
—Audiophile vinyl			

NAUTILUS
❑ NR-27	Cornerstone	1982	25.00
—Audiophile vinyl			
❑ NR-45	Paradise Theater	198?	30.00
—Audiophile vinyl			
❑ NR-15	Pieces of Eight	1981	30.00
—Audiophile vinyl			

RCA VICTOR
❑ AFL1-3597	Best of Styx	1979	12.00
❑ AYL1-4756	Best of Styx	1982	10.00
❑ AFL1-3594	Lady	1979	12.00
—Retitled version of "Styx II"			
❑ AYL1-4233	Lady	1981	10.00
—Retitled version of "Styx II"			
❑ AFL1-3596	Miracles	1979	12.00
—Retitled version of "Man of Miracles			
❑ AFL1-3595	Serpent	1979	12.00
—Retitled version of "The Serpent Is Rising			
❑ AFL1-3593	Styx	1979	12.00
❑ AYL1-3888	Styx	1980	10.00

WOODEN NICKEL
❑ BWL1-2250	Best of Styx	1977	15.00
❑ BWL1-0638	Man of Miracles	1974	30.00
—Original version contains "Lies"			
❑ BWL1-0638	Man of Miracles	1974	25.00
—Second version contains "Best Thing"			
❑ WNS-1008	Styx	1972	25.00
❑ BWL1-1008	Styx	1975	18.00
❑ WNS-1012	Styx II	1973	25.00
—With die-cut cover			
❑ BWL1-1012	Styx II	1975	18.00
❑ BWL1-0287	The Serpent Is Rising	1974	25.00

SUB-ZERO BAND, THE

SUB-ZERO
❑ 1172	The Sub-Zero Band	197?	200.00

SUDLER, MONETTE

INNER CITY
❑ IC-2062	Time for a Change	197?	18.00

STEEPLECHASE
❑ SCS-1087	Brighter Days for You	198?	15.00
❑ SCS-1102	Live in Europe	198?	15.00
❑ SCS-1062	Time for a Change	198?	15.00

SUEDE

WARNER BROS.
❑ SUELPX001 [B]	Bloodsports	2013	30.00

SUGAR

RYKO ANALOGUE
❑ RALP10300	File Under: Easy Listening	1994	15.00

SUGAR BEARS, THE

BIG TREE
❑ BTS-2009	Introducing the Sugar Bears	1972	25.00

SUGAR CREEK

METROMEDIA
❑ MD1020	Please Tell a Friend	1969	60.00

SUGAR HILL GANG

SUGAR HILL
❑ SH249 [B]	8th Wonder	1981	25.00
❑ SH9206 [B]	Livin' in the Fast Lane	1984	18.00
❑ SH245 [B]	Sugar Hill Gang	1980	30.00

SUGARCUBES, THE

ELEKTRA
❑ 60860	Here Today, Tomorrow, Next Week!	1989	15.00
❑ 60860 [DJ]	Here Today, Tomorrow, Next Week!	1989	18.00
—White label promo on audiophile vinyl			
❑ 60801	Life's Too Good	1988	15.00
❑ 60801 [DJ]	Life's Too Good	1988	18.00
—White label promo on audiophile vinyl			

SUGARLOAF

BRUT
❑ 6006	I Got a Song	1973	18.00

CLARIDGE
❑ 1000	Don't Call Us, We'll Call You	1975	15.00

LIBERTY
❑ LST-11010 [B]	Spaceship Earth	1971	25.00

Number	Title	Yr	NM
❑ LST-7640	Sugarloaf	1970	25.00

SUGARPLUM FAIRY AND CAST, THE

RCA CAMDEN
❑ CAL-1101 [M]	'Twas the Night Before Christmas	1968	18.00
❑ CAS-1101 [S]	'Twas the Night Before Christmas	1968	15.00

SUICIDAL TENDENCIES

CAROLINE
❑ CAROL1336	Join the Army	1987	18.00

EPIC
❑ 6E45244	Controlled by Hatred/Feel Like Shit...Deja Vu	1989	15.00
❑ FE44288	How Will I Laugh Tomorrow When I Can't Even Smile Today	1988	15.00
❑ E45389	Lights...Camera...Revolution	1990	15.00

FRONTIER
❑ 4604-1-L	Suicidal Tendencies	198?	18.00
❑ 1011	Suicidal Tendencies	1983	18.00

SUICIDE

ANTILLES
❑ AN-7080 [B]	Alan Vega-Martin Rev	1980	18.00

RED STAR
❑ RS-1 [B]	Suicide	1977	30.00
❑ RED-800	Suicide	1980	14.00
—Reissue of RS-1			

WAX TRAX!
❑ 7072 [B]	A Way of Life	1989	25.00

SUICIDE COMMANDOS

BLANK
❑ 002	The Suicide Commandos Make a Record	1977	30.00

TWIN/TONE
❑ TTR7906	The Commandos Commit Suicide Dance Concert	1979	75.00
—Limited edition of 1,000 copies			

SUKMAN, HARRY

LIBERTY
❑ LRP-3135 [M]	Command Performance	1959	25.00
❑ LST-7135 [S]	Command Performance	1959	30.00
❑ LRP-3005 [M]	Nightfall	1955	25.00
❑ LRP-3151 [M]	The Franz Liszt Story	1960	25.00
❑ LST-7151 [S]	The Franz Liszt Story	1960	30.00

SULIEMAN, IDREES

NEW JAZZ
❑ NJLP-8202 [M]	Roots	1958	60.00
—Purple label			
❑ NJLP-8202 [M]	Roots	1958	100.00
—Yellow label			
❑ NJLP-8202 [M]	Roots	1965	30.00
—Blue label, trident logo at right			

STEEPLECHASE
❑ SCS-1202	Bird's Grass	198?	15.00
❑ SCS-1052	Now Is the Time	198?	15.00

SULLIVAN, CHARLES

INNER CITY
❑ IC-1012	Genesis	1975	18.00

SULLIVAN, FRANK

REVELATION
❑ 34	First Impressions	1981	12.00

SULLIVAN, IRA

ATLANTIC
❑ 1476 [M]	Horizons	1967	30.00
❑ SD-1476 [S]	Horizons	1967	18.00

DELMARK
❑ DL-402 [M]	Blue Stroll	1961	30.00
❑ DS-402 [S]	Blue Stroll	1961	40.00
❑ DS-422	Nicky's Tune	1970	25.00

DISCOVERY
❑ 873	Horizons	1983	15.00
—Reissue of Atlantic SD 1476			

FLYING FISH
❑ FF-27075	Ira Sullivan	198?	12.00
—Reissue			
❑ FF-075	Ira Sullivan	1978	15.00

GALAXY
❑ 5137	Multimedia	198?	15.00
❑ 5114	Peace	1979	15.00

HORIZON
❑ SP-706	Ira Sullivan	1976	15.00

MUSE
❑ MR-5242	Ira Sullivan Does It All!	1981	18.00

PAUSA

Number	Title	Yr	NM
❑ 7169	Strings Attached	1985	15.00

STASH
❑ ST-208	The Incredible Ira Sullivan	1980	25.00

VEE JAY
❑ VJS-3003 [S]	Bird Lives!	198?	15.00
—Reissue with new prefix on thinner vinyl			
❑ LP-3003 [M]	Bird Lives!	1960	50.00
❑ SR-3003 [S]	Bird Lives!	1960	60.00

SULLIVAN, JIM

MERCURY
❑ MG-21137 [M]	Sitar Beat	1967	25.00
❑ SR-61137 [S]	Sitar Beat	1967	25.00

SULLIVAN, JOE

CAPITOL
❑ T636 [M]	Classics in Jazz	1955	40.00

DOWN HOME
❑ MGD-2 [M]	Mr. Piano Man: The Music of Joe Sullivan	1956	50.00

EPIC
❑ LG1003 [10]	Joe Sullivan Plays Fats Waller Compositions	1954	80.00

FOLKWAYS
❑ FJ-2851	Joe Sullivan Piano	197?	15.00

RIVERSIDE
❑ RLP 12-202 [M]	New Solos by an Old Master	1955	60.00

TIME-LIFE
❑ STL-J-27	Giants of Jazz	1982	25.00

VERVE
❑ MGV-1002 [M]	Mr. Piano Man: The Music of Joe Sullivan	1957	40.00
❑ V-1002 [M]	Mr. Piano Man: The Music of Joe Sullivan	1961	25.00

SULLIVAN, MAXINE, AND BOB WILBER

MONMOUTH-EVERGREEN
❑ 6917	Bob & Maxine	1969	18.00
❑ 6919	Maxine Sullivan and Bob Wilber	1969	15.00

SULLIVAN, MAXINE

ATLANTIC
❑ 81783	Together	1987	12.00

AUDIOPHILE
❑ AP-193	Good Morning, Life!	1986	12.00
❑ AP-185	It Was Great Fun	1984	12.00
❑ AP-167	Maxine	198?	12.00
❑ AP-154	Maxine Sullivan and the Ike Isaacs Trio	198?	12.00
❑ AP-128	We Just Couldn't Say Goodbye	1979	12.00

CIRCLE
❑ 47	Maxine Sullivan and John Kirby 1940	198?	12.00

CONCORD JAZZ
❑ CJ-288	Uptown	1986	12.00

EVEREST ARCHIVE OF FOLK & JAZZ
❑ 307	Maxine Sullivan with Jack Teagarden	197?	12.00

MONMOUTH-EVERGREEN
❑ 7038	Sullivan, Shakespeare and Hyman	197?	18.00

PERIOD
❑ SPL-1207 [M]	Maxine Sullivan, Volume 2	1956	50.00
❑ RL-1909 [M]	Maxine Sullivan 1956	1956	50.00

STASH
❑ ST-257	Maxine Sullivan Sings the Music of Burton Lane	1986	12.00
❑ ST-244	The Great Songs from the Cotton Club by Harold Arlen and Ted Koehler	1985	12.00

SUMAC, YMA

CAPITOL
❑ ST1169 [S]	Fuego del Andes	1959	50.00
❑ T1169 [M]	Fuego del Andes	1959	40.00
❑ L423 [10]	Inca Taqui	1953	100.00
❑ T770 [M]	Legend of the Jivaro	1956	50.00
—Turquoise label			
❑ T770 [M]	Legend of the Jivaro	1963	25.00
—Black colorband label, "Capitol" at top			
❑ SM-299 [M]	Legend of the Sun Virgin	197?	15.00
❑ L299 [10]	Legend of the Sun Virgin	1952	120.00
❑ T299 [M]	Legend of the Sun Virgin	1955	50.00
❑ M-11892	Mambo!	1979	15.00
❑ H564 [10]	Mambo!	1954	100.00
❑ T564 [M]	Mambo!	1955	50.00
❑ H244 [10]	Voice of the Xtabay	1952	100.00
❑ DW684 [R]	Voice of the Xtabay and Inca Taqui	1963	18.00
❑ SM-684	Voice of the Xtabay and Inca Taqui	197?	15.00
—On this reissue, Side 1 is in mono			
❑ W684 [M]	Voice of the Xtabay and Inca Taqui	1955	50.00
—Gray label			

Number	Title	Yr	NM
❑ W684 [M]	Voice of the Xtabay and Inca Taqui	1963	25.00
—Black colorband label, "Capitol" at top			

CORAL

Number	Title	Yr	NM
❑ CRL56058 [10]	Presenting Yma Sumac	1952	120.00

LONDON

Number	Title	Yr	NM
❑ XPS608	Miracles	1972	25.00

SUMMER, DONNA

ATLANTIC

Number	Title	Yr	NM
❑ 81987	Another Place and Time	1989	15.00

CASABLANCA

Number	Title	Yr	NM
❑ NBLP7150	Bad Girls	1979	15.00
❑ 822557-1	Bad Girls	1984	12.00
❑ NBLP7038	Four Seasons of Love	1976	12.00
❑ NBLP7201	Greatest Hits, Vol. 1	1979	10.00
❑ NBLP7202	Greatest Hits, Vol. 2	1979	10.00
❑ 822559-1	Greatest Hits, Vol. 2	1984	10.00
❑ NBLP7056	I Remember Yesterday	1977	12.00
❑ NBLP7119	Live and More	1978	15.00
❑ 811123-1	Live and More	1985	12.00
❑ NBLP7078	Once Upon a Time...	1977	15.00
❑ NBLP7191	On the Radio -- Greatest Hits Vols. 1 and 2	1979	15.00
❑ 822558-1	On the Radio -- Greatest Hits Vols. 1 and 2	1984	12.00
❑ NBPIX7119 [PD]	The Best of Live and More	1979	25.00
❑ 822560-1	Walk Away	1984	10.00
❑ NBLP7244	Walk Away -- Collector's Edition (The Best of 1977-1980)	1980	12.00

EPIC

Number	Title	Yr	NM
❑ E269910	Live and More Encore	1999	18.00

GEFFEN

Number	Title	Yr	NM
❑ GHS24102	All Systems Go	1987	12.00
❑ GHS24040 [DJ]	Cats Without Claws	1984	18.00
—Promo only on Quiex II vinyl			
❑ GHS24040	Cats Without Claws	1984	12.00
❑ GHS2005	Donna Summer	1982	12.00
❑ GHS2000	The Wanderer	1980	12.00

MERCURY

Number	Title	Yr	NM
❑ 812265-1	She Works Hard for the Money	1983	12.00
❑ 826144-1	The Summer Collection	1985	12.00

OASIS

Number	Title	Yr	NM
❑ OCLP5004	A Love Trilogy	1976	15.00
❑ OCLP5003	Love to Love You Baby	1975	15.00
—Add 50% if poster is included			
❑ 822792-1	Love to Love You Baby	1985	10.00

SUMMER SOUNDS, THE

LAUREL

Number	Title	Yr	NM
❑ 90973	Up Down	196?	1000.00

SUMMERHILL

TETRAGRAMMATON

Number	Title	Yr	NM
❑ T-114	Summerhill	1969	30.00

SUMMERLIN, ED

ECCLESIA

Number	Title	Yr	NM
❑ ER-101 [M]	Liturgical Jazz	1959	60.00

SUMMERS, ANDREW ROWAN

FOLKWAYS

Number	Title	Yr	NM
❑ FA-2348 [M]	Andrew Rowan Summers	1957	30.00
❑ FA-2002 [10]	Christmas Carols	195?	50.00
❑ FC7502 [M]	Christmas Carols	196?	18.00
❑ FA-2361 [M]	Hymns and Carols	195?	30.00
❑ FA-2021 [10]	Seeds of Love	1951	50.00
❑ FP-21 [10]	Seeds of Love	1951	50.00
❑ FA-2044 [10]	The Faulse Lady	1954	50.00
❑ FP-44 [10]	The Faulse Lady	1954	50.00
❑ FA-2041 [10]	The Lady Gay	1954	50.00
❑ FP-41 [10]	The Lady Gay	1954	50.00
❑ FA-2364 [M]	The Unquiet Grave and Other American Tragic Ballads	195?	30.00

SUMMERS, ANDY, AND ROBERT FRIPP

A&M

Number	Title	Yr	NM
❑ SP9-5011	Bewitched	1984	12.00
❑ SP-4913	I Advance Masked	1982	12.00
❑ SP-17299 [DJ]	Speak Out Interview	1982	30.00
—Issued in generic cover with sticker			
❑ SP-17299 [DJ]	Speak Out Interview	1982	30.00
—Issued in generic cover with sticker			

SUMMERS, ANDY

MCA

Number	Title	Yr	NM
❑ 42007	XYZ	1987	12.00

PRIVATE MUSIC

Number	Title	Yr	NM
❑ 2039-1-P	Mysterious Barricades	1988	12.00

SUMMERS, BILL

PRESTIGE

Number	Title	Yr	NM
❑ 10103	Cayenne	1977	18.00
❑ 10102	Feel the Heat	1977	18.00
❑ 10105	Straight to the Bank	1978	18.00

SUN RA

A&M

Number	Title	Yr	NM
❑ SP-5260	Blue Delight	1989	25.00

ABC IMPULSE!

Number	Title	Yr	NM
❑ AS-9245	Angels and Demons at Play	1974	40.00
❑ AS-9255	Astro Black	1973	60.00
❑ AS-9239	Atlantis	1973	40.00
❑ AS-9270	Fate in a Pleasant Mood	1974	50.00
❑ ASD-9265	Jazz in Silhouette	1974	50.00
❑ ASD-9298	Pathways to Unknown Worlds	1975	60.00
❑ AS-9271	Super Sonic Sounds	1974	50.00
❑ ASD-9276	The Bad and the Beautiful	1974	40.00
❑ AS-9243	The Magic City	1973	50.00
❑ AS-9242	The Nubians of Plutonia	1974	50.00
❑ 1974	Welcome to Saturn	1974	60.00
❑ ASD-9292	We Travel the Spaceways	1974	80.00
—May only exist as a promo or test pressing			

AFFINITY

Number	Title	Yr	NM
❑ AFF10	The Solar-Myth Approach Volume I	1978	40.00
❑ AFF76	The Solar-Myth Approach Volume II	1978	40.00

BASF

Number	Title	Yr	NM
❑ 20748	It's After the End of the World	1971	50.00

BLACK LION

Number	Title	Yr	NM
❑ 106	Pictures of Infinity	197?	40.00

BLACK SAINT

Number	Title	Yr	NM
❑ 120111	Hours After	1990	30.00
❑ 120101	Reflections in Blue	1987	25.00

BLUE THUMB

Number	Title	Yr	NM
❑ BTS-41 [Q]	Space Is the Place	1973	100.00
—All copies are quad			

DELMARK

Number	Title	Yr	NM
❑ DS-414 [R]	Sound of Joy	1968	25.00
❑ DL-411 [M]	Sun Song	1967	30.00
❑ DS-411 [R]	Sun Song	1967	25.00
—Reissue of Transition 10			

DIW

Number	Title	Yr	NM
❑ DIWP-2 [PD]	Cosmo Omnibus Imaginable Illusion: Live at Pit-Inn	1988	120.00
—Picture disc; limited to under 1,000 copies			
❑ 8024	Cosmo Omnibus Imaginable Illusion: Live at Pit-Inn	1988	60.00

ESP-DISK'

Number	Title	Yr	NM
❑ S-1045 [S]	Nothing Is	1969	30.00
❑ 1014 [M]	The Heliocentric Worlds of Sun Ra, Volume 1	1966	60.00
❑ S-1014 [S]	The Heliocentric Worlds of Sun Ra, Volume 1	1966	80.00
—Reproductions exist of this LP			
❑ 1017 [M]	The Heliocentric Worlds of Sun Ra, Volume 2	1966	40.00
—With voices overdubbed on "The Sun Myth			
❑ S-1017 [S]	The Heliocentric Worlds of Sun Ra, Volume 2	1966	80.00
—With voices overdubbed on "The Sun Myth			
❑ 1017 [M]	The Heliocentric Worlds of Sun Ra, Volume 2	1966	60.00
—Without voices overdubbed on "The Sun Myth			
❑ S-1017 [S]	The Heliocentric Worlds of Sun Ra, Volume 2	1966	100.00
—Without voices overdubbed on "The Sun Myth			

HAT ART

Number	Title	Yr	NM
❑ 2017	Sunrise in Different Directions	1986	40.00

HAT HUT

Number	Title	Yr	NM
❑ 17	Sunrise in Different Directions	1980	60.00

HORO

Number	Title	Yr	NM
❑ HDP-25/26	New Steps	1978	200.00
❑ HDP-23/24	Other Voices, Other Blues	1978	150.00
❑ HDP-19/20	Unity	1978	150.00

IAI

Number	Title	Yr	NM
❑ 373850	Solo Piano Volume 1	197?	30.00
❑ 373858	St. Louis Blues	1978	30.00

INNER CITY

Number	Title	Yr	NM
❑ IC-1020	Cosmos	1978	50.00
—Original edition; reproductions exist			
❑ IC-1039	Live at Montreux	1978	40.00

JIHAD

Number	Title	Yr	NM
❑ 1968 [S]	A Black Mass	1968	300.00
—Black and white cover			
❑ 1968 [S]	A Black Mass	1968	200.00
—Color cover			

LEO

Number	Title	Yr	NM
❑ LR-154	Love in Outer Space: Live in Utrecht	1988	25.00

MELTDOWN

Number	Title	Yr	NM
❑ MPA-1	John Cage Meets Sun Ra	1987	200.00

PHILLY JAZZ

Number	Title	Yr	NM
❑ PJ-666	Lanquidity	1978	250.00
—Reproductions exist			
❑ PJ-1007	Of Mythic Worlds	1980	250.00

PRAXIS

Number	Title	Yr	NM
❑ CM110	Live at Praxis 84 Volume 3	1985	80.00
❑ CM108	Live at Praxis Volume 1	1984	70.00
❑ CM109 [B]	Live at Praxis Volume 2	1985	80.00
❑ CM106	Sun Ra Arkestra Meets Salah Ragab in Egypt	1983	60.00

RECOMMENDED

Number	Title	Yr	NM
❑ RR-11	Nuits de la Fondation Maeght Volume I	1981	50.00
—Reissue of Shandar 10.001; plays at 45 rpm			

ROUNDER

Number	Title	Yr	NM
❑ 3035	Strange Celestial Road	1982	30.00
—Reproductions exist			

SATURN

Number	Title	Yr	NM
❑ A/B-1984SG-9	A Fireside Chat with Lucifer	1984	150.00
❑ 19841	A Fireside Chat with Lucifer	1984	150.00
❑ SR-9956-2/O/P [M]	Angels and Demons at Play	1965	80.00
—Red label; metallic gold cover			
❑ LP-407 [M]	Angels and Demons at Play	196?	40.00
—Chicago address on label; reproductions exist			
❑ SR-9956 [M]	Art Forms of Dimensions Tomorrow	1965	50.00
—Red label; reproductions exist			
❑ LP-404 [M]	Art Forms of Dimensions Tomorrow	1969	40.00
—Chicago address on label; reproductions exist			
❑ ESR-507 [S]	Atlantis	1969	80.00
—El Saturn" label			
❑ 10480	Aurora Borealis	1980	80.00
❑ 123180	Beyond the Purple Star Zone	1981	200.00
❑ C/D-1984SG-9	Celestial Love	1984	150.00
❑ 19842	Celestial Love	1984	150.00
❑ ESR-520	Continuation	1969	80.00
❑ LP-520	Continuation	1970	50.00
❑ LP-408 [S]	Cosmic Tones for Mental Therapy	1967	200.00
—Red label; Sun Ra art on cover; reproductions exist			
❑ KH-2772 [S]	Cosmic Tones for Mental Therapy	196?	80.00
—Blue cover; Chicago address on label			
❑ 1981	Dance of Innocent Passion	1981	150.00
❑ LP-485	Deep Purple	1973	150.00
❑ LP-538	Discipline 27-II	1973	150.00
❑ CMIJ78	Disco 3000	1978	150.00
❑ SR-9956-2/A/B [M]	Fate in a Pleasant Mood	1965	80.00
—Red label; reproductions exist			
❑ LP-202 [M]	Fate in a Pleasant Mood	196?	100.00
—Chicago address on label			
❑ 72579	God Is More Than Love Can Ever Be	1979	200.00
❑ 13188III/12988II	Hidden Fire 1	1988	80.00
❑ 13088A/12988B	Hidden Fire 2	1988	80.00
❑ 101185	Hiroshima	1985	150.00
❑ ESR-508 [S]	Holiday for Soul-Dance	1969	60.00
—El Saturn" label; reproductions exist			
❑ LP-849	Horizon	1974	150.00
❑ 1217718	Horizon	1974	150.00
❑ 6680	I, Pharaoh	1980	150.00
—El Saturn" label			
❑ LP-203 [M]	Interstellar Low Ways	1969	50.00
—Chicago address on label; reproductions exist			
❑ 144000	Invisible Shield	197?	200.00
❑ LP-5786 [M]	Jazz in Silhouette	1958	150.00
—Yellow label			
❑ LP-205 [M]	Jazz in Silhouette	1967	100.00
—Red label			
❑ LP-205 [M]	Jazz in Silhouette	1967	80.00
—Green label			
❑ 1984A/B	Just Friends	1984	150.00
❑ MS87976	Live at Montreux	1976	150.00
❑ 1272	Live in Egypt 1	1973	80.00
❑ 19783	Media Dream	1978	150.00
❑ 1978	Media Dream	1978	150.00
❑ LP-509 [M]	Monorails and Satellites	1968	100.00
—El Saturn" label; reproductions exist			
❑ LP-519 [S]	Monorails and Satellites, Vol. II	1969	80.00
—El Saturn" label			
❑ ESR-1970	My Brother the Wind	1970	150.00
❑ ESR-521	My Brother the Wind	1970	100.00
—Reproductions exist			
❑ LP-521	My Brother the Wind	197?	50.00
❑ SRA-2000	My Brother the Wind, Volume II	1971	150.00
❑ ESR-523	My Brother the Wind, Volume II	1971	100.00
—Reproductions exist			
❑ 77771	Nidhamu	197?	250.00
❑ 7771	Nidhamu	197?	150.00
❑ 1982	Nuclear War	1982	150.00
❑ IX SR72881	Oblique Parallax	1981	200.00
❑ 91379	Omniverse	1979	150.00
❑ 101679	On Jupiter	1979	150.00
—El Saturn" label			
❑ KH-98766 [M]	Other Planes of There	1966	100.00
—Red label; reproductions exist			
❑ LP-206 [M]	Other Planes of There	1967	100.00
—Chicago address on label			
❑ 61674	Out Beyond the Kingdom Of	1974	150.00

Number	Title	Yr	NM
❏ 9121385	Outer Reach Intensity-Energy	1985	200.00
❏ LP-530	Outer Spaceways Incorporated	1974	200.00
—Chicago address on label			
❏ LP-530	Outer Spaceways Incorporated	1974	150.00
—Philadelphia address on label			
❏ IX/1983-220	Ra to the Rescue	1983	150.00
❏ SR-9956-2-M/N [M]	Rocket #9 Take Off For the Planet Venus	1966	500.00
—Cover has "burning candle" logo			
❏ GH-9954-E/F [M]	Secrets of the Sun	1965	250.00
—Red label			
❏ LP-208 [M]	Secrets of the Sun	196?	100.00
—Chicago address on label			
❏ 11179	Sleeping Beauty	1979	80.00
❏ LP-747	Some Blues But Not the Kind That's Blue	1977	150.00
❏ 1014077	Some Blues But Not the Kind That's Blue	1977	150.00
❏ 101477	Some Blues But Not the Kind That's Blue	1977	150.00
❏ 7877	Somewhere Over the Rainbow	1977	150.00
❏ LP-487	Song of the Stargazers	1979	150.00
❏ 6161	Song of the Stargazers	1979	200.00
❏ 19782	Sound Mirror	1978	150.00
❏ LP-512	Sound Sun Pleasure!!	1970	60.00
—Reproductions exist			
❏ LP-527	Space Probe	197?	150.00
❏ 14200-A/B	Space Probe	197?	80.00
❏ LP-502 [S]	Strange Strings	1967	100.00
—Red label; reproductions exist			
❏ 92074	Sub Underground	1974	200.00
❏ IHNY-165	Sun Ra and His Arkestra Featuring Pharoah Sanders and Black Harold	1976	150.00
❏ SR-9956-11A/B [M]	Sun Ra Visits Planet Earth	1966	80.00
—Red label; reproductions exist			
❏ LP-207 [M]	Sun Ra Visits Planet Earth	1968	100.00
—Minneapolis address on label			
❏ LP-207 [M]	Sun Ra Visits Planet Earth	196?	80.00
—El Saturn" label			
❏ SRLP-0216 [M]	Super-Sonic Jazz	1957	300.00
—Blank cover			
❏ SRLP-0216 [M]	Super-Sonic Jazz	1957	600.00
—Silk-screened cover			
❏ SRLP-0216 [M]	Super-Sonic Jazz	1958	250.00
—Purple "keyboard" cover			
❏ SRLP-0216 [M]	Super-Sonic Jazz	1965	80.00
—Blue or green cover			
❏ LP-204 [M]	Super-Sonic Sounds	1968	80.00
—Blue or green cover; Chicago address on label			
❏ LP-772	Taking a Chance on Chances	1977	150.00
❏ 81774	The Antique Blacks	1974	200.00
❏ ESR-532	The Bad and the Beautiful	196?	50.00
—Chicago address on label; reproductions exist			
❏ LP-529	The Invisible Shield	1974	150.00
—Philadelphia address on label			
❏ LP-529	The Invisible Shield	1974	200.00
—Chicago address on label			
❏ SR-9956-11E/F [M]	The Lady with the Golden Stockings	1966	600.00
—Cover is generic and says "Tonal Views of Times Tomorrow			
❏ LPB-711 [M]	The Magic City	1966	80.00
—Red label; reproductions exist			
❏ LP-403 [M]	The Magic City	196?	60.00
—Chicago address on label			
❏ LP-522	The Night of the Purple Moon	197?	100.00
—Reproductions exist			
❏ LP-406 [M]	The Nubians of Plutonia	1969	100.00
—Chicago address on label; reproductions exist			
❏ LP-771	The Soul Vibrations of Man	1977	200.00
❏ ESR-5000	Universe in Blue	1972	150.00
❏ LP-200	Universe in Blue	197?	150.00
❏ 91780	Voice of the Eternal Tomorrow	1980	150.00
❏ HK-5445 [M]	We Travel the Spaceways	1966	120.00
—Red label			
❏ LP-409 [M]	We Travel the Spaceways	196?	60.00
—El Saturn" label; reproductions exist			
❏ LP-539	What's New?	197?	150.00
❏ 752	What's New?	197?	100.00
❏ 52375	What's New?	1975	125.00
❏ LP-405	When Angels Speak of Love	196?	40.00
❏ LP-1966 [M]	When Angels Speak of Love	1966	500.00
—Red cover with a "sideways" image of Sun Ra			
❏ 101485	When Spaceships Appear	1985	150.00
❏ LP-402	When Sun Comes Out	196?	40.00
❏ LP-2066 [M]	When Sun Comes Out	1963	400.00
—Blank cover			
❏ LP-2066 [M]	When Sun Comes Out	1963	500.00
—Green cover with yellow sun			
❏ LP-2066 [M]	When Sun Comes Out	1963	500.00
—Black ameboid figure on cover			
❏ LP-2066 [M]	When Sun Comes Out	1967	300.00
—Spaceman at piano cover; reproductions exist			

SATURN/RECOMMENDED

Number	Title	Yr	NM
❏ SRRD-1	Cosmo Sun Connection	1985	40.00

SAVOY

Number	Title	Yr	NM
❏ MG-12169 [M]	The Futuristic Sounds of Sun Ra	1961	100.00

SAVOY JAZZ

| ❏ SJL-1141 | We Are in the Future | 1984 | 40.00 |

SHANDAR

| ❏ SR 10.001 | Nuits de la Fondation Maeght Volume I | 1971 | 50.00 |
| ❏ SR 10.003 | Nuits de la Fondation Maeght Volume II | 1971 | 50.00 |

SWEET EARTH

| ❏ SER1003 | The Other Side of the Sun | 1979 | 150.00 |
| —Reproductions exist | | | |

THOTH INTERGALACTIC

❏ KH-2772 [S]	Cosmic Tones for Mental Therapy	1969	60.00
❏ KH-1272	Live in Egypt 1	1973	60.00
❏ 7771	Nidhamu	197?	60.00
❏ KH-98766 [M]	Other Planes of There	1969	60.00
❏ KH-5472 [M]	Strange Strings	196?	80.00
❏ LPB-711 [M]	The Magic City	1969	60.00
❏ IR-1972	The Night of the Purple Moon	1970	60.00

TOTAL ENERGY

❏ NER3029	It Is Forbidden	2001	15.00
—Green vinyl			
❏ NER3026	Life Is Beautiful	1999	15.00
❏ NER3021	Outer Space Employment Agency	1999	15.00

TRANSITION

| ❏ TLP-10 [M] | Jazz by Sun Ra | 1957 | 500.00 |
| —With booklet (deduct 1/5 if missing) | | | |

SUNDAY FUNNIES, THE

RARE EARTH

| ❏ RS-538 | Benediction | 1972 | 15.00 |
| ❏ RS-526 [B] | The Sunday Funnies | 1971 | 18.00 |

SUNDAYS, THE

DGC

| ❏ 24277 | Reading, Writing and Arithmetic | 1990 | 18.00 |

SUNDOWNERS, THE

LIBERTY

| ❏ LRP-3269 [M] | Folk Songs for the Rich | 1962 | 25.00 |
| ❏ LST-7269 [S] | Folk Songs for the Rich | 1962 | 30.00 |

SUNKEL, PHIL

ABC-PARAMOUNT

❏ ABC-225 [M]	Gerry Mulligan and Bob Brookmeyer Play Phil Sunkel's Jazz Concerto Grosso	1958	60.00
❏ ABCS-225 [S]	Gerry Mulligan and Bob Brookmeyer Play Phil Sunkel's Jazz Concerto Grosso	1958	50.00
❏ ABC-136 [M]	Jazz Band	1956	80.00

SUNNA

ASTRALWERKS

| ❏ ASW49708-1 | One Minute Science | 2000 | 30.00 |

SUNNY AND THE SUNLINERS

KEY-LOC

❏ 3008 [M]	Adelante	196?	30.00
❏ 3005 [M]	A Little Brown-Eyed Soul	196?	30.00
❏ 3004 [M]	Canta Sunny	196?	30.00
❏ 3002 [M]	No Te Chifles	196?	30.00
❏ 3009 [M]	Sky High	196?	30.00
❏ 3001 [M]	Smile Now, Cry Later	196?	30.00
❏ 3003 [M]	Sunny and the Sunliners Live in Hollywood	196?	30.00
❏ 3010 [M]	The Missing Link	196?	30.00
❏ 3006 [M]	This Is My Band	196?	30.00
❏ 3007 [M]	Versatile	196?	30.00

SUNGLOW

❏ SLP-101 [M]	Sunny Ozuna and the Sunglows	1963	100.00
—As "The Sunglows			
❏ SLP-102 [M]	The Fabulous Sunglows	1964	100.00
—As "The Sunglows			
❏ SLP-103 [M]	The Original Peanuts	1965	80.00
—As "The Sunglows			
❏ SLP-103S [S]	The Original Peanuts	1965	100.00
—As "The Sunglows			

TEAR DROP

❏ LPM-2001 [M]	Las Vegas Welcomes Sunny and the Sunliners	1964	40.00
❏ LPM-2000 [M]	Talk to Me	1963	100.00
❏ LPM-2008 [M]	Teardrop Presents Sunny and the Sunliners	196?	40.00

SUNNY DAY REAL ESTATE

SUB POP

❏ SP-246	Diary	1994	40.00
—Aqua vinyl			
❏ SP-246	Diary	1994	25.00
—Black vinyl			
❏ SP-409	How It Feels to Be Something On	1997	30.00
❏ SP-316	Sunny Day Real Estate	1995	25.00
❏ SP-485	Sunny Day Real Estate Live	1999	30.00

TIME BOMB

| ❏ 42541-1 | The Rising Tide | 2000 | 40.00 |

SUNNYLAND SLIM

BLUESVILLE

❏ BVLP-1016 [M]	Slim's Shout	1961	120.00
—Blue label, silver print			
❏ BVLP-1016 [M]	Slim's Shout	1964	30.00
—Blue label, trident logo at right			

PRESTIGE

| ❏ PRST-7723 | Slim's Shout | 1969 | 25.00 |

WORLD PACIFIC

| ❏ WPS-21890 | Slim's Got His Thing Goin' On | 1969 | 25.00 |

SUNRAYS, THE

TOWER

| ❏ T5017 [M] | Andrea | 1966 | 50.00 |
| ❏ ST5017 [S] | Andrea | 1966 | 60.00 |

SUNSET DRAGSTERS, THE

PALACE

| ❏ M-775 [M] | Hot Rod Rally | 196? | 80.00 |
| ❏ PST-775 [S] | Hot Rod Rally | 196? | 100.00 |

SUNSETS, THE (1)

PALACE

| ❏ M-752 [M] | Surfing with the Sunsets | 1963 | 40.00 |
| ❏ PST-752 [S] | Surfing with the Sunsets | 1963 | 50.00 |

SUNSHINE, MONTY

STOMP OFF

| ❏ SOS-1110 | New Orleans Hula | 1986 | 12.00 |

SUNSHINE BOYS, THE

DOT

| ❏ DLP-3189 [M] | Sing Unto Him | 1959 | 30.00 |
| ❏ DLP-25189 [S] | Sing Unto Him | 1959 | 40.00 |

STARDAY

❏ SLP-349 [M]	A Happy Home Up There	1965	30.00
❏ SLP-113 [M]	America's Number One Gospel Group	1960	40.00
❏ SLP-166 [M]	More Country Music Sing-Along	1962	30.00

SUNSHINE COMPANY, THE

IMPERIAL

❏ LP-9359 [M]	Happy Is the Sunshine Company	1967	25.00
❏ LP-12359 [S]	Happy Is the Sunshine Company	1967	25.00
❏ LP-12399	Sunshine and Shadows	1969	25.00
❏ LP-9368 [M]	The Sunshine Company	1968	30.00
—Mono copies are promo only			
❏ LP-12368 [S]	The Sunshine Company	1968	25.00

SUPER HEROINES, THE

CLEOPATRA

| ❏ 2243 [B] | L.A. Riot Grrrls - The Best Of 1982-1985 | | 25.00 |

SUPER STOCKS, THE

CAPITOL

❏ T1997 [M]	Hot Rod Rally	1963	50.00
❏ ST1997 [S]	Hot Rod Rally	1963	70.00
❏ T2190 [M]	School Is a Drag	1964	100.00
❏ ST2190 [S]	School Is a Drag	1964	120.00
❏ T2113 [M]	Surf Route 101	1964	100.00
—With bonus single, "Doin' the Surfink"/"Finksville, U.S.A." by Mr. Gasser and the Weirdos, in special pocket on front cover			
❏ T2113 [M]	Surf Route 101	1964	100.00
—Without bonus single			
❏ ST2113 [S]	Surf Route 101	1964	150.00
—With bonus single, "Doin' the Surfink"/"Finksville, U.S.A." by Mr. Gasser and the Weirdos, in special pocket on front cover			
❏ ST2113 [S]	Surf Route 101	1964	125.00
—Without bonus single			
❏ T2060 [M]	Thunder Road	1964	100.00
❏ ST2060 [S]	Thunder Road	1964	125.00
❏ (S)T2060	Thunder Road Bonus Poster	1964	50.00

SUPERBLUE

BLUE NOTE

| ❏ B1-91731 | Superblue | 1989 | 18.00 |

SUPERFINE DANDELION, THE

MAINSTREAM

| ❏ 56102 [M] | The Superfine Dandelion | 1967 | 100.00 |
| ❏ S-6102 [S] | The Superfine Dandelion | 1967 | 60.00 |

SUPERSAX

CAPITOL

| ❏ ST-11177 | Supersax Plays Bird | 1973 | 12.00 |

Number	Title	Yr	NM
❑ ST-11271	Supersax Plays Bird, Volume 2/Salt Peanuts	1974	12.00
❑ ST-11371	Supersax Plays Bird with Strings	1975	12.00

COLUMBIA

Number	Title	Yr	NM
❑ FC44436	Stone Bird	1989	15.00
❑ FC39140	Supersax and L.A. Voices	1984	12.00
❑ FC39925	Supersax and L.A. Voices, Vol. 2	1985	12.00
❑ FC40547	Supersax and L.A. Voices Volume 3: Straighten Up and Fly Right	1986	12.00

MOBILE FIDELITY

Number	Title	Yr	NM
❑ 1-511	Supersax Plays Bird	1981	40.00
—Audiophile vinyl			

PAUSA

Number	Title	Yr	NM
❑ 7038	Chasin' the Bird	1977	12.00
❑ 7082	Dynamite!	1979	12.00
❑ 9028	Supersax Plays Bird, Volume 2/Salt Peanuts	198?	10.00

SUPERSISTER

DWARF

Number	Title	Yr	NM
❑ PDLP-2001	Supersister	197?	30.00

SUPERTRAMP

A&M

Number	Title	Yr	NM
❑ SP-3708	Breakfast in America	1979	10.00
❑ SP-3730 [PD]	Breakfast in America	1979	500.00
—In-house picture discs featuring A&M staff members posing with the cover model			
❑ 2137081	Breakfast in America	2008	25.00
❑ SP-5013	Brother Where You Bound	1985	12.00
❑ SP-3647	Crime of the Century	1974	15.00
❑ 2136471	Crime of the Century	2008	25.00
❑ SP-4560	Crisis? What Crisis?	1975	15.00
❑ SP-3214	Crisis? What Crisis?	1982	10.00
—Budget-line reissue			
❑ SP-3215	Even in the Quietest Moments	1982	10.00
—Budget-line reissue			
❑ SP-4634	Even in the Quietest Moments…	1977	15.00
❑ SP-3732	…Famous Last Words…	1982	12.00
❑ SP-3284	…Famous Last Words…	1986	10.00
—Budget-line reissue			
❑ SP-5181	Free as a Bird	1987	12.00
❑ SP-4311 [B]	Indelibly Stamped	1971	30.00
—First edition with brown label			
❑ SP-3129	Indelibly Stamped	198?	10.00
—Budget-line reissue			
❑ SP-4311	Indelibly Stamped	197?	12.00
—Second edition with silverish label			
❑ SP-6702	Paris	1980	15.00
❑ SP-4274 [B]	Supertramp	1970	30.00
—First edition with brown label			
❑ SP-4665	Supertramp	1978	15.00
—Reissue of 4274			
❑ SP-3149	Supertramp	198?	10.00
—Budget-line reissue			
❑ SP-4274	Supertramp	197?	12.00
—Second edition with silverish label			

MOBILE FIDELITY

Number	Title	Yr	NM
❑ 1-045	Breakfast in America	1980	50.00
—Audiophile vinyl			
❑ 1-005 [B]	Crime of the Century	1979	60.00
—Audiophile vinyl			
❑ MFQR-005 [B]	Crime of the Century	1983	150.00
—Ultra High Quality Recording; in box			

SWEET THUNDER

Number	Title	Yr	NM
❑ 5 [B]	Even in the Quietest Moments…	198?	60.00
—Audiophile vinyl			

SUPREMES, THE, AND THE FOUR TOPS

MOTOWN

Number	Title	Yr	NM
❑ MS745	Dynamite	1971	18.00
❑ MS717	The Magnificent Seven	1970	18.00
❑ M5-123V1A	The Magnificent Seven	1981	15.00
—Reissue of Motown 717			
❑ MS736 [B]	The Return of the Magnificent Seven	1971	18.00

SUPREMES, THE, DIANA ROSS AND, AND THE TEMPTATIONS

MOTOWN

Number	Title	Yr	NM
❑ M679 [M]	Diana Ross and the Supremes Join the Temptations	1968	30.00
❑ MS679 [S]	Diana Ross and the Supremes Join the Temptations	1968	25.00
❑ M5-139V1	Diana Ross and the Supremes Join the Temptations	1981	15.00
—Reissue of Motown 679			
❑ MS699	On Broadway	1969	25.00
❑ MS682	TCB	1968	25.00
❑ M5-171V1	TCB	1981	15.00
—Reissue of Motown 682			

Number	Title	Yr	NM
❑ MS692	Together	1969	25.00

SUPREMES, THE

DORAL

Number	Title	Yr	NM
❑ DRL104	Doral Presents Diana Ross and the Supremes	1971	50.00
—Available through Doral cigarettes			

MOTOWN

Number	Title	Yr	NM
❑ 5381ML3	25th Anniversary	1986	25.00
—By "Diana Ross and the Supremes			
❑ M623 [M]	A Bit of Liverpool	1964	40.00
❑ MS623 [S]	A Bit of Liverpool	1964	50.00
❑ M9-794L3	Anthology (1962-1969)	1974	30.00
—By "Diana Ross and the Supremes			
❑ 5278ML	Captured Live on Stage	1982	10.00
—Reissue?			
❑ MS694	Cream of the Crop	1969	25.00
❑ M663 [M]	Diana Ross and the Supremes Greatest Hits	1967	30.00
❑ MS663 [S]	Diana Ross and the Supremes Greatest Hits	1967	40.00
❑ MS702	Diana Ross and the Supremes Greatest Hits, Volume 3	1970	25.00
❑ M5-203V1	Diana Ross and the Supremes Greatest Hits, Volume 3	1981	15.00
—Reissue of Motown 702			
❑ MT/MS663	Diana Ross and the Supremes Greatest Hits Poster	1967	12.00
❑ 5371ML	Diana Ross and the Supremes Sing Motown	1985	12.00
❑ MS708	Farewell	1970	30.00
—By "Diana Ross and the Supremes			
❑ M751L	Floy Joy	1972	18.00
❑ MS672 [S]	Funny Girl	1968	25.00
—The above LP came out before Motown 670			
❑ M672 [M]	Funny Girl	1968	30.00
—Mono appears to be promo only			
❑ M5-237V1	Greatest Hits	1982	12.00
—Reissue (unknown if it's the complete 2-record set or an edited version)			
❑ 5313ML	Great Songs and Performances That Inspired the Motown 25th Anniversary TV Special	1983	12.00
❑ M6-863S1	High Energy	1976	18.00
❑ M643 [M]	I Hear a Symphony	1966	30.00
❑ MS643 [S]	I Hear a Symphony	1966	30.00
❑ M5-147V1	I Hear a Symphony	1981	15.00
—Reissue of Motown 643			
❑ MS689	Let the Sunshine In	1969	25.00
❑ 5305ML	Let the Sunshine In	1983	10.00
—Reissue of MS 689			
❑ M670 [M]	Live at London's Talk of the Town	1968	30.00
—Mono is promo only			
❑ MS676 [S]	Live at London's Talk of the Town	1968	25.00
—The above LP came out before Motown 670 and 672			
❑ MS670	Love Child	1968	25.00
❑ 5245ML	Love Child	1982	10.00
—Reissue of MS 670			
❑ M6-873S1	Mary, Scherrie and Susaye	1976	18.00
❑ M606 [M]	Meet the Supremes	1963	900.00
—With group sitting on stools			
❑ M606 [M]	Meet the Supremes	1963	30.00
—With close-up of group's faces			
❑ MS606 [S]	Meet the Supremes	1964	40.00
—With close-up of group's faces			
❑ M5-223V1	Meet the Supremes	1982	10.00
—Reissue of Motown 606			
❑ MT638 [M]	Merry Christmas	1965	30.00
❑ MS638 [S]	Merry Christmas	1965	40.00
—Same as above, but in stereo			
❑ 5252ML	Merry Christmas	1982	12.00
—Reissue of MS 638			
❑ M627 [M]	More Hits by the Supremes	1965	30.00
❑ MS627 [S]	More Hits by the Supremes	1965	30.00
❑ 5361ML	Motown Legends	1985	12.00
❑ MS720	New Ways But Love Stays	1970	18.00
❑ M665 [M]	Reflections	1968	30.00
❑ MS665 [S]	Reflections	1968	25.00
❑ MS705	Right On	1970	18.00
—By "The Supremes"; the first LP after Diana Ross left			
❑ M5-101V1	Superstar Series, Vol. 1	1981	15.00
—By "Diana Ross and the Supremes			
❑ M756L	The Supremes	1972	18.00
❑ M6-828	The Supremes	1975	18.00
❑ M649 [M]	The Supremes A' Go-Go	1966	30.00
❑ MS649 [S]	The Supremes A' Go-Go	1966	30.00
❑ M5-138V1	The Supremes A' Go-Go	1981	15.00
—Reissue of Motown 649			
❑ M636 [M]	The Supremes at the Copa	1965	30.00
❑ MS636 [S]	The Supremes at the Copa	1965	30.00
❑ M5-162V1	The Supremes at the Copa	1981	15.00
—Reissue of Motown 636			
❑ M7-904R1	The Supremes at Their Best	1978	18.00
❑ MT-625 [M]	The Supremes Sing Country, Western & Pop	1965	30.00
❑ MS625 [S]	The Supremes Sing Country, Western & Pop	1965	30.00
❑ M5-158V1	The Supremes Sing Country Western and Pop	1981	10.00
—Reissue of Motown 625			
❑ M650 [M]	The Supremes Sing Holland-Dozier-Holland	1967	30.00
❑ MS650 [S]	The Supremes Sing Holland-Dozier-Holland	1967	30.00
❑ M5-182V1	The Supremes Sing Holland-Dozier-Holland	1981	15.00
—Reissue of Motown 650			
❑ M659 [M]	The Supremes Sing Rodgers & Hart	1967	30.00
❑ MS659 [S]	The Supremes Sing Rodgers & Hart	1967	30.00
❑ MS737	Touch	1971	18.00
❑ PR-102 [DJ]	Touch Interview	1971	30.00
❑ PR-102 [DJ]	Touch Interview	1971	30.00
❑ M629 [M]	We Remember Sam Cooke	1965	30.00
❑ MS629 [S]	We Remember Sam Cooke	1965	30.00
—The above LP came out before Motown 627			
❑ M621 [M]	Where Did Our Love Go	1964	30.00
❑ MS621 [S]	Where Did Our Love Go	1964	40.00
❑ 5270ML	Where Did Our Love Go	1982	10.00
—Reissue of MS 621			

NATURAL RESOURCES

Number	Title	Yr	NM
❑ NR4010	Merry Christmas	1978	15.00
—Reissue of Motown 638			
❑ NR4006T1	Where Did Our Love Go	1978	15.00
—Reissue of Motown 621			

PICKWICK

Number	Title	Yr	NM
❑ SPC-3383	Baby Love	197?	15.00
—Edited reissue of Motown 621			

UNIVERSAL MOTOWN

Number	Title	Yr	NM
❑ 5315839	I Hear a Symphony	2009	25.00

SURE!, AL B.

WARNER BROS.

Number	Title	Yr	NM
❑ 25662	In Effect Mode	1988	10.00
❑ 26005	Private Times...And the Whole 9!	1990	15.00

SURF STOMPERS, THE

DEL-FI

Number	Title	Yr	NM
❑ DFLP-1236 [M]	The Original Surfer Stomp	1963	60.00
❑ DFST-1236 [S]	The Original Surfer Stomp	1963	80.00
❑ DLF-1236	The Original Surfer Stomp	1997	15.00

SURF TEENS, THE

SUTTON

Number	Title	Yr	NM
❑ SU-339 [M]	Surf Mania	1963	50.00
❑ SSU-339 [S]	Surf Mania	1963	60.00

SURFARIS, THE (1)

DECCA

Number	Title	Yr	NM
❑ DL4560 [M]	Fun City, U.S.A.	1964	40.00
❑ DL74560 [S]	Fun City, U.S.A.	1964	60.00
❑ DL4487 [M]	Hit City '64	1964	40.00
❑ DL74487 [S]	Hit City '64	1964	60.00
❑ DL4614 [M]	Hit City '65	1965	40.00
❑ DL74614 [S]	Hit City '65	1965	60.00
❑ DL4663 [M]	It Ain't Me, Babe	1965	40.00
❑ DL74663 [S]	It Ain't Me, Babe	1965	60.00
❑ DL4470 [M]	The Surfaris Play Wipe Out	1963	40.00
❑ DL74470 [S]	The Surfaris Play Wipe Out	1963	30.00

DOT

Number	Title	Yr	NM
❑ DLP-3535 [M]	Wipe Out	1963	50.00
—With back cover photo featuring five Surfaris			
❑ DLP-3535 [M]	Wipe Out	1963	40.00
—With back cover photo featuring four Surfaris			
❑ DLP-3535 [M]	Wipe Out	1963	30.00
—With no back cover photo of the Surfaris			
❑ DLP-25535 [S]	Wipe Out	1963	80.00
—With back cover photo featuring five Surfaris			
❑ DLP-25535 [S]	Wipe Out	1963	50.00
—With back cover photo featuring four Surfaris			
❑ DLP-25535 [S]	Wipe Out	1963	40.00
—With no back cover photo of the Surfaris			

PICKWICK

Number	Title	Yr	NM
❑ SPC-3636	Wipe Out and Surfer Joe	1978	18.00

SURFARIS, THE (2)

DIPLOMAT

Number	Title	Yr	NM
❑ D-2309 [M]	Wheels-Shorts-Hot Rods	1963	30.00
—As "The Original Surfaris			
❑ DS-2309 [S]	Wheels-Shorts-Hot Rods	1963	30.00
—As "The Original Surfaris			

SUNDAZED

Number	Title	Yr	NM
❑ LP-5014	Bombora!	199?	12.00
—As "The Original Surfaris			

SURFERS, THE

HIFI

Number	Title	Yr	NM
❑ R-408 [M]	On the Rocks	1959	120.00
❑ SR-408 [S]	On the Rocks	1959	150.00

Number	Title	Yr	NM

SURFRIDERS, THE

VAULT
LP-105 [M]	Surfbeat, Volume 2	1963	30.00
VS-105 [S]	Surfbeat, Volume 2	1963	40.00

SURFSIDERS, THE

DESIGN
DLPS-208 [S]	The Surfsiders Sing The Beach Boys Songbook	1965	25.00
DLP-208 [M]	The Surfsiders Sing The Beach Boys Songbook	1965	18.00

SURMAN, JOHN

ANTILLES
AN-7004	Morning Glory	197?	15.00

ECM
1148	Reflection	197?	15.00
23795	Such Winters of Memory	1983	12.00
1193	The Amazing Adventures of Simon Simon	1981	15.00
1295	Withholding Pattern	1986	15.00

SURPRISE PACKAGE

LHI
S-12005 [B]	Free Up	1968	40.00

SURRATT, CECIL, AND SMITTY SMITH

AUDIO LAB
AL-1565 [M]	Songs Everybody Knows	1961	100.00

KING
860 [M]	Country Music from the Heart of the Country	1963	50.00
966 [M]	Good Country Singin' and Pickin'	1966	40.00

SURVIVOR

SCOTTI BROTHERS
QZ38791	Caught in the Game	1983	10.00
FZ38062	Eye of the Tiger	1982	10.00
ARZ37549	Premonition	1981	12.00
SB7107	Survivor	1980	15.00
OZ44282	Too Hot to Sleep	1988	10.00
FZ39578	Vital Signs	1984	10.00
FZ40457	When Seconds Count	1986	10.00

SUSSMAN, RICHARD

INNER CITY
IC-1045	Free Fall	1978	15.00
IC-1068	Tributaries	1979	15.00

SUTCH, SCREAMING LORD

COTILLION
SD9049	Hands of Jack the Ripper	1972	30.00
SD9015	Lord Sutch and Heavy Friends	1970	30.00
— With Jimmy Page, John Bonham and Jeff Beck

SUTHERLAND, JOAN

LONDON
5943 [M]	Joy of Christmas	1965	15.00
OS25943 [S]	Joy of Christmas	1965	18.00

SUTHERLAND BROTHERS

COLUMBIA
JC35293	Down to Earth	1978	12.00
JC35703	When the Night Comes Down	1979	12.00

ISLAND
SW-9315	The Sutherland Brothers Band	1972	15.00

SUTHERLAND BROTHERS AND QUIVER

COLUMBIA
PC33982	Reach for the Sky	1976	12.00
PC34376	Slipstream	1977	12.00

ISLAND
SW-9341	Dream Kid	1974	12.00
SW-9326	Lifeboat	1973	12.00

SUTTON, DICK

JAGUAR
JP-802 [10]	Jazz Idiom	1954	80.00
JP-804 [10]	Progressive Dixieland	1954	80.00

SUTTON, GLENN

MERCURY
SRM-1-5018	Close Encounters of the Sutton Kind	1979	12.00

SUTTON, RALPH

ANALOGUE PRODUCTIONS
AP 018	Partners in Crime	199?	30.00
— Audiophile vinyl

AUDIOPHILE
AP-163	Off the Cuff	198?	12.00

CIRCLE
L-413 [10]	Ralph Sutton	1951	80.00

COLUMBIA
CL6140 [10]	Piano Moods	1950	80.00

COMMODORE
XFL-16570	Bix Beiderbecke Suite and Jazz Portraits	198?	12.00
FL-30001 [M]	Ralph Sutton	1951	80.00

DECCA
DL5498 [10]	I Got Rhythm	1953	80.00

DOWN HOME
MGD-4 [M]	Backroom Piano: The Ragtime Piano of Ralph Sutton	1955	60.00
DH-1003 [10]	Ragtime Piano Solos	1953	80.00

HARMONY
HL7109 [M]	Tribute to Fats	1958	25.00

JAZZ ARCHIVES
JA-45	Ralph Sutton and the All-Stars	198?	12.00

JAZZOLOGY
JCE-92	Alligator Crawl	197?	12.00

OMEGA
OML-51 [M]	Jazz At the Olympics	196?	18.00
OSL-51 [S]	Jazz At the Olympics	196?	25.00

PROJECT 3
PR5040SD	Knocked Out Nocturne	1969	15.00

RIVERSIDE
RLP 12-212 [M]	Classic Jazz Piano	1956	60.00

ROULETTE
R-25232 [M]	Ragtime, U.S.A.	1963	18.00
SR-25232 [S]	Ragtime, U.S.A.	1963	25.00

SACKVILLE
2012	Piano Solos	198?	12.00

STORYVILLE
4013	Ralph Sutton Quartet	198?	12.00

VERVE
MGV-1004 [M]	Backroom Piano: The Ragtime Piano of Ralph Sutton	1956	50.00

SUZUKI, PAT

RCA VICTOR
LPM-1965 [M]	Broadway '59	1959	25.00
LSP-1965 [S]	Broadway '59	1959	30.00
LPM-2186 [M]	Looking at You	1960	25.00
LSP-2186 [S]	Looking at You	1960	30.00
LPM-2030 [M]	Pat Suzuki	1959	25.00
LSP-2030 [S]	Pat Suzuki	1959	30.00

VIK
LX-1147 [M]	Pat Suzuki	1958	30.00
LX-1127 [M]	The Many Sides of Pat Suzuki	1958	30.00

SVENSSON, REINHOLD

PRESTIGE
PRLP-155 [10]	New Sounds from Sweden, Volume 8	1953	200.00
PRLP-129 [10]	Reinhold Svensson, Volume 2: Favorites	1952	200.00
PRLP-106 [10]	Reinhold Svensson Piano	1951	200.00

SVENSSON, REINHOLD/BENGT HALLBERG

PRESTIGE
PRLP-174 [10]	Piano Moderns	1953	200.00

SWAGGART, JIMMY

JIM
24-141	Silver Jubilee Album: The Very Best of Jimmy Swaggart	1981	25.00
— One of the two records is a picture disc

SWAGMEN, THE

PARKWAY
P-7015 [M]	Meet the Swagmen	1962	40.00
SP-7015 [S]	Meet the Swagmen	1962	50.00

SWALLOW, STEVE

ECM
1160	Home	1979	15.00

SWAMP DOGG

CANYON
LP-7706	Total Destruction to Your Mind	1970	30.00

ELEKTRA
EKS-74089	Rat On	1971	25.00

SWAMPWATER

KING
KSD-1122	Swampwater	1971	18.00

RCA VICTOR
LSP-4572	Swampwater	1971	18.00

SWAN, BILLY

A&M
SP-4686	You're OK, I'm OK	1978	12.00

COLUMBIA
PZ34183	Billy Swan	1977	10.00
— Reissue of Monument 34183
| PC34473 | Four | 1977 | 12.00 |
| PZ33279 | I Can Help | 1977 | 10.00 |
— Reissue of Monument 33279
| PZ33805 | Rock 'n' Roll Moon | 1977 | 10.00 |
— Reissue of Monument 33805

EPIC
FE37079	I'm Into Lovin' You	1981	12.00

MONUMENT
PZ34183	Billy Swan	1976	12.00
7629	Billy Swan At His Best	1978	12.00
KZ33279	I Can Help	1974	12.00
PZ33805	Rock 'n' Roll Moon	1975	12.00

SWAN SILVERTONES, THE

SPECIALTY
SPS-2122	Love Lifted Me	1970	25.00
SPS-2148	My Rock	1971	25.00

UPFRONT
UPF-112	The Lord's Prayer	1968	25.00

VEE JAY
LP-5034 [M]	Blessed Assurance	1963	30.00
LP-5059 [M]	Let's Go to Church Together	1964	30.00
SR-5059 [S]	Let's Go to Church Together	1964	30.00
VJS-18008	Pray for Me	1975	25.00
LP-5013 [M]	Savior Pass Me Not	1962	30.00
LP-5006 [M]	Singing in My Soul	1960	30.00
LP-5052 [M]	The Best of the Swan Silvertones	1963	30.00
LP-5003 [M]	The Swan Silvertones	1959	40.00

SWANN, BETTYE

ABET
LP405 [B]	Make Me Yours	197?	25.00

CAPITOL
ST-270	Don't You Ever Get Tired of Hurting Me	1969	50.00
ST-190	The Soul View Now!	1969	100.00

COLLECTABLES
COL-5177	Make Me Yours	198?	12.00

MONEY
1103 [M]	Make Me Yours	1967	30.00
S-1103 [S]	Make Me Yours	1967	30.00

SWANSON, RIC

ARMERICAN GRAMAPHONE
AG-600	Urban Surrender	1985	12.00

OPTIMISM
OP-3220	Renewal	198?	15.00

SWARTZ, HARVIE

GRAMAVISION
8202	Underneath It All	198?	12.00
18-8503-1	Urban Earth	1986	12.00

SWEAT, ISAAC PAYTON

BELLAIRE
LP1100	Cotton Eyed Joe/Shottish	1980	15.00

PAID
2005	Cotton-Eyed Joe	1981	15.00

SWEAT, KEITH

ELEKTRA
61707	Keith Sweat	1996	15.00
ED5872 [DJ]	Keith Sweat	1996	18.00
— Promo-only sampler from LP of the same name

VINTERTAINMENT
60861	I'll Give All My Love to You	1990	15.00
60763	Make It Last Forever	1987	10.00

SWEATHOG

COLUMBIA
KC31144	Hallelujah	1972	15.00
C30601	Sweathog	1971	15.00

SWEDES FROM JAZZVILLE

EPIC
LN3309 [M]	Swedes from Jazzville	195?	50.00

SWEDISH JAZZ KINGS, THE

STOMP OFF
SOS-1188	After Midnight	1987	12.00
SOS-1122	What Makes Me Love You So?	1986	12.00

SWEENEY TODD

LONDON
PS694	If Wishes Were Horses	1977	60.00
— Possibly a Canadian import only

Number	Title	Yr	NM

SWEET, MATTHEW

A&M
| □ SP-5233 | Earth | 1989 | 18.00 |

COLUMBIA
| □ BFC40417 | Inside | 1986 | 18.00 |

ZOO
| □ 31130 | Blue Sky on Mars | 1997 | 18.00 |
— All copies authographed by Matthew Steel on the label

ZOO/CLASSIC
| □ 11081 | 100% Fun | 1995 | 25.00 |
| □ 11050 [B] | Altered Beast | 1995 | 30.00 |
— Audiophile vinyl pressing; released on CD in 1993
| □ 11015 | Girlfriend | 1995 | 50.00 |
— Audiophile vinyl pressing; released on CD in 1991

SWEET, RACHEL

COLUMBIA
| □ FC38342 | Blame It on Love | 1982 | 12.00 |

STIFF/COLUMBIA
□ ARC37077	...And Then He Kissed Me	1981	12.00
□ JC36101	Fool Around	1979	15.00
□ NJC36337	Protect the Innocent	1980	12.00
□ JC36337	Protect the Innocent	1980	12.00

SWEET, THE

CLEOPATRA
| □ 3955 [B] | Live In Denmark 1976 | | 25.00 |

SWEET, THE (1)

BEAT ROCKET
| □ BR125 | Hell Raisers! | 2000 | 15.00 |

BELL
| □ 1125 | The Sweet | 1973 | 30.00 |

CAPITOL
| □ ST-11929 | Cut Above the Rest | 1979 | 15.00 |
| □ SN-16118 | Cut Above the Rest | 1980 | 10.00 |
— Budget-line reissue
| □ PRO-11929 [DJ] | Cut Above the Rest | 1979 | 50.00 |
— Special promo box contains record, cassette, 8-track, photo, bio
| □ ST-11395 | Desolation Boulevard | 1975 | 15.00 |
| □ SN-16287 | Desolation Boulevard | 1981 | 10.00 |
— Budget-line reissue
□ SPRO-8371/2 [DJ]	For A.O.R. Radio Only	1976	30.00
□ ST-11496	Give Us a Wink	1976	15.00
□ SN-16115	Give Us a Wink	1980	10.00
— Budget-line reissue
| □ SKAO-11744 | Level Headed | 1978 | 15.00 |
| □ SN-16117 | Level Headed | 1980 | 10.00 |
— Budget-line reissue
| □ STAO-11636 | Off the Record | 1977 | 15.00 |
| □ SN-16116 | Off the Record | 1980 | 10.00 |
— Budget-line reissue
| □ SPRO-8849 [DJ] | Short and Sweet | 1978 | 30.00 |
| □ ST-12106 | Sweet VI | 1980 | 15.00 |

KORY
| □ 3009 | The Sweet | 1977 | 15.00 |
— Reissue of Bell LP

SWEET CREAM

SHADY BROOK
| □ SB-011 | Sweet Cream and Other Delights | 1978 | 18.00 |

SWEET INSPIRATIONS, THE

ATLANTIC
□ SD8182	Songs of Faith and Inspiration	1968	25.00
□ SD8253	Sweet, Sweet Soul	1970	25.00
□ SD8225	Sweets for My Sweet	1969	25.00
□ SD8155	The Sweet Inspirations	1968	25.00
□ 8201 [M]	What the World Needs Now	1969	50.00
— Mono is white label promo only; "d/j copy monaural" sticker on stereo cover
| □ SD8201 [S] | What the World Needs Now Is Love | 1969 | 25.00 |

RSO
| □ RS-1-3058 | Hot Butterfly | 1979 | 12.00 |

STAX
| □ STS-3017 | Estelle, Myrna and Sylvia | 1973 | 25.00 |

SWEET PANTS

BARKLEY
| □ 1141 | Fat Peter Presents Sweet Pants | 1969 | 200.00 |

SWEET SENSATION (1)

PYE
| □ 12110 | Sweet Sensation | 1975 | 12.00 |

SWEET SENSATION (2)

ATCO
| □ 90917 | Take It While It's Hot | 1988 | 12.00 |
| □ 91722 | Time to Jam! The Remix Album | 1991 | 18.00 |

SWEET THURSDAY

TETRAGRAMMATON
| □ T-112 | Sweet Thursday | 1969 | 25.00 |

SWEET TOOTHE

DOMINION
| □ NR-7360 | Testing | 1974 | 300.00 |

SWEETHEARTS OF THE RODEO

COLUMBIA
| □ FC40614 | One Time, One Night | 1988 | 10.00 |
| □ B6C40406 | Sweethearts of the Rodeo | 1986 | 10.00 |

SWEETWATER

REPRISE
□ RS6417	Just for You	1970	18.00
□ RS6473	Melon	1971	18.00
□ RS6313	Sweetwater	1968	18.00

SWENSON, INGA

LIBERTY
| □ LRP-3379 [M] | I'm Old Fashioned | 1964 | 30.00 |
| □ LST-7379 [S] | I'm Old Fashioned | 1964 | 30.00 |

SWIFT, DUNCAN

BLACK LION
| □ 301 | Piano Ragtime: Joplin and Morton | 197? | 15.00 |

SWIFT RAIN

HI
| □ SHL-32064 | Coming Down | 1971 | 30.00 |

SWIMMING POOL Q'S, THE

A&M
| □ SP-5107 | Blue Tomorrow | 1986 | 12.00 |

CAPITOL
| □ C1-91068 | World War Two Point Five | 1989 | 15.00 |

DB
| □ 87 [EP] | Firing Squad for God | 1985 | 10.00 |
| □ 55 | The Deep End | 1981 | 18.00 |

SWING OUT SISTER

FONTANA
| □ 838293-1 | Kaleidoscope World | 1989 | 15.00 |

MERCURY
| □ 832213-1 | It's Better to Travel | 1987 | 12.00 |

SWINGIN' MEDALLIONS

SMASH
| □ MGS-27083 [M] | Double Shot (Of My Baby's Love) | 1966 | 40.00 |
— First pressing contains the original 45 version of the title song
| □ MGS-27083 [M] | Double Shot (Of My Baby's Love) | 1966 | 30.00 |
— Later pressings contain a "censored" version of the title song
| □ SRS-67083 [S] | Double Shot (Of My Baby's Love) | 1966 | 50.00 |
— First pressing contains the original 45 version of the title song
| □ SRS-67083 [S] | Double Shot (Of My Baby's Love) | 1966 | 40.00 |
— Later pressings contain a "censored" version of the title song

SWINGING BLUE JEANS, THE

IMPERIAL
| □ LP-9261 [M] | Hippy Hippy Shake | 1964 | 100.00 |
| □ LP-12261 [R] | Hippy Hippy Shake | 1964 | 100.00 |

SWINGING SWEDES, THE

TELEFUNKEN
| □ LGX-66050 [M] | The Swinging Swedes | 195? | 50.00 |

SWINGING SWEDES, THE/THE COOL BRITONS

BLUE NOTE
| □ BLP-5019 [10] | New Sounds from the Olde World | 1951 | 300.00 |

SWITCH

GORDY
□ G8-993M1	Reaching for Tomorrow	1980	15.00
□ G7-980R1	Switch	1978	15.00
□ G7-988R1	Switch II	1979	15.00
□ G8-1007M1	Switch V	1981	15.00
□ G8-999M1	This Is My Dream	1980	15.00

TOTAL EXPERIENCE

| □ TEL-8-5701 | Am I Still Your Boyfriend? | 1984 | 12.00 |

SWITTEL, JIMMY

DECCA
| □ DL8618 [M] | Hymns to the Blessed Virgin Mary | 1957 | 25.00 |

SYKES, ROOSEVELT

BLUESVILLE
| □ BVLP-1014 [M] | The Honeydripper | 1961 | 100.00 |
— Blue label, silver print
| □ BVLP-1014 [M] | The Honeydripper | 1964 | 30.00 |
— Blue label, trident logo at right
| □ BVLP-1006 [M] | The Return of Roosevelt Sykes | 1960 | 100.00 |
— Blue label, silver print
| □ BVLP-1006 [M] | The Return of Roosevelt Sykes | 1964 | 30.00 |
— Blue label, trident logo at right

CROWN
| □ CLP-5287 [M] | Roosevelt Sykes Sings the Blues | 1962 | 50.00 |
| □ CST-287 [S] | Roosevelt Sykes Sings the Blues | 1962 | 50.00 |

DELMARK
| □ DL-607 | The Hard Driving Blues of Roosevelt Sykes | 1963 | 50.00 |

SYLVAIN SYLVAIN

RCA VICTOR
| □ DJL1-4062 [DJ] | RCA Special Radio Series XII | 1981 | 25.00 |
— Promo-only interviews and music
| □ AFL1-3913 | Syl Sylvain and the Teardrops | 1982 | 15.00 |
| □ AFL1-3475 | Sylvain Sylvain | 1980 | 15.00 |

SYLVERN, HANK

ABC-PARAMOUNT
| □ 146 [M] | Christmas in Hi-Fi | 1956 | 30.00 |

SYLVERS, FOSTER

PRIDE
| □ 0027 | Foster Sylvers | 1973 | 15.00 |

SYLVERS, THE

CAPITOL
□ ST-11868	Best of the Sylvers	1978	12.00
□ ST-11705	New Horizons	1977	12.00
□ ST-11465	Showcase	1976	12.00
□ ST 11580	Something Special	1976	12.00

CASABLANCA
| □ NBLP7151 | Disco Fever | 1979 | 12.00 |
| □ NBLP7103 | Forever Yours | 1978 | 12.00 |

GEFFEN
| □ GHS24039 | Bizarre | 1984 | 12.00 |

MGM
| □ SE-4930 | The Sylvers III | 1974 | 12.00 |

PRIDE
| □ 0007 | The Sylvers | 1972 | 15.00 |
| □ 0026 | The Sylvers II | 1973 | 15.00 |

SOLAR
| □ 22 | Concept | 1981 | 12.00 |

SYLVESTER, TERRY

EPIC
| □ KE33076 | Terry Sylvester | 1974 | 15.00 |

SYLVIA (1)

STANG
| □ 1010 | Sylvia | 197? | 25.00 |

SUGAR HILL
| □ 258 | Sylvia I | 1981 | 12.00 |

VIBRATION
□ 143	Brand New Funk	197?	15.00
□ 131	Lay It On Me	1977	15.00
□ 126	Pillow Talk	1973	18.00

SYLVIA (2)

RCA
| □ 5618-1-R | Greatest Hits | 1987 | 10.00 |

RCA VICTOR
□ AHL1-3986	Drifter	1981	10.00
□ AHL1-4312	Just Sylvia	1982	10.00
□ AHL1-5413	One Step Closer	1985	10.00
□ AHL1-4672	Snapshot	1983	10.00
□ AHL1-4960	Surprise	1984	10.00

SYLVIAN, DAVID

VIRGIN
| □ 2167 [DJ] | Ink in the Well -- A Conversation | 1987 | 25.00 |
— Promo-only interview album
| □ 90904 | Plight and Premonition | 1988 | 12.00 |
— With Holger Czukay
| □ 90677 | Secrets of the Beehive | 1987 | 12.00 |

Number	Title	Yr	NM

SYMPHONY JAZZ ENSEMBLE

QCA
❑ 364	Carmen	197?	18.00
❑ 378	Eastside Corridor	197?	18.00

SYMS, SYLVIA

20TH CENTURY FOX
❑ TFM-4123 [M]	The Fabulous Sylvia Syms	1963	30.00
❑ TFS-4123 [S]	The Fabulous Sylvia Syms	1963	30.00

ATLANTIC
❑ ALS-137 [10]	Songs by Sylvia Syms	1952	100.00
❑ 1243 [M]	Songs by Sylvia Syms	1956	50.00
— Black label
| ❑ 1243 [M] | Songs by Sylvia Syms | 1960 | 30.00 |
— Multicolor label, white "fan" logo at right

COLUMBIA
❑ CL1447 [M]	Torch Song	1960	30.00
— Red and black label with six "eye" logos
| ❑ CS8243 [S] | Torch Song | 1960 | 40.00 |
— Red and black label with six "eye" logos

DECCA
❑ DL8639 [M]	Songs of Love	1958	40.00
— Black label, silver print
| ❑ DL8188 [M] | Sylvia Syms Sings | 1955 | 50.00 |
— Black label, silver print

KAPP
❑ KL-1236 [M]	That Man -- Love Songs to Frank Sinatra	1961	30.00
❑ KS-3236 [S]	That Man -- Love Songs to Frank Sinatra	1961	40.00

MOVIETONE
❑ 2022 [M]	In a Sentimental Mood	1967	25.00
❑ 72022 [S]	In a Sentimental Mood	1967	18.00

PRESTIGE
❑ PRLP-7489 [M]	For Once in My Life	1967	30.00
❑ PRST-7489 [S]	For Once in My Life	1967	25.00
❑ PRLP-7439 [M]	Sylvia Is!	1965	25.00
❑ PRST-7439 [S]	Sylvia Is!	1965	30.00

VERSION
❑ VLP-103 [10]	After Dark	1954	80.00

SYNDICATE OF SOUND

BELL
❑ 6001 [M]	Little Girl	1966	50.00
❑ S-6001 [S]	Little Girl	1966	80.00

SUNDAZED
❑ LP5051	Little Girl	2001	15.00
— Reissue on 180-gram vinyl

SYNERGY

AUDION
❑ SYN204	Metropolitan Suite	1987	12.00

PASSPORT
❑ PB6005	Audion	1981	12.00
❑ PG-1	Computer Experiments Volume One	1981	18.00
❑ PB6000	Cords	1978	18.00
— First pressing on clear vinyl
| ❑ PB6000 | Cords | 1978 | 12.00 |
— Later pressings on black vinyl
| ❑ PPSD-98009 | Electronic Realizations for Rock Orchestra | 1975 | 15.00 |
| ❑ PB6001 | Electronic Realizations for Rock Orchestra | 1979 | 12.00 |
— Reissue of 98009
❑ PB6003	Games	1979	12.00
❑ P2B11002	Semi-Conductor	1984	15.00
❑ PPSD-98014	Sequencer	1976	15.00
❑ PB6002	Sequencer	1979	12.00
— Reissue of 98014

SYNTHESIS

CHIAROSCURO
❑ 172	Six by Six	197?	15.00

SZABO, GABOR

ABC IMPULSE!
❑ AS-9105	Gypsy 66	1968	15.00
❑ AS-9204	His Great Hits	1971	18.00
❑ AS-9128	Jazz Raga	1968	15.00
❑ AS-9159	Light My Fire	1968	18.00
❑ AS-9167	More Sorcery	1968	18.00
❑ AS-9123	Spellbinder	1968	15.00
❑ AS-9173	The Best of Gabor Szabo	1968	18.00
❑ AS-9146	The Sorcerer	1968	15.00
❑ AS-9151	Wind, Sky and Diamonds	1968	18.00

BLUE THUMB
❑ BTS-28	High Contrast	1972	15.00
— With Bobby Womack
| ❑ 6014 | Live | 1974 | 15.00 |
| ❑ BTS-8823 | Magical Connection | 1971 | 15.00 |

BUDDAH
❑ 20-SK	Blowin' Some Old Smoke	1971	15.00
❑ 18-SK	Watch What Happens	1970	15.00

CTI
❑ 6026	Mizrab	1973	15.00
❑ 6035	Rambler	1974	15.00

GRP/IMPULSE!
❑ IMP-211	The Sorcerer	199?	18.00
— Reissue on audiophile vinyl

IMPULSE!
❑ A-9105 [M]	Gypsy 66	1966	25.00
❑ AS-9105 [S]	Gypsy 66	1966	30.00
❑ A-9128 [M]	Jazz Raga	1967	30.00
❑ AS-9128 [S]	Jazz Raga	1967	25.00
❑ A-9123 [M]	Spellbinder	1966	25.00
❑ AS-9123 [S]	Spellbinder	1966	30.00
❑ A-9146 [M]	The Sorcerer	1967	30.00
❑ AS-9146 [S]	The Sorcerer	1967	25.00
❑ AS-9151	Wind, Sky and Diamonds	1968	30.00
— This exists on the pre-ABC Impulse! label, though theoretically it shouldn't. Other titles may exist on that label also.

MCA
❑ 4155	His Great Hits	198?	15.00

MERCURY
❑ SRM-1-1141	Faces	1977	12.00
❑ SRM-1-1091	Nightflight	1976	12.00

PEPITA
❑ 707	Femme Fatalo	198?	12.00

SALVATION
❑ 704	Macho	1975	15.00

SKYE
❑ SK-3 [S]	Bacchanal	1968	18.00
❑ MK-3 [M]	Bacchanal	1968	40.00
— Mono is promo only; "Monaural Promotion Copy" sticker on stereo cover
❑ SK-7	Dreams	1969	18.00
❑ SK-9	Gabor Szabo 1969	1969	18.00
❑ SK-15	Lena & Gabor	1970	18.00
— With Lena Horne

SZABO, RICH

BBW
❑ 2001	Best of Both Worlds	198?	15.00

SZAJNER, BOB

RMS
❑ 77004	Afterthoughts	198?	15.00
❑ 77003	Sound Ideas	198?	15.00

SEEDS & STEMS
❑ SSH-7802	Jazz Opus 20/40	1979	15.00

SZAKCSI

GRP
❑ GR-9577	Mystic Dreams	1989	15.00
❑ GR-1045	Sa-chi	1988	12.00

SZERYNG, HENRYK

MERCURY LIVING PRESENCE
❑ SR90466 [S]	Bach: Violin Concertos in A and E; Double Concerto in D	196?	70.00
— Maroon label, with "Vendor: Mercury Record Corporation
| ❑ SR90308 [S] | Brahms: Violin Concerto in D | 196? | 80.00 |
— With Antal Dorati/London Symphony Orchestra; maroon label, no "Vendor: Mercury Record Corporation
| ❑ SR90308 [S] | Brahms: Violin Concerto in D | 196? | 30.00 |
— With Antal Dorati/London Symphony Orchestra; maroon label, with "Vendor: Mercury Record Corporation
| ❑ SR90393 [S] | Khachaturian: Violin Concerto | 196? | 50.00 |
— With Antal Dorati/London Symphony Orchestra; maroon label, no "Vendor: Mercury Record Corporation
| ❑ SR90393 [S] | Khachaturian: Violin Concerto | 196? | 40.00 |
— With Antal Dorati/London Symphony Orchestra; maroon label, with "Vendor: Mercury Record Corporation
| ❑ SR90393 [S] | Khachaturian: Violin Concerto | 196? | 25.00 |
— With Antal Dorati/London Symphony Orchestra; third edition (dark red, not maroon, label)
| ❑ SR90348 [S] | Kreisler: Caprice Viennois and 12 Others | 196? | 30.00 |
— Maroon label, no "Vendor: Mercury Record Corporation
| ❑ SR90406 [S] | Mendelssohn: Violin Concerto in E; Schumann: Violin Concerto in D | 196? | 30.00 |
— With Antal Dorati/London Symphony Orchestra; maroon label, no "Vendor: Mercury Record Corporation
| ❑ SR90367 [S] | Treasures | 196? | 30.00 |
— Maroon label, no "Vendor: Mercury Record Corporation

RCA VICTOR RED SEAL
❑ LSC-2281 [S]	Brahms: Violin Concerto	1959	150.00
— With Pierre Monteux/London Symphony Orchestra; original with "shaded dog" label
| ❑ LSC-2421 [S] | In Recital | 1960 | 50.00 |
— Original with "shaded dog" label
| ❑ LSC-2456 [S] | Lalo: Symphonie Espagnole | 1961 | 200.00 |
— With Walter Hendl/Chicago Symphony Orch.; original with "shaded dog" label
| ❑ LSC-2363 [S] | Tchaikovsky: Violin Concerto in D | 1960 | 80.00 |

— With Charles Munch/Boston Symphony Orchestra; original with "shaded dog" label

SZERYNG, HENRYK / ARTUR RUBENSTEIN

RCA VICTOR RED SEAL
❑ LSC-2377 [S]	Beethoven: Kreutzer and Spring Sonatas	1960	40.00
— Original with "shaded dog" label
| ❑ LSC-2620 [S] | Beethoven: Violin Sonata No. 8; Brahms: Violin Sonata No. 1 | 1962 | 50.00 |
— Original with "shaded dog" label
| ❑ LSC-2619 [S] | Brahms: Violin Concertos 2 and 3 | 1962 | 50.00 |
— Original with "shaded dog" label

SZIGETI, JOSEF; MIECZYSLAW HORSZOWSKI; JOHN BARROWS

MERCURY LIVING PRESENCE
❑ SR90210 [S]	Brahms: Horn Trio; Violin Sonata No. 2	196?	180.00
— Maroon label, no "Vendor: Mercury Record Corporation
| ❑ SR90210 [S] | Brahms: Horn Trio; Violin Sonata No. 2 | 196? | 70.00 |
— Maroon label, with "Vendor: Mercury Record Corporation

SZIGETI, JOSEF

MERCURY LIVING PRESENCE
❑ SR90358 [S]	Beethoven: Violin Concerto in D	196?	100.00
— With Antal Dorati/London Symphony Orchestra; maroon label, no "Vendor: Mercury Record Corporation
| ❑ SR90225 [S] | Brahms: Violin Concerto in D | 196? | 180.00 |
— Maroon label, no "Vendor: Mercury Record Corporation
| ❑ SR90419 [S] | Prokofiev: Violin Concerto No. 1; Stravinsky: Duo Concertante | 196? | 30.00 |
— Maroon label, no "Vendor: Mercury Record Corporation
| ❑ SR90419 [S] | Prokofiev: Violin Concerto No. 1; Stravinsky: Duo Concertante | 196? | 50.00 |
— Maroon label, with "Vendor: Mercury Record Corporation" (second edition is more sought after than the first)
| ❑ SR90319 [S] | Prokofiev: Violin Sonatas No. 1 and 2 | 196? | 100.00 |
— Maroon label, no "Vendor: Mercury Record Corporation
| ❑ SR90442 [S] | Violin Sonatas | 1965 | 50.00 |
— Maroon label, with "Vendor: Mercury Record Corporation

SZOBEL, HERMANN

ARISTA
❑ AL4058	Szobel	1976	15.00

T

T, JEAN-CLAUDE

PHILADELPHIA INT'L.
❑ PZ34246 [B]	The Bicentennial Poet	1976	30.00

T. REX

CLEOPATRA
❑ 9625 [B]	Bang A Gong (Get It On)		25.00
❑ 1987 [B]	Electric Suicide		25.00

FAT POSSUM
❑ FP1244-1 [B]	Bolan's Zip Gun	2011	30.00
❑ FP1238-1 [B]	Tanx	2011	30.00
❑ FP1232-1 [B]	The Slider	2010	30.00
❑ FP1242-1 [B]	Zinc Alloy And The Hidden Riders of Tomorrow	2011	30.00

REPRISE
❑ PRO511 [DJ]	An Interview with Marc Bolan	1971	100.00

T. REX

A&M
❑ SP-3514	Tyrannosaurus Rex (A Beginning)	1972	18.00
— Compilation of early LPs Prophets, Seers & Sages and My People Were Fair and Had Sky in Their Hair But Now They're Content to Wear Stars on Their Brows

BLUE THUMB

— Add $5 for bonus single SP-6115/6, "Ride a White Swan"/"Is It Love." For reasons unknown, the single seems to be much more readily available than the LP

Number	Title	Yr	NM

Number	Title	Yr	NM
❑ BTS7 [B]	Unicorn	1969	30.00
CASABLANCA			
❑ NBLP7005	Light of Love	1974	15.00
—Reissue of 9006			
❑ NB9006	Light of Love	1974	18.00
—Original, distributed by Warner Bros.			
MARC ON WAX/RELATIVITY			
❑ 8249	Bolan's Zip Gun	198?	12.00
❑ 8251	Dandy in the Underworld	198?	12.00
❑ 8252	Futuristic Dragon	198?	12.00
❑ 8254	Tanx	198?	12.00
❑ 8253	The Slider	198?	12.00
❑ 8250	Zinc Alloy & The Hidden Riders of Tomorrow	198?	12.00
REPRISE			
❑ PRO511 [DJ]	An Interview with Marc Bolan	1971	100.00
❑ RS6466 [B]	Electric Warrior	1971	30.00
❑ MS2132 [B]	Tanx	1973	35.00
❑ MS2095 [B]	The Slider	1972	25.00
❑ RS6440	T. Rex	1971	16.00
RHINO			
❑ R1-76111	Electric Warrior	2003	18.00
—Reissue on 180-gram vinyl			
WARNER BROS.			
❑ 25333	T. Rextasy: The Best of T. Rex, 1970-1973	1985	12.00

T.A.T.U.

INTERSCOPE

❑ B0005382-01 [B]	Dangerous and Moving	2005	50.00

T-BONES, THE

LIBERTY

❑ LRP-3346 [M]	Boss Drag	1963	60.00
❑ LST-7346 [S]	Boss Drag	1963	100.00
❑ LRP-3363 [M]	Boss Drag at the Beach	1964	60.00
❑ LST-7303 [3]	Boss Drag at the Beach	1964	100.00
❑ LRP-3404 [M]	Doin' the Jerk	1965	40.00
❑ LST-7404 [M]	Doin' the Jerk	1965	60.00
❑ LRP-3471 [M]	Everyone's Gone to the Moon	1966	35.00
❑ LST-7471 [S]	Everyone's Gone to the Moon	1966	30.00
❑ LRP-3439 [M]	No Matter What Shape (Your Stomach's In)	1966	25.00
❑ LST-7439 [S]	No Matter What Shape (Your Stomach's In)	1966	30.00
❑ LRP-3446 [M]	Sippin' and Chippin'	1966	25.00
❑ LST-7446 [S]	Sippin' and Chippin'	1966	30.00
SUNSET			
❑ SUM-1119 [M]	Shapin' Things Up	196?	15.00
❑ SUS-5119 [S]	Shapin' Things Up	196?	18.00

T.C. ATLANTIC

DOVE

❑ LP-4459	T.C. Atlantic	1966	100.00

T.I.M.E.

LIBERTY

❑ LST-7605	Smooth Ball	1969	30.00
❑ LST-7558	T.I.M.E.	1968	30.00

T-MODEL FORD

FAT POSSUM

❑ 80303-1 [B]	Pee-Wee Get My Gun	1997	18.00

T.S.O.L.

CLEOPATRA

❑ 5569 [B]	Code Blue		25.00

T-SQUARE

PORTRAIT

❑ FR44193	Truth	1988	12.00

T.V. AND THE TRIBESMEN

HANNA-BARBERA

❑ HLP-9507 [S]	Barefootin'	1966	30.00

T2

LONDON

❑ PS583 [B]	It'll All Work Out in Boomland	1971	100.00

TABACKIN, LEW

INNER CITY

❑ IC-1028	Dual Nature	1976	15.00
❑ IC-6052	Rites of Pan	197?	18.00
❑ IC-1038	Tabackin	1977	15.00
❑ IC-6048	Tenor Gladness	197?	18.00
JAM			
❑ 5005	Black and Tan Fantasy	198?	15.00

TABOR, ERON

STUDIO ONE

❑ S-104	Eron Tabor	196?	25.00

TACO

RCA VICTOR

❑ AFL1-4818	After Eight	1983	10.00
❑ CPL1-4920	Let's Face the Music	1984	12.00

TACUMA, JAMAALADEEN

GRAMAVISION

❑ 18-8803	Jukebox	1988	12.00
❑ 18-0(# unk)	Music World	1986	12.00
❑ GR-8308	Renaissance Man	1984	12.00
❑ GR-8301	Showstopper	1983	15.00

TAD

SUB POP

❑ 89 [B]	8-Way Santa	1991	25.00
❑ 27 [B]	God's Balls	1989	30.00
—Next 500 with "Manzine			
❑ 27 [B]	God's Balls	1989	30.00
—First 2,000 with gatefold cover			
❑ 27 [B]	God's Balls	1989	25.00
—Others in standard cover			
❑ 49 [EP]	Salt Lick	1990	30.00

TAFF, RUSS

HORIZON

❑ SP-751	Medals	198?	15.00
❑ SP-671	Russ Taff	198?	15.00
MYRRH			
❑ 701-679206-4	Medals	1985	15.00
❑ MSB 6706	Walls of Glass	1983	15.00

TAILGATE RAMBLERS, THE

JAZZOLOGY

❑ J-32	Pause	1968	15.00
❑ J-43	Swing	197?	15.00

TALAS

COMBAT

❑ 8005	Live Speed On Ice	1984	18.00
EVENFALL			
❑ EF401 [B]	Talas	1979	25.00
RELATIVITY			
❑ EMCL8001	Sink Your Teeth Into That	1982	16.00

TALBERT, THOMAS

ATLANTIC

❑ 1250 [M]	Bix Fats Duke Interpreted by Thomas Talbert	1957	40.00
—Black label			
❑ SD1250 [S]	Bix Fats Duke Interpreted by Thomas Talbert	1958	40.00
—Green label			
❑ 1250 [M]	Bix Fats Duke Interpreted by Thomas Talbert	1961	25.00
—Multicolor label, white "fan" logo at right			
❑ SD1250 [S]	Bix Fats Duke Interpreted by Thomas Talbert	1961	25.00
—Multicolor label, white "fan" logo at right			
SEA BREEZE			
❑ SB-2038	Things As They Are	198?	12.00
—As "Tom Talbert"			

TALISMEN, THE

BLUE STAR

❑ M-6323 [M]	Treasury of American Railroad Songs and Ballads	1964	25.00
❑ MS-6323 [S]	Treasury of American Railroad Songs and Ballads	1964	30.00
PRESTIGE			
❑ PRLP-7406 [M]	Folk Swingers Extraordinaire	1965	25.00
❑ PRST-7406 [S]	Folk Swingers Extraordinaire	1965	30.00

TALK TALK

EMI AMERICA

❑ ST-17113	It's My Life	1983	12.00
❑ DLP-19001 [EP]	Talk Talk	1982	12.00
❑ ST-17179	The Colour of Spring	1986	12.00
❑ ST-17083	The Party's Over	1982	12.00
EMI MANHATTAN			
❑ E1-46977	Spirit of Eden	1988	18.00
❑ SPRO 04172 [EP]	Spirit of Eden -- Let the Music Speak	1988	25.00
—Promo-only sampler with edits of four of the six songs from the original LP on side 1 and the same four tracks again on Side 2			
❑ E1-46366	The Party's Over	1988	18.00
—Reissue of EMI America ST-17083; much scarcer than the original			

TALKING HEADS

RHINO VINYL

❑ R1-70802	Remain in Light	2006	18.00
—Reissue on 180-gram vinyl			
SIRE			
❑ SRK6076	Fear of Music	1979	12.00
❑ R153839	Little Creatures	1985	15.00
—RCA Music Service edition			
❑ 25305	Little Creatures	1985	12.00
❑ SR6058	More Songs About Buildings and Food	1978	15.00
❑ SRK6058	More Songs About Buildings and Food	1979	10.00
—Reissue with new prefix			
❑ R153810	Naked	1988	15.00
—BMG Direct Marketing edition			
❑ 25654	Naked	1988	12.00
❑ PRO01033 [DJ]	Psycho Killer/Life During Wartime/Take Me to the River/Houses in Motion	1982	18.00
—Promo-only 4-song sampler			
❑ SRK6095	Remain in Light	1981	12.00
❑ R150102	Speaking in Tongues	1983	15.00
—BMG Direct Marketing edition			
❑ 23771 [B]	Speaking in Tongues	1983	30.00
—Clear vinyl in oversize plastic container with Robert Rauschenberg artwork			
❑ 23883	Speaking in Tongues	1983	12.00
—Standard issue			
❑ R124560	Stop Making Sense	1984	15.00
—RCA Music Service edition			
❑ 25121 [B]	Stop Making Sense (Soundtrack)	1984	25.00
—First issue with booklet and black & white cover			
❑ 25186	Stop Making Sense (Soundtrack)	1984	12.00
—Second issue: No booklet, color cover			
❑ PRO0930 [DJ]	Talking Heads	1980	18.00
—Promo-only 4-song sampler from "Remain in Light			
❑ PRO-A-930 [DJ]	Talking Heads	1980	18.00
—Promo-only 4-song sampler from "Remain in Light			
❑ SR6036	Talking Heads '77	1977	15.00
❑ 2SR3590	The Name of This Band Is Talking Heads	1982	25.00
❑ PRO-A-1033 [DJ]	The Name of This Band Is Talking Heads Sampler	1982	18.00
—Promo only			
❑ 25512	True Stories	1986	12.00
WARNER BROS.			
❑ WBMS-104 [DJ]	Talking Heads Live on Tour	1979	30.00
—Part of "The Warner Bros. Music Show" series (has been counterfeited)			
❑ WBMS-104 [DJ]	The Warner Bros. Music Show -- Talking Heads Live on Tour	1979	30.00
—Promo-only radio show (has been counterfeited)			

TALLEY, JAMES

CAPITOL

❑ ST-11695	Ain't It Somethin'	1977	12.00
❑ ST-11605	Blackjack Choir	1977	12.00
❑ ST-11416	Got No Bread, No Milk, No Money, But We Sure Got a Lot of Love	1975	15.00
❑ ST-11494	Tryin' Like the Devil	1976	12.00

TAMBA 4, THE

A&M

❑ SP-3013	Samba Blim	1969	30.00
❑ SP-3004	We and the Sea	1968	30.00

TAMPA RED

BLUEBIRD

❑ AXM2-5501	Guitar Wizard	1975	18.00
BLUES CLASSICS			
❑ 25	Guitar Wizard (1935-53)	197?	15.00
BLUESVILLE			
❑ BVLP-1043 [M]	Don't Jive Me	1962	120.00
—Blue label, silver print			
❑ BVLP-1043 [M]	Don't Jive Me	1963	30.00
—Blue label, trident logo at right			
❑ BVLP-1030 [M]	Don't Tampa with the Blues	1961	120.00

Number	Title	Yr	NM
—Blue label, silver print			
❏ BVLP-1030 [M]	Don't Tampa with the Blues	1963	30.00
—Blue label, trident logo at right			
FANTASY			
❏ OBC-516	Don't Tampa with the Blues	198?	12.00
YAZOO			
❏ 1039	Bottleneck Guitar	197?	15.00

TAMS, THE

Number	Title	Yr	NM
1-2-3			
❏ ST-567	The Best of the Tams	1970	25.00
ABC			
❏ ABCS-627	A Little More Soul	1968	30.00
❏ ABCS-673	A Portrait of the Tams	1969	30.00
❏ ABCS-499 [S]	Hey Girl, Don't Bother Me	1964	25.00
—Reissue of ABC-Paramount 499			
❏ ABCS-481 [R]	Presenting the Tams	1968	25.00
—Reissue of ABC-Paramount 481			
❏ ABC-596 [M]	Time for the Tams	1967	40.00
❏ ABCS-596 [S]	Time for the Tams	1967	30.00
ABC-PARAMOUNT			
❏ ABC-499 [M]	Hey Girl, Don't Bother Me	1964	30.00
❏ ABCS-499 [S]	Hey Girl, Don't Bother Me	1964	40.00
❏ ABC-481 [M]	Presenting the Tams	1964	50.00
❏ ABCS-481 [R]	Presenting the Tams	1964	30.00
CAPITOL			
❏ SM-11839	The Best of the Tams	1979	15.00
COMPLEAT			
❏ CMLP-5001 [EP]	Beach Music from the Tams	198?	10.00
SOUNDS SOUTH			
❏ SO-16010	The Mighty, Mighty Tams	1977	18.00

TANEGA, NORMA

Number	Title	Yr	NM
NEW VOICE			
❏ NV-2001 [M]	Walkin' My Cat Named Dog	1966	60.00
❏ NVS-2001 [S]	Walkin' My Cat Named Dog	1966	80.00

TANGERINE DREAM

Number	Title	Yr	NM
CAROLINE			
❏ CAROL1349	Livemiles	1988	15.00
ELEKTRA			
❏ 5E-557	Exit	1981	12.00
❏ 5E-521	Thief	1981	12.00
EMI AMERICA			
❏ ST-17141	Flashpoint	1984	12.00
MCA			
❏ 6165	Legend	1986	10.00
❏ 2277	Sorcerer	1977	15.00
PRIVATE MUSIC			
❏ 2057-1-P	Lily on the Beach	1989	18.00
❏ 2047-1-P	Miracle Mile	1989	18.00
❏ 2042-1-P	Optical Race	1988	18.00
RELATIVITY			
❏ 865618069	Alpha Centauri	1986	15.00
❏ 865618071	Atam	1986	15.00
❏ 865618068	Electronic Meditation	1986	15.00
❏ 865618072	Green Desert	1986	15.00
❏ EMC8043	Le Parc	198?	15.00
❏ EMC8045	Poland	198?	18.00
❏ 865618113	Underwater Sunlight	1986	15.00
❏ 865618070	Zeit	1986	18.00
VIRGIN			
❏ PZG35014 [B]	Encore	1977	30.00
❏ VR 13-108 [B]	Phaedra	1974	30.00
❏ VR 13-116 [B]	Rubycon	1975	30.00
❏ PZ34427	Stratosfear	1976	18.00
VIRGIN INTERNATIONAL			
❏ VI2097 [B]	Cyclone	1979	15.00
—Reissue			
❏ VI2111	Force Majeure	1979	15.00
❏ VI2010	Phaedra	1979	12.00
—Reissue			
❏ VI2044 [B]	Ricochet	1975	30.00
❏ VI2025	Rubycon	1979	12.00
—Reissue			
❏ VI2068	Stratosfear	1979	15.00
—Reissue of 34427			

TANGERINE ZOO, THE

Number	Title	Yr	NM
MAINSTREAM			
❏ S-6116 [B]	Outside Looking In	1969	75.00
❏ S-6107 [B]	Tangerine Zoo	1968	60.00

TAPSCOTT, HORACE

Number	Title	Yr	NM
FLYING DUTCHMAN			
❏ FDS-107	The Giant Is Awakened	1969	25.00
❏ FD-10107	The Giant Is Awakened	197?	18.00
INTERPLAY			
❏ 7724	Horace Tapscott in New York	197?	15.00
❏ 7714	Songs of the Unsung	197?	15.00

TARANTULA

Number	Title	Yr	NM
A&M			
❏ SP-4202	Tarantula	1969	24.00

TARIKA BLUE

Number	Title	Yr	NM
CHIAROSCURO			
❏ 141	Blue Path	197?	18.00

TARRIERS, THE

Number	Title	Yr	NM
ATLANTIC			
❏ 8042 [M]	Tell the World	1960	30.00
❏ SD8042 [S]	Tell the World	1960	40.00
DECCA			
❏ DL4538 [M]	Gather 'Round	1964	30.00
❏ DL74538 [S]	Gather 'Round	1964	30.00
❏ DL4342 [M]	The Tarriers	1962	30.00
❏ DL74342 [S]	The Tarriers	1962	30.00
GLORY			
❏ PG-1200 [M]	The Tarriers	1958	60.00
KAPP			
❏ KL1349 [M]	The Original Tarriers	1963	30.00
❏ KS3349 [S]	The Original Tarriers	1963	30.00
UNITED ARTISTS			
❏ UAL-4033 [M]	Hard Travelin'	1959	30.00
❏ UAS-5033 [S]	Hard Travelin'	1959	40.00

TASTE

Number	Title	Yr	NM
ATCO			
❏ SD 33-322	On the Boards	1970	30.00
❏ SD 33-296	Taste	1969	30.00

TASTE OF HONEY, A

Number	Title	Yr	NM
CAPITOL			
❏ SOO-11951	Another Taste	1979	15.00
❏ ST-11754	A Taste of Honey	1978	12.00
❏ ST-12173	Ladies of the Eighties	1982	15.00
❏ ST-12089	Twice as Sweet	1980	15.00

TATE, BABY

Number	Title	Yr	NM
BLUESVILLE			
❏ BVLP-1072 [M]	What You Done	1963	80.00
—Blue label, silver print			
❏ BVLP-1072 [M]	What You Done	1963	30.00
—Blue label, trident logo at right			

TATE, BUDDY, AND DOLLAR BRAND

Number	Title	Yr	NM
CHIAROSCURO			
❏ 165	Buddy Tate and Dollar Brand	1977	15.00

TATE, BUDDY

Number	Title	Yr	NM
BASF			
❏ 20740	Unbroken	197?	18.00
BLACK LION			
❏ 312	Kansas City Woman	197?	18.00
CHIAROSCURO			
❏ 123	Buddy Tate and His Buddies	1973	18.00
CONCORD JAZZ			
❏ CJ-163	The Great Buddy Tate	1981	12.00
FANTASY			
❏ OJC-184	Tate-A-Tate	1985	12.00
FELSTED			
❏ 7004 [M]	Swinging Like Tate	1958	80.00
❏ 2004 [S]	Swinging Like Tate	1958	80.00
MASTER JAZZ			
❏ 8127	Swinging Like Tate	197?	15.00
❏ 8128	Texas Twister	197?	15.00
MUSE			
❏ MR-5198	Buddy Tate and the Muse All-Stars Live at Sandy's	1979	12.00
❏ MR-5249	Hard Blowin': Live at Sandy's	198?	12.00
PAUSA			
❏ 7030	Unbroken	198?	12.00
SACKVILLE			
❏ 3027	Buddy Tate Quartet	198?	12.00
❏ 3017	Sherman Shuffle	198?	12.00
❏ 3034	The Ballad of Artistry	198?	12.00
SWINGVILLE			
❏ SVLP-2029 [M]	Groovin' with Buddy Tate	1961	50.00
—Purple label			
❏ SVLP-2029 [M]	Groovin' with Buddy Tate	1965	30.00
—Blue label, trident logo at right			
❏ SVLP-2014 [M]	Tate-A-Tate	1960	50.00
—Purple label			
❏ SVLP-2014 [M]	Tate-A-Tate	1965	30.00
—Blue label, trident logo at right			
❏ SVLP-2003 [M]	Tate's Date	1960	50.00
—Purple label			
❏ SVLP-2003 [M]	Tate's Date	1965	30.00
—Blue label, trident logo at right			

TATE, GRADY

Number	Title	Yr	NM
ABC IMPULSE!			
❏ ASD-9330	The Master	197?	15.00
BUDDAH			
❏ BDS-5623	By Special Request	1973	15.00

Number	Title	Yr	NM
JANUS			
❏ 7010	Movin' Day	197?	15.00
❏ 3050	She Is My Lady	197?	15.00
SKYE			
❏ SK-17	After the Long Ride Home	197?	18.00
❏ SK-1007	Feeling Life	197?	18.00
❏ SK-4	Windmills of My Mind	1969	25.00

TATE, HOWARD

Number	Title	Yr	NM
ATLANTIC			
❏ SD8303	Howard Tate	1971	25.00
TURNTABLE			
❏ 5002	Reaction	1969	25.00
VERVE			
❏ V-5022 [M]	Get It While You Can	1967	25.00
❏ V6-5022 [S]	Get It While You Can	1967	30.00

TATRO, DUANE

Number	Title	Yr	NM
CONTEMPORARY			
❏ C-3514 [M]	Jazz for Moderns	1956	80.00

TATUM, ART, AND BUDDY DEFRANCO

Number	Title	Yr	NM
AMERICAN RECORDING SOCIETY			
❏ G-412 [M]	The Art Tatum-Buddy DeFranco Quartet	1956	40.00
VERVE			
❏ MGV-8229 [M]	The Art Tatum-Buddy DeFranco Quartet	1958	50.00
❏ V-8229 [M]	The Art Tatum-Buddy DeFranco Quartet	1961	25.00

TATUM, ART; BENNY CARTER; LOUIS BELLSON

Number	Title	Yr	NM
CLEF			
❏ MGC-643 [M]	Tatum-Carter-Bellson	1955	80.00
VERVE			
❏ MGV-8227 [M]	Makin' Whoopee	1958	50.00
❏ V-8227 [M]	Makin' Whoopee	1961	25.00
❏ MGV-8013 [M]	The Three Giants	1957	50.00
❏ V-8013 [M]	The Three Giants	1961	25.00

TATUM, ART; ROY ELDRIDGE; ALVIN STOLLER; JOHN SIMMONS

Number	Title	Yr	NM
CLEF			
❏ MGC-679 [M]	The Art Tatum-Roy Eldridge-Alvin Stoller-John Simmons Quartet	1955	120.00
VERVE			
❏ MGV-8064 [M]	The Art Tatum-Roy Eldridge-Alvin Stoller-John Simmons Quartet	1957	80.00
❏ V-8064 [M]	The Art Tatum-Roy Eldridge-Alvin Stoller-John Simmons Quartet	1961	30.00

TATUM, ART

Number	Title	Yr	NM
20TH CENTURY FOX			
❏ S-4162 [R]	This Is Art Tatum, Volume 1	196?	15.00
❏ 3162 [M]	This Is Art Tatum, Volume 1	196?	18.00
❏ S-4163 [R]	This Is Art Tatum, Volume 2	196?	15.00
❏ 3163 [M]	This Is Art Tatum, Volume 2	196?	18.00
20TH FOX			
❏ FTM-102-2 [M]	Piano Discoveries	1961	30.00
❏ FTS-102-2 [R]	Piano Discoveries	1961	25.00
❏ FTM-3029 [M]	Piano Discoveries Vol. I	1960	25.00
❏ FTS-3029 [R]	Piano Discoveries Vol. I	1960	18.00
❏ FTM-3033 [M]	Piano Discoveries Vol. II	1960	25.00
❏ FTS-3033 [R]	Piano Discoveries Vol. II	1960	18.00
AIRCHECK			
❏ 21	Radio Broadcasts	197?	12.00
ASCH			
❏ ALP-356 [10]	Art Tatum	1950	150.00
AUDIOPHILE			
❏ AP-88	The Remarkable Art Tatum	198?	12.00
BOOK-OF-THE-MONTH			
❏ 51-5400	The One and Only	1980	30.00
BRUNSWICK			
❏ BL58023 [10]	Art Tatum Piano Solos	1950	100.00
❏ BL58013 [10]	Art Tatum Trio	1950	100.00
❏ BL54004 [10]	Here's Art Tatum	1955	120.00
CAPITOL			
❏ H216 [10]	Art Tatum	1950	100.00
❏ T216 [M]	Art Tatum	1955	80.00
—Turquoise label			
❏ M-11028	Art Tatum	1972	15.00
❏ T216 [M]	Art Tatum	1959	40.00
—Black colorband label, logo at left			
❏ T216 [M]	Art Tatum	196?	25.00
—Black colorband label, logo at top			
❏ H269 [10]	Art Tatum Encores	1951	100.00
❏ H408 [10]	Art Tatum Trio	1953	100.00
CLEF			
❏ 0(no #) [M]	Art Tatum	1954	300.00
—Boxed set with volumes 2, 3, 4 and 5 of The Genius of Art Tatum			
❏ MGC-612 [M]	The Genius of Art Tatum #1	1954	80.00
❏ MGC-613 [M]	The Genius of Art Tatum #2	1954	80.00
❏ MGC-614 [M]	The Genius of Art Tatum #3	1954	80.00

Number	Title	Yr	NM
❑ MGC-615 [M]	The Genius of Art Tatum #4	1954	80.00
❑ MGC-618 [M]	The Genius of Art Tatum #5	1954	80.00
❑ MGC-657 [M]	The Genius of Art Tatum #6	1955	80.00
❑ MGC-658 [M]	The Genius of Art Tatum #7	1955	80.00
❑ MGC-659 [M]	The Genius of Art Tatum #8	1955	80.00
❑ MGC-660 [M]	The Genius of Art Tatum #9	1955	80.00
❑ MGC-661 [M]	The Genius of Art Tatum #10	1955	80.00
❑ MGC-712 [M]	The Genius of Art Tatum #11	1956	80.00
CMS/SAGA			
❑ 6915	The Rarest Solos	197?	12.00
COLUMBIA			
❑ CL6301 [10]	An Art Tatum Concert	1954	80.00
❑ GL101 [10]	Gene Norman Concert at Shrine Auditorium, May 1949	1952	150.00
❑ CS9655 [S]	Piano Starts Here	1968	25.00
—Red "360 Sound" label			
❑ CS9655	Piano Starts Here	1971	12.00
—Orange label			
❑ PC9655	Piano Starts Here	198?	10.00
—Reissue with new prefix			
❑ CS9655 [M]	Piano Starts Here	1968	40.00
—Mono is white label promo only with stereo number; "Special Mono Radio Station Copy" sticker on cover			
❑ CL2565 [10]	The Tatum Touch	1956	50.00
DECCA			
❑ DL5086 [10]	Art Tatum Piano Solos	1950	120.00
❑ DL8715 [M]	The Art of Tatum	1958	50.00
DIAL			
❑ LP-206 [10]	Art Tatum Trio	1950	250.00
EMARCY			
❑ 826129-1	20th Century Piano Genius	1986	15.00
FOLKWAYS			
❑ FL-33 [10]	Art Tatum Trio	1951	80.00
❑ F-12293	Footnotes to Jazz	197?	15.00
GNP CRESCENDO			
❑ GNP-9025	Art Tatum at the Crescendo, Vol. 1	197?	12.00
❑ GNP-9026	Art Tatum at the Crescendo, Vol. 2	197?	12.00
HARMONY			
❑ HL7006 [M]	An Art Tatum Concert	1957	30.00
JAZZ MAN			
❑ 5030	Get Happy	198?	12.00
❑ 5024	The Genius	198?	12.00
JAZZZ			
❑ 101	Works of Art	197?	15.00
MCA			
❑ 42327	Solos	1990	15.00
❑ 4019	Tatum Masterpieces	197?	15.00
MOVIETONE			
❑ 2021 [M]	The Legendary Art Tatum	1967	18.00
❑ 72021 [R]	The Legendary Art Tatum	1967	15.00
ONYX			
❑ 205	God Is in the House	197?	15.00
PABLO			
❑ 2310887	The Best of Art Tatum	198?	12.00
❑ 2405418	The Best of Art Tatum	198?	12.00
❑ 2625706	The Tatum Group Masterpieces	197?	60.00
—Boxed set with eight volumes (except 2310 775) included			
❑ 2310732	The Tatum Group Masterpieces with Benny Carter, Vol. 1	197?	12.00
❑ 2310733	The Tatum Group Masterpieces with Benny Carter, Vol. 2	197?	12.00
❑ 2310737	The Tatum Group Masterpieces with Ben Webster	197?	12.00
❑ 2310736	The Tatum Group Masterpieces with Buddy DeFranco	197?	12.00
❑ 2310735	The Tatum Group Masterpieces with Jo Jones	197?	12.00
❑ 2310720	The Tatum Group Masterpieces with Lionel Hampton, Buddy Rich	197?	12.00
❑ 2310775	The Tatum Group Masterpieces with Lionel Hampton, Buddy Rich, Vol. 2	198?	12.00
❑ 2310731	The Tatum Group Masterpieces with Lionel Hampton, Sweets Edison, Barney Kessel	197?	12.00
❑ 2310734	The Tatum Group Masterpieces with Roy Eldredge	197?	12.00
❑ 2625703	The Tatum Solo Masterpieces	1974	150.00
—Box set with all 13 volumes included			
❑ 2310723	The Tatum Solo Masterpieces, Vol. 1	197?	12.00
❑ 2310729	The Tatum Solo Masterpieces, Vol. 2	197?	12.00
❑ 2310730	The Tatum Solo Masterpieces, Vol. 3	197?	12.00
❑ 2310789	The Tatum Solo Masterpieces, Vol. 4	197?	12.00
❑ 2310790	The Tatum Solo Masterpieces, Vol. 5	197?	12.00
❑ 2310791	The Tatum Solo Masterpieces, Vol. 6	197?	12.00
❑ 2310792	The Tatum Solo Masterpieces, Vol. 7	197?	12.00
❑ 2310793	The Tatum Solo Masterpieces, Vol. 8	198?	12.00
❑ 2310835	The Tatum Solo Masterpieces, Vol. 9	198?	12.00
❑ 2310862	The Tatum Solo Masterpieces, Vol. 10	198?	12.00
❑ 2310864	The Tatum Solo Masterpieces, Vol. 11	198?	12.00
❑ 2310870	The Tatum Solo Masterpieces, Vol. 12	198?	12.00
❑ 2310875	The Tatum Solo Masterpieces, Vol. 13	198?	12.00
PAUSA			
❑ 9017	The Legend	198?	12.00
REM HOLLYWOOD			
❑ LP-3 [10]	Piano Virtuoso	1950	120.00
—The number "2" is on the front cover, but "LP-3" appears on the label			
STINSON			
❑ SLP-40 [M]	Art Tatum Solos and Trio	195?	40.00
❑ SLP-40 [10]	Art Tatum Trio	1950	150.00
STORYVILLE			
❑ 4108	Masters of Jazz, Vol. 8	199?	15.00
TIME-LIFE			
❑ STL-J-24	Giants of Jazz	1982	25.00
VARESE SARABANDE			
❑ VC81021	The Keystone Sessions	197?	18.00
VERVE			
❑ MGV-8101-5 [M]	Art Tatum, Volume 1	1957	200.00
—Boxed set with volumes 1-5 of The Genius of Art Tatum			
❑ MGV-8102-5 [M]	Art Tatum, Volume 2	1957	200.00
—Boxed set with volumes 6-10 of The Genius of Art Tatum			
❑ MGV-8347 [M]	More of the Greatest Piano of Them All	1959	50.00
❑ V-8347 [M]	More of the Greatest Piano of Them All	1961	25.00
❑ MGV-8118 [M]	Presenting the Art Tatum Trio	1957	50.00
❑ V-8118 [M]	Presenting the Art Tatum Trio	1961	25.00
❑ MGV-8360 [M]	Still More of the Greatest Piano of Them All	1960	50.00
❑ V-8360 [M]	Still More of the Greatest Piano of Them All	1961	25.00
❑ VSP-33 [M]	The Art of Art	1966	18.00
❑ VSPS-33 [R]	The Art of Art	1966	15.00
❑ MGV 8220 [M]	The Art Tatum-Ben Webster Quartet	1958	50.00
❑ V-8220 [M]	The Art Tatum-Ben Webster Quartet	1961	25.00
❑ V-8433 [M]	The Essential Art Tatum	1962	25.00
❑ MGV-8036 [M]	The Genius of Art Tatum #1	1957	50.00
❑ V-8036 [M]	The Genius of Art Tatum #1	1961	25.00
❑ MGV-8037 [M]	The Genius of Art Tatum #2	1957	50.00
❑ V-8037 [M]	The Genius of Art Tatum #2	1961	25.00
❑ MGV-8038 [M]	The Genius of Art Tatum #3	1957	50.00
❑ V-8038 [M]	The Genius of Art Tatum #3	1961	25.00
❑ MGV-8039 [M]	The Genius of Art Tatum #4	1957	50.00
❑ V-8039 [M]	The Genius of Art Tatum #4	1961	25.00
❑ MGV-8040 [M]	The Genius of Art Tatum #5	1957	50.00
❑ V-8040 [M]	The Genius of Art Tatum #5	1961	25.00
❑ MGV-8055 [M]	The Genius of Art Tatum #6	1957	50.00
❑ V-8055 [M]	The Genius of Art Tatum #6	1961	25.00
❑ MGV-8056 [M]	The Genius of Art Tatum #7	1957	50.00
❑ V-8056 [M]	The Genius of Art Tatum #7	1961	25.00
❑ MGV-8057 [M]	The Genius of Art Tatum #8	1957	50.00
❑ V-8057 [M]	The Genius of Art Tatum #8	1961	25.00
❑ MGV-8058 [M]	The Genius of Art Tatum #9	1957	50.00
❑ V-8058 [M]	The Genius of Art Tatum #9	1961	25.00
❑ MGV-8059 [M]	The Genius of Art Tatum #10	1957	50.00
❑ V-8059 [M]	The Genius of Art Tatum #10	1961	25.00
❑ MGV-8095 [M]	The Genius of Art Tatum #11	1957	50.00
❑ V-8095 [M]	The Genius of Art Tatum #11	1961	25.00
❑ MGV-8323 [M]	The Greatest Piano of Them All	1959	50.00
❑ V-8323 [M]	The Greatest Piano of Them All	1961	25.00
❑ MGV-8332 [M]	The Incomparable Music of Art Tatum	1959	50.00
❑ V-8332 [M]	The Incomparable Music of Art Tatum	1961	25.00

TATUM, ART/ERROLL GARNER

Number	Title	Yr	NM
JAZZTONE			
❑ J-1203 [M]	Kings of the Keyboard	1956	40.00
ROOST			
❑ LP-2213 [M]	Giants of the Piano	1956	50.00

TATUM, ART/JAMES P. JOHNSON

Number	Title	Yr	NM
MCA			
❑ 4112	Tatum Masterpieces Vol. 2/ Johnson Plays Fats Waller	197?	15.00

TATUM, ART/MARY LOU WILLIAMS

Number	Title	Yr	NM
HALL OF FAME			
❑ 607	King and Queen	197?	12.00
JAZZTONE			
❑ J-1280 [M]	The King and Queen	1958	40.00

TAUPIN, BERNIE

Number	Title	Yr	NM
ASYLUM			
❑ 6E-263	He Who Rides the Tiger	1980	15.00
ELEKTRA			
❑ EKS-75020	Bernie Taupin	1972	18.00
RCA			
❑ 64200RAB [DJ]	Interview Album	1987	25.00
❑ 6420-1-RAB [DJ]	Interview Album	1987	25.00
❑ 5922-1-R	Tribe	1987	12.00

TAVARES

Number	Title	Yr	NM
CAPITOL			
❑ ST-11258	Check It Out	1973	12.00
❑ SW-11719	Future Bound	1978	12.00
❑ SN-16207	Future Bound	1981	10.00
—Budget-line reissue			
❑ ST-11316	Hard Core Poetry	1974	12.00
❑ ST-11396	In the City	1975	12.00
❑ ST-12167	Loveline	1982	12.00
❑ ST-11628	Love Storm	1977	12.00
❑ SN-16206	Love Storm	1981	10.00
—Budget-line reissue			
❑ ST-12117	Love Uprising	1981	12.00
❑ SW-11874	Madam Butterfly	1979	12.00
❑ ST-11533	Sky-High!	1976	12.00
❑ ST-12026	Supercharged	1980	12.00
❑ ST-11701	The Best of Tavares	1977	12.00
RCA VICTOR			
❑ AFL1-4357	New Directions	1982	12.00
❑ AFL1-4700	Words and Music	1983	12.00

TAVENER, JOHN

Number	Title	Yr	NM
APPLE			
❑ SMAS-3369	The Whale	1972	25.00

TAX FREE

Number	Title	Yr	NM
POLYDOR			
❑ 24-4053 [B]	Tax Free	1971	30.00

TAXXI

Number	Title	Yr	NM
FANTASY			
❑ F-9603	Day for Night	1980	18.00
❑ F-9628	Foreign Tongue	1983	18.00
❑ F-9617	States of Emergency	1982	25.00
MCA			
❑ 5580	Expose	1985	12.00

TAYLES, THE

Number	Title	Yr	NM
CINEVISTA			
❑ US1001	Who Are These Guys -- Live at the Nitty Gritty	1972	80.00

TAYLOR, ALEX

Number	Title	Yr	NM
CAPRICORN			
❑ CP 0101	Dinnertime	1972	12.00
❑ 860	With Friends and Neighbors	1971	12.00

TAYLOR, ANDY

Number	Title	Yr	NM
MCA			
❑ R153322	Thunder	1987	15.00
—BMG Direct Marketing edition			
❑ 5837	Thunder	1987	12.00

TAYLOR, ART

Number	Title	Yr	NM
BLUE NOTE			
❑ BLP-4047 [M]	A.T.'s Delight	1960	150.00
—Deep groove" version (deep indentation under label on both sides)			
❑ BLP-4047 [M]	A.T.'s Delight	1960	80.00
—Regular version, W. 63rd St. address on label			
❑ BST-84047 [S]	A.T.'s Delight	1960	60.00
—W. 63rd St. address on label			
❑ BST-84047 [S]	A.T.'s Delight	1985	12.00
—The Finest in Jazz Since 1939" reissue			
FANTASY			
❑ OJC-094	Taylor's Wailers	198?	12.00
NEW JAZZ			
❑ NJLP-8219 [M]	Taylor's Tenors	1959	50.00
—Purple label			
❑ NJLP-8219 [M]	Taylor's Tenors	1965	30.00
—Blue label, trident logo at right			
PRESTIGE			
❑ PRLP-7117 [M]	Taylor's Wailers	1957	100.00

TAYLOR, BILLY

Number	Title	Yr	NM
ABC IMPULSE!			
❑ AS-71 [S]	My Fair Lady Loves Jazz	1968	18.00
ABC-PARAMOUNT			
❑ ABC-134 [M]	Billy Taylor At the London House	1956	50.00
❑ ABC-162 [M]	Billy Taylor Introduces Ira Sullivan	1957	50.00
❑ ABC-112 [M]	Evergreens	1956	50.00
❑ ABC-177 [M]	My Fair Lady Loves Jazz	1957	50.00
❑ ABC-226 [M]	The New Trio	1958	50.00
❑ ABCS-226 [S]	The New Trio	1958	40.00
ARGO			
❑ LP-650 [M]	Taylor Made Flute	1959	50.00

Number	Title	Yr	NM
❑ LPS-650 [S]	Taylor Made Flute	1959	40.00
ATLANTIC			
❑ 1329 [M]	One for Fun	1960	50.00
—Black label			
❑ SD1329 [S]	One for Fun	1960	50.00
—Green label			
❑ ALR-113 [10]	Piano Panorama	1951	150.00
❑ 1277 [M]	The Billy Taylor Touch	1958	50.00
—Black label			
❑ 1277 [M]	The Billy Taylor Touch	1961	30.00
—Multicolor label, white "fan" logo at right			
BELL			
❑ S-6049	OK Billy!	1970	18.00
CAPITOL			
❑ T2302 [M]	Midnight Piano	1965	25.00
❑ ST2302 [S]	Midnight Piano	1965	30.00
❑ T2039 [M]	Right Here, Right Now	1963	25.00
❑ ST2039 [S]	Right Here, Right Now	1963	30.00
CONCORD JAZZ			
❑ CJ-145	Where've You Been	1981	12.00
FANTASY			
❑ OJC-1730	Cross Section	198?	12.00
❑ OJC-015	The Billy Taylor Trio with Candido	1982	12.00
IMPULSE!			
❑ A-71 [M]	My Fair Lady Loves Jazz	1965	25.00
❑ AS-71 [S]	My Fair Lady Loves Jazz	1965	30.00
MERCURY			
❑ MG-20722 [M]	Impromptu	1962	25.00
❑ SR-60722 [S]	Impromptu	1962	30.00
MONMOUTH-EVERGREEN			
❑ 7089	Jazz Alive	1978	15.00
MOODSVILLE			
❑ MVLP-16 [M]	Interlude	1961	50.00
—Green label			
❑ MVLP-16 [M]	Interlude	1965	30.00
—Blue label, trident logo at right			
PAUSA			
❑ 7096	Sleeping Bee	198?	12.00
PRESTIGE			
❑ PRLP-7001 [M]	A Touch of Taylor	1955	80.00
❑ PRST-7664 [R]	A Touch of Taylor	1969	18.00
❑ PRLP-184 [10]	Billy Taylor Trio	1954	200.00
❑ PRLP-188 [10]	Billy Taylor Trio	1954	200.00
❑ PRLP-139 [10]	Billy Taylor Trio, Volume 1	1953	220.00
❑ PRLP-7015 [M]	Billy Taylor Trio, Volume 1	1956	80.00
❑ PRLP-165 [10]	Billy Taylor Trio, Volume 2	1953	250.00
❑ PRLP-7016 [M]	Billy Taylor Trio, Volume 2	1956	100.00
❑ PRLP-168 [10]	Billy Taylor Trio, Volume 3	1953	220.00
❑ PRLP-7093 [M]	Billy Taylor Trio at Town Hall	1957	80.00
❑ PRLP-194 [10]	Billy Taylor Trio In Concert at Town Hall, December 17, 1954	1955	200.00
❑ PRLP-7071 [M]	Cross Section	1956	80.00
❑ 16-2 [M]	Let's Get Away from It All	1957	500.00
—This album plays at 16 2/3 rpm and is marked as such; white label			
❑ PRLP-7051 [M]	The Billy Taylor Trio with Candido	1956	80.00
❑ PRST-7762	Today!	1970	18.00
RIVERSIDE			
❑ RLP 12-319 [M]	Billy Taylor Trio Uptown	1960	50.00
❑ RLP-1168 [S]	Billy Taylor Trio Uptown	1960	50.00
❑ RLP 12-306 [M]	Billy Taylor with Four Flutes	1959	50.00
❑ RLP-1151 [S]	Billy Taylor with Four Flutes	1959	50.00
❑ RLP 12-339 [M]	Warming Up	1960	50.00
❑ RLP-1195 [S]	Warming Up	1960	50.00
ROOST			
❑ R-406 [10]	Jazz at Storyville	1952	120.00
❑ R-409 [10]	Taylor Made Jazz	1952	120.00
SAVOY			
❑ MG-9035 [10]	Billy Taylor Piano	1953	120.00
SESAC			
❑ N-3001 [M]	Custom Taylored	1959	60.00
❑ SN-3001 [S]	Custom Taylored	1959	50.00
STATUS			
❑ ST-8313 [M]	Live! At Town Hall	1965	40.00
SURREY			
❑ S-1033 [M]	Easy Life	1966	30.00
❑ SS-1033 [S]	Easy Life	1966	30.00
TOWER			
❑ ST-5111 [S]	I Wish I Knew	1968	30.00
WEST 54			
❑ 8008	Live at Storyville	198?	15.00

TAYLOR, BOBBY, AND THE VANCOUVERS

Number	Title	Yr	NM
GORDY			
❑ G-930 [M]	Bobby Taylor and the Vancouvers	1968	80.00
—Mono is promo only			
❑ GS-930 [S]	Bobby Taylor and the Vancouvers	1968	60.00
❑ GS-942	Taylor Made Soul	1969	60.00

TAYLOR, BUCK

Number	Title	Yr	NM
JPL			
❑ 14098	That Man from Gunsmoke	197?	40.00

TAYLOR, CARMOL

Number	Title	Yr	NM
ELEKTRA			
❑ 7E-1069	Song Writer	1976	15.00

TAYLOR, CATHIE

Number	Title	Yr	NM
CAPITOL			
❑ T1359 [M]	A Little Bit of Sweetness	1960	25.00
❑ ST1359 [S]	A Little Bit of Sweetness	1960	30.00
❑ T1448 [M]	The Tree Near My House	1961	25.00
❑ ST1448 [S]	The Tree Near My House	1961	30.00

TAYLOR, CECIL

Number	Title	Yr	NM
A&M			
❑ 7502152861	In Florescence	1990	15.00
AMERICAN RECORDING SOCIETY			
❑ G-437 [M]	Modern Jazz	195?	40.00
ARISTA/FREEDOM			
❑ AF1038	Indent	197?	15.00
❑ AF1905	Nefertiti	197?	18.00
❑ AF1005	Silent Tongues	1975	15.00
BARNABY			
❑ Z30562	Cecil Taylor Quartet	1971	18.00
❑ KZ31035	New York City R&B	1972	18.00
BLUE NOTE			
❑ BLP-4260 [M]	Conquistador	1967	30.00
❑ BST-84260 [S]	Conquistador	1967	30.00
—With "A Division of Liberty Records" on label			
❑ B1-84260 [S]	Conquistador	1989	15.00
—The Finest in Jazz Since 1939" reissue			
❑ BST-84260 [S]	Conquistador	197?	18.00
—Reissue with newer label; with "A Division of United Artists Records" on label			
❑ BN-LA458-H2	In Transition	197?	18.00
❑ BLP-4237 [M]	Unit Structures	1966	30.00
❑ BST-84237 [S]	Unit Structures	1966	30.00
—With "New York, USA" on label			
❑ BST-84237 [S]	Unit Structures	1967	18.00
—With "A Division of Liberty Records" on label			
CANDID			
❑ CD-8006 [M]	The World of Cecil Taylor	1960	50.00
❑ CS-9006 [S]	The World of Cecil Taylor	1960	40.00
CONTEMPORARY			
❑ C-3562 [M]	Looking Ahead!	1959	50.00
❑ S-7562 [S]	Looking Ahead!	1959	40.00
FANTASY			
❑ 6014 [M]	Live At the Café Montmarte	1964	25.00
❑ 86014 [S]	Live At the Café Montmarte	1964	30.00
❑ OJC-452	Looking Ahead	1990	15.00
HAT ART			
❑ 1993/4	Garden	1986	18.00
—Reissue of Hat Hut 1993/4			
❑ 3011	One Too Many Salty Swift & Not Goodbye	1986	25.00
—Reissue of Hat Hut 02			
❑ 2036	The Eight	1987	18.00
HAT HUT			
❑ 3508	Calling It the 8th	1981	15.00
❑ 1993/4	Garden	198?	25.00
❑ 16	It Is In the Brewing Luminous	198?	18.00
❑ 02	One Too Many Salty Swift & Not Goodbye	197?	30.00
INNER CITY			
❑ IC-3021	Air Above Mountains (Buildings Within)	1977	18.00
❑ IC-3001	The Dark to Themselves	197?	18.00
JAZZ MAN			
❑ 5031	New York R & B	198?	12.00
❑ 5026	The World of Cecil Taylor	198?	12.00
JCOA			
❑ 1002	Cecil Taylor with the Jazz Composers Orchestra	197?	18.00
MOSAIC			
❑ MR6-127	The Complete Candid Recordings of Cecil Taylor and Buell Neidlinger	199?	100.00
NEW WORLD			
❑ 201	Cecil Taylor	1978	15.00
❑ 303	Three Phasis	197?	15.00
PAUSA			
❑ 7108	Fly! Fly! Fly!	198?	12.00
❑ 7053	Live in the Black Forest	198?	12.00
PRESTIGE			
❑ 34003	Great Concert	197?	25.00
SOUL NOTE			
❑ 121150	For Olim	199?	15.00
❑ SN-1089	Winged Serpent (Sliding Quadrants)	1986	15.00
TRANSITION			
❑ TRLP-19 [M]	Jazz Advance	1956	200.00
—With booklet (deduct 1/4 if missing)			
UNIT CORE			
❑ 30551	Spring of Two Blue-J's	197?	25.00
UNITED ARTISTS			
❑ UAL-4014 [M]	Hard Driving Jazz	1959	50.00
❑ UAL-4046 [M]	Love for Sale	1959	50.00
❑ UAS-5046 [S]	Love for Sale	1959	40.00
❑ UAS-5014 [S]	Stereo Drive	1959	40.00

TAYLOR, CHET

Number	Title	Yr	NM
BRYLEN			
❑ BN-4408	Pretty Words	1982	12.00

TAYLOR, CHIP

Number	Title	Yr	NM
BUDDAH			
❑ BDS-5118 [B]	Gasoline	1972	18.00
CAPITOL			
❑ ST-11909	Saint Sebastian	1979	12.00
COLUMBIA			
❑ KC34345	Somebody Shoot Out the Jukebox	1977	12.00
WARNER BROS.			
❑ BS2718	Last Chance	1973	15.00
❑ BS2824	Some of Us	1974	15.00

TAYLOR, CREED

Number	Title	Yr	NM
ABC-PARAMOUNT			
❑ ABC-308 [M]	Lonelyville "The Nervous Beat	1960	30.00
❑ ABCS-308 [S]	Lonelyville "The Nervous Beat	1960	30.00
❑ ABC-259 [M]	Shock Music in Hi-Fi	1958	40.00
❑ ABCS-259 [S]	Shock Music in Hi-Fi	1958	60.00
❑ ABC-317 [M]	The Best of the Barracks Ballads	1960	30.00
❑ ABCS-317 [S]	The Best of the Barracks Ballads	1960	30.00

TAYLOR, DEBBIE

Number	Title	Yr	NM
TODAY			
❑ TLP-1007	Comin' Down on You	1985	50.00

TAYLOR, DICK

Number	Title	Yr	NM
SKYLARK			
❑ SKLP-18 [10]	Blue Moon	1954	80.00

TAYLOR, EARL

Number	Title	Yr	NM
CAPITOL			
❑ T2090 [M]	Bluegrass Taylor-Made	1963	40.00
❑ ST2090 [S]	Bluegrass Taylor-Made	1963	50.00
UNITED ARTISTS			
❑ UAL-3049 [M]	Folk Songs from the Bluegrass	1960	30.00
❑ UAS-6049 [S]	Folk Songs from the Bluegrass	1960	30.00

TAYLOR, HOUND DOG

Number	Title	Yr	NM
ALLIGATOR			
❑ 4701	Hound Dog Taylor	1971	30.00
❑ 4704	Natural Boogie	1974	25.00

TAYLOR, JAMES

Number	Title	Yr	NM
APPLE			
❑ SKAO3352	James Taylor	1969	30.00
—With title in black print			
❑ SKAO3352	James Taylor	1970	25.00
—With title in orange print			
COLUMBIA			
❑ TC37009	Dad Loves His Work	1981	12.00
❑ PC37009	Dad Loves His Work	198?	10.00
❑ HC47009	Dad Loves His Work	1983	40.00
—Half-speed mastered edition			
❑ FC36058	Flag	1979	12.00
❑ PC36058	Flag	198?	10.00
❑ JC34811	JT	1977	12.00
❑ PC34811	JT	198?	10.00
❑ FC40851	Never Die Young	1988	12.00
❑ FC40052	That's Why I'm Here	1985	12.00
EUPHORIA			
❑ EST-2 [B]	James Taylor and the Original Flying Machine 1967	1971	18.00
NAUTILUS			
❑ NR-29	Gorilla	1981	40.00
—Audiophile pressing			
TRIP			
❑ TLP-9513	Rainy Day Man	197?	12.00
—Reissue of Euphoria album			
WARNER BROS.			
❑ BS2866	Gorilla	1975	12.00
—Burbank" label			
❑ BS2866	Gorilla	1979	10.00
—Cream label			
❑ BS42866 [Q]	Gorilla	1975	18.00
❑ BS2979	Greatest Hits	1976	15.00
—This and other variations of this title have re-recorded versions of "Carolina in My Mind" and "Something in the Way She Moves.			
❑ BSK3113	Greatest Hits	1977	12.00
—Burbank" label			
❑ BSK3113	Greatest Hits	1979	10.00
—Cream label			

Number	Title	Yr	NM
❏ BS2912	In the Pocket	1976	12.00
— Burbank" label			
❏ BS2912	In the Pocket	1979	10.00
— Cream label			
❏ BS2561	Mud Slide Slim and the Blue Horizon	1971	12.00
— Green "WB" label			
❏ BS2561	Mud Slide Slim and the Blue Horizon	1973	10.00
— Burbank" label or cream label			
❏ BS2660	One Man Dog	1972	12.00
— Green "WB" label			
❏ BS2660	One Man Dog	1973	10.00
— Burbank" label or cream label			
❏ BS42660 [Q]	One Man Dog	1975	18.00
❏ WS1843	Sweet Baby James	1970	30.00
— Very early pressings have green label with "W7" logo			
❏ WS1843	Sweet Baby James	1970	
— Green "WB" label with no reference to other songs on front cover			
❏ WS1843	Sweet Baby James	1970	12.00
— Green "WB" label with "Contains Fire and Rain and Country Road" added to front cover			
❏ ST-93138	Sweet Baby James	1970	25.00
— Capitol Record Club edition			
❏ WS1843	Sweet Baby James	1973	10.00
— Burbank" label or cream label			
❏ 274300	Sweet Baby James	2007	30.00
— Reissue on 180-gram vinyl with replica of original green "WB" label and lyric poster			
❏ BS2794	Walking Man	1973	12.00
— Burbank" label			
❏ BS2794	Walking Man	1979	10.00
— Cream label			

TAYLOR, JOE

PROJAZZ
❏ PAD-635	Mystery Walk	1988	12.00

TAYLOR, JOHNNIE

BEVERLY GLEN
❏ 10001	Just Ain't Good Enough	1982	15.00

COLUMBIA
❏ JC36548	A New Day	1980	15.00
❏ PC33951	Eargasm	1976	15.00
— Originals have no bar code			
❏ PCQ33951 [Q]	Eargasm	1976	25.00
❏ PC33951	Eargasm	1986	10.00
— Budget-line reissue with bar code			
❏ JC35340	Ever Ready	1978	15.00
❏ PC34401	Rated Extraordinaire	1977	15.00
❏ PCQ34401 [Q]	Rated Extraordinaire	1977	25.00
❏ JC36061	She's Killing Me	1979	15.00
❏ JC37127	The Best of Johnnie Taylor	1981	15.00

ICHIBAN
❏ ICH-1022	Stuck in the Mud	198?	12.00
❏ ICH-1042	Ugly Man	198?	12.00

MALACO
❏ MAL-7452	Crazy 'Bout You	1989	12.00
❏ MAL-7446	In Control	198?	12.00
❏ MAL-7400	Just Can't Do Right	1991	12.00
❏ MAL-7440	Lover Boy	198?	12.00
❏ MAL-7463	The Best of Johnnie Taylor on Malaco, Vol. 1	1992	12.00
❏ MAL-7421	This Is Your Night	190?	12.00
❏ MAL-7431	Wall to Wall	198?	12.00

STAX
❏ 88001	Chronicle	1977	25.00
❏ STS-2032	Johnnie Taylor's Greatest Hits	1970	30.00
❏ MPS-8558	Little Bluebird	1988	12.00
❏ STS-2030	One Step Beyond	1971	30.00
❏ STS-2012	Rare Stamps	1969	30.00
❏ STS-2008	Raw Blues	1969	30.00
❏ MPS-8508	Raw Blues	1982	12.00
❏ MPS-8520	Super Hits	1983	12.00
❏ STS-5509	Super Taylor	1974	25.00
❏ STS-3014	Taylored in Silk	1973	25.00
❏ MPS-8537	Taylored in Silk	1987	12.00
— Reissue of 3014			
❏ STS-5521	The Best of Johnnie Taylor	1975	25.00
❏ STS-2023	The Johnnie Taylor Philosophy Continues	1969	30.00
❏ ST-715 [M]	Wanted: One Soul Singer	1967	50.00
❏ STS-715 [S]	Wanted: One Soul Singer	1967	60.00
❏ STS-2005	Who's Making Love	1968	40.00
❏ STX-4115	Who's Making Love	198?	12.00
— Reissue of 2005			

TAYLOR, KATE

COLUMBIA
❏ JC36034	It's In There and It's Got to Come Out	1979	12.00
❏ JC35089	Kate Taylor	1978	12.00

COTILLION
❏ SD9045	Sister Kate	1971	12.00

TAYLOR, KINGSIZE, AND THE DOMINOES

MIDNIGHT
❏ HLP-2101 [M]	Real Gonk Man	1965	50.00

Number	Title	Yr	NM
❏ HST-2101 [S]	Real Gonk Man	1965	100.00

TAYLOR, KOKO

ALLIGATOR
❏ AL4754	An Audience with the Queen	1987	12.00
❏ AL4724	From the Heart of a Woman	1981	12.00
❏ AL4706	I Got What It Takes	1976	15.00
❏ AL4784	Jump for Joy	1990	18.00
❏ AL4740	Queen of the Blues	1985	12.00
❏ AL4711	The Earthshaker	1978	15.00

CHESS
❏ CH-50018 [B]	Basic Soul	1972	35.00
❏ LPS-1532	Koko Taylor	1969	30.00
❏ CH-9263	Koko Taylor	1987	15.00
— Reissue of 1532			

TAYLOR, LAURA

GOOD SOUNDS
❏ GS-105	Dancin' in My Feet	1979	30.00

TAYLOR, LITTLE JOHNNY, AND TED TAYLOR

RONN
❏ LSP-7533	The Super Taylors	1973	25.00

TAYLOR, LITTLE JOHNNY

FANTASY
❏ MPF-4510	Little Johnny Taylor's Greatest Hits	1982	12.00

GALAXY
❏ 203 [M]	Little Johnny Taylor	1963	100.00
❏ 8203 [S]	Little Johnny Taylor	1963	150.00
❏ 207 [M]	Little Johnny Taylor's Greatest Hits	1964	100.00
❏ 8207 [S]	Little Johnny Taylor's Greatest Hits	1964	150.00

RONN
❏ LPS-7530	Everybody Knows About My Good Thing	1972	30.00
❏ LSP-7535	L.J.T.	1975	25.00
❏ LSP-7532	Open House at My House	1973	30.00

TAYLOR, LIVINGSTON

ATCO
❏ SD 33-334	Livingston Taylor	1970	15.00

CAPRICORN
❏ 863	Liv	1971	12.00
❏ CP 0114	Over the Rainbow	1973	12.00

EPIC
❏ JE36153	Man's Best Friend	1979	12.00

TAYLOR, LYNN

GRAND AWARD
❏ GA-33-0(# unk) [M]	Lynn Taylor Sings	195?	300.00

TAYLOR, MARTIN

CONCORD JAZZ
❏ CJ-184	Skye Boat	198?	12.00

TAYLOR, MARY

DOT
❏ DLP-25987	Mary Taylor's Very First Album	1971	15.00

TAYLOR, MEL

WARNER BROS.
❏ W1624 [M]	Mel Taylor in Action	1966	30.00
❏ WS1624 [S]	Mel Taylor in Action	1966	40.00

TAYLOR, MICK

COLUMBIA
❏ JC35076 [B]	Mick Taylor	1979	18.00

TAYLOR, R. DEAN

RARE EARTH
❏ RS-522 [B]	I Think, Therefore I Am	1971	25.00

TAYLOR, RUSTY

STOMP OFF
❏ SOS-1082	Give Me a Call	1985	12.00
❏ SOS-1028	Good Old Bad Old Days	198?	12.00
❏ SOS-1186	Let's Misbehave	1988	12.00

TAYLOR, SAM "THE MAN

DECCA
❏ DL4417 [M]	It's a Blue World	1963	18.00
❏ DL74417 [S]	It's a Blue World	1963	25.00
❏ DL4302 [M]	Misty Mood	1962	18.00
❏ DL74302 [S]	Misty Mood	1962	25.00
❏ DL4573 [M]	Somewhere in the Night	1964	18.00
❏ DL74573 [S]	Somewhere in the Night	1964	25.00

LION
❏ L-70054 [M]	Sam "The Man" Taylor	1958	30.00

METROJAZZ
❏ E-1008 [M]	Jazz for Commuters	1958	50.00
❏ SE-1008 [S]	Jazz for Commuters	1958	40.00

Number	Title	Yr	NM
MGM			
❏ E-3292 [M]	Blue Mist	1955	60.00
— Yellow label			
❏ E-3973 [M]	Blue Mist	1961	30.00
❏ SE-3973 [S]	Blue Mist	1961	30.00
— Possibly a re-recording of 3292			
❏ E-3783 [M]	More Blue Mist	1959	30.00
❏ SE-3783 [S]	More Blue Mist	1959	40.00
❏ E-3482 [M]	Music for Melancholy Babies	1957	60.00
— Yellow label			
❏ E-293 [10]	Music with the Big Beat	195?	100.00
❏ E-3473 [M]	Music with the Big Beat	1956	80.00
— Yellow label			
❏ E-3380 [M]	Out of This World	1956	60.00
— Yellow label			
❏ E-3573 [M]	Prelude to Blues	1957	60.00
— Yellow label			
❏ E-3553 [M]	Rockin' Sax and Rollin' Organ	1957	60.00
— Yellow label			
❏ GAS-146	Sam "The Man" Taylor (Golden Archive Series)	1970	18.00
❏ E-3967 [M]	Sam "The Man" Taylor Plays Hollywood	1960	30.00
❏ SE-3967 [S]	Sam "The Man" Taylor Plays Hollywood	1960	40.00

MOODSVILLE
❏ MVLP-24 [M]	The Bad and the Beautiful	1962	50.00
— Green label			
❏ MVLP-24 [M]	The Bad and the Beautiful	1965	30.00
— Blue label, trident logo at right			

TAYLOR, TED

ALARM
❏ 1000	1976	1976	30.00

MCA
❏ 3059	Keepin' My Head Above Water	1978	15.00

OKEH
❏ OKM-12104 [M]	Be Ever Wonderful	1963	30.00
❏ OKS-14104 [S]	Be Ever Wonderful	1963	40.00
❏ OKM-12109 [M]	Blues and Soul	1965	30.00
❏ OKS-14109 [S]	Blues and Soul	1965	40.00
❏ OKM-12113 [M]	Ted Taylor's Greatest Hits	1966	30.00
❏ OKS-14113 [S]	Ted Taylor's Greatest Hits	1966	30.00

RONN
❏ LP-8003	Be Ever Wonderful	198?	12.00
❏ LPS-7528	Shades of Blue	1969	15.00
❏ LP-8004	Steal Away	198?	12.00
❏ LPS-7531	Taylor Made	1972	15.00
❏ LPS-7529	You Can Dig It!	197?	15.00

SOLPUGIDS
❏ 1001	Be Ever Wonderful	198?	18.00
❏ 1002	Taylor Made for You	198?	18.00

TAYLOR, TUT

WORLD PACIFIC
❏ WP-1816 [M]	12 String Dobro	1964	30.00
❏ ST-1816 [S]	12 String Dobro	1964	80.00
— Red vinyl			
❏ ST-1816 [S]	12 String Dobro	1964	30.00
— Black vinyl			
❏ WP-1829 [M]	Dobro Country	1964	30.00
❏ ST-1829 [S]	Dobro Country	1964	30.00

TAYLOR-GOOD, KAREN

MESA
❏ 1111	Karen	1984	15.00

TCHAIKOVSKY, ANDRE

RCA VICTOR RED SEAL
❏ LSC-2360 [S]	Chopin: Preludes; Barcarolle: Mazurkas, Etudes, Ballade 3	1960	60.00
— Original with "shaded dog" label			
❏ LSC-2354 [S]	Mozart: Fantasia in C; Sonata in C, K. 457; Sonata in C, K. 330	1960	70.00
— Original with "shaded dog" label			
❏ LSC-2287 [S]	Mozart: Piano Concerto No. 25	1959	100.00
— With Fritz Reiner/Chicago Symphony Orchestra; original with "shaded dog" label			

TCHAIKOVSKY, BRAM/BENNY MARDONES

POLYDOR
❏ PRO129 [DJ]	Two Stars Are Better Than One	1980	15.00
— Promo-only sampler			

TCHICAI, JOHN, AND PIERRE DERGE

STEEPLECHASE
❏ SCS-1174	Ball at Louisiana	1982	15.00

TCHICAI, JOHN

BLACK SAINT
❏ 120094	Timo's Message	1990	15.00

Number	Title	Yr	NM
STEEPLECHASE			
❑ SCS-1075	The Real Tchical	198?	15.00
TE KANAWA, KIRI			
PHILIPS			
❑ 412629-1	Ave Maria	1984	12.00
TEA COMPANY, THE			
SMASH			
❑ SRS-67105	Come and Have Some Tea	1968	50.00
TEAGARDEN, JACK			
AIRCHECK			
❑ 9	Jack Teagarden and Frankie Trumbauer	197?	12.00
❑ 24	Jack Teagarden on the Air	198?	12.00
BETHLEHEM			
❑ BCP-32 [M]	Jazz Great	1955	50.00
❑ BCP-6040	Meet Me Where They Play the Blues	1978	15.00
—*Distributed by Caytronics" reissue*			
BIOGRAPH			
❑ C-2	Great Soloist	197?	12.00
BLUEBIRD			
❑ 9986-1-RB	That's a Serious Thing	1990	15.00
CAPITOL			
❑ T1095 [M]	Big T's Dixieland Band	1959	25.00
❑ ST1095 [S]	Big T's Dixieland Band	1959	30.00
❑ T1143 [M]	Shades of Night	1959	25.00
❑ ST1143 [S]	Shades of Night	1959	30.00
❑ T820 [M]	Swing Low Sweet Spiritual	1957	40.00
❑ T721 [M]	This Is Teagarden	1956	40.00
COLUMBIA SPECIAL PRODUCTS			
❑ JSN6044 [M]	King of the Blues Trombone	197?	30.00
COMMODORE			
❑ 20015 [10]	Big T	195?	80.00
DECCA			
❑ DL8304 [M]	Big T's Jazz	1956	40.00
❑ DL4540 [M]	The Golden Horn of Jack Teagarden	1964	18.00
❑ DL74540 [R]	The Golden Horn of Jack Teagarden	1964	15.00
EPIC			
❑ SN6044 [M]	King of the Blues Trombone	1963	80.00
❑ LN24045 [M]	King of the Blues Trombone, Vol. 1	1963	30.00
❑ LN24046 [M]	King of the Blues Trombone, Vol. 2	1963	30.00
❑ LN24047 [M]	King of the Blues Trombone, Vol. 3	1963	30.00
EVEREST ARCHIVE OF FOLK & JAZZ			
❑ 352	Big Band Jazz	198?	12.00
❑ FS-335	Original Dixieland	198?	12.00
FOLKWAYS			
❑ FJ-2819	The Big Band Sound of Jack Teagarden and Bunny Berigan	198?	15.00
IAJRC			
❑ LP-19	Sincerely, Jack Teagarden	198?	18.00
JAZZTONE			
❑ J-1222 [M]	Big T	195?	30.00
—*Reissue of Period material*			
JOLLY ROGER			
❑ 5026 [10]	Jack Teagarden	1955	50.00
MCA			
❑ 227	The Golden Horn of Jack Teagarden	1973	12.00
—*Black rainbow label*			
MOSAIC			
❑ MQ6-168	The Complete Capitol Fifties Jack Teagarden Sessions	199?	100.00
PERIOD			
❑ SLP-1106 [10]	Meet Me Where They Play the Blues	1955	80.00
❑ SLP-1110 [10]	Original Dixieland	1955	80.00
RCA VICTOR			
❑ LPV-528 [M]	Jack Teagarden	1965	25.00
RONDO-LETTE			
❑ A-18 [M]	The Blues and Dixie	1958	30.00
ROULETTE			
❑ R-25177 [M]	Dixie Sound	1962	18.00
❑ SR-25177 [S]	Dixie Sound	1962	25.00
❑ R-25091 [M]	Jack Teagarden at the Round Table	1960	18.00
❑ SR-25091 [S]	Jack Teagarden at the Round Table	1960	25.00
❑ R-25119 [M]	Jazz Maverick	1961	18.00
❑ SR-25119 [S]	Jazz Maverick	1961	25.00
❑ R-25243 [M]	Portrait of Mr. T	1963	18.00
❑ SR-25243 [S]	Portrait of Mr. T	1963	25.00
ROYALE			
❑ 18156 [10]	The Blues	195?	80.00
SAVOY JAZZ			
❑ SJL-1162	Varsity Sides	1986	12.00
SOUNDS			
❑ S-1203	Jack Teagarden in Concert	197?	18.00

Number	Title	Yr	NM
TIME-LIFE			
❑ STL-J-08	Giants of Jazz	1979	25.00
TRIP			
❑ 6	Jack Teagarden	197?	12.00
URANIA			
❑ UJLP-1002 [10]	Jack Teagarden Sings and Plays	1954	100.00
❑ UJLP-1001 [10]	Meet the New Jack Teagarden	1954	100.00
VERVE			
❑ V-8495 [M]	Jack Teagarden!!	1962	18.00
❑ V6-8495 [S]	Jack Teagarden!!	1962	25.00
❑ V-8416 [M]	Mis'ry and the Blues	1961	18.00
❑ V6-8416 [S]	Mis'ry and the Blues	1961	25.00
❑ V-8465 [M]	Think Well of Me	1962	18.00
❑ V6-8465 [S]	Think Well of Me	1962	25.00
TEAGARDEN, JACK/BOBBY HACKETT			
COMMODORE			
❑ FL-30012 [M]	Jack Teagarden and Bobby Hackett	1959	30.00
TEAGARDEN, JACK/JONAH JONES			
AAMCO			
❑ ALP-309 [M]	Two Boys from Dixieland	196?	30.00
—*Reissue of Bethlehem material*			
BETHLEHEM			
❑ BCP-6042 [M]	Dixieland	1959	40.00
TEAGARDEN, JACK/MAX KAMINSKY			
COMMODORE			
❑ XFL-14940	Big T and Mighty Max	198?	12.00
HALL OF FAME			
❑ 616	Jack and Max	197?	12.00
TEAGARDEN, JACK/PEE WEE RUSSELL			
FANTASY			
❑ OJC-1708	Jack Teagarden's Big Eight / Pee Wee Russell's Rhythmakers	1985	12.00
RIVERSIDE			
❑ RLP 12-141	Jack Teagarden's Big Eight / Pee Wee Russell's Rhythmakers	1956	60.00
TEARDROP EXPLODES, THE			
MERCURY			
❑ SRM-1-4016	Kilimanjaro	1981	15.00
❑ SRM-1-4035	Wilder	1981	15.00
TEARDROPS, THE (U)			
20TH CENTURY FOX			
❑ FXG-5011 [M]	The Teardrops at Trinchi's	1963	30.00
TEARS FOR FEARS			
FONTANA			
❑ R133653	The Seeds of Love	1989	15.00
—*BMG Direct Marketing edition*			
❑ 838730-1	The Seeds of Love	1989	12.00
MERCURY			
❑ R143666	Songs from the Big Chair	1985	15.00
—*BMG Direct Marketing edition*			
❑ 824300-1	Songs from the Big Chair	1985	12.00
❑ 811039-1	The Hurting	1983	18.00
—*Child on cover (original)*			
❑ 811039-1	The Hurting	1983	12.00
—*Photo of group next to duck pond on cover (reissue)*			
TEBALDI, RENATA			
LONDON			
❑ OS26241	Christmas Festival	1971	15.00
TECHNOTRONIC			
SBK			
❑ K1-93422	Pump Up the Jam -- The Album	1989	25.00
❑ K1-95028	Trip On This -- The Remixes	1990	25.00
TEDDY AND THE PANDAS			
TOWER			
❑ ST-5125	Basic Magnetism	1968	30.00
TEDDY BEARS, THE			
IMPERIAL			
❑ LP-9067 [M]	The Teddy Bears Sing!	1959	400.00
❑ LP-12010 [S]	The Teddy Bears Sing!	1959	1500.00
TEDESCO, TOMMY			
DISCOVERY			
❑ 928	Hollywood Gypsy	1986	12.00
❑ 851	My Desiree	1982	12.00
❑ 789	When Do We Start	1978	15.00
IMPERIAL			
❑ LP-9321 [M]	Calypso Soul	1966	18.00
❑ LP-12321 [S]	Calypso Soul	1966	25.00

Number	Title	Yr	NM
❑ LP-9295 [M]	Guitars	1965	18.00
❑ LP-12295 [S]	Guitars	1965	25.00
❑ LP-9263 [M]	The Electric 12 String Guitar of Tommy Tedesco	1964	18.00
❑ LP 12263 [S]	The Electric 12 String Guitar of Tommy Tedesco	1964	25.00
TREND			
❑ TR-517	Alone at Last	1979	25.00
—*Direct-to-disc recording*			
❑ TR-514	Autumn	1978	25.00
—*Direct-to-disc recording*			
❑ TR-534 [B]	Carnival Time	1983	15.00
TEE, WILLIE			
CAPITOL			
❑ ST-199	I'm Only a Man	1969	18.00
UNITED ARTISTS			
❑ UA-LA655-G	Anticipation	1976	15.00
TEE SET, THE			
COLOSSUS			
❑ CCS-1001 [B]	Ma Belle Amie	1970	25.00
TEEGARDEN AND VAN WINKLE			
ATCO			
❑ 33-272 [M]	An Evening at Home with Teegarden and Van Winkle	1968	60.00
—*Mono is white label promo only*			
❑ SD 33-272 [S]	An Evening at Home with Teegarden and Van Winkle	1968	18.00
WESTBOUND			
❑ 2003	But Anyhow	1969	18.00
❑ 2010	On Our Way	1971	18.00
TEEMATES, THE			
AUDIO FIDELITY			
❑ AFLP-3042 [M]	Jet Set Dance Discotheque	1964	40.00
❑ AFSD-7042 [S]	Jet Set Dance Discotheque	1964	50.00
TEEN QUEENS, THE			
CROWN			
❑ CLP-5022 [M]	Eddie My Love	1956	250.00
—*Black label, all silver print*			
❑ CLP-5022 [M]	Eddie My Love	196?	100.00
—*Black label, "CROWN" in alternating colored letters*			
❑ CLP-5373 [M]	The Teen Queens	1963	50.00
❑ CST-373 [R]	The Teen Queens	1963	30.00
TEENA MARIE			
EPIC			
❑ FE40318	Emerald City	1986	12.00
❑ FE40318 [DJ]	Emerald City	1986	25.00
—*Promo only on green vinyl*			
❑ FE40872	Naked to the World	1988	12.00
❑ FE38882	Robbery	1983	12.00
❑ FE39528	Starchild	1984	12.00
GORDY			
❑ G8-997M1	Irons in the Fire	1980	15.00
❑ G8-1004M1	It Must Be Magic	1981	15.00
❑ G7-992R1	Lady T.	1980	15.00
❑ G7-986R1	Wild and Peaceful	1979	15.00
MOTOWN			
❑ 5370ML	Greatest Hits	1985	12.00
TEENAGE JESUS AND THE JERKS			
MIGRANE/LUST UNLUST			
❑ CC-336 [EP]	Teenage Jesus and the Jerks	1979	60.00
—*Pink vinyl*			
❑ CC-336 [EP]	Teenage Jesus and the Jerks	1979	50.00
—*Black vinyl*			
TEITELBAUM, RICHARD			
ARISTA/FREEDOM			
❑ AF1037	Time Zones	197?	15.00
TELEVISION			
4 MEN WITH BEARDS			
❑ 4M507LP [B]	Adventure		25.00
❑ 4M533LP [B]	Television		25.00
CAPITOL			
❑ SPRO-79456 [DJ]	Television	1992	30.00
—*Promo-only vinyl release (stock copies on CD and cassette only)*			
❑ SPRO-79456 [DJ]	Television	1992	30.00
—*Vinyl is promo only*			
ELEKTRA			
❑ 6E-133 [B]	Adventure	1978	25.00
❑ 7E-1098 [B]	Marquee Moon	1977	30.00
TEMIZ, OKAY			
FINNADAR			
❑ 9032	Drummer of Two Worlds	198?	18.00

Number	Title	Yr	NM

TEMPERLEY, JOE, AND JIMMY KNEPPER

HEP

Number	Title	Yr	NM
❏ 2003	Just Friends	198?	12.00

TEMPEST

WARNER BROS.

❏ BS2682	Tempest	1973	30.00

TEMPESTS, THE

SMASH

❏ MGS-27098 [M]	Would You Believe?	1966	30.00
❏ SRS-67098 [S]	Would You Believe?	1966	30.00

TEMPLE, PICK

PRESTIGE INT'L.

❏ PRLP-13008 [M]	Pick of the Crop	196?	30.00

X

❏ LXA-3022 [10]	Folk Songs of the People	1954	50.00

TEMPLE, SHIRLEY

20TH CENTURY FOX

❏ TFM-3102 [M]	The Best of Shirley Temple	1963	30.00
❏ TFM-3172 [M]	The Best of Shirley Temple, Vol. 2	1965	30.00

20TH FOX

❏ FOX-3006 [M]	Little Miss Wonderful	1959	40.00
—Shirley Temple pictured as an adult on cover			
❏ FOX-3006 [M]	Little Miss Wonderful	196?	40.00
—Shirley Temple pictured as a child on cover			
❏ FOX-3045 [M]	More Little Miss Wonderful	1961	40.00
❏ TCF-103 [M]	The Shirley Temple Songbook	1961	50.00

MOVIETONE

❏ MTM-71012 [M]	Curtain Call	1966	25.00
❏ MTM-71001 [M]	On the Good Ship Lollipop	1966	25.00

TEMPLETON, ALEC

ATLANTIC

❏ 1222 [M]	The Magic Piano	1956	40.00
—Black label			
❏ 1222 [M]	The Magic Piano	1961	25.00
—Multicolor label, white "fan" logo at right			

TEMPLIN, RAY

EUPHONIC

❏ 1219	A Flash at the Piano	198?	12.00

TEMPO, NINO, AND APRIL STEVENS

ATCO

❏ 33-156 [M]	Deep Purple	1963	40.00
❏ SD 33-156 [S]	Deep Purple	1963	50.00
❏ 33-180 [M]	Hey Baby	1966	30.00
❏ SD 33-180 [S]	Hey Baby	1966	40.00
❏ 33-162 [M]	Nino and April Sing the Great Songs	1964	30.00
❏ SD 33-162 [S]	Nino and April Sing the Great Songs	1964	40.00

RCA CAMDEN

❏ CAL-921 [M]	A Nino Tempo/April Stevens Program	1964	15.00
—Actually contains solo recordings by each, packaged together to capitalize on the success of "Deep Purple"			

WHITE WHALE

❏ WW-113 [M]	All Strung Out	1967	25.00
❏ WWS-7113 [S]	All Strung Out	1967	30.00

TEMPO, NINO

A&M

❏ SP-3629	Come See Me 'Round Midnight	1974	30.00

LIBERTY

❏ LRP-3023 [M]	Rock 'n' Roll Beach Party	1958	120.00

TEMPOS, THE

JUSTICE

❏ JLP-104	Speaking of the Tempos	1966	500.00

TEMPREES

WE PRODUCE

❏ 1903	Love Maze	1973	60.00
❏ 1901	Love Men	1972	60.00
❏ 1905	Temprees 3	1974	60.00

TEMPTATIONS, THE

ATLANTIC

❏ SD19188	Bare Back	1978	15.00
❏ SD19143	Hear to Tempt You	1977	15.00

GORDY

❏ G966V1	1990	1973	18.00
❏ G962L	All Directions	1972	25.00
❏ G6-969S1	A Song for You	1975	18.00
❏ 6085GL	Back to Basics	1984	15.00
❏ GS939	Cloud Nine	1969	25.00
❏ G918 [M]	Gettin' Ready	1966	30.00
❏ GS918 [S]	Gettin' Ready	1966	30.00

—Script "Gordy" at top of label			
❏ GS918 [S]	Gettin' Ready	1967	25.00
—Block "GORDY" inside "G" on left of label			
❏ G8-998M1	Give Love at Christmas	1980	18.00
❏ G6-973S1	House Party	1975	18.00
❏ GS953	Live at London's Talk of the Town	1970	25.00
❏ GS938	Live at the Copa	1968	25.00
❏ G965L	Masterpiece	1973	25.00
❏ G911 [M]	Meet the Temptations	1964	40.00
❏ GS911 [S]	Meet the Temptations	1964	50.00
—Script "Gordy" at top of label			
❏ GS911 [S]	Meet the Temptations	1967	30.00
—Block "GORDY" inside "G" on left of label			
❏ G8-994M1	Power	1980	15.00
❏ GS947	Psychedelic Shack	1970	25.00
❏ GS949	Puzzle People	1969	25.00
❏ 6008GL	Reunion	1982	15.00
❏ GS957	Sky's the Limit	1971	25.00
❏ G961L	Solid Rock	1972	25.00
❏ 6032GL	Surface Thrills	1983	15.00
❏ GS954	Temptations Greatest Hits II	1970	25.00
❏ G921 [M]	Temptations Live!	1967	30.00
❏ GS921 [S]	Temptations Live!	1967	30.00
—Script "Gordy" at top of label			
❏ GS921 [S]	Temptations Live!	1967	30.00
—Block "GORDY" inside "G" on left of label			
❏ G914 [M]	Temptin' Temptations	1965	30.00
❏ GS914 [S]	Temptin' Temptations	1965	30.00
—Script "Gordy" at top of label			
❏ GS914 [S]	Temptin' Temptations	1967	25.00
—Block "GORDY" inside "G" on left of label			
❏ G8-1006M1	The Temptations	1981	15.00
❏ GS951	The Temptations' Christmas Card	1969	30.00
❏ G7-975S1	The Temptations Do the Temptations	1976	18.00
❏ G919 [M]	The Temptations' Greatest Hits	1966	30.00
❏ GS919 [S]	The Temptations' Greatest Hits	1966	30.00
—Script "Gordy" at top of label			
❏ GS919 [S]	The Temptations' Greatest Hits	1967	25.00
—Block "GORDY" inside "G" on left of label			
❏ G924 [M]	The Temptations in a Mellow Mood	1967	30.00
❏ GS924 [S]	The Temptations in a Mellow Mood	1967	30.00
❏ GS933	The Temptations Show	1969	25.00
❏ G912 [M]	The Temptations Sing Smokey	1965	35.00
❏ GS912 [S]	The Temptations Sing Smokey	1965	45.00
—Script "Gordy" at top of label			
❏ GS912 [S]	The Temptations Sing Smokey	1967	25.00
—Block "GORDY" inside "G" on left of label			
❏ G927 [M]	The Temptations Wish It Would Rain	1968	60.00
—Mono is white-label promo only			
❏ GS927 [S]	The Temptations Wish It Would Rain	1968	25.00
❏ 6207GL	To Be Continued	1986	15.00
❏ 6164GL	Touch Me	1986	15.00
❏ 6119GL	Truly for You	1984	15.00
❏ G6-971S1	Wings of Love	1976	18.00
❏ G922 [M]	With a Lot o' Soul	1967	30.00
❏ GS922 [S]	With a Lot o' Soul	1967	30.00
—Script "Gordy" at top of label			
❏ GS922 [S]	With a Lot o' Soul	1967	25.00
—Block "GORDY" inside "G" on left of label			

MOTOWN

❏ 5389ML	25th Anniversary	1986	18.00
❏ M5-212V1	All the Million Sellers	1982	15.00
❏ M782	Anthology	1973	30.00
❏ 5279ML	Give Love at Christmas	1983	12.00
—Reissue of Gordy 998			
❏ M5-144V1	Masterpiece	1981	15.00
—Reissue of Gordy 965			
❏ M5-140V1	Meet the Temptations	1981	15.00
—Reissue of Gordy 911			
❏ M5-164V1	Psychedelic Shack	1981	15.00
—Reissue of Gordy 947			
❏ M5-172V1	Puzzle People	1981	15.00
—Reissue of Gordy 949			
❏ MOT-6275	Special	1989	15.00
❏ 5251ML	The Temptations Christmas Card	1982	12.00
—Reissue of Gordy 951			
❏ M5-205V1	The Temptations Sing Smokey	1981	15.00
—Reissue of Gordy 912			
❏ 6246ML	Together Again	1987	15.00

NATURAL RESOURCES

❏ NR4005T1	The Temptations in a Mellow Mood	1978	15.00
—Reissue of Gordy 924			

PICKWICK

❏ SPC-3540	Psychedelic Shack	197?	15.00
—Reissue of Gordy 947			

UNIVERSAL MOTOWN

❏ 5316011	Cloud Nine	2009	25.00
—Reissue of Gordy 939			

10CC

MERCURY

❏ SRM-1-3702	Deceptive Bends	1977	15.00
❏ SRM-1-1061 [B]	How Dare You!	1976	18.00
❏ SRM-2-8600	Live and Let Live	1977	18.00
❏ SRM-1-1029 [B]	The Original Soundtrack	1975	18.00

POLYDOR

❏ PD-1-6161 [B]	Bloody Tourists	1978	15.00
❏ PD-1-6244	Greatest Hits 1972-1978	1979	12.00

U.K.

❏ 53105 [B]	10cc	1973	25.00
❏ 53110 [B]	100cc	1975	18.00
❏ AUKS53107 [B]	Sheet Music	1974	25.00

WARNER BROS.

❏ BSK3442	Look Hear?	1980	12.00
❏ BSK3575	Ten Out of Ten	1981	12.00

10,000 MANIACS

AUDIO FIDELITY

❏ AFZTL1510 [B]	Our Time In Eden	2011	30.00

CHRISTIAN BURIAL

❏ P-2010 [EP]	Human Conflict #5	1983	80.00
❏ P-3001	Secrets of the I Ching	1984	120.00

ELEKTRA

❏ R130236	Blind Man's Zoo	1989	15.00
—BMG Direct Marketing edition			
❏ 60815	Blind Man's Zoo	1989	15.00
❏ 60815 [DJ]	Blind Man's Zoo	1989	18.00
—Promo-only audiophile pressing (white labels)			
❏ R100481	In My Tribe	1987	15.00
—BMG Direct Marketing edition			
❏ 60738 [DJ]	In My Tribe	1987	18.00
—Promo-only audiophile pressing			
❏ 60738	In My Tribe	1987	12.00
❏ ED5270 [DJ]	Interview	1987	30.00
—Lenny Kaye interviews Natalie Merchant; promo only			
❏ 60428	The Wishing Chair	1985	15.00

TEN WHEEL DRIVE

CAPITOL

❏ ST-11199	Ten Wheel Drive	1973	12.00

POLYDOR

❏ 24-4024	Brief Replies	1970	15.00
❏ 24-4008	Construction #1	1969	15.00
❏ 24-4062	Peculiar Friends	1971	15.00

TEN YEARS AFTER

CHRYSALIS

❏ F1-21722	About Time	1989	15.00
❏ PV41001	A Space in Time	1987	10.00
❏ F1-21001	A Space in Time	1989	10.00
❏ CHS1084	Cricklewood Green	1975	12.00
❏ PV41084	Cricklewood Green	1983	10.00
❏ F1-21084	Cricklewood Green	1989	10.00
❏ PV41573	Positive Vibrations	1987	10.00
❏ F1-21573	Positive Vibrations	1989	10.00
❏ FV41049	Recorded Live	1987	12.00
❏ PV41009	Rock and Roll Music to the World	1987	10.00
❏ F1-21009	Rock and Roll Music to the World	1989	10.00
❏ CHS1083	Ssssh	1975	12.00
❏ PV41083	Ssssh	1983	10.00
❏ F1-21083	Ssssh	1989	10.00
❏ FV41580	Universal	1988	12.00
❏ F1-21580	Universal	1989	10.00
❏ CHS1085	Watt	1975	12.00
❏ PV41085	Watt	1983	10.00
❏ F1-21085	Watt	1989	10.00

COLUMBIA

❏ KC30801	A Space in Time	1971	15.00
❏ CQ30801 [Q]	A Space in Time	1973	30.00
❏ PC30801	A Space in Time	1979	10.00
❏ PC34366	Classic Performances of Ten Years After	1976	12.00
❏ PC32851	Positive Vibrations	1974	12.00
❏ C2X32288 [B]	Recorded Live	1973	25.00
❏ KC31779	Rock and Roll Music to the World	1972	15.00
❏ C31779	Rock and Roll Music to the World	197?	12.00
—Reissue with new prefix			

DERAM

❏ XDES18064	Alvin Lee and Company	1972	15.00
❏ DES18038	Cricklewood Green	1970	18.00
❏ DES18072	Goin' Home! Their Greatest Hits	1975	15.00
❏ DES18029	Ssssh	1969	18.00
❏ DES18021	Stonedhenge	1969	18.00
❏ DES18009 [S]	Ten Years After	1968	25.00
❏ DE16009 [M]	Ten Years After	1968	100.00
❏ DES18016	Undead	1968	18.00
❏ XDES18050	Watt	1970	18.00
—With large "DERAM" on top half of label			
❏ SMAS-93428	Watt	1970	25.00
—Capitol Record Club edition			
❏ XDES18050	Watt	1970	30.00
—With "LONDON" under smaller "DERAM" at top of label			

Number	Title	Yr	NM
LONDON			
☐ LC50008	Greatest Hits	1977	12.00
☐ 820324-1	Greatest Hits	1986	10.00
TERRACE, PETE			
FANTASY			
☐ 3203 [M]	Going Loco	1956	60.00
—Red vinyl			
☐ 3203 [M]	Going Loco	195?	30.00
☐ 3215 [M]	Invitation to the Mambo	1956	60.00
—Red vinyl			
☐ 3215 [M]	Invitation to the Mambo	195?	30.00
☐ 3234 [M]	The Pete Terrace Quintet	1957	60.00
—Red vinyl			
☐ 3234 [M]	The Pete Terrace Quintet	195?	30.00
FORUM			
☐ F-9041 [M]	Cole Porter in Latin America	196?	18.00
☐ SF-9041 [S]	Cole Porter in Latin America	196?	15.00
TICO			
☐ LP-1023 [M]	A Night in Mambo Jazzland	1956	40.00
☐ SLP-1082 [S]	Bella Pachanga	1961	30.00
☐ LP-1082 [M]	Bella Pachanga	1961	30.00
☐ LP-1036 [M]	Cha Cha Cha in New York	1957	40.00
☐ LP-1063 [M]	Cole Porter in Latin America	1959	30.00
☐ LP-1057 [M]	My One and Only Love	1959	30.00
☐ LP-1050 [M]	Pete with a Latin Beat	1958	30.00
☐ LP-1028 [M]	The Nearness of You	1956	40.00
TERRACE, RAY			
TOWER			
☐ ST-5105	The Home of Boogaloo	1968	25.00
TERRELL, TAMMI			
MOTOWN			
☐ MS-652	Irresistible Tammi	1969	50.00
☐ M5-231V1	Irresistible Tammi	1982	12.00
TERRY, AL			
INDEX			
☐ 5001	This Is Al Terry	196?	18.00
TERRY, BUDDY			
MAINSTREAM			
☐ MRL-336	Awareness	1972	18.00
☐ MRL-391	Lean On Him	1974	15.00
☐ MRL-356	Pure Dynamite	1973	18.00
PRESTIGE			
☐ PRLP-7525 [M]	Electric Soul	1967	30.00
☐ PRST-7525 [S]	Electric Soul	1967	30.00
☐ PRLP-7541 [M]	Natural Soul	1967	30.00
☐ PRST-7541 [S]	Natural Soul	1967	30.00
TERRY, CLARK			
20TH CENTURY FOX			
☐ TFM-3137 [M]	What Makes Sammy Swing	1963	25.00
☐ TFS-4137 [S]	What Makes Sammy Swing	1963	30.00
ABC IMPULSE!			
☐ AS-9157 [S]	It's What's Happenin'	1968	25.00
☐ AS-9127 [S]	Spanish Rice	1968	18.00
☐ AS-64 [S]	The Happy Horn of Clark Terry	1968	18.00
ARGO			
☐ LP-620 [M]	Out on a Limb	1957	60.00
CAMEO			
☐ CS-1064 [S]	More	1964	40.00
☐ C-1064 [M]	More (Theme From Mondo Cane)	1964	30.00
☐ C-1071 [M]	Tread Ye Lightly	1964	30.00
☐ CS-1071 [S]	Tread Ye Lightly	1964	40.00
CANDID			
☐ CD-8009 [M]	Color Changes	1960	50.00
☐ CS-9009 [S]	Color Changes	1960	40.00
EMARCY			
☐ MG-36007 [M]	Clark Terry	1955	80.00
☐ MG-36093 [M]	The Jazz School	1956	60.00
ETOILE			
☐ CPR-1	Clark Terry's Big Bad Band	197?	25.00
FANTASY			
☐ OJC-229	Duke with a Difference	1990	15.00
☐ OJC-302	In Orbit	1988	15.00
☐ OJC-604	Memories of Duke	1991	15.00
☐ OJC-066	Serenade to a Bus Seat	198?	15.00
IMPULSE!			
☐ A-9127 [M]	Spanish Rice	1966	30.00
☐ AS-9127 [S]	Spanish Rice	1966	30.00
☐ A-64 [M]	The Happy Horn of Clark Terry	1964	30.00
☐ AS-64 [S]	The Happy Horn of Clark Terry	1964	30.00
JAZZ MAN			
☐ 5046	Color Changes	198?	12.00
MAINSTREAM			
☐ MRL-347	Angyumaluma	1972	18.00
☐ MRL-373	Clark Terry and the W.B. Brookmeyer Quintet	1973	18.00
☐ 56043 [M]	Clark Terry Tonight	1965	25.00
☐ S-6043 [S]	Clark Terry Tonight	1965	30.00

Number	Title	Yr	NM
☐ S-6086	Clark Terry with Bob Brookmeyer	196?	25.00
☐ 56066 [M]	Mumbles	1966	25.00
☐ S-6066 [S]	Mumbles	1966	30.00
☐ MRL-320	Straight No Chaser	1971	18.00
☐ 56054 [M]	The Power of Positive Swinging	1965	25.00
☐ S-6054 [S]	The Power of Positive Swinging	1965	30.00
☐ MRL-803	What'd He Say	197?	25.00
MILESTONE			
☐ 47032	Cruising	197?	18.00
MOODSVILLE			
☐ MVLP-20 [M]	Everything's Mellow	1961	50.00
—Green label			
☐ MVLP-20 [M]	Everything's Mellow	1965	30.00
—Blue label, trident logo at right			
☐ MVLP-26 [M]	The Jazz Version of "All American"	1962	50.00
—Green label			
☐ MVLP-26 [M]	The Jazz Version of "All American"	1965	30.00
—Blue label, trident logo at right			
PABLO TODAY			
☐ 2312105	Ain't Misbehavin'	1979	15.00
☐ 2312118	Memories of Duke	1980	15.00
☐ 2313127	Yes, the Blues	1981	15.00
PAUSA			
☐ 7131	Wham!	198?	12.00
POLYDOR			
☐ 24-5002	Clark Terry at Montreux Jazz Festival	1970	18.00
RIVERSIDE			
☐ 6167	Clark Terry and Thelonious Monk in Orbit	198?	15.00
☐ RM-3009 [M]	C.T. Meets Monk	1967	30.00
☐ RS-3009 [S]	C.T. Meets Monk	1967	25.00
☐ RLP 12-246 [M]	Duke with a Difference	1957	100.00
☐ RLP-1108 [S]	Duke with a Difference	1959	80.00
☐ RLP 12-271 [M]	In Orbit	1958	100.00
☐ RLP 12-237 [M]	Serenade to a Bus Seat	1957	300.00
—White label, blue print			
☐ RLP 12-237 [M]	Serenade to a Bus Seat	1957	100.00
—Blue label, microphone logo at top			
☐ 6209	Serenade to a Bus Seat	198?	15.00
☐ RLP 12-295 [M]	Top and Bottom Brass	1959	100.00
☐ RLP-1137 [S]	Top and Bottom Brass	1959	80.00
SWING			
☐ 8406	Paris 1960	1985	12.00
TRIP			
☐ 5528	Swahili	197?	12.00
VANGUARD			
☐ VSD-79365	Clark Terry and His Jolly Giants	197?	15.00
☐ VSD-79373	Clark Terry Big Band Live at Buddy's Place	1976	15.00
☐ VSD-79355	Clark Terry Big Band Live at Wichita Fest '74	1975	15.00
☐ VSD-79393	Globetrotter	1977	15.00
VERVE			
☐ V6-8836	Previously Unreleased Recordings	197?	18.00
WING			
☐ MGW-60002 [M]	The Jazz School	1955	80.00
TERRY, CLARK/COLEMAN HAWKINS			
COLPIX			
☐ CP-450 [M]	Eddie Costa Memorial Concert	1963	250.00
☐ SCP-450 [S]	Eddie Costa Memorial Concert	1963	50.00
TERRY, DON			
COLUMBIA			
☐ CL6288 [10]	Teen-Age Dance Session	1955	50.00
TERRY, GORDON			
LIBERTY			
☐ LRP-3218 [M]	Liberty Square Dance Club	1962	25.00
—With calls			
☐ LRP-3219 [M]	Liberty Square Dance Club	1962	25.00
—Without calls			
PLANTATION			
☐ 514	Disco Country	1977	15.00
TERRY, LILLIAN			
SOUL NOTE			
☐ SN-1047	A Dream Comes True	198?	15.00
☐ SN-1147	Oo-Shoo-Be-Doo-Be…Oo… Oo…Oo…Oo	1986	15.00
TERRY, PAT, JR.			
CIRCLE			
☐ C-54	All Jazzed Up	1981	12.00
TERRY, RON			
WING			
☐ MGW-12108 [M]	Polkas and Waltzes	1959	18.00

Number	Title	Yr	NM
☐ SRW-16108 [S]	Polkas and Waltzes	1959	25.00
TERRY, SONNY, AND BROWNIE MCGHEE			
A&M			
☐ SP-4379	Sonny & Brownie	1973	15.00
ARCHIVE OF FOLK MUSIC			
☐ 242	Brownie & Sonny	198?	15.00
BLUESVILLE			
☐ BVLP-1020 [M]	Blues All Around My Head	1961	80.00
—Bright blue label, no trident logo			
☐ BVLP-1020 [M]	Blues All Around My Head	1964	30.00
—Blue label with trident logo on right			
☐ BVLP-1005 [M]	Blues and Folk	1960	80.00
—Bright blue label, no trident logo			
☐ BVLP-1005 [M]	Blues and Folk	1964	30.00
—Blue label with trident logo on right			
☐ BVLP-1033 [M]	Blues in My Soul	1961	80.00
—Bright blue label, no trident logo			
☐ BVLP-1033 [M]	Blues in My Soul	1964	30.00
—Blue label with trident logo at right			
☐ BVLP-1002 [M]	Down Home Blues	1960	80.00
—Bright blue label, no trident logo			
☐ BVLP-1002 [M]	Down Home Blues	1964	30.00
—Blue label with trident logo on right			
☐ BVLP-1058 [M]	Live at the Second Fret	1962	80.00
—Bright blue label, no trident logo			
☐ BVLP-1058 [M]	Live at the Second Fret	1964	30.00
—Blue label with trident logo on right			
BLUESWAY			
☐ BLS-6059	Couldn't Believe My Eyes	1970	18.00
☐ BLS-6028	Long Way from Home	1969	18.00
COLLECTABLES			
☐ COL-5198	Golden Classics: Blowin' the Fuses	198?	12.00
EVEREST			
☐ 242	Brownie McGhee and Sonny Terry	1969	30.00
☐ 206	Sonny Terry	1968	30.00
FANTASY			
☐ 24708	Back to New Orleans	1972	18.00
☐ F-3317 [M]	Blues and Shouts	1962	150.00
—Red vinyl			
☐ F-3317 [M]	Blues and Shouts	1962	40.00
—Black vinyl			
☐ OBC-505	Brownie's Blues	1984	12.00
☐ 24723	California Blues	1981	18.00
☐ F-3296 [M]	Just a Closer Walk with Thee	1962	150.00
—Red vinyl			
☐ F-3296 [M]	Just a Closer Walk with Thee	1962	40.00
—Black vinyl			
☐ 24721	Midnight Special	1977	18.00
☐ F-3340 [M]	Sonny and Brownie at Sugar Hill	1962	150.00
—Red vinyl			
☐ F-3340 [M]	Sonny and Brownie at Sugar Hill	1962	40.00
—Black vinyl			
☐ FS-8091 [S]	Sonny and Brownie at Sugar Hill	1962	150.00
—Blue vinyl			
☐ FS-8091 [S]	Sonny and Brownie at Sugar Hill	1962	40.00
—Black vinyl			
☐ OBC-503	Sonny's Story	1984	12.00
☐ F-3254 [M]	Sonny Terry & Brownie McGhee	1961	150.00
—Red vinyl			
☐ F-3254 [M]	Sonny Terry & Brownie McGhee	1961	40.00
—Black vinyl			
FOLKLORE			
☐ FRLP-14013 [M]	Down Home Blues	1964	40.00
☐ FRST-14013 [S]	Down Home Blues	1964	50.00
FOLKWAYS			
☐ FA-2327 [M]	Blues and Folk Songs	1960	30.00
☐ F-2421 [M]	Traditional Blues, Volume 1	1961	30.00
☐ FS-2421 [S]	Traditional Blues, Volume 1	1961	40.00
☐ F-2422 [M]	Traditional Blues, Volume 2	1961	30.00
☐ FS-2422 [S]	Traditional Blues, Volume 2	1961	40.00
FONTANA			
☐ SGF-67599	Where the Blues Begin	1969	30.00
KIMBERLEY			
☐ 2017 [M]	Southern Meetin'	1963	25.00
☐ 11017 [S]	Southern Meetin'	1963	30.00
MAINSTREAM			
☐ M-6049 [M]	Hometown Blues	1966	25.00
☐ MS-6049 [S]	Hometown Blues	1966	30.00
MOBILE FIDELITY			
☐ 1-233	Sonny and Brownie	1996	25.00
—Audiophile vinyl			
MUSE			
☐ 5117	Hootin'	198?	15.00
☐ 5131	You Hear Me Talkin'	198?	15.00
OLYMPIC			
☐ 7108	Hootin' & Hollerin'	1972	15.00

Number	Title	Yr	NM

PRESTIGE

❑ PRLP-7715	Best of Sonny Terry and Brownie McGhee	1969	18.00
❑ PRLP-7803	Live at the Second Fret	1970	18.00

ROULETTE

❑ R-25074 [M]	The Folk Songs of Sonny & Brownie	1959	50.00
❑ RS-25074 [S]	The Folk Songs of Sonny & Brownie	1959	80.00

SAVOY

❑ SJL-1137	Climbin' Up	1984	12.00
❑ 12218	Down Home Blues	1973	15.00

SHARP

❑ 2003 [M]	Down Home Blues	195?	150.00

SMASH

❑ MGS-27067 [M]	Brownie McGhee at the Bunkhouse	1965	30.00
❑ SRS-67067 [S]	Brownie McGhee at the Bunkhouse	1965	40.00

SMITHSONIAN/FOLKWAYS

❑ SF-40011	Sing	198?	12.00

STORYVILLE

❑ 4007	Brownie & Sonny	1972	15.00

TOPIC

❑ T-29 [M]	Songs	1958	50.00

VEE JAY

❑ VJLP-1138	Coffee House Blues	198?	12.00

— With Lightnin' Hopkins

VERVE

❑ MGV3008 [M]	Blues Is My Companion	1961	80.00

VERVE FOLKWAYS

❑ FV9010 [M]	Get Together	1965	30.00
❑ FVS9010 [S]	Get Together	1965	30.00
❑ FV9019 [M]	Guitar Highway	1965	30.00
❑ FVS9019 [S]	Guitar Highway	1965	30.00

WASHINGTON

❑ W-702 [M]	Talkin' 'Bout the Blues	1961	50.00

WORLD PACIFIC

❑ WP-1294 [M]	Blues Is a Story	1960	50.00
❑ ST-1294 [S]	Blues Is a Story	1960	80.00
❑ WP-1296 [M]	Down South Summit Meetin'	1960	50.00
❑ ST-1296 [S]	Down South Summit Meetin'	1960	80.00

TERRY, SONNY

ALLIGATOR

❑ AL-4734	Whoopin'	198?	15.00

— With Johnny Winter, Willie Dixon and others

BLUE LABOR

❑ 101	Robbin' the Grave	197?	15.00

BLUESVILLE

❑ BVLP-1069 [M]	Sonny Is King	1963	80.00

— Bright blue label, no trident logo

❑ BVLP-1069 [M]	Sonny Is King	1964	30.00

— Blue label with trident logo on right

❑ BVLP-1025 [M]	Sonny's Story	1961	80.00

— Bright blue label, no trident logo

❑ BVLP-1025 [M]	Sonny's Story	1964	30.00

— Blue label with trident logo on right

COLLECTABLES

❑ COL-5195	Chain Gang Blues	198?	12.00
❑ COL-5307	Sonny Terry	198?	12.00

ELEKTRA

❑ EKL-15 [10]	City Blues	1954	150.00

— With Alec Stewart

❑ EKL-14 [10]	Folk Blues	1954	150.00

FANTASY

❑ OBC-521	Sonny Is King	198?	12.00

FOLKWAYS

❑ 3821	A New Sound	198?	15.00
❑ FP-35 [10]	Harmonica and Vocal Solos	1952	150.00
❑ FA-2035 [10]	Harmonica and Vocal Solos	1952	100.00
❑ FS-2369	On the Road	196?	18.00
❑ FP-2006 [10]	Sonny Terry's Washboard Band	1950	150.00

— Blue and white cover

❑ FA-2006 [10]	Sonny Terry's Washboard Band	195?	100.00

— Black and white cover (reissue)

PRESTIGE

❑ PRST-7802	Sonny Is King	1970	18.00

RIVERSIDE

❑ RLP-644 [M]	Sonny Terry and His Mouth Harp	195?	80.00

STINSON

❑ SLP-55 [10]	Sonny Terry and His Mouth Harp	1950	150.00
❑ 55	Sonny Terry and His Mouth Harp	197?	15.00

— Reissue of 10-inch LP

TESCHEMACHER, FRANK

BRUNSWICK

❑ BL58017 [10]	Tesch Plays Jazz Classics	1950	80.00

TIME-LIFE

❑ STL-J23	Giants of Jazz	1982	25.00

TEX, JOE

ACCORD

❑ SN-7174	J.T.'s Funk	1982	12.00

ATLANTIC

❑ SD8231	Buying a Book	1969	25.00
❑ SD8292	From the Roots Came the Rapper	1972	18.00
❑ SD8211	Happy Soul	1969	25.00
❑ 8106 [M]	Hold What You've Got	1965	40.00
❑ SD8106 [P]	Hold What You've Got	1965	50.00
❑ 8133 [M]	I've Got to Do a Little Better	1966	40.00
❑ SD8133 [S]	I've Got to Do a Little Better	1966	50.00
❑ SD8254	Joe Tex Sings with Strings and Things	1970	18.00
❑ SD8156	Live and Lively	1968	25.00
❑ SD8187 [S]	Soul Country	1968	25.00
❑ 8187 [M]	Soul Country	1968	40.00

— Mono is white label promo only; "d/j copy monaural" sticker on cover

❑ 8144 [M]	The Best of Joe Tex	1967	25.00
❑ SD8144 [P]	The Best of Joe Tex	1967	30.00
❑ 81278	The Best of Joe Tex	1985	12.00
❑ 8124 [M]	The Love You Save	1966	40.00
❑ SD8124 [S]	The Love You Save	1966	50.00
❑ 8115 [M]	The New Boss	1965	40.00
❑ SD8115 [S]	The New Boss	1965	50.00

CHECKER

❑ LP-2993 [M]	Hold On	1965	150.00

DIAL

❑ DL6100	He Who Is Without Funk Cast the First Stone	1979	12.00
❑ DL6002	I Gotcha	1972	18.00
❑ DL6004	Joe Tex Spills the Beans	1973	18.00

EPIC

❑ PE34666	Bumps and Bruises	1977	15.00

KING

❑ 935 [M]	The Best of Joe Tex	1965	100.00
❑ KS-935 [R]	The Best of Joe Tex	1965	75.00

LONDON

❑ LC-50017	Super Soul	1977	12.00

PARROT

❑ PA61002 [M]	The Best of Joe Tex	1965	50.00
❑ PAS71002 [R]	The Best of Joe Tex	1965	30.00

PRIDE

❑ PRD-0020	The History of Joe Tex	1973	12.00

RHINO

❑ RNLP-70191	I Believe I'm Gonna Make It: The Best of Joe Tex 1964-1972	1988	12.00

TEXAS BOYS CHOIR, THE

TURNABOUT (VOX)

❑ TV-S34544	Benjamin Britten: A Ceremony of Carols; Gregg Smith: Bible Songs for Young Voices	1973	15.00

TEXAS PLAYBOYS, THE

CAPITOL

❑ ST-11725	Live and Kickin'	1978	18.00
❑ ST-11612	Today	1977	18.00

TEXAS RANGERS, THE

CUMBERLAND

❑ SRC-69505 [S]	The Best of Western Swing	1963	30.00
❑ MGC-29507 [M]	The Best of Western Swing	1963	25.00

TEXAS RUBY

KING

❑ 840 [M]	Texas Ruby Sings His Favorite Songs	1963	50.00

TEXAS TROUBADOURS, THE

DECCA

❑ DL4644 [M]	Country Dance Time	1965	25.00
❑ DL74644 [S]	Country Dance Time	1965	30.00
❑ DL4745 [M]	Ernest Tubb's Fabulous Texas Troubadours	1966	25.00
❑ DL74745 [S]	Ernest Tubb's Fabulous Texas Troubadours	1966	30.00
❑ DL75017	The Terrific Texas Troubadours and Guests	1968	25.00
❑ DL4459 [M]	The Texas Troubadours	1964	30.00
❑ DL74459 [S]	The Texas Troubadours	1964	30.00

THA ALKAHOLICS

LOUD/RCA

❑ 66280	21 & Over	1993	18.00
❑ 66446	Coast II Coast	1995	18.00
❑ 67345	Likwidation	1997	15.00

THACKRAY, JAKE

PHILIPS

❑ PSH600-318 [B]	Jake's Progress	1969	25.00
❑ PHS600-275 [B]	The Last Will and Testament of	1967	30.00

THAT PETROL EMOTION

POLYDOR

❑ 833132-1	Babble	1987	12.00

VIRGIN

❑ 91354	Chemicrazy	1990	12.00
❑ 91019	End of the Millennium Psychosis Blues	1988	12.00

THAXTON, LLOYD

DECCA

❑ DL4594 [M]	Lloyd Thaxton Presents	1964	25.00
❑ DL74594 [S]	Lloyd Thaxton Presents	1964	30.00

THE THE

EPIC

❑ BFE40471	Infected	1987	15.00
❑ FE45241	Mindbomb	1989	15.00
❑ BFE39266	Soul Mining	1985	15.00

THE UGLY BEATS

❑ GH1126 [S]	Bring on the Beats!	2011	15.00

— Retail value of new LP. Also was released on CD.

❑ GH1156 [S]	Motor!	2010	18.00

— 180-gram vinyl with free download code.

❑ GH1140 [S]	Take A Stand	2007	15.00

THEE IMAGE

MANTICORE

❑ MA6506 [B]	Inside the Triangle	1975	25.00
❑ MA6504S1 [B]	Thee Image	1975	25.00

THEE MIDNITERS

CHATTAHOOCHIE

❑ C-1001 [M]	Thee Midniters	1965	70.00
❑ CS-1001 [S]	Thee Midniters	1965	85.00

WHITTIER

❑ W-5000 [M]	Bring You Love Special Delivery	1966	40.00
❑ WS-5000 [S]	Bring You Love Special Delivery	1966	50.00
❑ W-5002 [M]	Giants	1967	40.00
❑ WS-5002 [S]	Giants	1967	50.00
❑ W-5001 [M]	Unlimited	1966	40.00
❑ WS-5001 [S]	Unlimited	1966	50.00

ZYANYA/RHINO

❑ RNLP-063	The Best of Thee Midniters	1983	15.00

THEE MUFFINS

(NO LABEL)

❑ (no #)0	Thee Muffins Pop Up!	1967	200.00

THEE PROPHETS

KAPP

❑ KS-3596	Playgirl	1969	25.00

THEM

HAPPY TIGER

❑ HT-1004	Them	1969	50.00
❑ HT-1012	Them In Reality	1971	120.00

LONDON

❑ PS639 [P]	Backtrackin'	1974	12.00
❑ 820326-1	Them Featuring Van Morrison	1985	12.00
❑ LC-50001 [R]	The Story of Them	1977	12.00

PARROT

❑ PA61008 [M]	Them Again	1966	100.00
❑ PAS71008 [R]	Them Again	1966	50.00
❑ PA61005 [M]	Them Featuring "Gloria	1966	60.00

— Same album as above, but with slightly different title

❑ PAS71005 [R]	Them Featuring "Gloria	1966	40.00

— Same album as above, but with slightly different title

❑ PA61005 [M]	Them Featuring "Here Comes the Night	1965	100.00
❑ PAS71005 [R]	Them Featuring "Here Comes the Night	1965	70.00
❑ BP71053 [P]	Them Featuring Van Morrison	1972	15.00

— Gloria," "Here Comes the Night," "If You and I Could Be as Two," "One More Time" and "One Two Brown Eyes" are true stereo.

TOWER

❑ T5104 [M]	Now and Them	1967	60.00
❑ ST5104 [S]	Now and Them	1967	80.00
❑ ST5116 [S]	Time Out! Time In for Them	1968	100.00

THEODORE

CORAL

❑ CRL757322 [S]	Coral Records Presents Theodore in Stereo	1959	100.00

THESE TRAILS

SINERGIA

❑ SR4059	These Trails	1973	180.00

THESELIUS, GOSTA

BALLY

❑ BAL-12002 [M]	Swedish Jazz	1956	50.00

Number	Title	Yr	NM

THEUS, FATS

CTI
❏ 1005	Black Out	1972	18.00

THEY MIGHT BE GIANTS

BAR NONE
❏ A-HAON 004 [EP]	Don't Let's Start	1987	25.00
❏ A-HAON 005 [EP]	(She Was a) Hotel Detective	1988	25.00
❏ A-HAON 002	They Might Be Giants	1986	25.00

— *Original edition contains lyric sheet and no mention of Restless Records*

BAR NONE/RESTLESS
❏ 72605 [EP]	Don't Let's Start	1988	18.00

— *Reissue of A-HAON 004*

❏ 72600	Lincoln	1988	18.00
❏ 72611 [EP]	They'll Need a Crane	1989	12.00
❏ A-HAON 002	They Might Be Giants	1988	18.00

— *With mention of Restless Records*

ELEKTRA
❏ R114772	Flood	1990	18.00

— *BMG Music Service edition*

❏ 60907	Flood	1990	18.00
❏ E1-60907	Flood	1990	18.00

— *Columbia House edition*

THIELEMANS, TOOTS

A&M
❏ SP-3613	Yesterday and Today	1974	15.00

ABC-PARAMOUNT
❏ ABC-482 [M]	The Whistler and His Guitar	1965	30.00
❏ ABCS-482 [S]	The Whistler and His Guitar	1965	30.00

CHOICE
❏ 1007	Captured Alive	197?	18.00

COLUMBIA
❏ CL658 [M]	The Sound	1955	50.00

COMMAND
❏ RS 33-906 [M]	Contrasts	1967	25.00
❏ RS906SD [S]	Contrasts	1967	18.00
❏ RS 33-918 [M]	Guitars and Strings… And Things	1967	25.00
❏ RS918SD [S]	Guitars and Strings… And Things	1967	18.00
❏ RSSD978-2	The Salient One	1973	18.00
❏ RS930SD	Toots!	1968	18.00

CONCORD JAZZ
❏ CJ-355	Only Trust Your Heart	1988	12.00

DECCA
❏ DL9204 [M]	Time Out for Toots	1958	50.00
❏ DL79204 [S]	Time Out for Toots	1958	40.00

FANTASY
❏ OJC-1738	Man Bites Harmonica	198?	12.00

INNER CITY
❏ IC-1145	Live	198?	15.00
❏ IC-1146	Live 2	198?	15.00
❏ IC-1147	Live 3	198?	15.00
❏ IC-1148	Spotlight	198?	15.00

JAZZ MAN
❏ 5016	Slow Motion	198?	12.00

RIVERSIDE
❏ RLP 12-257 [M]	Man Bites Harmonica	1958	100.00

SIGNATURE
❏ SM-6006 [M]	The Soul of Toots Thielmans	1960	80.00
❏ SS-6006 [S]	The Soul of Toots Thielmans	1960	60.00

THIGPEN, ED

GNP CRESCENDO
❏ GNPS-2098	Action Re-Action	197?	12.00

VERVE
❏ V-8663 [M]	Out of the Storm	1966	25.00
❏ V6-8663 [S]	Out of the Storm	1966	30.00

THILO, JESPER

STORYVILLE
❏ 4065	Swingin' Friends	198?	12.00
❏ 4072	Tribute to Frog	198?	12.00

THIN LIZZY

LONDON
❏ LC-50004	The Rocker (1971-1974)	1977	14.00
❏ PS594	Thin Lizzy	1971	40.00
❏ PS636	Vagabonds of the Western World	1973	30.00

MERCURY
❏ SRM-1-1186	Bad Reputation	1977	15.00
❏ 5313416	Black Rose/A Rock Legend	2009	25.00
❏ SRM-1-1108	Fighting	1976	15.00

— *Reissue of Vertigo 2005*

❏ SRM-1-1081	Jailbreak	1976	15.00
❏ 5310376	Jailbreak	2008	25.00
❏ SRM-1-1119	Johnny the Fox	1976	15.00
❏ SRM-1-1107	Night Life	1976	15.00

— *Reissue of Vertigo 2002*

VERTIGO
❏ VEL-2005	Fighting	1975	18.00
❏ VEL-2002	Night Life	1974	18.00

VH1 CLASSICS
❏ VH132	Still Dangerous	2009	25.00

WARNER BROS.
❏ BSK3338	Black Rose/A Rock Legend	1979	12.00
❏ BSK3496	Chinatown	1980	12.00
❏ 23986	Life" -- Live	1984	18.00
❏ BS23213	Live and Dangerous	1978	15.00
❏ BSK3622	Renegade	1982	12.00
❏ 23831	Thunder and Lightning	1983	12.00

THINGS TO COME

SUNDAZED
❏ LP-5008	I Want Out	199?	12.00

THINK

LAURIE
❏ SLLP-2052	Encounter	1972	15.00

THIRD ESTATE, THE

THIRD ESTATE
❏ LP-1000	Years Before the Wine	1976	200.00

THIRD EYE BLIND

ELEKTRA
❏ 62415-1	Blue	1999	60.00
❏ 62012-1	Third Eye Blind	1997	40.00

THIRD POWER

VANGUARD
❏ VSD-6554 [B]	Believe	1970	35.00

THIRD RAIL, THE

EPIC
❏ LN24327 [M]	Id Music	1967	30.00
❏ BN26327 [S]	Id Music	1967	40.00

THIRTEENTH FLOOR ELEVATORS, THE

INTERNATIONAL ARTISTS
❏ 8	13th Floor Elevators Live	1968	100.00
❏ 8	13th Floor Elevators Live	1979	30.00

— *Repressing with "Masterfonics" in dead wax*

❏ 9	Bull of the Woods	1968	80.00
❏ 9	Bull of the Woods	1979	30.00

— *Repressing with "Masterfonics" in dead wax*

❏ 5 [M]	Easter Everywhere	1968	400.00

— *Mono is promo only*

❏ 5 [S]	Easter Everywhere	1968	150.00

— *With custom inner sleeve*

❏ 5 [S]	Easter Everywhere	1968	150.00

— *Without custom inner sleeve*

❏ 5 [S]	Easter Everywhere	1979	30.00

— *Repressing with "Masterfonics" in dead wax*

❏ 1 [M]	Psychedelic Sounds	1967	250.00

— *Green and yellow label*

❏ 1 [M]	Psychedelic Sounds	1968	150.00

— *All-yellow label*

❏ 1 [S]	Psychedelic Sounds	1968	200.00

— *All-yellow label*

❏ 1 [S]	Psychedelic Sounds	1979	30.00

— *Repressing with "Masterfonics" in dead wax*

❏ 1 [S]	Psychedelic Sounds	1968	200.00

— *Aqua-blue label*

31ST OF FEBRUARY, THE

VANGUARD
❏ VSD-6503	The 31st of February	1969	40.00

31 FLAVORS, THE

CROWN
❏ CST-592	Hair	1968	50.00

.38 SPECIAL

A&M
❏ SP-17402 [DJ]	10 From 38	1986	18.00

— *Promo-only compilation*

❏ SP-3164	.38 Special	198?	10.00

— *Budget-line reissue of 4638*

❏ SP-4638	.38 Special	1977	15.00
❏ SP-3910 [B]	Flashback	1987	12.00

— *Includes bonus 7-inch 33 1/3 rpm small hole single "Flashback Live EP"; deduct 40 percent if missing*

❏ SP-5218	Rock & Roll Strategy	1988	12.00
❏ SP-3216	Rockin' Into the Night	198?	10.00

— *Budget-line reissue of 4782*

❏ SP-4782 [B]	Rockin' Into the Night	1979	15.00
❏ SP-3165	Special Delivery	198?	10.00

— *Budget-line reissue of 4684*

❏ SP-4684	Special Delivery	1978	15.00
❏ SP-3299	Special Forces	198?	10.00

— *Budget-line reissue of 4888*

❏ SP-4888 [B]	Special Forces	1982	12.00
❏ SP-5115	Strength in Numbers	1986	12.00
❏ SP-3310	Tour de Force	198?	10.00

— *Budget-line reissue of 4971*

❏ SP-4971	Tour de Force	1983	12.00
❏ SP-3298	Wild-Eyed Southern Boys	198?	10.00

— *Budget-line reissue of 4835*

❏ SP-4835	Wild-Eyed Southern Boys	1981	12.00

THOMAS, B.J.

ABC
❏ ABCD-912	Help Me Make It to My Rockin' Chair	1976	12.00
❏ ABDP-858	Reunion	1975	12.00

ACCORD
❏ SN-7106	Lovin' You	198?	12.00

BUCKBOARD
❏ 1023	B.J. Thomas Sings Hank Williams and Other Favorites	198?	12.00

CLEVELAND INT'L.
❏ FC38561	New Looks	1983	12.00
❏ PC38561	New Looks	1984	10.00

— *Budget-line reissue*

❏ FC39337	Shining	1984	12.00
❏ FC39111	The Great American Dream	1983	12.00
❏ PC39111	The Great American Dream	1984	10.00

— *Budget-line reissue*

❏ FC40157	Throwing Rocks at the Moon	1985	12.00

COLUMBIA
❏ PC40148	All Is Calm, All Is Bright...	1985	12.00
❏ PC38400	Love Shines	1984	10.00

— *Reissue of Priority 38400*

❏ FC40496	Night Life	1986	12.00

DORAL
❏ (# unknown)0	Doral Presents B.J. Thomas	1971	25.00

— *Mail-order promotion from Doral cigarettes*

EVEREST
❏ 4104	Golden Greats	1981	12.00

HICKORY
❏ LPM-133 [M]	The Very Best of B.J. Thomas	1966	25.00
❏ LPS-133 [S]	The Very Best of B.J. Thomas	1966	30.00
❏ T90956 [M]	The Very Best of B.J. Thomas	1966	30.00

— *Capitol Record Club edition*

❏ ST90956 [S]	The Very Best of B.J. Thomas	1966	30.00

— *Capitol Record Club edition*

MCA
❏ 5296	As We Know Him	1982	12.00
❏ 2286	B.J. Thomas	1977	12.00
❏ 3035	Everybody Loves a Rain Song	1978	12.00
❏ 746	Everybody Loves a Rain Song	1980	10.00

— *Budget-line reissue*

❏ 3231	For the Best	1979	12.00
❏ 5155	In Concert	1980	12.00
❏ 27032	In Concert	198?	10.00

— *Reissue of MCA 5155*

❏ 5195	Some Love Songs Never Die	1980	12.00

MYRRH
❏ MSB-6593	A Happy Man	1979	12.00
❏ MSB-6675	Amazing Grace	1981	12.00
❏ WR-8200	Amazing Grace	1985	10.00

— *Reissue of 6675*

❏ MSB-6574	Home Where I Belong	1978	12.00
❏ MSB-6705	Miracle	1983	12.00
❏ WR-8153	Peace in the Valley	1985	12.00

— *Reissue of 6710*

❏ MSB-6710	Peace in the Valley	1983	12.00
❏ MSB-6653	The Best of B.J. Thomas	1980	12.00
❏ MSB-6725	The Best of B.J. Thomas, Volume 2	1984	12.00
❏ MSB-6633	You Gave Me Love	1979	12.00

PACEMAKER
❏ PLP-3001 [M]	B.J. Thomas and the Triumphs	1965	200.00

PAIR
❏ PDL2-1099	Greatest Hits	1986	15.00

PARAMOUNT
❏ PAS-6052	B.J. Thomas Songs	1973	15.00
❏ PAS1020	Longhorns & Londonbridges	1974	15.00

PICKWICK
❏ SPC-3623	The Best of B.J. Thomas	197?	12.00

PRIORITY
❏ JU38400	Love Shines	1982	12.00

REPRISE
❏ 25898	Midnight Minute	1989	15.00

SCEPTER
❏ 5101	Billy Joe Thomas	1972	15.00
❏ 5108	B.J. Thomas Country	1972	15.00
❏ SPS-582	Everybody's Out of Town	1970	15.00
❏ SRM-561 [M]	For Lovers and Losers	1967	25.00
❏ SPS-561 [S]	For Lovers and Losers	1967	18.00
❏ 5112	Greatest All-Time Hits	1973	18.00
❏ SPS-578	Greatest Hits, Volume 1	1969	15.00
❏ SPS-597	Greatest Hits, Volume Two	1971	15.00

Number	Title	Yr	NM
❑ SRM-535 [M]	I'm So Lonesome I Could Cry	1966	25.00
❑ SPS-535 [S]	I'm So Lonesome I Could Cry	1966	30.00
❑ SPS-586	Most of All	1970	15.00
❑ SPS-570 [S]	On My Way	1968	18.00
❑ SRM-570 [M]	On My Way	1968	30.00

— *Mono appears to be white label promo only; in stereo cover with "Promotional DJ Copy Monaural Not for Sale" sticker on front*

❑ SPS-580	Raindrops Keep Fallin' on My Head	1970	15.00

— *Remixed version; trail-off wax number on Side 1 is "SPS-580-A-1C" or "SPS-580-A-1D" and on Side 2 is "SPS-580-B-1C"*

❑ SPS-580	Raindrops Keep Fallin' on My Head	1970	18.00

— *Original "muddy mix"; trail-off wax number on Side 1 is "SPS-580-A-1B" and on Side 2 is "SPS-580-B-1A"*

❑ SRM-556 [M]	Tomorrow Never Comes	1966	18.00
❑ SPS-556 [S]	Tomorrow Never Comes	1966	25.00
❑ SPS-576	Young and In Love	1969	18.00
STARDAY			
❑ 992	The Best of B.J. Thomas	197?	12.00
UNITED ARTISTS			
❑ UA-LA389-E	The Very Best of B.J. Thomas	1974	15.00

THOMAS, CARLA

ATLANTIC

Number	Title	Yr	NM
❑ 8057 [M]	Gee Whiz	1961	100.00

— *With white "fan" logo*

❑ 8057 [M]	Gee Whiz	1963	40.00

— *With black "fan" logo*

❑ SD8057 [S]	Gee Whiz	1961	150.00

— *With white "fan" logo*

❑ SD8057 [S]	Gee Whiz	1963	50.00

— *With black "fan" logo*

❑ SD8232	The Best of Carla Thomas	1969	30.00
STAX			
❑ 709 [M]	Carla	1966	35.00
❑ 709 [S]	Carla	1966	50.00
❑ 706 [M]	Comfort Me	1966	35.00
❑ 706 [P]	Comfort Me	1966	50.00
❑ STS-2044	Love Means Carla Thomas	1971	35.00
❑ STS-2019	Memphis Queen	1969	35.00
❑ MPS-8538	Memphis Queen	1987	12.00

— *Budget-line reissue*

❑ 718 [M]	The Queen Alone	1967	35.00
❑ 718 [S]	The Queen Alone	1967	50.00

THOMAS, DANNY

COLUMBIA

Number	Title	Yr	NM
❑ XTV60818/9 [M]	An Evening with Danny Thomas	1960	30.00

— *Made for Post Cereals*

MGM

❑ E-201 [10]	An Evening with Danny Thomas	1954	100.00
MYRRH			
❑ MST-6522	I'll Still Be Loving You	197?	12.00
❑ MSA-6539	Jesus Is My Kind of People	197?	12.00
❑ MST-6520	Tomorrow Belongs to You	1973	12.00

THOMAS, DAVID

STOMP OFF

Number	Title	Yr	NM
❑ SOS 1072	Through the Bottomlands	1984	12.00

THOMAS, DYLAN

CAEDMON

Number	Title	Yr	NM
❑ TC1002 [M]	A Child's Christmas in Wales and Five Poems (Dylan Thomas, Volume 1)	1957	25.00

— *Number stamped into dead wax; "New York, 1, New York" address on label and cover*

THOMAS, GARY

ENJA

Number	Title	Yr	NM
❑ R1-79604	Code Violations	1989	15.00
JMT			
❑ 834432-1	By Any Means Necessary	198?	12.00

THOMAS, IAN

ATLANTIC

Number	Title	Yr	NM
❑ SD19167	Still Here	1978	12.00
CHRYSALIS			
❑ CHR1126	Goodnight Mrs. Calabash	1976	15.00
JANUS			
❑ JLS-3058	Ian Thomas	1973	15.00
❑ JXS-7005	Long Long Way	1974	15.00
MERCURY			
❑ 826030-1	Add Water	1985	15.00
❑ 822319-1	Riders on Dark Horses	1984	12.00

THOMAS, IRMA

BANDY

Number	Title	Yr	NM
❑ 70003	Irma Thomas Sings	197?	30.00

FUNGUS

Number	Title	Yr	NM
❑ FB-25150	In Between Tears	1973	40.00
IMPERIAL			
❑ LP-9302 [M]	Take a Look	1966	50.00
❑ LP-12302 [S]	Take a Look	1966	60.00
❑ LP-9266 [M]	Wish Someone Would Care	1964	50.00
❑ LP-12266 [S]	Wish Someone Would Care	1964	60.00
RCS			
❑ 1004	Safe with Me	1980	30.00

THOMAS, JEANNIE

STRAND

Number	Title	Yr	NM
❑ SL-1030 [M]	Jeannie Thomas Sings for the Boys	1961	40.00
❑ SLS-1030 [S]	Jeannie Thomas Sings for the Boys	1961	50.00

THOMAS, JOE (2), AND JAY MCSHANN

UPTOWN

Number	Title	Yr	NM
❑ 27.12	Blowin' In from Kansas City	198?	15.00

THOMAS, JOE (2)

UPTOWN

Number	Title	Yr	NM
❑ 27.01	Raw Meat	198?	15.00

THOMAS, JOE (3), AND BILL ELLIOTT

SUE

Number	Title	Yr	NM
❑ LP-1025 [M]	Speak Your Piece	1964	50.00

THOMAS, JOE (3)

CHIAROSCURO

Number	Title	Yr	NM
❑ 2018	Flash	1979	15.00
GROOVE MERCHANT			
❑ 504	Joy of Cookin'	197?	25.00
❑ 3310	Masada	197?	18.00

THOMAS, JON

ABC-PARAMOUNT

Number	Title	Yr	NM
❑ 351 [M]	Heartbreak	1960	30.00
❑ S-351 [S]	Heartbreak	1960	40.00
WING			
❑ MGW-12258 [M]	The Big Beat on the Organ	1963	25.00
❑ SRW-16258 [R]	The Big Beat on the Organ	1963	15.00

THOMAS, LEON

FLYING DUTCHMAN

Number	Title	Yr	NM
❑ FD-10155	Blues and the Soulful Truth	197?	18.00
❑ FD-10164	Facets	1973	18.00
❑ FD-10167	Full Circle	197?	18.00
❑ FD-10115	Spirits Known and Unknown	1969	25.00
❑ FD-10132	The Leon Thomas Album	197?	25.00
MEGA			
❑ M51-5003	Gold Sunrise on Magic Mountain	197?	25.00
PORTRAIT			
❑ FR44161	The Leon Thomas Blues Band	1988	12.00

THOMAS, MARLO, AND FRIENDS

A&M

Number	Title	Yr	NM
❑ SP-5196	Free to Be...A Family	1988	15.00

— *Includes a track by Soul Asylum*

THOMAS, PAT

MGM

Number	Title	Yr	NM
❑ E-4103 [M]	Desafinado	1962	18.00
❑ SE-4103 [S]	Desafinado	1962	25.00
❑ E-4206 [M]	Moody's Mood	1964	25.00
❑ SE-4206 [S]	Moody's Mood	1964	30.00
STRAND			
❑ SL-1015 [M]	Jazz Patterns	1961	40.00
❑ SLS-1015 [S]	Jazz Patterns	1961	50.00

THOMAS, RAY

THRESHOLD

Number	Title	Yr	NM
❑ THS16	From Mighty Oaks	1975	18.00
❑ THS17	Hopes Wishes & Dreams	1976	18.00
❑ THSX-102 [DJ]	Ray Thomas Discusses The Recording of His First Solo Album From Mighty Oaks	1975	50.00

THOMAS, RENE

FANTASY

Number	Title	Yr	NM
❑ OJC-1725	Guitar Groove	198?	12.00
JAZZLAND			
❑ JLP-27 [M]	Guitar Groove	1960	30.00
❑ JLP-927 [S]	Guitar Groove	1960	40.00

THOMAS, RUFUS

ALLIGATOR

Number	Title	Yr	NM
❑ AV-4769	That Woman Is Poison	1988	12.00
A.V.I.			
❑ 6046	I Ain't Gettin' Older, I'm Gettin' Better	1978	18.00
❑ 6015	If There Were No Music	1977	18.00

GUSTO

Number	Title	Yr	NM
❑ 0064	Rufus Thomas	1980	12.00
STAX			
❑ STS-3008	Crown Prince of Dance	1973	30.00
❑ STS-3004	Did You Hear Me	1972	30.00
❑ STS-2028	Do the Funky Chicken	1970	30.00
❑ STS-2039 [B]	Rufus Thomas Live/Doing the Push and Pull at P.J.'s	1971	30.00
❑ ST-704 [M]	Walking the Dog	1963	150.00

THOMAS, TIMMY

GLADES

Number	Title	Yr	NM
❑ 33-6501	Why Can't We Live Together	1973	18.00
GOLD MOUNTAIN			
❑ GM-80006	Gotta Give a Little Love	1984	12.00

THOMAS, WALTER "FOOTS"

PRESTIGE

Number	Title	Yr	NM
❑ PRST-7584	Walter "Foots" Thomas All-Stars	196?	18.00

THOMPSON, BOB

INTIMA

Number	Title	Yr	NM
❑ SJ-73284	7 In, 7 Out	1987	12.00

— *Reissue of Rainbow 2010*

❑ SJ-73238	Brother's Keeper	1987	12.00
❑ D1-73331	Say What You Want	1988	12.00
❑ D1-73519	Wilderness	1989	15.00
RAINBOW			
❑ 2010	7 In, 7 Out	1986	25.00

THOMPSON, BUTCH, AND CHET ELY

JAZZOLOGY

Number	Title	Yr	NM
❑ J-79	Jelly Rolls On	197?	12.00

THOMPSON, BUTCH, AND HAL SMITH

STOMP OFF

Number	Title	Yr	NM
❑ SOS-1075	Echoes from Storyville, Vol. 1: If You Don't Shake	1985	12.00
❑ SOS-1116	Echoes from Storyville, Vol. 2: Milenberg Joys	1986	12.00

THOMPSON, BUTCH

JAZZOLOGY

Number	Title	Yr	NM
❑ J-146	Butch Thompson and His Boys in Chicago	1986	12.00
STOMP OFF			
❑ SOS-1037	A' Solas	198?	12.00

THOMPSON, CHESTER

BLACK JAZZ

Number	Title	Yr	NM
❑ 6	Powerhouse	197?	30.00

THOMPSON, DON

CONCORD JAZZ

Number	Title	Yr	NM
❑ CJ-243	Beautiful Friendship	198?	12.00
PM			
❑ 008	Country Place	1976	15.00

THOMPSON, HANK

ABC

Number	Title	Yr	NM
❑ AB-1095	Brand New Hank	1978	15.00
ABC DOT			
❑ DOSD-2060	Back in the Swing of Things	1976	15.00
❑ DO-2091	Doin' My Thing	1977	15.00
❑ DOSD-2032	Hank Thompson Sings Nat King Cole	1975	15.00
❑ DOSD-2003	Moving On	1974	15.00
❑ DOSD-2069	The Thompson Touch	1977	15.00
CAPITOL			
❑ T1544 [M]	An Old Love Affair	1961	30.00

— *Black colorband label, logo at left*

❑ T1544 [M]	An Old Love Affair	1962	18.00

— *Black colorband label, logo at top*

❑ ST1544 [S]	An Old Love Affair	1961	30.00

— *Black colorband label, logo at left*

❑ ST1544 [S]	An Old Love Affair	1962	25.00

— *Black colorband label, logo at top*

❑ T2460 [M]	A Six Pack to Go	1966	25.00
❑ ST2460 [S]	A Six Pack to Go	1966	30.00
❑ T2274 [M]	Breakin' In Another Heart	1965	25.00
❑ ST2274 [S]	Breakin' In Another Heart	1965	30.00
❑ T2575 [M]	Breakin' the Rules	1966	25.00
❑ ST2575 [S]	Breakin' the Rules	1966	30.00
❑ T1775 [M]	Cheyenne Frontier Days	1962	25.00
❑ ST1775 [S]	Cheyenne Frontier Days	1962	30.00
❑ T1111 [M]	Favorite Waltzes	1959	80.00

— *Black colorband label, logo at left*

❑ T1111 [M]	Favorite Waltzes	1962	25.00

— *Black colorband label, logo at top*

❑ T2089 [M]	Golden Country Hits	1964	25.00
❑ ST2089 [S]	Golden Country Hits	1964	30.00
❑ T826 [M]	Hank!	1959	30.00

— *Black colorband label, logo at left*

❑ T826 [M]	Hank!	1962	25.00

— *Black colorband label, logo at top*

❑ T826 [M]	Hank!	1957	80.00

— *Turquoise or gray label*

Number	Title	Yr	NM
❑ T1632 [M]	Hank Thompson at the Golden Nugget	1961	30.00
—Black colorband label, logo at left			
❑ T1632 [M]	Hank Thompson at the Golden Nugget	1962	18.00
—Black colorband label, logo at top			
❑ ST1632 [S]	Hank Thompson at the Golden Nugget	1961	30.00
—Black colorband label, logo at left			
❑ ST1632 [S]	Hank Thompson at the Golden Nugget	1962	25.00
—Black colorband label, logo at top			
❑ T1955 [M]	Hank Thompson at the State Fair of Texas	1963	25.00
❑ ST1955 [S]	Hank Thompson at the State Fair of Texas	1963	30.00
❑ T911 [M]	Hank Thompson Favorites	1957	80.00
—Turquoise or gray label			
❑ T975 [M]	Hank Thompson's Dance Ranch	1958	80.00
—Turquoise or gray label			
❑ T975 [M]	Hank Thompson's Dance Ranch	1959	30.00
—Black colorband label, logo at left			
❑ T975 [M]	Hank Thompson's Dance Ranch	1962	25.00
—Black colorband label, logo at top			
❑ T2154 [M]	It's Christmas Time	1963	25.00
❑ ST2154 [S]	It's Christmas Time	1963	30.00
❑ T2826 [M]	Just an Old Flame	1967	30.00
❑ ST2826 [S]	Just an Old Flame	1967	25.00
❑ T2342 [M]	Luckiest Heartache in Town	1965	25.00
❑ ST2342 [S]	Luckiest Heartache in Town	1965	30.00
❑ T1360 [M]	Most of All	1960	30.00
—Black colorband label, logo at left			
❑ T1360 [M]	Most of All	1962	25.00
—Black colorband label, logo at top			
❑ ST1360 [S]	Most of All	1960	40.00
—Black colorband label, logo at left			
❑ ST1360 [S]	Most of All	1962	30.00
—Black colorband label, logo at top			
❑ T729 [M]	New Recordings of Hank's All-Time Hits	1959	30.00
—Black colorband label, logo at left			
❑ T729 [M]	New Recordings of Hank's All-Time Hits	1962	25.00
—Black colorband label, logo at top			
❑ H729 [10]	New Recordings of Hank's All-Time Hits	195?	120.00
❑ T729 [M]	New Recordings of Hank's All-Time Hits	1956	80.00
—Turquoise or gray label			
❑ H618 [10]	North of the Rio Grande	1953	120.00
❑ T618 [M]	North of the Rio Grande	1956	80.00
—Turquoise or gray label			
❑ T1246 [M]	Songs for Rounders	1959	30.00
❑ ST1246 [S]	Songs for Rounders	1959	40.00
❑ T418 [M]	Songs of the Brazos Valley	1959	30.00
—Black colorband label, logo at left			
❑ T418 [M]	Songs of the Brazos Valley	1962	25.00
—Black colorband label, logo at top			
❑ H418 [10]	Songs of the Brazos Valley	1953	120.00
❑ T418 [M]	Songs of the Brazos Valley	1956	80.00
—Turquoise or gray label			
❑ T1741 [M]	The #1 Country and Western Band	1962	30.00
—Black colorband label, logo at left			
❑ T1741 [M]	The #1 Country and Western Band	1962	25.00
—Black colorband label, logo at top			
❑ DT1741 [R]	The #1 Country and Western Band	1962	25.00
—Black colorband label, logo at left			
❑ DT1741 [R]	The #1 Country and Western Band	1962	15.00
—Black colorband label, logo at top			
❑ T1878 [M]	The Best of Hank Thompson	1963	25.00
❑ ST1878 [S]	The Best of Hank Thompson	1963	30.00
❑ T2661 [M]	The Best of Hank Thompson Vol. 2	1967	30.00
❑ ST2661 [S]	The Best of Hank Thompson Vol. 2	1967	25.00
❑ T1469 [M]	This Broken Heart of Mine	1960	30.00
—Black colorband label, logo at left			
❑ T1469 [M]	This Broken Heart of Mine	1962	25.00
—Black colorband label, logo at top			
❑ ST1469 [S]	This Broken Heart of Mine	1960	40.00
—Black colorband label, logo at left			
❑ ST1469 [S]	This Broken Heart of Mine	1962	30.00
—Black colorband label, logo at top			

DOT

❑ DOS-25996	Cab Driver (A Salute to the Mills Brothers)	1972	18.00
❑ DOS 2-2000	Hank Thompson's 25th Anniversary Album	1971	25.00
❑ DLP-25971	Hank Thompson Salutes Oklahoma	1969	18.00
❑ DOS-26004	Hank Thompson's Greatest Hits Vol. 1	1972	18.00
❑ DOS-26015	Kindly Keep It Country	1973	18.00
❑ DLP-25991	Next Time I Fall in Love (I Won't)	1971	18.00
❑ DLP-25894	On Tap, In the Can, or In the Bottle	1968	18.00
❑ DLP-25932	Smoky the Bar	1969	18.00

Number	Title	Yr	NM

HILLTOP

❑ JS-6085 [S]	You Always Hurt the One You Love	196?	15.00
—Five tracks are rechanneled, five are true stereo			

MCA

❑ 689	Brand New Hank	198?	10.00
❑ 3250	Take Me Back to Tulsa	1980	12.00

WARNER BROS.

❑ W1679 [M]	The Countrypolitan Sound of Hank Thompson	1967	18.00
❑ WS1679 [S]	The Countrypolitan Sound of Hank Thompson	1967	25.00
❑ W1686 [M]	The Gold Standard Collection of Hank Thompson	1967	18.00
❑ WS1686 [S]	The Gold Standard Collection of Hank Thompson	1967	25.00
❑ W1664 [M]	Where Is the Circus and Other Heart Breakin' Hits	1966	18.00
❑ WS1664 [S]	Where Is the Circus and Other Heart Breakin' Hits	1966	25.00

THOMPSON, HAYDEN

KAPP

❑ KL-1507 [M]	Here's Hayden Thompson	1966	30.00
❑ KS-3507 [S]	Here's Hayden Thompson	1966	40.00

THOMPSON, KAY

MGM

❑ E-3146 [M]	Kay Thompson Sings	1955	30.00

SIGNATURE

❑ SM-1017 [M]	Let's Talk About Russia	1959	30.00

THOMPSON, LES

RCA VICTOR

❑ LPT-3102 [10]	Gene Norman Presents "Just Jazz"	1952	150.00

THOMPSON, LINDA

WARNER BROS.

❑ 92 51641 [B]	One Clear Moment	1985	25.00
❑ 1-25164 [B]	One Clear Moment	1985	25.00

THOMPSON, LUCKY

51 WEST

❑ Q16072	Back to the World	198?	16.00

ABC IMPULSE!

❑ ASH-9307-2	Dancing Sunbeam	1975	30.00

ABC-PARAMOUNT

❑ ABC-111 [M]	Lucky Thompson Featuring Oscar Pettiford, Volume 1	1956	120.00
❑ ABC-171 [M]	Lucky Thompson Featuring Oscar Pettiford, Volume 2	1957	120.00

BIOGRAPH

❑ BLP-12061	Lullaby in Rhythm	1979	15.00

DAWN

❑ DLP-1113 [M]	Lucky Thompson	1957	100.00

FANTASY

❑ OJC-194	Lucky Strikes	1985	15.00

GROOVE MERCHANT

❑ GM-508	Goodbye Yesterday	1973	30.00
❑ GM-4411	Illuminations	197?	30.00
❑ GM-517	I Offer You	1974	30.00

INNER CITY

❑ IC-7016	Lucky Thompson	1976	18.00

LONDON

❑ D-93098 [10]	Recorded in Paris '56	1956	100.00

MOODSVILLE

❑ MVLP-39 [M]	Lucky Thompson Plays Jerome Kern and No More	1963	60.00
—Green label			
❑ MVST-39 [S]	Lucky Thompson Plays Jerome Kern and No More	1963	80.00
—Green label			
❑ MVLP-39 [M]	Lucky Thompson Plays Jerome Kern and No More	1965	30.00
—Blue label, trident logo at right			
❑ MVST-39 [S]	Lucky Thompson Plays Jerome Kern and No More	1965	40.00
—Blue label, trident logo at right			

NESSA

❑ N-13	Body and Soul	197?	30.00

PRESTIGE

❑ PRLP-7394 [M]	Happy Days Are Here Again	1965	50.00
—Blue label, trident logo at right			
❑ PRST-7394 [S]	Happy Days Are Here Again	1965	60.00
—Blue label, trident logo at right			
❑ PRLP-7365 [M]	Lucky Strikes	1965	50.00
—Blue label, trident logo at right			
❑ PRST-7365 [S]	Lucky Strikes	1965	60.00
—Blue label, trident logo at right			

RIVOLI

❑ 44 [M]	Kinfolk's Corner	1965	100.00
❑ S-44 [S]	Kinfolk's Corner	1965	120.00
❑ 40 [M]	Lucky Is Back!	1965	100.00
❑ S-40 [S]	Lucky Is Back!	1965	120.00

Number	Title	Yr	NM

SWING

❑ 8404	Paris 1956, Vol. 1	1985	12.00

TOPS

❑ I -928 [10]	Jazz at the Auditorium	1954	150.00

TRANSITION

❑ TRLP-21 [M]	Lucky Strikes	1956	500.00
—With booklet (deduct 1/5 if missing)			

URANIA

❑ UJLP-1206 [M]	Accent on Tenor Sax	1955	120.00

XANADU

❑ 204	Brown Rose	1985	18.00

THOMPSON, MALACHI

DELMARK

❑ DS-442	Spirit	1989	15.00

THOMPSON, MAYO

TEXAS REVOLUTION

❑ 2270	Corky's Debt to His Father	1969	80.00

THOMPSON, RICHARD

BONG LOAD

❑ BL52	Action Packed	2001	18.00
—1,000 copies pressed on "Coke-bottle green" vinyl			
❑ BL44 [B]	Mock Tudor	1999	30.00

CAPITOL

❑ C1-48845 [B]	Amnesia	1988	18.00
❑ C1-95713 [B]	Rumor & Sigh	1991	18.00

CARTHAGE

❑ CGLP-4405 [B]	Henry the Human Fly	1983	18.00
—Reissue of Reprise LP			
❑ CGLP-4413 [B]	Richard Thompson (Guitar/ Vocal)	1983	18.00
—Reissue of Island 9421 with original UK title			
❑ CGLP-4409 [B]	Strict Tempo	1983	18.00

DIVERSE

❑ DIV 009	Front Parlour Ballads	2005	30.00

HANNIBAL

❑ HNLP-1313	Heart of Kindness	1983	12.00
❑ HNLP-1316 [B]	Small Town Romance	1984	18.00

POLYDOR

❑ 825421-1 [B]	Across a Crowded Room	1985	15.00
❑ 829728-1 [B]	Daring Adventures	1986	18.00

REPRISE

❑ MS2112 [B]	Henry the Human Fly	1972	35.00

THOMPSON, RICHARD AND LINDA

4 MEN WITH BEARDS

❑ 4M139LP [B]	Shoot Out The Lights		25.00

CARTHAGE

❑ CGLP-4412 [B]	First Light	1983	18.00
—Reissue of Chrysalis 1177			
❑ CGLP-4408 [B]	Hokey Pokey	1983	18.00
—Reissue of Island 9305			
❑ CGLP-4407 [B]	I Want to See the Bright Lights Tonight	1983	18.00
—Reissue of Island 9266 (UK)			
❑ CGLP-4404 [B]	Pour Down Like Silver	1983	18.00
—Reissue of Island 9348			
❑ CGLP-4403 [B]	Sunnyvista	1983	25.00
—First U.S. issue of this LP			

CHRYSALIS

❑ CHR1177 [B]	First Light	1978	30.00

HANNIBAL

❑ HNBL1303 [B]	Shoot Out the Lights	1982	18.00

ISLAND

❑ ISLA9421 [B]	Bright Lights and Live! More or Less	1977	40.00
—First U.S. issue of "I Want to See the Bright Lights Tonight" plus an LP of unreleased material			
❑ ILPS9305 [B]	Hokey Pokey	1974	30.00
❑ ILPS9348 [B]	Pour Down Like Silver	1975	25.00

THOMPSON, SIR CHARLES

AMERICAN RECORDING SOCIETY

❑ G-447 [M]	Basically Swing	1957	30.00

APOLLO

❑ 103 [10]	Sir Charles Thompson and His All Stars	1951	400.00

COLUMBIA

❑ CL1663 [M]	Rockin' Rhythm	1961	30.00
❑ CS8463 [S]	Rockin' Rhythm	1961	30.00
❑ CL1364 [M]	Sir Charles Thompson and the Swing Organ	1959	30.00
❑ CS8205 [S]	Sir Charles Thompson and the Swing Organ	1959	30.00

EUPHONIC

❑ 1221	The Neglected Professor	198?	12.00

SACKVILLE

❑ 3037	Portrait of a Piano	199?	15.00

VANGUARD

❑ VRS-8009 [10]	Sir Charles Thompson and His Band	1954	150.00

Number	Title	Yr	NM
❑ VRS-8006 [10]	Sir Charles Thompson Quartet	1954	100.00
❑ VRS-8003 [10]	Sir Charles Thompson Sextet	1953	100.00
❑ VRS-8018 [10]	Sir Charles Thompson Trio	1955	100.00

THOMPSON, SONNY

KING

Number	Title	Yr	NM
❑ 655 [M]	Mellow Blues	1959	250.00
❑ 568 [M]	Moody Blues	1956	500.00

THOMPSON, SUE

HICKORY

Number	Title	Yr	NM
❑ H3G-4515	...And Love Me	1974	18.00
❑ LPM-104 [M]	Meet Sue Thompson	1962	50.00
❑ LPS-104 [S]	Meet Sue Thompson	1962	80.00
❑ LPM-121 [M]	Paper Tiger	1965	30.00
❑ LPS-121 [S]	Paper Tiger	1965	40.00
❑ LPM-111 [M]	Sue Thompson's Golden Hits	1963	30.00
❑ LPS-111 [S]	Sue Thompson's Golden Hits	1963	40.00
❑ LPM-130 [M]	Sue Thompson with Strings Attached	1966	30.00
❑ LPS-130 [S]	Sue Thompson with Strings Attached	1966	40.00
❑ H3F-4511	Sweet Memories	1974	18.00
❑ LPS-148	This Is Sue Thompson Country	1969	25.00
❑ LPM-107 [M]	Two of a Kind	1962	30.00
❑ LPS-107 [S]	Two of a Kind	1962	40.00

WING

Number	Title	Yr	NM
❑ MGW-12317 [M]	The Country Side of Sue Thompson	1965	25.00
❑ SRW-16317 [R]	The Country Side of Sue Thompson	1965	18.00

THOMPSON TWINS

ARISTA

Number	Title	Yr	NM
❑ R154479	Best of the Thompson Twins: Greatest Mixes	1988	15.00
—BMG Direct Marketing edition			
❑ AL8542	Best of the Thompson Twins: Greatest Mixes	1988	15.00
❑ R154307	Close to the Bone	1987	15.00
—BMG Direct Marketing edition			
❑ AL-8449	Close to the Bone	1987	12.00
❑ SP-137 [EP]	Extra Special Tuneful Twosome!	1982	15.00
—Promo-only remixes; Side 1 is "Identical Twin Side" and Side 2 is "Fraternal Twin Side			
❑ R144367	Here's to Future Days	1985	15.00
—RCA Music Service edition			
❑ AL8-8276	Here's to Future Days	1985	12.00
❑ ADP9586 [DJ]	Interview Sampler	1987	25.00
—One side of interviews, the other of music; promo only			
❑ ADP9586 [DJ]	Interview Sampler	1987	25.00
—One side of interviews, the other of music; promo only			
❑ AL6601	In the Name of Love	1982	15.00
❑ ALB6-8309	In the Name of Love	1985	10.00
—Reissue of AL8-8244			
❑ AL8-8244	In the Name of Love	1984	12.00
—Reissue of AL 6601			
❑ R124567	Into the Gap	1984	15.00
—RCA Music Service edition			
❑ AL8-8200	Into the Gap	1984	12.00
❑ AL6607	Side Kicks	1983	15.00
❑ ALB6-8310	Side Kicks	1986	10.00
—Reissue of AL8 8002			
❑ AL9624	Side Kicks	1983	12.00
—Reissue of 6607			
❑ AL8-8002	Side Kicks	1984	10.00
—Reissue of 9624			

WARNER BROS.

Number	Title	Yr	NM
❑ 25921	Big Trash	1989	12.00

THORINSHIELD

PHILIPS

Number	Title	Yr	NM
❑ PHS600251 [B]	Thorinshield	1968	30.00

THORNE, FRAN

TRANSITION

Number	Title	Yr	NM
❑ TRLP-27 [M]	Piano Reflections	1956	200.00
—With booklet (deduct 1/4 if missing)			

THORNHILL, CLAUDE

CIRCLE

Number	Title	Yr	NM
❑ CLP-19	Claude Thornhill and His Orchestra 1941 & 1947	1981	15.00

COLUMBIA

Number	Title	Yr	NM
❑ CL6164 [10]	Claude Thornhill Encores	1951	80.00
❑ CL6050 [10]	Dance Parade	1949	80.00
❑ CL709 [M]	Dancing After Midnight	1955	40.00
❑ CL6035 [10]	Piano Reflections	1949	80.00
❑ KG32906	The Memorable Claude Thornhill	1974	18.00
—Original issue			
❑ PG32906	The Memorable Claude Thornhill	197?	15.00
—Reissue with new prefix; some may have bar codes			

DECCA

Number	Title	Yr	NM
❑ DL8722 [M]	Claude on a Cloud	1958	30.00
❑ DL78722 [S]	Claude on a Cloud	1958	30.00
❑ DL8878 [M]	Dance to the Sound of Claude Thornhill	1958	30.00
❑ DL78878 [S]	Dance to the Sound of Claude Thornhill	1958	30.00

DESIGN

Number	Title	Yr	NM
❑ DLP-50 [M]	Sleepy Serenade	196?	12.00

HARMONY

Number	Title	Yr	NM
❑ HL7088 [M]	The Thornhill Sound	1957	30.00

HINDSIGHT

Number	Title	Yr	NM
❑ HSR-108	Claude Thornhill and His Orchestra 1947	198?	15.00

INSIGHT

Number	Title	Yr	NM
❑ IN-207	Claude Thornhill and His Orchestra	198?	15.00

KAPP

Number	Title	Yr	NM
❑ KL-1058 [M]	Two Sides of Claude Thornhill	1958	30.00
❑ KS-3058 [S]	Two Sides of Claude Thornhill	1958	30.00

MONMOUTH-EVERGREEN

Number	Title	Yr	NM
❑ 7024	Claude Thornhill at Glen Island Casino 1941	198?	12.00
❑ MR-6606	Snowfall -- A Memory of Claude Thornhill	197?	18.00

RCA CAMDEN

Number	Title	Yr	NM
❑ CAL-307 [M]	Dinner for Two	1958	30.00

TREND

Number	Title	Yr	NM
❑ TL-1002 [10]	Claude Thornhill Plays the Great Jazz Arrangements of Gerry Mulligan and Ralph Aldrich	1953	120.00
❑ TL-1001 [10]	Dream Stuff	1953	120.00

THORNTON, BIG MAMA

ARHOOLIE

Number	Title	Yr	NM
❑ F-1039 [M]	Ball and Chain	1968	30.00
❑ F-1028 [M]	Big Mama Thornton in Europe	1966	30.00
❑ F-1032 [M]	Chicago Blues: The Queen at Monterey	1967	30.00

BACK BEAT

Number	Title	Yr	NM
❑ BLP-68	She's Back	1970	30.00

MERCURY

Number	Title	Yr	NM
❑ SR-61225	Stronger Than Dirt	1969	30.00
❑ SR-61249	The Way It Is	1970	30.00

PENTAGRAM

Number	Title	Yr	NM
❑ PE-10005	Saved	1971	25.00

VANGUARD

Number	Title	Yr	NM
❑ VSD-79351	Jail	1974	18.00
❑ VSD-79354	Sassy Mama	1975	18.00

THORNTON, CLIFFORD

JCOA

Number	Title	Yr	NM
❑ 1008	Gardens of Harlem	197?	10.00

THIRD WORLD

Number	Title	Yr	NM
❑ 12372	Communications Network	197?	18.00
❑ 0600 [S]	Freedom and Unity	1969	30.00

THORNTON, TERI

COLUMBIA

Number	Title	Yr	NM
❑ CL2094 [M]	Open Highway	1963	30.00
❑ CS8894 [S]	Open Highway	1963	40.00

DAUNTLESS

Number	Title	Yr	NM
❑ DM-4306 [M]	Somewhere in the Night	1963	30.00
❑ DS-6306 [S]	Somewhere in the Night	1963	30.00

RIVERSIDE

Number	Title	Yr	NM
❑ RLP-352 [M]	Devil May Care	1961	40.00
❑ RS-9352 [S]	Devil May Care	1961	30.00
❑ 6142	Devil May Care	198?	15.00
❑ RM-3525 [M]	Lullabye of the Leaves	1964	30.00
❑ RS-93525 [S]	Lullabye of the Leaves	1964	30.00

THOROGOOD, GEORGE, AND THE DESTROYERS

EMI AMERICA

Number	Title	Yr	NM
❑ ST-17076	Bad to the Bone	1982	12.00
❑ ST-17214	Live	1986	12.00
❑ ST-17145	Maverick	1985	12.00

EMI MANHATTAN

Number	Title	Yr	NM
❑ E1-46973	Born to Be Bad	1988	12.00

MCA

Number	Title	Yr	NM
❑ 3091	Better Than the Rest	1979	12.00

ROUNDER

Number	Title	Yr	NM
❑ 3013	George Thorogood and the Destroyers	1977	15.00
❑ 3045	More George Thorogood and the Destroyers	1980	12.00
❑ 3024	Move It On Over	1978	15.00

THORPE, BILLY

CAPRICORN

Number	Title	Yr	NM
❑ CPN 0221	Children of the Sun	1979	25.00

ELEKTRA

Number	Title	Yr	NM
❑ 6E-294	21st Century Man	1980	12.00

PASHA

Number	Title	Yr	NM
❑ BFZ40682	Children of the Sun... Revisited	1987	12.00
❑ FZ38179	East of Eden's Gate	1982	12.00
❑ ARZ37499	Stimulation	1981	12.00

POLYDOR

Number	Title	Yr	NM
❑ PD-1-6228	Children of the Sun	1979	15.00

THRASHER BROTHERS, THE

MCA

Number	Title	Yr	NM
❑ 5352	Country in My Soul	1983	12.00

THREADGILL, HENRY

ABOUT TIME

Number	Title	Yr	NM
❑ 1005	Just the Facts and Pass the Bucket	198?	15.00
❑ 1004	When Was That?	198?	15.00

NOVUS

Number	Title	Yr	NM
❑ 3025-1-N	Easily Slip Into Another World	1988	12.00
❑ 3052-1-N	Rag, Bush and All	1989	12.00
❑ 3013-1-N	You Know the Number	1987	12.00

THREE

STEEPLECHASE

Number	Title	Yr	NM
❑ SCS-1201	Three	198?	15.00
—Khan Jamal; Johnny Dyani; Pierre Dorge			

THREE CATS AND A FIDDLE

REPEAT

Number	Title	Yr	NM
❑ S-150 [M]	Three Cats and a Fiddle	1964	18.00

THREE CHUCKLES, THE

VIK

Number	Title	Yr	NM
❑ LX-1067 [M]	The Three Chuckles	1956	250.00

THREE DEGREES, THE

ARIOLA AMERICA

Number	Title	Yr	NM
❑ SW-50044	New Dimensions	1978	12.00
❑ OL1501	Three D	1980	12.00

EPIC

Number	Title	Yr	NM
❑ PE34385	Standing Up for Love	1977	15.00

ICHIBAN

Number	Title	Yr	NM
❑ ICH-1041	Three Degrees...And Holding	198?	12.00

PHILADELPHIA INT'L.

Number	Title	Yr	NM
❑ KZ33162	International	1975	15.00
❑ KZ32406	The Three Degrees	1974	15.00
❑ PZ33840	The Three Degrees Live	1975	15.00

ROULETTE

Number	Title	Yr	NM
❑ SR-42050	Maybe	1970	40.00
❑ 3015	So Much Love	1975	12.00

THREE DEUCES, THE

STOMP OFF

Number	Title	Yr	NM
❑ SOS-1186	Stompin' 'n' Slidin'	1988	12.00

THREE DOG NIGHT

ABC

Number	Title	Yr	NM
❑ 928	American Pastime	1976	12.00
❑ 888	Coming Down Your Way	1975	12.00

ABC COMMAND

Number	Title	Yr	NM
❑ CQD-40018 [Q]	Coming Down Your Way	1975	25.00
❑ CQD-40014 [Q]	Hard Labor	1974	25.00

ABC DUNHILL

Number	Title	Yr	NM
❑ DSY-50138	Around the World with Three Dog Night	1973	18.00
❑ DSX-50158	Cyan	1973	15.00
❑ DSX-50098	Golden Bisquits	1971	15.00
—With detachable cardboard poster intact; interestingly, the label spells the LP title "Golden Biscuits			
❑ DSD-50168	Hard Labor	1974	30.00
—With uncensored "childbirth" front cover			
❑ DSD-50168	Hard Labor	1974	18.00
—With huge Band-Aid attached to jacket, covering the "childbirth			
❑ DSD-50168	Hard Labor	1974	12.00
—With huge Band-Aid as part of the LP artwork			
❑ DSX-50108	Harmony	1971	15.00
❑ DS-50078	It Ain't Easy	1970	100.00
—Original cover with band members in the nude			
❑ DS-50078	It Ain't Easy	1970	15.00
—Regular front cover with gatefold			
❑ SKAO-93211	It Ain't Easy	1970	18.00
—Capitol Record Club edition			
❑ DSD-50178	Joy to the World: Their Greatest Hits	1974	15.00
—With gatefold cover			
❑ DSD-50178	Joy to the World: Their Greatest Hits	1975	12.00
—With standard cover			
❑ DSX-50088	Naturally	1970	15.00
—With detachable cardboard poster intact			
❑ SMAS-93422	Naturally	1970	18.00
—Capitol Record Club edition			
❑ DSD-50118	Seven Separate Fools	1972	15.00
—With seven oversize playing cards included			

Number	Title	Yr	NM
❑ SVAS-94772	Seven Separate Fools	1972	18.00
—Capitol Record Club edition			
❑ DS-50058	Suitable for Framing	1969	15.00
❑ SKAO-92057	Suitable for Framing	1969	18.00
—Capitol Record Club edition			
❑ DS-50048	Three Dog Night "One	1969	15.00
—Same album as above, but with revised title on cover			
❑ DS-50048	Three Dog Night	1968	18.00
❑ DS-50068	Three Dog Night Was Captured Live at the Forum	1969	15.00

AT EASE

Number	Title	Yr	NM
❑ MD11109	Three Dog Night: Their Greatest Recordings	1978	25.00
—This Album Compiled Exclusively for Military Personnel" by ABC			

COLUMBIA SPECIAL PRODUCTS

Number	Title	Yr	NM
❑ P14769	Three Dog Night	1978	18.00

MCA

Number	Title	Yr	NM
❑ 37120	Joy to the World: Their Greatest Hits	1980	10.00
❑ 6018	The Best of Three Dog Night	1982	15.00

PASSPORT

Number	Title	Yr	NM
❑ PB5001 [EP]	It's a Jungle	1983	10.00

PICKWICK

Number	Title	Yr	NM
❑ SPC-3664	Golden Greats of Three Dog Night	1979	12.00

SESSIONS

Number	Title	Yr	NM
❑ ARI-1004	Sessions Presents Three Dog Night	1977	15.00

THREE D'S, THE (2)

CAPITOL

Number	Title	Yr	NM
❑ T2314 [M]	I Won't Be Worried Long	1965	25.00
❑ ST2314 [S]	I Won't Be Worried Long	1965	30.00
❑ T2171 [M]	New Dimensions in Folk Songs	1964	25.00
❑ ST2171 [S]	New Dimensions in Folk Songs	1964	30.00

THREE FACES WEST

OUTPOST

Number	Title	Yr	NM
❑ 1000	Three Faces West	197?	25.00

THREE FLAMES, THE

MERCURY

Number	Title	Yr	NM
❑ MG-20239 [M]	At the Ben Soir	1957	50.00

THREE JOLLY MINERS, THE

HISTORICAL

Number	Title	Yr	NM
❑ 23 [M]	The Three Jolly Miners 1925-28	1968	18.00

3M MUSIC MAKERS, THE

SOUNDMASTERS

Number	Title	Yr	NM
❑ E-1136	Holiday Happenings	198?	12.00

THREE MAN ARMY, THE

KAMA SUTRA

Number	Title	Yr	NM
❑ KSBS-2044	A Third of a Lifetime	1971	30.00
—Pink label, gatefold cover			

REPRISE

Number	Title	Yr	NM
❑ MS2150	Three Man Army	1973	25.00
❑ MS2182	Three Man Army Two	1974	25.00

311

CAPRICORN

Number	Title	Yr	NM
❑ 536181-1 [B]	Transistor	1997	15.00

THREE SOULS, THE

Number	Title	Yr	NM
❑ LP-4036 [M]	Dangerous Dan Express	1964	25.00
❑ LPS-4036 [S]	Dangerous Dan Express	1964	30.00
❑ LP-4044 [M]	Soul Sounds	1965	25.00
❑ LPS-4044 [S]	Soul Sounds	1965	30.00

THREE SOUNDS, THE

BLUE NOTE

Number	Title	Yr	NM
❑ BLP-4155 [M]	Black Orchid	1963	30.00
❑ BST-84155 [S]	Black Orchid	1963	30.00
—With "New York, USA" address on label			
❑ BST-84155 [S]	Black Orchid	1967	18.00
—With "A Division of Liberty Records" on label			
❑ BLP-4014 [M]	Bottoms Up	1959	250.00
—Deep groove" version (deep indentation under label on both sides)			
❑ BLP-4014 [M]	Bottoms Up	1959	80.00
—Regular version, W. 63rd St. address on label			
❑ BST-4014 [S]	Bottoms Up	1959	400.00
—Deep groove" version (deep indentation under label on both sides)			
❑ BST-4014 [S]	Bottoms Up	1959	60.00
—Regular version, W. 63rd St. address on label			
❑ BLP-4014 [M]	Bottoms Up	1963	30.00
—With "New York, USA" address on label			
❑ BST-4014 [S]	Bottoms Up	1963	25.00
—With "New York, USA" address on label			
❑ BST-84014 [S]	Bottoms Up	1967	18.00
—With "A Division of Liberty Records" on label			
❑ BST-84285 [S]	Coldwater Flat	1968	25.00
—With "A Division of Liberty Records" on label			
❑ BST-84301 [S]	Elegant Soul	1968	25.00
—With "A Division of Liberty Records" on label			
❑ BLP-4072 [M]	Feelin' Good	1961	80.00
—With W. 63rd St. address on label			
❑ BST-84072 [S]	Feelin' Good	1961	50.00
—With W. 63rd St. address on label			
❑ BLP-4072 [M]	Feelin' Good	1963	30.00
—With "New York, USA" address on label			
❑ BST-84072 [S]	Feelin' Good	1963	25.00
—With "New York, USA" address on label			
❑ BST-84072 [S]	Feelin' Good	1967	18.00
—With "A Division of Liberty Records" on label			
❑ BLP-4020 [M]	Good Deal	1959	300.00
—Deep groove" version (deep indentation under label on both sides)			
❑ BLP-4020 [M]	Good Deal	1959	80.00
—Regular version, W. 63rd St. address on label			
❑ BST-84020 [S]	Good Deal	1959	50.00
—With W. 63rd St. address on label			
❑ BLP-4020 [M]	Good Deal	1963	30.00
—With "New York, USA" address on label			
❑ BST-84020 [S]	Good Deal	1963	25.00
—With "New York, USA" address on label			
❑ BST-84020 [S]	Good Deal	1967	18.00
—With "A Division of Liberty Records" on label			
❑ BLP-4088 [M]	Here We Come	1961	80.00
—With 61st St. address on label			
❑ BST-84088 [S]	Here We Come	1961	50.00
—With 61st St. address on label			
❑ BLP-4088 [M]	Here We Come	1963	30.00
—With "New York, USA" address on label			
❑ BST-84088 [S]	Here We Come	1963	25.00
—With "New York, USA" address on label			
❑ BST-84088 [S]	Here We Come	1967	18.00
—With "A Division of Liberty Records" on label			
❑ BLP-4102 [M]	Hey! There	1962	30.00
❑ BST-84102 [S]	Hey! There	1962	30.00
—With "New York, USA" address on label			
❑ BST-84102 [S]	Hey! There	1967	18.00
—With "A Division of Liberty Records" on label			
❑ BLP-1600 [M]	Introducing the Three Sounds	1958	250.00
—Deep groove" version (deep indentation under label on both sides)			
❑ BLP-1600 [M]	Introducing the Three Sounds	1958	80.00
—Regular version, W. 63rd St. address on label			
❑ BST-1600 [S]	Introducing the Three Sounds	1959	350.00
—Deep groove" version (deep indentation under label on both sides)			
❑ BST-1600 [S]	Introducing the Three Sounds	1959	60.00
—Regular version, W. 63rd St. address on label			
❑ BLP-1600 [M]	Introducing the Three Sounds	1963	30.00
—With "New York, USA" address on label			
❑ BST-1600 [S]	Introducing the Three Sounds	1963	25.00
—With "New York, USA" address on label			
❑ BST-81600 [S]	Introducing the Three Sounds	1967	18.00
—With "A Division of Liberty Records" on label			
❑ BLP-4120 [M]	It Just Got To Be	1963	30.00
❑ BST-84120 [S]	It Just Got To Be	1963	30.00
—With "New York, USA" address on label			
❑ BST-84120 [S]	It Just Got To Be	1967	18.00
—With "A Division of Liberty Records" on label			
❑ BLP-4265 [M]	Live at the Lighthouse	1967	30.00
❑ BST-84265 [S]	Live at the Lighthouse	1967	25.00
—With "A Division of Liberty Records" on label			
❑ BLP-4044 [M]	Moods	1960	400.00
—Deep groove" version (deep indentation under label on both sides)			
❑ BLP-4044 [M]	Moods	1960	80.00
—Regular version, W. 63rd St. address on label			
❑ BST-84044 [S]	Moods	1960	50.00
—With W. 63rd St. address on label			
❑ BLP-4044 [M]	Moods	1963	30.00
—With "New York, USA" address on label			
❑ BST-84044 [S]	Moods	1967	18.00
—With "A Division of Liberty Records" on label			
❑ BST-84044 [S]	Moods	1963	25.00
—With "New York, USA" address on label			
❑ BLP-4197 [M]	Out of This World	1965	30.00
❑ BST-84197 [S]	Out of This World	1965	30.00
—With "New York, USA" address on label			
❑ BST-84197 [S]	Out of This World	1967	18.00
—With "A Division of Liberty Records" on label			
❑ BST-84197 [S]	Out of This World	1970	18.00
—With "Liberty/UA, Inc." on label			
❑ BST-84341 [S]	Soul Symphony	1969	25.00
—With "A Division of Liberty Records" on label			
❑ BLP-4248 [M]	Vibrations	1966	30.00
❑ BST-84248 [S]	Vibrations	1966	30.00
—With "New York, USA" address on label			
❑ BST-84248 [S]	Vibrations	1967	18.00
—With "A Division of Liberty Records" on label			

LIMELIGHT

Number	Title	Yr	NM
❑ LM-82026 [M]	Beautiful Friendship	1965	25.00
❑ LS-86026 [S]	Beautiful Friendship	1965	30.00
❑ LM-82014 [M]	Three Moods	1965	25.00
❑ LS-86014 [S]	Three Moods	1965	30.00

MERCURY

Number	Title	Yr	NM
❑ MG-20776 [M]	Jazz On Broadway	1963	30.00
❑ SR-60776 [S]	Jazz On Broadway	1963	30.00
❑ MG-20921 [M]	Live at the Living Room	1963	30.00
❑ SR-60921 [S]	Live at the Living Room	1963	30.00
❑ MG-20839 [M]	Some Like It Modern	1963	30.00
❑ SR-60839 [S]	Some Like It Modern	1963	30.00

VERVE

Number	Title	Yr	NM
❑ V-8513 [M]	Blue Genes	1963	30.00
❑ V6-8513 [S]	Blue Genes	1963	30.00

THREE STOOGES, THE

CORAL

Number	Title	Yr	NM
❑ CRL57289 [M]	Nonsense Song Book	1959	80.00
❑ CRL757289 [S]	Nonsense Song Book	1959	100.00

GOLDEN

Number	Title	Yr	NM
❑ GLP-43 [M]	Madcap Musical Nonsense	1962	80.00

PETER PAN

Number	Title	Yr	NM
❑ 8098	The Three Stooges	1970	30.00

VOCALION

Number	Title	Yr	NM
❑ VL3823 [M]	The Three Stooges Sing for Kids	196?	25.00
❑ VL73823 [S]	The Three Stooges Sing for Kids	196?	30.00

THREE SUNS, THE

GOLDEN TONE

Number	Title	Yr	NM
❑ 14094	In Orbit	195?	15.00

PICKWICK

Number	Title	Yr	NM
❑ SPC-3037	Twilight Time	197?	12.00

RCA CAMDEN

Number	Title	Yr	NM
❑ CAL-633 [M]	The Sound of Christmas	1964	15.00
❑ CAS-633(e) [R]	The Sound of Christmas	1964	15.00

RCA VICTOR

Number	Title	Yr	NM
❑ LSP-2054 [S]	A Ding Dong Dandy Christmas!	1959	30.00
❑ LPM-2054 [M]	A Ding Dong Dandy Christmas!	1959	25.00
❑ LPM-2963 [M]	A Swingin' Thing	1964	18.00
❑ LSP-2963 [S]	A Swingin' Thing	1964	25.00
❑ LPM-3040 [10]	Busy Fingers	1952	50.00
❑ LPM-52 [10]	Christmas Favorites	1951	50.00
❑ LPM-3056 [10]	Christmas Party	1952	50.00
❑ LPM-3354 [M]	Country Music Shindig	1965	18.00
❑ LSP-3354 [S]	Country Music Shindig	1965	25.00
❑ LPM-2307 [M]	Dancing on a Cloud	1961	25.00
❑ LSP-2307 [S]	Dancing on a Cloud	1961	30.00
❑ LPM-1316 [M]	Easy Listening	1956	30.00
❑ LPM-2715 [M]	Everything Under the Sun	1963	18.00
❑ LSP-2715 [S]	Everything Under the Sun	1963	25.00
❑ LPM-2310 [M]	Fever and Smoke	1961	25.00
❑ LSP-2310 [S]	Fever and Smoke	1961	30.00
❑ LPM-2437 [M]	Fun in the Sun	1961	25.00
❑ LSP-2437 [S]	Fun in the Sun	1961	30.00
❑ LPM-28 [10]	Hands Across the Table	1951	50.00
❑ LPM-1734 [M]	Having a Ball with the Three Suns	1959	25.00
❑ LSP-1734 [S]	Having a Ball with the Three Suns	1959	30.00
❑ LPM-1249 [M]	High Fi and Wide	1956	30.00
❑ LPM-1578 [M]	Let's Dance with the Three Suns	1958	25.00
❑ LSP-1578 [S]	Let's Dance with the Three Suns	1958	30.00
❑ LPM-1669 [M]	Love in the Afternoon	1959	25.00
❑ LSP-1669 [S]	Love in the Afternoon	1959	30.00
❑ LPM-1220 [M]	Malaguena	1956	30.00
❑ LPM-1333 [M]	Midnight for Two	1957	30.00
❑ LPM-3125 [10]	Mods	1953	50.00
❑ LPM-2532 [M]	Movin' 'N' Groovin'	1962	25.00
❑ LSP-2532 [S]	Movin' 'N' Groovin'	1962	30.00
❑ LPM-1173 [M]	My Reverie	1956	30.00
❑ LPM-2235 [M]	On a Magic Carpet	1960	25.00
❑ LSP-2235 [S]	On a Magic Carpet	1960	30.00
❑ LPM-2904 [M]	One Enchanted Evening	1964	18.00
❑ LSP-2904 [S]	One Enchanted Evening	1964	25.00
❑ LPM-3146 [10]	Polka Time	1954	50.00
❑ LPM-3113 [10]	Pops Concert Favorites	1953	50.00
❑ ANL1-1779(e)	Pure Gold	1974	12.00
❑ LPM-3174 [10]	Sacred Hymns	1954	50.00
❑ LPM-3075 [10]	Slumbertime	1953	50.00
❑ LPM-1219 [M]	Slumber Time	1956	30.00
❑ LPM-1041 [M]	Soft and Sweet	1955	30.00
❑ LPM-1132 [M]	Sounds of Christmas	1955	30.00
❑ LPM-1964 [M]	Swingin' on a Star	1959	25.00
❑ LSP-1964 [S]	Swingin' on a Star	1959	30.00
❑ LPM-3447 [M]	The Best of the Three Suns	1965	18.00
❑ LSP-3447 [S]	The Best of the Three Suns	1965	25.00
❑ LPM-1543 [M]	The Things in Love in Hi-Fi	1958	25.00
❑ LSP-1543 [S]	The Things in Love in Hi-Fi	1958	30.00
❑ LPM-3034 [10]	The Three Suns Present	1952	50.00
❑ VPS-6075	This Is the Three Suns	1972	18.00
❑ LPM-3 [10]	Three-Quarter Time	1951	50.00
❑ LPM-3130 [10]	Top Pops	1953	50.00
❑ LPM-2120 [M]	Twilight Memories	1960	25.00
❑ LSP-2120 [S]	Twilight Memories	1960	30.00
❑ LPM-3012 [10]	Twilight Moods	1952	50.00
❑ LPM-1171 [M]	Twilight Time	1956	30.00
❑ LPM-2617 [M]	Warm and Tender	1962	25.00
❑ LSP-2617 [S]	Warm and Tender	1962	30.00

Number	Title	Yr	NM
ROYALE			
❑ 29 [10]	Midnight Time	1951	50.00
❑ 1 [10]	Twilight Time	1951	50.00
SEARS			
❑ SPS-437	Twilight Time	1969	15.00
VARSITY			
❑ VLP-6048 [10]	Midnight Time	1950	50.00
❑ VLP-6001 [10]	Twilight Time	1950	50.00
THROCKMORTON, SONNY			
MERCURY			
❑ SRM-1-3736	Last Cheater's Waltz	1979	12.00
WARNER BROS.			
❑ 25374	Southern Train	1986	10.00
THROWING MUSES			
SIRE			
❑ 25710	House Tornado	1988	12.00
❑ 25855	Hunkpapa	1989	12.00
❑ 25640	The Fat Skier	1987	12.00
❑ 26489	The Real Ramona	1991	15.00
THUDPUCKER, JIMMY			
WINDSONG			
❑ BXL1-2589	Greatest Hits	1977	25.00
THUNDER, JOHNNY			
DIAMOND			
❑ D-5001 [M]	Loop De Loop	1963	100.00
❑ DS-5001 [S]	Loop De Loop	1963	150.00
THUNDER AND ROSES			
UNITED ARTISTS			
❑ UAS-6709	King of the Black Sunrise	1969	30.00
THUNDERBIRDS, THE			
RED FEATHER			
❑ TH-1 [M]	Meet the Fabulous Thunderbirds	1964	200.00
THUNDERCLAP NEWMAN			
MCA			
❑ 354	Hollywood Dream	1974	12.00
— Reissue of Track 354			
TRACK			
❑ SD8264 [B]	Hollywood Dream	1970	30.00
❑ 354	Hollywood Dream	1973	15.00
— Reissue of Track 8264			
THUNDERKLOUD, BILLY, AND THE CHIEFTONES			
20TH CENTURY			
❑ T-452	Off the Reservation	1974	15.00
❑ T-471	What Time of Day	1975	15.00
SUPERIOR			
❑ SR-103	All Through the Night	197?	18.00
❑ S-2010	Where Do I Begin to Tell the Story	1975	18.00
THUNDERPUSSY			
M.R.I.			
❑ 31748 [B]	Documents of Captivity	1973	150.00
THUNDERS, JOHNNY			
CLEOPATRA			
❑ 8200 [B]	Dawn Of The Dead: Live At Max's Kansas City (New York)		30.00
— picture disc			
REAL			
❑ RR-1 [B]	So Alone	196?	30.00
— ex-New York Dolls			
THUNDERTREE			
ROULETTE			
❑ SR-42038 [B]	Thundertree	1970	35.00
THURSDAY GROUP, THE			
PATHFINDER			
❑ PTF-8307	The Thursday Group	198?	15.00
❑ PTF-8807	Uncle Mean	198?	15.00
TIBBETTS, STEVE			
ECM			
❑ 1218	Northern Song	198?	12.00
❑ 25002	Safe Journey	1984	12.00
TIBOR BROTHERS, THE			
JOMAR			
❑ S80-744-3631	The Tibor Brothers	1979	18.00
TICHENOR, TREBOR			
DIRTY SHAME			
❑ 2001	King of Folk Ragtime	197?	15.00

Number	Title	Yr	NM
TIDE, THE			
MOUTH			
❑ 7237	Almost Live	1971	50.00
TIDES, THE			
MERCURY			
❑ MG-20714 [M]	Limbo Rock	1962	18.00
❑ SR-60714 [S]	Limbo Rock	1962	25.00
WING			
❑ MGW-12265 [M]	Surf City and Other Surfin' Favorites	1963	30.00
❑ SRW-16265 [S]	Surf City and Other Surfin' Favorites	1963	30.00
❑ MGW-12248 [M]	The Best of Bossa Nova	1963	18.00
❑ SRW-16248 [S]	The Best of Bossa Nova	1963	25.00
TIEKEN, FREDDIE, AND THE ROCKERS			
I.T.			
❑ 2301 [M]	By Popular Demand	1957	60.00
❑ 2304 [M]	Freddie Tieken and the Rockers	1958	60.00
TIFFANY			
MCA			
❑ 6267	Hold an Old Friend's Hand	1988	12.00
❑ 10030	New Inside	1990	18.00
❑ 5793	Tiffany	1987	10.00
TIFFANY SHADE, THE			
MAINSTREAM			
❑ S-6105	The Tiffany Shade	1968	100.00
TIJUANA VOICES WITH BRASS			
PICKWICK			
❑ SPCX-1005	Tijuana Voices Sing Merry Christmas	1970	15.00
TIKIS, THE			
MINARET			
❑ TLP-7001 [M]	The Tikis	196?	100.00
PHILIPS			
❑ PHM200043 [M]	The Tikis	1962	30.00
❑ PHS600043 [S]	The Tikis	1962	30.00
TIL, SONNY			
DOBRE			
❑ 1026	Back to the Chapel	1978	15.00
RCA VICTOR			
❑ LSP-4538	Old Gold/New Gold	1971	18.00
❑ LSP-4451	Sonny Til Returns	1970	25.00
'TIL TUESDAY			
EPIC			
❑ OE44041 [B]	Everything's Different Now	1988	12.00
❑ EAS1350 [EP]	Everything's Different Now Sampler	1988	15.00
— Promo only; few songs			
❑ BFE39458 [B]	Voices Carry	1985	15.00
❑ FE39458	Voices Carry	1985	10.00
— Reissue with new prefix			
❑ FE40314	Welcome Home	1986	12.00
TILLES, NURIT			
JAZZOLOGY			
❑ JCE-87	Ragtime, Here and Now!	1982	12.00
TILLIS, MEL, AND NANCY SINATRA			
ELEKTRA			
❑ 5E-549	Mel and Nancy	1981	15.00
TILLIS, MEL, AND SHERRY BRYCE			
MGM			
❑ SE-4937	Let's Go All the Way Tonight	1974	18.00
❑ SE-4800	Living and Learning/Take My Hand	1971	18.00
TILLIS, MEL			
COLUMBIA			
❑ C30253	Heart Over Mind	1970	15.00
❑ CL1724 [M]	Heart Over Mind and Other Big Country Hits	1962	30.00
❑ CS8524 [S]	Heart Over Mind and Other Big Country Hits	1962	40.00
ELEKTRA			
❑ 60016	It's a Long Way to Daytona	1982	12.00
❑ 6E-236	Me and Pepper	1979	12.00
❑ 60192	Mel Tillis' Greatest Hits	1982	12.00
❑ 6E-310	Southern Rain	1980	12.00
❑ 6E-271	Your Body Is an Outlaw	1980	12.00
HARMONY			
❑ KH31952	Mel	1972	15.00
❑ HS11170 [S]	The Great Mel Tillis Sings Walk On, Boy and Other Great Country Hits	196?	15.00
❑ HL7370 [M]	The Great Mel Tillis Sings Walk On, Boy and Other Great Country Hits	196?	18.00

Number	Title	Yr	NM
HILLTOP			
❑ JS-6153	Detroit City	197?	12.00
KAPP			
❑ KS-3543	Let Me Talk to You	1968	18.00
❑ KL-1514 [M]	Life Turned Her That Way	1967	18.00
❑ KS-3514 [S]	Life Turned Her That Way	1967	25.00
❑ KS-3589	Mel Tillis' Greatest Hits	1969	18.00
❑ KS-3639	Mel Tillis In Person	1970	18.00
❑ KS-3609	Mel Tillis Sings Old Faithful	1969	18.00
❑ KS-3535 [S]	Mr. Mel	1967	18.00
❑ KL-1535 [M]	Mr. Mel	1967	25.00
❑ KS-3630	She'll Be Hanging 'Round Somewhere	1970	18.00
❑ KS-3570	Something Special	1968	18.00
❑ KL-1493 [M]	Stateside	1966	18.00
❑ KS-3493 [S]	Stateside	1966	25.00
❑ KS-3594	Who's Julie	1969	18.00
MCA			
❑ 5378	After All This Time	1983	10.00
❑ 3077	Are You Sincere	1979	15.00
❑ 653	Are You Sincere	198?	10.00
— Reissue of 3077			
❑ 2252	Heart Healer	1977	15.00
❑ 650	Heart Healer	198?	10.00
— Reissue of 2252			
❑ 2364	I Believe in You	1978	15.00
❑ 652	I Believe in You	198?	10.00
— Reissue of 2364			
❑ 2204	Love Revival	1976	15.00
❑ 649	Love Revival	198?	10.00
— Reissue of 2204			
❑ 2288	Love's Troubled Waters	1977	15.00
❑ 651	Love's Troubled Waters	198?	10.00
— Reissue of 2288			
❑ 66	Mel Tillis' Greatest Hits	1973	15.00
— Reissue of Kapp 3589			
❑ 550	Mel Tillis In Person	197?	12.00
— Reissue of Kapp 3639			
❑ 3208	M-M-Mel Live	1980	15.00
❑ 789	M-M-Mel Live	198?	10.00
— Reissue of 3208			
❑ 3167	Mr. Entertainer	1979	15.00
❑ 37121	Mr. Entertainer	198?	10.00
— Reissue of 3167			
❑ 5472	New Patches	1984	10.00
❑ 4091	The Best of Mel Tillis	1975	18.00
❑ 3274	The Very Best of Mel Tillis	1980	12.00
MERCURY			
❑ 835310-1	Brand New Mister Me	1988	10.00
MGM			
❑ MG-2-5402	24 Great Hits	1977	18.00
❑ SE-4870	I Ain't Never/Neon Rose	1972	18.00
❑ MG-2-5404	Live at the Sam Houston Coliseum & Birmingham Municipal Auditorium	1978	18.00
— Combines 4788 and 4889 in one package			
❑ M3G-4987	Mel Tillis and the Statesiders	1975	15.00
❑ SE-4889	Mel Tillis and the Statesiders On Stage at the Birmingham Municipal Auditorium	1973	18.00
❑ M3O-4970	Mel Tillis' Greatest Hits	1974	15.00
❑ MG-1-5002	M-M-Mel	1975	15.00
❑ SE-4681	One More Time	1970	18.00
❑ SE-4780	Recorded Live at the Sam Houston Coliseum, Houston, Texas	1971	18.00
❑ SE-4907	Sawmill	1973	18.00
❑ M3F-4960	Stomp Them Grapes	1974	15.00
❑ SE-4757	The Arms of a Fool/Commercial Affection	1971	18.00
❑ MC-1-5021	The Best of Mel Tillis and the Statesiders	1976	15.00
❑ SE-4806	The Very Best of Mel Tillis and the Statesiders	1972	18.00
❑ MG-1-5022	Welcome to Mel Tillis Country	1976	15.00
❑ SE-4841	Would You Want Your World to End	1972	18.00
POWER PAK			
❑ PO-295	Mel Tillis & Friends	197?	12.00
RCA VICTOR			
❑ AHL1-5483	California Road	1985	10.00
STARDAY			
❑ SLP-471	Stateside	1972	15.00
TIME-LIFE			
❑ STW-111	Country Music	1981	12.00
VOCALION			
❑ VL73914	Big 'n' Country	1970	15.00
TILLIS, PAM			
WARNER BROS.			
❑ 23871	Above and Beyond the Doll of Cutey	1983	30.00
TILLMAN, FLOYD			
CIMARRON			
❑ C-2003 [M]	Let's Make Memories	1962	50.00
HARMONY			
❑ HL7316 [M]	Floyd Tillman's Best	1964	30.00
❑ HS11297	I'll Still Be Lovin' You	1969	30.00

Number	Title	Yr	NM
HILLTOP			
❑ JM-6017 [M]	Floyd Tillman Sings His Greatest Hits of Lovin'	196?	10.00
MUSICOR			
❑ MS-3157	Dream On	1968	25.00
❑ MM-2136 [M]	Floyd Tillman's Country	1967	25.00
❑ MS-3136 [S]	Floyd Tillman's Country	1967	30.00
RCA VICTOR			
❑ LPM-1686 [M]	Floyd Tillman's Greatest	1958	60.00
STARDAY			
❑ SLP-310 [M]	Let's Make Memories	1965	30.00

TILLOTSON, JOHNNY

Number	Title	Yr	NM
ACCORD			
❑ SN-7194	Scrapbook	1982	12.00
AMOS			
❑ AAS7006	Tears on My Pillow	1969	25.00
BARNABY			
❑ BR-4007	Johnny Tillotson's Greatest	1977	15.00
BUDDAH			
❑ BDS-5112	Johnny Tillotson	1972	18.00
CADENCE			
❑ CLP-3058 [M]	It Keeps Right On a-Hurtin'	1962	30.00
❑ CLP-25058 [S]	It Keeps Right On a-Hurtin'	1962	40.00
❑ CLP-3052 [M]	Johnny Tillotson's Best	1961	60.00
—Maroon and silver label			
❑ CLP-3052 [M]	Johnny Tillotson's Best	1962	30.00
—Red and black label			
❑ CLP-25052 [P]	Johnny Tillotson's Best	1961	50.00
—Maroon and silver label			
❑ CLP-25052 [P]	Johnny Tillotson's Best	1962	30.00
—Red and black label			
❑ CLP-3067 [M]	You Can Never Stop Me Loving You	1963	30.00
❑ CLP-25067 [P]	You Can Never Stop Me Loving You	1963	40.00
EVEREST			
❑ 4113	Johnny Tillotson's Greatest Hits	1982	12.00
METRO			
❑ M-561 [M]	Johnny Tillotson Sings Tillotson	1967	18.00
❑ MS-561 [S]	Johnny Tillotson Sings Tillotson	1967	25.00
MGM			
❑ E-4452 [M]	Here I Am	1967	25.00
❑ SE-4452 [S]	Here I Am	1967	30.00
❑ E-4395 [M]	No Love at All	1966	25.00
❑ SE-4395 [S]	No Love at All	1966	30.00
❑ E-4328 [M]	Our World	1965	25.00
❑ SE-4328 [S]	Our World	1965	30.00
❑ E-4270 [M]	She Understands Me	1965	25.00
❑ SE-4270 [S]	She Understands Me	1965	30.00
❑ E-4188 [M]	Talk Back Trembling Lips	1964	25.00
❑ SE-4188 [S]	Talk Back Trembling Lips	1964	30.00
❑ E-4302 [M]	That's My Style	1965	25.00
❑ SE-4302 [S]	That's My Style	1965	30.00
❑ SE-4532 [S]	The Best of Johnny Tillotson	1968	25.00
❑ E-4532 [M]	The Best of Johnny Tillotson	1968	30.00
—May be promo only (yellow label)			
❑ E-4402 [M]	The Christmas Touch	1966	30.00
❑ SE-4402 [S]	The Christmas Touch	1966	30.00
❑ E-4224 [M]	The Tillotson Touch	1964	25.00
❑ SE-4224 [S]	The Tillotson Touch	1964	30.00
❑ T90410 [M]	The Tillotson Touch	1965	30.00
—Capitol Record Club edition			
❑ ST90410 [S]	The Tillotson Touch	1965	30.00
—Capitol Record Club edition			
❑ SE-4814	The Very Best of Johnny Tillotson	1971	15.00
UNITED ARTISTS			
❑ UA-LA759-G	Johnny Tillotson	1977	12.00

TIMBER CREEK

Number	Title	Yr	NM
RENEGADE			
❑ 95014	Hellbound Highway	1975	150.00

TIMBERLAKE, JUSTIN

Number	Title	Yr	NM
JIVE			
❑ 82876-88062-1	Futuresex/Lovesounds	2006	25.00
❑ 01241-41823-1	Justified	2002	25.00

TIMBUK 3

Number	Title	Yr	NM
I.R.S.			
❑ 42124	Eden Alley	1987	12.00
❑ 82015	Edge of Allegiance	1989	15.00
❑ R143810	Greetings from Timbuk 3	1986	16.00
—RCA Music Service edition			
❑ 5739	Greetings from Timbuk 3	1986	14.00

TIMELESS ALL-STARS, THE

Number	Title	Yr	NM
TIMELESS			
❑ LPSJP-178	It's Timeless	1988	12.00

TIMMENS, JIM, AND HIS JAZZ ALL-STARS

Number	Title	Yr	NM
WARNER BROS.			
❑ W1278 [M]	Gilbert and Sullivan Revisited	1958	25.00
❑ WS1278 [S]	Gilbert and Sullivan Revisited	1958	30.00

TIMMONS, BOBBY

Number	Title	Yr	NM
FANTASY			
❑ OJC-364	Bobby Timmons In Person	198?	12.00
❑ OJC-104	This Here Is Bobby Timmons	198?	12.00
MILESTONE			
❑ MSP-9020	Do You Know the Way	1969	25.00
❑ MSP-9011	Got to Get It	1969	25.00
❑ 47031	Moanin'	197?	18.00
PRESTIGE			
❑ PRLP-7429 [M]	Chicken and Dumplin's	1966	30.00
❑ PRST-7429 [S]	Chicken and Dumplin's	1966	30.00
❑ PRLP-7351 [M]	Chun-King	1965	30.00
❑ PRST-7351 [S]	Chun-King	1965	30.00
❑ PRLP-7414 [M]	Holiday Soul	1966	30.00
❑ PRST-7414 [S]	Holiday Soul	1966	40.00
❑ PRLP-7335 [M]	Little Barefoot Soul	1964	30.00
❑ PRST-7335 [S]	Little Barefoot Soul	1964	30.00
❑ PRLP-7483 [M]	Soul Food	1967	60.00
❑ PRST-7483 [S]	Soul Food	1967	50.00
❑ PRLP-7465 [M]	Soul Man	1967	60.00
❑ PRST-7465 [S]	Soul Man	1967	50.00
❑ PRST-7780	The Best of Soul Piano	1970	25.00
❑ PRLP-7387 [M]	Workin' Out	1966	30.00
❑ PRST-7387 [S]	Workin' Out	1966	30.00
RIVERSIDE			
❑ R-6110	Bobby Timmons In Person	197?	18.00
❑ RLP-468 [M]	Born to Be Blue!	1963	50.00
❑ RS-9468 [S]	Born to Be Blue!	1963	40.00
❑ RLP-363 [M]	Easy Does It	1961	80.00
❑ RS-9363 [S]	Easy Does It	1961	60.00
❑ RS-3053	From the Bottom	196?	18.00
❑ RLP-334 [M]	Soul Time	1960	80.00
❑ RS-9334 [S]	Soul Time	1960	60.00
❑ RLP-422 [M]	Sweet and Soulful Sounds	1962	50.00
❑ RS-9422 [S]	Sweet and Soulful Sounds	1962	40.00
❑ RLP-391 [M]	The Bobby Timmons Trio In Person -- Recorded "Live" at the Village Vanguard	1961	120.00
❑ RS-9391 [S]	The Bobby Timmons Trio In Person -- Recorded "Live" at the Village Vanguard	1961	80.00
❑ RLP 12-317 [M]	This Here Is Bobby Timmons	1960	150.00
❑ RLP-1164 [S]	This Here Is Bobby Timmons	1960	120.00
❑ R-6050	This Here Is Bobby Timmons	197?	18.00

TIMMOTHY

Number	Title	Yr	NM
PEAR			
❑ (# unknown)0	Strange But True	1972	200.00

TIN HOUSE

Number	Title	Yr	NM
EPIC			
❑ E30511	Tin House	1971	25.00

TIN HUEY

Number	Title	Yr	NM
WARNER BROS.			
❑ BSK3297	Contents Dislodged During Shipment	1979	15.00

TIN MACHINE

Number	Title	Yr	NM
EMI			
❑ R164054	Tin Machine	1989	14.00
—BMG Direct Marketing edition			
❑ E1-91990	Tin Machine	1989	15.00
—Featuring David Bowie			

TIN TIN

Number	Title	Yr	NM
ATCO			
❑ SD 33-370	Astral Taxi	1971	18.00
❑ SD 33-350	Tin Tin	1970	18.00

TINGLING MOTHER'S CIRCUS

Number	Title	Yr	NM
MUSICOR			
❑ MS-3167	Circus of the Mind	1968	30.00

TINO AND THE REVLONS

Number	Title	Yr	NM
DEARBORN			
❑ 1004	By Request at the Sway-Zee	1966	200.00

TINY TIM

Number	Title	Yr	NM
BOUQUET			
❑ SLP-711 [B]	Love and Kisses from Tiny Tim	1968	25.00
REPRISE			
❑ RS6351	For All My Little Friends	1969	18.00
❑ RS6292 [S]	God Bless Tiny Tim	1968	18.00
❑ R6292 [M]	God Bless Tiny Tim	1968	60.00
—Mono copies may all be white label promos			
❑ RS6323	Tiny Tim's Second Album	1969	18.00

TIPPETTS, JULIE

Number	Title	Yr	NM
UTOPIA			
❑ BUL11248 [B]	Sunset Glow	1975	30.00

TIPTON, CARL

Number	Title	Yr	NM
SIMS			
❑ LP-143 [M]	The Carl Tipton Show	196?	40.00

TIRABASSO, JOHN

Number	Title	Yr	NM
DISCOVERY			
❑ DS-884	Live at Dino's	198?	12.00
DOBRE			
❑ 1022	Diamond Cuff Links and Mink	197?	18.00

TISO, WAGNER

Number	Title	Yr	NM
PHILIPS			
❑ 834632-1	Manu Carue	1989	15.00
VERVE			
❑ 831819-1	Giselle	1987	12.00

TITANS, THE

Number	Title	Yr	NM
MGM			
❑ E-3992 [M]	Today's Teen Beat	1961	30.00
❑ SE-3992 [S]	Today's Teen Beat	1961	40.00

TITUS GROAN

Number	Title	Yr	NM
JANUS			
❑ JLS-3024	Titus Groan	1971	30.00

TITUS OATES

Number	Title	Yr	NM
LIPS			
❑ (no #)0	Jungle Lady	1974	200.00

TJADER, CAL, AND CARMEN MCRAE

Number	Title	Yr	NM
CONCORD JAZZ			
❑ CJ-189	Heat Wave	1982	12.00

TJADER, CAL, AND CHARLIE BYRD

Number	Title	Yr	NM
FANTASY			
❑ 9453	Tambu	1974	15.00

TJADER, CAL, AND STAN GETZ

Number	Title	Yr	NM
FANTASY			
❑ 8348 [S]	Cal Tjader-Stan Getz Quartet	1963	15.00
—Reissue of 8005			
❑ 3266 [M]	Cal Tjader-Stan Getz Sextet	1958	50.00
—Red vinyl			
❑ 3266 [M]	Cal Tjader-Stan Getz Sextet	1958	30.00
—Black vinyl, red label, non-flexible vinyl			
❑ 3266 [M]	Cal Tjader-Stan Getz Sextet	196?	18.00
—Black vinyl, red label, flexible vinyl			
❑ 3348 [M]	Cal Tjader-Stan Getz Sextet	1963	18.00
—Reissue of 3266			
❑ 8005 [S]	Cal Tjader-Stan Getz Sextet	196?	30.00
—Blue vinyl			
❑ 8005 [S]	Cal Tjader-Stan Getz Sextet	196?	25.00
—Black vinyl, blue label, non-flexible vinyl			
❑ 8005 [S]	Cal Tjader-Stan Getz Sextet	196?	15.00
—Black vinyl, blue label, flexible vinyl			

TJADER, CAL

Number	Title	Yr	NM
CONCORD JAZZ			
❑ CJ-159	The Shining Sea	1981	12.00
CONCORD PICANTE			
❑ CJP-176	A Fuego Vivo	1981	12.00
❑ CJP-247	Good Vibes	1983	12.00
❑ CJP-133	Gozame! Pero Ya...	1980	15.00
❑ CJP-113	La Onda Va Bien	1979	15.00
CRYSTAL CLEAR			
❑ 8003	Huracan	1978	30.00
—Direct-to-disc recording			
FANTASY			
❑ 8416	Agua Dulce	1971	15.00
❑ 9502	Amazonas	1975	15.00
❑ 3283 [M]	A Night at the Blackhawk	1959	50.00
—Red vinyl			
❑ 3283 [M]	A Night at the Blackhawk	1959	30.00
—Black vinyl, red label, non-flexible vinyl			
❑ 3283 [M]	A Night at the Blackhawk	196?	18.00
—Black vinyl, red label, flexible vinyl			
❑ 8026 [S]	A Night at the Blackhawk	196?	30.00
—Blue vinyl			
❑ 8026 [S]	A Night at the Blackhawk	196?	25.00
—Black vinyl, blue label, non-flexible vinyl			
❑ 8026 [S]	A Night at the Blackhawk	196?	15.00
—Black vinyl, blue label, flexible vinyl			
❑ OJC-278	A Night at the Blackhawk	1987	12.00
—Reissue of 8026			
❑ 9521	At Grace Cathedral	1977	15.00
❑ 3253 [M]	Cal Tjader	1958	60.00
—Red vinyl			
❑ 3253 [M]	Cal Tjader	1958	40.00
—Black vinyl, non-flexible vinyl			
❑ 3315 [M]	Cal Tjader Live and Direct	1961	40.00
—Red vinyl			
❑ 3315 [M]	Cal Tjader Live and Direct	1961	30.00

Number	Title	Yr	NM
—Black vinyl, red label, non-flexible vinyl			
❑ 3315 [M]	Cal Tjader Live and Direct	196?	18.00
—Black vinyl, red label, flexible vinyl			
❑ 8059 [S]	Cal Tjader Live and Direct	1962	30.00
—Blue vinyl			
❑ 8059 [S]	Cal Tjader Live and Direct	1962	25.00
—Black vinyl, blue label, non-flexible vinyl			
❑ 8059 [S]	Cal Tjader Live and Direct	196?	15.00
—Black vinyl, blue label, flexible vinyl			
❑ 3330 [M]	Cal Tjader Plays the Harold Arlen Songbook	1961	40.00
—Red vinyl			
❑ 3330 [M]	Cal Tjader Plays the Harold Arlen Songbook	1961	30.00
—Black vinyl, red label, non-flexible vinyl			
❑ 3330 [M]	Cal Tjader Plays the Harold Arlen Songbook	196?	18.00
—Black vinyl, red label, flexible vinyl			
❑ 8072 [S]	Cal Tjader Plays the Harold Arlen Songbook	1962	30.00
—Blue vinyl			
❑ 8072 [S]	Cal Tjader Plays the Harold Arlen Songbook	1962	25.00
—Black vinyl, blue label, non-flexible vinyl			
❑ 8072 [S]	Cal Tjader Plays the Harold Arlen Songbook	196?	15.00
—Black vinyl, blue label, flexible vinyl			
❑ OJC-285	Cal Tjader Plays the Harold Arlen Songbook	1987	12.00
—Reissue of 8072			
❑ 3227 [M]	Cal Tjader Quartet	1956	100.00
—Red vinyl			
❑ 3307 [M]	Cal Tjader Quartet	1960	40.00
—Red vinyl			
❑ 3307 [M]	Cal Tjader Quartet	1960	30.00
—Black vinyl, red label, non-flexible vinyl			
❑ 3307 [M]	Cal Tjader Quartet	196?	18.00
—Black vinyl, red label, flexible vinyl			
❑ 8083 [R]	Cal Tjader Quartet	1962	30.00
—Blue vinyl			
❑ 8083 [R]	Cal Tjader Quartet	1962	25.00
—Black vinyl, blue label, non-flexible vinyl			
❑ 8083 [R]	Cal Tjader Quartet	1962	15.00
—Black vinyl, blue label, flexible vinyl			
❑ 3313 [M]	Cal Tjader Quintet	1961	40.00
—Red vinyl; evidently a different album than 3232			
❑ 3313 [M]	Cal Tjader Quintet	1961	30.00
—Black vinyl, red label, non-flexible vinyl			
❑ 3313 [M]	Cal Tjader Quintet	196?	18.00
—Black vinyl, red label, flexible vinyl			
❑ 8084 [S]	Cal Tjader Quintet	1962	30.00
—Blue vinyl; stereo version of 3313			
❑ 8084 [S]	Cal Tjader Quintet	1962	25.00
—Black vinyl, blue label, non-flexible vinyl			
❑ 8084 [S]	Cal Tjader Quintet	1962	15.00
—Black vinyl, blue label, flexible vinyl			
❑ 3366 [M]	Cal Tjader's Greatest Hits	1965	10.00
❑ 8366 [S]	Cal Tjader's Greatest Hits	1965	15.00
❑ MPF-4527	Cal Tjader's Greatest Hits	1987	12.00
—Reissue of 8366			
❑ 3374 [M]	Cal Tjader's Greatest Hits, Volume 2	1966	10.00
❑ 8374 [S]	Cal Tjader's Greatest Hits, Volume 2	1966	15.00
❑ MPF-4530	Cal Tjader's Greatest Hits, Volume 2	1987	12.00
—Reissue of 8374			
❑ 3275 [M]	Cal Tjader's Latin Concert	1958	50.00
—Red vinyl			
❑ 3275 [M]	Cal Tjader's Latin Concert	1958	30.00
—Black vinyl, red label, non-flexible vinyl			
❑ 3275 [M]	Cal Tjader's Latin Concert	196?	18.00
—Black vinyl, red label, flexible vinyl			
❑ 8014 [S]	Cal Tjader's Latin Concert	196?	30.00
—Blue vinyl			
❑ 8014 [S]	Cal Tjader's Latin Concert	196?	25.00
—Black vinyl, blue label, non-flexible vinyl			
❑ 8014 [S]	Cal Tjader's Latin Concert	196?	15.00
—Black vinyl, blue label, flexible vinyl			
❑ OJC-643	Cal Tjader's Latin Concert	1991	15.00
—Reissue of 8014			
❑ 3295 [M]	Concert by the Sea	1959	50.00
—Red vinyl			
❑ 3295 [M]	Concert by the Sea	1959	30.00
—Black vinyl, red label, non-flexible vinyl			
❑ 3295 [M]	Concert by the Sea	196?	18.00
—Black vinyl, red label, flexible vinyl			
❑ 8038 [S]	Concert by the Sea	196?	30.00
—Blue vinyl			
❑ 8038 [S]	Concert by the Sea	196?	25.00
—Black vinyl, blue label, non-flexible vinyl			
❑ 8038 [S]	Concert by the Sea	196?	15.00
—Black vinyl, blue label, flexible vinyl			
❑ 3341 [M]	Concert by the Sea, Volume 2	1962	40.00
—Red vinyl			
❑ 3341 [M]	Concert by the Sea, Volume 2	1962	30.00
—Black vinyl, red label, non-flexible vinyl			
❑ 3341 [M]	Concert by the Sea, Volume 2	196?	18.00
—Black vinyl, red label, flexible vinyl			

Number	Title	Yr	NM
❑ 8098 [S]	Concert by the Sea, Volume 2	1962	30.00
—Blue vinyl			
❑ 8098 [S]	Concert by the Sea, Volume 2	1962	25.00
—Black vinyl, blue label, non-flexible vinyl			
❑ 8098 [S]	Concert by the Sea, Volume 2	196?	15.00
—Black vinyl, blue label, flexible vinyl			
❑ 3299 [M]	Concert on the Campus	1960	40.00
—Red vinyl			
❑ 3299 [M]	Concert on the Campus	1960	30.00
—Black vinyl, red label, non-flexible vinyl			
❑ 3299 [M]	Concert on the Campus	196?	18.00
—Black vinyl, red label, flexible vinyl			
❑ 8044 [S]	Concert on the Campus	196?	30.00
—Blue vinyl			
❑ 8044 [S]	Concert on the Campus	196?	25.00
—Black vinyl, blue label, non-flexible vinyl			
❑ 8044 [S]	Concert on the Campus	196?	15.00
—Black vinyl, blue label, flexible vinyl			
❑ OJC-279	Concert on the Campus	1987	12.00
—Reissue of 8044			
❑ 3309 [M]	Demasiado Caliente	1960	40.00
—Red vinyl			
❑ 3309 [M]	Demasiado Caliente	1960	30.00
—Black vinyl, red label, non-flexible vinyl			
❑ 3309 [M]	Demasiado Caliente	196?	18.00
—Black vinyl, red label, flexible vinyl			
❑ 8053 [S]	Demasiado Caliente	196?	30.00
—Blue vinyl			
❑ 8053 [S]	Demasiado Caliente	196?	25.00
—Black vinyl, blue label, non-flexible vinyl			
❑ 8053 [S]	Demasiado Caliente	196?	15.00
—Black vinyl, blue label, flexible vinyl			
❑ 9533	Guarabe	1977	15.00
❑ 3241 [M]	Jazz at the Blackhawk	1957	50.00
—Red vinyl			
❑ 3241 [M]	Jazz at the Blackhawk	1957	30.00
—Black vinyl, red label, non-flexible vinyl			
❑ 3241 [M]	Jazz at the Blackhawk	196?	18.00
—Black vinyl, red label, flexible vinyl			
❑ 8096 [R]	Jazz at the Blackhawk	1962	30.00
—Blue vinyl			
❑ 8096 [R]	Jazz at the Blackhawk	1962	25.00
—Black vinyl, blue label, non-flexible vinyl			
❑ 8096 [R]	Jazz at the Blackhawk	196?	15.00
—Black vinyl, blue label, flexible vinyl			
❑ OJC-436	Jazz at the Blackhawk	1990	12.00
—Reissue of 8096			
❑ 9446	Last Bolero in Berkeley	1974	15.00
❑ 9482	Last Night When We Were Young	1975	15.00
❑ 8019 [S]	Latin for Dancers	196?	100.00
—Blue vinyl, the existence of this has been confirmed. Black vinyl copies of 8019 are unknown.			
❑ 8019 [S]	Latin for Dancers	196?	120.00
—A red vinyl copy with this number is known to exist also, probably pressed in error			
❑ 3279 [M]	Latin for Lovers	1958	50.00
—Red vinyl			
❑ 3279 [M]	Latin for Lovers	1958	30.00
—Black vinyl, red label, non-flexible vinyl			
❑ 3279 [M]	Latin for Lovers	196?	18.00
—Black vinyl, red label, flexible vinyl			
❑ 8016 [S]	Latin for Lovers	196?	30.00
—Blue vinyl			
❑ 8016 [S]	Latin for Lovers	196?	25.00
—Black vinyl, blue label, non-flexible vinyl			
❑ 8016 [S]	Latin for Lovers	196?	15.00
—Black vinyl, blue label, flexible vinyl			
❑ 3250 [M]	Latin Kick	1957	50.00
—Red vinyl			
❑ 3250 [M]	Latin Kick	1957	30.00
—Black vinyl, red label, non-flexible vinyl			
❑ 3250 [M]	Latin Kick	196?	18.00
—Black vinyl, red label, flexible vinyl			
❑ 8033 [S]	Latin Kick	196?	30.00
—Blue vinyl			
❑ 8033 [S]	Latin Kick	196?	25.00
—Black vinyl, blue label, non-flexible vinyl			
❑ 8033 [S]	Latin Kick	196?	15.00
—Black vinyl, blue label, flexible vinyl			
❑ OJC-642	Latin Kick	1991	15.00
—Reissue of 8033			
❑ 3339 [M]	Latino	1962	40.00
—Red vinyl			
❑ 3339 [M]	Latino	1962	30.00
—Black vinyl, red label, non-flexible vinyl			
❑ 3339 [M]	Latino	196?	18.00
—Black vinyl, red label, flexible vinyl			
❑ 8079 [S]	Latino	1962	30.00
—Blue vinyl			
❑ 8079 [S]	Latino	1962	25.00
—Black vinyl, blue label, non-flexible vinyl			
❑ 8079 [S]	Latino	196?	15.00
—Black vinyl, blue label, flexible vinyl			
❑ 9409	Live at the Funky Quarters	1970	15.00
❑ 24712	Los Ritmos Caliente	197?	18.00
❑ 3326 [M]	Mambo	1961	40.00

Number	Title	Yr	NM
—Red vinyl			
❑ 3326 [M]	Mambo	1961	30.00
—Black vinyl, red label, non-flexible vinyl			
❑ 3326 [M]	Mambo	196?	18.00
—Black vinyl, red label, flexible vinyl			
❑ 8057 [S]	Mambo	1962	30.00
—Blue vinyl			
❑ 8057 [S]	Mambo	1962	25.00
—Black vinyl, blue label, non-flexible vinyl			
❑ 8057 [S]	Mambo	196?	15.00
—Black vinyl, blue label, flexible vinyl			
❑ 3202 [M]	Mambo with Tjader	1955	100.00
—Red vinyl			
❑ 3202 [M]	Mambo with Tjader	1956	50.00
—Black vinyl, red label, non-flexible vinyl			
❑ 3202 [M]	Mambo with Tjader	196?	30.00
—Black vinyl, red label, flexible vinyl			
❑ 9424	Mambo with Tjader	1973	15.00
❑ OJC-271	Mambo with Tjader	1987	12.00
—Reissue of 3202			
❑ 3262 [M]	Mas Ritmo Caliente	1958	50.00
—Red vinyl			
❑ 3262 [M]	Mas Ritmo Caliente	1958	30.00
—Black vinyl, red label, non-flexible vinyl			
❑ 3262 [M]	Mas Ritmo Caliente	196?	18.00
—Black vinyl, red label, flexible vinyl			
❑ 8003 [S]	Mas Ritmo Caliente	196?	30.00
—Blue vinyl			
❑ 8003 [S]	Mas Ritmo Caliente	196?	25.00
—Black vinyl, blue label, non-flexible vinyl			
❑ 8003 [S]	Mas Ritmo Caliente	196?	15.00
—Black vinyl, blue label, flexible vinyl			
❑ 9422	Primo	1972	15.00
❑ 9463	Puttin' It Together	1974	15.00
❑ 3-17 [10]	Ritmo Caliente	1954	150.00
—Any of various non-black vinyl pressings			
❑ 3-17 [10]	Ritmo Caliente	1954	100.00
—Black vinyl			
❑ 3216 [M]	Ritmo Caliente	1956	100.00
—Red vinyl			
❑ 3216 [M]	Ritmo Caliente	1956	50.00
—Black vinyl, red label, non-flexible vinyl			
❑ 3216 [M]	Ritmo Caliente	196?	30.00
—Black vinyl, red label, flexible vinyl			
❑ 8077 [R]	Ritmo Caliente	1962	30.00
—Blue vinyl			
❑ 8077 [R]	Ritmo Caliente	1962	25.00
—Black vinyl, blue label, non-flexible vinyl			
❑ 8077 [R]	Ritmo Caliente	196?	15.00
—Black vinyl, blue label, flexible vinyl			
❑ 3271 [M]	San Francisco Moods	1958	50.00
—Red vinyl			
❑ 3271 [M]	San Francisco Moods	1958	30.00
—Black vinyl, red label, non-flexible vinyl			
❑ 3271 [M]	San Francisco Moods	196?	18.00
—Black vinyl, red label, flexible vinyl			
❑ 8017 [S]	San Francisco Moods	196?	30.00
—Blue vinyl			
❑ 8017 [S]	San Francisco Moods	196?	25.00
—Black vinyl, blue label, non-flexible vinyl			
❑ 8017 [S]	San Francisco Moods	196?	15.00
—Black vinyl, blue label, flexible vinyl			
❑ OJC-277	San Francisco Moods	1987	12.00
—Reissue of 8017			
❑ 3232 [M]	The Cal Tjader Quintet	1956	100.00
—Red vinyl			
❑ 3232 [M]	The Cal Tjader Quintet	1956	50.00
—Black vinyl, red label, non-flexible vinyl			
❑ 3232 [M]	The Cal Tjader Quintet	196?	30.00
—Black vinyl, red label, flexible vinyl			
❑ 8085 [R]	The Cal Tjader Quintet	196?	30.00
—Blue vinyl; stereo version of 3232			
❑ 8085 [R]	The Cal Tjader Quintet	196?	25.00
—Black vinyl, blue label, non-flexible vinyl			
❑ 8085 [R]	The Cal Tjader Quintet	196?	15.00
—Black vinyl, blue label, flexible vinyl			
❑ 3-9 [10]	The Cal Tjader Trio	1953	150.00
—Any of various non-black vinyl pressings			
❑ 3-9 [10]	The Cal Tjader Trio	1953	100.00
—Black vinyl			
❑ 8406	Tjader	1970	15.00
❑ 3289 [M]	Tjader Goes Latin	1959	50.00
—Red vinyl			
❑ 3289 [M]	Tjader Goes Latin	1959	30.00
—Black vinyl, red label, non-flexible vinyl			
❑ 3289 [M]	Tjader Goes Latin	196?	18.00
—Black vinyl, red label, flexible vinyl			
❑ 8030 [S]	Tjader Goes Latin	196?	30.00
—Blue vinyl			
❑ 8030 [S]	Tjader Goes Latin	196?	25.00
—Black vinyl, blue label, non-flexible vinyl			
❑ 8030 [S]	Tjader Goes Latin	196?	15.00
—Black vinyl, blue label, flexible vinyl			
❑ 3221 [M]	Tjader Plays Mambo	1956	100.00
—Red vinyl			
❑ 3221 [M]	Tjader Plays Mambo	1956	50.00
—Black vinyl, red label, non-flexible vinyl			
❑ 3221 [M]	Tjader Plays Mambo	196?	30.00
—Black vinyl, red label, flexible vinyl			

Number	Title	Yr	NM
❏ OJC-274	Tjader Plays Mambo	1987	12.00
—Reissue of 3221			
❏ 3-18 [10]	Tjader Plays Mambo	1954	150.00
—Red vinyl			
❏ 3211 [M]	Tjader Plays Tjazz	1956	100.00
—Red vinyl			
❏ 3211 [M]	Tjader Plays Tjazz	1956	50.00
—Black vinyl, red label, non-flexible vinyl			
❏ 3278 [M]	Tjader Plays Tjazz	1958	50.00
—Red vinyl; reissue of 3211			
❏ 3278 [M]	Tjader Plays Tjazz	1958	30.00
—Black vinyl, red label, non-flexible vinyl			
❏ 3278 [M]	Tjader Plays Tjazz	196?	18.00
—Black vinyl, red label, flexible vinyl			
❏ 8097 [R]	Tjader Plays Tjazz	1962	30.00
—Blue vinyl			
❏ 8097 [R]	Tjader Plays Tjazz	1962	25.00
—Black vinyl, blue label, non-flexible vinyl			
❏ 8097 [R]	Tjader Plays Tjazz	196?	15.00
—Black vinyl, blue label, flexible vinyl			
❏ 3310 [M]	West Side Story	1960	40.00
—Red vinyl			
❏ 3310 [M]	West Side Story	1960	30.00
—Black vinyl, red label, non-flexible vinyl			
❏ 3310 [M]	West Side Story	196?	18.00
—Black vinyl, red label, flexible vinyl			
❏ 8054 [S]	West Side Story	196?	30.00
—Blue vinyl			
❏ 8054 [S]	West Side Story	196?	25.00
—Black vinyl, blue label, non-flexible vinyl			
❏ 8054 [S]	West Side Story	196?	15.00
—Black vinyl, blue label, flexible vinyl			
❏ 8379	West Side Story	1967	15.00
—Reissue of 8054			
GALAXY			
❏ 5107	Breathe Easy	1977	15.00
❏ 5121	Here	1978	15.00
MGM			
❏ 10008	Sonido Nuevo	197?	18.00
PRESTIGE			
❏ 24026	The Monterey Concerts	1973	18.00
SAVOY			
❏ MG-9036 [10]	Cal Tjader -- Vibist	1954	100.00
SKYE			
❏ SK-10	Cal Tjader Plugs In	1969	25.00
❏ SK-1	Solar Heat	1968	25.00
❏ SK-19	Tjader-Ade	1970	18.00
VERVE			
❏ V-8671 [M]	Along Comes Cal	1966	18.00
❏ V6-8671 [S]	Along Comes Cal	1966	25.00
❏ V-8575 [M]	Breeze from the East	1964	25.00
❏ V6-8575 [S]	Breeze from the East	1964	30.00
❏ V-8651 [M]	El Soni Do Nuevo -- The New Soul Sound	1966	18.00
❏ V6-8651 [S]	El Soni Do Nuevo -- The New Soul Sound	1966	25.00
❏ V-8730 [M]	Hip Vibrations	1967	25.00
❏ V6-8730 [S]	Hip Vibrations	1967	18.00
❏ V-8419 [M]	In a Latin Bag	1961	25.00
❏ V6-8419 [S]	In a Latin Bag	1961	30.00
❏ V-8459 [M]	Saturday Night…Sunday Night at the Blackhawk	1962	25.00
❏ V6-8459 [S]	Saturday Night…Sunday Night at the Blackhawk	1962	30.00
❏ V-8507 [M]	Several Shades of Jade	1963	25.00
❏ V6-8507 [S]	Several Shades of Jade	1963	30.00
❏ V-8531 [M]	Sona Libre	1963	25.00
❏ V6-8531 [S]	Sona Libre	1963	30.00
❏ V-8626 [M]	Soul Bird: Whippenpoof	1965	25.00
❏ V6-8626 [S]	Soul Bird: Whippenpoof	1965	30.00
❏ V-8637 [M]	Soul Burst	1965	25.00
❏ V6-8637 [S]	Soul Burst	1965	30.00
❏ V-8614 [M]	Soul Sauce	1965	25.00
❏ V6-8614 [S]	Soul Sauce	1965	30.00
❏ 827756-1	Soul Sauce	1986	12.00
—Reissue of 8614			
❏ V-8725 [M]	The Best of Cal Tjader	1967	18.00
❏ V6-8725 [S]	The Best of Cal Tjader	1967	25.00
❏ V-8470 [M]	The Contemporary Music of Mexico and Brazil	1962	25.00
❏ V6-8470 [S]	The Contemporary Music of Mexico and Brazil	1962	30.00
❏ V6-8769	The Prophet	1969	18.00
❏ V-8585 [M]	Warm Wave	1964	25.00
❏ V6-8585 [S]	Warm Wave	1964	30.00

TJADER, CAL/DON ELLIOTT

SAVOY

❏ MG-12054 [M]	Vib-Rations	1956	40.00
—Reissue of 9036 and 9033			

TLC

LAFACE

❏ LFL6155 [DJ]	Fanmail	1999	18.00
—Promo-only "clean version" in company sleeve			
❏ 26055	Fanmail	1999	15.00

TOAD HALL

LIBERTY

❏ LST-7580	Toad Hall	1968	30.00

Number	Title	Yr	NM
TOAD THE WET SPROCKET			
COLUMBIA			
❏ FC45326 [B]	Bread and Circus	1989	18.00
❏ C47309	Fear	1991	25.00
❏ C46060	Pale	1990	30.00
—Marbled white (almost greenish) vinyl			

TOADS, THE

WIGGINS

❏ 64021 [M]	The Toads	1964	300.00

TOBY BEAU

RCA VICTOR

❏ DJL1-2994 [DJ]	3 You Missed. 1 You Didn't	1978	25.00
—Promo-only sampler			
❏ AFL1-3575	If You Believe	1980	15.00
❏ AFL1-3119	More Than a Love Song	1979	15.00
❏ AFL1-2771	Toby Beau	1978	12.00

TODD, ART AND DOTTY

DART

❏ D-444 [M]	Black Velvet Eyes	1959	40.00
DOT			
❏ DLP-3742 [M]	Chanson d'Amour (Song of Love)	1966	30.00
❏ DLP-25742 [S]	Chanson d'Amour (Song of Love)	1966	30.00

TODD, RICHARD

GM RECORDINGS

❏ 2010	New Ideas	1986	15.00

TOE FAT

RARE EARTH

❏ RS-511	Toe Fat	1970	30.00
❏ RS-525	Toe Fat Two	1971	30.00

TOGASHI, MASAHIKO

INNER CITY

❏ IC-6011	Spiritual Nature	197?	18.00

TOGAWA, PAUL

MODE

❏ LP-104 [M]	Paul Togawa Quartet	1957	80.00

TOKENS, THE

B.T. PUPPY

❏ BTPS-1014	December 5th	1971	200.00
❏ BTPS-1012	Greatest Moments	1970	30.00
❏ BTP-1000 [M]	I Hear Trumpets Blow	1966	25.00
❏ BTPS-1000 [P]	I Hear Trumpets Blow	1966	30.00
❏ BTPS-1027	Intercourse	1971	600.00
❏ BTPS-1006	Tokens of Gold	1969	30.00
BUDDAH			
❏ BDS-5059	Both Sides Now	1971	18.00
DIPLOMAT			
❏ D-2308 [M]	Kings of the Hot Rods	196?	30.00
❏ DS-2308 [S]	Kings of the Hot Rods	196?	30.00
RCA			
❏ 8534-1-R	Re-Doo-Wopp	1988	12.00
RCA VICTOR			
❏ LPM-2514 [M]	The Lion Sleeps Tonight	1961	80.00
❏ LSP-2514 [S]	The Lion Sleeps Tonight	1961	150.00
❏ LPM-3685 [M]	The Tokens Again	1966	40.00
❏ LSP-3685 [S]	The Tokens Again	1966	50.00
❏ LPM-2631 [M]	We, The Tokens, Sing Folk	1962	40.00
❏ LSP-2631 [S]	We, The Tokens, Sing Folk	1962	50.00
❏ LPM-2886 [M]	Wheels	1964	80.00
❏ LSP-2886 [S]	Wheels	1964	100.00
WARNER BROS.			
❏ W1685 [M]	It's a Happening World	1967	30.00
❏ WS1685 [S]	It's a Happening World	1967	25.00

TOKENS, THE AND THE HAPPENINGS

B.T. PUPPY

❏ BTP-1002 [M]	Back to Back	1967	25.00
—Half this LP is by the Tokens, the other half by the Happenings			
❏ BTPS-1002 [S]	Back to Back	1967	30.00

TOLBERT, ISRAEL

WARREN/STAX

❏ STS-2038	Popper Stopper	1971	30.00
—Cover says "Warren Records Distributed by Stax," label is Stax			

TOLKIEN, J.R.R.

CAEDMON

❏ TC1478	J.R.R. Tolkien Reads and Sings His "The Lord of the Rings	1975	25.00

TOLLIVER, CHARLES

ARISTA/FREEDOM

❏ AF1002	Paper Man	1975	15.00
❏ AF1017	The Ringer	1975	15.00

Number	Title	Yr	NM
STRATA-EAST			
❏ SES-8001	Compassion	1980	15.00
❏ SES-19757	Impact	1975	18.00
❏ SES-1972	Live at Slugs'	1972	25.00
❏ SES-19720	Live at Slugs', Vol. 2	1972	25.00
❏ SES-19740/1	Live at the Loosdrecht Jazz Festival	1974	30.00
❏ SES-19745	Live in Tokyo	1974	25.00
❏ SES-1971	Music Inc.	1971	25.00

TOLONEN, JUKKA

TERRA

❏ T-6	Touch Wood	1985	15.00

TOM AND JERRY (2)

MERCURY

❏ MG-20626 [M]	Guitar's Greatest Hits	1961	30.00
❏ SR-60626 [S]	Guitar's Greatest Hits	1961	40.00
❏ MG-20756 [M]	Guitar's Greatest Hits, Vol. 2	1962	30.00
❏ SR-60756 [S]	Guitar's Greatest Hits, Vol. 2	1962	40.00
❏ MG-20671 [M]	Guitars Play the Sound of Ray Charles	1962	30.00
❏ SR-60671 [S]	Guitars Play the Sound of Ray Charles	1962	40.00
❏ MG-20842 [M]	Surfin' Hootenanny	1963	40.00
❏ SR-60842 [S]	Surfin' Hootenanny	1963	50.00

TOM TOM CLUB

SIRE

❏ 25888	Boom Boom Chi Boom Boom	1989	12.00
❏ 23916	Close to the Bone	1983	12.00
❏ SRK3628	Tom Tom Club	1981	12.00
WARNER BROS.			
❏ WBMS-120 [DJ]	Wordy Rapping with the Tom Tom Club	1986	25.00
—Part of "The Warner Bros. Music Show"; promo only			

TOMITA

RCA RED SEAL

❏ ARL1-4019	A Voyage Through His Greatest Hits, Vol. 2	1981	12.00
❏ ARL1-5184	Canon of the 3 Stars	1984	12.00
❏ ARL1-1312	Firebird	1976	12.00
❏ ARD1-1312 [Q]	Firebird	1976	30.00
❏ ARL1-4317	Grand Canyon Suite	1982	12.00
❏ ARL1-3439	Greatest Hits	1980	12.00
❏ ARL1-1919	Holst: The Planets	1976	12.00
❏ ARL1-2616	Kosmos	1978	12.00
❏ ARL1-5461	Live at Linz, 1984 -- The Mind of the Universe	1985	12.00
❏ ARL1-0838	Moussorgsky: Pictures at an Exhibition	1975	12.00
❏ ARD1-0838 [Q]	Moussorgsky: Pictures at an Exhibition	1975	30.00
❏ ARL1-3412	Ravel: Bolero	1980	12.00
❏ ARL1-0488	Snowflakes Are Dancing	1974	12.00
❏ ATL1-4332	Snowflakes Are Dancing	1982	15.00
—Reissue with die-cut cover and custom innersleeve			
❏ ARD1-0488 [Q]	Snowflakes Are Dancing	1974	30.00
❏ ARL1-5037	Spacewalk -- Impressions of an Astronaut	1984	12.00
❏ ARL1-2885	The Bermuda Triangle	1979	12.00

TOMLIN, LILY

ARISTA

❏ AB4142	Lily Tomlin On Stage	1977	15.00
POLYDOR			
❏ PD5023	And That's the Truth	1972	12.00
❏ PD6051	Modern Scream	1976	15.00
❏ 24-4055	This Is a Recording	1971	12.00

TOMMY AND THE TWISTERS

REGENT

❏ MG-6104 [M]	Let's All Do the Twist	1961	40.00

TOMMY TUTONE

COLUMBIA

❏ FC38425	National Emotion	1983	12.00
❏ JC36372	Tommy Tutone	1980	15.00
❏ AS1461 [DJ]	Tommy Tutone	1982	25.00
—Three tracks from "Tommy Tutone-2" and the same three tracks live; promo-only			
❏ ARC37401	Tommy Tutone-2	1981	15.00
❏ PC37401	Tommy Tutone-2	198?	10.00
—Budget-line reissue			

TOMORROW

SIRE

❏ SES-97912	Tomorrow	1968	60.00

TOMPALL AND THE GLASER BROTHERS

DECCA

❏ DL4041 [M]	This Land Folk Songs	1960	30.00
❏ DL74041 [S]	This Land Folk Songs	1960	40.00
ELEKTRA			
❏ 60148	After All These Years	1982	12.00
❏ 5E-542	Lovin' Her Was Easier	1981	12.00

Number	Title	Yr	NM
MGM			
❏ SE-4775	Award Winners	1971	18.00
❏ SE-4888	Great Hits from Two Decades	1973	18.00
❏ SE-4620	Now Country	1969	18.00
❏ SE-4812	Rings and Things	1972	18.00
❏ SE-4510	Through the Eyes of Love	1968	18.00
❏ E-4465 [M]	Tompall & the Glaser Brothers	1967	30.00
❏ SE-4465 [S]	Tompall & the Glaser Brothers	1967	25.00
❏ SE-4976	Vocal Group of the Decade	1974	18.00

TOMPKINS, FRED

Number	Title	Yr	NM
FESTIVAL			
❏ 9001	Compositions	197?	15.00
❏ 9002	Somesville	1975	15.00
F.K.T.			
❏ 103	Cecile	1980	15.00
❏ 101	Compositions	1980	12.00
❏ 102	Somesville	1980	12.00

TOMPKINS, ROSS, AND JOE VENUTI

Number	Title	Yr	NM
CONCORD JAZZ			
❏ CJ-51	Live '77	1978	15.00

TOMPKINS, ROSS

Number	Title	Yr	NM
CONCORD JAZZ			
❏ CJ-117	Festival Time	198?	12.00
❏ CJ-46	Lost in the Stars	1977	15.00
❏ CJ-65	Ross Tompkins and His Good Friends	1978	15.00
❏ CJ-28	Scrimshaw	1976	15.00
FAMOUS DOOR			
❏ HL-153	In the Swing of Things	1987	12.00
❏ HL-151	L.A. After Dark	1986	12.00
❏ HL-143	Street of Dreams	198?	12.00
❏ HL-146	Symphony	198?	12.00

TOMS, GARY, EMPIRE

Number	Title	Yr	NM
MCA			
❏ 2289	Turn It Out	1977	12.00
MERCURY			
❏ SRM-1-3731	Do It Again	1978	12.00
P.I.P.			
❏ 6814	7-6-5-4-3-2-1 Blow Your Whistle	1975	12.00

TONE LOC

Number	Title	Yr	NM
DELICIOUS VINYL			
❏ 314-510609-1 [B]	Cool Hand Loc	1991	25.00
❏ DV3000 [B]	Loc-ed After Dark	1989	30.00

TONEY, OSCAR, JR.

Number	Title	Yr	NM
BELL			
❏ 6006 [M]	For Your Precious Love	1967	30.00
❏ S-6006 [S]	For Your Precious Love	1967	30.00

TONGUE

Number	Title	Yr	NM
HEMISPHERE			
❏ HIS-101	Tongue	1970	30.00

TONGUE AND GROOVE

Number	Title	Yr	NM
FONTANA			
❏ 3RF-6/593	Tongue and Groove	1968	25.00

TONI AND TERRY

Number	Title	Yr	NM
CAPITOL			
❏ ST-11137	Cross-Country	1973	15.00

TONSBERG CHORAL CHOIR

Number	Title	Yr	NM
HARMONY MUSIC			
❏ LP-18 [M]	Christmas Songs from Norway	196?	18.00

TONTO'S EXPANDING HEAD BAND

Number	Title	Yr	NM
EMBRYO			
❏ SD732 [B]	Zero Time	1971	35.00

TONY TONI TONE

Number	Title	Yr	NM
WING			
❏ 841902-1	Revival	1990	25.00
❏ 835549-1	Who?	1988	15.00

TOO MUCH JOY

Number	Title	Yr	NM
ALIAS			
❏ A-003	Son of Sam I Am	1988	12.00
GIANT			
❏	Besides	1991	15.00
PRO-A-5054 [DJ]			
— Promo-only collection			
STONEGARDEN			
❏ SGN-901	Green Eggs and Crack	1987	200.00

TOOL

Number	Title	Yr	NM
VOLCANO			
❏ 31160-1	Lateralus	2005	40.00
— Two picture discs; CD version issued in 2001			
ZOO			
❏ 11087-1	Aenima	1996	250.00
❏ 11027-1 [B]	Opiate	1992	25.00
❏ 11052-1 RE	Undertow	1993	30.00

TOOTS AND THE MAYTALS

Number	Title	Yr	NM
ISLAND			
❏ ILPS9330 [B]	Funky Kingston	1975	18.00
MANGO			
❏ MLPS9330	Funky Kingston	197?	12.00
— Reissue of Island 9330			
❏ MLPS9590	Just Like That	1980	12.00
❏ MLPS9670	Knock Out	1982	12.00
❏ MLPS9647	Live	1980	15.00
❏ MLPS9534	Pass the Pipe	198?	12.00
❏ MLPS9374	Reggae Got Soul	1976	15.00
❏ 9781	Reggae Greats	198?	12.00

TOP DRAWER

Number	Title	Yr	NM
WISH BONE			
❏ 721207	Solid Oak	1969	400.00

TOPS ORCHESTRA AND CHORISTERS

Number	Title	Yr	NM
TOPS			
❏ L1525 [M]	Christmas Favorites	195?	18.00

TOPSIDERS, THE

Number	Title	Yr	NM
JOSIE			
❏ JOZ-4000 [M]	Rock Goes Folk	1963	30.00

TOREADOR BRASS, THE

Number	Title	Yr	NM
HARMONY			
❏ HS-11352	Toreador Christmas	1968	15.00

TORFF, BRIAN

Number	Title	Yr	NM
AUDIOPHILE			
❏ AP-182	Manhattan Hoe-Down	1983	12.00
OPTIMISM			
❏ OP-2601	Hitchhiker of Karoo	198?	12.00

TORKANOWSKY, DAVID

Number	Title	Yr	NM
ROUNDER			
❏ 2090	Steppin' Out	198?	12.00

TORME, MEL, AND BUDDY RICH

Number	Title	Yr	NM
CENTURY			
❏ 1100	Together Again -- For the First Time	1978	30.00
— Direct-to-disc recording			
GRYPHON			
❏ G-903	Together Again -- For the First Time	1978	12.00

TORME, MEL

Number	Title	Yr	NM
ALLEGRO ELITE			
❏ 4117 [10]	Mel Torme Sings	195?	30.00
ATLANTIC			
❏ 8069 [M]	Comin' Home Baby	1962	30.00
❏ SD8069 [S]	Comin' Home Baby	1962	40.00
❏ SD18129	Live at the Maisonette	1975	15.00
❏ 8066 [M]	Mel Torme at the Red Hill Inn	1962	30.00
❏ SD8066 [S]	Mel Torme at the Red Hill Inn	1962	40.00
❏ 80078	Songs of New York	1982	12.00
❏ 8091 [M]	Sunday in New York	1963	30.00
❏ SD8091 [S]	Sunday in New York	1963	40.00
AUDIOPHILE			
❏ 67	Mel Torme Sings About Love	198?	25.00
BETHLEHEM			
❏ BCP6016 [M]	California Suite	1957	50.00
❏ BCP-34 [M]	It's a Blue World	1956	50.00
❏ BCP-52 [M]	Mel Torme and the Marty Paich Dektette	1956	50.00
❏ BCP6020 [M]	Mel Torme Live at the Crescendo	1958	50.00
❏ BCP6013 [M]	Mel Torme Sings Fred Astaire	1957	50.00
❏ BCP6031 [M]	Songs for Any Taste	1959	50.00
❏ BCP6042	The Torme Touch	1978	15.00
— Reissue of BCP 52			
CAPITOL			
❏ ST-313	A Time for Us	1969	15.00
❏ P200 [M]	California Suite	1950	100.00
❏ ST-430	Raindrops Keep Falling on My Head	1970	15.00
COLUMBIA			
❏ CL2535 [M]	Mel Torme Right Now	1966	15.00
❏ CS9335 [S]	Mel Torme Right Now	1966	18.00
❏ CL2318 [M]	That's All -- A Lush Romantic Album	1965	18.00
❏ CS9118 [S]	That's All -- A Lush Romantic Album	1965	25.00
COLUMBIA SPECIAL PRODUCTS			
❏ P13090	That's All	1976	15.00
CONCORD JAZZ			
❏ CJ-382	In Concert Tokyo	1989	12.00
— Above two with the Marty Paich Dek-Tette			
❏ CJ-306	Mel Torme with Rob McConnell and the Boss Brass	1986	12.00
❏ CJ-360	Reunion	1988	12.00
CORAL			
❏ CRL57012 [M]	Gene Norman Presents Mel Torme "Live" at the Crescendo	1955	50.00
❏ CRL57044 [M]	Musical Sounds Are the Best Songs	1956	50.00
DISCOVERY			
❏ 910	Sings His California Suite	1986	12.00
— Reissue of Capitol 200			
EVEREST ARCHIVE OF FOLK & JAZZ			
❏ 324	The Velvet Fog	1976	12.00
FINESSE			
❏ W2X37484	Mel Torme & Friends Recorded at Marty's, New York City	1981	15.00
GLENDALE			
❏ 6018	Easy to Remember	1979	12.00
❏ 6007	Mel Torme	1978	12.00
GRYPHON			
❏ G-916	A New Album	1980	12.00
LIBERTY			
❏ LST-7560 [S]	A Day in the Life of Bonnie and Clyde	1968	25.00
❏ LRP-3560 [M]	A Day in the Life of Bonnie and Clyde	1968	40.00
— Stock copy mono inside stereo cover with "Audition Mono LP Not for Sale" sticker			
METRO			
❏ M-532 [M]	I Wished on the Moon	1965	15.00
❏ MS-532 [S]	I Wished on the Moon	1965	18.00
MGM			
❏ E552 [10]	Mel Torme Sings	1952	100.00
MUSICRAFT			
❏ 2005	Gone with the Wind	1986	12.00
❏ 510	It Happened in Monterey	1983	12.00
❏ 508	Mel Torme, Volume 1	1983	12.00
STASH			
❏ ST-252	'Round Midnight	1985	12.00
STRAND			
❏ SL 1076 [M]	Mel Torme Sings	1960	25.00
❏ SLS-1076 [S]	Mel Torme Sings	1960	30.00
TIME-LIFE			
❏ SLGD-13	Legendary Singers: Mel Torme	1000	18.00
TOPS			
❏ L-1615 [M]	Prelude to a Kiss	1958	30.00
VENISE			
❏ 10021 [M]	The Touch of Your Lips	196?	25.00
— Yellow vinyl; reissue of Tops L-1615 without patter in between songs			
VERVE			
❏ MGV2120 [M]	Back in Town	1959	50.00
❏ V-2120 [M]	Back in Town	1961	25.00
— Reissue			
❏ MGVS6063 [S]	Back in Town	1960	50.00
❏ V6-2120 [S]	Back in Town	1961	30.00
— Reissue			
❏ UMV-2675	Back in Town	1982	12.00
❏ MGV2146 [M]	Broadway, Right Now	1961	50.00
❏ V-2146 [M]	Broadway, Right Now	1961	25.00
— Reissue			
❏ V6-2146 [S]	Broadway, Right Now	1961	30.00
❏ V-8491 [M]	I Dig the Duke! I Dig the Count!	1962	30.00
❏ V6-8491 [S]	I Dig the Duke! I Dig the Count!	1962	30.00
❏ MGV2132 [M]	Mel Torme Swings Schubert Alley	1960	50.00
❏ V-2132 [M]	Mel Torme Swings Shubert Alley	1961	25.00
— Reissue			
❏ MGVS6146 [S]	Mel Torme Swings Shubert Alley	1960	50.00
❏ V6-2132 [S]	Mel Torme Swings Shubert Alley	196?	30.00
— Reissue of 62132			
❏ UMV-2521	Mel Torme Swings Shubert Alley	1981	12.00
❏ MGVS62132 [S]	Mel Torme Swings Shubert Alley	196?	40.00
— Early reissue of 6146			
❏ V-8440 [M]	My Kind of Music	1962	30.00
❏ V6-8440 [S]	My Kind of Music	1962	30.00
❏ MGV2117 [M]	Ole Torme! Mel Torme Goes South of the Border with Billy May	1959	50.00

Number	Title	Yr	NM
❑ V-2117 [M]	Ole Torme! Mel Torme Goes South of the Border with Billy May	1961	25.00
—Reissue			
❑ MGVS6058 [S]	Ole Torme! Mel Torme Goes South of the Border with Billy May	1960	50.00
❑ V6-2117 [S]	Ole Torme! Mel Torme Goes South of the Border with Billy May	1961	30.00
—Reissue			
❑ MGV2144 [M]	Swingin' on the Moon	1960	50.00
❑ V-2144 [M]	Swingin' on the Moon	1961	25.00
—Reissue			
❑ V6-2144 [S]	Swingin' on the Moon	1961	30.00
—Reissue of 62144			
❑ MGVS62144 [S]	Swingin' on the Moon	1960	60.00
❑ 823248-1	The Duke Ellington and Count Basie Songbooks	1984	12.00
—Reissue of Verve 8491			
❑ MGV2105 [M]	Torme	1958	50.00
❑ V-2105 [M]	Torme	1961	25.00
—Reissue			
❑ MGVS6015 [S]	Torme	1960	50.00
❑ V6-2105 [S]	Torme	1961	30.00
—Reissue			
❑ V-8593 [M]	Verve's Choice -- The Best of Mel Torme	1964	15.00
❑ V6-8593 [S]	Verve's Choice -- The Best of Mel Torme	1964	18.00
VOCALION			
❑ VL73905	The Velvet Fog	197?	12.00

TORMENTORS, THE

ROYAL

Number	Title	Yr	NM
❑ RLP-111 [M]	Hanging Around	1967	200.00

TORN, DAVID, AND GEOFFREY GORDON

ECM

Number	Title	Yr	NM
❑ 1284	Best Laid Plans	1985	15.00

TORNADOES, THE (1)

LONDON

Number	Title	Yr	NM
❑ LL3279 [M]	Telstar	1963	200.00
❑ LL3293 [M]	The Sounds of the Tornadoes	1963	200.00
—Basically the same album as above, but with a new cover, one different track and the song order shuffled.			

TORNADOES, THE (2)

JOSIE

Number	Title	Yr	NM
❑ J-4005 [M]	Bustin' Surfboards	1963	200.00
❑ JS-4005 [S]	Bustin' Surfboards	1963	300.00
SUNDAZED			
❑ LP-5024	Bustin' Surfboards	1996	12.00

TOROK, MITCHELL

GUYDEN

Number	Title	Yr	NM
❑ GLP-502 [M]	Caribbean	1960	40.00
❑ ST-502 [S]	Caribbean	1960	50.00
REPRISE			
❑ R6223 [M]	Guitar Course	1966	25.00
❑ RS6223 [S]	Guitar Course	1966	30.00

TORQUES, THE

LEMCO

Number	Title	Yr	NM
❑ 604	The Torques Live	1966	200.00
WIGGINS			
❑ 64010	Zoom!	1967	200.00

TORRANCE, RICHARD

CAPITOL

Number	Title	Yr	NM
❑ SW-11660	Anything's Possible	1978	12.00
❑ SW-11610	Bareback	1977	12.00
❑ SW-11699	Double Take	1978	12.00
SHELTER			
❑ 2134	Belle of the Ball	1975	12.00
❑ 2112	Eureka	1974	15.00

TORRES, NESTOR

VERVE FORECAST

Number	Title	Yr	NM
❑ 839387-1	Morning Ride	1989	15.00

TOTO

COLUMBIA

Number	Title	Yr	NM
❑ 8C838685 [EP]	Africa/Rosanna	1983	25.00
—Africa-shaped picture disc; numbered like an LP although it has only these two songs on it and is (approximately) 7 inches			
❑ FC40273	Fahrenheit	1986	12.00
❑ FC36229	Hydra	1979	12.00
❑ PC36229	Hydra	198?	10.00
—Budget-line reissue with new prefix			
❑ 9C939911 [PD]	Isolation	1984	25.00
❑ QC38962	Isolation	1984	12.00
❑ C45369	Past to Present 1977-1990	1990	30.00
—Vinyl available only from Columbia House			
❑ AS577 [DJ]	Special Radio Interview	1979	25.00
❑ FC40873	The Seventh One	1988	12.00

Number	Title	Yr	NM
❑ JC35317	Toto	1978	12.00
❑ PC35317	Toto	198?	10.00
—Budget-line reissue with new prefix			
❑ HC47728	Toto IV	198?	40.00
—Half-speed mastered edition			
❑ FC37728	Toto IV	1982	12.00
❑ PD36813 [PD]	Turn Back	1981	30.00
—Promo-only picture disc			
❑ FC36813	Turn Back	1981	12.00
❑ PC36813	Turn Back	1984	10.00
—Budget-line reissue with new prefix			
MOBILE FIDELITY			
❑ 1-250	Toto IV	1996	40.00
—Audiophile vinyl			

TOUCH, THE

COLISEUM

Number	Title	Yr	NM
❑ DS-51004	The Touch	1968	30.00

TOUCH

GEAR FAB

Number	Title	Yr	NM
❑ GF105	Street Suite	1999	30.00
—Reissue of rare album plus bonus tracks			
MAINLINE			
❑ 2001	Street Suite	1969	2000.00
—VG value 1000; VG+ value 1500			

TOUCHSTONE

UNITED ARTISTS

Number	Title	Yr	NM
❑ UAS-5563	Tarot	1972	30.00

TOUFF, CY

ARGO

Number	Title	Yr	NM
❑ LP-606 [M]	Doorway To Dixie	1956	40.00
❑ LP-641 [M]	Touff Assignment	1959	30.00
❑ LPS-641 [S]	Touff Assignment	1959	30.00
PACIFIC JAZZ			
❑ PJ-1211 [M]	Cy Touff, His Octet and Quintet	1956	150.00
❑ PJ-42 [M]	Keester Parade	1962	60.00
WORLD PACIFIC			
❑ PJM-410 [M]	Havin' A Ball	1958	100.00

TOURISTS, THE

EPIC

Number	Title	Yr	NM
❑ NJE36757	Luminous Basement	1980	18.00
❑ JE36386	Reality Effect	1980	18.00
❑ PC39318	Should Have Been Greatest Hits	1984	15.00

TOUSSAINT, ALLEN

4 MEN WITH BEARDS

Number	Title	Yr	NM
❑ 4M213 [B]	Life, Love and Faith	2012	25.00
❑ 4M214LP [B]	Southern Nights		25.00
RCA VICTOR			
❑ LPM-1767 [M]	The Wild Sounds of New Orleans	1958	300.00
—As "Al Tousan"			
REPRISE			
❑ MS2062	Life, Love and Faith	1972	30.00
SCEPTER			
❑ 24003	Toussaint	1971	30.00
WARNER BROS.			
❑ BSK3142	Motion	1978	15.00

TOWER OF POWER

COLUMBIA

Number	Title	Yr	NM
❑ PC34302	Ain't Nothin' Stoppin' Us Now	1976	12.00
—No bar code on cover			
❑ PC34302	Ain't Nothin' Stoppin' Us Now	198?	10.00
—Budget-line reissue with bar code			
❑ PCQ34302 [Q]	Ain't Nothin' Stoppin' Us Now	1976	18.00
❑ JC35784	Back on the Streets	1979	12.00
❑ JC34906	We Came to Play!	1978	12.00
DIRECT DISC			
❑ SD16601	Back to Oakland	1980	30.00
—Audiophile vinyl			
SAN FRANCISCO			
❑ SD204	East Bay Grease	1971	50.00
SHEFFIELD LABS			
❑ 17	Direct	1982	30.00
—Direct-to-disc recording			
WARNER BROS.			
❑ BS2749	Back to Oakland	1974	18.00
—Burbank" palm trees label			
❑ BS2749	Back to Oakland	1979	10.00
—White or tan label			
❑ BS2616	Bump City	1972	18.00
—Green "WB" label			
❑ BS2880	In the Slot	1975	18.00

Number	Title	Yr	NM
—Burbank" palm trees label			
❑ BS2924	Live and In Living Color	1976	18.00
—Burbank" palm trees label			
❑ BS2924	Live and In Living Color	1979	10.00
—White or tan label			
❑ BS2681	Tower of Power	1973	18.00
—Green "WB" label			
❑ BS2681	Tower of Power	1973	15.00
—Burbank" palm trees label			
❑ BS2681	Tower of Power	1979	10.00
—White or tan label			
❑ BS2834	Urban Renewal	1975	18.00
—Burbank" palm trees label			

TOWNER, RALPH, AND GARY BURTON

ECM

Number	Title	Yr	NM
❑ 1056	Matchbook	1975	15.00
❑ 25038	Slide Show	1986	12.00

TOWNER, RALPH, AND GLEN MOORE

ECM

Number	Title	Yr	NM
❑ 1025	Trios/Solos	197?	15.00

TOWNER, RALPH, AND JOHN ABERCROMBIE

ECM

Number	Title	Yr	NM
❑ 1207	Five Years Later	198?	12.00

TOWNER, RALPH

ECM

Number	Title	Yr	NM
❑ 1121	Batik	1978	15.00
❑ 23788	Blue Sun	1983	12.00
❑ 1032	Diary	1973	18.00
❑ 1153	Old Friends, New Friends	197?	12.00
❑ 1173	Solo Concert	1979	12.00
❑ 1060	Solstice	197?	15.00
❑ ECM-1-1095	Sound and Shadows	1977	15.00

TOWNSEND, ED

CAPITOL

Number	Title	Yr	NM
❑ T1214 [M]	Glad to Be Here	1959	30.00
❑ ST1214 [S]	Glad to Be Here	1959	30.00
❑ T1140 [M]	New in Town	1959	30.00
❑ ST1140 [S]	New in Town	1959	30.00
CURTOM			
❑ 5006	Ed Townsend Now	1976	15.00

TOWNSEND, HENRY

BLUESVILLE

Number	Title	Yr	NM
❑ BVLP-1041 [M]	Tired Bein' Mistreated	1962	120.00
—Blue label, silver print			
❑ BVLP-1041 [M]	Tired Bein' Mistreated	1964	30.00
—Blue label, trident logo at side			

TOWNSHEND, PETE, AND RONNIE LANE

ATCO

Number	Title	Yr	NM
❑ 90097	Rough Mix	1983	10.00
—Reissue of MCA LP			
MCA			
❑ 2295 [B]	Rough Mix	1977	12.00

TOWNSHEND, PETE

ATCO

Number	Title	Yr	NM
❑ SD 38-149	All the Best Cowboys Have Chinese Eyes	1982	12.00
❑ 90539	Another Scoop	1987	15.00
❑ PR940 [EP]	Deep End Sampler	1986	25.00
—Promo-only sampler from Deep End Live			
❑ SD 32-100	Empty Glass	1980	12.00
❑ 90553	Pete Townshend's Deep End Live!	1986	12.00
❑ 90063	Scoop	1983	15.00
❑ 90473	White City -- A Novel	1985	12.00
ATLANTIC			
❑ 81996	The Iron Man: The Musical by Pete Townshend	1989	12.00
—Also includes tracks by John Lee Hooker, Simon Townshend, Nina Simone, The Who			
DECCA			
❑ 79189 [B]	Who Came First	1972	35.00
—With poster (deduct 50% if missing). Evidently a near-simultaneous release with Track 79189			
EEL PIE			
❑ EPR-0007	Another Scoop	2002	40.00
—Classic Records edition on "Quiex SV" vinyl			
❑ EPR-0013	Scoop 3	2001	50.00
—Classic Records edition on "Quiex SV" vinyl			
MCA			
❑ 2026	Who Came First	1973	15.00
—Reissue of 79189			
TRACK			
❑ PR0160 [DJ]	Pete Townshend Talks To and About Thunderclap Newman	1970	100.00
—One-sided promo-only interview record			

Number	Title	Yr	NM
❑ PR-A-160 [DJ]	Pete Townshend Talks To and About Thunderclap Newman	1970	100.00
— One-sided promo-only interview record			
❑ 79189 [B]	Who Came First	1972	35.00
— With poster (deduct 50% if missing)			

TOYS, THE

DYNOVOICE

Number	Title	Yr	NM
❑ 9002 [M]	The Toys Sing "A Lover's Concerto" and "Attack!	1966	40.00
❑ S-9002 [P]	The Toys Sing "A Lover's Concerto" and "Attack!	1966	50.00

T'PAU

VIRGIN

Number	Title	Yr	NM
❑ R133568	Bridge of Spies	1987	15.00
— BMG Direct Marketing edition			
❑ 90595	Bridge of Spies	1987	15.00

TRACEY, STAN, AND KEITH TIPPETT

EMANEM

Number	Title	Yr	NM
❑ 3307	TNT	1975	18.00

TRACEY, STAN

LONDON

Number	Title	Yr	NM
❑ LL3107 [M]	Showcase	195?	40.00

TRADE WINDS, THE

KAMA SUTRA

Number	Title	Yr	NM
❑ KLP-8057 [M]	Excursions	1967	30.00
❑ KLPS-8057 [S]	Excursions	1967	30.00

TRADER HORNE

JANUS

Number	Title	Yr	NM
❑ JLS-3012 [B]	Morning Way	1970	80.00

TRAFFIC

ASYLUM

Number	Title	Yr	NM
❑ 7E-1020	When the Eagle Flies	1974	15.00

ISLAND

Number	Title	Yr	NM
❑ 90058	John Barleycorn Must Die	1983	10.00
— Reissue			
❑ 8427801	John Barleycorn Must Die	2008	25.00
❑ 90060	Mr. Fantasy	1983	10.00
— Reissue			
❑ SW-9323	Shoot Out at the Fantasy Factory	1973	18.00
❑ ILPS9224	Shoot Out at the Fantasy Factory	197?	15.00
— Reissue			
❑ 90027	Shoot Out at the Fantasy Factory	1983	10.00
— Reissue			
❑ SW-9306	The Low Spark of High Heeled Boys	1971	18.00
❑ ILPS9180	The Low Spark of High Heeled Boys	197?	15.00
— Reissue			
❑ 90026	The Low Spark of High Heeled Boys	1983	10.00
— Reissue			
❑ 8427791	The Low Spark of High Heeled Boys	2008	25.00
❑ 90059	Traffic	1983	10.00
— Reissue			
❑ SMAS-9336	Traffic -- On the Road	1973	25.00
❑ ILSD2	Traffic -- On the Road	197?	18.00
— Reissue			
❑ 90028	Traffic -- On the Road	1983	15.00
— Reissue			

MOBILE FIDELITY

Number	Title	Yr	NM
❑ 1-209	The Low Spark of High Heeled Boys	1994	50.00
— Audiophile vinyl			

UNITED ARTISTS

Number	Title	Yr	NM
❑ UAS-5500	Best of Traffic	1969	25.00
— Originals have pink and orange labels			
❑ UAL-3651 [M]	Heaven Is In Your Mind	1967	150.00
❑ UAS-6651 [S]	Heaven Is In Your Mind	1967	50.00
❑ UA-LA421-G	Heavy Traffic	1975	18.00
❑ UAS-5504	John Barleycorn Must Die	1970	25.00
— Originals have black and orange labels			
❑ UAS-6702	Last Exit	1969	25.00
— Originals have purple and orange labels			
❑ ST-92018	Last Exit	1969	30.00
— Capitol Record Club edition; label is the old-style black with circles at the top!			
❑ UA-LA526-G	More Heavy Traffic	1975	18.00
❑ UAS-6651 [S]	Mr. Fantasy	1968	35.00
— Retitled version of "Heaven Is In Your Mind" with old title still on back cover			
❑ UAS-6651 [S]	Mr. Fantasy	1968	30.00
— Retitled version of "Heaven Is In Your Mind" with green strip across top of back with song titles			
❑ UAS-6676	Traffic	1968	25.00
— Originals have purple and orange labels			
❑ UAS-5550	Welcome to the Canteen	1971	18.00

TRAILER, REX, AND THE PLAYBOYS

CROWN

Number	Title	Yr	NM
❑ CLP-5158 [M]	Country & Western	1958	30.00

TRAMLINE

A&M

Number	Title	Yr	NM
❑ SP-4208	Somewhere Down the Line	1969	25.00

TRAMMELL, BOBBY LEE

ATLANTA

Number	Title	Yr	NM
❑ 1503 [M]	Arkansas Twist	1962	1000.00

SOUNCOT

Number	Title	Yr	NM
❑ SC-1102	I Dare America to Be Great	1971	25.00
❑ SC-1141	Love Isn't Love Till You Give It Away	1972	18.00

TRAMMPS, THE

ATLANTIC

Number	Title	Yr	NM
❑ SD18211	Disco Inferno	1977	12.00
❑ SD19267	Mixin' It Up	1980	12.00
❑ SD19290	Slipping Out	1981	12.00
❑ SD19194	The Best of the Trammps	1978	12.00
❑ SD19148	The Trammps III	1977	12.00
❑ SD19210	The Whole World's Dancing	1979	12.00
❑ SD18172	Where the Happy People Go	1976	12.00

BUDDAH

Number	Title	Yr	NM
❑ BDS-5641	The Legendary Zing Album Featuring the Fabulous Trammps	1975	15.00

GOLDEN FLEECE

Number	Title	Yr	NM
❑ KZ33163	Trammps	1975	12.00

PHILADELPHIA INT'L.

Number	Title	Yr	NM
❑ PZ33163	Disco Champs	1977	10.00
— Reissue of Golden Fleece LP			

TRANSIENTS, THE

HORIZON

Number	Title	Yr	NM
❑ WP-1633 [M]	The Funky 12 String Guitar	1963	25.00
❑ WPS-1633 [S]	The Funky 12 String Guitar	1963	30.00

TRANSVISION VAMP

UNI

Number	Title	Yr	NM
❑ 5	Pop Art	1988	15.00
❑ 605	Velveteen	1989	15.00

TRAPEZE

PAID

Number	Title	Yr	NM
❑ 2003	Hold On	1981	12.00

THRESHOLD

Number	Title	Yr	NM
❑ THS4	Medusa	1971	80.00
❑ THS11	The Final Swing	1974	40.00
❑ THS2	Trapeze	1970	40.00
❑ THS8	You Are the Music, We're Just the Band	1972	40.00

WARNER BROS.

Number	Title	Yr	NM
❑ BS2828	Hot Wire	1974	15.00
❑ BS2887	Trapeze	1975	15.00

TRAPP FAMILY SINGERS, THE

RCA CAMDEN

Number	Title	Yr	NM
❑ CAL-209 [M]	The Trapp Family Singers Present Christmas and Folk Songs	195?	25.00

TRASHMEN, THE

BEAT ROCKET

Number	Title	Yr	NM
❑ BR107	Surfin' Bird	1999	15.00
— Reissue on 180-gram vinyl			

GARRETT

Number	Title	Yr	NM
❑ GA-200 [M]	Surfin' Bird	1964	250.00
❑ GAS-200 [R]	Surfin' Bird	1964	350.00

SUNDAZED

Number	Title	Yr	NM
❑ LP5003 [B]	Great Lost Album	1991	12.00
❑ LP5002	Live Bird '65-'67	1991	12.00

TRASK, DIANA

ABC

Number	Title	Yr	NM
❑ ABDP-948	Believe Me Now or Believe Me Later	1976	15.00
❑ AC-30030	The ABC Collection	1976	15.00

ABC DOT

Number	Title	Yr	NM
❑ DOSD-2007	Diana Trask's Greatest Hits	1974	15.00
❑ DOSD-2024	The Mood I'm In	1975	15.00

COLUMBIA

Number	Title	Yr	NM
❑ CL1601 [M]	Diana Trask	1961	30.00
❑ CS8401 [S]	Diana Trask	1961	30.00
❑ CL1705 [M]	Diana Trask on TV	1961	30.00
❑ CS8505 [S]	Diana Trask on TV	1961	30.00

DOT

Number	Title	Yr	NM
❑ DOS-25989	Diana's Country	1971	18.00
❑ DOS-25999	Diana Trask Sings About Loving	1972	18.00
❑ DLP-25957	From the Heart	1969	18.00
❑ DOS-26016	It's a Man's World	1973	18.00
❑ DOS-26022	Lean It All on Me	1974	18.00
❑ DLP-25920	Miss Country Soul	1969	18.00

PICKWICK/HILLTOP

Number	Title	Yr	NM
❑ 6188	Miss Country Soul	197?	12.00

TRAUT, ROSS

HEADFIRST

Number	Title	Yr	NM
❑ 9709	Ross Traut	198?	18.00

TRAUT/RODBY

COLUMBIA

Number	Title	Yr	NM
❑ FC44472	The Great Lawn	1989	15.00

TRAVEL AGENCY, THE

VIVA

Number	Title	Yr	NM
❑ V-36017	The Travel Agency	1968	30.00

TRAVELERS 3, THE

ELEKTRA

Number	Title	Yr	NM
❑ EKL-236 [M]	Live! Live! Live!	1963	30.00
❑ EKL-226 [M]	Open House	1963	30.00
❑ EKL-216 [M]	The Travelers 3	1963	30.00

TRAVELING WILBURYS

WILBURY

Number	Title	Yr	NM
❑ 26324	Traveling Wilburys, Vol. 3	1990	25.00
❑ 25796	Traveling Wilburys (Volume One)	1988	25.00

TRAVELLERS, THE

KAPP

Number	Title	Yr	NM
❑ KL-1157 [M]	Journey with the Travellers	1960	30.00
❑ KS-3051 [S]	Journey with the Travellers	1960	30.00

TRAVERS, MARY

CHRYSALIS

Number	Title	Yr	NM
❑ CHR1168	It's In Everyone of Us	1978	12.00

WARNER BROS.

Number	Title	Yr	NM
❑ BS2677	All My Choices	1973	15.00
— Green "WB" label			
❑ BS2795	Circles	1974	15.00
— Burbank" palm-trees label			
❑ WS1907	Mary	1971	15.00
— Green "WB" label			
❑ BS2609	Morning Glory	1972	15.00
— Green "WB" label			

TRAVERS, PAT

CLEOPATRA

Number	Title	Yr	NM
❑ 9009 [B]	Blues On Fire		25.00

POLYDOR

Number	Title	Yr	NM
❑ PD-16103 [B]	Makin' Magic	1977	15.00
❑ PD-16079 [B]	Pat Travers	1976	12.00
❑ PD-16121 [B]	Putting It Straight	1977	12.00

TRAVIS, MERLE, AND JOE MAPHIS

CAPITOL

Number	Title	Yr	NM
❑ T2102 [M]	Merle Travis and Joe Maphis	1964	40.00
❑ ST2102 [S]	Merle Travis and Joe Maphis	1964	50.00

TRAVIS, MERLE

CAPITOL

Number	Title	Yr	NM
❑ T891 [M]	Back Home	1957	100.00
— Turquoise or gray label			
❑ T891 [M]	Back Home	1959	30.00
— Black colorband label, logo at left			
❑ T891 [M]	Back Home	1962	25.00
— Black colorband label, logo at top			
❑ T1956 [M]	Songs of the Coal Mines	1963	40.00
❑ ST1956 [S]	Songs of the Coal Mines	1963	50.00
❑ ST2938	Strictly Guitar	1968	30.00
❑ T2662 [M]	The Best of Merle Travis	1967	30.00
❑ DT2662 [R]	The Best of Merle Travis	1967	25.00
❑ T650 [M]	The Merle Travis Guitar	1956	120.00
— Turquoise or gray label			
❑ T650 [M]	The Merle Travis Guitar	1959	30.00
— Black colorband label, logo at left			
❑ T650 [M]	The Merle Travis Guitar	1962	25.00
— Black colorband label, logo at top			
❑ T1664 [M]	Travis	1962	40.00
— Black colorband label, logo at left			
❑ T1664 [M]	Travis	1962	25.00
— Black colorband label, logo at top			
❑ ST1664 [S]	Travis	1962	50.00
— Black colorband label, logo at left			
❑ ST1664 [S]	Travis	1962	30.00
— Black colorband label, logo at top			
❑ T1391 [M]	Walkin' the Strings	1960	80.00
— Black colorband label, logo at left			
❑ T1391 [M]	Walkin' the Strings	1962	25.00
— Black colorband label, logo at top			

TRAVIS, NICK

RCA VICTOR

Number	Title	Yr	NM
❑ LJM-1010 [M]	The Panic Is On	1954	120.00

Number	Title	Yr	NM

TRAVIS, RANDY

MUSIC VALLEY

Number	Title	Yr	NM
❑ 0(# unknown)	Randy Ray Live at the Nashville Palace	1982	300.00

— With no "Randy Travis" sticker on front cover

| ❑ 0(# unknown) | Randy Ray Live at the Nashville Palace | 1986 | 200.00 |

— With "Randy Travis" sticker on front cover; the records are the same as the first edition

WARNER BROS.

❑ 25568	Always & Forever	1987	12.00
❑ 25972	An Old-Fashioned Christmas	1989	15.00
❑ R174597	Heroes and Friends	1990	25.00

— Only released on vinyl through BMG Direct Marketing

❑ 25988	No Holdin' Back	1989	15.00
❑ 25738	Old 8x10	1988	12.00
❑ 25435	Storms of Life	1986	12.00

TRAVOLTA, JOHN

MIDLAND INT'L.

| ❑ BKL1-2211 | Can't Let You Go | 1977 | 15.00 |
| ❑ BKL1-1563 | John Travolta | 1976 | 15.00 |

MIDSONG INT'L.

| ❑ MTF 001 | Travolta Fever | 1978 | 18.00 |

— Reissue of his two LPs in one package

TREE

GOAT FARM

| ❑ 580 | Tree | 1970 | 70.00 |

TREMELOES, THE

DJM

| ❑ 2 | Shiner | 1974 | 15.00 |

EPIC

❑ LN24326 [M]	Even the Bad Times Are Good	1967	30.00
❑ BN26326 [P]	Even the Bad Times Are Good	1967	30.00
❑ LN24310 [M]	Here Comes My Baby	1967	30.00
❑ BN26310 [R]	Here Comes My Baby	1967	25.00
❑ LN24363 [M]	Suddenly You Love Me	1968	30.00
❑ BN26363 [R]	Suddenly You Love Me	1968	25.00
❑ BN26388 [S]	World Explosion '58/'68	1968	30.00
❑ LN24388 [M]	World Explosion '58/'68	1968	60.00

— White label promo only

TRENIERS, THE

DOT

| ❑ DLP-3257 [M] | Souvenir Album | 1960 | 100.00 |

EPIC

| ❑ LG3125 [M] | The Treniers on TV | 1955 | 200.00 |

TRENT, BUCK

ABC DOT

| ❑ DOSD-2058 | Bionic Banjo | 1976 | 12.00 |
| ❑ DO-2077 | Oh Yeah! | 1977 | 12.00 |

BOONE

| ❑ 1212 | Give Me Five | 1967 | 25.00 |

RCA VICTOR

| ❑ LSP-4705 | Sounds of Now and Beyond | 1972 | 15.00 |

SMASH

| ❑ MGS-27002 [M] | The Sound of a Bluegrass Banjo | 1962 | 25.00 |

— Smash LPs as "Charles Trent"

❑ SRS-67002 [S]	The Sound of a Bluegrass Banjo	1962	30.00
❑ MGS-27017 [M]	The Sound of a Five String Banjo	1962	25.00
❑ SRS-67017 [S]	The Sound of a Five String Banjo	1962	30.00

TRESVANT, RALPH

MCA

| ❑ 10116 | Ralph Tresvant | 1990 | 15.00 |

TREVOR, JEANNIE

MAINSTREAM

| ❑ 56075 [M] | Jeannie Trevor Sings!! | 1965 | 30.00 |
| ❑ S-6075 [S] | Jeannie Trevor Sings!! | 1965 | 30.00 |

TREVOR, VAN

BAND BOX

| ❑ (# unknown)0 | Come On Over to Our Side | 1967 | 25.00 |

DATE

| ❑ DES-4008 | You've Been So Good to Me | 1967 | 18.00 |

ROYAL AMERICAN

| ❑ 2800 | Funny Familiar Forgotten Feelings | 1969 | 18.00 |

TRIANGLE, THE

AMARET

| ❑ 5000 [B] | How Now Brown Cow | 1969 | 30.00 |

Number	Title	Yr	NM

TRICHT, EVERT VAN

MERCURY LIVING PRESENCE

| ❑ SR90403 [S] | Oboe Concerti | 196? | 30.00 |

— With Kurt Redel/Vienna Symphony Orchestra and Pro Arte Orchestra of Munich; maroon label, no "Vendor: Mercury Record Corporation

TRICYCLE

ABC

| ❑ S-674 | Tricycle | 1969 | 25.00 |

TRIGGER, VIC

SANCTUARY

| ❑ 12103 | Electronic Wizard | 1977 | 100.00 |

TRIMBLE, BOBB

(NO LABEL)

| ❑ (no #)0 | Harvest of Dreams | 1982 | 150.00 |

VENGEANCE

| ❑ BT-8458 | Iron Curtain Dream | 1980 | 800.00 |

TRIO, THE

SAVOY

| ❑ MG-12023 [M] | The Trio | 1955 | 100.00 |

TRIO

MERCURY

| ❑ 814320-1 | Trio and Error | 1983 | 25.00 |
| ❑ MX-1-509 [EP] | Trio (Contains the Hit Da Da Da) | 1982 | 18.00 |

TRIO A LA MODE

DTR

| ❑ 1001 | A Christmas Celebration | 1985 | 12.00 |

TRIPLETS, THE

ELEKTRA

| ❑ 60455 [EP] | Break the Silence | 1986 | 10.00 |

TRIPSICHORD MUSIC BOX, THE

JANUS

| ❑ JLS-3016 | The Tripsichord Music Box | 1971 | 200.00 |

TRISTANO, LENNIE; JO BUSHKIN; BOBBY SCOTT; MARIAN MCPARTLAND

SAVOY

| ❑ MG-12043 [M] | The Jazz Keyboards of Lennie Tristano, Joe Bushkin, Bobby Scott & Marian McPartland | 1955 | 80.00 |

TRISTANO, LENNIE

ATLANTIC

| ❑ 1224 [M] | Lennie Tristano | 1955 | 80.00 |

— Black label

| ❑ 1224 [M] | Lennie Tristano | 1960 | 30.00 |

— Multicolor label, white "fan" logo at right

| ❑ 1224 [M] | Lennie Tristano | 1964 | 18.00 |

— Multicolor label, black "fan" logo at right

❑ SD 2-7006	Lennie Tristano Quartet	198?	18.00
❑ SD 2-7003	Requiem	1980	18.00
❑ 1357 [M]	The New Tristano	1960	50.00

— Multicolor label, white "fan" logo at right

| ❑ 1357 [M] | The New Tristano | 196? | 18.00 |

— Red and purple label, black "fan" logo at right

ELEKTRA/MUSICIAN

| ❑ 60264 | New York Improvisations | 1984 | 15.00 |

INNER CITY

| ❑ IC-6002 | Descent Into the Maelstrom | 197? | 30.00 |

JAZZ

❑ JR-6	Continuity	1985	15.00
❑ JR-1	Live at Birdland 1949	198?	15.00
❑ JR-5	Live in Toronto 1952	198?	15.00

MOSAIC

| ❑ MQ10-174 | The Complete Atlantic Recordings of Lennie Tristano, Lee Konitz and Warne Marsh | 199? | 300.00 |

NEW JAZZ

| ❑ NJLP-101 [10] | Lennie Tristano with Lee Konitz | 1950 | 600.00 |

PRESTIGE

| ❑ PRLP-101 [10] | Lennie Tristano with Lee Konitz | 1951 | 500.00 |

TRISTANO, LENNIE/ARNOLD ROSS

EMARCY

| ❑ MG-26029 [10] | Holiday in Piano | 1953 | 400.00 |

TRISTANO, LENNIE/BUDDY DEFRANCO

CAPITOL

| ❑ M-11060 | Cross Currents | 1972 | 30.00 |

— Capitol Jazz Classics, Vol. 14"; original edition does not have an "All Rights Reserved" disclaimer in the perimeter print

---

Number	Title	Yr	NM
❑ M-11060	Cross Currents	1975	18.00

— Capitol Jazz Classics, Voil. 14"; yellow label with "Capitol" at bottom; "All Rights Reserved" in perimeter print

TRITT, TRAVIS

WARNER BROS.

| ❑ W1-26589 | It's All About to Change | 1991 | 25.00 |

— Vinyl available only from Columbia House

TRIUMPH

MCA

| ❑ MCA-5537 [B] | Thunder Seven | 1984 | 18.00 |

— Quiex II promo

TRIUMVIRAT

CAPITOL

| ❑ ST-11862 | A La Carte | 1978 | 15.00 |
| ❑ SN-16123 | A La Carte | 1980 | 10.00 |

— Budget-line reissue

| ❑ SN-16119 | Illusions on a Double Dimple | 1980 | 10.00 |

— Budget-line reissue

| ❑ ST-11551 | Old Loves Die Hard | 1976 | 15.00 |
| ❑ SN-16122 | Old Loves Die Hard | 1980 | 10.00 |

— Budget-line reissue

| ❑ ST-11697 | Pompeii | 1977 | 15.00 |
| ❑ SN-16120 | Pompeii | 1980 | 10.00 |

— Budget-line reissue

| ❑ ST-11392 | Spartacus | 1975 | 15.00 |
| ❑ SN-16121 | Spartacus | 1980 | 10.00 |

— Budget-line reissue

HARVEST

| ❑ ST-11311 | Illusions on a Double Dimple | 1974 | 18.00 |

TRIZO 50

CAVERN

| ❑ 740142 | Trizo 50 | 197? | 300.00 |

TROGGS, THE

ATCO

| ❑ 33-193 [M] | Wild Thing | 1966 | 50.00 |
| ❑ SD 33-193 [R] | Wild Thing | 1966 | 40.00 |

FONTANA

| ❑ SRF67576 [R] | Love Is All Around | 1968 | 30.00 |
| ❑ MGF27556 [M] | Wild Thing/With a Girl Like You | 1966 | 40.00 |

— Contents identical to the Atco LP; two slightly different cover variations are known; record has mono number and plays mono; number "27556" in trail-off

| ❑ SRF67556 [R] | Wild Thing/With a Girl Like You | 1966 | 30.00 |

— Contents identical to the Atco LP; two slightly different cover variations are known

| ❑ MGF27556 [R] | Wild Thing/With a Girl Like You | 1966 | 30.00 |

— Contents identical to the Atco LP; two slightly different cover variations are known; record has mono number but plays in rechanneled stereo; number "2/67556" in trail-off

MKC

| ❑ 214 | Live at Max's Kansas City | 1980 | 15.00 |

PRIVATE STOCK

| ❑ PS-2008 [B] | The Troggs Tapes | 1976 | 18.00 |

PYE

| ❑ 12112 | The Troggs | 1975 | 15.00 |

RHINO

| ❑ RNLP-118 | The Best of the Troggs | 1985 | 12.00 |
| ❑ R170118 | The Best of the Troggs | 1988 | 10.00 |

SIRE

| ❑ SASH-3714 | The Vintage Years | 1976 | 18.00 |

TROLL, THE

SMASH

| ❑ SRS-67114 | Animated Music | 1969 | 50.00 |

TROMBONES, INC., THE

WARNER BROS.

| ❑ W1272 [M] | They Met at the Continental Divide | 1959 | 50.00 |
| ❑ WS1272 [S] | They Met at the Continental Divide | 1959 | 60.00 |

TROMBONES UNLIMITED

LIBERTY

❑ LRP-3494 [M]	Big Boss Bones	1967	25.00
❑ LST-7494 [S]	Big Boss Bones	1967	18.00
❑ LST-7592	Grazing in the Grass	1968	18.00
❑ LRP-3527 [M]	Holiday for Trombones	1967	25.00
❑ LST-7527 [S]	Holiday for Trombones	1967	18.00
❑ LRP-3549 [M]	One of Those Songs	1968	30.00
❑ LST-7549 [S]	One of Those Songs	1968	18.00
❑ LRP-3449 [M]	These Bones are Made for Walking	1966	18.00
❑ LST-7449 [S]	These Bones are Made for Walking	1966	25.00
❑ LRP-3472 [M]	You're Gonna Hear From Me	1966	18.00
❑ LST-7472 [S]	You're Gonna Hear From Me	1966	25.00

Number	Title	Yr	NM
TROUBADOURS DE ROI BAUDOUIN			
PHILIPS			
❏ PCC606 [S]	Missa Luba	1963	18.00
— Released in '63, this didn't chart until 1969			
❏ PCC-206 [M]	Missa Luba	1963	18.00
TROUP, BOBBY			
AUDIOPHILE			
❏ AP-98	In a Class Beyond Compare	198?	12.00
BETHLEHEM			
❏ BCP-1030 [10]	Bobby Troup	1955	60.00
❏ BCP-19 [M]	Bobby Troup Sings Johnny Mercer	1955	50.00
❏ BCP-35 [M]	The Distinctive Style of Bobby Troup	1955	50.00
CAPITOL			
❏ H484 [10]	Bobby	1953	80.00
❏ T484 [M]	Bobby	1955	50.00
INTERLUDE			
❏ MO-501 [M]	Cool	1959	40.00
❏ ST-1001 [S]	Cool	1959	40.00
LIBERTY			
❏ LRP-3002 [M]	Bobby Troup and His Trio	1955	50.00
❏ LRP-3026 [M]	Do Re Mi	1957	50.00
❏ LRP-3078 [M]	Here's to My Lady	1958	50.00
MODE			
❏ LP-111 [M]	Bobby Swings Tenderly	1957	100.00
PAUSA			
❏ 9032	Bobby Troup	198?	12.00
RCA VICTOR			
❏ LPM-1959 [M]	Bobby Troup and His Jazz All-Stars	1959	40.00
❏ LSP-1959 [S]	Bobby Troup and His Jazz All-Stars	1959	50.00
TROWER, ROBIN			
ATLANTIC			
❏ 82080	In the Line of Fire	1990	15.00
❏ 81838	Take What You Need	1988	12.00
CHRYSALIS			
❏ FV41420	Back It Up	1983	12.00
❏ PV41420	Back It Up	1986	12.00
— Reissue			
❏ CHR1324	B.L.T.	1981	12.00
❏ PV41324	B.L.T.	1984	10.00
— Reissue			
❏ CHR1057	Bridge of Sighs	1974	15.00
— Green label, "3300 Warner Blvd." address			
❏ CHR1057	Bridge of Sighs	1977	12.00
— Blue label, New York address			
❏ FV41057	Bridge of Sighs	1984	12.00
— Reissue			
❏ PV41057	Bridge of Sighs	1986	10.00
— Reissue			
❏ CHR1189	Caravan to Midnight	1978	15.00
❏ PV41189	Caravan to Midnight	1984	10.00
— Reissue			
❏ CHR1073	For Earth Below	1975	15.00
— Green label, "3300 Warner Blvd." address			
❏ CHR1073	For Earth Below	1977	12.00
— Blue label, New York address			
❏ PV41073	For Earth Below	1984	10.00
— Reissue			
❏ CHR1148 [B]	In City Dreams	1977	15.00
❏ PV41148	In City Dreams	1984	10.00
— Reissue			
❏ CHR1107	Long Misty Days	1976	15.00
— Green label, "3300 Warner Blvd." address			
❏ CHR1107	Long Misty Days	1977	12.00
— Blue label, New York address			
❏ PV41107	Long Misty Days	1983	10.00
— Reissue			
❏ CHR1089	Robin Trower Live!	1976	15.00
— Green label, "3300 Warner Blvd." address			
❏ CHR1089	Robin Trower Live!	1977	12.00
— Blue label, New York address			
❏ PV41089	Robin Trower Live!	1983	10.00
— Reissue			
❏ CHR1039	Twice Removed from Yesterday	1973	15.00
— Green label, "3300 Warner Blvd." address			
❏ CHR1039	Twice Removed from Yesterday	1977	12.00
— Blue label, New York address			
❏ PV41039	Twice Removed from Yesterday	1983	10.00
— Reissue			
❏ CHR1215	Victims of the Fury	1980	15.00
❏ PV41215	Victims of the Fury	1983	10.00
— Reissue			
GNP CRESCENDO			
❏ 2187	Passion	1986	12.00
PASSPORT			
❏ PB-6049	Beyond the Mist	1985	12.00
TROY, DORIS			
APPLE			
❏ ST-3371	Doris Troy	1970	30.00

Number	Title	Yr	NM
ATLANTIC			
❏ 8088 [M]	Just One Look	1964	30.00
❏ SD8088 [P]	Just One Look	1964	50.00
— The title song is rechanneled			
TROYKA			
COTILLION			
❏ SD9020 [B]	Troyka	1970	40.00
TRUMAN, MARGARET			
RCA VICTOR			
❏ LM-145 [10]	A Margaret Truman Program	1952	80.00
❏ LM-57 [10]	American Songs	1951	80.00
TRUMPET KINGS, THE			
ANALOGUE PRODUCTIONS			
❏ APR-3010	Alternate Blues	199?	18.00
PABLO			
❏ 2310754	Montreux '75	1975	15.00
TRUMPET SUMMIT			
PABLO TODAY			
❏ 2312114	Trumpet Summit Meets the Oscar Peterson Big 4	198?	15.00
TRUMPETEERS, THE (1)			
GRAND			
❏ 7701 [M]	The Last Supper	195?	100.00
SCORE			
❏ SLP-4021 [M]	Milky White Way	1956	300.00
TRYFOROS, BOB			
PURITAN			
❏ 5002	Joplin on Guitar	197?	15.00
TRYNIN, JENNIFER			
PATHFINDER			
❏ PTF-8827 [EP]	Trespassing	1988	18.00
SQUINT			
❏ JT-101	Cockamamie	1994	15.00
TRYTHALL, GIL			
ATHENA			
❏ 6004	Nashville Gold	1970	15.00
❏ 6003	Switched On Nashville/Country Moog	1970	15.00
TUBB, ERNEST, AND LORETTA LYNN			
DECCA			
❏ DL75115	If We Put Our Heads Together	1969	30.00
❏ DL4639 [M]	Mr. and Mrs. Used to Be	1965	30.00
❏ DL74639 [S]	Mr. and Mrs. Used to Be	1965	40.00
❏ DL4872 [M]	Singin' Again	1967	30.00
❏ DL74872 [S]	Singin' Again	1967	30.00
MCA			
❏ 1000	The Ernest Tubb/Loretta Lynn Story	1973	10.00
TUBB, ERNEST			
CACHET			
❏ 33001	Ernest Tubb: The Legend and the Legacy, Volume One	1979	15.00
DECCA			
❏ DL75222 [B]	A Good Year for the Wine	1970	25.00
❏ DL4046 [M]	All Time Hits	1961	30.00
❏ DL74046 [S]	All Time Hits	1961	40.00
❏ DL4867 [M]	Another Story	1967	30.00
❏ DL74867 [S]	Another Story	1967	30.00
❏ DL75388	Baby, It's So Hard to Be Good	1972	25.00
❏ DL4518 [M]	Blue Christmas	1963	30.00
❏ DL74518 [S]	Blue Christmas	1963	30.00
❏ DL4746 [M]	By Request	1966	30.00
❏ DL74746 [S]	By Request	1966	30.00
❏ DL75072	Country Hit Time	1968	25.00
❏ DL5301 [10]	Ernest Tubb Favorites	1951	150.00
❏ DL8291 [M]	Ernest Tubb Favorites	1955	70.00
❏ DL4118 [M]	Ernest Tubb's Golden Favorites	1961	30.00
❏ DL74118 [S]	Ernest Tubb's Golden Favorites	1961	40.00
❏ DL75006 [S]	Ernest Tubb's Greatest Hits	1968	30.00
❏ DL5006 [M]	Ernest Tubb's Greatest Hits	1968	80.00
— White label promo only			
❏ DL75252	Ernest Tubb's Greatest Hits, Vol. 2	1970	25.00
❏ DL4772 [M]	Ernest Tubb Sings Country Hits Old & New	1966	30.00
❏ DL74772 [S]	Ernest Tubb Sings Country Hits Old & New	1966	30.00
❏ DL4957 [M]	Ernest Tubb Sings Hank Williams	1968	50.00
❏ DL74957 [S]	Ernest Tubb Sings Hank Williams	1968	30.00
❏ DL4681 [M]	Hittin' the Road	1965	30.00
❏ DL74681 [S]	Hittin' the Road	1965	30.00
❏ DL5336 [10]	Jimmie Rodgers Songs Sung by Ernest Tubb	1951	150.00

Number	Title	Yr	NM
❏ DL4385 [M]	Just Call Me Lonesome	1962	30.00
❏ DL74385 [S]	Just Call Me Lonesome	1962	30.00
❏ DL75114	Let's Turn Back the Years	1969	18.00
❏ DL4640 [M]	My Pick of the Hits	1965	30.00
❏ DL74640 [S]	My Pick of the Hits	1965	30.00
❏ DL75301	One Sweet Hello	1971	25.00
❏ DL4321 [M]	On Tour	1962	30.00
❏ DL74321 [S]	On Tour	1962	30.00
❏ DL75122	Saturday Satan, Sunday Saint	1969	25.00
❏ DL75345	Say Something Nice to Sarah	1972	25.00
❏ DL5497 [10]	Sing a Song of Christmas	1954	150.00
❏ DL4514 [M]	Thanks a Lot	1964	30.00
❏ DL74514 [S]	Thanks a Lot	1964	30.00
❏ DL8553 [M]	The Daddy of 'Em All	1956	70.00
❏ DL4064 [M]	The Ernest Tubb Record Shop	1960	40.00
❏ DL74064 [S]	The Ernest Tubb Record Shop	1960	50.00
❏ DXA159 [M]	The Ernest Tubb Story	1959	80.00
— Deduct 25 percent if book is missing			
❏ DXSA7159 [S]	The Ernest Tubb Story	196?	30.00
— Deduct 25 percent if book is missing			
❏ DL4397 [M]	The Family Bible	1963	30.00
❏ DL74397 [S]	The Family Bible	1963	30.00
❏ DL8834 [M]	The Importance of Being Ernest	1959	50.00
❏ DL78834 [S]	The Importance of Being Ernest	1959	60.00
❏ DL5334 [10]	The Old Rugged Cross	1951	150.00
FIRST GENERATION			
❏ LP-0002	The Legend and the Legacy	1979	50.00
— No ads on back cover			
❏ LP-0002	The Legend and the Legacy	1979	40.00
— With ad for Ernest Tubb Record Shop on back cover			
❏ TV-1033	The Legend and the Legacy	1979	30.00
— Mail-order version			
MCA			
❏ 512	Baby, It's So Hard to Be Good	197?	15.00
— Reissue of Decca 75388			
❏ 496	Ernest Tubb	1975	15.00
❏ 84	Ernest Tubb's Golden Favorites	1973	15.00
— Reissue of Decca 74118			
❏ 16	Ernest Tubb's Greatest Hits	1973	15.00
— Reissue of Decca 75006			
❏ 24	Ernest Tubb's Greatest Hits, Vol. 2	1973	15.00
— Reissue of Decca 75252			
❏ 341	I've Got All the Heartaches I Can Handle	1973	15.00
❏ 4040	The Ernest Tubb Story	197?	18.00
— Reissue of Decca DXSA 7159			
VOCALION			
❏ VL73684 [R]	Ernest Tubb and His Texas Troubadours	196?	12.00
❏ VL3684 [M]	Ernest Tubb and His Texas Troubadours	196?	10.00
TUBB, JUSTIN, AND LORENE MANN			
RCA VICTOR			
❏ LPM-3591 [M]	Together and Alone	1966	30.00
❏ LSP-3591 [S]	Together and Alone	1966	40.00
TUBB, JUSTIN			
CUTLASS			
❏ 123	Travelin' Singin' Man	1972	30.00
DECCA			
❏ DL8644 [M]	Country Boy in Love	1957	60.00
DOT			
❏ DLP-25922 [S]	Things I Still Remember Very Well	1969	18.00
❏ DLP-3922 [M]	Things I Still Remember Very Well	1969	50.00
— Record is black label stock copy; "Mounaural" sticker appears on stereo cover			
FIRST GENERATION			
❏ 1	What's Wrong with the Way We're Doing It Now	1979	15.00
PHONORAMA			
❏ 5565	What's Wrong with the Way We're Doing It Now	1983	10.00
RCA VICTOR			
❏ LPM-3339 [M]	Where You're Concerned	1965	25.00
❏ LSP-3339 [S]	Where You're Concerned	1965	30.00
STARDAY			
❏ SLP-160 [M]	Star of the Grand Ole Opry	1962	40.00
❏ SLP-334 [M]	The Best of Justin Tubb	1965	30.00
❏ SLP-198 [M]	The Modern Country Sound of Justin Tubb	1962	40.00
VOCALION			
❏ VL73802	That Country Style	196?	15.00
TUBES, THE			
A&M			
❏ SP-4632	Now	1977	15.00
❏ SP-3243	Now	198?	12.00
— Reissue of SP-4632			

Number	Title	Yr	NM
❏ SP-4751	Remote Control	1979	15.00
❏ SP-3242	Remote Control	198?	10.00
— Reissue of SP-4751			
❏ SP-4534	The Tubes	1975	15.00
❏ SP-3161	The Tubes	198?	10.00
— Reissue of SP-4534			
❏ SP-4870	T.R.A.S.H. (Tubes Rarities And Smash Hits)	1981	12.00
❏ SP-3244	T.R.A.S.H. (Tubes Rarities And Smash Hits)	198?	10.00
— Reissue of SP-4870			
❏ SP-17012 [DJ]	Tubes Live/Edited for Trouble-Free Airplay (The First "Clean" Tubes Album)	1978	25.00
— Generic cover with sticker; promo only			
❏ SP-6003	What Do You Want From Live!	1978	18.00
❏ SP-4580 [B]	Young and Rich	1976	15.00
❏ SP-3222	Young and Rich	198?	10.00
— Reissue of SP-4580			
CAPITOL			
❏ ST-12381	Love Bomb	1985	12.00
❏ SN-16446	Love Bomb	1987	10.00
— Reissue of ST-12381			
❏ ST-12260	Outside/Inside	1983	12.00
❏ SN-16360	Outside/Inside	1985	10.00
— Reissue of ST-12260			
❏ SOO-12151	The Completion Backward Principle	1981	12.00
❏ SN-16378	The Completion Backward Principle	1986	10.00
— Reissue of SOO-12151			

TUCK & PATTI

Number	Title	Yr	NM
WINDHAM HILL			
❏ WH-0116	Love Warriors	1989	15.00
❏ WH-0111	Tears of Joy	1988	12.00

TUCKER, FAYE

Number	Title	Yr	NM
TIME			
❏ 52108 [M]	Country & Western Soul	1963	25.00
❏ S-2018 [S]	Country & Western Soul	1963	30.00

TUCKER, MAUREEN

Number	Title	Yr	NM
50 SKIDILLION WATTS			
❏ MOE7 [B]	Life in Exile After Abdication	1989	30.00
❏ MOE1 [EP]	Moejadkatebarry	1987	25.00
TRASH			
❏ TLP-1001 [B]	Playin' Possum	1981	35.00

TUCKER, MICKEY

Number	Title	Yr	NM
MUSE			
❏ MR-5174	Mister Mysterious	1978	15.00
❏ MR-5223	The Crawl	1979	15.00
XANADU			
❏ 143	Sojourn	1977	15.00
❏ 128	Triplicity	1976	15.00

TUCKER, SOPHIE

Number	Title	Yr	NM
COLUMBIA			
❏ CL2604 [M]	Last of the Red Hot Mamas	1966	18.00
DECCA			
❏ DL5371 [10]	A Collection of Songs She Has Made Famous	1951	40.00
❏ DL4942 [M]	Greatest Hits	1968	30.00
❏ DL74942 [R]	Greatest Hits	1968	15.00
❏ DL8355 [M]	The Great Sophie Tucker	195?	30.00
MCA			
❏ 263	Greatest Hits	1973	12.00
MERCURY			
❏ MG20267 [M]	Bigger and Better Than Ever	1957	18.00
❏ MG20046 [M]	Cabaret Days	1955	25.00
❏ MG20073 [M]	Her Latest and Greatest Spicy Songs	1956	25.00
❏ MG20567 [M]	In Person -- Adults Only	1960	25.00
❏ SR60227 [S]	In Person -- Adults Only	1960	30.00
❏ MG20035 [M]	My Dream	1955	25.00
WING			
❏ MGW12176 [M]	Bigger and Better Than Ever	196?	15.00
❏ MGW12213 [M]	Cabaret Days	196?	15.00
❏ SRW16213 [R]	Cabaret Days	196?	12.00
❏ MGW12167 [M]	Her Latest and Greatest Spicy Songs	196?	15.00

TUCKER, TANYA

Number	Title	Yr	NM
ARISTA			
❏ AL9596	Changes	1982	12.00
❏ AL8381	Changes	1984	10.00
— Reissue of 9596			
CAPITOL			
❏ ST-12474	Girls Like Me	1986	12.00
❏ C1-91814	Greatest Hits	1989	15.00
❏ CLT-46870	Love Me Like You Used To	1987	12.00
❏ C1-48865	Strong Enough to Bend	1988	12.00
CAPITOL NASHVILLE			
❏ 1P8140	What Do I Do with Me	1991	25.00
— Only available on vinyl through Columbia House			

Number	Title	Yr	NM
COLUMBIA			
❏ KC31742	Delta Dawn	1972	18.00
❏ PC31742	Delta Dawn	198?	10.00
❏ KC33355	Greatest Hits	1975	15.00
❏ PC33355	Greatest Hits	197?	10.00
— No bar code on cover			
❏ KC32272	What's Your Mama's Name	1973	18.00
❏ KC32744	Would You Lay with Me (In a Field of Stone)	1974	15.00
❏ PC32744	Would You Lay with Me (In a Field of Stone)	197?	10.00
❏ PC34733	You Are So Beautiful	1977	15.00
— No bar code on cover			
❏ PC34733	You Are So Beautiful	197?	10.00
— With bar code on cover			
COLUMBIA SPECIAL PRODUCTS			
❏ P15770	The Best of Tanya Tucker	1981	15.00
MCA			
❏ 5140	Dreamlovers	1980	12.00
❏ 27030	Dreamlovers	198?	10.00
— Reissue of 5140			
❏ 37225	Greatest Hits	1984	10.00
— Reissue of 3032			
❏ 2213	Here's Some Love	1976	15.00
❏ 656	Here's Some Love	1980	10.00
— Reissue of 2213			
❏ 2167	Lovin' and Learnin'	1976	15.00
❏ 655	Lovin' and Learnin'	1980	10.00
— Reissue of 2167			
❏ 2253	Ridin' Rainbows	1977	15.00
❏ 657	Ridin' Rainbows	1980	10.00
— Reissue of 2253			
❏ 5228	Should I Do It	1981	12.00
❏ 2141	Tanya Tucker	1975	15.00
❏ 654	Tanya Tucker	1980	10.00
— Reissue of 2141			
❏ 5299	Tanya Tucker Live	1982	12.00
❏ 37242	Tanya Tucker Live	1984	10.00
— Reissue of 5299			
❏ 3032	Tanya Tucker's Greatest Hits	1978	15.00
❏ 5106	Tear Me Apart	1979	12.00
❏ 37158	Tear Me Apart	1981	10.00
— Reissue of 5106			
❏ 5357	The Best of Tanya Tucker	1983	12.00
❏ 3066	TNT	1978	15.00
— Original gatefold cover			
❏ 37075	TNT	1981	10.00
— Reissue of 3066; gatefold removed			

TUCKER, TOMMY

Number	Title	Yr	NM
CHECKER			
❏ LP-2990 [M]	Hi-Heel Sneakers	1964	250.00
— Black label			
❏ LP-2990 [M]	Hi-Heel Sneakers	1965	120.00
— Blue label with checkers			
CIRCLE			
❏ CLP-124	Tommy Tucker and His Californians 1933	1991	15.00
❏ C-15	Tommy Tucker and His Orchestra 1942-1947	198?	12.00

TUCKY BUZZARD

Number	Title	Yr	NM
CAPITOL			
❏ ST-787	Tucky Buzzard	1971	16.00
❏ ST-864	Warm Slash	1972	25.00
PASSPORT			
❏ 97001	Alright in the Night	1973	18.00
❏ 98002	Tucky Buzzard	1974	18.00

TUFF DARTS

Number	Title	Yr	NM
SIRE			
❏ SRK6048	Tuff Darts!	1978	15.00

TURBANS, THE

Number	Title	Yr	NM
HERALD			
❏ 5009	Presenting the Turbans	197?	25.00
— No such album was released in the 1950s; this is a bootleg that has some collector value.			
LOST-NITE			
❏ LLP-25 [10]	The Turbans	1981	12.00
— Red vinyl			
RELIC			
❏ 5009	The Turbans' Greatest Hits	198?	15.00

TURNER, GRANT

Number	Title	Yr	NM
CVS			
❏ 8008	Grant Turner Remembers the Grand Ole Opry	197?	18.00

TURNER, HANK

Number	Title	Yr	NM
COLUMBIA			
❏ CL1958 [M]	Golden Country and Western Hits	1963	25.00
❏ CS8758 [S]	Golden Country and Western Hits	1963	30.00

Number	Title	Yr	NM
TURNER, IKE			
CROWN			
❏ CLP-5367 [M]	Ike Turner Rocks the Blues	1963	200.00
❏ CST-367 [R]	Ike Turner Rocks the Blues	1963	100.00
FANTASY			
❏ F-9597	The Edge	1980	12.00
POMPEII			
❏ SD6003	A Black Man's Soul	1969	18.00
UNITED ARTISTS			
❏ UA-LA087-F	Bad Dreams	1973	18.00
❏ UAS-5576	Blues Roots	1972	18.00

Number	Title	Yr	NM
TURNER, IKE AND TINA			
A&M			
❏ SP-4178	River Deep -- Mountain High	1969	30.00
— Official release of Philles 4011			
❏ SP-3179	River Deep -- Mountain High	1982	12.00
— Budget-line reissue			
ABC			
❏ 4014	16 Great Performances	1975	15.00
ACCORD			
❏ SN-7147	Hot and Sassy	1981	12.00
BLUE THUMB			
❏ BTS5	Outta Season	1968	18.00
❏ BTS-8805	Outta Season	1971	15.00
— Early reissue of Blue Thumb 5			
❏ BTS49	The Best of Ike & Tina Turner	1973	15.00
❏ BTS11	The Hunter	1969	18.00
CAPITOL			
❏ ST-571	Her Man, His Woman	1971	18.00
COLLECTABLES			
❏ COL-5107	Golden Classics	198?	12.00
❏ COL-5137	It's Gonna Work Out Fine	198?	12.00
EMI AMERICA			
❏ ST-17212	It's Gonna Work Out Fine	1986	12.00
❏ SQ-17216	Workin' Together	1986	12.00
HARMONY			
❏ HS11360	Ooh Poo Pah Doo	1969	18.00
❏ H30567	Something's Got a Hold on Me	1971	18.00
KENT			
❏ KST-538	Festival of Live Performances	1969	30.00
❏ K3T-550	Please Please Please	1971	30.00
❏ K-5014 [M]	The Ike and Tina Turner Revue Live	1964	30.00
❏ KST-514 [S]	The Ike and Tina Turner Revue Live	1964	40.00
❏ K-5019 [M]	The Soul of Ike and Tina	1966	30.00
❏ KST-519 [S]	The Soul of Ike and Tina	1966	40.00
LIBERTY			
❏ LT-917	Airwaves	1981	10.00
❏ LST-7637	Come Together	1970	18.00
❏ LO-51156	Get Back!	1985	12.00
❏ LST-7650	Workin' Together	1970	18.00
LOMA			
❏ LS5904 [S]	Live! The Ike & Tina Turner Show, Vol. 2	1966	30.00
— Reissue of Warner Bros. 1579?			
❏ L5904 [M]	Live! The Ike & Tina Turner Show Vol. 2	1966	30.00
MINIT			
❏ 24018	In Person	1969	25.00
PHILLES			
❏ PHLP4011 [M]	River Deep -- Mountain High	1967	8000.00
— Value is for record alone; covers were not printed			
PICKWICK			
❏ SPC-3284	Too Hot to Hold	197?	12.00
POMPEII			
❏ SD6004	Cussin', Cryin' and Carryin' On	1969	30.00
❏ SD6006	Get It Together	1969	30.00
❏ SD6000 [S]	So Fine	1968	30.00
❏ 6000 [M]	So Fine	1968	60.00
— Mono is white label promo only; front cover has "d/j copy monaural" sticker on it			
STRIPED HORSE			
❏ SHL-2001	Golden Empire	1986	12.00
SUE			
❏ LP2005 [M]	Don't Play Me Cheap	1963	400.00
❏ LP2004 [M]	Dynamite	1963	400.00
❏ LP2003 [M]	Ike and Tina Turner's Kings of Rhythm Dance	1962	400.00
— Despite the title, this is an all-instrumental album (Tina's vocals do not appear)			
❏ LP2007 [M]	It's Gonna Work Out Fine	1963	400.00
❏ LP1038 [M]	The Greatest Hits of Ike and Tina Turner	1965	300.00
❏ LP2001 [M]	The Soul of Ike and Tina Turner	1961	400.00
SUNSET			
❏ SUS-5286	Ike & Tima Turner's Greatest Hits	1969	18.00
❏ SUS-5265	The Fantastic Ike & Tina Turner	1969	18.00

Number	Title	Yr	NM
UNART			
❑ S21021	Greatest Hits	197?	12.00
UNITED ARTISTS			
❑ UA-LA917-H	Airwaves	1978	15.00
❑ UA-LA707-G	Delilah's Power	1977	15.00
❑ UAS-5598	Feel Good	1972	15.00
❑ UA-LA592-G	Greatest Hits	1976	15.00
❑ UAS-5667	Ike & Tina Turner's Greatest Hits	1972	15.00
❑ UAS-5660	Let Me Touch Your Mind	1972	15.00
❑ UAS-9953	Live at Carnegie Hall/What You Hear Is What You Get	1971	18.00
❑ UAS-5530	'Nuff Said	1971	15.00
❑ UA-LA180-F	Nutbush City Limits	1973	15.00
❑ UA-LA312-G	Sweet Rhode Island Red	1974	15.00
❑ UA-LA203-G	The Gospel According to Ike & Tina Turner	1974	15.00
❑ UA-LA064-G	The World of Ike & Tina Live	1973	18.00
WARNER BROS.			
❑ WS1810	Ike & Tina Turner's Greatest Hits	1969	30.00
❑ W1579 [M]	Live! The Ike & Tina Turner Show	1965	30.00
❑ WS1579 [S]	Live! The Ike & Tina Turner Show	1965	40.00

TURNER, JIM

Number	Title	Yr	NM
EUPHONIC			
❑ 1222	Old Fashioned Love: A Tribute to James P. Johnson	198?	12.00

TURNER, JOE, AND PETE JOHNSON

Number	Title	Yr	NM
EMARCY			
❑ MG-36014 [M]	Joe Turner and Pete Johnson	1955	200.00

TURNER, JOE

Number	Title	Yr	NM
ARHOOLIE			
❑ 2004 [M]	Jumpin' the Blues	1962	25.00
ATCO			
❑ 33-376 [M]	Joe Turner -- His Greatest Recordings	1971	18.00
ATLANTIC			
❑ 8033 [M]	Big Joe Is Here	1959	120.00
— Black label			
❑ 8033 [M]	Big Joe Is Here	1960	100.00
— White "bullseye" label			
❑ 8033 [M]	Big Joe Is Here	1963	18.00
— Black "fan" logo on label			
❑ 8033 [M]	Big Joe Is Here	1960	40.00
— White "fan" logo on label			
❑ 1332 [M]	Big Joe Rides Again	1959	150.00
— Black label			
❑ SD1332 [S]	Big Joe Rides Again	1959	200.00
— Green label			
❑ 1332 [M]	Big Joe Rides Again	1963	18.00
— Black "fan" logo on label			
❑ SD1332 [S]	Big Joe Rides Again	1963	25.00
— Black "fan" logo on label			
❑ 1332 [M]	Big Joe Rides Again	1960	40.00
— White "fan" logo on label			
❑ SD1332 [S]	Big Joe Rides Again	1960	50.00
— White "fan" logo on label			
❑ SD8812	Boss of the Blues	1981	12.00
— Reissue of 1234			
❑ 81752	Greatest Hits	1987	12.00
❑ 8005 [M]	Joe Turner	1957	150.00
— Black label			
❑ 8005 [M]	Joe Turner	1963	18.00
— Black "fan" logo on label			
❑ 8005 [M]	Joe Turner	1961	40.00
— White "fan" logo on label			
❑ 8023 [M]	Rockin' the Blues	1958	120.00
— Black label			
❑ 8023 [M]	Rockin' the Blues	1963	18.00
— Black "fan" logo on label			
❑ 8023 [M]	Rockin' the Blues	1960	40.00
— White "fan" logo on label			
❑ 8081 [M]	The Best of Joe Turner	1963	50.00
❑ 1234 [M]	The Boss of the Blues	1956	120.00
— Black label			
❑ SD1234 [S]	The Boss of the Blues	1959	180.00
— Green label			
❑ 1234 [M]	The Boss of the Blues	1960	100.00
— White "bullseye" label			
❑ SD1234 [S]	The Boss of the Blues	1960	150.00
— White "bullseye" label			
❑ 1234 [M]	The Boss of the Blues	1963	18.00
— Black "fan" logo on label			
❑ SD1234 [S]	The Boss of the Blues	1963	25.00
— Black "fan" logo on label			
❑ 1234 [M]	The Boss of the Blues	1961	40.00
— White "fan" logo on label			
❑ SD1234 [S]	The Boss of the Blues	1961	50.00
— White "fan" logo on label			
BLUES SPECTRUM			
❑ BS-104	Great Rhythm and Blues Oldies Vol. 4	197?	18.00
BLUESTIME			
❑ 9002 [M]	The Real Boss of the Blues	196?	40.00
❑ 29002 [S]	The Real Boss of the Blues	196?	30.00
BLUESWAY			
❑ S-6060	Roll 'Em	1973	18.00
❑ BL6006 [M]	Singing the Blues	1967	25.00
❑ BLS-6006 [S]	Singing the Blues	1967	30.00
DECCA			
❑ DL8044 [M]	Joe Turner Sings Kansas City Jazz	1953	250.00
FANTASY			
❑ OJC-497	Trumpet Kings Meet Joe Turner	1991	15.00
INTERMEDIA			
❑ QS-5036	Everyday I Have the Blues	198?	12.00
❑ QS-5008	Rock This Joint	198?	12.00
❑ QS-5043	Roll Me Baby	198?	12.00
❑ QS-5030	The Blues Boss -- Live	198?	12.00
❑ QS-5026	The Very Best of Joe Turner -- Live	198?	12.00
KENT			
❑ KST-542	Joe Turner Turns On the Blues	1973	18.00
MCA			
❑ 1325	Early Big Joe	198?	12.00
MUSE			
❑ MR-5293	Blues Train	198?	12.00
— With Roomful of Blues and Dr. John			
PABLO			
❑ 2310818	Every Day I Have the Blues	198?	15.00
❑ 2310937	Flip, Flop and Fly	1989	15.00
❑ 2310863	Have No Fear, Joe Turner Is Here	1983	15.00
❑ 2310776	In the Evening	197?	15.00
❑ 2310760	Nobody in Mind	197?	15.00
❑ 2310913	Patcha, Patcha, All Night Long	198?	15.00
❑ 2310883	Singing the Same, Sad, Happy, Forever Blues	1983	15.00
❑ 2405404	The Best of "Big" Joe Turner	198?	15.00
❑ 2310848	The Best of Joe Turner	1980	15.00
❑ 2310800	Things That I Used to Do	197?	15.00
❑ 2310717	Trumpet Kings Meet Joe Turner	197?	15.00
SAVOY			
❑ MG-14012 [M]	Blues'll Make You Happy	1958	150.00
❑ MG-14106 [M]	Careless Love	1963	80.00
SAVOY JAZZ			
❑ SJC-406	Blues'll Make You Happy	1985	12.00
— Reissue of Savoy 14012			
❑ SJL-2223	Have No Fear	197?	18.00

TURNER, JOE (2)

Number	Title	Yr	NM
CHIAROSCURO			
❑ 147	King of Stride	1976	18.00
CLASSIC JAZZ			
❑ 138	Effervescent	1976	18.00
PABLO			
❑ 2310763	Another Epoch Stride Piano	197?	15.00

TURNER, NIK

Number	Title	Yr	NM
CLEOPATRA			
❑ CLP0601 [B]	Space Gypsy	2013	30.00

TURNER, RAY

Number	Title	Yr	NM
CAPITOL			
❑ H306 [10]	Kitten on the Keys	1952	50.00

TURNER, SAMMY

Number	Title	Yr	NM
BIG TOP			
❑ 12-1301 [M]	Lavender Blue Moods	1959	300.00
— May not exist in stereo			

TURNER, SPYDER

Number	Title	Yr	NM
MGM			
❑ E-4450 [M]	Stand By Me	1967	30.00
❑ SE-4450 [S]	Stand By Me	1967	30.00
WHITFIELD			
❑ BSK3124	Music Web	1978	12.00
❑ BSK3397	Only Love	1979	12.00

TURNER, TINA

Number	Title	Yr	NM
CAPITOL			
❑ PJ-12530	Break Every Rule	1986	10.00
❑ C1-91873	Foreign Affair	1989	10.00
❑ ST-12330	Private Dancer	1984	10.00
❑ 1P8192	Simply the Best	1991	25.00
— Columbia House edition (only US vinyl version)			
❑ C1-90126	Tina Live in Europe	1988	15.00
FANTASY			
❑ MFP-4520 [EP]	Mini	1984	10.00
SPRINGBOARD			
❑ SPB-4033	The Queen	1972	12.00
UNITED ARTISTS			
❑ UA-LA495-G	Acid Queen	1975	15.00
❑ UA-LA919-G	Rough	1978	15.00
❑ UA-LA200-F	Tina Turns the Country On	1973	18.00
WAGNER			
❑ 14108	Good Hearted Woman	1979	15.00

TURNER, TITUS

Number	Title	Yr	NM
JAMIE			
❑ JLP-3018 [M]	Sound Off	1961	25.00
❑ JLPS-3018 [S]	Sound Off	1961	30.00

TURNER, VELVERT, GROUP

Number	Title	Yr	NM
FAMILY PRODUCTIONS			
❑ FPS-2704 [B]	Velvert Turner Group	1972	60.00

TURNER, ZEB

Number	Title	Yr	NM
AUDIO LAB			
❑ AL-1537 [M]	Country Music in the Turner Style	1959	150.00

TURNQUIST REMEDY

Number	Title	Yr	NM
PENTAGRAM			
❑ PE-10004 [B]	Turnquist Remedy	1970	35.00

TURRENTINE, STANLEY

Number	Title	Yr	NM
BAINBRIDGE			
❑ BT-1038	Stan the Man	1981	15.00
BLUE NOTE			
❑ BLP-4150 [M]	A Chip Off the Old Block	1963	60.00
❑ BST-84150 [S]	A Chip Off the Old Block	1963	60.00
— With New York, USA address on label			
❑ BST-84150 [S]	A Chip Off the Old Block	1967	30.00
— With "A Division of Liberty Records" on label			
❑ LT-1095	Ain't No Way	1981	18.00
❑ BST-84298	Always Something There	1968	40.00
— A Division of Liberty Records" on label			
❑ BST-84336	Another Story	1969	40.00
— A Division of Liberty Records" on label			
❑ BLP-4057 [M]	Blue Hour	1961	150.00
— With W. 63rd St. addresss on label			
❑ BLP-4057 [M]	Blue Hour	1963	40.00
— With New York, USA address on label			
❑ BST-84057 [S]	Blue Hour	1961	120.00
— With W. 63rd St. addresss on label			
❑ BST-84057 [S]	Blue Hour	1963	40.00
— With New York, USA address on label			
❑ BST-84057 [S]	Blue Hour	1967	30.00
— With "A Division of Liberty Records" on label			
❑ BST-84057 [S]	Blue Hour	1971	25.00
— With "A Division of United Artists" on label			
❑ BST-84057	Blue Hour	1986	15.00
— The Finest in Jazz Since 1939" label reissue			
❑ B1-84065	Comin' Your Way	1988	18.00
— The Finest in Jazz Since 1939" label; first issue of LP			
❑ BST-84315	Common Touch!	1969	30.00
— A Division of Liberty Records" on label			
❑ BLP-4081 [M]	Dearly Beloved	1961	120.00
— With W. 63rd St. address on label			
❑ BLP-4081 [M]	Dearly Beloved	1963	40.00
— With New York, USA address on label			
❑ BST-84081 [S]	Dearly Beloved	1961	120.00
— With W. 63rd St. address on label			
❑ BST-84081 [S]	Dearly Beloved	1963	50.00
— With New York, USA address on label			
❑ BST-84081 [S]	Dearly Beloved	1967	30.00
— With "A Division of Liberty Records" on label			
❑ BLP-4268 [M]	Easy Walker	1967	100.00
— A Division of Liberty Records" on label			
❑ BST-84268 [S]	Easy Walker	1967	50.00
— A Division of Liberty Records" on label			
❑ BLP-4162 [M]	Hustlin'	1964	60.00
❑ BST-84162 [S]	Hustlin'	1964	60.00
— With New York, USA address on label			
❑ BST-84162 [S]	Hustlin'	1967	30.00
— With "A Division of Liberty Records" on label			
❑ BST-84162 [S]	Hustlin'	1970	18.00
— With "A Division of United Artists" on label			
❑ LT-1037	In Memory Of...	1980	30.00
❑ BLP-4201 [M]	Joyride	1965	50.00
❑ BST-84201 [S]	Joyride	1964	60.00
— With New York, USA address on label			
❑ BST-84201 [S]	Joyride	1967	30.00
— With "A Division of Liberty Records" on label			
❑ BST-84201	Joyride	1984	15.00
— The Finest in Jazz Since 1939" label reissue			
❑ BN-LA883-J2	Jubilee Shout!!	1977	30.00
❑ BST-84122	Jubilee Shout!!	1986	18.00
— The Finest in Jazz Since 1939" label; first issue of LP			
❑ B1-90261	La Place	1989	18.00
— The Finest in Jazz Since 1939" on label			
❑ BLP-4039 [M]	Look Out!	1960	400.00
— Deep groove" version; W. 63rd St. address on label			
❑ BLP-4039 [M]	Look Out!	1960	150.00
— Regular version with W. 63rd St. address on label			
❑ BLP-4039 [M]	Look Out!	1963	40.00
— With New York, USA address on label			
❑ BST-84039 [S]	Look Out!	1960	60.00
— With W. 63rd St. addresss on label			

Number	Title	Yr	NM
❏ BST-84039 [S]	Look Out!	1963	40.00
— *With New York, USA address on label*			
— BST-84039 [S]	Look Out!	1967	30.00
— *With "A Division of Liberty Records" on label*			
❏ LT-1075	Mr. Natural	1980	18.00
❏ BLP-4129 [M]	Never Let Me Go	1963	60.00
❏ BST-84129 [S]	Never Let Me Go	1963	60.00
— *With New York, USA address on label*			
❏ BST-84129 [S]	Never Let Me Go	1967	30.00
— *With "A Division of Liberty Records" on label*			
❏ LT-993	New Time Shuffle	1979	18.00
❏ BLP-4240 [M]	Rough 'n Tumble	1966	50.00
❏ BST-84240 [S]	Rough 'n Tumble	1966	50.00
— *With New York, USA address on label*			
❏ BST-84240 [S]	Rough 'n Tumble	1967	30.00
— *With "A Division of Liberty Records" on label*			
❏ BN-LA394-H2	Stanley Turrentine	1975	25.00
❏ BT-85105	Straight Ahead	1984	15.00
— *The Finest in Jazz Since 1939" on label*			
❏ BLP-4096 [M]	That's Where It's At	1962	120.00
— *With W. 63rd St. address on label*			
❏ BLP-4096 [M]	That's Where It's At	1963	60.00
— *With New York, USA address on label*			
❏ BST-84096 [S]	That's Where It's At	1962	120.00
— *With W. 63rd St. address on label*			
❏ BST-84096 [S]	That's Where It's At	1963	50.00
❏ BST-84096 [S]	That's Where It's At	1967	30.00
— *With "A Division of Liberty Records" on label*			
❏ BST-84096 [S]	That's Where It's At	1986	15.00
— *The Finest in Jazz Since 1939" reissue*			
❏ B1-93201	The Best of Stanley Turrentine	1989	18.00
— *The Finest in Jazz Since 1939" on label*			
❏ BST-84286	The Look of Love	1968	30.00
— *With "A Division of Liberty Records" on label*			
❏ BST-84286	The Look of Love	1971	25.00
— *With "A Division of United Artists" on label*			
❏ BLP-4256 [M]	The Spoiler	1967	80.00
— *A Division of Liberty Records" on label*			
❏ BST-84256 [S]	The Spoiler	1967	40.00
— *A Division of Liberty Records" on label*			
❏ BLP-4069 [M]	Up at Minton's, Volume 1	1961	120.00
— *With W. 63rd St. address on label*			
❏ BLP-4069 [M]	Up at Minton's, Volume 1	1963	40.00
— *With New York, USA address on label*			
❏ BST-84069 [S]	Up at Minton's, Volume 1	1961	120.00
— *With W. 63rd St. address on label*			
❏ BST-84069 [S]	Up at Minton's, Volume 1	1963	40.00
— *With New York, USA address on label*			
❏ BST-84069 [S]	Up at Minton's, Volume 1	1967	30.00
— *With "A Division of Liberty Records" on label*			
❏ BLP-4070 [M]	Up at Minton's, Volume 2	1961	120.00
— *With W. 63rd St. addresss on label*			
❏ BLP-4070 [M]	Up at Minton's, Volume 2	1963	40.00
— *With New York, USA address on label*			
❏ BST-84070 [S]	Up at Minton's, Volume 2	1961	120.00
— *With W. 63rd St. address on label*			
❏ BST-84070 [S]	Up at Minton's, Volume 2	1963	40.00
— *With New York, USA address on label*			
❏ BST-84070 [S]	Up at Minton's, Volume 2	1967	30.00
— *With "A Division of Liberty Records" on label*			
❏ BT-85140	Wonderland	1987	15.00
— *The Finest in Jazz Since 1939" on label*			
❏ BST-84424	Z.T.'s Blues	1985	15.00
— *The Finest in Jazz Since 1939" on label*			
CTI			
❏ 6017	Cherry	1972	25.00
❏ 8010	Cherry	1981	15.00
— *Reissue of 6017*			
❏ 6030	Don't Mess with Mister T.	1973	18.00
❏ 8011	Don't Mess with Mister T.	1981	15.00
— *Reissue of 6030*			
❏ CTSQ-6030 [Q]	Don't Mess with Mister T.	1973	80.00
❏ 6010	Salt Song	1971	25.00
❏ 8008	Salt Song	1981	15.00
— *Reissue of 6010*			
❏ 6005	Sugar	1971	25.00
❏ 8006	Sugar	1981	15.00
— *Reissue of 6005*			
❏ 6048	The Baddest Turrentine	1974	18.00
❏ 6052	The Sugar Man	1975	25.00
ELEKTRA			
❏ 6E-217	Betcha	1979	12.00
❏ 60201	Home Again	1982	15.00
❏ 6E-269	Inflation	1980	12.00
❏ 5E-534	Tender Togetherness	1981	15.00
FANTASY			
❏ F-9508	Everybody Come On Out	1976	18.00
❏ F-9493	Have You Ever Seen the Rain	1975	18.00
❏ F-9478	In the Pocket	1975	18.00
❏ F-9534	Nightwings	1977	18.00
❏ FPM-4002 [Q]	Pieces of Dreams	1974	30.00
❏ F-9465	Pieces of Dreams	1974	18.00
❏ F-9519	The Man with the Sad Face	1976	18.00
❏ F-9604	Use the Stairs	1980	15.00
❏ F-9548	West Side Highway	1978	18.00
❏ F-9563	What About You!	1978	15.00

Number	Title	Yr	NM
IMPULSE!			
❏ AS-9115 [B]	Let It Go	1967	30.00
MAINSTREAM			
❏ 56041 [M]	Tiger Tail	1965	40.00
❏ S-6041 [M]	Tiger Tail	1965	50.00
PHOENIX 10			
❏ PHX-317	Yester-Me, Yester-You	198?	15.00
SUNSET			
❏ SUS-5255	The Soul of Stanley Turrentine	196?	15.00
TIME			
❏ 52086 [M]	Stan the Man	1962	100.00
❏ S-2086 [S]	Stan the Man	1962	120.00
TRIP			
❏ TLX-5006	Yester-Me, Yester-You	197?	18.00
UPFRONT			
❏ UPF-147	Stanley Turrentine	197?	15.00
TURRENTINE, TOMMY			
BAINBRIDGE			
❏ BT-1047	Tommy Turrentine	198?	15.00
TIME			
❏ T-70008 [M]	Tommy Turrentine	1960	80.00
— *Reproductions exist*			
❏ ST-70008 [S]	Tommy Turrentine	1960	100.00
TURTLES, THE			
RHINO			
❏ RNPD901 [PD]	1968	1984	15.00
❏ RNPD900	1968	1984	10.00
❏ RNLP70155	Chalon Road	1986	12.00
❏ RNLP160	Greatest Hits	1983	12.00
❏ RNLP152	Happy Together	1983	12.00
❏ RNLP151	It Ain't Me Babe	1983	12.00
❏ RNLP70158	Shell Shock	1986	12.00
❏ RNLP70177	The Best of the Turtles (Golden Archives Series)	1987	12.00
❏ RNLP70156	The Turtles Present the Battle of the Bands	1986	12.00
❏ RNDF280 [EP]	Turtle-Sized	1984	15.00
— *Green vinyl turtle-shaped EP*			
❏ RNLP70157	Turtle Soup	1986	12.00
❏ RNLP70159	Turtle Wax: The Best of the Turtles, Vol. 2	1988	12.00
❏ RNLP154	Wooden Head	1983	12.00
❏ RNLP153	You Baby	1983	12.00
SIRE			
❏ SASH-3703	The Turtles' Greatest Hits/Happy Together Again	1974	25.00
WHITE WHALE			
❏ WW114 [M]	Happy Together	1967	40.00
❏ WWS7114 [S]	Happy Together	1967	30.00
❏ WW111 [M]	It Ain't Me Babe	1965	40.00
❏ WWS7111 [S]	It Ain't Me Babe	1965	40.00
❏ WW115 [M]	The Turtles! Golden Hits	1967	60.00
❏ WWS7115 [S]	The Turtles! Golden Hits	1967	25.00
❏ WW7127	The Turtles! More Golden Hits	1970	25.00
❏ WWS7118 [B]	The Turtles Present the Battle of the Bands	1968	30.00
❏ WW7124	Turtle Soup	1969	30.00
❏ WW7133	Wooden Head	1970	25.00
❏ WW112 [M]	You Baby	1966	40.00
❏ WWS7112 [S]	You Baby	1966	40.00
TUSA, FRANK			
ENJA			
❏ 2056	Father Time	197?	18.00
TUSKEGEE INSTITUTE CHOIR			
WESTMINSTER			
❏ XWM-18080 [M]	Spirituals	195?	50.00
TUXEDOMOON			
RALPH			
❏ TX8354	A Thousand Lives by Picture	1983	15.00
❏ TX8104	Desire	1981	15.00
❏ TX8004-L	Half-Mute	1980	15.00
TUXEDOMOON			
❏ EP79 [EP]	Scream with a View	1979	25.00
❏ EP45 [EP]	Tuxedomoon	1978	25.00
TV ON THE RADIO			
DGC			
❏ 1188201	Dear Science	2008	25.00
TV SMITH'S EXPLORERS			
EPIC			
❏ ARE37432 [B]	The Last Words of the Great Explorer	1981	30.00
— *promo*			
TWARDZIK, RICHARD			
PACIFIC JAZZ			
❏ PJ-37 [M]	The Last Set	1962	60.00

Number	Title	Yr	NM
TWENTIETH CENTURY ZOO, THE			
VAULT			
❏ LPS-122	Thunder on a Clear Day	1968	60.00
21ST CENTURY, THE			
RCA VICTOR			
❏ APL1-1189	Ahead of Our Time	1975	30.00
TWENTY MILES			
FAT POSSUM			
❏ 80302-1 [B]	Twenty Miles	1997	18.00
$27 SNAP-ON FACE			
HETERODYNE			
❏ 0001 [B]	$27 Snap-On Face	1977	100.00
— *Blue vinyl; with lyric sheet*			
TWIGGY			
MERCURY			
❏ SRM-1-1138	Please Get My Name Right	1977	15.00
❏ SRM-1-1093	Twiggy	1976	15.00
TWILLEY, DWIGHT			
❏ AB4214	Twilley	1979	12.00
❏ AB4140	Twilley Don't Mind	1977	12.00
CBS ASSOCIATED			
❏ BFZ40266	Wild Dogs	1986	10.00
EMI AMERICA			
❏ ST-17107	Jungle	1984	12.00
❏ ST-17064	Scuba Divers	1982	12.00
MCA			
❏ 688	Sincerely	1981	10.00
— *Reissue of Shelter LP*			
SHELTER			
❏ SA-52001	Sincerely	1976	12.00
TWIN CITIES CATHOLIC CHORALE, THE			
WANDERER FORUM			
❏ WFR103	Every Year at Christmas Comes the Holy Child	197?	15.00
TWINK			
SIRE			
❏ SES-97022 [B]	Think Pink	1970	250.00
TWINS, THE			
RCA VICTOR			
❏ LPM-1708 [M]	Teenagers Love the Twins	1958	50.00
TWISTED SISTER			
ATLANTIC			
❏ 81275	Come Out and Play	1985	10.00
❏ 81772	Love Is for Suckers	1987	10.00
❏ 80156	Stay Hungry	1984	10.00
❏ 81256	Under the Blade	1985	10.00
❏ 80074	You Can't Stop Rock 'n' Roll	1983	10.00
SECRET			
❏ SHH13712 [EP]	Ruff Cuts	1981	18.00
— *UK import*			
❏ SECX9	Under the Blade	1982	15.00
— *UK import*			
❏ SECXP9 [PD]	Under the Blade	1982	25.00
— *UK import*			
TWISTERS, THE			
TREASURE			
❏ TLP-890 [M]	Doin' the Twist	1962	30.00
TWISTIN' KINGS			
MOTOWN			
❏ M-601 [M]	Twistin' the World Around	1961	300.00
TWITTY, CONWAY, AND LORETTA LYNN			
DECCA			
❏ DL75326	Lead Me On	1972	25.00
❏ DL75251	We Only Make Believe	1971	25.00
HEARTLAND			
❏ HL-1059/60	The Best of Conway and Loretta	1987	25.00
MCA			
❏ 427	Country Partners	1974	18.00
❏ 2354	Country Partners	1978	12.00
— *Reissue of MCA 427*			
❏ 3190	Diamond Duet	1979	15.00
❏ 723	Diamond Duet	198?	12.00
— *Reissue of MCA 3190*			
❏ 2278	Dynamic Duo	1977	15.00
❏ 2143	Feelins'	1975	18.00
❏ 2372	Honky Tonk Heroes	1978	15.00
❏ 722	Honky Tonk Heroes	198?	12.00
— *Reissue of MCA 2372*			
❏ 9	Lead Me On	1973	15.00
— *Reissue of Decca 75326*			

Column 1

Number	Title	Yr	NM
❏ 335	Louisiana Woman, Mississippi Man	1973	18.00
❏ 42216	Making Believe	1988	10.00
❏ 3164	The Very Best of Loretta and Conway	1979	15.00
❏ 37237	The Very Best of Loretta and Conway	1983	10.00

— Budget-line reissue

Number	Title	Yr	NM
❏ 5178	Two's a Party	1981	15.00
❏ 2209	United Talent	1976	18.00
❏ 629	United Talent	198?	12.00

— Reissue of MCA 2209

Number	Title	Yr	NM
❏ 8	We Only Make Believe	1973	15.00

— Reissue of Decca 75251

MCA CORAL

Number	Title	Yr	NM
❏ CDL-8006	Never Ending Song of Love	1973	15.00

TWITTY, CONWAY

ACCORD

Number	Title	Yr	NM
❏ SN-7169	Early Favorites	1982	15.00

ALLEGIANCE

Number	Title	Yr	NM
❏ AV-5012	You Made Me What I Am	1983	18.00

DECCA

Number	Title	Yr	NM
❏ DL4913 [M]	Conway Twitty Country	1967	30.00
❏ DL74913 [S]	Conway Twitty Country	1967	30.00
❏ DL75352	Conway Twitty's Greatest Hits Vol. I	1972	25.00
❏ DL4724 [M]	Conway Twitty Sings	1965	30.00
❏ DL74724 [S]	Conway Twitty Sings	1965	30.00
❏ DL75105	Darling, You Know I Wouldn't Lie	1968	25.00
❏ DL75248	Fifteen Years Ago	1970	25.00
❏ DL75209	Hello Darlin'	1970	25.00
❏ DL4990 [M]	Here's Conway Twitty	1968	50.00
❏ DL74990 [S]	Here's Conway Twitty	1968	30.00
❏ DL75276	How Much More Can She Stand	1971	25.00
❏ ST-93776	How Much More Can She Stand	1971	30.00

— Capitol Record Club edition

Number	Title	Yr	NM
❏ DL75335	I Can't See Me Without You	1972	25.00
❏ DL75361	I Can't Stop Loving You/Last Date	1972	25.00
❏ DL75131	I Love You More Today	1969	25.00
❏ DL75292	I Wonder What She'll Think About Me Leaving	1971	25.00
❏ DL4828 [M]	Look Into My Teardrops	1966	30.00
❏ DL74828 [S]	Look Into My Teardrops	1966	30.00
❏ DL75062 [B]	Next in Line	1968	30.00
❏ DL75172	To See My Angel Cry	1970	25.00

ELEKTRA

Number	Title	Yr	NM
❏ 60115 [B]	#1 Classics, Volume 1	1982	12.00
❏ 60209	#1 Classics, Volume 2	1982	12.00
❏ 60182	Dream Maker	1982	12.00
❏ 60005	Southern Confort	1982	12.00

HEARTLAND

Number	Title	Yr	NM
❏ HL-1088/9	The Very Best of Conway Twitty	1989	25.00

MCA

Number	Title	Yr	NM
❏ 5817	A Night with Conway Twitty	1986	10.00
❏ 5969	Borderline	1987	10.00
❏ 5424	Classic Conway	1983	10.00
❏ 376	Clinging to a Saving Hand	1973	60.00
❏ 3063	Conway	1978	15.00
❏ 702	Conway	197?	12.00

— Reissue of MCA 3063

Number	Title	Yr	NM
❏ 52	Conway Twitty's Greatest Hits	1973	15.00

— Reissue of Decca 75352

Number	Title	Yr	NM
❏ 2345	Conway Twitty's Greatest Hits, Vol. 1	1978	15.00

— Reissue of Decca 75352

Number	Title	Yr	NM
❏ 37229	Conway Twitty's Greatest Hits, Vol. 1	1983	10.00

— Budget-line reissue

Number	Title	Yr	NM
❏ 2235	Conway Twitty's Greatest Hits, Vol. 2	1976	18.00
❏ 3086	Cross Winds	1979	15.00
❏ 37163	Cross Winds	198?	10.00

— Budget-line reissue

Number	Title	Yr	NM
❏ 2328	Georgia Keeps Pullin' on My Ring	1978	15.00
❏ 37081	Georgia Keeps Pullin' on My Ring	198?	10.00

— Budget-line reissue

Number	Title	Yr	NM
❏ 3210	Heart and Soul	1980	15.00
❏ 37227	Heart and Soul	1983	10.00

— Budget-line reissue

Number	Title	Yr	NM
❏ 19	Hello Darlin'	1973	15.00

— Reissue of Decca 75209

Number	Title	Yr	NM
❏ 625	High Priest of Country	197?	12.00

— Reissue of MCA 2144

Number	Title	Yr	NM
❏ 2144	High Priest of Country Music	1975	18.00
❏ 406	Honky Tonk Angel	1974	18.00
❏ 42297	House on Old Lonesome Road	1989	15.00
❏ 53	I Can't Stop Loving You/Last Date	1973	15.00

— Reissue of Decca 75361

Number	Title	Yr	NM
❏ 441	I'm Not Through Loving You Yet	1974	18.00
❏ 2293	I've Already Loved You in My Mind	1977	15.00
❏ 469	Linda on My Mind	1975	18.00

Column 2

Number	Title	Yr	NM
❏ 5204	Mr. T.	1981	15.00
❏ 2206	Now and Then	1976	18.00
❏ 5318	Number Ones	1982	15.00
❏ 2262	Play Guitar Play	1977	15.00
❏ 5138	Rest Your Love on Me	1980	15.00
❏ 37228	Rest Your Love on Me	1983	10.00

— Budget-line reissue

Number	Title	Yr	NM
❏ 303	She Needs Someone to Hold Her (When She Cries)	1973	18.00
❏ 5700	Songwriter	1986	10.00
❏ 42115	Still in Your Dreams	1988	10.00
❏ 3043	The Very Best of Conway Twitty	1978	15.00
❏ 18	To See My Angel Cry	1973	15.00

— Reissue of Decca 75172

Number	Title	Yr	NM
❏ 2176	Twitty (This Time I've Hurt Her More Than She Loves Me)	1975	18.00
❏ 359	You've Never Been This Far Before/Baby's Gone	1973	18.00

MCA CORAL

Number	Title	Yr	NM
❏ CB-20000	I'm So Used to Loving You	1973	15.00

METRO

Number	Title	Yr	NM
❏ M-512 [M]	It's Only Make Believe	1966	18.00
❏ MS-512 [S]	It's Only Make Believe	1966	25.00

MGM

Number	Title	Yr	NM
❏ SES-4844	20 Great Hits by Conway Twitty	1973	25.00
❏ GAS-110	Conway Twitty (Golden Archive Series)	1970	25.00
❏ SE-4799	Conway Twitty Hits	1971	18.00
❏ E-3849 [M]	Conway Twitty's Greatest Hits	1960	70.00
❏ E-3849 [M]	Conway Twitty's Greatest Hits	1960	40.00

— With poster

Number	Title	Yr	NM
❏ SE-3849 [P]	Conway Twitty's Greatest Hits	1960	80.00

— With poster

Number	Title	Yr	NM
❏ SE-3849 [P]	Conway Twitty's Greatest Hits	1960	50.00

— Without poster

Number	Title	Yr	NM
❏ E-3744 [M]	Conway Twitty Sings	1959	100.00

— Yellow label

Number	Title	Yr	NM
❏ E-3744 [M]	Conway Twitty Sings	1960	40.00

— Black label

Number	Title	Yr	NM
❏ E-3744 [M]	Conway Twitty Sings	196?	300.00

— Reissue with orange cover and a clean-cut photo of Conway

Number	Title	Yr	NM
❏ SE-3744 [S]	Conway Twitty Sings	1959	150.00

— Yellow label

Number	Title	Yr	NM
❏ SE-3744 [S]	Conway Twitty Sings	1960	50.00

— Black label

Number	Title	Yr	NM
❏ SE-3744 [S]	Conway Twitty Sings	196?	300.00

— Reissue with orange cover and a clean-cut photo of Conway

Number	Title	Yr	NM
❏ SE-4837	Conway Twitty Sings the Blues	1972	18.00
❏ E-4217 [M]	Hit the Road	1964	30.00
❏ SE-4217 [S]	Hit the Road	1964	30.00
❏ E-3818 [M]	Lonely Blue Boy	1960	70.00
❏ SE-3818 [S]	Lonely Blue Boy	1960	100.00
❏ E-4019 [M]	Portrait of a Fool and Others	1962	40.00
❏ SE-4019 [S]	Portrait of a Fool and Others	1962	50.00
❏ E-4089 [M]	R & B '63	1963	40.00
❏ SE-4089 [S]	R & B '63	1963	50.00
❏ E-3786 [M]	Saturday Night with Conway Twitty	1960	70.00
❏ SE-3786 [S]	Saturday Night with Conway Twitty	1960	100.00
❏ E-3943 [M]	The Conway Twitty Touch	1961	50.00
❏ SE-3943 [S]	The Conway Twitty Touch	1961	80.00
❏ E-3907 [M]	The Rock and Roll Story	1961	50.00
❏ SE-3907 [S]	The Rock and Roll Story	1961	80.00
❏ SE-4650	You Can't Take the Country Out of Conway	1969	18.00

PICKWICK

Number	Title	Yr	NM
❏ SPC-3360	Shake It Up	1973	15.00

TEE VEE

Number	Title	Yr	NM
❏ TV-1009	20 Certified #1 Hits	1978	18.00

— Alternate number is MCA Special Markets MSM-35003

WARNER BROS.

Number	Title	Yr	NM
❏ 60115	#1 Classics, Volume 1	1983	10.00

— Reissue of Elektra LP

Number	Title	Yr	NM
❏ 60209	#1 Classics, Volume 2	1983	10.00

— Reissue of Elektra LP

Number	Title	Yr	NM
❏ 25777	#1's -- The Warner Bros. Years	1988	10.00
❏ 25078	By Heart	1984	12.00
❏ 25294	Chasin' Rainbows	1985	12.00
❏ 25170	Conway's Latest Greatest Hits	1984	12.00
❏ 25207	Don't Call Him a Cowboy	1985	12.00
❏ 60182	Dream Maker	1983	10.00

— Reissue of Elektra LP

Number	Title	Yr	NM
❏ 25406	Fallin' for You for Years	1986	12.00
❏ 23869	Lost in the Feeling	1983	12.00
❏ 23971	Merry Twismas	1983	25.00

2 LIVE CREW, THE

EFFECT

Number	Title	Yr	NM
❏ E3003	Live in Concert	1990	12.00

Column 3

LIL' JOE

Number	Title	Yr	NM
❏ 286	Essential DJ 12" and Mega Mixes	2002	12.00
❏ XR-238	Greatest Hits Vol. 2	1999	18.00
❏ XR-239	Greatest Hits Vol. 2/Edit	1999	18.00
❏ 264	Private Personal Parts	2000	15.00
❏ XR-215	Shake a Lil' Somethin'	1996	18.00
❏ XR-227	The 2 Live Crew Goes to the Movies -- A Decade of Hits	1997	15.00
❏ XR-231	The Real One	1998	15.00

LUKE

Number	Title	Yr	NM
❏ 208	Back At You for '94	1994	25.00

— As "The New 2 Live Crew"; edited version

Number	Title	Yr	NM
❏ 207	Back at Your Ass for the Nine-4	1994	25.00

— As "The New 2 Live Crew

Number	Title	Yr	NM
❏ 91424	Banned in the U.S.A.	1990	18.00

— As "Luke Featuring The 2 Live Crew

Number	Title	Yr	NM
❏ 122	Greatest Hits	1992	25.00
❏ 123	Greatest Hits/Edit	1992	25.00
❏ DMD1760	Sports Weekend (As Nasty As They Wanna Be Part II)	1991	18.00

— Promo-only vinyl issue in generic black cardboard sleeve

LUKE SKYYWALKER

Number	Title	Yr	NM
❏ XR-108	As Clean As They Wanna Be	1989	18.00
❏ XR-107 [B]	As Nasty As They Wanna Be	1989	18.00
❏ XR-101	Move Somethin'	1988	15.00
❏ XR-100	The 2 Live Crew "Is What We Are	1987	18.00

2PAC

AMARU/JIVE

Number	Title	Yr	NM
❏ 41628	R U Still Down? (Remember Me)	1997	30.00

DEATH ROW

Number	Title	Yr	NM
❏ 63008	All Eyez on Me	2001	25.00

— Reissue

Number	Title	Yr	NM
❏ 63012	The Don Killuminati -- The 7 Day Theory	2001	18.00

— As "Makaveli"; reissue

DEATH ROW/INTERSCOPE

Number	Title	Yr	NM
❏ 524204-1 [B]	All Eyez on Me	1996	30.00
❏ INT4-90301	Greatest Hits	1998	30.00
❏ 490413-1	Still I Rise	1999	18.00

— As "2Pac + Outlawz

Number	Title	Yr	NM
❏ INT2-90039	The Don Killuminati -- The 7 Day Theory	1996	18.00

— As "Makaveli

Number	Title	Yr	NM
❏ 490840-1	Until the End of Time	2001	30.00

INTERSCOPE

Number	Title	Yr	NM
❏ 91767 [B]	2Pacalypse Now	1991	25.00
❏ 92399	Me Against the World	1995	25.00

RESTLESS

Number	Title	Yr	NM
❏ 72737	Strictly 4 My N.I.G.G.A.Z.	1998	18.00

— Vinyl reissue of 1993 album (we can't prove or disprove the existence of the original Interscope edition on vinyl)

TYLE, TEDDY

GOLDEN CREST

Number	Title	Yr	NM
❏ GC-3060 [M]	Moon Shot	1959	40.00

TYLER, ALVIN "RED

ACE

Number	Title	Yr	NM
❏ LP-1006 [M]	Rockin' and Rollin'	1960	150.00
❏ LP-1021 [M]	Twistin' with Mr. Sax	1962	120.00

ROUNDER

Number	Title	Yr	NM
❏ 2061	Graciously	1987	12.00
❏ 2047	Heritage	1986	15.00

TYLER, BONNIE

CHRYSALIS

Number	Title	Yr	NM
❏ CHR-1140	The World Starts Tonight	1976	18.00
❏ PV41140	The World Starts Tonight	1983	12.00

— Reissue of 1140

COLUMBIA

Number	Title	Yr	NM
❏ BFC38710	Faster Than the Speed of Night	1983	18.00

— Silver print on front cover

Number	Title	Yr	NM
❏ FC38710	Faster Than the Speed of Night	1983	10.00

— Blue-green print on front cover

Number	Title	Yr	NM
❏ FC44163	Notes from America	1988	15.00
❏ OC40312	Secret Dreams and Forbidden Fire	1986	10.00

RCA VICTOR

Number	Title	Yr	NM
❏ AFL1-3072	Diamond Cut	1979	12.00
❏ AFL1-2821	It's a Heartache	1978	12.00
❏ AYL1-4110	It's a Heartache	1984	10.00

— Best Buy Series" reissue

TYLER, CHARLES

ADELPHI

Number	Title	Yr	NM
❏ 5011	Sixty Minute Man	1980	15.00

ESP-DISK'

Number	Title	Yr	NM
❏ S-1059 [S]	Eastern Man Alone	1968	25.00

Number	Title	Yr	NM
❑ 1029 [M]	The Charles Tyler Ensemble	1966	25.00
❑ S-1029 [S]	The Charles Tyler Ensemble	1966	30.00

NESSA

Number	Title	Yr	NM
❑ N-16	Saga of the Outlaws	197?	18.00

SILKHEART

| ❑ SH-118 | Autumn in Paris | 199? | 15.00 |

STORYVILLE

| ❑ 4098 | Definite, Vol. 1 | 198? | 12.00 |

TYLER, T. TEXAS

CAPITOL

❑ T1662 [M]	Salvation	1962	30.00
❑ ST1662 [S]	Salvation	1962	30.00
❑ T2344 [M]	The Hits of T. Texas Tyler	1965	25.00
❑ ST2344 [S]	The Hits of T. Texas Tyler	1965	30.00

KING

❑ 734 [M]	Songs Along the Way	1962	80.00
❑ 689 [M]	The Great Texan	1960	120.00
❑ 664 [M]	T. Texas Tyler	1959	120.00
❑ 721 [M]	T. Texas Tyler	1961	80.00

SOUND

| ❑ 607 [M] | Deck of Cards | 1958 | 80.00 |

STARDAY

| ❑ SLP-379 [M] | The Man with a Million Friends | 1966 | 30.00 |

WRANGLER

| ❑ W-1002 [M] | T. Texas Tyler | 1962 | 40.00 |
| ❑ W-31002 [S] | T. Texas Tyler | 1962 | 50.00 |

TYLER, WILLIE, AND LESTER

TAMLA

| ❑ TM-265 [M] | Hello Dummy | 1965 | 200.00 |

TYMES, THE

ABKCO

| ❑ 4228 | The Best of Tymes | 1973 | 15.00 |

COLUMBIA

| ❑ CS9778 | People | 1969 | 18.00 |

PARKWAY

❑ P7049 [M]	18 Greatest Hits	1964	40.00
❑ P7039 [M]	Somewhere	1964	50.00
—Includes bonus single 7039 (deduct 20 percent if missing)			
❑ P7032 [M]	So Much in Love	1963	40.00
—With group standing in front-cover photo			
❑ P7032 [M]	So Much in Love	1963	200.00
—With head-and-shoulders group photo on front cover			
❑ P7038 [M]	The Sound of the Wonderful Tymes	1963	40.00
❑ SP7038 [S]	The Sound of the Wonderful Tymes	1963	50.00

RCA VICTOR

❑ APL1-2406	Diggin' Their Roots	1977	15.00
❑ APL1-0727	Trustmaker	1974	15.00
❑ APL1-1835	Turning Point	1976	15.00

U

U-GOD

PRIORITY

| ❑ 50086 | Golden Arms Redemption | 1999 | 18.00 |

U.K.

POLYDOR

❑ PD-1-6194 [B]	Danger Money	1979	12.00
❑ PD-1-6234	Night After Night	1979	12.00
❑ PD-1-6146	U.K.	1978	12.00

U.K. SUBS

CLEOPATRA

| ❑ 9860 [B] | Endangered Species | | 25.00 |
| ❑ 2970 [B] | Punk As Fuck | | 25.00 |

U-KREW, THE

ENIGMA

| ❑ 7735241 | The U-Krew | 1990 | 18.00 |

U-MEN

BLACK LABEL

| ❑ BLR 002 [B] | Step on a Bug The Red Toad Speaks | 1988 | 30.00 |

HOMESTEAD

| ❑ HMS 024 [EP] | Stop Spinning | 1985 | 30.00 |

U2

INTERSCOPE

| ❑ 1263001 | No Line on the Horizon | 2009 | 30.00 |

ISLAND

❑ 510347-1 [B]	Achtung Baby	1991	50.00
—U.S. LP covers are uncensored (Adam Clayton appears naked without any "X" or shamrock over his appendage)			
❑ R144636	Boy	1983	15.00
—RCA Music Service edition			

Number	Title	Yr	NM
❑ ILPS9646	Boy	1980	18.00
❑ 842296-1	Boy	1990	10.00
—Reissue; sticker with new number placed over bar code of leftover 90040 pressings			
❑ 90040	Boy	1983	15.00
—Reissue; first pressings have dark purple labels			
❑ 90040 [B]	Boy	1983	12.00
—Second pressings have light blue labels			
❑ 90040 [B]	Boy	1983	10.00
—Third pressings have black labels			
❑ 1084301	Boy	2008	25.00
❑ R114632	October	1983	15.00
—RCA Music Service edition			
❑ ILPS9680	October	1981	15.00
—Back cover has engineering credits, etc., in upper left			
❑ 842297-1	October	1990	10.00
—Reissue; sticker with new number placed over bar code of leftover 90092 pressings			
❑ 90092	October	1983	12.00
—Reissue; first pressings have dark purple labels			
❑ ILPS9680	October	1981	18.00
—Back cover is blank (no engineering credits, etc.) in upper left			
❑ 90092 [B]	October	1983	12.00
—Second pressings have light blue labels			
❑ 90092 [B]	October	1983	10.00
—Third pressings have black labels			
❑ 1082901	October	2008	25.00
❑ 524334-1 [B]	Pop	1997	50.00
❑ PR127545-1	PopMart Sampler	1997	80.00
—Promo-only 8-song collection of old and new U2 material			
❑ R200596	Rattle and Hum	1988	18.00
—BMG Direct Marketing edition			
❑ 91003	Rattle and Hum	1988	18.00
❑ 842299-1	Rattle and Hum	1990	15.00
—Reissue; sticker with new number placed over bar code of leftover 91003 pressings			
❑ R153501	The Joshua Tree	1987	15.00
—RCA Music Service edition; no lyric sheet			
❑ 90581	The Joshua Tree	1987	12.00
—With lyric sheet			
❑ 842298-1	The Joshua Tree	1990	10.00
—Reissue; sticker with new number placed over bar code of leftover 90581 pressings			
❑ PR2049 [DJ]	The Joshua Tree Interview... Their Words and Music	1987	40.00
❑ R154515	The Unforgettable Fire	1985	15.00
—RCA Music Service edition			
❑ 822898-1	The Unforgettable Fire	1990	10.00
—Reissue; new sticker placed on leftover Island/Atco pressings			
❑ 90231	The Unforgettable Fire	1984	12.00
❑ R153598 [EP]	Under a Blood Red Sky	1983	12.00
—BMG Direct Marketing edition			
❑ 90127-1-B [EP]	Under a Blood Red Sky	1983	30.00
—White labels with "Mini LP" logo; with version of "The Electric Co." in which Bono sings snippets of "A-Me-Ri-Ca" from West Side Story and "Send In The Clowns" during the instrumental break.			
❑ 818008-1 [EP]	Under a Blood Red Sky	1990	10.00
—Reissue; sticker with new number placed over bar code of leftover 90127 pressings			
❑ 90127-1-B [EP]	Under a Blood Red Sky	1983	12.00
—White labels with "Mini LP" logo; edited version of "The Electric Co."			
❑ 1095001 [EP]	Under a Blood Red Sky	2008	25.00
❑ R124619	War	1983	15.00
—BMG Direct Marketing edition			

❑ 90067 [B]	War	1983	15.00
—Original pressings have dark purple labels			
❑ 811148-1	War	1990	10.00
—Reissue; sticker with new number placed over bar code of leftover 90067 pressings			
❑ 90067 [B]	War	1983	12.00
—Second pressings have light blue labels			
❑ 90067 [B]	War	1983	10.00
—Third pressings have black labels			
❑ 1083201	War	2008	25.00

Number	Title	Yr	NM
❑ R140642 [EP]	Wide Awake in America	1985	15.00
—RCA Music Service edition			
❑ 90279-1-A [EP]	Wide Awake in America	1985	12.00
❑ 842479-1 [EP]	Wide Awake in America	1990	10.00
—Reissue; sticker with new number placed over bar code of leftover 90279 pressings			
❑ 518047-1 [B]	Zooropa	1993	35.00
—All "U.S." copies actually are British imports			

MOBILE FIDELITY

| ❑ 1-207 | The Unforgettable Fire | 1994 | 60.00 |
| —Audiophile vinyl | | | |

WARNER BROS.

| ❑ WBMS-117 [DJ] | Two Sides Live | 1981 | 200.00 |
| —Promo only, part of "The Warner Bros. Music Show"; legitimate copies are on black vinyl | | | |

UB40

A&M

❑ R144329	CCCP/Live in Moscow	1987	15.00
—BMG Direct Marketing edition			
❑ SP-5168	CCCP/Live in Moscow	1987	12.00
❑ SP-5033	Geffery Morgan	1984	12.00
❑ R100677	Labour of Love	1986	15.00
—BMG Direct Marketing edition			
❑ SP-6-4980	Labour of Love	1983	12.00
❑ SP-4980	Labour of Love	198?	10.00
—Reissue with altered prefix			
❑ SP-6-5090 [EP]	Little Baggariddim	1985	12.00
—Original copies are in a clear plastic sleeve			
❑ SP-5090 [EP]	Little Baggariddim	1985	10.00
—Second printings are in standard album cover			
❑ R134092	Rat in the Kitchen	1986	15.00
—RCA Music Service edition			
❑ SP-5137	Rat in the Kitchen	1986	12.00
❑ R100677	UB40	1988	15.00
—BMG Direct Marketing edition			
❑ SP-5213	UB40	1988	12.00
❑ SP-4955	UB40 1980-83	1983	15.00

VIRGIN

| ❑ 91324 | Labour of Love II | 1989 | 25.00 |

UBC, THE

EMI

| ❑ E1-93919 | 2 All Serious Thinkers | 1990 | 18.00 |

UBIQUITY

ELEKTRA

| ❑ 6E-120 | Starbooty | 1978 | 15.00 |

UFO

CHRYSALIS

❑ CHR1074	Force It	1975	15.00
❑ PV41074	Force It	1983	10.00
❑ CHR1127	Lights Out	1977	15.00
❑ FV41127	Lights Out	1983	10.00
❑ PV41127	Lights Out	1986	10.00
—Reissue of FV 41127			
❑ FV41402	Making Contact	1983	12.00
❑ PV41402	Making Contact	1986	10.00
—Reissue of FV 41402			
❑ CHR1360	Mechanix	1982	15.00
❑ PV41360	Mechanix	1983	10.00
❑ BFV41518	Misdemeanor	1986	12.00
❑ CHR1103	No Heavy Petting	1976	15.00
❑ PV41103	No Heavy Petting	1983	10.00
❑ CHR1239	No Place to Run	1980	15.00
❑ PV41239	No Place to Run	1983	10.00
❑ CHR1182	Obsession	1978	15.00
❑ PV41182	Obsession	1983	10.00
❑ CHR1059	Phenomenon	1974	18.00
—Green label			
❑ PV41059	Phenomenon	1983	10.00
❑ CHR1059	Phenomenon	1977	15.00
—Fading blue label			
❑ CHR1209	Strangers in the Night	1979	18.00
❑ V2X41209	Strangers in the Night	1983	14.00
❑ FV41644	The Best of the Rest	1988	15.00
❑ CHR1307	The Wild, the Willing and the Innocent	1981	15.00
❑ PV41307	The Wild, the Willing and the Innocent	1983	10.00

METAL BLADE/ENIGMA

| ❑ 7734041 [EP] | Ain't Misbehavin' | 1989 | 12.00 |

RARE EARTH

| ❑ RS624 | UFO 1 | 1971 | 30.00 |

UGGAMS, LESLIE

ATLANTIC

❑ SD8241	Just to Satisfy You	1969	18.00
❑ 8128 [M]	Time to Love	1967	18.00
❑ SD8128 [S]	Time to Love	1967	25.00
❑ SD8196 [S]	What's an Uggams?	1968	18.00
❑ 8196 [M]	What's an Uggams?	1968	40.00
—Mono is white label promo only; cover has "d/j copy monaural" sticker on front			

COLUMBIA

| ❑ CS9936 | Leslie | 1970 | 15.00 |

Number	Title	Yr	NM
❑ CL1706 [M]	Leslie Uggams on TV	1962	18.00
❑ CS8506 [S]	Leslie Uggams on TV	1962	25.00
❑ CS8665 [S]	More Leslie Uggams on TV	1963	25.00
❑ CL1865 [M]	More Leslie Uggams on TV	1963	18.00
❑ CL2071 [M]	So in Love	1963	18.00
❑ CS8871 [S]	So in Love	1963	25.00
MOTOWN			
❑ M6-846	Leslie Uggams	1975	15.00
SONDAY			
❑ 8000	Try to See It My Way	1972	15.00
ULANO, SAM			
LANE			
❑ LP-140 [M]	Sam Ulano	195?	50.00
❑ LP-151 [M]	Sam Ulano Is Mr. Rhythm	195?	50.00
ULLMAN, TRACEY			
MCA			
❑ 5471	You Broke My Heart in 17 Places	1984	12.00
ULMER, JAMES "BLOOD			
ARTISTS HOUSE			
❑ 13	Are You Glad to Be in America?	1980	25.00
❑ AH9407 [B]	Tales of Captain Black	1979	25.00
BLUE NOTE			
❑ BT-85136	America -- Do You Remember the Love?	1987	15.00
CARAVAN OF DREAMS			
❑ CDP85004	Live at the Caravan of Dreams	1986	18.00
COLUMBIA			
❑ ARC38285	Black Rock	1982	25.00
❑ ARC37493 [B]	Free Lancing	1981	25.00
❑ BFC38900	Odyssey	1983	15.00
IN+OUT			
❑ 7007	Revealing	1990	15.00
ULTIMATE			
CASABLANCA			
❑ NBLP-7128	Ultimate	1979	18.00
❑ NBLP-7208	Ultimate	1980	15.00
— These are different albums			
ULTIMATE SPINACH			
MGM			
❑ E-4570 [M]	Behold & See	1968	100.00
— Mono is promo only (yellow label)			
❑ SE-4570 [S]	Behold & See	1968	30.00
❑ E-4518 [M]	Ultimate Spinach	1968	60.00
❑ SE-4518 [S]	Ultimate Spinach	1968	30.00
❑ SE-4600	Ultimate Spinach	1969	30.00
ULTRA VIOLET			
CAPITOL			
❑ ST-11244	Ultra Violet	197?	30.00
ULTRAMAGNETIC MC'S, THE			
MERCURY			
❑ 510893-1	Funk Your Head Up	1991	25.00
NEXT PLATFAU			
❑ 5402	B-Sides Companion	1997	18.00
❑ 1013	Critical Beatdown	1988	30.00
❑ 5496	Critical Beatdown	199?	15.00
— Reissue			
TUFF CITY			
❑ 4023	Mo Love's Basement Tapes	1996	18.00
— Compilation of older material			
❑ 4021	New York What Is Funky	1996	18.00
— Compilation of older material			
❑ 624	Smack My Bitch Up	1998	25.00
— Compilation of older material			
❑ 618	The Basement Tapes 1984-1990	1994	18.00
— Compilation of older material			
WILD PITCH			
❑ WP2010	The Four Horsemen	199?	18.00
— Reissue			
❑ E1-89917	The Four Horsemen	1993	25.00
ULTRAVOX			
ANTILLES			
❑ AN7069	Systems of Romance	1978	18.00
❑ AN7079	Three Into One	1980	18.00
CHRYSALIS			
❑ FV41459	Lament	1984	12.00
❑ B6V41394	Quartet	1983	12.00
❑ CHR1338	Rage in Eden	1981	12.00
❑ FV41490	The Collection	1984	12.00
❑ CHR1296 [B]	Vienna	1980	18.00
❑ FV41296	Vienna	198?	10.00
— Reissue			
ISLAND			
❑ ILPS9449 [B]	Ultravox!	1977	18.00

Number	Title	Yr	NM
UMEKI, MIYOSHI			
MERCURY			
❑ MG-20568 [M]	Miyoshi	1958	25.00
❑ SR-60228 [S]	Miyoshi	1959	30.00
UNBEATABLES, THE			
DAWN			
❑ 5050 [M]	Live at Palisades Park	1964	150.00
UNCLE DOG			
MCA			
❑ 302 [B]	Old Hat	1973	25.00
UNCLE FESTIVE			
NOVA			
❑ 8703-1	Money's No Object	198?	12.00
OPTIMISM			
❑ OP-3107	Say Uncle	1988	12.00
UNCLE JOSH AND COUSIN JAKE			
COTTON TOWN			
❑ 101 [M]	Just Joshing	1958	100.00
UNCLE KRACKER			
ATLANTIC			
❑ 83279-1 [B]	Double Wide	2000	25.00
❑ 83542-1	No Stranger to Shame	2002	18.00
UNCLE LAR' AND LIL' TOMMY			
WLS			
❑ WLS-890	Animal Stories	1981	25.00
❑ WLS-947	Animal Stories Volume Three	1983	25.00
❑ WLS-1000	Animal Stories Volume Two	1982	25.00
UNCLE LOUIE			
MARLIN			
❑ 2228	Unclue Louie's Here	1979	25.00
UNCLE TUPELO			
ROCKVILLE			
❑ 6050-1 [B]	No Depression	1990	60.00
❑ 6110-1	Still Feel Gone/March 16-20, 1992	1992	150.00
SUNDAZED			
❑ LP-5153	89/93: An Anthology	2002	30.00
UNDEAD			
POST MORTEM			
❑ LP 002	Act Your Rage	1989	25.00
— Pink (white with red accents) vinyl			
❑ LP 002	Act Your Rage	1989	25.00
— Teal (white with blue accents) vinyl			
❑ LP 002	Act Your Rage	1989	30.00
— Blue vinyl			
❑ LP 002	Act Your Rage	1989	30.00
— Yellow vinyl			
❑ LP 002	Act Your Rage	1989	30.00
— Red vinyl			
❑ LP 002	Act Your Rage	1989	50.00
— Clear vinyl			
❑ LP 002	Act Your Rage	1989	100.00
— Green vinyl			
❑ LP 002	Act Your Rage	1989	100.00
— Orange vinyl			
❑ LP 002	Act Your Rage	1989	18.00
— Black vinyl			
❑ SHAG1001	Dawn of the Undead	1991	30.00
❑ LP 001 [EP]	Never Say Die!	1989	30.00
SKYCLAD/SKREAMIN' SKULL			
❑ LIVE119 [B]	Live Slayer	1992	18.00
UNDERWORLD			
❑ UWR 008	'Til Death!	1998	12.00
— Pressed on four different colors of vinyl (blue, green, yellow, red), each of equal value			
UNDERGROUND, THE			
WING			
❑ MGW-12337 [M]	Psychedelic Visions	1967	80.00
❑ SRW-16337 [S]	Psychedelic Visions	1967	100.00
UNDERGROUND KINGZ			
JIVE			
❑ 41502	Too Hard to Swallow	1992	18.00
— Issued in generic black cover			
UNDERGROUND SUNSHINE			
INTREPID			
❑ IT-74003	Let There Be Light	1969	30.00
UNDERTONES, THE			
CAPITOL			
❑ ST-12358	All Wrapped Up	1983	18.00

Number	Title	Yr	NM
HARVEST			
❑ ST-12159 [B]	Positive Touch	1981	18.00
SIRE			
❑ SRK6088	Hypnotised	1980	15.00
❑ SRK6071	The Undertones	1979	15.00
UNDERWORLD			
SIRE			
❑ 25945	Change the Weather!	1989	12.00
❑ 25627	Underneath the Radar	1988	15.00
UNDISPUTED TRUTH, THE			
GORDY			
❑ G6-970	Cosmic Truth	1975	25.00
❑ G6-968	Down to Earth	1974	25.00
❑ G5-959	Face to Face with the Truth	1972	25.00
❑ G6-972	Higher Than High	1975	25.00
❑ G5-963	Law of the Land	1973	25.00
❑ G955L	The Undisputed Truth	1971	30.00
WHITFIELD			
❑ BS2967	Method to the Madness	1977	25.00
❑ BSK3202	Smokin'	1979	18.00
UNFOLDING			
AUDIO FIDELITY			
❑ AFLP-2184 [M]	How to Blow Your Mind and Have a Freak-Out Party	1967	70.00
❑ AFSD-6184 [S]	How to Blow Your Mind and Have a Freak-Out Party	1967	100.00
UNFORGIVEN, THE			
ELEKTRA			
❑ 60461	The Unforgiven	1986	12.00
UNICORN			
CAPITOL			
❑ ST-11334 [B]	Blue Pine Trees	1974	18.00
— Produced by David Gilmour (Pink Floyd)			
❑ ST-11692	One More Tomorrow	1977	12.00
❑ ST-11453 [B]	Unicorn 2	1976	18.00
UNIFICS, THE			
KAPP			
❑ KS-3582 [B]	Sittin' In at the Court of Love	1968	30.00
UNIQUES, THE (1)			
PAULA			
❑ LPS-2208	Golden Hits	1970	30.00
❑ LP-2194 [M]	Happening Now	1967	30.00
❑ LPS-2194 [S]	Happening Now	1967	30.00
❑ LP-2199 [M]	Playtime	1968	30.00
❑ LPS-2199 [S]	Playtime	1968	30.00
❑ LPS-2204	The Uniques	1969	30.00
❑ LP-2190 [M]	Uniquely Yours	1966	30.00
❑ LPS-2190 [S]	Uniquely Yours	1966	30.00
UNIT FOUR PLUS TWO			
LONDON			
❑ LL3427 [M]	Unit Four Plus Two #1	1965	80.00
❑ PS427 [P]	Unit Four Plus Two #1	1965	60.00
UNITED STATES DOUBLE QUARTET			
B.T. PUPPY			
❑ BTS-1005	Life Is Groovy	1969	50.00
UNITED STATES OF AMERICA, THE			
COLUMBIA			
❑ CL2814 [M]	The United States of America	1968	100.00
— Mono is promo only			
❑ CS9614 [S]	The United States of America	1968	80.00
— With outer bag			
❑ CS9614 [S]	The United States of America	1968	40.00
— Without outer bag			
UNIVERSAL ROBOT BAND			
RED GREG			
❑ 1003	Freak in the Light of the Moon	1978	25.00
UNREST			
MATADOR			
❑ OLE 024	Fuck Pussy Galore (And All Her Friends)	1993	12.00
TEEN BEAT			
❑ 77 [B]	Imperial FFRR	1992	18.00
❑ 35	Kustom Karnal Blackxploitation	1990	18.00
❑ 21	Malcolm X Park	1988	18.00
❑ 14	Tink of S.E.	1987	18.00
UNSANE			
AMPHETAMINE REPTILE			
❑ Amrep 039	Scattered, Smothered and Covered	1995	18.00

Number	Title	Yr	NM

MATADOR
❑ OLE 074	Peel Sessions	1994	18.00
❑ OLE 047	Singles '89-'92	1993	18.00
❑ OLE 070	Total Destruction	1994	18.00
❑ OLE 009	Unsane	1991	18.00
❑ OLE 009	Unsane for Tennis	1991	100.00

—*Original title of this LP with a different cover; quickly pulled from release and replaced with a "less offensive" cover*

RELAPSE
| ❑ RR6976 | Occupational Hazard | 1998 | 18.00 |

—*Picture disc*

UNSPOKEN WORD, THE
ASCOT
| ❑ AS16028 | Tuesday, April 19th | 1968 | 25.00 |

UNTAMED YOUTH, THE
ESTRUS
| ❑ ES1223 | Live in Las Vegas | 1995 | 15.00 |
| ❑ ES1231 | Planet Mace | 1997 | 15.00 |

NORTON
❑ ED215	More Gone Gassers	1990	10.00
❑ ED207	Some Kinda Fun!!	1989	12.00
❑ ED223	The Untamed Youth Are the Sophisticated International Playboys	1992	50.00
❑ ED263	Youth Runs Wild!	199?	12.00

UNUSUAL WE
PULSAR
| ❑ 10608 [B] | Unusual We | 1969 | 35.00 |

UPCHURCH, PHIL
BLUE THUMB
| ❑ BTS-6005 | Darkness, Darkness | 1971 | 25.00 |
| ❑ BTS-59 | Lovin' Feelin' | 1973 | 15.00 |

BOYD
| ❑ B-398 [M] | You Can't Sit Down | 1961 | 80.00 |
| ❑ BS-398 [S] | You Can't Sit Down | 1961 | 100.00 |

CADET
| ❑ LPS-840 | The Way I Feel | 1970 | 18.00 |
| ❑ LPS-826 | Upchurch | 1969 | 18.00 |

JAM
| ❑ 007 | Free and Easy | 198? | 15.00 |

KUDU
| ❑ 22 | Phil Upchurch and Tennyson Stevens | 1975 | 15.00 |

MARLIN
| ❑ 2209 | Phil Upchurch | 1978 | 15.00 |

MILESTONE
| ❑ MSP-9010 | Feeling Blue | 1968 | 18.00 |

UNITED ARTISTS
❑ UAL-3175 [M]	Big Hit Dances	1962	30.00
❑ UAS-6175 [S]	Big Hit Dances	1962	30.00
❑ UAL-3162 [M]	You Can't Sit Down, Part 2	1961	30.00
❑ UAS-6162 [S]	You Can't Sit Down, Part 2	1961	40.00

URGE OVERKILL
GEFFEN
| ❑ GEF-24818 | Exit the Dragon | 1995 | 18.00 |
| ❑ GEF-24529 | Saturation | 1993 | 15.00 |

—*All copies on orange vinyl*

TOUCH & GO
❑ 52	Americruiser	1990	15.00
❑ 37	Jesus Urge Superstar	1989	15.00
❑ 86 [10]	Stull	1992	35.00

—*Whitish vinyl original*

| ❑ 86 [10] | Stull | 1992 | 12.00 |

—*Black vinyl*

| ❑ 70 [B] | The Supersonic Storybook | 1991 | 15.00 |

URGENT
MANHATTAN
| ❑ ST-53004 | Cast the First Stone | 1984 | 12.00 |
| ❑ MLT-46680 | Thinking Out Loud | 1987 | 15.00 |

URIAH HEEP
CHRYSALIS
| ❑ CHR1204 [B] | Fallen Angel | 1978 | 12.00 |

COLUMBIA
| ❑ BFC40132 | Equator | 1985 | 10.00 |

MERCURY
❑ SRM-1-4057	Abominog	1982	10.00
❑ SRM-1-630 [B]	Demons and Wizards	1972	18.00
❑ 812313-1	Head First	1983	10.00
❑ SRM-1-614	Look at Yourself	1971	12.00
❑ SR-61319	Salisbury	1970	15.00
❑ SRM-1-1070	The Best of Uriah Heep	1976	10.00
❑ 822476-1	The Best of Uriah Heep	1986	10.00

—*Reissue of Mercury 1070*

❑ SRM-1-652 [B]	The Magician's Birthday	1972	18.00
❑ SR-61294	Uriah Heep	1970	18.00
❑ SRM-2-7503 [B]	Uriah Heep Live	1973	25.00

WARNER BROS.
| ❑ BS3013 [B] | Firefly | 1977 | 12.00 |

❑ BS2949	High and Mighty	1976	12.00
❑ BSK3145	Innocent Victim	1978	12.00
❑ BS2869	Return to Fantasy	1975	12.00
❑ BS2724	Sweet Freedom	1973	12.00
❑ W2800	Wonderworld	1974	12.00

URSO, PHIL
REGENT
| ❑ MG-6003 [M] | Sentimental Journey | 1956 | 50.00 |

SAVOY
| ❑ MG-15041 [10] | Bob Brookmeyer with Phil Urso | 1954 | 150.00 |
| ❑ MG-12056 [M] | The Philosophy of Urso | 1956 | 50.00 |

USA-EUROPEAN CONNECTION
MARLIN
| ❑ 2212 | Come Into My Heart | 1978 | 15.00 |
| ❑ 2231 | USA-European Connection | 1979 | 15.00 |

USA FOR AFRICA
COLUMBIA
| ❑ USA40043 | We Are the World | 1985 | 15.00 |

—*Actually a various-artists LP, but listed here because it was credited to "USA For Africa"*

USHER
ARISTA
| ❑ 14715 | 8701 | 2001 | 18.00 |
| ❑ LFPL6043 [DJ] | My Way | 1997 | 18.00 |

—*Promo-only "clean" version*

| ❑ 26008 | Usher | 1994 | 15.00 |

USSELTON, BILLY
KAPP
| ❑ KL-1051 [M] | Bill Usselton -- His First Album | 1957 | 50.00 |

UTFO
JIVE
| ❑ 1326 | Bag It and Bone It | 1991 | 25.00 |

SELECT
❑ 21629	Doin' It!	1989	15.00
❑ 21619	Lethal	1987	15.00
❑ 21616	Skeezer Pleezer	1986	15.00
❑ 21614	UTFO	1985	30.00

UTOPIA
BEARSVILLE
❑ BRK6991	Adventures in Utopia	1979	15.00
❑ BRK3487	Deface the Music	1980	15.00
❑ BRK6970 [B]	Oops! Wrong Planet	1977	15.00
❑ BR6965	RA	1977	15.00
❑ BRK3666	Swing to the Right	1982	15.00
❑ BR6954	Todd Rundgren's Utopia	1974	15.00
❑ BR6961	Todd Rundgren's Utopia/ Another Live	1975	15.00

NETWORK
| ❑ 60183 | Utopia | 1982 | 18.00 |

—*The second record has the same five songs on both sides*

PASSPORT
❑ PB6029	Oblivion	1984	12.00
❑ PB6044	POV	1985	12.00
❑ PB6053	Trivia	1986	12.00

RHINO
❑ RNLP70872	Adventures in Utopia	1987	10.00
❑ R1-70892	Anthology (1974-1985)	1989	12.00
❑ RNLP70873	Deface the Music	1987	10.00
❑ RNLP70870	Oops! Wrong Planet	1987	10.00
❑ RNLP70869	RA	1987	10.00
❑ RNLP70875	Swing to the Right	1987	10.00
❑ RNLP70865	Todd Rundgren's Utopia	1987	10.00
❑ RNLP70867	Todd Rundgren's Utopia/ Another Live	1987	10.00

V

VACHE, WARREN
AUDIOPHILE
| ❑ AP-196 | First Time Out | 1986 | 12.00 |

CONCORD JAZZ
❑ CJ-323	Easy Going	1987	12.00
❑ CJ-153	Iridescence	1981	12.00
❑ CJ-87	Jillian	1979	12.00
❑ CJ-203	Midtown Jazz	1982	12.00
❑ CJ-98	Polished Brass	1980	12.00
❑ CJ-392	Warm Evenings	1989	15.00

DREAMSTREET
| ❑ 101 | Blues Walk | 197? | 18.00 |

MONMOUTH-EVERGREEN
| ❑ 7081 | First Time Out | 197? | 18.00 |

VAGABONDS, THE
UNIQUE
| ❑ LP-112 [M] | The Vagabonds | 1957 | 30.00 |

VAGRANTS, THE
ARISTA
| ❑ AL-8459 | The Great Lost Vagrants Album | 1987 | 25.00 |

VALE, JERRY
COLUMBIA
❑ KG31543	All-Time Greatest Hits	1972	15.00
❑ KC31716	Alone Again (Naturally)	1972	12.00
❑ CL1955 [M]	Arrivederci, Roma	1963	15.00
❑ CS8755 [S]	Arrivederci, Roma	1963	18.00
❑ CL2181 [M]	Be My Love	1964	15.00
❑ CS8981 [S]	Be My Love	1964	18.00
❑ CL2225 [M]	Christmas Greetings from Jerry Vale	1964	15.00
❑ CS9025 [S]	Christmas Greetings from Jerry Vale	1964	18.00
❑ CL2530 [M]	Everybody Loves Somebody	1966	15.00
❑ KC32829	Free As the Wind	1974	12.00
❑ KG31938	Great Italian Hits	1973	15.00
❑ CL2489 [M]	Great Moments on Broadway	1966	15.00
❑ CS9289 [S]	Great Moments on Broadway	1966	18.00
❑ CL2313 [M]	Have You Looked Into Your Heart	1965	15.00
❑ CS9113 [S]	Have You Looked Into Your Heart	1965	18.00
❑ C30799	I Don't Know How to Love Her	1971	12.00
❑ CL1797 [M]	I Have But One Heart	1962	15.00
❑ CS8597 [S]	I Have But One Heart	1962	18.00
❑ CS9634	I Hear a Rhapsody	1968	18.00
❑ CL1114 [M]	I Remember Buddy	1958	18.00
❑ CS8069 [S]	I Remember Buddy	1959	25.00

—*Originals have red and black "6 eye" labels*

| ❑ CL1164 [M] | I Remember Russ | 1958 | 18.00 |
| ❑ CS8016 [S] | I Remember Russ | 1958 | 25.00 |

—*Originals have red and black "6 eye" labels*

❑ CL2444 [M]	It's Magic	1966	15.00
❑ CS9244 [S]	It's Magic	1966	18.00
❑ CL1529 [M]	Jerry Vale's Greatest Hits	1961	18.00
❑ CS8778 [R]	Jerry Vale's Greatest Hits	1963	15.00
❑ CS9982	Jerry Vale Sings 16 Greatest Hits of the 60's	1970	15.00
❑ C31147	Jerry Vale Sings the Great Hits of Nat King Cole	1972	15.00
❑ KG32083	Jerry Vale Sings the Great Love Songs	1973	15.00
❑ KC32454	Jerry Vale's World	1973	12.00
❑ C31021	Let It Be	1970	15.00
❑ C32238	Love Is a Many-Splendored Thing	1973	12.00
❑ CL2371 [M]	Moonlight Becomes You	1965	15.00
❑ CS9171 [S]	Moonlight Becomes You	1965	18.00
❑ CL2659 [M]	More Jerry Vale's Greatest Hits	1967	18.00
❑ CS9459 [S]	More Jerry Vale's Greatest Hits	1967	15.00
❑ CL2273 [M]	Standing Ovation!	1965	15.00
❑ CS9073 [S]	Standing Ovation!	1965	18.00
❑ CL2583 [M]	The Impossible Dream	1967	15.00
❑ CS9383 [S]	The Impossible Dream	1967	18.00
❑ C30389	The Italian Album	1970	12.00
❑ CG33615	The Italian Album/Arrivederci, Roma	1974	15.00
❑ CL2043 [M]	The Language of Love	1963	15.00
❑ CS8843 [S]	The Language of Love	1963	18.00
❑ CL2387 [M]	There Goes My Heart	1965	15.00
❑ CS9187 [S]	There Goes My Heart	1965	18.00
❑ CS8175 [S]	The Same Old Moon	1960	18.00
❑ CL1380 [M]	The Same Old Moon	1959	18.00
❑ CS9694	This Guy's in Love with You	1968	18.00
❑ CS9757	Till	1969	18.00
❑ CL2116 [M]	Till the End of Time	1964	15.00
❑ CS8916 [S]	Till the End of Time	1964	18.00
❑ CL2684 [M]	Time Alone Will Tell	1967	15.00
❑ CS9484 [S]	Time Alone Will Tell	1967	18.00
❑ C30104	We've Only Just Begun	1971	12.00
❑ CS9838	Where's the Playground Susie?	1969	18.00
❑ GP16	With Love, Jerry Vale	1969	18.00
❑ CL2774 [M]	You Don't Have to Say You Love Me	1968	18.00
❑ CS9574 [S]	You Don't Have to Say You Love Me	1968	18.00

COLUMBIA LIMITED EDITION
| ❑ LE10164 | Christmas Greetings from Jerry Vale | 197? | 12.00 |

—*Reissue*

| ❑ LE10058 | Till | 197? | 12.00 |

—*Reissue of 9757*

HARMONY
❑ HS11298	As Long As She Needs Me	1969	12.00
❑ KH30345	Born Free	1971	12.00
❑ HS11376	Hey Look Me Over	1970	12.00
❑ KH30759	More	1971	12.00
❑ KH32478	What a Wonderful World	1973	12.00

VALE, RICKY, AND THE SURFERS
STRAND
| ❑ SL-1104 [M] | Everybody's Surfin' | 1963 | 40.00 |
| ❑ SLS-1104 [S] | Everybody's Surfin' | 1963 | 50.00 |

Number	Title	Yr	NM

VALENS, RITCHIE

DEL-FI
❑ DFLP1225 [M]	His Greatest Hits	1963	350.00
—Black cover			
❑ DFLP1225 [M]	His Greatest Hits	1963	150.00
—White cover			
❑ DFLP1247 [M]	His Greatest Hits, Volume 2	1965	200.00
❑ DFLP1214 [M]	In Concert at Pacoima Jr. High	1960	250.00
❑ DFLP1206 [M]	Ritchie	1959	150.00
❑ DFLP1201 [M]	Ritchie Valens	1959	250.00
—Blue label with black border			
❑ DFLP1201 [M]	Ritchie Valens	1959	150.00
—Black label with "diamonds" border			

GUEST STAR
❑ GS-1484 [M]	The Original La Bamba	1963	30.00
❑ GSS-1484 [R]	The Original La Bamba	1963	25.00
❑ GS-1469 [M]	The Original Ritchie Valens	1963	30.00
❑ GSS-1469 [R]	The Original Ritchie Valens	1963	25.00

MGM
❑ GAS-117	Ritchie Valens (Golden Archive Series)	1970	30.00

RHINO
❑ RNLP-70233	In Concert at Pacoima Jr. High	1987	12.00
❑ RNLP-70232	Ritchie	1987	12.00
❑ RNLP-70231	Ritchie Valens	1987	12.00
❑ RNDF-200	The Best of Ritchie Valens	1981	15.00
❑ RNLP-70178	The Best of Ritchie Valens (Golden Archive Series)	1987	12.00
❑ RNBC-2798	The History of Ritchie Valens	198?	30.00

VALENS, RITCHIE / JERRY KOLE

CROWN
❑ CLP-5336 [M]	Ritchie Valens and Jerry Kole	1963	30.00

VALENTE, BENITA, AND THE PHILADELPHIA SINGERS

RCA RED SEAL
❑ 6559-1-RC	Gloria! Gloria! Christmas with Benita Valente	1987	12.00

VALENTE, CATERINA

DECCA
❑ DL4051 [M]	Arriba	1959	30.00
❑ DL8755 [M]	A Toast to the Girls	1958	30.00
❑ DL4052 [M]	Catarina: The Greatest in Any Language	1959	30.00
❑ DL4050 [M]	Caterina A La Carte	1959	30.00
❑ DL4504 [M]	Golden Favorites	1964	25.00
❑ DL74504 [R]	Golden Favorites	1964	15.00
❑ DL4035 [M]	More Schlagerparade	1959	30.00
❑ DL8436 [M]	Ole Caterina	1957	30.00
❑ DL8440 [M]	Plenty Valente!	1957	30.00
❑ DL8852 [M]	Schlagerparade	1958	25.00
❑ DL8203 [M]	The Hi-Fi Nightingale	1956	30.00

LONDON
❑ LL3441 [M]	Caterina Valente's Greatest Hits	1965	15.00
❑ PO441 [S]	Caterina Valente's Greatest Hits	1965	18.00
❑ ST 03108 [S]	Caterina Valente's Greatest Hits	196?	25.00
—Capitol Record Club edition			
❑ TW01190 [M]	Continental Favorites	196?	18.00
❑ TW91253 [M]	Fire and Frenzy	196?	18.00
—With Edmundo Ros			
❑ SW99019 [S]	Fire and Frenzy	196?	25.00
—With Edmundo Ros			
❑ SW99025 [S]	German Evergreens	196?	25.00
—With Silvio Francesco			
❑ TW91267 [M]	German Evergreens	196?	18.00
—With Silvio Francesco			
❑ LL3471 [M]	Go Latin!	196?	15.00
—With Silvio Francesco			
❑ PS471 [S]	Go Latin!	196?	18.00
—With Silvio Francesco			
❑ LL3362 [M]	I Happen to Like New York	196?	15.00
❑ PS362 [S]	I Happen to Like New York	196?	18.00
❑ PS473 [S]	Intimate Valente	196?	18.00
❑ LL3473 [M]	Intimate Valente	196?	15.00
❑ PS275 [S]	I Wish You Love	196?	18.00
—With Stanley Black			
❑ LL3275 [M]	I Wish You Love	196?	15.00
—With Stanley Black			
❑ TW91260 [M]	Miss Personality	196?	18.00
❑ LL3355 [M]	Songs I've Sung on the Perry Como Show	196?	15.00
❑ PS355 [S]	Songs I've Sung on the Perry Como Show	196?	18.00
❑ SW99292 [S]	South of the Border	196?	25.00
❑ TW91292 [M]	South of the Border	196?	18.00
❑ LL3307 [M]	Strictly U.S.A.	196?	15.00
❑ PS307 [S]	Strictly U.S.A.	196?	18.00
❑ PS536 [S]	Sweet Beat	1969	18.00
❑ LL3363 [M]	Valente and Violins	196?	15.00
❑ PS363 [S]	Valente and Violins	196?	18.00

LONDON PHASE 4
❑ SP-44181	Love	197?	30.00
❑ SP-44125	Silk and Latin	197?	30.00

PETERS INT'L.
❑ PLD-7046	Caterina Valente	197?	15.00
❑ PLD-7021	Golden Days	197?	15.00

RCA VICTOR
❑ LPM-2119 [M]	Classics with a Chaser	1960	25.00
❑ LSP-2119 [S]	Classics with a Chaser	1960	30.00
❑ LPM-2241 [M]	Superfonics	1961	25.00
❑ LSP-2241 [S]	Superfonics	1961	30.00

VALENTI, DINO

EPIC
❑ LN24335 [M]	Dino Valenti	1967	25.00
❑ BN26335 [S]	Dino Valenti	1967	25.00

VALENTINE, HILTON

CAPITOL
❑ ST-330 [B]	All in Your Head	1969	35.00

VALENTINE, JIMMIE

JUBILEE
❑ LP-9 [10]	Music to Beat By	1954	40.00

VALENTINO, MARK

SWAN
❑ SLP-508 [M]	Mark Valentino	1963	50.00

VALENTYNE, RUDY

ROULETTE
❑ R-25299 [M]	And Now... Rudy Valentyne	1965	25.00
❑ SR-25299 [S]	And Now... Rudy Valentyne	1965	30.00

VALHALLA

UNITED ARTISTS
❑ UAS-6730 [B]	Valhalla	1969	30.00

VALIDS, THE

AMBER
❑ 802 [M]	Accapella	1966	30.00

VALJEAN

CARLTON
❑ LP-146 [M]	Mashin' the Classics	1963	25.00
❑ STLP-146 [S]	Mashin' the Classics	1963	30.00
❑ LP-143 [M]	The Theme from Ben Casey	1962	25.00
❑ STLP-143 [S]	The Theme from Ben Casey	1962	30.00

VALLEE, RUDY

RCA VICTOR
❑ LPM-2507 [M]	Young Rudy Vallee	1961	30.00
❑ LSP-2507 [R]	Young Rudy Vallee	196?	25.00

VALLEY, JIM

FIRST AMERICAN
❑ 7710	Dance Inside Your Head	1977	18.00

LIGHT
❑ L3-5564	Family	197?	18.00

PANORAMA
❑ 104-S	Jim "Harpo" Valley	1968	40.00

VALLI, FRANKIE

MCA
❑ 5134	Heaven Above Me	1979	12.00
❑ 743	Heaven Above Me	1982	10.00
—Reissue of 5134			
❑ 3198	The Very Best of Frankie Valli	1980	12.00
❑ 756	The Very Best of Frankie Valli	1982	10.00
—Reissue of 3198			

MOTOWN
❑ M6-852	Inside You	1975	18.00
❑ M5-104V1	Motown Superstar Series, Vol. 4	1981	12.00

PHILIPS
❑ PHM200247 [M]	Frankie Valli -- Solo	1967	40.00
❑ PHS600247 [S]	Frankie Valli -- Solo	1967	30.00
❑ PHS600274	Timeless	1968	30.00

PRIVATE STOCK
❑ PS-2000	Closeup	1975	15.00
❑ PS-2001	Frankie Valli Gold	1975	15.00
❑ PS-7012	Hits	1978	15.00
❑ PS-7002 [B]	Lady Put the Light Out	1977	15.00
❑ PS-2006	Our Day Will Come	1975	15.00
❑ PS-2017	Valli	1976	15.00

WARNER BROS.
❑ BSK3233	Frankie Valli…Is the Word	1978	12.00

VALLI, JUNE

AUDIO FIDELITY
❑ AFSD-6214 [S]	June Valli Today	1969	25.00

MERCURY
❑ SR-60145 [S]	Do-It-Yourself Wedding Album	1959	30.00
❑ MG-20463 [M]	Do-It-Yourself Wedding Album	1959	25.00

RCA VICTOR
❑ LPM-1120 [M]	The Torch	1955	40.00

VAMPIRES, THE

UNITED ARTISTS
❑ UAL-3378 [M]	The Vampires at the Monster Ball	1964	30.00
❑ UAS-6378 [S]	The Vampires at the Monster Ball	1964	30.00

VAN DAMME, ART

BASF
❑ 22016	Invitation	197?	18.00
❑ 21755	Squeezing Art and Tender Flutes	197?	18.00
❑ 25257	Star Spangled Rhythm	197?	25.00
❑ 25113	The Many Moods of Art Van Damme	197?	25.00

CAPITOL
❑ H178 [10]	Cocktail Capers	1950	50.00
❑ T178 [M]	Cocktail Capers	1954	40.00
❑ L300 [10]	More Cocktail Capers	1952	50.00
❑ T300 [M]	More Cocktail Capers	1954	40.00

COLUMBIA
❑ CL1563 [M]	Accordion A La Mode	1960	30.00
❑ CS8363 [S]	Accordion A La Mode	1960	30.00
❑ CL2013 [M]	A Perfect Match	1963	18.00
❑ CS8813 [S]	A Perfect Match	1963	25.00
❑ CL1794 [M]	Art Van Damme Swings Sweetly	1962	18.00
❑ CS8594 [S]	Art Van Damme Swings Sweetly	1962	25.00
❑ CL1382 [M]	Everything's Coming Up Music	1959	30.00
❑ CS8177 [S]	Everything's Coming Up Music	1959	30.00
❑ CL801 [M]	Manhattan Time	1956	30.00
❑ CL6265 [10]	Martini Time	1953	40.00
❑ CL630 [M]	Martini Time	1955	30.00
❑ CL876 [M]	The Art of Van Damme	1956	30.00
❑ CL2585 [10]	The Art Van Damme Quintet	1956	40.00
❑ CL2192 [M]	The New Sound Of the Art Van Damme Septet	1964	15.00
❑ CS8992 [S]	The New Sound Of the Art Van Damme Septet	1964	18.00
❑ CL544 [M]	The Van Damme Sound	1955	30.00
❑ C2L7 [M]	They're Playing Our Song	1958	40.00

DESIGN
❑ DLP-905 [M]	3 of a Kind	196?	15.00
❑ SDLP-905 [R]	3 of a Kind	196?	10.00

HARMONY
❑ HL-7439 [M]	Music for Lovers	196?	15.00
❑ HS-11439 [S]	Music for Lovers	196?	12.00

PAUSA
❑ 7151	Art Van Damme and Friends	198?	12.00
❑ 7027	Blue World	197?	12.00
❑ 7066	Invitation	197?	12.00
❑ 7104	Keep Going	198?	12.00
❑ 7126	Squeezing Art and Tender Flutes	198?	12.00

PICKWICK
❑ PC-3009 [M]	Lover Man!	196?	15.00
❑ PCS-3009 [R]	Lover Man!	196?	10.00

SONIC ARTS
❑ 12	By Request	1980	15.00

VAN DER GRAAF GENERATOR

4 MEN WITH BEARDS
❑ 4M217LP [B]	H To He, Who Am The Only One		25.00
❑ 4M218LP [B]	Pawn Hearts		25.00
❑ 4M216LP [B]	The Least We Can Do Is Wave To Each Other		25.00

ABC DUNHILL
❑ DS50097	H to He Who Am the Only One	1971	30.00

CHARISMA
❑ CAS-1051 [B]	Pawn Hearts	1971	30.00

MERCURY
❑ SRM-1-1069 [B]	Godbluff	1975	25.00
❑ SRM-1-1096 [B]	Still Life	1976	25.00
❑ SR-61238	The Aerosol Grey Machine	1969	100.00
❑ SRM-1-1116 [B]	World Record	1976	25.00

PROBE
❑ CPLP-4515	The Least We Can Do Is Wave to Each Other	1970	30.00

PVC
❑ 9901 [B]	Vital	1979	30.00

VAN DERBUR, MARILYN

DECCA
❑ DL8770 [M]	Miss America	1958	40.00

VAN DYKE, DICK

COMMAND
❑ RS860SD [S]	Songs I Like	1963	30.00

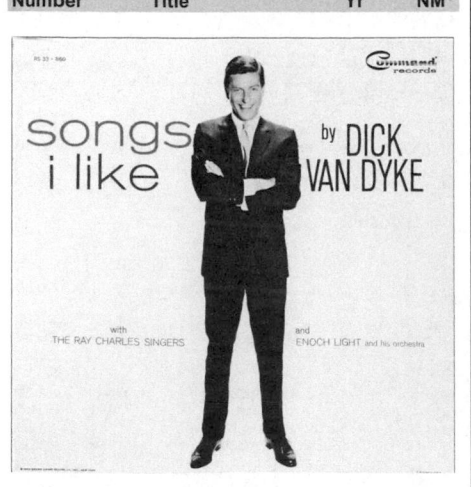

Number	Title	Yr	NM
☐ RS 33-860 [M]	Songs I Like	1963	30.00

VAN DYKE, EARL, AND THE SOUL BROTHERS

MOTOWN

☐ M-631 [M]	The Motown Sound	1965	40.00
☐ MS-631 [S]	The Motown Sound	1965	50.00

SOUL

☐ SS-715	The Earl of Funk	1970	40.00

VAN DYKE, LEROY

DOT

☐ DLP3693 [M]	Auctioneer	1966	25.00

HARMONY

☐ HS11308	I've Never Been Loved	196?	15.00

KAPP

☐ KS-3605	Greatest Hits	1969	18.00
☐ KS-3607	Just a Closer Walk with Thee	1969	18.00
☐ KS-3571	Lonesome Is	1968	18.00

MCA

☐ 145	Greatest Hits	1973	15.00

MERCURY

☐ MG-20950 [M]	Leroy Van Dyke at the Tradewinds	1964	12.00
☐ SR-60950 [S]	Leroy Van Dyke at the Tradewinds	1964	30.00
☐ MG-20716 [M]	Movin' Van Dyke	1963	25.00
☐ SR-60716 [S]	Movin' Van Dyke	1963	30.00
☐ MG-20922 [M]	Songs for Mom and Dad	1964	25.00
☐ SR-60922 [S]	Songs for Mom and Dad	1964	30.00
☐ MG-20802 [M]	The Great Hits of Leroy Van Dyke	1963	25.00
☐ SR-60802 [S]	The Great Hits of Leroy Van Dyke	1963	30.00
☐ MG-20682 [M]	Walk On By	1962	25.00
☐ SR-60682 [S]	Walk On By	1962	30.00

PLANTATION

☐ 516	Gospel Greats	1977	15.00

SUN

☐ 131	Golden Hits	1974	15.00

WARNER BROS.

☐ W1652 [M]	Country Hits	1966	18.00
☐ WS1652 [S]	Country Hits	1966	25.00
☐ W1618 [M]	The Leroy Van Dyke Show	1965	18.00
☐ WS1618 [S]	The Leroy Van Dyke Show	1965	25.00

WING

☐ MGW-12322 [M]	Movin'	196?	15.00
☐ SRW-16322 [S]	Movin'	196?	18.00
☐ MGW-12302 [M]	Out of Love	196?	15.00
☐ SRW-16302 [S]	Out of Love	196?	18.00

VAN DYKES, THE (2)

BELL

☐ 6004 [M]	Tellin' It Like It Is	1967	50.00
☐ S-6004 [S]	Tellin' It Like It Is	1967	60.00

VAN EATEN, LON AND DERREK

A&M

☐ SP-4507	Who Do You Outdo	1975	12.00

APPLE

☐ SMAS-3390	Brother	1972	18.00

VAN EPS, GEORGE

CAPITOL

☐ T2533 [M]	My Guitar	1966	18.00
☐ ST2533 [S]	My Guitar	1966	25.00
☐ ST2783	Seven String Guitar	1968	18.00
☐ ST-267	Soliloquy	1969	18.00

COLUMBIA

☐ CL929 [M]	Mellow Guitar	1956	40.00

CORINTHIAN

☐ 121	Mellow Guitar	198?	12.00

VAN HALEN

DCC COMPACT CLASSICS

☐ LPZ-2066	Van Halen	1998	40.00
—Audiophile vinyl			

WARNER BROS.

☐ 23985 [DJ]	1984	1984	40.00
—Promo on Quiex II vinyl			
☐ 23985 [B]	1984	1984	12.00
☐ 25394 [B]	5150	1986	12.00
☐ 45760	Balance	1995	30.00
☐ BSK3677 [B]	Diver Down	1982	12.00
☐ HS3540	Fair Warning	1981	12.00
☐ W1-26594	For Unlawful Carnal Knowledge	1991	30.00
—The only U.S. vinyl version was released through Columbia House			
☐ PRO705 [DJ]	Looney Tunes	1978	100.00
—Promo-only EP on red vinyl			
☐ 25732	OU812	1988	12.00
☐ BSK3075	Van Halen	1978	15.00
—Early pressings have "Burbank" labels			
☐ BSK3075	Van Halen	1979	12.00
—White/cream labels			
☐ HS3312	Van Halen II	1979	12.00
☐ HS3415	Women and Children First	1980	12.00

VAN HEUSEN, JIMMY

UNITED ARTISTS

☐ UAL-3494 [M]	Van Heusen Plays Van Heusen	1966	25.00
☐ UAS-6494 [S]	Van Heusen Plays Van Heusen	1966	30.00

VAN RONK, DAVE

CADET

☐ CA-50044	Songs for Aging Children	1973	25.00

FANTASY

☐ 24710	Dave Van Ronk	1972	25.00

FOLKLORE

☐ FRLP-14012 [M]	Dave Van Ronk, Folksinger	1963	30.00
☐ FRST-14012 [S]	Dave Van Ronk, Folksinger	1963	40.00
☐ FRLP-14025 [M]	Inside Dave Van Ronk	1964	30.00
☐ FRST-14025 [S]	Inside Dave Van Ronk	1964	40.00
☐ FRLP-14001 [M]	In the Tradition	1963	30.00
☐ FRST-14001 [S]	In the Tradition	1963	40.00

FOLKWAYS

☐ FTS31020	Black Mountain Blues	1968	30.00
☐ FS-3818 [M]	Dave Van Ronk Sings Ballads, Blues and Spirituals	1959	40.00
☐ FA-2383 [M]	Dave Van Ronk Sings Earthy Ballads and Blues	1961	40.00

MERCURY

☐ MG-20864 [M]	Dave Van Ronk and the Ragtime Jug Stompers	1964	30.00
☐ SR-60864 [S]	Dave Van Ronk and the Ragtime Jug Stompers	1964	30.00
☐ MG-20908 [M]	Just Dave Van Ronk	1964	30.00
☐ SR-60908 [S]	Just Dave Van Ronk	1964	30.00

POLYDOR

☐ 24-4052	Van Ronk	1972	25.00

VERVE FOLKWAYS

☐ FV-9006 [M]	Dave Van Ronk Sings the Blues	1965	30.00
☐ FVS-9006 [S]	Dave Van Ronk Sings the Blues	1965	30.00
☐ FV-9017 [M]	Gambler's Blues	1965	30.00
☐ FVS-9017 [S]	Gambler's Blues	1965	30.00

VERVE FORECAST

☐ FTS-3041 [M]	Dave Van Ronk and the Hudson Dusters	1968	30.00
☐ FT-3009 [M]	No Dirty Names	1967	30.00
☐ FTS-3009 [S]	No Dirty Names	1967	30.00

VAN VOOREN, MONIQUE

RCA VICTOR

☐ LPM-1553 [M]	Mink in Hi-Fi	1958	30.00

VAN ZANDT, TOWNES

POPPY

☐ PYS-40012	Delta Momma Blues	1970	18.00
☐ PYS-40001	For the Sake of a Song	1968	30.00
☐ PYS-5700	High, Low and In Between	1972	18.00
☐ PYS-40004	Our Mother, The Mountain	1969	18.00
☐ PP-LA004-F	The Late Great Townes Van Zandt	1973	18.00
☐ PYS-40007	Townes Van Zandt	1969	18.00

SUGAR HILL

☐ SH-1020	At My Window	1987	12.00
☐ SH-1026	Live and Obscure	1989	12.00

TOMATO

☐ 7013	Delta Momma Blues	1978	15.00
—Reissue of Poppy 40012			
☐ 7017 [B]	Flyin' Shoes	1978	15.00
☐ 7012	High, Low and In Between	1978	15.00
—Reissue of Poppy 5700			
☐ 7001	Live at the Old Quarter, Houston, Texas	1977	18.00
☐ 7015	Our Mother, The Mountain	1978	15.00
—Reissue of Poppy 40004			
☐ 7011	The Late Great Townes Van Zandt	1978	15.00
—Reissue of Poppy 004			
☐ 7014	Townes Van Zandt	1978	15.00
—Reissue of Poppy 40007			

VANCE, PAUL

SCEPTER

☐ SRM-557 [M]	Ma Vie (My Life)	1966	18.00
☐ SPS-557 [S]	Ma Vie (My Life)	1966	25.00

VANDALS, THE

KUNG FU

☐ 78762	Christmas with the Vandals: Oi to the World!	1996	12.00

VANDROSS, LUTHER

COTILLION

☐ SD9907	Luther	1976	50.00
—As "Luther			
☐ SD9916	This Close to You	1977	100.00
—As "Luther			

EPIC

☐ FE44308	Any Love	1988	10.00
☐ FE39196 [B]	Busy Body	1983	12.00
☐ FE38235	Forever, For Always, For Love	1982	12.00
☐ FE40415	Give Me the Reason	1986	10.00
☐ HE47451	Never Too Much	198?	30.00
—Half-speed mastered edition			
☐ FE37451	Never Too Much	1981	12.00
☐ E46789	Power of Love	1991	15.00
☐ E57775	Songs	1994	18.00
☐ E245320	The Best of Luther Vandross... The Best of Love	1989	15.00
☐ FE39882	The Night I Fell in Love	1985	10.00
☐ E57795	This Is Christmas	1995	15.00
☐ E67553	Your Secret Love	1996	15.00

VANGELIS

ARISTA

☐ AL-8545	Direct	1988	12.00

DEUTSCHE GRAMMAPHON

☐ 415196-1	Invisible Connections	1985	18.00
—All copies for U.S. distribution were pressed in West Germany			

POLYDOR

☐ 815732-1	Antarctica	198?	18.00
—Most copies may be imports			
☐ PD-1-6335	Chariots of Fire	1981	12.00
☐ 825384-1	Chariots of Fire	1985	10.00
—Reissue			
☐ PD-1-6199	China	1979	12.00
☐ 825245-1	Mask	1985	12.00
☐ 829663-1	Opera Sauvage	1986	10.00
—Reissue			
☐ 823396-1	Soil Festivities	1984	12.00
☐ 839518-1	Themes	1989	18.00

RCA VICTOR

☐ LPL1-5136	Albedo 0.39	1976	12.00
—Original prefix			
☐ AFL1-5136	Albedo 0.39	197?	10.00
—Reissue prefix			
☐ AFL1-3020	Beaubourg	1978	15.00
☐ AYL1-4387	Beaubourg	1982	10.00
—Best Buy Series" reissue			
☐ LPL1-5110	Heaven and Hell	1976	12.00
—Original prefix; tan label			
☐ AFL1-5110	Heaven and Hell	197?	10.00
—Reissue prefix; black label, dog near top			
☐ AFL1-2627	Spiral	1977	12.00
☐ DJL1-1849 [DJ]	The Vangelis Radio Special	1976	100.00
—Promo only music and interviews			
☐ AFL1-4397	To the Unknown Man	1982	10.00

VERTIGO

☐ VEL-1019	Earth	1974	50.00
—As "Vangelis O.			

VANILLA FUDGE

ATCO

☐ 90149	Mystery	1984	15.00
☐ SD 33-278	Near the Beginning	1969	18.00
☐ SD 33-244	Renaissance	1968	25.00
—Purple and brown label			
☐ SD 33-244	Renaissance	1969	15.00
—Yellow label			
☐ SD 33-303	Rock 'N' Roll	1969	18.00
☐ SD 33-237	The Beat Goes On	1968	25.00
—Purple and brown label			
☐ SD 33-237	The Beat Goes On	1969	15.00
—Yellow label			
☐ 33-237 [M]	The Beat Goes On	1968	80.00
☐ 90006	The Best of Vanilla Fudge	1982	12.00
☐ 33-224 [M]	Vanilla Fudge	1967	60.00
☐ SD 33-224 [S]	Vanilla Fudge	1967	25.00
—Purple and brown label			

Number	Title	Yr	NM
❏ SD 33-224 [S]	Vanilla Fudge	1969	15.00
— Yellow label			
❏ SD 33-224	Vanilla Fudge	197?	10.00
— Any later label			

SUNDAZED

❏ LP5168 [M]	Vanilla Fudge	2004	18.00
— Reissue on 180-gram vinyl			

VANILLA ICE

ULTRA

❏ ULT4019	Hooked	1990	40.00
— Basically the same album as "To the Extreme," which was not issued on vinyl in the United States			

VANITY FARE

PAGE ONE

❏ 2502 [B]	Early in the Morning	1970	35.00

VANNELLI, GINO

A&M

❏ SP-4664	A Pauper in Paradise	1977	12.00
❏ SP-4722	Brother to Brother	1978	12.00
❏ SP-3170	Brother to Brother	1981	10.00
— Reissue of 4722			
❏ SP-3139	Crazy Life	1981	10.00
— Reissue of 4395			
❏ SP-4395	Crazy Life	1973	15.00
❏ SP-3630	Powerful People	1974	12.00
❏ SP-3120	Powerful People	1981	10.00
— Reissue of 3630			
❏ SP-4533 [B]	Storm at Sunup	1975	12.00
❏ SP-3729	The Best of Gino Vannelli	1981	12.00
❏ SP-3260	The Best of Gino Vannelli	1982	10.00
— Reissue of 3729			
❏ SP-4596	The Gist of the Gemini	1976	12.00
❏ SP-3112	The Gist of the Gemini	1981	10.00
— Reissue of 4596			

ARISTA

❏ AB9539	Nightwalker	1981	12.00

CBS ASSOCIATED

❏ BFZ40337	Big Dreamers Never Sleep	1987	12.00

HME

❏ FZ40077	Black Cars	1985	12.00

MOBILE FIDELITY

❏ 1-041	Powerful People	1980	25.00
— Audiophile vinyl			

NAUTILUS

❏ NR-35	Brother to Brother	198?	30.00
— Audiophile vinyl			

VAN'T HOF, JASPER

PAUSA

❏ 7084	Live in Montreux	1979	12.00

VANWARMER, RANDY

16TH AVENUE

❏ D1-70553	I Am/Randy Vanwarmer	1988	12.00

BEARSVILLE

❏ BRK3561	The Beat of Love	1981	12.00
❏ BRK6988	Warmer	1979	12.00

VAPORS, THE

LIBERTY

❏ LT-1090	Magnets	1981	12.00
❏ LT-1049	New Clear Days	1981	12.00
— Reissue			

UNITED ARTISTS

❏ LT-1049	New Clear Days	1980	18.00

VARIATIONS, THE

JUSTICE

❏ JLP-212	Dig 'Em Up	196?	400.00

VAUGHAN, DENNY

BEVERLY HILLS

❏ BHS-19	Aberga-Denny	1969	18.00

CORAL

❏ CRL56038 [10]	Moonlight and Roses	1951	50.00

VAUGHAN, FRANKIE

PHILIPS

❏ PHM200006 [M]	Singin' Happy	1962	25.00
❏ PHS600006 [S]	Singin' Happy	1962	30.00

VAUGHAN, SARAH, AND BILLY ECKSTINE

EMARCY

❏ 822526-1	The Irving Berlin Songbook	1984	12.00

LION

❏ L-70088 [M]	Billy and Sarah	195?	30.00

MERCURY

❏ MG-20316 [M]	Sarah Vaughan and Billy Eckstine Sing the Best of Irving Berlin	1959	30.00
❏ SR-60002 [S]	Sarah Vaughan and Billy Eckstine Sing the Best of Irving Berlin	1959	40.00

VAUGHAN, SARAH, AND COUNT BASIE

PABLO

❏ 2312130	Send In the Clowns	1980	12.00

ROULETTE

❏ R52061 [M]	Count Basie and Sarah Vaughan	1960	30.00
❏ SR52061 [S]	Count Basie and Sarah Vaughan	1960	30.00
❏ SR42018	Count Basie and Sarah Vaughan	1968	18.00

VAUGHAN, SARAH; DINAH WASHINGTON; JOE WILLIAMS

ROULETTE

❏ R52108 [M]	We Three	1964	18.00
❏ SR52108 [S]	We Three	1964	25.00

VAUGHAN, SARAH

ACCORD

❏ SN-7195	Simply Divine	1981	12.00

ALLEGRO

❏ 3080 [10]	Early Sarah	195?	80.00
❏ 1592 [M]	Sarah Vaughan	1955	50.00
❏ 1608 [M]	Sarah Vaughan	1955	50.00

ALLEGRO ELITE

❏ 4106 [10]	Sarah Vaughan Sings	195?	30.00

ATLANTIC

❏ SD16037	Songs of the Beatles	1981	15.00

BRYLEN

❏ BN4411	Desires	198?	12.00
— Last name is misspelled "Vaughn"			

CBS MASTERWORKS

❏ FM42519	Brazilian Romance	1987	12.00
❏ FM37277	Gershwin Live!	1982	12.00
— With the Los Angeles Philharmonic Orchestra			

COLUMBIA

❏ CL660 [M]	After Hours with Sarah Vaughan	1955	50.00
❏ CL914 [M]	Linger Awhile	1956	50.00
❏ CL6133 [10]	Sarah Vaughan	1950	120.00
❏ CL745 [M]	Sarah Vaughan in Hi-Fi	1956	50.00

COLUMBIA SPECIAL PRODUCTS

❏ P14364	Linger Awhile	1978	12.00
— Reissue of Columbia 914			
❏ P13084	Sarah Vaughan in Hi-Fi	1976	12.00
— Reissue of Columbia 745			

CONCORD

❏ 0010 [M]	Sarah Vaughan Concert	1957	30.00

CORONET

❏ 277	Sarah Vaughan Belts the Hits	196?	18.00

EMARCY

❏ MG-26005 [10]	Images	1954	80.00
❏ MG-36058 [M]	In the Land of Hi-Fi	1956	80.00
❏ 826454-1	In the Land of Hi-Fi	1986	12.00
— Reissue of 36058			
❏ MG-36004 [M]	Sarah Vaughan	1955	80.00
❏ EMS-2-412	Sarah Vaughan Live	197?	15.00
❏ MG-36089 [M]	Sassy	1956	50.00
❏ MG-36109 [M]	Swingin' Easy	1957	50.00
❏ 814187-1	The George Gershwin Songbook	1983	15.00
❏ 824864-1	The Rodgers & Hart Songbook	1985	12.00

EVEREST ARCHIVE OF FOLK & JAZZ

❏ 250	Sarah Vaughan	197?	12.00
❏ 271	Sarah Vaughan, Volume 2	1973	12.00
❏ 325	Sarah Vaughan, Volume 3	197?	12.00

FORUM

❏ F-9034 [M]	Dreamy	196?	15.00
❏ SF-9034 [S]	Dreamy	196?	18.00

HARMONY

❏ HL7158 [M]	The Great Sarah Vaughan	196?	15.00

LION

❏ L70052 [M]	Tenderly	1958	30.00

MAINSTREAM

❏ MRL379	Feelin' Good	1973	18.00
❏ MRL419	More Sarah Vaughan from Japan	1974	18.00
❏ MRL2401	Sarah Vaughan "Live" In Japan	1973	25.00
❏ MRL404	Sarah Vaughan and the Jimmy Rowles Quintet	1974	18.00
❏ MRL361	Sarah Vaughan/Michel Legrand	1972	18.00
❏ MRL412 [B]	Send In the Clowns	1974	18.00
❏ MRL340	Time in My Life	1972	18.00

MASTERSEAL

❏ MS-55 [M]	Sarah Vaughan Sings	195?	30.00

MERCURY

❏ SR-60020 [S]	After Hours at the London House	1959	40.00
❏ MG-20383 [M]	After Hours at the London House	1958	40.00
❏ MG-20580 [M]	Close to You	1960	30.00
❏ SR-60240 [S]	Close to You	1960	40.00
❏ MG-25188 [10]	Divine Sarah	1955	100.00
❏ MGP-2-100 [M]	Great Songs from Hit Shows	1957	60.00
❏ MG-20244 [M]	Great Songs from Hit Shows, Vol. 1	1957	30.00
❏ SR-60041 [S]	Great Songs from Hit Shows, Vol. 1	1959	40.00
❏ MG-20245 [M]	Great Songs from Hit Shows, Vol. 2	1958	30.00
❏ SR-60078 [S]	Great Songs from Hit Shows, Vol. 2	1959	40.00
❏ MG-20223 [M]	In a Romantic Mood	1957	40.00
❏ MG-21122 [M]	It's a Man's World	1967	18.00
❏ SR-61122 [S]	It's a Man's World	1967	25.00
❏ MG-20617 [M]	My Heart Sings	1961	30.00
❏ SR-60617 [S]	My Heart Sings	1961	30.00
❏ MG-20441 [M]	No 'Count Sarah	1959	30.00
❏ SR-60116 [S]	No 'Count Sarah	1959	40.00
❏ MG-21069 [M]	Pop Artistry	1966	18.00
❏ SR-61069 [S]	Pop Artistry	1966	25.00
❏ MG-20326 [M]	Sarah Vaughan and Her Trio at Mr. Kelly's	1958	40.00
❏ MG-20094 [M]	Sarah Vaughan at the Blue Note	1956	40.00
❏ MG-20645 [M]	Sarah Vaughan's Golden Hits	1961	25.00
❏ SR-60645 [S]	Sarah Vaughan's Golden Hits	1961	30.00
— Original black label version			
❏ SR-60645 [S]	Sarah Vaughan's Golden Hits	1965	18.00
— Red label version with white "MERCURY" alone at top			
❏ SR-60645 [S]	Sarah Vaughan's Golden Hits	1968	15.00
— Red label with multiple Mercury logos along the label edge			
❏ MGP-2-101 [M]	Sarah Vaughan Sings George Gershwin	1957	60.00
❏ MG-20310 [M]	Sarah Vaughan Sings George Gershwin, Vol. 1	1958	30.00
❏ SR-60045 [S]	Sarah Vaughan Sings George Gershwin, Vol. 1	1959	40.00
❏ MG-20311 [M]	Sarah Vaughan Sings George Gershwin, Vol. 2	1958	30.00
❏ SR-60046 [S]	Sarah Vaughan Sings George Gershwin, Vol. 2	1959	40.00
❏ MG-21009 [M]	Sarah Vaughan Sings the Mancini Songbook	1965	18.00
❏ SR-61009 [S]	Sarah Vaughan Sings the Mancini Songbook	1965	25.00
❏ MG-21116 [M]	Sassy Swings Again	1967	18.00
❏ SR-61116 [S]	Sassy Swings Again	1967	25.00
❏ MG-20831 [M]	Sassy Swings the Tivoli	1962	25.00
❏ SR-60831 [S]	Sassy Swings the Tivoli	1962	30.00
❏ 826320-1	The Complete Sarah Vaughan on Mercury Vol. 1: Great Jazz years (1954-56)	1986	40.00
❏ 826327-1	The Complete Sarah Vaughan on Mercury Vol. 2: Great American Songs (1956-67)	1986	40.00
❏ 826333-1	The Complete Sarah Vaughan on Mercury Vol. 3: Great Show on Stage (1954-56)	1986	40.00
❏ 830721-1	The Complete Sarah Vaughan on Mercury Vol. 4 Part 1: Live in Europe (1963-64)	1987	40.00
❏ 830726-1	The Complete Sarah Vaughan on Mercury Vol. 4 Part 2: Sassy Swings Again	1987	40.00
❏ MG-25213 [10]	The Divine Sarah Sings	1955	100.00
❏ MG-20540 [M]	The Divine Sarah Vaughan	1960	30.00
❏ SR-60255 [S]	The Divine Sarah Vaughan	1960	30.00
❏ MG-20438 [M]	The Magic of Sarah Vaughan	1959	30.00
❏ SR-60110 [S]	The Magic of Sarah Vaughan	1959	40.00
❏ MG-21079 [M]	The New Scene	1966	18.00
❏ SR-61079 [S]	The New Scene	1966	25.00
❏ MG-20370 [M]	Vaughan and Violins	1958	40.00
❏ SR-60038 [S]	Vaughan and Violins	1959	40.00
❏ MG-20882 [M]	Vaughan with Voices	1963	25.00
❏ SR-60882 [S]	Vaughan with Voices	1963	30.00
❏ MG-20941 [M]	Viva Vaughan	1964	18.00
❏ SR-60941 [S]	Viva Vaughan	1964	25.00
❏ MG-20219 [M]	Wonderful Sarah	1957	40.00

METRO

❏ M-539 [M]	Tenderly	1965	15.00
❏ MS-539 [S]	Tenderly	1965	18.00

MGM

❏ E-3274 [M]	My Kinda Love	1955	60.00
— Combination of two 10-inch LPs on one 12-inch LP			
❏ E-544 [10]	Sarah Vaughan Sings	1951	120.00
❏ E-165 [10]	Tenderly	1950	120.00

MUSICRAFT

❏ 504	Divine Sarah	197?	12.00
❏ MVS-2006	Lover Man	1986	12.00
❏ MVS-2002	The Man I Love	1986	12.00

PABLO

❏ 2312125	Copacabana	1981	12.00
❏ 2310821	How Long	1978	12.00
❏ 2312101	I Love Brazil	1978	12.00
❏ 2310885	The Best of Sarah Vaughan	1983	12.00

Number	Title	Yr	NM
❑ 2405416	The Best of Sarah Vaughan	1990	12.00
❑ 2312111	The Duke Ellington Songbook One	1979	12.00
❑ 2312116	The Duke Ellington Songbook Two	1980	12.00

PABLO TODAY

Number	Title	Yr	NM
❑ 2312137	Crazy and Mixed Up	1982	12.00

PALACE

Number	Title	Yr	NM
❑ 5191 [M]	Sarah Vaughan Sings	195?	30.00

PICKWICK

Number	Title	Yr	NM
❑ PCS-3035	Fabulous Sarah Vaughan	197?	12.00

REMINGTON

Number	Title	Yr	NM
❑ RLP-1024 [10]	Hot Jazz	1953	200.00

RIVERSIDE

Number	Title	Yr	NM
❑ RLP2511 [10]	Sarah Vaughan Sings with John Kirby	1955	100.00

RONDO-LETTE

Number	Title	Yr	NM
❑ A-53 [M]	Sarah Vaughan Sings	1959	30.00
❑ A-35 [M]	Songs of Broadway	1958	30.00

ROULETTE

Number	Title	Yr	NM
❑ R52070 [M]	After Hours	1961	30.00
❑ SR52070 [S]	After Hours	1961	30.00
❑ R52060 [M]	Divine One	1960	30.00
❑ SR52060 [S]	Divine One	1960	30.00
❑ R52046 [M]	Dreamy	1960	30.00
❑ SR52046 [S]	Dreamy	1960	40.00
❑ RE-103	Echoes of an Era: The Sarah Vaughan Years	197?	18.00
❑ R52104 [M]	Lonely Hours	1963	18.00
❑ SR52104 [S]	Lonely Hours	1963	25.00
❑ R52118 [M]	Sarah Plus Two	1965	18.00
❑ SR52118 [S]	Sarah Plus Two	1965	25.00
❑ R52116 [M]	Sarah Sings Soulfully	1965	18.00
❑ SR52116 [S]	Sarah Sings Soulfully	1965	25.00
❑ R52123 [M]	Sarah Slightly Classical	1966	18.00
❑ SR52123 [S]	Sarah Slightly Classical	1966	25.00
❑ R52091 [M]	Snowbound	1962	25.00
❑ SR52091 [S]	Snowbound	1962	30.00
❑ R52100 [M]	Star Eyes	1963	18.00
❑ SR52100 [S]	Star Eyes	1963	25.00
❑ R52112 [M]	Sweet 'N Sassy	1964	18.00
❑ SR52112 [S]	Sweet 'N Sassy	1964	25.00
❑ R52092 [M]	The Explosive Side of Sarah	1962	25.00
❑ SR52092 [S]	The Explosive Side of Sarah	1962	30.00
❑ K-105 [M]	The Sarah Vaughan Years	196?	25.00
❑ SK-105 [S]	The Sarah Vaughan Years	196?	30.00
❑ K-105 [M]	The Sarah Vaughan Years	196?	25.00
❑ R52109 [M]	The World of Sarah Vaughan	1964	18.00
❑ SR52109 [S]	The World of Sarah Vaughan	1964	25.00
❑ R52082 [M]	You're Mine	1962	30.00
❑ SR52082 [S]	You're Mine	1962	30.00
—Black vinyl			
❑ SR52082 [S]	You're Mine	1962	60.00
—Red vinyl			

ROYALE

Number	Title	Yr	NM
❑ 18129 [10]	Sarah Vaughan and Orchestra	195?	30.00
❑ 18149 [10]	Sarah Vaughan and Orchestra	195?	30.00

—Includes recordings made on the Musicraft label in the 1940s

SCEPTER CITATION

Number	Title	Yr	NM
❑ CTN-18029	The Best of Sarah Vaughan	1972	15.00

SPIN-O-RAMA

Number	Title	Yr	NM
❑ 73 [M]	Sweet, Sultry and Swinging	196?	40.00
❑ S-73 [S]	Sweet, Sultry and Swinging	196?	50.00
❑ 114 [M]	The Divine Sarah Vaughan	196?	40.00
❑ S-114 [S]	The Divine Sarah Vaughan	196?	50.00

TIME-LIFE

Number	Title	Yr	NM
❑ SLGD-09	Legendary Singers: Sarah Vaughan	1985	18.00

TRIP

Number	Title	Yr	NM
❑ 5523	In the Land of Hi-Fi	197?	12.00
❑ 5501	Sarah Vaughan	197?	12.00
❑ 5517	Sassy	197?	12.00
❑ 5551	Swingin' Easy	197?	12.00

WING

Number	Title	Yr	NM
❑ MGW-12123 [M]	All Time Favorites	1963	15.00
❑ SRW-16123 [S]	All Time Favorites	1963	18.00
❑ MGW-12280 [M]	The Magic of Sarah Vaughan	1964	15.00
❑ SRW-16280 [S]	The Magic of Sarah Vaughan	1964	18.00

VAUGHAN, STEVIE RAY

EPIC

Number	Title	Yr	NM
❑ 8E839609 [PD]	Couldn't Stand the Weather	1984	200.00
❑ FE39304 [B]	Couldn't Stand the Weather	1984	18.00
❑ E66217	Greatest Hits	1995	18.00
❑ FE45024 [B]	In Step	1989	18.00
❑ E240511 [B]	Live Alive	1986	25.00
❑ FE40036 [B]	Soul to Soul	1985	18.00
❑ BFE38734 [B]	Texas Flood	1983	18.00
❑ E47390	The Sky Is Crying	1991	30.00

VAUGHAN BROTHERS, THE

CBS ASSOCIATED

Number	Title	Yr	NM
❑ Z46625	Family Style	1990	25.00

VAUGHN, BILLY

ABC

Number	Title	Yr	NM
❑ 4005	16 Great Performances	1974	12.00

DOT

Number	Title	Yr	NM
❑ DLP3625 [M]	12 Golden Hits from Latin America	1965	15.00
❑ DLP25625 [S]	12 Golden Hits from Latin America	1965	18.00
❑ DLP3497 [M]	1962's Greatest Hits	1963	15.00
❑ DLP25497 [S]	1962's Greatest Hits	1963	18.00
❑ DLP25882	A Current Set of Standards	1968	12.00
❑ DLP3751 [M]	Alfie	1966	15.00
❑ DLP25751 [S]	Alfie	1966	18.00
❑ DLP-25897	Alone with Today	1968	12.00
❑ DLP3593 [M]	Another Hit Album!	1964	15.00
❑ DLP25593 [S]	Another Hit Album!	1964	18.00
❑ DLP25841	As Requested	1968	12.00
❑ DLP3458 [M]	A Swingin' Safari	1962	18.00
❑ DLP25458 [S]	A Swingin' Safari	1962	25.00
❑ DLP3396 [M]	Berlin Melody	1961	18.00
❑ DLP25396 [S]	Berlin Melody	1961	25.00
❑ DLP3156 [M]	Billy Vaughn Plays	1959	18.00
❑ DLP25156 [S]	Billy Vaughn Plays	1959	25.00
❑ DLP3260 [M]	Billy Vaughn Plays Stephen Foster	1960	18.00
❑ DLP25260 [S]	Billy Vaughn Plays Stephen Foster	1960	25.00
❑ DLP3119 [M]	Billy Vaughn Plays the Million Sellers	1958	18.00
❑ DLP25119 [S]	Billy Vaughn Plays the Million Sellers	1959	25.00
❑ DLP3800 [M]	Billy Vaughn Presents Friends from Rio Playing "Something Stupid	1967	15.00
❑ DLP25800 [S]	Billy Vaughn Presents Friends from Rio Playing "Something Stupid	1967	12.00
❑ DLP3165 [M]	Blue Hawaii	1959	18.00
❑ DLP25165 [S]	Blue Hawaii	1959	25.00
❑ DLP3559 [M]	Blue Velvet & 1963's Great Hits	1964	15.00
❑ DLP25559 [S]	Blue Velvet & 1963's Great Hits	1964	18.00
❑ DLP3424 [M]	Chapel by the Sea	1962	18.00
❑ DLP25424 [S]	Chapel by the Sea	1962	25.00
❑ DLP3148 [M]	Christmas Carols	1958	18.00
❑ DLP25985	Everything Is Beautiful	1970	12.00
❑ DLP3578 [M]	Forever	1964	15.00
❑ DLP25578 [S]	Forever	1964	18.00
❑ DLP3201 [M]	Golden Hits	1959	18.00
❑ DLP25201 [S]	Golden Hits	1959	25.00
❑ DLP3811 [M]	Golden Hits/The Best of Billy Vaughn	1967	15.00
❑ DLP25811 [S]	Golden Hits/The Best of Billy Vaughn	1967	12.00
❑ DLP3205 [M]	Golden Saxophones	1959	18.00
❑ DLP25205 [S]	Golden Saxophones	1959	25.00
❑ DLP3280 [M]	Golden Waltzes	1961	18.00
❑ DLP25280 [S]	Golden Waltzes	1961	25.00
❑ DLP3698 [M]	Great Country Hits	1966	15.00
❑ DLP25698 [S]	Great Country Hits	1966	18.00
❑ DLP3558 [M]	Greatest Boogie Woogie Hits	1963	15.00
❑ DLP25558 [S]	Greatest Boogie Woogie Hits	1963	18.00
❑ DLP3409 [M]	Greatest String Band Hits	1962	18.00
❑ DLP25409 [S]	Greatest String Band Hits	1962	25.00
❑ DLP3288 [M]	Great Golden Hits	1960	18.00
❑ DLP25288 [S]	Great Golden Hits	1960	25.00
❑ DLP25899	Have Yourself a Merry Merry Christmas	1968	15.00
❑ DLP3813 [M]	I Love You	1967	15.00
❑ DLP25813 [S]	I Love You	1967	12.00
❑ DLP3045 [M]	Instrumental Souvenirs	1957	18.00
❑ DLP3796 [M]	Josephine	1967	15.00
❑ DLP25796 [S]	Josephine	1967	12.00
❑ DLP3140 [M]	La Paloma	1959	18.00
❑ DLP25140 [S]	La Paloma	1959	25.00
❑ DLP3275 [M]	Linger Awhile	1960	18.00
❑ DLP25275 [S]	Linger Awhile	1960	25.00
❑ DLP3322 [M]	Look for a Star	1960	18.00
❑ DLP25322 [S]	Look for a Star	1960	25.00
❑ DLP3064 [M]	Melodies in Gold	1957	18.00
❑ DLP25064 [R]	Melodies in Gold	196?	12.00
❑ DLP3628 [M]	Mexican Pearls	1965	15.00
❑ DLP25628 [S]	Mexican Pearls	1965	18.00
❑ DLP3679 [M]	Michelle	1966	15.00
❑ DLP25679 [S]	Michelle	1966	18.00
❑ DLP3654 [M]	Moon Over Naples	1965	15.00
❑ DLP25654 [S]	Moon Over Naples	1965	18.00
❑ DLP3086 [M]	Music for the Golden Hours	1958	18.00
❑ DLP25086 [R]	Music for the Golden Hours	196?	12.00
❑ DLP25911	Nashville Saxophones	1969	12.00
❑ DLP3540 [M]	Number One Hits, Vol. #1	1963	15.00
❑ DLP25540 [S]	Number One Hits, Vol. #1	1963	18.00
❑ DLP3828 [M]	Ode to Billy Joe	1967	15.00
❑ DLP25828 [S]	Ode to Billy Joe	1967	12.00
❑ DLP3366 [M]	Orange Blossom Special and Wheels	1961	18.00
❑ DLP25366 [S]	Orange Blossom Special and Wheels	1961	25.00
❑ DLP3605 [M]	Pearly Shells	1965	15.00
❑ DLP25605 [S]	Pearly Shells	1965	18.00
❑ DLP25837	Pretty Country	1968	12.00
❑ DLP5857	Quietly Wild	1968	12.00
❑ DLP3100 [M]	Sail Along Silv'ry Moon	1958	18.00
❑ DLP25100 [S]	Sail Along Silv'ry Moon	1959	25.00
❑ DLP3523 [M]	Sukiyaki and 11 Hawaiian Hits	1963	15.00
❑ DLP25523 [S]	Sukiyaki and 11 Hawaiian Hits	1963	18.00
❑ DLP3782 [M]	Sweet Maria	1967	15.00
❑ DLP25782 [S]	Sweet Maria	1967	12.00
❑ DLP3001 [M]	Sweet Music and Memories	1955	30.00
—Maroon label			
❑ DLP3001 [M]	Sweet Music and Memories	1957	18.00
—Black label			
❑ DLP25001 [R]	Sweet Music and Memories	196?	12.00
❑ DLP3788 [M]	That's Life & Pineapple Market	1967	15.00
❑ DLP25788 [S]	That's Life & Pineapple Market	1967	12.00
❑ DLP3016 [M]	The Golden Instrumentals	1956	30.00
—Maroon label			
❑ DLP3016 [M]	The Golden Instrumentals	1957	18.00
—Black label			
❑ DLP25016 [R]	The Golden Instrumentals	196?	12.00
❑ DLP3276 [M]	Theme from A Summer Place	1960	18.00
❑ DLP25276 [S]	Theme from A Summer Place	1960	25.00
❑ DLP3349 [M]	Theme from The Sundowners	1960	18.00
❑ DLP25349 [S]	Theme from The Sundowners	1960	25.00
❑ DLP3442 [M]	The Shifting, Whispering Sands	1962	18.00
❑ DLP25442 [S]	The Shifting, Whispering Sands	1962	25.00
❑ DLP25937	The Windmills of Your Mind	1969	12.00
❑ DLP25969	True Grit	1969	12.00
❑ DLP25975	Winter World of Love	1970	12.00

HAMILTON

Number	Title	Yr	NM
❑ HLP113 [M]	Golden Gems	196?	15.00
❑ HLP12113 [S]	Golden Gems	196?	15.00
❑ HLP162 [M]	Songs I Wrote	196?	15.00
❑ HLP12162 [S]	Songs I Wrote	196?	15.00
❑ HLP147 [M]	Strauss Waltz Concert	196?	15.00
❑ HLP12147 [S]	Strauss Waltz Concert	196?	15.00

MCA

Number	Title	Yr	NM
❑ 27018	Blue Hawaii	198?	10.00
—Budget-line reissue			
❑ 801	La Paloma	198?	10.00
—Budget-line reissue			
❑ 4164	The Best of Billy Vaughn	198?	15.00

PARAMOUNT

Number	Title	Yr	NM
❑ PAS-6025	An Old Fashioned Love Song	1972	12.00
❑ PAS-1031	Billy Vaughn Plays His Greatest Hits	1974	15.00
❑ PAS-6044	Country's Greatest Hits	1973	12.00
❑ PAS-1033	Electrified	1974	12.00
❑ PAS-5037	I Don't Know How to Love Him	1971	12.00
❑ PAS-6035	Soundstage!	1972	12.00
❑ PAS-5032	Theme from Love Story	1971	12.00

PICKWICK

Number	Title	Yr	NM
❑ SPC-3093	Embraceable You	197?	12.00
❑ SPC-3213	Moon River	197?	12.00
❑ SPC-3146	Up, Up and Away	197?	12.00

RANWOOD

Number	Title	Yr	NM
❑ 7025	Billy Vaughn and His Orchestra Play 22 Greatest Hits	1982	15.00

VAUGHN, FATHER TOM

CONCORD JAZZ

Number	Title	Yr	NM
❑ CJ-16	Joyful Jazz	1976	15.00

RCA VICTOR

Number	Title	Yr	NM
❑ LPM-3708 [M]	Cornbread (Meat Loaf, Greens and Deviled Eggs)	1967	25.00
❑ LSP-3708 [S]	Cornbread (Meat Loaf, Greens and Deviled Eggs)	1967	18.00
❑ LPM-3577 [M]	Jazz In Concert at the Village Gate	1966	18.00
❑ LSP-3577 [S]	Jazz In Concert at the Village Gate	1966	25.00
❑ LPM-3845 [M]	Motor City Soul	1967	25.00
❑ LSP-3845 [S]	Motor City Soul	1967	18.00

VAUGHN, ROBERT

MGM

Number	Title	Yr	NM
❑ E-4488 [M]	Readings from Hamlet	1962	30.00
❑ SE-4488 [S]	Readings from Hamlet	1962	30.00

VAUGHT, BOB, AND THE RENEGADES

GNP CRESCENDO

Number	Title	Yr	NM
❑ GNP-83 [M]	Surf Crazy	1963	30.00
❑ GNPS-83 [S]	Surf Crazy	1963	40.00

VEE, BOBBY

LIBERTY

Number	Title	Yr	NM
❑ LRP-3385 [M]	30 Big Hits From the 60's	1964	30.00
❑ LST-7385 [S]	30 Big Hits From the 60's	1964	30.00
❑ LRP-3448 [M]	30 Big Hits From the 60's, Volume 2	1966	30.00
❑ LST-7448 [S]	30 Big Hits From the 60's, Volume 2	1966	30.00
❑ LRP-3232 [M]	A Bobby Vee Recording Session	1962	30.00
❑ LST-7232 [S]	A Bobby Vee Recording Session	1962	40.00
❑ LRP-3181 [M]	Bobby Vee	1961	40.00

Number	Title	Yr	NM
❑ LST-7181 [S]	Bobby Vee	1961	50.00
❑ LRP-3393 [M]	Bobby Vee Live on Tour	1965	30.00
❑ LST-7393 [S]	Bobby Vee Live on Tour	1965	30.00
❑ LRP-3228 [M]	Bobby Vee Meets the Crickets	1962	40.00
❑ LST-7228 [S]	Bobby Vee Meets the Crickets	1962	50.00
❑ LRP-3289 [M]	Bobby Vee Meets the Ventures	1963	40.00
❑ LST-7289 [S]	Bobby Vee Meets the Ventures	1963	50.00
❑ LRP-3245 [M]	Bobby Vee's Golden Greats	1962	30.00
❑ LST-7245 [S]	Bobby Vee's Golden Greats	1962	40.00
❑ LM-51008	Bobby Vee's Golden Greats	198?	10.00
❑ LRP-3464 [M]	Bobby Vee's Golden Greats, Volume 2	1966	25.00
❑ LST-7464 [S]	Bobby Vee's Golden Greats, Volume 2	1966	30.00
❑ LRP-3205 [M]	Bobby Vee Sings Hits of the Rockin' 50's	1961	40.00
❑ LST-7205 [S]	Bobby Vee Sings Hits of the Rockin' 50's	1961	50.00
❑ LRP-3352 [M]	Bobby Vee Sings the New Sound from England!	1964	30.00
❑ LST-7352 [S]	Bobby Vee Sings the New Sound from England!	1964	30.00
❑ LRP-3165 [M]	Bobby Vee Sings Your Favorites	1960	50.00
❑ LST-7165 [S]	Bobby Vee Sings Your Favorites	1960	80.00
❑ LRP-3186 [M]	Bobby Vee With Strings and Things	1961	40.00
❑ LST-7186 [S]	Bobby Vee With Strings and Things	1961	50.00
❑ LRP-3534 [M]	Come Back When You Grow Up	1967	25.00
❑ LST-7534 [S]	Come Back When You Grow Up	1967	30.00
❑ LST-7592	Do What You Gotta Do	1968	30.00
❑ LST-7612	Gates, Grills and Railings	1969	30.00
❑ LRP-3336 [M]	I Remember Buddy Holly	1963	40.00
❑ LST-7336 [S]	I Remember Buddy Holly	1963	50.00
❑ LN-10223	I Remember Buddy Holly	198?	10.00
❑ LST-7554 [S]	Just Today	1968	30.00
❑ LST-3554 [M]	Just Today	1968	40.00

— Cover is stereo with "Audition Mono Not for Sale" sticker, but the label is regular stock mono

Number	Title	Yr	NM
❑ LRP-3480 [M]	Look at Me Girl	1966	25.00
❑ LST-7480 [S]	Look at Me Girl	1966	30.00
❑ LRP-3267 [M]	Merry Christmas from Bobby Vee	1962	30.00
❑ LST-7267 [S]	Merry Christmas from Bobby Vee	1962	40.00
❑ LRP-3211 [M]	Take Good Care of My Baby	1962	30.00
❑ LST-7211 [S]	Take Good Care of My Baby	1962	40.00
❑ LRP-3285 [M]	The Night Has a Thousand Eyes	1963	30.00
❑ LST-7285 [S]	The Night Has a Thousand Eyes	1963	40.00

SUNSET

Number	Title	Yr	NM
❑ SUM-1162 [M]	A Forever Kind of Love	1967	12.00
❑ SUS-5162 [S]	A Forever Kind of Love	1967	15.00
❑ SUM-1111 [M]	Bobby Vee	1966	12.00
❑ SUS-5111 [S]	Bobby Vee	1966	15.00
❑ SUM-1186 [M]	The Christmas Album	1967	15.00

— Reissue of Liberty album with two fewer tracks

Number	Title	Yr	NM
❑ SUS-5186 [S]	The Christmas Album	1967	15.00

UNITED ARTISTS

Number	Title	Yr	NM
❑ LT-1008	Bobby Vee's Golden Greats	1980	12.00
❑ UA-LA025-G2	Legendary Masters Series	1973	300.00

— Withdrawn before release, but a few copies survived

Number	Title	Yr	NM
❑ UAS-5656	Nothin' Like a Sunny Day	1972	15.00
❑ UA-LA085-G	Robert Thomas Velline	1973	25.00
❑ UA-LA332-E	The Very Best of Bobby Vee	1975	15.00

VEGA, AL

PRESTIGE

Number	Title	Yr	NM
❑ PRLP-152 [10]	Al Vega Piano Solos With Bongos	1953	150.00

VEGA, SUZANNE

A&M

Number	Title	Yr	NM
❑ 7502152931	Days of Open Hand	1990	15.00
❑ SP-17472 [DJ]	Portrait of an Artist	1987	18.00

— Promo-only 7-song sampler

Number	Title	Yr	NM
❑ SP-5136	Solitude Standing	1987	10.00
❑ SP-6-5072	Suzanne Vega	1985	12.00

VEGA, TATA

TAMLA

Number	Title	Yr	NM
❑ T6-347S1	Full Speed Ahead	1976	18.00
❑ T8-370M1	Givin' All My Love	1980	30.00
❑ T6-353S1	Totally Tata	1977	18.00
❑ T7-360R1	Try My Love	1978	18.00

VEGA BROTHERS, THE

MCA

Number	Title	Yr	NM
❑ 5686	The Vega Brothers	1986	10.00

VEGAS, PAT AND LOLLY

MERCURY

Number	Title	Yr	NM
❑ MG-21059 [M]	At the Haunted House	1966	30.00
❑ SR-61059 [S]	At the Haunted House	1966	40.00

VELASCO, VI

VEE JAY

Number	Title	Yr	NM
❑ VJ-1135 [M]	The Vi Velasco Album	1965	25.00

VELEZ, MARTHA

POLYDOR

Number	Title	Yr	NM
❑ PD5034	Hypnotized	1972	18.00

SIRE

Number	Title	Yr	NM
❑ SR6040	American Heartbeat	1977	12.00
❑ SASD-7515	Escape from Babylon	1976	12.00

— Produced by Bob Marley

Number	Title	Yr	NM
❑ SES-97008	Fiends and Angels	1969	30.00
❑ SES-7409	Matinee Weepers	1973	18.00

VELVET, JIMMY

UNITED ARTISTS

Number	Title	Yr	NM
❑ UAS-6653	A Touch of Velvet	1968	30.00

VELVET TONE

Number	Title	Yr	NM
❑ 501	A Touch of Velvet	1968	60.00

VELVET ELVIS

ENIGMA

Number	Title	Yr	NM
❑ 73300 [B]	Velvet Elvis	1988	15.00

VELVET MONKEYS

ROUGH TRADE

Number	Title	Yr	NM
❑ RUS102	Rake	1990	15.00

— Band includes Thurston Moore (Sonic Youth), J Mascis (Dinosaur Jr), etc.

VELVET NIGHT

METROMEDIA

Number	Title	Yr	NM
❑ MD-1028	Velvet Night	1970	30.00

VELVET REVOLVER

RCA

Number	Title	Yr	NM
❑ 59794-1	Contraband	2004	30.00

VELVET UNDERGROUND, THE

4 MEN WITH BEARDS

Number	Title	Yr	NM
❑ 4M137LP [B]	Another View		25.00
❑ 4M154LP [B]	The Velvet Underground & Nico		25.00
❑ 4M156LP [B]	Velvet Underground		25.00
❑ 4M136LP [B]	VU: A Collection of Previously Unreleased Recordings		25.00
❑ 4M155LP [B]	White Light/White Heat		25.00

COTILLION

Number	Title	Yr	NM
❑ SD9500 [DJ]	Live at Max's Kansas City	1972	75.00

White label promo with "d/j copy monaural" sticker on front cover, which in this case is odd because all copies are mono!

Number	Title	Yr	NM
❑ SD9500	Live at Max's Kansas City	1972	25.00

— Original pressing has a light blue label

Number	Title	Yr	NM
❑ SD9500	Live at Max's Kansas City	197?	18.00

— Reissue with purplish label

Number	Title	Yr	NM
❑ SD9500	Live at Max's Kansas City	198?	15.00

— Reissue with purplish label and bar code on back cover

Number	Title	Yr	NM
❑ SD9500	Live at Max's Kansas City	2001	12.00

— Rhino/Scorpio reissue; light blue label

Number	Title	Yr	NM
❑ SD9034 [S]	Loaded	1970	150.00

— White label promo; not the monaural version, this one has no sticker on the cover and has the "SD" prefix on the label

Number	Title	Yr	NM
❑ SD9034 [S]	Loaded	1970	25.00

— Original pressing has a light blue label

Number	Title	Yr	NM
❑ SD9034 [S]	Loaded	197?	18.00

— Reissue with purplish label

Number	Title	Yr	NM
❑ SD9034 [S]	Loaded	198?	15.00

— Reissue with purplish label and bar code on back cover

Number	Title	Yr	NM
❑ 9034 [M]	Loaded	1970	250.00

— Mono is white label promo only; "d/j copy monaural" sticker on front cover; no "SD" prefix on label

Number	Title	Yr	NM
❑ SD9034 [S]	Loaded	2001	12.00

— Rhino/Scorpio reissue; purplish label

Number	Title	Yr	NM
❑ R19034 [B]	Loaded	2014	40.00

MERCURY

Number	Title	Yr	NM
❑ SRM-2-7504 [B]	1969 (Live)	1974	18.00

— Reissues with Chicago skyline labels

Number	Title	Yr	NM
❑ SRM-2-7504	1969 (Live)	1974	50.00

— Originals with red labels

Number	Title	Yr	NM
❑ SRM-2-7504 [DJ]	1969 (Live)	1974	100.00

— White label promo

Number	Title	Yr	NM
❑ SRM-2-7504	1969 (Live)	1983	25.00

— Reissue with black labels; non-gatefold cover; no bar code on back

MGM

Number	Title	Yr	NM
❑ M3G4950	Archetypes	1974	25.00
❑ M3G4950 [DJ]	Archetypes	1974	40.00

— White label promo

Number	Title	Yr	NM
❑ SW-95722	Archetypes	1974	30.00

— Longines Symphonette edition

Number	Title	Yr	NM
❑ SE-4617	The Velvet Underground	1969	50.00

— With "BMI" publishing credit

Number	Title	Yr	NM
❑ SE-4617 [DJ]	The Velvet Underground	1969	400.00

— Yellow label promo

Number	Title	Yr	NM
❑ SE-4617 [DJ]	The Velvet Underground	1969	250.00

— White label promo

Number	Title	Yr	NM
❑ SE-4617	The Velvet Underground	1971	40.00

— With "ASCAP" publishing credit

Number	Title	Yr	NM
❑ GAS-131	The Velvet Underground (Golden Archive Series)	1970	40.00

— Blue and gold label stock copy

Number	Title	Yr	NM
❑ GAS-131 [DJ]	The Velvet Underground (Golden Archive Series)	1970	100.00

— Yellow label promo

Number	Title	Yr	NM
❑ GAS-131 [DJ]	The Velvet Underground (Golden Archive Series)	1970	100.00

— White label promo

POLYDOR

Number	Title	Yr	NM
❑ B0017649-01 [B]	Scepter Studios Sessions	2012	30.00
❑ 8232901 [S]	The Velvet Underground and Nico	2008	25.00

PRIDE

Number	Title	Yr	NM
❑ 0022	Lou Reed and the Velvet Underground	1973	18.00

— Tan label; label calls this "That's the Story of My Life

Number	Title	Yr	NM
❑ 0022 [DJ]	Lou Reed and the Velvet Underground	1973	50.00

— White label; label calls this "That's the Story of My Life

SUNDAZED

Number	Title	Yr	NM
❑ VU4002 [Mono]	The Quine Tapes	2010	200.00
❑ VU4003 [B]	The Verve/MGM Albums	2012	200.00
❑ LP5466 [B]	Velvet Underground	2014	30.00

VERVE

Number	Title	Yr	NM
❑ 826284-1	1969 (Live)	1985	15.00

— Reissue of Mercury SRM-2-7504

Number	Title	Yr	NM
❑ 829405-1	Another View	1986	15.00
❑ 815454-1	The Velvet Underground	1985	15.00

— Reissue of MGM SE-4617

Number	Title	Yr	NM
❑ V-5008 [M]	The Velvet Underground and Nico	1967	500.00

— Version 1: With peel-off banana peel, photo of band framed by a male torso (deduct 50% if banana sticker is gone)

Number	Title	Yr	NM
❑ V-5008 [M]	The Velvet Underground and Nico	1967	500.00

— Version 2: With peel-off banana peel, photo of torso obscured by a large black sticker (deduct 50% if stickers removed)

Number	Title	Yr	NM
❑ V-5008 [M]	The Velvet Underground and Nico	1967	400.00

— Version 3: With peel-off banana peel, torso is airbrushed off the cover (deduct 50% if banana sticker removed)

Number	Title	Yr	NM
❑ V6-5008 [S]	The Velvet Underground and Nico	1967	200.00

— Version 1: With peel-off banana peel, photo of band framed by a male torso (deduct 50% if banana sticker is gone)

Number	Title	Yr	NM
❑ V6-5008 [S]	The Velvet Underground and Nico	1967	200.00

— Version 2: With peel-off banana peel, photo of torso obscured by a sticker (deduct 50% if stickers removed)

Number	Title	Yr	NM
❑ V6-5008 [S]	The Velvet Underground and Nico	1967	150.00

— Version 3: With peel-off banana peel, torso is airbrushed off the cover, publishing on label is credited to "Three Prong Music" (deduct 50% if banana sticker removed)

Number	Title	Yr	NM
❑ V6-5008 [S]	The Velvet Underground and Nico	1970	80.00

— Version 5: With unpeelable banana; blue label with silver "T" shape on it; publishing on the label is credited to "Oakfield Avenue Music"

Number	Title	Yr	NM
❑ 823290-1	The Velvet Underground and Nico	1985	15.00

— Reissue of Verve V6-5008

Number	Title	Yr	NM
❑ V-5008 [M]	The Velvet Underground and Nico	1967	400.00

— Promo copy; white label

Number	Title	Yr	NM
❑ V-5008 [M]	The Velvet Underground and Nico	1967	400.00

— Promo copy; yellow label

Number	Title	Yr	NM
❑ V6-5008 [S]	The Velvet Underground and Nico	1968	100.00

— Version 4: With peel-off banana peel, torso is airbrushed off the cover, publishing on label is credited to "Oakfield Avenue Music," Side 2 trail-off wax has an "RE-1" (deduct 50% if banana sticker removed)

Number	Title	Yr	NM
❑ V6-5008 [S]	The Velvet Underground and Nico	1973	70.00

— Version 6: Same as Version 5 except the label is now white with "MGM" at left and "Verve" at right

Number	Title	Yr	NM
❑ V6-5008 [S]	The Velvet Underground and Nico	1975	50.00

— Version 7: Same as Version 5, but the label is now black with silver T-shape

Number	Title	Yr	NM
❑ V6-5008 [S]	The Velvet Underground and Nico	1978	30.00

— Version 8; The cover is no longer a gatefold

Number	Title	Yr	NM
❑ 823721-1	VU	1985	15.00
❑ V-5046 [M]	White Light/White Heat	1967	400.00

— White label promo

Number	Title	Yr	NM
❑ V-5046 [M]	White Light/White Heat	1967	800.00

— Version 1: "Skeleton" cover -- a black-on-black skeleton is visible when cover is viewed at an angle

Number	Title	Yr	NM
❑ V-5046 [M]	White Light/White Heat	1967	700.00

— Version 2: No "skeleton" on cover

Number	Title	Yr	NM
❑ V6-5046 [S]	White Light/White Heat	1967	250.00

— Yellow label promo

Number	Title	Yr	NM
❑ V6-5046 [S]	White Light/White Heat	1967	40.00

— Version 2: No "skeleton" on cover; publishing on label is

Number	Title	Yr	NM
credited to "Three Prong Music			
❑ V6-5046 [S]	White Light/White Heat	1967	80.00
— Version 1: "Skeleton" cover -- a black-on-black skeleton is visible when cover is viewed at an angle			
❑ 825119-1	White Light/White Heat	1985	15.00
— Reissue of Verve V6-5046			
❑ V-5046 [M]	White Light/White Heat	1967	300.00
— Yellow label promo			
❑ V6-5046 [S]	White Light/White Heat	1968	30.00
— Version 3: No "skeleton" on cover; publishing on label is credited to "Oakfield Avenue Music			

VENTURA, CAROL

PRESTIGE

Number	Title	Yr	NM
❑ PRLP-7358 [M]	Carol!	1965	30.00
❑ PRST-7358 [S]	Carol!	1965	30.00
❑ PRLP-7405 [M]	I Love to Sing!	1965	30.00
❑ PRST-7405 [S]	I Love to Sing!	1965	30.00

VENTURA, CHARLIE, AND MARY ANN MCCALL

Number	Title	Yr	NM
NORGRAN			
❑ MGN-20 [10]	An Evening with Mary Ann McCall and Charlie Ventura	1954	200.00
❑ MGN-1053 [M]	An Evening with Mary Ann McCall and Charlie Ventura	1955	100.00
❑ MGN-1013 [M]	Another Evening with Charlie Ventura and Mary Ann McCall	1954	120.00
VERVE			
❑ MGV-8143 [M]	An Evening with Mary Ann McCall and Charlie Ventura	1957	80.00
❑ V-8143 [M]	An Evening with Mary Ann McCall and Charlie Ventura	1961	30.00

VENTURA, CHARLIE

Number	Title	Yr	NM
BATON			
❑ 1202 [M]	New Charlie Ventura in Hi-Fi	1957	50.00
BRUNSWICK			
❑ BL54025 [M]	Here's Charlie	1957	80.00
CLEF			
❑ MGC-117 [10]	Charlie Ventura Collates	1953	250.00
CORAL			
❑ CRL56067 [10]	Open House	1952	150.00
CRAFTSMAN			
❑ 8039 [M]	Charlie Ventura Plays for the People	1960	30.00
CRYSTALETTE			
❑ 5000 [10]	Stomping With the Sax	1950	200.00
DECCA			
❑ DL8046 [M]	Charlie Ventura Concert	1954	100.00
EMARCY			
❑ MG-26028 [10]	F.Y.I. Ventura	1954	120.00
❑ MG-36015 [M]	Jumping with Ventura	1955	80.00
FAMOUS DOOR			
❑ 115	Chazz '77	1977	12.00
GENE NORMAN			
❑ GNP-1 [M]	Charlie Ventura In Concert	1954	100.00
GNP CRESCENDO			
❑ GNP-1 [M]	Charlie Ventura In Concert	196?	15.00
❑ GNPS-1 [R]	Charlie Ventura In Concert	196?	12.00
HALL OF FAME			
❑ 605	Charlie Ventura Quintet	197?	12.00
IMPERIAL			
❑ IM-3002 [10]	Charlie Ventura and His Sextet	1953	200.00
KING			
❑ 543 [M]	Adventure with Charlie Ventura	1958	80.00
MCA			
❑ 42330	Gene Norman Presents a Charlie Ventura Concert	1990	15.00
MERCURY			
❑ MGC-117 [10]	Charlie Ventura Collates	1952	250.00
MOSAIC			
❑ MQ9-182	The Complete Verve/Clef Charlie Ventura/Flip Phillips Studio Sessions	199?	150.00
NORGRAN			
❑ MGN-1075 [M]	Blue Saxophone	1956	120.00
❑ MGN-1103 [M]	Charley's Parley	1956	120.00
❑ MGN-1073 [M]	Charlie Ventura in a Jazz Mood	1956	120.00
❑ MGN-8 [10]	Charlie Ventura Quartet	1953	250.00
❑ MGN-1041 [M]	Charlie Ventura's Carnegie Hall Concert	1955	120.00
PHOENIX			
❑ 6	Charlie Boy	197?	12.00
RCA VICTOR			
❑ LPM-1135 [M]	It's All Bop to Me	1955	120.00
REGENT			
❑ MG-6064 [M]	East of Suez	1958	50.00
SAVOY JAZZ			
❑ SJL-2243	Euphoria	198?	15.00
TOPS			
❑ L-1528 [M]	Charlie Ventura Plays Hi-Fi Jazz	1958	30.00
TRIP			
❑ 5536	Jumping with Ventura	197?	12.00
VERVE			
❑ V-8165 [M]	Blue Saxophone	1961	30.00
❑ MGV-8165 [M]	Blue Saxophone	1957	60.00
❑ V-8132 [M]	Charlie Ventura'a Carnegie Hall Concert	1961	30.00
❑ MGV-8163 [M]	Charlie Ventura in a Jazz Mood	1957	60.00
❑ V-8163 [M]	Charlie Ventura in a Jazz Mood	1961	30.00
❑ MGV-8132 [M]	Charlie Ventura's Carnegie Hall Concert	1957	80.00
ZIM			
❑ 1004	Charlie Ventura in Chicago	197?	12.00

VENTURA, CHARLIE/CHARLIE KENNEDY

Number	Title	Yr	NM
REGENT			
❑ MG-6047 [M]	Crazy Rhythms	1957	60.00
SAVOY			
❑ MG-12200	Crazy Rhythms	197?	15.00

VENTURA, RAY

Number	Title	Yr	NM
ATLANTIC			
❑ 8011 [M]	Hi-Fi Music for Young Parisians	1956	50.00
— Black label			
DOT			
❑ DLP-3120 [M]	La Belle Bardot	1958	50.00
— Brigitte Bardot is the cover model			

VENTURAS, THE

Number	Title	Yr	NM
DRUM BOY			
❑ DBM-1003 [M]	Here They Are	1964	200.00
❑ DBS-1003 [S]	Here They Are	1964	300.00

VENTURES, THE

Number	Title	Yr	NM
COMPLEAT			
❑ 672013-1	The Best of the Ventures	1986	12.00
DOLTON			
❑ BLP2006 [M]	Another Smash!!!	1961	50.00
— Pale blue label with dolphins on top			
❑ BLP2006 [M]	Another Smash!!!	1963	25.00
— Dark label, logo on left			
❑ BST8006 [S]	Another Smash!!!	1961	60.00
— Pale blue label with dolphins on top			
❑ BST8006 [S]	Another Smash!!!	1963	30.00
— Dark label, logo on left			
❑ BLP2016 [M]	Beach Party	1963	25.00
— Retitled version of "Mashed Potatoes and Gravy			
❑ BST8016 [S]	Beach Party	1963	30.00
— Retitled version of "Mashed Potatoes and Gravy			
❑ BLP2010 [M]	Dance!	1963	25.00
— Dark label, logo on left; retitled version of "Twist with the Ventures			
❑ BST8010 [S]	Dance!	1963	30.00
— Dark label, logo on left; retitled version of "Twist with the Ventures			
❑ BLP2014 [M]	Dance with the Ventures	1963	25.00
— Dark label, logo on left' retitled version of "The Ventures' Twist Party, Vol. 2			
❑ BST8014 [S]	Dance with the Ventures	1963	30.00
— Dark label, logo on left' retitled version of "The Ventures' Twist Party, Vol. 2			
❑ BLP2017 [M]	Going to the Ventures Dance Party!	1962	30.00
❑ BST8017 [S]	Going to the Ventures Dance Party!	1962	40.00
❑ BLP2045 [M]	Go with the Ventures!	1966	25.00
❑ BST8045 [S]	Go with the Ventures!	1966	30.00
❑ BLP2050 [M]	Guitar Freakout	1967	25.00
❑ BST8050 [S]	Guitar Freakout	1967	30.00
❑ BLP2024 [M]	Let's Go!	1963	30.00
❑ BST8024 [S]	Let's Go!	1963	30.00
❑ BLP2016 [M]	Mashed Potatoes and Gravy	1962	30.00
❑ BST8016 [S]	Mashed Potatoes and Gravy	1962	40.00
❑ BLP16501 [M]	Play Guitar with the Ventures	1965	30.00
❑ BST17501 [S]	Play Guitar with the Ventures	1965	30.00
❑ BLP16502 [M]	Play Guitar with the Ventures, Vol. 2	196?	30.00
❑ BST17502 [S]	Play Guitar with the Ventures, Vol. 2	196?	30.00
❑ BLP16503 [M]	Play Guitar with the Ventures, Vol. 3	196?	30.00
❑ BST17503 [S]	Play Guitar with the Ventures, Vol. 3	196?	30.00
❑ BLP16504 [M]	Play Guitar with the Ventures, Vol. 4	196?	30.00
❑ BST16504 [S]	Play Guitar with the Ventures, Vol. 4	196?	30.00
❑ BLP2022 [M]	Surfing	1963	30.00
❑ BST8022 [S]	Surfing	1963	30.00
❑ BLP2008 [M]	The Colorful Ventures	1961	50.00
— Pale blue label with dolphins on top			
❑ BLP2008 [M]	The Colorful Ventures	1963	25.00
— Dark label, logo on left			
❑ BST8008 [S]	The Colorful Ventures	1961	60.00
— Pale blue label with dolphins on top			
❑ BST8008 [S]	The Colorful Ventures	1963	30.00
— Dark label, logo on left			
❑ BLP2029 [M]	The Fabulous Ventures	1964	30.00
❑ BST8029 [S]	The Fabulous Ventures	1964	30.00
❑ BLP2004 [M]	The Ventures	1961	50.00
— Pale blue label with dolphins on top			
❑ BLP2004 [M]	The Ventures	1963	25.00
— Dark label, logo on left			
❑ BST8004 [S]	The Ventures	1961	60.00
— Pale blue label with dolphins on top			
❑ BST8004 [S]	The Ventures	1963	30.00
— Dark label, logo on left			
❑ BLP2037 [M]	The Ventures A-Go-Go	1965	30.00
❑ BST8037 [S]	The Ventures A-Go-Go	1965	30.00
❑ BLP2042 [M]	The Ventures/Batman Theme	1966	30.00
❑ BST8042 [S]	The Ventures/Batman Theme	1966	40.00
❑ BLP-2038 [M]	The Ventures' Christmas Album	1965	30.00
❑ BST-8038 [S]	The Ventures' Christmas Album	1965	25.00
❑ BLP2027 [M]	(The) Ventures in Space	1964	40.00
❑ BST8027 [S]	(The) Ventures in Space	1964	50.00
❑ BLP2033 [M]	The Ventures Knock Me Out!	1965	30.00
❑ BST8033 [S]	The Ventures Knock Me Out!	1965	30.00
❑ BLP2035 [M]	The Ventures on Stage	1965	30.00
❑ BST8035 [S]	The Ventures on Stage	1965	30.00
❑ BLP2019 [M]	The Ventures Play Telstar, The Lonely Bull	1962	30.00
❑ BST8019 [S]	The Ventures Play Telstar, The Lonely Bull	1962	40.00
❑ BLP2023 [M]	The Ventures Play the Country Classics	1963	30.00
❑ BST8023 [S]	The Ventures Play the Country Classics	1963	30.00
❑ BLP2014 [M]	The Ventures' Twist Party, Vol. 2	1962	50.00
— Pale blue label with dolphins on top			
❑ BST8014 [S]	The Ventures' Twist Party, Vol. 2	1962	60.00
— Pale blue label with dolphins on top			
❑ BLP2010 [M]	Twist with the Ventures	1962	50.00
— Pale blue label with dolphins on top			
❑ BST8010 [S]	Twist with the Ventures	1962	60.00
— Pale blue label with dolphins on top			
❑ BLP2031 [M]	Walk, Don't Run, Vol. 2	1964	30.00
❑ BST8031 [S]	Walk, Don't Run, Vol. 2	1964	30.00
❑ BLP2003 [M]	Walk Don't Run	1960	50.00
— Pale blue label with dolphins on top			
❑ BLP2003 [M]	Walk Don't Run	1963	25.00
— Dark label, logo on left			
❑ BST8003 [S]	Walk Don't Run	1960	60.00
— Pale blue label with dolphins on top			

Number	Title	Yr	NM
❑ BST8003 [S]	Walk Don't Run	1963	30.00
— Dark label, logo on left			
❑ BLP2040 [M]	Where the Action Is	1966	25.00
❑ BST8040 [S]	Where the Action Is	1966	30.00
❑ BLP2047 [M]	Wild Things!	1966	25.00
❑ BST8047 [S]	Wild Things!	1966	30.00
LIBERTY			
❑ LRP-2054 [M]	$1,000,000.00 Weekend	1967	25.00
❑ LST-8054 [S]	$1,000,000.00 Weekend	1967	25.00
❑ LST-8052 [S]	Changing Times	1970	40.00
— Reissue of "Super Psychedelics			
❑ LRP-2055 [M]	Flights of Fancy	1968	30.00
❑ LST-8055 [S]	Flights of Fancy	1968	25.00
❑ LRP-2053 [M]	Golden Greats by the Ventures	1967	25.00
❑ LST-8053 [S]	Golden Greats by the Ventures	1967	25.00
❑ LTAO-8053	Golden Greats by the Ventures	1981	10.00
❑ LST-8061	Hawaii Five-O	1969	18.00
❑ LST-8023	I Walk the Line and Other Giant Hits	1970	25.00
— Reissue of "The Ventures Play the Country Classics			
❑ LST-8060	More Golden Greats	1970	18.00
❑ LST-8057	On the Scene	1970	18.00

Number	Title	Yr	NM
—Reissue of "The Horse			
❑ LST-8050	Revolving Sounds	1970	30.00
—Reissue of "Guitar Freakout			
❑ LRP-2052 [M]	Super Psychedelics	1967	25.00
❑ LST-8052 [S]	Super Psychedelics	1967	30.00
❑ LST-8062 [B]	Swamp Rock	1969	18.00
❑ LST-8057	The Horse	1968	25.00
❑ LN-10203	The Ventures	1984	10.00
❑ LST-35000	The Ventures 10th Anniversary Album	1970	25.00
❑ LN-10190	(The) Ventures in Space	1984	10.00
❑ LN-10155	The Ventures Play Telstar, The Lonely Bull	1981	10.00
❑ LN-10156	The Ventures Play the Country Classics	1981	10.00
❑ LN-10122	The Very Best of the Ventures	1981	10.00
❑ LN-10224	TV Themes	1984	10.00
❑ LST-8059	Underground Fire	1969	25.00
❑ LST-8031	Walk, Don't Run, Vol. 2	1970	30.00
—Reissue of Dolton 8031 with new cover			
❑ LN-10188	Walk, Don't Run, Vol. 2	1984	10.00
❑ LST-8003 [B]	Walk Don't Run	1970	18.00
—Reissue of Dolton 8003 with new front cover, original back cover			
❑ LST-8003	Walk Don't Run	1970	25.00
—Reissue of Dolton 8003 with new front and back covers			
❑ LT-8003	Walk Don't Run	1981	10.00
SUNDAZED			
❑ LP5398 [B]	Another Smash	2013	25.00
❑ LP5400 [B]	Mashed Potatoes and Gravy	2013	25.00
❑ LP5399 [B]	The Colorful Ventures	2013	25.00
❑ LP5397 [B]	The Ventures	2013	25.00
❑ LP5396 [B]	Walk Don't Run	2013	25.00
SUNSET			
❑ SUS-5317	A Decade with the Ventures	1970	15.00
❑ SUS-5270	Super Group	1969	15.00
❑ SUM-1160 [M]	The Guitar Genius of the Ventures	1967	15.00
❑ SUS-5160 [S]	The Guitar Genius of the Ventures	1967	18.00
UNITED ARTISTS			
❑ UAS-5575	Joy/The Ventures Play the Classics	1972	15.00
❑ UAS-6796	New Testament	1971	15.00
❑ UA-LA147-G	Only Hits	1973	18.00
❑ UAS-5649	Rock and Roll Forever	1972	15.00
❑ UA-LA586-F	Rocky Road	1976	15.00
❑ UA-LA217-E	The Jim Croce Songbook	1973	15.00
❑ UAS-5547	Theme from Shaft	1971	15.00
❑ UXS-80	The Ventures	1971	18.00
❑ UA-LA331-E	The Very Best of the Ventures	1974	15.00
❑ UA-LA717-F	TV Themes	1977	30.00
VENUTA, BENAY			
MERCURY			
❑ MG-25006 [10]	Old Time Favorites	1949	70.00
VENUTI, JOE, AND DAVE MCKENNA			
CHIAROSCURO			
❑ 100	Alone at the Palace	1977	15.00
VENUTI, JOE, AND EARL HINES			
CHIAROSCURO			
❑ 145	Hot Sonatas	1975	15.00
VENUTI, JOE, AND GEORGE BARNES			
CONCORD JAZZ			
❑ CJ-14	Gems	197?	15.00
❑ CJ-30	Live at the Concord Summer Festival	197?	15.00
VENUTI, JOE, AND LOUIS PRIMA			
DESIGN			
❑ DLP-54 [M]	Hi-Fi Lootin'	195?	25.00
VENUTI, JOE, AND MARIAN MCPARTLAND			
HALCYON			
❑ 112	Maestro and Friend	197?	15.00
VENUTI, JOE, AND ZOOT SIMS			
CHIAROSCURO			
❑ 128	Joe and Zoot	197?	18.00
❑ 142	Joe Venuti and Zoot Sims	1975	15.00
VENUTI, JOE			
AUDIOPHILE			
❑ AP-118	Incredible	197?	12.00
CHIAROSCURO			
❑ 134	Blue Four	1975	15.00
❑ 203	The Best of Joe Venuti	1979	12.00
EVEREST ARCHIVE OF FOLK & JAZZ			
❑ 349	Joe Venuti and the Dutch Swing College Band	197?	12.00
FLYING FISH			
❑ FF-077	Joe in Chicago, 1978	1979	15.00
GOLDEN CREST			
❑ GC-3100 [M]	Joe Venuti Plays Gershwin	1959	30.00

Number	Title	Yr	NM
❑ GC-3101 [M]	Joe Venuti Plays Jerome Kern	1959	30.00
GRAND AWARD			
❑ GA-33-351 [M]	Fiddle on Fire	1956	40.00
PAUSA			
❑ 7034	Doin' Things	197?	12.00
TOPS			
❑ L923 [10]	Twilight on the Trail	195?	30.00
VANGUARD			
❑ VSD-79405	Jazz Violin	197?	12.00
❑ VSD-79396	Joe Venuti in Milan	197?	12.00
YAZOO			
❑ 1062	Violin Jazz	198?	12.00
VENUTI, JOE/EDDIE LANG			
COLUMBIA			
❑ C2L24 [M]	Swinging the Blues	1965	25.00
—Red labels with "360 Sound Mono" on labels			
❑ C2L24 [M]	Swinging the Blues	1963	30.00
—Guaranteed High Fidelity" on labels			
COLUMBIA SPECIAL PRODUCTS			
❑ JC2L24 [M]	Swinging the Blues	1975	18.00
—Reissue of C2L 24			
X			
❑ LVA-3036 [M]	Joe Venuti and Eddie Lang	1955	40.00
VER PLANCK, BILLY			
SAVOY			
❑ MG-12101 [M]	Dancing Jazz	1957	40.00
❑ MG-12121 [M]	Jazz for Playgirls	1957	40.00
VER PLANCK, MARLENE			
AUDIOPHILE			
❑ AP-160	A New York Singer	1980	12.00
❑ AP-169	A Warmer Place	1981	12.00
❑ AP-186	I Like to Sing	1984	12.00
❑ AP-138	Marlene Ver Planck Loves Johnny Mercer	197?	12.00
❑ AP-218	Marlene Ver Planck Sings Alec Wilder	1986	12.00
❑ AP-235	Pure and Natural	1988	12.00
❑ AP-121	You'd Better Love Me	197?	12.00
MOUNTED			
❑ 108	A Breath of Fresh Air	1968	18.00
❑ 114	This Happy Feeling	197?	18.00
SAVOY			
❑ MG-12058 [M]	I Think of You with Every Breath I Take	1956	50.00
—As "Marlene			
VERA, BILLY, AND JUDY CLAY			
ATLANTIC			
❑ 8174 [M]	Storybook Children	1967	30.00
❑ SD8174 [S]	Storybook Children	1967	30.00
VERA, BILLY			
ALFA			
❑ 10001	Billy and the Beaters	1981	18.00
❑ 10012	Billy Vera	1982	15.00
ATLANTIC			
❑ SD8197 [S]	With Pen in Hand	1968	30.00
❑ 8197 [M]	With Pen in Hand	1968	40.00
CAPITOL			
❑ C1-46948	Retro Nuevo	1988	12.00
MACOLA			
❑ 0961	The Billy Vera Album	1987	12.00
—Reissue of Midsong Int'l. LP			
MIDSONG INT'L.			
❑ BKL1-2219	Out of the Darkness	1977	15.00
RHINO			
❑ RNLP70858	By Request -- The Best of Billy Vera and the Beaters	1986	15.00
❑ RNLP70185	The Atlantic Years	1987	12.00
THUNDER			
❑ TVLP 0018	The Hollywood Sessions	1987	12.00
VERDON, GWEN			
RCA VICTOR			
❑ LPM-1152 [M]	The Girl I Left Home For	1956	40.00
VERGARI, MADELINE			
SEA BREEZE			
❑ SB-108	This Is My Lucky Day	198?	12.00
VERHEYEN, CARL			
CMG			
❑ CML-8012	No Borders	198?	12.00
VERITY, JOHN, BAND			
ABC DUNHILL			
❑ DSX-50170	The John Verity Band	1974	25.00

Number	Title	Yr	NM
VERLAINE, TOM			
ELEKTRA			
❑ 6E-216	Tom Verlaine	1979	18.00
I.R.S.			
❑ 42050	Flash Light	1987	12.00
WARNER BROS.			
❑ 25144	Cover	1984	12.00
❑ BSK3539	Dreamtime	1981	12.00
❑ BSK3685 [B]	Words from the Front	1982	12.00
VERNE, LARRY			
ERA			
❑ 104 [M]	Mister Larry Verne	1961	60.00
VERNON, KENNY			
CAPITOL			
❑ ST-11227	Loversville	1973	15.00
CHART			
❑ CHS-1018	Country Happening	1969	18.00
❑ CHS-1038	Nashville Union Station Depot	1971	18.00
MERCURY			
❑ SRM-1-606	Country Giants	1970	18.00
VERNON, MILLI			
AUDIOPHILE			
❑ AP-178 [B]	Old Shoes	1989	12.00
—As "Millie Vernon			
STORYVILLE			
❑ STLP-910 [M]	Introducing Milli Vernon	1956	300.00
VERSATONES, THE			
RCA VICTOR			
❑ LPM-1538 [M]	The Versatones	1957	100.00
VERUCA SALT			
BEYOND			
❑ 78103	Resolver	2000	15.00
GEFFEN			
❑ 22121 [EP]	Blow It Out Your Ass, It's Veruca Salt	1996	15.00
MINTY FRESH			
❑ MF-7 [B]	American Thighs	1994	25.00
❑ MF-19	Eight Arms to Hold You	1997	18.00
❑ MF-9 [10]	Nunber One Blind	1995	15.00
—Pink vinyl			
VERY SPECIAL ENVOY			
ROULETTE			
❑ SR-42003	Very Special Envoy	1968	25.00
VESALA, EDWARD			
ECM			
❑ 1088	Satu	197?	15.00
VETTES, THE			
MGM			
❑ E-4193 [M]	Rev-Up	1963	100.00
❑ SE-4193 [S]	Rev-Up	1963	120.00
VIBRATION SOCIETY, THE			
STASH			
❑ ST-261	The Music of Rahsaan Roland Kirk	1986	12.00
VIBRATIONS, THE			
CHECKER			
❑ LP-2978 [M]	The Watusi	1961	200.00
MANDALA			
❑ 3006	Taking a New Step	1972	25.00
OKEH			
❑ OKM-12112 [M]	Misty	1966	30.00
❑ OKS-14112 [S]	Misty	1966	40.00
❑ OKM-12114 [M]	New Vibrations	1967	30.00
❑ OKS-14114 [S]	New Vibrations	1967	40.00
❑ OKM-12111 [M]	Shout	1965	30.00
❑ OKS-14111 [S]	Shout	1965	40.00
❑ OKS-14129	The Vibrations' Greatest Hits	1969	30.00
VIBRATORS, THE			
CLEOPATRA			
❑ 9152 [B]	Alaska 127		25.00
❑ 3670 [B]	Garage Punk		25.00
❑ 8201 [B]	Pure Mania		30.00
—picture disc			
❑ 6453 [B]	Pure Mania		25.00
❑ 7061 [B]	V2		25.00
VICE SQUAD			
CLEOPATRA			
❑ 3830 [B]	Fuck Authority		25.00

Number	Title	Yr	NM

VICEROYS, THE (3)

BOLO
❏ BLP-8000 [M]	The Viceroys at Granny's Pad	1963	40.00

VICK, HAROLD

BLUE NOTE
❏ BLP-4138 [M]	Steppin' Out	1963	40.00
❏ BST-84138 [S]	Steppin' Out	1963	50.00
—With "New York, USA" address on label			
❏ BST-84138 [S]	Steppin' Out	196?	18.00
—With "A Division of Liberty Records" on label			

MUSE
❏ MR-5054	Commitment	197?	15.00

RCA VICTOR
❏ LPM-3761 [M]	Straight Up	1967	25.00
❏ LSP-3761 [S]	Straight Up	1967	18.00
❏ LPM-3677 [M]	The Caribbean Suite	1966	18.00
❏ LSP-3677 [S]	The Caribbean Suite	1966	25.00

STRATA-EAST
❏ SES-7431	Don't Look Back	197?	25.00

VICKERY, MACK

MEGA
❏ 31-1002	Mack Vickery at the Alabama Women's Prison	1970	18.00

VICTIMS OF CHANCE, THE

CRESTVIEW
❏ CRS-3052	The Victims of Chance	197?	60.00

VICTORIA, C.B.

JANUS
❏ JXS-7029	Dawning Day	1976	15.00

VIDEO ALL STARS, THE

SOMERSET
❏ SF-8800 [M]	The Video All Stars Play TV Jazz Themes	1956	120.00

VIENNA ART ORCHESTRA

HAT HUT
❏ 1980/1	Concerto Piccolo	1980	25.00
❏ 1999/2000	From No Time to Rag Time	1982	25.00
❏ 2024	Perpetuum Mobile	1985	18.00
❏ 1991/2	Suite for the Green Eighties	1981	25.00
❏ 2005	The Minimalism of Erik Satie	1984	18.00

VIENNA BOYS CHOIR

CAPITOL
❏ T10164 [M]	Christmas in Austria	1959	18.00
—As "Wiener Sangerknaben"			

VIENNA CHOIR BOYS, THE, AND HERMANN PREY

RCA RED SEAL
❏ ARL1-2939	Christmas with the Vienna Choir Boys and Hermann Prey	1978	12.00

VIENNA CHOIR BOYS

RCA RED SEAL
❏ ARL1-3437	Britten: A Ceremony of Carols/Seven English Christmas Carols	1979	12.00

VIENNA PHILHARMONIC ORCHESTRA (FRITZ REINER, CONDUCTOR)

RCA VICTOR RED SEAL
❏ LSC-2077 [S]	Strauss: Till Eulenspiegel	1959	100.00
—Original with "shaded dog" label			
❏ LSC-2077 [S]	Strauss: Till Eulenspiegel	199?	30.00
—Classic Records reissue			

VIENNA PHILHARMONIC ORCHESTRA (PIERRE MONTEUX, CONDUCTOR)

RCA VICTOR RED SEAL
❏ LSC-2491 [S]	Beethoven: Symphonies No. 1 and 8	1961	40.00
—Original with "shaded dog" label			
❏ LSC-2316 [S]	Beethoven: Symphony No. 6	1959	50.00
—Original with "shaded dog" label			
❏ LSC-2362 [S]	Berlioz: Symphortie Fantastique	1960	40.00
—Original with "shaded dog" label			
❏ LSC-2394 [S]	Haydn: Symphonies No. 94 and 101	1960	30.00
—Original with "shaded dog" label			

VIENNA PHILHARMONIC ORCHESTRA (WILHELM FURTWANGLER, CONDUCTOR)

URANIA
❏ URLP-7095 [M]	Beethoven: Symphony No. 3	195?	600.00
—Withdrawn from the market when it was discovered that the record had been mastered slightly fast			

VIG, TOMMY

DISCOVERY
❏ 780	Encounter with Time	197?	12.00

DOBRE
❏ 1015	1978	1978	15.00

MILESTONE
❏ MSP-9007	Sounds of the Seventies	1968	25.00

VIGRASS AND OSBORNE

EPIC
❏ KE33077	Steppin' Out	1975	15.00

UNI
❏ 73129	Queues	1971	18.00

VILLA, PEPE

KING
❏ 660 [M]	Music of Mexico	1959	30.00

VILLAGE PEOPLE

CASABLANCA
❏ NBLP-7220	Can't Stop the Music (Soundtrack)	1980	12.00
—Also includes one song by the Ritchie Family and one song by David London			
❏ NBLP-7118	Cruisin'	1978	12.00
❏	Cruisin'	1978	25.00
NBPIX-7118 [PD]			
❏ NBLP-7144	Go West	1979	12.00
❏ NBLP-7183 [B]	Live and Sleazy	1979	15.00
❏ NBLP-7096	Macho Man	1978	12.00
❏	Macho Man	1978	25.00
NBPIX-7096 [PD]			
❏ NBLP-7064	Village People	1977	12.00
❏	Village People	1978	25.00
NBPIX-7064 [PD]			

RCA VICTOR
❏ AFL1-4105	Renaissance	1981	15.00

RHINO
❏ R1-70167	Greatest Hits	1988	18.00

VILLAGE STOMPERS, THE

EPIC
❏ LN24109 [M]	Around the World with the Village Stompers	1964	15.00
❏ BN26109 [S]	Around the World with the Village Stompers	1964	18.00
❏ LN24180 [M]	A Taste of Honey	1965	15.00
❏ BN26180 [S]	A Taste of Honey	1965	18.00
❏ LN24090 [M]	More Sounds of Washington Square	1964	18.00
❏ BN26090 [S]	More Sounds of Washington Square	1964	25.00
❏ LN24129 [M]	New Beat on Broadway!	1964	15.00
❏ BN26129 [S]	New Beat on Broadway!	1964	18.00
❏ LN24235 [M]	One More Time	1966	15.00
❏ BN26235 [S]	One More Time	1966	18.00
❏ LN24161 [M]	Some Folk, a Bit of Country and a Whole Lot of Dixie	1965	15.00
❏ BN26161 [S]	Some Folk, a Bit of Country and a Whole Lot of Dixie	1965	18.00
❏ LN24318 [M]	The Village Stompers' Greatest Hits	1967	15.00
❏ BN26318 [S]	The Village Stompers' Greatest Hits	1967	18.00
❏ LN24078 [M]	Washington Square	1963	18.00
❏ BN26078 [S]	Washington Square	1963	25.00

VILLEGAS

COLUMBIA
❏ CL787 [M]	Introducing Villegas	1956	30.00
❏ CL877 [M]	Very, Very Villegas	1956	30.00

VINCENT, GENE

CAPITOL
❏ T1059 [M]	A Gene Vincent Record Date	1958	1500.00
—Yellow label promo			
❏ T1059 [M]	A Gene Vincent Record Date	1958	1500.00
—Black label promo			
❏ T1059 [M]	A Gene Vincent Record Date	1958	400.00
—Turquoise label stock copy			
❏ T764 [M]	Bluejean Bop!	1957	1000.00
—Yellow label promo			
❏ T764 [M]	Bluejean Bop!	1957	1000.00
—Black label promo			
❏ T764 [M]	Bluejean Bop!	1957	600.00
—Turquoise label stock copy			
❏ T1342 [M]	Crazy Times	1960	300.00
—Black label with colorband, Capitol logo at left			
❏ ST1342 [S]	Crazy Times	1960	500.00
—Black label with colorband, Capitol logo at left			
❏ T811 [M]	Gene Vincent and the Blue Caps	1957	1000.00
—Yellow label promo			
❏ T811 [M]	Gene Vincent and the Blue Caps	1957	1000.00
—Black label promo			
❏ T811 [M]	Gene Vincent and the Blue Caps	1957	500.00
—Turquoise label stock copy			
❏ T970 [M]	Gene Vincent Rocks! And the Blue Caps Roll	1958	1000.00
—Yellow label promo			
❏ T970 [M]	Gene Vincent Rocks! And the Blue Caps Roll	1958	1500.00
—Black label promo			
❏ T970 [M]	Gene Vincent Rocks! And the Blue Caps Roll	1958	500.00
—Turquoise label stock copy			
❏ DKAO-380 [R]	Gene Vincent's Greatest	1969	50.00
❏ SM-380 [R]	Gene Vincent's Greatest	197?	18.00
—Abridged reissue of DKAO-380			
❏ N-16208	Gene Vincent's Greatest	198?	15.00
—Budget-line reissue			
❏ T1207 [M]	Sounds Like Gene Vincent	1959	300.00
—Black label with colorband, Capitol logo at left			
❏ SM-11287	The Bop That Just Won't Stop	1974	18.00
❏ N-16209 [B]	The Bop That Just Won't Stop	198?	18.00
—Budget-line reissue			

DANDELION
❏ 9-102	I'm Back and I'm Proud	1970	50.00

INTERMEDIA
❏ QS-5074	Rockabilly Fever	198?	15.00

KAMA SUTRA
❏ KSBS2019	Gene Vincent	1970	50.00
❏ KSBS2027	The Day the World Turned Blue	1971	50.00

ROLLIN' ROCK
❏ 022	Forever	1981	18.00

VINNEGAR, LEROY

CONTEMPORARY
❏ C-3542 [M]	Leroy Walks!	1957	80.00
❏ S-7003 [S]	Leroy Walks!	1959	50.00
❏ S-7542 [S]	Leroy Walks!	197?	15.00
❏ M-3608 [M]	Leroy Walks Again!	1962	30.00
❏ S-7608 [S]	Leroy Walks Again!	1962	40.00

FANTASY
❏ OJC-160	Leroy Walks!	198?	12.00
❏ OJC-454	Leroy Walks Again!	1990	12.00

LEGEND
❏ 1001	Glass of Water	197?	18.00

PBR
❏ 6	The Kid	197?	15.00

STEREO RECORDS
❏ S-7003 [S]	Leroy Walks!	1958	60.00

VEE JAY
❏ LP-2502 [M]	Jazz's Great Walker	1964	30.00
❏ LPS-2502 [S]	Jazz's Great Walker	1964	30.00

VINSON, EDDIE "CLEANHEAD"/JIMMY WITHERSPOON

KING
❏ 634 [M]	Battle of the Blues, Volume 3	1960	1500.00

VINSON, EDDIE "CLEANHEAD

AAMCO
❏ 312 [M]	Cleanhead's Back in Town	196?	40.00

BETHLEHEM
❏ BCP-6036	Back in Town	1978	18.00
❏ BCP-5005 [M]	Eddie "Cleanhead" Vinson Sings	1957	100.00

BLUESWAY
❏ BL-6007 [M]	Cherry Red	1967	30.00
❏ BLS-6007 [S]	Cherry Red	1967	30.00

CIRCLE
❏ CLP-57	Kidney Stew	1983	15.00

DELMARK
❏ 631	Old Kidney Stew Is Fine	1980	15.00

FLYING DUTCHMAN
❏ 31-1012	You Can't Make Love Alone	197?	18.00

KING
❏ KS-1087	Cherry Red	1969	30.00

MUSE
❏ MR-5282	Cleanhead and Roomful of Blues	1982	15.00
❏ MR-5243	Eddie "Cleanhead" Vinson and the Muse All-Stars: Hold It Right There	198?	15.00
❏ MR-5208	Eddie "Cleanhead" Vinson and the Muse All-Stars: Live at Sandy's	1979	15.00
❏ MR-5310	Eddie "Cleanhead" Vinson Sings the Blues	198?	15.00
❏ MR-5116	The Clean Machine	1978	18.00

PABLO
❏ 2310866	I Want a Little Girl	198?	15.00

REGGIES
❏ 1000	Rollin' Over the Devil	1981	15.00

RIVERSIDE
❏ RLP-502 [M]	Back Door Blues	1965	40.00
❏ RLS-9502 [S]	Back Door Blues	1965	40.00

VINTON, BOBBY

ABC

Number	Title	Yr	NM
❑ D-891	Heart of Hearts	1975	12.00
❑ X-851	Melodies of Love	1974	12.00
❑ D-957	Serenades of Love	1976	12.00
❑ D-924	The Bobby Vinton Show	1975	12.00
❑ AB-981	The Name Is Love	1977	12.00

COLUMBIA LIMITED EDITION

Number	Title	Yr	NM
❑ LE10016	Big Ones	197?	12.00
❑ LE10140	Blue Velvet	197?	12.00
—Reissue of Epic 26068			
❑ LE10052	Please Love Me Forever	197?	12.00
❑ LE10139	Roses Are Red	197?	12.00

COLUMBIA MUSICAL TREASURY

Number	Title	Yr	NM
❑ 6P6035	The Bobby Vinton Treasury	197?	30.00
—Columbia House" logo on upper right back cover			

EPIC

Number	Title	Yr	NM
❑ JE35605	Autumn Memories	1979	12.00
❑ LN24122 [M]	A Very Merry Christmas	1964	15.00
❑ BN26122 [S]	A Very Merry Christmas	1964	18.00
❑ LN24068 [M]	Blue On Blue	1963	150.00
—Promo only on blue vinyl			
❑ LN24068 [M]	Blue On Blue	1963	30.00
—Stock copy on black vinyl			
❑ BN26068 [S]	Blue On Blue	1963	30.00
❑ LN24068 [M]	Blue Velvet	1963	18.00
—Retitled version of "Blue On Blue			
❑ BN26068 [S]	Blue Velvet	1963	25.00
—Retitled version of "Blue On Blue			
❑ KEG31487	Bobby Vinton's All-Time Greatest Hits	1972	18.00
❑ PEG31487	Bobby Vinton's All-Time Greatest Hits	197?	15.00
—Reissue			
❑ LN24098 [M]	Bobby Vinton's Greatest Hits	1964	15.00
—Despite lower number, this came out after "Tell Me Why			
❑ BN26098 [S]	Bobby Vinton's Greatest Hits	1964	18.00
—Despite lower number, this came out after "Tell Me Why			
❑ PE26098	Bobby Vinton's Greatest Hits	198?	10.00
—Budget-line reissue			
❑ BN26517	Bobby Vinton's Greatest Hits of Love	1970	18.00
❑ LN24154 [M]	Bobby Vinton Sings for Lonely Nights	1965	15.00
❑ BN26154 [S]	Bobby Vinton Sings for Lonely Nights	1965	18.00
❑ LN24035 [M]	Bobby Vinton Sings the Big Ones	1962	18.00
❑ BN26035 [S]	Bobby Vinton Sings the Big Ones	1962	25.00
❑ KEG33468	Bobby Vinton Sings the Golden Decade of Love	1975	15.00
❑ LN24245 [M]	Bobby Vinton's Newest Hits	1967	15.00
❑ BN26245 [S]	Bobby Vinton's Newest Hits	1967	18.00
❑ LN24188 [M]	Country Boy	1966	15.00
❑ BN26188 [S]	Country Boy	1966	18.00
❑ LN3727 [M]	Dancing at the Hop	1961	30.00
❑ BN579 [S]	Dancing at the Hop	1961	50.00
❑ LN24170 [M]	Drive-In Movie Time	1965	15.00
❑ BN26170 [S]	Drive-In Movie Time	1965	18.00
❑ KE31286	Ev'ry Day of My Life	1972	15.00
❑ KEG33767	Greatest Hits/Greatest Hits of Love	1976	15.00
❑ BN26437	I Love How You Love Me	1968	18.00
❑ LN24203 [M]	Live at the Copa	1967	15.00
❑ BN26203 [S]	Live at the Copa	1967	18.00
❑ LN24187 [M]	More of Bobby Vinton's Greatest Hits	1966	15.00
❑ BN26187 [S]	More of Bobby Vinton's Greatest Hits	1966	18.00
❑ LN24136 [M]	Mr. Lonely	1965	15.00
❑ BN26136 [S]	Mr. Lonely	1965	18.00
❑ BN26540	My Elusive Dreams	1970	18.00
❑ LN24341 [M]	Please Love Me Forever	1967	18.00
❑ BN26341 [S]	Please Love Me Forever	1967	18.00
❑ LN24020 [M]	Roses Are Red	1962	18.00
❑ BN26020 [S]	Roses Are Red	1962	25.00
❑ LN24182 [M]	Satin Pillows and Careless	1966	15.00
❑ BN26182 [S]	Satin Pillows and Careless	1966	18.00
❑ KE31642	Sealed with a Kiss	1972	15.00
❑ JE35998	Spring Sensations	1979	12.00
❑ JE35999	Summer Serenade	1979	12.00
❑ BN26382	Take Good Care of My Baby	1968	18.00
❑ LN24113 [M]	Tell Me Why	1964	15.00
❑ BN26113 [S]	Tell Me Why	1964	18.00
❑ LN24049 [M]	The Greatest Hits of the Greatest Groups	1963	18.00
❑ BN26049 [S]	The Greatest Hits of the Greatest Groups	1963	25.00
❑ LN24081 [M]	There! I've Said It Again	1964	18.00
❑ BN26081 [S]	There! I've Said It Again	1964	25.00
❑ BN26471	Vinton	1969	18.00
❑ PE32921	With Love	1974	12.00
❑ LN3780 [M]	Young Man with a Big Band	1961	30.00
❑ BN597 [S]	Young Man with a Big Band	1961	50.00

HARMONY

Number	Title	Yr	NM
❑ KH11402	Vinton Sings Vinton	197?	12.00

PICKWICK

Number	Title	Yr	NM
❑ SPC-3353	Melodies of Love	197?	10.00

TAPESTRY

Number	Title	Yr	NM
❑ TRS-1001 [EP]	Santa Must Be Polish	1987	12.00

VIOLA, AL

LEGEND

Number	Title	Yr	NM
❑ 1002	Alone Again	197?	18.00

MODE

Number	Title	Yr	NM
❑ LP-121 [M]	Solo Guitar	1957	80.00

PBR

Number	Title	Yr	NM
❑ 11	Prelude to a Kiss	197?	15.00
❑ 7	Salutations F.S.	197?	15.00

VIOLENT FEMMES

RHINO

Number	Title	Yr	NM
❑ R1-79951 [B]	Violent Femmes	2003	18.00
—Reissue on 180-gram vinyl			

SLASH

Number	Title	Yr	NM
❑ 25819	3	1988	12.00
❑ 25094	Hallowed Ground	1984	15.00
❑ 25340	The Blind Leading the Naked	1986	12.00
❑ 23845	Violent Femmes	1983	18.00

WARNER BROS.

Number	Title	Yr	NM
❑ PRO-A-3519 [DJ]	3 On 3	1989	30.00
—Promo-only interviews and music			

VIOLINAIRES, THE

CHECKER

Number	Title	Yr	NM
❑ LP-10060	At His Command	1970	25.00
❑ LPS-10057	God's Creation	1969	25.00
❑ CK-10067	Groovin' with Jesus	197?	25.00
❑ LPS-10020 [S]	I'm Going to Serve the Lord	196?	30.00
❑ LP-10020 [M]	I'm Going to Serve the Lord	196?	25.00
❑ LPS-10045 [S]	Live the Right Way	196?	30.00
❑ LP-10045 [M]	Live the Right Way	196?	30.00
❑ LPS-10030 [S]	Move On Up	196?	30.00
❑ LP-10030 [M]	Move On Up	196?	25.00
❑ 2CK-10065	Please Answer This Prayer	197?	30.00
❑ LPS-10040 [S]	Shout!	196?	30.00
❑ LP-10040 [M]	Shout!	196?	25.00
❑ LP-10011 [M]	Stand By Me	1965	30.00
❑ LP-10017 [M]	The Fantastic Violinaires	1966	30.00
❑ LPS-10053	The Violinaires in Concert	1968	25.00

VIRGIN INSANITY

FUNKY

Number	Title	Yr	NM
❑ 71411	Illusions of the Maintenance Man	1970	200.00

VIRGINIANS, THE

MONUMENT

Number	Title	Yr	NM
❑ MLP-8031 [M]	Ballads and Bluegrass	1965	25.00
❑ SLP-18031 [S]	Ballads and Bluegrass	1965	30.00

UNITED ARTISTS

Number	Title	Yr	NM
❑ UAL-3293 [M]	The Wonderful World of Bluegrass Music	1963	25.00
❑ UAS-6293 [S]	The Wonderful World of Bluegrass Music	1963	30.00

VIRTUES, THE

FAYETTE

Number	Title	Yr	NM
❑ 1816 [M]	Frank Virtue and the Virtues	1964	60.00
—Blue cover			
❑ 1816 [M]	Frank Virtue and the Virtues	1964	40.00
—White cover			

STRAND

Number	Title	Yr	NM
❑ L-1061 [M]	Guitar Boogie Shuffle	1960	30.00
❑ SL-1061 [S]	Guitar Boogie Shuffle	1960	40.00

WYNNE

Number	Title	Yr	NM
❑ WLP-111 [M]	Guitar Boogie Shuffle	1960	120.00
❑ WLP-711 [S]	Guitar Boogie Shuffle	1960	180.00

VISAGE

POLYDOR

Number	Title	Yr	NM
❑ 823052-1	Beat Boy	1984	15.00
❑ 815347-1	Fade to Grey -- The Singles Collection	1983	15.00
❑ PD1-6350	The Anvil	1982	15.00
❑ PD1-6304	Visage	1981	15.00
❑ PX1-501 [EP]	Visage	1981	15.00

VISCOUNTS, THE (1)

AMY

Number	Title	Yr	NM
❑ 8008 [M]	Harlem Nocturne	1965	40.00
❑ S-8008 [S]	Harlem Nocturne	1965	50.00

MADISON

Number	Title	Yr	NM
❑ 1001 [M]	The Viscounts	1960	200.00

VISION

MUSIC IS MEDICINE

Number	Title	Yr	NM
❑ 9027	Vision	198?	15.00

VISION OF SUNSHINE

AVCO EMBASSY

Number	Title	Yr	NM
❑ 33007	Vision of Sunshine	1970	30.00

VISITORS, THE

COBBLESTONE

Number	Title	Yr	NM
❑ 9010	Neptune	197?	25.00

MUSE

Number	Title	Yr	NM
❑ MR-5024	In My Youth	197?	15.00
❑ MR-5094	Motherland	1976	15.00
❑ MR-5195	Neptune	197?	12.00
❑ MR-5047	Rebirth	197?	15.00

VOGUES, THE

CO & CE

Number	Title	Yr	NM
❑ LP-1230 [M]	Five O'Clock World	1966	50.00
—Stereo pressings of these two albums are not known to exist!			
❑ LP-1229 [M]	Meet the Vogues	1965	50.00

PICKWICK

Number	Title	Yr	NM
❑ SPC-3214 [R]	A Lover's Concerto	1971	12.00
❑ SPC-3188 [R]	Five O'Clock World	1971	12.00

REPRISE

Number	Title	Yr	NM
❑ RS6347	Memories	1969	18.00
—With "W7" and "r:" logos on two-tone orange label			
❑ RS6371	The Vogues' Greatest Hits	1969	18.00
—With "W7" and "r:" logos on two-tone orange label			
❑ SW-93040	The Vogues' Greatest Hits	1970	25.00
—Capitol Record Club edition			
❑ RS6395	The Vogues Sing the Good Old Songs	1970	15.00
❑ RS6326 [B]	Till	1969	18.00
—With "W7" and "r:" logos on two-tone orange label			
❑ RS6314	Turn Around, Look at Me	1968	18.00
—With "W7" and "r:" logos on two-tone orange label			
❑ ST-91559	Turn Around, Look at Me	1968	25.00
—Capitol Record Club edition			

SSS INTERNATIONAL

Number	Title	Yr	NM
❑ 34	The Vogues' Greatest Hits	1977	12.00

VOLLENWEIDER, ANDREAS

CBS/FM

Number	Title	Yr	NM
❑ FM42255	Down to the Moon	1986	12.00
❑ FM39963	White Winds	1985	12.00

CBS MASTERWORKS

Number	Title	Yr	NM
❑ FM37793	...Behind the Gardens... Behind the Wall...Under the Tree...	1984	12.00
❑ FM37827	Caverna Magica (...Under the Tree-In the Cave...)	1984	12.00

COLUMBIA

Number	Title	Yr	NM
❑ OC45154	Dancing with the Lion	1989	15.00

VOLTAGE BROTHERS, THE

LIFESONG

Number	Title	Yr	NM
❑ JZ35042	The Voltage Brothers	1978	25.00
❑ JZ35653	Throw Down	1978	25.00

MTM

Number	Title	Yr	NM
❑ ST-71055	The Voltage Brothers	1986	18.00

VON SCHMIDT, ERIC

FOLKLORE

Number	Title	Yr	NM
❑ FRLP-14005 [M]	Folk Blues	1964	30.00
❑ FRST-14005 [S]	Folk Blues	1964	40.00

PRESTIGE

Number	Title	Yr	NM
❑ PRLP-7384 [M]	Eric Sings Von Schmidt	1966	25.00
❑ PRST-7384 [S]	Eric Sings Von Schmidt	1966	30.00

SMASH

Number	Title	Yr	NM
❑ SRS-67124	Who Knocked the Brains Out of the Sky?	1969	25.00

W

WACKER, FRED

CADET

Number	Title	Yr	NM
❑ LPS-4050 [S]	Fred Wacker Swings Cool	1966	18.00
❑ LP-4050 [M]	Fred Wacker Swings Cool	1966	15.00

DOLPHIN

Number	Title	Yr	NM
❑ 9 [M]	Freddy Wacker and His Windy City Seven	195?	50.00

WADDELL, STEVE

STOMP OFF

Number	Title	Yr	NM
❑ SOS-1172	Frisco Comes to Melbourne	1987	12.00

WADE, ADAM

COED

Number	Title	Yr	NM
❑ LPC-903 [M]	Adam and Evening	1961	50.00
❑ LPCS-903 [S]	Adam and Evening	1961	60.00
❑ LPC-902 [M]	And Then Came Adam	1960	50.00
❑ LPCS-902 [S]	And Then Came Adam	1960	60.00

EPIC

Number	Title	Yr	NM
❑ LN24019 [M]	Adam Wade's Greatest Hits	1962	30.00
❑ BN26019 [S]	Adam Wade's Greatest Hits	1962	30.00
❑ LN24056 [M]	A Very Good Year for Girls	1963	30.00
❑ BN26056 [S]	A Very Good Year for Girls	1963	30.00

Number	Title	Yr	NM
❑ LN24026 [M]	One Is a Lonely Number	1962	30.00
❑ BN26026 [S]	One Is a Lonely Number	1962	30.00
❑ LN24044 [M]	What Kind of Fool Am I?	1963	30.00
❑ BN26044 [S]	What Kind of Fool Am I?	1963	30.00
KIRSHNER			
❑ PZ34919	Adam Wade	1977	15.00

WADSWORTH MANSION

Number	Title	Yr	NM
SUSSEX			
❑ SXBS-7008	Wadsworth Manison	1971	30.00
— Some copies of this LP have the above typographical error			
❑ SXBS-7008	Wadsworth Mansion	1971	25.00

WADUD, ABDUL

Number	Title	Yr	NM
RED RECORD			
❑ VPA-147	Straight Ahead/Free at Last	198?	15.00

WAGNER, DANNY, AND KINDRED SOUL

Number	Title	Yr	NM
IMPERIAL			
❑ LP-12405	The Kindred Soul of Danny Wagner	1968	30.00

WAGNER, JACK

Number	Title	Yr	NM
QWEST			
❑ 25089 [EP]	All I Need	1984	10.00
— Version with five songs on it			
❑ 25214	All I Need	1985	10.00
— Version with 10 songs on it			
❑ 25562	Don't Give Up Your Day Job	1987	10.00
❑ 25318	Lighting Up the Night	1985	10.00

WAGNER, LARRY

Number	Title	Yr	NM
A44			
❑ AP-501 [10]	Larry Wagner	1954	60.00

WAGNER, ROGER, CHORALE

Number	Title	Yr	NM
CAPITOL			
❑ P8332 [M]	Folk Songs of the Frontier	195?	30.00
❑ P8324 [M]	Folk Songs of the New World	195?	30.00
❑ PBR8345 [M]	Folk Songs of the Old World	195?	40.00
❑ P8387 [M]	Folk Songs of the World	195?	25.00
❑ STBB-488	Great Choral Music of Christmas	1970	18.00
❑ P8353 [M]	Joy to the World!	195?	18.00
— Original labels are green and gold			
❑ SP8353 [S]	Joy to the World!	195?	30.00
❑ P8267 [M]	Songs of Stephen Foster	195?	30.00
❑ T2591 [M]	The Best of the Roger Wagner Chorale Christmas Carols	1966	15.00
❑ ST2591 [S]	The Best of the Roger Wagner Chorale Christmas Carols	1966	18.00
— Originals have black "The Star Line" labels			

WAGONER, PORTER, AND DOLLY PARTON

Number	Title	Yr	NM
PAIR			
❑ PDL1-1013	Sweet Harmony	1986	15.00
RCA VICTOR			
❑ LSP-4186	Always, Always	1969	25.00
❑ LPM-3926 [M]	Just Between You and Me	1968	100.00
❑ LSP-3926 [S]	Just Between You and Me	1968	25.00
❑ LSP-4039	Just the Two of Us	1968	25.00
❑ APL1-0248	Love and Music	1973	18.00
❑ LSP-4388	Once More	1970	25.00
❑ APL1-0646	Porter 'N' Dolly	1974	18.00
❑ AHL1-3700	Porter Wagoner and Dolly Parton	1980	15.00
❑ AYL1-4251	Porter Wagoner and Dolly Parton	1982	10.00
— Best Buy Series" reissue			
❑ LSP-4305	Porter Wayne and Dolly Rebecca	1970	25.00
❑ APL1-1116	Say Forever	1975	18.00
❑ LSP-4556	The Best of Porter Wagoner and Dolly Parton	1971	25.00
❑ AHL1-4556	The Best of Porter Wagoner and Dolly Parton	1983	12.00
❑ LSP-4628	The Right Combination/ Burning the Midnight Oil	1972	18.00
❑ LSP-4761	Together Always	1972	18.00
❑ LSP-4490	Two of a Kind	1971	25.00
❑ LSP-4841	We Found It	1973	18.00

WAGONER, PORTER, AND SKEETER DAVIS

Number	Title	Yr	NM
RCA VICTOR			
❑ LPM-2529 [M]	Porter Wagoner and Skeeter Davis Sing Duets	1962	30.00
❑ LSP-2529 [S]	Porter Wagoner and Skeeter Davis Sing Duets	1962	30.00

WAGONER, PORTER

Number	Title	Yr	NM
ACCORD			
❑ SN-7179	Down Home Country	1982	15.00
DOT/MCA			
❑ 39053	Porter Wagoner	1986	12.00
RCA CAMDEN			
❑ CAL-861 [M]	An Old Log Cabin for Sale	1965	15.00
❑ CAS-861 [S]	An Old Log Cabin for Sale	1965	15.00
❑ CAL-769 [M]	A Satisfied Mind	1963	15.00
❑ CAS-769(e) [R]	A Satisfied Mind	1963	12.00
❑ CXS-9010	Blue Moon of Kentucky	1971	18.00
❑ CAS-2321	Country Feeling	1968	15.00
❑ CAL-2191 [M]	Green, Green Grass of Home	1967	15.00
❑ CAS-2191 [S]	Green, Green Grass of Home	1967	15.00
❑ CAS-2409	Howdy Neighbor	1970	15.00
❑ CAL-2116 [M]	I'm Day Dreamin' Tonight	1967	15.00
❑ CAS-2116 [S]	I'm Day Dreamin' Tonight	1967	15.00
❑ CAS-2478	Porter Wagoner Country	1971	15.00
❑ CAS-2588	The Silent Kind	1972	15.00
❑ CAL-942 [M]	Your Old Love Letters" And Other Country Hits	1966	15.00
❑ CAS-942 [S]	Your Old Love Letters" And Other Country Hits	1966	15.00
RCA VICTOR			
❑ LPM-1358 [M]	A Satisfied Mind	1956	200.00
❑ LPM-2447 [M]	A Slice of Life -- Songs Happy 'N' Sad	1962	30.00
❑ LSP-2447 [S]	A Slice of Life -- Songs Happy 'N' Sad	1962	30.00
❑ LSP-4734	Ballads of Love	1972	18.00
❑ AHL1-7000	Collector's Series	1985	12.00
❑ LPM-3593 [M]	Confessions of a Broken Man	1966	25.00
❑ LSP-3593 [S]	Confessions of a Broken Man	1966	30.00
❑ LSP-4386	Down in the Alley	1970	25.00
❑ LSP-4034	Gospel Country	1968	25.00
❑ LPM-3488 [M]	Grand Old Gospel	1966	25.00
❑ LSP-3488 [S]	Grand Old Gospel	1966	30.00
❑ APL1-0713	Highway Headin' South	1974	18.00
❑ APL1-0142	I'll Keep on Lovin' You	1973	18.00
❑ LPM-2840 [M]	In Person	1964	30.00
❑ LSP-2840 [S]	In Person	1964	30.00
❑ LSP-4181	Me and My Boys	1969	25.00
❑ LPM-3855 [M]	More Grand Old Gospel	1967	30.00
❑ LSP-3855 [S]	More Grand Old Gospel	1967	25.00
❑ LPM-3509 [M]	On the Road	1966	25.00
❑ LSP-3509 [S]	On the Road	1966	30.00
❑ AHL1-2432	Porter	1977	15.00
❑ LSP-4586	Porter Wagoner Sings His Own	1971	18.00
❑ LSP-4508	Simple As I Am	1971	25.00
❑ APL1-1056	Sing Love	1975	18.00
❑ LPM-3683 [M]	Soul of a Convict	1967	30.00
❑ LSP-3683 [S]	Soul of a Convict	1967	25.00
❑ LPM-3560 [M]	The Best of Porter Wagoner	1966	25.00
❑ LSP-3560 [S]	The Best of Porter Wagoner	1966	30.00
❑ ANL1-1213	The Best of Porter Wagoner	1975	15.00
❑ LSP-4321	The Best of Porter Wagoner, Volume 2	1970	25.00
❑ LPM-2960 [M]	The Bluegrass Story	1964	25.00
❑ LSP-2960 [S]	The Bluegrass Story	1964	30.00
❑ LPM-3968 [M]	The Bottom of the Bottle	1968	100.00
❑ LSP-3968 [S]	The Bottom of the Bottle	1968	25.00
❑ LSP-4116	The Carroll County Accident	1969	25.00
❑ LPM-3797 [M]	The Cold Hard Facts of Life	1967	30.00
❑ LSP-3797 [S]	The Cold Hard Facts of Life	1967	25.00
❑ APL1-0346	The Farmer	1974	18.00
❑ LSP-4810	The Porter Wagoner Experience	1973	18.00
❑ LPM-2650 [M]	The Porter Wagoner Show	1963	30.00
❑ LSP-2650 [S]	The Porter Wagoner Show	1963	30.00
❑ LPM-3389 [M]	The Thin Man from West Plains	1965	25.00
❑ LSP-3389 [S]	The Thin Man from West Plains	1965	30.00
❑ APL1-0496	Tore Down	1974	18.00
❑ LSP-4661	What Ain't to Be	1972	18.00
❑ LPM-2706 [M]	Y'All Come	1963	30.00
❑ LSP-2706 [S]	Y'All Come	1963	30.00
❑ LSP-4286	You Got-ta Have a License	1970	25.00
WARNER BROS.			
❑ 23783	Viva Porter Wagoner!	1983	12.00

WAIKIKIS, THE

Number	Title	Yr	NM
KAPP			
❑ KL-1484 [M]	A Taste of Hawaii	1966	18.00
❑ KS-3484 [S]	A Taste of Hawaii	1966	25.00
❑ KL-1437 [M]	Beach Party	1965	18.00
❑ KS-3437 [S]	Beach Party	1965	25.00
❑ KS-3612	Greatest Hits	1970	15.00
❑ KL-1432 [M]	Hawaii Honeymoon	1965	18.00
❑ KS-3432 [S]	Hawaii Honeymoon	1965	25.00
❑ KL-1366 [M]	Hawaii Tattoo	1964	18.00
❑ KS-3366 [S]	Hawaii Tattoo	1964	25.00
❑ KL-1473 [M]	Lollipops and Roses	1966	18.00
❑ KS-3473 [S]	Lollipops and Roses	1966	25.00
❑ KS-3575	Midnight Luau	1969	18.00
❑ KS-3593	Moonlight on Diamond Head	1969	18.00
❑ KL-1555 [M]	Pearly Shells from Hawaii	1968	30.00
— White label promo in stereo cover, "Mono" sticker on front			
❑ KS-3555 [S]	Pearly Shells from Hawaii	1968	18.00
MCA			
❑ 547	Greatest Hits	197?	12.00
❑ 544	Pearly Shells from Hawaii	197?	12.00

WAILERS, THE

Number	Title	Yr	NM
BELL			
❑ 6016	Walk Thru the People	1969	30.00
ETIQUETTE			
❑ ALB-026 [M]	Out of Our Tree	1966	200.00
❑ ALB-01 [M]	The Fabulous Wailers at the Castle	196?	200.00
❑ ALB-022 [M]	The Wailers and Company	196?	140.00
❑ 22296/7 [B]	The Wailers and Their Greatest Hits	1979	30.00
❑ ALB-023 [M]	Wailers, Wailers, Everywhere	196?	200.00
GOLDEN CREST			
❑ CR-3075 [M]	Fabulous Wailers	1959	300.00
— Full-color photo on cover			

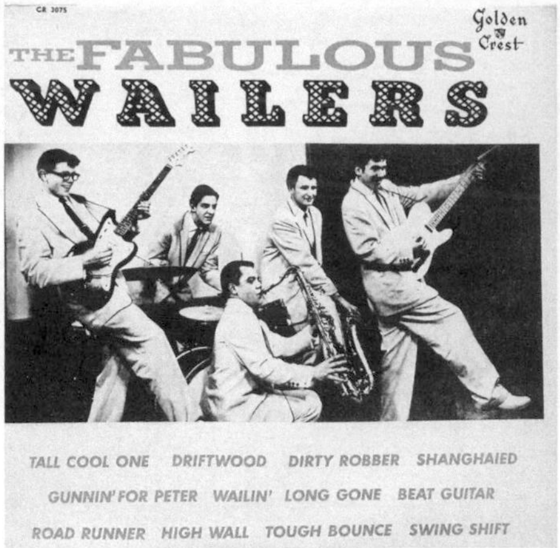

Number	Title	Yr	NM
❑ CR-3075 [M]	Fabulous Wailers	1962	300.00
— Black and white photo on cover			
❑ CR-3075 [M]	Fabulous Wailers	196?	80.00
— Title, no photo, on cover			
IMPERIAL			
❑ LP-9262 [M]	Tall Cool One	1964	80.00
❑ LP-12262 [S]	Tall Cool One	1964	120.00
UNITED ARTISTS			
❑ UAL-3557 [M]	Outburst!	1966	80.00
❑ UAS-6557 [S]	Outburst!	1966	120.00

WAINWRIGHT, LOUDON, III

Number	Title	Yr	NM
ARISTA			
❑ AB4173	Final Exam	1978	15.00
❑ AL4063	T Shirt	1976	15.00
ATLANTIC			
❑ SD8291	Album II	1971	25.00
❑ SD8260	Loudon Wainwright III	1970	25.00
COLUMBIA			
❑ KC31462	Album III	1972	18.00
❑ PC31462 [B]	Album III	198?	10.00
— Budget-line reissue			
❑ KC32710	Attempted Mustache	1973	18.00
❑ PC32710 [B]	Attempted Mustache	198?	10.00
— Budget-line reissue			
❑ PC33369	Unrequited	1975	15.00
— No bar code on cover			
❑ PC33369	Unrequited	198?	10.00
— Budget-line reissue with bar code			
ROUNDER			
❑ 3050	A Live One	1979	15.00
❑ 3076	Fame and Wealth	1983	15.00
❑ 3096	I'm Alright	1986	12.00
❑ 3106	More Love Songs	1987	12.00
SILVERTONE			
❑ 1203-1-J	Therapy	1989	15.00

WAITE, GENEVIEVE

Number	Title	Yr	NM
PARAMOUR			
❑ 5088 [B]	Romance Is on the Rise	1974	30.00

WAITE, JOHN

Number	Title	Yr	NM
CHRYSALIS			
❑ CHR-1376	Ignition	1982	12.00
❑ FV41376	Ignition	1983	10.00
— Reissue of 1376			
EMI AMERICA			
❑ ST-17164	Mask of Smiles	1985	10.00
❑ ST-517164	Mask of Smiles	1985	12.00
— Columbia House edition			
❑ ST-17124	No Brakes	1984	10.00
❑ ST-517124	No Brakes	1984	12.00
— Columbia House edition			
❑ PW-17227	Rover's Return	1987	10.00

WAITRESSES, THE

Number	Title	Yr	NM
POLYDOR			
❑ 810980-1	Bruiseology	1983	12.00
❑ 810980-1 [DJ]	Bruiseology	1983	30.00
— Promo only on purpleish vinyl			
❑ PX-1-507 [EP]	I Could Rule the World If I Could Only Get the Parts	1982	12.00

Number	Title	Yr	NM
❑ PD-1-6346	Wasn't Tomorrow Wonderful?	1982	12.00

WAITS, TOM

ASYLUM

Number	Title	Yr	NM
❑ 6E-162 [B]	Blue Valentine	1978	12.00
❑ SD5061	Closing Time	1973	15.00
❑ 7E-1117	Foreign Affairs	1977	12.00
❑ 6E-295	Heartattack and Vine	1980	12.00
❑ 7E-2008	Nighthawks at the Diner	1975	15.00
❑ 7E-1078 [B]	Small Change	1976	15.00
❑ 7E-1015	The Heart of Saturday Night	1974	15.00
—Original "clouds" label, no Warner Communications logo			
❑ 7E-1015	The Heart of Saturday Night	1984	10.00
—Reissue with black and yellow label			

ELEKTRA

Number	Title	Yr	NM
❑ 60416	Anthology of Tom Waits	1985	12.00

EPITAPH

Number	Title	Yr	NM
❑ 86547	Mule Variations	1999	15.00

ISLAND

Number	Title	Yr	NM
❑ 90987	Big Time	1988	12.00
❑ 90572	Franks Wild Years	1987	12.00
❑ 90299	Rain Dogs	1985	12.00
❑ 90095	Swordfishtrombones	1983	15.00
❑ 424691	Swordfishtrombones	2009	25.00

WAKEFIELD SUN

MGM

Number	Title	Yr	NM
❑ SE-4626	Wakefield Sun	1969	30.00

WAKELY, JIMMY

CAPITOL

Number	Title	Yr	NM
❑ H-9004 [10]	Christmas on the Range	1950	150.00
❑ H4008 [10]	Songs of the West	195?	120.00

DECCA

Number	Title	Yr	NM
❑ DL8680 [M]	Enter and Rest and Pray	1957	60.00
❑ DL75077	Heartaches	1969	18.00
❑ DL75192	Now and Then	1970	18.00
❑ DL8409 [M]	Santa Fe Trail	1956	80.00

DOT

Number	Title	Yr	NM
❑ DLP-3754 [M]	Christmas with Jimmy Wakely	1966	25.00
❑ DLP-25734 [S]	Christmas with Jimmy Wakely	1966	30.00
❑ DLP-3711 [M]	Slippin' Around	1966	25.00
❑ DLP-25711 [S]	Slippin' Around	1966	30.00

MCA CORAL

Number	Title	Yr	NM
❑ 20033	Blue Shadows	1973	12.00

MCR

Number	Title	Yr	NM
❑ 1254	Jimmy Wakely Revisits Country Western Swing with the Big Band Sound	1974	18.00
❑ 1250	Jimmy Wakely Sings a Tribute to Bob Wills	1974	18.00

SHASTA

Number	Title	Yr	NM
❑ 501	Country Million Sellers	195?	18.00
❑ 505	Jimmy Wakely Sings	196?	18.00
❑ 528	J.W. Country	196?	18.00
❑ 502	Merry Christmas	1959	18.00
❑ 512	The Jimmy Wakely Family Show	196?	18.00

TOPS

Number	Title	Yr	NM
❑ L-1601 [M]	A Cowboy Serenade	195?	30.00

VOCALION

Number	Title	Yr	NM
❑ VL73904	Big Country Songs	1970	15.00
❑ VL73857	Here's Jimmy Wakely	1968	15.00

WAKEMAN, RICK

A&M

Number	Title	Yr	NM
❑ SP-3621	Journey to the Centre of the Earth	1974	15.00
❑ QU-53621 [Q]	Journey to the Centre of the Earth	1974	40.00
❑ SP-3156	Journey to the Centre of the Earth	198?	10.00
—Budget-line reissue of 3621			
❑ SP-4583	No Earthly Connection	1976	15.00
❑ SP-6501 [B]	Rhapsodies	1979	25.00
❑ SP-4660	Rick Wakeman's Criminal Record	1977	15.00
❑ SP-4515	The Myths and Legends of King Arthur and the Knights of the Round Table	1975	15.00
❑ QU-54515 [Q]	The Myths and Legends of King Arthur and the Knights of the Round Table	1975	40.00
❑ SP-3230	The Myths and Legends of King Arthur and the Knights of the Round Table	1984	10.00
—Budget-line reissue of 4515			
❑ SP-4361	The Six Wives of Henry VIII	1973	15.00
—Originals have brown labels			
❑ QU-54361 [Q]	The Six Wives of Henry VIII	1974	40.00
❑ SP-4361	The Six Wives of Henry VIII	1974	12.00
—Silver label with "fading" A&M logo			
❑ SP-3229	The Six Wives of Henry VIII	1984	10.00
—Budget-line reissue of 4361			
❑ SP-4614	White Rock	1977	15.00

MOBILE FIDELITY

Number	Title	Yr	NM
❑ 1-230	Journey to the Centre of the Earth	1995	25.00
—Audiophile vinyl			

SWEET THUNDER

Number	Title	Yr	NM
❑ 1	Journey to the Centre of the Earth	1981	50.00
—Audiophile vinyl			

VARESE SARABANDE

Number	Title	Yr	NM
❑ STV-81162 [B]	The Burning (Soundtrack)	1982	25.00

WALCOTT, COLLIN

ECM

Number	Title	Yr	NM
❑ 1062	Cloud	1976	15.00
❑ 1096	Grazing	1977	15.00

WALD, JERRY

KAPP

Number	Title	Yr	NM
❑ KL-1043 [M]	Listen to the Music of Jerry Wald	1956	40.00

LION

Number	Title	Yr	NM
❑ L-70014 [M]	Tops in Pops -- Designed for Dancing	1958	30.00

WALDEN, NARADA MICHAEL

ATLANTIC

Number	Title	Yr	NM
❑ SD19222	Awakening	1979	12.00
❑ SD19351	Confidence	1981	12.00
❑ SD19141	I Cry, I Smile	1978	12.00
❑ SD19259	The Dance of Life	1979	12.00
❑ SD19279	Victory	1980	12.00
❑ 80058	You, Looking at Me	1982	12.00

REPRISE

Number	Title	Yr	NM
❑ 25694	Divine Emotion	1988	12.00

WARNER BROS.

Number	Title	Yr	NM
❑ 25176	The Nature of Things	1984	12.00

WALDO, TERRY

DIRTY SHAME

Number	Title	Yr	NM
❑ 1237	Snookums Rag	197?	15.00

STOMP OFF

Number	Title	Yr	NM
❑ SOS-1120	Terry Waldo and the Gotham City Band	1987	12.00
❑ SOS-1002	Wizard of the Keyboard	198?	12.00

WALDO'S GUTBUCKET SYNCOPATORS

BLACKBIRD

Number	Title	Yr	NM
❑ 12009	Jazz in the Afternoon	197?	15.00
❑ 6002	Ohio Theatre Concert	197?	12.00

STOMP OFF

Number	Title	Yr	NM
❑ SOS-1001	Foolin' Devilish	198?	12.00
❑ SOS-1036	Presents	198?	12.00

WALDO'S RAGTIME ORCHESTRA

STOMP OFF

Number	Title	Yr	NM
❑ SOS-1007	Smiles and Chuckles	198?	12.00
❑ SOS-1069	Spectacular Ragtime	198?	12.00

WALDRON, MAL, AND GARY PEACOCK

CATALYST

Number	Title	Yr	NM
❑ 7906	First Encounter	197?	15.00

WALDRON, MAL, AND STEVE LACY

HAT ART

Number	Title	Yr	NM
❑ 2038	Let's Call This	1987	18.00

INNER CITY

Number	Title	Yr	NM
❑ IC-3010	One-upsmanship	197?	15.00

SOUL NOTE

Number	Title	Yr	NM
❑ 121170	Sempre Amore	1990	18.00

WALDRON, MAL

ARISTA/FREEDOM

Number	Title	Yr	NM
❑ AF1013	Blues for Lady Day	1975	15.00
❑ AF1042	Signals	1977	15.00

BETHLEHEM

Number	Title	Yr	NM
❑ BCP-6045 [M]	Left Alone	1960	40.00
❑ SBCP-6045 [S]	Left Alone	1960	40.00

ENJA

Number	Title	Yr	NM
❑ 2004	Black Glory	197?	18.00
❑ 2050	Hard Talk	197?	18.00
❑ 3075	Mingus Lives	198?	15.00
❑ 2034	Up Popped the Devil	197?	18.00
❑ 4010	What It Is	198?	15.00

FANTASY

Number	Title	Yr	NM
❑ OJC-132	Impressions	198?	12.00
❑ OJC-611	Mal/1	1991	15.00
❑ OJC-082	The Quest	198?	12.00

INNER CITY

Number	Title	Yr	NM
❑ IC-3018	Moods	1979	18.00

MUSE

Number	Title	Yr	NM
❑ MR-5305	Encounters	198?	12.00

MUSIC MINUS ONE

Number	Title	Yr	NM
❑ 4005 [M]	Blue Drums	1961	25.00
❑ 4007 [M]	For Pianists Only	1961	25.00
❑ 1018 [M]	For Singers 'N Singer	1960	25.00
❑ 175 [M]	Fun With Brushes	1960	25.00
❑ 1017 [M]	Mal Waldron	1960	25.00
❑ 1012 [M]	Moonglow and Stardust	1960	25.00
❑ 1015 [M]	Music of Duke Ellington	1960	25.00
❑ 1016 [M]	Music of McHugh	1960	25.00
❑ 4008 [M]	They Laughed When I Sat Down to Play	1961	25.00

NEW JAZZ

Number	Title	Yr	NM
❑ NJLP-8242 [M]	Impressions	1960	50.00
—Purple label			
❑ NJLP-8242 [M]	Impressions	1965	30.00
—Blue label, trident logo at right			
❑ NJLP-8201 [M]	Mal/3: Sounds	1958	50.00
—Purple label			
❑ NJLP-8201 [M]	Mal/3: Sounds	1958	100.00
—Yellow label			
❑ NJLP-8201 [M]	Mal/3: Sounds	1965	30.00
—Blue label, trident logo at right			
❑ NJLP-8208 [M]	Mal/4: Trio	1958	50.00
—Purple label			
❑ NJLP-8208 [M]	Mal/4: Trio	1965	30.00
—Blue label, trident logo at right			
❑ NJLP-8269 [M]	The Quest	1962	50.00
—Purple label			
❑ NJLP-8269 [M]	The Quest	1965	30.00
—Blue label, trident logo at right			

PALO ALTO

Number	Title	Yr	NM
❑ PA-8014	One Entrance, Many Exits	1982	12.00

PAULA

Number	Title	Yr	NM
❑ LPS-4000	Mal Waldron on the Steinway	197?	15.00

PRESTIGE

Number	Title	Yr	NM
❑ 24107	After Hours	197?	18.00
❑ PRLP-7090 [M]	Mal/1	1957	80.00
❑ PRLP-7111 [M]	Mal/2	1957	80.00
❑ 24068	Mal Waldron/1 and 2	197?	18.00
❑ PRST-7579 [S]	The Quest	1969	25.00

SOUL NOTE

Number	Title	Yr	NM
❑ 121118	The Go-Go -- Live at the Vilalge Gate	1989	15.00
❑ 121148	The Seagulls of Kristiansund	1990	18.00
❑ 121130	Update	1989	15.00

STATUS

Number	Title	Yr	NM
❑ ST-8316 [M]	The Dealers	1965	40.00

WEST 54

Number	Title	Yr	NM
❑ 8010	Live/Left Alone	1980	15.00

WALES, HOWARD, AND JERRY GARCIA

DOUGLAS

Number	Title	Yr	NM
❑ Z30580	Hooteroll	1971	40.00

WALI AND THE AFRO-CARAVAN

SOLID STATE

Number	Title	Yr	NM
❑ SS 18000	Home Lost and Found	1969	25.00

WALKER, BILLY

COLUMBIA

Number	Title	Yr	NM
❑ CL1935 [M]	Billy Walker's Greatest Hits	1963	18.00
❑ CS8735 [S]	Billy Walker's Greatest Hits	1963	25.00
❑ CS9798	Billy Walker's Greatest Hits, Volume 2	1969	18.00
❑ CL1624 [M]	Everybody's Hits But Mine	1961	25.00
❑ CS8424 [S]	Everybody's Hits But Mine	1961	30.00
❑ C30226	Goodnight	1971	15.00
❑ CL2206 [M]	Thank You for Calling	1964	18.00
❑ CS9006 [S]	Thank You for Calling	1964	25.00
❑ CL2331 [M]	The Gun, the Gold and the Girl/Cross the Brazos at Waco	1965	18.00
❑ CS9131 [S]	The Gun, the Gold and the Girl/Cross the Brazos at Waco	1965	25.00

HARMONY

Number	Title	Yr	NM
❑ HL7306 [M]	Anything Your Heart Desires	1964	18.00
❑ HL7410 [M]	Big Country Hits	1967	18.00
❑ HS11210 [S]	Big Country Hits	1967	15.00
❑ HS11414	Charlie's Shoes	1970	15.00
❑ H31177	There May Be No Tomorrow	1972	12.00

MGM

Number	Title	Yr	NM
❑ SE-4887	Billy Walker's All Time Greatest Hits	1972	15.00
❑ SE-4756	I'm Gonna Keep On Lovin' You/She Goes Walking Through My Mind	1971	18.00
❑ SE-4789	Live!	1972	18.00
❑ SE-4863	The Billy Walker Show	1973	15.00
❑ SE-4938 [B]	Too Many Memories	1974	15.00
❑ SE-4682	When a Man Loves a Woman (The Way That I Love You)	1970	18.00

MONUMENT

Number	Title	Yr	NM
❑ MLP-8047 [M]	A Million and One	1966	15.00
❑ SLP-18047 [S]	A Million and One	1966	18.00
❑ SLP-18101	Billy Walker Salutes the Country Music Hall of Fame	1969	18.00
❑ KZ31912	Billy Walker's Greatest Hits	1972	15.00
❑ 6641	Billy Walker's Greatest Hits	1976	12.00
❑ SLP-18143	Darling Days	1970	18.00

Number	Title	Yr	NM
❑ SLP-18090	I Taught Her Everything She Knows	1968	18.00
❑ SLP-18116	Portrait of Billy	1969	18.00
❑ MLP-8072 [M]	The Walker Way	1967	25.00
❑ SLP-18072 [S]	The Walker Way	1967	18.00

RCA VICTOR

❑ APL1-1489	Alone Again	1976	15.00
❑ APL1-1160	Lovin' and Losin'	1975	15.00

WALKER, CHARLIE

COLUMBIA

❑ CL1691 [M]	Charlie Walker's Greatest Hits	1961	25.00
❑ CS8491 [S]	Charlie Walker's Greatest Hits	1961	30.00

EPIC

❑ LN24153 [M]	Born to Lose	1965	18.00
❑ BN26153 [S]	Born to Lose	1965	25.00
❑ BN26343 [S]	Charlie Walker's Greatest Hits	1968	18.00
❑ LN24343 [M]	Charlie Walker's Greatest Hits	1968	40.00
❑ LN24137 [M]	Close All the Honky Tonks	1965	18.00
❑ BN26137 [S]	Close All the Honky Tonks	1965	25.00
❑ LN24328 [M]	Don't Squeeze My Sharmon	1967	30.00
❑ BN26328 [S]	Don't Squeeze My Sharmon	1967	25.00
❑ BN26424	He Is My Everything	1969	18.00
❑ E30660	Honky Tonkin'	1971	18.00
❑ BN26483	Recorded Live in Dallas	1969	18.00
❑ LN24209 [M]	Wine, Women and Walker	1966	18.00
❑ BN26209 [S]	Wine, Women and Walker	1966	25.00

HARMONY

❑ HL7415 [M]	Golden Hits	1967	18.00
❑ HS11215 [S]	Golden Hits	1967	15.00

PLANTATION

❑ 535	Golden Hits	1978	12.00

RCA VICTOR

❑ APL1-0181	Break Out the Bottle	1973	15.00
❑ LSP-4737	Charlie Walker	1972	18.00

VOCALION

❑ VL73814	The Style of Charlie Walker	1968	15.00

WALKER, CINDY

MONUMENT

❑ MLP-8020 [M]	Words and Music by Cindy Walker	1964	25.00
❑ SLP-18020 [S]	Words and Music by Cindy Walker	1964	30.00

WALKER, CLINT

WARNER BROS.

❑ W1343 [M]	Inspiration	1959	30.00
❑ WS1343 [S]	Inspiration	1959	40.00

WALKER, DAVID T.

ODE

❑ SP-77011	David T. Walker	1971	12.00
❑ SP-77035	On Love	1976	12.00
❑ SP-77020	Press On	1974	12.00

ZEA

❑ 1000	Plum Happy	1970	18.00

WALKER, JERRY JEFF

ATCO

❑ SD 33-336	Bein' Free	1970	25.00
❑ SD 33-297	Five Years Gone	1969	30.00
❑ SD 33-259 [B]	Mr. Bojangles	1968	30.00

BAINBRIDGE

❑ 6222	Mr. Bojangles	198?	12.00

DECCA

❑ DL75384	Jerry Jeff Walker	1972	18.00

ELEKTRA

❑ 6E 163	Jerry Jeff	1978	12.00
❑ 6E-239	Too Old to Change	1980	12.00

MCA

❑ 8013	A Man Must Carry On	1977	15.00
❑ 6003	A Man Must Carry On	198?	12.00
—Budget-line reissue			
❑ 3041	Contrary to Ordinary	1978	12.00
❑ 37162	Contrary to Ordinary	198?	10.00
—Budget-line reissue			
❑ 5355	Cowjazz	1983	12.00
❑ 2202	It's a Good Night for Singin'	1976	12.00
❑ 27026	It's a Good Night for Singin'	198?	10.00
—Budget-line reissue			
❑ 510	Jerry Jeff Walker	1975	12.00
—Reissue of Decca LP			
❑ 2358	Jerry Jeff Walker	1977	10.00
—Reissue of MCA 510			
❑ 2156	Ridin' High	1975	12.00
❑ 37006	Ridin' High	198?	10.00
—Budget-line reissue			
❑ 5128	The Best of Jerry Jeff Walker	1980	12.00
❑ 382	Viva Terlingua!	1973	12.00
❑ 2350	Viva Terlingua!	1977	10.00
—Reissue of MCA 382			
❑ 450	Walker's Collectibles	1974	12.00
❑ 2355	Walker's Collectibles	1977	10.00

—Reissue of MCA 450

SOUTHCOAST

❑ 5199	Reunion	1981	12.00

VANGUARD

❑ VSD-6521	Driftin' Way of Life	1969	25.00
❑ VMS-73124	Driftin' Way of Life	1985	10.00

—Reissue of 6521

WALKER, JIMMIE

BUDDAH

❑ BDS5635 [B]	Dyn-O-Mite	1975	15.00

WALKER, JR., AND THE ALL STARS

MOTOWN

❑ 5297ML	All the Great Hits of Jr. Walker and the All Stars	1984	12.00
❑ M7-786	Anthology	1974	25.00
❑ 6053ML	Blow the House Down	1983	12.00
❑ M5-208V1	Greatest Hits	1981	12.00
—Reissue of Soul 718			
❑ M5-105V1	Motown Superstar Series, Vol. 5	1981	12.00
❑ M5-141V1	Shotgun	1981	12.00
—Reissue of Soul 701			

PICKWICK

❑ SPC-3391	Shotgun	197?	15.00

SOUL

❑ SS-726	A Gassss	1970	18.00
❑ SS-721	Gotta Hold on to This Feeling	1969	30.00
❑ SS-718	Greatest Hits	1969	25.00
❑ SS-710	Home Cookin'	1969	25.00
❑ S6-745	Hot Shot	1976	18.00
❑ 705 [M]	Live	1967	25.00
❑ SS-705 [S]	Live	1967	30.00
❑ SS-733	Moody Jr.	1971	18.00
❑ SS-738	Peace and Understanding Is Hard to Find	1973	18.00
❑ S-732L	Rainbow Funk	1971	18.00
❑ 703 [M]	Road Runner	1966	25.00
❑ SS-703 [S]	Road Runner	1966	30.00
❑ S6-747	Sax Appeal	1976	18.00
❑ 701 [M]	Shotgun	1965	60.00
—Mostly white label with vertical "Soul" at left			
❑ 701 [M]	Shotgun	1965	25.00
—Purple swirl label with "Soul" at top			
❑ SS-701 [S]	Shotgun	1965	30.00
❑ S7-750	Smooth	1978	18.00
❑ 702 [M]	Soul Session	1966	60.00
—Mostly white label with vertical "Soul" at left			
❑ 702 [M]	Soul Session	1966	25.00
—Purple swirl label with "Soul" at top			
❑ SS-702 [S]	Soul Session	1966	30.00
❑ SS-721	What Does It Take to Win Your Love	1970	25.00
—Retitled version of above			
❑ S6-748	Whopper Bopper Show Stopper	1977	18.00

WHITFIELD

❑ WHK3331	Back Street Boogie	1980	15.00

WALKER, KIT

WINDHAM HILL

❑ WH-0109	Dancing on the Edge of the World	1987	12.00
❑ WH-0117	Fire in the Lake	1989	15.00

WALKER, MARTIN

ABC-PARAMOUNT

❑ ABC-483 [M]	From Scotland with Love	1964	18.00
❑ ABCS-483 [S]	From Scotland with Love	1964	25.00

WALKER, NANCY

RCA CAMDEN

❑ CAL-501 [M]	I Hate Men	1960	30.00
❑ CAS-561 [S]	I Hate Men	1960	30.00

WALKER, PETER

VANGUARD

❑ VSD-79282	Second Poem to Karmela	1968	25.00

WALKER, SCOTT

4 MEN WITH BEARDS

❑ 4M149LP [B]	Scott		25.00
❑ 4M150LP [B]	Scott 2		25.00
❑ 4M151LP [B]	Scott 3		25.00
❑ 4M152LP [B]	Scott 4		25.00

SMASH

❑ SRS-67099	Aloner	1968	25.00
❑ SRS-67106	Scott, Volume 2	1968	25.00
❑ SRS-67121	Scott Walker 3	1969	25.00

WALKER, T-BONE

ATLANTIC

❑ 8020 [M]	T-Bone Blues	1959	250.00
—Black label			
❑ 8020 [M]	T-Bone Blues	1960	100.00
—Red and purple label			

❑ SD8256	T-Bone Blues	1970	25.00

BLUE NOTE

❑ BN LA533-H2	Classics	1975	25.00

BLUESTIME

❑ 29010	Blue Rocks	1969	30.00
❑ 29004	Everyday I Have the Blues	1968	30.00

BLUESWAY

❑ BLS-6058	Dirty Mistreater	1973	18.00
❑ BLS-6014	Funky Town	1968	30.00
❑ BLS-6008 [B]	Stormy Monday Blues	1968	40.00
—Reissue of Wet Soul LP?			

BRUNSWICK

❑ BL754126	The Truth	1968	30.00

CAPITOL

❑ H370 [10]	Classics in Jazz	1953	1000.00
❑ T370 [M]	Classics in Jazz	1953	300.00
❑ T1958 [M]	Great Blues Vocal and Guitar	1963	200.00
—Black "The Star Line" label (existence of black colorband label not confirmed)			

DELMARK

❑ D-633 [M]	I Want a Little Girl	1967	40.00
❑ DS-633 [S]	I Want a Little Girl	1967	50.00

IMPERIAL

❑ LP-9146 [M]	I Get So Weary	1961	300.00
❑ LP-9116 [M]	Singing the Blues	1960	250.00
❑ LP-9098 [M]	T-Bone Walker Sings the Blues	1959	300.00

MOSAIC

❑ MR9-130	The Complete Recordings of T-Bone Walker 1940-1954	199?	300.00
—Limited edition of 7,500			

POLYDOR

❑ PD-5521 [B]	Fly Walker Airlines	1973	25.00
❑ 24-4502 [B]	Good Feelin'	1972	25.00

REPRISE

❑ 2RS6483	Very Rare	1973	25.00

WET SOUL

❑ 1002	Stormy Monday Blues	1967	50.00

WALKER BROTHERS, THE

SMASH

❑ MGS-27076 [M]	Introducing the Walker Brothers	1965	70.00
❑ SRS-67076 [R]	Introducing the Walker Brothers	1965	50.00
❑ MGS-27082 [M]	The Sun Ain't Gonna Shine (Anymore)	1966	50.00
❑ SRS-67082 [P]	The Sun Ain't Gonna Shine (Anymore)	1966	60.00
—The Sun Ain't Gonna Shine (Anymore)" and "When the Lights Go Out" are rechanneled.			

TOWER

❑ T5026 [M]	I Only Came to Dance with You	1966	30.00
—As "Scott Engel and John Stewart			
❑ ST5026 [S]	I Only Came to Dance with You	1966	25.00
—As "Scott Engel and John Stewart			

WALL, DAN

AUDIOPHILE

❑ AP-143	Dan Wall Trio	198?	12.00

PROGRESSIVE

❑ PRO-7016	The Trio	198?	15.00

WALL OF VOODOO

INDEX/I.R.S.

❑ SP-70401 [EP]	Wall of Voodoo	1980	15.00

I.R.S.

❑ SP-70026	Call of the West	1982	15.00
❑ SP-70022	Dark Continent	1981	15.00
❑ 5997	Happy Planet	1987	12.00
❑ 5662	Seven Days in Sammystown	1985	15.00
❑ 42140	The Ugly American in Australia	1988	12.00

WALLACE, BENNIE

AUDIOQUEST

❑ AQLP-1017	The Old Songs	1993	18.00

BLUE NOTE

❑ BT-48014	Border Town	1988	15.00
❑ BT-85107	Twilight Time	198?	15.00

ENJA

❑ 4028	Bennie Wallace and Chick Corea	1982	15.00
❑ 4046	Big Jim's Tango	1982	15.00
❑ 3091	Wallace Plays Monk	198?	15.00

INNER CITY

❑ IC-3025	Fourteen Bar Blues	1979	15.00
❑ IC-3034	Live at the Public Theater	1979	15.00

WALLACE, GEORGE, JR.

PORTRAIT

❑ JR36579	Heroes Like You and Me	1981	30.00

Number	Title	Yr	NM

WALLACE, JERRY

CHALLENGE
2002	Greatest Hits	1969	18.00
CH619 [M]	In the Misty Moonlight	1964	25.00
CHS619 [S]	In the Misty Moonlight	1964	30.00
CHL606 [M]	Just Jerry	1959	60.00
CH616 [M]	Shutters and Boards	1962	30.00
CHS616 [S]	Shutters and Boards	1962	40.00
CH612 [M]	There She Goes	1961	30.00
CHS612 [S]	There She Goes	1961	40.00

DECCA
| DL75294 | This Is Jerry Wallace | 1971 | 18.00 |
| DL75349 | To Get to You | 1972 | 18.00 |

LIBERTY
LST-7564	Another Time, Another World	1968	25.00
LST-7597	Sweet Child of Sunshine	1968	25.00
LRP-3545 [M]	This One's on the House	1967	40.00
— Stock copy inside stereo cover; "Audition Mono LP Not for Sale" sticker on front
| LST-7545 [S] | This One's on the House | 1967 | 25.00 |

MCA
301 [B]	Do You Know What It's Like to Be Lonesome?	1973	15.00
408	For Wives and Lovers	1974	15.00
462	I Wonder Whose Baby (You Are Now)/Make Hay While the Sun Shines	1975	15.00
366	Primrose Lane/Don't Give Up on Me	1973	15.00

MERCURY
| MG-21072 [M] | The Best of Jerry Wallace | 1966 | 18.00 |
| SR-61072 [S] | The Best of Jerry Wallace | 1966 | 25.00 |

MGM
M3G-4995	Comin' Home to You	1976	15.00
M3G-4990	Greatest Hits	1975	12.00
M3G-5007	Jerry Wallace	1976	12.00

SUNSET
| SUS-5294 | Primrose Lane | 1969 | 15.00 |

UNITED ARTISTS
| UXS-95 | Jerry Wallace Superpak | 1972 | 25.00 |

WALLACE BROTHERS, THE

SIMS
| LP-128 [M] | Soul, Soul and More Soul | 1965 | 200.00 |
| LPS-128 [S] | Soul, Soul and More Soul | 1965 | 250.00 |

WALLER, FATS

BIOGRAPH
1002	Rare Piano Rolls	197?	12.00
1005	Rare Piano Rolls, Volume 2	197?	12.00
1015	Rare Piano Rolls, Volume 3	197?	12.00

BLUEBIRD
AXM2-5518	Piano Solos	197?	18.00
AXM2-5511	The Complete Fats Waller, Volume 1	197?	18.00
AXM2-5575	The Complete Fats Waller, Volume 2	198?	18.00
AXM2-5583	The Complete Fats Waller, Volume 3	198?	18.00
5905-1-RB	The Complete Fats Waller, Volume 4	1987	18.00
6288-1-RB	The Joint Is Jumpin'	1987	12.00
9983-1-RB	The Last Years: Fats Waller and His Rhythm, 1940-1943	198?	30.00

BULLDOG
| BDL-2004 | 20 Golden Pieces of Fats Waller | 198? | 12.00 |

EVEREST ARCHIVE OF FOLK & JAZZ
| 337 | Ain't Misbehavin' | 197? | 12.00 |
| 319 | Fats Waller Plays Fats Waller | 197? | 12.00 |

GIANTS OF JAZZ
| GOJ-1035 | Live, Volume 2 | 198? | 12.00 |
| GOJ-1029 | Live at the Yacht Club | 198? | 12.00 |

MUSICAL HERITAGE SOCIETY
| MHS4937 | Fats" Waller at the Organ | 1981 | 12.00 |

RCA VICTOR
LPV-562 [M]	African Ripples	1969	25.00
LPM-1246 [M]	Ain't Misbehavin'	1956	50.00
CPL1-2904	A Legendary Performer	1979	12.00
LPM-6000 [M]	Fats	1960	80.00
LPT-8 [10]	Fats Waller 1934-42	1951	150.00
LPV-516 [M]	Fats Waller '34/'35	1965	25.00
LPT-14 [10]	Fats Waller Favoites	1951	150.00
LPT-1001 [M]	Fats Waller Plays and Sings	1954	80.00
LPT-6001 [M]	Fats Waller Radio Transcriptions	1954	120.00
— Boxed set with booklet
LPM-1502 [M]	Handful of Keys	1957	50.00
LPM-1503 [M]	One Never Knows, Do One?	1959	50.00
LPV-550 [M]	Smashing Thirds	1968	25.00
LPT-3040 [10]	Swingin' the Organ	1953	120.00
LPV-473 [M]	The Real Fats Waller	1965	30.00
LPV-525 [M]	Valentine Stomp	1966	25.00

RIVERSIDE
RLP-1021 [10]	Fats Waller at the Organ	1953	150.00
RLP-1010 [10]	Rediscovered Fats Waller Piano Solos	1953	150.00
RLP 12-109 [M]	The Amazing Mr. Waller	1955	60.00

| RLP-1022 [10] | The Amazing Mr. Waller Vol. 2: Jivin' with Fats | 1953 | 150.00 |
— Black vinyl
| RLP-1022 [10] | The Amazing Mr. Waller Vol. 2: Jivin' with Fats | 1953 | 250.00 |
— Red vinyl
| RLP 12-103 [M] | The Young Fats Waller | 1955 | 60.00 |

STANYAN
| 10057 | The Undiscovered Fats Waller | 197? | 12.00 |

SWING
| SW-8442/3 | Fats Waller in London | 198? | 15.00 |

TIME-LIFE
| STL-J-15 | Giants of Jazz | 1980 | 25.00 |

TRIP
| 5042 | A Legend in His Lifetime | 197? | 15.00 |
| J-4 | Fats Waller on the Air | 197? | 12.00 |

X
| LVA-3035 [10] | The Young Fats Waller | 1955 | 150.00 |

WALLER, GORDON

ABC
| X-749 | And Gordon | 1972 | 18.00 |

WALLER, JIM, AND THE DELTAS

ARVEE
| A-432 [M] | Surfin' Wild | 1963 | 80.00 |
| AS-432 [S] | Surfin' Wild | 1963 | 100.00 |

WALLINGTON, GEORGE

ATLANTIC
| 1275 [M] | Knight Music | 1958 | 80.00 |
— Black label
| SD1275 [S] | Knight Music | 1958 | 80.00 |
— Green label
| 1275 [M] | Knight Music | 1961 | 30.00 |
— Multicolor label, white "fan" logo at right
| SD1275 [S] | Knight Music | 1961 | 25.00 |
— Multicolor label, white "fan" logo at right

BLUE NOTE
| BLP-5045 [10] | George Wallington and His All-Star Band | 1954 | 1000.00 |

EAST-WEST
| 4004 [M] | The Prestidigitator | 1958 | 250.00 |

FANTASY
| OJC-1704 | Jazz for the Carriage Trade | 1985 | 15.00 |
| OJC-1754 | The George Wallington Trios | 198? | 15.00 |

NEW JAZZ
| NJLP-8207 [M] | The New York Scene | 1958 | 250.00 |
— Purple label
| NJLP-8207 [M] | The New York Scene | 1965 | 60.00 |
— Blue label, trident logo at right

NORGRAN
| MGN-1010 [M] | George Wallington with Strings | 1954 | 120.00 |
| MGN-24 [10] | The Workshop of the George Wallington Trio | 1954 | 200.00 |

PRESTIGE
PRST-7820	At Café Bohemia '55	1971	18.00
PLP-1001 [M]	George Wallington Quintet at the Bohemia	1955	1500.00
PRLP-7032 [M]	Jazz for the Carriage Trade	1956	800.00
P-24093	Our Delight	197?	18.00
PRLP-136 [10]	The George Wallington Trio	1952	500.00
PRLP-158 [10]	The George Wallington Trio, Volume 2	1953	500.00
PRST-7587 [R]	The George Wallington Trios	1968	30.00

PROGRESSIVE
| PRO-7001 | The George Wallington Quintet at the Café Bohemia, 1955 | 198? | 12.00 |
| PLP-3001 [10] | The George Wallington Trio | 1952 | 500.00 |

SAVOY
MG-12122 [M]	Jazz at Hotchkiss	1957	100.00
MG-15037 [10]	The George Wallington Trio	1954	150.00
MG-12081 [M]	The George Wallington Trio	1956	100.00

SAVOY JAZZ
| SJL-1122 | Dance of the Infidels | 198? | 15.00 |

VERVE
| MGV-2017 [M] | Variations | 1956 | 80.00 |

WALLIS, RUTH

JUBILEE
| JGM-2050 [M] | Ruth Wallis Sings The Spice Is Right | 1963 | 25.00 |

KING
993 [M]	Bahama Mama	1966	30.00
987 [M]	Davy's Little Dinghy	1966	30.00
986 [M]	Here's Looking Up Your Hatch	1966	30.00
992 [M]	He Wants a Little...Pizza	1966	30.00
265-9 [10]	House Party	1952	120.00
395-507 [M]	House Party	1956	100.00
988 [M]	Marry Go Round	1966	30.00
991 [M]	Oil Man from Texas	1966	30.00
989 [M]	Red Lights	1966	30.00

265-6 [10]	Rhumba Party	1952	120.00
904 [M]	Saucy Hit Parade	1964	30.00
990 [M]	Ubangi Me	1966	30.00

MERCURY
| SR-61210 | How to Stay Sexy Tho' Married | 1969 | 25.00 |

WALLIS ORIGINAL
W-3 [10]	Cafe Party	195?	40.00
WLP-15 [M]	Cruise Party	195?	30.00
WLP-13 [M]	For Sophisticates Only	195?	30.00
WLP-14 [M]	French Postcards Set to Music	195?	30.00
W-5 [10]	Holiday Party	195?	40.00
— Black vinyl
| W-5 [10] | Holiday Party | 195? | 60.00 |
— Red vinyl
WLP-18 [M]	Hot Songs for Cool Knights	195?	30.00
W-6 [10]	Life of the Party	195?	40.00
WLP-17 [M]	Love Is for the Birds	195?	30.00
W-9 [M]	Men and Memories	195?	40.00
W-2 [M]	Ruth Wallis	195?	40.00
W-1 [10]	Ruth Wallis' Old Party Favorites	195?	40.00
WLP-16 [M]	Salty Songs for Underwater Listening	195?	30.00
WLP-11 [M]	Saucy Hit Parade	195?	30.00
W-4 [10]	Senorita Ruth Wallis and Her Latin Party Rhythms	195?	40.00
WLP-12 [M]	That Saucy Redhead	195?	30.00
WLP-10 [M]	Wallis on the Party Line	195?	30.00

WALLOWITCH, JOHN

SERENUS
| 22015 [B] | Now Appearing At The Dreamland Memory Ballroom | 197? | 40.00 |
| SEP2005 [B] | This Is | 1964 | 250.00 |
— Andy Warhol cover.
| SEP2006 [B] | This Is The Other Side Of | 1975 | 300.00 |
— Andy Warhol cover utilized same artwork as SEP 2005 but placed on the back cover - "the other side".

WALRATH, JACK

BLUE NOTE
| BT-46905 | Master of Suspense | 1987 | 15.00 |
| B1-91101 | Neohippus | 1989 | 15.00 |

GATEMOUTH
| 1002 | Demons in Pursuit | 1979 | 15.00 |

MUSE
| MR-5362 | Wholly Trinity | 198? | 12.00 |

RED RECORD
| VPA-182 | Live at Umbria Jazz Festival, Vol. 1 | 1986 | 15.00 |
| VPA-186 | Live at Umbria Jazz Festival, 1986 Vol. 2 | 1986 | 15.00 |

STASH
| ST-223 | A Plea for Sanity | 198? | 12.00 |
| ST-221 | Revenge of the Fat People | 198? | 12.00 |

STEEPLECHASE
| SCS-1172 | Jack Walrath in Europe | 1982 | 15.00 |

WALSH, JOE

ABC
| AA-1083 | The Best of Joe Walsh | 1978 | 12.00 |
— Also contains two James Gang tracks
| ABCD-932 | You Can't Argue with a Sick Mind | 1976 | 12.00 |
| QD-40016 [Q] | The Smoker You Drink, the Player You Get | 1974 | 25.00 |

ABC DUNHILL
| DS-50130 | Barnstorm | 1972 | 12.00 |
— Of the James Gang and the Eagles
| DS-51071 | So What | 1974 | 12.00 |
| DS-50140 [B] | The Smoker You Drink, the Player You Get | 1973 | 12.00 |

ASYLUM
| 6E-141 | But Seriously, Folks… | 1978 | 12.00 |
| 5E-523 | There Goes the Neighborhood | 1981 | 10.00 |

MCA
| 37053 | Barnstorm | 1979 | 10.00 |
— Reissue of ABC Dunhill 50130
| 37055 | So What | 1979 | 10.00 |
— Reissue of ABC Dunhill 50171
| 37052 | The Best of Joe Walsh | 1979 | 10.00 |
— Reissue of ABC 1083
| 37054 | The Smoker You Drink, the Player You Get | 1979 | 10.00 |
— Reissue of ABC Dunhill 50140
| 37051 | You Can't Argue with a Sick Mind | 1979 | 10.00 |
— Reissue of ABC 932

WARNER BROS.
25606	Got Any Gum?	1987	10.00
25281	The Confessor	1985	10.00
25281 [DJ]	The Confessor	1985	18.00
— Promo only on Quiex II vinyl
| 23884 | You Bought It -- You Name It | 1983 | 10.00 |

Number	Title	Yr	NM

WALSTON, RAY

VEE JAY

Number	Title	Yr	NM
☐ LP-1110 [M]	My Favorite Songs from "Mary Poppins" and Other Songs to Delight	1965	30.00
☐ SR-1110 [S]	My Favorite Songs from "Mary Poppins" and Other Songs to Delight	1965	30.00

WALT, SHERMAN

RCA VICTOR RED SEAL

☐ LSC-2353 [S]	Vivaldi: The Four Seasons Concertos	1960	30.00
— Original with "shaded dog" label			

WALTER, CY

ATLANTIC

☐ 1236 [M]	Rodgers Revisited	1956	40.00
— Black label			
☐ 1236 [M]	Rodgers Revisited	1961	25.00
— Multicolor label, white "fan" logo at right			

MGM

☐ E-4393 [M]	Cy Walter at the Drake	1966	15.00
☐ SE-4393 [S]	Cy Walter at the Drake	1966	18.00

WESTMINSTER

☐ WP-6120 [M]	Dry Martini, Please	195?	30.00
☐ WST-15054 [S]	Dry Martini, Please	195?	30.00

WALTON, CEDAR, AND HANK MOBLEY

MUSE

☐ MR-5132	Breakthrough	197?	15.00

WALTON, CEDAR

CLEAN CUTS

☐ 704	Solos	1980	18.00

COBBLESTONE

☐ 9011	Breakthrough	197?	18.00

COLUMBIA

☐ JC36285	Soundscapes	1980	12.00

FANTASY

☐ OJC-462	Cedar!	1990	12.00
☐ OJC-6002	Cedar Walton Plays Cedar Walton	1988	12.00

INNER CITY

☐ IC-6019	Pit Inn	198?	15.00
☐ IC-6009	The Pentagon	197?	15.00

MUSE

☐ MR-5010	A Night at Boomer's, Vol. 1	1973	15.00
☐ MR-5022	A Night at Boomer's, Vol. 2	1973	15.00
☐ MR-5059	Firm Roots	197?	18.00
☐ MR-5244	The Maestro	1981	12.00

PRESTIGE

☐ PRLP-7519 [M]	Cedar!	1967	30.00
☐ PRST-7519 [S]	Cedar!	1967	25.00
☐ PRST-7693	Soul Cycle	1970	25.00
☐ PRST-7591	Spectrum	1968	25.00
☐ PRST-7618	The Electric Boogaloo Song	1969	25.00

RCA VICTOR

☐ APL1-1435	Beyond Mobius	1976	25.00
☐ APL1-1009 [B]	Mobius	1975	25.00

RED RECORD

☐ VPA-179	Cedar's Blues	1986	15.00

STEEPLECHASE

☐ SCS-1085	First Set	198?	15.00
☐ SCS-1179	Third Set	198?	15.00

WALTON, FRANK

DELMARK

☐ DS-436	Reality	197?	12.00

WALTON, JON

GATEWAY

☐ 7006	Jon Walton Swings Again	1964	18.00

WALTON, WADE

BLUESVILLE

☐ BVLP-1060 [M]	Shake 'Em on Down	1963	100.00
— Blue label, silver print			
☐ BVLP-1060 [M]	Shake 'Em on Down	1964	30.00
— Blue label, trident logo at right			

WANDERERS THREE, THE

DOLTON

☐ BLP2021 [M]	We Sing Folk Songs	1963	25.00
☐ BST8021 [S]	We Sing Folk Songs	1963	30.00

WANDERLEY, WALTER

A&M

☐ SP-3022	Moondreams	1969	15.00
☐ SP-3018	When It Was Done	1969	15.00

CANYON

☐ 7711	Return of the Original Sound	196?	15.00

GNP CRESCENDO

☐ GNPS 2137	Brazil's Greatest Hits	197?	12.00
☐ GNPS-2142	Perpetual Motion Love	197?	12.00

MGM LATINO SERIES

☐ LAT10010 [S]	Cheganca	197?	18.00
— Reissue of Verve V6-8676			

PHILIPS

☐ PHM200227 [M]	Brazilian Blend	1967	15.00
☐ PHS600227 [S]	Brazilian Blend	1967	18.00
☐ PHM200233 [M]	Organ-ized	1967	15.00
☐ PHS600233 [S]	Organ-ized	1967	18.00

TOWER

☐ T5047 [M]	From Rio with Love	1966	18.00
☐ ST5047 [S]	From Rio with Love	1966	18.00
☐ T5058 [M]	Murmurio	1967	18.00
☐ ST5058 [S]	Murmurio	1967	18.00

VERVE

☐ V-8706 [M]	Batucada	1967	25.00
☐ V6-8706 [S]	Batucada	1967	18.00
☐ V-8676 [M]	Cheganca	1966	18.00
☐ V6-8676 [S]	Cheganca	1966	25.00
☐ V-8739 [M]	Kee-Ka-Roo	1967	25.00
☐ V6-8739 [S]	Kee-Ka-Roo	1967	18.00
☐ V-8658 [M]	Rain Forest	1966	18.00
☐ V6-8658 [S]	Rain Forest	1966	25.00

WORLD PACIFIC

☐ WP-1866 [M]	Quarteto Bossamba	1967	30.00
☐ ST-21866 [S]	Quarteto Bossamba	1967	18.00
☐ WP-1856 [M]	Samba So!	1967	25.00
☐ ST-21856 [S]	Samba So!	1967	18.00

WANG CHUNG

ARISTA

☐ AL6603	Huang Chung	1982	18.00
— As "Huang Chung"			

GEFFEN

☐ R163751	Mosaic	1986	15.00
— RCA Music Service edition			
☐ GHS24115	Mosaic	1986	12.00
☐ R144369	Points on the Curve	1983	15.00
— RCA Music Service edition			
☐ GHS4004	Points on the Curve	1983	12.00
☐ R101063	The Warmer Side of Cool	1989	15.00
— BMG Direct Marketing edition			
☐ GHS24222	The Warmer Side of Cool	1989	12.00

WAR

AVENUE

☐ R171706	Peace Sign	1994	18.00

BLUE NOTE

☐ BN-LA690-G [B]	Platinum Jazz	1977	18.00

LAX

☐ PW37111	All Day Music	1981	12.00
— Reissue of United Artists 5546			
☐ PW37112	The World Is a Ghetto	1981	12.00
— Reissue of United Artists 5652			
☐ PW37113	Why Can't We Be Friends?	1981	12.00
— Reissue of United Artists 441			

MCA

☐ 5362	Best of the Music Band	1982	12.00
☐ 3030	Galaxy	1977	12.00
☐ 745	Galaxy	1983	10.00
— Reissue of MCA 3030			
☐ 5411	Music Band Jazz	1983	12.00
☐ 3085	The Music Band	1979	12.00
☐ 747	The Music Band	1983	10.00
— Reissue of MCA 3085			
☐ 3193	The Music Band 2	1979	12.00
☐ 751	The Music Band 2	1983	10.00
— Reissue of MCA 3193			
☐ 5156	The Music Band Live	1980	12.00

PRIORITY

☐ SL9467	The Best of War…And More	1987	12.00

RCA VICTOR

☐ AFL1-4598	Life (Is So Strange)	1983	12.00
☐ AFL1-4208	Outlaw	1982	12.00

UNITED ARTISTS

☐ UAS-5546 [B]	All Day Music	1971	18.00
☐ UA-LA128-F [B]	Deliver the Word	1973	18.00
☐ UA-LA648-G	Greatest Hits	1976	12.00
☐ SP-103 [DJ]	Radio Free War	1974	30.00
— Promo only on blue vinyl			
☐ UAS-5652	The World Is a Ghetto	1972	15.00
☐ UAS-5508	War	1971	18.00
☐ UA-LA193-J [B]	War Live!	1974	25.00
☐ UA-LA441-G	Why Can't We Be Friends?	1975	12.00

WARBURTON, PAUL, AND DALE BRUNING

CAPRI

☐ 7986	Our Delight	198?	12.00

WARD, ALAN

RCA VICTOR RED SEAL

☐ LSC-2302 [S]	Gilbert and Sullivan Overtures	1959	25.00
— Original with "shaded dog" label			

WARD, ANITA

JUANA

☐ 200,004	Songs of Love	1979	12.00
☐ 200,006	Sweet Surrender	1979	12.00

WARD, BILLY, AND THE DOMINOES

DECCA

☐ DL8621 [M]	Billy Ward and the Dominoes	1958	250.00

FEDERAL

☐ 295-94 [10]	Billy Ward and His Dominoes	1955	15000.00
— VG value 6000; VG+ value 9500			
☐ 548 [M]	Billy Ward and His Dominoes	1958	1500.00
☐ 559 [M]	Clyde McPhatter with Billy Ward and His Dominoes	1958	1200.00

KING

☐ 5005	14 Hits	197?	15.00
☐ 5008	21 Hits	197?	15.00
☐ 952 [M]	24 Songs	1966	50.00
☐ 733 [M]	Billy Ward and His Dominoes Featuring Clyde McPhatter and Jackie Wilson	1961	600.00
☐ 559 [M]	Clyde McPhatter with Billy Ward and His Dominoes	1958	600.00
— Yellow cover			
☐ 559 [M]	Clyde McPhatter with Billy Ward and His Dominoes	196?	300.00
— Pink cover			

LIBERTY

☐ LRP-3113 [M]	Pagan Love Song	1959	60.00
☐ LST-7113 [S]	Pagan Love Song	1959	100.00
☐ LRP-3056 [M]	Sea of Glass	1957	60.00
☐ LRP-3083 [M]	Yours Forever	1958	60.00

WARD, HELEN

COLUMBIA

☐ CL-6271 [10]	It's Been So Long	1954	50.00

PAX

☐ 6004 [10]	Wild Bill Davison with Helen Ward	1954	60.00

RCA VICTOR

☐ LPM-1464 [M]	With a Little Bit of Swing	1957	40.00

WARD, JACKY

ASYLUM

☐ 60013	Night After Night	1982	10.00

MERCURY

☐ SRM-1-5009	A Lover's Question	1978	12.00
☐ SRM-1-1170	Jacky Ward	1977	15.00
☐ SRM-1-5030	More!	1980	12.00
☐ SRM-1-5013	Rainbow	1978	12.00
☐ SRM-1-5021	The Best of Jacky Ward … Up 'Til Now	1979	12.00

SUNBIRD

☐ SN50103	Big Blue Diamond	1980	15.00

TARGET

☐ 1315	Big Blue Diamond	1972	15.00

WARD, ROBIN

DOT

☐ DLP3555 [M]	Wonderful Summer	1963	200.00
☐ DLP25555 [S]	Wonderful Summer	1963	300.00

WARDELL, ROOSEVELT

RIVERSIDE

☐ RLP-350 [M]	The Revelation	1960	30.00
☐ RS-9350 [S]	The Revelation	1960	30.00

WARE, DAVID S.

HAT HUT

☐ W	Birth of a Being	1978	18.00

WARE, WILBUR; JOHNNY GRIFFIN; JUNIOR MANCE

JAZZLAND

☐ JLP-12 [M]	The Chicago Cookers	1960	40.00

WARE, WILBUR

FANTASY

☐ OJC-1737	The Chicago Sound	198?	12.00

RIVERSIDE

☐ RLP 12-252 [M]	The Chicago Sound	1957	80.00
☐ 6048	The Chicago Sound	197?	15.00

WARFIELD, WILLIAM

COLUMBIA MASTERWORKS

☐ ML2206 [M]	Old American Songs and Five Sea Chanties	195?	50.00

WARINER, STEVE

ARISTA

☐ AL8691	I Am Ready	1992	25.00
— Vinyl version available only from Columbia House			

Number	Title	Yr	NM
MCA			
❑ 42032	Greatest Hits	1987	10.00
❑ 42272	I Got Dreams	1989	12.00
❑ 42130	I Should Be with You	1988	10.00
❑ 5926	It's a Crazy World	1987	10.00
❑ 5672	Life's Highway	1985	10.00
❑ 5545	One Good Night Deserves Another	1985	10.00
RCA VICTOR			
❑ AHL1-7164	Down in Tennessee	1986	10.00
❑ AHL1-5326	Greatest Hits	1985	10.00
❑ AHL1-4859	Midnight Fire	1983	12.00
❑ AHL1-4154	Steve Wariner	1982	12.00
❑ AYL1-5440	Steve Wariner	1985	10.00
—Best Buy Series" reissue			

WARING, FRED, AND THE PENNSYLVANIANS

Number	Title	Yr	NM
CAPITOL			
❑ T936 [M]	All Through the Night	1959	18.00
—Black colorband label, logo at left			
❑ ST936 [S]	All Through the Night	1958	25.00
❑ T936 [M]	All Through the Night	1958	25.00
—Turquoise label			
❑ T1949 [M]	Alma Mater Memories	1963	15.00
❑ ST1949 [S]	Alma Mater Memories	1963	18.00
❑ WBO1079 [M]	Broadway Cavalcade	1958	30.00
—Black colorband labels, logo at left			
❑ SWBO1079 [S]	Broadway Cavalcade	1959	30.00
—Black colorband labels, logo at left			
❑ T1389 [M]	Broadway Cavalcade, Volume 1	1960	18.00
—Reissue of Side 1 and Side 2 of WBO 1079; black colorband label, logo at left			
❑ T1389 [M]	Broadway Cavalcade, Volume 1	1963	12.00
—Black colorband label, logo at top			
❑ ST1389 [S]	Broadway Cavalcade, Volume 1	1960	25.00
—Reissue of Side 1 and Side 2 of SWBO 1079; black colorband label, logo at left			
❑ ST1389 [S]	Broadway Cavalcade, Volume 1	1963	15.00
—Black colorband label, logo at top			
❑ T1390 [M]	Broadway Cavalcade, Volume 2	1960	18.00
—Reissue of Side 3 and Side 4 of WBO 1079; black colorband label, logo at left			
❑ ST1390 [S]	Broadway Cavalcade, Volume 2	1960	25.00
—Reissue of Side 3 and Side 4 of SWBO 1079; black colorband label, logo at left			
❑ STBB-347	Christmas Magic	1969	18.00
—Collects ST 1260 and ST 1610 in one package; green label original			
❑ STBB-347	Christmas Magic	1972	15.00
—Orange label reissue			
❑ T1208 [M]	Do You Remember?	1959	18.00
—Black colorband label, logo at left			
❑ ST1208 [S]	Do You Remember?	1959	25.00
—Black colorband label, logo at left			
❑ W845 [M]	Fred Waring and the Pennsylvanians in Hi Fi	1957	30.00
—Gray label (original)			
❑ W845 [M]	Fred Waring and the Pennsylvanians in Hi-Fi	1959	18.00
—Black colorband label, logo at left			
❑ SW845 [S]	Fred Waring and the Pennsylvanians in Hi-Fi	1958	25.00
—Black colorband label, logo at left; does not include "Way Back Home" or "So Beats My Heart for You," which are on mono versions			
❑ T1452 [M]	Keyboard Chorale	1960	18.00
—Black colorband label, logo at left			
❑ ST1452 [S]	Keyboard Chorale	1960	25.00
—Black colorband label, logo at left			
❑ TAO1504 [M]	Let Freedom Sing: An Album for Americans	1961	25.00
—Includes booklet; black colorband label, logo at left			
❑ STAO1504 [S]	Let Freedom Sing: An Album for Americans	1961	30.00
—Includes booklet; black colorband label, logo at left			
❑ T896 [M]	Now Is the Caroling Season	1957	25.00
—Originals have turquoise labels			
❑ ST896 [S]	Now Is the Caroling Season	1959	18.00
—Black colorband label, logo at left			
❑ T896 [M]	Now Is the Caroling Season	1959	18.00
—Black colorband label, logo at left			
❑ T896 [M]	Now Is the Caroling Season	1962	15.00
—Black colorband label, logo at top			
❑ ST896 [S]	Now Is the Caroling Season	1962	15.00
—Black colorband label, logo at top			
❑ T1122 [M]	Praise Him	1959	18.00
—Black colorband label, logo at left			
❑ ST1122 [S]	Praise Him	1959	25.00
—Black colorband label, logo at left			
❑ T1396 [M]	Rise Up Singin'	1960	18.00
—Black colorband label, logo at left			
❑ ST1396 [S]	Rise Up Singin'	1960	25.00
—Black colorband label, logo at left			
❑ T989 [M]	Selections from "The Music Man	1958	25.00
—Turquoise label			
❑ ST989 [S]	Selections from "The Music Man	1959	25.00
—Black colorband label, logo at left			
❑ T2625 [M]	The Best of Fred Waring and the Pennsylvanians	1967	15.00
❑ ST2625 [S]	The Best of Fred Waring and the Pennsylvanians	1967	18.00
❑ T1610 [M]	The Meaning of Christmas	1963	18.00
—Black colorband label, logo at left			
❑ ST1610 [S]	The Meaning of Christmas	1963	25.00
—Black colorband label, logo at left			
❑ SM-1610	The Meaning of Christmas	197?	10.00
—Reissue of ST 1610 with same contents			
❑ ST1610 [S]	The Meaning of Christmas	1963	15.00
—Black colorband label, logo at top			
❑ ST1610 [S]	The Meaning of Christmas	1963	18.00
—Black colorband label, logo at top			
❑ T1260 [M]	The Sounds of Christmas	1959	18.00
—Black colorband label, logo at left			
❑ ST1260 [S]	The Sounds of Christmas	1959	25.00
—Black colorband label, logo at left			
❑ T1298 [M]	The Time, the Place, the Girl	1960	18.00
—Black colorband label, logo at left			
❑ ST1298 [S]	The Time, the Place, the Girl	1960	25.00
—Black colorband label, logo at left			
❑ T1764 [M]	The Waring Blend	1962	15.00
❑ ST1764 [S]	The Waring Blend	1962	18.00
❑ T2054 [M]	This I Believe	1964	15.00
❑ ST2054 [S]	This I Believe	1964	18.00
CAPITOL CREATIVE PRODUCTS			
❑ L-6550 [M]	Fred Waring and the Pennsylvanians Sing of Faith, Home and Christmas	1967	18.00
—Compiled for the E.F. MacDonald Company, Dayton, Ohio			
CAPITOL PICKWICK SERIES			
❑ PC-3454 [M]	Some Enchanted Evening	196?	12.00
❑ SPC-3454 [S]	Some Enchanted Evening	196?	15.00
❑ PC-3451 [M]	The Romantic Sound	196?	12.00
❑ SPC-3451 [S]	The Romantic Sound	196?	15.00
DECCA			
❑ DL4809 [M]	A-Caroling We Go	1966	15.00
❑ DL74809 [S]	A-Caroling We Go	1966	18.00
❑ DL4875 [M]	Barbershop Sing	1967	15.00
❑ DL74875 [S]	Barbershop Sing	1967	15.00
❑ DL8172 [M]	Christmas Time	1955	25.00
❑ DL78172 [R]	Christmas Time	196?	15.00
❑ DL5295 [10]	Christmas Time	1950	40.00
❑ DLP5005 [10]	Cole Porter Songs	1950	50.00
❑ DL8222 [M]	College Memories	1956	18.00
❑ DL5202 [10]	Columbia, the Gem of the Ocean (Patriotic and Service Songs)	1950	40.00
❑ DL8708 [M]	Excerpts from Carousel and Oklahoma	1958	18.00
❑ DL8082 [M]	For Listening Only	1954	30.00
❑ DL4753 [M]	Fred Waring Showcase	1966	12.00
❑ DL74753 [S]	Fred Waring Showcase	1966	15.00
❑ DL4345 [M]	God's Trombones	1962	15.00
❑ DL74345 [S]	God's Trombones	1962	18.00
❑ DL8047 [M]	God's Trombones and Other Spirituals	195?	30.00
❑ DL8335 [M]	Harmonizin' the Old Songs	1956	18.00
❑ DL9031 [M]	Hear, Hear	195?	18.00
❑ DLP5004 [10]	Jerome Kern Songs	1950	50.00
❑ DL8005 [M]	Listening Time	1950	40.00
❑ DL8110 [M]	Lullaby Time	1955	25.00
❑ DL4759 [M]	Magic Music	1966	12.00
❑ DL74759 [S]	Magic Music	1966	15.00
❑ DL8829	Memorable Moments from Broadway Musicals	1959	18.00
❑ DLP5036 [10]	Pleasure Time	1951	40.00
❑ DL8026 [M]	Program Time	1950	30.00
❑ DL5292 [10]	Richard Rodgers and Oscar Hammerstein II Songs, Vol. 1	1950	40.00
❑ DL5293 [10]	Richard Rodgers and Oscar Hammerstein II Songs, Vol. 2	1950	40.00
❑ DLP5009 [10]	Selections from Miss Liberty	1950	50.00
❑ DL8033 [M]	Song of America	195?	40.00
❑ DL8084 [M]	Song of Christmas	1954	30.00
❑ DL4511 [M]	Song of Easter	1965	12.00
❑ DL74511 [S]	Song of Easter	1965	15.00
❑ DL8111 [M]	Songs in Reverence	1955	25.00
❑ DL8670 [M]	Songs of Devotion	1958	18.00
❑ DL5061 [10]	Songs of Devotion, Vol. 1	1950	40.00
❑ DL5062 [10]	Songs of Devotion, Vol. 2	1950	40.00
❑ DL4234 [M]	Songs of Faith	1962	15.00
❑ DL74234 [S]	Songs of Faith	1962	18.00
❑ DL8039 [M]	Songs of Faith, Vols. 1 and 2	195?	30.00
❑ DL8709 [M]	Songs of Inspiration	1958	18.00
❑ DL8710 [M]	Stars and Stripes Forever	1958	18.00
❑ DBX186 [M]	The Best of Fred Waring	1965	18.00
❑ DXSB7186 [S]	The Best of Fred Waring	1965	18.00
❑ DL4158 [M]	This Is My Country	1961	15.00
❑ DL74158 [S]	This Is My Country	1961	18.00
❑ DL5141 [10]	This Is My Country	1950	40.00
❑ DL8171 [M]	'Twas the Night Before Christmas	1955	25.00
❑ DL78171 [R]	'Twas the Night Before Christmas	196?	15.00
❑ DLP5021 [10]	'Twas the Night Before Christmas	1950	50.00
❑ DL75007	Two Sides of Fred Waring and the Pennsylvanians	1968	15.00
HARMONY			
❑ HS11363	In Concert	1970	12.00
MCA			
❑ 15009	A-Caroling We Go	1973	12.00
—Reissue of DL 74809; black label with rainbow			
❑ 15009	A-Caroling We Go	1980	10.00
—Blue label with rainbow			
❑ 15011	Christmas Time	1973	12.00
—Reissue of DL 78172; black label with rainbow			
❑ 15011	Christmas Time	1980	10.00
—Blue label with rainbow			
❑ 207	God's Trombones	1973	10.00
—Reissue of Decca 74345			
❑ 4008	The Best of Fred Waring and the Pennsylvanians	1973	15.00
—Reissue of Decca 7186; black labels with rainbow			
❑ 193	This Is My Country	1973	10.00
—Reissue of Decca 74158			
❑ 15016	'Twas the Night Before Christmas	197?	12.00
—Reissue of MCA 517; black label with rainbow			
❑ 15016	'Twas the Night Before Christmas	1980	10.00
—Blue label with rainbow			
❑ 517	'Twas the Night Before Christmas	1974	15.00
—Black rainbow label			
MEGA			
❑ 31-1005	Nashville	1971	12.00
REPRISE			
❑ R6148 [M]	Fred Waring and the Pennsylvanians in Concert	1964	15.00
❑ RS6148 [S]	Fred Waring and the Pennsylvanians in Concert	1964	18.00
❑ R6137 [M]	To You...Forever	1964	15.00
❑ RS6137 [S]	To You...Forever	1964	18.00
STASH			
❑ 126	Memorial Album	1985	12.00

WARLAND, DALE, SINGERS

Number	Title	Yr	NM
AUGSBURG			
❑ 23-1317	Carols of Christmas	1981	12.00
❑ 23-1621	Echoes of Christmas	1979	12.00

WARNES, JENNIFER

Number	Title	Yr	NM
ARISTA			
❑ AL4062	Jennifer Warnes	1977	12.00
❑ AB4217 [B]	Shot Through the Heart	1979	12.00
❑ AL9560	The Best of Jennifer Warnes	1982	10.00
CYPRESS			
❑ 661111-1 [B]	Famous Blue Raincoat	1987	40.00
PARROT			
❑ PAS-71020 [B]	I Can Remember Anything	1968	30.00
—As "Jennifer			
❑ PAS-71034 [B]	See Me	1970	30.00
—As "Jennifer			
ROCK THE HOUSE			
❑ RTH5052	Famous Blue Raincoat	1996	50.00
—Classic Records reissue			

WARRANT

Number	Title	Yr	NM
COLUMBIA			
❑ C45487	Cherry Pie	1990	18.00
❑ FC44383	Dirty Rotten Filthy Stinking Rich	1988	10.00

WARREN, EARLE

Number	Title	Yr	NM
MUSE			
❑ MR-5312	Earle Warren and the Count's Men	198?	12.00

WARREN, FRAN

Number	Title	Yr	NM
AUDIO FIDELITY			
❑ AFSD-6207	Come Into My World	1968	30.00
MGM			
❑ E-3394 [M]	Mood Indigo	1956	50.00
—Yellow label			
TOPS			
❑ L-1585 [M]	Hey There	195?	25.00
VENISE			
❑ 7019 [M]	Come Rain or Come Shine	195?	30.00
❑ 10019 [S]	Come Rain or Come Shine	195?	50.00
—Yellow vinyl			
WARWICK			
❑ W-2012 [M]	Something's Coming	1960	30.00

WARREN, PETER

Number	Title	Yr	NM
ENJA			
❑ 2018	Bass Is	197?	18.00

WARREN, RUSTY

Number	Title	Yr	NM
GNP CRESCENDO			
❑ 2103	Bottoms Up!	1976	15.00
❑ 2088	Knockers Up! '76	1976	15.00

Number	Title	Yr	NM
❑ 2079	Knockers Up!/Songs for Sinners	1975	18.00
❑ 2080	Rusty Warren Bounces Back/Sin-Sational	1975	18.00
❑ 2081	Rusty Warren Lays It on the Line	1975	15.00
❑ 2114	Sexplosion	1977	15.00

JUBILEE

Number	Title	Yr	NM
❑ JLP2049 [M]	Banned in Boston?	1963	30.00
❑ JGM2069 [M]	Bottoms Up!	1967	25.00
❑ JGS2069 [S]	Bottoms Up!	1967	25.00
❑ JGM-2029 [M]	Knockers Up!	1960	30.00
❑ JGM2074	Look What I've Got for You	1967	25.00
❑ JGM-2059 [M]	More Knockers Up!	1965	30.00
❑ JLP5025 [M]	Portrait of Life	196?	25.00
❑ JLPS5025 [S]	Portrait of Life	196?	25.00
❑ JGM-2064 [M]	Rusty Rides Again	1966	30.00
❑ JGM2039 [M]	Rusty Warren Bounces Back	1961	30.00
❑ JGM2044 [M]	Rusty Warren in Orbit	1962	30.00
❑ JGM-2054 [M]	Sex-X-Ponent	1964	30.00
—Cover has JGM prefix; label has JG prefix			
❑ JLP2034 [M]	Sin-Sational	1961	30.00
❑ JGM-2024 [M]	Songs for Sinners	1960	30.00

WARWICK, DEE DEE

ATCO

Number	Title	Yr	NM
❑ SD 33-337	Turnin' Around	1970	30.00

MERCURY

Number	Title	Yr	NM
❑ SR-61221	Foolish Fool	1968	30.00
❑ MG-21100 [M]	I Want to Be with You	1967	30.00
❑ SR-61100 [S]	I Want to Be with You	1967	30.00

WARWICK, DIONNE

ARISTA

Number	Title	Yr	NM
❑ AB4230 [B]	Dionne	1979	12.00
❑ AL8295	Dionne	1985	10.00
—Budget-line reissue			
❑ AL8573	Dionne Warwick Sings Cole Porter	1990	15.00
❑ AL8262	Finder of Lost Loves	1985	12.00
❑ AL8398	Friends	1985	12.00
❑ AL9585	Friends in Love	1982	12.00
❑ AL8358	Friends in Love	1985	10.00
—Budget-line reissue			
❑ AL8540	Greatest Hits 1979-1990	1989	15.00
❑ AL9609	Heartbreaker	1982	12.00
❑ AL8338 [B]	Heartbreaker	1985	10.00
—Budget-line reissue			
❑ A2L8605	Hot! Live and Otherwise	1981	15.00
❑ A2L8111	Hot! Live and Otherwise	1983	12.00
—Budget-line reissue			
❑ AL8104	How Many Times Can We Say Goodbye	1983	12.00
❑ AL9526	No Night So Long	1980	12.00
❑ AL8446	Reservations for Two	1987	12.00

EVEREST

Number	Title	Yr	NM
❑ 4103	Dionne Warwick	1981	12.00

MOBILE FIDELITY

Number	Title	Yr	NM
❑ 2-098	Hot! Live and Otherwise	1982	30.00
—Audiophile vinyl			

MUSICOR

Number	Title	Yr	NM
❑ 2501	Only Love Can Break a Heart	1977	15.00

PAIR

Number	Title	Yr	NM
❑ PDL2-1098	Masterpieces	1986	15.00
❑ PDL2-1043	The Dynamic Dionne Warwick	1986	15.00

PICKWICK

Number	Title	Yr	NM
❑ PTP-2056	Alfie	1973	15.00
—As "Dionne Warwicke			

RHINO

Number	Title	Yr	NM
❑ RNDA-1100	Anthology 1962-1971	1985	18.00

SCEPTER

Number	Title	Yr	NM
❑ S-517 [M]	Anyone Who Had a Heart	1964	18.00
❑ SS-517 [S]	Anyone Who Had a Heart	1964	25.00
❑ P2M5139 [M]	Dionne!	1967	25.00
—Columbia Record Club exclusive			
❑ P2S5140 [S]	Dionne!	1967	25.00
—Columbia Record Club exclusive			
❑ SRM-534 [M]	Dionne Warwick in Paris	1966	15.00
❑ SPS-534 [S]	Dionne Warwick in Paris	1966	18.00
❑ SPS-577	Dionne Warwick's Golden Hits, Part 2	1969	18.00
❑ SRM-565 [M]	Dionne Warwick's Golden Hits, Part One	1967	25.00
❑ SPS-565 [S]	Dionne Warwick's Golden Hits, Part One	1967	18.00
❑ SPS-575	Dionne Warwick's Greatest Motion Picture Hits	1969	18.00
❑ SPS-598	From Within	1972	25.00
—As "Dionne Warwicke			
❑ SRM-531 [M]	Here I Am	1965	18.00
❑ SPS-531 [S]	Here I Am	1965	25.00
❑ SRM-555 [M]	Here Where There Is Love	1966	15.00
❑ SPS-555 [S]	Here Where There Is Love	1966	18.00
❑ ST-91010 [S]	Here Where There Is Love	1966	25.00
—Capitol Record Club edition			
❑ SPS-581	I'll Never Fall in Love Again	1970	18.00
❑ LP-523 [M]	Make Way for Dionne Warwick	1964	18.00
❑ SPS-523 [S]	Make Way for Dionne Warwick	1964	25.00
❑ SRM-559 [M]	On Stage and in the Movies	1967	15.00
❑ SPS-559 [S]	On Stage and in the Movies	1967	18.00
❑ ST-91099 [S]	On Stage and in the Movies	1967	25.00
—Capitol Record Club edition			
❑ S-508 [M]	Presenting Dionne Warwick	1963	18.00
❑ SS-508 [S]	Presenting Dionne Warwick	1963	25.00
❑ SPS-571	Promises, Promises	1968	18.00
❑ SPS-573	Soulful	1969	18.00
❑ SPS 2-596	The Dionne Warwicke Story	1971	25.00
—As "Dionne Warwicke			
❑ SRM-567 [M]	The Magic of Believing	1968	30.00
❑ SPS-567 [S]	The Magic of Believing	1968	25.00
❑ LP-528 [M]	The Sensitive Sound of Dionne Warwick	1965	18.00
❑ SPS-528 [S]	The Sensitive Sound of Dionne Warwick	1965	25.00
❑ SRM-563 [M]	The Windows of the World	1967	15.00
❑ SPS-563 [S]	The Windows of the World	1967	18.00
❑ SRM-568 [M]	Valley of the Dolls	1968	50.00
—May only exist as a white label promo			
❑ SPS-568 [S]	Valley of the Dolls	1968	18.00
❑ SPS-587 [B]	Very Dionne	1970	18.00

SPRINGBOARD

Number	Title	Yr	NM
❑ SPS-4002	Dionne Warwicke Sings Her Very Best	1972	12.00
—As "Dionne Warwicke			
❑ SPS-4032	Greatest Hits, Vol. 2	197?	12.00
❑ SPS-4003	One Hit After Another	1972	12.00
—As "Dionne Warwicke			
❑ SPS-4001	The Golden Voice of Dionne Warwicke	1972	12.00
—As "Dionne Warwicke			

TIME-LIFE

Number	Title	Yr	NM
❑ SLGD-18	Legendary Singers: Dionne Warwick	1987	18.00

UNITED ARTISTS

Number	Title	Yr	NM
❑ UA-LA337-G	The Very Best of Dionne Warwicke	1974	15.00
—As "Dionne Warwicke			

WARNER BROS.

Number	Title	Yr	NM
❑ BS2585	Dionne	1971	15.00
—As "Dionne Warwicke			
❑ BS2658	Just Being Myself	1973	15.00
—As "Dionne Warwicke			
❑ BS3119	Love at First Sight	1976	15.00
❑ BS2846	Then Came You	1975	15.00
—As "Dionne Warwicke			
❑ BS42846 [Q]	Then Came You	1975	25.00
—As "Dionne Warwicke			
❑ BS2893	Track of the Cat	1975	15.00

WAS (NOT WAS)

CHRYSALIS

Number	Title	Yr	NM
❑ R100615	What's Up Dog?	1988	15.00
—BMG Direct Marketing edition			
❑ FV41664 [B]	What's Up Dog?	1988	15.00

GEFFEN

Number	Title	Yr	NM
❑ GHS4016	Born to Laugh at Tornadoes	1983	12.00
❑ PRO-A-2079 [DJ]	Shake Your Head + 3	1983	18.00
—Promo-only sampler from Born to Laugh at Tornadoes			

ISLAND

Number	Title	Yr	NM
❑ ILPS9666	Was (Not Was)	1981	15.00

WASHBOARD SAM

RCA VICTOR

Number	Title	Yr	NM
❑ LPV-577 [M]	Feeling Lowdown	196?	30.00

WASHINGTON, BABY

AVI

Number	Title	Yr	NM
❑ AV-6038	I Wanna Dance	1978	12.00

COLLECTABLES

Number	Title	Yr	NM
❑ COL-5108	Only Those in Love	198?	12.00
❑ COL-5124	That's How Heartaches Are Made	198?	12.00
❑ COL-5040	The Best of Baby Washington	198?	12.00

SUE

Number	Title	Yr	NM
❑ LP-1042 [M]	Only Those in Love	1965	150.00
❑ LPS-1042 [S]	Only Those in Love	1965	300.00
❑ LP-1014 [M]	That's How Heartaches Are Made	1963	150.00

TRIP

Number	Title	Yr	NM
❑ 8009	The One and Only Baby Washington	1971	18.00

VEEP

Number	Title	Yr	NM
❑ VPS-16528	With You in Mind	1968	30.00

WASHINGTON, DINAH, AND BROOK BENTON

MERCURY

Number	Title	Yr	NM
❑ MG-20588 [M]	The Two of Us	1960	30.00
❑ SR-60244 [S]	The Two of Us	1960	30.00
❑ 824823-1	The Two of Us	1985	10.00
—Reissue			

WASHINGTON, DINAH

ACCORD

Number	Title	Yr	NM
❑ SN-7207	Retrospective	1982	12.00

COLLECTABLES

Number	Title	Yr	NM
❑ COL-5200	Golden Classics	1989	12.00

DELMARK

Number	Title	Yr	NM
❑ DL-451	Mellow Mama	1992	25.00

EMARCY

Number	Title	Yr	NM
❑ MG-26032 [10]	After Hours with Miss D	1954	150.00
❑ MG-36028 [M]	After Hours with Miss D	1955	70.00
—Reissue of 26032			
❑ MG-36065 [M]	Dinah	1956	70.00
❑ MG-36000 [M]	Dinah Jams	1955	80.00
❑ MG-36130 [M]	Dinah Washington Sings Bessie Smith	1957	60.00
❑ MG-36119 [M]	Dinah Washington Sings Fats Waller	1957	60.00
❑ MG-36011 [M]	For Those in Love	1955	70.00
❑ MG-36073 [M]	In the Land of Hi-Fi	1956	60.00
❑ 826453-1	In the Land of Hi-Fi	1986	12.00
❑ EMS-2-401	Jazz Sides	197?	18.00
❑ 824883-1	Jazz Sides	198?	15.00
—Reissue of 401			
❑ MG-36141 [M]	Newport '58	1958	50.00
❑ 814184-1	Slick Chick (On the Mellow Side)	1983	15.00
❑ MG-36104 [M]	The Swingin' Miss "D	1956	60.00

EVEREST ARCHIVE OF FOLK & JAZZ

Number	Title	Yr	NM
❑ FS-297	Dinah Washington	197?	15.00

GRAND AWARD

Number	Title	Yr	NM
❑ GA 33-318 [M]	Dinah Washington Sings the Blues	1955	50.00
—Add 50% if removable wrap-around cover is still there			

HARLEM HIT PARADE

Number	Title	Yr	NM
❑ 8002	Finer Dinah	197?	12.00

MERCURY

Number	Title	Yr	NM
❑ MG-25140 [10]	Blazing Ballads	1952	150.00
❑ MG-21119 [M]	Dinah Discovered	1967	25.00
❑ SR-61119 [S]	Dinah Discovered	1967	18.00
❑ MG-25060 [10]	Dinah Washington	1950	150.00
❑ MG-20525 [M]	Dinah Washington Sings Fats Waller	1960	30.00
—Reissue of EmArcy 36119			
❑ SR-60202 [S]	Dinah Washington Sings Fats Waller	1960	40.00
❑ MG-25138 [10]	Dynamic Dinah	1952	150.00
❑ MG-20614 [M]	For Lonely Lovers	1961	30.00
❑ SR-60614 [S]	For Lonely Lovers	1961	30.00
❑ MG-20604 [M]	I Concentrate on You	1961	30.00
❑ SR-60604 [S]	I Concentrate on You	1961	30.00
❑ MG-20729 [M]	I Wanna Be Loved	1962	30.00
❑ SR-60729 [S]	I Wanna Be Loved	1962	30.00
❑ MG-20119 [M]	Music for a First Love	1957	50.00
❑ MG-20120 [M]	Music for Late Hours	1957	50.00
❑ MG-20523 [M]	Newport '58	1960	30.00
—Reissue of EmArcy 36141			
❑ SR-60200 [S]	Newport '58	1960	40.00
❑ MG-20638 [M]	September in the Rain	1961	30.00
❑ SR-60638 [S]	September in the Rain	1961	30.00
❑ MG-20661 [M]	Tears and Laughter	1962	30.00
❑ SR-60661 [S]	Tears and Laughter	1962	30.00
❑ MG-20247 [M]	The Best in Blues	1958	50.00
❑ MG-20829 [M]	The Good Old Days	1963	18.00
❑ SR-60829 [S]	The Good Old Days	1963	25.00
❑ MG-20439 [M]	The Queen	1959	30.00
❑ SR-60111 [S]	The Queen	1959	40.00
❑ MG-20928 [M]	The Queen and Quincy	1965	18.00
❑ SR-60928 [S]	The Queen and Quincy	1965	25.00
❑ MGP-2-103 [M]	This Is My Story	1963	30.00
—Combines 20788 and 20789 in one package			
❑ MGP-2-603 [S]	This Is My Story	1963	30.00
—Combines 60788 and 60789 in one package			
❑ MG-20788 [M]	This Is My Story -- Dinah Washington's Golden Hits, Volume 1	1963	18.00
❑ SR-60788 [S]	This Is My Story -- Dinah Washington's Golden Hits, Volume 1	1963	25.00
❑ 822867-1	This Is My Story -- Dinah Washington's Golden Hits, Volume 1	1985	10.00
—Reissue			
❑ MG-20789 [M]	This Is My Story -- Dinah Washington's Golden Hits, Volume 2	1963	18.00
❑ SR-60789 [S]	This Is My Story -- Dinah Washington's Golden Hits, Volume 2	1963	25.00
❑ MG-20572 [M]	Unforgettable	1961	30.00
❑ SR-60232 [S]	Unforgettable	1961	30.00
❑ MG-20479 [M]	What a Diff'rence a Day Makes!	1960	30.00
❑ SR-60158 [S]	What a Diff'rence a Day Makes!	1960	40.00
❑ 818815-1	What a Diff'rence a Day Makes!	198?	10.00
—Reissue			

PICKWICK

Number	Title	Yr	NM
❑ SPC-3043	Dinah Washington	196?	12.00
❑ SPC-3536	Greatest Hits	197?	12.00
❑ SPC-3230	I Don't Hurt Anymore	197?	12.00

ROULETTE

Number	Title	Yr	NM
❑ R25253 [M]	A Stranger on Earth	1964	18.00
❑ SR25253 [S]	A Stranger on Earth	1964	25.00
❑ R25189 [M]	Back to the Blues	1963	18.00
❑ SR25189 [S]	Back to the Blues	1963	25.00
❑ R25170 [M]	Dinah '62	1962	18.00
❑ SR25170 [S]	Dinah '62	1962	25.00
❑ R25220 [M]	Dinah '63	1963	18.00
❑ SR25220 [S]	Dinah '63	1963	25.00
❑ R25269 [M]	Dinah Washington	1964	18.00
❑ SR25269 [S]	Dinah Washington	1964	25.00
❑ R25183 [M]	Drinking Again	1962	18.00
❑ SR25183 [S]	Drinking Again	1962	25.00
❑ RE104	Echoes of an Era	196?	18.00
❑ R25180 [M]	In Love	1962	18.00
❑ SR25180 [S]	In Love	1962	25.00
❑ R25244 [M]	In Tribute	1963	18.00
❑ SR25244 [S]	In Tribute	1963	25.00
❑ RE117	Queen of the Blues	1971	18.00
❑ R25289 [M]	The Best of Dinah Washington	1965	18.00
❑ SR25289 [S]	The Best of Dinah Washington	1965	25.00
❑ 42014	The Best of Dinah Washington	1968	15.00
— Reissue of 25289			
❑ RE125	The Immortal Dinah Washington	1973	18.00

TRIP

Number	Title	Yr	NM
❑ 5516	After Hours	1973	12.00
❑ 5500	Dinah Jams	1973	12.00
❑ 5556	Dinah Washington Sings Bessie Smith	197?	12.00
❑ TLX9505	Sad Songs -- Blue Songs	197?	15.00
❑ 5524	Tears and Laughter	1974	12.00
❑ 5565	The Swingin' Miss D	197?	12.00

VERVE

Number	Title	Yr	NM
❑ 818930-1	The Fats Waller Songbook	1984	12.00

WING

Number	Title	Yr	NM
❑ MGW-12271 [M]	Dinah Washington Sings Fats Waller	1964	15.00
❑ SRW-16271 [S]	Dinah Washington Sings Fats Waller	1964	15.00
❑ MGW-12140 [M]	The Late Late Show	1963	15.00
❑ SRW-16140 [S]	The Late Late Show	1963	15.00
❑ PKW-2-121	The Original Queen of Soul	1969	25.00
❑ SRW-16386	The Original Soul Sister	196?	15.00

WASHINGTON, EARL

JAZZ WORKSHOP

Number	Title	Yr	NM
❑ JWS-202 [M]	All Star Jazz	1963	60.00
❑ JWS-213 [M]	Reflections	1963	60.00

WASHINGTON, ERNESTINE

DISC

Number	Title	Yr	NM
❑ DLP-712 [10]	Ernestine Washington with Bunk Johnson	195?	200.00

WASHINGTON, GINO

ATAC

Number	Title	Yr	NM
❑ 2730	Gino Washington's Golden Hits	1969	30.00

KAPP

Number	Title	Yr	NM
❑ KL-1415 [M]	Gino Washington's Ram Jam Band	1967	80.00
❑ KS-3415 [S]	Gino Washington's Ram Jam Band	1967	30.00

WASHINGTON, GROVER, JR.

COLUMBIA

Number	Title	Yr	NM
❑ C48530	Next Exit	1992	25.00
❑ FC40510	Strawberry Moon	1987	12.00
❑ OC44256	Then and Now	1988	12.00
❑ OC45253	Time Out of Mind	1989	12.00

ELEKTRA

Number	Title	Yr	NM
❑ 60415	Anthology of Grover Washington, Jr.	1985	12.00
❑ 5E-562	Come Morning	1981	12.00
❑ 60318	Inside Moves	1984	12.00
❑ 6E-182	Paradise	1979	12.00
❑ 60215	The Best Is Yet to Come	1982	12.00
❑ 6E-305	Winelight	1980	12.00

KUDU

Number	Title	Yr	NM
❑ KU-07	All the King's Horses	1972	15.00
❑ KU-32	A Secret Place	1976	15.00
❑ KU-24	Feels So Good	1975	15.00
❑ KU-03	Inner City Blues	1971	15.00
❑ KUX-3637	Live at the Bijou	1977	18.00
❑ KU-20	Mister Magic	1975	15.00
❑ KUX-1213	Soul Box	1973	18.00
— The two records also were issued separately			
❑ KSQX-1213 [Q]	Soul Box	1973	35.00
❑ KU-12 [B]	Soul Box, Vol. 1	1973	15.00
❑ KU-13	Soul Box, Vol. 2	1973	15.00

MOTOWN

Number	Title	Yr	NM
❑ M5-186V1	All the King's Horses	1981	10.00
— Reissue of Kudu 07			
❑ M9-961A2	Anthology	1981	18.00
❑ M5-165V1	A Secret Place	1981	10.00
— Reissue of Kudu 32			
❑ M9-940	Baddest	1980	18.00
❑ M5-177V1	Feels So Good	1981	10.00
— Reissue of Kudu 24			
❑ 5307ML	Greatest Performances	1983	12.00
❑ 6126ML	Grover Washington Jr. at His Best	198?	12.00
❑ M5-189V1	Inner City Blues	1981	10.00
— Reissue of Kudu 03			
❑ M8-239	Live at the Bijou	1982	15.00
— Reissue			
❑ M5-175V1	Mister Magic	1981	10.00
— Reissue of Kudu 20			
❑ M7-910	Reed Seed	1978	12.00
❑ 5236ML	Reed Seed	1982	10.00
— Reissue of 910			
❑ M7-933	Skylarkin'	1980	12.00
❑ 5232ML	Skylarkin'	1982	10.00
— Reissue of 933			
❑ M5-184V1	Soul Box, Vol. 1	1981	10.00
— Reissue of half of Kudu 1213			
❑ M5-187V1	Soul Box, Vol. 2	1981	10.00
— Reissue of half of Kudu 1213			

NAUTILUS

Number	Title	Yr	NM
❑ NR-39	Winelight	1981	50.00
— Audiophile vinyl			

WASHINGTON, TUTS

ROUNDER

Number	Title	Yr	NM
❑ 2041	New Orleans Piano Professor	198?	12.00

WASHINGTON, TYRONE

BLUE LABOR

Number	Title	Yr	NM
❑ 102	Do Right	197?	25.00

BLUE NOTE

Number	Title	Yr	NM
❑ BST-84274	Natural Essence	1968	30.00

WASSERMAN, ROB

MCA

Number	Title	Yr	NM
❑ 42131	Duets	1988	12.00

ROUNDER

Number	Title	Yr	NM
❑ 0179	Solo	198?	15.00

WATANABE, KAZUMI

GRAMAVISION

Number	Title	Yr	NM
❑ R1-79415	Kilowatt	1989	15.00
❑ 18-8506	Mobo Club	1985	12.00
❑ GR-8404	Mobo I	1984	15.00
❑ GR-8406	Mobo II	1984	15.00
❑ 18-8602	Mobo Splash	1986	12.00
❑ 18-8706	Spice of Life	1987	12.00
❑ 18-8810	Spice of Life Too	1988	12.00

INNER CITY

Number	Title	Yr	NM
❑ IC-6071	Mermaid Boulevard	198?	15.00

WATANABE, SADAO

CATALYST

Number	Title	Yr	NM
❑ 7911	Sadao Watanabe and Charlie Mariano	197?	15.00

COLUMBIA

Number	Title	Yr	NM
❑ C2X36818	How's Everything	1980	15.00
❑ FC37433	Orange Express	1981	12.00

ELEKTRA

Number	Title	Yr	NM
❑ 60748	Birds of Passage	1987	12.00
❑ 60816	Elis	1988	12.00
❑ 60906	Front Seat	1989	15.00
❑ 60431	Maisha	1986	12.00
❑ 60475	Parker's Mood	1986	12.00
❑ 60803	Selected Sadao Watanabe	1989	18.00

ELEKTRA/MUSICIAN

Number	Title	Yr	NM
❑ 60297	Fill Up the Night	1984	12.00
❑ 60371	Rendezvous	1985	12.00

INNER CITY

Number	Title	Yr	NM
❑ IC-6064	Autumn Blow	198?	15.00
❑ IC-6061	Bird of Paradise	198?	15.00
❑ IC-6062	California Shower	197?	15.00
❑ IC-6015	I'm Old Fashioned	1978	15.00
❑ IC-6060	Morning Island	198?	15.00
❑ IC-6063	My Dear Life	198?	15.00

VANGUARD

Number	Title	Yr	NM
❑ VSD-79344	Round Trip	1974	15.00

WATERBOYS, THE

CHRYSALIS

Number	Title	Yr	NM
❑ PV41542	A Pagan Place	1986	10.00
— Reissue			
❑ FV41589	Fisherman's Blues	1988	12.00
❑ PV41541	The Waterboys	1986	10.00
— Reissue of first U.K. LP			
❑ FV41543	This Is the Sea	1986	12.00
— Reissue			

ISLAND

Number	Title	Yr	NM
❑ 90190	A Pagan Place	1984	18.00
❑ 90147 [EP]	The Waterboys	1983	12.00
❑ 90457	This Is the Sea	1985	15.00

WATERGATE SEVEN PLUS ONE, THE

STOMP OFF

Number	Title	Yr	NM
❑ SOS-1165	Ostrich Walk and Alligator Crawl	1989	12.00

WATERS, BENNY

MUSE

Number	Title	Yr	NM
❑ MR-5340	From Paradise (Small's) to Shangri-La	1987	12.00

STOMP OFF

Number	Title	Yr	NM
❑ SOS-1210	Memories of the Twenties	1991	12.00

WATERS, CRYSTAL

MERCURY

Number	Title	Yr	NM
❑ 848894-1	Surprise	1991	15.00

WATERS, ETHEL

BIOGRAPH

Number	Title	Yr	NM
❑ 12022	Ethel Waters 1921/24	197?	12.00
❑ 12025	Jazzin' Babies Blues	197?	12.00

COLUMBIA

Number	Title	Yr	NM
❑ KG31571	Her Greatest Years	1972	18.00
❑ PG31571	Her Greatest Years	197?	15.00
— Reissue with new prefix			
❑ CL2792 [M]	On Stage and Screen 1925-1940	1968	18.00

GLENDALE

Number	Title	Yr	NM
❑ GL-9011	Ethel Waters	198?	12.00

MERCURY

Number	Title	Yr	NM
❑ MG-20051 [M]	Ethel Waters	1954	50.00

MONMOUTH-EVERGREEN

Number	Title	Yr	NM
❑ 6812	Miss Ethel Waters	1968	15.00

REMINGTON

Number	Title	Yr	NM
❑ RLP-1025 [10]	Ethel Waters	1950	50.00

WORD

Number	Title	Yr	NM
❑ WST-8044	His Eye Is On the Sparrow	197?	15.00
❑ W-3100LP [M]	His Eye Is On the Sparrow	196?	18.00

X

Number	Title	Yr	NM
❑ LVA-1009 [M]	Ethel Waters	1955	50.00

WATERS, JOE

NEW COLONY

Number	Title	Yr	NM
❑ 831	Harvest Moon	1983	12.00

WATERS, KIM

WARLOCK

Number	Title	Yr	NM
❑ WAR-2720	All Because of You	1990	15.00
❑ WAR-2713	Sweet and Saxy	1989	15.00

WATERS, MUDDY, AND HOWLIN' WOLF

CHESS

Number	Title	Yr	NM
❑ CH-9100	Muddy and The Wolf	1985	15.00

WATERS, MUDDY

BLUE SKY

Number	Title	Yr	NM
❑ PZ34449	Hard Again	1977	15.00
— No bar code on cover			
❑ PZ34449 [B]	Hard Again	198?	10.00
— Budget-line reissue with bar code			
❑ JZ34928	I'm Ready	1978	15.00
❑ PZ34928	I'm Ready	198?	10.00
— Budget-line reissue			
❑ JZ37064	King Bee	1981	15.00
❑ PZ37064	King Bee	198?	10.00
— Budget-line reissue			
❑ JZ35712	Muddy "Missisiippi" Waters Live	1980	15.00
❑ PZ35712	Muddy "Missisiippi" Waters Live	198?	10.00
— Budget-line reissue			

CADET CONCEPT

Number	Title	Yr	NM
❑ CS-320	After the Rain	1969	30.00
❑ CS-314	Electric Mud	1968	30.00

CHESS

Number	Title	Yr	NM
❑ LP-1533 [M]	Blues from Big Bill's Copacabana	1968	50.00
❑ CH-50023	Can't Get No Grindin'	1973	25.00
❑ CH-9319	Can't Get No Grindin'	1990	12.00
— Reissue of 50023			
❑ 127	Fathers and Sons	1969	30.00
❑ 2CH-50033	Fathers and Sons	1974	25.00
— Reissue of 127			
❑ LP-1483 [M]	Folk Singer	1964	120.00
❑ CH-9261	Folk Singer	1987	12.00
— Reissue of 1483			
❑ CH-60026	London Revisited	1974	18.00
❑ 2CH-60006	McKinley Morganfield, A.K.A. Muddy Waters	1971	30.00
❑ LP-1511 [M]	More Real Folk Blues	1967	50.00
❑ LPS-1511 [S]	More Real Folk Blues	1967	40.00
❑ CH-9278	More Real Folk Blues	1988	12.00
— Reissue of 1511			
❑ LP-1507 [M]	Muddy, Brass and Blues	1966	40.00
❑ LPS-1507 [S]	Muddy, Brass and Blues	1966	50.00
❑ CH-9286	Muddy, Brass and the Blues	1989	12.00
— Reissue of 1507			

Number	Title	Yr	NM

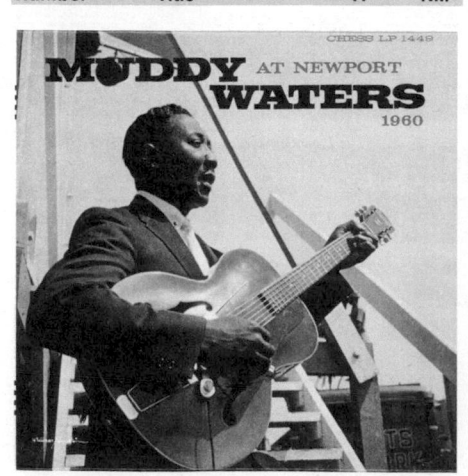

Number	Title	Yr	NM
□ LP-1449 [M]	Muddy Waters at Newport	1962	120.00
□ CH-9198	Muddy Waters at Newport	1986	12.00
—Reissue of 1449			
□ CH-50012	Muddy Waters Live	1972	25.00
□ LP-1444 [M]	Muddy Waters Sings Big Bill	1960	300.00
□ LP-1444 [DJ]	Muddy Waters Sings Big Bill	1960	1000.00
—White label promo			
□ CH-9197	Muddy Waters Sings Big Bill	1986	12.00
—Reissue of 1444			
□ LPS-1444 [R]	Muddy Waters Sings Big Bill	196?	18.00
—Rechanneled stereo reissue			
□ CH-9180	Rare and Unissued	1986	15.00
□ CH-9101	Rolling Stone	1985	15.00
□ LPS-1539	Sail On	1969	30.00
□ LP-1427 [M]	The Best of Muddy Waters	1957	500.00
—Black label			
□ LP-1427 [DJ]	The Best of Muddy Waters	1957	1500.00
—White label promo; VG value 500; VG+ value 1000			
□ CH-9255	The Best of Muddy Waters	1987	12.00
—Reissue of 1427			
□ LPS-1427 [R]	The Best of Muddy Waters	196?	15.00
—Black label			
□ CH6-80002	The Chess Box	1990	50.00
□ CH-60013	The London Muddy Waters Sessions	1972	25.00
□ CH-9298	The London Muddy Waters Sessions	1989	12.00
—Reissue of 60013			
□ CH-50035	The Muddy Waters Woodstock Album	1976	18.00
□ LP-1501 [M]	The Real Folk Blues of Muddy Waters	1965	60.00
□ CH-9274	The Real Folk Blues of Muddy Waters	1987	12.00
—Reissue of 1501			
□ LPS-1553	They Call Me Muddy Waters	1971	25.00
□ CH-9299	They Call Me Muddy Waters	1989	12.00
—Reissue of 1553			
□ CH-9291	Trouble No More: Singles 1955-1959	1989	15.00
□ CH-60031	Unk" in Funk	1975	18.00
INTERMEDIA			
□ QS-5071	Sweet Home Chicago	198?	12.00
MOBILE FIDELITY			
□ 1-201	Folk Singer	1994	50.00
—Audiophile vinyl			
MUSE			
□ MR-5008	Mud in Your Ear	198?	15.00
TESTAMENT			
□ 2210	Stovall's Plantation	197?	15.00

WATERS, PATTY

ESP-DISK'

□ 1055 [S]	Patty Waters College Tour	1968	60.00
□ 1025 [M]	Patty Waters Sings	1966	30.00
□ S-1025 [S]	Patty Waters Sings	1966	30.00

WATERS, ROGER

COLUMBIA

□ FC40795 [B]	Radio K.A.O.S.	1987	18.00
□ FC39290 [B]	The Pros and Cons of Hitch Hiking	1984	30.00
—Original nude cover			
□ FC39290 [B]	The Pros and Cons of Hitch Hiking	1984	15.00
—Revised cover with black rectangle over woman's naked rear end			
□ PC39290	The Pros and Cons of Hitch Hiking	1986	12.00
—Budget-line reissue with new prefix			

MERCURY

□ R209833 [B]	The Wall -- Live in Berlin	1990	30.00
—BMG Direct Marketing version			
□ 846611-1 [B]	The Wall -- Live in Berlin	1990	35.00

WATKINS, DOUG

NEW JAZZ

□ NJLP-8238 [M]	Soulnik	1960	60.00
—Purple label			
□ NJLP-8238 [M]	Soulnik	1965	30.00
—Blue label, trident logo at right			

PHILIPS

| □ PHM200001 [M] | French Horns for My Lady | 1962 | 25.00 |
| □ PHS600001 [S] | French Horns for My Lady | 1962 | 30.00 |

TRANSITION

| □ TRLP-20 [M] | Watkins at Large | 1956 | 1200.00 |
| —Deduct 1/10 if booklet is missing | | | |

WATKINS, JOE

GHB

| □ GHB-74 | Last Will and Testament | 197? | 12.00 |

WATKINS, JULIUS

BLUE NOTE

| □ BLP-5053 [10] | Julius Watkins Sextet | 1954 | 400.00 |
| □ BLP-5064 [10] | Julius Watkins Sextet, Volume 2 | 1955 | 400.00 |

WATKINS, LOVELACE

MGM

| □ E-3831 [M] | The Voice of Lovelace Watkins | 1960 | 30.00 |
| □ SE-3831 [S] | The Voice of Lovelace Watkins | 1960 | 40.00 |

WATKINS, MARY

OLIVIA

| □ LF-919 | Something Moving | 198? | 12.00 |

PALO ALTO

| □ PA-8030 | Wind of Change | 198? | 12.00 |

REDWOOD

| □ R-8506 | Spiritsong | 1985 | 12.00 |

WATKINS, MITCH

ENJA

| □ R1-79603 | Underneath It All | 1989 | 15.00 |

WATLEY, JODY

ATLANTIC

| □ 83087 | Flower | 1998 | 18.00 |

MCA

□ 10355	Affairs of the Heart	1991	15.00
□ 5898	Jody Watley	1987	12.00
□ 6276	Larger Than Life	1989	12.00
□ 6343	You Wanna Dance with Me?	1989	15.00

SOLAR

| □ D1-72561 | Beginnings | 1988 | 12.00 |

WATROUS, BILL

COLUMBIA

□ PC36977	Bill Watrous	1981	15.00
□ KC33090	Manhattan Wildlife Refuge	1974	25.00
□ PC33701	Tiger of San Pedro	1975	25.00

FAMOUS DOOR

□ HL-101	Bone Straight Ahead	1973	30.00
□ HL-136	Coronary Trombossa	1981	12.00
□ HL-134	I'll Play for You	1980	15.00
□ HL-137	La Zorra	1981	12.00
□ HL-144	Roarin' Back Into New York	1982	12.00
□ HL-147	The Best of Bill Watrous	198?	12.00
□ HL-127	Watrous in Hollywood	1979	15.00

SOUNDWINGS

| □ SW-2104 | Reflections | 1987 | 18.00 |
| □ SW-2100 | Someplace Else | 1986 | 18.00 |

WATSON, BOBBY

BLUE NOTE

| □ B1-90262 | No Question About It | 1988 | 15.00 |
| □ B1-91915 | The Inventor | 1990 | 15.00 |

RED RECORD

| □ VPA-184 | Appointment in Milano | 1986 | 15.00 |
| □ VPA-173 | Perpetual Groove (Live in Europe) | 198? | 15.00 |

WATSON, DOC

FLYING FISH

□ FF-301	Guitar Album	1983	15.00
□ FF-352	Pickin' the Blues	1985	12.00
□ FF-252	Red Rocking Chair	1981	15.00

FOLKWAYS

| □ FA-2366 [M] | Doc Watson and Family | 1963 | 30.00 |
| □ FA-31021 [S] | Doc Watson and Family | 196? | 18.00 |

INTERMEDIA

| □ QS-5031 | Out in the Country | 198? | 12.00 |

LIBERTY

□ LW-601	Doc and the Boys	1981	12.00
—Reissue of United Artists 601			
□ LT-943	Live and Pickin'	1981	12.00
—Reissue of United Artists 943			

□ LN-10027	Lonesome Road	1981	10.00
—Budget-line reissue			
□ LT-887	Look Away!	1981	12.00
—Reissue of United Artists 887			
□ LWB-423 [B]	Memories	1981	15.00
—Reissue of United Artists 423			

POPPY

□ PYS-5703	The Elementary Doc Watson	1972	18.00
□ PP-LA022-F	Then and Now	1973	18.00
□ PP-LA210-G	Two Days in November	1974	18.00

SMITHSONIAN/FOLKWAYS

| □ SF-40012 | The Doc Watson Family | 1990 | 15.00 |
| —Reissue of Folkways LP | | | |

SUGAR HILL

□ SH-3742	Down South	1985	12.00
□ SH-3759	Portrait	1987	12.00
□ SH-3752	Riding the Midnight Train	1986	12.00

UNITED ARTISTS

□ UA-LA601-G	Doc and the Boys	1976	15.00
□ UA-LA943-H	Live and Pickin'	1979	15.00
□ UA-LA725-G	Lonesome Road	1977	15.00
□ UA-LA887-H	Look Away!	1978	15.00
□ UA-LA423-G	Memories	1975	18.00

VANGUARD

□ VSD-6576	Ballads from Deep Gap	1971	18.00
□ VRS-9152 [M]	Doc Watson	1964	25.00
□ VSD-79152 [S]	Doc Watson	1964	30.00
□ VRS-9170 [M]	Doc Watson and Son	1965	25.00
□ VSD-79170 [S]	Doc Watson and Son	1965	25.00
□ VSD-9/10	Doc Watson on Stage	1970	25.00
□ VSD-79276	Good Deal	1968	18.00
□ VRS-9239 [M]	Home Again	1967	18.00
□ VSD-79239 [S]	Home Again	1967	25.00
□ VSD107/8	Old Timey Concert	1977	25.00
□ VRS-9213 [M]	Southbound	1966	18.00
□ VSD-79213 [S]	Southbound	1966	25.00
□ VSD79213 [B]	Southbound	2014	30.00
□ VSD45/46	The Essential Doc Watson	1973	25.00
□ VMS-73108	The Essential Doc Watson, Vol. 1	1985	12.00
□ VMS-73121	The Essential Doc Watson, Vol. 2	1985	12.00

WATSON, GENE

CAPITOL

□ ST-11715	Beautiful Country	1977	15.00
□ ST-11529	Because You Believe In Me	1976	15.00
□ ST-11443	Love in the Hot Afternoon	1975	15.00
□ ST-12102	No One Will Ever Know	1980	15.00
□ ST-11597	Paper Rosie	1977	15.00
□ SN-16124	Paper Rosie	198?	10.00
—Budget-line reissue			
□ SW-11805	Reflections	1978	15.00
□ SN-16304	Reflections	198?	10.00
—Budget-line reissue			
□ ST-11947	Should I Come Home	1979	15.00
□ ST-11782	The Best of Gene Watson	1978	15.00
□ C1-91641	The Best of Gene Watson	1989	15.00
□ SN-16241	The Best of Gene Watson, Vol. 2	198?	10.00

EPIC

□ FE40644	Honky Tonk Crazy	1987	10.00
□ BFE40076	Memories to Burn	1985	10.00
□ FE40306	Starting New Memories	1986	10.00

MCA

□ 5170	Between This Time and the Next Time	1981	12.00
□ 5572	Greatest Hits	1985	10.00
□ 5440	Little by Little	1984	12.00
□ 951	Little by Little	1985	10.00
—Reissue of 5440			
□ 5241	Old Loves Never Die	1981	12.00
□ 5384	Sometimes I Get Lucky	1983	12.00
□ 950	Sometimes I Get Lucky	1985	10.00
—Reissue of 5384			
□ 5302	This Dream's on Me	1982	12.00

MCA CURB

| □ 5520 | Heartaches, Love and Stuff | 1984 | 10.00 |
| □ 5670 | Texas Saturday Night | 1985 | 10.00 |

WARNER BROS.

| □ 25832 | Back in the Fire | 1989 | 12.00 |

WATSON, JOHNNY "GUITAR", AND LARRY WILLIAMS

OKEH

| □ OKM12122 [M] | Two for the Price of One | 1967 | 40.00 |
| □ OKS14122 [S] | Two for the Price of One | 1967 | 60.00 |

WATSON, JOHNNY "GUITAR

A&M

| □ SP-4880 | That's What Time It Is | 1981 | 12.00 |

CADET

| □ LP-4056 [M] | I Cried for You | 1967 | 30.00 |
| □ LPS-4056 [S] | I Cried for You | 1967 | 30.00 |

CHESS

| □ LP-1490 [M] | Blues Soul | 1965 | 70.00 |
| □ LPS-1490 [S] | Blues Soul | 1965 | 80.00 |

Number	Title	Yr	NM
DJM			
3	Ain't That a Bitch	1976	12.00
7	A Real Mother for Ya	1977	12.00
27 [B]	E.D.P. Extra Disco Perception	1979	12.00
— As "Watsonian Institute			
714 [B]	Funk Beyond the Call of Duty	1977	12.00
19	Giant	1978	12.00
501	Johnny "Guitar" Watson and the Family Clone	1981	12.00
31	Love Jones	1980	12.00
13	Master Funk	1978	12.00
— As "Watsonian Institute			
24	What the Hell Is This?	1979	12.00
FANTASY			
MPF-4503	Greatest Hits	1981	12.00
9484	I Don't Want to Be Alone Stranger	1975	15.00
9437	Listen	1973	15.00
KING			
857 [M]	Johnny Guitar Watson	1963	400.00
MCA			
5273	The Very Best of Johnny "Guitar" Watson	1981	12.00
OKEH			
OKM12118 [M]	Bad	1967	30.00
OKS14118 [S]	Bad	1967	40.00
OKM12124 [M]	In the Fats Bag	1967	30.00
OKS14124 [S]	In the Fats Bag	1967	40.00
POWER PAK			
306	Gangster of Love	1978	12.00

WATSON, ROBERT
ROULETTE

Number	Title	Yr	NM
SR-5009	Estimated Time of Arrival	1977	15.00

WATT, MIKE
COLUMBIA

Number	Title	Yr	NM
C66464	Ball-Hog Or Tugboat?	1995	15.00

WATT, TOMMY
BETHLEHEM

Number	Title	Yr	NM
BCP-6052 [M]	Watts Cooking	1961	30.00

WATTERS, LU

Number	Title	Yr	NM
MGC-503 [10]	Lu Watters Jazz	1954	100.00
DOWN HOME			
MGD-5 [10]	Lu Watters and His Yerba Buena Jazz Band	1955	60.00
GOOD TIME JAZZ			
L-12007 [M]	1942 Series	1955	40.00
L-12001 [M]	Dawn Club Favorites	1954	40.00
L-8 [10]	Lu Watters and His Yerba Buena Jazz Band	1952	50.00
L-12002 [M]	Originals and Ragtime	1954	40.00
L-0A [M]	San Francisco Style	195?	60.00
L 12003 [M]	Stomps, Etc. and the Blues	1954	40.00
HOMESPUN			
103	Live Recordings from Hambone Kelly's	197?	12.00
107	Lu Watters and the Yerba Buena Jazz Band, 1941	197?	12.00
101	Lu Watters and the Yerba Buena Jazz Band, Vol. 1	197?	12.00
102	Lu Watters and the Yerba Buena Jazz Band, Vol. 2	197?	12.00
104	Lu Watters and the Yerba Buena Jazz Band, Vol. 4	197?	15.00
106	Lu Watters and the Yerba Buena Jazz Band, Vol. 6	197?	12.00
105	Memories of the Bodega Battle	197?	15.00
MERCURY			
MGC-510 [10]	Lu Watters and His Yerba Buena Jazz Band	1952	120.00
MG-35013 [10]	Lu Watters and the Yerba Buena Jazz Band	1950	150.00
MGC-103 [10]	Lu Watters and the Yerba Buena Jazz Band	1950	120.00
MGC-503 [10]	Lu Watters Jazz	1951	120.00
RIVERSIDE			
RLP-2513 [10]	Lu Watters 1947	1955	120.00
RLP 12-213 [M]	San Francisco Style	1956	60.00
VERVE			
MGV-1005 [M]	Lu Watters and His Yerba Buena Jazz Band	1956	50.00
V-1005 [M]	Lu Watters and His Yerba Buena Jazz Band	1961	25.00

WATTERS, LU/SANTO PECORA
VERVE

Number	Title	Yr	NM
MGV-1008 [M]	Dixieland Jamboree	1956	50.00
V-1008 [M]	Dixieland Jamboree	1961	30.00

WATTS, ALAN
ASCENSION

Number	Title	Yr	NM
(# unknown)0	Dhyana: of the Art of Meditation, Vol. 1	1970	30.00
(# unknown)0	Dhyana: of the Art of Meditation, Vol. 2	1970	30.00

Number	Title	Yr	NM
MEA			
LP-1001 [M]	Haiku Poems	1962	50.00
LP-1007 [M]	This Is It	1962	60.00
LP-1002 [M]	Zen and Senryu	1962	50.00
TOGETHER			
1025	Why Not Now	1970	30.00
WARNER BROS.			
W1923	The Sounds of Hinduism	1968	30.00

WATTS, CHARLIE
COLUMBIA

Number	Title	Yr	NM
FC40570	The Charlie Watts Orchestra Live Fulham Town Hall	1986	18.00
CONTINUUM			
19308	From One Charlie	1990	30.00

— Box set with LP, book ("Ode to a High Flying Bird") and photo of Charlie Parker

WATTS, ERNIE
ELEKTRA

Number	Title	Yr	NM
6E-285	Look in Your Heart	1980	12.00
PACIFIC JAZZ			
PJ-20155	Planet Love	1969	30.00
QWEST			
25283	Musician	1985	12.00
VAULT			
LP-9011	Wonderbag	1968	25.00

WATTS, MARZETTE
ESP-DISK'

Number	Title	Yr	NM
1044 [S]	Marzette Watts and Company	1971	25.00
SAVOY			
MG-12193 [M]	The Marzette Watts Ensemble	1968	25.00

WAVE, THE
ATLANTIC

Number	Title	Yr	NM
81883	Second Wave	1988	12.00

WAVE CRESTS, THE
VIKING

Number	Title	Yr	NM
VKL-6606 [M]	Surftime U.S.A.	1963	60.00
VKS-6606 [S]	Surftime U.S.A.	1963	100.00

WAVERLY CONSORT, THE
COLUMBIA MASTERWORKS

Number	Title	Yr	NM
M34554	A Renaissance Christmas Celebration	1977	15.00

WAYBILL, FEE
CAPITOL

Number	Title	Yr	NM
ST-12369 [B]	Read My Lips	1984	15.00

WAYFARERS, THE
RCA VICTOR

Number	Title	Yr	NM
LPM-2666 [M]	Come Along with the Wayfarers	1963	30.00
LSP-2666 [S]	Come Along with the Wayfarers	1963	30.00
LPM-1213 [M]	The Wayfarers	1956	50.00
LPM-2735 [M]	The Wayfarers at the Hungry I	1963	30.00
LSP-2735 [S]	The Wayfarers at the Hungry I	1963	30.00
LPM-2946 [M]	The Wayfarers at the World's Fair	1964	30.00
LSP-2946 [S]	The Wayfarers at the World's Fair	1964	40.00

WAYLAND QUARTET, THE
4 CORNERS OF THE WORLD

Number	Title	Yr	NM
FCS-4249	Jazz Bach	1968	18.00

WAYLON AND JESSI
RCA VICTOR

Number	Title	Yr	NM
AAL1-3931	Leather and Lace	1981	12.00

WAYLON AND WILLIE
COLUMBIA

Number	Title	Yr	NM
FC38562	Take It to the Limit	1983	12.00
RCA VICTOR			
AFL1-2686	Waylon and Willie	1978	12.00
AAL1-2686	Waylon and Willie	198?	10.00
— Reissue with new prefix			
AYL1-5134	Waylon and Willie	198?	10.00
— Best Buy Series" reissue			
AFL1-2686 [DJ]	Waylon and Willie	1978	30.00
— Promo only on gold vinyl			
AHL1-4455	WW II	1982	12.00
AYL1-5138	WW II	198?	10.00
— Best Buy Series" reissue			

WAYNE, CHUCK, AND JOE PUMA
CHOICE

Number	Title	Yr	NM
1004	Interactions	197?	15.00

Number	Title	Yr	NM
WAYNE, CHUCK			
FOCUS			
FL-333 [M]	Tapestry	1964	30.00
FS-333 [M]	Tapestry	1964	30.00
PRESTIGE			
PRLP-7367 [M]	Morning Mist	1965	25.00
PRST-7367 [S]	Morning Mist	1965	30.00
PROGRESSIVE			
3003 [10]	The Chuck Wayne Quintet	1953	200.00
PRO-7008	Traveling	1976	15.00
SAVOY			
MG-12077 [M]	The Jazz Guitarist	1956	50.00
SAVOY JAZZ			
SJL-1144	Tasty Pudding	198?	12.00
VIK			
LX-1098 [M]	String Fever	1957	50.00

WAYNE, FRANCES
ATLANTIC

Number	Title	Yr	NM
1263 [M]	The Warm Sound	1957	50.00
— Black label			
1263 [M]	The Warm Sound	1961	25.00
— White "fan" logo at right of label			
BRUNSWICK			
BL54022 [M]	Frances Wayne	1958	40.00
CORAL			
CRL56019 [10]	Salute to Ethel Waters	195?	60.00
EPIC			
LN3222 [M]	Songs for My Man	1956	50.00

WAYNE, JOHN
RCA VICTOR

Number	Title	Yr	NM
LSP-4828	America, Why I Love Her	1973	30.00
AFL1-3484	America, Why I Love Her	1979	12.00
— Reissue of 4828			
AYL1-3959	America, Why I Love Her	1981	10.00
— Best Buy Series" reissue			

WAYNE, NANCY
20TH CENTURY

Number	Title	Yr	NM
T-442	Cheatin' Was the Last Thing on My Mind	1974	15.00
T-472	I Wanna Kiss You	1975	15.00

WAYNE, WEE WILLIE
IMPERIAL

Number	Title	Yr	NM
LP-9144 [M]	Travelin' Mood	1961	500.00

WAZOO
ZIG ZAG

Number	Title	Yr	NM
217	Wazoo	197?	20.00

WE FIVE
A&M

Number	Title	Yr	NM
SP-138 [M]	Make Someone Happy	1967	25.00
SP-4138 [S]	Make Someone Happy	1967	18.00
SP-4168	The Return of We Five	1969	18.00
SP-111 [M]	You Were On My Mind	1965	18.00
SP-4111 [S]	You Were On My Mind	1965	25.00
VAULT			
136	Catch the Wind	1970	18.00

WEASELS, THE
WING

Number	Title	Yr	NM
MGW-12282 [M]	The Liverpool Beat	1964	30.00
SRW-16282 [S]	The Liverpool Beat	1964	30.00

WEATHER REPORT
ARC

Number	Title	Yr	NM
PC236030	8:30	1979	18.00
JC35358	Mr. Gone	1978	12.00
— Original issue; no bar code on cover			
PC35358	Mr. Gone	1980	10.00
— Budget-line reissue; bar code on back cover			
JC36793	Night Passage	1980	12.00
PC36793	Night Passage	198?	10.00
— Budget-line reissue			
FC37616	Weather Report	1982	12.00
HC47616	Weather Report	1982	40.00
— Half Speed Mastered" on cover			
PC37616	Weather Report	198?	10.00
— Budget-line reissue			
COLUMBIA			
PC34099	Black Market	1976	15.00
— No bar code on cover			
PC34099	Black Market	1980	10.00
— With bar code on cover			
FC39147	Domino Theory	1984	12.00
PC34418	Heavy Weather	1977	12.00
— No bar code on cover			
PC34418	Heavy Weather	198?	10.00
— Budget-line reissue; bar code on back cover			
HC44418	Heavy Weather	198?	40.00

Number	Title	Yr	NM
—Half-Speed Mastered" on cover			
❑ KC31352	I Sing the Body Electric	1972	15.00
— Original edition; no bar code on cover			
❑ PC31352	I Sing the Body Electric	1977	10.00
—Reissue; with or without bar code on cover			
❑ KC32494	Mysterious Traveller	1974	15.00
—Original issue; no bar code on cover			
❑ PC32494	Mysterious Traveller	1977	10.00
—Reissue; with or without bar code on cover			
❑ CQ32494 [Q]	Mysterious Traveller	1974	30.00
❑ FC38427	Procession	1983	12.00
❑ FC39908	Sportin' Life	1985	12.00
❑ KC32210	Sweetnighter	1973	15.00
— Original edition; no bar code on back cover			
❑ PC32210	Sweetnighter	1977	10.00
—Reissue with new prefix; with or without bar code on cover			
❑ PC33417	Tale Spinnin'	1975	15.00
— Original edition; no bar code on cover			
❑ PC33417	Tale Spinnin'	1977	10.00
—Budget-line reissue; with or without bar code			
❑ PCQ33417 [Q]	Tale Spinnin'	1975	30.00
❑ FC40280	This Is This	1986	15.00
❑ C30661	Weather Report	1971	15.00
— Original edition; no bar code on cover			
❑ KC30661	Weather Report	1974	12.00
— Reissue of C 30661			
❑ PC30661	Weather Report	1977	10.00
— Reissue; with or without bar code on cover			

WEATHERBIRD JAZZ BAND, THE

STOMP OFF
❑ SOS-1034	Fireworks	198?	12.00

WEATHERBURN, RONN

STOMP OFF
❑ SOS-1107	After the Ball	198?	12.00

WEATHERLY, JIM

ABC
❑ ABCD-982	Pictures and Rhymes	1977	12.00
❑ ABCD-937	The People Some People Choose to Love	1976	12.00

BUDDAH
❑ BDS-5637	Magnolias & Misfits	1975	12.00
❑ BDS-5608	The Songs of Jim Weatherly	1974	12.00

RCA VICTOR
❑ APL1-0090	A Simpler Time	1973	15.00
❑ APL1-0267	Jim Weatherly	1974	15.00
❑ LSP-4747	Weatherly	1972	15.00

WEAVER, CHARLIE

COLUMBIA
❑ CL1345 [M]	Charlie Weaver Sings for His People	1959	30.00

STARLITE
❑ 6003 [10]	Charlie Weaver Sings	1954	50.00

WEAVER, DENNIS

ABC
❑ DP-847	People Songs	1974	15.00

IM'PRESS
❑ 1614	Dennis Weaver	1972	18.00

OVATION
❑ OVOD-1440	One More Road	1975	15.00

WEAVERS, THE

ANALOGUE PRODUCTIONS
❑ 005	Reunion at Carnegie Hall, 1963	199?	30.00
—Audiophile vinyl			

DECCA
❑ DL8909 [M]	Folk Songs Around the World	1959	40.00
❑ DL8893 [M]	Folk Songs Made Famous by the Weavers	196?	25.00
❑ DL78893 [R]	Folk Songs Made Famous by the Weavers	196?	18.00
❑ DL5285 [10]	Folk Songs of America and Other Lands	1951	100.00
❑ DL8893 [M]	The Best of the Weavers	1959	40.00
—Black label, silver print			
❑ DXB173 [M]	The Best of the Weavers	1965	30.00
❑ DXSB173 [R]	The Best of the Weavers	1965	25.00
❑ DL75169 [R]	The Weavers' Greatest Hits	1971	15.00
❑ DL4277 [M]	Weavers' Gold	1962	25.00
❑ DL74277 [R]	Weavers' Gold	1962	18.00
❑ DL-5373 [10]	We Wish You a Merry Christmas	1952	100.00

MCA
❑ 4052	The Best of the Weavers	197?	18.00
— Reissue of Decca 7173; black rainbow labels			
❑ 4052	The Best of the Weavers	1980	15.00
— Blue rainbow labels			

VANGUARD
❑ VRS9100 [M]	Almanac	1961	30.00
❑ VSD2101 [S]	Almanac	1961	40.00
❑ VMS-73122	Classics	1985	12.00

Number	Title	Yr	NM
❑ VRS9130 [M]	Reunion at Carnegie Hall, 1963	1963	25.00
❑ VSD2150 [S]	Reunion at Carnegie Hall, 1963	1963	30.00
❑ VRS9161 [M]	Reunion at Carnegie Hall, Part 2	1965	25.00
❑ VSD79161 [S]	Reunion at Carnegie Hall, Part 2	1965	30.00
❑ VRS9010 [M]	The Weavers at Carnegie Hall	1957	40.00
❑ VRS-6533 [R]	The Weavers at Carnegie Hall	1970	15.00
❑ VMS-73101	The Weavers at Carnegie Hall	1984	10.00
— Reissue of 6533			
❑ VRS9075 [M]	The Weavers at Carnegie Hall, Vol. 2	1960	30.00
❑ VSD2069 [S]	The Weavers at Carnegie Hall, Vol. 2	1960	40.00
❑ VRS9024 [M]	The Weavers at Home	1959	30.00
❑ VSD2030 [S]	The Weavers at Home	1959	40.00
❑ VSD-15/16	The Weavers' Greatest Hits	1971	18.00
❑ VRS9013 [M]	The Weavers on Tour	1957	40.00
❑ VRS-6537 [R]	The Weavers on Tour	1970	15.00
❑ VMS-73116	The Weavers on Tour	1985	10.00
— Reissue of 6537			
❑ SRV-3001 [M]	The Weavers Song Bag	1967	25.00
❑ SRV-73001 [S]	The Weavers Song Bag	1967	30.00
❑ VRS9043 [M]	Travelling on with the Weavers	1959	30.00
❑ VSD2022 [S]	Travelling on with the Weavers	1959	40.00

WEB, THE

DERAM
❑ DES18018 [B]	Fully Interlocking	1968	40.00

WEBB, ART

ATLANTIC
❑ SD18226	Love Eyes	197?	12.00
❑ SD18212	Mr. Flute	197?	12.00

WEBB, CHICK

CIRCLE
❑ CLP-81	Stompin' at the Savoy, 1936	198?	12.00

COLUMBIA
❑ CL2639 [M]	The Immortal Chick Webb	1967	30.00
❑ CS9439 [R]	The Immortal Chick Webb	1967	15.00

DECCA
❑ DL9223 [M]	Chick Webb 1937-39	1958	40.00
❑ DL79223 [R]	Chick Webb 1937-39	1958	30.00

FOLKWAYS
❑ FJ-2818	Chick Webb Featuring Ella Fitzgerald	197?	12.00

MCA
❑ 1327	Ella Swings the Band	198?	12.00
❑ 1303	Legend	198?	12.00
❑ 1348	Princess of the Savoy	198?	12.00
❑ 4107	The Best of Chick Webb	197?	15.00

TRIP
❑ J-5	On the Air	197?	12.00

WEBB, GEORGE

JAZZOLOGY
❑ J-122	George Webb's Dixielanders	1985	12.00

WEBB, JACK

RCA VICTOR
❑ LPM-3199 [10]	Dragnet -- The Christmas Story	1954	150.00
❑ LPM-1126 [M]	Pete Kelly's Blues	1955	50.00
— Webb narrates; jazz combo plays			
❑ LPM-2053 [M]	Pete Kelly's Blues	1959	30.00
—Reissue of 1126			
❑ LSP-2053(e) [R]	Pete Kelly's Blues	1959	25.00

WARNER BROS.
❑ W1207 [M]	You're My Girl	1958	30.00
❑ WS1207 [S]	You're My Girl	1958	40.00
❑ W1207 [M]	You're My Girl	1958	30.00
❑ WS1207 [S]	You're My Girl	1958	40.00

WEBB, JAY LEE

DECCA
❑ DL4933 [M]	I Come Home a-Drinkin'	1967	30.00
❑ DL74933 [S]	I Come Home a-Drinkin'	1967	25.00
❑ DL75121	She's Looking Better by the Minute	1969	25.00

WEBB, JIMMY

ASYLUM
❑ SD5070	Land's End	1974	18.00

ATLANTIC
❑ SD18218 [B]	El Mirage	1977	15.00

EPIC
❑ BN26401	Jim Webb Sings Jim Webb	1968	25.00

LORIMAR
❑ FC37695	Angel Heart	1982	15.00

REPRISE
❑ RS6448	And So: On	1971	18.00

Number	Title	Yr	NM
❑ MS2055	Letters	1972	18.00
❑ RS6421	Words and Music	1970	18.00

WEBB, ROGER

SWAN
❑ SLP-516 [M]	John, Paul and All That Jazz	1964	30.00

WEBER, EBERHARD

ECM
❑ 1288	Chorus	1985	15.00
❑ 1042	Colours of Chloe	197?	18.00
❑ 1137	Fluid Rustle	1979	12.00
❑ 1086	Following Morning	197?	15.00
❑ 1231	Later That Evening	198?	12.00
❑ 1188	Little Movements	1980	12.00
❑ 1107	Silent Feet	1978	12.00
❑ 1066	Yellow Fields	197?	15.00

WEBER, HAJO, AND ULRICH INGENBOLD

ECM
❑ 1235	Winterreise	198?	15.00

WEBSTER, BEN, AND COLEMAN HAWKINS

COLUMBIA
❑ KG32774	Giants of the Tenor Saxophone	1973	18.00

VERVE
❑ VE-2-2520	Tenor Giants	197?	18.00

WEBSTER, BEN, AND DON BYAS

COMMODORE
❑ XFL-14938	Kings of Tenor Sax	198?	12.00

WEBSTER, BEN, AND HARRY "SWEETS" EDISON

COLUMBIA
❑ CL1891 [M]	Ben Webster-Sweets Edison	1962	30.00
❑ CS8691 [S]	Ben Webster-Sweets Edison	1962	30.00

COLUMBIA JAZZ MASTERPIECES
❑ CJ40853	Ben and "Sweets	1987	12.00

COLUMBIA JAZZ ODYSSEY
❑ PC37036	Ben and "Sweets	1981	12.00

WEBSTER, BEN, AND JOE ZAWINUL

FANTASY
❑ OJC-109	Soulmates	198?	12.00

MILESTONE
❑ 47056	Trav'lin' Light	198?	15.00

RIVERSIDE
❑ RLP-476 [M]	Soulmates	1964	30.00
❑ RS-9476 [S]	Soulmates	1964	30.00

WEBSTER, BEN

ABC IMPULSE!
❑ AS-65 [S]	See You at the Fair	1968	18.00

ANALOGUE PRODUCTIONS
❑ AP 011	Ben Webster at the Renaissance	199?	30.00

BASF
❑ 20658	Ben Webster Meets Don Byas	197?	18.00

BLACK LION
❑ 111	Atmosphere for Lovers and Thieves	197?	18.00
❑ 190	Duke's in Bed!	197?	15.00
❑ 302	Saturday Montmartre	197?	15.00

BRUNSWICK
❑ BL58031 [10]	Tenor Sax Stylings	1952	600.00

CIRCLE
❑ 41	The Horn	198?	12.00
❑ 42	The Horn -- Alternate Takes	198?	12.00

DISCOVERY
❑ 818	The Warm Moods of Ben Webster	198?	12.00

EMARCY
❑ MG-26006 [10]	The Big Tenor	1954	300.00
❑ 824836-1	The Complete Ben Webster on EmArcy	1986	18.00

ENJA
❑ 2038	Live at Pio's	197?	15.00

FIDELIO
❑ FL-4475	Gentle Ben	198?	12.00

IMPULSE!
❑ A-65 [M]	See You at the Fair	1964	30.00
❑ AS-65 [S]	See You at the Fair	1964	30.00

INNER CITY
❑ IC-2008	My Man	197?	18.00

JAZZ ARCHIVES
❑ JA-15	Ben: A Tribute to a Great Jazzman	198?	12.00
❑ JA-35	Ben and the Boys	198?	12.00

JAZZ MAN
❑ 5007	Atmosphere for Lovers	198?	12.00

NESSA
❑ N-8	Did You Call?	197?	25.00

Number	Title	Yr	NM
NORGRAN			
❏ MGN-1039 [M]	Ben Webster Plays Music with Feeling	1955	200.00
❏ MGN-1089 [M]	King of the Tenors	1956	120.00
❏ MGN-1018 [M]	Music for Loving	1955	200.00
❏ MGN-1001 [M]	The Consummate Artistry of Ben Webster	1954	150.00
PRESTIGE			
❏ 24031	At Work in Europe	197?	18.00
REPRISE			
❏ R-2001 [M]	The Warm Moods of Ben Webster	1961	30.00
❏ R9-2001 [S]	The Warm Moods of Ben Webster	1961	30.00
STEEPLECHASE			
❏ SCS-1008	My Man	198?	15.00
TIME-LIFE			
❏ STL-J-21	Giants of Jazz	1981	25.00
VERVE			
❏ VE-2-2530	Ballads	197?	18.00
❏ 833550-1	Ballads	198?	15.00
❏ MGV-8318 [M]	Ben Webster and Associates	1959	50.00
❏ MGVS-6056 [S]	Ben Webster and Associates	1959	40.00
❏ V-8318 [M]	Ben Webster and Associates	1961	30.00
❏ V6-8318 [S]	Ben Webster and Associates	1961	25.00
❏ UMV-2515	Ben Webster and Associates	198?	15.00
❏ MGV-8349 [M]	Ben Webster Meets Oscar Peterson	1959	50.00
❏ MGVS-6114 [S]	Ben Webster Meets Oscar Peterson	1960	40.00
❏ V-8349 [M]	Ben Webster Meets Oscar Peterson	1961	30.00
❏ V6-8349 [S]	Ben Webster Meets Oscar Peterson	1961	25.00
❏ MGV-8020 [M]	King of the Tenors	1957	50.00
❏ V-8020 [M]	King of the Tenors	1961	30.00
❏ UMV-2081	King of the Tenors	198?	12.00
❏ MGV-8130 [M]	Music with Feeling -- Ben Webster with Strings	1957	50.00
❏ V-8130 [M]	Music with Feeling -- Ben Webster with Strings	1961	30.00
❏ MGV-2026 [M]	Sophisticated Lady -- Ben Webster with Strings	1956	50.00
❏ V-2026 [M]	Sophisticated Lady -- Ben Webster with Strings	1961	30.00
❏ MGV-8274 [M]	Soulville	1958	50.00
❏ V-8274 [M]	Soulville	1961	30.00
❏ VE-2-2536	Soulville	1980	18.00
❏ 833551-1	Soulville	198?	15.00
❏ MGV-8359 [M]	The Soul of Ben Webster	1960	50.00
❏ V-8359 [M]	The Soul of Ben Webster	1961	30.00
WEBSTER, MAMIE			
CUB			
❏ 8002 [M]	The Blues	1959	150.00
WECHTER, JULIUS			
JAZZ: WEST			
❏ LP-9 [M]	Linear Sketches	1956	200.00
WEDGES, THE			
TIME			
❏ 52090 [M]	Hang Ten (For Surfers Only)	1963	50.00
❏ S-2090 [S]	Hang Ten (For Surfers Only)	1963	70.00
WEED, BUDDY			
COLUMBIA			
❏ CL6160 [10]	Piano Moods	1951	50.00
CORAL			
❏ CRL57087 [M]	Piano Solos with Rhythm Accompaniment	1957	40.00
WEEKS, ANSON			
FANTASY			
❏ 3306 [M]	Cruisin' with Anson	1960	30.00
—Red vinyl			
❏ 3306 [M]	Cruisin' with Anson	1960	18.00
—Black vinyl			
❏ 8051 [S]	Cruisin' with Anson	1960	30.00
—Blue vinyl			
❏ 8051 [S]	Cruisin' with Anson	1960	15.00
—Black vinyl			
❏ 3333 [M]	Dancin' at Anson's	1961	15.00
—Black vinyl			
❏ 8076 [S]	Dancin' at Anson's	1961	18.00
—Black vinyl			
❏ 3333 [M]	Dancin' at Anson's	1961	30.00
—Red vinyl			
❏ 8076 [S]	Dancin' at Anson's	1961	30.00
—Blue vinyl			
❏ 3258 [M]	Dancin' with Anson	1958	30.00
—Red vinyl			
❏ 3258 [M]	Dancin' with Anson	1958	18.00
—Black vinyl			
❏ 8001 [S]	Dancin' with Anson	1960	30.00
—Blue vinyl			
❏ 8001 [S]	Dancin' with Anson	1960	15.00
—Black vinyl			
❏ 8001 [S]	Dancin' with Anson	1960	30.00
—Red vinyl (error pressing?)			

Number	Title	Yr	NM
❏ 3269 [M]	Memories	1958	30.00
—Red vinyl			
❏ 3269 [M]	Memories	1958	18.00
—Black vinyl			
❏ 8006 [S]	Memories	1960	30.00
—Blue vinyl			
❏ 8006 [S]	Memories	1960	15.00
—Black vinyl			
❏ 3297 [M]	More Dancin' with Anson	1959	30.00
—Red vinyl			
❏ 3297 [M]	More Dancin' with Anson	1959	18.00
—Black vinyl			
❏ 8043 [S]	More Dancin' with Anson	1960	30.00
—Blue vinyl			
❏ 8043 [S]	More Dancin' with Anson	1960	15.00
—Black vinyl			
❏ 3338 [M]	Old Favorites and New	1962	30.00
—Red vinyl			
❏ 3338 [M]	Old Favorites and New	1962	15.00
—Black vinyl			
❏ 8090 [S]	Old Favorites and New	1962	30.00
—Blue vinyl			
❏ 8090 [S]	Old Favorites and New	1962	18.00
—Black vinyl			
❏ 8355 [S]	Reminiscing at the Mark	1964	18.00
❏ 3355 [M]	Reminiscing at the Mark	1964	15.00
HINDSIGHT			
❏ HSR-146	Anson Weeks and the Hotel Mark Hopkins Orchestra 1932	198?	12.00
WEEN			
GRAND ROYAL			
❏ GR 010 [B]	Chocolate and Cheese	1994	30.00
—Cassette and CD on Elektra 61639			
WEEZER			
DGC			
❏ DGC-25007 [B]	Pinkerton	1996	45.00
GEFFEN			
❏ B0004520-01	Make Believe	2005	18.00
❏ 069-493241-1 [B]	Maladroit	2002	18.00
❏ 069-493045-1	Weezer	2001	25.00
—Green vinyl			
❏ 069-493045-1	Weezer	2001	18.00
—Black vinyl			
WEIGAND, JACK			
CAMEO			
❏ C-1012 [M]	Stairway to the Stars	1961	15.00
❏ SC-1012 [S]	Stairway to the Stars	1961	18.00
WYNCOTE			
❏ SW-9017 [S]	Shangri-La and Other Favorites	1964	15.00
❏ W-9017 [M]	Shangri-La and Other Favorites	1964	12.00
WEIN, GEORGE			
ATLANTIC			
❏ SD1533 [S]	George Wein and the Newport All-Stars	1969	18.00
❏ 1221 [M]	Wein, Women and Song	1955	50.00
—Black label			
❏ 1221 [M]	Wein, Women and Song	1961	30.00
—Multicolor label, white "fan" logo at right			
BETHLEHEM			
❏ BCP-6050 [M]	George Wein and the Storyville Sextet -- Jazz at the Modern	1960	40.00
❏ SBCP-6050 [S]	George Wein and the Storyville Sextet -- Jazz at the Modern	1960	40.00
COLUMBIA			
❏ CS9631 [S]	Alive and Well in Mexico	1968	18.00
IMPULSE!			
❏ A-31 [M]	George Wein and the Newport All-Stars	1963	25.00
❏ AS-31 [S]	George Wein and the Newport All-Stars	1963	30.00
RCA VICTOR			
❏ LPM-1332 [M]	The Magic Horn of George Wein	1956	40.00
WEINER SANGERKNABEN			
CAPITOL			
❏ T10164 [M]	Christmas in Austria	196?	18.00
WEIR, BOB			
ARISTA			
❏ AL9568	Bobby and the Midnites	1981	12.00
❏ AL8367	Bobby and the Midnites	1985	10.00
—Budget-line reissue			
❏ AL4155 [B]	Heaven Help the Fool	1978	12.00
❏ AL8366	Heaven Help the Fool	1985	10.00
—Budget-line reissue			

Number	Title	Yr	NM
WARNER BROS.			
❏ BS2627	Ace	1972	40.00
—Color photo on back cover			
❏ BS2627	Ace	1972	30.00
—Black and white photo on back cover			
WEIRD-OHS, THE			
MERCURY			
❏ MG-20976 [M]	The Sounds of the Weird-Ohs	1964	150.00
❏ SR-60976 [S]	The Sounds of the Weird-Ohs	1964	200.00
WEIRDOS			
BOMP!			
❏ 4007 [EP]	Who? What? When? Where? Why?	1979	18.00
FRONTIER			
❏ 4623-1-L [B]	Condor	1990	15.00
❏ 4630-1-L [B]	Weird World	1991	25.00
OUT OF DARKNESS			
❏ OTD 001 [DJ]	Message from the Underworld	198?	40.00
—Promo-only release			
RHINO			
❏ RNEP508 [EP]	Action Design	1980	25.00
WEISBERG, TIM			
A&M			
❏ SP-3045	Dreamspeaker	1973	12.00
❏ SP-4352	Hurtwood Edge	1972	15.00
❏ SP-4545	Listen to the City	1975	12.00
❏ SP-4600	Live at Last!	1976	12.00
❏ SP-4749	Smile/The Best of Tim Weisberg	1979	12.00
❏ SP-3261	Smile/The Best of Tim Weisberg	198?	10.00
—Budget-line reissue			
❏ SP-3039	Tim Weisberg	1971	15.00
❏ SP-3658	Tim Weisberg 4	1974	12.00
❏ SP-3121	Tim Weisberg 4	198?	10.00
—Budget-line reissue			
CYPRESS			
❏ 661112-1	High Risk	1986	12.00
❏ YL-0123	Outrageous Temptations	1989	15.00
DESERT ROCK			
❏ DR-001	High Risk	1985	18.00
LIBERTY			
❏ LN-10029	Rotations	198?	10.00
—Budget-line reissue			
❏ LN-10031	The Tim Weisberg Band	198?	10.00
—Budget-line reissue			
MCA			
❏ 3084	Night Rider!	1979	12.00
❏ 5125	Party of One	1980	12.00
❏ 5245	Travelin' Light	1981	12.00
NAUTILUS			
❏ NR-7 [B]	Tip of the Weisberg	1980	30.00
—Audiophile vinyl			
UNITED ARTISTS			
❏ UA-LA857-H	Rotations	1978	12.00
❏ UA-LA773-G	The Tim Weisberg Band	1977	12.00
WEISS, LARRY			
20TH CENTURY			
❏ T-428	Black and Blue Suite	1974	18.00
WEISSBERG, ERIC, AND DELIVERANCE			
WARNER BROS.			
❏ BS2720	Rural Free Delivery	1973	12.00
WEISSBERG, ERIC, AND MARSHALL BRICKMAN			
ELEKTRA			
❏ EKL-238 [M]	New Dimensions in Banjo and Bluegrass	1963	25.00
❏ EKS-7238 [S]	New Dimensions in Banjo and Bluegrass	1963	30.00
—Mandolin-player label			
❏ EKS-7238 [S]	New Dimensions in Banjo and Bluegrass	1967	25.00
—Tan label with large stylized "E" at top			
❏ EKS-7238 [S]	New Dimensions in Banjo and Bluegrass	1969	18.00
—Red label with large stylized "E" at top			
❏ EKS-7238 [S]	New Dimensions in Banjo and Bluegrass	1971	15.00
—Butterfly label			
❏ EKS-7238 [S]	New Dimensions in Banjo and Bluegrass	1980	12.00
—Red label with Warner Communications logo in lower right			
WEISSBERG, ERIC, AND STEVE MANDELL			
WARNER BROS.			
❏ BS2683	Dueling Banjos from Deliverance	1973	12.00
—Except for the title song and "End of a Dream," this is			

Number	Title	Yr	NM
actually a reissue of Elektra 7238; green label			
❏ BS2683	Dueling Banjos from Deliverance	1973	10.00
—Burbank" palm trees label			

WELCH, ELISABETH

DRG

Number	Title	Yr	NM
❏ SL-5202	Where Have You Been?	1987	12.00

WELCH, LENNY

CADENCE

Number	Title	Yr	NM
❏ CLP3068 [M]	Since I Fell for You	1963	30.00
❏ CLP25068 [S]	Since I Fell for You	1963	50.00

COLUMBIA

Number	Title	Yr	NM
❏ CL2430 [M]	Since I Fell for You	1965	25.00
—Reissue of Cadence 3068			
❏ CS9230 [S]	Since I Fell for You	1965	30.00
—Reissue of Cadence 25068			

KAPP

Number	Title	Yr	NM
❏ KL-1517 [M]	Lenny	1967	18.00
❏ KS-3517 [S]	Lenny	1967	25.00
❏ KL-1481 [M]	Rags to Riches	1966	18.00
❏ KS-3481 [S]	Rags to Riches	1966	25.00
❏ KL-1457 [M]	Two Different Worlds	1965	18.00
❏ KS-3457 [S]	Two Different Worlds	1965	25.00

WELCH CHORALE, THE

VANGUARD

Number	Title	Yr	NM
❏ VRS428 [M]	A Music Box of Christmas Carols	1954	25.00
—With Music Boxes from the Bornand Collection			

WELDON, MAXINE

MAINSTREAM

Number	Title	Yr	NM
❏ MRL-339	Chilly Wind	1972	15.00
❏ MRL-319	Right On	1971	15.00

WELK, LAWRENCE

CORAL

Number	Title	Yr	NM
❏ CRL57038 [M]	Bubbles in the Wine	1956	25.00
❏ CRL57226 [M]	Champagne Dancing Party	1958	18.00
❏ CRL757226 [S]	Champagne Dancing Party	1958	25.00
❏ CRL57078 [M]	Champagne Pops Parade	1956	25.00
❏ CRL57186 [M]	Jingle Bells	1957	25.00
❏ CRL757186 [R]	Jingle Bells	196?	15.00
❏ CRL57011 [M]	Lawrence Welk and His Sparkling Strings	1955	25.00
❏ CRL57066 [M]	Lawrence Welk at Madison Square Garden	1956	25.00
❏ CRL57262 [M]	Lawrence Welk Featuring Larry Hooper	1959	18.00
❏ CRL57260 [M]	Lawrence Welk Featuring the Lennon Sisters	1959	18.00
❏ CRL57023 [M]	Lawrence Welk Introduces the Girl Friends	1955	30.00
❏ CRL57146 [M]	Lawrence Welk Plays Dixieland	1957	25.00
❏ CRL57214 [M]	Lawrence Welk Presents Keyboard Kapers	1958	18.00
❏ CRL57383 [M]	Lawrence Welk Showcase	1962	15.00
❏ CRL757383 [S]	Lawrence Welk Showcase	1962	15.00
❏ CRL57093 [M]	Merry Christmas from Lawrence Welk	1956	25.00
❏ CRL757093 [R]	Merry Christmas from Lawrence Welk	196?	15.00
❏ CRL57068 [M]	Moments to Remember	1956	25.00
❏ CRL57353 [M]	My Golden Favorites	1961	15.00
❏ CRL757353 [S]	My Golden Favorites	1961	15.00
❏ CRL57178 [M]	Nimble Fingers	1957	25.00
❏ CRL56101 [10]	Nimble Fingers	195?	30.00
❏ CRL56043 [10]	On Moonlight Bay	195?	30.00
❏ CRL57067 [M]	Pick-A-Polka!	1956	25.00
❏ CRL757067 [R]	Pick-A-Polka!	1959	15.00
❏ CRL757041 [R]	Say It With Music	196?	15.00
❏ CRL57041 [M]	Say It With Music	1956	25.00
❏ CRL57036 [M]	Shamrocks and Champagne	1955	25.00
❏ CRL757036 [R]	Shamrocks and Champagne	196?	15.00
❏ CRL57111 [M]	Show Time	1957	25.00
❏ CRL56045 [10]	Songs About My Extraordinary Gal and Her Friends	195?	30.00
❏ CRL57439 [M]	Songs Everybody Knows	1964	15.00
❏ CRL757439 [S]	Songs Everybody Knows	1964	15.00
❏ CRL57191 [M]	Songs of Faith	1958	18.00
❏ CRL56088 [10]	Souvenir Album	195?	30.00
❏ CXB5 [M]	The Best of Lawrence Welk	196?	25.00
❏ 7CXSB5 [S]	The Best of Lawrence Welk	196?	18.00
❏ CRL57113 [M]	The World's Finest Music	1957	25.00
❏ CRL757113 [R]	The World's Finest Music	196?	15.00
❏ CRL57025 [M]	TV Favorites	1955	25.00
❏ CRL57267 [M]	TV Western Theme Songs	1959	18.00
❏ CRL757267 [S]	TV Western Theme Songs	1959	25.00
❏ CRL56120 [10]	Viennese Waltzes for Dancing	1954	30.00
❏ CRL57119 [M]	Waltz with Lawrence Welk	1957	25.00

CORONET

Number	Title	Yr	NM
❏ 275	Lawrence Welk and His Orchestra	196?	12.00

DECCA

Number	Title	Yr	NM
❏ DL8323 [M]	Around We Go	1956	18.00
❏ DL8213 [M]	Lawrence Welk's Polka Party	1956	18.00
❏ DL8324 [M]	Welktime	1956	18.00

DESIGN

Number	Title	Yr	NM
❏ 200	Champagne Time	196?	12.00
❏ 912	Three of a Kind	196?	12.00

DOT

Number	Title	Yr	NM
❏ DLP3510 [M]	1963's Early Hits	1963	12.00
❏ DLP25510 [S]	1963's Early Hits	1963	15.00
❏ DLP3629 [M]	Apples and Bananas	1965	12.00
❏ DLP25629 [S]	Apples and Bananas	1965	15.00
❏ DLP3544 [M]	A Tribute to the All-Time Greats	1963	12.00
❏ DLP25544 [S]	A Tribute to the All-Time Greats	1963	15.00
❏ DLP3457 [M]	Baby Elephant Walk and Theme from The Brothers Grimm	1962	12.00
❏ DLP25457 [S]	Baby Elephant Walk and Theme from The Brothers Grimm	1962	15.00
❏ DLP3489 [M]	Bubbles in the Wine	1962	12.00
❏ DLP25489 [S]	Bubbles in the Wine	1962	15.00
❏ DLP3359 [M]	Calcutta!	1961	12.00
❏ DLP25359 [S]	Calcutta!	1961	15.00
❏ DLP3688 [M]	Champagne on Broadway	1966	12.00
❏ DLP25688 [S]	Champagne on Broadway	1966	15.00
❏ DLP3224 [M]	Dance with Lawrence Welk	1959	15.00
❏ DLP25224 [S]	Dance with Lawrence Welk	1959	18.00
❏ DLP3395 [M]	Diamond Jubilee	1961	12.00
❏ DLP25395 [S]	Diamond Jubilee	1961	15.00
❏ DLP3318 [M]	Double Shuffle	1960	12.00
❏ DLP25318 [S]	Double Shuffle	1960	15.00
❏ DLP3572 [M]	Early Hits of 1964	1964	12.00
❏ DLP25572 [S]	Early Hits of 1964	1964	15.00
❏ DLP3812 [M]	Golden Hits/The Best of Lawrence Welk	1967	15.00
❏ DLP25812 [S]	Golden Hits/The Best of Lawrence Welk	1967	12.00
❏ DLP3779 [M]	Hymns We Love	1967	12.00
❏ DLP25779 [S]	Hymns We Love	1967	15.00
❏ DLP3248 [M]	I'm Forever Blowing Bubbles	1960	12.00
❏ DLP25248 [S]	I'm Forever Blowing Bubbles	1960	15.00
❏ DLP3350 [M]	Last Date	1960	12.00
❏ DLP25350 [S]	Last Date	1960	15.00
❏ DLP3317 [M]	Lawrence in Dixieland	1960	12.00
❏ DLP25317 [S]	Lawrence in Dixieland	1960	15.00
❏ DLP3238 [M]	Lawrence Welk Presents Great American Composers	1960	12.00
❏ DLP25238 [S]	Lawrence Welk Presents Great American Composers	1960	15.00
❏ DLP3247 [M]	Lawrence Welk Presents Great Overtures in Dance Time	1960	12.00
❏ DLP25247 [S]	Lawrence Welk Presents Great Overtures in Dance Time	1960	15.00
❏ DLP3790 [M]	Lawrence Welk's "Hits of Our Time	1967	12.00
❏ DLP25790 [S]	Lawrence Welk's "Hits of Our Time	1967	15.00
❏ DLP3412 [M]	Moon River	1961	12.00
❏ DLP25412 [S]	Moon River	1961	15.00
❏ DLP3164 [M]	Mr. Music Maker	1959	15.00
❏ DLP25164 [S]	Mr. Music Maker	1959	18.00
❏ DLP3616 [M]	My First of 1965	1965	12.00
❏ DLP25616 [S]	My First of 1965	1965	15.00
❏ DLP3302 [M]	Polkas	1960	12.00
❏ DLP25302 [S]	Polkas	1960	15.00
❏ DLP3528 [M]	Scarlett O'Hara	1963	12.00
❏ DLP25528 [S]	Scarlett O'Hara	1963	15.00
❏ DLP3397 [M]	Silent Night and 13 Other Best-Loved Christmas Songs	1961	15.00
❏ DLP25397 [S]	Silent Night and 13 Other Best-Loved Christmas Songs	1961	18.00
❏ DLP3432 [M]	Sing-a-Long Party	1962	12.00
❏ DLP25432 [S]	Sing-a-Long Party	1962	15.00
❏ DLP3251 [M]	Songs of the Islands	1960	12.00
❏ DLP25251 [S]	Songs of the Islands	1960	15.00
❏ DLP3274 [M]	Strictly for Dancing	1960	12.00
❏ DLP25274 [S]	Strictly for Dancing	1960	15.00
❏ DLP3296 [M]	Sweet and Lovely	1960	12.00
❏ DLP25296 [S]	Sweet and Lovely	1960	15.00
❏ DLP3342 [M]	The Champagne Music of Lawrence Welk	1960	12.00
❏ DLP25342 [S]	The Champagne Music of Lawrence Welk	1960	15.00
❏ DLP3611 [M]	The Golden Millions	1964	12.00
❏ DLP25611 [S]	The Golden Millions	1964	15.00
❏ DLP3653 [M]	The Happy Wanderer	1966	12.00
❏ DLP25653 [S]	The Happy Wanderer	1966	15.00
❏ DLP3218 [M]	The Lawrence Welk Glee Club	1959	15.00
❏ DLP25218 [S]	The Lawrence Welk Glee Club	1959	18.00
❏ DLP3591 [M]	The Lawrence Welk Television Show 10th Anniversary	1964	12.00
❏ DLP25591 [S]	The Lawrence Welk Television Show 10th Anniversary	1964	15.00
❏ DLP3200 [M]	The Voices and Strings of Lawrence Welk	1959	15.00
❏ DLP3663 [M]	Today's Great Hits	1966	12.00
❏ DLP25663 [S]	Today's Great Hits	1966	15.00
❏ DLP3284 [M]	To Mother	1960	12.00
❏ DLP25284 [S]	To Mother	1960	15.00
❏ DLP25200 [S]	Voices and Strings	1959	18.00
❏ DLP3499 [M]	Waltz Time	1963	12.00
❏ DLP25499 [S]	Waltz Time	1963	15.00
❏ DLP3774 [M]	Winchester Cathedral	1966	12.00
❏ DLP25774 [S]	Winchester Cathedral	1966	15.00
❏ DLP3552 [M]	Wonderful! Wonderful!	1963	12.00
❏ DLP25552 [S]	Wonderful! Wonderful!	1963	15.00
❏ DLP3389 [M]	Yellow Bird	1961	12.00
❏ DLP25389 [S]	Yellow Bird	1961	15.00
❏ DLP3428 [M]	Young World	1962	12.00
❏ DLP25428 [S]	Young World	1962	15.00

HAMILTON

Number	Title	Yr	NM
❏ HLP152 [M]	Mary Poppins	1965	12.00
❏ HLP12152 [S]	Mary Poppins	1965	15.00

HARMONY

Number	Title	Yr	NM
❏ HS11301	Champagne Dance Party	1969	12.00
❏ HL7394 [M]	Vintage Champagne	1966	15.00
❏ HS11194 [S]	Vintage Champagne	1966	15.00

HEARTLAND

Number	Title	Yr	NM
❏ 1006	Musical Family Reunion	198?	12.00

MCA

Number	Title	Yr	NM
❏ 733	Polka and Waltz Time	197?	10.00
—Reissue of Vocalion 73670			
❏ 4044	The Best of Lawrence Welk	197?	15.00
❏ 4026	The Best of Lawrence Welk, Volume 2	197?	15.00
❏ 4104	The Best Polkas	197?	15.00

MCA CORAL

Number	Title	Yr	NM
❏ 20100	Champagne Music	197?	10.00

MERCURY

Number	Title	Yr	NM
❏ MG-20092 [M]	Dance Party	1956	18.00

MISTLETOE

Number	Title	Yr	NM
❏ MLP-1215	Christmas with Lawrence Welk	197?	12.00

PICKWICK

Number	Title	Yr	NM
❏ SPC-3157	As Time Goes By	196?	12.00
❏ SPC-3212	Blue Hawaii	197?	12.00
❏ SPC-3143	If You Were the Only One	196?	12.00
❏ SPC-3092	I'll See You Again	196?	12.00
❏ SPC-3196	Love Is a Many-Splendored Thing	197?	12.00
❏ SPC-3252	Polkas!	197?	12.00
❏ SPC-3070	Save the Last Dance for Me	196?	12.00
❏ SPC-1019	The Christmas Song	197?	12.00
—Reissue of Coral LP "Jingle Bells" with shuffled running order			
❏ SPC-3116	You'll Never Walk Alone	196?	12.00

PREMIER

Number	Title	Yr	NM
❏ 9043	Lawrence Welk	196?	12.00

RANWOOD

Number	Title	Yr	NM
❏ 7023	22 All-Time Big Band Favorites	1983	15.00
❏ 7028	22 All-Time Favorite Waltzes	198?	15.00
❏ 7009	22 Great Songs for Dancing	1978	15.00
❏ 7016	22 Great Songs for Easy Listening	198?	15.00
❏ 7004	22 Great Waltzes	1977	15.00
❏ 7029	22 Merry Christmas Favorites	198?	15.00
❏ 5005	24 of the World's Greatest Polkas	197?	15.00
—With Myron Floren			
❏ 8145	25 Years on Television	1975	12.00
❏ 7002	200 Years of American Music	1976	15.00
❏ 8024	Calcutta!	1968	10.00
—Reissue of Dot 25359			
❏ 8083	Candida	1970	12.00
❏ 8079	Champagne Strings	1970	12.00
❏ 8211	Come Waltz with Me	1984	10.00
❏ 8027	Country Music's Great Hits	1968	12.00
❏ 8049	Galveston	1969	12.00
❏ 8091	Go Away Little Girl	1971	12.00
❏ 8028	Golden Hits/The Best of Lawrence Welk	1968	10.00
—Reissue of Dot 25812			
❏ 8184	Hallelujah!	1978	12.00
❏ 8042	Hymns We Love	1968	10.00
—Reissue of Dot 25779			
❏ 8060	Jean	1969	12.00
❏ 6002	Lawrence Welk and His Musical Family Celebrate 50 Years in Music	1974	12.00
❏ 6001	Lawrence Welk and His Musical Family in Concert	1973	15.00
❏ 8194	Lawrence Welk Plays Dixieland	1980	12.00
❏ 8130	Lawrence Welk Plays From That's Entertainment	1974	12.00
❏ 8053	Lawrence Welk Plays I Love You Truly and Other Songs of Love	1969	12.00
❏ 8201	Lawrence Welk Presents Anacani	1982	12.00
❏ 10001	Live at Lake Tahoe	1978	15.00
❏ 8003	Love Is Blue	1968	12.00
❏ 8044	Memories	1969	12.00
❏ 2000	Merry Christmas	197?	12.00
❏ 8016	Moon River	1968	10.00
—Reissue of Dot 25412			
❏ 8109	(More of) The Big Band Sound	1972	12.00
❏ 8140	Most Requested TV Favorites	1974	12.00
❏ 8210	Musical Memories with Lawrence Welk	1984	10.00
❏ 8183	My Personal Favorites	1978	12.00
❏ 8165	Nadia's Theme	1976	12.00
❏ 8087	No, No, Nanette	1971	12.00
❏ 4100	On Tour, Volume 1	198?	10.00
❏ 4101	On Tour, Volume 2	198?	10.00

Number	Title	Yr	NM
❑ 2004	Polkas	197?	10.00
—With Myron Floren			
❑ 8191	Remembering the Sweet and Swing Band Era, Vol. 1	1979	12.00
❑ 8192	Remembering the Sweet and Swing Band Era, Vol. 2	1979	12.00
❑ 5001	Reminiscing	1972	15.00
❑ 8195	Reminiscing, Vol. 2	1980	15.00
❑ 8020	Silent Night and 13 Other Best-Loved Christmas Songs	1968	10.00
—Reissue of Dot 25397			
❑ 8022	Songs of the Islands	1968	10.00
—Reissue of Dot 25251			
❑ 8162	The Best of Lawrence Welk: 20 Great Hits	1976	12.00
❑ 8077	The Big Band Sound	1970	12.00
❑ 8023	The Champagne Music of Lawrence Welk	1968	10.00
—Reissue of Dot 25342			
❑ 8068	The Golden 60's	1970	12.00
❑ 8114	The Good Life	1973	12.00
❑ 8034	The Lawrence Welk Singers and Orchestra	1968	12.00
❑ 8026	The Lawrence Welk Television Show	1968	10.00
—Reissue of Dot 25591			
❑ 10002	The Sweet and Swing Band Era	1979	15.00
❑ 8030	To America with Love	1968	12.00
❑ 8025	Waltz Time	1968	10.00
—Reissue of Dot 25499			
❑ 8017	Winchester Cathedral	1968	10.00
—Reissue of Dot 25774			
❑ 8021	Yellow Bird	1968	10.00
—Reissue of Dot 25389			

READER'S DIGEST

Number	Title	Yr	NM
❑ RDA156	Champagne Dance Time with Lawrence Welk	196?	12.00
❑ RDA95	Champagne Music Varieties	196?	30.00
❑ RDA-07-A	Merry Christmas from Lawrence Welk and His Champagne Music Makers	1970	30.00

SUNNYVALE

Number	Title	Yr	NM
❑ SVL-1015	Silent Night and 13 Other Best-Loved Christmas Songs	1978	10.00
—Same contents as Dot 25397			

THOMAS

Number	Title	Yr	NM
❑ 20052	The Magic of Color-Glo	196?	15.00

VOCALION

Number	Title	Yr	NM
❑ VL73865	Champagne Polkas	1969	12.00
❑ VL3671 [M]	Lawrence Welk and His Champagne Music	196?	12.00
❑ VL73671 [R]	Lawrence Welk and His Champagne Music	196?	12.00
❑ VL73783 [R]	Lawrence Welk and His Champagne Music Makers Play for You	1967	12.00
❑ VL3783 [M]	Lawrence Welk and His Champagne Music Makers Play for You	1967	15.00
❑ VL3670 [M]	Polka and Waltz Time	196?	12.00
❑ VL73670 [R]	Polka and Waltz Time	196?	12.00
❑ VL73888	Til the End of Time	1969	12.00
❑ VL73921	Wonderful Music	1970	12.00

WING

Number	Title	Yr	NM
❑ MGW-12214 [M]	Aragon Trianon Memories	196?	15.00
❑ SRW-16214 [R]	Aragon Trianon Memories	196?	12.00
❑ MGW-12119 [M]	Dance Party	196?	15.00
❑ SRW-16210 [S]	Music for Polka Lovers	196?	12.00
❑ MGW-12210 [M]	Music for Polka Lovers	196?	15.00
❑ SRW-16379	The Best of Welk	196?	12.00
❑ PKW-2-114	With a-One and a-Two	1969	18.00

WELLER, FREDDY

ABC DOT

Number	Title	Yr	NM
❑ DOSD-2026	Love You Back to Georgia	1975	15.00

COLUMBIA

Number	Title	Yr	NM
❑ CS9904	Games People Play/These Are Not My People	1969	18.00
❑ KC33883	Greatest Hits	1975	15.00
❑ KC34244	Liquor, Love and Life	1976	12.00
❑ CS1036	Listen to the Young Folks	1970	18.00
❑ KC35658	Love Got in the Way	1979	12.00
❑ PC34709	One Man Show	1977	12.00
❑ C30638	Promised Land	1971	15.00
❑ KC31769	Roadmaster	1972	15.00
❑ KC32958	Sexy Lady	1974	15.00
❑ KC32218	Too Much Monkey Business	1973	15.00

HARMONY

Number	Title	Yr	NM
❑ KH31784	Country Collection	1972	12.00

WELLES, ORSON

AUDIO FIDELITY

Number	Title	Yr	NM
❑ W-90366	War of the Worlds	1964	18.00
—Capitol Record Club edition; same edited version as Audio Rarities LPA 2355			

AUDIO RARITIES

Number	Title	Yr	NM
❑ LPA2355 [B]	War of the Worlds	1955	30.00
—Edited version of the October 30, 1938 Mercury Theatre radio broadcast			

EVOLUTION

Number	Title	Yr	NM
❑ 2 LPS4001 [B]	War of the Worlds	1971	30.00
—Complete version of the October 30, 1938 Mercury Theatre radio broadcast			

LONGINES SYMPHONETTE

Number	Title	Yr	NM
❑ SY-5251	War of the Worlds	197?	18.00
—Complete version of the October 30, 1938 Mercury Theatre radio broadcast, but on one record			

MEDIARTS

Number	Title	Yr	NM
❑ 41-2	The Begatting of the President	1970	18.00

MURRAY HILL

Number	Title	Yr	NM
❑ S44217	War of the Worlds	197?	15.00
—Complete version of the October 30, 1938 Mercury Theatre radio broadcast; reissue of Evolution LP			

UNITED ARTISTS

Number	Title	Yr	NM
❑ UAS-5521	The Begatting of the President	1971	15.00
—Reissue of Mediarts LP			

WELLS, DICKY

FELSTED

Number	Title	Yr	NM
❑ FAJ-7006 [M]	Bones for the King	1958	40.00
❑ SJA-2006 [S]	Bones for the King	1958	40.00
❑ FAJ-7009 [M]	Trombone Four in Hand	1958	40.00
❑ SJA-2009 [S]	Trombone Four in Hand	1958	40.00

MASTER JAZZ

Number	Title	Yr	NM
❑ 8118	Trombone Four-in-Hand	197?	15.00

PRESTIGE

Number	Title	Yr	NM
❑ PRST-7593 [R]	Dicky Wells in Pais 1937	1968	30.00

UPTOWN

Number	Title	Yr	NM
❑ 27.07	Lonesome Road	198?	12.00

WELLS, JUNIOR

BLUE ROCK

Number	Title	Yr	NM
❑ 64003	Live at the Golden Bear	1969	30.00
❑ 64002	You're Tuff Enough	1968	30.00

DELMARK

Number	Title	Yr	NM
❑ DS-640	Blue Hit Big Towns	1969	30.00
❑ DS-640	Blues Hit the Big Town	1969	30.00
❑ DL-612 [M]	Hoodoo Man Blues	1966	40.00
❑ DS-612 [S]	Hoodoo Man Blues	1966	50.00
❑ DS-628 [B]	Southside Blues Jam	1967	30.00

VANGUARD

Number	Title	Yr	NM
❑ VSD-79262	Comin' At You	1968	30.00
❑ VRS-9231 [M]	It's My Life Baby	1966	30.00
❑ VSD-79231 [S]	It's My Life Baby	1966	40.00

WELLS, KITTY, AND JOHNNY WRIGHT

DECCA

Number	Title	Yr	NM
❑ DL75028 [S]	We'll Stick Together	1968	30.00
❑ DL5028 [M]	We'll Stick Together	1968	50.00
—Mono appears to be white label promo only			

WELLS, KITTY, AND RED FOLEY

DECCA

Number	Title	Yr	NM
❑ DL4109 [M]	Golden Favorites	1961	30.00
❑ DL74109 [S]	Golden Favorites	1961	40.00
❑ DL4906 [M]	Together Again	1967	30.00
❑ DL74906 [S]	Together Again	1967	30.00

WELLS, KITTY

DECCA

Number	Title	Yr	NM
❑ DL8888 [M]	After Dark	1959	60.00
—Black label, silver print			
❑ DL8888 [M]	After Dark	1961	30.00
—Black label with color bars			
❑ DL75164	Bouquet of Country Hits	1969	25.00
❑ DL4612 [M]	Burning Memories	1965	30.00
❑ DL74612 [S]	Burning Memories	1965	30.00
❑ DL4349 [M]	Christmas Day with Kitty Wells	1962	30.00
❑ DL74349 [S]	Christmas Day with Kitty Wells	1962	30.00
❑ DL4776 [M]	Country All the Way	1966	30.00
❑ DL74776 [S]	Country All the Way	1966	30.00
❑ DL4554 [M]	Country Music Time	1964	30.00
❑ DL74554 [S]	Country Music Time	1964	30.00
❑ DL75067	Cream of Country Hits	1968	30.00
❑ DL8858 [M]	Dust on the Bible	1959	60.00
—Black label, silver print			
❑ DL8858 [M]	Dust on the Bible	1961	30.00
—Black label with color bars			
❑ DL78858 [R]	Dust on the Bible	196?	25.00
❑ DL4493 [M]	Especially for You	1964	30.00
❑ DL74493 [S]	Especially for You	1964	30.00
❑ DL4679 [M]	Family Gospel Sing	1965	30.00
❑ DL74679 [S]	Family Gospel Sing	1965	30.00
❑ DL75098	Guilty Street	1969	30.00
❑ DL4141 [M]	Heartbreak U.S.A.	1961	30.00
❑ DL74141 [S]	Heartbreak U.S.A.	1961	40.00
❑ DL75325	Heartwarming Gospel Songs	1972	25.00
❑ DL75382	I've Got Yesterday	1972	25.00
❑ DL8979 [M]	Kitty's Choice	1960	50.00
—Black label, silver print			
❑ DL78979 [S]	Kitty's Choice	1960	60.00
—Maroon label, silver print			
❑ DL8979 [M]	Kitty's Choice	1961	30.00
—Black label with color bars			
❑ DL78979 [S]	Kitty's Choice	1961	30.00
—Black label with color bars			
❑ DL8293 [M]	Kitty Wells' Country Hit Parade	1956	60.00
—Black label, silver print			
❑ DL8293 [M]	Kitty Wells' Country Hit Parade	1961	30.00
—Black label with color bars			
❑ DL78293 [R]	Kitty Wells' Country Hit Parade	196?	25.00
❑ DL4108 [M]	Kitty Wells' Golden Favorites	1961	30.00
❑ DL74108 [R]	Kitty Wells' Golden Favorites	196?	25.00
❑ DL5001 [M]	Kitty Wells' Greatest Hits	1968	50.00
—White label promo only			
❑ DL75001 [S]	Kitty Wells' Greatest Hits	1968	30.00
❑ DL74961	Kitty Wells Showcase	1968	30.00
❑ DL4741 [M]	Kitty Wells Sings Songs Made Famous by Jim Reeves	1966	30.00
❑ DL74741 [S]	Kitty Wells Sings Songs Made Famous by Jim Reeves	1966	30.00
❑ DL8732 [M]	Lonely Street	1958	60.00
—Black label, silver print			
❑ DL8732 [M]	Lonely Street	1961	30.00
—Black label with color bars			
❑ DL78732 [R]	Lonely Street	196?	25.00
❑ DL4658 [M]	Lonesome Sad and Blue	1965	30.00
❑ DL74658 [S]	Lonesome Sad and Blue	1965	30.00
❑ DL4857 [M]	Love Makes the World Go Around	1967	30.00
❑ DL74857 [S]	Love Makes the World Go Around	1967	30.00
❑ DL75313	Pledging My Love	1971	25.00
❑ DL4197 [M]	Queen of Country Music	1962	30.00
❑ DL74197 [S]	Queen of Country Music	1962	40.00
❑ DL4929 [M]	Queen of Honky Tonk Street	1967	40.00
❑ DL74929 [S]	Queen of Honky Tonk Street	1967	30.00
❑ DL4075 [M]	Seasons of My Heart	1961	30.00
❑ DL74075 [S]	Seasons of My Heart	1961	40.00
❑ DL75350	Sincerely	1972	25.00
❑ SW-94491	Sincerely	1972	30.00
—Capitol Record Club edition			
❑ DL75221	Singin' 'Em Country	1970	25.00
❑ DL4270 [M]	Singing on Sunday	1962	30.00
❑ DL74270 [S]	Singing on Sunday	1962	40.00
❑ DL4831 [M]	The Kitty Wells Show	1966	30.00
❑ DL74831 [S]	The Kitty Wells Show	1966	30.00
❑ DXB174 [M]	The Kitty Wells Story	1963	30.00
❑ DXSB7174 [P]	The Kitty Wells Story	1963	40.00
❑ DL75277	They're Stepping All Over My Heart	1971	25.00
❑ DL8552 [M]	Winner of Your Heart	1957	60.00
—Black label, silver print			
❑ DL8552 [M]	Winner of Your Heart	1961	30.00
—Black label with color bars			
❑ DL78552 [R]	Winner of Your Heart	196?	25.00
❑ DL75245	Your Love Is the Way	1970	25.00

WELLS, MARY

20TH FOX

Number	Title	Yr	NM
❑ TFM3178 [M]	Love Songs to the Beatles	1965	80.00
❑ TFS4178 [S]	Love Songs to the Beatles	1965	100.00
❑ ST-90790 [S]	Love Songs to the Beatles	1965	150.00
—Capitol Record Club edition			
❑ TFM3171 [M]	Mary Wells	1965	40.00
❑ TFS4171 [S]	Mary Wells	1965	60.00

ALLEGIANCE

Number	Title	Yr	NM
❑ AV-444	The Old, the New, and the Best of Mary Wells	1984	12.00

ATCO

Number	Title	Yr	NM
❑ 33-199 [M]	Two Sides of Mary Wells	1966	30.00
❑ SD 33-199 [S]	Two Sides of Mary Wells	1966	30.00

EPIC

Number	Title	Yr	NM
❑ ARE37540	In and Out of Love	1981	18.00

JUBILEE

Number	Title	Yr	NM
❑ JGS-8018	Servin' Up Some Soul	1968	30.00

MOTOWN

Number	Title	Yr	NM
❑ MLP-600 [M]	Bye Bye Baby/I Don't Want to Take a Chance	1961	300.00
—White label stock copy			
❑ MLP-600 [M]	Bye Bye Baby/I Don't Want to Take a Chance	1962	250.00
—With map; label address above the center hole			
❑ M5-161V1	Bye Bye Baby/I Don't Want to Take a Chance	1981	12.00
❑ M616 [M]	Greatest Hits	1964	40.00
❑ MS616 [S]	Greatest Hits	1964	40.00
❑ 5233ML	Greatest Hits	1982	12.00
❑ M617 [M]	Mary Wells Sings My Guy	1964	50.00
❑ M5-167V1	Mary Wells Sings My Guy	1981	12.00
❑ M611 [M]	Recorded Live on Stage	1963	120.00
—With map; label address above the center hole			
❑ M611 [M]	Recorded Live on Stage	1964	40.00
—With map; label address around lower part of label			
❑ M605 [M]	The One Who Really Loves You	1962	160.00
—With map; label address above the center hole			
❑ M605 [M]	The One Who Really Loves You	1964	40.00

Number	Title	Yr	NM
—With map; label address around lower part of label			
❏ M5-221V1	Two Lovers	1981	12.00
❏ M607 [M]	Two Lovers and Other Great Hits	1963	120.00
—With map; label address above the center hole			
❏ M607 [M]	Two Lovers and Other Great Hits	1964	40.00
—With map; label address around lower part of label			
❏ M653 [M]	Vintage Stock	1967	50.00
❏ MS653 [S]	Vintage Stock	1967	50.00
MOVIETONE			
❏ 71010 [M]	Ooh	1966	30.00
❏ 72010 [S]	Ooh	1966	30.00

WELLSTOOD, DICK, AND CLIFF JACKSON

SWINGVILLE
❏ SVLP-2026 [M]	Uptown and Downtown	1961	50.00
—Purple label			
❏ SVLP-2026 [M]	Uptown and Downtown	1965	30.00
—Blue label, trident logo at right			

WELLSTOOD, DICK

CHIAROSCURO
❏ 129	Dick Wellstood Featuring Kenny Davern	197?	15.00
❏ 109	From Ragtime On	197?	15.00
❏ 139	One-Man Jazz Machine	1975	15.00
CLASSIC JAZZ			
❏ 10	From Dixie to Swing	197?	12.00
JAZZOLOGY			
❏ JCE-73	Alone	197?	12.00
PICKWICK			
❏ SPC-3376	Music from "The Sting	197?	12.00
❏ SPC-3575	Ragtime Music of Scott Joplin	197?	12.00
RIVERSIDE			
❏ RLP-2506 [10]	Dick Wellstood	1955	100.00

WERNER, KEN

FINNADAR
❏ SR9019	The Piano Music of Bix Beiderbecke - Duke Ellington - George Gershwin - James P. Johnson	1978	12.00
INNER CITY			
❏ IC-3036	Beyond the Forest of Mirkwood	198?	15.00

WESLEY, FRED

ATLANTIC
❏ SD18214	A Blow for Me, A Toot to You	1977	15.00
❏ SD19254	Say Blow by Blow Backwards	1979	15.00
PEOPLE			
❏ PE-6604	Breakin' Bread	1974	25.00
❏ PE-6602	Damn Right I Am Somebody	1974	25.00
❏ PE-5603	Doing It to Death	1973	80.00
❏ PE-5601	Food for Thought	1972	80.00

WESS, FRANK, AND JOHNNY COLES

UPTOWN
❏ 27.14	Two at the Top	198?	12.00

WESS, FRANK, AND KENNY BURRELL

PRESTIGE
❏ PRLP-7278 [M]	Steamin'	1963	40.00
❏ PRST-7278 [R]	Steamin'	1963	30.00

WESS, FRANK, AND THAD JONES

STATUS
❏ ST-8310 [M]	Touche	1965	40.00

WESS, FRANK

COMMODORE
❏ FL-20032 [10]	Frank Wess	1952	120.00
❏ FL-20031 [10]	Frank Wess Quintet	1952	120.00
ENTERPRISE			
❏ 5001	To Memphis	197?	18.00
MAINSTREAM			
❏ 56033 [M]	Award Winner	1965	30.00
❏ S-6033 [R]	Award Winner	1965	15.00
MOODSVILLE			
❏ MVLP-8 [M]	Frank Wess Quartet	1960	50.00
—Green label			
❏ MVLP-8 [M]	Frank Wess Quartet	1965	30.00
—Blue label, trident logo at right			
PRESTIGE			
❏ PRLP-7231 [M]	Southern Comfort	1962	40.00
❏ PRST-7231 [S]	Southern Comfort	1962	50.00
❏ PRLP-7266 [M]	Yo Ho! Poor You, Little Me	1963	40.00
❏ PRST-7266 [S]	Yo Ho! Poor You, Little Me	1963	50.00
PROGRESSIVE			
❏ PRO-7057	Flute Juice	198?	12.00
SAVOY			
❏ MG-12022 [M]	Flutes and Reeds	1955	80.00

Number	Title	Yr	NM
❏ MG-12095 [M]	Jazz for Playboys	1956	80.00
❏ MG-12072 [M]	North, South, East, Wess	1956	80.00
SAVOY JAZZ			
❏ SJL-1136	I Hear Ya Talkin'	198?	12.00
STATUS			
❏ ST-7266 [S]	Yo Ho! Poor You, Little Me	1965	25.00

WEST, ALVY

COLUMBIA
❏ CL6062 [10]	Alvy West and His Little Band	1949	60.00

WEST, BRUCE & LAING

WINDFALL
❏ KC32899	Live 'N' Kickin'	1974	15.00
❏ KC32216	Whatever Turns You On	1973	15.00
❏ CQ32216 [Q]	Whatever Turns You On	1973	25.00
❏ KC31929	Why Dontcha	1972	15.00
❏ CQ31929 [Q]	Why Dontcha	1972	25.00

WEST, DOTTIE, AND DON GIBSON

RCA VICTOR
❏ LSP-4131	Dottie and Don	1969	25.00

WEST, DOTTIE

LIBERTY
❏ LT-860	Dottie	1981	10.00
—Reissue of United Artists 860			
❏ LT-51129	Full Circle	1982	12.00
❏ LT-51155	Greatest Hits	1984	12.00
❏ LT-51114	High Times	1982	12.00
❏ LT-51145	New Horizons	1983	12.00
❏ LT-1000	Special Delivery	1981	10.00
—Reissue of United Artists 1000			
❏ LT-740	When It's Just You and Me	1981	10.00
—Reissue of United Artists 740			
❏ LT-1062	Wild West	1981	12.00
POWER PAK			
❏ 274	Country Girl Singing Sensation	197?	12.00
RCA CAMDEN			
❏ CAS-2454	A Legend in My Time	1971	15.00
❏ ACL1-0482	Loving You	1974	12.00
❏ CAL-2155 [M]	The Sound of Country Music	1967	18.00
❏ CAS-2155 [S]	The Sound of Country Music	1967	15.00
❏ ACL1-0125	Would You Hold It Against Me	1973	12.00
RCA VICTOR			
❏ LSP-4482	Careless Hands	1971	18.00
❏ APL1-1041	Carolina Cousins	1975	15.00
❏ CPL1-7047	Collector's Series	1985	12.00
❏ LSP-4332	Country and West	1970	25.00
❏ LSP-4004	Country Girl	1968	30.00
❏ APL1-0344	Country Sunshine	1973	15.00
❏ ANL1-2327	Country Sunshine	1977	12.00
—Reissue of APL1-0344			
❏ LSP-4154	Dottie Sings Eddy	1969	25.00
❏ LPM-3490 [M]	Dottie West Sings	1966	30.00
❏ LSP-3490 [S]	Dottie West Sings	1966	30.00
❏ LPM-3784 [M]	Dottie West Sings Sacred Ballads	1967	30.00
❏ LSP-3784 [S]	Dottie West Sings Sacred Ballads	1967	30.00
❏ LSP-4095	Feminine Fancy	1969	25.00
❏ LSP-4433	Forever Yours	1970	25.00
❏ LSP-4606	Have You Heard	1971	18.00
❏ LPM-3368 [M]	Here Comes My Baby	1965	30.00
❏ LSP-3368 [S]	Here Comes My Baby	1965	30.00
❏ APL1-0543	House of Love	1974	15.00
❏ APD1-0151 [Q]	If It's All Right with You/Just What I've Been Looking For	1973	25.00
❏ APL1-0151	If It's All Right with You/Just What I've Been Looking For	1973	15.00
❏ LPM-3830 [M]	I'll Help You Forget Her	1967	30.00
❏ LSP-3830 [S]	I'll Help You Forget Her	1967	30.00
❏ LSP-4704	I'm Only a Woman	1972	18.00
❏ LSP-4276	Makin' Memories	1970	25.00
❏ AYL1-4302	Once You Were Mine	1982	10.00
❏ AHL1-4117	Once You Were Mine	1981	12.00
❏ LPM-3587 [M]	Suffer Time	1966	30.00
❏ LSP-3587 [S]	Suffer Time	1966	30.00
❏ LSP-4811	The Best of Dottie West	1973	18.00
❏ LPM-3932 [M]	What I'm Cut Out to Be	1968	50.00
❏ LSP-3932 [S]	What I'm Cut Out to Be	1968	30.00
❏ LPM-3693 [M]	With All My Heart and Soul	1967	30.00
❏ LSP-3693 [S]	With All My Heart and Soul	1967	30.00
STARDAY			
❏ SLP-302 [M]	Country Girl Singing Sensation	1964	40.00
UNITED ARTISTS			
❏ UA-LA860-G	Dottie	1978	12.00
❏ LT-1000	Special Delivery	1980	12.00
❏ UA-LA740-G	When It's Just You and Me	1977	12.00

WEST, HEDY

VANGUARD
❏ VRS-9126 [M]	Hedy West, Volume 2	1963	25.00
❏ VSD-2126 [S]	Hedy West, Volume 2	1963	30.00
❏ VRS-9124 [M]	Hedy West Accompanying Herself on the 5-String Banjo	1963	25.00

Number	Title	Yr	NM
❏ VSD-2124 [S]	Hedy West Accompanying Herself on the 5-String Banjo	1963	30.00

WEST, JIM

HOME COMFORT
❏ 1011	Good Things Goin' Down	1977	15.00

WEST, KANYE

DEF JAM
❏ 1219801	808s & Heartbreak	2008	30.00

WEST, LESLIE

I.R.S.
❏ 82016	Alligator	1989	18.00
PASSPORT			
❏ PB-6061	Theme	1987	15.00
PHANTOM			
❏ BPL1-0954	The Great Fatsby	1975	15.00
❏ BPL1-1258	The Leslie West Band	1976	15.00
WINDFALL			
❏ 4500	Mountain	1969	18.00

WEST, LUCRETIA

WESTMINSTER
❏ WP-6063 [M]	Spirituals	1957	40.00

WEST, MAE

DAGONET
❏ DG-4 [M]	Wild Christmas	1966	30.00
❏ DGS-4 [S]	Wild Christmas	1966	40.00
DECCA			
❏ DL9016 [M]	The Fabulous Mae West	1955	60.00
—All-black label with silver print			
❏ DL9016 [M]	The Fabulous Mae West	1960	30.00
—Black label with colorband			
❏ DL79016 [R]	The Fabulous Mae West	1960	18.00
❏ DL79176	The Original Voice Tracks from Her Greatest Movies	1970	18.00
MCA			
❏ 2053	The Fabulous Mae West	1974	15.00
—Reissue of Decca LP			
MEZZOTONE			
❏ 1 [10]	Mae West Songs, Vol. 1	1952	100.00
❏ 2 [10]	Mae West Songs, Vol. 2	1952	100.00
MGM			
❏ SE-4869	Great Balls of Fire	1972	25.00
ROUND			
❏ RS-100	Under the Mistletoe with Mae West	1977	25.00
TOWER			
❏ T5028 [M]	Way Out West	1966	30.00
❏ ST5028 [S]	Way Out West	1966	40.00

WEST, SHELLY

VIVA
❏ 25189	Don't Make Me Wait on the Moon	1985	10.00
❏ 23983	Red Hot	1983	10.00
WARNER BROS.			
❏ 23775	West by West	1983	10.00

WEST, SPEEDY, AND JIMMY BRYANT

CAPITOL
❏ H520 [10]	Two Guitars Country Style	1954	200.00
❏ T520 [M]	Two Guitars Country Style	1954	120.00

WEST, SPEEDY

CAPITOL
❏ T1835 [M]	Guitar Spectacular	1962	30.00
❏ ST1835 [S]	Guitar Spectacular	1962	40.00
❏ T1341 [M]	Steel Guitar	1960	40.00
❏ ST1341 [S]	Steel Guitar	1960	60.00
❏ T956 [M]	West of Hawaii	1958	80.00

WEST

EPIC
❏ BN26433	Bridges	1969	25.00
❏ BN26380	West	1968	25.00

WEST COAST POP ART EXPERIMENTAL BAND, THE

AMOS
❏ AAS-7004	Where's My Daddy	1969	50.00
FIFO			
❏ M101	West Coast Pop Art Experimental Band	1966	2000.00
—With regular cover; VG value 1000; VG+ value 1500			
❏ M101	West Coast Pop Art Experimental Band	1966	500.00
—With plain cardboard cover			
RAZZBERRY SAWFLY			
❏ 800	West Coast Pop Art Experimental Band	1980	100.00
—Reissue of Fifo LP			

Column 1

Number	Title	Yr	NM
REPRISE			
R6247 [M]	The West Coast Pop Art Experimental Band, Part One	1967	150.00
RS6247 [S]	The West Coast Pop Art Experimental Band, Part One	1967	100.00
R6270 [M]	The West Coast Pop Art Experimental Band, Vol. 2	1967	200.00
RS6270 [S]	The West Coast Pop Art Experimental Band, Vol. 2	1967	100.00
R6298 [M]	Vol. 3: A Child's Guide to Good and Evil	1968	200.00

—May exist only as a white label promo

Number	Title	Yr	NM
RS6298 [S]	Vol. 3: A Child's Guide to Good and Evil	1968	100.00
SUNDAZED			
LP5036	West Coast Pop Art Experimental Band, Volume One	1997	18.00

WEST END JAZZ BAND

Number	Title	Yr	NM
STOMP OFF			
SOS-1085	Chicago Breakdown	1985	12.00
SOS-1042	Red Hot Chicago	1982	12.00

WESTBROOK, FORREST

Number	Title	Yr	NM
REVELATION			
REV-11	This Is Their Time, Oh Yes	197?	18.00

WESTBROOK, MIKE

Number	Title	Yr	NM
HAT ART			
2031	Love for Sale	198?	18.00
2012	On Duke's Birthday	1986	18.00
2040	Westbrook-Rossini	1987	18.00

WESTCHESTER WORKSHOP, THE

Number	Title	Yr	NM
UNIQUE			
LP-103 [M]	Unique Jazz	1957	50.00

WESTERN, JOHNNY

Number	Title	Yr	NM
COLUMBIA			
CL1788 [M]	Have Gun, Will Travel	1962	40.00
CS8588 [S]	Have Gun, Will Travel	1962	50.00

WESTERN UNION BAND, THE

Number	Title	Yr	NM
SHAWN-DEL			
(# unknown)	The Western Union Band	1907	12.00

WESTERN WIND, THE

Number	Title	Yr	NM
MUSICAL HERITAGE SOCIETY			
MHS4077	Christmas in the New World	1979	15.00
NONESUCH			
79053	An Old-Fashioned Christmas: Caroling with the Western Wind	1983	12.00

WESTON, KIM

Number	Title	Yr	NM
MGM			
E-4477 [M]	For the First Time	1967	30.00
SE-4477 [S]	For the First Time	1967	40.00
SE 4601	This Is America	1968	40.00
VOLT			
VOS-6014	Kim, Kim, Kim	1971	30.00

WESTON, PAUL

Number	Title	Yr	NM
CAPITOL			
T1153 [M]	Floatin' Like a Feather	1959	15.00
T1154 [M]	Music for Dreaming	1959	15.00
ST1154 [S]	Music for Dreaming	1959	18.00
H222 [10]	Music for Dreaming	195?	40.00
T1222 [M]	Music for Memories	1959	15.00
ST1222 [S]	Music for Memories	1959	18.00
T1563 [M]	Music for My Love	1961	15.00
ST1563 [S]	Music for My Love	1961	18.00
T1192 [M]	Music for the Fireside	1959	15.00
ST1192 [S]	Music for the Fireside	1959	18.00
ST-91212	Romantic Reflections	196?	18.00

—Capitol Record Club exclusive

Number	Title	Yr	NM
COLUMBIA			
CL572 [M]	Caribbean Cruise	1955	18.00
CL977 [M]	Crescent City	1956	18.00
CL1112 [M]	Hollywood	1958	18.00
CL794 [M]	Love Music from Hollywood	1956	18.00
CL693 [M]	Mood for 12	1955	18.00
CL909 [M]	Moonlight Becomes You	1956	18.00
CL879 [M]	Solo Mood	1956	18.00
CL6232 [10]	Whispers in the Dark	195?	40.00
CORINTHIAN			
107	Cinema Cameos	198?	10.00
116	Crescent City	198?	10.00
109	Easy Jazz	198?	10.00
HARMONY			
KH31578	Paul Weston Plays Jerome Kern	1972	12.00
KH31603	Paul Weston Plays Jerome Kern, Vol. 2	1972	12.00

Column 2

WESTON, RANDY, AND CECIL PAYNE

Number	Title	Yr	NM
JAZZLAND			
JLP-13 [M]	Greenwich Village Jazz	1960	40.00

WESTON, RANDY

Number	Title	Yr	NM
1750 ARCH			
1802	Blue	198?	15.00
ARISTA/FREEDOM			
AF1026	Berkshire Blues	197?	15.00
AF1014	Blues Africa	197?	15.00
AF1004	Carnival	1975	15.00
ATLANTIC			
SD1609	African Cookbook	197?	18.00
COLPIX			
CP-456 [M]	Highlight	1963	30.00
SCP-456 [S]	Highlight	1963	60.00
CTI			
6016	Blue Moses	197?	15.00
DAWN			
DLP-1116 [M]	The Modern Art of Jazz	1957	80.00
FANTASY			
OJC-1747	Jazz A La Bohemia	1990	12.00
INNER CITY			
IC-1013	African Nite	1975	15.00
JAZZLAND			
JLP-4 [M]	Zulu!	1960	40.00
JUBILEE			
JLP-1060 [M]	Piano A La Mode	1957	40.00
MILESTONE			
7206	Zulu	197?	18.00
PAUSA			
PR7017	Randy Weston	198?	18.00
POLYDOR			
PD-5055	Tanjah	197?	15.00
RIVERSIDE			
RLP-2508 [10]	Cole Porter in a Modern Mood	1954	120.00
RLP 12-203 [M]	Get Happy	1956	60.00
6063	Get Happy	197?	15.00
RLP 12-232 [M]	Jazz A La Bohemia	1957	60.00
RLP-2515 [10]	Randy Weston Trio	1955	120.00
RLP 12-227 [M]	Randy Weston Trio and Solo	1957	60.00
6208	Trio and Solo	198?	12.00
RLP 12-214 [M]	With These Hands…	1956	60.00
ROULETTE			
R-65001 [M]	Uhuru Afrika	1960	100.00
RS-65001 [S]	Uhuru Afrika	1960	120.00
TRIP			
5033	Blues	197?	12.00
UNITED ARTISTS			
UAL-4045 [M]	Destry Rides Again	1959	40.00
UAS-5045 [S]	Destry Rides Again	1959	50.00
UAL-4011 [M]	Little Niles	1959	40.00
UAS-5011 [S]	Little Niles	1959	50.00
UAL-4066 [M]	Live at the Five Spot	1959	40.00
UAS-5066 [S]	Live at the Five Spot	1959	50.00

WESTON, RANDY/LEM WINCHESTER

Number	Title	Yr	NM
METROJAZZ			
E-1005 [M]	New Faces at Newport	1958	50.00
SE-1005 [S]	New Faces at Newport	1958	40.00

WESTPHALIAN CHORUS ENSEMBLE

Number	Title	Yr	NM
NONESUCH			
H-71242	Michael Praetorius: Polytonal Christmas Music	197?	15.00

WET WET WET

Number	Title	Yr	NM
UNI			
5000	Popped In Souled Out	1987	12.00

WET WILLIE

Number	Title	Yr	NM
CAPRICORN			
CP 0149	Dixie Rock	1975	12.00
CP 0113	Drippin' Wet/Live	1973	15.00
CP 0200	Greatest Hits	1978	12.00
CP 0128	Keep on Smilin'	1974	12.00
CP 0182	Left Coast Live	1977	12.00
CP 0166	The Wetter the Better	1976	12.00
SD861	Wet Willie	1971	18.00
CP 0138	Wet Willie	1974	12.00

—Reissue of 861

Number	Title	Yr	NM
CP 0109	Wet Willie II	1972	15.00
EPIC			
JE34983	Manorisms	1977	12.00
JE35794	Which One's Willie?	1979	12.00

WETMORE, DICK

Number	Title	Yr	NM
BETHLEHEM			
BCP-1035 [10]	Dick Wetmore	1955	250.00

WETTLING, GEORGE

Number	Title	Yr	NM
COLUMBIA			
CL2559 [10]	George Wettling's Jazz Band	1956	50.00

Column 3

—House Party Series" issue

Number	Title	Yr	NM
CL6189 [10]	George Wettling's Jazz Band	1951	80.00

—Original issue

Number	Title	Yr	NM
HARMONY			
HL7080 [M]	Dixieland in Hi-Fi	1957	25.00
KAPP			
KL-1028 [M]	Jazz Trios	1956	40.00
KL-1005 [M]	Ragtime Duo	1955	40.00
WEATHERS INDUSTRIES			
5501 [M]	High Fidelity Rhythms	1955	40.00

WHALEFEATHERS, THE

Number	Title	Yr	NM
NASCO			
9005	The Whalefeathers	1970	100.00
9003	The Whalefeathers Declare	1969	100.00

WHALUM, KIRK

Number	Title	Yr	NM
COLUMBIA			
FC40812	And You Know That!	1988	12.00
FC40221	Floppy Disk	1985	12.00
FC45215	The Promise	1989	15.00

WHAM!

Number	Title	Yr	NM
COLUMBIA			
BFC38911	Fantastic	1983	18.00

—Cover and label list artist as "Wham! U.K.

Number	Title	Yr	NM
FC38911 [B]	Fantastic	1985	12.00

—Reissue; cover and label list artist as "Wham!

Number	Title	Yr	NM
9C940062 [PD]	Make It Big	1985	30.00

—Picture disc

Number	Title	Yr	NM
FC39595	Make It Big	1984	12.00
OC40285	Music from the Edge of Heaven	1986	12.00

—With "removable sticker" list of song titles still on front cover

WHAT IS THIS

Number	Title	Yr	NM
L33-1174 [EP]	What Is This	1985	18.00

—Promo-only version with custom labels and sleeve

Number	Title	Yr	NM
5598	What Is This	1985	12.00

WHATNAUTS, THE

Number	Title	Yr	NM
STANG			
1005	The Whatnauts	1970	25.00

WHEELER, BILLY EDD

Number	Title	Yr	NM
FLYING FISH			
FF-085	Wild Mountain Flowers	1979	15.00
FOLKWAYS			
31014	When Kentucky Had No Union Men	196?	25.00
KAPP			
KL-1351 [M]	A New Bag of Songs Written and Sung by Billy Edd Wheeler	1964	18.00
KS-3351 [S]	A New Bag of Songs Written and Sung by Billy Edd Wheeler	1964	25.00
KL-1479 [M]	Goin' Town and Country	1966	18.00
KS-3479 [S]	Goin' Town and Country	1966	25.00
KS 3567	I Ain't the Worryin' Kind	1968	18.00
KL-1425 [M]	Memories of America/Ode to the Little Brown Shack Out Back	1965	18.00
KS-3425 [S]	Memories of America/Ode to the Little Brown Shack Out Back	1965	25.00
KL-1533 [M]	Paper Birds	1967	25.00
KS-3533 [S]	Paper Birds	1967	18.00
KL-1443 [M]	Wheeler Man	1965	18.00
KS-3443 [S]	Wheeler Man	1965	25.00
MONITOR			
MF-367 [M]	Billy Edd and Bluegrass	1962	30.00
MF-354 [M]	Billy Edd U.S.A.	1961	30.00
RCA VICTOR			
LSP-4491	Love	1971	18.00
UNITED ARTISTS			
UAS-6711	Nashville Zodiac	1969	18.00

WHEELER, CLARENCE

Number	Title	Yr	NM
ATLANTIC			
SD1551	Doin' What We Wanna	1970	50.00
SD1636	New Chicago Blues	1973	25.00
SD1585	The Love I've Been Looking For	1971	30.00

WHEELER, KENNY

Number	Title	Yr	NM
ECM			
1156	Around 6	1979	12.00
1102	Deer Wan	1977	12.00
25000	Double, Double You	1984	12.00
1069	Gnu High	197?	15.00

WHEELER, ONIE

Number	Title	Yr	NM
BRYLEN			
BN4448	Something New and Something Old	1982	12.00

Number	Title	Yr	NM

WHEELS, BURT, AND THE SPEEDSTERS

CORONET
❑ CX-216 [M]	Sounds of the Big Racers	1964	30.00
❑ CXS-216 [S]	Sounds of the Big Racers	1964	30.00

WHEELS, THE

MONTGOMERY WARD
❑ 010	Sounds of the Hot Rods	196?	120.00

WHEN IN ROME

VIRGIN
❑ 90994	When in Rome	1988	12.00

WHIGHAM, JIGGS

PAUSA
❑ 7134	Hope	198?	12.00

WHISPERS, THE

ACCORD
❑ SN-7100	I Can Remember	1981	12.00

ALLEGIANCE
❑ AV-5004	Excellence	1985	12.00

CAPITOL
❑ C1-92957	More of the Night	1990	15.00

DORE
❑ 338	Shhh	197?	15.00

INTERMEDIA
❑ QS-5075	Doctor Love	198?	12.00

JANUS
❑ 7006	Bingo	1974	40.00
❑ 7013	Greatest Hits	1975	30.00
❑ JLS-3046	Life and Breath	1973	40.00
❑ JLS-3041	The Whispers' Love Story	1972	50.00

SOLAR
❑ 60451 [B]	Happy Holidays to You	1985	15.00
❑ BXL1-2774	Headlights	1978	15.00
❑ BXL1-3578	Imagination	1980	15.00
❑ ST-72554	Just Gets Better with Time	1987	12.00
❑ 60216	Love for Love	1983	12.00
❑ S-27	Love Is Where You Find It	1982	12.00
❑ BXL1-2270	Open Up Your Love	1978	15.00
—Reissue of Soul Train 2270			
❑ AYL1-3839	Open Up Your Love	1981	10.00
—"Best Buy Series" reissue			
❑ 60356	So Good	1984	12.00
❑ BXL1-4242	The Best of the Whispers	1982	15.00
❑ BXL1-3521	The Whspers	1979	15.00
❑ BXL1-3976	This Kind of Lovin'	1981	15.00
❑ PZ75306	Vintage Whispers	1989	15.00
❑ BXL1-3105	Whisper in Your Ear	1979	15.00

SOUL CLOCK
❑ 22001	Planets of Life	1969	100.00

SOUL TRAIN
❑ BVL1-1450	One for the Money	1976	18.00
❑ BVL1-2270	Open Up Your Love	1977	18.00

WHITCOMB, IAN, AND DICK ZIMMERMAN

AUDIOPHILE
❑ AP-225	Steppin' Out	1987	12.00

STOMP OFF
❑ SOS-1017	Don't Say Goodbye Miss Ragtime	198?	15.00
❑ SOS-1049	My Wife Is Dancing Mad	198?	15.00

WHITCOMB, IAN

AUDIOPHILE
❑ AP-147	At the Ragtime Ball	1983	15.00
❑ AP-115	Treasures of Tin Pan Alley	197?	15.00

FIRST AMERICAN
❑ 7704	Crooner Tunes	1979	12.00
❑ 7789	In Hollywood	1982	12.00
❑ 7751	Instrumentals	1981	12.00
❑ 7725	Red Hot "Blue Heaven	1980	12.00
❑ 7729	The Rock and Roll Years	1981	12.00

RHINO
❑ RNLP-127	The Best of Ian Whitcomb (1964-1968)	1986	10.00

SIERRA
❑ 8708	Pianomelt	1980	12.00

TOWER
❑ T5042 [M]	Mod, Mod Music Hall	1966	18.00
❑ ST5042 [S]	Mod, Mod Music Hall	1966	25.00
❑ ST5100	Sock Me Some Rock	1968	25.00
❑ T5071 [M]	Yellow Underground	1967	18.00
❑ ST5071 [S]	Yellow Underground	1967	25.00
❑ T5004 [M]	You Turn Me On	1965	30.00
❑ DT5004 [R]	You Turn Me On	1965	25.00

UNITED ARTISTS
❑ UA-LA021-F	Under the Ragtime Moon	1972	12.00

WHITE, ANDREW

ANDREW'S MUSIC
❑ AM-1	Andrew Nathaniel White III	197?	25.00
❑ AM-33	Bionic Saxophone	1978	15.00
❑ AM-14	Collage	1975	18.00

Number	Title	Yr	NM
❑ AM-25	Countdown	1976	18.00
❑ AM-28	Ebony Glaze	1977	15.00
❑ AM-2	Live at the "New Thing"	197?	30.00
❑ AM-8	Live at the Foolery, Vol. 1	1975	18.00
❑ AM-9	Live at the Foolery, Vol. 2	1975	18.00
❑ AM-10	Live at the Foolery, Vol. 3	1975	18.00
❑ AM-11	Live at the Foolery, Vol. 4	1975	18.00
❑ AM-12	Live at the Foolery, Vol. 5	1975	18.00
❑ AM-13	Live at the Foolery, Vol. 6	1975	18.00
❑ AM-3	Live in Bucharest	197?	25.00
❑ AM-31	Live in New York Vol. 1	1977	15.00
❑ AM-32	Live in New York Vol. 2	1977	15.00
❑ AM-15	Marathon' 75, Vol. 1	1976	18.00
❑ AM-16	Marathon' 75, Vol. 2	1976	18.00
❑ AM-17	Marathon' 75, Vol. 3	1976	18.00
❑ AM-18	Marathon' 75, Vol. 4	1976	18.00
❑ AM-19	Marathon' 75, Vol. 5	1976	18.00
❑ AM-20	Marathon' 75, Vol. 6	1976	18.00
❑ AM-21	Marathon' 75, Vol. 7	1976	18.00
❑ AM-22	Marathon' 75, Vol. 8	1976	18.00
❑ AM-23	Marathon' 75, Vol. 9	1976	18.00
❑ AM-29	Miss Ann	1977	15.00
❑ AM-5	Passion Flower	197?	25.00
❑ AM-42	Profile: White	1983	15.00
❑ AM-26	Red Top	1977	15.00
❑ AM-36	Saxophonitis	1979	15.00
❑ AM-30	Seven Giant Steps for Coltrane	1977	18.00
❑ AM-6	Songs for a French Lady	197?	25.00
❑ AM-24	Spotts, Maxine and Brown	1976	18.00
❑ AM-7	Theme	1975	25.00
❑ AM-27	Trinkle, Trinkle	1977	15.00
❑ AM-37	Weekend at One Step, Vol. 1: Fonk Update	1980	15.00
❑ AM-38	Weekend at One Step, Vol. 2: I Love Japan	1980	15.00
❑ AM-39	Weekend at One Step, Vol. 3: Have Band Will Travel	1980	15.00
❑ AM-4	Who Got Da Funk?	197?	25.00

WHITE, BARRY

20TH CENTURY
❑ T-493	Barry White's Greatest Hits	1975	12.00
❑ T-599	Barry White's Greatest Hits, Volume 2	1981	12.00
❑ T-543	Barry White Sings for Someone You Love	1977	12.00
❑ T-571	Barry White The Man	1978	12.00
❑ T-444	Can't Get Enough	1974	12.00
❑ T-590	I Love to Sing the Songs I Sing	1979	12.00
❑ T-516	Is This Whatcha Wont?	1976	12.00
❑ T-407	I've Got So Much to Give	1973	12.00
❑ T-466	Just Another Way to Say I Love You	1975	12.00
❑ T-502	Let the Music Play	1976	12.00
❑ T-423	Stone Gon'	1973	12.00

A&M
❑ 7502153771	Put Me in Your Mix	1991	15.00
❑ SP-5256	The Man Is Back!	1990	12.00
❑ SP-5154	The Right Night and Barry White	1987	12.00

AUDIO FIDELITY
❑ AFZLP169 [B]	Can't Get Enough	2014	30.00

CASABLANCA
❑ 822782-1	Barry White's Greatest Hits	1984	10.00
❑ 822783-1	Barry White's Greatest Hits, Volume 2	1984	10.00

SUPREMACY
❑ SUP-8002	No Limit on Love	1974	15.00
—Compilation of older material			

UNLIMITED GOLD
❑ FZ36208	Barry White's Sheet Music	1980	12.00
❑ FZ37176	Beware	1982	12.00
❑ FZ38048	Change	1982	12.00
❑ FZ38711	Dedicated	1983	12.00
❑ Z2X36957	The Best of Our Love	1981	15.00
❑ JZ35763	The Message Is Love	1979	12.00

WHITE, BARRY AND GLODEAN

UNLIMITED GOLD
❑ FZ37054	Barry and Glodean White	1981	12.00

WHITE, BRIAN, AND ALAN GRESTY

JAZZOLOGY
❑ J-116	Muggsy Remembered	1988	12.00

WHITE, BUKKA

ARHOOLIE
❑ 1019 [M]	Sky Songs, Volume 1	1966	30.00
❑ 1020 [M]	Sky Songs, Volume 2	1966	30.00

BLUE HORIZON
❑ 4604	Blues Masters, Volume 4	1970	30.00

CLEOPATRA
❑ 9492 [B]	Aberdeen, Mississippi Blues		25.00

HERWIN
❑ 201	Sic 'em Dogs	196?	30.00

TAKOMA
❑ C-1001 [M]	Mississippi Blues	196?	30.00

WHITE, CARLA

STASH
❑ ST-237	Andruline	1983	12.00

Number	Title	Yr	NM

WHITE, DANNY

GRAND PRIX
❑ 101	Danny White Sings Country	1983	30.00

WHITE, JOHN

MAINSTREAM
❑ MRL-330	John White	1972	15.00

WHITE, JOSH

ABC-PARAMOUNT
❑ ABC-407 [M]	Josh White -- Live!	1962	30.00
❑ ABCS-407 [S]	Josh White -- Live!	1962	40.00
❑ T-90190 [M]	Josh White -- Live!	1964	30.00
—Capitol Record Club edition			
❑ ABC-124 [M]	Josh White Stories, Vol. 1	1956	60.00
❑ ABC-166 [M]	Josh White Stories, Vol. 2	1957	60.00

DECCA
❑ DL5062 [10]	Ballads and Blues	1949	150.00
❑ DL5247 [10]	Ballads and Blues, Vol. 2	195?	120.00
❑ DL8665 [M]	Josh White	1958	40.00
—Black label, silver print			

ELEKTRA
❑ EKL-123 [M]	25th Anniversary Album	1957	40.00
❑ EKL-158 [M]	Chain Gang Songs	1958	80.00
❑ EKS-7158 [S]	Chain Gang Songs	195?	100.00
❑ EKL-211 [M]	Empty Bed Blues	1962	30.00
❑ EKS-7211 [S]	Empty Bed Blues	1962	30.00
❑ EKL-114 [M]	Josh, Ballads and Blues	1957	40.00
❑ EKL-102 [M]	Josh at Midnight	1956	40.00
❑ EKL-193 [M]	Spirituals and Blues	1960	30.00
❑ EKS-7193 [S]	Spirituals and Blues	1960	40.00
❑ EKL-203 [M]	The House I Live In	1961	30.00
❑ EKS-7203 [S]	The House I Live In	1961	40.00
❑ EKL-701 [10]	The Story of John Henry/ Ballads, Blues and Other Songs	1955	50.00

EMARCY
❑ MG-26010 [10]	Strange Fruit	1954	120.00

LONDON
❑ LPB-338 [10]	A Josh White Program	195?	120.00
❑ LL1147 [M]	A Josh White Program	1956	50.00
❑ LPB-341 [10]	A Josh White Program, Vol. 2	195?	120.00
❑ LL1341 [M]	A Josh White Program, Vol. 2	195?	50.00

MERCURY
❑ MG-21022 [M]	I'm on My Own Way	1963	30.00
❑ SR-61022 [R]	I'm on My Own Way	1963	25.00
❑ MG-20203 [M]	Josh White's Blues	1957	60.00
❑ MG-25014 [10]	Josh White Sings Blues	1949	150.00
❑ MG-20821 [M]	The Beginning	1963	30.00
❑ SR-60821 [R]	The Beginning	1963	25.00

PERIOD
❑ SLP-1115 [10]	Josh White Comes a-Visiting	1956	60.00

STINSON
❑ SLP-15 [10]	Josh White Sings Folk Songs	1950	120.00
❑ SLP-14 [10]	Josh White Sings the Blues	1950	120.00

WHITE, KITTY

EMARCY
❑ MG-36020 [M]	A New Voice in Jazz	1955	50.00
❑ MG-36068 [M]	Kitty White	1955	50.00

PACIFICA
❑ PL-802 [10]	Kitty White	1955	100.00

WHITE, LENNY

ELEKTRA
❑ 6E-121	Adventures of Astral Pirates	1978	12.00
❑ 6E-223	Best of Friends	1979	12.00
❑ 5E-551	Just Like Dreamin'	1981	12.00
❑ 6E-164	Streamline	1978	12.00
❑ 6E-304	Twennynine with Lenny White	1980	12.00

NEMPEROR
❑ SD441	Big City	1977	15.00
❑ SD435	Venusian Summer	1975	15.00

WHITE, MACK

COMMERCIAL
❑ 782	Lonely in the Crowd	197?	18.00

WHITE, MAURICE

COLUMBIA
❑ FC39883	Maurice White	1985	12.00

WHITE, MICHAEL

ABC IMPULSE!
❑ AS-9268	Father Music, Mother Dance	1974	18.00
❑ ASD-9281	Go with the Flow	1974	18.00
❑ AS-9241	Land of Spirit and Light	1973	18.00
❑ AS-9221	Pneuma	197?	18.00
❑ AS-9215	Spirit Dance	197?	18.00

ELEKTRA
❑ 6E-138	X Factor	1978	12.00

WHITE, MIKE

SEECO

Number	Title	Yr	NM
❑ SLP-442 [M]	Dixieland Jazz	1960	25.00
❑ SLP-4420 [S]	Dixieland Jazz	1960	30.00

WHITE, STEVE

LIBERTY

Number	Title	Yr	NM
❑ LJH-6006 [M]	Jazz Mad -- The Unpredictable Steve White	1955	50.00

WHITE, TONY JOE

20TH CENTURY

Number	Title	Yr	NM
❑ T-523	Eyes	1977	15.00

CASABLANCA

Number	Title	Yr	NM
❑ NBLP7233	Real Thang	1980	12.00

COLUMBIA

Number	Title	Yr	NM
❑ FC38817	Dangerous	1983	12.00

MONUMENT

Number	Title	Yr	NM
❑ SLP-18114	Black and White	1969	18.00
❑ SLP-18133	...Continued	1969	18.00
❑ SLP-18142	Tony Joe	1970	18.00

WARNER

Number	Title	Yr	NM
❑ MOVLP1073 [B]	Tony Joe White	2014	30.00

WARNER BROS.

Number	Title	Yr	NM
❑ BS2708	Homemade Ice Cream	1973	15.00
❑ BS2580	The Train I'm On	1972	15.00
❑ WS1900	Tony Joe White	1971	15.00

WHITE BOY

TRADEWIND

Number	Title	Yr	NM
❑ MM-11761	The Average Rat Band	1976	150.00

WHITE EAGLE JAZZ BAND, THE

GHB

Number	Title	Yr	NM
❑ GHB-204	The White Eagle Jazz Band	1988	12.00

WHITE LIGHT

CENTURY

Number	Title	Yr	NM
❑ 39955	White Light	1968	300.00

WHITE LIGHTNIN'

ABC

Number	Title	Yr	NM
❑ S-690	File Under Rock	1969	25.00

WHITE NOISE

ANTILLES

Number	Title	Yr	NM
❑ AN-7011 [B]	An Electric Storm	1973	30.00

WHITE PLAINS

DERAM

Number	Title	Yr	NM
❑ DES18045 [B]	My Baby Loves Lovin'	1970	25.00

WHITE TIGER

E.M.C.

Number	Title	Yr	NM
❑ EMC-3653	White Tiger	1986	25.00

WHITE WITCH

CAPRICORN

Number	Title	Yr	NM
❑ CP 0129 [B]	A Spiritual Greeting	1974	30.00
❑ CP 0107 [B]	White Witch	1973	30.00

WHITE ZOMBIE

CAROLINE

Number	Title	Yr	NM
❑ 1362	Make Them Die Slowly	1989	25.00
❑ 1350	Soul Crusher	1988	25.00

GEFFEN

Number	Title	Yr	NM
❑ GEF24806	Astro-Creep: 2000	1995	18.00

SILENT EXPLOSION

Number	Title	Yr	NM
❑ 0(# unknown) [EP]	Psycho-Head Blowout	1986	60.00
❑ SE 002	Soul Crusher	1987	60.00

WHITEMAN, PAUL, ORCHESTRA

MONMOUTH-EVERGREEN

Number	Title	Yr	NM
❑ 7078	Live in '75	1975	15.00
❑ 7074	The Classic Arrangements of Challis, Satterfield, Hayton	197?	15.00

WHITEMAN, PAUL

CAPITOL

Number	Title	Yr	NM
❑ T622 [M]	Classics in Jazz	1955	50.00
❑ T1678 [M]	Paul Whiteman Conducts George Gershwin	1962	18.00
❑ DT1678 [R]	Paul Whiteman Conducts George Gershwin	1962	15.00

COLUMBIA

Number	Title	Yr	NM
❑ CL2830 [M]	Paul Whiteman Featuring Bing Crosby	1968	18.00

CORAL

Number	Title	Yr	NM
❑ CRL57021 [M]	The Great Gershwin	1955	25.00

GRAND AWARD

Number	Title	Yr	NM
❑ GA-33-412 [M]	Cavalcade of Music	1960	25.00
❑ GA-244SD [S]	Cavalcade of Music	1960	30.00
❑ GA-33-351 [M]	Fiddle on Fire	195?	30.00
❑ GA-33-502 [M]	Great Whiteman Hits	195?	30.00
❑ GA-33-356 [M]	Hawaiian Magic	1958	25.00
❑ GA-208SD [S]	Hawaiian Magic	1958	30.00
❑ GA-33-901 [M]	Paul Whiteman/50th Anniversary	1956	50.00
❑ GA-33-503 [M]	The Greatest Stars of My Life	195?	50.00
— In red velvet jacket			
❑ GA-33-409 [M]	The Night I Played at 666 Fifth Ave.	1960	25.00
❑ GA-241SD [S]	The Night I Played at 666 Fifth Ave.	1960	30.00

MARK 56

Number	Title	Yr	NM
❑ 761 [M]	Tribute to Gershwin 1936	197?	15.00

RCA VICTOR

Number	Title	Yr	NM
❑ LPV-555 [M]	Paul Whiteman, Volume 1	195?	18.00

SUNBEAM

Number	Title	Yr	NM
❑ 18 [M]	In Concert 1927-32	197?	15.00

X

Number	Title	Yr	NM
❑ LVA-3040 [10]	Paul Whiteman's Orchestra Featuring Bix Beiderbecke	1955	80.00

WHITES, THE

MCA CURB

Number	Title	Yr	NM
❑ 5820	Ain't No Binds	1987	10.00
❑ 5490	Forever You	1984	10.00
❑ 5717	Greatest Hits	1986	10.00
❑ 5562	Whole New World	1985	10.00

WARNER BROS.

Number	Title	Yr	NM
❑ 23872	Old Familiar Feeling	1983	10.00

WHITESNAKE

GEFFEN

Number	Title	Yr	NM
❑ GHS24167	Come an' Get It	1987	12.00
— Reissue of Mirage 16043			
❑ GHS24168	Live... In the Heart of the City	1987	12.00
— Reissue of Mirage 19292			
❑ GHS24176	Lovehunter	1988	12.00
— Reissue of United Artists 981			
❑ GHS24173	Saints & Sinners	1988	12.00
— First U.S. issue of 1982 U.K. LP			
❑ GHS4018 [B]	Slide It In	1984	12.00
❑ GHS24249	Slip of the Tongue	1989	12.00
❑ GHS24174	Snakebite	1988	12.00
— Reissue of United Artists 915			
❑ GHS24175	Trouble	1988	12.00
— Reissue of United Artists 937			
❑ GHS24099	Whitesnake	1987	12.00
❑ R163629	Whitesnake	1987	15.00
— BMG Direct Marketing version			

MIRAGE

Number	Title	Yr	NM
❑ WTG16043	Come an' Get It	1981	15.00
❑ WTG19292	Live... In the Heart of the City	1980	15.00
❑ WTG19276	Ready an' Willing	1980	15.00

PARLOPHONE

Number	Title	Yr	NM
❑ UAGR30305 [B]	Trouble	2014	30.00

UNITED ARTISTS

Number	Title	Yr	NM
❑ LT-981	Lovehunter	1979	15.00
❑ UA-LA915-H	Snakebite	1978	16.00
— As "David Coverdale's Whitesnake			
❑ UA-LA937-H	Trouble	1978	15.00

WHITFORD-ST. HOLMES BAND

COLUMBIA

Number	Title	Yr	NM
❑ FC37365	Whitford/St. Holmes Band	1981	12.00

WHITING, MARGARET, AND JIMMY WAKELY

HILLTOP

Number	Title	Yr	NM
❑ JM-6053 [M]	I'll Never Slip Around Again	196?	15.00
❑ JS-6053 [R]	I'll Never Slip Around Again	196?	15.00

WHITING, MARGARET

AUDIOPHILE

Number	Title	Yr	NM
❑ AP-173	Come a Little Closer	198?	12.00
❑ AP-207	This Lady's in Love with You	1986	12.00
❑ AP-152	Too Marvelous for Words	198?	12.00

CAPITOL

Number	Title	Yr	NM
❑ T685 [M]	For the Starry-Eyed	1955	40.00
❑ T410 [M]	Love Songs	1954	40.00
❑ H209 [10]	Margaret Whiting Sings Rodgers and Hart	1950	50.00
❑ H234 [10]	Songs	1950	50.00
❑ H163 [10]	South Pacific	1950	50.00

DOT

Number	Title	Yr	NM
❑ DLP3072 [M]	Goin' Places	1957	30.00
❑ DLP3337 [M]	Just a Dream	1960	18.00
❑ DLP25337 [S]	Just a Dream	1960	25.00
❑ DLP3113 [M]	Margaret	1958	18.00
❑ DLP25113 [S]	Margaret	1958	25.00
❑ DLP3176 [M]	Margaret Whiting's Great Hits	1959	18.00
❑ DLP25176 [S]	Margaret Whiting's Great Hits	1959	25.00
❑ DLP3235 [M]	Ten Top Hits	1960	18.00
❑ DLP25235 [S]	Ten Top Hits	1960	25.00

HAMILTON

Number	Title	Yr	NM
❑ HLP143 [M]	My Ideal	196?	15.00
❑ HLP12143 [S]	My Ideal	196?	18.00

LONDON

Number	Title	Yr	NM
❑ LL3510 [M]	Maggie Isn't Margaret Anymore	1967	25.00
❑ PS510 [S]	Maggie Isn't Margaret Anymore	1967	18.00
❑ PS527	Pop Country	1968	18.00
❑ LL3497 [M]	The Wheel of Hurt	1967	25.00
❑ PS497 [S]	The Wheel of Hurt	1967	18.00

MGM

Number	Title	Yr	NM
❑ E-4006 [M]	Past Midnight	1961	18.00
❑ SE-4006 [S]	Past Midnight	1961	25.00

VERVE

Number	Title	Yr	NM
❑ V-4038 [M]	The Jerome Kern Song Book	1960	18.00
❑ V6-4038 [S]	The Jerome Kern Song Book	1960	25.00

WHITLEY, KEITH

RCA

Number	Title	Yr	NM
❑ 6494-1-R	Don't Close Your Eyes	1988	12.00
❑ 9809-1-R	I Wonder Do You Think of Me	1989	15.00

RCA VICTOR

Number	Title	Yr	NM
❑ MHL1-8525 [EP]	A Hard Act to Follow	1984	15.00
❑ AHL1-7043	L.A. to Miami	1986	18.00
— Original issue, has 7 tracks			
❑ AEL1-5870	L.A. to Miami	1986	12.00
— Reissue of 7043, has 10 tracks			

WHITLOCK, BOBBY

ABC DUNHILL

Number	Title	Yr	NM
❑ DS-50121	Bobby Whitlock	1972	15.00
❑ DSX-50131	Raw Velvet	1972	15.00

CAPRICORN

Number	Title	Yr	NM
❑ CP 0160 [B]	One of a Kind	1975	12.00
❑ CP 0168	Rock Your Sox Off	1976	12.00

WHITMAN, SLIM

CLEVELAND INT'L.

Number	Title	Yr	NM
❑ JE36847	Christmas with Slim Whitman	1980	15.00
❑ FE37403	Mr. Songman	1982	12.00
❑ JE36768	Songs I Love to Sing	1980	12.00
❑ AS99-875 [DJ]	Songs I Love to Sing	1980	40.00
— Promo-only picture disc			

COLUMBIA SPECIAL PRODUCTS

Number	Title	Yr	NM
❑ P16323	Christmas with Slim Whitman	1981	12.00

EPIC

Number	Title	Yr	NM
❑ PE36847	Christmas with Slim Whitman	1981	10.00
— Reissue of Cleveland Int'l. JE 36847			
❑ PE36768	Songs I Love to Sing	198?	10.00
— Reissue of Cleveland Int'l. JE 36768			

IMPERIAL

Number	Title	Yr	NM
❑ LP-9342 [M]	15th Anniversary	1967	18.00
❑ LP-12342 [S]	15th Anniversary	1967	15.00
❑ LP-9252 [M]	All-Time Favorites	1964	30.00
— Black label with stars on top			
❑ LP-9252 [M]	All-Time Favorites	1964	18.00
— Black and pink label			
❑ LP-9252 [M]	All-Time Favorites	1966	15.00
— Black and green label			
❑ LP-3004 [10]	America's Favorite Folk Artist	1954	600.00
❑ LP-9333 [M]	A Time for Love	1966	15.00
❑ LP-12333 [S]	A Time for Love	1966	18.00
❑ LP-9313 [M]	A Travelin' Man	1966	15.00
❑ LP-12313 [S]	A Travelin' Man	1966	18.00
❑ LP-9356 [M]	Country Memories	1967	18.00
❑ LP-12356 [S]	Country Memories	1967	15.00
❑ LP-9268 [M]	Country Songs/City Hits	1964	18.00
— Black and pink label			
❑ LP-9268 [M]	Country Songs/City Hits	1966	15.00
— Black and green label			
❑ LP-12268 [S]	Country Songs/City Hits	1964	25.00
— Black and pink label			
❑ LP-12268 [S]	Country Songs/City Hits	1966	18.00
— Black and green label			
❑ LP-9003 [M]	Favorites	1956	50.00
— Maroon label			
❑ LP-9003 [M]	Favorites	1958	30.00
— Black label with stars on top			
❑ LP-9003 [M]	Favorites	1964	25.00
— Black and pink label			
❑ LP-9003 [M]	Favorites	1966	18.00
— Black and green label			
❑ LP-9171 [M]	Forever	1961	30.00
— Black label with stars on top			
❑ LP-9171 [M]	Forever	1964	18.00
— Black and pink label			
❑ LP-9171 [M]	Forever	1966	15.00
— Black and green label			
❑ LP-9308 [M]	God's Hand in Mine	1966	15.00
❑ LP-12411	Happy Street	1969	15.00

Number	Title	Yr	NM
❑ LP-9209 [M]	Heart Songs and Love Songs	1962	30.00
—Black label with stars on top			
❑ LP-9209 [M]	Heart Songs and Love Songs	1964	18.00
—Black and pink label			
❑ LP-9209 [M]	Heart Songs and Love Songs	1966	15.00
—Black and green label			
❑ LP-9088 [M]	I'll Walk with God	1960	30.00
—Black label with stars on top			
❑ LP-9088 [M]	I'll Walk with God	1964	25.00
—Black and pink label			
❑ LP-9088 [M]	I'll Walk with God	1966	18.00
—Black and green label			
❑ LP-12032 [S]	I'll Walk with God	1959	40.00
—Black label with silver top			
❑ LP-12032 [S]	I'll Walk with God	1964	30.00
—Black and pink label			
❑ LP-12032 [S]	I'll Walk with God	1966	25.00
—Black and green label			
❑ LP-9226 [M]	I'm a Lonely Wanderer	1963	30.00
—Black label with stars on top			
❑ LP-9226 [M]	I'm a Lonely Wanderer	1964	18.00
—Black and pink label			
❑ LP-9226 [M]	I'm a Lonely Wanderer	1966	15.00
—Black and green label			
❑ LP-12375	In Love, The Whitman Way	1968	15.00
❑ LP-9245 [M]	Irish Songs The Whitman Way	1963	30.00
—Black label with stars on top			
❑ LP-9245 [M]	Irish Songs The Whitman Way	1964	18.00
—Black and pink label			
❑ LP-9245 [M]	Irish Songs The Whitman Way	1966	15.00
—Black and green label			
❑ LP-9137 [M]	Just Call Me Lonesome	1961	30.00
—Black label with stars on top			
❑ LP-9137 [M]	Just Call Me Lonesome	1964	18.00
—Black and pink label			
❑ LP-9137 [M]	Just Call Me Lonesome	1966	15.00
—Black and green label			
❑ LP-9277 [M]	Love Song of the Waterfall	1964	18.00
—Black and pink label			
❑ LP-9277 [M]	Love Song of the Waterfall	1966	15.00
—Black and green label			
❑ LP-12277 [S]	Love Song of the Waterfall	1964	25.00
—Black and pink label			
❑ LP-12277 [S]	Love Song of the Waterfall	1966	18.00
—Black and green label			
❑ LP-9102 [M]	Million Record Hits	1960	30.00
—Black label with stars on top			
❑ LP-9303 [M]	More Than Yesterday	1965	18.00
—Black and pink label			
❑ LP-9303 [M]	More Than Yesterday	1966	15.00
—Black and green label			
❑ LP-12303 [S]	More Than Yesterday	1965	25.00
—Black and pink label			
❑ LP-12303 [S]	More Than Yesterday	1966	18.00
—Black and green label			
❑ LP-9156 [M]	Once in a Lifetime	1961	30.00
—Black label with stars on top			
❑ LP-9156 [M]	Once in a Lifetime	1964	18.00
—Black and pink label			
❑ LP-9156 [M]	Once in a Lifetime	1966	15.00
—Black and green label			
❑ LP-9288 [M]	Reminiscing	1965	18.00
—Black and pink label			
❑ LP-9288 [M]	Reminiscing	1966	15.00
—Black and green label			
❑ LP-12288 [S]	Reminiscing	1965	25.00
—Black and pink label			
❑ LP-12288 [S]	Reminiscing	1966	18.00
—Black and green label			
❑ LP-12436	Slim	1969	15.00
❑ LP-12100 [R]	Slim Whitman	1964	18.00
—Black and pink label			
❑ LP-12100 [R]	Slim Whitman	1966	15.00
—Black and green label			
❑ LP-9135 [M]	Slim Whitman's First Visit to Britain	1960	30.00
—Black label with stars on top			
❑ LP-9135 [M]	Slim Whitman's First Visit to Britain	1964	18.00
—Black and pink label			
❑ LP-9135 [M]	Slim Whitman's First Visit to Britain	1966	15.00
—Black and green label			
❑ LP-9026 [M]	Slim Whitman Sings	1957	50.00
—Maroon label			
❑ LP-9026 [M]	Slim Whitman Sings	1958	30.00
—Black label with stars on top			
❑ LP-9026 [M]	Slim Whitman Sings	1964	25.00
—Black and pink label			
❑ LP-9026 [M]	Slim Whitman Sings	1966	18.00
—Black and green label			
❑ LP-9056 [M]	Slim Whitman Sings	1958	50.00
—Maroon label			
❑ LP-9056 [M]	Slim Whitman Sings	1958	30.00
—Black label with stars on top			
❑ LP-9056 [M]	Slim Whitman Sings	1964	25.00
—Black and pink label			
❑ LP-9056 [M]	Slim Whitman Sings	1966	18.00
—Black and green label			
❑ LP-9064 [M]	Slim Whitman Sings	1959	30.00
—Black label with stars on top			
❑ LP-9064 [M]	Slim Whitman Sings	1964	25.00
—Black and pink label			
❑ LP-9064 [M]	Slim Whitman Sings	1966	18.00
—Black and green label			
❑ LP-9194 [M]	Slim Whitman Sings	1962	30.00
—Black label with stars on top			
❑ LP-9194 [M]	Slim Whitman Sings	1964	18.00
—Black and pink label			
❑ LP-9194 [M]	Slim Whitman Sings	1966	15.00
—Black and green label			
❑ LP-12194 [S]	Slim Whitman Sings	1962	30.00
—Black label with silver top			
❑ LP-12194 [S]	Slim Whitman Sings	1964	25.00
—Black and pink label			
❑ LP-12194 [S]	Slim Whitman Sings	1966	18.00
—Black and green label			
❑ LP-9163 [M]	Slim Whitman Sings Annie Laurie	1961	30.00
—Black label with stars on top			
❑ LP-9163 [M]	Slim Whitman Sings Annie Laurie	1964	18.00
—Black and pink label			
❑ LP-9163 [M]	Slim Whitman Sings Annie Laurie	1966	15.00
—Black and green label			
❑ LP-12077 [S]	Slim Whitman Sings Annie Laurie	1961	30.00
—Black label with silver top			
❑ LP-12077 [S]	Slim Whitman Sings Annie Laurie	1964	25.00
—Black and pink label			
❑ LP-12077 [S]	Slim Whitman Sings Annie Laurie	1966	18.00
—Black and green label			
❑ LP-9102 [M]	Song of the Old Waterwheel	1964	25.00
—Black and pink label; title changed			
❑ LP-9102 [M]	Song of the Old Waterwheel	1966	18.00
—Black and green label			
❑ LP-12102 [R]	Song of the Old Waterwheel	1964	18.00
—Black and pink label			
❑ LP-12102 [R]	Song of the Old Waterwheel	1966	15.00
—Black and green label			
❑ LP-12448	The Slim Whitman Christmas Album	1969	18.00
❑ LP-9235 [M]	Yodeling	1963	30.00
—Black label with stars on top			
❑ LP-9235 [M]	Yodeling	1964	18.00
—Black and pink label			
❑ LP-9235 [M]	Yodeling	1966	15.00
—Black and green label			

LIBERTY

Number	Title	Yr	NM
❑ SL-8128	All My Best	1981	15.00
—Mail-order album			
❑ LN-10153	Country Songs/City Hits	1981	10.00
—Budget-line reissue			
❑ LN-10124	Ghost Riders in the Sky	1981	10.00
—Budget-line reissue			
❑ LN-10152	God's Hand in Mine	1981	10.00
—Budget-line reissue			
❑ LN-10033	Red River Valley	1981	10.00
—Budget-line reissue			
❑ LN-10125	The Best of Slim Whitman, Vol. 2	1981	10.00
—Budget-line reissue			
❑ LM-1067	The Slim Whitman Christmas Album	1980	10.00
—Abridged reissue of Imperial 12448			
❑ LM-1005	The Very Best of Slim Whitman	1981	10.00
—Reissue of United Artists 1005			
❑ LN-10123	Till We Meet Again	1981	10.00
—Budget-line reissue			

PAIR

Number	Title	Yr	NM
❑ PDL2-1085	One of a Kind	1986	15.00

PICKWICK

Number	Title	Yr	NM
❑ SPC-3590	Happy Anniversary	1978	12.00

RCA CAMDEN

Number	Title	Yr	NM
❑ CAL-954 [M]	Birmingham Jail	1966	25.00
❑ CAS-954(e) [R]	Birmingham Jail	1966	15.00

RCA VICTOR

Number	Title	Yr	NM
❑ AYL1-3774	Birmingham Jail	1980	10.00
—Best Buy Series" reissue			
❑ LPM-3217 [10]	Slim Whitman Sings and Yodels	1954	300.00

SUNSET

Number	Title	Yr	NM
❑ SUM-1167 [M]	Lonesome Heart	1967	15.00
❑ SUS-5167 [R]	Lonesome Heart	1967	15.00
❑ SUS-5320	Ramblin' Rose	1970	12.00
❑ SUS-5267	Slim Whitman	1969	15.00
❑ SUM-1112 [M]	Unchain Your Heart	1966	15.00
❑ SUS-5112 [R]	Unchain Your Heart	1966	15.00

UNITED ARTISTS

Number	Title	Yr	NM
❑ UA-LA513-G	Everything Leads Back to You	1975	12.00
❑ UAS 6783	Guess Who	1970	15.00
❑ UA-LA319-G	Happy Anniversary	1974	12.00
❑ UA-LA787-G	Home on the Range	1978	12.00
❑ UA-LA046-F	I'll See You When I Get There	1973	12.00
❑ UAS-6819	It's a Sin to Tell a Lie	1971	15.00
❑ UA-LA752-G	Red River Valley	1977	12.00
❑ UAS-6832	The Best of Slim Whitman	1972	15.00
❑ UA-LA245-G	The Very Best of Slim Whitman	1974	12.00
❑ LM-1005	The Very Best of Slim Whitman	1980	12.00
❑ UA-LA386-E	The Very Best of Slim Whitman	1974	12.00
❑ UAS-6763	Tomorrow Never Comes	1970	15.00

WHITNEY, DAVE

JAZZOLOGY

Number	Title	Yr	NM
❑ J-68	Dave Whitney and His Jazz Band	198?	12.00

WHITNEY, MARVA

KING

Number	Title	Yr	NM
❑ KS-1053	I Sing Soul	1969	120.00
❑ KS-1062	It's My Thing	1969	120.00
❑ KS-1079	Live and Lowdown at the Apollo	1970	200.00

WHITNEY SUNDAY

DECCA

Number	Title	Yr	NM
❑ DL75239 [B]	Whitney Sunday	1970	30.00

WHITTAKER, ROGER

CAPITOL NASHVILLE

Number	Title	Yr	NM
❑ C1594058	World's Most Beautiful Christmas Songs	1990	18.00
—Available on vinyl through Columbia House only			

PAIR

Number	Title	Yr	NM
❑ PDL2-1111	Fire and Rain	1986	15.00
❑ PDL2-1039	Golden Tones	1986	15.00

RCA VICTOR

Number	Title	Yr	NM
❑ LSP-4505	A Special Kind of Man	1971	18.00
❑ AFL1-4505	A Special Kind of Man	1978	12.00
—Reissue of LSP-4505			
❑ AYL1-3946	A Special Kind of Man	1981	10.00
—Best Buy Series" reissue			
❑ AFL1-4129	Changes	1982	12.00
❑ AFL1-2525	Folk Songs	1978	15.00
❑ AQL1-2525	Folk Songs	198?	12.00
—Reissue of AFL1-2525			
❑ LSP-4405	I Don't Believe in It Any More	1970	18.00
❑ AFL1-4405	I Don't Believe in It Any More	1978	12.00
—Reissue of LSP-4405			
❑ AYL1-4177	I Don't Believe in It Any More	1982	10.00
—Best Buy Series" reissue			
❑ AFL1-3077	Imagine	1978	15.00
❑ AQL1-3077	Imagine	198?	10.00
—Reissue of AFL1-3077			
❑ APL1-0855	Last Farewell" and Other Hits, The	1975	15.00
❑ AFL1-0855	Last Farewell" and Other Hits, The	1978	12.00
—Reissue of APL1-0855			
❑ AQL1-0855	Last Farewell" and Other Hits, The	198?	10.00
—Reissue of AFL1-0855			
❑ CPL2-4057	Live in Concert	1981	15.00
❑ LSP-4652	Loose and Fiery	1972	18.00
❑ AFL1-3501	Mirrors of My Mind	1979	12.00
❑ AQL1-3501	Mirrors of My Mind	198?	10.00
—Reissue of AFL1-3501			
❑ LSP-4340	New World in the Morning	1970	18.00
❑ AFL1-4340	New World in the Morning	1978	12.00
—Reissue of LSP-4340			
❑ AYL1-4178	New World in the Morning	1982	10.00
—Best Buy Series" reissue			
❑ APL1-1853	Reflections of Love	1976	15.00
❑ AFL1-1853	Reflections of Love	1978	12.00
—Reissue of APL1-1853			
❑ ANL1-1405	Roger Whittaker	1976	15.00
❑ NFL1-8047	Take a Little -- Give a Little	1985	12.00
❑ APL1-2255	The Best of Roger Whittaker	1977	15.00
❑ AFL1-2255	The Best of Roger Whittaker	1978	12.00
—Reissue of APL1-2255			
❑ AQL1-2255	The Best of Roger Whittaker	198?	10.00
—Reissue of AFL1-2255			
❑ AFL1-5803	The Genius of Love	1986	12.00
❑ APL1-1313	The Magical World of Roger Whittaker	1976	15.00
❑ AFL1-1313	The Magical World of Roger Whittaker	1978	12.00
—Reissue of APL1-1313			
❑ AYL1-3670	The Magical World of Roger Whittaker	1980	10.00
—Best Buy Series" reissue			
❑ ANL1-2933	The Roger Whittaker Christmas Album	1978	15.00
❑ AFL1-4321	The Wind Beneath My Wings	1983	12.00

Number	Title	Yr	NM
❑ AFL1-0078	Traveling with Roger Whittaker	1978	12.00
—Reissue of APL1-0078			
❑ APL1-0078	Traveling with Roger Whittaker	1973	18.00
❑ AFL1-3518	Voyager	1980	12.00
❑ AQL1-3518	Voyager	198?	10.00
—Reissue of AFL1-3518			
❑ AFL1-3355	When I Need You	1979	12.00
❑ AYL1-3911	When I Need You	1981	10.00
—Best Buy Series" reissue			
❑ AFL1-3778	With Love	1980	12.00

WHO, THE

DECCA

Number	Title	Yr	NM
❑ DL4892 [M]	Happy Jack	1967	80.00
❑ DL4892 [M]	Happy Jack	1967	150.00
—White label promo			
❑ DL74892 [P]	Happy Jack	1967	60.00
—All stereo except that "Happy Jack" and "Don't Look Away" are rechanneled			
❑ DL74892 [P]	Happy Jack	1967	180.00
—White label promo			
❑ DL79175	Live at Leeds	1970	40.00
—With gatefold cover and numerous inserts			
❑ DL5064 [M]	Magic Bus -- The Who on Tour	1968	250.00
—White label promo; no stock copies were released in mono			

Number	Title	Yr	NM
❑ DL75064 [P]	Magic Bus -- The Who on Tour	1968	50.00
—All rechanneled except "Magic Bus" and "I Can't Reach You," which are true stereo.			
❑ DL75064 [P]	Magic Bus -- The Who on Tour	1968	150.00
—White label promo			
❑ DL79184 [B]	Meaty Beaty Big and Bouncy	1971	30.00
—With poster (deduct 1/3 if missing)			
❑ DL4950 [M]	The Who Sell Out	1967	150.00
❑ DL4950 [M]	The Who Sell Out	1967	300.00
—White label promo with songs in the same order as the stock copy			
❑ DL4950 [M]	The Who Sell Out	1967	500.00
—White label promo with side 1 banded for airplay and all the commercials on one side			
❑ DL74950 [S]	The Who Sell Out	1967	50.00
❑ DL74950 [S]	The Who Sell Out	1967	250.00
—White label promo with songs in the same order as the stock copy			
❑ DL74950 [S]	The Who Sell Out	1967	400.00
—White label promo with side 1 banded for airplay and all the commercials on one side			
❑ DL4664 [M]	The Who Sing My Generation	1966	150.00
❑ DL4664 [M]	The Who Sing My Generation	1966	250.00
—White label promo			
❑ DL74664 [R]	The Who Sing My Generation	1966	60.00
❑ DL74664 [R]	The Who Sing My Generation	1966	200.00
—White label promo			
❑ DL734586 [B]	The Who/The Strawberry Alarm Clock	1969	150.00
—Special Products release for Philco. One side has Who songs, the other, Strawberry Alarm Clock songs			
❑ DXSW7205 [B]	Tommy	1969	60.00
—With booklet			
❑ DXSW7205 [DJ]	Tommy	1969	200.00
—White label promo			
❑ DL79182	Who's Next	1971	30.00

DIRECT DISC

Number	Title	Yr	NM
❑ SD16610 [B]	Who Are You	1980	50.00
—Audiophile vinyl			

GEFFEN

Number	Title	Yr	NM
❑ 8136511	Who's Next	2008	25.00

LIFE

Number	Title	Yr	NM
❑ DL74664 [R]	The Who Sing My Generation	1967	150.00

MCA

Number	Title	Yr	NM
❑ 2-4067 [P]	A Quick One/The Who Sell Out	1976	25.00
—Black labels with rainbow			
❑ 2-4067 [P]	A Quick One/The Who Sell Out	1978	18.00
—Tan labels			
❑ 2-4067 [P]	A Quick One/The Who Sell Out	1980	15.00
—Blue labels with rainbow			
❑ 25987	Face Dances	1989	10.00
❑ 2045 [S]	Happy Jack	1974	50.00
❑ 2-12001	Hooligans	1981	12.00
❑ 25986	It's Hard	1989	10.00
❑ 3-19501	Join Together	1990	25.00
—Box set with booklet			
❑ 2022	Live at Leeds	1973	15.00
❑ 3023	Live at Leeds	1977	12.00
❑ 37000	Live at Leeds	1979	10.00
❑ 1577	Live at Leeds	1988	10.00
❑ 2-4068 [P]	Magic Bus/The Who Sing My Generation	1976	25.00
—Black labels with rainbow			
❑ 2-4068 [P]	Magic Bus/The Who Sing My Generation	1978	18.00
—Tan labels			
❑ 2-4068 [P]	Magic Bus/The Who Sing My Generation	1980	15.00
—Blue labels with rainbow			
❑ 2025	Meaty Beaty Big and Bouncy	1973	15.00
❑ 3025	Meaty Beaty Big and Bouncy	1977	12.00
❑ 37001	Meaty Beaty Big and Bouncy	1979	10.00
❑ 1578	Meaty Beaty Big and Bouncy	1988	10.00
❑ 37169	Odds and Sods	1980	10.00
❑ 2-10004 [B]	Quadrophenia	1973	25.00
—Black labels with rainbow			
❑ 8310741	Quadrophenia	2008	30.00
—Tan labels			
❑ 6895 [B]	Quadrophenia	1980	18.00
❑ 2-11005	The Kids Are Alright	1979	15.00
❑ 6899	The Kids Are Alright	1980	12.00
—Early versions have number stamped in gold on cover with 11005 records. No difference in value.			
❑ 2161	The Who By Numbers	1975	15.00
❑ 3026	The Who By Numbers	1977	12.00
❑ 37002	The Who By Numbers	1979	10.00
❑ 1579	The Who By Numbers	1988	10.00
❑ 2044 [R]	The Who Sing My Generation	1974	50.00
❑ 2-10005	Tommy	1973	18.00
—Black labels with rainbow			
❑ 2-10005	Tommy	1978	15.00
—Tan labels			
❑ 2-10005	Tommy	1980	12.00
—Blue labels with rainbow			
❑ 5712	Two's Missing	1987	12.00
❑ 3050	Who Are You	1978	12.00
❑ L33-1987 [DJ]	Who Are You	1978	30.00
—White label promo with sticker "Who Are You Edited for Broadcast" on cover -- the line "Who the fuck are you?" is deleted twice			
❑ 14950 [PD]	Who Are You	1978	18.00
—Picture disc			
❑ 37003	Who Are You	1979	10.00
❑ 1580	Who Are You	1988	10.00
❑ 8031	Who's Better, Who's Best	1989	18.00
❑ 5408	Who's Greatest Hits	1983	10.00
❑ 1496	Who's Greatest Hits	1987	10.00
❑ 8018	Who's Last	1984	12.00
❑ 5641	Who's Missing	1986	12.00
❑ 2023	Who's Next	1973	15.00
❑ 3024	Who's Next	1977	12.00
❑ 5220	Who's Next	1979	10.00
❑ 11164	Who's Next	1995	30.00
—Heavy Vinyl" reissue on 180-gram vinyl with gatefold cover			

MOBILE FIDELITY

Number	Title	Yr	NM
❑ 1-115	Face Dances	1984	50.00
—Audiophile vinyl			

TRACK

Number	Title	Yr	NM
❑ 2-4067 [P]	A Quick One/The Who Sell Out	1974	40.00
❑ 2-4068 [P]	Magic Bus/The Who Sing My Generation	1974	40.00
❑ 2126 [B]	Odds and Sods	1974	30.00
❑ 2-10004	Quadrophenia	1973	25.00

WARNER BROS.

Number	Title	Yr	NM
❑ HS3516	Face Dances	1981	10.00
❑ WBMS-116 [DJ]	Filling In the Gaps	1981	80.00
—With drawing on cover			
❑ WBMS-116 [DJ]	Filling In the Gaps	1981	50.00
—With generic "Warner Bros. Music Show" cover			
❑ 23731 [DJ]	It's Hard	1982	35.00
—Promo version on Quiex II vinyl			
❑ 23731	It's Hard	1982	10.00

WHYTE, RONNIE

AUDIOPHILE

Number	Title	Yr	NM
❑ AP-127	I Love a Piano	198?	12.00
❑ AP-151	Ronnie Whyte at the Conservatory	198?	12.00
❑ AP-204	Soft Whyte	1986	12.00

MONMOUTH-EVERGREEN

Number	Title	Yr	NM
❑ 7088	New York State of Mind	197?	15.00

PROGRESSIVE

Number	Title	Yr	NM
❑ PRO-7075	Something Wonderful	1986	12.00

WICHITA TRAIN WHISTLE, THE

DOT

Number	Title	Yr	NM
❑ DLP-25861	Mike Nesmith Presents/The Wichita Train Whistle Sings	1968	30.00

WICKLINE

CASCADE MOUNTAIN

Number	Title	Yr	NM
❑ 2	Wickline	198?	15.00

WIDESPREAD DEPRESSION ORCHESTRA, THE

STASH

Number	Title	Yr	NM
❑ ST-206	Boogie in the Barnyard	1980	12.00
❑ ST-203	Downtown Uproar	1979	12.00
❑ ST-212	Time to Jump and Shout	198?	12.00

WIDESPREAD JAZZ ORCHESTRA

ADELPHI

Number	Title	Yr	NM
❑ 5015	Swing Is the Thing	198?	12.00

COLUMBIA

Number	Title	Yr	NM
❑ FC40034	Paris Blues	1985	12.00

WIEDLIN, JANE

EMI MANHATTAN

Number	Title	Yr	NM
❑ R152262	Fur	1988	15.00
—BMG Direct Marketing edition			
❑ E1-48683	Fur	1988	12.00

I.R.S.

Number	Title	Yr	NM
❑ 5638	Jane Wiedlin	1985	12.00

WIER, RUSTY

20TH CENTURY

Number	Title	Yr	NM
❑ T-469	Don't It Make You Wanna Dance?	1975	12.00
❑ T-495	Rusty Wier	1975	12.00

ABC

Number	Title	Yr	NM
❑ D-820	Stoned, Slow and Rugged	1974	15.00

COLUMBIA

Number	Title	Yr	NM
❑ KC34319	Black Hat Saloon	1976	12.00
❑ PC34775	Stacked Deck	1977	12.00

MCA

Number	Title	Yr	NM
❑ 820	Stoned, Slow and Rugged	1980	10.00
—Reissue of ABC 820			

WIGGINS, GERALD

CHALLENGE

Number	Title	Yr	NM
❑ CHP-604 [M]	The King and I	1957	60.00

CLASSIC JAZZ

Number	Title	Yr	NM
❑ 117	Wig Is Here	198?	12.00

CONTEMPORARY

Number	Title	Yr	NM
❑ M-3595 [M]	Relax and Enjoy It	1961	30.00
❑ S-7595 [S]	Relax and Enjoy It	1961	40.00

DIG

Number	Title	Yr	NM
❑ LP-102 [M]	Gerald Wiggins Trio	1956	60.00

DISCOVERY

Number	Title	Yr	NM
❑ DL-2003 [10]	Gerald Wiggins Trio	1953	120.00

FANTASY

Number	Title	Yr	NM
❑ OJC-173	Relax and Enjoy It	198?	12.00

HIFI

Number	Title	Yr	NM
❑ J-618 [M]	Wiggin' Out	1961	30.00
❑ JS-618 [S]	Wiggin' Out	1961	40.00

MOTIF

Number	Title	Yr	NM
❑ 504 [M]	Reminiscin' with Wig	1956	60.00

SPECIALTY

Number	Title	Yr	NM
❑ SP-2101 [S]	Around the World	1969	25.00

TAMPA

Number	Title	Yr	NM
❑ TP-33 [M]	Gerald Wiggins Trio	1957	100.00
—Colored vinyl			
❑ TP-33 [M]	Gerald Wiggins Trio	1958	50.00
—Black vinyl			
❑ TP-1 [M]	The Loveliness of You	1957	100.00
—Colored vinyl			
❑ TP-1 [M]	The Loveliness of You	1958	50.00
—Black vinyl			

WIGGINS, ROY

DIPLOMAT

Number	Title	Yr	NM
❑ DPL2615 [M]	Songs I Played for Eddy Arnold	196?	18.00

STARDAY

Number	Title	Yr	NM
❑ SLP-188 [M]	Mister Steel Guitar	1962	30.00
❑ SLP-392 [M]	Nashville Steel Guitar	1965	30.00

Number	Title	Yr	NM
❏ SLP-259 [M]	The Fabulous Steel Guitar Artistry of Roy Wiggins	1963	30.00

WIGGS, JOHNNY, AND RAYMOND BURKE

S/D
❏ LP-1001 [10]	Chamber Jazz	1955	50.00

WIGGS, JOHNNY

GHB
❏ GHB-100	Johnny Wiggs and the New Orleans Kids	197?	12.00

NEW ORLEANS
❏ 7206	Congo Square	197?	12.00
❏ 47045	Congo Square	197?	12.00

PARAMOUNT
❏ CJS107 [10]	Johnny Wiggs' New Orleanians Playing Jazz Favorites and Featuring Ray Burke	195?	60.00

SOUTHLAND
❏ LP-200 [10]	Johnny Wiggs	1954	50.00
❏ LP-200 [M]	Johnny Wiggs	195?	30.00

WIGWAM

VERVE FORECAST
❏ FTS-3089 [B]	Tombstone Valentine	1970	30.00

WILBER, BOB, AND KENNY DAVERN

WORLD JAZZ
❏ WJLP-S-5	Soprano Summit	1974	18.00

WILBER, BOB, AND SCOTT HAMILTON

CHIAROSCURO
❏ 171	Bob Wilber and Scott Hamilton	1977	15.00

WILBER, BOB

CIRCLE
❏ L-406 [10]	Bob Wilbur Jazz Band	1951	50.00
❏ CLP-98	Reflections	1986	12.00

CLASSIC JAZZ
❏ 9	Blowin' the Blues Away	197?	12.00
❏ 8	New Clarinet in Town	197?	12.00
❏ 5	Spreadin' Joy	197?	12.00

JAZZOLOGY
❏ J-44	Bob Wilber and His Famous Jazz Band	198?	12.00
❏ J-141	Live at Bechet's	1986	12.00
❏ J-142	Ode to Bechet	1986	12.00

MONMOUTH-EVERGREEN
❏ 6917	The Music of Hoagy Carmichael	197?	15.00

RIVERSIDE
❏ RLP-2501 [10]	Young Men With Horns	1952	80.00

WILBOURN, BILL, AND KATHY MORRISON

UNITED ARTISTS
❏ UAS-6685	The Lovers	1969	18.00

WILBURN BROTHERS, THE

DECCA
❏ DL4211 [M]	City Limits	1961	30.00
❏ DL74211 [S]	City Limits	1961	40.00
❏ DL4871 [M]	Cool	1967	30.00
❏ DL74871 [S]	Cool	1967	25.00
❏ DL4615 [M]	Country Gold	1965	25.00
❏ DL74615 [S]	Country Gold	1965	30.00
❏ DL4225 [M]	Folk Songs	1962	25.00
❏ DL74225 [S]	Folk Songs	1962	30.00
❏ DL4645 [M]	I'm Gonna Tie One on Tonight	1965	25.00
❏ DL74645 [S]	I'm Gonna Tie One on Tonight	1965	30.00
❏ DL4954 [M]	It's Another World	1968	40.00
❏ DL74954 [S]	It's Another World	1968	25.00
❏ DL4764 [M]	Let's Go Country	1966	25.00
❏ DL74764 [S]	Let's Go Country	1966	30.00
❏ DL75173	Little Johnny from Down the Street	1970	25.00
❏ DL8959 [M]	Livin' in God's Country	1959	40.00
❏ DL78959 [S]	Livin' in God's Country	1959	60.00
❏ DL4544 [M]	Never Alone	1964	25.00
❏ DL74544 [S]	Never Alone	1964	30.00
❏ DL8774 [M]	Side by Side	1958	40.00
❏ DL78774 [S]	Side by Side	1959	60.00
❏ DL75214	Sing Your Heart Out Country Boy	1971	25.00
❏ DL4464 [M]	Take Up Thy Cross	1964	25.00
❏ DL74464 [S]	Take Up Thy Cross	1964	30.00
❏ DL75291	That She's Leaving Feeling	1972	25.00
❏ DL4058 [M]	The Big Heartbreak	1960	30.00
❏ DL74058 [S]	The Big Heartbreak	1960	40.00
❏ DL8576 [M]	The Wilburn Brothers	1957	40.00
❏ DL4721 [M]	The Wilburn Brothers Show	1966	60.00
—With guests Loretta Lynn, Ernest Tubb, Harold Morrison			
❏ DL74721 [S]	The Wilburn Brothers Show	1966	80.00
—With guests Loretta Lynn, Ernest Tubb, Harold Morrison			
❏ DL4142 [M]	The Wilburn Brothers Sing	1961	30.00
❏ DL74142 [S]	The Wilburn Brothers Sing	1961	40.00
❏ DL4391 [M]	Trouble's Back in Town	1963	25.00

Number	Title	Yr	NM
❏ DL74391 [S]	Trouble's Back in Town	1963	30.00
❏ DL4824 [M]	Two for the Show	1967	30.00
❏ DL74824 [S]	Two for the Show	1967	25.00

KING
❏ 746 [M]	The Wonderful Wilburn Brothers	1961	100.00

MCA
❏ 4011	Portrait	197?	18.00

MCA CORAL
❏ 20058	That Country Feeling	1973	12.00

VOCALION
❏ VL3691 [M]	Carefree Moments	1962	18.00
❏ VL73691 [S]	Carefree Moments	1962	18.00
❏ VL73889	I Walk the Line	197?	15.00
❏ VL73876	That Country Feeling	197?	15.00

WILCO

REPRISE
❏ 46236-1 [B]	Being There	1996	30.00

RHINO VINYL
❏ RI-76492	A Ghost is Born	2005	30.00

SIRE
❏ 45857	A.M.	1995	80.00
—Red vinyl in generic plastic sleeve with sticker in upper left corner			

SUNDAZED
❏ LP5161	Yankee Hotel Foxtrot	2002	30.00

WILCOX, HARLOW

PLANTATION
❏ PLP-12	Cripple Cricket and Other Country Critters	1971	18.00
❏ PLP-7	Groovy Grubworm and Other Golden Guitar Greats	1970	18.00

WILCOX, LARRY

COLUMBIA
❏ CL2147 [M]	Hot Rod Jazz	1964	30.00
❏ CS8947 [S]	Hot Rod Jazz	1964	40.00

COLUMBIA SPECIAL PRODUCTS
❏ CSRP8947 [M]	Hot Rod Jazz	196?	25.00

WILCOX THREE, THE

RCA CAMDEN
❏ CAL-669 [M]	The Greatest Folk Songs Ever Sung	1961	25.00

WILD, JACK

BUDDAH
❏ BDS-5110	A Beautiful World	1972	30.00
❏ BDS-5083	Everything's Coming Up Roses	1971	30.00

CAPITOL
❏ SKAO-545	The Jack Wild Album	1970	30.00

WILD-CATS, THE

UNITED ARTISTS
❏ UAL-3031 [M]	Bandstand Record Hop	1958	50.00

WILD BUTTER

UNITED ARTISTS
❏ UAS-6766	Wild Butter	1970	30.00

WILD CHERRY

EPIC
❏ PE34462	Electrified Funk	1977	12.00
❏ JE35011	I Love My Music	1978	12.00
❏ JE35760	Only the Wild	1979	12.00
❏ PE34195 [B]	Wild Cherry	1976	15.00

WILD MAN STEVE

DEALER'S CHOICE
❏ 780	Did He Really Say That	198?	18.00
❏ 777	Is It Good Baby	198?	18.00

DICK-ER
❏ D70	Do Not Disturb	1972	25.00

LAFF
❏ 181	Eatin' Ain't Cheatin'	1973	15.00
❏ 191	When You're Hot You're Hot	1976	15.00

RAW
❏ 7002	King of Them All	1971	18.00
❏ 7000	My Man! Wild Man!	1969	18.00
❏ 7001	Wild! Wild! Wild!	1970	18.00

WILD ONES, THE (1)

UNITED ARTISTS
❏ UAL-3450 [M]	The Arthur Sound	1965	30.00
❏ UAS-6450 [S]	The Arthur Sound	1965	30.00

WILD TURKEY

CHRYSALIS
❏ CHR1010	Turkey	1973	12.00

REPRISE
❏ MS2070	Battle Hymn	1972	15.00

Number	Title	Yr	NM

WILDE, KIM

EMI AMERICA
❏ SN-16351	Kids in America	198?	15.00
—Budget-line reissue of first LP			
❏ ST-17065	Kim Wilde	1981	12.00
❏ ST-517065	Kim Wilde	1981	15.00
—Columbia House edition			

MCA
❏ 5903	Another Step	1987	12.00
❏ 42230	Close	1988	12.00
❏ 5550	Teases and Dares	1985	12.00

WILDE, MARTY

EPIC
❏ LN3686 [M]	Bad Boy	1960	80.00
❏ LN3711 [M]	Wilde About Marty	1960	80.00
❏ BN575 [S]	Wilde About Marty	1960	100.00

WILDER, ALEC

COLUMBIA
❏ CL6181 [10]	Alec Wilder Octet	1951	60.00

MERCURY
❏ MG25008 [10]	Alec Wilder and His Octet	1949	60.00

WILDER, JOE

COLUMBIA
❏ CL1319 [M]	Jazz from "Peter Gunn"	1959	40.00
—Red and black label with six "eye" logos			
❏ CS8121 [S]	Jazz from "Peter Gunn"	1959	60.00
—Red and black label with six "eye" logos			
❏ CL1372 [M]	The Pretty Sound of Joe Wilder	1959	50.00
—Red and black label with six "eye" logos			
❏ CS8173 [S]	The Pretty Sound of Joe Wilder	1959	100.00
—Red and black label with six "eye" logos			

SAVOY
❏ MG-12063 [M]	'N' Wilder...	1956	50.00

SAVOY JAZZ
❏ SJL-1191	Softly with Feeling	1989	15.00

WILDER, MATTHEW

PRIVATE I
❏ FZ39879	Bouncin' Off the Walls	1984	12.00
❏ BFZ39112	I Don't Speak the Language	1983	12.00
❏ FZ39112	I Don't Speak the Language	1984	10.00
—Reissue with new prefix			

WILDERNESS ROAD

COLUMBIA
❏ C31118	Wilderness Road	1972	25.00

REPRISE
❏ MS2125	Sold for the Prevention of Disease Only	1973	25.00

WILDWEEDS, THE

VANGUARD
❏ VSD-6552	The Wildweeds	1970	30.00

WILEY, LEE

ALLEGRO ELITE
❏ 4019 [10]	Lee Wiley Sings -- Lennie Tristano Plays	195?	100.00

AUDIOPHILE
❏ AP-1	Lee Wiley Sings Ira and George Gershwin and Cole Porter	1986	12.00
❏ AP-10	Lee Wiley Sings the Songs of Richard Rodgers and Lorenz Hart and Harold Arlen	1990	15.00

COLUMBIA
❏ CL6216 [10]	Lee Wiley Sings Irving Berlin	1952	100.00
❏ CL6215 [10]	Lee Wiley Sings Vincent Youmans	1952	100.00
❏ CL6169 [10]	Night in Manhattan	1951	120.00
❏ CL656 [M]	Night in Manhattan	1955	80.00

JAZZTONE
❏ J-1248 [M]	The Songs of Rodgers and Hart -- Intimate Jazz	1956	50.00

JJC
❏ M-2003 [M]	The Classic Interpretations of the Immortal Cole Porter	195?	50.00
❏ M-2002 [M]	The One and Only Lee Wiley	195?	50.00

LIBERTY MUSIC SHOP
❏ 1003 [10]	Cole Porter Songs by Lee Wiley	195?	300.00
❏ 1004 [10]	George Gershwin Songs by Lee Wiley	195?	300.00

MONMOUTH-EVERGREEN
❏ 7041	Back Home Again	1971	15.00
❏ 6807	Lee Wiley Plays Rodgers & Hart/Harold Arlen	1968	18.00
❏ 7034	Lee Wiley Sings Gershwin & Porter	1970	15.00

Number	Title	Yr	NM
RCA VICTOR			
❑ LPM-1566 [M]	Touch of the Blues	1957	60.00
❑ LPM-1408 [M]	West of the Moon	1957	80.00
RIC			
❑ M-2002 [M]	The One and Only Lee Wiley	1964	25.00
❑ S-2002 [S]	The One and Only Lee Wiley	1964	30.00
STORYVILLE			
❑ STLP-312 [10]	Lee Wiley Sings Rodgers and Hart	1954	200.00
TOTEM			
❑ 1021	Lee Wiley on the Air	197?	12.00
❑ 1033	Lee Wiley on the Air, Vol. 2	198?	12.00

WILKERSON, DON

Number	Title	Yr	NM
BLUE NOTE			
❑ BLP-4121 [M]	Elder Don	1963	30.00
❑ BST-84121 [S]	Elder Don	1963	40.00
— With "New York, USA" address on label			
❑ BST-84121 [S]	Elder Don	1967	25.00
— With "A Division of Liberty Records" on label			
❑ BLP-4107 [M]	Preach, Brother!	1962	30.00
❑ BST-84107 [S]	Preach, Brother!	1962	40.00
— With "New York, USA" address on label			
❑ BST-84107 [S]	Preach, Brother!	1967	25.00
— With "A Division of Liberty Records" on label			
❑ BLP-4145 [M]	Shoutin'	1963	30.00
❑ BST-84145 [S]	Shoutin'	1963	40.00
— With "New York, USA" address on label			
❑ BST-84145 [S]	Shoutin'	1967	25.00
— With "A Division of Liberty Records" on label			
RIVERSIDE			
❑ RLP-332 [M]	Texas Twister	1960	40.00
❑ RLP-1186 [S]	Texas Twister	1960	40.00

WILKES, RAY

Number	Title	Yr	NM
INNER CITY			
❑ IC-1051	Dark Blue Man	197?	15.00

WILKINS, ERNIE

Number	Title	Yr	NM
EVEREST			
❑ LPBR-5077 [M]	Here Comes the Swingin' Mr. Wilkins	1959	30.00
❑ SDBR-1077 [S]	Here Comes the Swingin' Mr. Wilkins	1959	30.00
❑ LPBR-5104 [M]	The Big New Band of the '60s	1960	30.00
❑ SDBR-1104 [S]	The Big New Band of the '60s	1960	30.00
MAINSTREAM			
❑ MRL-305	Hard Mother Blues	1971	18.00
❑ MRL-806	Screaming Mothers	197?	18.00
RCA CAMDEN			
❑ CAL-543 [M]	The Greatest Songs Ever Swung	195?	18.00
SAVOY			
❑ MG-12044 [M]	Top Brass Featuring 5 Trumpets	1955	60.00
STEEPLECHASE			
❑ SCS-1190	Montreux	198?	15.00
STORYVILLE			
❑ 4051	Ernie Wilkins and the Almost Big Band	198?	12.00

WILKINS, JACK

Number	Title	Yr	NM
CHIAROSCURO			
❑ 156	Merge	1977	15.00
❑ 185	You Can't Live Without It	1978	15.00
MAINSTREAM			
❑ MRL-396	Windows	197?	15.00

WILKINS, LITTLE DAVID

Number	Title	Yr	NM
MCA			
❑ 2215	King of All the Taverns	1976	15.00
❑ 445	Little David Wilkins	1974	15.00
PLAYBOY			
❑ KZ35028	New Horizons	1977	15.00

WILKINSON TRI-CYCLE

Number	Title	Yr	NM
DATE			
❑ TES4016 [B]	Wilkinson Tri-Cycle	1969	60.00

WILL TO POWER

Number	Title	Yr	NM
EPIC			
❑ E46051	Journey Home	1991	15.00
❑ FE40940	Will to Power	1988	12.00

WILLET, SLIM

Number	Title	Yr	NM
AUDIO LAB			
❑ AL-1542 [M]	Slim Willet	1959	100.00

WILLETTE, BABY FACE

Number	Title	Yr	NM
ARGO			
❑ LP-749 [M]	Behind the 8-Ball	1965	30.00
❑ LPS-749 [S]	Behind the 8-Ball	1965	30.00
❑ LP-739 [M]	No Rock	1964	30.00
❑ LPS-739 [S]	No Rock	1964	30.00
BLUE NOTE			
❑ BLP-4068 [M]	Face to Face	1961	150.00
— With W. 63rd St. address on label			
❑ BST-84068 [S]	Face to Face	1961	120.00
— With W. 63rd St. address on label			
❑ BLP-4068 [M]	Face to Face	1963	30.00
— With "New York, USA" address on label			
❑ BST-84068 [S]	Face to Face	1963	25.00
— With "New York, USA" address on label			
❑ BST-84068 [S]	Face to Face	1967	18.00
— With "A Division of Liberty Records" on label			
❑ BLP-4084 [M]	Stop and Listen	1962	120.00
— With 61st St. address on label			
❑ BST-84084 [S]	Stop and Listen	1962	100.00
— With 61st St. address on label			
❑ BLP-4084 [M]	Stop and Listen	1963	30.00
— With "New York, USA" address on label			
❑ BST-84084 [S]	Stop and Listen	1963	25.00
— With "New York, USA" address on label			
❑ BST-84084 [S]	Stop and Listen	1967	18.00
— With "A Division of Liberty Records" on label			
CADET			
❑ LP-749 [M]	Behind the 8-Ball	1966	15.00
❑ LPS-749 [S]	Behind the 8-Ball	1966	18.00
❑ LPS-739 [S]	No Rock	1966	18.00
❑ LP-739 [M]	No Rock	1966	15.00

WILLIAMS, AL

Number	Title	Yr	NM
RENAISSANCE			
❑ 9565	Sandance	1976	15.00

WILLIAMS, ANDRE

Number	Title	Yr	NM
SDEG			
❑ 4020	Directly from the Streets	198?	12.00

WILLIAMS, ANDY

Number	Title	Yr	NM
ATCO			
❑ 90561	Close Enough for Love	1987	12.00
CADENCE			
❑ CLP1018 [M]	Andy Williams	1957	50.00
❑ CLP3002 [M]	Andy Williams	1958	50.00
— Cover depicts Andy standing			
❑ CLP3002 [M]	Andy Williams	1960	25.00
— Cover depicts Andy reclining			
❑ CLP3054 [M]	Andy Williams' Best	1962	25.00
❑ CLP25054 [S]	Andy Williams' Best	1962	30.00
❑ CLP3005 [M]	Andy Williams Sings Rodgers and Hammerstein	1958	40.00
— Cover depicts a café scene			
❑ CLP3005 [M]	Andy Williams Sings Rodgers and Hammerstein	1960	25.00
— Cover depicts a close-up of Andy's face			
❑ CLP3027 [M]	Andy Williams Sings… Steve Allen	1959	25.00
❑ CLP25027 [S]	Andy Williams Sings… Steve Allen	1959	18.00
❑ CLP3030 [M]	Lonely Street	1960	25.00
❑ CLP25030 [S]	Lonely Street	1960	30.00
❑ CLP3061 [M]	Million Seller Songs	1962	25.00
❑ CLP25061 [S]	Million Seller Songs	1962	30.00
❑ CLP3038 [M]	The Village of St. Bernadette	1960	25.00
❑ CLP25038 [S]	The Village of St. Bernadette	1960	30.00
❑ CLP3029 [M]	To You Sweetheart, Aloha	1959	25.00
❑ CLP25029 [S]	To You Sweetheart, Aloha	1959	30.00
❑ CLP3026 [M]	Two Time Winners	1959	25.00
❑ CLP25026 [S]	Two Time Winners	1959	30.00
— Black vinyl			
❑ CLP25026 [S]	Two Time Winners	1959	80.00
— Red vinyl			
❑ CLP3047 [M]	Under Paris Skies	1961	25.00
❑ CLP25047 [S]	Under Paris Skies	1961	30.00
CAPITOL			
❑ ST-12387	Greatest Love Classics	1984	12.00
COLUMBIA			
❑ KC31625	Alone Again (Naturally)	1972	12.00
❑ CQ31625 [Q]	Alone Again (Naturally)	1972	18.00
❑ PC34299	Andy	1976	12.00
❑ PCQ34299 [Q]	Andy	1976	18.00
❑ KCS9979	Andy Williams' Greatest Hits	1970	15.00
❑ KC32384	Andy Williams' Greatest Hits, Vol. 2	1973	12.00
❑ CL2383 [M]	Andy Williams' Newest Hits	1966	15.00
❑ CS9183 [S]	Andy Williams' Newest Hits	1966	18.00
❑ CL2680 [M]	Born Free	1967	15.00
❑ CS9480 [S]	Born Free	1967	18.00
❑ CL2324 [M]	Canadian Sunset	1965	15.00
— Reissue of Cadence 3054			
❑ CS9124 [S]	Canadian Sunset	1965	18.00
— Reissue of Cadence 25054			
❑ C33191	Christmas Present	1974	12.00
❑ CL1751 [M]	Danny Boy And Other Songs I Love to Sing	1962	18.00
❑ CS8551 [S]	Danny Boy And Other Songs I Love to Sing	1962	25.00
❑ CL2015 [M]	Days of Wine and Roses	1963	15.00
❑ CS8815 [S]	Days of Wine and Roses	1963	18.00
❑ CL2338 [M]	Dear Heart	1965	15.00
❑ CS9138 [S]	Dear Heart	1965	18.00
❑ CS9922	Get Together with Andy Williams	1969	18.00
— The Osmonds appear on three tracks			
❑ CS9844	Happy Heart	1969	15.00
❑ CL2323 [M]	Hawaiian Wedding Song	1965	15.00
— Reissue of Cadence 3029			
❑ CS9123 [S]	Hawaiian Wedding Song	1965	18.00
— Reissue of Cadence 25029			
❑ CS9662 [S]	Honey	1968	15.00
❑ CS2862 [M]	Honey	1968	25.00
❑ CL2533 [M]	In the Arms of Love	1967	15.00
❑ CS9333 [S]	In the Arms of Love	1967	18.00
❑ CL2766 [M]	Love, Andy	1967	18.00
❑ CS9566 [S]	Love, Andy	1967	15.00
❑ KC30497	Love Story	1971	12.00
❑ CQ30497 [Q]	Love Story	1972	18.00
❑ CG33597	Love Story/Born Free	1975	15.00
❑ KC31303	Love Theme from "The Godfather	1972	12.00
❑ CQ31303 [Q]	Love Theme from "The Godfather	1972	18.00
❑ CL2420 [M]	Merry Christmas	1965	15.00
❑ CS9220 [S]	Merry Christmas	1965	15.00
❑ CL1809 [M]	Moon River and Other Great Movie Themes	1962	15.00
❑ CS8609 [S]	Moon River and Other Great Movie Themes	1962	18.00
❑ CG33600	Moon River/Days of Wine and Roses	1975	15.00
❑ CS9896	Raindrops Keep Fallin' on My Head	1970	15.00
❑ KC32383	Solitaire	1973	12.00
❑ CL2171 [M]	The Academy Award Winning "Call Me Irresponsible" and Other Hits Songs from the Movies	1964	15.00
❑ CS8971 [S]	The Academy Award Winning "Call Me Irresponsible" and Other Hits Songs from the Movies	1964	18.00
❑ CL2087 [M]	The Andy Williams Christmas Album	1963	15.00
❑ CS8887 [S]	The Andy Williams Christmas Album	1963	15.00
❑ KC30105	The Andy Williams Show	1970	12.00
❑ GP5	The Andy Williams Sound of Music	1969	25.00
❑ CL2205 [M]	The Great Songs from "My Fair Lady" and Other Broadway Hits	1964	15.00
❑ CS9005 [S]	The Great Songs from "My Fair Lady" and Other Broadway Hits	1964	18.00
❑ CG31064	The Impossible Dream	1971	18.00
❑ PC33563	The Other Side of Me	1975	12.00
❑ CL2499 [M]	The Shadow of Your Smile	1966	15.00
❑ CS9299 [S]	The Shadow of Your Smile	1966	18.00
❑ KC32949	The Way We Were	1974	12.00
❑ CL2137 [M]	The Wonderful World of Andy Williams	1964	15.00
❑ CS8937 [S]	The Wonderful World of Andy Williams	1964	18.00
❑ CL1879 [M]	Warm and Willing	1962	15.00
❑ CS8679 [S]	Warm and Willing	1962	18.00
❑ KC33234	You Lay So Easy on My Mind	1974	12.00
❑ KC30797	You've Got a Friend	1971	12.00
❑ CQ30797 [Q]	You've Got a Friend	1971	18.00
COLUMBIA SPECIAL PRODUCTS			
❑ CSS966	Andy... & Company	1969	15.00
— Side 1 is Andy Williams; Side 2 has tracks by the Williams Brothers, Claudine Longet and the Osmond Brothers; sold only at Woolworth's			
HARMONY			
❑ KH30133	Andy Williams	1970	12.00
PAIR			
❑ PDL2-1103	The Best of Andy Williams	1986	15.00
TIME-LIFE			
❑ SLGD-11	Legendary Singers: Andy Williams	1986	18.00

WILLIAMS, ANN

Number	Title	Yr	NM
CHARLIE PARKER			
❑ PLP-807 [M]	First Time Out	1963	40.00
❑ PLP-807S [S]	First Time Out	1963	40.00

WILLIAMS, BETTY VAIDEN

Number	Title	Yr	NM
VANGUARD			
❑ VRS-9028 [M]	Folk Songs and Ballads of North Carolina	195?	30.00

WILLIAMS, BIG JOE

Number	Title	Yr	NM
BLUESVILLE			
❑ BVLP-1067 [M]	Big Joe Williams at Folk City	1963	100.00
— Blue label, silver print			
❑ BVLP-1067 [M]	Big Joe Williams at Folk City	1964	30.00
— Blue label with trident logo			
❑ BVLP-1056 [M]	Blues for 9 Strings	1962	100.00
— Blue label, silver print			
❑ BVLP-1056 [M]	Blues for 9 Strings	1964	30.00
— Blue label with trident logo			
❑ BVLP-1083 [M]	Studio Blues	1964	100.00
— Blue label, silver print			
❑ BVLP-1083 [M]	Studio Blues	1964	30.00
— Blue label with trident logo			

Number	Title	Yr	NM

DELMARK

❑ DL-604 [M]	Blues on Highway 49	1962	60.00
❑ DL-609 [M]	Starvin' Chain Blues	1966	30.00

FOLKWAYS

❑ FA-3820 [M]	Mississippi's Big Joe Williams	1962	30.00
❑ FAS-3820 [R]	Mississippi's Big Joe Williams	1962	25.00

MILESTONE

❑ 3001 [M]	Classic Delta Blues	1966	30.00

WILLIAMS, BILLY

CORAL

❑ CRL57184 [M]	Billy Williams	1957	60.00
❑ CRL57251 [M]	Half Sweet, Half Beat	1959	50.00
❑ CRL757251 [S]	Half Sweet, Half Beat	1959	80.00
❑ CRL57343 [M]	The Billy Williams Revue	1960	50.00
❑ CRL757343 [S]	The Billy Williams Revue	1960	60.00

MERCURY

❑ MG20317 [M]	Oh Yeah!	1958	60.00

MGM

❑ E-3400 [M]	The Billy Williams Quartet	1957	60.00

WING

❑ MGW-12131 [M]	Vote for Billy Williams	1959	40.00

WILLIAMS, BILLY DEE

PRESTIGE LIVELY ARTS

❑ 30001 [M]	Let's Misbehave	1962	40.00

WILLIAMS, BUSTER

BUDDAH

❑ BDS-5728	Dreams Come True	1980	15.00

MUSE

❑ MR-5171	Heartbeat	1979	15.00
❑ MR-5080	Pinnacle	1975	15.00
❑ MR-5101	Reflections	1976	15.00

WILLIAMS, CAMILLA

MGM

❑ E-156 [10]	Spirituals	1952	100.00

WILLIAMS, CHARLES

MAINSTREAM

❑ MRL-312	Charles Williams	1971	15.00
❑ MRL-381	Stickball	1973	15.00
❑ MRL-345	Trees and Grass and Things	1972	15.00

WILLIAMS, CLARENCE

BIOGRAPH

❑ 12038	Clarence Williams Volume 1, 1927-28	197?	12.00
❑ 12006	Clarence Williams Volume 1, 1927-29	197?	12.00

MCA

❑ 1349	Music Mann	198?	12.00

RIVERSIDE

❑ RLP-1033 [10]	Clarence Williams and Orchestra	1954	60.00

WILLIAMS, CLAUDE

CLASSIC JAZZ

❑ 135	Fiddler's Dream	198?	12.00

WILLIAMS, COOTIE

HALL OF FAME

❑ 602	The Big Challenge	197?	12.00

JARO

❑ JAM-5001 [M]	Around Midnight	1959	100.00
❑ JAS-8001 [S]	Around Midnight	1959	80.00

MOODSVILLE

❑ MVLP-27 [M]	The Solid Trumpet of Cootie Williams	1962	50.00
—Green label			
❑ MVLP-27 [M]	The Solid Trumpet of Cootie Williams	1965	30.00
—Blue label, trident logo at right			

PHOENIX

❑ 1	Cootie Williams Sextet and Orchestra	197?	12.00

RCA VICTOR

❑ LPM-1718 [M]	Cootie Williams in Hi-Fi	1958	80.00
❑ LSP-1718 [S]	Cootie Williams in Stereo	1958	150.00

WARWICK

❑ W-2027 [M]	Do Nothing Till You Hear From Me	1960	40.00
❑ W-2027ST [S]	Do Nothing Till You Hear From Me	1960	60.00

WILLIAMS, COOTIE/JIMMY PRESTON

ALLEGRO ELITE

❑ 4109 [10]	Rock 'N' Roll	195?	50.00

WILLIAMS, DANNY

UNITED ARTISTS

❑ UAL-3493 [M]	Magic Town	1966	18.00
❑ UAS-6493 [S]	Magic Town	1966	25.00
❑ UAL-3297 [M]	The Exciting Danny Williams	1963	18.00
❑ UAS-6297 [S]	The Exciting Danny Williams	1963	25.00
❑ UAL-3359 [M]	White on White	1964	18.00
❑ UAS-6359 [S]	White on White	1964	25.00
❑ UAL-3380 [M]	With You in Mind	1964	18.00
❑ UAS-6380 [S]	With You in Mind	1964	25.00

WILLIAMS, DAVID "FAT MAN"

NEW ORLEANS

❑ 7204	Apple Tree	197?	12.00

WILLIAMS, DENIECE

ARC

❑ FC37048	My Melody	1981	12.00
❑ PC37048	My Melody	198?	10.00
—Budget-line reissue			
❑ FC37952	Niecy	1982	12.00
❑ HC47952	Niecy	1983	50.00
—Half-speed mastered edition			
❑ PC37952	Niecy	198?	10.00
—Budget-line reissue			
❑ AS1432 [DJ]	Niecy	1982	30.00
—Promo-only picture disc			
❑ JC35568 [B]	When Love Comes Calling	1979	15.00

COLUMBIA

❑ FC44322	As Good As It Gets	1989	12.00
❑ FC40084	Hot on the Trail	1986	12.00
❑ FC38622 [B]	I'm So Proud	1983	12.00
❑ PC38622	I'm So Proud	198?	10.00
—Budget-line reissue			
❑ FC39366	Let's Hear It for the Boy	1984	12.00
❑ JC34911	Song Bird	1977	12.00
❑ PC34911	Song Bird	198?	10.00
—Budget-line reissue			
❑ PC34242	This Is Niecy	1976	15.00
—No bar code on cover			
❑ PC34242	This Is Niecy	198?	10.00
—Reissue with bar code on cover			
❑ FC40486	Water Under the Bridge	1987	12.00

MCA

❑ 6338	Special Love	1989	12.00

SPARROW

❑ SPR-1256	From the Beginning	1990	18.00
❑ ST-41039	So Glad I Know	198?	15.00
—Reissue of 1121?			
❑ SPR-1121	So Glad I Know	1986	15.00
❑ SPR-1174	Special Love	1989	15.00

WILLIAMS, DIANA

CAPITOL

❑ ST-11587	Diana Williams	1976	15.00

WILLIAMS, DON

ABC

❑ AA-1069 [B]	Expressions	1978	15.00

ABC/DOT

❑ DOSD-2018	Don Williams, Vol. 2	1974	15.00
—Reissue of JMI 4006			
❑ DOSD-2004	Don Williams, Vol. III	1974	15.00
❑ DOSD-2014	Don Williams, Volume One	1974	15.00
—Reissue of JMI 4004			
❑ DO-2035	Greatest Hits	1975	15.00
❑ DO-2049	Harmony	1976	15.00
❑ DO-2088	I'm Just a Country Boy	1977	15.00
❑ DO-2064	Visions	1976	15.00
❑ DOSD-2021	You're My Best Friend	1975	15.00

CAPITOL

❑ ST-12440	New Moves	1987	10.00
❑ C1-91444	Prime Cuts	1989	10.00
❑ CLT-48034	Traces	1988	10.00

JMI

❑ 4006	Don Williams, Volume 2	1974	25.00
❑ 4004	Don Williams, Volume One	1973	30.00

MCA

❑ 5493	Café Carolina	1984	12.00
❑ 5697	Don Williams Sings Bob McDill	1986	12.00
❑ 5210	Especially for You	1981	12.00
❑ 37233	Especially for You	198?	10.00
—Budget-line reissue			
❑ 3279	Expressions	1980	10.00
—Reissue of ABC 1069			
❑ 37135	Greatest Hits	198?	10.00
—Budget-line reissue			
❑ 5133	I Believe in You	1980	12.00
❑ 37234	I Believe in You	198?	10.00
—Budget-line reissue			
❑ 37232	I'm Just a Country Boy	198?	10.00
—Budget-line reissue			
❑ 5306	Listen to the Radio	1982	12.00
❑ 5803	Lovers and Best Friends	1986	12.00
❑ 3192	Portrait	1980	12.00
❑ 37231	Portrait	198?	10.00
—Budget-line reissue			
❑ 3096	The Best of Don Williams, Vol. 2	1979	12.00

❑ 37155	The Best of Don Williams, Vol. 2	198?	10.00
—Budget-line reissue			
❑ 5465	The Best of Don Williams, Vol. 3	1984	12.00
❑ 1442	The Best of Don Williams, Vol. 3	1985	10.00
—Budget-line reissue			
❑ 5671	The Best of Don Williams, Vol. 4	1985	12.00
❑ 37230	Visions	198?	10.00
—Budget-line reissue			
❑ 5407	Yellow Moon	1983	12.00

RCA

❑ 9656-1-R	One Good Well	1989	12.00
❑ R124814	True Love	1990	18.00
—BMG Music Service pressing; only US vinyl edition			

WILLIAMS, GEORGE

BRUNSWICK

❑ BL54020 [M]	The Fox	1957	50.00

RCA VICTOR

❑ LPM-1301 [M]	Rhythm Was His Business	1956	40.00
❑ LPM-1205 [M]	We Could Make Such Beautiful Music	1956	40.00

WILLIAMS, GRIFF

HINDSIGHT

❑ HSR-175	Griff Williams and His Orchestra 1946-1951	198?	12.00

WILLIAMS, HANK, AND HANK WILLIAMS, JR.

MGM

❑ E-4378 [M]	Again	1966	25.00
❑ SE-4378 [S]	Again	1966	30.00
❑ E-4276 [M]	Father and Son	1965	30.00
❑ SE-4276 [S]	Father and Son	1965	30.00
❑ 2SES-4865	Hank Williams: The Legend in Story and Song	1973	18.00
❑ M3HB4975	Insights Into Hank Williams in Song and Story	1974	18.00

WILLIAMS, HANK, JR., AND LOIS JOHNSON

MGM

❑ SE-4750	All for the Love of Sunshine	1971	25.00
❑ SE-4721	Removing the Shadow	1971	18.00
—The label has the word "Shadows" instead of "Shadow"			
❑ SE-4857	Send Me Some Lovin'/Whole Lotta Lovin'	1972	25.00

WILLIAMS, HANK, JR.

CAPRICORN

❑ W1-26806	Maverick	1992	25.00
—Columbia House edition (only U.S. vinyl release)			

ELEKTRA

❑ 6E-194	Family Tradition	1979	15.00
❑ 6E-278	Habits Old and New	1980	12.00
❑ 60193	Hank Williams, Jr.'s, Greatest Hits	1982	12.00
❑ 60100	High Notes	1982	12.00
❑ 5E-538	One Night Stands	1982	12.00
—Reissue			
❑ 6E-330	Rowdy	1981	12.00
❑ 60223 [B]	Strong Stuff	1983	18.00
❑ 5E-539	The New South	1982	12.00
—Reissue			
❑ 5E-535	The Pressure Is On	1981	12.00
❑ 6E-237	Whiskey Bent and Hell Bound	1979	12.00

MGM

❑ MG-1-5020	14 Greatest Hits	1976	15.00
❑ SE-4862	After You/Pride's Not Hard to Swallow	1973	15.00
❑ SE-4540	A Time to Sing	1968	30.00
❑ E-4316 [M]	Ballads of the Hills and Plains	1965	25.00
❑ SE-4316 [S]	Ballads of the Hills and Plains	1965	30.00
❑ E-4344 [M]	Blues My Name	1966	25.00
❑ SE-4344 [S]	Blues My Name	1966	30.00
❑ T-90695 [M]	Blues My Name	1966	30.00
—Capitol Record Club edition			
❑ ST-90695 [S]	Blues My Name	1966	30.00
—Capitol Record Club edition			
❑ M3G-4988	Bocephus	1974	15.00
❑ E-4391 [M]	Country Shadows	1966	25.00
❑ SE-4391 [S]	Country Shadows	1966	30.00
❑ T-90925 [M]	Country Shadows	1966	30.00
—Capitol Record Club edition			
❑ SE-4843	Eleven Roses	1972	15.00
❑ MG-1-5009	Hank Williams, Jr., and Friends	1975	40.00
❑ SE-4675	Hank Williams, Jr., Singing My Songs (Johnny Cash)	1970	18.00
❑ GAS-119	Hank Williams, Jr. (Golden Archive Series)	1970	18.00
❑ SE-4656	Hank Williams, Jr.'s Greatest Hits	1970	18.00
❑ SE-4822	Hank Williams, Jr.'s Greatest Hits, Volume 2	1972	15.00
❑ SE-4774	I've Got a Right to Cry/They All Used to Belong to Me	1971	18.00
❑ SE-4906	Just Pickin' -- No Singin'	1973	15.00

Number	Title	Yr	NM
❑ SE-4644	Live at Cobo Hall, Detroit	1969	25.00
❑ M3G-4971	Living Proof	1974	15.00
❑ SE-4559	Luke the Drifter, Jr.	1969	25.00
❑ SE-4632	Luke the Drifter, Jr. (Vol. 2)	1969	25.00
❑ SE-4673	Luke the Drifter, Jr. (Vol. 3)	1970	18.00
❑ E-4428 [M]	My Own Way	1967	25.00
❑ SE-4428 [S]	My Own Way	1967	30.00
❑ E-4527 [M]	My Songs	1968	40.00
❑ SE-4527 [S]	My Songs	1968	30.00
❑ E-4213 [M]	Sings the Songs of Hank Williams	1964	25.00
❑ SE-4213 [S]	Sings the Songs of Hank Williams	1964	30.00
❑ SE-4621	Songs My Father Left Me	1969	25.00
❑ SE-4657	Sunday Morning	1970	18.00
❑ SE-4798	Sweet Dreams	1972	15.00
—With the Mike Curb Congregation			
❑ E-4513 [M]	The Best of Hank Williams, Jr.	1967	25.00
❑ SE-4513 [S]	The Best of Hank Williams, Jr.	1967	30.00
❑ SE-4936	The Last Love Song	1973	15.00
❑ E-4260 [M]	Your Cheatin' Heart	1964	25.00
❑ SE-4260 [S]	Your Cheatin' Heart	1964	30.00

PAIR

Number	Title	Yr	NM
❑ PDL2-1164	I'm Walkin'	1987	15.00

POLYDOR

Number	Title	Yr	NM
❑ 825091-1	14 Greatest Hits	1985	10.00
❑ 833069-1	Blues My Name	1987	10.00
❑ 833070-1	Eleven Roses	1987	10.00
❑ 831575-1	Hank Williams, Jr., and Friends	1987	15.00
❑ 811903-1	Hank Williams, Jr.'s Greatest Hits	1983	10.00
❑ 811906-1	Hank Williams, Jr.'s Greatest Hits, Volume 2	1983	10.00
❑ 811902-1	Live at Cobo Hall, Detroit	1983	10.00
—Reissue			
❑ 835132-1	Standing in the Shadows	1988	10.00

WARNER BROS.

Number	Title	Yr	NM
❑ R120612	America (The Way I See It)	1990	25.00
—BMG Music Service edition (no regular vinyl release)			
❑ 25593	Born to Boogie	1987	10.00
❑ 6E-194	Family Tradition	1983	10.00
❑ 25267	Five-O	1985	12.00
❑ 25834	Greatest Hits III	1989	10.00
❑ 25328	Greatest Hits -- Volume 2	1985	10.00
❑ 6E-278	Habits Old and New	1983	10.00
❑ 25538	Hank "Live	1987	10.00
❑ 60193	Hank Williams, Jr.'s, Greatest Hits	1983	10.00
❑ 60100	High Notes	1983	10.00
❑ 26090	Lone Wolf	1990	15.00
❑ 25088	Major Moves	1984	12.00
❑ 23924	Man of Steel	1983	12.00
❑ 25412	Montana Café	1986	10.00
❑ 5E-538	One Night Stands	1983	10.00
❑ BS2988	One Night Stands	1977	15.00
❑ R160351	Pure Hank	1991	25.00
—BMG Music Service edition (no regular vinyl release)			
❑ 6E-330	Rowdy	1983	10.00
❑ 60223 [B]	Strong Stuff	1983	12.00
❑ 25514	The Early Years	1984	15.00
❑ PRO-A-2052 [DJ]	The Hank Williams, Jr., Interview	1983	30.00
❑ 5E-539	The New South	1983	10.00
❑ BS3127	The New South	1977	15.00
❑ 5E-535	The Pressure Is On	1983	10.00
❑ 6E-237	Whiskey Bent and Hell Bound	1983	10.00
❑ 25725	Wild Streak	1988	10.00

WILLIAMS, HANK

CANDELITE MUSIC

Number	Title	Yr	NM
❑ CMI-1951/2	The Golden Dream of Hank Williams	1976	18.00

COUNTRY MUSIC FOUNDATION

Number	Title	Yr	NM
❑ CMF-006	Just Me and My Guitar	198?	12.00
❑ CMF-007	The First Recordings	198?	12.00

METRO

Number	Title	Yr	NM
❑ M-509 [M]	Hank Williams	1966	25.00
❑ MS-509 [R]	Hank Williams	1966	15.00
❑ M-547 [M]	Mr. and Mrs. Hank Williams	1966	25.00
❑ MS-547 [R]	Mr. and Mrs. Hank Williams	1966	15.00
❑ M-602 [M]	The Immortal Hank Williams	1967	25.00
❑ MS-602 [R]	The Immortal Hank Williams	1967	15.00

MGM

Number	Title	Yr	NM
❑ E-4040 [M]	14 More of Hank Williams' Greatest Hits -- Vol. II	1962	40.00
❑ SE-4040 [R]	14 More of Hank Williams' Greatest Hits -- Vol. II	1963	18.00
—Black label			
❑ E-4140 [M]	14 More of Hank Williams' Greatest Hits (Volume 3)	1963	30.00
❑ SE-4140 [R]	14 More of Hank Williams' Greatest Hits (Volume 3)	1963	18.00
—Black label			
❑ SE-4140 [R]	14 More of Hank Williams' Greatest Hits (Volume 3)	1968	15.00
—Blue and gold label			
❑ SE-4755-2	24 Greatest Hits	1971	18.00
❑ MG-2-5401	24 Greatest Hits, Volume 2	197?	18.00
❑ SE240-2	24 Karat Hits	1969	30.00
❑ 3E-2 [M]	36 of His Greatest Hits	1957	300.00
—Yellow labels			
❑ 3E-2 [M]	36 of His Greatest Hits	1960	150.00
—Black labels			
❑ M3G-4954	Archetypes	1974	15.00
❑ E-4138 [M]	Beyond the Sunset	1963	30.00
❑ SE-4138 [R]	Beyond the Sunset	1963	18.00
—Black label			
❑ SE-4651	Essential Hank Williams	1969	15.00
❑ E-3928 [M]	First, Last and Always	1961	40.00
—Reissue of E-3605			
❑ SE-3928 [R]	First, Last and Always	1968	15.00
—Blue and gold label			
❑ MG-1-5019	Hank Williams, Sr., Live at the Grand Old Opry	1976	15.00
❑ E-4529 [M]	Hank Williams and Strings, Volume 3	1968	40.00
❑ SE-4529 [S]	Hank Williams and Strings, Volume 3	1968	25.00
❑ E-203 [10]	Hank Williams as Luke the Drifter	1953	500.00
❑ E-3267 [M]	Hank Williams as Luke the Drifter	1955	100.00
—Yellow label			
❑ E-3267 [M]	Hank Williams as Luke the Drifter	1960	40.00
—Black label			
❑ E-3927 [M]	Hank Williams as Luke the Drifter	1961	40.00
—Reissue of E-3267			
❑ SE-3927 [R]	Hank Williams as Luke the Drifter	1968	15.00
—Blue and gold label			
❑ E-3918 [M]	Hank Williams' Greatest Hits	1961	40.00
❑ SE-3918 [R]	Hank Williams' Greatest Hits	1963	25.00
—Black label			
❑ SE-3918 [R]	Hank Williams' Greatest Hits	1968	15.00
—Blue and gold label			
❑ SE-4040 [R]	Hank Williams' Greatest Hits, Volume 2	1968	15.00
—Blue and gold label			
❑ E-4576 [M]	Hank Williams in the Beginning	1968	40.00
❑ SE-4576 [R]	Hank Williams in the Beginning	1968	18.00
❑ E-3923 [M]	Hank Williams Lives Again	1961	40.00
—Reissue of E-3272 with new title			
❑ SE-3923 [R]	Hank Williams Lives Again	1968	15.00
—Blue and gold label			
❑ E-3999 [M]	Hank Williams on Stage Recorded Live	1962	40.00
—Note revised title			
❑ SE-3999 [R]	Hank Williams on Stage Recorded Live	1968	15.00
—Blue and gold label			
❑ E-107 [10]	Hank Williams Sings	1952	500.00
❑ 3E-4 [M]	Hank Williams Sings 36 More of His Greatest Hits	1958	250.00
—Yellow labels			
❑ 3E-4 [M]	Hank Williams Sings 36 More of His Greatest Hits	1960	150.00
—Black labels			
❑ E-242 [10]	Honky Tonkin'	1954	500.00
❑ E-3412 [M]	Honky Tonkin'	1957	100.00
—Yellow label			
❑ E-3412 [M]	Honky Tonkin'	1960	50.00
—Black label			
❑ E-3926 [M]	I'm Blue Inside	1961	40.00
—Reissue of E-3330			
❑ SE-3926 [R]	I'm Blue Inside	1968	15.00
—Blue and gold label			
❑ E-243 [10]	I Saw the Light	1954	500.00
❑ E-3331 [M]	I Saw the Light	1956	300.00
—Yellow label; green cover			
❑ E-3331 [M]	I Saw the Light	1959	100.00
—Yellow label; church on cover			
❑ E-3331 [M]	I Saw the Light	1960	40.00
—Black label			
❑ SE-3331 [R]	I Saw the Light	1968	15.00
—Blue and gold label			
❑ E-4481 [M]	I Won't Be Home No More	1967	30.00
❑ SE-4481 [S]	I Won't Be Home No More	1967	25.00
—Black label			
❑ SE-4481 [S]	I Won't Be Home No More	1968	18.00
—Blue and gold label			
❑ E-4300 [M]	Kaw-Liga and Other Humorous Songs	1965	30.00
❑ SE-4300 [R]	Kaw-Liga and Other Humorous Songs	1965	18.00
—Black label			
❑ SE-4300 [R]	Kaw-Liga and Other Humorous Songs	1968	15.00
—Blue and gold label			
❑ E-3924 [M]	Let Me Sing a Blue Song	1961	40.00
—Reissue of E-3560			
❑ SE-3924 [R]	Let Me Sing a Blue Song	1968	15.00
—Blue and gold label			
❑ SE-4680	Life to Legend	1970	15.00
❑ E-4254 [M]	Lost Highway (and Other Folk Ballads)	1964	40.00
❑ SE-4254 [R]	Lost Highway (and Other Folk Ballads)	1964	25.00
—Black label			
❑ SE-4254 [R]	Lost Highway (and Other Folk Ballads)	1968	15.00
—Blue and gold label			
❑ E-202 [10]	Memorial Album	1953	500.00
❑ E-3272 [M]	Memorial Album	1955	100.00
—Yellow label			
❑ E-3272 [M]	Memorial Album	1960	40.00
—Black label			
❑ E-3272 [M]	Memorial Album	1968	25.00
—Blue and gold label			
❑ E-168 [10]	Moanin' the Blues	1952	500.00
❑ E-3330 [M]	Moanin' the Blues	1956	100.00
—Yellow label			
❑ E-3330 [M]	Moanin' the Blues	1960	40.00
—Black label			
❑ E-4429 [M]	More Hank Williams and Strings	1966	25.00
❑ SE-4429 [S]	More Hank Williams and Strings	1966	30.00
—Black label			
❑ SE-4429 [S]	More Hank Williams and Strings	1968	18.00
—Blue and gold label			
❑ E-4380 [M]	Movin' on -- Luke the Drifter	1966	30.00
❑ SE-4380 [R]	Movin' on -- Luke the Drifter	1968	15.00
—Blue and gold label			
❑ ST-90884 [R]	Movin' on -- Luke the Drifter	1968	18.00
—Capitol Record Club edition; blue and gold label			
❑ E-3999 [M]	On Stage! Hank Williams Recorded Live	1962	60.00
❑ SE-3999 [R]	On Stage! Hank Williams Recorded Live	196?	25.00
—Black label			
❑ E-4109 [M]	On Stage Volume II/Hank Williams	1963	40.00
❑ SE-4109 [R]	On Stage Volume II/Hank Williams	1963	25.00
—Black label			
❑ SE-4109 [R]	On Stage Volume II/Hank Williams	1968	15.00
—Blue and gold label			
❑ E-291 [10]	Ramblin' Man	1954	500.00
❑ E-3219 [M]	Ramblin' Man	1955	200.00
—Yellow label			
❑ E-3219 [M]	Ramblin' Man	1960	40.00
—Black label			
❑ PRO-912 [DJ]	Reflections of Those Who Loved Him	1975	300.00
—Promo-only box set			
❑ E-3560 [M]	Sing Me a Blue Song	1957	100.00
—Yellow label			
❑ E-3560 [M]	Sing Me a Blue Song	1960	50.00
—Black label			
❑ E-4267-4 [M]	The Hank Williams Story	1965	60.00
❑ E-3605 [M]	The Immortal Hank Williams	1958	100.00
—Yellow label			
❑ E-3605 [M]	The Immortal Hank Williams	1960	40.00
—Black label			
❑ E-4377 [M]	The Legend Lives Anew -- Hank Williams with Strings	1966	25.00
❑ SE-4377 [S]	The Legend Lives Anew -- Hank Williams with Strings	1966	30.00
—Black label			
❑ SE-4377 [S]	The Legend Lives Anew -- Hank Williams with Strings	1968	18.00
—Blue and gold label			
❑ ST-91115 [S]	The Legend Lives Anew -- Hank Williams with Strings	1968	25.00
—Capitol Record Club edition; blue and gold label			
❑ E-3803 [M]	The Lonesome Sound of Hank Williams	1960	40.00
❑ E-3955 [M]	The Spirit of Hank Williams	1961	40.00
❑ SE-3955 [R]	The Spirit of Hank Williams	1968	15.00
—Blue and gold label			
❑ E-3733 [M]	The Unforgettable Hank Williams	1959	100.00
—Yellow label			
❑ E-3733 [M]	The Unforgettable Hank Williams	1960	40.00
—Black label			
❑ SE-3733 [R]	The Unforgettable Hank Williams	1968	15.00
—Blue and gold label			
❑ T-90511 [M]	The Very Best of Hank Williams	1965	40.00
—Capitol Record Club edition			
❑ ST-90511 [R]	The Very Best of Hank Williams	1965	25.00
—Capitol Record Club edition			
❑ E-4168 [M]	The Very Best of Hank Williams	1963	30.00
❑ SE-4168 [R]	The Very Best of Hank Williams	1963	18.00
—Black label			
❑ SE-4168 [R]	The Very Best of Hank Williams	1968	15.00
—Blue and gold label			
❑ E-4227 [M]	The Very Best of Hank Williams, Volume 2	1964	30.00
❑ SE-4227 [R]	The Very Best of Hank Williams, Volume 2	1964	18.00
—Black label			
❑ SE-4227 [R]	The Very Best of Hank Williams, Volume 2	1968	15.00
—Blue and gold label			
❑ E-3850 [M]	Wait for the Light to Shine	1960	40.00
❑ SE-3850 [R]	Wait for the Light to Shine	1968	15.00
—Blue and gold label			

Number	Title	Yr	NM
❑ E-3925 [M]	Wanderin' Around	1961	40.00

—Reissue of E-3219

Number	Title	Yr	NM
❑ SE-3925 [R]	Wanderin' Around	1968	15.00

—Blue and gold label

POLYDOR

Number	Title	Yr	NM
❑ 823293-1	24 Greatest Hits	1984	15.00
❑ 823294-1	24 Greatest Hits, Volume 2	1984	15.00
❑ 821233-1	40 Greatest Hits	1984	18.00
❑ 831574-1	Beyond the Sunset	1987	12.00
❑ 823291-1	Hank Williams' Greatest Hits	1984	10.00
❑ 831634-1	Hey, Good Lookin'	1987	12.00
❑ 825548-1	I Ain't Got Nothin' But Time	1985	12.00
❑ 825557-1	I'm So Lonesome I Could Cry	1986	12.00
❑ 833752-1	I Won't Be Home No More	1988	12.00
❑ 833749-1	Let's Turn Back the Years	1988	12.00
❑ 831633-1	Long Gone Lonesome Blues	1987	12.00
❑ 825554-1	Lost Highway	1986	12.00
❑ 825551-1	Lovesick Blues	1985	12.00
❑ 825531-1	On the Air	1985	12.00
❑ 823695-1	Rare Takes and Radio Cuts	1984	12.00
❑ 823292-1	The Very Best of Hank Williams	1984	10.00
❑ SE-4168	The Very Best of Hank Williams	1976	10.00

—Reissue of MGM SE-4168

TIME-LIFE

Number	Title	Yr	NM
❑ TLCW-01	Country and Western Classics	1981	30.00
❑ STW-118	Country Music	1981	12.00

WILLIAMS, HANK /ROY ACUFF

LAMB AND LION

Number	Title	Yr	NM
❑ LL-706	Hank Williams, Sr./Roy Acuff "Collector's Item!"	197?	40.00

—Sides 1-4 are reissues of Hank Williams; side 5-6 are Roy Acuff

WILLIAMS, HERBIE

WORKSHOP JAZZ

Number	Title	Yr	NM
❑ WSJ-216 [M]	The Soul and Sound of Herbie Williams	1963	60.00

WILLIAMS, JAMES

CONCORD JAZZ

Number	Title	Yr	NM
❑ CJ-104	Everything I Love	1980	12.00
❑ CJ-140	Images (Of the Things to Come)	1981	12.00
❑ CJ-192	The Arioso Touch	1982	12.00

EMARCY

Number	Title	Yr	NM
❑ 834368-1	Magical Trio 2	1989	15.00
❑ 832859-1	The Magical Trio	1988	12.00

SUNNYSIDE

Number	Title	Yr	NM
❑ SSC-1007	Alter Ego	1985	12.00
❑ SSC-1012	Progress Report	1986	12.00

ZIM

Number	Title	Yr	NM
❑ 2005	Flying Colors	1977	15.00

WILLIAMS, JASON D.

RCA

Number	Title	Yr	NM
❑ 9782-1-R	Tore Up	1989	15.00

WILLIAMS, JESSICA

ADELPHI

Number	Title	Yr	NM
❑ 5005	Portraits	197?	18.00
❑ 5003	The Portal of Antrim	1976	18.00

BLACKHAWK

Number	Title	Yr	NM
❑ BKH-51301	Nothin' But the Truth	1986	12.00

CLEAN CUTS

Number	Title	Yr	NM
❑ 703	Orgonomic Music	198?	15.00
❑ 701	Rivers of Memory	1979	15.00
❑ 706	Update	1982	15.00

WILLIAMS, JOE

BLUEBIRD

Number	Title	Yr	NM
❑ 6464-1-RB	The Overwhelming Joe Williams	1988	12.00

BLUE NOTE

Number	Title	Yr	NM
❑ BST-84355	Worth Waiting For	1970	18.00

DELOS

Number	Title	Yr	NM
❑ DMS-4001	Nothin' But the Blues	1984	15.00

FANTASY

Number	Title	Yr	NM
❑ F-9441	Joe Williams Live	1974	15.00
❑ OJC-438	Joe Williams Live	1990	12.00

FORUM

Number	Title	Yr	NM
❑ F-9033 [M]	That Kind of Woman	196?	15.00
❑ SF-9033 [S]	That Kind of Woman	196?	18.00

JASS

Number	Title	Yr	NM
❑ J-6	Chains of Love	198?	12.00

PAUSA

Number	Title	Yr	NM
❑ PR9008	Worth Waiting For	1982	12.00

RCA VICTOR

Number	Title	Yr	NM
❑ LPM-2762 [M]	Joe Williams at Newport '63	1963	30.00
❑ LSP-2762 [S]	Joe Williams at Newport '63	1963	30.00
❑ LPM-2713 [M]	Jump for Joy	1963	30.00
❑ LSP-2713 [S]	Jump for Joy	1963	30.00
❑ LPM-2879 [M]	Me and the Blues	1964	30.00
❑ LSP-2879 [S]	Me and the Blues	1964	30.00
❑ LPM-3461 [M]	The Exciting Joe Williams	1965	25.00
❑ LSP-3461 [S]	The Exciting Joe Williams	1965	30.00
❑ LPM-3433 [M]	The Song Is You	1965	25.00
❑ LSP-3433 [S]	The Song Is You	1965	30.00

REGENT

Number	Title	Yr	NM
❑ MG-6002 [M]	Everyday	1956	50.00

ROULETTE

Number	Title	Yr	NM
❑ R-52005 [M]	A Man Ain't Supposed to Cry	1958	30.00
❑ SR-52005 [S]	A Man Ain't Supposed to Cry	1958	40.00
❑ SR-42016	A Man Ain't Supposed to Cry	1968	18.00
❑ R-52071 [M]	Have a Good Time with Joe Williams	1961	30.00
❑ SR-52071 [S]	Have a Good Time with Joe Williams	1961	40.00
❑ R-52030 [M]	Joe Williams Sings About You!	1959	30.00
❑ SR-52030 [S]	Joe Williams Sings About You!	1959	40.00
❑ R-52105 [M]	New Kind of Love	1964	30.00
❑ SR-52105 [S]	New Kind of Love	1964	30.00
❑ R-52102 [M]	One Is a Lonesome Number	1963	30.00
❑ SR-52102 [S]	One Is a Lonesome Number	1963	30.00
❑ R-52066 [M]	Sentimental and Melancholy	1961	30.00
❑ SR-52066 [S]	Sentimental and Melancholy	1961	40.00
❑ R-52085 [M]	Swingin' Night at Birdland	1962	30.00
❑ SR-52085 [S]	Swingin' Night at Birdland	1962	30.00
❑ R-52039 [M]	That Kind of Woman	1960	30.00
❑ SR-52039 [S]	That Kind of Woman	1960	40.00
❑ R-52069 [M]	Together	1961	30.00
❑ SR-52069 [S]	Together	1961	40.00

—With Harry "Sweets" Edison

SAVOY

Number	Title	Yr	NM
❑ MG-12216 [M]	Joe Williams Sings	196?	18.00

—Reissue of Regent LP

SAVOY JAZZ

Number	Title	Yr	NM
❑ SJL-1140	Everyday I Have the Blues	198?	12.00

SHEBA

Number	Title	Yr	NM
❑ 102	Heart and Soul	197?	15.00

SOLID STATE

Number	Title	Yr	NM
❑ SM-17008 [M]	Presenting Joe Williams and the Jazz Orchestra	1967	30.00
❑ SS-18008 [S]	Presenting Joe Williams and the Jazz Orchestra	1967	25.00
❑ SS-18015 [S]	Something Old, New and Blue	1968	25.00

TEMPONIC

Number	Title	Yr	NM
❑ 29561	With Love	197?	18.00

VERVE

Number	Title	Yr	NM
❑ 833236-1	Every Night	1987	12.00
❑ 837932-1	In Good Company	1989	15.00

WILLIAMS, JOHN

EMARCY

Number	Title	Yr	NM
❑ MG-26047 [10]	John Williams	1955	100.00
❑ MG-36061 [M]	John Williams Trio	1956	50.00

WILLIAMS, JOHN TOWNER

BETHLEHEM

Number	Title	Yr	NM
❑ BCP-6025 [M]	World on a String	1958	50.00

WILLIAMS, KEITH

EDISON INTERNATIONAL

Number	Title	Yr	NM
❑ SDP-501 [S]	Big Band Jazz Themes	1960	30.00
❑ 501 [M]	Big Band Jazz Themes	1960	25.00

LIBERTY

Number	Title	Yr	NM
❑ LRP-3040 [M]	The Dazzling Sound	1957	30.00

WILLIAMS, LARRY

CHESS

Number	Title	Yr	NM
❑ LP-1457 [M]	Larry Williams	1961	200.00

OKEH

Number	Title	Yr	NM
❑ OKM-12123 [M]	Larry Williams' Greatest Hits	1967	30.00
❑ OKS-14123 [S]	Larry Williams' Greatest Hits	1967	40.00

SPECIALTY

Number	Title	Yr	NM
❑ SP-7002	Bad Boy	1990	25.00
❑ SP-2109 [M]	Here's Larry Williams	1959	200.00

—Original pressing on thick vinyl with no copyright information on back cover

Number	Title	Yr	NM
❑ SP-2109 [M]	Here's Larry Williams	198?	12.00

—Reissue with thinner vinyl and copyright information on back

WILLIAMS, LAWTON

MEGA

Number	Title	Yr	NM
❑ 1004	Between Truck Stops	1971	15.00

WILLIAMS, LENNY

ABC

Number	Title	Yr	NM
❑ AB-1023	Choosing You	1977	12.00
❑ AA-1073	Spark of Love	1978	12.00

MCA

Number	Title	Yr	NM
❑ 5147	Let's Do It Today	1980	12.00
❑ 3155	Love Current	1979	12.00
❑ 5253	Taking Chances	1982	12.00

MOTOWN

Number	Title	Yr	NM
❑ M6-843	Rise Sleeping Beauty	1975	15.00

WILLIAMS, LEONA

HICKORY

Number	Title	Yr	NM
❑ LPS-151	That Williams Girl	1971	18.00
❑ LPS-165	The Best of Leona Williams	1972	18.00

MCA

Number	Title	Yr	NM
❑ 2212	San Quentin's First Lady	1976	15.00

MERCURY

Number	Title	Yr	NM
❑ 822424-1	Someday When Things Are Good	1984	10.00

WILLIAMS, LOIS

STARDAY

Number	Title	Yr	NM
❑ SLP-448	A Girl Named Sam	1970	25.00

WILLIAMS, LUCINDA

FOLKWAYS

Number	Title	Yr	NM
❑ 31067	Happy Woman Blues	1980	150.00

—As "Lucinda

Number	Title	Yr	NM
❑ 31066	Ramblin' on My Mind	1979	200.00

—As "Lucinda

LOST HIGHWAY

Number	Title	Yr	NM
❑ B0002368-01	Live @ the Fillmore	2005	25.00
❑ B0006398-01 [B]	West	2007	18.00
❑ 088170255-1	World Without Tears	2003	18.00

ROUGH TRADE

Number	Title	Yr	NM
❑ 66 [EP]	Passionate Kisses	1989	12.00

SMITHSONIAN/FOLKWAYS

Number	Title	Yr	NM
❑ 40003	Happy Woman Blues	1990	15.00

—Reissue

WILLIAMS, MARY LOU, AND CECIL TAYLOR

PABLO LIVE

Number	Title	Yr	NM
❑ 2620108	Embraced	1978	18.00

WILLIAMS, MARY LOU, AND DON BYAS

GNP CRESCENDO

Number	Title	Yr	NM
❑ GNP-9030	Mary Lou Williams and Don Byas	197?	12.00

WILLIAMS, MARY LOU, AND DON BYAS/BUCK CLAYTON AND ALIX COMBELLE

STORYVILLE

Number	Title	Yr	NM
❑ STLP-906 [M]	Messin' 'Round in Montmarte	1956	50.00

WILLIAMS, MARY LOU

ASCH

Number	Title	Yr	NM
❑ ALP-345 [10]	Mary Lou Williams Trio	1950	200.00

ATLANTIC

Number	Title	Yr	NM
❑ ALR-114 [10]	Piano Panorama, Volume 2	1951	120.00

AUDIOPHILE

Number	Title	Yr	NM
❑ AP-8 [M]	Roll 'Em	1988	12.00

CHIAROSCURO

Number	Title	Yr	NM
❑ 103	From the Heart	197?	15.00
❑ 146	Live at the Cookery	197?	15.00

CIRCLE

Number	Title	Yr	NM
❑ 412 [10]	Piano Contempo	1951	120.00

CONCERT HALL JAZZ

Number	Title	Yr	NM
❑ 1007 [10]	A Keyboard History	1955	50.00

CONTEMPORARY

Number	Title	Yr	NM
❑ C-2507 [10]	Piano '53	1953	100.00

EMARCY

Number	Title	Yr	NM
❑ MG-26033 [10]	Mary Lou	1954	100.00

FOLKWAYS

Number	Title	Yr	NM
❑ FS-2860 [M]	History of Jazz	197?	15.00
❑ FS-32843 [R]	Mary Lou Williams	196?	15.00
❑ FS-2843 [M]	Mary Lou Williams	196?	18.00
❑ FP-32 [10]	Rehearsal -- Jazz Session/ Footnotes to Jazz, Vol. 3	1951	100.00
❑ FJ-2966	The Asch Recordings 1944-1947	197?	18.00
❑ FJ-32844	Zodiac Suite	196?	15.00

GNP CRESCENDO

Number	Title	Yr	NM
❑ GNPS-9029	Mary Lou Williams in London	198?	12.00

INNER CITY

Number	Title	Yr	NM
❑ IC-2043	Free Spirits	197?	18.00

JAZZTONE

Number	Title	Yr	NM
❑ J-1206 [M]	A Keyboard History	1955	40.00

KING

Number	Title	Yr	NM
❑ 295-85 [10]	Progressive Piano Stylings	1953	150.00

MARY

Number	Title	Yr	NM
❑ 32843 [M]	Black Christ of the Andes	1964	30.00
❑ 32843 [S]	Black Christ of the Andes	1964	30.00
❑ 101	Black Christ of the Andes	197?	18.00

—Reissue with new number

Number	Title	Yr	NM
❑ 102	Mary Lou's Mass	197?	18.00
❑ 282489 [M]	Music for Peace	1964	30.00
❑ 282489 [S]	Music for Peace	1964	30.00
❑ 103	Zoning	1974	18.00

Number	Title	Yr	NM
PABLO			
❏ 2310819	My Mama Pinned a Rose	1978	15.00
❏ 2405412	The Best of Mary Lou Williams	198?	12.00
PABLO LIVE			
❏ 2308218	Solo Recital/Montreux Jazz Festival 1978	1979	15.00
STEEPLECHASE			
❏ SCS-1043	Free Spirits	198?	15.00
STINSON			
❏ SLP-29 [10]	Jazz Variation	1950	150.00
❏ SLP-24 [M]	Mary Lou Williams	195?	30.00
❏ SLP-24 [10]	Mary Lou Williams	1950	150.00

WILLIAMS, MARY LOU/JUTTA HIPP

Number	Title	Yr	NM
SAVOY JAZZ			
❏ SJL-1202	First Ladies of Jazz	1990	15.00

WILLIAMS, MARY LOU/RALPH BURNS

Number	Title	Yr	NM
JAZZTONE			
❏ J-1255 [M]	Composers – Pianists	1956	40.00

WILLIAMS, MASON

Number	Title	Yr	NM
AMERICAN GRAMAPHONE			
❏ AG-800	Classical Gas	1987	12.00
— With Mannheim Steamroller			
EVEREST			
❏ 3265	Listening Matter	1969	15.00
FLYING FISH			
❏ FF-059	Fresh Fish	1978	12.00
VEE JAY			
❏ VJ-1103 [M]	Them Poems and Things	1964	25.00
❏ VJS-1103 [S]	Them Poems and Things	1964	30.00
WARNER BROS.			
❏ WS1838	Hand Made	1970	15.00
❏ WS1788	Music by Mason Williams	1969	15.00
❏ WS1941	Sharepickers	1971	15.00
❏ WS1776	The Mason Williams Ear Show	1968	15.00
❏ WS1729 [S]	The Mason Williams Phonograph Record	1968	15.00
— Green label with "W7" logo			
❏ WS1729	The Mason Williams Phonograph Record	1973	10.00
— "Burbank" palm trees label			
❏ WS1729	The Mason Williams Phonograph Record	1970	12.00
— Green label with "WB" logo			
❏ W1729 [M]	The Mason Williams Phonograph Record	1968	30.00
— Mono is white label promo only			

WILLIAMS, MAURICE, AND THE ZODIACS

Number	Title	Yr	NM
COLLECTABLES			
❏ COL-5021	The Best of Maurice Williams and the Zodiacs	198?	12.00
HERALD			
❏ HLP-1014 [M]	Stay	1961	500.00
RELIC			
❏ 5017	Greatest Hits	197?	18.00
SNYDER			
❏ 5586 [M]	At the Beach	196?	100.00
SPHERE SOUND			
❏ SR-7007 [M]	Stay	1965	120.00
❏ SSR-7007 [R]	Stay	1965	80.00

WILLIAMS, MEL

Number	Title	Yr	NM
DIG			
❏ LP-103 [M]	All Thru the Night	1956	600.00

WILLIAMS, NORMAN

Number	Title	Yr	NM
THERESA			
❏ 105	One for Bird	1980	15.00
❏ 101	The Bishop	1979	15.00
❏ 102	The Bishop's Bag	1979	15.00

WILLIAMS, OTIS, AND HIS CHARMS

Number	Title	Yr	NM
DELUXE			
❏ 570 [M]	Their All Time Hits	1957	1000.00
KING			
❏ 570 [M]	Their All Time Hits	1957	600.00
❏ 614 [M]	This Is Otis Williams and His Charms	1959	400.00
STOP			
❏ STLP-1022	Otis Williams and the Midnight Cowboys	1971	30.00

WILLIAMS, PATRICK

Number	Title	Yr	NM
ALLEGIANCE			
❏ AV-443	Dreams and Themes	1985	12.00
— Reissue of PCM album			
CAPITOL			
❏ ST-11242	Threshold	1974	12.00

Number	Title	Yr	NM
COLUMBIA			
❏ JC36318	An American Concerto	1979	12.00
PAUSA			
❏ 7060	Theme	1980	12.00
PCM			
❏ PAA1001	Dreams and Themes	1984	15.00
SOUNDWINGS			
❏ SW-2103	10th Avenue	1987	12.00
❏ SW-2107	Threshold	1988	12.00

WILLIAMS, PAUL

Number	Title	Yr	NM
A&M			
❏ SP-3655	A Little Bit of Love	1974	12.00
❏ SP-4701	Classics	1977	12.00
❏ SP-3606	Here Comes Inspiration	1974	12.00
❏ SP-4327	Just an Old Fashioned Love Song	1971	12.00
❏ SP-3131	Just an Old Fashioned Love Song	198?	10.00
— Budget-line reissue			
❏ SP-4367	Life Goes On	1972	12.00
❏ SP-4550	Ordinary Fool	1975	12.00
PORTRAIT			
❏ JR35610	Windy Side	1979	12.00
REPRISE			
❏ RS6401	Someday Man	1970	15.00

WILLIAMS, RICHARD

Number	Title	Yr	NM
BARNABY			
❏ BR-5014	New Horn in Town	197?	12.00
CANDID			
❏ CD-8003 [M]	New Horn in Town	1960	40.00
❏ CS-9003 [S]	New Horn in Town	1960	50.00

WILLIAMS, ROBERT PETE

Number	Title	Yr	NM
BLUESVILLE			
❏ BVLP-1026 [M]	Free Again	1961	100.00
— Blue label, silver print			
❏ BVLP-1026 [M]	Free Again	1964	30.00
— Blue label with trident logo			
FOLK/LYRIC			
❏ FL-109 [M]	Prison Blues	1960	100.00

WILLIAMS, ROD

Number	Title	Yr	NM
MUSE			
❏ MR-5380	Hanging in the Balance	198?	12.00

WILLIAMS, ROGER

Number	Title	Yr	NM
BAINBRIDGE			
❏ 8002	Ivory Impact	1982	15.00
❏ 6265	Somewhere in Time	1986	12.00
HOLIDAY			
❏ HDY1927	Golden Christmas	1981	10.00
KAPP			
❏ KLE-1 [M]	10th Anniversary/Limited Edition	1964	25.00
— Reissue of Kapp 1088, 1130 and 1172 in one package			
❏ SKLE-1 [S]	10th Anniversary/Limited Edition	1964	30.00
❏ KL-1406 [M]	Academy Award Winners	1964	12.00
❏ KS-3406 [S]	Academy Award Winners	1964	15.00
❏ KL-1483 [M]	Academy Award Winners, Vol. 2	1966	12.00
❏ KS-3483 [S]	Academy Award Winners, Vol. 2	1966	15.00
❏ KL-1063 [M]	Almost Paradise	1957	18.00
— Maroon and silver (or blue and silver) label			
❏ KL-1063 [M]	Almost Paradise	1962	15.00
— Any later label variation			
❏ KL-1172 [M]	Always	1960	18.00
— Maroon and silver (or blue and silver) labels			
❏ KL-1172 [M]	Always	1962	15.00
— Any later label variation			
❏ KS-3056 [S]	Always	1960	25.00
— Maroon and silver (or blue and silver) labels			
❏ KS-3056 [S]	Always	1962	18.00
— Any later label variation			
❏ KS-3549	Amore	1968	15.00
❏ KL-1012 [M]	Autumn Leaves	1956	25.00
— Retitled version of above; maroon and silver (or blue and silver) label			
❏ KL-1012 [M]	Autumn Leaves	1962	15.00
— Any later label variation			
❏ KL-1452 [M]	Autumn Leaves -- 1965	1965	12.00
❏ KS-3452 [S]	Autumn Leaves -- 1965	1965	15.00
❏ KL-1501 [M]	Born Free	1966	12.00
❏ KS-3501 [S]	Born Free	1966	15.00
❏ KL-3 [M]	By Special Request	196?	15.00
— Columbia Record Club exclusive			
❏ KL-4 [M]	By Special Request, Vol. 2	196?	15.00
— Columbia Record Club exclusive			
❏ KL-1164 [M]	Christmas Time	1959	18.00
— Merry Christmas" silver, red and green label			
❏ KL-1164 [M]	Christmas Time	1962	15.00
— Any later label variation			
❏ KS-3164 [S]	Christmas Time	196?	15.00
— Reissue of KS-3048 (new cover, no gatefold)			

Number	Title	Yr	NM
❏ KS-3048 [S]	Christmas Time	1959	25.00
❏ KL-1305 [M]	Country Style	1963	15.00
❏ KS-3305 [S]	Country Style	1963	18.00
❏ KL-1031 [M]	Daydreams	1956	18.00
— Maroon and silver (or blue and silver) label			
❏ KL-1031 [M]	Daydreams	1962	15.00
— Any later label variation			
❏ KL-1395 [M]	Family Album of Hymns	1964	12.00
❏ KS-3395 [S]	Family Album of Hymns	1964	15.00
❏ KL-1336 [M]	For You	1963	15.00
❏ KS-3336 [S]	For You	1963	18.00
❏ KL-1260 [M]	Greatest Hits	1962	15.00
❏ KS-3260 [S]	Greatest Hits	1962	18.00
❏ KS-3595	Happy Heart	1969	15.00
❏ KL-1470 [M]	I'll Remember You	1966	12.00
❏ KS-3470 [S]	I'll Remember You	1966	15.00
❏ KL-1008 [M]	It's a Big, Wide, Wonderful World	1955	30.00
— Maroon and silver (or blue and silver) labels			
❏ KL-1008 [M]	It's a Big, Wide, Wonderful World	1962	15.00
— Any later label variation			
❏ KS-3645	Love Story	1971	12.00
❏ KS-3610	Love Theme from "Romeo and Juliet"	1969	15.00
❏ KS-3665	Love Theme from "The Godfather"	1972	12.00
❏ KL-1266 [M]	Maria	1962	15.00
❏ KS-3266 [S]	Maria	1962	18.00
❏ KL-1130 [M]	More Songs of the Fabulous Fifties	1959	18.00
— Maroon and silver (or blue and silver) labels			
❏ KL-1130 [M]	More Songs of the Fabulous Fifties	1962	15.00
— Any later label variation			
❏ KS-3013 [S]	More Songs of the Fabulous Fifties	1959	25.00
— Maroon and silver (or blue and silver) labels			
❏ KS-3013 [S]	More Songs of the Fabulous Fifties	1962	18.00
— Any later label variation			
❏ KS-3550	More Than a Miracle	1968	15.00
❏ KL-1290 [M]	Mr. Piano	1962	15.00
❏ KS-3290 [S]	Mr. Piano	1962	18.00
❏ KL-1112 [M]	Near You	1959	18.00
— Maroon and silver (or blue and silver) labels			
❏ KL-1112 [M]	Near You	1962	15.00
— Any later label variation			
❏ KS-1112 [S]	Near You	1959	25.00
— Maroon and silver (or blue and silver) labels			
❏ KS-1112 [S]	Near You	1962	18.00
— Any later label variation			
❏ KS-3565	Only for Lovers	1969	15.00
❏ KS-3671	Play Me	1972	12.00
❏ KL-1512 [M]	Roger!	1967	12.00
❏ KS-3512 [S]	Roger!	1967	15.00
❏ KL-1012 [M]	Roger Williams	1956	30.00
❏ KL-1530 [M]	Roger Williams/Golden Hits	1967	15.00
❏ KS-3530 [S]	Roger Williams/Golden Hits	1967	15.00
❏ KS-3638	Roger Williams/Golden Hits, Volume 2	1970	15.00
❏ KL-1222 [M]	Roger Williams Invites You to Dance	1961	18.00
❏ KS-3222 [S]	Roger Williams Invites You to Dance	1961	25.00
❏ KL-1062 [M]	Roger Williams Plays Beautiful Waltzes	1962	15.00
— Any later label variation			
❏ KL-1062 [M]	Roger Williams Plays Beautiful Waltzes	1957	18.00
— Maroon and silver (or blue and silver) label			
❏ KL-1042 [M]	Roger Williams Plays Christmas Songs	1956	18.00
— Maroon and silver (or blue and silver) label; unbanded			
❏ KL-1088 [M]	Roger Williams Plays Gershwin	1958	18.00
— Maroon and silver (or blue and silver) labels			
❏ KL-1088 [M]	Roger Williams Plays Gershwin	1962	15.00
— Any later label variation			
❏ KL-1414 [M]	Roger Williams Plays the Hits	1965	12.00
❏ KS-3414 [S]	Roger Williams Plays the Hits	1965	15.00
❏ KL-1040 [M]	Roger Williams Plays the Wonderful Music of the Masters	1956	18.00
— Maroon and silver (or blue and silver) labels			
❏ KL-1040 [M]	Roger Williams Plays the Wonderful Music of the Masters	1962	15.00
— Any later label variation			
❏ KW-900 [M]	Roger Williams Showcase	196?	15.00
❏ SKW-900 [S]	Roger Williams Showcase	196?	18.00
❏ KXL-5005 [M]	Songs of the Fabulous Century	195?	25.00
— Maroon and silver (or blue and silver) labels			
❏ KXL-5005 [M]	Songs of the Fabulous Century	1962	18.00
— Any later label variation			
❏ KXS-5005 [S]	Songs of the Fabulous Century	1959	30.00
— Maroon and silver (or blue and silver) labels			
❏ KXS-5005 [S]	Songs of the Fabulous Century	1962	25.00
— Any later label variation			

Number	Title	Yr	NM
❑ KL-1211 [M]	Songs of the Fabulous Century, Volume 1	1960	15.00
❑ KS-3211 [S]	Songs of the Fabulous Century, Volume 1	1960	18.00
❑ KL-1212 [M]	Songs of the Fabulous Century, Volume 2	1960	15.00
❑ KS-3212 [S]	Songs of the Fabulous Century, Volume 2	1960	18.00
❑ KXL-5000 [M]	Songs of the Fabulous Fifties	1957	25.00
—Maroon and silver (or blue and silver) labels			
❑ KXL-5000 [M]	Songs of the Fabulous Fifties	1962	18.00
—Any later label variation			
❑ KXS-5000 [S]	Songs of the Fabulous Fifties	1959	30.00
—Maroon and silver (or blue and silver) labels			
❑ KXS-5000 [S]	Songs of the Fabulous Fifties	1962	25.00
—Any later label variation			
❑ KL-1209 [M]	Songs of the Fabulous Fifties, Volume 1	1960	15.00
❑ KS-3209 [S]	Songs of the Fabulous Fifties, Volume 1	1960	18.00
❑ KL-1210 [M]	Songs of the Fabulous Fifties, Volume 2	1960	15.00
❑ KS-3210 [S]	Songs of the Fabulous Fifties, Volume 2	1960	18.00
❑ KXL-5003 [M]	Songs of the Fabulous Forties	1957	25.00
—Maroon and silver (or blue and silver) labels			
❑ KXL-5003 [M]	Songs of the Fabulous Forties	1962	18.00
—Any later label variation			
❑ KXS-5003 [S]	Songs of the Fabulous Forties	1959	30.00
—Maroon and silver (or blue and silver) labels			
❑ KXS-5003 [S]	Songs of the Fabulous Forties	1962	25.00
—Any later label variation			
❑ KL-1207 [M]	Songs of the Fabulous Forties, Volume 1	1960	15.00
❑ KS-3207 [S]	Songs of the Fabulous Forties, Volume 1	1960	18.00
❑ KL-1208 [M]	Songs of the Fabulous Forties, Volume 2	1960	15.00
❑ KS-3208 [S]	Songs of the Fabulous Forties, Volume 2	1960	18.00
❑ KL-1251 [M]	Songs of the Soaring '60s	1961	18.00
❑ KS-3251 [S]	Songs of the Soaring '60s	1961	25.00
❑ KS-3650	Summer of '42	1971	12.00
❑ KL-1434 [M]	Summer Wind	1965	12.00
❑ KS-3434 [S]	Summer Wind	1965	15.00
❑ KL-1217 [M]	Temptation	1960	18.00
—Maroon and silver (or blue and silver) labels			
❑ KL-1217 [M]	Temptation	1962	15.00
—Any later label variation			
❑ KS-3217 [S]	Temptation	1960	25.00
❑ KL-1003 [M]	The Boy Next Door	1955	30.00
—Maroon and silver (or blue and silver) labels			
❑ KL-1003 [M]	The Boy Next Door	1962	15.00
—Any later label variation			
❑ KS-3629	Themes from Great Movies	1970	15.00
❑ KL-1354 [M]	The Solid Gold Steinway	1964	15.00
❑ KS-3354 [S]	The Solid Gold Steinway	1964	18.00
❑ KL-1081 [M]	Till	1962	15.00
—Any later label variation			
❑ KL-1081 [M]	Till	1958	18.00
—Maroon and silver (or blue and silver) label			
❑ K-1081-S [S]	Till	1959	25.00
—Maroon and silver (or blue and silver) labels			
❑ KS-1081 [S]	Till	1962	18.00
—Any later label variation			
❑ KXL-5008 [M]	Tonight! Roger Williams at Town Hall	196?	25.00
❑ KXS-5008 [S]	Tonight! Roger Williams at Town Hall	196?	30.00
❑ KS-3000 [S]	Waltzes in Stereo	1959	25.00
—Maroon and silver (or blue and silver) labels			
❑ KS-3000 [S]	Waltzes in Stereo	1962	18.00
—Any later label variation			
❑ KL-1147 [M]	With These Hands	1959	18.00
—Maroon and silver (or blue and silver) labels			
❑ KL-1147 [M]	With These Hands	1962	15.00
—Any later label variation			
❑ KS-3030 [S]	With These Hands	1959	25.00
—Maroon and silver (or blue and silver) labels			
❑ KS-3030 [S]	With These Hands	1962	18.00
—Any later label variation			
❑ KL-1244 [M]	Yellow Bird	1961	18.00
❑ KS-3244 [S]	Yellow Bird	1961	25.00
MCA			
❑ 20202	Autumn Leaves	198?	10.00
—Reissue of Kapp material			
❑ 15005	Christmas Time	197?	10.00
—Reissue of Kapp material			
❑ 2279	Evergreen	1977	12.00
❑ 539	Family Album of Hymns	1975	10.00
—Reissue of Kapp 3395			
❑ 63	Greatest Hits	1973	10.00
—Reissue of Kapp 3260			
❑ 438	I Honestly Love You	1974	12.00
❑ 324	Last Tango in Paris	1973	12.00
❑ 378	Live	1973	12.00
❑ 2237	Nadia's Theme	1976	12.00
❑ 76	Play Me	1973	10.00
—Reissue of Kapp 3671			
❑ 64	Roger Williams/Golden Hits	1973	10.00
—Reissue of Kapp 3530			
❑ 68	Roger Williams/Golden Hits, Volume 2	1973	10.00
—Reissue of Kapp 3638			
❑ 71	Somewhere My Love	1973	10.00
—Retitled reissue of unknown Kapp LP			
❑ 4106	The Best of Roger Williams	197?	15.00
❑ 403	The Way We Were	1974	12.00
❑ 5574	To Amadeus With Love	1985	12.00
❑ 2175	Virtuoso	1975	12.00
PICKWICK			
❑ PTP-2086	Roger Williams at the Piano	197?	15.00
❑ SPC-3367	Spanish Eyes	197?	10.00
❑ SPC-3511	Sunrise, Sunset	197?	10.00
VOCALION			
❑ VL73918	Moments to Remember	1970	12.00

WILLIAMS, TEX

Number	Title	Yr	NM
BOONE			
❑ LP-1210 [M]	The Two Sides of Tex Williams	1966	25.00
❑ LSP-1210 [S]	The Two Sides of Tex Williams	1966	30.00
CAPITOL			
❑ T1463 [M]	Smoke! Smoke! Smoke!	1960	30.00
❑ ST1463 [S]	Smoke! Smoke! Smoke!	1960	40.00
DECCA			
❑ DL4295 [M]	Country Music Time	1962	25.00
❑ DL74295 [S]	Country Music Time	1962	30.00
❑ DL5565 [10]	Dance-O-Rama #5	1955	300.00
IMPERIAL			
❑ LP-9309 [M]	The Voice of Authority	1966	25.00
❑ LP-12309 [S]	The Voice of Authority	1966	30.00
LIBERTY			
❑ LRP-3304 [M]	Tex Williams in Las Vegas	1963	25.00
❑ LST-7304 [S]	Tex Williams in Las Vegas	1963	30.00
MONUMENT			
❑ Z30909	A Man Called Tex	1971	25.00
RCA CAMDEN			
❑ CAL-363 [M]	Tex Williams' Best	1958	30.00

WILLIAMS, TONY

Number	Title	Yr	NM
MERCURY			
❑ MG-20454 [M]	A Girl Is a Girl Is a Girl	1959	50.00
❑ SR-60138 [S]	A Girl Is a Girl Is a Girl	1959	60.00
PHILIPS			
❑ PHM200051 [M]	The Magic Touch of Tony	1962	30.00
❑ PHS600051 [S]	The Magic Touch of Tony	1962	30.00
REPRISE			
❑ R-6006 [M]	His Greatest Hits	1961	30.00
❑ R9-6006 [S]	His Greatest Hits	1961	30.00

WILLIAMS, TONY (2)

Number	Title	Yr	NM
BLUE NOTE			
❑ BT-48494	Angel Street	1988	15.00
❑ BT-85138	Civilization	1987	15.00
❑ BT-85119	Foreign Intrigue	198?	15.00
❑ BLP-4180 [M]	Life Time	1964	30.00
❑ BST-84180 [S]	Life Time	1964	30.00
—With "New York, USA" address on label			
❑ BST-84180 [S]	Life Time	1967	18.00
—With "A Division of Liberty Records" on label			
❑ B1-93170	Native Heart	1990	15.00
❑ BLP-4216 [M]	Spring	1965	30.00
❑ BST-84216 [S]	Spring	1965	30.00
—With "New York, USA" address on label			
❑ BST-84216 [S]	Spring	1967	18.00
—With "A Division of Liberty Records" on label			
❑ BST-84216 [S]	Spring	1985	12.00
—The Finest in Jazz Since 1939" reissue			
COLUMBIA			
❑ PC33836	Believe It	1975	12.00
❑ HC45705	Joy of Flying	198?	50.00
—Half-speed mastered edition			
❑ JC35705	Joy of Flying	1979	12.00
❑ PC34263	Million Dollar Legs	1976	12.00
❑ JC36397	The Best of Tony Williams	1980	12.00
POLYDOR			
❑ PD-4065	Ego	197?	15.00
❑ 25-3001	Emergency	1969	25.00
❑ PD-4017	Emergency, Vol. 1	197?	15.00
❑ PD-5040	The Old Bum's Rush	1973	15.00
❑ PD-4021	Turn It Over	197?	15.00
VERVE			
❑ VE-2-2541	Once in a Lifetime	198?	15.00

WILLIAMS, VALDO

Number	Title	Yr	NM
SAVOY			
❑ MG-12188 [M]	New Advanced Jazz	1967	30.00

WILLIAMS, WENDY O.

Number	Title	Yr	NM
PASSPORT			
❑ PB-6034	W.O.W.	1984	15.00
PROFILE			
❑ PAL1230	Maggots: The Record	1987	18.00

WILLIAMSON, CLAUDE

Number	Title	Yr	NM
BETHLEHEM			
❑ BCP-54 [M]	Claude Williamson	1956	80.00
❑ BCP-69 [M]	'Round Midnight	1957	80.00
CAPITOL			
❑ H6502 [10]	Claude Williamson	1954	120.00
❑ H6511 [10]	Keys West	1955	120.00
❑ T6511 [M]	Keys West	1956	100.00
—Turquoise label			
CONTRACT			
❑ 15003 [M]	Theatre Party	196?	30.00
❑ 15001 [M]	The Fabulous Claude Williamson Trio	196?	30.00
CRITERION			
❑ 601 [M]	Claude Williamson Mulls the Mulligan Scene	1958	80.00
DISCOVERY			
❑ 862	La Fiesta	198?	12.00
INTERPLAY			
❑ 7708	Holography	1977	15.00
❑ 7727	La Fiesta	1979	15.00
❑ 7717	New Departure	1978	15.00

WILLIAMSON, SONNY BOY (1)

Number	Title	Yr	NM
BLUES CLASSICS			
❑ 3	Blues Classics by Sonny Boy Williamson	196?	30.00
❑ 20	Blues Classics by Sonny Boy Williamson, Vol. 2	196?	30.00
❑ BC24	Blues Classics by Sonny Boy Williamson, Volume 3	196?	30.00

WILLIAMSON, SONNY BOY (2), AND THE YARDBIRDS

Number	Title	Yr	NM
MERCURY			
❑ SR-61271 [R]	Eric Clapton and the Yardbirds Live with Sonny Boy Williamson	1970	25.00
—Reissue			
❑ MG-21071 [M]	Sonny Boy Williamson and the Yardbirds	1965	100.00
❑ SR-61071 [R]	Sonny Boy Williamson and the Yardbirds	1965	50.00
—First cover with a picture of the bluesman and the band			
❑ SR-61071 [R]	Sonny Boy Williamson and the Yardbirds	196?	30.00
—Later cover with cartoon artwork on the cover			

WILLIAMSON, SONNY BOY (2)

Number	Title	Yr	NM
ALLIGATOR			
❑ AL-4787	Keep It To Ourselves	1990	15.00
ARHOOLIE			
❑ 2020 [B]	King Biscuit Time	197?	15.00
CHECKER			
❑ LP-1437 [M]	Down and Out Blues	1959	350.00
CHESS			
❑ LPS-1536	Bummer Road	1969	30.00
❑ CH-9257	Down and Out Blues	1988	12.00
❑ LP-1509 [M]	More Real Folk Blues	1966	80.00
❑ CH-9277	More Real Folk Blues	1988	12.00
❑ CHV-417	One Way Out	1975	18.00
❑ CH-9116	One Way Out	198?	12.00
❑ 2ACMB-206	Sonny Boy Williamson	1976	25.00
—Reissue of 50027			
❑ LP-1503 [M]	The Real Folk Blues	1966	80.00
❑ CH-9272	The Real Folk Blues	1988	12.00
❑ 2CH-50027	This Is My Story	1972	30.00
GNP CRESCENDO			
❑ GNPS-10003	Sonny Boy Williamson in Chicago	198?	12.00
STORYVILLE			
❑ 4016	A Portrait in Blues	197?	15.00
❑ 4062	The Blues of Sonny Boy Williamson	197?	15.00

WILLIAMSON, STU

Number	Title	Yr	NM
BETHLEHEM			
❑ BCP-55 [M]	Stu Williamson	1956	120.00
❑ BCP-1024 [10]	Stu Williamson Plays	1955	250.00
❑ BCP-31 [M]	Stu Williamson Plays	1955	120.00

WILLING, FOY, AND THE RIDERS OF THE PURPLE SAGE

Number	Title	Yr	NM
CROWN			
❑ CLP-5306 [M]	Cool Water	196?	15.00
❑ CST-582	Country & Western Favorites	196?	12.00
CUSTOM			
❑ CS1017	Cool, Cool Water	197?	12.00
JUBILEE			
❑ JL-5028 [M]	The New Sound of American Folk	1962	25.00
❑ JLS-5028 [S]	The New Sound of American Folk	1962	30.00

Number	Title	Yr	NM
ROULETTE			
❑ R-25035 [M]	Cowboy	1958	40.00
ROYALE			
❑ 6032 [10]	The Riders of the Purple Sage	1952	100.00
VARSITY			
❑ 6032 [10]	The Riders of the Purple Sage	1950	120.00
WILLIS, CHUCK			
ATLANTIC			
❑ 8079 [M]	I Remember Chuck Willis	1963	150.00
❑ SD8079 [P]	I Remember Chuck Willis	1963	200.00
❑ 8018 [M]	The King of the Stroll	1958	300.00
—Black label			
❑ 8018 [M]	The King of the Stroll	1960	150.00
—Purple and orange label			
EPIC			
❑ LN3728 [M]	A Tribute to Chuck Willis	1960	300.00
❑ LN3425 [M]	Chuck Willis Wails the Blues	1958	500.00
WILLIS, LARRY			
GROOVE MERCHANT			
❑ 514	Inenr Crisis	197?	18.00
WILLIS, PETE			
CIRCLE			
❑ C-45	The One and Only Pete Willis	1982	12.00
PROGRESSIVE			
❑ PRO-7013	The One and Only Pete Willis	198?	12.00
WILLIS BROTHERS, THE			
STARDAY			
❑ SLP-403 [M]	Bob	1967	30.00
❑ SLP-442	Bummin' Around	1969	30.00
❑ SLP-229 [M]	Code of the West	1963	50.00
❑ SLP-472	For the Good Times	1971	25.00
❑ SLP-323 [M]	Give Me 40 Acres	1965	40.00
❑ SLP-387 [M]	Goin' to Town	1966	30.00
❑ SLP-428	Hey, Mister Truck Driver	1968	30.00
❑ SLP-306 [M]	Let's Hit the Road	1965	40.00
❑ SLP-353 [M]	Road Stop Juke Box Hits	1966	30.00
❑ SLP-466	The Best of the Willis Brothers	1970	25.00
❑ SLP-369 [M]	The Wild Side of Life	1966	30.00
❑ SLP-163 [M]	The Willis Brothers in Action	1962	60.00
WILLOUGHBY, LARRY			
ATLANTIC AMERICA			
❑ 90112	Building Bridges	1983	12.00
WILLS, BOB			
ANTONES			
❑ 6000 [10]	Old Time Favorites	195?	500.00
—Fan club release			
❑ 6010 [10]	Old Time Favorites	195?	500.00
—Fan club release			
CAPITOL			
❑ SKBB-11550	Bob Wills and His Texas Playboys in Concert	1976	25.00
COLUMBIA			
❑ KG32416	Anthology	1973	25.00
❑ CL9003 [10]	Bob Wills Round-Up	1949	300.00
DECCA			
❑ DL8727 [M]	Bob Wills and His Texas Playboys	1957	100.00
—Black label, silver print			
❑ DL8727 [M]	Bob Wills and His Texas Playboys	1961	40.00
—Black label with color bars			
❑ DL78727 [R]	Bob Wills and His Texas Playboys	196?	25.00
❑ DL5562 [10]	Dance-O-Rama #2	1955	300.00
DELTA			
❑ DLP-1149	Bob Wills and His Texas Playboys On Stage	1982	12.00
HARMONY			
❑ HL7036 [M]	Bob Wills Special	1957	40.00
—Maroon label			
❑ HL7036 [M]	Bob Wills Special	196?	25.00
—Black label			
❑ HL7304 [M]	The Best of Bob Wills	1963	30.00
❑ HL7345 [M]	The Great Bob Wills	1965	25.00
KAPP			
❑ KS-3639	Bob Wills in Person	1970	25.00
❑ KL-1506 [M]	From the Heart of Texas	1966	25.00
❑ KS-3506 [S]	From the Heart of Texas	1966	30.00
❑ KL-1542 [M]	Here's That Man Again	1966	50.00
—Mono is white label promo only; in stereo cover with "Mono" sticker			
❑ KS-3542 [S]	Here's That Man Again	1968	30.00
❑ KL-1523 [M]	King of Western Swing	1967	30.00
❑ KS-3523 [S]	King of Western Swing	1967	30.00
❑ KS-3641	The Best of Bob Wills	1971	25.00
❑ KS-3601	The Greatest String Band Hits	1969	25.00

Number	Title	Yr	NM
❑ KS-3587	The Living Legend	1969	25.00
❑ KS-3569	Time Changes Everything	1969	25.00
LIBERTY			
❑ LRP-3303 [M]	Bob Wills Sings and Plays	1963	30.00
❑ LST-7303 [S]	Bob Wills Sings and Plays	1963	40.00
❑ LRP-3182 [M]	Living Legend	1961	30.00
❑ LST-7182 [S]	Living Legend	1961	40.00
❑ LRP-3194 [M]	Mr. Words and Mr. Music	1961	30.00
❑ LST-7194 [S]	Mr. Words and Mr. Music	1961	40.00
❑ LRP-3173 [M]	Together Again	1960	30.00
❑ LST-7173 [S]	Together Again	1960	40.00
LONGHORN			
❑ LP-001 [M]	My Keepsake Album	1965	80.00
MGM			
❑ GAS-141	A Tribute (Golden Archive Series)	1971	30.00
❑ E-91 [10]	Ranch House Favorites	1951	300.00
❑ E-3352 [M]	Ranch House Favorites	1956	150.00
STARDAY			
❑ SLP-375 [M]	San Antonio Rose	1965	40.00
TIME-LIFE			
❑ STW-119	Country Music	1981	12.00
UNITED ARTISTS			
❑ LST-7303 [S]	Bob Wills Sings and Plays	1978	18.00
—Reissue of Liberty 7303 on "sunrise" label; tan label variations may exist but are unconfirmed			
❑ UA-LA216-J [B]	For the Last Time	1974	40.00
—Box set with booklet			
❑ UAS-9962	Legendary Masters	1971	30.00
VOCALION			
❑ VL3735 [M]	Western Swing Band	1965	25.00
WILLS, DAVID			
EPIC			
❑ KE33353	Barrooms to Bedrooms	1975	15.00
❑ KE33548	Everybody's Country	1975	15.00
RCA VICTOR			
❑ MHL1-8516 [EP]	New Beginnings	1984	10.00
WILLS, JOHNNIE LEE			
FLYING FISH			
❑ FF-069	Reunion	1978	15.00
ROUNDER			
❑ 1027 [B]	Tulsa Swing	1978	15.00
SIMS			
❑ LP-108 [M]	Johnny Lee Wills at the Tulsa Stampede	1963	30.00
❑ LPS-108 [S]	Johnny Lee Wills at the Tulsa Stampede	1963	50.00
❑ LP-101 [M]	Where There's a Wills, There's a Way	1962	40.00
❑ LPS-101 [S]	Where There's a Wills, There's a Way	1962	60.00
WILMER AND THE DUKES			
APHRODISIAC			
❑ 6001 [B]	Wilmer and the Dukes	1969	30.00
WILSON, AL			
PLAYBOY			
❑ PB410	I've Got a Feeling	1976	15.00
❑ JZ34744	I've Got a Feeling	1977	12.00
—Reissue of 410			
ROCKY ROAD			
❑ 3700 [B]	La La Peace Song	1974	18.00
❑ RR-3601	Show and Tell	1973	18.00
❑ RR-3600	Weighing In	1973	18.00
SOUL CITY			
❑ SCS-92006	Searching for the Dolphins	1969	30.00
WILSON, BRIAN			
ARISTA			
❑ 82876-70300-1	What I Really Want for Christmas	2005	15.00
RHINO			
❑ RI-76582	Brian Wilson Presents Smile	2004	30.00
❑ RI-76471	Gettin' In Over My Head	2004	25.00
SIRE			
❑ 25669	Brian Wilson	1988	12.00
❑	Words and Music	1988	30.00
PRO-A-3248 [DJ]			
—Promo-only music and interview			
WILSON, CARL			
CARIBOU			
❑ NJZ37010	Carl Wilson	1981	25.00
❑ ARZ37970	Youngblood	1982	25.00
WILSON, CASSANDRA			
JMT			
❑ 834419-1	Blue Skies	1988	12.00
❑ 834412-1	Days Aweigh	1987	12.00
❑ 860004-1	Point of View	1986	18.00
—Original edition			
❑ 834404-1	Point of View	1987	12.00

Number	Title	Yr	NM
WILSON, CLIVE			
NEW ORLEANS			
❑ NOR-7210	Clive Wilson Plays New Orleans Jazz	1986	12.00
WILSON, DENNIS			
CARIBOU			
❑ PZ34354 [B]	Pacific Ocean Blue	1977	30.00
WILSON, FLIP			
ATLANTIC			
❑ 8149 [M]	Cowboys and Colored People	1967	30.00
❑ SD8149 [S]	Cowboys and Colored People	1967	18.00
—Green and blue label			
❑ SD8149 [S]	Cowboys and Colored People	1969	15.00
—Red and green label			
❑ SD8179	You Devil You	1968	18.00
—Green and blue label			
❑ SD8179	You Devil You	1969	15.00
—Red and green label			
IMPERIAL			
❑ LP-9155 [M]	Flippin'	1961	30.00
LITTLE DAVID			
❑ LD1001 [M]	Geraldine/Don't Fight the Feeling	1972	30.00
—White label promo only; sticker on cover says "Promotional DJ Copy Monaural Not for Sale"			
❑ LD1001 [S]	Geraldine/Don't Fight the Feeling	1972	15.00
❑ LD1000	The Devil Made Me Buy This Dress	1970	15.00
❑ LD2000	The Flip Wilson Show	1970	15.00
MINIT			
❑ 24012	Flippin'	1968	18.00
—Reissue of Imperial LP			
SCEPTER			
❑ S-520	Flip Wilson's Pot Luck	1964	25.00
SPRINGBOARD			
❑ SPB-4004	Funny and Live at the Village Gate	1972	15.00
—Reissue of Scepter LP			
SUNSET			
❑ SUS-5297	Flipped Out	1970	15.00
—Reissue of Minit LP			
WILSON, GERALD			
AUDIO LAB			
❑ AL-1538 [M]	Big Band Modern	1959	150.00
DISCOVERY			
❑ 872	Corcovado	1983	12.00
❑ 833	Lomelin	1981	12.00
FEDERAL			
❑ 295-93 [10]	Gerald Wilson	1953	300.00
PACIFIC JAZZ			
❑ ST-20135 [S]	California Soul	1969	18.00
❑ ST-20160 [S]	Eternal Equinox	1969	18.00
❑ ST-20132 [S]	Everywhere	1968	18.00
❑ PJ-10099 [M]	Feelin' Kinda Blue	1964	18.00
❑ ST-20099 [S]	Feelin' Kinda Blue	1966	25.00
❑ LN-10101	Feelin' Kinda Blue	1981	10.00
—Budget-line reissue			
❑ PJ-88 [M]	Gerald Wilson on Stage	1964	30.00
❑ ST-88 [S]	Gerald Wilson on Stage	1964	30.00
❑ LN-10100	Gerald Wilson on Stage	1981	10.00
—Budget-line reissue			
❑ PJ-10111 [M]	Golden Sword	1966	18.00
❑ ST-20111 [S]	Golden Sword	1966	25.00
❑ PJ-10118 [M]	Live and Swinging	1967	25.00
❑ ST-20118 [S]	Live and Swinging	1967	18.00
❑ PJ-61 [M]	Moment of Truth	1962	30.00
❑ ST-61 [S]	Moment of Truth	1962	30.00
❑ LN-10098	Moment of Truth	1981	10.00
—Budget-line reissue			
❑ PJ-80 [M]	Portraits	1964	30.00
❑ ST-80 [S]	Portraits	1964	30.00
❑ ST-20174	The Best of Gerald Wilson	1970	18.00
❑ PJ-LA889-H	The Best of the Gerald Wilson Orchestra	1978	12.00
❑ PJ-34 [M]	You Better Believe It	1961	30.00
❑ ST-34 [S]	You Better Believe It	1961	30.00
❑ LN-10097	You Better Believe It	1981	10.00
—Budget-line reissue			
TEND			
❑ TR-537	Calafia	1985	15.00
WILSON, GLENN			
CADENCE JAZZ			
❑ CJR-1023	Impasse	198?	12.00
SUNNYSIDE			
❑ SSC-1030	Elusive	1988	12.00

WILSON, J. FRANK, AND THE CAVALIERS

JOSIE

Number	Title	Yr	NM
❑ JM-4006 [M]	Last Kiss	1964	75.00
❑ JS-4006 [S]	Last Kiss	1964	100.00

WILSON, JACK

ATLANTIC

Number	Title	Yr	NM
❑ 1406 [M]	Jack Wilson Quartet	1963	30.00
❑ SD1406 [S]	Jack Wilson Quartet	1963	40.00
❑ 1427 [M]	The Two Sides of Jack Wilson	1964	30.00
❑ SD1427 [S]	The Two Sides of Jack Wilson	1964	40.00

BLUE NOTE

Number	Title	Yr	NM
❑ BST-84270 [S]	Easterly Winds	1968	25.00
— With "A Division of Liberty Records" on label			
❑ BLP-4251 [M]	Something Personal	1967	40.00
❑ BST-84251 [S]	Something Personal	1967	30.00
— With "New York, USA" address on label			
❑ BST-84251 [S]	Something Personal	1967	25.00
— With "A Division of Liberty Records" on label			
❑ BST-84328 [S]	Song for My Daughter	1969	25.00
— With "A Division of Liberty Records" on label			

DISCOVERY

Number	Title	Yr	NM
❑ 872	Corcovado	198?	12.00
❑ 777	Innovations	1977	15.00
❑ 805	Margo's Theme	1979	15.00

VAULT

Number	Title	Yr	NM
❑ LP-9001 [M]	Brazilian Mancini	1964	30.00
❑ LPS-9001 [S]	Brazilian Mancini	1964	30.00
❑ LP-9008 [M]	Jazz Organs	1965	30.00
❑ LPS-9008 [S]	Jazz Organs	1965	30.00
❑ LP-9002 [M]	Ramblin'	1964	30.00
❑ LPS-9002 [S]	Ramblin'	1964	30.00

WILSON, JACKIE

BRUNSWICK

Number	Title	Yr	NM
❑ BL54059 [M]	A Woman, a Lover, a Friend	1961	50.00
— All-black label			
❑ BL754059 [S]	A Woman, a Lover, a Friend	1961	80.00
— All-black label			
❑ BL54059 [M]	A Woman, a Lover, a Friend	1964	25.00
— Black label with color bars			
❑ BL754059 [S]	A Woman, a Lover, a Friend	1964	30.00
— Black label with color bars			
❑ BL54110 [M]	Baby Workout	1963	50.00
— All-black label			
❑ BL754110 [S]	Baby Workout	1963	80.00
— All-black label			
❑ BL54110 [M]	Baby Workout	1963	25.00
— Black label with color bars			
❑ BL754110 [S]	Baby Workout	1963	30.00
— Black label with color bars			
❑ BL754185 [B]	Beautiful Day	1972	18.00
❑ BL54105 [M]	Body and Soul	1962	50.00
— All-black label			
❑ BL754105 [S]	Body and Soul	1962	80.00
— All-black label			
❑ BL54105 [M]	Body and Soul	1964	25.00
— Black label with color bars			
❑ BL754105 [S]	Body and Soul	1964	30.00
— Black label with color bars			
❑ BL54101 [M]	By Special Request	1961	50.00
— All-black label			
❑ BL754101 [S]	By Special Request	1961	80.00
— All-black label			
❑ BL54101 [M]	By Special Request	1964	25.00
— Black label with color bars			
❑ BL754101 [S]	By Special Request	1964	30.00
— Black label with color bars			
❑ BL754154	Do Your Thing	1969	25.00
❑ BL54042 [M]	He's So Fine	1959	120.00
— All-black label			
❑ BL54042 [M]	He's So Fine	1964	30.00
— Black label with color bars			
❑ BL54130 [M]	Higher and Higher	1967	30.00
❑ BL754130 [S]	Higher and Higher	1967	30.00
❑ BL754138 [S]	I Get the Sweetest Feeling	1968	25.00
❑ BL54138 [M]	I Get the Sweetest Feeling	1968	100.00
— Yellow label promo only; "Monaural" sticker over the word "Stereo" on cover			
❑ BL754158	It's All a Part of Love	1970	25.00
❑ BL54055 [M]	Jackie Sings the Blues	1960	150.00
— All-black label			
❑ BL754055 [S]	Jackie Sings the Blues	1960	200.00
— All-black label			
❑ BL54055 [M]	Jackie Sings the Blues	1964	25.00
— Black label with color bars			
❑ BL754055 [S]	Jackie Sings the Blues	1964	30.00
— Black label with color bars			
❑ BL54108 [M]	Jackie Wilson at the Copa	1962	50.00
— All-black label			
❑ BL754108 [S]	Jackie Wilson at the Copa	1962	80.00
— All-black label			
❑ BL54108 [M]	Jackie Wilson at the Copa	1964	25.00
— Black label with color bars			
❑ BL754108 [S]	Jackie Wilson at the Copa	1964	30.00
— Black label with color bars			
❑ BL754140	Jackie Wilson's Greatest Hits	1969	25.00
❑ BL54045 [M]	Lonely Teardrops	1959	150.00
— All-black label			
❑ BL54045 [M]	Lonely Teardrops	1964	30.00
— Black label with color bars			
❑ BL54134 [M]	Manufacturers of Soul	1968	50.00
— With Count Basie			
❑ BL754134 [S]	Manufacturers of Soul	1968	25.00
— With Count Basie			
❑ BL54112 [M]	Merry Christmas from Jackie Wilson	1963	30.00
❑ BL754112 [S]	Merry Christmas from Jackie Wilson	1963	40.00
❑ BL54058 [M]	My Golden Favorites	1960	60.00
— All-black label			
❑ BL54058 [M]	My Golden Favorites	1964	30.00
— Black label with color bars			
❑ BL54115 [M]	My Golden Favorites, Volume 2	1964	30.00
❑ BL754115 [S]	My Golden Favorites, Volume 2	1964	30.00
❑ BL754212	Nobody But You	1977	18.00
❑ BL754199	Nowstalgia	1974	18.00
❑ BL54113 [M]	Shake a Hand	1964	30.00
❑ BL754113 [S]	Shake a Hand	1964	30.00
❑ BL54117 [M]	Somethin' Else	1964	30.00
❑ BL754117 [S]	Somethin' Else	1964	30.00
❑ BL54050 [M]	So Much	1960	100.00
— All-black label			
❑ BL754050 [S]	So Much	1960	150.00
— All-black label			
❑ BL54050 [M]	So Much	1964	25.00
— Black label with color bars			
❑ BL754050 [S]	So Much	1964	30.00
— Black label with color bars			
❑ BL54120 [M]	Soul Galore	1966	30.00
❑ BL754120 [S]	Soul Galore	1966	30.00
❑ BL54118 [M]	Soul Time	1965	30.00
❑ BL754118 [S]	Soul Time	1965	30.00
❑ BL54119 [M]	Spotlight on Jackie	1965	30.00
❑ BL754119 [S]	Spotlight on Jackie	1965	30.00
❑ BL54106 [M]	The World's Greatest Melodies	1962	50.00
— All-black label			
❑ BL754106 [S]	The World's Greatest Melodies	1962	80.00
— All-black label			
❑ BL54106 [M]	The World's Greatest Melodies	1964	25.00
— Black label with color bars			
❑ BL754106 [S]	The World's Greatest Melodies	1964	30.00
— Black label with color bars			
❑ BL754167	This Love Is Real	1971	25.00
❑ BL54122 [M]	Whispers	1966	30.00
❑ BL754122 [S]	Whispers	1966	30.00
❑ BL54100 [M]	You Ain't Heard Nothin' Yet	1961	50.00
— All-black label			
❑ BL754100 [S]	You Ain't Heard Nothin' Yet	1961	80.00
— All-black label			
❑ BL54100 [M]	You Ain't Heard Nothin' Yet	1964	25.00
— Black label with color bars			
❑ BL754100 [S]	You Ain't Heard Nothin' Yet	1964	30.00
— Black label with color bars			
❑ BL754172	You Got Me Walking	1971	25.00

COLUMBIA

Number	Title	Yr	NM
❑ FC40866	Reet Petite: The Best of Jackie Wilson	1987	15.00

EPIC

Number	Title	Yr	NM
❑ EG38623	The Jackie Wilson Story	1983	25.00
❑ FE39408	The Jackie Wilson Story, Vol. 2	1985	15.00
❑ PE39408	The Jackie Wilson Story, Vol. 2	198?	10.00
— Budget-line reissue			

RHINO

Number	Title	Yr	NM
❑ RNLP-70230	Through the Years: A Collection of Rare Album Tracks and Single Sides	1987	15.00

WILSON, JOE LEE

INNER CITY

Number	Title	Yr	NM
❑ IC-1042	Secrets from the Sun	197?	15.00
❑ IC-1064	Without a Song	197?	15.00

OBLIVION

Number	Title	Yr	NM
❑ 5	Livin' High Off Nickels and Dimes	197?	18.00

SURVIVAL

Number	Title	Yr	NM
❑ 110	What Would It Be	1975	15.00

WILSON, JOEMY

DARGASON

Number	Title	Yr	NM
❑ DM-105	Gifts II: Traditional Christmas Carols	1987	12.00

WILSON, JULIE

ARDEN

Number	Title	Yr	NM
❑ B&S-1	Julie Wilson at Brothers and Sisters, Vol. 1	1976	25.00
❑ B&S-2	Julie Wilson at Brothers and Sisters, Vol. 2	1976	25.00

CAMEO

Number	Title	Yr	NM
❑ C-1021 [M]	Meet Julie Wilson	1962	30.00

DOLPHIN

Number	Title	Yr	NM
❑ 6 [M]	Love	1956	50.00

VIK

Number	Title	Yr	NM
❑ LX-1118 [M]	Julie Wilson at the St. Regis	1958	30.00
❑ LX-1095 [M]	My Old Flame	1957	30.00

WILSON, LARRY JON

MONUMENT

Number	Title	Yr	NM
❑ KZ34041	Let Me Sing My Song to You	1976	12.00
❑ 7615	Loose Change	1978	12.00
❑ KZ33382	New Beginnings	1975	12.00

WILSON, LESETTE

HEADFIRST

Number	Title	Yr	NM
❑ 9708	Now That I've Got Your Attention	198?	15.00

WILSON, LONNIE

STARDAY

Number	Title	Yr	NM
❑ SLP-217 [M]	The Playboy Farmer	196?	30.00

WILSON, MARIE

DESIGN

Number	Title	Yr	NM
❑ DLP-76 [M]	Gentlemen Prefer Marie Wilson	1959	40.00

STASH

Number	Title	Yr	NM
❑ ST-250	I Thought About You	1985	12.00

WILSON, MARTY

20TH CENTURY FOX

Number	Title	Yr	NM
❑ TF-3101 [M]	Young America Dances to Golden Goodies	1963	25.00
❑ TFS-4101 [S]	Young America Dances to Golden Goodies	1963	30.00

WILSON, MERI

GRT

Number	Title	Yr	NM
❑ 8023	First Take	1977	18.00

WILSON, MURRY

CAPITOL

Number	Title	Yr	NM
❑ T2819 [M]	The Many Moods of Murry Wilson	1967	60.00
❑ ST2819 [S]	The Many Moods of Murry Wilson	1967	50.00

WILSON, NANCY, AND CANNONBALL ADDERLEY

CAPITOL

Number	Title	Yr	NM
❑ T1657 [M]	Nancy Wilson/Cannonball Adderley	1962	30.00
— Black label with colorband, Capitol logo on left			
❑ ST1657 [S]	Nancy Wilson/Cannonball Adderley	1962	30.00
— Black label with colorband, Capitol logo on left			
❑ ST1657 [S]	Nancy Wilson/Cannonball Adderley	1962	25.00
— Black label with colorband, Capitol logo on top			
❑ T1657 [M]	Nancy Wilson/Cannonball Adderley	1962	18.00
— Black label with colorband, Capitol logo on top			
❑ SM-1657	Nancy Wilson/Cannonball Adderley	197?	12.00
— Reissue			

WILSON, NANCY

CAPITOL

Number	Title	Yr	NM
❑ ST-11317	All in Love Is Fair	1974	15.00
❑ T2495 [M]	A Touch of Today	1966	18.00
❑ ST2495 [S]	A Touch of Today	1966	25.00
❑ SM-2495	A Touch of Today	197?	12.00
— Reissue			
❑ T1828 [M]	Broadway My Way	1963	18.00
❑ ST1828 [S]	Broadway My Way	1963	25.00
❑ SM-1828	Broadway My Way	197?	12.00
— Reissue			
❑ SY-4575	Broadway My Way	197?	12.00
— Odd reissue			
❑ ST-798	But Beautiful	1971	18.00
❑ SM-798	But Beautiful	197?	12.00
— Reissue			
❑ ST-429	Can't Take My Eyes Off You	1970	18.00
❑ SM-12031	Can't Take My Eyes Off You	1980	12.00
— Reissue of 429			
❑ SWBB-256	Close-Up	1969	25.00
— Combines 1828 and 1934 into one package			
❑ ST-11386	Come Get to This	1975	15.00
❑ SM-11819	Come Get to This	1978	12.00
— Reissue of 11386			
❑ ST2909	Easy	1968	18.00
❑ SM-11802	Easy	1978	12.00
— Reissue of 2909			
❑ STBB-727	For Once in My Life/Who Can I Turn To	1971	25.00
❑ T2433 [M]	From Broadway with Love	1966	18.00
❑ ST2433 [S]	From Broadway with Love	1966	25.00
❑ T2351 [M]	Gentle Is My Love	1965	18.00
❑ ST2351 [S]	Gentle Is My Love	1965	25.00

Number	Title	Yr	NM
T1767 [M]	Hello Young Lovers	1962	25.00
ST1767 [S]	Hello Young Lovers	1962	30.00
T1934 [M]	Hollywood My Way	1963	18.00
ST1934 [S]	Hollywood My Way	1963	25.00
SM-1934	Hollywood My Way	197?	12.00
—Reissue			
T2155 [M]	How Glad I Am	1964	18.00
ST2155 [S]	How Glad I Am	1964	25.00
SM-11767	How Glad I Am	1978	12.00
—Reissue of 2155			
ST-353	Hurt So Bad	1969	18.00
ST-11131	I Know I Love Him	1972	15.00
ST-11659	I've Never Been to Me	1977	15.00
T2712 [M]	Just for Now	1967	18.00
ST2712 [S]	Just for Now	1967	25.00
ST-842	Kaleidoscope	1971	18.00
ST-11943	Life, Love and Happiness	1979	15.00
T1319 [M]	Like in Love	1960	30.00
—Black label with colorband, Capitol logo on left			
ST1319 [S]	Like in Love	1960	30.00
—Black label with colorband, Capitol logo on left			
T1319 [M]	Like in Love	1960	18.00
—Black label with colorband, Capitol logo on top			
ST1319 [S]	Like in Love	1960	25.00
—Black label with colorband, Capitol logo on top			
T2757 [M]	Lush Life	1967	25.00
ST2757 [S]	Lush Life	1967	18.00
SMAS-11786	Music on My Mind	1978	15.00
ST-148	Nancy	1969	18.00
T2634 [M]	Nancy -- Naturally	1967	18.00
ST2634 [S]	Nancy -- Naturally	1967	25.00
SM-11884	Nancy -- Naturally	1979	12.00
—Reissue of 2634			
ST-541	Now I'm a Woman	1970	18.00
T1440 [M]	Something Wonderful	1960	30.00
—Black label with colorband, Capitol logo on left			
ST1440 [S]	Something Wonderful	1960	30.00
—Black label with colorband, Capitol logo on left			
T1440 [M]	Something Wonderful	1960	18.00
—Black label with colorband, Capitol logo on top			
ST1440 [S]	Something Wonderful	1960	25.00
—Black label with colorband, Capitol logo on top			
ST-234	Son of a Preacher Man	1969	18.00
ST-12055	Take My Love	1980	15.00
T2555 [M]	Tender Loving Care	1966	18.00
ST2555 [S]	Tender Loving Care	1966	25.00
SKAO2947	The Best of Nancy Wilson	1968	18.00
SN-16128	The Best of Nancy Wilson	198?	10.00
—Budget-line reissue			
KAO2136 [M]	The Nancy Wilson Show!	1965	18.00
SKAO2136 [S]	The Nancy Wilson Show!	1965	25.00
ST-763	The Right to Love	1971	18.00
—Retitled reissue of 2757			
ST2970	The Sound of Nancy Wilson	1968	18.00
T1524 [M]	The Swingin's Mutual	1961	30.00
—Black label with colorband, Capitol logo on left			
ST1524 [S]	The Swingin's Mutual	1961	30.00
—Black label with colorband, Capitol logo on left			
T1524 [M]	The Swingin's Mutual	1961	18.00
—Black label with colorband, Capitol logo on top			
ST1524 [S]	The Swingin's Mutual	1961	25.00
—Black label with colorband, Capitol logo on top			
SM-1524 [S]	The Swingin's Mutual	1976	12.00
—With George Shearing; reissue			
ST-11518	This Mother's Daughter	1976	15.00
T2082 [M]	Today, Tomorrow, Forever	1964	18.00
ST2082 [S]	Today, Tomorrow, Forever	1964	25.00
T2321 [M]	Today -- My Way	1965	18.00
ST2321 [S]	Today -- My Way	1965	25.00
T2844 [M]	Welcome to My Love	1968	30.00
ST2844 [S]	Welcome to My Love	1968	18.00
T2012 [M]	Yesterday's Love Songs/ Today's Blues	1964	18.00
ST2012 [S]	Yesterday's Love Songs/ Today's Blues	1964	25.00

COLUMBIA

Number	Title	Yr	NM
FC40787	Forbidden Lover	1987	12.00
FC40330	Keep You Satisfied	1986	12.00
FC44464	Nancy Now!	1989	12.00

PAUSA

| PR-9041 | Nancy -- Naturally | 1985 | 12.00 |

PICKWICK

| SPC-3273 | Goin' Out of My Head | 197? | 12.00 |
| SPC-3348 | The Good Life | 197? | 12.00 |

WILSON, NORRO

SMASH

| SRS-67116 | Dedicated to: Only You | 1969 | 18.00 |

WILSON, PHIL, AND RICH MATTESON

ASI

203	Sound of Wasp	197?	15.00
5000	Sound of Wasp	197?	12.00
—Reissue of 203			

WILSON, PHIL

FAMOUS DOOR

| HL-133 | Boston-New York Axis | 1980 | 15.00 |
| HL-109 | That's All | 197? | 15.00 |

OUTRAGEOUS

| 1 | Getting It All Together | 197? | 18.00 |

WILSON, PHILLIP

HAT HUT

| 0Q | Esoteric | 197? | 18.00 |

WILSON, REG

HERALD

| HLP-0104 [M] | All By Himself | 1956 | 50.00 |

WILSON, REUBEN

BLUE NOTE

BST-84343	Blue Mode	1970	30.00
BST-84365	Groovy Situation	1971	30.00
BST-84317	Love Bug	1969	30.00
—With "A Division of Liberty Records" on label			
BST-84295	On Broadway	1968	30.00
—With "A Division of Liberty Records" on label			
BST-84377	Set Us Free	1972	30.00

CADET

| CA-60033 | Got to Get Your Own | 1975 | 18.00 |

GROOVE MERCHANT

4404	Bad Stuff	197?	25.00
511	Sweet Life	1973	25.00
523	The Cisco Kid	1974	18.00

WILSON, TEDDY, AND MARIAN MCPARTLAND

HALCYON

| 106 | Elegant Piano | 197? | 15.00 |

WILSON, TEDDY

ALLEGRO

| 4024 [10] | All Star Sextet | 1954 | 100.00 |
| 4031 [10] | All Star Sextet | 1954 | 100.00 |

BLACK LION

177	Moonglow	197?	15.00
209	Runnin' Wild Montreux	197?	15.00
308	Striding After Fats	197?	15.00

CAMEO

| C-1059 [M] | Teddy Wilson 1964 | 1964 | 30.00 |
| SC-1059 [S] | Teddy Wilson 1964 | 1964 | 30.00 |

CHIAROSCURO

168	Teddy Martin Revamps Rodgers and Hart	197?	15.00
150	Teddy Wilson and the All-Stars	197?	15.00
111	With Billie in Mind	1973	15.00

CLASSIC JAZZ

| 32 | Live at Santa Tecia | 1976 | 12.00 |
| 101 | Three Little Words | 197? | 12.00 |

CLEF

| MGC-156 [10] | Soft Moods with Teddy Wilson | 1954 | 200.00 |
| MGC 140 [10] | The Didactic Mr. Wilson | 1953 | 200.00 |

COLUMBIA

CL1442 [M]	And Then They Wrote	1960	30.00
CS8242 [S]	And Then They Wrote	1960	40.00
C80100 [3]	Gypsy	1959	40.00
CL1352 [M]	Gypsy in Jazz	1959	30.00
CL748 [M]	Mr. Wilson	1956	60.00
CL1318 [M]	Mr. Wilson and Mr. Gershwin	1959	40.00
CL6153 [10]	Piano Moods	1950	120.00
KG31617	Teddy Wilson and His All-Stars	1973	18.00
CL6098 [10]	Teddy Wilson and His Piano	1950	250.00
CL6040 [10]	Teddy Wilson Featuring Billie Holiday	1949	400.00

COMMODORE

| FL-20029 [10] | Town Hall Concert | 1952 | 200.00 |

DIAL

| LP-213 [10] | Teddy Wilson All Stars | 1950 | 300.00 |

GNP CRESCENDO

| GNP-9014 | Teddy Wilson | 197? | 12.00 |

JAZZ ARCHIVES

| JA-28 | Teddy Wilson Sextet 1944, Vol. 1 | 198? | 12.00 |
| JA-36 | Teddy Wilson Sextet 1944, Vol. 2 | 198? | 12.00 |

JAZZOLOGY

| J-86 | Teddy's Choice | 198? | 12.00 |

MERCURY

| MG-25172 [10] | Piano Pastries | 1953 | 120.00 |

MGM

| E-129 [10] | Runnin' Wild | 1951 | 200.00 |

MOSAIC

| MQ8-173 | The Complete Verve Recordings of the Teddy Wilson Trio | 199? | 150.00 |

MUSICRAFT

2007	As Time Goes By	1986	12.00
2008	Sunny Morning	1986	12.00
502	Teddy Wilson and His All Stars, Vol. 1	198?	12.00

NORGRAN

| MGN-1019 [M] | The Creative Teddy Wilson | 1955 | 100.00 |

PRESTIGE

| PRST-7696 [S] | The Teddy Wilson Trio in Europe | 1969 | 18.00 |

QUICKSILVER

| QS-9002 | Into the Sky | 198? | 12.00 |

ROYALE

| 18169 [10] | Teddy Wilson and His All Stars | 195? | 100.00 |

SACKVILLE

| 2005 | Teddy Wilson in Tokyo | 198? | 12.00 |

STORYVILLE

| 4046 | Teddy Wilson Revisits the Goodman Years | 198? | 12.00 |

TIME-LIFE

| STL-J-20 | Giants of Jazz | 1981 | 30.00 |

VERVE

MGV-2029 [M]	For Quiet Lovers	1956	60.00
V-2029 [M]	For Quiet Lovers	1961	30.00
MGV-2073 [M]	I Got Rhythm	1957	50.00
V-2073 [M]	I Got Rhythm	1961	25.00
MGV-2011 [M]	Intimate Listening	1956	50.00
V-2011 [M]	Intimate Listening	1961	25.00
MGV-8272 [M]	The Impeccable Mr. Teddy Wilson	1958	50.00
V-8272 [M]	The Impeccable Mr. Teddy Wilson	1961	25.00
MGV-8299 [M]	These Tunes Remind Me of You	1959	50.00
V-8299 [M]	These Tunes Remind Me of You	1961	25.00
MGV-8330 [M]	The Touch of Teddy Wilson	1959	50.00
V-8330 [M]	The Touch of Teddy Wilson	1961	25.00

WHO'S WHO IN JAZZ

| 21009 | Lionel Hampton Presents Teddy Wilson | 1979 | 12.00 |

WILSON, TEDDY/GERRY MULLIGAN

VERVE

V6-8827	Newport Years	197?	15.00
MGV-8235 [M]	The Teddy Wilson Trio and the Gerry Mulligan Quartet at Newport	1958	50.00
V-8235 [M]	The Teddy Wilson Trio and the Gerry Mulligan Quartet at Newport	1961	25.00
UMV-2622 [M]	The Teddy Wilson Trio and the Gerry Mulligan Quartet at Newport	198?	15.00

WILSON PHILLIPS

SBK

1P-8219	Shadows and Light	1992	80.00
—Only U.S. vinyl release was through Columbia House			
K1-93745	Wilson Phillips	1990	15.00

WINCHESTER, JESSE

AMPEX

| A10104 | Jesse Winchester | 1970 | 25.00 |

BEARSVILLE

BRK6984	A Touch on the Rainy Side	1978	12.00
BR2045	Jesse Winchester	1971	18.00
—Reissue of Ampex LP			
BR6953	Learn to Love It	1974	15.00
BR6964	Let the Rough Side Drag	1976	16.00
PRO-A-693 [DJ]	Live at the Bijou Café Plus a Live Interview at Media College in Montreal	1977	40.00
BR6968	Nothing But a Breeze	1977	12.00
BRK6989	Talk Memphis	1981	12.00
PRO560 [DJ]	The Jesse Winchester Radio Show	1976	40.00
BR2102	Third Down, 110 to Go	1972	18.00

RHINO

RNLP-70885	Jesse Winchester	1988	12.00
R1-70085	The Best of Jesse Winchester	1989	12.00
RNLP-70886	Third Down, 110 to Go	1988	12.00

SUGAR HILL

| SH-1023 | Humour Me | 1988 | 15.00 |

WINCHESTER, LEM

ARGO

| LPS-642 [S] | Lem Winchester with the Ramsey Lewis Trio | 1959 | 40.00 |
| LP-642 [M] | Lem Winchester with the Ramsey Lewis Trio | 1959 | 50.00 |

FANTASY

| OJC-1719 | Winchester Special | 198? | 12.00 |

METROJAZZ

| E-1005 [M] | New Faces at Newport | 1958 | 50.00 |

MOODSVILLE

MVLP-11 [M]	Lem Winchester with Feeling	1960	50.00
—Green label			
MVLP-11 [M]	Lem Winchester with Feeling	1965	30.00
—Blue label, trident logo at right			

NEW JAZZ

NJLP-8244 [M]	Another Opus	1960	50.00
—Purple label			
NJLP-8244 [M]	Another Opus	1965	30.00
—Blue label, trident logo at right			
NJLP-8239 [M]	Lem's Beat	1960	50.00

Number	Title	Yr	NM
—Purple label			
❑ NJLP-8239 [M]	Lem's Beat	1965	30.00
—Blue label, trident logo at right			
❑ NJLP-8223 [M]	Winchester Special	1959	80.00
—Purple label			
❑ NJLP-8223 [M]	Winchester Special	1965	30.00
—Blue label, trident logo at right			

WIND

LIFE

Number	Title	Yr	NM
❑ LLPS-2000	Make Believe	1969	25.00

WIND CHILL FACTOR

QCA

Number	Title	Yr	NM
❑ 372	City Streets	1978	15.00

WIND HARP, THE

UNITED ARTISTS

Number	Title	Yr	NM
❑ UAS-9963	Song from the Hill	1972	25.00

WIND IN THE WILLOWS, THE

CAPITOL

Number	Title	Yr	NM
❑ SKAO2956 [B]	The Wind in the Willows	1968	100.00

WINDHURST, JOHNNY

JAZZOLOGY

Number	Title	Yr	NM
❑ J-3	The Imaginative Johnny Windhurst	1963	18.00

TRANSITION

Number	Title	Yr	NM
❑ TRLP-2 [M]	Jazz at Columbus Ave.	1956	200.00
—Deduct 1/4 if booklet is missing			

WINDING, KAI, AND SONNY STITT

HALL OF FAME

Number	Title	Yr	NM
❑ 612	Early Modern	197?	12.00

WINDING, KAI

A&M

Number	Title	Yr	NM
❑ SP-3008	Israel	1969	15.00

ABC IMPULSE!

Number	Title	Yr	NM
❑ AS3 [S]	The Incredible Kai Winding Trombones	1968	15.00
—Black and red label			

COLUMBIA

Number	Title	Yr	NM
❑ CL1329 [M]	Dance to the City Beat	1959	40.00
❑ CS8136 [S]	Dance to the City Beat	1959	30.00
❑ CL1264 [M]	Swingin' State	1958	50.00
❑ CS8062 [S]	Swingin' State	1958	40.00
❑ CL999 [M]	Trombone Panorama	1957	50.00
❑ CL936 [M]	Trombone Sound	1956	50.00

GATEWAY

Number	Title	Yr	NM
❑ 7022	Jazz Showcase	1979	12.00

GLENDALE

Number	Title	Yr	NM
❑ 6004	Caravan	1977	12.00
❑ 6003	Danish Blue	1976	12.00

HARMONY

Number	Title	Yr	NM
❑ HL7341 [M]	The Great Kai Winding Sound	1962	18.00

IMPULSE!

Number	Title	Yr	NM
❑ A3 [M]	The Incredible Kai Winding Trombones	1960	30.00
❑ AS3 [S]	The Incredible Kai Winding Trombones	1960	30.00
—Orange and black label			

MCA

Number	Title	Yr	NM
❑ 29062	Incredible Kai Winding Trombones	198?	12.00
—Reissue of Impulse! 3			

PICKWICK

Number	Title	Yr	NM
❑ SPC-3004	Trombones	196?	15.00

RED RECORD

Number	Title	Yr	NM
❑ VPA-143	Duo Bones	198?	15.00

ROOST

Number	Title	Yr	NM
❑ LP408 [10]	Kai Winding All Stars	1952	120.00

SAVOY

Number	Title	Yr	NM
❑ MG-12119 [M]	In the Beginning	196?	18.00
❑ MG-9017 [10]	New Trends Of Jazz	1952	120.00

VERVE

Number	Title	Yr	NM
❑ V-8661 [M]	Dirty Dog	1966	15.00
❑ V6-8661 [S]	Dirty Dog	1966	18.00
❑ V-8427 [M]	Kai Ole	1962	30.00
❑ V6-8427 [S]	Kai Ole	1962	30.00
❑ V-8525 [M]	Kai Winding Solo	1963	30.00
❑ V6-8525 [S]	Kai Winding Solo	1963	30.00
❑ V-8602 [M]	Modern Country	1964	18.00
❑ V6-8602 [S]	Modern Country	1964	25.00
❑ V-8573 [M]	Mondo Cane #2	1964	30.00
❑ V6-8573 [S]	Mondo Cane #2	1964	30.00
❑ V-8551 [M]	More!!!	1963	30.00
❑ V6-8551 [S]	More!!!	1963	30.00
❑ V-8657 [M]	More Brass	1966	15.00
❑ V6-8657 [S]	More Brass	1966	18.00
❑ V-8691 [M]	Penny Lane and Time	1967	18.00
❑ V6-8691 [S]	Penny Lane and Time	1967	15.00
❑ V-8620 [M]	Rainy Day	1965	18.00
❑ V6-8620 [S]	Rainy Day	1965	25.00
❑ V-8493 [M]	Suspense Themes in Jazz	1962	30.00
❑ V6-8493 [S]	Suspense Themes in Jazz	1962	30.00
❑ V-8639 [M]	The "In" Instrumentals	1965	18.00
❑ V6-8639 [S]	The "In" Instrumentals	1965	25.00
❑ V-8556 [M]	The Lonely One	1963	30.00
❑ V6-8556 [S]	The Lonely One	1963	30.00

WHO'S WHO IN JAZZ

Number	Title	Yr	NM
❑ 21001	Lionel Hampton Presents Kai Winding	1978	12.00

WINDMILL SAXOPHONE QUARTET

PATHFINDER

Number	Title	Yr	NM
❑ PTF-8801	Very Scary	1988	12.00

WINDOWS

CYPRESS

Number	Title	Yr	NM
❑ YL-0214	The French Laundry	1989	15.00

INTIMA

Number	Title	Yr	NM
❑ SJ-73218	Is It Safe	1987	12.00
❑ D1-73298	Mr. Bongo	1988	12.00
❑ SJ-73219	Windows	1987	12.00
—Reissue of self-titled debut album			

(LABEL UNKNOWN)

Number	Title	Yr	NM
❑ (# unknown)0	Windows	1985	25.00

WINDY CITY BANJO BAND, THE

PINNACLE

Number	Title	Yr	NM
❑ 107	The Windy City Banjo Band	1963	18.00

WINGFIELD, PETE

ISLAND

Number	Title	Yr	NM
❑ ILPS9333	Breakfast Special	1975	15.00

WINKLER, MARK

CMG

Number	Title	Yr	NM
❑ CML-7207	Ebony Rain	1988	12.00
❑ CML-8021	Hottest Night of the Year	1989	15.00

WINNERS, THE

CROWN

Number	Title	Yr	NM
❑ CLP-5394 [M]	Checkered Flag	1963	30.00
❑ CST-394 [S]	Checkered Flag	1963	30.00

WINSLOW, STEPHANIE

WARNER BROS.

Number	Title	Yr	NM
❑ BSK3406	Crying	1980	12.00
❑ BSK3529	Dakota	1981	12.00

WINSTON, GEORGE

LOST LAKE ARTS

Number	Title	Yr	NM
❑ LL-0081	Ballads and Blues 1972	1981	12.00
—Reissue of Takoma recordings			

TAKOMA

Number	Title	Yr	NM
❑ 9016	Piano Solos	1973	18.00

WINDHAM HILL

Number	Title	Yr	NM
❑ WH-1012	Autumn	1984	12.00
—Reissue with A&M distribution			
❑ C-1012	Autumn	1980	15.00
—Original issue			
❑ WH-1025	December	1984	12.00
—Distributed by A&M Records; "December" in raised white letters			
❑ C-1025	December	1982	18.00
—NOT distributed by A&M Records; "December" in black letters			
❑ WH-1019	Winter Into Spring	1984	12.00
—Reissue, distributed by A&M Records			
❑ C-1019	Winter Into Spring	1982	15.00
—Original issue			

WINSTON, MURIEL

STRATA-EAST

Number	Title	Yr	NM
❑ SES-7411	A Fresh Viewpoint	197?	18.00

WINSTON, SHERRY

HEADFIRST

Number	Title	Yr	NM
❑ 634	Do It for Love	198?	12.00

WARLOCK

Number	Title	Yr	NM
❑ WAR-2724	Love Is	1991	15.00

WINSTONS, THE

METROMEDIA

Number	Title	Yr	NM
❑ MD-1010	Color Him Father	1969	50.00

WINTER, EDGAR

BLUE SKY

Number	Title	Yr	NM
❑ PZ33483 [B]	Jasmine Nightdreams	1975	15.00
❑ PZQ33483 [Q]	Jasmine Nightdreams	1975	30.00
❑ PZ34858	Re-Cycled	1977	15.00
❑ JZ36494	Standing on Rock	1981	15.00
❑ PZ33798	The Edgar Winter Group with Rick Derringer	1975	15.00
❑ PZQ33798 [Q]	The Edgar Winter Group with Rick Derringer	1975	30.00
❑ JZ35989	The Edger Winter Album	1979	15.00

EPIC

Number	Title	Yr	NM
❑ E30512	Edgar Winter's White Trash	1971	18.00
—Yellow label			
❑ KE30512	Edgar Winter's White Trash	1973	15.00
—Orange label			
❑ PE30512	Edger Winter's White Trash	1985	10.00
—Budget-line reissue; dark blue label			
❑ BN26503	Entrance	1970	18.00
—Yellow label			
❑ BN26503 [B]	Entrance	1973	15.00
—Orange label			
❑ BG33770	Entrance/White Trash	1975	18.00
—Combines 26503 and 30512 into one package			
❑ KEG31249	Roadwork	1972	25.00
—Yellow labels			
❑ KEG31249	Roadwork	1973	18.00
—Orange labels			
❑ EG31249	Roadwork	1987	12.00
—Budget-line reissue; dark blue labels			
❑ PE32461	Shock Treatment	1974	18.00
—Orange label			
❑ PEQ32461 [Q]	Shock Treatment	1974	40.00
❑ PE32461	Shock Treatment	1985	10.00
—Budget-line reissue; dark blue label			
❑ KE31584	They Only Come Out at Night	1972	18.00
—Yellow label			
❑ KE31584	They Only Come Out at Night	1973	15.00
—Orange label			
❑ EQ31584 [Q]	They Only Come Out at Night	1973	40.00
❑ PE31584	They Only Come Out at Night	197?	12.00
—Reissue with new prefix; orange label			
❑ PE31584	They Only Come Out at Night	1979	10.00
—Budget-line reissue; dark blue label			

RHINO

Number	Title	Yr	NM
❑ R1-70709	Mission Earth	1989	15.00
❑ R1-70895	The Edger Winter Collection	1989	12.00

WINTER, JOHNNY

ACCORD

Number	Title	Yr	NM
❑ SN-7135	Ready for Winter	1981	12.00

ALLIGATOR

Number	Title	Yr	NM
❑ 4735	Guitar Slinger	1984	12.00
❑ 4742	Serious Business	1985	12.00
❑ 4748	Third Degree	1986	12.00

BLUE SKY

Number	Title	Yr	NM
❑ PZ33944	Captured Live	198?	10.00
—Budget-line reissue with bar code on cover			
❑ PZ33944	Captured Live!	1976	15.00
—No bar code on cover			
❑ PZQ33292 [Q]	John Dawson Winter III	1974	25.00
❑ PZ33292	John Dawson Winter III	1974	15.00
❑ PZ34813	Nothin' But the Blues	1977	15.00
—No bar code on cover			
❑ PZ34813	Nothin' But the Blues	198?	10.00
—Budget-line reissue with bar code on cover			
❑ JZ36343 [B]	Raisin' Cain	1980	15.00
❑ JZ35475	White, Hot and Blue	1978	15.00

BUDDAH

Number	Title	Yr	NM
❑ BDS-7513	First Winter	1969	25.00

COLUMBIA

Number	Title	Yr	NM
❑ CS9826	Johnny Winter	1969	25.00
—360 Sound" label			
❑ CS9826	Johnny Winter	1970	15.00
—Orange label			
❑ PC9826	Johnny Winter	198?	10.00
—Budget-line reissue			
❑ C30221	Johnny Winter And	1970	25.00
—360 Sound" label			
❑ C30221	Johnny Winter And	1970	15.00
—Orange labels			
❑ PC30221	Johnny Winter And	198?	10.00
—Budget-line reissue			
❑ CG33651	Johnny Winter And//Live/ Johnny Winter And	1975	18.00
❑ C30475	Live/Johnny Winter And	1971	18.00
❑ PC30475	Live/Johnny Winter And	198?	10.00
—Budget-line reissue			
❑ CQ32715 [Q]	Saints and Sinners	1974	30.00
❑ KC32715	Saints and Sinners	1974	18.00
❑ PC32715	Saints and Sinners	197?	10.00
—Budget-line reissue			
❑ KCS9947	Second Winter	1969	30.00
—360 Sound" labels; record 2 has music on only one side (other side is blank)			
❑ KCS9947	Second Winter	1970	18.00
—Orange labels			
❑ PC9947	Second Winter	198?	12.00
—Budget-line reissue			
❑ KC32188	Still Alive and Well	1973	18.00
❑ CQ32188 [Q]	Still Alive and Well	1973	30.00
❑ PC32188	Still Alive and Well	198?	10.00
—Budget-line reissue			

Number	Title	Yr	NM
FRIDAY MUSIC			
❑ FRM41914 [B]	Live Bootleg Special Edition	2014	30.00
GRT			
❑ 10010	The Johnny Winter Story	1969	25.00
IMPERIAL			
❑ LP-12431	The Progressive Blues Experiment	1969	50.00
JANUS			
❑ 3008	About Blues	1970	25.00
❑ 3056	Before the Storm	197?	25.00
❑ 3023	Early Times	1970	30.00
LIBERTY			
❑ LN-10294	The Progressive Blues Experiment	1986	12.00
—Reissue of Imperial LP			
MCA/VOYAGER			
❑ 42241	The Winter of '88	1988	12.00
SONOBEAT			
❑ RS-1002	The Progressive Blues Experiment	1968	300.00
—Released in plain white cardboard jacket			
UNITED ARTISTS			
❑ UA-LA139-F	Austin, Tex.	1974	18.00

WINTER, JOHNNY AND EDGAR

Number	Title	Yr	NM
BLUE SKY			
❑ ASZ242 [DJ]	Johnny and Edgar Winter Discuss Together	1976	30.00
—Promo-only interview album			
❑ PZ34033	Together	1976	15.00

WINTER, PAUL, AND PAUL HALLEY

Number	Title	Yr	NM
LIVING MUSIC			
❑ LM-0013	Whales Alive!	1987	12.00

WINTER, PAUL

Number	Title	Yr	NM
A&M			
❑ SP-4698	Common Ground	1978	15.00
❑ SP-4653	Earthdance	1977	15.00
❑ SP-4207	Something in the Wind	1969	18.00
❑ SP-4279	The Road	1970	18.00
❑ SP-4170	The Winter Consort	1968	18.00
COLUMBIA			
❑ CL1925 [M]	Jazz Meets the Bossa Nova	1962	18.00
❑ CS8725 [S]	Jazz Meets the Bossa Nova	1962	25.00
❑ CL2155 [M]	Jazz Meets the Folk Song	1964	18.00
❑ CS8955 [S]	Jazz Meets the Folk Song	1964	25.00
❑ CL1997 [M]	Jazz Premiere: Washington	1963	18.00
❑ CS8797 [S]	Jazz Premiere: Washington	1963	25.00
❑ CL2064 [M]	New Jazz on Campus	1963	18.00
❑ CS8864 [S]	New Jazz on Campus	1963	25.00
❑ CL2315 [M]	Rio	1965	18.00
❑ CS9115 [S]	Rio	1965	25.00
❑ CL2272 [M]	The Sound of Ipanema	1965	18.00
❑ CS9072 [S]	The Sound of Ipanema	1965	25.00
EPIC			
❑ KE31643	Icarus	1972	15.00
❑ PE31610	Icarus	197?	12.00
—Reissue			
LIVING MUSIC			
❑ LMR-1	Callings	1980	25.00
—With 20 page booklet			
❑ LM-0001	Callings	198?	18.00
—Reissue of LMR-1			
❑ LMR-6	Canyon	1986	15.00
❑ LMR-5	Concert for the Earth Live at the United Nations	1985	15.00
❑ LM-0015	Earthbeat	1987	12.00
❑ LMR-4	Icarus	1985	15.00
—Reissue of Epic LP			
❑ LM-0004	Icarus	198?	12.00
—Reissue of LMR-4			
❑ LMR-2	Missa Gaia/Earth Mass	1983	25.00
❑ LMR-3	Sun Singer	1984	15.00
❑ LM-0003	Sun Singer	198?	12.00
—Reissue of LMR-3			
❑ LM-0012	Wintersong	1986	12.00

WINTER, RAYMOND

Number	Title	Yr	NM
INNER CITY			
❑ IC-1135	Tropic Woods	198?	15.00

WINTERHALTER, HUGO

Number	Title	Yr	NM
ABC-PARAMOUNT			
❑ ABCS-447 [S]	Season for My Beloved	1963	18.00
❑ ABC-447 [M]	Season for My Beloved	1963	15.00
HARMONY			
❑ HL7078 [M]	Music, Music, Music	195?	18.00
KAPP			
❑ KS3407 [S]	Best of '64, The	1964	18.00
❑ KL1407 [M]	Best of '64, The	1964	15.00
❑ KL1429 [M]	Big Hits of 1965	1965	15.00
❑ KS3429 [S]	Big Hits of 1965	1965	18.00
❑ KL-1426 [M]	Semi-Classical Favorites	196?	15.00
❑ KS-3426 [S]	Semi-Classical Favorites	196?	18.00

Number	Title	Yr	NM
MUSICOR			
❑ MDS-1036	Airport Love Theme	197?	12.00
❑ M2S3160	All Time Movie Greats	196?	18.00
❑ MS3190	Applause	1971	15.00
❑ MDS-1042	Best of the Motion Picture Hits	197?	15.00
❑ MS-3170	Classical Gas	1970	12.00
❑ MS-3196	Love Story	1971	12.00
❑ MDS-1029	Midnight Cowboy	197?	15.00
❑ MS-3184	My Favorite Broadway and Hollywood Music	197?	12.00
❑ MDS-1013	Pop Parade	197?	15.00
❑ M2S3168	Romanceable and Danceable	196?	18.00
❑ M2S3178	Your Favorite Motion Picture Music	197?	18.00
PICKWICK			
❑ CAS-2309	Hawaiian Wedding Song	197?	10.00
—Black label, multi-color "P" logo			
RCA CAMDEN			
❑ CAL-443 [M]	Big and Sweet with a Beat	1958	18.00
❑ CAL-449 [M]	Christmas Magic	1958	18.00
—Reissue of RCA Victor 3132 with two extra tracks			
❑ CAS-2309	Hawaiian Wedding Song	1969	12.00
❑ CAS-2546	Latin Gold	1972	12.00
❑ CAL-379 [M]	Magic Touch	195?	18.00
RCA VICTOR			
❑ LPM-1179 [M]	Always	1955	25.00
❑ LPM-3132 [10]	Christmas Magic	1954	30.00
❑ LPM-1020 [M]	Great Music Themes of TV	1954	30.00
❑ LPM-1400 [M]	Happy Hunting	1956	25.00
❑ LPM-2482 [M]	Hugo Winterhalter Goes... Continental	1961	18.00
❑ LSP-2482 [S]	Hugo Winterhalter Goes... Continental	1961	25.00
❑ LPM-2167 [M]	Hugo Winterhalter Goes... Gypsy	1960	18.00
❑ LSP-2167 [S]	Hugo Winterhalter Goes... Gypsy	1960	25.00
❑ LPM-2417 [M]	Hugo Winterhalter Goes... Hawaiian	1961	18.00
❑ LSP-2417 [S]	Hugo Winterhalter Goes... Hawaiian	1961	25.00
❑ LPM-1677 [M]	Hugo Winterhalter Goes... Latin	1957	25.00
❑ LSP-1677 [S]	Hugo Winterhalter Goes... Latin	1958	30.00
❑ LPM-2271 [M]	Hugo Winterhalter Goes... South of the Border	1960	18.00
❑ LSP-2271 [S]	Hugo Winterhalter Goes... South of the Border	1960	25.00
❑ LSP-2645 [S]	I Only Have Eyes for You	1964	18.00
❑ LPM-2645 [M]	I Only Have Eyes for You	1964	15.00
❑ LPM-3051 [10]	Music by Starlight	195?	30.00
❑ LPM-1185 [M]	Music by Starlight	1955	25.00
❑ ANL1-2483	Pure Gold	1977	12.00
❑ LPM-3050 [10]	Reminiscing	195?	30.00
❑ LPM-3101 [10]	Song Hits from "Peter Pan" and "Hans Christian Andersen	195?	30.00
❑ LPM-3379 [M]	The Best of Hugo Winterhalter	1965	15.00
❑ LSP-3379 [S]	The Best of Hugo Winterhalter	1965	18.00
❑ LPM-1338 [M]	The Eyes of Love	1956	25.00
❑ LPM-1905 [M]	Two Sides of Hugo Winterhalter	1958	25.00
❑ LSP-1905 [S]	Two Sides of Hugo Winterhalter	1958	30.00
❑ LPM-3100 [10]	Winterhalter Magic	195?	30.00
❑ LPM-1904 [M]	Wish You Were Here	1958	25.00
❑ LSP-1904 [S]	Wish You Were Here	1958	30.00

WINTERS, JERRI

Number	Title	Yr	NM
BETHLEHEM			
❑ BCP-76 [M]	Somebody Loves Me	1957	50.00
FRATERNITY			
❑ F-1001 [M]	Winter's Here	1955	60.00

WINTERS, JONATHAN

Number	Title	Yr	NM
COLUMBIA			
❑ KG31985	Jonathan Winters Laughs Live	1972	25.00
—Reissue of 9611 and 9799 in one package			
❑ PG31985	Jonathan Winters Laughs Live	197?	15.00
—Reissue with new prefix			
❑ CL2811 [M]	Jonathan Winters Wings It!	1968	30.00
❑ CS9611 [S]	Jonathan Winters Wings It!	1968	18.00
❑ CS9799	Stuff 'N' Nonsense	1969	18.00
VERVE			
❑ V-15032 [M]	Another Day, Another World	1962	30.00
❑ V6-15032 [R]	Another Day, Another World	196?	15.00
❑ MGV-15011 [M]	Down to Earth	1960	30.00
❑ MGVS-6155 [S]	Down to Earth	1960	30.00
❑ V-15011 [M]	Down to Earth	1961	25.00
❑ V6-15011 [S]	Down to Earth	1961	25.00
—Reissue of 6155			
❑ V-15047 [M]	Great Moments in Comedy	1965	25.00
❑ V6-15047 [R]	Great Moments in Comedy	196?	15.00
❑ V-15025 [M]	Here's Jonathan	1961	30.00
❑ V6-15025 [S]	Here's Jonathan	1961	30.00
❑ V-15035 [M]	Humor As Seen Through the Eyes of Jonathan Winters	1963	30.00
❑ V6-15035 [S]	Humor As Seen Through the Eyes of Jonathan Winters	1963	30.00

Number	Title	Yr	NM
❑ V-15041 [M]	Jonathan Winters' Mad, Mad, Mad, Mad World	1964	25.00
❑ V6-15041 [R]	Jonathan Winters' Mad, Mad, Mad, Mad World	196?	15.00
❑ V-15057 [M]	Movies Are Better Than Ever	1967	25.00
❑ V6-15057 [R]	Movies Are Better Than Ever	196?	15.00
❑ V-15052 [M]	The Best of Frickert and Suggins	1966	25.00
❑ V6-15052 [R]	The Best of Frickert and Suggins	196?	15.00
❑ MGV-15009 [M]	The Wonderful World of Jonathan Winters	1960	30.00
❑ MGVS-6099 [S]	The Wonderful World of Jonathan Winters	1960	30.00
❑ V-15009 [M]	The Wonderful World of Jonathan Winters	1961	25.00
❑ V6-15009 [S]	The Wonderful World of Jonathan Winters	1961	25.00
—Reissue of 6099			
❑ V-15037 [M]	Whistle Stopping with Jonathan Winters	1964	25.00
❑ V6-15037 [R]	Whistle Stopping with Jonathan Winters	196?	15.00

WINTERS, PINKY

Number	Title	Yr	NM
ARGO			
❑ LP-604 [M]	Lonely One	1956	40.00
CREATIVE			
❑ LP-604 [M]	Lonely One	1956	60.00
VANTAGE			
❑ VLP-3 [10]	Pinky Winters	1954	1000.00

WINTERS, SMILEY

Number	Title	Yr	NM
ARHOOLIE			
❑ 8004/5	Smiley Etc.	1969	25.00

WINWOOD, STEVE

Number	Title	Yr	NM
ISLAND			
❑ ILPS9576	Arc of a Diver	1981	12.00
❑ 5317713	Arc of a Diver	2009	25.00
❑ 25448	Back in the High Life	1986	10.00
❑ 25660	Chronicles	1987	10.00
❑ ILPS9387	Go	1976	15.00
—With Stomu Yamahita and Michael Shrieve			
❑ ILPS9494	Steve Winwood	1977	12.00
❑ ILPS9777	Talking Back to the Night	1982	12.00
SPRINGBOARD			
❑ SPB-4040	Winwood & Friends	197?	18.00
—Budget release with Winwood material on Side 1 and a collection of Jeff Beck, Yardbirds, Long John Baldry and Jack Bruce/Ginger Baker material on Side 2			
UNITED ARTISTS			
❑ UAS-9950	Winwood	1971	18.00
—Collection of tracks Winwood recorded with the Spencer Davis Group, Traffic and Blind Faith; without booklet			
❑ UAS-9950	Winwood	1971	30.00
—Collection of tracks Winwood recorded with the Spencer Davis Group, Traffic and Blind Faith; with booklet			
VIRGIN			
❑ 91405	Refugees of the Heart	1990	18.00
❑ 90946	Roll With It	1988	10.00
❑ R154633	Roll With It	1988	12.00
—BMG Direct Marketing edition			

WIPERS, THE

Number	Title	Yr	NM
PARK AVE.			
❑ 0(# unknown)	Is This Real?	1980	50.00
❑ 82802	Youth of America	1981	50.00
RESTLESS			
❑ 72194	Follow Blind	1987	15.00
❑ 72094	Land of the Lost	1986	15.00
❑ 72187	Over the Edge	1987	15.00
—Reissue			
❑ 72026	Wipers Live	1985	15.00
TIM/KERR			
❑ 31 [B]	Silver Sail	1993	25.00

WIRE

Number	Title	Yr	NM
4 MEN WITH BEARDS			
❑ 4M510LP [B]	154		25.00
❑ 4M509LP [B]	Chairs Missing		25.00
❑ 4M508LP [B]	Pink Flag		25.00
HARVEST			
❑ ST-11757 [B]	Pink Flag	1977	30.00
MUTE/ENIGMA			
❑ D1-73314 [B]	A Bell Is a Cup Until It Is Struck	1988	18.00
❑ D1-73516 [B]	It's Beginning to and Back Again	1989	18.00
❑ MLP-73273 [EP]	Snakedrill	1987	18.00
❑ SWAO-73270 [B]	The Ideal Copy	1987	18.00
WARNER BROS.			
❑ BSK3398 [B]	154	1979	25.00

WISE, CHUBBY, AND MAC WISEMAN

Number	Title	Yr	NM
GILLEY'S			
❑ 500	Give Me My Smokies and The Tennessee Waltz	197?	25.00

Number	Title	Yr	NM

WISE, CHUBBY

STARDAY

Number	Title	Yr	NM
❑ SLP-154 [M]	The Tennessee Fiddler	1961	50.00

WISEMAN, MAC

ABC

Number	Title	Yr	NM
❑ 4009	16 Great Performances	1974	15.00
❑ AC-30033	The ABC Collection	1976	15.00

CAPITOL

Number	Title	Yr	NM
❑ T1800 [M]	Bluegrass Favorites	1962	30.00
❑ ST1800 [S]	Bluegrass Favorites	1962	40.00

CMH

Number	Title	Yr	NM
❑ 6202	Country Memories	197?	15.00
❑ 4502	Greatest Bluegrass Hits	198?	12.00
❑ 6217	Mac Wiseman Sings Gordon Lightfoot	197?	15.00
❑ 9021	Songs That Made the Juke Box Play	197?	18.00
❑ 9001	The Mac Wiseman Story	197?	18.00

DOT

Number	Title	Yr	NM
❑ DLP-3313 [M]	12 Great Hits	1960	30.00
❑ DLP-25313 [S]	12 Great Hits	1960	40.00
❑ DLP-3730 [M]	A Master at Work	1966	25.00
❑ DLP-25730 [S]	A Master at Work	1966	30.00
❑ DLP-3135 [M]	Beside the Still Waters	1959	30.00
❑ DLP-25135 [S]	Beside the Still Waters	1959	40.00
❑ DLP-3373 [M]	Best Loved Gospel Hymns	1961	30.00
❑ DLP-25373 [S]	Best Loved Gospel Hymns	1961	40.00
❑ DLP-3731 [M]	Bluegrass	1966	25.00
❑ DLP-25731 [S]	Bluegrass	1966	30.00
❑ DLP-3408 [M]	Fireball Mail	1961	40.00
❑ DLP-25408 [R]	Fireball Mail	196?	25.00
❑ DLP-25896	Golden Hits of Mac Wiseman	1968	25.00
❑ DLP-3213 [M]	Great Folk Ballads	1959	30.00
❑ DLP-25213 [S]	Great Folk Ballads	1959	40.00
❑ DLP-3336 [M]	Keep on the Sunny Side	1960	40.00
❑ DLP-25336 [R]	Keep on the Sunny Side	196?	25.00
❑ DLP-3697 [M]	This Is Mac Wiseman	1966	25.00
❑ DLP-25697 [S]	This Is Mac Wiseman	1966	30.00
❑ DLP-3084 [M]	Tis Sweet to Be Remembered	1958	50.00
❑ DLP-25084 [R]	Tis Sweet to Be Remembered	196?	25.00

HAMILTON

Number	Title	Yr	NM
❑ HLP-12130 [M]	Sincerely	1964	25.00
❑ HLP-12167 [M]	Songs of the Dear Old Days	1965	25.00

HILLTOP

Number	Title	Yr	NM
❑ JM-6047 [M]	Mac Wiseman	1967	18.00
❑ JS-6047 [R]	Mac Wiseman	1967	15.00

MCA

Number	Title	Yr	NM
❑ 4009	16 Great Performances	198?	10.00
—Reissue of ABC 4009			

RCA VICTOR

Number	Title	Yr	NM
❑ LSP-4845	Concert Favorites	1972	18.00
❑ ANL1-1208	Concert Favorites	1975	12.00
—Reissue of 4845			
❑ LSP-4336	Johnny's Cash and Charley's Pride	1970	18.00

VETCO

Number	Title	Yr	NM
❑ 508	New Traditions, Vol. 1	197?	18.00
❑ 509	New Traditions, Vol. 2	197?	18.00

WISHBONE ASH

ATLANTIC

Number	Title	Yr	NM
❑ SD18164	Locked In	1976	12.00
❑ SD18200	New England	1976	12.00

DECCA

Number	Title	Yr	NM
❑ DL75437 [B]	Argus	1972	25.00
❑ DL75295	Pilgrimage	1971	18.00
❑ DL75249	Wishbone Ash	1971	18.00

FANTASY

Number	Title	Yr	NM
❑ 9629	Twin Barrels Burning	1983	12.00

I.R.S.

Number	Title	Yr	NM
❑ 82006	Here to Hear	1989	15.00
❑ 42101	Nouveau Calls	1988	15.00

MCA

Number	Title	Yr	NM
❑ 49	Argus	1973	15.00
—Reissue of Decca 75437			
❑ 2344	Argus	1978	12.00
—Reissue of MCA 49			
❑ 787	Argus	198?	10.00
—Reissue			
❑ 2311	Front Page News	1977	12.00
❑ 5283	Hot Ash	1981	12.00
❑ 3221	Just Testing	1980	12.00
❑ 770	Just Testing	198?	10.00
—Reissue			
❑ 8006	Live Dates	1973	18.00
❑ 3060	No Smoke Without Fire	1978	12.00
❑ 769	No Smoke Without Fire	198?	10.00
—Reissue			
❑ 36	Pilgrimage	1973	15.00
—Reissue of Decca 75295			
❑ 464	There's the Rub	1974	15.00
❑ 2343	Wishbone Ash	1978	12.00
—Reissue of Decca 75249			
❑ 327	Wishbone Four	1973	15.00
❑ 2348	Wishbone Four	1978	12.00
—Reissue of MCA 327			
❑ 786	Wishbone Four	198?	10.00
—Reissue			

WISHFUL THINKING

PAUSA

Number	Title	Yr	NM
❑ 7205	Think Again	1987	15.00
❑ 7187	Wishful Thinking	1986	12.00

SOUNDWINGS

Number	Title	Yr	NM
❑ SW-2109	Way Down West	1988	12.00

WISNER, JIMMY

CHANCELLOR

Number	Title	Yr	NM
❑ CHJ-5014 [M]	Aper-Sepshun	1960	30.00
❑ CHJS-5014 [S]	Aper-Sepshun	1960	30.00

COLUMBIA

Number	Title	Yr	NM
❑ CS9837	Love Theme from "Romeo and Juliet	1969	12.00

FELSTED

Number	Title	Yr	NM
❑ FL-7509 [M]	Blues for Harvey	1962	30.00
❑ FL-2509 [S]	Blues for Harvey	1962	30.00

WYNCOTE

Number	Title	Yr	NM
❑ W-9103 [M]	Cast Your Fate to the Wind	1965	12.00
❑ SW-9103 [S]	Cast Your Fate to the Wind	1965	15.00

WITHERS, BILL

COLUMBIA

Number	Title	Yr	NM
❑ FC37199	Bill Withers' Greatest Hits	1981	12.00
—Re-release of 36877 with "Just the Two of Us" added			
❑ JC35596	'Bout Love	1979	12.00
❑ PC40178	Just As I Am	1985	10.00
—Reissue of Sussex 7006			
❑ PC33704	Making Music	1975	12.00
❑ JC34903	Menagerie	1977	12.00
❑ PC34327	Naked and Warm	1976	12.00
❑ PC40177	Still Bill	1985	10.00
—Reissue of Sussex 7014			
❑ FC39887	Watching You Watching Me	1985	12.00

MOBILE FIDELITY

Number	Title	Yr	NM
❑ MFSL20446 [B]	Bill Withers Live At Carnegie Hall	2014	40.00

SUSSEX

Number	Title	Yr	NM
❑ SXBS-7025-2	Bill Withers Live at Carnegie Hall	1973	25.00
❑ SUX-8032	+'Justments	1974	18.00
❑ SXBS-7006 [B]	Just As I Am	1971	25.00
❑ SXBS-7014	Still Bill	1972	25.00
❑ SUX-8037	The Best of Bill Withers	1975	18.00

WITHERSPOON, JIMMY, AND BEN WEBSTER

VERVE

Number	Title	Yr	NM
❑ V6-8835	Previously Unreleased Recordings	197?	18.00

WITHERSPOON, JIMMY, AND GERRY MULLIGAN

EVEREST ARCHIVE OF FOLK & JAZZ

Number	Title	Yr	NM
❑ 264	Jimmy Witherspoon and Gerry Mulligan	197?	15.00

WITHERSPOON, JIMMY, AND RICHARD "GROOVE" HOLMES

OLYMPIC GOLD MEDAL

Number	Title	Yr	NM
❑ 7107	Groovin' and Spoonin'	1974	15.00

SURREY

Number	Title	Yr	NM
❑ S-1106 [M]	Blues for Spoon and Groove	1965	30.00
❑ SS-1106 [S]	Blues for Spoon and Groove	1965	30.00

WITHERSPOON, JIMMY

ABC

Number	Title	Yr	NM
❑ 717	Handbags and Gladrags	1970	30.00

ANALOGUE PRODUCTIONS

Number	Title	Yr	NM
❑ APR3008	Evenin' Blues	199?	18.00

BLUE NOTE

Number	Title	Yr	NM
❑ BN-LA534-G	Spoonful	1976	15.00

BLUESWAY

Number	Title	Yr	NM
❑ BLS-6026	Blues Singer	1969	30.00
❑ BLS-6040	Hunh	1970	30.00
❑ BLS-6051	The Best of Jimmy Witherspoon	1970	30.00

CAPITOL

Number	Title	Yr	NM
❑ ST-11360	Love Is a Five Letter Word	1975	15.00

CHESS

Number	Title	Yr	NM
❑ CH-93003	Spoon So Easy: The Chess Years	1990	15.00

CONSTELLATION

Number	Title	Yr	NM
❑ CM1422 [M]	Take This Hammer	1964	50.00
❑ CMS1422 [R]	Take This Hammer	1964	30.00

CROWN

Number	Title	Yr	NM
❑ CLP-5156 [M]	Jimmy Witherspoon	1959	80.00
—Black label, silver print			
❑ CLP-5156 [M]	Jimmy Witherspoon	1961	30.00
—Gray label, black print			
❑ CLP-5192 [M]	Jimmy Witherspoon Sings the Blues	1959	80.00
—Black label, silver print			
❑ CLP-5192 [M]	Jimmy Witherspoon Sings the Blues	1961	30.00
—Gray label, black print			
❑ CST-215 [S]	Jimmy Witherspoon Sings the Blues	1961	150.00
—Red vinyl; contrary to prior reports, this album -- at least the red vinyl version -- is in true stereo!			
❑ CST-215 [S]	Jimmy Witherspoon Sings the Blues	1961	100.00
—Black vinyl; this value assumes that this is in true stereo, as the red vinyl version is, but this has not been confirmed			

FANTASY

Number	Title	Yr	NM
❑ OBC-527	Baby, Baby, Baby	1990	15.00
—Reissue of Prestige 7290			
❑ OBC-511	Evenin' Blues	1988	15.00
—Reissue of Prestige 7300			
❑ 9660	Rockin' L.A.	1989	15.00
❑ 24701	The 'Spoon Concerts	1972	25.00

HIFI

Number	Title	Yr	NM
❑ R-421 [M]	At the Monterey Jazz Festival	1959	100.00
❑ SR-421 [S]	At the Monterey Jazz Festival	1959	60.00
❑ R-422 [M]	Feelin' the Spirit	1959	100.00
❑ SR-422 [S]	Feelin' the Spirit	1959	60.00
❑ R-426 [M]	Jimmy Witherspoon at the Renaissance	1959	100.00
❑ SR-426 [S]	Jimmy Witherspoon at the Renaissance	1959	60.00

JAZZ MAN

Number	Title	Yr	NM
❑ 5013	Jimmy Witherspoon Sings the Blues	1980	15.00

LAX

Number	Title	Yr	NM
❑ PW37115	Love Is a Five Letter Word	1981	12.00
—Reissue of Capitol LP			

MUSE

Number	Title	Yr	NM
❑ MR-5288	Jimmy Witherspoon Sings the Blues	1983	12.00
❑ MR-5327	Midnight Lady Called the Blues	1986	12.00

PRESTIGE

Number	Title	Yr	NM
❑ PRLP-7290 [M]	Baby, Baby, Baby	1963	40.00
❑ PRST-7290 [S]	Baby, Baby, Baby	1963	40.00
❑ PRLP-7314 [M]	Blues Around the Clock	1964	40.00
❑ PRST-7314 [S]	Blues Around the Clock	1964	40.00
❑ PRLP-7475 [M]	Blues for Easy Livers	1967	30.00
❑ PRST-7475 [S]	Blues for Easy Livers	1967	25.00
❑ PRLP-7327 [M]	Blue Spoon	1964	40.00
❑ PRST-7327 [S]	Blue Spoon	1964	40.00
❑ PRLP-7300 [M]	Evenin' Blues	1964	40.00
❑ PRST-7300 [S]	Evenin' Blues	1964	40.00
❑ 7855	Mean Old Frisco	1974	18.00
❑ PRLP-7356 [M]	Some of My Best Friends Are the Blues	1965	30.00
❑ PRST-7356 [S]	Some of My Best Friends Are the Blues	1965	30.00
❑ PRLP-7418 [M]	Spoon in London	1966	30.00
❑ PRST-7418 [S]	Spoon in London	1966	30.00
❑ PRST-7713	The Best of Jimmy Witherspoon	1969	25.00

RCA VICTOR

Number	Title	Yr	NM
❑ LPM-1639 [M]	Goin' to Kansas City Blues	1957	100.00
❑ ANL1-1048	Goin' to Kansas City Blues	1976	12.00
—Reissue			

REPRISE

Number	Title	Yr	NM
❑ R-6012 [M]	Hey, Mrs. Jones	1961	40.00
❑ R9-6012 [S]	Hey, Mrs. Jones	1961	60.00
❑ R-6059 [M]	Roots	1962	40.00
❑ R9-6059 [S]	Roots	1962	60.00
❑ R-2008 [M]	Spoon	1961	40.00
❑ R9-2008 [S]	Spoon	1961	60.00

UNITED

Number	Title	Yr	NM
❑ 7715	A Spoonful of Blues	197?	15.00

VERVE

Number	Title	Yr	NM
❑ V-5050 [M]	A Spoonful of Soul	1968	30.00
❑ V6-5050 [S]	A Spoonful of Soul	1968	25.00
❑ V-5007 [M]	Blue Point of View	1966	25.00
❑ V6-5007 [S]	Blue Point of View	1966	30.00
❑ V-5030 [M]	Blues Is Now	1967	30.00
❑ V6-5030 [S]	Blues Is Now	1967	25.00

WORLD PACIFIC

Number	Title	Yr	NM
❑ WP-1267 [M]	Singin' the Blues	1959	100.00
❑ WP-1402 [M]	There's Good Rockin' Tonight	1961	60.00
—Reissue of 1267			

WITTWER, JOHNNY

STINSON

Number	Title	Yr	NM
❑ SLP-58	Piano Rags	195?	25.00

WIXELL, INGVAR

CAPITOL

Number	Title	Yr	NM
❑ T10485 [M]	Christmas Music of Sweden	1965	15.00
❑ DT10485 [R]	Christmas Music of Sweden	1965	15.00
—Same as above, but in rechanneled stereo			
❑ SP-10485 [R]	Christmas Music of Sweden	1969	12.00
—Reissue with new prefix and label			
❑ SM-10485 [R]	Christmas Music of Sweden	197?	10.00
—Reissue with new prefix and label			

WIZARD

PEON

Number	Title	Yr	NM
❑ 1069	Original Wizard	1971	200.00

WIZARDS FROM KANSAS, THE

MERCURY

Number	Title	Yr	NM
❑ SR-61309	The Wizards from Kansas	1970	200.00

WOFFORD, MIKE

DISCOVERY

Number	Title	Yr	NM
❑ 784	Afterthoughts	1978	15.00
❑ 778	Bird of Paradise	1977	15.00
❑ 808	Mike Wofford Plays Jerome Kern	1979	12.00
❑ 816	Mike Wofford Plays Jerome Kern, Volume 2	1980	12.00
❑ 827	Mike Wofford Plays Jerome Kern, Volume 3	198?	12.00

EPIC

Number	Title	Yr	NM
❑ LN24225 [M]	Strawberry Wine	1967	25.00
❑ BN26225 [S]	Strawberry Wine	1967	18.00

FLYING DUTCHMAN

Number	Title	Yr	NM
❑ BDL1-1372	Joplin: Interpretations '76	1976	15.00

MILESTONE

Number	Title	Yr	NM
❑ MPS-9012	Summer Night	1968	25.00

TREND

Number	Title	Yr	NM
❑ TR-552	Funkalero	1988	12.00

WOFSEY, GARY

AMBI

Number	Title	Yr	NM
❑ 1521	Kef's Pool	198?	15.00
❑ 1520	Mel	198?	15.00
❑ 1519	My Grandfather's Clock	198?	15.00

WOLFE, NEIL, AND NOAH YOUNG

WK

Number	Title	Yr	NM
❑ 101	I Am Music/I Am Song	197?	18.00

WOLFE, NEIL

COLUMBIA

Number	Title	Yr	NM
❑ CL2378 [M]	Out of This World	1965	15.00
❑ CS9178 [S]	Out of This World	1965	18.00
❑ CS9600	Piano for Barbra	1968	15.00
❑ CL2239 [M]	Piano -- My Way	1964	15.00
❑ CS9039 [S]	Piano -- My Way	1964	18.00

IMPERIAL

Number	Title	Yr	NM
❑ LP-9169 [M]	Neil Swings Nicely	1962	18.00
❑ LP-12084 [S]	Neil Swings Nicely	1962	25.00
❑ LP-9192 [M]	One Order of Blues	1962	18.00
❑ LP-12192 [S]	One Order of Blues	1962	25.00

WOLFE, STEVE, AND NANCY KING

INNER CITY

Number	Title	Yr	NM
❑ IC-1049	First Date	197?	15.00

WOLFMAN JACK

BREAD

Number	Title	Yr	NM
❑ 0170	Wolfman Jack and the Wolf Pack	1965	400.00

WOODEN NICKEL

Number	Title	Yr	NM
❑ BWS1-0119	Fun and Romance Through the Ages	1974	30.00
❑ WN3-1009	Wolfman Jack	1972	30.00

WOLLMAN, TERRY

NOVA

Number	Title	Yr	NM
❑ 8706	Bimini	1987	12.00

WOMACK, BOBBY

ARISTA

Number	Title	Yr	NM
❑ AB4222 [B]	Roads of Life	1979	15.00

BEVERLY GLEN

Number	Title	Yr	NM
❑ 10000	The Poet	1981	12.00
❑ 10003	The Poet II	1984	12.00

COLUMBIA

Number	Title	Yr	NM
❑ PC34384	Home Is Where the Heart Is	1977	12.00
❑ JC35083	Pieces	1978	12.00

LIBERTY

Number	Title	Yr	NM
❑ LN-10171	Bobby Womack's Greatest Hits	198?	10.00
—Budget-line reissue of United Artists 346			
❑ LST-7645	The Womack "Live	1971	15.00

MCA

Number	Title	Yr	NM
❑ 5617	So Many Rivers	1985	10.00

MINIT

Number	Title	Yr	NM
❑ 24014	Fly Me to the Moon	1968	30.00
❑ 24027	My Prescription	1969	30.00

UNITED ARTISTS

Number	Title	Yr	NM
❑ UAS-5225	Across 110th Street	1972	15.00
❑ UA-LA346-G	Bobby Womack's Greatest Hits	1974	15.00
❑ UA-LA638-G	B.W. Goes C and W	1976	15.00
❑ UAS-5539	Communication	1971	15.00
❑ UA-LA043-F [B]	Facts of Life	1973	18.00
❑ UA-LA353-G	I Don't Know What the World Is Coming To	1975	15.00
❑ UA-LA199-G	Lookin' for a Love Again	1974	15.00
❑ UA-LA544-G	Safety Zone	1975	15.00
❑ UAS-5577	Understanding	1972	15.00
❑ LM-1002	Understanding	1980	10.00
—Reissue of 5577			

WOMB

DOT

Number	Title	Yr	NM
❑ DLP-25959 [B]	Overdub	1969	30.00
❑ DLP-25933 [B]	Womb	1969	30.00

WOMBLES, THE

COLUMBIA

Number	Title	Yr	NM
❑ KC33140	Remember You're a Womble	1974	15.00

WOMENFOLK, THE

RCA VICTOR

Number	Title	Yr	NM
❑ LPM-3527 [M]	Man Oh Man	1966	15.00
❑ LSP-3527 [S]	Man Oh Man	1966	18.00
❑ LPM-2919 [M]	Never Underestimate the Power of the Womenfolk	1964	15.00
❑ LSP-2919 [S]	Never Underestimate the Power of the Womenfolk	1964	18.00
❑ LPM-2832 [M]	The Womenfolk	1964	15.00
❑ LSP-2832 [S]	The Womenfolk	1964	18.00
❑ LPM-2991 [M]	The Womenfolk at the Hungry I	1965	15.00
❑ LSP-2991 [S]	The Womenfolk at the Hungry I	1965	18.00

WONDER, STEVIE

GORDY

Number	Title	Yr	NM
❑ GS932 [B]	Eivets Rednow	1968	40.00
—As "Eivets Rednow			

JOBETE

Number	Title	Yr	NM
❑ JSA-6253 [DJ]	The Wonder of Stevie	1988	40.00
—Publisher's demo with excerpts of 105 (!) Stevie Wonder songs			

MOTOWN

Number	Title	Yr	NM
❑ 6248ML	Characters	1987	12.00
❑ 31453 0238-1 [DJ]	Conversation Peace	1995	30.00
—Vinyl is promo only; white cover with custom sticker			
❑ M5-166V1	Down to Earth	1981	15.00
—Reissue of Tamla 272			
❑ M9-804A3	Looking Back	1977	30.00
—Withdrawn after Stevie Wonder objected to its release			
❑ 6291ML	Music from the Movie Jungle Fever	1991	25.00
❑ 10903141	Music of My Mind	2008	25.00
❑ M5-179V1	My Cherie Amour	1981	15.00
—Reissue of Tamla 296			
❑ M5-131V1	Recorded Live/Little Stevie Wonder/The 12 Year Old Genius	1981	15.00
—Reissue of Tamla 240			
❑ M5-176V1	Signed, Sealed and Delivered	1981	15.00
—Reissue of Tamla 304			
❑ 5255ML	Someday at Christmas	1982	12.00
—Reissue of Tamla 281			
❑ M5-210V1	The Jazz Soul of Little Stevie	1981	15.00
—Reissue of Tamla 233			
❑ 6108ML	The Woman in Red	1984	15.00
—With no sticker proclaiming "New Stevie Wonder Album			
❑ 6108ML	The Woman in Red	1984	12.00
—With sticker at top proclaiming "New Stevie Wonder Album			
❑ M5-173V1	Tribute to Uncle Ray	1981	15.00
—Reissue of Tamla 232			
❑ M5-183V1	Up-Tight Everything's Alright	1981	15.00
—Reissue of Tamla 268			
❑ M5-150V1	With a Song in My Heart	1981	15.00
—Reissue of Tamla 250			

TAMLA

Number	Title	Yr	NM
❑ T272 [M]	Down to Earth	1966	25.00
❑ TS272 [S]	Down to Earth	1966	30.00
❑ TS291	For Once in My Life	1968	25.00
❑ T6-332S1	Fulfillingness' First Finale	1974	18.00
❑ T282 [M]	Greatest Hits	1968	30.00
❑ TS282 [S]	Greatest Hits	1968	25.00
❑ T8-373S1	Hotter Than July	1980	15.00
❑ T326L	Innervisions	1973	18.00
❑ 6134TL	In Square Circle	1985	12.00
❑ T279 [M]	I Was Made to Love Her	1967	25.00
❑ TS279 [S]	I Was Made to Love Her	1967	30.00
❑ T13-371C2	Journey Through the Secret Life of Plants	1979	18.00
❑ T314L	Music of My Mind	1972	25.00
❑ TS296	My Cherie Amour	1969	25.00
❑ T240 [M]	Recorded Live/Little Stevie Wonder/The 12 Year Old Genius	1963	150.00
—The above three LPs as "Little Stevie Wonder			
❑ TS304	Signed Sealed and Delivered	1970	25.00
❑ T281 [M]	Someday at Christmas	1967	30.00
❑ TS281 [S]	Someday at Christmas	1967	40.00
❑ T7-362R1	Someday at Christmas	1978	25.00
—Unusual reissue of 281			
❑ T13-340C2	Songs in the Key of Life	1976	25.00
—With booklet and bonus 7-inch EP (deduct 25% if missing)			
❑ T255 [M]	Stevie at the Beach	1964	80.00
❑ TS298	Stevie Wonder Live	1970	25.00
❑ T313L	Stevie Wonder's Greatest Hits Vol. 2	1971	25.00
—Some, if not all, LP covers have the title mis-punctuated as "Stevie Wonders' Greatest Hits Vol. 2			
❑ 6002TL2	Stevie Wonder's Original Musiquarium I	1982	18.00
❑ T319L [B]	Talking Book	1972	30.00
—Original pressings have a braille note on cover			
❑ T319L	Talking Book	1973	12.00
—No braille note on cover			
❑ T233 [M]	The Jazz Soul of Little Stevie	1962	200.00
❑ T232 [M]	Tribute to Uncle Ray	1962	200.00
❑ T268 [M]	Up-Tight Everything's Alright	1966	30.00
❑ TS268 [S]	Up-Tight Everything's Alright	1966	30.00
❑ TS308	Where I'm Coming From	1971	25.00
❑ T250 [M]	With a Song in My Heart	1964	80.00
❑ T248 [M]	Workout Stevie, Workout	1963	1000.00
—Canceled; test pressings or acetates may exist			

UNIVERSAL MOTOWN

Number	Title	Yr	NM
❑ 5316422	Songs in the Key of Life	2009	30.00
—Two LP plus 7			

WONDERLAND BAND, THE

ROADSHOW

Number	Title	Yr	NM
❑ BXL1-3390	Wonderwoman	1979	18.00

WOOD, BOBBY

JOY

Number	Title	Yr	NM
❑ JL1001 [M]	Bobby Wood	1964	40.00

WOOD, BOOTY

MASTER JAZZ

Number	Title	Yr	NM
❑ 8102	Hang In There	197?	18.00

WOOD, BRENTON

BRENT

Number	Title	Yr	NM
❑ 5100 [M]	Introducing Brenton Wood! Boogaloo	1967	40.00
❑ S-100 [S]	Introducing Brenton Wood! Boogaloo	1967	60.00
—Four tracks by Brenton Wood, six by other artists			

CREAM

Number	Title	Yr	NM
❑ 1006	Come Softly	1977	18.00

DOUBLE SHOT

Number	Title	Yr	NM
❑ 1003 [M]	Baby You Got It	1967	30.00
❑ 5003 [S]	Baby You Got It	1967	30.00
—Black vinyl			
❑ 5003 [S]	Baby You Got It	1967	200.00
—Multi-color vinyl			
❑ 1002 [M]	Oogum Boogum	1967	30.00
❑ 5002 [S]	Oogum Boogum	1967	30.00

RHINO

Number	Title	Yr	NM
❑ RNLP-70223	The Best of Brenton Wood	1000	12.00

WOOD, DEL

COLUMBIA

Number	Title	Yr	NM
❑ CL2539 [M]	Upright, Low Down and Honky Tonk	1966	15.00
❑ CS9339 [S]	Upright, Low Down and Honky Tonk	1966	18.00

LAMB & LION

Number	Title	Yr	NM
❑ 1009	Rag Time Glory Special	197?	15.00

MERCURY

Number	Title	Yr	NM
❑ MG-20804 [M]	Piano Roll Blues	1963	15.00
❑ SR-60804 [S]	Piano Roll Blues	1963	18.00
❑ MG-20713 [M]	Ragtime Goes International	1962	15.00
❑ SR-60713 [S]	Ragtime Goes International	1962	18.00
❑ SR-60678 [S]	Ragtime Goes South of the Border	1962	18.00
❑ MG-20678 [M]	Ragtime Goes South of the Border	1962	15.00
❑ MG-20978 [M]	Roll Out the Piano	1964	15.00
❑ SR-60978 [S]	Roll Out the Piano	1964	18.00

RCA CAMDEN

Number	Title	Yr	NM
❑ CAL-684 [M]	Honky Tonk Piano	1962	15.00
❑ CAS-684 [R]	Honky Tonk Piano	1962	12.00
❑ CAL-796 [M]	It's Honky Tonk Time	1964	15.00
❑ CAS-796 [R]	It's Honky Tonk Time	1964	12.00

RCA VICTOR

Number	Title	Yr	NM
❑ LPM-2240 [M]	Buggies, Bustles and Barrelhouse	1960	18.00
❑ LSP-2240 [S]	Buggies, Bustles and Barrelhouse	1960	25.00
❑ LPM-1129 [M]	Down Yonder	1955	25.00
❑ LPM-2203 [M]	Flivvers, Flappers and Fox Trots	1960	18.00
❑ LSP-2203 [S]	Flivvers, Flappers and Fox Trots	1960	25.00
❑ LPM-1437 [M]	Hot, Happy and Honky	1957	25.00
❑ LPM-2091 [M]	Mississippi Show Boat	1959	18.00
❑ LSP-2091 [S]	Mississippi Show Boat	1959	25.00
❑ LPM-1633 [M]	Rags to Riches	1958	18.00
❑ LSP-1633 [S]	Rags to Riches	1958	25.00
❑ LPM-3907 [M]	The Best of Del Wood	1968	30.00

Number	Title	Yr	NM
❏ LSP-3907 [S]	The Best of Del Wood	1968	15.00
VOCALION			
❏ VL3609 [M]	There's a Tavern in the Town	196?	15.00

WOOD, HALLY

ELEKTRA

| ❏ EKL-10 [10] | O Lovely Appearance of Death | 1953 | 50.00 |

WOOD, JOHN

LOS ANGELES

| ❏ 1001 | Freeway of Love | 197? | 18.00 |
| ❏ 1002 | Until Goodbye | 1976 | 18.00 |

RANWOOD

| ❏ RLP-8036 | Introducing the John Wood Trio | 1969 | 18.00 |

WOOD, RONNIE

COLUMBIA

❏ FC37473	1234	1981	18.00
❏ JC35702	Gimme Some Neck	1979	18.00
❏ PC35702 [B]	Gimme Some Neck	198?	10.00
—Budget-line reissue			

WARNER BROS.

| ❏ BS2819 | I've Got My Own Album to Do | 1974 | 25.00 |
| ❏ BS2872 | Now Look | 1975 | 18.00 |

WOOD, ROY

TOWNHOUSE

| ❏ SN-7127 | One Man Band | 1981 | 15.00 |

UNITED ARTISTS

❏ UA-LA168-F [B]	Boulders	1973	18.00
❏ 0(# unknown) [DJ]	Boulders Folder	1973	40.00
—Promo version of 168 in 13x13 folder with press kit and postcards			
❏ UA-LA219-G [B]	Introducing Eddy and the Falcons	1974	15.00
❏ UA-LA575-G [B]	Mustard	1976	15.00
❏ UA-LA042-F [B]	Wizzard's Brew	1973	15.00

WARNER BROS.

| ❏ BSK3247 [B] | On the Road Again | 1979 | 15.00 |
| ❏ BS3065 [B] | Super Active Wizzo | 1977 | 15.00 |

WOODARD, LYMAN

STRATA

| ❏ 105-75 | Saturday Night Special | 197? | 18.00 |

WOODBURY, WOODY

STEREODDITIES

❏ 0BITOA	Booze Is the Only Answer	1961	40.00
—With record, paperback book and smaller booklets			
❏ MW6	The Best of Woody Woodbury	1963	25.00
❏ MW5	The Spice Is Right	1962	30.00
❏ MW7	Through the Keyhole	1964	25.00
❏ MW1	Woody Woodbury Looks at Love and Life	1960	30.00
❏ MW3	Woody Woodbury's Concert in Comedy	1961	30.00
❏ MW2	Woody Woodbury's Laughing Room	1960	30.00
❏ MW4	Woody Woodbury's Saloonatics	1961	30.00

WOODS, BILL

COUNTRY TOWN

| ❏ CTR-24803 [M] | Bill Woods from Bakersfield | 196? | 120.00 |

WOODS, CHRIS

DELMARK

| ❏ DS-437 | Modus Operandi | 1979 | 12.00 |
| ❏ DS-434 | Somebody Stole My Blues | 197? | 15.00 |

WOODS, JIMMY

CAPITOL

| ❏ ST-654 | Essence | 1971 | 18.00 |

CONTEMPORARY

❏ M-3605 [M]	Awakening	1962	30.00
❏ S-7605 [S]	Awakening	1962	30.00
❏ M-3612 [M]	Conflict	1963	30.00
❏ S-7612 [S]	Conflict	1963	30.00

WOODS, MACEO

VEE JAY

❏ LP-5001 [M]	Amazing Grace	1959	30.00
—Maroon label			
❏ LP-5001 [M]	Amazing Grace	1961	25.00
—Black colorband label			
❏ LP-5053 [M]	Garden of Prayer	1963	25.00
❏ SR-5053 [S]	Garden of Prayer	1963	30.00
❏ VJS-18002	Seeking Salvation	1975	18.00
❏ LP-5010 [M]	The Lord Will Make a Way	1960	30.00
—Maroon label			
❏ LP-5010 [M]	The Lord Will Make a Way	1961	25.00
—Black colorband label			

Number	Title	Yr	NM
VOLT			
❏ VOS-6009	Hello Sunshine	1970	25.00
❏ VOS-6013	Step to Jesus	1971	25.00

WOODS, PHIL, AND CHRIS SWANSON

SEA BREEZE

| ❏ SB-2008 | Crazy Horse | 198? | 12.00 |
| ❏ SB-2019 | Piper at the Gates of Dawn | 1984 | 12.00 |

WOODS, PHIL, AND GENE QUILL

COLUMBIA JAZZ ODYSSEY

| ❏ PC36806 | Phil Talks with Quill | 1980 | 12.00 |

EPIC

❏ LN3521 [M]	Phil Talks with Quill	1959	50.00
❏ BN554 [S]	Phil Talks with Quill	1959	40.00
❏ BN554 [S]	Phil Talks with Quill	199?	30.00
—Classic Records reissue on audiophile vinyl			

FANTASY

| ❏ OJC-215 | Phil and Quill with Prestige | 198? | 12.00 |

PRESTIGE

| ❏ 2508 | Four Altos | 198? | 15.00 |
| ❏ PRLP-7115 [M] | Phil and Quill with Prestige | 1957 | 80.00 |

RCA VICTOR

| ❏ LPM-1284 [M] | The Woods-Quill Sextet | 1956 | 80.00 |

WOODS, PHIL, AND GENE QUILL/JACKIE MCLEAN AND JOHN JENKINS/HAL MCKUSICK

NEW JAZZ

❏ NJLP-8204 [M]	Bird Feathers	1958	150.00
—Yellow Prestige label			
❏ NJLP-8204 [M]	Bird Feathers	1959	80.00
—Purple label			
❏ NJLP-8204 [M]	Bird Feathers	1965	40.00
—Blue label, trident logo at right			

WOODS, PHIL, AND LEW TABACKIN

OMNISOUND

| ❏ 1033 | Phil Woods and Lew Tabackin | 198? | 12.00 |

WOODS, PHIL

ABC IMPULSE!

| ❏ AS-9143 [S] | Greek Cooking | 1068 | 18.00 |

ADELPHI

| ❏ 5010 | More Live | 198? | 12.00 |

ANTILLES

| ❏ AN-1013 | At the Vanguard | 198? | 12.00 |
| ❏ AN-1006 | Birds of a Feather | 1982 | 12.00 |

BARNABY

❏ KZ31036	Rights of Swing	1972	15.00
❏ BR-5016	Rights of Swing	197?	12.00
—Reissue			

BLACKHAWK

| ❏ BKH-50401 | Heaven | 1986 | 12.00 |

CANDID

| ❏ CD-8016 [M] | Rights of Swing | 1960 | 40.00 |
| ❏ CS-9016 [S] | Rights of Swing | 1960 | 50.00 |

CENTURY

| ❏ 1050 | Songs for Sisyphus | 197? | 25.00 |

CLEAN CUTS

| ❏ 702 | Phil Woods Quartet, Vol. 1 | 1979 | 15.00 |

CONCORD JAZZ

❏ CJ-345	Bop Stew	1988	12.00
❏ CJ-377	Bouquet	1989	15.00
❏ CJ-361	Evolution	1988	12.00

EMBRYO

| ❏ SD530 | Phil Woods at the Frankfurt Jazz Festival | 197? | 18.00 |

ENJA

| ❏ 3081 | Three for All | 1981 | 15.00 |

EPIC

| ❏ LN3436 [M] | Warm Woods | 1958 | 250.00 |

FANTASY

❏ OJC-1735	Bird Feathers	198?	15.00
❏ OJC-092	Paring Off	198?	15.00
❏ OJC-1732	The Young Bloods	198?	15.00
❏ OJC-052	Woodlore	1982	15.00

GRYPHON

| ❏ 788 | I Remember | 1979 | 15.00 |
| ❏ 782 | Sisyphus | 1978 | 15.00 |

IMPULSE!

| ❏ A-9143 [M] | Greek Cooking | 1967 | 30.00 |
| ❏ AS-9143 [S] | Greek Cooking | 1967 | 30.00 |

INNER CITY

| ❏ IC-1002 | European Rhythm Machine | 197? | 18.00 |

JAZZ MAN

| ❏ 5001 | Rights of Swing | 1982 | 12.00 |

MGM

| ❏ SE-4695 | Phil Woods at the Montreux Jazz Festival | 197? | 18.00 |

Number	Title	Yr	NM
MOSAIC			
❏ MQ7-159	The Phil Woods Quartet/ Quintet 20th Anniversary Set	199?	120.00

MUSE

| ❏ MR-5037 | Musique de Bois | 1974 | 15.00 |

NEW JAZZ

❏ NJLP-1104 [10]	Phil Woods New Jazz Quintet	1954	500.00
❏ NJLP-8291 [M]	Pot Pie	1962	100.00
—Purple label			
❏ NJLP-8291 [M]	Pot Pie	1965	40.00
—Blue label, trident logo at right			

PALO ALTO/TBA

| ❏ PA-8084 | Live from New York | 1985 | 12.00 |

PRESTIGE

❏ 24065	Altology	197?	18.00
❏ PRST-7673 [R]	Early Quintets	1969	18.00
❏ PRLP-7046 [M]	Paring Off	1956	100.00
❏ PRLP-191 [10]	Phil Woods New Jazz Quartet	1954	400.00
❏ PRLP-204 [10]	Phil Woods New Jazz Quintet	1955	400.00
❏ PRLP-7080 [M]	The Young Bloods	1957	100.00
❏ PRLP-7018 [M]	Woodlore	1956	500.00
—Yellow label with W. 50th St. address			

QUICKSILVER

| ❏ QS-4011 | Live from New York | 1991 | 15.00 |

RCA VICTOR

❏ BGL1-1800	Floresta	1976	15.00
❏ BXL1-1800	Floresta	1978	12.00
—Reissue with new prefix			
❏ BGL1-1027	Images	1975	15.00
❏ BXL1-1027	Images	1978	12.00
—Reissue with new prefix			
❏ BGL2-2202	Live from the Showboat	1977	18.00
❏ BGL1-1391	The New Album	1976	15.00
❏ BXL1-1391	The New Album	1978	12.00
—Reissue with new prefix			

RED RECORD

| ❏ VPA-163 | European Tour Live | 198? | 15.00 |
| ❏ VPA-177 | Integrity | 1985 | 18.00 |

SAVOY JAZZ

| ❏ SJL-1179 | Bird Calls: Vol. 1 | 1987 | 12.00 |

STATUS

| ❏ ST-8304 [M] | Sugan | 1965 | 40.00 |

TESTAMENT

| ❏ 4402 | New Music | 197? | 18.00 |

VERVE

| ❏ V6-8791 | Round Trip | 1969 | 18.00 |

WOODY, BILL

ABC HICKORY

| ❏ HB-44009 | Just for You Babe | 1977 | 15.00 |
| —As "Woody | | | |

MCA

| ❏ 3095 | Organized Noise | 1979 | 12.00 |

WOODY'S TRUCK STOP

SMASH

| ❏ SRS-67111 [B] | Woody's Truck Stop | 1969 | 30.00 |

WOOFERS, THE

WYNCOTE

| ❏ W9011 [M] | Dragsville | 1964 | 40.00 |
| ❏ SW9011 [S] | Dragsville | 1964 | 50.00 |

WOOLEY, AMY

MCA

| ❏ 5240 | Amy Wooley | 1981 | 12.00 |

WOOLEY, SHEB

GUSTO

| ❏ GTV-110 | Greatest Hits of Sheb Wooley Or Do You Say Ben Colder | 1979 | 15.00 |

MGM

❏ E-4173 [M]	Ben Colder	1963	30.00
❏ SE-4173 [S]	Ben Colder	1963	40.00
—MGM 4173 as "Ben Colder			
❏ GAS-139	Ben Colder (Golden Archive Series)	1970	18.00
—As "Ben Colder			
❏ E-4421 [M]	Big Ben Strikes Again	1967	25.00
❏ SE-4421 [S]	Big Ben Strikes Again	1967	25.00
—MGM 4421 as "Ben Colder			
❏ SE-4614	Harper Valley P.T.A.	1968	25.00
—As "Ben Colder			
❏ SE-4629	Have One On	1969	18.00
—As "Ben Colder			
❏ E-4325 [M]	It's a Big Land	1965	25.00
❏ SE-4325 [S]	It's a Big Land	1965	30.00
❏ SE-4758	Live and Loaded	1971	18.00
—As "Ben Colder			
❏ E-3299 [M]	Sheb Wooley	1956	150.00

Number	Title	Yr	NM
❏ E-3904 [M]	Songs from the Days of Rawhide	1961	40.00
❏ SE-3904 [S]	Songs from the Days of Rawhide	1961	50.00
❏ E-4117 [M]	Spoofing the Big Ones	1961	40.00
❏ SE-4117 [S]	Spoofing the Big Ones	1961	50.00
— MGM 4117 as "Ben Colder			
❏ E-4136 [M]	Tales of How the West Was Won	1963	30.00
❏ SE-4136 [S]	Tales of How the West Was Won	1963	40.00
❏ E-4026 [M]	That's My Ma and That's My Pa	1962	30.00
❏ SE-4026 [S]	That's My Ma and That's My Pa	1962	40.00
❏ SE-4530	The Best of Ben Colder	1968	25.00
— As "Ben Colder			
❏ E-4275 [M]	The Very Best of Sheb Wooley	1965	25.00
❏ SE-4275 [S]	The Very Best of Sheb Wooley	1965	30.00
❏ SE-4876	The Wacky World of Ben Colder	1973	18.00
— As "Ben Colder			
❏ SE-4615	Warm and Wooley	1969	25.00
❏ SE-4807	Warming Up to Colder	1972	18.00
— As "Ben Colder			
❏ SE-4674	Wild Again	1970	18.00
— As "Ben Colder			
❏ E-4482 [M]	Wine, Women and Song	1967	25.00
❏ SE-4482 [S]	Wine, Women and Song	1967	25.00
— MGM 4482 as "Ben Colder			

WOOLIES, THE

SPIRIT

Number	Title	Yr	NM
❏ 9645-2001	Basic Rock	1971	40.00
❏ 9645-2005	Live at Lizards	1973	40.00

WOOLLEY, BRUCE, AND THE CAMERA CLUB

COLUMBIA

Number	Title	Yr	NM
❏ NJC36301	Bruce Woolley and the Camera Club	1980	18.00

WORLD BASS VIOLIN ENSEMBLE

BLACK SAINT

Number	Title	Yr	NM
❏ BSR-0063	Basically Yours	198?	15.00

WORLD FAMOUS CHORUS, A

KAYBANK-MUSICMASTERS

Number	Title	Yr	NM
❏ KB2698	Seasons Greetings	197?	15.00

WORLD OF OZ, THE

DERAM

Number	Title	Yr	NM
❏ DFS18022 [B]	The World of Oz	1969	60.00

WORLD PARTY

CHRYSALIS

Number	Title	Yr	NM
❏ F1-21654	Goodbye Jumbo	1990	15.00
❏ R134261	Private Revolution	1987	15.00
— RCA Music Service edition			
❏ BFV41552	Private Revolution	1986	12.00

WORLD RHYTHM BAND

DISCOVERY

Number	Title	Yr	NM
❏ 865	Ibex	198?	12.00

WORLD SAXOPHONE QUARTET

BLACK SAINT

Number	Title	Yr	NM
❏ BSR-0077	Live in Zurich	198?	15.00
❏ BSR-0056	Revue	198?	15.00
❏ BSR-0027	Steppin'	198?	15.00
❏ BSR-0046	W.S.Q.	198?	15.00

ELEKTRA/MUSICIAN

| ❏ 60864 | Rhythm and Blues | 1989 | 15.00 |

ELEKTRA/NONESUCH

| ❏ 79164 | Dances and Ballads | 1988 | 12.00 |
| ❏ 79137 | World Saxophone Quartet Plays Duke Ellington | 1987 | 12.00 |

WORLD'S GREATEST JAZZ BAND, THE

EVEREST ARCHIVE OF FOLK & JAZZ

Number	Title	Yr	NM
❏ 314	The World's Greatest Jazz Band	197?	12.00

FLYING DUTCHMAN

| ❏ BDL1-1371 | The World's Greatest Jazz Band In Concert | 1976 | 15.00 |

WORLD JAZZ

❏ 1	Century Plaza	197?	15.00
❏ 2	Hark the Herald Angels Swing	197?	15.00
❏ 3	The World's Greatest Jazz Band in Concert, Vol. 1	197?	15.00
❏ 4	The World's Greatest Jazz Band in Concert, Vol. 2	197?	15.00
❏ 8	The World's Greatest Jazz Band On Tour	197?	15.00
❏ 10	The World's Greatest Jazz Band On Tour II	197?	15.00
❏ 6	The World's Greatest Jazz Band Plays Cole Porter	197?	15.00

Number	Title	Yr	NM
❏ 9	The World's Greatest Jazz Band Plays Duke Ellington	197?	15.00
❏ 11	The World's Greatest Jazz Band Plays George Gershwin	1978	15.00
❏ 7	The World's Greatest Jazz Band Plays Rodgers and Hart	197?	15.00

WORTH, MARION, AND GEORGE MORGAN

COLUMBIA

Number	Title	Yr	NM
❏ CL2197 [M]	Slippin' Around	1964	25.00
❏ CS8997 [S]	Slippin' Around	1964	30.00

WORTH, MARION

COLUMBIA

Number	Title	Yr	NM
❏ CL2011 [M]	Marion Worth's Greatest Hits	1963	25.00
❏ CS8811 [S]	Marion Worth's Greatest Hits	1963	30.00
❏ CL2287 [M]	Marion Worth Sings Marty Robbins	1964	25.00
❏ CS9087 [S]	Marion Worth Sings Marty Robbins	1964	30.00

DECCA

| ❏ DL4936 [M] | A Woman Needs Love | 1967 | 30.00 |
| ❏ DL74936 [S] | A Woman Needs Love | 1967 | 25.00 |

WOULD

PERCEPTION

Number	Title	Yr	NM
❏ 24	Would	1972	30.00

WRAY, LINK

EPIC

Number	Title	Yr	NM
❏ LN3661 [M]	Link Wray and the Wraymen	1960	250.00

NORTON

❏ 211	Big City After Dark (Missing Links Vol. 2)	199?	12.00
❏ 210	Hillbilly Wolf (Missing Links Vol. 1)	199?	12.00
❏ 212	Some Kinda Nut (Missing Links Vol. 3)	199?	12.00
❏ 253	Streets of Chicago (Missing Links Vol. 4)	1995	12.00

POLYDOR

❏ PD-5047	Be What You Want To	1972	25.00
❏ 24-4064	Link Wray	1971	25.00
❏ PD-6025	The Link Wray Rumble	1974	25.00

RECORD FACTORY

| ❏ 1929 | Yesterday and Today | 1969 | 80.00 |

SWAN

| ❏ SLP-510 [M] | Jack the Ripper | 1963 | 150.00 |

VERMILLION

| ❏ 1924 | Great Guitar Hits | 196? | 80.00 |
| ❏ 1925 [M] | Link Wray Sings and Plays Guitar | 196? | 80.00 |

VISA

| ❏ 7009 | Bullshot | 1979 | 15.00 |
| ❏ 7010 | Live at the Paradiso | 1980 | 15.00 |

WRAY, VERNON

VERMILLION

Number	Title	Yr	NM
❏ 1972	Wasted	1972	100.00

WRECKLESS ERIC & AMY RIGBY

SOUTHERN DOMESTIC

Number	Title	Yr	NM
❏ SD005LP [B]	A Working Museum	2012	25.00

WRECKLESS ERIC

STIFF

Number	Title	Yr	NM
❏ USE1 [B]	Whole Wide World	1979	25.00

STIFF/EPIC

❏ E236463 [B]	Big Smash	1980	25.00
❏ AS785 [EP]	Wreckless Eric	1980	18.00
— Promo-only 5-song sample from E2 36463			

WRICE, LARRY "WILD"

PACIFIC JAZZ

Number	Title	Yr	NM
❏ PJ-24 [M]	Wild!	1961	30.00
❏ ST-24 [S]	Wild!	1961	30.00

WRIGHT, BERNARD

ARISTA

Number	Title	Yr	NM
❏ ALB8-8103	Funky Beat	198?	12.00

GRP/ARISTA

| ❏ GL5011 | 'Nard | 1980 | 15.00 |

MANHATTAN

| ❏ ST-53014 | Mr. Wright | 1985 | 12.00 |

WRIGHT, BETTY

ALSTON

Number	Title	Yr	NM
❏ 4410	Betty Travelin' in the Wright Circle	1979	15.00
❏ 4408	Betty Wright Live	1978	15.00
❏ 4400 [B]	Danger High Voltage	1974	15.00
❏ SD7026	Hard to Stop	1973	18.00
❏ SD 33-388 [B]	I Love the Way You Love	1972	18.00
❏ 4406	This Time for Real	1977	15.00

Number	Title	Yr	NM
ATCO			
❏ SD 33-260	My First Time Around	1968	30.00
COLLECTABLES			
❏ COL-5118	Golden Classics	198?	12.00
EPIC			
❏ JE36879	Betty Wright	1981	12.00
❏ FE38558	Wright Back at You	1983	12.00
FANTASY			
❏ 9644	Sevens	1986	12.00
MS. B.			
❏ 3301	Mother Wit	1988	12.00
❏ 3318	Passion and Compassion	198?	18.00

WRIGHT, BOBBY

ABC

| ❏ ABCD-842 | Seasons of Love | 1974 | 15.00 |

DECCA

| ❏ DL75319 | Here I Go Again | 1971 | 18.00 |

WRIGHT, CHARLES, AND THE WATTS 103RD STREET RHYTHM BAND

ABC

Number	Title	Yr	NM
❏ D-887	Lil' Encouragement	1975	15.00

ABC DUNHILL

| ❏ DS-50162 | Doin' What Comes Naturally | 1973 | 18.00 |
| ❏ DS-50187 | Ninety Day Cycle People | 1974 | 15.00 |

WARNER BROS.

❏ WS1864	Express Yourself	1970	18.00
❏ WS1801	In the Jungle, Babe	1969	25.00
— Green label with "W7" logo			
❏ WS1801	In the Jungle, Babe	1970	18.00
— Green label with "WB" logo			
❏ BS2620	Rhythm and Poetry	1972	18.00
— Green label with "WB" logo			
❏ BS2620	Rhythm and Poetry	1973	15.00
— Burbank" palm-trees logo			
❏ WS1741	The Watts 103rd Street Rhythm Band	1968	25.00
— Green label with "W7" logo			
❏ WS1761	Together	1969	25.00
— Green label with "W7" logo			
❏ WS1761	Together	1970	18.00
— Green label with "WB" logo			
❏ WS1904	You're So Beautiful	1971	18.00

WRIGHT, DEMPSEY

ANDEX

| ❏ A-3006 [M] | The Wright Approach | 1958 | 60.00 |
| ❏ AS-3006 [S] | The Wright Approach | 1958 | 50.00 |

WRIGHT, FRANK

CHIAROSCURO

| ❏ 2014 | Kevin, My Dear Son | 1979 | 13.00 |

ESP-DISK

❏ 1023 [M]	Frank Wright Trio	1966	30.00
❏ S-1023 [S]	Frank Wright Trio	1966	25.00
❏ 1053 [S]	Your Prayer	1968	25.00

WRIGHT, GARY

A&M

❏ SP-4277	Extraction	1970	18.00
❏ SP-4296	Footprint	1971	18.00
❏ SP-3528	That Was Only Yesterday	1976	18.00
— By "Gary Wright/Spooky Tooth			

CYPRESS

| ❏ 0111 | Who I Am | 1988 | 15.00 |

WARNER BROS.

❏ BSK3244	Headin' Home	1979	12.00
❏ BS2868	The Dream Weaver	1975	12.00
❏ BS2951	The Light of Smiles	1976	12.00
❏ BSK3511	The Right Place	1981	12.00
❏ BSK3137	Touch and Gone	1977	12.00

WRIGHT, GEORGE

ABC/WESTMINSTER GOLD

| ❏ WGDP-8305 | The Christmas Album | 1974 | 12.00 |
| — Reissue of Dot 25479 | | | |

DOT

| ❏ DLP3479 [M] | Christmas Time | 1962 | 15.00 |
| ❏ DLP25479 [S] | Christmas Time | 1962 | 18.00 |

HIFI

| ❏ R-706 [M] | Merry Christmas | 195? | 18.00 |
| ❏ R-705 [M] | Music for Christmas | 195? | 18.00 |

WRIGHT, JOHN

FANTASY

| ❏ OJC-1743 | South Side Soul | 1990 | 15.00 |

PRESTIGE

❏ PRLP-7212 [M]	Makin' Out	1961	80.00
❏ PRLP-7233 [M]	Mr. Soul	1962	80.00
❏ PRST-7233 [S]	Mr. Soul	1962	60.00
❏ PRLP-7197 [M]	Nice 'N' Nasty	1961	80.00
❏ PRLP-7190 [M]	South Side Soul	1960	100.00

Number	Title	Yr	NM

STATUS
❑ ST-8322 [M]	The Last Amen	1965	80.00

WRIGHT, JOHNNY

DECCA
❑ DL4770 [M]	Country Music Special	1966	30.00
❑ DL74770 [S]	Country Music Special	1966	30.00
❑ DL4846 [M]	Country the Wright Way	1967	30.00
❑ DL74846 [S]	Country the Wright Way	1967	25.00
❑ DL4698 [M]	Hello Vietnam	1965	30.00
❑ DL74698 [S]	Hello Vietnam	1965	30.00
❑ DL75019	Johnny Wright Sings Country Favorites	1968	25.00

WRIGHT, LEO

ATLANTIC
❑ 1358 [M]	Blues Shout	1960	30.00
—Multicolor label, white "fan" logo at right			
❑ SD1358 [S]	Blues Shout	1960	30.00
—Multicolor label, white "fan" logo at right			
❑ 1358 [M]	Blues Shout	196?	18.00
—Multicolor label, black "fan" logo at right			
❑ SD1358 [S]	Blues Shout	196?	25.00
—Multicolor label, black "fan" logo at right			
❑ 1393 [M]	Suddenly the Blues	1962	30.00
—Multicolor label, black "fan" logo at right			
❑ SD1393 [S]	Suddenly the Blues	1962	30.00
—Multicolor label, black "fan" logo at right			

ROULETTE
❑ SR-5007	Evening Breeze	1977	12.00

VORTEX
❑ 2011	Soul Talk	197?	25.00

WRIGHT, MARVIN "LEFTY"

X
❑ LXA-3028 [10]	Boogie Woogie Piano	1954	60.00

WRIGHT, NAT

WARWICK
❑ W-2040 [M]	The Biggest Voice in Jazz	1961	50.00
❑ W-2040ST [S]	The Biggest Voice in Jazz	1961	80.00

WRIGHT, O.V.

BACK BEAT
❑ 70	A Nickel and a Nail and Ace of Spade	1971	60.00
❑ 66	Eight Men, Four Women	1968	60.00
❑ 61 [M]	If It's Only for Tonight	1965	100.00
❑ S-61 [S]	If It's Only for Tonight	1965	150.00
❑ 72	Memphis Unlimited	1973	50.00
❑ 67 [B]	Nucleus of Soul	1969	60.00

HI
❑ 6008	Bottom Line	1978	30.00
❑ 6001	Into Something	1977	30.00
❑ 6011	We're Still Together	1979	30.00

WRIGHT, RICHARD

COLUMBIA
❑ JC35559 [B]	Wet Dream	1978	30.00

WRIGHT, SONNY (2)

KAPP
❑ KS-3614	I Love You, Loretta Lynn	1968	25.00

WRIGHT, WILLIE

ARGO
❑ LP-4024 [M]	I'm on My Way	1963	25.00
❑ LPS-4024 [S]	I'm on My Way	1963	30.00

CONCERT DISC
❑ 45 [S]	I Sing Folk Songs	1960	40.00
❑ 1045 [M]	I Sing Folk Songs	1960	30.00

WRIGHT BROTHERS, THE

MERCURY
❑ 818654-1	Easy Street	1984	10.00

WARNER BROS.
❑ 23736	Made in the U.S.A.	1982	12.00

WYLER, GRETCHEN

JUBILEE
❑ JLP-1100 [M]	Wild, Wyler, Wildest	1959	30.00
❑ SDJLP-1100 [S]	Wild, Wyler, Wildest	1959	30.00

WYLIE, RICHARD "POPCORN"

ABC
❑ ABCD-834	E.S.P.	1974	60.00

WYMAN, BILL

ROLLING STONES
❑ COC59102 [B]	Monkey Grip	1974	25.00
❑ COC79100 [B]	Monkey Grip	1974	18.00
—Reissue of 59102			
❑ QD79100 [Q]	Monkey Grip	1974	30.00
❑ COC79103	Stone Alone	1976	15.00
❑ QD79103 [Q]	Stone Alone	1976	30.00

Number	Title	Yr	NM

WYNDER K. FROG

UNITED ARTISTS
❑ UAS-5740 [B]	Into the Fire	1971	18.00
❑ UAS-6695 [B]	Out of the Frying Pan	1970	18.00

WYNETTE, TAMMY

COLUMBIA LIMITED EDITION
❑ LE10194	Tammy's Touch	197?	15.00
❑ LE10049	The First Lady	197?	15.00
❑ LE10193	The Ways to Love a Man	197?	15.00
❑ LE10195	We Sure Can Love Each Other	197?	15.00

COLUMBIA SPECIAL PRODUCTS
❑ P13261	Bedtime Story	1976	15.00
❑ P13259	My Man	1976	15.00
❑ P11228	Take Me to Your World	1973	15.00
❑ P13256	The Ways to Love a Man	1976	15.00
❑ P13611	Twenty Big Hits of Tammy Wynette	197?	18.00
❑ P11519	Your Good Girl's Gonna Go Bad	1973	15.00

EPIC
❑ EG40625	Anniversary: 20 Years of Hits	1987	18.00
❑ KE32745	Another Lonely Song	1974	15.00
❑ KE31285	Bedtime Story	1972	18.00
❑ FE38312	Biggest Hits	1984	12.00
❑ E30343	Christmas with Tammy	1970	25.00
❑ BN26392 [S]	D-I-V-O-R-C-E	1968	25.00
❑ LN24392 [M]	D-I-V-O-R-C-E	1968	50.00
—This has been confirmed to exist on yellow label stock copies			
❑ FE37344	Encore	1981	12.00
❑ PE37344	Encore	198?	10.00
—Budget-line reissue			
❑ FE38744	Even the Strong Get Lonely	1983	12.00
❑ FE38372	Good Love and Heartbreak	1983	12.00
❑ FE40832	Higher Ground	1987	12.00
❑ BN26423	Inspiration	1969	25.00
❑ KE33582	I Still Believe in Fairy Tales	1975	15.00
❑ KE36013	Just Tammy	1979	15.00
❑ KE31937	Kids Say the Darndest Things	1973	18.00
❑ PE34694	Let's Get Together One Last Time	1977	15.00
❑ KE31717	My Man	1972	18.00
❑ FE44498	Next to You	1989	15.00
❑ KE35044	One of a Kind	1977	15.00
❑ JE36485	Only Lonely Sometimes	1980	12.00
❑ FE37980	Soft Touch	1982	12.00
❑ FE39971	Sometimes When We Touch	1985	12.00
❑ BN26451	Stand By Your Man	1969	25.00
❑ BG33773	Stand By Your Man/Bedtime Story	1976	18.00
❑ LN24353 [M]	Take Me to Your World/I Don't Wanna Play House	1968	40.00
—May exist only as a white label promo			
❑ BN26353 [S]	Take Me to Your World/I Don't Wanna Play House	1968	25.00
❑ BN26486	Tammy's Greatest Hits	1969	25.00
❑ PE26486	Tammy's Greatest Hits	198?	10.00
—Budget-line reissue			
❑ E30733	Tammy's Greatest Hits, Volume II	1971	25.00
❑ PE30733	Tammy's Greatest Hits, Volume II	198?	10.00
—Budget-line reissue			
❑ KE33396	Tammy's Greatest Hits, Volume III	1975	15.00
❑ PE33396	Tammy's Greatest Hits, Volume III	198?	10.00
—Budget-line reissue			
❑ KE35630	Tammy's Greatest Hits, Volume IV	1978	15.00
❑ BN26549	Tammy's Touch	1970	25.00
❑ E30213 [B]	The First Lady	1970	25.00
❑ KEG30358	The First Songs of the First Lady	1970	25.00
❑ BN26519	The Ways to Love a Man	1970	25.00
❑ EGP503	The World of Tammy Wynette	1970	30.00
❑ PE34075	'Til I Can Make It on My Own	1976	15.00
❑ E30658	We Sure Can Love Each Other	1971	25.00
❑ EQ30658 [Q]	We Sure Can Love Each Other	1972	30.00
❑ KE35442	Womanhood	1978	15.00
❑ KE33246	Woman to Woman	1975	15.00
❑ PE34289	You and Me	1976	15.00
❑ FE37104	You Brought Me Back	1981	12.00
❑ LN24305 [M]	Your Good Girl's Gonna Go Bad	1967	30.00
❑ BN26305 [S]	Your Good Girl's Gonna Go Bad	1967	25.00

HARMONY
❑ KH30914	Just a Matter of Time	1971	15.00
❑ KH30096	Send Me No Roses	1970	15.00

PAIR
❑ PDL2-1073	From the Bottom of My Heart	1986	15.00

REALM
❑ 2V8047	The Queen Volume 1	1976	18.00
❑ 1V8048	The Queen Volume 2	1976	12.00

TIME-LIFE
❑ STW-116	Country Music	1981	15.00

Number	Title	Yr	NM

WYNN, ALBERT

RIVERSIDE
❑ RLP-426 [M]	Albert Wynn and His Gutbucket Seven	1962	30.00
❑ RS-9426 [R]	Albert Wynn and His Gutbucket Seven	1962	25.00

WYNTERS, GAIL

HICKORY
❑ LPS-138 [S]	A Girl for All Seasons	1967	18.00
❑ LPM-138 [M]	A Girl for All Seasons	1967	25.00

RCA VICTOR
❑ APL1-2285	Let the Lady Sing	1977	25.00

X

X-RAY SPEX

BLUE PLATE
❑ CAROL-1813-1	Germ Free Adolescents	1992	25.00
—Recorded in 1978, this is this classic new wave LP's first American issue			

EMI
❑ INS-3023	Germ Free Adolescents	1978	35.00
—British release only, no U.S. version until 1992			

X

ELEKTRA
❑ 60430	Ain't Love Grand	1985	15.00
❑ 60788	Live at the Whiskey A-Go-Go on the Fabulous Sunset Strip	1988	18.00
❑ 60283	More Fun in the New World	1983	15.00
❑ 60492	See How We Are	1987	12.00
❑ 60150 [B]	Under the Big Black Sun	1982	18.00

RHINO
❑ R1-74370	Los Angeles	2003	25.00
—Reissue on 180-gram vinyl			

SLASH
❑ SR-104 [B]	Los Angeles	1980	30.00
❑ 23930	Los Angeles	1983	15.00
—Reissue of Slash 104			
❑ SR-107 [B]	Wild Gift	1981	30.00
❑ 23931	Wild Gift	1983	15.00
—Reissue of Slash 107			

X CLAN

4TH & B'WAY
❑ 444019-1	To the East Blackwards	1990	18.00

POLYDOR
❑ 513225-1	Xodus — The New Testament	1992	18.00

XAVIER

LIBERTY
❑ LT-51116	Point of Pleasure	1981	18.00

XAVION

ASYLUM
❑ 60375	Burnin' Hot	1984	18.00

XIT

CANYON
❑ 7114	Entrance	197?	50.00
❑ C-7121	Relocation	1977	40.00

RARE EARTH
❑ R-536	Plight of the Redman	1972	30.00
❑ R-545 [B]	Silent Warrior	1973	30.00

WARRIOR
❑ WAR49	Plight of the Redman	1981	18.00
—Reissue of Rare Earth 536			

XSCAPE

SO SO DEF
❑ C57107	Hummin' Comin' At Cha	1993	15.00
❑ C67022	Off the Hook	1995	15.00

XTC

GEFFEN
❑ GHS4035	Black Sea	1984	12.00
—Reissue of Virgin/Epic 38150			
❑ GHS4034	Drums and Wires	1984	12.00
—Reissue of Virgin/Epic 38151			
❑ GHS4036	English Settlement	1984	18.00
—First release of British version of this album in U.S.			
❑ GHS4033	Go2	1984	12.00
—Reissue of Virgin/Epic 38152			
❑ GHS4027	Mummer	1983	12.00
❑ R201086 [B]	Oranges and Lemons	1989	18.00
—BMG Direct Marketing edition			
❑ GHS24218	Oranges and Lemons	1989	18.00

Number	Title	Yr	NM
❏ GHS24169	Psonic Psunspot	1987	18.00
—As "The Dukes of Stratosphear			
❏ GHS24117	Skylarking	1986	18.00
—First pressing, with "Mermaid Smiled" and without "Dear God			
❏ GHS24117	Skylarking	1986	12.00
—Second pressing, with "Dear God" and without "Mermaid Smiled			
❏ GHS24054	The Big Express	1984	12.00
❏ GHS4037	Waxworks (Some Singles, 1977-82)	1984	15.00
❏ GHS4032	White Music	1984	12.00
—Reissue of Virgin/Epic 38153			

VIRGIN

❏ VA13147	Black Sea	1980	30.00
—Promo only; label, jacket and innersleeve ALL must have this number			
❏ VA13134 [B]	Drums and Wires	1979	35.00
—With bonus 7-inch record (PR 344) enclosed -- deduct 40 percent if missing			

VIRGIN/EPIC

❏ PE38150	Black Sea	1982	12.00
—Reissue of Virgin/RSO 1001			
❏ PE38151	Drums and Wires	1982	12.00
—Reissue of Virgin 13134			
❏ ARE37943	English Settlement	1982	12.00
—Drastically edited version of U.K. original, which was a 2-record set			
❏ PE38152	Go2	1982	12.00
—Reissue of Virgin International VI-2108			
❏ PE38153	White Music	1982	12.00
—Reissue of Virgin International VI-2095			

VIRGIN INTERNATIONAL

❏ VI-2108	Go2	1979	18.00
❏ VI-2095 [B]	White Music	1979	25.00

VIRGIN/RSO

❏ VR-1-1000	Black Sea	1980	25.00
—With green outer bag and "VA 13147" on innersleeve			
❏ VR-1-1000	Black Sea	1980	15.00
—Without green outer bag; innersleeves may or may not have "VA 13147" reference			

WARNER BROS.

❏ WBMS-146 [DJ]	Skylarking Interview with Andy Partridge	1986	30.00
—Part of "The Warner Bros. Music Show" series			

XYMOX

RELATIVITY

❏ EMC8037	The Clan of Xymox	1985	30.00

WING

❏ 848516-1	Phoenix	1991	15.00
❏ 839233-1	Twist of Shadows	1989	15.00

XYZ

ENIGMA

❏ 7735251	XYZ	1989	12.00

YZIBIT

LOUD

❏ 1885	Restless	2001	18.00

LOUD/RCA

❏ 67578	40 Dayz & 40 Nightz	1998	18.00
❏ 66816-1	At the Speed of Life	1996	18.00

Y

Y KANT TORI READ

ATLANTIC

❏ 81845	Y Kant Tori Read	1989	200.00
—Deduct 20% for albums with a gold promo stamp and cut-out mark. Also, any picture disc of this album is a bootleg, no matter what it claims to be			

YA HO WA 13

HIGHER KEY

❏ 3304	All or Nothing at All	1974	400.00
—Above 4 as "Father Yod and the Spirit of '76			
❏ 3302	Contraction	1974	500.00
❏ 3303	Expansion	1974	500.00
❏ 3308	I'm Gonna Take You Home	1975	800.00
❏ 3301	Kohoutek	1973	300.00
❏ 3307	Penetration: An Aquarian Symphony	1974	400.00
❏ 3306	The Savage Sons of Ya Ho Wa	1974	400.00
❏ 3309	To the Principles for the Children	1975	800.00
❏ 3305	Ya Ho Wa 13	1974	500.00

YACHTSMEN, THE

BUENA VISTA

❏ BV-3310 [M]	High and Dry with the Yachtsmen	1961	30.00

YAGED, SOL

HERALD

❏ HLP-0103 [M]	It Might As Well Be Swing	1956	50.00

LANE

❏ LP-149 [M]	Live at the Gaslight Club	195?	50.00
❏ LP-154 [M]	One More Time	195?	50.00
❏ LPS-154 [S]	One More Time	195?	50.00
❏ LP-155 [M]	Sol Yaged at the Gaslight Club	195?	50.00
❏ LPS-155 [S]	Sol Yaged at the Gaslight Club	195?	50.00

PHILIPS

❏ PHM200002 [M]	Jazz at the Metropole	1961	18.00
❏ PHS600002 [S]	Jazz at the Metropole	1961	25.00

YALE DIXIELAND BAND, THE

COLUMBIA

❏ CL736 [M]	Eli's Chosen Six	1955	40.00

YAMA AND THE KARMA DUSTERS

MANHOLE

❏ 1 [B]	Up from the Sewers	1970	200.00

YAMA YAMA JAZZ BAND, THE

JAZZOLOGY

❏ J-78	New Orleans Jazz -- Australian Style, Vol. 1	198?	12.00
❏ J-79	New Orleans Jazz -- Australian Style, Vol. 2	198?	12.00

YAMAMOTO, TSUYOSHI

CONCORD JAZZ

❏ CJ-218	Zephyr	1981	12.00

THREE BLIND MICE

❏ TBM-23	Midnight Sugar	1995	30.00
—Audiophile vinyl			
❏ TBM-30	Misty	199?	30.00
—Audiophile vinyl			

YAMASHITA, STOMU

KUCKUCK

❏ KU-072	Sea and Sky	198?	15.00

YANCEY, JIMMY

ATLANTIC

❏ ALS-134 [10]	Piano Solos	1952	80.00
❏ 1283 [M]	Pure Blues	1958	50.00
—Black label			
❏ 1283 [M]	Pure Blues	1961	25.00
—Multicolor label, white "fan" logo at right			
❏ 1283 [M]	Pure Blues	1964	18.00
—Multicolor label, black "fan" logo at right			
❏ ALS-103 [10]	Yancey Special	1950	100.00
❏ ALS-130 [10]	Yancey Special	1952	80.00

JAZZOLOGY

❏ J-51	In the Beginning	197?	12.00

PARAMOUNT

❏ CJS-101 [10]	Yancey Special	1951	100.00

PAX

❏ LP-6011 [10]	1943 Mixture	1954	80.00
❏ LP-6012 [10]	Evening With the Yanceys	1954	80.00

RIVERSIDE

❏ RLP-1028 [10]	Lost Recording Date	1954	100.00
❏ RLP 12-124 [M]	Yancey's Getaway	1956	60.00

X

❏ LX-3000 [10]	Blues and Boogie	1954	100.00

YANCEY, MAMA, AND ART HODES

VERVE FOLKWAYS

❏ FVS-9015 [S]	Blues	1965	30.00
❏ FV-9015 [M]	Blues	1965	25.00

YANCY DERRINGER

HEMISPHERE

❏ H-15104	Openers	1975	50.00

YANKEE DOLLAR, THE

DOT

❏ DLP-25874 [B]	The Yankee Dollar	1968	120.00

YANKEE RHYTHM KINGS

GHB

❏ GHB-151	Classic Jazz of the 20s	1980	12.00
❏ GHB-97	Classic Jazz of the 20s	1978	12.00
❏ GHB-83	Yankee Rhythm Kings, Vol. 1	197?	12.00

YANKOVIC, "WEIRD AL"

ROCK N ROLL

❏ FZ40033	Dare to Be Stupid	1985	12.00
❏ FZ44149	Even Worse	1988	12.00
❏ FZ39221	In 3-D	1984	12.00
❏ BFZ38679	Weird Al	1983	12.00
❏ PZ38679	Weird Al	1985	10.00

Number	Title	Yr	NM
—Budget-line reissue			

YANKOVIC, FRANKIE

COLUMBIA

❏ CL2253 [M]	Christmas Party	1964	15.00
❏ CS9053 [S]	Christmas Party	1964	18.00

SMASH

❏ 830396-1	Christmas Memories	198?	12.00

YANOVSKY, ZALMAN

BUDDAH

❏ BDS-5019	Alive and Well in Argentina	1968	40.00

KAMA SUTRA

❏ KSBS-2030	Alive and Well in Argentina	1971	25.00

YARBROUGH, BOB

SUGAR HILL

❏ 002	Because You're Just More a Woman	1971	18.00

YARBROUGH, CAMILLE

VANGUARD

❏ VSD-79356	The Iron Pot Cooker	197?	15.00

YARBROUGH, GLENN

ELEKTRA

❏ EKL-135 [M]	Here We Go, Baby	1957	40.00

FIRST AMERICAN

❏ 7766	Just a Little Love	1981	12.00

RCA VICTOR

❏ LPM-3422 [M]	Baby the Rain Must Fall	1965	15.00
❏ LSP-3422 [S]	Baby the Rain Must Fall	1965	18.00
❏ ANL1-2138	Baby the Rain Must Fall	1977	12.00
—Reissue of LSP-3422			
❏ LPM-3301 [M]	Come Share My Life	1965	18.00
❏ LSP-3301 [S]	Come Share My Life	1965	25.00
❏ LPM-3801 [M]	For Emily, Whenever I May Find Her	1967	18.00
❏ LSP-3801 [S]	For Emily, Whenever I May Find Her	1967	18.00
❏ VPS-6018	Glenn Yarbrough Sings the Rod McKuen Songbook	1969	18.00
❏ LPM-3860 [M]	Honey and Wine	1967	25.00
❏ LSP-3860 [S]	Honey and Wine	1967	18.00
❏ LPM-3472 [M]	It's Gonna Be Fine	1905	15.00
❏ LSP-3472 [S]	It's Gonna Be Fine	1965	18.00
❏ LPM-3661 [M]	Live at the Hungry I	1966	15.00
❏ LSP-3661 [S]	Live at the Hungry I	1966	18.00
❏ LPM-2905 [M]	One More Round	1964	18.00
❏ LSP-2905 [S]	One More Round	1964	25.00
❏ LSP-4349	The Best of Glenn Yarbrough	1970	15.00
❏ LPM-3951 [M]	The Bitter and the Sweet	1968	30.00
❏ LSP-3951 [S]	The Bitter and the Sweet	1968	18.00
❏ LPM-3539 [M]	The Lonely Things	1966	15.00
❏ LSP-3539 [S]	The Lonely Things	1966	18.00
❏ LSP-2836 [S]	Time to Move On	1964	25.00
❏ LPM-2836 [M]	Time to Move On	1964	18.00
❏ LSP-4047	We Survived the Madness	1968	18.00

STAX

❏ STX-5506	My Sweet Lady	1975	12.00

TRADITION

❏ 1019 [M]	Come Sit By My Side	195?	25.00
❏ 2095	Looking Back	1970	15.00
❏ 2054	The Best of Glenn Yarbrough	1967	18.00

WARNER BROS.

❏ WS1911	Bend Down and Touch Me	1971	15.00
❏ WS1736	Each of Us Alone: Glenn Yarbrough Sings the Words and Music of Rod McKuen	1968	15.00
❏ WS1876	Jubilee	1970	15.00
❏ WS1832	Let Me Choose Life	1969	15.00
❏ WS1782	Somehow, Someway	1969	15.00
❏ WS1817	Yarbrough Country	1969	15.00

YARDBIRDS, THE

ACCORD

❏ SN-7143 [S]	For Your Love	1981	10.00
❏ SN-7237 [R]	Having a Rave Up with the Yardbirds	1981	10.00

COLUMBIA SPECIAL PRODUCTS

❏ P13311 [S]	Live Yardbirds Featuring Jimmy Page	1976	80.00

COMPLEAT

❏ CPL-2-2002	A Compleat Collection	1984	15.00

EPIC

❏ LN24167 [DJ]	For Your Love	1965	400.00
—White label promo			
❏ LN24167 [M]	For Your Love	1965	400.00
❏ BN26167 [P]	For Your Love	1965	200.00
—The album is in true stereo except for "Sweet Music"			
❏ PE34491 [P]	Great Hits	1977	12.00
❏ LN24177 [DJ]	Having a Rave Up with the Yardbirds	1965	400.00
—White label promo			
❏ LN24177 [M]	Having a Rave Up with the Yardbirds	1965	80.00

Number	Title	Yr	NM
❑ BN26177 [R]	Having a Rave Up with the Yardbirds	1965	50.00
❑ BN26177 [R]	Having a Rave Up with the Yardbirds	1973	30.00
—Reissue with orange label			
❑ LN24313 [DJ]	Little Games	1967	400.00
❑ LN24313 [M]	Little Games	1967	150.00
—Some copies with this number are stereo; look for the "XSB" prefix before the master number			
❑ BN26313 [S]	Little Games	1967	50.00
❑ E30615 [S]	Live Yardbirds Featuring Jimmy Page	1971	300.00
❑ LN24210 [DJ]	Over Under Sideways Down	1966	500.00
—White label promo			
❑ LN24210 [M]	Over Under Sideways Down	1966	60.00
❑ BN26210 [P]	Over Under Sideways Down	1966	80.00
—Over Under Sideways Down" is rechanneled			
❑ EG30135	The Yardbirds Featuring Performances by Jeff Beck, Eric Clapton, Jimmy Page	1970	50.00
❑ LN24246 [DJ]	The Yardbirds' Greatest Hits	1966	300.00
—White label promo			
❑ LN24246 [M]	The Yardbirds' Greatest Hits	1966	50.00
❑ BN26246 [P]	The Yardbirds' Greatest Hits	1966	30.00
❑ PE34490 [P]	Yardbirds Favorites	1977	12.00
❑ FE38455	Yardbirds (Roger the Engineer)	1982	30.00
❑ HE48455	Yardbirds (Roger the Engineer)	1982	250.00
—Half-Speed Mastered" edition			

PAIR

Number	Title	Yr	NM
❑ PDL2-1151	Best of British Rock	1988	15.00

PARLOPHONE

Number	Title	Yr	NM
❑ 825646335404 [B]	Little Games	2014	30.00

RHINO

Number	Title	Yr	NM
❑ RNDF253 [PD]	Afternoon Tea	1982	18.00
❑ RNLP70189 [M]	Five Live Yardbirds	1986	10.00
❑ RNLP70128 [M]	Greatest Hits, Volume 1: 1964-1966	1986	10.00

SPRINGBOARD

Number	Title	Yr	NM
❑ SPB-4036 [R]	Eric Clapton and the Yardbirds	1972	12.00
❑ SPB-4039 [R]	Shapes of Things	1972	12.00

SUNDAZED

Number	Title	Yr	NM
❑ 5368 [Mono]	Little Games	2010	25.00
❑ LP5181	Live! Blueswailing July '64	2004	15.00

YARROW, PETER

WARNER BROS.

Number	Title	Yr	NM
❑ BS2860	Hard Times	1975	15.00
❑ BS2599	Peter	1972	15.00
❑ BS2891	Peter Yarrow	1975	15.00
❑ BS2730	That's Enough for Me	1973	15.00

YAZ-KAZ

GRAMAVISION

Number	Title	Yr	NM
❑ 18-7013	Jonon-Sho	198?	15.00

YAZ

SIRE

Number	Title	Yr	NM
❑ 23737	Upstairs at Eric's	1982	25.00
—As "Yazoo			
❑ 23737	Upstairs at Eric's	1982	12.00
—As "Yaz			
❑ 23903	You and Me Both	1983	12.00

YEARWOOD, TRISHA

MCA

Number	Title	Yr	NM
❑ 1P-8161	Trisha Yearwood	1991	30.00
—Vinyl edition available only from Columbia House			

YELL CHASERS, THE

REALTIME

Number	Title	Yr	NM
❑ 822	I've Got My Fingers	197?	25.00
—Direct-to-disc recording; plays at 45 rpm			

YELLIN, PETE

MAINSTREAM

Number	Title	Yr	NM
❑ MRL-363	Dance of Allegra	197?	18.00
❑ MRL-397	It's the Right Thing	1974	18.00

YELLOW BALLOON, THE

CANTERBURY

Number	Title	Yr	NM
❑ CLPM-1502 [M]	The Yellow Balloon	1967	30.00
❑ CLPS-1502 [S]	The Yellow Balloon	1967	30.00

YELLOW PAYGES, THE

UNI

Number	Title	Yr	NM
❑ 73045	The Yellow Payges, Volume 1	1969	30.00

YELLOW SUNSHINE

GAMBLE

Number	Title	Yr	NM
❑ KZ32405 [B]	Yellow Sunshine	1973	35.00

YELLOWJACKETS

MCA

Number	Title	Yr	NM
❑ 5994	Four Corners	1987	12.00
❑ 6236	Politics	1988	12.00
❑ 5752	Shades	1986	12.00
❑ 6304	The Spin	1989	15.00

WARNER BROS.

Number	Title	Yr	NM
❑ 23813	Mirage A Trois	1983	12.00
❑ 25204	Samurai Samba	1985	12.00
❑ BSK3573	The Yellowjackets	1982	12.00

YES

ARISTA

Number	Title	Yr	NM
❑ AL8643	Union	1991	30.00
—U.S. vinyl available only through Columbia House			

ATCO

Number	Title	Yr	NM
❑ 90125 [B]	90125	1983	10.00
❑ 90474	9012Live: The Solos	1985	10.00
❑ 90522	Big Generator	1987	10.00

ATLANTIC

Number	Title	Yr	NM
❑ SD19320 [B]	Classic Yes	1982	30.00
—Original copies include a bonus 7-inch promo single			
❑ SD19320	Classic Yes	1982	12.00
—With bonus single missing			
❑ SD7244	Close to the Edge	1972	15.00
❑ SD19133	Close to the Edge	1977	10.00
❑ 7244 [DJ]	Close to the Edge	1972	80.00
—White label mono copies banded for airplay			
❑ SD16019	Drama	1980	12.00
❑ SD7211	Fragile	1972	15.00
❑ SD19132	Fragile	1977	10.00
❑ SD19106	Going for the One	1977	12.00
❑ SD18122	Relayer	1974	12.00
❑ SD18122 [DJ]	Relayer	1974	25.00
—Promo copies banded for airplay			
❑ SD19135	Relayer	1977	10.00
❑ SD 2-908	Tales from Topographic Oceans	1974	18.00
❑ SD 2-908 [DJ]	Tales from Topographic Oceans	1974	30.00
—Promo copies banded for airplay			
❑ SD8283	The Yes Album	1971	15.00
❑ SD19131	The Yes Album	1977	10.00
❑ 8283 [M]	The Yes Album	1971	80.00
—White label promo only; "DJ Copy Monaural" sticker on cover			
❑ SD8273	Time and a Word	1970	15.00
❑ SD19202 [B]	Tormato	1978	12.00
❑ SD8243	Yes	1969	15.00
❑ PR285 [DJ]	Yes Music: An Evening with Jon Anderson	1977	50.00
❑ SD 2-510	Yesshows	1980	15.00
❑ PR260 [DJ]	Yes Solo LP Sampler	1976	35.00
❑ SD 3-100 [B]	Yessongs	1973	30.00
❑ SD18103	Yesterdays	1975	12.00
❑ SD19134	Yesterdays	1977	10.00

CLEOPATRA

Number	Title	Yr	NM
❑ 8169 [B]	The BBC Recordings 1969-1970		30.00

FRIDAY MUSIC

Number	Title	Yr	NM
❑ 219004	Close to the Edge	2008	30.00

MOBILE FIDELITY

Number	Title	Yr	NM
❑ 1-077	Close to the Edge	1982	60.00
—Audiophile vinyl			

RHINO

Number	Title	Yr	NM
❑ R1-73788	The Yes Album	2003	25.00
—Reissue on 180-gram vinyl			

YESTERDAY'S CHILDREN

MAP CITY

Number	Title	Yr	NM
❑ 3012	Yesterday's Children	1969	75.00

YESTERDAY'S FOLK

BUDDAH

Number	Title	Yr	NM
❑ BDS-5035	U.S. 69	1969	25.00

YETTI-MEN, THE / THE UPPA TRIO

KAL

Number	Title	Yr	NM
❑ KB-4348	The Yetti-Men/The Uppa Trio	1967	600.00

YOAKAM, DWIGHT

OAK

Number	Title	Yr	NM
❑ OR2356 [EP]	Guitars, Cadillacs, Etc., Etc.	1984	80.00
—Six-song EP; cover is in black and white; the song "Guitars, Cadillacs" does NOT appear on this release			

REPRISE

Number	Title	Yr	NM
❑ R100009	Buenas Noches from a Lonely Room	1988	15.00
—BMG Direct Marketing edition			
❑ 25749	Buenas Noches from a Lonely Room	1988	12.00
❑ W1-25749	Buenas Noches from a Lonely Room	1988	15.00
—Columbia House edition			
❑ R150223	Guitars, Cadillacs, Etc., Etc.	1986	15.00
—RCA Music Service edition			
❑ 25372 [B]	Guitars, Cadillacs, Etc., Etc.	1986	12.00
—LP has 10 songs rather than the six on the Oak EP; front cover has color on it			
❑ W1-25372	Guitars, Cadillacs, Etc., Etc.	1986	15.00
—Columbia House edition			
❑ R164146	Hillbilly Deluxe	1987	15.00
—BMG Direct Marketing edition			
❑ 25567	Hillbilly Deluxe	1987	12.00
❑ W1-25567	Hillbilly Deluxe	1987	15.00
—Columbia House edition			
❑ R164310	If There Was a Way	1990	25.00
—BMG Direct Marketing edition; only U.S. vinyl version			
❑ 25989	Just Lookin' for a Hit	1989	12.00
❑ W1-25989	Just Lookin' for a Hit	1989	15.00
—Columbia House edition			
❑ R174052	Just Lookin' for a Hit	1989	15.00
—BMG Direct Marketing edition			

YORK, BETH

LADYSLIPPER

Number	Title	Yr	NM
❑ LR-104	Transformations	1986	15.00

YORK BROTHERS, THE

KING

Number	Title	Yr	NM
❑ 820 [M]	16 Great Country and Western Hits	1963	80.00
❑ 581 [M]	The York Brothers	1958	100.00
❑ 586 [M]	The York Brothers, Volume 2	1958	100.00

YOST, PHIL

TAKOMA

Number	Title	Yr	NM
❑ C-1016	Bent City	196?	25.00
❑ C-1021	Fog-Hat Ramble	196?	25.00

YOU KNOW WHO GROUP, THE

INTERNATIONAL ALLIED

Number	Title	Yr	NM
❑ 420 [M]	The "You Know Who" Group	1965	50.00

YOUNG, BARRY

DOT

Number	Title	Yr	NM
❑ DLP3672 [M]	One Has My Name	1965	25.00
❑ DLP25672 [S]	One Has My Name	1965	30.00

YOUNG, CATHY

MAINSTREAM

Number	Title	Yr	NM
❑ S-6121	A Spoonful of Cathy Young	1968	40.00

YOUNG, CECIL

AUDIO LAB

Number	Title	Yr	NM
❑ AL-1516 [M]	Jazz on the Rocks	1959	80.00

KING

Number	Title	Yr	NM
❑ 295-1 [10]	A Concert of Cool Jazz	1952	100.00

YOUNG, DAVID

MAINSTREAM

Number	Title	Yr	NM
❑ MRL-323	David Young	1972	18.00

YOUNG, ELDEE

ARGO

Number	Title	Yr	NM
❑ LP-1003 [M]	Eldee Young and Company	1962	30.00
❑ LPS-1003 [S]	Eldee Young and Company	1962	30.00
❑ LP-699 [M]	Just for Kicks	1962	25.00
❑ LPS-699 [S]	Just for Kicks	1962	25.00

YOUNG, FARON

ALLEGIANCE

Number	Title	Yr	NM
❑ AV-5008	The Sheriff	198?	12.00

CAPITOL

Number	Title	Yr	NM
❑ T2307 [M]	Falling in Love	1965	25.00
❑ ST2307 [S]	Falling in Love	1965	30.00
❑ T2037 [M]	Faron Young's Memory Lane	1964	30.00
❑ DT2037 [R]	Faron Young's Memory Lane	1964	25.00
❑ T1528 [M]	Hello Walls	1961	30.00
❑ ST1528 [S]	Hello Walls	1961	40.00
❑ T2536 [M]	If You Ain't Lovin' You Ain't Livin'	1966	30.00
❑ DT2536 [R]	If You Ain't Lovin' You Ain't Livin'	1966	25.00
❑ T1185 [M]	My Garden of Prayer	1959	40.00
❑ T778 [M]	Sweethearts or Strangers	1957	60.00
—Turquoise or gray label			
❑ T778 [M]	Sweethearts or Strangers	1959	30.00
—Black colorband label, logo at left			
❑ T1245 [M]	Talk About Hits	1959	30.00
❑ ST1245 [S]	Talk About Hits	1959	40.00
❑ T1876 [M]	The All-Time Great Hits of Faron Young	1963	30.00
❑ DT1876 [P]	The All-Time Great Hits of Faron Young	1963	25.00
❑ T1450 [M]	The Best of Faron Young	1960	30.00
❑ ST1450 [S]	The Best of Faron Young	1960	40.00
❑ T1004 [M]	The Object of My Affection	1958	50.00
❑ T1634 [M]	The Young Approach	1961	30.00
❑ ST1634 [S]	The Young Approach	1961	40.00
❑ T1096 [M]	This Is Faron Young	1959	50.00

HILLTOP

Number	Title	Yr	NM
❑ JM-6037 [M]	Faron Young	1966	18.00
❑ JS-6037 [S]	Faron Young	1966	15.00
❑ JS-6073	I'll Be Yours	1968	15.00

MARY CARTER

Number	Title	Yr	NM
❑ MC1000 [M]	Faron Young Sings on Stage for Mary Carter Paints	196?	60.00
— Promotional item for sponsor of The Faron Young Show			

MCA

Number	Title	Yr	NM
❑ 3092	Chapter Two	1979	15.00
❑ 757	Chapter Two	198?	10.00
— Budget-line reissue of 3092			
❑ 3212	Free and Easy	1980	15.00

MERCURY

Number	Title	Yr	NM
❑ SRM-1-1016	A Man and His Music	1974	15.00
❑ MG20931 [M]	Country Dance Favorites	1964	25.00
❑ SR60931 [S]	Country Dance Favorites	1964	30.00
❑ SR61359	Evening	1972	25.00
— Original title?			
❑ MG20840 [M]	Faron Young Aims at the West	1963	25.00
❑ SR60840 [S]	Faron Young Aims at the West	1963	30.00
❑ MG21047 [M]	Faron Young's Greatest Hits	1965	25.00
❑ SR61047 [S]	Faron Young's Greatest Hits	1965	30.00
❑ SR61354	Faron Young Sings "Leavin' and Sayin' Goodbye	1971	18.00
❑ SR61275	Faron Young Sings "Occasional Wife" and "If I Ever Fall in Love with a Honky Tonk Girl	1970	25.00
❑ SRM-1-698	Faron Young Sings "Some Kind of a Woman	1974	18.00
❑ MG21058 [M]	Faron Young Sings the Best of Jim Reeves	1966	25.00
❑ SR61058 [S]	Faron Young Sings the Best of Jim Reeves	1966	30.00
❑ SR61364	Faron Young Sings This Little Girl of Mine	1972	18.00
❑ SR61143	Greatest Hits Vol. 2	1968	25.00
❑ SR61174	Here's Faron Young	1968	25.00
❑ SRM-1-1075	I'd Just Be Fool Enough	1976	15.00
❑ SR61359	It's Four in the Morning	1972	18.00
— Revised title to reflect the hit?			
❑ SR61212	I've Got Precious Memories	1969	25.00
❑ SRM-1-674	Just What I Had in Mind	1973	18.00
❑ MG21007 [M]	Pen and Paper	1965	25.00
❑ SR61007 [S]	Pen and Paper	1965	30.00
❑ SR61337	Step Aside	1971	25.00
❑ MG20896 [M]	Story Songs for Country Folks	1964	25.00
❑ SR60896 [S]	Story Songs for Country Folks	1964	30.00
❑ MG20971 [M]	Story Songs of Mountains and Valleys	1965	25.00
❑ SR60971 [S]	Story Songs of Mountains and Valleys	1965	30.00
❑ SR61267	The Best of Faron Young	1970	25.00
❑ SRM-1-1130	The Best of Faron Young, Vol. 2	1977	15.00
❑ MG20785 [M]	This Is Faron	1963	25.00
❑ SR60785 [S]	This Is Faron	1963	30.00
❑ SR61376 [B]	This Time the Hurtin's on Me	1973	18.00
❑ MG21110 [M]	Unmitigated Gall	1967	30.00
❑ SR61110 [S]	Unmitigated Gall	1967	25.00
❑ SR61241	Wine Me Up	1969	25.00
❑ SRM-1-5005	Young Feelin'	1978	15.00

PICCADILLY

Number	Title	Yr	NM
❑ 3547	Hello Walls	196?	12.00

SEARS

Number	Title	Yr	NM
❑ SPS-124	Candy Kisses	1969	30.00

SESAC

Number	Title	Yr	NM
❑ (# unknown) [DJ]	Church Songs	196?	80.00

TOWER

Number	Title	Yr	NM
❑ T5022 [M]	It's a Great Life	1966	25.00
❑ DT5022 [R]	It's a Great Life	1966	15.00
❑ DT5121	The World of Faron Young	1968	18.00

YOUNG, JESSE COLIN

CAPITOL

Number	Title	Yr	NM
❑ T2070 [M]	The Soul of a City Boy	1964	50.00
❑ ST-11267	The Soul of a City Boy	1974	15.00
— Reissue of 2070			
❑ N-16129	The Soul of a City Boy	1981	10.00
— Budget-line reissue			

CYPRESS

Number	Title	Yr	NM
❑ 0103	The Highway Is for Heroes	1987	12.00

ELEKTRA

Number	Title	Yr	NM
❑ 6E-157	American Dreams	1978	12.00

MERCURY

Number	Title	Yr	NM
❑ MG21005 [M]	Young Blood	1965	30.00
❑ SR61005 [S]	Young Blood	1965	40.00

RACCOON

Number	Title	Yr	NM
❑ BS2588	Together	1972	15.00

WARNER BROS.

Number	Title	Yr	NM
❑ BS2790	Light Shine	1974	12.00
❑ BS3033	Love on the Wing	1977	12.00
❑ BS2913	On the Road	1976	12.00
❑ BS2845	Songbird	1975	12.00
❑ BS2734	Song for Juli	1973	12.00

YOUNG, JOHN

ARGO

Number	Title	Yr	NM
❑ LP-713 [M]	A Touch of Pepper	1962	30.00
❑ LPS-713 [S]	A Touch of Pepper	1962	30.00
❑ LP-692 [M]	Themes and Things	1962	30.00
❑ LPS-692 [S]	Themes and Things	1962	30.00
❑ LP-612 [M]	Young John Young	1957	40.00

CADET

Number	Title	Yr	NM
❑ LPS-692 [S]	Themes and Things	1966	18.00
❑ LP-692 [M]	Themes and Things	1966	15.00

DELMARK

Number	Title	Yr	NM
❑ DL-403 [M]	The John Young Trio	1961	30.00
❑ DS-403 [S]	The John Young Trio	1961	40.00

VEE JAY

Number	Title	Yr	NM
❑ VJS-3060	Opus de Funk	1974	25.00

YOUNG, JOHNNY

ARHOOLIE

Number	Title	Yr	NM
❑ F-1037	Chicago Blues	1966	30.00
❑ F-1029	Johnny Williams and His Chicago Blues Band	1965	30.00

BLUE HORIZON

Number	Title	Yr	NM
❑ BH-4609	Blues Masters, Volume 9	1969	25.00

YOUNG, KATHY, AND THE INNOCENTS

INDIGO

Number	Title	Yr	NM
❑ LP-504 [M]	The Sound of Kathy Young	1961	300.00

YOUNG, LARRY

ARISTA

Number	Title	Yr	NM
❑ AL4072	Spaceball	1976	15.00

BLUE NOTE

Number	Title	Yr	NM
❑ BLP-4266 [S]	Contrasts	1967	40.00
❑ BST-84266 [S]	Contrasts	1967	30.00
— With "A Division of Liberty Records" on label			
❑ BST-84304 [S]	Heaven on Earth	1968	30.00
— With "A Division of Liberty Records" on label			
❑ BLP-4187 [M]	Into Somethin'	1964	30.00
❑ BST-84187 [S]	Into Somethin'	1964	40.00
— With "New York, USA" address on label			
❑ BST-84187 [S]	Into Somethin'	1967	25.00
— With "A Division of Liberty Records" on label			
❑ LT-1038	Mother Ship	1980	15.00
❑ BLP-4242 [M]	Of Love and Peace	1966	30.00
❑ BST-84242 [S]	Of Love and Peace	1966	40.00
— With "New York, USA" address on label			
❑ BST-84242 [S]	Of Love and Peace	1967	25.00
— With "A Division of Liberty Records" on label			
❑ BLP-4221 [M]	Unity	1966	30.00
❑ BST-84221 [S]	Unity	1966	40.00
— With "New York, USA" address on label			
❑ BST-84221 [S]	Unity	1967	25.00
— With "A Division of Liberty Records" on label			
❑ BST-84221	Unity	198?	12.00
— The Finest in Jazz Since 1939" reissue			

MOSAIC

Number	Title	Yr	NM
❑ MR9-137	The Complete Blue Note Recordings of Larry Young	199?	200.00

NEW JAZZ

Number	Title	Yr	NM
❑ NJLP-8249 [M]	Testifying	1960	50.00
— Purple label			
❑ NJLP-8249 [M]	Testifying	1965	30.00
— Blue label, trident logo at right			
❑ NJLP-8264 [M]	Young Blues	1961	50.00
— Purple label			
❑ NJLP-8264 [M]	Young Blues	1965	30.00
— Blue label, trident logo at right			

PRESTIGE

Number	Title	Yr	NM
❑ PRLP-7237 [M]	Groove Street	1962	40.00
❑ PRST-7237 [S]	Groove Street	1962	40.00

YOUNG, LEON

ATCO

Number	Title	Yr	NM
❑ 33-163 [M]	Liverpool Sound for Strings	1964	30.00
❑ SD 33-163 [S]	Liverpool Sound for Strings	1964	30.00

YOUNG, LESTER, AND PAUL QUINICHETTE

EMARCY

Number	Title	Yr	NM
❑ MG-26021 [10]	Pres Meets Vice-Pres	1954	250.00

YOUNG, LESTER; ROY ELDRIDGE; HARRY "SWEETS" EDISON

VERVE

Number	Title	Yr	NM
❑ MGV-8298 [M]	Going for Myself	1959	60.00
❑ V-8298 [M]	Going for Myself	1961	30.00
❑ MGV-8316 [M]	Laughin' to Keep from Cryin'	1960	60.00
❑ V-8316 [M]	Laughin' to Keep from Cryin'	1961	30.00
❑ MGVS-6054 [S]	Laughin' to Keep from Cryin'	1960	70.00
❑ V6-8316 [S]	Laughin' to Keep from Cryin'	1961	30.00
❑ UMV-2694	Laughin' to Keep from Cryin'	198?	12.00
❑ MGVS-6054 [S]	Laughin' to Keep from Cryin'	199?	30.00
— Classic Records reissue on audiophile vinyl			

YOUNG, LESTER

ALADDIN

Number	Title	Yr	NM
❑ LP-706 [10]	Easy Does It	1954	300.00
❑ LP-801 [M]	Lester Young and His Tenor Sax, Volume 1	1956	120.00
❑ LP-802 [M]	Lester Young and His Tenor Sax, Volume 2	1956	120.00
❑ LP-705 [10]	Lester Young Trio	1953	300.00

AMERICAN RECORDING SOCIETY

Number	Title	Yr	NM
❑ G-417 [M]	Pres and Teddy	1957	50.00

BLUE NOTE

Number	Title	Yr	NM
❑ BN-LA456-H2	Pres: The Aladdin Sessions	1975	18.00

CHARLIE PARKER

Number	Title	Yr	NM
❑ CLP-402 [M]	Pres	1961	50.00
❑ CLP-405 [M]	Pres Is Blue	1961	50.00

CLEF

Number	Title	Yr	NM
❑ MGC-108 [10]	Lester Young Collates	1953	250.00
❑ MGC-124 [10]	Lester Young Collates No. 2	1953	250.00
— Some copies of this have Mercury covers; no difference in value			
❑ MGC-104 [10]	The Lester Young Trio	1953	250.00
❑ MGC-135 [10]	The Lester Young Trio No. 2	1953	250.00

COLUMBIA

Number	Title	Yr	NM
❑ JG33502	The Lester Young Story, Vol. 1	1975	18.00
❑ JG34837	The Lester Young Story, Vol. 2: Romance	1976	18.00
❑ JG34840	The Lester Young Story, Vol. 3: Enter Count	1976	18.00

COMMODORE

Number	Title	Yr	NM
❑ XFL-15352	A Complete Session	198?	12.00
❑ FL-20021 [10]	Kansas City Style	1952	300.00
❑ FL-30014 [M]	Kansas City Style	1959	100.00
❑ XFL-14937	The Kansas City Six and Five	198?	12.00

CROWN

Number	Title	Yr	NM
❑ CLP-5305 [M]	Nat "King" Cole Meets Lester Young	196?	30.00
❑ CST-305 [R]	Nat "King" Cole Meets Lester Young	196?	15.00

EMARCY

Number	Title	Yr	NM
❑ SRE-66010	Lester Young At His Very Best	1967	18.00

EPIC

Number	Title	Yr	NM
❑ LN3107 [M]	Lester Leaps In	1956	100.00
❑ SN6031 [M]	Lester Young Memorial Album	1959	150.00
❑ LN3576 [M]	Lester Young Memorial Album, Volume 1	1959	50.00
❑ LN3577 [M]	Lester Young Memorial Album, Volume 2	1959	50.00
❑ LN3168 [M]	Let's Go to Pres	1956	100.00

EVEREST ARCHIVE OF FOLK & JAZZ

Number	Title	Yr	NM
❑ 287	Pres	197?	12.00

IMPERIAL

Number	Title	Yr	NM
❑ LP-9187-A [M]	The Great Lester Young, Volume 2	1962	50.00
❑ LP-12187-A [R]	The Great Lester Young, Volume 2	196?	25.00
❑ LP-9181-A [M]	The Immortal Lester Young	1962	50.00
❑ LP-12181-A [R]	The Immortal Lester Young	196?	25.00

INTRO

Number	Title	Yr	NM
❑ LP-602 [M]	Swinging Lester Young	1957	100.00
❑ LP-603 [M]	The Greatest	1957	100.00

JAZZ ARCHIVES

Number	Title	Yr	NM
❑ JA-18	Jammin' with Lester, Vol. 1	198?	12.00
❑ JA-34	Jammin' with Lester, Vol. 2	198?	12.00
❑ JA-42	Lester Young and Charlie Christian 1939-40	198?	12.00

MAINSTREAM

Number	Title	Yr	NM
❑ 56009 [M]	52nd Street	1965	30.00
❑ S-6009 [R]	52nd Street	1965	15.00
❑ 56008 [M]	Chairman of the Board	1965	30.00
❑ S-6008 [R]	Chairman of the Board	1965	15.00
❑ 56012 [M]	Prez	1965	30.00
❑ S-6012 [R]	Prez	1965	15.00
❑ 56002 [M]	The Influence of Five	1965	30.00
❑ S-6002 [R]	The Influence of Five	1965	15.00
❑ 56004 [M]	Town Hall Concert	1965	30.00
❑ S-6004 [R]	Town Hall Concert	1965	15.00

MERCURY

Number	Title	Yr	NM
❑ MGC-108 [10]	Lester Young Collates	1951	300.00
❑ MGC-104 [10]	The Lester Young Trio	1951	300.00

NORGRAN

Number	Title	Yr	NM
❑ MGN-1071 [M]	Lester's Here	1956	100.00
❑ MGN-1093 [M]	Lester Swings Again	1956	100.00
❑ MGN-1022 [M]	Lester Young	1955	200.00
❑ MGN-1100 [M]	Lester Young	1956	100.00
❑ MGN-1074 [M]	Lester Young and the Buddy Rich Trio	1956	100.00
❑ MGN-5 [10]	Lester Young with the Oscar Peterson Trio No. 1	1954	200.00
❑ MGN-6 [10]	Lester Young with the Oscar Peterson Trio No. 2	1954	200.00
❑ MGN-1072 [M]	Pres	1956	100.00
❑ MGN-1043 [M]	Pres and Sweets	1955	200.00
❑ MGN-1005 [M]	The President	1954	200.00
❑ MGN-1054 [M]	The President Plays with the Oscar Peterson Trio	1955	100.00

ONYX

Number	Title	Yr	NM
❑ 218	Prez in Europe	197?	15.00

PABLO

Number	Title	Yr	NM
❑ 2405420	The Best of Lester Young	198?	12.00

PABLO LIVE

Number	Title	Yr	NM
❑ 2308219	Lester Young in Washington, D.C., at Olivia Davis', Vol. 1	1979	15.00
❑ 2308225	Lester Young in Washington, D.C., at Olivia Davis', Vol. 2	1980	15.00

Number	Title	Yr	NM
❏ 2308228	Lester Young in Washington, D.C., at Olivia Davis', Vol. 3	198?	12.00
❏ 2308230	Lester Young in Washington, D.C., at Olivia Davis', Vol. 4	198?	12.00

PICKWICK

❏ SPC-5015	Prez Leaps Again	197?	12.00

SAVOY

❏ MG-12068 [M]	Blue Lester	1956	80.00
❏ MG-9002 [10]	Lester Young (All Star Be Bop)	1951	300.00
❏ MG-12155 [M]	The Immortal Lester Young	1959	60.00
❏ MG-12071 [M]	The Master's Touch	1956	80.00

SAVOY JAZZ

❏ SJL-1133	Master Takes	198?	12.00
❏ SJL-1109	Pres Lives	1977	12.00
❏ SJL-2202	The Complete Lester Younbg (1944-49)	197?	18.00

SCORE

❏ SLP-4019 [M]	Lester Young / The King Cole Trio	1958	80.00
❏ SLP-4028 [M]	Swinging Lester Young	1958	80.00
❏ SLP-4029 [M]	The Great Lester Young	1958	80.00

SUNSET

❏ SUS-5181	Giant of Jazz	1967	15.00

TIME-LIFE

❏ STL-J-13	Giants of Jazz	1980	25.00

TRIP

❏ 5519	Pres at His Best	197?	12.00

VERVE

❏ VSP-30 [M]	Giants 3	1966	30.00
—With Buddy Rich and Nat King Cole			
❏ VSPS-30 [R]	Giants 3	1966	15.00
❏ MGV-8187 [M]	It Don't Mean a Thing (If It Ain't Got That Swing)	1957	60.00
❏ V-8187 [M]	It Don't Mean a Thing (If It Ain't Got That Swing)	1961	30.00
❏ VE-2-2527	Jazz Giants '56	197?	18.00
❏ MGV-8161 [M]	Lester's Here	1957	60.00
❏ V-8161 [M]	Lester's Here	1961	30.00
❏ VE-2-2516	Lester Swings	197?	18.00
❏ 833554-1	Lester Swings	198?	15.00
❏ MGV-8181 [M]	Lester Swings Again	1957	60.00
❏ V-8181 [M]	Lester Swings Again	1961	30.00
❏ MGV-8164 [M]	Lester Young and the Buddy Rich Trio	1957	60.00
❏ V-8164 [M]	Lester Young and the Buddy Rich Trio	1961	30.00
❏ VSPS-41 [R]	Lester Young at J.A.T.P.	196?	15.00
❏ VSP-41 [M]	Lester Young at J.A.T.P.	196?	18.00
❏ MGV-8378 [M]	Lester Young in Paris	1960	60.00
❏ V-8378 [M]	Lester Young in Paris	1961	30.00
❏ VE-2-2538	Mean to Me	197?	18.00
❏ VE-2-2502	Pres & Teddy & Oscar	197?	18.00
❏ MGV-8162 [M]	Pres	1957	60.00
❏ V-8162 [M]	Pres	1961	30.00
❏ UMV-2672	Pres	198?	12.00
❏ VSP-27 [M]	Pres and His Cabinet	1966	30.00
❏ VSPS-27 [R]	Pres and His Cabinet	1966	15.00
❏ MGV-8134 [M]	Pres and Sweets	1957	60.00
❏ V-8134 [M]	Pres and Sweets	1961	30.00
❏ UMV-2528	Pres and Sweets	198?	12.00
❏ MGV-8205 [M]	Pres and Teddy	1957	60.00
❏ V-8205 [M]	Pres and Teddy	1961	30.00
❏ MGV-8398 [M]	The Essential Lester Young	1961	60.00
❏ V-8398 [M]	The Essential Lester Young	1961	30.00
❏ MGV-8308 [M]	The Lester Young Story	1959	60.00
❏ V-8308 [M]	The Lester Young Story	1961	30.00
❏ MGV-8144 [M]	The President Plays with the Oscar Peterson Trio	1957	60.00
❏ V-8144 [M]	The President Plays with the Oscar Peterson Trio	1961	30.00

YOUNG, LESTER/CHU BERRY

JAZZTONE

❏ J-1218 [M]	Tops on Tenor: Pres and Chu	1956	70.00

YOUNG, LESTER/COUNT BASIE

MERCURY

❏ MG-25015 [10]	Lester Young Quartet/Count Basie Seven	1950	250.00

YOUNG, NEIL

GEFFEN

❏ GHS4013 [B]	Everybody's Rockin'	1983	50.00
—Promo on Quiex II audiophile vinyl			
❏ GHS4013	Everybody's Rockin'	1983	12.00
❏ R134125	Landing on Water	1986	18.00
—RCA Music Service edition			
❏ GHS24109	Landing on Water	1986	15.00
❏ R144439	Life	1987	18.00
—BMG Direct Marketing edition			
❏ GHS24154	Life	1987	15.00
❏ R163233	Old Ways	1985	18.00
—RCA Music Service edition			
❏ GHS24068	Old Ways	1985	15.00
❏ GHS2018 [DJ]	Trans	1982	40.00
—Promo on Quiex II audiophile vinyl			
❏ GHS2018 [B]	Trans	1982	35.00
—First pressings have a sticker on rear cover explaining the absence of "If You've Got Love"			
❏ GHS2018	Trans	1982	12.00
—Later pressings have neither sticker nor title of absent song			

MOBILE FIDELITY

❏ 1-252	Old Ways	1996	45.00
—Audiophile vinyl			

NAUTILUS

❏ NR-44 [B]	Harvest	1982	200.00
—Audiophile vinyl			

REPRISE

❏ RS6383 [B]	After the Gold Rush	1970	60.00
—Brown and orange label; photo of Marc Bolan (of T. Rex) appears erroneously in gatefold			
❏ RS6383	After the Gold Rush	1970	35.00
—Brown and orange label; photo of Neil Young appears erroneously printed upside down in gatefold			
❏ RS6383	After the Gold Rush	1970	18.00
—Brown and orange label; all photos correct			
❏ RS6383	After the Gold Rush	1970	12.00
—Brown "Reprise" label			
❏ MSK2283	After the Gold Rush	1978	40.00
—Contains remixed extended version of "When You Dance I Can Really Love." Title on cover in red, "RE 2" in trail-off vinyl			
❏ 531195-1 [B]	Americana	2012	50.00
❏ MSK2261	American Stars 'N' Bars	1977	12.00
❏ 527650-1 [B]	A Treasure	2011	50.00
❏ 46291	Broken Arrow	1996	40.00
❏ 311932-1 [B]	Chrome Dreams II	2007	60.00
❏ MSK2266	Comes A Time	1978	12.00
—With "Peace of Mind" as the last song on side 1. Covers can list either "Lotta Love" or "Peace of Mind."			
❏ MSK2266	Comes A Time	1978	75.00
—With "Lotta Love" listed and playing as the last song on side 1			
❏ 3RS2257 [DJ]	Decade	1977	500.00
—Test pressing; "Campaigner" contains extra verse deleted from the final version			
❏ 3RS2257 [DJ]	Decade	1977	500.00
—Test pressing; "Campaigner" contains extra verse deleted from the final version			
❏ 3RS2257	Decade	1977	25.00
❏ 511277-1 [B]	Dreamin' Man Live '92	2009	30.00
❏ RS6349 [DJ]	Everybody Knows This Is Nowhere	1969	75.00
—White label promo			
❏ RS6349 [DJ]	Everybody Knows This Is Nowhere	1969	75.00
—White label promo			
❏ RS6349	Everybody Knows This Is Nowhere	1969	30.00
—Brown and orange "Reprise/W7" label			
❏ RS6349	Everybody Knows This Is Nowhere	1970	18.00
—Brown "Reprise" label			
❏ MSK2282	Everybody Knows This Is Nowhere	1978	10.00
—Brown "Reprise" label; new number			
❏ 518040-1 [B]	Fork In The Road	2009	30.00
❏ 25899	Freedom	1989	18.00
❏ MSK2266 [DJ]	Give to the Wind	1978	1000.00
—Test pressing; plain white jacket with inserts and STOCK COPY LABEL. Title changed to "Comes A Time" for commercial release.			
❏ 48935-1	Greatest Hits	2005	40.00
—Distributed by Classic Records; 200-gram vinyl; with poster; also includes a bonus 7-inch single of "The Loner"/"Sugar Mountain" on either red, white or blue vinyl (not marked on packaging which color is inside; no difference in value)			
❏ R113998	Harvest	1972	15.00
—RCA Music Service edition			
❏ MS2032	Harvest	1972	18.00
—First pressings have textured cover and lyric insert			
❏ MS2032	Harvest	1972	12.00
❏ MSK2277	Harvest	1978	10.00
—Brown "Reprise" label; new number			
❏ SMAS-94285	Harvest	1972	30.00
—Capitol Record Club edition			
❏ HS2297	Hawks and Doves	1980	12.00
❏ 2XS6480	Journey Through the Past (Soundtrack)	1972	25.00
❏ 525956-1 [B]	Le Noise	2010	30.00
❏ 525956-1 [B]	Le Noise	2013	30.00
❏ 43328	Live at Massey Hall	2008	30.00
❏ 44429-1 [B]	Live At The Fillmore East	2006	30.00
❏ 2RX2296	Live Rust	1979	18.00
❏ 43265-1 [B]	Living With War "In The Beginning"	2007	30.00
❏ 44335-1 [B]	Living With War	2006	30.00
❏ 44335-1	Living with War	2006	30.00
—Distributed by Classic Records; 200-gram vinyl			
❏ 43328-1 [B]	Massey Hall 1971	2008	50.00
❏ 45934 [B]	Mirror Ball	1995	25.00
—With Pearl Jam (uncredited)			
❏ RS6317	Neil Young	1968	200.00
—Brown and orange "Reprise/W7" label, no name on front cover, no "RE-1" in trail-off wax			
❏ RS6317	Neil Young	1969	60.00
—Re-release: Brown and orange "Reprise/W7" label, no name on front cover, four tracks remixed ("RE 1" in trail-off wax)			
❏ RS6317	Neil Young	1970	18.00
—Reissue: Brown "Reprise" label, Neil Young's name is now on front cover			
❏ MSK2266 [DJ]	Ode to the Wind	1978	1000.00
—Test pressing; plain white jacket with inserts. Title changed to "Comes A Time" for commercial release			
❏ R2180	On the Beach	1974	25.00

❏ 49593-1	Prairie Wind	2005	40.00
—Distributed by Classic Records; 200-gram vinyl			
❏ 49593-1 [B]	Prairie Wind	2005	30.00
❏ 531980 [B]	Psychedelic Pill	2012	80.00
❏ 26315	Ragged Glory	1990	25.00
❏ HS2304 [B]	Re-Ac-Tor	1981	12.00
❏ HS2295	Rust Never Sleeps	1979	12.00
❏ 45749 [B]	Sleeps with Angels	1994	30.00
❏ 512563-1 [B]	Sugar Mountain - Live At Canterbury House 1968	2009	60.00
❏ R154182	This Note's for You	1987	15.00
—BMG Direct Marketing edition			
❏ 25719	This Note's for You	1988	15.00
❏ MS2151 [S-DJ]	Time Fades Away	1973	200.00
—With a cardboard inner sleeve, withdrawn after the earliest pressing.			
❏ M2151 [M]	Time Fades Away	1973	150.00
—Special mono pressing for radio stations only			
❏ MS2151 [S]	Time Fades Away	1973	200.00
—With a cardboard inner sleeve, withdrawn after the earliest pressing			
❏ MS2151	Time Fades Away	1973	12.00
❏ MS2221	Tonight's the Night	1975	12.00
❏ 46652 [B]	Year of the Horse	1997	50.00
❏ MS2242	Zuma	1975	12.00

THIRD MAN

❏ TMR245 [B]	A Letter Home	2014	30.00

VAPOR

❏ 48111	Are You Passionate?	2002	30.00
❏ 46171	Dead Man (Soundtrack)	1996	15.00
❏ VAP-1001	Greendale	2005	50.00
—Distributed by Classic Records; 140-gram vinyl with bonus 7-inch single, book, bumper sticker and stage bill			
❏ VAP-1001	Greendale	2005	80.00
—Distributed by Classic Records; 200-gram vinyl with bonus 7-inch single, book, bumper sticker and stage bill			

WARNER BROS.

❏ WBMS-107 [DJ]	The Warner Bros. Music Show	1979	50.00
—Promo-only interview album			
❏ WBMS-107 [DJ]	The Warner Bros. Music Show	1979	50.00
—Promo-only interview album			

YOUNG, NOAH

LAUGHING ANGEL

❏ LAR33	Unicorn Dream	1981	18.00

YOUNG, PAUL

COLUMBIA

❏ FC40543	Between Two Fires	1986	10.00
❏ BFC38976	No Parlez	1984	12.00
❏ FC38976	No Parlez	1985	10.00
—Reissue with new prefix			
❏ BFC39957	The Secret of Association	1985	12.00
❏ FC39957	The Secret of Association	1985	10.00
—Reissue with new prefix			

COMPLEAT

❏ 672006-1	London Dilemma	1986	18.00
—As "Paul Young and Street Band"			

YOUNG, STEVE

BLUE CANYON

❏ 505	Seven Bridges Road	197?	18.00

MOUNTAIN RAILROAD

❏ 52776	Honky-Tonk Man	197?	18.00

RCA VICTOR

❏ APL1-2510	No Place to Fall	1978	18.00
❏ APL1-1759	Renegade Picker	1976	18.00

REPRISE

❏ MS2081	Seven Bridges Road	1972	18.00

ROUNDER

❏ 3087	Honky-Tonk Man	198?	12.00
❏ 3058	Seven Bridges Road	198?	12.00
❏ 3057	To Satisfy You	198?	12.00

YOUNG, WEBSTER

FANTASY

❏ OJC-1716	For Lady	198?	12.00

PRESTIGE

❏ PRLP-7106 [M]	For Lady	1957	100.00

YOUNG-HOLT UNLIMITED

ATLANTIC

❏ SD1634	Oh Girl	1973	15.00

BRUNSWICK

❏ BL754141	Funky But!	1968	25.00
❏ BL754150	Just a Melody	1969	18.00
❏ BL54125 [M]	On Stage	1967	25.00
—As "Young-Holt Trio"			
❏ BL754125 [S]	On Stage	1967	25.00
—As "Young-Holt Trio"			
❏ BL754144	Soulful Strut	1968	18.00
❏ BL54128 [M]	The Beat Goes On	1967	30.00
❏ BL754128 [S]	The Beat Goes On	1967	25.00
❏ BL54121 [M]	Wack-Wack	1966	25.00

Number	Title	Yr	NM
—As "Young-Holt Trio"			
❑ BL754121 [S]	Wack-Wack	1966	25.00
—As "Young-Holt Trio			

CADET

Number	Title	Yr	NM
❑ LPS-791 [S]	Feature Spot	1967	25.00
—As "Eldee Young and Red Holt (of the Ramsey Lewis Trio)			
❑ LP-791 [M]	Feature Spot	1967	30.00

COTILLION

Number	Title	Yr	NM
❑ SD18004	Born Again	1972	15.00
❑ SD18001	Mellow Dreamin'	1971	15.00

PAULA

Number	Title	Yr	NM
❑ LPS-4002	Super Fly	1973	25.00

YOUNG AMERICANS, THE

ABC

Number	Title	Yr	NM
❑ S-626 [B]	The Wonderful World of the Young	1968	25.00
❑ S-659 [B]	Time for Livin'	1969	18.00
❑ 586 [M]	While We're Young	1967	30.00
❑ S-586 [S]	While We're Young	1967	25.00

YOUNG HEARTS, THE

MINIT

Number	Title	Yr	NM
❑ LP-40016 [M]	Sweet Soul Shakin'!	1968	30.00
❑ LP-24016 [S]	Sweet Soul Shakin'!	1968	30.00

YOUNG LIONS, THE (1)

TRIP

Number	Title	Yr	NM
❑ 5011	Lions of Jazz	197?	15.00

VEE JAY

Number	Title	Yr	NM
❑ VJS-3013 [S]	The Young Lions	197?	12.00
—Reissue on thinner, more flexible vinyl			
❑ LP-3013 [M]	The Young Lions	1960	40.00
❑ SR-3013 [S]	The Young Lions	1960	50.00

YOUNG LIONS, THE (2)

ELEKTRA/MUSICIAN

Number	Title	Yr	NM
❑ 60196	The Young Lions	1984	15.00

YOUNG MEN FROM MEMPHIS

UNITED ARTISTS

Number	Title	Yr	NM
❑ UAL-4029 [M]	Down Home Reunion	1959	50.00
❑ UAS-5029 [S]	Down Home Reunion	1959	40.00

YOUNG TUXEDO BRASS BAND, THE

ATLANTIC

Number	Title	Yr	NM
❑ 1297 [M]	Jazz Begins	1958	40.00
—Black label			
❑ SD-1297 [M]	Jazz Begins	1958	50.00
—Green label			
❑ 1297 [M]	Jazz Begins	1961	25.00
—Multicolor label, white "fan" logo at right			
❑ SD-1297 [M]	Jazz Begins	1961	18.00
—Multicolor label, white "fan" logo at right			
❑ 1297 [M]	Jazz Begins	1964	18.00
—Multicolor label, black "fan" logo at right			
❑ SD-1297 [M]	Jazz Begins	1964	15.00
—Multicolor label, black "fan" logo at right			

YOUNGBLOOD, LONNIE

RADIO

Number	Title	Yr	NM
❑ RR16045	Lonnie Youngblood	1981	18.00

TURBO

Number	Title	Yr	NM
❑ TU7019	Lonnie Youngblood	1977	25.00
❑ TU7011	Sweet Sweet Tootie	1972	50.00

YOUNGBLOODS, THE

MERCURY

Number	Title	Yr	NM
❑ SR-61273	Two Trips	1970	30.00
—Gold border on cover			
❑ SR-61273	Two Trips	1971	25.00
—Red border on cover			

RACCOON

Number	Title	Yr	NM
❑ BS2566	Good and Dusty	1971	15.00
❑ BS2653	High on a Ridge Top	1972	15.00
❑ BS2563	Ride the Wind	1971	15.00
❑ WS1878	Rock Festival	1970	15.00

RCA VICTOR

Number	Title	Yr	NM
❑ LPM-3865 [M]	Earth Music	1968	50.00
❑ LSP-3865 [S]	Earth Music	1968	30.00
❑ LSP-4150 [B]	Elephant Mountain	1969	18.00
—Orange label			
❑ AFL1-4150	Elephant Mountain	1977	12.00
—Reissue of LSP-4150			
❑ LSP-4150 [B]	Elephant Mountain	1975	15.00
—Tan label			
❑ LSP-3724	Get Together	1969	18.00
—Retitled version of "The Youngbloods			
❑ LSP-4561	Sunlight	1971	15.00
❑ LSP-4399	The Best of the Youngbloods	1970	18.00
❑ AFL1-4399	The Best of the Youngbloods	1977	12.00
—Reissue of LSP-4399			
❑ AYL1-3680	The Best of the Youngbloods	1980	10.00
—Best Buy Series" reissue			
❑ LPM-3724 [M]	The Youngbloods	1967	40.00
❑ LSP-3724 [S]	The Youngbloods	1967	30.00
❑ VPS-6051	This Is the Youngbloods	1972	18.00

YOUNGER, JAMES AND MICHAEL

MCA

Number	Title	Yr	NM
❑ 5391	James and Michael Younger	1983	12.00
❑ 900	James and Michael Younger	198?	10.00
—Budget-line reissue of 5391			

YOUNGER BROTHERS BAND, THE

HME

Number	Title	Yr	NM
❑ FW39978	The Younger Brothers Band	1985	10.00

YOUNGMAN, HENNY

URANIA

Number	Title	Yr	NM
❑ UR-9014 [M]	The Horse and Auto Race Game	195?	50.00

YUM YUM KIDS, THE

MGM

Number	Title	Yr	NM
❑ E-4396 [M]	Yummy in Your Tummy	1966	18.00
❑ SE-4396 [S]	Yummy in Your Tummy	1966	25.00

YURO, TIMI

LIBERTY

Number	Title	Yr	NM
❑ LRP-3208 [M]	Hurt	1961	40.00
❑ LST-7208 [S]	Hurt	1961	50.00
❑ LRP-3234 [M]	Let Me Call You Sweetheart	1962	18.00
❑ LST-7234 [S]	Let Me Call You Sweetheart	1962	25.00
❑ LRP-3319 [M]	Make the World Go Away	1963	18.00
❑ LST-7319 [S]	Make the World Go Away	1963	25.00
❑ LST-7594	Something Bad on My Mind	1968	15.00
❑ LRP-3212 [M]	Soul	1962	18.00
❑ LST-7212 [S]	Soul	1962	25.00
❑ LRP-3286 [M]	The Best of Timi Yuro	1963	18.00
❑ LST-7286 [S]	The Best of Timi Yuro	1963	25.00
❑ LRP-3263 [M]	What's a Matter Baby?	1963	18.00
❑ LST-7263 [S]	What's a Matter Baby?	1963	25.00

MERCURY

Number	Title	Yr	NM
❑ MG-20963 [M]	The Amazing Timi Yuro	1964	15.00
❑ SR-60963 [S]	The Amazing Timi Yuro	1964	18.00

SUNSET

Number	Title	Yr	NM
❑ SUM-1107 [M]	Timi Yuro	1966	12.00
❑ SUS-5107 [S]	Timi Yuro	1966	15.00

UNITED ARTISTS

Number	Title	Yr	NM
❑ UA-LA429-E	The Very Best of Timi Yuro	1974	15.00

Z

ZABACH, FLORIAN

DECCA

Number	Title	Yr	NM
❑ DL8158 [M]	Dream of Romance	195?	30.00
—Black label, silver print			
❑ DL8230 [M]	Hi-Fi Fiddle	195?	30.00
—Black label, silver print			
❑ DL8086 [M]	Hour of Love	195?	30.00
—Black label, silver print			
❑ DL5367 [10]	The Hot Canary	1951	60.00
❑ DL4425 [M]	The Hot Canary	196?	18.00

MERCURY

Number	Title	Yr	NM
❑ SR60145 [S]	Do-It-Yourself Wedding Album	1959	30.00
❑ MG20463 [M]	Do-It-Yourself Wedding Album	1959	25.00
❑ MG20436 [M]	It's Easy to Dance with Florian Zabach	1959	25.00
❑ SR60107 [S]	It's Easy to Dance with Florian Zabach	1959	30.00
❑ MG20305 [M]	Till the End of Time	1958	18.00
❑ SR60084 [S]	Till the End of Time	1958	25.00

VOCALION

Number	Title	Yr	NM
❑ VL3701 [M]	String Along	196?	15.00

WING

Number	Title	Yr	NM
❑ MGW12172 [M]	Golden Strings	196?	15.00
❑ SRW16172 [S]	Golden Strings	196?	18.00
❑ MGW12245 [M]	Till the End of Time	196?	15.00
❑ SRW16245 [S]	Till the End of Time	196?	18.00

ZACHARIAS, HELMUT

CAPITOL

Number	Title	Yr	NM
❑ ST-150	Zacharias Plays the Hits	1969	15.00

DECCA

Number	Title	Yr	NM
❑ DL8926 [M]	2,000,000 Strings	1960	15.00
❑ DL78926 [S]	2,000,000 Strings	1960	18.00
❑ DL8382 [M]	A Million Strings	195?	18.00
❑ DL8822 [M]	Hi-Fi Fiddler's Delight	195?	18.00
❑ DL8150 [M]	Holiday in Vienna	195?	18.00
❑ DL8431 [M]	Magic Violins	195?	18.00
❑ DL8982 [M]	Rendezvous for Strings	1960	15.00
❑ DL78982 [S]	Rendezvous for Strings	1960	18.00
❑ DL8949 [M]	Romantic Strings	1960	15.00
❑ DL78949 [S]	Romantic Strings	1960	18.00
❑ DL8753 [M]	Smorgasbord for Strings	195?	18.00
❑ DL8985 [M]	Strauss Waltzes	1960	15.00
❑ DL78985 [S]	Strauss Waltzes	1960	18.00
❑ DL8594 [M]	Strings, Moonlight and You	195?	18.00
❑ DL4083 [M]	Themes	196?	15.00
❑ DL74083 [S]	Themes	196?	18.00
❑ DL8089 [M]	Wine, Women and Waltzes	195?	18.00

PHILIPS

Number	Title	Yr	NM
❑ PHM200053 [M]	A Violin Sings	196?	15.00
❑ PHS600053 [S]	A Violin Sings	196?	18.00

RCA VICTOR

Number	Title	Yr	NM
❑ LPM-3597 [M]	Pop Goes Baroque	1966	15.00
❑ LSP-3597 [S]	Pop Goes Baroque	1966	18.00

ZACHERLEY, JOHN

CRESTVIEW

Number	Title	Yr	NM
❑ CR803 [M]	Zacherle's Monster Gallery	1963	40.00
❑ CRS7803 [S]	Zacherle's Monster Gallery	1963	50.00

ELEKTRA

Number	Title	Yr	NM
❑ EKL-190 [M]	Spook Along with Zacherle	1960	60.00
❑ EKS-7190 [S]	Spook Along with Zacherle	1960	80.00

PARKWAY

Number	Title	Yr	NM
❑ P7018 [M]	Monster Mash	1962	60.00
❑ P7023 [M]	Scary Tales	1963	60.00

ZACK, GEORGE

COMMODORE

Number	Title	Yr	NM
❑ FL-20001 [10]	Party Piano of the Roaring '20s	1950	50.00

ZADORA, PIA

CBS ASSOCIATED

Number	Title	Yr	NM
❑ BFZ40533	I Am What I Am	1986	12.00
❑ FZ40259	Pia and Phil	1986	10.00
❑ FZ45273	Pia Z.	1989	18.00

ELEKTRA

Number	Title	Yr	NM
❑ 60109	Pia	1982	15.00

ZAGER AND EVANS

RCA VICTOR

Number	Title	Yr	NM
❑ LSP-4214 [B]	2525 (Exordium and Terminus)	1969	25.00
❑ ANL1-1077	2525 (Exordium and Terminus)	1975	12.00
—Reissue of 4214			
❑ LSP-4302	Zager and Evans	1970	25.00

VANGUARD

Number	Title	Yr	NM
❑ VSD-6568	Food for the Mind	1971	18.00

WHITE WHALE

Number	Title	Yr	NM
❑ WWS-7123	The Early Writings of Zager and Evans (And Others)	1969	25.00
—Actually doesn't contain any music by Zager or Evans, but only songs they wrote; it remains here as it's usually considered a "Zager and Evans" LP			

ZAHARA

ANTILLES

Number	Title	Yr	NM
❑ AN-1011	Flight of the Spirit	198?	15.00

ZAMFIR

MERCURY

Number	Title	Yr	NM
❑ 822571-1	Christmas with Zamfir	1984	12.00

ZANIES, THE

DORE

Number	Title	Yr	NM
❑ 321	The Zanies	1969	30.00
❑ 337	The Zanies	1979	18.00

ZAPP

REPRISE

Number	Title	Yr	NM
❑ 25807	Zapp V (Vibe)	1989	15.00

WARNER BROS.

Number	Title	Yr	NM
❑ 25327	The New Zapp IV U	1985	10.00
❑ BSK3463	Zapp	1980	12.00
❑ 23583	Zapp II	1982	12.00
❑ 23875	Zapp III	1983	12.00

ZAPPA, DWEEZIL

BARKING PUMPKIN

Number	Title	Yr	NM
❑ ST-74204	Havin' a Bad Day	1987	12.00
—Reissue of Chrysalis 41581			

CHRYSALIS

Number	Title	Yr	NM
❑ BFV41581	Havin' a Bad Day	1986	15.00
❑ BFV41633	My Guitar Wants to Kill Your Mama	1988	12.00

ZAPPA, FRANK

ANGEL

Number	Title	Yr	NM
❑ DS-38170	Boulez Conducts Zappa: The Perfect Stranger	1983	15.00

BARKING PUMPKIN

Number	Title	Yr	NM
❑ BPRP-1115 [PD]	Baby Snakes	1983	30.00
—Picture disc			
❑ D1-74218	Broadway the Hard Way	1988	12.00
❑ ST-74202	Francesco Zappa	1985	12.00
❑ ST-74203	Frank Zappa Meets the Mothers of Prevention	1985	12.00

Number	Title	Yr	NM
❑ D1-74212	Guitar	1988	12.00
❑ ST-74205	Jazz from Hell	1986	12.00
❑ 74206	Joe's Garage, Acts 1, 2 and 3	1986	50.00
—Box set, two gatefolds, with insert			
❑ FW38820	London Symphony Orchestra	1983	15.00
❑ SJ-74207	London Symphony Orchestra, Volume 2	1987	12.00
❑ FW38403	Man from Utopia	1983	15.00
❑ BPR-1113 [B]	Return of the Son of Shut Up 'N' Play Yer Guitar	1981	40.00
—Mail-order item only			
❑ FW38066	Ship Arriving Too Late to Save a Drowning Witch	1982	15.00
❑ BPR-1111 [B]	Shut Up 'N' Play Yer Guitar	1981	40.00
—Mail-order item only			
❑ W3X-38289 [B]	Shut Up 'N' Play Yer Guitar	1982	50.00
—Box set containing all three "Shut Up 'N' Play Yer Guitar" albums			
❑ BPR-1112 [B]	Shut Up 'N' Play Yer Guitar Some More	1981	40.00
—Mail-order item only			
❑ SVBO-74200	Them Or Us	1984	18.00
❑ 7777 [B]	The Old Masters, Box 1	1984	80.00
—Boxed set			
❑ 8888 [B]	The Old Masters, Box 2	1986	80.00
—Another boxed set			
❑ 9999 [B]	The Old Masters, Box 3	1987	80.00
—Still another boxed set			
❑ 7X4-1 [B]	The Old Masters Sampler	1984	40.00
❑ 8888X [B]	The Old Masters Sampler 2	1986	40.00
❑ SWCO-74201	Thing-Fish	1984	25.00
❑ PW237336	Tinsel Town Rebellion	1981	25.00
❑ AS995 [DJ]	Tinsel Town Rebellion	1981	25.00
—Promo-only sampler			
❑ PW237537	You Are What You Is	1981	25.00
❑ AS1294 [DJ]	You Are What You Is Special Clean Cuts Edition	1981	25.00
❑ R174213	You Can't Do That on Stage Anymore Sampler	1988	15.00
❑ D1-74213	You Can't Do That on Stage Anymore Sampler	1988	12.00
❑ D1-74217	You Can't Do That on Stage Anymore Vol. 2	1988	12.00
❑ BPRP-1114 [PD]	Zappa	1982	30.00
—Picture disc with two songs			

BIZARRE

Number	Title	Yr	NM
❑ RS-6370 [B]	Burnt Weenie Sandwich	1970	30.00
—Blue label original; with booklet			
❑ RS-6370 [B]	Burnt Weenie Sandwich	1973	18.00
—Reissue with brown Reprise label			
❑ MS2030 [DJ]	Chunga's Revenge	1970	60.00
—White label promo			
❑ MS-2030	Chunga's Revenge	1970	30.00
—Blue label original			
❑ MS-2030	Chunga's Revenge	1973	18.00
—Reissue with brown Reprise label			
❑ MS-2042 [B]	Fillmore East, June 1971	1971	30.00
—Blue label original			
❑ MS-2042	Fillmore East, June 1971	1973	18.00
—Reissue with brown Reprise label			
❑ RS-6356	Hot Rats	1969	50.00
—Blue label original			
❑ RS-6356	Hot Rats	1973	18.00
—Reissue with brown Reprise label			
❑ MS2075 [B]	Just Another Band from L.A.	1972	40.00
—Blue label original			
❑ MS2075	Just Another Band from L.A.	1973	18.00
—Reissue with brown Reprise label			
❑ MS2093 [B]	The Grand Wazoo	1972	30.00
—Blue label original			
❑ MS2093	The Grand Wazoo	1973	18.00
—Reissue with brown Reprise label			
❑ MS-2024 [B]	Uncle Meat	1969	60.00
—Originals come with a booklet; blue label			
❑ MS-2024	Uncle Meat	1973	25.00
—Reissue with brown Reprise label			
❑ MS2094 [B]	Waka/Jawaka	1972	30.00
—Blue label original			
❑ MS2094 [B]	Waka/Jawaka	1973	18.00
—Reissue with brown Reprise label			
❑ MS-2028 [B]	Weasels Ripped My Flesh	1970	30.00
—Blue label original			
❑ MS-2028 [B]	Weasels Ripped My Flesh	1973	18.00
—Reissue with brown Reprise label			

COLUMBIA

Number	Title	Yr	NM
❑ (no #) [DJ]	Lather	1977	750.00
—Test pressing only; parts of this LP are on DSK 2291, 2292 and 2294; released as a whole only after Zappa's death, with vinyl only coming out in Japan			

DISCREET

Number	Title	Yr	NM
❑ DS2175	Apostrophe (')	1974	18.00
❑ DS42175 [Q]	Apostrophe (')	1974	35.00
❑ DS2175	Apostrophe (')	1974	50.00
—White label promo			
❑ DSK2289	Apostrophe (')	1977	15.00
—Reissue with new number			
❑ DS2234	Bongo Fury	1975	18.00
❑ DS2216	One Size Fits All	1975	18.00
❑ DSK2294	Orchestral Favorites	1978	18.00
❑ MS2149 [B]	Over-Nite Sensation	1973	40.00
❑ MS42149 [Q]	Over-Nite Sensation	1973	40.00
❑ DSK2288	Over-Nite Sensation	1977	15.00
—Reissue of DiscReet 2149 with new number			
❑ 2DS2202	Roxy and Elsewhere	1974	30.00
❑ DSK2292	Sleep Dirt	1978	18.00
❑ DSK2291	Studio Tan	1978	18.00
❑ 2D2290 [DJ]	Zappa in New York	1978	400.00
—Test pressing with "Punky's Whips			
❑ 2D2290	Zappa in New York	1978	250.00
—Stock copy with "Punky's Whips" erroneously listed on jacket			
❑ 2D2290	Zappa in New York	1978	25.00

FOO-EEE

Number	Title	Yr	NM
❑ R1-70372 [B]	Beat the Boots #2	1992	150.00
—Legitimate box-set release by Rhino of 11 bootlegged concerts			
❑ R1-70907 [B]	Beat the Boots	1991	200.00
—Legitimate box-set release by Rhino of eight bootlegged concerts			

MCA

Number	Title	Yr	NM
❑ 4183	200 Motels (movie soundtrack)	1986	18.00
—Reissue			

MGM

Number	Title	Yr	NM
❑ GAS-112 [DJ]	The Mothers of Invention	1970	100.00
—Yellow label promo			
❑ GAS-112	The Mothers of Invention	1970	50.00
❑ SE-4754 [DJ]	The Worst of the Mothers	1971	150.00
—Yellow label promo			
❑ SE-4754	The Worst of the Mothers	1971	50.00

RHINO/DEL-FI

Number	Title	Yr	NM
❑ RNEP-604	Rare Meat: The Early Productions of Frank Zappa	1984	40.00
—With original cover			

RYKO ANALOGUE

Number	Title	Yr	NM
❑ RALP40500 [B]	Strictly Commercial: The Best of Frank Zappa	1995	40.00
—Issued with obi			
❑ RALP10503 [B]	We're Only in It for the Money	1995	60.00
—Vinyl reissue; Frank Zappa/The Mothers of Invention			

UNITED ARTISTS

Number	Title	Yr	NM
❑ UAS-9956	200 Motels (movie soundtrack)	1971	50.00

VERVE

Number	Title	Yr	NM
❑ V-5013 [M]	Absolutely Free	1967	250.00
—White label promo			
❑ V-5013 [M]	Absolutely Free	1967	200.00
❑ V6-5013 [S]	Absolutely Free	1967	80.00
❑ V6-5055 [DJ]	Cruising with Ruben and the Jets	1968	200.00
—Yellow label promo			
❑ V6-5055	Cruising with Ruben and the Jets	1968	60.00
❑ V-5005-2 [M]	Freak Out!	1966	400.00
—White label promo			
❑ V-5005-2 [M]	Freak Out!	1966	200.00
—Cover version 1: Has blurb on inside gatefold on how to get a map of "freak-out hot spots" in L.A.			
❑ V-5005-2 [M]	Freak Out!	1966	250.00
—Cover version 2: Has no blurb inside on getting a map of "freak-out hot spots			
❑ V6-5005-2 [S]	Freak Out!	1966	300.00
—Yellow label promo			
❑ V6-5005-2 [S]	Freak Out!	1966	80.00
—Cover version 2: Has no blurb inside on getting a map of "freak-out hot spots			
❑ V6-5005-2 [S]	Freak Out!	1966	80.00
—Cover version 1: Has blurb on inside gatefold on how to get a map of "freak-out hot spots" in L.A.			
❑ V6-8741 [DJ]	Lumpy Gravy	1968	200.00
—Yellow label promo			
❑ V6-8741 [B]	Lumpy Gravy	1968	60.00
❑ V-8741 [M]	Lumpy Gravy	1968	350.00
—Yellow label promo; no stock copies were issued in mono			
❑ V6-5068 [DJ]	Mothermania -- The Best of the Mothers	1969	150.00
—Yellow label promo			
❑ V6-5068 [B]	Mothermania -- The Best of the Mothers	1969	80.00
❑ V6-5074 [DJ]	The XXXX of the Mothers	1969	150.00
—Yellow label promo			
❑ V6-5074	The XXXX of the Mothers	1969	50.00
❑ V-5045 [M]	We're Only in It for the Money	1968	500.00
—White label promo			
❑ V-5045 [M]	We're Only in It for the Money	1968	200.00
—With sheet of cut-outs a la "Sgt. Pepper's Lonely Hearts Club Band			
❑ V6-5045 [S]	We're Only in It for the Money	1968	60.00
—Un-censored version, with cut-outs			
❑ V6-5045 [S]	We're Only in It for the Money	1968	200.00
—Censored version: the songs "Who Needs the Peace Corps?" and "Let's Make the Water Turn Black" have lines deleted			

WARNER BROS.

Number	Title	Yr	NM
❑ BS-2970	Zoot Allures	1976	18.00

ZAPPA

Number	Title	Yr	NM
❑ SRZ-1-1603	Joe's Garage, Act I	1979	18.00
❑ SRZ-2-1502	Joe's Garage, Acts II and III	1980	25.00
❑ MK-129 [DJ]	Joe's Garage Acts I, II and III Sampler	1980	35.00
❑ SRZ-2-1501	Sheik Yerbouti	1979	25.00
❑ MK-78 [DJ]	Sheik Yerbouti Clean Cuts	1979	35.00

ZAVARONI, LENA

STAX

Number	Title	Yr	NM
❑ STS-5511	Ma! He's Making Eyes at Me	1974	15.00

ZAWINUL, JOE

ATLANTIC

Number	Title	Yr	NM
❑ SD1694	Concerto	1976	18.00
❑ 3004 [M]	Money in the Pocket	1966	25.00
❑ SD3004 [S]	Money in the Pocket	1966	30.00
❑ SD1579	Zawinul	1970	25.00

COLUMBIA

Number	Title	Yr	NM
❑ FC44316	Black Water	1989	15.00
❑ FC40081	Dialects	1986	12.00
❑ FC40969	Immigrants	1988	12.00

VORTEX

Number	Title	Yr	NM
❑ 2002 [S]	The Rise and Fall of the 3rd Stream	1968	25.00

ZAZU

WOODEN NICKEL

Number	Title	Yr	NM
❑ BWL1-0791 [B]	Zazu	1975	25.00

ZEBRA

ATLANTIC

Number	Title	Yr	NM
❑ 81692 [B]	3.V	1986	12.00
❑ PR1028 [DJ]	Interview/Questions and Answers	1987	25.00
—Promo-only music and interviews			
❑ 80159 [B]	No Tellin' Lies	1984	10.00
❑ 80054	Zebra	1983	10.00

ZEITLIN, DENNY, AND CHARLIE HADEN

ECM

Number	Title	Yr	NM
❑ 1239	Time Remembers One Time Once	1981	15.00

ZEITLIN, DENNY

1750 ARCH

Number	Title	Yr	NM
❑ 1758	Expansions	197?	18.00
❑ 1770	Soundings	1979	18.00
❑ 1759	Syzygy	197?	18.00

COLUMBIA

Number	Title	Yr	NM
❑ CL2340 [M]	Carnival	1965	25.00
❑ CS9140 [S]	Carnival	1965	30.00
❑ CL2182 [M]	Cathexis	1964	25.00
❑ CS8982 [S]	Cathexis	1964	30.00
❑ CL2463 [M]	My Shining Hour	1966	18.00
❑ CS9263 [S]	My Shining Hour	1966	25.00
❑ CL2748 [M]	Zeitgeist	1966	18.00
❑ CS9548 [S]	Zeitgeist	1966	25.00

LIVING MUSIC

Number	Title	Yr	NM
❑ LM-0011	Homecoming	1986	12.00

WINDHAM HILL

Number	Title	Yr	NM
❑ WH-0112	Denny Zeitlin Trio	1988	12.00
❑ WH-0121	In the Moment	1989	15.00

ZELL, JOHNNY

MANNA

Number	Title	Yr	NM
❑ MS-2065	Heralding Christmas	1979	12.00

ZENITH HOT STOMPERS, THE

STOMP OFF

Number	Title	Yr	NM
❑ SOS-1191	20th Anniversary Album	1991	15.00

ZENITH SIX, THE

GHB

Number	Title	Yr	NM
❑ GHB-12	The Zenith Six, Vol. 1	196?	15.00
❑ GHB-13	The Zenith Six, Vol. 2	196?	15.00

ZENITHS, THE

ATLANTIC

Number	Title	Yr	NM
❑ 8043 [M]	Makin' the Scene	1960	100.00
❑ SD8043 [S]	Makin' the Scene	1960	150.00

ZENO

MANHATTAN

Number	Title	Yr	NM
❑ ST-53025	Zeno	1986	12.00

ZENTNER, SI

LIBERTY

Number	Title	Yr	NM
❑ LMM-13009 [M]	A Great Band with Great Voices	1961	15.00
❑ LSS-14009 [S]	A Great Band with Great Voices	1961	18.00
❑ LMM-13017 [M]	A Great Band with Great Voices Swing the Great Voices of the Great Bands	1962	15.00

Number	Title	Yr	NM
❏ LSS-14017 [S]	A Great Band with Great Voices Swing the Great Voices of the Great Bands	1962	18.00
❏ LRP-3197 [M]	Big Band Plays the Big Hits	1961	15.00
❏ LST-7197 [S]	Big Band Plays the Big Hits	1961	18.00
❏ LRP-3350 [M]	Big Big Band Hits	1964	15.00
❏ LST-7350 [S]	Big Big Band Hits	1964	18.00
❏ LRP-3273 [M]	Desafinado	1963	15.00
❏ LST-7273 [S]	Desafinado	1963	18.00
❏ LRP-3353 [M]	From Russia with Love	1964	15.00
❏ LST-7353 [S]	From Russia with Love	1964	18.00
❏ LRP-3326 [M]	More	1963	15.00
❏ LST-7326 [S]	More	1963	18.00
❏ LRP-3457 [M]	The Best of Si Zentner	1966	15.00
❏ LST-7457 [S]	The Best of Si Zentner	1966	15.00
❏ LRP-3247 [M]	The Stripper and Other Big Band Hits	1962	15.00
❏ LST-7247 [S]	The Stripper and Other Big Band Hits	1962	18.00
❏ LRP-3216 [M]	Up a Lazy River (Big Band Plays the Big Hits: Vol. 2)	1962	15.00
❏ LST-7216 [S]	Up a Lazy River (Big Band Plays the Big Hits: Vol. 2)	1962	18.00
❏ LRP-3284 [M]	Waltz in Jazz Time	1963	15.00
❏ LST-7284 [S]	Waltz in Jazz Time	1963	18.00
SMASH			
❏ MGS-27007 [M]	Presenting Si Zentner	1961	18.00
❏ SRS-67007 [S]	Presenting Si Zentner	1961	25.00
❏ MGS-27013 [M]	Swing Fever	1962	18.00
❏ SRS-67013 [S]	Swing Fever	1962	25.00
SUNSET			
❏ SUM-1110 [M]	Big Band Brilliance	196?	12.00
❏ SUS-5110 [S]	Big Band Brilliance	196?	15.00

ZENTNER, SI AND MARTIN DENNY

LIBERTY

Number	Title	Yr	NM
❏ LMM-13020 [M]	Exotica Suite	1962	18.00
❏ LSS-14020 [S]	Exotica Suite	1962	25.00

ZEPHYR

PROBE

❏ 4510 [B]	Zephyr	1969	60.00

WARNER BROS.

❏ WS1897 [B]	Goin' Back to Colorado	1971	50.00
❏ BS2603 [B]	Sunset Ride	1972	30.00

ZERFAS

700 WEST

❏ 730710	Zerfas	1973	800.00

ZERO BOYS

LOOKOUT!

❏ LK-253	Vicious Circle	2000	12.00

—*Same reissue as on Panic Button except for the label and number*

NIMROD

❏ 1	Vicious Circle	1982	100.00

PANIC BUTTON

❏ PB286	Vicious Circle	2000	15.00

—*Reissue of Nimrod release with two bonus tracks*

TOXIC SHOCK

❏ TXLP11 [B]	Vicious Circle	1987	30.00

—*Reissue of Nimrod release*

ZEROS

BOMP!

❏ BLP4035 [B]	Don't Push Me Around	1991	25.00
❏ BLP4074	Right Now!	1909	12.00

ZETTERLUND, MONICA

INNER CITY

❏ IC-1082	It Only Happens Every Time	197?	18.00

ZEVON, WARREN

ARTEMIS

❏ 51156	The Wind	2004	25.00

—*180-gram version; CD was issued in 2003*

ASYLUM

❏ 60503	A Quiet Normal Life: The Best of Warren Zevon	1987	12.00
❏ 5E-509	Bad Luck Streak in Dancing School	1980	12.00
❏ 6E-118 [B]	Excitable Boy	1978	12.00
❏ 5E-519	Stand in the Fire	1980	12.00
❏ 60159	The Envoy	1982	12.00
❏ 7E-1060	Warren Zevon	1976	12.00

IMPERIAL

❏ LP-12456	Wanted Dead or Alive	1970	50.00

—*As "Zevon*

PICKWICK

❏ SPC-3715	Wanted Dead or Alive	1979	18.00

—*Reissue of Imperial album*

VIRGIN

❏ 90603	Sentimental Hygiene	1987	12.00
❏ 91068 [B]	Transverse City	1989	12.00

ZIG ZAG PEOPLE, THE

DECCA

❏ DL75110 [B]	The Zig Zag People Take Bubble Gum Music Underground	1969	30.00

ZINGARA

WHEEL

❏ 10001	Zingara	1981	18.00

ZIP CODES, THE

LIBERTY

❏ LRP-3367 [M]	Mustang	1964	150.00
❏ LST-7367 [S]	Mustang	1964	200.00

ZIPPERS, THE

RHINO

❏ RNEP601 [EP]	Six Song Mini Album	1981	30.00

ZIRCONS, THE

SNOWFLAKE

❏ 1003	The Crown Kings of Acappella	196?	60.00

ZITO, PHIL

COLUMBIA

❏ CL6110 [10]	International City Dixielanders	1950	50.00

ZITRO, JAMES

ESP-DISK'

❏ 1052 [S]	Zitro	1968	30.00

Z'LOOKE

ORPHEUS

❏ D1-75600	Take U Back to My Place	1988	15.00

ZODIAC MINDWARP & THE LOVE REACTION

VERTIGO

❏ 832729-1	Tattooed Beat Messiah	1988	15.00

ZOLLER, ATTILA

EMARCY

❏ SPE-66013 [S]	The Horizon Beyond	1968	30.00

EMBRYO

❏ SD523 [B]	Gypsy Cry	1970	25.00

INNER CITY

❏ IC-3008	Dream Bells	1976	18.00

ZOMBIE, ROB

1500 RECORDS

❏ 497201-1 [EP]	Remix-A-Go-Go	2000	10.00

—*Five-song remix EP in generic black sleeve with sticker*

GEFFEN

❏ 069490349-1	American Made Music to Strip By	1999	50.00
❏ GEF25212	Hellbilly Deluxe	1998	40.00

—*Picture disc in plastic sleeve with sticker*

❏ 069031471 [B]	The Sinister Urge	2001	50.00

ZOMBIES, THE

DATE

❏ TES-4013	Odessey and Oracle	1968	30.00

—*With no mention of "Time of the Season" on front cover*

❏ TES-4013 [B]	Odessey and Oracle	1969	25.00

—*With "Time of the Season" mentioned on front cover*

EPIC

❏ KEG32861 [B]	Time of the Zombies	1974	25.00

—*Record 1 is mono; Record 2 is stereo; orange labels*

❏ PEG32861 [B]	Time of the Zombies	1979	18.00

—*Later edition with blue labels*

LONDON

❏ PS557 [P]	Early Days	1969	25.00

—*All tracks in true stereo except "Tell Her No*

PARROT

❏ PA61001 [M]	The Zombies	1965	70.00
❏ PAS71001 [R]	The Zombies	1965	40.00

RHINO

❏ RNLP-120	Live on the BBC, 1965-67	1985	12.00
❏ RNLP70186 [S]	Odessy and Oracle	1986	10.00

VARESE SARABANDE

❏ 302 066 436 1 [B]	The Zombies	2013	30.00

ZOO, THE (1)

MERCURY

❏ SR-61300	The Zoo	1970	25.00

SUNBURST

❏ 7500 [B]	The Zoo Presents the Chocolate Moose	1968	50.00

ZOOM

MCA

❏ 5420	Blasting Off	1983	18.00

POLYDOR

❏ PD-1-6343	Saturday, Saturday Night	1981	25.00

ZOTTOLA, GLENN

DREAMSTREET

❏ 105	Live at Eddie Condon's	1980	15.00
❏ 107	Steamin' Mainstream	1986	12.00

FAMOUS DOOR

❏ HL-141	Secret Love	1981	15.00
❏ HL-149	Stardust	1983	15.00

ZULEMA

LEJOINT

❏ LEJ17000	Z-Licious	1978	18.00

RCA VICTOR

❏ APL1-1152	R.S.V.P.	1975	18.00
❏ APL1-1423	Suddenly There Was You	1976	18.00
❏ APL1-0819	Zulema	1975	18.00

SUSSEX

❏ SRA8029	Ms. Z.	1973	18.00
❏ SXBS7015	Zulema	1972	18.00

ZUNIGER, RICK

HEADFIRST

❏ 675	New Frontier	198?	15.00

ZURKE, BOB

RCA VICTOR

❏ LPM-1013 [M]	The Tom Cat on the Keys	1955	80.00

ZWOL

EMI AMERICA

❏ SW-17014	Effective Immediately	1979	12.00
❏ SW-17005	Zwol	1978	12.00

ZYTRON

PACIFIC ARTS

❏ B7-120	New Moon in Zytron	197?	18.00

ZZ TOP

LONDON

❏ PS656	Fandango!	1975	15.00
❏ PS612	Rio Grande Mud	1972	16.00
❏ PS-X-1001 [DJ]	Takin' Texas to the People	1976	60.00
❏ PS680	Tejas	1977	15.00
❏ PS706	The Best of ZZ Top	1977	15.00
❏ XPS631 [B]	Tres Hombres	1973	15.00
❏ PS584	ZZ Top's First Album	1971	15.00

RHINO/WARNER BROS.

❏ 308172	Fandango!	2008	25.00

WARNER BROS.

❏ 25342 [B]	Afterburner	1985	10.00
❏ HS3361	Deguello	1979	12.00
❏ 23774	Eliminator	1983	10.00
❏ BSK3593 [B]	El Loco	1981	12.00
❏ BSK3271	Fandango!	1979	10.00
❏ 26846	Greatest Hits	1992	25.00

—*U.S. vinyl available only through Columbia House*

❏ 26265	Recycler	1990	18.00
❏ BSK3269	Rio Grande Mud	1979	10.00
❏ BSK3272	Tejas	1979	10.00
❏ BSK3273	The Best of ZZ Top	1979	10.00
❏ BSK3270	Tres Hombres	1979	10.00
❏ 274492	Tres Hombres	2007	30.00

—*Reissue on 180-gram vinyl with gatefold, replica of "Burbank" WB label and insert*

❏ MOVLP1142 [B]	Tres Hombres	2014	30.00
❏ BSK3268	ZZ Top's First Album	1979	10.00

Number	Title	Yr	NM

Original Cast Recordings

AIN'T MISBEHAVIN'
- ☐ RCA Victor CBL2-2965 — 1978 — 15.00
  — *New recordings of the music of Fats Waller*

ALL AMERICAN
- ☐ Columbia Masterworks KOL5760 [M] — 1962 — 30.00
- ☐ Columbia Masterworks KOS2160 [S] — 1962 — 30.00

ALL NIGHT STRUT!
- ☐ Playhouse Square PHS-CLE 1S-1001 — 1976 — 80.00

ANKLES AWEIGHT
- ☐ Decca DL9025 [M] — 1955 — 40.00

ANNIE
- ☐ CBS Masterworks JS34712 — 197? — 10.00
  — *Reissue; cover is basically the same, but label has "CBS Masterworks" along the outer edge*
- ☐ Columbia Masterworks JS34712 — 1977 — 12.00
  — *Original; labels have "Columbia" circling the perimeter of the label*

ANNIE GET YOUR GUN
- ☐ Decca DL8001 [M] — 1949 — 50.00
  — *Original LP issue of the Broadway cast*
- ☐ Decca DL9018 [M] — 1955 — 40.00
  — *Early reissue of DL 8001; black label with silver print*
- ☐ Decca DL79018 [R] — 196? — 15.00
- ☐ RCA Victor LOC-1124 [M] — 1966 — 15.00
- ☐ RCA Victor LSO-1124 [S] — 1966 — 18.00
  — *Revival cast; black label, dog on top, "Stereo Dynagroove" at bottom*
- ☐ RCA Victor LSO-1124 [S] — 1969 — 12.00
  — *Revival cast; orange, tan or black "dog near top" label*

ANNIE'S CHRISTMAS
- ☐ Columbia CC38361 — 1982 — 15.00
  — *Based on the characters in the "Annie" Broadway play*

ANYA
- ☐ United Artists UAL-4133 [M] — 1965 — 25.00
- ☐ United Artists UAS-5133 [S] — 1965 — 50.00

APPLAUSE
- ☐ ABC ABCS-OC-11 — 1970 — 25.00

THE APPLE TREE
- ☐ Columbia Masterworks KOL6620 [M] — 1966 — 25.00
- ☐ Columbia Masterworks KOS3020 [S] — 1966 — 30.00

ARABIAN NIGHTS
- ☐ Decca DL9013 [M] — 1954 — 80.00

THE ATHENIAN TOUCH
- ☐ Broadway East OCM-101 [M] — 1964 — 150.00
- ☐ Broadway East OCS-101 [S] — 1964 — 200.00

BAJOUR
- ☐ Columbia Masterworks KOL6300 [M] — 1964 — 30.00
- ☐ Columbia Masterworks KOS2700 [S] — 1964 — 30.00

BAKER STREET (A MUSICAL ADVENTURE OF SHERLOCK HOLMES)
- ☐ MGM E-7000 [M] — 1965 — 30.00
- ☐ MGM SE-7000 [S] — 1965 — 30.00

A BALLAD FOR BIMSHIRE
- ☐ London AM48002 [M] — 1963 — 40.00
- ☐ London AMS78002 [S] — 1963 — 80.00

THE BALLAD OF BABY DOE
- ☐ MGM 3GC-1 [M] — 1958 — 150.00
  — *Box set*

THE BAND WAGON
- ☐ X LVA-1001 [M] — 1955 — 70.00

BELLS ARE RINGING
- ☐ Columbia Masterworks OL5170 [M] — 1957 — 30.00
  — *Gray and black label with six "eye" logos*
- ☐ Columbia Masterworks OS2006 [S] — 1959 — 30.00
  — *Re-recording in stereo of OL 5170*

BEN FRANKLIN IN PARIS
- ☐ Capitol VAS2191 [M] — 1964 — 30.00
- ☐ Capitol SVAS2191 [S] — 1964 — 30.00

BEST FOOT FORWARD
- ☐ Cadence CLP-4012 [M] — 1963 — 25.00
- ☐ Cadence CLP-24012 [S] — 1963 — 30.00
  — *1963 revival of 1941 play*

THE BEST LITTLE WHOREHOUSE IN TEXAS
- ☐ MCA 3049 — 1978 — 15.00
  — *Tan label original*
- ☐ MCA 37218 — 1980 — 10.00
  — *Reissue of MCA 3049*

BEYOND THE FRINGE
- ☐ Capitol W1792 [M] — 1962 — 30.00
- ☐ Capitol SW1792 [S] — 1962 — 30.00

BEYOND THE FRINGE '64
- ☐ Capitol W2072 [M] — 1964 — 25.00
- ☐ Capitol SW2072 [S] — 1964 — 30.00

BIG RIVER
- ☐ MCA 6147 — 1985 — 12.00
  — *Music written by Roger Miller*

THE BIRTHDAY OF A KING
- ☐ Hal Leonard Publishing HLP-42 — 1986 — 15.00
  — *Composers: John Jacobson and Ed Lojeski*

THE BOY FRIEND
- ☐ RCA Victor LOC-1018 [M] — 1954 — 30.00
  — *Originals have green labels*

THE BOYS IN THE BAND
- ☐ A&M SP-6001 — 1969 — 30.00

BRAVO, GIOVANNI
- ☐ Columbia Masterworks KOL5800 [M] — 1962 — 18.00
- ☐ Columbia Masterworks KOS2200 [S] — 1962 — 25.00

BRIGADOON
- ☐ RCA Victor LOC-1001 [M] — 1951 — 30.00
  — *Green front cover; green label*
- ☐ RCA Victor LOC-1001 [M] — 195? — 25.00
  — *Photos of kilted dancers on front cover; black "Long Play" label*
- ☐ RCA Victor LOC-1001 [M] — 1963 — 18.00
  — *Drawing of kilted dancers on front cover; black "Mono" label*
- ☐ RCA Victor LSO-1001(e) [R] — 1963 — 15.00
  — *Black label, dog on top*

BYE BYE BIRDIE
- ☐ Columbia Masterworks KOL5510 [M] — 1960 — 30.00
  — *Gray and black label with six "eye" logos; with gatefold cover*
- ☐ Columbia Masterworks OL5510 [M] — 196? — 25.00
  — *Gray and black label with six "eye" logos; with regular cover*
- ☐ Columbia Masterworks KOS2025 [S] — 1960 — 30.00
  — *Gray and black label with six "eye" logos; with gatefold cover*
- ☐ Columbia Masterworks OS2025 [S] — 196? — 30.00
  — *Gray and black label with six "eye" logos; with regular cover*

BY JUPITER
- ☐ RCA Victor LOC-1137 [M] — 1967 — 40.00
- ☐ RCA Victor LSO-1137 [S] — 1967 — 75.00
  — *Above is by a revival cast*

BY THE BEAUTIFUL SEA
- ☐ Capitol S531 [M] — 1954 — 70.00

CABARET
- ☐ Capitol KOL6640 [M] — 1966 — 18.00
- ☐ Columbia Masterworks KOS3040 [S] — 1966 — 25.00

CABIN IN THE SKY
- ☐ Capitol W2073 [M] — 1964 — 30.00
- ☐ Capitol SW2073 [S] — 1964 — 50.00
  — *Above is by a revival cast*

CALL ME MADAM
- ☐ RCA Victor LOC-1000 [M] — 1950 — 80.00
  — *Dinah Shore sings Ethel Merman's part for contractual reasons, otherwise it's by the entire original cast*

CAMELOT
- ☐ Columbia Masterworks KOL5620 [M] — 1960 — 25.00
  — *Gray and black label with six "eye" logos*
- ☐ Columbia Masterworks KOS2031 [S] — 1960 — 30.00
  — *Gray and black label with six "eye" logos; gatefold cover*

CAN-CAN
- ☐ Capitol S452 [M] — 1953 — 30.00
  — *Originals have red labels with Capitol logo at top*
- ☐ Capitol W452 [M] — 195? — 18.00
- ☐ Capitol DW452 [R] — 196? — 15.00

CANTERBURY TALES
- ☐ Capitol SW-229 — 1969 — 30.00

CAPTAIN JINKS OF THE HORSE MARINES
- ☐ RCA Victor ARL2-1727 — 1975 — 30.00
  — *Box set*

CARMEN JONES
- ☐ Decca DL8014 [M] — 1949 — 40.00
  — *Black label, gold print*
- ☐ Decca DL9021 [M] — 1955 — 25.00
  — *Reissue of 8014; black label, silver print*

CARNIVAL
- ☐ MGM E-3946 [M] — 1961 — 25.00
- ☐ MGM SE-3946 [S] — 1961 — 30.00
  — *Black label*
- ☐ MGM SE-3946 [S] — 1968 — 12.00
  — *Blue and gold label*

CAROUSEL
- ☐ Command RS 33-843 [M] — 1962 — 18.00
  — *Studio cast*
- ☐ Command RS-843SD [M] — 1962 — 25.00
  — *Studio cast with Alfred Drake and Roberta Peters, and Enoch Light's orchestra*

BEYOND THE FRINGE

BEYOND THE FRINGE '64

- ☐ Decca DL8003 [M] — 1949 — 40.00
  — *Original LP issue of the Broadway cast*
- ☐ Decca DL9020 [M] — 1955 — 30.00
  — *Early reissue of DL 8003; black label with silver print*
- ☐ Decca DL79020 [R] — 196? — 12.00
- ☐ MCA 1627 [R] — 198? — 10.00
  — *Reissue of MCA 37093*
- ☐ MCA 37093 [R] — 1980 — 10.00
  — *Reissue of MCA 2033*
- ☐ MCA 2033 [R] — 1973 — 10.00
  — *Reissue of Decca 79020; black label with rainbow*

CELEBRATE THE KING
- ☐ John W. Peterson Music JPLP 07013 — 1986 — 15.00
  — *"A Christmas Musical by John W. Peterson," who composed it*

A CHORUS LINE
- ☐ Columbia PS33581 — 1975 — 15.00
  — *Original edition; no bar code on back cover*
- ☐ Columbia PSQ33581 [Q] — 1976 — 25.00
- ☐ Columbia JS33581 — 197? — 12.00
  — *Second issue with new prefix; no bar code*
- ☐ Columbia JS33581 — 1981 — 10.00
  — *Third edition; bar code added to back cover*
- ☐ Columbia HS43581 — 1981 — 40.00
  — *Half-speed mastered edition*

CHRISTINE
- ☐ Columbia Masterworks OL5520 [M] — 1960 — 60.00
- ☐ Columbia Masterworks OS2026 [S] — 1960 — 100.00

CHRISTMAS FEVER
- ☐ Lillenas L-9022 — 1981 — 12.00

CHRISTMAS…IN SPLENDOR AND MAJESTY
- ☐ Light LS5833 — 1984 — 15.00
  — *Composed by Otis Skillings*

CINDY
- ☐ ABC-Paramount ABC-OC-2 [M] — 1964 — 30.00
- ☐ ABC-Paramount ABC-OCS-2 [S] — 1964 — 50.00

CLARA (BEG, BORROW OR STEAL)
- ☐ Commentary CYN-02 [M] — 1960 — 60.00

CLOWNAROUND
- ☐ RCA Victor LSP-4741 — 1972 — 250.00

CLUB 15
- ☐ Decca DL5155 [10] — 1949 — 60.00

THE COACH WITH THE SIX INSIDES
- ☐ ESP-Disk' 1019 [M] — 1967 — 30.00

COCO
- ☐ Paramount PMS-1002 — 1969 — 30.00

COME CELEBRATE JESUS: A CHRISTMAS INVITATION
- ☐ Word 7-01-896610-8 — 1985 — 15.00
  — *By Don Marsh and Claire Cloninger," the composers*

THE COMMITTEE
- ☐ Reprise F-2023 [M] — 1964 — 30.00
- ☐ Reprise FS-2023 [S] — 1964 — 40.00

COMPANY
- ☐ Columbia Masterworks SQ30993 [Q] — 1971 — 30.00
  — *Quadraphonic version has substantially different mixes than the original stereo LP*
- ☐ Columbia Masterworks OS3550 — 1970 — 15.00

THE CRADLE WILL ROCK
- ☐ MGM E-4289-2 [M] — 1964 — 30.00
- ☐ MGM SE-4289-2 [S] — 1964 — 30.00
  — *The above is by a revival cast*

THE CRITIC
- ☐ Decca DL9154 [M] — 1967 — 25.00
- ☐ Decca DL79154 [S] — 1967 — 25.00

CRY FOR US ALL
- ☐ Project 3 TS-1000SD — 1970 — 40.00

DAMES AT SEA
- ☐ Columbia Masterworks OS3550 — 1969 — 25.00

DAMN YANKEES
- ☐ RCA Victor LOC-1021 [M] — 1955 — 30.00
  — *Green cover*
- ☐ RCA Victor LOC-1021 [M] — 195? — 25.00
  — *Orange cover*
- ☐ RCA Victor LSO-1021(e) [R] — 1965 — 18.00
  — *Black label, dog on top, "Stereo Electronically Reprocessed" at bottom*
- ☐ RCA Victor AYL1-3948 — 1980 — 10.00
  — *"Best Buy Series" reissue*

THE DANCERS OF BALI
- ☐ Columbia Masterworks ML4618 [M] — 1952 — 40.00

DARLING OF THE DAY
- ☐ RCA Victor LOC-1149 [M] — 1968 — 40.00
- ☐ RCA Victor LSO-1149 [S] — 1968 — 60.00

DEAR WORLD
- ☐ Columbia Masterworks BOS3260 — 1969 — 25.00

Number	Title	Yr	NM

DEATH OF A SALESMAN
- ❏ Decca DX102 [M] — 1951 — 40.00
  — *Two-record boxed set with contents of 9007 and 9008*

DEATH OF A SALESMAN (PART 1)
- ❏ Decca DL9006 [M] — 1951 — 30.00
  — *Black label, gold print*

DEATH OF A SALESMAN (PART 2)
- ❏ Decca DL9007 [M] — 1951 — 30.00
  — *Black label, gold print*

DESTRY RIDES AGAIN
- ❏ Decca DL9075 [M] — 1959 — 30.00
- ❏ Decca DL79075 [S] — 1959 — 40.00

DOCTOR SELAVY'S MAGIC THEATRE
- ❏ United Artists UA-LA196-G — 1974 — 30.00

DO I HEAR A WALTZ?
- ❏ Columbia Masterworks KOL6370 [M] — 1965 — 18.00
- ❏ Columbia Masterworks KOS2770 [S] — 1965 — 25.00

DONNYBROOK!
- ❏ Kapp KDL-8500 [M] — 1961 — 25.00
- ❏ Kapp KD-8500-S [S] — 1961 — 30.00

DO RE MI
- ❏ RCA Victor LOCD-2002 [M] — 1961 — 30.00
  — *In black box with orange sleeve*
- ❏ RCA Victor LSOD-2002 [S] — 1961 — 40.00
  — *In black box with orange sleeve*
- ❏ RCA Victor LOC-1105 [M] — 1965 — 18.00
  — *Reissue of 2002 with standard red cover*
- ❏ RCA Victor LSO-1105 [S] — 1965 — 25.00
  — *Reissue of 2002 with standard red cover*

DRESSED TO THE NINES
- ❏ MGM E-3914 [M] — 1960 — 30.00
- ❏ MGM SE-3914 [S] — 1960 — 40.00

THE EARL OF RUSTON
- ❏ Capitol ST-465 — 1971 — 40.00

ERNEST IN LOVE
- ❏ Columbia Masterworks OL5530 [M] — 1960 — 60.00
- ❏ Columbia Masterworks OS2027 [S] — 1960 — 100.00

AN EVENING WITH RICHARD NIXON
- ❏ Ode SP-77015 — 1972 — 30.00

EVERLASTING LIGHT: A CHRISTMAS CAROL FOR A DARK WORLD
- ❏ Word 7-01-900810-0 — 1986 — 15.00
  — *By Claire Cloninger and Mark Hayes," the composers*

EVITA
- ❏ MCA 2-11003 — 1976 — 25.00
  — *London cast; white cover; with booklet*
- ❏ MCA 2-11007 — 1979 — 18.00
  — *New York cast; mostly black cover; with booklet*

FADE OUT-FADE IN
- ❏ ABC-Paramount ABC-OC-3 [M] — 1964 — 30.00
- ❏ ABC-Paramount ABCS-OC-3 [S] — 1964 — 30.00

A FAMILY AFFAIR
- ❏ United Artists UAL-4099 [M] — 1962 — 30.00
- ❏ United Artists UAS-5099 [S] — 1962 — 50.00

FANNY
- ❏ RCA Victor LOC-1015 [M] — 1954 — 30.00
  — *"Long Play" on label*
- ❏ RCA Victor LOC-1015 [M] — 196? — 18.00
  — *"Mono" on label*
- ❏ RCA Victor LSO-1015(e) [R] — 196? — 15.00
  — *"Stereo Electronically Reprocessed" on label*

THE FANTASTICKS
- ❏ MGM E-3872 [M] — 1963 — 25.00
  — *Original non-gatefold cover*
- ❏ MGM SE-3872 [S] — 1963 — 30.00
  — *Original non-gatefold cover*
- ❏ MGM E-3872 [M] — 196? — 12.00
  — *White gatefold cover*
- ❏ MGM SE-3872 [S] — 196? — 15.00
  — *White gatefold cover*
- ❏ MGM SE-3872 [S] — 196? — 12.00
  — *Black gatefold cover*

FIDDLER ON THE ROOF
- ❏ RCA Victor LOC-1093 [M] — 1964 — 18.00
- ❏ RCA Victor LSO-1093 [S] — 1964 — 25.00
  — *Black label, dog on top*

FINIAN'S RAINBOW
- ❏ Columbia Masterworks ML4062 [M] — 1948 — 30.00
  — *Original cover with no photo; green label*
- ❏ Columbia Masterworks OL4062 [M] — 196? — 15.00
  — *Reissue cover, either pink or green; gray label*
- ❏ Columbia Masterworks OS2080 [R] — 1963 — 15.00

Number	Title	Yr	NM

- ❏ RCA Victor LOC-1057 [M] — 1960 — 15.00
  — *Revival cast; "pot of gold" cover*
- ❏ RCA Victor LOC-1057 [M] — 1960 — 12.00
  — *Revival cast; cover shows co-stars hiding in the trees*
- ❏ RCA Victor LSO-1057 [S] — 1960 — 18.00
  — *Revival cast; "pot of gold" cover*
- ❏ RCA Victor LSO-1057 [S] — 1960 — 15.00
  — *Revival cast; cover shows co-stars hiding in the trees*

FIORELLO!
- ❏ Capitol WAO1321 [M] — 1959 — 25.00
- ❏ Capitol SWAO1321 [S] — 1959 — 30.00

FIRST IMPRESSIONS
- ❏ Columbia Masterworks OL5400 [M] — 1959 — 30.00
- ❏ Columbia Masterworks OS2014 [S] — 1959 — 60.00

FLAHOOLEY
- ❏ Capitol S284 [M] — 1951 — 150.00
- ❏ Capitol T-11649 [M] — 1977 — 18.00

FLORA, THE RED MENACE
- ❏ RCA Victor LOC-1111 [M] — 1965 — 30.00
- ❏ RCA Victor LSO-1111 [S] — 1965 — 30.00

FLOWER DRUM SONG
- ❏ Columbia Masterworks OL5350 [M] — 1958 — 25.00
  — *Gray and black label with six "eye" logos*
- ❏ Columbia Masterworks OS2009 [S] — 1958 — 30.00
  — *Gray and black label with six "eye" logos*

FLY BLACKBIRD
- ❏ Mercury OCM-2206 [M] — 1962 — 30.00
- ❏ Mercury OCS-6206 [S] — 1962 — 60.00

FUNNY GIRL
- ❏ Capitol VAS2059 [M] — 1964 — 18.00
- ❏ Capitol SVAS2059 [S] — 1964 — 25.00
  — *Both Barbra Streisand and Sydney Chaplin are pictured on the back cover*
- ❏ Capitol STAO2059 [S] — 196? — 15.00
  — *Only Barbra Streisand is pictured on the back cover*

A FUNNY THING HAPPENED ON THE WAY TO THE FORUM
- ❏ Capitol WAO1717 [M] — 1962 — 18.00
  — *Gatefold cover*
- ❏ Capitol SWAO1717 [S] — 1962 — 25.00
  — *Gatefold cover*

THE GAY LIFE
- ❏ Capitol WAO1560 [M] — 1961 — 30.00
- ❏ Capitol SWAO1560 [S] — 1961 — 50.00

GENTLEMEN PREFER BLONDES
- ❏ Columbia Masterworks ML4290 [M] — 1949 — 30.00
  — *Original with green label*
- ❏ Columbia Masterworks OL4290 [M] — 196? — 18.00
  — *Reissue with new prefix and various gray labels*
- ❏ Columbia Masterworks OS2310 [R] — 1963 — 12.00
  — *Gray label*
- ❏ Columbia Masterworks S32610 [R] — 1973 — 10.00

GEORGE M!
- ❏ Columbia Masterworks KOL6800 [M] — 1968 — 30.00
- ❏ Columbia Masterworks KOS3200 [S] — 1968 — 25.00

THE GIRL IN PINK TIGHTS
- ❏ Columbia Masterworks ML4890 [M] — 1954 — 60.00

THE GIRL WHO CAME TO SUPPER
- ❏ Columbia Masterworks KOL6020 [M] — 1963 — 30.00
- ❏ Columbia Masterworks KOS2420 [S] — 1963 — 30.00

GIVE 'EM HELL, HARRY!
- ❏ United Artists UA-LA540-H2 — 1975 — 25.00

THE GLORY OF CHRISTMAS
- ❏ Light LS-5775 — 1980 — 15.00
  — *A Cantata byt Jimmy & Carol Owens"; narrated by Efrem Zimbalist, Jr.*

THE GOLDEN APPLE
- ❏ RCA Victor LOC-1014 [M] — 1954 — 100.00

GOLDEN BOY
- ❏ Capitol VAS2124 [M] — 1964 — 30.00
- ❏ Capitol SVAS2124 [S] — 1964 — 30.00

GOLDILOCKS
- ❏ Columbia Masterworks OL5340 [M] — 1958 — 30.00
- ❏ Columbia Masterworks OS2007 [S] — 1958 — 60.00

GOODTIME CHARLEY
- ❏ RCA Victor ARL1-1011 — 1975 — 30.00

GREASE
- ❏ MGM 1SE-34 — 1972 — 15.00

THE GREAT WALTZ
- ❏ Capitol VAS2426 [M] — 1965 — 25.00
- ❏ Capitol SVAS2426 [S] — 1965 — 30.00

GREENWICH VILLAGE U.S.A.
- ❏ 20th Fox TCF-105-2 [M] — 1960 — 60.00
  — *With complete show*

Number	Title	Yr	NM

- ❏ 20th Fox TCF-105-2S [S] — 1960 — 100.00
  — *With complete show*
- ❏ 20th Fox FOX-4005 [M] — 1960 — 40.00
  — *With excerpts from the show*
- ❏ 20th Fox SFX-4005 [S] — 1960 — 50.00
  — *With excerpts from the show*

GREENWILLOW
- ❏ RCA Victor LOC-2001 [M] — 1960 — 25.00
- ❏ RCA Victor LSO-2001 [S] — 1960 — 50.00

GUYS AND DOLLS
- ❏ Decca DL8036 [M] — 1950 — 30.00
- ❏ Decca DL9023 [M] — 1955 — 25.00
  — *Reissue of 8036*
- ❏ Decca DL79023 [R] — 196? — 15.00
- ❏ MCA 2034 — 1973 — 12.00
  — *Reissue of 79023*
- ❏ MCA 37094 — 198? — 10.00
  — *Reissue of 2034*

GYPSY
- ❏ Columbia Masterworks OL5420 [M] — 1959 — 25.00
  — *Original covers are white with drawings*
- ❏ Columbia Masterworks OS2017 [S] — 1959 — 30.00
  — *Original covers are white with drawings*
- ❏ Columbia Masterworks OL5420 [M] — 1962 — 15.00
  — *Reissue covers are brown with show photos*
- ❏ Columbia Masterworks OS2017 [S] — 1962 — 18.00
  — *Reissue covers are brown with show photos*

HAIR
- ❏ Atco SD7002 — 1969 — 30.00
  — *Original London cast*
- ❏ Philips PHS600329 — 1969 — 30.00
  — *Original French cast*
- ❏ RCA Victor LOC-1143 [M] — 1967 — 18.00
  — *Off-Broadway cast*
- ❏ RCA Victor LSO-1143 [S] — 1967 — 15.00
  — *Off-Broadway cast; black label, dog at top, "Stereo" at bottom*
- ❏ RCA Victor LOC-1150 [M] — 1968 — 30.00
  — *Broadway cast*
- ❏ RCA Victor LSO-1150 [S] — 1968 — 25.00
  — *Broadway cast; black label, dog on top, "Stereo" at bottom*
- ❏ RCA Victor LSO-1150 [S] — 1968 — 12.00
  — *Broadway cast; orange label*
- ❏ RCA Victor ANL1-0986 — 1974 — 12.00
  — *Off-Broadway cast; reissue with new number*
- ❏ RCA Victor ABD1 0245 [Q] — 1973 — 25.00
  — *Broadway cast; quadraphonic remix*

HALF A SIXPENCE
- ❏ RCA Victor LOC-1110 [M] — 1965 — 25.00
- ❏ RCA Victor LSO-1110 [S] — 1965 — 30.00

HALF PAST WEDNESDAY
- ❏ Columbia CL1917 [M] — 1962 — 30.00
- ❏ Columbia CS8717 [S] — 1962 — 40.00

HAMLET
- ❏ Columbia Masterworks DOL302 [M] — 1964 — 30.00
  — *Boxed set with entire play (Broadway revival)*
- ❏ Columbia Masterworks DOS702 [S] — 1964 — 30.00
  — *Boxed set with entire play (Broadway revival)*
- ❏ Columbia Masterworks OL6220 [M] — 1964 — 18.00
  — *Highlights from the box set*
- ❏ Columbia Masterworks OS2620 [S] — 1964 — 18.00
  — *Highlights from the box set*

THE HAPPIEST GIRL IN THE WORLD
- ❏ Columbia Masterworks KOL5650 [M] — 1961 — 40.00
  — *Original covers are yellow*
- ❏ Columbia Masterworks KOL5650 [M] — 1961 — 30.00
  — *Second covers are white*
- ❏ Columbia Masterworks KOS2050 [S] — 1961 — 60.00
  — *Original covers are yellow*
- ❏ Columbia Masterworks KOS2050 [S] — 1961 — 40.00
  — *Second covers are white*

HAPPY HUNTING
- ❏ RCA Victor LOC-1026 [M] — 1956 — 40.00

HEAR! HEAR!
- ❏ Decca DL9031 [M] — 1955 — 50.00

HELLO, DOLLY!
- ❏ RCA Victor LOCD-1087 [M] — 1964 — 30.00
  — *Original cover is black and white on back and spotlights "Come and Be My Butterfly"; this song was deleted from the show, so the cover was changed*
- ❏ RCA Victor LOCD-1087 [M] — 1964 — 18.00
  — *New back cover is in color and has a photo of Carol Channing; "RE" is on cover*
- ❏ RCA Victor LSOD-1087 [S] — 1964 — 30.00
  — *Original cover is black and white on back and spotlights "Come and Be My Butterfly"; this song was deleted from the show, so the cover was changed*

Number	Title	Yr	NM

□ RCA Victor LSOD-1087 [S] — 1964 — 25.00
— *New back cover is in color and has a photo of Carol Channing; "RE" is on cover; black label, dog on top*

□ RCA Victor LSOD-1087 [S] — 1969 — 12.00
— *Orange or tan label*

HENRY, SWEET HENRY

□ ABC ABC-OC-4 [M] — 1967 — 30.00
□ ABC ABCS-OC-4 [S] — 1967 — 50.00

HERE'S LOVE

□ Columbia Masterworks KOL6000 [M] — 1963 — 30.00
□ Columbia Masterworks KOS2400 [S] — 1963 — 40.00

HIGH BUTTON SHOES

□ RCA Camden CAL-457 [M] — 1958 — 30.00
□ RCA Victor LOC-1107 [M] — 1964 — 40.00
□ RCA Victor LSO-1107 [R] — 1964 — 30.00

HIGH SPIRITS

□ ABC-Paramount ABC-OC-1 [M] — 1964 — 30.00
□ ABC-Paramount ABCS-OC-1 [S] — 1964 — 30.00

HOUSE OF FLOWERS

□ Columbia Masterworks ML4969 [M] — 1954 — 40.00
— *Blue label original*

□ United Artists UAS-5180 — 1968 — 40.00
— *Revival cast*

HOW NOW, DOW JONES

□ RCA Victor LOC-1142 [M] — 1967 — 30.00
□ RCA Victor LSO-1142 [S] — 1967 — 30.00

HOW TO SUCCEED IN BUSINESS WITHOUT REALLY TRYING

□ RCA Victor LOC-1066 [M] — 1961 — 25.00
□ RCA Victor LSO-1066 [S] — 1961 — 30.00
— *Black label, dog on top*

□ RCA Victor LSO-1066 [S] — 1969 — 12.00
— *Orange or tan label*

HUGHIE

□ Columbia Masterworks OL6260 [M] — 1965 — 30.00
□ Columbia Masterworks OS2760 [S] — 1965 — 30.00

I CAN GET IT FOR YOU WHOLESALE

□ Columbia Masterworks KOL5780 [M] — 1962 — 30.00
□ Columbia Masterworks KOS2180 [S] — 1962 — 30.00

ICE FOLLIES

□ Dot DLP-3757 [M] — 1967 — 30.00
□ Dot DLP-25757 [S] — 1967 — 30.00

I DO! I DO!

□ RCA Victor LOC-1128 [M] — 1966 — 18.00
□ RCA Victor LSO-1128 [S] — 1966 — 25.00
— *Black label, dog on top*

I HAD A BALL

□ Mercury OCM-2210 [M] — 1964 — 25.00
□ Mercury OCS-6210 [S] — 1964 — 30.00
□ Mercury OCM-2210 [M] — 1964 — 40.00
— *Promo-only two-record set with bonus interview record MGD-2-24*

ILLYA DARLING

□ United Artists UAL-8901 [M] — 1967 — 25.00
□ United Artists UAS-9901 [S] — 1967 — 25.00

I LOVE MY WIFE

□ Atlantic SD19107 — 1977 — 12.00

INTO THE WOODS

□ RCA 6796-1-RC — 1988 — 25.00

IRMA LA DOUCE

□ Columbia Masterworks OL5560 [M] — 1960 — 25.00
□ Columbia Masterworks OS2029 [S] — 1960 — 30.00

JACQUES BREL IS ALIVE AND WELL AND LIVING IN PARIS

□ Columbia Masterworks D2S779 — 1968 — 25.00
— *Box set; gray "360 Sound" labels*

J.B.

□ RCA Victor LD-6075 [M] — 1959 — 60.00
□ RCA Victor LDS-6075 [S] — 1959 — 70.00

JENNIE

□ RCA Victor LOC-1083 [M] — 1963 — 30.00
□ RCA Victor LSO-1083 [S] — 1963 — 50.00

JESUS CHRIST SUPERSTAR

□ Decca DL71503 — 1971 — 25.00
— *From the Broadway production; also see listings for this title in the VARIOUS ARTISTS COLLECTIONS sections.*

□ MCA 5000 — 1973 — 15.00
— *From the Broadway production; reissue*

JOSEPH AND THE AMAZING TECHNICOLOR DREAMCOAT

□ Scepter SPS-588X — 1968 — 25.00
— *With gatefold cover and libretto*

□ Scepter SMAS-93738 — 197? — 30.00
— *Capitol Record Club edition*

JOY

□ RCA Victor LSO-1166 — 1970 — 25.00

JUNO

□ Columbia Masterworks OL5380 [M] — 1959 — 40.00
□ Columbia Masterworks OS2013 [S] — 1959 — 70.00

KEAN

□ Columbia Masterworks KOL5720 [M] — 1961 — 30.00
□ Columbia Masterworks KSO2120 [S] — 1961 — 40.00

THE KING AND I

□ Decca DL9008 [M] — 1951 — 30.00
— *Black label, gold print*

□ Decca DL9008 [M] — 195? — 40.00
— *Drawing of Gertrude Lawrence and Yul Brynner on cover, with title on three lines*

□ Decca DL9008 [M] — 195? — 15.00
— *Drawing of Gertrude Lawrence and Yul Brynner on cover, with title on two lines*

□ Decca DL79008 [R] — 196? — 12.00

KWAMINA

□ Capitol W1645 [M] — 1962 — 30.00
□ Capitol SW1645 [S] — 1962 — 50.00

THE LADY'S NOT FOR BURNING

□ Decca DL9508/9 [M] — 1951 — 50.00
— *Oversize box set*

LAGINAPPE '59 PRESENTS BE MY GUEST

□ (no label) XCTV-10303 [M] — 1959 — 250.00
— *Custom pressing for New Trier High School, Illinois. Collectible because the future Ann-Margret sings one track on the LP!*

LEGS DIAMOND

□ RCA 7983-1-RC — 1989 — 30.00

LES MISERABLES

□ Geffen GHS24151 — 1987 — 18.00
— *Original Broadway cast recording*

□ Relativity 88561-8140-1 — 1985 — 25.00
— *Original London cast recording*

LET IT RIDE

□ RCA Victor LOC-1064 [M] — 1961 — 25.00
□ RCA Victor LSO-1064 [S] — 1961 — 40.00

LI'L ABNER

□ Columbia Masterworks OL5150 [M] — 1956 — 30.00

LITTLE ME

□ RCA Victor LOC-1078 [M] — 1962 — 25.00
□ RCA Victor LSO-1078 [S] — 1962 — 30.00

LITTLE SHOP OF HORRORS

□ Geffen GHSP-2020 — 1982 — 30.00

LOOK MA, I'M DANCIN'!

□ Decca DL5231 [M] — 1950 — 100.00

LORELEI

□ MGM M3G-55 — 1974 — 30.00
— *Second version, recorded with Broadway cast*

□ Verve MV-5097-OC — 1974 — 30.00
— *First version, recorded before the show hit Broadway*

LOST IN THE STARS

□ Decca DL8028 [M] — 1949 — 50.00
□ Decca DL9120 [M] — 1965 — 18.00
— *Reissue of 8028*

THE MAD SHOW

□ Columbia Masterworks OL6530 [M] — 1965 — 50.00
□ Columbia Masterworks OS2930 [S] — 1965 — 100.00

MAGGIE FLYNN

□ RCA Victor LSOD-2009 — 1968 — 30.00
□ RCA Victor LSOD-2009 — 1968 — 25.00

THE MAGIC SHOW

□ Bell 9003 — 1974 — 25.00

MAKE A WISH

□ RCA Victor LOC-1002 [M] — 1951 — 150.00

MAME

□ Columbia Masterworks KOS3000 [S] — 1966 — 25.00
— *Gray label with "360 Sound Stereo*

□ Columbia Masterworks KOL6600 [M] — 1966 — 18.00
□ Columbia Masterworks KOS3000 [S] — 1970 — 15.00
— *Olive label with orange "Columbia" around outside*

MAN OF LA MANCHA

□ Kapp KRL-4505 [M] — 1965 — 18.00
□ Kapp KRS-4505 [S] — 1965 — 25.00

MARK TWAIN TONIGHT!

□ Columbia Masterworks OL5440 [M] — 1959 — 15.00
□ Columbia Masterworks OS2019 [S] — 1959 — 18.00

ME AND JULIET

□ RCA Victor LOC-1012 [M] — 1953 — 70.00

MEDEA

□ Decca DLP9000 [M] — 1949 — 30.00

MEGILLA OF ITZIG MANGER

□ Columbia Masterworks OS3270 — 1968 — 40.00

MERRILY WE ROLL ALONG

□ RCA Victor CBL1-4197 — 1981 — 30.00

THE MERRY WIDOW

□ RCA Victor LOC-1094 [M] — 1964 — 25.00
□ RCA Victor LSO-1094 [S] — 1964 — 30.00

MESSIAH, BRIGHT MORNING STAR

□ Light LS5811 — 1982 — 15.00
— *Composers: Reba Rambo & Dony McGuire*

MEXICAN HAYRIDE

□ Decca DL5232 [10] — 1950 — 120.00

MILK AND HONEY

□ RCA Victor LOC-1065 [M] — 1961 — 30.00
— *With only credits (no picture) on front cover*

□ RCA Victor LOC-1065 [M] — 1961 — 25.00
— *With picture of Tommy Rall and two dancers on front cover*

□ RCA Victor LSO-1065 [S] — 1961 — 30.00
— *With only credits (no picture) on front cover*

□ RCA Victor LSO-1065 [S] — 1961 — 30.00
— *With picture of Tommy Rall and two dancers on front cover*

MISS LIBERTY

□ Columbia Masterworks ML4220 [M] — 1949 — 30.00
— *Originals have green labels*

MISS SAIGON

□ Geffen GHS24271 — 1990 — 25.00

THE MOST HAPPY FELLA

□ Columbia Masterworks OL5118 [M] — 1956 — 30.00
— *Gray and black label with six "eye" logos*

□ Columbia Masterworks OS2330 [R] — 196? — 18.00
□ Columbia Masterworks O3L240 [M] — 1956 — 50.00
— *Box set with entire show*

MR. PRESIDENT

□ Columbia Masterworks KOL5870 [M] — 1962 — 25.00
— *Gatefold with shiny silver cover*

□ Columbia Masterworks KOS2270 [S] — 1962 — 30.00
— *Gatefold with shiny silver cover*

MRS. PATTERSON

□ RCA Victor LOC-1017 [M] — 1954 — 150.00

MR. WONDERFUL

□ Decca DL9032 [M] — 1956 — 50.00

THE MUSIC MAN

□ Capitol WAO990 [M] — 1957 — 25.00
— *Gatefold cover, white with credits and drawing on front; gray label*

□ Capitol SWAO990 [S] — 1957 — 30.00
— *Gatefold cover, white with credits and drawing on front; gray label*

□ Capitol W990 [M] — 196? — 15.00
— *Regular cover with photo of Robert Preston as Harold Hill*

□ Capitol SW990 [S] — 196? — 18.00
— *Regular cover with photo of Robert Preston as Harold Hill*

MY FAIR LADY

□ Columbia Masterworks OL5090 [M] — 1956 — 30.00
— *Gray and black label with six "eye" logos*

□ Columbia Masterworks OS2015 [S] — 1959 — 25.00
— *Gray and black label with six "eye" logos; original London cast*

□ Columbia Masterworks OL5090 [M] — 1963 — 18.00
— *Gray label with "Guaranteed High Fidelity" at bottom*

□ Columbia Masterworks OL5090 [M] — 1956 — 12.00
— *Gray label, "Mono" at bottom*

□ Columbia Masterworks OS2015 [S] — 1959 — 15.00
— *Gray label, "Stereo" at bottom; original London cast*

□ Columbia Masterworks PS34197 — 1976 — 12.00
— *Revival cast*

MY PEOPLE

□ Contact C-1 [M] — 1966 — 25.00
□ Contact CS-1 [S] — 1966 — 30.00

THE NERVOUS SET

□ Columbia Masterworks OL5430 [M] — 1959 — 30.00
□ Columbia Masterworks OS2018 [S] — 1959 — 60.00

NEW FACES OF 1952

□ RCA Victor LOC-1008 [M] — 1952 — 30.00

NEW FACES OF 1956

□ RCA Victor LOC-1025 [M] — 1956 — 50.00

NEW FACES OF 1968

□ Warner Bros. BS2551 — 1968 — 30.00

THE NEW GIRL IN TOWN

□ RCA Victor LOC-1027 [M] — 1957 — 25.00
□ RCA Victor LSO-1027 [S] — 1958 — 50.00
□ RCA Victor LOC-1106 [M] — 1965 — 25.00
□ RCA Victor LSC-1106 [S] — 1965 — 30.00

THE NINA, THE PINTA AND THE SANTA MARIA

□ Dot DLP-9009 [M] — 1960 — 40.00
□ Dot DLP-29009 [S] — 1960 — 50.00

Number	Title	Yr	NM

NO STRINGS
- ❑ Capitol O1695 [M] — 1962 — 25.00
- ❑ Capitol SO1695 [S] — 1962 — 40.00

OF THEE I SING
- ❑ Capitol S350 [M] — 1952 — 150.00

OH, KAY!
- ❑ 20th Fox FOX-4003 [M] — 1960 — 30.00
- ❑ 20th Fox SFX-4003 [S] — 1960 — 50.00

OKLAHOMA!
- ❑ Decca DLP8000 [M] — 1949 — 30.00
—Black label, gold print; the first 12-inch LP on Decca
- ❑ Decca DL9017 [M] — 1955 — 25.00
—Reissue of 8000
- ❑ Decca DL9017 [M] — 196? — 25.00
—Reissue with new cover art
- ❑ Decca DL79017 [R] — 196? — 18.00
- ❑ Decca DL79017 [R] — 1968 — 25.00
—Special 25th Anniversary edition; cover has yellow drawing, inner sleeve has liner notes
- ❑ MCA 2030 — 1973 — 10.00
—Reissue of 79017; black label with rainbow
- ❑ MCA 37096 — 198? — 10.00
—Reissue of 2030

OLIVER!
- ❑ RCA Victor LOCD-2004 [M] — 1962 — 18.00
- ❑ RCA Victor LSOD-2004 [S] — 1962 — 25.00

ON A CLEAR DAY YOU CAN SEE FOREVER
- ❑ RCA Victor LOCD-2006 [M] — 1965 — 25.00
- ❑ RCA Victor LSOD-2006 [S] — 1965 — 30.00

ONCE UPON A MATTRESS
- ❑ Kapp KDL-7004 [M] — 1959 — 30.00
- ❑ Kapp KDL-7004-S [S] — 1959 — 30.00

110 IN THE SHADE
- ❑ RCA Victor LOC-1085 [M] — 1963 — 30.00
- ❑ RCA Victor LSO-1085 [S] — 1963 — 40.00

ONE TOUCH OF VENUS
- ❑ Decca DL9122 [M] — 1965 — 30.00
- ❑ Decca DL79122 [R] — 1965 — 30.00

ON YOUR TOES
- ❑ Decca DL9015 [M] — 1954 — 75.00

OVER HERE!
- ❑ Columbia Masterworks KS32961 — 1974 — 25.00
- ❑ Columbia Masterworks SQ32961 [Q] — 1974 — 30.00

PAINT YOUR WAGON
- ❑ RCA Victor LOC-1006 [M] — 1951 — 30.00
—Green label
- ❑ RCA Victor LOC-1006 [M] — 1955 — 25.00
—Black label, dog on top, "Long Play" at bottom
- ❑ RCA Victor LOC-1006 [M] — 1965 — 18.00
—Black label, dog on top, "Mono" at bottom
- ❑ RCA Victor LSO-1006 [R] — 1955 — 15.00
—Black label, dog on top
- ❑ RCA Victor LSO-1006 [R] — 1969 — 12.00
—Orange or tan label

PARADE
- ❑ Kapp KDL-7005 [M] — 1960 — 200.00
- ❑ Kapp KDS-7005 [S] — 1960 — 250.00

PARIS '90
- ❑ Columbia Masterworks ML4619 [M] — 1952 — 150.00

PEACE
- ❑ Metromedia MP-33001 — 1969 — 30.00

PETER PAN
- ❑ RCA Victor LOC-1019 [M] — 1954 — 40.00
- ❑ RCA Victor LSO-1019 [R] — 196? — 15.00
- ❑ RCA Victor AYL1-3762 [R] — 1980 — 10.00

THE PHANTOM OF THE OPERA
- ❑ Polydor 831273-1 — 1987 — 25.00
—With libretto
- ❑ Polydor 831563-1 — 1987 — 12.00
—One-record "highlights" release

PIPE DREAM
- ❑ RCA Victor LOC-1023 [M] — 1955 — 70.00
—With "Special Advance Edition" sticker on cover
- ❑ RCA Victor LOC-1023 [M] — 1955 — 50.00
—Without "Special Advance Edition" sticker on cover

PLAIN AND FANCY
- ❑ Capitol S603 [M] — 1955 — 30.00
—Red label

PLAYGIRLS
- ❑ Warner Bros. W1530 [M] — 1964 — 30.00
- ❑ Warner Bros. WS1530 [S] — 1964 — 30.00

PORGY AND BESS
- ❑ Decca DL7006 [10] — 1950 — 30.00
—Reissue of material first released on 78s

Number	Title	Yr	NM

- ❑ Decca DL8042 [M] — 1950 — 30.00
- ❑ Decca DL9024 [M] — 1955 — 30.00
—Reissue of 8042; drawing of Catfish Row on cover
- ❑ Decca DL9024 [M] — 196? — 18.00
—Photo of cast members on cover
- ❑ Decca DL79024 [R] — 196? — 12.00
—Photo of cast members on cover
- ❑ MCA 2035 [R] — 1973 — 10.00
—Reissue of 79024; black label with rainbow

THE PREMISE
- ❑ Vanguard VRS-9092 [M] — 1960 — 40.00

PUMP BOYS AND DINETTES
- ❑ CBS FM37790 — 1982 — 18.00

PURLIE
- ❑ Ampex A-40101 — 1970 — 30.00

RASHOMON
- ❑ Carlton LPX-5000 [M] — 1959 — 30.00
- ❑ Carlton STLPX-5000 [S] — 1959 — 30.00
—Not actually the original cast recording, but the play's incidental music

REDHEAD
- ❑ RCA Victor LOC-1048 [M] — 1959 — 25.00
- ❑ RCA Victor LSO-1048 [S] — 1959 — 50.00
—Without "Essie's Vision"
- ❑ RCA Victor LOC-1104 [M] — 1959 — 18.00
—Reissue of 1048
- ❑ RCA Victor LSO-1104 [S] — 1965 — 30.00
—Reissue adds "Essie's Vision" to stereo version

THE RIVER WIND
- ❑ London AM-48001 [M] — 1962 — 40.00
- ❑ London AMS-78001 [S] — 1962 — 80.00

THE ROAR OF THE GREASEPAINT -- THE SMELL OF THE CROWD
- ❑ RCA Victor LOC-1109 [M] — 1965 — 18.00
- ❑ RCA Victor LSO-1109 [S] — 1965 — 25.00

THE ROTHSCHILDS
- ❑ Columbia Masterworks S30337 — 1970 — 30.00

SAIL AWAY
- ❑ Capitol WAO1643 [M] — 1961 — 25.00
- ❑ Capitol SWAO1643 [S] — 1961 — 30.00

SARATOGA
- ❑ RCA Victor LOC-1051 [M] — 1959 — 30.00
- ❑ RCA Victor LSO-1051 [S] — 1959 — 50.00

SAY, DARLING
- ❑ RCA Victor LOC-1045 [M] — 1958 — 40.00
- ❑ RCA Victor LSO-1045 [R] — 1958 — 60.00

SELMA
- ❑ Cotillion SD 2-110 — 1976 — 25.00

SEVENTEEN
- ❑ RCA Victor LOC-1003 [M] — 1951 — 150.00

1776
- ❑ Columbia Masterworks BOS3310 — 1969 — 30.00
—The first edition has Howard DaSilva shown as Ben Franklin in credits and synopsis, though he does not appear on the LP
- ❑ Columbia Masterworks BOS3310 — 1969 — 15.00
—Revised (correct) edition has Rex Everhart shown as Ben Franklin in credits and synopsis

SEVENTH HEAVEN
- ❑ Decca DL9001 [M] — 1955 — 150.00

70 GIRLS, 70
- ❑ Columbia Masterworks S30589 — 1971 — 50.00

SHE LOVES ME
- ❑ MGM E4118OC-2 [M] — 1963 — 40.00
- ❑ MGM SE4118OC-2 [S] — 1963 — 50.00

SHOW BIZ (FROM VAUDE TO VIDEO)
- ❑ RCA Victor LOC-1011 [M] — 1954 — 40.00

SHOW BOAT
- ❑ Columbia Masterworks ML4058 [M] — 1948 — 30.00
—From the 1946 revival; paper envelope jacket with its opening on top
- ❑ Columbia Masterworks OL4058 [M] — 195? — 25.00
—From the 1946 revival; reissue of ML 4058

SHOW GIRL
- ❑ Roulette R-80001 [M] — 1961 — 25.00
- ❑ Roulette SR-80001 [S] — 1961 — 30.00

SIDE BY SIDE BY SONDHEIM
- ❑ RCA Victor CBL2-1851 — 1976 — 25.00

SILK STOCKINGS
- ❑ RCA Victor LOC-1016 [M] — 1955 — 40.00
- ❑ RCA Victor LOC-1102 [M] — 1965 — 25.00
—Reissue; regular cover
- ❑ RCA Victor LSO-1102 [R] — 1965 — 25.00

SIMPLY HEAVENLY
- ❑ Columbia Masterworks OL5240 [M] — 1957 — 30.00

Number	Title	Yr	NM

SING OUT, SWEET LAND!
- ❑ Decca DL8023 [M] — 1950 — 50.00
- ❑ Decca DL4304 [M] — 1963 — 25.00
- ❑ Decca DL74304 [R] — 1963 — 25.00

SKYSCRAPER
- ❑ Capitol VAS2422 [M] — 1965 — 25.00
- ❑ Capitol SVAS2422 [S] — 1965 — 30.00

SNOW WHITE AND THE SEVEN DWARFS
- ❑ Buena Vista STER-5009 — 1979 — 30.00

SONDHEIM: A MUSICAL TRIBUTE
- ❑ Warner Bros. 2WS2705 — 1973 — 25.00

SONG OF NORWAY
- ❑ Columbia CL1328 [M] — 1959 — 25.00
—1958 revival cast
- ❑ Columbia CS8135 [S] — 1959 — 50.00
—1958 revival cast
- ❑ Decca DL8002 [M] — 1949 — 30.00
- ❑ Decca DL9019 [M] — 1955 — 25.00
- ❑ Decca DL79019 [R] — 196? — 15.00
- ❑ MCA 2032 [R] — 1973 — 12.00
—Reissue of 79019; black label with rainbow

THE SOUND OF MUSIC
- ❑ Capitol DT91034 [R] — 1966 — 15.00
—Original London cast; Capitol Record Club exclusive
- ❑ Columbia Masterworks KOL5450 [M] — 1959 — 25.00
—Gray and black label with six "eye" logos
- ❑ Columbia Masterworks KOS2020 [S] — 1959 — 30.00
—Gray and black label with six "eye" logos
- ❑ Columbia Masterworks KOL5450 [M] — 1963 — 15.00
—Gray label with "Guaranteed High Fidelity" or "360 Sound Mono" on label
- ❑ Columbia Masterworks KOS2020 [S] — 1959 — 15.00
—Gray label with "360 Sound Stereo" at bottom
- ❑ Columbia Masterworks S32601 [S] — 1973 — 12.00
—Reissue of 2020

SOUTH PACIFIC
- ❑ Columbia Masterworks ML4180 [M] — 1949 — 30.00
—Green or blue label; large anchor on front cover
- ❑ Columbia Masterworks OL4180 [M] — 195? — 18.00
—Gray and black label with six "eye" logos; large anchor on front cover
- ❑ Columbia Masterworks OL4180 [M] — 195? — 15.00
—Gray and black label with six "eye" logos; glossy gatefold cover with Ezio Pinza and Mary Martin pictured
- ❑ Columbia Masterworks OL4180 [M] — 1963 — 12.00
—Gray label with "Guaranteed High Fidelity" or "360 Sound Mono"
- ❑ Columbia Masterworks OS2040 [S] — 196? — 12.00
—Gray label with "360 Sound Stereo
- ❑ Columbia Masterworks S32604 [R] — 1970 — 10.00
—Reissue of 2040

SOUTH PACIFIC, HITS FROM
- ❑ Columbia Masterworks A-1723 [PS] — 195? — 12.00

SOUTH PACIFIC, HITS FROM, VOL. 1 (HALL OF FAME SERIES)
- ❑ Columbia B-2579 [PS] — 195? — 10.00

ST. LOUIS WOMAN
- ❑ Capitol L355 [10] — 1952 — 80.00

STOP THE WORLD-I WANT TO GET OFF
- ❑ London AM58001 [M] — 1962 — 18.00
- ❑ London AMS88001 [S] — 1962 — 25.00

STREET SCENE
- ❑ Columbia Masterworks ML4139 [M] — 1949 — 30.00
—Paper envelope jacket with its opening on top

THE SUBJECT WAS ROSES
- ❑ Columbia Masterworks DOL308 [M] — 1964 — 25.00
- ❑ Columbia Masterworks DOS708 [S] — 1964 — 30.00

SUBWAYS ARE FOR SLEEPING
- ❑ Columbia Masterworks KOL5730 [M] — 1962 — 30.00
- ❑ Columbia Masterworks KOS2130 [S] — 1962 — 40.00

THE SURVIVAL OF ST. JOAN
- ❑ Paramount PAS-9000 — 1971 — 30.00

SWEENEY TODD-THE DEMON BARBER OF FLEET STREET
- ❑ RCA Victor CBL2-3379 — 1979 — 25.00

SWEET CHARITY
- ❑ Columbia Masterworks KOL6500 [M] — 1966 — 18.00
- ❑ Columbia Masterworks KOS2900 [S] — 1966 — 25.00

TAKE ME ALONG
- ❑ RCA Victor LOC-1050 [M] — 1959 — 18.00
- ❑ RCA Victor LSO-1050 [S] — 1959 — 25.00
—Black label

TAMALPAIS EXCHANGE
- ❑ Atlantic SD8263 — 1970 — 30.00

TAROT
- ❑ United Artists UAS-5563 — 1970 — 25.00

Number	Title	Yr	NM

TENDERLOIN
- ❏ Capitol WAO1492 [M] — 1960 — 30.00
  — *With program*
- ❏ Capitol SWAO1492 [S] — 1960 — 40.00
  — *With program*

TEVYA AND HIS DAUGHTERS
- ❏ Columbia Masterworks OL5225 [M] — 1957 — 30.00

TEXAS, LI'L DARLIN'
- ❏ Decca DL5188 [10] — 1950 — 80.00

THIS IS THE ARMY
- ❏ Decca DL5108 [10] — 1950 — 100.00

THIS WAS BURLESQUE
- ❏ Roulette R-25185 [M] — 1962 — 30.00
- ❏ Roulette SR-25186 [S] — 1962 — 30.00

THE THREEPENNY OPERA
- ❏ Columbia Masterworks PS34326 — 1976 — 25.00
  — *Another revival cast*
- ❏ MGM E-3121 [M] — 1954 — 30.00
  — *Revival cast; yellow label*
- ❏ MGM E-3121 [M] — 1959 — 18.00
  — *Revival cast; black label*
- ❏ MGM SE-3121 [R] — 196? — 15.00
  — *Revival cast; rechanneled stereo*
- ❏ Polydor 820260-1 — 198? — 10.00
  — *Revival cast; reissue*

THREE TO MAKE MUSIC
- ❏ RCA Victor LPM-2012 [M] — 1958 — 30.00
- ❏ RCA Victor LSP-2012 [S] — 1958 — 30.00

THREE WISHES FOR JAMIE
- ❏ Capitol S317 [M] — 1952 — 120.00

TIME CHANGES
- ❏ ABC ABCS-681 — 1969 — 30.00

A TIME FOR SINGING
- ❏ Warner Bros. W1639 [M] — 1966 — 40.00
- ❏ Warner Bros. WS1639 [S] — 1966 — 60.00

A TIME REMEMBERED
- ❏ Mercury MG-20380 [M] — 1957 — 30.00
- ❏ Mercury SR-60023 [S] — 1957 — 40.00
  — *Music from the dramatic play*

TO BROADWAY WITH LOVE
- ❏ Columbia Masterworks OL6030 [M] — 1964 — 30.00
- ❏ Columbia Masterworks OS2630 [S] — 1964 — 50.00

TOP BANANA
- ❏ Capitol S308 [M] — 1952 — 100.00

TOVARICH
- ❏ Capitol TAO1940 [M] — 1963 — 25.00
- ❏ Capitol STAO1940 [S] — 1963 — 30.00

A TREE GROWS IN BROOKLYN
- ❏ Columbia Masterworks ML4405 [M] — 1951 — 30.00
  — *Blue label*

TWO BY TWO
- ❏ Columbia Masterworks S30338 — 1970 — 25.00

TWO ON THE AISLE
- ❏ Decca DL8040 [M] — 1951 — 100.00
  — *Black label, gold print*
- ❏ Decca DL8040 [M] — 1955 — 60.00
  — *Black label, silver print*
- ❏ Decca DL8040 [M] — 196? — 60.00
  — *Black label with color bars*

TWO'S COMPANY
- ❏ RCA Victor LOC-1009 [M] — 1952 — 100.00

THE UNSINKABLE MOLLY BROWN
- ❏ Capitol WAO1509 [M] — 1960 — 25.00
- ❏ Capitol SWAO1509 [S] — 1960 — 30.00

UP IN CENTRAL PARK
- ❏ Decca DL8016 [M] — 1950 — 40.00
  — *Black label, gold print*
- ❏ Decca DL8016 [M] — 1955 — 30.00
  — *Black label, silver print*

WAITING FOR GODOT
- ❏ Columbia Masterworks O2L238 [M] — 1956 — 30.00

WEST SIDE STORY
- ❏ Columbia Masterworks OL5230 [M] — 1958 — 30.00
  — *Gray and black label with six "eye" logos*
- ❏ Columbia Masterworks OS2001 [S] — 1958 — 30.00
  — *Gray and black label with six "eye" logos*
- ❏ Columbia Masterworks OL5230 [M] — 1963 — 15.00
  — *Gray label with "Guaranteed High Fidelity" or "360 Sound Mono*
- ❏ Columbia Masterworks OS2001 [S] — 1963 — 18.00
  — *Gray label with "360 Sound Stereo*
- ❏ Columbia Masterworks S32603 [S] — 1973 — 12.00
  — *Reissue with new number*

WHAT MAKES SAMMY RUN?
- ❏ Columbia Masterworks KOI 6040 [M] — 1964 — 30.00
- ❏ Columbia Masterworks KSO2440 [S] — 1904 — 40.00

WILDCAT
- ❏ RCA Victor LOC-1060 [M] — 1961 — 30.00
- ❏ RCA Victor LSO-1060 [S] — 1961 — 40.00

WISH YOU WERE HERE
- ❏ RCA Victor LOC-1007 [M] — 1952 — 60.00

WONDERFUL TOWN
- ❏ Decca DL9010 [M] — 1953 — 30.00
  — *Black label, gold print*

WORDS AND MUSIC
- ❏ RCA Victor LRL1-5079 — 1974 — 25.00

YOU'RE A GOOD MAN, CHARLIE BROWN
- ❏ MGM 1E-9 [M] — 1967 — 25.00
- ❏ MGM S1E-9 [S] — 1967 — 25.00

YOUR OWN THING
- ❏ RCA Victor LOC-1148 [M] — 1968 — 30.00
- ❏ RCA Victor LSO-1148 [S] — 1968 — 25.00

ZORBA
- ❏ Capitol SO-118 — 1969 — 25.00

Soundtracks

AARON SLICK FROM PUNKIN CRICK
- ❏ RCA Victor LPM-3006 [10] — 1952 — 150.00

ABOUT LAST NIGHT...
- ❏ EMI America SV-17210 — 1986 — 12.00

ABSOLUTE BEGINNERS
- ❏ EMI America SV-17182 — 1986 — 15.00
- ❏ EMI America SV-517182 — 1986 — 15.00
  — *Columbia House record club edition*

ADVENTURES IN PARADISE
- ❏ ABC-Paramount ABC-329 [M] — 1960 — 30.00
- ❏ ABC-Paramount ABCS-329 [S] — 1960 — 40.00

ADVISE AND CONSENT
- ❏ RCA Victor LOC-1068 [M] — 1962 — 30.00
- ❏ RCA Victor LSO-1068 [S] — 1962 — 60.00

AN AFFAIR TO REMEMBER
- ❏ Columbia CL1013 [M] — 1957 — 40.00

AFRICA ADDIO
- ❏ United Artists UAL-4141 [M] — 1966 — 25.00
- ❏ United Artists UAS-5141 [S] — 1966 — 30.00

AGAINST ALL ODDS
- ❏ Atlantic 80152-1-E — 1984 — 12.00

THE AGONY AND THE ECSTASY
- ❏ Capitol MAS2427 [M] — 1965 — 60.00
- ❏ Capitol SMAS2427 [S] — 1965 — 80.00

AIRPORT
- ❏ Decca DL79173 — 1970 — 30.00

ALAKAZAM THE GREAT
- ❏ Vee Jay LP-6000 [M] — 1961 — 80.00

THE ALAMO
- ❏ Columbia CL1558 [M] — 1960 — 25.00
- ❏ Columbia CS8358 [S] — 1960 — 30.00

ALBERT PECKINPAW'S REVENGE
- ❏ Sidewalk T5907 [M] — 1967 — 30.00
- ❏ Sidewalk ST5907 [S] — 1967 — 30.00

ALEXANDER
- ❏ Polydor 24-7001 — 1970 — 40.00

ALEXANDER THE GREAT
- ❏ Mercury MG-20148 [M] — 1956 — 250.00

ALFIE
- ❏ ABC Impulse! AS-9111 [S] — 1968 — 18.00
- ❏ Impulse! A-9111 [M] — 1966 — 30.00
- ❏ Impulse! AS-9111 [S] — 1966 — 30.00

ALIEN
- ❏ 20th Century T-593 — 1979 — 30.00

ALIENS
- ❏ Varese Sarabande STV-81283 — 1986 — 30.00

ALIKI, MY LOVE
- ❏ Fontana MGF-27523 [M] — 1963 — 30.00
- ❏ Fontana SRF-67523 [S] — 1963 — 30.00

THE ALLNIGHTER
- ❏ Chameleon CHST9601 — 1987 — 18.00
- ❏ Chameleon CHPD9601 [PD] — 1987 — 30.00
  — *Picture disc*

ALL NIGHT LONG
- ❏ Epic LA16032 [M] — 1962 — 40.00
- ❏ Epic BA17032 [S] — 1962 — 50.00

ALL THAT JAZZ
- ❏ Casablanca NBLP-7198 — 1979 — 12.00

ALL THE LOVING COUPLES
- ❏ GNP Crescendo GNPS-2051 — 1969 — 40.00

ALL THE RIGHT MOVES
- ❏ Casablanca 814449-1 — 1983 — 15.00

ALL THE RIGHT NOISES
- ❏ Buddah BDS-5132 — 1971 — 30.00

ALL THIS AND WORLD WAR II
- ❏ 20th Century 2T-522 [B] — 1976 — 35.00
  — *Box set with booklet and flyer*

ALMOST FAMOUS
- ❏ Dreamworks RTH-2001 — 2001 — 40.00
  — *Album is called "Untitled"; contains five songs by Stillwater not on the CD version; 180-gram vinyl; with poster*

ALMOST SUMMER
- ❏ MCA 3037 — 1978 — 30.00

ALWAYS
- ❏ MCA 8036 — 1990 — 18.00

AMATEUR
- ❏ Matador OLE 098-1 — 1995 — 15.00

AMERICA, AMERICA
- ❏ Warner Bros. W1527 [M] — 1963 — 25.00
- ❏ Warner Bros. WS1527 [S] — 1963 — 30.00

AMERICAN ANTHEM
- ❏ Atlantic 81661 — 1986 — 12.00

AMERICAN FLYERS
- ❏ GRP 2001 — 1985 — 15.00

AMERICAN GIGOLO
- ❏ Polydor PD1-6259 — 1980 — 15.00

AMERICAN HOT WAX
- ❏ A&M SP-6500 — 1978 — 25.00

AN AMERICAN IN PARIS
- ❏ MGM E-93 [10] — 1951 — 40.00

AMERICAN POP
- ❏ MCA 5201 — 1981 — 30.00

AN AMERICAN TAIL
- ❏ MCA 39096 — 1986 — 18.00

AMERICATHON
- ❏ Lorimar JS36174 — 1979 — 15.00

THE AMOROUS ADVENTURES OF MOLL FLANDERS
- ❏ RCA Victor LOC-1113 [M] — 1965 — 40.00
- ❏ RCA Victor LSO-1113 [S] — 1965 — 80.00

ANASTASIA
- ❏ Decca DL8460 [M] — 1956 — 30.00

ANATOMY OF A MURDER
- ❏ Columbia CL1360 [M] — 1959 — 40.00
- ❏ Columbia CS8166 [S] — 1959 — 50.00

AND GOD CREATED WOMAN
- ❏ Decca DL8685 [M] — 1957 — 120.00

THE ANDROMEDA STRAIN
- ❏ Kapp KRS-5513 — 1971 — 40.00
  — *Regular cover*
- ❏ Kapp KRS-5513 — 1971 — 100.00
  — *Hexagonal cover glued onto silver cardboard*

ANGEL, ANGEL, DOWN WE GO
- ❏ Tower ST-5161 — 1970 — 30.00

ANGELS DIE HARD
- ❏ Uni 73091 — 1971 — 30.00

ANGELS FROM HELL
- ❏ Tower ST5128 — 1968 — 60.00

ANNIE
- ❏ CBS Masterworks JS38000 — 1982 — 12.00

THE ANONYMOUS VENETIAN
- ❏ United Artists UAS-5218 — 1971 — 30.00

ANOTHER TIME, ANOTHER PLACE
- ❏ Columbia CL1180 [M] — 1958 — 40.00

ANY WEDNESDAY
- ❏ Warner Bros. W1669 [M] — 1966 — 30.00
- ❏ Warner Bros. WS1669 [S] — 1966 — 40.00

ANY WHICH WAY YOU CAN
- ❏ Warner Bros. HS3499 — 1980 — 12.00

THE APARTMENT
- ❏ United Artists UAL-3105 [M] — 1960 — 30.00
- ❏ United Artists UAS-6105 [S] — 1960 — 40.00

APOCALYPSE NOW
- ❏ Elektra DP-90001 — 1979 — 30.00

THE APPLE
- ❏ Cannon 1001 — 1980 — 70.00

APRIL LOVE
- ❏ Dot DLP-9000 [M] — 1957 — 25.00

Number	Title	Yr	NM

ARMED AND DANGEROUS

❑ Manhattan SJ-53041 — 1986 — 12.00
— *Includes Sigue Sigue Sputnik*

ARMS AND THE GIRL

❑ Decca DL5200 [10] — 1950 — 100.00

AROUND THE WORLD IN 80 DAYS

❑ Decca DL9046 [M] — 1957 — 30.00
— *Black label, silver print*

❑ Decca DL79046 [S] — 1959 — 40.00
— *Maroon label, silver print; cover has "Full Stereo" banner*

❑ Decca DL79046 [S] — 196? — 15.00
— *Black label with color bars*

❑ Decca SW-94840 [S] — 1972 — 18.00
— *Capitol Record Club edition*

❑ MCA 2062 [S] — 1973 — 12.00
— *Reissue of 79046; black label with rainbow*

❑ MCA 37086 [S] — 198? — 10.00
— *Reissue of 2062*

AROUND THE WORLD UNDER THE SEA

❑ Monument MLP-8050 [M] — 1966 — 30.00
❑ Monument SLP-18050 [S] — 1966 — 50.00

ARRIVIDERCI, BABY!

❑ RCA Victor LOC-1132 [M] — 1966 — 25.00
❑ RCA Victor LSO-1132 [S] — 1966 — 40.00

ARTHUR

❑ Warner Bros. BSK3582 — 1980 — 12.00

ARTHUR 2: ON THE ROCKS

❑ A&M SP-3916 — 1988 — 12.00

ATHENA

❑ Mercury MG-25202 [10] — 1954 — 150.00

ATHENS, GA. -- INSIDE/OUT

❑ I.R.S. 6185 — 1987 — 12.00
— *Includes R.E.M. (2), Dreams So Real*

AT LONG LAST LOVE

❑ RCA Victor ABL2-0967 — 1975 — 25.00

AVIATOR

❑ Varese Sarabande STV-81240 — 1985 — 25.00

BABES IN TOYLAND

❑ Buena Vista BV-4022 [M] — 1961 — 30.00
❑ Buena Vista STER-4022 [S] — 1961 — 40.00

BABY, THE RAIN MUST FALL

❑ Ava A-53 [M] — 1965 — 40.00
❑ Ava AS-53 [S] — 1965 — 50.00
❑ Mainstream 56056 [M] — 1965 — 30.00
— *Reissue of Ava A-53*

❑ Mainstream S-6056 [S] — 1965 — 40.00
— *Reissue of Ava AS-53*

BABY DOLL

❑ Columbia CL958 [M] — 1956 — 60.00
— *Ads for other Columbia LPs on back cover*

❑ Columbia CL958 [M] — 195? — 50.00
— *No ads for LPs on back cover*

BABY FACE NELSON

❑ Jubilee JLP-2021 [M] — 1957 — 120.00

BACHELOR PARTY

❑ I.R.S. SP-70047 — 1984 — 15.00
— *Includes R.E.M., Oingo Boingo (2), The Fleshtones, The Alarm*

BACK STREET

❑ Decca DL9097 [M] — 1961 — 40.00
❑ Decca DL79097 [S] — 1961 — 80.00

BACK TO SCHOOL

❑ MCA 6175 — 1986 — 15.00

BACK TO THE BEACH

❑ Columbia SC40892 — 1987 — 12.00

BACK TO THE FUTURE

❑ MCA 6144 — 1985 — 12.00
— *Original issue*

❑ MCA 39300 — 198? — 10.00
— *Second edition; includes copies with 6144 labels and this number stamped on the front cover*

BACK TO THE FUTURE PART II

❑ MCA 6361 — 1989 — 18.00

THE BAD SEED

❑ RCA Victor LPM-1395 [M] — 1956 — 300.00

BAND OF ANGELS

❑ RCA Victor LPM-1557 [M] — 1957 — 100.00

BAND OF THE HAND

❑ MCA 6187 — 1986 — 15.00
— *Includes Andy Summers*

THE BAND WAGON

❑ MGM E-3051 [M] — 1953 — 30.00
— *Yellow label*

❑ MGM E-3051 [M] — 1960 — 25.00
— *Black label*

THE BANJOMAN

❑ Sire SA-7527 — 1977 — 25.00

BARABBAS

❑ Colpix CP510 [M] — 1962 — 40.00
❑ Colpix SCP510 [S] — 1962 — 80.00

BARBARELLA

❑ Dyno Voice DV-31908 — 1968 — 50.00

THE BARBARIAN AND THE GEISHA

❑ 20th Fox FOX-3004 [M] — 1958 — 250.00

BAREFOOT ADVENTURE

❑ Pacific Jazz PJ-35 [M] — 1961 — 40.00
❑ Pacific Jazz ST-35 [S] — 1961 — 60.00

BAREFOOT IN THE PARK

❑ Dot DLP-3803 [M] — 1967 — 25.00
❑ Dot DLP-25803 [S] — 1967 — 30.00

THE BARKLEYS OF BROADWAY

❑ MGM E-503 [10] — 1949 — 80.00

BARRY LYNDON

❑ Warner Bros. BS2903 — 1975 — 18.00

BATMAN

❑ Warner Bros. 25977 — 1989 — 25.00
— *Music composed and conducted by Danny Elfman*

BATMAN FOREVER

❑ Atlantic PR6339 [DJ] — 1995 — 30.00
— *Promo only; generic white cover with sticker*

BATTLE OF THE BULGE

❑ Warner Bros. W1617 [M] — 1965 — 40.00
❑ Warner Bros. WS1617 [S] — 1965 — 40.00

BEACH BLANKET BINGO

❑ Capitol T2323 [M] — 1965 — 30.00
❑ Capitol ST2323 [S] — 1965 — 60.00

BEAT STREET

❑ Atlantic 80154 — 1984 — 18.00
❑ Atlantic 80158 — 1984 — 30.00
— *Album called "Beat Street, Volume 2"*

BEAU JAMES

❑ Imperial LP-9041 [M] — 1957 — 40.00

BECKET

❑ Decca DL9117 [M] — 1964 — 30.00
❑ Decca DL79117 [S] — 1964 — 50.00

BEDAZZLED

❑ London MS-82009 — 1967 — 80.00

BEETLEJUICE

❑ Geffen R174166 — 1988 — 18.00
— *BMG Direct Marketing edition*

❑ Geffen GHS24202 — 1988 — 15.00
— *Music composed and conducted by Danny Elfman*

BEHOLD A PALE HORSE

❑ Colpix CP519 [M] — 1964 — 50.00
❑ Colpix SCP519 [S] — 1964 — 70.00

THE BELIEVERS

❑ Varese Sarabande STV-81328 — 1987 — 25.00

BELL, BOOK AND CANDLE

❑ Colpix CP502 [M] — 1959 — 60.00

BELLS ARE RINGING

❑ Capitol W1435 [M] — 1960 — 30.00
❑ Capitol SW1435 [S] — 1960 — 30.00

BELLY

❑ Def Jam 314-558925-1 — 1998 — 18.00

BENEATH THE PLANET OF THE APES

❑ Amos AAS-8001 — 1970 — 40.00

BEN-HUR

❑ MGM 1E1 [M] — 1959 — 40.00
— *Boxed edition with hardcover book*

❑ MGM S-1E1 [S] — 1959 — 50.00
— *Boxed edition with hardcover book*

❑ MGM 1E1 [M] — 196? — 15.00
— *Gatefold cover, no book*

❑ MGM S-1E1 [S] — 196? — 18.00
— *Gatefold cover, no book; black label*

❑ MGM S-1E1 [S] — 196? — 12.00
— *Gatefold cover, no book; blue and gold label*

THE BEST LITTLE WHOREHOUSE IN TEXAS

❑ MCA 6112 — 1982 — 12.00
❑ MCA 1499 — 198? — 10.00
— *Reissue of 6112*

BEST OF THE BEST

❑ Relativity 88561 0341 — 1989 — 25.00

BETRAYED

❑ Varese Sarabande 704.700 — 1988 — 30.00

BEVERLY HILLS COP

❑ MCA 5553 — 1984 — 12.00
— *Includes Danny Elfman*

BEVERLY HILLS COP II

❑ MCA R123346 — 1987 — 12.00
— *Includes George Michael ("I Want Your Sex")*

❑ MCA 6207 — 1987 — 10.00
— *Includes George Michael*

BEYOND THE GREAT WALL

❑ Capitol T10401 [M] — 1965 — 50.00

BEYOND THE VALLEY OF THE DOLLS

❑ 20th Century Fox TFS-4211 — 1970 — 200.00

THE BIBLE

❑ 20th Century Fox TF-3184 [M] — 1966 — 25.00
❑ 20th Century Fox TFS-4184 [S] — 1966 — 30.00

THE BIG CHILL

❑ Motown 6062ML — 1983 — 12.00
❑ Motown 6094ML — 1983 — 12.00
— *Subtitled "More Songs from the Original Soundtrack"*

THE BIG COUNTRY

❑ United Artists UAL-4004 [M] — 1958 — 30.00
❑ United Artists UAS-5004 [S] — 1958 — 50.00

THE BIG EASY

❑ Antilles AN-7087 — 1987 — 12.00

THE BIGGEST BUNDLE OF THEM ALL

❑ MGM E-4446 [M] — 1967 — 25.00
❑ MGM SE-4446 [S] — 1967 — 30.00

THE BIG GUNDOWN

❑ United Artists UAS-5190 — 1967 — 40.00

BILL & TED'S EXCELLENT ADVENTURE

❑ A&M SP-3915 — 1989 — 18.00

BILLIE

❑ United Artists UAL-4131 [M] — 1965 — 25.00
❑ United Artists UAS-5131 [S] — 1965 — 30.00

THE BILLION DOLLAR BRAIN

❑ United Artists UAL-4174 [M] — 1967 — 18.00
❑ United Artists UAS-5174 [S] — 1967 — 25.00

BILLY JACK

❑ Warner Bros. WS1926 — 1971 — 30.00
— *Original; green "WB" label*

❑ Warner Bros. BJS-1001 — 1973 — 18.00
— *Reissue; "Burbank" palm trees label*

BIRD

❑ Columbia SC44299 — 1988 — 18.00

THE BIRD WITH THE CRYSTAL PLUMAGE

❑ Capitol ST-642 — 1970 — 100.00

BLACK AND WHITE IN COLOR

❑ Buddah BDS-5698 — 1977 — 40.00

BLACKBIRDS OF 1928

❑ Columbia Masterworks OL6770 [M] — 1968 — 18.00
❑ Revue 1 [M] — 196? — 30.00
❑ Sutton SU-270 [M] — 196? — 25.00
❑ Sutton SSU-270 [R] — 196? — 15.00

BLACK GIRL

❑ Fantasy F-9420 — 1973 — 70.00

THE BLACK HOLE

❑ Buena Vista STER-5008 — 1979 — 50.00

THE BLACK ORCHID

❑ Dot DLP-3178 [M] — 1959 — 40.00
❑ Dot SLP-25178 [S] — 1959 — 50.00

BLACK ORPHEUS

❑ Epic LN3672 [M] — 1959 — 40.00
❑ Fontana MGF-27520 [M] — 1963 — 25.00
❑ Fontana SRF-67520 [R] — 1963 — 18.00

BLACK RAIN

❑ Virgin 91292 — 1989 — 12.00
— *Includes UB40, Iggy Pop*

BLACULA

❑ RCA Victor LSP-4806 — 1972 — 60.00

BLADE RUNNER

❑ Full Moon/Warner Bros. 23748 — 1982 — 25.00

BLESS THE BEASTS AND CHILDREN

❑ A&M SP-4322 — 1971 — 30.00

BLOOD AND SAND

❑ Decca DL5380 [10] — 1952 — 80.00

BLOOMER GIRL

❑ Decca DL8015 [M] — 1950 — 30.00

BLOW-UP

❑ MGM E-4447 [M] — 1967 — 40.00
❑ MGM SE-4447 [S] — 1967 — 50.00

THE BLUE MAX

❑ Mainstream 56081 [M] — 1966 — 40.00
❑ Mainstream S-6081 [S] — 1966 — 80.00

Number	Title	Yr	NM

BLUE VELVET
- ❏ Varese Sarabande STV-81292 — 1986 — 30.00

BOBO
- ❏ Warner Bros. W1711 [M] — 1967 — 25.00
- ❏ Warner Bros. WS1711 [S] — 1967 — 25.00

THE BODYGUARD
- ❏ Arista 18699 — 1992 — 15.00

BODY HEAT
- ❏ Label X LXSE-1-002 — 1983 — 120.00

BOEING, BOEING
- ❏ RCA Victor LOC-1121 [M] — 1965 — 30.00
- ❏ RCA Victor LSO-1121 [S] — 1965 — 30.00

BONNIE AND CLYDE
- ❏ Warner Bros. W1742 [M] — 1968 — 40.00
- ❏ Warner Bros. WS1742 [S] — 1968 — 30.00
- —*Originals have green labels with "W7" logo in a square at top*
- ❏ Warner Bros. ST-91414 [S] — 1968 — 30.00
- —*Capitol Record Club issue*

BORA, BORA
- ❏ American Int'l. STA-1029 — 1970 — 30.00

BORDER RADIO
- ❏ Enigma ST-73221 — 1987 — 15.00
- —*Includes John Doe*

BORN FREE
- ❏ MGM E-4368 [M] — 1966 — 18.00
- ❏ MGM SE-4368 [S] — 1966 — 25.00

BORN ON THE FOURTH OF JULY
- ❏ MCA 6340 — 1989 — 15.00
- —*Includes Edie Brickell and New Bohemians*

BORSALINO
- ❏ Paramount PAS-5019 — 1970 — 30.00

THE BOY FRIEND
- ❏ MGM 1SE-32 — 1971 — 25.00

A BOY NAMED CHARLIE BROWN
- ❏ Columbia Masterworks OS3500 — 1970 — 25.00

BOY ON A DOLPHIN
- ❏ Decca DL8580 [M] — 1957 — 60.00
- —*Black label with silver print, or pink label with black print (promo)*
- ❏ Decca DL8580 [M] — 196? — 25.00
- —*Black label with color bars*

THE BOYS FROM SYRACUSE
- ❏ Capitol TAO1933 [M] — 1963 — 30.00
- ❏ Capitol STAO1933 [S] — 1963 — 30.00

THE BOY WHO COULD FLY
- ❏ Varese Sarabande STV-81299 — 1986 — 25.00

BOYZ 'N THE HOOD
- ❏ Warner Bros. PRO-A-4996 [DJ] — 1991 — 25.00
- —*Promo-only vinyl release*

THE BRAVE ONE
- ❏ Decca DL8344 [M] — 1956 — 40.00

BREAKIN'
- ❏ Polydor 821919-1 — 1984 — 12.00
- —*Includes Re-Flex*

BRIGHT LIGHTS, BIG CITY
- ❏ Warner Bros. R100483 — 1988 — 15.00
- —*Includes M/A/R/R/S, Depeche Mode, New Order, Prince; BMG Direct Marketing edition*
- ❏ Warner Bros. 25688 — 1988 — 12.00
- —*Includes M/A/R/R/S, Depeche Mode, New Order, Prince*

BRIMSTONE & TREACLE
- ❏ A&M SP-4915 — 1982 — 12.00
- —*Includes Sting, The Police, Go-Go's, Squeeze*

BRONCO BILLY
- ❏ Elektra 5E-512 — 1980 — 12.00

BROTHER ON THE RUN
- ❏ Perception PLP-45 — 1973 — 40.00

THE BROTHERS
- ❏ Warner Bros. 48058-1 — 2001 — 25.00

BUCCANEER
- ❏ Columbia CL1278 [M] — 1958 — 30.00
- ❏ Columbia CS8096 [S] — 1958 — 40.00

BULL DURHAM
- ❏ Capitol C1-90586 — 1988 — 12.00
- —*Includes Los Lobos, The Blasters, House of Schock*

BULLITT
- ❏ Warner Bros. WS1777 — 1968 — 60.00

BUNDLE OF JOY
- ❏ RCA Victor LPM-1399 [M] — 1956 — 40.00

BUNNY LAKE IS MISSING
- ❏ RCA Victor LOC-1115 [M] — 1965 — 40.00
- ❏ RCA Victor LSO-1115 [S] — 1965 — 70.00

BUNNY O'HARE
- ❏ American Int'l. STA-1041 — 1971 — 25.00

BUONA SERA, MRS. CAMPBELL
- ❏ United Artists UAS-5192 — 1969 — 30.00

BURGLAR
- ❏ MCA 6201 — 1987 — 12.00
- —*Includes Belinda Carlisle, The Belle Stars, The Smithereens*

THE BURGLARS
- ❏ Bell 1105 — 1971 — 40.00

BUSTER
- ❏ Atlantic 81905 — 1988 — 12.00
- —*Includes The Searchers ("Sweets for My Sweet")*

BUTTERFIELD-8
- ❏ MGM E-3952 [M] — 1960 — 25.00
- ❏ MGM SE-3952 [S] — 1960 — 30.00

BYE BYE BIRDIE
- ❏ RCA Victor LOC-1081 [M] — 1963 — 30.00
- —*First cover without Ann-Margret on the front*
- ❏ RCA Victor LOC-1081 [M] — 196? — 25.00
- —*Second cover with Ann-Margret on front, but with no credits underneath*
- ❏ RCA Victor LOC-1081 [M] — 196? — 18.00
- —*Third cover with Ann-Margret on front and with credits underneath*
- ❏ RCA Victor LSO-1081 [S] — 1963 — 30.00
- —*First cover without Ann-Margret on the front*
- ❏ RCA Victor LSO-1081 [S] — 196? — 30.00
- —*Second cover with Ann-Margret on front, but with no credits underneath*
- ❏ RCA Victor LSO-1081 [S] — 196? — 25.00
- —*Third cover with Ann-Margret on front and with credits underneath*
- ❏ RCA Victor AYL1-3947 [S] — 1980 — 10.00
- —*Best Buy Series" reissue*

CABARET
- ❏ ABC ABCD-752 — 1972 — 25.00
- ❏ MCA 37125 — 198? — 10.00
- —*Reissue; blue label with rainbow*

THE CAINE MUTINY
- ❏ RCA Victor LOC-1013 [M] — 1954 — 10000.00
- —*VG value 4000; VG+ value 7000*
- ❏ RCA Victor LOC-1013 [M] — 1993 — 200.00
- —*Very limited edition (100 copies) reproduction of the original LP*

CALIFORNIA SUITE
- ❏ Columbia JC35727 — 1978 — 12.00
- —*Full name: "Neil Simon's California Suite"*

CALL ME MADAM
- ❏ Decca DL5465 [10] — 1953 — 50.00

CALL ME MISTER
- ❏ Decca DLP7005 [10] — 1950 — 100.00

CAMELOT
- ❏ Warner Bros. B1712 [M] — 1967 — 30.00
- ❏ Warner Bros. BS1712 [S] — 1967 — 25.00
- —*Gold label original*
- ❏ Warner Bros. SW-91347 — 1968 — 30.00
- —*Capitol Record Club edition*
- ❏ Warner Bros. BS1712 [S] — 1968 — 18.00
- —*Green label, "W7" box logo at top*
- ❏ Warner Bros. BS1712 [S] — 1970 — 15.00
- —*Green label, "WB" shield logo at top*
- ❏ Warner Bros. BS1712 [S] — 1973 — 12.00
- —*Burbank" palm trees label*
- ❏ Warner Bros. BSK3102 [S] — 1977 — 10.00
- —*Reissue with new number*

CAN-CAN
- ❏ Capitol W1301 [M] — 1960 — 25.00
- ❏ Capitol SW1301 [S] — 1960 — 30.00

CANDY
- ❏ ABC ABCS-OC-9 — 1968 — 30.00

CAPTIVE
- ❏ Virgin 90609 — 1987 — 18.00
- —*Music by The Edge and Larry Mullen of U2*

THE CARDINAL
- ❏ RCA Victor LOC-1084 [M] — 1963 — 40.00
- ❏ RCA Victor LSO-1084 [S] — 1963 — 60.00

THE CARE BEARS MOVIE
- ❏ Kid Stuff 3901 — 1985 — 25.00

THE CARETAKERS
- ❏ Ava A-31 [M] — 1963 — 25.00
- ❏ Ava AS-31 [M] — 1963 — 30.00

CAROUSEL
- ❏ Capitol W694 [M] — 1956 — 30.00
- —*Gray label*
- ❏ Capitol W694 [M] — 1959 — 25.00
- —*Black colorband label, logo at left*
- ❏ Capitol W694 [M] — 1962 — 18.00
- —*Black colorband label, logo at top*
- ❏ Capitol SW694 [S] — 1962 — 25.00
- —*Black colorband label*
- ❏ Capitol SW694 [S] — 1969 — 18.00
- —*Lime green label*
- ❏ Capitol SW694 [S] — 1973 — 15.00
- —*Orange label*

THE CARPETBAGGERS
- ❏ Ava A-45 [M] — 1964 — 30.00
- ❏ Ava AS-45 [S] — 1964 — 40.00

CARRY IT ON
- ❏ Vanguard VSD-79313 — 1971 — 30.00

CASINO ROYALE
- ❏ Colgems COMO-5005 [M] — 1967 — 30.00
- ❏ Colgems COSO-5005 [S] — 1967 — 100.00
- ❏ Colgems COSO-5005 [S] — 1999 — 30.00
- —*Classic Records reissue on audiophile vinyl*
- ❏ Colgems COSO-5005-45 — 199? — 40.00
- —*Classic Records reissue on four 12-inch 45 rpm records*

THE CATHERINE WHEEL
- ❏ Sire SRK3645 — 1981 — 15.00
- —*Includes David Byrne, who also composed all the music*

CAT PEOPLE
- ❏ Backstreet BSR6107 — 1982 — 25.00

A CERTAIN SMILE
- ❏ Columbia CL1194 [M] — 1958 — 40.00
- ❏ Columbia CS8068 [S] — 1958 — 80.00

THE CHAIRMAN
- ❏ Tetragrammaton T-5007 — 1969 — 30.00

CHARLOTTE'S WEB
- ❏ Paramount PAS-1008 — 1973 — 30.00

THE CHASE
- ❏ Columbia Masterworks OL6560 [M] — 1966 — 40.00
- ❏ Columbia Masterworks OS2960 [S] — 1966 — 60.00

CHINATOWN
- ❏ ABC ABDP-848 — 1974 — 40.00

CHITTY CHITTY BANG BANG
- ❏ United Artists UAS-5188 — 1968 — 30.00

CHRISTIANE F.
- ❏ RCA ABL1-4239 — 1981 — 18.00
- —*Includes David Bowie ("Helgen (Heroes)")*

THE CHRISTMAS THAT ALMOST WASN'T
- ❏ RCA Camden CAL-1086 [M] — 1966 — 30.00
- ❏ RCA Camden CAS-1086 [S] — 1966 — 40.00

CINDERELLA
- ❏ Disneyland WDL-4007 [M] — 1957 — 200.00
- —*Original issue, gatefold cover*
- ❏ Disneyland DQ-1207 [M] — 1959 — 40.00
- —*Second issue, white back cover with ads for nine other LPs*
- ❏ Disneyland DQ-1207 [M] — 1963 — 30.00
- —*Third issue, pink back cover*
- ❏ Disneyland DQ-1207 [M] — 1987 — 30.00
- —*Fifth issue, high gloss cover with prince putting slipper on Cinderella's foot*
- ❏ Disneyland 3107 [PD] — 1981 — 30.00
- —*Fourth issue, picture disc*

CINDERFELLA
- ❏ Dot DLP-8001 [M] — 1960 — 60.00
- ❏ Dot SLP-38001 [S] — 1960 — 100.00
- —*Gatefold cover with many extras including game board, spinner, booklet, music stand.*

CITY HEAT
- ❏ Warner Bros. 25219 — 1984 — 15.00
- —*Incidental music by Lennie Niehaus*

CLEOPATRA
- ❏ 20th Century Fox FXG-5008 [M] — 1963 — 30.00
- ❏ 20th Century Fox SXG-5008 [S] — 1963 — 40.00

CLEOPATRA JONES
- ❏ Warner Bros. BS2719 — 1973 — 30.00

CLOCKERS
- ❏ MCA 11304 — 1995 — 12.00
- —*Includes Seal*

CLOSE ENCOUNTERS OF THE THIRD KIND
- ❏ Arista AL9500 — 1977 — 30.00
- —*Includes one 12-inch record and one 7-inch record. Deduct 50 percent if the 7-inch record is missing.*

Number	Title	Yr	NM

COAL MINER'S DAUGHTER
- ❏ MCA 5107 — 1980 — 18.00

COFFY
- ❏ Polydor PD-5048 — 1973 — 100.00

THE COLLECTOR
- ❏ Mainstream 56053 [M] — 1965 — 30.00
- ❏ Mainstream S-6053 [S] — 1965 — 50.00

COLLEGE CONFIDENTIAL
- ❏ Chancellor CHL-5016 [M] — 1960 — 40.00
- ❏ Chancellor CHLS-5016 [S] — 1960 — 50.00

THE COLOR PURPLE
- ❏ Qwest 25336 — 1985 — 25.00
- —Regular gatefold edition; records are still on purple vinyl
- ❏ Qwest 25289 — 1985 — 30.00
- —Box set "limited edition" on purple vinyl with booklet

COLORS
- ❏ Sire R154136 — 1988 — 15.00
- —Includes Ice-T ("Colors")
- ❏ Warner Bros. 25713 — 1988 — 12.00
- —Includes Ice-T, Salt-N-Pepa

COMANCHE
- ❏ Coral CRL57046 [M] — 1956 — 400.00

COME BACK CHARLESTON BLUE
- ❏ Atco SD7010 — 1972 — 30.00

COME BLOW YOUR HORN
- ❏ Reprise R-6071 [M] — 1963 — 30.00
- ❏ Reprise R9-6071 [S] — 1963 — 50.00

COMETOGETHER
- ❏ Apple SW-3377 — 1971 — 25.00

THE CONNECTION
- ❏ Charlie Parker PLP-806 [M] — 1962 — 30.00
- ❏ Charlie Parker PLP-806S [S] — 1962 — 40.00
- ❏ Felsted 7512 [M] — 1960 — 200.00
- ❏ Felsted 2512 [S] — 1960 — 300.00

CONVOY
- ❏ United Artists UA-LA910-H — 1978 — 15.00

COOLEY HIGH
- ❏ Motown M7-840R2 — 1975 — 25.00

THE CORRUPT ONES
- ❏ United Artists UAL-4158 [M] — 1967 — 40.00
- ❏ United Artists UAS-5158 [S] — 1967 — 40.00

COTTON COMES TO HARLEM
- ❏ United Artists UAS-5211 — 1970 — 30.00

COURIER
- ❏ Virgin 90954 — 1989 — 15.00
- —Includes U2, Elvis Costello (as Declan MacManus), Hothouse Flowers

THE COURT JESTER
- ❏ Decca DL8212 [M] — 1956 — 70.00
- —Black label, silver print, or pink label, black print promo copy
- ❏ Decca DL8212 [M] — 190? — 30.00
- —Black label with color bars

THE COWBOY
- ❏ Decca DL8684 [M] — 1958 — 60.00
- —Black label, silver print, or pink label, black print promo copy
- ❏ Decca DL8684 [M] — 196? — 25.00
- —Black label with color bars

CRADLE 2 THE GRAVE
- ❏ Def Jam 44063615-1 — 2002 — 25.00

CRIME IN THE STREETS
- ❏ Decca DL8376 [M] — 1956 — 60.00
- —Black label, silver print, or pink label, black print promo copy
- ❏ Decca DL8376 [S] — 196? — 30.00
- —Black label with color bars

THE CROSS AND THE SWITCHBLADE
- ❏ Light LS-5550 — 1970 — 30.00

CRUISING
- ❏ Columbia JS36410 — 1980 — 40.00

CUSTER OF THE WEST
- ❏ ABC ABC-OC-5 [M] — 1968 — 80.00
- ❏ ABC ABCS-OC-5 [S] — 1968 — 100.00

CYCLE SAVAGES
- ❏ American Int'l. STA-1033 — 1970 — 30.00

CYRANO DE BERGERAC
- ❏ Capitol S283 [M] — 1951 — 30.00
- —Originals have red labels with Capitol logo at top

DAKTARI
- ❏ Leo the Lion CH-1043 [M] — 1967 — 25.00
- ❏ MGM CH-1043 [M] — 1967 — 25.00

THE DAMNED
- ❏ Warner Bros. WS1829 — 1969 — 30.00

DAMN THE DEFIANT!
- ❏ Colpix CP511 [M] — 1962 — 30.00
- ❏ Colpix SCP511 [S] — 1962 — 60.00

DAMN YANKEES
- ❏ RCA Victor LOC-1047 [M] — 1958 — 40.00
- —Original pressing with "Long Play" on label

DANCE CRAZE
- ❏ Chrysalis CHR1299 — 1981 — 25.00
- —Includes The Specials, The Selecter, Bad Manners, Madness, The English Beat, The Bodysnatchers; a great introduction to 2-Tone ska

DANGEROUSLY CLOSE
- ❏ Enigma SJ-73204 — 1986 — 12.00
- —Includes The Smithereens, Lords of the New Church

DARKMAN
- ❏ MCA 10094 — 1990 — 15.00
- —Composed and conducted by Danny Elfman

THE DARK OF THE SUN
- ❏ MGM SE-4544 — 1968 — 40.00

DARLING LILI
- ❏ RCA Victor LSPX-1000 — 1969 — 25.00

DAWN OF THE DEAD
- ❏ Varese Sarabande VC-81106 — 1979 — 30.00

DAYDREAMER
- ❏ Columbia Masterworks OL6540 [M] — 1966 — 30.00
- ❏ Columbia Masterworks OS2940 [S] — 1966 — 40.00

DAY OF ANGER
- ❏ RCA Victor LSO-1165 — 1969 — 25.00

THE DAY OF THE DOLPHIN
- ❏ Avco AV-11014 — 1973 — 30.00

DAYS OF HEAVEN
- ❏ Pacific Arts PAC8-128 — 1978 — 40.00

DAYS OF THUNDER
- ❏ DGC 24294 — 1990 — 25.00

THE DAY THE FISH CAME OUT
- ❏ 20th Century Fox TF-3194 [M] — 1967 — 30.00
- ❏ 20th Century Fox TFS-4194 [S] — 1967 — 40.00

DEADFALL
- ❏ 20th Century Fox S-4203 — 1968 — 60.00

THE DEADLY AFFAIR
- ❏ Verve V-8679 [M] — 1966 — 30.00
- ❏ Verve V6-8679 [S] — 1966 — 30.00

DEAD MAN WALKING
- ❏ Columbia C367989 — 1997 — 200.00

DEAR JOHN
- ❏ Dunhill OCD-55001 [M] — 1966 — 25.00
- ❏ Dunhill OCDS-55001 [S] — 1966 — 60.00

THE DECLINE OF WESTERN CIVILIZATION
- ❏ Slash 105 — 1981 — 25.00

THE DEEP
- ❏ Casablanca NBLP-7060 — 1977 — 10.00
  Blue vinyl

DEEP IN MY HEART
- ❏ MGM E-3153 [M] — 1955 — 40.00
- ❏ MGM E-3153 [M] — 1955 — 50.00

DE SADE
- ❏ Tower ST-5170 — 1969 — 30.00

DESIRE UNDER THE ELMS
- ❏ Dot DLP-3095 [M] — 1958 — 100.00

DESTINATION MOON
- ❏ Columbia CL6151 [10] — 1950 — 120.00
- ❏ Omega OL-3 [M] — 1959 — 40.00
- ❏ Omega OSL-3 [S] — 196? — 80.00

THE DEVIL AT 4 O'CLOCK
- ❏ Colpix CP509 [M] — 1962 — 40.00
- ❏ Colpix SCP509 [S] — 1962 — 70.00

THE DEVIL IN MISS JONES
- ❏ Janus JLS-3059 — 1973 — 30.00

DIAMONDS ARE FOREVER
- ❏ United Artists UAS-5520 — 1971 — 25.00
- ❏ United Artists UA-LA301-G — 1974 — 15.00
- —Reissue of 5520

THE DIARY OF ANNE FRANK
- ❏ 20th Fox FOX-3012 [M] — 1959 — 50.00
- ❏ 20th Fox SFX-3012 [S] — 1959 — 80.00

DIRTY DANCING
- ❏ RCA 6408-1-R — 1987 — 12.00
- ❏ RCA 6965-1-R — 1988 — 18.00
- —Album's title is "More Dirty Dancing"; original editions of the LP have instrumental selections entitled "Baby's Walk" and "The Lifts in the Lake Theme (Finale)"
- ❏ RCA 6965-1-R-A — 1988 — 12.00

—Album's title is "More Dirty Dancing"; revised editions of the LP have the two instrumental selections, but they are retitled "(I've Had) The Time of My Life (Instrumental Version)"

DIRTY GAME
- ❏ Laurie LLP-2034 [M] — 1966 — 30.00
- ❏ Laurie SLP-2034 [S] — 1966 — 30.00

DIVORCE AMERICAN STYLE
- ❏ United Artists UAL-4163 [M] — 1967 — 25.00
- ❏ United Artists UAS-5163 [S] — 1967 — 25.00

DIVORCE ITALIAN STYLE
- ❏ United Artists UAL-4106 [M] — 1962 — 40.00
- ❏ United Artists UAS-5106 [S] — 1962 — 50.00

D.O.A.
- ❏ Varese Sarabande 704.610 — 1988 — 40.00

DOCTOR DOLITTLE
- ❏ 20th Century Fox TCF-5101 [M] — 1967 — 25.00
- ❏ 20th Century Fox TCS-5101 [S] — 1967 — 25.00

DOCTOR GOLDFOOT AND THE GIRL BOMBS
- ❏ Tower T5053 [M] — 1966 — 25.00
- ❏ Tower DT5053 [R] — 1966 — 30.00

DOCTOR ZHIVAGO
- ❏ MCA 39042 — 198? — 10.00
- —Reissue
- ❏ MGM 1E-6 [M] — 1965 — 18.00
- ❏ MGM S1E-6ST [S] — 1965 — 25.00
- ❏ MGM SWAE-90620 [S] — 1965 — 25.00
- —Capitol Record Club issue

A DOG OF FLANDERS
- ❏ 20th Fox FOX-3026 [M] — 1959 — 80.00
- ❏ 20th Fox SFX-3026 [S] — 1959 — 300.00

DOGS IN SPACE
- ❏ Atlantic 81789 — 1987 — 15.00
- —Includes Iggy Pop, Michael Hutchense (of INXS), Brian Eno, etc.

$ (DOLLARS)
- ❏ Reprise MS2051 — 1971 — 25.00

DON'T MAKE WAVES
- ❏ MGM E-4483 [M] — 1967 — 30.00
- ❏ MGM SE-4483 [S] — 1967 — 30.00

THE DOORS
- ❏ Elektra E1-61047 — 1991 — 100.00
- —Only vinyl edition in US released through Columbia House

DO THE RIGHT THING
- ❏ Motown 6272 — 1989 — 12.00
- —Includes Public Enemy

DOWN AND OUT IN BEVERLY HILLS
- ❏ MCA 6160 — 1986 — 12.00
- —Includes Andy Summers (6)

DRAGNET
- ❏ MCA 6210 — 1987 — 12.00
- —Includes Art of Noise

DRANGO
- ❏ Liberty LRP-3036 [M] — 1957 — 150.00

A DREAM OF KINGS
- ❏ National General NG-1000 — 1969 — 30.00

DR. NO
- ❏ Liberty LT-50275 — 1981 — 10.00
- —Reissue of United Artists 275
- ❏ United Artists UAL-4108 [M] — 1963 — 40.00
- ❏ United Artists UAS-5108 [S] — 1963 — 50.00
- ❏ United Artists UA-LA275-G — 1974 — 12.00
- —Reissue of 5108

DR. PHIBES
- ❏ American Int'l. A-1040 — 1971 — 60.00

DUCK, YOU SUCKER
- ❏ United Artists UAS-5221 — 1972 — 40.00

DUDES
- ❏ MCA 6212 — 1987 — 12.00
- —Includes Jane's Addiction

DUEL AT DIABLO
- ❏ United Artists UAL-4139 [M] — 1966 — 30.00
- ❏ United Artists UAS-5139 [S] — 1966 — 30.00

DUMBO
- ❏ Disneyland WDL-4013 [M] — 1957 — 200.00
- —Original issue, gatefold cover
- ❏ Disneyland DQ-1204 [M] — 1959 — 30.00
- —Second issue, back cover has ads for nine other LPs
- ❏ Disneyland DQ-1204 [M] — 1963 — 18.00
- —Third issue, four black & white photos on back cover
- ❏ Disneyland 1204 [M] — 197? — 12.00
- —Fourth issue, yellow rainbow label, flying Dumbo on back cover
- ❏ Disneyland ST-4904 [M] — 1963 — 200.00
- —Special issue with pop-up figures in gatefold

Number	Title	Yr	NM

DUNE
- ❑ Polydor 823770-1 | 1984 | 30.00

THE DUNWICH HORROR
- ❑ American Int'l. STA-1028 | 1970 | 40.00

EARTH GIRLS ARE EASY
- ❑ Sire 25835 | 1989 | 12.00
- *—Includes The B-52's, Depeche Mode, The Jesus and Mary Chain, Julie Brown (2), Stewart Copeland*

EASTER PARADE
- ❑ MGM E-502 [10] | 1950 | 80.00

EAST SIDE, WEST SIDE
- ❑ Columbia CL2123 [M] | 1963 | 30.00
- ❑ Columbia CS8923 [S] | 1963 | 40.00

EASY MONEY
- ❑ Columbia JS38968 | 1983 | 12.00
- *—Includes Nick Lowe*

EASY RIDER
- ❑ ABC Dunhill DSX-50063 | 1969 | 30.00

EATING RAOUL
- ❑ Varese Sarabande STV81164 | 1982 | 15.00
- *—Includes Los Lobos*

ECCO
- ❑ Warner Bros. W1600 [M] | 1965 | 30.00
- ❑ Warner Bros. WS1600 [S] | 1965 | 30.00

THE EDDY DUCHIN STORY
- ❑ Decca DL8289 [M] | 1956 | 40.00
- *—Original cover with Tyrone Power and Kim Novak at a piano*
- ❑ Decca DL8289 [M] | 1959 | 25.00
- *—Reissue cover with Tyrone Power and Kim Novak kissing*
- ❑ Decca DL78289 [S] | 1959 | 25.00
- *—Maroon label, silver print, "Full Stereo" on front cover*
- ❑ Decca DL9121 [M] | 196? | 15.00
- *—Reissue of 8289*
- ❑ Decca DL79121 [S] | 196? | 18.00
- *—Reissue of 78289*
- ❑ MCA 2041 | 1973 | 12.00
- *—Reissue of 79121; black label with rainbow*
- ❑ MCA 37088 | 198? | 10.00
- *—Reissue of 2041*

THE EDUCATION OF SONNY CARSON
- ❑ Paramount PAS-1045 | 1974 | 25.00

THE EGYPTIAN
- ❑ Decca DL9014 [M] | 1954 | 60.00
- ❑ Decca DL79014 [R] | 196? | 25.00

EIGHT MEN OUT
- ❑ Varese Sarabande 704.600 | 1988 | 30.00

8 MILE, MORE MUSIC FROM
- ❑ Shady/Interscope 004450979-1 | 2002 | 30.00
- *—U.S. edition comes in generic black sleeve with center hole and sticker across top of cover*

84 CHARING CROSS ROAD
- ❑ Varese Sarabande STV81306 | 1987 | 15.00

EL CID
- ❑ MGM E-3977 [M] | 1962 | 40.00
- ❑ MGM SE-3977 [S] | 1962 | 50.00

EL DORADO
- ❑ Epic FLM-13114 [M] | 1967 | 50.00
- ❑ Epic LFS-15114 [S] | 1967 | 70.00

ELECTRA GLIDE IN BLUE
- ❑ United Artists UA-LA062-H | 1973 | 40.00
- *—With booklet and two posters*

ELEPHANT STEPS
- ❑ Columbia Masterwords M2X33044 | 1975 | 25.00

ELMER GANTRY
- ❑ United Artists UAL-4069 [M] | 1960 | 40.00
- ❑ United Artists UAS-5069 [S] | 1960 | 50.00

EL TOPO
- ❑ Apple SWAO-3388 | 1972 | 40.00

THE EMPIRE STRIKES BACK
- ❑ RSO RS-2-4201 | 1980 | 25.00
- *—With booklet*

ENTER THE DRAGON
- ❑ Warner Bros. BS2727 | 1973 | 60.00

E.T. THE EXTRA-TERRESTRIAL
- ❑ MCA 6109 | 1982 | 12.00
- ❑ MCA 6113 [PD] | 1982 | 30.00
- *—Picture disc in plastic envelope*
- ❑ MCA 16014 | 1982 | 40.00
- *—Audiophile edition*
- ❑ MCA 70000 | 1982 | 80.00
- *—Boxed version with booklet; story narrated by Michael Jackson*

EVERYTHING I HAVE IS YOURS
- ❑ MGM E-187 [10] | 1953 | 40.00

EVERY WHICH WAY BUT LOOSE
- ❑ Elektra 5E-503 | 1978 | 15.00

EVIL DEAD
- ❑ Varese Sarabande STV-81199 | 1984 | 25.00

EXODUS
- ❑ RCA Victor LOC-1058 [M] | 1960 | 25.00
- *—"Long Play" on label*
- ❑ RCA Victor LSO-1058 [S] | 1960 | 30.00
- *—"Living Stereo" on label*

THE EXORCIST
- ❑ Warner Bros. W2774 | 1974 | 30.00

A FACE IN THE CROWD
- ❑ Capitol W872 [M] | 1957 | 50.00

THE FALCON AND THE SNOWMAN
- ❑ EMI America SV-17150 | 1985 | 12.00
- *—Includes David Bowie ("This Is Not America")*

THE FALL OF THE ROMAN EMPIRE
- ❑ Columbia Masterworks OL6060 [M] | 1964 | 40.00
- ❑ Columbia Masterworks OS2460 [S] | 1964 | 60.00

THE FAMILY WAY
- ❑ London M76007 [M] | 1967 | 100.00
- *—No promo sticker on front cover (deduct 20 percent for promo)*
- ❑ London ST82007 [S] | 1967 | 120.00
- *—No promo sticker on front cover (deduct 20 percent for promo)*

FANNY
- ❑ Warner Bros. W1416 [M] | 1961 | 30.00
- ❑ Warner Bros. WS1416 [S] | 1961 | 30.00

FANTASIA
- ❑ Buena Vista WDX-101 [M] | 1961 | 30.00
- *—Second issue, blue labels, includes 24-page booklet*
- ❑ Buena Vista STER-101 [S] | 1961 | 40.00
- *—First stereo issue, black and yellow rainbow labels, includes 24-page booklet*
- ❑ Buena Vista 101 [S] | 1982 | 25.00
- *—Stereo reissue, two records, no booklet*
- ❑ Buena Vista V-104 | 1982 | 30.00
- *—Digitally re-recorded music track, Mickey Mouse as The Sorcerer on cover*
- ❑ Disneyland WDX-101 | 1957 | 60.00
- *—Original issue, maroon/red labels, includes 24-page booklet*

FANTASIA: NIGHT ON BALD MOUNTAIN; PASTORAL SYMPHONY; AVE MARIA
- ❑ Disneyland WDL-4101C [M] | 1958 | 25.00
- ❑ Disneyland STER-4101C [S] | 1958 | 30.00

FANTASIA: RITE OF SPRING; TOCCATA AND FUGUE
- ❑ Disneyland WDL-4101A [M] | 1958 | 25.00
- ❑ Disneyland STER-4101A [S] | 1959 | 30.00

FANTASIA: THE NUTCRACKER SUITE; DANCE OF THE HOURS
- ❑ Disneyland WDL-4101B [M] | 1958 | 25.00
- ❑ Disneyland STER-4101B [S] | 1959 | 30.00

THE FANTASTIC PLASTIC MACHINE
- ❑ Epic BN26469 | 1969 | 30.00

A FAREWELL TO ARMS
- ❑ Capitol W918 [M] | 1957 | 50.00

FAR FROM THE MADDING CROWD
- ❑ MGM 1E-11 [M] | 1967 | 18.00
- ❑ MGM S1E-11 [S] | 1967 | 30.00

THE FASTEST GUITAR ALIVE
- ❑ MGM SE-4475 | 1968 | 30.00

FAST TIMES AT RIDGEMONT HIGH
- ❑ Full Moon/Asylum 60158 | 1982 | 18.00
- *—Includes Go-Go's, Oingo Boingo*

FATHOM
- ❑ 20th Century Fox TFM-4195 [M] | 1967 | 40.00
- ❑ 20th Century Fox TFS-4195 [S] | 1967 | 50.00

FELLINI SATYRICON
- ❑ United Artists UAS-5208 | 1969 | 30.00

FELLINI'S ROMA
- ❑ United Artists UA-LA052-F | 1972 | 30.00

THE FEMALE PRISONER
- ❑ Columbia Masterworks OS3320 | 1969 | 30.00

FIDDLER ON THE ROOF
- ❑ United Artists UAS-10900 | 1971 | 25.00
- *—With booklet*

55 DAYS AT PEKING
- ❑ Columbia CL2028 [M] | 1963 | 40.00
- ❑ Columbia CS8828 [S] | 1963 | 70.00

THE FIGHTER
- ❑ Decca DL5414 [10] | 1952 | 80.00

THE FINAL COUNTDOWN
- ❑ Casablanca NBLP-7232 | 1980 | 40.00

A FINE MESS
- ❑ Motown 6180 | 1986 | 12.00
- *—Includes Los Lobos*

FINIAN'S RAINBOW
- ❑ Warner Bros. BS2550 | 1968 | 25.00

FIRE DOWN BELOW
- ❑ Decca DL8597 [M] | 1957 | 70.00

FIRSTBORN
- ❑ EMI America ST-517144 | 1984 | 15.00
- *—Includes Wang Chung, Talk Talk, Re-Flex; Columbia House edition*
- ❑ EMI America ST-17144 | 1984 | 12.00
- *—Includes Wang Chung, Talk Talk, Re-Flex*

A FISTFUL OF DOLLARS
- ❑ RCA Victor LOC-1135 [M] | 1967 | 25.00
- ❑ RCA Victor LSO-1135 [S] | 1967 | 30.00
- *—Black label, dog on top*
- ❑ RCA Victor LSO-1135 [S] | 1969 | 15.00
- *—Orange label, tan label, or black label with dog at 1 o'clock*

FIVE EASY PIECES
- ❑ Epic KE30456 | 1971 | 30.00

THE FIVE PENNIES
- ❑ Dot DLP-9500 [S] | 1959 | 30.00
- ❑ Dot DLP-29500 [S] | 1959 | 50.00

THE FLAMINGO KID
- ❑ Motown 6131ML | 1984 | 12.00
- *—Commonly distributed issue*
- ❑ Varese Sarabande STV-81232 | 1984 | 40.00
- *—Original issue*

FLASHDANCE
- ❑ Casablanca 811492-1 | 1983 | 12.00

A FLEA IN HER EAR
- ❑ 20th Century Fox TFS-4200 | 1968 | 30.00

FLETCH
- ❑ MCA 6142 | 1985 | 12.00
- *—Includes The Fixx, Kim Wilde*

FLOWER DRUM SONG
- ❑ Decca DL9098 [M] | 1961 | 25.00
- ❑ Decca DL79098 [S] | 1961 | 30.00
- ❑ MCA 2069 | 1973 | 12.00
- *—Reissue; black label with rainbow*

THE FOG
- ❑ Varese Sarabande STV-81191 | 1980 | 30.00

FOLIES BERGERE
- ❑ Decca DL8571 [M] | 1958 | 30.00

FOLLOW ME
- ❑ Uni 73056 | 1969 | 30.00

FOOTLOOSE
- ❑ Columbia JS39242 | 1984 | 12.00
- ❑ Columbia 9C939404 [PD] | 1984 | 25.00
- *—Picture disc version*

FOR A FEW DOLLARS MORE
- ❑ United Artists UAL-3608 [M] | 1967 | 25.00
- ❑ United Artists UAS-6608 [S] | 1967 | 30.00

FORBIDDEN ZONE
- ❑ Varese Sarabande STV81170 | 1983 | 15.00
- *—Includes Oingo Boingo (as The Mystical Knights of the Oingo Boingo); composed by Danny Elfman*

FOR LOVE OF IVY
- ❑ ABC SOC-7 | 1968 | 30.00

FOR THE FIRST TIME
- ❑ RCA Victor Red Seal LSC-2338 [S] | 1959 | 25.00
- *—"Shaded dog" and smaller "RCA Victor" lettering*
- ❑ RCA Victor Red Seal LSC-2338 [S] | 1965 | 18.00
- *—"White dog" and larger "RCA Victor" lettering*
- ❑ RCA Victor Red Seal LSC-2338 [S] | 1969 | 15.00
- *—Red label, no dog*
- ❑ RCA Victor Red Seal LM-2338 [M] | 1959 | 18.00

40 POUNDS OF TROUBLE
- ❑ Mercury MG-20784 [M] | 1963 | 30.00
- ❑ Mercury SR-60784 [S] | 1963 | 40.00

FOR YOUR EYES ONLY
- ❑ Liberty LOO-1109 | 1981 | 30.00

THE FOUR HORSEMEN OF THE APOCALYPSE
- ❑ MGM E-3993 [M] | 1962 | 25.00
- ❑ MGM SE-3993 [S] | 1962 | 30.00

FOUR IN THE MORNING
- ❑ Roulette OS805 [M] | 1966 | 40.00
- ❑ Roulette OSS805 [S] | 1966 | 50.00

Number	Title	Yr	NM

THE FOX
- ❏ Warner Bros. W1738 [M] — 1968 — 40.00
- ❏ Warner Bros. WS1738 [S] — 1968 — 30.00

THE FOX AND THE HOUND
- ❏ Disneyland 3106 [PD] — 1981 — 30.00
  — *Disney Picture Disc" series*
- ❏ Disneyland ST-3823 — 1981 — 25.00
  — *Non-picture disc version*

FOXY BROWN
- ❏ Motown M7-811 — 1974 — 25.00

FRANCIS OF ASSISI
- ❏ 20th Fox FOX-3053 [M] — 1961 — 200.00
- ❏ 20th Fox SFX-3053 [S] — 1961 — 250.00

THE FRENCH LINE
- ❏ Mercury MG-25182 [10] — 1954 — 80.00

FRIDAY
- ❏ Priority P1-53959 — 1995 — 18.00
  — *Includes Ice Cube, Dr. Dre, other gangsta rappers*

FRIENDLY PERSUASION
- ❏ RKO Unique LP-110 [M] — 1956 — 75.00

FRIGHT NIGHT
- ❏ Private I SZ40087 — 1985 — 15.00
  — *Includes Devo ("Let's Talk")*

FRITZ THE CAT
- ❏ Fantasy F-9406 — 1972 — 30.00

FROM RUSSIA WITH LOVE
- ❏ United Artists UAL-4114 [M] — 1964 — 25.00
- ❏ United Artists UAS-5114 [S] — 1964 — 30.00

THE FUGITIVE KIND
- ❏ United Artists UAL-4065 [M] — 1959 — 50.00
- ❏ United Artists UAS-5065 [S] — 1959 — 70.00

FUNERAL IN BERLIN
- ❏ RCA Victor LOC-1136 [M] — 1966 — 30.00
- ❏ RCA Victor LSO-1136 [S] — 1966 — 50.00

FUNNY GIRL
- ❏ Columbia Masterworks SQ30992 [Q] — 1971 — 40.00
- ❏ Columbia Masterworks BOS3220 — 1968 — 18.00
  — *Gray "360 Sound" label; record is removed from inside the gatefold; liner notes on a black background*
- ❏ Columbia Masterworks BOS3220 — 1968 — 15.00
  — *Gray "360 Sound" label; record is removed from inside the gatefold; liner notes on a tan background*
- ❏ Columbia Masterworks BOS3220 — 1970 — 12.00
  — *Olive label with "Columbia" encircling the edge*

A FUNNY THING HAPPENED ON THE WAY TO THE FORUM
- ❏ United Artists UAL-4144 [M] — 1966 — 15.00
- ❏ United Artists UAS-5144 [S] — 1966 — 18.00
- ❏ United Artists UA-LA284-G — 1974 — 12.00
  — *Reissue of 5144*

GAILY, GAILY
- ❏ United Artists UAS5202 — 1969 — 30.00

THE GAME IS OVER
- ❏ Atco 33-205 [M] — 1967 — 25.00
- ❏ Atco SD 33-205 [S] — 1967 — 30.00

THE GAMES
- ❏ Viking LPS-105 — 1970 — 200.00

GAY PURR-EE
- ❏ Warner Bros. B1479 [M] — 1963 — 25.00
- ❏ Warner Bros. BS1479 [S] — 1963 — 30.00

GEISHA BOY
- ❏ Jubilee JLP-1096 [M] — 1958 — 50.00
- ❏ Jubilee JGS-1096 [S] — 1959 — 80.00

THE GENE KRUPA STORY
- ❏ Verve MGV-15010 [M] — 1959 — 50.00
- ❏ Verve MGVS-6105 [S] — 1959 — 100.00
  — *Original issue*
- ❏ Verve V6-15010 [S] — 1963 — 80.00
  — *Early reissue*
- ❏ Verve V-15010 [M] — 1961 — 25.00

GENGHIS KHAN
- ❏ Liberty LRP-3412 [M] — 1965 — 40.00
- ❏ Liberty LST-7412 [S] — 1965 — 60.00

GENTLEMEN MARRY BRUNETTES
- ❏ Coral CRL57013 [M] — 1955 — 70.00

GENTLEMEN PREFER BLONDES
- ❏ MGM E-208 [M] — 1953 — 120.00

THE GENTLE RAIN
- ❏ Mercury MG-21016 [M] — 1966 — 25.00
- ❏ Mercury SR-61016 [S] — 1966 — 30.00

GET CRAZY
- ❏ Morocco 6065 — 1983 — 14.00
  — *Includes Ramones, Marshall Crenshaw, Lou Reed, Fear*

GETTING STRAIGHT
- ❏ Colgems COSO-5010 — 1970 — 30.00

GET YOURSELF A COLLEGE GIRL
- ❏ MGM E-4273 [M] — 1965 — 25.00
- ❏ MGM SE-4273 [S] — 1965 — 40.00

GHOSTBUSTERS
- ❏ Arista AL8-8246 — 1984 — 18.00
  — *First pressing has smaller print on front and eight photos on back*
- ❏ Arista AL8-8246 — 1984 — 12.00
  — *Later pressings have large print on front and seven photos on back*

GHOSTBUSTERS II
- ❏ MCA R151964 — 1989 — 15.00
  — *BMG Direct Marketing edition*
- ❏ MCA 6306 — 1989 — 12.00

GIANT
- ❏ Capitol W773 [M] — 1956 — 40.00
  — *Turquoise or gray label*
- ❏ Capitol W773 [M] — 1959 — 30.00
  — *Black colorband label, logo at left*
- ❏ Capitol W773 [M] — 1962 — 18.00
  — *Black colorband label, logo at top*
- ❏ Capitol DW773 [R] — 196? — 15.00

GIDGET GOES HAWAIIAN
- ❏ Colpix CP418 [M] — 1961 — 50.00

GIGI
- ❏ MCA 39045 — 1986 — 10.00
  — *Reissue*
- ❏ MGM W90523 [M] — 1965 — 15.00
  — *Capitol Record Club edition*
- ❏ MGM SW90523 [S] — 1965 — 18.00
- ❏ MGM E-3641 [M] — 1958 — 25.00
  — *Yellow label*
- ❏ MGM SE-3641 [S] — 1959 — 30.00
  — *Yellow label*
- ❏ MGM E-3641 [M] — 1960 — 15.00
  — *Black label*
- ❏ MGM SE-3641 [S] — 1960 — 18.00
  — *Black label*
- ❏ MGM SE-3641 [S] — 1968 — 15.00
  — *Blue and gold label*

GIGOT
- ❏ Capitol W1754 [M] — 1962 — 30.00
- ❏ Capitol SW1754 [S] — 1962 — 40.00

THE GIRL IN THE BIKINI
- ❏ Poplar PLP 33-1002 [M] — 1952 — 400.00

THE GIRL MOST LIKELY
- ❏ Capitol W930 [M] — 1957 — 60.00

GIRL ON A MOTORCYCLE
- ❏ Tetragrammaton T-5000 — 1969 — 30.00

GIRLS JUST WANT TO HAVE FUN
- ❏ Mercury 824510-1 — 1985 — 12.00
  — *Includes Animotion*

THE GLENN MILLER STORY
- ❏ Decca DL5519 [10] — 1954 — 40.00
- ❏ Decca DL8226 [M] — 1956 — 30.00
- ❏ Decca DL9123 [M] — 196? — 25.00
  — *Reissue of 8226*
- ❏ Decca DL79123 [R] — 196? — 18.00
- ❏ MCA 2036 — 1973 — 12.00
- ❏ MCA 1624 — 198? — 18.00
  — *This reissue is a bit more desirable because it was issued in true stereo*

GLORY
- ❏ Virgin 91329 — 1989 — 30.00
- ❏ Virgin 91329 — 1998 — 25.00
  — *Classic Records edition; audiophile reissue; cover is noticeably less sharp than the originals*

THE GLORY STOMPERS
- ❏ Sidewalk DT5910 [R] — 1968 — 50.00

GO, GO, GO WORLD
- ❏ Musicor MM-2059 [M] — 1965 — 40.00
- ❏ Musicor MS-3059 [S] — 1965 — 60.00

GO, JOHNNY, GO!
- ❏ (no label) (no number) [DJ] — 1959 — 1000.00
  — *Only exists as a promo*

THE GODFATHER
- ❏ Paramount PAS-1003 — 1972 — 25.00
  — *Original cover with triple gatefold*

THE GODFATHER PART II
- ❏ ABC ABDP-856 — 1975 — 25.00

THE GODFATHER PART III
- ❏ Columbia C47078 — 1990 — 25.00

GOD'S LITTLE ACRE
- ❏ United Artists UAL-4002 [M] — 1958 — 150.00

GOLD
- ❏ ABC ABCD-855 — 1975 — 30.00

GOLDEN BOY
- ❏ Colpix CP-478 [M] — 1964 — 25.00
- ❏ Colpix SCP-478 [S] — 1964 — 30.00

THE GOLDEN BREED
- ❏ Capitol ST2886 — 1967 — 30.00

THE GOLDEN COACH
- ❏ MGM E-3111 [M] — 1954 — 150.00

THE GOLDEN SCREW
- ❏ Atco 33-208 [M] — 1967 — 30.00
- ❏ Atco SD 33-208 [S] — 1967 — 40.00

GOLDFINGER
- ❏ United Artists UAL-4117 [M] — 1964 — 18.00
- ❏ United Artists UAS-5117 [S] — 1964 — 25.00

GOLIATH AND THE BARBARIANS
- ❏ American Int'l. 1001-M [M] — 1960 — 40.00
- ❏ American Int'l. 1001-S [S] — 1960 — 70.00

GONE WITH THE WAVE
- ❏ Colpix CP-492 [M] — 1965 — 40.00
- ❏ Colpix SCP-492 [S] — 1965 — 60.00

GONE WITH THE WIND
- ❏ MGM 1E-10 [M] — 1967 — 25.00
  — *Gatefold edition with 32-page booklet*
- ❏ MGM S1E-10 [M] — 1967 — 25.00
  — *Gatefold edition with 32-page booklet*

GOODBYE, CHARLIE
- ❏ 20th Century Fox TFM-3165 [M] — 1964 — 30.00
- ❏ 20th Century Fox TFS-4165 [S] — 1964 — 30.00

GOODBYE, MR. CHIPS
- ❏ MCA 39006 — 1986 — 10.00
  — *Reissue*
- ❏ MGM 1SE-19 — 1969 — 25.00

GOODBYE AGAIN
- ❏ United Artists UAL-4091 [M] — 1961 — 30.00
- ❏ United Artists UAS-5091 [S] — 1961 — 40.00

GOOD MORNING, VIETNAM
- ❏ A&M R154001 — 1987 — 15.00
  — *Includes The Searchers; BMG Direct Marketing edition*

GOOD NEWS
- ❏ MGM E-504 [10] — 1950 — 50.00

THE GOONIES
- ❏ Epic SE40067 — 1985 — 12.00
  — *Includes Cyndi Lauper (2), Bangles*

GORDON'S WAR
- ❏ Buddah BDS-5137 — 1973 — 40.00

THE GOSPEL ACCORDING TO ST. MATTHEW
- ❏ Mainstream 54000 [M] — 1966 — 30.00
- ❏ Mainstream 3-4000 [S] — 1966 — 100.00

GOTCHA!
- ❏ MCA Curb 5596 — 1985 — 15.00
  — *Includes Joan Jett and the Blackhearts, Bronski Beat*

GOTHIC
- ❏ Virgin 90607 — 1987 — 25.00

GOYA
- ❏ Decca DL8236 [M] — 1959 — 150.00

THE GRADUATE
- ❏ CBS Masterworks JS3180 [S] — 198? — 10.00
  — *CBS Masterworks" replaces "Columbia" along outer edge of label*
- ❏ Columbia Masterworks OS3180 [S] — 1968 — 15.00
  — *Original stereo edition: Gray label, "360 Sound Stereo" in white*
- ❏ Columbia Masterworks OL6780 [M] — 1968 — 50.00
  — *Mono" on label*
- ❏ Columbia Masterworks OS3180 [S] — 1971 — 12.00
  — *Olive label, "Columbia" along outer edge*
- ❏ Columbia Masterworks JS3180 [S] — 197? — 10.00
  — *Reissue with new prefix*

GRAND PRIX
- ❏ MGM 1E-8 [M] — 1967 — 25.00
- ❏ MGM 1SE-8 [S] — 1967 — 30.00

THE GREAT ESCAPE
- ❏ United Artists UAL-4107 [M] — 1963 — 30.00
- ❏ United Artists UAS-5107 [S] — 1963 — 30.00

THE GREATEST SHOW ON EARTH
- ❏ RCA Victor LPM-3018 [10] — 1952 — 200.00

THE GREATEST STORY EVER TOLD
- ❏ United Artists UAL-4120 [M] — 1965 — 30.00
- ❏ United Artists UAS-5120 [S] — 1965 — 30.00

Number	Title	Yr	NM

THE GREAT GATSBY
- ❏ Paramount 2-3001 — 1974 — 25.00

THE GREAT OUTDOORS
- ❏ Atlantic 81859 — 1988 — 12.00
- — *Includes Pop Will Eat Itself*

GREMLINS
- ❏ Geffen GHSP24044 [EP] — 1984 — 12.00
- — *Includes Peter Gabriel*

GROUNDS FOR MARRIAGE
- ❏ MGM E-536 [M] — 1950 — 80.00

GUESS WHO'S COMING TO DINNER
- ❏ Colgems COM-108 [M] — 1968 — 30.00
- ❏ Colgems COS-108 [S] — 1968 — 30.00

GULLIVER'S TRAVELS BEYOND THE MOON
- ❏ Mainstream 54001 [M] — 1965 — 30.00
- ❏ Mainstream S-4001 [S] — 1965 — 40.00

GUNS FOR SAN SEBASTIAN
- ❏ MGM SE-4565 — 1968 — 60.00

THE GUNS OF NAVARONE
- ❏ Columbia CL1655 [M] — 1961 — 25.00
- ❏ Columbia CS8455 [S] — 1961 — 50.00

GURU
- ❏ RCA Victor LSO-1158 — 1969 — 25.00

GYPSY
- ❏ Warner Bros. B1480 [M] — 1962 — 25.00
- ❏ Warner Bros. BS1480 [S] — 1962 — 30.00

GYPSY GIRL
- ❏ Mainstream 56090 [M] — 1966 — 30.00
- ❏ Mainstream S-6090 [S] — 1966 — 30.00

HALLELUJAH THE HILLS
- ❏ Fontana MGF-27524 [M] — 1964 — 30.00
- ❏ Fontana SRF-67524 [S] — 1964 — 30.00

THE HALLELUJAH TRAIL
- ❏ United Artists UAL-4127 [M] — 1965 — 25.00
- ❏ United Artists UAS-5127 [S] — 1965 — 30.00

HAMMERHEAD
- ❏ Colgems COS-110 — 1968 — 40.00

HAMMERSMITH IS OUT
- ❏ Capitol SW-861 — 1972 — 30.00

HANG 'EM HIGH
- ❏ United Artists UAS-5179 — 1968 — 30.00

THE HAPPENING
- ❏ Colgems COMO-5006 [M] — 1967 — 30.00
- ❏ Colgems COSO-5006 [S] — 1967 — 50.00

THE HAPPIEST MILLIONAIRE
- ❏ Buena Vista BV-5001 [M] — 1967 — 18.00
- ❏ Buena Vista STER-5001 [S] — 1967 — 25.00

HARD COUNTRY
- ❏ Epic SE37367 — 1981 — 12.00

THE HARD RIDE
- ❏ Paramount PAS-6005 — 1971 — 30.00

HARPER
- ❏ Mainstream 56078 [M] — 1966 — 25.00
- ❏ Mainstream S-6078 [S] — 1966 — 30.00

THE HARRAD EXPERIMENT
- ❏ Capitol ST-11182 — 1973 — 30.00

HARRAD SUMMER
- ❏ Capitol ST-11338 — 1974 — 30.00

HAWAII
- ❏ United Artists UAL-4143 [M] — 1966 — 25.00
- ❏ United Artists UAS-5143 [S] — 1966 — 30.00
- ❏ United Artists SW-90935 [S] — 1966 — 30.00
- — *Capitol Record Club issue*

THE HEART IS A LONELY HUNTER
- ❏ Warner Bros. WS1759 — 1968 — 30.00

HEART OF DIXIE
- ❏ A&M SP-3930 — 1989 — 25.00

HEAVENLY BODIES
- ❏ Private I SZ39930 — 1985 — 12.00
- — *Includes The Tubes*

HEAVENLY BODIES SAMPLER
- ❏ Private I AS1965 [DJ] — 1984 — 10.00
- — *Includes The Tubes; promo-only 4-song sampler*

HEAVY METAL
- ❏ Full Moon/Asylum DP-90004 — 1981 — 25.00
- — *Contains two LPs of pop/rock music*

HEAVY METAL, THE SCORE
- ❏ Full Moon/Asylum 5E-547 — 1981 — 50.00
- — *Contains Elmer Bernstein's instrumental music*

HEAVY TRAFFIC
- ❏ Fantasy F-9436 — 1973 — 30.00

HEIDI'S SONG
- ❏ K-Tel NU5310 — 1982 — 25.00

THE HELEN MORGAN STORY
- ❏ RCA Victor LOC-1030 [M] — 1957 — 60.00

HELLCATS
- ❏ Tower ST5124 — 1968 — 30.00

HELLO-GOODBYE
- ❏ 20th Century Fox S-4210 — 1970 — 40.00

HELL'S ANGELS '69
- ❏ Capitol SKAO-303 — 1969 — 30.00

HELL'S ANGELS ON WHEELS
- ❏ Smash MGS-27094 [M] — 1967 — 30.00
- ❏ Smash SRS-67094 [S] — 1967 — 30.00

HELL'S BELLS
- ❏ Sidewalk ST5919 — 1969 — 30.00

HELL TO ETERNITY
- ❏ Warwick W2030 [M] — 1960 — 120.00
- ❏ Warwick WST2030 [S] — 1960 — 200.00

HELL UP IN HARLEM
- ❏ Motown M802V1 — 1974 — 30.00

HEMINGWAY'S ADVENTURES OF A YOUNG MAN
- ❏ RCA Victor LOC-1074 [M] — 1962 — 40.00
- ❏ RCA Victor LSO-1074 [S] — 1962 — 70.00

HERCULES
- ❏ Varese Sarabande STV-81187 — 1983 — 25.00

THE HERO
- ❏ Capitol SW-11098 — 1972 — 25.00

A HERO AIN'T NOTHIN' BUT A SANDWICH
- ❏ Columbia PS35046 — 1978 — 25.00

HEROES OF TELEMARK
- ❏ Mainstream 56064 [M] — 1965 — 25.00
- ❏ Mainstream S-6064 [S] — 1965 — 30.00

HEY, LET'S TWIST
- ❏ Roulette R-25168 [M] — 1962 — 30.00
- ❏ Roulette SR-25168 [S] — 1962 — 30.00

HEY THERE, IT'S YOGI BEAR!
- ❏ Colpix CP-472 [M] — 1964 — 50.00
- ❏ Colpix SCP-472 [S] — 1964 — 80.00

HIDING OUT
- ❏ Virgin R163706 — 1987 — 12.00
- — *Includes Pretty Poison ("Catch Me I'm Falling"), Boy George ("Live My Life"); Public Image Ltd. ("Seattle")*
- ❏ Virgin 90661 — 1987 — 10.00
- — *Includes Pretty Poison ("Catch Me I'm Falling"), Boy George ("Live My Life"); Public Image Ltd. ("Seattle")*

HIGH SOCIETY
- ❏ Capitol W750 [M] — 1956 — 30.00
- — *Gray label original*
- ❏ Capitol W750 [M] — 1959 — 25.00
- — *Black colorband label, logo at left*
- ❏ Capitol W750 [M] — 1962 — 18.00
- — *Black colorband label, logo at top*
- ❏ Capitol SW750 [S] — 1959 — 30.00
- — *Black colorband label, logo at left*
- ❏ Capitol SW750 [S] — 1962 — 25.00
- — *Black colorband label, logo at top*

THE HOBBIT
- ❏ Buena Vista 103 — 1977 — 30.00
- ❏ Buena Vista 103A — 1977 — 40.00
- — *Special edition sold at Sears stores, with four decals and poster*
- ❏ Disneyland ST-3819 — 1978 — 30.00

HOLIDAY INN
- ❏ Decca DL4256 — 1962 — 30.00
- ❏ MCA 25205 — 1987 — 10.00
- — *Reissue of Decca LP*

HOMER AND EDDIE
- ❏ Apache D1-71654 — 1989 — 30.00

HONKYTONK MAN
- ❏ Warner Bros. 23739 — 1982 — 12.00

HOOSIERS
- ❏ Polydor 831475-1 — 1987 — 30.00

HOOTENANNY HOOT
- ❏ MGM E-4172 [M] — 1963 — 25.00
- ❏ MGM SE-4172 [S] — 1963 — 30.00

THE HORSEMEN
- ❏ Sunflower SNF-5007 — 1971 — 40.00

THE HORSE SOLDIERS
- ❏ United Artists UAL-4035 [M] — 1959 — 60.00
- ❏ United Artists UAS-5035 [S] — 1959 — 150.00

HOTEL PARADISO
- ❏ MGM E-4419 [M] — 1966 — 25.00
- ❏ MGM SE-4419 [S] — 1966 — 30.00

THE HOT ROCK
- ❏ Prophesy SD8055 — 1972 — 25.00

HOT ROD RUMBLE
- ❏ Liberty LRP-3048 [M] — 1957 — 150.00

THE HOUR OF THE GUN
- ❏ United Artists UAL-4166 [M] — 1967 — 40.00
- ❏ United Artists UAS-5166 [S] — 1967 — 70.00

HOUSEBOAT
- ❏ Columbia CL1222 [M] — 1958 — 50.00

A HOUSE IS NOT A HOME
- ❏ Ava A-50 [M] — 1964 — 30.00
- ❏ Ava AS-50 [S] — 1964 — 30.00

HOUSE PARTY
- ❏ Motown 9296 — 1990 — 15.00
- — *Includes L.L. Cool J, Flavor Flav (of Public Enemy)*

HOWARD THE DUCK
- ❏ MCA 6173 — 1986 — 25.00

HOW SWEET IT IS
- ❏ RCA Victor LSP-4037 — 1968 — 25.00

HOW THE WEST WAS WON
- ❏ MCA 39043 — 1986 — 10.00
- — *Reissue*
- ❏ MGM 1E-5 [M] — 1963 — 18.00
- ❏ MGM 1SE-5 [S] — 1963 — 25.00

HOW TO BEAT THE HIGH COST OF LIVING
- ❏ Columbia JS36741 — 1981 — 18.00

HOW TO MURDER YOUR WIFE
- ❏ United Artists UAL-4119 [M] — 1965 — 18.00
- ❏ United Artists UAS-5119 [S] — 1965 — 25.00

HOW TO SAVE A MARRIAGE AND RUIN YOUR LIFE
- ❏ Columbia Masterworks OS3140 — 1968 — 25.00

HOW TO STEAL A MILLION
- ❏ 20th Century Fox TFM-3183 [M] — 1966 — 40.00
- ❏ 20th Century Fox TFS-4183 [S] — 1966 — 50.00

HOW TO STUFF A WILD BIKINI
- ❏ Wand 671 [M] — 1965 — 30.00
- ❏ Wand S-671 [S] — 1965 — 40.00

HOW TO SUCCEED IN BUSINESS WITHOUT REALLY TRYING
- ❏ United Artists UAL-4151 [M] — 1967 — 25.00
- ❏ United Artists UAS-5151 [S] — 1967 — 30.00

HUGO THE HIPPO
- ❏ United Artists UA-LA637-G — 1976 — 25.00

THE HUNGER
- ❏ Varese Sarabande STV-81184 — 1984 — 12.00
- — *Includes David Bowie*
- ❏ Varese Sarabande STV-81184 — 1983 — 25.00

THE HUNT FOR RED OCTOBER
- ❏ MCA 6428 — 1990 — 30.00

HURRICANE
- ❏ Elektra 5E-504 — 1979 — 25.00

HURRY SUNDOWN
- ❏ RCA Victor LOC-1133 [M] — 1967 — 30.00
- ❏ RCA Victor LSO-1133 [S] — 1967 — 40.00

THE HUSTLER
- ❏ Kapp KL-1264 [M] — 1961 — 60.00
- ❏ Kapp KS-3264 [S] — 1961 — 120.00

ICEMAN
- ❏ Southern Cross SCRS-1006 — 1983 — 25.00

ICE STATION ZEBRA
- ❏ MGM S1E-14ST — 1968 — 40.00

IF HE HOLLERS, LET HIM GO
- ❏ Tower ST5152 — 1968 — 40.00

I'LL NEVER FORGET WHAT'S 'IS NAME
- ❏ Decca DL9163 [M] — 1967 — 30.00
- ❏ Decca DL79163 [S] — 1967 — 30.00

I LOVE MELVIN
- ❏ MGM E-190 [10] — 1953 — 50.00

I'M GONNA GIT YOU SUCKA
- ❏ Arista AL-8574 — 1988 — 12.00
- — *Includes Fishbone (with Curtis Mayfield)*

IMITATION OF LIFE
- ❏ Decca DL8879 [M] — 1959 — 50.00
- ❏ Decca DL78879 [S] — 1959 — 80.00

IN A SHALLOW GRAVE
- ❏ Varese Sarabande STV-81359 — 1988 — 40.00

INCHON
- ❏ Regency RI-8502 — 1982 — 30.00

INDIANA JONES AND THE TEMPLE OF DOOM
- ❏ Polydor 821592-1 — 1984 — 25.00

THE INDISCRETION OF AN AMERICAN WIFE
- ❏ Columbia CL6277 [10] — 1954 — 80.00

Number	Title	Yr	NM

I NEVER SANG FOR MY FATHER
| ❏ Bell 1204 | | 1970 | 40.00 |

IN HARM'S WAY
| ❏ RCA Victor LOC-1100 [M] | | 1965 | 40.00 |
| ❏ RCA Victor LSO-1100 [S] | | 1965 | 80.00 |

IN LIKE FLINT
| ❏ 20th Century Fox 4193 [M] | | 1967 | 40.00 |
| ❏ 20th Century Fox S-4193 [S] | | 1967 | 80.00 |

INNERSPACE
| ❏ Geffen GHS24161 | | 1987 | 12.00 |
| — Includes Wang Chung, Berlin | | | |

THE INN OF THE SIXTH HAPPINESS
| ❏ 20th Century Fox FOX-3011 [M] | | 1958 | 50.00 |
| ❏ 20th Century Fox SFX-3011 [S] | | 1958 | 70.00 |

IN SEARCH OF THE CASTAWAYS
| ❏ Disneyland ST-3916 [M] | | 1962 | 70.00 |

INSIDE DAISY CLOVER
| ❏ Warner Bros. W1616 [M] | | 1965 | 25.00 |
| ❏ Warner Bros. WS1616 [S] | | 1965 | 30.00 |

INSPECTOR CLOUSEAU
❏ MCA 25107		1986	10.00
— Reissue			
❏ United Artists UAS-5186		1968	30.00

INTERLUDE
| ❏ Colgems COSO-5007 | | 1968 | 40.00 |

THE INTERNS
| ❏ Colpix CP427 [M] | | 1962 | 30.00 |
| ❏ Colpix SCP427 [S] | | 1962 | 40.00 |

IN THE GOOD OLD SUMMERTIME
| ❏ MGM E-169 [10] | | 1949 | 100.00 |

IN THE HEAT OF THE NIGHT
| ❏ United Artists UAL-4160 [M] | | 1967 | 18.00 |
| ❏ United Artists UAS-5160 [S] | | 1967 | 25.00 |

INVITATION TO THE DANCE
| ❏ MGM E-3207 [M] | | 1956 | 50.00 |

THE IPCRESS FILE
| ❏ Decca DL9124 [M] | | 1965 | 30.00 |
| ❏ Decca DL79124 [S] | | 1965 | 40.00 |

IRMA LA DOUCE
| ❏ United Artists UAL-4109 [M] | | 1963 | 25.00 |
| ❏ United Artists UAS-5109 [S] | | 1963 | 30.00 |

THE ISLAND
| ❏ Varese Sarabande VC-81147 | | 1979 | 25.00 |

THE ISLAND AT THE TOP OF THE WORLD
| ❏ Disneyland ST-3814 | | 1974 | 30.00 |

ISLAND IN THE SKY
| ❏ Decca DL 7029 [10] | | 1953 | 300.00 |

IS PARIS BURNING?
| ❏ Columbia Masterworks OL6630 [M] | | 1966 | 30.00 |
| ❏ Columbia Masterworks OS3020 [S] | | 1966 | 40.00 |

THE ITALIAN JOB
| ❏ Paramount PAS-5007 | | 1969 | 40.00 |

IT'S ALWAYS FAIR WEATHER
❏ MCA 25018		1986	12.00
— Reissue			
❏ MGM E-3241 [M]		1955	50.00

IT'S A MAD, MAD, MAD, MAD WORLD
❏ MCA 39076		198?	10.00
— Reissue of United Artists 276			
❏ United Artists UAL-4110 [M]		1963	25.00
❏ United Artists UAS-5110 [S]		1963	30.00
❏ United Artists UA-LA276-G		1974	12.00
— Reissue of 5110			

IT STARTED IN NAPLES
❏ Dot DLP-3324 [M]		1960	60.00
❏ Dot DLP-25324 [S]		1960	100.00
❏ Varese Sarabande STV-81122		1982	18.00
— Reissue of Dot 25324			

I WANT TO LIVE
❏ United Artists UAL-4005 [M]		1958	30.00
— Orchestral music by Johnny Mandel			
❏ United Artists UAS-4005 [S]		1958	40.00
— Orchestral music by Johnny Mandel			
❏ United Artists UAL-4006 [M]		1958	30.00
— Jazz music by Gerry Mulligan, Shelly Manne and Art Farmer			
❏ United Artists UAS-4006 [S]		1958	40.00
— Jazz music by Gerry Mulligan, Shelly Mann and Art Farmer			
❏ United Artists UXL1 [M]		1958	60.00
— Combines 4005 and 4006 into one package			
❏ United Artists UXS51 [S]		1958	80.00
— Combines 5005 and 5006 into one package			

I WAS A TEENAGE ZOMBIE
| ❏ Enigma SJ-73296 | | 1987 | 15.00 |

Number	Title	Yr	NM

| — Includes The Fleshtones, The Del Fuegos, the dB's, The Dream Syndicate, Violent Femmes, The Waitresses, The Smithereens, Los Lobos | | | |

JACK THE RIPPER
| ❏ RCA Victor LPM-2199 [M] | | 1960 | 30.00 |
| ❏ RCA Victor LSP-2199 [S] | | 1960 | 50.00 |

JAMBOREE!
| ❏ Warner Bros. (no #) [M] | | 1957 | 1200.00 |
| — Album has been counterfeited. Originals have front cover slicks and back cover notes printed on the cardboard, and the records have "Jam 1" and "Jam 2" stamped (not etched) in the dead wax. | | | |

THE JAMES DEAN STORY
❏ Capitol W881 [M]		1957	60.00
❏ Kimberly 2016 [M]		1960	40.00
❏ Kimberly 11016 [S]		1960	50.00
— Reissue of World Pacific 2005			
❏ World Pacific P-2005 [M]		1958	100.00

JAWS
❏ MCA 2087		1975	25.00
❏ MCA 1660		198?	10.00
— Reissue of 2087			

JEAN DE FLORETTE
| ❏ TVT 3004 | | 1986 | 25.00 |

JEREMIAH JOHNSON
| ❏ Warner Bros. BS2902 | | 1972 | 25.00 |
| — Green label | | | |

JESSICA
| ❏ United Artists UAL-4096 [M] | | 1962 | 25.00 |
| ❏ United Artists UAS-5096 [S] | | 1962 | 30.00 |

THE JOE LOUIS STORY
| ❏ MGM E-221 [10] | | 1953 | 80.00 |

JOHNNY COOL
| ❏ United Artists UAL-4111 [M] | | 1963 | 25.00 |
| ❏ United Artists UAS-5111 [S] | | 1963 | 30.00 |

JOHNNY TREMAIN
| ❏ Disneyland WDL-4014 [M] | | 1957 | 50.00 |

JOHN PAUL JONES
❏ Varese Sarabande STV-81146		1981	18.00
— Reissue of Warner Bros. WS 1293			
❏ Warner Bros. W1293 [M]		1959	60.00
❏ Warner Bros. WS1293 [S]		1959	120.00

JUD
| ❏ Ampex A-50101 | | 1971 | 25.00 |

JUDGMENT AT NUREMBERG
❏ MCA 39055		198?	12.00
— Reissue of United Artists 5095			
❏ United Artists UAL-4095 [M]		1961	25.00
❏ United Artists UAS-5095 [S]		1961	50.00

JUDITH
| ❏ RCA Victor LOC-1119 [M] | | 1966 | 18.00 |
| ❏ RCA Victor LSO-1119 [S] | | 1966 | 30.00 |

JUICE
| ❏ MCA 10577 | | 1992 | 12.00 |
| — Includes Naughty By Nature, others; issue in generic sleeve with sticker | | | |

JULIET OF THE SPIRITS
| ❏ Mainstream 56062 [M] | | 1965 | 30.00 |
| ❏ Mainstream S-6062 [S] | | 1965 | 60.00 |

JULIUS CAESAR
| ❏ MGM E-3033 [M] | | 1953 | 40.00 |

JUMBO (BILLY ROSE'S)
| ❏ Columbia Masterworks OL5860 [M] | | 1962 | 25.00 |
| ❏ Columbia Masterworks OS2260 [S] | | 1962 | 30.00 |

JUMPIN' JACK FLASH
| ❏ Mercury 830545-1 | | 1986 | 12.00 |
| — Includes Bananarama | | | |

THE JUNGLE BOOK
❏ Buena Vista BV-4041 [M]		1967	18.00
❏ Buena Vista STER-4041 [S]		1967	30.00
❏ Disneyland 3105 [PD]		1981	30.00
— Disney Picture Disc" series			

JURASSIC PARK
| ❏ MCA/BMG (no #) [PD] | | 1993 | 1500.00 |
| — Custom-made picture disc; promo only | | | |

JUSTINE
| ❏ Monument SLP-18123 | | 1969 | 30.00 |

JUST ONE OF THE GUYS
| ❏ Elektra 60426 | | 1985 | 12.00 |
| — Includes Berlin | | | |

KALEIDOSCOPE
| ❏ Warner Bros. W1663 [M] | | 1966 | 25.00 |
| ❏ Warner Bros. WS1663 [S] | | 1966 | 30.00 |

THE KARATE KID
| ❏ Casablanca 822213-1 | | 1984 | 15.00 |
| — Includes The Flirts (with Jan & Dean), Gang of Four | | | |

Number	Title	Yr	NM

KELLY'S HEROES
| ❏ MGM S1E-23 | | 1970 | 30.00 |

THE KEY
| ❏ Columbia CL1185 [M] | | 1958 | 80.00 |

KILLERS THREE
| ❏ Tower ST-5141 | | 1968 | 25.00 |

THE KING AND I
❏ Capitol W740 [M]		1956	30.00
— Gray label			
❏ Capitol W740 [M]		1959	18.00
— Black colorband label, logo at left			
❏ Capitol W740 [M]		1962	15.00
— Black colorband label, logo at top			
❏ Capitol SW740 [S]		1959	25.00
— Black colorband label, logo at left			
❏ Capitol SW740 [S]		1962	18.00
— Black colorband label, logo at top			
❏ Capitol SW740 [S]		1969	15.00
— Lime green label			
❏ Capitol SW740 [S]		1973	12.00
— Orange label			
❏ Capitol SW740 [S]		1978	10.00
— Purple label			

KING KONG
| ❏ Reprise MS2260 | | 1976 | 25.00 |

KING KONG LIVES
| ❏ MCA 6203 | | 1987 | 30.00 |

THE KING OF COMEDY
| ❏ Warner Bros. 23765 | | 1983 | 12.00 |
| — Includes The Pretenders ("Back on the Chain Gang"), Talking Heads, Ric Ocasek | | | |

KING OF KINGS
❏ MCA 39056		198?	10.00
— Reissue of MGM S1E-2			
❏ MGM 1E-2 [M]		1961	30.00
— Boxed version with hardbound book and four 8x10 photos			
❏ MGM S1E-2 [S]		1961	40.00
— Boxed version with hardbound book and four 8x10 photos			
❏ MGM 1E-2 [M]		1961	18.00
— Standard cover			
❏ MGM S1E-2 [S]		1961	25.00
— Standard cover			

KING RAT
| ❏ Mainstream 56061 [M] | | 1965 | 30.00 |
| ❏ Mainstream S-6061 [S] | | 1965 | 50.00 |

KINGS GO FORTH
| ❏ Capitol W1063 [M] | | 1958 | 150.00 |

KING SOLOMON'S MINES
| ❏ Restless 72106 | | 1985 | 25.00 |

KISMET
❏ MCA 1424		1987	10.00
— Reissue of MGM 3201			
❏ Metro M-526 [M]		1965	15.00
— Reissue of MGM E-3281 with one fewer track			
❏ Metro MS-526 [R]		1955	12.00
— Rechanneled reissue of MGM E-3281 with one fewer track			
❏ MGM E-3281 [M]		1955	25.00
— Yellow label			
❏ MGM E-3281 [M]		1960	18.00
— Black label			

KISS ME, KATE
❏ MCA 25003		1986	12.00
— Reissue of MGM 3077			
❏ Metro M-525 [M]		1965	15.00
— Reissue of MGM 3077, but with only 10 songs			
❏ Metro MS-525 [R]		1965	12.00
— Rechanneled reissue of MGM 3077, but with only 10 songs			
❏ MGM E-3077 [M]		1953	25.00
— Yellow label			
❏ MGM E-3077 [M]		1959	18.00
— Black label			

KRULL
| ❏ Southern Cross SCRS-1004 | | 1983 | 25.00 |

KRUSH GROOVE
| ❏ Warner Bros. 25295 | | 1985 | 12.00 |
| — Includes Beastie Boys, L.L. Cool J, Krush Groove All-Stars, Debbie Harry | | | |

KWAMINA
| ❏ Mercury MG-20654 [M] | | 1961 | 30.00 |
| ❏ Mercury SR-60654 [S] | | 1961 | 30.00 |

LA BAMBA
❏ Slash/Warner Bros. R120062		1987	15.00
— BMG Direct Marketing version			
❏ Slash/Warner Bros. 25605		1987	12.00

Number	Title	Yr	NM

LABYRINTH
- ❏ EMI America SV-17206 — 1986 — 12.00
  — *Includes David Bowie*

LADY AND THE TRAMP
- ❏ Decca DL5557 [10] — 1955 — 60.00
- ❏ Decca DL8462 — 1957 — 70.00
- ❏ Disneyland 3103 [PD] — 1981 — 30.00
  — *Disney Picture Disc" edition*

LADYHAWKE
- ❏ Atlantic 81248 — 1985 — 25.00

THE LANDLORD
- ❏ United Artists UAS-5209 — 1970 — 25.00

THE LAST AMERICAN VIRGIN
- ❏ Columbia JS38279 — 1982 — 40.00

THE LAST EMBRACE
- ❏ Varese Sarabande STV-81166 — 1983 — 25.00

THE LAST EMPEROR
- ❏ Virgin 90690 — 1987 — 12.00
  — *One side of music by David Byrne*

THE LAST OF THE SECRET AGENTS
- ❏ Dot DLP-3714 [M] — 1966 — 25.00
- ❏ Dot DLP-25714 [S] — 1966 — 30.00

THE LAST RUN
- ❏ MCA 25116 — 1986 — 10.00
  — *Reissue of MGM 1SE-30*
- ❏ MGM 1SE-30 — 1971 — 30.00

THE LAST STARFIGHTER
- ❏ Southern Cross SCRS-1007 — 1984 — 30.00

LAST SUMMER
- ❏ Warner Bros. WS1791 — 1969 — 25.00

THE LAST VALLEY
- ❏ ABC-Dunhill DSX-50102 — 1971 — 40.00

LAWRENCE OF ARABIA
- ❏ Arista ABM-4009 — 1975 — 12.00
  — *Reissue of Bell 1205*
- ❏ Bell 1205 — 1971 — 12.00
  — *Reissue of Colgems COSO-5004*
- ❏ Colgems COMO-5004 [M] — 1967 — 15.00
  — *Reissue of Colpix CP-514*
- ❏ Colgems COSO-5004 [S] — 1967 — 18.00
  — *Reissue of Colpix SCP-514*
- ❏ Colpix CP-514 [M] — 1962 — 25.00
- ❏ Colpix SCP-514 [S] — 1962 — 30.00

LEAN ON ME
- ❏ Warner Bros. 25843 — 1987 — 12.00
  — *Includes Guns N' Roses ("Welcome to the Jungle")*

LENNY
- ❏ United Artists UA-LA359-H — 1974 — 25.00

THE LEOPARD
- ❏ 20th Century Fox FXG-5015 [M] — 1963 — 30.00
- ❏ 20th Century Fox SXG-5015 [S] — 1963 — 40.00
- ❏ Varese Sarabande STV-81190 — 1982 — 18.00
  — *Reissue of 20th Century Fox SXG-5015*

LES LIAISONS DANGEREUSES
- ❏ Charlie Parker PLP-813 [M] — 1962 — 30.00
- ❏ Charlie Parker PLP-813S [S] — 1962 — 30.00
- ❏ Epic LA16022 [M] — 1961 — 40.00
- ❏ Epic BA17022 [S] — 1961 — 30.00
- ❏ Fontana MGF-27539 [M] — 1965 — 25.00
- ❏ Fontana SRF-67539 [R] — 1965 — 18.00

LESS THAN ZERO
- ❏ Def Jam SC44042 — 1987 — 12.00
  — *Includes Bangles, Joan Jett and the Blackhearts, Glenn Danzig, Publ;Ic Enemy, L.L. Cool J, Oran "Juice" Jones*

LETHAL WEAPON
- ❏ Warner Bros. 25561 — 1987 — 12.00
  — *Includes Honeymoon Suite*

LET'S MAKE LOVE
- ❏ Columbia CL1527 [M] — 1960 — 30.00
- ❏ Columbia CS8327 [S] — 1960 — 50.00

LETTER TO BREZHNEV
- ❏ MCA/London 6162 — 1985 — 12.00
  — *Includes Fine Young Cannibals, Bronski Beat*

LET THE GOOD TIMES ROLL
- ❏ Bell 9002 — 1973 — 30.00

LEVIATHAN
- ❏ Varese Sarabande VS-5226 — 1989 — 25.00

THE LIFE AND TIMES OF JUDGE ROY BEAN
- ❏ Columbia Masterworks S31948 — 1972 — 30.00

LIFEFORCE
- ❏ Varese Sarabande STV-81249 — 1985 — 30.00

LIGHT FANTASTIC
- ❏ 20th Century Fox FXG-5016 [M] — 1963 — 25.00
- ❏ 20th Century Fox SXG-5016 [S] — 1963 — 30.00

LIGHT OF DAY
- ❏ Blackheart SZ40654 — 1986 — 15.00
  — *Includes The Barbusters (Joan Jett and the Blackhearts), Dave Edmunds*

LI'L ABNER
- ❏ Columbia Masterworks OL5460 [M] — 1959 — 30.00
  — *Credits within photo*
- ❏ Columbia Masterworks OL5460 [M] — 196? — 25.00
  — *Credits in red strip at bottom of photo*
- ❏ Columbia Masterworks OS2021 [S] — 1959 — 40.00
  — *Credits within photo*
- ❏ Columbia Masterworks OS2021 [S] — 196? — 30.00
  — *Credits in red strip at bottom of photo*

LILIES OF THE FIELD
- ❏ Epic LN24094 [M] — 1964 — 25.00
- ❏ Epic BN26094 [S] — 1964 — 30.00

THE LION
- ❏ London M-76001 [M] — 1962 — 400.00

LIONHEART
- ❏ Varese Sarabande STV-81304 — 1987 — 25.00

LIONHEART (MORE MUSIC FROM THE FILM)
- ❏ Varese Sarabande STV-81311 — 1987 — 50.00

THE LION IN WINTER
- ❏ Columbia Masterworks OS3250 — 1969 — 25.00

LITTLE BIG MAN
- ❏ Columbia Masterworks S30545 — 1970 — 25.00

LITTLE SHOP OF HORRORS
- ❏ Geffen GHS-24125 — 1986 — 25.00

LIVE AND LET DIE
- ❏ Liberty LMAS-100 — 1981 — 15.00
  — *Gray label; reissue of United Artists 100 with gatefold cover*
- ❏ Liberty LT-50100 — 1982 — 15.00
  — *Gray label; reissue of Liberty 100 with standard cover*
- ❏ United Artists UA-LA100-G — 1973 — 25.00
  — *Tan label; cover corner is not clipped off*
- ❏ United Artists SWAO-95120 — 1973 — 30.00
  — *Longines (formerly Capitol) Record Club edition*
- ❏ United Artists UA-LA100-G — 1973 — 12.00
  — *Tan label; cover corner is clipped*
- ❏ United Artists UA-LA100-G — 1977 — 12.00
  — *Sunrise" label with this number on both jacket and label*
- ❏ United Artists LMAS-100 — 1979 — 12.00
  — *Sunrise" label with this number on label (jacket still has UA-LA100-G)*

LIVE FOR LIFE
- ❏ United Artists UAL-4165 [M] — 1967 — 25.00
- ❏ United Artists UAS-5165 [S] — 1967 — 25.00

THE LIVELY SET
- ❏ Decca DL9119 [M] — 1964 — 30.00
- ❏ Decca DL79119 [S] — 1964 — 40.00

LOGAN'S RUN
- ❏ MGM MG-1-5302 — 1976 — 30.00

LOLITA
- ❏ MCA 39067 — 198? — 10.00
  — *Reissue of MGM SE-4050*
- ❏ MGM E-4050 [M] — 1962 — 25.00
- ❏ MGM SE-4050 [S] — 1962 — 30.00

THE LOLLIPOP COVER
- ❏ Mainstream 56067 [M] — 1966 — 25.00
- ❏ Mainstream S-6067 [S] — 1966 — 30.00

THE LONGEST DAY
- ❏ 20th Century Fox FXG-5007 [M] — 1962 — 25.00
- ❏ 20th Century Fox SXG-5007 [S] — 1962 — 30.00

THE LONG HOT SUMMER
- ❏ Roulette R-25026 [M] — 1958 — 75.00

LONG JOHN SILVER
- ❏ RCA Victor LPM-3279 [10] — 1954 — 300.00

THE LONG SHIPS
- ❏ Colpix CP-517 [M] — 1964 — 50.00
- ❏ Colpix SCP-517 [S] — 1964 — 60.00

LORD JIM
- ❏ Colpix CP-521 [M] — 1965 — 30.00
- ❏ Colpix SCP-521 [S] — 1965 — 40.00

LORD LOVE A DUCK
- ❏ United Artists UAL-4137 [M] — 1966 — 25.00
- ❏ United Artists UAS-5137 [S] — 1966 — 30.00

THE LORD OF THE RINGS
- ❏ Fantasy LOR-1 — 1978 — 25.00
- ❏ Fantasy LOR-PD2 — 1978 — 30.00
  — *Two picture discs*

THE LORDS OF FLATBUSH
- ❏ ABC ABCD-828 — 1974 — 30.00

A LOSS OF INNOCENCE
- ❏ Colpix CP-508 [M] — 1961 — 40.00

LOST ANGELS
- ❏ A&M SP-3926 — 1989 — 15.00
  — *Includes The Cure, Soundgarden, The Pogues, Soul Ayslum, Happy Mondays*

THE LOST BOYS
- ❏ Atlantic 81767 — 1987 — 12.00
  — *Includes INXS and Jimmy Barnes, Echo and the Bunnymen*

THE LOST CONTINENT
- ❏ MGM E-3635 [M] — 1957 — 200.00

LOVE IN 4 DIMENSIONS
- ❏ Request RLP-8090 [M] — 1966 — 30.00
- ❏ Request SRLP-8090 [S] — 1966 — 30.00

LOVE LIFE
- ❏ Heritage 600 [M] — 195? — 60.00

LOVERS AND OTHER STRANGERS
- ❏ ABC ABCS-OC-15 — 1970 — 25.00
- ❏ ABC SW-93479 — 1971 — 30.00
  — *Capitol Record Club edition*

M*A*S*H
- ❏ Columbia Masterworks OS3520 — 1970 — 25.00
  — *Original copies do not have the theme song done by Ahmad Jamal*
- ❏ Columbia Masterworks S32753 — 1973 — 12.00
  — *Reissue with the movie's theme performed by Ahmad Jamal*

MACARTHUR
- ❏ MCA 2287 — 1977 — 25.00

THE MAD ADVENTURES OF RABBI JACOB
- ❏ London PS652 — 1974 — 25.00
  — *Cover is intact with no cut-out markings*
- ❏ London PS652 — 1974 — 12.00
  — *Cover has cut-out markings (usually a hole punch or a cut-off corner)*

MADAME BOVARY
- ❏ MGM E-3507 [M] — 195? — 150.00

MADE IN USA
- ❏ Chrysalis OV41566 — 1987 — 12.00
  — *Includes Timbuk 3, World Party, Sonic Youth, Mojo Nixon & Skid Roper*

THE MAGIC CHRISTIAN
- ❏ Commonwealth United CU-6004 — 1970 — 30.00

MAGNIFICENT OBSESSION
- ❏ Decca DL8078 [M] — 1954 — 60.00
  — *Black label, gold print*
- ❏ Decca DL8078 [M] — 1955 — 50.00
  — *Black label, silver print*
- ❏ Decca DL8078 [M] — 196? — 30.00
  — *Black label with color bars*
- ❏ Varese Sarabande STV-81118 — 1981 — 15.00
  — *Reissue of Decca 8078*

MAJOR DUNDEE
- ❏ Columbia Masterworks OL6380 [M] — 1965 — 25.00
- ❏ Columbia Masterworks OS2780 [S] — 1965 — 30.00

MAJOR LEAGUE
- ❏ Curb 10402 — 1989 — 15.00
  — *Includes X, Beat Farmers, Lyle Lovett*

MALAMONDO
- ❏ Epic LN24126 [M] — 1964 — 30.00
- ❏ Epic BN26126 [S] — 1964 — 40.00

MALLRATS
- ❏ MCA 11294 — 1995 — 12.00
  — *Includes Weezer, Elastica, Belly, etc.*

MAME
- ❏ Warner Bros. W2773 — 1974 — 18.00
- ❏ Warner Bros. PRO580 [DJ] — 1973 — 50.00
  — *Promo-only gatefold edition with Lucille Ball in Christmas hat on the cover*

A MAN AND A WOMAN (UN HOMME ET UNE FEMME)
- ❏ United Artists UAL-4147 [M] — 1966 — 18.00
- ❏ United Artists UAS-5147 [S] — 1966 — 25.00
- ❏ United Artists SW-91032 [S] — 1967 — 30.00
  — *Capitol Record Club edition*

A MAN CALLED ADAM
- ❏ Reprise R6180 [M] — 1966 — 18.00
- ❏ Reprise RS6180 [S] — 1966 — 25.00

A MAN CALLED DAGGER
- ❏ MGM E-4516 [M] — 1967 — 18.00
- ❏ MGM SE-4516 [S] — 1967 — 25.00

A MAN CALLED FLINTSTONE
- ❏ Hanna-Barbera HLP-2055 [M] — 1967 — 100.00

A MAN COULD GET KILLED
- ❏ Decca DL4750 [M] — 1966 — 18.00
- ❏ Decca DL74750 [S] — 1966 — 25.00

Number	Title	Yr	NM

A MAN FOR ALL SEASONS
- ❑ RCA Victor VDM-116 [M] — 1966 — 30.00

MAN FROM SHAFT
- ❑ MGM SE-4836 — 1972 — 30.00

MANIAC
- ❑ Varese Sarabande STV-81143 — 1980 — 25.00

MAN IN THE MIDDLE
- ❑ 20th Century Fox TFM-3128 [M] — 1965 — 30.00
- ❑ 20th Century Fox TFS-4128 [S] — 1965 — 50.00

THE MAN OF A THOUSAND FACES
- ❑ Decca DL8623 [M] — 1957 — 50.00
  —*Black label, silver print, or pink label, black print promos*
- ❑ Decca DL8623 [M] — 196? — 30.00
  —*Black label with color bars*
- ❑ Varese Sarabande STV-81121 — 1981 — 15.00
  —*Reissue of Decca 8623*

MAN OF LA MANCHA
- ❑ United Artists UAS-9906 — 1972 — 25.00
  —*Cover is intact with no cut corners*
- ❑ United Artists UAS-9906 — 1972 — 12.00
  —*Cover has cut-out marking such as a cut-off corner*

THE MAN WHO WOULD BE KING
- ❑ Capitol SW-11474 — 1975 — 25.00

THE MAN WITH THE GOLDEN ARM
- ❑ Decca DL8257 [M] — 1956 — 40.00
- ❑ Decca DL78257 [R] — 196? — 25.00
- ❑ MCA 2043 [R] — 1973 — 12.00
  —*Reissue of Decca 78257; black label with rainbow*
- ❑ MCA 1528 — 198? — 10.00
  —*Reissue of MCA 2043*

THE MAN WITH THE GOLDEN GUN
- ❑ United Artists UA-LA358-G — 1974 — 25.00

MARACAIBO
- ❑ Decca DL8756 [M] — 1958 — 40.00
  —*Black label, silver print, or pink label, black print promos*
- ❑ Decca DL8756 [M] — 196? — 25.00
  —*Black label with color bars*

MARCO THE MAGNIFICENT
- ❑ Columbia Masterworks OS2870 [S] — 1966 — 40.00
- ❑ Columbia Masterworks OL6470 [M] — 1966 — 30.00

MARIE WARD
- ❑ Varese Sarabande STV-81268 — 1985 — 50.00

MARJORIE MORNINGSTAR
- ❑ RCA Victor LOC-1044 [M] — 1958 — 40.00
  —*RE" next to label number*
- ❑ RCA Victor LOC-1044 [M] — 1958 — 60.00
  —*An Original Soundtrack Recording" on spine*

MARRIED TO THE MOB
- ❑ Reprise 25763 — 1988 — 15.00
  —*Includes New Order, Sinead O'Connor, Chris Isaak, Debbie Harry, Brian Eno, The Feelies, Tom Tom Club*

MARRY ME, MARRY ME
- ❑ RCA Victor LSO-1160 — 1969 — 25.00

MARY, QUEEN OF SCOTS
- ❑ Decca DL79186 — 1972 — 30.00

MARY POPPINS
- ❑ Buena Vista BV-4026 [M] — 1964 — 15.00
  —*Originals have gatefold covers*
- ❑ Buena Vista STER-4026 [S] — 1964 — 18.00
  —*Originals have gatefold covers*
- ❑ Buena Vista STER-5005 [S] — 1973 — 12.00
  —*Reissue with new number and no gatefold*
- ❑ RCA Victor COP-111 [M] — 1964 — 18.00
  —*With gatefold; RCA Record Club edition*
- ❑ RCA Victor CSO-111 [S] — 1964 — 25.00
  —*With gatefold; RCA Record Club edition*

THE MASK
- ❑ Chaos 6455 [DJ] — 1994 — 25.00
  —*Generic cover; no other U.S. vinyl*

MASKED AND ANONYMOUS
- ❑ Columbia has CSK90618-1 — 2006 — 30.00
  —*Classic Records issue on 140-gram vinyl; CD issued in 2003*

MASTER OF THE WORLD
- ❑ Varese Sarabande VC-81070 — 1978 — 18.00
  —*Reissue of Vee Jay 4000*
- ❑ Vee Jay LP-4000 [M] — 1961 — 30.00
- ❑ Vee Jay SR-4000 [S] — 1961 — 40.00

MASTERS OF THE UNIVERSE
- ❑ Varese Sarabande STV-81333 — 1987 — 25.00

MCLINTOCK!
- ❑ United Artists UAL-4112 [M] — 1963 — 60.00
- ❑ United Artists UAS-5112 [S] — 1963 — 80.00

ME AND THE COLONEL
- ❑ RCA Victor LOC-1046 [M] — 1958 — 50.00

MEDITERRANEAN HOLIDAY
- ❑ London M-76003 [M] — 1964 — 50.00
- ❑ London MS-82003 [S] — 1964 — 80.00

MEET ME IN ST. LOUIS
- ❑ AEI 3101 — 1978 — 15.00
  —*Reissue of Decca LP*
- ❑ Decca DL8498 [M] — 1957 — 30.00
  —*LP reissue of 78 rpm album from 1944; B-side of LP is "The Harvey Girls.*

MEMORIES AUX BRUXELLES
- ❑ Carlton LP-112 [M] — 1959 — 30.00
- ❑ Carlton LP-12112 [S] — 1959 — 40.00

MENACE II SOCIETY
- ❑ Jive 41522 [DJ] — 1993 — 25.00
  —*Vinyl is promo only*

MEN IN WAR
- ❑ Imperial LP-9032W [M] — 1957 — 150.00

MERRY ANDREW
- ❑ Capitol T1016 [M] — 1958 — 50.00

MERRY CHRISTMAS, MR. LAWRENCE
- ❑ MCA 6125 — 1983 — 15.00
  —*Includes David Sylvian*
- ❑ MCA 6125 — 1983 — 12.00
  —*Music by Ryuichi Sakamoto. David Bowie stars in the movie, but does not sing on the LP.*

METROPOLIS
- ❑ Columbia JS39526 — 1984 — 12.00
  —*Includes Adam Ant*

MICKEY ONE
- ❑ MGM E-4312 [M] — 1965 — 25.00
- ❑ MGM SE-4312 [S] — 1965 — 30.00

MIDNIGHT COWBOY
- ❑ United Artists UAS-5198 — 1969 — 25.00

MIDNIGHT EXPRESS
- ❑ Casablanca NBLP-7114 — 1978 — 25.00

THE MIGHTY QUINN
- ❑ A&M SP-3924 — 1989 — 12.00
  —*Includes UB40, Yello*

A MILANESE STORY
- ❑ Atlantic 1388 [M] — 1962 — 25.00
- ❑ Atlantic SD1388 [S] — 1962 — 30.00

THE MINX
- ❑ Amsterdam 12007 — 1970 — 120.00

THE MISFITS
- ❑ United Artists UAL-4087 [M] — 1961 — 50.00
- ❑ United Artists UAS-5087 [S] — 1961 — 100.00
- ❑ United Artists UA-LA273-G [S] — 1974 — 15.00
  —*Reissue of 5087*

THE MISSOURI BREAKS
- ❑ MCA 25113 — 1986 — 12.00
  —*Reissue of United Artists UA-LA623-G*
- ❑ United Artists UA-LA623-G — 1976 — 30.00

MISS SADIE THOMPSON
- ❑ Mercury MG-25181 [10] — 1954 — 75.00
- ❑ Mercury MG-20123 [M] — 1956 — 150.00

MOBY DICK
- ❑ RCA Victor LPM-1247 [M] — 1956 — 120.00

MODERN GIRLS
- ❑ Warner Bros. 25526 — 1986 — 12.00
  —*Includes Depeche Mode, Toni Basil, Icehouse, The Jesus and Mary Chain*

MODERN TIMES
- ❑ United Artists UAL-4049 [M] — 1959 — 30.00
- ❑ United Artists UAS-5049 [R] — 196? — 25.00

MODESTY BLAISE
- ❑ 20th Century Fox TFM-3182 [M] — 1966 — 30.00
- ❑ 20th Century Fox TFS-4182 [S] — 1966 — 50.00

MOHAMMAD, MESSENGER OF GOD
- ❑ Namara 79001 — 1977 — 30.00

MONDO CANE
- ❑ United Artists UAL-4105 [M] — 1963 — 18.00
- ❑ United Artists UAS-5105 [S] — 1963 — 25.00

MONDO CANE NO. 2
- ❑ 20th Century Fox TFM-3147 [M] — 1964 — 30.00
- ❑ 20th Century Fox TFS-4147 [S] — 1964 — 40.00

MOON OVER PARADOR
- ❑ MCA 6249 — 1988 — 30.00

THE MOON SPINNERS
- ❑ Buena Vista BV-3323 [M] — 1964 — 40.00

MORE AMERICAN GRAFFITI
- ❑ MCA MCA2-11006 — 1979 — 25.00
  —*Tan labels*

MR. BUDDWING
- ❑ Verve V-8638 [M] — 1965 — 18.00
- ❑ Verve V6-8638 [S] — 1965 — 30.00

MR. MAGOO: 1001 ARABIAN NIGHTS
- ❑ Colpix CP-410 [M] — 1959 — 50.00
- ❑ Colpix SCP-410 [S] — 1959 — 150.00

MURDER INC.
- ❑ Canadian American CALP-1003 [M] — 1960 — 100.00

MUSCLE BEACH PARTY PLUS MERLIN JONES AND THE SCRAMBLED EGGHEAD
- ❑ Buena Vista BV-3314 [M] — 1964 — 60.00
- ❑ Buena Vista STER-3314 [S] — 1964 — 120.00

THE MUSIC MAN
- ❑ Warner Bros. B1459 [M] — 1962 — 18.00
- ❑ Warner Bros. BS1459 [S] — 1962 — 25.00
  —*Gold label originals*
- ❑ Warner Bros. BS1459 [S] — 1968 — 15.00
  —*Green label with "W7" box logo at top*
- ❑ Warner Bros. BS1459 [S] — 1970 — 12.00
  —*Green label with "WB" shield logo at top*
- ❑ Warner Bros. BS1459 [S] — 1973 — 10.00
  —*Burbank" palm trees label or later white label*

MUTINY ON THE BOUNTY
- ❑ MCA 25007 — 1986 — 10.00
  —*Reissue of MGM 1SE-4*
- ❑ MGM 1E-4 [M] — 1962 — 30.00
  —*Boxed set with book and painting*
- ❑ MGM S1E-4 [S] — 1962 — 40.00
  —*Boxed set with book and painting*
- ❑ MGM 1E-4 [M] — 196? — 15.00
  —*Standard cover*
- ❑ MGM S1E-4 [S] — 196? — 18.00
  —*Standard cover*

MY FAIR LADY
- ❑ Columbia Masterworks KOL8000 [M] — 1964 — 15.00
- ❑ Columbia Masterworks KOS2600 [S] — 1964 — 18.00

MY GEISHA
- ❑ RCA Victor LOC-1070 [M] — 1962 — 50.00
- ❑ RCA Victor LSO-1070 [S] — 1962 — 100.00

MY SIDE OF THE MOUNTAIN
- ❑ Capitol ST-245 — 1969 — 30.00

MY STEPMOTHER IS AN ALIEN
- ❑ Polydor 837798-1 — 1988 — 12.00
  —*Includes Animotion, M/A/R/R/S*

MY WILD IRISH ROSE
- ❑ RCA Victor LPM-3036 [10] — 1952 — 40.00

NAKED ANGELS
- ❑ Straight STS-1056 — 1969 — 30.00

THE NAKED MAJA
- ❑ United Artists UAL-4031 [M] — 1959 — 30.00
- ❑ United Artists UAS-5031 [S] — 1959 — 40.00

NANCY GOES TO RIO
- ❑ MGM F-508 [10] — 1950 — 60.00

NASHVILLE
- ❑ ABC ABCD-893 — 1975 — 25.00

NATIONAL LAMPOON'S ANIMAL HOUSE
- ❑ MCA 3046 — 1978 — 15.00
  —*Tan label original*
- ❑ MCA 3046 — 1980 — 12.00
  —*Blue label with rainbow*
- ❑ MCA 1692 — 198? — 10.00
  —*Reissue; blue label with rainbow*

NATIONAL LAMPOON'S VACATION
- ❑ Warner Bros. 23909 — 1983 — 25.00

NATIVE SON
- ❑ MCA 6198 — 1986 — 25.00

NAVAJO JOE
- ❑ United Artists UA-LA292-G — 1974 — 30.00

NED KELLY
- ❑ United Artists UAS-5213 — 1970 — 30.00
- ❑ United Artists UA-LA300-G — 1974 — 15.00
  —*Reissue of 5213*

NEVADA SMITH
- ❑ Dot DLP-3718 [M] — 1966 — 30.00
- ❑ Dot DLP-25718 [S] — 1966 — 40.00

THE NEVER ENDING STORY
- ❑ EMI America ST-17139 — 1984 — 25.00

NEVER ON SUNDAY
- ❑ United Artists UAL-4070 [M] — 1960 — 18.00
- ❑ United Artists UAS-5070 [S] — 1960 — 25.00
- ❑ United Artists SW-90834 [S] — 196? — 25.00
  —*Capitol Record Club edition*

THE NEW INTERNS
- ❑ Colpix CP-473 [M] — 1964 — 30.00
- ❑ Colpix SCP-473 [S] — 1964 — 40.00

Number	Title	Yr	NM

NEW JACK CITY
- ❏ Giant 24409 — 1991 — 15.00
  —*Includes Ice-T*

A NEW KIND OF LOVE
- ❏ Mercury MG-20859 [M] — 1963 — 18.00
- ❏ Mercury SR-60859 [S] — 1963 — 25.00

THE NEW MESSIAH
- ❏ Columbia KC31713 — 1972 — 25.00

NEW YORK STORIES
- ❏ Elektra Musician 60857 — 1988 — 15.00
  —*Includes Kid Creole and the Coconuts, Transvision Vamp*

NICHOLAS AND ALEXANDRA
- ❏ Bell 1103 — 1971 — 30.00

A NIGHT IN HEAVEN
- ❏ A&M SP-4966 — 1983 — 15.00
  —*Includes The English Beat*

A NIGHTMARE ON ELM STREET
- ❏ Varese Sarabande STV-81236 — 1984 — 18.00

A NIGHTMARE ON ELM STREET 2: FREDDY'S REVENGE
- ❏ Varese Sarabande STV-81275 — 1986 — 15.00

A NIGHTMARE ON ELM STREET 3: DREAM WARRIORS
- ❏ Varese Sarabande STV-81314 — 1987 — 18.00

A NIGHTMARE ON ELM STREET 4: THE DREAM MASTER
- ❏ Chrysalis R100504 — 1988 — 18.00
  —*BMG Direct Marketing edition*
- ❏ Chrysalis OV41673 — 1988 — 18.00
  —*Various-artists song collection*
- ❏ Varese Sarabande VS-5203 — 1988 — 18.00
  —*Orchestral and incidental music*

A NIGHTMARE ON ELM STREET 5: THE DREAM CHILD
- ❏ Jive 1258-1-J — 1989 — 15.00
  —*Various-artists song collection*

NIGHT OF THE GENERALS
- ❏ Colgems COMO-5002 [M] — 1967 — 40.00
- ❏ Colgems COSO-5002 [S] — 1967 — 70.00

THE NIGHT OF THE HUNTER
- ❏ RCA Victor LPM-1136 [M] — 1955 — 250.00

THE NIGHT THE LIGHTS WENT OUT IN GEORGIA
- ❏ Mirage SD16051 — 1981 — 12.00

9 1/2 WEEKS
- ❏ Capitol SV-12470 — 1986 — 12.00
- ❏ Capitol SV-512470 — 1986 — 18.00
  —*Columbia House edition*

NINE HOURS TO RAMA
- ❏ London M-76002 [M] — 1963 — 300.00

1969
- ❏ Polydor R100724 — 1988 — 12.00
  —*Includes Pretenders ("Windows of the World")*

9 TO 5
- ❏ 20th Century T-627 — 1980 — 12.00

NOTHING BUT THE BEST
- ❏ Colpix CP-477 [M] — 1964 — 25.00
- ❏ Colpix SCP-477 [S] — 1964 — 30.00

NOT WITH MY WIFE, YOU DON'T
- ❏ Warner Bros. W1668 [M] — 1966 — 18.00
- ❏ Warner Bros. WS1668 [S] — 1966 — 25.00

NO WAY TO TREAT A LADY
- ❏ Dot DLP-25846 — 1968 — 30.00

A NUN'S STORY
- ❏ Warner Bros. B1306 [M] — 1959 — 60.00
- ❏ Warner Bros. BS1306 [S] — 1959 — 100.00

O BROTHER, WHERE ART THOU?
- ❏ Lost Highway 088170069-1 — 2003 — 25.00

OBSESSION
- ❏ London Phase 4 SPC-21160 — 1976 — 30.00

OCTOPUSSY
- ❏ A&M SP-4967 — 1983 — 25.00

THE ODD COUPLE
- ❏ Dot DLP-25862 — 1968 — 25.00

ODDS AGAINST TOMORROW
- ❏ United Artists UAL-4061 [M] — 1959 — 30.00
- ❏ United Artists UAS-5061 [S] — 1959 — 50.00

OF LOVE AND DESIRE
- ❏ 20th Century Fox FXG-5014 [M] — 1963 — 30.00
- ❏ 20th Century Fox SXG-5014 [S] — 1963 — 30.00

OH, ROSALINDA!
- ❏ Mercury MG-20145 [M] — 1957 — 50.00

OH DAD, POOR DAD, MAMMA'S HUNG YOU IN THE CLOSET AND I'M FEELIN' SO SAD
- ❏ RCA Victor LPM-3750 [M] — 1967 — 25.00
- ❏ RCA Victor LSP-3750 [S] — 1967 — 30.00

OIL TOWN, U.S.A.
- ❏ RCA Victor LFM-2000 [10] — 1953 — 60.00

OKLAHOMA!
- ❏ Capitol WAO595 [M] — 1955 — 30.00
  —*Purple or dark red label*
- ❏ Capitol WAO595 [M] — 1956 — 25.00
  —*Gray label*
- ❏ Capitol WAO595 [M] — 1959 — 18.00
  —*Black colorband label, logo at left*
- ❏ Capitol WAO595 [M] — 1962 — 15.00
  —*Black colorband label, logo at top*
- ❏ Capitol SWAO595 [S] — 1959 — 25.00
  —*Black colorband label, logo at left*
- ❏ Capitol SWAO595 [S] — 1962 — 18.00
  —*Black colorband label, logo at top*
- ❏ Capitol SWAO595 [S] — 1969 — 15.00
  —*Lime green label*
- ❏ Capitol SWAO595 [S] — 1973 — 12.00
  —*Orange label*

OLD BOYFRIENDS
- ❏ Columbia Masterworks JS36072 — 1979 — 50.00

THE OLD MAN AND THE SEA
- ❏ Columbia CL1183 [M] — 1958 — 30.00
- ❏ Columbia CS8013 [S] — 1958 — 60.00

OLD YELLER
- ❏ Disneyland WDL-3024 [M] — 1957 — 50.00
  —*First edition*
- ❏ Disneyland WDL-1024 [M] — 1960 — 40.00
  —*Second edition*
- ❏ Disneyland 1024 [M] — 1974 — 30.00
  —*Reissue with no prefix*

OLIVER AND COMPANY
- ❏ Disney 64101 — 1988 — 30.00

ONCE UPON A TIME IN THE WEST
- ❏ RCA Victor LSP-4736 — 1969 — 30.00

THE ONE AND ONLY, GENUINE, ORIGINAL FAMILY BAND
- ❏ Buena Vista BV-5002 [M] — 1968 — 18.00
- ❏ Buena Vista STER-5002 [S] — 1968 — 25.00

THE ONE-EYED JACKS
- ❏ Liberty LOM-16001 [M] — 1961 — 30.00
- ❏ Liberty LOS-17001 [S] — 1961 — 50.00

ONE FLEW OVER THE CUCKOO'S NEST
- ❏ Fantasy F-9500 — 1975 — 25.00
- ❏ Fantasy MPF-4531 — 198? — 12.00
  —*Budget-line reissue of 9500*

101 DALMATIONS
- ❏ Disneyland ST-4903 [M] — 1963 — 150.00
  —*Gatefold cover with pop-up scene in center*
- ❏ Disneyland ST-3931 [M] — 1965 — 40.00
- ❏ Disneyland DQ-1308 [M] — 1966 — 25.00
- ❏ Disneyland ST-1908 [M] — 1960 — 30.00

ON HER MAJESTY'S SECRET SERVICE
- ❏ United Artists UAS-5204 — 1969 — 25.00
- ❏ United Artists UA-LA299-G — 1974 — 15.00
  —*Reissue of 5204*

ON THE BEACH
- ❏ Roulette R-25098 [M] — 1959 — 80.00
- ❏ Roulette SR-25098 [S] — 1959 — 150.00

THE OPTIMISTS
- ❏ Paramount PAS-1015 — 1973 — 30.00

ORCHESTRA WIVES
- ❏ RCA Victor LPT-3065 [10] — 1954 — 60.00

THE OSCAR
- ❏ Columbia Masterworks OL6550 [M] — 1966 — 25.00
- ❏ Columbia Masterworks OS2950 [S] — 1966 — 30.00

OTLEY
- ❏ Colgems COS-112 — 1969 — 30.00

OUR MAN FLINT
- ❏ 20th Century Fox TFM-3179 [M] — 1966 — 40.00
- ❏ 20th Century Fox TFS-4179 [S] — 1966 — 60.00

OUTLAND
- ❏ Warner Bros. HS3551 — 1981 — 30.00

OUTLAW BLUES
- ❏ Capitol ST-11691 — 1977 — 18.00

THE OUTLAW JOSEY WALES
- ❏ Warner Bros. BS2956 — 1976 — 30.00

THE OUTLAW RIDERS
- ❏ MGM 1SE-26 — 1970 — 25.00

OUT OF AFRICA
- ❏ MCA 6158 — 1985 — 25.00
- ❏ MCA 11327 — 1995 — 25.00
  —*Limited edition on "Heavy Vinyl"*

OUT OF SIGHT
- ❏ Decca DL4751 [M] — 1966 — 25.00
- ❏ Decca DL74751 [S] — 1966 — 30.00

OVER THE EDGE
- ❏ Warner Bros. HS3335 — 1979 — 12.00
  —*Includes The Ramones, The Cars*

PAGAN LOVE SONG
- ❏ MGM E-534 [M] — 1950 — 40.00

PAINT YOUR WAGON
- ❏ MCA 37099 — 198? — 10.00
  —*Reissue of Paramount 1001*
- ❏ Paramount PMS-1001 — 1969 — 25.00
  —*With booklet*

THE PAJAMA GAME
- ❏ Columbia Masterworks OL5210 [M] — 1957 — 30.00
  —*Gray and black label with six "eye" logos*

PAL JOEY
- ❏ Capitol W912 [M] — 1957 — 25.00
  —*Gray label*
- ❏ Capitol W912 [M] — 1959 — 18.00
  —*Black colorband label, logo at left*
- ❏ Capitol W912 [M] — 1962 — 15.00
  —*Black colorband label, logo on top*
- ❏ Capitol DW912 [R] — 196? — 12.00
  —*Black colorband label*
- ❏ Capitol SM-912 [R] — 1977 — 10.00
  —*Reissue with new prefix*

PANIC BUTTON
- ❏ Musicor MM-2026 [M] — 1964 — 80.00
- ❏ Musicor MS-3026 [S] — 1964 — 120.00

PAPER MOON
- ❏ Paramount PAS-1012 — 1973 — 25.00

PAPER TIGER
- ❏ Capitol SW-11475 — 1975 — 25.00

PAPILLON
- ❏ Capitol ST-11260 — 1973 — 25.00

THE PARENT TRAP!
- ❏ Buena Vista BV-3309 [M] — 1961 — 40.00
- ❏ Buena Vista STER-3309 [S] — 1961 — 60.00
  —*B-side of the above two: Camerata Conducts Themes from Great Motion Pictures*

PARIS BLUES
- ❏ United Artists UAL-4092 [M] — 1961 — 30.00
- ❏ United Artists UAS-5092 [S] — 1961 — 30.00

PARIS HOLIDAY
- ❏ United Artists UAL-4001 [M] — 1958 — 50.00

PARIS WHEN IT SIZZLES
- ❏ Reprise R6113 [M] — 1964 — 30.00
- ❏ Reprise RS6113 [S] — 1964 — 40.00

PARRISH
- ❏ Warner Bros. W1413 [M] — 1961 — 30.00
- ❏ Warner Bros. WS1413 [S] — 1961 — 80.00
  —*B-side of the above two: Popular Piano Concertos by George Greeley*

PARTY PARTY
- ❏ A&M SP-3212 — 1982 — 18.00
  —*Includes Elvis Costello, Dave Edmunds ("Run Rudolph Run"), Bananarama, Midge Ure, Bad Manners, etc.*

A PATCH OF BLUE
- ❏ Mainstream 56068 [M] — 1965 — 25.00
- ❏ Mainstream S-6068 [S] — 1965 — 30.00
- ❏ Mainstream ST-90805 [S] — 1965 — 30.00
  —*Capitol Record Club edition*

PATTON
- ❏ 20th Century Fox S-4208 — 1970 — 25.00

PATTY
- ❏ Stang 1026 — 1976 — 25.00

PENELOPE
- ❏ MGM E-4426 [M] — 1966 — 25.00
- ❏ MGM SE-4426 [S] — 1966 — 30.00

PENTHOUSE
- ❏ United Artists UAL-4170 [M] — 1967 — 25.00
- ❏ United Artists UAS-5170 [S] — 1967 — 25.00

THE PEOPLE NEXT DOOR
- ❏ Avco AV-11002 — 1970 — 30.00

PEPE
- ❏ Colpix CP-507 [M] — 1960 — 25.00
- ❏ Colpix SCP-507 [S] — 1960 — 30.00

PERFECT
- ❏ Arista R163614 — 1985 — 15.00
  —*Includes Wham! ("Wham Rap")*

Number	Title	Yr	NM
❏ Arista AL98278		1985	12.00
—Includes Wham! ("Wham Rap")			

PERFORMANCE
❏ Warner Bros. WS1846		1970	1500.00
—Original issue; has a completely different cover to the more common 2554			
❏ Warner Bros. BS2554		1970	25.00
—Second issue			

PERMANENT RECORD
❏ Epic E40879		198?	15.00
—Includes Joe Strummer (5 tracks), Lou Reed, The Stranglers			

PETE KELLY'S BLUES
❏ Columbia CL690 [M]		1955	40.00
❏ Decca DL8166 [M]		1955	50.00
—Black label, silver print			

PETE'S DRAGON
❏ Capitol SW-11704		1977	25.00

PET SEMATARY
❏ Varese Sarabande VS-5227		1989	18.00

PETULIA
❏ Warner Bros. WS1755		1968	30.00

PEYTON PLACE
❏ RCA Victor LOC-1042 [M]		1958	30.00
—"Long Play" at bottom of label			
❏ RCA Victor LOC-1042 [M]		1965	30.00
—"Monaural" at bottom of label			
❏ RCA Victor LSO-1042 [S]		1958	100.00
—"Living Stereo" at bottom of label			
❏ RCA Victor LSO-1042 [S]		1965	60.00
—"Stereo" at bottom of label			

PHAEDRA
❏ United Artists UAL-4102 [M]		1962	25.00
❏ United Artists UAS-5102 [S]		1962	30.00

THE PHILADELPHIA EXPERIMENT
❏ Rhino RNSP-306		1984	30.00

PICNIC
❏ Decca DL8320 [M]		1956	30.00
—Black label, silver print			
❏ Decca DL8320 [M]		196?	18.00
—Black label with color bars			
❏ Decca DL78320 [S]		1959	30.00
—Maroon or all-black label			
❏ Decca DL78320 [S]		196?	18.00
—Black label with color bars			
❏ MCA 2049		1973	12.00
—Reissue of Decca 78320; black label with rainbow			
❏ MCA 1527		198?	10.00
—Reissue of 2049			

A PIECE OF THE ACTION
❏ Curtom CU5019		1977	25.00

PINK CADILLAC
❏ Warner Bros. 25922		1989	12.00

PINOCCHIO
❏ Disneyland WDL 4002 [M]		1956	250.00
—Original edition			
❏ Disneyland ST-4905 [M]		1963	150.00
—Gatefold cover with pop-up center graphics			
❏ Disneyland DQ-1202 [M]		1959	30.00
—Second edition			
❏ Disneyland DQ-1202MO [M]		1963	25.00
—Third edition			
❏ Disneyland 3102 [PD]		1981	30.00
—"Disney Picture Disc" edition			

PIRANHA
❏ Varese Sarabande STV-81126		1979	25.00

THE PIRATE
❏ MGM E-21 [10]		1951	70.00

PLANET OF THE APES
❏ Project 3 PR-5023SD		1968	30.00
—Gatefold cover			
❏ Project 3 PR-5023SD		1968	25.00
—Regular cover			

PLAYING FOR KEEPS
❏ Atlantic 81678		1986	12.00
—Includes Arcadia			

THE PLEASURE SEEKERS
❏ RCA Victor LOC-1101 [M]		1964	50.00
❏ RCA Victor LSO-1101 [S]		1964	100.00

POLLYANNA
❏ Disneyland ST-1906 [M]		1960	50.00
❏ Disneyland DQ-1307 [M]		1967	30.00

POLTERGEIST
❏ MGM MG-1-5408		1982	40.00

POLTERGEIST III
❏ Varese Sarabande 704.620		1988	80.00

PORGY AND BESS
❏ Columbia Masterworks OL5410 [M]		1959	18.00
❏ Columbia Masterworks OS2016 [S]		1959	25.00

PORKY'S REVENGE
❏ Columbia CAS2034 [DJ]		1985	15.00
—Promo-only sampler; includes Dave Edmunds, Jeff Beck and George Harrison			
❏ Columbia JS39983		1985	15.00
—Includes Dave Edmunds			

THE POWER
❏ Cerberus CST-0211		1984	25.00

PRET-A-PORTER
❏ Miramax CAS6700 [DJ]		1994	30.00
—Promo only vinyl			

PRETTY BOY FLOYD
❏ Audio Fidelity AFLP-1936 [M]		1960	60.00
❏ Audio Fidelity AFSD-5936 [S]		1960	80.00

PRETTY IN PINK
❏ A&M R144487		1986	12.00
—Includes Orchestral Manoeuvres in the Dark ("If You Leave"); Psychedelic Furs ("Pretty in Pink"); etc.			

PRETTY WOMAN
❏ EMI E1-93492		1990	15.00
—Includes David Bowie, Go West, Red Hot Chili Peppers, Jane Wiedlin			

THE PRIDE AND THE PASSION
❏ Capitol W873 [M]		1957	60.00

THE PRINCESS BRIDE
❏ Warner Bros. 25610		1987	25.00

THE PRISONER OF ZENDA
❏ United Artists UA-LA374-G		1974	25.00

PRIVATE HELL 36
❏ Coral CRL56122 [10]		1954	100.00

THE PRODUCERS
❏ RCA Victor LPM-4008 [M]		1968	50.00
❏ RCA Victor LSP-4008 [S]		1968	30.00
❏ RCA Victor ANL1-1132		1975	12.00
—Reissue of LSP-4008			

THE PROFESSIONALS
❏ Colgems COMO-5001 [M]		1966	60.00
❏ Colgems COSO-5001 [S]		1966	150.00

A PROMISE AT DAWN
❏ Polydor 24-5502		1970	30.00

THE PROPER TIME
❏ Contemporary M-3587 [M]		1960	30.00
❏ Contemporary S 7587 [S]		1960	40.00

PROVIDENCE
❏ DRG SL-9502		1977	25.00

PRUDENCE AND THE PILL
❏ 20th Century Fox S 4199		1968	25.00

PSYCHO II
❏ MCA 6119		1983	25.00

Q THE WINGED SERPENT
❏ Cerberus CST-0206		1983	25.00

QUEST FOR FIRE
❏ RCA Victor ABL1-4274		1982	25.00

THE QUIET MAN
❏ Decca DL5411 [10]		1952	120.00

THE QUILLER MEMORANDUM
❏ Columbia Masterworks OL6660 [M]		1966	30.00
❏ Columbia Masterworks OS3060 [S]		1966	60.00

QUO VADIS?
❏ MCA 39075		198?	10.00
—Reissue of MGM 3524			
❏ MGM E-103 [10]		1951	40.00
—Music soundtrack only			
❏ MGM E-134 [10]		1951	60.00
—Box set of two discs; includes dialogue			
❏ MGM E-3524 [M]		1957	30.00
—Yellow label; has both music and dialogue			

RAGTIME
❏ Elektra 5E-565		1981	25.00

RAIDERS OF THE LOST ARK
❏ Columbia JS37373		1981	15.00
—Original issue; music only			
❏ Columbia JS37696		1981	15.00
—Music and dialogue			
❏ DCC Compact Classics LPZ 2-2009		1995	30.00
—Audiophile edition; includes music not on other releases of the soundtrack			

Number	Title	Yr	NM
❏ Polydor 821583-1		1984	12.00
—Reissue			

THE RAILWAY CHILDREN
❏ Capitol SW-871		1972	25.00

THE RAINMAKER
❏ RCA Victor LPM-1434 [M]		1956	100.00

RAINTREE COUNTY
❏ RCA Victor LOC-6000 [M]		1957	120.00
❏ RCA Victor LOC-1038 [M]		1958	30.00
❏ RCA Victor LSO-1038 [S]		1958	50.00

RAN
❏ Fantasy FSP-21004		1985	25.00

THE RAT RACE
❏ Dot DLP-3306 [M]		1960	40.00
❏ Dot DLP-25306 [S]		1960	50.00

RED DAWN
❏ Intrada RVF-6001		1985	40.00

RED GARTERS
❏ Columbia CL6282 [10]		1954	50.00

RED HEAT
❏ Virgin Movie Music 90891		1988	30.00

THE RED PONY
❏ Columbia Masterworks ML5983 [M]		196?	30.00
❏ Columbia Masterworks MS6583 [R]		196?	30.00
❏ Varese Sarabande STV-81259		1986	30.00

REDS
❏ Columbia Masterworks BJS37960		1981	25.00

THE RED TENT
❏ Paramount PAS-6019		1971	30.00

RENT-A-COP
❏ Intrada MAS-7002		1988	25.00

THE REPORTER
❏ Columbia CL2269 [M]		1963	30.00
❏ Columbia CS9069 [S]		1963	40.00

THE RESCUERS
❏ Disneyland ST-3816		1977	25.00

RETURN OF SUPERFLY
❏ Capitol C1-94244		1990	15.00
—Includes Ice-T			

RETURN TO PARADISE
❏ Decca DL5489 [10]		1953	200.00

THE REVOLUTION
❏ United Artists UAS-5185		1968	30.00
❏ United Artists UA-LA296-G		1974	15.00
—Reissue of 5185			

RHAPSODY OF STEEL
❏ U.S. Steel JB-502/3		1958	100.00

RICH, YOUNG AND PRETTY
❏ MGM E-86 [10]		1951	40.00

RIDER ON THE RAIN
❏ Capitol ST-584		1970	30.00

RIKKI AND PETE
❏ DRG SBL-12593		1988	15.00
—Includes Crowded House			

RIOT ON SUNSET STRIP
❏ Tower T5065 [M]		1967	25.00
❏ Tower DT5065 [R]		1967	30.00

ROADIE
❏ Warner Bros. 2HS3441		1980	18.00
—Includes Blondie			

ROAD TO HONG KONG
❏ Liberty LOM-16002 [M]		1962	25.00
❏ Liberty LOS-17002 [S]		1962	40.00

THE ROBE
❏ Decca DL9012 [M]		1953	30.00
—Maroon label			
❏ Decca DL79012 [R]		196?	15.00
❏ MCA 1529		198?	10.00
—Reissue of MCA 2052			
❏ MCA 2052		1973	12.00
—Reissue of Decca 79012; black label with rainbow			

ROBIN AND THE SEVEN HOODS
❏ Reprise F2021 [M]		1964	50.00
❏ Reprise FS2021 [S]		1964	60.00

ROBIN HOOD
❏ Disneyland ST-3810		1973	30.00

ROCK, PRETTY BABY
❏ Decca DL8429 [M]		1957	120.00
—Black label, silver print; also includes pink label promo			
❏ Decca DL8429 [M]		196?	30.00
—Black label with color bars			

Number	Title	Yr	NM
ROCK, ROCK, ROCK			
❑ Chess LP-1425 [M]		1958	200.00
❑ (no label) (no #) [M]		1958	1500.00
— Demo version, 20 tracks			
ROCK ALL NIGHT			
❑ Mercury MG-20293 [M]		1957	100.00
ROCK 'N' ROLL HIGH SCHOOL			
❑ Sire QSR-6070		1980	18.00
— Includes The Ramones (title song), Devo			
ROMANCE OF A HORSETHIEF			
❑ Allied Artists AAS-110-100		1971	50.00
ROME ADVENTURE			
❑ Warner Bros. W1458 [M]		1962	25.00
❑ Warner Bros. WS1458 [S]		1962	30.00
ROMEO AND JULIET			
❑ Capitol SWDR-289		1969	30.00
— From the 1968 Franco Zeffirelli remake; contains dialogue and music			
❑ Capitol ST-2993		1968	15.00
— From the 1968 Franco Zeffirelli remake; contains the music; black label with colorband			
❑ Capitol ST-400		1970	18.00
— From the 1968 Franco Zeffirelli remake; edited version of 289			
❑ Epic LC3126 [M]		1954	60.00
❑ Epic FLM13104 [M]		1966	30.00
— Reissue of 3126			
❑ Epic FLS15104 [R]		1966	30.00
ROOTS OF HEAVEN			
❑ 20th Fox FOX-3005 [M]		1958	300.00
ROSE MARIE			
❑ MGM E-229 [10]		1954	40.00
ROSEMARY'S BABY			
❑ Dot DLP-25875		1968	25.00
THE ROSE TATTOO			
❑ Columbia CL727 [M]		1955	50.00
THE ROYAL WEDDING			
❑ MGM E-543 [10]		1951	50.00
THE RULING CLASS			
❑ Avco AV-11003		1972	30.00
RUMBLE FISH			
❑ A&M SP-6-4983		1983	12.00
— Includes Stewart Copeland (ex-Police)			
RUN, ANGEL, RUN			
❑ Epic BN26474		1969	25.00
THE RUN OF THE ARROW			
❑ Decca DL8620 [M]		1957	60.00
— Black label, silver print, or pink label, black print promo			
❑ Decca DL8620 [M]		196?	30.00
— Black label with color bars			
RUN WILD, RUN FREE			
❑ SGC SD5003		1969	25.00
RUSTLERS' RHAPSODY			
❑ Warner Bros. 25284		1985	12.00
RYAN'S DAUGHTER			
❑ MGM 1SE-27		1970	30.00
SACCO AND VANZETTI			
❑ RCA Victor LSP-4612		1971	25.00
THE SACRED IDOL			
❑ Capitol T1293 [M]		1960	30.00
❑ Capitol ST1293 [S]		1960	30.00
THE SAINT			
❑ Virgin SPRO-12261 [DJ]		1997	30.00
SAINT JOAN			
❑ Capitol W865 [M]		1957	30.00
SALLAH			
❑ Philips PHM200177 [M]		1965	25.00
❑ Philips PHS600177 [S]		1965	30.00
SALOME			
❑ Decca DL6026 [10]		1953	120.00
SALVATION			
❑ Giant GR-16002		1988	15.00
— Includes New Order, Cabaret Voltaire			
SAMSON AND DELILAH			
❑ Decca DL6007 [10]		1952	60.00
THE SAND CASTLE			
❑ Columbia CL1455 [M]		1961	18.00
❑ Columbia CS8249 [S]		1961	25.00
THE SAND PEBBLES			
❑ 20th Century Fox 3189 [M]		1966	30.00
❑ 20th Century Fox S-4189 [S]		1966	50.00

Number	Title	Yr	NM
THE SANDPIPER			
❑ Mercury MG-21032 [M]		1965	30.00
❑ Mercury SR-61032 [S]		1965	30.00
SANTA AND THE 3 BEARS			
❑ Mr. Pickwick SPC1501		196?	25.00
— With "Santa" cutout intact			
SANTA CLAUS THE MOVIE			
❑ EMI America SJ-17177		1985	12.00
SATAN IN HIGH HEELS			
❑ Charlie Parker PLP-406 [M]		1962	50.00
— Gatefold cover			
❑ Charlie Parker PLP-406S [S]		1962	60.00
— Gatefold cover			
❑ Charlie Parker PLP-406 [M]		1962	30.00
— Standard cover			
❑ Charlie Parker PLP-406S [S]		1962	40.00
— Standard cover			
SATAN'S SADISTS			
❑ Smash SRS-67127		1969	30.00
SATURDAY NIGHT FEVER			
❑ RSO RS-2-4001		1977	18.00
— First editions have the studio version of "Jive Talkin'" by the Bee Gees on side 3			
❑ RSO RS-2-4001		1978	15.00
— Later editions have a live version of "Jive Talkin'" by the Bee Gees on side 3 ("REV" is in the Side 3 trail-off wax)			
❑ RSO 825389-1		198?	12.00
— Reissue with new number			
SATURDAY NIGHT FEVER/GREASE			
❑ RSO RPO1011 [DJ]		1978	30.00
— Side 1 has "The Best of Saturday Night Fever" (side 1 of original LP); Side 2 has "The Best of Grease" (side 1 of original LP)			
THE SAVAGE SEVEN			
❑ Atco 33-245 [M]		1968	30.00
❑ Atco SD 33-245 [S]		1968	30.00
SAVAGE WILD			
❑ American Int'l. STA-1032		1970	25.00
SAYONARA			
❑ RCA Victor LOC-1041 [M]		1957	50.00
❑ RCA Victor LSO-1041 [S]		1957	70.00
SAY ONE FOR ME			
❑ Columbia CL1337 [M]		1959	40.00
❑ Columbia CS8147 [S]		1959	80.00
THE SCALPHUNTERS			
❑ MCA 25042		1986	12.00
— Reissue of United Artists 5176			
❑ United Artists UAL-4176 [M]		1968	30.00
❑ United Artists UAS-5176 [S]		1968	40.00
SCARFACE			
❑ MCA 6126		1984	25.00
THE SCARLET AND THE BLACK			
❑ Cerberus CEM-0120		1983	30.00
SCENT OF MYSTERY			
❑ Ramrod T-6001 [M]		1960	50.00
❑ Ramrod T-6001 [S]		1960	100.00
SCROOGE			
❑ Columbia Masterworks S30258		1970	30.00
❑ Columbia Special Products P14077		1977	15.00
— Special Products reissue			
SCROOGED			
❑ A&M SP-3921		1988	12.00
— Includes the following Christmas songs:			
SEARCH FOR PARADISE			
❑ RCA Victor LOC-1034 [M]		1957	40.00
SEASIDE SWINGERS			
❑ Mercury MG-21031 [M]		1965	25.00
❑ Mercury SR-61031 [S]		1965	30.00
SEBASTIAN			
❑ Dot DLP-3845 [M]		1968	50.00
❑ Dot DLP-25845 [S]		1968	25.00
THE SECRET OF SANTA VITTORIA			
❑ MCA 25034		1986	12.00
— Reissue of United Artists 5200			
❑ United Artists UAS-5200		1969	30.00
SERGEANTS 3			
❑ Reprise R-2013 [M]		1962	30.00
❑ Reprise RS-2013 [S]		1962	50.00
THE SERPENT AND THE RAINBOW			
❑ Varese Sarabande STV-81362		1988	40.00
SERPICO			
❑ Paramount PAS-1016		1973	30.00
SEVEN BRIDES FOR SEVEN BROTHERS			
❑ MGM E-244 [10]		1954	40.00

Number	Title	Yr	NM
SEVEN GOLDEN MEN			
❑ United Artists UAS-5193		1969	30.00
THE SEVEN LITTLE FOYS			
❑ RCA Victor LPM-3275 [10]		1955	70.00
1776			
❑ Columbia S31741		1972	25.00
THE 7TH DAWN			
❑ United Artists UAL-4115 [M]		1964	30.00
❑ United Artists UAS-5115 [S]		1964	40.00
THE SEVENTH DAWN			
❑ United Artists UAL-4115 [M]		1964	30.00
❑ United Artists UAS-5115 [S]		1964	40.00
THE 7TH VOYAGE OF SINBAD			
❑ Colpix CP-504 [M]		1958	200.00
❑ Varese Sarabande STV-81135		1983	25.00
SEX AND THE SINGLE GIRL			
❑ Warner Bros. W1572 [M]		1964	18.00
❑ Warner Bros. WS1572 [S]		1964	25.00
SHAFT IN AFRICA			
❑ ABC ABCX-793		1973	30.00
SHAFT'S BIG SCORE			
❑ MGM 1SE-36		1972	30.00
SHAG			
❑ Sire 25800		1989	12.00
— Includes k.d. lang, Chris Isaak			
SHAKE HANDS WITH THE DEVIL			
❑ United Artists UAL-4043 [M]		1959	30.00
❑ United Artists UAS-5043 [S]		1959	50.00
SHALAKO			
❑ Philips PHS600286		1968	30.00
SHEBA BABY			
❑ Buddah BDS-5634		1975	30.00
SHE-DEVIL			
❑ Polydor 841583-1		1989	30.00
SHENANDOAH			
❑ Decca DL9125 [M]		1965	30.00
❑ Decca DL79125 [S]		1965	40.00
SHE'S OUT OF CONTROL			
❑ MCA 6281		1989	12.00
— Includes Oingo Boingo			
THE SHINING			
❑ Warner Bros. HS3449		1980	25.00
THE SHOP ON MAIN STREET			
❑ Mainstream 56082 [M]		1966	30.00
❑ Mainstream S-6082 [S]		1966	40.00
SHORT EYES			
❑ Curtom CU5017		1977	30.00
THE SHOW			
❑ Def Jam 529021-1		1995	15.00
— Includes L.L. Cool J, etc.			
SHOW BOAT			
❑ MGM E-559 [10]		1951	30.00
THE SICILIAN CLAN			
❑ 20th Century Fox S-4209		1970	50.00
SID & NANCY			
❑ MCA 6181		1986	12.00
— Includes Joe Strummer (ex-Clash), John Cale, The Pogues, Steve Jones (ex-Pistols)			
THE SIDEHACKERS			
❑ Amaret ST-5004		1969	25.00
THE SILENCERS			
❑ RCA Victor LOC-1120 [M]		1966	30.00
❑ RCA Victor LSO-1120 [S]		1966	50.00
SILENT RUNNING			
❑ Decca DL79188		1972	40.00
❑ Varese Sarabande STV-81072		1980	18.00
— Reissue			
SILK STOCKINGS			
❑ MCA 39074		198?	12.00
— Reissue			
❑ MGM E-3542 [M]		1957	30.00
SILVERADO			
❑ Geffen GHS24080		1985	25.00
SINGIN' IN THE RAIN			
❑ MCA 39044		198?	12.00
❑ Metro M-599 [M]		1966	18.00
— Reissue of MGM LP			
❑ Metro MS-599 [R]		1966	15.00
❑ MGM E-113 [10]		1952	30.00
SINGLE ROOM FURNISHED			
❑ Sidewalk ST-5917		1968	40.00

Number	Title	Yr	NM

THE 633 SQUADRON
- ❏ United Artists UA-LA305-G — 1974 — 30.00

SKATEDANCER
- ❏ Mira LP-3004 [M] — 1966 — 25.00
- ❏ Mira LPS-3004 [S] — 1966 — 30.00

SKI ON THE WILD SIDE
- ❏ MGM E-4439 [M] — 1967 — 30.00
- ❏ MGM SE-4439 [S] — 1967 — 50.00

SLAUGHTERHOUSE-FIVE
- ❏ Columbia Masterworks S31333 — 1972 — 30.00

SLAUGHTER ON 10TH AVENUE
- ❏ Decca DL8657 [M] — 1957 — 30.00
  — *Black label, silver print*
- ❏ Decca DL78657 [S] — 1957 — 30.00
  — *Black label, silver print*
- ❏ Decca DL8657 [M] — 1960 — 15.00
  — *Black label with color bars*
- ❏ Decca DL78657 [S] — 1960 — 18.00
  — *Black label with color bars*

SLAVES
- ❏ Skye SK-11 — 1969 — 30.00

THE SLAVE TRADE IN THE WORLD TODAY
- ❏ London M-76006 [M] — 1964 — 200.00

SLEEPING BEAUTY
- ❏ Disneyland WDL-4018 [M] — 1959 — 30.00
- ❏ Disneyland STER-4018 [S] — 1959 — 40.00
- ❏ Disneyland STER-4036 [S] — 1970 — 25.00
  — *Reissue of STER-4018*

SLEUTH
- ❏ Columbia Masterworks S32154 — 1973 — 25.00

SLIPPERY WHEN WET
- ❏ World Pacific WP-1265 [M] — 1959 — 50.00

SLUMBER PARTY '57
- ❏ Mercury SRM-1-1097 — 1976 — 30.00

A SMASHING TIME
- ❏ ABC ABC-OC-6 [M] — 1967 — 25.00
- ❏ ABC ABCS-OC-6 [S] — 1967 — 30.00
- ❏ ABC SW-91399 [S] — 1967 — 30.00
  — *Capitol Record Club edition*

SMOKEY AND THE BANDIT
- ❏ MCA 2099 — 1977 — 15.00

SMOKEY AND THE BANDIT 2
- ❏ MCA 6101 — 1980 — 12.00

SMOKEY AND THE BANDIT 3
- ❏ MCA 36006 — 1983 — 12.00

SNOOPY COME HOME
- ❏ Columbia Masterworks S31451 — 1972 — 25.00

THE SNOW QUEEN
- ❏ Decca DL8977 [M] — 1959 — 40.00
- ❏ Decca DL78977 [S] — 1959 — 60.00

SNOW WHITE AND THE SEVEN DWARFS
- ❏ Buena Vista 102 — 1975 — 50.00
  — *Entire movie on three LPs; TV mail-order item*
- ❏ Disneyland WDL-4005 [M] — 1956 — 200.00
  — *Gatefold cover*
- ❏ Disneyland DQ-1201 [M] — 1959 — 50.00
  — *Reissue of 4005; whirlpool-like designs on cover*
- ❏ Disneyland DQ-1201 [M] — 1968 — 30.00
  — *Reissue, with same cover as 4005, but no gatefold*
- ❏ Disneyland DQ-1201 [M] — 1987 — 30.00
  — *Reissue; high-gloss cover with cel photos on back*
- ❏ Disneyland 3101 [PD] — 1981 — 30.00
  — *Disney Picture Disc" edition*

SNOW WHITE AND THE THREE STOOGES
- ❏ Columbia CL1650 [M] — 1961 — 60.00
- ❏ Columbia CS8450 [S] — 1961 — 100.00

SODOM AND GOMORRAH
- ❏ RCA Victor LOC-1076 [M] — 1963 — 80.00
- ❏ RCA Victor LSO-1076 [S] — 1963 — 100.00

SOL MADRID
- ❏ MGM SE-4541ST — 1968 — 30.00

SOLOMON AND SHEBA
- ❏ MCA 1425 — 198? — 10.00
  — *Reissue*
- ❏ United Artists UAL-4051 [M] — 1959 — 50.00
  — *First cover with silky finish*
- ❏ United Artists UAL-4051 [M] — 1959 — 30.00
  — *Second, regular cover*
- ❏ United Artists UAS-5051 [S] — 1959 — 120.00
  — *First cover with silky finish*
- ❏ United Artists UAS-5051 [S] — 1959 — 60.00
  — *Second, regular cover*

SOMEBODY LOVES ME
- ❏ RCA Victor LPM-3097 [10] — 1952 — 50.00

SOME CAME RUNNING
- ❏ Capitol W1109 [M] — 1958 — 30.00
- ❏ Capitol SW1109 [S] — 1958 — 80.00

SOME LIKE IT HOT
- ❏ United Artists UAL-4030 [M] — 1959 — 50.00
- ❏ United Artists UAS-5030 [S] — 1959 — 75.00
- ❏ United Artists UA-LA272-G — 1974 — 15.00
  — *Reissue of 5030*

SOMETHING WILD
- ❏ MCA 6194 — 1986 — 12.00
  — *Includes New Order*

SOMEWHERE IN TIME
- ❏ MCA 5154 — 1980 — 25.00

SONG OF THE SOUTH
- ❏ Disneyland WDL-4001 [M] — 1956 — 300.00
  — *Yellow label (first pressing)*
- ❏ Disneyland WDL-4001 [M] — 1957 — 200.00
  — *Red/maroon label (second pressing)*

SONG OF THE SOUTH (UNCLE REMUS)
- ❏ Disneyland DQ-1205 [M] — 1959 — 30.00

SONG WITHOUT END
- ❏ Colpix CP-506 [M] — 1960 — 25.00
- ❏ Colpix SCP-506 [S] — 1960 — 30.00

THE SONS OF KATIE ELDER
- ❏ Columbia Masterworks OL6420 [M] — 1965 — 50.00
- ❏ Columbia Masterworks OS2820 [S] — 1965 — 100.00

SO THIS IS LOVE
- ❏ RCA Victor LOC-3000 [10] — 1953 — 80.00

SO THIS IS PARIS
- ❏ Decca DL5553 [10] — 1955 — 50.00

SOUL MAN
- ❏ A&M SP-3903 — 1986 — 10.00
  — *Includes Lou Reed, Martha Davis*

THE SOUL OF NIGGER CHARLEY
- ❏ MGM 1SE-46 — 1973 — 25.00

THE SOUND AND THE FURY
- ❏ Decca DL8885 [M] — 1959 — 30.00
- ❏ Decca DL78885 [S] — 1959 — 70.00

THE SOUND OF MUSIC
- ❏ RCA Victor LOCD-2005 [M] — 1965 — 18.00
  — *With booklet; back cover lists "I Have Confidence" as "I Have Confidence in Me*
- ❏ RCA Victor LSOD-2005 [S] — 1965 — 25.00
  — *With booklet; back cover lists "I Have Confidence" as "I Have Confidence in Me*
- ❏ RCA Victor LOCD-2005 [M] — 1965 — 15.00
  — *With booklet; back cover lists "I Have Confidence" correctly*
- ❏ RCA Victor LSOD-2005 [S] — 1965 — 18.00
  — *With booklet; back cover lists "I Have Confidence" correctly*
- ❏ RCA Victor LOOD-2005 [S] — 1969 — 15.00
  — *No booklet; gatefold cover, record comes out from inside; orange or tan label*
- ❏ RCA Victor LSOD-2005 [S] — 1977 — 12.00
  — *Gatefold cover, record comes out from outside; black label with dog at 1 o'clock*

SOUTH CENTRAL
- ❏ Hollywood 61403 [DJ] — 1992 — 25.00
  — *Vinyl is promo only*

SOUTHERN STAR
- ❏ Colgems COSO-5009 — 1969 — 60.00

SOUTH PACIFIC
- ❏ RCA Victor LOC-1032 [M] — 1958 — 25.00
  — *Long Play" on label; no "Academy Award Winner" on front cover*
- ❏ RCA Victor LSO-1032 [S] — 1958 — 30.00
  — *Living Stereo" on label; no "Academy Award Winner" on front cover*
- ❏ RCA Victor LOCD-2000 [M] — 1958 — 40.00
  — *Gatefold cover with photos inside*
- ❏ RCA Victor LOC-1032 [M] — 196? — 15.00
  — *Long Play" or "Mono" on label; with "Academy Award Winner" on front cover*
- ❏ RCA Victor LSO-1032 [S] — 196? — 18.00
  — *Living Stereo" or "Stereo" on black label; with "Academy Award Winner" on front cover*
- ❏ RCA Victor LSO-1032 [S] — 1958 — 15.00
  — *Orange label*
- ❏ RCA Victor AYL1-3681 — 1981 — 10.00
  — *Best Buy Series" reissue*

SPACEBALLS
- ❏ Atlantic 81770 — 1987 — 12.00
  — *Includes Berlin*

SPACECAMP
- ❏ RCA Victor ABL1-5856 — 1986 — 40.00

SPACE JAM, MUSIC FROM AND INSPIRED BY
- ❏ Warner Sunset/Atlantic 82961 — 1997 — 18.00

A SPANISH AFFAIR
- ❏ Dot DLP-3078 [M] — 1958 — 100.00

SPARKLE
- ❏ Atlantic SD18176 — 1976 — 25.00

SPARTACUS
- ❏ Decca DL9092 [M] — 1960 — 25.00
  — *Black label, silver print*
- ❏ Decca DL79092 [S] — 1960 — 30.00
  — *Maroon label, silver print*
- ❏ Decca DL9092 [M] — 1961 — 15.00
  — *Black label with color bars*
- ❏ Decca DL79092 [S] — 1961 — 18.00
  — *Black label with color bars*
- ❏ MCA 2068 — 1973 — 15.00
  — *Reissue of 79092; black label with rainbow*
- ❏ MCA 1534 — 198? — 12.00
  — *Reissue of 2068*

THE SPIRIT OF ST. LOUIS
- ❏ RCA Victor LPM-1472 [M] — 1957 — 50.00

SPLASH
- ❏ Cherry Lane 00301 — 1984 — 30.00
  — *With poster of Daryl Hannah*

THE SPY WHO CAME IN FROM THE COLD
- ❏ RCA Victor LOC-1118 [M] — 1965 — 25.00
- ❏ RCA Victor LSO-1118 [S] — 1965 — 40.00

THE SPY WITH A COLD NOSE
- ❏ Columbia Masterworks OL6670 [M] — 1966 — 25.00
- ❏ Columbia Masterworks OS3070 [S] — 1966 — 30.00

STAGECOACH
- ❏ Mainstream 56077 [M] — 1966 — 25.00
- ❏ Mainstream S-6077 [S] — 1966 — 30.00
- ❏ Mainstream T-90802 [M] — 1966 — 30.00
  — *Capitol Record Club edition*
- ❏ Mainstream ST-90802 [S] — 1966 — 30.00
  — *Capitol Record Club edition*

STAR!
- ❏ 20th Century Fox DTCS 5102 — 1968 — 25.00

THE STARS AND STRIPES FOREVER
- ❏ MGM E-176 [10] — 1952 — 30.00

STAR TREK -- THE MOTION PICTURE
- ❏ Columbia JS36334 — 1979 — 25.00

STATE FAIR
- ❏ Dot DLP-9011 [M] — 1962 — 30.00
- ❏ Dot DLP-29011 [S] — 1962 — 30.00

THE STERILE CUCKOO
- ❏ Paramount PAS-5009 — 1970 — 25.00

STILETTO
- ❏ Columbia Masterworks OS3360 — 1969 — 25.00

THE STING
- ❏ MCA 2040 — 197? — 12.00
- ❏ MCA 37091 — 1981 — 10.00
- ❏ MCA 390 — 1973 — 15.00
  — *Original edition*

ST. LOUIS BLUES
- ❏ Capitol W993 [M] — 1958 — 50.00
  — *Turquoise or gray label*
- ❏ Capitol W993 [M] — 1959 — 30.00
  — *Black colorband label, logo at left*
- ❏ Capitol W993 [M] — 196? — 25.00
  — *Black colorband label, logo at top*

ST. LOUIS WOMAN
- ❏ Capitol L355 [10] — 1955 — 80.00

THE STRANGE ONE
- ❏ Coral CRL57132 [M] — 1957 — 70.00

THE STRAWBERRY STATEMENT
- ❏ MGM 2SE-14 — 1970 — 30.00

A STREETCAR NAMED DESIRE
- ❏ Capitol L289 [10] — 1951 — 50.00

STREETS OF FIRE
- ❏ MCA 5492 — 1984 — 12.00
  — *Includes The Fixx, The Blasters*

STRICTLY BUSINESS
- ❏ MCA 10428 — 1991 — 12.00
  — *Includes L.L. Cool J*

A STUDY IN TERROR
- ❏ Roulette OS 801 [M] — 1965 — 40.00
- ❏ Roulette OSS-801 [S] — 1965 — 80.00

THE STUNT MAN
- ❏ 20th Century T-626 — 1980 — 30.00

Number	Title	Yr	NM

THE SUBTERRANEANS
☐ MGM E-3812ST [M] — 1960 — 40.00
☐ MGM SE-3812ST [S] — 1960 — 80.00

SUMMER AND SMOKE
☐ RCA Victor LOC-1067 [M] — 1961 — 50.00
☐ RCA Victor LSO-1067 [S] — 1961 — 70.00

SUMMER HOLIDAY
☐ Epic LN24063 [M] — 1963 — 30.00
☐ Epic BN26063 [S] — 1963 — 30.00

SUMMER LOVE
☐ Decca DL8714 [M] — 1958 — 60.00
— Black label, silver print, or pink label, black print promo
☐ Decca DL8714 [M] — 196? — 30.00
— Black label with color bars

SUMMER MAGIC
☐ Buena Vista BV-4025 [M] — 1963 — 40.00
☐ Buena Vista STER-4025 [S] — 1963 — 60.00

SUMMER STOCK
☐ MGM E-519 [10] — 1950 — 40.00

THE SUN ALSO RISES
☐ Kapp KDL-7001 [M] — 1957 — 60.00

THE SUNNY SIDE OF THE STREET
☐ Mercury MG-25100 [10] — 1951 — 60.00

SUN VALLEY SERENADE
☐ RCA Victor LPT-3064 [10] — 1954 — 60.00

SURFER GIRLS
☐ Oakwood SUS-1001 — 1978 — 100.00

SURF PARTY
☐ 20th Century Fox TFM-3131 [M] — 1964 — 30.00
☐ 20th Century Fox TFS-4131 [S] — 1964 — 30.00

THE SWAN
☐ MCA 25086 — 1986 — 12.00
— Reissue of MGM 3399
☐ MGM E-3399 [M] — 1956 — 70.00

THE SWARM
☐ Warner Bros. BSK3208 — 1978 — 30.00

SWEDISH HEAVEN AND HELL
☐ Ariel ARS-15000 — 1969 — 30.00

SWEET CHARITY
☐ Decca DL71502 — 1969 — 25.00

SWEET LOVE, BITTER
☐ ABC Impulse! AS-9141 [S] — 1968 — 18.00
☐ Impulse! A-9141 [M] — 1967 — 40.00
☐ Impulse! AS-9141 [S] — 1967 — 30.00

THE SWEET RIDE
☐ 20th Century Fox S-4198 — 1968 — 25.00

THE SWEET SMELL OF SUCCESS
☐ Decca DL8610 [M] — 1957 — 60.00

SWEET SWEETBACK'S BADASSSSSS SONG
☐ Stax STS-3001 — 1971 — 30.00

SWEPT AWAY
☐ Peters International PLD1005 — 1957 — 40.00

THE SWIMMER
☐ Columbia Masterworks OS3210 — 1968 — 30.00

SWINGER'S PARADISE
☐ Epic LN24145 [M] — 1965 — 25.00
☐ Epic BN26145 [S] — 1965 — 30.00

A SWINGIN' SUMMER
☐ Hanna-Barbera HLP-8500 [M] — 1966 — 30.00
☐ Hanna-Barbera HST-9500 [S] — 1966 — 30.00

SYLVIA
☐ Mercury MG-21004 [M] — 1965 — 25.00
☐ Mercury SR-61004 [S] — 1965 — 30.00

TAKE THIS JOB AND SHOVE IT!
☐ Epic SE37177 — 1981 — 15.00

TAPEHEADS
☐ Island 91030 — 1988 — 12.00
— Includes Devo ("Baby Doll" sung in Swedish!), Fishbone

TARAS BULBA
☐ United Artists UAL-4100 [M] — 1962 — 30.00
☐ United Artists UAS-5100 [S] — 1962 — 50.00

TAXI DRIVER
☐ Arista AL4079 — 1976 — 25.00
☐ Arista AL8179 — 198? — 18.00
— Reissue of 4079

TEENAGE CRUISERS
☐ Rhino RNLP-016 — 197? — 18.00
— Includes The Blasters, many others

TEENAGE REBELLION
☐ Sidewalk T-5903 [M] — 1967 — 25.00
☐ Sidewalk ST-5903 [S] — 1967 — 30.00

TELL ME THAT YOU LOVE ME, JUNIE MOON
☐ Columbia Masterworks OS3540 — 1970 — 25.00

THE TEN COMMANDMENTS
☐ Dot DLP-3054 [M] — 1956 — 40.00
☐ Dot DLP-25054 [S] — 1959 — 30.00
— Re-recording of the original soundtrack in stereo
☐ MCA 4159 — 198? — 18.00
— Reissue of Paramount set
☐ Paramount PAS-1006 — 1973 — 25.00
— Reissue of Dot 25054

TENDER IS THE NIGHT
☐ 20th Century Fox FOX-3054 [M] — 1962 — 150.00
☐ 20th Century Fox SFX-3054 [S] — 1962 — 200.00

THE TENTH VICTIM
☐ Mainstream 56071 [M] — 1965 — 40.00
☐ Mainstream S-6071 [S] — 1965 — 50.00

TEQUILA SUNRISE
☐ Capitol C1-91185 — 1988 — 15.00
— Includes Crowded House, Duran Duran

THANK GOD IT'S FRIDAY
☐ Casablanca NBLP-7099-3 — 1978 — 25.00
— Two full-length LPs plus a bonus 12-inch single by Donna Summer with blank B-side

THAT DARN CAT
☐ Buena Vista BV-3334 [M] — 1965 — 25.00
☐ Buena Vista STER-3334 [S] — 1965 — 30.00

THAT MAN IN ISTANBUL
☐ Mainstream 56072 [M] — 1966 — 25.00
☐ Mainstream S-6072 [S] — 1966 — 30.00

THAT'S ENTERTAINMENT!
☐ MCA 11002 — 1974 — 25.00
— Film credits in small print on back cover, and list of songs omits "That's Entertainment"
☐ MCA 11002 — 1976 — 18.00
— Film credits in larger print on back cover, and list of songs includes "That's Entertainment"

THERE'S NO BUSINESS LIKE SHOW BUSINESS
☐ Decca DL8091 [M] — 196? — 25.00
— Black label with color bars
☐ Decca DL8091 [M] — 1954 — 30.00
— Black label with silver print

THEY CALL IT AN ACCIDENT
☐ Island ILPS9757 — 1982 — 12.00
— Includes U2 (two versions of "October")

THEY SHOOT HORSES, DON'T THEY?
☐ ABC ABCS-OC-10 — 1969 — 25.00

THIEF OF HEARTS
☐ Casablanca 822942-1 — 1984 — 25.00

THE THIN BLUE LINE
☐ Nonesuch 79209-1 — 1988 — 25.00

THIS COULD BE THE NIGHT
☐ MGM E-3530 [M] — 1957 — 50.00

THIS EARTH IS MINE
☐ Decca DL8915 [M] — 1959 — 80.00
☐ Decca DL78915 [S] — 1959 — 100.00
☐ Varese Sarabande VC-81076 — 1979 — 18.00
— Reissue of Decca 78915

THIS PROPERTY IS CONDEMNED
☐ Verve V-8664 [M] — 1966 — 25.00
☐ Verve V6-8664 [S] — 1966 — 30.00

THE THOMAS CROWN AFFAIR
☐ United Artists UAS-5182 — 1968 — 25.00
☐ United Artists UA-LA295-G — 1974 — 15.00
— Reissue of 5182

THOROUGHLY MODERN MILLIE
☐ Decca DL1500 [M] — 1967 — 25.00
— With bound-in booklet
☐ Decca DL71500 [S] — 1967 — 25.00
— With bound-in booklet

THOSE GLORIOUS MGM MUSICALS: DEEP IN MY HEART/WORDS AND MUSIC
☐ MGM 2-SES-54-ST — 1973 — 25.00

THOSE GLORIOUS MGM MUSICALS: EVERYTHING I HAVE IS YOURS/SUMMER STOCK/I LOVE MELVIN
☐ MGM 2-SES-52-ST — 1973 — 25.00

THOSE GLORIOUS MGM MUSICALS: GOOD NEWS/IN THE GOOD OLD SUMMERTIME/TWO WEEKS WITH LOVE
☐ MGM 2-SES-49-ST — 1973 — 25.00

THOSE GLORIOUS MGM MUSICALS: LOVELY TO LOOK AT/BRIGADOON
☐ MGM 2-SES-50-ST — 1973 — 25.00

THOSE GLORIOUS MGM MUSICALS: NANCY GOES TO RIO/RICH, YOUNG AND PRETTY/ROYAL WEDDING
☐ MGM 2-SES-53-ST — 1973 — 25.00

THOSE GLORIOUS MGM MUSICALS: ROSE MARIE/SEVN BRIDES FOR SEVEN BROTHERS
☐ MGM 2-SES-41-ST — 1973 — 25.00

THOSE GLORIOUS MGM MUSICALS: SHOW BOAT/ANNIE GET YOUR GUN
☐ MGM 2-SES-42-ST — 1973 — 25.00

THOSE GLORIOUS MGM MUSICALS: SINGIN' IN THE RAIN/EASTER PARADE
☐ MGM 2-SES-40-ST — 1973 — 25.00

THOSE GLORIOUS MGM MUSICALS: THE BAND WAGON/KISS ME, KATE
☐ MGM 2-SES-44-ST — 1973 — 25.00

THOSE GLORIOUS MGM MUSICALS: THE BARKLEYS OF BROADWAY/LES GIRLS
☐ MGM 2-SES-51-ST — 1973 — 25.00

THOSE GLORIOUS MGM MUSICALS: THE PIRATE/PAGAN LOVE SONG/HIT THE DECK
☐ MGM 2-SES-43-ST — 1973 — 40.00

THOSE GLORIOUS MGM MUSICALS: TILL THE CLOUDS ROLL BY/THREE LITTLE WORDS
☐ MGM 2-SES-45-ST — 1973 — 25.00

THREE BITES OF THE APPLE
☐ MCA 25010 — 198? — 10.00
— Reissue of MGM SE-4444
☐ MGM E-4444 [M] — 1967 — 30.00
☐ MGM SE-4444 [S] — 1967 — 25.00

THREE FOR THE SHOW
☐ Mercury MG-25204 [M] — 1955 — 60.00

THREE IN THE ATTIC
☐ Sidewalk ST-5918 — 1968 — 30.00

THREE LITTLE WORDS
☐ MGM E-516 [10] — 1959 — 60.00

THE THREEPENNY OPERA
☐ RCA Victor LOC-1086 [M] — 1964 — 150.00
— With rare original cover: White background, pink and black drawing, characters underneath
☐ RCA Victor LOC-1086 [M] — 1964 — 18.00
— Reissue cover: White background, orange drawing, Sammy Davis Jr. in foreground, "RE" at bottom
☐ RCA Victor LSO-1086 [S] — 1964 — 200.00
— With rare original cover: White background, pink and black drawing, characters underneath
☐ RCA Victor LSO-1086 [S] — 1964 — 25.00
— Reissue cover: White background, orange drawing, Sammy Davis Jr. in foreground, "RE" at bottom

THE THREE WORLDS OF GULLIVER
☐ Colpix CP-414 [M] — 1960 — 60.00

THUNDER ALLEY
☐ Sidewalk T-5902 [M] — 1967 — 25.00
☐ Sidewalk ST-5902 [S] — 1967 — 30.00

THUNDERBALL
☐ United Artists UAL-4132 [M] — 1965 — 25.00
☐ United Artists UAS-5132 [S] — 1965 — 30.00
☐ United Artists SW-90820 [S] — 1965 — 40.00
— Capitol Record Club edition

TICK…TICK…TICK
☐ MGM SE-4667 [M] — 1970 — 30.00

TILL THE CLOUDS ROLL BY
☐ MCA 25000 — 1986 — 12.00
☐ Metro M-578 [M] — 1966 — 15.00
— Reissue of MGM 501
☐ Metro MS-578 [R] — 1966 — 12.00
☐ MGM E-501 [10] — 1950 — 50.00

TIMES SQUARE
☐ RSO RS-2-4203 — 1980 — 18.00
— Includes The Ramones ("I Wanna Be Sedated"), Talking Heads ("Life During Wartime"), XTC, Patti Smith, The Cure, etc.

TIMES SQUARE SAMPLER
☐ RSO RPO1026 [DJ] — 1980 — 15.00
— Includes Talking Heads, Roxy Music, Pretenders, two others

A TIME TO LOVE AND A TIME TO DIE
☐ Decca DL8778 [M] — 1958 — 100.00
☐ Varese Sarabande VC-81075 — 1979 — 18.00
— Reissue of Decca 8778

TO BED… OR NOT TO BED
☐ London M-76005 [M] — 1963 — 40.00

TO KILL A MOCKINGBIRD
☐ Ava A-20 [M] — 1962 — 30.00
☐ Ava AS-20 [S] — 1962 — 30.00

TOKYO OLYMPIAD
☐ Monument MLP-8046 [M] — 1966 — 18.00
☐ Monument SLP-18046 [S] — 1966 — 25.00

TOM JONES
☐ United Artists UAL-4113 [M] — 1963 — 25.00
☐ United Artists UAS-5113 [S] — 1963 — 30.00

Number	Title	Yr	NM

TOMMY
- ❏ Polydor PD 2-9502 — 1975 — 25.00

TOM SAWYER
- ❏ United Artists UA-LA057-F — 1973 — 25.00

TOO MUCH TOO SOON
- ❏ Mercury MG-20381 [M] — 1958 — 30.00
- ❏ Mercury SR-60019 [S] — 1958 — 80.00

TOP GUN
- ❏ Columbia SC40323 — 1986 — 12.00

TOPKAPI
- ❏ MCA 25118 — 1986 — 12.00
- ❏ United Artists UAL-4118 [M] — 1964 — 25.00
- ❏ United Artists UAS-5118 [S] — 1964 — 30.00

TO SIR, WITH LOVE
- ❏ Fontana MGF-27569 [M] — 1967 — 25.00
- ❏ Fontana SRF-67569 [S] — 1967 — 30.00

THE TOUCHABLES
- ❏ 20th Century Fox S-4206 — 1969 — 25.00

TO WONG FOO, THANKS FOR EVERYTHING! JULIE NEWMAR
- ❏ MCA 11231 — 1995 — 15.00
- — Includes Cyndi Lauper, Salt-N-Pepa

THE TRAIN
- ❏ United Artists UAL-4122 [M] — 1965 — 25.00
- ❏ United Artists UAS-5122 [S] — 1965 — 40.00

TRANSYLVANIA 6-5000
- ❏ Varese Sarabande STV-81267 — 1985 — 25.00

THE TRAP
- ❏ Atco 33-204 [M] — 1966 — 40.00
- ❏ Atco SD 33-204 [S] — 1966 — 70.00

TRAPEZE
- ❏ Columbia CL870 [M] — 1956 — 30.00

THE TRAPP FAMILY
- ❏ 20th Fox FOX-3044 [M] — 1961 — 30.00
- ❏ 20th Fox STX-3044 [S] — 1961 — 40.00

THE TREASURE OF SAN GENNARO
- ❏ Buddah BDS-5011 — 1968 — 40.00

THE TRIP
- ❏ Sidewalk T-5908 [M] — 1967 — 30.00
- ❏ Sidewalk ST-5908 [S] — 1967 — 40.00

TRIPLE CROSS
- ❏ United Artists UAL-4162 [M] — 1967 — 25.00
- ❏ United Artists UAS 5162 [S] — 1967 — 30.00

TROUBLE IN MIND
- ❏ Island 90501 — 1986 — 12.00
- — Includes Marianne Faithfull

THE TROUBLE WITH ANGELS
- ❏ Mainstream 56073 [M] — 1966 — 40.00
- ❏ Mainstream S 6073 [S] — 1966 — 80.00

TRUE GRIT
- ❏ Capitol ST-263 — 1969 — 30.00
- ❏ Capitol ST-8-0263 — 1969 — 40.00
- — Capitol Record Club edition

TRUE LIFE ADVENTURES
- ❏ Disneyland WDL-4011 [M] — 1957 — 70.00

TRUE STORIES, SOUNDS FROM
- ❏ Sire 25515 — 1986 — 12.00
- — Includes individual members of Talking Heads...not to be confused with the Talking Heads album True Stories.

THE TRUE STORY OF THE CIVIL WAR
- ❏ Coral CRL59100 [M] — 1958 — 80.00

TWO MULES FOR SISTER SARA
- ❏ Kapp KRS-5512 — 1970 — 30.00

TWO WEEKS WITH LOVE
- ❏ MGM E-530 [10] — 1950 — 40.00

ULYSSES
- ❏ RCA Victor LOC-1138 [M] — 1967 — 30.00
- ❏ RCA Victor LSO-1138 [S] — 1967 — 30.00

THE UMBRELLAS OF CHERBOURG (LES PARAPLUIES DE CHERBOURG)
- ❏ Philips PCC216 [M] — 1965 — 25.00
- ❏ Philips PCC616 [S] — 1965 — 30.00

THE UNBEARABLE LIGHTNESS OF BEING
- ❏ Fantasy FSP-21006 — 1988 — 25.00

UNCLE TOM'S CABIN
- ❏ Philips PHS600272 — 1968 — 40.00

THE UNFORGIVEN
- ❏ United Artists UAL-4068 [M] — 1960 — 40.00
- ❏ United Artists UAS-5068 [S] — 1960 — 70.00

THE UNSINKABLE MOLLY BROWN
- ❏ MCA 25011 — 1986 — 12.00
- — Reissue of MGM 4232

- ❏ MGM E-4232 [M] — 1964 — 18.00
- ❏ MGM SW-90048 [S] — 1964 — 18.00
- — Capitol Record Club edition
- ❏ MGM W-90048 [M] — 1964 — 15.00
- — Capitol Record Club edition
- ❏ MGM SE-4232 [S] — 1964 — 25.00

UP IN THE CELLAR
- ❏ American Int'l. A-1036 — 1970 — 25.00

UP THE DOWN STAIRCASE
- ❏ United Artists UAL-4169 [M] — 1967 — 25.00
- ❏ United Artists UAS-5169 [S] — 1967 — 40.00

UP THE JUNCTION
- ❏ Mercury SR-61159 — 1968 — 30.00

URBAN COWBOY
- ❏ Full Moon/Asylum DP-90002 — 1980 — 15.00

URBAN COWBOY II (MORE MUSIC FROM THE ORIGINAL SOUNDTRACK)
- ❏ Full Moon/Epic SE36291 — 1980 — 12.00

URGH! A MUSIC WAR
- ❏ A&M SP-6019 — 1981 — 15.00
- — Includes live tracks by The Police, Joan Jett and the Blackhearts, Wall of Voodoo, XTC, Go-Go's, Orchestral Manouvres in the Dark, Pere Ubu, Devo, Gary Numan, X, Gang of Four, The Cramps, etc.

VALENTINO
- ❏ United Artists UA-LA810-H — 1977 — 30.00

VALLEY GIRL
- ❏ Epic FE38623 — 1983 — 80.00
- ❏ Roadshow RS-101 — 1983 — 120.00

VALLEY OF THE DOLLS
- ❏ 20th Century Fox TF-4196 [M] — 1968 — 30.00
- ❏ 20th Century Fox TFS-4196 [S] — 1968 — 30.00
- ❏ 20th Century Fox SW-91374 [S] — 1968 — 30.00
- — Capitol Record Club edition

VANILLA SKY
- ❏ Reprise RTH-2002 — 2002 — 40.00
- — Classic Records edition on 180-gram vinyl ; contains a packet with a piece of film from the movie

THE VANISHING POINT
- ❏ Amos AAS-8002 — 1971 — 25.00

THE VANISHING PRAIRIE
- ❏ Columbia CL6332 [10] — 1954 — 80.00

VERTIGO
- ❏ Mercury MG-20384 [M] — 1958 — 150.00

THE VICTORS
- ❏ Colpix CP-516 [M] — 1963 — 25.00
- ❏ Colpix SCP-516 [S] — 1963 — 30.00

VICTOR/VICTORIA
- ❏ MGM MG-1-5407 — 1982 — 80.00
- ❏ Polydor MG-1-5407 — 198? — 12.00
- — Reissue of MGM release

A VIEW TO A KILL
- ❏ Capitol SJ-12413 — 1985 — 25.00

THE VIKINGS
- ❏ United Artists UAL-4003 [M] — 1958 — 30.00
- ❏ United Artists UAS-5003 [S] — 1958 — 40.00

VILLA RIDES!
- ❏ Dot DLP-25870 — 1968 — 40.00

THE V.I.P.S
- ❏ MGM E-4184 [M] — 1963 — 25.00
- ❏ MGM SE-4184 [S] — 1963 — 30.00
- — Music by Bill Evans

VISION QUEST
- ❏ Geffen R153920 — 1985 — 12.00
- — Includes Madonna ("Crazy for You," "Gambler")

VIVA MARIA!
- ❏ United Artists UAL-4135 [M] — 1965 — 25.00
- ❏ United Artists UAS-5135 [S] — 1965 — 30.00

VIVA MAX!
- ❏ RCA Victor LSP-4275 — 1969 — 25.00

THE VIXEN
- ❏ Beverly Hills BHS-22 — 1968 — 50.00

VOYAGE EN BALLON
- ❏ Philips PHM200029 [M] — 1960 — 30.00
- ❏ Philips PHS600029 [S] — 1960 — 40.00

WALK DON'T RUN
- ❏ Mainstream 56080 [M] — 1966 — 25.00
- ❏ Mainstream S-6080 [S] — 1966 — 40.00

WALK ON THE WILD SIDE
- ❏ Ava A-4-ST [M] — 1962 — 25.00
- ❏ Ava AS-4-ST [S] — 1962 — 40.00
- ❏ Choreo A-4-ST [M] — 1962 — 30.00
- ❏ Choreo AS-4-ST [S] — 1962 — 50.00

A WALK WITH LOVE AND DEATH
- ❏ Citadel CT-6025 — 1969 — 80.00

THE WANDERERS
- ❏ Warner Bros. BSK3359 — 1979 — 30.00

WAR AND PEACE
- ❏ Columbia CL930 [M] — 1956 — 30.00
- ❏ Melodiya/Capitol SWAO2918 — 1968 — 40.00

THE WARLOCK
- ❏ Intrada MAF-7003 — 1990 — 25.00

THE WAR LORD
- ❏ Decca DL9149 [M] — 1965 — 30.00
- ❏ Decca DL79149 [S] — 1965 — 50.00

WARNING SHOT
- ❏ Liberty LRP-3498 [M] — 1967 — 30.00
- ❏ Liberty LST-7498 [S] — 1967 — 40.00

WATERLOO
- ❏ Paramount PAS-6003 — 1971 — 30.00
- ❏ Paramount SW-93729 — 1971 — 30.00
- — Capitol Record Club edition

WATERMELON MAN
- ❏ Beverly Hills BHS-26 — 1970 — 30.00

WATERSHIP DOWN
- ❏ Columbia JS35707 — 1978 — 30.00

WAY...WAY OUT
- ❏ 20th Century Fox 3192 [M] — 1966 — 30.00
- ❏ 20th Century Fox S-4192 [S] — 1966 — 40.00

WEDDING IN MONACO
- ❏ Mercury MG-20149 [M] — 1956 — 250.00

WEST SIDE STORY
- ❏ Columbia Masterworks OL5670 [M] — 1961 — 25.00
- — Originals have gatefold covers and gray and black labels with six "eye" logos
- ❏ Columbia Masterworks OS2070 [S] — 1961 — 30.00
- — Originals have gatefold covers and gray and black labels with six "eye" logos
- ❏ Columbia Masterworks OS2070 [S] — 1963 — 18.00
- — Gatefold cover; gray "360 Sound Stereo" label
- ❏ Columbia Masterworks OS2070 [S] — 196? — 15.00
- — Regular cover; gray "360 Sound Stereo" label
- ❏ Columbia Masterworks OS2070 [S] — 1971 — 12.00
- — Regular cover; olive label with "Columbia" continuously around edge
- ❏ Columbia Masterworks OL5670 [M] — 1963 — 15.00
- — Gatefold cover; gray "360 Sound Stereo" label
- ❏ Columbia Masterworks OL5670 [M] — 196? — 12.00
- — Regular cover; gray "360 Sound Stereo" label

WHAT A WAY TO GO!
- ❏ 20th Century Fox TFM-3143 [M] — 1964 — 25.00
- ❏ 20th Century Fox TFS-4143 [S] — 1964 — 40.00

WHAT'S NEW PUSSYCAT?
- ❏ United Artists UAL-4128 [M] — 1965 — 25.00
- ❏ United Artists UAS-5128 [S] — 1965 — 30.00
- ❏ United Artists UA-LA278-G — 1974 — 15.00
- — Reissue of 5128

WHEN HARRY MET SALLY...
- ❏ Columbia SC45319 — 1989 — 15.00

WHEN THE BOYS MEET THE GIRLS
- ❏ MCA 25013 — 1986 — 12.00
- — Reissue of MGM 4334
- ❏ MGM E-4334 [M] — 1965 — 18.00
- ❏ MGM SE-4334 [S] — 1965 — 30.00

WHEN THE WIND BLOWS
- ❏ Virgin 90599 — 1987 — 12.00
- — Includes David Bowie, Squeeze

WHERE EAGLES DARE
- ❏ MCA 25082 — 1986 — 12.00
- — Reissue of MGM S1E-16
- ❏ MGM S1E-16ST — 1969 — 30.00

WHERE'S JACK?
- ❏ Paramount PAS-5005 — 1969 — 30.00

WHERE'S POPPA?
- ❏ United Artists UAS-5216 — 1970 — 30.00

WHERE THE BUFFALO ROAM
- ❏ Backstreet 5126 — 1980 — 15.00
- — Includes Neil Young

THE WHISPERERS
- ❏ MCA 25041 — 1986 — 12.00
- — Reissue of United Artists 5161
- ❏ United Artists UAL-4161 [M] — 1967 — 25.00
- ❏ United Artists UAS-5161 [S] — 1967 — 30.00

WHITE CHRISTMAS
- ❏ Decca DL8083 — 1954 — 50.00

WHO FRAMED ROGER RABBIT?
- ❏ Buena Vista 64100 — 1988 — 25.00

Number	Title	Yr	NM

WHO'S AFRAID OF VIRGINIA WOOLF?
❑ Warner Bros. B1656 [M]		1966	30.00
❑ Warner Bros. BS1656 [S]		1966	30.00
❑ Warner Bros. 2B1657 [M]		1966	40.00

—*Above (1657) is the complete film, not just the music and some dialogue*

WHO'S THAT GIRL
❑ Sire R100761		1987	12.00

—*Includes Madonna ("Who's That Girl," "Causing a Commotion," "The Look of Love," "Can't Stop"); Scritti Politti ("Best Thing Ever")*

WILD, WILD WINTER
❑ Decca DL4699 [M]		1966	25.00
❑ Decca DL74699 [S]		1966	30.00

THE WILD BUNCH
❑ Varese Sarabande STV-81145		1981	18.00

—*Reissue of Warner Bros. 1814*

| ❑ Warner Bros. WS1814 | | 1969 | 100.00 |

THE WILD EYE
❑ RCA Victor LSP-4003		1968	30.00

WILD GEESE
❑ A&M SP-4730		1978	25.00

WILD IN THE STREETS
❑ Tower SKAO5099		1968	30.00

WILD IS THE WIND
❑ Columbia CL1090 [M]		1957	30.00

THE WILD ONE
❑ Decca DL5515 [10]		1954	80.00
❑ Decca DL8349 [M]		1956	40.00

WILD ON THE BEACH
❑ RCA Victor LPM-3441 [M]		1965	30.00
❑ RCA Victor LSP-3441 [S]		1965	40.00

THE WILD RACERS
❑ Sidewalk ST-5914		1968	30.00

WILD WHEELS
❑ RCA Victor LSO-1156		1969	25.00

WILLIE DYNAMITE
❑ MCA 393		1974	25.00

WILLOW
❑ Virgin Movie Music 90939		1988	30.00

WILLY WONKA AND THE CHOCOLATE FACTORY
❑ MCA 37124		198?	12.00

—*Reissue of Paramount 6012*

| ❑ Paramount PAS-6012 | | 1971 | 40.00 |

THE WITCHES OF EASTWICK
❑ Warner Bros. 25607		1987	30.00

WITH A SONG IN MY HEART
❑ Capitol L309 [10]		1952	40.00
❑ Capitol T309 [M]		195?	30.00

THE WIZARD OF OZ
❑ MCA 39046		198?	12.00

—*Reissue of MGM 3996*

| ❑ MGM E-3464 [M] | | 1956 | 50.00 |

—*Yellow label*

| ❑ MGM E-3996 [M] | | 1962 | 18.00 |

—*Gatefold cover, black label*

| ❑ MGM SE-3996 [R] | | 196? | 18.00 |

—*Gatefold cover, black label*

WOMEN OF THE WORLD
❑ Decca DL9112 [M]		1963	25.00
❑ Decca DL79112 [S]		1963	30.00

WONDERFUL COUNTRY
❑ United Artists UAL-4050 [M]		1959	50.00
❑ United Artists UAS-5050 [S]		1959	100.00

WONDERFUL TO BE YOUNG
❑ Dot DLP-3474 [M]		1962	30.00
❑ Dot DLP-25474 [S]		1962	40.00

THE WONDERFUL WORLD OF THE BROTHERS GRIMM
❑ MGM 1E-3 [M]		1962	30.00

—*With box and hardback book*

| ❑ MGM S1E-3 [S] | | 1962 | 40.00 |

—*With box and hardback book*

WORDS AND MUSIC
❑ MCA 25029		1986	15.00

—*Reissue of MGM 505 with the addition of "Slaughter on Tenth Avenue," which does not appear on either the 10-inch LP or the budget-line Metro reissues*

❑ Metro M-580 [M]		1966	15.00
❑ Metro MS-580 [R]		1966	12.00
❑ MGM E-505 [10]		1950	50.00

THE WORLD OF SUZIE WONG
❑ RCA Victor LOC-1059 [M]		1960	25.00
❑ RCA Victor LSO-1059 [S]		1960	50.00

THE WRAITH
❑ Scotti Bros. SZ40429		1986	12.00

—*Includes Honeymoon Suite*

WRITTEN ON THE WIND
❑ Decca DL8424 [M]		1956	40.00

—*Black label, silver print, or pink label, black print promo*

| ❑ Decca DL8424 [M] | | 196? | 25.00 |

—*Black label with color bars*

| ❑ Varese Sarabande VC-81074 | | 1979 | 15.00 |

—*Reissue of Decca 8424*

THE WRONG BOX
❑ Mainstream 56088 [M]		1966	100.00
❑ Mainstream S-6088 [S]		1966	150.00

WUTHERING HEIGHTS
❑ American Int'l. A-1039		1971	30.00

W.W. AND THE DIXIE DANCEKINGS
❑ 20th Century ST-103		1975	30.00

THE YELLOW CANARY
❑ Verve V-8548 [M]		1963	25.00
❑ Verve V6-8548 [S]		1963	30.00

THE YELLOW ROLLS-ROYCE
❑ MGM T90424 [M]		1965	18.00

—*Capitol Record Club edition*

| ❑ MGM ST90424 [S] | | 1965 | 18.00 |

—*Capitol Record Club edition*

| ❑ MGM E-4292 [M] | | 1965 | 25.00 |
| ❑ MGM SE-4292 [S] | | 1965 | 30.00 |

YES, GEORGIO
❑ London PDV9001		1982	12.00

—*Contains one Christmas song:*

YESTERDAY, TODAY AND TOMORROW
❑ Warner Bros. W1552 [M]		1964	40.00
❑ Warner Bros. WS1552 [S]		1964	50.00

YOJIMBO
❑ MGM E-4096 [M]		1962	100.00
❑ MGM SE-4096 [S]		1962	150.00

YOU ARE WHAT YOU EAT
❑ Columbia Masterworks OS3240		1968	25.00

YOUNG BILLY YOUNG
❑ MCA 25031		1986	12.00

—*Reissue of United Artists 5199*

| ❑ United Artists UAS-5199 | | 1969 | 30.00 |

YOUNG DOCTORS IN LOVE
❑ Regency RI-8501		1982	25.00

YOUNG EINSTEIN
❑ A&M SP-3929		1988	12.00

—*Includes Mental As Anything, The Saints, Icehouse, Models*

YOUNG FRANKENSTEIN
❑ ABC ABCD-870		1975	25.00

THE YOUNG GIRLS OF ROCHEFORT
❑ Philips PCC 2-226 [M]		1968	25.00
❑ Philips PCC 2-626 [S]		1968	30.00

THE YOUNG LIONS
❑ Decca DL8719 [M]		1958	30.00
❑ Decca DL78719 [S]		1958	80.00
❑ Varese Sarabande STV-81115		1981	18.00

—*Reissue of Decca 78719*

YOUNG LOVERS
❑ Columbia Masterworks OL7010 [M]		1964	25.00
❑ Columbia Masterworks OS2510 [S]		1964	30.00

YOUNG MAN WITH A HORN
❑ Columbia CL6106 [10]		1950	100.00
❑ Columbia CL582 [M]		1950	40.00

THE YOUNG SAVAGES
❑ Columbia CL1672 [M]		1961	30.00
❑ Columbia CS8472 [S]		1961	100.00

YOUNG WINSTON
❑ Angel SFO-36901		1972	30.00

YOU ONLY LIVE TWICE
❑ United Artists UAL-4155 [M]		1967	25.00
❑ United Artists UAS-5155 [S]		1967	30.00
❑ United Artists UA-LA289-G		1974	15.00

—*Reissue of 5155*

YOURS, MINE AND OURS
❑ MCA 1434		198?	10.00

—*Reissue of United Artists 5181*

| ❑ United Artists UAS-5181 | | 1968 | 25.00 |

Z
❑ Columbia Masterworks OS3370		1970	25.00

ZABRISKIE POINT
❑ MCA 25032		1986	12.00

—*Reissue of MGM 4468*

| ❑ MGM SE-4468 | | 1970 | 25.00 |

ZACHARIAH
❑ ABC ABCS-OC-13		1970	30.00

ZOOT SUIT
❑ MCA 5267		1981	25.00

ZORBA THE GREEK
❑ 20th Century T-903		1973	15.00

—*Reissue of 20th Century Fox 4167*

❑ 20th Century Fox TFM-3167 [M]		1965	25.00
❑ 20th Century Fox TFS-4167 [S]		1965	30.00
❑ Casablanca 826245-1		198?	10.00

—*Reissue of 20th Century 903*

ZULU
❑ United Artists UAL-4116 [M]		1964	40.00
❑ United Artists UAS-5116 [S]		1964	70.00

Various Artists Collections

ACCENT ON TROMBONE
❑ Urania UJLP-1205 [M]		1955	30.00

AC-DC BLUES
❑ Stash ST-106		197?	12.00

ACE STORY, VOLUME ONE
❑ Ace 2031		1982	15.00

ACE STORY, VOLUME TWO
❑ Ace 2032		1982	15.00

ADD-A-PART JAZZ
❑ Columbia CL908 [M]		1956	30.00

THE ADVANCE GUARD OF THE '40S
❑ EmArcy MG-36016 [M]		1955	50.00

AFRO-COOL
❑ GNP Crescendo GNP-48 [M]		1959	25.00

AFRO-CUBAN JAZZ
❑ Verve 833561-1		198?	15.00
❑ Verve VE-2-2522		197?	18.00

AFRO SUMMIT
❑ BASF 20675		197?	25.00
❑ Pausa 7026		198?	12.00

AFTER HOUR JAZZ
❑ Epic LN(# unk) [M]		1955	30.00

AFTER HOURS
❑ King 395-528 [M]		1956	500.00
❑ King KLP-528		1987	15.00

—*With "Highland Music" on label*

AFTER HOURS BLUES, 1949
❑ Biograph 12010		1969	15.00

AIN'T THAT GOOD NEWS
❑ Specialty SPS-2115		1969	25.00

A LA CARTE
❑ Warner Bros. PRO-A-794		1978	25.00

ALAN FREED'S GOLDEN PICS
❑ End LP-313 [M]		1961	60.00

ALAN FREED'S MEMORY LANE
❑ End LP-314 [M]		1962	60.00

ALAN FREED'S TOP 15
❑ End LP-315 [M]		1962	60.00
❑ Roulette SR42042 [R]		1970	18.00

—*Reissue of End LP-315*

ALIVEMUTHERFORYA
❑ Columbia JC35349		1977	15.00

—*With Billy Cobham, Alphonso Johnson, Steve Khan, Tom Scott*

ALL-AMERICAN COWBOYS
❑ Kat Family FZ38126		1983	12.00

ALL DAY LONG
❑ Prestige PRLP-7081 [M]		1957	100.00

—*Reissued as Prestige 7277; see KENNY BURRELL.*

ALL DAY THUMB SUCKER REVISITED
❑ Blue Thumb BT3-7002		1995	25.00

—*Boxed set*

ALL GIRL MILLION SELLERS
❑ Ascot AM-13007 [M]		1964	40.00
❑ Ascot AS-16007 [P]		1964	40.00

ALL MEAT
❑ Warner Bros. PRO604		1975	25.00

ALL NIGHT LONG
❑ Prestige PRLP-7073 [M]		1957	100.00

—*Reissued as Prestige 7289; see KENNY BURRELL.*

ALL SINGING -- ALL TALKING -- ALL ROCKING
❑ Warner Bros. PRO573		1973	30.00

ALL STAR COUNTRY
❑ MGM SE-4690		1970	18.00
❑ RCA Victor PRS-387		1970	15.00

Number	Title	Yr	NM

ALL-STAR COUNTRY AND WESTERN
- Diplomat DS2623 — 196? — 15.00

ALL STAR COUNTRY HITS
- MGM SE-4787 — 1971 — 15.00

ALL-STAR DATES
- RCA Victor LPT-21 [10] — 1951 — 50.00

ALL STAR JAZZ
- Halo 50223 [M] — 195? — 30.00

ALL STAR ROCK, VOLUME 1
- Original Sound Recordings OSR-1 — 1972 — 12.00

ALL STAR ROCK, VOLUME 2
- Original Sound Recordings OSR-2 — 1972 — 12.00

ALL STAR ROCK, VOLUME 3
- Original Sound Recordings OSR-3 — 1972 — 12.00

ALL STAR ROCK, VOLUME 4
- Original Sound Recordings OSR-4 — 1972 — 12.00

ALL STAR ROCK, VOLUME 5
- Original Sound Recordings OSR-5 — 1972 — 12.00

ALL STAR ROCK, VOLUME 6
- Original Sound Recordings OSR-6 — 1972 — 12.00

ALL STAR ROCK, VOLUME 7
- Original Sound Recordings OSR-7 — 1972 — 12.00

ALL STAR ROCK, VOLUME 8
- Original Sound Recordings OSR-8 — 1972 — 12.00

ALL STAR ROCK, VOLUME 9
- Original Sound Recordings OSR-9 — 1972 — 12.00

ALL STAR ROCK, VOLUME 10
- Original Sound Recordings OSR-10 — 1972 — 12.00

ALL STAR ROCK, VOLUME 11
- Original Sound Recordings OSR-11 — 1972 — 40.00
— *This volume has an Elvis track on it, thus the higher price*

ALL STAR ROCK AND ROLL REVUE
- King 395-513 [M] — 1956 — 400.00
- King 638 [M] — 1959 — 200.00
— *Reissue of King 395-513*

ALL STAR SESSIONS
- Capitol M-11031 — 1973 — 15.00

ALL-STAR STOMPERS
- Circle L-402 [M] — 1951 — 40.00

ALL STAR SWING GROUPS
- Savoy Jazz SJL-2218 — 198? — 15.00

ALL STAR TRIBUTE TO TATUM
- American Recording Society G-424 [M] — 1957 — 30.00

ALL THE HITS BY ALL THE STARS
- Parkway P7013 [M] — 1962 — 40.00

ALL THE HITS BY ALL THE STARS, VOL. 2
- Parkway P7016 [M] — 1963 — 30.00

ALL THESE THINGS
- Instant LP-71000 — 1969 — 30.00

ALL THE STARS' BIGGEST HITS
- Parkway P-7033 [M] — 1963 — 50.00
— *With "pull-off pix" still intact on cover*

ALL THE STARS' BIGGEST HITS, VOLUME 2
- Parkway P-7034 [M] — 1963 — 50.00
— *With "pull-off pix" still intact on cover*

ALL-TIME ALL-STAR COUNTRY HITS: 48 HISTORIC PERFORMANCES
- RCA Victor CWS 0002 — 196? — 30.00
— *Box set*

ALL-TIME CHRISTMAS FAVORITES
- Capitol Special Markets SL-6931 — 1973 — 15.00
— *Sold only at Sylvania dealers*

ALL TIME COUNTRY AND WESTERN
- Decca DL4010 [M] — 1960 — 30.00
- Decca DL74010 [R] — 196? — 25.00

ALL TIME COUNTRY AND WESTERN, VOL. 2
- Decca DL4090 [M] — 1961 — 30.00
- Decca DL74090 [R] — 196? — 18.00

ALL TIME COUNTRY AND WESTERN, VOL. 3
- Decca DL4134 [M] — 1961 — 30.00
- Decca DL74134 [R] — 196? — 18.00

ALL TIME COUNTRY AND WESTERN, VOL. 4
- Decca DL4359 [M] — 1963 — 30.00
- Decca DL74359 [R] — 196? — 18.00

ALL TIME COUNTRY AND WESTERN, VOL. 5
- Decca DL4549 [M] — 1964 — 30.00
- Decca DL74549 [R] — 1964 — 18.00

ALL TIME COUNTRY AND WESTERN, VOL. 6
- Decca DL4657 [M] — 1965 — 25.00
- Decca DL74657 [R] — 1965 — 15.00

ALL TIME COUNTRY AND WESTERN, VOL. 7
- Decca DL4775 [M] — 1966 — 25.00
- Decca DL74775 [R] — 1966 — 15.00

ALL TIME COUNTRY AND WESTERN, VOL. 8
- Decca DL4881 [M] — 1967 — 25.00
- Decca DL74881 [S] — 1967 — 25.00

ALL TIME COUNTRY AND WESTERN, VOL. 9
- Decca DL75025 [S] — 1968 — 25.00
- Decca DL5025 [M] — 1968 — 50.00
— *Mono is white label promo only; cover is stereo with "Monaural" sticker*

ALL TIME COUNTRY AND WESTERN HITS
- King 537 [M] — 1956 — 150.00
- King 710 [M] — 1961 — 100.00
— *Not a reissue of King 537, but a different collection*

ALL TIME HIT SACRED AND GOSPEL SONGS
- King 1023 [M] — 1967 — 30.00

THE ALTERNATIVES
- Epic AS710 [DJ] — 1979 — 15.00
— *Includes Ian Dury, The Clash*

ALTERNATIVES
- Warner Bros. BS1873 — 1970 — 15.00

ALTO ALTITUDE
- EmArcy MG-36018 [M] — 1955 — 50.00

ALTO ARTISTRY
- Trip 5543 — 197? — 12.00

ALTO SAXES
- Norgran MGN-1035 [M] — 1955 — 80.00
- Verve MGV-8126 [M] — 1957 — 30.00
- Verve V-8126 [M] — 1961 — 25.00

ALTO SUMMIT
- Prestige PRLP-7684 — 1969 — 18.00

THE AMAZING METS
- Buddah 1969 — 1969 — 30.00

THE AMERICAN FAMILY ALBUM OF FAVORITE CHRISTMAS MUSIC
- RCA Red Seal VCS-7060 — 1970 — 18.00

AMERICAN FOLK BLUES FESTIVAL
- Excello LPS-8029 — 1972 — 25.00
- Exodus EX-302 — 1966 — 25.00
- Exodus EXS-302 [S] — 1966 — 30.00

AMERICANS ABROAD, VOL. 1
- Pax LP-6009 [10] — 1955 — 40.00

AMERICANS ABROAD, VOL. 2
- Pax LP-6015 [10] — 1955 — 40.00

AMERICANS IN EUROPE, VOL. 1
- ABC Impulse! AS-36 [S] — 1968 — 15.00
- Impulse! A-36 [M] — 1963 — 25.00
- Impulse! AS-36 [S] — 1963 — 30.00

AMERICANS IN EUROPE, VOL. 2
- ABC Impulse! AS-37 [S] — 1968 — 15.00
- Impulse! A-37 [M] — 1963 — 25.00
- Impulse! AS-37 [S] — 1963 — 30.00

AMERICA'S GREATEST COUNTRY STARS LIVE AND IN PERSON
- Harmony HL7414 [M] — 1967 — 18.00
- Harmony HS11214 [S] — 1967 — 18.00

AMERICA'S GREATEST JAZZMEN PLAY COLE PORTER
- Moodsville MVLP-34 [M] — 1963 — 40.00
— *Green label*
- Moodsville MVST-34 [S] — 1963 — 40.00
— *Green label*
- Moodsville MVLP-34 [M] — 1965 — 25.00
— *Blue label, trident logo at right*
- Moodsville MVST-34 [S] — 1965 — 25.00
— *Blue label, trident logo at right*

AMERICA'S GREATEST JAZZMEN PLAY GEORGE GERSHWIN
- Moodsville MVLP-33 [M] — 1963 — 40.00
— *Green label*
- Moodsville MVST-33 [S] — 1963 — 40.00
— *Green label*
- Moodsville MVLP-33 [M] — 1965 — 25.00
— *Blue label, trident logo at right*
- Moodsville MVST-33 [S] — 1965 — 25.00
— *Blue label, trident logo at right*

AMERICA'S GREATEST JAZZMEN PLAY RICHARD RODGERS
- Moodsville MVLP-35 [M] — 1963 — 40.00
— *Green label*
- Moodsville MVST-35 [S] — 1963 — 40.00
— *Green label*
- Moodsville MVLP-35 [M] — 1965 — 25.00
— *Blue label, trident logo at right*
- Moodsville MVST-35 [S] — 1965 — 25.00
— *Blue label, trident logo at right*

AMERICA'S GREATEST JAZZMEN PLAY THE BROADWAY SCENE
- Moodsville MVLP-38 [M] — 1963 — 40.00
— *Green label*
- Moodsville MVST-38 [S] — 1963 — 40.00
— *Green label*
- Moodsville MVLP-38 [M] — 1965 — 25.00
— *Blue label, trident logo at right*
- Moodsville MVST-38 [S] — 1965 — 25.00
— *Blue label, trident logo at right*

THE ANATOMY OF IMPROVISATION
- Verve MGV-8230 [M] — 1958 — 30.00
- Verve V-8230 [M] — 1961 — 25.00

...AND SO THIS IS CHRISTMAS (SOAP STARS SING OUT FOR SAVE THE CHILDREN)
- TVT 3006 — 1989 — 15.00

ANIMAL LIBERATION
- Wax Trax! 025 — 1987 — 15.00
— *Includes Lene Lovich & Nina Hagen, Howard Jones, etc.*

ANNIVERSARY
- Xanadu 201 — 1986 — 12.00

ANOTHER MONDAY NIGHT AT BIRDLAND
- Roulette R52022 [M] — 1959 — 30.00
- Roulette SR52022 [S] — 1959 — 30.00

AN ANTHOLOGY OF BRITISH BLUES, VOL. 1
- Immediate Z1252006 — 1968 — 30.00

AN ANTHOLOGY OF BRITISH BLUES, VOL. 2
- Immediate Z1252014 — 1968 — 30.00

ANTHOLOGY OF BRITISH ROCK
- Compleat 672011 — 1985 — 18.00
— *Includes David Bowie (6), The Searchers (2)*

AN ANTHOLOGY OF CALIFORNIA MUSIC
- Jazz: West Coast JWC-500 [M] — 1955 — 150.00

AN ANTHOLOGY OF CALIFORNIA MUSIC, VOL. 2
- Jazz: West Coast JWC-501 [M] — 1956 — 150.00

ANTHROPOLOGY
- Zim 1002 — 197? — 15.00

APOLLO SATURDAY NIGHT
- Atco 33-159 [M] — 1964 — 40.00
- Atco SD 33-159 [S] — 1964 — 50.00

APPETIZERS
- Warner Bros. PRO569 — 1973 — 30.00

APPROVED BY 10,000,000
- Teem LP-5004 — 196? — 30.00

ARISTA: A 15-YEAR HISTORY OF HITS
- Arista AL8655 — 1991 — 15.00
— *Includes Lisa Stansfield, Aretha Franklin and George Michael*

ARISTA AOR SAMPLER
- Arista ALS 06 [DJ] — 1978 — 25.00

THE ARISTA RECORDS FALL SAMPLER
- Arista ALS 01 [DJ] — 1976 — 15.00
— *Includes Patti Smith, Lou Reed*

ARISTA'S GREATEST HITS: PORTRAIT OF A DECADE 1975-1985
- Arista/Silver Eagle SE10383 — 1985 — 25.00

AROMA DISC PRESENTS CHRISTMAS HARMONIES
- CBS Special Products Q18403 — 1985 — 12.00
— *Designed to accompany certain Aroma Disc records*

AROMA DISC PRESENTS SOUNDS & SCENTS OF THE HOLIDAY SEASON
- CBS Special Products PQ17819 — 1984 — 15.00
— *Designed to accompany certain Aroma Disc records; label says title of LP is "Christmas Joy"*

AROUND THE CHRISTMAS TREE
- Decca DL38170 [M] — 196? — 15.00

THE ARTISTS AND MUSIC THAT STARTED IT ALL
- Motown PR-84 [DJ] — 1981 — 200.00
— *Promo-only box set; five of the records appeared as "The Motown Story: The First Twenty-Five Years" two years later*

THE ART OF JAZZ PIANO
- Epic LN3295 [M] — 1956 — 30.00

THE ART OF THE BALLAD
- Verve VSP-17 [M] — 1966 — 18.00
- Verve VSPS-17 [R] — 1966 — 12.00

THE ART OF THE BALLAD 2
- Verve VSP-38 [M] — 1966 — 18.00
- Verve VSPS-38 [R] — 1966 — 12.00

Number	Title	Yr	NM

THE ART OF THE JAM SESSION: MONTREUX '77
- ❏ Pablo Live 2620106 — 1978 — 70.00

ASSORTED FLAVORS OF PACIFIC JAZZ
- ❏ Pacific Jazz HFS-1 [M] — 1956 — 50.00

ATLANTIC BLUES
- ❏ Atlantic 81713 — 1987 — 50.00
—*Boxed set; also available as four 2-LP sets*

THE ATLANTIC FAMILY LIVE AT MONTREUX
- ❏ Atlantic SD-2-3000 — 1977 — 18.00

ATLANTIC JAZZ
- ❏ Atlantic 81712 — 1987 — 250.00
—*Boxed set with 12 volumes in 15 records, liner notes and credits*

THE ATLANTIC NEW ORLEANS JAZZ SESSIONS
- ❏ Mosaic MQ6-179 — 199? — 120.00

ATLANTIC RECORDS: CLASSIC ROCK
- ❏ Atlantic 81908 — 1989 — 30.00
—*Boxed set*

ATLANTIC RECORDS: GREAT MOMENTS IN JAZZ
- ❏ Atlantic 81907 — 1989 — 30.00

ATLANTIC RHYTHM AND BLUES
- ❏ Atlantic 81620 — 1986 — 100.00
—*Boxed set; also available as seven 2-LP sets*

ATTACK OF THE KILLER B'S
- ❏ Warner Bros. 23837 — 1983 — 15.00
—*Includes The Blasters, Marshall Crenshaw, Gang of Four, Peter Gabriel, The Ramones, Pretenders, Talking Heads, Laurie Anderson*

AT THE HOOTENANNY
- ❏ Kapp KL-1330 [M] — 1963 — 25.00
- ❏ Kapp KS-3330 [S] — 1963 — 30.00

AT THE HOOTENANNY, VOL. 2
- ❏ Kapp KL-1343 [M] — 1963 — 25.00
- ❏ Kapp KS-3343 [S] — 1963 — 30.00

AT THE HOOTENANNY, VOL. 3
- ❏ Kapp KL-1344 [M] — 1963 — 25.00
- ❏ Kapp KS-3344 [S] — 1963 — 30.00

AUDIO MASTER PLUS SAMPLER
- ❏ A&M SP6-3000 — 1983 — 15.00

AUDIO MASTER PLUS SAMPLER II
- ❏ A&M SP6-3021 — 1984 — 15.00

AN AUSTIN RHYTHM & BLUES CHRISTMAS
- ❏ Epic PE40576 — 1986 — 12.00

AUTOBIOGRAPHY IN JAZZ
- ❏ Debut DEB-198 [M] — 1955 — 150.00
- ❏ Fantasy OJC-115 — 198? — 12.00

AWARD ALBUM JAZZ VOCALS
- ❏ Bethlehem BCP-6060 [M] — 1961 — 30.00

AWARD WINNERS
- ❏ RCA Victor APL1-2262 — 1977 — 15.00

BACKGROUNDS OF JAZZ, VOL. 1: THE JUG BANDS
- ❏ X LX-3009 [10] — 1954 — 80.00

BACKGROUNDS OF JAZZ, VOL. 2: COUNTRY & URBAN BLUES
- ❏ X LVA-3016 [10] — 1954 — 80.00

BACKGROUNDS OF JAZZ, VOL. 3: KINGS OF THE BLUES
- ❏ X LVA-3032 [10] — 1955 — 80.00

BACK IN THE SADDLE AGAIN: AMERICAN COWBOY SONGS
- ❏ New World 314/5 — 198? — 18.00

BACK TO SCHOOL
- ❏ Epic AS1279 [DJ] — 1981 — 15.00
—*Includes Adam and the Ants, Orchestral Manoeuvres in the Dark, Lene Lovich, others; promo sent to college radio stations*

BACK TO SCHOOL WITH A BEAT
- ❏ A&M SP-17204 [DJ] — 1982 — 12.00
—*Includes Joe Jackson, Oingo Boingo*

BACKWOOD BLUES
- ❏ Riverside RLP-1039 [10] — 1954 — 80.00

BALLADS AND BREAKDOWNS OF THE GOLDEN ERA
- ❏ Columbia CS9660 — 1968 — 25.00

BALLROOM BANDSTAND
- ❏ Columbia CL611 [M] — 1955 — 30.00

BANDED TOGETHER
- ❏ Epic JE36177 — 1979 — 12.00
- ❏ Epic PE36177 — 198? — 10.00
—*Budget-line reissue*

BANG AND SHOUT SUPER HITS
- ❏ Bang BLPS-220 [P] — 1969 — 25.00

BANJO COUNTRY STYLE
- ❏ Audio Lab AL-1569 [M] — 1962 — 80.00

BARGAIN DAY
- ❏ EmArcy MG-36087 [M] — 1956 — 40.00

BARRELHOUSE BOOGIE
- ❏ Bluebird 8334-1-RB — 198? — 12.00

BARREL HOUSE PIANO
- ❏ Brunswick BL58022 [10] — 1951 — 60.00

BARRELHOUSE PIANO 1927-36
- ❏ Yazoo 1028 — 197? — 12.00

A BARREL OF OLDIES
- ❏ Del-Fi DFLP-1219 [M] — 1961 — 50.00

BARRY MANN AND CYNTHIA WEIL: SOLID GOLD
- ❏ Screen Gems/Columbia CPL-712 [DJ] — 1975 — 25.00
—*Promo-only compilation of oldies sent to radio to spur airplay on songs owned by this publishing house*

THE BASS
- ❏ ABC Impulse! AS-9284 — 197? — 25.00

BATTLE OF BANDS
- ❏ Capitol H235 [10] — 1950 — 50.00

BATTLE OF JAZZ, VOL. 3
- ❏ Brunswick BL58039 [10] — 1953 — 50.00

BATTLE OF THE BIG BANDS
- ❏ Capitol T667 [M] — 1956 — 30.00

BATTLE OF THE GARAGES
- ❏ Voxx 200.006 — 1981 — 15.00
—*Includes Slickee Boys, others*

BATTLE OF THE GROUPS
- ❏ End LP-305 [M] — 1960 — 60.00

BATTLE OF THE GROUPS, VOLUME 2
- ❏ End LP-309 [M] — 1960 — 60.00
- ❏ Trip 5527 — 197? — 12.00

BATTLE OF THE SAXES-TENOR ALL STARS
- ❏ EmArcy MG-36023 [M] — 1955 — 50.00

THE BEAT: SOUND WAVE OF THE 80'S
- ❏ K-Tel TU5040 — 1982 — 25.00

BEAT THE RETREAT: SONGS BY RICHARD THOMPSON
- ❏ Capitol C195929 [B] — 1994 — 25.00
—*Includes X, R.E.M., Bob Mould, Los Lobos, Graham Parker, David Byrne*

BEBOP BOYS
- ❏ Savoy Jazz SJL-2225 — 198? — 15.00

THE BEBOP ERA
- ❏ Columbia Jazz Masterpieces CJ40972 — 1988 — 12.00

THE BE-BOP ERA
- ❏ RCA Victor LPV-519 — 1965 — 25.00
- ❏ Prestige PRST-7828 — 1971 — 15.00

THE BELLS OF CHRISTMAS
- ❏ Book-of-the-Month Club 90-5677 — 1973 — 25.00
—*Sold through Book-of-the-Month Records; secondary number is "P3 11972*

BE OUR GUEST
- ❏ Gene Norman GNP-20 [M] — 1955 — 30.00

BESERKLEY'S BACK
- ❏ Beserkley 0067 — 1978 — 18.00
—*Includes Jonathan Richman and the Modern Lovers*

BEST COAST JAZZ
- ❏ EmArcy MG-36039 [M] — 1955 — 80.00

THE BEST FOR '89 FROM THE ENTIRE CAPITOL FAMILY
- ❏ Capitol SPRO79471 [DJ] — 1988 — 18.00
—*Includes Crowded House, dozens of others; personal seasons' greetings*

BEST FROM THE WEST: MODERN SOUNDS FROM CALIFORNIA, VOL. 1
- ❏ Blue Note BLP-5059 [10] — 1955 — 200.00

BEST FROM THE WEST: MODERN SOUNDS FROM CALIFORNIA, VOL. 2
- ❏ Blue Note BLP-5060 [10] — 1955 — 200.00

THE BEST OF ARGO JAZZ
- ❏ Argo ALPS-1 — 1961 — 30.00

BEST OF BAKERSFIELD
- ❏ Capitol ST-11111 — 1972 — 18.00

BEST OF BLUEGRASS
- ❏ Wing MGW-12267 [M] — 1964 — 18.00
- ❏ Wing SRW-16267 [S] — 1964 — 18.00

THE BEST OF BLUE NOTE, VOL. 1
- ❏ Blue Note BST-84429 — 197? — 25.00

THE BEST OF BLUE NOTE, VOL. 2
- ❏ Blue Note BST-84433 — 197? — 25.00

THE BEST OF BOMP! VOLUME ONE
- ❏ Bomp! 4002 — 1978 — 25.00
—*First pressings on white vinyl.*

BEST OF BRITAIN
- ❏ K-Tel TU2380 — 1974 — 15.00
—*20 tracks: Cilla Black/Dave Clark Five/Donovan/Adam Faith/Georgie Fame/Wayne Fontana & Mindbenders/Freddie & Dreamers/Gerry & Pacemakers/Honeycombs/Kinks/Billy J. Kramer & Dakotas/New Vaudeville Band/Searchers/Sandie Shaw/Swinging Blue Jeans/Zombies+*

THE BEST OF BRITISH ROCK
- ❏ Vee Jay VJS1209 — 198? — 15.00
—*Includes Marianne Faithfull*

THE BEST OF CHRISTMAS
- ❏ Capitol STBB2979 — 1968 — 25.00

THE BEST OF COTILLION
- ❏ Atlantic PR505 [DJ] — 1983 — 18.00
—*Includes Neil Young (snippets)*

THE BEST OF COUNTRY DUETS
- ❏ RCA Victor LSP-4082 — 1968 — 18.00

THE BEST OF DISNEY VOL. I
- ❏ Disneyland 2502 — 1978 — 30.00

THE BEST OF DISNEY VOL. II
- ❏ Disneyland 2503 — 1978 — 30.00

BEST OF DIXIELAND
- ❏ RCA Victor ANL1-1431 — 1976 — 12.00

THE BEST OF DIXIELAND
- ❏ RCA Victor LPM-2982 [M] — 1965 — 25.00
- ❏ RCA Victor LSP-2982 [R] — 1965 — 15.00

BEST OF LIMP, REST OF LIMP
- ❏ Limp 1004 — 1980 — 40.00
—*Numbered edition of 1,000*

BEST OF RALPH
- ❏ Ralph RR8251-2 — 1982 — 25.00

BEST OF RHYTHM AND BLUES
- ❏ Jubilee JLP-1014 [M] — 1956 — 500.00
   Pink label, red vinyl
- ❏ Jubilee JLP-1014 [M] — 1956 — 200.00
—*Pink label, black vinyl*
- ❏ Jubilee JLP-1014 [M] — 1956 — 150.00
—*Blue label, black vinyl*

THE BEST OF RHYTHM AND BLUES
- ❏ Warwick W2026 [M] — 1961 — 80.00

BEST OF THE '50S, '60S AND '70S
- ❏ RCA Victor AEL1-5838 — 1986 — 18.00

BEST OF THE '50S
- ❏ RCA Victor AEL1-5800 — 1986 — 18.00

BEST OF THE '60S
- ❏ RCA Victor AEL1-5802 — 1986 — 18.00

BEST OF THE '70S
- ❏ RCA Victor AEL1-5837 — 1986 — 18.00

BEST OF THE 80'S... SO FAR!
- ❏ RCA Victor AHL1-5058 — 198? — 12.00

BEST OF THE BIG NAME BANDS
- ❏ RCA Camden CAL-368 [M] — 1958 — 30.00

BEST OF THE BLUES, VOLUME 1
- ❏ Imperial LP-9257 [M] — 1964 — 30.00
- ❏ Imperial LP-12257 [R] — 1964 — 25.00

BEST OF THE BLUES, VOLUME 2
- ❏ Imperial LP-9259 [M] — 1964 — 30.00
- ❏ Imperial LP-12259 [R] — 1964 — 25.00

BEST OF THE BRITISH INVASION
- ❏ Pye 506 — 1975 — 15.00
—*12 tracks: Long John Baldry/Lonnie Donegan/Honeycombs/ Ivy League/Kinks/Rockin' Berries/Searchers/Sandie Shaw (2) +*

BEST OF THE GREAT SONGS OF CHRISTMAS (ALBUM 10)
- ❏ Columbia Special Products CSS1478 — 1970 — 15.00
—*Sold only at Goodyear tire dealers*

THE BEST OF THE KING BISCUIT FLOWER HOUR
- ❏ Silver Eagle SE10674 — 1988 — 30.00

BEST OF THE MUSICAL SOUNDS OF CHRISTMAS
- ❏ Capitol Creative Products SL-6713 — 1971 — 15.00

BEST OF THE NEW
- ❏ Warner Bros. PRO-A-1083 [DJ] — 1982 — 25.00
—*Promo-only collection of mixes from 12-inch singles; this was the first album to include a song by Madonna, the 12-inch version of "Everybody," before her debut LP was issued*

THE BEST OF THE R AND B GROUPS
- ❏ Warwick W2025 [M] — 1961 — 100.00

Number	Title	Yr	NM

BEST OF THE SOUNDTRACKS
- ❏ Tower ST-5148 — 1969 — 30.00

THE BEST VOCAL GROUPS IN ROCK 'N' ROLL
- ❏ Dooto DL-224 [M] — 1957 — 100.00
  — *Yellow label*
- ❏ Dooto DL-224 [M] — 196? — 30.00
  — *Multi-color label*

BETHLEHEM'S BEST
- ❏ Bethlehem EXLP-6 [M] — 1958 — 70.00
  — *Box set of 82, 83, and 84*

BETHLEHEM'S BEST, VOLUME 1
- ❏ Bethlehem BCP-82 [M] — 1958 — 30.00

BETHLEHEM'S BEST, VOLUME 2
- ❏ Bethlehem BCP-83 [M] — 1958 — 30.00

BETHLEHEM'S BEST, VOLUME 3
- ❏ Bethlehem BCP-84 [M] — 1958 — 30.00

BETHLEHEM'S GRAB BAG
- ❏ Bethlehem EXLP-2 [M] — 1958 — 40.00

THE BIG 18 -- LIVE ECHOES OF THE SWINGING BANDS
- ❏ RCA Victor LSP-1921 [S] — 1959 — 50.00
- ❏ RCA Victor LPM-1921 [M] — 1959 — 40.00

THE BIG BALL
- ❏ Warner Bros. PRO358 — 1970 — 30.00
  — *Originals have green labels*

BIG BAND CONTRAST
- ❏ Bethlehem BCP-6037 [M] — 1960 — 30.00

BIG BAND JAZZ
- ❏ Brunswick BL58050 [10] — 1953 — 50.00

BIG BAND JAZZ: TULSA TO HARLEM
- ❏ Delmark DL-439 — 1989 — 12.00

BIG BANDS
- ❏ Capitol STFL-293 — 1969 — 30.00
  — *One album each by Les Brown, Glen Gray, Duke Ellington, Benny Goodman, Harry James and Woody Herman*

BIG BANDS!
- ❏ Onyx 202 — 197? — 15.00

BIG BANDS: BIG BAND BASH
- ❏ Time-Life STBB-15 — 1984 — 18.00

BIG BANDS: ON THE ROAD
- ❏ Time-Life STBB-18 — 1985 — 18.00

BIG BANDS: THE SMALL GROUPS
- ❏ Time-Life STBB-21 — 1985 — 18.00

BIG BANDS: UPTOWN
- ❏ Time-Life STBB-20 — 1985 — 18.00

BIG BANDS: WORLD WAR II
- ❏ Time-Life STBB-28 — 1986 — 18.00

THE BIG BANDS 1000
- ❏ Prestige PRLP-7645 — 1969 — 18.00

BIG BANDS ARE BACK
- ❏ Commodore J2-15596 — 198? — 15.00

BIG BANDS' GREATEST HITS
- ❏ Columbia G30009 — 1970 — 25.00
  — *Red "360 Sound" labels*
- ❏ Columbia G30009 — 1970 — 18.00
  — *Orange labels*
- ❏ Columbia CG30009 — 197? — 15.00
  — *CG" prefix is a reissue of "G*

BIG BANDS' GREATEST HITS, VOL. 2
- ❏ Columbia G31213 — 1972 — 18.00
- ❏ Columbia G31213 — 197? — 15.00
  — *CG" prefix is a reissue of "G*

BIG BANDS OF THE SINGING YEARS, VOLUME 1
- ❏ Collectables COL-5096 — 198? — 12.00

BIG BANDS OF THE SINGING YEARS, VOLUME 2
- ❏ Collectables COL-5097 — 198? — 12.00

BIG BANDS OF THE SWING YEARS
- ❏ Everest Archive of Folk & Jazz 359 — 198? — 12.00

BIG BAND STEREO
- ❏ Capitol SW1055 [S] — 1959 — 30.00

BIG BANDS UPTOWN
- ❏ MCA 1323 — 198? — 12.00

BIG BANDS UPTOWN, VOL. 1
- ❏ Decca DL79242 — 1969 — 15.00

THE BIG BEAT
- ❏ Milestone 47016 — 1990 — 18.00

BIG COUNTRY HITS
- ❏ Pickwick JS-6166 — 1975 — 30.00

BIG COUNTRY HITS, VOL. 1
- ❏ RCA Victor LPM-3606 [M] — 1966 — 18.00
- ❏ RCA Victor LSP-3606 [S] — 1966 — 25.00

THE BIG HITS
- ❏ Columbia CL1353 [M] — 1959 — 30.00
- ❏ Columbia CS8161 [S] — 1959 — 40.00

THE BIG HITS OF MID-AMERICA
- ❏ Soma MG-1245 [M] — 1965 — 80.00

THE BIG HITS OF MID-AMERICA, VOLUME 2
- ❏ Soma MG-1246 [M] — 1965 — 80.00

BIG HITS OF MID-AMERICA VOLUME THREE
- ❏ Twin/Tone TTTR7907/8 — 1979 — 25.00

BIG LITTLE BANDS
- ❏ Onyx 220 — 197? — 15.00

BIG NAME DIXIE
- ❏ Score SLP-4024 [M] — 1958 — 50.00

THE BIG ONES FROM DUKE AND PEACOCK RECORDS
- ❏ Peacock PLP-2000 [M] — 1967 — 25.00

BIG RED MUSIC
- ❏ Columbia AS536 [DJ] — 1978 — 18.00
  — *Includes Boomtown Rats; red vinyl*

THE BIG SOUNDS OF THE DRAGS!
- ❏ Capitol T2001 [M] — 1963 — 25.00
- ❏ Capitol ST2001 [S] — 1963 — 30.00

BIG SUR FESTIVAL/ONE HAND CLAPPING
- ❏ Columbia KC31138 — 1972 — 25.00

BIG SURF HITS
- ❏ Del-Fi DFLP-1249 [M] — 1964 — 50.00
- ❏ Del-Fi DFST-1249 [S] — 1964 — 75.00

THE BIG TIME SYNDROME
- ❏ Big Time 6050-1-B — 1987 — 12.00
  — *Includes Love and Rockets, Redd Kross, Dream Syndicate*

BILLBOARD GREATEST CHRISTMAS HITS, 1935-1954
- ❏ Rhino R170637 — 1989 — 18.00

BILLBOARD GREATEST CHRISTMAS HITS, 1955-PRESENT
- ❏ Rhino R170636 — 1989 — 18.00

BILL EVANS: A TRIBUTE
- ❏ Palo Alto PA-8028 — 1982 — 18.00

BILL HARD SAMPLER
- ❏ Epic AS725 [DJ] — 1979 — 12.00
  — *Includes The Clash, Lene Lovich, The Romantics*

BILLIE, ELLA, LENA, SARAH!
- ❏ Columbia Jazz Odyssey PC36011 — 198? — 12.00

BILLIE HOLIDAY REVISITED
- ❏ Mainstream MRL-409 — 197? — 15.00

BING CROSBY AND ROSEMARY CLOONEY: WHITE CHRISTMAS
- ❏ Holiday/Collector's Gold 598 — 1980 — 12.00
  — *Crosby recordings are from a radio broadcast*

BIRDLAND ALL STARS AT CARNEGIE HALL
- ❏ Roulette RE-127 — 197? — 15.00

BIRDLANDERS
- ❏ Everest Archive of Folk & Jazz 275 — 197? — 12.00

THE BIRDLAND STARS ON TOUR, VOL. 1
- ❏ RCA Victor LPM-1327 [M] — 1956 — 40.00

THE BIRDLAND STARS ON TOUR, VOL. 2
- ❏ RCA Victor LPM-1328 [M] — 1956 — 40.00

THE BIRDLAND STORY
- ❏ Roulette RB-2 [M] — 1961 — 40.00
- ❏ Roulette SRB-2 [S] — 1961 — 40.00

BIRD'S NIGHT: A CELEBRATION OF THE MUSIC OF CHARLIE PARKER, LIVE AT THE FIVE SPOT
- ❏ Savoy Jazz SJL-2257 — 198? — 15.00

BIRD'S NIGHT -- THE MUSIC OF CHARLIE PARKER
- ❏ Savoy MG-12138 [M] — 1958 — 50.00

THE BIRTH OF BOP, VOL. 1
- ❏ Savoy MG-9022 [10] — 1953 — 150.00

THE BIRTH OF BOP, VOL. 2
- ❏ Savoy MG-9023 [10] — 1953 — 150.00

THE BIRTH OF BOP, VOL. 3
- ❏ Savoy MG-9024 [10] — 1953 — 150.00

THE BIRTH OF BOP, VOL. 4
- ❏ Savoy MG-9025 [10] — 1953 — 150.00

THE BIRTH OF BOP, VOL. 5
- ❏ Savoy MG-9026 [10] — 1953 — 150.00

BIRTH OF SOUL
- ❏ Decca DL79245 — 1969 — 15.00

BLACK AND WHITE RAGTIME, 1921-39
- ❏ Biograph 12047 — 197? — 15.00

BLACKBERRY JAM 1943-45
- ❏ Sunbeam 214 — 197? — 12.00

BLACK CALIFORNIA, VOL. 1
- ❏ Savoy Jazz SJL-2215 — 198? — 15.00

BLACK CALIFORNIA, VOL. 2
- ❏ Savoy Jazz SJL-2242 — 198? — 15.00

BLACK GIANTS
- ❏ Columbia CG33402 — 197? — 18.00

BLACK LION AT MONTREUX
- ❏ Black Lion 213 — 197? — 18.00

THE BLACK SWING TRADITION
- ❏ Savoy Jazz SJL-2246 — 198? — 15.00

THE BLASTING CONCEPT, VOL. II
- ❏ SST 043 — 1986 — 15.00
  — *Includes Black Flag, Husker Du, Meat Puppets, Minutemen, etc.*

BLEECKER AND MACDOUGAL: THE FOLK SCENE OF THE 1960S
- ❏ Elektra 60381 — 1984 — 25.00

BLOWIN' SESSIONS
- ❏ Blue Note BN-LA521-H2 — 1975 — 25.00

BLOWOUT AT MARDI GRAS
- ❏ Cook LP-1084 [M] — 1955 — 40.00

BLUE CHRISTMAS
- ❏ Welk Music Group WM-3002 [DJ] — 1984 — 80.00
  — *Promo only; compiled by the publisher of "Blue Christmas" and other holiday tunes for radio use*

BLUEGRASS: THE WORLD'S GREATEST SHOW
- ❏ Sugar Hill SH-2201 — 198? — 18.00

THE BLUEGRASS ALBUM
- ❏ Rounder 0140 — 198? — 12.00

THE BLUEGRASS ALBUM, VOL. 2
- ❏ Rounder 0164 — 198? — 12.00

THE BLUEGRASS ALBUM, VOL. 3
- ❏ Rounder 0180 — 198? — 12.00

THE BLUEGRASS ALBUM, VOL. 4
- ❏ Rounder 0210 — 198? — 12.00

BLUEGRASS OLDIES BUT GOODIES
- ❏ Cumberland MGC-29520 [M] — 1965 — 18.00
- ❏ Cumberland SRC-69520 [S] — 1965 — 18.00
- ❏ Smash MGS-27028 [M] — 1963 — 25.00
- ❏ Smash SRS-67028 [S] — 1963 — 25.00

BLUEGRASS SPECTACULAR
- ❏ CMH 5902 — 198? — 18.00
- ❏ Starday SLP-232 [M] — 1963 — 30.00

THE BLUE NOTE 50TH ANNIVERSARY COLLECTION VOL. 1: FROM BOOGIE TO BOP, 1939-1956
- ❏ Blue Note B1-92465 — 1989 — 18.00

THE BLUE NOTE 50TH ANNIVERSARY COLLECTION VOL. 2: THE JAZZ MESSAGE, 1956-1965
- ❏ Blue Note B1-92468 — 1989 — 18.00

THE BLUE NOTE 50TH ANNIVERSARY COLLECTION VOL. 3: FUNK AND BLUES, 1956-1967
- ❏ Blue Note B1-92471 — 1989 — 18.00

THE BLUE NOTE 50TH ANNIVERSARY COLLECTION VOL. 4: OUTSIDE IN, 1964-1989
- ❏ Blue Note B1-92474 — 1989 — 18.00

THE BLUE NOTE 50TH ANNIVERSARY COLLECTION VOL. 5: LIGHTING THE FUSE, 1970-1989
- ❏ Blue Note B1-92477 — 1989 — 18.00

BLUE NOTE '86: A GENERATION OF JAZZ
- ❏ Blue Note BQ-85127 — 1986 — 15.00

BLUE NOTE CLASSICS
- ❏ Blue Note B-6509 [M] — 1969 — 18.00

BLUE NOTE LIVE AT THE ROXY
- ❏ Blue Note BN-LA663-J2 — 1976 — 18.00

BLUE NOTE MEETS THE L.A. PHILHARMONIC
- ❏ Blue Note BN-LA870-H — 1977 — 18.00

BLUE RIBBON COUNTRY
- ❏ Capitol STBB2969 — 1968 — 30.00

BLUE RIBBON COUNTRY, VOL. 2
- ❏ Capitol STBB-217 — 1969 — 30.00

THE BLUES
- ❏ Vee Jay LP-1020 [M] — 1960 — 40.00
- ❏ Vee VJS-2-1007 — 1974 — 25.00

THE BLUES, VOL. 2
- ❏ Pacific Jazz JWC-502 [M] — 1956 — 50.00
- ❏ World Pacific JWC-502 [M] — 1958 — 40.00

Number	Title	Yr	NM

THE BLUES, VOL. 2: HAVE BLUES, WILL TRAVEL
- ❏ World Pacific JWC-509 [M] — 1958 — 40.00

THE BLUES, VOL. 3: BLOWIN' THE BLUES
- ❏ World Pacific JWC-512 [M] — 1958 — 40.00
- ❏ World Pacific ST-1029 [S] — 1959 — 30.00

THE BLUES, VOLUME 1
- ❏ Argo LP-4026 [M] — 1963 — 30.00

THE BLUES, VOLUME 2
- ❏ Argo LP-4027 [M] — 1963 — 30.00

THE BLUES, VOLUME 3
- ❏ Argo LP-4034 [M] — 1964 — 30.00

THE BLUES, VOLUME 4
- ❏ Argo LP-4042 [M] — 1964 — 30.00

THE BLUES, VOLUME 5
- ❏ Cadet LP-4051 [M] — 1966 — 30.00

THE BLUES AND ALL THAT JAZZ
- ❏ MCA 1353 — 198? — 12.00

BLUES FOR TOMORROW
- ❏ Fantasy OJC-030 — 1982 — 12.00
- ❏ Riverside RLP 12-243 [M] — 1957 — 40.00

BLUES FROM BIG BILL'S COPACABANA
- ❏ Chess LP1533 [M] — 1969 — 30.00
- *— Possibly a reissue of "Folk Festival of the Blues," Argo 4031*

BLUES IN CONCERT
- ❏ Groove Merchant 4405 — 197? — 25.00

THE BLUES IN MODERN JAZZ
- ❏ Atlantic 1337 [M] — 1961 — 25.00
- *— Multicolor label, white "fan" logo at right*
- ❏ Atlantic 1337 [M] — 1963 — 18.00
- *— Multicolor label, black "fan" logo at right*
- ❏ Atlantic SD1337 [R] — 1969 — 15.00

THE BLUES IN STEREO
- ❏ World Pacific ST-1021 [S] — 1959 — 30.00

BLUES LIVE IN BATON ROUGE
- ❏ Excello I PS-8021 — 1971 — 30.00

BLUES 'N' FOLK
- ❏ Bethlehem BCP-6071 [M] — 1963 — 60.00

THE BLUES PROJECT
- ❏ Elektra EKL-264 [M] — 1964 — 30.00
- ❏ Elektra EKS-7264 [S] — 1964 — 30.00
- *— No relation to the band of the same name; on one track, Bob Dylan plays piano under the name "Bob Landy"*

BLUES THAT GAVE AMERICA SOUL
- ❏ ABC Duke DLPX-82 [S] — 1974 — 18.00
- ❏ Duke DLP-82 [M] — 1966 — 25.00
- ❏ Duke DLPS-82 [S] — 1966 — 30.00

BLUES UPTOWN: URBAN BLUES, VOLUME 1
- ❏ Imperial LP-94002 — 1968 — 25.00

BLUESVILLE
- ❏ Bethlehem BCP-6038 [M] — 1960 — 30.00

BODY AND SOUL
- ❏ RCA Victor LPV-501 — 1964 — 25.00

BONING UP ON 'BONES
- ❏ EmArcy MG-36038 [M] — 1955 — 50.00

BOOGIE WOOGIE
- ❏ Decca DL5248 [10] — 1950 — 50.00

BOOGIE WOOGIE KINGS AND QUEENS
- ❏ Decca DL5249 [10] — 1950 — 50.00

BOOGIE WOOGIE PIANO
- ❏ Brunswick BL58018 [10] — 1950 — 60.00

BOOGIE WOOGIE PIANOS
- ❏ Columbia KC32708 — 197? — 12.00

BOOGIE WOOGIE RARITIES (1927-43)
- ❏ Milestone M-2009 — 197? — 15.00

BOOGIE WOOGIE TRIO
- ❏ Storyville 4006 — 198? — 12.00

BOOTY
- ❏ Mainstream MRL-413 — 1974 — 30.00

BOP CITY: EVIDENCE
- ❏ Boplicity BOPM-12 — 198? — 12.00

BOP CITY: MIDNIGHT
- ❏ Boplicity BOPM-9 — 198? — 12.00

BOP CITY: STRAIGHT AHEAD
- ❏ Boplicity BOPM-10 — 198? — 12.00

BOP CITY: THINGS ARE GETTING BETTER
- ❏ Boplicity BOPM-11 — 198? — 12.00

BOP LIVES
- ❏ Pickwick SPC-5011 — 197? — 12.00

BOPPIN'
- ❏ Jubilee JGM-1118 [M] — 1960 — 150.00

BORN AGAIN: 20 MOST LOVED SONGS OF FAITH & INSPIRATION
- ❏ Sufflok Marketing SMI-5K — 1977 — 12.00

BOSS GOLDIES -- SOUNDS FROM THE GROOVEYARD
- ❏ Columbia CL2559 [M] — 1966 — 25.00
- ❏ Columbia CS9339 [S] — 1966 — 30.00

BOWLING BALLS FROM HELL
- ❏ Clone CL-010 — 1980 — 18.00
- *— Includes The Waitresses; compilation of Akron, Ohio bands*

BOWLING BALLS II
- ❏ Clone CL-013 — 1981 — 18.00
- *— Includes The Waitresses, Tin Huey, more Akron bands*

BOY MEETS GIRL
- ❏ Stax STS 2-2024 — 1969 — 25.00

BRASS FEVER
- ❏ ABC Impulse! AS-9308 — 1975 — 18.00

BRASS FEVER: TIME IS RUNNING OUT
- ❏ ABC Impulse! AS-9319 — 197? — 18.00

BREAKERS
- ❏ A&M SP-17271 [DJ] — 1984 — 15.00
- *— Includes UB40, Simple Minds, The Alarm*

BREAKING THE RULES
- ❏ Columbia A2S881 [DJ] — 1980 — 25.00

THE BRIDGE SCHOOL CONCERTS, VOL. ONE
- ❏ Reprise 46824-1 — 1997 — 25.00
- ❏ Reprise 46824-1 — 1997 — 25.00

THE BRIGHTEST STARS OF CHRISTMAS
- ❏ RCA Special Products DPL1-0086 — 1974 — 25.00
- *— Sold only at JCPenney department stores*

BRIGHT LIGHTS AND HONKY TONKS
- ❏ Starday SLP-239 [M] — 1963 — 30.00

THE BRISTOL SESSIONS
- ❏ Country Music Foundation CMF-011 — 198? — 18.00

BRITISH FESTIVAL OF JAZZ CONCERT
- ❏ Decca DL5422 [10] — 1952 — 50.00

BRITISH GOLD
- ❏ Sire R224095 — 1978 — 25.00
- *— RCA Music Service edition*

BRITISH INVASION -- THE HISTORY OF BRITISH ROCK, VOL. 2
- ❏ Rhino R1-70321 — 1988 — 12.00
- *— Includes The Searchers*

BRITISH INVASION -- THE HISTORY OF BRITISH ROCK, VOL. 3
- ❏ Rhino R1-70322 — 1988 — 12.00
- *— Includes The Searchers*

BRITISH JAZZ FESTIVAL
- ❏ Decca DL5424 [10] — 1952 — 50.00

BRITISH ROCK CLASSICS
- ❏ Sire R234021 — 1978 — 25.00
- *— RCA Music Service edition*

BRITISH STERLING
- ❏ Lakefront LSM811 — 1981 — 30.00

BROADWAY CHRISTMAS SONGS
- ❏ Broadway BLP-XMAS-1001 — 19?? — 15.00
- *— Performed by anonymous musicians*

BROTHERS AND OTHER MOTHERS
- ❏ Savoy Jazz SJL-2210 — 198? — 15.00

BROTHERS AND OTHER MOTHERS, VOL. 2
- ❏ Savoy Jazz SJL-2236 — 198? — 15.00

BRUNSWICK'S GREATEST HITS
- ❏ Brunswick BL754186 — 1973 — 25.00

BUBBLE GUM MUSIC IS THE NAKED TRUTH, VOLUME 1
- ❏ Buddah BDA5032 — 1969 — 30.00

BUDDAH'S 360 DEGREE DIAL-A-HIT
- ❏ Buddah BDA5039 — 1969 — 30.00
- *— With rotating wheel under the front LP cover*

A BUMPER CROP OF ALL STARS
- ❏ King 753 [M] — 1961 — 100.00

BUNCH OF GOODIES
- ❏ Chess LP1441 [DJ] — 1960 — 600.00
- *— Multi-color splash vinyl*
- ❏ Chess LP1441 [M] — 1960 — 120.00
- *— Black vinyl*

BURBANK
- ❏ Warner Bros. PRO529 — 1972 — 30.00
- *— Originals have green labels*

BURBANK'S GREATEST HITS
- ❏ Warner Bros. PRO548 — 1973 — 25.00

BUSHKIN-SAFRANSKI-WILSON GROUPS
- ❏ Allegro 1590 [10] — 1955 — 50.00

BYE BYE BIRDIE
- ❏ Colpix CP-454 [M] — 1963 — 80.00
- ❏ Colpix SCP-454 [S] — 1963 — 100.00
- *— Studio version performed by Paul Petersen, Shelley Fabares, James Darren, the Marcels and others*

CAFÉ SOCIETY
- ❏ Onyx 210 — 197? — 15.00

CALIFORNIA CONCERT
- ❏ CTI CTX2+ 2 — 197? — 18.00

CALIFORNIA JAM 2
- ❏ Columbia PC235389 — 1978 — 25.00

CAN YOU HEAR ME? MUSIC FROM THE DEAF CLUB
- ❏ Optional/Walking Dead 001 — 1980 — 30.00
- ❏ PVC 7920 — 1980 — 25.00

THE CAPITOL DISC JOCKEY ALBUM MARCH 1967
- ❏ Capitol SPRO-4291/2 [DJ] — 1967 — 15.00

THE CAPITOL DISC JOCKEY ALBUM APRIL 1967
- ❏ Capitol SPRO-4316/7 [DJ] — 1967 — 15.00

THE CAPITOL DISC JOCKEY ALBUM JUNE 1967
- ❏ Capitol SPRO-4344/5 [DJ] — 1967 — 15.00

THE CAPITOL DISC JOCKEY ALBUM JULY 1967
- ❏ Capitol SPRO-4359/60 [DJ] — 1967 — 15.00

THE CAPITOL DISC JOCKEY ALBUM AUGUST 1967
- ❏ Capitol SPRO-4370/1 [DJ] — 1967 — 15.00

THE CAPITOL DISC JOCKEY ALBUM JANUARY 1968
- ❏ Capitol SPRO-4469/70 [DJ] — 1968 — 15.00

THE CAPITOL DISC JOCKEY ALBUM APRIL 1968
- ❏ Capitol SPRO-4520/1 [DJ] — 1968 — 15.00

THE CAPITOL DISC JOCKEY ALBUM SEPTEMBER 1968
- ❏ Capitol SPRO-4621/2 [DJ] — 1968 — 15.00

THE CAPITOL DISC JOCKEY ALBUM JULY 1969
- ❏ Capitol SPRO-4774/5 [DJ] — 1969 — 15.00
- *— Label calls this "Disc Jockey Sampler*

THE CAPITOL DISC JOCKEY ALBUM NOVEMBER 1969
- ❏ Capitol SPRO-4883/4 [DJ] — 1969 — 15.00

THE CAPITOL DISC JOCKEY ALBUM JANUARY 1970
- ❏ Capitol SPRO-4920/1 [DJ] — 1970 — 15.00

THE CAPITOL DISC JOCKEY ALBUM FEBRUARY 1970
- ❏ Capitol SPRO-4934/5 [DJ] — 1970 — 15.00

THE CAPITOL DISC JOCKEY ALBUM FOR CHRISTMAS 1967
- ❏ Capitol SPRO-4456/7 [DJ] — 1967 — 18.00

CAPITOL HITS SAMPLER
- ❏ Capitol SPRO-9481 [DJ] — 1985 — 18.00
- *— Includes The Power Station, The Motels, etc.*

CAPITOL IN-STORE SAMPLER
- ❏ Capitol SPRO9867/8 [DJ] — 1982 — 18.00
- *— Includes Missing Persons (2), Duran Duran -- also includes "Love Me Do" by the Beatles*

CARLOAD O' HITS
- ❏ Muse M-500 [M] — 1959 — 200.00

A CARNIVAL OF SONGS
- ❏ King 819 [M] — 1963 — 100.00

CAROLS AND CANDLELIGHT
- ❏ Columbia Special Products P12525 — 1974 — 12.00
- *— Sold only at Goodyear tire dealers*

THE CATS
- ❏ Fantasy OJC-079 — 198? — 12.00
- ❏ New Jazz NJLP-8217 [M] — 1959 — 80.00
- *— Purple label*
- ❏ New Jazz NJLP-8217 [M] — 1965 — 30.00
- *— Blue label, trident logo at right*

CATS AND JAMMER KIDS
- ❏ Angel ANG-60007 [10] — 1955 — 50.00

CATS VS. CHICKS
- ❏ MGM E-255 [10] — 1954 — 50.00

CBS RECORDS NASHVILLE SUPER HITLINE '88
- ❏ Columbia AS1424 [DJ] — 1988 — 15.00
- *— Includes Roseanne Cash (snippet)*

CBS TWO-FERS ARE GREAT MUSICAL VALUES!
- ❏ CBS A2S143/4 [DJ] — 1975 — 25.00

Number	Title	Yr	NM

CELEBRATE THE SEASON WITH TUPPERWARE
- ❑ RCA Special Products DPL1-0803 — 1987 — 25.00
— *Sold only at Tupperware parties*

A CELEBRATION OF DUKE
- ❑ Fantasy OJC-605 — 1991 — 15.00
- ❑ Pablo Today 2312119 — 197? — 18.00

CENTRAL AVENUE BREAKDOWN, VOL. 1
- ❑ Onyx 212 — 197? — 15.00

CENTRAL AVENUE BREAKDOWN, VOL. 2
- ❑ Onyx 215 — 197? — 15.00

CHA CHA CHA CARNIVAL
- ❑ Forum F9051 [M] — 196? — 12.00
- ❑ Forum FS9051 [S] — 196? — 15.00
— *Caney; Neil Lewis; Joe Lustig; Machito; Tito Puente; Tito Rodriguez; Pete Terrace*

THE CHANGING FACE OF HARLEM
- ❑ Savoy Jazz SJL-2208 — 198? — 15.00

THE CHANGING FACE OF HARLEM, VOL. 2
- ❑ Savoy Jazz SJL-2224 — 198? — 15.00

CHARLIE PARKER 10TH MEMORIAL CONCERT
- ❑ Limelight LM-82017 [M] — 1965 — 18.00
- ❑ Limelight LS-86017 [S] — 1965 — 25.00
- ❑ Trip 5510 — 197? — 12.00

CHARLIE PARKER MEMORIAL CONCERT
- ❑ Cadet 2CA-60002 — 1971 — 25.00
- ❑ Chess CH-92510 — 198? — 15.00

CHARTBUSTERS, VOL. 2
- ❑ Capitol T1945 [M] — 1963 — 30.00
- ❑ Capitol ST1945 [S] — 1963 — 40.00

CHARTBUSTERS, VOL. 3
- ❑ Capitol T2006 [M] — 1963 — 30.00
- ❑ Capitol ST2006 [S] — 1963 — 40.00

CHARTBUSTERS, VOL. 4
- ❑ Capitol T2094 [M] — 1964 — 40.00
- ❑ Capitol ST2094 [S] — 1964 — 60.00

CHARTBUSTERS: THE BEST OF BESERKLEY RECORDS 1975-1978
- ❑ Rhino RNLP70096 — 1986 — 12.00
— *Includes Jonathan Richman and the Modern Lovers (3)*

CHART BUSTERS '62
- ❑ Capitol T1837 [M] — 1963 — 30.00
- ❑ Capitol ST1837 [S] — 1963 — 40.00

CHESS IS BACK!
- ❑ Chess CH-333 [DJ] — 1982 — 25.00
— *Promo only, distributed by Sugar Hill*

CHICAGO: THE LIVING LEGENDS, VOL. 1
- ❑ Riverside RLP-389 [M] — 196? — 25.00
- ❑ Riverside RS-9389 [R] — 196? — 15.00

CHICAGO: THE LIVING LEGENDS, VOL. 2
- ❑ Riverside RLP-390 [M] — 196? — 25.00
- ❑ Riverside RS-9390 [R] — 196? — 15.00

CHICAGO AND ALL THAT JAZZ!
- ❑ Verve V-8441 [M] — 1961 — 30.00
- ❑ Verve V6-8441 [S] — 1962 — 30.00

THE CHICAGOANS
- ❑ Decca DL79231 — 1968 — 15.00

CHICAGO / AUSTIN HIGH SCHOOL
- ❑ RCA Victor LPM-1508 [M] — 1957 — 30.00

CHICAGO BLUES ANTHOLOGY
- ❑ Chess 2CH-60012 — 1972 — 25.00

CHICAGO JAZZ, 1923-29
- ❑ Biograph 12005 — 1968 — 15.00

CHICAGO JAZZ, VOLUME 2, 1925-29
- ❑ Biograph 12043 — 197? — 15.00

CHICAGO JAZZ ALBUM
- ❑ Decca DL8029 [M] — 1954 — 40.00

CHICAGO'S BOSS TENORS
- ❑ Chess CHV-414 — 1970 — 18.00

A CHILD'S CHRISTMAS
- ❑ Harmony HS14563 — 197? — 15.00

CHOCOLATE DANDIES, 1928-1933
- ❑ Swing SW-8448 — 198? — 12.00

CHRISTMAS -- A GIFT OF MUSIC
- ❑ Capitol Special Markets SL-6687 — 197? — 15.00
— *Reissue of "Zenith Presents Chrirsmas, A Gift of Music, Vol. 4" with almost identical cover*

A CHRISTMAS ALBUM
- ❑ Columbia PC39466 — 1984 — 12.00
— *Abridgement of "The Christmas Album," Columbia G 30763*

THE CHRISTMAS ALBUM
- ❑ Columbia G30763 — 1972 — 18.00

CHRISTMAS ALBUM
- ❑ Power Pak PO-507 — 1974 — 12.00

CHRISTMAS AMERICA
- ❑ Capitol Special Markets SL-6884 — 1973 — 15.00
— *Sold only at Firestone tire dealers (add 50% for sticker that says "Season's Greetings Firestone")*

CHRISTMAS AMERICA, ALBUM TWO
- ❑ Capitol Special Markets SL-6950 — 1974 — 15.00
— *Sold only at Firestone tire dealers (add 50% for sticker that says "Season's Greetings Firestone")*

CHRISTMAS AS IT HAPPENED
- ❑ Mennonite Hour TR4H-5299/5300 [DJ] — 1966 — 15.00
— *A series of seven 'newscasts' of the memorable events leading up to the birth of Jesus Christ; tracks have locked grooves; possibly issued without a cover*

CHRISTMAS AT HOME
- ❑ Capitol Creative Products SL-6530 — 1967 — 15.00

CHRISTMAS AT LUKE'S HOUSE
- ❑ Luke XR205-1 — 1993 — 15.00

CHRISTMAS AT LUKE'S SEX SHOP
- ❑ Luke XR206-1 — 1993 — 18.00
— *Featuring Luke, 2 Live Crew, Poison Clan, Home Team & Jiggle Gee (individual tracks not credited)*

CHRISTMAS AT OUR HOUSE
- ❑ Impact R3381 — 1975 — 15.00
— *Also contains narration by John T. Benson*

A CHRISTMAS CAROL/MUSIC OF CHRISTMAS
- ❑ MGM E3222 [M] — 1955 — 30.00
— *Expanded version of 10-inch LP. Also see LIONEL BARRYMORE.*

CHRISTMAS CAROUSEL
- ❑ Capitol SQBE-94406 — 1972 — 18.00
— *Available only through the Capitol Record Club*

CHRISTMAS CELEBRATION, A
- ❑ Vox Turnabout TV34869 — 1984 — 12.00

CHRISTMAS CHORUS
- ❑ Columbia Special Products CSS932/3 — 1969 — 18.00
— *Produced for NORM/A Step Ahead*

CHRISTMAS CLASSICS
- ❑ WCI UN-540 — 1985 — 25.00
— *Records individually numbered: 1. Capitol Special Markets SL-9309; 2. CBS Special Products P-18335; 3. CBS Special Products P-18334; 4. Capitol Special Markets SL 9308*

CHRISTMAS CLASSICS 1963
- ❑ E.F. MacDonald EFMX-63 — 1963 — 25.00
— *Special album done by the E.F. MacDonald Company, Dayton, Ohio*

CHRISTMAS CLASSICS (GOLDEN ARCHIVE SERIES)
- ❑ Rhino R170192 — 1988 — 18.00

CHRISTMAS COUNTRY
- ❑ Elektra 5E-554 — 1981 — 15.00

CHRISTMAS DAY
- ❑ Pickwick SPC1010 — 197? — 15.00

CHRISTMAS DAY IN THE COUNTRY
- ❑ Columbia Special Products P11887 — 1973 — 12.00

CHRISTMAS DAY WITH COLONEL SANDERS
- ❑ RCA Victor PRS-274 — 1968 — 25.00
— *Sold only at Kentucky Fried Chicken restaurants*

A CHRISTMAS DEDICATION FROM…
- ❑ Chess CH9717 — 1984 — 15.00

CHRISTMAS DOWN HOME
- ❑ Columbia Special Products P15849 — 1981 — 15.00
— *Sold only at Radio Shack stores; additional number is Realistic 51-7003*

CHRISTMAS DREAMS AND HOLIDAY WISHES
- ❑ RCA Special Products DPL1-0630 — 1983 — 12.00
— *Produced for the Fuller Brush Company*

CHRISTMAS ENCORES
- ❑ Columbia Special Products P15430 — 1981 — 12.00

CHRISTMAS EVE WITH COLONEL SANDERS
- ❑ RCA Victor PRS-256 — 1967 — 25.00
— *Sold only at Kentucky Fried Chicken restaurants*

CHRISTMAS FAVORITES
- ❑ RCA Victor PR-115-A [M] — 1961 — 18.00
— *Sold only at Acme markets (Mid-Atlantic states)*

A CHRISTMAS FESTIVAL
- ❑ Columbia Special Products P15429 — 1981 — 12.00
- ❑ RCA Record Club CCS-0145 — 1970 — 18.00

A CHRISTMAS FESTIVAL OF SONGS AND CAROLS
- ❑ RCA Victor PRM-170 [M] — 1964 — 15.00
— *Sold only at JCPenney department stores*
- ❑ RCA Victor PRS-170 [S] — 1964 — 18.00
— *Sold only at JCPenney department stores*

A CHRISTMAS FESTIVAL OF SONGS AND CAROLS, VOLUME 2
- ❑ RCA Victor PRM-195 [M] — 1965 — 15.00
— *Sold only at JCPenney department stores*
- ❑ RCA Victor PRS-195 [S] — 1965 — 18.00
— *Sold only at JCPenney department stores*

CHRISTMAS FOR THE 90'S, VOLUME 1
- ❑ Capitol Nashville 1P8117 — 1990 — 18.00
— *Available on vinyl through Columbia House only*

CHRISTMAS FOR THE 90'S, VOLUME 2
- ❑ Capitol Nashville 1P8118 — 1990 — 18.00
— *Available on vinyl through Columbia House only*

A CHRISTMAS GIFT FOR YOU FROM PHILLES RECORDS
- ❑ Philles PHLP-4005 [M] — 1963 — 150.00
— *First edition of this group of songs; blue and black labels*
- ❑ Philles PHLP-4005 [M] — 1964 — 80.00
— *Second edition of this group of songs; yellow and red labels; both first and second editions have "Marshmellow [sic] World" typo on front cover; also see PHIL SPECTOR'S CHRISTMAS ALBUM*

A CHRISTMAS GIFT FOR YOU FROM PHIL SPECTOR
- ❑ Phil Spector/Abkco D1-4005 [M] — 1989 — 25.00
— *Eighth edition of this group of songs*
- ❑ Phil Spector/Rhino RNLP70235 [M] — 1987 — 15.00
— *Seventh edition of this group of songs; title and cover design restored to one similar to the original, with the typo on "Marshmallow World" corrected*

CHRISTMAS GIFT 'RAP
- ❑ Motown MS-725 — 1970 — 25.00
— *Reissue of "Merry Christmas from Motown," MS-681*

CHRISTMASGLOW
- ❑ RCA Special Products DPL1-0178 — 1976 — 12.00

CHRISTMAS GREETINGS
- ❑ Columbia Special Products CSS1433 — 1970 — 12.00
- ❑ Columbia Special Products CSS1499 — 1970 — 12.00
— *Sold only at A&P grocery stores*

CHRISTMAS GREETINGS, VOL. 2
- ❑ Columbia Special Products C10399 — 1971 — 12.00
— *Sold only at A&P grocery stores*

CHRISTMAS GREETINGS, VOL. 3
- ❑ Columbia Special Products P11383 — 1972 — 12.00
— *Sold only at A&P grocery stores*

CHRISTMAS GREETINGS, VOL. 4
- ❑ Columbia Special Products P11987 — 1973 — 15.00
— *Sold only at A&P grocery stores*

CHRISTMAS GREETINGS FROM NASHVILLE
- ❑ Columbia PC39467 — 1984 — 12.00
- ❑ RCA Victor APL1-0262 — 1973 — 15.00
- ❑ RCA Victor ANL1 1053 — 1976 — 12.00
— *Reissue of APL1-0262*

CHRISTMAS HITS FROM WARNER BROS.
- ❑ Warner Bros. 8467/8 [DJ] — 1959 — 50.00

CHRISTMAS IN CALIFORNIA
- ❑ RCA Victor PRS-276 — 1968 — 15.00
— *Available only from Bank of America*

CHRISTMAS IN ENGLAND
- ❑ Capitol T10097 [M] — 195? — 18.00

CHRISTMAS IN ITALY
- ❑ Capitol T10093 [M] — 196? — 18.00
- ❑ Capitol SM-10093 [R] — 197? — 12.00

CHRISTMAS IN NEW YORK
- ❑ RCA Victor PRM-257 [M] — 1967 — 15.00
- ❑ RCA Victor PRS-257 [S] — 1967 — 18.00

CHRISTMAS IN NEW YORK VOLUME 2
- ❑ RCA Victor PRS-270 — 1968 — 15.00

CHRISTMAS IN NORWAY
- ❑ Capitol T10377 [M] — 196? — 18.00

CHRISTMAS IN SAINT LOUIS
- ❑ (no label) TS77-558/9 — 1977 — 18.00
— *Record is not banded, but here are the titles and artists:*

CHRISTMAS IN SAN FRANCISCO
- ❑ Embarcadero Center EC-101 — 1974 — 18.00
— *Featuring members of the San Francisco, Oakland ans San Jose Symphonies, the San Francisco and Western Operas, etc.; not all tracks have artists identified*

CHRISTMAS IN THE AIR
- ❑ RCA Special Products DPL1-0133 — 1975 — 12.00

CHRISTMAS IN THE STARS: STAR WARS CHRISTMAS ALBUM
- ❑ RSO RS-1-3093 — 1980 — 18.00

Number	Title	Yr	NM

—Concept album with Meco, Anthony Daniels as C3PO, Maury Yeston, Ron McBrien and John Bongiovi (later Jon Bon Jovi!)

CHRISTMAS IS...
❑ Columbia Special Products P11417 — 1972 — 15.00
—Sold only at Goodyear tire dealers

CHRISTMAS MEMORIES
❑ Columbia Special Products P15426 — 1980 — 12.00

CHRISTMAS MEMORIES PLAYED ON ANTIQUE MUSICAL BOXES
❑ Classic Christmas CC1934 — 1977 — 12.00
—Also see "Ford, Rita." These, from anonymous sources, apparently are not from Ms. Ford's collection.

A CHRISTMAS MESSAGE
❑ Lection 847310-1 — 1990 — 15.00

A CHRISTMAS MUSIC FESTIVAL
❑ Capitol Creative Products SL-6688 — 1970 — 12.00

CHRISTMAS NIGHT IN BETHLEHEM: THE MIDNIGHT CEREMONY AT ST. CATHERINE'S CHURCH
❑ ABC Dunhill DS-55002 — 1968 — 18.00
—Recording of the 1967 midnight Mass in the Holy Land; with 24-page booklet

CHRISTMAS ON DEATH ROW
❑ Death Row/Interscope INT2-90108 — 1996 — 18.00

CHRISTMAS PROGRAMMING FROM RCA VICTOR
❑ RCA Victor SP-33-66 [DJ] — 1959 — 1000.00
—Promo-only collection; has been counterfeited, but originals have color covers

CHRISTMAS RAP
❑ Profile PRO-1247 — 1987 — 12.00

A CHRISTMAS RECORD
❑ Ze/Passport PB6020 — 1982 — 25.00

THE CHRISTMAS ROCK ALBUM
❑ Priority SL9465 — 1986 — 18.00

THE CHRISTMAS SONG AND OTHER FAVORITES
❑ Columbia Special Products P12446 — 1974 — 12.00

THE CHRISTMAS SONGS
❑ Capitol SLB-57074 — 1988 — 18.00

THE CHRISTMAS SONGS, VOLUME II
❑ Capitol SL-57065 — 1989 — 15.00

CHRISTMAS SOUL SPECIAL
❑ QAG 1600 — 1982 — 18.00
❑ Varrick 015 — 1985 — 12.00
—Reissue of QAG album; new label, same cover, sticker on back cover with "Varrick" on it

THE CHRISTMAS SOUND OF MUSIC
❑ Capitol Special Markets SL-6996 — 1975 — 12.00

THE CHRISTMAS SOUNDS OF MUSIC
❑ Capitol Creative Products SL-6643 — 1969 — 15.00
—Sold only at B.F. Goodrich tire dealers

CHRISTMAS STARS: SUTHERLAND/TEBALDI/ PRICE SING BEST LOVED CHRISTMAS FAVORITES
❑ London OS26408 — 1974 — 15.00

CHRISTMAS STAR TIME
❑ Columbia Special Products P15756 — 1981 — 12.00

CHRISTMAS STOCKING
❑ Capitol NP90494 [M] — 1965 — 18.00
—Available only through the Capitol Record Club
❑ Capitol SNP90494 [S] — 1965 — 18.00
—Available only through the Capitol Record Club

CHRISTMAS -- THE SEASON OF MUSIC
❑ Capitol Creative Products SL-6679 — 1970 — 15.00
—Reissue of "Zenith Presents Christmas, A Gift of Music, Vol. 3" with almost identical cover

CHRISTMAS THROUGH THE YEARS
❑ MCA Special Markets DL734596 — 197? — 15.00
—Produced for First Financial Marketing Group
❑ Reader's Digest RDA-143 — 1984 — 25.00
—Available only through Reader's Digest magazine by mail order

CHRISTMAS TIME
❑ Decca DL34037 [M] — 196? — 18.00

CHRISTMASTIME IN CAROL AND SONG
❑ RCA Victor PRM-271 [M] — 1968 — 25.00
❑ RCA Victor PRS-271 [S] — 1968 — 15.00
❑ RCA Victor PRS-289 — 1969 — 15.00

A CHRISTMAS TO REMEMBER
❑ Columbia Special Products P13845 — 1977 — 12.00

A CHRISTMAS TRADITION
❑ Warner Bros. 25630 — 1987 — 15.00

A CHRISTMAS TRADITION, VOLUME II
❑ Warner Bros. 25762 — 1988 — 12.00

A CHRISTMAS TREASURY OF CLASSICS FROM AVON
❑ RCA Special Products DPL1-0716 — 1985 — 12.00
—Sold only through Avon dealers

CHRISTMAS TRIMMINGS
❑ Columbia Special Products P12795 — 1975 — 12.00

CHRISTMAS WISHES
❑ Columbia Special Products P13844 — 1977 — 12.00

CHRISTMAS WITH ANDY WILLIAMS AND THE WILLIAMS BROTHERS
❑ Columbia Special Products C10105 — 1971 — 12.00

CHRISTMAS WITH COLONEL SANDERS
❑ RCA Victor PRS-291 — 1969 — 25.00
—Sold only at Kentucky Fried Chicken restaurants

CHRISTMAS WITH EDDY ARNOLD/CHRISTMAS WITH HENRY MANCINI
❑ RCA Special Products DPL1-0079 — 1974 — 15.00

CHRISTMAS WITH GLEN CAMPBELL AND THE HOLLYWOOD POPS ORCHESTRA
❑ Capitol Creative Products SL-6699 — 1971 — 15.00
❑ Capitol Special Markets SL-6699 — 197? — 12.00
—Reissue on renamed label

CHRISTMAS WITH JOHNNY MATHIS AND PERCY FAITH
❑ Columbia Special Products P11805 — 1973 — 12.00

CHRISTMAS WITH JULIE ANDREWS (FEATURING THE YULETIDE CHORISTERS)
❑ RCA Victor PRS-290 — 1969 — 15.00

CHRISTMAS...WITH LOVE FROM JIM & TAMMY
❑ PTL RLP-1824 — 1980 — 15.00

CHRISTMAS WITH NAT KING COLE AND FRED WARING & THE PENNSYLVANIANS
❑ Capitol Special Markets SL-6883 — 197? — 12.00

CHRISTMAS WITH THE STARS
❑ Capitol Special Markets SL-6931 — 1973 — 12.00

CHRYSALIS 65 HITS
❑ Chrysalis VAS2677 [DJ] — 1087 — 18.00
—Includes edits of songs by David Bowie, Billy Idol, Icehouse, Blondie, many others

THE CHRYSALISTENER
❑ Chrysalis AS1602 [DJ] — 1982 — 15.00
—Includes Divinyls, Ultravox

CHUNKS
❑ New Alliance 003 — 1981 — 18.00
—Includes Minutemen, etc.

CLAMBAKE ON BOURBON STREET
❑ Cook LP-1085 [10] — 1955 — 50.00

CLASSIC BLUES ACCOMPANISTS
❑ Riverside RLP-1052 [10] — 1955 — 80.00

CLASSIC CAPITOL JAZZ SESSIONS
❑ Mosaic MQ19-170 — 199? — 400.00

THE CLASSIC COLLECTION -- CONTEMPORARY: THE GREAT JAZZ MEN/VOL. 2
❑ Dot DLP-25879 — 1968 — 18.00

THE CLASSIC COLLECTION -- TRADITIONAL: THE GREAT JAZZ MEN/VOL. 1
❑ Dot DLP-25878 — 1968 — 18.00

CLASSIC COUNTRY
❑ Epic FE38630 — 1983 — 12.00
❑ Epic PE38630 — 1985 — 10.00
—Budget-line reissue

CLASSIC COUNTRY MUSIC
❑ Columbia Special Products P815640 — 1981 — 50.00
—Boxed set; sold only by the Smithsonian; original version
❑ RCA Special Products DML6-0914 — 1990 — 50.00
—Boxed set; sold only by the Smithsonian; revised version

CLASSIC JAZZ PIANO STYLES
❑ RCA Victor LPV-544 [M] — 1967 — 25.00

CLASSIC LOVE SONGS
❑ RCA Victor AEL1-7195 — 1986 — 10.00

CLASSIC PIANOS
❑ Doctor Jazz FW38851 — 198? — 12.00

CLASSIC ROCK -- 1964
❑ Time-Life SCLR-03 — 1987 — 18.00
—Includes The Searchers

CLASSIC ROCK -- 1964: SHAKIN' ALL OVER
❑ Time-Life SCLR-16 — 1989 — 18.00
—Includes The Searchers

CLASSIC ROCK -- 1964: THE BEAT GOES ON
❑ Time-Life SCLR-09 — 1988 — 18.00
—Includes The Searchers

CLASSIC ROCK -- ROCK RENAISSANCE
❑ Time-Life SCLR-17 — 1989 — 18.00
—Includes MC5

CLASSIC ROCK -- ROCK RENAISSANCE II
❑ Time-Life SCLR-21 — 1990 — 18.00
—Includes The Velvet Underground

CLASSIC ROCK -- ROCK RENAISSANCE III
❑ Time-Life SCLR-26 — 1990 — 18.00
—Includes The Searchers

CLASSIC ROCK -- ROCK RENAISSANCE IV
❑ Time-Life SCLR-30 — 1991 — 18.00
—Includes MC5, The Velvet Underground and Nico

CLASSICS IN JAZZ
❑ Capitol T320 [M] — 1954 — 40.00

CLASSICS IN JAZZ: COOL AND QUIET
❑ Capitol H371 [10] — 1953 — 50.00

CLASSICS IN JAZZ: DIXIELAND STYLISTS
❑ Capitol H321 [10] — 1952 — 50.00

CLASSICS IN JAZZ: SMALL COMBOS
❑ Capitol H322 [10] — 1952 — 50.00

CLASSIC TENORS, VOL. 2
❑ Doctor Jazz FW39519 — 198? — 12.00

CLAY COLE PRESENTS BLASTS FROM THE PAST
❑ Blast BLP6803 [M] — 196? — 50.00

CLAY COLE'S BIN OF ORIGINAL GOLDEN OLDIES
❑ Jubilee JGM-5026 [M] — 1964 — 100.00

CLUB MTV PARTY TO GO
❑ Tommy Boy TB1037 — 1991 — 15.00
—Includes Digital Underground, Depeche Mode

A COLLECTION OF 16 ORIGINAL BIG HITS, VOLUME 3
❑ Motown MS624 [S] — 1966 — 30.00

A COLLECTION OF 16 ORIGINAL BIG HITS, VOLUME 5
❑ Motown MS651 [S] — 1966 — 25.00

A COLLECTION OF 16 ORIGINAL BIG HITS, VOLUME 6
❑ Motown MT655 [M] — 1967 — 25.00
❑ Motown MS655 [S] — 1967 — 25.00

A COLLECTION OF 16 ORIGINAL BIG HITS, VOLUME 7
❑ Motown M661 [M] — 1967 — 25.00
❑ Motown MS661 [S] — 1967 — 25.00

A COLLECTION OF 16 ORIGINAL BIG HITS, VOLUME 8
❑ Motown M666 [M] — 1967 — 25.00
❑ Motown MS666 [S] — 1967 — 25.00

A COLLECTION OF 16 ORIGINAL BIG HITS, VOLUME 9
❑ Motown MS668 [S] — 1968 — 25.00
❑ Motown MT668 [M] — 1968 — 50.00
—Mono is white label promo only; "Monaural Record DJ Copy" sticker on stereo cover

A COLLECTION OF 16 ORIGINAL BIG HITS, VOLUME 10
❑ Motown MS684 — 1969 — 25.00

A COLLECTION OF 16 ORIGINAL BIG HITS, VOLUME 11
❑ Motown MS693 — 1969 — 25.00

A COLLECTION OF CHRISTMAS FAVORITES
❑ Columbia Special Products P14988 — 1979 — 12.00

COLLECTORS' ITEMS, 1922-30
❑ Historical 11 — 1967 — 12.00

COLLECTORS' ITEMS, 1925-29
❑ Historical 20 — 1968 — 12.00

COLLECTORS ITEMS, VOL. 2
❑ Riverside RLP-1040 [10] — 1954 — 80.00

COLLECTOR'S JACKPOT, VOL. 1
❑ Jazz Archives JA-21 — 198? — 12.00

COLLECTOR'S JACKPOT, VOL. 2
❑ Jazz Archives JA-40 — 198? — 12.00

COLLECTOR'S SERIES: DUETS
❑ RCA Victor CPL1-7059 — 1985 — 10.00

COLLECTOR'S SERIES: DUETS DUETS
❑ RCA Victor CPL1-7130 — 1985 — 10.00

COLLECTOR'S SERIES SAMPLER RECORD
❑ London LCX1004 [DJ] — 1977 — 25.00

COLLECTUS INTERRUPTUS
❑ Warner Bros. PRO726 — 1977 — 25.00

COLLEGE JAZZ: DIXIELAND
❑ Columbia CL736 [M] — 1956 — 25.00

Number	Title	Yr	NM

COLORADO JAZZ PARTY
❏ BASF 25099 ... 197? ... 25.00

COLOR ME OBG: STATION WDRC
❏ Roulette R25347 [M] ... 1967 ... 25.00

COLUMBIA FALL '82 NEW ARTISTS SAMPLER
❏ Columbia AS1563 [DJ] ... 1982 ... 15.00
—Includes Men At Work, Romeo Void, Psychedelic Furs

COLUMBIA JAZZ FESTIVAL
❏ Columbia JJ-1 [M] ... 1959 ... 30.00

COLUMBIA PICTURES MUSIC GROUP
❏ Columbia Pictures (# unknown) [DJ] ... 1987 ... 15.00
—Includes Peter Gabriel, Kid Creole, etc.

COLUMBIA'S 24 HITS IN THE TOP 20 FOR 1982!
❏ Columbia A2S1588 [DJ] ... 1982 ... 30.00

COLUMBIA'S ALL NEW TIME-RELEASE CAPSULE
❏ Columbia AS247 [DJ] ... 1977 ... 18.00
—Promo-only sampler

COLUMBIA SLOW JAMS II
❏ Columbia CAS5640 [DJ] ... 1993 ... 12.00
—Includes Terence Trent D'Arby

COMBO JAZZ
❏ Jazztone J-1221 [M] ... 1956 ... 30.00

COME, WINTER; COME, LORD/SONGS FOR ADVENT AND THE EVE OF CHRISTMAS
❏ North American Liturgy Resources 29541 ... 1976 ... 18.00

COME CLOSER TO GOD
❏ Vee Jay LP-5061 [M] ... 1964 ... 30.00

COME TOGETHER: AMERICA SALUTES THE BEATLES
❏ Liberty 31712 ... 1995 ... 25.00

COMPARATIVE BLUES
❏ Hall of Fame 603 ... 197? ... 12.00
❏ Jazztone J-1258 [M] ... 1957 ... 30.00

THE COMPLETE COMMODORE JAZZ RECORDINGS, VOLUME I
❏ Mosaic M23-123 ... 199? ... 400.00

THE COMPLETE COMMODORE JAZZ RECORDINGS, VOLUME II
❏ Mosaic M23-128 ... 199? ... 400.00

THE COMPLETE COMMODORE JAZZ RECORDINGS, VOLUME III
❏ Mosaic M20-134 ... 199? ... 300.00

THE COMPLETE KEYNOTE COLLECTION
❏ Keynote 830121-1 ... 1986 ... 250.00

THE COMPLETE MASTER JAZZ PIANO SERIES
❏ Mosaic M6-140 ... 199? ... 100.00

COMPOSERS AT PLAY: HAROLD ARLEN AND COLE PORTER
❏ X LVA-1003 [M] ... 1955 ... 40.00

THE COMPOSITIONS OF BENNY GOLSON
❏ Riverside RLP-3505 [M] ... 1962 ... 18.00
❏ Riverside RS-93505 [S] ... 1962 ... 25.00

THE COMPOSITIONS OF BOBBY TIMMONS
❏ Riverside RLP-3512 [M] ... 1962 ... 18.00
❏ Riverside RS-93512 [S] ... 1962 ... 25.00

THE COMPOSITIONS OF CHARLIE PARKER
❏ Riverside RLP-3506 [M] ... 1962 ... 18.00
❏ Riverside RS-93506 [S] ... 1962 ... 25.00

THE COMPOSITIONS OF COLE PORTER
❏ Riverside RM-3515 [M] ... 1963 ... 18.00
❏ Riverside RS-93515 [S] ... 1963 ... 25.00

THE COMPOSITIONS OF DIZZY GILLESPIE
❏ Riverside RLP-3508 [M] ... 1962 ... 18.00
❏ Riverside RS-93508 [S] ... 1962 ... 25.00

THE COMPOSITIONS OF DUKE ELLINGTON
❏ Riverside RLP-3507 [M] ... 1962 ... 18.00
❏ Riverside RS-93507 [S] ... 1962 ... 25.00

THE COMPOSITIONS OF DUKE ELLINGTON, VOL. 2
❏ Riverside RLP-3510 [M] ... 1962 ... 18.00
❏ Riverside RS-93510 [S] ... 1962 ... 25.00

THE COMPOSITIONS OF GEORGE GERSHWIN
❏ Riverside RM-3517 [M] ... 1963 ... 18.00
❏ Riverside RS-93517 [S] ... 1963 ... 25.00

THE COMPOSITIONS OF HAROLD ARLEN
❏ Riverside RM-3518 [M] ... 1963 ... 18.00
❏ Riverside RS-93518 [S] ... 1963 ... 25.00

THE COMPOSITIONS OF HORACE SILVER
❏ Riverside RLP-3509 [M] ... 1962 ... 18.00
❏ Riverside RS-93509 [S] ... 1962 ... 25.00

THE COMPOSITIONS OF IRVING BERLIN
❏ Riverside RM-3519 [M] ... 1963 ... 18.00
❏ Riverside RS-93519 [S] ... 1963 ... 25.00

THE COMPOSITIONS OF JEROME KERN
❏ Riverside RM-3516 [M] ... 1963 ... 18.00
❏ Riverside RS-93516 [S] ... 1963 ... 25.00

COMPOSITIONS OF LIONEL HAMPTON
❏ Crown CLP-5107 [M] ... 195? ... 30.00

THE COMPOSITIONS OF MILES DAVIS
❏ Riverside RLP-3504 [M] ... 1962 ... 18.00
❏ Riverside RS-93504 [S] ... 1962 ... 25.00

THE COMPOSITIONS OF RICHARD RODGERS
❏ Riverside RM-3514 [M] ... 1963 ... 18.00
❏ Riverside RS-93514 [S] ... 1963 ... 25.00

THE COMPOSITIONS OF TADD DAMERON
❏ Riverside RLP-3511 [M] ... 1962 ... 18.00
❏ Riverside RS-93511 [S] ... 1962 ... 25.00

THE COMPOSITIONS OF THELONIOUS MONK
❏ Riverside RLP-3503 [M] ... 1962 ... 18.00
❏ Riverside RS-93503 [S] ... 1962 ... 25.00

CONCEPTION
❏ Prestige PRLP-7013 [M] ... 1956 ... 100.00

A CONCERT: BEHIND PRISON WALLS
❏ Pointed Star PS10178 ... 1978 ... 12.00
—Compiled for Napa auto parts dealers; has Johnny Cash, Roy Clark and Linda Ronstadt

CONCERT IN ARGENTINA
❏ Halcyon 113 ... 197? ... 18.00

CONCERT IN JAZZ
❏ Tops L-1532 [M] ... 1958 ... 25.00

CONCERT JAZZ
❏ Brunswick BL54027 [M] ... 1956 ... 30.00

CONCERTS FOR THE PEOPLE OF KAMPUCHEA
❏ Atlantic SD 2-7005 ... 1981 ... 25.00

A CONCORD JAM
❏ Concord Jazz CJ-142 ... 1981 ... 12.00

A CONCORD JAM, VOL. 2
❏ Concord Jazz CJ-180 ... 1982 ... 12.00

A CONCORD JAM, VOL. 3: A GREAT AMERICAN EVENING
❏ Concord Jazz CJ-220 ... 1984 ... 12.00

CONCORD JAZZ GUITAR COLLECTION, VOL. 1 AND 2
❏ Concord Jazz CJ-160 ... 198? ... 15.00

THE CONCORD SOUND, VOL. 1
❏ Concord Jazz CJ-278 ... 1985 ... 12.00

CONNECTED
❏ Limp 1005 ... 1981 ... 25.00

CONSPIRACY OF HOPE
❏ Mercury 830617-1 ... 1986 ... 15.00
—Includes Peter Gabriel, Tears for Fears, Howard Jones, Sting, Simple Minds

CONTEMPORARY CHRISTMAS CLASSICS
❏ Myrrh 7-01-077000-0 ... 1983 ... 12.00

COOK BOOK
❏ Warner Bros. PRO660 ... 1976 ... 25.00

COOL AND CAREFREE
❏ Columbia Special Products CSP119 [M] ... 1963 ... 15.00
—Sold only by Carrier air conditioner dealers

COOL CALIFORNIA
❏ Savoy Jazz SJL-2254 ... 198? ... 15.00

COOL EUROPE
❏ MGM E-3157 [M] ... 1955 ... 30.00

COOL GABRIELS
❏ Groove LG-1003 [M] ... 1956 ... 800.00
—Andy Warhol cover.

COOLIN'
❏ New Jazz NJLP-8216 [M] ... 1959 ... 60.00
—Purple label
❏ New Jazz NJLP-8216 [M] ... 1965 ... 30.00
—Blue label, trident logo at right

COOL JAZZ
❏ Seeco CELP-465 [M] ... 1960 ... 25.00

COOL JAZZ FROM HOLLAND
❏ Epic LN1126 [10] ... 1955 ... 40.00

COOL YULE
❏ Rhino RNLP-70073 ... 1986 ... 15.00

COOL YULE, VOLUME 2
❏ Rhino R170193 ... 1988 ... 15.00
—Same as above, but in stereo

COPULATIN' BLUES
❏ Stash ST-101 ... 197? ... 18.00

COPULATIN' BLUES, VOL. 2
❏ Stash ST-122 ... 198? ... 18.00

COPULATIN' RHYTHM
❏ Jass J-3 ... 198? ... 18.00

COPULATIN' RHYTHM, VOL. 2
❏ Jass J-5 ... 198? ... 18.00

THE CORE OF JAZZ
❏ MGM SE-4737 ... 1970 ... 15.00

COTTON CLUB STARS
❏ Stash ST-124 ... 198? ... 15.00

COUNTRY & WESTERN CLASSICS 1955
❏ Economic Consultants 1955 ... 1973 ... 25.00

COUNTRY & WESTERN CLASSICS 1956
❏ Economic Consultants 1956 ... 1973 ... 25.00

COUNTRY & WESTERN CLASSICS 1957
❏ Economic Consultants 1957 ... 1973 ... 25.00

COUNTRY & WESTERN CLASSICS 1958
❏ Economic Consultants 1958 ... 1973 ... 25.00

COUNTRY AFTER DARK
❏ Intermedia QS-5073 ... 198? ... 12.00

COUNTRY AND WESTERN, VOLUME 1
❏ Dot DLP-3700 [M] ... 1966 ... 18.00

COUNTRY AND WESTERN, VOLUME 2
❏ Dot DLP-3701 [M] ... 1966 ... 18.00

COUNTRY AND WESTERN, VOLUME 3
❏ Dot DLP-3702 [M] ... 1966 ... 18.00

COUNTRY AND WESTERN, VOLUME 4
❏ Dot DLP-3703 [M] ... 1966 ... 18.00

COUNTRY AND WESTERN AWARD WINNERS 1964
❏ Decca DL4622 [M] ... 1965 ... 25.00
❏ Decca DL74622 [S] ... 1965 ... 30.00

COUNTRY AND WESTERN AWARD WINNERS 1966
❏ Decca DL4837 [M] ... 1967 ... 25.00
❏ Decca DL74837 [S] ... 1967 ... 18.00

COUNTRY AND WESTERN FAVORITES
❏ Metro M-530 [M] ... 1965 ... 15.00
❏ Metro MS-530 [R] ... 1965 ... 12.00

COUNTRY AND WESTERN FAVORITES, VOLUME 2
❏ Metro M-572 [M] ... 1966 ... 15.00
❏ Metro MS-572 [R] ... 1966 ... 12.00

COUNTRY AND WESTERN JAMBOREE
❏ King 697 [M] ... 1961 ... 150.00

COUNTRY BONANZA
❏ Columbia Musical Treasury P2S5372 ... 1969 ... 18.00

COUNTRY BOY -- COUNTRY GIRL
❏ Decca DL4201 [M] ... 1962 ... 30.00
❏ Decca DL74201 [S] ... 1962 ... 30.00

COUNTRY CHRISTMAS
❏ Columbia CS9888 ... 1968 ... 18.00

A COUNTRY CHRISTMAS
❏ Columbia Special Products CSS1434 ... 1970 ... 15.00

COUNTRY CHRISTMAS
❏ Columbia Special Products/Sessions P16365 ... 1981 ... 12.00
❏ Epic JE36823 ... 1980 ... 12.00
❏ King 811 [M] ... 1962 ... 100.00
❏ Monument SLP-18125 ... 1969 ... 25.00

A COUNTRY CHRISTMAS
❏ RCA Victor CPL1-4396 ... 1982 ... 12.00
❏ RCA Victor AYL1-4812 ... 1983 ... 10.00
—Reissue of CPL1-4396

COUNTRY CHRISTMAS
❏ Time-Life STL-109 ... 1988 ... 25.00
—Available from Time-Life by mail order only; boxed set

A COUNTRY CHRISTMAS, VOLUME 2
❏ RCA Victor AYL1-4809 ... 1983 ... 15.00

A COUNTRY CHRISTMAS, VOLUME 3
❏ RCA Victor CPL1-5178 ... 1984 ... 12.00

A COUNTRY CHRISTMAS, VOLUME 4
❏ RCA Victor CPL1-7012 ... 1985 ... 12.00

COUNTRY CHRISTMAS FAVORITES
❏ Columbia 3C36088 ... 1979 ... 10.00
❏ Columbia Special Products C10876 ... 1972 ... 12.00

A COUNTRY CHRISTMAS WITH LORETTA LYNN AND FRIENDS
❏ MCA Special Markets 34979 ... 197? ... 15.00

COUNTRY CLASSICS
❏ RCA Victor LPM-2313 [M] ... 1961 ... 30.00
❏ RCA Victor LSP-2313(e) [R] ... 1962 ... 25.00

COUNTRY CREAM
❏ QMO Q-110 ... 197? ... 12.00
—Alternate number is Columbia Special Products C 10422

Number	Title	Yr	NM

COUNTRY EXPRESS
❏ Starday SLP-109 [M] — 1959 — 40.00
COUNTRY FAIR
❏ Capitol SWBB-562 — 1970 — 30.00
COUNTRY GIRLS SING COUNTRY SONGS
❏ RCA Camden CAL-959 [M] — 1966 — 15.00
❏ RCA Camden CAS-959 [S] — 1966 — 18.00
COUNTRY GOLD
❏ RCA Special Products DPL1-0561 — 1980 — 25.00
COUNTRY GOLD, VOL. 1
❏ Plantation PL-5 — 1969 — 15.00
COUNTRY GREATS
❏ Sessions/CSP P213769 — 1977 — 18.00
COUNTRY HIT PARADE
❏ Starday SLP-110 [M] — 1959 — 40.00
COUNTRY HITS BY COUNTRY STARS
❏ Capitol T1912 [M] — 1963 — 25.00
❏ Capitol ST1912 [S] — 1963 — 30.00
COUNTRY HITS PARADE
❏ RCA Victor LPM-3452 [M] — 1966 — 18.00
❏ RCA Victor LSP-3452 [S] — 1966 — 25.00
COUNTRY HOLIDAY
❏ Columbia Musical Treasury DS467 — 1968 — 18.00
COUNTRY JUBILEE
❏ Decca DL4172 [M] — 1961 — 30.00
COUNTRY MEMORIES
❏ Reader's Digest RBA-066-A — 1989 — 50.00
COUNTRY MUSIC BY THE WAYSIDE
❏ Wayside 1013 — 1968 — 25.00
COUNTRY MUSIC CLASSICS
❏ Columbia Special Products P213773 — 1976 — 15.00
COUNTRY MUSIC HALL OF FAME
❏ Starday SLP-164 [M] — 1962 — 30.00
COUNTRY MUSIC HALL OF FAME, VOL. 2
❏ Starday SLP-190 [M] — 1963 — 30.00
COUNTRY MUSIC HALL OF FAME, VOL. 3
❏ Starday SLP-256 [M] — 1963 — 30.00
COUNTRY MUSIC HALL OF FAME, VOL. 4
❏ Starday SLP-295 [M] — 1964 — 30.00
COUNTRY MUSIC HALL OF FAME, VOL. 5
❏ Starday SLP-360 [M] — 1966 — 30.00
COUNTRY MUSIC HALL OF FAME, VOL. 6
❏ Starday SLP-390 [M] — 1967 — 30.00
COUNTRY MUSIC HALL OF FAME, VOL. 7
❏ Starday SLP-409 — 1969 — 25.00
COUNTRY MUSIC HALL OF FAME, VOL. 8
❏ Starday SLP-430 — 1969 — 25.00
COUNTRY MUSIC HALL OF FAME, VOL. 9
❏ Starday SLP-449 — 1970 — 25.00
COUNTRY MUSIC HITS BY COUNTRY MUSIC STARS
❏ RCA Camden CAL-689 [M] — 1962 — 25.00
❏ RCA Camden CAS-689 [R] — 196? — 18.00
COUNTRY MUSIC HOOTENANNY
❏ Capitol ST2009 [S] — 1963 — 30.00
❏ Capitol T2009 [M] — 1963 — 30.00
COUNTRY MUSIC JAMBOREE
❏ Mercury MG-20350 [M] — 1958 — 40.00
COUNTRY MUSIC SPECTACULAR
❏ Starday SLP-117 [M] — 1961 — 40.00
COUNTRY MUSIC STAR SPECTACULAR
❏ Hickory LPM-116 [M] — 1963 — 30.00
COUNTRY MUSIC WHO'S WHO
❏ Starday SLP-304 [M] — 1964 — 30.00
—With 52-page booklet
❏ Starday SLP-304 [M] — 1964 — 25.00
—Without booklet
COUNTRY OLDIES BUT GOODIES
❏ Smash MGS-27016 [M] — 1962 — 25.00
❏ Smash SRS-67016 [S] — 1962 — 25.00
A COUNTRY SALUTE TO HANK WILLIAMS
❏ Harmony HL7265 [M] — 1960 — 25.00
THE COUNTRY'S BEST
❏ Capitol T1179 [M] — 1959 — 30.00
COUNTRY'S GREATEST HITS
❏ Power Pak PO-227 — 197? — 12.00
THE COUNTRY SIDE OF CHRISTMAS/ALL-TIME FAVORITES IN THE TRADITIONAL STYLE
❏ Capitol Creative Products SL-6586 — 1968 — 15.00
COUNTRY SOFT AND MELLOW
❏ Reader's Digest RB4-200 — 1989 — 50.00

COUNTRY SPECIAL
❏ Capitol STBB-402 — 1969 — 30.00
COUNTRY SPECTACULAR
❏ Columbia CL894 [M] — 1956 — 50.00
COUNTRY STAR PARADE, VOL. 2
❏ Vocalion VL3804 [M] — 1967 — 18.00
❏ Vocalion VL73804 [R] — 1967 — 15.00
COUNTRY STAR PARADE VOL. 1
❏ Vocalion VL3768 [M] — 1966 — 15.00
❏ Vocalion VL73768 [R] — 1966 — 15.00
COUNTRY STARS, COUNTRY HITS
❏ RCA Camden CAL-793 [M] — 1964 — 25.00
❏ RCA Camden CAS-793 [S] — 1964 — 25.00
COUNTRY STARS OF TODAY
❏ Power Pak PO-287 — 197? — 12.00
COUNTRY STARS SING SACRED SONGS
❏ RCA Camden CAL-2136 [M] — 1967 — 18.00
❏ RCA Camden CAS-2136 [S] — 1967 — 15.00
A COUNTRY STYLE CHRISTMAS
❏ Columbia Musical Treasury 3P6316 — 1975 — 18.00
COUNTRY USA: 1950
❏ Time-Life CTR-23 — 1991 — 25.00
COUNTRY USA: 1951
❏ Time-Life CTR-22 — 1991 — 25.00
COUNTRY USA: 1952
❏ Time-Life CTR-16 — 1990 — 18.00
COUNTRY USA: 1953
❏ Time-Life CTR-20 — 1990 — 18.00
COUNTRY USA: 1954
❏ Time-Life CTR-15 — 1990 — 25.00
COUNTRY USA: 1955
❏ Time-Life CTR-19 — 1990 — 25.00
COUNTRY USA: 1956
❏ Time-Life CTR-13 — 1990 — 25.00
COUNTRY USA: 1957
❏ Time-Life CTR-02 — 1988 — 18.00
COUNTRY USA: 1958
❏ Time-Life CTR-07 — 1989 — 25.00
COUNTRY USA: 1959
❏ Time-Life CTR-09 — 1989 — 18.00
COUNTRY USA: 1960
❏ Time-Life CTR-12 — 1989 — 18.00
COUNTRY USA: 1961
❏ Time-Life CTR-01 — 1988 — 18.00
COUNTRY USA: 1962
❏ Time-Life CTR-03 — 1988 — 18.00
COUNTRY USA: 1963
❏ Time-Life CTR-11 — 1989 — 18.00
COUNTRY USA: 1964
❏ Time-Life CTR-14 — 1990 — 18.00
COUNTRY USA: 1965
❏ Time-Life CTR-10 — 1989 — 18.00
COUNTRY USA: 1966
❏ Time-Life CTR-21 — 1991 — 25.00
COUNTRY USA: 1967
❏ Time-Life CTR-17 — 1990 — 18.00
COUNTRY USA: 1968
❏ Time-Life CTR-06 — 1989 — 18.00
COUNTRY USA: 1969
❏ Time-Life CTR-08 — 1989 — 25.00
COUNTRY USA: 1970
❏ Time-Life CTR-04 — 1988 — 18.00
COUNTRY USA: 1971
❏ Time-Life CTR-05 — 1989 — 18.00
COUNTRY USA: 1972
❏ Time-Life CTR-18 — 1990 — 18.00
COUNTY LINE
❏ K-Tel WU3450 — 1979 — 12.00
CRACKS IN THE SIDEWALK
❏ New Alliance 001 — 1980 — 18.00
—Includes Minutemen, Black Flag, others
CRAWLING FROM WITHIN
❏ 77 Records (# unknown) — 1987 — 15.00
—Includes Lemonheads
THE CRINK CHRONICLES
❏ CBS Associated AS1120 [DJ] — 1988 — 15.00
—Includes Midnight Oil, Prefab Sprout, Terence Trent D'Arby
CRITICS' CHOICE
❏ Dawn DLP-1123 [M] — 1958 — 80.00

CROSSROADS: WHITE BLUES IN THE 1960S
❏ Elektra 60383 — 1984 — 25.00
CRUISIN'
❏ Jazzland JLP-7 [M] — 1960 — 30.00
❏ Jazzland JLP-97 [S] — 1960 — 30.00
CTI SUMMER JAZZ AT THE HOLLYWOOD BOWL: LIVE ONE
❏ CTI 7076 — 197? — 15.00
CTI SUMMER JAZZ AT THE HOLLYWOOD BOWL: LIVE THREE
❏ CTI 7078 — 197? — 15.00
CTI SUMMER JAZZ AT THE HOLLYWOOD BOWL: LIVE TWO
❏ CTI 7077 — 197? — 15.00
CURRENT EVENTS
❏ Arista SP-150 [DJ] — 1983 — 18.00
—Includes Ministry, Heaven 17, Thompson Twins, etc.
CURTAIN UP! AMERICAN DANCE FAVORITES
❏ Mercury Living Presence SR90326 [S] — 196? — 40.00
—Maroon label, no "Vendor: Mercury Record Corporation
CURTAIN UP! FAVORITE CONCERT OVERTURES
❏ Mercury Living Presence SR90323 — 196? — 60.00
—Maroon label, no "Vendor: Mercury Record Corporation
CURTAIN UP! OPERA BALLET FAVORITES
❏ Mercury Living Presence SR90327 [S] — 196? — 30.00
—Maroon label, no "Vendor: Mercury Record Corporation
CYLINDER JAZZ
❏ Saydisc SDL-334 — 198? — 12.00
DANCE, BE HAPPY!
❏ Columbia CL967 [M] — 1957 — 25.00
DANCE BAND HITS
❏ RCA Victor LPT-2 [10] — 1951 — 40.00
DANCE DISCOTHEQUE
❏ Decca DL4556 [M] — 1964 — 18.00
❏ Decca DL74556 [S] — 1964 — 25.00
DANCE II IT, VOLUME 1
❏ A&M SP-4970 — 1983 — 12.00
—Includes Simple Minds, The Police, The Cure, etc.
DANCE ON THE WILD SIDE
❏ Chancellor CHL-5028 [M] — 1962 — 30.00
❏ Chancellor CHLS-5028 [S] — 1962 — 30.00
DANCE RHYTHM 'N' ROCK NEW MUSIC SEMINAR MIXER
❏ Warner Bros. PRO-A-2061 [DJ] — 1983 — 80.00
DANCE THE ROCK & ROLL
❏ Atlantic 8013 [M] — 1957 — 80.00
DANCE TO THE BANDS
❏ Capitol TBO727 [M] — 1956 — 40.00
❏ Capitol T977 [M] — 1958 — 25.00
DANCE TRAXX
❏ Atlantic R263754 — 198? — 15.00
—Includes INXS
DANCE TUNES FROM THE VAULT, VOLUME 2
❏ Chess LP1476 [M] — 1962 — 40.00
DANCING WITH THE STARS
❏ Epic LN3136 [M] — 1955 — 30.00
DANGERHOUSE VOLUME ONE
❏ Frontier 4629-1-L — 1991 — 15.00
—Includes X, Weirdos, many others
DARK MUDDY BOTTOM BLUES
❏ Specialty SPS-2149 — 1971 — 25.00
DAS IS JAZZ!
❏ Decca DL8229 [M] — 1956 — 30.00
A DATE WITH GREATNESS
❏ Imperial LP-12188A [R] — 1962 — 30.00
❏ Imperial LP-9188A [M] — 1962 — 50.00
—Features Aladdin tracks by Coleman Hawkins, Howard McGhee and Lester Young
A DATE WITH RIVERSIDE
❏ Riverside S-4 [M] — 195? — 40.00
A DAY IN THE COUNTRY
❏ Audio Lab AL-1519 [M] — 1959 — 80.00
DAYS OF WINE AND VINYL
❏ Warner Bros. PRO540 — 1973 — 30.00
DECADE OF JAZZ, VOLUME 1, 1939-49
❏ Blue Note BN-LA158-G2 — 1974 — 18.00
DECADE OF JAZZ, VOLUME 2, 1949-59
❏ Blue Note BN-LA159-G2 — 1974 — 18.00
DECADE OF JAZZ, VOLUME 3, 1959-69
❏ Blue Note BN-LA160-G2 — 1974 — 18.00

Number	Title	Yr	NM

DEEP EAR

| ❏ Warner Bros. PRO591 | 1974 | 30.00 |

DEEP SIX

| ❏ C/Z CZ 001 | 1985 | 50.00 |

THE DEFINITIVE JAZZ SCENE, VOL. 1

❏ ABC Impulse! AS-99 [S]	1968	15.00
❏ Impulse! A-99 [M]	1966	18.00
❏ Impulse! AS-99 [S]	1966	25.00

THE DEFINITIVE JAZZ SCENE, VOL. 2

❏ ABC Impulse! AS-100 [S]	1968	15.00
❏ Impulse! A-100 [M]	1966	18.00
❏ Impulse! AS-100 [S]	1966	25.00

THE DEFINITIVE JAZZ SCENE, VOL. 3

❏ ABC Impulse! AS-9101 [S]	1968	15.00
❏ Impulse! A-9101 [M]	1966	18.00
❏ Impulse! AS-9101 [S]	1966	25.00

DEF JAM RECORDINGS -- RETAIL TRACKS

| ❏ Def Jam CAS2715 [DJ] | 1987 | 25.00 |

DEL-FI ALBUM SAMPLER

| ❏ Del-Fi (no #) [DJ] | 1959 | 500.00 |
— *Green vinyl, promo only, with paper sleeve*

DEL-FI RECORD HOP

| ❏ Del-Fi DFLP-1210 [M] | 1959 | 80.00 |

DEMAND PERFORMANCES

| ❏ Monument MLP-8010 [M] | 1963 | 30.00 |
| ❏ Monument SLP-18010 [S] | 1963 | 40.00 |

DEMONSTRATION RECORD -- DISC JOCKEYS -- JAN.-FEB. 1955

| ❏ Capitol PRO-213 [DJ] | 1955 | 40.00 |

DESTINATION STEREO

| ❏ RCA Victor Red Seal LSC-2307 [S] | 1959 | 30.00 |

THE DEVOTEES ALBUM

| ❏ Rhino RNSP-301 | 1980 | 15.00 |
— *Includes Devo sound-alike contest winners...sort of a tribute to Devo?*

DIAL A HIT

| ❏ Bell 6030 | 1969 | 25.00 |

A DIAMOND HIDDEN IN THE MOUTH OF A CORPSE

| ❏ Giorno Poetry Systems 035 | 1985 | 30.00 |

DICK CLARK: 20 YEARS OF ROCK N' ROLL

| ❏ Buddah BDS5133 | 1973 | 25.00 |
— *Gatefold cover with booklet and bonus 7-inch cardboard record*
| ❏ Buddah BDS5133 | 1974 | 12.00 |
— *With none of the extras*

DIESEL SMOKE, DANGEROUS CURVES AND OTHER TRUCK DRIVERS FAVORITES

| ❏ Starday SLP-250 [M] | 1963 | 30.00 |

DIGITAL III AT MONTREUX

| ❏ Pablo Live 2308223 | 1980 | 15.00 |

DISCO-TEEN '66

| ❏ Columbia Record Club C155 [M] | 1966 | 25.00 |
| ❏ Columbia Record Club DS155 [S] | 1966 | 50.00 |
— *Sought-after for its otherwise unavailable extended stereo mix of Bob Dylan's "Positively 4th Street*

DISCOTHEQUE AU GO GO

| ❏ Design DLP-194 [M] | 1964 | 15.00 |
— *Cover calls this "Johnny Rivers Discotheque Au Go Go," but only one Johnny Rivers song is on the LP*
| ❏ Design SDLP-194 [R] | 1964 | 12.00 |
— *Cover calls this "Johnny Rivers Discotheque Au Go Go," but only one Johnny Rivers song is on the LP*

DISNEY'S CHRISTMAS ALL-TIME FAVORITES

| ❏ Disneyland 1V8150 | 1981 | 18.00 |

DISNEY'S CHRISTMAS FAVORITES

| ❏ Disneyland 2506 | 1979 | 15.00 |

DISPLAY CASE #8

| ❏ Warner Bros. PRO532 | 1972 | 30.00 |

DISPLAY CASE #9

| ❏ Warner Bros. PRO538 | 1972 | 30.00 |

DISPLAY CASE #10

| ❏ Warner Bros. PRO542 | 1973 | 30.00 |

DIXIE, LONDON STYLE

| ❏ London LL1337 [M] | 1956 | 25.00 |

DIXIELAND AT CARNEGIE HALL

❏ Forum SF-9011 [S]	196?	30.00
❏ Forum F-9011 [M]	196?	25.00
❏ Roulette R25038	1958	30.00
— *Originals have a black label*
| ❏ Roulette R25038 [M] | 1959 | 25.00 |
— *Second pressings have a white label with colored spokes*

DIXIELAND AT ITS BEST

| ❏ RCA Camden CAL-838 [M] | 1964 | 15.00 |
| ❏ RCA Camden CAS-838 [R] | 1964 | 12.00 |

DIXIELAND AT JAZZ, LTD.

| ❏ Atlantic 1261 [M] | 1957 | 40.00 |
— *Black label*
| ❏ Atlantic 1261 [M] | 1961 | 30.00 |
— *Multicolor label, white "fan" logo at right*

DIXIELAND AT JAZZ, LTD., VOL. 1

| ❏ Atlantic ALS-139 [10] | 1952 | 60.00 |

DIXIELAND AT JAZZ, LTD., VOL. 2

| ❏ Atlantic ALS-140 [10] | 1952 | 60.00 |

DIXIELAND CLASSICS

| ❏ Jazztone J-1216 [M] | 1956 | 30.00 |

DIXIELAND CONTRASTS

| ❏ Jazzman LJ-334 [M] | 1954 | 30.00 |

DIXIELAND FESTIVAL, VOL. 1

| ❏ Vik LX-1057 [M] | 1956 | 30.00 |

DIXIELAND HITS

| ❏ Swingville SVLP-2040 [M] | 1962 | 40.00 |
— *Purple label*
| ❏ Swingville SVLP-2040 [M] | 1965 | 25.00 |
— *Blue label, trident logo at right*

DIXIELAND IN OLD NEW ORLEANS

| ❏ Golden Crest GC-3021 [M] | 1958 | 25.00 |

DIXIELAND JAZZ

❏ Audiophile XL-325 [M]	1954	30.00
❏ Audiophile XL-330 [M]	1954	30.00
❏ Grand Award GA 33-310 [M]	1955	60.00
— *With wrap-around outer cover*
| ❏ Grand Award GA 33-310 [M] | 1955 | 30.00 |
— *Without wrap-around outer cover*

DIXIELAND JAZZ CLASSICS

| ❏ Herwin H-116 | 1980 | 15.00 |

DIXIELAND JAZZ GEMS

| ❏ Commodore FL-20010 [10] | 1950 | 50.00 |

DIXIELAND MAIN STREAM

| ❏ Savoy MG-12213 [M] | 196? | 25.00 |

DIXIELAND -- NEW ORLEANS

| ❏ Mainstream 56003 [M] | 1965 | 30.00 |
| ❏ Mainstream S-6003 [R] | 1965 | 15.00 |

DIXIELAND RHYTHM KINGS

| ❏ Paradox LP-6002 [10] | 1951 | 50.00 |

DIXIELAND SERIES, VOL. 1

| ❏ Savoy MG-15005 [10] | 1952 | 80.00 |

DIXIELAND SERIES, VOL. 2

| ❏ Savoy MG-15009 [10] | 1952 | 80.00 |

DIXIE LAND U.S.A.

| ❏ Promenade 2134 [M] | 195? | 18.00 |

DIXIELAND VS. BIRDLAND

| ❏ MGM E-231 [10] | 1954 | 80.00 |

THE D.I.Y. ALBUM

| ❏ D.I.Y./JW Productions DIY-0001 | 1982 | 50.00 |
— *Band copies on black vinyl*
| ❏ D.I.Y./JW Productions DIY-0001A | 1982 | 30.00 |
— *Store copies on clear vinyl (3-D pressing was planned but never done)*

DIZZY ATMOSPHERE

| ❏ Specialty LP-2110 [M] | 1957 | 40.00 |
— *Original edition, heavier vinyl*
| ❏ Specialty LP-2110 [M] | 198? | 25.00 |
— *Reissue on lighter vinyl*

DOCTOR DEATH'S VOLUME 1

| ❏ C'est La Mort 001 | 1986 | 30.00 |

D'OES CRAZY OLDIES

| ❏ Oldies 33 OL-8007 [M] | 1964 | 30.00 |

DO IT NOW - 20 GIANT HITS

| ❏ Ronco LP-1001 | 1971 | 25.00 |

DOO WOP

| ❏ Specialty SPS-2114 | 1969 | 25.00 |

DOUBLE BARREL JAZZ

| ❏ Bethlehem BCP-87 [M] | 1958 | 30.00 |

DOWN BEAT JAZZ CONCERT

| ❏ Dot DLP-9003 [M] | 1958 | 30.00 |
| ❏ Dot DLP-29003 [S] | 1958 | 30.00 |

DOWN BEAT JAZZ CONCERT, VOL. 2

| ❏ Dot DLP-3188 [M] | 1959 | 30.00 |
| ❏ Dot DLP-25188 [S] | 1959 | 30.00 |

DOWN BEAT'S HALL OF FAME, VOL. 1

| ❏ Verve MGV-8320 [M] | 1959 | 50.00 |
| ❏ Verve V-8320 [M] | 1961 | 25.00 |

A DOWN-HOME COUNTRY CHRISTMAS

| ❏ Columbia Special Products P14992 | 1979 | 10.00 |
| ❏ SeaShell P14992 | 1981 | 10.00 |
— *Reissue of Columbia Special Products P 14992*

DOWN HOME STOMP: RURAL BLUES, VOLUME 3

| ❏ Imperial LP-94006 | 1968 | 25.00 |

DR. DEMENTO PRESENTS THE GREATEST NOVELTY RECORDS OF ALL TIME VOLUME VI: CHRISTMAS

| ❏ Rhino RNLP825 | 1985 | 18.00 |

DREAMING ON THE RIVER TO NEW ORLEANS

| ❏ Southland SLP-238 | 1963 | 18.00 |

THE DRUMS

| ❏ ABC Impulse! AS-9272 | 197? | 25.00 |

DRUMS ON FIRE

| ❏ World Pacific WP-1247 [M] | 1958 | 40.00 |

DUDES & DOLLS

| ❏ Blaine House BHP1001 | 1975 | 18.00 |
— *Alternate number is Columbia Special Products P2 12939*

THE DUTCH EXPLOSION

| ❏ White Whale WWS-7130 | 1970 | 30.00 |

DYNAMITE

| ❏ K-Tel TU2360 | 1974 | 12.00 |

THE EARL BAKER CYLINDERS

| ❏ Jazz Archives JA-43 | 198? | 12.00 |

THE EARLY '60S: THESE WERE OUR SONGS

| ❏ Reader's Digest RC4-100 | 1989 | 50.00 |

EARLY AND RARE: CLASSIC JAZZ "COLLECTORS ITEMS

| ❏ Riverside RLP 12-134 [M] | 1957 | 40.00 |

THE EARLY DAYS OF BLUEGRASS, VOL. 1

| ❏ Rounder 1013 | 198? | 12.00 |

THE EARLY DAYS OF BLUEGRASS, VOL. 2

| ❏ Rounder 1014 | 198? | 12.00 |

THE EARLY DAYS OF BLUEGRASS VOL. 3: NEW SOUNDS RAMBLIN' FROM COAST TO COAST

| ❏ Rounder 1015 | 198? | 12.00 |

EARLY JAZZ GREATS, VOL. 1

| ❏ Jazztone J-1249 [M] | 1957 | 30.00 |

EARLY JAZZ GREATS, VOL. 2

| ❏ Jazztone J-1252 [M] | 1957 | 30.00 |

EARLY MODERN

| ❏ Milestone M-9035 | 197? | 15.00 |

EARLY VIPER JIVE

| ❏ Stash ST-105 | 197? | 12.00 |

EARTHY!

| ❏ Prestige PRLP-7102 [M] | 1957 | 100.00 |

THE EAST COAST JAZZ SCENE, VOL. 1

| ❏ Coral CRL57035 [M] | 1956 | 50.00 |

EASY LISTENING

❏ Audiophile AP-27 [M]	1953	30.00
❏ Audiophile AP-38 [M]	1953	30.00
❏ Audiophile XL-327 [M]	1954	30.00

EASY LISTENING HITS OF THE '60S AND '70S

| ❏ Reader's Digest RBA-040A | 1989 | 50.00 |

ECHOES OF AN ERA

| ❏ Elektra 60021 | 1982 | 12.00 |
— *With Stanley Clarke, Chick Corea, Chaka Khan and Joe Henderson*

ECHOES OF AN ERA VOLUME 2: THE CONCERT

| ❏ Elektra/Musician 60165 | 1983 | 12.00 |

ECHOES OF ENJA

| ❏ Enja 4000 | 197? | 15.00 |

ECHOES OF NEW ORLEANS

| ❏ Southland SLP-239 | 1963 | 18.00 |

ECLIPSE

| ❏ Warner Bros. PRO-A-828 | 1978 | 25.00 |

18 ALL TIME COUNTRY AND WESTERN HITS

| ❏ King 1027 [M] | 1968 | 30.00 |

18 ALL TIME RHYTHM 'N' BLUES HITS

| ❏ King 1026 [M] | 1968 | 30.00 |

18 KING-SIZE COUNTRY HITS

| ❏ Columbia CL2668 [M] | 1967 | 25.00 |
| ❏ Columbia CS9468 [R] | 1967 | 25.00 |

18 KING-SIZE RHYTHM AND BLUES HITS

| ❏ Columbia CL2667 [M] | 1967 | 30.00 |
| ❏ Columbia CS9467 [R] | 1967 | 25.00 |

EIGHT WAYS TO JAZZ

| ❏ Riverside RLP 12-272 [M] | 1958 | 30.00 |

ELEKTRA NEW FOLK SAMPLER

| ❏ Elektra SMP2 | 1956 | 30.00 |

ELEKTRA'S BEST, VOLUME 1: 1966-1968

| ❏ Elektra EB-1 | 1969 | 30.00 |
— *Promo only, red labels*

Number	Title	Yr	NM
ELEKTROCK: THE SIXTIES			
❑ Elektra 60403		1985	30.00
THE ELVIS PRESLEY YEARS			
❑ Reader's Digest RBA-236A		1991	50.00
EMI AMERICA HOLIDAY SAMPLER			
❑ EMI America SPRO9883/4 [DJ]		1986	18.00
—*Includes Pet Shop Boys, Stray Cats*			
ENCYCLOPEDIA OF JAZZ IN THE '60'S, VOL. 1			
❑ Verve V-8677 [M]		1966	18.00
❑ Verve V6-8677 [S]		1966	25.00
THE ENCYCLOPEDIA OF JAZZ IN THE 70S			
❑ RCA Victor APL2-1984		1977	18.00
THE ENCYCLOPEDIA OF JAZZ ON RECORDS			
❑ Decca DXF140 [M]		1957	100.00
—*Box set; individually issued as Decca 8398, 8399, 8400 and 8401*			
THE ENCYCLOPEDIA OF JAZZ ON RECORDS, VOL. 1: JAZZ OF THE TWENTIES			
❑ Decca DL8398 [M]		1957	25.00
THE ENCYCLOPEDIA OF JAZZ ON RECORDS, VOL. 1 AND 2: JAZZ OF THE TWENTIES/JAZZ OF THE THIRTIES			
❑ MCA 4061		197?	18.00
THE ENCYCLOPEDIA OF JAZZ ON RECORDS, VOL. 2: JAZZ OF THE THIRTIES			
❑ Decca DL8399 [M]		1957	25.00
THE ENCYCLOPEDIA OF JAZZ ON RECORDS, VOL. 3: JAZZ OF THE FORTIES			
❑ Decca DL8400 [M]		1957	25.00
THE ENCYCLOPEDIA OF JAZZ ON RECORDS, VOL. 3 AND 4: JAZZ OF THE FORTIES/JAZZ OF THE FIFTIES			
❑ MCA 4062		197?	18.00
THE ENCYCLOPEDIA OF JAZZ ON RECORDS, VOL. 4: JAZZ OF THE FIFTIES			
❑ Decca DL8401 [M]		1957	25.00
THE ENCYCLOPEDIA OF JAZZ ON RECORDS, VOL. 5: JAZZ OF THE SIXTIES			
❑ MCA 4063		197?	18.00
END OF AN ERA: RHYTHM 'N' BLUES, VOLUME 1			
❑ Imperial LP-94003		1968	25.00
ENERGY ESSENTIALS			
❑ ABC Impulse! ASD-9228		197?	25.00
ENGLAND'S GREATEST HIT MAKERS			
❑ London LL3430 [M]		1965	30.00
❑ London PS430 [R]		1965	25.00
ENGLAND'S GREATEST HITS			
❑ Fontana MGF27570 [M]		1967	50.00
—*With poster*			
❑ Fontana MGF27570 [M]		1967	40.00
—*Without poster*			
❑ Fontana SRF67570 [R]		1967	30.00
—*With poster*			
❑ Fontana SRF67570 [R]		1967	25.00
—*Without poster*			
THE ENIGMA VARIATIONS			
❑ Enigma 72001		1985	25.00
—*Includes Redd Kross, many more*			
THE ENIGMA VARIATIONS 2			
❑ Enigma SQBB-73247		1987	18.00
ERA OF THE CLARINET			
❑ Mainstream S-6011 [R]		1965	15.00
❑ Mainstream 56011 [M]		1965	30.00
ESCAPADE REVIEWS THE JAZZ SCENE			
❑ Liberty SL-9005 [M]		1957	30.00
ESCAPE			
❑ Gene Norman GNP-27 [M]		1958	30.00
ESQUIRE'S 2ND ANNUAL ALL-AMERICAN JAZZ CONCERT			
❑ Sunbeam 219		197?	15.00
ESQUIRE'S ALL-AMERICAN HOT JAZZ			
❑ RCA Victor LPV-544 [M]		1967	25.00
ESQUIRE'S WORLD OF JAZZ			
❑ Capitol TBO1970 [M]		1963	25.00
❑ Capitol STBO1970 [S]		1963	25.00
THE ESSENTIAL JAZZ VOCALS			
❑ Verve V-8505 [M]		1963	25.00
❑ Verve V6-8505 [R]		1963	15.00
AN EVENING OF JAZZ			
❑ Norgran MGN-1065 [M]		1956	80.00
❑ Verve MGV-8155 [M]		1957	30.00
❑ Verve V-8155 [M]		1961	25.00
EVERYBODY ROCKS!			
❑ Capitol T1025 [M]		1957	40.00
—*Turquoise label*			

Number	Title	Yr	NM
EVERYBODY'S FAVORITE BLUES			
❑ King 875 [M]		1963	70.00
EVERYBODY'S GONE SURFIN'			
❑ Parkway P-7035 [M]		1963	50.00
EVERY DAY IS A HOLLY DAY			
❑ Emergo EM9465		1989	15.00
—*Includes Slickee Boys*			
EVERY MAN HAS A WOMAN			
❑ Polydor 823490-1		1984	12.00
—*Includes Elvis Costello, Roseanne Cash; tribute album to Yoko Ono*			
THE EXCELLO STORY			
❑ Excello LPS-8025		1972	30.00
THE EXCITING NEW LIVERPOOL SOUND			
❑ Columbia CL2172 [M]		1964	30.00
EXPLOSIVE!			
❑ Liberty MM-412 [DJ]		1962	50.00
—*Promo-only release*			
EXPOSED: A CHEAP PEEK AT TODAY'S PROVOCATIVE NEW ROCK			
❑ CBS X237124		1981	12.00
—*Includes Adam and the Ants, Ian Gomm, Roseanne Cash, The Romantics, The Boomtown Rats, Garland Jeffreys*			
EXPOSED II			
❑ CBS X237601		1981	12.00
—*Includes Tommy Tutone, Gary Myrick and the Figures, Psychedelic Furs, Orchestral Manoeuvres in the Dark, Jo Jo Zep and the Falcons, etc.*			
FABULOUS FAVORITES OF OUR TIME			
❑ Liberty LRP-3223 [M]		1962	25.00
❑ Liberty LST-7223 [S]		1962	30.00
THE FAMILY CHRISTMAS COLLECTION			
❑ Time-Life STL-131		1990	30.00
—*Available from Time-Life by mail order only*			
FAMILY CHRISTMAS FAVORITES FROM BING CROSBY AND THE COLUMBUS BOYCHOIR			
❑ Decca DL34487		1967	18.00
—*Sold only at Safeway grocery stores*			
FAMILY PORTRAIT			
❑ A&M SP-19002		1968	25.00
FANFARE OF HITS			
❑ Argo LP-656 [M]		1960	30.00
FANTASTIC COUNTRY			
❑ RCA Victor PRS-423		1972	15.00
FANTASY SAMPLER			
❑ Fantasy FS-654 [M]		195?	25.00
—*Red vinyl*			
FAST MUTANT POP			
❑ PVC 7912		1980	16.00
—*Includes Human League, Gang of Four, Mekons, others*			
FAVORITE CHRISTMAS CAROLS FROM THE VOICE OF FIRESTONE			
❑ Firestone MLP7005 [M]		1962	15.00
—*Sold only at Firestone tire dealers; actually Volume 1 of the "Firestone Presents..." series*			
FAVORITE SACRED SONGS			
❑ King 556 [M]		1956	150.00
THE FEMININE TOUCH			
❑ Decca DL5486 [10]		1953	50.00
❑ Decca DL8316 [M]		1956	30.00
FESTIVAL JAZZ, VOL. 1			
❑ Jim Taylor Presents 106		197?	15.00
FESTIVAL JAZZ, VOL. 2			
❑ Jim Taylor Presents 107		197?	15.00
FIDDLER'S HALL OF FAME			
❑ Starday SLP-209 [M]		1963	30.00
FIDDLIN' COUNTRY STYLE			
❑ Nashville NLP-2015 [M]		1965	25.00
❑ Power Pak PO-296		197?	12.00
❑ Starday SLP-114 [M]		1960	40.00
15 FAVORITES			
❑ Hickory LPM-105 [M]		1962	30.00
15 GOLDEN HITS			
❑ United Artists UAL-3192 [M]		1962	30.00
❑ United Artists UAS-6192 [S]		1962	30.00
15 HITS: THE ORIGINAL RECORDINGS (THE ORIGINAL HITS, VOLUME 5)			
❑ Liberty LRP-3235 [M]		1962	25.00
FIFTEEN STAR SAXOPHONES			
❑ Bethlehem BCP-6035 [M]		1959	30.00
52ND STREET, VOL. 1			
❑ Onyx 203		197?	15.00

Number	Title	Yr	NM
52ND STREET, VOL. 2			
❑ Onyx 217		197?	15.00
52ND STREET JAZZ			
❑ Waldorf Music Hall MH 33-148 [10]		195?	100.00
50 BELOVED SONGS OF FAITH			
❑ Reader's Digest BMR3-100		1990	30.00
FIFTY CHRISTMAS FAVORITES			
❑ RCA Camden CXS-9025		1972	18.00
50 STARS! 50 HITS! OF COUNTRY MUSIC			
❑ Great Country Music CMS1/2/3/4		196?	25.00
—*Labels call this "50 Country Music Greats"; a Starday product*			
50 YEARS OF BLUEGRASS HITS, VOL. 1			
❑ CMH 9033		198?	18.00
50 YEARS OF BLUEGRASS HITS, VOL. 2			
❑ CMH 9034		198?	18.00
50 YEARS OF BLUEGRASS HITS, VOL. 3			
❑ CMH 9035		198?	18.00
50 YEARS OF BLUEGRASS HITS, VOL. 4			
❑ CMH 9036		198?	18.00
50 YEARS OF FILM			
❑ Warner Bros. 3XX2737		1973	30.00
—*Box set with 60-page booklet*			
50 YEARS OF FILM MUSIC			
❑ Warner Bros. 3XX2736		1973	30.00
—*Box set with 28-page booklet*			
50 YEARS OF JAZZ GREATS			
❑ Columbia Musical Treasury P3S5932		197?	25.00
50 YEARS OF JAZZ GUITAR			
❑ Columbia CG33566		1973	18.00
FILLET OF SOUL			
❑ Stax STS3021		1972	25.00
FILLMORE: THE LAST DAYS			
❑ Fillmore Z3X31390		1972	50.00
—*With booklet and bonus 7-inch single*			
FILL YOUR HEAD WITH JAZZ			
❑ Columbia G30217		1971	18.00
FILM MUSIC FROM FRANCE			
❑ Philips PHM200071 [M]		1962	25.00
❑ Philips PHS600071 [S]		1962	30.00
THE FINEST OF FOLK BLUESMEN			
❑ Bethlehem BCP-6017		197?	25.00
—*Despite lower number, this is a reissue of Bethlehem 6071, distributed by RCA*			
FINK ALONG WITH MAD			
❑ Big Top 12-1306 [M]		1962	100.00
FIRE & ICE			
❑ Realistic/Warner 51-3000(OP 1525)		1982	15.00
—*Includes Blondie, Pretenders*			
FIRE INTO MUSIC			
❑ CTI CTS-2		197?	18.00
FIRE ON THE STRINGS			
❑ Starday SLP-221 [M]		1963	30.00
FIRESTONE PRESENTS YOUR CHRISTMAS FAVORITES, VOLUME 3			
❑ Firestone MLP7008 [M]		1964	12.00
—*Sold only at Firestone tire dealers*			
❑ Firestone SLP7008 [S]		1964	12.00
—*Sold only at Firestone tire dealers*			
FIRESTONE PRESENTS YOUR CHRISTMAS FAVORITES, VOLUME 7			
❑ Firestone CSLP7015		1968	12.00
—*Sold only at Firestone tire dealers*			
FIRESTONE PRESENTS YOUR FAVORITE CHRISTMAS CAROLS, VOLUME 2			
❑ Firestone MLP7006 [M]		1963	12.00
—*Sold only at Firestone tire dealers*			
❑ Firestone SLP7006 [S]		1963	12.00
—*Sold only at Firestone tire dealers*			
FIRESTONE PRESENTS YOUR FAVORITE CHRISTMAS MUSIC, VOLUME 4			
❑ Firestone MLP7011 [M]		1965	12.00
—*Sold only at Firestone tire dealers*			
❑ Firestone SLP7011 [S]		1965	12.00
—*Sold only at Firestone tire dealers*			
FIRESTONE PRESENTS YOUR FAVORITE CHRISTMAS MUSIC, VOLUME 5			
❑ Firestone MLP7012 [M]		1966	12.00
—*Sold only at Firestone tire dealers*			
❑ Firestone SLP7012 [S]		1966	12.00
—*Sold only at Firestone tire dealers*			

Number	Title	Yr	NM

FIRESTONE PRESENTS YOUR FAVORITE CHRISTMAS MUSIC, VOLUME 6
- ❏ Firestone MLP7014 [M] — 1967 — 12.00
  — *Sold only at Firestone tire dealers*
- ❏ Firestone SLP7014 [S] — 1967 — 12.00
  — *Sold only at Firestone tire dealers*

FIRST ALBUM OF JAZZ
- ❏ Folkways FP-712 [10] — 1951 — 50.00

FIRST CHRISTMAS RECORD FOR CHILDREN
- ❏ Harmony HS14554 — 197? — 15.00

FIRST DECADE
- ❏ WEA 10 [DJ] — 1981 — 150.00
  — *Only 1,000 were made paying tribute to WEA's 10th anniversary*

THE FIRST GREAT ROCK FESTIVALS OF THE SEVENTIES: ISLE OF WIGHT/ATLANTA POP FESTIVAL
- ❏ Columbia G3X30805 — 1971 — 30.00

FIRST OF THE FAMOUS
- ❏ Capitol T2275 [M] — 1965 — 30.00

FIVE BIRDS AND A MONK
- ❏ Galaxy 5134 — 1979 — 15.00

FIVE FEET OF SWING
- ❏ Decca DL8045 [M] — 1954 — 40.00

5-STRING BANJO PICKIN' AND SINGIN'
- ❏ King 994 [M] — 1966 — 40.00

FLASHBACK! ROCK CLASSICS OF THE '70S
- ❏ Realm 1P8075 — 1991 — 18.00
  — *Includes The Cars*

FLEX YOUR HEAD
- ❏ Dischord 7 — 1982 — 50.00

THE FOLK BOX
- ❏ Elektra EKL-9001 — 1964 — 50.00

FOLK FESTIVAL OF THE BLUES
- ❏ Argo LP-4031 [M] — 1964 — 40.00

FOLK POPS 'N JAZZ SAMPLER
- ❏ Elektra SMP3 [M] — 1957 — 30.00

FOLK SAMPLER FIVE
- ❏ Elektra SMP5 [M] — 196? — 30.00

THE FOLK SCENE
- ❏ Elektra SMP6 [M] — 196? — 50.00

FOLKSONG '65
- ❏ Elektra SMP8 [M] — 1965 — 25.00
- ❏ Elektra S78 [S] — 1965 — 30.00

FOLKWAYS: A VISION SHARED
- ❏ Columbia OC44034 — 1988 — 15.00
  — *Includes U2 ("Jesus Christ"), Little Richard with Fishbone*

FOLLOW OUR TRACKS
- ❏ Warner Bros. PRO-A-3503 [DJ] — 1989 — 15.00
  — *Includes Elvis Costello, New Order, Ramones, Violent Femmes, R.E.M., Lou Reed, etc.*

FOLLOW OUR TRAX, VOL. 2
- ❏ Reprise PRO-A-3655 [DJ] — 1989 — 15.00
  — *Includes Morrissey, The B-52's, Tom Tom Club, Chris Isaak, others*

FOOTNOTES TO JAZZ, VOL. 2: ANATOMY OF A JAZZ COMPOSITION
- ❏ Folkways FP-31 [10] — 1951 — 50.00

FOOTPRINTS IN TIME
- ❏ White Whale WWS-7125 — 1970 — 30.00

FOR A MUSICAL MERRY CHRISTMAS
- ❏ RCA Victor PR-149A [M] — 1963 — 15.00
  — *Sold only at Acme Markets (Mid-Atlantic states)*
- ❏ RCA Victor PRM-163 [M] — 1964 — 15.00
  — *Sold at B.F. Goodrich dealers*
- ❏ RCA Victor PRS-163(e) [S] — 1964 — 15.00
  — *Sold at B.F. Goodrich dealers*

FOR A MUSICAL MERRY CHRISTMAS, VOL. TWO
- ❏ RCA Victor PRM189 [M] — 1965 — 15.00
  — *Sold at B.F. Goodrich dealers*
- ❏ RCA Victor PRS189 [S] — 1965 — 18.00
  — *Sold at B.F. Goodrich tire dealers*

FOR A MUSICAL MERRY CHRISTMAS, VOLUME 3
- ❏ RCA Victor PRM-221 [M] — 1966 — 15.00
  — *Sold at B.F. Goodrich dealers*
- ❏ RCA Victor PRS-221 [S] — 1966 — 18.00
  — *Sold at B.F. Goodrich dealers*

FOR A MUSICAL MERRY CHRISTMAS, VOLUME 4
- ❏ RCA Victor PRS-253 — 1967 — 15.00
  — *Sold at B.F. Goodrich dealers*

THE FORCE
- ❏ Warner Bros. PRO593 — 1974 — 25.00
- ❏ Warner Bros. PRO596 — 1974 — 30.00

FOR CHRISTMAS SEALS…A MATTER OF LIFE AND BREATH
- ❏ Decca Custom StyleE [DJ] — 1968 — 25.00
  — *Promo-only album for Christmas Seals*
- ❏ Decca Custom StyleF [DJ] — 1968 — 30.00
  — *Promo-only album for Christmas Seals; four five-minute programs*

FOR DANCERS ONLY
- ❏ Epic LN3120 [M] — 1955 — 30.00

FORD HOOTENANNY
- ❏ RCA Victor PRM-152 [M] — 1964 — 25.00
  — *Sold only at Ford dealers*

FOREMOST!
- ❏ Onyx 201 — 197? — 15.00

FOREPLAY #16
- ❏ A&M SP-17071 [DJ] — 1979 — 15.00
  — *Includes The Dickies, The Tubes*

FOREPLAY #17
- ❏ A&M SP-17074 [DJ] — 1979 — 12.00
  — *Includes U.K. Squeeze*

FOREPLAY #26
- ❏ A&M SP-17102 [DJ] — 1979 — 18.00
  — *Includes The Police, Joe Jackson; one-sided, with booklet*

FOREPLAY #27
- ❏ A&M SP-17107 [DJ] — 1979 — 18.00
  — *Includes Squeeze; with booklet*

FOREPLAY #42
- ❏ A&M SP-17150 [DJ] — 1981 — 12.00
  — *Includes Magazine, Split Enz*

FOREPLAY #43
- ❏ A&M SP-17154 [DJ] — 1981 — 15.00
  — *Includes Oingo Boingo, Squeeze*

FOREPLAY #44
- ❏ A&M SP-17159 [DJ] — 1981 — 15.00
  — *Includes Oingo Boingo, Magazine*

FOREPLAY #45
- ❏ A&M SP-17162 [DJ] — 1981 — 30.00
  — *Includes 20-minute collage of music from "Urgh! A Music War*

FOREPLAY #46
- ❏ A&M SP-17166 [DJ] — 1981 — 12.00
  — *Includes Wall of Voodoo*

FOREPLAY #47
- ❏ A&M SP-17174 [DJ] — 1981 — 15.00
  — *Includes The Police, The Cure*

FOREPLAY #48
- ❏ A&M SP-17177 [DJ] — 1981 — 12.00
  — *Includes Split Enz, The Fleshtones, Humans*

FOREPLAY
- ❏ A&M SP-17000 [DJ] — 1978 — 15.00
  — *Includes The Tubes*
- ❏ A&M SP-17146 [DJ] — 1981 — 12.00
  — *Includes The Cramps, John Cale*
- ❏ A&M SP-17018 [DJ] — 1978 — 18.00
  — *Includes U.K. Squeeze, The Stranglers; with booklet*

FORGOTTEN MILLION SELLERS
- ❏ King 792 [M] — 1962 — 100.00

FOR JAZZ LOVERS
- ❏ EmArcy MG-36086 [M] — 1956 — 40.00

FOR TWISTERS ONLY
- ❏ Ace LP-1020 [M] — 1962 — 70.00

FORTY GOSPEL GREATS
- ❏ Vee Jay VJS-2-19000 — 1975 — 30.00

FOUNDATIONS
- ❏ MCA 4153 — 198? — 15.00

FOUNDATIONS OF MODERN JAZZ
- ❏ Everest Archive of Folk & Jazz 229 — 196? — 12.00

FOUR ALTOS
- ❏ Prestige PRLP-7116 [M] — 1957 — 100.00

FOUR DECADES OF JAZZ
- ❏ Xanadu 5001 — 197? — 18.00

FOUR FRENCH HORNS
- ❏ Savoy MG-12173 [M] — 1961 — 50.00

THE FOUR MOST GUITARS
- ❏ ABC-Paramount ABC-109 [M] — 1956 — 30.00
- ❏ Paramount LP-109 [10] — 1954 — 60.00

FOUR OLD 7" ON A 12
- ❏ Dischord 14 — 1985 — 15.00
  — *Includes Teen Idles, S.O.A., Government Issue, Youth Brigade*

THE FOUR ROSES DANCE PARTY
- ❏ Columbia Special Products XTV68933/4 [M] — 1961 — 18.00

14 #1 COUNTRY HITS
- ❏ RCA Victor AHL1-7004 — 1985 — 15.00

14 GOLDEN RECORDINGS FROM THE HISTORIC VAULTS OF DUKE-PEACOCK RECORDS
- ❏ ABC ABCX-784 — 1973 — 25.00

14 GOLDEN RECORDINGS FROM THE HISTORIC VAULTS OF DUKE-PEACOCK RECORDS, VOLUME 2
- ❏ ABC ABCX-789 — 1973 — 25.00

14 GREAT ALL TIME C&W WALTZES
- ❏ King 890 [M] — 1964 — 70.00

14 HIT FLASHBACKS FROM THE GOLDEN GROUP ERA
- ❏ King 893 [M] — 1964 — 70.00

14 MORE NEWIES BUT GOODIES
- ❏ Mercury MG-20493 [M] — 1960 — 30.00
- ❏ Mercury SR-60241 [S] — 1960 — 40.00

14 NEWIES BUT GOODIES
- ❏ Mercury MG-20493 [M] — 1960 — 30.00
- ❏ Mercury SR-60172 [S] — 1960 — 40.00

14 OF THE WORLD'S BEST-LOVED CHRISTMAS SONGS
- ❏ Columbia Special Products CSP122 [M] — 1963 — 18.00
  — *Sold only at Walgreens drug stores. Title on record is "Music of Christmas"; number on record is "XTV 88672" on Side 1, "XTV 88673" on Side 2*

FOUR TO GO
- ❏ Columbia CL2018 [M] — 1963 — 25.00
- ❏ Columbia CS8818 [S] — 1963 — 30.00

FOUR TROMBONES… THE DEBUT RECORDINGS
- ❏ Prestige 24097 — 197? — 18.00

FRANK BULL AND GENE NORMAN PRESENT DIXIELAND JUBILEE
- ❏ Decca DL7022 [10] — 1952 — 50.00

FRANKENSTEIN AND OTHER ROCK MONSTERS!
- ❏ CBS Associated FZ39257 — 1984 — 12.00
  — *Includes The Romantics, David Johansen*

FRANK JOHNSON'S FAVORITES
- ❏ Ralph 8110 — 1981 — 25.00

FRENCH FESTIVAL
- ❏ Classic Jazz 133 — 197? — 15.00

FRENCH TOAST
- ❏ Angel ANG-60009 [10] — 1956 — 50.00

FRIDAY THE 13TH, COOK COUNTY JAIL
- ❏ Groove Merchant 515 — 197? — 18.00

FROM CANADA WITH LOVE
- ❏ PM 011 — 198? — 12.00

FROM DAVID FROST AND BILLY TAYLOR…MERRY CHRISTMAS
- ❏ Bell 6053 — 1970 — 18.00

FROM SPIRITUALS TO SWING
- ❏ Vanguard VMS-73131 — 197? — 12.00
- ❏ Vanguard VSD-47/48 — 197? — 18.00

FROM UNDER THE CHRISTMAS TREE
- ❏ Capitol Creative Products SL-6589 — 1968 — 15.00

FULL TILT
- ❏ K-Tel TU2770 — 1981 — 12.00
  — *Includes Blondie, Devo*

FUNKY BLUES NO. 2
- ❏ American Recording Society G-404 [M] — 1956 — 30.00

FUNKY CHRISTMAS
- ❏ Cotillion SD9911 — 1976 — 18.00

FUN ON THE FRETS: EARLY JAZZ GUITAR
- ❏ Yazoo 1061 — 197? — 12.00

THE FUTURE LOOKS BRIGHT
- ❏ SST/Posh Boy PBS120 [DJ] — 1981 — 30.00
  — *Vinyl is promo only*

GALA FAVORITES
- ❏ Mercury Living Presence SR90339 [S] — 196? — 30.00
  — *Maroon label, no "Vendor: Mercury Record Corporation*

GARDEN OF DELIGHTS
- ❏ Elektra S310 — 1971 — 25.00
  — *Butterfly labels, possibly promo only*

GARY MOORE PRESENTS "MY KIND OF MUSIC
- ❏ Columbia CL717 [M] — 1956 — 30.00

GEMS OF JAZZ, VOL. 1
- ❏ Decca DL5133 [10] — 1950 — 50.00
- ❏ Decca DL8039 [M] — 1954 — 40.00

Number	Title	Yr	NM

GEMS OF JAZZ, VOL. 2
| ❏ Decca DL5134 [10] | | 1950 | 50.00 |
| ❏ Decca DL8040 [M] | | 1954 | 40.00 |

GEMS OF JAZZ, VOL. 3
| ❏ Decca DL5383 [10] | | 1952 | 50.00 |
| ❏ Decca DL8041 [M] | | 1954 | 40.00 |

GEMS OF JAZZ, VOL. 4
| ❏ Decca DL5384 [10] | | 1952 | 50.00 |
| ❏ Decca DL8042 [M] | | 1954 | 40.00 |

GEMS OF JAZZ, VOL. 5
| ❏ Decca DL8043 [M] | | 1954 | 40.00 |

GENUINE MISSISSIPPI BLUES
| ❏ Ace 2028 | | 1981 | 15.00 |

GERRY GOFFIN AND CAROLE KING: SOLID GOLD
| ❏ Screen Gems/Columbia CPL-713 [DJ] | | 1975 | 25.00 |
—Promo-only compilation of oldies sent to radio to spur airplay on songs owned by this publishing house

GET HOT OR GO HOME: VINTAGE RCA ROCKABILLY '56-'59
| ❏ Country Music Foundation CMF-014 | | 1990 | 18.00 |

GET IT TOGETHER
| ❏ Mainstream MRL-350 | | 197? | 15.00 |

GIANTS OF BOOGIE WOOGIE
| ❏ Riverside RLP 12-106 [M] | | 1956 | 40.00 |

GIANTS OF JAZZ
| ❏ American Recording Society G-401 [M] | | 1956 | 30.00 |

THE GIANTS OF JAZZ
| ❏ Columbia CL1970 [M] | | 1963 | 30.00 |

GIANTS OF JAZZ
| ❏ George Wein Collection GW-3004 | | 198? | 12.00 |

GIANTS OF JAZZ, VOL. 2
| ❏ Who's Who in Jazz 21014 | | 197? | 12.00 |

GIANTS OF JAZZ, VOLUME 1
| ❏ Who's Who in Jazz WWLP21012 | | 1977 | 12.00 |

GIANTS OF JAZZ: THE GUITARISTS
| ❏ Time-Life STL-J-12 | | 1980 | 18.00 |

GIANTS OF JAZZ ORGAN
| ❏ King 837 [M] | | 1963 | 120.00 |

GIANTS OF JAZZ VOL. 2
| ❏ American Recording Society G-444 [M] | | 1957 | 30.00 |

GIANTS OF SMALL BAND SWING, VOL. 1
| ❏ Fantasy OJC-1723 | | 1990 | 12.00 |
| ❏ Riverside RLP 12-143 [M] | | 1957 | 40.00 |

GIANTS OF SMALL BAND SWING, VOL. 2
| ❏ Fantasy OJC-1724 | | 1990 | 12.00 |
| ❏ Riverside RLP 12-145 [M] | | 1957 | 40.00 |

GIANTS OF THE BLUES TENOR SAX
| ❏ Prestige 24101 | | 197? | 18.00 |

GIANTS OF THE FUNK TENOR SAX
| ❏ Prestige 24102 | | 197? | 18.00 |

GIANTS OF TRADITIONAL JAZZ
| ❏ Savoy Jazz SJL-2251 | | 198? | 15.00 |

THE GIFT OF CHRISTMAS
| ❏ Columbia Special Products C10018 | | 1971 | 15.00 |
—Sold only at Ace hardware stores (sticker on lower right front cover)
| ❏ Columbia Special Products P11648 | | 1973 | 12.00 |
—Same contents and order as "The Gift of Christmas," C 10018; oddly, the record calls this "The Gift of Christmas -- Volume II"!

THE GIFT OF CHRISTMAS, VOLUME I
| ❏ Columbia Special Products CSS706 | | 1968 | 15.00 |
—Produced for First Financial Marketing Group

THE GIFTS OF CHRISTMAS
| ❏ Guideposts P15954 | | 1981 | 15.00 |
—An exclusive Guideposts collection

THE GIRLS SING
| ❏ Savoy MG-12220 [M] | | 196? | 25.00 |

THE GLORY OF CHRISTMAS
| ❏ Columbia Musical Treasury P3S5356 | | 196? | 18.00 |
—Performed by anonymous musicians

GOD REST YE MERRY, JAZZMEN
| ❏ Columbia FC37551 | | 1981 | 15.00 |
—7-inch 33 1/3 rpm single with small hole; distributed by various banks
| ❏ Columbia PC37551 | | 198? | 10.00 |
—Budget-line reissue

GOIN' UP THE COUNTRY: RURAL BLUES, VOLUME 1
| ❏ Imperial LP-94000 | | 1968 | 25.00 |

GOLD & PLATINUM
| ❏ Realm 1P7679 | | 1985 | 12.00 |
—Includes Cyndi Lauper, The Police, Men At Work, The Cars, Nena

GOLD & PLATINUM, VOLUME FIVE
| ❏ Realm 1P7898 | | 1989 | 12.00 |
—Includes Midnight Oil, U2, INXS, Bangles

GOLD & PLATINUM, VOLUME FOUR
| ❏ Realm 2P7826 | | 1988 | 18.00 |
—Includes Beastie Boys ("Fight for Your Right"); Billy Idol ("Mony Mony")

GOLD & PLATINUM, VOLUME SIX
| ❏ Realm 1P7899 | | 1989 | 12.00 |
—Includes Terence Trent D'Arby, George Michael, Icehouse

GOLD & PLATINUM, VOLUME THREE
| ❏ Realm 1P7765 | | 1987 | 12.00 |
—Includes Bangles ("If She Knew What She Wants"), Belinda Carlisle ("Mad About You"), Hooters, The Outfield

GOLD & PLATINUM, VOLUME TWO
| ❏ Realm 1P7726 | | 1986 | 12.00 |
—Includes Wham! ("Careless Whisper"); Ciyndi Lauper, Tears For Fears, Sade, 'Til Tuesday

GOLDEN AGE OF COUNTRY MUSIC 1940-1970
| ❏ Reader's Digest RBA-005-A | | 1987 | 40.00 |

THE GOLDEN AGE OF RHYTHM AND BLUES
| ❏ Chess 2CH-50030 | | 1972 | 30.00 |

THE GOLDEN COUNTRY COLLECTION
| ❏ Homestead 1001 | | 1975 | 18.00 |
—Alternate number is Capitol Special Markets SLC-6964

GOLDEN COUNTRY GROUPS
| ❏ Reader's Digest RBA-201-A | | 1988 | 40.00 |

GOLDEN COUNTRY HITS
❏ Harmony HL7362 [M]		1966	15.00
❏ Harmony HS11162 [S]		1966	18.00
❏ United Artists UAL-3327 [M]		1964	18.00
❏ United Artists UAS-6327 [S]		1964	25.00

THE GOLDEN DAYS OF BRITISH ROCK
| ❏ Sire V6046 | | 1976 | 40.00 |

GOLDEN ECHOES
| ❏ Arvee A-433 [M] | | 1962 | 30.00 |
| ❏ Arvee SA-433 [S] | | 1962 | 30.00 |

GOLDEN ENCORES
| ❏ Cadence CLP-3043 [M] | | 1960 | 40.00 |

THE GOLDEN ERA OF JAZZ, VOL. 1
| ❏ Savoy MG-15015 [10] | | 1952 | 80.00 |

THE GOLDEN ERA OF JAZZ, VOL. 2
| ❏ Savoy MG-15018 [10] | | 1952 | 80.00 |

GOLDEN GASSERS
| ❏ Chess LP1458USA [M] | | 1961 | 120.00 |
—National version; see listings in this section under "KYA," "Murray the K" and "WAMO" for regional releases

THE GOLDEN GLOW OF CHRISTMAS
| ❏ Columbia Special Products C10925 | | 1972 | 15.00 |
—Sold only at JCPenney department stores

GOLDEN GOODIES, VOL. 1
| ❏ Roulette R25207 [M] | | 1963 | 30.00 |

GOLDEN GOODIES, VOL. 2
| ❏ Roulette R25210 [M] | | 1963 | 30.00 |

GOLDEN GOODIES, VOL. 3
| ❏ Roulette R25218 [M] | | 1963 | 30.00 |

GOLDEN GOODIES, VOL. 4: GOODIES FOR A DANCE PARTY
| ❏ Roulette R25209 [M] | | 1963 | 30.00 |

GOLDEN GOODIES, VOL. 5
| ❏ Roulette R25215 [M] | | 1963 | 30.00 |

GOLDEN GOODIES, VOL. 6
| ❏ Roulette R25216 [M] | | 1963 | 30.00 |

GOLDEN GOODIES, VOL. 7
| ❏ Roulette R25212 [M] | | 1963 | 30.00 |

GOLDEN GOODIES, VOL. 8
| ❏ Roulette R25214 [M] | | 1963 | 30.00 |

GOLDEN GOODIES, VOL. 9
| ❏ Roulette R25213 [M] | | 1963 | 30.00 |

GOLDEN GOODIES, VOL. 10
| ❏ Roulette R25217 [M] | | 1963 | 30.00 |

GOLDEN GOODIES, VOL. 11
| ❏ Roulette R25219 [M] | | 1963 | 30.00 |

GOLDEN GOODIES, VOL. 12
| ❏ Roulette R25211 [M] | | 1963 | 30.00 |

GOLDEN GOODIES, VOL. 14
| ❏ Roulette R25239 [M] | | 1964 | 25.00 |

GOLDEN GOODIES, VOL. 15
| ❏ Roulette R25240 [M] | | 1964 | 25.00 |

GOLDEN GOODIES, VOL. 16
| ❏ Roulette R25241 [M] | | 1964 | 25.00 |

GOLDEN GOODIES, VOL. 17
| ❏ Roulette R25242 [M] | | 1964 | 25.00 |

GOLDEN GOODIES OF 1963, VOL. 18
| ❏ Roulette R25247 [M] | | 1964 | 25.00 |

GOLDEN GREATS
| ❏ Liberty LRP-3500 [M] | | 1967 | 18.00 |
| ❏ Liberty LST-7500 [P] | | 1967 | 25.00 |

THE GOLDEN GROUPS
| ❏ Specialty SPS-2155 | | 1972 | 25.00 |

GOLDEN HITS FROM THE GANG AT BANG
| ❏ Bang BLP-215 [M] | | 1967 | 25.00 |
| ❏ Bang BLPS-215 [P] | | 1967 | 30.00 |

GOLDEN INSTRUMENTALS
| ❏ Dot DLP-3820 [M] | | 1967 | 30.00 |
| ❏ Dot DLP-25820 [S] | | 1967 | 30.00 |

GOLDEN INSTRUMENTALS COUNTRY STYLE
| ❏ Wing MGW-12261 [M] | | 1964 | 25.00 |
| ❏ Wing SRW-16261 [S] | | 1964 | 25.00 |

GOLDEN JAZZ INTRSUMENTALS
| ❏ Bethlehem BCP-6065 [M] | | 1962 | 30.00 |

GOLDEN MOMENTS IN COUNTRY AND WESTERN MUSIC
| ❏ Capitol SQBO-90985 [S] | | 196? | 25.00 |
—Capitol Record Club exclusive

GOLDEN SOUVENIRS
| ❏ United Artists UAL-3317 [M] | | 1963 | 30.00 |
| ❏ United Artists UAS-6317 [S] | | 1963 | 30.00 |

GOLDEN TEEN HITS
| ❏ Liberty L-5505 [M] | | 1962 | 40.00 |

GOLDEN TREASURE CHEST
| ❏ United Artists UAL-3314 [M] | | 1963 | 30.00 |
| ❏ United Artists UAS-6314 [S] | | 1963 | 30.00 |

GOLD HITS
| ❏ Warwick W2008 [M] | | 1959 | 80.00 |
—Reissue of "Goodies But Oldies, Volume 2"; this title still appears on the label

GOLD MEDAL
| ❏ Warner Bros. PRO-A-841 [DJ] | | 1980 | 15.00 |
—Includes Pearl Harbour and the Explosions, The Undertones, Pretenders

GOLD SOUL
| ❏ Stax STS2031 | | 1970 | 25.00 |

GONE BUT NOT FORGOTTEN
| ❏ Class LP-5004 [M] | | 1959 | 100.00 |
| ❏ Rendezvous M-1314 [M] | | 196? | 40.00 |
—Reissue of Class 5004

GOOD GUY JACK SPECTOR PRESENTS 22 ORIGINAL WINNERS
| ❏ Roulette R25254 [M] | | 1964 | 25.00 |

GOODIES BUT OLDIES VOLUME 2
| ❏ Warwick W2008 [M] | | 1959 | 120.00 |
—Original title of LP appears on both cover and label; reissued as "Gold Hits" -- and there was no Volume 1!

THE GOOD OLD 50'S
| ❏ Atco 33-118 [M] | | 1960 | 60.00 |

GOODYEAR PRESENTS THE GREAT SONGS OF CHRISTMAS
| ❏ RCA Special Products DPL1-0285 | | 1977 | 12.00 |
—Sold only at Goodyear tire dealers

GOOFY GREATS
| ❏ K-Tel NU9030 | | 1975 | 15.00 |

GOSPEL HOOTENANNY
| ❏ Imperial LP-9240 [M] | | 1963 | 25.00 |
| ❏ Imperial LP-12240 [S] | | 1963 | 30.00 |

GOSPEL STARS IN CONCERT
| ❏ Specialty SPS-2153 | | 1971 | 25.00 |

GRAFFITI GOLD
| ❏ Vee Jay VJS-2-9000 | | 1974 | 25.00 |

GRAND OLE OPRY HITS
| ❏ RCA Camden CAL-737 [M] | | 1963 | 25.00 |
| ❏ RCA Camden CAS-737 [R] | | 1966 | 18.00 |

GRAND OLE OPRY SPECTACULAR
| ❏ Starday SLP-242 [M] | | 1963 | 30.00 |

THE GREAT BAND ERA
| ❏ Reader's Digest RD-25 [M] | | 1965 | 25.00 |
—Box set with flip-open top
| ❏ Reader's Digest RD-25 [R] | | 1965 | 18.00 |
—Box set with flip-open top

THE GREAT BANDS
| ❏ Columbia Musical Treasury P2M5267 | | 1968 | 25.00 |

GREAT BLUES
| ❏ Riverside RLP-1074 [10] | | 1955 | 80.00 |

Number	Title	Yr	NM

GREAT BLUES SINGERS
- ❑ Riverside RLP 12-121 [M] — 1957 — 40.00

THE GREAT BLUES SINGERS
- ❑ Riverside RLP-1032 [10] — 1954 — 80.00

GREAT COUNTRY
- ❑ Capitol Special Markets SLB-8088 — 1977 — 15.00

GREAT COUNTRY AND WESTERN STARS
- ❑ Wing MGW-12268 [M] — 1964 — 25.00
- ❑ Wing SRW-16268 [S] — 1964 — 25.00

GREAT COUNTRY FAVORITES
- ❑ MGM E-4211 [M] — 1964 — 25.00
- ❑ MGM SE-4211 [S] — 1964 — 30.00

GREAT COUNTRY GOSPEL GROUPS
- ❑ Wing MGW-12262 [M] — 1964 — 18.00
- ❑ Wing SRW-16262 [S] — 1964 — 18.00

GREAT COUNTRY HITS
- ❑ United Artists UAL-3159 [M] — 1961 — 30.00

GREAT COUNTRY MUSIC, VOLUME 1
- ❑ Dot DLP-3732 [M] — 1966 — 15.00
- ❑ Dot DLP-25732 [S] — 1966 — 18.00

GREAT COUNTRY MUSIC, VOLUME 2
- ❑ Dot DLP-3733 [M] — 1966 — 15.00
- ❑ Dot DLP-25733 [S] — 1966 — 18.00

THE GREATEST 15 HITS ON ACE RECORDS
- ❑ Ace LP-1012 [M] — 1960 — 70.00

GREATEST CHILDREN'S CHRISTMAS HITS
- ❑ Columbia PC44411 — 1988 — 15.00

GREATEST COUNTRY AND WESTERN HITS NO. 3
- ❑ Columbia CL1816 [M] — 1962 — 25.00
- ❑ Columbia CS8616 [S] — 1962 — 30.00

GREATEST COUNTRY AND WESTERN HITS NO. 4
- ❑ Columbia CL2081 [M] — 1963 — 25.00
- ❑ Columbia CS8881 [S] — 1963 — 30.00

GREATEST COUNTRY HITS FROM THE MOVIES
- ❑ Epic FE39001 — 1984 — 12.00

GREATEST COUNTRY HITS OF THE 70'S
- ❑ Columbia PC36549 — 198? — 10.00
—*Budget-line reissue*
- ❑ Columbia JC36549 — 1980 — 12.00

GREATEST COUNTRY HITS OF THE 70'S, VOL. 2
- ❑ Columbia PC36802 — 198? — 10.00
—*Budget-line reissue*
- ❑ Columbia JC36802 — 1980 — 12.00

GREATEST COUNTRY HITS OF THE 70'S, VOL. 3
- ❑ Columbia PC36969 — 198? — 10.00
—*Budget-line reissue*
- ❑ Columbia JC36969 — 1981 — 12.00

GREATEST COUNTRY HITS OF THE '80S: 1980
- ❑ Columbia FC44281 — 1988 — 12.00

GREATEST COUNTRY HITS OF THE '80S: 1981
- ❑ Columbia FC44431 — 1988 — 12.00

GREATEST COUNTRY HITS OF THE '80S: 1982
- ❑ Columbia FC44430 — 1988 — 12.00

GREATEST COUNTRY HITS OF THE '80S: 1983
- ❑ Columbia FC44429 — 1988 — 12.00

THE GREATEST GOLDEN GOODIES
- ❑ Laurie LLP-2014 [M] — 1962 — 30.00
- ❑ Laurie SLP-2014 [R] — 196? — 18.00

GREATEST GOSPEL SONGS, VOLUME 1
- ❑ Specialty SPS-2144 — 1970 — 25.00

GREATEST GOSPEL SONGS, VOLUME 2
- ❑ Specialty SPS-2145 — 1970 — 25.00

GREATEST GOSPEL SONGS OF OUR TIMES
- ❑ Vee Jay LP-5043 [M] — 1963 — 30.00

THE GREATEST GREATEST HITS
- ❑ RCA Victor AHL1-7185 — 1986 — 10.00

THE GREATEST GROUPS OF THE 50'S
- ❑ Ace 2027 — 1981 — 15.00

GREATEST HITS
- ❑ Harmony HL7255 [M] — 1960 — 18.00

THE GREATEST HITS, VOL. 1
- ❑ Power Pak PO-248 — 197? — 12.00

THE GREATEST HITS, VOL. 2
- ❑ Power Pak PO-249 — 197? — 12.00

THE GREATEST HITS FROM ENGLAND
- ❑ Parrot PA61010 [M] — 1967 — 30.00
- ❑ Parrot PAS71010 [R] — 1967 — 25.00

THE GREATEST HITS FROM ENGLAND, VOLUME 2
- ❑ Parrot PA61017 [M] — 1968 — 30.00
- ❑ Parrot PAS71017 [R] — 1968 — 25.00

THE GREATEST JAZZ CONCERT EVER
- ❑ Prestige 24024 — 197? — 18.00

THE GREATEST JAZZ CONCERT IN THE WORLD
- ❑ Pablo 2625704 — 197? — 30.00

THE GREATEST NAMES IN JAZZ
- ❑ Verve PR2-3 — 196? — 25.00
—*Box set*

GREATEST RAP HITS, VOL. 1
- ❑ Sugar Hill 9132 — 1984 — 25.00

GREATEST RAP HITS, VOL. 2
- ❑ Sugar Hill 9133 — 1984 — 15.00
—*Includes Grandmaster Flash, Sugar Hill Gang*

THE GREATEST ROCK & ROLL
- ❑ Atlantic 8001 [M] — 1956 — 120.00

THE GREATEST SONGS OF WOODY GUTHRIE
- ❑ Vanguard VSD-35/36 — 1972 — 18.00

THE GREATEST TEENAGE HITS OF ALL TIME!
- ❑ Teem LP-5003 [M] — 196? — 30.00

GREATEST WESTERN HITS
- ❑ Columbia CL1257 [M] — 1959 — 30.00
- ❑ Columbia CS8776 [R] — 1963 — 25.00

GREATEST WESTERN HITS NO. 2
- ❑ Columbia CL1408 [M] — 1960 — 30.00
- ❑ Columbia CS8777 [R] — 1963 — 25.00

THE GREAT GROUP GOODIES
- ❑ Atco 33-143 [M] — 1962 — 80.00

GREAT GROUP OLDIES
- ❑ Oldies 33 OL-8003 [M] — 1963 — 30.00

GREAT GROUP OLDIES, VOL. 2
- ❑ Oldies 33 OL-8006 [M] — 1964 — 30.00

GREAT GROUPS, GREAT RECORDS
- ❑ Laurie LLP-2010 [M] — 1961 — 30.00

GREAT GUITARS AT THE WINERY
- ❑ Concord Jazz CJ-131 — 1980 — 15.00
—*Original issue*

GREAT GUITARS OF JAZZ
- ❑ MGM SE-4691 — 1970 — 15.00

THE GREAT HITS OF 1964 AND SOME GOLDEN OLDIES
- ❑ Vee Jay LP-1112 [M] — 1965 — 30.00
—*Not known to exist in stereo*

GREAT INSTRUMENTAL R&B HITS
- ❑ Imperial LP-9271 [M] — 1964 — 30.00
- ❑ Imperial LP-12271 [R] — 1964 — 25.00

GREAT JAZZ
- ❑ Rondo-lette A-31 [M] — 195? — 30.00

THE GREAT JAZZ ALBUM
- ❑ Project 3 PR6009/10 — 197? — 10.00

THE GREAT JAZZ ALBUM, VOLUME 2
- ❑ Project 3 PR6023/24 — 197? — 18.00

GREAT JAZZ BRASS
- ❑ RCA Camden CAL-383 [M] — 1958 — 30.00

GREAT JAZZ PIANISTS
- ❑ RCA Camden CAL-328 [M] — 1958 — 30.00

GREAT JAZZ PIANISTS OF OUR TIME
- ❑ RCA Camden CAL-882 [M] — 1965 — 18.00
- ❑ RCA Camden CAS-882 [R] — 1965 — 12.00

GREAT JAZZ REEDS
- ❑ RCA Camden CAL-339 [M] — 1958 — 30.00

THE GREAT JAZZ SINGERS
- ❑ Halo 50269 [M] — 1957 — 18.00

GREAT MOMENTS AT THE GRAND OLE OPRY
- ❑ RCA Victor CPL2-1904 — 1977 — 25.00

GREAT MOTION PICTURE THEMES
- ❑ United Artists UAL-3122 [M] — 1960 — 18.00
- ❑ United Artists UAS-6122 [S] — 1960 — 25.00

GREAT MOTION PICTURE THEMES (MORE ORIGINAL SOUND TRACKS AND HIT MUSIC)
- ❑ United Artists UAL-3158 [M] — 1961 — 18.00
- ❑ United Artists UAS-6158 [S] — 1961 — 25.00

THE GREAT ONES
- ❑ Capitol T1718 [M] — 1962 — 30.00
- ❑ Capitol ST1718 [S] — 1962 — 30.00

THE GREAT SONGS OF CHRISTMAS
- ❑ Columbia Special Products XTV69406/7 [M] — 1961 — 18.00
—*Sold only at Goodyear tire dealers*
- ❑ Columbia Special Products XTV69406/7 [M] — 1962 — 15.00
—*Reissue with no reference to Goodyear on the cover*

THE GREAT SONGS OF CHRISTMAS, ALBUM TWO
- ❑ Columbia Special Products XTV86100/1 [M] — 1962 — 18.00
—*Sold only at Goodyear tire dealers*

THE GREAT SONGS OF CHRISTMAS, ALBUM THREE
- ❑ Columbia Special Products CSP117 [M] — 1963 — 18.00
—*Sold only at Goodyear tire dealers. The number listed is on the jacket; on the record, the number is "XTV 86656" on Side 1 and "XTV 86657" on Side 2*

THE GREAT SONGS OF CHRISTMAS, ALBUM FOUR
- ❑ Columbia Special Products CSP155M [M] — 1964 — 18.00
—*Sold only at Goodyear tire dealers*
- ❑ Columbia Special Products CSP155S [S] — 1964 — 25.00
—*Sold only at Goodyear tire dealers*

THE GREAT SONGS OF CHRISTMAS, ALBUM FIVE
- ❑ Columbia Special Products CSP238M [M] — 1965 — 15.00
—*Sold only at Goodyear tire dealers*
- ❑ Columbia Special Products CSP238S [S] — 1965 — 18.00
—*Sold only at Goodyear tire dealers*

THE GREAT SONGS OF CHRISTMAS, ALBUM SIX
- ❑ Columbia Special Products CSM388 [M] — 1966 — 15.00
—*Sold only at Goodyear tire dealers*
- ❑ Columbia Special Products CSS388 [S] — 1966 — 18.00
—*Sold only at Goodyear tire dealers*

THE GREAT SONGS OF CHRISTMAS, ALBUM SEVEN
- ❑ Columbia Special Products CSS547 — 1967 — 15.00
—*Sold only at Goodyear tire dealers*

GREAT SONGS OF CHRISTMAS, ALBUM EIGHT
- ❑ Columbia Special Products CSS888 — 1968 — 15.00
—*Sold only at Goodyear tire dealers*

GREAT SONGS OF CHRISTMAS, ALBUM NINE
- ❑ Columbia Special Products CSS1033 — 1969 — 15.00
—*Sold only at Goodyear tire dealers; version 1 has a 10 1/2-inch flap on right inner gatefold (part of record is exposed)*
- ❑ Columbia Special Products CSS1033 — 1969 — 15.00
—*Sold only at Goodyear tire dealers; version 2 has a 12 1/4-inch flap on right inner gatefold (record is completely covered)*

THE GREAT SOUL HITS
- ❑ Brunswick BL54129 [M] — 1968 — 30.00
- ❑ Brunswick BL754129 [S] — 1968 — 18.00

THE GREAT SWING BANDS
- ❑ Jazztone J-1245 [M] — 1957 — 30.00

GREAT SWING BANDS OF THE FORTIES
- ❑ Audio Lab AL-1530 [M] — 1959 — 80.00

THE GREAT TENOR JAZZMEN
- ❑ Allegro 1634 [M] — 195? — 40.00

GREAT TRUMPET ARTISTS
- ❑ RCA Victor LPT-26 [10] — 1951 — 50.00
- ❑ RCA Victor LPT-06 [10] — 1952 — 50.00

GREENPEACE
- ❑ A&M SP-5091 — 1985 — 15.00
—*Includes Peter Gabriel, Kate Bush, Thomas Dolby, Pretenders, Depeche Mode, etc.*

GREENPEACE RAINBOW WARRIORS
- ❑ Geffen GHS24236 — 1989 — 15.00
—*Includes U2, Belinda Carlisle, Sting, Terence Trent D'Arby, World Party, Lou Reed, Eurythmics, Pretenders, INXS, Thompson Twins, Talking Heads, Simple Minds, The Waterboys, R.E.M., Peter Gabriel, Sade, etc.*

GRETSCH DRUM NIGHT, VOLUME 2
- ❑ Roulette R52067 [M] — 1961 — 30.00
- ❑ Roulette SR52067 [S] — 1961 — 30.00

GRETSCH DRUM NIGHT AT BIRDLAND
- ❑ Roulette R52049 [M] — 1960 — 30.00
- ❑ Roulette SR52049 [S] — 1960 — 30.00

THE GRIFFITH PARK COLLECTION
- ❑ Elektra/Musician 60025 — 1982 — 12.00
—*All-star session with STANLEY CLARKE; CHICK COREA; JOE HENDERSON; FREDDIE HUBBARD; LENNY WHITE*

THE GRIFFITH PARK COLLECTION VOL. 2: THE CONCERT
- ❑ Elektra/Musician 60262 — 198? — 15.00

GROOVY GOODIES
- ❑ Colpix CP-466 [M] — 1964 — 80.00
- ❑ Colpix SCP-466 [S] — 1964 — 100.00

GROUP OF GOODIES
- ❑ Chess LP1478 [M] — 1963 — 50.00
- ❑ Chess LPS1478 [R] — 196? — 25.00

GROUP OF GOODIES, VOLUME 2
- ❑ Chess LP1491 [M] — 1965 — 50.00

A GRP CHRISTMAS COLLECTION
- ❑ GRP GR-9574 — 1988 — 15.00

GRP LIVE IN SESSION
- ❑ GRP GR-1023 — 1985 — 12.00

GRP SAMPLER, VOL. 1
- ❑ GRP F-7701 — 198? — 12.00

Number	Title	Yr	NM

GRP SUPER LIVE IN CONCERT
❏ GRP GR-2-1650 — 1988 — 15.00

GUARANTEED TO PLEASE
❏ Teem LP-5002 [M] — 196? — 30.00

THE GUIDEPOSTS 1978 TREASURY OF CHRISTMAS HYMNS
❏ Guideposts GPR-005 — 1978 — 15.00

GUIDE TO JAZZ
❏ RCA Victor LPM-1393 [M] — 1956 — 30.00

GUITAR BOOGIE
❏ Pickwick ACL-7041 — 197? — 12.00
— Reissue of RCA Victor LSP-4624(e)
❏ RCA Victor LSP-4624(e) — 1971 — 18.00
— Includes tracks by Eric Clapton, Eric Clapton and Jimmy Page, The Allstars Featuring Jeff Beck, The Allstars Featuring Jimmy Page; orange label original
❏ RCA Victor AYL1-3768(e) — 1980 — 10.00
— Another reissue of RCA Victor LSP-4624(e)

GUITAR PLAYER
❏ MCA 6002 — 197? — 18.00
❏ MCA 8012 — 197? — 18.00

GUITAR PLAYER PRESENTS JAZZ GUITAR CLASSICS
❏ Fantasy OJC-6012 — 1990 — 18.00

GUITAR PLAYERS
❏ Mainstream MRL-410 — 197? — 15.00

GUITAR SESSION
❏ Inner City IC-6050 — 198? — 15.00

GUITAR STARS
❏ MCA 42126 — 1988 — 12.00

GUITAR WORKSHOP
❏ Pausa 7089 — 198? — 12.00

GUT BUCKET BLUES AND STOMPS
❏ Herwin 112 — 197? — 15.00

HALLMARK PRESENTS: CAROLS OF CHRISTMAS
❏ Hallmark 629 — 1080 — 15.00
— With the Mormon Tabernacle Choir, Sarah Vaughan and Samuel Ramey; sold only at Hallmark Cards dealers

HALLMARK PRESENTS: CHRISTMAS -- LISTEN TO THE JOY
❏ Hallmark 626 — 1986 — 12.00
— With Placido Domingo, The London Symphony Orchestra, The Vienna Choir Boys; sold only at Hallmark Cards dealers

HALLMARK PRESENTS: JOY TO THE WORLD
❏ Hallmark 628 — 1988 — 12.00
— With Placido Domingo, Leona Mitchell, Placido Domingo Jr., The London Symphony Orchestra and London Voices; sold only at Hallmark Cards dealers

HALLMARK PRESENTS: SONGS FOR THE HOLIDAYS
❏ Hallmark 627 — 1987 — 12.00
— With Peter Hoffmann, Deborah Sasson, The London Symphony Orchestra and Chorus; sold only at Hallmark Cards dealers

HANDFUL OF COOL JAZZ
❏ Bethlehem BCP-90 [M] — 1959 — 30.00

HAPPY BIRTHDAY, BABY JESUS
❏ Sympathy For The Record Industry SFTRI271 [10] — 1993 — 18.00

HAPPY BIRTHDAY, BABY JESUS: THE SECOND COMING
❏ Sympathy For The Record Industry SFTRI349 [10] — 1995 — 18.00
— White vinyl

HAPPY HOLIDAY
❏ Mistletoe 1243 — 1978 — 12.00

HAPPY HOLIDAYS
❏ Columbia Special Products CSP242 [M] — 1965 — 18.00
— Sold only at True Value Hardware stores

HAPPY HOLIDAYS, VOLUME 1
❏ RCA Special Products DPL1-0411 — 1979 — 15.00
— Sold only at V&S Variety Stores; for contents, see "Happy Holidays, Volume 14"

HAPPY HOLIDAYS, VOLUME II
❏ Columbia Special Products CSM348 [M] — 1966 — 18.00
— Sold only at True Value Hardware stores
❏ Columbia Special Products CSS348 [S] — 1966 — 15.00
— Sold only at True Value Hardware stores

HAPPY HOLIDAYS, VOL. III
❏ RCA Victor PRS-255 — 1967 — 18.00
— Sold only at True Value Hardware stores

HAPPY HOLIDAYS, VOLUME IV
❏ RCA Victor PRS-267 — 1968 — 18.00
— Sold only at True Value Hardware stores

HAPPY HOLIDAYS, VOL. 5
❏ Capitol Creative Products SL-6627 — 1969 — 15.00
— Sold only at True Value Hardware stores

HAPPY HOLIDAYS, ALBUM 6
❏ Capitol Creative Products SL-6669 — 1970 — 15.00
— Sold only at True Value Hardware stores

HAPPY HOLIDAYS, ALBUM SEVEN
❏ Capitol Creative Products SL-6730 — 1971 — 15.00
— Sold only at True Value Hardware stores

HAPPY HOLIDAYS, ALBUM 8
❏ Columbia Special Products C11086 — 1972 — 12.00
— Sold only at True Value Hardware stores

HAPPY HOLIDAYS, ALBUM NINE
❏ Columbia Special Products P11793 — 1973 — 12.00
— Sold only at True Value Hardware stores

HAPPY HOLIDAYS, ALBUM 10
❏ Columbia Special Products P12344 — 1974 — 12.00
— Sold only at True Value Hardware stores

HAPPY HOLIDAYS, VOLUME 13
❏ RCA Special Products DPL1-0319 — 1978 — 12.00
— Sold only at True Value Hardware stores

HAPPY HOLIDAYS, VOLUME 14
❏ RCA Special Products DPL1-0376 — 1979 — 12.00
— Sold only at True Value Hardware stores

HAPPY HOLIDAYS, VOLUME 15
❏ RCA Special Products DPL1-0453 — 1980 — 12.00
— Sold only at True Value Hardware stores

HAPPY HOLIDAYS, VOLUME 16
❏ RCA Special Products DPL1-0501 — 1981 — 12.00
— Sold only at True Value Hardware stores

HAPPY HOLIDAYS, VOLUME 17
❏ RCA Special Products DPL1-0555 — 1982 — 12.00
— Sold only at True Value Hardware stores

HAPPY HOLIDAYS, VOLUME 18
❏ RCA Special Products DPL1-0608 — 1983 — 12.00
— Sold only at True Value Hardware stores

HAPPY HOLIDAYS, VOLUME 19
❏ RCA Special Products DPL1-0689 — 1984 — 12.00
— Sold only at True Value Hardware stores

HAPPY HOLIDAYS, VOL. 20
❏ RCA Special Products DPL1-0713 — 1985 — 15.00
— Sold only at True Value Hardware stores

HAPPY HOLIDAYS, VOL. 21
❏ RCA Special Products DPL1-0739 — 1986 — 15.00
— Sold only at True Value Hardware stores

HAPPY HOLIDAYS, VOL. 22
❏ RCA Special Products DPL1-0777 — 1987 — 12.00
— Sold only at True Value Hardware stores

HAPPY HOLIDAYS, VOL. 23
❏ MCA Special Products 15042 — 1988 — 15.00
— Sold only at True Value Hardware stores

HAPPY HOLIDAYS VOL. 25
❏ RCA Special Products DPL2-0936 — 1990 — 30.00
— Sold only at True Value Hardware stores; the last one on vinyl LP -- and it contains an Elvis track among its 25 selections

HAPPY HOLLY DAYS
❏ Capitol Creative Products SL-6761 — 1971 — 12.00
❏ Capitol Creative Products SL-6654 — 1969 — 15.00

HAPPY JAZZ
❏ Jazztone J-1215 [M] — 1956 — 30.00

HARD GOODS
❏ Warner Bros. PRO583 — 1974 — 30.00

THE HARD SWING
❏ Pacific Jazz JWC-508 [M] — 1957 — 50.00
❏ World Pacific JWC-508 [M] — 1958 — 40.00

HARD TO BELIEVE -- A KISS COVERS COMPILATION
❏ C/Z CZ 024 — 1990 — 30.00

HARLEM COMES TO LONDON
❏ Swing SW-8444 — 198? — 12.00

HARLEM JAZZ 1930
❏ Brunswick BL58024 [10] — 1951 — 50.00

HARLEN ODYSSEY
❏ Xanadu 112 — 197? — 12.00

HAVE A HAPPY HOLIDAY
❏ Columbia Special Products CSS1432 — 1970 — 12.00

HAVE A JEWISH CHRISTMAS…?
❏ Tower T-5081 [M] — 1967 — 18.00
— Comedy sketches narrated by Lennie Weinrib and acted by Christine Nelson, Benny Rubin, Reginald X. Carlisle and Naomi Lewis

HAVE A MERRY CHESS CHRISTMAS
❏ Chess/MCA CH-25210 — 1988 — 15.00

HAVE YOURSELF A MERRY LITTLE CHRISTMAS
❏ Reprise R50001 [M] — 1963 — 30.00
— Wreath cover; titled on back cover "Top Hollywood Stars Want You to...
❏ Reprise R50001 [M] — 1963 — 30.00
— Christmas tree cover; titled "Frank Sinatra and His Friends Want You to...
❏ Reprise R9-50001 [S] — 1963 — 30.00
— Christmas tree cover; titled "Frank Sinatra and His Friends Want You to..."; stereo version of above
❏ Reprise 50001 — 1963 — 30.00
— Red and green cover with ornaments at top; titled on back cover "Top Hollywood Stars Want You to...
❏ Rhino R170911 — 198? — 15.00

HAVING A BALL
❏ End LP-302 [M] — 1958 — 500.00
— Original cover with groups pictured on a record

HEAD START -- BOB THIELE EMERGENCY
❏ Flying Dutchman FDS-104 — 1969 — 30.00

HEARTS OF GOLD: THE POP COLLECTION
❏ Foundation K1-96427 — 1991 — 18.00
— Includes George Michael, Bangles, Sinead O'Connor; only U.S. vinyl release through Columbia House

HEAVY HAULERS
❏ Power Pak PO-290 — 197? — 12.00

HEAVY HEADS
❏ Chess LP1522 [M] — 1967 — 30.00
❏ Chess LPS1522 [P] — 1967 — 30.00

HEAVY HEADS, VOYAGE 2
❏ Chess LP1528 [M] — 1969 — 25.00

HEAVY HITS!
❏ Columbia CS9840 — 1969 — 18.00

HEAVY METAL (SUPERSTARS OF THE 70S, VOLUME 2)
❏ Warner Special Products SP-2001 — 1974 — 25.00

HEAVY SOUNDS
❏ Columbia CS9952 — 1970 — 18.00

HELL COMES TO YOUR HOUSE
❏ Bemis Brain 123/124 — 1981 — 18.00
— Includes Social Distortion, Red Cross (Redd Kross), etc.

HELL COMES TO YOUR HOUSE, VOL. 2
❏ Bemis Brain E1049 — 1982 — 15.00
— Includes Minutemen, etc.

HENRY MANCINI SELECTS GREAT SONGS OF CHRISTMAS
❏ RCA Special Products DPL1-0148 — 1975 — 12.00
— Sold only at Goodyear tire dealers

HERALD THE BEAT
❏ Herald HLP-0110 [M] — 1957 — 300.00
— Black label
❏ Herald HLP-0110 [M] — 195? — 150.00
— Yellow label

HERE AND NOW
❏ Catalyst 7613 — 197? — 12.00

HERE ARE THE HITS!
❏ Fire FLP-100 [M] — 1959 — 400.00
— Reissued as "Memory Lane, Hits by the Original Groups" with the same label and number

HERE COME THE GIRLS
❏ Verve MGV-2036 [M] — 1956 — 40.00
❏ Verve V-2036 [M] — 1961 — 25.00

HERE COME THE SWINGING BANDS
❏ Verve MGV-8207 [M] — 195? — 30.00
❏ Verve V-8207 [M] — 1961 — 25.00

HI-FI JAZZ
❏ Brunswick BL58058 [10] — 1954 — 50.00

HI-FI JAZZ SESSION
❏ Masterseal MSLP5013 [M] — 1957 — 30.00

A HI-FI SALUTE TO THE GREAT ONES
❏ MGM E-3325 [M] — 1956 — 30.00

A HI-FI SALUTE TO THE GREAT ONES, VOL. 2
❏ MGM E-3354 [M] — 1956 — 30.00

HIGHLIGHTS IN JAZZ: TWELFTH ANNIVERSARY CONCERT
❏ Stash ST-254 — 1985 — 12.00

HILLBILLY HEAVEN
❏ Capitol Special Markets SL-8118 — 1979 — 15.00

HILLBILLY HIT PARADE
❏ Mercury MG-20282 [M] — 1957 — 50.00
❏ Starday SLP-102 [M] — 1956 — 100.00

Number	Title	Yr	NM

HILLBILLY HOLIDAY
- ❑ Rhino R170195 | 1988 | 15.00

HILLBILLY HOUSE PARTY
- ❑ Imperial LP-9214 [M] | 1963 | 30.00
- ❑ Imperial LP-12214 [R] | 1963 | 25.00

THE HISTORIC DONAUESCHINGEN JAZZ CONCERT 1957
- ❑ Pausa 7081 | 198? | 12.00

HISTORIC JAZZ CONCERT AT MUSIC INN
- ❑ Atlantic 1298 [M] | 1958 | 40.00
  — Black label
- ❑ Atlantic 1298 [M] | 1961 | 30.00
  — Multicolor label, white "fan" logo at right
- ❑ Atlantic 1298 [M] | 1963 | 25.00
  — Multicolor label, black "fan" logo at right

HISTORY OF BRITISH BLUES, VOLUME 1
- ❑ Sire SASH-3701 | 1973 | 25.00

HISTORY OF BRITISH ROCK
- ❑ Sire SASH-3702 | 1974 | 25.00
- ❑ Sire 2P6547 | 1975 | 25.00
  — Columbia House edition

HISTORY OF BRITISH ROCK, VOLUME 1
- ❑ Rhino R170319 | 1988 | 12.00

HISTORY OF BRITISH ROCK, VOLUME 2
- ❑ Rhino R170320 | 1988 | 12.00
- ❑ Sire SASH-3705 | 1974 | 25.00

HISTORY OF BRITISH ROCK, VOLUME 3
- ❑ Rhino R170321 | 1988 | 12.00
- ❑ Sire SASH-3712 | 1975 | 25.00

HISTORY OF BRITISH ROCK, VOLUME 4
- ❑ Rhino R170322 | 1988 | 12.00

HISTORY OF CLASSIC JAZZ
- ❑ Riverside SDP-11 [M] | 1956 | 300.00
  — Five-record set in leatherette album with booklet; records were available separately as Riverside 112, 113, 114, 115 and 116.

HISTORY OF CLASSIC JAZZ, VOL. 1
- ❑ Riverside RLP 12-112 [M] | 1957 | 40.00

HISTORY OF CLASSIC JAZZ, VOL. 2
- ❑ Riverside RLP 12-113 [M] | 1957 | 40.00

HISTORY OF CLASSIC JAZZ, VOL. 3
- ❑ Riverside RLP 12-114 [M] | 1957 | 40.00

HISTORY OF CLASSIC JAZZ, VOL. 4
- ❑ Riverside RLP 12-115 [M] | 1957 | 40.00

HISTORY OF CLASSIC JAZZ, VOL. 5
- ❑ Riverside RLP 12-116 [M] | 1957 | 40.00

HISTORY OF JAZZ, VOL. 1: NEW ORLEANS ORIGINS
- ❑ Capitol T793 [M] | 1956 | 30.00

HISTORY OF JAZZ, VOL. 1: THE SOLID SOUTH
- ❑ Capitol H239 [10] | 1950 | 50.00

HISTORY OF JAZZ, VOL. 2: THE GOLDEN ERA
- ❑ Capitol H240 [10] | 1950 | 50.00

HISTORY OF JAZZ, VOL. 2: THE TURBULENT '20S
- ❑ Capitol T794 [M] | 1956 | 30.00

HISTORY OF JAZZ, VOL. 3: EVERYBODY SWINGS
- ❑ Capitol T795 [M] | 1956 | 30.00

HISTORY OF JAZZ, VOL. 3: THEN CAME SWING
- ❑ Capitol H241 [10] | 1950 | 50.00

HISTORY OF JAZZ, VOL. 4: ENTER THE COOL
- ❑ Capitol H242 [10] | 1950 | 50.00
- ❑ Capitol T796 [M] | 1956 | 30.00

THE HISTORY OF NEW ORLEANS ROCK 'N' ROLL VOLUME I
- ❑ Ace 7184 | 1984 | 25.00
  — Sold only at the Louisiana World's Fair in New Orleans, May 12-Nov. 11, 1984

THE HISTORY OF NEW ORLEANS ROCK 'N' ROLL VOLUME II
- ❑ Ace 7284 | 1984 | 25.00
  — Sold only at the Louisiana World's Fair in New Orleans, May 12-Nov. 11, 1984

THE HISTORY OF NEW ORLEANS ROCK 'N' ROLL VOLUME III
- ❑ Ace 7384 | 1984 | 25.00
  — Sold only at the Louisiana World's Fair in New Orleans, May 12-Nov. 11, 1984

THE HISTORY OF NEW ORLEANS ROCK 'N' ROLL VOLUME IV
- ❑ Ace 7484 | 1984 | 25.00
  — Sold only at the Louisiana World's Fair in New Orleans, May 12-Nov. 11, 1984

HISTORY OF RHYTHM & BLUES, VOLUME 1/THE ROOTS 1947-52
- ❑ Atlantic SD8161 | 1968 | 25.00

HISTORY OF RHYTHM & BLUES, VOLUME 2/THE GOLDEN YEARS 1953-55
- ❑ Atlantic SD8162 [S] | 1968 | 25.00
- ❑ Atlantic 8162 [M] | 1968 | 40.00

HISTORY OF RHYTHM & BLUES, VOLUME 3/ ROCK & ROLL 1956-57
- ❑ Atlantic SD8163 | 1968 | 25.00

HISTORY OF RHYTHM & BLUES, VOLUME 4/THE BIG BEAT 1958-60
- ❑ Atlantic SD8164 | 1968 | 25.00

HISTORY OF RHYTHM & BLUES, VOLUME 5/THE BEAT GOES ON, 1961-62
- ❑ Atlantic 8193 [M] | 1968 | 40.00
  — Mono is promo only; "DJ Copy Monaural" sticker on front cover
- ❑ Atlantic SD8193 [S] | 1968 | 25.00

HITCHHIKER 2
- ❑ Columbia CAS1826 [DJ] | 1989 | 30.00

THE HITCHHIKER COLLEGE RADIO HOUR
- ❑ Columbia CAS1598 [DJ] | 1989 | 30.00

HITCHHIKER EXAMPLER
- ❑ Columbia CAS2011 [DJ] | 1990 | 18.00
  — Includes Mary Chapin Carpenter, Indigo Girls, Roseanne Cash

THE HIT MAKERS AND THEIR RECORD BREAKERS
- ❑ King 737 [M] | 1961 | 100.00

HIT PARADE OF COUNTRY MUSIC
- ❑ Starday SLP-184 [M] | 1962 | 30.00

THE HITS ARE ON VERVE
- ❑ Verve V-201 [M] | 1964 | 18.00
- ❑ Verve V6-201 [S] | 1964 | 25.00

HITS FROM THE SOUTH PRESENTED BY NICK CHARLES
- ❑ Stax 702 [M] | 1962 | 100.00
  — Has the same number as "Walk Right In" by Gus Cannon, but this LP doesn't have any mention of Atlantic distribution

HITS I FORGOT TO BUY
- ❑ Swan SLP-512 [M] | 1963 | 50.00

THE HITS OF '86
- ❑ RCA Victor 5768-1-R | 1987 | 10.00

THE HITS OF '87
- ❑ RCA 6496-1-R | 1987 | 10.00

HITS OF THE HOPS
- ❑ Warner Bros. W1448 [M] | 1962 | 30.00
- ❑ Warner Bros. WS1448 [S] | 1962 | 40.00

HITS OF THE MERSEY ERA, VOLUME 1
- ❑ EMI M-11690 | 1977 | 15.00
  — 10 tracks: Cilla Black (2)/Freddie & Dreamers (2)/Gerry & Pacemakers (2)/Hollies/Billy J. Kramer & Dakotas (2)/ Swinging Blue Jeans

HIT SOUNDS OF MERRIE MELODIES
- ❑ Warner Bros. PRO550 | 1973 | 30.00

HITS THAT JUMPED
- ❑ Checker LP2975 [M] | 1959 | 120.00

HITSVILLE
- ❑ Coral CRL57269 [M] | 1959 | 80.00
- ❑ Coral CRL757269 [S] | 1959 | 100.00

HITSVILLE U.S.A.
- ❑ Imperial LP-9084 [M] | 1959 | 40.00

HITSVILLE U.S.A., VOLUME 2
- ❑ Imperial LP-9099 [M] | 1960 | 40.00

HODGE PODGE OF OFF-BEAT JAZZ
- ❑ Sunbeam 1 | 197? | 12.00

HODGE PODGE OF OFF-BEAT JAZZ, VOL. 2
- ❑ Sunbeam 5 | 197? | 12.00

A HOLIDAY GIFT JUST FOR YOU
- ❑ Songbird SBLP-235 | 1973 | 15.00

HOLIDAY GREETINGS FROM EPA
- ❑ CBS CAS2664 [DJ] | 1987 | 15.00
  — Includes holiday greetings from Aimee Mann and "Weird Al" Yankovic, among others

HOLIDAY IN SAX
- ❑ EmArcy MG-26019 [10] | 1954 | 80.00

HOLIDAY IN TRUMPET
- ❑ EmArcy MG-26015 [10] | 1954 | 80.00

HOLIDAY MAGIC
- ❑ Capitol Creative Products SL-6728 | 1971 | 15.00
- ❑ Capitol Special Markets SL-6728 | 197? | 12.00
  — Same as above, but reissue on renamed label

HOLLAND-DOZIER-HOLLAND: YESTERDAY, TODAY AND FOREVER
- ❑ Jobete PRO-9 [DJ] | 1977 | 50.00
  — Promo-only publisher's demo

HOLLYWOOD CONFIDENTIAL
- ❑ GNP Crescendo 2132 | 1980 | 15.00
  — Includes The Runaways; a collection of Kim Fowley productions

HOME FOR CHRISTMAS
- ❑ Book-of-the-Month Club 91-6561 | 1982 | 18.00
- ❑ Columbia Musical Treasury P3S5608 | 1971 | 18.00
- ❑ Realm 2V8101 | 1977 | 18.00

HOME FOR CHRISTMAS: A JOYOUS EVENING OF YULETIDE MUSIC
- ❑ RCA Victor CPM-109 [M] | 1964 | 18.00
  — Label reads "RCA Victor Club Recording Selected by the Editors of Reader's Digest Music Guide
- ❑ RCA Victor CSP-109 [S] | 1964 | 25.00

HOME FOR THE HOLIDAYS
- ❑ Columbia Special Products P12014 | 1973 | 12.00
  — Sold only at Big N discount department store
- ❑ MCA MSM-35007 | 1978 | 15.00
  — Sold only at Firestone tire dealers (add 50% for sticker that says "Season's Greetings Firestone")

HOME OF THE BLUES
- ❑ Minit LP-0001 [M] | 1961 | 50.00

HOME OF THE BLUES, VOLUME 2
- ❑ Minit LP-0004 [M] | 1963 | 50.00
- ❑ Minit LP-40004 [M] | 1964 | 30.00
  — Reissue of 0004
- ❑ Minit LP-24004 [R] | 1964 | 25.00

HOMESPUN HUMOR
- ❑ King 726 [M] | 1961 | 100.00

HONEST TO GOODNESS COUNTRY MUSIC HITS
- ❑ RCA Victor LPM-2564 [M] | 1962 | 25.00
- ❑ RCA Victor LSP-2564 [S] | 1962 | 30.00

THE HONEST-TO-GOODNESS COUNTRY MUSIC HITS!!!! VOLUME 2
- ❑ RCA Victor LPM-2633 [M] | 1963 | 25.00
- ❑ RCA Victor LSP-2633(e) [R] | 1963 | 18.00

HONKERS AND BAR WALKERS
- ❑ Delmark DL-438 | 198? | 12.00

HOT CANARIES
- ❑ Columbia CL2534 [10] | 1954 | 30.00

HOT CLARINETS
- ❑ Historical 25 | 1969 | 12.00

HOT HITS TO WARM YOUR WINTER
- ❑ Polygram SA 054 [DJ] | 1985 | 18.00
  — Includes Big Country

HOT NO. 1 COUNTRY HITS
- ❑ Realm 1P8196 | 1992 | 18.00
  — Only available on vinyl through Columbia House

HOT NO. 1 HITS!
- ❑ Realm 1P8195 | 1992 | 18.00
  — Includes George Michael (with Elton John)

THE HOT ONES
- ❑ Columbia Special Products CSP-107 [M] | 1963 | 25.00
  — Available only from Johnson Sea Horse boat dealers

HOT ONES
- ❑ EMI America SPRO9865/6 [DJ] | 1982 | 12.00
  — Includes Stray Cats

HOT PIANOS
- ❑ Historical 29 | 1969 | 12.00

HOT PLATTERS
- ❑ Warner Bros. PRO474 | 1971 | 30.00
  — Originals have green labels

HOT TRACKS FROM ARISTA
- ❑ Arista SP-127 [DJ] | 1982 | 15.00
  — Includes Thompson Twins, Haircut One Hundred, A Flock of Seagulls

HOT TRUMPETS
- ❑ Historical 28 | 1969 | 12.00

HOT VS. COOL: A BATTLE OF JAZZ
- ❑ MGM E-211 [10] | 1953 | 50.00

HOUSE RENT PARTY
- ❑ Savoy MG-12199 [M] | 1961 | 50.00

HOW BLUE CAN YOU GET? GREAT BLUES VOCALS IN THE JAZZ TRADITION
- ❑ Bluebird 6758-1-RB | 1989 | 15.00

HOW HIGH THE MOON
- ❑ Clef MGC-Vol.1 [M] | 1955 | 50.00
  — Reissue of 608
- ❑ Clef MGC-608 [M] | 1955 | 40.00
  — Reissue of Mercury 608
- ❑ Mercury MGC-608 [M] | 1953 | 80.00
  — Reissue of Vol. 1

Number	Title	Yr	NM
❑ Mercury MG-35001 [10]		1950	80.00
❑ Mercury MGC-Vol.1 [10]		1951	60.00
— *Reissue of 35001*			

HOW THE GRINCH STOLE CHRISTMAS

❑ Random House/Scholastic 0-394-05008-8		1975	18.00

— *Not the original soundtrack, but placed here to avoid confusion (we hope). B-side is a condensation of Folkways FC-7750 (1956).*

HUM-N-STRUM: THE BEST OF FOLK AND COUNTRY

❑ Columbia Special Products CSP309 [M]		1966	18.00
— *For General Electric*			

HYMNS OF FAITH

❑ Colpix CP-408 [M]		1959	30.00

I DIDN'T KNOW THEY STILL MADE RECORDS LIKE THIS

❑ Warner Bros. PRO608		1975	25.00

I DIG ROCK AND ROLL

❑ Score SLP-4002 [M]		1957	200.00
— *Reissue of "Rock & Roll with Rhythm & Blues," Aladdin 710*			

IF YOU CAN'T PLEASE YOURSELF, YOU CAN'T PLEASE ANYONE ELSE

❑ Capitol ST-12439		1985	15.00
— *Includes The The, Yello, etc.*			

(I GOT NO KICK AGAINST) MODERN JAZZ

❑ GRP GR-9827		1995	18.00
— *Jazz artists do songs made famous by the Beatles*			

I LIKE JAZZ!

❑ Columbia JZ1 [M]		1955	30.00

I'LL BE HOME FOR CHRISTMAS

❑ Pickwick SPC-1009		197?	12.00

I LOVE THE SMELL OF NAPALM

❑ Creation 001		1986	18.00
— *Includes early Primal Scream, among others*			

IMAGINE THE JOYS OF CHRISTMAS. PRESENTED BY SYLVANIA.

❑ Capitol Creative Products SL-6700		1971	15.00
— *Sold only at Sylvania dealers; label calls this "A Sylvania Christmas*			

IMPERIAL MOVES

❑ Imperial MM-428 [DJ]		1966	40.00

IMPERIAL SAMPLER

❑ Imperial DJLP-1 [10]		195?	100.00
— *Promo-only item*			

THE IMPOSSIBLE DREAM -- THE STORY OF THE 1967 BOSTON RED SOX

❑ Fleetwood FCLP3024		1967	25.00

IMPULSE ARTISTS ON TOUR

❑ ABC Impulse! AS-9264		197?	15.00

IMPULSIVELY!

❑ ABC Impulse! AS-9266		197?	18.00

I'M WILD ABOUT MY LOVIN'

❑ Historical 32		1969	12.00

IN A MELLOW MOOD

❑ Elektra 5188 [DJ]		1986	15.00
— *Includes Simply Red*			

INCENSE AND OLDIES

❑ Buddah BDS5014		1969	25.00

IN CONCERT

❑ RCA Victor CPL2-1014		1975	25.00

IN CONCERT, VOL. 2

❑ CTI 6049		197?	15.00

THE INCREDIBLE COLLECTION -- DR. KNEW'S MUSIC

❑ RCA Victor DJL1-4860 [DJ]		1983	15.00
— *Includes Hayzi Fantayzee, Eurythmics, etc.*			

INDIVIDUALS

❑ Columbia CG36213		197?	15.00

INFORMAL SESSION AT SQUIRREL'S BY THE SONS OF BIX

❑ Paramount LP-104 [10]		1954	80.00

IN FROM THE STORM: THE MUSIC OF JIMI HENDRIX

❑ RCA Victor 68233-1 [PD]		1995	15.00
— *Includes Sting (with many jazz and rock musicians); limited edition picture disc (no regular U.S. vinyl exists)*			

IN HARMONY 2

❑ Columbia PC37461		1981	18.00
— *Contains one Christmas song:*			

IN LOVING MEMORY

❑ Motown M642 [M]		1968	250.00
— *Without song titles on cover*			

Number	Title	Yr	NM
❑ Motown M642 [M]		1968	150.00
— *With song titles on cover*			
❑ Motown MS642 [S]		1968	250.00
— *Without song titles on cover*			
❑ Motown MS642 [S]		1968	150.00
— *With song titles on cover*			
❑ Motown M642 [DJ]		1969	500.00
— *With custom silver cover; Loucye Gordy Wakefield Scholarship Fund benefit giveaway*			

IN-STORE SAMPLER VOL. 2

❑ EMI America SPRO-9842 [DJ]		1982	18.00
— *Includes Stray Cats (2), Kim Wilde, etc.*			

THE INSTRUMENTAL CHRISTMAS FAVORITES

❑ Capitol STBB-349		1969	18.00

INSTRUMENTAL GOLDEN GOODIES, VOL. 13

❑ Roulette R25238 [M]		1964	25.00

INSTRUMENTALLY YOURS

❑ RCA 6492-1-R		1987	10.00

INTERCOLLEGIATE MUSIC FESTIVAL, VOL. 1

❑ ABC Impulse! AS-9145 [S]		1968	15.00
❑ Impulse! A-9145 [M]		1967	25.00
❑ Impulse! AS-9145 [S]		1967	18.00

INTERNATIONAL JAM SESSIONS

❑ Xanadu 122		197?	12.00

INTERNATIONAL JAZZ WORKSHOP

❑ EmArcy MGE-26002 [M]		1964	30.00
❑ EmArcy SRE-66002 [S]		1964	30.00

INTERPLAY FOR TWO TRUMPETS AND TWO TENORS

❑ Fantasy OJC-292		1988	12.00
❑ Prestige PRLP-7112 [M]		1957	100.00

INTRODUCTION TO JAZZ

❑ Decca DL8244 [M]		1956	30.00

INTRODUCTION TO RARE EARTH RECORDS

❑ Rare Earth RS-505to 509 [DJ]		1969	200.00
— *Promo-only box set with rounded top; contains the first five LPs on the Rare Earth label*			

I REMEMBER BEBOP

❑ Columbia C235381		197?	18.00

IRREPRESSIBLE IMPULSES

❑ ABC Impulse! IMP-1972		1972	18.00

I.R.S. GREATEST HITS VOLUME 1

❑ I.R.S. SP-70950		1980	15.00
— *Includes Berlin, Buzzcocks, Oingo Boingo, Klark Kent, The Stranglers*			

I.R.S. GREATEST HITS VOLUMES 2 & 3

❑ I.R.S. SP-70800		1981	18.00
— *Includes Buzzcocks, John Cale, The Cramps, The Damned, The Fall, The Fleshtones, Klark Kent, The Humans, Oingo Boingo, The Police, Tom Robinson, Squeeze, The Stranglers*			

THE ISLAND STORY

❑ Island R243395		1988	25.00
— *BMG Direct Marketing edition*			
❑ Island 90684		1988	25.00

ISLES OF JAZZ

❑ Discovery DL-2010 [10]		1954	50.00

ITAL CHRISTMAS

❑ Top Ranking (no #)		197?	30.00
— *Jamaican import*			

ITALIAN JAZZ STARS

❑ Angel ANG-60001 [10]		1955	50.00

IT CAME FROM HOLLYWOOD!

❑ Capitol SPRO79199 [DJ]		1987	18.00
— *Includes Flesh For Lulu*			

IT'S CHRISTMAS

❑ Columbia Special Products C10040		1971	15.00

IT'S CHRISTMAS!

❑ Columbia Special Products P15761		1981	12.00

IT'S CHRISTMAS TIME!

❑ Columbia Special Products P14990		1979	10.00

IT'S CHRISTMASTIME!

❑ Columbia Special Products CSM429 [M]		1966	15.00
— *Sold only at A&P grocery stores*			

IT'S CHRISTMAS TIME!

❑ SeaShell P14990		1981	10.00
— *Reissue of Columbia Special Products P 14990*			

IT'S CHRISTMAS TIME AGAIN

❑ Stax MPS-8519		1982	15.00

IT'S DANCE TIME

❑ Cameo C-1068 [M]		1964	30.00

IT WILL STAND: MINIT RECORDS 1960-1963

❑ EMI America ST-17202		1986	15.00

IVY LEAGUE JAZZ

Number	Title	Yr	NM
❑ Decca DL8282 [M]		1956	30.00
❑ Golden Crest GC-3039 [M]		1958	25.00

JACKPOT OF HITS

❑ Apollo LP-490 [M]		1959	150.00

JAMES BOND -- 10TH ANNIVERSARY

❑ United Artists UXS-91		1972	30.00

JAMMING AT RUDI'S, VOL. 1

❑ Circle L-407 [M]		1951	40.00

JAMMING AT RUDI'S, VOL. 2

❑ Circle L-410 [M]		1951	40.00

JAMMIN' IN SWINGVILLE

❑ Prestige 24051		197?	18.00

JAM SESSION #1

❑ Clef MGC-4001 [M]		1953	50.00
❑ Clef MGC-601 [M]		1954	40.00
❑ Clef MGC-651 [M]		1955	40.00
— *Reissue of 4001*			
❑ Mercury MGC-601 [M]		1953	80.00

JAM SESSION #2

❑ Clef MGC-4002 [M]		1953	50.00
❑ Clef MGC-652 [M]		1955	40.00
— *Reissue of 4002*			
❑ Clef MGC-602 [M]		1954	40.00
❑ Mercury MGC-602 [M]		1953	80.00

JAM SESSION #3

❑ Clef MGC-653 [M]		1955	40.00
— *Reissue of 4003*			
❑ Clef MGC-4003 [M]		1953	50.00

JAM SESSION #4

❑ Clef MGC-654 [M]		1955	40.00
— *Reissue of 4004*			
❑ Clef MGC-4004 [M]		1953	50.00

JAM SESSION #5

❑ Clef MGC-655 [M]		1955	40.00
— *Reissue of 4005*			
❑ Clef MGC-4005 [M]		1953	50.00

JAM SESSION #6

❑ Clef MGC-656 [M]		1955	40.00
— *Reissue of 4006*			
❑ Clef MGC-4006 [M]		1953	50.00

JAM SESSION #7

❑ Clef MGC-677 [M]		1955	40.00

JAM SESSION #8

❑ Clef MGC-711 [M]		1955	40.00

JAM SESSION

❑ Clef MGC-4001/7 [M]		1953	300.00
— *Boxed set containing 4001-4007*			
❑ EmArcy MG-36002 [M]		1954	50.00

JAM SESSION, VOL. 2

❑ Skylark SKLP-12 [10]		1954	250.00

JAM SESSION AT CARNEGIE HALL

❑ Columbia CL557 [M]		1954	30.00

JAM SESSION AT COMMODORE

❑ Commodore FL-30006 [M]		1951	40.00

JAM SESSION COAST TO COAST

❑ Columbia CL547 [M]		1954	30.00

THE JAM SESSIONS: MONTREUX '77

❑ Fantasy OJC-385		1989	12.00
❑ Pablo Live 2620105		1978	18.00

JAZZ

❑ Halo 50242 [M]		1957	18.00
❑ Mainstream MRL-408		197?	15.00
❑ Royale 1883 [10]		195?	30.00

JAZZ, SKIFFLE AND JUG STYLE

❑ Herwin 113		197?	15.00

JAZZ, VOL. 1: THE SOUTH

❑ Folkways FP-53/4 [M]		1951	30.00
❑ Folkways FJ-2801 [M]		197?	15.00

JAZZ, VOL. 2: THE BLUES

❑ Folkways FP-55/6 [M]		1951	30.00
❑ Folkways FJ-2802 [M]		197?	15.00

JAZZ, VOL. 3: NEW ORLEANS

❑ Folkways FP-57/8 [M]		1951	30.00
❑ Folkways FJ-2803 [M]		197?	15.00

JAZZ, VOL. 4: JAZZ SINGERS

❑ Folkways FP-59/60 [M]		1951	30.00
❑ Folkways FJ-2804 [M]		197?	15.00

JAZZ, VOL. 5: CHICAGO

❑ Folkways FP-63/4 [M]		1951	30.00
❑ Folkways FJ-2805 [M]		197?	15.00

JAZZ, VOL. 6: CHICAGO #2

❑ Folkways FP-65/6 [M]		1951	30.00

Number	Title	Yr	NM
☐ Folkways FJ-2806 [M]		197?	15.00

JAZZ, VOL. 7: NEW YORK 1922-1934

Number	Title	Yr	NM
☐ Folkways FP-67/8 [M]		1951	30.00
☐ Folkways FJ-2807 [M]		197?	15.00

JAZZ, VOL. 8: BIG BANDS BEFORE 1938

| ☐ Folkways FP-69/70 [M] | | 1951 | 30.00 |
| ☐ Folkways FJ-2808 [M] | | 197? | 15.00 |

JAZZ, VOL. 9: PIANO

| ☐ Folkways FP-71/2 [M] | | 1951 | 30.00 |
| ☐ Folkways FJ-2809 [M] | | 197? | 15.00 |

JAZZ, VOL. 10: BOOGIE WOOGIE, JUMP, KANSAS CITY

| ☐ Folkways FP-73/4 [M] | | 1951 | 30.00 |
| ☐ Folkways FJ-2810 [M] | | 197? | 15.00 |

JAZZ, VOL. 11: ADDENDA

| ☐ Folkways FP-75/6 [M] | | 1951 | 30.00 |
| ☐ Folkways FJ-2811 [M] | | 197? | 15.00 |

JAZZ: THE 60S, VOLUME 1

| ☐ Pacific Jazz PJ-LA893-H | | 1977 | 12.00 |

JAZZ: THE 60S, VOLUME 2

| ☐ Pacific Jazz PJ-LA895-H | | 1977 | 12.00 |

JAZZ A LA MIDNIGHT

| ☐ Hall of Fame 608 | | 197? | 12.00 |
| ☐ Jazztone J-1282 [M] | | 1957 | 30.00 |

JAZZ A LA MOOD

| ☐ Jazztone J-1254 [M] | | 1957 | 30.00 |

JAZZ ALL STARS, VOL. 1

| ☐ Who's Who in Jazz 21010 | | 197? | 15.00 |

JAZZ AMERICANA

☐ Tampa TP-11 [M]		1957	100.00
—Colored vinyl			
☐ Tampa TP-11 [M]		1958	40.00
—Black vinyl			

JAZZ AND POPS FROM THE SOVIET UNION

| ☐ Colosseum CRLP-171 [M] | | 1955 | 30.00 |

JAZZ ANTHOLOGY OF WEST COAST JAZZ

| ☐ Jazztone J-1243 [M] | | 1957 | 30.00 |

JAZZ AT CARNEGIE HALL

☐ Arco AL-4 [10]		1950	80.00
☐ Mercury MG-35002 [10]		1950	80.00
—Reissue of Arco 4			

JAZZ AT CARNEGIE HALL, VOLUME 2

| ☐ Arco AL-8 [10] | | 195? | 80.00 |

JAZZ AT COLUMBIA -- COLLECTORS ITEMS

| ☐ Columbia CB-16 [M] | | 195? | 25.00 |
| —Columbia Record Club "bonus record" in generic sleeve with die-cut circle in middle | | | |

JAZZ AT COLUMBIA -- DIXIELAND

| ☐ Columbia CB-8 [M] | | 195? | 25.00 |
| —Columbia Record Club "bonus record" in generic sleeve with die-cut circle in middle | | | |

JAZZ AT JAZZ LTD.

| ☐ Atlantic 1338 [M] | | 1961 | 30.00 |
| —Multicolor label, white "fan" logo at right | | | |

JAZZ AT PRESERVATION HALL

| ☐ Atlantic 1408 [M] | | 1964 | 15.00 |
| ☐ Atlantic SD1408 [S] | | 1964 | 18.00 |

JAZZ AT PRESERVATION HALL, VOL. 2

| ☐ Atlantic 1409 [M] | | 1964 | 15.00 |
| ☐ Atlantic SD1409 [S] | | 1964 | 18.00 |

JAZZ AT PRESERVATION HALL, VOL. 3

| ☐ Atlantic 1410 [M] | | 1964 | 15.00 |
| ☐ Atlantic SD1410 [S] | | 1964 | 18.00 |

JAZZ AT STORYVILLE

☐ Paradox LP-6003 [10]		1951	50.00
☐ Savoy MG-15001 [10]		1952	80.00
☐ Savoy MG-15014 [10]		1952	80.00
☐ Storyville STLP-319 [10]		1955	80.00

JAZZ AT STORYVILLE, VOL. 2

| ☐ Savoy MG-15016 [10] | | 1952 | 80.00 |

JAZZ AT STORYVILLE, VOL. 3

| ☐ Savoy MG-15019 [10] | | 1953 | 80.00 |

JAZZ AT STORYVILLE, VOL. 4

| ☐ Savoy MG-15020 [10] | | 1953 | 80.00 |

JAZZ AT THE BOSTON ARTS FESTIVAL

| ☐ Storyville STLP-311 [10] | | 1954 | 80.00 |

JAZZ AT THE HOLLYWOOD BOWL

| ☐ Verve MGV-8231-2 [M] | | 1958 | 50.00 |
| ☐ Verve V-0231-2 [M] | | 1961 | 30.00 |

JAZZ AT THE NEW SCHOOL

| ☐ Chiaroscuro 110 | | 197? | 18.00 |

JAZZ AT THE PHILHARMONIC

| ☐ Stinson SLP-23 [10] | | 195? | 80.00 |
| —Black vinyl | | | |

Number	Title	Yr	NM
☐ Stinson SLP-23 [10]		195?	80.00
—Opaque red vinyl			
☐ Stinson SLP-23 [10]		1950	120.00
—See-through red vinyl; the first pressing of the first volume to be issued			
☐ Stinson SLP-23 [M]		195?	25.00

JAZZ AT THE PHILHARMONIC, NEW VOLUME 2

| ☐ Clef MGC-Vol.2 [M] | | 1955 | 50.00 |
| —Side 1 is the 10-inch Vol. 2; Side 2 is the 10-inch Vol. 3 | | | |

JAZZ AT THE PHILHARMONIC, NEW VOLUME 3

| ☐ Clef MGC-Vol.3 [M] | | 1955 | 50.00 |
| —Side 1 is the 10-inch Vol. 4; Side 2 is the 10-inch Vol. 5 | | | |

JAZZ AT THE PHILHARMONIC, NEW VOLUME 4

| ☐ Clef MGC-Vol.4 [M] | | 1955 | 50.00 |
| —Combines the 10-inch Vol. 6 and Vol. 14 on one record | | | |

JAZZ AT THE PHILHARMONIC, NEW VOLUME 5

| ☐ Clef MGC-Vol.5 [M] | | 1955 | 50.00 |
| —Combines the 10-inch Vol. 7, 10 and 11 on one record | | | |

JAZZ AT THE PHILHARMONIC, NEW VOLUME 6

| ☐ Clef MGC-Vol.6 [M] | | 1955 | 50.00 |
| —Combines the 10-inch Vol. 8 and Vol. 9 on one record | | | |

JAZZ AT THE PHILHARMONIC, NEW VOLUME 7

| ☐ Clef MGC-Vol.7 [M] | | 1955 | 50.00 |
| —Combines the 10-inch Vol. 12 and 13 on one record | | | |

JAZZ AT THE PHILHARMONIC, VOLUME 2

☐ Arco AL-1 [10]		1950	80.00
☐ Clef MGC-Vol.2 [10]		1953	60.00
—Reissue of Mercury Vol. 2			
☐ Mercury MGC-Vol.2 [10]		1951	60.00
—Reissue of 35003			
☐ Mercury MG-35003 [10]		1950	80.00
—Reissue of Arco 1			

JAZZ AT THE PHILHARMONIC, VOLUME 3

☐ Arco AL-2 [10]		1950	80.00
☐ Clef MGC-Vol.3 [10]		1953	60.00
—Reissue of Mercury Vol. 3			
☐ Mercury MGC-Vol.3 [10]		1951	60.00
—Reissue of 35004			
☐ Mercury MG-35004 [10]		1950	80.00
—Reissue of Arco 2			

JAZZ AT THE PHILHARMONIC, VOLUME 4

☐ Clef MGC-Vol.4 [10]		1953	60.00
—Reissue of Mercury Vol. 4			
☐ Mercury MGC-Vol.4 [10]		1951	60.00
—Reissue of 35005			
☐ Mercury MG-35005 [10]		1950	80.00

JAZZ AT THE PHILHARMONIC, VOLUME 5

☐ Clef MGC-Vol.5 [10]		1953	60.00
—Reissue of Mercury Vol. 5			
☐ Mercury MGC-Vol.5 [10]		1951	60.00
—Reissue of 35006			
☐ Mercury MG-35006 [10]		1950	80.00

JAZZ AT THE PHILHARMONIC, VOLUME 6

☐ Clef MGC-Vol.6 [10]		1953	60.00
—Reissue of Mercury Vol. 6			
☐ Mercury MGC-Vol.6 [10]		1951	60.00
—Reissue of 35007			
☐ Mercury MG-35007 [10]		1950	80.00

JAZZ AT THE PHILHARMONIC, VOLUME 7

☐ Clef MGC-Vol.7 [10]		1953	60.00
—Reissue of Mercury Vol. 7			
☐ Mercury MGC-Vol.7 [10]		1951	60.00
—Reissue of 35008			
☐ Mercury MG-35008 [10]		1950	80.00

JAZZ AT THE PHILHARMONIC, VOLUME 8

☐ Clef MGC-Vol.8 [10]		1953	60.00
—Reissue of Mercury Vol. 8			
☐ Mercury MGC-Vol.8 [10]		1951	60.00
—Reissue of 35000			
☐ Mercury MG-35000 [10]		1950	80.00

JAZZ AT THE PHILHARMONIC, VOLUME 9

☐ Clef MGC-Vol.9 [10]		1953	60.00
—Reissue of Mercury Vol. 9			
☐ Mercury MGC-Vol.9 [10]		1951	60.00
—Reissue of 35009			
☐ Mercury MG-35009 [10]		1950	80.00

JAZZ AT THE PHILHARMONIC, VOLUME 10

☐ Clef MGC-Vol.10 [10]		1953	60.00
—Reissue of Mercury Vol. 10			
☐ Mercury MGC-Vol.10 [10]		1951	60.00
—Reissue of 35010			
☐ Mercury MG-35010 [10]		1950	100.00

Number	Title	Yr	NM

JAZZ AT THE PHILHARMONIC, VOLUME 11

☐ Clef MGC-Vol.11 [10]		1953	60.00
—Reissue of Mercury Vol. 11			
☐ Mercury MGC-Vol.11 [10]		1951	60.00
—Reissue of 35011			
☐ Mercury MG-35011 [10]		1950	80.00

JAZZ AT THE PHILHARMONIC, VOLUME 12

☐ Clef MGC-Vol.12 [10]		1953	60.00
—Reissue of Mercury Vol. 12			
☐ Mercury MGC-Vol.12 [10]		1951	60.00

JAZZ AT THE PHILHARMONIC, VOLUME 13

☐ Clef MGC-Vol.13 [10]		1953	60.00
—Reissue of Mercury Vol. 13			
☐ Mercury MGC-Vol.13 [10]		1951	60.00

JAZZ AT THE PHILHARMONIC, VOLUME 14

☐ Clef MGC-Vol.14 [10]		1953	60.00
—Reissue of Mercury Vol. 14			
☐ Mercury MGC-Vol.14 [10]		1951	60.00

JAZZ AT THE PHILHARMONIC, VOLUME 15

☐ Clef MGC-Vol.15 [M]		1954	80.00
—Boxed set of new material with program			
☐ Clef MGC-Vol.15 [10]		1953	60.00
—Reissue of Mercury Vol. 15			
☐ Mercury MGC-Vol.15 [10]		1951	60.00

JAZZ AT THE PHILHARMONIC, VOLUME 16

| ☐ Clef MGC-Vol.16 [M] | | 1954 | 80.00 |
| —Boxed set of new material with program | | | |

JAZZ AT THE PHILHARMONIC, VOLUME 17

| ☐ Clef MGC-Vol.17 [M] | | 1955 | 80.00 |
| —Boxed set of new material with photo booklet | | | |

JAZZ AT THE PHILHARMONIC, VOLUME 18

| ☐ Clef MGC-Vol.18 [M] | | 1955 | 80.00 |
| —Boxed set of new material with booklet | | | |

JAZZ AT THE PHILHARMONIC: BIRD & PRES, CARNEGIE HALL 1949

| ☐ Verve 815150-1 | | 1984 | 12.00 |

JAZZ AT THE PHILHARMONIC: BIRD & PRES, THE '46 CONCERTS

| ☐ Verve 833565-1 | | 198? | 15.00 |
| ☐ Verve VE-2-2518 | | 197? | 18.00 |

JAZZ AT THE PHILHARMONIC: BLUES IN CHICAGO, 1955

| ☐ Verve 815151-1 | | 1984 | 12.00 |

JAZZ AT THE PHILHARMONIC: CARNEGIE BLUES

| ☐ Verve 825101-1 | | 1985 | 12.00 |

JAZZ AT THE PHILHARMONIC: HARTFORD 1953

| ☐ Pablo Live 2308240 | | 198? | 12.00 |

JAZZ AT THE PHILHARMONIC: HISTORIC RECORDINGS

| ☐ Verve VE-2-2504 | | 197? | 18.00 |

JAZZ AT THE PHILHARMONIC: IN TOKYO 1983

| ☐ Pablo Live 2620117 | | 1984 | 25.00 |

JAZZ AT THE PHILHARMONIC: LONDON 1969

| ☐ Pablo Live 2620119 | | 198? | 15.00 |

JAZZ AT THE PHILHARMONIC: MONTREUX '75

| ☐ Pablo 2310748 | | 197? | 18.00 |

JAZZ AT THE PHILHARMONIC: NORGRAN BLUES 1950

| ☐ Verve 815151-1 | | 1984 | 12.00 |

JAZZ AT THE PHILHARMONIC: ONE O'CLOCK JUMP 1953

| ☐ Verve 815153-1 | | 1984 | 12.00 |

JAZZ AT THE PHILHARMONIC: THE 1940S

| ☐ Verve UMV-9070/2 | | 197? | 30.00 |

JAZZ AT THE PHILHARMONIC: THE CHALLENGES, 1954

| ☐ Verve 815154-1 | | 1984 | 12.00 |

JAZZ AT THE PHILHARMONIC: THE COLEMAN HAWKINS SET

| ☐ Verve 815148-1 | | 1984 | 12.00 |

JAZZ AT THE PHILHARMONIC: THE DRUM BATTLE

| ☐ Verve 815146-1 | | 1984 | 12.00 |

JAZZ AT THE PHILHARMONIC: THE ELLA FITZGERALD SET

| ☐ Verve 815147-1 | | 1984 | 12.00 |

JAZZ AT THE PHILHARMONIC: THE EXCITING BATTLE -- STOCKHOLM '55

| ☐ Pablo 2310713 | | 197? | 15.00 |

JAZZ AT THE PHILHARMONIC: THE GETZ & J.J. SET

| ☐ Verve 825100-1 | | 1985 | 12.00 |

Number	Title	Yr	NM
JAZZ AT THE PHILHARMONIC: THE OSCAR PETERSON SET			
❏ Verve 825099-1		1985	12.00
JAZZ AT THE PHILHARMONIC: THE RAREST CONCERTS			
❏ Verve 815149-1		1984	12.00
JAZZ AT THE PHILHARMONIC: TRUMPET BATTLE, 1952			
❏ Verve 815152-1		1984	12.00
JAZZ AT THE PHILHARMONIC ALL STARS			
❏ American Recording Society G-416 [M]		1957	30.00
JAZZ AT THE PHILHARMONIC IN EUROPE			
❏ Verve V6-8823		197?	25.00
JAZZ AT THE PHILHARMONIC IN TOKYO			
❏ Pablo Live 2620104		198?	30.00
JAZZ AT THE SANTA MONICA CIVIC '72			
❏ Pablo 2625701		197?	30.00
JAZZ BAND BALL			
❏ Good Time Jazz L-12005 [M]		1954	25.00
JAZZ BANDS 1926-30			
❏ Historical 16		1967	12.00
JAZZ CITY PRESENTS			
❏ Bethlehem BCP-80 [M]		1957	30.00
JAZZ COMMITTEE FOR LATIN AMERICAN AFFAIRS			
❏ FM LP-303 [M]		1963	50.00
❏ Vee-Jay LP-303 [S]		196?	25.00
—All-black label with Vee Jay "brackets" logo and "STEREO" on label; most likely a reissue			
JAZZ CONCERT			
❏ Jazztone J-1219 [M]		1956	30.00
❏ Mercury MGJC-1 [M]		1953	120.00
—Combines 601 and 602 in a box			
JAZZ CONCERT WEST COAST			
❏ Savoy MG-12012 [M]		1955	80.00
❏ Savoy MG-12196 [M]		1961	50.00
JAZZ CONFIDENTIAL			
❏ Crown CLP-5056 [M]		1959	25.00
JAZZ CORNUCOPIA			
❏ Coral CRL57149 [M]		1958	30.00
JAZZ CRITICS' CHOICE			
❏ Columbia Jazz Odyssey PC36807		198?	12.00
JAZZ CRITICS' CHOICE: GREAT JAZZ CRITICS CHOOSE HISTORIC PERFORMANCES			
❏ Columbia CL2126 [M]		1964	15.00
JAZZ CRYSTALLIZATIONS			
❏ Pausa 7020		198?	12.00
JAZZ DANCE			
❏ Jaguar JP-801 [10]		1954	50.00
JAZZ DUPLEX			
❏ Pax LP-6006 [10]		1954	30.00
JAZZ FESTIVAL			
❏ Imperial LP-9233 [M]		1963	25.00
❏ Imperial LP-12233 [S]		1963	30.00
❏ Kapp KS-1 [M]		1956	25.00
JAZZ FESTIVAL, VOLUME 2			
❏ Imperial LP-9238 [M]		1963	25.00
❏ Imperial LP-12238 [S]		1963	30.00
JAZZ FESTIVAL IN HI-FI: NEAR IN AND FAR OUT			
❏ Warner Bros. W1281 [M]		1959	40.00
JAZZ FESTIVAL IN STEREO: NEAR IN AND FAR OUT			
❏ Warner Bros. WS1281 [S]		1959	30.00
JAZZ FOR ART'S SAKE			
❏ Dotted Eighth 101 [M]		195?	40.00
JAZZ FOR A SUNDAY AFTERNOON			
❏ Solid State SS-18027		1968	18.00
JAZZ FOR A SUNDAY AFTERNOON, VOL. 2			
❏ Solid State SS-18028		1968	18.00
JAZZ FOR A SUNDAY AFTERNOON, VOL. 3			
❏ Solid State SS-18037		1968	18.00
JAZZ FOR A SUNDAY AFTERNOON, VOL. 4			
❏ Solid State SS-18052		1969	18.00
JAZZ FOR HI-FI LOVERS			
❏ Dawn DLP-1124 [M]		1958	80.00
JAZZ FOR LOVERS			
❏ Riverside RLP 12-244 [M]		1957	40.00
JAZZ FOR PEOPLE WHO HATE JAZZ			
❏ RCA Victor LJM-1008 [M]		1954	50.00
JAZZ FOR PLAYBOYS			
❏ Savoy Jazz SJC-412		1985	12.00
JAZZ FOR PLAYGIRLS			
❏ Savoy Jazz SJC-413		1985	12.00
JAZZ FOR SURF-NIKS			
❏ Bethlehem BCP-6073 [M]		1961	30.00
JAZZ FROM DOWN UNDER			
❏ Jaguar JP-803 [10]		1954	50.00
JAZZ FROM NEW YORK, 1928-32			
❏ Historical 33		1969	12.00
JAZZ FROM SWEDEN			
❏ Discovery DL-2002 [10]		1953	50.00
JAZZ FROM THE FAMOUS DOOR			
❏ GHB GHB-116		197?	12.00
JAZZ GALA CONCERT			
❏ Atlantic SD1693		197?	15.00
JAZZ GIANTS			
❏ Biograph 3002		196?	15.00
THE JAZZ GIANTS			
❏ Norgran MGN-1056 [M]		1956	80.00
JAZZ GIANTS, VOL. 1			
❏ EmArcy MG-36048 [M]		1955	40.00
❏ Trip 5504		197?	12.00
JAZZ GIANTS, VOL. 2: THE PIANO PLAYERS			
❏ EmArcy MG-36049 [M]		1955	40.00
JAZZ GIANTS, VOL. 2 (REEDS)			
❏ Trip 5518		197?	12.00
JAZZ GIANTS, VOL. 3			
❏ Trip 5538		197?	12.00
JAZZ GIANTS, VOL. 3: REEDS, PART 1			
❏ EmArcy MG-36050 [M]		1955	40.00
JAZZ GIANTS, VOL. 3: REEDS, PART 2			
❏ EmArcy MG-36051 [M]		1955	40.00
JAZZ GIANTS, VOL. 3 (REEDS)			
❏ Trip 5555		197?	12.00
JAZZ GIANTS, VOL. 4: FOLK BLUES			
❏ EmArcy MG-36052 [M]		1955	40.00
JAZZ GIANTS, VOL. 5: BRASS			
❏ EmArcy MG-36053 [M]		1955	40.00
JAZZ GIANTS, VOL. 6: MODERN SWEDES			
❏ EmArcy MG-36054 [M]		1955	40.00
JAZZ GIANTS, VOL. 7: DIXIELAND			
❏ EmArcy MG-36055 [M]		1955	40.00
JAZZ GIANTS, VOL. 8: DRUM ROLE			
❏ EmArcy MG-36071 [M]		1956	40.00
JAZZ GIANTS '56			
❏ Verve UMV-2511		197?	15.00
THE JAZZ GIANTS '56			
❏ Verve MGV-8146 [M]		1957	30.00
❏ Verve V-8146 [M]		1961	25.00
JAZZ GIANTS '58			
❏ Verve MGV-8248 [M]		1958	50.00
❏ Verve V-8248 [M]		1961	30.00
❏ Verve UMV-2540		197?	15.00
JAZZ GOES TO BROADWAY			
❏ Kapp KL-1007 [M]		1956	25.00
JAZZ GREATS			
❏ Gateway 10111		197?	15.00
❏ Tops L-1508 [M]		1958	25.00
JAZZ GREATS!			
❏ Allegro 737 [M]		1958	30.00
JAZZ GREATS, VOL. 2			
❏ Columbia Special Products P13230		1976	12.00
—Custom manufactured for Radio Shack			
JAZZ GREATS 2			
❏ Gateway 10112		197?	15.00
JAZZ GREATS 3			
❏ Gateway 10113		197?	15.00
JAZZ HALL OF FAME, VOL. 2			
❏ Design DLP-113 [M]		196?	25.00
A JAZZ HOLIDAY			
❏ MCA MCA2-4018		1973	18.00
—Black label with rainbow			
THE JAZZ HOUR			
❏ Savoy MG-12126 [M]		1957	50.00
JAZZ IN A VERTICAL GROOVE, 1925-28			
❏ Biograph 12057		197?	12.00
JAZZ IN HOLLYWOOD			
❏ Liberty LJH-6001 [M]		1955	30.00
JAZZ INTERPLAY			
❏ Prestige PRLP-7341 [M]		1964	40.00
❏ Prestige PRLP-7341 [R]		1964	30.00
JAZZ IN THE THIRTIES			
❏ Swing SW-8457/8		198?	15.00
JAZZ IN TRANSITION			
❏ Transition TRLP-30 [M]		1956	200.00
—With booklet (deduct 1/4 if missing)			
JAZZ IS BUSTING OUT ALL OVER			
❏ Savoy MG-12123 [M]		1957	50.00
❏ Savoy Jazz SJC-408		198?	12.00
JAZZ JAMBOREE			
❏ Halo 50229 [M]		1957	25.00
JAZZ LAB			
❏ Starlite ST-7003 [M]		1955	50.00
THE JAZZ LIFE			
❏ Candid CD-8019 [M]		1960	40.00
❏ Candid CS-9019 [S]		1960	30.00
JAZZ LIFE!			
❏ Barnaby BR-5021		197?	15.00
JAZZ LTD.			
❏ Regal LP-11 [10]		1951	50.00
THE JAZZ MAKERS			
❏ Columbia CL1036 [M]		1957	25.00
JAZZMEN -- DETROIT			
❏ Savoy MG-12083 [M]		1956	80.00
JAZZ MONTAGE			
❏ Liberty LRP-3292 [M]		1963	18.00
❏ Liberty LST-7292 [S]		1963	25.00
JAZZ MUSIC FOR BIRDS			
❏ Bethlehem BCP-6039 [M]		1959	30.00
JAZZ MUSIC FOR PEOPLE WHO DON'T CARE ABOUT MONEY			
❏ Bethlehem BCP-88 [M]		1958	30.00
JAZZ ODYSSEY: THE SOUND OF CHICAGO			
❏ Columbia C3L32 [M]		1964	40.00
JAZZ ODYSSEY: THE SOUND OF HARLEM			
❏ Columbia C3L33 [M]		1964	40.00
JAZZ ODYSSEY: THE SOUND OF NEW ORLEANS			
❏ Columbia C3L30 [M]		1964	40.00
JAZZ OFF THE AIR, VOL. 1			
❏ Esoteric ESJ-2 [10]		1952	80.00
JAZZ OFF THE AIR, VOL. 2			
❏ Esoteric ESJ-3 [10]		1952	80.00
JAZZ OF THE FORTIES, VOL. 1			
❏ Folkways FJ-2841		197?	15.00
JAZZ OF THE ROARING 20'S			
❏ Riverside RLP 12-801 [M]		195?	50.00
JAZZ OF THE ROARING TWENTIES: DANCE MUSIC OF THE CHARLESTON ERA			
❏ Riverside RLP 12-108 [M]		1956	40.00
JAZZ OF THE SIXTIES			
❏ Vee Jay VJS-2-1008		1974	25.00
JAZZ OF TWO DECADES			
❏ EmArcy DEM-2 [M]		1956	40.00
THE JAZZOLOGY POLL WINNERS 1964			
❏ GHB GHB-200		1986	12.00
JAZZ OMNIBUS			
❏ Columbia CL1020 [M]		1957	25.00
JAZZ ON THE AIR			
❏ Brunswick BL58048 [10]		1953	50.00
JAZZ ON THE SCREEN			
❏ Fontana MGF-27532 [M]		1965	40.00
❏ Fontana SRF-67532 [S]		1965	40.00
JAZZ PIANISTS GALORE			
❏ Jazz: West Coast JWC-506 [M]		1956	150.00
THE JAZZ PIANO			
❏ RCA Victor LPM-3499 [M]		1966	25.00
❏ RCA Victor LSP-3499 [S]		1966	30.00
A JAZZ PIANO ANTHOLOGY			
❏ Columbia PG32355		197?	18.00
JAZZ PIANO GREATS			
❏ Folkways FJ-2852		197?	15.00
JAZZ PIONEERS 1933-36			
❏ Prestige PRLP-7647		1969	18.00
JAZZ POLL WINNERS			
❏ Columbia CL1610 [M]		1960	25.00
JAZZ POTPOURRI			
❏ Audiophile AP-24 [M]		1953	30.00
THE JAZZ RECORD STORY			
❏ Jazzology J-82		197?	12.00
THE JAZZ-ROCK-SOUL PROJECT			
❏ Riverside 3048		197?	25.00

Number	Title	Yr	NM
THE JAZZ ROUND			
❑ Verve VSP-24 [M]		1966	18.00
❑ Verve VSPS-24 [R]		1966	12.00
A JAZZ SALUTE TO FREEDOM			
❑ Core 100 [M]		196?	30.00
THE JAZZ SCENE			
❑ American Recording Society G-419 [M]		1957	30.00
❑ Clef MGC-674 [M]		1955	40.00
—Reissue of 4007			
❑ Clef MGC-4007 [M]		1953	50.00
❑ Clef Special Edition (no #) [10]		1953	100.00
— Two 10-inch LPs in box. Buyers had the option of purchasing a collection of photos that had been used in the original 78 rpm album; add another 50 percent if these photos are included			
JAZZ SET			
❑ Columbia Special Products CSP-217S [S]		1965	12.00
— Special item for Zenith			
❑ Columbia Special Products CSP-217M [M]		1965	15.00
THE JAZZ SINGERS			
❑ Prestige 24113		197?	18.00
JAZZ SOUL OF "CLEOPATRA			
❑ New Jazz NJLP-8292 [M]		1962	40.00
—Purple label			
❑ New Jazz NJLP-8292 [M]		1965	25.00
—Blue label, trident logo at right			
THE JAZZ SOUND			
❑ Columbia Special Products CSP298 [M]		1966	12.00
THE JAZZ STORY			
❑ Coral CJE-100 [M]		195?	100.00
—Box set; narrated by Steve Allen			
JAZZ SUPER HITS			
❑ Atlantic SD1528		1969	30.00
JAZZ SUPER HITS, VOL. 2			
❑ Atlantic SD1559		1970	25.00
JAZZ SURPRISE			
❑ Crown CLP-5008 [M]		1957	25.00
JAZZ SWINGS BROADWAY			
❑ Pacific Jazz PJM 404 [M]		1956	50.00
❑ World Pacific PJM-404 [M]		1958	40.00
JAZZTIME, U.S.A.			
❑ MCA 4113		197?	15.00
JAZZ TIME U.S.A. -- VOLUME 1			
❑ Brunswick BL54000 [M]		1952	30.00
JAZZ TIME U.S.A. -- VOLUME 2			
❑ Brunswick BL54001 [M]		1953	30.00
JAZZ TIME U.S.A. -- VOLUME 3			
❑ Brunswick BL54002 [M]		1954	30.00
JAZZTONE SAMPLER			
❑ Jazztone J-SPEC-100 [10]		1955	50.00
— With booklet			
JAZZ TRUMPET, VOL. 1			
❑ Prestige 24111		198?	18.00
THE JAZZ TRUMPET, VOL. 2			
❑ Prestige 24112		198?	18.00
JAZZ VARIATIONS, VOL. 1			
❑ Stinson SLP-20 [10]		195?	60.00
❑ Stinson SLP-20 [M]		196?	30.00
JAZZ VARIATIONS, VOL. 2			
❑ Stinson SLP-29 [M]		196?	30.00
JAZZVILLE, VOL. 1			
❑ Dawn DLP-1101 [M]		1956	80.00
JAZZ VIOLINS OF THE 40S			
❑ Folkways FJ-2854		197?	15.00
JAZZVISIONS: ALL STRINGS ATTACHED			
❑ Verve 841291-1		1989	15.00
JAZZVISIONS: BRIZILIAN KNIGHTS AND A LADY			
❑ Verve 841292-1		1989	15.00
JAZZVISIONS: ECHOES OF ELLINGTON, VOL. 1			
❑ Verve 841288-1		1989	15.00
JAZZVISIONS: ECHOES OF ELLINGTON, VOL. 2			
❑ Verve 841289-1		1989	15.00
JAZZVISIONS: JUMP THE BLUES AWAY			
❑ Verve 841287-1		1989	15.00
JAZZVISIONS: LATIN FAMILIA			
❑ Verve 841290-1		1989	15.00
JAZZVISIONS: RIO REVISITED			
❑ Verve 841286-1		1989	15.00
JAZZVISIONS: THE MANY FACES OF BIRD			
❑ Verve 841285-1		1989	15.00

Number	Title	Yr	NM
JAZZ VOCALS AWARD ALBUM			
❑ Bethlehem BCP-6068 [M]		1963	30.00
JAZZ WEST COAST, VOL. 1			
❑ Pacific Jazz JWC-500 [M]		1956	50.00
❑ World Pacific JWC-500 [M]		1958	40.00
JAZZ WEST COAST, VOL. 2			
❑ Pacific Jazz JWC-501 [M]		1956	50.00
❑ World Pacific JWC-501 [M]		1958	40.00
JAZZ WEST COAST, VOL. 3			
❑ Pacific Jazz JWC-507 [M]		1957	50.00
❑ World Pacific JWC-507 [M]		1958	40.00
JAZZ WEST COAST, VOL. 4			
❑ World Pacific JWC-510 [M]		1958	40.00
❑ World Pacific ST-1009 [S]		1959	30.00
JAZZ WEST COAST, VOL. 5			
❑ World Pacific JWC-511 [M]		1958	40.00
JAZZ -- WEST COAST VOL. III			
❑ Jazztone J-1274 [M]		195?	30.00
JAZZ WIZARDS, VOL. 1			
❑ Herwin 106		197?	15.00
JAZZ WIZARDS, VOL. 2			
❑ Herwin 107		197?	15.00
JAZZ WOMEN: A FEMINIST RETROSPECTIVE			
❑ Stash ST-109		197?	18.00
THE JAZZ WORLD			
❑ Columbia Special Products CSS524 [S]		1967	12.00
JAZZ YEARS: 25TH ANNIVERSARY			
❑ Atlantic SD-2-316		197?	18.00
A JAZZY WONDERLAND			
❑ Columbia 1P8120		1990	18.00
—Available on vinyl through Columbia House only			
JESUS CHRIST SUPERSTAR			
❑ Decca DXSA7206		1970	30.00
—Gatefold cover with booklet			
❑ Decca DXA7206		1970	30.00
—Box set with booklet			
❑ Decca MCA 2-10000		1973	15.00
—Gatefold cover with booklet; reissue; same custom labels as Decca issue			
❑ MCA 10000		197?	15.00
—Gatefold cover with booklet; reissue; generic MCA labels			
JINGLE BELL JAZZ			
❑ Columbia CL1893 [M]		1962	25.00
❑ Columbia CS8693 [S]		1962	18.00
❑ Columbia PC36803		1980	12.00
—Reissue of Harmony KH 32529 on the "Jazz Odyssey" series			
❑ Harmony KH32529		1973	15.00
—Reissue of CS 8693 with one track changed			
JINGLE BELL ROCK			
❑ Time-Life SRNR-XM		1987	25.00
—Available from Time-Life by mail order only; boxed set			
JOHN COLTRANE IN THE WINNER'S CIRCLE			
❑ Bethlehem BCP-6066 [M]		1961	30.00
—Reissue of 6024 with new title			
JOHN HAMMOND PRESENTS "FROM SPIRITUALS TO SWING" AT CARNEGIE HALL 1938			
❑ Vanguard VRS-8523 [M]		1959	40.00
JOHN HAMMOND PRESENTS "FROM SPIRITUALS TO SWING" AT CARNEGIE HALL 1939			
❑ Vanguard VRS-8524 [M]		1959	40.00
JOURNEYS INTO JAZZ, VOL. 1			
❑ GHB GHB-65		197?	12.00
JOURNEYS INTO JAZZ, VOL. 2			
❑ GHB GHB-66		197?	12.00
THE JOYFUL SOUND OF CHRISTMAS			
❑ RCA Record Club CSP-0601		1969	25.00
—Available only through the RCA Record Club			
THE JOY OF CHRISTMAS			
❑ Capitol SP8693		1968	15.00
❑ Capitol Creative Products SL-6580		1968	15.00
❑ Columbia Special Products P12042		1973	15.00
—Sold only at Strawbridge & Clothier stores (Philadelphia area)			
❑ RCA Victor PRM-197 [M]		1965	18.00
—Created for the National Tea Company			
❑ RCA Victor PRS-429		1972	15.00
THE JOY OF CHRISTMAS, FEATURING MARTY ROBBINS AND HIS FRIENDS			
❑ Columbia Special Products C11087		1972	18.00
THE JOY OF CHRISTMAS, VOLUME II			
❑ RCA Victor PRM-230 [M]		1966	18.00
—Created for the National Tea Company			

Number	Title	Yr	NM
❑ RCA Victor PRM-230-A [M]		1966	18.00
—Sold only at Acme markets (Mid-Atlantic area); same contents as PRM-230			
JOYOUS CHRISTMAS			
❑ Columbia Special Products CSS(# unk)		1967	15.00
—Produced for the Beneficial Finance System			
JOYOUS CHRISTMAS, VOLUME 2			
❑ Columbia Special Products CSS808		1968	15.00
—Produced for the Beneficial Finance System			
JOYOUS CHRISTMAS, VOLUME 3			
❑ Columbia Special Products CSS(# unk)		1969	15.00
—Produced for the Beneficial Finance System			
JOYOUS CHRISTMAS, VOLUME 4			
❑ Columbia Special Products CSS1485		1970	15.00
—Produced for the Beneficial Finance System			
JOYOUS CHRISTMAS, VOLUME 6			
❑ Columbia Special Products C11083		1972	12.00
—Produced for the Beneficial Finance System			
JOYOUS CHRISTMAS, VOLUME V			
❑ Columbia Special Products C10398		1971	12.00
—Produced for the Beneficial Finance System			
JOYOUS MUSIC FOR CHRISTMAS TIME			
❑ Reader's Digest RD45-M [M]		1963	25.00
❑ Reader's Digest RD45-S [S]		1963	25.00
—Available only through Reader's Digest magazine by mail order			
JOYOUS NOEL			
❑ Reader's Digest RDA-57A		1966	25.00
—Available only through Reader's Digest magazine by mail order			
THE JOYOUS SONGS OF CHRISTMAS			
❑ Columbia Special Products C10400		1971	12.00
—Sold only at Goodyear tire dealers			
JOYS OF CHRISTMAS			
❑ Capitol Creative Products SL-6610		1969	15.00
❑ Capitol Special Markets SL-6610		197?	12.00
—Reissue with revised label name			
JOY TO THE WORLD			
❑ Columbia Special Products P11647		1973	12.00
❑ Reader's Digest RBA-218/D		1985	18.00
JOY TO THE WORLD (30 CLASSIC CHRISTMAS MELODIES)			
❑ Columbia Special Products P314654		1978	25.00
—Box set; produced for Murray Hill Records			
JUBILEE MONAURAL SAMPLER. VOCALS AND INSTRUMENTALS			
❑ Jubilee MSJLP-803 [M]		1959	30.00
JUBILEE STEREOSONIC VOCAL SAMPLER, VOLUME 2			
❑ Jubilee SSJLP-802 [S]		1959	40.00
JUBILEE SURPRISE PARTY			
❑ Jubilee JGM-1107 [M]		1959	150.00
❑ Jubilee JGS-1107 [S]		1959	200.00
JUST FOUR LAUGHS VOLUME I			
❑ Scepter SPS5104		1972	15.00
—Contains routines by Bill Cosby, Dick Gregory, Redd Foxx and Flip Wilson			
JUST FOUR LAUGHS VOLUME II			
❑ Scepter SPS5105		1972	15.00
—Contains routines by Bill Cosby, Dick Gregory, Redd Foxx and Flip Wilson			
JUST JAZZ			
❑ Imperial LP-9246 [M]		1963	25.00
❑ Imperial LP-12246 [S]		1963	30.00
KANSAS CITY IN THE '30S			
❑ Capitol T1057 [M]		1958	30.00
KANSAS CITY JAZZ			
❑ Decca DL8044 [M]		1954	40.00
KANSAS CITY PIANO			
❑ Decca DL9226 [M]		1967	30.00
❑ Decca DL79226 [R]		1967	15.00
KATS KARAVAN (OLD FAVORITES WITH JIM LOWE)			
❑ Vee Jay LP-100 [M]		1957	50.00
—Gold label, black print			
KBIG CHOICES			
❑ World Pacific KBIG-1 [S]		1964	30.00
K-BOX DUSTY DISCS			
❑ Roulette R25338 [M]		1966	25.00
KEATS RIDES A HARLEY			
❑ Happy Squid HS 002		1981	25.00

Number	Title	Yr	NM

KELLOGG'S PRESENTS...BIG BAND CLASSICS

☐ RCA Special Products DPL1-0438(e) — 1980 — 12.00

KEYBOARD KINGS

☐ MGM E-100 [10] — 1951 — 50.00

KEYBOARD KINGS OF JAZZ

☐ RCA Victor LPT-4 [10] — 1951 — 40.00

KGFJ SOUNDS OF SUCCESS

☐ Roulette R25349 [M] — 1967 — 25.00

KIDS & CHRISTMAS '83

☐ Sound Approach/CSP P17621 — 1983 — 12.00
— *Presented by WEZW FM 104; benefit for Milwaukee Children's Hospital*

KILL ROCK STARS

☐ Kill Rock Stars KRS201 [B] — 1991 — 30.00
— *Includes Nirvana, etc.*

KINGS AND QUEENS OF IVORY

☐ MCA 1329 — 198? — 12.00

KINGS OF CLASSIC JAZZ

☐ Riverside RLP 12-131 [M] — 1957 — 40.00

KINGS OF SWING

☐ Pickwick PTP-2072 — 197? — 15.00

KINGS OF THE KEYBOARD

☐ American Recording Society G-406 [M] — 1956 — 30.00

THE KINGS SING THE BLUES

☐ Teem LP-5005 [M] — 196? — 30.00

KISS MY ASS -- CLASSIC KISS REGROOVED

☐ Mercury 522123-1 — 1994 — 40.00
— *All copies on red vinyl*

KNEBWORTH

☐ Polydor 847042-1 — 1990 — 18.00
— *Includes Tears For Fears*

KNOW YOUR JAZZ

☐ ABC-Paramount ABC-115 [M] — 1956 — 30.00

KPOI'S BATTLE OF THE SURFING BANDS

☐ Del-Fi DFST-1235 [S] — 1964 — 100.00
— *Honolulu version of the above LP*

☐ Del-Fi DFLP-1235 [M] — 1964 — 60.00

KTLA'S BATTLE OF THE SURFING BANDS

☐ Del-Fi DFLP-1235 [M] — 1964 — 50.00
☐ Del-Fi DFST-1235 [S] — 1964 — 80.00
— *Los Angeles version of the above LP*

KVIL CHRISTMAS VOL. III

☐ FairWest Enterprises FW-KVIL-84 — 1984 — 12.00
— *Recordings by musicians in the Dallas-Fort Worth area; tracks unspecified except as noted*

KYA GOLDEN GATE GREATS

☐ Chess LP1458SF [M] — 1961 — 150.00
— *San Francisco version of "Golden Gassers," Chess 1458*

KYA'S BATTLE OF THE SURFING BANDS

☐ Del-Fi DFLP-1235 [M] — 1964 — 50.00
☐ Del-Fi DFST-1235 [S] — 1964 — 80.00
— *San Francisco version of the above LP, with slightly different contents*

KYA'S MEMORIES OF THE COW PALACE

☐ Autumn LP101 [M] — 1963 — 70.00

LADIES GET THE BLUES

☐ Mercury 834199-1 — 1988 — 10.00

L.A. IN

☐ Rhino RNLP 009 — 1979 — 18.00
— *Includes The Knack, Motels, Oingo Boingo, others*

THE LAST COMPILATION ALBUM

☐ Stiff USE-3 — 1980 — 18.00
— *Includes The Cure, The Damned, Dexy's Midnight Runners, Madness, Wreckless Eric, etc.*

THE LAST RECORD ALBUM

☐ A&M (# unknown) — 1989 — 40.00

LATE MUSIC, VOLUME I

☐ Columbia CL541 [M] — 1954 — 30.00

LATE MUSIC, VOLUME II

☐ Columbia CL542 [M] — 1954 — 30.00

LATE MUSIC, VOLUME III

☐ Columbia CL543 [M] — 1954 — 30.00

THE LAUGHTOUR

☐ Sire PRO-A-3931 [EP] — 1990 — 25.00
— *Promo-only sampler*

LAURIE GOLDEN GOODIES

☐ Laurie LLP-2041 [M] — 1967 — 18.00
☐ Laurie SLLP-2041 [P] — 1967 — 30.00

LEGENDARY BLACK JAZZ STARS IN THEIR FIRST FILMS

☐ Biograph M-3 — 198? — 12.00

THE LEGEND OF JESSE JAMES

☐ A&M SP-3718 — 1980 — 15.00

LE GRAN MAMOU: A CAJUN MUSIC ANTHOLOGY, THE HISTORIC VICTOR AND BLUEBIRD SESSIONS 1928-1941

☐ Country Music Foundation CMF-013 — 1990 — 18.00

LENNY TRISTANO MEMORIAL CONCERT

☐ Jazz Records JR-3 — 198? — 40.00

LEONARD FEATHER'S ENCYCLOPEDIA OF JAZZ

☐ Vee Jay VJSP-400 — 1977 — 30.00

LEONARD FEATHER'S ENCYCLOPEDIA OF JAZZ, VOLUME ONE: GIANTS OF THE SAXOPHONE

☐ Vee Jay LP-2501 [M] — 1964 — 25.00
☐ Vee Jay VJS-2501 [S] — 1964 — 30.00

LEONARD FEATHER'S ENCYCLOPEDIA OF JAZZ OF THE '60S: BLUES BAG

☐ Vee Jay LP-2506 [M] — 1964 — 25.00

LET'S CELEBRATE CHRISTMAS

☐ Capitol Special Markets SL-6923 — 1973 — 15.00

LET'S HAVE A DANCE PARTY

☐ Ace LP-1019 [M] — 1961 — 70.00

LET'S SING ABOUT FREEDOM

☐ Vee Jay LP-5044 [M] — 1963 — 30.00

LET THEM EAT JELLYBEANS

☐ Alternative Tentacles VIRUS4 — 1982 — 30.00

LIBERTY PREMIER SERIES SPECTACULAR

☐ Liberty L-5504 [M] — 1962 — 25.00
☐ Liberty S-6604 [S] — 1962 — 30.00

LIBERTY PROUDLY PRESENTS STEREO -- THE VISUAL SOUND

☐ Liberty LST-100 [S] — 1959 — 40.00

LIFE IN THE EUROPEAN THEATER

☐ Elektra 60179 — 1982 — 18.00
— *Includes The Clash, The Jam, The [English] Beat, The Specials, XTC, Peter Gabriel, Madness, Bad Manners, The Stranglers, The Undertones, Echo & The Bunnymen, The Au Pairs*

LIFE IS BEAUTIFUL, SO WHY NOT EAT HEALTH FOOD?

☐ New Underground 44 — 1981 — 25.00

LIFE IS UGLY, SO WHY NOT KILL YOURSELF?

☐ New Underground 11 — 1981 — 25.00

THE LIFE TREASURY OF CHRISTMAS MUSIC

☐ Project/Capitol TL100 [M] — 1963 — 25.00
— *Designed as a supplement to the Life Book of Christmas; selections performed by anonymous chorus and orchestra and Boy Choristers from the Church of the Transfiguration (NY)*

LIGHTS OUT SAN FRANCISCO

☐ Blue Thumb BT6004 — 1970 — 30.00

LIKE 'ER RED HOT

☐ ABC Duke DLPX-73 [M] — 1974 — 18.00
☐ Duke DLP-73 [M] — 1960 — 120.00
— *Purple and yellow label*

☐ Duke DLP-73 [M] — 196? — 50.00
— *Orange label*

☐ Duke DLP-73 [M] — 196? — 30.00
— *Green label, "Distributed by ABC-Dunhill"*

LIMO

☐ Warner Bros. PRO691 — 1977 — 25.00

LISTEN TO OUR STORY

☐ Brunswick BL59001 [10] — 1950 — 60.00

LISTEN TO OUR VISION

☐ Gramavision 18-8509 — 1986 — 12.00

THE LITTLE DRUMMER BOY

☐ Capitol/Pickwick SPC-3462 — 197? — 12.00

A LITTLE ROCK AND ROLL FOR EVERYBODY

☐ Audio Lab AL-1567 [M] — 1960 — 200.00

THE LITTLEST ANGEL/LULLABY OF CHRISTMAS

☐ Decca DLP8009 [M] — 1949 — 40.00

LIVE AT BILL GRAHAM'S FILLMORE WEST

☐ Columbia CS9893 — 1969 — 18.00

LIVE AT CBGB'S

☐ Atlantic SD2-508 — 1976 — 25.00
— *Same album as CBGB/Omfug release*

☐ CBGB/Omfug 315 — 1976 — 30.00

LIVE AT TARGET

☐ Subterranean 3 — 1980 — 30.00

LIVE AT THE FESTIVAL

☐ Enja 2030 — 197? — 18.00

LIVE AT THE WHISKEY A-GO-GO

☐ Vee Jay LP-1100 [M] — 1964 — 30.00
— *Not known to exist in stereo*

LIVE FOR IRELAND

☐ MCA 42113 — 1987 — 12.00
— *Includes U2, The Boomtown Rats, Elvis Costello, The Pogues*

LIVE! FOR LIFE

☐ I.R.S. 5731 — 1986 — 12.00
— *Includes Stewart Copeland, R.E.M., The Alarm, General Public, Sting, Bangles, Oingo Boingo, Go-Go's, Squeeze*

THE LIVELY SOUND OF UNIVERSITY

☐ Capitol Custom (no #) [M] — 1966 — 25.00
— *Mustang Sweepstakes Prize Winner" on front cover*

THE LIVING CHRISTMAS TREE (DR. JERRY FALWELL PRESENTS)

☐ Old Time Gospel Hour TRB-11 — 197? — 15.00

LIVING MUSIC COLLECTION '86

☐ Living Music LM-0006 — 1986 — 12.00

LOADED

☐ Savoy MG-12074 [M] — 1956 — 50.00

LONDON BROIL

☐ Angel ANG-60004 [10] — 1955 — 50.00

THE LONG HIT SUMMER

☐ Epic AS2118 [DJ] — 1985 — 15.00
— *Includes Dead Or Alive, Sade*

A LOOK AT YESTERDAY

☐ Mainstream 56025 [M] — 1965 — 30.00
☐ Mainstream S-6025 [R] — 1965 — 15.00

LOOK WHO'S SURFIN' NOW!

☐ King 882 [M] — 1964 — 150.00

LOONEY TUNES AND MERRIE MELODIES

☐ Warner Bros. PRO423 — 1970 — 100.00
— *Box set with booklet of liner notes; originals have green labels*

LOST IN THE STARS

☐ A&M SP-9-5104 — 1985 — 15.00
— *Includes Marianne Faithfull, Sting, Lou Reed*

A LOT OF YARN BUT A WELL-KNITTED JAZZ ALBUM

☐ Bethlehem BCP-91 [M] — 1958 — 30.00

LOVE ME TENDER

☐ Time-Life STL-133 — 1991 — 30.00

LOVE THOSE GOODIES

☐ Checker LP2973 [DJ] — 1959 — 500.00
— *White label, multi-color splash vinyl*

☐ Checker LP2973 [M] — 1959 — 120.00

LULLABY OF BIRDLAND

☐ RCA Victor LPM-1146 [M] — 1955 — 50.00

LUSTY MOODS

☐ Moodsville MVLP-37 [M] — 1963 — 40.00
— *Green label*

☐ Moodsville MVST-37 [S] — 1963 — 40.00
— *Green label*

☐ Moodsville MVLP-37 [M] — 1965 — 25.00
— *Blue label, trident logo at right*

☐ Moodsville MVST-37 [S] — 1965 — 25.00
— *Blue label, trident logo at right*

☐ Status ST-8319 [M] — 1965 — 30.00

MAD "TWISTS" ROCK 'N' ROLL

☐ Big Top 12-1305 [M] — 1962 — 100.00

THE MAGICAL MUSIC OF WALT DISNEY

☐ Ovation OV-5000 — 1978 — 60.00
— *Box set*

THE MAGIC HORN

☐ RCA Victor LPM-1332 [M] — 1956 — 40.00

THE MAGIC OF CHRISTMAS

☐ Capitol SWBB-93810 — 1971 — 18.00
— *Available only through the Capitol Record Club*

☐ Columbia Musical Treasury P3S5806 — 1972 — 25.00
☐ Columbia Musical Treasury P2M5245 — 196? — 18.00
— *No artists mentioned*

THE MAGIC OF CHRISTMAS WITH CHILDREN

☐ Capitol Creative Products L6517 [M] — 196? — 18.00
— *Sold only at Safeway stores (In Association with Jon M. Huntsman Inc., Continental Production Company)*

MAGNAVOX ALBUM OF CHRISTMAS MUSIC

☐ Columbia Special Products CSQ11093 [Q] — 1972 — 25.00
— *Sold only at Magnavox dealers; yes, this is in quadraphonic!*

MAGNAVOX PRESENTS A REPRISE OF GREAT HITS

☐ Reprise PRO578 — 1973 — 12.00

MAHALIA (JACKSON) AND FRIENDS AT CHRISTMASTIME

☐ Columbia Special Products P11804 — 1973 — 15.00
— *Side 2 is all rechanneled stereo; Side 1 is true stereo*

Number	Title	Yr	NM

MAIDEN AUSTRALIA
- ❏ A&M SP-4952 — 1983 — 12.00
— *Includes Split Enz, Mental As Anything, Jo Jo Zep, etc.*

MAMBO JAZZ
- ❏ Prestige PRLP-135 [10] — 1952 — 150.00

MANASSAS JAZZ FESTIVAL
- ❏ Jazzology J-17 — 196? — 12.00

THE MAN WITH A HORN
- ❏ Decca DL5191 [10] — 1950 — 50.00

THE MANY FACES OF THE BLUES
- ❏ Savoy MG-12125 [M] — 1957 — 50.00

THE MANY MOODS OF CHRISTMAS
- ❏ Columbia Special Products P12013 — 1973 — 15.00
— *Sold only at Goodyear tire dealers*
- ❏ RCA Special Products DPL1-0085 — 1974 — 12.00

MARCH '84 IN-STORE SAMPLER
- ❏ Capitol SPRO9089 [DJ] — 1984 — 12.00
— *Includes Duran Duran, Thomas Dolby, Missing Persons*

MAR Y SOL
- ❏ Atco SD-2-705 — 1972 — 18.00

MASTER JAZZ PIANO
- ❏ Master Jazz 8105 — 197? — 15.00

MASTER JAZZ PIANO, VOL. 2
- ❏ Master Jazz 8108 — 197? — 15.00

MASTER JAZZ PIANO, VOL. 3
- ❏ Master Jazz 8117 — 197? — 15.00

MASTER JAZZ PIANO, VOL. 4
- ❏ Master Jazz 8129 — 197? — 15.00

MASTERS OF THE MODERN PIANO
- ❏ Verve VE-2-2514 — 197? — 18.00

MAX'S KANSAS CITY 1976
- ❏ Ram 1213 — 1976 — 25.00

MAX'S KANSAS CITY PRESENTS NEW WAVE HITS FOR THE '80S
- ❏ Max's Kansas City 19801 — 1981 — 25.00
— *Compilation of first two Max's Kansas City albums plus new tracks*

MAX'S KANSAS CITY VOL. 2, 1977
- ❏ Ram 2213 — 1977 — 15.00

MEGA HITS 1986
- ❏ MCA 5985 — 1987 — 12.00
— *Includes Belinda Carlisle, The Outfield*

THE MELLOW MOODS
- ❏ RCA Victor LPM-1365 [M] — 1956 — 40.00

MELLOW THE MOOD/JAZZ IN A MELLOW MOOD
- ❏ Blue Note BLP-5001 [10] — 1951 — 200.00

THE MELTING POT
- ❏ SST 249 — 1987 — 15.00
— *Includes Sonic Youth*

MEMORABLE SESSIONS IN JAZZ
- ❏ Blue Note BLP-5026 [10] — 1953 — 200.00

MEMORIES ARE MADE OF HITS
- ❏ Liberty LRP-3200 [M] — 1961 — 30.00
— *Reissued as "The Original Hits, Volume 4*

MEMORY LANE, HITS BY THE ORIGINAL GROUPS
- ❏ Fire FLP-100 [M] — 1959 — 200.00
— *Reissue of "Here Are the Hits!" with the same label and number*

MEMPHIS COUNTRY
- ❏ Sun 120 — 1970 — 18.00

MEMPHIS GOLD
- ❏ Stax 710 [M] — 1966 — 30.00
- ❏ Stax S710 [S] — 1966 — 30.00

MEMPHIS GOLD VOLUME 2
- ❏ Stax 726 [M] — 1967 — 25.00
- ❏ Stax S726 [S] — 1967 — 30.00

MEMPHIS JAZZ FESTIVAL
- ❏ Jazzology J-134 — 198? — 12.00

MEMPHIS MILLIONS
- ❏ Stax STS3023 — 1973 — 18.00

THE MERCURY 40TH ANNIVERSARY V.S.O.P. ALBUM
- ❏ Mercury 824116-1 — 1985 — 40.00

MERCURY LIVING PRESENCE
- ❏ Mercury Living Presence SR90293 [S] — 196? — 120.00
— *Maroon label, no "Vendor: Mercury Record Corporation"; contains music by groups conducted by Paul Paray, Antal Dorati and Frederick Fennell*

MERRY CHRISTMAS
- ❏ Columbia Musical Treasury 3P6306 — 1975 — 18.00
- ❏ Coral CRL56080 [10] — 1952 — 80.00
- ❏ Rainbow Sound R-5032-LPS — 198? — 12.00
- ❏ RCA Victor PRS-168 — 1964 — 18.00

MERRY CHRISTMAS BABY
- ❏ Gusto/Hollywood K-5018-X — 1978 — 15.00

MERRY CHRISTMAS BABY (CHRISTMAS MUSIC FOR YOUNG LOVERS)
- ❏ Hollywood HLP501 [M] — 1956 — 120.00

MERRY CHRISTMAS FROM...
- ❏ King 680 [M] — 1959 — 200.00
- ❏ Reader's Digest RD4-83 — 1969 — 25.00
— *Available only through Reader's Digest magazine by mail order*

MERRY CHRISTMAS FROM COKESBURY BOOKSTORES
- ❏ Columbia Special Products P14277 — 1977 — 12.00
— *Sold only at Cokesbury bookstores (duh)*

MERRY CHRISTMAS FROM CORAL RECORDS
- ❏ Coral CRL57355 [M] — 1960 — 25.00

MERRY CHRISTMAS FROM MOTOWN
- ❏ Motown MS-681 — 1968 — 30.00

MERRY CHRISTMAS FROM SESAME STREET
- ❏ CRA CTW25516 — 1975 — 15.00

MERRY CHRISTMAS MUSIC/CHRISTMAS FAVORITES
- ❏ Plymouth P12-59 [M] — 1952 — 25.00
— *Artists not mentioned on jacket or label*

MERRY CHRISTMAS TO YOU
- ❏ Capitol T9030 [M] — 1955 — 50.00

MERRY CHRISTMAS WITH NAT KING COLE/FRED WARING AND THE PENNSYLVANIANS
- ❏ Capitol Special Markets SL-6883 — 1973 — 12.00

A MERRY MERRY CHRISTMAS
- ❏ Columbia Special Products CSP161 — 1964 — 18.00
— *Number on record is "XTV 86094" on Side 1 and "XTV 86095" on Side 2*

THE METRONOME ALL-STARS
- ❏ Columbia CL2528 [10] — 1954 — 30.00

METRONOME ALL-STARS
- ❏ Harmony HL7044 [M] — 1957 — 30.00
- ❏ RCA Camden CAL-426 [M] — 1958 — 30.00

METRONOME ALL STARS 1956
- ❏ Clef MGC-743 [M] — 1956 — 40.00
- ❏ Verve MGV-8030 [M] — 1957 — 40.00
- ❏ Verve V 8030 [M] — 1961 — 25.00

MGM MILLION SELLERS: COUNTRY & WESTERN HITS, VOLUME 1
- ❏ MGM E-3825 [M] — 1960 — 30.00

MGM RECORDS PARADE OF STARS
- ❏ MGM NP90569 [M] — 1965 — 25.00
— *Capitol Record Club sampler of 12 MGM artists and soundtracks*

MICHIGAN ROCKS
- ❏ Seeds and Stems 77001 — 1977 — 30.00

MICKEY MOST PRESENTS BRITISH GO-GO
- ❏ MGM E4306 [M] — 1965 — 30.00
- ❏ MGM SE4306 [R] — 1965 — 30.00

MICKEY MOST PRESENTS ENGLISH IN-GROUPS
- ❏ Metro M-577 [M] — 1966 — 25.00
- ❏ Metro MS-577 [R] — 1966 — 25.00

MIDDLE OF THE ROAD
- ❏ Warner Bros. PRO525 — 1972 — 30.00
— *Originals have green labels*

MIDNIGHT JAMBOREE
- ❏ Decca DL4041 [M] — 1961 — 30.00
- ❏ Decca DL74041 [S] — 1961 — 30.00

MIDNIGHT JAZZ AT CARNEGIE HALL
- ❏ Verve MGV-8189-2 [M] — 1957 — 50.00
- ❏ Verve V-8189-2 [M] — 1961 — 30.00

MILESTONE JAZZSTARS IN CONCERT
- ❏ Milestone M-55006 — 198? — 18.00

MILESTONE TWOFER GIANTS
- ❏ Milestone MSP-1 — 197? — 18.00

THE MILLION-AIRS
- ❏ Coral CRL57310 [M] — 1959 — 30.00

A MILLION OR MORE
- ❏ ABC-Paramount ABC-216 [M] — 1959 — 80.00

MILLION PERFORMANCE SONGS, VOLUME 1
- ❏ Jobete JSA-6251 [DJ] — 1988 — 25.00
— *Promo-only publisher's demo*

MILLION PERFORMANCE SONGS, VOLUME 2
- ❏ Jobete JSA-6252 [DJ] — 1988 — 25.00
— *Promo-only publisher's demo*

MILLION SELLER DANCE HITS
- ❏ Parkway P-7028 [M] — 1963 — 30.00

MISS AMERICA PRESENTS A COLLECTOR'S ALBUM
- ❏ Columbia Special Products XTV68873/4 — 1961 — 18.00
— *With photo of Nancy Anne Fleming, Miss America 1961, on the cover; specially pressed for Philco*

MISSING LINKS
- ❏ MCA 42206 — 1988 — 12.00

MISTLETOE AND MEMORIES
- ❏ RCA 8372-1-R — 1988 — 18.00

THE MODERN IDIOM
- ❏ Capitol H325 [10] — 1952 — 60.00

MODERN JAZZ
- ❏ London LL1185 [M] — 1955 — 25.00
- ❏ Tops L-1521 [M] — 1958 — 25.00

MODERN JAZZ CONCERT
- ❏ Adventures in Sound WL-127 [M] — 1958 — 40.00

MODERN JAZZ FESTIVAL
- ❏ Harmony HL7196 [M] — 1958 — 25.00

MODERN JAZZ GALLERY
- ❏ Kapp KXL-5001 [M] — 195? — 25.00

MODERN JAZZ GREATS
- ❏ Crown CLP-5212 [M] — 196? — 18.00

MODERN JAZZ HALL OF FAME
- ❏ Design DLP-29 [M] — 196? — 15.00
- ❏ Design DLPS-29 [R] — 196? — 10.00

MODERN JAZZ PIANO
- ❏ RCA Camden CAL-384 [M] — 1958 — 30.00

MODERN JAZZ PIANO ALBUM
- ❏ Savoy Jazz SJL-2247 — 198? — 15.00

MODERN JAZZ SPECTACULAR
- ❏ Jazztone J-1231 [M] — 1956 — 30.00

MODERN JAZZ SURVEY 1: NEW YORK JAZZ
- ❏ Prestige 16-5 — 1957 — 600.00
— *This album plays at 16 2/3 rpm and is marked as such; white label*

MODERN JAZZ SURVEY 2: BARITONES AND FRENCH HORNS
- ❏ Prestige 16-6 — 1957 — 600.00
— *This album plays at 16 2/3 rpm and is marked as such; white label*

MODERN JAZZ TRUMPETS
- ❏ Prestige PRLP-113 [10] — 1951 — 200.00

MODERN MOODS
- ❏ Moodsville MVLP-2 [M] — 1961 — 40.00
— *Green label*
- ❏ Moodsville MVLP-2 [M] — 1965 — 25.00
— *Blue label, trident logo at right*

MOMENTS OF MOTOWN
- ❏ Motown PR-122 [DJ] — 1983 — 50.00
— *Promo only item with narration and song snippets*

MONARCH ALL STAR JAZZ, VOL. 1
- ❏ Monarch LP-201 [10] — 1952 — 50.00

MONARCH ALL STAR JAZZ, VOL. 2
- ❏ Monarch LP-202 [10] — 1952 — 50.00

MONARCH ALL STAR JAZZ, VOL. 3
- ❏ Monarch LP-203 [10] — 1952 — 50.00

MONARCH ALL STAR JAZZ, VOL. 4
- ❏ Monarch LP-204 [10] — 1952 — 50.00

MONARCH ALL STAR JAZZ, VOL. 5
- ❏ Monarch LP-205 [10] — 1952 — 50.00

MONDAY NIGHT AT BIRDLAND
- ❏ Roulette R52015 [M] — 1958 — 30.00
- ❏ Roulette SR52015 [S] — 1959 — 30.00

MONSTERS
- ❏ Warner Bros. PRO-A-796 — 1978 — 25.00

MONTAGE
- ❏ Savoy MG-12029 [M] — 1955 — 80.00

MONTGOMERY WARD PRESENTS A CHRISTMAS TO REMEMBER
- ❏ Capitol Creative Products SL-6573 — 1968 — 15.00
— *Sold only at Montgomery Ward stores*

MONTGOMERY WARD PRESENTS A CHRISTMAS TO REMEMBER VOL. 2
- ❏ Capitol Creative Products SL-6610 — 1969 — 15.00
— *Sold only at Montgomery Ward stores*

MONTGOMERY WARD PRESENTS A CHRISTMAS TO REMEMBER VOL. 3
- ❏ Capitol Creative Products SL-6681 — 1970 — 12.00
— *Sold only at Montgomery Ward stores*

MONTGOMERY WARD PRESENTS CHRISTMAS FAVORITES
- ❏ Montgomery Ward W-101 — 1965 — 18.00
— *No artists mentioned on label or jacket*

Number	Title	Yr	NM

THE MONTREUX '77 COLLECTION
❏ Pablo Live 2620107 — 1978 — 70.00
THE MONTREUX COLLECTION
❏ Pablo 2625707 — 197? — 18.00
MONTREUX SUMMIT
❏ Columbia JG35005 — 1978 — 18.00
MONTREUX SUMMIT, VOLUME 2
❏ Columbia JG35090 — 1978 — 18.00
MONUMENTAL COUNTRY HITS
❏ Monument SLP-18095 — 1968 — 25.00
MONUMENTAL POP HITS
❏ Monument SLP-18096 — 1968 — 25.00
MOOD IN BLUE
❏ Urania UJLP-1209 [M] — 1955 — 30.00
MOOD TO BE WOOED
❏ Cadet LP-784 [M] — 1967 — 25.00
❏ Cadet LPS-784 [S] — 1967 — 18.00
MORE COUNTRY CLASSICS
❏ RCA Victor LPM-2467 [M] — 1961 — 30.00
❏ RCA Victor LSP-2467 [S] — 1961 — 30.00
MORE COUNTRY MUSIC SPECTACULAR
❏ Starday SLP-140 [M] — 1961 — 40.00
MORE DRUMS ON FIRE
❏ World Pacific WP-1261 [M] — 1960 — 40.00
❏ World Pacific ST-1022 [S] — 1960 — 30.00
MORE FOR YOUR MONEY
❏ Bell 6009 — 1968 — 25.00
MORE GOLDEN GREATS
❏ Liberty LRP-3548 [M] — 1967 — 25.00
❏ Liberty LST-7548 [P] — 1967 — 18.00
MORE GOLD HITS, VOLUME 2
❏ Warwick W2044 [M] — 1961 — 80.00
MORE GREAT HITS OF 1964 AND OTHER GOLDEN GOODIES
❏ Vee Jay LP 1136 [M] — 1965 — 30.00
— Not known to exist in stereo
MORE HOT COUNTRY REQUESTS
❏ Epic FE44279 — 1988 — 10.00
MORE HOT COUNTRY REQUESTS, VOL. 2
❏ Epic FE44280 — 1988 — 10.00
MORE LIVE ECHOES OF THE SWINGING BANDS
❏ RCA Victor LSP-1983 [S] — 1959 — 50.00
❏ RCA Victor LPM-1983 [M] — 1959 — 40.00
MORE SOLID GOLD PROGRAMMING
❏ Screen Gems/Columbia CPL-716/7 [DJ] — 1975 — 30.00
— Promo-only compilation of oldies sent to radio to spur airplay on songs owned by this publishing house; contains three Beatles recordings
THE MOST
❏ Forum Circle FC-9079 [M] — 1963 — 15.00
❏ Forum Circle FCS-9079 [S] — 1963 — 15.00
THE MOST, VOLUME 1
❏ Roulette R52050 [M] — 1960 — 25.00
❏ Roulette SR52050 [S] — 1960 — 30.00
THE MOST, VOLUME 2
❏ Roulette R52053 [M] — 1960 — 25.00
❏ Roulette SR52053 [S] — 1960 — 30.00
THE MOST, VOLUME 3
❏ Roulette R52057 [M] — 1961 — 25.00
❏ Roulette SR52057 [S] — 1961 — 30.00
THE MOST, VOLUME 4
❏ Roulette R52062 [M] — 1961 — 25.00
❏ Roulette SR52062 [S] — 1961 — 30.00
THE MOST, VOLUME 5
❏ Roulette R52075 [M] — 1961 — 25.00
❏ Roulette SR52075 [S] — 1961 — 30.00
THE MOST OF THE TWIST
❏ Roulette R25176 [M] — 1962 — 30.00
— Originals have a white label with colored spokes
MOTOR CITY SCENE
❏ Bethlehem BCP-6056 [M] — 1961 — 200.00
THE MOTOR-TOWN REVIEW, VOL. 1
❏ Motown MT609 [M] — 1963 — 40.00
THE MOTOR-TOWN REVIEW, VOL. 2
❏ Motown MT615 [M] — 1964 — 30.00
THE MOTORTOWN REVIEW IN PARIS
❏ Tamla T264 [M] — 1965 — 30.00
❏ Tamla TS264 [S] — 1965 — 30.00
THE MOTORTOWN REVUE LIVE!
❏ Motown MS-688 — 1969 — 30.00
MOTOWN AT THE HOLLYWOOD PALACE
❏ Motown MS703 — 1970 — 18.00
❏ Motown MS-703 — 1970 — 18.00

MOTOWN CHARTBUSTERS, VOLUME 1
❏ Motown MS-707 — 1970 — 18.00
MOTOWN CHARTBUSTERS, VOLUME 2
❏ Motown MS-715 — 1970 — 18.00
A MOTOWN CHRISTMAS
❏ Motown M-795V2 — 1973 — 25.00
❏ Motown 5256ML2 — 1982 — 18.00
— Reissue of Motown 795V2 with same contents
❏ Motown R271663 — 1983 — 16.00
— Same as above, but RCA Music Service edition
MOTOWN CHRISTMAS ALBUM -- CHRISTMAS CHEERS FROM MOTOWN
❏ Motown MOT-6292 — 1989 — 18.00
MOTOWN INSTRUMENTALS
❏ Natural Resources NR4002T1 — 1978 — 25.00
MOTOWN'S GREAT INTERPRETATIONS
❏ Natural Resources NR4001T1 — 1978 — 25.00
MOTOWN SHOW TUNES
❏ Natural Resources NR4003T1 — 1978 — 25.00
MOTOWN SPECIAL
❏ Motown M603 [M] — 1962 — 80.00
THE MOTOWN STORY: THE FIRST 25 YEARS
❏ Motown PR-121 [DJ] — 1983 — 250.00
— Promo-only box set with extra record not on the commercial release; labels are white
THE MOTOWN STORY: THE FIRST DECADE
❏ Motown MS-726 — 1971 — 30.00
THE MOTOWN STORY: THE FIRST TWENTY-FIVE YEARS
❏ Motown 6048ML5 — 1983 — 30.00
MOTOWN WINNER'S CIRCLE: #1 HITS, VOL. 1
❏ Gordy GS-935 — 1969 — 30.00
MOTOWN WINNER'S CIRCLE: #1 HITS, VOL. 2
❏ Gordy GS-936 — 1969 — 30.00
MOTOWN WINNER'S CIRCLE: #1 HITS, VOL. 3
❏ Gordy GS-943 — 1969 — 30.00
MOTOWN WINNER'S CIRCLE: #1 HITS, VOL. 4
❏ Gordy GS-946 — 1969 — 30.00
MOTOWN WINNER'S CIRCLE: #1 HITS, VOL. 5
❏ Gordy GS-950 — 1970 — 30.00
MOUNTAIN FROLIC
❏ Brunswick BL59000 [10] — 1950 — 60.00
MTV, BET, VH-1 POWER PLAYERS
❏ EMI R100737 — 1988 — 12.00
— Includes L.L. Cool J ("I Need Love"), Cutting Crew ("I Just Died in Your Arms"); BMG Direct Marketing edition
MTV HIGH PRIORITY
❏ RCA Victor 6396-1-R — 1987 — 12.00
— Includes Bangles ("Manic Monday"), Cyndi Lauper ("Time After Time"), Belinda Carlisle ("I Feel the Magic"), Bananarama ("More Than Physical")
MTV'S ROCK 'N ROLL TO GO
❏ Elektra 60399 — 1985 — 12.00
— Includes The Cars, The Fixx, Billy Idol, Cyndi Lauper, Madonna, The Police, Thompson Twins, Wang Chung
MURRAY THE "K'S" SING ALONG WITH THE ORIGINAL GOLDEN GASSERS
❏ Roulette R25159 [M] — 1961 — 30.00
MURRAY THE K -- LIVE FROM THE BROOKLYN FOX
❏ KFM 1001 [M] — 1963 — 40.00
MURRAY THE K PRESENTS GOLDEN GASSERS FOR A DANCE PARTY
❏ Roulette R25192 [M] — 1962 — 30.00
MURRAY THE K PRESENTS GOLDEN GASSERS FOR HAND HOLDERS
❏ Roulette R25191 [M] — 1962 — 30.00
MURRAY THE K'S BLASTS FROM THE PAST
❏ Chess LP1461 [M] — 1961 — 40.00
MURRAY THE K'S GASSERS FOR SUBMARINE RACE WATCHERS
❏ Chess LP1470 [M] — 1962 — 40.00
MURRAY THE K'S GOLDEN GASSERS
❏ Chess LP1458NYC [M] — 1961 — 150.00
— New York version of "Golden Gassers," Chess 1458
MURRAY THE K'S NINETEEN-SIXTY TWO BOSS GOLDEN GASSERS
❏ Scepter SP-510 [M] — 1963 — 25.00
❏ Scepter SPS-510 [P] — 1963 — 30.00
A MUSICAL HISTORY OF JAZZ
❏ Grand Award GA 33-322 [M] — 1955 — 25.00

MUSIC AND PLUNK, TINKLE, TING-A-LING
❏ Mercury Living Presence SR90338 [S] — 196? — 50.00
— Maroon label, no "Vendor: Mercury Record Corporation
MUSIC AND RHYTHM SAMPLER
❏ PVC EP2 [DJ] — 1982 — 30.00
— Includes XTC, Peter Gabriel, David Byrne, The (English) Beat; one-LP sampler of two-record set
MUSIC BOX
❏ A&M SP-19006 — 196? — 15.00
— Created for BankAmericard
MUSIC BOX MELODIES OF CHRISTMAS
❏ Pickwick SPC-1014 — 197? — 12.00
— Also see "Ford, Rita." These, from anonymous sources, apparently are not from Ms. Ford's collection.
MUSIC FOR FRUSTRATED CONDUCTORS
❏ RCA Victor Red Seal LSC-2325 [S] — 1959 — 50.00
— Original with "shaded dog" label
MUSIC FOR THE BOY FRIEND…HE REALLY DIGS JAZZ
❏ Decca DL8314 [M] — 1956 — 30.00
MUSIC FROM THE DANCING YEARS
❏ RCA Victor PR-112 [M] — 1961 — 18.00
— Created for Dole Pineapple
MUSIC FROM THE SOUTH, VOL. 1: COUNTRY BRASS BANDS
❏ Folkways FA-2650 [M] — 195? — 25.00
THE MUSIC OF NEW ORLEANS, VOL. 1
❏ Folkways FA-2461 [M] — 1959 — 25.00
THE MUSIC OF NEW ORLEANS, VOL. 2
❏ Folkways FA-2462 [M] — 1959 — 25.00
THE MUSIC OF NEW ORLEANS, VOL. 3: DANCE HALLS
❏ Folkways FA-2463 [M] — 1959 — 25.00
THE MUSIC OF NEW ORLEANS, VOL. 4: THE BIRTH OF JAZZ
❏ Folkways FA-2464 [M] — 1959 — 25.00
THE MUSIC OF NEW ORLEANS, VOL. 5: NEW ORLEANS JAZZ
❏ Folkways FA-2465 [M] — 1959 — 25.00
THE "MUSIC OF YOUR LIFE" CHRISTMAS
❏ The "Music of Your Life P17169 — 1983 — 12.00
THE MUSIC PEOPLE
❏ Columbia C3X31280 — 1972 — 30.00
MUSIC TO READ JAMES BOND BY
❏ United Artists UAL-3415 [M] — 1965 — 25.00
❏ United Artists UAS-6415 [S] — 1965 — 30.00
MUSIC TO READ JAMES BOND BY, VOL. 2
❏ United Artists UAL-3541 [M] — 1966 — 25.00
❏ United Artists UAS-6541 [S] — 1966 — 30.00
MUSIC TO TRIM YOUR TREE BY
❏ RCA Victor PRS225 [S] — 1966 — 18.00
❏ RCA Victor PRM225 [M] — 1966 — 15.00
MUTANT POP
❏ PVC 7912 — 1980 — 15.00
— Includes Gang of Four, Human League, several others
MUZAK STIMULUS PROGRESSION NUMBER THREE: CHRISTMAS
❏ Muzak S-2563 — 196? — 15.00
— Instrumental versions by anonymous musicians
❏ Status ST-8315 [M] — 1965 — 30.00
MY SON THE SURF NUT
❏ Capitol T1939 [M] — 1963 — 50.00
❏ Capitol ST1939 [S] — 1963 — 60.00
THE NAMES OF DIXIELAND
❏ Baronet B-108 [M] — 195? — 25.00
NARADA: THE CHRISTMAS COLLECTION
❏ Narada N-63902 — 1988 — 15.00
NASCAR GOES COUNTRY
❏ MCA 474 — 1975 — 30.00
NASHVILLE BANDSTAND
❏ King 813 [M] — 1962 — 100.00
NASHVILLE BANDSTAND, VOLUME 2
❏ King 847 [M] — 1963 — 80.00
THE NASHVILLE CHRISTMAS ALBUM
❏ Epic PE40418 — 1986 — 12.00
NASHVILLE SATURDAY NIGHT
❏ Columbia House 1P6215 — 1975 — 12.00
❏ Nashville NLP-2009 [M] — 1965 — 25.00
❏ Starday SLP-128 [M] — 1961 — 40.00
NASHVILLE'S GREATEST CHRISTMAS HITS
❏ Columbia PC44412 — 1988 — 12.00

Number	Title	Yr	NM

NASHVILLE'S GREATEST CHRISTMAS HITS, VOLUME II
- ❏ Columbia PC44413 — 1988 — 12.00

NASHVILLE STEEL GUITAR
- ❏ Nashville NLP-2017 [M] — 1965 — 25.00
- ❏ Starday SLP-138 [M] — 1961 — 30.00

NATIVE NEW ORLEANS JAZZ
- ❏ Dot DLP-3009 [M] — 1956 — 30.00

NEIGHBORHOOD RHYTHMS
- ❏ Freeway 213 — 1984 — 40.00

NEW AMERICAN MUSIC VOL. 1: JAZZ
- ❏ Folkways FA-33901 — 197? — 15.00

NEW BLUE HORNS
- ❏ Fantasy OJC-256 — 198? — 12.00
- ❏ Riverside RLP 12-294 [M] — 1958 — 30.00

THE NEW BREED
- ❏ ABC Impulse! IA-9339 — 197? — 18.00
- ❏ RCA Victor CPL1-5491 — 1986 — 10.00

NEW CHAMBER JAZZ
- ❏ Epic LN1124 [10] — 1955 — 30.00

NEW FACES AT NEWPORT
- ❏ Metrojazz E-1005 [M] — 1958 — 50.00
- ❏ Metrojazz SE-1005 [S] — 1958 — 30.00

NEW MUSIC: SECOND WAVES
- ❏ Savoy Jazz SJL-2235 — 198? — 15.00

NEW MUSIC SEMINAR '84
- ❏ Capitol SPRO9216 [DJ] — 1984 — 12.00
- *—Includes Duran Duran, Thomas Dolby, etc.*

NEW MUSIC SEMINAR SAMPLER
- ❏ Columbia AS1521 [DJ] — 198? — 15.00
- *—Includes Boomtown Rats, Dave Edmunds, Nina Hagen, Romeo Void, many more*

NEW ORLEANS, OUR HOME TOWN
- ❏ Imperial LP-9260 [M] — 1964 — 30.00
- ❏ Imperial LP-12260 [R] — 1964 — 25.00

NEW ORLEANS: THE LIVING LEGENDS
- ❏ Riverside RLP-356/7 [M] — 196? — 50.00
- *— Two records in gatefold jacket*

NEW ORLEANS: THE LIVING LEGENDS, VOL. 1
- ❏ Riverside RLP-356 [M] — 196? — 25.00
- ❏ Riverside RS-9356 [R] — 196? — 15.00

NEW ORLEANS: THE LIVING LEGENDS, VOL. 2
- ❏ Riverside RLP-357 [M] — 196? — 25.00
- ❏ Riverside RS-9357 [R] — 196? — 15.00

NEW ORLEANS ALL-STARS
- ❏ GHB GHB-35 — 196? — 15.00

NEW ORLEANS BOUNCE: URBAN BLUES, VOLUME 2
- ❏ Imperial LP-94004 — 1968 — 25.00

NEW ORLEANS BRASS BANDS: DOWN YONDER
- ❏ Rounder 2062 — 198? — 12.00

NEW ORLEANS DIXIELAND
- ❏ Southland SLP-216 [M] — 1955 — 30.00

NEW ORLEANS ENCORE
- ❏ Riverside RLP-2503 [10] — 1954 — 80.00

NEW ORLEANS EXPRESS
- ❏ EmArcy MG-36022 [M] — 1955 — 50.00

NEW ORLEANS HORNS
- ❏ Riverside RLP-1005 [10] — 1953 — 80.00

NEW ORLEANS JAZZ
- ❏ Decca DL5483 [10] — 1953 — 50.00
- ❏ Decca DL8283 [M] — 1956 — 30.00

NEW ORLEANS JAZZ AND HERITAGE FESTIVAL, 10TH ANNIVERSARY
- ❏ Flying Fish FF-089 — 198? — 12.00

NEW ORLEANS JAZZ AND HERITAGE FESTIVAL, 1976
- ❏ Rhino R1-71111 — 1989 — 18.00

NEW ORLEANS JAZZ AT THE KITTY HALLS
- ❏ Arhoolie 1013 — 198? — 12.00

NEW ORLEANS JAZZ BABIES
- ❏ Southland SLP-214 [M] — 1955 — 30.00

NEW ORLEANS JAZZ KINGS
- ❏ Southland SLP-217 [M] — 1955 — 30.00

NEW ORLEANS JAZZ STARS
- ❏ Southland SLP-211 [M] — 1955 — 30.00

NEW ORLEANS LEGENDS
- ❏ Riverside RLP 12-119 [M] — 1957 — 40.00

NEW ORLEANS REVIVAL
- ❏ Riverside RLP-1047 [10] — 1954 — 80.00

NEW ORLEANS RHYTHM KINGS
- ❏ Riverside RLP 12-102 [M] — 195? — 60.00
- *—Also see NEW ORLEANS RHYTHM KINGS in the main A-Z listings.*

NEW ORLEANS STYLE
- ❏ X LVA-3029 [10] — 1954 — 80.00

NEW ORLEANS TO LOS ANGELES
- ❏ Southland SLP-215 [M] — 1955 — 30.00

NEWPORT JAZZ FESTIVAL
- ❏ RCA Victor LPM-3369 [M] — 1965 — 18.00
- ❏ RCA Victor LSP-3369 [S] — 1965 — 25.00

NEWPORT JAZZ FESTIVAL: LIVE
- ❏ Columbia C238262 — 198? — 15.00

NEWPORT JAZZ FESTIVAL ALL STARS
- ❏ Atlantic SD1331 [S] — 1961 — 30.00
- *—Multicolor label, white "fan" logo at right*

NEWPORT JAZZ FESTIVAL ALL-STARS
- ❏ Atlantic 1331 [M] — 1961 — 30.00
- *—Multicolor label, white "fan" logo at right*

NEW SOUNDS FROM SWEDEN, VOL. 1: THE DARING YOUNG SWEDES
- ❏ Prestige PRLP-119 [10] — 1951 — 400.00

THE NEW SPIRIT OF CAPITOL
- ❏ Capitol SNP-6 — 1970 — 15.00

THE NEW TRADITION SINGS THE OLD TRADITION
- ❏ Warner Bros. R124450 — 1989 — 18.00
- *—BMG Direct Marketing edition*

A NEW VISION FROM GRAMAVISION
- ❏ Gramavision 18-8510 — 1986 — 12.00

NEW VOICES
- ❏ Dawn DLP-1125 [M] — 1956 — 80.00

THE NEW WAVE IN JAZZ
- ❏ ABC Impulse! AS-90 [S] — 1968 — 15.00
- ❏ Impulse! A-90 [M] — 1966 — 18.00
- ❏ Impulse! AS-90 [S] — 1966 — 25.00

NEW YORK JAZZ OF THE TWENTIES
- ❏ Riverside RLP-1048 [10] — 1954 — 80.00

A NIGHT AT THE BOULEVARD
- ❏ Felsted FL-7503 [M] — 1960 — 40.00

THE 1930S, VOL. 1
- ❏ Aircheck 1 — 197? — 12.00

1944 ESQUIRE JAZZ ALL-STARS
- ❏ Aircheck 27 — 197? — 12.00

1947 WNEW SATURDAY NIGHT SWING SESSION
- ❏ Everest Archive of Folk & Jazz 231 — 196? — 12.00

1959 MONTEREY JAZZ FESTIVAL
- ❏ Everest Archive of Folk & Jazz 239 — 196? — 12.00

1966 COUNTRY & WESTERN AWARD WINNERS
- ❏ Decca DL74837 [S] — 1967 — 25.00
- ❏ Decca DL4837 [M] — 1967 — 25.00

THE 1969 WARNER/REPRISE RECORD SHOW
- ❏ Warner Bros. PRO336 — 1969 — 30.00
- *—Originals have "W7" logos on labels*
- ❏ Warner Bros. PRO336 — 197? — 18.00
- *—With "WB" logos on labels*

THE 1969 WARNER/REPRISE SONGBOOK
- ❏ Warner Bros. PRO331 — 1969 — 30.00
- *—The first of the famous Warner/Reprise "Loss Leaders" mail-order series; originals have "W7" logos on labels*
- ❏ Warner Bros. PRO331 — 197? — 18.00
- *—With "WB" logos on labels*

1984 ON THE DANCE FLOOR
- ❏ EMI America SPRO9077/8 [DJ] — 1984 — 15.00
- *—Includes Kate Bush*

19 HOT COUNTRY REQUESTS
- ❏ Epic FE39597 — 1985 — 10.00

19 HOT COUNTRY REQUESTS, VOL. 2
- ❏ Epic FE40175 — 1985 — 10.00

19 HOT COUNTRY REQUESTS, VOL. 3
- ❏ Epic FE40479 — 1986 — 10.00

THE NITTY GRITTY
- ❏ Vee Jay LP-1084 [M] — 1964 — 30.00
- *—Not known to exist in stereo*

NO AGE
- ❏ SST 102 — 198? — 12.00
- *—Includes Black Flag, etc.*

NO 'COUNT
- ❏ Savoy MG-12078 [M] — 1956 — 60.00

NO ENERGY CRISIS
- ❏ ABC Impulse! AS-9267 — 1974 — 25.00

NON DAIRY CREAMER
- ❏ Warner Bros. PRO443 — 1971 — 30.00
- *—Originals have green labels*

A NONESUCH CHRISTMAS
- ❏ Nonesuch H-71232 — 197? — 15.00
- *—Second pressings have Warner Communications logo*
- ❏ Nonesuch H-71232 — 1971 — 18.00
- *—First pressings have no reference to Warner Communications*

NO NEW YORK
- ❏ Antilles AN-7067 — 1978 — 15.00
- *—Includes Teenage Jesus and the Jerks, etc.*

NO NUKES: THE MUSE CONCERTS FOR A NON-NUCLEAR FUTURE
- ❏ Asylum ML-801 — 1979 — 30.00

NORMAN GRANZ JAM SESSION
- ❏ Verve VE-2-2508 — 197? — 18.00

NORMAN GRANZ JAZZ CONCERT
- ❏ Norgran MGN-2502 [M] — 1954 — 80.00
- ❏ Norgran MGN-2501 [M] — 1954 — 80.00

THE NORTHWEST BATTLE OF THE BANDS VOLUME 1: FLASH AND CRASH
- ❏ Beat Rocket BR128 — 2001 — 15.00

THE NORTHWEST BATTLE OF THE BANDS VOLUME 2: KNOCK YOU FLAT!
- ❏ Beat Rocket BR129 — 2001 — 15.00

NO SOUR GRAPES, JUST PURE JAZZ
- ❏ Bethlehem BCP-92 [M] — 1958 — 30.00

NOTHING CHEESY ABOUT THIS JAZZ
- ❏ Bethlehem BCP-85 [M] — 1958 — 30.00

NOT SO QUIET ON THE WESTERN FRONT
- ❏ Alternative Tentacles VIRUS14 — 1982 — 30.00
- *—Includes Dead Kennedys, Flipper, lots of others*

NOVA SCOTIA FOLK SONGS
- ❏ Elektra EKL-23 [10] — 1954 — 40.00

NO WAVE
- ❏ A&M SP-4738 — 1978 — 18.00
- *—First pressing on watercolor blue vinyl*
- ❏ A&M SP-4738 — 1978 — 10.00
- *—Black vinyl*
- ❏ A&M PR4738 [DJ] — 1978 — 30.00
- *—White label promo on watercolor blue vinyl; numbered sticker on generic cover*

NUGGETS
- ❏ Elektra 7E-2006 — 1972 — 40.00

OCEAN DRIVE
- ❏ Beach Beat/Warner Special Products OP2528W — 1981 — 25.00

OCTOBER '61 POP SAMPLER
- ❏ RCA Victor SPS-33-141 [DJ] — 1961 — 600.00
- *—Promo-only collection*

OCTOBER 1960 POPULAR STEREO SAMPLER
- ❏ RCA Victor SPS-33-96 [DJ] — 1960 — 600.00
- *—Promo-only collection*

OCTOBER CHRISTMAS SAMPLER 59-40-41
- ❏ RCA Victor SPS-33-54 [DJ] — 1959 — 600.00
- *—Promo-only collection*

THE OFFICIAL GRAMMY AWARDS ARCHIVE COLLECTION (ALBUM OF THE YEAR)
- ❏ Franklin Mint GRAM-14 — 1985 — 60.00

THE OFFICIAL GRAMMY AWARDS ARCHIVE COLLECTION (ALL-TIME WINNERS)
- ❏ Franklin Mint GRAM-2 — 1985 — 60.00

THE OFFICIAL GRAMMY AWARDS ARCHIVE COLLECTION (BEST NEW ARTIST)
- ❏ Franklin Mint GRAM-6 — 1985 — 60.00

THE OFFICIAL GRAMMY AWARDS ARCHIVE COLLECTION (FOLK PERFORMANCES)
- ❏ Franklin Mint GRAM-10 — 1985 — 60.00

THE OFFICIAL GRAMMY AWARDS ARCHIVE COLLECTION (GREAT PERFORMANCES OF THE ROCK ERA, VOL. 1)
- ❏ Franklin Mint GRAM-3 — 1985 — 60.00

THE OFFICIAL GRAMMY AWARDS ARCHIVE COLLECTION (JAZZ VOCALISTS)
- ❏ Franklin Mint GRAM-13 — 1985 — 60.00

THE OFFICIAL GRAMMY AWARDS ARCHIVE COLLECTION (POP PERFORMANCES, VOL. 1)
- ❏ Franklin Mint GRAM-5 — 1985 — 60.00

THE OFFICIAL GRAMMY AWARDS ARCHIVE COLLECTION (RECORD OF THE YEAR)
- ❏ Franklin Mint GRAM-1 — 1985 — 60.00

Number	Title	Yr	NM

THE OFFICIAL GRAMMY AWARDS ARCHIVE COLLECTION (RHYTHM AND BLUES, VOL. 1)
❏ Franklin Mint GRAM-8 — 1985 — 70.00

THE OFFICIAL GRAMMY AWARDS ARCHIVE COLLECTION (SONG OF THE YEAR)
❏ Franklin Mint GRAM-9 — 1985 — 60.00

THE OFFICIAL GRAMMY AWARDS ARCHIVE COLLECTION (STAGE & ORIGINAL CAST RECORDINGS)
❏ Franklin Mint GRAM-11 — 1985 — 120.00

THE OFFICIAL GRAMMY AWARDS ARCHIVE COLLECTION (THE BIG BAND SOUND)
❏ Franklin Mint GRAM-7 — 1985 — 60.00

THE OFFICIAL GRAMMY AWARDS ARCHIVE COLLECTION (THE GREAT SINGERS)
❏ Franklin Mint GRAM-4 — 1985 — 150.00

THE OFFICIAL GRAMMY AWARDS ARCHIVE COLLECTION (THE PRODUCER'S CHOICE)
❏ Franklin Mint GRAM-12 — 1985 — 60.00

O. HENRY'S THE GIFT OF THE MAGI
❏ E.F. MacDonald EFMX-62 — 1962 — 25.00
—*Special album done by the E.F. MacDonald Company, Dayton, Ohio*

OLD AND HEAVY GOLD 1955
❏ Economic Consultants 1955 — 1973 — 25.00

OLD AND HEAVY GOLD 1956
❏ Economic Consultants 1956 — 1973 — 30.00

OLD AND HEAVY GOLD 1957
❏ Economic Consultants 1957 — 1973 — 30.00

OLD AND HEAVY GOLD 1958
❏ Economic Consultants 1958 — 1973 — 30.00

OLD AND HEAVY GOLD 1959
❏ Economic Consultants 1959 — 1973 — 25.00

OLD AND HEAVY GOLD 1960
❏ Economic Consultants 1960 — 1973 — 30.00

OLD AND HEAVY GOLD 1961
❏ Economic Consultants 1961 — 1973 — 30.00

OLD AND HEAVY GOLD 1962
❏ Economic Consultants 1962 — 1973 — 30.00

OLD AND HEAVY GOLD 1963
❏ Economic Consultants 1963 — 1973 — 25.00

OLD AND HEAVY GOLD 1964
❏ Economic Consultants 1964 — 1973 — 25.00
—*Original magazine ads claimed that six Beatles tracks would appear on this LP; they were replaced before release*

OLD AND HEAVY GOLD 1965
❏ Economic Consultants 1965 — 1973 — 25.00
—*Original magazine ads claimed that three Beatles tracks would appear on this LP; they were replaced before release*

OLD AND HEAVY GOLD 1966
❏ Economic Consultants 1966 — 1973 — 25.00

OLD AND HEAVY GOLD 1967
❏ Economic Consultants 1967 — 1973 — 25.00
—*Original magazine ads claimed that a Beatles track would appear on this LP; it was replaced with another track before release*

OLD AND HEAVY GOLD 1968
❏ Economic Consultants 1968 — 1973 — 25.00
—*Original magazine ads claimed that a Beatles track would appear on this LP; it was replaced with another track before release*

OLD AND HEAVY GOLD 1969
❏ Economic Consultants 1969 — 1973 — 25.00
—*Original magazine ads claimed that a Beatles track would appear on this LP; it was replaced with another track before release*

OLD AND HEAVY GOLD 1970
❏ Economic Consultants 1970 — 1973 — 25.00
—*Original magazine ads claimed that a Beatles track would appear on this LP; it was replaced with another track before release*

OLD AND HEAVY GOLD 1971
❏ Economic Consultants 1971 — 1973 — 25.00
—*Original magazine ads claimed that a Paul McCartney track would appear on this LP; it was replaced with another track before release*

AN OLD FASHIONED CHRISTMAS
❏ Reader's Digest RDA216-A — 197? — 25.00
—*Available only through Reader's Digest magazine by mail order*

AN OLD-FASHIONED CHRISTMAS
❏ Longines Symphonette LS214 [S] — 196? — 15.00
—*Record label has the number SYS 5422*

OLDIES BUT GOODIES
❏ Original Sound LPM-5001 [M] — 1959 — 50.00
—*Original pressing with no reference to other volumes on the back cover*
❏ Original Sound LPM-5001 [M] — 1960s — 15.00
—*Later editions with later volumes in the series on the back cover*

OLDIES BUT GOODIES, VOL. 2
❏ Original Sound LPM-5003 [M] — 1960 — 40.00
—*Original pressing with no reference to later volumes on the back cover*
❏ Original Sound LPM-5003 [M] — 1960s — 15.00
—*Later editions with later volumes in the series on the back cover*

OLDIES BUT GOODIES, VOL. 3
❏ Original Sound LPM-5004 [M] — 1961 — 30.00
—*Original pressing with no reference to later volumes on the back cover*
❏ Original Sound LPM-5004 [M] — 1960s — 15.00
—*Later editions with later volumes in the series on the back cover*

OLDIES BUT GOODIES, VOL. 4
❏ Original Sound LPM-5005 [M] — 1962 — 30.00
—*Original pressing with no reference to later volumes on the back cover*
❏ Original Sound LPM-5005 [M] — 1960s — 15.00
—*Later editions with later volumes in the series on the back cover*

OLDIES BUT GOODIES, VOL. 5
❏ Original Sound LPM-5007 [M] — 1963 — 25.00
—*Original pressing with no reference to later volumes on the back cover*
❏ Original Sound LPM-5007 [M] — 1960s — 15.00
—*Later editions with later volumes in the series on the back cover*

OLDIES BUT GOODIES, VOL. 6
❏ Original Sound LPM-5011 [M] — 1963 — 25.00
—*Original pressing with no reference to later volumes on the back cover*
❏ Original Sound LPM-5011 [M] — 1960s — 15.00
—*Later editions with later volumes in the series on the back cover*

OLDIES BUT GOODIES, VOL. 7
❏ Original Sound LPM-5012 [M] — 1964 — 25.00
—*Original pressing with no reference to later volumes on the back cover*
❏ Original Sound LPM-5012 [M] — 1960s — 15.00
—*Later editions with later volumes in the series on the back cover*

OLDIES BUT GOODIES, VOL. 8
❏ Original Sound LPM-5014 [M] — 1966 — 18.00
—*Original pressing with no reference to later volumes on the back cover*
❏ Original Sound LPM-5014 [M] — 1960s — 12.00
—*Later editions with later volumes in the series on the back cover*

OLDIES BY THE DOZEN
❏ Parkway P-7035 [M] — 1963 — 30.00

OLDIES BY THE DOZEN, VOLUME 2
❏ Parkway P-7041 [M] — 1964 — 50.00
—*With bonus 45 of "The Twist" by Chubby Checker on on side and "Mashed Potato Time" by Dee Dee Sharp on the other; deduct 40 percent if missing*

OLDIES DANCE PARTY, VOLUME 1
❏ Oldies 33 OL-8001 [M] — 1963 — 25.00

OLDIES DANCE PARTY, VOLUME 2
❏ Oldies 33 OL-8002 [M] — 1963 — 25.00

OLDIES IN HI-FI
❏ Chess LP1439 [M] — 1959 — 300.00
—*Black vinyl*
❏ Chess LP1439 [DJ] — 1959 — 600.00
—*Multi-color splash vinyl*

OLD 'N GOLDEN
❏ Jamie JLPS-3031 — 1968 — 25.00

OLD TIME BANJO PROJECT
❏ Elektra EKL-276 [M] — 1964 — 25.00
❏ Elektra EKS-7276 [S] — 1964 — 30.00

OLEO
❏ Pausa 7025 — 198? — 12.00

OLIO
❏ Prestige PRLP-7084 [M] — 1957 — 250.00
—*Yellow label with W. 50th St. address*

O LOVE IS TEASIN': ANGLO-AMERICAN MOUNTAIN BALLADRY
❏ Elektra 60402 — 1985 — 25.00

ONE DOZEN GOLDIES
❏ Carlton LP 12-121 [M] — 1960 — 50.00

100 HALL OF FAME OLDIES
❏ Vee-Jay HHF-6833/4/5/6/7 — 197? — 100.00
—*Mail-order offer that was sent to buyers in a cardboard mailer; price includes mailer; no other cover was issued*

ONE NIGHT STAND: A KEYBOARD EVENT
❏ Columbia KC237100 — 198? — 15.00
—*"Half-Speed Mastered" edition*
❏ Columbia HC247100 — 198? — 50.00

ONE NIGHT WITH BLUE NOTE PRESERVED
❏ Blue Note BTDK-85117 — 1985 — 60.00

ONE NIGHT WITH BLUE NOTE PRESERVED, VOL. 1
❏ Blue Note BT-85113 — 1985 — 15.00

ONE NIGHT WITH BLUE NOTE PRESERVED, VOL. 2
❏ Blue Note BT-85114 — 1985 — 15.00

ONE NIGHT WITH BLUE NOTE PRESERVED, VOL. 3
❏ Blue Note BT-85115 — 1985 — 15.00

ONE NIGHT WITH BLUE NOTE PRESERVED, VOL. 4
❏ Blue Note BT-85116 — 1985 — 15.00
—*Box set containing all 4 volumes*

ONE WORLD JAZZ
❏ Adventures in Sound WL-162 [M] — 1959 — 50.00
❏ Adventures in Sound WS-314 [S] — 1959 — 40.00

ON STAGE AT THE GRAND OLE OPRY
❏ Decca DL4393 [M] — 1964 — 30.00
❏ Decca DL74393 [S] — 1964 — 30.00

ON THE FIRST DAY OF CHRISTMAS
❏ Columbia Special Products P15425 — 1980 — 12.00

ON-THE-ROAD JAZZ
❏ Riverside RLP 12-127 [M] — 1957 — 40.00

ON THE TRAIL
❏ Pausa 7024 — 198? — 12.00

ON THIS CHRISTMAS NIGHT
❏ Songbird MCA-3184 — 1979 — 18.00

ON THIS DAY EARTH SHALL RING…
❏ Hogeye HOG 007 — 1985 — 12.00

OPENING NIGHTS AT THE MET
❏ RCA Victor Red Seal LM-6171 [M] — 1966 — 25.00

OPERA FOR PEOPLE WHO HATE OPERA
❏ RCA Victor Red Seal LSC-2391 [S] — 1960 — 25.00
—*Original with "shaded dog" label*

OPRY OLD TIMERS
❏ Starday SLP-182 [M] — 1962 — 30.00

OPRY TIME IN TENNESSEE
❏ Starday SLP-177 [M] — 1962 — 30.00

OPUS DE BLUES
❏ Savoy MG-12142 [M] — 1959 — 60.00

OPUS DE JAZZ
❏ Savoy MG-12036 [M] — 1955 — 80.00

OPUS IN SWING
❏ Savoy MG-12085 [M] — 1956 — 60.00

THE ORCHESTRA "HOUSE OF SOUND
❏ Brunswick BL54003 [M] — 1954 — 30.00

THE ORGAN PLAYS MUSIC FOR A MERRY CHRISTMAS
❏ Reader's Digest RDA42-A — 1966 — 25.00
—*Available only through Reader's Digest magazine by mail order*

ORIGINAL BLUE NOTE JAZZ, VOL. 1
❏ Blue Note B-6504 — 1969 — 25.00

ORIGINAL BLUE NOTE JAZZ, VOL. 2
❏ Blue Note B-6506 — 1970 — 25.00

THE ORIGINAL COUNTRY HITS #1
❏ Liberty LRP-3305 [M] — 1963 — 25.00

THE ORIGINAL COUNTRY HITS #2
❏ Liberty LRP-3345 [M] — 1964 — 25.00

THE ORIGINAL COUNTRY HITS #3
❏ Liberty LRP-3382 [M] — 1964 — 25.00

ORIGINAL GOLDEN BLUES GREATS, VOL. 1
❏ Liberty LST-7572 [R] — 1968 — 15.00
—*Reissue of "The Original R&B Hits, Volume 1," Liberty 3381, in rechanneled stereo*

ORIGINAL GOLDEN COUNTRY GREATS, VOLUME 1
❏ Liberty LST-7569 [R] — 1968 — 15.00
—*Reissue of "The Original Country Hits #1," Liberty 3305, in rechanneled stereo*

ORIGINAL GOLDEN COUNTRY GREATS, VOLUME 2
❏ Liberty LST-7570 [R] — 1968 — 15.00
—*Reissue of "The Original Country Hits #2," Liberty 3345, in rechanneled stereo*

ORIGINAL GOLDEN COUNTRY GREATS, VOLUME 3
❏ Liberty LST-7571 [R] — 1968 — 15.00
—*Reissue of "The Original Country Hits #3," Liberty 3382, in rechanneled stereo*

Number	Title	Yr	NM

ORIGINAL GOLDEN GREATS, VOLUME 3
- ❑ Liberty LST-7573 [R] — 1968 — 15.00
— *Reissue of "The Original Hits, Volume 7," Liberty 3274, in rechanneled stereo*

ORIGINAL GOLDEN GREATS, VOLUME 4
- ❑ Liberty LST-7574 [R] — 1968 — 15.00
— *Only one track, "Surf City" by Jan and Dean, is true stereo*

ORIGINAL GOLDEN GREATS, VOLUME 5
- ❑ Liberty LST-7575 [R] — 1968 — 15.00
— *Three tracks are in true stereo: "Hurt" (Timi Yuro), "Tower of Strength" (Gene McDaniels) and "The Night Has a Thousand Eyes" (Bobby Vee)*

ORIGINAL GOLDEN GREATS, VOLUME 6
- ❑ Liberty LST-7576 [R] — 1968 — 15.00
— *Four tracks are in true stereo*

ORIGINAL GOLDEN GREATS, VOLUME 7
- ❑ Liberty LST-7577 [R] — 1968 — 15.00
— *Three tracks are in true stereo*

ORIGINAL GOLDEN GREATS, VOLUME 8
- ❑ Liberty LST-7578 [R] — 1968 — 15.00

ORIGINAL GOLDEN GREATS, VOLUME 9
- ❑ Liberty LST-7579 [R] — 1968 — 15.00

ORIGINAL GOLDEN GREATS, VOLUME 10
- ❑ Liberty LST-7619 — 1969 — 18.00

ORIGINAL GOLDIES FROM THE FABULOUS '50S, VOLUME 1
- ❑ Josie JM-4002 [M] — 1963 — 60.00

ORIGINAL GOLDIES FROM THE FABULOUS '50S, VOLUME 2
- ❑ Josie JM-4003 [M] — 1963 — 60.00

ORIGINAL GOLDIES FROM THE FABULOUS '50S, VOLUME 3
- ❑ Josie JM-4004 [M] — 1963 — 60.00

THE ORIGINAL GREATEST HITS OF THE GREAT COUNTRY AND WESTERN STARS
- ❑ Mercury MG-20825 [M] — 1963 — 25.00
- ❑ Mercury SR-60825 [S] — 1963 — 30.00

ORIGINAL HIT RECORDS
- ❑ Roulette R25106 [M] — 1960 — 30.00
— *Originals have a white label with colored spokes*

THE ORIGINAL HITS, PAST & PRESENT
- ❑ Liberty LRP-3178 [M] — 1960 — 25.00

THE ORIGINAL HITS, VOLUME 3: PAST & PRESENT
- ❑ Liberty LRP-3187 [M] — 1961 — 25.00

THE ORIGINAL HITS, VOLUME 4
- ❑ Liberty LRP-3200 [M] — 1962 — 25.00
— *Reissue of "Memories Are Made of Hits;" for "The Original Hits, Volume 5," see "15 Hits: The Original Recordings*

THE ORIGINAL HITS, VOLUME 6
- ❑ Liberty LRP-3260 [M] — 1962 — 25.00

THE ORIGINAL HITS, VOLUME 7: ALL-TIME HIT INSTRUMENTALS
- ❑ Liberty LRP-3274 [M] — 1963 — 25.00

THE ORIGINAL HITS, VOLUME 8
- ❑ Liberty LRP-3288 [M] — 1963 — 25.00

THE ORIGINAL HITS, VOLUME 9
- ❑ Liberty LRP-3325 [M] — 1963 — 25.00

THE ORIGINAL HITS, VOLUME 10
- ❑ Liberty LRP-3344 [M] — 1964 — 25.00

THE ORIGINAL HITS, VOLUME 11
- ❑ Liberty LRP-3418 [M] — 1965 — 25.00
- ❑ Liberty LST-7418 [P] — 1965 — 25.00

THE ORIGINAL HITS, VOLUME TWO: PAST & PRESENT
- ❑ Liberty LRP-3180 [M] — 1961 — 25.00

THE ORIGINAL HOOTENANNY
- ❑ Crestview CRV806 [M] — 1963 — 25.00
- ❑ Crestview CRS7806 [S] — 1963 — 30.00

ORIGINAL MEMPHIS ROCK AND ROLL, VOLUME 1
- ❑ Sun 116 — 1974 — 25.00

ORIGINAL MOTION PICTURE HIT THEMES
- ❑ United Artists UAL-3197 [M] — 1962 — 18.00
- ❑ United Artists UAS-6197 [S] — 1962 — 25.00

THE ORIGINAL R&B HITS, VOLUME 1
- ❑ Liberty LRP-3381 [M] — 1964 — 25.00

ORIGINAL RECORDINGS BY THE ARTISTS WHO MADE THEM HITS
- ❑ Flip 1002 [M] — 1960 — 400.00

ORIGINAL ROCK OLDIES, VOLUME 1
- ❑ Specialty SPS-2129 — 1970 — 25.00

ORIGINAL ROCK OLDIES, VOLUME 2
- ❑ Specialty SPS-2130 — 1970 — 25.00

THE ORIGINAL SOUND OF THE 20'S
- ❑ Columbia C3L35 — 1965 — 40.00

ORIGINAL SURFIN' HITS
- ❑ GNP Crescendo GNP-84 [M] — 1963 — 40.00
— *With bonus photos; deduct 25-50 percent if missing*
- ❑ GNP Crescendo GNPS-84 [S] — 1963 — 50.00
— *With bonus photos; deduct 25-50 percent if missing*

OUR BEST
- ❑ Clef MGC-639 [M] — 1955 — 50.00
- ❑ Norgran MGN-1021 [M] — 1955 — 80.00

OUR BEST TO YOU
- ❑ Everlast ELP-201 [M] — 1960 — 200.00

OUR SIGNIFICANT HITS
- ❑ Specialty SP-2112 [M] — 1960 — 120.00
— *Gold and black label*

OUR SINGING HERITAGE, VOL. 1
- ❑ Elektra EKL-151 [M] — 1958 — 30.00

OUR SINGING HERITAGE, VOL. 2
- ❑ Elektra EKL-152 [M] — 1958 — 30.00

OUT CAME THE BLUES
- ❑ MCA 1352 — 198? — 12.00

OUTSTANDING JAZZ COMPOSITIONS OF THE 20TH CENTURY
- ❑ Columbia C2L31 [M] — 1964 — 25.00

PABLO ALL-STARS JAM: MONTREUX '77
- ❑ Fantasy OJC-380 — 1989 — 12.00
- ❑ Pablo Live 2308210 — 197? — 18.00

A PACKAGE OF 16 BIG HITS
- ❑ Motown MT614 [M] — 1964 — 100.00
— *"Package" cover*
- ❑ Motown MT614 [M] — 1966 — 25.00
— *No "package" on cover*
- ❑ Motown MS614 [S] — 1966 — 30.00
— *No "package" on cover; contains alternate stereo versions of "Please Mr. Postman" by the Marvelettes and "Do You Love Me" by the Contours*

PAJAMA PARTY
- ❑ Forum F-9006 [M] — 196? — 30.00
— *Reissue of Roulette 25021*
- ❑ Forum SF-9006 [R] — 196? — 25.00
- ❑ Roulette R25021 [M] — 1958 — 40.00
— *Originals have a black label*
- ❑ Roulette R25021 [M] — 1959 — 30.00
— *Second pressings have a white label with colored spokes*
- ❑ Roulette SR25021 [R] — 196? — 15.00

PANORAMA OF BRITISH JAZZ
- ❑ Discovery DL-2001 [10] — 1953 — 50.00

PARAMOUNT CORNET BLUES RARITIES CHICAGO 1924-27
- ❑ Herwin 111 — 197? — 15.00

PARAMOUNT HOT JAZZ RARITIES 1926-28
- ❑ Herwin 110 — 197? — 15.00

PARLOR PIANO: BLUES AND STOMPS
- ❑ Biograph 1001 — 197? — 12.00

PARTY AFTER HOURS
- ❑ Aladdin LP-703 [10] — 1950 — 8000.00
— *Red vinyl*
- ❑ Aladdin LP-703 [10] — 1950 — 4000.00
— *Black vinyl*

PEACE ON EARTH
- ❑ Capitol S?B?-585 — 1970 — 18.00

PEACHES: "PICK OF THE CROP
- ❑ Capricorn PRO588 — 1974 — 30.00

THE PEOPLE'S RECORD
- ❑ Warner Bros. PRO645 — 1976 — 25.00

PERCUSSION PROFILES
- ❑ ECM 19002 — 1977 — 15.00

PERCUSSION UNABRIDGED
- ❑ Kimberly 2022 [M] — 1963 — 25.00
- ❑ Kimberly 11022 [S] — 1963 — 30.00

PERFECT FOR DANCING: ALL TEMPOS
- ❑ RCA Victor LPM-1072 [M] — 1954 — 30.00

PERFECT FOR DANCING: FOX TROTS
- ❑ RCA Victor LPM-1070 [M] — 1954 — 30.00

PERFECT FOR DANCING: JITTERBUG OR LINDY
- ❑ RCA Victor LPM-1071 [M] — 1954 — 30.00

PERIOD'S JAZZ DIGEST
- ❑ Period SPL-302 [M] — 1956 — 50.00

PERIOD'S JAZZ DIGEST VOL. 2
- ❑ Period SPL-304 [M] — 1955 — 50.00

PETAL PUSHERS
- ❑ Chess LP1520 [M] — 1967 — 30.00
- ❑ Chess LPS1520 [S] — 1967 — 30.00

THE PHILCO ALBUM OF HOLIDAY MUSIC
- ❑ Columbia Special Products CSM431 — 1966 — 18.00
— *Sold only at Philco dealers*

PHIL SPECTOR: BACK TO MONO 1958-1969
- ❑ Phil Spector/Abkco 7118-1 [B] — 1991 — 120.00
— *Box set; Sides 9 and 10 are the final vinyl reissue of A Christmas Gift for You from Phil Spector*

PHIL SPECTOR'S CHRISTMAS ALBUM
- ❑ Apple SW3400 [M] — 1972 — 30.00
— *Reissue of A CHRSTMAS GIFT FOR YOU FROM PHILLES RECORDS; third edition of this group of songs; completely different cover with Phil Spector dressed as Santa Claus and wearing a "Back to Mono" button*
- ❑ Passport PB3604 [S] — 1984 — 15.00
— *Sixth edition of this group of songs; Phil Spector-as-Santa Claus' "Back to Mono" button is airbrushed off the cover; the last version of this LP to appear in true stereo*
- ❑ Pavillion PZ37686 [S] — 1981 — 18.00
— *Fifth edition of this group of songs; Phil Spector-as-Santa Claus' "Back to Mono" button is airbrushed off the cover; once again, this LP is true stereo*
- ❑ Warner/Spector SP9103 [S] — 1974 — 25.00
— *Fourth edition of this group of songs; similar cover to third edition; despite the cover's "Authentic Mono" statement and Phil Spector-as-Santa Claus' "Back to Mono" button, this album is in true stereo!*

PHIL SPECTOR'S GREATEST HITS
- ❑ Warner/Spector 2SP9104 — 1977 — 40.00

THE PHIL SPECTOR SPECTACULAR
- ❑ Philles PHLP100 [DJ] — 1972 — 1500.00
— *Not issued with cover*

PIANISTS GALORE
- ❑ Pacific Jazz JWC-506 [M] — 1957 — 50.00
- ❑ World Pacific JWC-506 [M] — 1958 — 40.00

PIANO ARTISTRY
- ❑ Audiophile AP-28 [M] — 1953 — 30.00

PIANO GIANTS
- ❑ Prestige 24052 — 197? — 18.00

PIANO IN STYLE
- ❑ MCA 1332 — 198? — 12.00

PIANO INTERPRETATIONS
- ❑ Norgran MGN-1036 [M] — 1955 — 80.00
- ❑ Verve MGV-8125 [M] — 1957 — 30.00
- ❑ Verve V-8125 [M] — 1961 — 25.00

PIANO JAZZ, VOLUME 1
- ❑ Brunswick BL54014 [M] — 1955 — 30.00

PIANO JAZZ, VOLUME 2
- ❑ Brunswick BL54015 [M] — 1955 — 30.00

PIANO MODERN
- ❑ Verve VSP-13 [M] — 1966 — 18.00
- ❑ Verve VSPS-13 [M] — 1966 — 12.00

PIANO MUSIC FOR PARTIES
- ❑ Columbia CL603 [M] — 1955 — 30.00

PIANO MUSIC FOR TWO
- ❑ Columbia CL602 [M] — 1955 — 30.00

PIANO ONE
- ❑ Private Music 2004-1-P — 1986 — 12.00

THE PIANO PLAYERS
- ❑ Xanadu 171 — 197? — 15.00

PIANO RAGTIME OF THE FORTIES
- ❑ Herwin 403 — 197? — 15.00

PIANO RAGTIME OF THE TEENS, TWENTIES AND THIRTIES
- ❑ Herwin 402 — 197? — 15.00

PIANO RAGTIME OF THE TEENS, TWENTIES AND THIRTIES, VOL. 2
- ❑ Herwin 405 — 197? — 15.00

PIANO RAGTIME OF THE TEENS, TWENTIES AND THIRTIES, VOL. 3
- ❑ Herwin 406 — 197? — 15.00

PIANO ROLL HALL OF FAME
- ❑ Sounds 1202 — 196? — 15.00

PIANO ROLL TRANSCRIPTIONS
- ❑ Riverside RLP 12-110 [M] — 1956 — 40.00
- ❑ Riverside RLP 12-126 [M] — 1957 — 40.00

PIANO STYLISTS
- ❑ Capitol H323 [10] — 1952 — 50.00

PIANO TWO
- ❑ Private Music 2027-1-P — 1988 — 12.00

PICK HITS OF THE RADIO GOOD GUYS
- ❑ Laurie LLP-2021 [M] — 1963 — 30.00
- ❑ Laurie SLP-2021 [R] — 196? — 18.00

PICK HITS OF THE RADIO GOOD GUYS, VOLUME 2
- ❑ Laurie LLP-2026 [M] — 1964 — 30.00
- ❑ Laurie SLP-2026 [R] — 196? — 18.00

Number	Title	Yr	NM

PICK OF THE COUNTRY
- ❏ RCA Victor LPM-2094 [M] — 1960 — 30.00
- ❏ RCA Victor LSP-2094 [S] — 1960 — 30.00

THE PICK OF THE COUNTRY, VOLUME 2
- ❏ RCA Victor LPM-2956 [M] — 1964 — 25.00
- ❏ RCA Victor LSP-2956(e) [R] — 1964 — 18.00

PICK UP THE BEAT
- ❏ Epic LN3127 [M] — 1955 — 30.00

PIONEERS OF BOOGIE WOOGIE
- ❏ Riverside RLP-1009 [10] — 1953 — 80.00

PIONEERS OF BOOGIE WOOGIE, VOL. 2
- ❏ Riverside RLP-1034 [10] — 1954 — 80.00

PIONEERS OF THE JAZZ GUITAR
- ❏ Yazoo 1057 — 197? — 12.00

PITTSBURGH'S GREATEST HITS
- ❏ Itzy 101 — 1966 — 50.00

PLAYBOY ALL STARS VOLUME 1
- ❏ Playboy PB-1957 [M] — 1957 — 40.00

PLAYBOY ALL STARS VOLUME 2
- ❏ Playboy PB-1958 [M] — 1958 — 40.00

PLAYBOY ALL STARS VOLUME 3
- ❏ Playboy PB-1959 [M] — 1959 — 60.00

PLAYBOY MUSIC HALL OF FAME WINNERS
- ❏ Playboy PB-7473 — 1978 — 200.00
- — One of very few compilation LPs to contain both an Elvis and a Beatles track!

THE PLAYERS' ASSOCIATION
- ❏ Vanguard VSD-79384 — 197? — 15.00

PLAZA HOUSE PRESENTS MUSIC HALL
- ❏ Capitol Creative Products SL-6719 — 1971 — 15.00
- — One side by Merle Haggard; one side by Sonny James

PLENTY GOOD MUSIC
- ❏ Capitol SPRO9937 [DJ] — 1983 — 15.00
- — Includes The Tubes, Duran Duran

POLKAS
- ❏ Audio Lab AL-1543 [M] — 1959 — 40.00

POLYDOR DANCE CLASSICS -- BRITISH EDITION
- ❏ Polydor 885004-1 — 1986 — 18.00
- — Includes Level 42, Visage

POLYGRAM RADIO INSTORE SAMPLER
- ❏ Polygram 051 [DJ] — 1983 — 15.00
- — Includes Big Country, The Style Council

POP COUNTRY HITS
- ❏ RCA Victor LPM-2949 [M] — 1964 — 18.00
- ❏ RCA Victor LSP-2949 [S] — 1964 — 25.00

POP HIT PARTY
- ❏ Columbia CL1237 [M] — 195? — 25.00

POP ORIGINS
- ❏ Chess LP1544 [M] — 1969 — 30.00

POP PARADE
- ❏ MGM E-194 [10] — 1953 — 50.00

POP SHOPPER
- ❏ RCA Victor SPL-12/13 [M] — 1955 — 30.00

POPULAR CHRISTMAS CLASSICS
- ❏ Capitol Special Markets SL-8100 — 1977 — 15.00

POPULAR FAVORITES
- ❏ Columbia CL6057 [10] — 1949 — 40.00

THE POPULAR GOLD ALBUM
- ❏ Capitol T972 [M] — 1958 — 30.00

PORGY AND BESS
- ❏ Bethlehem EXLP-1 [M] — 1956 — 70.00
- ❏ Bethlehem BCP-6040 [M] — 1959 — 30.00

PORTRAITS IN JAZZ
- ❏ Reprise R-6084 [M] — 1963 — 15.00
- ❏ Reprise R9-6084 [S] — 1963 — 18.00

THE POSSE, CHAPTER 2
- ❏ Macola 1080 — 1988 — 15.00
- — Includes Ice-T, Digital Underground

POT, SPOON, PIPE AND JUG
- ❏ Stash ST-102 — 197? — 12.00

A POT OF FLOWERS
- ❏ Mainstream S-6100 [S] — 1967 — 100.00
- ❏ Mainstream 56100 [M] — 1967 — 80.00

POT OF GOLDEN GOODIES
- ❏ Herald HLP-1015 [M] — 1962 — 150.00

A POTPOURRI OF JAZZ
- ❏ Verve MGV-2032 [M] — 1956 — 40.00
- ❏ Verve V-2032 [M] — 1961 — 25.00

POWER, GLORY AND MUSIC
- ❏ Salvation 1000 — 197? — 18.00

THE POWER AND THE MAJESTY: RAIN 'N' TRAIN DEMONSTRATION DISC
- ❏ Mobile Fidelity 1-004 — 1979 — 50.00
- — Audiophile vinyl

PRESTIGE CLASSIC JAM SESSIONS, VOL. 1
- ❏ Prestige 24107 — 198? — 18.00

PRESTIGE GROOVY GOODIES, VOL. 1
- ❏ Prestige PRLP-7298 [M] — 1964 — 30.00
- ❏ Prestige PRST-7298 [R] — 1964 — 25.00

PRESTIGE SOUL MASTERPIECES
- ❏ Fantasy OJC-1201 — 1988 — 15.00

PRESTIGE TWOFER GIANTS, VOL. 1
- ❏ Prestige PRP-1 — 197? — 18.00

PRESTIGE TWOFER GIANTS, VOL. 2
- ❏ Prestige PRP-2 — 197? — 18.00

PRIMITIVE PIANO
- ❏ Tone 1 [M] — 195? — 30.00

THE PRINCE'S TRUST 10TH ANNIVERSARY BIRTHDAY PARTY
- ❏ A&M SP-3906 — 1987 — 12.00
- — Includes Howard Jones ("No One Is to Blame"), Midge Ure, Big Country, Level 42
- ❏ A&M R144451 — 1987 — 18.00
- — Same as SP-3906; BMG Direct Marketing edition

PROGRESSIVE PIANO
- ❏ RCA Victor LJM-3001 [10] — 1952 — 50.00

THE PROGRESSIVE RECORDS ALL STAR TENOR SAX SPECTACULAR
- ❏ Progressive PRO-7019 — 1978 — 15.00

THE PROGRESSIVE RECORDS ALL STAR TROMBONE SPECTACULAR
- ❏ Progressive PRO-7018 — 1978 — 15.00

THE PROGRESSIVE RECORDS ALL STAR TRUMPET SPECTACULAR
- ❏ Progressive PRO-7015 — 1978 — 15.00

THE PROGRESSIVE RECORDS ALL STAR TRUMPET SPECTACULAR, VOL. 2
- ❏ Progressive PRO-7017 — 1978 — 15.00

THE PROGRESSIVES
- ❏ Columbia KG31574 — 1973 — 25.00
- ❏ Columbia CG31574 — 197? — 15.00
- — "CG" prefix is a reissue of "KG"

PROPAGANDA
- ❏ A&M SP-4786 — 1979 — 25.00
- — Includes poster

PUMPING VINYL
- ❏ Warner Bros. PRO-A-773 — 1977 — 25.00

PUNK AND DISORDERLY
- ❏ Posh Boy PBS-131 — 1982 — 18.00
- — Includes Dead Kennedys, more

PURE MAGIC: THE SONGS OF PAM SAWYER & MARILYN MCLEOD
- ❏ Jobete PRO-1A [DJ] — 1978 — 40.00
- — Promo-only publisher's demo with short excerpts of songs

QSP PRESENTS A GIFT OF MUSIC
- ❏ RCA Special Products QSP1-0034 — 1984 — 50.00

QUAD CITY ALL-STAR CHRISTMAS
- ❏ Big Beat 82970 — 1996 — 15.00

QUEENS OF COUNTRY
- ❏ Columbia KC32719 — 1974 — 15.00

RADAR BLUES
- ❏ King KLP-1050 [M] — 1969 — 30.00

RADIO RADIO/SOUL TWIST/YOU'VE GOTTA BE CRUEL TO BE KIND
- ❏ Columbia AS443 [DJ] — 1979 — 40.00
- — Includes Elvis Costello, Mink DeVille, Nick Lowe; promo-only 3-song sampler on orange vinyl

RADIO SMASH FLASHBACKS: DRIVE TIME
- ❏ Laurie LLP-2028 [M] — 1964 — 30.00
- ❏ Laurie SLP-2028 [R] — 196? — 18.00

RADIO SMASH FLASHBACKS: PRIME TIME
- ❏ Laurie LLP-2029 [M] — 1964 — 30.00
- ❏ Laurie SLP-2029 [R] — 196? — 18.00

RADIO TOKYO TAPES, VOL. 2
- ❏ Enigma E1086 — 1984 — 15.00

RADIO TOKYO TAPES, VOL. 3
- ❏ PVC 8931 — 1985 — 15.00
- — Includes Minutemen, Henry Rollins

RADIO U.
- ❏ Epic AS1742 [DJ] — 1983 — 15.00
- — Includes Cyndi Lauper, Altered Images, Nena, etc.

RAGTIME PIANO ROLL, VOL. 1
- ❏ Riverside RLP-1006 [10] — 1953 — 100.00

RAGTIME PIANO ROLL, VOL. 2
- ❏ Riverside RLP-1025 [10] — 1954 — 80.00

RAGTIME PIANO ROLL, VOL. 3
- ❏ Riverside RLP-1049 [10] — 1954 — 80.00

RAGTIMERS' IMMORTAL PERFORMANCES
- ❏ RCA Victor LPT-1000 [M] — 1954 — 30.00

RAILROAD SONGS
- ❏ King 869 [M] — 1963 — 70.00

RAINY DAY
- ❏ Enigma E1024 — 1983 — 15.00
- — Includes Susanna Hoffs (early solo track)

RAMBLIN' COUNTRY
- ❏ Columbia Special Products P12484 — 1974 — 15.00

RARE BANDS OF THE 20S, VOL. 1
- ❏ Historical ASC-3 — 1966 — 15.00

RARE BANDS OF THE 20S, VOL. 2
- ❏ Historical ASC-6 — 1966 — 15.00

RARE BANDS OF THE 20S, VOL. 3
- ❏ Historical ASC-7 — 1966 — 15.00

RARE HOT CHICAGO JAZZ
- ❏ Herwin 109 — 197? — 15.00

RARE VERTICAL JAZZ
- ❏ Historical ASC-8 — 1966 — 15.00

RAREWERKS
- ❏ Astralwerks ASW50717 — 2001 — 25.00

RAT MUSIC FOR RAT PEOPLE
- ❏ Go 003 — 1982 — 25.00

REACH OUT AND TOUCH
- ❏ Reader's Digest RBA-037A — 1991 — 50.00

THE REAL AMBASSADORS
- ❏ Columbia CL5850 [M] — 1962 — 25.00
- ❏ Columbia OS2250 [S] — 1902 — 30.00

THE REAL BLUES
- ❏ Excello LPS-8011 [R] — 1969 — 25.00

REBIRTH OF BEALE STREET
- ❏ Beale Street BS-1 — 1983 — 200.00
- — Limited edition of 1,000 made for the city of Memphis

RECORDED IN NEW ORLEANS, VOL. 1
- ❏ Good Time Jazz L-12019 [M] — 1955 — 25.00

RECORDED IN NEW ORLEANS, VOL. 2
- ❏ Good Time Jazz L-12020 [M] — 1955 — 25.00

RECORDED ON LOCATION AT THE FIVE SPOT CAFE IN NEW YORK CITY...A MEMORIAL CONCERT DEDICATED TO THE MUSIC OF CHARLIE PARKER
- ❏ Signal S-1204 [M] — 1957 — 200.00

RECORD HOP
- ❏ Decca DL8067 [M] — 1955 — 30.00

RED BIRD GOLDIES
- ❏ Red Bird LP 20-102 [M] — 1965 — 80.00

RED HOT & BOTHERED 1
- ❏ Kinetic/Reprise 45954 [10] — 1995 — 12.00
- — With booklet "The Indie Rock Guide to Dating"; limited edition of 5,000

RED HOT & BOTHERED 2
- ❏ Kinetic/Reprise 45982 [10] — 1995 — 12.00
- — With booklet "The Indie Rock Guide to Dating 2"; limited edition of 5,000

RED HOT AND BLUE JAZZ
- ❏ Waldorf Music Hall MH 33-141 [10] — 195? — 200.00

REEFER SONGS
- ❏ Stash ST-100 — 197? — 18.00

A REGGAE CHRISTMAS
- ❏ Real Authentic Sound RAS3101 — 1984 — 15.00

REGGAE CHRISTMAS BY THE JOE GIBBS FAMILY OF ARTISTS
- ❏ Joe Gibbs Music 8077 — 1982 — 25.00

RELAXED SAXOPHONE MOODS
- ❏ Prestige PRLP-141 [10] — 1953 — 100.00

REMEMBER HOW GREAT, VOLUME 1
- ❏ Roulette SR42027 [R] — 1968 — 15.00

REMEMBER HOW GREAT, VOLUME 2
- ❏ Roulette SR42028 [R] — 1968 — 15.00

REMEMBER HOW GREAT, VOLUME 3
- ❏ Roulette SR42029 [R] — 1968 — 15.00

REMEMBER HOW GREAT, VOLUME 4
- ❏ Roulette SR42031 [R] — 1969 — 15.00

REMEMBER HOW GREAT, VOLUME 5
- ❏ Roulette SR42032 [R] — 1969 — 15.00

Number	Title	Yr	NM

REMEMBERING CHRISTMAS WITH THE BIG BANDS
- ❏ RCA Special Products DPM1-0506 [M] — 1981 — 15.00

REMEMBER THE OLDIES
- ❏ Argo LP-649 [M] — 1963 — 40.00
- ❏ Argo LP-649 [M] — 1963 — 400.00
— *Multi-color splash vinyl; white label promo*

REPRISE ALL STAR SPECTACULAR!
- ❏ Reprise R-6028 [M] — 1962 — 40.00

REQUESTED BY YOU
- ❏ Columbia CL607 [M] — 1955 — 30.00

RESTLESS VARIATIONS
- ❏ Restless 72101 — 1985 — 15.00
— *Includes The Dead Milkmen, Mojo Nixon and Skid Roper, etc.*

RETAIL IN-STORE SAMPLER
- ❏ Columbia AS1912 [DJ] — 1984 — 12.00
— *Includes Elvis Costello, Bangles, Dave Edmunds*

REVENGE OF THE KILLER B'S
- ❏ Warner Bros. 25068 — 1984 — 12.00
— *Includes Madonna ("Ain't No Big Deal"), The B-52's, The Pretenders, Marshall Crenshaw, Aztec Camera, Echo and the Bunnymen*

RFD CHRISTMAS
- ❏ Columbia Special Products P15427 — 1981 — 12.00

RHYTHM & BLUES
- ❏ RCA Camden CAL-371 [M] — 1958 — 30.00

RHYTHM & BLUES CHRISTMAS
- ❏ United Artists UA-LA654-R — 1976 — 15.00

RHYTHM, BLUES AND BOOGIE-WOOGIE
- ❏ Decca DL4011 [M] — 1960 — 30.00

RHYTHM AND BLUES
- ❏ Savoy MG-15008 [10] — 1952 — 80.00

RHYTHM PLUS ONE
- ❏ Epic LN3297 [M] — 1956 — 30.00

THE RHYTHM SECTION
- ❏ Epic LN3271 [M] — 1956 — 30.00

RICHARD NADER/LET THE GOOD TIMES ROLL
- ❏ Bell 9002 — 1973 — 25.00

RIDIN' IN RHYTHM
- ❏ Swing SW-8453/4 — 198? — 15.00

RINGSIDE AT CONDON'S
- ❏ Savoy MG-15029 [10] — 1954 — 80.00

RINGSIDE AT CONDON'S VOL. 2
- ❏ Savoy MG-15030 [10] — 1954 — 80.00

RIVERBOAT JAZZ
- ❏ Brunswick BL58026 [10] — 1951 — 50.00

RIVERSIDE DRIVE
- ❏ Riverside RLP 12-267 [M] — 1958 — 30.00

RIVERSIDE MODERN JAZZ SAMPLER
- ❏ Riverside S-3 [M] — 1956 — 40.00

THE ROARING 20'S
- ❏ Saydisc SDL-344 — 198? — 12.00
— *Compilation of seven versions of the title song, released not long after the movie of the same name*

ROBERT W. SARNOFF -- 25 YEARS OF RCA LEADERSHIP
- ❏ RCA Victor RWS-0001 [DJ] — 1973 — 2000.00
— *Souvenir record handed out at Sarnoff's retirement party; VG value 1000; VG+ value 1500*

ROCK & ROLL FOREVER
- ❏ Atlantic 1239 [M] — 1956 — 150.00

ROCK & ROLL WITH RHYTHM & BLUES
- ❏ Aladdin LP-710 [M] — 195? — 1500.00

ROCK 80
- ❏ K-Tel TU2780 — 1980 — 12.00
— *Includes Gary Numan, Pretenders, Sniff 'N' The Tears, Nick Lowe, Joe Jackson, Blondie, The Ramones, The Knack, Ian Gomm, M*

ROCK-A-BALLADS
- ❏ Cadence CLP-3041 [M] — 1960 — 40.00

ROCK-A-HITS
- ❏ Cadence CLP-3042 [M] — 1960 — 40.00

ROCK AND ROLL: THE EARLY DAYS
- ❏ RCA Victor AFM1-5463 — 1985 — 25.00

ROCK AND ROLL BANDSTAND
- ❏ Roulette R25093 [M] — 1959 — 30.00
— *Originals have a white label with colored spokes*

ROCK AND ROLL CHRISTMAS
- ❏ Ace 2040 — 198? — 15.00

ROCK AND ROLL DANCE PARTY
- ❏ King 536 [M] — 1956 — 300.00
- ❏ RPM LRP-3001 — 195? — 500.00

ROCK AND ROLL RECORD HOP
- ❏ Roulette R25059 [M] — 1959 — 30.00
— *Originals have a white label with colored spokes*

ROCK AND ROLL REVUE, VOLUME 2
- ❏ King 654 [M] — 1959 — 150.00

ROCK AND ROLL VS. RHYTHM AND BLUES
- ❏ Dooto DTL-223 [M] — 1957 — 100.00

ROCK AT THE EDGE
- ❏ Arista R114791 — 1986 — 15.00
— *Includes Patti Smith Group, Iggy Pop, Blondie, Lou Reed...*
- ❏ Arista AL8436 — 1986 — 12.00
— *Includes Patti Smith Group, Iggy Pop, Blondie, Lou Reed., Television, Ian Dury, Richard Hell, Graham Parker*

A ROCKIN' CHRISTMAS
- ❏ Columbia Special Products P12445 — 1974 — 18.00

ROCKIN' CHRISTMAS -- THE '50S
- ❏ Rhino RNLP-066 — 1984 — 18.00

ROCKIN' CHRISTMAS -- THE '60S
- ❏ Rhino RNLP-067 — 198? — 18.00
— *Sold by Elder Beerman Stores in the Dayton, Ohio area*

A ROCKING CHRISTMAS STOCKING
- ❏ Capitol SPRO9303/4/5/6 [DJ] — 1984 — 25.00

ROCKIN' LITTLE CHRISTMAS
- ❏ MCA 25084 — 1986 — 18.00
- ❏ MCA R154275 — 1986 — 18.00
— *Same as above, but BMG Music Service edition*

ROCKIN' SLUMBER PARTY
- ❏ Famous LP-501 [M] — 1961 — 30.00

ROCKIN' TOGETHER
- ❏ Atco 33-103 [M] — 1958 — 100.00

ROCK N' ROLL JAMBOREE
- ❏ End LP-302 [M] — 1959 — 120.00
— *Second cover and title with puppet and a guitar*

ROCK 'N' ROLL SOCK HOP
- ❏ Score SLP-4018 [M] — 1958 — 200.00

ROCK-O-RAMA
- ❏ Abkco AB4222 — 1972 — 25.00

ROCK-O-RAMA, VOLUME 2
- ❏ Abkco AB4223 — 1972 — 25.00

ROCK'S GREATEST HITS
- ❏ Columbia GP11 — 1969 — 25.00

RODGERS AND HART GEMS
- ❏ Pacific Jazz JWC-504 [M] — 1956 — 50.00
- ❏ World Pacific JWC-504 [M] — 1958 — 40.00

RODNEY ON THE 'ROQ
- ❏ Posh Boy PBA-106 — 1980 — 15.00
— *Includes Black Flag, lots of others; with special edition of Flipside, a fanzine (add 50% if magazine is included)*

RODNEY ON THE 'ROQ, VOL. 2
- ❏ Posh Boy PBS-123 — 1981 — 18.00
— *Includes Black Flag, Minutemen, Red Cross (Redd Kross), etc.; with special edition of Flipside (#28) (add 50%)*

THE ROMANTICS AND FRIENDS: MIDWEST POP EXPLOSION
- ❏ Quark CATCH3 — 1981 — 18.00
— *Includes The Romantics, Stiv Bators*

RONCO PRESENTS A CHRISTMAS GIFT
- ❏ Ronco/CSP P12430 — 1974 — 18.00
— *Gatefold with pop-up manger scene*

RONCO PRESENTS A CHRISTMAS PRESENT
- ❏ Ronco/CSP P11772 — 1973 — 18.00
— *Gatefold with pop-up North Pole scene*

ROOST 5TH ANNIVERSARY ALBUM
- ❏ Roost RST-1201 [M] — 1955 — 50.00

ROOTS OF BRITISH ROCK
- ❏ Sire SASH-3711 — 1975 — 25.00

THE ROOTS OF DIXIELAND JAZZ
- ❏ Everest Archive of Folk & Jazz 274 — 197? — 12.00

THE ROOTS OF DIXIELAND JAZZ, VOL. 2
- ❏ Everest Archive of Folk & Jazz 320 — 198? — 12.00

ROULETTE PRESENTS A DEMONSTRATION OF THE NEW DIMENSIONAL SOUND OF DYNAMIC STEREO
- ❏ Roulette SR-100 [S] — 1958 — 30.00

'ROUND MIDNIGHT
- ❏ Milestone M-9144 — 1986 — 15.00

RUMBLE
- ❏ Jubilee JGM-1114 [M] — 1959 — 150.00

SAMPLER III
- ❏ American Gramaphone AG-366 — 1984 — 15.00

SATURDAY MORNING -- CARTOONS' GREATEST HITS
- ❏ MCA 11348 — 1995 — 15.00
— *Includes Liz Phair, Matthew Sweet, Collective Soul, Butthole Surfers, The Ramones, Reverend Horton Heat, Violent Femmes, etc.*

SATURDAY NIGHT AT THE UPTOWN
- ❏ Atlantic 8101 [M] — 1964 — 30.00
- ❏ Atlantic SD8101 [S] — 1964 — 30.00

SATURDAY NIGHT FUNCTION: RURAL BLUES, VOLUME 2
- ❏ Imperial LP-94001 — 1968 — 25.00

SATURDAY NIGHT GRAND OLE OPRY
- ❏ Decca DL4303 [M] — 1962 — 30.00
- ❏ Decca DL74303 [S] — 1962 — 30.00

SATURDAY NIGHT GRAND OLE OPRY, VOL. 2
- ❏ Decca DL4539 [M] — 1964 — 25.00
- ❏ Decca DL74539 [S] — 1964 — 30.00

SATURDAY NIGHT GRAND OLE OPRY, VOL. 3
- ❏ Decca DL4671 [M] — 1965 — 25.00
- ❏ Decca DL74671 [S] — 1965 — 30.00

SATURDAY NIGHT MOOD
- ❏ Columbia CL599 [M] — 1954 — 30.00

SATURDAY NIGHT POGO
- ❏ Rhino RNLP 003 — 1978 — 18.00
— *Includes Motels, other L.A. bands*

SAXES, INC.
- ❏ Warner Bros. W1336 [M] — 1959 — 50.00
- ❏ Warner Bros. WS1336 [S] — 1959 — 80.00

SAX GREATS
- ❏ Everest Archive of Folk & Jazz 331 — 198? — 12.00

SAXOMANIAC
- ❏ Apollo LP-477 [M] — 1958 — 100.00

THE SAXOPHONE
- ❏ ABC Impulse! AS-9253 — 197? — 25.00

SAXOPHONE REVOLT
- ❏ Riverside RLP 12-284 [M] — 1958 — 150.00

THE SAX SECTION
- ❏ Epic LN3278 [M] — 1956 — 40.00

SAX STYLISTS
- ❏ Capitol H328 [10] — 1952 — 50.00

SCHLAGERS!
- ❏ Warner Bros. PRO359 — 1970 — 30.00
— *Originals have green labels*

SEASON'S GREETINGS FROM BARBRA STREISAND...AND FRIENDS
- ❏ Columbia Special Products CSS1075 — 1969 — 25.00
— *Created exclusively for Maxwell House Coffee*

SECOND SESSION AT SQUIRREL'S
- ❏ Paramount LP-108 [10] — 1954 — 60.00

THE SECRET POLICEMAN'S OTHER BALL
- ❏ Island ILPS9698 — 1982 — 15.00
— *Includes Sting ("Message in a Bottle"), Bob Geldof ("I Don't Like Mondays")*

THE SECRET POLICEMAN'S THIRD BALL
- ❏ Virgin 90643 — 1987 — 15.00
— *Includes Kate Bush, Duran Duran, Lou Reed, Bob Geldof, Erasure, Peter Gabriel (live recordings)*

SEIZE THE BEAT
- ❏ Ze ILPS-9667 — 1981 — 15.00
— *Includes Kid Creole and the Coconuts (i.e., Don Armando's 2nd Avenue Rumba Band), Was (Not Was)*

SELECTIONS FROM APRIL 1956 ALBUMS FOR RADIO-TV PROGRAM USE
- ❏ Capitol PRO-252/3 [DJ] — 1956 — 40.00

SELECTIONS FROM FEBRUARY 1956 POPULAR ALBUMS FOR RADIO-TV PROGRAM USE
- ❏ Capitol PRO-240/1 [DJ] — 1956 — 40.00

SELECTIONS FROM JANUARY 1956 ALBUMS FOR RADIO-TV PROGRAM USE
- ❏ Capitol PRO-238/9 [DJ] — 1956 — 40.00

SELECTIONS FROM MARCH 1956 ALBUMS FOR RADIO-TV PROGRAM USE
- ❏ Capitol PRO-246/7 [DJ] — 1956 — 40.00

SELECTIONS FROM THE VINTAGE SERIES
- ❏ RCA Victor SP-33-322 [DJ] — 196? — 18.00
— *Promo-only sampler from albums issued in the LPV-500 series*

SELECTIONS FROM URGH! A MUSIC WAR
- ❏ A&M SP-17169 [DJ] — 1981 — 18.00
— *Promo-only sampler; Includes Devo, Echo and the Bunnymen, Go-Go's, Oingo Boingo, The Police, XTC*

Number	Title	Yr	NM

SESAME STREET CHRISTMAS SING-A-LONG
- ❏ Sesame Street CTW22112 — 1984 — 12.00

SESSION AT MIDNIGHT
- ❏ Capitol T707 [M] — 1956 — 30.00

SESSION AT RIVERSIDE
- ❏ Capitol T761 [M] — 1956 — 30.00

THE SEVEN AGES OF JAZZ
- ❏ Metrojazz 2-E-1009 [M] — 1959 — 60.00
- ❏ Metrojazz 2-SE-1009 [S] — 1959 — 50.00

SHARP CUTS
- ❏ Planet P-6 — 1980 — 12.00
- —Includes Suburban Lawns, Single Bullet Theory, The dB's, etc.

SHOUTIN', SWINGIN' AND MAKIN' LOVE
- ❏ Chess CHV-412 — 1970 — 18.00

SHUT DOWN
- ❏ Capitol T1918 [M] — 1963 — 40.00
- ❏ Capitol DT1918 [R] — 1963 — 40.00

SHUT DOWNS AND HILL CLIMBS
- ❏ Liberty LRP-3366 [M] — 1964 — 40.00
- ❏ Liberty LST-7366 [S] — 1964 — 50.00

SIGNALS
- ❏ Savoy Jazz SJL-2231 — 198? — 15.00
- —pecial Products P 14989

SILLY SONGS
- ❏ Imperial House 9240 — 1977 — 18.00

SILVER BLUE
- ❏ Xanadu 137 — 197? — 15.00

THE SINATRA FAMILY WISH YOU A MERRY CHRISTMAS
- ❏ Reprise FS-1026 — 1969 — 50.00

SING A SONG OF SOUL
- ❏ Checker LP2998 [M] — 1966 — 80.00
- ❏ Checker LPS2998 [S] — 1966 — 100.00

THE SINGER-SONGWRITER PROJECT
- ❏ Elektra FKL-299 [M] — 1965 — 30.00
- —With 13 tracks
- ❏ Elektra EKL-299 [M] — 1965 — 25.00
- —With 11 tracks, though the label and cover claim there are 13
- ❏ Elektra EKS-7299 [S] — 1965 — 30.00
- —With 13 tracks
- ❏ Elektra EKS-7299 [S] — 1965 — 25.00
- —With 11 tracks, though the label and cover claim there are 13
- ❏ Savoy MG-12217 [M] — 196? — 25.00

SINGIN' THE BLUES
- ❏ MCA 4064 — 197? — 15.00

THE SIREN
- ❏ Posh Boy PBS-103 — 1980 — 25.00

SITTIN' IN
- ❏ Verve MGV-8225 [M] — 1958 — 50.00
- ❏ Verve V-8225 [M] — 1961 — 30.00

16 GOODIES -- BLASTS FROM THE PAST
- ❏ Blast BLP-6803 [M] — 1964 — 40.00

16 ORIGINAL BIG HITS, VOLUME 2
- ❏ Tamla TM256 [M] — 1964 — 25.00

$64,000 JAZZ
- ❏ Columbia CL777 [M] — 1955 — 50.00

60 CHRISTMAS CLASSICS
- ❏ Sessions DVL2-0723 — 1985 — 25.00
- —Record 3 is numbered "P18827" and Record 4 is numbered "P18828"

60 FLASH-BACK GREATS OF THE SIXTIES
- ❏ K-Tel TU229 — 1972 — 40.00
- —One of the few sought-after K-Tel collections, among its contents is a Beatles track ("My Bonnie")

60 YEARS OF COUNTRY MUSIC
- ❏ RCA Victor CPL2-4351 — 1982 — 25.00

60 YEARS OF MUSIC AMERICA LOVES BEST
- ❏ RCA Victor LM-6074 — 1959 — 30.00

60 YEARS OF MUSIC AMERICA LOVES BEST, VOLUME II
- ❏ RCA Victor LM-6088 — 1960 — 30.00

60 YEARS OF MUSIC AMERICA LOVES BEST, VOLUME III (POPULAR)
- ❏ RCA Victor LOP-1509 — 1961 — 25.00

60 YEARS OF MUSIC AMERICA LOVES BEST, VOLUME III (RED SEAL)
- ❏ RCA Victor Red Seal LM-2574 — 1961 — 25.00

60 YEARS OF THE GRAND OLE OPRY
- ❏ RCA Victor CPL2-9507 — 1986 — 18.00

A SLICE OF LEMON
- ❏ Columbia Special Products CSM-389 [M] — 1966 — 30.00

- —Manufactured for Dr. Pepper; contains a spoken-word introduction by Dick Clark, plus tracks by Bob Dylan, Simon & Garfunkel, the Dave Clark Five, the Brothers Four, Percy Faith, Dave Brubeck, the New Christy Minstrels, Tony Bennett and Doris Day

SMALL COMBO HITS
- ❏ RCA Victor LPT-3 [10] — 1951 — 40.00

SMART, LUSCIOUS, BEAUTIFUL
- ❏ Bethlehem BCP-6034 [M] — 1960 — 30.00

THE SMITHSONIAN COLLECTION OF CLASSIC JAZZ
- ❏ Smithsonian/CSP P611891 — 1973 — 40.00
- ❏ Smithsonian/CSP P719477 — 1987 — 40.00
- —Revised version of 1973 original

SMOKE RINGS
- ❏ RCA Victor LPT-13 [10] — 1951 — 40.00

SMOOTH & SWINGING JAZZ
- ❏ Verve PM-12 [M] — 1964 — 18.00
- —Custom edition for Whyte & Mackay's Blended Scotch Whiskey

SOFT PEDAL
- ❏ Columbia CL2511 [10] — 1954 — 30.00

SOLID COUNTRY GOLD
- ❏ RCA Victor CPL1-4841 — 1983 — 12.00

SOLID GOLD HITS
- ❏ Imperial LP-9230 [M] — 1963 — 30.00
- ❏ Imperial LP-12230 [R] — 1963 — 25.00

SOLID GOLD PROGRAMMING
- ❏ Screen Gems/Columbia CPL-711 [DJ] — 1975 — 25.00
- —Promo-only compilation of oldies sent to radio to spur airplay on songs owned by this publishing house
- ❏ Screen Gems/Columbia CPL-715 [DJ] — 1975 — 25.00
- —Same concept as above album, but completely different contents, and mostly in stereo

SOLID GOLD SONGS INSTRUMENTALLY
- ❏ Screen Gems/Columbia CPL-714 [DJ] — 1975 — 25.00
- —Promo-only compilation of oldies sent to radio to spur airplay on songs owned by this publishing house

SOLID GOLD SOUL
- ❏ Atlantic 8116 [M] — 1966 — 18.00
- ❏ Atlantic SD8116 [S] — 1966 — 25.00

SOLID STATE DEMONSTRATION RECORD
- ❏ Solid State SS93 [DJ] — 1966 — 18.00
- —Sampler from six Solid State LP releases

SOLO FLIGHT
- ❏ Pacific Jazz JWC-505 [M] — 1956 — 50.00
- ❏ World Pacific JWC-505 [M] — 1958 — 40.00

SOLO SPOTLIGHTS
- ❏ King 745 [M] — 1961 — 100.00

THE SOMA RECORDS STORY, VOLUME 2: BRIGHT LIGHTS, BIG CITY!
- ❏ Beat Rocket BR112 — 1999 — 15.00

THE SOMA RECORDS STORY, VOLUME 3: A MAN'S GOTTA BE A MAN!
- ❏ Beat Rocket BR113 — 1999 — 15.00

THE SOMA RECORDS STORY VOLUME 1: SHAKE IT FOR ME!
- ❏ Beat Rocket BR111 — 1999 — 15.00

SOME LIKE IT COOL
- ❏ United Artists X-71 [M] — 1959 — 40.00
- ❏ United Artists SX-71 [S] — 1959 — 40.00

SOMETHING FESTIVE!
- ❏ A&M SP-19003 — 1968 — 18.00
- —Sold only at B.F. Goodrich tire dealers

SOMETHING FOR BOTH EARS
- ❏ World Pacific HFS-2 [S] — 1958 — 40.00
- —Stereo sampler

SOMETHING NEW, SOMETHING BLUE
- ❏ Columbia CL1388 [M] — 1959 — 25.00

SONGS BY RODGERS AND HART AND JOHNNY GREEN
- ❏ Discovery DL-3014 [10] — 1951 — 50.00

SONGS FOR A SUMMER NIGHT
- ❏ Columbia PM2 [M] — 1963 — 25.00
- ❏ Columbia PMS2 [S] — 1963 — 30.00

SONGS FOR CHRISTMAS -- THE OLD AND THE NEW
- ❏ RCA Victor PR-132-A [M] — 1962 — 18.00
- —Sold only at Jewel food stores

SONGS FOR THE CHRISTMAS SEASON
- ❏ Capitol Creative Products SL-6541 — 1967 — 15.00

THE SONGS OF ASHFORD AND SIMPSON
- ❏ Jobete PRO-3 [DJ] — 1974 — 40.00
- —Promo-only publisher's demo with short excerpts of songs

SONGS OF CHRISTMAS
- ❏ Singcord ZLP998S — 1977 — 12.00

SONGS OF FAITH
- ❏ Audio Lab AL-1504 [M] — 1959 — 80.00

SONGS OF FAITH AND INSPIRATION
- ❏ Time-Life STL-127 — 1989 — 30.00

SONGS OF FAITH VOLUME 2
- ❏ Audio Lab AL-1523 [M] — 1959 — 80.00

THE SONGS OF HOLLAND-DOZIER-HOLLAND
- ❏ Jobete PRO-4 [DJ] — 1974 — 40.00
- —Promo-only publisher's demo with short excerpts of songs

THE SONGS OF JOHN LENNON AND PAUL MCCARTNEY
- ❏ 20th Century T2-540 — 1977 — 18.00
- —Includes Peter Gabriel; reissue of soundtrack of "All This and World War II"

THE SONGS OF JOHNNY BRISTOL-FRANK WILSON-MICKEY STEVENSON AND FREDDIE PERREN
- ❏ Jobete PRO-8 [DJ] — 1976 — 40.00
- —Promo-only publisher's demo with short excerpts of songs

THE SONGS OF MARVIN GAYE
- ❏ Jobete PRO-6 [DJ] — 1974 — 40.00
- —Promo-only publisher's demo with short excerpts of songs

THE SONGS OF NORMAN WHITFIELD
- ❏ Jobete PRO-7 [DJ] — 1976 — 40.00
- —Promo-only publisher's demo with short excerpts of songs

SONGS OF RIVERS, OCEANS AND SEAS
- ❏ King 871 [M] — 1963 — 70.00

THE SONGS OF SMOKEY ROBINSON
- ❏ Jobete PRO-2 [DJ] — 1972 — 40.00
- —Promo-only publisher's demo with short excerpts of songs; there are two versions of this LP, both with the same number; each is of equal value

THE SONGS OF STEVIE WONDER
- ❏ Jobete PRO-5 [DJ] — 1974 — 40.00
- —Promo-only publisher's demo with short excerpts of songs

SONGS OF THE HILLS
- ❏ Audio Lab AL-1515 [M] — 1959 — 80.00

SOUL CHRISTMAS
- ❏ Atco SD 33-269 — 1968 — 30.00

SOULED OUT
- ❏ Chess LPS1546 [S] — 1969 — 50.00

SOUL EXPLOSION
- ❏ Stax STS 2-2007 — 1969 — 25.00

SOULFUL CHRISTMAS
- ❏ Mistletoe MLP-1213 — 197? — 15.00

SOULFUL OLDIES
- ❏ Oldies 33 OL-8005 [M] — 1964 — 30.00

SOUL JAZZ, VOL. 1
- ❏ Bluesville BVLP-1009 [M] — 1960 — 50.00
- —Blue label, silver print
- ❏ Bluesville BVLP-1009 [M] — 1965 — 30.00
- —Blue label, trident logo at right

SOUL JAZZ, VOL. 2
- ❏ Bluesville BVLP-1010 [M] — 1960 — 50.00
- —Blue label, silver print
- ❏ Bluesville BVLP-1010 [M] — 1965 — 30.00
- —Blue label, trident logo at right

SOUL JAZZ GIANTS
- ❏ Prestige PRST-7791 — 1970 — 18.00

SOUL MEETING SATURDAY NIGHT HOOTENANNY STYLE
- ❏ Vee Jay LP-1074 [M] — 1963 — 30.00
- —Not known to exist in stereo

THE SOUL OF JAZZ
- ❏ Riverside S-5 [M] — 1957 — 40.00
- ❏ World Wide MGS-20002 [S] — 1958 — 80.00

THE SOUL OF JAZZ PERCUSSION
- ❏ Warwick W5003 [M] — 1961 — 30.00
- ❏ Warwick W5003ST [S] — 1961 — 40.00

THE SOUL OF JAZZ PIANO
- ❏ Riverside 9S-7 [M] — 196? — 30.00

SOUL OLDIES VOLUME I
- ❏ Unart M20022 [M] — 1967 — 18.00
- ❏ Unart S21022 [S] — 1967 — 15.00

SOUL OLDIES VOLUME II
- ❏ Unart M20023 [M] — 1967 — 18.00
- ❏ Unart S21023 [S] — 1967 — 15.00

THE SOUND OF BIG BAND JAZZ IN HI-FI
- ❏ World Pacific WP-1257 [M] — 1960 — 40.00

Number	Title	Yr	NM

THE SOUND OF BIG BAND JAZZ IN STEREO
| ❑ World Pacific ST-1015 [S] | 1960 | 30.00 |

THE SOUND OF GENIUS
| ❑ Columbia Masterworks SGM1 [M] | 1963 | 25.00 |
| ❑ Columbia Masterworks SGS1 [S] | 1963 | 30.00 |

THE SOUND OF HOLYWOOD
| ❑ Mystic MLP33128 | 198? | 18.00 |
| — Includes Black Flag, Government Issue, more |
| ❑ Mystic MLP33124 | 1983 | 18.00 |
| — Includes Bad Religion, a lot more |

THE SOUND OF JAZZ
| ❑ Columbia CL1098 [M] | 1957 | 25.00 |

THE SOUND OF PICANTE
| ❑ Concord Picante CJP-295 | 1986 | 12.00 |

SOUNDS IN SPACE
| ❑ RCA Victor SP-33-13 [S] | 1958 | 25.00 |
| — Narrated by Ken Nordine with songs by various artists |

THE SOUNDS OF CHRISTMAS
| ❑ Capitol STBB-93245 | 1970 | 18.00 |
| — Available only through the Capitol Record Club |

SOUNDS OF CHRISTMAS
| ❑ Columbia Special Products P12474 | 1974 | 15.00 |
| — Sold only through Amway dealers |

THE SOUNDS OF CHRISTMAS
| ❑ MCA Special Markets DL734735 | 197? | 15.00 |

SOUNDS OF SUCCESS
| ❑ Jamie JLP-3017 [M] | 1961 | 30.00 |
| ❑ Jamie JLPS-3017 [S] | 1961 | 30.00 |

SOUNDTRACK SMASHES
| ❑ MCA 6435 | 1990 | 12.00 |
| — Includes Oingo Boingo |

SOUND WAVES
| ❑ K-Tel TU2690 | 1980 | 12.00 |
| — Includes Prince |

SOUTHERN COMFORT
| ❑ Sessions/CSP P212897 | 1975 | 15.00 |

SOUTHERN MEETIN'
| ❑ Kimberly 2017 [M] | 1963 | 25.00 |
| ❑ Kimberly 11017 [S] | 1963 | 30.00 |

SOUTH SIDE JAZZ
| ❑ Chess CHV-415 | 1971 | 15.00 |

SOUVENIR/PROGRAMMING RECORD -- DEALERS/DISC JOCKEYS -- OCT.-NOV. 1955
| ❑ Capitol PRO-232 [DJ] | 1955 | 40.00 |

THE SPANISH SIDE OF JAZZ
| ❑ Roulette SR-42001 | 1968 | 25.00 |

SPECIAL CHRISTMAS LP FOR DISC JOCKEYS
| ❑ Capitol PRO-201 [DJ] | 1954 | 50.00 |

SPECIAL COLLECTOR'S EDITION ALBUM FROM ROCKIN' RECORDS
| ❑ Sun 1032 | 1986 | 30.00 |
| — Limited edition of 600 copies |

SPIN TIME WITH LIBERTY
| ❑ Liberty MM-417 [DJ] | 1962 | 50.00 |
| — Promo-only release |

SPIRITUALS
| ❑ King 951 [M] | 1966 | 50.00 |
| — Reissue of "Spirituals, Volume 5," King 576 |

SPIRITUALS, VOLUME 5
| ❑ King 576 [M] | 1957 | 150.00 |

SPIRITUALS TO SWING: JOHN HAMMOND'S 30TH ANNIVERSARY CONCERT 1967
| ❑ Columbia G30776 | 1971 | 18.00 |
| ❑ Columbia CG30776 | 197? | 15.00 |
| — CG" prefix is a reissue of "G |

SQUARES BLOT OUT THE SUN
| ❑ DB 72 | 1990 | 12.00 |
| — Includes Swimming Pool Q's, Pylon, The Brains |

STABLE MATES
| ❑ Savoy MG-12115 [M] | 1957 | 50.00 |

A STARLIGHT CHRISTMAS
| ❑ MCA 10066 | 1990 | 12.00 |

STARS
| ❑ Sun 148 | 1982 | 25.00 |
| — Includes two early Alabama tracks |

THE STARS ARE OUT IN TEXAS
| ❑ RCA Victor CPL1-7165 | 1986 | 10.00 |

STARS FOR A SUMMER NIGHT
| ❑ Columbia PM1 [M] | 1961 | 30.00 |
| ❑ Columbia PMS1 [S] | 1961 | 30.00 |

STARS OF BLUEGRASS MUSIC
| ❑ CMH 5903 | 198? | 18.00 |

THE STARS OF CHRISTMAS
| ❑ RCA Special Products DPL1-0842 | 1988 | 25.00 |
| — Sold only through Avon dealers |

THE STARS OF HEE HAW
| ❑ Capitol ST-437 | 1970 | 25.00 |

STARS OF JAZZ '61
| ❑ Jazzland JLP-1001 [M] | 1961 | 30.00 |

STARS OF THE APOLLO
| ❑ Columbia G30788 | 1971 | 18.00 |
| ❑ Columbia CG30788 | 197? | 15.00 |
| — CG" prefix is a reissue of "G |

STARS OF THE GRAND OLE OPRY 1926-1974
| ❑ RCA Victor CPL2-0466 | 1974 | 25.00 |

START SWIMMING
| ❑ Stiff SINK1 | 1981 | 25.00 |

START THE PARTY VOL. 1
| ❑ Big Beat/Atlantic 92425 | 1994 | 18.00 |
| — Includes Simply Red |

THE STASH CHRISTMAS ALBUM
| ❑ Stash 125 | 1980 | 18.00 |

STAX...ONCE YOU'VE BEEN THERE, YOU KNOW YOU'RE HOME
| ❑ Stax STS1 [DJ] | 1971 | 40.00 |
| — Promo only in blank white gatefold cover |

THE STAX/VOLT REVUE -- LIVE IN LONDON
| ❑ Stax 721 [M] | 1967 | 25.00 |
| ❑ Stax S721 [S] | 1967 | 30.00 |

THE STAX/VOLT REVUE -- LIVE IN LONDON, VOLUME 2
| ❑ Stax 722 [M] | 1967 | 25.00 |
| ❑ Stax S722 [S] | 1967 | 30.00 |

STAY AWAKE
| ❑ A&M R100600 | 1988 | 18.00 |
| — Same as A&M SP-3918; BMG Direct Marketing edition |
| ❑ A&M SP-3018 | 1988 | 15.00 |
| — Includes Bonnie Raitt and Was (Not Was); Natalie Merchant, Michael Stipe, Mark Bingham and The Roches, Sinead O'Connor; Buster Poindexter; The Replacements, etc/ |

STAY IN SCHOOL -- DON'T BE A DROP OUT
| ❑ Stax A-11 [DJ] | 1967 | 500.00 |

STEREOSONIC JUBILEE SAMPLER, VOLUME 1
| ❑ Jubilee SSJLP-001 [S] | 1959 | 40.00 |

STERLING BALL 1971
| ❑ Motown M739 [DJ] | 1971 | 250.00 |
| — Loucye Gordy Wakefield Scholarship Fund benefit giveaway |

STIFFS LIVE
| ❑ Stiff/Arista STF-0001 | 1978 | 12.00 |
| — Includes Elvis Costello, Ian Dury and the Blockheads, Nick Lowe, Wreckless Eric |

STILL MORE GOLD HITS, VOLUME 3
| ❑ Warwick W2048 [M] | 1962 | 80.00 |

ST. LOUIS JAZZ, 1925-27
| ❑ Herwin 114 | 197? | 15.00 |

STRAIGHT NO CHASER
| ❑ Blue Note B1-28263 | 1994 | 30.00 |
| — Compilation of original recordings that were sampled by US3, plus others |

STREET BEAT
| ❑ Sugar Hill 9228 | 1984 | 30.00 |

STRETCHING OUT
| ❑ United Artists UAL-4023 [M] | 1959 | 400.00 |
| ❑ United Artists UAS-5023 [S] | 1959 | 300.00 |

STRICTLY BEBOP
| ❑ Capitol M-11059 | 1973 | 15.00 |

STRICTLY FROM DIXIE
| ❑ MGM E-3262 [M] | 1956 | 30.00 |

THE STRING BAND PROJECT
| ❑ Elektra EKL-292 [M] | 1965 | 25.00 |
| ❑ Elektra EKS-7292 [S] | 1965 | 30.00 |

A STRING OF SWINGIN' PEARLS
| ❑ RCA Victor LPM-1373 [M] | 1956 | 30.00 |

STUFF THIS IN YOUR STOCKING! ELVES IN ACTION
| ❑ Veebltronics/Skyclad 68 | 1990 | 15.00 |

SUB POP 100
| ❑ Sub Pop 10 [B] | 1986 | 250.00 |

SUB POP 200
| ❑ Sub Pop 25 [EP] | 1988 | 150.00 |

SUMMER COOLERS
| ❑ EMI America SPRO9448/9 [DJ] | 1985 | 12.00 |
| — Includes Limahl, Red Hot Chili Peppers |

SUMMER FESTIVAL
| ❑ RCA Victor Red Seal LM-6097 [M] | 1962 | 25.00 |
| ❑ RCA Victor Red Seal LSC-6097 [S] | 1962 | 30.00 |

SUMMER'S BEST MUSIC (IN-STORE SAMPLER)
| ❑ Columbia CAS2089 [DJ] | 1985 | 12.00 |
| — Includes Hooters, Alison Moyet, Cock Robin |

SUMMER SOUVENIRS
| ❑ Bell 6035 | 1969 | 25.00 |

SUMMIT MEETING
❑ Vanguard VSD-79390	1977	15.00
❑ Vee Jay LP-3026 [M]	1961	25.00
❑ Vee Jay SR-3026 [S]	1961	30.00

SUNDAY MORNING
| ❑ Vee Jay LP-5016 [M] | 1961 | 30.00 |

SUN ROCKABILLY'S, VOLUME 1
| ❑ Sun 1010 | 1978 | 18.00 |

SUN'S GOLD HITS
| ❑ Sun LP-1250 [M] | 1961 | 200.00 |

THE SUN STORY
| ❑ Rhino RNDA-71103 | 1986 | 25.00 |

SUPER GOLDEN HITS
| ❑ Jubilee JGS-8019 | 1968 | 100.00 |
| — Despite the stereo prefix, this LP is mono |

SUPER GOLDEN HITS, VOLUME 2
| ❑ Jubilee JGS-8023 | 1969 | 100.00 |
| — Reissue of "Clay Cole's Bin of Original Golden Oldies," Jubilee 5026; again, despite the stereo prefix, this LP is mono |

THE SUPER GROUPS
| ❑ Atco SD 33-279 | 1969 | 25.00 |

SUPER GROUPS
| ❑ Warner Bros. PRO630 | 1976 | 25.00 |

THE SUPER GROUPS FROM HOLLAND
| ❑ White Whale WWS-7129 | 1970 | 30.00 |

THE SUPER HITS
| ❑ Atlantic Group 501 [M] | 1967 | 25.00 |
| ❑ Atlantic Group SD501 [S] | 1967 | 25.00 |

THE SUPER HITS, VOL. 2
| ❑ Atlantic SD8188 [S] | 1968 | 25.00 |
| ❑ Atlantic 8188 [M] | 1968 | 40.00 |
| — Mono is white label promo only; cover has "d/j copy monaural" sticker on it |

THE SUPER HITS, VOL. 3
| ❑ Atlantic SD8203 [S] | 1968 | 25.00 |
| ❑ Atlantic 8203 [M] | 1968 | 40.00 |
| — Mono is white label promo only |

THE SUPER HITS, VOL. 4
| ❑ Atlantic SD8224 | 1969 | 25.00 |

THE SUPER HITS, VOL. 5
| ❑ Atlantic SD8274 [S] | 1970 | 25.00 |
| — This was the first album to contain "Ohio" by Crosby, Stills, Nash and Young and the only LP to contain the 3:11 version of "Whole Lotta Love" by Led Zeppelin |
| ❑ Atlantic 8274 [M] | 1970 | 50.00 |
| — Mono is white label promo only |

SUPER OLDIES/VOL. 1
| ❑ Capitol T2562 [M] | 1966 | 25.00 |
| ❑ Capitol ST2562 [S] | 1966 | 30.00 |

SUPER OLDIES/VOL. 2
| ❑ Capitol T2565 [M] | 1966 | 25.00 |
| ❑ Capitol ST2565 [S] | 1966 | 30.00 |

SUPER OLDIES/VOL. 3
| ❑ Capitol STBB2910 | 1968 | 25.00 |

SUPER OLDIES/VOL. 4
| ❑ Capitol STBB-149 | 1969 | 25.00 |

SUPER OLDIES/VOL. 5
| ❑ Capitol STBB-216 | 1969 | 25.00 |

SUPER ROCK
| ❑ Columbia G30121 | 1970 | 18.00 |

THE SUPER SOUL-DEES
| ❑ Capitol T2798 [M] | 1967 | 25.00 |
| ❑ Capitol ST2798 [S] | 1967 | 25.00 |

THE SUPER SOUL-DEES, VOL. 2
| ❑ Capitol STBB-2911 | 1968 | 25.00 |

THE SUPER SOUL-DEES, VOL. 3
| ❑ Capitol STBB-178 | 1969 | 25.00 |

SUPERSTAR IN-STORE SAMPLER
| ❑ Epic EAS2495 [DJ] | 1986 | 18.00 |
| — Includes Joan Jett and the Blackhearts, 'Til Tuesday, Cyndi Lauper |

Number	Title	Yr	NM

SUPERSTARS OF THE '70S
- ❑ Warner Special Products SP-4000 — 1973 — 40.00
  — *Box set with booklet of liner notes*

SURFIN' ON WAVE NINE
- ❑ King 855 [M] — 1963 — 80.00

SURF'S UP AT BANZAI PIPELINE
- ❑ Northridge NM-101 [M] — 1963 — 200.00
  — *Original pressing of LP reissued on Reprise*
- ❑ Reprise R6094 [M] — 1963 — 100.00
- ❑ Reprise RS6094 [S] — 1963 — 150.00

SURF'S UP! AT BANZAI PIPELINE
- ❑ Northridge NM-101 [M] — 1963 — 150.00

SURVIVAL SAMPLER
- ❑ Warner Bros. PRO-A-2161 [DJ] — 1984 — 10.00
  — *Includes The Church, Scritti Politti*

SWAMP BLUES VOLUME 1
- ❑ Excello LPS-8015 [R] — 1970 — 25.00

SWAMP BLUES VOLUME 2
- ❑ Excello LPS-8016 [R] — 1970 — 25.00

SWEDES FROM JAZZVILLE
- ❑ Epic LN3309 [M] — 1957 — 50.00

SWEDISH PASTRY
- ❑ Discovery DL-2008 [10] — 1954 — 50.00

SWEET ADELINES MEDALIST QUARTETS OF 1958
- ❑ Cadence CLP-3018 [M] — 1959 — 40.00

SWEET ADELINES MEDALISTS OF 1957
- ❑ Cadence CLP-3009 [M] — 1958 — 40.00

SWEET DREAMS OF COUNTRY
- ❑ Reader's Digest RBA-049A — 1990 — 50.00

SWEET 'N GREASY: RHYTHM 'N' BLUES, VOLUME 2
- ❑ Imperial LP-94005 — 1968 — 25.00

SWING 1946
- ❑ Prestige PRLP-7604 — 1969 — 18.00

SWING AGAIN!
- ❑ Capitol T1386 [M] — 1960 — 25.00
- ❑ Capitol DT1386 [R] — 196? — 15.00

SWING BILLIES
- ❑ Audio Lab AL-1546 [M] — 1960 — 120.00

SWING BILLIES VOLUME 2
- ❑ Audio Lab AL-1566 [M] — 1960 — 120.00

SWING CLASSICS 1935
- ❑ Prestige PRLP-7646 — 1969 — 18.00

THE SWING ERA, VOL. 1
- ❑ X LVA-3030 [10] — 1955 — 80.00

SWING GOES DIXIE
- ❑ American Recording Society G-420 [M] — 1957 — 30.00

SWING GUITARS
- ❑ Norgran MGN-1033 [M] — 1955 — 80.00
- ❑ Verve MGV-8124 [M] — 1957 — 30.00
- ❑ Verve V-8124 [M] — 1961 — 25.00

SWING HI, SWING LO
- ❑ Blue Note BLP-5027 [10] — 1953 — 200.00
- ❑ Blue Note B-6507 [M] — 1969 — 18.00

SWINGIN': BIG BAND SWING AND JAZZ FROM THE 1930S AND 1940S
- ❑ Folkways FJ-2861 — 1986 — 15.00

SWINGING BROADWAY
- ❑ Kimberly 2024 [M] — 1963 — 25.00
- ❑ Kimberly 11024 [S] — 1963 — 30.00

SWINGING FOR THE KING
- ❑ Mercury MG-20133 [M] — 1956 — 50.00

A SWINGIN' GIG
- ❑ Tampa TP-2 [M] — 1957 — 100.00
  — *Colored vinyl*
- ❑ Tampa TP-2 [M] — 1958 — 50.00
  — *Black vinyl*

SWINGING SMALL BANDS
- ❑ MCA 1324 — 198? — 12.00

SWINGING SOUNDTRACK
- ❑ Kimberly 2016 [M] — 1963 — 25.00
- ❑ Kimberly 11016 [S] — 1963 — 30.00

SWINGIN' LIKE SIXTY, VOL. 1
- ❑ World Pacific WP-1289 [M] — 1960 — 30.00
- ❑ World Pacific ST-1289 [S] — 1960 — 30.00

SWINGIN' LIKE SIXTY, VOL. 2
- ❑ World Pacific ST-1290 [S] — 1960 — 30.00

SWINGIN' LIKE SIXTY, VOL. 3
- ❑ World Pacific ST-1291 [S] — 1960 — 30.00

SWINGIN' SOUNDS
- ❑ Columbia Special Products XTV82030 [M] — 1962 — 30.00
  — *Issued for the W.A. Sheaffer Pen Co.*

SWING LIGHTLY
- ❑ Jazztone J-1265 [M] — 1957 — 30.00

SWING… NOT SPRING!
- ❑ Savoy MG-12062 [M] — 1956 — 50.00

SWING POTPOURRI
- ❑ Audiophile AP-23 [M] — 1953 — 30.00

SWINGTIME JIVE
- ❑ Stash ST-108 — 197? — 12.00

THE SWINGVILLE ALL-STARS
- ❑ Swingville SVLP-2010 [M] — 1960 — 40.00
  — *Purple label*
- ❑ Swingville SVLP-2010 [M] — 1965 — 25.00
  — *Blue label, trident logo at right*

SWITCHED ON BLUES
- ❑ Soul SS-720 — 1969 — 150.00

TAKE THE LIBERTY
- ❑ Liberty MM-427 [DJ] — 1966 — 40.00

TAME YOURSELF
- ❑ Rhino 90082 — 1991 — 30.00

TAMLA SPECIAL #1
- ❑ Tamla TM224 [M] — 1962 — 150.00
  — *White label*
- ❑ Tamla TM224 [M] — 1963 — 70.00
  — *Yellow label*

A TASTE OF JAZZ
- ❑ Concord Jazz CJ-93 — 1979 — 12.00

A TASTE OF MCA
- ❑ MCA L33-1803 [DJ] — 1979 — 18.00
  — *Includes Joe Ely*

TASTE TEST #1 -- LIVE FROM BRAIN COOKIES
- ❑ New Alliance 045 — 1990 — 30.00

TEA PAD SONGS, VOL. 1
- ❑ Stash ST-103 — 197? — 12.00

TEA PAD SONGS, VOL. 2
- ❑ Stash ST-104 — 197? — 12.00

TEENAGE PARTY
- ❑ Gee GLP-702 [M] — 1958 — 200.00
  — *Red label*
- ❑ Gee GLP-702 [M] — 196? — 60.00
  — *Gray label*

TEEN DELIGHTS
- ❑ Vee Jay LP-1021 [M] — 1960 — 30.00

TEEN DELIGHTS, VOLUME 2
- ❑ Vee Jay LP-1036 [M] — 1961 — 30.00

THE TEEN SOUND
- ❑ Columbia Special Products CSS523 — 1967 — 15.00

TEENSVILLE
- ❑ Liberty L-5503 [M] — 1962 — 40.00

TENNESSEE
- ❑ Design DLP-611 [M] — 1962 — 25.00
  — *CA Music Service edition*

TENNESSEE MOUNTAIN BLUEGRASS FESTIVAL
- ❑ CMH 9014 — 198? — 18.00

TENOR CONCLAVE
- ❑ Prestige PRLP-7074 [M] — 1957 — 100.00
  — *Reissued as Prestige 7249; see JOHN COLTRANE.*

TENOR JAZZ
- ❑ Mercury MG-20016 [10] — 1950 — 100.00
  — *Issued in a paper sleeve*

TENORS ANYONE?
- ❑ Dawn DLP-1126 [M] — 1958 — 120.00

TENOR SAX
- ❑ Concord 3012 [M] — 195? — 40.00

TENOR SAXES
- ❑ Norgran MGN-1034 [M] — 1955 — 80.00
- ❑ Verve MGV-8127 [M] — 1957 — 30.00
- ❑ Verve V-8127 [M] — 1961 — 25.00

TENOR SAX SOLOS, VOL. 1
- ❑ Savoy MG-9008 [10] — 1952 — 150.00

TENOR SAX SOLOS, VOL. 2
- ❑ Savoy MG-9013 [10] — 1952 — 150.00

TENOR SAX SOLOS, VOL. 3
- ❑ Savoy MG-9021 [10] — 1953 — 150.00

TEN TUNES OF CHRISTMAS
- ❑ Candee 50-50 — 195? — 25.00
  — *Sold through "The 50-50 Club," a Cincinnati radio and TV show; all the artists have Cincinnati ties*

THAT'S THE WAY I FEEL NOW
- ❑ A&M SP-6600 — 1984 — 18.00
  — *Includes Joe Jackson*

THAT'S THE WAY I FEEL NOW (A TRIBUTE TO THELONIOUS MONK)
- ❑ A&M SP-6006 — 198? — 18.00

THAT'S TRUCKDRIVIN'
- ❑ Starday DT-90617 [R] — 196? — 25.00
  — *Capitol Record Club edition*
- ❑ Starday T-90617 [M] — 196? — 30.00
  — *Capitol Record Club edition*

THEMES LIKE OLD TIMES
- ❑ Viva 36018 — 1969 — 25.00

THEME SONGS
- ❑ Columbia CL6016 [10] — 1949 — 40.00
- ❑ RCA Victor LPT-1 [10] — 1951 — 40.00

THESAURUS OF CLASSIC JAZZ
- ❑ Columbia C4L18 — 1961 — 50.00

THEY ALL PLAYED RAGTIME
- ❑ Jazzology JCE-52 — 197? — 12.00

THEY ALL PLAYED THE MAPLE LEAF RAG
- ❑ Herwin 401 — 197? — 15.00

3RD ANNIVERSARY ALBUM -- 25 COUNTRY MUSIC GREATS
- ❑ Homestead AC-1 — 196? — 15.00

A THIRD SESSION AT SQUIRREL'S
- ❑ Paramount LP-110 [10] — 1954 — 60.00

30X30: 30 GREAT HITS BY 30 GREAT COUNTRY ARTISTS, VOL. 1
- ❑ Columbia Musical Treasuries P2S5218 — 1968 — 25.00

30X30: 30 GREAT HITS BY 30 GREAT COUNTRY ARTISTS, VOL. 2
- ❑ Columbia Musical Treasuries P2S5220 — 1968 — 25.00

30 FAVORITE SONGS OF CHRISTMAS WITH CHIMES AND CHORUS
- ❑ Disneyland DQ-1329 [M] — 1963 — 25.00
  — *Performed by anonymous musicians*

30 GOLDEN COUNTRY HITS
- ❑ RCA Special Products DVL2-0447 — 1980 — 15.00
  — *Mail-order offer from Sessions*

30 SECONDS OVER D.C.
- ❑ Limp 1001 — 1978 — 18.00
  — *Includes Slickee Boys; issued on orange vinyl*

30 YEARS OF NO. 1 COUNTRY HITS
- ❑ Reader's Digest RBA-215-A — 1986 — 50.00

THIS COULD LEAD TO LOVE
- ❑ Riverside RLP 12-808 [M] — 195? — 50.00

THIS IS CHRISTMAS
- ❑ RCA Victor VPS-6046 — 1971 — 18.00

THIS IS FORT APACHE
- ❑ MCA 11179 — 1995 — 15.00
  — *Includes Belly, The Lemonheads, Throwing Muses, Radiohead, Juliana Hatfield*

THIS IS HOW IT ALL BEGAN: THE SPECIALTY STORY, VOLUME 1
- ❑ Specialty SPS-2117 — 1970 — 25.00

THIS IS HOW IT ALL BEGAN: THE SPECIALTY STORY, VOLUME 2
- ❑ Specialty SPS-2118 — 1970 — 25.00

THIS IS SOUL
- ❑ Atlantic 8170 [M] — 1968 — 40.00
- ❑ Atlantic SD8170 [S] — 1968 — 25.00

THIS IS STEREO
- ❑ Liberty LST-101 [S] — 1960 — 40.00
  — *Black vinyl*
- ❑ Liberty LST-101 [S] — 1960 — 120.00
  — *Red vinyl*

THIS IS THE BIG BAND ERA
- ❑ RCA Victor VPM-6043 — 197? — 18.00

THIS IS THE BLUES
- ❑ Kimberly 2020 [M] — 1963 — 25.00
- ❑ Kimberly 11020 [S] — 1963 — 30.00

THIS IS THE BLUES, VOL. 1
- ❑ Pacific Jazz PJ-13 [M] — 1961 — 30.00

THIS IS THE BLUES, VOL. 2
- ❑ Pacific Jazz PJ-30 [M] — 1962 — 30.00
- ❑ Pacific Jazz ST-30 [S] — 1962 — 30.00

THIS IS THEIR TIME, OH YEAH
- ❑ Revelation REV-11 — 1970 — 18.00

THIS IS YOUR COUNTRY
- ❑ Realm 1P8126 — 1991 — 18.00
  — *Only available on vinyl through Columbia House*

Number	Title	Yr	NM

THREADS OF GLORY -- 200 YEARS OF AMERICA IN WORDS & MUSIC
- ❏ London Phase 4 6SP14000 — 1975 — 30.00

THREE DECADES OF MUSIC, 1939-49, VOL. 1
- ❏ Blue Note BST-89902 — 1969 — 30.00

THREE DECADES OF MUSIC, 1949-59, VOL. 1
- ❏ Blue Note BST-89903 — 1969 — 30.00

THREE DECADES OF MUSIC, 1959-69, VOL. 1
- ❏ Blue Note BST-89904 — 1969 — 30.00

THREE ROADS TO JAZZ
- ❏ American Recording Society LP-100 [M] — 1956 — 30.00

A TIME FOR PRAYER
- ❏ Audio Lab AL-1518 [M] — 1959 — 80.00

THE TIME-LIFE TREASURY OF CHRISTMAS
- ❏ Time-Life STL-107 — 1986 — 25.00
- — *Available from Time-Life by mail order only; boxed set*
- ❏ Time-Life STL-107 — 1989 — 18.00
- — *Available from Time-Life by mail order only; same as above, except in wide sleeve rather than box*

THE TIME-LIFE TREASURY OF CHRISTMAS, VOLUME TWO
- ❏ Time-Life STL-108 — 1987 — 18.00
- — *Available from Time-Life by mail-order only; all known copies are boxed sets*

TODAY'S HITS
- ❏ Philles PHLP4004 [M] — 1963 — 400.00
- — *First pressings have blue and black labels*
- ❏ Philles PHLP4004 [M] — 1964 — 200.00
- — *Second pressings have yellow and red labels*

TOGETHER
- ❏ Warner Bros. PRO486 — 1972 — 25.00
- — *Originals have green labels*

TOGETHER AT CHRISTMAS (READER'S DIGEST FAMILY ALBUM OF CHRISTMAS MUSIC)
- ❏ Reader's Digest RDA151-A — 1974 — 25.00
- — *Available only through Reader's Digest magazine by mail order*

TOMMY BOY GREATEST BEATS: THE FIRST FIFTEEN YEARS 1981-1996, VOLUME 1
- ❏ Tommy Boy TB1115 — 1998 — 25.00

TOMMY BOY GREATEST BEATS: THE FIRST FIFTEEN YEARS 1981-1996, VOLUME 2
- ❏ Tommy Boy TB1165 — 1998 — 25.00

TOMMY BOY GREATEST BEATS: THE FIRST FIFTEEN YEARS 1981-1996, VOLUME 3
- ❏ Tommy Boy TB1117 — 1998 — 25.00

TOMMY BOY GREATEST BEATS: THE FIRST FIFTEEN YEARS 1981-1996, VOLUME 4
- ❏ Tommy Boy TB1166 — 1998 — 25.00

TOMORROW'S HITS
- ❏ Vee Jay LP-1042 [M] — 1962 — 30.00

TOOTIN' THROUGH THE ROOF, VOL. 1
- ❏ Onyx 209 — 197? — 15.00

TOOTIN' THROUGH THE ROOF, VOL. 2
- ❏ Onyx 213 — 197? — 15.00

THE TOP 10 STORY IN SOUND
- ❏ Jobete PRO-1 [DJ] — 1972 — 40.00
- — *Promo-only publisher's demo with short excerpts of songs*

TOP HITS OF '54 VOLUME II
- ❏ Capitol H9119 [10] — 1954 — 50.00

TOP R&B ARTISTS SING COUNTRY SONGS
- ❏ King 884 [M] — 1964 — 80.00

A TOTAL EXPERIENCE CHRISTMAS
- ❏ Total Experience TEL8-5707 — 1984 — 15.00

TOWN HALL CONCERT
- ❏ Mainstream S-6004 [R] — 1965 — 15.00
- ❏ Mainstream 56004 [M] — 1965 — 30.00

A TOWN SOUTH OF BAKERSFIELD
- ❏ Enigma 72059-1 — 1985 — 15.00
- — *Includes Dwight Yoakam*

TRADITIONAL CHRISTMAS SONGS
- ❏ Audio Lab AL-1517 [M] — 1959 — 80.00

TRADITIONAL JAZZ
- ❏ London LL1242 [M] — 1955 — 25.00

TRADITIONAL JAZZ AT THE ROYAL FESTIVAL HALL
- ❏ London LL1184 [M] — 1955 — 25.00

TREASURE ALBUM
- ❏ Hickory LPS-154 — 1970 — 40.00

TREASURE CHEST GOODIES
- ❏ Stax 703 [M] — 1963 — 40.00
- — *National version of "Hits from the South Presented by Nick Charles" with rearranged contents*

TREASURE CHEST OF HITS
- ❏ Swan LP-501 [M] — 1960 — 80.00

A TREASURE CHEST OF SONG HITS
- ❏ Columbia CL613 [M] — 1955 — 30.00

TREASURE TUNES FROM THE VAULT (AS ADVERTISED ON WLS)
- ❏ Chess LP1474 [M] — 1962 — 40.00

A TREASURY OF CHRISTMAS
- ❏ Columbia Record Club P4S5022 — 1965 — 30.00

A TREASURY OF GOLDEN CHRISTMAS SONGS
- ❏ Vee Jay LP-5045 [M] — 1963 — 30.00

TRIBUTE TO CHARLIE PARKER FROM THE NEWPORT JAZZ FESTIVAL
- ❏ RCA Victor LPM-3738 [M] — 1967 — 30.00
- ❏ RCA Victor LSP-3738 [S] — 1967 — 25.00

A TRIBUTE TO DUKE
- ❏ Concord Jazz CJ-50 — 197? — 15.00

TRIBUTE TO MONK AND BIRD
- ❏ Tomato TOM-9002 — 1979 — 18.00

TROMBONE BAND STAND
- ❏ Bethlehem BCP-6036 [M] — 1960 — 30.00

TROMBONES
- ❏ Savoy MG-12086 [M] — 1956 — 60.00

TROMBONE SCENE
- ❏ Vik LX-1087 [M] — 1957 — 30.00

TROUBLEMAKERS
- ❏ Warner Bros. PRO-A-857 — 1978 — 25.00

TRUCK DRIVER SONGS
- ❏ King 866 [M] — 1963 — 70.00

TRUMPETER'S HOLIDAY
- ❏ Epic LN3252 [M] — 1956 — 30.00

TRUMPET INTERLUDE
- ❏ EmArcy MG-36017 [M] — 1955 — 50.00
- ❏ Savoy MG-12096 [M] — 1957 — 60.00

TRUMPET STYLISTS
- ❏ Capitol H326 [10] — 1952 — 50.00

TRUMPET TRIBUTE TO FATS NAVARRO, CLIFFORD BROWN, BOOKER LITTLE
- ❏ Trip 5036 — 197? — 15.00

TUNES TO BE REMEMBERED
- ❏ Excello LP-800I [M] — 1960 — 150.00
- — *Original cover is green with black records that list the title and artist of each selection*

TURN BACK THE CLOCK
- ❏ King 859 [M] — 1963 — 70.00

TV COUNTRY JAMBOREE
- ❏ RCA Camden CAL-925 [M] — 1965 — 15.00
- ❏ RCA Camden CAS-925 [S] — 1965 — 18.00

THE 12 DAYS OF CHRISTMAS
- ❏ Pickwick SPC-1021 — 1976 — 12.00

12 FLIP HITS
- ❏ Flip 1001 [M] — 1959 — 300.00

THE 12 GREATEST OLDIES IN THE WHOLE WORLD, EVER
- ❏ Parkway P-7031 [M] — 1963 — 30.00

THE 12 HITS OF CHRISTMAS
- ❏ United Artists UA-LA669-R — 1976 — 15.00

12 MILLION SELLERS
- ❏ Forum F-9057 [M] — 1963 — 25.00
- ❏ Forum SF-9057 [R] — 1963 — 18.00

12 + 3 = 15 HITS
- ❏ End LP310 [M] — 1961 — 60.00

12 SONGS OF CHRISTMAS
- ❏ Reprise F-2022 [M] — 1964 — 25.00
- ❏ Reprise FS-2022 [S] — 1964 — 18.00

12 TOP TEEN DANCES 1961-1962
- ❏ Cameo C-1016 [M] — 1962 — 30.00

22 HIGH-BALLIN' HITS!
- ❏ GRT 2103-709 — 1976 — 15.00

24 KARAT GOLD FOR GROOVIN'
- ❏ Verve V6-6654 — 1968 — 25.00

24 SACRED SONGS
- ❏ King 965 [M] — 1966 — 50.00

25 SONGS OF CHRISTMAS, VOLUME II
- ❏ Birdwing BWR2076 — 1985 — 18.00

25 SONGS OF CHRISTMAS FROM SPARROW
- ❏ Birdwing BWR2042 — 1982 — 18.00

25 YEARS OF C&W HITS
- ❏ King 1006 [M] — 1966 — 30.00

25 YEARS OF COUNTRY AND WESTERN SACRED SONGS
- ❏ King 807 [M] — 1962 — 100.00

25 YEARS OF POPULAR MUSIC
- ❏ King 1008 [M] — 1966 — 30.00

25 YEARS OF PRESTIGE
- ❏ Prestige 24046 — 197? — 18.00

25 YEARS OF R&B HITS
- ❏ King 1004 [M] — 1966 — 30.00

25 YEARS OF R&B HITS, VOLUME 1
- ❏ King 725 [M] — 1961 — 100.00

25 YEARS OF R&B HITS, VOLUME 2
- ❏ King 749 [M] — 1961 — 100.00

20 ALL TIME NO. 1 HITS
- ❏ Roulette R25290 [M] — 1965 — 25.00
- ❏ Roulette SR25290 [R] — 1965 — 15.00

20 BIG BOSS FAVORITES: 10 GREAT HITS OF 1964 -- 10 GREAT OLDIES HITS
- ❏ Roulette R25304 [M] — 1965 — 25.00
- ❏ Roulette SR25304 [R] — 1965 — 18.00
- — *Of the 20 tracks, only "Laugh, Laugh" by the Beau Brummels and "El Watusi" by Ray Barretto are true stereo*

20 SOULFUL OLDIES, VOLUME 1
- ❏ Vee Jay VJVS-1001 [R] — 1972 — 25.00

20 SOULFUL OLDIES, VOLUME 2
- ❏ Vee Jay VJVS-1002 [R] — 1972 — 25.00

20 SOULFUL OLDIES, VOLUME 3
- ❏ Vee Jay VJVS-1003 [R] — 1972 — 25.00

20 SOULFUL OLDIES, VOLUME 4
- ❏ Vee Jay VJVS-73-1006/7 [R] — 1973 — 25.00

20 SOULFUL OLDIES, VOLUME 5
- ❏ Vee Jay VJVS-73-1008/9 [R] — 1973 — 25.00

20 SOULFUL OLDIES, VOLUME 6
- ❏ Vee Jay VJVS-73-1010/11 [R] — 1973 — 25.00

20 YEARS OF NO. 1 HITS (1956-1975)
- ❏ Reader's Digest RBA-243A — 1986 — 50.00

TWISTIN' ALL NIGHT LONG
- ❏ Swan LP-506 [M] — 1962 — 120.00

2 X 5
- ❏ Red Star RED-100 — 1980 — 18.00
- — *Includes The Fleshtones, etc.*

TWO ROOMS: CELEBRATING THE SONGS OF ELTON JOHN & BERNIE TAUPIN
- ❏ Polydor P1-47570 [M] — 1990 — 30.00
- — *U.S. vinyl available only through Columbia House*

THE UNAVAILABLE 16
- ❏ Vee Jay LP-1051 [M] — 1962 — 40.00

UNDERGROUND GOLD
- ❏ Liberty LST-7625 — 1969 — 18.00

UNDER ONE ROOF
- ❏ EmArcy MG-36088 [M] — 1956 — 40.00

UNEXPURGATED JAZZ
- ❏ Audiophile AP-43 [M] — 1953 — 30.00

THE UNFORGETTABLE FIFTIES
- ❏ Heartland 1072 — 1988 — 25.00

THE UP ANOTHER OCTAVE TRANSMISSION
- ❏ Up Another Octave (no #) — 1981 — 30.00
- — *Includes early Berlin*

UPRIGHT AND LOWDOWN
- ❏ Columbia CL685 [M] — 1955 — 25.00

UP SWING
- ❏ RCA Victor LPT-12 [10] — 1951 — 40.00

URBAN EXPOSURE
- ❏ K-Tel NU1990 — 1986 — 15.00
- — *Includes Run-D.M.C.*

A VARIETY OF COUNTRY SACRED SONGS
- ❏ Audio Lab AL-1557 [M] — 1960 — 60.00

THE VERVE COMPENDIUM OF JAZZ, NO. 1
- ❏ Verve MGV-8194 [M] — 1957 — 30.00
- ❏ Verve V-8194 [M] — 1961 — 25.00

THE VERVE COMPENDIUM OF JAZZ, NO. 2
- ❏ Verve MGV-8195 [M] — 1957 — 30.00
- ❏ Verve V-8195 [M] — 1961 — 25.00
- — *markets (Mid-Atlantic states)*

VERY SAXY
- ❏ Fantasy OJC-458 — 1990 — 15.00
- ❏ Prestige PRST-7790 — 1971 — 25.00
- — *Reissue of 7167*
- ❏ Prestige PRLP-7167 [M] — 1959 — 60.00

VARIOUS ARTISTS COLLECTIONS

Number	Title	Yr	NM
A VERY SPECIAL CHRISTMAS			
❏ A&M SP-3911		1987	18.00
— Benefit album for Special Olympics			
VICEROY CIGARETTES CAMPUS JAZZ FESTIVAL			
❏ RCA Custom KO7P-1544 [M]		1959	30.00
— Available thorugh Viceroy cigarettes			
THE VIEW FROM HERE			
❏ Medical MR2707		1987	12.00
— Includes Camper Van Beethoven			
WALKIN' BY MYSELF			
❏ Chess LP1446 [M]		1960	80.00
THE WALTONS' CHRISTMAS ALBUM			
❏ Columbia KC33193		1974	18.00
— Only one of the actors who appeared on the show appears on the album, thus it's listed here under Various Artists rather than Soundtracks or Television Albums			
WAMO'S GOLDEN GASSERS			
❏ Chess LP1458PGH [M]		1961	150.00
— Pittsburgh version of "Golden Gassers," Chess 1458			
WANNA BUY A BRIDGE?			
❏ Rough Trade ROUGH US3		1980	25.00
— Same as above; green cover			
❏ Rough Trade ROUGH US3		1980	25.00
— Includes Scritti Politti, The Slits, Cabaret Voltaire, Stiff Little Fingers, many others; blue cover			
WARNER BROS. 20TH ANNIVERSARY LP			
❏ Warner Bros. PRO775 [DJ]		1979	15.00
— Includes Neil Young			
THE WARNER/REPRISE RADIO SHOW			
❏ Warner Bros. PRO463		1971	30.00
— Originals have green labels			
WASHBOARD RHYTHM KINGS, VOL. 1			
❏ X LVA-3021 [10]		1954	80.00
WAVES			
❏ Bomp! 4003		1979	30.00
— Includes The Romantics; originals on blue vinyl			
WE CUT THIS ALBUM FOR BREAD			
❏ Bethlehem BCP-86 [M]		1958	30.00
WEED: A RARE BATCH			
❏ Stash ST-107		197?	15.00
WE KILLED MCKINLEY			
❏ Maxwell MXC3630		1988	12.00
— Includes an early Goo Goo Dolls track			
WELCOME TO MUSIC CITY U.S.A.			
❏ Columbia CL2590 [M]		1966	15.00
❏ Columbia CS9390 [S]		1966	18.00
WE LIKE BANDS			
❏ Coral CRL57229 [M]		195?	15.00
WE LIKE BOYS/GREAT BOY OLDIES			
❏ Oldies 33 OL-8004 [M]		1964	30.00
WE SING THE BLUES			
❏ Minit LP-0003 [M]		1962	50.00
WEST COAST JAZZ, VOL. 2			
❏ Jazztone J-(# unk) [M]		1957	30.00
WEST COAST VS. EAST COAST			
❏ MGM E-3390 [M]		1956	30.00
WESTERN STAR PARADE			
❏ Vocalion VL3805 [M]		1967	18.00
❏ Vocalion VL73805 [R]		1967	15.00
WESTERN SWING			
❏ King 876 [M]		1963	70.00
WESTERN SWING IN HI-FI			
❏ Decca DL8730 [M]		1958	40.00
WE'VE BUILT A JAZZ ALBUM FOR YOU			
❏ Bethlehem BCP-89 [M]		1958	30.00
WE'VE GOT YOUR MUSIC			
❏ Atlantic PR273 [DJ]		1977	18.00
— Includes Peter Gabriel			
WE WISH YOU A COUNTRY CHRISTMAS			
❏ Columbia Special Products P14991		1979	10.00
❏ SeaShell P14991		1981	10.00
— Reissue of Columbia Special Products P 14991			
WE WISH YOU A MERRY CHRISTMAS			
❏ CBS/FM FM39093		1985	12.00
❏ Harmony KH31536		1972	12.00
❏ Natural Resources NR4011T1		1978	18.00
❏ Warner Bros. W1337 [M]		1960	30.00
❏ Warner Bros. WS1337 [S]		1960	30.00

Number	Title	Yr	NM
WE WISH YOU A MERRY CHRISTMAS!			
❏ Pickwick PC-1004 [M]		196?	15.00
❏ Pickwick SPC-1004 [S]		196?	18.00
WFUN GOOD GUYS			
❏ Roulette R25273 [M]		1965	25.00
WHAT'S NEW? ON CAPITOL STEREO, VOL. 1			
❏ Capitol SN-1 [S]		1959	30.00
WHAT'S SHAKIN'			
❏ Elektra EKL-4002 [M]		1966	40.00
— Deduct 25 percent if booklet is missing			
❏ Elektra EKS-74002 [S]		1966	50.00
— Deduct 25 percent if booklet is missing			
WHEELIN' AND DEALIN'			
❏ Prestige PRLP-7131 [M]		1957	100.00
— Reissued as Status 8327; see JOHN COLTRANE.			
WHERE THE ACTION IS -- BOMP!			
❏ Bomp! 3001 [DJ]		1980	18.00
— Includes Romantics, Stiv Bators, Weirdos, others			
WHIO RADIO CHRISTMAS FEELINGS			
❏ Sound Approach/CSP P16366		1981	15.00
WHITE BOY BLUES -- CLASSIC GUITARS OF CLAPTON, BECK AND PAGE			
❏ Compleat 672005-1		1984	15.00
— Includes Eric Clapton, Eric Clapton & Jimmy Page, John Mayall & the Bluesbreakers, The All Stars featuring Jimmy Page, The All Stars featuring Jeff Beck, The All Stars featuring Nicky Hopkins, Cyril Davies and the All Stars, Santa Barbara Machine Head, and Jeremy Spencer; yet another compilation of material included in the LP "Guitar Boogie" and elsewhere			
WHITE MANSIONS			
❏ A&M SP6004		1978	25.00
WHK GOOD GUYS			
❏ Roulette R25295 [M]		1965	25.00
THE WHOLE BURBANK CATALOG			
❏ Warner Bros. PRO512		1972	25.00
— Originals have green labels			
A WHOLE LOT OF BLOWIN'			
❏ Audio Lab AL-1539 [M]		1959	60.00
WHOPPERS			
❏ Jubilee JGM-1119 [M]		1960	100.00
— Reissue of "Best of Rhythm and Blues," Jubilee 1014			
THE WHO'S WHO OF COUNTRY AND WESTERN MUSIC			
❏ Capitol T2538 [M]		1966	25.00
❏ Capitol ST2538 [S]		1966	25.00
WHY STUDY?			
❏ Columbia AS1765 [DJ]		1983	15.00
— Includes Elvis Costello, Wham! U.K., Midnight Oil; comes in plain black sleeve			
THE WIDE, WIDE WORLD OF JAZZ			
❏ RCA Victor LPM-1325 [M]		1956	30.00
WILD WILDWOOD RECORDED LIVE			
❏ Chancellor CHL-5017 [M]		1960	30.00
❏ Chancellor CHLS-5017 [S]		1960	30.00
WING LIVELY GUYS			
❏ Roulette R25307 [M]		1965	25.00
WINNERS ALL! THE DOWN BEAT JAZZ POLL '64			
❏ Verve V-8579 [M]		1964	25.00
❏ Verve V6-8579 [S]		1964	30.00
WINNER'S CIRCLE			
❏ Bethlehem BCP-6024 [M]		1958	40.00
WINNERS CIRCLE LIMITED EDITION			
❏ Columbia GB-4 [M]		1959	30.00
A WINNING SEASON OF JAZZ FROM CBS RECORDS			
❏ Columbia AS374 [DJ]		1977	18.00
— Promo-only sampler			
A WINTER'S SOLSTICE			
❏ Windham Hill WH-1045		1985	15.00
A WINTER'S SOLSTICE II			
❏ Windham Hill WH-1077		1988	15.00
WINTER'S WARMTH			
❏ Columbia Special Products CSP315/6		1965	18.00
— Produced for NORM/A Step Ahead			
WINTER WARNERLAND			
❏ Warner Bros. PRO-A-3328		1988	40.00
— Promo-only set; Record 1 is red vinyl, Record 2 is green vinyl			
THE WOMEN IN JAZZ			
❏ Storyville STLP-916 [M]		1956	50.00

Number	Title	Yr	NM
WONDERFUL MEMORIES FROM THE FAMILY PRAYER BOOK			
❏ Vee Jay LP-5066 [M]		1964	30.00
WOODSTOCK			
❏ Cotillion SD 3-500		1970	25.00
— Pale blue labels			
❏ Cotillion SD 3-500		1977	18.00
— Reissue on purplish labels			
❏ Mobile Fidelity 5-200		1985	200.00
— Audiophile vinyl			
WOODSTOCK TWO			
❏ Cotillion SD 2-400		1971	25.00
WORKING CLASS HERO -- A TRIBUTE TO JOHN LENNON			
❏ Hollywood ED-62015-1 [DJ]		1995	18.00
— Promo only on white vinyl; includes Red Hot Chili Peppers, Candlebox, Blues Traveler, Screaming Trees, The Flaming Lips, Collective Soul, Toad The Wet Sprocket, Mary Chapin Carpenter, etc.			
THE WORLD'S GREATEST MUSIC SERIES 'POP' -- JAZZ			
❏ Artia-Parliament WGM2AB		196?	100.00
— Box set of material from the Roulette label; also issued as two five-record boxes			
❏ Artia-Parliament WGM2B		196?	50.00
— Second of two five-record sets			
❏ Artia-Parliament WGM-2A [M]		196?	50.00
❏ Artia-Parliament WGM(S)-2A [S]		196?	60.00
WRCA PLAYS THE HITS FOR YOUR CUSTOMERS			
❏ RCA Victor DJL1-1785 [DJ]		1976	200.00
WWIN ASTRO JOCKS			
❏ Roulette R25337 [M]		1966	25.00
— Same LP as "WOL Soul Brothers			
YES L.A.			
❏ Dangerhouse EW79 [PD]		1979	80.00
— Includes X, The Germs, etc.; one-sided clear picture disc			
YOU CAN'T RESIST IT			
❏ MCA L33-1005 [DJ]		1986	15.00
— Includes Steve Earle, Lyle Lovett			
THE YOU'LL HATE THIS RECORD RECORD			
❏ The Only Label LP 001		1983	25.00
— Includes GG Allin, etc.			
THE YOUNG AT BOP			
❏ EmArcy MG-26001 [10]		1954	80.00
THE YOUNG ONES OF JAZZ			
❏ EmArcy MG-36085 [M]		1956	40.00
YOUR FAVORITE GROUPS AND THEIR GOLDEN GOODIES, VOL. 19			
❏ Roulette R25248 [M]		1964	25.00
YOUR FAVORITE SINGING GROUPS			
❏ Hull 1002 [M]		1962	1500.00
YOUR INTRODUCTION TO THE SOUND OF THE 'SIXTIES			
❏ Liberty MM-403 [DJ]		1960	30.00
— Promo-only release			
YOUR MUSICAL SOUVENIR FROM QSP			
❏ RCA Special Products QSP1-0042		1986	60.00
YOUR OLD FAVORITES ON OLD TOWN			
❏ Old Town LP-101 [M]		1959	200.00
YOURS			
❏ Harmony HL7042 [M]		1957	25.00
YOUR SPECIAL MUSICAL SOUVENIR FROM QSP			
❏ RCA Special Products QSP1-0047		1986	60.00
YOU'VE GOT TO HEAR IT TO BELIEVE IT			
❏ Solid State SS-94		1966	25.00
ZENITH PRESENTS ALL STAR HOOTENANNY			
❏ Columbia Special Products CSP149 [M]		1963	50.00
— With three early Bob Dylan tracks credited to "Bobby Dylan." Also has tracks by Pete Seeger (2), Orriel Smith (2) and The Clancy Brothers with Tommy Makem (3)			
ZENITH PRESENTS HOOTENANNY SPECIAL			
❏ Columbia Special Products CSP216M [M]		1965	30.00
❏ Columbia Special Products CSP216S [S]		1965	30.00
ZENITH SALUTES THE SWINGIN' BANDS			
❏ Columbia Special Products CSS525 [M]		1967	18.00
— Available from Zenith dealers			
ZIG ZAG FESTIVAL			
❏ Mercury SRD-2-29 [DJ]		1970	30.00